Encyclopedia of Southern Culture

Encyclopedia of Southern Culture

CHARLES REAGAN WILSON & WILLIAM FERRIS

COEDITORS

ANN J. ABADIE & MARY L. HART

ASSOCIATE EDITORS

SPONSORED BY

THE CENTER FOR THE STUDY OF SOUTHERN CULTURE

AT THE UNIVERSITY OF MISSISSIPPI

THE UNIVERSITY OF NORTH CAROLINA PRESS

CHAPEL HILL & LONDON

The paper in this book meets the guidelines for permanence and durability of the Committee on Production Guidelines for Book Longevity of the Council on Library Resources.

Printed in the United States of America

93 92 91 90 89 5 4 3

Library of Congress Cataloging-in-Publication Data

Encyclopedia of Southern culture / Charles Reagan Wilson and William Ferris, coeditors; Ann J. Abadie and Mary L. Hart, associate editors.

p. cm.

Includes index.

ISBN 0-8078-1823-2 (alk. paper)

1. Southern States—Civilization—Dictionaries. 2. Southern States—Dictionaries and encyclopedias. I. Wilson, Charles Reagan. II. Ferris, William R.

F209.E53 1989 88-17084

975'.003'21—dc19 CIP

Both the initial research and the publication of this work were made possible in part through a grant from the Division of Research Programs of the National Endowment for the Humanities, an independent federal agency whose mission is to award grants to support education, scholarship, media programming, libraries, and museums, in order to bring the results of cultural activities to a broad, general public.

"Tell about the South. What's it like there.
What do they do there. Why do they live there.
Why do they live at all."

WILLIAM FAULKNER

Absalom, Absalom!

The Encyclopedia of Southern Culture was
produced through major grants from the Program
for Research Tools and Reference Works of the
National Endowment for the Humanities, the
Ford Foundation, the Atlantic-Richfield
Foundation, and the Mary Doyle Trust.

The publication of this volume
was made possible by the
Fred W. Morrison Fund of the
University of North Carolina Press.

Contents

Consultants

Agriculture
Thomas D. Clark
248 Tahoma Road
Lexington, Ky. 40503

Art and Architecture
Jessie Poesch
Department of Art
Tulane University
New Orleans, La. 70118

Black Life
Thomas C. Holt
Department of History
University of Chicago
Chicago, Ill. 60637

Education
Thomas G. Dyer
Associate Vice President for Academic Affairs
University of Georgia
Old College
Athens, Ga. 30602

Environment
Martin V. Melosi
Department of History
University of Houston
Houston, Tex. 77004

Ethnic Life
George E. Pozzetta
Department of History
University of Florida
Gainesville, Fla. 32611

Folklife
William Ferris
Center for the Study of Southern Culture
University of Mississippi
University, Miss. 38677

Geography
Richard Pillsbury
Department of Geography
Georgia State University
Atlanta, Ga. 30303

History and Manners
Charles Reagan Wilson
Center for the Study of Southern Culture
University of Mississippi
University, Miss. 38677

Industry
James C. Cobb
Honors Program
P.O. Box 6233
University of Alabama
Tuscaloosa, Ala. 35487-6322

Language
Michael Montgomery
Department of English
University of South Carolina
Columbia, S.C. 29208

Law
Maxwell Bloomfield
Department of History
The Catholic University of America
Washington, D.C. 20017

Literature
M. Thomas Inge
Randolph-Macon College
Ashland, Va. 23005

Media
Edward D. C. Campbell, Jr.
Virginia State Library
11th Street at Capitol Square
Richmond, Va. 23219

Music
Bill C. Malone
Department of History
Tulane University
New Orleans, La. 70118

Mythic South
George B. Tindall
Department of History
University of North Carolina
Chapel Hill, N.C. 27599

Politics
Numan Bartley
Department of History
University of Georgia
Athens, Ga. 30602

Recreation
John Shelton Reed
Department of Sociology
University of North Carolina
Chapel Hill, N.C. 27599

Religion
Samuel S. Hill
Department of Religion
University of Florida
Gainesville, Fla. 32611

Science and Medicine
James O. Breeden
Department of History
Southern Methodist University
Dallas, Tex. 75275

Social Class
J. Wayne Flynt
Department of History
Auburn University
Auburn, Ala. 36830

Urbanization
Blaine A. Brownell
School of Social and Behavioral Sciences
University of Alabama at Birmingham
Birmingham, Ala. 35294

Violence
Raymond D. Gastil
48 E. 21st Street
New York, N.Y. 10010

Women's Life
Carol Ruth Berkin
Baruch College
City University of New York
17 Lexington Avenue
New York, N.Y. 10010

Foreword

Can you remember those southern elder men who "jes' set" on their favored chair or bench for hours, every day—and a year later they could tell you at about what time of day someone's dog had trotted by? And the counterpart elderly ladies, their hands deeply wrinkled from decades of quilting, canning, washing collective tons of clothing in black cast-iron pots, in which at other seasonal times pork fat was rendered into lard, or some of that lard into soap? These southern ancestors, black and white, have always struck me as the Foundation Timbers of our South, and I think that we who were reared and raised by them, and amongst them, are blessed that we were.

I consider this *Encyclopedia of Southern Culture* the answer to a deep need that we resuscitate and keep alive and fresh the memories of those who are now bones and dust, who during their eras and in their respective ways contributed toward the social accretion that has entered legend as "the southern way of life," which we continue today.

It is a culture resulting from the antebellum mixture of social extremes based on the chattel slavery that supported an aristocratic gentility; in between the slaves and planters a vast majority struggled for their own survival. Centuries of slavery were abolished by an indelible war whose legacies continue to haunt us. The southern memory is of generations of life, of the good and the bad, the humor and the suffering from the past. The southerner does not sentimentalize but only remembers.

Out of the historic cotton tillage sprang the involuntary field hollers, the shouts, and the moanin' low that have since produced such a cornucopia of music, played daily, on every continent, where I have been astounded at how much I heard of the evolved blues, jazz, and gospel—as well as bluegrass and country—all of them of direct southern origin.

Equally worldwide is southern literature. Writers took the oral traditions of the South—the political rhetoric, preaching, conversational wordplay, and lazy-day storytelling—and converted them into art. The latest addition to southern literature is this *Encyclopedia*, no small part of whose greatness, I think, is that it is compiled by many researchers who did not simply read books but who rubbed shoulders with those whom they interviewed and recorded and studied. They walked and talked with the sharecropper farmers, the cooks, the quiltmakers, the convicts, the merchants, the fishermen, and all the others who make these pages a volume of living memories.

The region and its people have undergone dramatic changes in the last decades, overcoming much, although not all, of the poverty of the past, and they are now sharing in the nation's prosperity. Old ways that divided the people have fallen away to be replaced by new dreams. The hard lessons from the past are not forgotten in this *Encyclopedia*. I testify that this *Encyclopedia of Southern Culture* mirrors the very best of what has lately come to be called "the new South." Never before has such a volume been produced by a team so committed to distilling and presenting our southern distinctiveness.

Alex Haley

Acknowledgments

This volume could never have been completed without the assistance of countless individuals. The coeditors and associate editors wish to thank our consultants and contributors for their planning, researching, and writing of articles. We should note that Raven McDavid helped to plan the Language section before his untimely death in 1984. Clarence Mohr's work on the early design of the *Encyclopedia* provided the basic organizational structure for the volume. Many scholars reviewed articles, made suggestions for improvements, and verified factual material. Richard H. Brown, of the Newberry Library in Chicago, advised wisely on *Encyclopedia* matters, as with other projects of the Center for the Study of Southern Culture. Howard Lamar offered sage counsel on the *Encyclopedia* from its earliest planning stages. Research assistants Elizabeth Makowski and Sharon A. Sharp supervised the review and verification of entries, assisted by numerous teaching assistants and volunteers, and also served as staff writers. Editorial assistants Ann Sumner Holmes, Ginna Parsons, and Karen McDearman Cox supervised final production of copy and served as endless sources of good advice and varied skill. Lolly Pilkington read the entire manuscript with a skilled eye. Teaching assistants in the Department of History and the Southern Studies program spent much time in the library checking and rechecking information and reading galley proof. Personnel in the John Davis Williams Library of the University of Mississippi often came to our rescue, and we are grateful to the many archivists and librarians across the nation who assisted us with obtaining illustrations. Special thanks are due the staff of the University of North Carolina Press, especially its director Matthew Hodgson, editor-in-chief Iris Tillman Hill, managing editor Sandra Eisdorfer, and Ron Maner, Pamela Upton, and Paula Wald.

The *Encyclopedia of Southern Culture* was produced with financial support from the National Endowment for the Humanities, the Ford Foundation, the Atlantic-Richfield Foundation, and the Mary Doyle Trust. The Graduate School and alumni and friends of the University of Mississippi donated required funds for a matching NEH grant in 1983, and the editors are grateful for their assistance. Donors include: The James Hand Foundation by Kathleen Hand Carter; Mrs. R. R. Morrison, Jr.; Mrs. Hester F. Faser; David L. May; James J. Brown, Jr.; Lynn Crosby Gammill; First National Bank of Vicksburg, Mississippi; The Goodman Charitable and Educational Trust, Hallie Goodman, Trustee; Dr. F. Watt Bishop; Robert Travis; Mrs. Dorothy Crosby; Christopher Keller, Jr.; Worth I. Dunn; and Wiley Fairchild.

Introduction

The American South has long generated powerful images and complex emotions. In the years since World War II, the region has undergone dramatic changes in race relations, political institutions, and economic life. Those changes have led some observers to forecast the eventual end of a distinctive southern region. Other scholars and popular writers point to continuities with past attitudes and behavior. The *Encyclopedia of Southern Culture* appears during a period of major transition in the life of the South and is in part a reflection of these changes. It examines both the historical and the contemporary worlds of southern culture. The *Encyclopedia*'s editors have sought to assemble authoritative, concise, thoughtful, substantive, and interesting articles that will give scholars, students, and general readers a useful perspective on the South.

Southern Culture

The *Encyclopedia*'s definition of "the South" is a cultural one. The geographical focus is, to be sure, on the 11 states of the former Confederacy (Alabama, Arkansas, Florida, Georgia, Louisiana, Mississippi, North Carolina, South Carolina, Tennessee, Texas, and Virginia), but this tidy historical definition fails to confront the complexities of studying the region. Delaware, Kentucky, Maryland, and Missouri were slave states at the beginning of the Civil War, and many of their citizens then and after claimed a southern identity. Social scientists today use statistical data covering the "census South," which includes Delaware, Maryland, West Virginia, Oklahoma, and the District of Columbia. The Gallup public opinion polling organization defines the South as the Confederate states plus Oklahoma and Kentucky.

Moreover, the realities of cultural areas require a broadened definition. Cultural areas have core zones, where distinctive traits are most concentrated, and margins, where the boundaries of the culture overlap with other cultural areas. The *Encyclopedia*'s articles explore the nature of both these core areas and margins in the South. The borders of the South have surely varied over time. In the colonial era Delaware was an agricultural slave state with a claim of being southern. Maryland was a southern state, sharing much with its neighbor, Virginia, in a Chesapeake subculture. Maryland did not join the Confederacy, but soldiers from the state fought in the Confederate armies and one finds Confederate monuments in Baltimore. St. Louis was a midwestern city and the gateway to the West, but southerners have also claimed it. The Mississippi River culture tied St. Louis to areas of the Lower South, and southerners have often been associated with it. John F. Kennedy once said that Washington, D.C., was known for its southern efficiency and northern charm. Carved from an area of Virginia as a concession to southerners, Washington was a slaveowning area and was once a center for slave auctions. Later, under Woodrow Wilson, a southern-born president, the nation's capital became a racially segregated bastion reflecting southern regional mores. Washington has also long been a center for southern black migration, an educational mecca for blacks, and a center for black musicians, artists, and writers. Most recently, geographical proximity to Appalachia has made Washington a center for the performance of such other expressions of southern culture as bluegrass music. Contemporary Washington, however, appears to be less and less "southern," and urban historians consequently omit it from the list of regional cities (and thus there is no separate entry on Washington in this volume).

Contributors to the *Encyclopedia* at times transcend geography and history when examining questions of regional consciousness, symbolism, mythology, and sectional stereotyping. The "South" is found wherever southern culture is found, and that culture is located not only in the Deep South, the Upper South, and border cities, but also in "little Dixies" (the southern parts of Ohio, Indiana, Illinois, and parts of Missouri and Oklahoma), among black Mississippians who migrated to south Chicago, among white Appalachians and black Alabamians who migrated to Detroit, and among former Okies and Arkies who settled in and around Bakersfield, California. This diaspora of southern ethnic culture is also found in the works of expatriate southern artists and writers. Although Richard Wright and Tennessee Williams lived in Paris and New York, respectively, they continued to explore their southern roots in their writing.

The South exists as a state of mind both within and beyond its geographical boundaries. Recent studies of mythology suggest that the New York theater in the late 19th century and Hollywood in the 20th century have kept alive images, legends, and myths about the South in the national consciousness. One can view the American South and its culture as international property. The worlds of *Roots*, *Gone with the Wind*, blues, country music, rock and roll, William Faulkner, and Alice Walker are admired and closely studied throughout the world. The South has nurtured important myths, and their impact on other cultures is a vital aspect of the *Encyclopedia*'s perspective. In the end, then, the *Encyclopedia*'s definition of the South is a broad, inclusive one, based on culture.

This volume focuses specifically on exploring the culture of the South. In the 1950s anthropologists Alfred Kroeber and Clyde Kluckholn cataloged 164 definitions of culture, suggesting the problems then and now of a precise definition. To 19th-century intellectuals culture was the best of civilization's achievements. Matthew Arnold was perhaps the best-known advocate of this Victorian-era ideal, and H. L. Mencken—the South's nastiest and most entertaining critic in the early 20th century—was also a believer in it. Mencken argued in his essay "The Sahara of the Bozart" (1920) that the upper-class, aristocratic southerner of the early 19th century "liked to toy with ideas. He was hospitable and tolerant. He had the vague thing that we call culture." Mencken found the South of his era severely wanting, though, in this ideal of culture. He saw in the South "not a single picture gallery worth going into, or a single orchestra capable of playing the nine symphonies of Beethoven, or a single opera-house, or a single theater devoted to decent plays, or a single public monument (built since the war) that is worth looking at, or a single workshop devoted to the making of beautiful things." Mencken allowed that the region excelled "in the lower reaches of the gospel hymn, the phonograph and the chautauqua harangue."

The South of Mencken's day did trail the rest of the nation in the development of important cultural institutions; but today the South, the nation, and the world celebrate the "lower reaches" of southern culture. This judgment on the value of the sounds and words coming from the region reflects 20th-century understandings of culture. Anthropologists have taken the lead in exploring the theoretical aspects of cultures. Edward Burnett Tylor gave a classic definition of culture as "that complex whole which includes knowledge, belief, art, morals, law, customs, and any other capabilities and habits" acquired by the members of a society. For students of culture, the goal was to study and outline discrete cultural traits, using this definition to convey the picture of a culture. During the 20th century another major anthropological theory of culture emerged. Kroeber, Bronislaw Malinowski, and Ruth Benedict stressed the study of pattern, form, structure, and organization in a culture rather than the simple listing of observed traits. Patterns could include customs associated with food, labor, and manners as well as more complex social, political, and economic systems.

Recently culture has been viewed as an abstraction, consisting of the inherited models and ideas with which people approach their experiences. The theory of social structure, first developed by British anthropologist Alexander Reginald Radcliffe-Brown in the 1930s and 1940s, stressed that culture must include recognition of the persistence of social groups, social classes, and social roles. The structuralist theories of Claude Lévi-Strauss attempt to apply abstract mathematical formulae to society. Although social anthropologists avoid the term *culture*, they have insured that the study of culture not neglect social background.

The theoretical work of Clifford Geertz is especially significant in understanding the definition of culture developed for the *Encyclopedia of Southern Culture*. Geertz defines *culture* as "an historically transmitted pattern of meanings embodied in symbols, a system of inherited conceptions expressed in symbolic forms." Through culture, humans "communicate, perpetuate, and develop their knowledge about and attitudes toward life." This contemporary definition stresses mental culture, expressed through symbol systems, which gives human beings a framework for understanding one another, themselves, and the wider world. Culture patterns, including material, oral, mental, and social systems, are blueprints for organizing human interaction.

The *Encyclopedia of Southern Culture* is not intended as a contribution to the general study of culture theory, although awareness of theories of culture has been useful background in the conceptualization of the volume and in the selection of topics. The volume attempts to study within the southern context what 20th-century humanist T. S. Eliot said, in *Notes towards the Definition of Culture*, was culture—"all the characteristic activities and interests of a people." Articles in the volume deal with regional cultural achievements in such areas as music, literature, art, and architecture. The broader goal of the volume is to chart the cultural landscape of the South, addressing those aspects of southern life and thought that have sustained either the reality or the illusion of regional distinctiveness. The volume details specific cultural traits, suggests the cultural patterns that tie the region together, points out the internal diversity within the South, and explores with special attention the importance of social structure and symbolism. Above all, the volume has been planned to carry out Eliot's belief that "culture is not merely the sum of several activities, but a *way of life*."

Eliot's definition of culture, then, can be seen as a working definition for the *Encyclopedia of Southern Culture*. In order to foster interdisciplinary communication, the editors have included the full range of social indicators, trait groupings, literary concepts, and historical evidence commonly used by students of regionalism. The criteria for the all-important selection of topics, however, have been consistently to include the characteristic traits that give the South a distinctive culture.

A special concern of the *Encyclopedia* has been to identify distinctive regional characteristics. It addresses those aspects of southern life and thought—the individuals, places, ideas, rituals, symbols, myths, values, and experiences—which have sustained either the reality or the illusion of regional distinctiveness. The comparative method has been encouraged as a way to suggest contrasts with other American regions and with other societies. One lesson of earlier regional scholarship has been the need to look at the South in the widest possible context. The editors of this volume have assumed that the distinctiveness of southern culture does not lie in any one trait but rather in the peculiar combination of regional cultural characteristics. The fundamental uniqueness of southern culture thus emerges from the *Encyclopedia's* composite portrait of the South. The editors asked contributors to consider individual traits that clearly are unique to the region. Although some topics may not be uniquely southern in themselves, contributors have been asked to explore particular regional aspects of those topics. Subjects that suggest the internal diversity of the region are also treated if they contribute to the overall picture of southern distinctiveness. The Cajuns of Louisiana, the Germans of Texas, and the Jews of Savannah, for example, contribute to the distinctive flavor of southern life. Their adaptations, and resistance, to southern cultural patterns suggest much about the region's distinctiveness.

The question of continuity and change in southern culture is another central concern of this volume. Contributors have examined themes and topics in an evolutionary framework. Historians represent by far the largest group of contributors to the project. The volume does not attempt to narrate the region's history in a systematic way, a task ably achieved in the *Encyclopedia of Southern History* (1979), but contributors from all disciplines have developed material within an appropriate time perspective. As Clifford Geertz has written, culture is "historically transmitted," a fact that is especially relevant for the study of the South, where the apogee of cultural distinctiveness may well have been in an earlier period. Because the *Encyclopedia* focuses on culture rather than history, historical topics were chosen because they are relevant to the origin, development, or decline of an aspect of southern culture. Given the historical shape of southern cultural development, one would expect less material on the colonial era (before there was a self-conscious "South") and increased concentration of material in the Civil War and postbellum eras (perhaps the high points of southern cultural distinctiveness). Nearly all articles include historical material, and each overview essay systematically traces the development of a major subject area. In addition, such selected historical entries as "Colonial Heritage," "Frontier Heritage," and "Civil War" are included with a cultural focus appropriate to the volume.

Study of Southern Regionalism

The *Encyclopedia of Southern Culture* reflects a broad intellectual interest in regionalism, the importance of which in the United States is far from unique when seen in a global context. The struggle to accommodate regional cultures within a larger nation is an experience common to many Western and Third World peoples. Despite the contemporary developments in transportation and communication that promise the emergence of a "global village," regionalism is an enduring reality of the modern world. The Basques in Spain, the Scots in Britain, the Kurds in the Middle East, and Armenians in the Soviet Union are only a few examples of groups that have recently reasserted their regional interests.

Although public emphasis on the United States as a cultural melting pot has sometimes obscured the nation's enduring regional heritage, the study of regionalism has long been a major field of scholarship involving leading authorities from many academic disciplines both in the United States and abroad. The *Encyclopedia* is part of the broader field of American Studies, which has dramatically evolved in recent years from a focus on such regional types as the New England Yankees, the southern Cavaliers, and the western cowboys and Indians. Since the 1960s studies of black life, ethnic life, and women's life have significantly changed the definition of American culture. In the 1980s the study of American region, place, and community—whether it be a Brooklyn neighborhood or a county in rural Mississippi—is essential to understanding the nation. In the context of this American Studies tradition, the *Encyclopedia* focuses on the American South, a place that has influenced its people in complex and fascinating ways.

Significant bodies of research exist for all major regions of the United States, but by almost any standard the American South has received the most extensive scholarly attention. Since the 1930s virtually all aspects of southern life have come under increasingly rigorous, systematic intellectual scrutiny. The *Encyclopedia of Southern Culture* is a collaborative effort that combines intellectual perspectives that reflect the breadth of Southern Studies. Sociologists, historians, literary critics, folklorists, anthropologists, political scientists, psychologists, theologians, and other scholars have written on the region, and all of these fields are represented by contributors to the *Encyclopedia*. Journalists, lawyers, physicians, architects, and other professionals from outside the academy have also studied the South, and their contributions appear in this volume as well.

Students of the South operate within a well-developed institutional framework. The proliferation of academic journals that focus on the South has mirrored expanding disciplinary boundaries in regional scholarship. The *Journal of Southern History*, the *Southern Review*, the *Southern Economic Journal*, *Social Forces*, the *Southern Folklore Quarterly*, the *Virginia Quarterly Review*, the *South Atlantic Quarterly*, and the *Southwestern Political Science Quarterly* are only a few of the titles that have specialized in publishing material on the region. The contemporary era has witnessed a dramatic expansion in the publication of books on the South. The University of North Carolina Press was the first southern university press to publish an extensive list of titles on the South, and by the early 1950s the press alone had produced some 200 studies. Works on the region are now published by university presses in every southern state and find a ready market with national publishers as well.

Research on the South has led to greater appreciation of the region's internal diversity, which is reflected in the study of smaller geographical areas or specialized themes. Such recent periodicals as the *Appalachian Journal*, *Mid-South Folklore*, and *South Atlantic Urban Studies* illustrate the narrowing geographical and topical focus of recent scholarship on the South. Overlapping interests and subject matter shared among regional scholars have exerted a steady pressure toward broadening disciplinary horizons. Meaningful cooperation among disciplines is complicated by differences of vocabulary and method, but students of the American South demonstrate a growing awareness that they are engaged in a common endeavor that can be furthered as much by cooperation as by specialization. Such periodicals as *Southern Quarterly*, *Southern Studies*, and *Perspectives on the American South* have established forums for interdisciplinary study.

In recent years regional scholarship has also influenced curriculum development in colleges and universities. Leading institutional centers for the study of the

South include the Center for the Study of Southern Culture at the University of Mississippi, the Institute for Southern Studies at the University of South Carolina, the Institute for Southern Studies at Durham, N.C., and the Center for the Study of Southern History and Culture at the University of Alabama. Appalachian study centers are located at, among other places, the University of Kentucky, East Tennessee State University, Appalachian State University, Mars Hill College, and Berea College. The Institute for Texan Cultures is in San Antonio, and Baylor University launched a Texas Studies Center in 1987. The Center for Arkansas Studies is at the University of Arkansas at Little Rock, while the University of Southwestern Louisiana's Center for Louisiana Studies concentrates on Cajun and Creole folk culture. These developments are, again, part of a broader interest in regional studies programs at universities in other regions, including the Center for the Study of New England Culture at the University of Massachusetts at Amherst and the Great Plains Center at the University of Nebraska.

The *Encyclopedia of Southern Culture* grows out of the work of the University of Mississippi's Center for the Study of Southern Culture, which was established in 1977 to coordinate existing university resources and to develop multidisciplinary teaching, research, and outreach programs about the South. The center's mission is to strengthen the university's instructional program in the humanities, to promote scholarship on every aspect of southern culture, and to encourage public understanding of the South through publications, media productions, lectures, performances, and exhibitions. Center personnel administer a Southern Studies curriculum that includes both B.A. and M.A. degree programs; a Ford Foundation–funded, three-year (1986–89) project aimed at incorporating more fully the experiences of blacks and women into the teaching of Southern Studies; an annual United States Information Agency–sponsored project for international scholars interested in regional and ethnic cultures; such annual meetings as the Porter L. Fortune Chancellor's Symposium on Southern History, the Faulkner and Yoknapatawpha Conference, and the Barnard-Millington Symposium on Southern Science and Medicine; and a variety of periodicals, films, and media presentations. The center administers these programs in cooperation with the on-campus departments in the College of Liberal Arts, the Afro-American Studies program, and the Sarah Isom Center for Women's Studies. The University of Mississippi and its Center for the Study of Southern Culture provided the necessary institutional setting for coordinating the diverse needs of the *Encyclopedia*'s hundreds of participants.

Recognizing both the intellectual maturity of scholarship on the American South and the potential role of regional study in consolidating previously fragmented academic endeavors, the *Encyclopedia* planners conceived the idea of an interdisciplinary reference work to bring together and synthesize current knowledge about the South. Scholars studying the South have been served by a number of reference works, but none of these has had the aims and perspective of the *Encyclopedia of Southern Culture*. The 13-volume series, *The South in the Building of the Nation* (1909–13), which attempted a comprehensive survey of the region's history, was the closest predecessor to this encyclopedia. Other major works include the 16-volume *Library of Southern Literature* (1908–13), Howard W. Odum's monumental *Southern Regions of the United States* (1936), W. T. Couch's edited *Culture in the South* (1936), and, more recently, the *Encyclopedia of Southern History* (1978), the *Encyclopedia of Religion in the South* (1984), and the *History of Southern Literature* (1986).

Like any major reference work, the *Encyclopedia* addresses the long-range needs and interests of a diverse reading audience. Before launching the project the editors consulted extensively with leading authorities in all areas of American Studies and Southern Studies and sought additional advice from directors of comparable projects. Planning for the volume began in 1978 with the compilation of a working outline of subjects that had received frequent attention in major studies of regional culture. During the fall of 1979 some 270 U.S. and international scholars received copies of the preliminary topical list, together with background information about the project. Approximately 150 of these scholars, representing a variety of disciplines, responded to this mailing, commenting upon the potential value of the proposed volume and making suggestions concerning its organization and content.

In 1980 the Center for the Study of Southern Culture commissioned several scholars to prepare detailed lists of topics for major sections of the volume, and to write sample articles as well. The National Endowment for the Humanities supported the *Encyclopedia of Southern Culture* with a 1980–81 planning grant and grants covering 1981–83 and 1984–86. The Ford Foundation, the Atlantic-Richfield Foundation, and the Mary Doyle Trust also provided major funding. Full-time work on the *Encyclopedia* began in September 1981. The content of the volume was divided into 24 major subject areas, and the editors selected a senior consultant to assist in planning the topics and contributors for each section. During the fall and winter of 1981–82, the consultants formulated initial lists of topics and recommended appropriate contributors for entries. In general, the consultants were actively involved in the initial stages of planning and less involved in later editorial work. Project staff handled the paperwork for assignments. The editors sent each contributor a packet of information on the project, including the overall list of topics, so that contributors could see how their articles fit into the volume as a whole. Authors were encouraged to make suggestions for additional entries, and many of them did so. When contributors were unable to write for the volume, they often suggested other scholars, thus facilitating the reassignment of articles. The editors assumed the responsibility for editing articles for style, clarity, and tone appropriate for a reference book. They reviewed all entries for accuracy, and research assistants verified the factual and bibliographical veracity of each entry. The senior consultants, with their special expertise in each subject area, provided an additional check on the quality of the articles.

Organization and Content of the Encyclopedia

The *Encyclopedia of Southern Culture* is a synthesis of current scholarship and attempts to set new directions for further research. The *Encyclopedia*'s objectives are fourfold: (1) The volume provides students and general readers with convenient access to basic facts and bibliographical data about southern cultural patterns and their historical development. (2) By bringing together lucid analyses of modern scholarship on southern culture from the humanities and the social sciences, the *Encyclopedia* is intended to facilitate communication across disciplinary lines and help stimulate new approaches to regional study. It attempts to integrate disparate intellectual efforts and represents an innovative organization and presentation of knowledge. (3) The volume can serve as a curriculum component for multidisciplinary courses on the American South and provide a model for scholars wishing to assemble similar research tools in other regions. (4) Viewed in its totality, the *Encyclopedia* locates the specific components of regional culture within the framework of a larger organic whole. At this level, the volume attempts to illuminate the nature and function of regionalism in American culture.

The editors considered an alphabetical arrangement of articles but concluded that organization of information into 24 major sections more accurately reflects the nature of the project and would provide a fresh perspective. Cross-references to related articles in other sections are essential guides to proper use of the *Encyclopedia*, enabling readers to consult articles written on a common topic from different perspectives. Sections often reflect an academic field (history, geography, literature), but at times the academic division has been rejected in favor of a section organized around a cultural theme (such as social class) that has become a central scholarly concern. In general, the sections are designed to reflect the amount and quality of scholarship in particular areas of regional study. Articles within each section are arranged in three divisions. The overview essay is written by the *Encyclopedia*'s consultant in that section and provides an interpretive summary of the field. That essay is followed by alphabetically arranged thematic articles and then by alphabetically arranged, brief topical-biographical sketches.

Although the editors and consultants conceived each section as a separate unit, sections are closely connected to one another through cross-references. The titles of major sections are brief, but the editors have grouped together related material under these simple rubrics. The Agriculture section thus includes rural-life articles, the Black Life section includes articles on race relations, Social Class includes material on social structure and occupational groups, and Industry includes information on commercial activity.

Several sections deserve special comment in regard to their organization and content. The Black Life section contains most, though not all, of the separate entries on southern black culture. The editors placed Richard Wright and Ralph Ellison in Literature to honor their roles as central figures in *southern* (as well as black) literature, and most blues musicians are similarly found in Music. But the list of biographies in Black Life is intended to stand on its own, including individuals representing music, literature, religion, sports, politics, and other areas of black achievement. The *Encyclopedia* claims for southern culture such individuals as Mary McLeod Bethune, Ida Wells-Barnett, Arna Bontemps, and James Weldon Johnson, who traditionally have been seen as part of black history but not southern culture. The separate Black Life section is intended to recognize the special nature of southern black culture—both black and southern. Black culture is central to understanding the region and the *Encyclopedia*'s attempt to explore this perspective in specific, detailed topics may be the most significant contribution of the volume toward understanding the region. Although the terms *Afro-American* and *Euro-American* are sometimes used, *black* and *white* are more often used to refer to the two major interrelated cultures of the South. These terms seem the clearest, most inclusive, and most widely accepted terms of reference.

The Women's Life section has similar aims. Many thematic articles and biographies of women of achievement appear in this section, which is designed to stand on its own. Scholars in the last 20 years have explored southern women's cultural values and issues, and their work provides a distinctive perspective on the region. Gender, like race and social class, has set parameters for cultural life in the South. The section includes articles on family life, childhood, and the elderly, reflecting the major responsibilities and concerns of women. The inclusion of these topics in this section is not meant to suggest that family responsibilities were the sole concern of women or that men were uninvolved with family, children, and the elderly. The articles usually discuss both male and female activities within the family. Scholarship on family life has often focused on women's roles, and family matters traditionally have played a significant part in women's lives. Most of the Women's Life section is concentrated, however, on concerns beyond the family and household, reflecting the contemporary scholarship in this area.

The Education section presented especially difficult choices of inclusion, and again, a selective approach was adopted. The flagship state public university in each southern state is included, but beyond that, institutions have been selected that represent differing constituencies to suggest the diversity of educational activity in the region. Berea College, Commonwealth College, the University of the South, and Tuskegee Institute each reflect an important dimension of southern education. The inclusion of additional school entries would have departed from the *Encyclopedia*'s overall guidelines and made a one-volume reference work impossible.

The History and Manners section contains a mix of articles that focus on cultural and social dimensions of the South. Combining topics in history and manners reflects the editors' decision that in a reference work on cultural concerns, history entries should deal with broad sociocultural history. There are, thus, no separate, detailed entries on Civil War battles, but, instead, long thematic articles on the cultural meaning of battlefields, monuments, and wars. The article on Robert E. Lee discusses the facts of Lee's life but also the history of his image for southerners and Americans.

Overview essays in each section are interpretive pieces that synthesize modern scholarship on major aspects of southern culture. The consultants who have written them trace historical developments and relate their broad subjects to regional cultural concerns. Many specific topics are discussed within overview essays rather than through separate entries, so readers should consult the index in order to locate such material. As one might expect, major subject areas have developed at a different pace. In such fields as literature, music, religion, folklife, and political culture, a vast body of scholarship exists. In these areas, the *Encyclopedia* overview essays provide a starting point for those users of this reference work interested in the subject. Such other fields as law, art, science, and medicine have only recently emerged as separate fields of Southern Studies. In these areas, the overview essays should help define the fields and point toward areas for further research.

Most thematic, topical, and biographical entries fall clearly within one section, but some articles were appropriate for several sections. The Scopes trial, for example, could have been placed in Religion, Law, or Science and Medicine. Consultants in Black Life, Music, and Women's Life all suggested Bessie Smith as an entry in their categories. The article on cockfighting clearly related to the Recreation section but was placed in Violence to suggest how recreational activities reflect a culture of violence. The gospel music articles could have appeared in Religion, but the editors decided that Music was the most appropriate category for them. Much consideration and consultation with authorities in relevant fields occurred before such decisions were made on topics that did not fit perfectly into any one section. Readers should rely on the index and the cross-references between sections to lead them to desired entries.

Biographies focus on the cultural significance of key individuals. The volume does not claim to be exhaustive in its biographical entries. Rather than attempt to include all prominent people in a subject area, the editors decided to treat representative figures in terms of their contributions to, or significance for, southern culture. In selecting individuals, the goal was to include biographies of those iconic individuals associated with a particular aspect of the region's culture. Consultants identified those major figures who have immediate relevance to the region. The editors and consultants also selected individuals who illuminate major themes and exemplify southern cultural styles. Persons in this category may have made special contributions to southern distinctiveness, to cultural achievements, or to the development of a characteristic aspect of southern life. The Music and Literature categories have been given somewhat fuller biographical attention than other subject areas, a decision that is warranted by southern achievements in those areas. In addition to the separate biographical entries, many individuals are discussed in such thematic articles as "Linguists" or "Historians," which outline contributions of key persons to certain fields. Readers should consult the index to locate biographical information on southerners who appear in the volume.

The *Encyclopedia* includes biographies of living persons as well as the deceased. The volume is especially concerned with regional cultural issues in the contemporary South, and the inclusion of living individuals was crucial to establishing continuities between past and present. Entries on Bill Moyers and Charles Kuralt, for example, help readers to understand that the journalistic traditions of the South have been extended into the television age.

Selecting approximately 250 individuals for inclusion in the *Encyclopedia of Southern Culture* was no easy task. The list of potential individuals was widely circulated, and the choices represent the informed judgment of our consultants and contributors, leading scholars in the field of Southern Studies. The selection of biographies was made in light of the volume's overall definition of culture. The goal was not to list every cultural trait or include every prominent individual in the South but to explore *characteristic* aspects of the region's life and culture and to show their interrelationships. The biographical entries are not simply descriptive, factual statements but are instead intimately related to the broader thematic and overview essays. Biographical entries were meant to suggest how a representative individual is part of a broader pattern, a way of life, in the American South.

Interdisciplinary study has become prominent in a number of scholarly areas, but in few is it as useful as in the study of region. The interrelatedness of such specific fields as politics, religion, economics, cultural achievement, and social organization becomes especially obvious when scholars study a region. Interdisciplinary study of the South is a means of exploring humanity in all its aspects. The intellectual specialization of the modern world often makes this study difficult, but the editors of the *Encyclopedia* hope this volume will promote that goal. Scholars exploring various aspects of the South's life now compose a distinct field of interdisciplinary Southern Studies, and this volume joins those scholars in common effort to extend the present bounds of knowledge about the South.

The Editors
Center for the Study of Southern Culture
University of Mississippi

Editors' Note

The *Encyclopedia* is divided into 24 major subject areas, arranged in alphabetical order. A table of contents listing articles in each section is found at the beginning of the section. An overview essay is followed by a series of alphabetically arranged thematic essays and then brief, alphabetically arranged topical-biographical entries. Readers are urged to consult the index, as well as the tables of contents, in locating articles.

When appropriate, articles contain cross-references to related articles in other sections. Material is cross-referenced only to similar-length or shorter material. Thematic articles, for example, are cross-referenced to thematic articles or to short topical articles in other sections but not to longer overview essays. Topical-biographical entries are cross-referenced to topical-biographical articles in other sections but not to longer overview or thematic essays. Each cross-reference to related material lists the section in small capital letters, followed by the article title. If the entry is a short topical-biographical article, the title is preceded by a slash. The following example is a cross-reference to, first, a thematic article and, then, a topical-biographical entry, both in the Folklife section:

See also FOLKLIFE: Storytelling; / Clower, Jerry

Every effort was made to update material before publication. However, changes in contributors' affiliations, in biographical data because of the death of an individual, and in the names of institutions, for example, could not be made after the book went to press.

Agriculture

THOMAS D. CLARK
Lexington, Kentucky
CONSULTANT

Sharecropper, Warren County, Miss., 1972

Agriculture

The basic and historic industry in the South has been agriculture. This fact has had an enormous bearing on the development of a distinctive regional culture and economy. From the first English settlement at Jamestown in the opening decade of the 17th century to the present the South's principal economic focus has been upon agriculture. Throughout its history agriculture in the South has experienced four or five distinctive phases of change. Each new era made social, cultural, and economic impressions upon the southern people.

Most British emigrants who approached the American shores were ambitious to reestablish in the New World an Old World pastoral society and agricultural economy. Soil and climate conditions, the forest cover, and difficult access to transportation all contributed to the shaping of distinctive agrarian fortunes and fresh ways of life in the early colonial South. Imperative from the outset was the necessity to develop both subsistence farming and commercial planting. For both types of farmers land became the necessary foundation for economic and social wellbeing. It was the catalyst that spread Anglo-American civilization over the wide expanse of virgin southern hinterlands.

Soon after initial English settlement the great baronial, river valley plantations appeared, with access to water transportation. Almost simultaneously the great land companies came into existence, hoping to encourage immigration and to speculate in almost unlimited claims of backcountry lands. Land policies were a major factor shaping the spreading settlements. With the expansion of the Atlantic coastal civilization a mixture of plantations and yeoman farms came to characterize the economy. Both depended heavily upon four basic staple crops: corn, tobacco, rice, and indigo. The latter was soon succeeded by Sea Island, or black-seeded, cotton. These crops, with the exception of corn, either took a heavy toll on the thin Tidewater lands or were too regionally and environmentally restricted to permit successful transmission to the upcountry. In time, however, tobacco was transported beyond the Appalachians to become an important cash crop in pioneer Kentucky and Tennessee. Short-staple cotton supplanted the Sea Island variety and was ideally suited to the lands of the developing South.

By the mid-18th century an ever-increasing proportion of the southern population shifted their dependence from commercial crops to the subsistence ones. Two exciting chapters in southern agricultural history involve the growing of corn and the rolling back of the cattle- and hog-droving frontiers. The early Anglo-American immigrants developed a fondness for corn and pork products.

The spread of agrarian culture is reflected in modern geographic and economic studies, which materially revise early notions about the maturing of the agricultural economy across the South. Sam B. Hilliard's recent *Atlas of Antebellum Southern Agriculture* (1984) conveys a dramatic sense of the changing phases of regional farming and labor. This and other recent studies sharply revise earlier ones that did not do justice to the region's production of livestock and foodstuffs.

Advance of Agricultural Frontiers. The opening of the trans-Appalachian frontier in the Upper South in the latter quarter of the 18th century drew a stream of agricultural emigrants away from the depleted Tidewater and lower Piedmont lands of the Atlantic Seaboard. The western rivers and their valleys held fresh promise for farmers. Traditional agricultural patterns were spread across the mountains but were adapted to a distinctive new way of agrarian life. In Kentucky, for instance, commercial, staple-crop farming was devoted to grain, tobacco, hemp, and livestock production. This pattern also prevailed in the Bluegrass region of Tennessee.

During the first half of the 19th century a major migration to the recently vacated Indian lands of the Atlantic and Gulf coastal South occurred. This movement was stimulated by opportunities to exploit the cotton producing lands of the Old Southwest, the quieting of Indian and international claims, and the ready adaptation of staple crops. Cotton became the principal staple cash crop because of both the nature of the land and the recent invention and perfection of the mechanical cotton gin. On this sprawling, fertile southern frontier at least three layers of human economic and pastoral history existed by the time of the Civil War. All across the region herdsmen or cattle grazers and hog drovers pursued a moderately labor-intensive way of life and pastured their herds and droves on the vast virginal domain. Some of these low-caste forerunners of Anglo-American civilization moved on with the expanding frontier until no more public lands remained to be exploited; others settled down to become yeoman farmers or sharecroppers.

As the southern agricultural frontiers advanced, plain dirt farmers laid claim to modest landholdings, peopled the emigrant trails, opened fields and pastures in the virgin forests, built simple dwellings and barns, and established rural communities. All across new regions these yeomen established subsistence farming, created an uncomplicated economy, held fast to family ties and folkways, personified the image of much of the antebellum South, and formed the bulk of the population. Modern statistical charts and illustrative maps portray the pattern of economic and agricultural expansion in the South to 1860 and convey a sense of the vibrant dynamics of the southern agricultural civilization during these formative years.

Plantations and Farms. In sharp contrast to the panorama of the yeoman-farmer background and the limited production of commercial crops were the plantations, with their extensive landholdings and slave labor force. These sprang up principally in areas with more fertile and productive lands. Of necessity the plantation was a staple-crop, slave-labor, semicommercial enterprise. This type of farming in the South generated its own social, economic, and cultural characteristics. To a large extent the way of life on southern cotton, rice, sugar, and tobacco plantations tended to break much of the isolation in the region. In economic terms, the plantation required extensive management, the opening and maintenance of domestic and foreign markets, the organization of both supply and credit systems, and ready access to transportation facilities. The staple crops were readily adaptable to large landholdings, intensive use of labor, and commercial farming methods.

While rice, tobacco, and sugarcane growing were important regionally, short-staple cotton growing was central to most southern plantations after 1890. Highly adaptable to land, climate, and casual methods of cultivation and harvesting, cotton enjoyed the advantage of having both a domestic and an international market. The yeoman farm was also a producer of cotton, a fact that became more central to its operation after the Civil War.

In recent years economists, sociologists, and historians who have reexamined the available contemporary documentary sources have sharply revised older notions about the nature and diversity of antebellum crop production and its bearing upon earlier forms of rural farm life. The most important areas of regional self-sufficiency that have been reconsidered are the production of consumable crops, the volume of livestock, and the importance of the small and middle-sized farmer.

Whatever role the larger plantation and its more affluent owners may have played in regional commerce, politics, and social and cultural life, it was the yeoman farmer who opened large areas of the land, helped create counties and towns, "lived largely at home," and gave body and soul to southern rural life. From backcountry Virginia and the Carolinas to east Texas there sprang up a homogeneity of racial, social, and cultural agrarian organization. Remarkably, the South before 1860 nurtured two systems of agricultural economy and modes of life—the yeoman farm and the plantation.

The Civil War was a historical watershed of southern farming. Slavery was abolished, and the rural labor situation experienced drastic changes. Though plantations survived, they operated on a different scale. Their labor supply was disrupted, as they had to employ wage workers or sharecroppers. Time was required to reclaim the great cotton markets, and dramatic changes occurred in the financing of this type of farming.

Postbellum Agricultural System. In the postwar years the southern yeoman farmer was caught up in what almost amounted to an economic straitjacket. He was forced by a usurious credit-granting system to turn more and more to production of cash crops, especially cotton and tobacco. All farmers, large and small, were severely pressed to secure sufficient operating capital. A new form of agricultural production credit appeared, based upon crop liens and dependent upon merchants who furnished farm supplies. Both farmer and merchant in turn were thrown largely upon the mercy of wholesalers, manufacturers, extraregional grain and meat producers, and fertilizer distributors.

Between 1865 and 1925 most southern farmers were thrust upon a treadmill, producing sufficient staple crops to pay both inflated prices for supplies and the extortionate interest on crop liens. Both white and black farmers rapidly sank into the economic peonage of the staple-crop system of rising debts and falling prices. The farming operations of the individual tenant or sharecropper became almost primitive in nature. This system of southern farming was ultimately disastrous. Cotton was the predominant cash crop, and its days in the Upland South were numbered after 1920. The crop laid a heavy burden upon its impoverished producers and exacted a heavy toll from the land. Within three-quarters of a century the flagrantly careless methods of cotton cultivation destroyed an enormous amount of topsoil and left behind a deeply gullied landscape. So serious was this loss that by 1933 much of the South was a disaster area. Even more serious, however, each year more and more farmers were forced into the ranks of sharecroppers and tenants, a trend that continued until the New Deal.

Tobacco, sugarcane, and rice were more regionally confined. They never equaled financially and socially the importance of cotton for the southern population. They, like cotton, depended upon widespread domestic and foreign markets, and in the case of dark tobacco, farmers were sorely pressed by the dominance of outside buyers. In the opening decade of this century the dark-tobacco farmers resorted to vigilante tactics in an effort to improve marketing conditions of their crops, resulting in the Black Patch War in Kentucky.

Editors of southern country weeklies and the regional farm journals cajoled and scolded farmers for their failure to grow more foodstuffs. They preached monotonous editorial sermons on the themes of increasing crop diversification, halting the wastage of the soil, and eliminating blind dependence upon nonconsumable crops. Stern critics were Charles Otken, George K. Holmes, W. H. Skaggs, and a score of later authors. Farmers themselves attempted to better their lots by creating organizations to exert political and economic pressures in alleviating oppressive conditions. Vain efforts were made by such groups as the "white cappers" of the cotton belt and the nightriders of the dark-tobacco areas.

Change in Southern Farming. The spread of the boll weevil menace across the cotton belt after 1900 raised bitter winds of change. World War I and the sequent depression in 1921 sounded further warnings that the old cash-crop system was a failure. The socially and economically devastating sharecropping system and the Great Depression of the 1930s hastened the demise of southern staple-crop farming.

The problems of sharecropping and ruinous credit granted by general stores and fertilizer trusts are no longer factors in southern farming. The multiplication of banks and savings and loan companies has made credit available on other bases. The introduction of the tractor, mechanical cotton picker, combine, haying machine, and the nonrow system of cultivation along with vastly improved chemical fertilizers has revolutionized southern farming. Added to the chemical and mechanical advances are the genetically improved plants adapted to southern soils and climate. The importation of new varieties of hardy grasses and the conversion of old cotton fields to grazing lands have dramatically reduced cotton production in the South. Following the eradication of the Texas fever tick and the screw worm, the region has become a major cattle producing section. Introduction of large-volume hay balers has eliminated the use of a large labor force, and hay has now become a major southern crop.

After 1930 the southern agricultural economy underwent an almost miraculous change. None of the doomsayers of the old Farm Security days of the New Deal could have envisioned what was about to occur on the eroded acres of impoverished tenant-dredged farms. Never in the history of agriculture had there occurred such a sharp breaking away from the past. The problems of share and tenant farming largely vanished after 1940, and no economic, social, or cultural institution in the South was left untouched by the post-Depression and World War II revolution. The good roads movement, begun in 1916, was fully developed, the increasing influence of the federal aid programs was felt, the extension and experimental services became more effective agencies, and the old furnishing mercantile system gave way to cash grocery and chain-discount stores and to town and city merchants and implement dealers.

At last the great editorial and farm-agent dream of crop diversification in the South became a reality. The general application of the new sciences to farming ushered in a new age of agrarianism and transformed the rural way of life. A fast-growing and highly mobile segment of the southern population now classified by the U.S. Census Bureau as "rural non-farm" appeared, and the southern black population migrated from the farms to towns and cities. Today part-time farmers with the aid of the new machines and genetically improved crops can produce more with far less time and labor than their forebears could with endless toil.

See also EDUCATION: Rural and Agricultural Education; ENVIRONMENT: Land Use; Natural Resources; Soil and Soil Conservation; GEOGRAPHY: Plantation Morphology; / Cotton Gins; Sugar Plantations; HISTORY AND MANNERS: Frontier Heritage; INDUSTRY: Chain and Specialty Stores; SCIENCE AND MEDICINE: Agriculture, Scientific; / Ruffin, Edmund; SOCIAL CLASS: Migrant Workers; Socialism; Tenant Farmers; / Farmers' Alliance; Mitchell, H. L.; Sharecroppers Union; Southern Tenant Farmers' Union

Thomas D. Clark
Lexington, Kentucky

Agricultural History (January 1979); Thomas D. Clark, *Journal of Southern History* (February 1946), *Pills, Petticoats, and Plows: The Southern Country Store* (1944); Pete Daniel, *Breaking the Land: The Transformation of Cotton, Tobacco, and Rice Cultures since 1880* (1985); Gilbert C. Fite, *Cotton Fields No More: Southern Agriculture, 1865–1980* (1984); Lewis C. Gray, *History of Agriculture in the Southern United States to 1860*, 2 vols. (1933); Matthew Brown Hammond, *The Cotton Industry: An Essay in American Economic History*, Part I (1897); Sam B. Hilliard, *Atlas of Antebellum Southern Agriculture* (1984); Charles S. Johnson, Edwin R. Embree, and Will W. Alexander, *The Collapse of Cotton Tenancy: A Summary of Field Studies and Statistical Surveys, 1933–1935* (1935); Jack Temple Kirby, *Rural Worlds Lost: The American South, 1920–1960* (1987); Howard W. Odum, *Southern Regions of the United States* (1936); Charles Otken, *The Ills of the South: Or Related Causes Hostile to the General Prosperity of the Southern People* (1894); Frank L. Owsley, *Plain Folk of the Old South* (1949); Arthur F. Raper, *Tenants of the Almighty* (1943); Ira De A. Reid, *Sharecroppers All* (1941); William H. Skaggs, *The Southern Oligarchy: An Appeal in Behalf of the Silent Masses of Our Country against the Despotic Rule of the Few* (1924); *Statistical Abstract of the United States*, 1900, 1910, 1920, 1960, 1984 (1901, 1911, 1921, 1961, 1985); Rupert B. Vance, *Human Geography of the South: A Study in Regional Resources and Human Adequacy* (1932), *Human Factors in Cotton Culture: A Study in the Social Geography of the American South* (1929).

Cotton scene on Popular Street, Macon, Georgia, early 1900s

Rural Life

Just as a truly solid South never existed in an overall regional sense, there has never prevailed a hard and fast pattern of rural life across the region. Much of the developing South, and especially that part designated the Old Southwest, spawned and nurtured an arrested form of frontier American culture that reflected the particular environmental influences to which people were exposed. Southerners were not the only Americans set adrift in such a large mass of virgin land; none, however, implanted this experience more indelibly in their folkways and modes of rural life. The availability of a seemingly inexhaustible amount of reasonably fertile land, a wide variety of trees, generous rainfall and water resources, and a benign climate supplied the natural ingredients for the development of a distinctive culture. Rural southerners, as much by individual choice as by circumstance, made dual responses to the land. Some came as land-greedy plantation masters, but more remained yeoman subsistence farmers. Both created an isolated regional folk culture that sustained almost two centuries of social continuity with definite intrasectional variations.

Southern geographical isolation was a central influence in sustaining one of the most pronounced broad-patterned cultural lags in American history. This powerful and pervasive influence shaped folkways by blending old human forms and customs with necessary adaptations mandated in the new country. Though the southern way of rural life for individual families and communities appeared simple and uncomplicated, in fact the regional pattern was highly complex.

Folk Culture. From the beginnings of English settlement to the present, the modes of rural southern life have been compared and measured against those of older, more mature civilizations, nearly all of which were industrially and technologically oriented. Internally the southern rural way of life included social classes with subtle boundaries, but common to all of them was a taste for regional foods, the prevalence of folk customs, the importance of blood relationships, and a sense of Old World origins. Much of the so-called aristocratic or patrician planter class rose from the common yeoman folk masses and brought up with them many of their tastes and manners. Only after the Civil War and the rise of cities, industries, and diversified commercialization did class distinctions become more sharply defined and divisive.

Perhaps it was a tragic lapse in southern history that the rich regional folk culture was denied sufficient time to mature intellectually and economically before its progress was rudely disrupted by war. Few if any of the regional decision makers of the antebellum South truly comprehended, though, the dynamics of their emerging folk society. In large areas of the developing South in 1860, much of the population had only begun to make transitions from the primitive log-cabin frontier stage to a more mature and intensified social and economic pattern of life. In some areas an inordinately long interval prevailed between stages. The stifling barriers of the great landed hinterland had barely been breached with roads, stream channels and crossings, and railroads. The rural population remained almost wholly dependent upon the small yeoman subsistence farm as its main source of livelihood.

Rich natural resources remained only partially explored and exploited. The necessary human talents and skills had not been developed, nor were there facilities, to bring the resources into profitable production. Two primary resources, the great forest belt and the coal and iron seams, had begun to make miniscule contributions to the economic and cultural advancement of the earlier rural South. Of greater significance was the lag in institutional developments. Rural southerners lacked the necessary vision and entrepreneurial leadership to generate ample institutional support to bring into fruitful production the rich natural bounties of the land. Paradoxically, the rural southern population lived frugal, if not impoverished, lives in many places atop some of the richest resources in America. The agrarian population generated insufficient capital to do more than organize and sustain struggling institutions. It developed no important universities, supported no notable libraries, and sustained only a limited number of banks.

The earlier emigrants who pursued with frenetic passion and expectation the public-land frontier in the Lower South moved almost entirely within a virtually impregnable folk culture. They clung tenaciously to blood relationships. Predominantly these people were of Anglo- and Afro-American origins. Yeoman farmer and planter alike transported in their cultural baggage a defined set of folkways and ancient traditions. For instance, a Mississippi countryman would not have felt awkwardly out of place among country folk of rural hinterland Virginia. He would have readily recognized family names and those of country churches and their denominations, the limited nature of rural schools, common tastes in foods, modes of entertainment and sports, and, most of all, the general social customs. Most likely his people had relatives who remained behind in the great migration. This was even more true in those other wellsprings of southern population, the Carolinas and Georgia.

Religion, Women, Family, Community. No social force had greater or more diverse impact on the rural southern way of life than religion. The Protestant church, whatever denominational label it bore, was a durable institutional bedrock. Within a loosely defined theological context, rural southern Protestants were exposed to a strong folk mix of biblical fundamentalism, sabbatarianism, emotional conversion experiences, and periodic spiritual rejuvenation. The great wave of unbridled emotional revivalism that occurred in Virginia, the Carolinas, and Kentucky in the mid-18th century and the early part of the 19th spread throughout the rural South. No recurring social event in the lives of most southern countrymen became more fixed institutionally than the annual revivals and camp meetings. The sustained spiritual results of these gatherings are hard to measure beyond the general observations that they no doubt served mightily to keep the church and denominational torches aflame. Conversions, backslidings, and spiritual rebirths were frequent and fervent.

The social influence of the annual revivals was more discernible. They were recurrent punctuations between the growing and harvesting seasons when either the bounteous grace of nature was visible or the will of God was evident in crop failure. Both were occasions for earnest supplication. In some vague historical manner the annual southern country revival meetings almost seemed to be a link with Old World pagan harvest festivals—the sometimes unrestrained emotional atmosphere even offered a trace of the ancient Grecian seasonal rites of the Eleusinian Mysteries.

Although the ways of rural southern life had a sharply masculine tone, the role of women in regional history has been vital. Homemaking alone involved a multiplicity of onerous tasks for most of two centuries. Not only did the country woman perform all the functions of mother, nurse, family counselor, and spiritual leader, she was as well spinner and weaver, knitter, seamstress, quilter, fruit and vegetable preserver, butcher, and supplemental field hand. She busied herself in soapmaking, tending livestock, and looking after the garden and orchard. No doubt, as many or more women and children worked in the rural South from 1820 to 1920 as in any other section of the United States. As late as 1930 the South had the largest number of women, white and black, engaged in agricultural work of any region in the nation.

In addition to her numerous labors, the country woman kept track of kinships and relatives, remembered ancient folk rhymes, ballads, party games, and the ingredients and applications of folk remedies. She was the main preserver of the Sabbath, lent a softness of tone to the raw frontier, and in a humble way encouraged certain social refinements. However much rural southern women appeared in the background in abstract historical documentation, they provided the solid warping of the social fabric of the rural South in all its ages.

Although the rural southern family was of a strongly patriarchal nature, where the grandfather and father assumed predominant roles in most matters, the mother supplied the human adhesive that held the family together. Generally rural families were close knit and numerous. In the newer areas of the region emigrants moved and settled down as family units, and one still finds southern communities where common family names predominate. Historically, the more isolated neighborhoods were the most cohesive because of family ties, and especially so in the Highland South.

Rural southern families were unified, but members became widely dispersed as they followed the moving frontier westward. Literally hundreds of families in time had members living all across the western part of the country. Travelers repeatedly commented upon the restlessness and constant movement of people in search of new and cheaper lands. Americans are now diligently searching for their blood roots in older settled areas, and southern genealogists, in particular, have produced sizable collections of books, family trees, and guides in tracing an astonishing dispersement of people of common ancestral roots. Throughout the South almost numberless small or private cemeteries dot the landscape, serving as mute repositories of personal historical information that rival the records of county clerks, the census schedules, and collections of family papers. Regardless of the social and economic fortunes of the deceased, in historical perspective they become a vital link in the human history of this age.

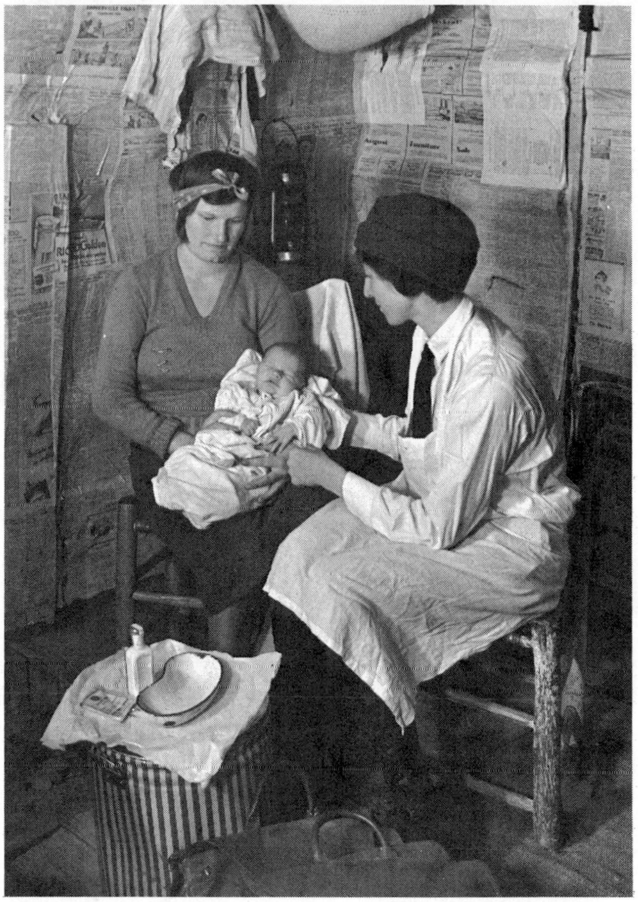

Nurse with new-born baby and mother, Kentucky, early 1900s

Local neighborhoods are just as important an influence in unifying yet dividing the rural South. Modernizing influences such as improved transportation, the introduction of specialized skills and services, the availability of scientific medical care, new types of merchandising, and the rise of urban centers all worked to make the rural southern community a place of both warmhearted, generous neighborliness and of bitter personal strife.

No more appealing nostalgic chapters can be found in the history of the rural South than those describing neighborly common workings such as logrollings, the harvesting and processing of field crops, and the assisting of neighbors fallen victims to misfortunes. Of an even more human nature was communal aid in births, in sickness, and in death and disaster. Whatever country neighbors lacked in skill and sophistication, they made up for in human concern for the welfare of neighbors in need.

Conversely, rural southern neighborhood rifts could be

violent, senseless, and irreconcilable, with the old bitterness sometimes lingering on for generations to come. Few, if any, southern communities escaped their fusses and violent incidents. Columns of southern country weekly newspapers and court dockets are filled with accounts of squabbles ranging from disputes over land boundaries and religious beliefs to straying livestock, women, dogs, and politics. The rural southern temper could become overheated with suddenness, and rural memories of injuries were long and brooding.

In a pleasanter vein rural southerners of all ages generated and passed on an impressive body of folklore. Indian-like, they handed down by word of mouth customs, traditions, superstitions, and wild yarns. In a region subjected to serious educational and cultural lags the spoken word was of historical importance, and the folktale of local origin was well adapted to giving a living sense of time and place. In the passing decades it became rich grist for the writers who created a more durable published form of literature. This rural frontier heritage has been important in the development of a regional literature.

Rural Institutions. The southern rural way of life sustained several institutions common to all parts of the South: the local county seat, the country church, the one-room country school, the general store, the weekly newspaper, and the fourth-class post office. The county seat with its court days was at once a center of justice after a fashion and of public administration, a market town, a local gathering place, and a limited professional center. For vast numbers of rural southerners the county seat was the nearest they ever came to visiting an urban community. Country churches were as varied in forms and rituals as they were numerous. Scarcely any community was without at least one church. The southern landscape from the Potomac to the Trinity was dotted with Calvaries, Bethels, Enons, Shilohs, Mt. Sinais, Hebrons, Lebanons, Mount Pleasants, Rocky Hills, Shady Groves, and Campgrounds. These were as much social centers as spiritual founts. Possibly more communicants took home from church notions of crop prospects, cotton and tobacco prices, coon dogs, squirrel hunting, and local news than impressions of what the preachers had said in their interminable sermons on the subject of eternal damnation.

No rural southern institution gathered about itself a warmer aura of human nostalgia than the general or country store. Seated at crossroads all across the South, the stores were combination merchandising and farmers' markets; sources of credit, medicine, and simple bits of luxury; newscenters; resorts for sage advice; and eternal places for gossiping and yarn spinning. Southern crops planted and grown in words around country-store stoves and on their porches far surpassed those actually planted in neighboring fields and ultimately listed in the tables of decennial censuses. Had the store crops ever reached maturity, the South would have made a fabulous showing against the rest of the nation.

In a region largely without access to banks, the general or furnishing store was a life-sustaining source of credit for the maintenance of an informal type of cash flow. Without this, much of the rural southern agricultural system would have been even more seriously handicapped. In large measure general stores in hundreds of isolated rural southern communities shaped the lives of their customers and served as a cardinal link between southern countrymen and the outside world of capital, industry, and contemporary technological and material advances. Stoveside and porch forums were places where every subject of interest to an agrarian society was discussed, and southern mankind's most complex problems were settled with authoritative certainty.

If older southerners have recalled with a certain romantic nostalgia the country store with its heterogeneous mixture of merchandise, smells, and excitement, they have even more fondly recalled one-room country schools and angelic or martinet teachers. For many parts of the South, the primitive schoolroom tucked away in an obscure corner was the only real intellectual gesture people made in a raw country environment. Emphasis on the "three r's" prepared rural youth to function in a plain and unsophisticated society where technical and industrial challenges were absent. Commercial intercourse in most communities seldom was more demanding than simply understanding merchants' accounts at settling-up time at the end of crop seasons. If an individual became literate enough to read the Scriptures, then he had achieved one of the main objectives of an education. There was doubtless reward enough in a countryman's signing his name to a land deed, an application for a marriage license, a mortgage, or any other formal document filed permanently in a county clerk's office. He could also form a vague and partisan political opinion from reading the local country weekly newspaper.

Wherever a new county seat was located, an editor-printer appeared to claim the honor of publishing an official organ. The modest four-page southern weekly was essentially a bulletin of legal notices, the voice of the Democratic county officials, and a broadside for the advertising of worthless proprietary medicines. Nevertheless, the modest news and editorial columns reflected the turnings and workings of the rural southern mind and, almost universally, the partisan and prejudiced opinions of the editors. News columns, especially those called "locals," while astonishingly puerile, reflected the folkways and the sterility of life in rural communities where little of interest happened except birthing and dying. With an authority backed by printer's ink, editors commented on all subjects, upheld public morals, lectured readers on their decorum or lack of it, and discussed politics, religion, and the weather with the certainty that there was only one side to every question. Many of them crusaded effectively for or against public issues. They preached diversification of field crops without being able to suggest solutions to credit, transportation, and marketing dilemmas.

Literary Images. Country weekly papers portrayed rural southerners in their changing moods and in varying social and economic conditions, and they also welcomed them into the world with birth notices and ushered them out of it with eloquent obituaries. Historically, they preserved the countryman's personality and image as raw material for more formal writers. As southern backwoods emigrants pushed deeper inland, they evolved into a new genre of backwoodsmen. Often far removed from the seasoning influences of refining institutions, they regressed culturally. Early regional authors found the country greenhorns captivating subjects for their essays and books. Such natives as Augustus Baldwin Longstreet, William Tappan Thompson, John Jones Hooper, Joseph Glover Baldwin, and George Washington Harris gave immortality to an assortment of southern backcountry types. While these authors distorted descriptions of their fictional characters, they conveyed a strong realistic sense of an important segment of southern life. At the time the genre authors were writing and publishing their books, the country newspapers ran space-filler stories of a kindred nature partly under the guise of semihumorous news items. Foreign and domestic travelers in the antebellum South left accounts of their experiences, many of which were as distorted as the writings of the professed regional humorists.

The rural southerner and his way of life with its crises and triumphs survived the Civil War and Reconstruction as a literary theme. In the writings of George Washington Cable, James Lane Allen, Mary Noailles Murphree, Ellen Glasgow, and Joel Chandler Harris, he appeared in many guises ranging from sophisticated plantation gentry to lowly field hands living close to the footstool of nature and the land. Whatever his role, he exhibited color out of proportion to his condition. Whether it be mountain feudist, sharecropping peasant, tobacco-stained constituent of political demagogues, narrow-minded communicant of a rural evangelical church, or just plain yeoman subsistence farmer, he personified a rural region of the nation floundering against diversity and change, almost always being confronted by the uncertainties of time and fortune.

A later generation of southern writers peopled their books with similar countrymen. William Faulkner gave evidence in his writings that he was conversant with the earlier chroniclers of the backwoods. So did Thomas Wolfe, Erskine Caldwell, Thomas Stribling, and Elizabeth Maddox Roberts. Eudora Welty's characters are rural Mississippians who have direct blood relationship with the pioneers who moved from the Carolinas to settle that state.

In the field of nonfiction, state and local libraries bulge with personal memoirs and regional histories that collectively detail a major portion of the southern rural experience. In a more formal manner Benjamin B. Kendrick and Alex M. Arnett, *The South Looks at Its Past* (1935); Rupert B. Vance, *The Human Geography of the South: A Study in Regional Resources and Human Adequacy* (1932); W. T. Couch, ed., *Culture in the South* (1949); Herman C. Nixon, *Possum Trot: Rural Community, South* (1941); and Howard W. Odum, *Southern Regions of the United States* (1936) are largely about rural southerners. Even the U.S. census reports reveal graphically the unfolding fortunes of the rural South and its people over almost two centuries.

The tempo of life in earlier years was set by recurring crop seasons, plantings, workings, and harvestings, each separated from the other by intervals suggesting a chronic state of laziness and idleness. The agrarian life in its natural rhythms allowed time for neighborliness and the exercise of a distinctive form of rural civility in both social and business intercourse. Even the drawling speech of the rural southerner in some measure reflected the impact of time and the land, the homogeneity of human origins, the cultural lags, racial mixture, geographical isolation, and stubborn resistance to change. These, however, in time were subjected to the inevitable revisions born of lowering old barriers.

Change and Continuity since 1920. The folkways of life in the rural South underwent marked changes in the decade following 1920. Already the boll weevil invasion had shaped the future for one segment of regional agriculture. The rise of towns and industries, the acute depression at the outset of that decade, the impact of consolidated schools and of higher education, the coming of new systems of merchandising, and then the later Great Depression and the New Deal with its various rural problem-solving agencies—all revised, if they did not destroy, the old patterns and customs of southern rural life. Added to these were the scientific breakthroughs in wood-using industries, the spread of modern highway systems, the creation of the Tennessee Valley Authority, the introduction of the Rural Electrification Administration, and the enormous impact of mechanized farming. Within two decades these forces practically erased the bolder outlines of the traditional approaches and patterns of rural life.

For more than a century the course of rural life in the South was unplanned. After 1920 most of the old rural institutions were caught in the web of failure. The system of sharecropping and tenant farming that had flourished from 1865 to 1920 was on the brink of abject failure. No longer could the South survive this waste of

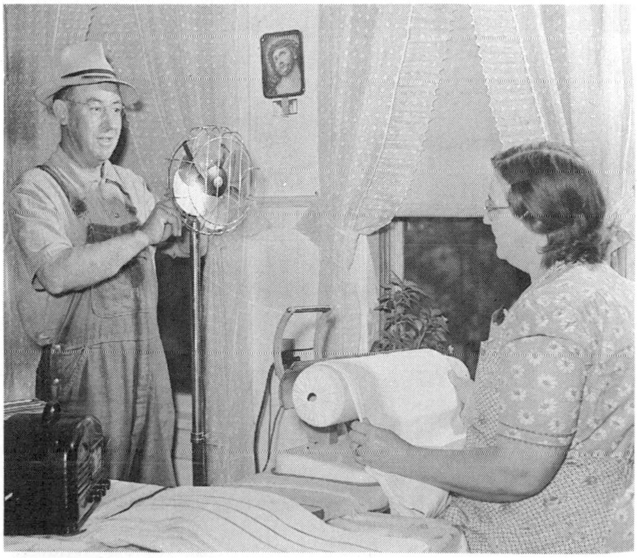

By the 1940s, electricity brought fans, radios, and other conveniences to rural southerners, such as this couple in Knox County, Tenn.

human energy and soils. Both white and black tenants deserted the farm by hundreds of thousands, driven away by biting poverty. In fact one of the most dramatic social and economic changes that occurred in the rural South in this century was the almost complete departure from the land by black farmers.

In reality the cherished dream of a self-sufficient rural America never materialized at any period in southern history. Neither did Henry W. Grady's eloquent oratorical fantasy of a contented agrarian southern population living off the land ever come even remotely near realization. As late as 1930 Howard W. Odum could ask the rhetorical question about the human condition of the rural South: "Are not its white people still more than 90 per cent of the earlier stock? Are they not of Protestant faith, sabbath observing, family loving and patriarchal, of religious intensity, quarreling with the government, individualists taking their politics, their honors, and their drinking hard? Their attitudes toward work and play, toward women and property, toward children and their work, toward the dominant leaders are still much the same as was the early vintage. Both Southeast and Southwest are still frontier folk; the Southeast, parts of which are the oldest of the United States culture, reflecting a sort of arrested frontier pattern of life." This, he thought, still formed a baseline for recovering in the South what might have been.

Southern folk stubbornly held onto cherished standards of conservative Protestant beliefs and personal relationships even in the face of urban modernity. The linkage with frontier political concepts was not broken. Though severely strained, the once viable spirit of obliging neighborliness survived in isolated rural islands in more tentative forms. Change has come most completely, though, in the loss of neighborhood-centering institutions, especially with standardization of the schools at all levels. The crusaders of the late 19th and early 20th centuries who declared war on the lethargic rural ways of life wrought more thoroughly than they knew. The consolidation of schools practically obliterated neighborhood boundaries by removing core centers, and what this revolution in education failed to accomplish the good roads crusade finished.

In this latter quarter of the 20th century, the social, cultural, and statistical patterns of the rural South bear only fading resemblances to the past. Thousands of old and cherished country homesteads have been smashed to earth to make way for pastures and woodlands. Beloved old churches once serving thriving congregations now stand vacant with most of their strict sabbatarian communicants lying in nearby, neglected cemeteries. Sites of the famous campgrounds long ago fell victims to the pines, and few people can now point out the places where country schools, stores, and fourth-class post offices stood. Even villages and towns have succumbed to the ravages of time and progress, forgotten except as names on the pages of local histories.

Nonetheless, southerners strive for continuity. Incessantly searching, blacks and whites on the trail of ancestors have turned genealogy into an important southern industry. Weed-grown and abandoned graveyards, like earlier regional Indian mounds, have become rich informational sources linking present descendants with the past. Four identifiable human interest areas survive from the earlier southern rural way of life: a love of sports, a taste for regional foods and cooking, an all but inerasable streak of religious fundamentalism, and the love of a good folksy yarn.

There lingers on in the southern psyche a yearning to escape into some simplistic air-conditioned and cellophane-wrapped Jeffersonian valhalla, located conveniently near a modern shopping mall, not too far from a football stadium, with free access to a good color television set to relieve the mind of serious concern with social and cultural lags and deficient showings in economic statistical tables. Large areas of the old rural South have fallen victim either to urban sprawl, super highway rights-of-way, airports, or industrial sites. Each year 200,000 more acres of land are gobbled up in this way. The old southern rural pattern of life has been broken beyond hope of restitution. Sunbelt invaders have offered it ruthless competition.

See also ART AND ARCHITECTURE: Farm Buildings; EDUCATION: Rural and Agricultural Education; / *Foxfire*; ENVIRONMENT: Climate and Weather; / Soil and Soil Conservation; FOLKLIFE articles; GEOGRAPHY articles; INDUSTRY: / Chain and Specialty Stores; LANGUAGE: Folk Speech; LITERATURE: Agrarianism in Literature; MYTHIC SOUTH: Plantation Myth; RELIGION: Folk Religion; SCIENCE AND MEDICINE: Health, Rural; / Country Doctor; SOCIAL CLASS: Tenant Farmers; / Farmers' Alliance; Sharecroppers Union; Southern Tenant Farmers' Union; Timber Workers; Tobacco Workers.

Thomas D. Clark
Lexington, Kentucky

John B. Boles, *The Great Revival, 1787–1805: The Origins of the Southern Evangelical Mind* (1972); Thomas D. Clark, *Pills, Petticoats, and Plows: The Southern Country Store* (1944), *The Southern Country Editor* (1948), ed., *Travels in the Confederate States* (1948), *Travels in the New South*, 2 vols. (1962), *Travels in the Old South*, 3 vols. (1959); W. T. Couch, *These Are Our Lives* (1939); Virginius Dabney, *Below the Potomac: A Book about the New South* (1942); Pete Daniel, *Standing at the Crossroads: Southern Life in the Twentieth Century* (1986); James D. B. De Bow, *Statistical View of the United States, Embracing Its Territory, Population—White, Free, Colored and Slave—Moral and Social Condition* (1854); J. Wayne Flynt, *Dixie's Forgotten People: The South's Poor Whites* (1979); Margaret J. Hagood, *Mothers of the South: Portraiture of the White Tenant Farm Woman* (1939); C. Hugh Holman, *Three Modes of Modern Fiction: Ellen Glasgow, William Faulkner, Thomas Wolfe* (1966); Arthur Palmer Hudson, *Humor in the Old Deep South* (1939), *Folklore Keeps the Past Alive* (1961); Benjamin Burks Kendrick and Alex Matthews Arnett, *The South Looks at Its Past* (1935); Jack Temple Kirby, *Rural Worlds Lost: The American South, 1920–1960* (1986); Herman C. Nixon, *Possum Trot: Rural Community, South* (1941); Howard W. Odum, *Folk, Region, and Society: Selected Papers of Howard W. Odum*, ed. Katherine Jocker, Guy B. Johnson, George L. Simpson, and Rupert B. Vance (1964), *Southern Regions of the United States*

(1936), *The Way of the South* (1947); Frederick Law Olmsted, *A Journey in the Back Country* (1860); Frank L. Owsley, *Plain Folk of the Old South* (1949); A. E. Parkins, *The South: Its Economic-Geographical Development* (1938); Ben Robertson, *Red Hills and Cotton: An Upcountry Memory* (1942); Theodore Rosengarten, *All God's Dangers: The Life of Nate Shaw* (1975); Louis D. Rubin, Jr., *Writers of the Modern South: The Faraway Country* (1966), with Robert D. Jacobs, *The Southern Renascence: The Literature of the Modern South* (1953); Rupert B. Vance, *Human Factors of Cotton Culture: A Study in the Social Geography of the American South* (1929).

Agribusiness

In the 1930 symposium *I'll Take My Stand* Andrew Lytle criticized southerners who said, "Industrialize the farm; be progressive; drop old fashioned ways and adopt scientific methods." Conversion of farms into scientific, purely commercial endeavors "means the end of farming as a way of life." In the years since Lytle wrote, southern agriculture has been fundamentally restructured, leading to a decline in the number of southerners on the land and the increasing dominance of farming by fewer and fewer large operations. In the spring of 1986 the Congressional Office of Technology Assessment forecast that in the year 2000 about 50,000 large farms would produce 75 percent of America's food and warned that half of the nation's current 2.2 million farmers would be off the land. Contemporary southern agriculture is part of this national trend.

John H. Davis, a former assistant secretary of agriculture, coined the term *agribusiness* in 1955 to describe the vertical integration of agriculture through a company's control of the production, processing, and marketing of farm products. Agribusiness relies heavily on contract farming, whereby an agricultural business contracts with individual farmers for the delivery of produce at a set price. The company then processes the farm commodity and distributes it for sale. The term *agribusiness* gained a new visibility in the early 1970s, with the increasing dominance of American agriculture by corporations. The *Reader's Guide to Periodical Literature* did not use *agribusiness* as a category for indexing until 1971, when national attention was increasingly focused on it.

Southerners have engaged in agriculture as a commercial activity, of course, since the colonial era, when tobacco became North America's leading export. In the antebellum era cotton was not only the centerpiece of the mythic romantic plantation but also a part of the world economy, as Confederates discovered with their failed policy of cotton diplomacy. For generations after 1865, however, southern farmers grew mostly cotton, corn, tobacco, and peanuts on small, relatively inefficient and nonproductive farms. Low income and widespread poverty characterized the system, which required labor-intensive cultivation. Once established, the system held on tenaciously. Markets, transportation, health and educational services, and credit were all inadequate to promote change, despite efforts of reformers.

The southern agricultural system began to change in the 1930s, and especially during and after World War II. By the 1960s a revolution was completed and millions of southerners had left the land. The mid-20th-century transformation of southern agriculture led to the emergence of agribusiness in the contemporary South.

The federal government played a major role in the restructuring of southern agriculture. Farmers fighting the boll weevil welcomed federal government agents and supported Seaman A. Knapp's programs in the early 20th century to discourage the insect. Knapp's demonstration farms, formalized as the Federal Extension Service in 1914, became a source of expertise for farmers interested

Chicken "factory"—a major agribusiness enterprise

in change. In the 1930s, government policies reducing crop acreage in exchange for cash payments promoted a reduction in the surplus population of farm workers. Congressional farm policy over the years rewarded large growers, rather than small operators, and made attractive increased capitalization and expansion. During the early 1960s, for example, government payments went to the top producers of major southern crops. Twenty percent of cotton growers in the Southeast gained 61 percent of payments, while 20 percent of Louisiana sugarcane growers received 72 percent of subsidy payments and 20 percent of rice growers got 64 percent of the government money. In the three decades after World War II direct government subsidies represented a major source of corporate farm income; in 1970, almost $5.2 billion was handed out.

The loss of labor during and after the 1930s also promoted fundamental agricultural change. By reducing farm acreage, the federal government had stimulated migration of displaced rural southerners to cities, and World War II was a spur, as the armed services and factories needed workers. After the war, southerners continued to seek opportunities out of the South. Almost a fifth of southerners left the region in the 1940s. More than 1 million blacks alone migrated in that decade. Southern agriculture had traditionally suffered from a labor surplus, according to economic historians, but between 1940 and 1960 the decline of the region's farm population was so drastic, almost 60 percent, that major changes in cultivation patterns occurred. Mechanization of farms also promoted labor decline and the growth of agribusiness. Machines were more efficient on large land acreages than small and reduced the need for human workers. With farm mechanization came the displacement of sharecroppers and tenants. Many sharecroppers were black, and the protests of the civil rights movement provided the last pretext for many landowners to dismiss, without earlier paternalistic concern, former tenants whose families, in some cases, had worked on the land for generations. The displaced tenants scattered, but some remained behind. By the 1970s wide gaps in income and lifestyle existed in southern rural areas between the prosperous agribusiness landowners and managers, on the one hand, and the unemployed or underemployed black poor on the other.

Mechanization laid the basis for agribusiness in the South in other ways as well. Although the first tractors appeared on farms during World War I, most farms in the South were too small or unprofitable for the machines. Southern farmers were comparatively slow to mechanize. In 1940 the value of machinery per Mississippi farm was $138, compared to $795 in the Middle West. International Harvester developed a mechanical picker in the early 1940s, but less than 50 of them were produced during the war years. After the war, the machine, combined with the use of preemergent and postemergent herbicides, helped to change permanently southern farming, allowing farmers to cultivate and harvest the cotton crop with fewer and fewer workers. The tractor, in turn, enabled farmers of many different crops to cultivate larger acreage in a less labor-intensive way. Tractors assisted southern farmers as they switched from cotton and corn to nonrow crops.

Southerners, in fact, increasingly turned from cotton to other farm commodities. By the 1960s much land that once grew cotton was woodland or pasture. By 1970 more than a third of crop acreage in Alabama, Florida, Mississippi, and Virginia was pasture, which promoted the raising of livestock. Cattle, hogs, and poultry assumed greater economic significance. Soybeans, though, were the clear beneficiary of the switch from cotton. Soybeans are extremely versatile in their uses and are not as labor intensive in cultivation as cotton. In 1940 southerners raised 7.6 million bales of cotton and 5.4 million bushels of soybeans, but by 1975 the equivalent figures were 3 million bales and 523 million bushels. The soybean through the 1970s was the centerpiece of southern agribusiness.

The emergence of large farm units made agribusiness possible in the South. The small plots cultivated by sharecroppers and tenants were anathema to centralized farming, but this had changed by the 1960s. In 1950 there were 2.1 million farms in the South, but by 1975 the number was only 720,000. The average farm size in these decades climbed from 93 to 216 acres. Sharecropper shacks symbolically vanished, and modern centralized operations appeared. Farmowners and part owners became typical agricultural figures. In the 1940s and 1950s the percentage of land operated by *full* owners actually decreased. Many farmers now owned some land and rented additional acreage. Farm management became a crucial factor to success, and capitalization in equipment was more important for some farmers than the amount of land owned.

Geographer Merle Prunty, Jr., has used the term *neoplantation* to describe this agricultural operation where an owner or manager runs a farm using hired workers. It resembled an antebellum southern plantation in spatial arrangements but lacked the earlier paternalistic concern of planters for workers. Large-scale farmers were the only ones who could profit from this scale of operation. The Delta and Pine Land Company plantation at Scott, Miss., embodied these changes. In the late 1930s the plantation's 5,000 tenants raised 16,000 acres of cotton. By 1970 the plantation land area had expanded to 25,000 acres, but the work force of laborers had declined to 500. Cotton grew on 7,000 acres of land, with the rest devoted to soybeans, corn, and grazing land for 3,000 head of cattle.

Changes in government farm policy, the mechanization of southern agriculture, the loss of farm labor, the diversification of farming, the appearance of large farm units all were factors in nurturing agribusiness operations in the South. Vertical integration gradually appeared in new agricultural sectors after World War II, and demographic patterns in the South promoted this. Increasing urbanization and an accompanying mass market for prepared food brought the centralization of food production and distribution. Women were increasingly employed outside the home and households needed new food services. Dairy and poultry producers, among others, in turn, found the delivery of their commodities to consumers concentrated in sometimes far-off cities to be difficult without marketing assistance. Agribusiness offered a valuable economic service, and agribusiness companies made profits, often large, because of economies of scale from the new vertical integration. Critics charged, though, that individual family farmers—once celebrated by Thomas Jefferson as "God's chosen people"—had lost independence and management control, making them subservient to multimillion-dollar corporations.

In the 1970s agribusiness became one of the major foundations for the economic prosperity of the Sunbelt. By the mid-1970s Florida was the nation's second leading producer of fruits and vegetables, and Texas was number one in the size of cattle and sheep herds. Georgia led the nation in the value of its poultry crop, with Arkansas third, and Georgia topped the nation's agriculturalists in peanut production. In 1970 corporate farms were more pervasive in the South than anyplace in the nation except in the western states of California, Nevada, and Arizona. Corporations owned one-fifth of Florida's farm acreage, and 10 companies controlled 119,000 of Florida's 636,000 acres of citrus. Among the leading corporate producers, processors, and distributors in the South during the 1970s were the Coca-Cola Company, Southdown (a Houston sugar corporation), Tropicana (the Florida orange juice giant), Gold Kist (the Atlanta corporation dealing in poultry), and Southland (the Texas convenience store operators). The Associated Milk Producers of Texas was a billion-dollar a year agribusiness firm. Energy-producing companies diversified into agribusiness in the early 1970s. Tenneco, for example, was a Houston-based natural gas company whose subsidiaries also produced crops and fertilizers and marketed and distributed agricultural products. Much of agribusiness wealth coming from exploitation of southern resources went out of the South, but, in any event, agribusiness was a key sector of Sunbelt prosperity.

Southern agribusiness operators have faced increasing difficulties in the 1980s. Problems developed in the production of certain southern crops and southerners suffered generally from the national farm crisis. As far back as the 1950s, farmers had faced a cost-price squeeze. In order to increase their efficiency, southern farmers used machinery, fertilizer, gasoline and diesel fuel, hybrid seed, and herbicides, and the costs of large-scale production meant that commodity prices had to keep up with costs. The increased exports of the late 1960s and early 1970s created the best of times. Southerners shared in prosperity as the national net farm income rose from $18 billion to $33 billion in 1973. Optimistic farmers borrowed money to buy more land and more expensive equipment. Declining prices for crops in the mid-1970s and general discontent led to the formation of a protest group—the American Agriculture Movement—in the Great Plains states. Southern farmers who had once aspired to agribusiness success had joined the protest by October of 1977. In November a nine-mile-long parade of tractors drove through President Jimmy Carter's hometown of Plains, Ga., to dramatize the cause. Difficulties grew worse during the 1980s as Ronald Reagan's Administration cut back on federal government aid to farmers. The likely result was the increased dominance of fewer and fewer agribusiness operators and the final end of farming as a southern way of life.

Charles Reagan Wilson
University of Mississippi

William Adams, *Georgia Review* (Winter 1986); *Agricultural History* (January 1979); Pete Daniel, *Breaking the Land: The Transformation of Cotton, Tobacco, and Rice Cultures since 1880* (1985), *Standing at the Crossroads: Southern Life in the Twentieth Century* (1986); Gilbert C. Fite, *American Farmers: The New Minority* (1981), *Cotton Fields No More: Southern Agriculture, 1865–1980* (1984); David R. Goldfield, *Promised Land: The South since 1945* (1987); Jack Temple Kirby, *Rural Worlds Lost: The American South, 1920–1960* (1987); *Progressive Farmer* (February 1986); Ingolf Vogeler, *The Myth of the Family Farm: Agribusiness Dominance of U.S. Agriculture* (1981).

Country Store

From 1865 to 1930 no institution influenced the South's economy, politics, and the daily life of its people more than the crossroads store. Hundreds, maybe thousands, of these stores were scattered throughout the region.

The history of the southern country store begins with the merchant. He was initially an outsider who brought a cost-accounting mentality and objectivity believed to be more or less foreign to the people among whom he settled. In the post–Civil War South he found ways and means of exchanging goods and services with a minimum of cash, for in those times few people had much cash. The storekeeper had to connect with northern and western manufacturers in order to stock his store with goods. The connection ran from alleged Wall Street monied interests through the meat packers, fertilizer manufacturers, wholesale houses, and the feed, grain, and cotton speculators down to the local country-store merchant.

Merchants always existed in the South, but their rise to power came after the Civil War. The storekeeper's fate was linked with that of both whites and blacks. Before the war the slave's needs had been at least minimally met by his owner, the planter, and his labor was coerced, but after 1865 this system of control was ended. Freedom, however, did not bring financial security, and destitute blacks and many poor whites were forced to find food from any source and under any condition. By means of "stomach discipline," through the medium of the commissary on the plantation and the store at the crossroads, it was possible to acquire an effective leverage over black and white labor. The commissary and the store were both political and economic institutions.

One aspect of the legal machinery by which the merchants operated was the strict application of lien laws enacted by state legislatures. The liens were crop liens or mortgages not on land only, as was generally true before the Civil War, but also on livestock and on "all growing crops." But often the crops were not "growing"; liens might be placed on them even before they were planted. These laws originally were designed to give planters security for food and other supplies furnished their freed black tenants and sharecroppers whom they were not now required to support as slaves. But the laws were quickly used by merchants as well as planters. The lien system meant that the purchaser of a crop, usually cotton, was determined at the beginning of the crop year, and often the purchaser came to be the local merchant.

In the post–Civil War period credit was a critical problem throughout the South. Because only a few farmers could borrow money from a bank, if, indeed, there was a bank in the community, and because of the low value of land, the lien laws made it possible for a merchant to offer credit in small amounts to the hundreds and thousands needing it. The system created an interdependence between the storekeeper and both the landed and landless black and white farmers and tenants of the area served by his store. The credit often took the form of coupon books, which were valid for trade only at his store, thus effectively restricting competition for their trade. In addition to his monopoly over trade the merchant charged interest on credit that sometimes ranged as high as 40 percent. On commissary accounts planters often charged as much if not more. Many merchants accumulated large fortunes, but there were great risks involved in merchandising at the crossroads. Merchants had financial obligations to their suppliers, and there were losses incident to weather, depression, crop failures, and overextended credit. When rumors spread that crops were not doing well, merchants often sent out inspectors or went out themselves to the farms to ascertain if their fears were warranted.

Country stores can be found throughout the United States and their counterparts exist in other parts of the world. What, if anything, was especially distinctive and significant about the southern country store? Above all, there was the "furnish" system incident to the lien laws, but beyond this was the central role played by the country store in the social organization of most southern communities outside the mountain areas. It appears to have been the chief community organizer and builder, particularly in the old plantation and biracial areas, for a significant period of time after the Civil War. Probably every village and town community anywhere requires some specific institution that attracts, in the words of sociologist Everett C. Hughes, "a configuration of other institutions about them so that they create a community of a certain kind." Population clusters from hamlets to cities have grown up around fortresses, castles, cathedrals, *cabildos*, and monasteries. A study of such central community institutions might well lead through the marketplace of the Greek city, the forum of republican Rome, the salons of Paris, the coffee and ale houses of old London, the churches of New England, and the schools of the Midwest.

After the Civil War a new series of population concentrations appeared in the South, necessitating new community organizations. Here and there a county courthouse generated a town of lawyers and county officials around it. The southern county seems to have been almost as much a social as a governmental unit. Other communities sometimes emerged around a church, a trading post, an academy, or an inn. Despite the small concentrations of population, in predominantly rural areas a fair number of country stores had been scattered across the South before the war, serving largely white farmers, but their numbers dramatically increased after the war. Towns that grew up around country stores sometimes took the name of the local storekeeper.

In the postbellum South three factors interacted to cause the country store to emerge into a position of much greater strength and significance than it had had in the antebellum South. The first was sheer geographic isolation. Roads were unbelievably poor; to travel five miles from the crossroads over dirt roads almost unpassable in bad weather was a problem for every farmer and sharecropper with his mule and wagon. Not until the coming of the Ford automobile did roads improve much, although many discussions and complaints were heard about them. High railroad freight rates added to the isolation. The second factor was the dominance of cotton in the economy. A botanical annual, cotton so occupied the lives and plans of those on the land that it became in effect an institutional perennial, the crop traditionally, easily, and unskillfully produced, transported, stored, and marketed. Under the circumstances, to have shifted from one crop to another would have required much more credit from money-lending sources than most farmers had access to. The third factor was the biracial structure of a society steadily moving from the racial controls of the antebellum South to the segregation of the postwar era. Whites and blacks came to live in two different but complementary social worlds. It was a situation ripe for trade and for new marketplaces to emerge.

Trade dictates a certain kind of relationship for those involved in it, and this had significance for the biracial agricultural South, especially in the decades following the Civil War. Local churches were divided racially as well as denominationally, and they were used, ordinarily, only one day in the week. Schools were racially segregated and used only seasonally and for limited times during the day and the week. Courthouses were few and far between, and none of these played an important communitywide integrating role. So the full force of the community's population could and did focus on the store, which was open for business every day, except Sunday, throughout the year. Blacks and whites in the postbellum South more nearly approached equality in the store than anywhere else. Never completely equalitarian, it was more so than other institutions where Jim Crow laws and customs effectively separated the races. Blacks patronized the white store along with whites and often were at liberty to try on hats, garments, and shoes as they fancied. A white customer might spend much time in banter with blacks or with whites of lower class than himself at the store, but he would never think of inviting such people to his home. There was an air of familiarity and tolerance at the store rarely matched elsewhere.

The country store also played an important role in meeting daily needs. The store stocked a bewildering variety of items such as hats, corsets, gloves, blouses, stockings, and cheap perfumes for women; blue jeans, overalls, brogans, broad-brimmed hats, and "pridarita" (Pride of Readsville) smoking tobacco for the men; peppermint candy and crackers for the children; and rat cheese for all. Axle grease, lard, kerosene, and other such smelly items gave a characteristic odor to the place. When someone was born, married, or died, the store provided the items needed for these rituals of life and death. The country store was no orderly department store; its goods were not likely to be very systematically arranged and displayed. Almost everything was to be found behind something else.

The country store flourished in the days before the coming of modern brick-store civilization and provided a characteristic feature of the southern landscape. The store was a barnlike wood frame structure to which additions were made as trade expanded. A wing or shed added on one side might be used for machinery, tools, and other heavy items, along with kerosene for home lamps. A wing added on the other side stored seed, fertilizers, stock feed, horse collars, trace chains, and general hardware. A second floor above the main floor was often added. Here among the coffins and caskets the local Masons and Woodmen of the World met on designated evenings. These were rural male fraternities; modern urban service and luncheon clubs, such as Rotary and Kiwanis, had not yet arrived. An office at the rear of the building could be added for desks, account books, and the big iron safe. To this inner sanctum, sharecroppers and tenants, as well as small landowning farmers, were admitted one at a time to go over accounts, to make or receive payments, or to arrange credit against next year's crop. The "drummer," or traveling salesman, representing a jobbing house in Baltimore, Cincinnati, or St. Louis met the store owner at least once a year to take his order for wholesale supplies. The drummer was much more than a salesman; he was a visitor from another world bringing exciting news and opinions from the outside and a fund of racy stories sure to go the rounds and to be repeated many times until he came again.

After the invention of the telephone the store often possessed the only such instrument in the community. The big colorful catalogs of Montgomery Ward and Sears, Roebuck and Company, both of which were national country stores or country-store extensions of sorts, were put to considerable use through the medium of the store. Frequently, the merchant himself mailed or telephoned orders for his customers. The telephone made it possible as never before to get in touch with people in Chicago or any other place in the United States. More important for local people was the opportunity to make quick contact with the local doctor, if there was one, and relatives of a sick member of the family.

In the absence of a local doctor or a drugstore and druggist, who often served as a doctor or medical advisor, the country store reaped much profit from the sale of patent medicines. After food, probably the greatest demand by the rural population was for medicine. Prescriptions came by way of wall, fence, tree, or local newspaper advertising or from the satisfactory experience of neighbors and fellow church members. Historian Thomas D. Clark once noted that the manufacturer of Plantation Bitters claimed an annual sale throughout the South of $5 million worth of the product. Lydia Pinkham's Vegetable Compound for Women made, as Clark puts it, "advanced matronhood a positive joy" and also provided a means of getting one's picture along with a testimonial in a newspaper or an advertising leaflet.

The store operated as a general gathering place every day except Sunday (and sometimes even then if a church service was being held there) and in all seasons of the year. Weather and seasonal conditions nurtured two characteristic scenes played in the country store as theater. One was a summer scene. On the unpaved sidewalk in front men gathered on a hot day to loaf, whittle, play checkers, or pitch horseshoes and to comment on the attractions of passing women. In the winter scene men and boys and sometimes a few women sat around the potbellied stove swapping yarns, arguing politics or religion, and recounting details of farming operations. There was a philosophy present in the assumptions underlying this talk, which would now be called a "cracker-barrel philosophy." The weighty matters under discussion required a sawdust-filled box for the benefit of tobacco chewers. It was a spitting society; everyone spat, even snuff-dipping women, if any were present.

The country store with its southern flavor is still to be found here and there in rural, isolated areas. Certain old-fashioned items of merchandise may still be found there, but now its line of merchandise tends to make it approach the convenience store. A gasoline pump is likely to be found out front along with an opportunity to pick

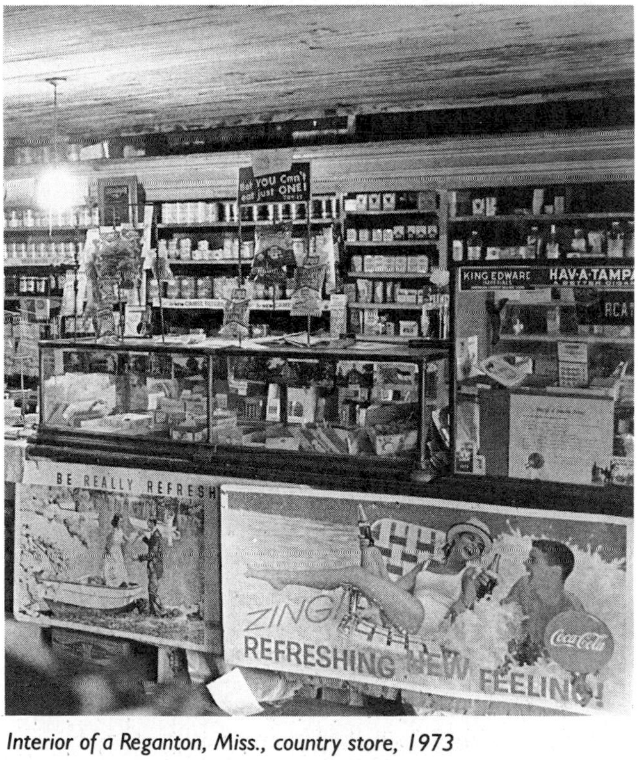

Interior of a Reganton, Miss., country store, 1973

up some trade from passing motorists. Striped candy no longer comes in by the barrel; candy bars and vending machines have been substituted. Cash sales have increased, for banks have taken away the crop-lien credit business. Loafers still gather there consuming quantities of bottled drinks. Between growing towns and cities has come the decline of other towns so that many places, bypassed by the superhighways, are reverting to the level of villages and villages to the level of hamlets. In these villages and hamlets something like the old-time country store tends to hang on, and this accounts, possibly more than any other single institution except the school, for the persistence of such villages and hamlets. In altered form the general store appears to have lasted longer as a pioneer institution in the South than in any other part of the United States.

Edgar T. Thompson
Duke University

Lewis E. Atherton, *The Southern Country Store, 1800–1860* (1949); Jacqueline P. Bull, *Journal of Southern History* (February 1952); Gerald Carson, *The Old Country Store* (1954); Thomas D. Clark, *Journal of Southern History* (February 1946), *Pills, Petticoats, and Plows: The Southern Country Store* (1944); J. Evetts Haley, *Charles Schreiner: General Merchandise* (1945); Arthur F. Raper, *Preface to Peasantry: The Tale of Two Black Belt Counties* (1936); Francis Butler Simkins, *North Carolina Historical Review* (April 1930); T. S. Stribling, *The Store* (1932); Harold D. Woodman, *King Cotton and His Retainers: Financing and Marketing the Cotton Crop of the South, 1800–1925* (1968).

Crops

Southern culture and commerce have been shaped by a basic dependence upon agricultural production. Cotton, tobacco, corn, peanuts, pumpkins, squash, beans, Irish potatoes, sweet potatoes, chili peppers, and tomatoes are crops indigenous to the United States and were cultivated by Indians and later by colonists in the southern states. These crops continue to be major food and fiber crops. Wheat, rice, indigo, and sugarcane were introduced by Europeans and have become major commercial crops. Seed grain crops, such as soybeans and hybrid sorghums, today surpass all other crops in total acreage and were generally developed in the modern era from European and African stock. Major southern crops now in cultivation, ranked by acreage in production, are soybeans, cotton, rice, tobacco, and sugarcane. Soybean acreage for the past two decades has exceeded acreage in cotton twofold.

During the colonial era, tobacco, rice, and indigo comprised the major commercial crops. However, throughout the colonial and antebellum periods, acreage in corn exceeded that of any other single crop. Most corn never reached the marketplace; instead it provided sustenance for farm families and their animals.

Tobacco was the most valuable colonial crop. John Rolfe, of the Virginia colony, successfully cultivated and cured a West Indian variety of tobacco, which he first shipped to a British market in 1613. Exports from Virginia rose from 20,000 pounds in 1618 to over 500,000 in 1627. By the 1630s overproduction caused a slump in tobacco prices from luxury levels to those of a general commodity. The tobacco market subsequently became a mass market. Exports reached 18 million pounds by 1860. Tobacco farming has historically involved smaller acreages and more intensive labor than other crops. Today, southern farm income from tobacco regularly exceeds $1 billion per year.

Commercial rice production began in South Carolina about 1694 with seed imported from Madagascar. First planted in tidal marshes, rice was soon cultivated along inland river marshes. Cultivation by flooding from ponds and then from tidal rivers employing an ingenious system of locks and dams facilitated rising production within a well-defined coastal region of the Carolinas and Georgia. Antebellum rice production involved large investments in land, mills, and slaves. The Civil War marked the end of a flourishing rice culture in the Carolinas, after which rice cultivation shifted to the Mississippi Delta and to the prairies of southwest Louisiana and Texas.

Rice farming became mechanized in the coastal prairies of Texas and Louisiana where reapers, combines, tractors, hydraulic pumps, rail transportation, cheap land, and improved plant varieties combined to virtually revolutionize the industry. In the 20th century rice growing expanded in Arkansas and Mississippi and developed in Tennessee and California. The 3 million acres of rice in cultivation in 1980 generated approximately $1.3 billion in farm income. Rice ranked sixth in farm value among all U.S. crops. Although the nation's rice production accounts for only 2 percent of the world total, American rice comprises one-third of the total world trade in rice.

Indigo was introduced into the Carolinas from the West Indies by Eliza Lucas about 1739. Parliament exempted indigo from import duties and offered a price subsidy that remained in effect until 1777. The American Revolution and the introduction of chemical dyes terminated this once-profitable industry. Wheat production was commercially significant before the Civil War, with Virginia the leading wheat producer of the southern states. Wheat production and milling continued on a limited basis in most southern states into the 20th century. Texas remains one of the leading wheat producers in the United States.

Cotton became commercially significant after the development of Eli Whitney's gin in 1793. One thousand pounds of cotton were shipped to England in 1789 and 4.5 million bales in 1861. Cotton became synonymous with slavery and the plantation system. The plantation survived the Civil War with the sharecrop and crop-lien systems. Until the 1920s acreage in cotton continued to climb. In 1926 production peaked when the 44.5 million acres in cotton produced 18 million bales. Declining prices, depression, war, government farm programs, and alternative employment opportunities resulted in the rapid demise of the Cotton Kingdom, so that by the 1970s acreage in cotton had declined to about 10 million

Children picking cotton at an unidentified location, early 20th century

acres yielding approximately 10 million bales annually, and much of that production was in the irrigated lands of the Southwest, outside the traditional cotton belt.

Corn has been a pervasive crop in the South since frontier days. A large portion of the nation's total corn crop is still grown and consumed on southern farms and in local markets. Commercial production increased appreciably between 1970 and 1980, when U.S. corn production doubled. Kentucky, Georgia, and Texas led in acreage planted in 1980, with the value of the Texas crop $402 million, the Kentucky crop $347 million, and the Georgia crop $188 million.

Despite rapid declines in farm population in the South since World War II, production of most crops has actually increased through the application of scientific farming techniques. Food crops, predominantly those indigenous to the region, continue to be widely produced and consumed. Agriculture and the agrarian heritage continue to play a dominant role in the economic and cultural development of the South.

See also SCIENCE AND MEDICINE: Agriculture, Scientific

Henry C. Dethloff
Texas A&M University

Stuart Bruchey, *Cotton and the Growth of the American Economy* (1967); Pete Daniel, *Breaking the Land: The Transformation of Cotton, Tobacco, and Rice Cultures since 1880* (1985); Gilbert C. Fite, *American Farmers: The New Minority* (1981); Paul W. Gates, *The Farmer's Age: Agriculture, 1815–1860* (1960); Duncan C. Heyward, *Seed from Madagascar* (1937); Sam B. Hilliard, *Hog Meat and Hoecake: Food Supply in the Old South, 1840–1860* (1972); Joseph C. Robert, *The Story of Tobacco in America* (1949); John T. Schlebecker, *Whereby We Thrive: A History of American Farming, 1607–1972* (1975); Fred A. Shannon, *The Farmer's Last Frontier: Agriculture, 1860–1897* (1945); J. Carlyle Sitterson, *Sugar Country: The Cane Sugar Industry in the South, 1753–1950* (1953); James H. Street, *New Revolution in the Cotton Economy: Mechanization and Its Consequences* (1967).

Diversification

The history of the American South has been inextricably bound to the agricultural development of the region. In spite of growing industrialization, especially since World War II, the land and farmer have consistently remained among the most influential forces in the shaping of the southern economic, political, and cultural heritage. Almost as pervasive, too, has been the unceasing call for diversification of agricultural activities—a call whose limited success also reveals a significant quality of the southern farmer.

Prior to the Civil War, small, family-owned farms most often typified southern agriculture. These subsistence units were diversified and self-sufficient, producing corn, wheat, dairy products, fruits, sweet potatoes, and livestock. This diversification stemmed mainly from necessity, not from any consciously well-planned effort. Southern farmers toiled long hours to produce what they needed to survive, frequently growing small amounts of the already important cash crops—tobacco or cotton—to supplement their limited incomes. They were, however, generally unaware of (or ignored) calls by agrarian leaders to practice more progressive farming methods. Instead, through trial and error they developed their own farming system—often employing backward methods—which soon became ingrained and handed down from father to son. This system proved difficult to change. Faced with both limited leisure and money, these modest landholders found their cultural opportunities restricted to a basic level, far different from those available to the planter class. They enjoyed quilting bees, corn huskings, family reunions, church events, and traditional folk music sometimes provided by a fiddler. These activities reflected their strong devotion to family, religion, and the land. They were proud, independent, and self-reliant, but lacking in opportunities to learn about more progressive farming methods then being introduced in the 1840s elsewhere in the nation, especially in the North.

Tobacco plantations, with their accompanying slave labor, were self-sufficient in the 17th- and 18th-century South. In the 19th century, also, the great plantations of tobacco and cotton primarily remained self-sufficient. A growing emphasis upon producing more and more of the cash crops, however, proved a detriment to the land and to efforts for diversification. Both farsighted southern agrarian leaders and regional farm publications warned repeatedly of the dangers to the soil and to the overall development of the South in becoming so dependent upon cash crops. Such prominent 19th-century agricultural spokesmen as Edmund Ruffin and John Taylor of Virginia, Dr. Martin W. Phillips of South Carolina, and George W. Jeffreys of North Carolina urged the growing of grain crops, the adoption of fertilizers, the raising of livestock, and other progressive methods to stop the depletion of the southern soil. At the same time the Augusta, Ga., *Southern Cultivator* expressed the concern of many agrarian journals in contrasting the exhausted soil, inefficient methods of production, and general decay of southern farms to the more productive soils, higher land values, and diversification of northern farms. Southern agricultural fairs and societies reiterated that message. Some plantation owners, especially those in Maryland and Virginia, did move to wheat and cattle production but only because tobacco could no longer be economically produced there. Plantation owners generally refused to adopt newer agrarian methods and thereby helped instill a resistance to change that was a portent of darker days for southern farming.

The Civil War and Reconstruction left most southern farmers, black and white, without the capital necessary for economic independence. To secure credit for equipment, food, seed, and other necessities, they pledged in advance to landowners and merchants part of the crops they helped produce. A crop-lien system evolved, with its accompanying tenant and sharecropping farmers, and dominated the South until the 1930s. It marked the nadir of southern agriculture. As decades passed, more and more farmers slipped into the sharecropper-tenant class and destitution dogged their every step. Southern agrarian spokesmen pointed out the obvious—the agricultural system devastated the people and the region. But farmers could do little to change conditions. They lacked, most importantly, the capital to institute basic changes necessary to alleviate their oppression. Because of a lack of schools or inadequate ones illiteracy spread and health conditions deteriorated as balanced diets became as rare as balanced agricultural practices. Stubborn farmers further exacerbated conditions by using backward methods handed down from previous generations. Sometimes they spoke out against their plight. Organizations and political parties including the Farmers' Alliance and the Populists advocated such ideas as agricultural cooperatives where farmers would control production and pricing. Lacking capital and effective leadership, farmers failed to effect changes.

The 20th century witnessed a continuation of these deplorable conditions. Many vigorous attempts to end sharecropping and tenant farming occurred: experiment stations set up by land-grant colleges introduced new farming methods; farm journals such as Clarence H. Poe's *Progressive Farmer* constantly stressed the benefits of diversified plant and animal production; Dr. Seaman A. Knapp did yeoman work by going directly to poor farmers and demonstrating progressive, scientific methods; fairs, agricultural societies, and cooperative extension programs proposed new ways to confront old problems; the U.S. Department of Agriculture blanketed the South with free literature and spokesmen urging diversification—but all of these efforts failed. Conditions remained strikingly similar to those of the 1880s, and southern farmers of the 1920s were the poorest group in the nation. Not surprisingly, their cultural pursuits reflected their meager circumstances and consisted of whatever they could create or imagine in their poor surroundings: self-trained musicians provided accompaniment to homegrown songs that described the plight of the people; the ever-present church and its strong message of eventual salvation provided solace against the bleak economic horizon. Ironically, the southern farmers' inability to change was accompanied by a strange, but bountiful, crop of writers. William Faulkner, Erskine Caldwell, Robert Penn Warren, Flannery O'Connor, Eudora Welty, and others graphically portrayed the farmers' destitution and in so doing established careers that led to international literary acclaim. From a region that wore out soil and soul rose one of the greatest literary blossomings in America.

The Great Depression of the 1930s, along with World War II in the 1940s, ended the crippling economic system that had characterized southern farming since Reconstruction. The federal government, through New Deal enactments, especially the Agricultural Adjustment Act, accomplished crop reduction by paying landowning farmers to restrict their production. These federal payments provided the capital that had been so lacking for decades, and farmers began the slow, steady process of adopting many of the progressive, scientific measures proposed throughout the region's history. World War II and its aftermath witnessed millions of poor farmers leaving the region for better economic opportunities elsewhere in the nation. The events of the 1930s and 1940s effectively eliminated from southern agriculture the small, family farmer who for centuries had played an overwhelmingly important role in the region.

A true revolution became apparent in the region after 1945: farmers acquired larger tracts of land, tractor power replaced animal muscle, livestock production increased dramatically, new crops such as soybeans and peanuts grew where cotton once had grown, and scientific farming became accepted and necessary for survival in the new environment. Rising farm incomes provided a better way of life and decent housing; schools and health facilities now became available to southern farmers. Outside forces finally reshaped the southern farmer into the modern agricultural producer long yearned for by agrarian leaders.

Diversification came to the South only after all internal attempts failed. This development helps underscore the South's reluctance to change, its tendency to continue with older, more conservative ways, even in the face of viable alternatives. For those farmers who survived the incredible decades of destitution to arrive at a new, better level of life, the most constant of all cultural heritages—the love of the land—still endures.

See also HISTORY AND MANNERS: New Deal; Populism; SCIENCE AND MEDICINE: Agriculture, Scientific; / Ruffin, Edmund; SOCIAL CLASS: Tenant Farmers; / Farmers' Alliance

Joseph A. Coté
University of Georgia Library

Gilbert C. Fite, *Agricultural History* (January 1979), *Cotton Fields No More: Southern Agriculture, 1865–1980* (1984); Lewis

C. Gray, *History of Agriculture in the Southern United States to 1860*, 2 vols. (1933); Clarence Hamilton Poe Papers, North Carolina Department of Archives and History, Raleigh; Gavin Wright, *The Political Economy of the Cotton South: Households, Markets, and Wealth in the Nineteenth Century* (1978).

Garden Patch

In addition to maintaining decorative formal gardens, southerners have a tradition of functional gardens providing, especially, vegetables for the table. They are called garden patches, garden plots, kitchen gardens, provision gardens, or simply vegetable gardens. They have been locales for intercultural exchange between the American Indian, European, and African ways of growing.

The first people of the Southeast to keep garden patches were the Indians. As anthropologist Charles Hudson has noted, "In Creek towns, and probably in Indian settlements throughout the Southeast, the women cultivated kitchen gardens in addition to the large fields in the river bottoms, and these were located in and around the town itself." From early times, then, the garden patch was frequently associated with women and with essential provision of food for the table. Corn, beans, and squash, the three principal agricultural crops, were grown in such areas. Land for these garden patches would gradually become exhausted and this sometimes led to relocation of entire towns, in the search for better land for these essential garden areas.

Gardening to colonial European settlers meant not only working on well-planned, formal designs of trees, shrubbery, and flowers, but also the growing of food. The gentry imported plants and seeds from Europe and experimented with native plants. Robert Beverley noted that vegetable gardens were productive in Virginia, where the people had most of the "culinary plants" from England as well as indigenous ones. In North Carolina gardens, said Julia Cherry Spruill, "were parsnips, carrots, turnips, beets, artichokes, radishes, several kinds of potatoes, leeks, onions, shallots, chives, and garlic." Salads included cabbage, savoy, lettuce, fennel, spinach, mint, rhubarb, sorrel, and purslane. Asparagus thrived under natural conditions, and celery, cucumbers, and squash were abundant.

An Afro-American gardening tradition took root in the colonial Southeast as well. Yams, okra, tanniers, collards, benne, and other plants from West Africa all grew in the South in small "provision gardens," which slaveowners sometimes encouraged and other times ignored. Some African plants and growing techniques entered Cherokee agriculture in the 17th century and were adapted by German immigrants in North Carolina and elsewhere and by English settlers. African plant stocks were frequently difficult to transplant, but southerners sometimes imported Caribbean plants or experimented with New World plant substitutes from the Indians.

The techniques of growing vegetables, as well as the plants grown, were another aspect of the Afro-American tradition. A 19th-century planter on the Sea Islands off the coast of Georgia described a slave's garden as "a small patch where arrowroot, long collards, sugar cane, tanniers, ground nuts, beene, gourds, and watermelons grew in comingled luxuriance." The "comingled" look was the key, a form inherited from West Africa and still seen frequently in the American South. The mixture of plant types together, rather than separated out in orderly rows, seems to create an effective "garden climate," explaining the endurance of the form. By layering plants, through planting two or three plants growing to different heights next to each other, the insect population apparently can be reduced, weeds decreased through shading them out, and soil nutrients and water conserved.

The garden patch was a common part of life for blacks and whites on the antebellum southern plantation. The plantation mistress sometimes supervised work on garden plots and kept detailed records of her plantings. One 1834 diary reported that Eliza Mitchell was growing cabbage, strawberries, raspberries, snap beans, corn, cymblings, and sugar beets. Large plantations devoted acreage to the growing of such vegetables, which were used to feed the black work force. Slaveowners, according to most recent studies, let many slaves have garden patches. The bondsmen looked after their crops at the end of the work day, on Saturday afternoon, and on Sunday. Planters often gave slaves some weekend time to work on these and purchased fresh vegetables from their slaves as a way of providing incentive for their work, keeping up morale, and giving the workers extra money for occasional luxuries. If allowed, slaves would market their produce on Saturdays at crossroad stores or in towns. This trade was never as large in the South as in the Caribbean, but it was significant. Most vegetables grown by slaves in their gardens were, however, for consumption by the families that grew them. The ability to control their garden patch and practice gardening skills promoted self-worth among the slaves. This was a family activity, and the family meal of homegrown and prepared vegetables became a simple but significant ritual reinforcing kinship.

Southern tenant farmers after the Civil War and into the 20th century found vegetable garden plots to be especially significant in their lives. Most of their time was devoted to raising cotton or other cash crops, for which they received minimal compensation. The garden plot was widespread among tenants and common among mill town people, whenever the land was available. Some landlords did not want tenants raising vegetables, feeling it took away from their cotton work, but most seem not to have discouraged it. James Agee in *Let Us Now Praise Famous Men* (1941) described an Alabama garden plot. He said it was close to the rear of the house, "about the shape and about two-thirds the size of a tennis court, and is caught within palings against the hunger and damage of animals." The palings were thin slats of pine, which were strung together with wire. Weeds stood outside these fence walls, while inside "the planting is concentrated to the utmost possible, in green and pink-veined wax and velvet butter beans, and in hairy buds of okra." Insects were a continual torment, with beetles and other pests a potential threat to vegetables at every step of the way.

As in earlier times, the fresh vegetables from the garden patch were an important part of the rural southerner's nutrition, especially for the tenants and sharecroppers. By the 1930s government investigations had identified problems with the southern diet, with its heavy reliance on starchy foods and supposed lack of fresh vegetable consumption. Howard W. Odum pointed in 1936 to statistics that showed the South was considerably above the national average and also above every other region in the nation in the amount of farm vegetables raised, suggesting changes in the dietary habits of the people of the region. He concluded that the statistics "indicate the relatively large dependence of the farm folk upon home produce." Novelist Richard Wright, in *Black Boy* (1945), recalled from his Mississippi and Arkansas childhood, "the delight I caught in seeing long straight rows of red and green vegetables stretching away in the sun to the bright horizon."

In the modern South the raising of vegetables, fruits, and other items in small garden plots is a continuing tradition. *New York Times* reporter Wayne King has noted that "one of the pleasures of gardening, particularly in the South, is reading the seed packets. Among radishes, as a mundane example, there are Crimson Giants, Red Princes and Scarlet Globes. One can plant Southland's Louisiana Green Velvet Okra, Mississippi Sunshine Mammoth Edible All-Star Selection Blackeye Peas, Sweet Slice Burpless Hybrid Cucumbers, Dixie Hybrid Crookneck Squash, watermelons called Fat Boy or tomatoes called Big Boy." In addition to a diversity of plants to grow, there is progress on fighting the insects that always plagued the region. Individual gardeners go into their yards with spray tanks of insecticides strapped to their backs, wearing rain slickers, boots, and maybe even goggles, prepared to destroy threats to their summer salads.

Organic gardening has become fashionable in the region today. One practitioner prefers to call it "biologically grown" food, because that phrase conveys the soil-building process and the holistic relationship between the plant and its environment. *Organic farming* generally is defined as farming that uses natural biological methods. It can be more difficult in the South than in the North because the hot climate dries up the organic matter in the soil, making it hard to build it up. The long growing season and mild winters through much of the South mean more insect pests and weeds to fight, lessons learned by every generation and type of southern farmer sooner or later. Southern organic farmers fertilize with natural rock powder, seaweed, fish emulsion, compost, and manure. They plant legumes as crop covering and they believe in crop rotation. Organic farming has become a business in parts of the South, but it is also important in terms of the suburban and city southerners who set aside land in their yards or on their small farms to raise vegetables.

The growth of interest in regional cooking among the middle class has also promoted the growing of vegetable patches. Southerners in the modern South, even those in cities, are not far removed in historical time from the rural farm South, and those southerners who continue to plant their garden patches and grow favorite southern vegetables seem to hold on to a long southern tradition that unites the people of the region.

See also ETHNIC LIFE: Indian Cultural Contributions; HISTORY AND MANNERS: Foodways

Charles Reagan Wilson
University of Mississippi

John B. Boles, *Black Southerners, 1619–1869* (1983); Catherine Clinton, *The Plantation Mistress: Woman's World in the Old South* (1982); Tom Hatley, *Southern Changes* (October–November 1984); Howard W. Odum, *Southern Regions of the United States* (1936); Julia Cherry Spruill, *Women's Life and Work in the Southern Colonies* (1938); Debby Wechsler, *Southern Exposure* (November–December 1983); Peter Wood, *Black Majority: Negroes in Colonial South Carolina from 1670 through the Stono Rebellion* (1974).

Good Roads Movement

The good roads movement in the South was at first primarily an attempt to convince farmers that road improvements would not be detrimental to their interests. Behind the campaign for better roads was the League of American Wheelmen, an organization of bicyclists, which drew its membership almost exclusively from the Northeast. During the late 19th century the league spent considerable time and money attempting to convince farmers in the South, and elsewhere in the country, that good roads would bring them greater economic and cultural rewards. The league also lobbied hard for a federal program aiding road building, and in 1893 Congress earmarked $10,000 as part of an agricultural appropriation bill establishing the Office of Roads Inquiry (ORI).

Limited funding and a need to gain grass-roots support for a good roads movement mandated an investigative and educational role for the new federal agency. Campaigns to survey road conditions, win over opponents of road reforms, and demonstrate the proper techniques in road construction commenced. As part of this effort the ORI launched an assault on the notoriously poor roads in the South. In cooperation with the national Good Roads Association and the Southern Railway, the ORI sponsored a Good Roads Train, which toured the states of Virginia, North Carolina, South Carolina, Georgia, Alabama, and Tennessee during the 1901–2 winter months. At each of 18 stops, southerners listened to speakers explain the advantages of good roads and watched "object-lesson" demonstrations in proper road construction methods. At the train's last stop in Charlottesville, Va., on 3 April 1902, Samuel Spencer, president of the Southern Railway, observed that the train had aroused enthusiasm for an improvement that he regarded "as the most important now before us in the development of the South."

Eighteen local good roads associations were soon located in the six-state area. Members of these vanguard organizations and others that sprang up across the South during the first two decades of the 20th century translated the message of good roads into language that not only farmers but businessmen, educators, ministers, boosters, and politicians could understand. Their efforts were so extensive and unrelenting that historian Francis Butler Simkins considered the good roads movement in the South "the third god [along with industrial and educational projects] in the Trinity of southern progress."

Southern state legislatures were slow, though, to appropriate money for road improvements. Prior to 1906, not one state in the South had started a state aid-for-roads program or established a highway department. Road improvements in the South were made by local good roads organizations, by county bond issues, or occasionally by states like North Carolina, which sponsored "Good Road Days" where citizens actually labored to grade or resurface a stretch of road in their community. There was little understanding of the proper techniques necessary to insure that improvements would last.

When the automobile arrived on the scene, southerners called attention to the poor road conditions in the South by employing reliability runs and interstate tours. In 1909, in conjunction with the Atlanta Automobile Show, the Atlanta *Journal* and the New York *Herald* sponsored a reliability run from Broadway south to Peachtree Street. During the next two years Charles J. Glidden directed two separate tours into the South. These contests received wide attention and gave rise to hundreds of similar efforts in every southern state.

By 1914, when 1,600 good roads delegates assembled in Atlanta at the fourth annual convention of the American Road Congress, it was evident that the question of good roads alone was no longer the single most important issue. Many southerners now envisioned good roads as a means of uniting North and South, bringing money and jobs into the South. The Capital Highway Association (1909), the Dixie Highway Association (1915), the Jackson Highway Association (1915), the Lee Highway Association (1918), the North and South Bee Line Highway Association (1917), and the Bankhead Highway Association (1920), among others, were all organized to promote the construction of new routes between the North and South.

In 1916 Congress passed the Federal Aid Road Act and funds for the first time became available to southern states for road construction. Among its provisions the new law required that all expenditures take place through state highway departments. By 1917 every southern state had a highway department, thus bringing state governments for the first time clearly into the good roads picture. The 1916 law, however, provided money for the construction of post roads only and had little impact on the overwhelming number of miles of ungraded, unpaved roads throughout the South. These tortuous roads hampered the mobility of thousands of soldiers stationed in camps in southern states during World War I, and good roads advocates were quick to point out the national defense benefits of further road improvements. Article after article appeared in the two most widely circulated promotional magazines of the good roads movement in the South, *Dixie Highway* (1915–20) and *Southern Good Roads* (1910–20). These publications urged Congress to address the problem with additional legislation and more money.

Following the war, Congress passed the Federal Aid Highway Act of 1921. A system of interstate and intercounty roads was designated to constitute the Federal Aid Highway Road System. The Dixie Highway, the Lee Highway, and the Atlantic Coastal Highway became part of this trunk-line system, but federal dollars had to be matched by states on a 50–50 basis, and southern state legislatures rarely appropriated enough money to get the South out of the mud and onto hard-surfaced highways. As late as the 1960s roads in the South remained inferior to those in the North and Midwest. Nevertheless, the efforts of good roads advocates helped not only to increase the urban population of the South but to end much of the sectional isolation southerners had experienced throughout their history.

See also GEOGRAPHY: Roadside; HISTORY AND MANNERS: Automobile; RECREATION: Tourism, Automobile

Howard L. Preston
Spartanburg, South Carolina

John Hollis Bankhead, Sr., Papers, Alabama Department of Archives and History, Montgomery; Cecil K. Brown, *The State Highway System of North Carolina: Its Evolution and Present Status* (1931); Dewey W. Grantham, *Southern Progressivism: The Reconciliation of Progress and Tradition* (1983); Philip P. Mason, *The League of American Wheelmen and the Good Roads Movement, 1880–1905* (1958); Josephine Anderson Pearson Papers, Tennessee State Archives, Nashville; Joseph H. Pratt, *South Atlantic Quarterly* (January 1910).

Livestock

Livestock rivaled cotton in economic importance in the colonial, early national, and antebellum South. Historians, however, have largely ignored the topic. Southern historians and the public have been fascinated with slavery and the Civil War, both of which are closely associated with the cotton culture. Frontier historians remain preoccupied with the cowboy-Indian, rancher-farmer epic enacted on the Great Plains in the post–Civil War era. These topics consequently are richly documented, while data on southern livestock is more elusive.

The first known European to comment on the suitability of the South for stock raising was Cabeza de Vaca, who survived the disastrous 1527 Narvaez expedition to Florida and who eventually made his way across the continent. Throughout the colonial period explorers and settlers constantly noted either the potential for livestock or the manner in which imported animals thrived. Because animals flourished equally well in English, French, and Spanish colonies, the movement of Old

World bloodlines from the Atlantic Seaboard into and beyond the Mississippi Valley was multidirectional and continuous through the colonial and early national periods. Spanish beef cattle predominated by the end of the colonial period, but colonists from numerous European nations introduced a variety of breeds. The same applies to the pedigrees of hogs, horses, and sheep, though the latter were not nearly so abundant.

Cattle and pigs were ubiquitous and valuable. From Virginia to Florida this industry—at first unanticipated by founders of the colonies—flourished during the colonial era, though nowhere as extensively as in South Carolina. By the early 18th century vast herds were reported—some numbering in the thousands. Much remains to be discovered about the sale of live animals, meat, and related products. The West Indies provided a lucrative market for stock raisers, and consequently there was an early introduction of Spanish institutions and breeding stock into the English colonies. From the Carolinas cattle raising quickly spread into Georgia, where a further exchange of bloodlines and herding techniques took place along the Florida border.

Meanwhile, a livestock industry was emerging in the Old Southwest. By the second half of the 18th century vast herds of cattle grazed on the luxuriant prairies to the northwest of New Orleans in the Opelousas region. Had not travelers and officials referred so often to the extensive herds of cattle, one might be tempted to question the credibility of their figures, which frequently ranged into the thousands. Spanish census data of the 1780s and 1790s as well as territorial tax records of the early 1900s tend to substantiate the evidence. Indeed, there are strong indications that the raising of cattle and swine accounted for the most prevalent use of the land in the Old South at the turn of the 19th century.

All the tribes of the American Southeast quickly emulated the stock raising of the European intruders. Though Indians owned some pigs, most accounts mention sizable herds of cattle tended by the Native Americans, at times in fenced pastures. Early herdsmen, whose lifestyle kept them in the vanguard of settlement, frequently found themselves in conflict with the tribesmen. Indians resented the destruction of their crops by livestock; whites complained frequently about the theft of stock, especially cattle and horses. Such charges and countercharges were exchanged until the policy of Indian removal was effected. Although all tribes acquired some horses, the Chickasaw and Seminole developed particularly hardy, agile breeds, which were prized by cowboys and cavalrymen. Ironically, stock raising proved to be an important economic activity of the tribes after they were removed to the Indian Territory.

Mounted slaves—some of whom came from African tribes with long herding traditions—tended cattle for generations, often becoming expert horsemen. Though the use of blacks as cattle hunters, or cowboys, first was prevalent in the Carolinas, generations of their descendants watched over livestock as the culture of their masters spread across the South and into Texas. Considering this experience, it is not surprising that free blacks in significant numbers became cowboys in the trans-Mississippi West after the Civil War.

Although cattle raising in the South did not exactly parallel the trans-Mississippi experience, the similarities were surprising. Roundups, branding, long drives, open ranges, and numerous stock regulations all were a part of both the southern and southwestern scene. Most differences related to the ranging of cattle in the pine forests and, farther to the South, among the palmettos. Hence, in many locales the whip either replaced the lariat or was used in addition to it. Long rawhide whips in skillful hands produced a cracking noise that traveled great distances—cracks that most likely are the roots of the appellation "cracker" as in "Georgia cracker."

Though ascertaining accurately the profitability of stock raising prior to the mid-19th century is difficult, ample evidence suggests that cattle, horses, and swine maintained relatively high values. Because both cows and pigs at times roamed out of sight in the piney woods or on stretches of prairie, the wealth of the herders was not readily apparent. However, estate inventories and other manuscripts indicate that the value of stock was surprisingly high, especially in comparison to other property such as slaves. Cattle, horses, and pigs were favorite targets of thieves, suggesting their worth. In addition to the value of animals on the hoof and of fresh or preserved meat, a ready market existed for hides, horns, and tallow. The local, national, and international market for leather was tremendous in a preindustrial society dependent on horses, mules, and oxen for transportation, plowing, and power to operate various machines. Many personal and household items now made of fiber, plastic, or metal were fashioned of leather or horn.

With the invention of the cotton gin and the resumption of a brisk international trade after the War of 1812, cultivation of cotton increased annually until that crop was crowned "king" on the eve of the Civil War. Nevertheless, herding of cattle and swine remained important, although historians widely disagree about just how important. Nor do historians concur on the relationship of herders and planters. Indeed, much remains to be learned about the interdependency of the herdsmen, farmers, and planters. Prior to the War of 1812 many of the so-called planters were in fact ranchers, and their production of livestock—draft animals, beef cattle, and swine—was of sufficient importance to lead them to experiment with the introduction of superior bloodlines of all types of animals, including sheep. (Efforts to improve bloodlines of beef cattle generally proved unsuccessful, probably because of the lack of resistance to "Texas fever," which was endemic among cattle native to the region.) Sheep herding was not a significant factor in the Lower South until the late 19th and early 20th centuries when greater effort was made to market wool. In the Upper South and border states sheep raising was always more important.

In 1860 there were approximately 8 million cattle and 10 million swine in the Lower South. According to some estimates, the value of southern livestock in 1860 was twice that of that year's cotton crop and roughly equal to the combined value of all southern crops. Regardless of the accuracy of these figures, the point is well made; livestock in the South was far more important economically and culturally than heretofore recognized.

Little scholarship exists concerning the status of live-

Farmer in his Sunday best, feeding his pigs, Benton, Miss., 1975

stock in the postbellum period. The devastation of meat-producing herds and stables of riding and draft animals during the Civil War is well documented. Historians disagree as to why herding by the plain folk never regained its prewar prominence. Most likely the answer relates to the crop-lien system and the rapid repeal of laws protecting the running of stock on the open range. Nevertheless, stock raising continued to be a way of life in the piney woods and coastal areas. Drives of cattle to the various Gulf Coast ports continued well into the 20th century. With the advances in veterinary science and the development of disease-resistant cattle breeds, cattle raising has reappeared, after a hiatus of a century, as a major industry in the Lower South in the decades since World War II. While many of the herds and feedlots are operated under local ownership, some of the largest ranches are in the hands of national and international corporate investors.

See also MYTHIC SOUTH: / "Crackers"

John D. W. Guice
University of Southern
Mississippi

Donald B. Dodd and Wynelle S. Dodd, *Historical Statistics of the South, 1790–1970* (1973); Lewis C. Gray, *History of Agriculture in the Southern United States*, 2 vols. (1933); John D. W. Guice, *Western Historical Quarterly* (April 1977); Sam B. Hilliard, *Hog Meat and Hoecake: Food Supply in the Old South, 1840–1860* (1972); Terry G. Jordan, *Trails to Texas: Southern Roots of Western Cattle Ranching* (1981); Forrest McDonald and Grady McWhiney, *Journal of Southern History* (May 1975), *American Historical Review* (December 1980); Frank L. Owsley, *Plain Folk of the Old South* (1949).

Mechanization

During the antebellum period the institution of slavery, the ignorance of many farmers, the lack of local markets where farmers could inspect and purchase implements, and the reluctance of plantation owners to invest in quality tools retarded the mechanization of southern agriculture. From the colonial period until the early 19th century, local artisans or plantation blacksmiths usually crafted the tools used in southern agriculture, and few implements were standardized. Technological change came slowly, and, prior to the Civil War, the sickle, cradle scythe, and shovel plow remained basic implements for cultivating and harvesting. By the late 1840s, however, more progressive farmers were beginning to use a variety of improved plows, harrows, and cultivators, many of which had been developed and manufactured in the North. By the mid-19th century better farmers also used horse-powered threshing machines, corn shellers, feed mills, and fodder choppers. After the Civil War an abundance of cheap labor, limited capital, inadequate credit institutions, and the large number of small farms limited technological change in the South. Southern farmers did not use the grain drill, corn planter, or reaper extensively until the late 19th century.

By the early 1880s Louisiana and Texas farmers were applying midwestern wheat-growing technology on their rice lands. Although small fields and numerous drainage ditches slowed mechanization, grain binders enabled rice farmers to harvest 15 acres per day. In the late 1890s some rice farmers experimented with steam traction engines for plowing and used elevators for loading rice into railroad cars and storage facilities.

Sugarcane growers replaced the plow with the disc cultivator during the 1890s and doubled the acreage one man could weed per day. The adoption of the disc cultivator was the most important technological change among sugarcane growers during the last half of the 19th century. By the turn of the 20th century growers also were using slings, hooks, and derricks to lift the sugarcane onto wagons and railway cars. On the eve of World War I cane loading machines were in general use throughout the sugar region.

Further technological change lagged until the 1930s when the Great Depression stimulated agricultural mechanization. At that time many landowners preferred to accept government payments from the Agricultural Adjustment Administration for taking land out of production rather than receive rent or cotton from tenants and sharecroppers. Frequently, that money was used to purchase tractors, milking machines, corn pickers, and grain combines. Bankrupt small farmers also sold their lands to larger, more prosperous farmers, and land consolidation enabled more efficient use of mechanized equipment. World War II stimulated mechanization, because industrial jobs and the armed forces drew men and women away from agricultural work. Southern farmers who could afford to do so responded to resulting labor shortages by using more tractors, combines, peanut pickers, hay balers, and dairy equipment.

While southern farmers gradually made technological adjustments during the 1930s and early 1940s, agricultural engineers and tinkerers worked independently or for farm implement companies to solve the most perplexing technological problem in southern agriculture—mechanization of the cotton harvest. During the 1920s Texas and Oklahoma farmers on the southern Plains began using sleds that stripped the cotton bolls from the plants, but mechanical pickers were not efficient until the International Harvester Company built the first practical spindle picker in 1941. Continued labor shortages after the end of World War II and technological improvements during the 1950s made the mechanical picker a commercial success. By the late 1960s mechanical pickers harvested approximately 96 percent of the cotton crop. Because each two-row picker replaced approximately 80 workers, the machine displaced at least a million men and women in the harvest fields after the mid-1940s.

The development of the tractor hastened the mechanization of southern agriculture. Although only 1 percent of the farmers in the 11 cotton states owned tractors in 1920, the later small, general-purpose tractor produced after the mid-1920s was well suited for the southern farm. Great Plains farmers in Texas and Oklahoma adopted the tractor first, and southern farmers gradually turned to it as well. During World War II Arkansas, Mississippi, Alabama, Georgia, and North and South Carolina farmers increased their supply of tractors by 100 percent. Until the end of World War II, however, the adoption of tractors and other mechanized equipment was a response to a declining labor supply rather than a cause of flight from the land. Even so, by 1945 less than 20 percent of the nation's 2 million tractors were located in the cotton states.

By the mid-20th century the most mechanized southern farms were located on the Yazoo Delta or Basin, the Coastal Plain of Texas, and the southern Great Plains in Texas and Oklahoma. In those areas level terrain, large fields, and few obstructions made the farms ideal for the efficient application of mechanization. By the early 1970s southern farmers had begun to use airplanes to dust their crops with pesticides, and the mechanical tobacco picker was practical in certain limited economic situations. Mechanical pickers also harvested citrus fruits and eight-row planters seeded the cotton crop. By the late 1970s tractors, combines, corn pickers or picker-shellers, pickup balers, and field forage harvesters were common implements on southern farms, and all major aspects of southern agriculture were mechanized.

Technological change has contributed to the decline of the southern farm population and agricultural work force. Mechanization also has encouraged the consolidation of farms, stimulated a neoplantation movement, and enabled southern farmers to produce more food and fiber than ever before. By so doing, mechanization has helped improve the quality of southern farm life.

See also SCIENCE AND MEDICINE: Technology

R. Douglas Hurt
State Historical Society of Missouri
Columbia, Missouri

Driver of a combine thrashing oats, Thomastown, La., 1940

Gilbert C. Fite, *Agricultural History* (January 1950 and January 1980), *Cotton Fields No More: Southern Agriculture, 1865–1980* (1984); Mildred Kelly Ginn, *Louisiana Historical Quarterly* (April 1940); Lewis C. Gray, *History of Agriculture in the Southern United States to 1860*, 2 vols. (1933); J. Carlyle Sitterson, *Sugar Country: The Cane Sugar Industry in the South, 1753–1950* (1953); James H. Street, *The New Revolution in the Cotton Economy* (1957); Bell Irvin Wiley, *Agricultural History* (April 1939).

Plantations

During the 16th and 17th centuries Englishmen established plantations, also called colonies, in Ireland, Virginia, Bermuda, Plymouth, Massachusetts Bay, Jamaica, and elsewhere. During the 17th century, however, the term *plantation* gradually came to mean an extensive agricultural enterprise where proprietors or managers directed large labor forces in the production of export crops. Thereafter plantations remained colonial only in the important sense of their economic relationship to faraway markets.

Plantations of this sort developed first in North America on the Virginia peninsula between the James and York rivers, the first tobacco kingdom, and then spread throughout Tidewater Virginia and Maryland. As white indentured labor gave way to black slavery in the final decades of the 17th century, plantations in the Chesapeake Bay region came to resemble those that Europeans had earlier founded in the Caribbean and northeastern Brazil. South Carolina was from the 1670s a plantation society concentrating on rice and indigo production. Georgia followed suit during the middle of the next century. The plantations of the Carolina-Georgia Low Country fostered the greatest personal fortunes in the North American colonies at the time of the Revolution, and Virginia planters numbered disproportionately among the ranks of the founders of the Republic. George Washington, Patrick Henry, Richard Henry Lee, Thomas Jefferson, James Madison, and George Mason were all planters.

The westward surge of plantations began early. Thomas Jefferson grew tobacco in Virginia's Piedmont before the Revolution. The culture of upland (short staple) cotton, however, was the incentive for expansion both of plantations and black slavery. Eli Whitney's famous gin, invented in 1793, was rapidly duplicated and deployed. Both old and newly made planters pressed into Cherokee and other Indian lands. Andrew Jackson planted cotton and grew wealthy as a pioneer in the Nashville basin. Huge plantations and fortunes were created early in the Mississippi Delta hinterlands and near Natchez. A mature Cotton Kingdom did not appear, however, until the fierce Creeks and Seminoles were subdued and were moved (with the Cherokees and other tribes) farther west. This agricultural empire stretched in a great crescent from south central Virginia, southwesterly around the Appalachians through the central Carolinas, Piedmont Georgia, the Black Belt of south central Alabama and central Mississippi, up and down the wetlands of the lower Mississippi, and westward into eastern Texas. The latter area comprised a cotton frontier during the 1850s. There were also tobacco (and tobacco-cotton) plantations in Virginia and North Carolina, hemp plantations in central Kentucky, rice and Sea Island (long staple) cotton plantations in the Carolina-Georgia lowlands, and enormous sugar estates in southeastern Louisiana. In addition to these great export staples plantations produced, both for consumption and sale, corn, Irish and sweet potatoes, peanuts, and legumes.

Geographers and historians have characterized the plantation as a frontier institution, a flung-out settlement form tied to and dependent upon "metropolitan" capital, industry, and markets. Metropolises for antebellum planters were the textile manufacturing and financial centers of New England, Britain, and Europe. Agents, or factors, arranged sales and shipment of crops and purchases of both durable and luxury consumer goods for planters, their families, and slaves. Frontier estates were sometimes imposing examples of foreign sophistication. The interior walls of Andrew Jackson's Hermitage, for instance, were covered with French wallpaper, and guests drank from expensive, imported crystal. Some riverside mansions in Mississippi and Louisiana were furnished even more lavishly. Most plantation headquarters were more modestly appointed, however. The typical frontier "big house" probably evolved from a simple open-hallway log or board home, which gradually acquired a second story, a prefabricated portico, and columns, all crudely resembling the neoclassical style.

During the three decades before the Civil War a planter was defined by the number of slaves owned—20 or more—rather than by acres of land possessed or pounds of crops grown and shipped. Labor directly affected the amount of land that might be worked and crops that might be grown. Agriculturists believed that 20 or more slaves enabled farmers to achieve certain economies of scale on good, extensive acreage. By this measure there were not many planters or plantations in the Old South. Of 8,039,000 whites living in the 15 slave states in 1850, only 384,884 owned any slaves at all. Of these, 46,274 possessed 20 or more. Only about 2,500 had 30 or more. Only a handful of "great planters" owned 100 or more slaves. Wade Hampton III, the greatest of all and a Confederate general, held about 3,000 blacks in bondage on plantations in South Carolina and Mississippi.

Historians are agreed that, despite their relatively small numbers, planters largely directed antebellum economic, political, and social life. About half of all slaves worked on plantations, and their products dominated southern exports and conferred power upon planters. States adopted the federal ratio method of counting three-fifths of slave populations in determining representation in legislatures, and taxes on slaves were generally low. It is no wonder that the status of planter was the region's *beau ideal* and that the yeomanry and professional men alike aspired to own plantations.

The Civil War destroyed slavery, but not plantations. Ownership of large entailments persisted. Various historians estimate that about half of all plantations were still held by the same families 15 years after Appomattox. The most dramatic changes wrought by emancipation were in the tenure of labor and the occupancy pattern on plantations. Sharecropping replaced legal bondage in much of the South, and sharecroppers, who were former slaves during early postbellum decades, lived in cabins on subdivided tenant farms, instead of in centrally grouped quarters. What geographers term the *fragmented plantation* was born. Sharecroppers, especially blacks, submitted to nearly as much supervision from owners and overseers as during slave times. Sharecroppers had no rights to crops under their care, and, despite technical and legal differences, their situation resembled that of hired laborers. In districts where whites predominated, fragmented plantations were often worked by white tenants who occupied the higher statuses of share tenant or cash renter, and who tolerated less supervision by planters and their agents. From the 1880s until about 1935, however, thousands of white farmowners and tenants fell into the status of sharecropper, while many blacks fled the countryside. By the 1930s most sharecroppers were white.

Fragmented plantations came gradually and painfully to an end between 1935 and 1955. The boll weevil ruined many cotton plantations, particularly in the older regions where the land, owners, and tenants alike were poorer than elsewhere. Laborers fled, and scattered tenant houses were vacated. New Deal crop reduction and subsidy programs for cotton and tobacco had dramatic results: planters evicted thousands of tenants and then began to invest in labor-saving machinery. As mechanical cotton harvesters, herbicides, and pesticides became available during the 1940s, the reconsolidation of plantations gathered momentum. Sharecroppers became hired workers and then were unemployed, as machines and chemicals performed their wonders. Millions fled the countryside in this new American enclosure movement. Bulldozers finally demolished tenant cabins to clear ever-larger fields.

What emerged from this radical transformation was the neoplantation. Superficially it resembled the antebellum model: the owner-manager's power over labor and equipment was centralized once more; and workers (now but a handful on each plantation) once more lived in centrally grouped housing. Neoplantations are more capital-intensive and less labor-intensive than were earlier ones. On the modern plantation there is little reason or opportunity for the paternalism that characterized antebellum plantations and subsequent sharecropper estates. Present agricultural approaches are altogether different. By 1955 the West (especially California and Arizona) had established ascendancy in cotton production, while much of the old plantation South was abandoning the crop. Cotton still grows in the lower Mississippi Delta districts and in Texas, but typical neoplantations are more likely sown with soybeans, grain, sorghum, peanuts, and increased amounts of corn. During the 1960s innovative planters in Mississippi's Delta counties also adopted rice culture from neighboring Louisiana and Arkansas's Grand Prairie and later developed catfish ponds. Many neoplantations produce beef cattle, others are huge dairy operations, and some specialize in pecans. A few score of former fragmented cotton and corn plantations with poor, sandy soil—many of them in southern Georgia and northwestern Florida—have evolved into hunting preserves that also contain timber.

Most neoplantations differ little from large farms in Iowa or California ranches—except, of course, where peculiarly southern crops such as sugar are grown. The term *plantation* remains applicable because neoplantations are concentrated in the historical plantation region and because use of the word persists.

See also GEOGRAPHY: Plantation Morphology; MYTHIC SOUTH: Plantation Myth

Jack Temple Kirby
Miami University of Ohio

P. P. Courtenay, *Plantation Agriculture* (2d ed., 1980); Francis Pendleton Gaines, *The Southern Plantation: A Study in the Development and the Accuracy of a Tradition* (1925); Lewis C. Gray, *History of Agriculture in the Southern United States to 1860*, 2 vols. (1933); Merle C. Prunty, Jr., *Geographical Review* (October 1955); Arthur F. Raper, *Preface to Peasantry: A Tale of Two Black Belt Counties* (1936); Edgar T. Thompson, ed., *The Plantation: An International Bibliography* (1983).

Poultry

Poultry is a common item in the food consumption patterns of southerners today, and the regional taste for southern fried chicken is one that has persisted for many years. Poultry, especially chicken, has served as a regular but supplementary meat to pork, which dominated southern diets during the 1800s and early 1900s.

Chicken was most common in the diets of well-to-do farmers and was regarded among the less affluent population as a semiluxury item. It was a popular Sunday dish and was often served to visitors, including the local preacher. Humorous tales about the preacher's love for chicken abound in both black and white folklore.

Chickens were kept on practically every farm and often ran loose in the barnyard area. As a result farmers virtually lived with their chicken flock. Chickens could be kept on a minimum of feed and were much more convenient to slaughter and prepare for eating than either pork or beef. Predators such as the fox and the hawk were a constant problem for the farmer's barnyard flock, thus requiring the farmer to keep both his dog and shotgun handy.

Since 1900 the per capita rate of consumption of chicken has increased markedly, outstripping the growth in demand for other meats such as beef and pork. During this period, and especially in recent decades, very important changes have occurred in the production of chickens, and these had an effect on both the economy and culture of the South. A few decades ago the rural population of the South was largely self-sufficient in terms of supplying its chicken and egg needs. Farmers maintained small flocks of chickens for their own use. Often the demand by city dwellers for chickens and eggs was met by farmers who sold excess production to town merchants. This trade furnished butter-and-egg money for farm housewives. Today it is rare indeed to find farm families that produce chickens and eggs. In place of this production system have come the large-scale and highly specialized mass production techniques involving the utilization of the latest technological advancements.

This modern era of poultry production dates from the 1930s; its methods had almost totally replaced the previous production techniques by the 1950s. The modern poultry farmer has one or more chicken houses growing 10,000 to 20,000 birds per house. Ordinarily each batch is grown under contract with large agribusiness firms during a period of 7 to 10 weeks. Market-ready chickens are taken to processing plants for slaughtering, dressing, and packing, and are later transported by refrigerated truck to widely dispersed markets. The poultry industry is characterized by a vertical integration in which an agribusiness firm, either through direct ownership or contract, controls the entire production process. Such firms own processing plants, feed mills, and hatcheries, and contract with farmers to raise the chickens. Because of these arrangements the farmer has little voice in the industry. Some observers label this type of poultry farming a modern version of sharecropping. However, one advantage of this production system to the farmer is that it reduces the capital needed to start poultry farming.

Today a large proportion of southern poultry is produced by farmers who derive only a part of their total income from this source. The chief wage earner may have a full-time industrial or commercial job while the family raises chickens as a supplementary source of income, or chicken farming may be ancillary to other agricultural pursuits. Labor needs of poultry farming are minimal because of the automation of the process. The management of two chicken houses of 10,000 to 20,000 chickens each can usually be accomplished during the evenings and on weekends by family members.

Several of the nation's main poultry-growing areas are located in the South. Northeast Georgia was one of the first areas to begin large-scale commercial chicken production, with Gainesville serving as a processing plant center and location of feed mills and hatcheries. Both northeast Georgia and northwest Arkansas began to develop as poultry centers in the late 1930s and early 1940s. They were followed in the 1940s by centers in south central Mississippi and central North Carolina, and in the 1950s by northern Alabama, around Cullman County. Today a trip through these areas provides visible indications of the industry's impact on the landscape with the long, narrow chicken houses on farms and the specialized feed trucks and poultry-transport vehicles that operate between feed mills, farms, and processing plants.

The emergence of chicken production in these areas largely reflects changing conditions of traditional subsistence farming. Many of these regions were from the beginning of settlement poor farm areas. They were populated by low-income farm families who had lost a previous source of farm revenue from cotton in northeast Georgia, northern Alabama, and south central Mississippi; tobacco in North Carolina; and fruit in northwest Arkansas. Any new source of farm income such as chicken raising was welcomed enthusiastically by these farmers. Local entrepreneurs and agricultural officials were largely instrumental in establishing this industry. J. D. Jewell, for instance, played an important role in establishing production in northeast Georgia. He owned a small feed store in Gainesville in the 1930s and encouraged neighboring farmers to grow chickens, affording him a market outlet for feed and other supplies. Because cash with which to buy baby chicks and feed was seriously limited among farmers, Jewell supplied his customers with credit until their chickens were marketed. However, when the chickens reached the proper age and size for marketing, the farmer had no way to get them to market. Jewell provided transportation to haul the live chickens to urban markets. Later his company became one of the major vertical integrators in northeast Georgia, and he became nationally recognized as an industry leader.

Today southern poultry raisers dominate national chicken production, accounting for 61 percent of total output. The five leading states are Arkansas, Georgia, Alabama, North Carolina, and Mississippi. Four of the five most profitable chicken companies (in 1984) are in the South: Tyson Foods in Springdale, Ark.; Gold Kist, a farm-cooperative business in Atlanta; Holly Farms in North Wilkesboro, N.C.; and Perdue Farms Inc., in Salisbury, Md. Chicken has become the fastest-growing part of the fast-food business, profiting such southern companies as Kentucky Fried Chicken, Church's Fried Chicken, Popeyes, and Bojangles.

J. Dennis Lord
University of North Carolina
at Charlotte

J. Fraser Hart, *Annals of the Association of American Geographers* (December 1980); Sam B. Hilliard, *Hog Meat and Hoecake: Food Supply in the Old South, 1840–1860* (1972); Edward Karpoff, *Agricultural Situation* (March 1959); N. R. Kleinfield, *New York Times* (9 December 1984); J. Dennis Lord, "Regional Marketing Patterns and Locational Advantages in the United States Broiler Industry" (Ph.D. dissertation, University of Georgia, 1970), *Southeastern Geographer* (April 1971); Irene A. Moke, *Journal of Geography* (October 1967); Malden C. Nesheim, *Poultry Production* (1979).

Sharecropping and Tenancy

Since the post–Civil War years the plantation landlord and the tenant farmer have been among the most prominent figures in the nation's perception of the South. They have been graphic symbols of the region's ruralism, poverty, and cultural backwardness and have exemplified the paternalism, exploitation, and social-class dimensions of southern agriculture. And, indeed, until the mid-20th century these images reflected the reality of several million southerners whose lives were blighted by crop-lien tenancy.

Tenancy was a response to the disorganization and poverty of southern agriculture following the Civil War. Former slaves and landless whites needed access to land and compensation as laborers, but landlords lacked money for wages. To organize production, landowners allowed these workers to farm plots of 20 to 40 acres on a crop-sharing basis. They also undertook the support of their tenants during the crop season by extending credit for food and living necessities, secured by a lien on their portions of the crop. Often this credit was arranged through rural store owners, or furnish merchants, who were also general suppliers of feed, fertilizer, and implements. Landlords with many tenants, however, frequently furnished them directly, through plantation commissaries. This crop-sharing and lien-financing system was necessitated by the South's dearth of farm-production credit. It reflected the limitations of agricultural technology; this system sustained the large force of unskilled labor that was needed as long as cotton and tobacco remained unmechanized.

Although few of the South's landless farmers were independent cash renters, most were share tenants and

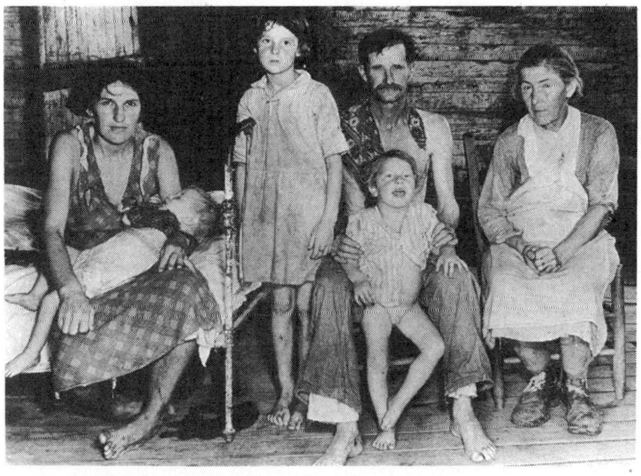

Sharecropper family at home in Alabama, 1935

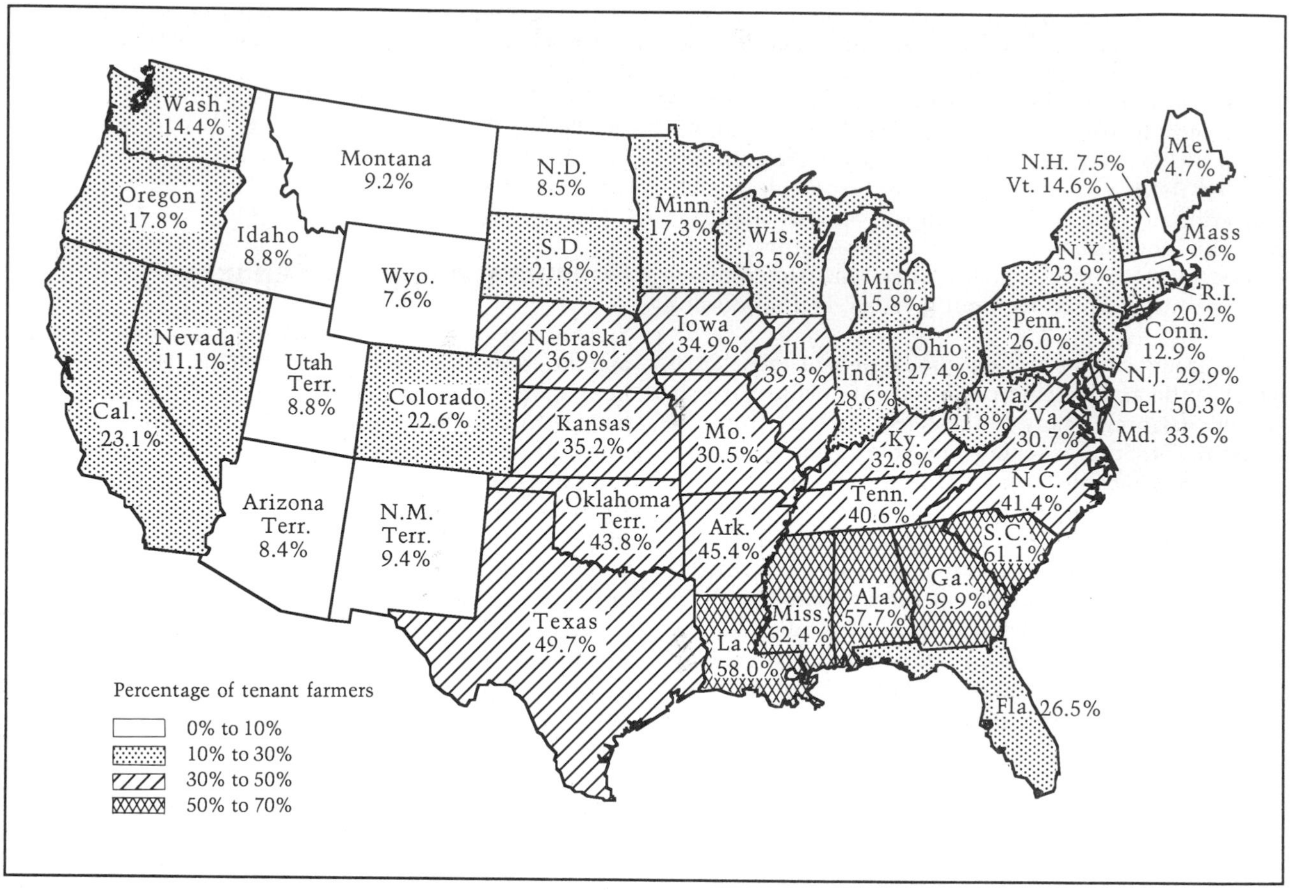

Farm Tenancy, 1890

Source: George B. Tindall, *America: A Narrative History*, 2d ed., vol. 2 (1988).

sharecroppers. These two levels of tenancy were defined by the farmers' contributions to production, their need for subsistence credit, and how closely they were supervised by landlords. Share tenants often owned mules or equipment and might be able to supply some seed or fertilizer. Their furnishing needs varied, as did their supervision. Accordingly, their portion of the crop could be as much as two-thirds or three-fourths, less, of course, advances and interest. Sharecroppers, on the other hand, usually possessed no workstock or tools and contributed only labor. Dependent on lien credit for nearly all living necessities, and working under much supervision, they ordinarily received no more than half the crop, from which "furnishing" and interest was deducted.

In the chronically depressed southern agriculture of the late 19th century and the early 20th, tenancy increased steadily as many farmers lost their land. It reached its peak in 1930, when the census counted 228,598 cash tenants, 772,573 sharecroppers, and 759,527 other tenants (mostly share tenants) in 13 southern and border states. Tenancy was the dominant pattern in staple-crop production. In 1937 the President's Committee on Farm Tenancy estimated that tenants and croppers were 65 percent of all farmers in the cotton belt and 48 percent in tobacco regions. Approximately two-thirds of southern tenants were white, although among croppers, the lowest tenure group, the numbers of whites and blacks were about equal. Tenants and their families easily comprised nearly half the 1930 southern farm population of 15.5 million.

Southern tenancy was the context for a culture of rural poverty. Tenants and croppers received some of the lowest incomes in America, rarely clearing more than a few hundred dollars per year. Their more common experience, especially in years of low crop prices, was to receive no net income at all because their shares of crops could not cover high-interest furnishing debts. These scant earnings kept rural southerners living right at the bottom of the national scale. Cotton and tobacco tenants lived in the fields they worked in pine-board cabins that lacked window glass, screens, electricity, plumbing, and even wells and privies. Thousands of families were without common household furnishings, stoves, mattresses, or adequate clothing and shoes. The poorest croppers subsisted on a furnish-store diet that relied heavily on salt pork, flour, and meal. Owning no cows or poultry and tending no gardens, they seldom consumed milk, eggs, or fresh vegetables. Malnutrition compounded wretched living conditions to make chronic illness a major feature of rural life, as malaria, pellagra, and hookworm infection stunted the development of children, shortened lives, and lowered the economic productivity of the poor.

Crop-lien tenancy was both exploitive and paternalistic. One of the familiar figures of southern rural lore was the tight-fisted landlord who kept all accounts, charged exorbitant interest on advances, and took over his tenants' cotton for debts. As part of the local power structure, planters were in a position to make whatever settlements they wished, without challenge from poor and illiterate tenants. Perhaps the greatest tragedy of this system was that exploitation was built into it. A landlord who was hard-pressed by mortgage and tax obligations, production costs, and low crop prices, often could not profit without cutting as deeply as possible into his tenants' shares. Moreover, as planters extended credit, they also supervised tenants' farming, leaving the least skilled, especially, with little opportunity to develop competence and self-direction. Tenancy thus bred dependency among the poor.

Tenants had little security on the land. They worked under year-to-year verbal agreements that left landlords free to dispense with their services at settling time. With a great surplus of unskilled labor at hand, planters usually felt little need to hold dissatisfied or unwanted tenants. Most landless farmers were highly mobile, moving as often as every year or two. This transience was socially and economically wasteful; it deprived tenants of any role in their communities and reinforced illiteracy by preventing regular schooling of their children. It destroyed incentives to maintain farm property and contributed greatly to soil erosion.

The southern public's perception of tenancy conformed to traditional American views of poverty, which have been highly judgmental toward the poor. Rural poverty was so pervasive as to be the expected condition of landless farmers. Moreover, tenants and croppers were often seen as unworthy and shiftless people who had neither the ability nor the desire for self-improvement. Yet, at the same time, the assumption frequently expressed in the 1930s was that any ambitious, industrious farmer could work his way up an agricultural ladder, progressing from sharecropping to securer levels of tenancy to small landownership. These persistent views were a major impediment to efforts to reduce rural poverty.

The Great Depression focused national attention on southern tenancy. Ironically this public notice came as the system was beginning to break down. As hard times intensified, many landlords cut their own expenses by abandoning crop sharing, discontinuing furnishing, and converting to wage labor. This trend grew during the New Deal. Under the Agricultural Adjustment Administration (AAA) acreage-reduction contracts decreased labor needs and, in effect, encouraged landlords to dispense with tenants to avoid sharing government payments with them. This impact of the AAA was brought forcefully to public attention after 1935 by the protests of the Southern Tenant Farmers' Union. Tenancy continued as a national issue as the New Deal attempted to alleviate rural poverty through federal relief, the Bankhead Tenancy Act of 1937, and the Farm Security Administration.

In the decades after the 1930s southern agriculture underwent massive changes that swept away tenancy. Mechanization was the most revolutionary development. From the 1930s onward the number of tractors on southern farms increased dramatically, and after World War II the cotton picker came into general use. Landlords employed wage workers to meet their more limited labor needs and discarded outmoded crop-sharing arrangements. Crop and livestock diversification and chemical weed control also made farming less labor-intensive. This transformation of southern agriculture was a major cause of the great postwar exodus of the rural poor from the land and, in many cases, from the region.

See also HISTORY AND MANNERS: New Deal; SOCIAL CLASS: Poverty; Tenant Farmers

Paul E. Mertz
University of Wisconsin
Stevens Point

David E. Conrad, *The Forgotten Farmers: The Story of Sharecroppers in the New Deal* (1965); Charles S. Johnson, Edwin R. Embree, and Will W. Alexander, *The Collapse of Cotton Tenancy: A Summary of Field Studies and Statistical Surveys* (1935); Paul E. Mertz, *New Deal Policy and Southern Rural Poverty* (1978); Arthur F. Raper, *Preface to Peasantry: A Tale of Two Black Belt Counties* (1936); U.S. National Resources Committee, *Farm Tenancy: Report of the President's Committee* (1937); Rupert B. Vance, *Human Factors in Cotton Culture: A Study in the Social Geography of the American South* (1929); Thomas Jackson Woofter, Jr., *Landlord and Tenant on the Cotton Plantation* (1936).

Agricultural Extension Services

The development of scientific agriculture to increase southern farmer productivity and profits has been crucial. Scientific advancement requires experimentation, which brings both failures and successes, and few southern farmers could afford the risks. In the antebellum period the problem was not serious, however, because the availability of virgin land and cheap labor decreased the costs of soil depletion.

The Civil War marked a turning point in agricultural development. Not only did southern conditions drastically change, but earlier individual and state attempts at scientific agriculture were given a boost by new federal legislation—the Morrill Acts of 1862 and 1890, which provided federal aid to state agricultural colleges, and the Hatch Act of 1887, which funded agricultural experiment stations. In the South much of the early experimentation of the land grant colleges and experiment stations centered on the most important cash crop—cotton.

Researchers soon learned that their work was futile without effective means to communicate their findings to farmers. Thus, a wide variety of extension activities was undertaken, including the publication of bulletins, farmers' institutes and conferences, short courses in agriculture, and agricultural fairs. Such programs still reached only a small number of farmers, usually those who were more literate and in close proximity to agricultural schools.

The spread of the boll weevil and the relative backwardness of agricultural methods increased the need for direct contact with more farmers. The idea of demonstration farms was implemented in 1902 when Seaman A. Knapp was placed in charge of a pilot program that included five model farms in Texas and Louisiana. The effectiveness of taking agricultural instruction to the farmer was recognized in 1914 with the passage of the Smith-Lever Act. This legislation provided the basis for a large-scale, federally sponsored extension progam with local farm and home demonstration agents in each county. Significantly, pioneering extension activities at Tuskegee Institute led to the appointment of black agents from the beginning of the program, although they continued to be victims of pay discrimination until the 1960s. By the 1980s the extension network served a declining number of farmers, in part because of U.S. Department of Agriculture policies favoring the growth of agribusiness, but it also administered such programs as 4-H, which reached larger audiences.

Linda O. McMurry
Raleigh, North Carolina

Gladys Baker, *The County Agent* (1939); Jim Hightower, *Hard Tomatoes, Hard Times: The Hightower Report* (1972); H. C. Knoblauch et al., *State Agricultural Experiment Station* (1962); Roy V. Scott, *The Reluctant Farmer: The Rise of Agricultural Extension to 1914* (1970).

Boll Weevil

The cotton boll weevil, *Anthonomous grandis* (Boheman), migrated from Mexico across the Rio Grande River near Brownsville, Tex., in 1892. The weevil's annual fall dispersal carried it to Louisiana in 1903, to Mississippi in 1907, and to the far reaches of the cotton belt in the early 1920s.

By depositing eggs in the cotton square, the boll weevil prevented development of the locks of fiber. Farmers relied on the cultural method—a series of adjustments in growing practices—to reduce the weevil's damage. As farmers adopted parts of this system, especially planting earlier with early maturing varieties, the production figures inched upward, but recovery was usually short of preweevil levels.

During the initial infestation many communities exclusively dependent on cotton underwent boll weevil panics or depressions similar to other economic depressions. When landlords decided not to plant during the coming year, black and white tenants often migrated in advance of the weevil—to the west, north, and east. The weevil, along with industrial opportunities available during World War I, spurred movement to northern cities, as did the severe infestations in Georgia and South Carolina in the early 1920s. The insect, meanwhile, entered southern folklore, as Huddie "Leadbelly" Ledbetter popularized the well-known "Boll Weevil" song, and the town of Enterprise, Ala., in 1919 erected the Boll Weevil Monument to honor the pest that dramatically affected southern life.

Several factors favorable to growing cotton under weevil conditions—drier climate, colder winters, and fertile land—accelerated shifts in cotton production to west Texas, the northern part of the cotton belt, and the Yazoo-Mississippi Delta. Natural and human factors kept some areas out of cotton production long after the weevil's arrival. In Alabama's Black Belt clay-ridden soils prevented early crops. Absentee owners of the old Natchez District no longer wished to risk a cotton crop. The weevil compounded problems of soil erosion and depleted soils in the Piedmont plantation belt of Georgia. The finest of America's cottons, Sea Island, was eliminated.

The agriculturalists who had long summoned the southern farmer to diversify welcomed the weevil as a blessing in disguise. For most farmers, the blessing was indeed well disguised. Basic farm crops, corn and other grains, increased, but supplied little income. The lack of a good marketing system and unfamiliarity with growing, grading, and packing methods beset productive truck farmers. Southerners tried to create markets for peanut oil and sweet potatoes, with little success. Local markets were insufficient for the many who tried dairy farming.

Some boll weevil–induced agricultural developments endured. Farmers of southwest Georgia and southeast Alabama substituted peanuts for cotton. Local plants processed the peanut-fed hogs. Southern farmers converted cotton fields to pasture and upgraded cattle herds—especially in Alabama's Black Belt.

Insecticides, beginning with calcium arsenate in 1919 and followed by a new generation of synthetic ones after World War II, provided some relief. But this increased investment in the crop, along with fertilizers and machinery, brought a shift from extensive planting under the tenant system to planting cotton on the better lands under attentive management.

Cotton continued as an important crop, but the boll weevil destroyed faith in it as a certain source of income and revealed the dangers of reliance on a single crop. Southern farmers and businessmen, mindful that the persistent weevil could strike repeatedly, became more receptive to new crops and industries. Although the boll weevil had some beneficial long-term effects, such present-day interpretations should not overshadow the human plight it caused the tenants and small-farm owners at the bottom of the agricultural ladder.

Douglas Helms
Soil Conservation Service, USDA

Douglas Helms, "Just Lookin' for a Home: The Cotton Boll Weevil and the South" (Ph.D. dissertation, Florida State University, 1977); Walter D. Hunter and Warren E. Hinds, *Mexican Cotton-Boll Weevil*, Bureau of Entomology Bulletin No. 114, S. Doc. 305, 62d Congress, 2d sess., 1912; Arthur F. Raper, *Preface to Peasantry: A Tale of Two Black Belt Counties* (1936).

Communal Farms

Scholarly attention has focused on the large, successful, and well-known communal farms of the Northeast—including those of the Shakers, the Harmony Society, and Oneida. There have been, however, a number of significant communities in the South. The Shakers established Pleasant Hill and South Union in Kentucky in the early 1800s. Nashoba, an interracial Tennessee commune, was founded east of Memphis on the Wolf River in 1825 by Frances Wright, a reformer from Scotland. The name for the community derived from the Indian word for wolf. The experiment lasted until 1828 and was intended as a model society for slaves, whom Wright and her followers purchased and prepared for freedom, and for whites, who lived in a cooperative arrangement based on the ideas of reformer Robert Dale Owen. Wright left Nashoba in 1828 for Owen's New Harmony commune in Indiana, and the Tennessee settlement was gradually phased out. Another notable communal farm was founded by Cyrus R. Teed at Estero, Fla. Its basis was the philosophy of Koreshanity, which claimed to explain the astronomical and religious principles of the universe, and it lasted from about 1900 to 1917.

Clarence Jordon, a Georgia Baptist preacher, conceived the idea for Koinonia Farms, a Christian community that began operations near Americus, Ga., in 1942. The name for the farm came from the Greek word for "fellowship" or "communism," and the intent of its founders was for the community to share its worldly goods. It was to be a religious and a material inspiration to the surrounding impoverished rural areas of south Georgia.

The residents experimented with new scientific techniques for raising poultry and livestock and taught them to other farmers. The farm later successfully grew grapes, pecans, and peanuts, providing an adequate income for the group. Despite its economic success, Koinonia Farms became controversial in the 1950s and 1960s because of the vocal support of its members for racial equality and pacifism. Physical violence and an economic boycott from nearby whites challenged its survival, but it outlasted these threats. The community, which in the early 1980s included about 50 people living at Koinonia, has most recently launched a program to provide low-cost housing to Georgia's rural poor.

In the late 1960s and early 1970s a new wave of community building began. These communal experiments grew out of the counterculture. Many of these latter-day communards were veterans of the civil rights movement, Vietnam War protests, and campus-reform struggles. Of the modern communes in the South, two are especially noteworthy.

The first of these is called Twin Oaks, a commune near Louisa, Va. Inspired by B. F. Skinner's novel *Walden Two* (1948), Twin Oaks was started by eight people committed to the principles of behaviorist psychology. In June of 1967 they moved onto a 123-acre farm purchased from a retired tobacco farmer. Farming supplies food for the group, and their income is supplemented by the sale of handwoven hammocks. Although many other communes have not worked, Twin Oaks is a thriving enterprise in large part because of firm rules on work and cooperation. As of 1983 the community had grown to include some 80 members.

Another intriguing escape from the mainstream of American life is The Farm in Summertown, Tenn., about 80 miles southwest of Nashville. In 1970 Stephen Gaskin led a group of San Francisco hippies from California to this 1,750-acre farm. Like Twin Oaks, The Farm is based on a mixture of idealism and practicality. The Farm has a number of businesses—including a book-publishing company, a mail-order food store, and a CB-repair operation. The Farm has its own international relief organization, called PLENTY, which is recognized by the United Nations. The Farm is organized along the lines of a religious group, following the teachings of Stephen Gaskin, which are based on a combination of Judaeo-Christian ethics and Eastern mysticism. By 1983 The Farm had 950 members in Summertown, making it easily the largest working commune in America. In the future the South may continue to attract more social experiments like communes because of the benign agricultural climate, the relatively low price of land, and the increasingly tolerant attitude of southerners toward alternative lifestyles.

See also RELIGION: / Shakers

Angus K. Gillespie
Rutgers University

Stephen Gaskin, *Monday Night Class* (1974); Rosabeth Moss Kanter, *Commitment and Community: Communes and Utopias in Sociological Perspective* (1972); Kathleen Kinkade, *A Walden Two Experiment: The First Five Years of Twin Oaks Community* (1973).

Corn

Corn today has over 500 industrial uses, most of them little known. For nearly three centuries maize or Indian corn had scores of everyday uses in the South, far more than all other crops combined. The area devoted to corn production in the South in 1920 was 46 million acres, the high point in acreage. That represented 44.6 percent of the nation's total. As food it was basic to survival. Southerners, like other rural Americans, ate it as roasting ears, popcorn, hominy grits, cornbread, dodgers, hoecake, johnny cake, pone, mush, fritters, spoon bread, pudding, porridge, parched corn, fish-frying batter, Hoppin' John (with peas), succotash (with beans), cornstarch, and in the Southwest, tamales, tortillas, atole, and posole. They consumed it with meats and sweets and washed it down with corn liquor. This staple grain was on the southern table in some form at practically every meal.

The horses, mules, and oxen that helped to produce crops ate their share of corn, as did the hogs and poultry so vital to southern diets. As animal feed, corn topped all other crops by a wide margin. It was fed green in growing season and as dried grain, fodder, and silage during other months.

Southerners employed corn for nonfood purposes that

all but stagger the imagination. They used cobs for pipes, torches, corn shellers, tool handlers, jug stoppers, fishing corks, back scratchers, litter, hair curlers, missiles (for the popular corncob fights), salt and pepper shakers (hollowed), knothole plugs, and, above all, kindling. Other Americans certainly used corn products in the same ways, but probably not to the same extent for so long a time as southerners.

Corn, cornmeal, and whiskey served as money to pay millers, weavers, preachers, and taxes, and whiskey was a universal home medicine. Ears of corn were used as darning eggs and as ornaments. Grains served as jewelry and as popcorn Christmas tree strings and were used in games such as bingo and hully gully.

Not to be outdone by the grains they yielded, husks (shucks) had a wide range of uses. They became dolls, dusters, writing paper, weaving material for chair backs, padding for pillows and mattresses, packing for fruits, vegetables, and fragiles, and wrapping for sausages, tamales, ash cakes, and cigarettes. Even silks were useful. Settlers smoked them as tobacco, formed them as hair for dolls, and steeped them to make medicines. Stalks and leaves were adapted for use as scarecrows, bamboo-like fences, thatching, and for erosion stoppage. Fodder became insulation in and outside cabins, and fodder stacks and shocks occasionally served as shelter for families at nights and during bad weather or as places for drunks to sleep off their corn-liquor overdose.

Corn was, without serious rival, the universal plant of the South. Little wonder that southerners fashioned around it a culture of language, literature, poetry, music, art, and humor.

Nicholas P. Hardeman
California State University

Nicholas P. Hardeman, *Shucks, Shoes, and Hominy Blocks: Corn as a Way of Life in Pioneer America* (1981); Sam B. Hilliard, *Hog Meat and Hoecake: Food Supply in the Old South, 1840–1860* (1972); Paul Weatherwax, *Indian Corn in Old America* (1954).

Cotton Culture

After the invention of the cotton gin in 1793, cotton spread southwestward. It was cultivated on plantations using slave labor and on small farms. The South produced 2,982,634 bales in 1855 and harvested 4,861,292 in 1859. The Civil War ended slavery, and after a struggle over tenure arrangements, a sharecropping and crop-lien system emerged that absorbed not only former slaves but also increasing numbers of white farmers who had lost their land. Between World War I and the Great Depression, cotton production shifted dramatically to the West. Cotton plantings in the eastern part of the cotton belt declined from 12 million acres in the 1910–14 years to 8.8 million by 1932. Depression and federal acreage-control policies marked the beginning of a new era as planters dismissed sharecroppers, replaced them with wage hands, and later turned to tractors. During World War II the mechanical cotton picker came on the market and pushed millions of farmers off the land. Cotton acreage dropped from 25 million acres in 1940 to 17.5 in 1945. In 1860 approximately two-thirds of all American cotton was produced in the area east of the Mississippi River, but a century later this area was producing only a third of the national total. Currently more cotton is grown west of the Mississippi River than in the old areas of production in the Southeast.

Cotton farmers began their work in the spring, breaking the land, running rows, and planting. After the plants emerged, constant chopping and hoeing continued until lay-by time in midsummer. In the autumn when the bolls matured and opened into fluffy locks, workers picked the seed cotton; then it was ginned for sale. Under slavery, the plantation owner or a white overseer supervised the cultivation of the crop, and a black driver served as field foreman. Some plantations operated a task system that allowed slaves to complete a set amount of work each day, and others used a gang system that required all slaves to work together. After emancipation sharecroppers made verbal contracts during the Christmas season, sometimes received an advance in wages from the landlord, and arranged for credit at a local store. This furnishing arrangement customarily ran only to lay-by time, so sharecroppers had to work at odd jobs to supplement their incomes. At settlement time, much of their share of the crop paid back the exorbitant interest charged by "time" furnishing merchants. Many sharecroppers drifted into a state of peonage, a form of debt bondage that bound them to the land. Croppers moved often, usually within the same community. Most lived in primitive and unsanitary shacks, and the condition of their lives was characterized by illiteracy, poor health, and inadequate food.

In the last decade of the 19th century, the Mexican cotton boll weevil crossed the Rio Grande River and began eating its way northeastward through the cotton belt. All attempts to halt its march failed, but by utilizing cultivation practices developed by the extension service, farmers continued to grow adequate yields. The weevil did not infest western areas as much as the older growing region, and the cost of production in the latter area increased and put farmers in a poor competitive position. As much as any single factor, the weevil hastened cotton's march westward, although mechanization and the lack of a sharecropping system in western areas were also important in the shift.

In the early years of the New Deal, the Agricultural Adjustment Administration (AAA) drastically reduced acreage, and millions of farmers were forced off the land, despite AAA contracts that forbade displacement of tenants. As small owners and sharecroppers attempted to cope with acreage reduction, federal money fueled the drive toward mechanization. Before complete mechanization occurred after World War II, landowners utilized wage laborers to perform the seasonal chopping and picking chores. Many former sharecroppers survived by securing relief from government programs, and large numbers of exfarmers fled to northern cities in search of work and survival.

After 1945, with the perfection of the mechanical picker, there was little need for large numbers of farm workers in the cotton area. The old southern cotton-area farmers could not take advantage of mechanization as well as those of the West. Largely replacing cotton as a southern staple were soybeans, cattle, peanuts, and other crops. Whereas the old cotton culture was highly exploitative, the changes set in motion by the New Deal and by mechanization exacted a high human cost. In some respects it was a mechanical enclosure movement that forced farmers off the land into cities. By 1968 about 94 percent of the cotton crop was machine harvested. The cotton culture that had epitomized the slave and post–Civil War South continued its migration to the West, leaving behind diversified farming on enlarged units. The term *cotton South* became almost solely historical in its meaning.

Pete Daniel
Smithsonian Institution
Washington, D.C.

David E. Conrad, *The Forgotten Farmers: The Story of Sharecroppers in the New Deal* (1965); Pete Daniel, *Breaking the Land: The Transformation of Cotton, Tobacco, and Rice Cultures since 1880* (1985); Gilbert C. Fite, *Agricultural History* (January 1980); Eugene D. Genovese, *Roll, Jordan, Roll: The World the Slaves Made* (1974); Donald H. Grubbs, *Cry from the Cotton: The Southern Tenant Farmers' Union and the New Deal* (1971); Henry I. Richards, *Cotton and the Agricultural Adjustment Administration* (1936); Theodore Rosengarten, *All God's Dangers: The Life of Nate Shaw* (1974); James H. Street, *The New Revolution in the Cotton Economy* (1957); Harold D. Woodman, *Journal of Southern History* (November 1977).

Dairy Industry

Production of milk and dairy products in the early South differed insignificantly from that in the North. Considerable divergence appeared in the 19th century, though, because of slower urban growth in the South. While the old dairy belt emerged in the North to supply milk for commercially manufactured dairy products in a national market and fluid milk to large cities, southerners haphazardly supplied their towns with fluid milk, made their own butter, and at times bought canned milk and cheese produced in the North.

The dairy picture in the South changed surprisingly little from the 19th century until about World War II. During that era all across the region many small farmers kept and milked a few, often mixed-breed cows, separated the milk, fed the skim to the hogs, made their own butter, and sold the surplus cream in town or shipped it on the railroad to market. Along with the sale of a few eggs, this trade allowed them a small but steady cash flow. By the 1930s an increasing number of small cheese-manufacturing plants had appeared in the South, and better roads brought motor-truck carriers to pick up whole grade B milk from many small unspecialized producers. Near the towns, dairy specialists milked cows, bottled fluid milk, and sold it to town residents. At the same time, dairymen near larger cities were selling fluid milk to processors who pasteurized it and sold it on the local market.

From World War II onward the growth of highways and urban centers in the South transformed dairy production, processing, and marketing. The small grade B, or manufacturing, milk producer swiftly disappeared, and dairy farming in the South became more specialized than in any place other than California and the Far West. By the 1960s the average cow population of Texas dairy farms was roughly twice that of Wisconsin, a state whose total dairy production dwarfed that of any other state in the Union. During the 1970s efforts toward market rationalization and integration, carried on by large merged milk-producer cooperatives, increasingly blurred distinctions between dairy farming in the South and the rest of the nation.

E. Dale Odom
North Texas State University

Lewis C. Gray, *History of Agriculture in the Southern United States to 1860*, 2 vols. (1933); Thomas R. Pirtle, *History of the Dairy Industry* (1926); John T. Schlebecker, *History of American Dairying* (1967).

Farm Security Administration

During the Great Depression the New Deal administration wrestled with the problem of massive and chronic rural poverty. Between 1935 and 1946 the Farm Security Administration (FSA) was the federal agency that worked to uplift some of America's poorest people.

The FSA began as the Resettlement Administration (RA), created by President Franklin D. Roosevelt's executive order in May 1935. The RA consolidated federal programs for classifying rural land, retiring submarginal farms, and resettling their residents. Also transferred to the RA were rural subsistence homesteads for surplus industrial workers, pilot suburban housing projects, and several cooperative farm communities started with federal relief funds. But the largest responsibility assigned to the new agency was the rural rehabilitation work of the Federal Emergency Relief Administration (FERA). Faced with the urgent needs of destitute farmers, especially southern tenants and sharecroppers, the FERA had attempted to keep them on the land with a combination of production and living credit and close supervision of their farming. Acquiring this rapidly growing program made the RA an antipoverty agency.

The RA's responsibilities expanded in July 1937, when Congress passed the Bankhead-Jones Farm Tenancy Act providing a modest lending program to help tenants buy farms. President Roosevelt assigned this new work to the RA, which was renamed the Farm Security Administration.

Even though the FSA never reached a majority of the poor, and often bypassed the most impoverished, its programs gave substantial aid to many farmers during its peak years of 1937–42. The largest program was always rural rehabilitation. The FSA's 1941 report, for example, indicated loans or grants (typically a few hundred dollars per case) being received by more than 600,000 southern families. County FSA supervisors helped clients write farm- and home-management plans and gave technical advice. At its best this supervision improved the farming skills, self-direction, nutrition, and health of the poor. Among other programs the FSA promoted for low-income farmers were cooperatives for marketing produce and purchasing supplies, joint ownership of breeding livestock or machinery, farm-improvement loans, prepaid health-care plans, and debt-adjustment loans. However, farm-purchase lending under the Bankhead-Jones Act was so poorly funded that the FSA could serve only a few thousand borrowers per year, making little impact on tenancy.

Under southern administrators Will W. Alexander (1936–40) and Calvin B. Baldwin (1940–43), the FSA attempted a comprehensive attack on rural poverty, but its efforts were short-lived. Congress slashed the FSA's funds during World War II and disbanded it in 1946. A few of the FSA's credit functions survive in a successor agency, the Farmers' Home Administration.

Paul E. Mertz
University of Wisconsin
Stevens Point

Sidney Baldwin, *Poverty and Politics: The Rise and Decline of the Farm Security Administration* (1968); Paul E. Mertz, *New Deal Policy and Southern Rural Poverty* (1978).

Fertilizer

In the 1840s and 1850s an agricultural reform movement occurred in the South as planters and farmers sought some means of restoring their worn-out fields. Farm journals of the period recommended increased use of lime and manures. At the same time superphosphate and Peruvian guano were introduced as commercial fertilizers. By 1860 their use had spread from Maryland and Virginia into the Carolinas and Georgia.

After the Civil War the problems of exhausted land and quick returns on cotton and tobacco crops combined to greatly accelerate the use of fertilizers. To meet this demand the fertilizer industry began to move southward. In 1868 development of the South Carolina phosphate deposits began, and Charleston soon became an important fertilizer center. In the 1890s new phosphate mines in Florida and Tennessee came into production.

Fertilizer was in most demand for use on cotton, and a

Billboard advertising fertilizer, Laurinburg, N.C., 1938

mixed product (in 200-pound bags) containing the three principal plant nutrients (nitrogen, phosphorus, and potassium) was popular with southern farmers. Many farmers commonly prepared their own mixtures by combining superphosphate and kainit (a potash salt) with cottonseed meal. The general use of fertilizers had several effects on southern culture. The cotton and tobacco belts were extended into areas where their cultivation was previously unprofitable. The old compost heap was abandoned, and farmers tended to limit cultivation to old upland fields. Commercial fertilizers stimulated intensive farming, particularly in trucking areas, and assured higher yields per acre. Finally, the use of commercial fertilizers was responsible for bringing the fertilizer industry to the South.

During the 1880s the South benefited from the Morrill Act of 1862, which provided for state colleges of agriculture, and later from the Hatch Act (1887), which provided for agricultural experiment stations. Since 1933 the Tennessee Valley Authority (TVA) has operated fertilizer research facilities at Muscle Shoals, Ala., to develop new and improved products and processes. About 64 percent of fertilizers in this nation today are made with technology developed by TVA.

The South continues to supply most of the phosphate, sulfur, and ammonia used in fertilizer production; but vast changes have occurred in the industry during the last 25 years. Consumption of fertilizer, particularly outside the South, has increased greatly. Concentrated fertilizers have replaced traditional low-analysis materials. Bagged fertilizers are being rapidly replaced by fluids and bulk-blended solids. Mechanical handling and custom application is now common. In 1980 southerners used

17.5 million tons of commercial fertilizer (one-third of national consumption), an increase of 83 percent since 1955.

See also ENVIRONMENT: Tennessee Valley Authority

Richard C. Sheridan
Tennessee Valley Authority

Norman L. Haggett and Janice T. Berry, *1980 Fertilizer Summary Data* (1981); Richard C. Sheridan, *Agricultural History* (January 1979); Rosser H. Taylor, *North Carolina Historical Quarterly* (July–October 1953).

Fruit Production

From Florida orange groves to Georgia peach orchards, fruit production has held an important position in the agricultural South. Pecans, tree fruit, citrus, and several types of berries have gained in popularity and status as cash crops, particularly in the past several decades. As row-crop agriculture has become dominated by huge, corporate enterprises, many small-acreage farmers have turned to labor-intensive fruit crops, which yield high returns.

In colonial days wild berries were cultivated and highly prized. Grapes and the native muscadine were used primarily for winemaking, and several hybridized varieties became widely planted. The late 19th century, however, saw a decline in southern vineyards due primarily to the increased competition from California grape production. The industry all but disappeared during the Prohibition era.

With many new "native wine" laws being enacted, a renewed interest in winemaking has appeared in the Southeast, from Virginia all the way to Texas. Government research stations have developed many high-yielding, quality varieties that have replaced the older ones due to their increased sugar content and heavy production. This has, in turn, led to a resurgence in popularity of muscadines for the fresh market, pick-your-own vineyards, and southern wineries.

Bunch grapes, even the French-American hybrids, are highly susceptible to serious insect and disease problems in the Deep South. Much research and interest exist in developing pest-resistant varieties, but, in spite of the good quality of grapes being harvested in the South, no varieties have survived the problems for long. As a result, vinifera and hybrid grapes in the South have yet to become economically competitive with California ones.

Blueberries have become a cash crop in the South. Highbush blueberries generally thrive only as far south as north Arkansas to North Carolina, but many southern research stations have, for several decades, worked with the native rabbiteye blueberries to produce varieties much better adapted and more productive than either highbush or wild plants. Breeding in virtually all southern states has made possible blueberry bushes that have heavy yields of bigger and better-flavored berries. The pick-your-own market has, as with muscadines, helped increase the acreage now planted with blueberries. In addition, blueberry growers' associations in Georgia, Florida, Arkansas, and Mississippi-Louisiana, have begun marketing blueberries by the hundreds of thousands of tons.

A single county in Florida has more acres of oranges than does the entire state of California. By far, most of the oranges, grapefruits, limes, tangelos, and tangerines consumed in the United States (whole or juiced) come from Florida. Until consecutive hard freezes destroyed the last of its citrus groves by the mid-1930s, Mississippi had what was called the "satsuma coast"; the current uppermost limit for citrus has been moved south to the lower half of Florida and south Texas.

Many of the South's citrus groves have been all but ruined by unusually severe freezes in the 1980s, but most of the crops were salvaged through juice processing, and many groves are currently being replanted.

Peaches have been a commercial crop in the South for well over 100 years. Seedling trees were used extensively until such grafted varieties as Belle of Georgia, named in 1875, became available. South Carolina now produces more peaches than Georgia, having sustained less winter damage to its orchards in the last decade. Over 135,000 tons of peaches were harvested from the Southeast in 1984.

Another fruit for the South is the strawberry, with Florida leading its neighbors with over 83 million pounds harvested in 1984. Labor problems are a major limiting factor in strawberry production, with migrant workers performing most of the back-bending harvest work.

Apples and pears have been grown in the mountainous regions of North Carolina, Tennessee, Virginia, and Arkansas for well over half a century. Breeding programs at research stations have produced disease-resistant and mild-climate varieties, which are becoming popular throughout the South. Southern apple production is still concentrated in the cooler regions of the Upper South.

Since the early 1950s small-scale fruit growers have found themselves increasingly under-priced by larger, corporate operations. Migrant workers have constituted the backbone of the large fruit orchards and vineyards, while family farms have had to employ local, seasonal help. Pick-your-own markets, roadside stands, and a general population becoming more interested in the healthful consumption of fresh and processed fruit have all helped develop a stronger fruit industry. With rising long-haul transportation costs and new varieties of fruit adapted for the southern climate, fruit production has become an attractive industry for the South.

Felder Rushing
Mississippi Cooperative
Extension Service

Eugene C. Auchter, *Orchard and Small Fruit Culture* (1929); Norman F. Childers, *Modern Fruit Science: Orchard and Small*

Fruit Culture (5th ed., 1975); Economic Research Service, U.S. Department of Agriculture, *Fruit Outlook and Situation* (March 1984); *Fruit South* (1977–79).

Grange

In November of 1867 Oliver H. Kelley, the father of the Patrons of Husbandry, returned to Washington, D.C., after a tour of the South and a summer working on a farm in Minnesota. Struck by the despair of southern farmers in South Carolina and Mississippi, Kelley conceived the notion of a national organization for the moral and educational uplift of the agricultural community. The Patrons, commonly called the Grange, pioneered as the first national farm organization and admitted women as equal members. The Grange was also innovative in sending out paid propagandists to spread its gospel. Later radical agrarian organizations in the South admitted women and sent out lecturers.

At first southerners resisted the Grange. Politically, the South was struggling with Reconstruction, and most white farmers feared any organization that originated in the North and especially in Washington, D.C. Moreover, males recoiled at rumors that the Grange advocated women's suffrage. Consequently, the national organization enlisted important men within the southern community to organize the ex-Confederate states and assuage potential white hostility. For example, D. Wyatt Aiken, a well-known southern agriculturalist who edited the *Rural Carolinian* (Columbia, S.C.), served as National Lecturer to the South; John T. Jones of Arkansas, who served as Worthy Master of the National Grange (1876–77), recruited in Texas and Tennessee; and A. J. Vaughan of Mississippi traveled for the Grange in Louisiana, Arkansas, and Mississippi. These organizers, all ex-Confederate officers, were closely identified with the end of Reconstruction and the New South.

The Grange, unlike the later Farmers' Alliance, grew from the top down and was not a grass-roots organization. It entered South Carolina and Mississippi in 1872 and eventually claimed, in 1875, 228,000 members throughout the ex-Confederate states. The organization endorsed typically agrarian aims. In the new state constitutions, after Reconstruction, its members supported such goals as financial retrenchment and railroad regulation. The organization, although technically not political, tended to be composed of traditional Democrats, who feared that a third party would either perpetuate, or bring back, Republican political successes. The Grange leadership supported the Ku Klux Klan and was able to attract few if any black members to its Council of Laborers, a separate organization created for blacks.

The appeal of the Grange to the South was economic and not political. Local and state affiliates formed economic cooperatives throughout the southern states, which extended credit to their members—local stores, warehouses, gins, insurance companies, and individual agents. When the price of cotton did not increase, these overextended and underfinanced cooperatives collapsed. Their demise hastened that of the Grange, and by 1878 the organization was defunct in most of the South.

See also SOCIAL CLASS: / Farmers' Alliance

Robert A. Calvert
Texas A&M University

Solon J. Buck, *The Granger Movement, 1870–1880* (1913); Robert A. Calvert, "Search for Identity: The Grange in the Southwest" (Ph.D. dissertation, University of Texas, 1967); D. Sven Nordin, *Rich Harvest: A History of the Grange, 1867–1900* (1974); Theodore Saloutos, *Farmer Movements in the South, 1865–1933* (1960).

Knapp, Seaman A.

(1833–1911) Agricultural reformer.

Seaman Asahel Knapp brought many experiences to his goal of improving southern agriculture. As editor, college president, essayist, teacher, and organizer, he acquired the skills necessary to secure acceptance of his most important idea—the Farmers' Cooperative Demonstration Work program.

Reared in Essex County, N.Y., Knapp graduated from Union College. Acting upon a physician's advice to seek outdoor activities, he moved to Iowa in 1866 and began a lifelong study of agriculture. As professor and president of Iowa State College (now University), he urged farmers to adopt scientific farming practices. Knapp also edited the *Western Stock Journal and Farmer*, emphasizing the use of better livestock and the diversification of crops. In 1885 he became head of the North American Lumber and Timber Company and moved to Louisiana. For the next decade he convinced farmers that rice could be grown by using modern agricultural practices. In 1898 Knapp joined the U.S. Department of Agriculture, which sent him to Japan where he discovered a rice strain more suitable to America's mechanized demands.

Panic struck Texas cotton farmers in 1903 as the boll weevil devastated wide areas. Knapp's effort to combat this insect gained for him a national reputation and set into motion an agricultural program that promised hope for the South. Backed by financial guarantees from local citizens to compensate for any losses, Knapp persuaded farmers to try methods on their own lands that few had been willing previously to employ. They began using crop rotation, deeper plowing, better livestock, diversification, improved seed selection, and fertilizers. Initially, 7,000 to 8,000 farmers joined the program. The results were impressive. Cotton yields increased 50 to 100 percent over yields on farms using older methods. The boll weevil remained, but Knapp's ideas offset losses from the insect and the Farmers' Cooperative Demonstration Work program was born. Impressed by Knapp's success, the U.S. Department of Agriculture and later the General Education Board provided funds to spread the program throughout the region. The General Education Board's commitment stemmed from its belief that as the economic status of rural taxpayers increased, better schools would result. Farmers' Cooperative Demonstration projects also contained educational programs including boys' and girls' farm groups—the forerunners of the 4-H clubs.

By the time of Knapp's death in 1911, the Farmers' Cooperative Demonstration Work program was firmly established in the South. A fitting tribute to Knapp's efforts occurred in 1914 with the passage of the Smith-Lever Act, which incorporated the Farmers' Cooperative Demonstration Work ideas into national law.

See also EDUCATION: / General Education Board

Joseph A. Coté
University of Georgia Library

Rodney Cline, *The Life and Work of Seaman A. Knapp* (1936).

Naval Stores

The naval stores industry, whose principal products were tar, pitch, and turpentine, derives its name from the use of these products for waterproofing the rigging and hulls of early wooden sailing vessels. The industry was based on the exploitation of the pine woods for resinous juices and is one of the oldest industries in the South. It was developed at Jamestown in 1608 but is associated especially with North Carolina because of the highly resinous long-leaf pine (*Pinus palustris*), whose natural habitat is the approximately 100-mile-wide Coastal Plain from Virginia to Texas.

Until 1835 the people of North Carolina were often referred to, somewhat derisively, as "tar, pitch, and turpentine folk." At the time of the American Revolution, North Carolina produced in value three-fifths of all the naval stores exported from the continental colonies. The naval-stores industry continued throughout the antebellum period, and its uniqueness ultimately bequeathed to the state and its people the nickname "Tar Heels."

Tar was produced by a process of dry distillation in an earthen kiln of pieces of dead long-leaf pine. Lengths of dead wood, called lightwood, omnipresent in the forest, were gathered, split into short pieces, placed in a kiln, covered with earth, and subjected to a slow fire that forced out the resinous matter. The tar was dipped from a pit outside of the kiln and poured into barrels. Pitch was obtained by boiling tar to a thicker consistency.

After 1820 production of tar declined, and by 1835 the production of turpentine and its derivatives, spirits of turpentine and rosin, became the main focus of the industry. This developed from improved processes of distilling and from new uses for spirits of turpentine and rosin. Spirits of turpentine was used as a paint thinner and preserver of wood, but after 1835 it was used also as a solvent in the burgeoning rubber industry, particularly as an illuminant. Camphene lamps were the chief form of light in homes and businesses after the decline of whale oil and prior to the development of kerosene. Camphene (spirits of turpentine mixed with alcohol) provided a bright light, was relatively inexpensive, but was highly inflammable. Rosin, a residue from distilling, found new uses in the manufacture of soap, lamp black, ink, and in sizing paper for printing.

With the development of the second phase of the industry, planters entered the business on a large scale, employing slave labor. Once trained in turpentine operations, blacks preferred turpentining to other forms of farm labor because it was based on the task system and they were somewhat more independent in their work. One man could attend a "crop" of 10,000 boxes spread over 50 to 100 acres of land. The industry required a number of specialized workers: "boxers" cut holes in the base of the tree as a container for the resin; "chippers" periodically reopened the wound in the tree above the box to increase the flow of resin; "dippers" removed the resin from the boxes every 10 days; distillers refined the product at a nearby distillery into spirits of turpentine and rosin; and coopers made barrels for the products.

With the development of this phase of the industry, North Carolina's economy boomed. Until the Civil War the state remained the preeminent naval-stores producer, with production of all forms of naval-stores products valued in 1860 at approximately $12 million.

A turpentine orchard was exhausted in 5 to 10 years of cultivation, and the industry was necessarily migratory. In the post–Civil War period it spread rapidly southward into South Carolina and the Gulf states. The exploitation of the long-leaf pine forest of the Deep South between 1870 and 1920 was one means by which southerners recouped their capital after the war. Factors in Savannah, Jacksonville, Pensacola, and Mobile obtained control of large tracts of pine land and controlled the trade. They leased timber to operators, advanced the capital in the form of goods and tools, and subsequently marketed the products. Savannah became the leading naval-stores port from 1880 to 1920 and continued to set the world price of naval stores until 1950.

In the surge southward North Carolina procedures were followed, and skilled turpentine workers were sought from the Carolinas. Sometimes entire communities of people, plus their household goods, cattle, cats, dogs, chickens, and other property, were transported by train to Georgia, Alabama, or Mississippi. A new community was born in the piney woods of the Deep South, complete with dwellings, distillery, commissary, and a combination church-school. The overseer was operations supervisor, enforcer of law and order, director of the commissary and distillery, and physician. It was a primitive, isolated, lonely, destructive, and unique way of life. In approximately two generations, from 1870 to 1930, most of the original stands of long-leaf pine, covering 130,000,000 acres, were consumed.

The industry underwent little change until the 20th century when the imminent exhaustion of the timber supply prompted the use of clay and metal cups to receive the resin and avoid the premature destruction of the trees. Producers were reluctant to change methods until forced to do so in 1908 by the factors. The federal government attempted to improve techniques and quality by establishing a Naval Stores Experiment Station at Olustee, Fla., in 1932, and by providing a cost-sharing subsidy to producers after 1936.

In the post–World War II period the development of the sulphate process for making paper led to the production of turpentine and rosin as by-products, and the old man-and-axe turpentine industry fell prey to the more efficient competition of modern chemistry and chainsaw technology. Instead of weekly trips to the woods to chip the trees, the operator removed the entire tree, transported it to the mill, and mechanically and chemically separated it into its component products for subsequent use. Between 1967 and 1972 the federal government liquidated its stocks of naval stores, ceased its subsidy, and in 1973 closed the Olustee Station. Like the village blacksmith, the trail-driving cowboy, and the one-horse shay, the "turpentine man" had had his day.

See also ENVIRONMENT: / Lightwood; SOCIAL CLASS: / Timber Workers

Percival Perry
Wake Forest University

Charles C. Crittenden, *The Commerce of North Carolina, 1763–1789* (1936); Thomas Gamble, ed., *Naval Stores: History, Production, Distribution and Consumption* (1920); Percival Perry, "Naval Stores" (Ph.D. dissertation, Duke University, 1947), *Journal of Southern History* (November 1968).

Peanuts

Peanuts, *pinders*, *groundpeas*, and *goobers* are names applied to a nutritious food that has been a part of southern culture since colonial times. Groundpea is most descriptive, as the plant is a legume and belongs to the pea family, botanically known as *Arachis hypogaea*. Peanuts were known in South America around 2,800 years ago. Spanish explorers carried them to Spain in the 16th century, and traders carried them to Africa. Peanuts possibly arrived in the South on slave-trading vessels, which carried them as food for slaves. The Congo name for peanuts, *nguba*, became *goober* in the South.

Originally produced by slaves and free blacks for local use and sale, peanuts were exported from South Carolina soon after the Revolution. In the antebellum period they were grown locally in most southern states, but Wilmington, N.C., was the principal commercial market from 1830 to 1860. Nicholas N. Nixon of New Hanover County was the largest producer and promoter of scientific cultivation. Lack of commercial development in other southern areas was due in part to competition from cotton and in part to the tedious hand labor required in peanut production.

The Civil War created a national market for peanuts. Soldiers of both armies fighting in Virginia found locally grown peanuts a portable, nourishing food, confirmed by the Civil War song "Eating Goober Peas." Soldiers who returned home wrote to Virginia for more peanuts, and the commercial industry was born. Between 1865 and 1868 production tripled each year, and the 1869 crop was estimated at over 600,000 bushels. From 1868 to 1900 Norfolk was the peanut capital of the United States and was succeeded after 1900 by Suffolk, Va.

For 30 years after the Civil War peanuts, roasted in the shell, were a treat sold by street vendors. Boiled peanuts were a delicacy associated with cotton-picking and -ginning season. Neighborhood "peanut boilings" were a form of social intercourse in southern communities. Farmers in the Lower South planted peanuts for fall fattening of swine, a practice known in Georgia as "hogging off."

In the decade from 1889 to 1899 commercial production and consumption of peanuts increased over 300 percent. George Washington Carver's research in the 1890s revealed their high nutritional value as food and over 300 uses for peanuts. Devastation to the cotton crop by the boll weevil after 1905 persuaded farmers to change to peanuts. Increased mechanization between 1900 and 1910 reduced labor costs and increased production and consumption.

From 1899 to 1919 peanut production increased eightfold, and World War I established peanuts as a continuing factor in the southern economy. After World War II production became highly mechanized. Peanuts today are the ninth most valuable farm crop in the United States, valued at over $1 billion, with a record 1981 crop of 3.98 billion pounds. Seven states dominate production, with Georgia producing almost one-half, followed by Alabama, North Carolina, Texas, Virginia, Oklahoma, and Florida. Four major types are produced: larger kerneled Virginias, the medium-sized Runner in the Lower South, small Spanish peanuts in Texas-Oklahoma, and Valencias in New Mexico.

The United States makes greater use of peanuts for food than any other country, with annual consumption of nine pounds per person. Two-thirds goes into peanut butter, salted and roasted peanuts, and confectionary products. The remainder is exported or crushed for oil and animal feed. Boiled peanuts are still particularly identified with rural areas of the South, found for sale at roadside stands and eaten as a plain snack. The United States's production of peanuts today is only 10 percent of world production, but accounts for more than one-third of world exports, principally to Canada, Europe, and Japan. Except for the period from 1942 to 1948, production has been controlled since 1934 by various regulations of the U.S. Department of Agriculture.

Percival Perry
Wake Forest University

Frank Selman Arant, ed., *The Peanut, The Unpredictable Legume* (1981); F. Roy Johnson, *The Peanut Story* (1977).

Pecans

Among the various images that summon to mind the South, pecans take first place in the category of edible nuts. When European settlers first arrived in the New World they found black walnuts, hickory nuts, chestnuts, chinquapins, and pecans growing wild in the South. All of these, except the chestnut (killed by a blight around 1920), continue to grow, but only the pecan is commercially important. The pecan is synonymous with the South because its natural habitat is the nine southern states from the Carolinas to Texas. Because of the high quality of the nut meat, the quantity of pecans produced annually, and the relative ease of propagating improved varieties, the pecan has become the "queen of nuts" in the United States. It is, moreover, the fifth most important nut tree in the world, and the southern states are the only substantial producers other than Mexico.

More than one-half the total crop of pecans comes from wild and seedling trees, principally in Texas, Oklahoma, and Louisiana. The region from South Carolina to Louisiana is important for improved varieties, developed since 1890, with Georgia the chief producer. Seedlings are as flavorful as improved varieties, but yield of the latter is twice as great. Production is shifting toward the Southwest (New Mexico) with concentration in larger orchards, increasing mechanization, and preservation by cold storage. Although the number of individual pecan farmers is decreasing, the number of trees bearing and being planted is increasing.

From approximately 1 million pounds in 1900, the pecan crop increased to an average of 10 million in the 1920s; to 20 million in the early 1930s; to 40 million by the late 1930s; and to 60 million around 1945. Since 1960 the average annual crop has approximated 220 million pounds, valued at over $74 million. Great fluctuation in yields and price occur because of the tree's tendency to produce larger crops biennially. Since 1949 the federal government and growers' cooperative associations have attempted to stabilize prices.

Currently 94 percent of pecans are marketed commercially in shelled form. The largest users are bakeries (36 percent of the total), suppliers of unsalted retail packages (24 percent), confectioners (19 percent), and ice cream makers (6 percent). Fewer than 40 firms dominate marketing.

Ground pecan shells have found numerous uses: as mulches for plants and as poultry litter; as filler in feeds and fertilizer; as abrasives in soap and polishes; and as filler in plastic wood, including artistic use in molded figures of birds and animals.

Pecans have a long association with southern life. Many Deep South residents plant pecan trees in the yard because the trees are both ornamental and productive. Pecans have contributed extensively to the culinary aspects of southern life, from pralines, which appeared in Louisiana as early as 1762, to recipes for cakes, notably fruit cakes, for which Claxton, Ga., is famous; in the ubiquitous pecan pie; in cookies; in salad, meat, and bread recipes; as roasted-and salted-nut treats for special occasions; or when consumed directly from the shell around the family hearth at evening, especially as a tradition of the Thanksgiving and Yuletide seasons.

Percival Perry
Wake Forest University

USDA, *Agricultural Statistics* (annual); Jasper G. Woodroof, *Tree Nuts: Production, Processing, Products* (1967).

Pest Control

Temperate climates and continuous planting made staple crops susceptible to numerous pests and diseases. In the 19th century farmers tried any number of means and substances to destroy or repel insect pests. Southerners with a mechanical bent applied their talents to devising machines to collect pests. Under the plantation system, labor-intensive methods were sometimes feasible. To drive rice birds away, slaves stationed on platforms fired old muskets, snapped noisemaking plaited whips of white oak, or laid carrion about the field borders to attract buzzards that the birds mistook for hawks. Cotton growers carried torches through fields to attract and destroy moths of cottonworms. Hand picking crawling insects was a well-known and often-used method where effective. The extensive cultivation of staple crops on low fertility soils generally made labor-intensive pest control unprofitable. Arsenical compounds such as London purple and Paris green were the main insecticides for chewing insects in the late 19th and early 20th centuries, but they were generally too expensive to compensate for the increased production. However, on valuable fruit crops, Bordeaux mixture became a standard poison.

Plant diseases, often soil borne, plagued crops, especially on the Coastal Plain. Tobacco growers found, as had ancient farmers, that rotating crops provided some relief. In 1892 a scientist at the Alabama Agricultural Experiment Station, George F. Atkinson, first described cotton wilt and its transmission. The notion of observing and selecting wilt-resistant varieties of plants probably occurred to many farmers, but some of the first scientific work in selection was done by a U.S. Department of Agriculture scientist, W. A. Orton, on Sea Island cotton in South Carolina beginning in 1899. The first wilt-resistant Sea Island cotton, Rivers, became available in 1902, and the first upland variety, Dillon, followed in 1905. Insect-transmitted diseases such as malaria brought debilitation; yellow fever epidemics brought death and the disruption of trade and social life. In a regional sense, the diseases—or fear of them—contributed to poor land use by discouraging settlement of the river bottoms and deltas in favor of the erosion-susceptible hills. Josiah Nott of Mobile, Ala., recognized that mosquitoes carried yellow fever, but he did not supply the scientific proof. Later discoveries enabled cleanup and spraying activities to eliminate breeding pools.

The 20th-century southern cattle industry rests primarily on eliminating the Texas fever–carrying cattle tick. The tick prevented improvement of southern herds because imported purebreds succumbed to the fever. It deprived cattlemen of northern markets where southern cattle were shunned. In the South cattle brought one-half the price of cattle in tick-free states. When a combination of federal quarantines and state-mandated dipping laws started in 1906, the South was losing an estimated $40 million annually. Of the infested 725,565 square miles, 312,012 had been cleaned and released from quarantine by 1917. The pest was confined to the Texas border by 1943. With the possible exception of fence laws, it was the most pervasive intrusion of state powers into the activities of farmers yet. Some farmers displayed their displeasure by dynamiting dipping vats. Tick riders now patrol the Mexican border to prevent reintroduction.

Alterations in growing methods provided some relief in the early 1900s from the boll weevil, which threatened southern cotton from the 1890s on, but farmers still hoped for an effective insecticide. A University of North Carolina graduate, William C. Piver, formulated calcium arsenate in 1912. It rapidly became the primary boll weevil poison until it was replaced after World War II. Scientists at USDA's Tallulah, La., laboratory pioneered in the use of airplanes for crop dusting. One crop-dusting company based in Monroe, La., evolved into Delta Airlines, and the company's stockholder meetings are still held in Monroe. Yazoo-Mississippi Delta farmers were often receptive to agricultural innovations, and the airplane was no exception. They were the first to use aerial crop dusting on a wide scale. Southern manufacturers provided the animal-drawn equipment for earthbound insect chasers.

World War II accelerated herbicide research that would change agriculture significantly. The South, like other agricultural areas, accepted 2-4D as a herbicide to eliminate weed competition. As more selective herbicides became available, they reduced weed-control costs and gradually eliminated much of the hoeing and chopping. The prospect of control with herbicides made southerners more receptive to introduced grasses for conservation and pasture.

A group of synthetic organic insecticides that killed a broad spectrum of insects became available in the late 1940s and early 1950s. Unlike the arsenical insecticides that had to be ingested, the organochlorine and organophosphate ones killed on contact. As per-acre cotton production increased, the share of insecticide treatment as a cost of production decreased. Insecticides became an integral part of the mechanization of acriculture. Farmers, bankers, and other creditors viewed the pesticides as an umbrella of insurance to protect other investments in the crop—machinery, land, fertilizer, and improved seed. Too often, farmers sprayed on a schedule without regard to insect infestation levels. During the 1970s cotton consumed one-half the insecticides used in the United States. The South accounted for two-thirds of the insecticides used. The South was also the major regional user of nematocides and defoliants.

Cotton insect control has not been without problems and controversies. In the early 1950s the boll weevil became immune to one of the chlorinated hydrocarbon insecticides, benzene hexachloride. Also, the so-called broad-spectrum insecticides killed friend and foe alike. With the demise of natural parasites and predators, incidental cotton pests came to the fore. The most striking example occurred in the Rio Grande Valley in Texas. Predators and parasites controlled the budworm, but the budworm became resistant to the organophosphorous insecticide used on the boll weevil. The insecticide also killed the parasites and predators of the budworm, releasing destructive budworm populations on the valley's cotton crops.

Faced with increasing problems of insect immunity, entomologists looked to eliminating insects from an area as a solution. As in the case of the cattle tick, the life history of an insect occasionally, but not often, provided the opportunity for a single effective control method or the possibility of early elimination. Early destruction of cotton stalks and plowing provided the means to control the pink boll worm in Texas, when farmers chose to use it on a community basis. A method of elimination employed has been sterilizing male insects by irradiation and then releasing them into the insect population. The successful elimination of the cattle screwworm from Curacao in 1954 led to the successful implementation of the technique in the Southeast in 1959. In 1980 the screwworm was eliminated from the United States. Release of sterile males has been utilized as a technique, along with insecticides and lures, in eliminating the Mediterranean fruit fly from Florida. Mississippi and North Carolina hosted USDA pilot projects to eliminate the boll weevil.

Despite these successes insects persisted as an important limitation on crop production. The methods to deal with them moved from being solely the concern of farmers and agriculturalists to matters of public debate and policy. During the two decades since the publication of Rachel Carson's *Silent Spring* (1962) the debates have intensified. The controversy over the areawide programs using insecticides, such as the boll weevil project in North Carolina and fire ant control with mirex, are but two examples. Traditionally in the South, any agricultural or industrial development that promised to raise incomes and alleviate chronic poverty went unquestioned. Southerners are now more often questioning the balance between benefits and costs in environmental terms.

Early problems with resistance and environmental concerns led to research efforts emphasizing a myriad of complementary control measures that reduced reliance on insecticides. The integrated pest-management approach stressed cultural controls, biological controls, alternate plant varieties, trap plants, insect growth regulators, behavioral-modification chemicals, and timely applications of chemical insecticides. Monitoring of insect populations, or scouting, was essential to reducing unnecessary sprayings.

Some recent developments promised safer and more effective controls: 10 species of sweet potato plants have been selected for resistance to insects; vetch grown under pecan trees harbored predators of pecan pests. After the citrus black fly arrived in Florida, entomologists imported predators from the Rio Grande Valley to control it. Synthetic pyrethoids became the primary cotton insecticide, and residue problems have been lessened because only one-tenth the volume of previous insecticides was required for control.

Douglas Helms
Soil Conservation Service, USDA

Animal Diseases, Yearbook of Agriculture, 1965 (1965); Dale G. Bottrell and Perry L. Adkisson, *Annual Review of Entomology* (1977); Thomas R. Dunlap, *DDT: Scientists, Citizens, and Public Policy* (1981); *Farmer's World, Yearbook of Agriculture, 1964* (1964); Lewis C. Gray, *History of Agriculture in the Southern United States to 1860*, 2 vols. (1933); Douglas Helms, *Agricultural History* (January 1979, January 1980); *Insects, Yearbook of Agriculture, 1952* (1952); John H. Perkins, *Insects, Experts, and the Insecticide Crisis: The Quest for New Pest Management Strategies* (1982); *Plant Diseases, Yearbook of Agriculture, 1953* (1953); John T. Schlebecker, *Whereby We Thrive: A History of American Farming, 1607–1972* (1975).

Poe, Clarence Hamilton

(1881–1964) Agricultural journalist.

The life of North Carolina journalist Clarence Hamilton Poe affords insight into the evolution of southern farming from the 1890s into the 1960s. Beginning in 1897 as a "printer's devil" for the Raleigh-based *Progressive Farmer*, he achieved national prominence first as editor, then as owner—positions he held until his death. In the process he built the *Progressive Farmer* into the largest farm journal in the United States. Today it continues to be one of the nation's most significant farm publications.

Using the *Progressive Farmer* as a podium, Poe championed a myth long dominant in southern history—that agrarian life was morally and culturally superior to other types of existence. Poe believed that small, family-owned farms engendered unique cultural and character-building traits. Farm life developed stong, independent individuals with a respect for nature, a sense of community, a dedication to family, a clear understanding of life, a reverence for the earth, and a devotion to God. The farmer tilling the soil, with devoted wife at home rearing the children, created a society superior to that of northern cities where a modern industrial system robbed labor of its dignity and where unrest and half-suppressed rebellion were constant undercurrents.

Poe feared, however, that backward southern farming methods would doom that agrarian lifestyle. Accordingly, he advocated such changes as improved educational facilities, the creation of agricultural cooperatives, and the diversification of farming. With these reforms Poe envisioned idyllic communities "untouched by town influences" where farmers would own and operate grain elevators, livestock associations, and rural credit organizations. Community life would center around educational, religious, social, and intellectual activities. Successful farmers could purchase their own homes and fields and thereby end absentee landlordism. Finally, these communities would remain small, avoiding the problems associated with cities and towns.

Poe's advocacy of the preservation of a supposed superior southern agricultural life underscores one of the region's most persistent myths. Reality, however, was much different. Sharecropping and tenant farming dominated the South throughout the late 19th and early 20th centuries. Eventually southern farming did change, but not because of Poe's influence. Rather, New Deal legislation favored large agricultural farm units, while World War II uprooted untold numbers of farmers. In the 1950s Poe reluctantly concluded that the family farm was a thing of the past—but he still believed in the superiority of rural life.

Joseph A. Coté
University of Georgia Library

Clarence Hamilton Poe, *How Farmers Co-Operate and Double Profits* (1915), Papers, North Carolina Department of Archives and History, Raleigh; *Progressive Farmer*, 1899–1964.

Progressive Farmer

The first issue of *Progressive Farmer* appeared 10 February 1886. Colonel Leonidas L. Polk, a former Confederate officer and a farmer from Anson County, N.C., conceived the newspaper, which later became a monthly magazine, as a forum for promoting the goals of a better rural way of life, a more scientific agriculture, and an improved educational system for farm people. The *Progressive*

Farmer's son in Carroll County, Ga., 1941

Farmer became a successful North Carolina institution whose efforts led in the early 1890s to a reorganization of that state's department of agriculture and the founding of a new agricultural college, North Carolina State University. Polk, meanwhile, became president of the Farmers' Alliance and North Carolina's first agricultural commissioner.

Polk died in 1892, and Clarence Poe and four colleagues bought *Progressive Farmer* in 1903 for $7,500. Poe was a self-educated farmboy who, as editor of the magazine and a leader in the country life movement, helped to transform southern rural life. Tait Butler, a veterinary medicine professor at Mississippi State University, also contributed to the shape of *Progressive Farmer*. He began publishing a rural life newspaper called *Southern Farm Gazette* in 1895, sold it in 1898, and joined Poe's editorial team on *Progressive Farmer* in 1908. Together they purchased *Southern Farm Gazette* and made it the basis for a new western edition of *Progressive Farmer*. The magazine's headquarters moved from Raleigh, N.C., to Birmingham, Ala., in 1911, and the staff was publishing five locally oriented, regional editions by 1928.

Tait Butler's son Eugene became an assistant editor in the Memphis office of *Progressive Farmer* in 1917 and eventually replaced Clarence Poe as president of the Progressive Farmer Company in 1953. Monthly circulation of the magazine hit 1,400,000 in 1959, although it had declined to 850,000 by 1986. The Progressive Farmer Network provides agricultural news to 50 radio stations. Under Butler the magazine's "Country Living" section was expanded into a separate periodical, *Southern Living*. Time Inc. bought Southern Progress Corp., the parent company of *Progressive Farmer*, in 1985.

Charles Reagan Wilson
University of Mississippi

Progressive Farmer, 1899–1964.

Rice Culture

As the Carolina and Georgia rice culture made adjustments to post-Civil War labor demands and farmers along the Mississippi River started growing rice using labor-intensive methods, a highly mechanized rice culture developed in the southwest Louisiana prairie. The completion of the transcontinental Southern Pacific Railroad in the early 1880s opened the area, and real estate promoters encouraged midwestern farmers to settle there. These transplanted midwesterners discovered a similarity of Cajun Providence rice to wheat and adapted wheat binders to the soggy rice fields. After several dry years in the early 1890s wilted Providence stands of rice, canal companies organized to furnish water while other farmers dug wells for irrigation. By the turn of the century this highly mechanized rice culture eclipsed the troubled East Coast and Mississippi River growing areas.

The prairie stretched into Texas, and farmers there utilized the same irrigation and growing principles as their Louisiana neighbors. In the early part of the 20th century Arkansas prairie farmers discovered technology and started growing rice. From the beginning these rice farmers utilized the latest machinery, and by World War I many owned binders, tractors, threshers, and irrigation pumps. Unlike many southern crops, rice was capital and machine intensive rather than labor intensive. The tenure system also varied radically from that of other cash crops. Corporations purchased large tracts, sold part, and rented other sections to tenants. A form of sharecropping emerged, and a cropper would pay a portion of his crop to the canal company for water, pay the landlord another portion for rent, and keep the remainder. The tenant furnished all the machinery used in growing and harvesting the crop.

As in farm areas throughout the country, the boom-and-bust cycle of World War I stunted the rice-growing industry. During the 1920s the formerly expansive rice culture stabilized as farmers attempted to pay off loans for machinery bought during the war. By this time, tractors had become universal on the prairies, and this varied dramatically from other areas of the South that remained labor intensive.

Rice prices declined, as did those of other commodities, during the early years of the Great Depression. When Congress established the Agricultural Adjustment Administration (AAA) in 1933, rice was included as a basic commodity. Even before a rice program had been set up, prices climbed to a parity level. For the first two years, the rice section of the AAA fumbled with marketing agreements with millers, but in 1935 it set up a program that paralleled other commodity sections. In one important respect the rice section proved innovative; it gave allotments to producers—not to landlords. It reasoned that because tenants had such large investments in machinery, they deserved allotments. Also, crop-rotation customs dictated that often a man farmed his land one year and sharecropped with a neighbor the next.

Throughout the 1930s the rice culture remained stable, and during World War II rice became a valuable food to feed the world. Rice farmers meanwhile turned to combines, making another technological jump. Prosperity continued until the early 1950s, when the end of the Korean War caused a sharp decline in international demand. Rice allotments were cut drastically. The effects in the rice areas of the South paralleled those in the cotton culture 20 years earlier. The allotment system also was changed in parts of Louisiana and Arkansas, for Agriculture Stabilization and Conservation state committees, without calling for a vote from growers, changed from producer to farm allotments, awarding allotments to landlords.

Louisiana rice farmers felt the forces of change most drastically, but in Arkansas the culture continued to expand. In 1972, the first year since 1956 that no quota was in effect, rice again became an expanding commodity; production increased by 25 percent between 1972 and 1974. With higher prices and no quotas in effect, rice production spread quickly to new lands in Arkansas and the Yazoo-Mississippi Delta. Despite all the changes in the rice culture, many rice farmers continued to lease land or farm on shares. Even as similar crop-sharing practices disappeared in other areas of the South, mechanized rice farmers continued them. The expansive nature of the culture can be seen in the increased farm price that rose from $359 million in 1964 to $1.2 billion in 1973. Because rice culture was highly mechanized by the 1930s, rice farmers suffered much less from the forces of acreage reduction and human displacement than did those in other farm areas of the South. Rice was agribusiness from its origin in the prairies, and new opportunities only meant refinements in the culture—not the agonizing transformation that accompanied mechanization in other areas of the South.

Pete Daniel
Smithsonian Institution
Washington, D.C.

Lawson P. Babineaux, "A History of the Rice Industry in Southwestern Louisiana" (M.A. thesis, University of Southwestern Louisiana, 1967); Pete Daniel, *Breaking the Land: The Transformation of Cotton, Tobacco, and Rice Cultures since 1880* (1985); Henry C. Dethloff, *Arkansas Historical Quarterly* (1970); John N. Efferson, *The Production and Marketing of Rice* (1952); Rudolph Carrol Hammack, "The New Deal and Louisiana Agriculture" (Ph.D. dissertation, Tulane University, 1973); Seaman A. Knapp, *The Present Status of Rice Culture in the United States,* USDA Bulletin No. 22 (1899).

Rural Electrification Administration

When the Rural Electrification Administration (REA) was created in 1935, less than 4 percent of the farms in the southern states had electricity. Without it, many of the comforts of modern life were unavailable, and for that reason the South enthusiastically welcomed the REA. In 1936, when Congress gave the REA statute authority, southern congressmen were among the agency's most ardent supporters. The Southern Policy Association, a group of southern congressmen anxious to promote southern development, endorsed the REA bill and regarded electrification as an important step in that direction.

As the REA began operation, southern farmers quickly established electric cooperatives, and the percentage of farms with service slowly grew. By 1941 the national average had climbed to 30 percent, and, although the southern percentage was lower, the South moved steadily ahead. At the end of World War II the REA started a massive construction program to finish the job, and by 1955 virtually 90 percent of the South's farmers had electrical service. Although the effects of electrification were evident nationwide, they had the most dramatic impact in the South, owing probably to the region's higher number of substandard homes when the REA started.

By providing running water and indoor toilets, the REA finally helped bring an end to the hookworm that had ravaged the South for over a century. Refrigeration had a similar beneficial effect on diets through the storage of perishable foods. In some small towns cold-storage cooperatives were started. Incandescent lighting improved the quality of life in homes and schools, and radio became a regular feature in southern homes. Electrification stimulated diversification: the Bureau of Agriculture Economics reported an increase in dairy farming, and the South became a major poultry-producing region. Most important, however, was the greater comfort and sense of satisfaction that southerners felt as they began to enjoy the numerous conveniences provided through electricity. Electrification must be considered one of the most significant stimulants for modernization of the rural South.

D. Clayton Brown
Texas Christian University

Erma Angevine, ed., *People. Their Power: The Rural Electric Fact Book* (1980); Marquis William Childs, *The Farmer Takes a Hand: The Electric Power Revolution in Rural America* (1952); Louis J. Goodman, John N. Hawkins, and Ralph N. Love, eds., *Small Hydroelectric Projects for Rural Development: Planning and Management* (1981).

Rural Free Delivery

Although the free delivery of mail service was commonplace in the nation's cities and towns in 1900, American farmers were still going, usually once a week, to small fourth-class post offices for their mail. That year the farmers in the 11 states of the old Confederacy and Kentucky had nearly 21,000 such post offices, over one-third of all those in the nation, to which the mail was carried from central post offices over more than 94,000 miles of star mail routes.

Slow and inefficient, this mail service offered little relief for the southern farmer's isolation, and in the 1890s, when Postmaster General John Wanamaker suggested delivering mail to farmers, southern members of Congress enthusiastically supported the proposal. In four successive years Leonidas Livingston, Tom Watson, and Charles Moses, all Georgia congressmen, and North Carolina's Senator Marion Butler offered amendments to appropriation bills allocating money for a rural free-delivery experiment. Finally, in 1896, Postmaster General Wilson L. Wilson, acting upon Senator Butler's amendment, began a rural-delivery experiment in West Virginia with an appropriation of $40,000. During the next six years southern members of Congress labored to keep the experiment alive, and in 1902, following the lead of Congressman Claude Swanson of Virginia, Congress made the rural free delivery of mail a permanent postal service.

In spite of the support southern congressional delegations had given, however, the South never received as much rural free-delivery mail service as did the midwestern states largely because of postal regulations and politics. According to postal regulations, rural free-delivery routes were first established where the density and literacy of the population seemed likely to make the route pay for itself, and fewer such places existed in the South than in the Midwest. More importantly, the rural routes were first established when the Republicans controlled the government, and midwestern Republican congressmen found it much easier to secure mail routes for political reasons than did their Democratic counterparts from the South. By 1950, therefore, there was one rural mail route for every 1,278 rural inhabitants in the five midwestern states of Ohio, Illinois, Iowa, Kansas, and Indiana, and only one for every 2,038 people in the 11 Confederate states and Kentucky.

Nevertheless, the rural free delivery of mail revolutionized communication in the South. Daily newspapers became commonplace in southern farm homes, more letters were written and received, more advertising filled the mails, and, more importantly, the rural South was brought into increasing contact with the North. Rural free delivery paved the way for the establishment of a modern parcel post system, which was also supported by southern members of Congress and which helped to break the country storekeeper's monopoly on the southern farmer's trade.

Rural free delivery inspired a good roads movement throughout the South, led southerners to argue for government aid for building farm-to-market roads, and lured them away from their traditional stand on states' rights.

Wayne E. Fuller
University of Texas at El Paso

Daniel J. Boorstin, *The Americans: The Democratic Experience* (1973); Wayne E. Fuller, *Journal of Southern History* (November 1959), *Mississippi Valley Historical Review* (June 1955), *R.F.D.: The Changing Face of Rural America* (1964).

Sears, Roebuck Catalog

"Without that catalog," writes Harry Crews in his 1978 autobiography of a Bacon County, Ga., boyhood, "our childhood would have been radically different. The federal government ought to strike a medal for Sears, Roebuck Company for sending all those catalogs to farming families, for bringing all that color and all that mystery and all that beauty into the lives of country people."

A genuine piece of Americana, the "Farmer's Bible" or "Wish Book" had a special impact on the South. Predominantly rural for so much longer than their Yankee counterparts, southerners relied on the Sears catalog for glimpses of urban life or light reading as well as order blanks. In many one-room schoolhouses it served as a primer and reference book. The catalog might even be credited with standardizing material-culture terminology. When a southern farmer needed a new "sling-blade" or "slam-bang," he was forced to order it from Sears as a "weed cutter."

Company policy as well as copy directly affected the region. By locating a major stove supplier in ore-rich Alabama in 1902, Sears became one of the first northern firms to recognize the South's industrial potential. In 1906 Sears's first mail-order branch was established in Dallas, and within the next 20 years both the Atlanta, Ga., and Memphis, Tenn., plants opened regional warehouses stocking items particularly suited to southern trade.

Well into the 19th century country stores provided their rural customers with virtually all their needs. Beginning in the last decades of the century, further extension of the railroads, good roads campaigns, the introduction of rural free delivery (1896), and, eventually, parcel post (1913) dramatically changed conditions that had kept southern farmers isolated and, whatever their dissatisfactions, loyal to the local merchant. Richard Sears's Big Book challenged the retail monopoly.

Sears by no means originated the mail-order business. Rooted in the colonial period (Benjamin Franklin's promotion of his Pennsylvania stoves was one of the original schemes), numerous mail-order firms existed by the end of the Civil War. Montgomery Ward, in operation since 1872 and distributing a wide variety of goods exclusively by mail, had even succeeded in getting his firm named the official supply house for the Grange. Yet by 1900 Sears Roebuck had become the clear leader in the mail-order world, and it has conceded its edge to none of its competitors since.

Catalogs were designed for hours of fireside reading with woodcuts and flamboyant descriptions to encourage cover-to-cover browsing. Rooted in the principle of "never omitting the obvious" the description of the "Long Range Wonder Double Barrel Breech Loading Hammerless Shotgun, the World's Wonder" totaled some 3,000 words. If there was not something among the stereoscopes and bicycles, buggies and mackintoshes, dry goods, furniture and gramophones to catch the buyer's fancy, the final testimonials, glowing recommendations of satisfied customers, and most convincingly the famous money-back guarantee usually did.

Sears's successful tactics gave rise to an all-out campaign against the mail-order companies. Shopkeepers lit bonfires in town squares and offered bounties for every new catalog turned in for fuel. Some merchants offered prizes and free admissions to movies in trade for the books. Newspaper editors, dependent on the advertising revenues of local retailers, originated epithets (Monkey Ward, Rears and Soreback, Shears and Sawbuck) and helped circulate accusations about cheap, damaged goods and "sewing machines" that turned out to be a needle and thread. No one had ever *seen* Richard Sears or Ward, so it was not hard to convince many southerners that both men were black—a rumor given added credibility by the later philanthropy of Sears president Julius Rosenwald in the cause of black education.

Ultimately, the automobile, urban growth, and the chain store did more than catalog buying to undermine the economic viability of small local retailers. As urbanization continued and its customers grew more sophisticated, Sears accommodated to the changing market.

With the passage of the Pure Food and Drug Act in 1906, highly profitable, if suspect, patent medicines were dropped from the catalog. Gone were the superlatives: "World's Largest," "cheapest," and "America's strongest," unless justified by fact. Catalog vocabulary was simplified ("lachrimal secretions" became tears, "nutrition," food) and descriptions streamlined. In 1976 Sears switched to the "segmented people-oriented approach," to copy that "required the end of any pretension that the catalog is a work of literature."

Little in the 1984 catalog is reminiscent of the extravagant puffery of Richard Sears's "Wish Books"; little about the diversified billion-dollar Sears corporation reflects its humble origins as a watch wholesaler. Yet some fundamentals remain: serviceable, affordable merchandise, a large rural clientele, and loyal customers. In the words of Georgia Governor Eugene Talmadge, "God Almighty, Sears, Roebuck, and Eugene Talmadge" are names to count on.

Elizabeth M. Makowski
University of Mississippi

Louis E. Asher and Edith Heal, *Send No Money* (1942); Lewis E. Atherton, *The Southern Country Store, 1800–1860* (1949); Thomas D. Clark, *Pills, Petticoats, and Plows: The Southern Country Store* (1944); Boris Emmet and John E. Jeuck, *Catalogues and Counters: A History of Sears, Roebuck and Company* (1950); Jack Salzman, ed., *Prospects*, vol. 7 (1982); Sears, Roebuck & Co., *Merchant to the Millions: A Brief History of the Origins and Development of Sears, Roebuck and Co.* (1959); *Time* (20 August 1984); Gordon L. Weil, *Sears, Roebuck U.S.A.* (1977).

Soybeans

Soybean production in the United States increased from 13.9 million bushels in 1930 to 2.3 billion bushels in 1982. The acreage devoted to the crop increased from 1 million to 71 million acres in the same period. Introduced as a novelty as early as 1804, the soybean was first used in the United States primarily for forage, beginning about 1900. Although many people saw its potential as a source of oil, less than one-fourth of the planted acreage in the mid-1930s was harvested for beans, which were then pressed for the oil for industrial uses and for meal for livestock feeding. Then a group of German chemists developed refining processes that removed from the oil its unpalatable flavor and odor, making soybean oil usable in products for human consumption.

Since then soybeans have had an impact on every part of the United States, but this impact has been particularly notable in the post–World War II South. As early as 1917 the U.S. Department of Agriculture published bulletins urging southern farmers to consider replacing cotton with soybeans. Not until World War II, though, with its patriotic appeals, high prices, and exodus of labor from southern farms, did many farmers turn from cotton to soybeans. After the war, production declined when farmers found the new crop was highly susceptible to damage from weather and insects. Shifts in cotton production, research, and government policies were among factors bringing soybeans back to prominence.

Cotton production shifted to the West and Southwest where the land and climate were suited to mechanization and where irrigation reduced the chances of crop failure. Research led to the realization that many southern farmers could double crop their land by planting in succession oats or winter wheat and then soybeans. While the development of the solvent extraction of the oil was particularly beneficial to southern farmers, new varieties of soybeans, which were less susceptible to weather and insect damage, were developed by the southern state agricultural experiment stations. The cultural significance of this was clear from the names given to the favorite strains raised in the South—the Davis, Lee, Bragg, Forrest, Pickett, Jackson, and Rebel. E. E. Hartwig, USDA soybean breeder at Stoneville, Miss., deliberately named his varieties after Confederate heroes.

The postwar accumulation of cotton surpluses led the federal government to cut back the acreage of cotton farmers could grow with price supports, leading many southern farmers to turn their land from cotton to soybeans. In 1945 the nine southern and border states of Georgia, Alabama, North Carolina, South Carolina, Tennessee, Mississippi, Missouri, Arkansas, and Louisiana produced 6 million bales of cotton and 18 million bushels of soybeans. In 1982 these same states produced 4.6 million bales of cotton and 757 million bushels of soybeans. A quiet revolution brought about by a single new crop had changed the face of the South.

Wayne D. Rasmussen
U.S. Department of Agriculture

Edward J. Dies, *Soybeans: Gold from the Soil* (1943); Harry D. Fornari, *Agricultural History* (January 1979); W. J. Morse and J. L. Carter, *Yearbook of Agriculture* (1937).

Sugar Industry

Cane sugar is a key commodity in international trade and an important component of the modern diet. At one time or another, sugarcane was grown commercially in Alabama, Georgia, South Carolina, Texas, Louisiana, and Florida. However, during the 19th century south Louisiana became the focal point of this dynamic industry.

Between 1880 and 1910 the Louisiana sugar industry experienced a scientific and technological revolution in methods, process apparatus, and scale of operation. The animal-powered mills and open evaporation kettles characteristic of the antebellum period were supplanted by large, technically designed, and scientifically controlled central factories. One commentator of the period, Mark Twain, described the modern sugar factory as "a wilderness of tubs and tanks and vats and filters, pumps, pipes, and machinery." This new industrial world, which emerged in rural Louisiana, was brought about in large part by a variety of local institutions working in alliance with certain agencies of the federal government. They included the Louisiana Sugar Planters' Association (LSPA), the Louisiana Sugar Experiment Station, the Audubon Sugar School, Louisiana State University, and the U.S. Department of Agriculture. These institutions facilitated the introduction of a progressive chemical and engineering technology, derived in part from the European beet-sugar industry, into this traditional plantation culture of the Deep South.

The late 19th-century modernization of the Louisiana sugar industry took place within an international context. Louisiana sugar planters, confronted with competition from the European beet-sugar manufacturers, responded not only to an economic challenge but a scientific and technological one as well. They met this foreign threat by creating local institutions for coordinating planters' activities, conducting research, and supplying the scientific and technical expertise necessary for the modernization of their industry.

Of these local organizations, the LSPA made the crucial contribution to this agricultural and manufacturing transformation. Established in 1877 and led by many of the wealthiest and most politically powerful sugar planters in Louisiana, the LSPA systematically developed connections with federal government officials, practical engineers, and academic scientists to gain its organizational objectives.

As a result of changes in national party policies concerning the sugar tariff and the concurrent emergence of sugar-producing areas in Hawaii, Puerto Rico, Cuba, and Java, the Louisiana sugar industry entered into a period of decline after 1900. Subsequently, a number of sugar planters and investors channeled their energies and capital into south Florida, where they attempted to apply the practices of the Louisiana industry to the completely different environment found in the Everglades. The economic feasibility of the Florida industry became a reality only after USDA scientists at Canal Point, Fla., and research scientists from the United States Sugar Corporation discovered new varieties of cane, established specific fertilizer requirements, and introduced cultivation techniques appropriate for the region's unique soil, drainage, and climatic conditions. By 1940 Florida's sugarcane industry surpassed Louisiana's not only in terms of yield, but also in quality of raw sugar produced.

The Florida and Louisiana sugar industries supply only a fraction of the sugar consumed in the United States today, but they continue to have a significant impact upon their respective local economies.

John A. Heitmann
University of Dayton

Nöel Deerr, *The History of Sugar* (1949); John A. Heitmann, *The Modernization of the Louisiana Sugar Industry, 1830–1910* (1987); Emile A. Maier, *A Story of Sugar Cane Machinery* (1952); J. Carlyle Sitterson, *Sugar Country: The Cane Sugar Industry in the South, 1753–1950* (1953).

Tobacco Culture, Flue-cured

Commercial tobacco production in this country dates to the Jamestown colony in the early 17th century, and the expansion and contraction of plantings varied with international demand and prices. Over the years farmers developed a host of varieties that they cultivated throughout the country. After the Civil War bright tobacco, so called because of its golden color produced by intense heat during curing, became a favorite of manufacturers. As the demand for cigarette tobacco increased in the late 19th century, growers changed the work culture by harvesting several leaves from the stalk at a time instead of cutting the entire stalk, tied bundles of these leaves to a stick, and cured them in barns that had flues. Increased demand set in motion a massive expansion of the flue-cured culture from its northeastern North Carolina seedbed into eastern North and South Carolina and by World War I to Georgia. Imperialistic growers spread the secrets of flue-curing and cloned tobacco barns, packhouses, and auction warehouses as they conquered new territory.

The flue-cured culture was extremely labor intensive. It was more than a clever saying that it took 13 months to cultivate, harvest, cure, and grade a crop for market. Because of the intense labor requirements of the crop, most tobacco farmers planted only three to six acres, the amount that a family could cultivate. The work routine began in the winter when farmers cut wood to heat the curing barns. In January they cleared land for a plantbed and seeded it before breaking the land and running rows. In May they transplanted seedlings to the fields, plowed, chopped, and as the tobacco grew, picked off hornworms and suckers and broke off the flowery tops. When harvest season arrived in July, they harvested three to four ripe leaves each week, and the process continued for five or six weeks. Harvesters were called "primers," and they put the leaves into sleds pulled by mules that then drew the sleds to a scaffold where women and children handed the leaves to stringers who tied them to sticks. At dusk primers returned from the fields and hung the leaves in the barns for curing. After harvest season each leaf was graded and tied into "hands" for market. It was sometimes Christmas before all the tobacco had been graded and sold.

By 1930 tobacco farmers, like other southern farmers, felt the slump in prices generated by the Great Depression. The Agricultural Adjustment Act (AAA) recognized tobacco as a basic commodity, and growers, warehousemen, manufacturers, and politicians attempted to conclude a marketing agreement with AAA representatives. When the markets opened in 1933, prices remained low, but a marketing agreement that promised parity prices for the 1933 crop in exchange for acreage reduction the next year succeeded. Over 90 percent of flue-cured growers voted for this plan. The AAA stabilized the flue-cured area, and the number of tobacco farms increased during the 1930s and the 1940s. During these years the hand-labor system changed little.

In the 1950s tobacco farmers cut back acreage, and this forced many farmers, especially sharecroppers, out of farming. At the same time, farmers cultivated their land

North Carolina tobacco farmers, Chatham County, 1930s

more intensely, increasing production per acre from 922 pounds in 1939 to 2,200 pounds in 1964. Only in the 1960s did the flue-cured tobacco culture mechanize to any extent. In addition to tractors used for plowing and hauling sleds to the scaffold, a mechanical topper covered 20 acres a day and not only removed the tops but at the same time sprayed for suckers and hornworms. By the mid-1960s farmers insisted on intracounty leasing of allotments, and many small-allotment holders leased out acreage to larger growers. In 1968 Congress extended loose-leaf marketing, which had been customary in Georgia, to all areas, ending the labor-intensive grading and tying tasks. By the 1970s farmers were using bulk barns, an innovation that ended the banding and tying tasks at the scaffold. Meanwhile, a mechanical tobacco harvester began cutting out primers. The hand scale ended as machines handled the crop in bulk.

The forces set in motion in the 1950s plus increasing mechanization disrupted the old tenure arrangements in the tobacco area and led to massive displacement of farmers. Because the flue-cured culture mechanized so late, many exfarmers found work in the emerging factories of the area, easing the transition from farming by preserving communities, churches, and schools. In 1982, largely because of the controversy over smoking and health, Congress changed the price-support program, instituting a no-net-cost-to-taxpayers scheme that shifted the cost to tobacco farmers. Also, nonfarm allotment holders such as corporations and educational institutions had until December 1983 to sell their allotments to active farmers. Like other commodity cultures, tobacco farming became a large-scale and capital-intensive operation that bore little resemblance to the intense hand-and-mule culture that originated in the 19th century.

See also INDUSTRY: / Tobacco Industry; SOCIAL CLASS: / Tobacco Workers

Pete Daniel
Smithsonian Institution
Washington, D.C.

Anthony Badger, *Prosperity Road: The New Deal, Tobacco, and North Carolina* (1980); Pete Daniel, *Breaking the Land: The Transformation of Cotton, Tobacco, and Rice Cultures since 1880* (1985); William R. Finger, ed., *The Tobacco Industry in Transition: Policies for the 1980s* (1981); J. Fraser Hart and Ennis L. Chestang, *Geographical Review* (October 1978); Harold B. Rowe, *Tobacco under the AAA* (1935); Nannie May Tilley, *The Bright-Tobacco Industry, 1860–1929* (1948).

Truck Farming

Truck farming is a form of agriculture that is national in scale, but it has left a significant imprint on the South. It involves the sale of annual fruit crops—as distinguished from orchard crops—and vegetables in commercial markets in fresh condition. This enterprise matured as an agricultural industry because of the development and growth of American cities. During the years following the Civil War, the expansion of the nation's urban population created a year-round demand for fresh produce. Essential to the successful conduct of the industry is the fast and efficient delivery of produce to market by refrigerated transport. During the formative stage following 1865, railroads provided this vital service.

Truck farming emerged as a factor in the economic life of the South during the period of its national evolution. By 1900 it engaged the energies of southerners in scattered segments of the region stretching from the Eastern Shore of Virginia to the lower Rio Grande Valley of Texas. Its spread is attributed to the promotional efforts of railway companies operating in the South, the immigration of northern and European farmers familiar with this type of farming, and low returns from cotton, which prompted some southerners to seek more dependable profits in a new venture. A listing of southern counties containing pockets of intensive production includes Norfolk and Northampton in Virginia, Seminole and Palm Beach in Florida, Copiah in Mississippi, and Cameron and Hidalgo in Texas. By the second half of the 20th century, however, the producing areas in Texas and Florida clearly dominated southern output. Although the southern farmer has produced a wide variety of truck produce, the primary crops have been potato, watermelon, tomato, and cabbage.

In those regions where southerners pursued truck farming energetically a form of agriculture different from that of the prevailing cotton culture emerged. The production of truck crops was not totally free from tenancy, but the landowning small farmer remained the primary producer until the mid-20th century when he was replaced by large agribusiness units. The cultivation of these crops required more intensive and careful effort than that needed for cotton. Migratory workers were often utilized, and extensive use was made of labor furnished by members of the producer's family. In some localities public school schedules were dictated by the planting and harvesting of crops. Distinctive features included packing sheds where local produce was prepared for rail shipment, ice plants that provided refrigeration for the freight cars carrying the produce, and "hot spots" adjacent to the packing sheds where producers and buyers met to transact their business.

In those portions of the South with proper soil and climate conditions in combination with transportation facilities direct to urban markets, truck farming provided the southern farmer with an alternative to dependence on the dominant cash crop.

James L. McCorkle, Jr.
Northwestern State University
of Louisiana

Gilbert C. Fite, *Cotton Fields No More: Southern Agriculture, 1865–1980* (1984); James L. McCorkle, Jr., "The Mississippi Vegetable Industry: A History" (Ph.D. dissertation, University of Mississippi, 1966); Bruce McKinley and W. C. Funk, *An Economic Study of Truck Farming in the Plant City Area, Hillsborough County, Florida* (1926); Wells A. Sherman, *Merchandising Fruits and Vegetables: A New Billion Dollar Industry* (1928).

Art and Architecture

JESSIE POESCH
Tulane University
CONSULTANT

Carroll Cloar, Where the Southern Cross the Yellow Dog *(1965)*

Architecture

Most of the houses in the United States today were probably built after the beginning of World War I. A large number of public buildings, office towers, and industrial structures were also built after that date. What is true of the nation as a whole is equally true of the South, especially in urban centers such as Atlanta, Jackson, Birmingham, Nashville, New Orleans, and others that have greatly expanded in size and population in the last 25 years. We are still perhaps too close in time to this recent rash of building to see it in historical perspective and to see how and if it has distinct regional qualities. A present consensus would probably be that the majority of styles and building types represent national rather than regional choices. Art and architecture are often by their nature national and international in character, but with regional accents. Modern technology and materials (including air-conditioning), modern communication systems, and a highly mobile population have abetted this tendency.

The large hotel with central multistory lobby or atrium is a characteristic modern building type. The spectacular open spaces of hotels of this kind lend a sense of drama and theater to one's visit to a strange city. The Hyatt-Regency Hotel in Atlanta, designed by John C. Portman and Associates and completed in 1967, was the first of this genre. The fashion for and appreciation of a variety of such open, interior public spaces have now spread throughout the land. Though originating in the South (scholars can always identify precedents for each new building type—the much earlier Brown Palace Hotel in Denver is a case in point), one would not identify this fashion as specifically southern. Rather, it seems to represent an innovative impulse in design and form associated with a place undergoing great commercial and economic expansion.

Where once church towers and public buildings, such as schools, county courthouses, or state capitols, were the dominant features of town and city landscapes, now office towers, hotels, and high-rise apartment houses shape the skylines of cities and many towns. Other new building types and new arrangements of buildings and community spaces are changing living patterns. An obvious example is the development of the shopping mall, which is replacing, or has replaced, main street. This is one of many changes brought about by widespread use of the automobile and by population growth.

The advent of air-conditioning, especially from the 1940s onward, when it began to be affordable both in workplaces and in residences even of many poorer people, has done much to cause the built environment of the South to conform even more closely to national patterns. Earlier, the long, hot summers virtually forced the builders of southern homes to find ways of coping with the heat—dogtrots, wide central halls, porches, verandas, piazzas, galleries, cupolas on large houses, attic vents, raised cottages with air circulation underneath, and T-shaped house plans, to name a few. These devices were often concealed so that a given building might appear in shape and detail to conform to a particular style or taste. Although summers are hot in other parts of the country and many of these devices were used elsewhere—the porch, for example, was a ubiquitous feature on houses in the United States during the second half of the 19th century—the porches, swings, hammocks, and other accoutrements were important for longer periods of time in the South. Air-conditioning has thus been a factor in changing the pace of American life and especially life in the South, in ways both overt and subtle. Life in summer is more enclosed and private. New houses seldom have the porches or the overhanging roofs formerly typical. Where once businesses, schools, and colleges closed down or operated at a much slower pace for four months in the summer, they now follow the same schedules as their counterparts throughout the nation.

Despite the fact that a high proportion of the buildings in the South today are relatively new, the survival of older buildings plays an important role both in how southerners interpret their own environment and in how others see and interpret it. Most surviving older buildings are still in use and are therefore part of contemporary life and culture. Some few have been set aside as museums. In both cases they help to give distinctive and particular character to specific places.

Though a few 17th-century structures survive, those older buildings extant and in use date largely from the 18th and 19th centuries. These include the rather sober early Georgian, the more exuberant high Georgian, the neoclassical of the Federal period, the "columnar" style where late Georgian and Greek Revival sometimes blend, the austere "pure" Greek revival, the Gothic, the Italianate of the post–Civil War period, the various picturesque tastes of the late 19th century, and the beaux arts formalism of the early 20th century. Also included now as older and historic are such relatively recent modes as the art deco and moderne of the 1920s and 1930s.

Buildings completed in the modish style of a given time are important not only for the functions they serve but also for the way they demonstrate the shared tastes of an era. They are important symbols or visual statements of what both the owner or patron and the designer or architect conceive to be the role of the building in that time and place. They reflect in turn the status and role of those who live in or use the building. Furthermore, the buildings reflect not only the status of the occupants or users of the building but also the aspirations and achievements of the entire community.

There are conspicuous southern examples in each of the stylistic phases that have enjoyed popularity in this country. Among the most familiar are Drayton Hall in South Carolina, an example of an architectural choice and symbol of the wealthy landed planters on the 18th-century Atlantic Seaboard whose lifestyle had close parallels with English counterparts; the Virginia Capitol in Richmond and the complex of buildings at the University of Virginia, deliberately designed to serve and to symbolize the functions of democratic governance and learning in the new Republic; the Tennessee Capitol, another "temple of democracy" of a slightly later date; and the great columnar houses found in Natchez, Miss., the result of the prosperity of a slaveowning class of cotton planters and merchants in the Deep South. The extraordinary cluster of art deco hotels and residences in Miami is a reminder of that area's spectacular growth in the 1920s and 1930s.

In addition to these conspicuous structures other modest examples exist, less familiar to a wide public but well known within a limited area. The distinctive "Virginia house" developed in the early 17th century and the T-shaped plantation or farm houses found in the Carolinas (which provide an abundance of cross-ventilation) are cases in point. The raised cottages of the Deep South, sometimes called "mosquito" cottages in the Carolinas and "Creole" cottages on the Gulf Coast and in Louisiana, are of several different types and hence different plans but constitute a recognizable genre. They include humble one- or two-room structures lived in by poor blacks and whites as well as cottages of considerably larger scale. Among urban structures the "singles" and "doubles" of Charleston represent particular types, as do the distinctive row houses of Baltimore, the French-influenced cottages of New Orleans, and the long, narrow shotgun houses of the late 19th century. In some cases the consistent or distinctive use of materials identifies, in a general way, other characteristic regional building traditions. The stone houses of Kentucky and the varieties of log structures, particularly in the Upper South, are examples. Many of these were built by frontiersmen as sturdy utilitarian structures in the late 18th and early 19th centuries and have since become symbols of an era.

In some cases different building traditions in different regions developed out of the traditions familiar to the earliest settlers such as the English, French, German, Spanish, and Scottish. Certain construction methods were also assimilated from the Indian and African populations.

A growing body of research into the nature and uses of vernacular structures exists. Such research is fueled by a desire to formulate a more accurate picture of the nature of the built environment and to study more than structural types and architectural modes. Farm buildings and industrial and commercial buildings are, and were, a conspicuous part of the built environment of the South, as elsewhere. Here, too, the study of the variety of forms, tastes, and traditions needs further exploration.

Much of the interest in older structures and the realization of their importance and relevance to understanding ourselves and our past have been stimulated by the movement for historic preservation. Various forces have motivated this interest in architectural preservation. These include respect and love for major historical figures or for buildings associated with historical events; a nostalgia for the past; respect and feeling for distinctive architecture and buildings of a place or period, be it elaborate mansion or simple log cabin or dogtrot; and a desire to preserve the consistent appearance or fabric of a section of a community. In recent years architectural preservation has been seen as a tourist lure for a city, town, or area, and hence an economic asset. Also, the preservation of extant buildings is often economically sensible. Hence old warehouses or factory buildings are being converted into apartment buildings and old railroad stations into restaurants.

The South has actively participated in the historic preservation movement. The earliest successful effort of this kind in the United States is generally identified as the effort to preserve Mount Vernon, the home of George Washington, and to open it to the public, an effort initiated in 1853. The most conspicuous and perhaps most extensive example of historic preservation is Colonial Williamsburg, where an entire community has been restored to its 18th-century ambience. This project was inaugurated in the 1930s. Thanks to relatively little change there during the 19th century, there were 81 intact 18th-century buildings that needed little more than a sprucing up and the removal of additions. At the same time several of the more important buildings, such as the Capitol and the Governor's Palace, both of which had totally disappeared, were reconstructed on the basis of careful study of documents and archaeological research.

The Capitol and the Governor's Palace are among the most impressive buildings at Williamsburg, but the restoration as a whole is significant for its inclusion of a wide range of forms—small and medium-sized houses, outbuildings, shops, and gardens. Increasingly, emphasis has been placed on interpretations of the lifestyle and values of the inhabitants as well as on the physical nature of the built environment. Moreover, although it was once true that only the roles of the political, social, and intellectual leaders of the community were examined, there is now a more evenhanded approach in which the lives of all classes, including slaves and servants, are studied and interpreted. Williamsburg, because of the scale of the restoration and the disciplined research that has characterized the organization, has had a profound effect on the standards of historic preservation and also on the consciousness of both the nation's and the region's architectural history. Other restored areas that have had a similar, if more limited, influence include the Old Salem restoration at Winston-Salem, N.C., which helped to bring to the fore the Germanic heritage of the South, and Westville, near Lumpkin, Ga., a re-creation of the buildings, sights, and smells of a rural mid-19th-century village. Cities with distinct architectural characters in which there have been controlled preservation and restoration include Charleston, Savannah, and New Orleans. They are among the most attractive cities in the country and are seen as emblems of the rich and complex history of the South.

The influence of Williamsburg and the enthusiasm for architecture in a historical idiom go far beyond simple historic preservation. Reinforcing the slightly earlier Colonial Revival architectural style, the Williamsburg work is echoed throughout modern suburbs and in numerous historic architecture projects.

Despite the dicta of early and mid-20th-century architectural theorists and practitioners concerning purity and simplicity of form and the need to build for a machine age, a large number of builders and developers in the South (and elsewhere) opted for modifications of traditional architecture, particularly in residential architecture. In some cases the plans may have changed significantly—front-door access but also side- and back-door access through garages, more "family" rooms, a high proportion of one- or one-and-a-half-story ranch houses—but the surface embellishment is an interpretation of traditional forms, albeit sometimes very free. Among these traditional types in the South is what could be called antebellum revival, that is, the columnar-fronted mansion. More recently, popular magazines have shown examples and plans of vernacular types, such as Louisiana colonial structures with double-pitched sheltering roofs. The recent "postmodern" architectural movement has in a sense taken cognizance of what developers and builders have understood—that a certain amount of ornament and embellishment and playful manipulation of spaces is pleasing to the eye and the spirit. They in turn are trying to create buildings in which some traditional forms and ornament are used in both functional and appealing ways. This is a very self-conscious movement.

Less self-conscious artistically is another new trend that may or may not have an important effect on the nature of architecture and the built environment in the South and elsewhere—the increased awareness of the need for energy conservation. A notable example of the way in which the shape and appearance of the building have been determined by energy and environmental considerations is the Jones Bredge Headquarters of the Simmons Company in Atlanta, Ga., designed by Thompson, Hancock, Witte and Associates and completed in 1975. This building, roughly the shape of a parallelogram, rests on steel trusses (thus it is raised from the ground—a traditional southern practice) and is designed to take advantage of solar and ecological factors. The need to make specific adaptations in order to save energy and materials may reshape, once again, the forms of our shelters.

Whether in vernacular idioms or in more self-conscious architectural styles and designs, whether serving private or public, commercial or industrial needs, buildings are important statements of status, symbols of cultural aspirations, and statements of community pride. Some are personal statements by architect or patron and some now seem to be distinctive period statements. The architecture of the South, as elsewhere, is complex and many layered.

See also BLACK LIFE: Architecture, Black; FOLKLIFE: Aesthetics, Afro-American; Aesthetics, Anglo-American; House Types; / Bungalow House; Dogtrot House; I House; Pyramidal House; Saddlebag House; Shotgun House; T House; GEOGRAPHY: Log Housing; RECREATION: / Colonial Williamsburg

Jessie Poesch
Tulane University

Wayne Andrews, *Pride of the South: A Social History of Southern Architecture* (1979); Edward A. Chappell, "Cultural Change in the Shenandoah Valley: Northern Augusta County Houses before 1861" (M.A. thesis, University of Virginia, 1977); Barbara H. Church, "The Early Architecture of the Lower Valley of Virginia" (M.A. thesis, University of Virginia, 1978); Mary Wallace Crocker, *Historic Architecture in Mississippi* (1973); Henry Glassie, *Folk Housing in Middle Virginia: A Structural Analysis of Historic Artifacts* (1975); Charles B. Hosmer, Jr., *Presence of the Past: A History of the Preservation Movement in the United States before Williamsburg* (1965); John Linley, *The Georgia Catalog: Historic American Buildings Survey, A Guide to the Architecture of the State* (1982); Lewis Mumford, *The South in Architecture* (1941); James Patrick, *Architecture in Tennessee, 1768–1897* (1981); Jessie Poesch, *The Art of the Old South: Painting, Sculpture, Architecture and the Products of Craftsmen, 1560–1860* (1983); Leland M. Roth, *A Concise History of American Architecture* (1979); Kenneth Severens, *Southern Architecture: 350 Years of Distinctive American Buildings* (1981); Dell Upton, "Early Vernacular Architecture in Southeastern Virginia" (Ph.D. dissertation, Brown University, 1980), with John Michael Vlach, eds., *Common Places: Readings in American Vernacular Architecture* (1986).

Drayton Hall in South Carolina (1738–42), an exemplary Palladian design on the Ashley River

Visual Arts

The works of art created in the South and their creators are part and parcel of the broader national and international artistic milieu but at the same time are rooted in the specific time, place, and person of their creation. In any given period, not just in the recent "modern" era, the arts have seldom reflected regional or national distinctiveness. For example, in the 12th century one finds surprisingly similar sculptural motifs from France to Poland; at the same time an astute scholar can determine the different "hands" in a given sculptural program. In studying the visual arts of the American South, especially the region's 20th-century culture, one gains more by examining and objectively describing what exists than by trying to categorize what is or is not uniquely southern.

Currently interest in the arts is growing in the South. The number of working artists in the region is now in the thousands, and those who support or attend art events surely number in the millions in any given year. Still, a relatively small proportion of the total population is concerned with painting and the visual arts and their role in society. Every city of any size has its museum, its art galleries and dealers, its art classes in institutions of learning or those given by free-lance instructors, its workshops and special exhibitions. Though these activities are still centered in larger cities, the tentacles reach into smaller communities through arts and humanities programs as well as through the media of television, radio, magazines, and newspapers. Whereas artists once felt they could succeed only if their works were shown in New York, more now find a sufficient outlet in their own region. New York is still the center of the art world, but some dealers and museum directors in that city now feel it necessary to keep abreast of what is happening in other regions. Those who are involved in such visual arts as painting and photography may not agree as to what they are all about or what is "good" or what grasps and holds the mind and spirit, yet their numbers are legion.

The emergence and proliferation of the arts, especially during the last 30 years or so, has also to do with the growth of population, the relative affluence of a substantial number of people, the growth of the national economy, the tilt of that economy toward the South, and the growth of a network of museums and schools at all levels. This has made for rich diversification.

Most artists in the South have embraced the tenets of what is loosely called modernism; these tenets include varieties of abstractionism as well as the relatively new realism. The diversity to be found among the works of recent and contemporary artists almost defies description, yet critics have sensed some common elements that have influenced, and are reflected in, the arts in today's South. William A. Fagaly, in a perceptive essay accompanying the exhibit *Southern Fictions*, held at the Contemporary Arts Museum in Houston in 1983, touched upon some of these: a strong sense of place and obsession with the earth; a volatile society given to strong expression and vibrant color; uncontrolled emotional release resulting in violence and tragedy; the mix of cultures—African, English, and Latin; indulgent appetites for indigenous foods and music; a penchant for storytelling and for social interchange; and also a persistent inferiority complex. These "regional" qualities are not necessarily expressed in the work of all artists in the South and, when they are expressed in one way or another, are not necessarily the aspect that most contributes to the success of any given work; nonetheless, they are clearly important. These factors have in fact had more influence on writers and musicians than on productions of the visual arts. Donald Kuspit, in his selection of contemporary paintings for the Virginia Museum of Fine Arts exhibition *Painting in the South: 1564–1980*, which circulated among six museums from 1983 to 1985, sought those works that expressed a southern sensibility. These included works suggesting both southerners' relationship to the land and the conflict between this relationship and such facets of modernization as the streaking highways that cut across this land. He emphasized that regionalism is not necessarily the most relevant element in any single work. Some southern painters' works reflect the influence of popular culture—and the South is one of the nurseries of modern pop culture—the struggle to grasp inherent contradictions in southern culture, the myths that still envelop the South but are dead or dying, a feeling for the absurdities of modern times, and a movement toward decorative abstraction.

Recent historical exhibits and studies of artists in the South reflect a growing sense of the diversity of regional history and of the importance of region itself. Building on the work of William Dunlap in the 1830s, J. Hall Pleasants and Anna Wells Rutledge pioneered in the southern study of art. Pleasants examined the careers of artists who worked in the 18th and 19th centuries in Maryland and produced a series of monographs in the 1940s. A file of his unpublished research is now in the possession of the Maryland Historical Society. Rutledge's 1949 study, *Artists in the Life of Charleston*, is indispensable to anyone interested in the art of South Carolina. Since the work of these and other pioneers, a small but steady flow of regional studies and studies of individual southern artists has appeared. Notable among these is the exhibition mentioned previously, *Painting in the South: 1564–1980*. Its accompanying scholarly catalog is a permanent record of this important exhibition. Even so, the historical study of the visual arts in the South is only in its beginnings.

In the largely agricultural and sparsely settled South, the relatively few who worked in the visual arts often had to struggle for patronage and for opportunities to show and sell their works. Patronage was important in the colonial period, and some of the most distinguished patrons were to be found in the South. The delineation of the flora and fauna of this nation had its roots in the American South—the artists include John White, Mark Catesby, William Bartram, John James Audubon, and Maria Martin—yet development of landscape painting was slow. The hot climate, the great distances, and perhaps even the persistence of a culture whose members preferred to live out-of-doors rather than paint it militated against this. In both the portraits and genre paintings that survive from the 18th and 19th centuries, the biracial, indeed multiracial nature of southern life (and hence American life) is revealed more forcefully than can be discerned from any but the most recent studies of painting in America. What is being done today builds, knowingly or otherwise, on the traditions, practices, and struggles of the past.

See also BLACK LIFE: Art, Black; ENVIRONMENT: Naturalists; / Audubon, John James; FOLKLIFE: Folk Painting; WOMEN'S LIFE: / Martin, Maria

Jessie Poesch
Tulane University

Bruce W. Chambers, *Art and Artists of the South: The Robert P. Coggins Collection* (1984); Corcoran Gallery of Art, *American Painters of the South* (1960); David C. Driskell, *Two Centuries of Black American Art* (1976); Ula Milner Gregory, in *Culture in the South*, ed. W. T. Couch (1935); F. Jack Hurley, Nancy Hurley, and Gary Witt, eds., *Southern Eye, Southern Mind* (1981); James C. Kelly and Estill Curtis Pennington, *The South on Paper: Line, Color and Light* (1985); Donald B. Kuspit, *Art in America* (July–August 1976), *Art Voices South* (January 1979); David Madden, *Southern Quarterly* (Winter 1984); Jessie Poesch, *The Art of the Old South: Painting, Sculpture, Architecture and the Products of Craftsmen, 1560–1860* (1983), in *The Cultural Legacy of the Gulf Coast*, ed. Lucius F. Ellsworth and Linda K. Ellsworth (1976); *Southern Quarterly* (Fall–Winter 1985); Virginia Museum of Fine Arts, *Painting in the South: 1564–1980* (1983).

Architects of Colonial Williamsburg

From its beginning in the late 1920s, Colonial Williamsburg has been conceived as a place where Americans learn about their history. As early as 1932 benefactor John D. Rockefeller, Jr., preferred the motto "That the future may learn from the past," to more esoteric statements of purpose, and few fourth graders or museum administrators have regarded Williamsburg as merely a preservation project since. For more than 50 years, the town has maintained a powerful grip on the national consciousness. Consider for example Lee Iacocca's stated purpose of making the Statue of Liberty and Ellis Island "an ethnic Williamsburg" and modern art curator Henry Geldzahler's somewhat eccentric assessment of Andrew Wyeth as "the Williamsburg of American painting—charming, especially when seen from a helicopter." Such references, as well as countless American buildings carried out in a "Williamsburg" style, reveal that the restored town is widely seen as an expression of American rather than regional culture. Some of the reasons for this lie in its Depression-era origins.

Just how the re-created community of Williamsburg achieved its present evocative condition is worth considering. The essential roles of Rockefeller and the visionary rector of Bruton Parish Church, W. A. R. Goodwin, are well known, but those of the people who most directly created the place are much less so. Chief financial decisions were made by Rockefeller himself, advised by his corporate lieutenants and influenced by Goodwin and restoration architects. Certainly Rockefeller's perception of history and politics affected the emerging museum, but there is little evidence that this perception was not shared by all the principals.

In the beginning, design decisions were made on a variety of levels by three groups: partners in the Boston firm of Perry, Shaw, and Hepburn, their representatives in residence at Williamsburg, and an advisory committee. Largely because of a chance meeting between Goodwin and architect William G. Perry in 1926, the Perry, Shaw, and Hepburn firm was hired in 1927 to prepare proposals for restoration of principal parts of the town. The following year, the identity of the benefactor was revealed and Perry, Shaw, and Hepburn began plans for a number of buildings.

The firm had been established in 1922 and had primarily produced relatively modest New England buildings in competent, restrained renditions of historical modes. In 1927, for example, it was involved with a Bulfinch-inspired classroom building for Radcliffe, an Elizabethan or perhaps Jacobean academic building in Brookline, Mass., and a Norman-style Episcopal church in the south end of Boston. At that time, the firm was small (about five draftsmen in addition to the three principals) and the partners were intimately involved in design. As in other architectural offices, varied personalities and talents resulted in the partners' pursuing different parts of the firm's work. Employees remember Perry as a successful promoter, Shaw as a rational space planner, and Hepburn as the talented designer. Nonetheless, surviving drawings show that all three men had some drafting talent,

Old courthouse, erected in 1770, Williamsburg, Virginia

and Perry's story of staying up until 4:00 A.M. in a New York hotel room doing bird's-eye presentation drawings for Goodwin and the still-anonymous Rockefeller reinforces the impression that he could turn out reasonably convincing images when the situation demanded. Daily management of various projects was carried out by job captains drawn from the drafting room.

With the advent of the Williamsburg restoration, the firm expanded significantly, and much administration and design work shifted to Virginia. In 1928 the firm hired Walter Macomber as "resident architect" and promptly shipped him off to Williamsburg. Largely self-educated through a series of jobs in New England architectural offices and a nearly obsessive recording of traditional buildings, Macomber brought to the project a concern for detail in craftsmanship that long outlived his tenure. For Macomber, the essence of colonial buildings lay in the subtleties of their moldings rather than in their planning, and he encouraged a quickly assembled group of draftsmen to look for design inspiration in the countryside around Williamsburg.

The draftsmen were primarily young, imaginative, hard-drinking men with different backgrounds. Best known today (because of his later publications) is Thomas Waterman, who like Macomber had a nonacademic education. Waterman had worked for Boston ecclesiastical architect Ralph Adams Cram and with William Sumner Appleton, founder of the Society for the Preservation of New England Antiquities. He was on the island of Mallorca preparing measured drawings of Palma Cathedral for Cram in 1928 when the call came from Perry, Shaw, and Hepburn. David Hays, a young draftsman also without memories of college architectural classes, was already working for the partners in Boston, and John Barrows came from a Norfolk firm. They were joined by Sammy MacMurtrie, who was finishing architecture school at MIT, and John Henderson from Georgia Tech. The quality of draftsmanship, as well as the spice of life in Williamsburg, was enhanced by George Campbell, who had recently graduated from a Dublin technical school and had left Ireland because of his antirepublican sentiments. Campbell had a grasp of 18th-century details learned in the streets of Dublin and, when found staying in Boston with William Perry's chauffeur, was sent south. Late in 1928 the group was joined by draftsman Singleton Peabody Moorehead, a young Harvard graduate who had had experience at archaeological sites in the Southwest, had practiced with Macomber's old Boston firm of Strickland, Blodgett, and Law, and had developed skills at sketching old buildings on a grand tour of Europe.

The partners, Macomber, and the draftsmen all expected to have an initial period of time for study and design, but upon arriving they found representatives of the New York construction firm of Todd and Brown already present and anxious for working drawings. Antagonism with Todd and Brown, the necessity of dealing with an astonished but strong-willed Virginia community, and the rapid pace of work in what was largely a new idiom put extraordinary pressure on Macomber and the draftsmen. Early difficulties were exacerbated by the partners' insistence on living in Boston. The development of designs from schematics to final drawings, not to mention the resolution of political issues, was slowed by Perry, Shaw, and Hepburn's general absence.

A stabilizing influence appeared in the autumn of 1929, when the partners sent A. Edwin Kendrew to organize the architectural work. Systematic and eminently reasonable, Kendrew began to bring order out of chaos, and he hired additional staff to deal with the increasing work load. For a majority of them—like Finlay Ferguson, Jr., Francis Duke, Everette Fauber, and Milton Grigg, all from the University of Virginia—this was their first full-time job.

Despite Kendrew's efforts, working conditions contributed to disagreements over professional roles. Thomas Waterman was perhaps the most talented member of the group, and by almost all accounts he became the most aggressive. Drawings show that he produced a large percentage of the designs for reconstruction of the Governor's Palace, Capitol, and Raleigh Tavern, as well as the substantial restoration of the main building at the College of William and Mary. The drawings reinforce suggestions that other draftsmen were sometimes pushed aside to deal with less exciting subjects. Yet everyone present was involved in design development to some degree. Waterman's prominent role in the Palace project notwithstanding, for example, the principal outside elevations were developed from the now-famous Bodleian copperplate by Macomber and John Barrows, most of the paint colors were chosen by Boston interior designer Susan Nash, and the rather lavish entrance hall was designed by Moorehead. Ultimately, Moorehead was the most resilient presence. His tenure at Williamsburg outlasted both Waterman's and Macomber's by 30 years. Kendrew remained even longer; he finally retired, as senior vice president, in 1968.

Arthur Shurcliff, a Boston landscape architect who developed garden and street planting schemes for the historic zone until 1941, further enlivened the hectic early scene. Shurcliff was a dramatic, Wildean character whose independence often overcame his official deference to Perry, Shaw, and Hepburn. Zealous enthusiasm led him to Williamsburg executives Arthur Woods and Kenneth Chorley, or directly to Rockefeller.

From 1928 until 1948 an advisory committee of nationally and regionally prominent architects reviewed projects and helped set architectural standards for the Williamsburg effort. Increasingly this committee came to rely on the local staff for most answers. Initially it helped resolve issues involving the extent of the work and lent support to the architects' efforts. In delicate matters involving the preferences of administrators and donors at the state-run College of William and Mary, for example, the committee occasionally nudged the parties toward a better standard of authenticity. This was particularly helpful in the first several years when the extent of future restorations remained very nebulous. In 1928 only buildings on the main street were considered crucial, and uncertainty existed about how to handle areas that had lost their 18th-century buildings. Even then Goodwin and Rockefeller were thinking in terms of a general environment for the principal buildings—Goodwin called it "the frame of the picture"—but the picture was still much smaller than it ultimately became.

As restoration proceeded, the committee came to rely on the local staff for most answers, because their research at the site had made them more expert than even outspoken committee member Fiske Kimball in evaluating building techniques of colonial Virginia. Somehow between the hours of drafting and drinking, the architects found sufficient time to explore the Tidewater countryside. As Macomber had done earlier in New England and George Campbell in Ireland, they carefully observed the details of traditional buildings and recorded their observations in drawings rather than text. By gradually developing an encyclopedic familiarity with early Virginia design, they were following a 19th-century historicist view that one could become entirely conversant in an ancient style, and thereafter design in it much like its original practitioners did. In many ways, this approach reflected an arts and crafts fascination with local, indigenous character. Old vernacular design was seen as important because it embodied a preindustrial, *regional* personality.

Williamsburg held an appeal for these designers that ran somewhat counter to a vernacular mode. The buildings did not stand in an informal pattern like those in a picturesque English village, but rather were arranged in a precise order along parallel streets broken by public spaces and designed with a strong sense of axis. This simple American Baroque plan brought order to the various vernacular parts, creating a coherent system that seemed very much like the studio projects Moorehead and other students had observed and executed in long, late-night charettes. In many ways, the restored and recreated public buildings and vistas in Williamsburg seemed to offer an American antecedent for grander beaux-arts designs in cities like Chicago and Washington.

The partners in Boston and the respected review committee members, as well as the young draftsmen in Williamsburg, had a shared educational background, formal or not. It emphasized immersion in historical styles and their skillful use for modern buildings. Regional styles were viewed with favor, and modest hand-crafted details were still seen as wholesome. Countering the picturesqueness of vernacular building was a fondness for grand, balanced beaux-arts planning.

All involved were unusually careful in following details of existing buildings and in employing specific evidence when it was available for reconstructions. When direct evidence could not be found, they drew on their understanding of the local style to create plausible reconstructions. They saw life in the 18th-century South as more homogeneous and certainly more genteel than late 20th-century historians do. As a result, their observations among the venerable buildings of Tidewater Virginia were selective, focusing on pleasant, well-resolved design rather than the confusion and cheapness that existed alongside it. The fine products of a slave economy were presented, but the system was romanticized or left unacknowledged. Complex history was thus screened and sanitized and delivered to a nation receptive to its optimistic, patriotic message.

This is not entirely the way it would be done today; provocative economic theory, social history, and the civil rights movement would make that impossible. Yet the grand project that began in 1928 and continued along the same lines for the next 50 years holds an unusual appeal. Substantially the product of a particular time and educational system, Colonial Williamsburg is commonly seen as a graceful effort, a seamless whole. Perhaps it could not have been accomplished at another time. Yet because of its size and complexity, it clearly offers continuing opportunities for development and change.

See also RECREATION: / Colonial Williamsburg

Edward A. Chappell
Williamsburg, Virginia

Charles B. Hosmer, Jr., in *The Colonial Revival in America*, ed. Alan Axelrod (1985), *Preservation Comes of Age: From Williamsburg to the National Trust, 1926–1949* (1981); Fay Campbell Kaynor, *Winterthur Portfolio* (Summer–Autumn 1985); Michael Wallace, *Radical History Review* (1981).

Colonial Revival Architecture

The Colonial Revival subsumes what can be called the "antebellum revival." This would include 20th-century houses built in the Greek Revival or columnar styles of the 1840s and 1850s. By the 1930s and 1940s these original structures had become emblems of the image—real or imagined—of the South's white antebellum "aristocratic" culture, which by this time had gained national acceptance. It had some basis in fact but was considerably nourished by popular novels and films. In England the Queen Anne style revived vernacular English domestic architecture of the medieval period, but in America the style was related to colonial architecture. Beginning roughly in 1867, gathering force in the early 1870s, and growing in favor from 1874 on, the Colonial Revival enjoyed a nostalgic and antiquarian popularity in the South as well as in the rest of the United States.

In 1867 Donald G. Mitchell in his book *Rural Studies* examined old American houses with "a character of their own" that should be respected. However, his proposals for new houses were scarcely influenced by colonial precedents except for his advocacy of half-timbering, which he observed was rarely found in the North but commonly existed in Florida and Louisiana. Illustrated in the book was an old small building that he sketched near New Orleans; he would later propose that Louisiana erect a similar one at the Centennial Exhibition in Philadelphia in 1876.

In 1869 Richard Upjohn, noted architect and the first

president of the American Institute of Architects, wrote "Colonial Architecture of New York and the New England States," one of the first such articles in a professional publication. In the 1870s laymen as well as architects enjoyed seaside vacations, which focused attention upon seaside resort towns, many of which had not changed since colonial days. This widespread exposure to colonial architecture helped to promote the style's popularity.

The Colonial Revival, wrote one architect in 1876, is "no feeble copy of foreign styles of questionable fitness and in little sympathy with our institutions but distinctly American." Despite the interest in the American colonial past generated by the 1876 Centennial Exhibition, no structure at that exhibit replicated any colonial structure. The Connecticut State Building came the closest. It was certainly not a strict copy of a Connecticut saltbox but was intended to evoke thoughts of the state's early history, according to architect Donald Mitchell.

In March of 1876 the *American Architect* suggested that architects spend their holidays making notes of colonial architecture because it, "with all its faults of formality and meagerness, was, on the whole, decidedly superior in style and good building, if we may say so, to most that has followed it." The following year noted architects Charles McKim, William Mead, Stanford White, and William Bigelow made a walking tour of colonial New England buildings that were attracting attention in the professional journals (such as the *American Architect*, which published Robert Peabody's "Georgian Homes of New England" in 1877). Sketching their way along the coast of Massachusetts and New Hampshire, they seemed to be searching for a national heritage on which to build an American architectural style. In later years eclectic devotees would claim this trip as the "discovery" of the colonial. The subsequent architectural firm of McKim, Mead, and White would dominate American architecture for years.

The Colonial Revival style began at first as an addition to the Queen Anne vocabulary; details such as Adamesque garlands, classical pilasters, and Palladian windows were common. But by 1879, the style had emerged in its own right. Shingles yielded to clapboards, picturesque massing to symmetry. The playful roof of the Queen Anne was replaced by a standard hipped or gabled roof. At the center of the facade, the symmetrical axis, was an elaborate doorway flanked by big broad windows with a single sheet of plate glass below and many smaller panes above arranged in a pseudo-Georgian pattern. Details and massing in this initial phase were larger than their original colonial counterparts, with many of the elements oversized or exaggerated.

The 20th century brought a more academic approach, perfectly symmetrical, correctly proportioned, and more widely accepted. At first only Georgian and Federal precedents were used; however, as various regions of the country explored their colonial architecture, numerous variations became popular. In the Southwest the mission style (characterized by semicircular arches, low-pitched tiled roofs, and stucco surfaces) and the pueblo style (characterized by massive-looking battered walls with round corners, flat roofs, and projecting roof beams called "viga") evolved. In Florida, Texas, and California the Spanish past was romanticized in the Spanish Colonial Revival style popularized by the 1915 San Diego Exposition. The Mar-A-Lago by Addison Mizner in Palm Beach, Fla., is a superb example of the style. White stuccoed Spanish-style cottages and churches and schools built in the Spanish mission styles are also to be found in Louisiana and Alabama, where the earlier Spanish period of domination was relatively short but nonetheless important. In Louisiana, Mississippi, and Alabama, the Creole colonial heritage was borrowed, while from New York came the Dutch colonial, and from Cape Cod came the style that bore its name. From Virginia came the Williamsburg style after the reconstruction of that capital in the 1930s. Versions of Williamsburg-Georgian houses have appeared throughout the country, North and South, East and West, since the 1930s. Whether these have enjoyed more popularity in the South since that time is difficult to say. Certainly they appear in significant numbers in affluent suburbs and sections of cities from Baton Rouge to Norfolk. Alongside the plans and external architectural features of Williamsburg-Georgian, the interior paneling and the "Williamsburg colors," such as soft muted blues and greens, have been used in numerous interiors.

All of these styles were very popular in the South in early 20th-century neighborhoods, as housing demands created enormous pressures. The strong national sentiment, which resulted in the introduction of variations of what were originally regional forms into all parts of the country, served in part to blur the sense of regional architecture.

Robert J. Cangelosi
New Orleans, Louisiana

Alan Axelrod, ed., *The Colonial Revival in America* (1985); Donald W. Curl, *Mizner's Florida: American Resort Architecture* (1984); Robert B. Harmon, *The Colonial Revival in American Architecture: A Brief Study Guide* (1983); Marian Page, *Historic Houses Restored and Preserved* (1976); William H. Pierson, Jr., *American Buildings and Their Architects: The Colonial and Neo-Classical Styles* (1970); Carole Rifkind, *A Field Guide to American Architecture* (1980); Leland M. Roth, *A Concise History of American Architecture* (1979).

Decorative Arts

In 1949 the American curator at the Metropolitan Museum of Art, speaking at the First Antiques Forum at Williamsburg, noted that "very little of artistic merit was made south of Baltimore." The history of southern decorative art is not, however, one of underachievement but of underappreciation. Much of this neglect was at the hands of native sons and daughters until this century.

Well-assembled collections of antiques appeared in New England by 1793, but such collections were largely unknown in the South at that time except for the occasional preservation of inherited family pieces or items belonging to Revolutionary War heroes.

Generally speaking, old furniture in the region was thrown or given away or was stored and forgotten. Heat, humidity, and insects have taken their toll as have fires, earthquakes, hurricanes, tornadoes, and wars. Charleston, S.C., for example, experienced so-called great fires in 1740, 1828, and 1861. Ironically, when the city was under seige in 1863 to 1865, Charlestonians who could moved prized family pieces to Columbia for safekeeping only to see their state capitol torched in 1865. Looting during the war contributed to the dearth of surviving southern-made objects. Economic depression followed the Civil War, forcing some southerners to move away and others to sell heirlooms that had survived the war. Continuing regional poverty in the 20th century discouraged interest in preserving craftsmen's products.

A new era of respect for southern handiwork began in 1952 when the Virginia Museum of Fine Arts at Richmond, the magazine *Antiques*, and Colonial Williamsburg jointly organized a major exhibition, *Southern Furniture, 1640–1820*. It was the first show of its kind and spawned many exhibits and studies thereafter. The Virginia Museum exhibit has been overshadowed by only one development—the founding of the Museum of Early Southern Decorative Arts (MESDA) in 1965 in Winston-Salem, N.C. MESDA has fostered a systematic approach to the study of regional decorative arts. Its 15 period rooms are arranged chronologically from 1690 to 1820, and it has four galleries and an outstanding collection. More ambitious, though not as visible, are MESDA's ongoing, long-range projects such as the survey of regional decorative arts in public and private collections, to be published as the *Catalogue of Early Southern Decorative Arts* and the *Index of Early Southern Artists and Artisans*. The latter contains data on a wide spectrum of individuals from cabinetmakers to silversmiths and addresses questions regarding identification of craftspeople, use of technology, design and materials sources, education, apprenticeship experiences, and social customs. Since 1975 the public has been informed of MESDA's work through its quarterly periodical, the *Journal of Early Southern Decorative Arts*.

The scholarship of the last 30 years has promoted development of a comprehensive picture of the South's decorative arts, which have been geographically widespread and culturally diverse. Though fewer "schools" of artisans have been identified than in the Northeast, distinguishing design and construction techniques have been established.

The dominant influence upon the decorative arts along the southeastern seaboard and in many island areas was English. However, the region's decorative arts are richer because of contributions from Moravians, Shakers, Swiss Protestants, Afro-Americans, and French and Caribbean immigrants. In whatever period craftsmen have been active in the South, they have generally taken contemporary concepts of aesthetics and combined them with ideas remembered or inherited from their homelands, using available materials and tools. This has been true of goldsmiths, carriagemakers, potters, needleworkers, and many other craftspeople.

Valuable discoveries have been made regarding the location and output of individuals and workshops, and we now have a growing tabulation of southern-made objects. This research refutes earlier assumptions that southern production was meager and unrefined or that fine crafted things in the South were imported from Europe in general and England in particular.

Decorative arts are often born more from necessity than from the urge to display. This was true for household items in the early South. After shelter, furniture was the most pressing need. Imported furniture was expensive, and only a limited amount could be brought with colonists by ship. Initially, the simplest of devices passed as furniture—benches, stools, chests, and trunks. These were made by carpenters, joiners, and turners or by homeowners themselves. Resourcefulness was a necessity, and comfort was secondary.

When colonists settled the Tidewater sections of Maryland, Virginia, and the Carolinas, they found abundant hardwoods and soon favored oak and walnut for furniture. Secondary woods included yellow pine, maple, red cedar, and in South Carolina, cypress. The need for storage and the absence of closets dictated the production of cupboards, clothespresses, and blanket chests. More complex but not at all beyond the abilities of turners was the gateleg table particularly popular from 1675 through the early 1700s. Its side leaves could be raised when needed or dropped for placement against a wall, providing more space in modest-sized rooms.

The chair, so common and indispensable today, was less common in the 17th century than stools and benches. No single type of chair in the South may be called typical, but armchairs resembling the Brewster or Great chairs of New England were known. They featured turned architectural elements throughout, caging the sitter upon a rush seat. Beds from the early colonial period are as rare as colonial-era chairs, and when equipped with bedstead curtains and valances, they were valued even then at more than their weight in tobacco.

From the 17th century to the early 18th century southerners' desire for luxury goods was not substantial enough to support specialized artisans, but as farmers and traders began to prosper they sought goods such as table services. Silver pieces, sometimes engraved, survive from the Charleston, S.C., area. They approximate the form and embellishment of contemporary English work. Earthenware pottery from the mid-17th century has been found in Virginia. Utilitarian rather than ornate, it was made from Virginia clay banks, which later yielded good brick for permanent homes and civic buildings.

By the middle of the 18th century dramatic changes had come to southern decorative arts. The colonies of the preceding century survived and stabilized, and some settlements even prospered. Soon some southerners desired to improve personal possessions and had the means to do so. English culture became even more dominant. Colonists, emulating prosperous merchant and manufacturing classes in England who aspired to aristocratic values, constructed imposing homes and purchased generous furnishings.

Baltimore and Annapolis, Md., Norfolk and Williamsburg, Va., Edenton, N.C., and Charleston, S.C., boasted active cabinet production. Colonial furniture workshops usually had English-trained craftsmen who instructed and supervised colonial apprentices or local artisans using English copybooks, the most influential being *The Gentleman and Cabinet-Maker's Directory* (London, 1754) by Thomas Chippendale. Southern artisans soon achieved high levels of stylistic and technical ability. Their work and reputation led to sales in New England and exports to Europe. That success coincided with a proliferation of furniture forms more service- and comfort-oriented—easy chairs, tea tables, and several types of desks/secretaries.

Remarkable information has been pieced together concerning outstanding workshops in Williamsburg where craftsmen like Peter Scott, Anthony Hay, and Benjamin Bucktrout sharpened their skills in the 1700s. They created household furniture and ceremonial pieces using mahogany when possible. Durable and easy to carve, mahogany could be polished, revealing superb graining; and though not a native material, it was easily imported from the Caribbean.

Eighteenth-century furniture from eastern Virginia mixed refinements with sound construction. Especially noticeable on case furniture and otherwise elaborate items were the standard features of full dust boards between drawers, paneled backs, and composite feet. Emphasis upon high-quality construction was a trait of southern furniture and contributed to the long-standing perception of it as "plain but neat." By contrast, northern furniture was more flamboyant. In Virginia and elsewhere Chippendale was followed by furniture resembling English Sheraton, Hepplewhite, and Regency styles. Production increased, yet standards remained high.

If Virginia had an 18th-century rival in the decorative arts, it was indeed Charleston, S.C. Not only was Charleston the commercial, political, legal, and social center of South Carolina, but it rivaled Philadelphia culturally and was deservedly known as the jewel of the Southeast. Furniture had been produced in Charleston since soon after its founding in 1670. High English tariffs (33 percent duty on imports by 1822) on finished products encouraged the resourceful Carolinians in their domestic arts.

Charleston furniture almost presumes mahogany. So much of it came from the West Indies that by 1740 all duties on it were repealed. A Charleston chair, for example, was easily distinguished from English imports by the amount of mahogany, by its thicker rails, and by heavier corner blocks. A Charleston double chest of drawers, a bookcase, or a secretary might be exceptionally tall, scaled to high ceilings. Likewise, Charleston beds sometimes had nine-foot posts and had removable headboards to facilitate nocturnal breezes. By 1810 a Charleston directory listed 81 cabinetmakers, and the city's furniture making was at a high point. It declined in the mid-1820s because of the acceptance of cheaper mass-produced pieces from England and New England.

Furniture making followed settlers as they pushed inland, upland, and over the tall line of mountain ranges. From the Germans in the North Carolina Piedmont to the French in lower Louisiana, national craft traditions were retained at least in spirit. Moravian furniture, for example, redefined the term *spartan*. Sawbuck tables and conservatively designed chairs met the utilitarian needs of a simple lifestyle. French settlements in the lower Mississippi Valley also produced rather austere furniture. Large armoires distinctive to the area were made from fine-grained walnut that responded to polishing and from abundant supplies of cypress. Delicately carved, cloven-hoofed doe's feet supported tables, bedsteads, and case furniture alike. Louisiana furniture has only recently been studied, and few pieces have survived. Its difference from French or French Canadian work has been noted, but its similarity to furniture from the French islands of the West Indies has increasingly been recognized.

Late 18th-century silver from the southern colonies is a rarer commodity than furniture because it could be melted for other purposes. Fighting occurred in Charleston, S.C., and the surrounding countryside during the Revolutionary War, and it is a small miracle that any silver survived at all. The British forcibly took it by the rice barrelful, with one account suggesting 500 rice barrels of silver were taken.

At least 35 silversmiths were active at the time, producing mugs, bowls, tankards, and coffee pots as well as occasional unusual items for the table. Craftsmen of note included Daniel and Thomas You and Alexander Petrie. The work of James Geddy II of Williamsburg is well known, too, and can still be appreciated through his re-created home and workshop at Williamsburg.

By the early 19th century silversmith Charles Burnett of Georgetown in the District of Columbia was forming vessels that reflected the growing identification by the American Republic with ancient Greek institutions and aesthetics. An affinity for things Greek was even more noticeable in American furniture. French Empire styles also gained popularity, and American craftsmen synthesized English Regency and French Empire by looking at imported pieces and poring over fashion books like Thomas Hope's *Household Furniture*.

Baltimore was an active center during this period. Fine work also came from Alexandria, Va. Beyond chairs in the manner of Herculaneum and Pompeii, the most conspicuous changes could be seen in chests of drawers often termed "bureaus" or "consol bureaus." Emblematic features included highly figured mahogany veneers accented by brass hardware, carved scrolls of bold proportion, and columns supporting an overhanging top drawer. Scrolls animated sofas on back rails and writhing arm rests. The scale was generally masculine and vigorously imposing, all compatible with Greek Revival architecture, the best examples of which are in the South. This furniture was remarkably inexpensive.

The pendulum of taste eventually swung from classi-

Secretary, brought to Greene County, Ga., in 1802, a typical southern antique by the time this photograph was made in 1941

cal to other revival styles by the mid-1800s. Rococo revival was especially represented in the South by the successful New Orleans firm of Prudent Mallard. Mallard was at various times listed as a furniture dealer, cabinetmaker, and upholsterer. Rococo furniture could be fancifully ornate with seemingly endless pierced and carved vinework. Mallard's bedroom sets were eagerly sought by those living great distances upriver from New Orleans. His half-testers featured dowels in the footboard finials that could be raised to support tentlike gauze protection against mosquitoes. Such pragmatic adoption of a high style to local conditions of climate was typical of southern ingenuity.

The Civil War and the Reconstruction period that followed disrupted patronage of most of the decorative arts in the South. But progress did not end altogether, as evidenced by the innovative Newcomb pottery works at Tulane University.

Research into the decorative arts of the South is still in its infancy. Yet current scholarly interest is very encouraging, and the titles of recent studies and exhibition catalogs reveal increased specificity and focus. Valuable resources include *Furniture of Williamsburg and Eastern Virginia, 1710–1790*; *Furniture of the Georgia Piedmont before 1830*; *John Shaw: Cabinetmaker of Annapolis*; *Early Furniture of Louisiana*; and currently in preparation *Mississippi-Made Furniture, 1790–1865*. Magazines such as *Southern Accents* and *Texas Homes* are popular forums for the decorative arts in the South, and national periodicals such as the magazine *Antiques* frequently publish stories on the South.

Thomas Dewey
University of Mississippi

E. Milby Burton, *Charleston Furniture, 1700–1825* (1955); George B. Cutten, *Silversmiths of North Carolina, 1696–1860* (2d ed., 1984); Marshall B. Davidson, E. Milby Burton, and Helen Comstock, *South Furniture* (1952); William Voss Elder III and Lu Bartlett, *John Shaw: Cabinetmaker of Annapolis* (1983); Henry D. Green, *Furniture of the Georgia Piedmont before 1830* (1976); William Griffin et al., *Neat Pieces: The Plain-Style Furniture of Nineteenth-Century Georgia* (1983); Wallace B. Gusler, *Furniture of Williamsburg and Eastern Virginia, 1710–1790* (1979); Jessie Poesch, *The Art of the Old South: Painting, Sculpture, Architecture and the Products of Craftsmen, 1560–1860* (1983), *Early Furniture of Louisiana* (1972); Gregory R. Weidman, *Furniture in Maryland, 1740–1940* (1984).

Farm Buildings

Farm buildings are working buildings. The number, kind, and arrangement of buildings on a farm vary regionally according to the type of agriculture practiced in a given locality and inherited ethnic and traditional ideas. Geographical diversity is complicated by change over time. Alterations in the agricultural system of a locality may result in nearly complete replacement of older farm buildings with newer ones. In some parts of eastern Virginia, for example, the change from tobacco to corn, peanut, and hog farming resulted in the nearly complete destruction of the area's 18th- and early 19th-century farm buildings. More commonly, changes in farming practices have altered the preferred types of farm buildings even though the crop has remained the same. Colonial tobacco-growing practices required different kinds of tobacco barns from those used since the early 19th century, so few tobacco barns survive from before 1800.

The most conspicuous farm building to lay observers is the barn. In English tradition, a barn was a place to store unthreshed grain and to process it by threshing. Its plan consisted of large storage bays alternating with narrower runways fitted with doors at one or both ends for wagon entry and with wooden floors for threshing. The smallest version, consisting of a storage bay on either side of a runway, was known by the 18th century as an English barn. Large examples might extend seven to nine parts, with four to five storage bays alternating with threshing floors and runways. After threshing, the grain might be stored in chests in the barn or in separate granaries. Animals lived not in the barn but in other buildings.

There is little evidence that barns of this sort were built in the earliest Tidewater southern settlements. Little need existed for such large buildings for grain storage; other crops, notably tobacco and maize, or Indian corn, occupied more of the farmers' time and resources. Where they were used, barns tended to be small. Grain was most commonly threshed in the field by horses or on portable threshing floors in the farmyard and only occasionally on permanent threshing floors in the barn.

Early barns are more common in the Upland South, and they have attracted considerably more study. Geographers and folklorists have labeled the most common of them single-crib, double-crib, and transverse-crib barns.

All are one-story buildings, commonly augmented by open sheds on one or more sides to shelter animals and equipment. The single-crib barn contains one enclosed space; the double-crib barn has two enclosures, separated by a runway. In form it resembles the traditional English barn, although Terry G. Jordan has associated it with central-runway hay barns in Austria, and Martin Wright believes it has a Scandinavian ancestry. Surviving examples seem to have been built for mixed use, with grain storage in one bay, animal housing in another, and the dirt-floored runway used for vehicle loading and shelter below, with hay storage on poles above. The form is an additive one, and examples with three cribs and two runways exist. Single-crib and double-crib barns normally have gable roofs with their ridges running parallel to the entry facades. The transverse-crib barn, on the other hand, has its entrances on the gable ends, as do other southern farm buildings of all sorts. It consists of three or more adjacent cribs, or enclosures, on either side of a wide runway. There are many theories about the origin of the transverse-crib barn, none conclusively established. Henry Glassie's hypothesis is the simplest; he has suggested that the transverse-crib barn was created in the early 19th-century Tennessee Valley through the construction of two parallel double-crib barns separated to create two runways at right angles. Ultimately one of the runways was filled in, creating the transverse-crib barn. Whatever its origin, it seems likely that the transverse-crib barn is a creation of the Upland South. Like the double-crib barn, it was a mixed-use building, housing animals, hay, and farm implements.

In the eastern uplands between the late 18th and the early 20th centuries, farmers also built forebay (also bank, or Pennsylvania) barns, a hybrid of English and Germanic traditions probably created in Pennsylvania in the 18th century. Others used English barns, bank barns without forebays, and hybrids like the cantilever barns of east Tennessee and western North Carolina. In the latter, an upper level was deeply cantilevered beyond a lower on two or four sides of a double- or transverse-crib barn. Few examples survive and their precise origins are uncertain, but they represent a localized combination of the crib barn with the cantilevered appearance and framing of the forebay barn as a way of increasing hay-storage capacity.

Specialized buildings on southern farms tended to be few and small. Even barns were unnecessary. The most common buildings other than barns were small storage houses for field crops. Granaries about 20 feet wide and 20 to 40 feet long were used in the Tidewater for the storage of grain and field crops. The survivors, few of which date before 1800, tend to contain a single open space, sealed inside with flush boards about waist high to permit bulk storage. Most have gable-end entries. Equally prevalent are small, freestanding "cribs" (not to be confused with the cribs that are parts of a barn) for storing corn. One common form, which can be found all over the United States, is made of log or of frame covered with narrow, widely spaced slats. It is 3 or 4 feet high, about the same width, and 10 feet long. The entry is from the gable, and the sides slant in toward the bottom, giving the ends a pentagonal appearance. Along the Atlantic Coast, somewhat larger, gable-end, vertical-walled buildings, about 10 by 20 feet, were constructed. Usually they could be partitioned with loose boards into three parts for ease of loading. Since the late 19th century, many farmers have preferred tall, thin, slatted structures, loaded from the top. Frequently, "drive-through" cribs are created by placing under a single roof one or more cribs that alternate with wagonways for loading them.

Another important class consists of farm buildings that serve for processing agricultural products. Most common are small square buildings, 8 to 12 feet on a side, used in smoking or chemically curing meat and for storing dairy products and keeping them cool. These are usually included in the domestic complex, standing close to the house. From North Carolina south, cotton gins in large buildings built for that purpose are common. Farther north, small gins can sometimes be found installed in a corner of a granary or storage shed, indicating that cotton had been a minor crop for the farmer.

The most recognizable and carefully studied of the processing and storage buildings found on southern farms are the tobacco "barns" scattered throughout the region. Southern farmers have cultivated tobacco as a market crop since the early 17th century, and a variety of barn forms have been created in response to changing methods of cultivation and curing. Before the early 19th century tobacco farmers in the Tidewater and Piedmont regions prepared and partially dried their tobacco in open sheds before hanging it in long, narrow barns to finish curing. The tobacco leaves were tied in bunches, or "hands," and draped over sticks a little over five feet long. The inside of the barn was fitted with horizontal poles, running front to back, set at intervals of about five feet horizontally and vertically. The sticks carrying the tobacco leaves were draped across these tier poles, which filled the barn from the ridge of the roof to within a few feet of the floor. There the tobacco was left to be dried by the air. Then it was taken down and pressed into enormous barrels, or hogsheads, for sale and shipping.

Methods of curing by heat have been used since the 18th century, when tobacco was exposed to damped open fires whose smoke was allowed to drift out through holes in the barn. Fire curing of dark tobaccos is still common in the Virginia Piedmont and in Kentucky, where square or oblong barns, respectively, are used for the process. About 1820 a technique was developed for curing bright tobaccos, grown in eastern Virginia and North Carolina, in small barns using the heat from enclosed fires. These "flue-cured" barns, which are still widely used, are cubical structures 16 to 24 feet on a side. Many are built of log, though frame and more recently concrete-block structures can also be found. The earliest survivors are heated from long, low, open-topped, floor-level stone furnaces, resembling barbecue pits, which are stoked from the outside. From the far end of the furnace a metal flue protrudes, carried horizontally to the far corner and then up through the roof of the barn. This flue, together with the piece of sheet metal that covers the open top of the furnace, helps to diffuse the heat evenly through the barn, which like its colonial predecessors is filled with tier poles to carry the tobacco sticks. Flue-cured barns are customarily scattered over the farm, convenient to the fields. Open sheds on one or more sides provide shelter for the workers who strip the plants and prepare the tobacco to be hung. In North Carolina one occasionally sees long rows of these barns connected by a continuous arcade of open worksheds, but more often the barns stand singly or in pairs. In the 20th century, fuel-oil furnaces, recognizable by the fuel-oil tanks next to the barn, replaced coal- and wood-fired furnaces as the preferred heating method, and they in turn were supplanted by propane heating devices, identifiable by the sheet-metal monitor on the ridge of the roof. Most recently, "bulk curing" in small, tightly sealed metal boxes resembling trailers has begun to replace flue curing.

Air curing continues to be used for some tobaccos. In southern Maryland, long, narrow barns are used. These are usually covered with vertical-board siding in which every other board is hinged to allow the sides to be opened for greater air penetration when the building is full. In the Appalachian uplands hay barns are often adapted to the purpose simply by pulling off most of their exterior siding.

A farm is an economic entity. Except, perhaps, for a small yard in front of the house, the farm buildings are a unit with the farmhouse, the yards, and the fields. Together, they constitute a continuous group of related spaces carefully designed for the production, processing, and storage of agricultural products. The farmer must decide which necessary tasks require special buildings, which can be performed in multipurpose buildings, and which can be accomplished in the open. Thus, the open sheds that cluster around all southern farm buildings cannot be overlooked in an account of the architecture of the farm. They form transitional spaces between the tightly enclosed farmhouse and farm buildings and the open yards and fields; their use is encouraged by the mild climate of the region, which allows storage, equipment shelter, and even animal housing in sheds rather than fully enclosed buildings.

The largest divisions of the farmstead are the yards and fields themselves. Here space is differentiated by the

Outbuilding on a farm, Sharon, Miss., 1972

varied fences and walls that are in many cases the oldest forms to be seen on the southern farm. Picket fences for front yards and gardens and post-and-rail fences for gardens and farmyards were first recorded in the 17th century, and they are still used for these purposes. The snake, or Virginia, fence and its stake-and-rider variants have been used to enclose pastures and fields since the late 17th century. Their advantage is that they can be disassembled and moved as land use changes. Horizontal-board fences, a 19th-century innovation, are also common in prosperous areas of the South. In limestone regions of the Upland South stone, or "rock," fences were popular. A striking form of Kentucky stone wall, in which the horizontal courses are capped by a row of jagged stones set on edge, is known as the Bluegrass fence, but it is a northern European form. As in other parts of the country, wire fencing and electric fencing have replaced wood and stone, particularly for farm fields; but the diligent observer can still find all of the traditional fence types.

See also AGRICULTURE: / Tobacco Culture; FOLKLIFE: / Smokehouse; GEOGRAPHY: Plantation Morphology; / Cotton Gins

Dell Upton
University of California
at Los Angeles

Eric Arthur and Dudley Witney, *The Barn: A Vanishing Landmark in North America* (1972); Ligon Flynn and Roman Stankus, in *Carolina Dwelling: Towards Preservation of Place: In Celebration of the North Carolina Vernacular Landscape*, ed. Doug Swaim (1978); Henry Glassie, *Mountain Life and Work* (Spring 1964, Summer 1965), *Pattern in the Material Folk Culture of the Eastern United States* (1969), *Pennsylvania Folklife* (Winter 1965–66, Summer 1966); J. Fraser Hart and Eugene Cotton Mather, *Annals of the Association of American Geographers* (September 1961); Terry G. Jordan, *American Log Buildings: An Old World Heritage* (1985); Marian Moffett and Lawrence Wodehouse, *The Cantilever Barn in East Tennessee* (1984); Karl B. Raitz, *Landscape* (Spring 1978); Orlando V. Ridout, in *Perspectives in Vernacular Architecture*, ed. Camille Wells (1982); Laura Scism, in *Carolina Dwelling: Towards Preservation of Place: In Celebration of the North Carolina Vernacular Landscape*, ed. Doug Swaim (1978).

French Architecture

Although France's colonial domination of Louisiana lasted only from 1682 to the 1760s, its influence upon the architecture and culture of the region was profound. Encompassing all the territory drained by the Mississippi River, Louisiana was claimed by LaSalle, who in 1682 had descended the river from the French holdings in Canada. Not until 1698, however, did Pierre le Moyne de Iberville sail from France to build the first French outpost on the Gulf Coast. Situated on the eastern shore of Biloxi Bay, Fort Maurepas was a modest example of a system of fortifications developed by the French military engineer Sebastien Vauban (1633–1707). Built entirely of timber, it consisted of a square palisade with pointed bastions at the corners designed to eliminate blind spots on the wall. Thus, the pattern of fortifications was strongly influenced by French military engineering theory. Many other forts followed, all employing the Vauban system to some degree.

In addition to fortifications, military engineers laid out towns (usually on a grid plan) and designed buildings for the crown, often guided by French precedent published in books such as *La Science des Ingenieurs* (Paris, 1729). Their designs were usually simplified adaptations of current Louis XV forms. The larger colonial structures were outwardly symmetrical and generally rectangular, with high-pitched roofs usually hipped at the ends. Moulded stucco details such as quoins at the corners and horizontal bands were often used to imitate stone masonry construction. In massing and detail they were similar to French buildings elsewhere, but the subtropical climate had a marked influence upon the local buildings. Unlike France and Canada, the southern colony had frequent, heavy rains and a long summer. Because traditional French building forms were better suited to northern latitudes, roofed galleries were added to shade the walls and provide sheltered outdoor living space. The gallery roofs were often framed from the tops of the turned or chamfered wood posts to a point about halfway up the slope of the main roof, giving the roof an unusual double pitch (e.g., The Intendance, 1749).

The heavy timber building frame known as *colombage* was brought from France, where it had been in wide use since medieval times. It consisted of squared timbers pinned together at mortise-and-tenon joints. Continuous sills were laid upon the ground, and posts were set at the corners of the building and at the sides of all windows and doors. Across the tops of these posts, horizontal members formed the top of the walls. In order to add stability, diagonal members were added, and to achieve some insulation, the walls were filled with either soft bricks or with *bouzillage* (a mixture of mud and moss or straw) and covered on the outside with wide boards or stucco. The roof-framing systems of even small French colonial buildings were usually well-crafted trusses pinned at the joints with wooden pegs. Dormers were small and attics were most often used only for storage.

French influence did not cease when colonial Louisiana was ceded to Spain in 1763. Although the government changed, many of those who designed and constructed the buildings were born of French parents, and they carried on the tradition that had already been established.

The greatest influence that the Spanish had on architecture was their enactment of laws governing building construction in the city of New Orleans. Until then, owners were free to build as they chose, which usually meant frame buildings roofed with flammable wood shingles. In 1788 and again in 1794, catastrophic fires leveled large portions of the city. After the second great fire, the Cabildo, or city government, specified that all roofs be covered with slate or tile, that walls be of brick or brick between posts covered with stucco, and that buildings be built up to the front property line, thus creating a sort of fire wall and giving the city its intensely urban character.

During the Spanish period, Americans began to filter into the former French colony, and many of them continued to build in the adapted French style. By responding to the problems of climate and limited available materials, the "typical" French house became an accepted form that survived long after the Louisiana Purchase of 1803. This type of house was rectangular, usually of two stories, and the rooms opened onto one another without halls. The first story was built entirely of stuccoed brick and was used for utility purposes; the second story was of colombage filled with brick or bouzillage and covered on the outside with stucco or wide ship-lapped boards. Interior walls were invariably plastered and painted. All wood, except the floors, was painted. Access to the second floor was by exterior stairs under the sheltering gallery roofs. Openings were protected by solid wooden shutters hung on strap hinges, and the first floor was paved with brick if it was paved at all. The second-floor ceiling joists and floorboards formed the ceiling of the first floor. The principal floor was usually well finished, with French doors and casement windows hung on decorative wrought-iron hinges. Top and bottom bolts, slide latches, and knob-operated bar latches completed the door and window hardware. The exposed second-floor ceiling joists (always beaded on the corners) supported the beaded attic floorboards. The plastered walls were usually adorned with a baseboard, chair rail, and cornice (always of wood). Ceilings on the principal floor were generally high (10 to 12 feet) to allow the summer heat to rise so that cross-ventilation could carry it out of the house.

The principal architectural feature of most rooms was the mantel. Fireplaces in buildings of this type were invariably on interior walls, and they were often paired back to back. Consequently, the fireboxes and breasts projected into the rooms. Mantels were paneled on the sides, and the shelf always wrapped around the breast, returning against the wall. Ornament on these "Creole" mantels varied from engaged turned posts to fluted pilasters. The more elaborate gougework on some Creole mantels was probably a result of influence from the American North. Sometimes, the breasts were also encased in paneling and the room cornice was carried out around them.

Variations of this perfectly adapted building form were used in towns and suburbs and in the country until the middle of the 19th century. The popularity of the great national building styles—Greek Revival, Gothic, and Italianate—ultimately overwhelmed the traditional local style, but even these were somewhat affected by the adapted French forms.

Combining as it did elements of Louis XV design and climatic adaptations to the southern latitude, expressed in indigenous materials, French colonial architecture left a unique and enduring impression upon the South—one that exists in no other place in quite the same way.

See also ETHNIC LIFE: / French; Spanish

Frank W. Masson
New Orleans, Louisiana

Jessie Poesch, *The Art of the Old South: Painting, Sculpture, Architecture and the Products of Craftsmen, 1560–1860* (1983); Italo W. Ricciuti, *New Orleans and Its Environs: The Domestic Architecture, 1727–1870* (1938); Samuel Wilson, Jr., *Bienville's New Orleans: A French Colonial Capital, 1718–1768* (1968).

Georgian Revival Architecture

Within the space of a quarter century, from the 1920s to the beginning of World War II, a body of truly distinguished domestic architecture was produced in the South. These Georgian Revival houses, distinctive from those of the early 20th century and those of the post–World War II period, occupy a place in the architectural history of the South—and particularly the Upland South—not unlike that of the houses of the mid-19th-century antebellum period. Both were products of a rapidly developing economy, and both were places on which their owners had lavished money in the creation of a handsome home. Both were also brought to a halt by war: in the first instance, by the Civil War; in the second, by the prolonged economic effects of the Great Depression and then by World War II.

The Georgian Revival of the interwar period was separate and distinct from the Colonial Revival of the early 20th century. At the same time, it grew from many of the same impulses that had fostered the earlier effort and was the final or mature phase of the Colonial Revival. The character of the houses of the period is specific, definable, and discrete; they are also extraordinarily beautiful buildings.

The personality of the houses of the Georgian Revival is dominated by the architecture of the 18th century of Virginia and Maryland, which by a confluence of natural and contrived circumstances, came to be seen as an exemplar of the finest design. This borrowing represents one of the earliest instances in this country of a contemporary adaptation of older indigenous architecture. The upper middle class and the aspiring aristocrats of the early 20th century—some of whom were the descendants of the middle class and aristocracy of the 18th century—were anxious to assume the trappings of their own, or collateral, ancestry and saw the houses of the 18th century as appropriate settings.

The image of the Virginia house was strong and desirable, and its adaptation as a model was a deliberate decision by 20th-century southerners. Much was written about the 18th-century houses of Virginia in the period. They were more celebrated than those of any other southern state. A few books were written about the houses of South Carolina, Charleston, Georgia, and Alabama, and Thomas Tileston Waterman's *Early Architecture of North Carolina* appeared, but none was so exhaustive an investigation of 18th-century houses as Thomas Tileston Waterman's *The Mansions of Virginia*. Published in 1945, it did not influence the designs of the 1920s and 1930s, but it showed the degree of scrutiny applied in that era to 18th-century houses.

An appreciation of the mansions of the James River is well stated and purposefully crafted in remarks that William Lawrence Bottomley (1883–1951), a leading architect of the Georgian Revival country house, made on the topic during an interview in 1929. Speaking principally of the great James River plantations, he said,

> . . . they have a marvelous natural advantage because of their location in a beautiful, in many ways romantic, country; but the point is . . . that this natural advantage has been turned to full account through the development of a splendidly sound architectural tradition . . . the direct outcome of a distinguished civilization, built up in two centuries or more of country life. . . . The Virginia families who maintained this tradition were careful to nourish it and to enrich it as much as possible, by drawing on inspiration outside. . . . But the importations were so thoroughly absorbed into the Virginia tradition that it remained absolutely American   American of the Old South. I believe we should do everything possible to preserve this old southern ideal of country house architecture because it is one of the finest things we have and it is still vital.

Bottomley was foremost among a group of architects, mainly from New York and Philadelphia, who designed buildings—mostly Georgian Revival—for southern clients from 1910 to 1940, mostly in the 1920s. This group included Harrie T. Lindeberg, Robert Rodes McGoodwin, Charles Barton Keene, Aymar Embury, Hobart Upjohn, William Adams Delano, Chester Holmes Aldrich, John Russell Pope, and Dwight James Baum. Each specialized in house types and styles related to the matter of "personality," a frequent topic of architectural writing of the period. The houses of these architects were important in themselves, but their deeper significance lies in their influence. In Richmond, where the largest single group of Georgian Revival houses by William Lawrence Bottomley is located, and throughout Virginia, Bottomley's houses were emulated by local and regionally important architects, including Henry Baskervill (1867–1946) among others. Bottomley designed one of his finest Georgian Revival houses in the 1930s, Tatton Hall in Raleigh, N.C., for N. E. Edgerton. In Winston-Salem, the houses of Charles Barton Keene were often the particular models for houses by the local architectural firm of Northrup and O'Brien and by C. Gilbert Humphries. In Atlanta and the state of Georgia the work of Neel Reid, distinguished by a lavish hand heavily influenced by an affection for Italy and the classical devices of the Italian Renaissance, saw wide admiration and emulation there and in the states of the Lower South.

Other architects throughout the South also designed

Interior hallway in a Virginia home designed by architect William T. Bottomley

in the Georgian Revival style. In Virginia, perhaps the greatest local practitioner of the style, after Bottomley, was Duncan Lee (1884–1954), who took Carter's Grove, one of the landmark houses of the 18th century, and transformed it into one of the landmark houses of the Georgian Revival. He connected the wings to the main block, raised the roof, and added ranges of dormers, one of the hallmarks of the Georgian Revival. Stanhope S. Johnson was another Virginia architect who achieved great acclaim for his Georgian houses, including Galliston Hall in Farmington at Charlottesville.

Architects elsewhere in the South were also specialists in the Georgian Revival. Among them were James R. Edmunds and Herbert G. Crisp, who operated as the Office of Joseph Evans Sperry in Baltimore. One of their landmark houses is located not in Maryland but outside Chapel Hill, N.C. It was designed for David St. Pierre Du Bose, of a distinguished South Carolina family, and his wife who, having lived for some time in Baltimore, chose architects of that city to create a house for their Meadowmont estate. It obviously borrows from Maryland houses, including the Hammond-Harwood House doorway, one of the most frequently copied features of the period, which appears at Meadowmont on the east entrance.

The Georgian Revival houses of these architects were found most commonly in two places in the South. They were located on large multiacre lots in the upper-level suburban developments of the period, such as Windsor Farms in Richmond and Biltmore Forest in Asheville; or they were the seats of large suburban or rural estates, where they were often accompanied by complementary outbuildings that, in Keene's work, create a harmonious assembly. These architects designed houses and other buildings that were not only built in the South but that, in numerous ways, reflected the southern climate, geography, society, and strong traditions. Those traditions and their imagery, illusionary or real, accounted for the success of Edmunds and Crisp's work.

The principal Georgian Revival restoration project in the 1920s and 1930s was the restoration of Williamsburg, Virginia's colonial capital. Word of this project spread rapidly among the architectural community, and progress on the various buildings was widely reported in both professional and decorator magazines. Williamsburg was but the largest of many such efforts, including the restoration of Stratford Hall by the Robert E. Lee Memorial Association; of Gunston Hall by the Colonial Dames of America; and of Monticello, on which Fiske Kimball advised. Other projects were Kenmore in Fredericksburg; Wilton in Richmond; and Christ Church, Lancaster County, Va. Among the last of these was the reconstruction of Tryon Palace in New Bern, N.C.

Coinciding with these architectural restorations was an associated and closely related series of garden restorations by one of a series of men, including, principally, Charles Gillette (1886–1969), Arthur Shurcliffe, Umberto Innocenti of New York, or Thomas Sears of Boston. In 1923 the James River Garden Club published a seminal work, *Historic Gardens of Virginia*, which included period and documentary photographs of Virginia gardens, together with restored gardens of the 1910–20 period and the early 1920s. It remains one of the most important works of the period, which also saw the publication of *Carolina Gardens* and *The Garden History of Georgia* (1933).

The success of the Georgian Revival was also influenced and enhanced by developments in brickwork. Herbert Claiborne, Sr. (1886–1957) was an acknowledged historian of Virginia brickwork, and his firm, Claiborne & Taylor, had executed work on a number of restorations. He brought his knowledge of 18th-century Virginia brickwork and his experience in repairing it to the construction of houses in Richmond and other parts of Virginia. As did the architects, Claiborne & Taylor set a high standard of excellence that became a model for emulation.

The people who commissioned Georgian Revival houses in Virginia and elsewhere in the South were of two types. Some, including most of those in Richmond, were prominent individuals in their states and the region, many having second-generation ancestors in Virginia. This group looked back locally to their 18th-century origins and tried to downplay the industrial 19th-century sources of their wealth and any associated Victorian manifestations. Another group of clients during the interwar period included non-southerners or relocated southerners for whom farm seats and hunting boxes were expanded, overbuilt, or designed anew in Virginia, North Carolina, South Carolina, Maryland, and Georgia. Because of the social status of these housebuilders and the professional status of the architects, much of the best work in the Georgian Revival style was published, mainly in the 1920s and 1930s, in such national trade, professional, and related magazines as *House Beautiful*, *Architect*, *Architectural Record*, *House and Garden*, and *Country Life*.

One of the lasting contributions of the Georgian Revival to southern and American architectural history was the publication *Great Georgian Houses of America*. The Great Depression led to much retrenchment in the architectural profession. The chief response to the rising unemployment of draftsmen and apprentice architects was the organization of Architects Emergency Committee beginning in 1930. In 1932 trained architects and draftsmen began producing measured drawings of the plans, plats, elevations, and details of America's historic houses, which were published in 1933 in *Great Georgian Houses of America* for the benefit of the Architects Emergency Committee.

Great Georgian Houses was published by subscription, with the names of subscribers listed at the front in the fashion of 18th-century English architectural book publishing, suggesting a parallel to the social status of the subscribers. Forty-four houses, representing 14 states and the District of Columbia, were illustrated in the first volume. Not unexpectedly, more houses were included from Virginia (9 of the 44) than from any other state. Maryland houses were second in number. Sixteen pages were given to Mount Vernon, the largest section devoted to a single building, and their inclusion was the first time that the Mount Vernon Ladies Association had given permission for their publication. Bremo, the Cocke family estate in Fluvanna County, Va., is shown on 11 pages. The prominence of the Virginia and Maryland houses reflected their significance as exemplars of the finest Georgian and Federal work. Volume 2 of *Great Georgian Houses of America* was published in 1937 and included illustrations of six houses in both Virginia and New York; otherwise, no single state was represented by more than three houses.

The seeds of change were, however, already in the wind. For architects who practiced after World War II and for the clients of those architects, *Great Georgian Houses* had a broad appeal and did serve as the inspiration and source book for the design of numerous revival houses. But distinct changes in both the scale and character of these postwar houses set them apart from those of the interwar period. The careers of most of the architects who had designed Georgian Revival houses in the interwar period were largely over by 1937, and few had work of any consequence after 1941. *Great Georgian Houses* is a fitting epitaph for their careers and for the Georgian Revival of the interwar period.

See also HISTORY AND MANNERS: Historic Preservation; RECREATION: / Colonial Williamsburg

Davyd Foard Hood
North Carolina Department of Cultural Resources
Raleigh, North Carolina

Mary Wallace Crocker, *Historic Architecture in Mississippi* (1973); Charles B. Hosmer, Jr., *Presence of the Past: A History of the Preservation Movement in the United States before Williamsburg* (1965); Marian Page, *Historic Houses Restored and Preserved* (1976); William H. Pierson, Jr., *American Buildings and Their Architects: The Colonial and Neo-Classical Styles* (1970); Leland M. Roth, *A Concise History of American Architecture* (1979); Kenneth Severens, *Southern Architecture: 350 Years of Distinctive American Buildings* (1981).

German Architecture

Germanic settlement in the South had two main sources: movement south from Pennsylvania in the 18th century and immigration to Texas in the mid-19th century. The eastern Germans abandoned their distinctive architectural traditions early in the 19th century, while the Texas Germans maintained theirs only until the end of the century. Nevertheless, the diversity of Germanic regional traditions in Europe is reflected in the very different buildings that can still be seen in the two regions.

Germans settled in the South in the 17th century, and their names can be found in the record books from an early date. Architecturally, however, the Germanic groups who settled in Pennsylvania in the 1680s made the first notable marks on the landscape. In the 1720s the descendants of those colonists, augmented by fresh arrivals from Europe, began to migrate down the Shenandoah Valley along the Great Valley Road, which stretches from south-central Pennsylvania through Maryland, Virginia, and Tennessee, with a branch into North Carolina. Although they have been called Germans, they were of diverse central and western European origins, including emigrants from the present-day nations of Germany, Switzerland, the Netherlands, France, Czechoslovakia, and Poland. Scholars and antiquarians have given most attention to the architecture of those groups with origins near the Rhine River. They created a distinctive material legacy.

Central to their traditions was a kind of house, imported by German and Swiss immigrants, called the *Flurkuchenhaus* (hall-kitchen house), or Continental house. It was one or two stories tall and had two to four rooms in the main story. Its distinctive feature was an off-center interior chimney. To one side was a long, narrow kitchen (*Küche*), into which the front and rear outside doors opened. It had a large fireplace for cooking, and the stairs were located in one corner. Sometimes a secondary room was partitioned off at the rear of the kitchen or in an entrance vestibule at the front. On the opposite side of the central chimney a square or nearly square parlor (*Stube*) was heated by a metal or ceramic stove that was attached to the chimney and fed through a stokehole in the rear from the kitchen fireplace. By the end of the 18th century, iron Franklin-type stoves or small fireplaces were more common. Some builders installed a fixed table and benches in the front outside corner of the *Stube*, although none now survive. Often, there was a narrow sleeping and storage room (*Kammer*) behind the *Stube*.

The Continental house was very much a farmhouse: the cellar and the upper floors were as important as the main level. The cellar was devoted to food preparation and storage. Cellars were usually dug under only part of the house and, in large examples, included an outer room and an inner one that might be vaulted or otherwise insulated for use as a cool storage space. If possible, the house was built over a spring to provide a water source. In recognition of the active use of the cellar, the house was frequently located on a bank in such a way that both the main floor and the basement could be entered at grade. The loft area of the *Flurkuchenhaus* was traditionally used for the storage of grain and other farm produce. Loose boards laid over the collar beams of the roof trusses increased the attic's storage capacity, and a fixed stair on one gable end gave access to this uppermost level. Some houses had small pent roofs that sheltered working spaces close to the outside walls, and others had large porches or piazzas in which, according to 19th-century accounts, saddles, bridles, and other equipment were hung. The domestic space might be extended farther into the yard by an outdoor bake oven. As the description suggests, the Germanic house was a rural building, although a few urban examples could be found in the South.

The *Flurkuchenhaus* was not the only dwelling used by Germanic farmers in the 18th-century South. Single-room houses were common but are not as conspicuous to the modern observer. Most of the survivors were sturdily built and bank sited in the customary fashion and had two full stories of living space. At the other extreme, a few very large houses separated the traditional ground-floor rooms with a narrow entry passage that might contain the stair. In the best surviving example, Schifferstadt (mid-18th century) in Frederick, Md., the passage runs through the middle of the chimney stack. Fireplaces opening onto the passage were used to stoke the iron stoves in the living rooms.

Germanic farmers used distinctive structural systems to create their farmhouses and farm buildings. Among the surviving structures, log walls are most common. Log building was brought to America from central Europe, and Germans in the South maintained the tradition. Early German structures tended to use massive logs with full-dovetail notching, although half-dovetail and V-notched buildings can also be found. Finer buildings employed rubble, sometimes coursed, limestone walls. The German method of framing, or *Fachwerk*, was rare in the South. *Fachwerk* is a timber-framing system distinguished by the use of square posts linked by intermediate horizontal rails about the same size as the posts. No studs are used in *Fachwerk*. The most recognizable feature is the diagonal bracing that connects horizontal members at the top and bottom of the wall rather than running from a vertical to a horizontal timber as in English traditional building. Although the term is usually translated as half-timbering, and the frame might be filled with brick or wattle and daub and exposed to view on the exterior, southern examples were usually covered with weatherboards.

Most Germanic buildings in the 18th-century South were built by individual farmers, yet the largest and most conspicuous groups of survivors are those of the Moravian communalists at Salem and Bethabara in the North Carolina Piedmont. The Moravians arrived at Bethabara in November 1753, but the principal Moravian settlement at Salem was begun in 1766. Although the Moravians carefully regulated building in their communities, traditional structural systems and traditional forms characterized their work. The early buildings were built of *Fachwerk* or log; after the 1780s brick was common. Special plans were devised for the enormous communal dwellings that housed the single men and women, but the smaller 18th-century dwellings used the traditional plans employed by German farmers in Maryland, Virginia, and North Carolina. Eighteenth-century public buildings like the tavern, the boys' school, and the Vorsteher's house used Anglo-American two-room-deep, central-passage plans.

Germanic ideas were also major components of a distinctive barn type brought into the Upland South. Called a bank barn, a forebay barn, a Pennsylvania barn, or a Switzer barn, it combined Continental siting and use with English interior arrangements. In Switzerland a barn with its upper level overhanging the lower along one long side was used to house farm animals below and the hay to feed them above. In Pennsylvania in the 18th century the upper floor of the Swiss barn began to be arranged like an English barn, with openings in the center of both long sides affording access to a central threshing floor flanked by storage bays for grain. The bank barn was set into a hillside like the Continental house, so that both levels could be approached at grade. In the Upland South the Pennsylvania barn was occasionally built in brick, but more often in log or stone with frame overhangs, or forebays. The heyday of the bank barn in the South was the first half of the 19th century, although it continued to be built until the end of the century.

In the 18th century, Germanic groups in the South were known for avoiding contact with Anglo-Americans; but after the Revolution they were drawn into the larger society, and their architecture began to show signs of assimilation. The forebay barn is the most obvious example of this fusion, although its effects can be observed in Continental houses as well. They were made to appear more like large Anglo-American houses by increasing the number of openings, spacing them regularly, and sometimes moving the door closer to the center either to achieve or to give the impression of symmetry. Other builders moved the chimneys to the ends. Household work was moved out of the house into separate kitchens and other domestic outbuildings. They substituted freestanding meat houses and smokehouses for vaulted cellars, and they built small houses over springs to cool their dairy products instead of constructing their dwellings over the springs. With the importance of the house as a working building reduced, many builders abandoned bank siting and set their houses flat on the ground. The old narrow room that was once the kitchen was now used as a sitting room or dining room. Finally, the Continental plan itself was abandoned. After 1830 it was difficult to recognize any distinctive features in the architecture of those whose ancestors had come from central Europe in the 18th century.

There was a fresh German contribution to southern architecture in the mid-19th century, when emigrants from many parts of present-day Germany came to Texas as part of a larger migration of Germans to the central regions of the United States. The first few arrived in 1831 and began to settle in the region between Austin and Houston. A larger group arrived between 1845 and 1860, settled in east Texas near their predecessors, and also went to the hill country of west-central Texas northwest of San Antonio. Impelled by overpopulation, the mechanization of German agriculture, and crop failures in the 1840s and 1850s, about 30,000 Germans immigrated to Texas before 1860. In Texas they abandoned some distinctive architectural customs, including the building of house-barns, courtyard farmsteads, and tightly clustered agricultural villages, although Fredericksburg and New Braunfels in the hill country were envisioned as traditional farm villages. They tended to settle in dispersed farmsteads similar to other Texans, but their preference for mixed farming led to the construction of capacious barns that distinguished their farmsteads.

The Texas Germans built in log, frame, and stone. Their timber structures used *Fachwerk* frames similar to those found in the eastern South. Many were covered on the exterior with weatherboards, as in the 18th-century examples; but exposed and whitewashed frames, with either a rendered plaster protecting wattle and daub or pieces of limestone between the timbers, were more common than elsewhere in the South. In the hill country limestone construction dominated after the Civil War.

Although the agricultural practices and structural systems of Texas Germans had European origins, this was less true with respect to their house forms. On farms and in towns Germans built one- and two-room houses with central entries and three-opening facades. Often there was a rear kitchen lean-to roof and a gable-end stair to the second story. When German farmers abandoned Fredericksburg to live on their agricultural tracts in the late 19th century, very small versions of these one-room houses were built as "Sunday houses" for use by the family when in town. The plan and appearance of Texas German houses are similar to those of Anglo-American Texans and very different from the postmedieval European farmhouses to which they have been compared.

See also ETHNIC LIFE: / Germans; FOLKLIFE: House Types; GEOGRAPHY: Log Housing; RELIGION: / Moravians

Dell Upton
University of California at
Los Angeles

Edward A. Chappell, *Proceedings of the American Philosophical Society* (February 1980); Bernard L. Herman, in *Carolina Dwelling: Towards Preservation of Place: In Celebration of the North Carolina Vernacular Landscape*, ed. Doug Swaim (1978); Terry G. Jordan, *German Seed in Texas Soil: Immigrant Farmers in Nineteenth-Century Texas* (1966), *Texas Log Building: A Folk Architecture* (1978); William J. Murtagh, *Moravian Architecture and Town Planning: Bethlehem, Pennsylvania, and Other Eighteenth-Century American Settlements* (1967); Dell Upton, *Notes on Virginia* (Summer 1979), in *Material Culture of the Wooden Age*, ed. Brooke Hindle (1981).

Gothic Revival Architecture

Despite a preoccupation with classical architecture and culture, the South has always flirted with a Gothic identity. The concepts of chivalry, feudalism, and aristocracy are so deeply embedded in the southern psyche that they remain there today. To truly understand the southern Gothic Revival buildings, one must see them as part of a larger phenomenon, social as well as architectural.

Southern interest in the Middle Ages expressed itself in numerous ways. One was an extravagant admiration for romantic-antiquarian literature such as Sir Walter Scott's Waverley novels. A host of minor southern writers before the Civil War emulated Scott's style, and southern families even named their children after the titles and characters of Gothic novels.

Southerners wrote of themselves as if they were describing heroes of Gothic romance. In contrasting the northern and southern characters, Richmond newspaper editor and historian Edward Pollard spoke of a lack of congeniality between the Puritan colonists who established themselves on the "rugged and cheerless soil of New England" and the colonists of Virginia and the Carolinas who were, he said, "distinguished by their polite manners, their fine sentiments, their attachment to a sort of feudal life, . . . and the prodigal and improvident aristocracy that dispersed its stores in constant rounds of hospitality and gaiety."

Other 19th-century writers were less enthusiastic about the South's Camelot-like self-image. Mark Twain commented caustically on the phenomenon and blamed it on Sir Walter Scott, who "with his enchantments . . . sets the world in love with dreams and phantoms; with decayed and swinish forms of religion; with decayed and degraded systems of government . . . and the sham chivalrys of a brainless and worthless long-vanished society. . . . Most of the world has now outlived a good part of these harms, . . . but in our South they flourish pretty forcefully still." Twain blamed "the Sir Walter disease" for what he considered the worst traits of the southern character and manners, from jejune romanticism to duels, inflated speeches, and inflexible patterns of rank and caste. Twain concluded that but for the influence of Scott, the southern character "would be wholly modern, in place of modern and medieval mixed."

If Twain felt that Scott's romantic-chivalric attitudes had retarded the South, he also did not fail to link Scott

Louisiana state capitol, Baton Rouge, 1847–49

with southern Gothic architecture. One building he specifically attacked was the Louisiana State Capitol at Baton Rouge, by architect James Dakin. The Capitol, anathematized by Twain as "this little sham castle," was, in fact, the largest and most conspicuous Gothic public building in the antebellum South. As such, it was probably a more potent symbol than Twain realized. In addition to literary associations, it conjured up the image of a South with fortified castles as statehouses, suggesting decentralized, feudal governments and an individualistic-separatist mentality. Although only two castellated statehouses were built in the United States, both were in the Deep South (Louisiana and Georgia). It is difficult to suppose that southerners—and northerners as well—did not read political as well as literary symbolism into them.

Another context in which medieval imagery might have seemed symbolically appropriate was the southern plantation: the only true nonurban, decentralized, self-sustaining (i.e., "feudal") social unit in 19th-century America. But Gothic plantation houses were a comparative rarity. The image of planters living like feudal lords in Gothic castles surrounded by a class of humans linked in an unending bond to the soil was perhaps too stark to be palatable. The Greek Revival plantation house, with its symbolic ambiguity, seemed to divert notice from the moral problems of a slave economy, whereas the Gothic would have called attention to them. Waverley (1852), near Columbus, Ga., seems to underscore the literary appeal but moral unsuitability of the Gothic castle for plantation architecture. It is a Greek Revival plantation house with a romantic name derived from Scott.

Despite the general reservations, however, a few planters had romantic enthusiasm enough to opt for Gothic. One example is Belmead, in Powhatan County, Va., the castellated villa of Philip St. George Cocke, whose very name tells us about his family's pretensions to an aristocratic-chivalric ideal (he had a cousin named Richard Ivanhoe Cocke). Belmead, designed in 1845 by New York architect Alexander Jackson Davis, is situated above the James River, from which it is meant to be viewed. More than any other southern Gothic house, it resembles the Gothic villas along the Hudson River in New York State. This resemblance may help to explain the scarcity of Gothic castles in the South. Large Gothic villas may have been stigmatized by wealthy yet socially conservative southerners because of their implied connections to liberal and progressive patrons in New York and the Northeast. Romanticism in the South seemed to be of a nostalgic, backward-looking, Sir Walter Scott type, while northern Romanticism was of a progressive, forward-looking character, expressing itself in transcendentalism, the Hudson River school of painting, and the American park movement.

By choosing castellated Gothic for Belmead, Philip St. George Cocke exhibited a less regional, more cosmopolitan sensibility than most southern planters were willing to evince. Yet despite its architectural cosmopolitanism, Belmead had regional touches, such as window glass decorated with southern plantation crops: cotton, tobacco, wheat, and Indian corn. These, used in place of medieval heraldic devices, made the point that any claims the planter class had to being a "hereditary aristocracy" rested entirely on the land.

A Gothic plantation house of an alternate type was Afton Villa, at St. Francisville, La., built for the Barrow family. Rather than build a castellated villa, an unknown architect skillfully adapted the functional requirements of the plantation house to a vastly expanded version of a Gothic cottage. This symmetrical villa, with its steep overhanging roofs, wooden ornamentation, and inset galleries, was organized behind a regular vertical and horizontal grid not unlike a classical portico and used many of the climate-control devices of the southern Greek villas.

Despite the claim made by some 19th-century critics that Gothic, as a "northern" architectural style, was inappropriate to a southern geography, symmetrical Gothic villas and cottages proved a popular residential type in the South. These "pointed-style" houses were smaller, less expensive, and less "feudal" than the castles and also did not seem to have the negative associations with northern liberalism that the larger villas did. Executed in a variety of sizes and materials, they appealed to a great socioeconomic range and, like Greek country villas, were usually found in rich agricultural regions of the South. Southern builders adapted the cottage designs from northern journals and architectural pattern books such as Andrew Jackson Downing's *The Horticulturist, A Journal of Rural Art and Rural Taste*, or his better-known *The Architecture of Country Houses* (1850). These pattern-book designs were aimed at a rural audience, which explains their popularity in the predominantly agrarian South. Downing, although a New Yorker, was careful not to alienate his southern readers, and his writings on architecture, horticulture, and picturesque landscape became the model for many southern agricul-

Afton Villa, a Gothic plantation house near St. Francisville, La., built 1849–early 1850s

tural journals. Aside from these, the early 19th-century South had few architectural publications of its own.

Despite the numerous smaller Gothic residences, it was in ecclesiastical architecture that the South seemed most comfortable with its Gothic identity. Two churches in the South, the Episcopal and the Roman Catholic, had liturgical traditions reaching back to the Middle Ages, and, by reference, to the architectural traditions of the English parish church and the European Gothic cathedral.

Episcopal congregations could look to the resources of the Cambridge Camden Society in England and its bimonthly publication on church building and ritual, *The Ecclesiologist*. The ecclesiological movement was, in one sense, the religious arm of British colonial expansionism, and *The Ecclesiologist* reviewed and criticized new church construction, not only in Britain but in the New World as well. Consequently, the use by the American Episcopal church of "approved" Gothic architecture was an inescapable reality.

Southern Episcopal congregations frequently employed northern architects approved by the New York Ecclesiological Society, the American counterpart of the English ecclesiologists. The two architects who had the most influence on southern Episcopal churches were Richard Upjohn and Frank Wills, both of New York. Of the two, Wills was less well known but was perhaps the more sensitive architect. Among the southern churches Wills designed is Trinity Episcopal Church (1833–53) in Mobile, Ala., a fine version of the English 14th-century parish churches revived by British architect Augustus Welby Pugin and favored as models by the ecclesiologists.

Upjohn, renowned for designs such as Trinity Church in New York, had a major impact on southern Episcopal church building both through commissioned designs and through his 1852 publication, *Upjohn's Rural Architecture*. This church pattern book provided modest wooden designs for rural parishes too poor to afford elaborate masonry structures and the fees of a professional architect. As a result of Upjohn's own designs and his pattern book, there are southern Episcopal churches by him in Alabama, North and South Carolina, Florida, Georgia, Maryland, Mississippi, and Texas.

Unlike the humble models for Episcopal parishes were the Gothic churches designed for southern Catholic congregations. The Catholic churches were larger, grander, cathedral-type structures, usually found in urban settings because of the large numbers of Irish, German, and other European Catholic immigrants who settled in southern cities. Between 1830 and 1850 the number of Catholics in America rose from 600,000 to 3.5 million. This vast increase in the Catholic population was given conspicuous physical expression in southern port cities by such Gothic monuments as James Dakin's St. Patrick's Cathedral in New Orleans. These huge Catholic

Trinity Episcopal Church, Mobile, Ala., 1853–55

churches were being erected at a time when antiimmigrant sentiment was at its height. There were anti-Catholic riots in some southern cities, and nativist political parties such as the Know-Nothings sprang up on antiforeign platforms. It was no coincidence that the vast new Catholic cathedrals, often the most conspicuous monuments on 19th-century southern skylines, were raised in the very teeth of this discrimination as impressive statements in brick and stone of the solidarity of Roman Catholicism.

Medieval forms were also used to house southern institutions. Architect James Renwick and Senator Robert Dale Owen, in their plan for the Smithsonian Institution, Washington, D.C., and Owen in his book *Hints on Public Architecture* (1849) proposed making an amalgam of picturesque Gothic and Romanesque into a "national style" for public buildings. One of Owen's principal arguments for the revival of medieval architecture was its relative economy of construction. Medieval buildings were cheaper on a large scale because they did not require marble, their masonry could be roughly finished, and their walls were a simple two-dimensional "skin" thrown around the interior, with token pointed arches, towers, and crenelations to give "historical style." By contrast, classical public buildings required a high degree of finish, expensive materials, and dozens of carved steps, columns, and capitals.

The cheapness of castellated Gothic, combined with its planning flexibility, made it popular for large southern institutional structures where cost was a decisive factor. James Dakin cited cost as one of the reasons for his selection of Gothic for the Louisiana statehouse, and the style was used for orphanages, schools for the deaf and mute, military academies, jails, prisons, and lunatic asylums. Frequently to be found in juxtaposition with these great, stripped-down Gothic institutional buildings were grounds landscaped in romantic or picturesque fashion, like English 18th-century parks. The picturesque grounds, in addition to being appropriate to Gothic Revival architecture, may have been seen as having therapeutic value for inmates of such institutions as the Nashville, Tenn., Hospital for the Insane, built between 1851 and 1854, by architect Adolphus Heiman. In any case, "institutional Gothic" was used to house many of 19th-century southern society's disenfranchised: the needy, the deaf, the dumb, the blind, the insane, the penalized, and in the case of picturesque cemeteries, the dead.

Gothic was also used for southern educational institutions, a role that hints at Gothic scholasticism and English medieval campus planning. This trend continued into the 20th century, in such fine examples of collegiate Gothic architecture as those of architect Horace Trumbauer at Duke University, Durham, N.C.

Both Greek and Gothic in the South were aspects of a larger search for an architectural and regional identity. It was a quest not merely to house southern people and institutions but to achieve for southern civilization a parity with the great civilizations of the past, whether classical or medieval. As a southern writer for the Columbia, Tenn., *Guardian* put it in 1842, "We shall have our troubadours and our minstrels—and the banks of our Mississippi will become in song as classic as the Tiber, and in Romance as famous as the Danube."

See also MYTHIC SOUTH: Romanticism

Patrick A. Snadon
University of Kentucky

Francis Kervick, *Architects in America of Catholic Tradition* (1962); Caulder Loth and J. T. Sadler, *The Only Proper Style: Gothic Architecture in America* (1975); James Patrick, *Winterthur Portfolio* (Summer 1980); William H. Pierson, Jr., *American Buildings and Their Architects: Technology and the Picturesque, The Corporate and Early Gothic Styles* (1978); Phoebe B. Stanton, *The Gothic Revival and American Church Architecture: An Episode in Taste, 1840–1856* (1968); David B. Warren and Katherine S. Howe, *The Gothic Revival Style in America, 1830–1870* (1976).

Greek Revival Architecture

In the popular imagination, Greek Revival architecture, especially the great plantation house, is symbolic of the antebellum South. The potency of this image has discouraged not only analysis of its origins but also consideration of its validity. Most frequently, such architecture has been discussed in the context of romantic beauty, as the residue of an aristocratic culture somehow akin to the "Athenian Golden Age." At its best, this myth has created such visions as the neoromantic photographic studies of Clarence John Laughlin—themselves masterpieces of 20th-century southern art. At its worst, the image has obscured the complex forces that were at work in the South in the decades before the Civil War, producing diverse and expressive architectural forms overlaid with rich and often enigmatic meanings.

By the time of the American Revolution, neoclassicism held sway in the countries of western Europe. Highly educated and well-traveled men of the revolutionary generation, such as Thomas Jefferson, employed Federal-style architecture as one means of expressing their status as creators of a new nation. Provincial only in its superficial native and patriotic motifs, this style's geometry, planning, and overall articulation reflected forms that had originated in Europe.

As Jefferson and his colleagues were replaced by younger men, the sense of a permanent and self-assured America increased. Americans felt confident enough to take a more myopic view in their search for aesthetic inspiration, with one result being the Greek Revival style in architecture, still attuned to international neoclassicism, but now a more effervescent, innovative, idealistically chauvinistic, and diverse variation on that theme. Buoyant American nationalism was crystallized in the form of templed dwellings, churches, courthouses, and capitols.

This phenomenon was not identical in the North and South, however. The South continued to be agrarian in reality and aristocratic in aspiration; but it also continued to be necessarily international in outlook due to its emphasis on direct European trading connections. The North, on the other hand, looked toward industrialization, egalitarianism, and urbanized self-sufficiency. Furthermore, the South's distinctive agricultural circumstance included regional variation, and it experienced a considerable evolution over the course of time. The 18th century was dominated by the coastal enclaves of tobacco-raising Virginia and rice-growing South Carolina and Georgia, but the 19th century saw the rising importance of sugar-producing Louisiana and later the inland "cotton kingdom." Here, as the frontier moved westward, the boom periods of the early 19th century produced the many great white-columned buildings amidst an even greater number of crude, one-room log cabins and dogtrot houses.

The philosophical differences between North and South were not profound before 1820. Only as southerners felt compelled to defend the institution of slavery did their region become isolated and their position intransigent. The southern mind became progressively sectional, then regionally nationalistic, and finally unilaterally expansionistic, culminating in the Confederacy and plans to annex Mexico, Cuba, and the rest of the Caribbean. As one concrete manifestation of this attitude, there appeared a nationalistic architecture. Slavery, considered by many to be the central theme of antebellum southern culture, upset the equilibrium of southern life, creating an aberration that transfixed both North and South. The architectural parallel was a kind of fetish, what J. Frazier Smith has called the "white-pillared architecture." A paradox was created: the Orders, or columns with entablatures, were the formal basis of classicism and neoclassisicm and were physical evidence of the ancient conception of proportion and balance in life as well as in art; in southern, antebellum, columnar architecture, however, that balance proved elusive. Rather than an ordering element, the column became a device of exhibitionism, a sectional emblem, and a symbol of paternalistic and chivalrous society, aristocratic rule, and hierarchical rigidity. This white-columned architecture might well have been exported, along with slavery, to any new lands the South claimed as it fulfilled its belligerent conception of manifest destiny. The Greek Revival style, declining in the North on the eve of the Civil War, remained integral to southern culture when apocalyptic external forces terminated its development.

An old mansion in Natchez, Miss., photographed in 1940

Columnar plantation houses were being built in the South through the 1850s, although their details were becoming less archaeologically "Grecian" and more "baroque." While competing with other styles such as Gothic and Italian, the concept of the columned facade remained in favor in the South a decade after its demise in the North; and though acquiring a newer, more eclectic, ornamental, and aggressive vocabulary, the basic syntax was still in evidence and perhaps would have survived had the South been the victor in the Civil War.

Southern residential buildings displayed columns as profusely as did public architecture. In a decentralized, agrarian economy the plantation house was as much a symbol of stability and authority as was any seat of religion or government. That southern domestic architecture so universally appropriated the column did not, however, seem to reduce the significance of public buildings. If anything, the societal status of the domestic architecture was elevated well above that prevalent in the North, and that of public architecture was at least equivalent.

In molding public opinion and housing southern institutions, architects and patrons viewed Greek Revival public structures as eminently practical, modern buildings that made virile collective statements about southern cultural and economic attainment. To this end, of the 13 southern states, 8 had capitols planned by legislative fiat (a much higher percentage than in any other region), itself a telling comment on the search for preordained order within the culture. Similarly, 8 of these 13 had one or more capitols in Greek-temple form. Rivaling the capitols in size and importance were such buildings as hotels, which served the same purpose as Roman triumphal arches—to act as symbolic gateways and to impress travelers with the economic progress and cultural accomplishments of southern cities. The temple form was ubiquitous; but alternative Greek building types could serve with at least equal appropriateness—a stoa for a commercial block or a Greek treasury for a bank. Many of the most successful and least archaeological of the southern public buildings, far from being only "Grecian," included imaginative combinations of elements from other architectural vocabularies: Renaissance massing and wall division, Roman vaulting and domes, and more primitive Egyptian forms—all used not to supplant but to elaborate and energize the somewhat limited trabeated vocabulary of the Greeks.

This Greek Revival public architecture has been even less well investigated than domestic work. If this important, monumental neoclassical architecture is to be satisfactorily understood, it must be more carefully assessed within its southern context, and it must be compared to the European models created by such 19th-century classicists as J. N. L. Durrand and Karl Fredrick Schinkel.

The proliferation in recent years of books pretending to address southern domestic architecture, but most often recapitulating pallid myth, has certainly done more harm than good. Even noted scholars have often purveyed anachronistic confusion. William H. Pierson, Jr., in *American Buildings and Their Architects: The Colonial and Neo-Classical Styles* (1970), has written that southern domestic architecture "was dominated almost entirely by the peripteral colonnade"; but this simply was not the case. The three original southern enclaves each developed distinctive domestic schemes. Throughout the 18th century, Virginians preferred the Georgian, two-story, two-room-deep residence having a brick mass of Palladian inspiration covered by a hipped roof and often provided with a two-story central pedimented bay or portico. During the Greek Revival period this form was made more classically correct in both spirit and detail, and the result spread throughout the South as Virginians migrated into newly developing lands. In North Carolina and Georgia a wide, one-room deep, two-story block with a low-pitched, transverse-gabled roof was the most common form, unself-conscious at first, but gradually being furnished with a more pretentious one- or two-story porch or piazza across the long side; this piazza often employed columns with extremely wide intercolumniations to support a deep entablature, typically hiding the sloping roof behind. In Louisiana the Norman French peasant's house, transported to and developed first in the West Indies and possibly in Canada, was enlarged and outfitted with galleries, often, but not always, on all four sides. To these three prototypes must be added the pattern-book buildings and those designed to individual specifications by professionally trained architects. All of these types were then intermingled with one another, producing almost endless variants.

In addition to stylistic developments there were extensive environmental adaptations. Once again, many published materials have created confusion. Wayne Andrews, in his *Pride of the South: A Social History of Southern Architecture* (1979), has suggested that in the South there were "not too many inventions that served the particular demands of Southern climate." This observation could hardly be more inaccurate. The list of sun- and heat-control devices perfected by southern designers and builders was impressive. These included raised first floors, high ceilings, belvederes, and stair-tower plenums to take advantage of air stratification and natural convection; windows, jib-windows, doors, transoms, and longitudinal and transverse halls, all carefully located to encourage cross-ventilation; and roof overhangs, shutters, and latticework positioned to prevent solar heat gain. Such features have been verified, using modern testing procedures, to conform to current scientific energy conservation theory and application. Significantly the Georgian, Federal, and Queen Anne styles, which preceded and followed the Greek Revival, never displayed an equivalent degree of environmental modification; these styles tended to be quite homogeneous in both North and South. And, after all, ancient Greek architecture was created for a hot, sunny climate; it was the North that never came to grips with environmental adaptation.

Some authors have attributed environmental features such as the gallery to the influence of slaves' building experiences in Africa or the West Indies. The effects of slavery on the form of the southern plantation were, however, manifested in a much more calculated fashion. Planters sought to minimize or to conceal architecturally the negative aspects of slavery while calling attention to the number of slaves they owned, the primary indicator of their economic success. This complex pattern of behavioral control was accomplished by means of site planning, landscaping, spatial form and placement, and horizontal and vertical circulation elements, all subtly interconnecting layers and zones of family, guest, and servant spaces. Perhaps the greatest success of the southern Greek Revival plantation was its careful and tenuous accommodation of stressful social and environmental circumstances.

Finally, although southerners rarely spoke explicitly about their architecture, they built prolifically and on a grand scale. If one searches for incisive documentary evidence, especially among published materials, one searches almost in vain. This vacuum suggests not that southerners never thought seriously about architecture, but rather that very subtle attitudes were at work that valued most not a house but a home, not buildings as volumetric space but buildings as stages for human action, not landscape design but land itself, and so on. In the South certain matters pertaining to taste, culture, and manners have traditionally been neither questioned nor spoken about openly, so much so that they may, to an outside observer, appear to have been unimportant or even unknown. The southerner, however, would probably prefer the term unself-conscious behavior—a code of unspoken but ever-present decorum in patterns of thought and personal interaction, ultimately much like the modular regularity of classical architecture itself. Both, however, were systems that allowed adequate flexibility of expression within a carefully defined grammar and syntax. In the end, the resolution of the enigma of southern life and the architecture that reflected and supported it must be sought through an understanding of these peculiar attitudes and institutions that blossomed and faded in the South like a strange, hybrid flower.

See also EDUCATION: Classical Tradition; ENVIRONMENT: Climate and Weather; HISTORY AND MANNERS: Manners; MYTHIC SOUTH: Plantation Myth

Michael W. Fazio
Mississippi State University

Patrick A. Snadon
University of Kentucky

James Robert Bienvenu, "Two Greek Revival Hotels in New Orleans: The St. Charles by James Gallier, Sr., and the St. Louis by J. N. B. de Pouilly" (M.A. thesis, Tulane University, 1961); Talbot Hamlin, *Greek Revival Architecture in America: Being an Account of Important Trends in American Architecture and American Life prior to the War between the States* (1944); W. Darrell Overdyke, *Louisiana Plantation Homes: Colonial and Antebellum* (1965); William H. Pierson, Jr., *American Buildings and Their Architects: The Colonial and Neo-Classical Styles* (1970); Jessie Poesch, *The Art of the Old South: Painting, Sculpture, Architecture and the Products of Craftsmen, 1560–1860* (1983); J. Frazier Smith, *White Pillars: Early Life and Architecture of the Lower Mississippi Valley Country* (1941).

Historiography of Southern Architecture

Many historians of southern culture have been at least touched by the heavy air of nostalgia that threatens to stifle the region, but architectural historians have been even less willing or able than scholars in related fields to break through this layer of illusion and expose the reality beneath.

The origins of this tendency can be traced to a group of writers who created a mythical southern kingdom, complete with architectural setting, casting themselves as literary priests without whom an initiation into the mysteries of southern life would have been impossible. Writing before the Civil War, Virginia novelists such as John Pendleton Kennedy (*Swallow Barn*, 1832) and John Esten Cooke (*The Virginia Comedians*, 1854) began the tradition. Subsequently, southern writers developed a rhetoric of reconstruction, using as a forum such popular literary magazines as *Scribner's Monthly* (later *Century Magazine*), *Lippincott's Magazine*, and *Harper's*. Authors like Joel Chandler Harris and Sherwood Bonner fashioned an image of a southern civilization to serve their ends as apologists and propagandists for a prostrate South bent on rehabilitating its reputation. Thomas Nelson Page polished the facets of this southern romantic legend to virtual perfection.

Contemporary with these mythmakers, late 19th-century architectural writer-critics such as Mariana Van Rensselaer, Russell Sturgis, and Montgomery Schuyler (often writing, ironically, in the same literary magazines as Harris, Bonner, and Page) virtually ignored the South in their examinations of American building. Even the first historical studies of the country's architecture, which appeared in the 1920s, ventured only into Virginia and sometimes Charleston and New Orleans. The foremost of these publications were *Domestic Architecture of the American Colonies* (1922) and *American Architecture* (1928), both by Fiske Kimball, *American Colonial Architecture* (1924) by Joseph Jackson, and *The Story of American Architecture* (1927) by Thomas Tallmadge. Fiske Kimball's monograph, *Thomas Jefferson; Architect*, appeared in 1916 and Helen Pierce Gallagher's *Robert Mills* in 1935.

In 1941 the Society of Architectural Historians was founded, and its *Journal* was immediately dominated by American materials—a situation that has changed radically. Subsequently, additional general surveys of American building history were added, each containing sections devoted to the South: Talbot Hamlin's *Greek Revival Architecture in America* (1944), primarily a formal analysis and now badly dated; James Marston Fitch's *American Building: The Historical Forces That Shaped It* (1948), which included a perspective on social and intellectual factors; and Hugh Morrison's *Early American Architecture* (1952). Also appearing were two more studies of nationally renowned architects who practiced in the South—*Benjamin Henry Latrobe* (1955) by Talbot Hamlin and *William Strickland, Architect and Engineer, 1788–1854* (1950) by Agnes Gilchrist.

This same period saw the creation of a type of book that looked to the earlier popular propagandists for its inspiration—the limited-edition picturebook with short, often flowery text. The earliest of these appeared in Virginia, including Robert A. Lancaster, Jr.'s *Historic Virginia Houses and Churches* (1915), Edith Tunis Sale's *Manors of Virginia in Colonial Times* (1909), and Francis A. Christian and Suzanna W. Massie's *Homes and Gardens in Old Virginia* (1930); the latter was assembled for the Garden Club of America, one important supporter of the genre. Similar are the *History of Homes and Gardens in Tennessee* (1935), edited by Robert Seawell Brandau; Archibald Henderson and Bayard Wootten's *Old Homes and Gardens of North Carolina* (1939); Elizabeth Simpson's *Bluegrass Houses and Their Traditions* (1933); and J. Wesley Cooper's *Natchez, A Treasure of Antebellum Homes* (1957). In South Carolina the buildings of Charleston have dominated interest, leading to the production of such specialized titles as Elizabeth Curtis's *Gateways and Doorways of Charleston: South Carolina in the Eighteenth and Nineteenth Centuries* (1926). Louisiana authors have developed a particularly ethereal point of view, the most imaginative being that of Clarence John Laughlin in *Ghosts along the Mississippi* (1948).

A more substantive type of regional work began in South Carolina with *Dwelling Houses of Charleston, South Carolina* (1917) by Alice Ravenel, Huger Smith, and Daniel Elliott Huger Smith, and *Charleston, South Carolina* (1929) by Albert Simonds and Samuel Lapham. Further studies with scholarly aspirations appeared in the subsequent decades. Thomas Tileston Waterman's work is exemplary, including his *Mansions of Virginia, 1706–1776* (1946). Also active in the Tidewater were Henry Chandlee Forman, best known for his *The Architecture of the Old South: The Medieval Style, 1585–1850* (1948), and Frederick Nichols, whose interests extended to Georgia as well. In Kentucky, Clay Lancaster has published widely, primarily in journals, as has Rexford Newcomb, author of *Architecture in Old Kentucky* (1953). Likewise, Samuel Wilson, Jr., has conducted studies of the architecture of New Orleans and nearby parishes in Louisiana, and Samuel Gaillard Stoney and Beatrice St. Julien Ravenel have continued the tradition established earlier in Charleston and its environs with *Plantations of the Carolina Low Country* (1955) and *Architects of Charleston* (1945), respectively.

A more general work of significance is J. Frazier Smith's *White Pillars* (1941) with its emphasis on the Orders, or columns with entablature, as symbols of the southern Greek Revival style. Also cited often is Lewis Mumford's *The South in Architecture* (1941); however, this small volume provides little real insight into regional issues and architectural solutions. The frequent citation of James C. Bonner's "Plantation Architecture of the Lower South on the Eve of the Civil War," in the *Journal of Southern History* (August 1945), a study of forces at cross-purposes with neoclassicism, reflects not so much the absolute quality of that article as the celebrity that has met any imaginative examination of the nature of southern architecture. Also not to be ignored are the state guidebooks produced during the Depression years by the Federal Writers' Project.

Contemporary scholarship has begun to show signs of maturation. Albert Manucy's *The Houses of St. Augustine* (1962) represents a model of its type—a detailed technical analysis of building types in a specific location. John Linley's *Architecture of Middle Georgia* (1972) and Frederick Nichol's more substantive *The Architecture of Georgia* (1976) cover that state reasonably well, if not exhaustively. Much less analytical but still useful are Mary Wallace Crocker's *Historic Architecture in Mississippi* (1973) and D. Gregory Jeane and Douglas C. Purcell's *The Architectural Legacy of the Lower Chattahoochee Valley in Alabama and Georgia* (1976). Likewise, Thomas Brumbaugh's *Architecture of Middle Tennessee* (1974) is a picture book in the lineage of garden club publications. Arthur Scully has produced the only carefully researched study of a southern practitioner, *James Dakin, Architect* (1973); also noteworthy is the less comprehensive *William Nichols, Architect* (1979) by C. Ford Peatross. An unusual and significant work is Clay Lancaster's extensively documented *Eutaw: The Builders and Architecture of an Antebellum Southern Town* (1979). Wayne Andrews's *Pride of the South: A Social History of Southern Architecture* (1979) has magnificent photography but is more of a social register than a social history. Likewise, Kenneth Severens's *Southern Architecture* (1981) promises in its title much more than it delivers. The groundwork has simply not yet been sufficiently laid for such a sweeping view of southern architecture. Finally, James Patrick's *Architecture in Tennessee, 1768–1897* (1981) contains a thought-provoking text, with overtones of religious philosophy. His work addresses social and aesthetic issues and strives for an understanding of the continuity of southern architectural development.

More such studies are needed, studies that view southern architecture intellectually and analytically and not simply romantically. Researchers must address all stylistic periods and not overemphasize antebellum neoclassicism. Also, more detailed works on specific communities and areas and on specific designers are required before a comprehensive regional history can be successfully compiled.

Michael W. Fazio
Mississippi State University

Industrial 19th-Century Architecture

No cohesive southern industrial architecture emerged during the 19th century. Despite the growth of sectionalism, the ornamentation and construction techniques of southern mills revealed that they were part of a national movement. The millwrights, engineers, and, in a few cases, architects who planned these structures copied earlier northern models and rarely incorporated any innovations. The configuration of many 19th-century factories was dictated by their manufacturing process, so that specific types of industries developed distinctive buildings with little regional variation. A company's wealth usually determined the degree of embellishment. Stone, wood, or brick covered early mills, but over time brick exteriors became nearly universal, and a standardized industrial style became ubiquitous. Bays separated by brick pilasters, windows and doors crowned with segmental arches, and corbelled cornices and gables characterized warehouses, factories, and related buildings throughout the nation. Larger edifices exhibited the influence of current Victorian styles with Romanesque, Gothic, or Second-Empire features.

Given these national forces, most southern factories resembled those of their northern competitors. The construction of blast furnaces in North Carolina, Tennessee, Georgia, and Alabama mirrored that of earlier ones in New England and Pennsylvania. The walls of Richmond's Tredegar Iron Works, one of the region's most significant antebellum industries, showed no southern characteristics. Similar brick structures topped by monitors and flanked by squatty chimneys housed iron foundries in cities throughout the North and South. Tobacco factories in Statesville and Mount Airy, N.C., and in Lynchburg, Va., processed a southern product, but their rectangular, multistoried buildings with embellished stepped-gabled fronts might have sheltered a myriad of other manufactories throughout the nation.

Perhaps the southern economic and physical environment influenced the architecture of some mills. The lack of capital after the Civil War and the abundance of yellow pine caused some southern builders to continue using hand-hewn timbers with mortise-and-tenon joints after they had been superseded by iron or machined posts. These earlier framing methods were employed in rural grist mills, other small factories, and wooden bridges—both covered ones and deck-truss railroad trestles. In some cases black craftsmen preserved these traditional techniques: Horace King, an exslave, and his sons built such structures in Alabama, Mississippi, and Georgia through the first decade of the 20th century. Climate probably dictated the configuration of the region's open-sided turpentine stills and sawmills.

Larger urban mills displayed more distinctive styling, which tended to reflect local influences; such individuality disappeared with the onslaught of standardization. Richmond's Dunlop Mills structure (1853) rose seven stories above the James River. Its vertical emphasis typified flour mills, but its parapet end walls, with lunettes over each bay, gave the appearance of a late 18th- or early 19th-century Virginia building. Twenty years later, the Piedmont Mills building (c. 1875) in Lynchburg, Va., with its pilasters and arched windows resembled grist mills in any other American city. This uniformity increased as national companies that manufactured milling equipment began designing and constructing complete mills.

Lacking any national models, the architecture of Charleston's three antebellum rice mills evoked the classical mood of the city. The most magnificent of these was Governor Thomas Bennett's Italian Renaissance "palace," which began milling rice in 1844. Its rusticated lower level, large Palladian windows on the front and sides, and the Greek and Roman details on the other fenestration were all copied from various Italian palaces. Its elaborate surface contrasted starkly with the plain, massive timbers that supported it. The interior and exterior bays did not even correspond, and some of the rows of inside columns ended in window openings. Such an exuberant facade might have been an inappropriate screen for a steam engine and milling equipment, and it might have been emblematic of the region's, or Charleston's, hostility toward industry, but its grand style was an appropriate reflection of the importance of rice to the city's economy.

Among the South's—and the nation's—grandest structures were those associated with railroads. Viewed both as a gateway to a community and as a symbol of a town's urban status, railroad stations, train sheds, and shop buildings were conceived with special attention to fanciful details. In Nashville the antebellum Louisville & Nashville depot stood as a fortress with battlements along the roof and the corner towers, and trains entered through Tudor arches. In Savannah's Central of Georgia complex, normally mundane structures—privies, a water tower, and a smokestack—were combined into an ornamental column. The Central of Georgia's depot, offices, warehouses, and shops were built between 1850 and 1890 and contained classical, Gothic, and Italianate components. Despite their stylistic differences, they collectively illustrated the continuing importance of the railroad to the city and asserted, in brick, the goal of making Savannah the leading cotton center. By the turn of the century, railroad stations in major southern cities resembled Romanesque cathedrals, Gothic castles, and Roman "baths." This railroad architecture was national, not southern: it revealed that southern cities shared the urban ethos that pervaded the rest of the nation.

Textile mills became symbolic of the South's drive to industrialize during the 19th century. Early southern entrepreneurs employed northern-trained millwrights, so the first southern factories repeated the characteristics of Rhode Island spinning mills—narrow buildings, three to five stories in height, with a front stair tower capped by a cupola. With exceptions like the Augusta Factory (1847), which resembled the massive structures of Lowell, most antebellum and the initial postbellum mills remained austere in decoration and limited in volume. After 1880 the scale of factories increased substantially because of improvements in motive power and illumination, but few innovations occurred in the system of interior supports; more wooden posts and beams were simply added to span the greater lengths. Mill engineers gave little attention to improving working conditions.

The design emphasis by the 1880s focused on the exterior of these mills. Decorative brickwork embellished many of their features, but especially the cornices and the Romanesque arches of the massive towers that dominated most of these structures. The heavily ornamented mills conveyed a civic dimension by embodying the pride and aspirations of entire communities. The ornamentation, although Victorian in tone and similar to that on northern mills, may also have been an expression of the New South creed (or cotton mill crusade), which promised to transform the region. Ironically, like the corbelled and arched masonry, the impact of industrialism on the South—and its poverty—was superficial.

Stylistically, the most distinctive New South mills appeared in Georgia and especially in Augusta. Having led the region in textile production for four decades, the Georgia corporations had sufficient internal expertise to design their own plants in the 1880s. Probably the South's most imposing industrial facade was Augusta's Sibley Mill (1880). Because of its crenellated parapet and decorative stair towers and pavilions topped with finials, some historians have speculated that it was modeled after the British Houses of Parliament, but it probably was intended to imitate, and thereby memorialize, the Confederate Powder Works, which had earlier stood on the site. At the same time, its exuberance appeared to have been inspired by the optimism of the New South creed.

By contrast, the Carolina and Alabama mills of the

1880s were built by national engineering firms such as Lockwood and Greene with more restrained and more uniform designs. They planned the Columbia (S.C.) Duck Mill (1893), the world's first textile factory to be powered by electricity, but its architecture failed to suggest its uniqueness. It resembled all the other mills along the Atlantic Seaboard. The 1890s publications of Daniel Tompkins, a southern mill engineer, reflected this standardization; his mills varied only in scale. By that decade, the exuberance of the New South was waning; as plants grew in size, windowed areas expanded, and less corbelling appeared on the smaller brick areas of these more utilitarian structures. By 1900 the factory was a permanent part of the southern landscape: the triad of brick smokestack, water tank, and mill tower rising above a pine forest marked the location of a textile factory and its surrounding village. The workers and often their houses remained southern in style, but the architecture of the mill building was national in style. Southern sectionalism had been unable to stem the homogenizing force of the national economy.

See also INDUSTRY: / Textile Industry; MYTHIC SOUTH: New South Myth

John S. Lupold
Columbus College

Keith L. Bryant, Jr., *Journal of Urban History* (February 1976); Stephen Goldfarb, *Industrial Archeology in Georgia* (1978); Samuel Lapham, Jr., *Architectural Record* (August 1924); Theodore A. Sande et al., *Journal of the Society of Architectural Historians* (December 1976).

Nonresidential 20th-Century Architecture

The nonresidential southern architectural styles of the early 20th century can be divided into the same two categories as residential architecture—historic and nonhistoric.

Period revivals were very popular in the conservative South. The same styles that adorned residential structures could also be found on nonresidential ones. The French, Spanish, Dutch, and English Colonial Revival styles, as well as the Federal and Georgian, were very popular, as were the Renaissance, Tudor, and neo-Italianate styles. In addition, four other historical styles were commonly employed for nonresidential structures—the Gothic Revival, neoclassical, stripped-down classical, and beaux arts.

The Gothic Revival style (1900–1940) of the early 20th century was primarily used on public buildings, churches in particular. Precedents favored were the English perpendicular and Tudor styles, but the French Gothic was occasionally employed alone or combined with the English style. The silhouettes of these buildings are very complex, although symmetry is common. These Gothic Revival structures are generally built of masonry stone when available. In commercial buildings terra cotta is often used. The most renowned Gothic architects of this period were Ralph Adams Cram and Bertram Grosvenor Goodhue. Cram had developed the theory that Gothic architecture had "not suffered a natural death," therefore, he intended to "take up English Gothic at the point where it was cut off." The Gothic Revival style was particularly popular for southern universities. Loyola of the South in New Orleans and the University of Florida in Gainesville are two such examples.

Neoclassical, stripped-down classical, and beaux arts styles were used for monumental buildings in cities and towns throughout the South. All three are derived from the same source—classical Greek and Roman prototypes—but the manner in which the elements are used distinguishes each style.

Neoclassicism (1900–1940) encompassed Greek, Roman, and Renaissance elements and characteristics composed in the classical manner, with a monumental scale. The 1929 New Orleans Criminal Court Building by Diboll & Owen Architects is a typical example of the style.

Stripped-down classicism, sometimes referred to as fascist moderne, employed the same massing and scale as neoclassicism but made little or no use of historically derived details. Many such public structures throughout the South were built as Depression-era projects by the WPA and PWA. The 1939 State Fair Exhibit Museum in Shreveport, La., is a good example of this style.

Beaux arts classicism (1890–1920) employs classical elements in a theatrical or baroque manner. The École des Beaux Arts in Paris was directly responsible for the reemergence of classicism, but exhibitions such as the World's Columbian Exposition (Chicago, 1893), the Louisiana Purchase Exposition (St. Louis, 1904), and the Panama-Pacific Exposition (San Francisco, 1915) propagated the style in the public's mind. Cities of white marble were sought in the national City Beautiful movement.

All three classical styles were popular in the South for governmental and civic buildings, libraries, museums, colleges, theaters, banks, railway terminals, monuments, and memorials.

Nonhistorically inspired styles popular during the early 20th century include the commercial, the decorative brick, storefront modern, art deco, and streamline moderne.

The commercial style (1890–1910) arose out of the ashes of the great Chicago fire to spread across the nation. An anonymous editor of *Industrial Chicago* wrote in 1891, "The Commercial Style is the title suggested by the great office and mercantile buildings now found here. The requirements of commerce and the business principles of real estate owners called this style into life. Light, space, air and strength were demanded by such requirements and principles as the first objects and exterior ornamentation as the second."

Commercial-style buildings were an early development of the high-rise office complex, and at least one example can be found in every southern city. They are generally 5 to 16 stories, with flat skylines, large windows, and an external structural expression. This style was made possible through technological advances such as steel-frame construction, the passenger elevator, fireproofing techniques, and mechanical ventilation. The Mills Building, designed by Frost and Frost Architects in 1910 in El Paso, Tex., and the Wainwright Building, designed by Adler and Sullivan in St. Louis in 1890, are typical examples.

The decorative brick style was an outgrowth of the commercial style. Whereas the commercial style shunned ornamentation, the decorative brick style used masonry products in an innovative decorative manner. Patterns of masonry pinwheels, sinkages, and polychromatic motifs were employed. The spandrels were generally recessed slightly behind the piers, and the skyline was often broken. Terra cotta ornaments were sometimes incorporated. Examples of this style can be found in New Orleans's Historic Warehouse District. The Woodward-Wright warehouse by Emile Weil is a typical example there.

Many small commercial buildings and stores in small towns are in this idiom. Such buildings are the hallmark of main streets throughout the nation including, of course, the South. In many county seats, such as Oxford, Miss., these are among the buildings that front the streets and the square where the county courthouse is situated. The core of small-town life was once centered here.

The storefront modern style developed simultaneously with strip shopping developments. The style, as its name implies, was one that simply addressed the front of the structure, ignored the unseen rear, and had no sides to contend with, except on corner buildings. Intended to be seen from the passing auto, the style used slick, clean materials with bold details and lots of neon lights. Opaque glass and baked-enamel panels were often used. The versatility and boldness of the style made it perfect for widespread usage by chain stores. By its standardized design of red opaque glass and gold lettering, one recognized a Woolworth store in New Orleans as easily as in Macon.

Art deco (1920–30) was popularly used for high-rise buildings and movie theaters. Stylized ornamentation was perhaps its most recognizable feature. Motifs based on pure geometry, abstracted naturalistic forms, or stripped-down ancient decorative elements manifested themselves in hard-edged, low-relief ornamentation.

As a style of ornamentation, art deco evolved in France during the early 1920s as a reaction to the art nouveau. The 1925 L'Exposition des Arts Decoratif in Paris diffused a sentiment in America that there could be modern ornamentation. This concept bridged the gap between the beaux arts philosophy, which contended historical ornamentation was essential, and the Bauhaus philosophy, which renounced all ornamentation. Art deco structures are alive with bold colors, dramatic massing, picturesque skylines, and an emphasis on the vertical, making this style popular for resort areas such as the Miami Beach Art Deco District.

Streamline moderne (1930–40) developed during a period of rapid social change. The worldwide Depression had caused disillusionment and confusion. The common desire to "get things moving again" demanded drastic solutions. Out of this confusion a new profession emerged—industrial design—which literally reshaped everything in order to stimulate a devastated economy.

Industrial designers promoted streamlining as a symbol of the future—a future that combined art, engineering, design, processing, packaging, and sales. Instead of the applied art of the art deco, streamlining preferred subtle meaningful forms of ornament. Although buildings were static, the principles of fluid dynamics were applied. Architects had to settle for an abstraction of motion, resulting in slick, curved surfaces. The style was very popular for Greyhound bus stations and gas stations throughout the South.

The architect Theodore Flaxman, of Shreveport, La., was among those Americans who early studied and responded to this modern "international" style. A municipal incinerator built in the 1930s in Shreveport, and since destroyed, was cited at the 1937 World's Fair in Paris as one of the best examples of modern architecture in America. The Mayer House in Shreveport, built in 1930, is a fine surviving example of this genre.

The Louisiana State Capitol Building, designed by the New Orleans firm of Weiss, Dreyfous and Seiferth, was one of two skyscraper capitols in the United States (the other is in Nebraska) built in the early 1930s. The architects called it modern classic, and it used a restrained modern idiom, including symbolic low-relief sculpture on the outside and richly colored marble panels, with echoes of art deco detailing, on the inside. Built while Huey Long was the governor of the state, it is, in a sense, his monument, and a monument to his individual brand of populist politics.

Robert J. Cangelosi
New Orleans, Louisiana

William H. Jordy, *American Buildings and Their Architects*, vol. 3 (1972); Walter C. Kidney, *The Architecture of Choice: Eclecticism in America, 1880–1930* (1974); Carole Rifkind, *A Field Guide to American Architecture* (1980); Leland M. Roth, *A Concise History of American Architecture* (1979); G. E. K. Kidder Smith, *The Architecture of the United States: The South and Midwest* (1981).

Painting and Painters, 1564–1790

The first two important, but unsuccessful, European attempts to establish colonies in that part of North America that is now the United States were in the South. In each of these an artist-draftsman accompanied the expeditions and was charged with recording impressions of the peoples, the flora, and the fauna of the region, as well as with mapmaking. Thus, Jacques Le Moyne de Morgues in 1564 and 1565 accompanied the French expedition that established a short-lived Huguenot settlement on the St. Johns River in Florida, and John White served as cartographer and draftsman to Sir Walter Raleigh's 1585 expedition that established the Roanoke colony.

Only one of the original 42 watercolors by Le Moyne survives (in the New York Public Library), while a portfolio of White's work, including 59 watercolors, has survived (British Museum). Among these are delicately rendered depictions of the Indian inhabitants, showing them at tasks such as cooking, fishing, and cultivating crops, as well as renderings of plants and creatures. The Indians are made to appear somewhat Europeanized, but there is nonetheless valuable ethnological information. These works were disseminated in Europe by Théodore De Bry, who published in Germany a series of volumes on the New World, reproducing the drawings of White and Le Moyne as engraved illustrations. De Bry's first volume, *A Briefe and True Report of the New Found Land of Virginia*, published in 1590, had engravings based on White's drawings and was accompanied by Thomas Hariot's narrative, a somewhat optimistic account of a land with a mild climate like Persia. This was followed by German, Latin, and French editions. Between 1590 and 1620 this volume went through 17 printings. The volume with engravings based on Le Moyne's drawings and his text was published in German, French, and Latin some years after the artist's death in 1591. Thus, in the years between 1590 and 1620, when permanent colonies had been established, these volumes and engravings formed the English and European visions of America. Moreover, subsequent books, such as John Smith's *The Generall Historie of Virginia* of 1624, had illustrations based on De Bry's engravings. Images representing America and extending well into the 18th century, such as that on an 18th-century Spanish tile, were drawn from Smith's *Generall Historie*.

Virtually no paintings or drawings survive from the first 60 or so years of permanent settlement in the South, years in which the settlers suffered from disease, high mortality rates, poor planning, inability to adjust to the hot climate, and poor relations with the Indians. It was far from a Persian paradise. Likewise, very few artifacts, such as furniture or silver, survive from this period.

One cannot identify surviving paintings and graphic arts created in the South and find records of artists and their patrons before the early years of the 18th century, which brought the development of the plantation society and the growth of towns. Patrons were largely of the planter and merchant classes, and their choice was for portraits. This preference was shared with fellow colonists in the North and indeed with many English people.

A German-born artist, Justus Engelhardt Kühn (died 1717), recorded the likenesses of several Maryland and Virginia planter families, often showing them posed in elegant settings whose source lay in remembered European scenes or in prints. In Charleston, Henrietta Johnston (died 1728 or 1729) used pastels to render delicate interpretations of her patrons. She was the wife of a minister and supplemented her husband's income with her work. Charles Bridges was an agent for the missionary Society for Promoting Christian Knowledge and earned part of his income by painting portraits of notables in the Williamsburg area. An unidentified artist working in the Jamestown area recorded the likenesses of members of the Brodnax and Ambler families. William Dering also worked in and around Williamsburg.

Another Englishman, John Wollaston, lived in Maryland, Virginia, and South Carolina intermittently from 1753 to at least 1767. His elegant, graceful renditions of his subjects helped to introduce the rococo taste. The Swedish-born artist Gustavus Hesselius (1682–1755) is known to have worked in Maryland, and possibly in Virginia, before settling in Philadelphia. His son, John (1728–78), found patrons in Virginia and in 1763 settled permanently in Maryland. With these three artists one can begin to trace more clearly some of the interactions and interrelationships among artists in the southern colonies. Wollaston appears, for example, to have influenced in part the style of Gustavus Hesselius. The latter no doubt taught his son something of the art and craft of painting. John Hesselius in turn is known to have been the first teacher of Charles Willson Peale (1741–1821), who was born in Maryland and was among the slowly growing number of aspiring young American-born artists who spent a year or more studying in England. Peale was taught, as were a number of his generation, by his fellow American, Benjamin West, only a few years his senior but well established in London. Peale returned and settled for a time in Annapolis; some of his finest portraits show Marylanders and Virginians. He later moved to Philadelphia and made some visits to the southern states. Several of his children and his nieces and nephews, who also became artists, visited the South in search of patrons. His son Rembrandt Peale (1778–1860) lived for a time in Baltimore, where he established the short-lived Peale Museum in 1797.

In Charleston the artist Jeremiah Theüs (c. 1719–74) enjoyed something of a monopoly of patronage from 1739 until his death in 1774. Born to a Protestant family in Switzerland, he immigrated with them as a youth to South Carolina, to escape religious persecution. There is a certain stiffness in many of his portraits, but this is often redeemed by his skillful use of color and his feeling for elegance of fabrics. During the 18th century southerners living on the Atlantic Seaboard often maintained close business and personal ties with England; young men were sometimes sent there for their education. During visits to the homeland they had their portraits painted, thus carrying artistic patronage beyond the borders of the region.

As one examines these portraits of the 18th century, it is fair to say that patron and artist alike wished for an image that was a likeness and a statement of the status of the sitter. Rich fabrics, satins, velvets, and laces were fashionable and are depicted. Often several members of a family were painted as a group, thus emphasizing the importance and continuity of family ties.

The first renderings of flora and fauna of the present United States, as done by Le Moyne and White, were based on those in the Southeast. Likewise, the first systematic study and publication of natural history in North America, Mark Catesby's two-volume *Natural History of Carolina, Florida, and the Bahama Islands* (published 1731–43), drew upon this verdant region for most of its material. Catesby, an Englishman, first visited the American continent from 1712 to 1719. His interest in the natural history of the New World and his collection of its specimens led a group of naturalists to sponsor a second trip from 1722 to 1725. Upon his return to England, he learned to do engravings and embarked upon publication. His illustrations are among the first to depict animals and birds in their natural habitats. In his engraved depictions he deliberately eschewed shadows, both because he felt they were beyond his competence and because he believed greater accuracy could be achieved without them. To the modern eye his illustrations have an appealing, slightly naive quality. A three-folio collection of his natural history drawings on which his plates are based is now in the Royal Collection at Windsor Castle.

Two other artist-draftsmen who may have hoped to achieve publications such as those given to White, Le Moyne, and Catesby are Alexandre De Batz and Philip Georg Friedrich Von Reck. De Batz was connected with the French military forces in Louisiana, and a small group of his surviving drawings, dated between 1731 and 1735, are in the Peabody Museum in Boston. They include a drawing of a temple and chief of the Acolapissas Indians and one showing Choctaw warriors and children. These are among the earliest surviving visual documents from the Deep South. (The numerous architectural plans and elevations done by the French engineers in connection with the colonies in Mobile, New Orleans, and the adjacent areas represent another group.)

Von Reck's journal and drawings have only recently come to light; they have been stored in the Royal Library of Denmark apparently since the 18th century. A Protestant German, Von Reck accompanied a group of Salzburgers who established a settlement in Georgia in 1734 and again in 1736. He stayed only a few weeks on his first visit and a few months on his second, but during these times he made a number of drawings of flora and fauna found in that region as well as several straightforward drawings of the Yuchi Indians. Some of these drawings are captioned in several languages—Yuchi, Greek, German, and French or English. The works of both Von Reck and De Batz are valuable documentaries of the first encounters of Europeans and the native peoples in the New World.

See also ENVIRONMENT: Naturalists

Jessie Poesch
Tulane University

Francis W. Bilodeau and Mrs. Thomas J. Tobias, eds., *Art in South Carolina, 1670–1970* (1970); Bruce W. Chambers, *Art and Artists of the South: The Robert P. Coggins Collection* (1984); David C. Driskell, *Two Centuries of Black American Art* (1976); James T. Flexner, *First Flowers of Our Wilderness: American Painting, the Colonial Period* (1969); Caroline M. Hickman, *Southern Quarterly* (Fall–Winter 1985); Jessie Poesch, *The Art of the Old South: Painting, Sculpture, Architecture and the Products of Craftsmen, 1560–1860* (1983); Virginia Museum of Fine Arts, *Painting in the South: 1564–1980* (1983); Carolyn J. Weekly, *Antiques* (November 1976, February 1977); Ben F. Williams, *Two Hundred Years of the Visual Arts in North Carolina* (1976).

Painting and Painters, 1790–1860

Portraiture was the most popular art form, both North and South, during the early years of the rapidly expanding new Republic. Portrait painters were legion, and the careers of many have not been examined. Even though the South was less densely populated than the North, many artists practiced their skills in local communities, both large and small. Thomas Cantwell Healy worked in Port Gibson, Miss., in the 1850s, and a number of French-born artists, such as J. J. Vaudechamp and Jacques Amans, established themselves in New Orleans during the 1830s through 1850s. Artists such as Matthew Harris Jouett and Ralph E. W. Earl found their patrons in relatively new communities west of the Appalachians, such as Lexington, Ky., and Nashville, Tenn.

The many portraits reflect changing tastes and values. The 18th-century feeling for elegance is seen in paintings by Thomas Sully's student, Thomas S. Officer, who was in Mobile and Richmond in the 1830s and 1840s. In general, however, painters moved toward the austerity of the neoclassical and an ever-greater emphasis on the very realistic. There was little idealizing. Though some paintings exist of young and beautiful women who might qualify as "southern belles," considerably more are of unpretentious matrons, such as a stern-looking portrait of the wife of Isaac Shelby, a governor of Kentucky, painted in 1827 by Patrick Henry Davenport (Kentucky Historical Society).

During this period one can trace a developing iconography of national and regional heroes. Gilbert Stuart was one of several artists who helped make George Washington's image familiar through the many copies of his portraits. Some of these found their way into the South, adorning county courthouses or city halls. Legislative bodies commissioned portraits. North Carolina commissioned two full-length portraits of Washington from Thomas Sully. A misunderstanding occurred, and Sully produced a dramatic canvas of *Washington Crossing the Delaware* that was too large for the space. It was refused and now is in the Boston Museum of Fine Arts. The city of Charleston still owns a handsome full-length portrait of Washington, which was commissioned from John Trumbull and was completed in 1792. Charleston also has an excellent miniature painting of the Marquis de Lafayette by Charles Fraser. The city of Richmond and the state legislature of Kentucky were among other political bodies that commissioned portraits of the renowned general Lafayette when he made his grand return visit to the United States in 1825. Ralph E. W. Earl became the virtual court painter of Andrew Jackson after he attained fame. Other heroes who were painted a number of times include Jefferson, Calhoun, Clay, and Daniel Boone.

The painting of miniatures—small, intimate portraits in watercolor on ivory—enjoyed a special popularity in the early decades of the 19th century. One of the finest of the practitioners of this art was Charles Fraser of Charleston. In 1857 he was given a retrospective exhibition in his native city, and over 400 of his miniatures were shown. He was particularly adept in painting the elderly, showing them in honest yet sympathetic likenesses.

Several artists, such as Jacob Frymire, Joshua Johnston, and Charles Peale Polk, all of whom worked in the late 18th or early 19th centuries, might be classified as slightly naive painters. Polk and Johnston worked in and around Baltimore. Johnston is important as the first known professional black painter in the European tradition. Both Polk and Frymire traveled in western Maryland and Virginia as itinerant painters.

The biracial and multiracial nature of southern society is visible in a number of paintings from this era. Several portraits of free people of color, such as one attributed to Francois Fleischbein (c. 1860, New Orleans Museum of Art), or the portrait of James Armistead Lafayette by John R. Martin (c. 1824, Valentine Museum, Richmond), show dignified, attractive individuals. George Catlin included Seminole Indians among the subjects he recorded in the 1830s. A handsome, full-length portrait of the Creek Indian chief William McIntosh (c. 1820–23, Alabama Department of Archives and History) is attributed to Nathan and Joseph Negus. The Seminole leader Osceola was painted both by Robert R. Curtis of Charleston and by Catlin in 1838. Among the most poignant of paintings of blacks is the large *Plantation Burial* (1860, Historic New Orleans Collection) done by John Antrobus in Louisiana. It is a sympathetic depiction of a moment in the private lives of members of a slave community.

During the late 18th and early 19th centuries landscape painting gained importance as a genre in the United States, particularly in New York State and New England. George Beck painted several picturesque views of Baltimore in the late 1790s (Maryland Historical Society). George Washington was one of his patrons. The meticulously rendered scenes by Francis Guy (c. 1800–1805, Maryland Historical Society) qualify more as portraits of cities than as landscapes proper. Both Beck and Guy helped launch the development of landscape painting. In general, however, this development in the South was fitful until after the Civil War. George Cooke, working in the 1830s, and T. Addison Richards were among artists who wrote on the virtues of scenery in the South, and each did some cityscapes and landscapes. Richards, however, candidly admitted that the terrain was difficult, distances too great, transportation poor, and access to urban centers limited. William Charles Anthony Frerichs was one who caught the drama of the North Carolina mountains on his canvasses. James Cameron, working in Chattanooga in the late 1850s, recorded the dramatic terrain of that area. In an impressive painting showing Colonel and Mrs. James A. Whiteside, their children, and their servants, this artist combined group portraiture and landscape (Hunter Museum of Art, Chattanooga). A large

View of Mount Vernon, looking toward the southwest

and richly detailed painting of the New Orleans waterfront done in 1853 by Hippolyte Sebron (Tulane University) is another that is more cityscape than landscape. Influenced by Daguerre, it has an open-ended "slice-of-life" quality that presages compositional concepts of the Impressionists.

The most famous of all American painters of natural history, John James Audubon, did many of his preliminary studies for his *Birds of America* in the Deep South, particularly in Louisiana, Mississippi, and South Carolina. Outdoor life, sports, and horse racing were popular in the South, so it is no surprise that the most popular animal or horse painter in the United States in the 19th century, Edward Troye, spent most of his time in the South. Troye lived for some time in Kentucky and Alabama and traveled throughout the region. Many of his works, which often include depictions of jockeys and trainers, are still in private collections.

The lives of a number of painters were abruptly changed with the advent of the Civil War. Some left the region, others joined the military forces, and those who remained found few patrons in the years 1860 to 1865.

See also BLACK LIFE: Art, Black; ENVIRONMENT: / Audubon, John James

Jessie Poesch
Tulane University

Bruce W. Chambers, *Art and Artists of the South: The Robert P. Coggins Collection* (1984); Corcoran Gallery of Art, *American Painters of the South* (1960); James H. Craig, *The Arts and Crafts in North Carolina, 1699–1840* (1965); David C. Driskell, *Two Centuries of Black American Art* (1976); David Moltke-Hansen, *Art in the Lives of South Carolinians: Nineteenth-Century Chapters* (1979); Estill Curtis Pennington, *William Edward West, 1788–1857: Kentucky Painter* (1985); Jessie Poesch, *The Art of the Old South: Painting, Sculpture, Architecture and the Products of Craftsmen, 1560–1860* (1983); *Southern Quarterly* (Fall–Winter 1985); Virginia Museum of Fine Arts, *Painting in the South: 1564–1980* (1983).

Painting and Painters, 1860–1920

The differences in circumstances between the South and its peoples and the rest of the nation were probably felt most acutely by southerners during and after the Civil War, extending until World War I. In many cases these differences lasted until World War II and, in part, still exist. They affected artists and their choices of subject matter in subtle ways and significantly reduced their chances for showing and selling their works. Nevertheless, artists who worked in the South were influenced by the same artistic trends that influenced artists in other parts of the country.

During the Civil War Winslow Homer, Edwin A. Forbes, Henry Mosler, Alfred R. Waud, and William Waud were among artists who followed the troops and recorded day-to-day events for popular journals. Homer also created oil paintings based on his observations in the South at this time, including his *Defiance: Inviting a Shot Before Petersburg, Virginia* (1864) and his *At the Cabin Door* (1865–66). The first suggests the courage and sometimes foolhardiness of soldiers in that conflict; the second indicates the proud, quiet hopes and subtle defiance of blacks at this time. Conrad Wise Chapman joined the Confederate army and, after being wounded, was reassigned to Charleston, S.C., and ordered to illustrate the city's fortifications. The 31 small oil-on-board paintings, though most frequently viewed for their historical content, are noteworthy for their freshness and clarity.

In Richmond, William D. Washington painted the *Burial of Latané* in 1864, recording an incident of 1862 and showing white women and slaves performing a young war hero's burial service, a service attended by white children but by no adult white males. In 1869 Everett B. D. Fabrino Julio painted a large-scale double equestrian portrait showing the imagined conference of General Lee and Stonewall Jackson on the eve of the battle of Chancellorsville—a battle in which Jackson was struck down, dying shortly thereafter. Prints based on these two paintings subsequently enjoyed wide circulation among white southerners and became symbols of the Lost Cause—the death of heroes and the role of women who carried on nobly in the absence of their men. Henry Mosler's painting *The Lost Cause*, first exhibited in 1868, showed a weary infantryman returning to his ruined cabin, thus focusing on the effect of the war on ordinary yeoman farmers of the highlands. This Mosler painting was reproduced in chromolithographs and widely circulated. In the late 1860s John Adams Elder's *Battle of the Crater* and a notable posthumous portrait of Stonewall Jackson (Corcoran Gallery of Art) were well known. In the decades after the war still other artists, among them William Gilbert Gaul and Xanthus R. Smith, painted imaginary episodes of the conflict. Alfred Waud was one of several artists whose drawings record the South during Reconstruction, and Forbes and Waud later contributed illustrations for late 19th-century publications on the war. Thus, a group of now little-known paintings and drawings formed an iconography of noble defeat, an ethos that helped salve the pride of white southerners during years of poverty and reconstruction.

Winslow Homer returned to Virginia in the 1870s and did a group of paintings of southern blacks, all characterized by quiet dignity and forthright depiction. John James Elder, Richard Norris Brooke, and Lucien Whiting Powell were Virginia artists who painted everyday life of blacks in the 1870s and 1880s. Lyell E. Carr did a similar series of rural black Georgia life in the 1890s. The intent of the artists was to show "sober and truthful" depictions of these impoverished peoples. All of these artists were influenced in part by changing European choices of subject matter; the southern black, for example, was equated with the picturesque laboring peasant and thus became an emblem of the South. To the 20th-century eye some of these depictions have a sentimental quality—though they are a far cry from the caricature seen on minstrel-show, music-sheet illustrations. They record blacks as a

Conrad Wise Chapman, Camp Near Corinth, Mississippi *(1862)*

passive, untroubled people, a view shared by both northern and southern whites. They record the role of blacks in the life of the South, and many are painted with great skill and present their subjects with great dignity. William Aiken Walker's small paintings of blacks and their cabins frequently served as picturesque mementoes, which northern visitors to the southern resorts took home. Less than successful artistically, they too are known for their depictions of black rural southerners and their heritage.

The southern landscape—particularly the quiet, rural life along the bayous and streams of south Louisiana and the Gulf Coast—became the favorite subject matter for artists Richard Clague, Marshall Smith, and William Buck. Joseph Rusling Meeker, who had served with the Union navy, returned again and again to the Deep South to paint the verdure and humid atmosphere of the wetlands. Flavius Fisher, living in Lynchburg, Va., made the open spaces of the Dismal Swamp his theme. Further north, artists such as Carl Brenner and Clarence Boyd painted the characteristic woodlands of Kentucky in a style that has roots both in the Barbizon school of France and in the reverent and meticulous response to nature articulated by Asher B. Durand of New York. Though their paintings were based on the world around them, these artists were not self-consciously regional in the later spirit of the 1930s.

Occasionally their critics expressed a strongly regional attitude. Praising Richard Clague's work on 21 January 1871, a reviewer in the *Commercial Bulletin* of New Orleans spoke of his ability to capture "the characteristics of our peculiar scenery," and, in perhaps an oblique reference to the dramatic works of artists such as Bierstadt, said that "there is no meretricious glare about these fine studies, no straining after effect." In the early 20th century Ellsworth Woodward of New Orleans, following the precepts of the arts and crafts movement and of John Dewey, exhorted artists of the region to draw from their own environment for the subjects of their works.

During the 1870s Florida began to attract visitors. It was the "new Eden," the still-unspoiled paradise of the expanding industrial nation. Northern artists such as Winslow Homer, with his brilliant late watercolors of the tropics (including Florida), Thomas Moran, and William Morris Hunt were among those who spent one or more winters there. Martin J. Heade first came to Florida in 1883 and later settled in St. Augustine, where he led a small artists' colony until his death in 1904. His glowing landscapes of the wetlands of Florida show a still-primitive wilderness. George Inness, and then his son, George Inness, Jr., found warmth and a sense of union with nature in Tarpon Springs, Fla. Elliot Daingerfield, a native of North Carolina, was a close friend and associate of the elder Inness in New York. In his mature years he returned regularly to his summer home in Blowing Rock, N.C., where he painted the familiar contours of the land in muted tonalities, which also suggest his deep, religious feeling for the spiritual quality of the natural world.

Knowledge of women artists practicing in America in the late 19th and early 20th centuries is still somewhat limited, but in this period several women artists from the South emerged. Clara Weaver Parrish and Anne Goldthwaite, both of Alabama, were among artists who received their training and spent much of their artistic careers in New York, though each returned to the South with some regularity and included southern subjects in their works. This emergence of women artists coincided with the women's suffrage movement and the slow access to higher education gained by women at this time. Newcomb College of Tulane University, founded in 1886–87, was one of the first women's colleges in the South to have an extensive art training program. Gertrude Roberts Smith, painter, and Mary Sheerer, ceramic designer, were both teachers at Newcomb College and important artists in their own right and helped to shape a generation of women artists after the college's founding.

Artistic organizations, formed from time to time in various southern communities, provided opportunities for meetings among artists, instructed aspiring artists, and provided occasions for exhibits. In New Orleans, for example, the Southern Art Union was organized around 1881 and lasted until sometime after 1883. The Southern Arts League was organized in 1885, changed its name to the Artists' Association of New Orleans, and was officially incorporated in 1886; by 1899 it had 63 members. In the late 1890s the Arts and Exhibition Club was founded, and by 1905 merged with the Artists' Association, thus forming the Art Association of New Orleans, a group that still exists but is now one among many art groups in the city. The Arts and Crafts Club of New Orleans was founded in 1922 and continued as an exhibiting and teaching organization until March 1951. Similar organizations were formed in other cities and areas, some short lived, others surviving for considerably longer times, such as the Nashville Art Association, the Waco Art League in Texas, the Carolina Art Association in Charleston, and the Mississippi Art Association.

One national culmination of this local and regional artistic activity was the formation at a meeting held in Washington, D.C., in May 1909 of the American Federation of Arts, an organization that aimed to include "all institutions, societies, city and village improvement associations, and schools and other organizations in the United States, whose purpose is to promote the study of art, the cultivation of the public taste, and the application of art to the development of material conditions in our country." Though the majority of those attending the founding meeting were from New York, Boston, and Philadelphia, delegates included those from the Art Association of New Orleans, the Carolina Art Association, and the Waco Art League, as well as a number from Maryland organizations and a sizable group from private and public organizations based in Washington, D.C., then still a very southern city. William Woodward, representing both the Art Association of New Orleans and Tulane University, was one of the principal speakers.

Despite the efforts of local and regional organizations, artists in the South still found it difficult to find patrons and exhibit their works. The area was still essentially rural, and the art groups were quite small. Another organization designed to help artists reach a wider audience was the Southern States Art League, founded in 1921. One of its founders, Ellsworth Woodward, bemoaned the fact that so many of the South's best artists had found it necessary to leave the area and had achieved success only in the North. The Southern States Art League regularly sponsored exhibits and meetings until its virtual demise in 1946. Its most successful exhibit was held in Nashville in 1935, when over 12,000 people attended.

Despite many artists' seeming isolation, the influence of the Impressionists and the Symbolists found its way into the South during the last decade of the 19th and the first two decades of the 20th centuries through the network of communication in the artistic world. Evidence of this influence is seen in the works of artists such as Ellsworth and William Woodward, Alexander Drysdale, and Gertrude Roberts Smith, all of New Orleans; Robert Loftin Newman, whose roots were in Tennessee; William Posey Silva, who depicted landscapes of Tennessee and Georgia; J. Gari Melchers in Virginia; and Julian Onderdonk in San Antonio.

See also BLACK LIFE: Art, Black; ENVIRONMENT: / Homer, Winslow; MYTHIC SOUTH: / Lost Cause Myth

Jessie Poesch
Tulane University

Bruce W. Chambers, *Art and Artists of the South: The Robert P. Coggins Collection* (1984), *Southern Quarterly* (Fall–Winter 1985); Corcoran Gallery of Art, *American Painters of the South* (1960); David C. Driskell, *Two Centuries of Black American Art* (1976); Max Kozloff, *Artforum* (May 1973); David Moltke-Hansen, *Art in the Lives of South Carolinians: Nineteenth-Century Chapters* (1979); Pauline Pinckney, *Painting in Texas: The Nineteenth Century* (1967); Virginia Museum of Fine Arts, *Painting in the South: 1564–1980* (1983); Ben F. Williams, *Two Hundred Years of the Visual Arts in North Carolina* (1976).

Painting and Painters, 1920–1960

The modern period in southern painting can be said to begin in the early 1920s with the activities of the Fugitive group at Vanderbilt University in Nashville. Although the Fugitives were essentially a literary group, they were also concerned with theories of artistic expression in general, especially with regard to the South. Their importance lies in their cosmopolitan attitude toward creative expression. The four major figures in the movement were Donald Davidson, John Crowe Ransom, Allen Tate, and Robert Penn Warren. Although respecting the new modernism that spanned national boundaries, they regretted that southern culture, as they had known it, appeared to be dissolving under the pressure of the new industrial age. Like the modern artist in general, the Fugitives struggled with the rift between reason and the imagination, between science and faith; they assumed the mantle of the modern sensibility but set out to make it uniquely southern as well. Donald Davidson, always the Fugitive with the strongest sense of his southern roots, wrote an essay for the *Saturday Review* in May 1926 titled "The Artist as Southerner." He felt that any artist who chose his materials exclusively from his surroundings was provincial, not innovative or modern, yet he recognized the peculiar clash between modernism and tradition that marked the dilemma of the southern artist.

The Fugitives were not the only group to recognize that a new period of expression was at hand. The circle of the *Double Dealer* magazine, published in New Orleans from 1921 to 1926, sought to end the artistic backwardness that they, like the Fugitives, had perceived as the South's lot since the end of the Civil War. William Faulkner, who would best exemplify the new southern artist, was among the younger southerners this magazine featured. Another magazine, the *New South*, begun in Chattanooga in 1927, turned matters in its first issue more expressly to art. In a spirited essay on "The South in American Art," a writer extolled the southern artists who painted the local yet American scene. "We must build and maintain schools wherein Southern talent may be educated and trained," he wrote, "and thereby interpret the spirit and traditions of the South, which can only be expressed by native artists."

The call for painters of the southern scene was sparked by the activities of Thomas Hart Benton, who traveled extensively in 1928 and 1929 over the back roads of the Deep South, gathering material for his major mural programs in New York in the early 1930s on American history and culture. The paintings that Benton produced on his trip through the South were prophetic of the kind of work many southern painters would turn to in the 1930s. One southern artist who echoed Benton's activity in the same period was Conrad Albrizio, who completed an important mural cycle in 1930 for the Louisiana State Capitol Building in Baton Rouge. The building was the brainchild of the flamboyant governor Huey P. Long and was one of the most successfully designed and decorated public buildings of its time. Albrizio's cycle of paintings, done for the governor's reception room, has unfortunately been lost; however, complete sketches survive to show that the artist executed a series of narrative scenes of the daily life of the state, including a panel depicting industrial activity.

Likewise, the artist Roderick MacKenzie, working in Birmingham, Ala., completed four large panels depicting the history of that commonwealth for the domed central portion of the statehouse. This kind of artistic activity in the South increased markedly with the onset of the Depression and the art programs of Franklin D. Roosevelt's New Deal. Between January 1933 and April 1939 the social service wings of the New Deal poured nearly $2 billion into the southern states, providing large-scale relief and resulting in many wide-ranging physical improvements. The federal art programs had a direct and profound effect on painting activity in the South. One result was the rapid emergence of an even greater sectional feeling with regard to the development of the arts. By encouraging a regional focus, the New Deal programs had the effect of turning many southern artists and communities inward.

In order to comprehend fully the nature of painting in the South in the 1930s, it is necessary to understand the Agrarian and regionalist movements. The Agrarian philosophy, which grew out of the earlier Fugitive movement in Nashville, had to do with the desire, in Allen Tate's words, for "getting back to the roots" of the southern experience. The Agrarians posited a duality between agrarian and industrial society, with the latter viewed as a threat to southern civilization. However, this movement was far from simplistic; the arguments of its best writers were often impassioned and stimulating. Donald Davidson again set the tone in an article titled "A Mirror for Artists," where he maintained that the duty of the southern artist was first to be an active member of his community. Seen in this context, one can understand the participation of an artist like Conrad Albrizio in a symposium in 1936 titled "The Arts in the Community." Albrizio echoed the aims of other southern painters of this period by calling for work that would "appraise the people of the community, their spirit, and their degree of culture." He went on to execute mural programs in several southern cities throughout the decade, maintaining that the artist's role was to help the average southerner understand that "the real values of everyday life" and "the beauty of simple things" were the keys to lasting artistic expression.

Albrizio's beliefs were typical of the regionalist movement as a whole in the decade of the 1930s. Richard Coe, who painted the Birmingham steel mills in this period, had identical views. He headed the Alabama section of the WPA, saying that "American art for and by the American people is a slogan worth heeding." Another Alabama artist who was equally active along these lines was Kelly Fitzpatrick, who helped establish the Alabama Art League in Montgomery in 1930. Three years later on the banks of the Coosa River in Elmore County he founded the Poka-Hutchi Art Colony, which flourished during the summers until 1948, attracting some of the South's leading artists, many of whom were keenly interested in depicting the lives of the rural people, black or white. Artists like Howard Cook followed Thomas Hart Benton's footsteps and traveled through the region in order to portray the southern worker realistically, yet with sympathy and dignity. In many respects, the concerns of artists like Cook mirrored those of major regionalist thinkers like Howard W. Odum of the University of North Carolina at Chapel Hill, who steered the old southern sectionalism into a constructive investigation of local culture as a part of a larger national picture.

In 1936 a young painter named Lamar Dodd was appointed to the art faculty of the University of Georgia after winning an award at the annual exhibition of the Art Institute of Chicago for a painting depicting a slag dump and railroad cut near Wylan, Ala. Such a subject was typical for Dodd, who preferred to paint things that captured, in his words, "the mood of the place," the everyday South. Like many southern artists in this period, Dodd was trained at the Art Students League in New York before returning to his native area to paint and teach. He soon gained a reputation as the outstanding artist in Georgia, and he was active in many educational, civic, and professional groups, including the Association of Georgia Artists and the Southeastern Art Association. Thus, an energetic artist like Lamar Dodd was able to found a large and important center for art at the University of Georgia, and the South began to have a generation of young artists trained largely in their native region.

Activity was under way in Mississippi as well. The Mississippi Art Association, founded in 1911, was followed by the Gulf Coast Art Association of Biloxi, with William Woodward of New Orleans as president. Individual painters in Mississippi, while not as numerous as in the neighboring states of Alabama and Louisiana, nevertheless mirrored similar social concerns in their work, as in Marie Hull's paintings of sharecroppers that she painted after her return from extensive study in New York and Europe. Again, such depictions were meant to dignify the individual, not demean him. One contemporary newspaper account of Hull's sensitive portraits recognized their "clear sharp eye and indomitable spirit," where the subjects were "slightly stooped by [their] toiling decades but strengthened rather than broken by them." The Mississippi artist who gained greatest recognition in the 1930s was John McCrady, who initially worked in Oxford, where he became friends with William Faulkner. McCrady was vocal about wanting to paint southern subjects and soon set up a studio in New Orleans, where he achieved a national reputation as a regionalist while completing work for the WPA. In 1937 he was featured in *Life* magazine, and the following year he helped found an association of artists called A New Southern Group. In 1939 McCrady and Robert Penn Warren were awarded Guggenheim fellowships; McCrady's intent was to paint a series of works on "The Life and Faith of the Southern Negro."

Clearly, the regionalist movement had an overriding effect on the painting of the South in this period, and just as clearly, regionalism to the artists was less a matter of blind nativism than cultural growth. This was nowhere more apparent than in Dallas, Tex., where strong new artistic activity centered around the events of the Texas State Centennial in 1936. A group of talented younger artists, who were informally labeled "The Nine," rose to prominence and developed what became one of the most notable and original regional schools of southern painting. Dallas stood at the boundary of the Southeast and Southwest, and the paintings of The Nine reflected that duality. The principal artists in the group were Alexandre Hogue, Jerry Bywaters, Otis Dozier, William Lester, and Everett Spruce. All but Spruce, who hailed from Arkansas, had been raised in Texas in rural communities. Their paintings depicted rural and urban subjects, set against the Texas landscape, and were characterized by clarity and openness of space and light. No single artist dominated this important group, and they all were intensely active in community affairs, teaching, writing, and working with local galleries and the newly built Dallas Museum of Fine Arts. This group was active until the events of World War II forced them to go their separate ways; yet they exemplified the enormous impact that a regionalist aesthetic had on the development of southern culture.

Throughout the Depression era many southern painters, including the members of the Dallas Nine, felt compelled to portray the southern black as a way of coming to grips with the reality of their own environment. In a similar way, the decade of the 1930s witnessed the expanding struggles of the Afro-American artist's search for his own roots—roots far deeper and harder to trace. As early as 1921 W. E. B. Du Bois, writing in the *Crisis*, had maintained that "the transforming hand and seeing eye of the artist, white or black," were needed to help in the search for Afro-American identity. Alain Locke's *The New Negro*, published in 1925, began to spur interest in Afro-American folklore and art as a method of turning social disillusionment into racial pride. In 1931 Locke, then professor of philosophy at Howard University, published an article in the *American Magazine of Art* titled "The American Negro as Artist," where he surveyed the work of the major Afro-American artists of the period, many of whom had come from the South. He had warm words of praise for a younger generation of artists who aimed to express in their art the "race, spirit, and background as well as the individual skill and temperament of the artist." One of these artists was William H. Johnson, who was just then beginning his remarkable career. Born in Florence, S.C., but associated with Charleston, he studied at the Art Students League in New York and was awarded a William E. Harmon Foundation Prize for further study abroad. In 1938 he began teaching at the Harlem Community Center in New York and exhibited his works to increasingly wide acclaim; yet it was not to last. His color denied him the opportunity and recognition that he deserved, and his later life was marked by tragic circumstances. However, other artists could turn such prejudices to their advantage. Aaron Douglas, who founded the department of art at Fisk University in Nashville and taught generations of students, is an example. Douglas was trained in New York and was an active member of the Harlem Renaissance; he furnished the illustrations for Locke's book *The New Negro*. With the help of Edwin Harleston, another Afro-American artist from Charleston, Douglas completed a series of highly significant murals depicting the course of "Negro history" for the library at Fisk University. As an artist, Douglas maintained that he wanted to "place himself where the people are," and his selfless contributions to the development of Afro-American art in the South cannot be overemphasized.

A number of young white southern painters were also interested in the sympathetic portrayal of blacks along the lines suggested by Douglas and were committed to change during this period. Charles Shannon, who was born and raised in Montgomery, Ala., studied at the Cleveland School of Art and returned in 1935 to Butler County, where he built a log cabin and proceeded to paint a number of expressionistic works about southern blacks. "I came to love this land," the artist wrote, "the plants and people that grew from it." In 1938 Shannon received a Julius Rosenwald Fellowship "for Southerners who are working on problems distinctive to the South." The following year Shannon and a group of friends organized a cooperative venture in Montgomery that they called New South, which was designed to enrich the cultural life of the area by gathering together artists and artisans to work in a gallery and theater, and to teach workshops and classes.

In Virginia a similar effort was made by Julien Binford, who had returned from his study in New York to buy a piece of land in Fine Creek, where he busily converted the ruins of an old foundry into a house and studio. Binford was one of the first recipients of the Virginia Artist Fellowships instituted by the Virginia Museum of Fine Arts in Richmond, and he used it to conduct classes at the Craig House Negro Art Center. In 1942 he produced a much-heralded mural for the black congregation of the Shiloh Baptist Church near his home. Binford's contemporary, Robert Gwathmey, a native of Richmond, infused social commentary into his work in a more overt fashion. In 1946 he told a writer for *Art News* that he would return to his home every summer after teaching in New York and see anew the deep social problems that affected his native South. Yet his paintings seemed to exude more pathos than hate. As a southern painter he was angry and critical, but he also seemed to shoulder some of the guilt.

The period of World War II activated a broad cycle of change in the South. The region was on the move, shifting, growing, and changing old and seemingly entrenched patterns. Sometimes the change was strongly resisted, often for the sake of an increasingly outmoded sectionalism. Southern painters became more concerned not with a sense of place, but with a sensibility. Romare Bearden, originally from Charlotte, studied and worked in New York and Europe before coming to the realization that his most evocative images came from "the people I knew and remembered down South." His work represents the essence of the migration of the southern black from the rural areas and traditions to postwar urban society. "I paint out of the tradition of the Blues, of call and recall," the artist has written. "I never left Charlotte, except physically."

Remembrances, visions, the mythology of place—these elements underlie much postwar southern painting. Carroll Cloar, an artist originally from Arkansas, moved to Memphis in 1955 and began a series of paintings based on his boyhood in the Arkansas Delta. "There is a joy in the sense of belonging, of possessing and being possessed, by the land where you were born." His meticulous, vibrant works evoke the spirit of folk art yet with a power that derives from sophisticated study of his surroundings. Likewise, Hobson Pittman's paintings seem like dream worlds of southern myths and impressions. Raised on a plantation near Epworth, N.C., Pittman became a noted artist and teacher outside his native South, but the imagery and spirit of the region never left his work. All three of these artists—Bearden, Cloar, and Pittman—have created evocations, dreams, and remembrances of an otherworldly South that seems to exist mostly as fiction.

Some southern artists in the postwar period withdrew to create a world wholly their own yet inextricably part of southern culture. Walter Inglis Anderson, after studying art in Pennsylvania and in Europe, moved to a tiny cottage in Ocean Springs, Miss., where, in virtual seclusion, he painted the local flora and fauna. Throughout the 1950s Anderson spent most of his time on Horn Island, a small, ever-changing sandbar rich in plants and wildlife. He produced thousands of watercolors of this southern version of Walden Pond and kept detailed journals of his feelings and impressions as he explored every inch of its terrain throughout the seasons. Like Anderson, Will Henry Stevens also adopted a uniquely personal vision, but one that embodied two separate styles. He taught at Newcomb College in New Orleans from 1921 until his retirement in 1948 and spent nearly all his summers in western North Carolina, painting the woods and hillsides. His "pastel paintings" of these southern woodlands, using a nonrubbing chalk of his own invention, were praised when they were first exhibited in 1941. Curiously, Stevens also painted in a more nonobjective style and exhibited those works separately. In December 1941 he went so far as to have two simultaneous exhibitions in separate galleries, which may suggest the dilemma that some southern artists faced regarding a search for a meaningful style in a period when southern culture was undergoing profound changes.

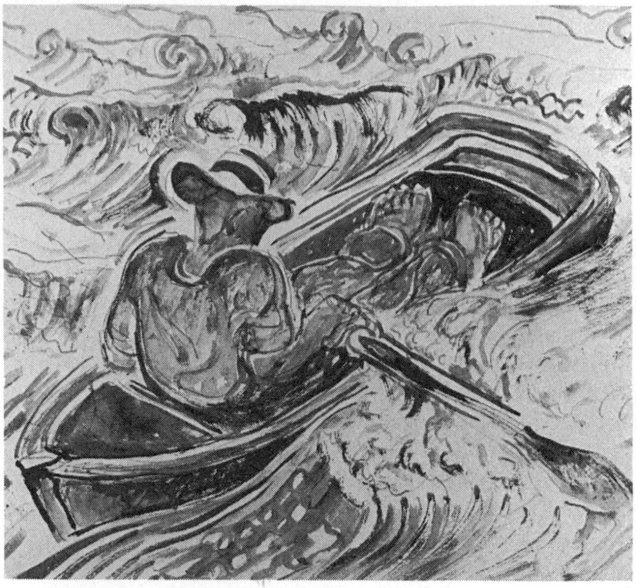

Walter Anderson, Walter Anderson Rowing His Boat *(c. 1950s)*

Stevens spent his summers close to an enormously influential school that had been founded in 1933 near Black Mountain, N.C. It was an entirely experimental community, with shifting ideas and goals, but it attracted some of the brightest and most fertile artistic minds of the postwar era, including Josef Albers, Walter Gropius, Willem de Kooning, Robert Motherwell, Clement Greenberg, Beaumont Newhall, and Buckminster Fuller. The only southern painter to receive an invitation to teach at this isolated outpost was Robert Gwathmey; for the most part, the effect of Black Mountain College on the immediate development of painting in the South was minimal. Yet the artistic climate in the South changed drastically in this period, in part because of the influence of the New York School and of the art centers that had been established at southern colleges and universities. For the first time the impetus for artistic change was generated from within the South itself.

The activity of artists like Ralston Crawford, based in New Orleans, is an example of the newer acceptance of modernist styles in the region. Crawford, who had adapted a style of nonrepresentational geometric abstraction, began teaching at Louisiana State University at Baton Rouge in 1949. In his paintings of New Orleans, which were done in a series, he conveyed the hard light and busy rhythms of the city's industrial and maritime activity in color-filled forms and shapes that revealed his passion for jazz. Like Crawford, George Cress developed his art within the new idiom. Cress attended Emory University and then studied art under Lamar Dodd and Jean Charlot at the University of Georgia and was thus a member of the new generation of artists trained within the South. He began teaching at the University of Chattanooga and has served in the Southeastern College Art Conference, as well as the Tennessee Arts Council. His painting style evolved out of the context of the second generation of the New York School, as he depicted the layered bluffs of his region in an abstract pattern of loose patches of color and texture. Cress's contemporary Claude Howell, who has taught at the University of North Carolina in his native Wilmington since 1953, works in a more representational style, painting structured, austere views of his locale. Michael O'Brien, in his stimulating book, *The Idea of the American South*, has written of the artist's need to see "the South itself as an idea, used to organize and comprehend disparate facts of social reality." Certainly the modern southern artist has assumed a southern sensibility in his work and has developed out of that position. Thus, an artist like William Halsey of Charleston could turn from early, representational paintings of his surroundings to ones that became increasingly abstract without relinquishing the uniquely southern sensibility that some have sensed in his work.

Throughout the period herein reviewed, southern artists sought to preserve a regional aesthetic as opposed to a more national one. It was a period of paradox and change, when older sectional desires clashed with national, and eventually international, artistic influences. Artists in the South in the period prior to World War II could not be classified in the avant-garde sense as independent; in the more traditional sense, they thought of themselves as integral members of—even interpreters for—their own southern society. Only after the establishment of a comprehensive cultural network of museums and universities does one find the growth of the independent sensibility, the open acceptance of the broader framework of American culture with the southern artist fully a part of the international art world.

See also BLACK LIFE: Art, Black; EDUCATION: / Black Mountain College; HISTORY AND MANNERS: Modernism; New Deal Cultural Programs; LITERATURE: Agrarianism in Literature; / Davidson, Donald; Ransom, John Crowe; Tate, Allen; Warren, Robert Penn; MYTHIC SOUTH: Regionalism; / Agrarians, Vanderbilt

Rick Stewart
Dallas Museum of Art

Amon Carter Museum, *Texas Painting and Sculpture: The Twentieth Century* (1971); Bruce W. Chambers, *Art and Artists of the South: The Robert P. Coggins Collection* (1984); Corcoran Gallery of Art, *American Painters of the South* (1960); David C. Driskell, *Two Centuries of Black American Art* (1976); Ralph H. Hudson, *Black Artists / South* (1979); Huntsville Museum of Art, *Contemporary Painting in Alabama* (1980); James C. Kelly and Estill Curtis Pennington, *The South on Paper: Line, Color and Light* (1985); Jack Morris, *Contemporary Artists of South Carolina* (1970); Virginia Museum of Fine Arts, *Painting in the South: 1564–1980* (1983).

Painting and Painters, 1960–1980

In studying contemporary art in the South, one must explore signs and symbols associated with the region in the popular imagination and pay particular attention to how these have emerged in the visual arts.

If one is indeed shaped by the environment, daily life, and early experiences, then the concept of a "southern" type of art is as inevitable as history. The internal characteristics of southern art, especially when it comes to modern and contemporary paintings, present a far from tidy field, partly because the region itself is so heterogeneous. One can distinguish between the Deep South (South Carolina, Georgia, Alabama, Mississippi, and Louisiana) and the Southern Rim (Tennessee, Virginia, North Carolina, Florida, Texas, and sometimes Arkansas and others) on the basis of historical, sociocultural, and economic factors, all of which affect art and artists.

The *American Heritage Dictionary* defines the term *regionalism* in three ways, and art from the Southeast fits all three understandings. The first is of, pertaining to, or characteristic of a large geographical region, and Nellie Mae Rowe, Sam Doyle, Robert Gordy, and Elizabeth Shannon are southern artists who are regional in this sense of the term. The second definition is of, pertaining to, or characteristic of a particular region or localized district, and Donald Roller Wilson, Carroll Cloar, Romare Bearden, and Juan Gonzales represent southern art in this aspect. *Regionalism* can also mean something characterized by a particular language dialect in an area. The religious, social, and ethnic localism of Sister Gertrude Morgan, the Reverend Howard Fenster, Jesse Poimboeuf, and Rise Delmar Ochsner exemplify regional art of this type.

To the extent that distinct regional subcultures exist, some aspects might be used by regional artists to evoke a sense of place, time, and geographical identity, e.g., Sam Doyle's "first black midwife, she was a slave." With respect to such factors in contemporary southern painting, one must look outside the field of art for clues. In *The*

Enduring South (1975) John Shelton Reed isolates four influences he considers important in this region: familism, religiosity, localism, and a greater tolerance for violence than the rest of the country. To these one might add the isolationism of the "old folks at home" mentality or what should be classified as the "South of the mind," which holds true in the social localism of such cities as Charleston, Mobile, and Savannah.

In southeastern painting regional imagery abounds, as in the works of Patty Whitty Johnson, Sue Moore, and Douglas Bourgeois. A respect for custom and the past is still prevalent, affecting newcomers in a variety of ways, and a certain inclination remains toward representational images and a decorative unity of form that appears to be a consistent shaping force in the art of such southerners as Jasper Johns, Kenneth Noland, Dorothy Gillespie, and Ida Kohlmeyer. Thus, a basis seems to exist for positing clearly identifiable qualities when it comes to southern art.

In the visual arts the term *regionalism* presents additional problems. According to conventional wisdom, provincials are those people who do not live in or receive artistic truth from New York City. Much of the art produced outside of New York has its own roots, references, and traditions. When outsiders—mainstream critics, artists, and others—are brought in to judge exhibitions of "southern" art, they more often than not ignore these sharp differences, applying their own standards to the art they see. The problem with this, for example, may clearly be seen in the case of south Florida, which is the tropics, the gateway to the Latin Americas and the Caribbean. It is inconceivable that such factors would not exert considerable influence on the art of an impressionable generation of younger creators in the state. To ignore these realities on the grounds of mainstream standards would neither be responsible criticism nor a fair assessment of the surrealist-style art.

Doubtless the setting of the South conjures up pictures in the popular imagination of weeping willows, cypresses, Spanish moss, plantations, and Afro-Americans—not tropical iconography. The overall impression, as noted previously, can be deceptive. The art of this region is undeniably the product, like any serious art, of a search for meaning. Explicit in this definition is a decided concern with irrationality, ineptitude, banality, and deceitful fragility on the one hand, and, on the other hand, a refined literary picturesqueness with a special emphasis on representation and decorative embellishments. To these qualities one might add whimsicality; sly, humorous exaggerations concerning both Christian and pagan themes; and dashes of charm, irony, magic, quaintness, directness, naiveté; a startlingly crude, powerful, and often unexpectedly brutal primitivism.

Clearly, southern artists have been suspicious of established fashions and accepted fundamentals of modern style, i.e., mathematical absolutes, a reliance on science and technology, and rational thought processes. Perhaps in terms of Realism and neo-expressionism, their suspicion of the latter has been prophetic.

While there is at present no definitive southern school of painting, recent exhibitions such as *Black Folk Art in America 1930–1980* (Corcoran Gallery of Art), *More Than Land or Sky: Art from Appalachia* (National Museum of American Art), and *Painting in the South: 1564–1980* (Virginia Museum of Fine Arts) have focused critical attention on southern art. The reality is simply this: before one can begin to discuss southern art, it has to be seen and written about. In this context the efforts of the Southeastern Center for Contemporary Art, the New Orleans Center for Contemporary Art, Nexus, the Atlanta Art Workers Coalition, the Southeast College Art Conference, the Southeastern Women's Caucus for Art, and a host of other art support systems are crucial. Primary among the regional journals is *Art Papers*, which gives serious review to states in the Southeast. These regional resources represent much more than a mere reflection of a mainstream with tributaries that once reached no further than New York, Chicago, and California.

Today's art offers a fascinating array of styles and attitudes, and nowhere more so than in the southeastern region. The problem is that there are not enough trained and motivated critics to pay serious attention to art in the South. Recent issues of *Art News* and *Arts Magazine* have begun to pay some attention, but sweepingly superficial overviews and individual profiles are hardly a remedy for the neglect of regional artists.

See also BLACK LIFE: Art, Black; FOLKLIFE: Folk Painting; HISTORY AND MANNERS: Modernism

Sandra Langer
New York City

Art News (February 1983); Elizabeth C. Baker, *Art in America* (July–August 1976); Bruce W. Chambers, *Art and Artists of the South: The Robert P. Coggins Collection* (1984); Corcoran Gallery of Art, *American Painters of the South* (1960); David C. Driskell, *Two Centuries of Black American Art* (1976); Walter Gabrielson, *Art in America* (January–February 1974); James C. Kelly and Estill Curtis Pennington, *The South on Paper: Line, Color and Light* (1985); Terry Smith, *Artforum* (September 1974); Virginia Museum of Fine Arts, *Painting in the South: 1564–1980* (1983); *Women Artists News* (February 1980).

Photography and Photographers

From 1839, when the first photographic processes were publicly introduced, until the 1880s, photography in the South was virtually indistinguishable from photography practiced elsewhere in America. The daguerreotype, a unique image made upon a sensitized silver plate, was the popular early photographic medium; its first commercial application was for the production of portraits. There was a great deal of mobility among the first daguerreotypists, especially on the Atlantic Seaboard. Realizing the commercial potential of this revolutionary medium, dozens of opportunists labored to make improvements in equipment. Henry Fitz, Jr. (1808–63), a pioneer American telescope manufacturer, developed the lens for Alexander Wolcott's portrait camera, which received the first American photographic patent in May 1840. Fitz operated a portrait gallery in Baltimore, Md., from 1840 to 1842. In New Orleans, Jules Lion (1816–66), a black lithographer, was working with a daguerreotype camera he had brought directly from Paris. Whether or not Lion tried to make portraits at that time is conjectural; he did succeed in making and exhibiting views of the city in March of 1840.

The nation's capital, with its constant parade of statesmen and visiting dignitaries, offered the greatest possibilities for the development of a portrait trade. John Plumbe, Jr. (1808–57), a Welshman, learned daguerreotyping from a student of Wolcott in Washington, D.C., in 1840. His success there led to the establishment of offices in 18 cities by 1846, an unprecedented venture. Plumbe located branches in Baltimore, Md.; Louisville, Ky.; Petersburg, Alexandria, and Richmond, Va.; St. Louis, Mo.; and New Orleans, La.; as well as in other major U.S. cities, Liverpool, and Paris. Understandably, overexpansion and mismanagement led to his financial collapse in 1847. Following the demise of the Plumbe operations, Jesse H. Whitehurst (c. 1820–75) dominated the Washington trade. Whitehurst, a native of Virginia, who had opened his first establishment in Norfolk in 1844, added galleries in Richmond and Lynchburg and in Baltimore, Md., to his operations.

During the winter of 1851–52, Marcus A. Root (1808–88), author of *The Camera and the Pencil* (1864) and numerous articles and photographic journals, purchased a Washington gallery in partnership with John Hawley Clarke (1831–1914). James A. Cutting of Boston prepared applications for patents to the collodion processes in Root and Clarke's gallery in 1853 and 1854. These new processes enabled the introduction of the ambrotype, a collodion negative on glass, and the tintype, a collodion negative upon a thin, coated iron sheet. These photos were much cheaper and quicker to produce than daguerreotypes, but the most important use of the collodion process was for the production of glass negatives from which many positives could be made, thus introducing a means of rapid production of inexpensive images.

In 1857 and 1858 a unique opportunity fell to the Washington galleries when a succession of American Indian dignitaries came to negotiate treaties with Congress. The most extensive series of portraits was made in the newly opened studio of James E. McClees, which was operated by Julian Vannerson and Samuel H. Cohen. The tribal chieftains, with their exotic dress, language, and rituals, appealed to the romanticism of the age. The portraits were exhibited in their studio, and copies were offered for sale. Whitehurst and Mathew Brady also made and exhibited Indian portraits that winter. In New York City, Brady had learned daguerreotyping from Samuel F. B. Morse, the inventor and painter who became acquainted with the process directly from Daguerre in Paris.

Another student of Morse was Frederick A. P. Barnard (1809–89), a native of Connecticut. Barnard opened a gallery in October 1841 in Tuscaloosa, Ala., where he was a professor of mathematics at the state university. With his partner William H. Harrington (c. 1810–61), a native of Pennsylvania, he conducted experiments using chlorine as a chemical accelerator, descriptions of which were published in the *American Journal of Science and Arts* (July 1841). Barnard later became the first chancellor of the University of Mississippi and subsequently president of Columbia College in New York City, but he maintained a scientific interest in photography, publishing articles in photographic journals of the day. Harrington relocated in New Orleans, where he maintained a leading daguerreotype gallery until the commencement of the Civil War.

George Smith Cook (1819–1902), also of Connecticut, had a most estimable record in the history of southern photography. Cook learned daguerreotyping in New Orleans about 1843 and remained there until 1845, when he embarked on his four-year odyssey through the South. Cook reportedly spread the art from St. Louis, Mo., to Charleston, S.C., where he finally settled in 1849. He was so renowned that Brady chose him to operate his own New York studio during his absence in 1851 and 1852. Cook moved to Richmond, Va., in 1880, where he operated a gallery until his death.

From historical and sociological standpoints, the most important early galleries were those, like Cook's in Charleston and Richmond, that created a consistent visual chronicle of a developing community, in some instances for a half century. These photographers made thousands of formal studio portraits of prominent and ordinary citizens, their children, and family functions. Some specialized in architectural views, recording the outward and upward growth of the southern cities, or views of commerce along the rivers, especially the great steamboats of the Ohio and Mississippi rivers. Interior and exterior views of these steamboats are beautifully preserved in the glass negatives of J. Mack Moore, who worked in Vicksburg, Miss.

With the advent of the war, the demand for collodion photography accelerated, especially for the manufacture of portraits of departing soldiers and their loved ones. Tintypes and paper prints in the fashionable *carte-de-visite* size, approximately 2½″ × 4″, were cheap, and multiple images could be made from a single exposure. Even the tintype, when made with a multilens camera, could yield several images on a single plate.

The war gave the photographer a new role—as recorders of the tragic American drama. Wartime photographers who remain famous today, Mathew Brady (c. 1823–96) and Alexander Gardner (1821–82), are remembered particularly for their disturbing views of the scarred battlefields of Maryland and Virginia. In 1866 Gardner published a two-volume *Sketch Book of the War*, which contained over 100 views by 11 photographers. But the volumes were not well received by a public eager to forget the pain and anguish of the war. Similarly, George N. Barnard (1819–1902) offered a portfolio of his war photography without success. Barnard, appointed official photographer for the Chief Engineer's Office, Military Division of the Mississippi in 1863, followed General William T. Sherman's troops on the "march to the sea" through Tennessee, Georgia, and South Carolina. Barnard recorded the aftermath of battle, without the violence of Brady's or Gardner's work but with a disciplined artistic style. Barnard more than any other portrayed the "gentleman's war," as the southerner would prefer to remember it for generations. The photographs that were popular after the war were those of the Confederate commanders. For instance, the most popular photographs of Robert E. Lee were made by Michael Miley (1841–1918), a Lexington, Va., operator. Miley made numerous portraits of Lee, who also lived in Lexington as president of Washington College.

Several more obscure southern photographers were responsible for significant images of the war. Jay D. Edwards (1831–1900), a native of New Hampshire, was a New Orleans operator specializing in view photography at the outset of the war. In the spring of 1861 Edwards went to Pensacola, Fla., where he photographed New Orleans regiments, as well as federal gunboats and fortifications. Edwards, accused of making reconnaissance photos for the Confederacy, had his negatives confiscated. Andrew David Lytle was also accused of making spy prints of federal encampments in the occupied city of Baton Rouge, La. William D. McPherson and his partner Mr. Oliver apparently refrained from clandestine activities and allied themselves with the Union. The pair made views of battlesites at Port Hudson, Miss.; in northern Louisiana; and on contract with the Chief Engineer's Office, recorded the ruins of Fort Morgan, Ala., in 1864.

After the war McPherson settled in New Orleans, where he produced an exceptionally fine series of *carte-de-visite* views of the city. About the same time, the D. R. Stiltz Company of Baltimore produced views of public buildings. These pursuits were indicative of an increasing interest in view photographs, which were issued in several formats. The most widely distributed were the stereographic cards, which appeared three-dimensional when seen through a special viewing device. After the war local publishers in the major southern cities began publishing stereographs. A series of stereo cards, forming a panoramic view of a city, was a specialty of these houses. Both Theodore Lilienthal and Samuel T. Blessing offered panoramic series of New Orleans during 1866–1867. J. F. Jarvis and the firm of Bell and Brother produced views of Washington, D.C.; and O. Pierre Havens and J. N. Wilson specialized in views of Savannah, Ga. In 1866 J. Mullen of Lexington, Ky., produced an unusually early series on agriculture and rural life in Kentucky, including pictures of newly emancipated black farmers. C. Seaver, Jr., photographed in Florida, especially in St. Augustine; J. G. Mangold also worked there, "The land of flowers and tropical scenery." The number of stereos printed each year was prodigious, stereographic stores opened in every major city in the South, and every Victorian parlor boasted a viewer of one design or another. The business was soon dominated by firms that published cards in great quantity and sold them cheaply. Eventually the independent southern publishers were put out of business by a succession of large firms with networks for national distribution.

Several technical advances changed the nature of photography about 1880. The dry plate process, developed by

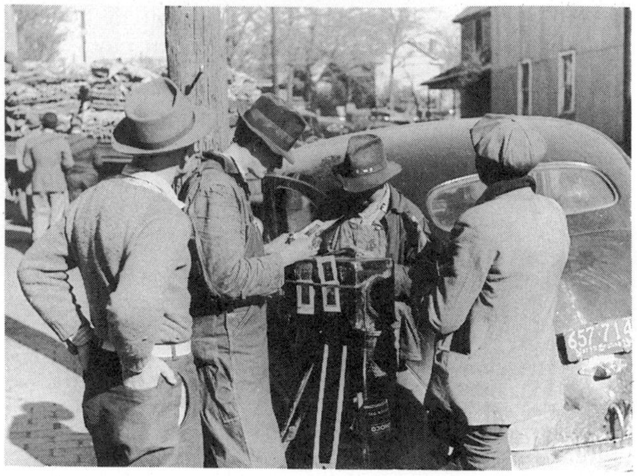

A traveling photographer in Durham, N.C., 1939

an Englishman in 1871, finally gained acceptance with American operators. This process, which used gelatin rather than collodion as the negative support, simplified laboratory work. Secondly, the invention of photolithographic systems for newspapers and journals created new commercial markets for photographs. Agriculture and early industrial communities were photographed for news and promotional services.

At the turn of the century photographers such as J. W. Stephenson of Wilkes County, Ga., focused on the cotton production and sorghum mill operations. Equally important, however, was their documentation of the small southern town: the family reunions, pageants, parades, traveling carnival shows, community baseball teams, bicycle clubs, church meetings, Confederate veterans' parades, and dedications of the ubiquitous memorials. What characterized most of the South between the Civil War and World War I was its agrarian nature. Life for the southerner, both black and white, centered on the family and the church, institutions that nurtured an elemental respect for the cyclical rituals, which gave one a sense of belonging and surviving within his community. Family stories preserved the folk culture, while photographs, neatly tacked in the photo albums, preserved traditions of ancestors and their ceremonies. These became virtually iconic, reinforcing the customs and entrenching the southerner in a romantic conception of the past as he coped with the intrusions of industry and urbanization.

By the turn of the century, northern industrialists were opening factories and mills in southern cities where raw materials and cheap labor were available, and photographers preserved these activities on film. Oscar V. Hunt of Birmingham, Ala., documented the early operations of the U.S. Steel Company at nearby Fairfield, Ala. Caufield and Shook and the Royal Photo Company in Louisville, Ky., photographed the shipbuilding, automobile, and rubber-tire industries from 1903 until the mid-1970s. In Memphis, Tenn., the major inland cotton trade center, J. C. Coovert photographed every aspect of cotton production from the mid-1890s until his death in 1937. About 1900 George Beach and F. J. Schleuter chronicled the early oil and gas operations near Houston, Tex. These firms documented the development of industry and the concomitant prosperity of the communities, the ceremonial openings of banks and stores, the mansions of the businessmen, as well as the storekeepers and clerks on the porches of their "carpenter gothic" cottages.

Railroads expanded into a complicated network connecting the southern market towns, and the rail companies commissioned photographers to depict, in an appealing style, the towns and countryside along their routes, to encourage immigration and travel. The Texas-Ohio Company produced a remarkable folio of sites along the Southern Pacific Line through Texas in 1902. Independent companies, such as the Detroit Publishing Company and the Albertype Company, also specialized in the mass publication of travel views, producing postcards and souvenir books of such picturesque places as Biltmore (the Vanderbilt chateau at Asheville, N.C.), the boardwalks of Florida beaches, or the harbors at Savannah, Ga., and Charleston, S.C.

With the introduction of the box camera and flexible roll film by George Eastman in 1888, inexpensive photographs became available to everyone. Everyday events could be recorded with a new spontaneity. The concept of the amateur was not new. One of the finest early southern amateurs was George Coales of Baltimore, Md., who about 1860 wrote a *Manual on Photography Adapted to Amateur Practice*. Coale made exquisite salt prints of Maryland's waterways and countryside. From the Eastman era, George H. Johnson of Charleston, S.C., recorded events in his city from the earthquake of 1886 to the victory parades of 1918, as well as casual views of his family and genre scenes of black children and sharecroppers, much in the mood of William Aiken Walker's paintings.

With the enthusiasm caused by dry plate photography, camera clubs were formed all over the country. Half a dozen photographic magazines and texts and manuals with instructions for new printing processes were being published at the turn of the century. Some clubs combined the new rage for cycling with the mobility of the box camera. Others took themselves more seriously, renouncing the casual nature of "kodaking," and forming sizable clubs, such as the Kentucky-Tennessee Photographers Association, begun about the turn of the century, which had 140 active members by 1906. Surprisingly, the rage for art also supported a number of schools; one was the Southern School of Photography of McMinnville, Tenn., which claimed in 1906 to have the "Largest Building in the World Devoted to the Teaching of the Art of Photography."

The pictorialist style, as practiced in England, particularly suited the southerner, with his predilection for romance, theatricality, and nostalgia. With a large-view camera, he posed friends or sought picturesque scenes to imitate contemporary paintings or illustrations of Victorian literature. He printed in a technique that resembled a fine art print, each layer more complex than the last.

In Louisville, Ky., Kate Matthews (1870–1957) photographed in the pictorialist style, portraying women and children in ideal domestic settings or posing friends to illustrate novels, such as *The Little Colonel*. Matthews's work was published by *Ladies' Home Journal*, *Vogue*, and *Cosmopolitan* magazines. Arnold Genthe (1869–1942) was primarily known for portraits of celebrities and views of San Francisco's Chinatown. Influenced by the writings of George Washington Cable, Lafcadio Hearn, and Grace King, Genthe photographed the vanishing colonial architecture of New Orleans in the soft-focus manner of pictorialism. His book, *Old New Orleans*, was published in 1926.

While some photographers were imitating painting, a few were discovering the camera's ability to record dispassionately. Frances Benjamin Johnston (1864–1952), a native of West Virginia, began her career as a photojournalist within the inner circles of Washington politics in 1889. Johnston's unprecedented course included essays on black education at Hampton Institute in Virginia in 1899, and, periodically from 1902 to 1906, at Tuskegee Institute in Alabama. Her most significant achievement was the survey of southern colonial architecture for the Carnegie Foundation from 1933 to 1940. Johnston made over 6,000 negatives of every aspect of historic buildings and gardens from Maryland to Louisiana.

Lewis Hine compiled the earliest photographic essay for social reform in the South. In 1907 Hine, hired by the National Child Labor Committee to dramatize the tragedy of child labor abuses, photographed in the textile mills of the Carolinas and in the agricultural and fishing industries of the South. In 1933 Hine documented for state and federal agencies the building of the Tennessee Valley Authority dams and nearby communities.

Apart from the photojournalists and social reformers, a succession of documentary photographers have worked in the South, motivated by a respect for the distinctive regional characteristics of the folk cultures, crafts, farming traditions, the storytellers and ballad singers. Doris Ullman (1884–1934), though from a wealthy New York family, was drawn to the qualities of simplicity and devotion she found in the craftsmen of Appalachia and the black people living in isolated rural communities. In

A Frances Benjamin Johnston photograph of Edgemont, Albemarle County, Va., c. 1935

contrast to the sentimentalizing manner of some genre photographers, Ullman conveyed the inner strength and religious nature of her subjects. William A. Barnhill, a native of Arkansas, was interested in the handicrafts and local technology of the highlanders of North Carolina. His photographs, taken from 1914 to 1917, though less well known, are of equal significance. Prentice Hall Polk, a black professional photographer, has been recording life at Tuskegee Institute in Alabama since 1927. Polk has created a valuable historical record of the students, educators, and residents of this cultural center for black Americans. A less known, but very important black photographer, Reverend L. O. Taylor of Memphis, photographed and filmed churches, black businesses, and homes of the black middle-class community.

The largest documentary to include the South was that of the Resettlement Administration, later the Farm Security Administration (FSA). From 1935 to 1943 Roy Emerson Stryker directed his staff to gather picture stories, which would persuade Congress to aid the depressed farming communities of America. A significant portion of these photographs was made in the South, where, in some areas, 75 percent of the people were tenant farmers. Dorothea Lange's strong sympathies for the migrant workers and tenant farmers are evident in her photos of the Mississippi River Delta region taken from 1935 to 1938. Marion Post Wolcott and Arthur Rothstein photographed the migrant laborers of the truck farms. Ben Shahn and Russell Lee's forte lay in the portrayal of small-town life and resettlement camps. Walker Evans's disciplined and carefully composed photos portrayed the poverty of the tenant farmers. Evans took a leave of absence to prepare a document on southern sharecroppers for *Fortune* magazine with James Agee. Though *Fortune* rejected the material, it was finally published in 1941 as *Let Us Now Praise Famous Men*, a classic vision of three tenant families in Alabama, portrayed with dignity and honesty. Eudora Welty made a similar photographic portrait of her home state, Mississippi, while working with the Farm Security Administration. Her work was later published in *One Time, One Place* (1971).

In 1943 Stryker embarked on a project for Standard Oil Company (New Jersey). This time he concentrated not on poverty but on the prosperity that the oil industry was bringing to the country. Because the focus of the ESSO project was upon the largest oil-producing states, much emphasis was placed upon Texas and Louisiana, where Russell Lee and Todd Webb gathered stories of small towns and bayou settlements affected by off-shore exploration and drilling. Edwin Rosskam documented the stories of oil transport along the Mississippi River. In North Carolina, Esther Bubly photographed the towns that lay in the path of the pipeline, and Sol Libsohn produced the story of exploration and drilling off Cape Hatteras.

At the time Stryker's photographers were working in the South, Clarence John Laughlin (1905–85) began exploring his native Louisiana. Laughlin's early fascination with European symbolist writers formalized his reactions against the Depression-era environment and created an enigmatic style that suited his romanticism. Laughlin photographed the plantation houses, the Creole cemeteries, and the streets and characters of New Orleans. Ironically, Laughlin accompanied Edward Weston on the Louisiana portion of his cross-country tour in 1941. Weston's photographs, commissioned for a special publication of Walt Whitman's *Leaves of Grass*, were composed with absolute discipline and in the sharpest focus, while Laughlin's photos were gothic, mystical equivalents of dreams. Laughlin published his work in *Ghosts along the Mississippi* in 1948 and began his long career of lecturing and producing traveling exhibitions.

Todd Webb photograph of an unnamed Louisiana community, 1940s

Photo documentaries of the scope of the FSA and ESSO projects will probably never be attempted again. These are major sociological and historical records of the South in rapid transition from an agrarian to an industrialized society, documents of a people witnessing the collapse of social and religious traditions and experiencing the disintegration of the extended family unit.

Outside of these monumental projects, few have conveyed so forcefully as Roland L. Freeman (b. 1936) the complexity of the urbanization of the South. In the 1960s Freeman, a black photographer and a native of Baltimore, documented the restructuring of a black Maryland tobacco-farming community, following its members from the simple existence in the country to the frustrating anonymous life in city tenements. Like Ullman and Barnhill, Freeman was also inspired by southern folk cultures. In the early 1970s he photographed the black quilters, basketmakers, blacksmiths, and carpenters of southern Mississippi in his own style, celebrating the self-sufficiency of the rural black farmers. Writer Ernest J. Gaines has made similar photographic portraits of his home in rural Louisiana. These photos, like those of Eudora Welty, add an interesting dimension to his craft as a writer of fiction.

Also in the documentary tradition, Alex Harris, a native of Atlanta and an associate of Duke University, has collaborated with psychologist Robert Coles on projects in Alaska and New Mexico, but he has also produced essays on the poor living conditions of tenant families in North Carolina. For several years Debbie Fleming Caffrey has been photographing the resident workers on sugarcane plantations at Franklin, La. With an affection rooted in familiarity, she has recorded them each season with sympathy and dignity.

Recent photography in the South has been called southern only by accident of place. Since the 1930s, southern writing has explored the urbanization of the region and the destruction of its identities. Urbanization was well under way before southern artists became aware of photography's potential for interpreting that experience. When the art did find its proponents on southern campuses in the 1960s, photography there was essentially indistinguishable from the national school. Present education encourages exposure to many visions and techniques, and the highly mobile students of Minor White, Aaron Siskind, and Henry Holmes Smith, to name a few, have spread their diverse talents through the best institutions of the South. John Menapace, at Duke University, transforms the North Carolina landscape into highly disciplined and elegant design abstractions; Jaromir Stephany at the University of Maryland, Baltimore County, uses the *cliché verre* technique to invent nonrepresentational images of dynamic energy; Jerry Uelsmann, at the University of Florida, uses a multiple printing technique to develop mirrors of his imagination. These are photographers whose works are of abstract formalism, of psychic invention, and not of a regional nature. But there are photographers working in the South who have been so moved by the geography, culture, and history of the environment that they have chosen to create art from its raw material.

John McWilliams at Georgia State University produces austerely formal landscapes, some with an underlying outrage against the barbarous intrusions of industry. Emmet Gowin's early work in his native Danville, Va., is presented, not in the symbolism of Uelsmann, but with an immediate and elemental response to the drama of family rituals, celebrations, and tragedies. Gowin's work suggests the theatricality and ambiguity of contemporary storytellers such as Flannery O'Connor. With decidedly greater obscurity and a gently gothic mien, Ralph Eugene Meatyard (1925–72) of Lexington, Ky., enlisted his family and neighbors to devise a private state for his imagined conversations, creating photographs reminiscent of the fiction of Carson McCullers, with its grotesque and symbolic overtones.

William Eggleston (b. 1939), a resident of Memphis, Tenn., uses images from his private experience as a son of a Mississippi Delta farming family to symbolize the erosion of the traditional culture that nurtured him. Eggleston uses the dye transfer method, which produces color of dazzling luminosity, to photograph the incongruous juxtapositions of city and country, suburbia and wilderness. Atlanta photographer Michael Turner evokes the essence of the history of the southern white middle class in his photos of timeworn homes with peeling paint and torn screens. His subjects seem to be the symbols of southern gentility beset by altered economic systems. There is a sense of loss and change. Since 1974, Paul Kwilecki of Decatur County, Ga., has also worked with the landmarks and characters of his immediate surroundings. Kwilecki's intuitive vision is comparable to that of the French masters Atget and Brassai.

Using the camera in a straightforward reportorial manner, Geoffrey L. Winningham (b. 1943) concentrates on the rituals and pastimes of his fellow Texans, especially the fanatically loyal sportsmen, both participants and spectators. Lyle Bongé of Biloxi, Miss., and New York observes selectively the humor and human foibles and vulnerabilities of Mardi Gras maskers in New Orleans. The portraits of George Dureau of New Orleans and Gay Block of Houston also capture the complex humanity of their subjects. Dureau, a painter, first used photographs as aids to composition but shortly perceived their separate merits. His subjects are the street people of Esplanade Avenue and the lower wards of the city, mostly young blacks photographed against a simple seamless background, creating classical portraits reminiscent of Degas or Velázquez. Amid the largest Jewish community in the South, Block (b. 1942) specializes in photographing middle-class families within their own homes, against the setting of their possessions. She produces portraits of brilliant insight, which enable her subjects to know themselves more clearly.

Several southern women, however, seem dissatisfied with the factual nature of the straight photograph. Though a resident of Rochester, N.Y., Bea Nettles (b. 1946) creates photographs infused with references to her upbringing in Florida, the abundant green of landscapes, dreams and memories of childhood, and a strong attachment to family. Nettles continually experiments with nonsilver processes, reinventing the concept of the photograph. Her highly subjective creations, while unconventional in method, employ constant images of familiarity, which give her work cohesiveness. Rita deWitt of the University of Southern Mississippi and Merri Moor Winnett of North Carolina both print multiple negative montages on paper and fabric, creating highly complex photo-drawings expressing personal experiences. Nancy Rexroth uses an inexpensive plastic Diana camera; her casual approach to her subject, combined with the unpredictable focus of the plastic lens, produces dreamlike snapshots.

One of the most significant southern photographers is William Christenberry (b. 1936), a resident of Washington, D.C., who photographs in color. Each summer he returns to his native Alabama to record familiar places from his youth, compiling a notebook of rural Alabama architecture and social history. Christenberry's exquisitely simple views subtly evoke the presence of former inhabitants.

Christenberry teaches at the Corcoran School of Art in Washington, D.C., one of several schools that nurture photography in the South. Others with strong photographic departments are the University of Maryland, at both its College Park and Catonsville locations, the University of Florida at Gainesville, Georgia State University in Atlanta, and Rice University in Houston, Tex. The Light Factory in Charlotte, N.C., and Nexus, Inc., in Atlanta, Ga., provide workshops of outstanding merit. The finest archival collections in the region are the Gernsheim Collection at the University of Texas, Austin; the Photographic Archives at the University of Louisville (Ky.); and, of course, the Photographs and Prints Division of the Library of Congress. Public collections of historical and contemporary interest are located at the Corcoran Gallery in Washington, D.C.; the Museum of Fine Arts in Houston, Tex.; the New Orleans Museum of Art; and the High Museum of Atlanta, Ga.

Mary Louise Tucker
New Orleans, Louisiana

A. D. Coleman, *The Southern Ethic* (1975); F. Jack Hurley, Nancy Hurley, and Gary Witt, eds., *Southern Eye, Southern Mind* (1981); David Madden, *Southern Quarterly* (Winter 1984); Margaret D. Smith and Mary Louise Tucker, *Photography in New Orleans: The Early Years, 1840–1865* (1982); Robert Taft, *Photography and the American Scene: A Social History, 1839–1899* (1938).

Queen Anne and Eastlake Styles of Architecture

The Queen Anne style of architecture was conceived in England by Richard Norman Shaw during the 1860s, though the term is a misnomer. Shaw at first borrowed details from the rural manor houses of Queen Elizabeth's reign, not Queen Anne's. The erroneous designation seems attributable to the English architect J. J. Stevenson in the 1870s.

Shaw's houses were widely published in the architectural press and thus came to be imitated in the United States in the early 1870s. However, the popular acceptance of the Queen Anne in America can be attributed to the Centennial Exhibition of 1876 in Philadelphia. For this fair the British government erected in the Queen Anne style two buildings that received a good deal of critical acclaim.

The style flourished in America during the 1880s and 1890s and represented a renewed interest in the picturesque. The present "epoch of Queen Anne is a delightful insurrection against the monotonous era of rectangular buildings," declared an 1880s magazine. Irregular planning and massing accompanied by a variety of color, texture, and structural expressionism characterized the style.

Americans nationalized the style by the use of Colonial Revival details and regional materials such as shingles and siding. Although the Queen Anne was a mix of architectural details, the main theme was classical and is sometimes called free classic. Frequently the style was combined with Eastlake and Romanesque detailing, creating unique designs. For extra interest, details were sometimes borrowed from Islamic and Oriental precedents.

The impact of the Queen Anne on the southern housing stock was enormous because of the rapid growth of the southern economy during the post-Reconstruction period and because a Queen Anne residence could be erected inexpensively and quickly. The majority of the Queen Anne residences were made of wood, so the developing southern timber industry, such as that in the area around Pensacola, Fla., provided an abundance of materials from which to draw. The Queen Anne house can be found throughout the South, particularly in the Savannah Victorian District, the New Orleans Uptown District, East End Historic District in Galveston, the Historic District of Pensacola, and Atlanta's "Sweet Auburn" Historic District.

Because Queen Anne house designs were often chosen from pattern books of the period such as Holly's *Modern Dwellings*, and details were mass produced thanks to technological advances, a certain consistency in the style was achieved. Externally, Queen Anne houses are massive, irregular, and picturesque. Projecting elements such as cylindrical towers with conical roofs; polygonal turrets with distinctive roofs; tall, elaborate, decorative chimneys with large corbelled tops; and well-detailed entrance porches, verandas, and bay windows are featured elements.

Every surface of the Queen Anne house is textured or has applied ornament, making the house's exterior finishing the dominant decorative element. Windows come in a profusion of shapes but tend to be tall, thin, large, and double-hung. Frequently, the windows have the top sash divided into small colored panes of glass surrounding a larger central field. The lower sash is a single large pane of glass or is divided by a single vertical muntin. This type of window has been designated "Queen Anne window." Stained-glass windows are common, as are Palladian windows and other forms of grouped windows. Doors are usually deeply recessed under porch roofs and vestibules or second-story overhangs and have a large glass area. Roofs are steep and complex with moderate overhangs, polychromatic slates, or patterned metal shingles and elaborate terra cotta ridge tiles. Gables are common and often include a large porch gable, adding to the picturesque effect of the total design.

The floor plans are informal and asymmetrical. The featured room—the "living hall"—was introduced for the style and was designed to impress. This room was generally finished in dark oak or other wood and had an elaborate wooden staircase illuminated by staggered stained-glass windows. Often a large fireplace occupied a place of prominence. The dining room, parlor, and study were connected to the entrance hall by large sliding doors, which permitted a relatively open place that could be divided into private rooms as necessary. The kitchen, with its accessory pantry and storage, opened to the dining room. Projecting and inserted verandas and terraces were integral parts of the total design. Bedrooms and baths were generally relegated to the second story, but were sometimes confined to a rear wing.

The ubiquitous long, narrow cottages of New Orleans, a vernacular form popularly called "shotgun" cottages, were frequently decorated with patterned shingles on their gables and with scroll brackets or courses of turnings supporting the porch roofs. The style is superficial, the plan essentially the same as on earlier structures with Greek Revival porticoes. But even here the builders sometimes achieved a sense of irregular massing by putting small triangular caps over side doors or by adding a small projecting bay on a front porch.

The Eastlake style coexisted with the Queen Anne and shared many of its planning and massing characteristics; but this style is distinguished from the Queen Anne by its detailing, much of which can be traced to the neo-Greco style. Under the auspices of neo-Greco, the round forms and foliated ornament of the Italianate style took on a rectangularity and precision thought to be expressive of an increasingly mechanized and industrial society. Incised ornament was a hallmark. Stylized single-line flowers and long, parallel, narrow channels were favorite details.

The Eastlake style was named after Charles Locke Eastlake, an English architect who is more noted for his books than his architecture. Eastlake's *Hints on Household Taste* was first published in London in 1868 and made its American debut in Boston in 1872. The book was immensely popular, with six editions in the next 11 years. Eastlake promoted a style of furniture and interior detailing that was angular, notched, and carved. He wrote, "It is an established principle in the theory of design that decorative art is degraded when it passes into a direct imitation of natural objects. Nature may be typified or symbolized, but not actually imitated."

Other books, such as *Gothic Forms* by Bruce Talbert, which appeared in America in 1873, helped to formulate the style. While Eastlake concentrated on details, Talbert showed whole interiors.

American architectural designers found their own interpretation of the style. Their ornament was largely the product of the chisel, the gouge, and the lathe. Details were massive, oversized, and robust. Designers placed no limits on the arrangement of forms or the amount of ornamentation on the exterior of the Eastlake house, much to the chagrin of Charles Eastlake, who wrote, "I regret . . . that [I] should be associated . . . with a phase of taste in architecture and industrial art with which I can have no real sympathy and by all accounts seems to be extravagant and bizarre."

The Eastlake style was the product of industrialization, but, ironically, it was named for a leader of the arts and crafts movement who advocated a return to the craftsmanship of the past. Factory-made decorative elements could be ordered by mail from catalogs or bought from local distributors. The Orleans Manufacturing and Lumber Company published one such catalog in 1891. Even entire houses could be ordered prefabricated. The multitude of ornamentations resulted in a wide variety of combinations. Both small cottages in places like Biloxi, Miss., and large houses in New Orleans commonly employed the Eastlake style.

Robert J. Cangelosi
New Orleans, Louisiana

Alan Gowans, *Images of American Living: Four Centuries of Architecture and Furniture as Cultural Expression* (1964); Carole Rifkin, *A Field Guide to American Architecture* (1980); Leland M. Roth, *A Concise History of American Architecture* (1979); G. E. K. Kidder Smith, *The Architecture of the United States: The South and Midwest* (1981).

Residential 20th-Century Architecture

The rapidly expanding middle class and the enormous mobility offered by the automobile created demands for suburban housing. Houses had to be flexible enough to accommodate a changing society and inexpensive enough to be affordable. Consequently, 20th-century houses differed immensely from 19th-century houses in scale and floor plan. Southern housing of the early 20th century can be divided into two categories—those free from historical precedents and those that rely on historical eclecticism.

The most popular nontraditional architectural style of the period was the California style (1900–1940), sometimes referred to as the bungalow style. "California" seemed to be the preferred term during the heyday of the style, while "bungalow" simply referred to a small residence. The California style was an honest, bold expression of architecture that synthesized precedents from many sources without mimicking any one. These houses were basically wooden with masonry complements such as porches, chimneys, piers, and retaining walls.

The style is unpretentious and distinguished by its clever use of wooden structural members as ornamentation. Building elements seem to flow from one to the next, with one element being an integral part of that which immediately precedes and follows. The massing of the style is very picturesque, with low lines. Roofs are generous, with broad sloping overhangs. Windows are commonly short and grouped together to take advantage of breezes. The floor plan is very informal, with spaces flowing from one to another, rendering a feeling of openness. Typically, circulation is through the living room, which often has a large fireplace setting the tone of the decor. Interior details reflect a strong "crafts" orientation. Front, side, rear, and sleeping porches are common in order to keep interior spaces cool.

The architects of California formulated the style, giving it its innovative features and design. The Greene brothers, Charles and Henry, were its most influential architects. The style was a builders' style, which was promoted through numerous periodicals, including *Craftsman Magazine*, *Bungalow Magazine*, and *Ladies' Home*

Journal. Even the Sears and Roebuck catalog carried California bungalow house plans, "direct from bungalow land," for the meager price of five dollars. With such inexpensive prices, identical houses can be found in widely separated locales.

Southerners eagerly accepted the bungalow, which had been designed for a similar climate, and it was built throughout the region for middle- to low-income housing, in small towns and large. One can readily date the period of growth and expansion of certain sections of cities by the presence of whole groups of these bungalows in a neighborhood. One such subdivision is Gentilly Terrace in New Orleans.

Another popular nonhistorical style was the craftsman style (1900–1920). It had its roots in the English arts and crafts movement, as a solution to the "corrupt" values of the Victorian styles. The movement's chief advocate was the English architect turned artist, William Morris. Morris realized that he was unsuccessfully competing with machine art and began to write articles opposing the machine. In 1888 the English Arts and Crafts Exhibition Society was formed, which published articles and held exhibitions extolling the virtues of handcrafted art.

In Boston the first American Society of Arts and Crafts was organized in 1897. But it was from Gustav Stickley's *Craftsman Magazine* and his two *Craftsman Home* books that the movement received its widespread acceptance in the South. Young architects took up the cause, rejecting machine aesthetics as impersonal. Their solution advocated greater honesty and sincerity in architecture with artful attention to every detail. Southern homes using this style tend to be modest in scale. Some of these are found among Gulf Coast cottages and in some summer houses in the mountains of North Carolina, Georgia, and Virginia.

Other early 20th-century nonhistorical styles found in the South include the prairie, art deco, streamline moderne, and international styles. The prairie style (1900–1920) evolved on the prairies of the Midwest. It explored new ways of relating building to the landscape and new concepts of interior space. The master of the style was Frank Lloyd Wright, who described the prairie style house as "having sloping roofs, low proportions, quiet skylines, suppressed heavy-set chimneys and sheltering overhangs, low terraces and out-reaching walls sequestering private gardens." Wright, who has been described as a 20th-century Jeffersonian agrarian, had only one prairie house in the South, the Ziegler House (1909–10) in Frankfort, Ky., but two of his Usonian houses (a variation of the prairie house) are in Falls Church, Va. (the Pope-Leighey House, 1939–41), and Florence, Ala. (the Rosenbaum House, 1939–40).

Art deco (1920–30), which was characterized by a vertical emphasis with highly stylized ornamentation, was commonly employed in commercial architecture but could also be found in large residences and apartment complexes. In the South the style was most popular in southern Florida.

Streamline moderne (1930–40) was inspired by America's love for the machine. Its shapes were guided by the principles of aerodynamics and hydrodynamics. Smooth white curvilinear shapes were used to try to capture the spirit of frozen motion.

The international style (1910–40), which originated in Europe, had limited acceptance in the South, chiefly in metropolitan areas. Henry-Russell Hitchcock and Philip Johnson described it as "first, a new concept of architecture as volume rather than as mass." In addition, "regularity rather than axial symmetry" was the main way of achieving orderly design. The style, finally, "proscribes arbitrary applied decoration." The 1938 Feibleman residence in Metarie, La., is a good example of this style.

Although 20th-century revivals can be found for almost every previous architectural style, the Tudor, neo-Italianate, Renaissance, and Colonial Revival styles have been the most common in the South. The Tudor style (1900–1930) was originally based on both English Elizabethan and Jacobean styles and, as a consequence, it is sometimes referred to as the "Jacobethan" style. As the style matured, it began to imitate the English medieval period with greater accuracy. Its most distinguishing feature is half-timbering with stucco or masonry infill. It was used on both modest and expensive houses throughout the South. The Wymond House in Louisville, Ky., is an outstanding example of a large Tudor Revival residence.

The neo-Italianate (1910–30) was a revival of the Italian villas of the Mediterranean, distinguished by shallow brackets and a large umbrella-type roof with barrel roofing tiles. It was very popular for large residences along the Gulf Coast because of its large protective roof and large windows and its air of opulence. The Rostrevor House in Louisville, Ky., is a good example.

The Renaissance revival (1890–1940) developed as an academic reaction to the free spirit of the late 19th-century styles. It borrowed Renaissance elements, details, and composition from England, France, Spain, and Italy. These residences tended to be large and elaborate and were more often than not designed by architects. The style's primary advocate was the New York architectural firm of McKim, Mead, and White. Many such large residences can be found in the Swiss Avenue Historic District in Dallas, Tex.; and Audubon Place in New Orleans. Outstanding individual examples include the Alexander House (1906), Dallas, Tex., the Hills House (1899), St. Louis, Mo.; and the Armstrong House (1917), Savannah, Ga.

See also FOLKLIFE: / Bungalow House

Robert J. Cangelosi
New Orleans, Louisiana

William H. Jordy, *American Buildings and Their Architects*, vol. 2 (1972); Walter C. Kidney, *The Architecture of Choice: Eclectism in America, 1880–1930* (1974); Clay Lancaster, *The American Bungalow, 1880–1930* (1985); Leland M. Roth, *A Concise History of American Architecture* (1979); Dell Upton and John Michael Vlach, eds., *Common Places: Readings in American Vernacular Architecture* (1986); Leila Wilburn, *Southern Homes and Bungalows* (1914).

Resort Architecture

Attractive scenery, accessibility, and wealthy clients with leisure time—all the necessary endowments for a resort area—belonged to the South in the 18th century. Many plantation owners in the eastern Tidewater, an area that includes Virginia, Maryland, North Carolina, South Carolina, and Georgia, grew rich planting tobacco, rice, and indigo to trade with England. The Tidewater area consequently emerged as the first part of America to produce wealthy residents with leisure time.

However elegant many of the plantation homes were, they were hot, humid, unhealthy, and uncomfortable during long summers. As transportation developed, the gentry began to escape the unpleasant climate and recurring epidemics by hiding away in the cool mountains of Virginia. Southerners sought resorts that offered simple, close-to-nature living with carefree, healthful, cool environments. Until then, the lack of passable roads actually made it easier for Americans to go to Europe or the West Indies.

Travelers in the 18th and early 19th centuries used inns and taverns located on main highways and toll roads during their journeys. Some of these travelers left descriptive, often derogatory, accounts of their accommodations. Sir August Foster, an Englishman, reported in his travels through Virginia that Gadsby's Tavern in Alexandria "kept the best house of entertainment in America." An inventory of 1802 showed 10 buildings at Gadsby's, including stables, kitchen, and laundry. All of Foster's lodgings were not comfortable, however. He mentioned a few intolerable inns, a wretched log house, and a "mean looking tavern with fare equally so." Phillip Nicklin, under his pseudonym Peregrine Prolix, had a happier stay "at the sign of the Swan" in New Market, Va., on his way back from the springs of Virginia. He wrote that he was "very comfortable . . . fared sumptuously, and lay in fine linen." Equally hospitable inns in Charleston, S.C., often served guests their meals in the summerhouses among the gardens. Taverns and hotels all over the South had ballrooms for community social events.

Tidewater planters and their families endured the crude mountain roads in stagecoaches or on horseback for that singular lure of the resorts—that ancient, mysterious, and magical phenomenon of a natural spring. Since the dawn of history, springs have had widespread appeal. The American Indians believed such waters contained healing qualities and sought springs as they traveled. English colonists brought with them to America a long tradition of using therapeutic waters, as did the German settlers.

A cluster of mineral springs, hot, warm, and tepid, discovered in the early 18th century, developed into America's first resorts. In an area about 75 miles in diameter, the springs bordered what is now the Virginia–West Virginia line. In 1748 George Washington mentioned one, Bath Springs, also known as Alum Springs, in his diary, when he camped in a field near what later became a major resort.

Stagecoach lines began making runs to these resorts, located in "pleasant, accessible mountain valleys, always cool in the summer." Visitors especially liked to tour the "waters"; the whole circuit of the Virginia–West Virginia springs could be made in less than 170 miles. "To the Springs! Leave the heat and the misery behind . . . seek cool air, clean water, relaxing baths, sparkling company!"

The European concept of a spa eventually filtered to these mountain resorts. Primitive resorts quickly offered "hydro-therapy" cures to make guests feel good by bathing and by drinking the water. Springs competed with one another in having a slightly different temperature and mineral content. Water analysis was the focal point for a spring's advertisement in the 19th century. Brochures outlined chemical properties of the waters and listed the diseases that could be cured, documented by testimonials from patrons. In 1846 John J. Moorman, physician-in-residence at White Sulphur Springs, started publishing books on the Virginia springs, other springs in the South, and springs elsewhere in the country. His book, *The Mineral Springs of North America* (1873), is an important source for spring lore, culture, and advertisements for different resorts. He detailed the sundry cures and explained how bottled water sold from many springs produced an important source of revenue.

As the spring resorts rose in prominence, their architecture became more and more sophisticated. The first abodes were tents pitched in fields close to the waters. They gave way to clusters of log cabins gradually replaced by frame buildings. Descriptions from early travelers revealed how similar were the buildings, layouts, and overall plans for the spring resorts, most of which flaunted summerhouses, pavilions, belvederes, kiosks, garden houses, and teahouses amidst their spacious grounds. A 19th-century traveler named Edward Pollard wrote about the ambience of Montgomery's White Sulphur Springs: "The lawn of the springs . . . a large elliptical plain planted with ornamental trees . . . the ground divided by a stream . . . a pleasant architectural effect for the practical designs of comfort."

Early 19th-century architecture of the spring resorts reflected the fashionable Greek Revival style. A classical columned porch, two or three stories high, was common. Spring resort buildings repeatedly used this form, which originated in the 1830s in southern residential architecture. In 1856 when Botetourt Springs resort became Hollins Institute, the forerunner of Hollins College, a dormitory building was built in the Greek Revival style with its plan and porches still in the spring resort manner. Architecture in the later 19th century tended to follow prevalent styles of that time.

The center of attraction of every spring resort was its spring covering, often an octagon with classical columns supporting a dome to make a gazebo form. Rustic touches abounded with branch furniture, log cabins, and informal landscaping, in sharp contrast with the severe Greek Revival architecture.

Southern hospitality played a great part in the ambience of the springs. In the South the absence of large cities left families isolated on their plantations. Resorts, therefore, offered families opportunities for meeting

Alabama Row at the Greenbrier in West Virginia

other families and were ideally suited for courting places and marriage markets. Belles arrived with trunks of clothing for summer activities. Genial hosts purposefully tried to create a romantic atmosphere to attract visitors. Ballrooms flourished, as did porches with cozy nooks, bowers, and lover's lanes. The amenities of a good hotel included music, dancing, wine, good company, and the water of the springs.

This aura of southern hospitality at spring resorts continues today, as best exemplified by White Sulphur Springs and its hotel, the Greenbrier. Known from Indian times, these springs attracted development between 1778 and 1783 when tents were first erected on the site. Subsequently, between 1784 and 1786, log cabins were built. By 1800 there were cottages. In 1835 a ballroom and a kitchen were added to a tavern to form the nucleus of a great resort. When Prolix visited in 1835, he reported that the valley had been cleared, except for a few trees left for ornament and shade. He tallied a frame dining room 120 feet long, a kitchen with attached bakery, two large stables with 80 stalls each, a grand ballroom, and rows of cabins built of various materials. All the cabins had porches. Prolix observed that White Sulphur's spring was "covered with a handsome dome supported on columns, and contained in an octagonal marble case . . . the bottom formed of the rock from which the water gushes." Prolix rhapsodized about the charm of the resort and its delightful society that came "to see and be seen, to chat, laugh, and dance."

The most famous buildings at White Sulphur were designed by J. H. B. Latrobe, son of the well-known American architect Benjamin Henry Latrobe. Visiting many of the Virginia springs, he left watercolor sketches that document spring architecture. In 1850 the erstwhile builder designed a row of cottages, today called the Baltimore Cottages. Latrobe noted that they were very up-to-date—"papered, supplied with water, gas, speaking tubes, and all the modern arrangements for comfort."

Each row of cottages had its own social distinction. Bachelors, for example, lived in Wolf Row. Guests walked Lover's Lane, danced in the ballroom, courted on Baltimore Row, heard music from the bandstand in the center of the grounds, ate in the large dining rooms where everyone gathered at mealtime, and attended chapel in the barroom, which was converted for that purpose on Sundays.

In the 19th century the White Sulphur Springs Hotel was renovated with arcades, porticoes, domes, and more guest homes. By 1870 the Chesapeake & Ohio Railroad served the resort. In the 20th century the old main building was torn down and replaced. A central portico, reminiscent of the White House, and a five-story colonnade, reminiscent of a southern mansion, were added after 1922. Today, the Greenbrier survives as one of the most impressive resort complexes left in the South.

The other prime extant example of a spring resort is Hot Springs, Va., with its major hotel, the Homestead. As early as 1766, Thomas Bullitt built a primitive hostel at the Hot Springs. Like the Greenbrier, the Homestead has seen continuous use despite fires, rebuilding, and changing economic conditions. Guests still enjoy the famous hot baths, popular since the 18th century, but their use for hydrotherapy has waned.

The Homestead was rebuilt in "baronial" style after a fire in 1901; a 12-story tower added in 1929 forms "one of America's few Georgian–Colonial Revival high rises." The Cavalier Hotel in Virginia Beach, Va., built in 1927, is another Colonial Revival high-rise structure. The Homestead now has a modern addition in severe geometric forms, as the Cavalier similarly sports a steel frame, glass-walled motel across the street.

The Warm Springs, Ga., resort, like most of its contemporaries, did not flourish in the 20th century, yet it was very popular in the 19th century. Thomas Jefferson visited these springs in 1818 and again in 1825. Prolix stayed in the Warm Springs Hotel, while his two traveling companions stayed in a "most ancient log cabin," consoled by the fact that Jefferson had spent three weeks there. In 1835 Prolix reported that the Warm Springs Hotel was a two-story, brick structure, 100 feet long with a porch on the front. He noted that there was a room for dancing, a parlor, a large and airy eating room, and a tenpin alley. The springs flowed into a wooden, octagonal, men's bathhouse, which was 120 feet in circumference and reputedly built in 1761. A similar women's bathhouse built in 1836 stands nearby. The two bathhouses and a few small cottages are all that remain of this resort.

Careful records of spring architecture and culture in Virginia and West Virginia were left by German artist Edward Beyer, who visited America about 1848 and spent three years drawing and painting. His *Album of Virginia*, printed in Germany, contains 40 lithographs of resorts and other natural attractions in the area. Meticulously drawn "panoramas and accurate architectural projections give details of dress, artifacts, and people." In five of his pictures he added some "future and proposed improvements." Beyer painted not only the big popular springs, but many of the smaller, less fashionable resorts frequented by people who could not afford the big ones.

Each spring possessed some special characteristic. The

buildings of Sweet Springs, Va., in Monroe County (now West Virginia), for instance, have always been associated with a Thomas Jefferson design. The "Jefferson" building at Sweet Springs is made of brick with columns and classical detail. It has a 160-foot-long dining room and a 17-foot-wide porch running the length of the building. As yet, no evidence beyond local lore has surfaced to credit the building to Jefferson. The structure today serves as a home for the aged. Rockbridge Alum Springs in Virginia had a central hotel with "Italianate ceilings and a Gothic structure on the grounds." An 1880s description portrayed the atmosphere of this resort in its post–Civil War glory: ". . . lovely skimmed-milk blue bandstand with its crimson touches on the central lawn where brass bands delighted the scattered spectators with marches; the fashionable yellow furniture with black stripes covering the chairs."

Allegheny Springs, Va., featured a remarkable gazebo made of rustic cedar branches, decorated with gnarled, twisted laurel branches and roots. Supposedly built by German immigrants in the 1890s using the art nouveau style, it has been preserved by private owners. In 1872 Yellow Sulphur Springs, Va., erected a building with a French mansard roof, but a year later it burned, to be replaced by a structure in the high Victorian eclectic style with an onion dome tower, which was torn down in 1960. Salt Sulphur Springs Hotel in Monroe County, Va., had a huge dining room in the 1830s, as did most spring resorts, but its distinction was a long line of fans on the ceiling. All the fans were connected to a rope so that they could be pulled by one person. Another Virginia resort, Craig Healing Springs, touted rooms of claw-footed bathtubs filled with spring water.

After the Civil War easy railroad access boosted business at the spring resorts. The southern social elite delighted in staying at the same resorts with former leaders of the Confederacy, but increasing numbers of visitors were northerners. Installation of bathrooms helped revive the popularity of some resorts as the 20th century opened. Yet many hotels were unable to keep up with modern conveniences such as screening, refrigeration, and air-conditioning. Fire continued to take its toll, and many resort structures were not rebuilt after they burned. The 1929 Depression sent numerous resorts into bankruptcy. Rapid transportation by automobile bypassed most of them. The last popular national attention given to a spring resort occurred in the 1940s when President Franklin D. Roosevelt visited Warm Springs in Georgia for hydrotherapy in its 95-degree water. Most of the remaining spring hotels are in a state of decay with the exception of a few that have adapted to new conditions. Religious organizations and similar groups operate some of the survivors.

The deathblow came to the resorts when railroads completely supplanted stagecoach lines. Although railroads first ran to the spring resorts, they later extended to undeveloped areas further south where a warm climate beckoned winter tourists. In the 1880s and 1890s the railroads enhanced resort and real estate development in Florida to such an extent that they created a boom in that state.

Two remarkable railroad men spearheaded the push into Florida. Henry B. Plant went south from his native New England to become president of the Southern Express Company. First laying track for the Atlantic Coast Line into western Florida, he consolidated his railroad business with his land sales. Likewise, Henry M. Flagler developed his railroad lines down the untouched east coast of Florida with accompanying hotel-resorts. Flagler, a partner in Rockefeller, Andrews, and Flagler oil refiners, predecessors of the Standard Oil Company, wanted to develop Florida real estate.

The Tampa Bay Hotel, opened in 1891 on 20 acres of landscaped grounds, best typifies Florida west coast development by Henry B. Plant. At a cost of $3 million, architect J. A. Wood created a hotel in the Moorish style with minarets, domes, wooden horseshoe designs, and crescent-shaped moons "nailed everywhere." A 1917 visitor to the hotel saw it filled with a wildly eclectic collection. It was "the Alhambra . . . furnished in the late Victorian manner." In 1930 the hotel became the University of Tampa, and today it is well preserved. The Tampa Bay Hotel was the architectural wonder of Plant's Florida development, even though his Belleview Hotel in Clearwater, opened in 1895, remained for a long while the largest hotel-resort on Florida's west coast.

On the east coast Henry M. Flagler inaugurated his railroad-resort development with the spectacular Ponce de Leon Hotel in St. Augustine, which had been designed by the New York architectural firm of Carrère and Hastings with the assistance of Bernard Maybeck. According to legend, Flagler looked to Spain for ideas for his Spanish Renaissance–style structure. At a cost of $1.25 million for 540 rooms, he created one of the first buildings in America made of poured concrete. The hotel was later converted to Flagler College.

Moving south from St. Augustine with his railroad and land development schemes, Flagler chose Palm Beach, 70 miles north of Miami, for a new city. "I shall build upon this spot a magnificent playground," he said. With his development of Palm Beach, Flagler also proposed to build churches and private gambling clubs to go with his hotels. In 1894 he set out to build the Royal Poinciana Hotel and raced to complete the railroad to it at the same time. The hotel won! It was the largest wooden structure ever built—six stories high, holding 1,750 guests who were entertained in a park of 32 acres with gardens, tennis courts, and golf courses. The building was a combination of late Victorian eclectic and Queen Anne forms. The Royal Poinciana Hotel was destroyed by the 1934 hurricane, leaving the Breakers, Flagler's other Palm Beach hotel. After an 1893 fire, the Breakers had been rebuilt in 1896 in a Spanish style.

If Flagler and Plant were developers, Addison Cairns Mizner, who also left his mark on Florida, was an adventurer-architect. Moving to Palm Beach in 1918, he quickly stamped his personal interpretation of Spanish architecture on the city and its neighbor, Boca Raton. In 1919 Mizner designed the courtyard for Paris Singer's Everglades Club, a private social club in the city of Palm Beach. Mizner "turned the Spanish style inside out like a glove, making all the openings face a patio." A contemporary description of the club caught the flavor of Mizner's Spanish-Florida style: "Seville, the Alhambra, a dash of Madeira and Algiers, an Italian lagoon and terraced garden and the incomparable Florida sunshine." With many commissions for private homes costing over a million dollars, Mizner used his fake Spanish style to develop Palm Beach architecture. He also developed Worth Avenue, Palm Beach's main shopping street, a rival to Fifth Avenue in New York City. His designs for fake Spanish buildings with little side streets and alleys for shops all served the great hotels and houses at this resort.

Addison Mizner's masterpiece was a resort complex now called the Boca Raton Club. On an inlet on the inland waterway in Boca Raton, he built the first hotel, the Cloister Inn, in a Spanish medieval style. Expanding his concept, he created a scheme for the largest hotel complex in the world. The inn on which he started was executed in Spanish style with pink and white walls surrounded by gardens with thousands of tropical plants and flowers. A dock on the waterway accommodated patrons' yachts. Unfortunately, in 1926 the Florida land-speculation boom ended, leaving only the small inn, completed in February 1926, a few outbuildings, and the docks. Since that time the Boca Raton Club has added a golf course, tennis courts, many other buildings, and a beach club.

Further south, what was to become the city of Miami was reached by the railroad in 1897. The site served as a troop camp during the Spanish-American War. In the 1921–25 Florida land boom automobile access gave the low-lying island considerable prominence and bay-bottom land sold quickly. The boom ended with the 1926 hurricane. Miami's subsequent development slowly gathered momentum until the 1980s. In the 1930s Miami and Miami Beach became fashionable places to escape both the Depression and northern winters. Small hotels in the art deco style were built in a 125-block district of the city. The art deco–Mediterranean Revival style, streamlined and exotic in decoration, was used on more than 800 buildings. Developers of the 1980s, seeking to build high-rise hotels and condominiums, face opposition from these early, small art deco hotels, which are trying to preserve the initial atmosphere of the resort city.

Miami skyrocketed to success as sun-seeking, wealthy tourists and conventioneers descended upon the city. The hotels of Morris Lapidus, whose Fountainbleau Hotel of 1954 is probably the best example of Florida kitsch-baroque architecture, epitomize the extravagance of Miami Beach architecture in the 1950s.

While Flagler and Plant were pushing into Florida to provide seaside resorts, similar resorts sprang up in other areas of the South. Saltwater bathing was never as popular in the 19th century as spring bathing, but by the late 1880s the first cottages opened for business at Virginia Beach, Va., and stilt houses appeared on the Outer Banks of North Carolina.

One of the most unusual island resorts in the South developed on Jekyll Island, a 12-by-2-mile island off the coast at Brunswick, Ga. Organized as a club in 1888 by families like Morgan, Astor, Gould, Vanderbilt, and Rockefeller, Jekyll Island became a winter refuge from January to March for the super-rich. A small clubhouse-restaurant was built, and each family had its own house on the island. The club closed in 1942. In 1954 a highway was built to the island, formerly accessible only by boat.

A parallel development took place at Sea Island, Ga., where the Gulf Stream moderates the climate. In 1928 Howard E. Coffin had Addison Mizner build a hotel complex, called the Cloister, in the Mediterranean style. Originally only 46 rooms, the Cloister now occupies the center of a large beach resort. Beautiful beaches also attracted big resort development on Hilton Head Island off South Carolina and at Kiawah Island near Charleston.

Beach resort development continued at Virginia Beach, Va. In the 1930s cottages were built both in residential areas near the water and on stilts along the waterfront. Motels, beginning in the 1920s and the 1930s, supplanted big Victorian hotels of the late 19th century. Today condominiums, with time-sharing arrangements, represent the wave of the future at seaside resorts.

The Gulf Coast of the southern United States has traditionally featured a long saltwater bathing season. Early in the 19th century the Gulf Coast from Mobile to Lake Pontchartrain enjoyed popularity as a resort area for residents from Natchez and New Orleans who wished to escape the heat. Southern plantation architectural styles were transplanted to the beachfront at Biloxi, Ocean Springs, Bay St. Louis, and Pass Christian, Miss. Gulf Coast resort houses rested on brick piers for coolness and floodproofing. Decorative cutout work, often larger than necessary, softened the sunlight and wide verandas provided cross-ventilation. Long wooden piers projecting into the shallow water adjoined the Gulf Coast hotels.

Louis Sullivan, one of America's foremost architects, found inspiration while at Ocean Springs, Miss., vacationing from his Chicago office. He felt so at home that he had a local carpenter build two bungalows between 1890 and 1891. Whether Sullivan or his most famous pupil, Frank Lloyd Wright, actually designed the two vacation cottages is a matter of speculation.

As the 20th century dawned, the great resorts of the 19th century faced doom, precipitated by the economic, social, and transportation revolutions. Transportation, as always, engendered new developments. Private railroad-car sidings were replaced by parking lots. Cheap automobile transportation over interstate highways, with overnight stops in chain motels, became the norm. Resorts in the South gradually adapted to new transportation patterns and sports preferences of the 20th century. Resorts were no longer the domain only of the rich. Wealth became diffused, and new recreational activities gained momentum.

Southern resorts with their moderate climate offer a variety of outdoor sporting activities for long seasons. In the 20th century tennis courts dot many lawns, and ski trails, with the advent of artificial snow, abound along mountain paths. Spectator sports such as horse racing have grown in popularity since 1931, when Hialeah Racetrack in Miami opened, complete with flamingoes. The Tides Inn, started in 1946 on the eastern shore of Virginia, shines as a major resort for yacht owners.

More than any other sport, golf altered the layout of

resort complexes. With its need for beautifully manicured courses on expansive tracts, golf changed the look of the 20th-century leisure landscape. By an accident of geology, Pinehurst, in central North Carolina, with its mild, dry climate, sand hills, and piney woods, became the golf capital of the South.

In the late 1800s New England developer James W. Tufts hired landscape architect Frederick Law Olmsted to create a special community. Olmsted laid out a complete village with shopping area, hotel, boardinghouses, some 16 cottages, and a meeting house–chapel based on a New England model. Olmsted's design featured curving streets and lavish landscaping within a protected community. By 1898 Tufts, completing his first course and later adding an appropriate clubhouse in 1899, had introduced the game of golf to Pinehurst. Pinehurst remains a famous southern golfing center with five featured 18-hole championship courses and numerous others in the immediate area. The location of Pinehurst did not depend on water to attract its customers, either for bathing or for drinking. What water was to one generation of tourists, the desire to play a game in a pleasant climate became to the next. Automobiles and airplanes make the contemporary resort easily accessible.

One of the most innovative southern resort communities to be developed in recent years is Seaside, a project near Point Washington, Fla., which has been carefully planned to capture the atmosphere of a small southern town during the late 1800s and early 1900s. Owners Robert and Daryl Davis cooperated with architects to design between 1978 and 1983 a detailed planning and zoning code that not only requires certain structural elements but also encourages such features of southern vernacular architecture as front porches and wood-shingle or metal roofs. Combined with these features are Victorian-style decorative latticework and brackets. The Seaside community further evokes images of small-town life by centering businesses around a town square, incorporating gazebos, and building narrow, tree-lined streets.

Since the early 18th century the spacious layouts and carefully designed environments for leisure in the South have represented the relationship between pleasure-seeking customers and an easy-going atmosphere. Taking advantage of pleasant weather for recreation, southern leisure sites developed innovative environments. Southern craving for socializing spurred a tradition of resort visiting. As transportation and technology opened new areas for leisure pursuits, visitors continued frequenting the great resorts, whose everlasting fame was propagated by southern weather, southern charm, and always "southern hospitality."

See also ETHNIC LIFE: Caribbean Influence; HISTORY AND MANNERS: Automobile; Railroad; / Olmsted, Frederick Law; INDUSTRY: / Flagler, Henry; RECREATION: Tourism; / Hilton Head; URBANIZATION: / Miami

W. L. Whitwell and
Lee Winborne
Hollins College

Cleveland Amory, *The Last Resorts* (1952); Edward Beyer, *Album of Virginia: or, Illustration of the Old Dominion* (1980); Stan Cohen, *Historic Springs of the Virginias: A Pictorial History* (1981); Marshall Fishwick, *Springlore in Virginia* (1978); Sir Augustus John Foster, *Jeffersonian America: Notes on the United States of America, Collected in the Years 1805–6–7 and 1811–12* (1954); Brendan Gill and Dudley Witney, *Summer Places* (1978); Constance M. Greiff, *Lost America: From the Atlantic to the Mississippi* (1971); Andrew Hepburn, *Great Resorts of North America* (1965); James M. Jordan IV, *Virginia Beach* (1974); Louis Joyner, *Southern Living* (June 1984, July 1986); Harnett T. Kane, *The Golden Coast* (1959); Russell Lynes, *The Tastemakers* (1954); Peregrine Prolix, *Letters Descriptive of Virginia Springs* (1835); Perceval Reniers, *The Springs of Virginia* (1941); Ishbel Ross, *Taste in America: An Illustrated History of the Evolution of Architecture, Furnishings, Fashions, and Customs of the American People* (1967); Paul M. Sachner, *Architectural Record Houses 1986* (1986).

Sculpture

The lack of sculpture was one item in H. L. Mencken's indictment of culture in the early 20th-century South, and scholars have generally echoed his sentiments. The South has had, however, a twofold tradition of sculpture—monumental works on the grand scale and folk sculpture on a more humble scale, in the form of stonecarving, woodcarving, ironworking, and other crafts. Although the monumental work in the region is not categorized with the highest artistic achievements, it is a notable reflection of southern cultural values. The folk sculpture of the region is likewise rooted in regional life, and its aesthetic value is increasingly appreciated by critics.

The South has a long tradition of honoring its heroes through monuments. The South Carolina assembly authorized a statue of William Pitt, erected in Charleston in 1766, to commemorate the English hero of the French and Indian War, while Virginia officially honored its governor, Norborne Berkeley, in 1773 in Williamsburg. This tendency was even more pronounced after the American Revolution. Virginia took the lead in honoring heroes from that conflict. The Virginia Legislature commissioned French sculptor Jean Antonine Houdon to do a bust of Lafayette and, later, a marble statue of George Washington dressed in the uniform of the Continental army, which was placed in the Virginia State Capitol Building in Richmond in 1796. In the Old State House in Raleigh, N.C, stands a statue from 1821 by Antonio Canova, depicting Washington in another popular pose of the time—dressed as an ancient Roman, seated on a grand chair. Washington was the very image of Cincinnatus, an image reflecting the early southern, as well as American, attempt to see the new nation's culture in classical terms.

Hiram Powers was not a southerner, but he executed works immortalizing many southern heroes. He did a bust of the aging Andrew Jackson in 1835 and, while living in Washington, D.C., fashioned works of southerners John Marshall and John C. Calhoun. He enjoyed the patronage of southerners, especially the Preston family of South Carolina, who authorized him to do a portrait statue of that state's Calhoun. Henry Clay was the subject of Kentuckian Joel Tanner Hart's full-length statue, completed in 1859, for the Ladies' Clay Association of Virginia.

There are two famed equestrian statues dating from the antebellum era. Clark Mills's bronze monument of Andrew Jackson was unveiled amid much fanfare in Washington in 1853, and replicas were soon ordered for Nashville and New Orleans. It was placed in the heart of New Orleans, in an area known thereafter as Jackson Square. A second equestrian statue was Thomas Crawford's homage to George Washington, placed near the Capitol in Richmond. It was a sculptural group of Washington and other Virginia heroes. Frederick Law Olmsted called it "the highest attainment of American plastic arts."

Many of these works were by non-southern artists. John Cogdell (1778–1847), on the other hand, was a Charleston lawyer who exemplified the southerner interested in sculpture as an avocation. Cogdell dabbled in painting but concentrated by the late 1830s on sculpture. He visited Italy for inspiration and later was one of the few native-born Americans to exhibit in the Pennsylvania Academy in Philadelphia and the National Academy of Design in New York. He did busts of Lafayette and Sir Walter Scott. Most aspiring American artists, including a few southerners, lived in Italy, to be near ancient works, a supply of marble, skilled assistants, and the European appreciation of sculpture.

After the Civil War poverty discouraged the commissioning of monumental sculpture. By the turn of the 20th century, however, a movement was under way to honor the Confederacy by erecting monuments to its heroes. For most towns and cities in the region, this meant the erection of a rather standardized monument of a Confederate soldier. These ubiquitous statues represented the idea of sculpture to most southerners. Their artistic merits were few, but culturally they were most significant in using artwork to convey regional values. Typically located on town squares, Confederate monuments were shafts topped by the image of an average soldier. Inscriptions at the base of monuments pledged loyalty to the Lost Cause, "Lest We Forget."

Some monuments to the Confederacy were more artistic than others in conception and execution. Sir Moses Ezekiel and Augustus Lukeman were among the best Lost Cause sculptors, but the most famous was Edward Virginius Valentine, who was born in Richmond in 1838, studied abroad, and then returned to the South in 1865. He became the most renowned artist of the Lost Cause, specializing in sculpting works to honor such Confederate heroes as Robert E. Lee, Thomas "Stonewall" Jackson, Jeb Stuart, and P. G. T. Beauregard. His best-known work is a recumbent statue of Lee in the chapel at Washington and Lee University. Richmond, Va., saw itself as the Rome of the South in nurturing monumental art, with statues to Jeb Stuart, Matthew F. Maury, and Hunter H. McGuire; its Monument Boulevard has statues to Confederate heroes Lee, Davis, and Jackson, as well as one to George Washington. Stone Mountain in Georgia is the most grandiose monument to the Confederacy. The United Daughters of the Confederacy commissioned a carving of the images of Lee, Davis, and Jackson into the mountain, which is a huge marble outcropping. The monument was not completed until 1970.

The South has honored through sculpture cultural heroes other than the Confederates. Elisabet Ney was a German-born artist who came to Texas in the 19th century and produced monuments to such Texas heroes as Sam Houston, Stephen Austin, and Confederate General Albert Sidney Johnston. New Orleans was the home to many monuments, including the Wounded Stag near the Delgado Museum of Art and the symbolic fountain at Audubon Park. Thomas P. Minns executed a series of studies for Nashville honoring blacks, farmers, and rural Tennesseans, while William M. McVey contributed a James Bowie statue in Texarkana and decorative sculpture on the San Jacinto Monument. Clyde Chandler's Sidney Smith Memorial Fountain is in Dallas, and southern gardens provide an attractive setting for much statuary. South Carolina's Brookgreen Gardens have over 300 pieces, by Archer M. and Anna Hyatt Huntington, all in an appropriate southern setting, surrounded by live oaks and Spanish moss. Classical figures were executed for turn-of-the-century expositions at New Orleans, Atlanta, and Nashville; the Parthenon in Nashville is a lasting monument to such fairs.

Fewer monuments have been dedicated to World War I and World War II veterans than to those of earlier conflicts. Needed structures such as roads and bridges have often served as memorials instead. However, one of the region's most original pieces of sculpture was dedicated as a World War I monument on the University of Virginia campus—the McConnell Statue by Gutzon Borglum (the original carver of Stone Mountain and later Mount Rushmore). It is the bronze image of a World War I flying ace, who sits poised on a globe, ready for flight. Charleston's memorial to World War I is a nude male figure adorning Battery Park.

In the contemporary South modern art, including modern sculpture, is found in cities such as Atlanta, Miami, Dallas, and Houston. There are examples of works by international sculptors such as Alexander Calder, Joan Miró, or Henry Moore. Among the most prominent black sculptors from the South, or those using southern themes, are Richmond Barthé, Francis Marion Marche, Augusta C. Savage, William E. Artis, Selma Burke, Margaret T. Burroughs, Elizabeth Catlett, and Marion Perkins.

In addition to creating a regional tradition of monumental sculpture, black and white southerners have produced a wide variety of folk sculpture. The South has had many craftsmen who produced work that transcended the merely functional to become folk sculpture. They are sometimes called primitive, eccentric, naive, or most commonly, folk artists. This category of sculpture includes commercial art, items with both utilitarian and aesthetic dimensions. It also includes the home sculptor who executes works for pleasure. Home sculpture is seen at craft stores, Christmas fairs, and flea markets.

A frequent southern image in film and literature is the whittler on a porch. Whittling, in fact, has had social, educational, and economic facets that make it a common activity, especially in the rural South. A representative of this tradition, Earnest Bennett (originally from Fairplay, Ky.), was recognized with a National Heritage Award from the National Endowment for the Arts in 1986. The pocketknife, sometimes called a jacknife, was the simple, basic tool needed, and whittling encouraged qualities of resourcefulness and ingenuity in its use. Pocketknives are valued material culture artifacts among carvers, who sometimes collect and trade them. The skill of carving was typically passed from one generation to another, frequently from an elderly family member or neighbor to a young man coming of age.

The inspiration for such folk sculpture comes from the tasks, materials, and skills of everyday life; farmers and carpenters make art while working with wood, quarry workers while working in limestone. Often these are communally shared skills applied to expressive forms, and they enhance the pride and prestige of the maker. A distinctive regional dimension comes also from the use of local materials. Southern folk sculpture has traditionally been in wood, stone, iron, or clay.

Because the South has been a heavily forested area, the use of timber as a material for sculpture was natural, and the skills associated with carving were valued in the southern economy. Sometimes the folk artist used a knife, sometimes a chisel; the wood object might be painted or it might be left unfinished. Some wood carvings were functional, others simply for show, and still others were novelty items. Carved objects included musical instruments, apothecary mortars, barber poles, weathervanes, whirligigs, toys, shop signs, shop carvings, wildfowl decoys, furniture accessories, walking canes, and larger-than-life-size rifles.

Pierre Joseph Landry (1770–1843) was an antebellum southern folk artist who carved in wood apparently as a pastime. He carved works that told stories, especially allegorical ones and those with echoes of religious themes from medieval art. Other antebellum artists carved wooden dolls and toys with movable parts. Religion has served as a prime theme for southern carvers, who have produced many church steeples topped by upward-pointing fingers.

Three-dimensional carved human figures were found in the South, many serving as shop signs. The carved Indian was a nationally popular wooden piece, displayed outside tobacco shops, and was one of the most common full-figured wooden pieces produced in the pre–Civil War South. Matthew S. Kahle, a Lexington, Va., furniture maker, produced a full-figured, standing George Washington for the Washington College Chapel in 1840. A carved black man stood as a symbol outside the New Orleans slave auction. Carved human figures also adorned the bows of ships.

Walking canes have often been carved. They were highly functional products for the elderly and handicapped, and folk artists gave them ornamental touches to make them artistic. Snake canes have been common, with serpents' bodies wrapped around the length of the stick and a head topping off the cane. Three-dimensional animals have also been carved into canes, as have politicians (shops near Monticello in Virginia sell Thomas Jefferson canes). Ceremonial staffs for lodges and fraternal groups have also been produced by folk sculptors.

Carved animals, in the form of domestic pets, livestock, and small animal wildlife, are commonly found in southern homes. They are a modern survival of the traditional southern pastoral ideal. Eagles are popular for interior decoration. Snakes are a favorite image, and the South has its fair share of carved serpents. A common form is a slithering toy—a jointed snake, with carved wooden pieces held together by string or wire. Carving wildfowl decoys began as a folk art by hunters who had a practical use for them. Ned Burgess of Currituck, N.C., for example, turned carving decoys into an art. He made more decoys between 1920 and 1945 than any other North Carolina carver, creating his works for hunters in sportsmen's clubs, for market hunters, and for subsistence hunters. He did many species of local waterfowl, including swans, geese, canvasbacks, redheads, blackheads, pintails, pigeons, black ducks, mallards, ruddy ducks, and coots. Carved ducks are now a ubiquitous presence through much of the South, thanks to commercial marketing.

Among the South's first folk sculptors were the stone carvers who cut gravestones from slate, granite, marble, sandstone, or fieldstone. Limestone seems to have been the most popular rock form. Stone carvers have usually been seen more as craftsmen than as artists, but many gravestones in the region exhibit aesthetic dimensions. Most, to be sure, repeat standard shapes and designs, such as weeping willow trees, cherubic angels, hearts and hands, crosses, skull and bones, flowers, and lambs for children. Scholars have documented, though, the stylized, innovative work of creative stonemasons, such as Laurence Krone, who carved tombstones for customers in southwestern Virginia in the early 19th century. Much stonecarving for graves was, however, anonymous. In the modern South, Nashville, Tenn., carver William Edmondson achieved fame for his stone carvings of animals, angels, flowerpots, religious figures, and garden statuary. He died in 1951, by which time his work had been displayed at the Museum of Modern Art in New York City.

Appalachian folk craftsmen have sometimes carved in a distinctive regional material—coal. Around the turn of the 20th century, for example, a Bell County, Ky., miner created a replica of the Bible from coal. Coal carvings are available at mountain craft fairs and have become a commercialized product for sale at tourist stores.

Ironworkers frequently decorated their practical creations with artistic touches. One type of ironwork in the South involved casting, whereby molten metal was poured into a mold. Not all casting, to be sure, would be classified as sculpture, but the production of a prototype enabled a caster to produce an object for widespread duplication. Iron furnaces turned out a variety of designs for such objects as andirons, stove plates, cast animals, and various household ornaments and cooking utensils. Most cast iron in the South, however, was imported from the North and was more an industrial form than a fine or folk art.

Another form of southern ironwork was wrought iron. Blacksmiths were an essential figure in both rural and city life, and sometimes they embellished their creations with artistic touches. The blacksmith shaped his metal into functional objects of daily living such as andirons, pokers, gates, commercial signs, grave markers, and kitchen implements. Folk sculptors working in both cast and wrought iron used the same themes and designs as other southern sculptors—animal forms, especially snakes, the human form, and scenes of nature and of religious life. The cities of Charleston and New Orleans contain the highest achievements of southern ironwork sculpture—in the lacelike gates and ornamental metal flourishes used in construction. South Carolinian Philip Simmons (b. 1912) is one of the most famous and skilled of many black artisans who invested their utilitarian craft with artistic dimensions.

Sheet metal was another medium for southern metal sculptors. Tin and copper objects were common in southern households, and those with imaginative decorations of design or motif qualify as folk art. Weathervanes, among the most popular of sheet metal objects that have been documented and collected, were common everywhere. In the form of chickens, horses, cows, sheep, or hogs, they topped barns; angels adorned churches; fish and gulls appeared along coastal areas; and arrows, Indians with drawn bows and arrows, and patriotic eagles were frequent.

Stoneware became the dominant form for traditional ceramics in the South by the early 1800s. Potter dynasties—such as those of the Cole, Brown, and Meaders families—provide continuity in the tradition today. Much pottery would not rank as folk sculpture, given that its objects are purely functional or decorated only through painting. Nonetheless, many potters created artistic sculpture in the form of face jugs and highly decorated vessels. Some pots were mainly utilitarian, designed for storing food, churning butter, or watering plants, but potters would decorate even those by incising distinctive designs. Flowerpots and gravemarkers were inscribed with fluted rims and flaring forms. Potters sometimes had stamps with which they made whimsical designs, their signatures, or Masonic or lodge symbols. Potters in the Shenandoah Valley of Virginia were particularly noted for creating molds in the form of animals and birds, fish and flowers, or human figures, and then attaching them to pitchers, bowls, flowerpots, vases, and other vessels to create elaborate, three-dimensional works. Other artists in clay, such as James "Son" Thomas of Leland, Miss., rely on dreams and visions for inspiration. Thomas creates sculptured images of animals and distinctive human skulls.

See also FOLKLIFE articles; HISTORY AND MANNERS: Monuments; / Stone Mountain; MYTHIC SOUTH: / Lost Cause Myth

Charles Reagan Wilson
University of Mississippi

Kate Langley Bosher, in *The South in the Building of the Nation*, vol. 10, ed. Samuel C. Mitchell (1909); Carl Bridenbaugh, *The Colonial Craftsman* (1961); Simon J. Bronner, *Chain Carvers: Old Men Crafting Meaning* (1985), *Grasping Things: Folk Material Culture and Mass Society in America* (1986); John A. Burrison, *Brothers in Clay: The Story of Georgia Folk Pottery* (1983); Charles Camp, ed., *Traditional Craftsmanship in America: A Diagnostic Report* (1983); Allen H. Eaton, *Handicrafts of the Southern Highlands* (1937); John Ezell, *The South since 1865* (2d ed., 1975); William Ferris, ed., *Afro-American Folk Art and Crafts* (1983); Henry Glassie, *Pattern in the Material Folk Culture of the Eastern United States* (1968); Donald Van Horn, *Carved in Wood: Folk Culture in the Arkansas Ozarks* (1979); Cynthia Elyce Rubin, ed., *Southern Folk Art* (1985); Robert Sayers, *Festival of American Folklife 1981*, ed. Jack Santino (1981); Allen Tullos, ed., *Southern Exposure* (Summer–Fall 1977); John Michael Vlach, *The Afro-American Tradition in Decorative Arts* (1977), *Charleston Blacksmith: The Life and Work of Philip Simmons* (1981); Charles G. Zug III, *Turners and Burners: The Folk Potters of North Carolina* (1986).

Vernacular Achitecture (Lowland South)

The vernacular, or common, architecture of a region is an indicator of its economic development and changing social values. The realities of life in the 17th-century Lowland South shaped builders' choices of plan types and building technologies, and these have remained at the core of the region's vernacular architecture. The vernacular building system of the Lowland South has been greatly weakened since World War I, but it has never disappeared. Recent historians of the early South have emphasized the area's social instability. A high mortality rate during the first century of settlement, coupled with a high demand for agricultural workers in the labor-intensive tobacco economy, absorbed economic resources and altered social relationships as planters attempted to extract as much labor as possible from their employees. These strains affected southern architectural traditions in two ways.

First, because most early southerners preferred to devote their resources to agricultural production, they developed building systems that capitalized on plentiful supplies of timber to minimize the human investment in building. Crude buildings characterized the beginnings of all the colonies, but in the South they continued to be built long after the Chesapeake and Albemarle settlements were securely under way. The earliest structures were commonly made of rough timbers driven into the ground and covered with split boards nailed to them. Later, 17th-century builders used mortise-and-tenon frames, simplifying them by omitting foundations and sinking the wooden uprights directly into the ground. There were several variations of the "post" building, as recent scholars have called it, ranging from the driven "puncheons" of the first buildings to carefully framed structures set on wooden-block foundations. Post building made it possible to build quickly and cheaply, conserving labor and capital for other uses. It was common even for public structures like churches and courthouses in the 17th-century South. Post building required frequent repairs, and few post-built structures survived more than 20 years after their initial construction. Only two colonial post-built houses—Cedar Park in Anne Arundel County, Md., and Sotterley in St. Mary's County, Md.—still exist, and both owe their preservation to a protective casing of durable materials added early in their existence. In the early 18th century wealthy southerners began to build their homes more substantially, but post-built houses were erected for poor whites and blacks until the end of the colonial period, and post, or "pole," construction is still widely used in southern agricultural buildings.

Although post building was no longer used for finer homes after the 17th century, a distinctive southern framing system grew out of it that embodied the labor-saving intention of post building in the use of a small number of relatively standardized parts, assembled with the simplest of mortise-and-tenon and notch joints. Whereas traditional Anglo-American frames of the type used in New England employ large timbers tied together by complex joints, southern frames consist of pairs of light walls linked at the top. Relatively small major timbers—about four by eight inches in houses—were set at 10-foot intervals, with the spaces between filled by three-by-four-inch studs. Often these were simply nailed into shallow notches chipped into the outer surfaces of the frame. Two long walls constructed in this manner were tilted up, and ceiling joists notched at their undersides were dropped on to hold the walls upright. The roof was most commonly formed of light three-by-four-inch rafters pegged at the top. A light board laid across the ends of the ceiling joists enabled the builder to nail the rafters anywhere along it, eliminating the need for cutting joints to seat the rafters. In the southern frame the parts were relatively unspecialized and could be cut out quickly and in numbers and assembled with equal ease. Yet the system was versatile enough that buildings as small as a smokehouse or as large as a mansion could be built using essentially the same approach. The southern framing system changed little between about 1720 and the Civil War and was used in some areas until the 20th century. It was carried west by southerners into the middle western and south central states, and its influence is apparent in 19th-century buildings as far west as California.

Thus, despite the stereotype of the South as a land of brick buildings, masonry walls have always been rare in the Lowland South, even for large structures; wood has been the characteristic building material. Although timber has most commonly been used in joined frames, log construction entered the Lowland South in the late 17th century. By the end of the 18th century small log houses, often with wooden chimneys, were widely used by poor planters in the Tidewater South—George Washington reported seeing almost nothing else on a trip South through Virginia and North Carolina in 1791—and they were the standard form of slave housing as well. In low-lying sections of east Texas and the Gulf Coast states log construction came with the early settlers and was a common vernacular building technology through the 19th and early 20th centuries. In some parts of the East Coast, however, logs never made much headway, except in small agricultural buildings constructed in the late 19th and early 20th centuries. In those areas the frame tradition was nearly universal and prevailed even where logs were used. For example, late 18th- and early 19th-century builders in northern Maryland were fond of a hybrid log-frame system, in which horizontal logs were tenoned into corner posts.

The 17th century gave the Lowland South its principal domestic plan forms as well as its building technology. At first, immigrants to the Chesapeake and Albemarle regions built many kinds of traditional English houses, but by about 1680 single-story, one-room-deep houses had become the standard. Poorer colonists, constrained by a barebones existence, had no choice about house size. For middling or wealthy people, the choice of small houses was a product of the relation between planters and their workers. Where most English agriculturalists in the 17th century were accustomed to employing familiar locals, who lived and worked in the farmers' own large houses, the presence of a constantly changing labor force of strangers prompted southern planters to abandon the custom and to move their laborers' working and resting areas to outbuildings. Thus, most planters' houses were reduced to one- or two-room dwellings standing at the center of a large domestic complex. From the late 17th century on, this fragmentation of domestic functions into a complex of small buildings was one of the most striking aspects of the southern landscape to outsiders, whose published commentaries repeatedly compared planters' residences to small villages. The creation of the southern domestic complex in the 17th century arose from altered relationships among English people. Although it later became a distinguishing mark of slave society, the separation of house and domestic outbuildings antedated the adoption of slave labor throughout the Lowland South.

A typical domestic complex included a kitchen, usually a building similar in size and appearance to a one-room house; a milkhouse or dairy for the cool storage of dairy products, and a smokehouse for the preservation of meats. Larger complexes in the 18th and 19th centuries contained a laundry, often attached to the kitchen; an office; and, in a few instances, a sunken icehouse, a school, or a small storehouse. Servants lived in the work buildings or in separate houses. In the 17th century cellars were customarily separate from the house and were only moved under the dwelling in the 18th century. Even then they were often thought of as outbuildings and were provided with outside entrances facing the other outbuildings, but with no access from inside the house.

At the core of the complex was the house itself. Two-room, or hall-parlor, houses (the name is a modern one) consisted of a large main room, called the hall by its occupants, which was the principal center of activity. It was used for sitting and eating, and the head of the household sometimes slept there. Off from it was a smaller room, usually called the parlor or chamber, which shared many of the hall's functions. Its more secluded location made it the preferred sleeping room. The parlor often had a door in the end or rear wall leading to the outbuildings at the side or rear of the house. A few very large hall-parlor houses had projecting entry rooms that were called porches, although they were enclosed. Some, like Bacon's Castle (1665) in Surry County, Va., one of the finest houses in the colony when it was built, had a rear tower for the stairs as well.

The relative homogeneity of house size and plan in the late 17th and early 18th centuries dissolved in the mid-18th century. One- and two-room houses remained the staple of the housing stock, but wealthier southerners began to add other spaces to these. A room called the dining room, but serving as many different functions as the earlier hall and parlor, could be found in many large houses. The addition of rooms led many builders in the 18th century to build houses two rooms deep, although others preferred to maintain the traditional single-room depth and to attach the added rooms in ells at right angles to the main house. More important than the use of added rooms and the increased depth of large houses was the use of a passage into which the main door opened. The passage, which usually contained the stair as well, served as a buffer between the outside and the public rooms of the house and allowed circulation to each room of the house without the necessity of passing through any other. Passages made slow headway at first, but by the early 19th century they were common in most houses with more than two rooms and could even be found appended to one-room houses.

The use of passages, extra rooms, and two-room (or double-pile) depths is most striking in the so-called Georgian-plan house, a structure with two rooms on either side of a central passage and usually two stories tall. Georgian plans were first used in the Lowland South in large mansions of the second decade of the 18th century. The smaller houses that used passages or two-room depths have been thought of as derivations of the Georgian form, but, in fact, a more complex process was involved in which traditional builders adapted the new ideas to traditional forms rather than merely imitating upper-class buildings.

Henry Glassie discusses the formal relationships between old and new ideas as they affected an area of Piedmont Virginia in his study *Folk Housing in Middle Virginia*. There were clearly social components to the Georgian idea as well, although these have not received the same attention. Fieldwork suggests, however, that many areas of the South underwent a period of intense experimentation in house forms either just before or just after 1800. During that period, in addition to the traditional forms, houses with odd and unique plans were constructed. At the end of the period of experimentation, each area seems to have selected the same solution to rural housing, based on the central-passage idea. New houses were built with passages, and both older and experimental houses were converted to the newly popular forms. The most conspicuous of the new dwelling types of the early 19th century was a two-story, one-room-deep house with a central passage. Although I houses, as the geographers call them, were built by a few wealthy southerners as early as the 1730s, they were not common until the 1820s. After that, they enjoyed a nationwide popularity, although one-room versions of the same plan were probably more numerous in the Lowland South.

The high visibility of the I house has obscured the continuing presence of single-room and hall-parlor houses. Moreover, the I house is only one of many possible ways to arrange four rooms and a passage. In the Chesapeake-Albemarle region a two-story, double-pile house, one room wide with a passage at the side was popular between 1790 and 1850. In the region stretching south from southern North Carolina, a one-story house with a central passage and four rooms was built from the mid-19th century into the 20th century. This is often called a Creole cottage in the Gulf Coast states, and in 20th-century hipped-roof versions, a pyramidal cottage. The renowned Charleston single house is in effect an I house turned sideways, although it apparently emerged only after a period of experimentation with traditional urban house plans. All of these houses have been identified as distinctive regional forms, but all incorporate more widespread architectural elements in superficially different ways. Scholars must await an investigation of the reasons such regional choices were made.

In the 19th century southern vernacular builders adopted another nationally popular house form. This was a T- or L-plan building, consisting of two wings set at right angles to one another. One section contained two rooms, one in front of the other, while the other wing contained one room and sometimes an entry passage. This form was adaptable to a large, stylish house or a very modest one. T-plan houses were commonly built in large numbers to house tenants and industrial workers in the late 19th and early 20th centuries. These present another opportunity for study, but their room uses appear to have been traditional; only the picturesque appearance of the perpendicular wings was novel.

See also FOLKLIFE: House Types; / Bungalow House; Dogtrot House; I House; Pyramidal House; Saddlebag House; Shotgun House; T House; GEOGRAPHY: Log Housing

Dell Upton
University of California
at Los Angeles

Cary Carson, in *Material Culture and the Study of American Life*, ed. Ian M. G. Quimby (1978); Cary Carson, Norman F. Barka, William M. Kelso, Garry Wheeler Stone, and Dell Upton, *Winterthur Portfolio* (Summer–Autumn 1981); Brent Glass, in *Carolina Dwelling: Towards Preservation of Place: In Celebration of the North Carolina Vernacular Landscape*, ed. Doug Swaim (1978); Henry Glassie, *Folk Housing in Middle Virginia:*

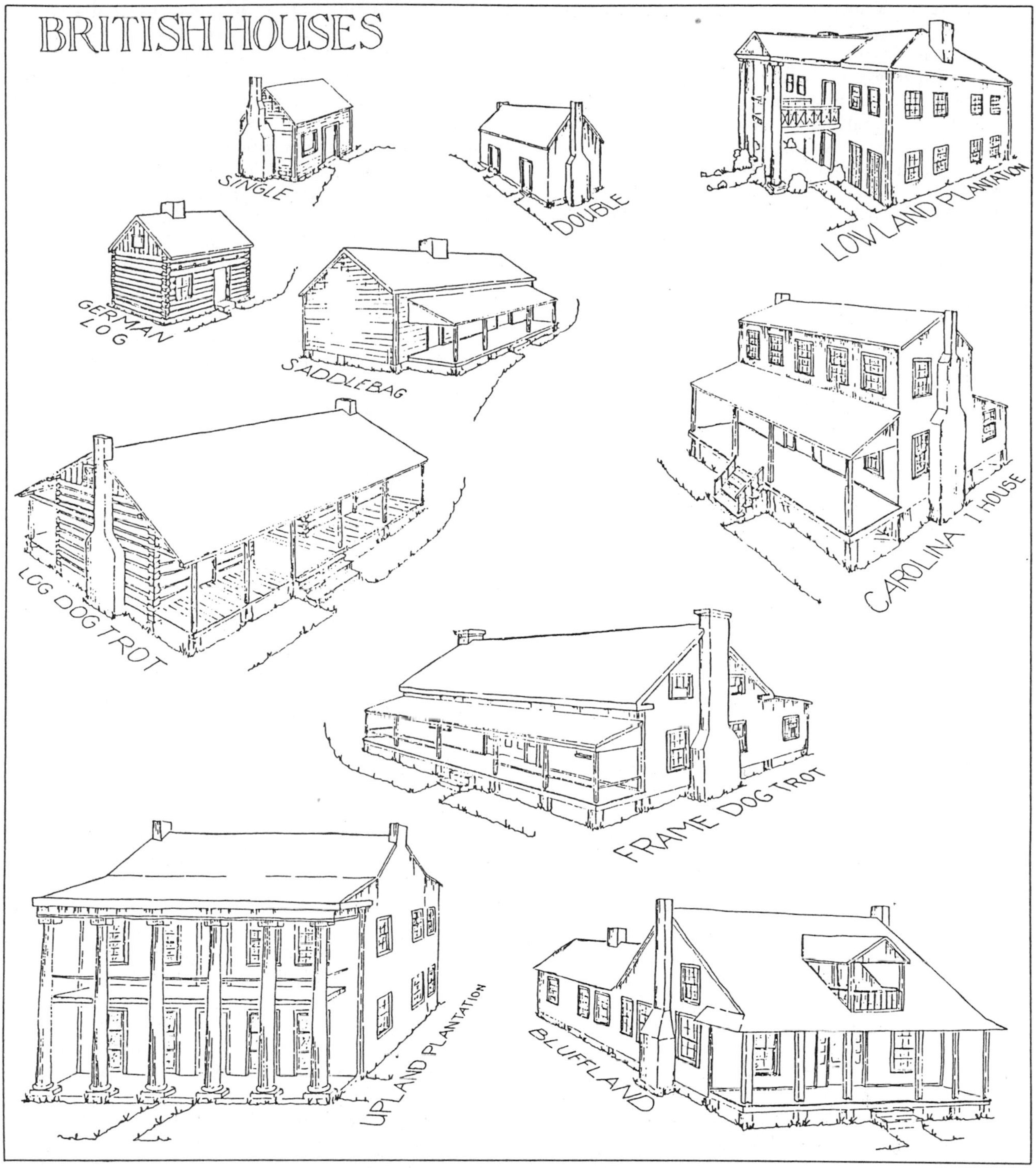

A drawing of types of British houses found in the South

A Structural Analysis of Historic Artifacts (1975), *Pattern in the Material Folk Culture of the Eastern United States* (1969); Lisa Howorth, "Popular Vernacular: The One-Story T House in the South" (M.A. thesis, University of Mississippi, 1984); Dell Upton, in *Material Culture of the Wooden Age*, ed. Brooke Hindle (1981), *Winterthur Portfolio* (Summer–Autumn 1982); Thomas T. Waterman, *The Dwellings of Colonial America* (1950).

Vernacular Architecture (Upland South)

Architecturally, the Upland South can be defined as the area lying between the Ohio River on the north, the Blue Ridge and Smoky Mountains on the east, the northern portions of the Gulf states on the south, and the Ozark Mountains on the west. Since the early 20th century this region has been depicted as a repository of antiquated cultural forms. Students of architecture have tended to concentrate on exotic or archaic forms there, such as log construction, dogtrot- and saddlebag-plan houses, and double-crib barns, and to neglect consideration of more ordinary vernacular buildings and particularly the patterns of architectural change. However, vernacular building in this part of the South, as in the Lowland South, is largely a product of the national popular culture of the 19th century.

Much of the distinctive architecture in the Upland South was brought into the region in the 18th century by the first European colonists, who entered the uplands through the great valley that stretches from central Pennsylvania into Tennessee or who crossed the Blue Ridge and Smoky Mountains from the east. Their architecture included log construction, several small house plans derived from English and Scotch-Irish traditions, and Germanic architectural designs. Popular building types and technologies began in the early 19th century, through new migrants, popular publications, and in rare cases the direct importation of building parts and materials.

The best-known building technology of the Upland South is log construction. The origins of log building in the United States are uncertain. The dominant theory is Fred Kniffen's and Henry Glassie's. They suggest that log construction was brought from Europe to Pennsylvania by Germanic and central European settlers. In Pennsylvania it was rapidly adopted by Anglo-American and Scotch-Irish builders. More recently, Terry G. Jordan has returned to the earlier 20th-century theory that log construction was introduced into the Delaware Valley by Finns and Swedes in the mid-17th century. Although his argument is not entirely convincing, he has demonstrated that the log architecture of Europe is more varied and its patterns are less clear than Kniffen and Glassie thought. In America the phrase "log building" conceals a complex group of independent traits that must be examined more closely than they have been.

Structurally, the distinctive characteristic of log building is the horizontal courses locking together at the corners to stand up; in the standard form, where there are interstices of several inches between the individual logs, their only vertical support is at the corners. Consequently, log structures are often described according to the shapes of the notches that link them at the corners. The most common notching forms in the Upland South are the V-notch and the full- and half-dovetail notches. Saddle, diamond, square, and half notches are less common. A log structure is really only stable if there are four log sides that brace each other. This four-sided unit is traditionally called a pen or (in farm buildings) a crib and is the basic unit for the analysis of log building plans. Log construction has continued in the Upland South since the first settlement; traditional builders still construct and repair log houses and farm buildings.

Other building methods were equally early, if not as conspicuous. A few frame houses survive from the last quarter of the 18th century. Framing, using pit-sawn and water-mill-sawn materials, was common for large houses throughout the 19th century. In those parts of the uplands where timbering was commercially practiced in the late 19th century, steam-sawn, balloon-framed houses became common after the 1880s. Poorer builders took advantage of cheap mill-sawn materials to build single-wall (box or plank) buildings. These light structures lacked most standard framing members; they were supported by thick, closely set planks. Small horizontal pieces nailed to their inner faces at the top and bottom, and sometimes light vertical sticks at the corners, held the structural planks together. In houses, an outer covering of weatherboards was usually nailed directly to the supporting planks, and any interior finish—whitewash, paper, or plaster—was also applied directly to the structure. Box framing has been studied in Arkansas and Kentucky and undoubtedly was even more widespread, if unreported, in other parts of the South.

Masonry construction was preferred for the largest vernacular structures. Much of the Upland South contains rich stores of easily worked limestone, which was used for chimneys, foundations, and many large houses in the fertile valleys. Large houses and farm buildings built as early as the mid-18th century survive in upland Maryland, Virginia, North Carolina, and Tennessee. Brick structures survive from the 1790s, but they were rare before the second decade of the 19th century.

Vernacular house types were as varied as building technology in the Upland South. Among the earliest surviving houses there are small *cabins*, or houses of a single structural unit, one story high. The definition is Henry Glassie's, but the term was already identified in the 18th century as one favored by the English-speaking settlers in the Upland South. Glassie distinguishes two types of cabins—one with a gable roof parallel to the front, end chimney, a single front entry, and a square plan that is derived from English traditions; and another that may derive from Scotch-Irish traditions and also has a parallel gable roof and end chimney, but has both front and rear entries and a rectangular plan. The interior is sometimes partitioned into a large room with a fireplace and a smaller one without heat. In addition, some early southerners built traditional Anglo-American hall-parlor (or hall-chamber) houses consisting of a large room, the hall, into which the front door opened, and a smaller room—the parlor or chamber—adjacent to it. Unlike the partitioned rectangular cabin, in the hall-parlor house both rooms were provided with fireplaces.

Other traditional house types are of less certain origin. These include the so-called saddlebag and dogtrot houses, and the double-pen-plan house. The saddlebag house is distinguished by the "draping" of its rooms on either side of a large central chimney like saddlebags on a horse. Unlike central-chimney houses in the Lowland South or the northeastern United States, the rooms on either side form separate structural pens that lean against the chimney, rather than enclosing the stack within a single unified structure. The units may resemble one or more of the simple cabin forms: a saddlebag house might consist of a square unit and a rectangular one, or a square and a two-room rectangular one, or two square or two rectangular units. Many saddlebag houses were built in stages. In the dogtrot house there are also two major sections, built at the same time, and in most cases containing a single room each. They are separated by a passageway that has no front or rear walls, and all three sections are covered by a continuous roof. The enclosed rooms are entered from the passage—the dogtrot proper—rather than from the front of the house. Many dogtrot houses were altered by enclosing the open passage, creating a central-passage plan of a type familiar all over the 19th-century United States. In the third two-part form, the double-pen house, the pens or units are built adjacent to one another without an intervening passage or chimney. Unlike the hall-parlor house, both rooms are approximately equal in size; more striking, each has its own front door. All three of these Upland South plans were most commonly built in one-story or story-and-a-half heights, although two-story dogtrot houses can be found. All are stereotyped as log buildings, though they were built in frame, and occasionally in brick and stone.

The origins of these three distinctive plans remain in dispute. The saddlebag house has been associated with Anglo-American central-chimney traditions as adapted to the exigencies of log-pen building. The double-pen house has similarly been attributed to the peculiarities of the log-pen structure. Another theory is that the double-pen house is an attempt to Anglicize the appearance of a four-bay facade deriving from Germanic building traditions. A third attributes its identical pens to Scandinavian antecedents.

The dogtrot house has been the object of the most speculation. One of the earliest explanations was that of Martin Wright, who argued that, like the double-pen house, the dogtrot derived from Fenno-Scandinavian traditions brought to the Delaware Valley in the 17th century. Others see it as a poor person's version of the Georgian central-passage house. Climatic explanations—that the open "breezeway" is an accommodation to the southern climate—are also popular. Unfortunately, the study of Upland South architecture has concentrated on the identification of typological examples through often-superficial field examination. No careful study of the physical histories of individual, closely dated examples, of archival sources, and of socioeconomic or room-use patterns has been made, nor has there been direct field study of the proposed precedents. Consequently, scholars do not know how old these Upland South types are or what their history in the region is. All hypotheses about their origins are speculative, and none of the proposed theories seems convincing.

At the same time small house types appeared, several larger vernacular house plans were also imported into the Upland South. These include the so-called Quaker-plan house, another form of uncertain origins. The name derives from a description of an ideal house plan published by William Penn for the benefit of Quaker settlers in Pennsylvania, but no researcher has established any firm link between the 17th-century description and surviving examples, few of which date from before 1790 or after 1830. Quaker-plan houses are similar in plan to hall-parlor houses except that two small square rooms, one in front of the other, take the place of the parlor. These usually share a single chimney with fireplaces set diagonally in the corners of each room.

Central-passage-plan houses, one or two stories high and occasionally two rooms deep, representing the popular culture of the Lowland South and Middle Atlantic source areas, were also introduced to the Upland South in the late 18th century. A few were built in log and limestone, but brick and especially frame were the favored materials. In the 19th century, central-passage, one-room-deep houses—the ubiquitous I houses described by geographers and folklorists—were the most common houses for prosperous farmers and townfolk. As in the Lowland South, the traditional forms continued to be built even as popular house types and new methods of manufacturing building materials and constructing houses and farm buildings spread through the Upland South after 1830.

See also FOLKLIFE: House Types; / Dogtrot House; I House; Pyramidal House; Saddlebag House; Shotgun House; GEOGRAPHY: Log Housing

Dell Upton
University of California
at Los Angeles

Henry Glassie, *Mountain Life and Work* (Winter 1963, Spring 1964, Summer 1965), *Pattern in the Material Folk Culture of the Eastern United States* (1969), in *The Study of American Folklore: An Introduction*, by Jan Harold Brunvand (2d ed., 1978); Terry G. Jordan, *American Log Buildings: An Old World Heritage* (1985); Fred Kniffen, *Annals of the Association of American Geographers* (December 1965), with Henry Glassie, *Geographical Review* (January 1966); Charles E. Martin, *Hollybush: Folk Building and Social Change in an Appalachian Community* (1984); William Lynwood Montell and Michael Lynn Morse, *Kentucky Folk Architecture* (1976); James Patrick, *Architecture in Tennessee, 1768–1897* (1981); Karl B. Raitz, *Landscape* (Spring 1978); Dell Upton and John Michael Vlach, eds., *Common Places: Readings in American Vernacular Architecture* (1986); Thomas T. Waterman, *The Dwellings of Colonial America* (1950).

Amisano, Joseph

(b. 1917) Architect.

Born in New York in 1917, Amisano became a leading designer of modern architecture in the South. He received his architecture degree from Pratt Institute in New York in 1940, was a Fourth Year Design Medalist from that institution, and in 1950 won a Prix de Rome. In 1978 he was elected to the National Academy of Design as an associate member. Before joining the Atlanta firm of Toombs, Amisano, and Wells in 1954, he was associated with the firm of Harrison, Foulhoux, and Abramovitz in New York and in the Canal Zone. Later he joined the New York firm of Walter Sanders, where he met and worked with Buckminster Fuller.

Amisano's first national recognition came in 1942 with his design for proposed row apartments in New York. His major recognition as a designer came with his work in Atlanta in the late 1950s and the early 1960s. He played the major role in the design of Lenox Square, built in Atlanta in 1958 and soon recognized as one of the nation's most successful shopping malls. This "space for people," as Amisano called it, reflected Atlanta's growing importance as a major business center. The mall contained 58 shops, most of them branches of Atlanta's established institutions, including Rich's and Davison-Paxon. The key to the design was the 1,014-foot-long central mall, which provided shoppers with an insulation from automobile traffic. The open mall with its shops seemed to be very much in the spirit of the sunny Italian plazas Amisano had come to know and love during the time he spent in Rome as a Fellow at the American Academy. Spanning the 55-foot width of the mall are arches of white concrete, folded and arched into shapes more sculptural than architectural. Plantings in boxes and pots mask the long perspective of the mall so that shoppers see only four or five storefronts at one time. The design was restrained by its basically stern and classical character and by the economy of the construction. Lavish as the design seemed at the time, the cost was 20 to 25 percent below that of comparable malls.

Amisano's firm designed the Village Shopping Center in Cleveland, Tenn. His design for the Science Center at the University of Georgia in Athens was completed in 1957, and his designs for the Pharmacy Building and the Visual Arts Building on that campus were completed in 1962, the same year Harper High School was built in Atlanta from his design. In 1965 Amisano's plans for the Peachtree Palisades Building, a totally black structure, were completed in Atlanta.

During the period of the late 1960s Amisano designed two distinctive churches in Atlanta. The John Knox Presbyterian Church was completed in 1967 in suburban Atlanta, and the Unitarian Church was completed in 1968. Both were recognized for their distinctive central design. The decade of the 1960s was climaxed, however, by his design for the Atlanta Memorial Arts Center, which was dedicated in October of 1968. The center housed the High Museum of Art, the Atlanta College of Art, Symphony Hall, and the Alliance Theatre. Again the design of the buildings was distinguished by the stern classical character of its massively simple forms. The most important large structure designed by Amisano in the 1970s was the Peachtree Summit Building, completed in 1975.

Amisano's design of the Atlanta University Center Library was completed in the spring of 1983, and his design for the MARTA Peachtree Center station was completed and won a Georgia A.I.A. award in that year. The unique feature of the design is the exposed granite of the tunnel, which was left unfinished as the main decorative element of the station.

Marie Huper Pepe
Agnes Scott College

American Architects Directory (3d ed., 1970); *Antiques* (July 1970); Rob Beauchamp, Atlanta *Journal*/Atlanta *Constitution Weekend* (10 August 1985); *Progressive Architecture* (April 1959).

Anderson, Walter

(1903–1965) Painter.

Walter Inglis Anderson was born 29 September 1903 in New Orleans, La., and grew up in the Mississippi Gulf Coast region. Anderson's artistic curiosity, imagination, and love of nature were strongly influenced by his mother's interest in art, music, and literature. His professional art training began at the Parsons Institute in New York City when he was 20. From 1924 to 1928 Anderson studied at the Pennsylvania Academy of the Fine Arts under the supervision of Henry McCarter, an artist who had worked with the impressionists in Paris. The Cressen Award he received from the Academy in 1928 allowed Anderson to travel in France, where he studied the primitive cave paintings at Les Eyzies. McCarter's guidance and these cave paintings contributed to Anderson's strong sense of design and color.

In 1933 Anderson married Agnes Grinstead, and the couple settled down in an antebellum cottage nestled in the woods of Ocean Springs, Miss. The Andersons spent a delayed honeymoon trip canoeing down the Mississippi River two years later. During the mid-1930s he completed a WPA mural in the Ocean Springs High School and produced award-winning pottery for Shearwater Pottery, a business founded by his older brother, Peter, in 1928. Torn between the exacting demands of his job at Shearwater Pottery and his desire to pursue his own artistic career, Anderson suffered a nervous breakdown in 1937. He spent the next three years in and out of mental institutions.

Anderson rejoined his family in 1940 at the Oldfields Plantation near Gautier, Miss., where his father-in-law lived. While at Oldfields, Anderson reread classic books and transformed the texts into a series of block prints and line images. By 1946 his interest in epic illustration had faded, and he left his wife and three children at Oldfields in 1947 to return alone to his cottage in Ocean Springs.

Anderson spent most of the remainder of his life at the cottage fulfilling his fantasy of becoming an "alienado" and revitalized his naturalist painting through numerous jaunts to Horn Island off the Mississippi coast. Anderson often slept on the beach under a small, overturned skiff and sketched in the open. The Brooklyn Museum in New York featured his block prints and children's book illustrations in a 1949 exhibition, but his work entered many public collections as a result of a 1967–68 traveling exhibition organized by the Brooks Memorial Gallery in Memphis.

In 1951 he began one of his most complicated works, *Creation at Sunrise*, a 12-by-14-foot mural painted on the walls of his cottage. The theme of the mural is centered on Psalm 104. The animals, woods, and plants featured in the mural are modeled on those found in the Mississippi Gulf Coast. Light is used impressionistically in several phases of sunrise, morning, storm, noon, sunset, and night. The mural provides art historians with valuable insights into Anderson's often-misunderstood artistic spirit.

Since his death in New Orleans in 1965 Anderson's art has become more visible. Artist, voyager, and naturalist, Anderson created art for art's sake. A great body of his art has yet to be examined or cataloged.

Elizabeth McGehee
Salem College

Susan V. Donaldson, *Southern Quarterly* (Fall–Winter, 1985); Mary Anderson Stebly, *Sea, Earth, Sky: The Art of Walter Anderson* (1980); Redding S. Sugg, Jr., *The Horn Island Logs of Walter Inglis Anderson* (1973), *A Painter's Psalm: The Mural in Walter Anderson's Cottage* (1978), *Walter Anderson's Illustrations of Epic and Voyage* (1980).

Art Museums

Museums open to the public and displaying a wide range of arts have roots in royal and ecclesiastical collections going back before the Middle Ages. Not until the 18th century, growing out of the educational ideals of the Enlightenment, did museums as known today begin to take shape. Peale's Museum in Philadelphia and the Charleston Museum, both of which display works of art and a variety of natural history objects, are among the earliest of such institutions in the United States. In the second half of the 19th century, however, the great private or quasi-private art museums such as the Metropolitan Museum of Art in New York and the Boston Museum of Fine Arts, both founded in 1870, were established in the United States. Other distinguished art museums in this country founded before 1900 include the Brooklyn Museum (1823), the Albright-Knox Art Gallery in Buffalo (1862), the Philadelphia Museum of Art (1876), the Chicago Art Institute (1879), and the Cincinnati Art Museum (1881). In the South the three museums whose foundations go back to the 19th century are the Gibbes in Charleston (1858), the Telfair Academy in Savannah (1875), and the Valentine in Richmond (1892). (The Smithsonian Institution in Washington, D.C., was founded in 1846, but the subdivisions in which works of art and craft are the major focus mostly date from after 1937, when the National Gallery of Art was founded.)

In the 20th century, museums began to play an important role in the cultural and artistic life of communities in the South; before that time the relatively small size of the cities and the poor economy mitigated against their establishment. Artists, educators, and community leaders were among those who encouraged the founding of such museums. In the early years of this century, and even up to World War II, the opportunities for artists to exhibit their works were few, and they looked to museums as artistic centers where this could take place. Most of the major museums in the South still hold annual or biennial exhibits featuring local or regional artists. With the proliferation of private galleries and art dealers, especially since the 1950s, the need for museums to serve this function is less urgent but still important.

Both artists and educators were eager for the establishment of museums in which they would be able to see, without traveling great distances, something of the artistic heritage of the past. Artists learn much from other artists, both directly from their teachers and colleagues and indirectly from their study and perception of earlier works of art, and they supported efforts to establish museums. Educators, particularly those who taught art and art history, felt the need for their students and the general public to have the opportunity to see original works of art from other periods and places. Community leaders have shared these desires and have, in addition, perceived art museums as civic assets. Even so, the growth and development of museums in the South were slow and sporadic. Virtually all major southern cities now have a fine arts museum. These include Houston (1900), Dallas (1903), Atlanta (1905), New Orleans (1910), Jackson, Miss. (1911), Memphis (1913), Baltimore (1914), Louisville (1925), San Antonio (1926), Sarasota (1930), Montgomery (1930), Richmond (1934), West Palm Beach (1940), Columbia, S.C. (1950), Birmingham (1951), Columbus, Ga. (1952), Raleigh (1956), Nashville (1957), Little Rock (1960), Fort Worth (1961), and Mobile (1964). In addition to developing permanent collections, most of these museums now have lively educational programs of lectures, films, concerts, special tours, and children's programs. They also host traveling exhibitions, such as the extremely popular one of treasures from King Tut's tomb. New buildings for Atlanta's High Museum of Art, which opened in November of 1983, and Dallas's Museum of Art, which opened in January of 1985, have been hailed as major architectural achievements and as signs of growing public, especially commercial, support for arts in the South. Altogether these varied institutions offer a rich and diverse mix of education and recreation available to young and old alike.

Jessie Poesch
Tulane University

American Association of Museums, *Official Museum Directory* (1986).

Bearden, Romare

(1914–1988) Painter.

Born 2 September 1914 in Charlotte, N.C., Bearden attended public schools in New York and Pittsburgh but came back south to spend summers with his great-grandparents in Mecklenburg County, N.C. He received a B.S. in mathematics from New York University in 1935, studied at the Art Students League in New York (1936–37), worked on advanced mathematics at Columbia University (1943), served in the U.S. Army (1942–45), and went to Paris after the war to study philosophy and art at the Sorbonne (1951). He worked for the New York Department of Social Services off and on in the late 1930s and late 1940s, and then from 1952 to 1966. He traveled widely and tried his hand at songwriting in the early 1950s. He was art director of the Harlem Cultural Council for years beginning in 1964 and worked with the Alvin Ailey Ballet Company as artistic adviser. His works were exhibited at the Carnegie Museum in Pittsburgh, the Institute of Modern Art in Boston, and the Corcoran Gallery in Washington, D.C., among other places. He was the author of *The Painter's Mind* (with Carl Holty, 1969) and *Six Black Masters of American Art* (with Harry Henderson, 1972). Bearden died 11 March 1988.

Bearden applied cubist techniques to portraying the life of American blacks. He used large collages and montages, combining African imagery with the spatial dimensions of cubism. Sophisticated and modern in structure, his work also contains a decidedly traditional narrative story line. His themes are not exclusively southern, but many of his paintings treat the South explicitly. Typical subjects are jazz and blues, farm life, the rituals of baptism and voodoo, and perhaps above all, homecoming. His works on the South tend to be lyrical and evocative, to portray mythic characters, and to deal with elemental human concerns. *Sunset-Moonrise with Maudell Sleet* pictures a real-life North Carolina woman from his youth as a godlike figure in her garden. *Miss Bertha and Mr. Seth*, which portrays an elderly black couple posing, is again based on individuals he knew in North Carolina. Critic Ralph Pomeroy has observed that Bearden's thematic interests are so universal that he can "equate a field hand with a god" and mix the races so that "it is no surprise in his work to come upon, say, a hand that has both black and white fingers."

Charles Reagan Wilson
University of Mississippi

Julia Markus, *Smithsonian* (March 1981); Albert Murray, in *Romare Bearden, 1970–1980: An Exhibition Organized by the Mint Museum, Department of Art, Charlotte, North Carolina*, ed. Jerald L. Melbert and Milton J. Bloch (1980); Ralph Pomeroy, *Artnews* (October 1967); John Williams and Bundie Washington, *The Art of Romare Bearden* (1974).

Binford, Julien

(b. 1908) Painter and sculptor.

Binford, much acclaimed artist of Virginia, was born in Powhatan in 1908, the son of parents who traced their ancestry in America back many generations. At the age of 15 he moved with his family to Atlanta and eventually entered the premedical program at Emory University. He decided to become an artist and found encouragement from Roland McKinney, the newly appointed director of the High Museum of Art. On his recommendation Binford went to Chicago and enrolled in classes at the Art Institute of Chicago under the Russian artist and stage designer Boris Anisfeld, who was known as an expressive colorist. In 1932 Binford won the institute's coveted Ryerson Traveling Fellowship, and after three years of classes in Chicago the young artist was on his way to Paris. There he began experimenting with a variety of mediums and approaches, producing numerous pen-and-ink sketches, as well as a series of evocative gouaches that attracted the favor of French critics. His associates in Paris in this period included the writer Lucien Fabre and the poet Leon Paul Fargue. In 1934 the dealer Paul Guillaume saw the artist's work and declared that Binford possessed "the qualities of a painter and his gouaches show great imagination, spirit, and originality." Binford was subsequently given a one-man show at the Galerie Jean Charpentier and was able to sell some of his work.

Buoyed by his success, Binford ignored the advice of many of his Paris friends and returned to America in 1936. In May of that year he was given a one-man show at the Karl Freund Galleries in New York. One enthusiastic critic wrote that Binford's works displayed a "deep religious spirit, curiosity tinctured, we felt, with satire, their glowing color and extraordinary sensitivity, make them definitely worthy of your attention." Unfortunately, Binford's work attracted no buyers, and he and his French wife, Elizabeth, bought a patch of land in Powhatan, Va., with their savings. The land was verdant with swamp laurel and jewel weed, cedar and sycamore; on the banks of a stream named Fine Creek were the ruins of an old foundry, which the artist would later convert to a studio. He began painting the people and landscape of the area, mostly the black farmers who lived in relative poverty.

In March 1938 the struggling artist signed on with the Federal Arts Project of the Works Progress Administration, which paid him to produce paintings. He completed approximately 40 works prior to his termination with the project in August 1940. That year his work was featured in one of the Virginia Artists Series exhibitions hosted by the Virginia Museum. The artist was lauded for his portrayal of the life of his native state by the museum's director, Thomas Colt. "Return to America has meant a return to realism, which, to him, possesses all the color, all the structure, and all the emotional content of abstraction," he wrote. Binford was awarded the first Senior Fellowship given by the museum, and he established an art class at the Craig House Negro Art Center and taught classes in mural painting at the Richmond School of Art.

During World War II Binford occupied a studio in Hell's Kitchen in New York City and established a lifelong relationship with Midtown Galleries, which subsequently exhibited his work. He was assigned to the navy as a war correspondent for *Life* magazine and executed a number of sketches of New York Harbor in wartime and of convoy activities at sea, which today hang in the Pentagon in Washington, D.C. More significant, however, was his activity as a muralist in the same period. During his WPA tenure he had completed a mural depicting a logging scene in his native South for a post office in Forest, Miss. In 1942 the artist finished a powerful mural titled *The River Jordan* for the Shiloh Baptist Church, a black congregation in his native area. His paintings from this fertile period often portrayed the powerfully expressive gestures of the simple rural people he had grown to appreciate and respect. As one critic tellingly wrote in 1943, "For us it is a record of a people and a time and a place which is part of the heritage of America."

After the war Binford was appointed professor of art at Mary Washington College in Fredericksburg, Va., where he organized a series of exhibitions that helped form the university collection. In 1951 he completed a mural depicting the signing of the Virginia Declaration of Rights for the State Library in Richmond. Since that time the artist has completed several mural commissions and has been given numerous one-man shows. He restored the ruins of the old mill at Fine Creek into a livable structure, where he set up a spacious studio within its three-foot-thick blue granite walls. In his later work he reverted to limpid, yet colorful renditions of the cyclamens, iris, daisies, and violets that abounded around his house in the backwoods country that served as his source of artistic inspiration.

Rick Stewart
Dallas Museum of Art

Art Digest (August 1951); *Artnews* (15 November 1942); Elizabeth Binford, *American Artist* (April 1953); Virginia Museum of Fine Arts, *Painting in the South: 1564–1980* (1983).

Bottomley, William Lawrence

(1883–1951) Architect.

William Lawrence Bottomley made unique contributions to the practice of country house architecture in the South. Through the Georgian Revival houses he designed and through the publication of *Great Georgian Houses of America*, he exerted a distinctive and marked impression on country house design. Bottomley designed houses for clients throughout the South in the states of North Carolina, South Carolina, Florida, Alabama, Louisiana, Maryland, and West Virginia; his reputation was made through his commissioned houses for clients in Virginia.

Bottomley was born on 22 February 1883 in New York City. He received his B.S. in architecture from Columbia University in 1906. For a period he worked in the office of Heins and LaFarge in New York and in July 1907 was awarded the McKim Fellowship in Architecture at the American Academy in Rome. He remained in Rome for just over six months before leaving in March 1908 for Paris, where he succeeded on his entrance exam for the École des Beaux Arts. He returned to the United States in 1909 and married Harriet Townsend, an architectural writer whose mother was from Lexington, Va. Shortly thereafter he formed a partnership, Hewitt and Bottomley, which lasted until 1919, and then had a series of associates, including Edward C. Dean, with whom he worked on the Turtle Bay project. In 1928 he became the principal architect in the firm of Bottomley, Wagner, and White—which was formed largely to handle the design of River House in New York. Bottomley was made a fellow of the American Institute of Architects in 1944. He died on 1 February 1951.

Bottomley's early work had an eclectic flavor (influenced by his travels in Italy, France, and Spain), which can be seen in Turtle Bay Gardens and his stucco-covered houses. Another product of the early 1920s was *Spanish Details* (1924), which included photographs and drawings of portals, courtyards, windows, loggias, doors, ceilings, and ironwork and became a sourcebook for other architects.

His first house in Virginia, designed in 1915, was a classical five-bay house, covered in stucco; its form and organization reflected Georgian principles, which would dominate his work for the next 20 years. The following year he designed a house for H. L. Golsan on Richmond's Monument Avenue, the first of his red-brick Georgian houses in Virginia and the first of seven town houses he would design for this prestigious residential avenue. After these two houses, he gained a series of commissions in Richmond for other country houses and estates, including a beautiful range of houses at Windsor Farms on the hill above the James River, culminating in Milburne, designed in 1934 and completed in 1935.

The Richmond houses became well known in Virginia and helped to secure commissions for Bottomley throughout the state and the South. His designs for farm seats and hunting boxes in the Warrenton-Middleburg area and in Albemarle County, Va., were also published and led to new commissions. Most of the Georgian Revival houses were executed in red brick but notable exceptions included Lockerbie in Birmingham, Ala., and the William E. Chilton House in Charleston, W.Va., which are distinguished stone buildings. Tatton Hall in Raleigh, N.C., one of his important Georgian Revival houses of the mid-1930s, has a soft salmon-colored brick.

Bottomley's work was a product of early 20th-century interest in the architecture and gardens of the 18th and 19th centuries. His fame rests on the creation of the "ideal" Georgian Revival country house, especially in Virginia. Although the great 18th-century Virginia houses were his models, he reinterpreted them in a manner appropriate to the 20th century. Bottomley also served as chairman of the editorial committee under whose auspices the two-volume *Great Georgian Houses of America* (1933, 1937) was compiled. In the hands of younger architects these two volumes inspired a subsequent generation of houses.

Davyd Foard Hood
North Carolina Department of Cultural History
Raleigh, North Carolina

Davyd Foard Hood, "William Lawrence Bottomley in Virginia: The 'Neo-Georgian' House in Richmond" (M.A. thesis, University of Virginia, 1975); William B. O'Neal and Christopher Weeks, *The Work of William Lawrence Bottomley in Richmond* (1985).

Chapman, Conrad Wise

(1842–1910) Painter.

Chapman was born in Washington, D.C., where his father, Virginia-born John Gadsby Chapman, painted murals in the Capitol. He grew up in Rome, Italy, where the elder Chapman settled in 1848. His early instruction in art was provided by his father. Fired with devotion to Virginia, young Chapman returned to America with the outbreak of the Civil War in 1861 and enlisted in the Confederate army. He prepared numerous sketches of war scenes, especially in Virginia and South Carolina. In 1863 and 1864 he was assigned to depict the batteries and forts at Charleston, S.C. There he executed his unique and celebrated series of paintings of the Charleston defenses. In 1864 Chapman went briefly to Rome because of his mother's illness. When he returned, he landed in Texas, only to learn that the Civil War had ended.

Chapman joined Confederate General John B. Magruder in supporting Emperor Maximilian in Mexico. Magruder's group, however, soon disbanded. Enamored of the Mexican landscape, Chapman painted an impressive 14-foot-long canvas, the *Valley of Mexico,* a panoramic view of the entire valley. Some critics believe it to be the finest painting by an American of the Mexican landscape and have compared it with works by José Maria Velasco, Mexico's greatest 19th-century landscapist. In later years, Chapman resided in France, Italy, England, New York, and Virginia. Though he lived until 1910 (he died in Hampton, Va.), he completed his most memorable work by the early 1870s.

Conrad Wise Chapman is best known as the principal painter of the Confederacy. His small landscapes of Charleston are some of the most brilliant paintings associated with the Civil War. Each a masterpiece, these paintings—the result of Chapman's private romantic response to the call of sectional patriotism—are characterized by a freshness of color, an excellent use of the effects of light, a deftness of brushstroke, and a skillful use of minute detail. The Charleston paintings also demonstrate a rather extraordinary attitude toward the subject they depict. Though an ardent partisan of the Confederate cause, Chapman revealed in these paintings none of the propaganda elements that dominate many pictorial representations of wartime scenes. For his Charleston work and for his masterpiece, the *Valley of Mexico,* Chapman deserves increased recognition as an important American landscape artist.

L. Moody Simms, Jr.
Illinois State University

Louise F. Catterall, ed., *Conrad Wise Chapman, 1842–1910* (1962); L. Moody Simms, Jr., *Virginia Cavalcade* (Spring 1971).

Christenberry, William

(b. 1936) Photographer.

Born in Tuscaloosa, Ala., Christenberry's lifelong photographic preoccupation arose from a chance encounter with Walker Evans and James Agee's book, *Let Us Now Praise Famous Men*. Written largely about his native Hale County, Ala., the book, and a subsequent friendship with Evans, motivated Christenberry to make records of places familiar from his childhood: houses, barns, churches, graveyards, general stores, and commercial signs advertising such goods as snuff and cola. Christenberry teaches at the Corcoran Gallery in Washington, D.C., and returns each summer to photograph and to collect remnants of rural buildings, clapboard, rusted tin, and fading signs, which he reassembles into giant collages.

Christenberry photographs in color with subtlety and gentle restraint, as though with a bit of nostalgia for a South that has all but vanished. Christenberry's exqui-

A William Christenberry photograph of a new-made grave, north Mississippi, 1970s

sitely simple views evoke the presence of the inhabitants of 40 years ago.

Mary Louise Tucker
New Orleans, Louisiana

William Christenberry, *Southern Photographs* (1983); Frances Fralin, *Washington Photography: Images of the Eighties* (1982).

Cloar, Carroll

(b. 1913) Painter.

As a young boy growing up in Earle, Ark., Carroll Cloar remembered the regional stories and folktales that his parents and others told him. "I could actually remember how I visualized those things when I was told about them, and I painted that way," Cloar later recalled. "I've tried to keep a child's point of view, the simplicity, the wonder."

Cloar graduated from Southwestern College in Memphis, and after two years as a student at the Memphis Academy of Arts, he journeyed to New York and enrolled in the Art Students League, studying under Harry Sternberg and Ernest Fiene. In 1939, after nearly four years of study, he was awarded a MacDowell Traveling Fellowship from the league and used it to travel through Mexico. After service in the air force during World War II, Cloar received a Guggenheim Fellowship for 1946–47 and spent another year in Mexico painting in oil. Afterwards Cloar adopted tempera as his preferred medium, and between 1950 and 1954 he traveled to Central and South America and to Europe, intermittently living and working in New York. The European trip caused a significant change in his career. While there, the artist later recounted, "I just painted, copied things I thought were visually interesting—and then I began to have ideas for my paintings from childhood." Upon his return to America the artist moved to Memphis and began to explore the roots of his upbringing, examining old photographs and reacquainting himself with earlier memories.

Cloar adapted his painting style to one based on the expressive color and linear design of folk paintings, but with very sophisticated results. "I had a whole series of ideas, which I called Childhood Imagery, remembering how I thought of things as a child. The first one was *My Father Was as Big as a Tree.*" The work depicted his father, a burly former logger, standing alongside a stylized tree of similar height, while the artist was shown as a grim-faced child in a soapbox racer, far smaller and distant. Cloar's colors grew luminescent and dreamlike, while natural features were rendered with otherworldly uniformity. He exhibited at the Alan Gallery in New York and was praised by several critics as having a rare gift for observation and imagery. "The fact is, the image in art has neither beginning nor ending," Cloar wrote five years later. "It is a moment in time, isolated from the hours and days that surround it, and the vision comes to the artist whole." Cloar evoked vivid memories of his family and friends, their faces, dress, and customs locked in the eerie stillness of his paintings. Titles such as *Panthers Chasing the Little Girls*, *Brother Hinsley Wrestling with the Angel*, or *Charlie Mae and the Racoon Tree* are indicative of the rich lore of subject matter that Cloar tapped with his art. In 1959 he purchased an old frame house in Memphis and remodeled part of it into a studio and gallery. Next to the front entrance on the outside of the house the artist created a 14-foot-high mosaic depicting figures of children against a patterned background of flowers, which he titled *A Garden of Love*.

Much of Cloar's work since 1960 has portrayed the inhabitants of his native region in seemingly everyday tasks, such as laboring in a cotton field, killing time in front of a local store, or walking along a narrow country road; they are portrayed in such a way as to make the ordinary become extraordinary. One loses a sense of time, even a sense of specific place in these paintings. The viewer's own senses are sharpened by Cloar's use of rhythmic stroke and pattern, his intensified light and color. Shadows seem as palpable as solid forms, and the scenes take on a visionary resonance. Paintings such as *Where the Southern Cross the Yellow Dog* re-create, in an unforgettable way, the legacy of an incident in southern culture.

In 1969 he was given a priceless hoard of photographs taken by a black photographer in his hometown, and he began to incorporate some of the unidentified, haunting images into his work. All kinds of people, from WPA quilters to anonymous wedding guests, were transposed into the artist's dreamlike vision. "Cloar's real power, and it enables him to transcend mere eclecticism, derives from his feeling for time, especially past time," the painter and critic Sidney Tillim has written. "It is an identification so strong that even contemporary events or portraits, when represented by Cloar in his fastidious style, appear to have occurred long ago or seem to be passing into timelessness." Certainly Carroll Cloar, like William Faulkner, has evoked a South far beyond the mere commonplace and has elevated it to art.

Rick Stewart
Dallas Museum of Art

Catalog of Paintings by Carroll Cloar, Southwestern University Burrow Library Monograph #6 (1963); Paul Cummings, ed., *Dictionary of Contemporary American Artists* (4th ed., 1983); Guy Northrup, *Hostile Butterflies and Other Paintings by Carroll Cloar* (1977).

Dodd, Lamar

(b. 1909) Painter.

Lamar Dodd, one of the preeminent painters of Georgia, was born in Fairburn and received a five-year Certificate of Art and diploma from LaGrange High School in 1926.

After a short period as a student in the School of Architecture at the Georgia Institute of Technology, Dodd enrolled in the Art Students League of New York. He studied with Charles Bridgeman and Boardman Robinson and privately with George Luks, who had achieved his reputation as a member of Robert Henri's circle of urban realists. After a year back in LaGrange devoted entirely to painting, Dodd had his first one-man exhibition at the High Museum of Art in Atlanta. He then returned to the Art Students League for a period of further study with Jean Charlot and John Steuart Curry. The young Georgia artist was thus exposed to a range of gifted teachers who worked in traditional representative modes, most of whom believed in an art that depicted and elevated the everyday scene.

Dodd returned to the South in 1934 and spent the next three years honing his abilities, while holding down a job at an art supply store in Birmingham, Ala. His efforts were rewarded when he received an award at the annual national exhibition at the Art Institute of Chicago in 1936. His paintings in this period were portrayals of ordinary things in his environment that most people would overlook. For example, he made sketches of a slag dump, which he transported into evocative paintings that seemed to convey more than just an outward appearance. "I wanted to create a feeling of solid forms," he recalled of this period, "to capture the mood of a place."

In 1937 Lamar Dodd was named to the faculty of the art school at the University of Georgia at Athens. A short time later he was made head of the art department, and he embarked on a distinguished career as a teacher active in many educational, civic, and professional groups. Within a few years he was named one of the outstanding artists in America, with successful one-man exhibitions in New York at the Ferargil Galleries and in Washington at the Corcoran Gallery. He accepted a visiting professorship at the University of Southern California in 1942 and traveled through the Southwest. Similar jaunts in the Midwest followed, and he became president of the Association of Georgia Artists and of the Southeastern Art Association in 1946. Meanwhile, his painting continued to receive high praise. "What he portrays of Georgia is a more elusive and deeper quality, a turn of mind, a design for living, that may seem clannish to outsiders, but is rich in rewards for those born to it," his friend and former teacher Jean Charlot wrote in 1944. In 1948 Dodd was named Regents Professor of Art at the University of Georgia and assumed the presidency of the Southern States Art League. Many painting awards followed, as the artist gained fame as one of the outstanding painters of the South. By 1950 he had been awarded two Carnegie grants and was elected president of the College Art Association of America.

Lamar Dodd's painting had developed from an initial style of realism based on the language of forms to a more abstract version where formal considerations began to predominate. His paintings depicting cotton pickers toiling in a field, for example, conveyed their mood and situation by means of an expressionistic handling of form and color. "Dodd is a realist in that he finds his inspiration in his environing world," one critic wrote in 1949, "but his translation of his personal reactions to it reveal his subtle perception of the character of his visual experiences and of the relation of the things observed to one another." He was cited as a bold and vigorous colorist who achieved "poetry in the plastic language of the paint itself." Dodd continued to exhibit and lecture widely, including a stint in Europe for the United States Information Service in 1956. He was appointed a charter member of the U.S. Advisory Committee in the Arts the following year and participated in the first cultural exchange between the United States and the Soviet Union in 1958.

Perhaps one of the artist's most interesting honors was his appointment in 1963 as an official NASA artist for the Mercury Astronaut project; he covered Gordon Cooper's orbital spacecraft launching at Cape Canaveral. His resulting work was included in the landmark *Eyewitness to Space* exhibition at the National Gallery of Art in 1965. He again served as NASA artist in 1968 and 1969 for the *Apollo 7* and *Apollo 10* launchings. From this experience the artist produced a series of abstract works, some of which indicate his fascination with the idea described by one reviewer as the "poetic experience of men standing many thousands of miles outside the earth and looking back upon it as persons who are at once infinitely detached and yet very much of the earth." Dodd culminated his outstanding career by painting a frontier that is as yet unexplored; he had succeeded in translating his southern environment into the universal language of art.

Rick Stewart
Dallas Museum of Art

Lamar Dodd, *Lamar Dodd: A Retrospective Exhibition* (1970).

Douglas, Aaron

(1898–1979) Painter.

Aaron Douglas is widely regarded as one of the most important figures in the history of Afro-American art in the South, but his achievement is part of the larger history of American art as well. Born in Topeka, Kan., Douglas graduated from the University of Nebraska School of Fine Arts in 1925. A short time after that he moved to New York City, where he immediately came under the influence of Winold Reiss, who had done work based on a study of racial and folk types. Illustrations by both men appeared in Alain Locke's pioneering study, *The New Negro*, which was published that same year and among many other things called for the reexploration of African motifs in black art. Douglas's work appeared in many periodicals during the full flower of the Harlem Renaissance, including *Vanity Fair*, *Opportunity*, *Theatre Arts Monthly*, and important but short-lived little magazines like *Fire* and *Harlem*. In 1927 James Weldon Johnson published his book of sermons in verse titled *God's*

Trombones, with striking illustrations by Douglas, whose modernist style had been firmly established. The artist reexamined African and Egyptian forms and interpreted them by means of interlocking forms and colors based on a careful study of cubism and other modernist art movements. His paintings frequently depicted symbolic figures intertwined with planes and shafts of modulated light and subdued, yet rich color. Douglas attempted to convey the mystical or spiritual union of American blacks with their ancestral past through formal techniques that were richly evocative.

The most important work Douglas finished in this period was a series of murals, completed in 1934 under the auspices of the Public Works of Art Project, that portrayed the entire Afro-American experience. Four panels that the artist titled *Song of the Towers* depict, in succession, the African heritage, the Emancipation, life in the rural South, and urban dilemma. Douglas had been invited to execute a series of murals on black life for the library at Fisk University in Nashville, Tenn. In 1937 the artist accepted a teaching position there as head of the art department, a post he held until his retirement in 1966. Douglas's previous associations and friendships, as well as his outstanding ability as a teacher, enabled him to enrich the lives of generations of students. Aaron Douglas was one of the most respected, yet self-effacing, artists of the South in the modern period. To date there has been no adequate study or exhibition of his work, leaving a large gap in the art history of the South.

See also BLACK LIFE: / Johnson, James Weldon

Rick Stewart
Dallas Museum of Art

David C. Driskell, Gregory D. Ridley, and D. L. Graham, *Retrospective Exhibition: Paintings by Aaron Douglas* (1971); Nathan I. Huggins, *Harlem Renaissance* (1971).

Eggleston, William

(b. 1939) Photographer.

Eggleston was born in Memphis, Tenn., where he still resides. Eggleston photographs in color, using the dye transfer method, which produces colors of such richness and density that the subjects seem palpable; the very atmosphere is perceived—the clarity of a sky, dustiness of a country road, the heat of a fire, or the mustiness of a motel room. He is a master of detecting subject matter that will maximize the characteristics of his medium.

Images from his own cultural experiences as a member of a Delta farming family in northern Mississippi portray the encroachment of the urban-industrial spirit upon a community rooted in the habits and values of cotton farming. Eggleston pictures the abrupt boundaries between city pavements and country roads, suburban houses and rolling fields. His photos are about country people living in the city, and the imposition of urban customs upon them. His images also, conversely, affirm the tenacity of the Delta folkways. Eggleston has exhibited widely, including a one-man color show at the Museum of Modern Art, New York, in 1976. Eggleston photographed John Huston's production of *Annie*, and his work appeared in the 1982 book *Annie on Camera*. He also collaborated with David Byrne and the Talking Heads in the production of the film *True Stories*, and Eggleston's photographs will accompany descriptions of the making of the film in a forthcoming book.

Mary Louise Tucker
New Orleans, Louisiana

John Szarkowski, *William Eggleston's Guide with Essay* (1976).

Gwathmey, Robert

(b. 1903) Painter.

Gwathmey is a major exception to the generalization that the 20th-century renaissance in southern culture had little impact on the visual arts. His paintings reflected the same fascination with the South, its people, and its tradition that was found in the writing of novelists, poets, journalists, and historians of the Southern Renaissance. Like many of them, Gwathmey also felt the need to break free of the oppressiveness of the inherited southern culture and social order. Because his art often depicted sharecroppers and white planters in juxtaposition, it was first characterized as merely a southern version of the social realist painting of the 1930s. Only a few southern museums included his works in their collections, compounding the general problem that paintings were not very accessible to most southerners. This created the phenomenon of an artist who was better known and recognized in New York than in his native region.

Gwathmey, however, always considered himself a southerner. He was born in 1903 in Richmond, Va., where he was educated through high school. By the time he began attending North Carolina State in 1924, he had already had several jobs as a laborer. He received his first formal training in art at the Maryland Institute in Baltimore in 1925 and 1926, but he soon transferred to the prestigious Pennsylvania Academy of Fine Arts. While there, he learned art technique well enough to be awarded two European summer study fellowships. He taught at Beaver College and the Carnegie Institute in Pennsylvania and at the Cooper Union in New York City. A Rosenwald Fellowship enabled him to spend part of 1944 living and sketching on a farm in North Carolina. In the late 1930s he destroyed all his previous paintings and began to focus on southern themes. Some, such as *Poll Tax County* (1945), were bitter critiques of the white-controlled caste and political systems. Others, like *Painting of a Smile* (1953), were more subtle examinations of the vitality of black culture and the decadence of the white ruling class.

Gwathmey believed the South provided an ideal source

Robert Gwathmey, Hoeing *(1943)*

of inspiration for the visual artist because of the region's colorful vegetation and soil and its striking contrasts of black and white and of past and present. His complex painting *Space* (1964) incorporates commentary on southern involvement in space exploration as well as on the Freedom Rides and a decaying Confederate cannon and monument. Gwathmey's acceptance in the art world of New York led to a comfortable later life on Long Island with his North Carolina-born wife. His political activism brought him under FBI surveillance during the post–World War II period, and he remained a dissenter, particularly during the Vietnam War era. The largest public collection of his works is at the Hirshhorn Museum of the Smithsonian Institution in Washington, D.C.

Charles K. Piehl
Mankato State University

Paul Robeson, *Robert Gwathmey* (1946).

Johnson, William Henry

(1901–1970) Painter.

Johnson was an extremely prolific artist whose most important paintings, drawings, and prints concentrated on the history and culture of black people in the United States and especially the South.

Johnson was born in Florence, S.C., the oldest of four children (he had two sisters and a brother). His mother was black and part Sioux Indian, and his father was white. His name was taken from a stepfather, William Johnson, a sharecropper who became infirm while William Henry was still a boy. The young Johnson left school to work and help support his family. His teacher recalled that he was too poor to afford pencils and paper, but he would draw pictures in the dirt.

At age 17 he left Florence against the wishes of his family, determined to become a painter. He arrived in New York City and worked odd jobs, saving his money and sending some home to his family. In 1921 he was the first Afro-American to enroll in the National Academy of Design. During the next five years he won prizes for his achievements while studying with the noted American painter Charles Hawthorne. In 1926 he left for Europe to paint and remained there until 1938, except for one visit to the United States in 1930.

In 1930 he married Halcha Krake, a Danish ceramicist and weaver, and settled in Odense, Denmark. Together, for the next eight years, they worked in their studios and exhibited their artworks throughout Scandinavia and North Africa. By 1938 Johnson felt he had to return home to the United States to paint the history of his people. Living in Europe was becoming more difficult as World War II approached. He and his wife settled in

Harlem, where he began to produce his most important body of work. Most of his paintings, such as *Chain Gang* (1939–40), drew on the southern black experience.

In Europe his work was expressionistic, influenced most by the works of Soutine, Van Gogh, Munch, and Gauguin. Once Johnson returned to New York, his style shifted to pseudo narrative, almost cartoonish in its simplicity. Works such as *Jesus and Three Marys* and *Folk Family* particularly distinguish his style at this time, but the public was shocked by this seemingly radical change.

By the time of his wife's death in 1945, Johnson had already begun to show signs of his own illness in his work and in periods of irrational behavior. After his wife's death, he left the United States with all his works and was found wandering on the streets of Oslo, Norway. He was sent home to the United States and hospitalized at Central Islip, Long Island, suffering from syphillis. Johnson died in 1970. His entire collection represents one of the three largest holdings of a single American artist in the Smithsonian Institution, Washington, D.C.

Leslie King-Hammond
The Maryland Institute,
College of Art

Adelyn D. Breeskin, *William H. Johnson, 1901–1970* (1971); Alain Locke, *The American Magazine of Art* (July–December 1931).

Johnston, Frances Benjamin

(1864–1952) Photographer.

A native of Grafton, W.Va., Johnston studied art in Paris and at the Art Students League in New York but became dissatisfied with the state of academic American art and turned to newspaper illustration. She sensed the potential of photography in journalism, as it was "the more accurate medium." Johnston acquired a camera and studied under the direction of Thomas William Smillie, then in charge of the Division of Photography at the Smithsonian Institution.

Her first essays concerned political events in the capital. She also photographed the Kohinoor coal mines of Pennsylvania, the Mesabe iron ore range on Lake Superior, and female factory workers in Massachusetts. Johnston did not approach her assignments in the spirit of Jacob Riis, the social reformer, but as an objective reporter. In 1899 she was invited by Hampton Institute, an industrial school for blacks, to dramatize the progress of educated, upwardly mobile students and graduates. That public relations and fund-raising project led to an invitation to Tuskegee Institute in Alabama in 1902; she returned there and through 1906 photographed the students and their renowned educators Booker T. Washington and George Washington Carver. While in the area she also photographed, with dignity and sensitivity, poor, rural folk of Alabama. Throughout her career Johnston made portraits of outstanding Americans, such as Susan B. Anthony, Joel Chandler Harris, Theodore Roosevelt and his family, Samuel Clemens, Andrew Carnegie, Alexander Graham Bell, and Jacob Riis.

An interest in architecture and horticulture led to Johnston's greatest commission; she obtained a grant from the Carnegie Foundation to record southern colonial architecture. From 1933 to 1940, when Johnston was in her late sixties and early seventies, she traveled the Atlantic and Gulf Coast states, documenting every aspect of historic buildings and gardens, from mansions to farm buildings in every condition of repair. Her photographs convey a familiarity with the places and an appreciation for the former inhabitants. Several books resulted from the Carnegie survey, *The Early Architecture of North Carolina* (1941) and *Plantations of the Carolina Low Country* (1938) among them. In 1945 Johnston was awarded an honorary membership in the American Institute of Architects. Johnston lived in semiretirement in New Orleans during her last years and died there in 1952.

Mary Louise Tucker
New Orleans, Louisiana

Pete Daniel and Raymond Smock, *A Talent for Detail: The Photographs of Miss Frances Benjamin Johnston, 1889–1910* (1974).

Koch, Richard

(1889–1971) Architectural designer.

During a 55-year career, Koch established a practice diverse in its design approaches and pioneering in its efforts to preserve and adapt the unique architectural heritage of the South. His knowledge of various styles was clearly seen in his reinterpretation of early 19th-century Louisiana building forms. His fusion of then-current ideas of modern design with traditional forms resulted in his being awarded the Silver Medal of the Architectural League of New York in 1938.

Koch was born in New Orleans on 9 June 1889, the son of Anna Frotscher and Julius Koch, an architect-builder from Germany. In 1910 Richard Koch received his architectural degree from Tulane University and then studied at Atelier Bernier in Paris (1911–12). Between 1913 and 1915 he worked in the offices of Aymar Embury II in New York, John Russell Pope, who designed in Washington, D.C., and William Wells Bosworth in Boston. During this period he came to appreciate the architecture of colonial New England and New York.

In 1916 Koch returned to New Orleans and formed a partnership with Charles R. Armstrong, an association that lasted until 1935, interrupted only by Koch's duty as a first lieutenant in the Air Service of the U.S. Army from 1916 to 1918.

Early in his career Richard Koch established a reputation with his sensitive renovations of several important buildings in the Vieux Carré of New Orleans and followed these with work on two noted plantation houses

(Shadows-on-the-Teche in 1922 and Oak Alley in 1926). At Le Petit Theatre du Vieux Carré in 1922 he designed a new auditorium in a carefully detailed rendition of an earlier style—one of the first modern buildings in the French Quarter to be designed in this way.

The period 1933 to 1938 seems to have been a watershed in Koch's career; in 1933 he was appointed district officer for the Historic American Buildings Survey in Louisiana. In this capacity he directed teams of architects in making measured drawings of some of the finest early buildings in the state. This close examination of local historic buildings purged his original designs of elements not typical of the Creole and American Federal traditions—notably the Spanish influence seen in much of his work during the 1920s. His sensitivity to the historic environment led him to design quite differently in the Garden District of New Orleans from the way he did in the French Quarter, and to work in the Anglo-American tradition in Mississippi and the French tradition in south Louisiana.

In 1935 Armstrong left the partnership, and in the same year a new associate, Samuel Wilson, Jr., joined his firm; Wilson became a partner in 1955. Together, these two executed many more restorations, renovations, and new designs (some frankly modern, some in Koch's fusion style, and some in strictly historical styles). Koch's practice was always diverse—ranging from fine residences to offices, shops, banks, hospitals, and warehouses.

Koch served as president of the National Architectural Accrediting Board in 1954, and he was made a fellow of the American Institute of Architects in 1938. Koch continued to practice until his death on 20 September 1971.

Frank W. Masson
New Orleans, Louisiana

Hermande de Bachelleseebold, *Old Louisiana Plantation Homes and Family Ties*, vol. 2 (1941); William R. Cullison, *Louisiana History* (Fall 1977); New Orleans *Times-Picayune* (21 September 1971).

Laughlin, Clarence John

(1905–1985) Photographer.

Laughlin was born near New Iberia, La., in 1905. Five years later his family moved to New Orleans. Laughlin's early interest in the works of the pre-Raphaelite school led to a stronger intellectual commitment to the French symbolist writers—Baudelaire, Mallarmé, and Bergson. Their works confirmed his disillusion with the state of post-Depression society, an environment of decay, corruption, and poverty of spirit. Remnants of the past grandeur of Louisiana—the plantation houses, the mausoleums and tombs of its cemeteries, the colonial architecture of the city—became the constructs of his imagination and served his preference for an age that had vanished and his reaction against realism in an age of industrialization. Through contemporary magazines, Laughlin became aware of the work of Stieglitz, Strand, Atget, and Man Ray; the latter two artists especially reinforced his impulses for symbolism and surrealism. Laughlin's photographic vision was completely at odds with the popular pictorial style or the straight photography of artists such as Edward Weston or Ansel Adams. But Laughlin gained national recognition when his photographs were exhibited in New York in 1940 with those of Atget. The following year he published *New Orleans and the Living Past*.

During World War II Laughlin worked for the signal corps. After his discharge he returned to photography, working especially as a free-lance architectural photographer. In 1948 he published the monumental *Ghosts along the Mississippi*, began a long career of lecturing, and produced seven traveling photo exhibitions. *Ghosts along the Mississippi* was reissued in 1968.

Prior to his death in 1985, Laughlin remained active with his photography, book collecting, and writing. He did not feel the visual image self-sufficient, and added his own captions to amplify or clarify specific symbolism. Laughlin felt that his images provide clues to the mysterious forces that energize all living things.

Mary Louise Tucker
New Orleans, Louisiana

Mary Louise Tucker, *Modern Photography* (April 1977).

McCrady, John

(1911–1968) Painter.

John McCrady, best known as a painter of life in the South in the period between the two world wars, was born in the rectory of Grace Church in Canton, Miss. Soon after, his family moved first to Greenwood, Miss., and then to Hammond, La., where his father served as rector of the Episcopal church. In 1928 the family moved to Oxford, Miss., where the young McCrady eventually entered the University of Mississippi. His interest in art was already apparent, and during the summers in 1931 and 1932, he visited his brother in Philadelphia, where he enrolled in courses at the Pennsylvania Academy of Fine Arts. In 1932 he went to New Orleans and prepared for classes in the Arts and Crafts Club. After only a year's study he received a coveted scholarship to the Art Students League in New York City. There he studied very briefly with Thomas Hart Benton and much longer, and with more effect on his art, with Kenneth Hayes Miller. The influence of Miller's weighty figural style can be seen clearly on McCrady's subsequent work, and it was Miller as well who introduced the young southern artist to the multistage technique of painting, which used thin oil glazes over a tempera ground to achieve a brilliance and depth of surface.

McCrady returned to New Orleans in 1934 and within a year exhibited his work at the landmark exhibition *Thirty-Five Painters of the Deep South* at the Boyer Galleries in Philadelphia. The following year he was given his first one-man exhibition at the same galleries and had joined the Federal Arts Project of the Works Progress Administration. In 1937 the artist received national acclaim when his works, including the famous painting titled *Swing Low, Sweet Chariot,* were shown in New York. He was given a five-page spread in *Life* magazine, was praised by Stark Young in the pages of the *New Republic,* and was singled out by *Time* as "the purest example of regional art that turned up during the year." Such praise was high indeed in an age when regionalism was elevated to the status of a national religion, but in terms of southern culture McCrady was one of many talented artists in the period who chose to return to their own surroundings as inspiration for their art. McCrady was instrumental in the formation in 1938 of A New Southern Group, a New Orleans association of painters, sculptors, and graphic artists. He was commissioned by *Life* to paint "the second in a series of dramatic scenes in 20th Century American History," and chose the shooting of Huey Long. The same year, 1939, he received a Guggenheim fellowship to travel throughout the South to record the life and faith of the southern black, a trip that resulted in many notes and sketches.

In 1942 McCrady opened an art school in the Vieux Carré in New Orleans and began to receive the many commissions that would come to him throughout his artistic life. Although McCrady was praised by the American Institute of Arts and Letters in 1949 for his "warm poetic vision of life in the South," his work did not escape criticism as a "flagrant example of racial chauvinism." To contemporary eyes, McCrady's works do occasionally suffer from an overabundance of stereotype and caricature, but he was a product of his time, wrapped securely in the folk mythology of his native region. In his later years McCrady devoted much of his time to teaching and writing. As late as 1963 he pioneered what was termed the carbon acrylic method of painting, where a carbon sketch on a watercolor board served as the ground, over which were layered a number of acrylic glazes.

Rick Stewart
Dallas Museum of Art

Keith Marshall, *John McCrady, 1911–1968* (1975); *New Republic* (3 November 1937).

Mills, Robert

(1781–1855) Architect.

Born in Charleston, S.C., Robert Mills is often said to be the first native-born American to train specifically for a career in architecture. He served (c. 1799–1801) as an apprentice and draftsman under James Hoban during the construction of the White House, then enjoyed the use of Jefferson's architectural library and executed drawings for the new president. With letters of introduction from Jefferson, Mills toured the seaboard as far north as Boston. In 1803 he entered the office of Benjamin Henry Latrobe and worked in and about Philadelphia until 1809. In that year he married Eliza Barnwell Smith of Winchester, Va., and began his own practice as an architect and engineer in Philadelphia.

While still with Latrobe, Mills proved his competence with the plans for the South Carolina College (Columbia, 1802), the Circular Church (Charleston, 1804), the First Presbyterian Church (Augusta, Ga., 1807), and the Sansom Street Church and wings for Independence Hall (Philadelphia, 1808). His reputation was established in 1812 when he won the design competition for the Monumental Church in Richmond, Va. Here, and in his Burlington Jail (Mount Holly, N.J., 1808), his commitment to fireproof construction was manifest.

His design for the Washington Monument in Baltimore (1814) brought national acclaim. Based upon Trajan's Column, it was the first major monument to George Washington. A depression slowed construction of the monument, and in 1820 Mills moved his family to South Carolina, where he became the civil and military engineer of the state. During the ensuing decade he built canals, published an atlas and a description of the state, worked as a cartographer, and designed the South Carolina Insane Asylum (Columbia, 1821), the fireproof County Records Office (Charleston, 1822), and numerous less notable structures. This interlude in South Carolina may be viewed as a period of preparation for his return to Washington (1830) and his subsequent service to the federal government.

Although busy, he skirted poverty for five years. Then in 1836 the final phase of his career began auspiciously with the design for the U.S. Treasury and his appointment by Andrew Jackson as federal architect, a post he held until 1842. For the federal government he developed a series of customs houses and marine hospitals from Newburyport, Mass., to Mobile, Ala.; he designed the Patent Office (1839) and worked on various modifications of the U.S. Capitol. He also found time for private clients and for writing about municipal waterworks, navigation, railroads, and a route to the Pacific. In 1846 his design for the Washington Monument in Washington, D.C., was published. Despite significant modifications during construction (it was not completed until 1884), this remains his most famous work.

Robert Mills's career mirrored the early evolution of architecture as a profession in America. Aesthetically, his work reflected the growing impact of American pragmatism upon the revival styles of the 19th century. He was a major force in shaping the architectural landscape of the South and, like other southerners in the early Republic, he made vital contributions to the cultural form of the new nation.

John Morrill Bryan
University of South Carolina

John Morrill Bryan, *An Architectural History of the South Carolina College, 1801–1855* (1976), *Robert Mills, Architect, 1781–1855* (1976); Helen Mar Pierce Gallagher, *Robert Mills: Architect of the Washington Monument, 1781–1855* (1935).

Mizner, Addison

(1872–1933) Architect.

Born in Benicia, Calif., Addison Cairns Mizner revived a Spanish-style architecture in Florida and exerted a major influence on the development of Palm Beach. Although he had no formal training in architecture and, in fact, earned no degrees, he did study design in Guatemala and at the University of Salamanca, Spain. More importantly for his architectural career, he acquired practical experience while apprenticed from 1893 to 1896 to the architect Willis Polk in San Francisco and gained a broad knowledge of architecture from his extensive travels in China, Central America, and Europe. While in Guatemala, Mizner began trading in antiques and art. He finally received his license to practice architecture in 1919 from the state of Florida on the basis of the state's grandfather clause.

In 1904 Mizner settled in New York. From his society connections he soon had an active practice consisting principally of additions, renovations, and the design of new residences in New York State and throughout the Northeast. But most of his work, and the part on which his fame rests, was done in the South. In 1918 Mizner went to Florida to convalesce from an accident. That same year he designed the Everglades Club in Palm Beach for Paris Singer. The design of this exclusive club, Spanish-inspired with a flavor of Islam, was a grand architectural success. The club set the style for the rapidly growing winter resort and established Mizner's reputation. During the 1920s Mizner designed more than 100 buildings including clubs, theaters, hotels, entertainment complexes, and some of the grandest estates and mansions in the country. His designs are characterized by the the integration of interior rooms with exterior patios and courtyards, richly ornamented interiors, and elaborate portals.

In order to build his designs exactly, Mizner established his own factories for the manufacture of terra cotta, cast-iron, and cast-stone ornament and of new and "antique" furniture. Mizner also ventured into the field of city planning. He was responsible for the layout of the new resort of Boca Raton. These recreational facilities and hotels were finished before the Florida land collapse of 1926, which left Mizner bankrupt. While he continued to receive some commissions, he spent the last years of his life writing *The Many Mizners* (1932), an entertaining biography of his family.

Mizner single-handedly gave form and style to Palm Beach; his theatrical and picturesque architecture embodied the extravagant vacation lifestyle of the famous and wealthy. In the 1920s Mizner ranked as one of the United States's most prominent architects.

Karen Kingsley
Tulane University

Donald W. Curl, *Mizner's Florida: American Resort Architecture* (1984); Addison Cairns Mizner and Ida M. Tarbell, *The Florida Architecture of Addison Mizner* (1928); Anona Christina Orr-Cahall, "An Identification and Discussion of the Architecture and Decorative Arts of Addison Mizner (1872–1933)" (Ph.D. dissertation, Yale University, 1979).

Southern States Art League

The Southern States Art League, first named the All Southern Art Association, was created in 1921 to make possible the comprehensive exhibition of art about the South, including the best efforts of southern artists. Those artists judged excellent enough to represent the South did so at annual exhibitions, which were held in major southern cities, and at traveling circuit exhibitions that moved throughout the South.

The goals of the Southern States Art League were to increase public awareness of the talent of southern artists, to improve the artists' status, to encourage patronage and sales of members' works, to educate the public through traveling exhibitions of members' art, to hold a yearly conference to address issues important to the artists, and to publish a monthly newsletter to keep the membership informed. The league hoped to further art education in the South and therefore to assist the southern public in developing a sense of art values. It encouraged the formation of art programs at various southern schools and universities and stressed the need to develop southern art colonies. The league also hoped to enter the political arena and support legislation in Congress that would benefit the artist.

Although the Southern States Art League was chartered in 1921 in Charleston, S.C., administrative offices moved to New Orleans in 1923. Ellsworth Woodward (chairman of the Newcomb College School of Art) was at that time elected president, an office he held until his death in 1939. Ethel Hutson of New Orleans served as secretary until 1947. Membership grew steadily each year, although many members became inactive during the Depression and World War II. The Southern States Art League's records list membership as topping 600 in 1933, but actual names of artists in the records only number 425.

Yearly conventions in major southern cities provided a place for artists to meet, discuss pertinent issues, and exhibit and sell their works, and for the public to view and purchase southern art. The annual convention's exhibition drew increasing numbers of visitors every year, totaling 12,000 at the annual exhibition in Nashville, Tenn., in 1935. The traveling circuit exhibitions were the most effective means of making southern art available to southerners. Two circuits traveled every year, each displaying 30 or so works in large cities and small towns alike. Sales at conventions and traveling circuit exhibitions were usually quite low.

Evaluating the quality of the works shown is difficult; records indicate some titles, but few photographs survive, nor have more than a handful of originals been traced. Landscapes, flower paintings, and genre scenes seem to have dominated. League President Ellsworth Woodward regularly exhorted members to submit only top-quality works of art, but his admonitions often were not heeded.

With the death of Ellsworth Woodward in 1939 the league was weakened. James Chillman, director of the Houston Museum of Fine Arts, became president, but the headquarters remained in New Orleans. When Chillman retired in 1947, Benjamin E. Shute of Atlanta became president. The last conference was held in Richmond, Va., in the same year. Shute resigned within one year, and then Lamar Dodd took over, followed by Joseph Hutchinson of the Mint Museum in Charlotte, N.C. The league was officially dissolved in 1950.

Amy Kirschke
Tulane University

Amy Kirschke, "The Southern States Art League: An Overview" (M.A. thesis, Tulane University, 1983).

Valentine, Edward Virginius

(1838–1930) Sculptor.

The son of a prosperous merchant and a member of a family that had lived in Virginia since the middle of the 17th century, Valentine was born in Richmond, where he received his early education from tutors and private schools. He later attended the University of Virginia. Awarded a silver medal for a bust of the Apollo Belvedere in 1855, he began studying anatomy at the Medical College of Virginia the following year. After exhausting the resources of local artists, Valentine went abroad for further study. He studied in London in 1859, in Paris in 1859 and 1860, and in Italy in 1861. In 1861 Valentine went to Berlin, where he studied with the eminent August Kiss until the latter's death four years later. He then returned to Richmond and opened a studio as the Civil War was drawing to an end.

Though Reconstruction Richmond would seem to have been an unlikely place for a sculptor to practice his art, Valentine was successful in obtaining commissions and in selling genre sculptures. After Robert E. Lee's death late in 1870, Valentine received his most inspiring commission—the creation of a recumbent memorial statue of the general for the mausoleum attached to the Lee Chapel at Washington and Lee University. This work is undoubtedly Valentine's finest and most highly acclaimed work.

Valentine's Richmond studio teemed with activity during the 1880s and 1890s. During that period he was the South's best-known sculptor, and numerous examples of his work survive. In addition to his recumbent statue of Lee, among his best are his bronze standing figure of Lee for the Capitol's Statuary Hall in Washington; his statue of Thomas Jefferson for Richmond's Jefferson Hotel; and his bronze statue of Jefferson Davis atop the Davis monument in Richmond. Valentine remained active until his death in Richmond in 1930.

Post–Civil War southerners, by necessity, emphasized the practical and thereby tended to neglect—and sometimes even to smother—the creative spirit. Sculpture especially suffered from this mood and from the poverty that provoked it. Frequently viewed as exotic, sculpture was also expensive. Much of the more elaborate and impressive statuary executed in the postwar South was the work of imported hands. In Edward Virginius Valentine, however, the South produced a native-born sculptor who created works worthy of note. Valentine and his fellow sculptors taught a later generation of southerners that statuary could be an important source of inspiration. Through his sculpture Valentine hoped to give his ideals to the world and to remind southerners of the best of their heritage.

L. Moody Simms, Jr.
Illinois State University

L. Moody Simms, Jr., *Virginia Cavalcade* (Summer 1970); Elizabeth G. Valentine, *Dawn to Twilight: Work of Edward V. Valentine* (1929).

West, William Edward

(1788–1857) Painter.

West was born in Lexington, Ky., on 10 December 1788 to Edward West, Jr., a Virginian who had moved to Kentucky in 1784, and Maria Creed Brown. At an early age William Edward West traveled the Ohio and Mississippi rivers to Natchez and New Orleans and began an association with the Evans and Turner families of the Natchez region, whose relations and friends would provide his most important commissions.

West visited Philadelphia, possibly as early as 1808, where he met Washington Irving and Thomas Sully, two lifelong friends and influences. Although it seems unlikely that he actually studied with Sully, West undoubtedly observed Sully's painting techniques, absorbing those technical aspects of coloration Sully had witnessed in Gilbert Stuart's work. While in Philadelphia, West painted several members of the Gratz family. In the second decade of the 19th century West worked and traveled between Philadelphia and New Orleans. He had studios in Philadelphia (1809–17) and in New Orleans (1817–19) but was most productive in Natchez (1817–19).

West undertook more formal art study in Florence, Italy, and while he was there, George K. Bruen of New York commissioned a portrait of Lord Byron, the English romantic poet, for the American Academy in New York. West went to the poet's villa in Pisa and did the portrait. West lived in Florence until 1825, when he moved to Paris. One of West's best works, an allegorical portrait called *The Muses*, was painted there in 1825, the year West departed Paris for London.

Having gained notoriety as the last portraitist of Byron, West embarked upon a 12-year career as a highly successful Anglo-Saxon painter. He painted many of the most prominent members of the American financial and diplomatic community, and several of the genre or literary paintings that West exhibited at the Royal Academy were well received, especially *Annette Delarbre*, drawn from a story of Washington Irving. West also painted the English poetess Felicia Hemans, with whom he enjoyed a warm correspondence.

From 1832 to 1837 West was involved in financial speculations that left him bankrupt. He returned to Baltimore and opened a studio on Baltimore Street. The young Robert E. Lee, stopping en route to military engineering duties at St. Louis, was painted by West in 1838. West's Baltimore retrenchment was the most productive and successful period in his life. He repaid all his debts in England and amassed enough money to move into semiretirement in New York in 1841.

Throughout the 1840s West lived in New York City, painting various members of the Delano and Astor families and occasionally other New York society figures. He visited and traveled with Washington Irving and exhibited at the American Artist's Union. *The Confessional*, a religious picture, was much admired by Irving and was acquired by Thomas Jefferson Bryan for his "Christian Art" collection. In the late 1840s and early 1850s West painted the last of his Natchez commissions. In 1855 West moved to Nashville, Tenn., to live among his family, and there he died on 2 November 1857. He is buried in the old city cemetery.

West's early work has the spare elegance of the neoclassical portraits of Stuart and Sully. He was a superb colorist, and his portraits were marked by strong characterization and freshness and by deep and richly luminous eyes. A maturing of his style occurred during the years in Italy. An infatuation with mannerist composition revealed itself in his literary and allegorical pictures, especially *The Muses* and *The Present*, two of his finest works. His mature portraits, especially that of Lee, rank among the best work of the 19th century.

Estill Curtis Pennington
Lauren Rogers Museum of Art

William Dunlap, *History of the Rise and Progress of the Arts of Design in the United States* (1834; reprint 1969); Estill Curtis Pennington, *William Edward West (1788–1857): Kentucky Painter* (1985); Henry T. Tuckerman, *Book of the Artists, American Artist Life* (1867; reprint 1940); William Edward West Papers, Catalog of American Portraits, National Portrait Gallery, Smithsonian Institution, Washington, D.C.

Wiener, Samuel G.

(1896–1977) Architect.

Wiener was one of the earliest practitioners of modern architecture (the international style) in the United States and introduced the style to the South. Born in Monroe, La., Wiener received his bachelor of architecture degree from the University of Michigan in 1920 and attended the Atelier Gromort, Paris, in 1922 and 1923. He was the Shreveport partner in the Louisiana architectural firm of Jones, Roessle, Olschner, and Wiener from 1925 to 1940, after which he established a separate practice. Wiener's work of the 1920s employs a wide range of then-fashionable historical styles as well as art deco, of which the Municipal Auditorium, Shreveport (1929), is a particularly splendid example. In 1928 Wiener published *Venetian Houses and Details*. An increasing interest in the new European architecture he saw illustrated in architectural journals inspired a study visit to Europe for several months in 1931. Wiener's work after his return to Shreveport shows a complete break with the past and a total commitment to the ideals and forms of European modernism. During the 1930s Wiener was responsible for all his firm's work in the modern idiom. Wiener also accepted private commissions and sometimes worked in collaboration with his younger brother, William Wiener (1907–81), a 1929 graduate of the University of Michigan with an architectural practice in Shreveport.

Among the residences designed by Sam Wiener are the Wile-Schober House (1934) and the Flesh-Walker-Guillot House (1936), both in Shreveport, and a weekend house on Cross Lake (1933) in collaboration with his brother William. Particularly noteworthy is Sam Wiener's own residence designed in 1937. Other work includes the El Karubah Club on Cross Lake (1931); the Big Chain Store (1940); and several schools, including Bossier High School (1938–40). The very fine Shreveport Orthopedic Clinic (1936) was demolished in the 1970s. Wiener's major work was the Shreveport Municipal Incinerator built in 1935 from Public Works Aministration funds. Photographs of the incinerator were exhibited in the U.S. Pavilion at the Paris International Exposition of 1937 as one of the best examples of modern architecture in the United States and in exhibits organized by the Museum of Modern Art, New York. The incinerator photographs, also published extensively in major international and national architectural journals, brought Wiener much acclaim.

Although in startling formal contrast to traditional southern architecture, Wiener's buildings were designed for regional climatic conditions. His use of linear plans and wrap-around corner windows allows cross-ventilation; the light-colored walls have a cooling effect on the buildings; and planar overhangs protect interiors from the sun. Wiener's designs acquired a local character without reducing the ideals and formal qualities of modernism. Although Wiener maintained an active practice after 1940, his later work never matched the originality and boldness of his 1930s designs. Sam Wiener was a major contributor to and advocate of modern architecture in the United States.

Karen Kingsley
Tulane University

Architectural Forum (November 1935); Karen Kingsley, *Modernism in Louisiana: A Decade of Progress, 1930–1940* (1984).

Black Life

THOMAS C. HOLT
University of Chicago
CONSULTANT

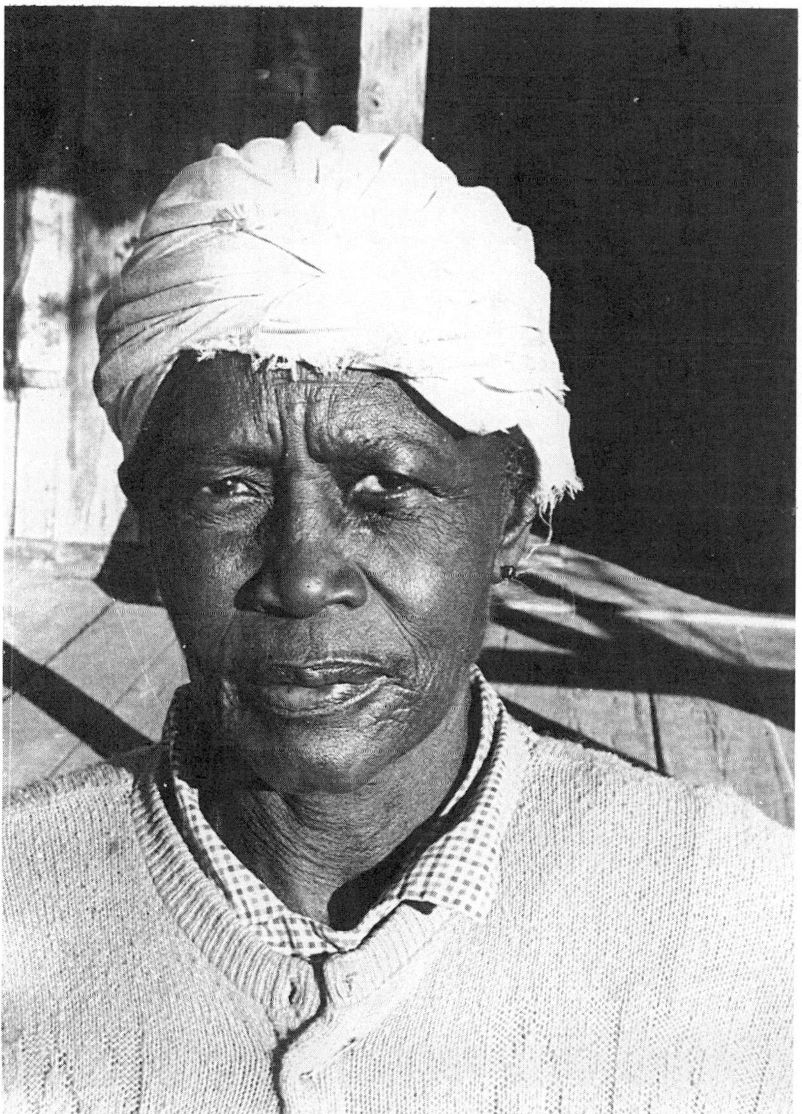

Rural Mississippi woman, 1970s

Black Life

Pre–Civil War Slave-Master Relations. On the eve of the Civil War the overwhelming majority of black Americans were southerners. They were an essential part of the South's labor force, raising its tobacco, cotton, hemp, and rice; mining its coal, salt, and gold; manning its few modern industries, such as textiles and ironworks; and building its railroads. Most performed these jobs as slaves. A minority were free. These free blacks worked in cities of the Lower South as craftsmen and as menial laborers and as owners or hired laborers on the farms of the Upper South. Slavery required a docile and cheap labor force; but at its margins it also permitted skilled black artisans, who claimed a proud, if tenuous, economic independence.

Civil War to World War I: Sharecroppers, Tenants, and Planters. In the decades between the Civil War and World War I, the overwhelming majority of black Americans remained in the rural South, working its farms and mines, while a growing minority labored in its cities. Black farm workers found themselves enmeshed in a system of tenancy and sharecropping that made a mockery of the freedom promised by the abolition of slavery. Black urban dwellers found themselves excluded from many of the crafts their fathers had worked before the war and from the newly developing southern industries. In both the cities and the countryside, blacks were subjected to a virulent racism, excluded from public institutions, denied normal social intercourse, and victimized by racist violence. During the century following emancipation, these economic and social structures of exploitation and exclusion decisively shaped northern as well as southern black life and culture.

Sharecropping and tenancy evolved after the Civil War and tied both blacks and whites to the land until the 1930s, giving way finally under economic and political pressures of New Deal agricultural reforms and war-induced demographic shifts. Well over 80 percent of black Americans lived on farms in the rural South in the late 19th century, and sharecropping touched their social, political, and economic lives.

Sharecropping and tenancy took shape during the first decade after the Civil War as the result of a standoff in the struggle between planters and their former slaves. Planters sought to maintain maximum control over their laborers, a control in which blacks saw uncomfortable similarities to slavery. For their part, the newly freed blacks wanted to escape the plantation, to have a farm and to make their own choices about where, when, and how their families lived and worked. But in order to achieve these goals they needed land.

Unfortunately, all government efforts at land reform for the benefit of the former slaves had failed. During the final months of the war, thousands of 40-acre plots had been distributed to black families along the South Carolina and Georgia coasts, and Congress passed legislation to facilitate permanent purchases by these settlers. But in the ensuing political struggle between Congress and President Andrew Johnson over Reconstruction policy, the settlers were eventually evicted. In 1866 a homestead law was passed to assist blacks in purchasing public land in the South; but the indifference and incompetence of federal officials charged with administering the law, the poor quality of the land, and the lack of material assistance to the settlers in clearing and developing the plots severely limited the law's effectiveness.

Despite the failure of these governmental initiatives, many blacks were able to purchase farms. Indeed, by 1900 one of every four black farmers owned his land. These successes occurred outside the major plantation areas of the Deep South. For the overwhelming majority of black people just emerging from the rigors of slavery, even the relatively low land prices of the postwar era were beyond their means. Furthermore, those who could scrape together the money experienced great difficulty getting white landowners to sell to them. In fact, black landowners were often targets of racial violence in the 1860s and 1870s.

Following emancipation there was a substantial reduction in the work force—as much as 37 percent by some economists' estimate—primarily because women, children, and the elderly greatly reduced the labor they gave to white estates. There were also collective work stoppages every year between 1865 and 1867. These "job actions," in which workers refused to sign or renew their contracts for the following year, panicked planters and forced wages up and improved working conditions.

Planters, despite their expressed preferences for a wage-and-gang labor system, were hard pressed to actually meet a payroll. Workers complained of not receiving the pay due them or receiving it late. The planters, who had always operated on credit in slavery days, simply did not command the credit to obtain cash for day-to-day operations. After emancipation they lost an important source of wealth and credit, because slaves represented as much as half the value of their property. The value of their other main asset, land, fell to historic lows. The planter—whatever his preferences regarding labor arrangements to replace slavery—found himself in a difficult position. He still had his land, but it was worth less than before the war and, in fact, was worthless if he could not get labor to work it.

Although southerners experimented with a number of other tenure and pay arrangements during the first decade following the Civil War, by the 1880s sharecropping and share tenancy were the dominant practices on tobacco and cotton farms. In this system the planter paid the worker with a share of the crop (usually half) at the end of the year rather than cash every day, week, or month. The worker and his family were assigned a plot of land to till and did not have to work in labor gangs under the direct supervision of the planter or his overseer, a practice they associated with slavery. The situation *looked like* a family farm even though blacks did not own the land.

But appearances were deceiving. In time the sharecropping arrangement came more and more to resemble a wage labor system with wages paid in kind. The planter controlled all matters related to the production and marketing of the crop. Indeed, the cropper could easily recognize his demeaned status by contrasting it with the situation of the share tenant. Southern tenants were mostly white, while black farmers were mostly croppers. Unlike croppers, tenants supplied their own tools, animals, and provisions and paid a share of the crop (usually a fourth of the cotton and a third of the corn) as rent. On rice and sugarcane properties the racial differences were sharper still: blacks worked for wages and tenancy was a status reserved for whites only.

Neither tenants nor sharecroppers prospered under the system. The landowner had solved his immediate credit problems by paying for labor in kind rather than in cash, but the farmer still needed credit to buy food, clothing, fertilizer, and other necessities for himself and his family until the crop came in. He received this credit from local merchants either directly or through the planter, but at an inflated cost. There were high markups on goods purchased on credit as compared to those bought with cash. A recent study found records from the 1880s showing markups, that is credit costs, ranging from 44 percent to 75 percent and averaging 59 percent. This was at a time when short-term interest rates in New York City were between 4 and 6 percent.

Given these extraordinary credit costs, it is easy to see how southern sharecroppers found it difficult to make ends meet. When the system was inaugurated in the 1870s, cotton prices were relatively high—around 30 and 40 cents a pound—but in the 1880s and 1890s the bubble of King Cotton burst on the world market, and by the 1890s depression it was down to 5 cents a pound. Farmers fell deeper in debt, and their debts were simply carried over from one year to another.

The plantation landlord and tenant farmer, historian Paul E. Mertz writes, became "graphic symbols of the South's ruralism, poverty, and cultural backwardness." They were symbols too of its paternalism, exploitation, and class oppression. The alliance formed between planters and merchants—sometimes cemented by marriages, family ties, or land purchases and defaulted mortgages—achieved a control over black labor and society that even slaveholders might have envied.

The sharecropping system and its attendant institutions imposed white supremacy on rural blacks, but a growing, significant minority of blacks lived in southern cities. Although most were menial day laborers, laundresses, and domestics, others continued prewar traditions of black craftsmanship. In cities like Charleston and New Orleans free blacks had dominated certain trades before the Civil War. Often they had been targets of protests by white workers resenting their competition. In the racial climate of the late 19th century, these protests bore fruit as blacks were increasingly excluded from their traditional trades, like carpentry, and denied access to skilled occupations tied to new technologies such as electricity. Black laborers were also turned away from cotton mills, the hope and symbol of the New South renaissance.

Excluded from the southern economic mainstream, blacks were also denied basic amenities of social life and opportunities for personal development. By the early 1900s public accommodations, transportation, schools, and the ballot box were either inaccessible or were accessible only under degrading and demeaning conditions. Blacks resisted the imposition of this American-style apartheid with bus and streetcar boycotts and court actions and by attempting political and economic alliances with various white dissidents, like the Populists and the Knights of Labor. But most of their traditional allies in the North, influenced by the rising racist tide, had deserted them; the national government was hostile, and the federal courts endorsed the southern system. Black initiatives and challenges brought forth greater violence as race rioters and lynch mobs terrorized black communities. In this setting, men who counseled acquiescence and accommodation, like Booker T. Washington, gained support from blacks and whites; while those insisting upon renewed and militant resistance, like W. E. B. Du Bois and Ida Wells-Barnett, made little headway before the massive demographic changes of World War I and the interwar years set in motion the winds of social change.

Post–World War I Struggles for Racial Equality. The economic opportunities created by World War I and World War II stimulated a dramatic exodus of blacks away from their ancestral roots in the rural South to the cities of the North and West. At the turn of the century, 90 percent of American blacks were southerners, an overwhelming majority of whom lived on farms. By 1960 only one of every two remained in the South, and only one of four lived in rural areas.

In addition to the attractions of industrial jobs and a seemingly more liberal racial climate in the North, blacks were driven out of the rural South by a massive transformation of southern agriculture. The Great Depression brought national attention to the problems associated with sharecropping and tenancy. But government policies intended to solve the problem of depressed commodity prices by reducing production had the effect of encouraging mechanization, farm consolidation, and the reduction of farm labor. Increasingly planters turned to seasonal wage laborers and turned their tenants off the land.

These changes facilitated the greatest political mobilization of black Americans since the Reconstruction era. Freed from the constraints of the rural South, blacks organized in both formal and informal political arenas. Beginning in the North during the 1920s, but spreading to southern cities by the 1940s and 1950s, blacks organized to protest segregation, Jim Crow, and job discrimination. With the advent of the New Deal, blacks became an important factor in national politics, and federal executive and judicial policies reflected the change. These political changes, together with a greatly augmented black intelligentsia and the revival of racial liberalism in the aftermath of Nazism, were essential precursors to the southern civil rights movement, which emerged full-blown in the late 1950s. When that movement had run its course, the face of southern institutions was radically transformed, as blacks voted and held office in unprecedented numbers, decisively influenced presidential politics, and enticed traditional white foes, like Governor George Wallace of Alabama, to recant their earlier racist views.

Cultural Support Systems among Blacks. The resources for this black militancy were not only in the demographic and geopolitical changes of post–World War II America, but in the inner recesses of the black community—in its institutions and its culture. In "freedom" as in slavery black people depended on cultural support systems provided by community and kin to survive degradation and oppression. In the rural South black families were the essential units embedded within an extended, intergenerational network of kin and friends that embraced secular and religious institutions. Churches, mutual aid associations, and schools were all peopled by parents, grandparents, aunts, cousins, and fictive kinfolk. Even in slavery blacks created customs, ceremonies, and rituals that reinforced their communal values and institutional ties. In freedom these cultural practices multiplied as weddings, funerals, church "homecomings," and family reunions provided occasions for renewing ties between individuals and their communities.

After kinship, religion was the most important value in southern black life. Slaves were not converted to Christianity in significant numbers until the era of the American Revolution and the creation of the Republic. But the specific content of religious doctrine mattered less than the institution of the independent black church. Free blacks established their own churches almost from the outset. Although slaves worshipped with their masters, they also held separate services led by their own slave preachers. With emancipation religious separation became open and formal as former slaves left their masters' churches to establish their own houses of worship. Churches provided venues for self-expression, affirmation of self-worth, and leadership in the black community from Reconstruction to the civil rights movement.

Closely associated with the church, and usually having overlapping membership, was the mutual benefit society.

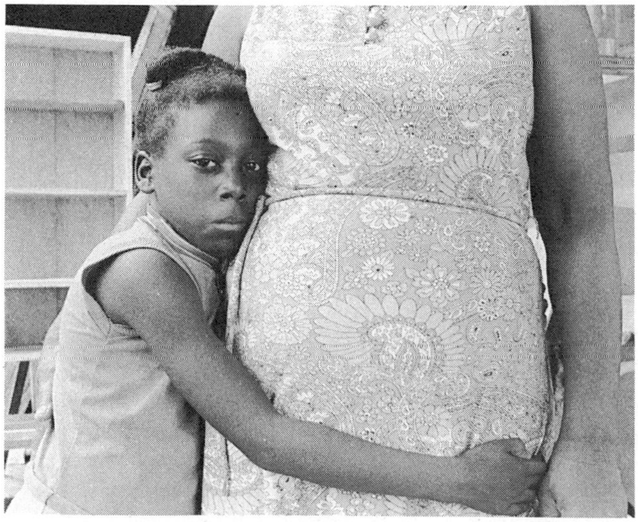

Young girl clinging to mother, 1970s

Indeed, a mutual aid association, the Free African Society, had been the precursor of the earliest black church, the A.M.E.'s Mother Bethel in Philadelphia. Fraternal orders and mutual benefit societies complemented the secular mission of the churches, pooling limited individual resources to provide a kind of social safety net. After slavery such organizations multiplied in the South, some of them providing the basis for business enterprises like banking and insurance. Maggie Lena Walker's leadership in the Independent Order of St. Luke, which sponsored a savings bank, a newspaper, and a variety of other community institutions, was one of the more prominent examples of this trend.

Creative Expressions of the Black Experience. The traditional black family, churches, and secular organizations provided for black southerners a sense of connectedness, of rootedness, which helps explain certain black cultural values and expressions, a special creativity that thrived despite oppression. There is a tension between tradition and innovation. Throughout black history African patterns of speech have been creolized, mixing features of the Old World with those of the New. The deep structure of an "African grammar," historian-folklorist Charles Joyner suggests, is blended with an English vocabulary to create something that is at once entirely new and yet still familiar.

Evidence of these patterns can be found in such cultural creations as language, religion, music, and folklore. Black aesthetic values, folklorist John Michael Vlach argues, are common in expressive arts as diverse as music, dance, quilting, and ironworking. These values emphasize experimentation, improvisation, and playfulness. Compositions are unbalanced, familiar motifs are combined in novel ways, and the results are often "crazy quilt" patterns that often test or invert the norm.

Performance is also a central feature of black oral tradition. Rapping, toasting, "signifying," and playing "the dozens" are as much a part of that performance tradition as folktales and music. The growth of black literacy in the 20th century created an audience for literary expression. Black poets, novelists, and playwrights drew on traditional oral forms grounded in southern black culture. Poets like Langston Hughes developed blues and jazz idioms, James Weldon Johnson celebrated spirituals and sermons, and Sterling Brown reshaped folklore, tall tales, and history.

Although a majority of black literary works were conceived and published outside the South, the region exerted a powerful influence on their themes, content, and forms. The South provided the cultural template for forms as diverse as jazz and rock and roll, spirituals and gospels, Brer Rabbit and Stagolee. The South provided the essential psychological landscape for a collective memory of suffering and survival. Like Quentin Compson in William Faulkner's *The Sound and the Fury*, black Americans have always had a love-hate relationship with the South. On the one hand, it symbolizes the worst that America has offered to blacks—racism, poverty, and oppression. But it also represents the roots of black culture, history, and "home." It is "down home" to blacks not

Martin Luther King, Jr. (in hat), and Stokely Carmichael (right) during civil rights march, Coldwater, Miss., 1966

born there; a "homeplace" for people whose fathers and mothers left decades ago. In community lore and joking it is a place to be escaped from; and yet a place that cannot be escaped. And finally, after the civil rights movement, it became a place to embrace: embraced less in optimism than in pride, because yet another generation had staked a blood-drenched claim to its equivocal legacy; embraced both for a sense of the possibilities it offered and in historical vindication for the many thousands gone.

See also AGRICULTURE: Sharecropping and Tenancy; ART AND ARCHITECTURE: Sculpture; Vernacular Architecture (Lowland South); EDUCATION: Desegregation; / Busing; Fisk University; Jackson State University; Piney Woods School; Tuskegee Institute; FOLKLIFE articles; INDUSTRY: Civil Rights and Business; LANGUAGE: Gullah; LAW: Civil Rights Movement; / Black Codes; *Brown* v. *Board of Education*; Greensboro Sit-in; Little Rock Crisis; *Plessy* v. *Ferguson*; Robinson, Spottswood W., III; Scott, Dred; Scottsboro Case; Slave Codes; MEDIA: Film, Blaxploitation; MUSIC articles; MYTHIC SOUTH: Racial Attitudes; SCIENCE AND MEDICINE: Racism, Scientific; URBANIZATION: Segregation, Residential; VIOLENCE: Literature and Song, Violence in Black; Race Riots; WOMEN'S LIFE: Race Relations and Women

Thomas C. Holt
University of Chicago

Ira Berlin, *Slaves without Masters: The Free Negro in the Antebellum South* (1974); Mary Frances Berry and John Blassingame, *Long Memory: The Black Experience in America* (1981); John Blassingame, *The Slave Community: Plantation Life in the Antebellum South* (1972); John B. Boles, *Black Southerners, 1619–1869* (1983); Dan T. Carter, *Scottsboro: A Tragedy of The American South* (1969); Robert Cruden, *The Negro in Reconstruction* (1969); John Hope Franklin, *From Slavery to Freedom: A History of Negro Americans* (1947; 5th ed., 1980); Eugene D. Genovese, *Roll, Jordan, Roll: The World the Slaves Made* (1974); Herbert G. Gutman, *The Black Family in Slavery and Freedom, 1750–1925* (1976); Louis R. Harlan, *The Maryland Historian* (Spring/Summer 1985); Darlene Clark Hine, ed., *The State of Afro-American History* (1986); Thomas C. Holt, *Black over White: Negro Political Leadership in South Carolina during Reconstruction* (1977); Winthrop D. Jordan, *White over Black: American Attitudes toward the Negro, 1550–1812* (1968); Charles Joyner, *Down by the Riverside: A South Carolina Slave Community* (1984); Lawrence W. Levine, *Black Culture and Black Consciousness: Afro-American Folk Thought from Slavery to Freedom* (1976); Sar A. Levitan, William B. Johnson, and Robert Taggart, *Still a Dream: The Changing Status of Blacks since 1960* (1975); Leon F. Litwack, *Been in the Storm So Long: The Aftermath of Slavery* (1979); Rayford W. Logan, *The Negro in American Life and Thought: The Nadir* (1954); Jay Mandle, *The Roots of Black Poverty: The Southern Plantation Economy after the Civil War* (1978); James M. McPherson et al., *Blacks in America: Bibliographical Essays* (1971); August Meier, *Negro Thought in America, 1880–1915* (1963), with Elliot M. Rudwick, *From Plantation to Ghetto* (1966); Howard N. Rabinowitz, *Race Relations in the Urban South, 1865–1900* (1978); Albert J. Raboteau, *Slave Religion: The "Invisible Institution" in the Antebellum South* (1978); Willie Lee Rose, *Rehearsal for Reconstruction: The Port Royal Experiment* (1964); Eileen Southern, *The Music of Black Americans: A History* (1971); Robert Farris Thompson, *Flash of the Spirit: African and Afro-American Art and Philosophy* (1983); John Michael Vlach, *The Afro-American Tradition in the Decorative Arts* (1978); Raymond Wolters, *Negroes and the Great Depression: The Problem of Economic Recovery* (1970); Peter Wood, *Black Majority: Negroes in Colonial South Carolina from 1670 through the Stono Rebellion* (1974); C. Vann Woodward, *The Strange Career of Jim Crow* (1955; 3d ed., 1974).

African Influences

In 1935 Melville J. Herskovits asked in the pages of the *New Republic* "What has Africa given America?" In his answer, a radical response for the time, he briefly mentioned the influence of blacks on American music, language, manners, and foodways. He found most of his examples, however, in the South. Fifty years later the answer to this question could be longer, perhaps less radical, but still surprising to many. Much of what people of African descent brought to the United States since 1619 has become so familiar to the general population, particularly in the South, that the black origins of specific customs and forms of expression have become blurred or forgotten altogether.

Consider, for example, the banjo. Not only is the instrument itself of African origin but so is its name. Although the banjo is encountered today chiefly in bluegrass ensembles where it is considered an instrument of the Appalachians, it was first played by slaves on Tidewater plantations in the 17th and 18th centuries. It was only taken up into the Piedmont and mountains during the 19th century by blacks working on railroad gangs. Although the contemporary banjo is physically quite different from its Afro-American folk antecedent, it retains nonetheless the unique sounds of its ringing high drone string and its drum head. These are the acoustic reminders of the instrument's African origins.

Linguists have noted that southern speech carries a remarkable load of African vocabulary. This assertion is all the more remarkable when we recall that white southerners have often claimed to have little interaction with blacks. Some regional words have murky origins, but there is no controversy for such terms as: *boogie, gumbo, tote, benne, goober, cooter, okra, jazz, mumbo-jumbo, hoodoo, mojo, cush,* and the affirmative and negative expressions *uh-huh* and *unh-uh*. All are traceable to African languages and usages. The term *guinea* is used as an adjective for a number of plants and animals that were imported long ago from Africa. Guinea hens, guinea worms, guinea grass, and guinea corn, now found throughout the South, are rarely thought of as exceptional, even though their names directly indicate their exotic African origins.

Beyond basic words blacks have created works of oral literature that have become favorite elements of southern folklore. Looking at the whole cycle of folktales with animal tricksters—those put into written form by Joel Chandler Harris and others—some may have European analogies but most appear to have entered the United States from Africa and the West Indies. The warnings they provide concerning the need for clever judgment and social solidarity are lessons taken to heart by both whites and blacks. The legacy of artful language in Afro-American culture is manifested further in other types of performance such as the sermon, the toast, and contests of ritual insult. For people who are denied social and economic power, verbal power provides important compensation. This is why men of words in the black community—the good talkers—are highly esteemed. The southern oratorical style has generally been noted as distinctive because of its pacing, and imagery and the demeanor of the speaker. Some of these traits heard in speeches and sermons are owed to black men of words who of necessity refined much of what is today accepted as standard southern "speechifying" into a very dramatic practice.

In the area of material culture blacks have generally been assumed to have made few contributions to southern life, but such an assessment is certainly in error. There have, over the last four centuries, existed distinctive traditions for Afro-American basketry, pottery, quilting, blacksmithing, boatbuilding, woodcarving, carpentry, and graveyard decoration. These achievements have gone unrecognized and unacknowledged. Take, for example, the shotgun house. Several million of these structures can be found all across the South, and some are now lived in by whites, although shotgun houses are generally associated with black neighborhoods. The first of these distinctive houses with their narrow shapes and gable entrances were built in New Orleans at the beginning of the 19th century by free people of color who were escaping the political revolution in Haiti. In the Caribbean such houses are used both in towns and the countryside; they were once used as slave quarters. Given its history, the design of the shotgun house should be understood as somewhat determined by African architectural concepts as well as Caribbean Indian and French colonial influences. Contemporary southern shotgun houses represent the last phase of an architectural evolution initiated in Africa, modified in the West Indies, and now in many southern locales dominating the cultural landscape.

The cultural expressions of the southern black population are integral to the regional experience. Although the South could still exist without banjos, Brer Rabbit, goobers, and shotgun houses, it would certainly be less interesting. The black elements of southern culture make the region more distinctive.

See also ETHNIC LIFE: Caribbean Influence; FOLKLIFE articles; LITERATURE: / Harris, Joel Chandler; MUSIC: / Banjo

John Michael Vlach
George Washington University

J. L. Dillard, *Black English* (1972); Dena J. Epstein, *Ethnomusicology* (September 1975); Melville J. Herskovits, *New Republic* (4 September 1935); Robert Farris Thompson, *Flash of the Spirit: African and Afro-American Art and Philosophy* (1983); John Michael Vlach, *Pioneer America* (January 1976), *The Afro-American Tradition in Decorative Arts* (1978).

Appalachians, Black

Black Appalachians are distinctive within southern culture because their historical and contemporary realities set them apart from other black southerners as well as from the millions of black migrants to northern industrial cities. Moreover, they are among the few blacks in

America to have existed as a racial minority in the midst of a cultural minority referred to as part of the culture of persistent poverty in America.

Despite the "discovery" of Appalachian whites by scholars, folklorists, and local color journalists in the late 19th century and the "rediscovery" of their incipient poverty during the Second Reconstruction of Lyndon Johnson's Great Society, little attention has focused on the blacks in their midst. The urbanization and migration of blacks from the South to the North has captured most attention from students of black life, as this became the central theme of the black experience for nearly a century. While Appalachian blacks share the same southern heritage as the millions of black urban migrants, their culture, work history, social homogeneity, and present status amidst considerable white poverty make them distinct from urban blacks and other rural nonfarm blacks in the South. Blacks in Appalachia are unlike other southern blacks for several reasons: (1) their migration was from one rural South area to another; (2) blacks in Appalachia are a very small proportion of the total population; and (3) poverty among black Appalachians is more severe than it is among other blacks—a fact of singular importance in a region characterized as culturally distinct and peripheral to national economic development.

The central and southern highlands of Appalachia cut a diagonal swath from northeast Alabama through Tennessee, Virginia, Georgia, Kentucky, across North and South Carolina, up to West Virginia. In 1980 blacks comprised nearly 9 percent of the estimated 12 million persons in this section of Appalachia. Though the Appalachian Regional Commission established boundaries that extend as far as upstate New York, Pennsylvania, and western Maryland, the central and southern sectors listed are commonly designated as Appalachia.

Black people have been in the southern region of Appalachia since it was colonized by the Scotch-Irish and German immigrants. Though not central to the subsistence agriculture of the highlands, blacks (more slave than free) comprised no less than 15 percent of the regional population between 1800 and 1870. After 1870 the number of blacks in Appalachia grew precipitously (as did the rest of the population) with the industrialization that followed the advent of railroads and the opening of coal mines. Coal mining—with its evolution from a labor-intensive to machine-intensive industry—had the greatest impact on Appalachian blacks in the Cumberland and Allegheny plateaus. Between 1880 and 1930 the growth rate of black populations in the coal-mining region followed the expansion of the industry itself. One study revealed that blacks constituted 53 percent of the miners in Alabama in 1930, and 27 percent in West Virginia, and they numbered nearly 10,000 in Kentucky. The role of blacks in the ranks of the United Mine Workers of America has yet to be clearly delineated, as black participation in antiunion activities during the 1900 to 1930 period overshadowed their strong commitment to labor.

The high emigration from Appalachia since the mid-1950s came in the wake of the decline of coal as an energy source. The mechanization of the industry led to

Black coal miners in Appalachia, date unknown

massive loss of jobs, and the rate of black movement away from the region was five times that of the general population. West Virginia blacks, for example, lost more than 15,000 coal-related jobs during the 1950–70 decades, and nearly 50 percent of the black population left the state. Blacks in the Harlan County, Ky., population were reduced by 75 percent during this same period. Although blacks in some portions of Appalachia, such as the South Carolina, Tennessee, and Alabama urban piedmonts, show stable and growing populations, few blacks in current remigration streams to the South are settling in rural Appalachia. Black emigration from the Allegheny and Cumberland plateaus from 1950 to 1970, then, seems to have had a lasting and final effect: the composition of the remaining black population in the coal regions portends a continuing decline and projection of "no blacks at all" in certain areas of eastern Kentucky, southwestern Virginia, eastern Tennessee, and southern West Virginia within a generation.

Blacks have been moving out of Appalachia steadily since 1930. Over the past half century they have resettled in many of the same cities chosen by the initial wave of blacks moving northward: Cincinnati, Cleveland, and Dayton, Ohio; Indianapolis, Gary, and Fort Wayne, Ind.; Detroit and other areas of employment related to the car industry; and the mills and manufacturing communities around metropolitan Chicago. To a lesser extent, black Appalachians have moved to the northeast corridor between Richmond, Va., and Boston, Mass. Eastern Kentucky's blacks cut a migratory stream to Lexington and Louisville in the state, though more can be found in northern Ohio and Michigan. The same applies to the thousands of West Virginia blacks who left since 1950. Smaller numbers of black Applachians in the southern highlands left the mountains to seek opportunities in nearby urban areas of Appalachia including Winston-Salem, N.C.; Knoxville, Tenn.; Roanoke, Va.; and Birmingham, Ala.; many went to the dominant city in the area, Atlanta, Ga.

Kinship networks, chronicled as the sustainers of white Applachian migratory streams, have also been of vital importance to blacks. The long-standing southern extended-family pattern was not generally interrupted in the move into Appalachia (as was the case for blacks moving to the cities at the turn of the century). Its stability has been noted as a life-sustaining link between mountain enclaves and the urban communities of the Midwest. Though generally well adjusted and assimilated in the industrial centers and suburbs, three generations of mountain blacks have developed strong family and community-of-origin networks. One exemplary case, the Eastern Kentucky Social Club, with large chapters in Illinois, Michigan, New York, Ohio, and Indiana sponsors yearly reunions and has hosted an average of 3,500 "homefolk" each Labor Day since 1970. In addition, these sojourners to eastern Kentucky's coalfields practice mutual assistance in the form of providing social and employment contacts for relocating persons and a variety of other civic, educational, and benevolent charities for "members."

Black Appalachians made notable contributions to mountain culture. Black slaves, for example, introduced an adaptation of an African musical instrument known as a "banjar" (banjo) to mountain life in the highlands as they crossed the Alleghenies with the first wave of white settlers in the 17th century. Clogging, that very popular form of mountain dance, was derived, at least in part, from slave dances such as the "Buck." Piedmont blues have remarkable parallels to the form of country and western music popularized in Nashville. Finally, shape-note singing of hymns was popular among black and white Appalachians as well.

A number of black Appalachians became "persons of note" outside the region. Booker T. Washington is perhaps the best known. Historian Carter G. Woodson, also born in West Virginia, was an early graduate of Kentucky's Berea College. Bill Withers, a popular black balladeer, is from a mountain family in West Virginia, as is television producer Tony Brown. Odetta, the well-known black folk singer, hails from northern Alabama; and black political activist Angela Davis comes from Birmingham. Nikki Giovanni, a prominent writer and poetess during the 1960s, is from Knoxville, which is also home to Sparky Rucker, one of the handful of contemporary black folk artists. Roberta Flack was raised in western North Carolina, and Chicago-based entrepreneur Gloria Proctor was born and raised in Black Mountain, N.C.

Appalachia was the locale for much of the ideological and political brainstorming that led to the momentous changes for blacks in American life. Capron Springs, W.Va., was the site of numerous meetings between northern industrialists-philanthropists and southern missionaries-educators to whom credit is given for carving out the "separate-but-equal" industrial colleges of the South. Sojourner Truth's Underground Railroad had some of its most reliable "stops" in the southern highlands. John Brown's coterie of abolitionists traced their roots to Appalachian emancipationists; the first antislavery newspaper, *The Emancipator*, was founded in Tennessee. Of course, Berea College has the distinction of holding the first biracial educational experiment in the South—the school was predominantly black up to the institutionalization of Jim Crow school systems. On the other hand, sleepy Clinton, Tenn., in the very heart of Appalachia, was the nation's test tube for public school desegregation. Finally, the world-shaking social revolutions sparked by the civil rights movement were begun as a series of community workshops on adult education for black southerners directed by Myles Horton at Tennessee's Highlander Center.

Any comparison of Appalachian blacks with the total Appalachian population shows their socioeconomic plight: they have a higher recent migration rate from the region; higher percentages of dependent persons; a higher percentage of female-headed families with children; lower educational levels; higher unemployment rates; lower job status; and higher incidences of poverty. Since half of all blacks in central and southern Appalachia are urban, they fall between rural blacks and urban blacks on most social indicators. Thus, they are generally "better off" than rural blacks—those concentrated in the Deep South—and are "worse off" than urban blacks. The prospects for blacks in Appalachia's coalfields are not good, although those in the southernmost states may stabilize and insure viable livelihoods.

The experiences of black Appalachians pose intriguing questions in regard to southern culture. How much have they borrowed from Appalachian whites in the form of peculiarly white Appalachian value patterns? How much of what is called Appalachian culture represents white assimilation of traits brought to the mountains by blacks as bondsmen? How much of the southern culture persists among black Appalachians today? Have they evolved a separate, though unrecognized, culture, either from the influence of white Appalachian culture or from isolation from other blacks? In what ways do race relations in Appalachia differ from those in the Deep South and northern industrial cities to which blacks migrated? Whether answers to such questions become important depends on the interest of Appalachian and southern scholars, policymakers, and citizens in examining a most unique case of southern ethnography, demography, and human ecology.

See also ENVIRONMENT: / Appalachian Mountains; ETHNIC LIFE: Mountain Culture; / Appalachians; MYTHIC SOUTH: Appalachian Culture; / Appalachian Myth

William H. Turner
University of Kentucky

Darold T. Barnum, *The Negro in the Bituminous Coal Mining Industry* (1970); David Bellows, "Appalachian Blacks: A Demographic Analysis" (M.A. thesis, Rutgers University, 1974); Michael Bruland, *The Status of Black People in Appalachia; A Statistical Profile* (1971); David A. Corbin, *Life, Work, and Rebellion in the Coal Fields: Southern West Virginia Coal Miners, 1880–1922* (1980); Ronald D. Eller, *Miners, Millhands, and Mountaineers: The Modernization of the Appalachian*

South (1982); Gloria Jackson and Ester Piovia, *Appalachia and Its Black Population: Selected Social and Economic Characteristics* (1972); Carter G. Woodson, *Journal of Negro History* (April 1916).

Architecture, Black

The African slave brought only the products of his mind to the New World, including the skills of ironworking and woodcarving and proficiency in the use of earth and stone. His innovations in the application of these skills qualified him as an architect alongside many other early American craftsmen.

The colonial plantation system relied upon its slave craftsmen to produce furniture, tools, and often buildings. In 1934, for example, historian Leila Sellers wrote about the Charleston, S.C., area: "Slaves had become proficient in every craft, even that of jeweler . . . the white artisan was virtually eliminated by 1790."

It was slaves who built the 10-room, two-and-a-half-story plantation called Magnolia in Plaquemines Parish, La., in 1795. Records and building technology reveal slave involvement in most early plantation construction throughout Louisiana. A few notable examples include Oakland in Bermuda, Cherokee in Natchez, and Kate Chopin's house, now the Bayou Folk Museum, in Cloutierville. When John Sims's house at Gippy Plantation in South Carolina was destroyed by fire, it was rebuilt in 1852 by slave artisans. Winsor Hall, the oldest landmark in Greenville, Ga., was designed and built in 1836 by Isaiah Wimbush, a slave artisan. Architectural characteristics such as steep, sloping hip roofs, central fireplaces, porches with wide overhanging roofs, and the use of earth and moss to construct walls suggest how elements of African architecture may have been introduced by slave builders.

Plantation records show that these slave artisans were also "hired out" or lent to other plantations. One example was James Bell, a Virginia slave who was brought to Huntsville, Ala., to design and build three spiral staircases for the Watkins-Moore Grayson mansion. Hiring out, however, seems to have been more widely practiced by urban slaveowners.

The papers of 19th-century entrepreneur Robert Jemision, Jr., of Alabama indicate he operated a school for slave artisans. His records of about 1830 show he had in his employ "two slave architects, Horace and Napoleon." Jemision, apparently pleased with Horace's work, introduced a bill in the 1845–46 session of the Alabama legislature to emancipate the slave architect. Horace King, as be became known, built some of Alabama's best constructed covered bridges. His 614-foot bridge spanning the Chattahoochee River was the longest of its type in the United States when it was built in 1873.

A contract drawn up in 1787 between Robin deLogny and "Charles," a free black carpenter, woodworker, and mason, indicated the existence of free black "architects" even before Horace King. The contract empowered Charles to construct Destrehan Plantation in St. Charles Parish, La., and specified that he be paid "one brute Negro, one cow and her calf, 50 quarts corn husks, and upon completion, 100 peastros." Because the contract only specified "a home 60 feet in length by 35 feet in width," we can assume the design was also by the builder Charles.

Besides free black artisans there were also free black planters who, often in efforts to emulate their white counterparts, built large plantation homes. In Louisiana there was Arlington (built in 1850 by Mignon Carlin), Cazelar house (built by Pierre Cazelar), and Parish Plantation (built by Andrew Drumford). After traveling through the 19th-century South, Frederick Law Olmsted wrote that the best houses and the most beautiful grounds that he had visited in Louisiana belonged to a nearly full-blooded black.

It is quite possible that the house Olmsted was referring to belonged to a son of Marie Therese, an exslave who gained her freedom in 1778, received two land grants from the Spanish government, and by 1803 had acquired at least 4,000 acres. Here she established Melrose Plantation, which became the center of the Metoyer landholdings of 13,000 acres, which, in turn, became known as Isle Brevelle, a settlement of "free people of color."

Louis Metoyer, one of Marie's 14 children, studied architecture in Paris and is responsible for the design of the Melrose mansion and many of the later buildings in Isle Brevelle. The main buildings of Melrose and its church, also built by Louis Metoyer, remain standing today. The most unusual of these buildings is the African house, built around 1800. Of purely African design, it is the only structure of its type now standing in the United States and recently was designated a national landmark.

By the end of the Reconstruction period, industrialization, trade unions, racism, and economic depression had dethroned the free black planter class and with it the black craftsman from his domination of the building trades. With the establishment of America's first school of architecture at the Massachusetts Institute of Technology in 1960, architecture began to be professionalized. The distinction between builder and architect was further sharpened in 1897 when Illinois required architects to be licensed by the state.

By 1890 there were 8,090 architects in the United States, 677 of whom were in the South. In 1910 there were 16,613, with 1,462 located in the southern states. Carter G. Woodson, using U.S. census figures, states in his book, *The Negro Professional and the Community*, that in 1890 there were 44 black architects, draftsmen, and inventors and in 1910 there were 54. His list for 1930 contains 45 black architects, none of whom were in southern states. Research has clearly shown that there were black architects in the South prior to 1930, and one can safely speculate that race played a role in determining who was classified as "architect."

In the South, at Booker T. Washington's Tuskegee Institute in Alabama, the first movement of black professional architecture was orchestrated. A closer examination of Washington's "normal school," which had been established to train teachers, reveals a most complete school of architecture within the department of mechanical industries. Tuskegee's early buildings were designed by department faculty members and were built under their supervision by students with student-made bricks. School records indicate that the department was established to make a profit and that it took on design and construction jobs outside the school. Course work included freehand drawing, drafting, and bookkeeping.

Almost without exception, early black architects began at Tuskegee, either as students or faculty members. Booker T. Washington recruited Robert R. Taylor in 1892 to develop the mechanical industries department. Taylor had been among the first blacks to graduate in architecture from MIT, and during his 41 years' tenure at Tuskegee, Taylor designed many of its major buildings, supervised overall campus planning and later became vice president of the Institute. He died suddenly on 13 December 1942, in the Institute's Butler Chapel, his favorite among his own early designs.

John A. Lankford, one of Taylor's earliest pupils, established the first known black professional architectural office in Jacksonville, Fla., in 1899. Prior to opening his office, Lankford had served as superintendent of Shaw University's Mechanical Industries Department, where he was responsible for the design of several buildings. In 1898 he designed and supervised the construction of the $100,000 Coleman Cotton Mill in Concord, N.C. Moving to Washington, D.C., in about 1901, Lankford became one of the leading black architects. He served as the national supervising architect to the A.M.E. church, for which he designed Big Bethel, a landmark of Atlanta's Auburn Avenue, and a church in Capetown, South Africa.

At least three members of Robert Taylor's Mechanical Industries Department faculty at Tuskegee made substantial architectural contributions. Wallace Rayfield, an 1899 graduate of the Pratt School of Architecture, established the first black architectural office in Birmingham, Ala. As with Lankford, much of his work was for churches. He later became the national architect for the A.M.E. Zion church. His designs include Ebenezer Baptist in Chicago and Birmingham's 16th Street Church, the church in which four little girls were killed in the mid–1960s bombing.

William Pittman, also a Tuskegee faculty member under Robert Taylor, moved to Washington, D.C., and worked with John Lankford before establishing his own office there in 1906. Architect Pittman gained the commission to design the Negro Building for the Jamestown Tricentennial in 1907. It was designed and built entirely by blacks and contained exhibits of "progress by the race."

A third Tuskegee faculty member and architect was Vertner A. Tandy. Graduating from Cornell University in 1908, he became the first black architect in New York state and was a leading resident of Harlem's famed Strivers' Row.

Among the black architects who did not attend Tuskegee was Julian Abele, who graduated from the University of Pennsylvania in 1902 and became the chief designer for Horace Trumbauer & Associates in Philadelphia. He was responsible for most of the firm's later work including the design for Duke University and the Duke family mansions in New York and New Jersey.

World War II had a profound effect on the development of black architects in America. In 1941 the War Department awarded a $4.2 million contract to the black architectural, engineering, and construction firm of McKissack & McKissack for the construction of Tuskegee Air Base. Hilyard Robinson, a Washington, D.C., architect, was awarded the architectural design contract. The project is seen today by many senior black architects as a milestone, since it was the only architectural work available to some of them. America's first black fighter squadron was trained at the Tuskegee base, and an organization of the Tuskegee airmen still exists today.

With funds available through the GI bill, black veterans received educational opportunities far exceeding those of previous generations. Racial segregation, however, limited their choices, creating unprecedented high enrollments at such black schools as Howard, Hampton, and Tuskegee, and contributed to the expansion of their faculty and programs.

Many veterans had first been exposed to these schools and their programs while in military training. Thus, John Spencer, AIA (now dean of Hampton's School of Architecture) returned to Hampton to study architecture after his U.S. Navy training there. David Byrd, AIA, president of the Huron Valley, Mich., chapter/AIA, and John Chase, AIA past president of the National Organization of Minority Architects, are also GI bill graduates of Hampton. Most significant, perhaps, was the growth of Howard's program in architecture, which resulted from GI bill enrollments.

The accreditation of Howard's School of Architecture in 1950, taken together with Washington's large black population, made the city the capital of black architects. The most recent AIA listing shows that the District of Columbia is the home of 32 black architects, 21 of whom are members of AIA. Another listing completed in 1971 notes 385 "minority persons" in architecture located in 38 different states and a total of 92 minority-owned firms. This listing shows that 40 percent of black architects and 46 percent of black-owned firms are in California, New York, and the District of Columbia. While there are fewer black architects in the southern states, there are more black-owned firms in the South.

Since 1967 there has been a considerable increase in the involvement of the black architect in AIA. At the 1968 Chicago convention, Taylor Culver was elected president of the Association of Student Chapters/AIA. At the 1970 Boston convention, Robert Nash, FAIA, of Washington, D.C., was elected vice president of the institute and became the first black to hold national office. The National Organization of Minority Architects (NOMA) was established in 1972 in Chicago, and Wendell Campbell, AIA, of Chicago was elected president of the new organization. A forerunner of NOMA was the National Technical Association, which was established in 1925 to bring together various black professionals, including architects and engineers.

Although blacks have inadequate representation in the profession, they are making significant strides toward full participation in America's architecture. There are now seven fully accredited predominantly black schools of architecture, and both black students and black faculty members can be seen at most schools of architecture.

See also ART AND ARCHITECTURE: Sculpture; Vernacular Architecture (Lowland South)

Richard K. Dozier
Tuskegee Institute

Charles A. Brown, *Biography of Wallace Rayfield* (1972); Richard K. Dozier, *Black Enterprise* (September 1976), *Black World* (May 1974), *AIA Journal* (July 1976); *Negro History Bulletin* (April 1940); William Quinn, *Tuesday Mazagine* (May and June 1972); Anson P. Stokes, *Tuskegee Institute: The First Fifty Years* (1931); Max Bennett Thrasher, *Tuskegee: Its Story and Its Work* (1900); Charles Wesley, *History of Alpha Phi Alpha Fraternity* (1975), *Crisis Magazine* (September 1916).

Art, Black

Many important black artists have come from the South. Some have shown influence of the region in their work, while others have shown no regional or ethnic tendency at all. Black artists were not recorded by name in the South during slavery. However, the works of anonymous craftsmen of that time have long been recognized for their quality. These works were found principally in Louisiana and the Carolinas, where architecture, balconies, wrought-iron gates, stairs, and columns of wood, as well as baskets, were made by blacks. The art of these craftsmen revealed the strong influence of West African imagery and technical skill that African slaves brought and passed down to later generations.

The earliest prominently known black artist in the South was Joshua Johnson. He became a very successful portrait painter in Baltimore soon after 1800 and worked there until at least 1827. Most of Johnson's patrons and subjects were white. His style of painting followed the popular limner tradition of the day: standardized formats, formulas of poses and accessories to which the face of the sitter was added. No other black artist of the time is known to have achieved his success or to have followed in his tradition. He was forgotten after his death and was not rediscovered until the 1940s.

Early in the 20th century black artists of the South became very influential. Because of their limited resources several developed multiple skills as artists, educators, art curators, and art critics. One of the first of these versatile persons was James Herring, who founded the art department at Howard University, Washington, D.C., in 1925 and the art gallery of the same university in 1930—the first such institutions established by black people. Over the years Howard has provided education for an impressive number of highly regarded black artists. The Howard University Art Gallery also provided exhibiting opportunities for many of the most respected white American artists of the 1930s and 1940s. In 1943 in Washington, D.C., James Herring and curator Alonzo Aden founded the Barnett-Aden Gallery, the first commercial black gallery in America and one of the most important galleries south of New York. Like the Howard Art Gallery, the Barnett-Aden showed an interracial mixture of artists, including some of the most respected white artists in the country. The gallery functioned until Herring's death in 1969.

In 1931 Hale Woodruff, a native of Cairo, Ill., moved from New York to teach at Atlanta University. He established the "Atlanta Annual," a competitive exhibition that was open to black artists throughout the country. The exhibition served as a major source of exposure for black artists, helped to improve black peoples' understanding of their art, and provided the South with another major center of art by blacks. Also in the 1930s Fisk University in Nashville, Tenn., started an art department, where the noted New York painter Aaron Douglas taught for many years.

Although Howard, Atlanta, and Fisk universities provided varying degrees of art education, few other opportunities existed for black artists to develop in the South. Many moved to the North either to begin or to further their study, yet many retained native regional sensibilities in their work in ways that reveal tendencies peculiar to black artists.

One such tendency is the use of satire to describe a black subculture. The tendency might have arisen in slavery as a social code that was permitted by whites who dismissed it as the harmless ways of a simple people. It is a satire that is self-deprecating, embracing insulting stereotypes with irony. Thus, blacks found wry humor in the comical exaggerations of their large lips, bulging eyes, large hands and feet, awkward movement, gaudy clothes, and love of watermelon. They relished this perversity not because they believed it, but because they wearied of escaping its stigma; so a negative definition became a common bond.

One artist who in the 1920s satirized the comical image of blacks through double entendre was Archibald Motley. His grotesque expressions of the stereotypical image of blacks and their life of debauchery created a surreal surface of glitter that camouflaged private loneliness. Motley's popularity declined by 1950, but his work regained attention in the late 1960s when black artists once again became fascinated with satirizing insulting stereotypes that others had created of them. Another painter from the South of Motley's generation whose work was in the same vein was Palmer Hayden. His sensibility was more rural than Motley's, and his art was less witty. Hayden used the stereotypes as a basis for abstraction. In his work large hands and feet, for example, became a basis for a new approach to figurative form. The massive and rough-hewn features Hayden depicted took his art in a direction that was both "naive" and "African"—naive in terms of its structural informality and pictorial inconsistencies, African in terms of its positive translation of West African sculptural character into painting.

Other southern black artists of the time transposed African forms into a black American imagery that played with the stereotypes of black features whites had created. Thus, a black American art began to emerge that was also related to cubism. Black artists of the South came from an environment that caused them to perceive their own bodies as a source of expression and stylization. Further, racial segregation forced their recognition of a cultural and artistic relationship to Africa.

Another artist of the time who discovered a relationship between black America and Africa was Augusta Savage, a realist sculptor whose forms were massive and brooding. A sculptor whose forms and subjects were pronouncedly African in sensibility was Richmond Barthé. Many of the artists who followed them took the black American relationship to African art as a point of departure, moving their ideas further into the realm of a "pan-African abstraction," in which the expressive structure of African art transcended the temporal subject matter to become the essence of their art. The stolid sculptural forms of Selma Burke fit this mold, too, as did the sculpture of Marion Perkins. Elizabeth Catlett's sculpture has been more angular but no less imbued with a feeling of African form. Eldzier Cortor, a painter, developed an elongated figure with African-American facial types in brooding surreal environments.

Some black artists from the South drew ideas from the evolved folk culture of Afro-Americans in the region. One such artist was William Henry Johnson, who had become a highly sophisticated painter before moving to Europe in the 1920s. When he returned to the United States in the late 1930s, he abandoned his international style and developed a simplified, two-dimensional form that reflected the vision of a naive. Through this form he explored the black folk experience in America, expressing themes of the family, religion, and war.

Romare Bearden, whose work began to mature around 1940, developed in a similar way. A master of collage, he shapes prismatic, two-dimensional images of black experiences, often reflecting an iconic character of his people's facial types and the psychology of their deprivation. Bearden extends Afro-American associations to Africa through the use of mask-type imagery and African patterns in his compositions. He has created another form of pan-Africanness even though his work has been profoundly affected by modernism, especially cubism and Matisse. Artists like Bearden and Johnson shaped a highly sophisticated art from the iconography of black folk culture.

The unschooled folk artists drew on and depicted folk visions. Because blacks were deprived of formal art training in the South, it is no surprise that many worked outside formal traditions. Each worked from a personal vision and improvised individualistic symbols, forms, and techniques. These artists include David Butler, Minnie Evans, William Edmundson, Clementine Hunter, and Elijah Pierce.

The art of other black artists from the South reveals no conspicuous ethnic tendency. Hughie Lee-Smith's subjects are black and white people set in desolate, surreal environments. Painter-printmaker James Wells is another who has developed a radiant expression and buoyant, figurative forms with which he explores religious themes. Alma Thomas gained international stature in the early 1970s for her abstract forms. In the late 1960s Leo Twiggs developed another range of abstraction through the use of fabrics, while Sam Gilliam extended the modern concept of painting by removing the canvas from the stretcher. Gilliam is credited with developing the concept of draped painting. Martin Puryear's work in wood has inspired a renewed sense of oneness between craftsmanship and the intrinsic expressive potential of the natural material. Other black artists include painters William T. Williams and Joe Overstreet; Merton Simpson has founded an important art gallery in New York. Benny Andrews, the son of sharecroppers in Madison, Ga., attended Ft. Valley State College and the University of Chicago before taking a B.F.A. from the Art Institute of Chicago in 1958. His paintings of the South stress rural living and contrast black and white life.

See also ART AND ARCHITECTURE: Painting and Painters; / Bearden, Romare; Douglas, Aaron; Johnson, William Henry; FOLKLIFE: Folk Painting; / Hunter, Clementine

Keith A. Morrison
University of Maryland

Theresa Dickason Cederholm, *Afro-American Artists: A Bio-bibliographical Directory* (1973); David C. Driskell, *Two Centuries of Black American Art* (1976); Elsa Honig Fine, *The Afro-American Artist* (1971); Lynda Roscoe Hartigan, *Sharing Traditions* (1985); Jane Livingston and John Beardsley, *Black Folk Art in America, 1930–1980* (1982); Keith A. Morrison, *Art in Washington and Its Afro-American Presence, 1940–1970* (1985); James A. Porter, *Modern Negro Art* (1943, reprint 1969); Virginia Museum of Fine Arts, *Painting in the South, 1954–1980* (1983).

Business, Black

West African slaves came from commercial economies and, wherever permitted in the New World, engaged in trade. The "Sunday markets" of the West Indies and South America were often dominated by Africans who filled them with produce from their garden plots. Such commercial activity, although less flourishing in North America, certainly existed, especially in colonial South Carolina. In fact a subeconomy carried on by slaves and free blacks in 18th-century South Carolina became so vigorous that the master class legislated against what it feared could become a political as well as an economic underground.

This tightening of the slave system against communication and assembly, the essence of trading activity, intensified during the 19th century, while simultaneously the number of new Africans became proportionately smaller after the closing of the slave trade in 1807. The tendency, then, was for American slaves to become increasingly socialized and assimilated into a dependent and isolated plantation life, while free blacks were squeezed into the bleakest margins of the southern economy. Unlike Latin America, the American South never had a black majority who out of demographic necessity would come to occupy many of the more favorable niches in the economy.

There were, of course, exceptions. Free blacks in South Carolina, where blacks were a majority, established in Charleston a small elite dealing in goods and services for a white clientele. Skilled craftsmen, especially masons, along with barbers, fishermen, grocers, and caterers constituted this specialized business class not only in Charleston but in New Orleans, Baltimore, Washington, D.C., and other southern cities. After emancipation, only the barbers retained a firm hold on these traditional black occupations. Black artisans, many of them ex-slaves, found themselves displaced by white workers and closed out of craft unions. Displacement and exclusion, however, did not dim the hopes of a rising class of black professionals and entrepreneurs who represented what Booker T. Washington called the "New Negro for a New Century," casting down their buckets in a New South.

Washington believed that business, above all else, could lift his people up from slavery. Beneath his rhetoric, Washington was no devotee of plantations and paternalism. He was bourgeois to the bone, a historical materialist on the right, who counseled that capitalism would neutralize racism and deliver from slavery all those who would attach themselves to its mighty engine. For black workers this ineluctable force might not work its magic overnight, but in the meantime they were well advised to invest their labor in the development of the New South, while the black middle class would "take advantage of the disadvantages" and build a duplicate black economy behind the walls of segregation.

Racial solidarity and black capitalism became watchwords in the face of an all-powerful Jim Crow. Benjamin J. Davis, a leading black businessman from Atlanta, reminded his colleagues in 1921 that "the white man does nothing with us that he can with a white man. He builds businesses for the employment of white boys and girls; we must build businesses for the employment of black boys and girls. We must have more producers of wealth." For the disciples of Washington, the black business movement amounted to middle-class millenarianism, with Washington presiding as the high priest, and the conventions of the National Negro Business League (founded by Washington in 1900) serving as camp meetings of the faithful testifying to salvation through enterprise.

In retrospect the business movement appears important mostly as myth and symbol, a bittersweet synthesis of two mainstays in American culture—capitalism and racism. But also there was substance. Black doctors, dentists, bankers, lawyers, journalists, and entrepreneurs, many of them educated in black institutions, took their places in black communities and served a black clientele. The highest statement of racial solidarity came from all-black southern towns, over 50 of which existed by 1910, each theoretically connected with the commercial life of the New South, but otherwise separate—each symbolizing a kind of utopian apartheid. By all odds the most famous was Mound Bayou, Miss., "a town owned and operated by our people," exulted a black reporter in 1912, a town where "a black mayor with his black aldermen sit in the council chambers making laws," where "a black marshall carries the billy, a black postmaster passes out the mail, a black ticket agent sells the tickets and the white man's waiting room is in the rear."

Although important ideologically, the black towns could not compete economically or culturally with the "Negro Mainstreets" of southern cities, such as Beale Street in Memphis or "Sweet Auburn" Avenue in Atlanta. In these ethnic enclaves, not unlike those of European immigrants in northern cities, a vibrant combination of commercial and cultural life gave black business a larger meaning in the everyday lives of the people. Without Booker T. Washington's faith in American capitalism, these black southerners nonetheless affirmed what had come to be theirs in every community large enough to support a commercial district. Business institutions ranged from "mom and pop" stores and juke joints to modern retail stores and essential services, and in the largest cities, newspapers, theaters, hotels, banks, and insurance companies.

The insurance firms deserve special mention because they formed the heart of black financial networks, the cultural beginnings of which can be traced to mutual benefit societies and the church. By the turn of the 20th century the burial insurance offered by the semisacred benefit societies and fraternal lodges increasingly gave way to industrial and ordinary insurance offered by secular enterprises like the North Carolina Mutual (1898) and Atlanta Life (1905). This process of modernization warmed the heart of Washington, and had he lived into the 1920s he would have joined in the celebration of Durham, N.C., as the "Capital of the Black Middle Class," the "Black Wall Street of America." By 1924 the North Carolina Mutual had spawned in Durham a commercial bank, a savings and loan institution, a fire insurance company, and along with a cotton mill and lesser enterprises, a national financial clearinghouse and chamber of commerce, the National Negro Finance Corporation (NNFC).

Symbolically, the failure of the NNFC in 1929 may have marked a turning point in the dream of black capitalism. The onset of the Great Depression, trenchant criticism from a new generation of leftist black academics, continuing black migration out of the South, and the impact of World War II and the civil rights movement on the accommodationist ideas of self help all played a part in the replacement of the dream of Booker T. Washington with the dream of Martin Luther King. The two were not necessarily mutually exclusive, however, and ambivalence on the liberating potential of black capitalism has continued to express itself. Ironically, integration in the South spelled doom for many black businesses whose customers chose to shop in white-owned stores, previously closed to them.

Future case studies may show that black business as culture and history has to be analyzed in subtle, creative ways outside the familiar models of protest and accommodation or neoclassical economics and Marxian theory. From the perspective of women's history, preliminary evidence would suggest that black women, less protected as they were than white women by the Victorian cult of domesticity, may have faced fewer internal barriers to entrepreneurial activity. The best 20th-century example of a black woman who apparently felt no such cultural restraints was Madame C. J. Walker, who took her cosmetics industry North and garnered great fame and fortune. But in the long run scholars may decide that the intimate association between black business and black culture, all within a poignant sense of community, went the way of Beale Street; and that it will be the creative music and the social memory that outlive the commercial meaning of these main streets.

See also INDUSTRY: / Insurance; MUSIC: / Beale Street; URBANIZATION: Segregation; Residential / Charleston; Memphis; New Orleans

Walter B. Weare
University of Wisconsin–Milwaukee

John H. Burrows, "The Necessity of Myth: A History of the National Negro Business League, 1900–1945" (Ph.D. dissertation, Auburn University, 1977); Louis R. Harlan, *Booker T. Washington: The Making of a Black Leader, 1856–1901* (1972), *Booker T. Washington: The Wizard of Tuskegee* (1983); Abram L. Harris, *The Negro as Capitalist: A Study of Banking and Business among American Negroes* (1936); Alexa B. Henderson, "A Twentieth-Century Black Enterprise: The Atlanta Life Insurance Company, 1905–1975" (Ph.D. dissertation, Georgia State University, 1975); August Meier, *Negro Thought in America, 1880–1915* (1963); Howard N. Rabinowitz, *Race Relations in the Urban South, 1865–1890* (1978); Arnold Taylor, *Travail and Triumph: Black Life and Culture in the South since the Civil War* (1976); David M. Tucker, *Lieutenant Lee of Beale Street* (1971); Walter B. Weare, *Black Business in the New South: A Social History of the North Carolina Mutual Life Insurance Company* (1973).

Creolization

Gullah is a creole language developed by the descendants of enslaved Africans in the Low Country and on the Sea Islands of South Carolina and Georgia. The earliest African slaves in these areas did not constitute a speech community as the term is used by sociolinguists. Their various African languages were often mutually unintelligible. The common language that they acquired was an English-based pidgin. Pidgin languages develop as a means by which speakers of diverse languages may communicate with one another. A pidgin has no native speakers: it is a second language by definition. But it became a native tongue when it was passed on to the American-born children of those enslaved Africans. Once a pidgin acquires native speakers, it is no longer considered a pidgin but is said to be a creole language. As a native tongue it must serve not merely the restricted functions of a pidgin, but all the functions of a language.

The process of linguistic change in which two or more languages converge to form a new native tongue is called by students of linguistic change "creolization." The creole language of Afro-American slaves in South Carolina and Georgia, Gullah, continued to develop—both in inner form and extended use—in a situation of language contact. There was reciprocal influence of African and English features upon both the creole and the regional standard. The English contribution was principally lexical; the African contribution was principally grammatical.

The process of linguistic change provides a model for explaining other aspects of the transformation from African to Afro-American culture. What might be called the "creolization of black culture" involves the unconscious "grammatical" principles of culture, the "deep structure" that generates specific cultural patterns. Such "grammatical" principles survived the Middle Passage and governed the selective adaptation of elements of both African and European culture. Herded together with others with whom they shared a common condition of servitude and some degree of cultural overlap, enslaved Africans were compelled to create a new language, a new religion, indeed a new culture.

Not only was the structure of the new language a result of the creolization process, but the structure of language use as well. The African preference for using indirect and highly ambiguous speech—for speaking in parables—was adapted by American-born slaves to a new natural, social, and linguistic environment. This aspect of the creolization process is strikingly evident in their proverbs. By employing the *grammar* of African proverb usage and the largely English *vocabulary* of the new creole language, Afro-Americans were able to transform older African proverbs into metaphors of their collective experience in the New World. Some African proverbs were simply translated into the new vocabulary; others underwent minor changes. Still others retained the semantics of the African proverbs but completely transmuted the rhetoric into metaphors more meaningful to the new environment.

Naming patterns exemplify another way in which Gullah-speaking slaves preserved their African linguistic heritage while also combining aspects of it with English. The traditional African custom of "basket-naming," or bestowing of private names, continued into the 20th century. As late as the Civil War, all seven West African day names, as well as other African basket names, appeared on slave lists in the South Carolina Low Country. But African continuities were not manifested solely in the static retentions of easily recognized African names. On the contrary, behind many of the apparently English names of the slaves were African naming patterns. In many cases African meanings were retained behind direct translation of names into English. Day names, in particular, were frequently translated into their English equivalents. But the creolization process, by which African *means* of using language were applied to a new tongue, produced such fresh seasonal basket names as *Christmas*. Similarly, black names revealed the adaptation to new places of the African pattern of naming after localities.

The creolization process was vividly exemplified in

black storytelling. The folk narrative tradition of Afro-Americans, like that of their African ancestors, was eclectic and creative. They took their sources where they found them, remembered what they found memorable, used what they found usable, and forgot the forgettable. Both inherited aesthetic grammars and the realities of the new environment played mediating roles in that process. Animal trickster tales constituted the most numerous type of folk narrative among Afro-Americans as among Africans, but Afro-Americans did not merely retain African trickster tales unchanged. On the contrary, the African narrative tradition was itself creative and innovative both in Africa and in America, where it encountered a strikingly different natural and social environment. Afro-American trickster tales indicate the black response to that new environment and efforts to manipulate it verbally and symbolically. In addition to animal trickster tales, the slaves narrated a cycle of human trickster tales in which the trickster role was not played by a surrogate slave—the rabbit—but by a real slave—John. Both animal and human trickster tales manifested continuities with African themes and with African traditions of indirect speech.

One of the most striking manifestations of the transformation of African cultures into Afro-American culture was in black religion. The slaves did not so much adapt to Christianity (at least not to the selective Christianity preached by their masters) as adapt Christianity to themselves. Just as the masters adapted Christianity to their own culture, so the slaves converted Christianity to theirs. God the judge of human behavior—God the master or overseer—was not the object of worship in Afro-Christianity, but a god more like African deities was: God the transcendent spirit. Blacks worshipped this new Christian deity in traditional African ways, and they made European religious forms serve traditional African religious functions. African religious beliefs and practices continued to flourish, however, in three distinct streams. One stream, including such practices as ecstatic trances and spirit possession as part of religious behavior, merged with Christianity, giving Afro-Christianity a distinctive touch. A second stream, which included belief in hags and witches, as well as in certain malign spirits, continued to exist among slave Christians as a sort of parallel consciousness, neither part of their Christianity nor completely outside of it. A third stream, including conjuration and sorcery, flourished as an underground alternative religious system in ways that ran quite counter to the doctrines of Christianity. What had been a unified religious outlook in Africa, in which virtually all experience was religious, had become fragmented and diversified in the new environment.

Creolization was illustrated as well in both the vocal and instrumental music of Afro-Americans. Their singing of secular songs as well as spirituals remained quite close to West African singing styles, their words often making incisive comments on the world of the local plantations. In instrumental music, the creolization process was exemplified both by continuities in instrumental preference with Africa—the banjo and the drums—and by the adaptation of such European instruments as the fiddle to Afro-American styles. Music, both vocal and instrumental, continued to serve African functions.

Afro-Americans adopted the grains, fruits, vegetables, and meats of the New World environment, but to those foodstuffs they applied an African culinary grammar—methods of cooking and spicing, remembered recipes, ancestral tastes. They added the *soul* ingredients. They not only maintained cultural continuity with West African cuisine, but adapted the African tradition creatively to the opportunities and necessities of a new culinary environment.

The clothing worn by the earliest generations of Afro-Americans, the slaves, served as an outward symbol of group identity and of the individual's place within the group. Just as in a folk community individuals are not completely free to express their individuality in dress, slaves were not completely free to express group consciousness and solidarity in their dress. If clothing is examined in relation to black community life as a whole, then how clothing is worn is seen to be as important as what is worn. A significant function of costume is that of differentiating between the workaday world and the festive world. The rhythmic alteration between work and festivity evident in the temporal life of the community was symbolized in Afro-American costume. For black slaves, that alternation distinguished between weekdays in the plantation fields and the festive air they gave to the weekends—the distinction between the time owed to the master and the time available for their purposes. They made Sundays the occasion for displaying not merely cleanliness but such finery as they possessed. During the week they might belong to the master, but on Sundays they emerged as self-respecting men and women.

Housing, too, reflected the creolization process. Many surviving slave cabins reflect the convergence of elements of African and European architecture. With facades that exemplify the vocabulary of European symmetry and control, they conceal floor plans marked by African spatial orientations. The long, narrow shotgun house type, which has emerged in the 20th century as a signpost of Afro-American culture, illustrates a similar convergence of cultures.

The creolization process was evident even in Afro-American work patterns. The early technological expertise that made possible rice cultivation on the South Carolina and Georgia coasts had come from Africans rather than Europeans, and numerous African continuities in planting, cultivation, threshing, and winnowing rice underlay the developing Euro-American economic networks and management techniques. The preference of black workers for communal labor, for hoeing in a line to the rhythm of work songs, strikingly exemplified continuity with African tradition. In many cases skilled black plantation craftsmen drew upon highly developed African technologies in metalwork, pottery, woodwork, leatherwork, and weaving. Even house servants played significant roles in the creolization of culture by serving as cultural intermediaries, taking African cultural patterns into the "big house" and European cultural patterns to the quarters. Blacks were not, after all, the only participants in the creolization process in South Carolina and Georgia Low Country, where blacks outnumbered whites by majorities of up to 10 to 1 in some places.

The study of linguistic creolization is a relatively recent phenomenon; the application of creolization theory to the study of Afro-American culture is in its infancy. It is but one explanation of cultural change; it is not the whole story. But it does represent a promising approach to understanding the transformation of diverse African cultures into Afro-American culture.

See also FOLKLIFE: Aesthetics, Afro-American; Clothing; Storytelling; / Proverbs; Shotgun House; HISTORY AND MANNERS: / Soul Food; LANGUAGE: Gullah; Indian Languages; / Indian Trade Languages; MUSIC: Spirituals; / Banjo; Fiddle

Charles Joyner
University of South Carolina—
Coastal Carolina College

Melville J. Herskovits, *The Myth of the Negro Past* (1941); Charles Joyner, *Down by the Riverside: A South Carolina Slave Community* (1984); Lawrence W. Levine, *Black Culture and Black Consciousness: Afro-American Folk Thought from Slavery to Freedom* (1978); Robert Farris Thompson, *Flash of the Spirit: African and Afro-American Art and Philosophy* (1983); John Michael Vlach, *The Afro-American Tradition in Decorative Arts* (1978); Peter Wood, *Black Majority: Negroes in Colonial South Carolina from 1670 through the Stono Rebellion* (1974).

Slave couple dancing, as portrayed in The Century Magazine, *February 1886*

Dance, Black

An enduring expressiveness, even during the oppression of slavery, marks the history of black dance in America, and through dance many aspects of the African heritage of black Americans thrive. As Lynne Fauley Emery in her seminal work *Black Dance in the United States from 1619 to 1970* (1972) explains, "A fundamental element of African aesthetic expression was the dance." When slave-traders plundered Africa, dance assumed new meaning. Aboard slaveships the traders frequently forced their captives to dance either for entertainment for the crew or for exercise (healthy slaves brought higher prices). Even under such conditions the slaveship dances served expressive purposes, too.

A strong African heritage flourished among slaves in the West Indies and spread to plantations of the American South. Among the dances carried over were the Calenda, the Chica, and the Juba or Jumba. The beat of the drum, an integral part of black dance, largely died out in the South after the so-called Stono insurrection in South Carolina in 1739, when escaping slaves beat drums to rally participants. Fearing a secret drum communication system among blacks, slaveowners pressed for prohibitions of slave assemblies and the use of drums. Except in the Georgia Sea Islands and Louisiana, slaves replaced the drum accompaniment to dances by slapping and patting their bodies, stomping their feet, and blowing reed pipes.

On southern plantations slaves danced both freely and under duress. Plantation owners often brought slaves to "the big house" to entertain through dance and music. Many owners prized slaves who danced well, and they sponsored dancing contests. Some owners allowed slave dances on their own plantations, and some gave written passes for slaves to attend dances on other plantations. Whites held conflicting views about black dance, however. Even those who enjoyed the slave entertainment tended to characterize black dances as heathen, lewd, and wild. Black dances, including ones such as the Ring Shout, which were part of religious services, met with particularly strong disapproval from white Protestants.

Occasions for dancing included funerals, weddings, quiltings, corn shuckings, Saturday evenings, and holidays such as Christmas and St. John's Day (June 24). Funeral dances in particular retained African elements, whereas wedding dances (called such despite prohibition of legal slave marriages on plantations) showed stronger European influences. Popular dances included the Buck, the Pigeon Wing, the Jig, the Cake-Walk, the Ring Dance, the Buzzard Lope, Water Dances, and the Juba. Agnes de Mille notes that the rhythm of such dances infused American dance and music with a new lifeblood through the accent on the offbeat or upbeat, a rhythm completely different from European styles. The cotillions, reels, and quadrilles of whites influenced black dances later in the antebellum period.

Black dance in New Orleans had its own character and

importance. New Orleans was one of the river-port cities where the Coonjine, or Counjaille, dance sprang up among the slaves who were hired out by their masters as stevedores or roustabouts. In the late 1700s and early 1800s quadroon women—those born to a mulatto mother and white father—sought to become the mistresses of upper-class white men and staged elaborate dances in order to form liaisons. The dances, however, represented white American and European trends rather than black ones. The dances of slaves at Congo Square, an open field "northwest of the city limits," contrasted sharply. Seeking to curb the influence of West Indian immigrants in the early 1800s, the New Orleans city council prohibited assemblies of slaves for dancing and other purposes except on Sundays in an open place. Congo Square, or Congo Plains, became that site. Drums were allowed as accompaniment to such popular dances as the Chica, the Babouille, the Cata, the Voudou, and the Congo. New Orleans blacks also witnessed special, frenzied voodoo ceremonial dances incorporating many African elements, and whites envisioned such dances as cannibalistic rituals. New Orleans's Mardi Gras began as a segregated event, and black participants devised their own festivities and incorporated dances in their parades.

Meanwhile, the minstrelsy tradition spread nationwide. "Even before the Revolutionary War," states Emery, "Americans were being entertained by impersonations of Negroes, and particularly of Negro dancing." In 1828 T. D. Rice, a northern performer, donned blackface and performed as Jim Crow, supposedly mimicking the dance of a crippled, elderly black groom he had seen. Historians generally agree with Emery that "Rice . . . rather than giving audiences a true picture of Negro dance, may have created the first clear-cut, long-lasting caricature of that dance: that grotesque, shuffling, peculiar, eccentric, jumping, loose-limbed, awkward, funny and, of course, rhythmic dance."

One outstanding exception among minstrel performers was the great black dancer William Henry Lane, known as Master Juba, who in his brief lifetime introduced a style that blended Irish and Afro-American dance. In general, though, minstrel shows parodied black life through incorporation of such dances as the Walk-Around and the Cake-Walk. Stereotypes of happy, naturally rhythmic, dancing blacks lingered long afterward. Even black minstrel performers of the 1860s felt compelled to wear wigs and paint exaggerating features to conform to white audiences' views of blacks. Among the black minstrel dancers who achieved great fame were Billy Kersands, member of the Georgia Minstrel troupe and master of the Virginia Essence dance, and Ernest Hogan, member of the Georgia Graduates minstrel troupe and originator of the Pasmala dance step.

In the 1890s increasing numbers of black performers entered the stage. In 1891 dancer Bill Robinson, a native of Richmond, Va., moved from Louisville, Ky., to New York with the popular show *The South before the War*. Robinson, later known as "Bojangles" and "The King of Tapology," broke barriers as the first black star of the Ziegfeld Follies but gained more recognition—and criticism—for film roles late in his career as the kindly, shuffling servant in scenes with Shirley Temple. Robinson's ability to create rhythmic sound through dance markedly shaped later tap-dancing trends. Throughout the 1920s black tap dancers such as Robinson and Clayton "Peg-Leg" Bates, a native of South Carolina, drew applause. Tap became associated with black dancers despite its origins in Irish and English clogging.

While groundbreaking shows such as *Darktown Follies* and *Shuffle Along* enthralled northern audiences with black song and dance, small black minstrel troupes continued to tour the South, eventually forming a vaudeville circuit called the Theatre Owners' Booking Association (TOBA). After the Civil War blacks in the South turned primarily to the churches as a social center. Many churches strongly disapproved of dance, yet traditions lived on. Emery describes one important trend: "There also developed a peculiar institution called the jook, or juke house. . . . Jook came to mean a Negro pleasure house: either a bawdy house or house for dancing, drinking, and gambling. It is in these jooks that 'the Negro dances circulated over the world' were created. Before being seen on the stage by the outside world, these dances made the rounds of Southern jukes."

Two highly popular dances that had such beginnings were the Black Bottom, which originated in Nashville, Tenn., and the Big Apple, which originated near Columbia, S.C. As masses of southern blacks moved to the North, particularly to Harlem, in the early 1900s, they took or influenced such dances as the Charleston, Ballin' the Jack, the Shimmy, and the Mooche. Other dances with black roots evolved, too, such as the Lindy Hop, Jitterbug, Shag, Suzi-Q, Camel Walk and Truckin'.

Progress came slowly in concert dance and classical ballet. Black dancers were long scorned because of American and European whites' standards of grace, beauty, and aesthetic purity. On an amateur level, however, The Hampton Institute Creative Dance Group (Hampton, Va.) pioneered in exploring black dance traditions in the South. Its student performers toured the country and emphasized dances based on both African and southern plantation traditions. The Hampton Institute programs both directly and indirectly influenced black dance trends, and Emery notes that "black concert dance companies were formed throughout the segregated institutions of the South, including Spellman College in Atlanta, Fisk University, Howard University, and Tuskegee Institute." Particularly at the South's predominantly black institutions strong programs in black dance still thrive.

In the realm of professional dance, black southerners have faced limited opportunities, though the black southern dance heritage has definitely influenced nationwide trends. By the 1970s black dancers and choreographers had made many inroads across the country. Alvin Ailey, a native of Texas who moved as a youth to Los Angeles, formed in 1958 the Alvin Ailey American Dance Theatre, one of the most highly acclaimed and widely known companies in the United States. Various famous productions have focused on themes of black experiences in the South, such as *District Storyville*, focusing on the early black jazz musicians who played in brothels in New Orleans, and Pearl Primus's *Strange Fruit*, dealing with lynchings of blacks in the South. Currently the South boasts such excellent showcases for dance performance as the Spoleto U.S.A. Festival in Charleston, S.C., and the American Dance Festival in Durham, N.C. Dance companies in the South include some that focus on black dance, such as the African-American Dance Ensemble of North Carolina, and many dance leaders encourage more exploration of forms that uniquely express all realms of black experience.

Blacks continue to influence popular dance styles, and singers such as James Brown often introduce a new dance with an accompanying song. Memphian Rufus Thomas began his musical career on the minstrel circuit and later recorded his "Funky Chicken," the title of both his song and the dance he popularized. Most recently, Michael Jackson has achieved international fame for his music and accompanying dance step, the "Moon Walk," a "post-modern" example of black dance no longer rooted in southern black culture.

See also FOLKLIFE: Voodoo; MUSIC: Dance, Development of; Minstrelsy; RECREATION: Mardi Gras; URBANIZATION: / Charleston; New Orleans

Sharon A. Sharp
University of Mississippi

Barbara N. Cohen-Stratymer, *Biographical Dictionary of Dance* (1982); *Dance Magazine* (May 1984, March 1985); Lynne F. Emery, *Black Dance in the United States from 1619 to 1970* (1972); Jane Goldberg, *Dance Scope* (Summer 1981); Cobbett Steinberg, ed., *The Dance Anthology* (1980); Ellen Switzer, *Dancers! Horizons in American Dance* (1982); Julinda L. Williams, *Dance Scope* (Spring 1980).

Education, Black

Formal education has been of vital importance to the status and aspirations of southern blacks. Denied to all but a few before the Civil War, it later became a barometer of discrimination, subject to successful court action and political protest. To individual black people throughout America it has been a main institutional means to gain personal respect, economic security, and racial progress. Its importance has long made black schooling the focus of much historical research by Carter G. Woodson, Horace Mann Bond, and other black scholars. Recent years have seen a new generation of highly critical scholarship that has placed the South in the context of the national political economy as it has probed reform movements, the southern class structure, and the role of schooling in "social control" by powerful interests, some of which have operated globally.

Beginning with mid-18th-century South Carolina legislation, the years prior to the Civil War witnessed the virtual elimination of formal education and literacy training for southern blacks, both slave and free. Although slavemasters might instruct one or two slaves to read in order to study the Scriptures, the idea of formal schools was another matter. Religious attitudes, some of which portrayed the black as subhuman, rationalized this situation and reinforced attitudes on the potential dangers of educated blacks to southern society, a theme that became a persistent phobia in southern history.

The Civil War spurred the growth of formal education. In 1868 the Hampton Institute was founded with the aid of the Union army. In 1865 the Bureau of Refugees, Freedmen, and Abandoned Lands was established by the federal government to provide general welfare. Within a year its mandate was extended to schooling and it began to provide a wide range of educational opportunities for blacks and poor whites. For five years it attracted teachers from the North and cooperated with missionary and religious organizations, assisting newly founded institutions, including Hampton, Fisk University (1865), Berea College (1855), and Atlanta University (1865). In 1867 Howard University, which was named after General O. O. Howard, the commissioner of the Freedmen's Bureau, was chartered in Washington, D.C., by the federal government. Immediately after the war most states set up school funds, although in many instances blacks had to pay special taxes in addition to those required of all citizens. In sum, there was a widespread black enthusiasm for education and a recognition that it was a key to economic and political power—a belief not usually shared by even those whites interested in black schooling.

Black legislators played an important role in the establishment of public education systems throughout the South, but their influence waned dramatically after the end of Reconstruction. The Ku Klux Klan had found schools a ready target in that era, and afterwards the forces of disfranchisement, discrimination, and segregation soon began to flourish. Attitudes that reinforced black inferiority were institutionalized in the work of Hampton and the Tuskegee Institute (1881), particularly after the 1895 "Atlanta Compromise" address by the latter's principal, Booker T. Washington. An internationally known advocate of industrial education and vocational labor, Washington became a leading symbol of black accommodation to political disfranchisement and exercised considerable influence over the quality of segregated and underfunded black educational institutions and systems throughout the South.

In 1896 the U.S. Supreme Court ruled in favor of "separate-but-equal" facilities for blacks in *Plessy* v. *Ferguson*. This decision legalized segregation and led to increased patterns of underfunding for black education even though white middle-class "progressive" politicians, often in concert with populist allies, soon improved all public education, partly to accommodate and pacify poor whites. Black colleges, which in many cases were little more than secondary schools, received unequal funding from state or, under land-grant provisions, federal sources. Many remained controlled by whites who believed in black inferiority and who consequently administered them in highly authoritarian fashion, a mode of control shared by some black college presidents. Although Hampton, Tuskegee, Fisk, and many other institutions trained black teachers, very few opportunities for graduate study or professional training existed in the South, and only Meharry Medical College (1876) in Nashville and Howard in Washington offered training in medicine, and the latter in law, of a quality comparable to that available in white universities. Black medical education faced the additional burden of a Carnegie Foundation report by Abraham Flexner in 1910, which recommended that medical needs among blacks be treated as community health issues, thereby affecting the quality of training and reinforcing fears about blacks as a "health menace." The legacy of the black medical schools is still very evident. As of 1983 almost half of all black physicians and dentists practicing in the United States had completed their professional training at Meharry.

By the early years of the 20th century protest was under way, expressed through the Niagara Movement and the founding of the National Association for the Advancement of Colored People. W. E. B. Du Bois, a Harvard-trained professor at Atlanta University, visibly opposed black accommodation and Booker T. Washington's "Tuskegee Machine." He encouraged research on black life, challenged black students to demand changes in collegiate conditions, and corrected stereotypes of black people and their African ancestry. Du Bois edited the NAACP's *Crisis*, a journal of signal importance to blacks and to white sympathizers. Consistent with his call for a black "talented tenth," a new generation of leaders, many of whom were trained at Howard University's Law School, used the courts successfully to challenge unequal resources, inferior conditions, disfranchisement, and, in the landmark *Brown* v. *Board of Education* (1954), de jure segregation itself. The pages of the *Journal of Negro Education*, founded in 1932 at Howard, published the research and political ideas of educators who documented the status of black education throughout the United States and, indeed, in other parts of the world.

The development of a public educational system for southern blacks was plagued by their rural status, inferior facilities, poorly trained teachers and administrators, white hostility, and a new technology that permitted whites to bus their children away from blacks. In cities like Atlanta, high schools came very late and their peculiar "vocational" and "industrial" emphasis was of little relevance to an increasingly urbanized industrial economy. To make matters worse, black educators frequently faced discrimination from white counterparts and their unions, which played the race issue to economic advantage.

The 1920s and 1930s saw educational psychology and other manifestations of educational science come to the South. Here, too, blacks faced problems, for they were subjected to culturally biased tests that portrayed them as intellectually deficient and to guidance and counseling programs that slotted them into menial jobs. Black professional associations such as the National Association of Teachers in Colored Schools and the Association of Colleges and Secondary Schools for Negroes strove to improve standards with only mixed results. White philanthropies, including the General Education Board and the Carnegie Corporation, continued to invest disproportionately in the modernization of white education. Blacks were discriminated against by the National Education Association. The American Federation of Teachers, which took a lead nationally in challenging segregation, maintained separate southern chapters. The "progressive" curriculum reform movements that swept the South in the late 1920s and early 1930s kept blacks at a disadvantage, using modern ideas about the differentiated "needs-oriented" course of study to promote nonacademic training. Attempts to gain higher education showed but fitful progress, and economic collapse in the 1930s made blacks suffer inordinately throughout America. Most Depression-era federal programs, including the Tennessee Valley Authority, the Civilian Conservation Corps, and the National Youth Adminstration, put the New Deal's stamp on segregation and inequality.

Blacks played a visible and important role in fighting racism and totalitarianism through their bravery in World War II and many wartime industries depended on their labor. For these reasons, and because headway was being made in the courts against separate and unequal provisions, southern states began to increase and even equalize expenditures on black schooling. Much of this spending, however, was intended to protect segregation so that even after the 1954 *Brown* decision the regional edifice of legalized segregation failed to crumble. President Eisenhower used federal troops to protect black students who were admitted to Little Rock Central High School in 1957, but the main progress came as the result of protest marches in the early 1960s and from the passage of the Civil Rights Acts of 1957, 1960, and 1964.

Results in the ensuing years have shown the lingering impact of centuries of racism and discrimination. The outer manifestations of legalized racial segregation have disappeared from the South, but integration has contributed to the establishment of an elaborate informal network of private white schools, many of which are Christian academies conducted under fundamentalist religious auspices. Many southern systems of public higher education contain colleges and universities that remain somewhat separate and unequal, while historically black colleges continue their struggle for survival and quality. A generation of black principals and administrators, as well as many teachers, lost their jobs in the reorganization of southern education. In some states, such as Florida, the education of blacks is mired in controversies over competency tests for students and teachers.

Black leaders began to argue in the early 1980s that the main problems facing a majority of blacks were found in deep-seated structural problems of a political and economic nature. Blacks remain grossly underrepresented at all levels of southern government. National income statistics suggest that in spite of the growth of a prosperous middle class, blacks are becoming poorer relative to the rest of the population. Due partly to continued concentration in decayed—northern and southern—urban areas there are disproportionately high unemployment levels, particularly among young people. In Texas and Florida, moreover, blacks face increasing competition from Latin American immigrants, a situation that has spilled over into violence. "Sunbelt" prosperity, which held out much hope, has not been distributed equally, nor is southern economic activity as robust in relation to other parts of the nation as it was in the 1970s.

Other major problems lie in the limited number of blacks who serve as school superintendents or school board members, even when public school systems are predominantly black. As of 1986, Georgia, for example, had only four black school superintendents, although 52 of the 187 school districts were predominantly black. With 32 predominantly black school districts among its total of 128 districts, Alabama had eight black superintendents. Among North Carolina's 141 school districts were four with a black school superintendent and four school boards with a black majority. Tensions have arisen, too, because it is common for white superintendents of predominantly black school systems to send their own children to segregated private schools. The imbalances have arisen for a variety of reasons: whites' control of political and tax structures, and thereby of school boards, low voting rates among blacks, and a shortage of blacks with administrative experience in the schools. In recent years, however, blacks increasingly have pressed for changes, particularly through legal means. Controversy erupted in Indianola, Miss., in 1986 when a white administrator was hired to succeed the retiring superintendent (also white) of the 93 percent black school district. Indianola's black residents boycotted the schools and white-owned businesses for 37 days, leading to a buy out of the new superintendent's contract coupled with his resignation and unanimous approval by the school board of Robert Merritt, a black administrator. Overall, however, assessments show that blacks' strides as administrators and school board members will probably be limited in the near future.

The federal role has been of assistance to blacks, but bureaucratization, persistent antifederal attitudes among conservative whites, and shifting federal priorities have meant a mixed return. National discussion about the overall condition of American education has not included a significant black presence, making it difficult to determine how changes will affect their relative condition, particularly as the national industrial and agricultural bases erode in the face of new technologically based industries. As in the years following the Civil War, black education faces regional and national conditions, most of which may well be beyond the power of the school to influence significantly.

See also EDUCATION articles; LAW: / *Brown* v. *Board of Education*; *Plessy* v. *Ferguson*; SCIENCE AND MEDICINE: Medical Education

Ronald K. Goodenow
Trinity College
Hartford, Connecticut

Horace Mann Bond, *The Education of the Negro in the American Social Order* (1934); Henry A. Bullock, *A History of Negro Education in the South: From 1619 to the Present* (1967); Dudley Clendinen, *New York Times* (23 June 1986); Vincent P. Franklin and James D. Anderson, eds., *New Perspectives on Black Educational History* (1978); Ronald K. Goodenow and Arthur O. White, eds., *Education and the Rise of the New South* (1981); National Alliance of Business, *Directory of Historically Black Colleges and Universities in the United States* (1983); Diane Ravitch, *The Troubled Crusade: American Education, 1945–1980* (1983); Meyer Weinberg, *A Chance to Learn: A History of Race and Education in the United States* (1977); Carter G. Woodson, *The Education of the Negro Prior to 1861* (1919).

Family, Black

In American culture, mention of "the family" suggests the ideal of a nuclear family household, which includes a legally married man and woman and their children. Many Americans might mention other family members, but seldom others beyond primary relatives with whom they have shared a household either as children (parents and siblings) or as adults (children and spouses). This family ideal has been popular in the United States for at least a century and is reflected in most of the family literature, in the media, in public policies regarding the family, and in the philosophy underlying human service programs oriented toward families.

The southern black family includes more than a household of primary relatives. A history of economic and political marginality has made it necessary for southern blacks to depend on support systems beyond the household for their survival. Although friendship bonds and patron-client relationships with whites and other higher status individuals contributed to southern black survival, rights and obligations within these relationships are not usually thought of as being as dependable as kinship bonds during times of need. Thus, early in their history, the concept of family for southern blacks began to extend beyond the residential unit to include not only parents, siblings, and children, but also biologically related kinsmen such as parents' parents and siblings, siblings' children, and children's children, as well as people who are not related at all. Such extension has facilitated survival for blacks in the South by increasing the size and range (including people of different social, ethnic, and racial categories) of the "family."

Although protection, care, instruction, and discipline of children are the primary responsibilities of the parents in the nuclear ideal, southern blacks have utilized shifting residences, fosterage, and informal adoptions to spread these obligations among other "family" members. Children may grow up within a number of households within the family groupings, or they might grow up entirely in a household other than that of their parents. The relatives or friends with whom a child resides might become foster parents of the child, or they might informally adopt the child. In either case, the child's relationship with his biological parents is usually not severed.

As a way to extend the rights and privileges of the family relationship, southern blacks used kinship terms in addressing nonkinsmen. Thus, when someone is addressed with specific kinship terms such as "mother" or "brother," the user of the term is stating that he or she will behave respectively like a son (or daughter) or brother (or sister) in his or her relationship to the person addressed, and that he or she is expecting a motherly or brotherly type of behavior in return. Southern blacks strengthened their links with distant relatives and nonkin relations by upgrading kinship terms, referring, for example, to a third cousin as an aunt or a wife's cousin as a brother-in-law.

In addition to the extended family relationship, the possession of land has given the southern black family a distinctive character. Landownership was a symbol of freedom for the free black during slavery and for the freedman following emancipation. Although land was always difficult for blacks to obtain, many of them did manage to do so. Among blacks in some southern communities, land was not a commodity to be sold but a resource to be used by kinsmen and to be passed down from generation to generation. In some families, the right to land and land use is controlled by one of the oldest and/or the dominant family members. Although black families are rapidly losing their land in the South, family land that resembles small villages with multiple households of related units is still visible in many places.

In an extended black family there is often a dominant dyad or individual, around whom many extended-family activities revolve. One of the family group's oldest couples or persons—often a widow—typically assumes this role. If there is family land, the dominant couple or individual usually lives on it, in many cases controlling its use. If multiple households live on the family land, the dominant person's household is the hub of local extended family activity, and nonlocal family members come first to that household when visiting. When the dominant family figure dies, another family member (usually an offspring) takes this role.

Another key to understanding the southern black family is its relationship to the church. In many rural areas and small towns of the South, churches are made up of a number of extended families. The church also provides rules regarding marriage, male and female behavior, childhood socialization, and respect for the elders. The church provides a community that blacks control. Some churches have "missionary societies" whose primary function is to visit the sick and "shut-in." Churches respond to some of the economic needs of poorer black families through gifts during special times such as Christmas and through special collections of money during Sunday services. Close kinship terms such as father or mother are sometimes used to refer to all elderly people in the church.

Communal occasions reconfirm the extended social support systems of the southern black family. Sunday dinner is a weekly "small feast," which brings together local primary relatives who do not reside together. Large dinners on Thanksgiving and Christmas bring together primary relatives who live in the same area as well as relatives who live elsewhere. Relatives also get together during other holidays such as Memorial Day, the Fourth of July, and Labor Day. "Cookouts," picnics, and barbecues are main events at such occasions. Larger extended family groupings come together at annual family reunions, and even larger groupings come together at church homecomings. Family reunions bring together the descendants of an ancestor or ancestral parents. A church homecoming brings together the present and past membership of a church. The overlapping between kinship and church memberships frequently results in church homecomings resembling large family reunions. Extended family and nonfamily friends also come together for weddings and funerals. These events bring people together and also serve to repay obligations, establish rights to new relationships, and reconfirm old links of rights and obligations.

Although blacks might have wanted to retain African family patterns in their pure form, the slave environment would not allow it. Unilineal descent as it was known in Africa was impossible to maintain because the slavemasters would not allow the development of large corporate groups based on ties as strong as kinship. The slave, in the meantime, needed social support wherever he could get it. Thus, not only did they most likely practice fosterage and adoption at that time, but they also attached kin terms to nonkinsmen and upgraded the kin terms of distant relatives.

By the end of slavery, black family life was becoming stabilized. But emancipation brought new pressures. Because freed slaves knew how to do little else but farm, the lack of opportunities to buy land and to get employment outside the plantation made it difficult for the vast majority of freed slaves to maintain a nuclear family, let alone an extended family. Southern postemancipation problems led to black migration in search of a better life, the emergence of a legal system that imprisoned a disproportionate number of black males, and a host of factors that contributed to the shortened life span of blacks, particularly males. All these factors contributed to an imbalance in local black sex ratios, which in turn affected the structure and function of the southern black family.

One pattern of migration, which accelerated during and after World War I, was to the urban North. For the first one or two generations, black migrants to northern cities maintained their southern kinship systems. They also developed support systems in the North similar to those that they knew in the South. In the absence of kin, they substituted friends. In some cases, supportive friends were treated as kinsmen. Those networks, though, had fewer kin involved than those in the South. After two generations, some urban black families tended to form new extended families. However, the lack of access to land in the urban North prevented black families from organizing themselves around landownership or from residing in multiple households of close proximity as in the South. As a consequence, land eventually lost some of its symbolic significance for northern blacks. When urban heirs sell family land in the South upon the deaths of their parents, the southern black extended family can be affected.

A growing reliance on social services, instead of kin and friends, has taken place in the South, as among southern migrants to the North, particularly with mechanization of southern farms and displacement of farm workers. Southern blacks, however, have managed to maintain to a considerable degree their attachment to the traditional kinship system, family land, and the church.

See also FOLKLIFE: Family Folklore; Funerals; Weddings; MYTHIC SOUTH: Family; WOMEN'S LIFE: / Elderly; Family Reunion

Tony L. Whitehead
University of North Carolina at Chapel Hill

Allison Davis, Burleigh B. Gardner, and Mary R. Gardner, *Deep South: A Social Anthropological Study of Caste and Class* (1941); K. Y. Day, in *Holding On to the Land and the Lord: Kinship, Ritual, Land Tenure and Social Policy in the Rural South*, ed. Robert L. Hall and Carol B. Stack (1982); John Hope Franklin, *From Slavery to Freedom: A History of Negro Americans* (1947; 5th ed., 1980); E. Franklin Frazier, *Negro Family in the United States* (1939); Herbert G. Gutman, *The Black Family in Slavery and Freedom, 1750–1925* (1977); Melville J. Herskovits, *The Myth of the Negro Past* (1941); Jacqueline Jones, *Labor of Love, Labor of Sorrow: Black Women, Work, and the Family from Slavery to the Present* (1985); E. P. Martin and J. M. Martin, *The Black Extended Family* (1978); D. B. Shimkin, E. M. Shimkin, and Dennis A. Frate, eds., *The Extended Family in Black Societies* (1978).

Film Images, Black

Between World Wars I and II, a small film industry outside the circle of Hollywood studios produced more than 200 "race movies"—feature films intended for a market composed of the black populations in the centers of American cities. Most of these films engaged their audiences depicting situations and characters that reversed the Hollywood portrayal of blacks. Instead of black servants, comedians, and musicians, there were black doctors, policemen, cowboys, judges, gangsters, and soldiers.

During its history from about 1916 through World War II, the race movie industry presented its audiences with a remarkably consistent image of the South as a spiritual home of the most deeply felt values of Afro-American life. This benign vision of life in the South derived from two circumstances. First, race movies usually featured all-black casts and situations, thereby precluding interracial dramatic conflict; and second, many black moviegoers, North and South, shared a memory of the rural South as a family home to be spoken of in only the most sentimental terms.

This black version of southern nostalgia differed from the Hollywood model in that the major studios often sentimentalized not the region but its race relations. Beginning with *Uncle Tom's Cabin* (1903) and extending through *Birth of a Nation* (1915) to *Gone with the Wind* (1939), such films formed a clearly defined genre.

Rarely did Hollywood attempt to present the South from a black perspective. Among the more successful of a handful of departures from cinematic convention were *Hallelujah!* (1929) and *Hearts in Dixie* (1929), both of which exploited a black musical idiom; *The Green Pastures* (1936), based upon Roark Bradford's *Ol' Man Adam an' His Chillun* (1928), a collection of tales told as though from the point of view of a rural black preacher, which, in turn, had been the source of Marc Connelly's Pulitzer Prize play entitled *The Green Pastures* (1929). In 1937 two black collaborators, Clarence Muse and Langston Hughes, contributed to the script of *Way Down South*, a B-movie treatment of the South as a "downhome" source of black virtues. Along with these few features, Hollywood produced occasional short films that ranged from "the usual old southern cabin setting" to the evocative *Yamacraw* (1930), which *Film Daily* characterized as "a jazz symphony of Negro life that is arresting in movement as well as in dramatic idea."

The earliest surviving race movie set in a southern locale was *The Birth of a Race* (1918), an intended antidote to the racial propaganda in D. W. Griffith's *Birth of a Nation*. Originally an ambitious history of mankind that gave due recognition to blacks, it soon passed from the hands of its black creators as costs mounted and grew into a pacifist movie in which blacks had only a small place. Nevertheless, in the last reel blacks are seen as an enduring presence in southern life and as willing volunteers during World War I.

In several black films throughout the 1920s, the southern image was of nurturing, rural permanence, an area in which blacks challenged the reigning social order and promoted racial unity. Among the best were Oscar Micheaux's *Within Our Gates* (1920), which dramatized the lynching of Leo Frank in Atlanta "as witnessed by the author"; *The Brute* (1920), in which the black boxer, Sam Langford, fought against a lynch mob in a film condemned in several southern towns as "a very dangerous picture to show in the South"; Micheaux's *Body and Soul* (1924), an exposé of corrupt preachers and bootleggers in "Tatesville," Ga.; and Micheaux's *Birthright* (1924), a story of a black Ivy Leaguer whose return to the South combined the themes of personal aspiration, racial solidarity, and a return to familial roots.

Several producers of race movies not only took up southern themes and locales in their films, but actually located in the South. Among them were Cotton Blossom and Lone Star in San Antonio, Ben Strasser in Winston-Salem, C. B. Campbell in Pensacola, and Ker-Mar in Baltimore. During the era of soundfilm, at least two companies established combined production and distribution centers in the South—Ted Toddy's Dixie National Pictures in Atlanta and Alfred Sack's Sackamuse Company in Dallas.

At least two black innovators developed a unique southern genre of visual proselytizing. Eloyce Gist of Washington and Kiefer Jackson of Baltimore were traveling evangelists and lecturers on religious subjects who combined film with oratory. Jackson's show had shots of the Holy Land and reportorial film of ministerial conventions, but Gist included at least one film in her presentation which graphically depicted an allegorical railroad train hurtling toward heaven or hell—depending on whether the passengers decide in time to change their secular ways to live lives of faith and good works.

By the opening of World War II, the black audience had migrated northward, thereby stimulating a trend toward more urbane formulas that emphasized cops-and-robbers "action" rather than homely values. Thereafter, only Spencer Williams, an actor-director-writer who worked for Sack, produced films that catered to southern black audiences. His *Go Down Death*, a film indebted to James Weldon Johnson's poem of the same title, and his *Blood of Jesus* closed out the Depression decade, the latter film earning, in the estimation of Sack's bookkeeper, more than any black film ever made. Both films were shot on southern ground and were deeply rooted in traditional regional values.

With the demise of race movies after World War II, Hollywood products ranged over a broad spectrum of attitudes toward the South. *Song of the South* (1946) and *Saratoga Trunk* (1946) celebrated or romanticized traditional white southern values. A spate of movies derived from the works of William Faulkner, Hamilton Basso, and other southerners portrayed the South as sexually repressed and cruel. Still others—*Band of Angels, The Foxes of Harrow, Drum, Mandingo*—were laden with social and political messages that required depicting antebellum times with undisguised rage. In recent years only a handful of black-centered films have treated the South in the warmly sentimental idiom of Spencer Williams's movies. Among them are *Nothing but a Man*, *Sounder*, *Conrack*, and *The Autobiography of Miss Jane Pittman*—the latter a film made for television, a medium that seemed to trade on sentimentality and even to magnify it in such grandiose projects as the incredibly popular *Roots*. Recent films, such as *The Color Purple* (1985) and *Crossroads* (1986), suggest a renewed interest in southern black life.

Paul Winfield (left) and Kevin Hooks (right) in a scene from* Sounder *(1972)

See also MEDIA: Film, Blaxploitation; / *Birth of a Nation*; *The Color Purple*; *Gone with the Wind*; *Mandingo*; *Roots*; *Uncle Tom's Cabin*

Thomas Cripps
Morgan State University

Donald Bogle, *Toms, Coons, Mulattoes, Mammies, & Bucks: An Interpretive History of Blacks in American Films* (1973); Thomas Cripps, *Slow Fade to Black: The Negro in American Films, 1900–1942* (1977); Phyllis Rauch Klotman, *Frame by Frame—A Black Filmography* (1979); Daniel J. Leab, *From Sambo to Superspade: The Black Experience in Motion Pictures* (1975); Henry T. Sampson, *Blacks in Black and White: A Source Book on Black Films* (1977).

Folklore, Black

The folklore of black southerners is a process of artistic communication, exemplified in recurring performances of music, folktales, and material culture. These performances reflect both continuity with Africa and creativity in the New World.

The oral traditions of black southerners include creole languages such as Gullah and a variety of dialects generally known as "black speech." Southern black folk speech has also included special linguistic forms such as jive talk, with African-derived slang words such as "guy," "jive," "hip," and "dig." Especially notable are such marked forms as rapping and toasting and ritualized linguistic interactions such as signifying and playing the dozens. Black southern proverbs strongly reflect the African preference for speaking by indirection.

Black southern folktales have been told since Africans first arrived in the South. The tales have even influenced the narratives of whites and Native Americans in the region. The tales include legends or folk narratives told as though true. Black southern legends include memorates, or personal experience narratives, as well as local legends and hero tales of such characters as "Old Nat" (Turner), "Moses" (Harriet Tubman), Shine, Jack Johnson, and Joe Louis. Other legends explain why buzzards are bald and why rabbits have long ears and short tails. Southern humor is also exemplified in the outrageous tall tales of black southerners.

The most popular folktales among black southerners have been trickster tales, with their theme of the struggle for mastery between the trickster—a small but sly animal such as Brer Rabbit—and his bigger, more powerful adversary. The trickster defeats his rival not by superior physical strength, but by superior intellect. Folklorists such as J. Mason Brewer and Richard Dorson collected a cycle of trickster stories featuring the never-ending contest of the slave trickster John and Old Marster.

Black southern music had its origins in the field hollers of plantation laborers and the street cries of urban peddlers. A special form of work songs was preserved in southern prisons. John and Alan Lomax collected many such songs from the remarkable Huddie Ledbetter, who after release from prison attained fame as "Leadbelly," the "king of the twelve-string guitar players." From the haunting spirituals of slaves, black gospel music was developed by such singers as Blind Gary Davis and Mahalia Jackson and composers such as Thomas A. Dorsey and the Reverend Herbert Brewster. The blues evolved from rural performers such as Tommy Johnson, Charley Patton, Mississippi John Hurt, and Blind Lemon Jefferson through female performers like Bessie Smith, Ma Rainey, and Chippie Hill to the modern urban blues of Mississippi Delta expatriates like Muddy Waters (McKinley Morganfield), Howlin' Wolf (Chester Burnett), and B. B. King. The reels and buck dances of slave fiddlers and banjo pickers evolved through fife and drum bands of northern Mississippi, jug bands of Memphis and Charleston, and brass bands of New Orleans into early jazz.

Black southern music has proved enormously influential on white southern musicians. Country music stars Jimmie Rodgers, Hank Williams, Maybelle Carter of the famous Carter Family, Bob Wills (the pioneer of jazz-tinged western swing), and Bill Monroe (the father of bluegrass), all acknowledged the influence of black southern music on them. In the 1950s Elvis Presley stepped into a Memphis recording studio, and out of the integration of white country music and black rhythm and blues ignited the new phenomenon of rock and roll.

Black southern folk belief is strongly influenced by African patterns of folk belief. African folk medicine of both the pharmaceutical and psychological varieties continues to be practiced in the South. Natural phenomena serve as signs foretelling either changing weather or approaching death. Ghosts or haunts—the spirits of the dead—return to trouble the living in the New World as in the Old, and their unwelcome visits can be warded off by various charms. Black religion incorporates the African religious phenomenon of spirit possession, called forth by the black preacher. But other African religious traditions, such as voodoo or hoodoo, exist apart from black Christianity. Many black southerners still take their problems to local conjurers. With the aid of mojo hands, goopher dust, John the Conqueror root, and other substances held to be magical, such conjurers can protect one from misfortune and cast spells upon one's enemies.

Among black southerners, as in cultures around the world, long days of toil alternate with periods of ritual festivity. Harvest time is such an occasion in the rural South; Mardi Gras is another in urban New Orleans. Mamie Garvin Fields in her *Lemon Swamp* recalls the Fourth of July celebrations in Charleston on the Battery, from which blacks were barred the rest of the year. The holiday was marked by barbecue and fried fish, music and speeches, and a recitation of the Emancipation Proclamation. Black southerners, following African tradition, still give a festive air to funerals as well as to weddings and such holidays as Christmas. In antebellum North Carolina (as in Jamaica) the John Canoe festival was an exotic part of slave Christmas celebrations in which bands of dancers, keeping time to the beat of the "gumbo box," triangles, and jawbones, begged donations from spectators.

From slavery to the present, black southern artists have created beautiful folk arts. On rice plantations in South Carolina, men and women made baskets in the African style of coiled basketry. Today black basketmakers in South Carolina are internationally acclaimed for continuing the tradition. Slave potters such as the renowned Dave of South Carolina's Edgefield District produced remarkable alkaline glazed stoneware. Their tradition continues in the clay sculpture of Mississippi's James "Son" Thomas. The gourd fiddles, sheep-hide banjos, beef-rib bones, and willow-stalk quills of slave instrument makers formed a tradition that continues today in Eli Owens's mouth-bows and Othar Turner's cane flutes. Throughout the South the achievements of slave seamstresses and quilters are seen in the cross-stitch embroidery of Mamie Garvin Fields and the quilts of Harriet Powers and Pecolia Warner. Slave blacksmiths not only shod horses and other livestock but also made the striking wrought-iron gates and grilles that were especially prized in South Carolina and Louisiana. Charleston's Phillip Simmons has been nationally recognized for his 20th-century wrought iron artistry.

From slave cabins to the modern shotgun house, black southerners have made unique contributions to the nation's architectural heritage. In its classic form the shotgun house is small and rectangular, one room wide by three rooms deep, with doors at each end and its gable end to the street.

Black southern foodways also exemplify folk cultural expression. Slaves in the Old South ate the foodstuffs of the plantation environment; but slave cooks applied to them African methods of cooking and spicing, remembered recipes, and ancestral tastes—the *soul* ingredients. They thus maintained cultural continuity with Africa, and introduced African foods—such as okra and yams—to the New World. The fusion of Old World and New World traditions continues in black southern recipes for preparing barbecue, gumbo, and other delicacies.

There were important parallels in the folk culture of southerners whose ancestors came from Africa and that of southerners whose ancestors came from Europe. These parallels fostered widespread cultural exchanges and enriched both groups. Today black southerners have a European folk heritage as well as an African one, and white southerners have an African folk heritage as well as a European one.

The South was the principal arena in which various African cultural traditions were transformed into an Afro-American culture. Black southerners kept alive traditions of their African ancestors and adopted traditions from white southerners. Throughout the South, folklore has been at the center of community life. That folklore has kept alive the shadows and ghosts of the past in the present and expresses a common cultural identity.

See also ETHNIC LIFE: Indian Cultural Contributions; FOLKLIFE articles; HISTORY AND MANNERS: Foodways; MUSIC articles

Charles Joyner
University of South Carolina—
Coastal Carolina College

John Blassingame, *The Slave Community: Plantation Life in the Antebellum South* (1972); Judith Wragg Chase, *Afro-American Arts and Crafts* (1971); W. E. B. Du Bois, *The Souls of Black Folk* (1903); Dena J. Epstein, *Sinful Tunes and Spirituals: Black Folk Music to the Civil War* (1977); William Ferris, *Journal of American Folklore* (April–June 1975); Mamie Garvin Fields and Karen Fields, *Lemon Swamp* (1983); Melville J. Herskovits, *The Myth of the Negro Past* (1941); Charles Joyner, *Down by the Riverside: A South Carolina Slave Community* (1984); Lawrence W. Levine, *Black Culture and Black Consciousness: Afro-American Folk Thought from Slavery to Freedom* (1977); Albert J. Raboteau, *Slave Religion: The "Invisible Institution" in the Antebellum South* (1978); Eileen Southern, *The Music of Black Americans: A History* (1971); Robert Farris Thompson, *Flash of the Spirit: African and Afro-American Art and Philosophy* (1983); Lorenzo Dow Turner, *Africanisms in the Gullah Dialect* (1949); John Michael Vlach, *The Afro-American Tradition in Decorative Arts* (1978); William Wiggins, *Black People and Their Culture* (1976).

Fraternal Orders, Black

The Afro-American fraternal orders and mutual benefit societies that proliferated throughout the South following emancipation evolved over several generations. They emerged from a rich underground of "invisible" institutions and folkways that slaves had created in their plantation communities; and insofar as they represented a folk culture, they owed their origins and style in part to Africa. They also resembled mutual benefit societies among European immigrants and often began out of purely pragmatic necessity. Melville J. Herskovits possibly exaggerated when he argued for a direct link with African cults and secret societies; and W. E. B. Du Bois probably strained the spiritual connection when he argued for a lineal descent from the West African Obeah worship. During slavery these voluntary associations were doubly clandestine, evolving out of a tradition of secret societies and the need to conceal organized behavior from the master class. As a consequence scholars know very little about the existence of orders and lodges among slaves, although Vincent Harding has identified the Twelve Knights of Tabor as a secret network of 40,000 slaves organized in 1846 with the aim of overthrowing slavery.

Among free blacks a more conspicuous tradition accounted for the formal or "visible" side of institutional development. As early as the 18th century, free blacks formed "African Societies" in the northern and southern urban communities, most notably the Free African Society of Philadelphia, founded in 1787. The Free African Society is more often remembered as the parent organization of the African Methodist Episcopal Church, but its own origins were decidedly secular, designed to provide a system of cooperative social welfare for the struggling black community of Philadelphia. This example of the mutual benefit society preceding the church points to the primacy of these societies and to the hazy distinction between the spiritual and the secular in Afro-American culture.

The program of mutual assistance among urban free blacks, especially the elite of Charleston and New Orleans, often reflected biases of class and color as well as a European orientation. Founded in 1790, Charleston's Brown Fellowship Society, for example, limited its membership to mulattoes, a practice that prompted the darker-skinned free blacks to launch their own equally exclusive society, the Free Dark Men of Color. In other cases, most obviously the black Masons (1787) and the Odd Fellows (1843), separate lodges grew out of their exclusion from the mainstream of white societies. Similar black counterpart groups, like the Elks and the Knights of Pythias, were founded after the Civil War.

Indeed the Civil War and emancipation set off an explosion in the number and variety of Afro-American societies. Four million exslaves seeking social and economic expression valued only the family and possibly the church above the benefit society in their hierarchy of basic institutions. In many cases the mutual aid society, the church, the school, and rudimentary insurance and business enterprises were linked by a common founder and a common set of buildings. Du Bois, writing in 1906 about the social phenomenon as a whole, concluded that "no complete account of Negro beneficial societies is possible, so large is their number and so wide their ramification. Nor can any hard and fast line between them and industrial insurance societies be drawn." Their mixed function, he continued, was "partly social intercourse and partly insurance. They furnish pastime from the monotony of work, a chance for parade, and insurance against misfortune. Next to the church they are the most popular organizations among Negroes."

However pressing the force of discrimination in the drive to establish separate black institutions, it would be a mistake to interpret these expressions of black culture as merely a response to exclusion. Black fraternal and mutual benefit societies took on a life and style of their own, tantamount to a southern folkway in the estimation of anthropologists Hylan Lewis and Hortense Powdermaker. In their respective studies of communities in South Carolina and Mississippi, Lewis and Powdermaker agreed that the "insurance envelope" was an omnipresent feature in humble cabins, and that "insurance" along with "church going, hunting and fishing" was a cultural staple. Doubtless, the vast array of lodges and societies provided an outlet for leadership and an avenue for status, respect, and recreation in compensation for what the larger society denied. In remembering his father as the Grand Marshall of the New Orleans Odd Fellows parade, Louis Armstrong may have caught the essence of this positive function: "I was very proud to see him in his uniform and his high hat with the beautiful streamer hanging down . . . Yes, he was a fine figure of a man, my dad. Or at least that is the way he seemed to me as a kid when he strutted by like a peacock at the head of the Odd Fellows Parade."

Finally it should be emphasized that black women served as role models playing key parts as both members and organizers in black fraternal and benefit societies. Most conspicuous among the leaders was Maggie Lena Walker, who in 1899 assumed leadership of the Independent Order of St. Luke, a Richmond fraternal society founded in 1867 by an exslave, Mary Prout. Under Walker's administration, the Order of St. Luke, like its larger Richmond rival, the Grand United Order of True Reformers, embraced an ideology of self-help and racial solidarity, attempting to organize and uplift the entire black community through a broad range of institutions, including a savings bank, a newspaper (the St. Luke *Herald*), and the St. Luke Emporium. The True Reformers added a utopian vision in its retirement community and cooperative farm. Walker's organization did not survive the Great Depression, but as an illustration of its cultural legitimacy, and hence the cultural depth of black fraternal societies, black women in the final years of the 20th century continue to organize under its banner, even in northern cities.

See also HISTORY AND MANNERS: Fraternal Groups; INDUSTRY: / Insurance; WOMEN'S LIFE: / Walker, Maggie Lena

Walter B. Weare
University of Wisconsin—Milwaukee

W. E. B. Du Bois, *Economic Cooperation among Negro Americans* (1907), *Efforts for Social Betterment among Negro Americans* (1909); Vincent Harding, in *The Making of Black America*, ed. August Meier and Elliot M. Rudwick (1969); Melville J. Herskovits, *The Myth of the Negro Past* (1941); Lawrence W. Levine, *Black Culture and Black Consciousness: Afro-American Folk Thought from Slavery to Freedom* (1977); Hylan Lewis, *Blackways of Kent* (1955); August Meier, *Negro Thought in America, 1880–1915* (1963); William J. Muraskin, *Middle Class Blacks in a White Society: Prince Hall Freemasonry in America* (1975); Hortense Powdermaker, *After Freedom: A Cultural Study in the Deep South* (1939); Walter B. Weare, *Black Business in the New South: A Social History of the North Carolina Mutual Life Insurance Company* (1973).

Freedom Movement, Black

The series of black protests that began with the Montgomery bus boycott of 1955–56 became during the following decade the most significant southern social movement of the 20th century. Although subsequent studies of this black movement usually stressed its civil rights goals and national leadership, the movement generated its own local institutions and leadership seeking economic and political reforms that went beyond the legislation sought by the major preexisting civil rights organizations. Indeed, black participants often called their movement a freedom struggle in order to express its broad range of goals. Rather than simply continuing long-term civil rights efforts by the National Association for the Advancement of Colored People (NAACP) and other national reform organizations, the southern black freedom movement can best be seen as a tactical and, ultimately, an ideological departure from those efforts. The southern movement was characterized by unconventional and increasingly militant tactics, locally initiated protest activity, decentralized control, and an increasing sense of racial consciousness among participants.

The first major phase of the modern black freedom struggle was the Montgomery bus boycott. Although blacks had protested against racial oppression throughout American history, the Montgomery boycott signaled the beginning of a period during which widely shared racial discontent was expressed through mass movements. Existing civil rights organizations did not initiate the movement, although Rosa Parks, whose arrest prompted the boycott, had been secretary of the local NAACP chapter. Parks's unplanned refusal on 1 December 1955 to give up her bus seat to a white man was both an outgrowth of the gradual rise of black political influence in the city and a stimulus for further mobilization of black community resources. On 5 December a group of local leaders established the Montgomery Improvement Association (MIA) to coordinate the boycott and chose as its leader the Reverend Martin Luther King, Jr., who had come to the city in 1954. King, who had received his divinity doctorate from Boston University, was one of the many new leaders who would reflect the increasing confidence and militancy of the movement, and his inspired oratory, filled with references to Christian and Gandhian concepts of nonviolent resistance, attracted widespread, favorable publicity. Despite the bombing of King's house and other acts of intimidation, the boycott continued until December 1956, when Montgomery officials reluctantly obeyed a Supreme Court order to desegregate the bus system.

The Montgomery bus boycott served as a model for black protest movements in other cities, for it demonstrated the ability of black communities to unite and struggle collectively for change. In 1957 King and his supporters founded the Southern Christian Leadership Conference (SCLC) to provide an institutional framework that would allow blacks to go beyond the NAACP's strategy of litigation and lobbying. As SCLC's leader, King moved cautiously, however, and did not initiate any major protest movements during the next five years. Nevertheless, King's presence in a community often increased black enthusiasm and attracted publicity. In addition, ministers and staff members associated with SCLC played crucial roles in many local movements.

The second major phase of the southern black struggle began on 1 February 1960, when four black college students in Greensboro, N.C., sat at a lunch counter reserved for whites. The students had been affiliated with NAACP youth chapters, but they initiated their protest without consulting adult leaders. Other students in Greensboro and elsewhere soon followed their example, finding that the sit-in tactic offered an appealing way for young blacks without special skills and resources to display their discontent. There had been previous sit-ins, but the Greensboro protest ignited a social movement because it was well publicized and occurred in a region containing many black students. Thousands of students in at least 60 communities, mostly in the Upper South, joined the sit-in movement during the winter and spring of 1960. In a few instances, violent clashes between protesters and white onlookers occurred, but student-led local protest organizations usually succeeded in maintaining nonviolent discipline while also displaying greater militance than the more cautious adult-led organizations. Despite efforts of the NAACP, SCLC, and the Congress of Racial Equality (CORE) to impose some control over the sit-in movement, the student protest leaders typically insisted on maintaining their independence. Even when student leaders formed the Student Nonviolent Coordinating Committee (SNCC) to coordinate the movement, the new civil rights organization was not given authority to set policy for its constituent groups. SNCC would remain the most decentralized, antiauthoritarian, and militant of the major civil rights organizations.

The third phase of the southern struggle, involving the Freedom Rides of 1961, was initiated by a civil rights organization—CORE—but this new form of protest activity did not become a social movement until CORE abandoned its initial campaign. In May 1960 CORE sent 13 riders through the southern states on a bus trip that was designed to expose the extent of segregation in bus terminals. After white mobs viciously attacked the riders near Anniston and at the Birmingham bus station, CORE leaders decided to discontinue their effort. At this point, however, student activists, many of whom had participated in the sit-ins, announced their determination to continue the rides. After encountering further mob violence in Montgomery, a group of riders went to Jackson, Miss., where they were promptly arrested after ignoring Jim Crow rules. Despite Attorney General Robert Kennedy's plea for a "cooling-off" period, other young activists also came to Jackson to join the students already in jail. In addition, the rides into Mississippi encouraged students elsewhere in the South to stage similar protests against segregated transportation facilities during the remaining months of 1961. Participation in the Freedom Rides allowed young students to display their militancy in places distant from their homes and campuses and to form a community of militant activists who saw themselves as the spearhead of the southern movement. This was particularly the case among the several hundred students who spent part of the summer of 1961 in Mississippi jails.

Some of the veterans of the Freedom Rides played important roles in the fourth phase of the southern struggle that began in the fall of 1961. Unlike the previous phases, this one was consciously initiated by civil rights activists who entered communities in order to begin social movements. These activists sought to mobilize poor and working-class blacks who had rarely been involved in previous protests, and during the following two years they were able to increase dramatically the size of the southern struggle. "Freedom songs," often based on traditional religious music, and feelings of racial solidarity that were strengthened through common experiences became the basis of a distinctive movement culture. In the urban and Upper South, activists organized massive demonstrations to achieve desegregation of public facilities, better housing and job opportunities for blacks, and the elimination of discriminatory governmental policies. First in Albany, Ga., during late 1961 and 1962, and then in many other urban areas, marches and rallies were held to demonstrate black resolve and to prod the federal government to intervene on behalf of blacks. Learning from the largely unsuccessful Albany movement, King and other SCLC leaders initiated, during the spring of 1963, a tumultuous protest movement in Birmingham that led President John Kennedy to introduce legislation that became the Civil Rights Act of 1964. The protests of 1963 culminated in August with a march on Washington that attracted over 200,000 participants.

While media attention was focused on the urban demonstrations, the voter registration campaign in the Deep South achieved more gradual gains. Although only a small proportion of eligible black voters had been registered by the end of 1963, local residents had begun to work with a group of full-time civil rights workers (mostly affiliated with SNCC). To coordinate the work of the various national civil rights groups and independent local organizations, Mississippi blacks created the Council of Federated Organizations (COFO), directed by Bob Moses. In 1964 the Mississippi Freedom Democratic party was formed as an alternative to the all-white regular Democratic party. During the summer of 1964 hundreds of northern white volunteers assisted the black organizers and local leaders in the state. Although the MFDP failed in its attempt to unseat the regular delegation at the 1964 national Democratic convention, the summer project and the series of protests the following year in Selma, Ala., publicized the disenfranchisement of blacks in the South and prompted President Lyndon Johnson to introduce voter rights legislation that was enacted during the summer of 1965.

The Selma to Montgomery march was one of the last major demonstrations of the southern struggle. The passage of voting rights legislation, the decline of white support for the black struggle, and the related upsurge in northern urban racial violence made southern blacks more likely to see conventional political tactics rather than mass protest as the most effective way to achieve their goals. Furthermore, the militant racial consciousness of black activists made some of them less interested in working for civil rights reforms and more determined to achieve political power through building autonomous, black-controlled institutions, such as the Black Panther party in Alabama. Ideological conflict between proponents of "black power," such as SNCC chairman Stokely Carmichael, and more conventional civil rights leaders

Police dog attacking civil rights demonstrators, Birmingham, 1963

such as King came into public view during the Mississippi march held in June 1966 after the shooting of James Meredith.

The era of mass demonstrations came to an end in 1965, but the long-term gains of the southern black freedom struggle can be seen in the subsequent rapid growth in the number of black elected officials, the disappearance of humiliating Jim Crow practices, and the increased sense of racial pride and potency felt by many southern blacks. Although most scholarly studies of the southern movement continue to interpret it as an outgrowth of the inexorable trend toward the entry of blacks into the American mainstream, the movement was also a product of Afro-American culture and institutional development and its distinctive emergent ideas have continued to influence black thought and political life.

See also LAW: Civil Rights Movement; MEDIA: Civil Rights and Media; VIOLENCE: Civil Rights, Federal Enforcement; WOMEN'S LIFE: / Parks, Rosa

Clayborne Carson
Stanford University

Clayborne Carson, *In Struggle: SNCC and the Black Awakening of the 1960s* (1981); William H. Chafe, *Civilities and Civil Rights: Greensboro, North Carolina, and the Black Struggle for Freedom* (1980); Charles W. Eagles, ed., *The Civil Rights Movement in America* (1986); James Forman, *The Making of Black Revolutionaries: A Personal Account* (1972); David L. Lewis, *King: A Critical Biography* (1970); Howell Raines, *My Soul Is Rested: Movement Days in the Deep South Remembered* (1977).

Funerary Customs, Black

If the southern way of death has become a remarkable ritual, the funerary customs of black southerners are even more so. While there is some overlap in the way both southern blacks and whites handle the terminal rite of passage, in Afro-American communities a funeral will generally have some distinctive features. Funerals are important social events all across the South, but among blacks funerals assume an especially high level of signifi-

Funeral at Rose Hill Baptist Church, Vicksburg, Miss., 1968

cance. In black society it would be very bad form for a funeral not to be a lavish, even extravagant, event. The conclusion of one's life is regarded as a highly charged occasion and many blacks make careful plans throughout their lives for the moment of death. Sociologist Hortense Powdermaker noted in her classic study of Indianola, Miss., that "no Negro . . . can live content unless he is assured of a fine funeral when he dies."

Because southern blacks have found themselves chronically held at the lowest economic levels, the custom of elaborate funerals has usually struck outsiders as an unwise use of limited funds or as a peculiar habit. The rationale for giving such a high priority to death rites, however, derives from reasonable political and cultural motives. Before emancipation of slaves in the mid-19th century, the only sure way to acquire one's freedom was to die. In death slaves escaped their masters and attained the dignity of either heavenly salvation if they were Christians or the joy of reconnection with the lost ancestors if they retained African beliefs. While those who lived after them mourned their passing, they also rejoiced in the new status of the deceased. Moreover, although slaves were often closely supervised when working, they were not usually checked carefully when they buried their dead. Funerals came then, over time, to be associated with autonomy and to be regarded as positive, even celebratory, events.

Because slaves were generally free to dispose of their dead as they saw fit, some distinctive beliefs and practices of an African origin were retained. These have over the last century and a half blended with standard Christian observance to give southern blacks their own approach to death and funerals. It has been widely held, for example, that the spirit of the deceased does not leave the domain of living but lingers on earth where it may intrude in daily affairs. That spirit must be placated or it might maliciously cause misfortune, pain, or even death. As a consequence of this precept an elaborate system of folk beliefs was developed that offers specific strategies to still an agitated "haint" or ghost. These beliefs follow the general principle that a spiritual being can be dealt with in the same manner as a human being. An expensive funeral thus confers on the spirit of the deceased, by means of a material display, a prominent social status. Another black custom is the so-called second burial, a formal ceremony held several months after interment during which the deceased is eulogized. Such commemorative events are held in part to assure the spirit that his or her family and friends still care. In traditional black graveyards bodies are interred with the objects used by the person in life, and often personal items like razors, lamps, clocks, toys, medicine bottles, glasses, cups, and so forth are clustered on top of the grave mound. These items are placed there to provide the spirits with material comforts so they might "rest easy" and not roam outside the cemetery. While such practice keeps the spirit where it belongs, it also connects the mourners to one they have lost and thus diminishes to a degree their sorrow.

See also FOLKLIFE: Cemeteries; Funerals; Grave Markers

John Michael Vlach
George Washington University

Newbell Niles Puckett, *Folk Beliefs of the Southern Negro* (1926; reprint ed. 1969); Robert Farris Thompson, *Flash of the Spirit: African and Afro-American Art and Philosophy* (1983); John Michael Vlach, *The Afro-American Tradition in Decorative Arts* (1978).

A Mississippi rural life scene, 1968

Genealogy, Black

Spurred on by a 1976 bicentennial celebration that called on all Americans to be proud of their immigrant ancestry and by the publication of Alex Haley's immensely popular book *Roots* in 1976, genealogy became the third leading hobby in the United States. Haley's establishment of the African source of his ancestry and the story of his family during the slavery and postslavery periods was a personal achievement in which black Americans took great pride, and they joined white Americans in the passion of ancestor hunting.

Ancestor hunting is filled with many difficulties. The most frequently used records are state and county vital statistics, particularly birth, marriage, and death records, but most states did not begin collecting such records until the latter half of the 19th century, and those providing the information for these records did not always have accurate knowledge. Probate records including wills, estate papers, guardianship records, depositions, records of law suits, and other court actions frequently did not have uniform collection and recording procedures. Moreover, most probate records are simply abstracts with only summary, and sometimes incomplete, information. Deeds, tax lists, and mortgage records are other sources used by genealogists. Such local records are plagued by shifting county and state boundaries over time, and many of them were destroyed by fire, particularly during the Civil War.

Although the difficulties listed above are problematic for all southerners who are interested in ancestor hunting, it is particularly problematic for blacks because of their history of slavery and the persistence of their economic and political marginality. The date sources mentioned above are oriented towards recording life events of citizens and property owners. During the slavery period most blacks in the United States were neither citizens nor property owners. Black ancestor hunters, therefore, cannot approach these records in the same way as their white counterparts.

In the early post-emancipation period, the majority of blacks were not landowners, and those who were rarely made out wills. The practice of dying intestate is still a problem among blacks in many parts of the rural South. As vital statistics began to be collected more systematically, the public recording of most rural, lower-income black (and white) births and deaths was haphazardly done. Birth certificate dates and names of elderly blacks are not always correct. The use of nicknames, the prevalence of illiteracy, and the common practice of giving two or more children within the same generation of an extended family cluster the same name also complicates black ancestor hunting.

Another problem in the search for black genealogy is the traditionally popular practice among southern blacks of informal adoption. To take in children, related and unrelated, was survival strategy for blacks during the slave period and a way of helping needy children in the post-emancipation slave period. Because of this, oral traditions of a family may contain information of an adoption, but not the names of the biological parents of the adoptee. In addition, finding records on a slave's parent now may be difficult because the parents' records could be under a name held when the parent was the property of an owner prior to ownership by the child's master.

Another problem resulting from slave breeding practices was multiple breeding unions, which contributed to difficulties in establishing biological fatherhood. Historically, when a black woman had children by more than one mate, the child had greater familiarity with maternal relatives while paternal relatives were less well known, if known at all. The high geographical mobility, north and west, by blacks during the latter part of the 19th century and the first half of the 20th century also creates gaps in the genealogical record.

Before going to the records, one must try to exhaust the memories of relatives and, in some cases, family friends, particularly elders who can carry the ancestor hunter back three or four generations. However, older and/or more genealogically knowledgeable family members may be hesitant to provide information, and in some cases may be downright opposed to ancestor hunting, viewing it as "digging up skeletons that should remain buried." These are sentiments found among all racial and ethnic groups, but for some older blacks ancestor hunting is especially problematic because of the concerns about "respectability" and "sin." The symbols of respectability are expressed in family life and include such notions as marital stability, sexual purity on the part of women (of which children by one man is an example), and maternal possessions. Because of the hardships of life in the South, some black families have struggled a long time to achieve these symbols of respectability, but once they are achieved, they try to forget the "sins" of the past.

Ancestor hunting becomes a threat because it might reveal in some cases that "sinful acts" formed the foundation upon which respectability was achieved. For example, higher socioeconomic status might have been achieved through illegal activities (such as selling bootleg whiskey) or illicit sexual activity. One area of sexual activity that may be interpreted as undesirable by some blacks, but at an earlier period provided a foundation upon which family respectability was achieved, is interracial mating. Both black and white family members may be opposed to the documentation of such interracial kinship ties, and they are sometimes kept private.

A devastating revelation is to uncover an incidence of incest within a family cluster, particularly if a child were born from such a union. Uncovering such examples of incest is possible, particularly in rural isolated populations. The probability of unknown incestuous unions is also increased with the instability of black family life that has been fostered by slavery, economic marginality, and residential mobility. There is a strong sentiment that one should not marry one's cousin, but the concept of cousin for some southern blacks is a *classifying kinship term* including not only first cousins (children of parents' siblings) but second, third, and even as distant as seventh cousins. Thus, when a relative opposes ancestor hunting because of a fear of the ancestor hunter's uncovering an ancestral incident of incest, the union may have occurred among persons who would be considered unrelated by most Americans.

The various problems (nonexistent and faulty records and family resistance) have been insurmountable for many a black family historian. But those who have experienced some success state that interviewing relatives has yielded very positive rewards, including becoming better acquainted with relatives beyond the immediate family, broadening the *functional* quality of the family network, and spending more time with older relatives and finding that these people are greater reservoirs of historical information, particularly community and family history, than history books or public documents. They found that Alex Haley was not alone in having older relatives who told stories that were passed down from generation to generation.

Black families not only have oral histories, but some also record their histories as part of family reunion celebrations. One set of North Carolina family reunion records goes back to 1822. In addition to family reunion journals other sources of family information are family Bibles, personal diaries, and mementos such as family albums, scrapbooks, and old letters. In the 18th, 19th, and early 20th centuries, blacks, as well as whites, frequently gave Bibles to newlywed couples. In the covers of these Bibles were written the names of the couple, the date of the marriage, the names and births of each child, and similar genealogical information.

Records kept by various organizations in which family members held membership can also yield significant data for black genealogists. Foremost among such sources are church records of marriage, some of which extend back as much as 150 years. Sources of black genealogical data also include the records of fraternal organizations, professional or occupational associations, and records of organizations that have given awards, honors, and medals to family members. Military organizations are also a good source of records. And, finally, probate records including arrests and convictions have provided genealogical data for some black ancestor hunters.

The records of the Freedman's Bureau have data on thousands of black families. Black genealogists working in the slave period find that it matters whether one's ancestors were slave or free. Some information on free black ancestors might appear in the usual sources of tax lists, marriage records, wills, estate records, and court materials; military records of the Civil and Revolutionary wars contain useful information, and apprentice lists have details on those free blacks who were bound out to learn a trade. Free blacks also appear in the federal census of 1850 and the first census in 1790.

The records of slaveowners are important sources of genealogical data for descendants of slaves. For example, the best (and sometimes only) source of vital statistics on slaves was the property account of the slaveowners. The births and deaths of slaves were important to slaveowners because their labor supply was affected by such events. Most large plantations kept slave birth registers and some also maintained slave death registers as part of their property inventory listings. Some states and territories did not allow slave marriages, but public documentation of preemancipation breeding unions was established by an 1866 cohabitation law. This law allowed exslaves who still cohabitated to acquire a *cohabitation certificate* so as not to be tried for a misdemeanor. These certificates contained preemancipation genealogical data as it recorded the date that the couple started living together.

Other sources of information concerning slaves included bills of sales, manumission records, property inventories, and the tax records, wills, deeds, and various probate records associated with the slave owner as a person of property. Genealogical materials on blacks also appear in plantation journals and the personal diaries of plantation masters and mistresses and the church records of slave baptisms.

See also FOLKLIFE: Family Folklore; MYTHIC SOUTH: Family; WOMEN'S LIFE: Family, Modernization of; Genealogy

Tony L. Whitehead
Forest Hazel
University of North Carolina
at Chapel Hill

Andrew Billingsley, *Black Families in White America* (1968); Herbert G. Gutman, *The Black Family in Slavery and Freedom, 1750–1925* (1976); Robert B. Hill, *Informal Adoption among Black Families* (1977); Debra L. Newman, *List of Free Black Heads of Families in the United States in 1790* (1973); Minnie K. Peebles, *North Carolina Historical Review* (April 1978); Carter G. Woodson, *Free Negro Owners of Slaves in the United States in 1830 together with a Brief Treatment of the Free Negro* (1925), *Free Negro Owners of Slaves in the United States in 1830 together with Absentee Ownership of Slaves in The United States in 1830* (1924).

Health, Black

In the post–Civil War era white southern physicians noted the rise of disease among newly emancipated blacks and predicted the eventual extinction of blacks from the United States despite all that medicine could do to prevent it. Many white laymen in the South held similar views. In fact, issues of black health have always concerned southern whites. Interest in the subject constitutes a minor theme in the region's history. It is paradoxical that so politically voiceless and socially invisible a group as southern blacks has received so much attention with regard to health, medical care, and disease characteristics. But there are important reasons for this trend, rooted in southern medical, racial, and intersectional history.

First, because southern whites for so long either subjugated or segregated blacks, they have never been able to escape taking at least partial responsibility for black health. Second, because of certain external physical characteristics, especially skin color, blacks in a white-dominated society have been visible and thus easily observed and studied with regard to health. Third, because race has been important in the South and in relations between the South and the rest of the nation, whites have used black medical distinctiveness, real and imagined, for political purposes.

Blacks brought with them from Africa to the New World a heritage of disease and medical care differing in many ways from that of the dominant Euro-American society. Some African health problems (e.g., sleeping sickness) and practices (e.g., use of certain herbs and tribal rites) disappeared for environmental reasons. Yet genetic maladies (sickle-cell anemia), disease susceptibilities (tuberculosis, respiratory diseases) and resistances (malaria, yellow fever), medical treatments (herbs, voodoo), and medical theories (supernatural causes of disease) remained, influencing the lives of both blacks and their white neighbors. White medicine dominated, but slaves, ostensibly not the owners of their bodies, could and did choose to invoke, covertly when necessary, their own medical systems. Some white masters condoned or reluctantly accepted these subtle statements of black independence because they saw no alternatives, felt their slaves should enjoy some freedoms, or noted that the black healing approaches worked. Some of these practices and remedies actually passed from the black to the white medical world.

A number of factors influenced the health status of Afro-Americans during the slavery period (1620–1865). Living conditions played an important role because plantation slave quarters, though located in rural areas, developed many public health characteristics of a village or small town. Infectious disease epidemics, parasitic infestations, and human- and other organic-waste disposal problems resulted from life in slave communities. Nutritionally unbalanced or nutrient-deficient food caused, at the least, weakness and, at worst, death from malnutrition or infection. Hard, unsafe working and living conditions; whipping and other physical punishments; pregnancy, childbirth, and gynecological problems among physically laboring women; and the psychological stresses of a life of servitude also contributed to poor health among slaves.

When slaves needed medical attention, owners usually insisted blacks turn to the Euro-American curing system rather than caring for themselves. Most states required that masters provide for proper maintenance of their human chattel. Some fulfilled this responsibility better than others, depending on widely varying factors including personality, number of slaves, financial status, master-slave relationship, presence or absence of owner, and threat of an epidemic to property (slaves) and to white lives. As a general rule, masters, mistresses, overseers, or overseers' wives used their own medical knowledge and skills on ailing slaves first; then, if these resources failed to reverse the course of disease or injury, they called the local physician. Whites handled illnesses within their own families in a similar manner, applying home remedies before calling in the physician, with one difference. They generally sought professional help sooner for white family members than for slaves.

As southern whites cared for more and more blacks, observed how slaves fared in the southern disease environment, and noted the effectiveness on bondsmen of various medical treatments, they began to notice trends. Blacks seemed much more prone to some diseases, less susceptible or even immune to others, and more or less responsive to one or another remedy. A belief developed, particularly between 1830 and 1860, that the South possessed different health conditions from the North or West, that southern medical care differed from that in the North, that blacks were medically different from whites, and that southern physicians were uniquely suited and trained to handle the region's health problems. Blacks, they further argued, were medically suited for the labor and environment of the South. With mounting antislavery pressure from the North, these observations became political points in the proslavery argument. However, no southern physician ever proved any of these ideas.

Emancipation in 1865 ostensibly released southern whites from the responsibility of providing medical care to blacks. Freedmen were on their own and had to rely on their own resources for the basic necessities of food, clothing, housing, and health. In reality, however, blacks generally did not have the wherewithal to survive without help. White predictions that blacks were doomed as a race because of innate physical inferiority and a dissolute lifestyle now that they were free seemed to be justified. Black health did decline, the result of poor housing, malnourishment, overcrowding, and the psychological stresses of a new environment and lifestyle. Whites noted rises in tuberculosis, syphilis, and insanity. Even federal intervention by the medical department of the Freedmen's Bureau brought only temporary and not always reliable assistance. The bureau's goal was to ease the transition from slavery to freedom for both blacks and whites. Though it employed physicians in key areas to provide hospital and dispensary care, the bureau failed in its medical mission on two counts. It established no mechanisms whereby blacks could either continue to receive medical care or learn to care for themselves. Once the bureau left a state (1868–71), blacks were left to their own devices or to the largess of local white authorities and white physicians. Once again, whites had responsibility for black health, at least in part. Some labor and shareholding contracts contained provisions for medical care paid for by the white landowner. City and county government authorities worried about the spread of infectious diseases from blacks to whites, especially as the black population of cities and towns was rising and their physical movements were less restricted. By the 1890s the larger urban areas established hospitals and clinics to care for both black and white poor. Some northern medical schools and several newly founded black schools (e.g., Meharry, Howard, Leonard) produced a small number of black physicians, many of whom opened practices in southern black communities, but the health and medical care of blacks remained at a lower level than that of whites.

As long as black health was primarily a southern problem, the nation as a whole ignored or remained ignorant of the black's plight. But the post–World War I "great migration" of rural southern blacks in search of better jobs and living conditions to northern and border state cities altered the nation's perception. Now money to study and remedy the poor health situations of blacks came from federal, state, and local governments as well as from private sources like the Rosenwald and Rockefeller foundations. They supported public health campaigns (the annual National Negro Health Week), the building of hospitals, medical education for blacks at white and black institutions, health improvement programs (tuberculosis, child and maternal health, syphilis [including the notorious Tuskegee Syphilis Study]), and overall assessments of black health status and needs (Gunnar Myrdal's classic *An American Dilemma*). The result of all this activity was the desegregation of health facilities, a better awareness of black health problems, the provision of assistance to pay for the high cost of medical care through government programs, the reduction of black mortality rates, and an increase in the number of blacks in the healing professions. Problems remain in the South, where state and local government funds are inadequate to pay for black health needs, rural life and traditional Afro-American healing practices persist, and blacks often cannot afford private medical care.

See also FOLKLIFE: Folk Medicine; Voodoo; HISTORY AND MANNERS: Philanthropy, Northern; SCIENCE AND MEDICINE: Health, Public; Education, Medical; Medicine, States' Rights

Todd L. Savitt
East Carolina University

Gaines M. Foster, *Journal of Southern History* (August 1982); James H. Jones, *Bad Blood: The Tuskegee Syphilis Experiment* (1981); *Journal of the National Medical Association* (numerous articles on the history of blacks in medicine in issues from the 1950s to the present); Kenneth F. Kiple and Virginia Himmelsteib King, *Another Dimension to the Black Diaspora: Diet, Disease, and Racism* (1981); Herbert M. Morais, *The History of the Negro in Medicine* (1967); Todd L. Savitt, *Medicine and Slavery: The Diseases and Health Care of Blacks in Antebellum Virginia* (1978).

Immigrants and Blacks

Compared to other regions the South has attracted few immigrants. Whites, already uncomfortable with the large and visible African presence, have generally opposed an influx of strangers from Europe and Asia. Prospective settlers have been deterred from establishing new homes in the area by the image of the South's inhospitable climate and by the prospect of competing with black labor. Yet Cubans, Haitians, and Southeast Asians have migrated to the South in the past generation, and other groups, in fact, came in earlier years.

Black Americans have not been especially receptive to those who looked to the South as a refuge from hunger and oppression. As the least advantaged of native-born Americans, they were the first to experience competition from foreigners for scarce jobs, housing, and education. When newcomers arrived, tensions occasionally erupted into violence; the Miami riot of May 1980, which was caused in part by black resentment at assistance given Cuban refugees, was but one of the latest and worst manifestations of this phenomena.

Whereas in the North immigration was sizable enough to attract public attention and to elicit organized resistance in the generation preceding the Civil War, in the South the reluctance of aliens to compete with slave labor limited the flow of newcomers to negligible numbers. Of those who came, some became slaveowners. More often, they sought work in border state cities such as Baltimore, Louisville, and St. Louis, although New Orleans, Mobile, and Savannah were popular destinations as well. Travelers reported that on occasion slaveowners employed cheap and expendable immigrants to do tasks that might endanger their valuable slave property.

As was to be the case in later years in the North, both slaves and free blacks in the South were sometimes used as "scabs" to destroy early attempts by white workers, many of them recent arrivals from Ireland and Germany, to improve wages and conditions of employment. The difficulty in finding stable and peaceful workers among the immigrants also led many managers of southern industries to prefer native black workers over the newcomers. Yet despite their reputation as unreliable and union prone, white native and immigrant laborers made inroads into a few occupations traditionally dominated by nonplantation slave and free black workers in the 1850s, notably in the textile industry and as longshoremen. In many industries blacks and whites worked alongside each other or in close physical proximity. Although some black employees encountered violence, as did the young Frederick Douglass, who nearly lost his life as a result of attacks by white workers in the Baltimore shipyards in the late 1830s, interracial cooperation rather than hostility was the norm in most integrated industries.

As rural slaves, the bulk of black southerners in the antebellum era had little contact with immigrants. Indeed, not until after emancipation did the issue of immigration receive the attention of large numbers of blacks. And then the subject became important not because of an influx of aliens and heightened competition and conflict, but rather as a result of whites who blamed Afro-Americans for the region's failure to recruit many immigrant workers. Successful recruitment schemes would have imperiled the newly acquired political power of the freedmen and perhaps even their physical survival in their land of birth. Northern blacks who had experienced occupational displacement by immigrants as early as the second quarter of the 19th century and who had roots in the South joined with their southern kin in deploring attempts by white opponents to drive blacks out of the region—and thus intensify economic competition in the

North—or to reduce the exslaves to a condition of semiservitude.

Blacks responded to the possibility of massive immigration to the South by exploiting the fears whites held of those who differed in language, values, and religious traditions. They warned that the bulk of newcomers would not be hard-working peasants but the "riff-raff" of Europe who would pollute the South with violence, labor discontent, and dangerous ideologies. Rather than expose the region to the evils too readily apparent in Europe and the North, whites would be wise to do as Booker T. Washington counseled in his Atlanta Exposition Address of 1895 and "cast down their buckets" among their familiar, faithful, and devoted black fellow citizens.

Most black leaders were uneasy if not alarmed at the prospect of large-scale immigration, but some professed indifference; they either doubted that aliens would come, saw a possibility of Afro-Americans and disgruntled aliens working together to reform the South, or felt confident that black workers could meet the challenge of greater competition. Indeed, Booker T. Washington and his followers used the specter of immigrant competition to promote the doctrine of racial pride, self-help, landownership, and industrial education. Competition and the example immigrants provided as they overcame adversity in a strange and often hostile environment could actually help in the advancement of the race, they claimed.

Open conflict between blacks and immigrants continued to be rare in postbellum southern society. Instead of expanding, the percentage of southerners born elsewhere actually declined in the late 19th and early 20th centuries. Those foreigners who came were more likely to settle in cities or in agricultural colonies such as Sunnyside, Ark., than to compete directly with black field hands. Afro-Americans could have hardly attributed their persistent plight to the relatively few aliens in Dixie, and they seldom sought to do so. True, they held many of the negative stereotypes of foreigners common among white southerners, especially regarding Italians and Jews. They also resented newcomers being accorded opportunities and rights denied them. And on occasion, blacks served as handy scapegoats for the frustrations immigrants experienced in their new home. Nevertheless, tension and hostility between blacks and white outsiders in the South have never approached that associated with the North and West. The more overt forms of discrimination from native whites in the South helped blacks remember that it was white racism and not immigration that caused their degradation, whereas in the North and West the larger numbers of aliens and the more subtle forms of discrimination often resulted in Afro-Americans seeing the immigrant as their enemy.

See also ETHNIC LIFE articles; URBANIZATION: / Mobile; New Orleans; Savannah

David J. Hellwig
St. Cloud State University

David J. Hellwig, *Filson Club History Quarterly* (April 1980), *Mississippi Quarterly* (Fall 1978); James L. Roark, *Masters without Slaves: Southern Planters in the Civil War and Reconstruction* (1977); Arnold Shankman, *Ambivalent Friends: Afro-Americans View the Immigrant* (1982), in *"Turn to the South": Essays on Southern Jewry*, ed. N. M. Kagonoff and Melvin I. Urofsky (1979), *Mississippi Quarterly* (Winter 1977–78); Robert S. Starobin, *Industrial Slavery in the Old South* (1970).

Indians and Blacks

Native Americans first observed Africans in company with the early European explorers, but there was little intensive contact between blacks and Indians until the establishment of Charleston in 1670. The South Carolinians enslaved Indians as well as Africans, but after the Tuscarora War (1711) and the Yamassee War (1715) almost destroyed the colony, the Carolinians changed tactics. Fearful that the enslaved Africans and Indians would unite to overthrow the white minority, they began a divide-and-rule policy to keep the two peoples separated. Indians were paid to capture escaping blacks and punish rebellious slaves; blacks were used to fight against Indians. And, lastly, further enslavement of Indians was discouraged. Most of the enslaved Native Americans were sold to the West Indies. Nevertheless, the considerable previous intermarriage between the two enslaved groups resulted in Afro-Americans having considerable Indian ancestry and absorbing Native American culture.

The southern Indians who had the closest contact with blacks were the Seminoles. This multiethnic people migrated to Florida in the late 1700s to get away from white settlers, and when the United States annexed Florida in 1819, the Seminoles resisted. They welcomed escaping black slaves, whose knowledge of white ways and commitment to freedom made them valuable warriors. Blacks served as interpreters in negotiations with the army, and their advice was respected. Though the Seminole blacks were called "slaves," they had complete freedom to live in their own independent black settlements or to intermarry with Seminoles. They fought fiercely in the Seminole War, as both Indians and blacks resisted removal and reenslavement. White fears of a red-black alliance came true in the 1835–42 war. The United States was forced to accept the Seminole demand that their black allies remain with them before they would move west. The threat to southern slavery, rather than land hunger, was the primary motive for the Seminole conflict. Once the Seminoles were removed to Indian Territory (Oklahoma), however, many of the blacks were kidnapped by slave catchers and sold into slavery in nearby states. In response, during the 1850s many Seminole blacks and Indians migrated to northern Mexico, where their descendants live today.

Chattel slavery was unknown among the aboriginal southeastern Indians, though it may have existed in some of the pre-Columbian Mississippian societies. Among the Cherokees, a captive could be "possessed" by his captor, but such persons were not used for labor purposes. The Cherokees and other Indians who used blacks as plantation slaves clearly adopted the practice from whites. Indeed, many of the earliest and largest Indian slaveholding families were really those with mostly white intermarriage. These mixed-blood families, with their slave-based economy, led in the acculturation of Cherokee, Chickasaw, Choctaw, and Creek. Slavery helped make the previously egalitarian native societies into class-based cash economies, with the nonslaveowning traditionalists on the bottom.

Once they were removed to Indian Territory in the 1830s, class resentments flared up. The slaveowning upper class gained considerable influence in the tribal governments and tightened the slave codes so that the institution became almost as oppressive as among whites. These proslavery factions led the Choctaw, Chickasaw, and Cherokee governments to adopt an alliance of friendship with the Confederate States of America in 1861, and even the Creeks and Seminoles were forced to do likewise. This alliance prompted the antislavery traditionalists to resist. Internal civil war raged in Indian Territory at the same time the national war was going on. The southern tribes were decimated.

Though the antislavery Cherokees got control of their government in 1863 and passed their own Emancipation Act, the victorious United States forced all Indians to end slavery in 1865. Furthermore, before the Union enfranchised blacks in the South, it forced Indian nations to adopt the freed blacks as equal citizens in their tribal governments. This question about whether to agree to adopt their former slaves divided and weakened the Indian governments at a crucial time. The question was complicated by the migration into Indian Territory of more blacks fleeing from white oppression in the South. Though many of the blacks won their fight for recognition of land allotments, both they and their Indian antagonists were largely dispossessed of those lands after the abolition of Indian Territory and the creation of the state of Oklahoma in 1907. Blacks who remained in the state tended to congregate in all-black towns, just as the Indians did in all-Indian areas, so there has not been as much mingling among the two groups as earlier. Their disunity cost them both.

Meanwhile, among the remnant Indians left in the Southeast after the removal era, a new white attitude emerged. Once the major Indian nations were out of the area, Southern whites began trying to lump all nonwhites into a subordinate "colored" category. This was especially true if the remnant group was not recognized by treaty and had largely lost its aboriginal culture. The rights of these people defined as "colored" were progressively restricted as the South moved ever more aggressively toward a black-versus-white biracial society. Into the 1870s the Lumbees in North Carolina resisted such trends by guerrilla warfare. But most such groups were too small to resist, and their only option was to isolate themselves from all outsiders, white and black.

Such isolated communities struggled to stay together as land losses and population increases forced them into the cash economy. To establish their Indian identity, they even resisted white attempts at educational integration, accounting for high illiteracy rates among southern Indians. Although both blacks and Indians faced similar discrimination, Indians continued to hope for a less restrictive social status. This allowed whites to formulate a new divide-and-rule policy, and a three-tier segregation policy emerged in counties with Indian communities.

As long as the black community remained powerless, there were no incentives for Indians to identify with it. Intermarriage was discouraged; Indians who did so were generally ostracized and merged into the black community.

Black-Indian relations began to change with the civil rights movement. Not only did black activism provide an inspiring example to dissatisfied Indians, but civil rights legislation sometimes helped Indians as well. As the segregation system began to break down, some Indians considered allying with blacks for further change, especially concerning education. The two groups, however, remain more separated today than in the pre-1840 era.

See also ETHNIC LIFE: Indians; / Cherokees; Chickasaws; Choctaws; Creeks; Lumbees; Seminoles

Walter L. Williams
University of Cincinnati

Daniel F. Littlefield, *Africans and Creeks: From the Colonial Period to the Civil War* (1979), *Africans and Seminoles: From Removal to Emancipation* (1976), *The Cherokee Freedmen: From Reconstruction to American Citizenship* (1978); Theda Perdue, *Slavery and the Evolution of Cherokee Society, 1540–1866* (1979); Walter L. Williams, ed., *Southeastern Indians since the Removal Era* (1979); J. Leitch Wright, Jr., *The Only Land They Knew: The Tragic Story of the American Indians in the Old South* (1981).

Landownership, Black

The evolution of land tenure patterns in the South has shaped the contours of Afro-American life and culture. The acquisition and use of land or real property as a commodity has been a basis for all other forms of wealth. In addition, land has been the physical space on which successive generations of Afro-Americans have organized themselves. Land has thus served an economic and a social role. The link between the use of land to provide food, shelter, and sources of income, and the perception of land as the cornerstone of one's cultural "homeplace" abound in the folkways of southern blacks.

Landownership has translated into economic autonomy, political assertiveness, and social independence for most Americans, and blacks were no exception to this. In the period prior to the Civil War a small number of free blacks acquired a modest amount of real property. It was commonplace for blacks who owned and worked their own farms during this period to have been trained through apprenticeships in other occupations as well. Enslaved blacks were not permitted by law, however, to own or exercise control over property. Though some free blacks owned land they often saw their control over real and personal property abridged by extralegal and illegal practices designed to circumvent black assertiveness and to promote white supremacy.

Still, a sizable number of "quasi-free" blacks remained living and working in the South. Southern free blacks tended to live in urban areas and owned property with an estimated value of $25 million. The Union victory that ended the Civil War emancipated approximately 4 million Afro-American men, women, and children, who joined the ranks of close to a half million free, mostly southern blacks. Most newly freed Afro-Americans knew and understood the significance that the ownership of 40 acres of land, a mule, the acquisition of literacy, and the exercise of the vote held for participation in a "New South," which the demise of chattel slavery offered.

Some blacks who were previously enslaved participated in attempts to demonstrate their serious commitment and expertise in commodities production and land management. During the war almost 800,000 acres of abandoned and confiscated land was amassed under the administration of the Freedmen's Bureau, and much of it was cultivated by blacks with the belief, and sometimes the promise, that following the war they would have the opportunity to own farmsteads. Indeed, many of the 183,000 freedmen, women, and children in contraband camps between 1863 and 1864 cultivated lands producing agricultural settlements such as the ones at Davis Bend, Miss., Port Royal, S.C., and Roanoke Island, N.C.

Although 40 acres and a mule had long been on the black agenda, the events of the Reconstruction era would betray that aspiration for the majority of blacks. Instead of creating independent landowning black family farmers, capable of playing a valuable role in the American economy, the Reconstruction period saw a betrayal of the progressive agenda for social change. Still, despite reactionary white supremacy political campaigns, black codes, vagrancy laws, the Ku Klux Klan, lynchings, and Jim Crow segregation, most black people remained in the South occupied primarily in agriculture.

In the 35 years following the failure of Reconstruction politics to enact a viable land resettlement and purchase plan for the newly emancipated freedmen, one-fourth of the black farmers of the South did acquire land. A relatively small number inherited land from parents who had acquired property either as free blacks or after their emancipation. There are documented instances of land being given to some of the interracial children born of the union of enslaved black women and white men. Clearly, though, the majority of Afro-Americans who acquired land worked to acquire it in parcels. By 1910 this success, which had been achieved against overwhelming odds, culminated in blacks owning more than 15 million acres of land.

About 91 percent of the country's 9.8 million blacks were still in the rural South in 1910. Approximately 890,000 blacks operated farms, 175,000 of which were full owners and another 43,000 of which were part owners. About 218,972 of these farmers were black owner-operators, and 670,000 were tenants who participated in the crop-lien system. The average size of black-owned farms was about 10–20 acres. By 1910 throughout most of the South blacks had been politically disfranchised and the majority were increasingly limited to participation in a cashless debt peonage cycle.

Land's importance as a commodity and as the basis for familial and social organization is reflected in the role it has played in the formation of capital and the creation and maintenance of black institutions. The steady decline in black ownership and the escalating increase in the out-migration of rural Afro-Americans to southern and northern cities between 1910 and 1940, and again from 1950 to most recently, 1975, seriously threatened the work of such black self-help institutions as colleges, churches, lodges, associations, and fraternities and sororities. Clearly, had it not been for the diligent work of blacks who worked in and through the black self-help agricultural experiment stations—such as at Tuskegee Institute—black farm agents, and the cadre of home demonstration agents, much of the multifaceted aid that many black farm families received would have been nonexistent.

"Separate and unequal" describes decades of disproportionate and unequal access to education, banking, credit, and political and legal rights. Black farm families often found themselves obliged to work and where feasible purchase land in areas where the soil was depleted and poor to marginal in quality. Many black farm families could not withstand the combination of these legal and extralegal mechanisms of social control. Gradually, the acquisition of farm acreage, which had steadily increased between 1870 and 1910, began to decline.

The acquisition of black-owned land, which served as the infrastructure supporting the economic stability of southern black rural institutional growth, reached an apex in the early 20th century and has been declining ever since. Consequently, many chose to leave the land and seek a "homeplace" and economic opportunity in other parts of the country. Some were pushed out by poverty, racism, the lack of opportunities, or by the opportunities of urban life.

The persistence of monoculture, or dependency on a single cash crop, continued despite the toll it exacted from both the black and white family farm population. Dependency on nonedible cash crops, malnutrition, low fertility, high infant mortality, pellagra, rickets, nutritional anemia, scurvy, and influenza were but a few of the maladies that, along with the destruction brought on by the boll weevil, cotton boll worm, tobacco bud worm, cattle tick, erosion, under-fertilized and poor soil, low cotton prices, inadequate and often unreasonable credit, governmental policies and tax structures designed to promote large-scale agricultural production, Jim Crow segregation, and often a virulent racism, all contributed to undermining the black presence on the land.

Moreover, except for the relative economic stability of the World War II years, the chronicle of black landownership in the 20th century is captured in a statistical depiction of black land loss, black out-migration, and the high turnover of black-owned land through foreclosures, duress sales, partition sales, or old age liens. In terms of the quality of life, most rural black residents are poor and live at the subsistence scale, survival level for most of their lives.

Between 1910 and 1960 approximately 3 million blacks left the South seeking a new "place" and despite the civil rights movement, between 1960 and 1970 roughly another 1.5 million blacks left the region. However, between 1975 and 1980 this 60-year process of relocating was reversed; about 222,000 blacks left the region while approximately 415,000 blacks moved to the South, though not necessarily as owners of equity in the form of landownership.

Between 1950 and 1970 southern blacks lost control of approximately 6 million acres of land, reducing the number of full and part owners from 193,000 to less than 67,000. Clearly, while not every transaction involving land transfer can be said to have resulted from the oppressive economic and social conditions under which black men, women, and children lived, it would be inaccurate to underestimate the economic consequences of racial oppression in circumventing the expansion of black-owned family farms.

By 1981, 4 percent of the black population lived on farms, representing 222,000 people, whereas 349,000 blacks had lived on farms in 1978. By comparison the white farm population declined 25 percent between 1970 and 1981, while the black farm population dropped 67 percent. Rural population unemployment rates in 1981 for blacks were 11.4 percent and for whites 2.5 percent, while nearly twice as many black farm residents lived in poverty, 30.2 percent versus 16.5 percent of whites.

Black-owned family farms have been a relatively small percentage of the overall black rural and agricultural presence in the South, but their existence has conferred a certain permanence on communities in which black sharecroppers were more easily exploited and at times driven from the land. Landowning blacks have served as a role model for those whose aspirations focused on acquiring land and the security that managing one's own farm generates.

See also AGRICULTURE: Sharecropping and Tenancy; / Agricultural Extension Services; Boll Weevil; HISTORY AND MANNERS: Reconstruction; LAW: / Black Codes; SOCIAL CLASS: Poverty; Tenant Farmers

Marsha Jean Darling
Wellesley College

Marsha Jean Darling, "The Growth and Decline of the Afro-American Family Farm in Warren County, North Carolina, 1910–1960" (Ph.D. dissertation, Duke University, 1982); John Hope Franklin, *From Slavery to Freedom: A History of Negro Americans* (1947; 5th ed., 1980); Leo McGee and Robert Boone, eds., *The Black Rural Landowner—Endangered Species: Social, Political and Economic Implications* (1979); Claude O. Oubre, *Forty Acres and a Mule: The Freedmen's Bureau and Black Land Ownership* (1978); George B. Tindall, *The Emergence of the New South, 1913–1945* (1967); University of California at Davis, Agricultural History Center, *A List of References for the History of Black Americans in Agriculture* (1981); U.S. Commission on Civil Rights, *The Decline of Black Farming in America* (1982); U.S. Department of Commerce, Bureau of the Census, *Census of Population: 1910, 1920, 1930, 1940, 1950, 1960, 1970, 1980; Census of Agriculture: 1910, 1920, 1930, 1940, 1945, 1959, 1969, 1974, 1982; The Social and Economic Status of the Black Population in the United States: 1790–1978*, Special Studies, P-23 (1980); *America's Black Population: 1970–1982, A Statistical View* (1983); Monroe Work, ed., *The Negro Yearbook, 1914–1915* (1915).

Literary Portrayals of Blacks

The American South inherited most of its early attitudes toward blacks and its means of portraying them in art and in literature from Europe. The "noble savage" and the "comic servant" had already appeared in European novels. Paintings had included the idea of the exotic primitive long before he appeared in the literature of America.

Following Goldsmith's and Burns's pastoral tradition of happy menials in bucolic settings, such poets as Henry Timrod and Edward Coote Pinkney described dusky peasants happily at work in the cotton patches of the antebellum South, dancing and singing around the campfires at night, delighted with their carefree, childlike existence. Like such religious and political apologists as Albert Taylor Bledsoe and John C. Calhoun, these authors assumed that the "sons of Ham" were appointed by God and fitted by nature to be hewers of wood and drawers of water.

The "peculiar institution" of slavery engendered little artistic expression; following the Civil War, however, Thomas Nelson Page, John Pendleton Kennedy, and others used garrulous old darkies to lament the passing of the old order in sentimental and defensive stories.

This contented slave stereotype was to cast its shadow well into the 20th century. Faulkner used it in *The Unvanquished*, and Margaret Mitchell popularized it in *Gone with the Wind*. Sometimes the figure is a comic young servant, but more often it is a gentle aged retainer. The "mammy" achieved mythic status both as the residual image of loving ties within slavery and as a reflection of continuing historical realities. Over the years, southern whites continued to engage black women to serve as nurses and cooks in white homes. Faulkner's Dilsey is a conscious tribute to his own mammy, Caroline Barr, a person he celebrated for her faith and her love of children. Such moderns as Truman Capote and Carson McCullers show comforting black servants as the mainstays of white children. In their wisdom, they have archetypal qualities; Faulkner even suggests for the role of Nancy in *Requiem for a Nun* a black madonna.

The black male has had a less consistent career in fiction. Uncle Remus, the old narrator of fables, is unusually authentic for the period. Joel Chandler Harris combined an interest in dialect with an ear for Afro-American folktales that shrewdly celebrate rebellion, making Uncle Remus realistic in spite of his sentimental context.

As opposed to this aged and sexless patriarch, the "brute Negro" was a projection of the sexual and political fears that accompanied the Reconstruction. Thomas Dixon, Jr., a violent white supremacist, portrayed blacks as apelike creatures intent on raping innocent young white maidens, thereby justifying the violence of the Klansmen. This image is more than of a rebellious slave, ungrateful and unmanageable. W. J. Cash and others insist that it was part of the spiral of lust and fear that led to the center of the southern psyche. It reflected the myth of the black's sexual potency and the fear of retaliation by black men for white men's use of black women. The myths of southern white womanhood, white supremacy, and racial purity were confronted with the threat of growing black power. The brute Negro is a far cry from the heroic noble savage.

The black male is a less popular subject for southern fiction than the black female because he is less a part of the white community. As farm laborer, butler, or handyman, he is a background figure and an alien. For a time during and after World War I, when blacks migrated in large numbers to northern industrial centers, he was cast as the runaway father or the sharecropper held in peonage.

In the 1920s and 1930s, socially conscious writers such as T. S. Stribling and Erskine Caldwell turned him into a Christ figure. As the Depression deepened and lynchings escalated, sympathy for this victim grew and the heroism of his persecutors disappeared. Redneck whites became the villains.

The self-sufficient black man occasionally emerged as the older, wilder "black prince"—a mythic figure who was magical, footloose, and amoral. Caroline Gordon pictured him as the mystical wanderer; William Styron turned him into a black prophet and rebel. The metamorphosis of the brute Negro into the black prince has been one of the most remarkable indicators of social change in the South. "Uncle Tom," at the same time, has changed from a term of approbation to one of denigration.

Although both male and female victims were at times black in color, the more popular choice has been the "tragic mulatto." This symbol of the perils of miscegenation was guaranteed to win white sympathy in stories as late as *Light in August* and *Band of Angels*. Other authors have used the same figures to signify upward mobility, particularly among the "talented tenth" who became the first professionals from the American black community. They sometimes went north and passed for white, or joined the growing black middle class in urban centers, occasionally returning to the South to help the black folk and to inspire social unrest. This figure sometimes emerges as the "black Anglo-Saxon" who is despised for his mindless aping of white culture or as the "black Babbitt" who is caricatured for his pompous delight in middle-class materialistic values. But in other novels, this "new Negro"—the rebel—uses his education to help his race.

These images have changed with the themes and the language, reflecting the rapid transformation of the black community in the past century. Just as black men and women have moved from illiterate, ragged slaves, to sharecroppers and landowners, to educated business men and women, teachers, lawyers, and doctors, so too the literature has changed. Faulkner portrayed a black veteran of World War I as an ignorant and comic "uppity nigger." He later pictured a black veteran of World War II as a brave and sophisticated politician.

The rise of black authors has also had its impact on the tone and quality of southern white authors. For a time, early in the 20th century, white local colorists affectionately portrayed black cabins filled with quaint folk whose lives were replete with exotic customs. This primitivism broke into more heroic images with Paul Green's Abraham and DuBose Heyward's Porgy. But the "exotic primitives" disappeared as *objects d'art* when black writers like W. E. B. Du Bois, James Weldon Johnson, Jean Toomer, Richard Wright, Ralph Ellison, Zora Neale Hurston, and Alice Walker began publishing.

When William Styron in 1967 tried to incorporate the black point of view into his epic presentation of *The Confessions of Nat Turner*, the black and white liberal community attacked him violently for presuming to speak for blacks. The responses, which addressed issues far more complex than the racial identity of the author or the point of view employed, have cast a pall over the creation of or publication of stories by white authors about blacks. Yet the southern writer, black or white, can hardly write about the South without writing about blacks. The slave over the years has gone from "darky" to "nigger" to "Nigra" to "Negro," from "person of color" to "colored" to "black," from "boy" and "gal" to "man" and "woman." The shift is clearly from a stereotype to an individualized human being. The authors have finally moved from defining noun to descriptive adjective in their use of "black."

In the later fiction of Faulkner, Robert Penn Warren, Eudora Welty, Flannery O'Connor, and in the plays of Tennessee Williams and Lillian Hellman, black characters embody human vanity, heroism, comedy, tragedy, and endurance.

See also LITERATURE articles; MYTHIC SOUTH: Plantation Myth; Racial Attitudes; / "Mammy"; "Moonlight-and-Magnolias" Myth; "Sambo"

Nancy M. Tischler
Pennsylvania State University

Robert A. Bone, *The Negro Novel in America* (1958); John M. Bradbury, *Renaissance in the South: A Critical History of the Literature* (1963); Sterling Brown, *The Negro in American Fiction* (1937); Hugh Gloster, *Negro Voices in American Fiction* (1948); Seymour L. Gross and John Edward Hardy, eds., *Images of the Negro in American Literature* (1966); John Herbert Nelson, *The Negro Character in American Literature* (1926); Nancy M. Tischler, *Black Masks: Negro Characters in Modern Southern Fiction* (1969).

Literature, Black

Over the past century southern black literature has evolved from a relatively sparse body of writings, mainly imitative of Euro-American literary forms and thematically focused on the plight of blacks in the South, to a sophisticated literary canon whose forms and meanings coalesce to give it a distinct identity.

Southern black poetry was basically undistinguished before the 1920s. Slave poet George Moses Horton and abolitionist Frances Ellen Watkins Harper were the most prominent southern black voices in antebellum poetry. Some poets, such as Horton, adopted standard Euro-American poetic techniques and seldom wrote about racial issues. Still others, like Harper, used these standard forms primarily to concentrate on issues germane to southern black life. Post–Civil War poets Albery A. Whitman, George M. McClellan, and Joseph S. Cotter, Sr., at times wrote skillfully about racial and nonracial topics in conventional poetic forms.

Before the 1920s the South produced few black poets who had mastered the art form on a level equal to that of blacks elsewhere in the country. Southern blacks emerged, though, as the dominant voices in the poetry of the Harlem Renaissance of the 1920s, and thereafter they remained in the vanguard of black poets in America. One wing of the Harlem Renaissance arts movement looked to the black South for aesthetic inspiration and artistic direction. Langston Hughes's *The Weary Blues* (1926) and James Weldon Johnson's *God's Trombones: Seven Negro Sermons in Verse* (1927) drew heavily from southern black folk culture and the experiences of the black masses within and outside the South. Hughes tapped an essentially secular component of southern black life—its music. Grounding his poetic technique in musical forms whose origins were southern and black and which, to a large extent, had evolved from the religious orientation of southern blacks, Hughes used blues and jazz to shape the form and meaning of his poetry. Johnson tapped the sacred side of the southern black experience. Choosing the black folk sermon as the embodiment of a southern black worldview and as an indigenous art form, Johnson elevated folk art to the level of high art. Poets, novelists, and playwrights after the 1920s (blacks and whites) followed the example of Hughes, Johnson, and others of the Harlem Renaissance by deriving artistic inspiration from the social and cultural life of the black South.

In the 1920s black poets' use of dialects became more refined as poetic form merged with content. Black dialect gave way to black idiom, and poets made even more extensive uses of features from the southern black oral tradition. Many southern black poets of the Harlem Renaissance also built their poetic canons with forms and themes not exclusively or predominantly black or southern. The lyricism of Jean Toomer's poetry and the intricate patterns of imagery drawn from nature by Anne Spencer revealed that a poetic voice originating from the black South could adopt the Euro-American literary heritage and yet remain relatively free of its constraints.

In the decades following the Harlem Renaissance, southern blacks continued to be major influences on black American poetry. Southerners Sterling Brown, Arna Bontemps, Margaret Walker, and Melvin B. Tolson were among black America's leading poets between the end of the Harlem Renaissance and the 1960s. A native of the District of Columbia, Sterling Brown in his *Southern Road* (1932) captured the spirit of the southern black folk character in the language, form, and personae of his poetry. Between the 1930s and the 1960s Walker and Tolson exhibited in their poetry an intricate blending of the Euro-American and Afro-American heritages. Tolson became one of the best American poets of his time.

As the movement toward a black aesthetic gained impetus in the 1960s, southern black writers, many of them poets, were again among the leaders. During the 1960s and after, the poetry of southern blacks lost many of its more obvious regional qualities and merged with the larger body of black American poetry. The focus shifted from the rural South to the urban North with southern settings, themes, and female personae being replaced by northern settings, themes, and male personae. Nikki Giovanni, Etheridge Knight, Don L. Lee, Naomi Madgett, Sterling Plumpp, and Lance Jeffers are only a few of the widely read contemporary black poets whose origins are southern.

Southern blacks wrote few plays before the 1920s. William Wells Brown's *Escape, or A Leap for Freedom* (1858) and Joseph S. Cotter, Sr.'s, *Caleb, the Degenerate* (1903), both dramatic tracts, are notable now chiefly for their historical value. Before the Harlem Renaissance, southern blacks wrote minstrel shows, musical comedies, and a few serious social dramas, but the significance of these works in black American theater arts is also mainly historical. As an outgrowth of the Renaissance, however, Langston Hughes (*Mulatto*, *When the Jack Hollers*, and *Little Ham*), Zora Neale Hurston (*Great Day*), Hal Johnson (*Run, Little Children*), and Arna Bontemps (*St. Louis Woman*) emerged as successful southern black playwrights. In the 1930s the Works Progress Administration's support of black theater arts—plays, playwrights, actors, and actresses—provided for the writing and production of several dramas of social realism by and about southern blacks.

After 1940 the number of southern black playwrights and plays about southern black life declined. Randolph Edmonds, Theodore Ward, and Alice Childress have, however, produced works in this period that rank with the best American plays. From the 1930s through the early 1960s southern black playwrights, like their northern counterparts, used the music, folklore, religion, social history, and other components of southern black life as a major source for their art, but after about 1960 the use of distinctly southern materials decreased sharply in plays by northern and southern blacks. Settings, themes, and characters associated with the urban North became predominant. Still, Alice Childress's *Wedding Band* (1966) and Samm-Art Williams's *Home*, distinctly southern black works, were among the most successful post-1960 plays.

In another genre, southerners were among the earliest (if not the first) black short-fiction writers in America.

Until well past 1900 southern black short fiction in the main was thematically about the slave experience and its aftermath and conformed largely to changes and developments in the short story as an American art form. William Wells Brown, Frederick Douglass, Frances W. Harper, and a few other southern blacks wrote various types of short prose fiction during the 19th century. Near the turn of the century Charles Waddell Chesnutt elevated southern black short fiction to the level of literary art. Many of Chesnutt's stories incorporated characteristics of the American local color movement and, regionally, several were classified as plantation literature. The tales of white southerner Thomas Nelson Page and those of Chesnutt exemplified the essential differences between black writers and white writers in approaches to the plantation South. Through characterization, theme, and incident black writers of the South repudiated the romantic image of the plantation. Chesnutt's Uncle Julius, for instance, contradicted the white portrayal of the faithful black servant, epitomized by Page's Sam and Joel Chandler Harris's Uncle Remus. The idyllic portrait of plantation life created by white writers was in stark contrast to the image Chesnutt and other blacks showed of a system infested with greed, inhumanity, deception, and cruelty.

Southern black writers also embellished conventional short-fiction forms by adding features that reflected black life in the South. One such feature was the double entendre, a characteristic of narrative expression rooted especially in the secular and sacred music of the black South. A part of the trickster motif, it helped shape not only characterization but also plot structure, language, and meaning in the different forms of southern black short fiction. Chesnutt's *The Conjure Woman* (1899) exemplified the black writer's skillful use of double entendre.

The Conjure Woman was also an early example of the use of the short-story cycle. The cycle is a fictional narrative that combines techniques of the novel and the short story. Among other collections of short fiction, Langston Hughes's *The Ways of White Folks* (1934) and the Simple series (1950–65); Richard Wright's *Uncle Tom's Children* (1938) and *Eight Men* (1961); Alice Childress's *Like One of the Family*; James A. McPherson's *Hue and Cry* (1969) and *Elbow Room* (1977); and Ernest J. Gaines's *Bloodline* (1975) demonstrated the consistent expertise of southern black writers' use of the cycle. Hal Bennet, Toni Cade Bambara, and Henry Dumas are among the best contemporary black short-fiction writers of southern origin to have produced superior short-story cycles as well as excellent individual stories.

Between 1900 and the 1970s the novel has been the most widely read and critically acclaimed genre in southern black literature. The manner in which it has concerned itself with the past distinguished it from the general black American novel, the southern white novel, and the Anglo-American novel. The southern white novel has generally dealt with the effects of a real or an imagined past on a present generation, with characters grappling to come to terms with that past. Typically, the southern black novel made the physical and psychological landscapes of the past a living part of the novel; it recreated, repopulated, and critically examined the past as physical setting. Surprisingly, though, southern blacks produced few novels that can be strictly defined as historical novels. Arna Bontemps (*Black Thunder*, 1936), Frank Yerby (*The Foxes of Harrow*, 1946), Waters Turpin (*The Rootless*, 1957), and Margaret Walker (*Jubilee*, 1966) were exceptions.

Those novels concerned with the past, particularly the slave past, used a rather distinct thematic structure. Characteristically, the southern black novel was structurally tripartite—usually beginning in the present, shifting to the recent or remote past, and returning to the present. There were frequent variations: a flight-rejection-return pattern evident in Chesnutt's *The House Behind the Cedars* (1900) and in other novels in the "passing" vein; a South-North-South pattern in Jean Toomer's *Cane* (1923) and in a host of novels that concerned the southern black migrant in the North, from James Weldon Johnson's *The Autobiography of an Ex-Coloured Man* (1912) to Ralph Ellison's *Invisible Man* (1952); a fear-flight-fate pattern in Richard Wright's *Native Son* (1940), William Attaway's *Blood on the Forge* (1941), and several novels whose settings were almost exclusively northern or whose themes were grounded in the violence of living black in America.

Prior to the mid-1970s southern black novels characteristically were concerned with blacks' identity and their process of self-definition. This overarching theme remained prominent over the generations: the 19th-century novels often focused on the plight of the mulatto; the early 20th-century novels that frequently recount the aborted attempts of black characters to "pass" as white; the Harlem Renaissance novels affirmed blackness as a key to identity; the protest-era novels followed in the tradition of *Native Son*; post-1960 novels that dwelt on the effects of black affirmation in a drastically changed, but still white-dominated, society.

For its form and its content, the southern black novel found one of its most influential prose models in the Afro-American slave narrative, which itself was essentially a southern product. Various features of the southern version of the black American novel have their antecedents in the genre: the concentration on generic black experiences and incidents; the tendency toward representative central characters; the emphasis on the protagonist's process of self-definition; the use of the autobiographical mode and the portrayal of an exemplary life; the analysis of society by an author (or narrator) removed from that society. Indeed, the first black American novelist, William Wells Brown, was himself a fugitive slave, and he cast his first novel, *Clotel* (1853), solidly in the traditions of the slave-narrative genre.

As the southern black novel evolved, from the 19th into the 20th century, its use of narrative voice blended with other features of southern black narrative prose to produce a particularly (but not exclusively) southern point of view in the black novel. For more than a century southern blacks wrote numerous prose narratives, which in their variety conformed to the autobiographical mode. There have been the fugitive-slave narratives and the exslave narratives; the spiritual, social, political, and personal autobiographies; the confessionals, exemplary lives, the diary-type and journal-type autobiographies; as well as the autobiographical novel. At times, real-life experiences and incidents were the backdrop for fictional characters; at other times real-life characters become the nucleus around which true-to-life (fictional) experiences and incidents are presented. Southern black prose writers were so attracted to the autobiographical mode that in numerous prose narratives they drew a very thin line between fiction and fact.

One group of prose narratives used the techniques of fiction—a group that includes Richard Wright's *Black Boy* (1945), Will Thomas's *The Seeking* (1953), H. Rap Brown's *Die Nigger Die!* (1970), and Alex Haley's *The Autobiography of Malcolm X* (1965) and *Roots* (1976). In another group the novels (fictional autobiographies) employed nonfiction techniques—Johnson's *The Autobiography of an Ex-Coloured Man* and Ernest J. Gaines's *The Autobiography of Miss Jane Pittman* (1971). Finally, in still another group there are novels such as Toomer's *Cane* and Ellison's *Invisible Man* that contain varying degrees and uses of autobiographical material.

Folktales and aphorisms, sacred and secular music, and the religious orientation or worldview of southern blacks all influenced language, undergirded imagery and symbolism, delineated characterization, and motivated plot structure in the southern black novel. This tendency was evident in the polemical, propagandistic, and apologetic novels that preceded World War I; it increased and became more refined in the novels between World War I and the 1930s; it pervaded such 1930s folk novels as Zora Neale Hurston's *Their Eyes Were Watching God* (1937) and George W. Henderson's *Ollie Miss* (1935); it shaped themes and characterization in the social-protest novels of the 1940s; and it pervaded Ellison's *Invisible Man* and several other novels in the post–World War II period. Southern black novelists as a group have thus made wide and varied uses of the cultural traditions of their region.

The merits of southern black literature have been widely acclaimed nationally and internationally. Ellison's *Invisible Man* won a National Book Award; McPherson's collection of short fiction, *Elbow Room*, was awarded a Pulitzer Prize, as was Alice Walker's novel *The Color Purple* (1982). The numerous awards, prizes, and distinctions accorded to works by blacks of southern origin throughout this century testify to the place they hold within the larger world of American literature.

See also GEOGRAPHY: Expatriates and Exiles; LITERATURE articles

J. Lee Greene
University of North Carolina
at Chapel Hill

Doris Abramson, *Negro Playwrights in the American Theatre* (1969); Richard K. Barksdale and Keneth Kinnamon, eds., *Black Writers of America: A Comprehensive Anthology* (1972); Robert A. Bone, *Down Home: A History of Afro-American Short Fiction from Its Beginnings to the End of the Harlem Renaissance* (1975); Arthur P. Davis and J. Saunders Redding, eds., *Cavalcade: Negro American Writing from 1760 to the Present* (1971); Addison Gayle, *The Way of the New World: The Black Novel in America* (1975); Hugh M. Gloster, *Negro Voices in American Fiction* (1948); James V. Hatch, *Black Playwrights, 1823–1977: An Annotated Bibliography of Plays* (1977); M. Thomas Inge, Maurice Duke, and Jackson R. Bryer, eds., *Black American Writers: Bibliographical Essays*, 2 vols. (1978); Blyden Jackson and Louis D. Rubin, Jr., *Poetry in America: Two Essays in Historical Interpretation* (1974).

Lynching

Lynching is part of the American, especially southern, tradition of vigilante terrorism. Vigilantism has taken several forms, depending on purpose: whitecappers usually flogged, or made threatening night visits, to "regulate" or intimidate their enemies; the charivari was usually a semifestive ritual (such as tar-and-feathering or merely serenading with "rough music") meant to humiliate transgressors of community standards; lynch mobs killed their victims. Thus lynching is the deadliest form of vigilantism.

Colonel Charles Lynch of Virginia, whose extralegal "court" sentenced Tories to floggings during the American Revolution, apparently provided the origin of the term "lynch-law." Until the 1850s lynch-law (lynching) was commonly associated with corporal and extralegal punishment, but not killing. Then, during the last decade before the Civil War, southern vigilantes, particularly in Louisiana and Texas, routinely inflicted death upon outlaws and on individuals suspected of plotting slave insurrections. That is when lynching took on its lethal connotation.

The Civil War and Reconstruction intensified southern lynching activity. Vigilantism in Texas alone during the war probably accounted for over 150 deaths. Lynching became more widespread in the Reconstruction years and was directed mostly at exslaves, because the free blacks, no longer valued as property, were often viewed as threatening the existence of white civilization. The specter of Haiti, and its bloody slave rebellion of the 1790s, white fear, and predictions of race war helped multiply acts of terrorism.

Not until 1882 were efforts made to gather data on lynching across the United States. During the 70 years from 1882 to the early 1950s, by which time lynching had virtually ended, a total of 4,739 persons reportedly died at the hands of lynch mobs in the United States. (Since these figures were compiled solely from lynching stories printed in leading urban newspapers of each state, it is likely the actual total was nearer 6,000.) Lynching statistics do not, of course, include those blacks or whites who died in race riots; nor would ordinary interracial homicides, where a person of one race killed someone of another race, be listed.

Reported lynchings for the entire United States averaged 150.4 per year during the last 19 years of the 19th century (1882 through 1900). The all-time peak lynch-law year was 1892, with 230. During the first decade of the 20th century (1901–10), lynchings nationally averaged 84.6 per year and dropped further for 1911–20 (to an average of 60.6 annually for the decade). After 1920 reported lynchings continued to decline, with the decade of 1921–30 averaging 27.5 per year. For 1931–40 there were 114 total lynchings (11.4 annual average). The decade of 1941–50 averaged 3 per year. Then lynching virtually ceased. From 1951 to 1985 only 10 lynching deaths were reported in the United States. Approximately 82 percent of all lynchings listed since 1882 took place in the South ("the South" defined here as being the 15 slave states of 1860). Western and midwestern states account for nearly all the remainder. Nationally, 72 percent of all lynch-mob victims have been black; in the South, 84 percent were black. Over 95 percent of the victims, both nationally and regionally, were males. Among the states, Mississippi ranks first in lynching from 1882 to the present, with 581 deaths (539 of them black); Georgia is second with 530 (491 black); Texas third with 493 (352 black); and Louisiana fourth with 391 (335 black). Very few participants in lynch mobs were prosecuted in any state, and prior to World War II almost none ever served time in prison.

Lynch-law was supposed to be, in the blunt words of one advocate of the practice, "the white woman's guarantee against rape by niggers." Ridding society of "black brutes" who violated Caucasian females was indeed the most often mentioned justification for lynching. "Whenever the Constitution comes between me and the virtue of the white women of South Carolina," exclaimed Governor Cole Blease, "then I say 'to hell with the Constitution.'" Since an accused black rapist of Blease's time and place would almost certainly face quick legal execution, why was mob action deemed necessary? Because, according to the rationale of lynching, a ravished white woman must be spared the agony of testifying in court, while the accused presumably would enjoy and be flattered by "the pomp and ceremony of formal justice."

In fact only about one-third of all lynching victims were suspected of rape or attempted rape. Murder or attempted murder was more often the alleged crime. Others who died at the hands of lynch mobs were accused of transgressions of descending importance, such as arson, burglary, slapping a white person, stealing chickens, chronic impudence, or simply being "vagrant and lewd." Whatever the supposed crime, lynching was widely assumed by whites to be a significant deterrent to black criminality. Black males were thought to be more afraid of lynch mobs than anything else. And rape, despite its secondary place in lynch-law statistics, was of prime importance in justifying the concept of vigilante action. Whenever lynching was discussed, rape became the central theme. Whites who objected to lynching ran the risk of being accused of sympathy for black rapists.

Most lynch mobs killed swiftly. The typical victim, after being hoisted with a rope tossed over a tree limb, trestle, or utility pole, would have his death throes ended by a fusillade of bullets. But some lynchings involved prolonged torture and fire. Mississippi, Georgia, and Texas were most likely to witness scenes of medieval horror during the 1890–1920 years. Nearly all torture-lynching victims were blacks accused of both raping and murdering whites. Most were burned at the stake, after preliminary tortures. One accused murderer in Louisiana, a white man, was slowly skinned alive.

Lynching of Gus Goodman, Bainbridge, Ga., 1905

Lynch mobs are not easily categorized. The larger throngs were probably made up of people who thought of themselves more as observers than as participants, such as the "hundreds of the best men in Atlanta" who, in 1899, boarded "excursion trains" bound for Newnan, Ga., to see accused rapist-murderer Sam Hose burn at the stake. Sometimes lynch mobs were racially integrated, as were most of the crowds who watched legal executions. Occasionally, black mobs lynched blacks accused of crimes against members of their race. There is one reported case of a white South Carolinian, in jail for molesting and murdering a black child, being handed over to an enraged black mob.

The stereotyped image of poor "redneck" whites making up the mobs who lynched blacks is only partially true. White vigilantes came from all strata of society. Middle- and upper-class participation in lynch mobs was especially common in Louisiana. True, most of the vocal opposition to lynchings came from prominent whites, notably religious leaders, lawyers, and judges. But without the tacit approval of most of the dominant elements in the white community, lynching could not have been so frequent. The South, after all, was essentially a hierarchical society.

Southern newspapers prior to 1920 usually hedged on the question of lynching and seldom condemned it if the mob victim was a black male accused of raping a white female. An outspoken defender of vigilante murder was Henry J. Hearsey (1840–1900), editor-publisher of the New Orleans *Daily States*, the official journal of that city's government. The question of actual guilt, Hearsey admitted, did not really concern him; he was sure lynching deterred black crime, and that was the important thing. Other journalists, not as bloodthirsty, sometimes became so desensitized to lynching that they reported such events with sly humor. As one example, the Port Gibson (Miss.) *Reveille* in 1892 thus described the death of John Robinson, black, who had robbed and killed a white man: "He offered to lead the mob to a railroad trestle under which the money lay buried. John and the money have now exchanged locations."

Antilynching crusaders, both nationally and within the South, began to see public opinion drift in their favor after 1920. Women such as Jessie Daniel Ames and Ida Wells-Barnett and groups such as the Association of Southern Women for the Prevention of Lynching were especially significant. Also, growing fear of legal consequences probably discouraged many would-be lynchers.

See also HISTORY AND MANNERS: Sexuality; MYTHIC SOUTH: / Rednecks; VIOLENCE: Crime, Attitudes toward; Outlaw-Heroes; / Ku Klux Klan; Mob Violence; WOMEN'S LIFE: / Ames, Jessie Daniel

William I. Hair
Georgia College

Edward L. Ayers, *Vengeance and Justice: Crime and Punishment in the 19th-Century American South* (1984); Ray Stannard Baker, *Following the Color Line* (1908, reprint 1969); Richard Maxwell Brown, *Strain of Violence: Historical Studies of American Violence and Vigilantism* (1975); James H. Chadbourn, *Lynching and the Law* (1933); James E. Cutler, *Lynch-Law: An Investigation into the History of Lynching in the United States* (1905); George C. Rable, *But There Was No Peace: The Role of Violence in the Politics of Reconstruction* (1984); Arthur F. Raper, *The Tragedy of Lynching* (1933); Walter White, *Rope and Faggot* (1929).

Migration, Black

To black southerners, migration has symbolized both the limitations and opportunities of American life. As slaves, many suffered forced migrations with the attendant heartbreaks of separation from family and community. As freed men and women they seized upon spatial mobility as one of the most meaningful manifestations of their newly won emancipation. Subsequently, black southerners sought to better their conditions by moving within the rural South, to southern cities, and finally to northern cities in a frustrating quest for equality and opportunity. Simultaneously, white southerners acted to restrict such movement, because until the mechanization of cotton culture, black geographic mobility—like black social and economic mobility—threatened the racial assumptions and labor relations upon which the southern economy and society rested.

The first significant migration of black southerners followed the American Revolution and the subsequent opening of the trans-Appalachian West to settlement by slaveholders. The enormous expansion of cotton cultivation in the early 19th century, combined with the closing of the foreign slave trade (1808), soon transformed a forced migration dominated by planters carrying their own slaves westward to one increasingly characterized by the professional slavetrader. Although the Chesapeake remained the major source for the interstate slave trade, after 1830 North and South Carolina, Kentucky, Tennessee, Missouri, and eventually Georgia also became "exporters" of slaves. The plantations of Alabama, Mississippi, Louisiana, Florida, Arkansas, and Texas were worked largely by these early black "migrants" and their children. Although it is difficult to determine the volume of the domestic slave trade, one historian has recently estimated that over 1 million black southerners were forcibly relocated between 1790 and 1860.

The forced migrations of the antebellum South were complemented by barriers against voluntary movement. Although each year hundreds of slaves escaped, they represented but a fraction of the southern black population. Even free black southerners were hemmed in, and by the 1830s their movement across state lines was either restricted or prohibited.

During the Civil War white fears and black hopes generated opposing migration streams. Many slaveowners responded to the approach of Union troops by taking their slaves west, either to the western, upcountry areas of the eastern states, or from the Deep South to Texas and Arkansas. Thousands of slaves, on the other hand, fled toward the advancing army.

Exslaves continued to move away from plantations after the war ended. For many, like Ernest J. Gaines's fictional Miss Jane Pittman, the act of moving constituted a test of the meaning of emancipation. Others sought to reunite with family separated by antebellum forced migration. Much of the movement grew out of a search for favorable social, political, and economic conditions, especially the chance for "independence," which was closely associated with landownership. The flurry of migration generally involved short distances, often merely to the next plantation or a nearby town or city.

Southern cities offered exslaves the protection of the Freedmen's Bureau and the Union army, higher wages, black institutions, political activity, and freedmen's schools. But under pressure from whites—and often faced with the prospect of starvation—many of the thousands who moved cityward soon returned to the plantations. Urban whites considered the black city dweller a threat to social order, and planters sought to stabilize and reassert dominance over their labor force. Vagrancy laws provided a temporary mechanism, and even after the legislative reforms during Reconstruction, the economic structure of the cities limited the urbanization of the black population. Few jobs outside the service sector were available to blacks, and black men especially found that survival was easier in the countryside. Black southerners continued to migrate to cities in modest numbers; by 1910 less than one-fourth lived in communities larger than 2,500. Some people moved back and forth, mainly between farm and small town, following seasonal labor patterns. This kind of mobility also characterized rural nonfarm labor and established what one historian has called a "migration dynamic," which later facilitated movement to northern cities.

Most black southerners who migrated longer distances in the 19th century headed for rural destinations, generally toward the south and west. During the 1870s and 1880s rumors and labor agents drew blacks living in the Carolinas and Georgia to the Mississippi Delta and other areas in the Gulf states with promises of higher wages and better living conditions. Usually, migrants found social and economic relations similar to what they had left behind. The search for "independence" continued, with black southerners trying Kansas in the 1870s and then Arkansas and Oklahoma between 1890 and 1910. Movement became as central to southern black life as it has been to the American experience in general. Because blacks for so long had been unable to move freely, however, it acquired a special mystique manifested as a major theme in black music and symbolized by the recurrent image of the railroad as a symbol of the freedom to move and start life anew. By the 1890s one black southerner in 12 would cross state lines during the decade in search of the still unfulfilled promise of emancipation. Local moves remained even more frequent.

The direction and historical impact of black migration shifted dramatically during World War I. Northern industrialists, previously reluctant to hire blacks when they could draw upon the continuing influx of white immigrants, turned their attention southward as immigration ceased and production orders began pouring in. Some sent labor agents into the South, but news about opportunities and conditions in the North traveled more often via an emerging black communications network comprising letters from earlier migrants, northern newspapers (especially the Chicago *Defender*), and railroad workers. Observers and subsequent scholars offered various catalogues of "economic" and "social" factors that "pushed" migrants from the South and "pulled" them toward the North. Floods, boll weevil infestations, and credit contractions contributed to the urge to move to northern cities offering higher wages than those available to black southerners. Jim Crow, lynching, disfranchisement, and discrimination in the legal and educational systems contrasted with seemingly more equitable and flexible race relations in the North. Most migrants left because of a combination of motivations, which they often summarized as "bettering my condition." For the first time, however, thousands of black southerners looked to industrial work, rather than landownership, in their hopes to enjoy the prerogatives of American citizenship.

Nearly one-half million black southerners headed north between 1916 and 1920, setting off a long-term demographic shift, which would leave only 53 percent of black Americans in the South by 1970, compared with 89 percent in 1910. Nearly all of these migrants went to cities, first in the Northeast and Midwest, and later in the West. Most followed the longitudinal routes of the major railroads, although by World War II, California was drawing thousands of migrants from Texas, Oklahoma, Arkansas, and Louisiana. At the same time, black southerners moved to southern cities, which by 1970 contained two-thirds of the region's black population. Even the massive urban unemployment of the Great Depression only moderately slowed the continuing flow northward, and movement accelerated to unprecedented levels during World War II and the following decades. Since 1970 migration has leveled off, and there has been some evidence of a return to the South.

Many white southerners initially responded to this "Great Migration" by continuing the tradition of constructing barriers in the paths of black migrants. As always, landlords and employers feared the diminution of their labor supply, a threat that in the 19th century had stimulated the enaction of a corpus of legislation designed to limit labor mobility. As a social movement and a series of individual decisions, however, the Great Migration also constituted a direct—although unacknowledged—threat to the fiber of social and economic relations in the South. The system rested upon the assumption that blacks were by nature docile, dependent, and unambitious. The decision to migrate and the evolution of a "movement" suggested dissatisfaction, ambition, and aggressive action. As they had in the past, white southerners tended to blame the movement on "outside forces" (in this case, labor agents), and localities ineffectively sought to stem the tide by tightening "enticement" laws and forcibly preventing blacks from leaving.

The Great Migration transformed both American urban and Afro-American society, as migrants adapted to urban life while retaining much of their southern and rural culture. It was not unusual for southern communities to reconstitute themselves and their institutions in northern cities. Frequent visiting between relatives in the South and North has contributed to this interchange between regional cultures, and the South is still "down home" to some northern black urbanites.

As a historical process, black migration within and from the South suggests some important continuities suffusing much of southern history: the coercive implications of white dependence on black labor; the refusal of blacks to accept their "place" as defined by whites; and the search for identity and opportunity articulated by black writer Richard Wright, whose personal migration experience began with the hope that "I might learn who I was, what I might be."

See also GEOGRAPHY: Migration Patterns; Population

James Grossman
University of Chicago

Florette Henri, *Black Migration: Movement North, 1900–1920* (1975); Allan Kulikoff, in *Slavery and Freedom in the Age of the American Revolution*, ed. Ira Berlin and Ronald Hoffman (1983); Nell Irvin Painter, *Exodusters: Black Migration to Kansas after Reconstruction* (1976); Arvarh Strickland, *Missouri Historical Review* (July 1975); Carter G. Woodson, *A Century of Negro Migration* (1918).

Miscegenation

This word first appeared in 1863 in an unsigned pamphlet written, it was later learned, by two New York City journalists, David G. Croly and George Wakeman, in collusion with Ohio Congressman Samuel S. Cox. From the Latin words *miscere*, to mix, and *genus*, race, it was created by these three Democrats to be a political weapon to stigmatize the Republican party and the Emancipation Proclamation as promoting sexual mixing of races, particularly of whites and blacks. From 1863 to the present, despite miscegenation's actual infrequency in the United States—especially in comparison with other multiracial societies like Latin America and South Africa—the word has served to conjure a threat to the continuation of white supremacy. Throughout history, racial purity has been more of an idea than a reality. Africans brought to the New World already had mixed with Europeans and Asians. Race mixing has been viewed by Afro-Americans as both a positive symbol of integration and assimilation into a white society and as an undermining of black identity and racial pride.

Well before 1863 the term *racial amalgamation* was commonly used to denote sexual intercourse between members of different races but also could include production of children from this liaison. Although somewhat less pejorative in intent than the word *miscegenation*, it also has reflected widespread negative white American attitudes about black-white sexual relations.

In the Chesapeake Bay area during the 17th century, black male slaves were imported while indentured lower-class single English women came to the colonies as household servants. The shortage of partners of the same race and relatively little prejudice about racial purity among the poorer classes stimulated race mixing.

The Lower South differentiated the status of mulattoes and blacks. Charleston and New Orleans exemplified the racial mixing made possible by urban anonymity. On the other hand, the lack of a large white indentured class on South Carolina plantations, where blacks were both domestic and field slaves, accounts for the absence of racial amalgamation.

In the 17th and early 18th centuries the growth of a relatively free and privileged mulatto class was resisted more in the British colonies than in any other slave society in the Americas. North Carolina and Georgia passed laws opposing racial amalgamation in the 18th century. Pennsylvania and Massachusetts, with relatively small black populations and minimal amounts of slavery, banned intermarriage. The fear of losing a homogeneous white culture in cities like Philadelphia and Boston helps explain the origin of northern laws.

By the beginning of the 18th century the female indentured white servant class diminished throughout the South, and the female-to-male ratio among black slaves became more equal. Although race mixing was less likely to occur between white females and black males, the prohibition of racial amalgamation continued. Laws against racial amalgamation now served to enforce the belief that only blacks could be slaves and that the freedom and independence of whites depended upon this racial distinction.

From the 18th century to the Civil War liaisons between white slave masters and black female slaves did occur, and many of their children were removed from the Lower South. The census of 1850 indicated that the Upper South contained two-thirds of the mulattoes in the entire South.

Except for the time of the American Revolution, when ideas of equality moved some northern states to abolish slavery and rescind their prohibition on racial amalgamation, such laws continued to proliferate in the North up to the Civil War. Both free and slave states entering the Union usually legally prohibited intermarriage, and some of the older states made interracial marriage not merely punishable but null and void. A person was defined as black if he/she had a black or mulatto ancestor in the previous three generations. Not until 1843 did Massachusetts's antislavery sentiment bring the abolition of the state's laws opposing interracial marriage—laws that had not only banned intermarriage but had fined clergymen performing such marriages.

The abolition of slavery, accompanied by the creation of the word *miscegenation* in 1863, raised the specter of increased race mixing—especially between black men and white women. White supremacy under slavery had assumed the childlike, docile quality of male slaves and the aggressiveness of freed blacks; the end of slavery transformed this image of male slaves into one of sexually potent men who wished to rape the daughters of white men. Adding to these deep fears were Victorian images of white women as alternately pure and vulnerable or as creatures of their own uncontrolled sexual passions. Criticism of post–Civil War Radical Reconstruction was replete with this imagery, and the end of Reconstruction brought more state laws against racial intermarriage than ever before. Slavery's abolition ended the relationship of the white master and black female slave, and thus caused a sharp decline in interracial mixing. Less miscegenation occurred than under slavery—a common contrast between slave and free societies. Yet the worst incidents of mob rule and lynching of blacks occurred in the late 19th and early 20th centuries under the guise of preventing racial mixing.

By 1850 a mulatto elite developed, and the importance of this group was dramatically evident in South Carolina during Radical Reconstruction (1868–76) where some 13 percent of the politicians were mulatto. Whether they descended from New Orleans and Charleston mulatto society, from illicit plantation liaisons, or, as a large fraction were, from antebellum free Afro-Americans, mulattoes provided a cadre of race leadership well into the 1920s. But 1880–1920 was also the age of passing, when many light-skinned Afro-Americans chose to identify themselves as whites to avoid the disadvantages of being black in a racist society. Passing and its meaning for black identity were major social and literary concerns in the 1920s for writers and leaders of the Harlem Renaissance.

As recently as 1930, 20 states still outlawed intermarriage between whites and Afro-Americans, and mixed

Yvonne De Carlo after her character, Amantha Starr, in Band of Angels *(1957), discovers black ancestry*

marriages (because of social disapproval) were rare in other states. Despite the 1967 Supreme Court decision *Loving* v. *Virginia*, declaring unconstitutional all laws against intermarriage, the number of marriages between whites and Afro-Americans remains as few as 2 in 1,000. Most mixing has occurred between blacks and mulattoes, and it is estimated that three-fourths of Afro-Americans in the 20th century are of mixed ancestry. White-black intermarriage rates are not likely to exceed soon even 1 percent. In the foreseeable future, miscegenation, therefore, will not bring racial assimilation. Since the 1960s, Afro-Americans mostly have turned toward asserting their racial identity and sense of black pride while seeking equal rights with whites.

See also ETHNIC LIFE: Caribbean Influence; Indian Cultural Contributions; HISTORY AND MANNERS: Sexuality; MYTHIC SOUTH: Racial Attitudes

Tilden G. Edelstein
Rutgers University

Ira Berlin, *Slaves without Masters: The Free Negro in the Antebellum South* (1974); Carl N. Degler, *Neither Black nor White: Slavery and Race Relations in Brazil and the United States* (1971); George M. Fredrickson, *White Supremacy: A Comparative Study in American and South African History* (1981); Laurence J. Friedman, *The White Savage: Racial Fantasies in the Postbellum South* (1970); Thomas C. Holt, *Black over White: Negro Political Leadership in South Carolina during Reconstruction* (1977); Winthrop D. Jordan, *White over Black: American Attitudes toward the Negro, 1550–1812* (1968); Joel Williamson, *New People: Miscegenation and Mulattoes in the United States* (1980); Forrest G. Wood, *Black Scare: The Racist Response to Emancipation and Reconstruction* (1970).

Music, Black

Black musical life was never limited to a single style or musical tradition. In the 19th century American popular songs found their way into the repertoire of black folk musicians, European fiddle tunes appeared in medleys performed by itinerant fiddlers, and shape-note singing was adopted by black congregations in imitation of the colonial traditions developed in the North but transplanted to the South in the 1830s. Black musicians were aware of various ethnic musical traditions; and the process of musical acculturation, forced on blacks because of their need to accommodate themselves to a sometimes hostile culture or accepted by them because the other music fitted in so well with their own, led them to learn repertories acceptable to both races.

Two great periods of musical acculturation have been preserved on records. The first occurred during the pre–World War II era when the radio and phonograph made the quick transmission of personal and regional styles possible, the second immediately following the war when Afro-American music was brought to the attention of a larger audience. Some of the evidence needed for studying black southern music comes from those commercial recordings classified as "blues" and marketed as "race records" in the 1920s and 1930s by producers who sought to profit from the sales of phonographs to black families, more of whom owned a record player than a musical instrument. Because those producers and the major record companies limited their "race" catalogs to those items likely to have strong sales among blacks, the other major recordings come from the fieldwork of folklorists employed by the Library of Congress, the Works Progress Administration, and a few major universities, evidence that includes examples dating back to the styles of the Civil War era.

Black musicians created in a variety of forms, from art songs to zydeco music (blues-influenced dance music

Othar Turner playing a black folk instrument, the fife, Gravel Springs, Miss., 1971

performed by French-speaking creole blacks). Many black musicians were musically bilingual, capable of absorbing and mastering (1) the Afro-Caribbean rhythms and dance forms brought to the Gulf Coast by emigrants from Haiti, Jamaica, and Cuba; (2) the many ethnic musical styles practiced by Cajun, German, French and Spanish Creole, Mexican, and French performers; and, after emancipation, (3) the new styles of American and European art and popular music from the North. Studies of the Afro-American style tend to emphasize folk music and jazz, but southern blacks also had a repertoire of material that they shared with whites, a "common heritage" known widely throughout the United States.

The multiethnic character of some antebellum southern cities contributed greatly to the opportunities for musical acculturation. Over 40 percent of the population of New Orleans (116,375 in 1850), 24 percent of Mobile (20,515 in 1850), and 30 percent of Charleston (42,985 in 1840) were foreign born. Each of these cities and its various ethnic groups provided music for urban blacks to learn and, through the "hiring out" practice, opportunities for slaves to join free blacks for performances at dances and other social events.

Following the rage for brass band music that began in Europe and spread to the United States in the late 1830s, brasswind ensembles, such as the Richmond Light Infantry Blues (ca. 1840) and Allen's Brass Band (Wilmington, N.C.), were established in the South. Bandbooks of both the pre–Civil War and postbellum periods reveal a repertoire consisting of everything from transcribed fiddle tunes and popular hymns to selections from European operas and American musical theater. The Negro Philharmonic Society of New Orleans (ca. 1838) presented concerts for many years, and one of its directors, Richard Lambert, headed a family that included several generations of famous musicians. Each of the cities of the South seemed to have both slave and free blacks who earned strong vocal reputations for their musicianship. Simeon Gilliat and George Walker were considered the finest musicians in early 19th-century Richmond, and the roster of famous New Orleans musicians at the end of the century features "legends" such as "Klondike," "John the Baptist," Ferdinand "Jelly Roll" Morton, and Anthony Jackson ("the World's Greatest Single-Handed Entertainer").

After 1865 some black artists and composers adopted European aesthetic values and performance traditions. Inspired by the success of the first group of Fisk Jubilee Singers (1871–78), the brilliant career of Mississippi-born Marie Smith Selika, and the many gifted instrumentalists, dancers, and singers who appeared with postbellum minstrel, vaudeville, and tent shows, blacks moved beyond the folk and traditional styles with which they were associated before the war. Trained by such distinguished black educators as John Wesley Work (Fisk University) and Robert Nathaniel Dett (Hampton Institute and Bennett College), many sought professional training for careers as performers or teachers. Few were to realize the dream of international recognition and personal artistic success, but southern-born artists such as Roland Hayes, William Grant Still, W. C. Handy, Leontyne Price, Mahalia Jackson, and many others have made outstanding contributions to the world of music.

The major features of black performance styles are communal singing with call-and-response patterns; polyrhythmic percussive accompaniments to both religious and secular vocal and choral music—foot tapping, hand clapping, and drumming performed in ways similar to known African practices, and the intense, sometimes ecstatic emotional participation of the audience or congregation in the performance.

A number of vocal techniques distinguish Afro-American singing from the popular, operatic, and theatrical styles of the 19th century. Black performers are described in literary sources as capable of producing a wide variety of vocal effects: ascending or descending glides or runs, frequent use of the head or falsetto voice (especially in quick leaps from low robust tones to high piercing ones), vocal imitations of natural and animal sounds. Devices commonly found in reports about and recordings of black storytellers include subtle pitch variations that follow the natural inflections of black speech, changes in pitch and dynamics directly related to the emotional content of a musical phrase, and a sometimes completely arhythmic vocalizing in the manner of an extended free-form sung meditation. Most of these stylistic traits are well-known to black and white audiences today, but they were virtually unknown in the popular music of the North prior to the 1920s, even in the minstrel shows that claimed to be "authentic" imitations of black behavior.

These characteristics can be found in the field cries and hollers, chants, lullabies, ritual songs, ring shouts, and religious songs in which a call-and-response pattern served as a framework for improvising melodies and texts. That ability to spontaneously create texts, tales, and songs has been documented in folklore studies and is a characteristic of almost all Afro-American music such as blues, jazz, and religious song.

Religious institutions, fraternal associations, and traditional seasonal festivals encouraged music making. From the colonial John Canoe or John Conny festivals in North Carolina and Virginia to the regularly scheduled dances in the Place Congo in New Orleans; from the corn shucking parties in Virginia, the Carolinas, and Texas to the cane songs of Mississippi and Louisiana; and from the voodoo ceremonies in Georgia and Florida to the sacred dances of Alabama and Arkansas, music played an important role in black social life. It accompanied dancing and singing and provided a background for an escape from the routines of life.

Three major 20th-century forms of Afro-American music are associated with the South: blues, ragtime piano, and New Orleans jazz. Classic ragtime—the syncopated and carefully structured piano and band music of Scott Joplin, James Scott, and Joseph Lamb—evolved from a combination of the rhythmically irregular Afro-American melodic style and the regular background rhythms of postbellum band music to which should be added the common black folk practice of treating melody, design, and rhythm very flexibly. Ragtime songs and dances were introduced by southern-born blacks who picked up the techniques of ragging tunes by ear, and the wide distribution of various types of rags in southern folk and popular music suggests that blacks and whites shared many musical ideas well before ragtime became popular in the North.

The blues, described by Paul Oliver as "arguably the most significant form of folk music to have emerged in this century," is deeply embedded in the black musical experience. Rich in its use of language and poetic imagery, varied in its multiple attraction to the deepest tragedies and most ribald comedies of human existence, and, musically, the source for the chord structures and harmonic patterns used in much American popular music and jazz, the blues is as important to the musical history of this century as black spirituals were to the 19th. Two major blues forms—urban and rural—are widely recognized by blues scholars. The performance of the blues involves very subtle communications processes. The music is a vehicle for sharing complaints, exorcising sorrow, laughing at the world's absurdities, mocking whites, and maintaining the integrity of black culture.

Dixieland jazz is one of the major forms of ensemble jazz. It was not the exclusive possession of blacks or the South, however, because early New Orleans jazz was played by nearly as many Creoles as blacks, especially after the segregation laws passed by New Orleans in 1894 and 1897 brought Afro-American and Creole cultures together in the uptown section. Still, southern blacks such as Louis Armstrong are inextricably linked with the birth of jazz. The role of black, white, and Creole musicians in creating and developing jazz makes it a classic case of musical amalgamation.

Black southerners, like black Americans elsewhere, adopted many of the same values as whites, but the Afro-American musical style reflects most vividly the inherent dichotomies blacks have faced in being Americans. The tendency to view the style in terms of its various genres—spirituals, blues, ragtime, gospel songs—sometimes obscures the fact that black musicians still treat music as an oral rather than a written art because black culture is still largely an oral culture in both North and South. The real strength of *southern* black music is its diversity, its ability to capture the tensions as well as the achievements of blacks, its indebtedness as well as its contribution to other forms of southern music, and its heritage of preserving older performance practices after the great black exodus from the South. Without southern culture as a stimulant to music acculturation, the Afro-American style would not have produced the unique fusion of traditions that have made it a potent force in this century's popular music.

See also MUSIC articles

William J. Mahar
Pennsylvania State University—
Capitol Campus

Dominique-Rene De Lerma, *Bibliography of Black Music*, 4 vols. (1981–84); Sam Dennison, *Scandalize My Name: Black Imagery in American Popular Music* (1982); Dena Epstein, *Sinful Tunes and Spirituals: Black Folk Music to the Civil War* (1977); David Horn, *The Literature of American Music in Books and Folk Music Collections: A Fully Annotated Bibliography* (1981); Bill C. Malone, *Southern Music—American Music* (1979); Paul Oliver, *Songsters and Saints: Vocal Traditions on Race Records* (1984); JoAnn Skowronski, *Black Music in America: A Bibliography* (1981); Eileen Southern, *Biographical Dictionary of Afro-American and African Musicians* (1982), *The Music of Black Americans: A History* (1971; 2d. ed., 1983); Jeff Todd Titon, *Early Downhome Blues: A Musical and Cultural Analysis* (1977).

Northern Cities, Blacks in

The most distinctive feature of black life in the South in the first half of the 20th century was the crystallization of a distinct Afro-American nationality. The sense of identity among the masses of black people based on a shared culture and common experiences in institutions such as churches provided the matrix sustaining life in the South and laying a foundation that was later transferred to newer settings in the North and West.

Pushed by the ravages of the boll weevil, floods, unemployment after the collapse of an exploitative tenancy-sharecropping system, and surging racism, black people were eager to escape the South. But not until these factors were combined with the pull of better jobs and a better life, especially in the war-stimulated, labor-starved industries of northern cities, did a mass migration begin. The move was facilitated by black newspapers like the Chicago *Defender*, by labor recruiters offering free train tickets, and by word of mouth.

The Afro-American move from the South to the North, from country to city, and from farm to factory is one of the most significant social transformations in the history of the United States. No aspect of the lives of black people was left unchanged. The dynamic interaction of a southern-based, rural Afro-American nationality and northern, urban experiences is key to understanding this process.

In 1900, 9 of every 10 black people lived in the South and about 8 of every 10 lived in rural areas. Although only 170,000 blacks migrated from the South in the first decade of the 20th century, that number increased to 454,000 between 1910 and 1920 and to 749,000 between 1920 and 1930. Between 1930 and 1950 black out-migrants from the South, and mainly *to* the North and cities, totaled 1.9 million. As a result, the percentage of blacks living in the North in 1950 increased to 34 percent, and the percentage living in cities had increased to 62 percent.

In 1940 over a million of the 3 million black people in the North lived in four cities—New York, Chicago, Philadelphia, and Detroit, increasing their black populations from 7 to 30 fold. Between 1910 and 1940, for example, New York's black population increased from 91,709 to 458,444, while Chicago's population grew from 44,103 to 277,731 during the same period.

A definite pattern existed to black migration, with

proximity to settlement sites and established transportation routes playing important roles. In 1930, 22 percent of Cleveland's blacks were born in Ohio, but 36 percent came from Georgia and Alabama. In Detroit, more blacks came from Georgia (21 percent) and Alabama (just over 14 percent) than were born in Michigan (14 percent). For Philadelphia, 32 percent were born in Virginia and South Carolina while only 30 percent were natives of the state. Finally, almost as many black Chicagoans had been born in Mississippi (17 percent) as in Illinois. Moreover, there was a distinct age and gender selectivity to the migrations: between 1920 and 1930, 45 of every 100 black males between 15 and 34 left Georgia, and between 1940 and 1950, Mississippi lost almost one-half of its young black adults.

The settlement patterns of southern blacks, especially the compactness and segregation of the black community, encouraged the survival of southern culture. Racial segregation existed in the North as well as in the South. A 1940 study of 109 cities using a residential segregation index with 100 as a maximum score, revealed a score of 83.2 for the Northeast (e.g., New York) and 88.4 for the North Central region (e.g., Chicago), as compared to 89.9 for the South. More specifically, the concentration of blacks increased between 1910 and 1950—from 66.8 to 79.7 in Chicago, from 46.0 to 74.0 in Philadelphia, from 64.1 to 80.9 in Boston, and from 60.6 to 86.6 in Cleveland. The result of this concentration was to promote the retention of older southern habits and customs.

The most profound change was in the world of work. Where 60 percent of black men worked in agriculture in 1910, by 1950 only 18.4 percent of blacks were employed as farm workers. By 1950 also, 38 percent of blacks in general were employed as blue-collar workers in the factories and 34 percent as service workers such as maids and janitors. Although blacks were still on the lowest rungs of the northern economic ladder, and constrained by racially discriminatory "job ceilings," which confined them to "Negro jobs," these low-status jobs were usually higher than those on the upper rungs of southern sharecropping tenancy. They brought higher pay, new skills, greater association with whites, and new organizational participation such as in unions.

In addition, a cultural transformation occurred, necessitated by new conditions and the pace of urban life with its greater freedom. Although racial segregation existed, black life in northern cities was less isolated and intimate than in the rural South. Soul food was commercial, available in numerous restaurants, and, as poet Sterling Brown said, "leisurely yarn-spinning" and "slowpaced aphoristic conversation became lost arts."

Religious life underwent profound changes. The rise of the "storefront" church in the city represented the adaptation of the small rural church to city life. In Chicago in the 1940s, 75 percent of the 500 churches in the black community were storefronts. These churches were clustered in the poorer areas of the black community in which migrants were concentrated. Storefronts provided a more intimate context for self-expression and social contacts than the larger, more bureaucratized city churches.

Holiness and spiritualist sects helped solve personal crises and facilitated the adjustment to disruption in family life, loss of social status, and other changes resulting from the transition. Practices such as faith healing were common in some of these churches and similar to practices found in the South. Among the most widely known were the Father Divine Peace Mission Movement and the Moorish Science Temple of America, a forerunner of the Nation of Islam.

While black membership in churches decreased in the urban North and while the significance of the church as a center of social life declined as it competed with other institutions, including movies, concerts, and other forms of recreation, the church nevertheless remained a key institution in the social life of black people in northern cities and provided a context for sustaining other aspects of rural southern life.

Urban life influenced the form, tempo, and lyrics of black music. The blues had long dealt exclusively with "despair and sadness" over wretched rural conditions, both natural and social: "Don't you see how them creatures, now have done me wrong? Boll weevil's got my cotton and the merchant's got my corn." Mirroring the urban reality of Motown (Detroit), the form remained, but the words were appropriately refocused: "Please Mr. Foreman, slow down your assembly line. I don't mind working, but I do mind dying."

The disruptive impact of the migrations and the harshness of the post–World War I and Depression era caused the producers of the new gospel music to consciously incorporate into black church music the sounds and the forms of earlier black musical traditions, including blues and jazz. According to the "Father of Gospel," Thomas A. Dorsey, the music helped "to give [black people] something to lift them out of that Depression . . . out of the muck and mire of poverty and loneliness, of being broke." In the face of dispersal from the black belt South, integration into the urban industrial economy, and racism, black migrants from the South "could go back home" through the blues and other southern musical traditions.

Black family life was affected by the trek north. Initially, urban families retained many of the basic characteristics of their rural counterparts—a larger proportion of children (relative to whites) and more grandchildren living with grandparents (the extended family). Since 1950, however, the number of husband-wife families has declined and the number of divorces increased. The number of female-headed households and the number of black children living in these households increased dramatically. Whether these developments represent the "disorganization" of the black family or show its strength in adapting to a hostile environment is much debated. In moving from the South to the North, from rural to urban, the black family clearly, in any event, changed in both form and function. Compounded by other developments, such as high unemployment among black youth, the problems created by this shift remain unsolved.

One issue that has not been sufficiently researched is the vibrant interchange that goes on between black people in the North and their southern kin. Black newspapers report on visits and reunions in almost every issue.

Social movements among black people in northern cities showed their southern roots. The Universal Negro Improvement Association of Marcus Garvey, one of the largest, is said to have been successful in large measure because of its appeal to newly arrived black southerners who were won over by the movement's emphasis on independent land-ownership and institutional development, reflecting their nation-like aspirations. Similarly, the increased popularity of the newly organized Communist party in the 1930s was related to its claims that the black belt region of the South was a black homeland and that blacks had the right to national self-determination and a government of their own choosing. More importantly, Communists were active organizers of several key campaigns, which touched the sentiment of transplanted black southerners. One example was the international defense of the Scottsboro (Ala.) boys, nine black youths unjustly accused and given the death sentence for raping two white women who later admitted to false testimony. The appeal of such later leaders as Martin Luther King, Jr., Malcolm X, and other civil rights activists also reflected the sustained interest of northern blacks in conditions in the South—a region defined by Malcolm X as "everything below Canada."

See also GEOGRAPHY: Expatriates and Exiles; Migration Patterns; / Northern Cities, Whites in; SOCIAL CLASS: Communism; LAW: / Scottsboro Case

Ronald Bailey
University of Mississippi

Abdul Alkalimat, *Introduction to Afro-American Studies: A Peoples College Primer* (1986); St. Clair Drake and Horace Cayton, *Black Metropolis: A Study of Negro Life in a Northern City* (1945); E. Franklin Frazier, *The Negro in the United States* (1949); Gunnar Myrdal, *An American Dilemma: The Negro Problem and Modern Democracy* (1944); Joe William Trotter, Jr., *Black Milwaukee: The Making of an Industrial Proletariat, 1915–1945* (1984).

Politics, Black

Black southerners heralded as a second emancipation the momentous 1944 U.S. Supreme Court decision in *Smith* v. *Alwright* outlawing the Texas white primary. In 1923 the Texas Legislature had enacted a law holding that the Democratic party was a private organization possessed of the authority to restrict membership and voting privileges to whites only in Democratic party primary elections. With alacrity, all southern states adopted similar forms of white primary legislation. Although black southerners retained the right to vote in general elections, in the one-party South such participation proved meaningless. Nomination in the primary was tantamount to election because the general elections merely rubber-stamped primary returns.

Few southern blacks enjoyed unfettered access even to general election voting booths. Legislation enacted by southern white politicians in the wake of the collapse of radical Reconstruction (1877) effectively disfranchised the vast majority of the region's black citizens. Poll tax laws, literacy clauses, restrictive voter registration tests, along with fear, intimidation, and violence erected an impenetrable barrier that denied blacks access to both the ballot box and political office. The white primary was a capstone to white supremacy and black powerlessness.

The *Smith* ruling, culminating two decades of litigation and struggle, dealt a shattering blow to black disfranchisement. The U.S. Supreme Court had declared that the right to participate fully in the electoral process could not be "nullified by a state through casting its electoral process in a form which permits a private organization to practice racial discrimination." The Democratic party's exclusion of blacks from voting in primary elections was viewed as a direct violation of the Fifteenth Amendment of the U.S. Constitution.

The *Smith* decision signaled the reentry of hundreds of thousands of blacks into southern politics. Moreover, it established a solid legal foundation through which the National Association for the Advancement of Colored People (NAACP) launched a massive assault on black second-class citizenship, housing segregation, and educational discrimination, giving rise to the modern civil rights movement.

After the landmark Supreme Court decision in *Brown* v. *Board of Education* (1954) prohibiting racial segregation in the schools, the black political revolution was well under way. In 1940 only 5 percent of voting-age black southerners were registered, whereas on the heels of *Smith* black registration increased to 12 percent. Two years after *Brown*, 25 percent of eligible southern blacks were enrolled on voting lists.

This modest growth in black political participation aroused the ire and determined opposition of southern white politicians. Throughout the late 1940s and 1950s Governor Eugene Talmadge of Georgia, Congressman E. C. Boswell of Alabama, Senator Theodore G. Bilbo of Mississippi, and others, initiated strategies designed to thwart black advancement and to preserve white supremacy.

Southern white politicians failed, however, to stem the tide of the political reform impulse unleashed, in part, by a liberal Supreme Court. Indeed, all remaining legal barriers to black voting and office holding fell before the onslaught of subsequent Supreme Court decisions on reapportionment and the strong leadership of Presidents Dwight D. Eisenhower, John F. Kennedy, and Lyndon Baines Johnson. Not to be outdone, the U.S. Congress enacted far-reaching legislation, including the civil rights laws of 1957, 1960, and 1964.

The Voting Rights Act passed by the Congress in 1965 represented a major victory in the black rights quest. It suspended the literacy tests that had been used to bar blacks from the polls, banned the poll tax as a state suffrage requirement, and gave the president the authority to send examiners into the South to register blacks. Not only did black registration and participation in the region's elections increase, but white southerners did also. In 1952 and 1956 fewer than 8 million southerners voted for president, but in 1980 over 20 million voted. Whites made up 9.7 million voters of that increase, blacks 3.1 million.

The significance of the dismantling of voter registration barriers for black political participation in the South cannot be overstated. Of equal importance were the unrelenting pressure and intense voter registration campaigns of civil rights organizations such as the Student Nonviolent Coordinating Committee, the Southern Christian Leadership Conference, the Congress of Racial Equality, and the NAACP.

The increase in black voter registration and office holding during the 1960s altered the South's political landscape. At the beginning of the decade 1,414,052, or 28 percent, of eligible black adults voted. By 1969 a record 64.3 percent participated in the electoral process. The three states registering the greatest percentage of blacks were Tennessee, 92.1 percent; Arkansas, 77.9 percent; and Texas, 73.1 percent.

In 1975 the number of black elected public officials in the South stood at 1,600. Within five years the number had jumped to nearly 2,500, and by January 1985 there were 3,233 black elected officials in the South. For the first time since Reconstruction southern blacks were elected to offices of power in city and county governments, state legislatures, and the U.S. House of Representatives, and they were appointed to prominent positions on the national level. Black mayors have served in scores of small southern towns, such as Tuskegee, Ala.; Fayette, Miss.; and Madison, Ark.; large southern metropolises have also boasted black mayors, including Ernest Morial of New Orleans, La., and Andrew Young of Atlanta, Ga., successor to Maynard Holbrook Jackson, who served as mayor from 1973 to 1982. Blacks now sit as state supreme court justices in Mississippi (Reuben Anderson), South Carolina (Ernest Finney), Virginia (John Charles Thomas), and North Carolina (Henry Frye).

On the national level, southern black politicians have achieved widespread acclaim. Barbara Jordan represented Texas in the Congress. Following Jordan's resignation in 1973, Mickey Leland, a former member of the Texas House of Representatives, was elected to serve. Andrew Young of Georgia was appointed U.S. ambassador to the United Nations during Jimmy Carter's presidency.

Jesse Jackson's 1984 bid for the presidency of the United States showcased the importance of the black vote in the South and promoted increased voter registration. Jackson's national campaign relied on southern black votes and the organizational power of the black churches in the region. Jackson received over 3 million votes in the primaries and became the central black political figure of the 1980s. The Voter Education Project in Atlanta had registered 750,000 new black voters in the 11 states of the old Confederacy by the summer of 1984.

In spite of impressive gains in black voter registration and office holding, politics has not proven to be a panacea. Persistent inequalities between black and white southerners continue. By 1980 blacks held 3 percent of elected offices in a region where they constituted 20 percent of the population. Over half of the 100 counties in the South with majority black populations still have no black elected officials. Jesse Jackson fought the southern winner-take-all primary system in 1984, pressing for reforms to go beyond the *Smith* decision. The changes wrought since the *Smith* decision indicate significant transformation in black political participation, but the black political revolution is still far from complete, and political parity remains a dream.

See also POLITICS articles

Darlene Clark Hine
Purdue University

Numan Bartley, *The Rise of Massive Resistance: Race and Politics in the South during the 1950s* (1969); Andrew Buni, *The Negro in Virginia Politics, 1902–1965* (1967); Ward E. Y. Elliott, *The Rise of Guardian Democracy: The Supreme Court's Role in Voting Rights Disputes, 1845–1969* (1974); Darlene Clark Hine, *Black Victory: The Rise and Fall of the White Primary in Texas* (1979); William R. Keech, *The Impact of Negro Voting: The Role of the Vote in the Quest for Equality* (1968); Steven F. Lawson, *Black Ballots: Voting Rights in the South, 1944–1969* (1976); Manning Marable, *Black American Politics: From the Washington Marches to Jesse Jackson* (1985); Donald R. Matthews and James W. Prothro, *Negroes and the New Southern Politics* (1966); August Meier and Elliot M. Rudwick, *CORE: A Study of the Civil Rights Movement, 1942–1968* (1973); Harvard Sitkoff, *The Struggle for Black Equality, 1954–1980* (1981).

Preacher, Black

During the Great Awakening of 1800 and for years after, many itinerant preachers found that their listeners for religious services often numbered in the thousands. To accommodate such large congregations, the camp meeting was institutionalized. These large-scale worship services were especially successful in the border states of Kentucky and Tennessee, where many clergymen from the North traveled. This new form of divine worship, sometimes attracting as many as 20,000 or more at events such as the one held at Cane Ridge, Ky., included black as well as white worshipers. Although this form of worship never caught on in the Northeast, it was highly successful in the South and Southwest. Many black ministers were inspired to preach at such gatherings, though at first only to other blacks, and a characteristic oral style of delivery emerged from this experience.

These sermons were characterized by the preacher's chanting the Word of God rather than delivering it conventionally. The sermon began traditionally enough with a statement of the day's text and its application to contemporary morals. Then, as the preacher got further into the day's message, he began to chant his lines, the metrics and time intervals of the lines became more and more regular and consistent, and as he became further imbued with the Holy Spirit, the preacher's delivery slid into song. The sermons were—and still are—characterized by an increase in emotional and spiritual intensity, expressed by the gradual transition from conventional pulpit oratorical style, through chanting, to highly emotional singing. Many black folk preachers are excellent singers and have had several years' experience with church choirs, if not on the professional stage. Quite a number have been choirmasters, and nearly all these men have from an early age attended church services in which music played a major role. A musical sense has thus been acquired, and its rhythms, intonations, timbres, and verbal phrasing are inextricable parts of the tradition.

Foreign visitors to black church services in the early 19th century remarked not only on the minister's chanting but on the congregation's equally emotional responses. Such witnesses were appalled by the unbridled emotionalism of such services.

The African heritage of black preachers influenced the style of their performances and of the congregations' responses. The African folksong tradition of call-and-response was carried over; not only was the preacher directly in this tradition, but in holy services the congregants felt free to call out to the preacher, or to the other congregants, as the Spirit moved them. The service became, and is still, however, something more than the regulated, orchestrated, and patterned response of one individual or group to another; in black services each member of the congregation actually creates his or her own sacred communion simultaneously with the holy service that is proceeding. Members of the congregation call out spontaneously, and such exclamations may not have been anticipated by the minister.

During a service in which the preacher has been successful in arousing the Spirit of the Lord or in bringing his congregation to a high emotional level, individual cries are frequent, some of the congregation will enter an altered state during which they may lose consciousness or dance seemingly involuntarily, and the preacher will be visibly ecstatic as well. Many people laugh aloud; a few cry unashamedly. When the service is over, they will say that they have had a happy time.

Research on this phenomenon suggests that while much of the sermon cannot possibly be heard distinctly, something is being communicated, and the congregation will feel that it has received God's Word. This may happen because many of the congregation know the Bible almost as thoroughly as does the preacher, and they creatively anticipate his message; also, in these services the congregation participates actively and creatively in the service, and may for long periods be "hearing" their own celebrations.

Both preacher and flock share many common traditions, not only inherited Christianity but also an Afro-American interpretation of that faith flavored by the experience of living in the South. Few preachers have had extensive seminary training; and many of their beliefs, like those of their congregations, are derived from popular traditions. For instance, many preachers prefer to use popular, folk versions of stories and parables in Scripture. Hence, although their Christianity is in the main "official," it is heavily influenced by folkloric elements. In some urban areas these preachers are often known as "old-time country preachers," though many of them have migrated away from the rural South to the urban North. The Reverend C. L. Franklin, for instance, became most famous after he left the South and moved to Detroit.

The ministers do not use manuscripts but believe that when they are in front of congregations the Holy Ghost is using them to communicate His message to the people. This spontaneous preaching style is accurately and movingly reproduced by William Faulkner in the last portion of *The Sound and the Fury*. In those pages the Reverend Shegog from St. Louis delivers a moving sermon in a style indistinguishable from the authentic oral performance. Significantly, this sermon is placed near the novel's conclusion; Faulkner recognized the great emotive and spiritual power that is the potential of this medium and chose to end his book on an affirming note.

Some white preachers also still preach in this mode; the style is not the exclusive property of one ethnic group. But the practitioners are mostly black and usually Methodist or Baptist. The practice is characteristically southern, though many preachers have now moved to the cities of the North and to the Pacific Southwest. These preachers continue to evoke the South in their services. Many professional black singers have vocal qualities that carry heavy echoes of this preaching style. Examples are Aretha Franklin (daughter of the Reverend C. L. Franklin), Sarah Vaughn, and Lou Rawls. Much of the "Motown sound" owes a debt to southern country preaching.

The influence of black folk preachers on the nation extends well beyond the contributions of musical entertainment and the popular arts. The Reverend Martin Luther King, Jr., was a "spiritual" preacher whose "I Have a Dream" speech was in large measure a sermon on racial equality; he is well known for this oral performance, which profoundly moved his listeners, regardless of their race or ethnic backgrounds. Today, this art is most prominently practiced by Chicago's Jesse Jackson, a southerner by birth and raising. His address to the Democratic National Convention (1984) was a spontaneous sermon, a moving oration delivered by electronic media to the nation and the world.

See also FOLKLIFE: Storytelling; RELIGION: Folk Religion

Bruce A. Rosenberg
Brown University

Richard Allen, in *Black American Literature, 1760–Present*, ed. Ruth Miller (1971); Paul C. Brownlow, *Quarterly Journal of Speech* (December 1972); Gerald L. Davis, *"I Got The Word in Me and I Can Sing It, You Know": A Study of the Performed Afro-American Sermon* (1986); Charles V. Hamilton, *The Black Preacher in America* (1972); Albert J. Raboteau, *Slave Religion: The "Invisible Institution" in the Antebellum South* (1978); Joseph R. Washington, Jr., *Black Religion: The Negro and Christianity in the United States* (1964).

Press, Black

The first black newspaper, *Freedom's Journal*, appeared in New York City 51 years after the Declaration of Independence, 36 years before the Emancipation Proclamation. It was edited by John B. Russwurm and Samuel E. Cornish. In its first editorial, *Freedom's Journal* outlined an objective that is still symbolic of the black press: "We wish to plead our cause. Too long have others spoken for us." Although it had the format of a newspaper this black weekly resembled a magazine more than a newspaper. In the South, the first black newspaper was *L'union*, established in New Orleans, La., on 27 September 1862.

Until the end of the Civil War, black newspapers were published exclusively in northern communities where blacks were literate and had the freedom to publish. But after the emancipation, scores of new newspapers appeared throughout America, particularly in the ex-Confederate states where the majority of blacks lived. The black press had found a new constituency.

After the Civil War, black newspapers such as the Arkansas *Freedman* (1869), the *Colored Tennessean* (1865), the South Carolina *Leader* (1865), the Vicksburg *Colored Citizen* (1867), and the Texas *Freedman's Press* (1868) helped the newly freed slaves to bridge the gap between bondage and freedom by serving as instruments of promotion for suffrage, education, religion, and economic self-help. But overt racism and the increased social restriction of blacks in the South paralleled the return of Democratic rule and indirectly spawned the birth of the Gainesville *New Era* (1873), the Savannah *Tribune* (1875), the Missouri *Negro World* (1875), the Bennettsville (S.C.) *Pee Dee Educator* (1879), and the Galveston *Spectator* (1873). On the other hand, a few of the black papers were not politically active. For example, the North Carolina *Journal of Industry* (1879) in its premiere editorial, "Our Position," promised to "stay clear of politics" and addressed itself to the white people of the South because it viewed the "welfare" of whites and blacks as being inextricably interwoven. Other black newspapers devoted themselves to the "intellectual, moral, and financial interest of colored people."

The themes of land, education, suffrage, race relations, violence, and economic self-help characterized the black press after Reconstruction and until the early 1900s. The Baptist *Vanguard* (1882), Gainesville, Fla., *Sentinel* (1887) Jacksonville *Peoples Journal* (1883), Raleigh *Gazette,* North Carolina *Republican and Civil Rights Advocate* (1884), *Star of Zion* (1876), Charleston *Messenger* (1890s), Richmond *Planet*, Petersburg *Lancet* (1882), the Dallas *Express* (1892), and others circulated widely throughout their respective regions and mirrored these themes during this period. They recorded the bitterness, indignation, and disillusionment of the newly freed blacks with the democratic system. At the same time, "they fought to elevate humanity" and to allay the fears of whites. Jesse Duke's Montgomery *Herald* (1886), Mansfield E. Bryant's Selma *Southern Independent* (1886), L. H. Harrison's Birmingham *Wide-Awake* (1888), and R. C. O. Benjamin's Birmingham *Negro American* (1886) exemplified black protest journalism in the Deep South, whereas John Mitchell's Richmond *Planet* reflected advocacy journalism in the Upper South.

Almost 100 black papers appeared in the 1890s in Alabama alone, followed by more than 70 from 1900 to 1910. But most of them were short-lived weeklies that were prevailingly Republican, financially insecure, and located in urban areas with large black populations. Men, especially ministers, dominated black journalism during the 19th century. A few black women, such as Maggie Lena Walker, Charlotte Hawkins Brown, and Josephine T. Washington, became prominent editors and journalists during this period.

Perhaps the Petersburg *Lancet* and the North Carolina *Republican and Civil Rights Advocate* (1884) best mirrored the advertising, layout, design, and subscription policies of the black press in the post-Reconstruction South. The *Advocate's* motto, "I Take No Step Backward" was carried under the masthead. Subscriptions were 50 cents for 3 months, 90 cents for 6 months, and $1.50 for 12 months. Advertisers included grocers, drug stores, barber shops, hairdressers, butchers, hardware and five-and-dime stores, Sunday school book suppliers, and cigarette and insurance companies. And like the Petersburg *Lancet*, columns were devoted to poems and short stories that dramatized the complexities of marriage and family and the glory of the Old West. The social page was dominated by "brilliant marriages," "large funerals," and "sermons." The black press gave its readers an organic sense of community life.

During the age of Booker T. Washington (1895–1915), the Kansas City *Call*, the Raleigh *Gazette*, the Savannah *Tribune*, the Charleston *Messenger*, the Norfolk *Journal and Guide* (1910), among others, effectively carried Washington's philosophy of economic self-help and racial accommodation, as did the *Colored American* magazine and the New York *Age*, two journals controlled directly by Washington.

On the other hand, however, the Nashville *Globe* (1905) was financially independent and openly contemptuous of Washington's philosophy. The *Globe*, the Richmond *Planet*, and later the Norfolk *Journal and Guide* and the Kansas City *Call* observed that Washington's philosophy was inconsistent with the economic and political realities of life in 20th-century America. The black press was also sensitive to the increased support of the National Association for the Advancement of Colored People (NAACP) among the South's rising black middle class. Black journalist P. B. Young founded the NAACP chapter in Norfolk, Va., in 1917 as an act of "self-preservation."

The event that forced black newspapers to abandon both Washington's philosophy and the Republican party was World War I. The black press supported the war effort, but expressed concern about the disparity between the quest for democracy abroad and the inequities at home. Black editors had hoped that loyalty and patriotism among blacks at home would result in increased political patronage and fair treatment. Instead, the Negrophobes and white supremacists in the South continued racial tyranny through lynching, disfranchisement, and racial segregation.

Although the Great Depression decimated most of the black press, the *Journal and Guide*, the St. Louis *Argus*, the Kansas City *Call*, the Carolina *Times*, the Atlanta *Daily World* (1928), and the Birmingham *World* not only survived but expanded throughout their respective regions. The *Journal and Guide* and the *Call* published national editions as well. Ironically, Mississippi, one of the first states to inaugurate the segregation movement during the 1890s, spawned more black newspapers between 1920 and 1940 than at any other comparable time in its history. Examples include the *Delta Leader* (1929), the *Southern Advocate* (1933), the Mississippi *Enterprise* (1939), and the Jackson *Advocate* (1938). Several publishers, according to historian Julius Thompson, "risked everything and cried out for civil rights," while others sent false signals to the masses and "failed to tell the truth as they saw it."

Collectively, the black press was politically ineffective before World War II. Although the black press complained about the inherent discrimination in many New Deal programs and the discriminatory hiring practices on military bases, A. Philip Randolph's threatened March on Washington in July of 1941 finally prompted President Franklin Roosevelt to issue Executive Order 8802, which banned discrimination in federal employment. The black papers were divided on the infamous Scottsboro case of the 1930s in which nine blacks were charged with the rape of two white females. Although black publisher P. B. Young (*Journal and Guide*), the titular head of the black press, spearheaded a defense fund drive and sought to arouse public sentiment in the South with weekly editorials such as "Darrow, The Communist and Scottsboro," "What Scottsboro Means to America," "Scottsboro vs. Dred Scott," and "The Verdict at Decatur," the Communist International Labor Defense (ILD) actually defended the accused. Locally, however, the *Journal and Guide* was more successful. Young's writings and political acumen saved the life of William Harper, a black man who had been sentenced to death for the crime of rape, and his serialized account of dilapidated schools in several Tidewater Virginia counties led to a state investigation and new schools for blacks.

The themes of equalization, crime, health care, better housing, migration, desegregation of the military, and suffrage predominated in the black press during World War II. The black press supported America's entry into the war and urged blacks to "close ranks," end debate, and suspend bickering. Perhaps the *Journal and Guide* best epitomized the black press when it declared, "We are Americans—we're at war." The *Guide* also reflected the sentiment of the black press when it rejected black activist A. Philip Randolph's proposed March on Washington, noting in a headline, "What Will They Think In Berlin?"

Black newspapers are an invaluable reference if used properly. They sometimes provide the only evidence that a particular incident (especially protest) even occurred. They recorded the births of the most lowly blacks and offered consoling words upon death. How else could families announce the graduation of their children from high school or impending social events? How else could black colleges disseminate information about tuition, schedule of courses, and athletic events? The black press publicized information about communicable diseases and the weather, and it explained controversial racial incidents to the community. Between 1865 and 1945, the black press was a mirror, crusader, advocate, and recorder of black life and culture in the South.

See also MEDIA: Newspapers; / Young, P. B.

Henry Lewis Suggs
Clemson University

Penelope L. Bullock, *The Afro-American Periodical Press, 1838–1909* (1981); Walter C. Daniel, *Black Journals of the United States* (1982); Frederick G. Detweiler, *The Negro Press in the United States* (1922); Vishnu V. Oak, *The Negro Newspaper* (1948); I. Garland Penn, *The Afro-American Press and Its Editors* (1891); Henry Lewis Suggs, *The Black Press in the South, 1865–1979* (1984); Roland E. Wolseley, *The Black Press, U.S.A.* (1971).

Race Relations

Throughout southern history, from the mid-17th century down to crucial changes in the 1970s, the region's ruling class dedicated itself to one overriding principle—white supremacy. Its large-scale employment of black labor must not be permitted to threaten the South's character as a white man's country. White racism was thus the driving force, the great first cause of southern race relations. Yet the pattern of those relations was complex, changing considerably over the centuries. Although the virulence of racism also grew more or less intense, on the whole it seems most realistic to treat it as a constant. The culture of racism was sufficient to sanction and support the whole range of discrimination that has characterized white supremacy in its successive stages. It follows that those stages themselves cannot be attributed to racism alone. Secondary causes—economic, political, intellectual—must also be considered. So must the fact that southern race relations did not exist in a vacuum. Especially after 1865, the southern ruling class had to operate within broad and changing limits of what the rest of the country would permit.

Under slavery the dominant pattern of white supremacy had been vertical, resting on the use of influence and force. The cruelty of the slave system had been direct, and so had been its sometimes genuinely affectionate paternalism. Black people necessarily developed their personalities, their family relations, their religion, and to an impressive extent their cultural autonomy by exploiting contradictions and opportunities within a complex fabric of dependency. These concessions enabled a profitable and rational economic system to function. There were exceptions to the rule of direct dominance of white over black, notably the free black populations of Charleston, New Orleans, and other southern communities. Moreover, the majority of southern whites had not owned slaves at all, and even fewer whites qualified as plantation owners. Still, the antebellum South's dominant mode of production, the economic foundation that supported its unchallenged planter ruling class, was slavery.

In rural areas, in the sharecropping system that came to replace slavery as the dominant mode of agrarian production after 1865, the dominant means of white control was the crop lien, in which a furnishing merchant (who was often a planter) provided land, seeds, fertilizer, tools, a mule, and credit for purchases of food and clothing in return for a portion (usually half) of the harvested crop. White farmers also engaged in sharecropping, including the crop lien, and a huge literature has examined the extent to which this transitional agrarian system was inherently discriminatory. The verdict seems to be that it was not—indeed, in the circumstances it is hard to conceive of an alternative—but that it provided planters and furnishing merchants who wished to discriminate with abundant opportunities to do so.

In cities, to which blacks as well as whites came in growing numbers, the problem of maintaining a workable system of white supremacy was far more complicated. City blacks were apt to be better educated and less directly dependent on whites. They included merchants, lawyers, teachers, journalists, craftsmen, and funeral directors—what came to be called the black bourgeoisie. Black quarters, where white faces were seldom seen, sometimes stretched for miles. In cities there were more opportunities for contact outside the complex etiquette that governed interracial associations on the plantation. Direct dominance of white over black no longer worked. In urban areas race relations were more impersonal, less paternal, and more competitive.

The 20th-century form of white supremacy was segregation. Although the antebellum and Reconstruction South had certainly known many of its aspects in practice, the usage of the word itself was new. According to the *Oxford English Dictionary*, the relevant "S" volume of which was compiled between 1910 and 1914, *segregation* was not part of the 19th-century vocabulary of race relations. The use of *segregation* as a key word in southern race relations is an indication that white supremacy was moving from one stage to another.

The 1890s were the crucial years when the South moved into this final stage of white supremacy. White southerners in that decade constructed a system and an ideology of race relations that were essentially new.

Why did white southerners create this system and ideology? And why at this time? Many reasons have been proposed, all of which probably have some validity and no combination of which seems quite sufficient. First, the 1890s were a period of political turmoil, centering on the Populist revolt. Everywhere Populists challenged the hegemony of the Democratic party establishment. In several states they worked with Republicans to drive Democrats from power. Equating the maintenance of white supremacy with the survival of their own party, Democrats took the vote away from blacks—and from many poor whites as well. Second, the drive toward segregation centered on cities and industry, which are associated with forces ordinarily considered to be progressive. Without legal segregation, industrialization and urbanization would probably have enabled blacks to threaten white supremacy. Third, this was a period of strong black assertiveness—strikes, boycotts, increased voting—so that to some extent whites were reacting to what they feared or imagined. On the whole the most satisfactory explanation is that the American nation, including the South, was undergoing rapid and massive change. Segregation was a means of placing the race question on hold while substantial parts of the South industrialized and while the nation as a whole modernized, expanded to what it considered its natural limits, and became one of the world's great imperial powers. Not for the first time, nor for the last, black people paid a heavy price for national reconciliation and progress.

Segregation covered the whole range of southern experience. In politics, beginning with the Mississippi plan in 1890, state after state invented or copied various ways—poll taxes, white party primaries, the understanding requirement (in which a prospective voter had to interpret a passage of the U.S. Constitution to the satisfaction of a registrar), as well as the more traditional means of fraud and terror—to exclude all but a tiny minority of black men, and after 1920 of black women, from the franchise. To some degree this was a new departure. Not only during Reconstruction, when federal troops enforced the Fifteenth Amendment, but for more than a decade after the Compromise of 1877, when the North acquiesced in home rule under local conservatives—an event quaintly referred to in southern history books as "Redemption"—blacks had voted in large numbers. Sometimes they had gained political office. More often white politicians and parties had competed for their votes.

In economics, segregation focused not on rural black belt or coastal areas, where the pattern of direct dominance through the crop-lien system largely continued, but on the industrializing Piedmont: the band that stretches from Danville, Va., through Greensboro and Charlotte, N.C., to Greenville, S.C., and Atlanta, Ga., and on to Birmingham, Ala. Black slaves had often worked in the few factories the South possessed before the Civil War. Now they were excluded entirely, as in cotton manufacturing, or restricted to dirty, low-paying jobs that were classified as unskilled, as in tobacco, coal mining, or iron and steel. Throughout the South, which in effect included the nation's capital during the Wilson Administration, blacks in services, retail, or civil administration were not found "above a certain level." The only significant exceptions were in business or industries owned by blacks in the segregated sector—insurance companies, banks, or small manufacturing establishments.

In education, from kindergarten through postgraduate levels, the South provided separate educational streams. According to the classic separate-but-equal argument, which justified segregation and which the Supreme Court accepted in a series of decisions including the landmark *Plessy* v. *Ferguson* (1896), schools were supposed to be equal. In terms of money spent per pupil (the ratio in favor of whites often being 10 to 1 or even higher), available programs, qualifications of teachers,

Street scene, Birmingham, 1940s

quality of buildings—and not surprisingly, results—the systems were rarely comparable, let alone equivalent.

Segregation, which was called Jim Crow and was the American equivalent of South African apartheid, covered all areas of life, love, work, leisure, and even death. Whenever black people left "their own" areas, they were confronted at every turn by demeaning and often debilitating restrictions. Housing was segregated not only by custom, as it largely remains, but by law. The few blacks whose parents could afford it were born in black hospitals (whose administrators and better-paid doctors and even nurses were apt to be white). They went to black schools. When they rode public transportation, they sat in the black section in the rear. If they wanted to drink, eat, or go to the toilet, they might be lucky enough to find facilities reserved for them; otherwise they had to do without. Parks, beaches, golf courses, tennis courts, and swimming pools excluded them; again comparatively rarely they might find separate but undoubtedly inferior facilities. If they ran afoul of the law, they were sworn on separate-but-equal Bibles and, if convicted by usually all-white juries, were sentenced by white judges to segregated jails. When they died, they were embalmed in black funeral parlors (one of the most promising businesses for the black bourgeoisie) and buried in black cemeteries.

The central theme running through much of the discrimination in jobs was the classic southern taboo concerning the mixture of race and sex. White females and black males were simply not supposed to meet, study, or work together except under the most rigid of protocol, lest sexual contact be the result. It has often been remarked that the concern of southern white people about miscegenation increased in inverse proportion to its actual incidence. It was very frequent during slavery, when owners had power over black women; it decreased markedly after 1865, when black men were at last able to protect black women. Perhaps James Baldwin's sarcastic comment to a southern white man reflects this history: "I've been marrying your daughter for centuries."

This vast, complex system of segregation, which covered every aspect of southern life, was built and enforced by white power. Sometimes that power was exercised more or less evenhandedly, according to something approaching a rule of law, albeit a law that was itself discriminatory. Sometimes it was arbitrary and, though rarely punished, exercised outside lawful channels. And it was at times exceedingly violent. Major race riots occurred in Atlanta, New Orleans, Memphis, Wilmington, and many other places. Most of these took place in cities but by no means all, the Phoenix Riot in South Carolina being an important rural example. The ebb and flow of violence followed a curve of real or imagined black "uppitiness": the 1890s when segregation was being established; the years just after World Wars I and II, when black soldiers came home; and the civil rights campaign of the 1960s being the peaks of racial violence. But the valleys were very deep. Hundreds of blacks were lynched, often by mobs transported to the scene by advertised special trains; frequently a town's most "respectable" citizens were unofficially known to have participated. Blacks in the thousands were beaten. At one time or another, all blacks were terrorized.

The rhetoric of racist literature was even more violent than the fact. There seems no useful point in repeating the "black beast" language of the novelist Thomas Dixon, Jr., or of such prominent politicians as Ben Tillman and Cole Blease of South Carolina or James Vardaman of Mississippi. As the moderate minister Edgar Gardner Murphy complained, the racial fanatics progressed "from the contention that no negro shall vote, to the contention that no negro shall learn, that no negro shall labor, and (by implication) that no negro shall live." The threat of extermination was by no means always left to implication. Indeed, it is hard to imagine any measure white people might have taken with respect to blacks that would not have been supported and sanctioned by the racist culture that prevailed from 1890 to 1915 and perhaps beyond.

Indeed, if one takes that literature seriously—and the example of Adolf Hitler and the Jewish Holocaust suggests that what fanatics in the 20th century say does indeed have to be taken literally—then segregation was not the worst of all possible "solutions" that white people might have devised. The late 19th century, after all, was the period when the United States brought to a logical and terrible conclusion its campaign of extermination and removal of the American Indians. Black leader Booker T. Washington used that example often in his speeches, as an example of what might happen to people who could not come to terms with the white man's economic and political system.

Segregation was not at first proposed by racial fanatics, but by moderates and liberals. It was not southern racists who developed black colleges, but northern philanthropists; without the latter there would have been none at all. In time segregation would come to be identified with the extreme right of the racial spectrum. In the 1890s, however, segregation was a moderate compromise. So long as there was no social mixing, then blacks could pursue their separate identity at their own pace and in their own way. "Separate but equal" was largely a fiction; but if there had been *nothing* in it, then ordinary people of good conscience, especially in the North, would never have accepted it. And they did.

The violence of the white power that lay behind segregation, as well as the threat of racist literature of the period, explains much about how the system worked. To some extent segregation was self-enforcing. Substantial sections of the black community, notably the much and unfairly maligned black bourgeoisie, had a stake in the system and even benefited from having a protected market in which to operate. They had more to lose from the breakdown of law and order, even when that law was discriminatory. Like any other people faced with power they correctly perceived to be irresistible, blacks created mechanisms through which they collaborated. They also resisted. Sometimes they fought violence with violence. Time and again they employed the methods of peaceful protest—boycotts, strikes, sit-ins, demonstrations—that would ultimately succeed in the 1960s.

Scholars have identified three broad approaches by which black people tried to contend with segregation. The first, associated with Booker T. Washington of Tuskegee Institute in Alabama, was accommodation and economic self-sufficiency. The second, identified with W. E. B. Du Bois of Atlanta University and the National Association for the Advancement of Colored People, was militant and organized resistance, especially in the courts. The third, led by Bishop Henry McNeal Turner of the African Methodist Episcopal church and later by the West Indian Marcus Garvey, was black nationalism and the so-called back-to-Africa movement. All of these approaches combined elements of collaboration and resistance. Even Du Bois accepted that blacks must live with some aspects of segregation, at least for the time being. Despite their often heated controversy, significant interchange took place between these leaders and movements. Their ultimate goal was the same—black power.

Why did the mid-20th century civil rights movement succeed when others had failed? Partly because blacks of all ages—Rosa Parks, whose refusal to leave her seat in a white section of a bus sparked the Montgomery boycott; the recent graduates of Atlanta and other universities, inspired by such educators as Benjamin Mays, who led the Southern Christian Leadership Conference under Martin Luther King, Jr.; the students who sat in at lunch counters in Greensboro and organized voter registration drives in Mississippi—were more numerous and better organized than ever before. As abolitionist Frederick Douglass had said, power concedes nothing without a struggle. Also, discrimination in the South proved increasingly embarrassing to American foreign policy after World War II. Gunnar Myrdal's *An American Dilemma* (1944) argued that Americans could not indefinitely postpone acting to correct such a blatant contradition of the democratic dream. The pivotal Supreme Court decision *Brown* v. *Board of Education* (1954) represented a national judgment on the South's racial system.

But the white South had not been converted. Virtually everywhere it resisted, sometimes violently and massively, sometimes more subtly (and probably more successfully). The civil rights campaign gathered strength and speed, and it would not be denied. Eventually, in place after place, white corporate and political leaders made the decision that though economic, political, and educational discrimination was far from ended, the career of white supremacy as a legal system was over. The South was no longer dedicated to being a white man's domain.

See also EDUCATION: Athletics and Education; Desegration; / Busing; Christian Academies; HISTORY AND MANNERS: Manners; Sexuality; INDUSTRY: Civil Rights and Business; LAW: Civil Rights Movement; / Black Codes; Slave Codes; MYTHIC SOUTH: Racial Attitudes; RELIGION: Civil Rights and Religion; SCIENCE AND MEDICINE: Racism, Scientific; VIOLENCE: Race Riots; / Mob Violence

John W. Cell
Duke University

John W. Cell, *The Highest Stage of White Supremacy: The Origins of Segregation in South Africa and the American South* (1982); Carl N. Degler, *Neither Black nor White: Slavery and Race Relations in Brazil and the United States* (1971); George Fredrickson, *White Supremacy: A Comparative Study in American and South African History* (1981); Marvin Harris, *Pattern of Race in the Americas* (1964); Winthrop D. Jordan, *White over Black: American Attitudes toward the Negro, 1550–1812* (1968); Edmund S. Morgan, *American Slavery, American Freedom: The Ordeal of Colonial Virginia* (1975); Willis D. Weatherford and Charles S. Johnson, *Race Relations: Adjustment of Whites and Negroes in the United States* (1934); Joel Williamson, *The Crucible of Race: Black-White Relations in the American South since Emancipation* (1985), ed. *The Origins of Segregation* (1968); C. Vann Woodward, *The Strange Career of Jim Crow* (1955; 3d ed. 1974).

Religion, Black

The religious life of the majority of black southerners originated in both traditional African religions and in Anglo-Protestant evangelicalism. The influence of Africa was more muted in the United States than in Latin America, where African-derived theology and ritual were institutionalized in the communities of Brazilian candomblé, Haitian voodoo, and Cuban santeria. Nevertheless, in the United States, as in Latin America, slaves did transmit to their descendants styles of worship, funeral customs, magical ritual, and medicinal practice based upon the religious systems of West and Central African societies.

Although some slaves in Maryland and Louisiana were baptized as Catholics, most had no contact with Catholicism and were first converted to Christianity in large numbers under the preaching of Baptist and Methodist revivalists in the late 18th century. The attractiveness of the evangelical revivals for slaves was due to several factors: the emotional behavior of revivalists encouraged the type of religious ecstasy similar to the danced religions of Africa; the antislavery stance taken by some Baptists and Methodists encouraged slaves to identify evangelicalism with emancipation; blacks actively participated in evangelical meetings and cofounded churches with white evangelicals; evangelical churches licensed black men to preach.

By the 1780s pioneer black preachers had already begun to minister to their own people in the South, and as time went on black congregations, mainly Baptist in denomination, increased in size and in number, despite occasional harassment and proscription by the authorities. However, the majority of slaves in the antebellum South attended church, if at all, with whites.

Institutional church life did not exhaust the religion of the slaves. An "invisible institution" of secret and often forbidden religious meetings thrived in the slave quarters. Here slaves countered the slaveholding gospel of the master class with their own version of Christianity in which slavery and slaveholding stood condemned by God. Slaves took the biblical story of Exodus and applied it to their own history, asserting that they, like the children of Israel, would be liberated from bondage. In the experience of conversion individual slaves affirmed their personal dignity and self-worth. In the ministry, black men exercised authority and achieved status nowhere else available to them. Melding African and Western European traditions, the slaves created a religion of great vitality.

Complementing Christianity in the quarters was conjure, a sophisticated combination of African herbal medicine and magic. Based on the belief that illness and misfortune have personal as well as impersonal causes, conjure offered frequently successful therapy for the mental and physical ills of generations of Afro-Americans and simultaneously served as a system for venting social tension and resolving conflict.

The Civil War, Emancipation, and Reconstruction wrought an institutional transformation of black churches in the South. Northern denominations—black as well as white—sent aid to the freedmen and missionaries to educate and bring them to church. Freedmen, eager to learn to read and write, flocked to schools set up by the American Missionary Association and other freedmen's aid societies. These freedmen's schools laid the foundation for major black colleges and universities such as Fisk, Morehouse, Dillard, and others. Eager to exercise autonomy, freedmen swarmed out of white churches and organized their own. Some affiliated with black denominations of northern origin, others formed their own southern associations.

Black ministers actively campaigned in Reconstruction politics and in some cases were elected to positions of influence and power. Richard H. Cain, for example, was elected to the U.S. House of Representatives from North Carolina and Hiram R. Revels to the Senate from Mississippi. With the failure of Reconstruction and the disfranchisement of black southerners, the church once again became the sole forum for black politics, as well as the economic, social, and educational center of black communities across the South.

By the end of the century, black church membership stood at an astounding 2.7 million out of a population of 8.3 million. Most numerous were the Baptists who succeeded in 1895 in creating a National Baptist Convention, followed numerically by the black Methodists, as institutionalized in the African Methodist Episcopal church and the African Methodist Episcopal Zion church, both founded in the North early in the century, and the Colored Methodist Episcopal church, formed by an amicable withdrawal from the Southern Methodist church, in 1870.

Though too poor to mount a full-fledged missionary campaign, the black churches turned to evangelization of Africa as a challenge to Afro-American Christian identity. The first black missionaries, David George and George Liele, had sailed during the Revolution, George to Nova Scotia and then to Sierra Leone, Liele to Jamaica. Daniel Coker followed in 1820 and Lott Carey and Colin Teague in 1821. But in the 1870s and 1880s the mission to Africa seemed all the more urgent. As race relations worsened, as lynching mounted in frequency, as racism was legislated in Jim Crow statutes, emigration appeared to black clergy like Henry McNeal Turner the only solution. Others saw the redemption of Africa as the divinely appointed destiny of black Americans, God's plan for drawing good out of the evil of slavery and oppression.

Connections between southern black churches and northern ones developed as blacks from the South migrated or escaped north, and as northern missionaries came to the South after the Civil War. Several southern blacks assumed positions of leadership in northern churches. Josiah Bishop, a Baptist preacher from Virginia, became pastor of the Abyssinian Baptist Church in New York, and Daniel Alexander Payne and Morris Brown, both of Charleston, became bishops of the A.M.E. church. Beginning in the 1890s and increasing after the turn of the century, rural southern blacks migrated in larger and larger numbers to the cities of the North. Frequently their ministers traveled with them and transplanted, often in storefront or house churches, congregations from the South.

In the cities, southern as well as northern, black migrants encountered new religious options that attracted some adherents from the traditional churches. Catholicism, through the influence of parochial schools, began attracting significant numbers of blacks in the 20th century. Black Muslims and Jews developed new religio-racial identities for Afro-Americans disillusioned with Christianity. The Holiness and Pentecostal churches stressed the experiential and ecstatic dimensions of worship while preaching the necessity of sanctification and the blessings of the Spirit. They also facilitated the development of gospel music by allowing the use of instruments and secular tunes in church services.

Though urbanization and secularization led to criticism of black religion as accommodationist and compensatory, the church remained the most important and effective public institution in southern black life. The religious culture of the black folk was celebrated by intellectuals like W. E. B. Du Bois and James Weldon Johnson, who acclaimed the artistry of the slave spirituals and black preaching.

In the late 1950s and 1960s the civil rights movement drew heavily upon the institutional and ethical resources of the black churches across the South. Martin Luther King, Jr., brought to the attention of the nation and the world the moral tradition of black religion. Today, black religion is more pluralistic than ever. Although the church is no longer the only institution that blacks control, it still exerts considerable power in black communities.

See also ETHNIC LIFE: Caribbean Influence; FOLKLIFE: Folk Medicine; Voodoo; RELIGION articles

Albert J. Raboteau
Princeton University

Hans A. Baer, *The Black Spiritual Movement: A Religious Response to Racism* (1984); James Cone, *For My People: Black Theology and the Black Church* (1984); W. E. B. Du Bois, *The Souls of Black Folk* (1903); Samuel S. Hill, ed., *Religion in the Southern States: A Historical Study* (1983); C. Eric Lincoln, ed., *The Black Experience in Religion* (1974); Donald G. Mathews, *Religion in the Old South* (1977); Albert J. Raboteau, *Slave Religion: The "Invisible Institution" in the Antebellum South* (1978); Clarence Walker, *A Rock in a Weary Land: The African Methodist Episcopal Church during the Civil War and Reconstruction* (1982); James M. Washington, *Frustrated Fellowship: The Black Baptist Quest for Social Power* (1986); Joseph R. Washington, Jr., *Black Religion: The Negro and Christianity in the United States* (1964).

Slave Culture

Torn from their native land and cast into the caldron of New World slavery, 10 million Africans were brought to the Americas during the four centuries of the Atlantic slave trade. The vast majority of those who survived the squalor and degradation of the "middle passage" and the early years of captivity—what Europeans called "the seasoning process"—suffered physical pain, psychological despair, and mental anguish. Many clung to their traditional languages, values, beliefs, and religions, but everywhere in the New World blacks found that in order to survive they would have to adjust to a new and alien environment.

In the southern colonies (later, states) the cultural transformation among slaves was relatively rapid. A majority of those who arrived in the colonies during the 17th century came from the West Indies and had already spent several years or more in the New World. During the 18th century those who came directly from Africa—called "outlandish" by the colonists—were either separated from the more "assimilated" slaves until they had accommodated themselves to the work routine or, as was the case in Virginia, sold to small slaveholders who worked alongside their bondsmen. Even as the proportion of Africans rose and the number of blacks spiraled upward—from 28,000 in 1700 (11 percent of the total colonial population) to 91,000 in 1730 (14 percent)—slaveowners established procedures to reward those who learned English, acquired new skills, and embraced Christianity. Those who most readily accepted new values, called "New Negroes," and those born on American soil, called creoles, could expect preferential treatment, special privileges, and more prestigious jobs. With the closing of the Atlantic slave trade to the United States in 1808, only a tiny fraction of the total slave population could claim any direct connection with West Africa.

Despite these demographic changes, many aspects of slave culture reflected the influence of Africa. In their family relationships slaves developed broad kinship patterns reminiscent of the familial patterns among various ethnic groups in their ancestral homeland. Even when families were broken by sale, blacks quickly reestablished kin networks whenever possible. Although most children lived with two parents and most adults lived in long-lasting marriages, slaves developed their own, unique family mores. They rarely, if ever, married first cousins; they engaged in sex prior to "marriage," usually with a future partner; they frequently gave their children names of blood kin outside the immediate family; and they had a much broader concept of "family" than most white southerners. "It was months before I learned their family relations," a teacher in South Carolina among the Sea Island slaves observed. "The terms 'bubber' for brother and 'titty' for sister, with 'nanna' for mother and 'mother' for grandmother, and 'father' for all the leaders in church and society, were so generally used I was forced to believe that they all belonged to one immense family."

If most slaveowners showed little interest in slave families, other than encouraging childbearing, they similarly allowed blacks to practice their own brand of Christianity. One of the most distinctive cultural transformations among blacks was their adaptation of various African beliefs and rites to American Protestantism. Slaves dwelt on the Old Testament, not only because they identified with the children, but, as Nathan Huggins points out, "because those books conformed more to their own instincts for tribal and clan deities." In their use of the New Testament they focused on the story of Jesus, the parables, and the Crucifixion. Moreover, slaves ignored the doctrinal disputes between various Protestant sects, believed evil was a force of the universe rather than man's natural condition, and accepted Christianity as fundamentally collective and social rather than individualistic. Revealing their ancestral heritage, slave preachers filled their messages with cosmic imagery and played on the feelings and emotions of the congregation; and, unlike whites (except in a few evangelical sects), slaves actively participated in each religious service, shouting ecstatic prayers, singing deeply felt spirituals, clapping their hands, and fervently entreating, "Come Jesus, Come Lord. Be among us now."

Language, music, and folktales were also important in slave culture. These were, as Lawrence W. Levine indicates, "instruments of life, of sanity, of health, and of self-respect." In communicating with one another slaves sometimes retained elements of speech acquired in West Africa. Along the Sea Island Coast of South Carolina and Georgia blacks spoke Gullah (sometimes known as Geechee), a black dialect that blended various African words, names, and sounds with English. African equivalents were substituted for *tooth*, *pregnancy*, *alcohol*, *sweet potato*; other nouns as well as adverbs, verbs, and adjectives were frequently changed by using groups of words in the African style: *day clean* meant "dawn"; *to sweet mouth* meant to flatter. Blacks also used various forms of ironic or sardonic humor when discussing whites. At the same time a number of slave words crept into the English language— *tote*, *banjo*, *cooter*, *chigger*, *yam*, *okra*, and *juke*.

Slave music was an especially distinctive cultural form. Blacks did not draw a clear line between secular and sacred music and, like many of their ancestors in West Africa, sang a great variety of work songs and spirituals. Their lyrics, intonations, and singing style were marked by poetic beauty, emotional intensity, and rich imagery:

Breddren, don' git weary,
Breddren, don' git weary,
Breddren, don' git weary,
Fo d work is most done.

De ship is in de harbor, harbor, harbor,
De ship is in de harbor,
To wait upon de Lord. . . .

'E got 'e ca'go raidy, raidy, raidy,
'E got 'e ca'go raidy,
Fo' to wait upon de Lord.

Passed down from parents to children or from conjurers to other slaves, folktales and folk beliefs were important vehicles for transmitting social values and attitudes. Some stories came directly from Africa; others evolved out of circumstances in the New World; still others were a blending of the two. Almost all the tales involved a lesson of one type or another, lessons about mercy, prestige, patience, greed, wealth, strength, success, honor, and sexual prowess. In most instances slaves used an animal trickster to convey a portrait or to teach a lesson. In the famous Brer Rabbit and the Wolf tale, Rabbit discovers a tar baby at the side of the road (placed there by Wolf). When Rabbit's curiosity gets the better of him, he strikes the tar baby and becomes enmeshed in the tar. Wolf comes to claim his prize. Realizing that Wolf will do exactly what he thinks Rabbit desires least, Rabbit begs not to be thrown into the briar patch, which is, of course, exactly what Wolf does, and wily Rabbit gains his freedom. Such tales were greatly enhanced by the manner of their delivery and the response of the audience. During the telling of a tale slaves chanted, mimicked, acted, and sang. "I don't know how they do it," one observer wrote, "but they will say 'lipity clipity, lipity clipity,' so you can almost hear a rabbit coming through the woods."

Although a distinct slave culture developed in America, relying on extended kinship networks, a different form of Christianity, and a rich folk heritage, many slaves rejected aspects of this culture. Overt resistance to slavery came primarily in two forms—individual acts of violence and running away. A close study of black rebelliousness in Virginia points to how African-born slaves typically ran away in groups and attempted to establish villages on the frontier whereas American-born slaves, who tried to escape in far greater numbers, ran away alone and tried to pass as free persons in the most settled areas of the state. The small number of large-scale revolts—compared to the hundreds of major revolutions in the Caribbean and South America—reveals the breakdown of West African communalism. Slaves who sought to improve their situation on the plantation and slaves who lived in towns and cities often sought to cast off the manners and attitudes of field hands. They dressed differently, learned to speak and act comfortably around whites, and whenever possible saved money and acquired personal possessions. In addition, as the doors to legal emancipation slowly closed during the antebellum decades, an increasing number of slaves, by one means or another, moved into what contemporaries called "quasi-freedom"—halfway between bondage and liberty. While legally enslaved, these blacks lived independent, sometimes completely autonomous lives, securing their own employment, maintaining their own families, and moving about from place to place. At the same time slaves who lived on small plantations or farms, along the frontier, or on plantations owned by French Creoles in Louisiana developed cultural mores and attitudes peculiar to their unique circumstances. In St. Landry Parish, for example, many slaves spoke French. The Civil War and general emancipation did not destroy slave culture, but more and more blacks saw the folkways of the past as a legacy of bondage and sought different values as a symbol of the future and freedom.

See also FOLKLIFE: Aesthetics, Afro-American; / Brer Rabbit; HISTORY AND MANNERS: Colonial Heritage; LANGUAGE: Gullah; LAW: / Slave Codes; MUSIC: Spirituals

Loren Schweninger
University of North Carolina
at Greensboro

John Blassingame, *The Slave Community: Plantation Life in the Antebellum South* (1972); Eugene D. Genovese, *Roll, Jordan, Roll: The World the Slaves Made* (1974); Herbert G. Gutman, *The Black Family in Slavery and Freedom, 1750–1925* (1976); Charles Joyner, *Down by the Riverside: A South Carolina Slave Community* (1984); Lawrence W. Levine, *Black Culture and Black Consciousness: Afro-American Folk Thought from Slavery to Freedom* (1977); Gerald W. Mullin, *Flight and Rebellion: Slave Resistance in Eighteenth-Century Virginia*

(1972); Leslie Owens, *This Species of Property: Slave Life and Culture in the Old South* (1976); Albert J. Raboteau, *Slave Religion: The "Invisible Institution" in the Antebellum South* (1978); George Rawick, *From Sundown to Sunup: The Making of the Black Community* (1972); Sterling Stuckey, *Massachusetts Review* (Summer 1968); Thomas Webber, *Deep Like the Rivers: Education in the Slave Quarter Community, 1831–1865* (1978); Peter Wood, *Black Majority: Negroes in Colonial South Carolina from 1670 through the Stono Rebellion* (1974).

Speech, Black

Black English is the term most often used to describe the dialect of lower-class blacks. Although many blacks use varieties of English identical to those used by whites, some linguists suggest that the speech of lower-class blacks is different structurally from any white variety. The relationship of black speech to white speech and the origins of black English are still matters of controversy, but the linguistic features of the dialect are well established. These include such features as invariant *be* (as in *we be working*) for long-term or continuous actions, absence of the *be* verb (as in *they sick*) to convey short-term actions, absence of the suffix *-s* on third-person singular present tense verbs (as in *he run*) and of the suffix *-ed* on past tense verbs (as in *he walk to school yesterday*), among others, and a higher frequency of some processes such as deletion of final consonants (as when *test* is pronounced *tes'*).

Despite the agreement about these features, black English is easily the most controversial topic in the study of southern speech, because attitudes toward it are often bound up with the political and social aspirations of laymen and the scholarly predispositions of linguists. Those who emphasize the essential similarities of all Americans deny that "black English," a dialect with ethnicity as its primary social correlate, exists. Those who emphasize the African heritage of American blacks, on the other hand, stress not only the differences between black and white speech but also the affinities between black speech and Anglophone creoles in the Caribbean and Africa. Linguists who adhere to each position work within different disciplines and use different methodologies, further complicating the problem. Many of the linguists who argue that black and white speech are qualitatively alike are dialect geographers whose primary area of research is English, while many of those who argue that black English is a radically different language are creolists studying Caribbean languages.

Both sides of the controversy, however, are responses to earlier attitudes toward black speech. During the last century, differences between black and white speech were often attributed to differences in physiology and in mental abilities, to the black's "thick lips and lazy tongue," and to his childlike mind. Others maintained that black speech was merely an archaic form of English, preserving relic forms that had their origins in rural British dialects but preserving nothing from Africa. More recently, some educators have suggested that the academic difficulties of black children are a consequence of deficiencies in their language. Maintaining that black English lacks grammatical categories such as tense that are necessary for logical thought, these educators claim that the language itself inhibits cognitive operations necessary for academic success. Modern linguistic research on black English confronts and refutes each of these, even as linguists themselves dispute the relationship between black and white speech, especially in the South, and the origins of black English.

Dialect geographers were the first to provide data on black speech, with McDavid and McDavid (1951) the most important of the early studies. Making use of field records of the *Linguistic Atlas of the Middle and South Atlantic States* and of Lorenzo Dow Turner's work on Gullah, the McDavids debunked the myths that black speech is the product of physiology and mental ability and that it preserves nothing of its African heritage. The study documented some two dozen words of African origin (including *okra*, *goober*, and *gumbo*) and suggested that some grammatical tendencies (such as the use of *for* as the sign of the infinitive in *he come for tell you*) and some features of pronunciation (such as a higher frequency of consonant cluster simplification) may reflect African influence, too. Yet the McDavids and other dialect geographers maintained that black and white speech were not radically different—that the range of variants was the same in both varieties, although statistical differences existed.

A decade later creolists such as William Stewart began to challenge the assertion that black and white speech differed only quantitatively. Pointing to similarities between black speech and Caribbean creoles in their use of such features as invariant *be* and zero copula, these creolists suggested that black English differed structurally as well as statistically from white varieties and that the differences were a result of the dialect's peculiar history. Dillard (1972) used literary attestations of creole-like forms and observations of early travelers to support the hypothesis that black English is actually a development of a creole language, much like those spoken in the Caribbean, which had its ultimate origins in a West African pidgin, a simplified admixture of English and a variety of African languages used in the absence of a common tongue. Black English maintains vestiges of its creole history; these account for many of the differences between black and white speech, although Dillard noted that "some Southern white dialects have been strongly influenced by Negro dialect."

Because the creolists lacked solid comparative data to confirm their hypotheses, dialect geographers continued to caution against the notion of "racial" dialects, with ethnicity as the primary social correlate; but these linguists also lacked sufficient data, especially on some crucial grammatical features such as invariant *be*, to establish their conclusion that black and white speech differ only quantitatively. The bitter debate between creolists and dialect geographers over the origin of black English and its relation to white speech became the central focus of scholarship in the field.

The solution to the controversy, however, lay not in polemics but in fieldwork. Sociolinguists using the methods developed by William Labov provided part of the solution. In research that refutes those educators who claim that black English represents a deficient form of English and is itself a barrier to logical thought, Labov and his associates provide extensive data on black speech in New York City, including data on crucial features such as invariant *be* and explicit comparisons with similar white speakers. After examining a number of linguistic features, Labov takes a position somewhere between that of the creolists and the dialect geographers. While he suggests that a number of features are unique to black speech, he concludes that black English is "best seen as a distinct subsystem within the larger grammar of English." Wolfram's (1974) extension of this methodology into the South allows both him and Fasold (1981) to modify Labov's conclusions so that they encompass the relationship between black and white English in the South, where the varieties are much closer than in the North. Both assert that some differences between black and white speech do persist even in the South but that these "by no means indicate widespread deep differences in grammar and phonology." Both also suggest that the creole hypothesis is the most likely explanation for this variation, although they believe that decreolization has eliminated most of the original creole features.

During the last five years, however, work on southern English has challenged even these conclusions. Data from the Linguistic Atlas of the Gulf States project, made available in 1981, provides a much broader range of informants than previous work (Wolfram's sample included primarily children) and suggests that Fasold's conclusions about black-white speech relationships are too restrictive. All the forms that blacks use appear in the speech of at least some whites, although the most stigmatized forms generally are used only by the elderly and most insular. Furthermore, recent work of a number of scholars indicates that the very question of black-white speech relations is too simplistic. For example, Pederson (1972) provides evidence of subregional variation in black English and of the complicated ways in which black speech relates to various dialects spoken by whites, while the essays in Montgomery and Bailey (1985) show that such factors as age, sex, and educational background play as important a role as ethnicity in language variation. The work of Bailey and Maynor (1985) in Texas and Mississippi on the present tense of *be*, particularly the subsystem that includes the features invariant *be* and zero copula, which have generated the most discussion, provides some indication of these complexities. These researchers demonstrate that black and white folk speech structures are quite similar: both varieties use the same forms in the same ways, although differences in the frequency of occurrence of forms do exist. Among younger speakers, however, the situation is quite different, with forms such as invariant *be* disappearing among whites but actually increasing among blacks so that the form is more frequent among children than adults. Moreover, Bailey and Maynor suggest that the speech of black adolescents is structurally different from that of both black and white folk speakers. If black English did not exist as a distinct ethnic dialect in the past, current developments suggest that it certainly may in the future as the speech of lower-class blacks continues to diverge from white varieties.

Even as new research on southern speech has shown the complexities of black-white speech relations, new work in creole studies is providing the kind of knowledge of Caribbean languages that will enable scholars to determine the precise relationship of black English to those creoles. Although most scholars now agree that at least some aspects of black English, including some features incorporated into white speech, show evidence of development from an earlier creole, much of the history of black English is obscure. Reconstructing that history is a major task.

In spite of the fact that these basic questions about black English remain unanswered, two things have been clearly established. First, black English cannot be explained on the basis of physiology, mental ability, or linguistic deficiency. Second, the importance of black English lies not so much in its linguistic features as in the attitudes that the larger society and its speakers have toward it.

Guy Bailey
Texas A&M University

Guy Bailey and Natalie Maynor, *American Speech* (Summer 1985); J. L. Dillard, *Black English: Its History and Usage in the United States* (1972); Ralph W. Fasold, *American Speech* (Fall 1981); William Labov, *Language in the Inner City: Studies in the Black English Vernacular* (1972); Raven I. McDavid, Jr., and Virginia G. McDavid, *American Speech* (February 1951); Michael Montgomery and Guy Bailey, *Language Variety in the South: Perspectives in Black and White* (1985); Lee Pederson, *Studies in Linguistics in Honor of Ravin I. McDavid, Jr.* (1972); Walt Wolfram, *Language* (September 1974).

Sports, Blacks in

Competition has never been simple for the black athlete in the South. Nor has he always had control over his own athletic destiny. Competition traditionally has functioned on two levels, the simplest of which is the competition in the arena of play, the give-and-take between athletes. More difficult and more complex has been the competition to be allowed to compete. In this battle black athletes in the South have been matched against a southern racial policy that emphasized segregation in all areas of life. In some sports the policy occasionally gave way, in others it remained fixed until the second half of the 20th century.

Blacks on the antebellum plantations fished, hunted, and watched cockfights; they boxed in matches promoted by their owners, and they even served as crews for boating regattas. Between 1865 and the 1890s there was no clear policy covering interracial competition in athletics. Although black athletes normally competed on a racially segregated basis, there were times when they vied with whites. In New Orleans, Memphis, and other parts of the South blacks and whites occasionally played baseball together in the 1870s and 1880s. And a few black athletes even gained fortune and fame competing against whites. From 1875 through 1902 black riders won 13 times at the Kentucky Derby. The most famous of the black jockeys, Isaac Murphy, won three times. When Murphy died in 1896, the estimated value of his estate was $50,000.

The most prominent arena of competition, however, was the boxing ring. During the late 1880s and early 1890s, when the national center of boxing was in New Orleans, several important interracial matches were staged. On 6 September 1892 the Olympic Club of New Orleans matched George "Little Chocolate" Dixon, a black, against a white named Jack Skelly. Dixon was the world's featherweight champion and a great boxer. Skelly was unheralded. The result was thoroughly predictable. Dixon administered a brutal beating of his white opponent.

The public reaction to the Dixon-Skelly bout symbolized what was happening to interracial competition throughout the South. A reporter for the Chicago *Tribune* noted that many white spectators "winced every time Dixon landed on Skelly. The sight was repugnant to some of the men from the South. A darky is all right in his place here, but the idea of sitting quietly by and seeing a colored boy pommel a white lad grates on Southerners." Even more to the point, the editor of the New Orleans *Times-Democrat* declared that it was "a mistake to match a negro and a white man, a mistake to bring the races together on any terms of equality, even in the prize ring." After the fight, the Olympic Club announced that it would never again promote an interracial bout.

In the prize ring, the most important area of southern athletic integration, segregation soon became the standard policy. Promoters turned against interracial bouts, and white southerners applauded their action. In one case where an interracial bout was promoted in Mississippi, it was stopped by a man described as "a loyal Southerner" who remarked: "The idea of niggers fighting white men. Why, if that darned scoundrel would beat that white boy the niggers would never stop gloating over it, and, as it is, we have enough trouble with them."

So Jim Crow came to the southern prize ring. He also came to southern baseball diamonds, race tracks, billiard halls, cockpits, and sporting clubs. In most sports Jim Crow was almost as strong above the Mason-Dixon line as below, for athletic segregation was not unique to the South. During the late 19th century professional baseball flirted with an interracial ideal, and a few blacks played on integrated teams. In 1887 the League of Colored Base Ball Clubs was recognized as a minor league under the National Agreement between professional baseball teams, a development that ultimately might have produced a vehicle for black advancement to the major leagues. However, after that year blacks were systematically excluded from "organized" professional baseball, and by 1892 the color line was firmly in place.

Black southern athletes still excelled, although they were hampered considerably by Jim Crow restrictions. Three black southern athletes gained particular fame during the first half of the 20th century. The first was Jack Johnson, the first black heavyweight champion. Born in Galveston, Tex., he was forced to leave the South to practice his trade. In 1908 he defeated Tommy Burns for the championship, but his defiant lifestyle generated only hatred in the white South. Again, white southern attitudes differed little from white northern opinion. In 1913 Johnson was forced to flee the country in order to escape a prison term resulting from a trumped up conviction under the Mann Act.

The other two black southern athletes were Jesse Owens and Joe Louis. They were born only months apart, both sons of Alabama sharecropper parents. Both were also products of the black southern migration to the North. Owens's family moved to Cleveland, Ohio; Louis's to Detroit, Mich. Owens developed into the greatest track-and-field athlete of the first half of the 20th century, achieving his greatest triumphs at the 1936 Olympic Games in Berlin. Louis became the second black to hold the heavyweight boxing title, reigning from 1937 to 1949. Unlike Johnson, both Owens and Louis projected accommodationist images, and thus both were relatively popular in North and South.

Athletes in this era became heroes of black life and folklore. North Carolina blacks sang, for example, of Jack Johnson, "Amaze an' Grace, how sweet it sounds,/Jack Johnson knocked Jim Jeffries down." Joe Louis was especially important in promoting a sense of pride among southern blacks. Writer Maya Angelou has written in *I Know Why the Caged Bird Sings* of the black farmers and workers around Stamps, Ark., gathering in her grandmother's general store to listen to the radio broadcast of a Louis fight, savoring each moment of victory.

After World War II integration became the touchstone in northern sports. In 1945 Branch Rickey, owner of the Brooklyn Dodgers, broke the color line in professional baseball by signing Jackie Robinson. Born in Georgia and raised in California, Robinson admirably responded to the challenge, winning acclaim on and off the playing field. The integration of baseball overshadowed the integration of professional football, which occurred in 1945. Slowly over the next two decades the other major sports followed football and baseball's lead. The National Basketball Association admitted blacks for the first time in 1950, the same year Althea Gibson was allowed to compete at Forest Hills in the U.S. tennis championships. By 1960 the major sports had been integrated in the North.

Integration in the South lagged behind the North. Few professional teams existed in the South, so the major focus of action was in the South's colleges and universities. Some southern states prohibited their universities from competing in athletics with northern schools that had blacks on their teams. As Governor Marvin Griffin of Georgia remarked in 1956, "The South stands at Armageddon. The battle is joined. There is no more difference in compromising the integrity of race on the playing field than in doing so in the classroom. One break in the dike and the relentless seas will rush in and destroy us."

As a result of this attitude, the Southeastern Conference (SEC) was the last major intercollegiate conference to integrate its athletic teams.

During the 1960s and 1970s, however, integration came to southern athletics. The major professional and college football, basketball, and baseball teams in the South accepted blacks. The first black athletes in the SEC were signed to scholarships in 1966, and integration of varsity teams began in the 1967–68 season. Even professional golf, the "whitest" of all sports, accepted integration. In 1974 Lee Elder became the first black golfer to participate in the Masters Tournament in Augusta, Ga. By the late 1970s, black athletes had at last won the right to compete in athletics in the South.

Sports, in fact, has come to play a prominent role in recent southern race relations. Participation in high school and college athletics has made black athletes such as Georgia's Herschel Walker into superheroes of whites as well as blacks, has promoted assimilation, and has undoubtedly been important in providing examples of high-achievement blacks. Critics such as sociologist Harry Edwards argue, however, that black involvement in sports has reinforced stereotypical images of blacks as physical performers and caused too many young blacks unrealistically to seek sports stardom at the expense of other career goals.

See also EDUCATION: Athletics and Education; RECREATION: Baseball; Basketball; Boxing; Football; Golf; / Aaron, Hank; Paige, Satchel; Robinson, Eddie; Walker, Herschel

Randy Roberts
Sam Houston State University

William J. Baker, *Jesse Owens: An American Life* (1986); Elliot Gorn, "The Manly Art: Bare Knuckle Prize Fighting and the Rise of American Sports" (Ph.D. dissertation, Yale University, 1983); John A. Lucas and Ronald A. Smith, *Saga of American Sports* (1978); Joan Paul, Richard V. McGhee, and Helen Fant, *Phylon* (December 1984); Randy Roberts, *Papa Jack: Jack Johnson and the Era of White Hopes* (1983); Dale A. Somers, *The Rise of Sports in New Orleans, 1850–1900* (1972); Jules Tygiel, *Baseball's Great Experiment: Jackie Robinson and His Legacy* (1983).

Theater, Black

The theorists and artists of the black arts movement of the 1960s saw the South as the matrix of black culture as well as the place where the struggle for civil rights began. From the days of slavery blacks developed unique forms of entertainment, including satires of slaveowners' society and humorous representations of their own situation that blended storytelling techniques, mimed songs, call-and-response patterns, and that encouraged verbal virtuosity and audience participation. Other rituals emerged at religious gatherings or within the black church, eliciting the involvement of the congregation and assuming a highly dramatized form. All these cultural manifestations were examples of black talent for performance and of the potential for active involvement by black audiences.

These early theatrical activities established both the reputation and the stereotype of blacks as accomplished entertainers, but their political, subversive function has never been properly assessed. Southern blacks were long barred from the legitimate theater as performers. Only free blacks, "free persons of color," were admitted as spectators. When blacks were finally accepted in minstrel troupes, they had to submit to the will of white producers and to the conventions of a genre that perpetuated negative images of their race.

The black renaissance of the 1960s and 1970s brought a theatrical revival to the South. The creation of the Free Southern Theater (FST) in 1963 opened a new era, aiming to develop a black, rural, and urban audience and to support the civil rights movement. The FST participated in the national black theater renaissance of the 1960s and 1970s but nevertheless remained distinctively southern. It was one of the few theaters in the United States (El Teatro Campesino in California is another) that was at one time wholly dedicated to its rural audiences.

The FST emerged as the leading theater troupe, but other groups have also been very active, notably in Louisiana (the Dashiki Project, the Ethiopian Theater, and Dillard and Southern universities in New Orleans) and in Georgia (Carlton Molette at Atlanta University). These groups have reinforced the FST in establishing a strong theatrical tradition; black plays were produced and festivals organized. Black theatrical groups offered workshops on acting and playwriting, and on music and dance, which are now considered essential parts of the theatrical experience.

Recent productions show greater concern for the dramatization of black life and history, a growing interest in folklore and its relationship to African and West Indian oral traditions, and an attention to black women's experience. Plays like *Dark Cowgirls and Prairie Queens*, presented by the Carpetbag Theatre for its 1985–86 season, capture the search of seven black women in the American West for freedom in the pre–Civil War era. Other plays like *Jus' Cumin' Home* and *Sing 'til the Song is Mine*, which were combined in a Jomandi Productions (Florida) tour play called *Voices in the Rain*, explore the interaction of black men and black women. *Junebug Jabbo Jones* by John O'Neal, one of the former directors of the FST, is a celebration of the wealth and diversity of the Afro-American oral tradition. In a long dramatic monologue the storyteller Junebug narrates the happenings of numerous characters and provides his own humorous comments.

Although these groups remain anchored in a tradition of black experience and speech that is distinctively southern, they also maintain contacts with other regions and abroad (John O'Neal's one-man show was presented in a theater festival in Paris at the American Center for Artists and at the Nancy Festival). These productions, imaginative and professional, establish the reputation of a unique southern black theater both regionally and nationally.

See also LITERATURE: Theater

Geneviève Fabre
University of Paris

Tom Dent, Gilbert Moses, and Richard Schechner, *The Free Southern Theatre by the Free Southern Theatre* (1969); Geneviève Fabre, *Drumbeats, Masks, and Metaphor: Contemporary Afro-American Theatre* (1983); Martha Jones, *Black Creation* (Fall 1972); Mance Williams, *Black Theatre in the 1960s and 1970s: A Historical-Critical Analysis of the Movement* (1985).

Towns, Black

The South after 1860 spawned towns with names like New Africa, New Rising Star, Slabtown, Acreville, Promised Land, and others now lost to the historical record. These towns, established by newly emancipated slaves, were uniquely southern. Their origins were rooted in the events of Reconstruction and efforts by freedpeople to claim a complex and multifaceted freedom. All the black towns established during this period were shaped by broad historical forces, a long-standing awareness among blacks that personal freedom was bound inextricably to residential separation from whites, and the policies that emerged from the federal government between 1861 and 1863 that designated slaves as contraband of war.

The antebellum South did not directly foster residential integrity for black people, yet both slaves and free blacks devised strategies for claiming some degree of independence in their living arrangements. Plantation life offered its own kind of residential autonomy and opportunities to forge a folk culture independent of whites. Free blacks established churches, schools for their children, fraternal orders, and mutual aid societies. Institutional structures and collective identities drawn from both experiences were easily adapted to the black town settings of the postwar South.

Slavery decayed wherever invading Union troops solidified their military position, beginning at Fortress Monroe, Va., in June 1861. As blacks deserted the plantations, they sought protection with the Union army. Otherwise preoccupied with military concerns, the army was faced with the problem of feeding, clothing, and housing the human contraband. Specific solutions to this dilemma varied but were guided by two general aims—restoration of the southern economy, primarily its agricultural production, and maintenance of social order.

General Benjamin Butler mobilized the blacks who came to Fortress Monroe as laborers. He set the precedent for federal policy by establishing contraband camps, temporary villages where freedpeople were provided seed and farming tools in return for a portion of their crops as repayment. Brigadier General Rufus Saxon devised a plan to reorganize the cotton economy of the Sea Islands by subdividing plantation lands and thereby establishing the basis for a black peasantry in that location. John Eaton created a black freeholding class at Davis Bend, Miss., parceling out land in his charge in small tracts to be cultivated by individual families. The results of these land experiments were clear. The freedpeople worked harder and the lands were more productive when farmed by families rather than by gang labor. The unintended consequences of the experiments were also clear. Contiguous collections of black-owned land were rapidly elaborated into communities as the freedpeople established the churches, schools, and mutual aid societies that formed the core of community life.

These initial postwar arrangements heightened the expectations of other blacks in the South who were also demanding the opportunity to own land and, in the words of former slave Garrison Frazier, to "live by ourselves rather than scattered among the whites." Economic self-sufficiency, landownership, and community were interconnected and inseparable. As community building continued and blacks found various ways to acquire their own land, the average number of land holdings in the South doubled between 1860 and 1880, and the average size of farm tracts fell from 365 to 157 acres. In some cases these towns began with cooperative purchases of whole plantations, arrangements guided from the outset by principles of mutual aid and reciprocity. In South Carolina, the only state in the defeated Confederacy with a black majority in both its Constitutional Convention and Reconstruction legislature, black land purchases were fostered by the Land Commission. This state agency settled approximately 14,000 black families on farms that they owned. Whatever the strategies used to create the towns during the 1860s and 1870s, they were rarely incorporated political units. Yet, with the institutional structures of church and school firmly entrenched, these stable rural communities survived well into the 20th century.

The intentional land developments of the West that began in the 1870s contrast sharply with the casual black communities of the postwar South. Racial violence, combined with crop failures, instigated a black exodus from the southern states to the West, where inexpensive land was available for homesteading. The establishment of Nicodemus, Kan., in 1877, reflected this movement. Mound Bayou, Miss., which was the easternmost of these towns, was established by Isaiah Montgomery in 1888. Montgomery, with land development and management experience at Davis Bend and business experience in Vicksburg during the mid-1880s, planned the Mound Bayou settlement to coincide with the opening of a new Louisville, New Orleans, and Texas railroad line. One of the early Nicodemus settlers, Edward P. McCabe, who enjoyed a successful career as a Kansas state politician, quit the town when the unassigned lands of Oklahoma were opened for settlement in 1889. McCabe envisioned the creation of an all-black state when he established Langston, Okla., in 1890, and although his dream was not realized, Langston became the home of the state's Colored Agricultural and Normal University.

More than 20 black towns were established in Oklahoma during the late 19th and early 20th centuries. The largest of these was Boley, opened for settlement in 1904. Like Mound Bayou, Boley was created with the intention of capitalizing on the expanding railroad industry and for a time enjoyed a degree of economic prosperity. Boley was a prototype of many other black towns. It adhered to Booker T. Washington's conservative philosophy of moral and economic race development, and it suffered from the predictable disadvantages of marginal capitalism and race discrimination.

Resources in the intentionally developed black towns in the West never matched the expectation of the entrepreneurs who established them. Unable to meet the challenges of change, primarily the mechanization of agriculture and the migration of blacks from rural to urban areas, these towns fell into decline during the first quarter of the 20th century. The heritage of the black towns, the solidarity of race, and the centrality of church and mutual aid in community life were retained and translated into new forms of community in the urban centers of black life by the mid-20th century.

See also URBANIZATION: Segregation, Residential

Elizabeth Rauh Bethel
Lander College

Elizabeth Rauh Bethel, *Promiseland: A Century of Life in a Negro Community* (1981); John Blassingame, *The Slave Community: Plantation Life in the Antebellum South* (1972); Norman L. Crockett, *Black Towns* (1979); Louis S. Gerteis, *From Contraband to Freedman: Federal Policy toward Southern Blacks, 1861–1865* (1973); Edward Magdol, *A Right to the Land: Essays on the Freedmen's Community* (1977); Nell Irvin Painter, *Exodusters: Black Migration to Kansas after Reconstruction* (1976); Hortense Powdermaker, *After Freedom: A Cultural Study in the Deep South* (1939); Willie Lee Rose, *Rehearsal for Reconstruction: The Port Royal Experiment* (1964).

Workers, Black

By 1754 the plantation system, based principally on crops of tobacco, rice, and indigo, was well established in the five southern English colonies—Maryland, Virginia, North Carolina, South Carolina, and Georgia. Over 36 percent of the population in these colonies were black slaves—220,000 out of 609,000.

Many Americans, including some southerners, believed that the spirit of the American Revolution, combined with the economic stagnation in tobacco, rice, and indigo planting, would force slavery to die out in the South, just as it was disappearing in the North. But in 1793 Eli Whitney invented the cotton gin, and planters began to take acreage out of other crops and enter the cotton market. The demand for slaves grew. Not even the prohibition by Congress of the importation of slaves from Africa after 1807 could keep cotton from becoming king. The plantation system spread westward, and slavery became solidly rooted in 15 southern states. By 1860 there were 4 million slaves in these states.

Although the economy of the antebellum South was basically agricultural, by 1861 industrialization had forged ahead to such an extent that the slave states accounted for more than 15 percent of the capital invested in the nation's industry. Some establishments employed both whites and slaves at the same factory, mine, or transportation project. But most of the industrial enterprises in the South employed slave labor almost exclusively. In the 1850s about 200,000 slaves—nearly 5 percent of the total slave population—worked in industry.

In 1860 there were more free blacks in the South than in the North—250,787 against 238,268. The absence of white immigrant artisans in the South and the general shortage of workers in the cities forced southern communities to depend on free black craftsmen. Despite repeated efforts of white workers to drive them out of trades, the needs of the community prevailed, and the free black became an indispensable part of the southern skilled labor force, especially in the Lower South. Unlike free blacks in the North, many in the South were able to work at their trades and to hand on their skills to their children.

A call was issued for a national labor convention of black workers to be held in December 1869 at Washington, D.C. It was issued by a group of black workers headed by Isaac Myers, a Baltimore ship caulker who became the first important black labor leader in America. The call noted that legal freedom had not yet brought economic freedom for the black workers. "Colored Men are excluded from the workshops on account of color." In the South the black worker was "unjustly deprived of the price of his labor," and in areas far from courts of justice, "forced to endure wrongs and oppressions worse than slavery."

The Colored National Labor Union, organized at the convention in Washington, attempted to change the conditions of southern black workers. So, too, did the Knights of Labor, organized in 1869, and the Industrial Workers of the World, founded in 1905. But none of these efforts were successful. The vast majority of black workers in the South lived in communities where even the attempt to unionize often brought wholesale arrests, imprisonments, and lynchings.

In 1914 the vast majority of blacks in the United States still lived in the South and were still the chief cultivators of the South's staple crops, enmeshed in a farm tenantry and sharecropping system that consigned them to a life of tilling the soil under conditions almost as restrictive and pernicious as chattel slavery, in rural isolation and a state of perpetual indebtedness.

Jobs in the new textile, iron, and steel factories in the South fell to the poor whites. There were black miners, especially in Alabama, where 46.2 percent of the coal miners in 1889 were blacks. But many of them worked under the convict-lease system. Blacks were arrested for trivial reasons or for no reason at all and sentenced to work out their penalty in the mines. In other southern states, especially Georgia, the convict-lease system supplied cheap black labor to companies building railroads or cutting timber.

The blacks who gravitated in increasing numbers to southern cities moved into personal and domestic service, traditionally regarded as the province of the black. They found employment in urban districts throughout the South as waiters, saloonkeepers, bartenders, janitors, bellhops, barbers, laundresses, and housekeepers. Black women found domestic work one of the few occupations open to the black.

Blacks in the South were gradually eliminated from skilled positions they had held since slavery. Beginning in the 1890s, white workers, most of them members of the American Federation of Labor (AFL) and the Railroad Brotherhoods, steadily eliminated black labor from jobs in the shipping, railroad, and building industries in the older southern seaboard cities. The jobs of electricians, plumbers, gasfitters and steamfitters, railroad engineers and firemen, stationary engineers, cranemen, hoistmen, machinists, and hundreds of other skilled and semiskilled occupations were labeled "for whites only." Black electricians, plumbers, pipefitters, and carpenters had constituted a fair percentage of those crafts at the turn of the century. A generation later, black building-trades work had become "almost marginal," and by 1950 blacks accounted for only 1 percent of the electricians and 3.2 percent of the carpenters. The figures on black participation in apprenticeship programs were even bleaker: 1 percent for plumbers and pipefitters, and 6 percent for carpenters. In Atlanta the proportion of black carpenters decreased from 36.3 percent in 1890 to 2.5 percent in 1920.

Writing in 1936, George Sinclair Mitchell observed that "the Southern trade unionism of the last thirty-odd years has been in good measure a protective device for the march of white artisans in places held by Negroes." Blacks who had spent years acquiring the skill needed for craftsmen's work were denied membership in white unions, which had signed closed-shop or union-shop agreements with employers, and were forced into menial service at low wages.

The same year that Mitchell's criticism of southern trade unionism was published, a labor organization was emerging that was to change the picture for black workers in the South. This was the Committee for Industrial Organization, which became in 1938 the Congress of Industrial Organizations (CIO). Despite bitter opposition of employers and vicious Red-baiting, in which AFL unions participated, the CIO organized thousands of workers in the South—workers in mining, oil, textiles, tobacco, the pulp and paper industry, transportation, and automobile manufacturing. Several southern industries, especially textiles, were white preserves, and this kept down the number of blacks organized. Still, wherever they were employed, black workers streamed into the CIO. In 1945 Lucy Randolph Mason, who did organizing work for the CIO in the South, noted: "Today CIO unions are found in every Southern state and are growing steadily in the region's basic industries and their by-products. Among the many hundreds of thousands of CIO members there are a vast number of Negroes."

The CIO did little to break down the discriminatory lines in industries where blacks were employed, which made it impossible for blacks to advance into better jobs. Moreover, the CIO's constitutional provisions barring discrimination were sometimes openly flouted in the South. But with all its limitations, the CIO marked a significant step forward for the black worker in the South. Lucy Randolph Mason attended a meeting of black women in Richmond, Va., members of the CIO Tobacco Stemmers' and Laborers' Industrial Union. "I asked the secretary what was the most important thing she gained through the union," she wrote later. "'Respect,' she replied in a flash. 'The boss can't come out in the plant any more and yell at us, or fire us if we answer him. The union takes care of all that now.'"

See also AGRICULTURE: Plantations; Sharecropping and Tenancy; / Cotton Culture; SOCIAL CLASS articles; VIOLENCE: / Convict Leasing

Philip S. Foner
Philadelphia, Pennsylvania

Horace R. Cayton and George Sinclair Mitchell, *Black Workers and the New Unions* (1939); Philip S. Foner, *History of Black Americans: From Africa to the Emergence of the Cotton Kingdom* (1975), *History of Black Americans: From Emergence of the Cotton Kingdom to the Eve of the Compromise of 1850* (1983), *Organized Labor and the Black Worker, 1969–1981* (1981); Gerald D. Jaynes, *Branches without Roots: Genesis of the Black Working Class in the American South, 1862–1882* (1986); F. Ray Marshall, *The Negro and Organized Labor* (1965); George Sinclair Mitchell, *Southern Economic Journal* (January 1936); Sterling D. Spero and Abram L. Harris, *The Black Worker: The Negro and the Labor Movement* (1931); Charles G. Wesley, *Negro Labor in the United States, 1850–1925: A Study in American Economic History* (1927); Carter G. Woodson and Lorenzo J. Greene, *The Negro Wage Earner* (1930); Billy Hall Wyche, "Southern Attitudes toward Industrial Unions, 1933–1941" (Ph.D. dissertation, University of Georgia, 1969).

Bethune, Mary McLeod

(1875–1955) Educator.

On 10 July 1875 educator, federal government official, and club woman Mary McLeod Bethune was born near Mayesville, S.C. She was one of 17 children born to former slaves and farm workers, Samuel and Patsy (McIntosh) McLeod. In 1882 Bethune abandoned many of her farm chores to attend the newly opened Presbyterian mission school for blacks near Mayesville. Aided with a scholarship, she left South Carolina in 1888 and continued her education at Scotia Seminary (later Barber-Scotia College) in Concord, N.C., completing the high school program in 1892 and the Normal and Scientific Course two years later. Hoping to become a missionary in Africa, she studied at the Moody Bible Institute in Chicago, but in 1895 the Presbyterian Mission Board turned down her application for a missionary post.

A disappointed Mary McLeod returned to her native South Carolina and began her first teaching job at Miss Emma Wilson's Mission School, where she had once been a student. Shortly thereafter, the Presbyterian Board appointed her to a teaching position at Haines Normal and Industrial Institute, and later transferred her to Kindell Institute in Sumter, S.C.

Following her marriage to Albertus Bethune in May 1898, the Bethunes moved to Savannah, Ga., where their only child, Albert McLeod Bethune, was born in 1899. Later that year, the family relocated in Palatka, Fla., where Mary McLeod Bethune established a Presbyterian missionary school. Five years later, after she separated from her husband, Bethune's lifelong ambition to build a school for black girls in the South led her and her son to Daytona Beach, Fla., where, in October 1904 the Daytona Literary and Industrial School for Training Negro Girls opened with Bethune as its president. Like most black educators in the post-Reconstruction South, Bethune emphasized industrial skills and Christian values, and appealed to both the neighboring black community and white philanthropists for financial support. As a consequence of Bethune's unwavering dedication, business acumen, and intellectual ability, the Daytona Institute grew from a small elementary school to incorporate a high school and teacher training program. In 1923 Bethune's school merged with Cookman Institute, a Jacksonville, Fla., college for men, and became the Daytona-Cookman Collegiate Institute. Six years later, the school's name was changed to Bethune-Cookman College in recognition of the important role that Mary McLeod Bethune had played in the school's growth and development.

As an educator in the South, Bethune had concerns that extended beyond campus life. In the absence of a municipally supported medical facility for blacks, the Daytona Institute, under Bethune's guidance, maintained a hospital for blacks from 1911 to 1927. During much of this same period she also operated the Tomoka Mission Schools for the children of black families working the Florida turpentine camps. Ignoring threats made by members of the Ku Klux Klan, Bethune organized a black voter registration drive in Florida, decades before the voter registration drive of the 1960s. As a delegate to the first meeting of the Southern Conference for Human Welfare, Bethune voiced her opposition to degrading southern racial customs.

Bethune joined and held official positions in a number of organizations, but she is best known among club women and the public at large for her monumental work with the National Council of Negro Women, which she founded at age 60 in 1935. Bethune served as its president until 1949. Dedicated to meeting the myriad needs of blacks in all walks of life, the council grew under Bethune's leadership to become the largest federation of black women's clubs in the United States. Headquartered in Washington, D.C., and with chapters located throughout the country and abroad, this association published the *Aframerican Woman's Journal*, established health and job clinics throughout the South, and educated a number of black youths from poor families in the South.

In 1935 President Franklin D. Roosevelt appointed Bethune as one of his special advisers on racial affairs, and four years later she served as the director of black affairs for the National Youth Administration. In May 1955 at the age of 79, one of the South's most well-known women died. The unveiling of a statue of Bethune in a federal park located in the nation's capital in 1974 and the opening of the Mary McLeod Bethune Museum and Archives for Black Women's History in Washington, D.C. in 1979 are lasting testaments to Bethune's intelligence and determination.

See also SOCIAL CLASS: / Southern Conference for Human Welfare

Sharon Harley
University of Maryland

James J. Flynn, *Negroes of Achievement in Modern America* (1970); Rackham Holt, *Mary McLeod Bethune: A Biography* (1964); Barbara Sicherman and Carol Hurd Green, eds., *Notable American Women: The Modern Period: A Biographical Dictionary* (1980); Emma Sterne, *Mary McLeod Bethune* (1957).

Bond, Julian

(b. 1940) Civil rights activist and politician.

Horace Julian Bond was born 14 January 1940 in Nashville, Tenn. Both Bond's parents had graduate degrees; his father, Horace Mann Bond, was a noted educator and administrator and was acquainted with such prominent black leaders as W. E. B. Du Bois. Bond spent his first years with his family in Chester County, Penn., where his father was president of Lincoln University. At the age of 12, Bond transferred to a private Quaker-run school near Philadelphia, a predominantly white school where he made average grades and was an outstanding athlete.

At 17 Bond moved to Atlanta with his family and attended Morehouse College, part of Atlanta University where his father was a faculty member. While in college from 1957 to 1961, Bond developed talents for writing poetry and for activism, particularly in the area of civil rights. In March 1960 he helped organize and participated in the first sit-in in the Atlanta City Hall. This action led to the formation of the Committee on Appeal for Human Rights, which, for a time, maintained a separate identity from a larger group with which it worked closely—the Student Nonviolent Coordinating Committee (SNCC), founded in Raleigh, N.C., in the spring of 1960. Bond proved to be a charismatic leader and activist and was a key figure in many SNCC activities, including voter-registration drives, picketing demonstrations, and boycotts. He also worked as reporter, feature writer, and managing editor for the Atlanta *Inquirer*, a newspaper started by several Morehouse students and faculty members to give the protest movement a voice in the black community.

Bond left school in 1961 and did not earn his B.A. degree until 1971. Since then, he has been the recipient of numerous honorary degrees. After leaving Morehouse, Bond married Alice Clopton and went to work for SNCC on a full-time basis as communications director. In 1965 he ran as a SNCC candidate for the Georgia Legislature from the 136th district in Atlanta and won the seat. Bond was prevented from taking his seat until 1967, however, because of political reaction to his outspoken opposition to U.S. involvement in Vietnam. Following a Supreme Court ruling in his favor, Bond did take his seat and served in the lower house until 1974.

Bond came to national attention at the national Democratic convention in Chicago in 1968, when he was nominated as a vice-presidential candidate after a split in the Georgia delegation. In 1974 he was elected to the Georgia Senate from the fifth district and was reelected in 1980. His bid for a third term ended in September 1986 with his loss in the primary to former city councilman, SNCC chairman, and Bond's ally, John Lewis. Political observers suggested that the district's white minority bloc vote for Lewis (80 percent of white voters supported him) stemmed from their perception of Bond as more militant on racial issues than Lewis and was responsible for Bond's defeat.

Bond remains active on political and social issues and has hinted that he will run for public office again. As of 1987 he was president of the Institute for Southern Studies in Durham, N.C., a research and publication center focused on the South.

Karen M. McDearman
University of Mississippi

W. Augustus Low and Virgil A. Clift, eds., *Encyclopedia of Black America* (1981); John Neary, *Julian Bond: Black Rebel* (1971); *Newsweek* (15 September 1986); Thomas Rose and John Greenya, *Black Leaders: Then and Now* (1984).

Bontemps, Arna

(1902–1973) Writer and scholar.

Arnaud Wendell Bontemps was three years old when his father decided to move his family from his son's birthplace in Alexandria, La., to California. The elder Bontemps hoped to escape the prejudice and intimidation that tormented his and other black families. Trying to protect his son, he later warned Arna never to act black.

Having read *Harlem Shadows*, a book of poems by black author Claude McKay, Arna Bontemps became aware of the emergence of black voices from Harlem. After he graduated from Union Pacific College in 1923 and with the first publication of one of his own poems, Bontemps moved from Los Angeles to Harlem, where he taught at the Harlem Academy. He continued to write and, subsequently, became identified with the Harlem Renaissance. In 1931 he published his first novel, *God Sends Sunday*, which was later adapted as *St. Louis Woman*, the musical in which Pearl Bailey made her Broadway acting debut.

A few years of teaching and writing in Alabama, a master's degree from the University of Chicago, and work with the Illinois Writers Project marked Bontemps's career until the beginning of his 22-year tenure as librarian at Fisk University in Nashville, Tenn. In 1968 he resumed teaching, first at the University of Illinois and then at Yale, where he served also as curator of the James Weldon Johnson Collection of Negro Arts and Letters. He had moved back to Nashville when he died of a heart attack in 1973.

Bontemps devoted much time to writing about black life, wanting, as he said in *Harper's*, "to write something about the changes I have seen in my lifetime, and about the Negro awakening and regeneration." Short stories portraying southern black life (*The Old South: "A Summer Tragedy and Other Stories of the Thirties"*), historical novels about black uprisings (*Black Thunder*), children's literature about black leaders (*Free at Last: The Life of Frederick Douglass*), and anthologies of works by black authors (*American Negro Poetry*) represent the range of his writings. He also edited W. C. Handy's autobiography, *Father of the Blues*, and collaborated with fellow writers Langston Hughes, Jack Conroy, and Countee Cullen.

Arna Bontemps spent much of his life exploring the culture of his race and his southern black heritage. In doing so, he became a primary force in the development and promotion of black literature in America.

See also EDUCATION: / Fisk University

Jessica Foy
Cooperstown Graduate Programs
Cooperstown, New York

Robert A. Bone, *Down Home: A History of Afro-American Short Fiction from Its Beginnings to the End of the Harlem Renaissance* (1975); Arna Bontemps, *Harper's* (April 1965); Arthur P. Davis, *From the Dark Tower: Afro-American Writers, 1900–1960* (1974).

Chesnutt, Charles W.

(1858–1932) Writer.

Charles Waddell Chesnutt, an Afro-American man of letters, was born in Cleveland, Ohio, on 20 June 1858, the son of free blacks who had emigrated from Fayetteville, N.C. When he was eight years old, Chesnutt's parents returned to Fayetteville, where Charles worked part-time in the family grocery store and attended a school founded by the Freedmen's Bureau. In 1872 financial necessity forced him to begin a teaching career in Charlotte, N.C. He returned to Fayetteville in 1877, married a year later, and by 1880 had become principal of the Fayetteville State Normal School for Negroes. Meanwhile he continued to pursue private studies of the English classics, foreign languages, music, and stenography. Despite his successes, he longed for broader opportunities and a chance to develop the literary skills that by 1880 led him toward an author's life. In 1883 he moved his family to Cleveland. There he passed the state bar examination and established his own court reporting firm. Financially prosperous and prominent in civic affairs, he resided in Cleveland for the remainder of his life.

"The Goophered Grapevine," an unusual dialect story that displayed intimate knowledge of black folk culture in the South, was Chesnutt's first nationally recognized work of fiction. Its publication in the August 1887 issue of the *Atlantic Monthly* marked the first time that a short story by a black had appeared in that prestigious magazine. After subsequent tales in this vein were accepted by other magazines, Chesnutt submitted to Houghton, Mifflin a collection of these stories, which was published in 1899 as *The Conjure Woman*. His second collection of short fiction, *The Wife of His Youth and Other Stories of the Color Line* (1899), ranged over a broader area of southern and northern racial experience than any previous writer on black American life had attempted. These two volumes were popular enough to convince Houghton, Mifflin to publish Chesnutt's first novel, *The House Behind the Cedars*, in 1900. This story of two blacks who pass for white in the postwar South revealed Chesnutt's sense of the psychological and social dilemmas facing persons of mixed blood in the region. His second novel, *The Marrow of Tradition* (1901), is based on the Wilmington, N.C., race riot of 1898. Hoping to write the *Uncle Tom's Cabin* of his generation, Chesnutt made a plea for racial justice that impressed William Dean Howells as a work of "great power," though with "more justice than mercy in it." The failure of the book to sell widely forced Chesnutt to give up his dream of supporting his family as a professional author. In 1905 he published his final novel, *The Colonel's Dream*, a tragic story of an idealist's attempt to revive a depressed North Carolina town through a socioeconomic program much akin to the New South creed of Henry W. Grady and Booker T. Washington. The novel received little critical notice.

During the latter years of his life Chesnutt continued to write and publish occasional short stories, but he was largely eclipsed in the 1920s by the writers of the Harlem Renaissance. He was awarded the Spingarn Medal in 1928 by the National Association for the Advancement of Colored People for his pioneering literary work on behalf of the Afro-American struggle. Today Chesnutt is recognized as a major innovator in the tradition of Afro-American fiction, an important contributor to the deromanticizing trend in post–Civil War southern literature, and a singular voice among turn-of-the-century realists who treated the color line in American life.

See also INDUSTRY: / Grady, Henry W.; VIOLENCE: / Wilmington Race Riot

William L. Andrews
University of Wisconsin

William L. Andrews, *The Literary Career of Charles W. Chesnutt* (1980); Helen M. Chesnutt, *Charles Waddell Chesnutt: Pioneer of the Color Line* (1952); Frances Richardson Keller, *An American Crusade: The Life of Charles Waddell Chesnutt* (1978).

Citizens' Councils

This group and allied organizations—the Virginia Defenders of State Sovereignty and Individual Liberties, the Tennessee Federation for Constitutional Government, the North Carolina Patriots, and the Georgia States' Rights Council—were formed by white supremacists in the South to resist school desegregation. Appearing first in Mississippi in July 1954, this movement of "white-collar" or "country club" Klans spread rapidly into each of the 11 former Confederate states. Dedicated to "states' rights and racial integrity," the council movement, like the Confederacy itself, failed to overcome southern parochialism and thus never forged a united front. Yet a semblance of regional unity was provided in 1956 by the formation of the Mississippi-based Citizens' Councils of America, an informal confederation of the more viable southern organized resistance groups.

The councils' natural habitats were the old plantation areas of the Lower South, where the black population was most heavily concentrated and where white racial fears were highest. Except in Virginia, where organized resistance was endorsed by the Byrd machine, and Little Rock, where Governor Orval Faubus was a supporter, councils or council-like groups enjoyed little success in the so-called rim-South states. In Florida, North Carolina, Tennessee, and Texas, members of the white power structure rarely became closely identified with the groups. But in the Deep South—in Alabama, Louisiana, Mississippi, and South Carolina—councils won the support of high elected officials and of business and professional leaders. Here, where their power and prestige were greatest, Citizens' Councils officially eschewed violence. Individual members were sometimes implicated in terrorist acts, however, and the movement was instrumental in creating a climate of fear and reprisal in which few whites and even fewer blacks dared challenge the status quo. In Alabama and Mississippi, councils functioned as shadow governments.

There are no reliable membership figures, but the Southwide total probably never exceeded 250,000, though non-dues-paying sympathizers surely numbered many thousands more. Having rapidly expanded in the years immediately after *Brown* v. *Board of Education*, white resistance organizations gradually declined following the federal-state confrontation at Little Rock. In growing numbers whites recognized that some degree of school desegregation was inevitable. Remobilization campaigns in the 1960s failed, and by mid-decade membership even in Mississippi had dwindled to insignificance. Thereafter, diehard movement leaders turned their support to all-white private schools.

See also LAW: / *Brown* v. *Board of Education*; POLITICS: / Byrd machine; Faubus, Orville; VIOLENCE: / Ku Klux Klan

Neil R. McMillen
University of Southern Mississippi

Numan Bartley, *The Rise of Massive Resistance: Race and Politics in the South during the 1950s* (1969); Hodding Carter, *The South Strikes Back* (1959); Neil R. McMillen, *The Citizens' Council: Organized Resistance to the Second Reconstruction* (1971).

Commission on Interracial Cooperation (CIC)

The CIC was founded in Atlanta in 1919 in an effort to ameliorate racial tension growing out of World War I. Seeking to bring "the best" whites and blacks together, the CIC, under the leadership of Executive Director Will W. Alexander, organized some 800 state and local interracial committees throughout the South. By the early 1920s a press service was sending releases concerning black achievements and race relations to about 1,200 newspapers and magazines. Through both local committees and the press service the CIC during its first decade worked to combat the Ku Klux Klan and lynching. In 1930 the organization established the Southern Commission on the Study of Lynching (SCSL) to examine all lynchings in that year and to formulate an effective preventive program. CIC Research Secretary Arthur Raper headed the SCSL's investigations, which were published in 1933 as *The Tragedy of Lynching*. In 1932 CIC Woman's Director Jessie Daniel Ames established the Association of Southern Women for the Prevention of Lynching (ASWPL) as an additional mechanism for opposing the practice.

As a result of the Great Depression of the early 1930s, the commission was forced to modify its program. No longer able to support its field staff, most of the state and local committees (with the exception of North Carolina and Virginia) ceased to maintain active groups. The commission instead, with funding from the Carnegie Foundation, developed a subsidiary group, the Conference on Education and Race Relations (CERR), which sponsored workshops, seminars, and publications to encourage the teaching of race relations in southern colleges. By 1942 CIC records indicated that about 500 southern colleges and 1,000 high schools were utilizing CERR materials. During the 1930s the commission also sought the inclusion of blacks in the various programs of Franklin D. Roosevelt's New Deal. Will W. Alexander headed a CIC committee, funded by the Rockefeller Foundation, which not only persuaded government agencies to hire black advisors on minority affairs but also sponsored several studies concerning the New Deal's impact on blacks. Among these studies were Arthur Raper's *A Preface to Peasantry* and Horace R. Cayton and George Sinclair Mitchell's *Black Workers and the New Unions*. The CIC Committee also was an influential force in bringing passage of the 1937 Bankhead-Jones Farm Tenancy Act, which established the Farm Security Administration (FSA). Will Alexander, though nominally still the CIC director, headed this agency. In Alexander's absence, leadership of the commission largely fell to Jessie Daniel Ames, who began in 1937 to revive state and local interracial committees. In 1940 she established *The Southern Frontier*, a monthly publication designed to keep these groups abreast of race relations news and CIC activities.

Will W. Alexander and other CIC leaders, especially University of North Carolina sociologist Howard W. Odum, concluded by the late 1930s that the commission needed to adopt a new strategy in order to address the South's racial problems. Influenced by Odum's theories of regional development, they envisioned an organization that would confront the inequities of segregation and attack the South's economic problems as a necessary prerequisite to solving its racial difficulties. To carry out their regional plan, they established the Southern Regional Council, with which the commission merged in 1944.

The CIC itself had never attacked the system of segregation, preferring to work within the system to improve the condition of blacks. By 1944 its program seemed conservative and outmoded. In many ways, however, it was, in Arthur Raper's phrase, a "frontier movement," which played an important role in educating southern whites to racial injustice, in examining the economic problems of the South's poor, and in making lynching an unacceptable practice.

See also EDUCATION: / Odum, Howard W.; SOCIAL CLASS: / Southern Regional Council; WOMEN'S LIFE: / Ames, Jessie Daniel

Ann Wells Ellis
Kennesaw College

W. E. Cole, *Social Forces* (May 1943); Wilma Dykeman and James Stokely, *Seeds of Southern Change: The Life of Will Alexander* (1962); Ann Wells Ellis, *Atlanta Historical Journal* (Spring 1980).

Congress of Racial Equality (CORE)

Rooted in the 1930s pacifist movements, the Congress of Racial Equality (CORE) was formed in Chicago in 1942 to oppose racial discrimination and encourage integration. For many years the group emphasized interracial membership and Gandhian nonviolent direct action. James

Farmer served as CORE's first national chairman and as its dynamic national director from 1961 to 1966.

From 1942 to 1961 CORE focused on integration of public accommodations and in 1946 tested compliance with the Supreme Court's ruling of that year declaring unconstitutional Virginia's laws requiring segregation on interstate motor carriers. To do so, CORE launched the Journey of Reconciliation, an integrated bus trip from Washington, D.C., to Kentucky. The ride elicited little attention, but it boosted CORE morale and served as the model for the Freedom Ride of 1961.

Late-1940s efforts to establish affiliates in the Deep South failed because of fear of brutal reprisals, though in southern border states affiliates slowly grew. After the success of the Southern Christian Leadership Conference's (SCLC) Montgomery bus boycott, CORE increased its southern projects. Its voter registration campaign in Virginia in the late 1950s proved disappointing, but such projects fared better in South Carolina, where in the 1960s CORE also actively supported efforts to integrate lunch counters.

CORE catapulted to national attention in 1961 when it spearheaded the Freedom Ride, an integrated bus trip from Washington, D.C., through the Deep South to test the South's response to the 1960 Supreme Court decision prohibiting segregation in bus- and train-terminal accommodations. Suffering violent reprisals in Anniston and Birmingham, Ala., the CORE riders stopped in Birmingham, where Student Nonviolent Coordinating Committee (SNCC) riders resumed the effort. Further violence occurred in Montgomery, and the CORE-SCLC-SNCC Freedom Ride Coordinating Committee recruited thousands of riders, 360 of whom were arrested and jailed in Jackson, Miss. The campaign resulted in the Interstate Commerce Commission's September 1961 ruling prohibiting segregated facilities in interstate travel. Many Deep South locales ignored the ruling, but a major battle had been won.

Subsequently, CORE's leaders played major roles in the surge of direct action in Mississippi, Alabama, Georgia, and Louisiana. More working-class blacks joined CORE, and attention turned to community development projects. Among civil rights groups CORE's influence waned between 1962 and 1964, partly because CORE-supported activities—such as demonstrations in Gadsden, Ala., and Plaquemine, La.—received little publicity, even when the protesters met with violence.

CORE established a regional office in Louisiana in 1964, but major voter registration campaigns there met with limited success and much harassment. Frustrated black residents armed for self-defense, and CORE accepted such actions as necessary. The murder of CORE workers Michael Schwerner and James Chaney and SNCC volunteer Andrew Goodman in Neshoba County, Miss., in 1964 elicited a national outcry for protection of civil rights workers. Subsequently CORE established "freedom schools" for black youth, community centers, and political programs throughout Mississippi and supported creation of the Mississippi Freedom Democratic party.

Problems and schisms within CORE increased; and by the 1965 CORE convention in Durham, N.C., James Farmer had decided to resign, and CORE's interracial focus had been rejected. Still in operation, CORE now promotes inner-city community-development projects in black neighborhoods.

Sharon A. Sharp
University of Mississippi

Inge Powell Bell, *CORE and the Strategy of Nonviolence* (1968); C. Eric Lincoln, in *The American Negro Reference Book*, ed. John P. Davis (1966); August Meier and Elliott M. Rudwick, *CORE: A Study in the Civil Rights Movement, 1942–1968* (1973).

Douglass, Frederick

(1808–1895) Black leader.

Frederick Douglass was the most important black American leader of the 19th century. He was born Frederick Augustus Washington Bailey, in Talbot County, on Maryland's Eastern Shore in 1808, the son of a slave woman, and in all likelihood, her white master. Upon his escape from slavery at age 20, Douglass adopted a new surname from the hero of Sir Walter Scott's *The Lady of the Lake.* Douglass immortalized his formative years as a slave in the first of three autobiographies, *Narrative of the Life of Frederick Douglass, An American Slave*, published in 1845. This and two subsequent autobiographies, *My Bondage and My Freedom* (1855) and *The Life and Times of Frederick Douglass* (1881), mark Douglass's greatest contributions to southern culture. Written both as antislavery propaganda and as personal revelation, they are universally regarded as the finest examples of the slave narrative tradition and as classics of American autobiography.

Douglass's public life ranged from his work as an abolitionist in the early 1840s to his attacks on Jim Crow segregation in the 1890s. Douglass lived the bulk of his career in Rochester, N.Y., where for 16 years he edited the most influential black newspaper of the mid-19th century, called successively *The North Star* (1847–51), *Frederick Douglass' Paper* (1851–58), and *The Douglass Monthly* (1859–63). Douglass achieved international fame as an orator with few peers and as a writer of persuasive power. In thousands of speeches and editorials Douglass levied an irresistible indictment against slavery and racism, provided an indomitable voice of hope for his people, embraced antislavery politics, and preached his own brand of American ideals.

Douglass welcomed the Civil War in 1861 as a moral crusade to eradicate the evil of slavery. During the war he labored as a fierce propagandist of the Union cause and emancipation, as a recruiter of black troops, and on two occasions as an advisor to President Abraham Lincoln. Douglass made a major contribution to the intellectual tradition of millennial nationalism, the outlook from which many Americans, North and South, interpreted

Frederick Douglass, abolitionist and black leader, date unknown

the Civil War. During Reconstruction and the Gilded Age Douglass's leadership became less activist and more emblematic. He traveled and lectured widely on racial issues, but his most popular topic was "Self-Made Men." By the 1870s Douglass had moved to Washington, D.C., where he edited the newspaper *The New National Era* and became president of the ill-fated Freedmen's Bank. As a stalwart Republican, he was appointed marshall (1877–81) and recorder of deeds (1881–86) for the District of Columbia, and chargé d'affaires for Santo Domingo and minister to Haiti (1889–91). Douglass had five children by his first wife Anna Murray, a free black woman from Baltimore who followed him out of slavery in 1838. Less than two years after Anna died in 1882, the 63-year-old Douglass married Helen Pitts, his white former secretary, an event of considerable controversy. Thus by birth and by his two marriages, Douglass is one of the South's most famous examples of the region's mixed racial heritage.

Douglass never lost a sense of attachment to the South. "Nothing but an intense love of personal freedom keeps us [fugitive slaves] from the South," Douglass wrote in 1848. He often referred to Maryland as his "own dear native soil." Brilliant, heroic, and complex, Douglass became a symbol of his age and a unique American voice for humanism and social justice. His life and thought will always speak profoundly to the dilemma of being black in America. Douglass died of heart failure in 1895, the year Booker T. Washington rose to national prominence with his Atlanta Exposition speech suggesting black accommodation to racial segregation.

David W. Blight
North Central College
Naperville, Illinois

John Blassingame et al., *The Frederick Douglass Papers*, 2 vols. (1979–1982); Philip S. Foner, *Life and Writings of Frederick Douglass*, 4 vols. (1955); August Meier, *Negro Thought in America, 1880–1915* (1963); Benjamin Quarles, *Frederick Douglass* (1948).

Du Bois, W. E. B.

(1868–1963) Historian, sociologist, editor, and novelist.

William Edward Burghardt Du Bois was born 23 February 1868 in Great Barrington, Mass. A New Englander in thought and conduct, as he put it, he entered the South in 1885, after a promising high school career, to attend Fisk University in Nashville, Tenn. He found the South deeply humiliating. "No one but a Negro," he wrote, "going into the South without previous experience of color caste can have any conception of its barbarism." Nevertheless, Fisk itself was challenging, even exhilarating, and summer teaching in rural counties sealed his attachment to the black masses and his determination to champion their cause. Graduating in 1888, he trained further at Harvard University (Ph.D. 1895) and the University of Berlin. His doctoral dissertation on the suppression of the slave trade was published in 1896. He held positions briefly with the University of Pennsylvania and Wilberforce in Ohio before returning to the South in 1897 to teach sociology, economics, and history at Atlanta University.

His third book, *The Souls of Black Folk* (1903), was a collection of hauntingly beautiful essays on every important aspect of black culture in the South; perhaps its most famous insight concerned the "double-consciousness" of the black American: "One ever feels his twoness—an American, a Negro; two souls, two thoughts, two unreconciled strivings; two warring ideals in one dark body, whose dogged strength alone keeps it from being torn asunder." With this book he secured preeminence among all Afro-American intellectuals and became the leader of those opposed to the powerful and conservative Booker T. Washington of Tuskegee. His yearly (1897–1914) Atlanta University Studies of black social conditions and a biography of John Brown (1909) added to his reputation.

Increasingly controversial, he moved to New York in 1910 to found and edit *The Crisis*, the monthly magazine of the fledgling NAACP. For 24 years he sustained an assault on all forms of racial injustice, especially in the South. In 1934 he published *Black Reconstruction in America*, a grand Marxist-framed reevaluation of the much-maligned role of blacks in the Civil War and its aftermath. That year he returned to Atlanta University after grave disagreements with the NAACP leadership over strategies during the Depression; Du Bois favored a program of voluntary self-segregation stressing economics that many people found similar to the old program of Booker T. Washington. At Atlanta University he found little support for his projected scheme to organize the study of sociology among black colleges and other institutions in the South. In 1944 he rejoined the NAACP in New York, but soon found himself again at odds with the leadership, this time over his growing interest in radical socialism. He left the NAACP finally in 1948. By this time his attitude toward the South had changed somewhat. Influenced no doubt by the aims of the leftist Southern Negro Youth Congress, he declared in 1948 that "the future of American Negroes is in the South. . . . Here is the magnificent climate; here is the fruitful earth under the beauty of the southern sun; and here . . . is the need of the thinker, the worker, and the dreamer." His Socialist activities culminated in his arrest and trial in 1951 as an unregistered agent of a foreign principal; the presiding judge heard the evidence, then directed his acquittal.

Unpopular and even shunned in some quarters, he turned to fiction to express his deepest feelings. In a trilogy set mainly in the South, *The Black Flame (The Ordeal of Mansart)*, 1957; *Mansart Builds a School*, 1959; *Worlds of Color*, 1961, he told the story of a black southerner, born at the end of Reconstruction, who rises slowly and patiently to the leadership of a small southern school, witnessing in his long lifetime the important events of modern American and world history. In October 1961 Du Bois was admitted to membership in the Communist party of the United States; that month he left his country to live in Ghana at the invitation of Kwame Nkrumah. In February 1963 he renounced his American citizenship and became a Ghanaian. He had made little progress on the task for which Nkrumah had summoned him, the editing of an "Encyclopedia Africana," when he died of natural causes 27 August 1963.

See also EDUCATION: / Fisk University; Tuskegee Institute

Arnold Rampersad
Stanford University

Herbert Aptheker, *Annotated Bibliography of the Published Writings of W. E. B. Du Bois* (1973); Arnold Rampersad, *The Art and Imagination of W. E. B. Du Bois* (1976).

Evers, Medgar

(1926–1963) Civil rights leader.

During the 1950s and 1960s Medgar Wiley Evers dedicated his life to the racial integration of Mississippi. He taught black Mississippians about the power of the ballot and he organized economic boycotts. At his urging, thousands of black customers refused to buy soft drinks, bread, and clothes sold by white-owned businesses that perpetuated segregation in Jackson, Miss. In the guise of a field hand in 1955, he gathered evidence on the lynching of Emmett Till, a black teenager. With force and clarity, Evers spoke out, shaming blacks and whites alike into taking steps to end racial separation.

Born 2 July 1926 Evers grew up in the small, east-central Mississippi town of Decatur. His father worked for a sawmill and on the railroads; his mother was a domestic worker. They raised cows, pigs, chickens, vegetables, and cotton on the small plot of land around their house on the edge of town. As a boy, Medgar learned about self-respect from his father, who did not follow the custom of stepping off the sidewalk when whites approached, and Medgar learned religious values from his mother, who required her children to attend church every Sunday.

Childhood experiences of brutality against blacks embittered Evers, and for a time, after serving in the U.S. Army during World War II, he idolized Jomo Kenyatta of Africa and dreamed of forming a band of fighters, similar to Kenyatta's, who would right the wrongs whites had inflicted on blacks. After the war, he enrolled at Alcorn Agricultural and Mechanical College in southwestern Mississippi. He married Myrlie Beasley on Christmas Eve 1951, and the next year the Magnolia Mutual Life Insurance Company hired him as a salesman. In February 1954, he tried to upgrade his education and break the color barrier at the University of Mississippi Law School, but was rejected. Evers decided not to pursue it, although later, in 1962, he assisted James H. Meredith in becoming the first black to enroll in the university. Evers's volunteer work for the National Association for the Advancement of Colored People turned into a full-time job: he was appointed in late 1954 as the first Mississippi field secretary of the NAACP, a post he held until his death.

He eventually rejected his notions of a Kenyatta-style revolution, though he did name one of his sons after Kenyatta. Evers traveled through Mississippi, inspiring blacks to fight segregation in every nonviolent way possible. Myrlie Evers said her husband amazed the journalists when he would tell them he stayed in Mississippi because he loved it. "It was part of him," she wrote in *For Us, the Living*, a book about their life together. "He loved to hunt and fish, to roam the fields and woods. . . . He had visited many places . . . but always he came back to Mississippi as a man coming home."

This sense of place and Evers's sense of justice led him to fight for change in Mississippi's capital city of Jackson. During the historic spring of 1963 Evers and other civil rights leaders pushed for blacks to be hired on the Jackson police force and as school crossing guards. Evers wanted public facilities and restaurants to be open to everyone, regardless of race. And he sought an end to the signs that segregated white and black races at drinking fountains and restrooms.

Mass meetings, demonstrations at segregated lunch counters, and boycotts of white businesses in Jackson began to force changes. Police arrested black teenagers who demonstrated and corralled them for days at the fairgrounds. Evers remained at the forefront of the city's boycotts, which were attracting national publicity.

On the night of 11 June 1963 President John F. Kennedy

told the nation in a televised address that he was sending a bill to Congress to ensure racial justice. The bill was to become the Civil Rights Act of 1964. After seeing Kennedy's speech, Evers drove to his Jackson home. Just after midnight on 12 June a bullet from a high-powered rifle felled him as he stepped from his car. Within an hour, he died at the University of Mississippi Medical Center, three weeks before his 37th birthday. After services in Jackson, Evers's body was flown to the National Cemetery in Arlington, Va., for a military burial.

Berkley Hudson
Providence, Rhode Island

Cleveland Donald, in *Mississippi Heroes*, ed. Dean Faulkner Wells and Hunter Cole (1980); Mrs. Medgar Evers with William Peters, *For Us, the Living* (1967); John R. Salter, Jr., *Jackson, Mississippi: An American Chronicle of Struggle and Schism* (1979).

Franklin, John Hope

(b. 1915) Historian.

Franklin stands in the first rank of professional historians and also in the first rank of those blacks who work actively on behalf of the modern civil rights movement. Born in Rentiesville, Okla., in 1915, Franklin embodies the ethnic and racial complexities of the South: his family was part Cherokee and part black, and some of its members served as slaves to the Cherokees in the antebellum decades. His father, Buck Franklin, became a successful lawyer in Tulsa and saw his legal offices destroyed in one of the anti-black riots after the Armistice of 1918. Buck Franklin quietly rebuilt his legal practice, for a time actually operating inside a tent, and this experience became vital to the spirit of John Hope Franklin's own protests and achievements.

Given the chance to attend college, young Franklin studied at Fisk (A.B. 1935) and then entered the Harvard graduate program (A.M. 1936, Ph.D. 1941) at a time when there were few black historians in the country. He taught at Fisk University, Howard University, Saint Augustine's College, Brooklyn College, and the University of Chicago. In the field of civil rights, Franklin was instrumental in integrating the Southern Historical Association and the Mississippi Valley Historical Association (now the Organization of American Historians), both of which he eventually served as president; he also contributed background research for the National Association for the Advancement of Colored People in the campaign to integrate the public schools, culminating successfully in the legal case, *Brown* v. *Board of Education* (1954).

In the study of black history Franklin published three major works: *From Slavery to Freedom: The History of Negro Americans* (1947; 5th ed., 1980) was an encyclopedic mapping of the path of black progress in America, optimistic in its style; *The Militant South, 1800–1861* (1956) was a bolder, more pessimistic interpretation, which traced both a self-destructive urge among the antebellum southern leaders who produced the Civil War and a continuing tendency to violence after the war; and *Reconstruction after the Civil War* (1963) was one of the early efforts to revise the mythic white view of the horrors of Reconstruction, as embodied in historian William A. Dunning's works, and to focus on black participation and achievement in the post–Civil War period.

See also LAW: *Brown* v. *Board of Education*

John Herbert Roper
St. Andrews Presbyterian College

John Hope Franklin, *Free Negroes in North Carolina, 1790–1860* (1943); Earle E. Thorpe, *Black Historians: a Critique* (1971); and interviews with Franklin, August Meier, C. Vann Woodward, and LeRoy Graf, typescripts filed in Southern Historical Collection, University of North Carolina, Chapel Hill.

Free Southern Theater

The early phase of southern black protest efforts depended heavily on the involvement of whites, including many northerners who served as "freedom riders" and in political action and voter registration projects. The rallying cry of "black and white together" gave way in the mid-1960s to calls for awareness of the unique black experience, which led to the emergence of groups such as the Student Nonviolent Coordinating Committee (SNCC) and its chairman, Stokely Carmichael.

A cultural and artistic complement to the political struggles of the civil rights movement in the early 1960s, the history of Free Southern Theater recapitulates, in most of its essentials, that of the larger movement. Free Southern Theater resulted from the collaboration, in the summer of 1963, of SNCC student directors Gilbert Moses and John O'Neal. O'Neal was a playwright, and Moses had had theatrical experience at Cleveland's Karuma Playhouse and off-Broadway with the Living Theater. Both had come to Mississippi intent on political activity but reluctant to divorce that action from their artistic concerns.

Headquartered at Tougaloo College in Jackson, the Free Southern Theater was an attempt to bridge the gap between art and politics. Its 1963 prospectus emphasized the dual significance of its name: the free development of black talent and self-expression and free-of-cost accessibility to theater, which would present an undistorted image of black society.

With the help of Richard Schechner, then editor of the *Tulane Drama Review*, the New York theater community was tapped for funds. Artistic assistance came from across the country. Training sessions were held at the

Guthrie, lighting equipment was loaned by Joseph Papp, and improvisational acting classes were conducted by Second City's Paul Sills. In 1964 the Free Southern Theater moved its base of operations to New Orleans and began a full-time touring schedule, playing 21 towns in 6 states in its first season. With Moses as artistic director, the 25-member company presented plays ranging from Beckett's *Waiting for Godot* to Langston Hughes's *Don't You Want to Be Free*, Ossie Davis's *Purlie Victorious*, and Martin Duberman's documentary drama *In White America*. In addition to workshops in writing and acting, designed to support collective creativity, efforts were made to produce original scripts ("Bogalusa," "Jonesburg Story") that reflected the complexities of local black experience.

Although the goals of the Free Southern Theater were similar to those of other black theater groups throughout the country, the circumstances under which the company worked stamped it as uniquely southern. Bringing plays to rural areas of Mississippi, Louisiana, Georgia, and Alabama, performances were staged by necessity in church auditoriums, schools, and at times in cotton fields. Refused publicity by the local press, unable to find rehearsal or living space, or targeted for violence by police, the performers often had to cancel appearances. Cast members were arrested and charged with vagrancy, evicted from apartments, and otherwise harassed. As late as 1973 an acrimonious debate was sparked by a New Orleans City Council grant of $15,000 to a group that critics claimed "called for the overthrow of the U.S. government," "encouraged violence against whites," and otherwise contributed to racial disharmony.

By the middle 1960s, a period of self-examination, which paralleled the civil rights movement on the national level, led the Free Southern Theater toward a recognition of black consciousness. Questioning the continued relevance of bringing Broadway, off-Broadway, or even radical white theater to the southern black community, some cast members wanted far more emphasis on local forms and idioms. Others doubted the validity of black theater that was not performed and managed exclusively by blacks. The resignation, in 1966, of both Moses and Schechner capped this period of upheaval.

Reorganized (the troup moved its base to the all-black neighborhood of Desire and transferred controlling interest to its black board members) and stabilized financially by grants from the Rockefeller Foundation and the National Endowment for the Arts, the Free Southern Theater continued for more than a decade to mount large-scale productions, offer summer youth workshops, and produce original material. Much of this material was written by cofounder John O'Neal. With plays like *Our Lan', When the Opportunity Scratches, Itch It* (1974) and the most recent, *Don't Start Me to Talking or I'll Tell Everything I Know* (1980), the Free Southern Theater demonstrated its commitment to theater that distinguished between an audience to be served and a market to be exploited—theater free from the often restrictive aesthetics of the commercial. In the face of decreased financial support and new goals of John O'Neal and other central troupe members, the Free Southern Theater officially ceased operations in November 1985, when a traditional New Orleans funeral service was held to mark its demise.

Elizabeth Makowski
University of Mississippi

Thomas Dent, Richard Schechner, and Gilbert Moses, eds., *The Free Southern Theater by the Free Southern Theater* (1969); Geneviève Fabre, *Drumbeats, Masks, and Metaphor: Contemporary Afro-American Theatre* (1983); James Flannery, *Performing Arts Journal* (October 1985); John O'Neal, *Southern Exposure* (Spring 1981); *Times-Picayune* (27 October 1973; 31 October 1973; 2 November 1973; 6 November 1973); Mance Williams, *Black Theater in the 1960s and 1970s: A Historical Critical Analysis of the Movement* (1985).

Gaines, Ernest J.

(b. 1933) Writer.

Born in Oscar, near New Roads, La., Gaines lived in the plantation quarters and worked in the fields as a boy. Most of the old people were illiterate, and Augustine Jefferson, the crippled aunt who reared Gaines, encouraged him to read and write letters for them. This was his first literary apprenticeship and started him on a career of bridging the gap between the spoken and the written word. "I came up in a place that was oral," he explains, "we *talked* stories." He has characterized all his books as attempts to capture "the sound of my people talking."

As neither high schools nor libraries were open to blacks in Pt. Coupee Parish, he moved to California in 1948, joining his mother and stepfather in Vallejo, where he finished high school and attended two years of junior college. Homesick, he searched libraries for books about rural life, finding few positive images of blacks in the American South, but responding warmly to accounts of peasant life in the works of Russian writers, particularly Turgenev, and to the lyrics of country blues singers, especially Lightnin' Hopkins.

After serving in the army, he enrolled at San Francisco State College and was graduated in 1957. In 1958 he won a Wallace Stegner Creative Writing Fellowship for graduate study at Stanford.

Six short stories appeared in magazines before Gaines published *Catherine Carmier* (1964), a novel of color-caste discrimination within the black Creole community. *Of Love and Dust* followed (1967), a novel of the convict-lease system in Louisiana, then *Bloodline* (1968), a collection of five stories, including "A Long Day in November," also issued separately as a children's book, and *The Sky is Gray*, televised in the National Endowment for the Humanities American Short Story series (1980). The novel Gaines characterized as his "folk autobiography," *The Autobiography of Miss Jane Pittman*, was published in 1971 and in 1974 was shown on CBS television in an ambitious production starring Cicely Tyson. *In My Father's House* (1978) is a grim novel exploring future roads open to black Americans in the years after the civil rights movement. In *A Gathering of Old Men* (1983) Gaines returns to the tragi-comic Jane Pittman world of strong, old, enduring, still feisty black plantation folk. Gaines is also a gifted photographer, and his photographs of his childhood world in Louisiana have been published in *Callaloo*.

Black oral tradition, the Creole culture, and love between white and black characters are richly portrayed in the fiction of Ernest Gaines. Both black and white characters are treated with sympathy and understanding. Since 1982 Gaines has been Professor of English and Writer in Residence at the University of Southwestern Louisiana, dividing his time between Lafayette and San Francisco.

Patricia K. Rickels
University of Southwestern Louisiana

Michel Fabre, *Callaloo* (May 1978); Patricia K. Rickels, *Southwestern Review* (1979); Charles H. Rowell, *Southern Review* (July 1985).

Greensboro Sit-in

See LAW: / Greensboro Sit-in

Haley, Alex

(b. 1921) Writer.

Alexander Palmer Haley was born 11 August 1921 in Ithaca, N.Y. At the time, both of his parents were in graduate school—his mother, Bertha Palmer, at the Ithaca Conservatory of Music and his father, Simon, at Cornell University. When he was six weeks old, Alex and his mother moved to Henning, Tenn., where they lived at her family home (later rejoined by his father) until 1929.

Haley graduated from high school in Normal, Ala., at age 15, enrolled at Alcorn A&M College in Mississippi, and then transferred to Elizabeth City State Teachers College in North Carolina. After two years he left college and enlisted in the U.S. Coast Guard in 1939. He served initially as a mess boy aboard a cargo-ammunition ship in the southwest Pacific. He devoted much of his free time to reading, writing letters, and writing adventure stories. In 1949 the Coast Guard created for him the position of chief journalist, which he held until he retired from military service in 1959 to become a full-time writer.

Haley then moved to New York where he struggled for several years to become a successful writer. Occasionally, magazines would buy his stories, but often they would not. At one low point, Haley says, he had only 18 cents and two cans of sardines. The following day, however, a check for one of his stories arrived in the mail. He kept and framed the 18 cents and cans of sardines as a reminder of the perseverance and determination required for him to achieve the status of an independent writer. In 1962 *Playboy* magazine hired him to conduct a series of interviews. His first was with jazz trumpeter Miles Davis. A subsequent interview with Malcolm X led him to write *The Autobiography of Malcolm X* (1964), which became a best-seller.

Alex Haley, best-selling author of Roots, *1980s*

Having established himself, Haley embarked upon a 12-year effort to trace the lineage of his mother's family. His search eventually took him to Gambia in West Africa, where his fourth great-grandfather, Kunte Kinte, had been born and then kidnapped in 1767 by slave traders en route to America. Combining fictional dialogue with the factual information he had uncovered, Haley wrote *Roots: The Saga of an American Family*. The novel, published in the fall of 1976, brought the author immediate fame.

By April 1977 nearly 2 million hardcover copies of *Roots* had been sold, a total that has since increased several times. For the novel, Haley received a Pulitzer Prize, a National Book Award, and numerous other honors. Haley's South in *Roots* is not a pleasant one for blacks as is Margaret Mitchell's in *Gone with the Wind*. It portrays instead the harsh aspects of slavery. For many blacks, this story of one family's ancestry captures the essence of their heritage in America.

Early in 1977 the ABC television network broadcast the story in an eight-episode miniseries, of which an estimated 130 million viewers watched at least one episode. A television sequel, *Roots: The Next Generations*, aired in 1979. Although the *Roots* programs had generated much interest in Haley's works, the TV series he created, *Palmerstown U.S.A.*, did not fare well, airing only briefly in 1980 and again in 1981.

See also MEDIA: / *Gone with the Wind; Roots*

Jessica Foy
Cooperstown Graduate Programs
Cooperstown, New York

Robert Bain, Joseph M. Flora, and Louis D. Rubin, Jr., eds., *Southern Writers: A Biographical Dictionary* (1979); Hans J. Massaquoi, *Ebony* (April 1977); Charles Moritz, ed., *Current Biography* (1977).

Hamer, Fannie Lou

(1917–1977) Civil rights activist.

Fannie Lou Townsend Hamer was the last of 20 children born to Jim and Ella Townsend, sharecroppers in Montgomery County, Miss. The family moved two years after her birth to Sunflower County, where she worked in the cotton fields from the age of six and attended public school through junior high. In 1945 she married Perry Hamer, a tractor driver on the W. D. Marlon plantation located four miles east of Ruleville. She labored as a field hand on the Marlon plantation until it was discovered that she could read and write. Then she was promoted to timekeeper. She was fired in 1962 because she had attempted to register to vote. Forced to leave the plantation, she received shelter in the home of William Tucker in Ruleville, but had to flee from there after the house was attacked and riddled with bullets.

In 1963 she passed the Mississippi literacy test and became a registered voter. She then became a field secretary for the Student Nonviolent Coordinating Committee, organizing voter registration campaigns and working to obtain welfare and other benefits for underprivileged black families. While returning by bus from a voter registration workshop, she was arrested and severely beaten for attempting to use the restroom in a bus station in Winona. Meanwhile, she had worked with the National Council of Churches in creating Delta Ministry, an extensive community development program in Mississippi.

Because the regular Democratic party of Mississippi refused to accept black members, Hamer joined with black and white protesters in 1964 to form the Mississippi Freedom Democratic party (MFDP). She was a member that year of the MFDP delegation that challenged the seating of the regular Mississippi delegation to the National Democratic Convention, and in her testimony before the credentials committee she vividly described the brutal reprisals she and other blacks had suffered in Mississippi because of their efforts to vote and to exercise other civil rights. Her testimony was dramatically presented to the nation by television. Thereafter, she was in great demand, both as a speaker and as a performer of civil rights songs and spirituals.

The MFDP was unsuccessful in replacing the regular Democratic delegation in 1964, but that convention pledged that no delegation that barred blacks would be seated in future conventions. Hamer became a member of the delegation of the Mississippi Loyalist Democratic party (the successor of MFDP), which unseated Mississippi's regular delegation at the National Democratic Convention. Meanwhile, in 1964 she had attempted to run as the MFDP candidate for the U.S. House of Representatives from Mississippi's Second Congressional District, but her name was not allowed on the ballot. Consequently, she, along with Victoria Gray and Annie Devine, on 4 January 1965, challenged the entire Mississippi delegation in the House of Representatives as unrepresentative of the people of the state. Their challenge failed.

In 1965 Hamer was the plaintiff in a suit that resulted in the U.S. Fifth Circuit of Appeals' setting aside the local elections in Sunflower and Moorhead counties because blacks had not been allowed to vote. She served on the Democratic National Committee from 1968 to 1971. In 1969 she founded and became vice president of Freedom Farms Corporation, a nonprofit venture designed to provide social services, to help needy black and white families produce food, to promote minority business opportunities, and to provide scholarships. She became chairperson of the board of directors of Fannie Lou Hamer Day Care Center founded in Ruleville by the National Council of Negro Women in 1970. She also served as a director of the Sunflower County Day Care and Family Service and the Garment Manufacturing Plant, as chairperson of the Sunflower County Voter's League, as a member of the policy council of the National Women's Political Caucus, as a trustee of the Martin Luther King Center for Social Change, and as a member of the state executive committee of the United Democratic party of Mississippi.

Fannie Lou Hamer received honorary degrees from Tougaloo College, Shaw University, Morehouse College, Columbia College, and Howard University. She also received the Mary Church Terrell Award from Delta Sigma Theta Sorority and the Paul Robeson Award from Alpha Phi Alpha Fraternity. In 1976 the mayor of Ruleville declared a Fannie Lou Hamer Day. She died of cancer in Mound Bayou Hospital the following March 14.

Clifton H. Johnson
Amistad Research Center
New Orleans, Louisiana

Black Enterprise (May 1977); John Egerton, *Progressive* (May 1977); Fannie Lou Hamer Papers, Amistad Research Center, New Orleans, Louisiana; Susan Johnson, *The Black Law Journal* (Summer 1972); June Jordan, *Fannie Lou Hamer* (1972); *Never Turn Back: The Life of Fannie Lou Hamer* (Rediscovery Productions film, 1983); *Sojourners* (December 1982); C. J. Wilson, *New South* (Spring 1973).

Hancock, Gordon Blaine

(1884–1970) Educator and social activist.

Gordon Blaine Hancock, born in Greenwood County, S.C., of exslave parents, attended Benedict College (B.A. 1911, B.D. 1912), Colgate University (B.A. 1919, B.D. 1920), and Harvard University (M.A. 1921). Seneca (South Carolina) Institute principal (1912–18), Virginia Union University professor (1921–52), Richmond's Moore Street Baptist Church pastor (1925–63), and Associated Negro Press columnist (1929–68), he became probably the most peripatetic and popular black spokesman in the Old Dominion and the Upper South during the three decades before the Supreme Court's *Brown* decision in 1954. A politically conscious educator, Hancock is significant as a symbol of black aspiration and dilemma.

Hancock's generation confronted the problem of ending black exclusion and initiating integration without abandoning cultural identity or sacrificing values of self-help and solidarity. Hancock, who offered one of the first courses in race relations at a southern school, merged accommodation and protest ideologies. Doubting that poverty and racism ever would be eliminated through mere militancy, he argued that blacks must seek to advance themselves and try to win white support by learning, saving, and voting. His dual message of autonomous development and interracial cooperation appeared weekly in 114 black newspapers. Throughout the Great Depression and the New Deal, he delivered speeches entitled "Back to the Farm," "Double Duty Dollar," and "Hold Your Job" to hundreds of church, civic, and college groups. Annoyed by what they called his "constant yapping," which allegedly exaggerated racial suffering, critics dubbed Hancock the "Gloomy Dean." Even so, he directed the 1942 Durham conference of black leaders whose far-reaching statement inspired the Southern Regional Council. Disappointed by that body's reluctance to condemn segregation, but less open about it (for fear of alienating liberals) than his fellow educator Benjamin E. Mays, the dean declared: "Like you, I am opposed to further research, and like you I am looking and pressing for action. And, if the Southern Regional Council cannot give this action, like you I want to see it pass. However, let's give it a good chance." After 1954, knowing well the pitfalls of interracialism, the old professor deplored blacks' pursuit of desegregation without a self-help strategy. Aged, infirm, and isolated, unlike the highly visible Mays, he died publicly unheralded.

See also SOCIAL CLASS: / Southern Regional Council

Raymond Gavins
Duke University

Raymond Gavins, *Perils and Prospects of Southern Black Leadership* (1977), *Virginia Magazine of History and Biography* (October 1977).

Hurston, Zora Neale

(1901?–1960) Writer and folklorist.

Born either in 1891 or 1901—the latter is normally given as the date of birth but recent studies suggest an earlier date—in the all-black town of Eatonville, Fla., Hurston became a distinguished novelist, folklorist, and anthropologist. She was next to the youngest of eight children, born the daughter of a Baptist minister who was mayor of Eatonville. Her mother died when Hurston was nine, and she left home at 14 to join a traveling show. She later attended Howard University, where she studied under Alain Locke and Lorenzo Dow Turner, and she earned an A.B. degree from Barnard College in 1928, working with Franz Boas. She became a well-known figure among the New York intellectuals of the Harlem Renaissance in the mid-1920s and then devoted the years 1927 to 1932 to field research in Florida, Alabama, Louisiana, and the Bahamas. *Mules and Men* (1935) was a collection of black music, games, oral lore, and religious practices. *Tell My Horse* (1938) was a similar collection of folklore from Jamaica and Haiti.

Hurston published four novels—*Jonah's Gourd Vine* (1934), *Their Eyes Were Watching God* (1937), *Moses, Man of the Mountain* (1939), and *Seraph on the Sewanee* (1948). Her autobiography, *Dust Tracks on a Road*, appeared in 1948. Married and divorced twice, she worked for the WPA Federal Theatre project in New York (1935–36) and for the Federal Writers' Project in Florida (1938). She taught briefly at Bethune-Cookman College in Daytona Beach, Fla. (1934), and at North Carolina College in Durham (1939), and she received Rosenwald and Guggenheim fellowships (1934, 1936–37).

Hurston was noteworthy for her portrayal of the strength of black life in the South. In her essay "The Pet Negro System," she assured her readers that not all black southerners fit the illiterate sharecropper stereotype fostered by the northern media. She pointed to the seldom-noted black professionals who, like herself, remained in the South because they liked some things about it. Most educated blacks, Hurston insisted, preferred not to live up North because they came to realize that there was "segregation and discrimination up there, too, with none of the human touches of the South." One of the "human touches" to which Hurston referred was the "pet Negro system" itself, a southern practice that afforded special privileges to blacks who met standards set by their white benefactors. The system survived, she said, because it reinforced the white southerner's sense of superiority. Clearly, it was not a desirable substitute for social, economic, and political equality, but Hurston's portrayal of the system indicated her affirmative attitude toward the region, despite its dubious customs.

Hurston had faith in individual initiative, confidence in the strength of black culture, and strong trust in the ultimate goodwill of southern white people, all of which influenced her perceptions of significant racial issues. When she saw blacks suffering hardships, she refused to acknowledge that racism was a major contributing factor, probably because she never let racism stop her. Hurston's biographer, Robert E. Hemenway, notes that "in her later life she came to interpret all attempts to emphasize black suffering . . . as the politics of deprivation, implying a tragedy of color in Afro-American life."

After working for years as a maid in Miami, Hurston suffered a stroke in early 1959 and, alone and indigent, died in the Saint Lucie County Welfare Home, Fort Pierce, Fla., 28 January 1960. Alice Walker has led a recent "rediscovery" of Hurston, whose works have become inspiration for black women writers.

See also LITERATURE: / Walker, Alice

Elvin Holt
University of Kentucky

Robert E. Hemenway, *Zora Neale Hurston: A Literary Biography* (1977); Zora Neale Hurston, *I Love Myself*, ed. Alice Walker (1979); Alice Walker, *In Search of Our Mothers' Gardens* (1983).

Jackson, Jesse

(b. 1941) Civil rights activist, minister, politician.

Called "the most famous Black man in America today" by one admiring biographer, a position confirmed by the more scientific conclusions of major national polls, Jesse Louis Jackson was born 8 October 1941 in Greenville, S.C. His mother was Helen Burns, and his father was Noah Louis Robinson, to whom his mother was never married. Charles Henry Jackson became the husband of Jesse's mother, and young Jackson's stepfather provided him with a comfortable home and stable family life.

Jackson grew up in Greenville, where he was sensitive to the racism and segregation of the times and exhibited an inquisitive mind, street savvy, athletic ability, and discipline. He left the University of Illinois after one year when he was told by coaches that a black man could not play quarterback, and he turned down a professional baseball contract when he was offered less than a white counterpart. He became active in the sit-in demonstrations organized by the Congress of Racial Equality (CORE) in Greensboro, N.C., where he had come to enter all-black North Carolina A&T University on a football scholarship. At A&T, he was a star quarterback, honor student, student body president, and fraternity leader. He was elected president of the North Carolina Inter-Collegiate Council on Human Rights, and by his senior year assumed broader responsibilities as the southeastern field director of CORE. Jackson accepted a Rockefeller scholarship to the Chicago Theological Seminary, having decided that the pulpit was a better platform than the courtroom to realize his developing ambitions and commitments.

Jackson's prominence in the civil rights movement is tied to his apprenticeship under Dr. Martin Luther King, Jr. Jackson met King while in college, but he did not join the staff of the Southern Christian Leadership Conference (SCLC) until 1965, helping to organize the Selma marches and demonstrations just prior to King's Chicago campaign. King later appointed Jackson as director of SCLC's Operation Breadbasket, an economic development coalition of ministers and business people using such direct action tactics as boycotts and mass demonstrations.

The assassination of King on 4 April 1968 led Jackson to assume national leadership, an opportunity he seized with vigor. Jackson emerged as the aggressive spokesperson of a movement in disarray. Operation Breadbasket moved away from its parent organization, SCLC, and proclaimed itself the leading civil rights organization in the nation. After a flurry of boycotts in which "covenants"—agreements to provide jobs, develop businesses, place deposits in black banks, and advertise in the black media—were signed, Operation Breadbasket was renamed Operation PUSH in December 1971. Jackson's tactics were reminiscent of the "Buy Black Campaign" and the "Don't Buy Where You Can't Work" protests of the 1930s in Chicago and other cities.

Jesse Jackson's greatest achievement was his 1984 presidential campaign. Jackson had run for mayor of Chicago in 1971 and had been active in such national political forums as the National Black Political Assembly in 1972 and 1973. He showed himself to be knowledgeable on a wide range of issues, articulate in televised debates, and adept in seizing media attention with such feats as his extrication of a black navy pilot from Syria. Jackson galvanized black community sentiment, and the results were quite unexpected. With a very small campaign war chest, Jackson gathered almost 20 percent of the vote in the Democratic primaries and won 465.5 convention votes. More important, his campaign spurred voter registration, stirred local debate and activity, and challenged Democratic party rules that seemed unfair. His achievement led to an invitation to deliver a keynote to the Democratic National Convention in San Fransisco. Looking toward the 1988 campaign, Jackson sought to fashion his "rainbow coalition" into a more viable organization.

Ronald Bailey
University of Mississippi

Rod Bush, ed., *The New Black Vote: Politics and Power in Four American Cities* (1984); Adolph Reed, Jr., *The Jesse Jackson Phenomenon: The Crisis of Purpose in Afro-American Politics* (1986); Barbara A. Reynolds, *Jesse Jackson: America's David* (1985); Hanes Walton, *Invisible Politics: Black Political Behavior* (1986).

Jim Crow

This term used to describe Afro-Americans probably originated in 19th-century minstrelsy. It has also been suggested that the term referred to a slave trader or an escaped slave, but the most generally accepted explanation credits a white minstrel entertainer, Thomas "Daddy" Rice, with popularizing the term. He performed a song-and-dance routine called "Jump Jim Crow" beginning in 1828. With face blackened from burnt cork and dressed in the rags of a beggar, Rice skipped on stage doing a shuffling dance, comically singing "I jump jis' so / An' ev'y time I turn about I jump Jim Crow." He cited an old Louisville slave belonging to a Mr. Crow as the inspiration for the act, having observed him entertain other workers in a livery stable. By the late 1830s Rice had made "Jim Crow" a part of his promotional name. He helped to put the blackface character into American entertainment and introduced a term to the language.

The story of the term *Jim Crow* is apparently more complicated than this traditional explanation of its origins. Jim Crow was probably first used outside of minstrelsy, to describe segregated facilities in the North. Mitford M. Mathews in *A Dictionary of Americanisms* (1951) cites a reference to a separate railroad car for blacks in Massachusetts in 1841, and Mathews also notes an 1842 item from *The Liberator* referring to the "negro pew" and the "Jim Crow car." Leon Litwack in *North of Slavery* (1961) used the term to describe segregated facilities in the pre–Civil War North.

In the late 19th century the name *Jim Crow* took on a new meaning, symbolizing the southern system of legal segregation that emerged after the Civil War. "Jim Crow law" first appeared in the *Dictionary of American English* in 1904, but laws requiring racial segregation had appeared briefly in the South during Reconstruction. They had generally disappeared by 1868, although the persistent custom of segregation did not disappear. Tennessee passed a Jim Crow statute in 1875, and increasingly in the following years blacks and whites were segregated throughout the South on trains, streetcars, steamboats, and port facilities. In the mid-1880s Afro-Americans were barred from white hotels, restaurants, barber and beauty shops, and theaters. By 1885 most states in the South were legally mandating segregated schools. The state constitutional reforms in Mississippi in 1890 and South Carolina in 1895 codified segregation laws, and other southern states soon followed. In 1896 the U.S. Supreme Court upheld the Jim Crow "separate-but-equal" principle in *Plessy* v. *Ferguson*.

These Jim Crow segregation laws were, according to historian C. Vann Woodward, "the public symbols and constant reminders" of the Afro-American's inferior position in the South. "That code lent the sanction of law to a racial ostracism that extended to churches and schools, to housing and jobs, to eating and drinking," concluded Woodward. It separated the races in sport and recreational activities, on all forms of public transportation, in prisons, asylums, orphanages, hospitals, and even in funeral homes and cemeteries. The term *Jim Crow* came to stand for racial segregation and was physically embodied in separate water fountains, eating places, bathrooms, Bibles in courtrooms, and pervasive signs stating "Colored" and "White" that gave the term a concrete meaning for southerners.

Sign at a bus station, Rome, Ga., 1953

See also LAW: / *Plessy* v. *Ferguson*

Charles Reagan Wilson
University of Mississippi

Robert C. Toll, *Blacking Up: The Minstrel Show In Nineteenth-Century America* (1974); William L. Van DeBurg, *Slavery and Race in Popular Culture* (1984); C. Vann Woodward, *The Strange Career of Jim Crow* (1955; 3d ed., 1974).

Johnson, Charles S.

(1893–1956) Sociologist.

Johnson successfully combined research on southern black life with leadership in the field of race relations. Under Johnson's direction (1928–47) the Fisk University Department of Social Sciences became the focal point for empirical research on the black South. Black scholars beginning with W. E. B. Du Bois made attempts to create a comprehensive body of objective research, but Johnson was the first black academic to secure the funding necessary to undertake ambitious projects. Johnson's vision and resources attracted and gave valuable experience to many young black social scientists including E. Franklin Frazier, Horace Mann Bond, and John Hope Franklin. The recognition given the studies of Johnson and his associates helped to discredit the belief that blacks were unable to undertake objective, scientific research. At the same time, the presence of respected white social scientists such as Robert Park, Eli Marks, and Kenneth Little on the Fisk faculty provided a model of interracial cooperation and reinforced the legitimacy of the Fisk approach to both scholarship and race relations.

Johnson received his sociological training at the University of Chicago (1917–22) where his methods were deeply influenced by the work of Robert Park. However, the fundamental assumption that undergirds Johnson's analysis, and is most fully stated in *The Negro in American Civilization* (1930), was his belief that the problems of blacks were demonstrably socioeconomic and historical in origin and not due to any inherent racial difference. As a consequence of this belief Johnson felt that black status would improve only with the removal of social, economic, and psychological obstacles.

A native southerner who spent only one decade outside the South, Johnson was especially sympathetic to the plight of rural blacks. He used an ethnographic approach to reveal both the isolation and the integrity of the rural black. Among the first to consider the impact of segregation and poverty upon black personality development, Johnson proposed the concept of the "folk Negro" as an alternative to the caste theory of southern race relations. A seemingly indefatigable author, editor, and contributor, Johnson in his most original and enduring contributions, *Shadow of the Plantation* (1934) and *Growing up in the Black Belt* (1941), deftly weaves the striking testimony of rural blacks.

In the history of southern race relations Johnson's only peer in terms of longevity and white confidence was Booker T. Washington. Johnson's nonpolemical approach, which did not sanction segregation, was endorsed and financially supported by the philanthropic and social welfare community beginning with his tenure as director of research and editor of *Opportunity* magazine for the National Urban League (1921–28). Johnson worked closely for three decades with white southern moderates such as Will W. Alexander, Willis Duke Weatherford, and Howard W. Odum to institutionalize the notion of interracial cooperation within the South, and he was the first black to be elected president of the Southern Sociological Society (1945). After he became president of Fisk University (1946–56), Johnson was increasingly called upon to apply his techniques for decreasing racial tensions to international situations, serving as delegate to UNESCO committees and on an American team of advisors on the postwar reorganization of Japan's educational system. But after the 1954 Supreme Court school desegregation decision Johnson was bitterly disappointed in the failure of white southern moderates to forcefully support the early civil rights movement. Shortly before his death in 1956 Johnson made his first public repudiation of white southern racial attitudes, characterizing the southern way of life as antidemocratic and at odds with the national interest.

See also EDUCATION: / Fisk University; Odum, Howard W.

Francille Rusan Wilson
University of Michigan

Patrick Gilpin, "Charles S. Johnson: An Intellectual Biography" (Ph.D. dissertation, Vanderbilt University, 1973); Charles S. Johnson, *New York Times Magazine* (23 September 1956); Richard Robbins, *Journal of Social and Behavioral Sciences* (Fall/Winter 1971–72); Preston Valien, *Sociology and Social Research* (March/April 1958).

Johnson, James Weldon

(1871–1938) Writer, civil rights leader, diplomat.

To James Weldon Johnson writing was a serious but secondary interest. Johnson's main concern was the NAACP, and he served from 1916 until 1930 as its field secretary. Johnson also had other interests and even a variety of careers.

Born in 1871 in Jacksonville, Fla., he was the principal of a primary school there. He was the founder of *The Daily American*, the first black daily newsletter, and was admitted to the Florida bar in 1897. Johnson and his brother, Rosamond, wrote successful Broadway musicals; he served as consul to Venezuela and Nicaragua during the administrations of Presidents Roosevelt and Taft. He edited *The Book of American Negro Poetry* (1922) and *The Book of American Negro Spirituals* (with Rosamond, in 1925), created the seven black sermons in verse that make up *God's Trombones* (1927), and wrote his autobiography, *Along This Way* (1933). He also authored *The Autobiography of an Ex-Coloured Man* (1912). In 1930 Johnson was named the Adam K. Spence Professor of Creative Literature at Fisk University, a position he held until his death in 1938.

James Weldon Johnson drew upon both black folklore and his own experiences as a southern black for the subject matter of his writing. Johnson collected spirituals and in *God's Trombones* clearly suggests southern black church speech through his reproduction of the southern black minister's characteristic rhetorical devices—the repetitions, the alliterations, the pauses, the echoes from the King James Bible, and the folk images. Johnson's ability to create the effect of dialect is one of his greatest skills as an artist.

Johnson's fiction evidences a similar skill. Like earlier black and white southern writers—Cable, Twain, Chesnutt—Johnson dramatized the plight of the mulatto. The central issue confronting the hero of *The Autobiography of an Ex-Coloured Man* is his identity in a society where racial caste determines one's identity. In spirit and in form, however, Johnson's work is much closer to Ellison's *Invisible Man* than it is to anything that preceded it. Ellison's conceit of a narrator who is invisible is a logical extension of Johnson's conceit of a narrator who passes for white. Both chronologically and artistically Johnson stands between earlier writers such as Chesnutt, who were beginning to create a black voice, and later writers, such as Ellison, who fully mastered their instrument.

See also EDUCATION: / Fisk University; LITERATURE: / Ellison, Ralph

Ladell Payne
Randolph-Macon College

M. Thomas Inge, Maurice Duke, and Jackson R. Bryer, eds., *Black American Writers: Bibliographical Essays*, vol. 1 (1978); Eugene Levy, *James Weldon Johnson: Black Leader, Black Voice* (1973); W. Augustus Low and Virgil A. Clift, eds., *Encyclopedia of Black America* (1981).

Johnson, Robert

(1912–1938) Blues singer.

Robert Johnson was the most celebrated and legendary of the blues artists who emerged from the Mississippi Delta prior to World War II. He was born near Hazelhurst, Miss., in 1912 and raised at a sharecroppers' settlement called Commerce. While still a youngster, he was drawn to the blues he had heard around him, learning to play the music on a harmonica and then a guitar. While still in his teens, he left home to become an itinerant bluesman, traveling throughout the Delta and then up the Mississippi River to Helena, Ark., Saint Louis, Mo., and finally to Chicago, Ill. In the mid-1930s he also traveled to Dallas and San Antonio, Tex., where he made a series of 29 blues recordings that were his legacy to the blues.

Johnson's blues repertoire has proved to be one of the most provocative in the entire history of the music. He was not only a gifted musician, but also a visionary poet. His vision of Afro-American life in the Delta is a haunting one. Songs like "Hellhound on My Trail" and "Me and the Devil Blues" point to his fatalistic assessment of the human condition and the supernatural powers in control of that condition. He saw no way out for blues musicians like himself. Such a choice of vocations necessitated making a pact with the forces of darkness because blues was the Devil's music.

The themes that dominated the landscape of Robert Johnson's blues were erotic, unrequited love, the urge to constantly move and explore new places, and the omnipotent powers of the supernatural. "Love in Vain" was his masterpiece on unrequited love; it was a theme he was obsessed with, appearing in about one-third of his songs. Erotic love was his counterpoint to heartbreak, and in songs like "Traveling Riverside Blues" he portrayed it with graphic and savory delight. Among his best-known travel songs were "Dust My Broom," "Rambling on My Mind," and "Walkin' Blues." The recurring message in these pieces was epitomized in the line—"Travel on poor Bob, just can't turn you 'round."

Robert Johnson's restless spirit reflected the changing social consciousness of the times, especially among the rural black population living in the South. Paradoxically, he was always drawn back to the Delta region he was so obsessed with leaving until, as fate would have it, he was tragically poisoned to death in a Greenwood, Miss., juke joint in 1938. He was in his twenties when he died, and with his passing the legend of Robert Johnson was born. Today he is considered one of the most popular and mysterious bluesmen of the century.

See also ENVIRONMENT: / Delta

Bill Barlow
Howard University

Samuel Charters, *Robert Johnson* (1973); Alan Greenburg, *Love in Vain: The Life and Legend of Robert Johnson* (1983); Robert Palmer, *Deep Blues* (1981); *Robert Johnson: King of the Delta Blues*, vols. I (CL 1654) and II (C30034), Columbia Records.

Juneteenth

Juneteenth is the popular name among black people in Texas for their emancipation day, which they celebrate on 19 June. On that day in 1865 Major General Gordon Granger officially announced the freedom of slaves when he arrived at Galveston to command the District of Texas following the Civil War.

Three black folktales provide other explanations of the date. In one version Texas landowners refused to announce emancipation until the 1865 harvest had been gathered by the slaves. According to a second story, a black man journeyed by mule from Washington to Texas and arrived in June 1865 with word of the abolition of slavery. The other legend has the end of slavery declared as late as June because an earlier messenger was killed on the way to Texas.

The celebration of 19 June as emancipation day spread to the neighboring states of Louisiana, Arkansas, and Oklahoma, and later to California as black Texans migrated west. It has appeared occasionally in Alabama and Florida, also as a result of migration.

Large celebrations began in 1866 and continued to be held regularly into the early 20th century, although blacks in some Texas towns honored emancipation on 1 January or 4 July—days favored in some other states. Observations of Juneteenth declined in the 1940s during World War II but revived with 70,000 black people on the Texas State Fair grounds at Dallas during 1950. As school desegregation and the civil rights movement focused attention on the expansion of freedom in the late 1950s and early 1960s, Juneteenth celebrations declined again, although small towns still observed Texas's emancipation day. In the 1970s Juneteenth was revived in some communities, especially after two black members convinced the Texas Legislature to declare Juneteenth an unofficial "holiday of significance . . . particularly to the blacks of Texas."

Typical celebrations over the years included parades, picnics, baseball games or other competitive contests, speeches on freedom and future goals, and dances. Leaders in the black community normally organized the events, although occasionally in the 20th century a business or a black fraternal group assumed that role.

Alwyn Barr
Texas Tech University

Ebony (June 1951); Wendy Watriss, *Southern Exposure* (No. 1, 1977); William Wiggins, " 'Free at Last!': A Study of Afro-American Emancipation Day Celebrations" (Ph.D. dissertation, Indiana University, 1974).

King, Martin Luther, Jr.

(1929–1968) Minister and civil rights leader.

Born on 15 January 1929 in Atlanta, Ga., Martin Luther King, Jr., came to symbolize the black freedom struggle that dominated the South from 1955 to 1968. He attended Morehouse College and graduated from Crozer Theological Seminary in June 1951. Emerging at the age of 27 as the principal leader of the Montgomery, Ala., bus boycott that initiated a new era of nonviolent protest against racial discrimination, King brought a strong family heritage in the Baptist church and excellent graduate training in philosophy and theology at Boston University to his role as spokesman for a movement that in little more than a decade transformed southern life.

In the early years of his public career King stressed two beliefs: that black southerners had to employ mass action as well as lawsuits if they were to win their constitutional rights as American citizens and that many white southerners would respond positively once they were shown that Christian morality supported the goals of the civil rights cause. The tactics of "direct action" led to protest efforts such as the "sit-ins" of 1960, the Freedom Ride of 1961, and the community-based demonstration campaigns that King's Southern Christian Leadership Conference mounted in Albany, Ga., Birmingham, Ala., St. Augustine, Fla., and Selma, Ala., in the years 1962–65. King's early optimism about the white South, and especially the white church, all but vanished as confrontation after confrontation demonstrated that few white southerners would stand up for racial justice.

King's 1963 "I Have A Dream" oration at the March on Washington and his 1964 receipt of the Nobel Peace Prize catapulted him to national and international fame at much the same time that civil rights protests were leading the federal government to enact the landmark Civil Rights Act of 1964 and Voting Rights Act of 1965. Achievement of these milestones and realization of their limitations led King to focus increasingly on the serious problems of his country and world that had not been ameliorated by those racial reform statutes: poverty and economic powerlessness that oppressed many white as well as black Americans, North as well as South; militarism and materialism that led to international violence and economic imperialism. King's desire to attack the former set of problems led him to mount a largely unsuccessful attack upon economic injustice in Chicago's ghettos in 1966; his realization of the need to speak out against international violence and oppression led him in 1967 to denounce America's involvement in Vietnam.

Before his murder, King was articulating a vision far distant from that with which he had begun. America, and the South, required thoroughgoing economic and structural change, and not merely the elimination of racial discrimination, if real human justice were to be attained. That struggle for a more just society would have to employ coercive and disruptive tactics, not simply persuasive ones, for the preceding 12 years had shown that white America was far less interested in social justice than King had imagined in 1956. At the time of his assassination in Memphis on 4 April 1968, Martin Luther King, Jr., believed that the road ahead was still far longer than the road he himself had traveled. As of 1986 the Martin Luther King, Jr., Papers Project, directed by Clayborne Carson at Stanford University, was well underway. The goal of the 15-year project is publication of 12 annotated volumes of selections from the broad range of King's writings, many of which will be available to the public for the first time. Plans are for the first volume to be available in 1990. In January 1986 King's birthday was declared a national holiday, the first such tribute to a black American.

Martin Luther King, Jr., as portrayed on a paper fan produced by the Dillon Funeral Homes and Burial Association, Leland, Vicksburg, Greenville, Indianola, and Cleveland, Miss., 1968

David J. Garrow
City College of New York
CUNY Graduate Center

Gaynelle Evans, *Chronicle of Higher Education* (3 September 1986); David J. Garrow, *Bearing the Cross: Martin Luther King, Jr., and the Southern Christian Leadership Conference, 1955–1968* (1986); Martin Luther King, Jr., *Where Do We Go From Here: Chaos or Community?* (1967); David L. Lewis, *King: A Critical Biography* (1970); Stephen B. Oates, *Let the Trumpet Sound: The Life of Martin Luther King, Jr.* (1982); Kenneth L. Smith and Ira G. Zepp, Jr., *Search for the Beloved Community: The Thinking of Martin Luther King, Jr.* (1974).

Lynch, John Roy

(1847–1939) Politician and lawyer.

Lynch was born on 10 September 1847 in Concordia Parish, La., the son of an Irishman, Patrick Lynch, and a slave, Catherine White. His father bought and sought to free his whole family, but death and the treachery of a friend intervened, so that Lynch was not freed until 1863 by the Union army in Natchez. Lynch was self-educated, except for four months of formal schooling in 1866. He early became active as a Republican, and in 1869 Governor Adelbert Ames appointed him a justice of the peace. That same year Lynch was elected to the Mississippi House of Representatives. Reelected in 1871, Lynch was chosen as speaker of the House, which he ruled, according to a unanimously passed resolution, "with becoming dignity, with uniform courtesy and impartiality, and with marked ability." The occasion of the resolution was Lynch's departure from the Mississippi House for the U.S. House of Representatives, where he took his seat in December 1873, after handily defeating the Democratic candidate. In all, he served three terms, though his third term was cut short by the necessity of having to contest the election of his Democratic opponent; Lynch was finally declared the winner.

Following defeat for reelection in 1882, Lynch went home to Adams County to run his plantation. Still active as a Republican, he was a delegate to the Republican national conventions of 1884, 1888, 1892, and 1900; earlier, in 1872, while a member of the Mississippi House, he was a delegate to the Republican convention of that year. Democrat Grover Cleveland offered Lynch a minor appointive office, which he turned down; but in 1889 he accepted from Republican President Benjamin Harrison the position of fourth auditor of the Treasury and served until the return of Democrats to national power in 1893.

About this time Lynch began the study of law, and in 1896 he was admitted to the Mississippi bar. From 1893 till 1896, though, Lynch largely busied himself with his Adams County plantation and with real estate speculation in Natchez. From 1896 to 1898 he practiced law in Mississippi and in Washington, D.C., with the firm of Robert H. Terrell. With the outbreak of the Spanish American War in 1898, Republican President William McKinley appointed Lynch as a paymaster of volunteer forces, with the rank of major; in 1901 he was appointed to the same position and rank in the regular army, in which he served till 1911, when he retired.

Lynch then settled in Chicago, where he practiced law and traded in real estate. In 1913 he published his *Facts of Reconstruction*, which is commonly regarded as the best account of Reconstruction by a black participant. His last years were spent writing *Reminiscences of an Active Life*, which was not published till 1970, under the editorship of John Hope Franklin. Lynch was married twice. His 1884 marriage to Ella Somerville, by whom he had one daughter, ended in divorce, and in 1911 he married Cora Williams, who survived him.

Charles E. Wynes
University of Georgia

John Hope Franklin, ed., *Reminiscences of an Active Life: The Autobiography of John Roy Lynch* (1970).

Mardi Gras Indians

The Mardi Gras Indians have the richest of folk rituals associated with Carnival in New Orleans. Groups of blacks, mostly from impoverished neighborhoods, fashion Indian costumes and parade through the streets on Mardi Gras, on the St. Joseph's Day feast on March 19, and in recent years on "Super Sunday," which falls shortly before the late April Jazz and Heritage Festival. For weeks before Mardi Gras the tribes meet in neighborhood bars to rehearse the chants sung on Carnival Day.

The earliest English language reference to the Indians is found in a memoir by Elise Kirsch, who described "a band of men (about 60) desguised as Indians . . . shouting and screaming war hoops." The Mardi Gras mentioned is apparently 1883, which coincides with the time frame fixed by the most reliable informant of the oral tradition, Allison "Tuddy" Montana, chief of the Yellow Pocahontas. Montana's grand-uncle, a plasterer named Becate Batiste, founded the tribe known as Creole Wild West in the early 1880s. The tribe eventually moved to another neighborhood across town, and the Yellow Pocahontas took its place in the downtown Seventh Ward. Since then tribes have come and gone, but a nucleus of about a dozen gathers annually. They have names such as the Ninth Ward Hunters, Golden Blades, Wild Squatoolas, Black Eagles, White Eagles, and the Red, White, and Blues. Afro-Caribbean dance steps and hand percussions among participants meld with the Indian persona. Similar rituals have long flourished in the carnivals of Haiti, Trinidad, and Brazil.

Until the Depression, tribes often fought with each other and with policemen; however, today's competition is ritualized. Costume making is a point of distinction among the Indians. The costumes are resplendent with

The Wild Tchoupitoulas, in Les Blank's film Always for Pleasure *(1978)*

billowing ostrich plumes, feathers, beaded vests, and knee pads. New costumes are usually made each year.

Each tribe is led by a Big Chief, and below him are other chiefs. Women of a Big Chief's entourage in this preponderantly masculine tradition are called Queens. The brave who scouts ahead for each tribe is called Spy Boy. Flag Boy carries the tribal pendant.

In the 1970s street chants moved from the streets into recording studios. Jazz composer Wilson Turbinton arranged the 1973 *Wild Magnolias* LP (Polydor), while *The Wild Tchoupitoulas* (1976, Island) was a collaboration of the Meters, the Neville Brothers, and their uncle, George Landry, who as Big Chief Jolley led the tribe. Landry's warm vocals are the heartbeat of the disc. In addition, two documentaries feature the Wild Tchoupitoulas, *Always for Pleasure* (Les Blank, Flower Films, 1978) and *Up From the Cradle of Jazz* (Davis Frentz, director, Jason Berry and Jonathan Foose, distributors, 1980).

Jason Berry
New Orleans, Louisiana

Jason Berry, Jonathan Foose, and Tad Jones, *Up from the Cradle of Jazz: New Orleans Music since World War II* (1987).

Mason, Charles Harrison

(1866–1961) Minister.

Mason, son of Jerry and Elisa Mason, was born 8 September 1866 on Prior Farm, near Memphis, Tenn. His early education was obtained in the public schools of Memphis, though his attendance at school was infrequent. His major educational experiences, primarily religious, were provided by his mother, replicating her own experiences that followed her conversion to Christianity during the period of American slavery. These experiences were augmented by teachings she received in the Missionary Baptist church, of which she and her husband were members.

In November of 1878, when Mason was 12 years old, the family moved to Plumersville, Ark., where Mason's education continued in the context of a religious home. A prolonged and intense fever overtook him in 1880, and following a healing experience in September of that year, he was converted and later baptized by his brother, I. S. Nelson, pastor of Mt. Olive Missionary Baptist Church, located near Plumersville.

Mason continued in faithful service in the Baptist church as a layman until 1893, when, at Preston, Ark., he preached his first sermon, which attracted many in attendance to his beliefs. To prepare himself for the ministry, on 1 November of that year he entered Arkansas Baptist College at Little Rock, remaining there for only three months before he left to become a traveling evangelist. In this capacity, he met in 1895 with Charles Price Jones of Jackson, Miss., J. A. Jeter of Little Rock, Ark., and Walter S. Pleasant of Hazelhurst, Miss., and became a member of a small body of Baptist ministers who were seeking a greater spiritual involvement than their church offered. At a meeting in Jackson, Miss., in 1896, they decided to organize churches under their own leadership, and a Church of God in Christ was established at Lexington, Miss., in 1897, "in an old gin on the bank of a little creek." The congregation based its faith on the doctrine of the apostles as recorded on Pentecost (Acts 2:4) and believed that the church's name was revealed to Mason in 1879 from a reference in First Thessalonians 2:14.

In 1906 a report came to the mid-South area that at meetings being conducted by the Reverend William J. Seymour in Los Angeles, Calif., one could receive the baptism of the Holy Ghost, according to Matthew 10:12. Mason, along with J. A. Jeter and D. J. Young of Pine Bluff, Ark., traveled to Los Angeles to the Azusa Street Revival (1906–9), where Mason received the Holy Ghost in March of 1907. They returned to Memphis later that year and began a series of services that attracted a large following. In August of 1907 a General Assembly of the Church of God in Christ was convened in Jackson, Miss., where Mason was elected chief overseer (the term was later replaced by bishop) and D. J. Young was elected editor of their official organ, the *Whole Truth*. By 1934 the denomination had a membership of 25,000, and in 1971 the membership was listed as 425,000, reaching 4.5 million in 1985.

Mason encouraged music and music making in his church and is credited with the composition of several songs, including "I'm a Soldier in the Army of the Lord" and "My Soul Loves Jesus." His congregation is responsible for contributions to black gospel music through such performers as Sister Rosetta Tharpe, Ernestine B. Washington, Andrae Crouch, Edwin and Walter Hawkins, The O'Neal Twins, the Boyer Brothers, and Vanessa Bell Armstrong. The presiding bishop of the Church of God in Christ is J. O. Patterson, with its headquarters in Memphis, Tenn.

Horace Clarence Boyer
Smithsonian Institution

Horace Clarence Boyer, "An Analysis of Black Church Music, with Examples Drawn from Services in Rochester, New York" (Ph.D. dissertation, University of Rochester, 1973); Otho B. Cobbins, *History of Church of Christ (Holiness) U.S.A.* (1966); J. O. Patterson, German R. Ross, and Julia Mason Atkins, *History and Formative Years of the Church of God in Christ with Excerpts from the Life and Works of Its Founder-Bishop C. H. Mason* (1969); German R. Ross, *Yes, Lord!* (1982).

Mays, Benjamin

(1894–1984) Educator and minister.

Son of Greenwood County, S.C., exslaves, alumnus of Bates College (B.A. 1920) and the University of Chicago (M.A. 1925, Ph.D. 1935), dean of the Howard University School of Religion (1934–40), and president of Morehouse College (1940–62), Benjamin Elijah Mays had become a world-renowned academician and churchman when he eulogized the slain Martin Luther King, Jr., on national television in 1968. Despite his advanced age, he presided over the Atlanta Board of Education during the next decade, as it implemented school desegregation and improved classroom instruction. Recipient of numerous honors—including the recent opening of Atlanta's Benjamin E. Mays High School, induction into the South Carolina Hall of Fame, and a joint resolution of tribute from the U.S. Congress—Mays is one of the most scholastically decorated southerners of this century.

But his historical importance rests upon more than public visibility since the 1960s. Like others whose names are not as well known, Mays had long been a community leader in the struggle for equality, and he exemplified the courage of politically oriented educators under a legal Jim Crow system. Although he refused Booker T. Washington's call to "Cast down your bucket where you are" and united with W. E. B. Du Bois's post–World War I "talented tenth," hoping "that someday I would be able to do something about a situation that had shadowed my early years and had killed the spirit of all too many of my people," Mays preached familiar ideals. He talked of character, Christianity, education, independence, and pride to blacks, while whites heard his denunciations of caste and his demands for change. Active during the 1930s in antiracist campaigns conducted by the Association of Southern Women for the Prevention of Lynching, Commission on Interracial Cooperation, National Association for the Advancement of Colored People, National Association of Negro Women's Clubs, National Council of Churches, National Urban League, Southern Conference on Human Welfare, and Young Men's Christian Association, he joined the black-liberal coalition that in 1944 formed the Southern Regional Council. A director, he criticized the organization's early failure to oppose segregation. As president of Morehouse College, Mays encouraged the questioning of the segregation system, as individuals such as writer Lillian Smith, a close associate, lectured at the school and criticized laws separating the races. Her largely student audience included several future civil rights crusaders, among them young Martin Luther "Mike" King. Mays's antisegregation views soon created much trouble for the outspoken president, whom witch-hunters labeled a Communist and occasionally picketed. When the council did break its silence, pledging in 1951 to build a segregated South, Mays could already foresee the 1954 *Brown* decision. Fittingly, Atlanta chose the former pioneer to help implement it.

Mays wrote several books, including *The Negro's God as Reflected in His Literature* (1938), *Seeking to be Christian in Race Relations*, with Joseph W. Nicholson (1965), *Negro's Church* (1969), *Born to Rebel* (1971), and *Lord the People Have Driven Me On* (1981). He died 28 March 1984.

See also SOCIAL CLASS: / Southern Regional Council; WOMEN'S LIFE: / Smith, Lillian

Raymond Gavins
Duke University

David L. Lewis, *King: A Critical Biography* (1970); Benjamin E. Mays, *Born to Rebel: An Autobiography of Benjamin E. Mays* (1987); Frank L. Prial, *New York Times* (29 March 1984).

Meredith, James

(b. 1933) Civil rights activist.

James Howard Meredith achieved international renown in 1962 when his admission to the University of Mississippi sparked a night-long riot during which two people were killed. Meredith's admission to the all-white university climaxed 18 months of legal and political resistance by both university and state officials, particularly from Governor Ross Barnett, who physically barred Meredith's admission on two occasions. The racial tension that accompanied his admission soon subsided, and Meredith graduated from the University in August of 1963. He described his experiences in *Three Years in Mississippi* (1965).

James H. Meredith's parents, Moses and Roxie Meredith, owned an 84-acre farm near Kosciusko, in Attala County, Miss. Meredith was born on that farm on 25 June 1933. After graduating from a St. Petersburg, Fla., high school, Meredith enlisted in the U.S. Air Force. While in the air force, he conceived a plan to return to his native state to gain admission to the University of Mississippi and break the color barrier in Mississippi.

In the years following his graduation from the university, Meredith pursued a variety of interests and causes. He took graduate courses in economics at the University of Ibadan, Nigeria, in 1964–65 and received a law degree from Columbia University in 1968. In 1966 Meredith was shot and wounded during a walk from Memphis, Tenn., to Jackson, Miss., which he called a "March Against Fear." He has conducted several unsuccessful political campaigns and has served as consultant and lecturer at colleges and universities in America and Africa. Meredith's business interests are as varied as his social and educational pursuits. He owned an apartment building in the Bronx and was a stock broker before returning to Jackson, Miss., in the early 1970s. While in Mississippi, he was self-employed and spent much of his time promoting business ties between American black entrepreneurs and black Africa. Meredith is married to Mary Jane Wiggins and has five children. He served as visiting professor at the University of Cincinnati during the 1984–85 academic year, and in the fall of 1986 he ran unsuccessfully for a position on the Cincinnati, Ohio, school board.

David Sansing
University of Mississippi

James W. Loewen and Charles Sallis, eds., *Mississippi: Conflict and Change* (1974); James H. Meredith, *Three Years in Mississippi* (1965).

Murray, Pauli

(1910–1985) Social reformer.

A thirst for learning, the ability to maintain personal directions while setting goals that were greater than she, and "a passion for equality" are the attributes that shaped the life of Pauli Murray, civil rights activist, lawyer, educator, author, and feminist. From early childhood until she entered Hunter College in New York, Murray lived with her aunt, Pauline Fitzgerald Dame, in Durham, N.C. During those years she refined her sense of self-worth and independence and became preconditioned to feminism.

Seeking to return to the "old family ancestral home" in Durham to care for her elderly aunts, Murray became actively involved during the years 1938 to 1941 in the struggle for civil and human rights. According to Murray, her involvement was "me trying to plod along toward some particular, specific objectives." Feeling handicapped with only a B.A. degree, she decided to enroll at the University of North Carolina for graduate studies; her efforts were unsuccessful. Similarly, in 1940, her refusal to sit on a broken seat led to her arrest and conviction for resisting segregation on an interstate bus. Those personal racial confrontations and a national tour in 1941 on behalf of a black man convicted of killing his white landlord prompted her decision to enter Howard University's Law School. Her goal was to become a civil rights lawyer in order to join the legal staff of the NAACP. She continued to protest segregation while a student at Howard by organizing sit-ins against restaurants.

In 1944 she was rejected because of her gender from Harvard's Law School. She attended the University of California School of Law at Berkeley, earning in 1945 the L.L.M. With a J.S.D. from Yale University (1965), Murray had completed her legal training. The sexual and racial barriers she encountered while pursuing her education reinforced her goals to seek better race relations, to eliminate sexism, and to improve the human condition.

She practiced law in New York and California (1946–60), held academic posts in the United States and Ghana (1960–73), was a member of the Committee on Civil and Political Rights of the President's Commission on the Status of Women (1962–63), and cofounded the National Organization for Women (1966). On 8 January 1977 she became one of the first women to be regularly ordained by the Episcopal church.

Murray's book *Proud Shoes: The Story of an American Family* (1956) was a family memoir, a genealogical record of her ancestors in Delaware, Pennsylvania, and North Carolina and especially her grandparents, Robert and Cornelia Fitzgerald. Upon her retirement on 1 January 1983, her first project was to work on a sequel to *Proud Shoes*. She continued to address herself to "the problem of 'psychic violence' in pursuit of the Martin Luther King, Jr., tradition of nonviolence," before her death in July of 1985.

Cynthia Neverdon-Morton
Coppin State College

Pauli Murray interview, Southern Oral History Program, University of North Carolina, Chapel Hill; Pauli Murray, *Southern Exposure* (Winter 1977); *Who's Who among Black Americans* (1980–81).

National Association for the Advancement of Colored People (NAACP)

Disheartened by a race riot in 1908 in Springfield, Ill.—the home of President Abraham Lincoln—by the spread of legalized Jim Crow, and by the accommodationist leadership of Booker T. Washington, an interracial group including W. E. B. Du Bois met in New York City in 1910 to establish the NAACP. The organization spent the next few decades in court challenges to the 1896 *Plessy* v. *Ferguson* decision, which sanctioned the separate-but-equal doctrine.

Beginning with *Guinn* v. *the United States* (1915), the NAACP convinced the Supreme Court to outlaw the use of the "grandfather clause" as a means to disfranchise black voters. In 1917 success came in *Buchanan* v. *Warley*, which ended municipal ordinances that sanctioned residential segregation. The NAACP attained further success in the 1930s and 1940s in cases that involved the removal of restrictions on blacks' participation in primary elections and compelled some southern and border states to admit blacks to their law and graduate schools. The culmination of these efforts came in 1954 in *Brown* v. *Board of Education*, which reversed *Plessy* and outlawed racial segregation in public schools.

The NAACP was also an activist organization, especially in its local chapters. In 1915 various NAACP locals picketed theaters showing the racially demeaning movie *Birth of a Nation*. Most major southern cities including Little Rock, Atlanta, Greensboro, and Montgomery had active NAACP chapters, although southern states like Alabama moved to ban the organization during the 1950s. A few southern chapters were especially militant. The president of the Monroe, N.C., NAACP in 1959 vowed self-defense with arms, if necessary, in response to white segregationist violence. The national office suspended him for this breach of policy.

During the civil rights movement, under the leadership of executive director Roy Wilkins and Washington, D.C., representative Clarence Mitchell, the NAACP played a crucial role in the successful lobbying for the 1964 Civil Rights Act and the 1965 Voting Rights Act. A Memphis judge, minister, and Federal Communications Commission member, Benjamin L. Hooks, succeeded Wilkins in 1977.

See also LAW: / *Brown* v. *Board of Education*; *Plessy* v. *Ferguson*; MEDIA: / *Birth of a Nation*

Dennis C. Dickerson
Rhodes College

John Hope Franklin, *From Slavery to Freedom: A History of Negro Americans* (1947; 5th ed., 1980); Charles F. Kellogg,

NAACP: A History of the National Association for the Advancement of Colored People, Volume I, 1909–1920 (1967); *Records of the NAACP, Branch Files*, Library of Congress, Manuscript Division, Washington, D.C.; B. Joyce Ross, *J. E. Spingarn and the Rise of the NAACP, 1911–1939* (1972); Roy Wilkins with Tom Matthews, *Standing Fast: The Autobiography of Roy Wilkins* (1982).

Negro Baseball Leagues

Under segregation, by custom and sometimes by law, interracial sports encounters were prohibited in the South. As a direct result black southerners developed their own sports world, and baseball was by far the most popular sport of the period.

Each town or rural area had a black baseball team that competed against other local black teams in games that had great cultural importance and entertainment value in those communities. The larger towns had better teams and the very best players became professionals. The top of the black baseball hierarchy was the Negro League—sometimes called the Negro Major Leagues.

Though headquartered in the North for economic reasons, the Negro League had a distinctly southern accent. The league's founder, Rube Foster, was an expatriate Texan; and the majority of players, always southerners, were recruited from southern teams during spring training or during regular Negro League barnstorming forays into the South. In addition, the Negro League contained a smattering of southern teams at various times including the Birmingham Black Barons, Memphis Red Sox, Atlanta Black Crackers, Jacksonville Red Caps, and Nashville Elite Giants. A Southern Negro League functioned as the strongest Negro minor league. Supplementing the professional and semiprofessional teams of the South were church teams and teams organized around the workplace.

The movement of black athletic talent from South to North mirrored the migration of blacks in general from the South during segregation. Yet the visibility of the black baseball stars and their association with the communities from whence they came provided a unifying influence for all black Americans. Southern blacks were able to follow their baseball heroes through the national black newspapers that circulated throughout the South, and northern black teams appealed to the still strong southern loyalties of the black fans through promotions such as "Texas Day," "Alabama Day," or "North Carolina Day."

The life of the traveling black ball player was difficult. Players were on the road constantly seeking a ball game and a payday, and they augmented the league schedule with exhibitions whenever possible. Sometimes they played three or four games in a single day. At the same time, in an age before television and air-conditioning, the ballplayers provided eagerly sought entertainment and were treated as bona fide celebrities in the black community. When the black players competed against and frequently defeated white major league players during postseason exhibitions in the North and West, they became genuine heroes in black America.

After Jackie Robinson became the first black to enter the major leagues in the 1947 season, black baseball rapidly declined as the black fans deserted their teams to watch integrated baseball. Southern-born Negro Leaguers who achieved prominence in the major leagues after integration include Willie Mays, Hank Aaron, Jackie Robinson, Ernie Banks, and Satchel Paige; but as recounted in the rich folklore that sprang up about Negro baseball, many of the greatest black players never played in the major leagues.

See also RECREATION: / Aaron, Hank; Paige, Satchel

Donn Rogosin
Austin, Texas

John Holway, *Voices from the Great Black Baseball Leagues* (1975); Robert Peterson, *Only the Ball Was White* (1970); Donn Rogosin, *Invisible Men: Life in Baseball's Negro Leagues* (1983).

Sea Islands

The area known as the Sea Islands, or the Low Country, includes all of the southeastern coastal region together with the adjacent islands extending from southern North Carolina to Florida. Apart from the inhabited and arable lands, the islands consist of brackish and salt marshes, beaches, and wooded areas. The three main ethnic groups are Afro-American, Euro-American, and a triethnic (Native American, Afro-American, and Euro-American) mixed group known as "Brass Ankles." Some of the better-known islands are Johns, James, and Wadmalaw (the so-called Bible Islands) near Charleston, S.C.; Edisto, where there is a palm-lined beach; and Ladies and St. Helena islands near Beaufort, S.C., where Penn Center, founded as a school for the islanders near the end of the Civil War, is located. Daufuskie, known through the photographic work of Jean Moutassamy-Ashe, Sapelo, and St. Mary's in Georgia are three islands still reached only by boat. Jekyll has been developed into a conference center; Ossabaw is a privately owned writers' colony. St. Simon has been suburbanized since the 1950s, and Sea Island, developed as a luxury resort, has been in and out of the news as various prominent people have honeymooned there.

Until the 1930s the Sea Islands were accessible only by boat. Causeways and bridges, which now connect some of the islands to the mainland, have had a major impact on the life of the islanders. Inhabited originally by Yamassee and other Native Americans, the area was invaded, explored, marched through, settled on, and written about successively by the Spanish, English, and French. Africans were brought to work the land, making possible large single-crop economies such as the prerevolutionary indigo, rice, and cotton and in later years potatoes, tomatoes, soybeans, and cabbage.

During the mosquito season the islands' Euro-American residents moved away to escape malaria, leaving behind the enslaved Africans, many of whom had the sickle-cell gene that protected them from the disease. Because of their isolation, the Afro-Americans preserved many of their African customs in their material folk culture and life, as evident in the distinctive patterning of their quilts, the construction of baskets, womens' modes of hair tying, cookery, the making of fishnets, and the practice of fishing. The African influence persists, too, in the Sea Islanders' insurance and burial societies, praying bands, and lodges. The Sea Island creole language (also known as Gullah or Geechee), like the folklore, exudes Africanness, as Lorenzo Dow Turner demonstrated in an epochal study. Much of Turner's work was based on naming customs, some of which are still practiced today.

Books have been written about the area—travel accounts, novels, folklore collections, explorers' journals, educational and religious missionaries' diaries, military records, and studies in history, language, and sociology. Charlotte Forten Grimké, W. F. Allen, Lucy McKim Garrison, Thomas Wentworth Higginson, William Gilmore Simms, Abigail Christensen, Charles Colcock Jones, Elsie Clews Parsons, Julia Peterkin, Guy B. and Guion Griffis Johnson, Guy and Candie Carawan, and many others have written with fascination about the area and its people, whose folkways command attention and respect.

The formerly high concentration of Afro-American residents has changed in recent years for two main reasons: northward migration of the Afro-American islanders in search of better economic opportunity and the influx of Euro-Americans through suburban, resort, and commercial developments. Recent developments on Kiawah, Hilton Head, and Daufuskie islands (S.C.) threaten the serene beauty of the islands as well as the cultural integrity of their Afro-American folkways, which have few defenses against the advance of mainland-originated technology.

See also RECREATION: / Hilton Head

Mary Ann Twining
Buffalo, New York

Edith McBride Dabbs, *Sea Island Diary: A History of St. Helena Island* (1983); Bessie Jones and Bess Lomax Hawes, *Step it Down: Games, Plays, Songs, and Stories from the Afro-American Heritage* (1972); Elsie Clews Parsons, *Folk-lore of the Sea Islands, South Carolina* (1923); Lorenzo Dow Turner, *Africanisms in the Gullah Dialect* (1949); Mary Ann Twining and Keith E. Baird, eds., *Journal of Black Studies* (June 1980).

Selma March

Throughout the first nine weeks of 1965 Martin Luther King, Jr., and the Southern Christian Leadership Conference (SCLC) helped local civil rights activists in and around Selma, Ala., organize demonstrations to protest discriminatory voter registration practices that had long blocked black citizens from casting ballots. In late February, following the fatal shooting of one protester, Jimmie Lee Jackson, by an Alabama state trooper, civil rights workers proposed a march from Selma to the Alabama state capitol in Montgomery, 54 miles away.

On Sunday, March 7, some 600 civil rights marchers headed east out of Selma on U.S. 80. State and local lawmen blocked the route and attacked the peaceful column with tear gas and billy clubs. News photographers and television cameras filmed the violent scene as the club-swinging lawmen chased the terrified demonstrators back into Selma. National outrage ensued when the film footage and dramatic photographs were featured on television stations and newspaper front pages all across America.

King announced a second march attempt, and civil rights sympathizers from around the nation flocked to Selma to join the effort. Lawmen peacefully turned back that second procession, and SCLC went into federal court seeking government protection for a third, full-scale march to Montgomery. Court hearings delayed a resolution of the question for a week, but on Sunday, March 21, with King and other dignitaries in the lead, 3,200 marchers set out for Montgomery as federal troops and officials furnished careful protection.

Walking some 12 miles a day and camping in fields at night, the marchers' ranks swelled to more than 25,000 when their procession entered Montgomery on Thursday, March 25. The march climaxed with a mass rally at the Alabama state capitol, culminating a three-week set of events that represented the emotional and political peak of the 1960s civil rights era. In the weeks following the march President Lyndon B. Johnson and bipartisan congressional supporters speeded passage of the Voting Rights Act of 1965, a comprehensive statute that remedied most of the injustices the Selma demonstrations had been designed to highlight.

See also URBANIZATION: / Montgomery

David J. Garrow
City College of New York
CUNY Graduate Center

David J. Garrow, *Protest at Selma: Martin Luther King, Jr., and the Voting Rights Act of 1965* (1978).

Silas Green Show

"Silas Green from New Orleans" was a traveling minstrel show that was owned, written, managed, and performed by black people. For over a half century (1907–58), the Silas Green Company toured urban and rural communities exclusively in the South and established itself as an institution among its black and white segregated audiences. Approximately 10 months a year, 6 nights a week, the show traveled throughout Florida, Georgia, North and South Carolina, Virginia and West Virginia, Tennessee, Kentucky, Mississippi, Arkansas, Louisiana, and Alabama.

The family-oriented comedy and musical show combined the theatrical traditions of minstrelsy and black musical comedy. White minstrelsy created the "blackface" and the writers of Silas Green retained the use of the burnt cork makeup for the main characters of their show. The comedy, however, *was* acted out in the context of a loosely woven plot that had continuity—a break with minstrelsy that was pioneered by Cole and Johnson in 1898 with *A Trip to Coontown*, the first black musical comedy. The comic story of the Silas Green show was interspersed with several chorus line numbers, one or two blues singers, and specialty acts that displayed a wide range of versatile talents. The musical sounds of "Silas Green from New Orleans" echoed the creative and innovative talents of black Americans. The band played ragtime, jazz, and swing tunes composed by southern and northern blacks, heralding and disseminating the music of its people throughout the South.

During the show's most successful years in the 1930s and 1940s, the troupe numbered up to 75, and the tent in which the production was performed nightly had the capacity to accommodate an audience of more than 2,500 people. Buses, automobiles, and a Pullman car were utilized to transport the troupe, for it was important in the hostile racial environment of the South that the show travel as a unit. Furthermore, most of the local black communities could not provide all of the sleeping and eating facilities for the members of the company; therefore, the Pullman car and trailers fulfilled these necessities.

Throughout its existence, "Silas Green from New Orleans" was black owned and controlled. The first owner of the company was "Professor" Eph Williams, a former circus performer and owner. Eph Williams acquired the show known as the "Jolly Ethiopians" from S. H. Dudley, Sr., and Salem Tutt Whitney and renamed it the Silas Green Company. After Williams's death in 1921, Charles Collier, a protégé of Williams, bought the show and is credited with reorganizing and rejuvenating it. Collier died in 1942; his wife, Hortense maintained the company until 1944 when she sold it to a partnership of Rodney Harris, Charles Morton, and Wilbur Jones. Jones soon bought out his partners and was the sole owner until he took it off the road in 1958. According to Jones the three main factors contributing to the show's demise were increased overhead expenses, the popularity of television, and heightened racial tensions in the South brought on by the 1954 Supreme Court decision in *Brown* v. *Board of Education* declaring segregation in public schools unconstitutional.

"Silas Green from New Orleans" was probably the longest-running black-owned minstrel show in the United States. Noted personalities such as "Ma" Rainey, Bessie Smith, Dewey "Pigmeat" Markham, Mamie Smith, Nipsey Russell, Johnny Huggins, and the comedy team of Butterbeans and Susie were members of the cast for varying lengths of time.

See also MUSIC: / Smith, Bessie

Eleanor J. Baker
Bloomington, Indiana

Chicago *Defender* (2 July 1921, 24 June 1922, 16 April 1932); James W. Johnson, *Black Manhattan* (1968); John Johnson, *Ebony* (September 1954); Major Robinson, *Our World* (April 1949).

Southern Christian Leadership Conference (SCLC)

The SCLC was founded in 1957 in Atlanta's Ebenezer Baptist Church, which was pastored by the Reverend Martin Luther King, Sr. Local protest movements, mostly bus boycotts, had occurred between 1953 and 1956 in such southern cities as Baton Rouge, New Orleans, Montgomery, Tallahassee, and Birmingham. Informal meetings took place among local movement leaders, mostly black ministers, including Joseph Lowery of Mobile, Fred Shuttlesworth of Birmingham, and Martin Luther King, Jr., of Montgomery, and among interested northern activists such as A. Philip Randolph, Bayard Rustin, Ella Baker, and Stanley Levison (the only white); the consensus was that a new federated organization could organize and focus growing black militancy in the South. Moreover, the NAACP had been barred legally from some southern states, and SCLC might fill the void left by this activist civil rights group.

Martin Luther King, Jr., largely because of his able leadership of the successful Montgomery bus boycott of 1955–56, became the first president of SCLC. SCLC was synonymous with King. Under the organization's auspices, he became involved in major demonstrations in Albany, Ga. (1961–62), Birmingham, Ala. (1963), St. Augustine, Fla. (1964), and Selma, Ala. (1965). The Birmingham and Selma marches dramatized the need for the Civil Rights Act of 1964 and the Voting Rights Act of 1965. King and SCLC also ventured north to Boston and Chicago to focus attention on racial and urban issues that produced de facto segregation and discrimination for blacks outside the South. He later spoke out strongly against the Vietnam War.

King operated SCLC with able lieutenants including the Reverends Ralph D. Abernathy, Andrew Young, Wyatt T. Walker, and Jesse Jackson. SCLC grew to 275 affiliates in both the North and South, although in many cases these locals were individual Baptist congregations. SCLC also had a Department of Economic Affairs, which for a time operated tutorial centers in 16 Alabama towns and tried to upgrade the occupational status of black steelworkers at an Atlanta plant. A large foundation grant in 1967 established a SCLC-sponsored educational project for black church leaders in 15 selected cities.

Just before King's assassination in 1968 in Memphis, he led that city's black sanitation workers in a fight for better wages and union recognition. King had hoped this effort would precede a massive Poor People's campaign in Washington, D.C. His successor, Abernathy, carried out the plan. Abernathy was eventually succeeded by a black United Methodist clergyman, the Reverend Joseph Lowery.

See also POLITICS: / Young, Andrew; URBANIZATION: / Birmingham; Montgomery; WOMEN'S LIFE: / Baker, Ella Jo

Dennis C. Dickerson
Rhodes College

Southern Christian Leadership Conference Records, Department of Economic Affairs, 1965 folder, 37:2, Martin Luther King, Jr., Center for Nonviolent Social Change Archives, Atlanta, Ga.; Adam Fairclough, *To Redeem the Soul of America: The Southern Christian Leadership Conference and Martin Luther King, Jr.* (1987); Grant Files, Southern Christian Leadership Conference, PA67–580, Ford Foundation Archives, Ford Foundation, New York, N.Y.; David L. Lewis, *King: A Critical Biography* (1970); Aldon D. Morris, *The Origins of the Civil Rights Movement: Black Communities Organizing for Change* (1984); Stephen B. Oates, *Let the Trumpet Sound: The Life of Martin Luther, King, Jr.* (1982).

Storyville

From 1 October 1897 until midnight 12 November 1917 New Orleans had a legally established district for prostitution. Although most often referred to by those who frequented it as "the District," the press called it Storyville for Alderman Sidney Story, who introduced Ordinance Number 13032 that created it.

The boundaries of Storyville were Customhouse (later renamed Iberville) Street, Basin Street, St. Louis Street, and North Robertson Street. This area—today almost totally covered by a federal housing project—lies just east (or downriver) of Canal Street and north (toward Lake Pontchartrain) of the French Quarter. A separate district, meant for blacks, was bounded by Perdido, Gravier, Franklin, and Locust Streets (now covered by government buildings). Storyville itself, however, was inhabited by both blacks and whites.

Prostitution has a long history in New Orleans. French methods of colonization included sending shipments of women from correctional institutions. The French did not stress the importance of sending family groups of settlers, who presumably would have set a higher moral tone. Additionally, the city was first and foremost a port, with the waterfront hell-raising of the usual port city.

Storyville was in some ways the result of a reform movement; unable to eliminate vice, the idea was to control prostitution by organizing it. Storyville could only have flourished, though, in a corrupt environment. Police were underpaid and not well disciplined, and political ward bosses—the Old Regular organization—had great authority to do as they pleased. Above all, the profits were high—for landlords, bar and cafe owners, liquor distributors, and even clothing stores. Storyville, in 1897, seemed to be an idea whose time had come.

In the beginning there were some 230 houses of prostitution and about 2,000 working prostitutes in Storyville. There was a directory, the Blue Book, issued from about 1901 to 1915 in at least 12 editions. The Blue Books listed prostitutes (sometimes divided into blacks and whites, and even Jews and Christians) and carried advertisements: for houses such as Madam Lulu White's Mahogany Hall, for cafes and dance halls, and even for venereal disease cures. Newspapers such as the *Mascot* and the *Sunday Sun* had lurid gossip columns (sometimes detailing peccadillos of New Orleans socialites as well as Storyville regulars). There was an annual Storyville Mardi Gras ball and even a Storyville photographer, Ernest J. Bellocq, whose work has received just praise in recent years and served as the model for Louis Malle's movie *Pretty Baby* (1978).

Storyville may have been many things, but it was not the birthplace of jazz. The main business of the district was prostitution. The pianist, or professor, might entertain the customers in the parlor or play for "naked dances," and the cafes and dance halls did have bands. But jazz, that amalgam of African musical traditions and European instruments and melodies, was evolving before Storyville and was heard at picnics, parades, and dances throughout the city. Jazz fans in New Orleans did not have to go to Storyville to hear it.

Jazz musicians, however, did work there. Tony Jackson (composer of "Pretty Baby") and Ferdinand "Jelly Roll" Morton played piano in houses. Joseph "King" Oliver, Edward "Kid" Ory, Johnny St. Cyr, Freddie Keppard, and Charles "Buddy" Bolden all played there. Louis Armstrong was old enough to sneak in and listen in his youth but not old enough to play in Storyville.

Although Storyville had ornate houses and beautiful women, it was also tough, dirty, and dangerous. The suicide rate was high. Venereal disease was ever present. Opium dens existed and cocaine, or "nose candy," was sold at drugstores. White slavery, child prostitution, lewd performances or "circuses," illegitimacy, and poverty were common. All conceivable crimes of violence—murders, attacks, rapes, robberies, general shoot-outs, poisonings, burnings, knife fights, eye-gougings—were committed in Storyville.

In the last years of the district the population dwindled. Some madams relocated in New Orleans; many moved upriver to Chicago or to other, more fertile economic fields. Finally, with World War I approaching and the morals of sailors at a nearby naval installation in mind, Secretary of the Navy Josephus Daniels suggested and New Orleans Mayor Martin Behrman concurred that Storyville be closed at midnight, 12 November 1917. Only 100 houses and 400 prostitutes remained.

Already dying, Storyville was killed by public opinion. There was a consensus that an officially organized vice district just did not work. As a marketplace, Storyville ceased to exist, but its commodity did not.

"You can make prostitution illegal in Louisiana," Mayor Behrman said, "but you can't make it unpopular."

See also HISTORY AND MANNERS: Sexuality; MUSIC: / Armstrong, Louis; Bolden, Buddy; Morton, Jelly Roll; Oliver, King; URBANIZATION: / New Orleans

Carolyn Goldsby Kolb
New Orleans, Louisiana

Russell Levy, "Of Bards and Bawds: New Orleans Sporting Life before and during the Storyville Era, 1897–1917" (M.A. thesis, Tulane University, 1967); Alan Lomax, *Mr. Jelly Roll* (1950); Al Rose, *Storyville, New Orleans: Being an Authentic, Illustrated Account of the Notorious Red-Light District* (1974); T. Harry Williams, *Huey Long* (1969).

Student Nonviolent Coordinating Committee (SNCC)

Formed in April 1960, the Student Nonviolent Coordinating Committee (SNCC) drew heavily from Nashville student activists committed to nonviolent direct action. In 1961 Congress of Racial Equality (CORE) leaders asked SNCC to help black students who were waging unsuccessful lunch counter sit-ins in Rock Hill, S.C. Fifteen SNCC members joined the efforts and initiated the "jail-no bail" protest strategy.

SNCC's next major wave of activity came during the CORE-initiated Freedom Ride of 1961. When in the face of violence in Alabama CORE leaders called off the project, SNCC members resumed the trip and traveled to Montgomery, where further violence erupted. SNCC, CORE, and the Southern Christian Leadership Conference (SCLC) formed the Freedom Riders Coordinating Committee, which solicited more participants to extend the rides to Jackson, Miss. Clayborne Carson notes that SNCC workers gained a reputation as the "shock troops" of the civil rights movement.

In 1961 SNCC developed both a protest wing and a voter registration one. Robert Moses headed SNCC's voter registration efforts in Mississippi, and James Forman became the group's new executive secretary. As the Mississippi efforts floundered in the face of resistance, other SNCC staff members launched massive protests of blacks in Albany, Ga., between fall 1961 and summer 1962.

In 1962 and 1963 SNCC staff members became increasingly effective as community organizers, and membership grew. James Forman recruited many notable young black leaders, such as Julian Bond, and activists such as Fannie Lou Hamer joined SNCC's staff. SNCC built support among northerners and expanded its community organization efforts in southwest Georgia and Mississippi. SNCC members increasingly criticized the Kennedy Administration and black groups such as the SCLC and only reluctantly supported the coalition that planned the 1963 March on Washington.

In 1964 SNCC leaders initiated the Mississippi Summer Project, a plan to enlist a massive force of white student volunteers as field-workers. All of the other major civil rights organizations supported the plan, and SNCC vied to maintain its leadership role. One 1964 effort was formation of the Mississippi Freedom Democratic party, an alternate Democratic political organization that hoped to challenge the regular party in Mississippi for seating at the Democratic national convention. Through separate voter registration procedures, over 80,000 blacks participated in the SNCC-organized "freedom vote." Though the MFD party challenge gained national support, it ultimately failed. The other major thrust of the Summer Project was establishment of "freedom schools" to educate young blacks in Mississippi. Over 2,000 students attended classes in the 41 schools.

After the murder of SNCC volunteer Andrew Goodman and CORE workers James Chaney and Michael Schwerner in Mississippi in 1964, SNCC moved toward approval of armed self-defense and helped black residents near Selma and Montgomery form the Lowndes County Freedom Organization (LCFO), known as the Black Panther party, headed by Stokely Carmichael.

Ambivalent about SCLC's 1965 voting rights campaign in Selma, Ala., SNCC became active in the Alabama protests after SNCC and SCLC marchers were attacked outside Selma in early spring. Following the Selma to Montgomery march led by Martin Luther King, Jr., SNCC recruited many black college students in Alabama, strengthened its militant focus, and targeted economic reforms and black pride themes. In 1966 Carmichael became chairman, leaders such as Robert Moses and Julian Bond left, and whites were virtually expelled. A tumultous period followed, and by 1970 SNCC had disintegrated amidst internal conflict and widespread criticism.

Sharon A. Sharp
University of Mississippi

Inge Powell Bell, *CORE and the Strategy of Nonviolence* (1968); Clayborne Carson, *In Struggle: SNCC and the Black Awakening of the 1960s* (1981); James Forman, *The Making of Black Revolutionaries: A Personal Account* (1972); C. Eric Lincoln, in *The American Negro Reference Book*, ed. John P. Davis (1966); Howard Zinn, *SNCC: The New Abolitionists* (1964).

Toomer, Jean

(1894–1967) Writer.

The only child of Nina Pinchback and Nathan Toomer, Nathan Eugene Toomer, also known as Jean Toomer, was born in the Washington, D.C., home of his grandparents, Nina Emily Hethorne and P. B. S. Pinchback. Born into a socially and politically prominent family—Pinchback was the first black lieutenant governor of Louisiana during Reconstruction—Toomer enjoyed the advantages and privileges of a middle-class family.

Toomer received his primary and secondary education in the public schools of the District of Columbia. After graduating from M Street High School (now known as Paul Laurence Dunbar High) in 1914, Toomer studied scientific agriculture at the University of Wisconsin, sociology at the University of Chicago, and law at the City College of New York. Toomer's range of interests was impressive, but it revealed not so much the possibilities of an expansive intellect as the workings of an anxious mind in search of what he would later call an "intelligible scheme." The chaotic years between 1914 and 1919, described by Toomer as the "years of wandering," were not completely devoid of order. During this period, Toomer experimented with writing and discovered such writers as Walt Whitman, George Bernard Shaw, and Waldo Frank. These writers exercised an extraordinary influence over Toomer: from Whitman, Toomer sensed the potentialities of ordinary speech; from Shaw, he discovered the didactic uses of art; in Frank, he found a friend and mentor who was instrumental in publishing the single work on which his reputation as an imaginative artist rests—*Cane* (1923).

A collection of verse, prose, and drama, *Cane* was the outcome of a two-month sojourn in the fall of 1921 in Sparta, Ga., where Toomer was acting principal of the Sparta Normal and Industrial Institute. Toomer responded passionately to the black folk culture whose dissolution is the subject of *Cane*. Toomer's sensual portrayal of black life, his emphasis on black folk culture, his experimentation with jazz forms and imagist techniques forged new artistic possibilities for the writers of the New Negro movement.

Toomer's southern sojourn had personal as well as artistic consequences. Long in search of a sense of wholeness, the young author of *Cane* achieved a unity of art and being while in the South never matched by his conversion to Quakerism, his involvement in Dianectics, and most important of all his work as a teacher of the psychological theories of George I. Gurdjieff. Gurdjieff's theories did not impart to the large body of fiction, verse, and drama written after 1923 the depth of feeling and the complexity of thought so characteristic of *Cane*. This fact explains why so much of the writing after *Cane* remains unpublished and why Toomer died in Doylestown, Penn., in obscurity and isolation.

Rudolph P. Byrd
Los Angeles, California

Brian Joseph Benson and Mabel Mayle Dillard, *Jean Toomer* (1980); Nellie Y. McKay, *Jean Toomer, Artist: A Study of His Literary Life and Work, 1894–1936* (1984); Darwin Turner, *In a Minor Chord: Three Afro-American Writers and Their Search for Identity* (1971).

Turner, Nat

(1800–1831) Slave.

Born in Southampton County, Va., Turner was a black American slave who led the Southampton insurrection, which has often been seen as the most effective slave rebellion in the South. In recent years, Turner has been a focus of cultural and historical debate.

Turner is the dominant figure among a trio of insurrectionists who led major uprisings, beginning in 1800 with Gabriel Prosser, continuing with Denmark Vesey in 1822, and ending with Turner in 1831. Famous in the folklore and oral history of black Americans, these rebels expressed the powerful urges of blacks to be free. Called "Ol' Prophet Nat" and leader of the most violent of the rebellions, Turner became an especially vivid figure in the underground history of American slavery.

Turner was born to a black woman owned by a plantation aristocrat also named Turner. Transported from Africa in her youth, Nat Turner's mother imbued in him a passion for freedom. Always dreamy and visionary, he learned to read, probably taught by his master's son, and early displayed strong religious feelings. As an adult he became a preacher among the slaves. Sold by the Turner family to a less prosperous farmer and sold again to a Southampton craftsman named Joseph Travis, Turner bitterly withdrew into religious fantasies marked by omens, signs, and visions. Turner burned for his freedom, but he also saw himself as a savior of his people. Following an eclipse of the sun, taken as a sign from the Lord, Turner and four trusted lieutenants embarked upon the bloody insurrection on the night of 21 August 1831, beginning with the slaughter of the Travis family. By 23 August, when the rebellion was thwarted by militia, Turner's rebels had killed almost 60 white men, women, and children. Turner escaped capture for six weeks, but eventually was caught, tried, and executed, as were some 16 others involved with him.

The cultural debate over Turner was sparked in 1967 by the publication of William Styron's novel *The Confessions of Nat Turner*. Though Daniel Panger published *Ol' Prophet Nat* (1967), it was Styron's best seller that challenged black Americans, historians, and social critics, for it raised questions on Turner, black history, and the "true" character ("Sambo" or "rebel") of the slave in the South. The co-opting of Turner by a white author prompted, for example, a polemical outcry called *William Styron's Nat Turner: Ten Black Writers Respond* (1968). Coming in the midst of the social revolution of the 1960s, Panger's, Styron's, and many others' works devoted to the Southampton Revolt soon made Turner a symbol of "Black Power and social liberation."

See also LITERATURE: / Styron, William

James M. Mellard
Northern Illinois University

John B. Duff and Peter M. Mitchell, *The Nat Turner Rebellion: The Historical Event and the Modern Controversy* (1971); Stephen B. Oates, *The Fires of Jubilee: Nat Turner's Fierce*

Rebellion (1975); Henry L. Tragle, *The Southampton Slave Revolt of 1831: A Compilation of Source Material* (1971).

Walker, Margaret

(b. 1915) Writer.

One of the first Afro-American writers to return to the region for a career after establishing a national literary reputation, Margaret Walker occupies an important transitional position in the history of southern letters. Born in Birmingham, Ala., on 27 July 1915, Walker left the South to earn her B.A. at Northwestern University (1935) and her M.A. at Iowa (1940). While a student, she worked with the Federal Writers' Project and began work on the poems included in *For My People* (1942), which won the Yale Award for Younger Poets. Pursuing her career in education, Walker taught at Livingstone College (North Carolina) and West Virginia State College before joining the faculty of Jackson State (Mississippi) in 1949. Married and the mother of four children, she has taught English, directed the Institute for the Study of the History, Life, and Culture of Black People, and conducted research for a biography of Richard Wright since that time. Her novel *Jubilee* (1966) solidified her literary reputation and has been translated into numerous languages.

Margaret Walker, Mississippi writer, 1976

Walker's writing is significant both for its celebration of Afro-American folklife and for its challenge to the romanticized plantation tradition of Thomas Nelson Page and Margaret Mitchell. "For My People," the poem that provided both the title and the central themes for Walker's first collection, traces the history of Afro-Americans from the rural South to the urban North and culminates in a vision of racial assertion and transcendence that anticipated and inspired many younger Afro-American poets. A brilliant reader of her own poetry, Walker draws heavily on the Afro-American oral tradition in poems such as "Kissie Lee" and "Molly Means." Walker's decision to publish two chapbooks—*Prophets for a New Day* (1970) and *October Journey* (1970)—with the black-operated Broadside Press reflects the evolution of Walker's voice evident in poems such as "For Malcolm X" and "Lineage," which has become a minor feminist classic. Similarly, as Walker explains in the monograph *How I Wrote Jubilee* (1971), *Jubilee* relies on materials derived from oral history to counter the romantic image of slavery propagated by works such as *Gone with the Wind*. In addition to presenting an Afro-American vision of the real nature of slavery and Reconstruction, the novel emphasizes the special perspective of the Afro-American woman who must suffer the main effects of violence from whites and blacks. *A Poetic Equation: Conversations between Nikki Giovanni and Margaret Walker* (1974) demonstrates Walker's continuing concern with the racial and sexual issues raised in her poetry and fiction.

See also LITERATURE: / Wright, Richard; MEDIA: / *Gone with the Wind*

Craig Werner
University of Wisconsin

Adrianne Baytop, in *American Women Writers: A Critical Reference Guide from Colonial Times to the Present*, vol. 4, ed. Lina Mainiero (1982); Maxine Block, ed., *Current Biography* (November 1943); Michael L. Edwards, *The Rhetoric of Afro-American Poetry: A Rhetorical Analysis of Black Poetry and the Selected Poetry of Margaret Walker and Langston Hughes* (1980); Elaine M. Newsome, in *Southern Writers: A Biographical Dictionary*, ed. Robert Bain, Joseph M. Flora, and Louis D. Rubin, Jr. (1979).

Washington, Booker T.

(1856–1915) Educator.

Booker Taliaferro Washington was the foremost black educator of the late 19th and early 20th centuries. He also had a major influence on southern race relations and was the dominant figure in black public affairs from 1895 until his death in 1915. Born a slave on a small farm in the Virginia backcountry, he moved with his family after

Booker T. Washington, black educator, c. 1900

emancipation to work in the salt furnaces and coal mines of West Virginia. After a secondary education at Hampton Institute, he taught an upgraded school and experimented briefly with the study of law and the ministry, but a teaching position at Hampton decided his future career. In 1881 he founded Tuskegee Normal and Industrial Institute on the Hampton model in the Black Belt of Alabama.

Though Washington offered little that was innovative in industrial education, which both northern philanthropic foundations and southern leaders were already promoting, he became its chief black exemplar and spokesman. In his advocacy of Tuskegee Institute and its educational method, Washington revealed the political adroitness and accommodationist philosophy that were to characterize his career in the wider arena of race leadership. He convinced southern white employers and governors that Tuskegee offered an education that would keep blacks "down on the farm" and in the trades. To prospective northern donors and particularly the new self-made millionaires such as Rockefeller and Carnegie he promised the inculcation of the Protestant work ethic. To blacks living within the limited horizons of the post-Reconstruction South, Washington held out industrial education as the means of escape from the web of sharecropping and debt and the achievement of attainable, *petit-bourgeois* goals of self-employment, landownership, and small business. Washington cultivated local white approval and secured a small state appropriation, but it was northern donations that made Tuskegee Institute by 1900 the best-supported black educational institution in the country.

The Atlanta Compromise Address, delivered before the Cotton States Exposition in 1895, enlarged Washington's influence into the arena of race relations and black leadership. Washington offered black acquiescence in disfranchisement and social segregation if whites would encourage black progress in economic and educational opportunity. Hailed as a sage by whites of both sections, Washington further consolidated his influence by his widely read autobiography *Up From Slavery* (1901), the founding of the National Negro Business League in 1900, his celebrated dinner at the White House in 1901, and control of patronage politics as chief black advisor to Presidents Theodore Roosevelt and William Howard Taft.

Washington kept his white following by conservative policies and moderate utterances, but he faced growing black and white liberal opposition in the Niagara Movement (1905–9) and the NAACP (1909–), groups demanding civil rights and encouraging protest in response to white aggressions such as lynchings, disfranchisement, and segregation laws. Washington successfully fended off these critics, often by underhanded means. At the same time, however, he tried to translate his own personal success into black advancement through secret sponsorship of civil rights suits, serving on the boards of Fisk and Howard universities, and directing philanthropic aid to these and other black colleges. His speaking tours and private persuasion tried to equalize public educational opportunities and to reduce racial violence. These efforts were generally unsuccessful, and the year of Washington's death marked the beginning of the Great Migration from the rural South to the urban North. Washington's racial philosophy, pragmatically adjusted to the limiting conditions of his own era, did not survive the change.

See also EDUCATION: / Fisk University; Hampton Institute; Tuskegee Institute

Louis R. Harlan
University of Maryland

Louis R. Harlan, *Booker T. Washington*, 2 vols. (1972, 1983), with Raymond W. Smock, eds., *The Booker T. Washington Papers*, 12 vols. (1972–); August Meier, *Negro Thought in America, 1880–1915* (1963).

Wells-Barnett, Ida

(1862–1931) Journalist and social activist.

On 16 July 1862, Ida Bell Wells-Barnett, a future journalist, club woman, and militant antilynching crusader, was born a slave in Holly Springs, Miss. The oldest daughter of slave parents James and Elizabeth (Bowling) Wells, she received her public school education in Holly Springs and attended Rust College, which was founded in

1866 as an industrial school for blacks in Holly Springs. A yellow fever epidemic took the lives of Wells's parents, leaving her, at the age of 14, in charge of her younger brothers and sisters. In order to support herself and her siblings, Wells began teaching at a nearby rural school, while attending Rust College.

In 1884 Wells moved her family to Memphis, Tenn., to be near an aunt and to obtain a better-paying teaching position. Before passing the teaching examination for the Memphis public schools, Ida Wells taught at a rural school outside Memphis. In Tennessee she began her lifelong public crusade against injustice and inequality, successfully suing in 1884 the Chesapeake and Ohio Railroad Company for attempting to force her to sit in the smoking car that had been designated for blacks. The lower court decision in Wells's favor was subsequently overruled by the Tennessee Supreme Court.

While in Tennessee, Wells became part owner and editor of a local black newspaper, the Memphis *Free Speech and Headlight* (shortened by Wells to *Free Speech*). Her previous journalistic experience included occasional articles, primarily on race relations in the South, under the pen name "Iola," for religious publications and black newspapers. In 1891 Wells lost her teaching job in Memphis, following the publication in the *Free Speech* of articles critical of the school system's unequal allocation of resources to black schools. The next year a Wells editorial denouncing lynching in general and the lynching of three Memphis blacks in particular resulted in the destruction of the *Free Speech* building and threats on her life.

Although forced thereafter to live outside the South, Wells continued her campaign against racial injustice, especially the lynchings of blacks, as a columnist for the *New York Age*, as an author, and as a prominent lecturer on racial injustice in the United States and abroad. In 1895 she published a pamphlet entitled *A Red Record: Tabulated Statistics and Alleged Causes of Lynchings in the United States, 1892–1893–1894*, which later appeared in London under the title *United States Atrocities*. In her crusade against lynching, the articulate Wells delivered numerous lectures, aided in the formation of antilynching societies in England, and met with President William McKinley in 1898, along with other blacks, to protest the lynchings of blacks. Her fight against injustice also led to the denunciation of black exclusion from the Chicago World's Fair in 1893. She collaborated with Frederick Douglass, Ferdinand L. Barnett (whom she later married), and I. Garland Penn on a publication entitled *The Reason Why the Colored American Is Not in the World's Columbian Exposition—The Afro-American's Contribution to Columbian Literature*.

In 1895 Ida married Ferdinand Lee Barnett, Assistant State's Attorney for Cook County and editor of the Chicago *Conservator*, the first black newspaper in Chicago. Wells then turned her attention to local civic activities. She founded and served as an officer in numerous women's groups, earning the title among some as the "Mother of Clubs." With money provided by some of the organizations she was active in, as well as with her own personal funds, Wells-Barnett traveled to Arkansas and Illinois to investigate race riots during World War I and in the postwar years reported on them for various black newspapers. Up to the time of her death in Chicago on 25 March 1931, Ida B. Wells-Barnett devoted her life to fighting for full equality for blacks and women throughout the United States, but especially in the South.

Sharon Harley
University of Maryland

Alfreda M. Duster, *Crusade for Justice: The Autobiography of Ida B. Wells* (1970); Ida B. Wells-Barnett, *On Lynchings* (1969).

"We Shall Overcome"

"We Shall Overcome" began as a labor song and became the anthem of the black freedom movement of the 1960s. The song was first used during a drive by the Congress of Industrial Organizations in the 1940s to organize Piedmont Carolina textile workers. Black tobacco workers in Charleston, S.C., used the song on the picket lines in 1945, and they brought it to the Highlander Folk School in Tennessee. From there it was conveyed to union leaders across the South.

Highlander was a training center in the 1950s for labor organizers and for civil rights workers, especially activists who later founded the Student Nonviolent Coordinating Committee. For six years before the first sit-ins in 1960, blacks and whites had held workshops at Highlander, with singing a part of the activities. "We Shall Overcome" was already identified with Highlander, and Guy Carawan, a white Californian (of southern-born parents), taught the song to the mostly young activists in the late 1950s. The song was copyrighted in 1960, by Ludlow Music, Inc., with words and music credited to Zelphia Horton, Frank Hamilton, Guy Carawan, and Pete Seeger. In fact, "We Shall Overcome" was an adaptation of an old black church tune, "I'll Overcome Someday."

According to Carawan, the first use of "We Shall Overcome" as part of a mass civil rights protest may have been outside the mayor's office in Nashville, Tenn., in the early 1960s. He led a group singing of the song in April 1960, in Raleigh, N.C., as part of a meeting at Shaw University on sit-ins. Jane Stembridge, an activist in the audience, later wrote that the song conveyed an inspiring "common vision" to the protestors. "We Shall Overcome" was widely used during the 1961 protest in Albany, Ga. Bernice Reagon recalled that the song "released a kind of power and required a level of concentrated energy I did not know I had." It was the official theme song of the 1963 March on Washington.

"We Shall Overcome" was the best known of the freedom songs that were a vital part of the black freedom movement. Often based on spirituals or black church music, freedom songs were one of the most emotionally moving aspects of the culture of protest. Civil rights activists testified to the power of those songs to stir the soul and to awaken the power of the black religious tradition and focus it on righteous protest. The SNCC Freedom Singers began touring the nation in 1962, singing freedom songs to raise money, and many freedom songs were later adapted by other protest movements in this nation and overseas.

Charles Reagan Wilson
University of Mississippi

Frank Adams, with Myles Horton, *Unearthing Seeds of Fire: The Idea of Highlander* (1975); Guy Carawan and Candie Carawan, compilers, *Songs of the Southern Freedom Movement: We Shall Overcome!* (1963); Josh Dunson, *Freedom in the Air: Song Movements of the 60's* (1965), *Sing Out* (September 1964); Bernice Reagon, *Sing Out* (January–February 1976).

Williams, Robert F.

(b. 1925) Black activist.

Williams was typical of the generation of southern blacks who launched the civil rights movement in the 1950s. Born in Monroe, N.C., in 1925, Williams grew up in a segregated society, served in the Marines during the Korean War, and after living briefly in Detroit, returned to North Carolina in 1955. He was active in the Monroe black community, and as president of the Union County NAACP led a series of demonstrations against Jim Crow practices and racial discrimination in hiring. In 1957 Williams organized a black rifle club, whose first public activity was to repel an armed Ku Klux Klan attack. When an all-white jury in 1959 acquitted a white man charged with attempted rape of a pregnant black woman, Williams angrily called for blacks to take up arms, to meet "violence with violence" (which he later clarified to mean "the right of armed self-defense against attack"). This outburst resulted in a six-month suspension by the national NAACP office and made him something of a pariah with the civil rights establishment, which then strongly supported Martin Luther King's nonviolent philosophy.

Williams's problems were only beginning. In the summer of 1961 Monroe was on the brink of race war, with the picketing of the public all-white swimming pool triggering armed conflict between the races. In the midst of the melee a white couple drove into a black neighborhood. A crowd of angry blacks marched the whites to Williams's home, where he held them for a few hours before releasing the couple unharmed. Charged with kidnapping, Williams fled the country with his wife and two children.

Williams spent the critical years of the civil rights movement in exile, first in Cuba and later in China. His book, *Negroes with Guns*, appeared in 1962. While in Cuba he broadcast a weekly radio message beamed at the South over "Radio Free Dixie" and edited his newsletter, *The Crusader*. As the movement in this country intensified, so did Williams's militancy; he called for revolution and urged blacks not to fight in Vietnam. While in China he was elected president-in-exile of the separatist Republic of New Africa. Increasingly frustrated by his inability to participate directly in the black struggle, Williams returned to the United States in 1963, living in Michigan while fighting extradition to stand trial in North Carolina. The state finally dropped the kidnapping charges in 1976, allegedly because the surviving white witness was too ill to testify.

Robert Williams's transformation from local NAACP leader to Third World revolutionary underscores the rapid and turbulent evolution of the civil rights movement in the South. His call for blacks to arm themselves, at first so shocking, had by the mid-1960s won support among many southern blacks, who knew from experience that violence had historically defined race relations in their region, and who—like Williams—were now unwilling to turn the other cheek.

John Dittmer
DePauw University

Harold Cruse, *The Crisis of the Negro Intellectual* (1967); James Forman, *The Making of Black Revolutionaries: A Personal Account* (1972); Robert F. Williams, *Negroes with Guns* (1962).

Woodson, Carter G.

(1875–1950) Historian

In 1915 Carter G. Woodson, who was born in New Canton, Va., a son of former slaves, organized the Association for the Study of Negro Life and History. He began publishing the *Journal of Negro History* 1 January 1916 and remained its editor until his 1950 death. Through the *Journal* and through his Associated Publishers, in Washington, D.C., he countered the bias permeating many contemporary accounts of slavery and the black man.

Woodson's 1922 *The Negro in Our History* went through 10 editions and was for many years the most widely used college text on the subject. But as time went on, Woodson turned more and more to racial propaganda in an effort to uplift his people. As one who had risen from a six-year stint in the coalfields of West Virginia to study at Berea College (1896–98), earn B.A. and M.A. degrees at the University of Chicago, take a 1912 Harvard Ph.D. in history, and become dean of liberal arts at Howard University (1919) and West Virginia State College (1920), he had an understandably sure sense of his own abilities. A self-made man, he was successful as an academician and publisher, and he believed in the need to present successful role models to black schoolchildren. As a result he wrote race history, emphasizing examples of individual success. His program for solving the problems of blacks in America was not unlike that of Booker T. Washington, whom he greatly admired.

Woodson became an entrenched member of the "black bourgeoisie." He adopted its mid-19th-century middle-class (white) values. He never learned to think in terms of black power—whether it be labor-union power or mass voting power.

Whatever his shortcomings as a historian and as a theorist, Carter G. Woodson was able to create, through his *Journal* and his Associated Publishers, vehicles for an alternative definition of the black situation to those that dominated American publishing throughout his lifetime.

S. P. Fullinwider
Arizona State University

Frank Klingberg, *Journal of Negro History* (January 1956); Michael Winston, *Journal of Negro History* (October 1975); James O. Young, *Black Writers of the Thirties* (1973).

Education

THOMAS G. DYER
University of Georgia
CONSULTANT

Schoolbus, Medora School, southwestern Jefferson County, Ky., c. 1930

Education

In recent years a resurgence of interest in the history of American education has yielded a sizable body of scholarship that alters many traditional ideas about the educational process in the South and its relationship to the broader social fabric. Although this research is not extensive enough to permit a thoroughgoing reinterpretation of southern educational history, a foundation has been laid to provide the basis for a broad overview. Scholars and laymen still have no useful modern guide to the evolution of the southern system of education and no interpretation that locates the regional experience within the broader national context.

Education in the American South has been characterized by an incessant quest for equality with educational systems outside the region. In many ways the region has been engaged in an unstinting effort for at least two centuries to develop an educational apparatus of quality comparable to that of the remainder of the nation. This self-conscious quest to obtain educational equality with more progressive systems elsewhere has been strongly inhibited by the region's peculiar values and culture. Furthermore, the most significant changes in schooling processes in the South have occurred in response to non-southern influences.

Early Educational Patterns. During the colonial era southerners accepted the English notion of education as a private responsibility. As a result, a stigma surrounded publicly supported education and led to a disparagement of those individuals who were unable to pay for instruction. Sparseness of settlement and a lack of effective governmental apparatus also inhibited the growth of schools in the South. Thus, the socializing effects of education were usually confined to areas where sufficient collective wealth existed to pay tutors for the education of children or where the means of an individual planter or merchant permitted the underwriting of his children's education.

As much interest existed in higher education in the prerevolutionary South as in the lower levels. Some southerners sent their sons to one of the nine colonial colleges located from Virginia northward, while a very few arranged for their education abroad. The attempt to found colleges in the region also reflected interest in higher education. The College of William and Mary, established in 1696, achieved true collegiate status by the third decade of the 18th century, but no other college came into existence in the South prior to the American Revolution. A few other attempts had been made, most notably perhaps the effort mounted by the trustees of Georgia to transfer a college planned for Bermuda to Georgia and a later plan, designed by the evangelist George Whitefield, which pointed toward the establishment of what would have been a denominational, provincial college in Savannah.

The revolutionary era produced significant interest in both common schools and colleges, and the libertarian forces unleashed by the Revolution contributed to a new interest in state systems of education. In several southern states plans evolved for designing unitary systems of education with state universities at the top supported by a system of academies and common schools. Most of these plans failed, although in several southern states universities did emerge prior to 1800, as did a few scattered colleges with no direct ties to the states.

In many respects, the South's educational system for the remainder of the period before the Civil War reflected the region's society and its conservative philosophy. Wealthy southerners hired private tutors for their children's instruction, while the middle class and moderately well-to-do created private contract schools and academies. For much of the period public education, in the contemporary sense of the term, was a foreign concept. The only tax-supported schools were the "poor" schools, which were set aside for those youths who would take a demeaning pauper's oath. Higher education catered to the children of the elite, and the collegiate curricula reflected the fondness of the privileged for classicism and the values of an earlier age. The region also rejected formal schooling for its black population.

This picture of southern education tends to perpetuate stereotypical notions of antebellum society without disclosing the strengths of southern education. Like their northern counterparts, southern primary and secondary schools grew and improved substantially during the pre–Civil War period. Although most of the region's schools remained privately supported, important strides were taken toward establishing tax-supported systems before the Civil War intervened. By 1861 literacy rates among whites had risen to approximately the same level as those of the midwestern states.

In still other ways the South felt the effects of the mid-19th-century educational revival. Southern colleges experimented with the introduction of collateral courses of study in the natural sciences and foreign languages. Colleges also began to admit older students of lower social station who either worked their way through school or received financial aid. Graduates of southern colleges, regardless of their social origins, played influential roles in the region's affairs both before and after the Civil War. The region also succeeded in establishing higher education for women on approximately the same level as that of the region's colleges for men. Although only a few women's colleges emerged, Wesleyan College in Macon, Ga., and several others offered a level of education that was genuinely collegiate. The sectional struggle and the coming of war negated many of these gains, as southern colleges increasingly became tools for the confirmation of regional values.

Civil War and Beyond. The Civil War disrupted education in the South, just as it thoroughly disrupted the activities of other social institutions. After the war, education resumed rather quickly at both lower and higher levels. Colleges that had been forced to close during the war now reopened, as did academies and other lower schools. During Reconstruction some state governments made appropriations for education. Perhaps the most significant question addressed during Reconstruction, however, related to the availability of education for newly freed slaves. Agents of the Freedmen's Bureau and representatives of northern churches began educational efforts in parts of the South even before the close of hostilities. With the coming of peace, large numbers of these groups began to educate the freedmen. Blacks greeted the prospect of education with great enthusiasm, viewing education as a ticket to equality in the white man's society. During Radical Reconstruction educational provisions found their way into the new state constitutions, where for the first time in southern history universal education was recognized as a right of all citizens. In addition to the constitutional provisions, state legislators passed laws that established in every southern state a state superintendent of public instruction, made provisions for the training of teachers, and authorized taxes in support of education. The region's poverty, persistent white resistance to educating blacks, and corruption in the management of state government limited the achievements of the educational reforms introduced during Reconstruction. Nevertheless, Reconstruction awakened the region to the concept of universal education and to the hope of state support for public education.

By the turn of the century, southern schools had fallen further and further behind the rest of the nation. In 1900, when the average amount expended per child for education in the United States was slightly less than three dollars, Alabama and North Carolina (at the lower end of the southern scale) provided only 50 cents per child, while Florida and Texas (at the upper end) provided slightly less than $1.50 per child. School terms in the South were less than 100 days in length as opposed to 145 days for the United States. Teachers remained very poorly trained and were pitifully paid, averaging only about one-half the amount paid teachers elsewhere in the nation. Only one southern state required school attendance, and as a result, only about 40 percent of the region's children went to school on a regular basis. Of those who did, only 1 in 10 completed the fourth grade. Schoolhouses were unbelievably primitive in the rural areas and in black areas within the cities. Secondary education throughout the region was virtually nonexistent. Illiteracy rates for the southern states greatly exceeded those in any other part of the nation. Census statistics indicated that at least half of the region's blacks could not read. Undoubtedly, even larger numbers could have been classified as functionally illiterate.

Southern colleges and universities made some progress from the close of Reconstruction until the turn of the century, but by and large they suffered from problems generated by the region's poverty. The Morrill Act of 1862 provided federal funds to designated institutions in the southern states, but state appropriations to public institutions remained quite low and, in some cases, nonexistent, as conservative southern legislators clung to a laissez-faire philosophy toward higher education. Private institutions struggled to survive on gifts from sponsoring denominations and tuition from students. Separate black colleges that opened soon after the close of the Civil War, with assistance from northern agencies like the American Missionary Association, had difficulty surviving in an atmosphere of white hostility.

For the most part, both black and white colleges adhered to classical liberal arts curricula, although a few state universities and some of the black institutions sought to incorporate agricultural and industrial training into their programs of study. There were a few efforts to introduce modern technological education, most notably at the newly founded Georgia School of Technology. Widespread education of teachers in a collegiate setting would await the second decade of the 20th century.

Reform Efforts. The beginnings of a southern educational reform movement could be discerned during the last two decades of the 19th century. A crusading spirit was brought by state leaders such as Charles B. Aycock and Edwin A. Alderman of North Carolina, Thomas U. Dudley of Kentucky, Charles W. Dabney of Tennessee, James L. Dillard of Louisiana, William N. Sheats of Florida, Oscar Cooper of Texas, J. J. Doyne of Arkansas, Braxton B. Comer of Alabama, Walter B. Hill of Georgia, and William H. Hand of South Carolina.

Funds provided by George F. Peabody, a Massachusetts banker, for the improvement of education at the elementary and secondary levels promoted the establishment of model schools and the improvement of individual schools. J. L. M. Curry, administrator of the Peabody Fund, proselytized throughout the region on behalf of education. Another eastern philanthropist, Robert C. Ogden, with the aid of people like Curry, established a series of educational conferences held throughout the region. These conferences, which coincided with an awakening of Progressivism in the region, brought an outpouring of interest in public education. Progressive southern governors sponsored legislation and constitutional revisions that led to dramatic increases in school revenues, a lengthening of the school terms, increases in the salaries of teachers, and decreases in the illiteracy rate. In addition, consolidation of rural schools followed, and by 1920 important strides had been taken toward establishing widespread public secondary education. During the first three decades of the 20th century, appropriations for education in all the southern states rose dramatically but stayed well below the national average.

Blacks by no means participated fully in the improvements of that era. Black education did benefit somewhat, however, from the introduction of Morrill funds, support of vocational education, and agencies like the Peabody Fund, the General Education Board, the John F. Slater Fund, and the Anna T. Jeanes Fund. In addition, philanthropies like the Rosenwald Foundation contributed millions of dollars toward the construction of black schools.

Despite the improvements in both black and white education during the Progressive era, the region's schools remained woefully inadequate. A few centers of achievement did appear, most notably in higher education, and the South committed an increasingly large percentage of its resources to the support of education. Southern schools, however, made relatively little progress in the

Mother teaching children in a sharecropper home, Transylvania, La., 1939

game of catch-up, which they would play for decades to come. The agricultural depression of the 1920s and the Great Depression of the 1930s compounded an already difficult fiscal situation. Also, the region's largely rural culture placed a low premium on education for both whites and blacks. Whites refused to acknowledge that blacks should receive equal education, or for that matter be educated beyond even the barest rudiments. State legislators throughout the region saw that black schools received only a fraction of the meager support that flowed to all of education.

Expansion of Education after World War II. As the Depression closed and World War II began, the southern economy entered a period of growth and increasing prosperity. A high birthrate during the war and rapid urbanization helped create a stronger demand for quality education. The growing prosperity of the region promoted increases in funding for education. Consolidation of schools became a hallmark in rural education, while in cities and suburbs massive construction programs were made possible by steadily increasing appropriations from state legislators. In addition to physical growth the region also turned its attention to salaries of teachers and requirements for teacher certification. Libraries and curricula grew, and secondary schools increasingly provided not only college preparatory education but also vocational-technical education.

In addition to the massive infusion of funds into elementary and secondary education, large amounts were also spent on improving the region's public colleges and universities. Long hampered by pitiful support from the states and by inferior facilities and faculties, these institutions now benefited from a growing awareness of the importance of higher education to the modernization of southern society. The appearance of large numbers of veterans on southern campuses following World War II added a much-welcomed source of revenue. The veterans' presence on campus helped to change the orientation of

Table 1. *Doctoral Programs at Southern Universities, 1879–1962*

			Average Doctorates Per Year 1953–62	
State	University	First Earned Doctorate Awarded	Arts and Sciences Only	Including Education
Alabama	Auburn	1955	4	9
	U. Alabama	1952	12	17
Arkansas	U. Arkansas	1953	7	16
Florida	Florida State	1952	31	43
	U. Florida	1934	65	79
	U. Miami	1962	1	1
Georgia	Emory	1948	15	15
	Georgia Inst. of Tech.	1950	10	10
	U. Georgia	1940	5	9
Kentucky	U. Kentucky	1930	23	30
	U. Louisville	1953	6	6
Louisiana	Louisiana State U.	1935	52	58
	Tulane	1887	27	27
Mississippi	Mississippi State U.	1960	1	1
	U. Mississippi	1950[1]	1	5
North Carolina	Duke	1928	69	73
	N.C. State U.	1948	31	31
	U. North Carolina	1883	82	93
Oklahoma	Oklahoma State U.	1948	23	33
	U. Oklahoma	1929	32	49
South Carolina	U. South Carolina	1891[2]	3	4
Tennessee	George Peabody	1919	9	33
	U. Tennessee	1886[3]	33	45
	Vanderbilt	1879	37	37
Texas	Baylor	1954	6	7
	North Texas State U.	1954	1	5
	Rice	1918	20	20
	Texas A&M	1940	35	35
	Texas Tech U.	1953	3	7
	Texas Women's U.	1953	4	7
	U. Houston	1947	9	19
	U. Texas	1915	125	152
Virginia	U. Virginia	1885	39	45
	Virginia Polytechnic Inst.	1942	13	13

Table I. *continued*

State	University	First Earned Doctorate Awarded	Average Doctorates Per Year 1953–62: Arts and Sciences Only	Including Education
West Virginia	U. West Virginia	1902	6	7
Average		—	23	30
Median		—	13	19

[1]One doctorate was granted in 1893, but none during the next 57 years.
[2]Nineteen doctorates were granted in the 60-year period 1891–1951.
[3]Four doctorates were granted in the 1886–1948 period.
Source: Allan M. Cartter, "Qualitative Aspects of Southern University Education," *Southern Economic Journal* (July 1965).

the institutions away from a strict *in loco parentis* posture. Enrollments in many southern institutions more than doubled during the late 1940s as a result of the presence of the veterans.

The southern record in higher education, however, remained well below that of the nation. Institutions such as the University of North Carolina or the University of Texas occasionally achieved national recognition for individual programs, but the achievements of most public and private universities in the region were not compatible with national norms. Indeed, southern *universities* remained little more than large liberal arts *colleges* with a modicum of professional education and little substantial graduate education.

In the early 1950s academicians and politicians developed an enlarged awareness of the importance of research in a university environment. There was a nascent recognition of the availability of federal and foundation funds for the support of research. Accordingly, in the 1950s many state and private institutions hired faculty who had both instructional and research skills. Their research led to a growth in outside funding for university programs during the late 1950s. With the 1958 National Defense Education Act, in the wake of the Russian launching of Sputnik, federal support increased exponentially, even though southern institutions did not share in the increased federal funding as greatly as colleges and universities in other parts of the nation.

The new dollars strengthened research and instructional areas of the universities. For the next 30 years southern universities steadily built their research components and worked to achieve the comprehensiveness that had marked the nation's better research universities. Institutions like the University of Florida and the University of Georgia as well as private institutions like Duke and Vanderbilt now appear with increasing frequency in various national rankings of research universities.

The spurt in the growth of southern education after World War II by no means brought the region to parity with other parts of the United States. Without a concomitant move toward establishing equal educational opportunities for blacks and whites, southern education was doomed to remain grossly inferior. During the 1950s southern whites and blacks realized that educational and racial equality were inextricably intertwined. After World War II improvements and increased funds flowed to black schools as white southerners attempted to avert integration through achieving closer approximation of the separate-but-equal formula prescribed in the 1896 Supreme Court decision *Plessy* v. *Ferguson*. Whites' hopes that integration could be avoided were derailed with the *Brown* v. *Board of Education* decision in 1954.

Race Relations and Educational Quality. A program of "massive resistance" and state interposition of federal authority became hallmarks of resistance to racial change in schools. Strong pressures for change came from outside the region as federal officials, the press, and other segments of society pressed for compliance with the court's directive. The schools became a primary focus of civil rights activity as blacks and whites chose to work out many of the region's most serious problems within the schoolroom. White resistance dragged on until the early 1970s when the pressures of legal decisions and federal legislation brought integration of the region's public schools.

White and black southerners finally turned to the problem of bringing the region's schools to a level approximating national norms. Although the region still lagged behind, some progress had been made in the years since the civil rights era had begun. Virtually all areas of educational activity reflected the great increases in funds, and southern spokesmen prophesied that the region would one day become an example to the rest of the nation in the pursuit of academic excellence and equality.

By the early 1980s racial issues had largely taken second place to issues of quality at all levels of southern education. The region now has a full panoply of educational programs ranging from preschool through postsecondary to a wide variety of adult programs. A new awareness of the importance of sound education in attracting business and industry to the region has inspired a resurgence of educational reform efforts. As a result of such efforts most southern schools are now on a par with other systems across the nation. Yet the parity has resulted from a convergence of southern progress and national backsliding in educational quality. Studies such as the 1985 report *A Nation at Risk* have documented a general lowering of national educational standards and thus have provided a new benchmark against which southern educational reforms must be judged.

Beginning in 1983 most southern legislatures inaugurated far-reaching educational reforms aimed at upgrading elementary and secondary education, with special attention given to such quality indicators as teacher salaries and qualifications. So extensive and so thoroughgoing were the reforms that a former U.S. secretary of education offered the judgment that the South might prove to be the leader in a revitalization of American education.

Such reforms depend upon continued economic prosperity in the region and upon the willingness of southerners to tax themselves at higher rates than have been historically acceptable. Whether the region will be able to finance the reforms seems in doubt in some states where growth has slowed and economic recession threatens implementation of reforms. It is not clear, moreover, what effect the reforms will have upon public *higher* education, which has enjoyed considerable progress in the region. The outcome of the reform movement of the 1980s remains in doubt.

Education has been one of the main mechanisms by which southern cultural norms have been maintained and transmitted. In the antebellum era, for example, spokesmen for southern sectionalism saw a continuing struggle against the North for cultural independence, and they attempted to use the southern schools to nurture an explicitly "southern" outlook in the young. Professor J. D. B. De Bow of the University of Louisiana (and editor of *De Bow's Review*) admitted that southern schools were inferior to those elsewhere in scholarly achievement but saw it better that "our sons remained in honest ignorance and at the plough-handle" than full of "doctrines subversive of their country's peace and honor." Delegates to commercial conventions before the Civil War frequently urged the use of native-born southern teachers in schools and a home press publishing textbooks appropriate to southern traditions and interests. The persistent call for a central southern university, training students in regional values, led one group of southerners to found the University of the South at Sewanee, Tenn., in the late 1850s.

American schools have traditionally been seen as institutions of the "melting pot," assimilating children from diverse ethnic backgrounds into the dominant American culture. Studies of mass education in the 20th century now suggest, though, that the process has not worked automatically. Sociologist John Shelton Reed has concluded that the schools have been less powerful in the South than elsewhere. The schools reflect a large degree of community control, "with the culturally conservative function such control implies." Historian Francis Butler Simkins once noted that "among Southerners there is the education which does not educate." Schools have been staffed primarily by southerners who shape the interpretation of educational information in textbooks, and southern students are subject to powerful local influences that make them attuned to receive and believe certain information but not all. Simkins concluded that "the home, not the school, determines the cultural outlook of Southerners," but it is likely, in many cases, that the two reinforced each other.

Elementary school in Warren County, Miss., 1962

Certain universities have served as, in effect, regional institutions educating an elite in southern traditions or promoting regional scholarship. The University of the South, Washington and Lee University, the University of North Carolina, and the University of Virginia are only a few examples of schools promoting regionalism in one way or another. Boys' military academies have likely played a similar role at the secondary school level, although much work remains to be done in exploring this topic.

By the mid-1980s it was also unclear how extensively southern cultural norms and beliefs would affect the future course of education in the region. Much evidence existed, however, to suggest that the attenuation of cultural boundaries was proceeding apace and that the South was losing much of its distinctiveness as a result of a significant in-migration, the revolution in race relations, and the systematic exposure of the region through the mass media to dominant national values. The enthusiasm with which political leaders embraced educational reforms as a passport to economic improvement (although in some ways a reenactment of earlier regional flirtations with boosterism) suggested that the region had a stronger commitment to educational improvement than had previously characterized the culture. That southern politicians now longed for a well-trained, educated labor force (as well as a docile one) also offered at least some evidence that the region had embraced national values in that area as well.

See also AGRICULTURE: / Agricultural Extension Services; BLACK LIFE: Education, Black; HISTORY AND MANNERS: Philanthropy, Northern; Progressivism; POLITICS: Segregation, Defense of; SCIENCE AND MEDICINE: Medical Education; Professionalization of Science; / Scopes Trial; SOCIAL CLASS: Poverty; WOMEN'S LIFE: Education of Women

Thomas G. Dyer
University of Georgia

Henry A. Bullock, *A History of Negro Education in the South: From 1619 to the Present* (1967); Thomas D. Clark, *The Emerging South* (1961); Charles W. Dabney, *Universal Education in the South*, 2 vols. (1936); Irving Gershenberg, *History of Education Quarterly* (Winter 1970); Ronald K. Goodenow and Arthur O. White, eds., *Education and the Rise of the New South* (1982); Louis R. Harlan, *Separate and Unequal: Public School Campaigns and Racism in the Southern Seaboard States, 1901–1915* (1958); Diane Ravitch, *The Troubled Crusade: American Education, 1945–1980* (1983); John Shelton Reed, *One South: An Ethnic Approach to Regional Culture* (1982); Charles P. Roland, *The Improbable Era: The South since World War II* (1975); David Tyack, *Managers of Virtue: Public School Leadership in America, 1820–1980* (1982), *Public Schools in Hard Times: The Great Depression and Recent Years* (1984), ed., *Turning Points in American Educational History* (1967); William Preston Vaughn, *Schools for All: The Blacks and Public Education in the South, 1865–1877* (1974); Thomas L. Webber, *Deep Like the Rivers: Education in the Slave Quarter Community, 1831–1865* (1978).

Academic Freedom

Southern culture has presented distinctive problems for academic freedom. Sectional characteristics of religion, race relations, political conservatism, and history have sometimes brought conflicts so violent that physical safety was threatened along with freedom of thought.

More than in any other section, the people of the Bible Belt had a personal and emotional contact with their religion rather than a mere institutional membership. Believers were expected to defend their faith and did so with passions frequently dividing towns, families, and educational institutions into hostile camps. As the mission of the church was to proselytize and to educate its members in its doctrine, so the free exercise of religion demanded the ability to create educational institutions to train preachers and lay readers. The absence of tax-supported public schools in the region motivated the growth of institutes, academies, and colleges with denominational affiliation. As naturally as the churches chose only members of their own religion to be their ministers, they chose only like-minded teachers for their institutions. The proprietary nature of such schools so conflicted with the theory of academic freedom that their character as institutions of higher education has been called into doubt, although many carried on with distinction the development of intellects. The conflicting claim of academics to the right of intellectual freedom and of the churches to the right to establish and maintain colleges is one of the abiding paradoxes of southern culture.

Instances of direct conflict of intellectual freedom with institutional purpose arose when professors changed their beliefs or when they found themselves caught in one of the frequent doctrinal splits in the denominations. The situation could be alleviated if the sect had a powerful central body that could exercise rigid control over the institutions. The upper offices tended to be held by the more liberal elements, which protected the institutions from the radical conservatism sometimes found in the pew. Where government remained on the congregational level, as it did among the Baptists, the Pentecostals, and the Churches of Christ, it was harder for the ecclesiastical hierarchy of the churches to closely supervise the institutions, which sometimes fell under the control of special interests, especially those led by a powerful preacher or those people or factions that could offer large financial incentives. Although many southern colleges and universities continue to have denominational ties, the tendency has been to weaken the sectarian contribution and control so that it is rare to find religious requirements for faculty membership, except in departments such as religion or Bible.

With the rise of the scientific method and the influence of Darwinism, an attempt to accommodate theology to new discoveries became common on religious campuses. In some cases the new theories were so contrary to the older doctrines that charges of heresy could be brought, as in the case of the general assembly's 1888 judgment against James Woodrow in the South Carolina Presbyterian synod. At the same time, and from the opposite direction, a new spirit of hostility toward theological concepts was manifesting itself, tending to claim an exclusive right to the title "intellectualism," and in a few cases going so far as to create a new outlook actively hostile to orthodox Christianity. In a number of cases the men who espoused the new ideas gained control of institutions created under the denominations and separated them from the churches, as at Vanderbilt.

The rise of the public schools in the early 20th century provided a new competition for the church schools, which they were not completely willing or able to face. Tax-supported education would, it was assumed, be religiously neutral because of the separation of church and state mandated by the U.S. Constitution. The new Darwinian theories presented a problem for that neutrality insofar as they dealt directly with the religiously pivotal issues of the nature and origin of man. Moderates in most denominations had already accommodated evolution to the Scriptures by using figurative interpretations of the Old Testament and including a reservation that the human soul, at least, was a special creation of God. They were willing for the tax-supported schools to teach the theories of evolution so long as they handled the matter of human development (and especially the nature of the human soul) with discretion and made no reference to the Bible.

By the 1920s, however, there were reports that a few teachers were using the classrooms to attack the Bible and to inculcate new religious doctrines based upon Darwinism. Such violations of the religious neutrality of the public school motivated appeals to the antiestablishment clause of the First Amendment. Fundamentalists wanted to prohibit all teaching of the evolution of man, while moderates proposed only a clarification of the constitutional infringement involved in a tax-supported assault on some religious beliefs. Proposals in several states were defeated by the divisions between these factions. When a law was proposed in Tennessee, its heading was worded so as to satisfy the fundamentalists, while its body prohibited only the teaching that used the theory of the evolution of man in expressed contradiction to the Bible. Even the opponents were mollified, because the wording was so vague that they did not believe it enforceable. The Scopes Trial in June 1925 was supposed to decide the constitutionality of the law, but the tactics of the defense turned it into a contest between the Bible and evolution. The result was that many southerners who had previously accepted both were now convinced the two were mutually exclusive and rejected Darwin to keep God. The South-baiting of the 1920s, so prevalent in the prosecution case and in the reporting of the trial, made many loyal southerners espouse antiintellectualism and made it harder for the moderates to continue to control denominations and institutions; academic freedom thereby suffered. The present attempts in some states to force "creationism" into the classroom or the textbooks have the same roots.

U.S. Supreme Court rulings since the 1950s on Bible reading, prayer, and integration in the public schools have provided new incentives for the formation of church-related primary and high schools, which tend to be under the control of the most conservative local churches and to have associations with the fundamentalist or "religious right" wing of the denominations. The lack of academic freedom in these Christian academies has not received the attention it would in higher education. The main controversies instead are over teacher qualifications, certification, and tuition tax credits.

Political and economic conservatism has created serious problems for academic freedom, especially in the periods of the reinstitution of Democratic control after the Civil War (during the years of Ku Klux Klan domination), the Red Scare, and the McCarthy era. Other sections suffered from the same turmoils, though perhaps not to the same extent.

The most emotional issue for southerners has been that of race relations. Even before the Civil War the controversy had become a struggle for freedom of thought and expression. Almost from the beginning, relations with the slaves and the exslaves took on the volatile mixture of racism, political interests, religious concerns, and sectional pride, and the bloody tragedy engulfed the section for years. After Reconstruction and the reestablishment of white political supremacy, black students and faculty were routinely denied academic freedom as well as civil rights, and the occasional white who defended them was in peril of ostracism, loss of position, and even violence. As the civil rights campaign of the 1950s and 1960s grew, it frequently found its leadership on the campuses. Especially during the integration conflicts, southern campuses witnessed the presence of marshalls, militiamen, tear gas, and even death. Although not all questions are settled, the basic issues have moved toward resolution so that freedom of thought and expression is no more an issue for the South than for other regions.

See also RELIGION: Civil Rights and Religion; Theological Orthodoxy; SCIENCE AND MEDICINE: Science and Religion; / Scopes Trial

Charles F. Ogilvie
University of Tennessee
at Martin

Clement Eaton, *The Freedom-of-Thought Struggle in the Old South* (1964); Richard Hofstadter and Walter P. Metzger, *Development of Academic Freedom* (1955); James W. Silver, *Mississippi: The Closed Society* (1964).

Adult Education

Historically, adult education has been characterized by the same limitations as public school and postsecondary education in the South. At least three patterns can be distinguished in the analysis of education of adults: the first is provided by the more urbanized trading centers of the interior and coastal areas such as Charleston, Natchez, New Orleans, Memphis, and Savannah; a second pattern, overlaying the first, is derived from the aristocratic plantation society of the East Coast Tidewater and Mississippi Delta areas; finally, the third pattern is developed from the vast interior stretches of the region from the Coastal Plains, the Piedmont, and the mountains that were populated by the relatively isolated, small family farmers.

The education provided to adults in southern trading centers such as Charleston and Natchez was not historically unlike that of the rest of the nation. The second pattern was unique to the region, but only a few thousand people were involved in educating adults on the plantations. In contrast, the distinguishing character of education of adults in the South derived from focusing on small farmers in the southern interior.

The general absence of anything but the most rudimentary provisions for childhood education in a small, often subsistence, farm environment provided little encouragement for many southern adults or children to achieve educationally. Consequently, illiteracy became a pervasive characteristic of thousands of adults in the period from colonial settlement to the Civil War. After the war illiteracy was a problem for more than just newly freed black adults. Thus, for the past one hundred years the battle for literacy has provided a distinctive character to adult education in the states of the old Confederacy.

Responses to the pervasiveness of illiteracy in the 50 years from 1875 to 1925 were diverse and numerous. They included local efforts and external efforts to provide education for adults, black and white. The battle was joined by philanthropists, industrialists, educators, and politicians. They created lay-by schools, moonlight schools, evening schools in textile communities, and a number of socially sensitive educational institutions such as Berea College, the Highlander Folk School, Martha Berry College, Rabun Gap–Nacoochee School, the South Carolina Opportunity School, and Ruskin College.

Rabun Gap–Nacoochee School in Georgia and the South Carolina Opportunity School are two 20th-century institutions that emerged shortly after the turn of the century when the situation concerning adult illiteracy was recognized as being acute. Both institutions continue to this day with modified curricula and missions.

Originally, both were designed to provide instruction to families in their areas. The founders of the institutions, Andrew J. Ritchie of the Rabun Gap–Nacoochee School and Wil Lou Gray of the South Carolina Opportunity School, perceived a need to enroll entire families in their programs providing a variety of educational opportunities. In the case of the South Carolina Opportunity School, instruction was limited to a short time during the lay-by period in the summer months. In contrast, families were permitted to move into one of the 21 cottages on the 1,800-acre school farm at Rabun Gap, where they could live for up to 10 years. The heads of each family and all adult children above school age were required to attend school sessions and meetings held for their benefit and improvement. Children of public school age were required to attend a school provided for them for nine months of the year.

By the third decade of the current century, state governments through their systems of public education had begun to make contributions of varying kinds to literacy programs. These programs alternately languished and flourished until 1964 when the federal government, through the Civil Rights Act, began to support adult basic-education programs in the various states. *Adult education* in many southern states is a term now used to refer to adult basic education. The increased prosperity of the southern region has reduced the relative prevalence of adult illiteracy, and a variety of additional provisions exists for meeting other educational needs of adults. Nevertheless, the pressure of approximately 2 million illiterate adults and continuing high levels of attrition in the public schools of the South indicate that, despite various strategies and campaigns and millions of dollars, the problem persists.

Other educational activities for adults exist in varying degrees across the South. Many states now contain at least one university with continuing-education facilities, including programs designed to meet the continuing professional-education needs of various groups from dentists to veterinarians. Technical institutes and community colleges provide a wide range of educational opportunities for adults with different levels of previous educational achievement.

See also BLACK LIFE: Education, Black; SOCIAL CLASS: Poverty; / Highlander Folk School

Huey Long
University of Georgia

Clyde N. Ginn, Frances Karnes, and Beverley B. Maddon, eds., *Issues and Trends in Adult Basic Education: Focus on Reading* (1979); Ronald K. Goodenow and Arthur O. White, eds., *Education and the Rise of the New South* (1981); Malcolm Knowles, *The Adult Learner: A Neglected Species* (1973); Huey Long et al., *Changing Approaches to Studying Adult Education* (1980); Ralph M. Lyon, *The Basis for Constructing Curricular Materials in Adult Education for Carolina Mill Workers* (1937); Joel H. Magisos and Anne E. Stakelon, compilers, *Adult Vocational Education: An Annotated Bibliography of Publications and Projects* (1975); John Ohlinger, *Media and Adult Learning: A Bibliography with Abstracts, Annotations, and Quotations* (1975).

Athletics and Education

Modern American athletics emerged in the years between 1880 and 1920. Beginning with a concern for nurturing "the strenuous life" in an urban, industrial society, Americans created a highly organized spectator and participant system of athletic activities for the young. These developments began in the Northeast, spread then to the Middle West, and came late to the South. Athletics, though, became an important part of southern education and helped to define a distinctive southern culture.

Americans at the turn of the 20th century articulated a sports ideology that spoke of "muscular Christianity," which stressed the religious significance of manliness and the importance of play for proper physical, spiritual, and mental development. The Young Men's Christian Association, city playground associations, church leagues, business-sponsored community leagues, and the public school athletic leagues all reflected the ideology that had come to the South by the 1920s. The ideology was an urban-centered concern, and the South's relative lack of urban areas in the early 20th century limited the importance of the interest in organized athletics until after 1920. The South's predominantly rural schools, oriented to the seasonal farm cycle, had little interest in, or ability to nurture, extracurricular activities such as athletics. Sports had long been important to rural southerners, but they were in the form of outdoor hunting and fishing. Eventually, though, southerners became convinced of the need for adult management of youthful athletics as a way to nurture cultural values. The emergence of "comprehensive" high schools encouraged adult management of youth sports. Athletics were said to help channel adolescent sexual energy into constructive social and moral habits and to help potentially rebellious students.

High school athletics slowly became an integral part of southern education. Schools, whether urban or rural, have competed since the 1920s in interscholastic leagues designed to allow relatively equal competition between schools of similar enrollment. High school sports in the South helped to give an identity and sense of common purpose to neighborhoods, towns, and cities. Historian Thomas D. Clark has noted that the enthusiasm for school athletics has placed schools "in a curious kind of public domain." "Even hardened old rednecks," Clark notes, "who have wandered in from the cotton fields have caught the fever. Fifty years ago they would have regarded these sports as either effeminate or juvenile. Not so the modern southerner." The emphasis on athletics has brought the general population into close association "with the forms if not the substance of education."

Football is a prime focus for school athletics. Friday night in the autumn is the time for a major southern ritual occasion. Football is the center of a complex cultural event involving more than players on the field. Cheerleaders, baton twirlers, trainers, and marching bands are actively involved, while the stands are filled with students, former players who have graduated and returned to cheer for their team, and parents and friends of parents. As historian Lawrence Goodwyn has written of Texas, schoolboy football "was an instrument of psychic survival and, as such, a centerpiece of the regional culture."

When the local high school team was having a bad season, an "uneasiness" settled over the entire community. Journalist James J. Kilpatrick has noted that while high school athletics are also taken seriously in the Midwest, in the South "they're a religion." Local people read in their Saturday papers or their weeklies of "the feats of Panthers, Rebels, Bisons, Rockets, Trojans, Bulldogs, Wildcats, Warriors, Whippets, Raiders, and Tigers."

Basketball was a rallying point for communities whose schools were too poor and/or too small to field football teams. In Kentucky, where basketball so dominates the culture that local storytellers joke that "a Kentucky homosexual is a boy who likes girls more than basketball," many small towns have enjoyed lasting distinction on the basis of their high school team's accomplishments in the state tournament. Girls' basketball was deeply rooted in the schools there long before the recent growth in women's sports.

Although the appearance of comprehensive high schools was an early 20th-century necessity for the development of extracurricular athletic activities, school athletics contributed in more recent times to southern reluctance to accept large, consolidated county high schools. In many rural southern counties a local community maintained its identity as a result of a small school where the boys and girls who comprised the varsity basketball teams were genuine community heroes and heroines. In this setting, the basketball games became the major social activity throughout most of the school year for both the adults and children of the community. These get-togethers provided inexpensive, family-oriented socialization for the rural populace and were carefully scheduled so as not to conflict with church activities—the other focal point of small-town community life.

By the 1960s most rural southern counties contained a "big school"—a county-seat high school with 500 to 2,000 students. However, the county was also still dotted with "country schools," which contained 300 to 600 students in grades 1 through 12. By the late 1960s and early 1970s consolidation and "progress" terminated most of these small, country high schools. The "farmers" rode the big yellow school buses for several hours each day to attend bigger and, ostensibly, better schools. Many of these rural youngsters, who had been "top dog" at their small school, were either too timid or too untalented to participate in extracurricular activities and sports at their new school. Others wanted to be involved but had to ride the bus home in order to assist with daily chores.

In exchange for a broader curriculum and other big-school amenities, many rural youngsters lost an opportunity to build confidence and leadership abilities through participation in sports, clubs, and other extracurricular activities. On the positive side, big-school education unquestionably led more rural youngsters to attend college.

By the 1980s some of the little high schools that once pumped lifeblood into local communities had become grade schools. Many others stood as empty and crumbling monuments to a part of southern life that had been lost forever. The dissolution of the small country high school led to a concomitant disappearance of community spirit and identity and left a rural populace frustrated, disoriented, and nostalgic for the good old days when a last-minute victory over an archrival lit fires of community pride that were rekindled by generations of storytellers. As University of Alabama football coach Paul "Bear" Bryant once observed, "It's hard to rally 'round a math class." For rural southerners, it was hard to rally around an empty building.

The stress on athletics has glorified success on the playing field at the expense of other forms of educational achievement in the South, as across the nation. In the high school social structure the athlete ranks near the top. Texas has led a recent movement to reduce the role of athletics in high schools. In 1984 the state board of education passed a rule, which was authorized by the state legislature, barring students from extracurricular activities if they did not pass every subject they took in the previous six-week examining period. The "no pass, no play" provision was promoted by businessman H. Ross Perot, who headed an advisory committee on educational excellence. The *New York Times* (28 April 1985) said the rule had "stirred about as much emotion in Texas as anything since Santa Anna overran the Alamo." The state's business and political leaders expressed strong commitment to it, but coaches and parents expressed concern over its fundamental challenge to athletic values in Texas schools. The other southern states have recently enacted programs to promote educational improvement, but none at the state level have adopted the Texas model.

Athletics has played a role in the desegregation of southern schools. A particularly skilled black athlete, such as Marcus Dupree in Philadelphia, Miss., can become a hero of the community. The stress on school athletics, however, has channeled black achievement disproportionately into sports at the expense of other activities, according to critics. Moreover, the achievements of black athletes do not always translate into later success for the athletes once they have graduated.

Southern schools have long produced outstanding women athletes, such as Mildred "Babe" Didriksen Zaharias and Wilma Rudolph. The region has a tradition of good girls' basketball, but the culture has only recently encouraged a general interest by girls in organized sports. Victorian ideas on femininity, which stressed passivity and fragility, held on longer in the South than elsewhere in this country and were reinforced by specifically regional notions of the lady and the belle. While the South is above the national average in support of sports such as football and basketball and in the production of talent in those areas, it ranks well below the national average in financial support of women's sports in the schools. Women's sports did expand in the 1920s, thanks to Amateur Athletic Union programs in swimming, track and field, basketball, and gymnastics. Tennis, golf, and swimming were encouraged in the schools rather than more vigorous sports such as softball or basketball. However, industrial sports leagues, which were sponsored by businesses, were important in providing athletic opportunities for women. Bowling is the most popular participant sport among women today in all regions, and the industrial league teams from the South and the Midwest have been strong in that sport and have long dominated in basketball. The late 1960s and 1970s witnessed a revolution in women's sports. Title IX of the Educational Amendments Act of 1972 outlawed sexual discrimination by school districts and institutions of higher learning. The hope was to force improved funding for women's athletics while avoiding the high-pressure, competitive problems of men's sports. Women's sports, though, have developed along the same lines as men's, stressing winning, the recruiting of the best high school athletes, the giving of athletic scholarships, and a predominantly spectator orientation.

College and university athletics have reflected many of the same patterns found in the schools. College football, for example, began in the Northeast in the late 19th century, but southern teams earned little national acclaim until the 1920s. The hot climate, regional provincialism, and wide distribution of good players in many small colleges supposedly prevented the emergence of powerful teams. The 1920–45 period witnessed a dramatic change. On 1 January 1926 Coach Wallace Wade's University of Alabama team defeated Washington State in a landmark intersectional game. The University of Georgia defeated Yale three times in a four-year period, and southern teams by the post–World War II years were frequently winning national championships. Southerners responded to these triumphs with an outburst of regional enthusiasm. "Indeed, pride in the strength of sectional football teams took its place along with pride in the valor of the Confederate army as a major source of Southern chauvinism," wrote historians Francis Butler Simkins and Charles Roland in *A History of the South* (1972). The athlete became a glamorous new southern hero and his coach the best-known university figure to the general populace. Athletics was soon a sometimes-consuming affair for students and alumni. Bonfires, cheerleaders, pep bands, and other ingredients of a new ritualism led one writer in 1930 to remark on the football South's "medieval pageantry long forgotten outside the South."

See also BLACK LIFE: Education, Black; Sports, Black; GEOGRAPHY: Sports, Geography of; RECREATION: Basketball; Cheerleading and Twirling; Football; / Bryant, Bear; Manning, Archie; Walker, Herschel

James M. Gifford
Appalachian Development Center
Appalachian State University

Charles Reagan Wilson
University of Mississippi

Jack Berryman, *Journal of Sport History* (Fall 1975); Ellen Gerber et al., *The American Woman in Sport* (1974); James A. Montgomery, "The Development of the Interscholastic Athletics Movement in the United States, 1890–1940" (Ph.D. dissertation, George Peabody College for Teachers, 1960); Tema Okun and Peter Wood, eds., *Southern Exposure* (Fall 1979); Benjamin G. Rader, *American Sports: From the Age of Folk Games to the Age of Spectators* (1983).

Black Education

See BLACK LIFE: Education, Black

Classical Tradition

From its beginnings the intellectual culture of the South reflected the influence of the Greek and Latin classics. In this respect southerners of the 17th and 18th centuries were hardly different from their British and European relatives. New England learning was also based upon a classical curriculum, but—as John Gould Fletcher observed—the Puritans "regarded education primarily as a means of training theological students." The settlers of Virginia and the Carolinas embraced the classics not so much for spiritual and pragmatic reasons but because they were the vehicle of English and European civilization. It is a remarkable coincidence that the first major work of literature produced in the South (or in America, for that matter) was George Sandys's translation of Ovid's *Metamorphoses*. Sandys's version—one of the most influential poetical works of 17th-century England—was composed in Jamestown during the poet's tenure as treasurer (1621–26).

The classical tradition had taken root in all the American colonies by the time of the American Revolution. Students at the College of William and Mary, like their counterparts at Harvard, learned their Latin (still out of Lily's grammar) before matriculation. Greek studies were less the rule than the ideal. This common background provided an important link between sections that had already begun to diverge in other respects. The political thinkers of the Revolution and the Constitution—Jefferson as much as Adams, Madison as much as Hamilton—had constant recourse in their writings to the principles and examples of the ancients. The Greek Revival style of 18th-century public buildings is a vivid testimony to the impact of classical ideals upon the Founding Fathers. Jefferson, in his earlier days, might have deplored the exclusivity of the classical regime, but at his University of Virginia graduates were expected "to be able to read the highest classics in the language with ease, thorough understanding, and just quantity," and Jefferson warned his fellow countrymen against following the example of Europeans, who—in his view—were abandoning Latin and Greek.

The classical tradition did not go unchallenged. The American Revolution bred expectations of a Golden Age in which the shackles of the centuries would be cast aside. The past, it was frequently argued, could not provide useful examples for the American experiment in republican self-government. The classics, which had already been dismissed by Locke and Rousseau as impractical, were now impugned as undemocratic. Northerners like Benjamin Rush and Noah Webster argued that a democratic society should not burden itself with the fripperies of decadent Europe. Such arguments were addressed by the Marylander Samuel Knox in his essay "On

Liberal Education" (1799), in which he slyly suggested that opposition to the classics was the result of "vitiated taste and the negligence or indulgence of parents."

In Charleston the battle lines of the ancients and the moderns had been drawn even before the Revolution in debates at the cosmopolitan city's library. In the 1820s Thomas Grimké took up the moderns' case, but Grimké's bold attacks were countered by no less than Roman Catholic Bishop John England and by statesman Hugh S. Legaré. Legaré printed his defense of the classics as the first article of the first issue of his new journal, the *Southern Review*. In the decades to come, the moderns were to have their triumph in the North, but Charleston—like the South as a whole—was to remain devoted to the classics for another century and a half. The College of Charleston maintained a Latin requirement for all arts degrees until 1966. That college's most illustrious student, Basil L. Gildersleeve, became unquestionably the greatest classical scholar America has produced. In 1854—seven years before the war that found the scholar riding with Jeb Stuart—Gildersleeve published an essay on "The Necessity of the Classics." To his defense of classical learning, he added the consideration that classical philology was a good field for southerners because it was "a harvest untouched by the sickle" of northern writers.

The sectionalist note struck by Gildersleeve (half a century before he wrote *The Creed of the Old South*) was one symptom of the growing cultural isolation that the South was imposing upon itself. The lust for modernity was regarded—like Unitarianism and the factory system—as a Yankee invention. Jefferson Davis was one of many prominent southerners who made a plea for keeping southern students at southern colleges. Most of these schools maintained stiff requirements until the turn of the century. Students at the University of Georgia were expected "to read, translate, and parse Cicero, Virgil, and the Greek Testament, and to write true Latin in prose" *before* admission. Similar requirements were imposed by William and Mary, South Carolina College, and Transylvania University (Kentucky), which a young Jefferson Davis attended. Classical requirements did not mean, necessarily, a contempt for more modern disciplines. At the University of Virginia in 1857, 249 students were enrolled in Latin, 248 in chemistry, 168 in Greek, and 171 in natural philosophy. The study of Latin (and Greek) was, however, regarded as necessary instruction. Frederick A. P. Barnard (before becoming president of the University of Mississippi) insisted that students at the University of Alabama needed classical training much more than the usual survey courses in science, even though Barnard was himself a science teacher.

By 1861 the South could be distinguished from the North by its attachment to the classics as much as by its agrarian ideals or its peculiar institution. At a time when the North was priding itself on the progress of the modern age, southern orators were continuing to model their speeches on Cicero and Demosthenes—albeit with the addition of Romantic flourishes—and planters in Mississippi were constructing their houses—not always in the best of taste—on the lines of ancient temples. Even the defense of slavery was justified by classical precedents and argued from ancient authorities. George Fitzhugh discovered, somewhat belatedly, that his *Sociology for the South* (1854) was Aristotelian, while Thomas Roderick Dew was made president of the University of Virginia largely on the strength of his famous proslavery argument, based in large measure on classical sources.

The hundred years following Reconstruction have seen a slow but constant ebbing of classical influences. The New South, envisioned by Henry W. Grady and realized by populists like Ben Tillman, was to be a practical sort of place whose citizens needed engineering and business skills more than the ability to write Latin prose. Southern politics came under the dominion of men who gloried in their identification with the common man and were inclined to hide what learning they possessed as a shameful secret. There were remarkable exceptions, like Sam Ervin of North Carolina, who larded his speeches with allusions to Cicero as well as Burke and Jefferson. Paradoxically, it was the exceptional old-fashioned orators like Ervin or Senator James Eastland of Mississippi who were still regarded as the typical southern statesmen. Even so, despite the South's commitment to modernization, its schools continued to offer Latin, either as a requirement or as a college preparatory elective, into the 1960s, and professional classicists were able to reassure themselves that southern high school graduates were still coming to college able to read a page of Caesar and to tell who fought whom and why under the walls of Troy.

To the extent that the South remains aware of its past, it will remain under the influence of the classics. Most of the major southern writers were schooled in the classics, even though they wrote as men of their own time. Nineteenth-century poets like Poe and Timrod wrote, like their English models, in the Romantic manner, and few attempts were made in a classical or neoclassical idiom. (Louisa McCord's *Caius Gracchus* is a partial exception.) Nonetheless, ancient literature was generally taken for granted by southern writers to an extent that is hard to realize. William Gilmore Simms is the exception that proves the rule: he was always keenly aware of his educational deficiencies. To understand the impact of the classics upon the southern intelligence, one need only browse through the pages of the literary reviews of the last century—*De Bow's Review*, the *Southern Literary Messenger*, and the *Southern Review*—for the countless articles and essays on ancient and modern oratory, classical poets, and even manuscripts of ancient authors. Although only 5 percent of the *Southern Quarterly Review*'s articles were actually devoted to the ancient world, the general impression is of a literary culture that took Greek and Latin for granted.

Indeed, classical themes and allusions abounded in southern literature even until the period after World War II. John Gould Fletcher's contribution to *I'll Take My Stand*, the Agrarian manifesto of 1930, was "Education, Past and Present," a reasoned defense of the old schooling; and the essays and verses of other Agrarians—Allen Tate, Robert Penn Warren, and Donald Davidson—seem to assume the classics as a common ground in a manner quite distinct from the self-conscious allusiveness of Ezra Pound and T. S. Eliot. What the future holds for the classical tradition in southern education and literature is uncertain.

See also: HISTORY AND MANNERS: / Davis, Jefferson; Jefferson, Thomas; Madison, James; INDUSTRY: / *De Bow's Review*; Grady, Henry W.; LAW: / Ervin, Sam; LITERATURE: Agrarianism in Literature; / Davidson, Donald; Poe, Edgar Allan; Simms, William Gilmore; Tate, Allen; Warren, Robert Penn; MYTHIC SOUTH: New South Myth; / Agrarians, Vanderbilt; Fitzhugh, George

Thomas Fleming
McClellanville, South Carolina

Richard Beale Davis, *Intellectual Life in the Colonial South, 1585–1763*, 3 vols. (1978); Clement Eaton, *The Mind of the Old South* (1964); Michael O'Brien, *A Character of Hugh Legaré* (1985), ed., *All Clever Men Who Make Their Way* (1982); *Southern Humanities Review* (Special Issue 1977); Twelve Southerners, *I'll Take My Stand: The South and the Agrarian Tradition* (1930).

Desegregation

Rigid segregation was the prior condition for southern white acceptance of tax-supported schools, even before the U.S. Supreme Court sanctioned separate-but-equal public accommodations in *Plessy* v. *Ferguson* (1896). With the collapse of two brief, but notable, biracial experiments in the New Orleans public schools (1870–77) and at the University of South Carolina (1873–77), racially dual school systems would be required by law in 17 "southern" states—the 11 former Confederate states, plus Delaware, Kentucky, Maryland, Missouri, Oklahoma, and West Virginia—and the District of Columbia (where Congress had provided separate black schools). Although perceived largely as a southern problem, segregated schools had existed in the North since the early 1800s and increased in reaction to the Great Migration of blacks (1890–1930) in such cities as Chicago, Indianapolis, and Philadelphia, which routinely assigned blacks to separate schools by gerrymandering, transfers, and ability testing.

The desegregation of southern education spanned 50 years and had four phases: (1) 1930–45, inauguration of the NAACP's desegregation campaign, which ended the era of virtually unchallenged Jim Crowism; (2) 1945–54, overturning the separate-but-equal doctrine, first in graduate and professional education and then in elementary and secondary schools; (3) 1955–64, massive southern white resistance countered by escalating federal intervention to enforce court-ordered desegregation and by passage of the 1964 Civil Rights Act; and (4) 1965–85, extensive desegregation of southern school districts by court decisions, civil rights enforcement, and threats of withholding large federal education grants.

Initially, Charles Hamilton Houston and Thurgood Marshall, NAACP Legal Defense and Education Fund attorneys, decided to attack segregation indirectly through lawsuits aimed at equalizing black and white schools in terms of curricula, teachers' salaries, and physical equipment. At the graduate and professional levels, states would be forced either to establish new schools for blacks or to admit them to existing white universities. In 1936 the Maryland Court of Appeals ordered Donald G. Murray admitted to the state university's law school, because none existed for blacks. Two years later, the U.S. Supreme Court ruled that Missouri could not meet the Fourteenth Amendment's equal-protection requirement by giving plaintiff Lloyd Gaines a tuition grant to study law in a nonsegregated state; after Gaines's unaccounted disappearance, Missouri established a Jim Crow law school. Other reverses followed in Kentucky and Tennessee, although West Virginia in 1938 voluntarily admitted blacks to its graduate and professional schools.

To achieve greater returns for the NAACP's time and limited financial resources, Marshall shifted, in 1945, to a direct attack on separate-but-equal education. Between 1948 and 1950 this new strategy opened doors of graduate and/or law schools at the universities of Oklahoma, Kentucky, Texas, Virginia, Missouri, and at Louisiana State University, while Delaware and Arkansas voluntarily admitted blacks. In the pivotal 1950 *Sweatt* v. *Painter* and *McLaurin* v. *Oklahoma State Regents for Higher Education*, the U.S. Supreme Court unanimously ruled, first, that the University of Texas Law School had to admit Heman Sweatt because the new black law school was inferior in academic traditions and prestige, and it then ordered the University of Oklahoma to accord George McLaurin equal, nonsegregated treatment in the classrooms, cafeteria, and library.

Buoyed by victories and supported by reports of President Truman's Committee on Civil Rights and Commission on Higher Education, the NAACP directly attacked segregated public elementary and secondary schools. On 17 May 1954 the U.S. Supreme Court unanimously ruled in five cases, collectively known as *Brown* v. *Board of Education*, that "separate educational facilities are inherently unequal" and that segregation deprived plaintiffs of equal protection of the laws. The Supreme Court's 1955 implementation decree remanded these cases to federal district courts, which would order desegregation "with all deliberate speed." Such delay did not apply to graduate and professional schools, according to the Supreme Court's decision in a University of Florida Law School case.

Swept up by massive white resistance, southern states enacted a barrage of new laws to prohibit or indefinitely postpone integration: pupil-placement laws, freedom-of-choice amendments, tuition grants, repeal of compulsory attendance laws, modification of teacher tenure, closing of public schools (Norfolk and Prince Edward County, Virginia), state interposition and nullification of the *Brown* decision, and mob violence (University of Alabama, February 1956; Little Rock Central High School, September 1957; University of Georgia, January 1961; and University of Mississippi, September–October 1962). Federal supremacy ultimately triumphed—paratroopers returned nine black students to Little Rock Central High School, while the army secured James Meredith's enrollment at Ole Miss. Both the U.S. Court of Appeals and the Supreme Court refused to allow integration to be suspended.

Where local leadership committed itself to keeping public schools open, integration was peaceful: District of Columbia, St. Louis, Baltimore, Greensboro, Charlotte, Winston-Salem, Dade County, Atlanta, and Dallas. In June 1963, despite Governor George C. Wallace's televised stand in the "schoolhouse door," responsible University of Alabama leadership registered two black students. Heeding the lessons of Mississippi and Alabama, both Clemson and the University of South Carolina integrated with dignity.

Significant desegregation occurred, nevertheless, only after the 1964 Civil Rights Act empowered the U.S. attorney general to bring lawsuits on behalf of black plaintiffs and prohibited, under Title VI, spending federal funds—appropriated under the Elementary and Secondary Education and Higher Education Acts of 1965—in segregated schools and colleges. In *Alexander* v. *Holmes County Board of Education* (1969) the U.S. Supreme Court unanimously ordered all school segregation ended immediately. Methods of creating unitary schools included busing, magnet schools, open enrollments, and rezoning. Meanwhile, traditionally white public colleges and universities in 10 southern and border states, including Oklahoma and Pennsylvania, were required to submit to the Office for Civil Rights comprehensive desegregation plans for increasing the number of black students and faculty, expanding financial-aid and remedial programs, and electing black trustees (*Adams* v. *Richardson*, 1973). Although overwhelmingly black public schools and colleges persist in the South, especially in Alabama, Mississippi, Louisiana, Texas, and the District of Columbia, segregated education is no longer distinctively a southern problem. In many locales new patterns of segregation have evolved as whites, sometimes in large numbers, have left public school settings rather than accept busing and other school-desegregation plans. Various court rulings since the mid-1980s have supported voluntary rather than mandatory efforts to achieve racial balancing in schools, and the implications in the South, as elsewhere in the nation, have yet to be seen.

See also BLACK LIFE: Education, Black; / Meredith, James; National Association for the Advancement of Colored People; LAW: Civil Rights Movement; / *Brown* v. *Board of Education*; Fifth Circuit Court of Appeals; Little Rock Crisis; *Plessy* v. *Ferguson*; POLITICS: Segregation, Defense of

Marcia G. Synnott
University of South Carolina

Russell H. Barrett, *Integration at Ole Miss* (1965); Numan Bartley, *Arkansas Historical Quarterly* (Summer 1966); Augustus M. Burns III, *Journal of Southern History* (Spring 1980); Richard Kluger, *Simple Justice: The History of Brown v. Board of Education and Black America's Struggle for Equality* (1975); Thurgood Marshall, *Journal of Negro Education* (Summer 1952); Gary Orfield, *The Reconstruction of Southern Education: The Schools and the 1964 Civil Rights Act* (1969); J. W. Peltason, *Fifty-eight Lonely Men: Southern Federal Judges and School Desegregation* (1961); President's Commission on Higher Education, *Higher Education for American Democracy: A Report* (1947); President's Committee on Civil Rights, *To Secure These Rights: The Report of the President's Committee on Civil Rights* (1947); Calvin Trillin, *An Education in Georgia: The Integration of Charlayne Hunter and Hamilton Holmes* (1964); Stephen L. Wasby, Anthony A. D'Amato, and Rosemary Metrailer, *Desegregation from Brown to Alexander: An Exploration of Supreme Court Strategies* (1977).

Federal-State Relations

Quality and equality have been dominant themes in the interaction of state and federal governments on the issue of education in the South. The federal government first became substantially involved with southern education when the Freedmen's Bureau allocated over $5 million to private schools that taught former slaves. Though southern state governments founded the first public universities in the United States long before joining the Confederacy, the interaction of state and federal governments following the Civil War assisted in the development of educational opportunities in the South.

At the end of the Civil War the southern states faced challenges to rebuild their society and to educate formerly enslaved citizens. Delegates who met to draft new state constitutions contended with the newly passed Thirteenth, Fourteenth, and Fifteenth Amendments to the U.S. Constitution that confirmed the freedmen's citizenship and mandated that no state could deny equal opportunity to its citizens. The delegates therefore adopted constitutional planks that proclaimed equal educational opportunity.

Despite constitutional language and limited attempts to provide nonsegregated education in some states, southern legislators soon enacted Jim Crow statutes that mandated separate educational facilities for whites and blacks. Motivated by misunderstanding and deep-seated prejudices and buoyed by purported scientific evidence that blacks constituted an inferior race, every southern state institutionalized a separate system for blacks and whites by the end of Reconstruction in 1877.

The decades after Reconstruction saw actions by both state and federal governments that legally sanctioned one educational system for whites and another for blacks. The infusion of nearly $2 million as a result of the 1862 Morrill Act helped revive public higher-education institutions in the South. To receive these funds, southern states agreed to provide opportunities for blacks to learn about the agricultural and mechanical arts. Federal authorities, however, acquiesced in state decisions to offer instruction in separate facilities. Federal courts approved these actions when the Supreme Court rendered its infamous 1896 *Plessy* v. *Ferguson* decision that legalized separate-but-equal facilities.

Having chosen to finance two educational systems, southern states offered black citizens schools increasingly inferior to those in other regions of the United

States. By 1915 southern states had invested over $145 million in public educational facilities. Of that, however, less than 10 percent was committed to black schools. This investment grew over the years, but the percentage provided black institutions remained proportionately the same. Although white systems of education fared better than black institutions, facilities and support for both lagged behind national standards.

This situation deteriorated steadily until the U.S. Supreme Court reversed itself in 1954 and declared separate-but-equal facilities inherently unequal and therefore unconstitutional. Although the *Brown* v. *Board of Education* decision heralded the demise of dual educational systems in the South, the Court's injunction that states move "with all deliberate speed" to achieve desegregation opened the door for states to stall.

Faced with state intransigence and increasing black unrest, the federal government enacted civil rights laws and education assistance programs in the 1960s that tied receipt of funds to nondiscrimination pledges. Southern states slowly acquiesced. In the 1970s and 1980s progressive state leaders cooperated with federal efforts to remove resistance to desegregation. Finally, blacks and whites began to receive instruction together.

State financing of the single educational system brought significant improvement. By 1985 southern states could boast that per capita expenditures for higher education exceeded the national average. Several states, though, continue under federal orders to eliminate vestiges of segregation in public educational institutions. Nonetheless, state and federal governments now jointly support efforts to expand and improve educational opportunities for all southern citizens.

See also BLACK LIFE: Education, Black; LAW: Supreme Court; / *Brown* v. *Board of Education*; *Plessy* v. *Ferguson*; POLITICS: Segregation, Defense of

Paul S. Baker
Hampden-Sydney College

Frank W. Blackmar, *The History of Federal and State Aid to Higher Education in the United States* (1890); John S. Brubacher and Willis Rudy, *Higher Education in Transition: A History of American Colleges and Universities, 1636–1976* (3d rev. ed., 1976); Henry A. Bullock, *A History of Negro Education in the South: From 1619 to the Present* (1967); Frederick Mosteller and Daniel P. Moynihan, eds., *On the Equality of Educational Opportunity* (1972); Gary Puckrein, *The Wilson Quarterly* (Spring 1984); Frederick Rudolph, *The American College and University: A History* (1962); Reed Sarratt, *The Ordeal of Desegregation: The First Decade* (1966); Kenneth M. Stampp, *The Era of Reconstruction, 1865–1877* (1965); C. Vann Woodward, *The Strange Career of Jim Crow* (1955; 2d rev. ed., 1966).

Fraternities and Sororities

The first Greek-letter society, Phi Beta Kappa, was founded in Virginia at the College of William and Mary on 5 December 1776 as a secret social organization; only later did it become the nation's leading scholastic honor society. It succeeded the earlier Flat Hat Club at William and Mary, to which Thomas Jefferson had belonged. Phi Beta Kappa members went on to found the original Kappa Alpha at the University of North Carolina in 1812. Before it became defunct in 1855, this fraternity had 12 "circles," all in the South.

Despite these beginnings, progenitors of today's college fraternities are considered to be the three fraternities of the "Union Triad," founded at Union College, Schenectady, N.Y., between 1825 and 1827. By 1850 there were 16 men's fraternities in the country, all founded in the North, but 12 of which had chapters established on southern campuses before secession. First to come south was the Mystical Seven, founded at Wesleyan University in 1837, which established a chapter at the University of Georgia in 1839 and later merged with Beta Theta Pi. The first college fraternity founded in the South was the Rainbow Fraternity, or "W.W.W.," established at the University of Mississippi in 1849. In 1886 it merged with Delta Tau Delta, itself established in 1858 at Bethany College, Va. (now West Virginia). Neither Epsilon Alpha at the University of Virginia nor Alpha Kappa Phi at Kentucky's Centre College survived the Civil War.

The first Greek-letter society founded in Dixie to take permanent root was Sigma Alpha Epsilon, begun in 1856 at the University of Alabama. Sigma Alpha, or the Black Badge Society, founded at Roanoke College in Salem, Va., in 1859, and eventually having eight southern chapters, was disbanded in 1882. The fraternity system flourished in the South before the Civil War, so that at the University of Mississippi, for example, 11 fraternities could be found among a small male student body at the time of secession. When the Civil War began, fraternities folded on nearly every southern college campus as the male students left for battle. However, war did not kill southern Greek-letter societies. During the Atlanta Campaign, five Sigma Chis from various colleges formed the Constantine Chapter of Sigma Chi in Gen. Joseph E. Johnston's Army of Tennessee and initiated two other Confederate soldiers on the night of 17 September 1864 near Jonesboro, Ga., where a monument commemorates the event.

After the Civil War, southern students, mainly Confederate veterans or military-college cadets, organized several new fraternities in the South: Alpha Tau Omega in 1865, Kappa Sigma Kappa (which merged with Theta Xi in 1962) in 1867, and Sigma Nu in 1869 at the Virginia Military Institute; Kappa Alpha Order, at what is now Washington and Lee, in 1865; and Phi Kappa Alpha in 1868 and Kappa Sigma in 1869 at the University of Virginia. Other southern fraternities that appeared later were Sigma Phi Epsilon, founded at the University of Richmond in 1901, and Phi Kappa Phi at the College of Charleston in 1904.

The first Greek-letter women's social organization in the United States was Alpha Delta Pi, begun at Wesleyan College in Macon, Ga., in 1851, closely followed there the next year by Phi Mu. Chi Omega started at the University of Arkansas in 1895. Virginia State Normal School (now Longwood College) in Farmville gave birth to four sororities: Kappa Delta in 1897, Sigma Sigma Sigma and Zeta Tau Alpha in 1898, and Alpha Sigma Alpha in 1901.

Early in this century, black college fraternities and sororities also appeared. The first black men's Greek-letter society was Alpha Phi Alpha at Cornell in 1906, followed by Kappa Alpha Psi at Indiana in 1911. As might be expected, Howard University in Washington, D.C., was the incubator for two black fraternities and three black sororities. For men there were Omega Psi Phi in 1911 and Phi Beta Sigma in 1914, and for women there were Alpha Kappa Alpha in 1908, Delta Sigma Theta in 1913, and Zeta Phi Beta in 1920. Sigma Gamma Rho became a black collegiate sorority at Butler University in Indianapolis in 1929. All these groups are found on southern campuses.

Southern social fraternities and sororities have had their ups and downs, as have others across the nation, in peace as well as in war. Secret societies were eventually suppressed at military colleges, such as VMI and The Citadel. Yet at some southern land-grant colleges once run on military lines there were social organizations such as Lee Guard and George Rifles at Mississippi A&M (now Mississippi State University) that later became chapters of national men's social fraternities. Early in this century, southern Populist governors and legislatures succeeded in banning Greek-letter societies on public campuses, such as in South Carolina from 1897 to 1929 and in Mississippi from 1912 to 1926. However, they continued to exist *sub rosa* in some cases and eventually returned stronger than ever.

Certain southern campuses have long been noted for their hospitality to "the Greeks," most notably the University of Alabama, which in 1963 on the eve of the Vietnam War was the home of 26 men's and 16 women's Greek-letter social organizations. The wave of social protest that swept over American campuses during the 1960s and 1970s was heralded in some quarters as dooming fraternities and sororities. Although the Greek system suffered elsewhere in the country, especially in the Northeast and Far West, it was not damaged noticeably in the South.

The national leadership of Greek organizations has reacted to increasing pressure by parents and college officials concerned about the brutality of certain hazing and initiation rituals. The resistance by Greek organizations to the alteration of these practices stems from the emphasis members place on secrecy of rituals and loyalty, both to each other and to the traditions of their groups. As a result of the recent deaths of some fraternity pledges during hazing rituals and the publicity the deaths received, the campaign against hazing has progressed in the South as elsewhere. The national fraternities, as well as the National Interfraternity Conference, have rules prohibiting hazing, and 18 states have laws against hazing practices. Many campuses, such as the University of Texas at Austin, have taken strong stands against the rituals, expelling students and on occasion suspending fraternity charters for violations of hazing prohibitions.

Fraternity and sorority participation at southern schools appears to be increasing, consistent with the national trend. College students join Greek organizations looking for camaraderie, social status, and the feeling of group unity. The gregariousness, conviviality, and love of ritualistic pomp and hierarchical status usually associated with southerners may account for the seemingly enduring popularity of Greek organizations in the region. Some college students are influenced by members of their families to join a particular Greek society.

Since the 1970s membership in both fraternities and sororities has risen steadily nationwide. In the last five years, national membership has grown by more than 150,000 to about 400,000. The percentage of students in Greek organizations varies widely on southern college campuses, though the percentage involvement is not necessarily indicative of the strength of the Greek system on any given campus. Fraternity participation in the South ranges from 70 percent of male students at Louisiana State University in Baton Rouge and at Centre College in Kentucky, to 5 percent of male students at East Carolina University and Tuskegee Institute. Sorority participation on southern campuses ranges from 65 percent of the female students at Shorter College in Georgia, to 4 percent of females at Tuskegee Institute and at North Carolina State University.

Although a strong Greek system has sometimes been associated with a "party campus" and considered antithetical to a serious academic emphasis, several southern institutions with excellent academic reputations have flourishing Greek organizations, among them Birmingham-Southern College in Alabama, Duke University in North Carolina, Emory University in Georgia, Millsaps College in Mississippi, and Vanderbilt University in Tennessee. Some southern schools have no fraternities and sororities at all. These include Berea College in Kentucky, the University of Dallas, Eckerd College in Florida, and Texas A&M University.

John Hawkins Napier III
Montgomery, Alabama

Allen Cabaniss, *A History of the University of Mississippi* (1949); Clyde S. Johnson, *Fraternities in Our Colleges* (1972); Thomas J. Meyer, *Chronicle of Higher Education* (12 March 1986); John Hawkins Napier III, *The Mississippian* (20 February 1948); John Robson, ed., *Baird's Manual of American College Fraternities* (19th ed., 1977), *The College Fraternity and Its Modern Role* (1966).

Illiteracy

Inability to read and write in any language has been the conventional definition of illiteracy and the basis of most illiteracy statistics. The concept of "functional" illiteracy was advanced during World War II as a result of the U.S. Army experience with soldiers who "could not understand written instructions about basic military tasks." The South has exceeded the rest of the nation in illiteracy, whether defined in functional terms or as the inability to read and write in any language. Information from the U.S. Census of 1870 illustrated the South's heritage of illiteracy. No area of the region had less than 12 percent illiteracy. The cotton-culture subregions, particularly the river-valley and delta areas and the Piedmont and Coastal Plain, were 40 percent or more illiterate. The South was agricultural, and agriculture then depended not upon science but upon traditional practice—learning by doing rather than by reading. The 1870 census found in the nation 4.53 million persons 10 years of age and over unable to read; 73.7 percent of them resided in the South. Four-fifths of blacks were then illiterate.

The agricultural economy rested upon a sparsely distributed population, the use of child labor that discouraged school attendance, and a prejudiced and often fatalistic people who lacked the means for upward mobility in the expanding industrial system of the nation. The church was more important as a social institution than the school; word of mouth, song, and story were prominent means of cultural transmission. Under these conditions illiteracy served to conserve tradition and retard cultural change, whereas a more general literacy would have accelerated adaptation and change. Said a Jasper County, Miss., man: "My grandfather—he raised me—figured going to school wouldn't help me pick cotton any better."

A decline in illiteracy has occurred in the South and the nation. As educational benefits were extended to blacks through both public and private schools (including schools sponsored by religious groups, such as the Congregational church, and by private foundations, such as the Rosenwald Fund), illiteracy rates dropped.

When the education of a generation of children is neglected, the deficiency persists throughout a lifetime. Teaching adults to read has not been as effective in eliminating illiteracy as have mortality and out-migration from the South. The neglect of a generation of school children during the Civil War (those 5 to 14 years of age in 1860) resulted in higher illiteracy rates for the native white population in 1900 (who then were 45 to 54 years of age) than for either the preceding or succeeding generation. The illiteracy rates by age of the black population of Louisiana, from 1890 to 1930, shown in Table 2, illustrate the persistence of the "cohort effect." By tracing the cohort diagonally across the table, one can discern the dogged tenacity of illiteracy, despite mortality and out-migration. The population represented below the diagonal line lived under pre–Civil War conditions. The older the population in 1890, the lower the rate of change in illiteracy to the terminal age group. As time progressed, reductions in illiteracy among the 10 to 14 age group accelerated.

The change in illiteracy in Georgia from 1960 to 1970 illustrates the source of gains and losses of illiterates in a state. The number of Georgia illiterates in 1960 was reduced by 45 percent in 1970. Some 22,530 were estimated to have died during the decade, and 23,840 were lost through out-migration. The Adult Basic Education Program of the state taught 14,380 to read during the period. However, 6,290 new illiterates, aged 14 to 24 years in 1970, entered the illiterate category. This new group testifies to the failure of the family and the school to inculcate literacy skills.

Table 2. *Illiteracy Rates Among Blacks in Louisiana, by Age, 1890–1930*

Ages	1890	1900	1910	1920	1930
10–14	60.3	49.7	40.0	25.4	7.7
15–24	66.3	54.3	41.5	31.5	14.7
25–34	70.7	58.7	43.9	34.6	21.3
35–44	78.7	65.7	51.0	41.7	26.7
45–54	86.0	76.7	60.5	51.2	34.7
55–64	89.5	84.8	72.4	63.5	45.6
65-up	92.6	89.9	81.4	77.5	64.4

Source: U.S. Bureau of the Census, *Population Reports*, 1900, 1910, 1920, 1930.

The most extensive recent testing of reading and writing has been conducted by the National Assessment of Educational Progress. In tests of 17-year-olds, the Southeast (which differs from the Census South by excluding Texas, Oklahoma, Maryland, Delaware, and the District of Columbia) scored lower than any other region; the results illustrate functional, rather than conventional, illiteracy. This is especially revealing because the 17-year-old is the product of the present school system.

Although some industrial plants will not hire illiterates, the prevalence of illiteracy in the South apparently has not affected plant location. Following World War II, as more oil, chemical, atomic energy, and other technological industries located in the South, educational requirements for employment rose and, except for common labor, the illiterate worker was less likely to find employment in them (indeed, the unemployment rate of illiterates is higher than that of literate workers). Southern migrants to the North who found jobs in the automobile industry were able to perform the work but often encountered off-the-job difficulties: overextending themselves in credit installment purchases, failing to adjust to city life, or returning home without receiving permission from supervisors. Their absentee rates were higher than those of other workers. Similar employment difficulties evidently plague the Spanish-American in the Southwest.

In general, illiterates have lower learning capacity, are more likely to be welfare recipients, and have higher rejection rates for military service. If female, they have higher fertility rates, and the instances of infant mortality among illiterates are always higher. There is more illiteracy in rural than in urban areas.

The South has approximately 398,000 illiterates, according to estimates based upon the 1980 census and the November 1979 Current Population Survey. The distribution by color is: white, 44.9 percent; black, 51.4 percent; other nonwhite, 3.7 percent. By age, illiterates are distributed as follows: 14–24 years, 9.2 percent; 25–44 years, 17.0 percent; 45–64 years, 32.2 percent; and 65 years and over, 41.6 percent. These are individuals unable to read and write, according to census definitions; functional illiterates are more numerous.

See also: RELIGION: / Fatalism; SOCIAL CLASS: Poverty

Abbott L. Ferriss
Emory University

Sterling G. Brinkley, *Journal of Experimental Education* (September 1957); John K. Folger and Charles B. Nam, *Education of the American Population* (1967); Eli Ginzberg and Douglas W. Bray, *The Uneducated* (1953); *Historical Statistics of the United States to 1970* (1975); Carman St. John Hunter with David Harman, *Adult Illiteracy in the United States: A Report to the Ford Foundation* (1979); National Assessment of Educational Progress, Report No. 11-R-02 (1982), Report No. 10-W-01 (1980); U.S. Bureau of the Census, *Current Population Reports*, Series P-23, No. 6 (November 1959), No. 8 (February 1963), No. 116 (March 1982); Series P-20, No. 99 (March 1959), No. 217 (March 1971); Sanford Winston, *Illiteracy in the United States* (1930).

Innovations in Education

Education in the South, as in other sections of the United States, is more than schooling. It is, in Bernard Bailyn's words, "the entire process by which a culture transmits itself across the generations," a process that has been deeply and irrevocably influenced by ideas and events originating outside the region. The most prominent shaping forces have been industrialization, urbanization, democratization, and shifts in the class, status, and power structures. Southern educators have had to cope in recent times with such national problems as accelerated rates of social change, greater differentiation in social and occupational roles, the decline of the local community, alterations in the family structure, and increased centralization and bureaucratization of social, political, and economic control. Solutions to these problems have been neither easy nor close at hand.

Throughout the South and the rest of the country individuals and organizations have sought to implement reforms not only in education but also in municipal government, the civil service, capital-labor relations, conservation, and international relations. Industrialization surely created standardized national norms, institutions, and individuals, and education became linked to "human resource development" and "wealth creation." Distinctive differences in education between the South and the rest of the nation have declined under the pressures of creating an efficient industrial state.

The educational responses to industrialization and urbanization nevertheless occurred with different emphases and intensity in the South than in the North. Southern educational reformers used the rhetoric of national educational reformers, but the impulses for change were rooted in southern traditions and some changes were altered to suit regional values and institutions. At least one important result of the southern educational reform movement had no northern equivalent. By the 1950s the South had *two* complete public and segregated school systems, a remarkable organizational achievement. The two systems were gradually and grudgingly fused into one during the 1960s and 1970s.

Alternatives to the modern industrial state and its preferred educational patterns always have been readily available in southern culture. Southern populism, for example, frequently challenged modernism and reaffirmed the values of the local community that were threatened by impersonal and remote forces. Populist theory deplored the erosion of the individual's control over his or her own destiny; it preferred a social order in which power was accessible in close and familiar institutions. Conservative Protestant theology also has helped isolate southern intellectual life and culture from prevailing trends of American society. And the antimodernism exemplified by the Agrarian manifesto *I'll Take My Stand*, which included an essay on education by John Gould Fletcher, persists today in many currents of southern thought.

Contradictions and paradoxes abound in southern educational development. Support for innovations coexisted with a desire for the status quo. Industrialization and urbanization developed along with a longing for an agrarian culture. Commercialism conflicted with religious antimaterialism. Individualism and a striving for liberty contrasted with the values of community and social responsibility. Nationalism was opposed by regionalism. Educators had to hold these conflicting trends in uneasy balance, and innovation was never easy.

When revivals or reactions occur, they are sometimes called innovations, and in these terms the South has frequently been in the forefront. The "New Conservatism" that emerged in the late 1970s addressed such southern political, moral, and social concerns as states' rights, reduced involvement of the federal government in business and educational activities, abortion, gun control, school prayer, and busing. The more recent "back-to-basics" movement in education—a reform of reforms—asserts a position many southern educators never abandoned. It claims the decisive factors in higher levels of academic achievement are pedagogical, not financial: an emphasis in schools on order and discipline, excellence, regular homework, and a high degree of teacher involvement and control. These characteristics are more frequently found in private and parochial schools than in public schools. Paradoxically, this very traditional position may lead to innovations in the use of education vouchers and tuition tax credits, and may dictate the amount of financial support public schools can expect to receive in the future. Similarly, innovative methods and materials for teaching evolution may emerge from religious conservatism.

Innovation occurred within the limits of the three principal models of formal schooling that developed in the South. The *inclusive model* envisions an all-embracing institution providing not only education but a wide variety of social and vocational services as well. This type of school has distinctive roles to play in social, cultural, political, and economic affairs. It is based on the assumptions and proposals of John Dewey.

The *exclusive model* gives the school a severely restricted role. Assigned the task of providing intellectual training for the pupils, the school does not function as a broad social service agency. This kind of institution generally reflects traditionalist assumptions about knowledge, individuals, and society, and is found frequently in the private sector of education.

A *central model* espouses a middle position. It attributes to the school a double role: teaching academic disciplines and arranging for other agencies to provide specialized vocational training and to assist with personal development. This type of institution has gained considerable support since the 1970s.

Innovations in southern education have taken place both within this institutional framework and beyond it throughout the 20th century. Education came to be seen as an ongoing process, flexible in structure, timing, place, and content. In the 1960s a cult of constant innovation appeared, supported nationally by a southern president. Education, health, housing, and other social services were regarded as parts of a whole. There was much easy talk about systems management, designs for change, and change agents; and there was an abundance of educational experiments, movements, reforms, and "breakthroughs." The South has not always led the way in proposing changes in school organization (Head Start and Upward Bound, alternative schools, magnet schools, mainstreaming), use of school personnel (team teaching, collective negotiations, teacher aides), curriculum, (community resources, bilingual education, sex education), and learning techniques (individualized instruction, multimedia centers, computer-assisted instruction), but the region has been profoundly changed by application of such developments.

Higher education in the South did not change dramatically until after World War II, when it was affected by the growth in the number of students, the addition of many new buildings, changes in the balance of subjects, and different emphases on undergraduate, professional, and postgraduate studies. The traditional moderation of higher education was replaced by the less-restrained social service ideology of the multiversity. In the 1960s open admission policies and new study programs were tried (e.g., black and ethnic studies). Distance learning systems were put into operation, with the University of Maryland a member of the vanguard. In general, though, southern universities were not leaders in such developments, and some of the changes adopted in the 1950s, the 1960s, and the 1970s currently are being reassessed.

No single point of view permits easy interpretation of these innovations in southern education. Proponents claimed they would make learning more relevant, or more liberal and humane, or more efficient and cost-effective. Some critics merely said the new ideas and practices did not produce their intended results. Other critics accused the innovators of using the rhetoric of reform for conservative purposes. According to this view, the innovations were intended to increase the school's hold on its pupils and enhance its effectiveness as an instrument of socialization, surveillance, and social control. The cosmetic innovations, these critics said, had the effect of maintaining existing social, political, and economic structures while giving the appearance of changes.

Edgar B. Gumbert
Georgia State University

Bernard Bailyn, *Education in the Forming of American Society: Needs and Opportunities for Study* (1960); Robert Church and Michael W. Sedlak, *Education in the United States: An Interpretive History* (1976); Lawrence A. Cremin, *The Transformation of the School: Progressivism in American Education, 1876–1957* (1961); Henry Ehlers, ed., *Crucial Issues in Education* (6th ed., 1977); Ronald K. Goodenow and Arthur O. White, eds., *Education and the Rise of the New South* (1981); Theodore W. Hipple, ed., *The Future of Education, 1975–2000* (1974); Henry J. Perkinson, *The Imperfect Panacea: American Faith in Education, 1865–1976* (1977); Herbert I. Von Haden and Jean Marie King, *Innovations in Education: Their Pros and Cons* (1971).

Learned Societies

An agrarian region marked by far-flung plantation settlement and hampered by climate, intellectual traditionalism, and, ultimately, a sectional suspicion of northern imports, the antebellum South lagged far behind the rest of the nation in the development of learned societies. Those societies that did exist sprang up in port cities with strong European connections and relatively dense populations. Characterized as "one of the liveliest intellectual centers in colonial America," Charleston supported a Library Society (1748), the Charleston Museum (1773), which was dedicated to providing "an accurate natural history of the province," the South Carolina Literary and Philosophical Society (1813), and the Elliot Society of Natural History (1853).

Drawing little distinction between the theoretical and the practical, and committed to establishing the new nation on a respectable international footing, early organizers both North and South favored the founding of scientific societies that would name and study unique American resources. The two preeminent scientific societies in the Old South, the Elliot Society and the New Orleans Academy of Sciences (1853), attempted to rival their older eastern counterparts and succeeded in attracting the attention of such noted naturalists as John Bachman and Harvard's Louis Agassiz. In 1856 the Elliot Society had a membership comparable to scientific academies in Boston and Philadelphia.

In the late 19th and early 20th centuries the vast majority of national learned societies came into existence, and many of them established branches in the South. The American Philosophical Association, the Modern Language Association, the Society of Biblical Literature, and the American Academy of Religion all formed southern sections. At the same time, societies with a more specifically regional character grew up: the Southern

Historical Association (1934), the Southern Society for Philosophy and Psychology (1904), the Southern Sociological Society (1935), and the Southern Speech Communication Association (1930). Since 1947 the Southern Humanities Conference has drawn those scholarly organizations specializing in the humanities into closer association.

Institutes committed to benefiting specific industries or sponsors, commercially oriented research organizations, and traditional learned societies now cover the South. Embracing education (International Studies Association, South Carolina), science (American Society of Biological Chemists, Florida), and the humanities (Pythagorean Philosophical Society, Texas), the list of national societies headquartered, or active, in the southern states reflects New South diversity.

See also HISTORY AND MANNERS: / Southern Historical Association

Elizabeth M. Makowski
University of Mississippi

Joseph C. Kiger, *American Learned Societies* (1963); Alexander Oleson and Sanborn Brown, eds., *The Pursuit of Knowledge in the Early American Republic* (1976); Michael Zils, ed., *World Guide to Scientific Associations* (1982).

Legal Education

See LAW: Legal Education

Libraries

Books came with the first English settlers to the New World. The artist John White, after returning in 1590 to Roanoke Island off the coast of North Carolina, found little more remaining than, in his own words, "my books torn from the covers." A generation later, when the permanent colonies had been established, books and libraries became integral parts of southern life.

Although printing in the southern colonies was an 18th-century development, individual and even institutional libraries emerged earlier. A substantial supply of devotional titles was imported for these early ventures, but examination of book titles reveals that southern colonists paid less attention to theology than did their New England counterparts. In fact, most titles were in applied science, the need for agrarian and medical practical manuals being imperative from the colonies' earliest days. Literature took second place, with theology and history trailing.

Private libraries were common in the 18th-century South, the most famous being those of the Virginians William Byrd II, John Mercer, and Robert Carter of Nomini Hall. Byrd's was perhaps the first great collector's library in the British colonies developed for purely bibliophilic reasons. The library of Arthur Dobbs, colonial governor of North Carolina, was replete with travel books, natural histories, and works on architecture.

Institutional libraries also appeared in the colonial era. In addition to the collegiate collections at Henrico, the library that began at the College of William and Mary in the 1690s was, by the close of the 18th century, one of the most distinguished in the nation, with approximately 3,000 volumes. Financed by a grant from Princess Anne, the Bibliotheca Provinciales, or Annapolitan Library, was organized in Maryland about 1696, serving as a model for later collections sent to New York, Boston, Philadelphia, and Charleston. At approximately the same time the Reverend Thomas Bray instituted his program for the establishment of parochial and provincial libraries to assist both clergy and laity in their duties. These were established not only in Maryland but at Bath, N.C., and in Charleston. A later development in Charleston, with much more lasting impact, was the formation in 1748 of arguably the most influential of all southern public-club libraries—the Charleston Library Society. In Georgia the most distinguished library by far was that formed by George Whitefield and bequeathed to the Bethesda Orphanage, with the primary goal of transforming that institution into a college.

Libraries in the first two centuries of the South's development were more significant than formal education because reading habits were utilitarian and broadly based. More importantly, the lack of local printing in the South meant that the thirst for reading materials was satisfied by imports. At least until the 1850s, the white southerner had his or her mind, in the words of Richard Beale Davis, "shaped and directed by the world from which he or a recent ancestor had come."

The advent of American independence, the opening of Georgia western lands, the Louisiana Purchase, and the popularization of the cotton gin, all in the decades surrounding the turn of the 19th century, worked to bring additional opportunities to the southern planter. This same period saw the first attempts at establishing state universities in the region in Georgia and North Carolina. Libraries were still, for the most part, considered a private responsibility. Thus, although a number of fine library societies were established, they were rarely free or particularly accessible and hence had little impact on the average rural southerner. Such attitudes became even more apparent as sectional animosities rose. In a survey of 154 American libraries completed in 1849 by Charles Coffin Jewett only 21 were southern and only 7 of those held the national average of 10,580 volumes.

Collections of distinction were formed, however. The library of South Carolina College, one of the most distinguished of all educational institutions in the country, had its own building—an unusual phenomenon for any university of that day. Literary coteries in Charleston and Richmond supported existing library societies in those cities. On most campuses the libraries of strength were those owned by the debating and literary societies, with their holdings oriented toward the political, historical, and theological. Also, Thomas Jefferson played a key role in the creation and support of the Library of Congress, which was established in 1800. After the library's collection was ravaged by fire in 1814, Jefferson contributed his own library, which formed the core of the Library of Congress's collection until its decimation by another fire in 1851.

The gains made in library services were effectively lost with the onset of war in 1861. New libraries were established at a much lower rate than in the earlier decades. Always a luxury, libraries became virtually unnecessary when simple survival was in question. Private libraries, too, suffered. The distinguished libraries amassed by William Gilmore Simms in South Carolina and Joseph Davis in Mississippi fell under the torch of federal troops. The end of war and the beginning of Reconstruction brought little change immediately. Of the 226 libraries in the United States holding at least 10,000 volumes in 1876, only 29 were in the South. The situation for southern libraries was bleak: personal income was both low and uncertain due to the decreasing agricultural potential; population was sparse and scattered in rural areas, limiting accessibility for the clientele; illiteracy was high; and the race problem affected all aspects of southern life and led to the creation of dual systems of education, as well as other public institutions, when the region lacked resources to provide adequately for even one. Library services remained a low priority when public welfare, health, and education cried for assistance and provided more visible results.

The development of these other programs, however, facilitated the later development of libraries in the region by making governmental projects more acceptable to the populace. Public endeavors in library service were anticipated and better understood. Libraries profited from experiences of agricultural extensionists and others whose public-contact activities provided precedents.

The growth of land-grant colleges and agricultural schools, teacher education, and the general establishment of the public school system led to a more positive image for libraries in the South, lessening elitist tendencies and emphasizing the public responsibility. In 1895 the Cotton States and International Exhibition in Atlanta served to bring into clear focus much of the activity in this regard. Visitors had the opportunity to examine a model library, to view equipment used in libraries, and, most importantly, to see that libraries possessed enough value to be given a place in an exposition calling attention to southern progress. By 1897 Georgia, at the instigation of the staff of the Young Men's Library Association of Atlanta, became the first southern state to establish a statewide library association. Two years later the American Library Association held its first convention in the South, also in Atlanta. This served two significant purposes for the South: local librarians were stimulated by national library concerns, and the visitors to the South were able to realize the seriousness of purpose that characterized southern librarians.

Also in 1899, the first contribution from Andrew Carnegie to a library building in the South was made public. The grant to the city of Atlanta transformed its subscription library, in existence since 1867, into a free public facility. At the same time library apprentice classes, the first in the Southeast, were begun in connection with the Atlanta library, and a later contribution made possible, in 1905, the establishment of the Southern Library School at the Carnegie Library of Atlanta. Library awareness was growing. In 1901 North Carolina enacted a law providing for state support of rural school libraries. Virginia by 1923 had a supervisor of school libraries charged with expanding the number and capabilities of school libraries in that state. With the founding in 1920 of the Southeastern Library Association came an organization for coordinating interests and efforts of librarians within the region. Further developments through the Tennessee Valley Authority and various Works Progress Administration agencies provided opportunities for new buildings and expanded activities.

Bookmobile in Jefferson County, Ala., early 20th century

Since World War II, libraries and library services in the South have dramatically expanded. The concept of "networking"—libraries cooperating to share materials and services—has been quite popular throughout the South, increasing potential for future development. On-line cooperative efforts such as SOLINET in the Southeast and AMIGOS in the Southwest have made sophisticated access tools available even to small regional libraries. In addition, state library operations have benefited from collaborative and cooperative programs of interlibrary loans, multiunit purchasing, and shared costs for on-line searching.

It is, however, in the university library that the greatest growth has occurred. Through the leadership of Harry Ransom and others, the University of Texas and its Humanities Research Center has become one of the premier facilities of its type in the nation. The universities of Virginia, North Carolina, Georgia, Florida, and Texas, plus Louisiana State and Duke universities all have holdings in excess of 2 million volumes. The rapid growth rate of the Sunbelt South and the gradual increase in sophistication in the needs of users made broad-based, extensive information services imperative.

See also HISTORY AND MANNERS: / Byrd, William, II; Jefferson, Thomas

Robert M. Willingham, Jr.
University of Georgia

Mary Edna Anders, *Southeastern Librarian* (Spring 1956); Richard Beale Davis, *Intellectual Life in the Colonial South, 1585–1763*, 3 vols., (1978); John David Marshall, ed., *An American Library History Reader* (1961); Frances Lander Spain, "Libraries of South Carolina: Their Origins and Early History, 1700–1830" (Ph.D. dissertation, University of Chicago, 1944); Louis Round Wilson and Edward A. Wight, *County Library Services in the South* (1935).

Medical Education

See SCIENCE AND MEDICINE: Medical Education

Military Schools

Why are military schools associated with the South, when the most famous of all military preparatory schools is Culver in Indiana? None of the nation's four uniformed service academies is in the South, although Annapolis might demur. Yet popular culture loves southern military-school settings, as in the movie *Taps* (1982), Terence Fugate's 1961 novel *Drum and Bugle*, and Pat Conroy's *Lords of Discipline* (1980), which had as its thinly disguised locale his alma mater, The Citadel, in Charleston, S.C.

The association may be simply the popular perception of the South as America's Sparta, or it may be that the South produces more "Peck's Bad Boys" in need of military discipline. More important is British historian Marcus Cunliffe's argument that military academies have come to be regarded as a feature of "the *idea* of the South," whereas northern military schools are less visible in the culture. Military schools are not just in the South, they are of it as well.

The South has not been famed for its preparatory schools. Aside from Henry Tutwiler's antebellum Green Springs Academy in Havana, Ala., the Webb School at Bell Buckle, Tenn., Episcopal High School in Alexandria, Va., and Woodberry Forest School, also in Virginia, no civilian prep schools readily come to mind, unlike the prestigious ones of the Northeast: Choate, Groton, Hotchkiss, St. Paul's, Middlesex, Hill, and the three Phillipses—Andover, Exeter, and Brooks. Instead, military prep schools thrive, having withstood the reaction against them during the Vietnam War and despite the proliferation of private "segregation" academies in the South, which hurt military-school enrollment in the same period.

Although some military schools have shed uniforms and gone coed, others are still staunch traditionalists. In Alabama's Black Belt, Marion Military Institute is thriving once more with a healthy enrollment, one of only three or four military junior colleges in the United States. Southern military academies, such as Fishburne, Fork Union, and Hargrave in Virginia, Camden in South Carolina, Chamberlain-Hunt in Mississippi, and Riverside in Georgia continue to train boys in hopes of producing soldiers. The Florida Air Academy in Lakeland and the Marine Military Academy in Harlingen, Tex., specialize in training for nonarmy military service. Virginia's Massanutten and Randolph-Macon academies are still military, but have coed day students. Some of the old standbys are gone, though—Mississippi's Gulf Coast Military Academy and Tennessee's Sewanee Military Academy. Tennessee Military Institute is now "TMI Academy," and Georgia Military Academy became the civilian and coed Woodward Academy in 1966.

Montgomery, Ala., once had two private boys' day military prep schools, Starke and Hurt. Both are long since gone, but junior ROTC units are flourishing at all four public high schools, with a choice of army at Sidney Lanier and George Washington Carver, air force at Robert E. Lee, or the marines at Jefferson Davis.

How did all this enthusiasm for military schooling in the South begin? Captain Alden Partridge, a member of the U.S. Military Academy's first graduating class of 1806, founded Vermont's Norwich University on the West Point model in 1819 as the nation's first private military college. He and his Norwich alumni popularized military schooling, founding private and public military academies, institutes, and colleges along West Point lines, both in the North and the South.

These early academies took root and flourished in Dixie at a time of growing sectional consciousness and conflict. The 1831 Nat Turner slave rebellion in Southampton County, Va., and the 1832 nullification crisis in South Carolina, both challenges to southern social order, were followed by the establishment of the Virginia Military Institute (VMI) (1839) and the South Carolina Military Academy at The Citadel in Charleston (1842). In fact, the Palmetto State also supported a second military academy, The Arsenal, in Columbia, until the Civil War. Both these institutions became better known than New England's Norwich and served as exemplars for other southern military schools, as well as furnishing trained officers to their states' militias.

By the time of secession every southern state, except the newest one, Florida, either supported its own military colleges or extended state aid, including arms and accouterments, to private military schools. Federal assistance was also given, as when the U.S. Army detailed a regular officer to teach military theory and tactics at St. John's College in Annapolis in 1824, at Norwich and VMI in the 1830s, and at the University of Tennessee in 1840.

In 1845 Col. Robert T. P. Allen, known affectionately

to his cadets as "Rarin' Tarin' Pitchin' Allen," founded the Kentucky Military Institute (KMI). Although it was a private school, that commonwealth's governor was designated its "Inspector," and the state's adjutant general was a member of its board of visitors. It flourished until 1861, when its faculty and students marched off to war, some south and others north.

Major George Alexander founded the Arkansas Military Institute at Tulip in 1850, and it too flourished until its people went to war. Also in 1850 Mississippi's oldest chartered college, Jefferson, founded in 1802 near Natchez and attended by Jefferson Davis, resumed its military program earlier adopted in 1829 after the Alden Partridge plan. The state of Mississippi furnished it with muskets, and thus had its military academy without having to tax itself to maintain it.

In 1851 West Pointer Arnoldus V. Brumby organized Marietta's Georgia Military Institute, which received state aid until Georgia bought it in 1857 and turned it into a state college. In Tennessee the Western Military Institute at Tyree was merged with the ailing University of Nashville in 1855. Historian John Hope Franklin has written that "no State approached Alabama's feverish interest in military education displayed just before the Civil War." That state extended generous support to two military academies at La Grange and Glenville, providing scholarships to two cadets from each county. Alabama also furnished arms and drill manuals to eight other military schools at various times in the decade of the 1850s and introduced compulsory military training into the University of Alabama in 1860. Texas called Col. R. T. P. Allen from KMI to found the Texas Military Institute at Bastrop.

Not only did these schools produce southern subalterns (VMI had produced more than 400 officers by the time of the Civil War), but some of their faculty gained fame as Civil War generals. Bushrod R. Johnson, the military superintendent at the University of Nashville, became a Confederate major general. Major Daniel H. Hill, later a Confederate lieutenant general, opened the North Carolina Military Institute at Charlotte in 1859, and by the time Fort Sumter surrendered, 150 cadets were enrolled. Incidentally, Citadel cadets claim to have fired the first shot on Fort Sumter, so it was they who began the war. In 1860 the first superintendent of the new Louisiana State Seminary of Learning and Military Academy, now LSU and still known as "the Old War Skule," was that future scourge of the South, William Tecumseh Sherman. The immortal Thomas "Stonewall" Jackson was teaching at VMI during John Brown's raid and commanded a company of cadets that stood guard over the courthouse and jail at Harpers Ferry during Brown's trial and hanging. All these "West Points of the South" (a term VMI has since claimed for itself) established a relationship between military education and southern policy that was proven when the call to arms came. Also, all this time, southern representation at West Point itself remained disproportionately high, and many of its former cadets became Confederate leaders, the most famous being Jefferson Davis, class of 1828, and Robert E. Lee, class of 1829.

After Appomattox and during Reconstruction, practically all southern military schools disappeared, except for VMI and The Citadel. However, during the Civil War, in 1862, the U.S. Congress had passed the Morrill Land Grant Act, which provided for federal land grants to fund the establishment of state agricultural and mechanical colleges that were also required to furnish military instruction. The act did not make such training mandatory, but all the "aggie" schools became military. When such colleges were founded in the defeated and impoverished South, they revived the military-school tradition—at Arkansas in 1871; at Auburn and the Virginia Polytechnic Institute in 1872; at Starkville, Miss., in 1878, where the first president was ex-Confederate Lt. Gen. Stephen D. Lee; at the Georgia Institute of Technology in 1885; at Raleigh, N.C., in 1887; at Clemson, S.C., in 1889; at the revived Louisiana State University, which later boasted the largest barracks in the world; and above all, at Texas A&M, which by World War II had furnished more regular army officers than West Point (seniors there still wear breeches, boots, and spurs). In addition to the land-grant institutions, some of the older state universities began to offer military instruction after the Reserve Officer Training Corps Acts of 1916 and 1920 extended ROTC to other than military institutes and land-grant colleges. At times, it was even compulsory, as at the universities of Mississippi and Alabama and at private colleges such as Davidson. Meanwhile, the southern military preparatory schools began reviving by the 1880s and became fashionable by the Gay Nineties, especially in Virginia's Shenandoah Valley.

Some who argue for the existence of a peculiarly southern martial tradition, such as sociologist Morris Janowitz, suspect that it really came into its own after the Confederacy's defeat; by 1910, 90 percent of the U.S. Army's general officers had southern affiliations. Douglas MacArthur first donned a uniform at a Texas military institute; George Catlett Marshall graduated from VMI to lead the U.S. Army and Air Corps into victory in World War II; the U.S. Marine commander in the Pacific War against Japan, Holland M. "Howlin' Mad" Smith, started his martial career as an Auburn cadet; and General William Westmoreland, commander of U.S. forces in Vietnam, attended The Citadel before receiving an appointment to West Point. During the Vietnam War, when public support for the military reached its nadir, military programs suffered less on southern university campuses than in any other part of America. At Chapel Hill an antiwar protest rally during the Cambodian invasion of 1970 fizzled out, and the following year enrollment applications at VMI and The Citadel rose from previous declines. ROTC programs continued to be maintained on southern civilian college campuses as well. In the 1980s support for military education has increased nationwide, but the South remains the region most committed to it.

See also HISTORY AND MANNERS: Civil War; Military Tradition; Vietnam War; MYTHIC SOUTH: Fighting South

John Hawkins Napier III
Montgomery, Alabama

Army Information Digest (December 1964); William Chapman, *Washington Post* (13 April 1970); Shelby Coffey III, *Washington Post's Potomac Magazine* (9 August 1970); Marcus Cunliffe, *Soldiers and Civilians: The Martial Spirit in America, 1775–1865* (1968); John Hope Franklin, *The Militant South* (1956); Morris Janowitz, *The Professional Soldier: A Social and Political Portrait* (1960); Patricia Linden, *Town and Country* (August 1976); Guy Martin, *Esquire* (June 1985); Drew Middleton, *New York Times* (18 April 1971); John Hawkins Napier III, *Alabama Historical Quarterly* (Fall–Winter 1967), *Alabama Review* (October 1980); William E. Schmidt, *New York Times* (9 April 1984).

Politics of Education

As a vehicle for socializing youth, education is usually seen as a liberalizing and enlightening force. However, education is often a force for oppression, mystification, and enslavement. Any objective evaluation of the historic role of education in the South reveals consistent theoretical and practical examples of the use of education as an oppressive force. Southern educational structure, financing, content, and expansion/development patterns have reflected the region's racist, elitist, patriarchal, paternalistic, and isolationist politics.

In the antebellum period educational policies and practices were woefully inequitable, combining exclusionary education with little or no governmental involvement. In most cases, rich white male children were sent to England for schooling or taught by tutors. Education for blacks was viewed as dangerous for both the slaves and the white elite. Education for women was seen as damaging to their health and to the natural order of society. Women, like slaves, were presumed incapable of, as well as uninterested in, attaining more than minimal academic training. Education for poor white males was rendered problematic because of the exclusive and costly nature of education in the South.

After the Civil War, educational opportunities improved for all groups, especially for those previously excluded. Reconstruction politics led to new educational systems stemming from government involvement in the southern educational process. However, the removal of federal troops from the South heralded the beginning of political segregation, which was reflected in segregated and unequal educational institutions, financing, and opportunities.

Blacks, women, and poor whites were allowed access to academic training, but clearly the education available to them was designed to reinforce their subordinate roles. The black precollegiate and collegiate institutions that began during the period of Reconstruction were forced to function with limited human and material resources. Educational opportunities for women were geared toward gender-biased training and sex-stereotyped careers. Poor white males consistently faced economic barriers to educational goals. The basic theoretical and practical character of southern education continued to reflect a racist, patriarchal, and class-biased political culture.

The civil rights era ushered in some changes, but the basic relationship between the ruling elite and subordinate groups remained. Positive gains such as increased financial support for blacks, women, and poor whites, and less social rigidity—a consequence of minority pressure on the ruling group—must be viewed in conjunction with the reduction in the number of black principals, reduced control over precollegiate educational institutions in the black community, vocational tracking by white counselors and administrators, curricula changes that deemphasized the importance and richness of a distinct black culture, and creation of an illusion of equality that continues to impede positive changes in the South.

Recent political moves toward decentralization, revenue sharing, and block grants to the states provide the South with another opportunity to reimpose and reinforce the political values of the Old South on the New South. Whatever the final outcome, the politics of the South will likely be reflected in the politics of southern education.

See also BLACK LIFE: Education, Black; LAW: Civil Rights Movement; POLITICS: Ideology, Political; SOCIAL CLASS: Politics and Social Class

Shelby Lewis
Atlanta University

Charles W. Dabney, *Universal Education in the South*, 2 vols. (1936); Winifred Green, *New South* (Fall 1970); Patrick McCauley and Edward D. Ball, eds., *Southern Schools: Progress and Problems* (1959); M. Hayes Mizell, *New South* (Winter 1971); Gary Orfield, *The Reconstruction of Southern Education: The Schools and the 1964 Civil Rights Act* (1969).

Quality of Education

The quality of southern education has improved significantly in the years following racial desegregation of southern schools and colleges. The quality of education is more obvious at all levels of elementary, secondary, and postsecondary schooling. Improvement has been made and continues to be made, but the need for appreciable improvement remains.

The improved quality of education can be attributed in large measure to the growth and expansion of educational opportunity in the southern region as southerners have struggled to achieve the national level of educational quality. Census figures show that southerners now complete more years of formal schooling than they previously did. High school students now graduate at a rate much closer to the national average. College enrollments indicate that southerners now attend college at a rate and in a manner more closely approximating that of the nation and its other regions. Educational statistics at all levels and in all areas suggest convergence with national norms and indices of educational progress. Large differences between the regions existed in 1971, but these had diminished considerably by 1980. For example, in 1971 the Southeast had the largest proportion (36 percent) of nine-year-old students in the lowest achievement group, and the Central States had the smallest proportion (19 percent), a difference of 17 percentage points. By 1980 the Southeast still had the largest proportion in the lowest achievement group (30 percent) and the Northeast had the smallest (21 percent), but the difference was only eight percentage points. The same was true for the 13- and 17-year-old students. The South has accomplished much in its concerted efforts to "catch up."

Significant progress has been made in the preschool and kindergarten years of public education. Among those states with increased rates of participation in preprimary programs, the increase for some was quite dramatic. Eleven states, eight of which were in the Southeast, showed increases of 50 percentage points or more over the period. Arkansas (3 percent in 1971 and 83 percent in 1981) and North Carolina (10 percent in 1971 and 88 percent in 1981) experienced the largest increases. Southern children now generally begin their formal schooling at an earlier age than they did a decade ago, and their chances for success at each subsequent level of education have been appreciably enhanced. Middle schools have replaced junior high schools in most progressive school districts, and opportunities for vocational, technical, or career-related forms of education have greatly expanded at secondary and postsecondary levels. The years of schooling have thus been extended on both ends, while substantive, qualitative changes have been made in the form and content of the education southerners receive.

The improved quality of southern education is evident not only in the quantitative indices of attendance, access, and years completed, but also in the impressions and viewpoints of visitors, the professional judgment of educators, and the national images created by the news media. The location of corporate business and industry in the South remains dependent upon "the quality of the schools" the children of executives, middle managers, and skilled technicians will attend—and upon local schools and colleges as a source of trained, technically competent manpower. Once the prototype of regional branch-office cities, Atlanta enjoys a national reputation as "the nation's most desirable location" for the relocation of national offices; its public schools are depicted nationally as one of education's remarkable success stories.

The South remains a distinctive region educationally by virtue of the composition of its population. Relatively speaking, the South is still younger than other regions and thus has a larger proportion of its population to educate. Between 1950 and 1980 the per capita personal income of southerners increased greatly although it was still only 90 percent of the national figure in 1980. Southerners, despite their belief in education as a means of economic and technological development, continue to tax themselves at a lower rate than other states and regions. Although southerners spend a larger proportion of their tax revenues on higher education, the expenditure per capita falls well below the national average. The salaries of public school teachers and college faculty continue to compare unfavorably with those of their national counterparts.

Other regional differences bearing indirectly on the quality of education include a lower level of urbanization and the South's racial composition. In 1984 only 69 percent of southerners lived in a metropolitan area, as compared to the 76 percent national average. The percentage of blacks in a state's total population ranged from 35.2 percent in Mississippi to 3.3 percent in West Virginia. The combination of the region's urban-rural mix and its racial composition continued in 1985 to produce great tension between schools in the inner city and public schools in suburban areas. The effects on educational quality of establishing private academies in small towns and semirural areas are as yet unclear.

Despite the improved quality of education in the South, there are still lingering, persistent gaps between regional and national achievements. Some gaps may be narrower because of the decline in national standards and norms, and it is distinctly possible that the South did not—or could not—catch up as much as it might have. National efforts to expand educational opportunities for a growing and increasingly pluralistic society have resulted in the side effects of test-score decline, grade inflation, and a crisis in literacy. To many social critics such by-products reflect a genuine decline in the quality of American education and a serious erosion of educational norms and values.

Regional differences in the reading, writing, and computational skills of public school children have been documented by the National Assessment of Educational Progress. Despite noticeable gains by students in the South, National Assessment findings tell an old and embarrassing story of educational deficits. A large proportion of public school students do not meet national expectations in basic learning skills or educational achievement; for most skills and accomplishments the proportion of failing students in the southern region is larger than the proportion reported for other regions of the nation.

Irrespective of lingering regional differences, however, the quality of southern education in the 1980s is directly and immediately affected by national trends and developments. Few questions of quality peculiar to the South have been raised about schools and colleges, and no unique challenge has been identified for southern education. National concerns and issues have focused directly on projected declines in high school and college enrollments, the inadequacies of academic preparation at the secondary school level, and the urgent need for schools and colleges to work more closely on a host of mutual problems. Many southern high schools, like their national peers, have diversified their curricula at the expense of educational substance and content. A large majority have been seeking means of implementing concepts of competency-based education or minimal competency testing mandated by state legislators. The national concern with quality has included a growing dissatisfaction with the last two years of high school and the first two years of college. Colleges have increasingly found it necessary to teach students basic skills not acquired in 12 years of public schooling. National panels and task forces have addressed once again the nation's need for general education, core curricula, and advanced learning skills. Funding priorities and commitments of the federal government have again undergone major shifts or alterations. Education at all levels has been suspected of diminished quality, eroded standards, or loss of integrity. For the first time, southern educators have been able to address questions of quality in a national context of mutual concern and understanding.

See also BLACK LIFE: Education, Black

Cameron Fincher
University of Georgia

Simon S. Johnson, *Update on Education: A Digest of the National Assessment of Educational Progress* (1975); Michael M. Myers, ed., *Fact Book on Higher Education in the South: 1981 and 1982* (1982); National Education Association, *Estimates of School Statistics, 1984–85* (1985).

Religion and Education

Religious institutions and individuals have used education to influence southern culture. Churches have established denominational schools and colleges, interdenominational academies, and theology schools. They have conducted weekly Sunday schools and annual Vacation Bible School classes. All of these institutions have communicated the specific teachings and ways of individual denominations, but they have typically also been standard-bearers of southern regional ways as well. They reflected the dominant evangelical approach of the region's numerically and culturally dominant Protestant groups. The ties between religion, education, and the broader culture were especially apparent in the role of religion in the public schools.

The Anglican church established the College of William and Mary in 1693, and it remained the only religious college in the South until well into the 18th century. Religious groups in the colonial period trained ministers through apprenticeship programs. The number of denominational colleges, many of which also had theology schools, increased markedly in the late 1700s and early 1800s. Roman Catholics established the South's first school of theology—St. Mary's in 1791 in Maryland. By the early 1800s Catholics operated seminaries in Charleston, St. Louis, New Orleans, and Bardstown, Ky.

After the Great Revival at the turn of the 1800s, evangelical churches—especially the Baptists, Methodists, and Presbyterians—became increasingly prominent in the South and established their own schools. Many congregations and worshipers believed that education was less important than "the call" to the ministry, and many southerners since then have been suspicious of formally trained clergy, favoring religious zeal as the prime crite-

Southern Baptist Theological Seminary, Louisville, Ky., 1931

rion for a successful preacher. Nonetheless, the southern churches have not been so antiintellectual that they did not support educational institutions.

Presbyterians have a long tradition of supporting education, and this was reflected in the South. They established Hampden-Sydney in Virginia in 1776, with a seminary added in 1807, and the Union Theological Seminary in Richmond in 1812. They supported Transylvania University in Kentucky, the first college west of the Appalachian Mountains, but withdrew assistance in 1818. Centre College of Kentucky was a cooperative effort of the church and the state; in 1824 the school became fully affiliated with the Presbyterians. Davidson College, which was named for General William Lee Davidson, began near Charlotte in 1836.

In the 1830s the Methodists launched Randolph-Macon in Virginia, Emory in Georgia, Emory and Henry in Virginia, and Holston in Tennessee. The Baptists founded Furman in South Carolina in 1826, Mercer in Georgia in 1833, and Wake Forest in North Carolina in 1834. These were founded by state conventions or regional conferences and assemblies. The University of Richmond in Virginia (1832) was the first attempt of Baptists in the South to establish a school to train their preachers. The Southern Baptist Theological Seminary was set up in Greenville, S.C., in 1859, and moved to Louisville, Ky., in 1877. Some antebellum colleges began as denominational institutions but later became public schools—Auburn University in Alabama started as the Methodist-supported East Alabama Male College (opening in 1859), and the University of Kentucky traces its history back to Kentucky University (1865), a Disciples of Christ school.

The Civil War was as devastating to southern denominational schools as to other aspects of life in the region. The schools and their personnel had assisted in the religious justification of the Old South and offered institutional moral support to the Confederacy. After the war some religious schools became central institutions in tying Christian and southern values together. The University of the South at Sewanee, Tenn., was officially founded in the late 1850s, but it did not offer programs until its resurrection after the war. Washington College became forever identified with southern tradition when Robert E. Lee chose to spend his postwar years there as president, until his death in 1870; the school was soon renamed Washington and Lee.

Following the Civil War large numbers of religiously supported or affiliated black schools emerged. The American Missionary Association was a nondenominational (though mostly supported by Congregationalists) agency that worked among the freedmen during Reconstruction and after. By 1870 it helped to support 170 colleges. The African Methodist Episcopal church, the African Methodist Episcopal Zion church, and other northern Methodist churches also played an important role in religious education in the South after the war. Schools dating from this period include Fisk in Tennessee, Hampton Institute in Virginia, Tuskegee and Talladega in Alabama, Atlanta University in Georgia, and Tougaloo and Rust in Mississippi. Baptists founded Roger Williams University in Nashville in 1863, and the Presbyterian and Reformed churches set up Biddle University in Charlotte in 1867 and Knoxville College in Tennessee in the 1870s. Episcopalians established St. Augustine's in Raleigh, N.C., in 1867.

Church work, especially by evangelical groups, expanded during the late 19th and early 20th centuries as a part of the effort to impose religious values on the South. The Methodists had high hopes for Vanderbilt, which began as that denomination's central college in 1873. The church broke ties in 1914, after the school's governing board became increasingly independent. Emory, Southern Methodist University, and later Duke became important church-supported liberal arts colleges. The Disciples of Christ began financial assistance to the Add-Ran Male and Female College in 1889, and that assistance continued when the school became Texas Christian University in 1902. A closely related religious group, the Churches of Christ, emerged in the early 20th century and now operates 17 schools of higher education, mostly in the South, including David Lipscomb in Nashville, Tenn., Freed-Hardeman in Henderson, Tenn., Harding University in Searcy, Ark., Oklahoma Christian College in Oklahoma City, Lubbock Christian College in Lubbock, Tex., and Abilene Christian University in Abilene, Tex. These institutions are located in areas of the greatest strength of the Churches of Christ.

The South's financial resources could not always match the interest of its religious people in maintaining denominational schools. In 1874 the Methodist Episcopal Church, South, supported 50 colleges, but by 1902 the number had been reduced to 18. A Southern Baptist Convention committee insisted that the "disease of starting Baptist Colleges has been sporadic, endemic, and epidemic." Nonetheless, the churches were not abandoning educational work. Many former colleges were simply reclassified as secondary schools, still under church sponsorship at a reduced cost level. The *Report of the Commissioner of Education, 1899–1900* from the federal government revealed that of 26,237 young people in educational institutions in the 11 former Confederate states plus Kentucky and Oklahoma, 13,859 were attending schools sponsored in some way by churches.

Denominational schools have continued to fulfill a number of vital functions for the churches in the 20th century. The evangelical groups are particularly concerned with missionary activity, and schools are a way to convey that interest to the young. Schools train lay people to work in counseling, publishing, and administration; they provide expertise in adult education, music, and recreational work. Faculties of these institutions are resources for local churches, offering workshops, institutes, and lectures.

The chief concern of denominational schools is the training of the clergy, and major church groups operate important theological schools. The southern Presbyterians maintain four seminaries: Union in Richmond (1823), Louisville in Kentucky (1901), Austin in Texas (1902), and Columbia in Decatur, Ga. (1928). The Cumberland Presbyterian church has Bethel College, McKenzie, Tenn., and the Memphis Theological Seminary. The theological school at Baylor University (established 1901) evolved into the Southwestern Baptist Theological Seminary in Fort Worth (1908). The Baptists also sponsor the Southern Baptist Theological Seminary, which has been in Louisville, Ky., since 1877; the New Orleans seminary (1917); and Southeastern at Wake Forest, N.C. (1951). Important Methodist theological schools are the Perkins School at SMU, the Candler School at Emory, and the Duke Divinity School. The Protestant Episcopal Theological Seminary of Virginia is in Alexandria, and the Episcopal Seminary of the Southwest is in Austin, Tex. St. Luke's School of Theology at the University of the South was the home to one of the South's most accomplished theologians, William Porcher DuBose.

Theological seminaries were rarely well endowed, and they had to face what historian Kenneth K. Bailey has called "a stifling popular distrust of scholarship." When scholarly findings revised traditional beliefs, "ancient myth was often acclaimed over present truth." A writer in the *Southern Methodist Review* in 1887 warned that requiring college training for itinerant preachers would "sound the death-knell of the Church." There were numerous celebrated attempts to remove professors at southern seminaries for teaching "dangerous" ideas—Alexander Winchell at Vanderbilt, James Woodrow at the Presbyterians' Columbia Seminary, Crawford H. Toy and William H. Whitsitt at the Baptist seminary in Louisville, and later, in the 1920s, John A. Rice at Southern Methodist University.

The Fundamentalist movement led to increasing questioning of the teachings of seminary professors during the 1920s. All southern white churches faced conflict over the issue, although the Presbyterian Church in the United States had fewer challenges than did the southern Methodists and the Southern Baptist Convention. Theological seminaries in the South have frequently faced challenges to their academic freedom, but their presidents and faculty have just as often stood up for free intellectual expression. They have represented religious humanism and ecumenicism within denominations that have sometimes not championed those ideas in general.

The relationship between religion and education involves more than the training of preachers and the establishment of denominational schools. A good measure of the influence of southern religion on the overall regional culture is the importance of religion in public education. After the Civil War, southern churches and religious leaders crusaded to impose their moral values on society and also worked to insure religious influence in schools. At first the churches were suspicious of public education. The 1871 General Assembly of the southern Presbyterian church insisted that education was "too dear, too vital to us as a Church, to be remitted to the State." Other church groups agreed, and the Methodists, especially, embarked on an ambitious plan to establish church boarding schools and other institutions for mass education. By the turn of the century the results were disappointing, because few such efforts were adequately supported financially.

The major denominations in the South came to champion the idea of public elementary and secondary schools; they worked to insure religious influences within public education. Vanderbilt University Chancellor James H. Kirkland noted in 1910 that in the South "no unfriendly attitude has been shown to religion either in the lower schools or in the State universities. The Bible is generally read in the public schools, and often school is opened with a song and prayer." In the 1960s historian Francis Butler Simkins wrote that "the implementation of universal education by the southern states bids fair to be the means of making Christianity universal." Schools and colleges across the region "resound with daily prayers, hymns, and Bible reading." University faculty senates began their proceedings with prayers in some places through the 1970s, and sporting events often still begin with invocations (which sometimes are thinly veiled supplications to the gods for assistance to the home team).

Religion's place in public education has become an important issue in the contemporary period because of the church-state relationship. Although national in scope, the debate has focused especially on the South because of the region's tradition of close ties between religion and education. In the 1960 presidential campaign Democratic party nominee John F. Kennedy spoke in Houston before a Protestant ministerial alliance, assuring the preachers that he would not support federal government funds for parochial schools; 20 years later southern fundamentalists were eager to receive tax credits for parents sending children to the Christian academies that increasingly dot the southern landscape.

Challenges to inclusion of prayers in public schools have come from the South. Madalyn Murray O'Hair was in the border South—Maryland—when she filed the lawsuit that led to the 1963 Supreme Court decision outlawing prayer in the public schools. She later moved to Austin, Tex., where she has since established an archives of the American atheist movement and has continued to campaign against church-state ties. In the 1980s a black father in Alabama challenged that state's laws permitting moments of silence in the schools. The South's role in this controversy is complicated. The Southern Baptist Convention has long advocated a strict separation of religion and public education and has generally opposed government aid to schools as well as opposing school prayers. Baylor University has been a leader in studying the issue and has a *Journal of Church and State*. The Virginia-based Moral Majority, on the other hand, has led national efforts to ratify a school-prayer amendment to the Constitution.

Religious leaders and organizations have also played a major role in influencing textbook adoptions in the South. They have testified before state textbook commissions and persuaded many of them to exclude books discussing theories of evolution. Religious leaders and individuals were also prominent in efforts in the early and mid-20th century to adopt only textbooks that positively portrayed southern history and white supremacy. The intimate ties between region and religion were especially clear here.

Finally, the humble Sunday school deserves mention for its role in southern culture. It is not uniquely southern nor even American. Robert Raikes, a printer and publisher in England, is normally considered the founder of the Sunday school movement, which caught on in the United States in the early 1800s. The first Sunday school in the South was apparently established in 1803 in the Second Baptist Church in Baltimore. Many religious people opposed the school idea at first as unbiblical, and Sunday schools were long a local congregational, lay effort more than an official tool of denominations. Sunday schools typically were regarded as missionary work—the Southern Baptist Convention at first included them as part of its Domestic Mission Board; that denomination's present Sunday School Board, headquartered in Nashville, was not set up until 1891. The major denominations embarked on campaigns after World War II to expand their Sunday school work so that it soon involved extensive organization, participation by adults as well as children, increased funding, and elaborate publications. The Sunday schools and related Vacation Bible Schools in the summer may not have been uniquely southern, but they have been fondly remembered institutions of regional life, effectively introducing children not only to the tenets of the region's dominant evangelical churches but also to the dominant cultural attitudes on race relations, child rearing, male-female roles, and countless other topics.

Charles Reagan Wilson
University of Mississippi

Donald S. Armentrout, *The Quest for the Informed Priest: A History of the School of Theology* (1979); Kenneth K. Bailey,

Southern White Protestantism in the Twentieth Century (1964); Ben C. Fisher, in *Encyclopedia of Religion in the South*, ed. Samuel S. Hill (1984); Thomas C. Hunt, James C. Carper, Charles R. Kniker, eds., *Religious Schools in America: A Selected Bibliography* (1986); Charles D. Johnson, *Higher Education of Southern Baptists: An Institutional History, 1826–1954* (1955); Lynn E. May, *Sunday School Leadership* (October 1980); Alan Peshkin, *God's Choice: The Total World of a Fundamentalist Christian School* (1986); Edward J. Power, *Catholic Higher Education in America* (1972); Joe M. Richardson, *Christian Reconstruction: The American Missionary Association and Southern Blacks, 1861–1890* (1986).

Rural and Agricultural Education

When the "Boll Weevil Special" of the Illinois Central Railway pulled into stations throughout the lower Mississippi River Valley, farmers turned out to see the latest in seed, fertilizer, and machinery, all displayed in the boxcars. They turned out, too, to hear lectures from state agriculture agents and university agronomists, who told farmers of the best methods for combating the weevil and other pests. Agents, professors, and displays all traveled in the "Special" during its two-week run through the rural South.

What the farmers got from the "Special" and the other "educational trains" was a continuing agricultural education, delivered in an unusual but fitting way. The trains operated in the South during the first decades of the 20th century and were both a symbolic and practical response by state education officials, state agricultural officials, the U.S. Department of Agriculture, and private interests to the unusual needs and problems of the rural South. During the 19th and early 20th centuries observers from all political points of view agreed that these problems and needs, particularly as they applied to agricultural and rural education, were great.

"Since the war," said Populist L. F. Livingston, "our people have had less opportunity for thought and study than any people in modern history; outside our cities, popular education has largely been a farce." U.S. Commissioner of Education N. H. R. Dawson devoted 50 pages of his *Report of the Commissioner of Education, 1887–88* to chronicling the paucity of educational opportunity in the rural South. Dawson found that in every possible measure of educational progress, the South lagged behind the North and West.

School terms ran 50 to 60 days in the rural South and 100 to 150 in the North and West. Massachusetts spent, in 1880, an average of $14.93 per pupil enrolled in its common schools, the highest in the nation. The lowest level of per capita expenditure by a non-southern state was New Jersey's $3.23. Louisiana's $1.53 was the highest in the South and still a princely sum compared to Alabama's $.96 spent for each pupil enrolled in the common schools. This lack of educational opportunity resulted in a staggering rate of adult illiteracy. In 1902 the U.S. Commissioner of Education found a 13.2 percent rate of illiteracy among adult white males living in the rural counties of New Hampshire. In Virginia the comparable rates were 35.4 percent for whites and 65.7 percent for blacks, figures that were typical of the region.

Dawson, in his 1887–88 report, admitted that the idea of the common school, of a schoolhouse in every hamlet and town, had never caught on in the South as it had in the North. Looking back, it is possible to see why this was so. First, settlement patterns in the southern colonies and states created a population more dispersed than in the North and even more dispersed than on the western frontier. The communities that evolved in the rural South were plantation centered, and bonds between families were personal rather than political or legal. In terms of both logistics and custom, the dispersion of the population discouraged the creation of government-sponsored schools.

Second, the South suffered under the double burden of a high population of school-age children and a low level of taxable wealth in the years after the Civil War. For every one child per adult in Massachusetts in 1890, there were two in South Carolina. In the same year, a 1 percent tax in Massachusetts raised five times the revenue as the same tax in the Palmetto State. So southerners were faced with large numbers of children to educate and few financial resources with which to accomplish the task. For rural producers this was asking too much. In times of agricultural depression, the provision of schooling became a near financial impossibility in most communities if left to their own revenue-producing ability.

Third, state political leaders were unwilling to provide centralized support for schooling in the South. Many agreed with the editor of the Scotland Neck *Democrat* who argued in 1887 that "[e]ducation had ruined a great many more men than it has helped." What ruined men, black and white, was the tendency of education to "fire the mind of the ignorant with dreams." "To educate a fellow above the station he moves in," claimed the editorial, "ruins his value as a citizen and destroys his usefulness as a member of society." The experience of Reconstruction, particularly the efforts of the Freedmen's Bureau and of local black school societies, reinforced for many white southerners the dangers of education for any but the elite. The New Orleans *Bulletin* in 1874 railed against northerners teaching in the bureau's schools and argued that under such tutelage blacks would soon demand social and political equality. The *Bulletin* urged its readers not to hire educated blacks, as they were "the most intelligent, therefore the most dangerous." As long as the prevailing view connected education and social instability, white support for schooling for the rural inhabitants of the region remained weak.

Deepening contact between northerners and southerners in the fields of business, education, and politics accompanied the growth of the New South. With that contact came revised notions concerning the social function of education that put agricultural education at the center of a movement to reform rural southern culture.

The model for the "new education" for the New South grew from two sources. In philosophy, the movement to establish schools in the rural South rested on the unlikely example of Samuel C. Armstrong's Hampton Institure. Armstrong, a Freedmen's Bureau agent, founded Hampton in 1868, with assistance from the American Missionary Association, as a white-controlled school for blacks. At Hampton, Armstrong combined training in agriculture with academic courses and rigid discipline to educate blacks to achieve within the narrowly defined limits of their social and economic sphere. The Hampton experiment proved to some southern leaders what northern educators had been saying and practicing for decades: namely, that education could be a powerful force in preserving social stability among blacks and whites alike.

The curriculum of the "new education" owed much to the success of the land-grant colleges, established by the passage of the Morrill Act in 1862. In the South the colleges quickly became centers of research in agriculture. Knowledge of new methods and techniques promised to "readjust agriculture and place it upon a plane of greater profit, reconstruct the rural home, and give attraction and dignity to country life," wrote Seaman A. Knapp, a leader of the "new education." But standing in the way of this revolution in rural living was the illiteracy, the poverty, and the lack of educational means for disseminating the discoveries made in the colleges. Southern educational leaders began in the last decades of the 19th century to push for educational reform based on the Hampton model of skill-centered, "appropriate" education, but with limited success.

Help came in the form of political clout, ideas, organization, and hard cash from the North, and from northern associates of the shapers of the New South. At the center of the northern effort was Robert C. Ogden, New York businessman, philanthropist, and churchman. Ogden had business interests in the South, but his main connection to the region was through his friend Armstrong. Ogden served as a Hampton trustee for 40 years and during that time was instrumental in raising funds for the school. In 1898 he turned his talents and energies to the broader task of organizing a campaign for southern education and, at the urging of J. L. M. Curry, Charles W. Dabney, and others, took the chairmanship of a loose confederation of educational reformers and welded them into the powerful Southern Education Board (1901).

The board began its work as a publicity machine, sending speakers, letters, and circulars to southern politicians, teachers' organizations, and communities. This public campaign sought to encourage support for, and funding of, schools at every level. Ogden recruited able spokesmen to the cause, including Charles B. Aycock, Edwin A. Alderman, Seaman A. Knapp, Albert Shaw, and Charles McIver. Together and separately they canvassed the South, building support for public schooling and the idea of individual and social progress through education.

In 1902 Ogden announced that a generous gift from John D. Rockefeller made it possible for the board to take more direct action. As the General Education Board, Ogden and his group sponsored teachers in rural areas, paid for a regionwide system of rural school inspectors, supported agricultural extension work, funded agricultural experiment stations, helped the "education trains" to carry their message, and managed, through the donation of equipment and supplies, the creation of an agricultural curriculum in southern schools. By 1920 the General Education Board had disbursed over $14 million, most of it raised in the North, in its efforts to build up rural education in the South.

More than simply injecting needed money and manpower into the cause of rural and agricultural education, though, the Campaign for Education in the South recast the idea of education in such a way that it gained the support of southern political leaders and the public in general. To rural producers and their families, education in agricultural methods and the dissemination of new techniques, whether adult education or vocational education for children, promised more productive farms and a better quality of life. To southern policymakers, as Henry W. Grady promised, schools offered "an efficient system of drilling the children to the habits of discipline and the customs of obedience which make for public order."

By the time the "Special" made its last run in 1925, the effort to build schools in the rural South, at least for whites, had succeeded. Southern school reform, in the 1920s, became an element of the national Progressive movement and lost much of its regional tone. Like the "Boll Weevil Special," rural educational development in the South owed much to northern initiative, took education to farmers and their families, and focused on skill training within the agricultural economy of the region. The combination promised a new century of educational growth for the rural South.

See also AGRICULTURE: Diversification; / Agricultural Extension Services; Knapp, Seaman A.; HISTORY AND MANNERS: Philanthropy, Northern; MYTHIC SOUTH: New South Myth

Theodore R. Mitchell
Dartmouth College

James D. Anderson, in *Work, Youth, and Schooling: Historical Perspectives on Vocationalism in American Education*, ed. Harvey Kantor and David Tyack (1982); Charles W. Dabney, *Universal Education in the South*, 2 vols. (1936); Paul Gaston, *The New South Creed: A Study in Southern Mythmaking* (1970); Carl Kaestle, *Pillars of the Republic: Common Schools and American Society, 1780–1860* (1983); A. C. True, in U.S. Department of Agriculture, *Miscellaneous Publications*, no. 15 (1923); C. Vann Woodward, *Origins of the New South, 1877–1913* (1951).

Teachers

Teaching in the South began as an uncertain, insecure, and temporary calling. Most antebellum teachers were men with no special qualifications who taught for irregular terms in scattered rural schools. Ranging from prospective ministers to itinerant ne'er-do-wells, these teachers worked for miserable wages and often "boarded 'round" with the parents of their students. The South's private academies, which sometimes received public funds, offered more stable employment and attracted better-qualified teachers.

The Civil War and Reconstruction devastated public and private education in the region. Black education did advance, thanks to the support of the Freedmen's Bureau and northern philanthropic and religious organizations. Northern teachers came south to assist in many states, but generally southern teachers struggled along in academies or in ill-supported public schools, where conditions were bad for white teachers and students and worse for blacks.

The development of statewide public school systems at the turn of the century changed teaching dramatically. Faced with booming enrollments, school officials hired a new breed of teachers—young, unmarried women. In addition to the belief that they embodied virtue, complacency, and reliability, women were said to make ideal employees because they would work for lower wages. More than in any other region, teaching became stereotyped as "women's work." Today the South has the highest percentage of female teachers in the nation.

Well into the 20th century, many southern teachers could boast of little formal education themselves. School officials built a variety of specialized teacher-education programs using northern models, including teacher institutes, which were periodic "in-service" meetings, and normal schools, which evolved by the 1930s into teachers' colleges and, by the 1950s, into state colleges and universities. Virtually all southern teachers now have college degrees, although urban teachers, white teachers, and high school teachers still go to school longer than their rural, black, and elementary counterparts.

Teacher associations in the South grew up independent of the national organizations with which they are now affiliated. Dominated by male administrators, state and local associations were for many years "teacher" organizations in name only. Teachers joined, not because they wanted to, but because their principals and superintendents demanded it. The associations were friendly to state and local school boards, uninvolved in politics, and indifferent to teachers' salaries and working conditions.

Gradually, the South's teacher organizations underwent three significant transformations. The first occurred after 1920 as they became more responsive to the needs of their members, working in a steady if nonmilitant way to improve teacher welfare. The organizations waged polite campaigns for tenure laws, pension and retirement benefits, and health and sick-leave provisions. During this period they also affiliated with the National Education Association (NEA). Southern teachers continued to think of themselves primarily as members of state and local associations, but gradually they began to see themselves as part of a unified national organization.

The black counterpart of the NEA was the American Teachers Association (ATA), composed of 10 state associations for black teachers. The South's teacher organizations experienced a second transformation with the merger of the ATA and the NEA in 1966. Responding to the civil rights movement, teachers in long-segregated associations joined hands, but often with reluctance and misgivings.

A third transformation occurred during the 1960s and 1970s as teacher associations became militant and politically active, a development in which the South lagged 5 to 10 years behind other regions. Administrators left teacher organizations in droves as they began to behave like teacher unions.

Actually, this was not the South's first experience with teacher unionism. Since the World War I era a very few teachers had joined locals affiliated with the American Federation of Teachers (AFT). Perceived as far too radical by most southern teachers, the AFT caught on only in larger cities, most notably Atlanta and New Orleans, where there was a relatively strong labor movement to lend support.

Collective bargaining for teachers, a common practice in the rest of the country, remains unacceptable to most state legislatures in the South. As of 1985 the average salary of teachers in the South was $20,523 as compared to the national average of $23,500, and the salaries and working conditions are still among the poorest in the nation. Yet southern teachers find their militancy restrained by politics and tradition. The wildcat Mississippi teachers' strike of 1985 signaled a new militancy among the nation's lowest-paid teachers, who gained higher salaries as a result of their protests.

See also BLACK LIFE: Education, Black

Joseph W. Newman
University of South Alabama

Ellwood P. Cubberley, *Public Education in the United States: A Study and Interpretation of American Educational History* (1919); Willard S. Elsbree, *The American Teacher: Evolution of a Profession in a Democracy* (1939); Edgar W. Knight, *Public Education in the South* (1922); Joseph W. Newman, "A History of the Atlanta Public School Teachers' Association" (Ph.D. dissertation, Georgia State University, 1978), *History of Education Quarterly* (Winter 1984), *Journal of Thought* (Fall 1983).

Technological Education

During the 20th century the South, along with the rest of the nation, has become increasingly aware of technology and its impact. Automobiles, computers, and hydroelectric power represent three of the most obvious examples of revolutionary change brought about by technology. Only in recent decades, however, has southern technological education kept pace with these changes or evidenced a high level of achievement.

Southern higher education before the Civil War was little different from that in the North. Focusing on the classical curriculum, a university education prepared the student for life as a cultured gentleman. Training in the sciences and practical fields such as engineering or agriculture had no place in the university experience. Southern education suffered greatly during the Civil War, with almost all institutions closing for the duration.

After the war, southern universities continued to stress the traditional liberal arts, but because of the region's economic difficulties, these institutions failed to approach parity with northern schools.

During the 1880s, however, the recovering South began to reevaluate the role of higher education. The success of contemporary businessmen led commentators to stress the importance of practical education as the means to economic enrichment. Latin, Greek, and esoteric sciences were supplanted by curricula designed to prepare the student for a place in the world of business, industry, and agriculture. Many southern states began establishing schools to supply such practical education. Auburn, which was Alabama Polytechnic from 1899 until 1960, Georgia Tech (founded as Georgia School of Technology in 1885), Clemson (1889), Texas A&M (1876), and Virginia Polytechnic Institute (1872) all owed their existence or continuation to the "practical" mentality of state legislators and businessmen, as well as to federal support through the Morrill Act.

The cultural and intellectual change represented by these new schools, however, may have been more apparent than real. As Thomas D. Clark argued in 1965, southern agricultural and mechanical colleges aimed at improving the farming community's way of life. By focusing on land policy and management and agricultural and general engineering, these institutions represented a commitment to the region's agrarian society. The South was apparently not yet ready to mimic the industrial outlook of its northern neighbors.

Another example of cultural inertia in education may be found in the development of separate black schools during the late 19th and early 20th centuries. Both northern philanthropists (guided by the recommendations of George F. Peabody) and state legislators supported the idea of "industrial education" for blacks. Yet this education, even at George Washington Carver's famous experiment station at Tuskegee Institute (1881), was designed to train efficient and contented black laborers for the semiindustrialized southern agricultural economy. Although the region's interest in education had increased markedly by the early 20th century, schools of science and technology to rival northern institutions such as MIT and Rensselaer Polytechnic failed to appear.

The first half of the 20th century witnessed little improvement in southern technological education. The number of institutions providing appropriate instruction grew to include such schools as Louisiana Polytechnic Institute (originally Louisiana Industrial Institute), Tennessee Polytechnic Institute (founded in 1915, but not a degree-granting school until 1928), and Texas Technological College (chartered in 1923); but few major improvements in curricula or equipment took place. The Great Depression hit state-supported institutions especially hard and further thwarted the growth of southern technological education. With 23 percent of the nation's population, the South in the 1930–31 academic year could claim only 17 percent of American engineering graduates. There had been no change a decade later.

The end of World War II signaled the beginning of a major change in technological education throughout the United States, a change in which the South participated. World War II had been a total technological endeavor, symbolized by the development and use of the atomic bomb. Students entering college after the war (with or without the GI Bill) naturally found engineering and science courses attractive. Compared to prewar levels, engineering enrollments doubled by the end of the decade, even though the number of engineering schools remained virtually constant in both the South and the nation as a whole.

The war experience had emphasized the practical value of government support for research and development, and that value remained substantial during the early years of the Cold War. Defense-related research, whether performed in government or university laboratories, enjoyed generous federal funding. Because of their relative lack of expertise, however, southern schools received little of this federal largesse, preventing significant growth of the region's technological education base. Although large sums flowed from Washington to such southern outposts as Redstone Arsenal (Huntsville, Ala.) and Oak Ridge, Tenn., southern education received few of the benefits.

The national shock of the successful launches of *Sputnik I* and *Sputnik II* in late 1957 precipitated another, and by far the most significant, change in America's educational history. For the next decade the nation focused on improving the scientific and technological base of American culture, with education receiving great attention and massive federal funding. Here, at last, the South began to enter the mainstream of technological and scientific development. The need for improved science education became immediately apparent, with southern schools at every level receiving federal funds to establish new programs and to improve existing ones. Aerospace research facilities, frequently cooperating with local universities, grew rapidly in Georgia, Florida, Alabama, Texas, and Louisiana. Schools such as the University of Alabama-Huntsville, Florida Institute of Technology, and Rice University worked closely with the National Aeronautics and Space Administration to guide the Apollo program to its successful lunar landing.

The flight of *Apollo XI* in July 1969, however, was a crucial turning point. Suddenly federal funding for programs involving science and technology began to evaporate. In part a reaction to growing environmental concerns, this lack of interest in science and technology made itself painfully obvious to undergraduate and graduate students who found it increasingly difficult to secure financial aid. The aerospace industry in the South, which had been the region's major path to its share in the technological renaissance of the Space Age, withered perceptibly, removing employment opportunities in many technical fields. By the early 1970s technological education in the South was in a precarious position.

Within a few years, southern technological education had resumed, but the recovery was due to market pressures and self-sustaining technological developments, rather than government support. The revolution associated with rapid developments in computers led not only to an increased demand for computer programmers and engineers, but also to a heightened appreciation for all technological fields. Although the aerospace industry had not fully recovered from the post-Apollo letdown, almost all other "high-tech" fields enjoyed profound growth. With high salaries available to engineers with undergraduate degrees, schools of engineering found themselves deluged with applications. In the South the region's population growth further reinforced this trend, with undergraduate engineering enrollment during the 1981–82 academic year approaching 100,000 students, distributed among 70 schools.

The rapid growth of southern engineering enrollments, however, was not without difficulties. Beginning in the late 1970s, southern states, as those elsewhere, found it increasingly difficult to fund higher education to any significant level. As a result, faculty strength and salaries rarely kept pace with the growing demands of higher enrollment. Facilities and equipment were similarly difficult to obtain, leading many of the region's technological schools to consider limiting enrollment. A less obvious difficulty concerned the place of traditional programs in those schools with growing technological curricula. Increasingly, English, history, physics, and mathematics departments found themselves pressured to become service departments, providing only those courses required for the engineering program's accreditation.

Despite the current healthy status of technological education in the South, sufficient problems exist to cause concern. Present demand for high-tech training may not be a permanent phenomenon, raising the possibility of an oversupply of trained personnel in the near future. Further, despite legislators' encouragement of practical education, state governments are not, at this time, providing the funds to offer that education. Finally, the emphasis on technological education has frequently led to the atrophy of programs in the arts, humanities, and social sciences. These problems are national, rather than strictly regional, in scope. Until they are addressed by governments and universities alike, the role of technological education in the South will remain an important, but unresolved, issue.

See also BLACK LIFE: Education, Black; HISTORY AND MANNERS: Automobile; Philanthropy, Northern; World War II; SCIENCE AND MEDICINE: Aerospace; Technology; / Carver, George Washington

George E. Webb
Tennessee Technological University

James D. Anderson, *History of Education Quarterly* (Winter 1978); Allan M. Cartter, *Southern Economic Journal* (July 1965); Thomas D. Clark, *Three Paths to the Modern South: Education, Agriculture, and Conservation* (1965); John S. Ezell, *The South since 1865* (1963); Lawrence P. Grayson, *Engineering Education* (December 1977); Daniel S. Greenberg, *The Politics of Pure Science* (1967); C. Vann Woodward, *Origins of the New South, 1877–1913* (1951).

Urbanization and Education

Scholars have given a variety of explanations for why education in the South differs from education in other regions of the United States. Some have emphasized geography as the causal factor, others economics, others ideology, others social structure, and still others some combination of these factors. Southern differences frequently are attributed simply to the rural nature of life. The urbanization of southern education took place mainly in the New South period and after (roughly 1875 to the present), and this fact provides one more angle from which the South's educational distinctiveness may be considered.

In broad outline, educational developments in southern cities were similar to those in other American cities. Southern cities experienced a progressive reform movement in education in the early 20th century, just as nonsouthern cities did; city schools in all regions were racked by the Great Depression of the 1930s as well as by the other economic gyrations of the 20th century; and educational institutions have grown more numerous and diverse in this century, both in the South and out of it. Since the 1954 *Brown* v. *Board of Education* decision of the U.S. Supreme Court, southern and non-southern school systems have been faced with the challenge of desegregation. Urban public universities in Charlotte, Birmingham, Tampa, Atlanta, New Orleans, and other southern cities have recently entered the competition for students and funds with nonurban southern public and private colleges and universities, just as newer public universities in Boston, Cleveland, Detroit, Chicago, and Milwaukee have begun to challenge the primacy of their regions' nonurban public universities and private colleges.

Yet, given this overall similarity from region to region, variations in the South's urban educational experience have distinguished it from the experiences of other regions. Changes regarded as innovations elsewhere have different meanings in the South. For example, the school system in Atlanta, Ga., in the late 19th and early 20th centuries selectively adopted educational innovations such as the introduction of technical subjects into the curriculum. Atlantans at first resisted the new subjects and then slowly accepted them, but only as new avenues of preparatory study for higher education. The reformist motive of providing true vocational education as an alternative offering was slow to be realized.

This hesitancy to embrace innovation wholeheartedly was characteristic of urban higher education as well. In the late 19th century and the early 20th, two of the region's urban institutions of higher education, Emory and Vanderbilt, were caught up in a struggle between utilitarian curricular reformers and traditional opponents of that reform. At Emory, which originally was in the small-town setting of Oxford, Ga., the conservatism of President Warren A. Candler (1888–98) undid vocational reforms achieved by his two immediate predecessors. Two decades later, Emory moved from Oxford to the urban setting of Atlanta, a move that was part of a plan by Candler, who by then was a Methodist bishop, to make Emory one of two universities closely tied to the Methodist Episcopal Church, South, and its traditional beliefs and values. Candler and his church had bitterly quarreled with its former affiliate university, Vanderbilt, which under the leadership of Chancellor James H. Kirkland chose secularism over Southern Methodism in order to receive a grant for its medical school from the Carnegie Foundation for the Advancement of Teaching.

At Vanderbilt, even after its divorce from the church and during several decades in which it was led by New South advocates like Kirkland and his successors, opposition to social and educational change was strong. A notable defense of traditional southern values came from the famous Vanderbilt Agrarians who published their manifesto *I'll Take My Stand* in 1930. Ironically, this defense of the values of the rural countryside came from one of the South's preeminent urban universities. One of the Agrarians, Donald Davidson, taught at Vanderbilt for over four decades from the 1910s to the 1950s, defending traditionalism in education and social life during that entire period. Davidson's rabid defense of segregation in the 1950s, however, showed the darker side of southern cultural traditionalism.

The urban South's experience with school desegregation since 1954 has run counter to the prophecies of doom made by Davidson and the antiintegration politicians. Desegregation has taken place with relative success in Florida's major cities—Jacksonville, Miami, and Tampa–St. Petersburg—as well as in other southern cities such as Charlotte, N.C., and Richmond, Va. Thus, by the 1970s most of the images of hate and fear that accompanied desegregation of urban schools came from such northern cities as Boston, Chicago, Buffalo, and Cleveland, rather than from the South. Explanations for this difference vary, but whatever the cause, the South's urban experience clearly contains something that has allowed it to meet the challenge of school desegregation without collapsing into spasms of hate. Nevertheless, the success of desegregation efforts must be interpreted in light of so-called white flight from urban public school systems. For example, in 1985 about 94 percent of Atlanta's public school students were black and in Memphis approximately 77 percent were black. Although some school systems are successfully turning around such trends, the new patterns of segregation will persist in many locales in the foreseeable future.

Comparisons of the southern urban educational experience with that in other regions are almost always made with the Northeast or the Midwest, but southern cities, with the exception of Birmingham and a few others, have little in common with the industrial centers of those areas. As 20th-century commercial, regional, and governmental centers, most of the South's cities have more in common with western cities such as Los Angeles than they do with the older industrial centers. Fruitful results should emerge when southern urban educational development is compared to the situation in western urban centers, as well as to the North and Midwest.

See also MYTHIC SOUTH: / Agrarians, Vanderbilt; URBANIZATION articles

Wayne J. Urban
Georgia State University

Mark K. Bauman, "Warren Akin Candler: Conservative Amidst Change" (Ph.D. dissertation, Emory University, 1975); John Kohler, "Donald Davidson, a Critique from the Losing Side: The Social and Educational Views of a Southern Conservative" (Ph.D. dissertation, Georgia State University, 1982); William E. Schmidt, *New York Times* (25 May 1985); Twelve Southerners, *I'll Take My Stand: The South and the Agrarian Tradition* (1930); Wayne J. Urban, in *The Age of Urban Reform: New Perspectives on the Progressive Era*, ed. Michael H. Ebner and Eugene M. Tobin (1977), in *Education and the Rise of the New South*, ed. Ronald K. Goodenow and Arthur O. White (1981).

Women's Education

See WOMEN'S LIFE: Education of Women

Alabama, University of

Chartered in 1820, the University of Alabama opened in 1831 in Tuscaloosa, physically and academically modeled on the University of Virginia. Serious antebellum disciplinary problems turned the university into a military academy by 1860. During the Civil War academic classes and military training continued until federal troops burned the university in 1865.

When only one student registered in 1865, trustees decided to rebuild the school before reopening in 1869. State political turmoil paralyzed the school during Reconstruction, resulting in frequent leadership changes, few students, and little money. Beginning in the mid-1870s when state appropriations rose, student numbers and faculty strength increased, although the university remained a military one. Student unrest returned, now against the military system, which was discontinued in 1903. By the end of the 19th century three of the university's best-known traditions—women students, a flourishing Greek system, and an expanding athletic program—were established.

The 20th century saw the university transformed from a small southern military college to a multicollege university. Programs such as law and medicine that had earlier languished now flourished along with the new graduate school and extension centers. Integration efforts in 1956 failed when a campus riot occurred. Segregation ended in 1963 with the successful enrollment of two black students, and as of 1985 blacks constituted approximately 10 percent of the student body. Student unrest, political instead of racial, returned in 1970 in protests over the killing of four students at Kent State and Jackson State universities.

In 1969 extension centers at Huntsville and Birmingham became autonomous, and in 1975 university trustees combined these two campuses with that at Tuscaloosa to create the University of Alabama system. By the 1970s the medical school in Birmingham achieved international recognition.

The national success of the athletic program in the 1970s overshadowed escalating faculty discontent on the Tuscaloosa campus over administrative neglect of academic programs. The president of that campus resigned after two "no confidence" votes of the faculty. New leadership in the 1980s both in the University of Alabama system and on the Tuscaloosa campus, as well as renewed efforts of university trustees, restored student and faculty confidence and won additional financial support from the state legislature. Joab L. Thomas became president of the university on 1 July 1981, and fall semester 1985 enrollment was 15,163.

See also RECREATION: / Bryant, Bear

Sarah Woolfolk Wiggins
University of Alabama

James B. Sellers, *History of the University of Alabama, 1819–1902* (1953); Suzanne Rau Wolfe, *The University of Alabama: A Pictorial History* (1983).

Arkansas, University of

The University of Arkansas, located at Fayetteville in the northwest corner of the state, was created by the legislature in 1871 as one of the universities in the land-grant system authorized by Congress in the Morrill Act of 1862. The school's early years were marked by adversity as it struggled to survive inadequate financing, caused in part by the antiintellectualism pervading Arkansas politics in the 1880s.

Like the other land-grant institutions, the University of Arkansas was committed to research and public service as well as teaching. An agricultural experiment station was established in 1888 and an agricultural extension service in 1914. These programs proved to be greatly beneficial to the state's agricultural economy.

In the early 20th century the university began to receive greater support from the citizens and more generous funding from the legislature. The school's "middle period" of development—during the tenures of presidents John C. Futrall, J. William Fulbright, and Arthur M. Harding—was characterized by growth in enrollment, strengthening of the faculty, expansion of the physical plant, and broadening of the curriculum.

At present the university offers degrees in many areas of study, including agriculture, home economics, arts and sciences, business administration, education, engineering, architecture, law, and medical sciences. Graduate instruction was initiated in 1927, and a broad range of programs is now offered leading to master's and doctor's degrees. In the 1984–85 academic year nearly 3,000 undergraduate and graduate degrees were awarded—74 associate's, 1,852 bachelor's, 808 master's, and 124 doctor's degrees. Total enrollment at the Fayetteville campus was 13,773 at the beginning of the fall 1985 semester.

In addition to the complex at Fayetteville, the university operates its medical sciences program and the Graduate Institute of Technology at Little Rock; these campuses offer master's and doctor's degrees in a variety of fields. In the 1970s three colleges were merged into the university—the University of Arkansas at Little Rock, the University of Arkansas at Pine Bluff, and the University of Arkansas at Monticello.

See also AGRICULTURE: / Agricultural Extension Services

William Foy Lisenby
University of Central Arkansas

Robert A. Leflar, *First 100 Years: Centennial History of the University of Arkansas* (1972).

Auburn University

Auburn began as a Methodist liberal arts college chartered as the East Alabama Male College by the Alabama Legislature over Governor John A. Winston's veto on 1 February 1856. Winston questioned the creation of a second Methodist college since the legislature had just chartered Southern University at Greensboro, which had the support of the Methodist Conference. Both institutions opened in 1859; Auburn had a faculty of 6, a student body of 80 men, and a board of trustees of 51. During the Civil War Auburn closed, but it reopened in 1866. In 1872, with no money to operate the school, the Methodist church transferred ownership to the state, and Auburn became the Agricultural and Mechanical College of Alabama, the first land-grant institution in the South. From this point there was conflict between the traditional and land-grant philosophies. Another continuing problem was the meager or inadequate financing from

Students at Auburn University, 1930s

the state, a situation common in the postwar and, later, the depression South.

Two early presidents, Isaac Taylor Tichenor and William Leroy Broun, led in the development of Auburn's physical plant, scientific curriculum, agricultural education, and experiment stations, but Broun's greater contribution was to recruit a core of brilliant young faculty who shaped the university for 50 years after his death. Two of these dynamic men were George Petrie, a young Johns Hopkins Ph.D. holder, who first came to Auburn in 1887 and who served the university as a history and Latin professor, academic dean, and football coach, and L. N. Duncan, who became president in 1935 and guided the university out of debt to financial stability. In 1899 the school's expanding academic program influenced the legislature to rename the college the Alabama Polytechnic Institute, and in 1960, in recognition of the name by which it had been commonly known and to emphasize the diversity and breadth of its academic programs, the school officially became Auburn University.

Auburn University's accomplishments must begin with its agricultural research and extension service contributions, which have improved the economy of the state of Alabama and helped to feed people everywhere, especially in Third World countries. Auburn's superior ROTC program has produced many outstanding officers, and its School of Engineering has graduates all over the world, particularly in the aerospace industry.

A second campus was created by the legislature in 1967 in Montgomery, and by the 1980s the Auburn campus had more students than any other university campus in Alabama. Auburn's athletic teams compete as "Tigers" to a cheer of "War Eagle," and the student newspaper is "The Plainsman"—a reference to the name "Auburn," which came from a line by poet Oliver Goldsmith, "Sweet Auburn, loveliest village of the plain." Although Auburn has attracted a large group of foreign and out-of-state students, the majority remain Alabama Baptists and Methodists with conservative political views and traditional values. The first black student enrolled in 1964, yet despite a vigorous minority recruitment program and scholarships, blacks remain a small but well-integrated part of the student body and a high percentage of the athletes. James E. Martin became president in 1984. The fall 1985 enrollment was 19,056 students.

See also AGRICULTURE: / Agricultural Extension Services

Leah Rawls Atkins
Auburn University

The College Blue Book, Narrative Descriptions (20th ed., 1985); Ralph B. Draughon, *Alabama Polytechnic Institute* (1954); Mickey Logue and Jack Simms, *Auburn: A Pictorial History of the Loveliest Village* (1981); Malcolm McMillan and Allen Jones, *Auburn University through the Years, 1856–1973*, Auburn University Bulletin, No. 68 (May 1973).

Barnard, Frederick A. P.

(1809–1889) Educator and scientist.

Born in Sheffield, Mass., Frederick Augustus Porter Barnard spent half of his professional life in the South. Barnard received his A.B. degree from Yale in 1828 and, suffering from increasing deafness, he taught mathematics and geography at institutions for the deaf from 1831 to 1837. In 1838 he accepted a teaching position at the University of Alabama, where he hoped to pursue his developing interest in the sciences, especially astronomy, and higher mathematics.

Barnard taught mathematics, natural philosophy, and chemistry at Alabama. He was instrumental in the establishment of an observatory at the university, although he had to struggle with the board of trustees, the administration, and the state government for the funds. While in Alabama, Barnard cultivated an interest in early photographic techniques. He learned daguerrotypy from Samuel F. B. Morse and opened a gallery in Tuscaloosa in 1841. He maintained a scientific interest in photography and published articles in photographic journals throughout his career. During the years 1853–54 Barnard opposed a reorganization of the Alabama curriculum that would have implemented the same type of broad elective system used at the University of Virginia and Brown University. Barnard favored retaining a traditional discipline-oriented system in which the student would be allowed a few elective courses. The board of trustees, as well as Basil Manly, the president of the university, supported the Virginia plan and it was adopted. Barnard refused to work under the new system and resigned in 1854.

Barnard then went to the University of Mississippi, which had opened in 1848. The university badly needed

Frederick A. P. Barnard, educator and scientist, c. 1860

instructors, and Barnard taught courses in mathematics, chemistry, physics, civil engineering, and astronomy. An ordained Episcopal minister, he also accepted a job as rector of the Oxford church. In 1856, only two years after his arrival, Barnard became president of the university. As president, his work was hampered by local residents, who saw no practical purpose for the university and regarded it with varying degrees of suspicion and dislike. Barnard was somewhat successful in his efforts to improve instruction and to acquire more sophisticated equipment for the school. Barnard's main interest at the University of Mississippi, as at Alabama, was the sciences, and his critics charged that he emphasized the study of science too heavily, to the exclusion of more traditional studies. As sectional differences intensified, suspicion of Barnard's northern roots pursued him. In March 1860 he was tried by the board of trustees on the charge of being "unsound on the slavery question." His supporters rallied behind him, however, and Barnard was cleared of the charges. Although Barnard was increasingly unhappy with his situation and attempted several times to secure positions elsewhere, poverty kept him from leaving Mississippi.

After Mississippi seceded from the Union early in 1861, university business was interrupted by the enlistment of many students in the military. Barnard left Mississippi in late 1861 and lived in Norfolk, Va., until Union troops captured that city in May 1862. Confederate president Jefferson Davis offered to hire Barnard to conduct a survey of the natural resources of the Confederacy, but Barnard refused because of his Union sympathies.

After working for two years with the U.S. Coastal Survey, Barnard was elected president of Columbia College, now Columbia University. During his 25 years at Columbia (1864–89), Barnard instituted standard entrance exams, introduced the concept of elective courses, and strengthened and enlarged the graduate and professional schools. His interest in science continued, and he was instrumental in founding the National Academy of Sciences in 1863.

Although Barnard later said that his years in Mississippi were among his worst, he seems to have genuinely loved the South and its people. His influence at the southern universities where he worked was felt long after his departure, especially in the area of science, and his hopes for upgrading the quality of education at Alabama and Mississippi were eventually fulfilled.

Karen M. McDearman
University of Mississippi

William J. Chute, *Damn Yankee!: The First Career of Frederick A. P. Barnard* (1977); John Fulton, *Memoirs of Frederick A. P. Barnard* (1896).

Baylor University

Chartered by the last Congress of the Republic of Texas on 1 February 1845, Baylor University is the oldest institution of higher education in Texas and is the world's largest Baptist university. Eponym and one of the chief founders was District Judge Robert Emmett Bledsoe Baylor, who also was an ordained minister. Twenty-four young men and women comprised the opening class of the school at Independence, Tex., on 18 May 1846. The first president, Henry Lee Graves, resigned in 1851 and was followed by Rufus C. Burleson, whose 10-year tenure saw 55 students graduate, including the first graduate, Stephen Decatur Rowe, in 1854. The Civil War years were naturally lean for Baylor, especially during the two-year administration of George W. Baines, great-grandfather of U.S. President Lyndon B. Johnson. Baines was followed by William Carey Crane, who led the institution from 1864 until his death in February 1885.

The Baptist State Convention voted in 1886 to consolidate Baylor and Waco universities at Waco, with the new home to be Baylor University at Waco. Rufus C. Burleson was named president of the unified school, and Reddin Andrews became vice president. Burleson opened the new Baylor University in the facilities of the former Waco University, but within two years new facilities were constructed on a 23-acre site given the institution by the city of Waco. At first the university's degrees for females, who pursued a slightly different curriculum from males, carried the title of "maid" while the men received "bachelor's" degrees. Before the turn of the century all courses were offered to both sexes and all undergraduate degrees were designated "bachelor." Graduate degrees were also available by 1894.

Samuel Palmer Brooks assumed operational control of the university in 1902. A former faculty member and a graduate of both Baylor and Yale, Brooks initiated programs to move the university from its regional parochial level to a complete university status. During Brooks's 29 years as president, several different schools were established as well as a college of arts and sciences. In addition, the university opened a theological seminary (which moved to Fort Worth in 1910 to become Southwestern Baptist Theological Seminary) and began to offer medical degrees through a college of medicine. That college was given independent status in 1969.

Upon Brooks's death in 1931, Pat M. Neff, a former Texas governor (1920–24) was elected president. The Depression caused numerous hardships on the faculty and staff, but the stringent operational measures of Neff enabled the institution to emerge from the period debt free. In 1948 Neff was replaced by William R. White, who immediately embarked upon a building program to meet the post–World War II boom. This was continued and greatly enlarged with the coming of Judge Abner V. McCall to the helm of the institution in 1961. During McCall's 20-year administration, Baylor's campus expanded from 40 acres to 350 acres and the physical structures increased to total more than 50. Enrollment reached the 10,000 mark with students from all 50 states and numerous foreign countries. In June 1981 Dr. Herbert H. Reynolds became president.

The university currently has a college of arts and sciences and schools of law, music, business, education, nursing, and graduate studies. It also operates the Baylor University Medical Center in Dallas and has an affiliate degree program with the United States Army Academy of Health Sciences in San Antonio. The 10,990-member student body (1984–85) has a 22 : 1 student-teacher ratio, and national fraternities and sororities are among the approximately 200 social, service, honorary, and professional student organizations. Baylor is one of six Texas schools with a Phi Beta Kappa chapter, and the percentage of National Merit Scholars enrolled is among the highest in the country.

Eugene W. Baker
Baylor University

Eugene W. Baker, *Nothing Better Than This* (1985); Lois Smith Murray, *Baylor at Independence* (1972).

Berea College

In 1853 Kentucky politician Cassius Marcellus Clay and others persuaded abolitionist John Fee to preach a series of sermons in the Cumberland foothills of Madison County. The following year Fee built a home there on a ridge he called Berea, after the town cited in Acts 17 : 10. The next year a one-room school was built, which doubled as an antislavery church. Fee hoped to create a college that would educate "all colors, classes, cheap and thorough." Some of their neighbors resented and feared farsighted educational leaders such as Fee. The inflammatory effect of John Brown's raid caused armed men to drive Fee and the other Berea leaders out of the state in January 1860. However, the intrepid group returned after the war and incorporated Berea College. The Reverend Henry Fairchild of Oberlin became its first president in 1869, and college classes began in 1870.

For the next century, under the presidential leadership of Henry Fairchild (1869–89), William B. Stewart (1890–92), William G. Frost (1892–1920), William J. Hutchins (1920–39), Francis J. Hutchins (1939–67), and Willis D. Weatherford, Jr. (1967–84), Berea College emerged as an institution with major commitments to educating poor Appalachian youth, to providing a liberal arts education in an atmosphere of Christian service, to maintaining the early founder's goals of interracial education, and to continuing a labor program that allows all students "to work their way through school." Berea's educational philosophy has paid rich dividends to southern Appalachia. Almost 50 percent of Berea's graduates have returned to their mountain homeland to provide significant service in many professional and business fields. Its enrollment in the 1984–85 academic year was 1,554 students.

James M. Gifford
Appalachian Development Center
Morehead State University

Richard B. Drake, *One Apostle Was a Lumberman: John G. Hanson and Berea's Founding Generation* (1975); William Goodell Frost, *For the Mountains: An Autobiography* (1937); Elizabeth Peck, *Berea's First Century, 1855–1955* (1955); John A. R. Rogers, *Birth of Berea College* (1903).

Black Mountain College

Thoroughly southern in its origins, though less so in its style, Black Mountain College was founded in 1933 by the volatile South Carolina classics scholar John Rice. The college began in buildings rented from the Blue Ridge Assembly of the Baptist church three miles outside Black Mountain, N.C.; in 1941 it moved a few miles to its permanent site at Lake Eden, N.C. Black Mountain became one of the least orthodox but most influential institutions in American educational history—influential out of all proportion to its short life and the size of its enrollment, which never went above 75. The history of the college breaks down into three periods: the first concluding with Rice's resignation in 1940; the second concluding with the 1949 departure of the painter Josef Albers, a powerful figure in the college after 1933 and especially so after Rice left; the third concluding with the closing of the college in 1956. Many documents charting this history are preserved in the state archives in Raleigh, N.C.

Prophetic of many of the experimental social and educational communities of the 1960s, Black Mountain College from its beginning broke with tradition. The community was largely self-supporting, performing much of its own labor and raising its own livestock and crops. The arts occupied the center of an unprecedentedly flexible curriculum; the college had no requirements, minimal bureaucracy, and never received accreditation. Contrary to the legalized segregation of the 1940s and 1950s, it admitted blacks. The Black Mountain community was probably more diverse than historian Martin Duberman's description of it as "a Yankee island in a Southern sea" suggests, but the college community's members were outside the mainstream of both national and regional culture and politics because of their lifestyles and views of education.

Black Mountain College saw its most creative years, those for which it is best known, under the direction of the poet Charles Olson. Between Olson's arrival in 1951 (after a short visit in 1949) and the school's closing in 1956 because of falling enrollment, lack of faculty, and financial problems, Black Mountain had as students or instructors people who have since become recognized as major innovators in virtually every art: Olson, Robert Creeley, Robert Duncan, and Edward Dorn in poetry; Merce Cunningham in dance; John Cage and David Tudor in music; Robert Rauschenberg in painting. The school also sponsored one of the most important avant-garde literary journals of the post–World War II period, the *Black Mountain Review*, of which seven issues appeared between 1954 and 1957. Black Mountain College survived only 23 years—in late 1954 its enrollment had plunged to nine students—but its impact on the arts in America is still being felt and measured.

Alan Golding
University of Mississippi

Fielding Dawson, *The Black Mountain Book* (1970); Martin Duberman, *Black Mountain: An Exploration in Community* (1972); *OLSON: A Journal of the Charles Olson Archives* (Spring 1974–Fall 1978).

Bob Jones University

Bob Jones University (BJU) is a nondenominational fundamentalist institution that styles itself "the world's most unusual university." Founded in 1927 by itinerant Methodist evangelist Robert Reynolds Jones, Sr. (1883–1968), the school outgrew early facilities near Panama City, Fla., and moved in 1933 to Cleveland, Tenn., and then, in 1947, to its present 200-acre campus in Greenville, S.C.

Still directed by the Jones family, BJU refuses to seek accreditation by regional or state agencies, fearing outside interference with its ability to stand "without apology for the old-time religion and the absolute authority of the Bible." The university's approximately 5,000-member student body (4,287 students in 1984–85) comes from virtually every state and many foreign countries for studies in Bible, missions, preaching, literature, foreign languages, education, business, and cinematography. BJU boasts a large collection of religious art and stages elaborate Shakespearean productions, seeking to combine the best of Western culture with strict Christian orthodoxy.

Graduates constitute a significant element in America's fundamentalist community. Known for their rigorous separatism, many serve as pastors and teachers in a myriad of independent (mostly Baptist and Bible) churches throughout the United States. They usually maintain close ties with the university and often carry BJU's fervent "Americanism" and conservative politics with them. Several graduates achieved prominence in the early 1980s as leaders of the New Christian Right.

Perhaps the university is best known for its rigid student code, largely unchanged since the 1920s. Students must dress conservatively, avoid off-campus dating, refrain from "griping," not patronize stores where liquor is sold, and observe other stringent regulations. A provision proscribing interracial dating became the subject of prolonged litigation in the 1970s, as the Internal Revenue Service challenged the school's tax-exempt status, claiming that the rule discriminated against minorities. This issue resulted in a Supreme Court case in 1982 and a national controversy over the Reagan Administration's effort to restore the exemption. The university lost the case yet has remained unbending in its commitment to the "old-time religion."

James Guth
Furman University

Gregory Jaynes, *New York Times* (14 January 1982); Melton Wright, *Fortress of Faith: The Story of Bob Jones University* (1960).

Busing

During the 1970s busing achieved more urban desegregation in the South, especially in Florida, Kentucky, North Carolina, and Tennessee, than it did in the North and the West. Legally, southern cities were more vulnerable to court-ordered remedies because of their past records of school segregation. Administratively, it was easier to implement metropolitan busing in southern communities, where the county was the "basic educational unit" (Florida and Kentucky), the number of school districts was relatively small, and "white flight" to suburbia had not undermined the possibility of creating reasonable black-white pupil ratios in city schools.

In the first major and decisive southern busing case, *Swann* v. *Charlotte-Mecklenburg Board of Education* (1971), the U.S. Supreme Court upheld an extensive busing order—of more than 43,000 children—for the largest school system in the Carolinas and the 43d largest in the nation. Under a proportional plan, black pupils would be transported from central-city to suburban schools, so that each school in the consolidated system would have a balanced black-white ratio. Busing between noncontiguous zones, the Supreme Court ruled, was a permissible remedy, if the school closest to home was racially segregated.

Although metropolitan solutions were implemented in Florida (statewide) and in Charlotte-Mecklenburg, Nashville-Davidson, and Louisville-Jefferson, busing was legally stopped at the city line in Richmond (by a divided Supreme Court) and exchanged in Atlanta for the appointment of more—over half—black school administrators (compromise of 1973).

The Supreme Court extended to northern and western communities (*Keyes* v. *School District No. 1, Denver, Colorado*, 1973) *Swann*'s school-desegregation requirement, but Detroit and similar cities thwarted metropolitan busing plans. In the absence of proof of prior official discrimination and its "inter-district effect" on suburban areas, "an inter-district remedy" was not legally justified (*Milliken* v. *Bradley*, 1974).

Opposition to busing became a heated political issue in the 1972 presidential campaign, when antibusing candidate Governor George C. Wallace of Alabama won the Florida and Michigan Democratic primaries. The Nixon Administration championed the neighborhood school concept and opposed busing. During the past decade, opponents repeatedly argued that busing neither improved the educational achievements of minority pupils nor increased racial tolerance. A 1982 Senate bill (#5951) proposed to prohibit the round-trip busing of pupils in excess of 10 miles or 30 minutes and to allow the attorney general to seek the dissolution of busing orders at the request of local school boards. The measure died in the House, but the debate continues.

Various southern cities have reformulated busing plans that they instituted in the 1970s. For example, in Memphis in 1982 the city and the NAACP Legal Defense and Education Fund, Inc., reached an agreement that allowed the city to limit busing and restore neighborhood status to a number of schools, though as of May 1985 approximately 16,000 black students and 3,500 white students were still being bused to achieve racial balance. The revamped busing plans coupled with aggressive school-improvement efforts enabled the Memphis public schools between 1981 and 1985 to lure back some 3,500 students who had fled the city system in the wake of earlier desegregation plans. Supported by the Reagan Administration, many southern cities are emphasizing alternatives to busing such as magnet schools, which are supposed to offer enriched public school opportunities and encourage voluntary integration. Such approaches may be used increasingly as court requirements for busing are eased or reversed. In 1986, for example, the Fourth Circuit Court of Appeals ruled that Norfolk, Va., could curtail the court-ordered busing that had been instituted in 1971 to achieve integration of the public schools. Throughout the South and the nation busing remains a highly controversial issue as efforts are made to achieve and maintain both racial balancing and educational quality.

Marcia G. Synnott
University of South Carolina

Thomas J. Cottle, *Busing* (1976); Ellie McGrath, *Time* (6 February 1984); Nicolaus Mills, *The Great School Bus Controversy* (1973), ed., *Busing U.S.A.* (1979); *Newsweek* (17 December 1984); Gary Orfield, *Must We Bus?: Segregated Schools and National Policy* (1978); Andy Paztor, *Wall Street Journal* (10 February 1986); William E. Schmidt, *New York Times* (25 May 1985).

Campbell, John C.

(1867–1919) Educator.

John Charles Campbell was born in LaPorte, Ind., 14 September 1867. He attended Williams College and Andover Newton Theological Seminary, graduating from the latter institution in 1895. That same year he married Grace Buckingham and moved to Joppa, Ala., where he headed a mountain academy. After serving there three years, he taught in the public schools of Stevens Point, Wis., and then in 1900 moved to Tennessee, where he served as principal of the Pleasant Hill Academy. From 1901 to 1907 he was superintendent of secondary education, dean, and president of Piedmont College, Demorest, Ga. In 1905, during his tenure at Piedmont, Campbell's wife died. Two years later, in 1907, he married Olive A. Dame of Medford, Mass., and spent several months traveling with her in Sicily and Italy.

In 1908 Campbell attended a meeting of the National Conference of Charities and Correction in Richmond, one session of which was devoted to benevolent work in Appalachia. This led directly to the work for which he is now best remembered. Inspired by a paper at the conference, Campbell approached Mary Glenn, a prominent figure in social work circles, with a proposal to conduct a survey of the social, industrial, educational, and religious problems of the Appalachian mountaineers, which would aid in ascertaining what resources were needed or available. Campbell's proposal was presented to the trustees of the Russell Sage Foundation on 25 May 1908. Funding for the survey was approved annually until October 1912, when he was appointed secretary of a newly established Southern Highland Division of the foundation. Campbell then carried out his plans for Appalachia. In an effort to foster cooperation among agencies working in Appalachia, he helped organize the Conference of Southern Mountain Workers (later known as the Council of the Southern Mountains) and for many years served as the group's leader. At Campbell's suggestion the southern Presbyterian church centralized its school work in the mountains and formed the Synod of Appalachia in 1914—the first formal acknowledgement by that denomination that Appalachia formed a natural, distinctive unit of organization.

Campbell worked for years on a book utilizing the information gathered in his survey of mountain problems, but *The Southern Highlander and His Homeland* (1921) did not appear until two years after his death. Although polemical, it is generally considered the best early study of Appalachia. Campbell's greatest difficulty in finishing the volume was that Appalachia was not a coherent region with a uniform culture and a homogeneous population, but was instead a complex portion of America that could not be easily generalized.

Campbell died in Asheville, N.C., 2 May 1919. With his passing the Russell Sage Foundation's work in the mountains came to an end, although for several years the organization continued to fund the annual meeting of the Conference of Southern Mountain Workers. Campbell's widow, herself a major figure in Appalachian cultural work, helped establish the John C. Campbell Folk School at Brasstown, N.C., in honor of her husband, who was one of the early American advocates of the Scandinavian folk school as an alternative to the traditional rural school. This school is still in existence.

W. K. McNeil
Ozark Folk Center
Mountain View, Arkansas

Isaac Messler, *Mountain Life and Work* (April 1928); Henry D. Shapiro, *Appalachia on Our Mind: The Southern Mountains and Mountaineers in the American Consciousness, 1870–1920* (1978); David E. Whisnant, *All That Is Native and Fine: The Politics of Culture in an American Region* (1983), *Modernizing the Mountaineer: People, Power and Planning in Appalachia* (1979).

Chautauqua

From its start in 1874 at a Methodist Sunday school assembly in Lake Chautauqua, N.Y., this movement had a southern flavor, and its felicitously packaged blend of semiclassical culture, popular religion, and self-improvement was widely welcomed in the Bible Belt. One cofounder, John Heyl Vincent, a Methodist minister born in Tuscaloosa, Ala., hailed the Chautauqua as a way to "mitigate sectional antipathies" in the post–Civil War years.

Although the circuit or tent Chautauquas still made their rounds of the southern hinterlands until the early 1930s, the independent Chautauquas, which met annually at the same site, had the most lasting influence. Independent Chautauquas were founded at Hillsboro, Va., 1877; Purcell, Va., 1878; Mountain Lake Park, Md., 1883; Monteagle, Tenn., 1883; DeFuniak Springs, Fla., 1884; Siloam Springs, Ark., 1886; Lexington, Ky., 1887; and the Piedmont Chautauqua at Lithia Springs (then Salt Springs), Ga., 1888. The spectacular Piedmont Chautauqua was the brainchild of Henry W. Grady, who called it the "Saratoga of the South." With the assistance of Marion C. Kiser and the Atlanta business community, an 8,000-seat tabernacle, two Italian Renaissance-style hotels, and a summer college building were constructed in about a month by an army of workers. In its heyday, the Piedmont Chautauqua's Summer College was headed by W. R. Harper, dean at Yale College, and included faculty from Harvard, Johns Hopkins, and the University of Virginia.

The circuit Chautauquas began in the Midwest in 1903 and soon spread to the South, where two systems, Alkahest of Atlanta and Radcliffe Attractions of Washington, D.C., handled most of the bookings. Alkahest, boasting that it "covered Dixie like the dew," had a principal seven-day circuit that played 40 towns per year. Radcliffe had three circuits that were scheduled for weeks and split weeks in well over 200 towns. The onset of the Depression and the popularity of radios combined to bring on the demise of the circuit Chautauqua.

The programs in both the independent and circuit Chautauquas were similar, offering something for all tastes and ages. Most popular were the inspirational addresses by such well-known speakers as Russell H. Conwell and William Jennings Bryan, but also widely enjoyed were the dramas, marching music, symphonic concerts, lectures on science, Gilbert and Sullivan operas, Cossack choirs, and magic shows. Many southerners remember the tent shows fondly for first bringing "culture" and entertainment to rural areas.

Benjamin W. Griffith
West Georgia College

Victoria Case and Robert O. Case, *We Called It Culture: The Story of Chautauqua* (1948); Benjamin W. Griffith, *Georgia Historical Quarterly* (Summer 1971), *Georgia Review* (Spring 1972); Theodore Morrison, *Chautauqua* (1974); Hugh A. Orchard, *Fifty Years of Chautauqua* (1923).

Christian Academies

Because of their central role in the socialization process, public schools have often been a focus of conflict in the United States. The gradual but inexorable application of the Bill of Rights to the states in matters of education, race, and religion since the 1940s prompted many white southerners to create alternate school systems.

The late 1960s saw the courts and the Internal Revenue Service finally demand compliance with *Brown* v. *Board of Education* (1954). One immediate reaction was the creation of secular private segregated (white) schools, often calling themselves "Christian academies."

As the Supreme Court turned its attention from basically Catholic issues (state aid to parochial schools) to more general religious questions (prayer and devotional Bible reading), the character of the "Christian" school changed. By the mid 1970s, integration became much less a factor than secularism, and a bona fide evangelical Christian school movement was born. These private schools are primarily, but not exclusively, white. They are attached to a wide variety of conservative Protestant churches, but particularly to those that identify themselves as independent and fundamentalist. Virtually all the churches that have played a leading role in the "New Christian Right" (such as the Moral Majority) of the 1980s run their own schools. Their philosophy is based upon the claim that churches and parents exclusively have the right and responsibility of education. The schools see themselves preserving *the* Christian and American way of life based upon the moral absolutes found in the Bible.

Curriculum designed specifically for Christian schools stresses providential guidance of American history and the necessity of moral purity in order to retain God's blessing. Some materials display a decidedly (almost caricatured) southern evangelical viewpoint. Slavery is seen in some as an accidental development resulting more from the actions of the North than of the South. Fervent anticommunism characterizes all, while a few display blatant anti-Catholicism as well. Some offer little information about the Civil War other than the fact that revivals took place among the Confederate troops. The civil rights movement of the 1950s and 1960s may be discussed in terms of its attending violence, to the exclusion of almost every other topic. Although all the texts affirm the separation of church and state, a vision of America as a Christian nation under assault by the forces of secularism, humanism, and anti-Christianity predominates.

Christian schools have become a crucial ingredient in the evangelical resurgence and its attempt to define and maintain an American Christian civilization. These schools provide many of the leaders and issues that have mobilized the New Christian Right.

See also LAW: / *Brown* v. *Board of Education*; RELIGION: / Moral Majority

Dennis E. Owen
University of Florida

David Nevin and Robert Bills, *The Schools That Fear Built: Segregationist Academies in the South* (1976), *Southern Exposure* (Summer 1979); Alan Peshkin, *The Total World of a Fundamentalist Christian School* (1986); John Whitehead, *The Separation Illusion: A Lawyer Examines the First Amendment* (1977).

Citadel, The

The origins of The Citadel may be traced to the alleged plot by Denmark Vesey, a free black, and 34 slaves to murder the white population of Charleston and set fire to the city in 1822. The accused conspirators were tried, convicted, and executed. Real or imagined, the specter of an insurrection terrified white Charlestonians. The city government petitioned the South Carolina Legislature to establish an arsenal or "citadel" to "insure domestic tranquility." The state provided the funds, and by 1825 a "citadel" was under construction at a site bounded by King, Boundary (later Calhoun), Meeting, and Inspection streets. A municipal guard was assigned to oversee the care and disposition of the arms and ammunition. The Citadel was only one of several local agencies established to provide racial and social control.

By an act of the legislature in 1841 a corps of young men assumed the duties of the guard while undertaking "a broad and practical education" at The Citadel, or South Carolina Military Academy. An imposing two-story brick, fortresslike building with turrets was designed and constructed. Over time two additional stories and wings were added. The highly visible, heavily armed cadets who frequently drilled on the parade ground were conducive to the "public order." The cadets and institution reflected the white southerners' liking for military trappings, guns and horses, camaraderie, and ceremony.

In early January 1861 the federal government sent the *Star of the West* to reinforce Fort Sumter in Charleston harbor. Hidden among the sand dunes on nearby Morris Island, cadets from The Citadel directed howitzer fire at the vessel. These were the opening salvos of the American Civil War. The vessel turned about, its mission aborted. In July 1863 The Citadel closed so that the cadets could take up military duties around Charleston.

In February 1865 the commander of the 21st First Colored Troops of the Union army accepted the surrender of the city and established his headquarters at The Citadel. The federal government released the institution to the state in 1882 and the school reopened. In 1922 The Citadel was relocated in the northwestern section of the city along the banks of the Ashley River. The architectural models for the new buildings were those of the old.

Today, the state-supported four-year college is flourishing. In the 1984–85 academic year The Citadel enrolled 3,001 male students in a corps of cadets. Black cadets were admitted for the first time in the 1960s, but to date no women have been accepted into the corps. Perhaps more than any other institution of higher education, The Citadel best reflects the cultural values of the Old South.

A special relationship has developed between Charleston and The Citadel. On Friday afternoons the cadets stage a weekly parade for townspeople and tourists. With unit flags fluttering and cannons booming, the cadets, dressed in uniforms of pre–Civil War design, step out to bagpipers and their band playing tunes like "Scotland the Brave." Invariably they conclude with "Dixie." When a Confederate flag painted on the institution's water tower was painted over in the late 1970s, students and alumni alike were outraged.

The Citadel's mission is to educate the "whole man" within a military setting. The rigors of the "knob," or plebe year, are supposed to foster a camaraderie that lasts a lifetime. Pat Conroy, the school's best-known graduate, is infamous in the eyes of some alumni for his characterization of The Citadel in his *The Lords of Discipline* (1980). Conroy writes that "the plebe system gave cruelty a good name." But for those like Conroy who become seniors, the ceremony of the ring is their most memorable experience. The ring binds them "to the brotherhood" of Citadel men and represents "passage through the system." There are chivalric overtones during graduation ceremonies when a ring is awarded to the cadet selected by his classmates as "the manliest, purest and most courteous."

In 1979 Admiral James B. Stockdale, neither a graduate of the institution nor a southerner, was selected by The Citadel's board of visitors as president. He was a winner of the Medal of Honor for heroic resistance during eight years as a prisoner of war in Hanoi; he was also a scholar. As president of the Naval War College, Admiral Stockdale had instituted electives in the humanities and had taught a course in moral philosophy.

For nearly a year Admiral Stockdale sought to minimize hazing during the plebe year at The Citadel, to change the school's "macho image," to attract scholarly students, and to reorganize the command structure. The board of visitors, however, all Citadel graduates, thought that the admiral was "moving too fast." In September 1980 Stockdale resigned, saying in dismay, "The place is locked in pre–Civil War concrete." The new president, Major General James A. Grimsley, a native South Carolinian, Citadel graduate, and retired U.S. Army major general, promised upon taking office that he planned no changes. That was the wish of the board of visitors, the students, and most of the faculty.

See also URBANIZATION: / Charleston

Walter J. Fraser, Jr.
Georgia Southern College

Oliver James Bond, *The Story of The Citadel* (1936); Pat Conroy, *The Lords of Discipline* (1980); *Newsweek* (1 September 1980).

Clemson University

Clemson began as Clemson Agricultural College, 27 November 1889. Founded by the will of Thomas Green Clemson (1807–88), first Superintendent of Agricultural Affairs and John C. Calhoun's son-in-law, it is the land-grant university of South Carolina. The campus encompasses Fort Hill, the Calhoun-Clemson home, which is located in the Piedmont. The school has, since its inception, been governed by 13 trustees, of whom seven are life trustees. The original seven were named by Thomas Clemson. Upon the death of one of the seven, the remaining six select the successor. Six other trustees are elected by the legislature.

Clemson opened 7 July 1893, on 854 acres with a main building, a chemical laboratory, machine hall, heating and lighting plant, one dormitory to house the 446 students, an infirmary, residences for the 15 faculty, two barns, and six silos. By 1986 the main campus consisted of 1,400 acres, and the total university land, including forests, experiment stations, and other tracts totaled 33,700 acres. There were 1,100 faculty, and student enrollment had grown to 12,926 (including 2,500 graduate students). About 65 percent of the students were from South Carolina, and the remainder were from 46 states, the District of Columbia, Puerto Rico, the Virgin Islands, and 79 countries.

Like many of its land-grant counterparts, Clemson Agricultural College began as a male-only military college and remained so until 1955. After that and until 1971 male students spent the first two years in ROTC; in 1971 the ROTC program became optional. Female students were first housed on campus in 1963. Clemson's racial integration was accomplished with dignity in the winter of 1963.

With the addition of undergraduate programs in most fields in arts and humanities, and master's and doctoral degrees in most scientific and technological areas, the school's name was changed to Clemson University on 1 July 1964. In 1986 nine colleges (Agricultural Sciences, Architecture, Commerce and Industry, Education, Engineering, Forest and Recreation Resources, Liberal Arts, Nursing, and Sciences) and the Graduate School made up the university. In keeping with its mission of public service and through its extension and experimental work, Clemson is involved in every county of South Carolina.

Jerome V. Reel, Jr.
Clemson University

The College Blue Book, Narrative Descriptions (20th ed., 1985).

College of William and Mary

The second college begun in British North America, William and Mary received a royal charter in 1693. Although some Virginia planters continued to educate their children in England, an increasing percentage economized by sending their sons to the less expensive Williamsburg institution, which included grammar and Indian schools in addition to a liberal arts college modeled on the British universities where most of the professors had studied. With a faculty that included such intellectuals as legal scholar George Wythe and the poet Goronwy Owen, William and Mary emerged in the late colonial period as a thriving intellectual center.

The Revolution was disastrous for William and Mary, which suspended classes for almost two years. In 1781 the school suffered a devastating fire. More important, the separation from England deprived the school of crucial income from British sources. There followed a century-long cycle of decline during which William and Mary failed to win even minimal assistance from a state government that turned its attention to the new university in Charlottesville. Although the pre–Civil War faculty included such luminaries as scientist John Millington and jurist St. George Tucker, the presidency of Thomas R. Dew from 1836 to 1846 offered the only hint of true resurgence.

The Civil War very nearly destroyed William and Mary, which again suspended classes as faculty and students alike rushed to join the southern forces. In 1862 the school once more suffered the ravages of fire when Union troops looted and burned the Main Building. President Benjamin S. Ewell returned from the war determined to reopen the college and managed to keep it in operation until it closed for want of funds in 1881. In 1888 the legislature provided a small sum to reopen William and Mary as an institution to train public school teachers. Ewell's successor, Lyon G. Tyler, then undertook the imposing task of reviving the school as a state-supported college. By the time he stepped down as president in 1919, William and Mary was an undistinguished institution, but it was also in no immediate danger.

College of William and Mary, Williamsburg, Va., c. 1840

During the 1920s John D. Rockefeller, Jr., became interested in restoring the town of Williamsburg to its 18th-century character. The college's location beside Colonial Williamsburg fostered interest in the school's heritage and helped to usher in a dramatic renaissance on the Williamsburg campus. Approaching the end of its third century, the College of William and Mary has regained the standard set when Thomas Jefferson was a student there in the 1760s. Its full-time enrollment in the 1984–85 academic year was 6,640.

See also HISTORY AND MANNERS: / Jefferson, Thomas; RECREATION: / Colonial Williamsburg

James P. Whittenburg
College of William and Mary

Herbert Baxter Adams, *The College of William and Mary: A Contribution to the History of Higher Education* (1887); Jack Eric Morpurgo, *Their Magesties Royall Colledge: William and Mary in the Seventeenth and Eighteenth Centuries* (1976); Lyon Gardiner Tyler, *The College of William and Mary in Virginia: Its History and Work, 1693–1907* (1907).

Commonwealth College

One of the South's few attempts at resident labor education, Commonwealth was established in 1923 at Newllano Cooperative Colony near Leesville, La. After one turbulent year at Newllano, the faculty moved the tiny school to Polk County, Ark. The director of the college was utopian Socialist William E. Zeuch, who supported theoretical labor education and communal living rather than active participation in radical reform movements. Zeuch established as Commonwealth's original mission the production of sophisticated, literate, and idealistic leaders for the labor movement. Given its southern location and avowed aims, the school was remarkably devoid of controversy.

This placid scenario changed abruptly with the Great Depression, however, when in June 1931 a student-staff revolt headed by longtime Commoner Lucian Koch seized control of the college, ousted Zeuch, and plunged Commonwealth into aggressive labor activity. Delegations of Commoners were sent to Harlan, Ky., and Franklin County, Ill., to support coal miners in their strikes for union recognition. Other Commoners involved themselves in farm-labor organization, supporting the National Farmer's Holiday Association and participating in strike activities in Corinth, Miss., and Paris, Ark. College faculty and staff were prominent in the formation of a new Socialist party in Arkansas in 1931, and Clay Fulks, an instructor, was the party's nominee for governor in 1932. All this activity generated a new reputation for the tiny school, with charges of atheism, free love, and, most frequently, communism being heard around the South.

In spite of the change in direction, Commonwealth always maintained the same pattern of day-to-day existence on campus. Located in rural Polk County, Ark., the school strove to be self-sufficient by requiring four hours of labor per day from staff and students in return for subsistence and, in the case of students, instruction. Faculty were not paid and were expected to participate in every campus activity, including farm work, maintenance, and anything else necessary to escape from "bourgeois interests." Women worked primarily in the kitchen, the library, the laundry, and the school office; men completed chores on the wood crew, carpentry crew, farm crew, masonry crew, or hauling crew.

Classes began at 7:30 each morning and were usually held in the instructor's cottage. The unvarying format was group discussion—occasionally heated. The college operated on a vague quarter system, and students were limited to three courses per quarter. Commonwealth assigned no grades, conferred no degrees, and had no class-attendance requirements. Classes seldom exceeded 6 students, and the total student body never numbered more than 55. The college community, though small, was extremely cosmopolitan and included Americans from various ethnic groups, all geographic sections, and every educational level. The only entrance requirements were intelligence and dedication to the labor movement.

The last five years of Commonwealth's existence were hallmarked by a frequently acrimonious association with the Southern Tenant Farmers' Union. Organizational activities on behalf of the union focused a considerable amount of unwelcome attention on the school; the old charges of free love and communism were revived in the press. In 1936 the union attempted to reorganize the college, oust the radicals, and make it a legitimate place to train labor leaders. The Communist faction was not dislodged, however, and after two stormy years the STFU and other labor groups withdrew their support; this was a fatal blow to the little college. Commonwealth ceased to operate in September of 1940.

See also SOCIAL CLASS: / Southern Tenant Farmers' Union

William H. Cobb
East Carolina University

William H. Cobb, *Arkansas Historical Quarterly* (Summer 1964, Summer 1973); Donald H. Grubbs, *Cry from the Cotton: The Southern Tenant Farmers' Union and the New Deal* (1971).

Couch, W. T.

(b. 1901) Publisher.

"I have found it necessary to compromise and to be cautious, but I do not compromise or exercise caution merely to avoid criticism." Writing to Walter Lippmann in 1927, on the heels of publishing a controversial edition of the *Congaree Sketches*, William Terry Couch summed up a philosophy that would guide his editorial decisions throughout a 20-year tenure at the University of North Carolina Press.

Born in 1901 in Pamplin, Va., to a Baptist country preacher and the daughter of erstwhile planters, Couch spent his childhood in a variety of small southern towns. When he was 17 the family settled in Hope Creek, a few miles from Chapel Hill, N.C., and Couch worked at part-time and summer jobs to supplement their farming income. Entering the University of North Carolina, he became editor of the student magazine and attracted the attention of Louis Round Wilson, then director of the university press. At 25 Couch became his assistant and in 1932 assumed directorship.

Couch regarded argument and criticism as essential to scholarship. He departed from the guarded, conservative policies of the press and felt that the publication of "nice inoffensive books" did not fulfill the promise of the new social science research that addressed substantive issues like religion, race, and economics.

Of the 450 titles brought out under Couch's direction, 170 dealt primarily with southern topics. A core list included studies such as Arthur F. Raper's *The Tragedy of Lynching* (1933) and Duane McCracken's *Strike Injunctions in the New South* (1931) issued by Howard W. Odum's Institute for Research in Social Science. Such classics as *These Are Our Lives* (1939) and Virginius Dabney's *Liberalism in the South* (1932) appeared, and in 1934 the symposium *Culture in the South*, edited and contributed to by Couch, ambitiously surveyed "the broad stream of southern life" in order to "sound its depths, measure its strengths, discover its complexity and ultimately find ways to remove the debris which now infests its waters."

Couch underscored the need for southern publishing, claiming that "any people that leaves its thinking . . . to minds elsewhere is doomed to subservience." He repeatedly stressed that scholarship was not a frill to be jettisoned in hard times; it was as fundamental to the region's educational process as up-to-date machinery was to farming. As an antidote to what he saw as the failure of southerners to look to books for information and entertainment from an early age, he also published elementary and high school texts, a book for adult illiterates, and work on farming techniques, gardening, and local architecture.

By producing books designed to be of regional interest and by creating a tolerance for diverse and often critical studies of the South, Couch turned the University of North Carolina Press into a prime force for intellectual growth in the region. By 1934 the press was receiving national recognition for its pioneering work, and university presses throughout the country changed directions to follow its lead, producing high-quality books aimed at the general reader in conjunction with specialized scholarship.

A New Deal liberal, in the vanguard of progressive thought on questions of race, Couch had encouraged candid studies on race, and the press maintained a consistent policy of publishing the work of black authors. Nevertheless, he was troubled, as his introduction suggests, by the demand for an end to segregation in Rayford Logan's *What the Negro Wants*. In 1945, a year after its publication, Couch resigned to take up the directorship of the University of Chicago Press. From 1952 to 1959 he served as editor-in-chief of *Collier's Encyclopedia*. His most recent book, *The Human Potential*, was published in 1974.

Elizabeth M. Makowski
University of Mississippi

W. T. Couch, *Sewanee Review* (Winter 1945), *Southwest Review* (Winter 1934); Daniel J. Singal, *The War Within: From Victorian to Modernist Thought in the South, 1919–1945* (1982).

Curry, J. L. M.

(1825–1903) Educator, minister, and politician.

A transitional figure between Old South and New, Jabez Lamar Monroe Curry displayed elements of both cultural traditions in his versatile public career. Born into a socially prominent, economically secure family and steeped in John C. Calhoun's constitutional doctrines, Curry studied law at Harvard. Horace Mann's example impressed upon him the value of universal education, and from his first term in the Alabama Legislature in 1847 to his final role in the Conference for Education in the South at the end of his life, Curry forcefully articulated the essential social, moral, and political functions of public education.

Elected to the U.S. House of Representatives in 1857, Curry resigned to defend secession and to serve in the Confederate Congress, but after 1865 he accepted emancipation when he embraced the racial paternalism of the New South. An ordained Baptist minister, he briefly assumed the presidency of Howard College in Alabama before joining the faculty of Virginia's Richmond College. In 1881 the Peabody Fund, established through the generosity of George Peabody of Massachusetts, named him general agent for its southern education campaign. Except for a three-year period (1885–88) as U.S. minister to Spain, Curry held the position until his death and became the incomparable orator-administrator of the late-19th-century education awakening.

Prodigious traveler, prolific correspondent, and author of numerous reports, he repeatedly addressed southern legislatures and citizens' groups to appeal for tax-supported schools. After 1890 he also represented the Slater Fund, endowed by John F. Slater of Connecticut to educate southern blacks. Because he defined universal education to include blacks and women, Curry championed coeducation, industrial education, teachers' institutes, and normal schools for teacher training.

In spite of his states' rights principles, Curry advocated enactment of the unsuccessful Blair education bill, a measure sponsored in the 1880s by Senator Henry Blair of New Hampshire to appropriate federal funds to fight illiteracy. Curry artfully identified enhanced literacy with the promotion of personal independence, the preservation of limited government, and the protection of individual liberties. Although he remained committed to black advancement, he grew increasingly pessimistic about it, and his inherent white-supremacist racism triumphed over his sense of noblesse oblige. More derivative than original in his ideas, Curry personified southern implementation of northern philanthropy and energetically crusaded for education as the paramount force of social and cultural stability.

See also POLITICS: / Calhoun, John C.

Betty Brandon
University of South Alabama

J. L. M. Curry Papers, Manuscripts Division, Library of Congress and Alabama Department of Archives and History, Montgomery; Merle Curti, *The Social Ideas of American Educators* (1935); Jessie Pearl Rice, *J. L. M. Curry: Southerner, Statesman, and Educator* (1949).

Duke University

Duke University in Durham, N.C., traces its origins to a local academy organized by a group of Methodists and Quakers under the leadership of Brantley York in Randolph County, N.C., in 1838. Known initially as Union Institute, it was reorganized in 1851 for the training of teachers and named Normal College before it became affiliated with the Methodist church in North Carolina and was renamed Trinity College in 1859. Continuing to operate during the harrowing years of the Civil War, the college, long presided over by Braxton Craven, acquired a northern-born, Yale-trained president, John F. Crowell, in 1887. In 1892, inspired by generous support offered by Durham Methodists grown prosperous in the tobacco industry, particularly Washington Duke and Julian S. Carr, Trinity College moved to Durham.

A spellbinding Methodist preacher and dynamic administrator, John C. Kilgo, succeeded Crowell as president in 1894 and greatly increased the interest of the Duke family in Trinity. In 1896 Washington Duke offered an endowment of $100,000 provided that Trinity admit women "on equal footing with men," and the college, which even earlier had some women students, quickly accepted the offer. Other gifts from the Duke family followed, with Benjamin N. Duke, Washington Duke's son, serving as a leading benefactor and the principal liaison between the college and the family.

Thanks to support from the Dukes and to an able, relatively young, and ambitious faculty recruited from the new graduate schools at Johns Hopkins, Columbia, and other northern universities, Trinity College had developed by the time of World War I into one of the leading liberal arts colleges in the South. Despite the clamor of powerful Democrats in North Carolina, the trustees of the college refused in 1903 to oust historian John Spencer Bassett, who had publicly deplored the racist politics of the "White Man's Party." Trinity thus achieved one of the pioneering victories for academic freedom in the United States and strengthened its belief in and reputation for independent thought and scholarship.

Dreams of a university organized around Trinity College dated back to Crowell and the 1890s, but President William Preston Few launched a serious effort to realize the dream in the early 1920s. Because Benjamin N. Duke was in failing health after about 1915, Few began with Duke's blessings and assistance to focus his efforts on

Chapel at Duke University, Durham, N.C.

James B. Duke, Benjamin Duke's younger brother and by far the richest member of the family. In 1919 and again in 1921 Few sketched out his plans to James B. Duke and proposed that, because several educational institutions in the United States were already named Trinity, if and when funds became available to enlarge the institution in Durham it should be named Duke University. James B. Duke was not ready to go along in 1921, but by December 1924, he was.

Naming Duke University as one of the prime beneficiaries of the perpetual philanthropic foundation he then established as the Duke Endowment, James B. Duke also provided around $19 million for the rebuilding of the old Trinity campus, for the creation of a new campus with Tudor Gothic buildings, and for the acquisition of some 8,000 acres of adjoining forest land. In 1930, when the first buildings on the new campus were completed, the old Trinity campus became the site of the coordinate Woman's College, which in 1972 was merged back into Trinity College as the liberal arts college for both men and women. Training in engineering was available in Trinity College after 1903, and in 1939 a separate School of Engineering was organized. In addition to Divinity and Law schools, the Medical School and Hospital were opened in 1930 and a School of Nursing in 1931. What eventually became the School of Forestry and Environmental Studies was established in 1938, and the School of Business Administration opened in 1969.

With 9,285 students enrolled in degree programs in the 1984–85 academic year, Duke University continues by choice to be one of the smaller, voluntarily supported, major universities in the nation. Terry Sanford, former governor of North Carolina, became its sixth president in 1970 and served until his retirement in 1984. As of 1986 Keith H. Brodie served as president.

See also INDUSTRY: / Duke, James B.; Tobacco Industry

Robert F. Durden
Duke University

Nora C. Chaffin, *Trinity College, 1839–1892: The Beginnings of Duke University* (1950); Earl W. Porter, *Trinity and Duke, 1892–1924: Foundations of Duke University* (1964); University Archives, Duke University Library.

Emory University

Emory College, chartered by the Georgia Methodist Conference in 1836, admitted students in 1838 to its Oxford, Ga., campus. Except when closed briefly during the Civil War, Emory strove through its traditional classical curriculum—in the words of an early president, Augustus Baldwin Longstreet—"to raise up a race of men who shall be fitted for the pulpit or the plow, the court or the camp, the Senate or the shop."

When the General Conference of the Methodist Episcopal Church, South, lost the power to control selections to the trustees of Vanderbilt University in 1913, the conference decided it needed a new university in the Southeast. A former Emory president, Warren A. Candler, now a bishop, persuaded the church commission to make Emory College the nucleus of such a university. The bishop's brother Asa, wealthy from promoting Coca-Cola, would provide a million-dollar endowment and a new campus, a wooded and hilly 75-acre tract northeast of Atlanta.

Chartered in 1915, Emory University first opened theology and law schools on the new campus, with the undergraduate college moving from Oxford in 1919. Later, business, dental, graduate, library, medical, and nursing schools were added. In 1953 the trustees opened college enrollment to women on equal terms with men. In 1962 Emory took the initiative to end racial restrictions by asking the courts to declare unconstitutional provisions in the Georgia constitution and statutes that denied tax-exempt status to private universities and colleges that integrated their student bodies; the state supreme court decided in Emory's favor.

Emory deliberately refrained from intercollegiate competition in major sports, instead emphasizing student participation in an intramural setting. From the 1920s onward, Emory's "athletics for all" program gained national renown and spurred much imitation. Other extracurricular activities of strength included debate, journalism, and choral singing.

Doctoral study began in 1946. Emory's steady strengthening of graduate and professional education, with a strong interdisciplinary thrust, received impetus from the gifts of its most generous benefactor, Robert W. Woodruff, a former student who took over the helm of Coca-Cola in the 1920s. His endowment gift of over $100 million, announced in 1979, was the largest benefaction at one time to a single educational institution in the history of American philanthropy. During the 1984–85 academic year, 8,533 students were enrolled. By its sesquicentennial in 1986, Emory had been accorded a role of increasing national stature in higher education.

See also INDUSTRY: / Coca-Cola; RELIGION: / Methodist Episcopal Church, South

James Harvey Young
Emory University

Mark K. Bauman, *Warren Akin Candler: The Conservative as Idealist* (1981); Henry Morton Bullock, *A History of Emory University* (1936); Charles Howard Candler, *Asa Griggs Candler* (1950); Thomas H. English, *Emory University, 1915–1965* (1966); James Harvey Young, "A Brief History of Emory College," *Emory College 1982/1983* [catalog].

Fisk University

Fisk University, a leading black educational institution for more than a century, opened in Nashville, Tenn., in 1866. A private, coeducational, liberal arts school, Fisk offers the bachelor's and master's degrees. Fisk began with commendable and lofty—some thought impractical—aims. Its founders, E. M. Cravath, John Ogden, and E. P. Smith, proposed to provide a free school of grades from primary to normal based upon a "broad Christian foundation." Fisk was designed to supply desperately needed, qualified black teachers and ultimately to become a first-class college giving black youth the same educational opportunities and advantages enjoyed by whites.

At first, all students were in primary grades, but a normal class was enrolled in 1867. In 1871 four students were accepted into the college department. Nevertheless, the college preparatory and college classes remained the smallest in the school for several years. Because public schools for black children were generally poor, Fisk was compelled to prepare its own students for advanced training.

The period 1870 to 1915 was critical for Fisk. Black poverty, white indifference, and the popularity of vocational education threatened Fisk's aspiration of becoming a major liberal arts college. But, with the $150,000 earned by the Fisk Jubilee Singers, President E. M. Cravath, supported by a determined faculty and loyal students, built a new campus, improved the faculty, and developed a solid college department.

When students joined alumni in 1925 to oust Fayette A. McKenzie, a white president whom they considered dictatorial, a new era began in Fisk history. Under the leadership of President Thomas E. Jones and noted scholar Charles S. Johnson, who was to become Fisk's first black president in 1946, the university experienced unprecedented growth. By the 1940s it had an endowment of several million dollars and had become an outstanding center of scholarship and culture. Faculty members Charles S. Johnson, James Weldon Johnson, Arna Bontemps, and John W. Work, Jr., all achieved international recognition in their fields. In 1931 Edwin R. Embree, president of the Rosenwald Fund, claimed that Fisk was probably the finest black college in the land. It had the "pick of the country" for its faculty and student body.

One mark of a great university is the degree to which its students are equipped to cope with the demands of life. Judging by their successes, Fisk students have been unusually well prepared. The alumni have distinguished themselves in almost every field of endeavor. Hundreds of Fiskites have become physicians, college presidents, professors, writers, statesmen, and community leaders. Physician George Sheppard Moore, scholar W. E. B. Du Bois, historian John Hope Franklin, and poet Nikki Giovanni are just a few of the famous graduates of Fisk University.

Since the early 1980s, however, Fisk has grappled with the specter of bankruptcy. Under the leadership of Henry Ponder, who became president in 1984, the university reduced its debt from approximately $4 million in 1985 to $600,000 as of May 1986, primarily through financial support from alumni and philanthropies. Nevertheless, Fisk's enrollment has declined steadily in recent years (550 in fall 1984, 506 in fall 1985), and in 1984 President Reagan appointed a special advisory board to evaluate the university's future. Released in May 1986, the board's report, *A Future for Fisk—A Fisk University Five-Year Strategic Plan 1986–1991*, recommended that the institution decrease its reliance on federal funds, strengthen retention efforts, and broaden its recruitment strategies to encourage attendance by whites as well as blacks.

See also BLACK LIFE: / Bontemps, Arna; Du Bois, W. E. B.; Franklin, John Hope; Johnson, Charles S.; Johnson, James Weldon; MUSIC: / Fisk Jubilee Singers

Joe M. Richardson
Florida State University

Chronicle of Higher Education (21 May 1986); Lester C. Lamon, *Journal of Southern History* (May 1974); *New York Times* (29 April 1986); Gustavus D. Pike, *The Jubilee Singers, and Their Campaign for Twenty Thousand Dollars* (1873); Joe M. Richardson, *A History of Fisk University, 1865–1946* (1980).

Florida, University of

The University of Florida is the oldest unit of the Florida university system of higher education. Located in Gainesville in the north-central part of Florida, it traces its roots to the East Florida Seminary, founded in 1853 in Ocala, and the Florida Agricultural College, which began in Lake City in 1884. The first baccalaureate degrees were awarded at the East Florida Seminary in 1882. In 1905 the Florida Legislature passed the Buckman Act consolidating higher-education facilities in the state. The legislation established a college for women (now Florida State University) and a university for men (now the University of Florida). The university began holding classes on the Gainesville campus in September 1906 with an enrollment of 102, and it remained largely a men's school until 1947.

All academic programs are located on a single campus, so that the professional skills represented in the various departments can be combined for interdisciplinary studies. The university includes colleges of agriculture, architecture, building construction, business administration, dentistry, education, engineering, fine arts, forest resources and conservation, health-related professions, journalism and communications, law, liberal arts and sciences, medicine, nursing, pharmacy, physical education, health and recreation, and veterinary medicine. The J. Hillis Miller Health Center includes a teaching hospital, Shands, whose physicians also staff the Veterans' Hospital in Gainesville. The health center is noted for its community-health program, which provides medical and nursing services for a 16-county area.

The university library has more than 3 million volumes, in addition to large collections of manuscripts, maps, rare books, documents, and newspapers. The major special collections relate to Florida and Spanish borderlands history and Latin American and Caribbean studies. The famous Howe Collection on early American literature is at the university, together with the papers and manuscripts of Marjorie Kinnan Rawlings, Zora Neale Hurston, and other noted novelists, poets, and playwrights from Florida and the South. The library also has the largest collection—some 60,000 volumes—of Judaica in the South. The Florida State Museum contains a large collection of North American Indian material and artifacts of the prehistoric period in Florida and the Caribbean. A television station and three radio stations are also located on campus.

The university is governed by a president appointed by the Board of Regents. Marshall M. Criser is president of the University of Florida. There were 35,496 students enrolled as of the 1984–85 academic year.

Samuel Proctor
University of Florida

A. H. Adams, "Public Higher Education in Florida, 1821–1961" (Ph.D. dissertation, Florida State University, 1962); *The College Blue Book, Narrative Descriptions* (20th ed., 1985); Samuel Proctor, "University of Florida, 1853–1906" (Ph.D. dissertation, University of Florida, 1958).

Foxfire

In March 1967, 600 copies of an offset magazine named *Foxfire* appeared on the streets of rural Clayton, Ga., the end result of three months of work by 9th- and 10th-grade students and their English teacher, B. Eliot Wigginton. Paid for by $440 in donations collected by the students from merchants and parents in the area, the magazine would certainly have passed from the scene virtually unnoticed had it not been that embedded in the collection of juvenile poetry and short stories were several pages of traditional Appalachian home remedies and superstitions that the Rabun Gap–Nacoochee School students had collected from their older relatives at home. Included, too, was one magical tale (related into a used tape recorder) by Luther Rickman, the retired county sheriff, about the 1936 robbing of the Bank of Clayton by the Zade Sprinkle gang. Transcribed by the four students and their teacher who conducted the interview one evening after school, the story appeared, word for word, in the magazine, and the demand for copies of "that magazine that's got Luther's story in it" was such that all 600 copies disappeared within days, and a second printing of 600 more was ordered to meet the demand.

As reactions to that issue came in, the students, with the support of the principal, decided to keep the magazine going, focusing on the local customs and traditions the readership obviously wanted. By 1971 a large body of material had been collected, and Doubleday offered to publish a book bringing the best of that material together for a broader audience. *The Foxfire Book*, published in March 1972, sold over 3 million copies—more than any book in that company's publishing history. It was followed by the numbered series of *Foxfire* volumes, the latest being *Foxfire 8* (1984), which covers topics ranging from folk pottery to mule swapping. All of the books are compilations of high school students' work and all have been enormously successful—an authentic publishing phenomenon.

The royalty money flowed into the nonprofit, tax-exempt corporation that had been set up in 1968 to solicit donations in support of the project. Wigginton, with the permission of the principal and school board, began to hire other adults (many of whom were former students who had since graduated from college) to work with him inside the public school system to broaden the number of community-based, experiential offerings available to new generations of high school students. By 1982 students were operating a television studio, a record company, a publishing company, a photography division, and a major environmental education program that included both a log home built on campus as a classroom and a full-scale experimental passive solar home. Schools across the country were copying the curricular designs. One hundred and ten acres had been purchased on which students and community carpenters reconstructed 27 historic log structures to serve as a working base of operations. It included staff and guest housing, an archive, a museum, offices, and a recreation area for community celebrations. A scholarship program was initiated that gave over $35,000 a year in college-scholarship assistance. In the fall of 1982 the play *Foxfire,* based on materials from the books and starring Hume Cronyn, Jessica Tandy, and Keith Carradine, became a hit on Broadway.

The staff, regarding all this as prelude, was, by 1982, preparing to play an even larger role in the educational and economic picture of Rabun County—a rural county that had seen a $440 investment pay off. It was an investment that linked the public school curriculum and the area's traditions and culture together in powerful and magical ways.

B. Eliot Wigginton
Foxfire

Richard M. Dorson, *North Carolina Folklore Journal* (November 1973); *Newsweek* (12 April 1982); B. Eliot Wigginton, *Moments: The Foxfire Experience* (1975), *North Carolina Folklore Journal* (May 1974), *Sometimes a Shining Moment: The Foxfire Experience* (1985), ed., *The Foxfire Book* (1972).

General Education Board

After a tour of southern black schools led by Robert C. Ogden, John D. Rockefeller, Jr., convinced his father to make a financial contribution to education in the South. The following year the Rockefellers pledged $1 million to be spent over a 10-year period and created the General Education Board (GEB). Chartered by the U.S. Congress in 1903 for "the promotion of education in the United States of America, without distinction of race, sex, or creed," the GEB by 1964 had appropriated more than $325 million, approximately 20 percent of which was earmarked for black education.

At the turn of the century the poverty of the post–Civil War period still restricted education in the South, and the region supported two school systems—one for black children and one for white. Because many rural areas were without schools, the GEB designated much of its initial support to developing rural schools. One of its first grants was to Berea College, located in an impoverished area of Kentucky. Berea was also the recipient of the GEB's last appropriation when, in 1964, the board contributed to the establishment of a Special Student Aid Program. The GEB funded training in agricultural economics and community development, believing that the southern economy had to improve before educational advancements could develop.

The GEB worked nationally to raise teachers' salaries, to support natural science and humanities studies, to provide research fellowships, and to improve medical school facilities and staffs. Its continuing focus, however, was on the South, and from 1940 to 1964 the GEB concentrated its work there. Universities such as Atlanta, Duke, and Tulane benefited, as did black students aspiring to teach and black educators who received GEB fellowships for further training.

The GEB strengthened black education enormously. Black universities such as Fisk and Dillard received millions of dollars in GEB grants. Rather than attacking the South's system of school segregation, the board tried to improve the quality of education by working through the predominantly white structure. Because the GEB was a northern institution, its members believed they had to proceed cautiously if their efforts were to succeed. The General Education Board raised the level of education for both blacks and whites by fighting the inequality of education, not between the races, but between the South and other regions of the United States.

Jessica Foy
Cooperstown Graduate Programs
Cooperstown, New York

Raymond B. Fosdick, Henry F. Pringle, and Katharine D. Pringle, *Adventure in Giving: The Story of the General Education Board* (1962); *General Education Board: An Account of Its Activities, 1902–1914* (1915); *General Education Board Review and Final Report, 1902–1964* (1964).

Georgia, University of

The University of Georgia became America's first state-chartered university in 1785. After prolonged debate the campus was built in Athens, Ga., approximately 65 miles from Atlanta. Franklin College, as it was then called, opened in 1801, under the direction of several Yale graduates including Josiah Meigs, its first president.

The school attempted to remain open during the Civil War, but was forced to close when the Union seizure of Chattanooga early in 1864 caused most of the university community to join the military. After reopening in 1866 Franklin College became the University of Georgia in 1869 under Chancellor Andrew A. Lipscomb.

Through World War II the university was plagued by the same problems that retarded the growth of other southern state schools. The university received inadequate financial support and competed with other state schools for recognition and programs. In 1919 the University of Georgia admitted women, whose presence immediately boosted the College of Agriculture's Department of Home Economics and the Peabody School of Education. The Georgia university system was reorganized in 1932 under the governance of a board of regents.

Since World War II the university's teaching staff, research programs, and public service function have been expanded. The growth of both professional schools and graduate programs rapidly escalated during the 1960s. The first black students were admitted to the university in 1961. By the fall of 1984, 24,371 students were enrolled, 13 schools and colleges existed within the university, and the campus had expanded to cover 3,500 acres. As of 1984 Georgia's president was Frederick C. Davison. In 1986 the university drew national attention when one of its professors, Jan Kemp, won a lawsuit against school administrators accused of compromising academic standards for athletes.

Karen M. McDearman
University of Mississippi

Robert Preston Brooks, *The University of Georgia under Sixteen Administrations* (1956); E. Merton Coulter, *College Life in the Old South* (1928); Thomas G. Dyer, *The University of Georgia: A Bicentennial History, 1785–1985* (1985).

Georgia Institute of Technology

Georgia Tech was chartered in 1885 and opened its doors in 1888. Interest in a school of technology in Georgia had been stimulated by the campaign for southern industrialization led by men like Henry W. Grady, editor of the Atlanta *Constitution*. In 1883 a legislative committee settled on the Worcester Free Institute in Massachusetts as an appropriate model. Worcester had pioneered the "commercial shop" system of technical education, in which students shared time between academic studies and work in the shops producing goods for sale.

When the school opened in Atlanta in 1888, it offered degrees only in mechanical engineering. The first professor of that subject, John Saylor Coon, was a founding member of the American Society of Mechanical Engineers. The rapid addition of programs in electrical and civil engineering, industrial chemistry, and textiles reflected both the development of modern engineering practice in America and the economic needs of the state. After the turn of the century architecture and commerce were added to the curriculum. Although the commercial shop system was scrapped in the 1890s, Tech retained a heavy emphasis on practical application.

Football began to play a major role in the school in 1904, when Tech hired its first full-time coach, John Heisman. Under Heisman and his successors, W. A. Alexander and Bobby Dodd, Tech for over half a century enjoyed a reputation as a national powerhouse.

Georgia Tech first won national recognition in engineering in 1930 when it received one of six awards made by the Guggenheim Foundation—and the only one in the South—to support a program in aeronautical engineering. World War II radically transformed Georgia Tech, as it did other colleges. Under the leadership of President Blake Van Leer, Tech responded to the need for a more science- and mathematics-based engineering program and for postgraduate training by shifting its curriculum decisively away from the shop approach, by strengthening programs in the sciences and mathematics, and by establishing its first Ph.D. programs. In 1948 Tech's name was changed from Georgia School of Technology to the Georgia Institute of Technology. It remained part of the university system of Georgia.

The post–World War II era also witnessed the growth of applied research, particularly in the electronics field, with most of the work being done through the Engineering Experiment Station (renamed in 1984 the Georgia Tech Research Institute). Research and development in electronics have in more recent years provided a base for high-technology "spin-off" firms in and near Atlanta.

In 1972 Joseph Mayo Pettit, then dean of engineering at Stanford University, became Georgia Tech's eighth president. Under his leadership Tech continued to move forward in research and graduate education in engineering, science, and related fields.

As of 1984–85 Georgia Tech's total enrollment was 10,958 students. Its campus had grown from the original two buildings to 128 buildings situated on over 310 acres near downtown Atlanta. Among its alumni are numerous presidents of major corporations and leading practitioners in Tech's areas of expertise. Former President Jimmy Carter, who attended Tech before enrolling in the Naval Academy, is recipient of the only honorary doctorate awarded by the Institute.

See also INDUSTRY: / Grady, Henry W.; POLITICS: / Carter, Jimmy

Robert C. McMath, Jr.
Georgia Institute of Technology

Marion L. Brittain, *The Story of Georgia Tech* (1948); Robert C. McMath, Jr., et al., *Engineering the New South: Georgia Tech, 1885–1985* (1985); Robert B. Wallace, Jr., *Dress Her in White and Gold: A Biography of Georgia Tech and of the Men Who Led Her* (1969).

Gildersleeve, Basil

(1831–1924) Classical scholar.

Born 23 October 1831 in Charleston, S.C., Basil Lanneau Gildersleeve became the most renowned American classicist of the late 19th century. Founder of the *American Journal of Philology* in 1880, Gildersleeve taught classics at Johns Hopkins for almost four decades and became a central figure in the professionalization of Greek and Latin studies in the American university.

Gildersleeve grew up in a home of pronounced southern loyalties. His father, Benjamin, was a northerner by birth but adopted the southern antebellum sectional cause with enthusiasm. A Presbyterian minister and editor of a denominational paper, Benjamin Gildersleeve supervised his son's early education and introduced him, somewhat unsystematically, to the classics. Basil Gildersleeve went on to attend the College of Charleston, Jefferson College in Pennsylvania, and Princeton, where he graduated in 1849. He taught classics at a private academy in Richmond and then spent 1850 to 1853 in Germany at Berlin, Göttingen, and Bonn, before taking his Ph.D. at Göttingen. He spent three years in Charleston writing and teaching. He became a professor at the University of Virginia in 1856, staying there until he went to Johns Hopkins in 1876. His service in the Confederate army left him with a crippling leg injury received in fighting in the Shenandoah Valley campaign. He died 9 January 1924.

Gildersleeve's *The Creed of the Old South* (1915) was a work celebrating the antebellum South. Southerners after the war produced many apologies for the romanticized plantation society, but Gildersleeve's stood out for its perspective on southern history. Although proud of the South's wartime heroism and unquestioning of southern ideals, he did not portray the South as the center of the universe. He did compare the Civil War to the Peloponnesian War—the North was Athens, the South, Sparta—but he knew the ultimate judgment of southern history would come far in the future. His long perspective on history enabled him to escape the anger and bitterness so prevalent in the first generation of southern intellectual life after the war.

Gildersleeve was also significant as a representative of southern intellectual ties with German culture. Gildersleeve inherited a dislike for British culture, stemming from family memories of the British occupation of Charleston during the War of 1812, and his reading of the Scottish Carlyle reinforced the aversion to the English and pointed Gildersleeve toward an interest in Goethe. Gildersleeve called the German author "the most important of all the teachers I ever had." He studied Goethe endlessly for a time when young. "This was the era of my Teutomania," he recalled later. His youthful interest in Germany proved to be enduring. German philology—and that nation's system of university education and scholarly research—became his model for the United States. He hoped, particularly, to give studies of Greece and Rome a new vigor through application of rigorous scholarly methods pioneered in Germany.

Charles Reagan Wilson
University of Mississippi

Basil Gildersleeve, *Forum* (February 1891); Fred Hobson, *Tell about the South: The Southern Rage to Explain* (1983); C. W. E. Miller, *American Journal of Philology* (January 1924); *Selections from the Brief Mention of Basil Lanneau Gildersleeve*, ed. C. W. E. Miller (1930).

Graham, Frank Porter

(1886–1972) Educator and statesman.

Frank Porter Graham, president of the University of North Carolina (1930–49)

Professor and president of the University of North Carolina, U.S. senator, and United Nations mediator, Frank Porter Graham was born in Fayetteville, N.C., in 1886. He received both undergraduate and law degrees from the University of North Carolina and a master's degree from Columbia, afterwards studying at the University of Chicago, the London School of Economics, and elsewhere. He left a position as instructor in history at the University of North Carolina for service in the Marine Corps during World War I but returned to rise to the rank of professor by 1927.

In 1930 Graham became president of the University of North Carolina; and in 1932, when that institution was consolidated with the North Carolina College for Women and North Carolina State College, he became president of the larger institution, the Consolidated University of North Carolina. Graham worked diligently during the period of economic depression to increase the university's scholarship funds for needy students and often was involved in intense controversy over political, social, and economic policies. All the while he defended the freedom of the university to seek, learn, believe, speak, and publish. Sometimes he was the object of personal attacks for his support of unpopular causes or persons, yet he never wavered in his faith in the young and in the future of a free, democratic society.

Beyond the university Graham was concerned with the needs of the poor and underprivileged, and he supported racial justice. Twice he was president of the North Carolina Conference for Social Service, and at President Franklin D. Roosevelt's appointment he served on federal boards and commissions, including the National Advisory Council on Social Security, of which he was chairman. During World War II he served on the National Defense Mediation Board and the National War Labor Board. President Harry Truman appointed him to the President's Committee on Civil Rights, for which Graham made a historic report on the country's racial problems and presented proposals for their solution. At Truman's request he served as the representative of the United States on the United Nations committee on the Dutch-Indonesian dispute. He also helped organize, and was the first president of, the Oak Ridge Institute of Nuclear Studies. In 1949 he was appointed by the governor of North Carolina to fill an unexpired term in the U.S. Senate, but in a bid for nomination for reelection he failed to win a majority in the primary. In a second primary the racial issue was injected to Graham's disadvantage, and he was rejected by his party.

Service on the President's Committee on Civil Rights and his well-known commitment to human rights and association with liberal causes contributed to Graham's defeat. Nevertheless, he continued his public service: as defense manpower administrator for the U.S. Department of Labor, as United Nations representative to mediate the dispute between India and Pakistan over Kashmir, and as assistant secretary general of the United Nations. Graham, a deeply religious man, worked diligently for human betterment not only at home but also throughout the world. He died in Chapel Hill, N.C., in 1972.

William S. Powell
University of North Carolina
at Chapel Hill

Frank P. Graham Papers, Southern Historical Collection, University of North Carolina, Chapel Hill.

Hampden-Sydney College

A private liberal arts college enrolling some 750 young men as of the 1984–85 academic year, Hampden-Sydney is situated on a 566-acre rural campus in Virginia's tobacco-growing southside, that part of the Old Dominion most reminiscent of the Old South. The college has been in continuous operation since January of 1776 and is the country's 10th-oldest institution of higher learning. Hanover Presbytery founded the college "as a southern replica of Princeton," according to historian Lawrence A. Cremin, intending both to nurture an educated commitment to public service and to promote the Presbyterian faith in the heavily Scotch-Irish counties of south-central Virginia. The name Hampden-Sydney was apparently chosen as symbolic proclamation of the founders' devotion to the principles of political and religious liberty for which John Hampden and Algernon Sydney had struggled in 17th-century England. The college's first board of trustees included such revolutionary luminaries as James Madison and Patrick Henry; and the school colors, garnet and gray, derive from the uniform of purple hunting shirts (dyed with the juice of pokeberries) and grey trousers, which the students' militia company wore while helping to defend Williamsburg and Petersburg during the late 1770s. At the outbreak of the Civil War the student body organized another company of militia, and the "Hampden-Sydney Boys" fought for the Confederacy in a losing effort at Rich Mountain on 10 June 1861.

The college has always drawn the overwhelming majority of its students from Virginia and the neighboring states of the Upper South. Although since 1980 increasing numbers of freshmen have come from both the Deep South and the Northeast, Virginians made up 60 percent of the student body in the 1984–85 academic year. Today Hampden-Sydney is most distinguished for an ambience that blends latter-day preppiness with gentlemanly traditions that hearken back to the 19th-century South. Prominent facets of that ambience, wrote Zöe Ingalls in 1985, are "the prevalence on campus of late-model BMW's and crudely laundered khaki trousers"; a strict student-run honor system; a social life dominated by fraternities; and a liberal arts curriculum that has made, in the words of one faculty member, "few adaptations to the fashion of vocationalism," although far and away the most popular major—economics—is one that students consider likely to facilitate success in the business world.

The most obvious aspect of the college's traditionalism is its firm commitment to continuing as all-male, Hampden-Sydney being the oldest of this country's few remaining all-male colleges. Entering freshmen receive copies of a booklet entitled "To Manner Born, To Manner Bred: A Hip-pocket Guide to Etiquette for the Hampden-Sydney Man," which exemplifies the college's partiality for traditional standards of genteel deportment that strike some observers as elitist or anachronistic. At the same time, however, Hampden-Sydney has been strongly affected by the dramatic changes in technology and race relations that have transformed much of the South and America at large in recent years. The college is integrating a computer laboratory and an audiovisual "International Communications Center" into its academic program; and the second Rhodes Scholar in the school's history, selected in December of 1985, is a black student from southside Virginia, who was also elected president of the student government.

See also ETHNIC LIFE: / Scotch-Irish; HISTORY AND MANNERS: / Madison, James

Shearer Davis Bowman
Hampden-Sydney College

Herbert C. Bradshaw, *History of Hampden-Sydney College, Volume I: From the Beginnings to the Year 1856* (1976); Lawrence A. Cremin, *American Education: The Colonial Experience, 1607–1783* (1970), *American Education: The National Experience, 1783–1876* (1980); Zöe Ingalls, *Chronicle of Higher Education* (18 September 1985).

Hampton Institute

In the mid-1800s northern missionary teachers worked vigorously to establish permanent educational institutions for free blacks, and in 1868 the American Missionary Association and the Freedmen's Bureau provided funding for establishment of the Hampton Normal and Agricultural Institute at Hampton, Va. Samuel C. Armstrong, the school's founder and first principal, developed a lifelong interest in education for blacks after commanding black regiments in the Civil War. Armstrong viewed blacks as intellectually inferior to whites, however, and emphasized "industrial works" programs, a widely accepted stance. The school's elementary- through college-level students received training in agriculture and skilled trades, and many pursued teaching careers in black schools, though opportunities were limited. Commitment to moral virtues, respect for discipline in the military tradition, and compromise and accommodation toward whites were emphasized. Such an approach clashed sharply with the growing demand in the 1890s for black liberal arts programs and drew scathing criticism from leaders such as W. E. B. Du Bois.

The rift between Du Bois and Booker T. Washington stemmed in large part from Washington's dedication to the traditions of Hampton Institute, his alma mater. Washington and Robert R. Moton, another Hampton Institute graduate and Washington's successor at Tuskegee Institute, championed the emphasis on vocational education for blacks. Nevertheless, Hampton Institute gradually phased out its elementary and secondary programs, deemphasized its vocational component, and began offering courses leading to a bachelor of science degree in 1922. By 1933 it received accreditation as a four-year college, and its graduate programs began in 1956. Weathering the strife of a white-supremacist "racial purity" campaign in Virginia in the 1920s and 1930s, the institute finally obtained black leadership when Alonzo G. Moron assumed the presidency from 1947 through 1959.

For many reasons Hampton Institute is recognized, according to Mary F. Berry and John W. Blassingame, as "one of the most influential schools in the history of black education." One of the first colleges to accept Native Americans and to invite African students, the institute has also had world-renowned choirs, a dance company focusing on black traditions, research projects to preserve black folklore, training programs in Africa, and a variety of publications and conferences on issues important to blacks. Its library houses an outstanding collection of materials on black history. The private, coeducational, independent institution currently combines liberal arts, teacher education, and vocational curricula. Both its faculty and student body are interracial and intercultural. Its 1984–85 enrollment was 4,260 students.

See also BLACK LIFE: / Du Bois, W. E. B.; Washington, Booker T.

Sharon A. Sharp
University of Mississippi

Mary Frances Berry and John W. Blassingame, *Long Memory: The Black Experience in America* (1982); W. Augustus Low and Virgil A. Clift, eds., *Encyclopedia of Black America* (1981); August Meier and Elliott Rudwick, *From Plantation to Ghetto* (1966); Alrutheus A. Taylor, *The Negro in the Reconstruction of Virginia* (1926); Raymond Wolters, *The New Negro on Campus: Black College Rebellions of the 1920s* (1975).

Jackson State University

Founded in Natchez, Miss., as a private church school by the American Baptist Home Missionary Society in 1877, Jackson State was established to serve the people of the Mississippi Valley between Memphis and the Gulf Coast. Twenty students were enrolled when the school opened on 23 October. Its first president, Charles Ayer of New York, resigned in 1894, and Luther G. Barrett succeeded him. In that same year the school relocated in Jackson and in 1903 moved to its present location in the city.

Zachary Taylor Hubert of Atlanta became the institution's first black president in 1911. His administration broadened the course of study and awarded the first college-level degree (B.A.) in 1924 to Annie Mae Brown Magee. Major educational activities during this time were directed toward teacher education. The Home Missionary Society withdrew its support in 1938, and the college moved from private control into the state system of higher education.

Jacob L. Reddix became president in 1940. Initially, the state assumed support of the college for the purpose of training rural and elementary schoolteachers, and in 1942 the Board of Trustees raised the curriculum to a four-year teacher's education program. A division of graduate studies and a program of liberal arts was organized in 1953.

On 2 March 1967 John A. Peoples, Jr., became the sixth president and the first alumnus to serve in that capacity. The academic program of the university was greatly expanded and the entire curriculum was reorganized with a newly established Graduate School and schools of Liberal Studies, Education, Science and Technology, and Business and Economics. Margaret Walker became director of the Institute for the Study of the History, Life, and Culture of Black People in 1968. Since that time the Institute has sponsored distinguished lectures, readings, and symposia on the black experience. Upon the completion of People's tenure in April 1984, the physical plant had also undergone significant change with the construction of six major buildings.

Jackson State received national publicity on 14 May 1970 when 2 students were killed and 12 wounded on campus as local authorities and national guardsmen confronted students during civil rights demonstrations. The incident occurred 10 days after the death of students at Kent State University.

James A. Hefner became the seventh president of Jackson State on 1 May 1984. Jackson State University's special mission as an urban university has sensitized the faculty to increased involvement in services to the community, serving the citizens of Mississippi with a broad array of public service, continuing education, and research programs.

Lelia G. Rhodes
Jackson State University

Lelia G. Rhodes, *Jackson State University: The First Hundred Years, 1877–1977* (1978).

Junior Colleges

One of the most notable developments in American higher education in this century has been the explosion in the number of two-year or junior colleges. The forces that spawned this movement in the North and West were also at work in the South.

William Rainey Harper, first president of the University of Chicago, is usually credited with being the founder of the movement when, at the turn of the century, he encouraged Chicago-area high schools to offer college courses that could be transferred to that university. But it was Alexis F. Logan, dean of the School of Education at the University of California, and David Starr Jordan, president of Leland Stanford Junior University, who seized upon Harper's concept and set the pattern for a junior college movement, not only for California but for the rest of the nation. The motives of these early pioneers centered less on the democratization of American higher education than on preserving the integrity of existing universities. By channeling the less-able student into two-year colleges, they hoped to reserve the universities for only the brightest secondary school graduates.

Logan, Jordan, and other proponents of the movement were heavily influenced by German educational institutions. They saw the two-year college as an extension of the high school, an American counterpart to the German *gymnasium*, rather than as an additional component of higher education. Ironically, with these elite objectives, one of the most vigorous instruments for the democratization of American higher education in this century emerged.

Although the roots of the community college movement are generally considered to be in the North, with its puritan passion for literacy and 19th-century emphasis on expansion of educational opportunity, it was a southerner, Thomas Jefferson, in the late 18th century, who envisioned something similar to the two-year college. He certainly spoke for its later advocates when he wrote: "If a nation expects to be ignorant and free in a state of civilization, it expects what never was and never will be." Yet for the South the transition was not always an easy one. The rural way of life and the remnants of a tradition that saw education as a prerogative of the elite retarded state involvement. Consequently, the weaker private colleges and the manual or trade schools were the first to see the advantages of a two-year college program. Many found that by dropping the junior and senior years, they could prevent or delay impending financial disaster.

With the exception of Texas, which became an early national leader in state support for the two-year college, private two-year colleges were the rule in the South until after World War II. Afterwards, the demands of a new and increasingly urban South resulted in growing community pressure for the establishment of more public two-year institutions.

Educational leaders who argued for an expansion of two-year college programs drew support in 1947 from the report of President Truman's Commission on Higher Education and in 1956 from President Eisenhower's Committee on Education Beyond the High School. As a result, the decades of the 1950s and 1960s saw the establishment of dozens of state-supported two-year colleges throughout the region.

Today, the two-year colleges of North Carolina, Texas, and Florida are among the most numerous and progressive in the nation. Other southern states are also making substantial gains in their attempts to make the first two years of college available to all. Approximately 33 percent of the nation's two-year colleges were located in the 13 southern states (the 11 states of the Confederacy plus West Virginia and Kentucky) as of 1983.

Gerald L. Cates
Truett McConnell College

American Association of Junior Colleges, *Junior College Directory* (1965, 1969, 1971, 1981); Thomas Jefferson, *The Writings of Thomas Jefferson*, 10 vols., ed. Paul Leicester (1892–99); Charles R. Monroe, *Profile of the Community College* (1972); Southern Association of Colleges and Schools, *Proceedings* (1895–1975); Roger Yarrington, ed., *Junior Colleges: 50 States/ 50 Years* (1969).

Kappa Alpha Order

Kappa Alpha Order, a national social fraternity for men, preserves in its basic principles and traditions the southern ideal of character its early members feared might perish with the society that existed in the South prior to the Civil War. Founded in the immediate aftermath of war, on 21 December 1865 at Washington College (now Washington and Lee University) in Lexington, Va., Kappa Alpha Order refined its ideals beginning in 1866. Samuel Zenas Ammen, a member of the order and later editor of the Baltimore *Sun*, realized that the initial ideals of the fraternity were too vague and weak. In an effort to establish a strong foundation for the continuing existence of Kappa Alpha Order, the members under the guidance of Ammen began a reformation and elaboration of the Order's principles that resulted in a clearly southern-oriented fraternity.

The Order's outlook drew on the idea of the southern gentleman. The ideal of a gentleman, wrote Ammen, is "that of the chivalrous warrior of Christ, the knight who loves God and country, honors and protects pure womanhood, practices courtesy and magnanimity of spirit and prefers self-respect to ill-gotten wealth." Ammen and early members considered these virtues and graces to be distinctively southern. General Robert E. Lee, who was president of the college during the Order's formative period (1865–70), was perceived by them to be the perfect expression of the southern gentleman, and the members looked to him as the spiritual founder of Kappa Alpha Order.

In perpetuating southern traditions of gentlemanly conduct, Kappa Alpha Order distinguishes itself from all other college social organizations. Although at first the Order preferred to remain exclusively in the South, it exists today with chapters on university and college cam-

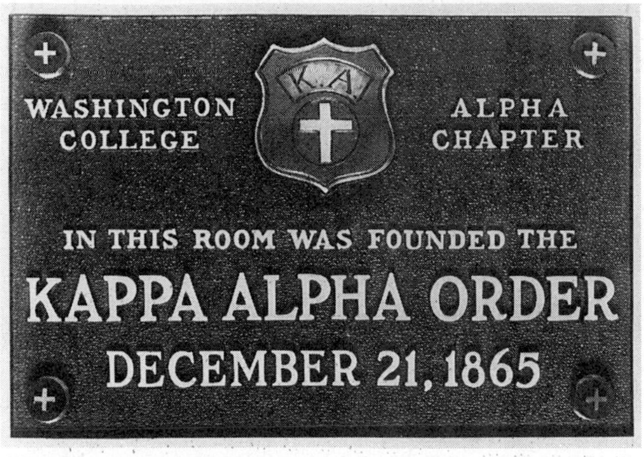

Plaque commemorating the founding of the Kappa Alpha Order, Washington College, Lexington, Va., 1865

puses from coast to coast. The group has initiated about 100,000 members since its founding, and there are now 114 active undergraduate chapters. The characteristics of the southern gentleman preserved by the Order appeal to men across the nation. The Kappa Alpha Order today celebrates its southern heritage on college campuses through spring festivities known as Old South, which includes a week of parties, cookouts, movies, parades, lawn parties, and the annual Old South Ball.

See also HISTORY AND MANNERS: / Lee, Robert E.

Newell Turner
New York, New York

Samuel Z. Ammen, *History of the Kappa Alpha Fraternity, 1865–1900* (1900); William K. Doty, *Samuel Zenas Ammen and the Kappa Alpha Order* (1922); Gary T. Scott, "The Kappa Alpha Order, 1865–1897; How It Came to Be and How It Came to Be Southern" (M.A. thesis, University of North Carolina, Chapel Hill, 1968).

Kentucky, University of

Founded in 1865 in Lexington, the state's land-grant agricultural and mechanical college was at first an uneasy component of the Disciples of Christ's Kentucky University. The college was separated in 1878 from the faction-torn university, and in 1882 James K. Patterson, president since 1869, led students and faculty across town to the new campus donated by the city. Patterson persuaded a divided legislature to retain a state property tax for the college.

In 1908, noting the coeducational enrollment of 500, the legislature renamed it State University, Lexington, Kentucky, thereby initiating a collegiate infrastructure, including Arts and Science, Agriculture, Law, three engineering colleges, and the existing Agriculture Experiment Station. His mission accomplished, Patterson resigned in 1910, and Judge Henry Stites Barker left the bench to become president. Renamed the University of Kentucky in 1916, the institution underwent an investigation that demanded drastic reforms and replacement of Barker. In August 1917 Frank LeRond McVey, an experienced outside academic, accepted the presidency though warned against Kentucky's "damnedest politics." He retired in 1940 from an academically improved university with 6,000 students, 500 staff, and an annual income of $3 million. The university awarded 791 degrees in that year. Morale was good despite discouragements suffered during the Depression.

Compared with similar institutions, the university under Herman L. Donovan (1941–56) and Frank G. Dickey (1956–63) gained no academic ground even with its greater emphasis upon research, publication, and graduate study; the creation of a complete medical center; and development of an unusual university-administered community college system (which by 1985 included 13 colleges). A 1960 state 3 percent sales tax promised adequate funding; the promise was fulfilled for the first (and last) time during the presidency of John W. Oswald (1963–68), and the institution grew in academic reputation as emphasis upon research and graduate and professional education imparted a university character.

Student unrest, energy crises, and inflation have clouded Otis A. Singletary's (1969–) administration. An overgrown state system of higher education has overburdened a poor state whose regionalisms, traditional indifference toward education, and "damnedest politics" have, according to critics, held back the university. It meets the physical criteria of greatness, though, with 20,421 students and 1,842 faculty in Lexington as of fall 1985 and approximately 24,000 students and 600 faculty in the community colleges. The university has achieved prominence in local and regional studies, where the university library has collected purposefully, the university press publishes fruitfully, and sociologists and historians have made significant contributions.

Carl Cone
Lexington, Kentucky

Charles G. Talbert, *The University of Kentucky: The Maturing Years* (1965).

Key, V. O., Jr.

(1908–1963) Political scientist.

A leading scholar of American politics, Valdimer Orlando Key, Jr., was a prolific writer who greatly influenced the study of political science in the 20th century. He was born in Austin, Tex., and spent his childhood in west Texas, where his father was involved in local politics. Key learned a great deal from observing his father's political dealings and developed a sensitivity to political processes that he employed in his studies.

Key attended McMurray College in Abilene, Tex., from 1925 to 1927, received his A.B. degree from the University of Texas in 1929, and studied under Charles E. Merriam at the University of Chicago, where he earned a Ph.D. in 1934. He taught at UCLA, Johns Hopkins, and Yale and in 1951 became Jonathan Trumbull Professor at Harvard, where he remained until his death in 1963. His most important work was *Southern Politics in State and Nation* (1949), which won the Woodrow Wilson Foundation Award. He also authored a widely used textbook, *Politics, Parties, and Pressure Groups* (1942).

Key's work is regarded as significant because he linked the empirical study of politics to the larger issues of democratic government, thereby shifting the traditional focus of students of political processes. He stressed the importance of American politics in determining many other aspects of life. Key's research dealt with three areas of political science: party politics, public administration, and public opinion. His *Southern Politics* is a well-researched analysis of regional political evolution. It relies on legal and statistical data, as well as extensive field interviews, which Key supervised closely. Because of Key's influential work, the discipline of political science became more specialized and empirical, elements that were tempered in Key's own studies by a recognition of politics essentially as an effective *human* activity.

Karen M. McDearman
University of Mississippi

Merle Black and John Shelton Reed, eds., *Perspectives on the American South*, vol. 2 (1984).

Louisiana State University

The Louisiana State Seminary of Learning, forerunner of Louisiana State University, opened on 2 January 1860 near the central Louisiana village of Pineville and admitted only male students. Its first superintendent was William Tecumseh Sherman, of later Civil War fame, who reluctantly departed for the North after Louisiana's secession in 1861. After several abortive attempts were made to keep the institution open, classes were suspended for the duration in 1863 as federal forces approached during an invasion of the Red River Valley. The seminary reopened in 1865 with four students under the superintendency of David French Boyd, a prewar faculty member and ex-Confederate colonel who was to remain at the helm for 17 of the next 21 years.

Despite financial stresses typical of the Reconstruction era, the seminary was beginning to flourish when fire destroyed the main building in October 1869 and brought it close to extinction; Boyd presided over its transfer to Baton Rouge, where the seminary shared until 1886 a large structure housing the State Institute for the Deaf, Dumb, and Blind. During his long tenure David Boyd presided over two watershed events: the legislatively mandated merger in 1877 with the Louisiana A&M College, previously located in New Orleans, and the move in 1886 to the former grounds of the U.S. Arsenal in Baton Rouge—LSU's first permanent home in 17 years and the springboard for its eventual development into a large modern university.

David Boyd's younger brother, Thomas Duckett Boyd, was elected president in 1896 and his 31-year tenure—longest of any LSU president—was to encompass several further historical landmarks: the admission of women to the student body in 1906; the utilization by the state of oil severance taxes during the 1920s to provide the university with a solid, permanent support base; and the move to the present campus, beginning in 1925 and pointing the way to the university's most spectacular period of growth. During the decade of the 1930s Governor, later Senator, Huey P. Long adopted LSU as a pet project and channeled state funds into construction and faculty expansion at a time when most universities were retrenching; one result was a quadrupling of enrollment before World War II, making LSU at the time the second-largest university in the former Confederate states. The university became a major center of southern literary and scholarly activity in the 1930s, focused on the *Southern Review*, which was established by Robert Penn Warren and Cleanth Brooks in 1935.

During the post–World War II era LSU expanded into a statewide system including eight separate administrative entities in five cities, with the "flagship" campus in Baton Rouge attaining an enrollment of more than 30,000 students before a leveling off in the mid-1980s. Its 1984–85 enrollment was 28,979 students. Court-ordered desegregation brought the first black graduate student to LSU in 1950, and all levels have been desegregated since the 1960s. In 1978 LSU was awarded status as the nation's 13th sea-grant university, matching its land-grant status of long standing. The current president of the LSU system is Allen Copping, who assumed the office on 15 March 1985. The chancellor of the Baton Rouge campus is James H. Wharton, who has been in the position since 1981.

See also LITERATURE: / Brooks, Cleanth; Warren, Robert Penn; POLITICS: / Long, Huey P.

Jack Fiser
Louisiana State University

Vergil L. Bedsole and Oscar Richard, eds., *Louisiana State University: A Pictorial Record of the First Hundred Years* (1959); Germaine M. Reed, *David French Boyd, Founder of Louisiana State University* (1977).

Mississippi, University of

Located at Oxford in the north-central section of Mississippi, the University of Mississippi was chartered by the legislature in 1844 and opened in 1848. As Mississippi's only state-supported institution of higher learning, the university offered both undergraduate liberal arts degrees and professional degrees. Early presidents included author Augustus Baldwin Longstreet (1849–56) and his successor Frederick A. P. Barnard, who initiated pioneering scientific research and teaching programs. Even after specialized colleges and universities were established in the state, the University of Mississippi continued to offer a comprehensive program including graduate and undergraduate degrees. Currently the university encompasses both the main campus at Oxford and a school of medicine, which opened in 1903 in Oxford and moved to Jackson in 1955.

In 1861 the entire student body withdrew to enroll in the Confederate army. The university suspended operation during the Civil War but reopened in the fall of 1865, becoming coeducational in 1882 and adding its first woman faculty member, Sarah Isom, in 1885. In addition to the normal trials any southern state university might experience, the University of Mississippi suffered two significant crises in its troubled history. In 1928 Governor Theodore G. Bilbo urged the legislature to relocate the state university from Oxford to Jackson, the state capital. His plans called for a gigantic increase in the state appropriation (from $1 million to $25 million), a restructuring of the university's curriculum, and sweeping personnel changes. All the governor's plans went awry, and in the process the university lost its accreditation for two years. Recent scholarship has somewhat tempered the criticism of Governor Bilbo, whose motives were less political and punitive than formerly believed.

A second major crisis came in 1962 when James Howard Meredith became the first black student to enroll at the university. Governor Ross Barnett led the state's white power structure in resisting Meredith's admission and delayed his enrollment for nearly 18 months by a series of legal maneuvers. When the courts at last ordered his admission, legal proceedings gave way to violence. Throughout the night of 31 September 1962 rioters surged across the university campus in a vain effort to prevent his enrollment. James Meredith did enroll and graduated from the university in August 1963.

The University of Mississippi is known universally as Ole Miss. This name became associated with the university during the 1896–97 academic year when the student body began publishing an annual, which was styled *The Ole Miss*. Within less than a decade alumni, students, and the media routinely referred to the university as Ole Miss. Although it has never been formally or officially adopted, the name Ole Miss has become a synonym for the University of Mississippi.

The university provides an institutional focus for interdisciplinary study of the American South through its Center for the Study of Southern Culture (established in 1977), Afro-American Studies program, Sarah Isom Center for Women's Studies, and the resources of the John Davis Williams Library, which includes a comprehensive William Faulkner collection and the Blues Archive. Annual conferences include the Faulkner Conference (since 1974) and the Chancellor's Symposium on Southern History (since 1975).

Barnard Observatory, University of Mississippi, c. 1859

R. Gerald Turner assumed the office of chancellor in 1984. Enrollment at the Oxford campus as of fall 1985 was 9,004 students.

See also BLACK LIFE: / Meredith, James; POLITICS: / Barnett, Ross; Bilbo, Theodore

David Sansing
University of Mississippi

Allen Cabaniss, *The University of Mississippi: Its First Hundred Years* (2d ed., 1971).

Mississippi State University

Mississippi State University is located in the eastern part of north-central Mississippi near the town of Starkville. It was chartered by the legislature in 1878 as the Agricultural and Mechanical College of the state of Mississippi to serve as the land-grant institution for white youths. The legislation establishing the college passed after considerable pressure from state Grange leaders who had agitated for several years to have the land-grant education function moved from its original location, the University of Mississippi at Oxford. Grangers preferred a separate institution, one that would better fulfill the mission of the Morrill Act, an 1862 federal law providing college training in scientific agriculture and industrial technology for the children of farmers.

Classes began in October 1880 under the presidency of former Confederate General Stephen D. Lee. Enrollment the first year totaled 354 men; female students were admitted two years later. The college awarded its first baccalaureate degrees in 1883 to eight students. Enrollment now totals 11,663; nearly 10,000 of these students study on the main campus. On-campus enrollment is the largest in the state. There are three off-campus branches;

two of these are degree-granting centers located in Meridian and Jackson.

In 1932 the legislature renamed the college Mississippi State College, and it became Mississippi State University in 1958. By then it had developed into a comprehensive, doctoral-degree-granting university committed to fulfilling the land-grant college functions of instruction, research, and service. The university includes 11 academic units: the Graduate School; the schools of Accountancy, Architecture, and Forest Resources; the Division of Continuing Education; and the colleges of Agriculture and Home Economics, Arts and Sciences, Business and Industry, Education, Engineering, and Veterinary Medicine. The Agricultural and Forestry Experiment Station, the Cooperative Extension Service, and numerous specialized units such as the John C. Stennis Institute of Government and the Center for International Security and Strategic Studies are also integral components of the university.

The university's library houses valuable collections of manuscripts, documents, maps, newspapers, and periodicals. A Special Collections department devoted to collecting materials of local, state, regional, and general histories also houses the papers of distinguished Mississippians such as Senator John C. Stennis, Congressman G. V. "Sonny" Montgomery, and newspaper editors Hodding Carter and Turner Catledge.

Donald Zacharias became the university's 15th chief executive officer when he assumed its presidency in August 1985.

Robert L. Jenkins
Mississippi State University

John K. Bettersworth, *People's College: A History of Mississippi State* (1953); Dean W. Colvard, *The "Land Grant" Way in Mississippi: The Story of Mississippi State University* (1962); James D. McComas, *Mississippi State University: A New Century, a New Dimension* (1978).

National Humanities Center

In an essay on "Education and the Southern Potential" (1966) sociologist Rupert B. Vance observed, "Beyond the level of graduate training, a new pattern in American intellectual life has been the emergence of centers for advanced study, such as the Institute for Advanced Study at Princeton and the Center for Advanced Study in the Behavioral Sciences at Stanford. There is no comparable institution in the South and none in sight." In 1976, however, the American Academy of Arts and Sciences in Boston, after considering more than 15 potential sites across the United States, accepted the invitation of the Triangle Universities Center for Advanced Studies, Inc. (TUCASI), a consortium of Duke University, the University of North Carolina at Chapel Hill, and North Carolina State University, to locate the newly conceived National Humanities Center in the Research Triangle Park of North Carolina. TUCASI raised funds from North Carolina corporations and foundations for a 30,000-square-foot building, and it assured library support and partial administrative funding for the new center from the three universities. Among the North Carolinians who formed TUCASI and helped establish the National Humanities Center were John Caldwell, Archie K. Davis, William Friday, C. Hugh Holman, and Terry Sanford.

The Center opened in 1978 and each academic year admits as fellows 40 to 50 scholars in the humanities to pursue individual research and to exchange ideas in daily conversation, lectures, interdisciplinary seminars, and conferences. A class of fellows includes young scholars (3 to 10 years beyond the doctorate), scholars in mid-career, and distinguished senior scholars; fellows have private studies and are given fellowship stipends, library assistance, and manuscript typing. Most fellows are chosen in an open competition, for which the Center receives applications from all parts of the United States and also from other nations. Scholars of southern history and culture who have been fellows of the Center include Cleanth Brooks, Richard Beale Davis, John Hope Franklin, Dewey Grantham, and John Shelton Reed. The Center also publishes a quarterly newsletter and produces a weekly radio program on the humanities. A 35-member national board of trustees, composed of leaders from education, the professions, and public life, oversees the Center, and a director is in charge of its administration. Directors have been Charles Frankel (1977–79), William J. Bennett (1979–81), and Charles Blitzer (1983–). Support for the Center has come from private foundations, corporations, the National Endowment for the Humanities and other federal agencies, the Triangle Universities, the state of North Carolina, individual donors, and an endowment fund. The Center's stated purpose is "to encourage scholarship in the humanities and to enhance the influence of the humanities in the United States."

See also BLACK LIFE: / Franklin, John Hope; LITERATURE: / Brooks, Cleanth

Kent Mullikin
National Humanities Center

Terry Eastland, *Change* (April 1980); Melvin Maddocks, *Time* (14 May 1979); Peter Riesenberg, *Christian Science Monitor* (7 May 1979); Malcolm G. Scully, *Chronicle of Higher Education* (28 April 1980).

North Carolina, University of

The University of North Carolina at Chapel Hill was authorized by the state constitution of 1776 and chartered by the General Assembly in 1789. The cornerstone of Old East Building, today the oldest state-university building in America, was laid on 12 October 1793. The first student arrived on 12 February 1795, and the first class was graduated in 1798. The university survived sectarian and political attacks, public apathy, and continued poverty. It began its slow emergence from obscurity as it strengthened its faculty and liberalized its curriculum. The natural sciences gained equal status with classical studies. After constitutional reforms of 1835 and the success attained by many alumni in state and federal government, a more favorable political climate for the university was accompanied by greater emphasis on education for public service. Three 18th-century and five 19th-century buildings, still standing, met campus needs before 1861 when it was second only to Yale in number of students enrolled. Although the university remained open through the Civil War, it was forced by general economic ruin and political bitterness to close from 1870 to 1875.

First to open a summer "normal school" for teachers (1877), the university introduced regular courses in education as early as 1885. Other guideposts to the future included the beginning of medical and pharmaceutical studies (1879), the first regular legislative appropriation (1881), announcement of graduate studies leading to degrees (1876), organization of scientific laboratories and discoveries of major significance in industrial chemistry (1880–1900), administrative integration of the semi-independent School of Law (1894), and admission of the first women students (1897).

The period before World War I was marked by significant gains in academic standards and productive scholarship of the faculty, reorganization and orderly expansion of library services, and increased emphasis on the applied and social sciences. During the 1920s the state successfully met the needs of the university through enlargement of its physical plant. The University Press was incorporated in 1922, the Institute for Research in Social Science was organized in 1924, and the Southern Historical Collection was established in 1930. From 1930 to 1949 the university was led by former history professor (1915–30) Frank P. Graham, who gained national recognition as an educator, statesman, and social activist. Expansion was halted by the Depression and by World War II but since 1947 has continued apace. A Division of Health Affairs was created that year and has resulted in greatly expanded schools of Medicine, Pharmacy, and Public Health, while new schools of Dentistry and Nursing and the North Carolina Memorial Hospital were established. A planetarium and astronomical observatory, a museum of art, a new library building, enlarged chemistry laboratories, and an indoor sports arena are among later additions to the campus. As of fall 1985 its full-time enrollment was 22,066 students.

William S. Powell
University of North Carolina
at Chapel Hill

R. D. W. Connor, ed., *Documentary History of UNC, 1776–1799*, 2 vols. (1953); William S. Powell, *First State University: A Pictorial History of the University of North Carolina* (1972); Phillips Russell, *These Old Stone Walls* (1972); Louis Round Wilson, *University of North Carolina, 1900–1930* (1957).

North Carolina School of the Arts

The North Carolina School of the Arts in Winston-Salem, N.C., is a state-supported school designed to train performing artists. Programs of study range from seventh grade through graduate school. The institution incorporates schools of Dance, Design and Production, Drama, and Music. All schools include an undergraduate program; the schools of Dance and Music and the Visual Arts program of the School of Design and Production provide training on the secondary level as well. In addition, a program leading to the Master of Fine Arts degree is offered in the School of Design and Production. There is also a complementary academic program at both the secondary and undergraduate levels. The current enrollment of 787 students represents 54 of North Carolina's counties, 48 states, and 13 foreign countries. The school employs 100 faculty, many of whom are recognized professional artists, and guest artists.

The enabling legislation establishing the school was passed by the North Carolina General Assembly in 1963, with the strong support of Governor Terry Sanford. Winston-Salem was chosen as the site of the campus because an existing structure, the Gray High School building, and the surrounding 40 acres were available, and because Winston-Salem had a reputation for audience and financial support of the arts. Vittorio Giannini, a Juilliard composer, was chosen as the first president of the school, which opened in 1965 with 226 students.

Upon the death of Giannini in 1967, Robert Ward, Pulitzer Prize–winning composer, was selected as president of the school. In the 1972–73 academic year the school became one of the 16 components of the reorganized University of North Carolina system, and in 1974 Robert Suderburg, also a composer, became the chancellor of the school. Jane Elizabeth Milley succeeded him as chancellor in September 1984.

Besides the 40-acre Gray High School campus, which has undergone much renovation, the school has restored the old Carolina Theater in downtown Winston-Salem. The theater has been renamed the Roger L. Stevens Center for the Performing Arts and has been important in the revitalization of downtown Winston-Salem.

The school also has several professional affiliates, including the North Carolina Dance Theater, the North Carolina Shakespeare Festival, the North Carolina Scenic Studios, and the Piedmont Opera Theatre.

Elaine Doerschuk Pruitt
North Carolina School of the Arts

Gary D. Ford, *Southern Living* (October 1983); Frank Getlein, *Smithsonian* (March 1981); Selwa Roosevelt, *Town and Country* (March 1981).

Odum, Howard W.

(1884–1954) Sociologist.

Howard Washington Odum (born in Georgia in 1884, died in North Carolina in 1954) was the South's best-known social scientist in the first half of the 20th century. In more than 20 books and 200 articles he assessed the level of the region's economic and cultural achievements, explored the forces that inhibited progress, and exhorted his fellow southerners to use their material, intellectual, and spiritual resources to rebuild their region. Odum's work was well known beyond academic circles, and he became an important symbol of the movement to use science and scientific open-mindedness as tools to unlock the region's potential and inspire a new sectional self-confidence.

Odum was educated during the height of the Progressive era. He received his bachelor's degree in 1904 from Emory University, a master's degree in classics from the University of Mississippi in 1906, and Ph.D. degrees from Clark University (psychology) in 1909 and Columbia University (sociology) in 1910. As a young man he absorbed the spirit of the great Progressive-era teachers and orators who believed that science could reveal the secrets of social phenomena and pave the way for major leaps forward in the human condition. Odum brought this spirit to the University of Georgia, where he was on the faculty in the School of Education from 1913 to 1919. During this period he campaigned actively to improve rural education in Georgia and began a lifelong effort to encourage diversification of southern agriculture by developing the dairy industry (Odum later received national awards as a breeder of Jersey cows). In 1919 Odum became the dean of Emory College, but his vision of Emory as an instrument of social services clashed with the philosophy of the school's conservative chancellor. When the University of North Carolina offered Odum a post as chair of the sociology department and dean of the School of Public Welfare, he moved to Chapel Hill, where he remained for the duration of a remarkably productive career.

At Chapel Hill Odum concentrated on using the resources of social science to study the South's problems and to suggest solutions. Toward these ends he founded the *Journal of Social Forces* and the Institute for Research in Social Science. Between 1924 and 1954 Odum persuaded northern philanthropists to contribute hundreds of thousands of dollars to support institute studies of regional economic conditions, labor relations, race problems, welfare programs, and penal reforms. The most notable of the many products of this work was a massive statistical portrait of the South that Odum published in 1936 under the title *Southern Regions of the United States*. This book was used extensively by contemporary journalists and political leaders in campaigns for regional self-improvement.

Over the course of his career Odum also made major contributions to preserving the cultural history of southern blacks. He published collections of black folksongs in 1911 (in the *Journal of American Folklore*) and in 1925 and 1926 (in book form, with Guy B. Johnson), and between 1928 and 1931 he wrote a trilogy of books based on the life of a wandering black laborer.

Howard W. Odum, renowned sociologist, c. 1930s

Howard W. Odum also participated directly in many social service programs. He helped lead three penal-reform movements in North Carolina, served as assistant director of President Hoover's Commission on Recent Social Trends, was a director of the North Carolina Welfare Commission, and helped found the Southern Regional Council. During the last two decades of his life Odum worked to develop a theory of regionalism that would encourage holistic analysis of all aspects of the South's condition and to devise means to ease the transition to a racially integrated society.

See also SOCIAL CLASS: / Southern Regional Council

Wayne D. Brazil
Hastings College of the Law

Katherine Jocher, Guy B. Johnson, George L. Simpson, and Rupert B. Vance, eds., *Folk, Region, and Society: Selected Papers of Howard W. Odum* (1964); Howard W. Odum, *An*

American Epoch (1930), *American Regionalism* (1938), *Cold Blue Moon* (1931), *Rainbow Round My Shoulder* (1928), *Southern Regions of the United States* (1936), *The Way of the South* (1947), *Wings on My Feet* (1929).

Phillips, U. B.

(1877–1934) Historian.

Ulrich Bonnell Phillips has recently been described by historian Eugene D. Genovese as perhaps the greatest historian America has produced. Author of six major works and 55 factual articles, Phillips almost singlehandedly directed the social and economic history of the antebellum South from pietistic antiquarianism to many of the major concerns of contemporary historians. An indefatigable discoverer and user of primary sources, especially plantation records, Phillips was undoubtedly the preeminent historian of the South in the first half of the 20th century. Still, his pervasive, if paternalistic, racism and his insistence that the plantation system was *the* social/economic system of the antebellum South caused his work to be virtually unread until his recent rediscovery.

Phillips was born 4 November 1877 in the small upland Georgia town of LaGrange. He received both his B.A. and M.A. from the University of Georgia and then went to Columbia, where he took his doctorate in 1902 under William Dunning. Phillips taught for short periods at both Wisconsin and Tulane and from 1911 to 1929 at the University of Michigan. On 21 January 1934, four years after leaving Michigan for Yale, Phillips died.

Phillips had four major ideas about the antebellum South: (1) its environment was an essential contributing factor to its development and Frederick Jackson Turner's hypothesis of the frontier worked perfectly for the South of prewar years; (2) the region's political economy was a combination of geography, economics, politics, social structure, race, and ideology and dominated all aspects of southern life; (3) the key to antebellum political economy was the plantation, which was not a mere economic institution but an entire way of life; and, finally, (4) the plantation was primarily a method of social control of a "stupid," genetically inferior race and the necessary first step in what Phillips unabashedly regarded as the continuing, essential task of preserving the South as "a white man's country."

Phillips incorporated Turner's regionalism into his 1902 dissertation "Georgia and States Rights," ostensibly a history of Georgia political thought. During the early 1900s he further developed the frontier thesis in numerous articles in major journals, the 13-volume *The South in the Building of the Nation*, and his introduction to the documentary collection *Plantation and Frontier*. Phillips's first attempt to view political economy as an interrelated system was his 1908 study of the development of the railroad industry, *A History of Transportation in the Eastern Cotton Belt to 1860*, which showed how the needs of the planter class created the type of railroads built in the South. Phillips then concentrated largely upon a systematic study of the plantation economy and produced two classic and highly influential works, *American Negro Slavery* (1918) and *Life and Labor in the Old South* (1929). In the late 1920s Phillips related his ideas of black social control to political history in such essays as "The Central Theme of Southern History" and was preparing a book on the subject at the time of his death.

Mark Smith
University of Texas at San Antonio

Merton Dillon, *Ulrich Bonnell Phillips: Historian of the Old South* (1985); Richard Hofstadter, *Journal of Negro History* (April 1944); John Herbert Roper, *U. B. Phillips: A Southern Mind* (1984).

Piney Woods School

Piney Woods Country Life School is a private boarding institution in Rankin County, Miss. The campus is surrounded by a 2,000-acre pine forest along Highway 49 between Jackson and Hattiesburg. It was founded in 1909 by a Missourian, Laurence Clifton Jones (1882–1975). After graduating from the University of Iowa in 1907 and teaching at Utica Institute in Mississippi, he decided to start his own school. One day as he sat on the end of a log, a teenage male came and sat on the other end. Jones discovered that the youth could not read because his family had bound him out to work. Each day as Jones taught him to read, more children came.

By the time of the first high school graduating class in 1918, Piney Woods had become known for the opportunity that it provided Afro-American boys and girls who had no money. They made bricks for buildings, worked in the office, and did carpentry, cooking, laundering, cleaning, and farming. In the past as well as today, the work program emphasized educating the head, the heart, and the hand. Students acquired three skills that were to help them earn a living or further their education.

After the 1920s the Piney Woods School included a school for the blind, which was moved to Jackson under the control of the state in the 1950s. Its musical programs included the Rays of Rhythm, Sweet Hearts of Rhythm, a marching band, a stage band, and a glee club. Visitors were treated with the best of black spirituals as they enjoyed southern hospitality on the Piney Woods campus.

In 1931 the school's elementary and secondary curriculum was enhanced by a junior college that focused on secretarial and teacher training. Numerous graduates from these programs have gone on to receive terminal degrees in their chosen fields. A positive work ethic is instilled in the students not only by the work program but by mottos posted on campus, such as "Will prepare myself and maybe my chance will come," "Devote yourself to a worthy task [and] you can't fail to have a worthy life," and "Work is the mother of contentment."

From the very beginning, Piney Woods has been a suc-

Story hour at the Piney Woods School, Mississippi, c. 1940s

cess story of interracial cooperation. Black and white citizens from Mississippi and the nation have given their time, talents, and financial resources to the institution. Also, in the early days Jones's wife, Grace Allen Jones (1876–1928), initiated the traveling singers who spent summers on the road introducing Piney Woods to the nation and soliciting funds. In 1953 Jones appeared on the *This Is Your Life* television program. The program and its successive showings helped the school establish the largest endowment of any high school for Afro-Americans in the nation.

Today the school provides an accredited curriculum for approximately 300 students in kindergarten through the 12th grade. In 1985 Charles Beady succeeded James S. Wade as its third president. An integrated board of trustees manages the school and plans for its future.

Alferdteen Harrison
Jackson State University

Alferdteen Harrison, *Piney Woods School: An Oral History* (1982).

Randolph-Macon College

Randolph-Macon College began with the desire of the Virginia Conference of the Methodist Episcopal church to have a clergy educated in the liberal arts and the desire of the leading citizens of Mecklenburg County to have a college. Fund-raising began in 1825, and a charter was acquired from the legislature of Virginia on 3 February 1830. The eponymous John Randolph and Nathaniel Macon, both well-known politicians, had no connection with the institution. The college was erected west of Boydton, Va., near the North Carolina border, then at the center of the conference.

At first the curriculum of Randolph-Macon followed the unique elective system of the University of Virginia, but the first formal president, Stephen Olin, persuaded the faculty in 1834 to adopt the rigid curriculum common to colleges at the time. In 1859 Randolph-Macon reverted to the elective system. The college achieved financial stability under President William A. Smith (1846–66). Smith taught a formal course defending slavery, and the college at one time owned two slaves. He and board of trustees chairman John Early, Methodist ministers both, were principals in the formation of the Methodist Episcopal Church, South.

The Civil War cut off the supply of students and forced the brief closing of the school. More damaging was the investment of much of the endowment in Confederate and southern municipal bonds. The war wrecked the regional transportation system and devastated the segment of the population that supported the school and sent sons to it. The board of trustees, pushed by the college president, Thomas Johnson, moved the college in 1868 to Ashland, Va., which had the virtue of being on a railroad line connecting the college with the Maryland Conference of the Methodists.

The college remained small, with 100 to 200 students, but pioneered educational reforms in the teaching of English literature (1870) and physical education (1886). Under the leadership of the college president, William Waugh Smith, the board of trustees established Randolph-Macon Woman's College in Lynchburg, Va., and three preparatory schools (at Bedford, Front Royal, and Danville, Va.), thus forming the Randolph-Macon system.

Modernizing the college in Ashland took more money than its rural, Methodist supporters could afford, and there was an appeal to northern financiers, especially Andrew Carnegie. When the Woman's College met the exacting standards of his pension fund (the first school in the South to do so), the money came with a stipulation that meant the board would cease to be entirely Methodist. This stipulation raised the question, voiced by alumnus James Cannon, of whether the board or the Virginia Conference would own and control the system. After a protracted, debilitating quarrel, the Virginia courts supported the trustees, but the moral victory was with the church. Very little changed at the college until after World War II.

Many of the subsequent improvements at the college reflect the growing prosperity of Virginia. In the postwar presidency of J. Earl Moreland, the college expanded its student body from 300 in the 1930s to 900, with concomitant increases in buildings, curricula, and faculty. In 1964 the college decided to admit students regardless of race and in 1971, during the presidency of Luther W. White III, began to admit residential women students. The student body of nearly 1,000 (964 as of the 1984–85 academic year) is drawn primarily from Virginia (65 percent) and Maryland. The college resolutely emphasizes the liberal arts but also embraces the sciences, including computer science. Its graduates frequently move into the professions (especially law and medicine) and business.

See also RELIGION: / Cannon, James; Methodist Episcopal Church, South

James Edward Scanlon
Randolph-Macon College

Richard Irby, *History of Randolph-Macon College, Virginia* (1898); James Edward Scanlon, *Randolph-Macon College: A Southern History* (1983).

Rice University

Rice University, a private, independent, coeducational university located in Houston, Tex., opened its doors to students in 1912 as the William Marsh Rice Institute. It was chartered in 1891 by former Houston merchant William Marsh Rice with a $200,000 interest-bearing note payable to the institute upon his death. Subsequently Rice made other gifts to the institute, all payable after his death. When the estate was settled in 1904, approximately $3 million was given to the institute as a separate capital fund, added to the original endowment that had grown to almost $3.3 million. At the time the institute opened in 1912, the endowment stood at approximately $9 million, allowing all students to attend without paying tuition—a privilege not ended until 1965.

The Board of Trustees in Houston appointed mathematician and astronomer Edgar Odell Lovett of Princeton University as president in 1907 with directions to plan the new institution. After worldwide travel, discussions, and faculty recruitment, Lovett oversaw the opening in 1912 marked by an international convocation of scholars. The entering class of 77 students had an international faculty of 10 (Julian Huxley was the first professor of biology), one major academic building (with an elaborate plan for additional buildings by the Boston architectural firm of Cram, Goodhue, and Ferguson), and a large endowment. The honor code, a cherished Rice tradition, was adopted by the student body in 1916. By 1924 the entering freshman class was limited to approximately 450, and undergraduate enrollment has been carefully controlled ever since. In 1985 it was approximately 3,800. The graduate enrollment has grown gradually to almost 1,200.

Under Lovett's direction the Rice Institute first developed major strength in the sciences and engineering, though distinguished instruction was offered from the beginning in the humanities and architecture. The curriculum broadened and the faculty increased greatly in size after World War II under the administration (1946–60) of physicist William V. Houston, as the name change in 1960 to Rice University acknowledged. Moral, social, and economic imperatives drove the university successfully to seek legal authority in 1964 to break the founder's charter in two regards: permission to admit students without regard to race and to charge (a modest) tuition. Further expansion, especially in the humanities and social sciences, came in the 1960s and 1970s during the administrations of chemists Kenneth S. Pitzer (1961–68) and Norman Hackerman (1970–85). In 1961 the National Aeronautics and Space Administration located the Manned Space Flight Center (now Johnson Space Center) on land made available by Rice, and in 1962 the university established the nation's first department of space science. The *Journal of Southern History* has been published at Rice since 1959; *Studies in English Literature* was founded at Rice in 1961; and the *Papers of Jefferson Davis* project has been headquartered at Rice since 1963. In July 1985 *Rice University Studies* (formerly *Rice Institute Pamphlet*) became Rice University Press. The Sheperd School of Music and the Jones School of Administration were added in 1973 and 1976, respectively.

In 1985, the year theologian George E. Rupp of Harvard Divinity School became Rice's fifth president, the endowment passed the half-billion-dollar mark, the largest of any private university in the South. The small undergraduate student body (3,813 enrollment in the 1984–85 academic year) is among the nation's most select, with average SAT scores over 1300 and one of the highest percentages of National Merit Scholarship winners.

See also URBANIZATION: / Houston

John B. Boles
Rice University

Stephen Fox, *The General Plan of the William M. Rice Institute and Its Architectural Development* (1980); Fredericka Meiners, *A History of Rice University: The Institute Years, 1907–1963* (1982); Andrew Forest Muir, in *William Marsh Rice and His Institute*, ed. Sylvia Stallings Morris, Rice University Studies (Spring 1972).

Sheats, William N.

(1851–1922) Educator.

During his lifetime William N. Sheats became variously known as Florida's "Little Giant of Education," "Florida's Progressive Educator," and the "Father of Florida's Public School System." His fame grew during more than two decades as superintendent of public instruction, and his efforts set the foundations for a modern state system of public education.

Born 5 March 1851 on a small cotton farm in the red clay foothills of the Appalachians near Auburn, Gwinnett County, Ga., Sheats was proud of his roots and often referred to himself as a Georgia cracker. His inspiration in life was his widowed mother, who though beaten down by sickness and poverty made every effort to get her children to school. Adopting her creed, Sheats worked his way through Emory College, eventually attaining a master's degree, and, while principal of a Georgia high school, he completed by correspondence an accounting course from Moore's Business College. Believing that Florida had a healthful climate, he accepted an offer as vice principal of the East Florida seminary at Gainesville in 1876.

A very popular teacher, Sheats was induced to run for superintendent of Alachua County Schools. He developed his philosophy of administration during three terms as county school superintendent. Reading journals, consulting with educators, and touring school facilities convinced Sheats to emphasize centralization of authority and uniformity of procedure. He revoked all teaching licenses, forcing teachers to take his examination based on a series of textbooks. Facing reexamination every one, two, or three years, teachers flocked to Sheats's institutes on pedagogy. He led the county school board in adopting a rigorous code of conduct for teachers, uniformity of textbooks, and consolidation of schools. He believed so strongly in the separate-but-equal doctrine that he provided excellent teacher training for blacks and attempted to establish for them an industrial training school comparable to Booker T. Washington's Tuskegee Institute. After 12 years of his leadership Alachua County schools went from near the bottom in school quality to near the top.

Sheats gained statewide recognition at the 1885 constitutional convention. The only school man present, he dominated debates that shaped the education article destined to remain in effect for 84 years. The document included provisions that special tax districts be developed for high school education, that the state superintendent of public instruction be elected, that racial integration in the public schools be prohibited, and that the state organize teacher training colleges, one for each race.

In 1892 Sheats became Florida's first elected state superintendent of public instruction. He soon showed the same passion for centralization and regimentation that had characterized his earlier work. He shocked teachers by revoking their licenses as a means to get them to sit for his long and difficult examination. He proposed a uniform course of study, an effort at consolidating schools into larger units, and a state-aid formula for high schools. In black education he caused a national sensation by having the sheriff close a Congregationalist school and arrest the teachers for instructing blacks and whites in the same school.

Educators from around the nation read about "Mr. Sheats" in a *National Education Association* article on the ideal chief state school officer, but his opponents, referring to "Tsar Sheats," schemed for his election defeat. They succeeded in 1904 by portraying him as too liberal on the race question. He was turned out by the voters, even though during his administration 32,000 additional children registered in school, raising the proportion of registered children from 66 percent in 1892 to 71 percent in 1904, and per student expenditures had increased from $4.25 to $8.10.

Sheats made an election comeback in 1912, and during his last years he put a personal stamp on Florida's compulsory attendance law and administered one of the South's most effective uniform textbook laws. On 19 July 1922 he died in office.

Arthur O. White
University of Florida

William N. Sheats, "Journal," William N. Sheats Papers, Southern Historical Collection, University of North Carolina, Chapel Hill; Arthur O. White, *One Hundred Years of State Leadership in Florida Public Education* (1979).

South Carolina, University of

Founded in 1801 as the South Carolina College, the University of South Carolina opened in 1805. The college received financial appropriations from the state government, enabling it to build a physical plant, which included the first separate college library building in the United States. The school attracted a faculty that included Francis Lieber, perhaps the most distinguished scholar in the antebellum South. The classical curriculum reached its peak in the 1850s during the presidency of James Henley Thornwell, who declared that the college existed "for Latin and Greek." At that time there were approximately 200 students, with eight professors on the faculty.

Although the era from 1801 to 1861 was prosperous, the next 60 years brought disaster, and the institution was closed on two occasions and reorganized six times. The Civil War forced it to suspend operations in June 1862, and the physical plant was converted into a Confederate military hospital, a status that saved it from the fire that destroyed much of Columbia when Sherman's army occupied the city in February 1865. In January 1866 the school was reopened as a university, but economic distress following the war prevented the state government from providing adequate support. The situation was further complicated when the Radical Republicans gained control of the state government in 1868 and two blacks were elected to the board of trustees. During Reconstruction several blacks were awarded A.B. and LL.B. degrees, and one, Richard T. Greener, became a member of the faculty.

Whites were appalled by events at the "Reconstruction University," and Governor Wade Hampton promptly closed it when the Democrats regained control in April 1877. The school remained closed until October 1880, when it reopened as the South Carolina College of Agriculture and Mechanic Arts. In 1890 Benjamin R. Tillman directed scathing attacks at the institution as the "seedbed of the aristocracy" and led his agrarian followers in a political revolution, which resulted in the founding of rival Clemson and Winthrop colleges.

After Tillman's attacks in 1890, 30 lean years followed during which the school was plagued by economic hardships, Tillmanite legislators, and hostile governors, such as Cole L. Blease. In 1906 it was again allowed to assume the name of university, and in the 1920s under the vigorous leadership of President William D. Melton, appropriations increased sufficiently to place the university in a position of equality with its state rivals. The same was true of enrollment, which grew from 600 to 1,800.

The post–World War II years brought tremendous growth, as the university became by far the largest institution in the state. Enrollment, which was 2,000 in 1940, has increased on the Columbia campus to 23,000, of which almost one-half are women and 8,000 are graduate students. There are also nine regional campuses with an enrollment of 12,000 undergraduates. The doctorate is offered in 50 fields and the master's degree in 104. Blacks were readmitted in 1963, peacefully, and approximately 14 percent of current students are black. The new Thomas Cooper Library is a major research center, while the South Caroliniana Library has become an outstanding repository of materials pertaining to state history.

In the 1980s President James B. Holderman has launched an ambitious program in international studies that operates through the James F. Byrnes International Center. The Institute for Southern Studies sponsors conferences, workshops, publications, and research on the region and especially the state of South Carolina.

Daniel W. Hollis
University of South Carolina

E. L. Green, *History of University of South Carolina* (1916); Daniel W. Hollis, *University of South Carolina*, 2 vols. (1951, 1956); Thomas T. Jones, *The University of South Carolina: Faithful Index to the Ambitions and Fortunes of the State* (1964).

Southern Methodist University

Celebrating its 75th year of founding in 1986, Southern Methodist University (SMU) in Dallas, Tex., has grown from a college with a theology school to a university of 9,000 students in four undergraduate and two graduate professional schools. Its denominational but nonsectarian nature early led to a liberal arts orientation. At the same time, the needs of Dallas led to the creation of schools of law, engineering, business, and the arts as well as theology and to SMU's early embrace of big-time football.

SMU was established in 1911 by a special educational commission of the five annual conferences of the Methodist Episcopal Church, South, in Texas, and it is now owned by the South Central Jurisdiction of the United Methodist Church. Vanderbilt University had severed its connection with the church in the early 20th century, and SMU became the sole Methodist-affiliated institution of higher learning west of the Mississippi River. Both Dallas and Fort Worth were under consideration as sites; the gift of a 133-acre campus and the promise of sustaining funds by Dallas citizens brought SMU to Dallas. It opened its doors in 1915, with 706 students, 35 faculty, and $279,178 in endowment.

The first president was a Georgian and graduate of Emory College, Robert S. Hyer, who came from another Methodist college, Southwestern of Georgetown, Tex. A physicist who had early experimented with wireless communication, he had a vision for SMU. He chose *veritas liberabit vos* as its motto, selected Harvard's and Yale's colors, and borrowed from the University of Virginia the neo-Georgian architectural pattern that still unifies SMU's 80-building campus.

Other SMU leaders, Umphrey Lee (1938–54) and Willis M. Tate (1954–72), were both SMU graduates. Lee, a minister and scholar who had been dean of Vanderbilt's School of Religion, steered SMU through World War II and toward research and scholarship as well as teaching. Tate was a genius at interpreting a university to the business leadership of Dallas and a strong defender of SMU as a "free marketplace of ideas." For his defense of academic freedom he was awarded the Alexander Meikeljohn award of the American Association of University Professors in 1967. Among those whom SMU invited to speak on campus during the times of McCarthyism and of 1960s social unrest were John Gates and Martin Luther King, Jr.

SMU began publishing the *Southwest Review* in 1925. It became respected through the contributions of John H. McGinnis, Henry Nash Smith, J. Frank Dobie, Lon Tinkle, and others. For a brief time just before the founding of the *Southern Review*, the *Southwest Review* was edited jointly by McGinnis at SMU and Cleanth Brooks and Robert Penn Warren at LSU. The SMU Press was established in 1937.

SMU integrated several of its schools in the 1950s, ahead of most other universities in the region, and was the first Southwest Conference school to have black athletes on its teams. The faculty of Perkins School of Theology had a key leadership role in integration in Dallas.

Marshall Terry
Southern Methodist University

Mary Martha Thomas, *Southern Methodist University: Founding and Early Years* (1974).

Tennessee, University of

The University of Tennessee enrolls more than 40,000 students on four campuses: the major campus at Knoxville, the Center for the Health Sciences at Memphis, and the predominantly undergraduate campuses at Chattanooga and Martin.

Established in 1794 as Blount College, a private, nonsectarian, coeducational school, it was rechartered by the Tennessee Legislature in 1807 as East Tennessee College, a male-only institution, and endowed with a land grant of 50,000 acres. Often condemned by frontier politicians as a school for rich men's sons, it was a small, struggling institution with never more than 169 students in the antebellum period.

During the Civil War the faculty generally supported the Union, while the loyalties of the students were divided. The university buildings were badly damaged in the conflict. The Confederate army occupied the campus first; later it was used as a military hospital by northern troops.

In 1869, largely because of the Union sentiments of trustees and faculty, it was designated the land-grant university under the Morrill Act. For the next generation a debate ensued within the university over the significance of the land-grant designation. Most of the faculty and the president looked upon agricultural and mechanical arts as merely a branch of the university; the trustees generally supported its transformation into a predominantly agricultural and scientific institution. The victory of the agricultural forces was completed in 1887 with the election of President Charles W. Dabney. Until then the university had been an all-male military school with drills, military government, and mandatory uniforms patterned after West Point. Military government was abandoned in 1890, and women returned in 1892.

From 1901 to 1917 the university was a leading institution in support of campaigns in behalf of universal public schooling in the South. With the aid of the Southern and General Education boards it conducted the Summer School of the South for teachers from throughout the region from 1902 to World War I, with 22,000 teachers attending during the first decade.

The university experienced phenomenal growth after World War II with veterans entering under the GI Bill, followed soon after by their sons and daughters. The first black students enrolled—under court order—in 1952. In 1968, shortly after the University of Chattanooga merged with the university, it was reorganized into a university system with a president as the highest officer and a chancellor over each campus.

Clinton B. Allison
University of Tennessee

Clinton B. Allison, in *Three Schools of Education: Approaches to Institutional History*, ed. Agnes Bagley (1984); James Riley Montgomery, Stanley J. Folmsbee, and Lee Seifert Green, *To Foster Knowledge: A History of the University of Tennessee, 1794–1970* (1984); The University of Tennessee Office of Management Services, *A Graphic View of the University of Tennessee* (7th ed., 1985).

Texas, University of

For many years Texas lawmakers considered the establishment of a state university. Finally, the Constitutional Convention of 1875 decided that "the Legislature shall, as soon as practicable, establish, organize and provide for the maintenance, support and direction of a university of the first class, to be located by a vote of the people of this State, and styled, 'The University of Texas,' for the promotion of literature, and the arts and sciences, including an agricultural and mechanical department." On 28 March 1881 the legislature passed a bill establishing the university, and Governor Oran M. Roberts signed the measure on 30 March. Later that year, Texans voted to locate the school in Austin. In November 1882 the cornerstone of the west wing of the original main building was laid in place on 40 acres of land one mile north of the Capitol; and in September 1883 the first students began classes in the temporary Capitol at the corner of Congress Avenue and Eleventh Street. Until 1895 the university was without a president, the chairman of the faculty serving as the chief executive officer. President William L. Prather (1899–1905), in addressing the students, uttered the now-famous words, "The eyes of Texas are upon you." Later the words were matched to the tune of "I've Been Working on the Railroad" and became the school song.

At the cornerstone ceremony, Ashbel Smith declaimed prophetically, "Smite the earth, smite the rock with the rod of knowledge, and fountains of unstinted wealth will gush forth." In 1923 oil was discovered on UT's west

Tower, University of Texas at Austin, c. 1940s

Texas lands. The money generated goes into the Permanent University Fund, which in 1982 was worth approximately $1.7 billion. UT receives two-thirds of the income from this fund and Texas A&M University one-third. Although still referred to as "the Forty Acres," the present campus occupies 300 acres and has more than 110 buildings. There were 47,838 students enrolled in the fall of 1985. UT has been merged with 13 other institutions to form the University of Texas system.

UT is the only southwestern member of the Association of American Universities. The latest assessment of doctoral education ranked the school 14th among the nation's universities in overall academic quality. Graduate programs in law, education, and business rank in the top 10 among public institutions. UT has long been a world leader in energy-related education and research.

The Lyndon Baines Johnson Presidential Library is located on the campus. The UT library, with almost 5 million volumes, is the eighth-largest academic library in the United States and is internationally known for its collection in Latin American history and culture and 20th-century British and American literature.

Norman D. Brown
University of Texas at Austin

Margaret Berry, *The University of Texas: A Pictorial Account of Its First Century* (1980); Ronnie Dugger, *The Invaded Universities: Form, Reform and New Starts* (1974); Roger A. Griffin, *Southwestern Historical Quarterly* (October 1982).

Texas A&M University

Texas Agricultural and Mechanical (A&M) University was the first public institution of higher education in Texas. The Texas Legislature authorized the establishment of the institution under the terms of the Morrill Act in November 1866. The act organizing the Agricultural and Mechanical College of Texas was approved on 17 April 1871; it appropriated $75,000 for the erection of buildings and bound the state to defray all expenses of the college exceeding the annual interest from the endowment. Proceeds from the sale of 180,000 acres of land, located in Colorado and authorized under the Morrill Act, were invested in $174,000 of gold frontier defense bonds of Texas. A locating commission accepted the offer of 2,146 acres of land from Brazos County, and the college opened on 4 October 1876. With an initial enrollment of some 50 students in the fall term of 1876, the institution grew to an enrollment exceeding 37,000 students in the mid-1980s.

The college began as an all-male agricultural and mechanical college with required military training and enrollment in the Corps of Cadets. Participation in military training and membership in the Corps of Cadets became voluntary in 1965. Although fewer than 10 percent of the students are now in the Corps of Cadets, the school continues to furnish more reserve officers than any other institution in the United States and offers ROTC programs leading to commissions in all four branches of the service. Women attended intermittently as special students over the years, but the institution officially admitted women students on a qualified basis after 1963 and adopted an open admissions policy in 1971. The 58th Legislature of Texas, on 23 August 1963, changed the name of the Agricultural and Mechanical College to Texas A&M University.

Texas A&M University offers graduate study in most fields, with a doctorate in many. It supports a College of Veterinary Medicine, established in 1916, and a College of Medicine, authorized in 1971, which graduated its first class in 1981. The Texas A&M University system, whose present chancellor is Arthur G. Hansen, provides administrative direction for Texas A&M University at Galveston, Prairie View A&M University, Tarleton State University, Texas Forest Service, Texas Agricultural Extension Service, Texas Agricultural Experiment Station, Texas Engineering Experiment Station, Texas Engineering Extension Service, Texas Transportation Institute, Texas Veterinary Medical Diagnostic Laboratory, and numerous other agencies and divisions. In 1971 Texas A&M University became one of the first four sea-grant designated institutions. Its current president is southern historian Frank E. Vandiver.

The university offers leadership in many of the newer technological areas, including space, nuclear research, computers, oceanography, chemistry, and the traditional areas of agriculture, engineering, architecture, education, geosciences, business, and liberal arts. Research expenditures first exceeded $100 million in 1982, and Texas A&M University now ranks in the top 20 universities in research expenditures. Under the authority of the Texas Constitution of 1876, Texas A&M is a branch of the University of Texas, which was established in 1883, and participates in the Permanent University Fund of the State of Texas. Texas A&M University aspires to preeminence in teaching, research, and public service.

Henry C. Dethloff
Texas A&M University

Henry C. Dethloff, *A Centennial History of Texas A&M University, 1876–1976*, 2 vols. (1975), *The Pictorial History of Texas A&M University, 1876–1976* (1975); George Sessions Perry, *The Story of Texas A. and M.* (1951).

Tulane University

Tulane University was founded in 1834, when seven New Orleans physicians, alarmed by the lack of a local medical school in those times of cholera and yellow fever epidemics, pooled their expertise to found the Medical College of Louisiana at New Orleans. A few years later it became the medical department of the newly established, state-supported University of Louisiana. In 1847 a law department was added; continuing progress, however, was interrupted by the closing of the university during the Civil War. After it reopened in 1878, a liberal arts department was added, later called the Academic Department, now the College of Arts and Sciences.

In 1822 Paul Tulane, a bachelor from Princeton, N.J., arrived in New Orleans to embark upon what would become a highly successful career as a merchant. He remained in New Orleans off and on for more than 50 years before returning to Princeton and retirement. Always a secretive, private person, Tulane in 1881 disclosed to General Randall Lee Gibson of New Orleans that he had for years been contemplating the creation of an institution of higher education to be located in New Orleans for the white youth of Louisiana. Tulane and Gibson went over the details involved in such an endeavor with the result that Gibson was asked to present the idea to 17 prominent New Orleans men whom Tulane wished to comprise his university's governing body. (The first board of administrators of the Tulane Educational Fund included such notables as Gibson himself, Charles Erasmus Fenner, the Reverend Benjamin Morgan Palmer, Edward Douglass White, and others of similar stature.)

As the specifics of Tulane's gift were completed, officials of the University of Louisiana let it be known that they would welcome inclusion in the plans for the new university. Because it was common knowledge that the older institution had fallen upon lean years, they invited James McConnell, Paul Tulane's New Orleans attorney and himself a member of the board of administrators, to meet with their board to discuss the possible advantages of such an arrangement. After careful investigation, it was agreed that the public University of Louisiana would henceforth be the private "Tulane University of Louisiana," and its doors were opened in 1884.

In 1886 Josephine Louise Newcomb, a native of Baltimore but a resident of New Orleans, sent a letter to the board of administrators expressing her desire to establish an appropriate memorial to her daughter, Harriott Sophie, who had died at the age of 15. Newcomb donated $100,000 to establish the H. Sophie Newcomb Memorial College—the first women's coordinate college in the United States. At her death Newcomb bequeathed to the college the residue of her estate, a sum in excess of $2 million.

In 1894, the year that the College of Technology (later the College of Engineering) was added, Tulane University moved from its downtown campus to its present location on more than 100 acres in uptown New Orleans. The medical department (later school) remained downtown and added schools of dentistry and pharmacy, these last two being closed for lack of students in 1928 and 1934, respectively. Today the Tulane Medical Center encompasses the School of Medicine, the School of Public Health and Tropical Medicine, outpatient clinics, and a full-service teaching hospital. Rounding out the academic components of the university on the uptown campus there followed the School of Architecture, the School of Commerce/Business Administration, the Graduate School, the School of Social Work, and the University College (evening division).

Although both Paul Tulane and Josephine Newcomb specified that the student body was to be composed of young white men and women, in 1962 a federal judge ruled that while the university could not be forced to integrate, it was no longer bound by the racial restrictions of the original gifts, and in 1963 Tulane University voluntarily admitted black students.

The W. R. Hogan Jazz Archive is now a premiere collection on a southern musical form, and the Amistad Collection is a world-renowned archives on black life. In the 1984–85 academic year Tulane had a full-time enrollment of 10,232 students, and Newcomb College of Tulane had 1,737 female students.

Doris H. Antin
Tulane University

John Percy Dyer, *Tulane, 1825–1950* (1954), *Tulane: The Biography of a University, 1834–1965* (1966).

Tuskegee Institute

Tuskegee was founded in 1881, the result of an accommodation between local blacks and whites after white political control of Macon County, Ala., was secured. Booker T. Washington, its first principal, established at the secondary level a curriculum of industrial and agricultural education modeled after his alma mater, Hampton Institute. Unlike Hampton and other new black schools, Tuskegee was staffed entirely by blacks. Washington's growing fame and influence attracted both northern philanthropic and southern conservative support.

George Washington Carver, its most famous teacher, brought national acclaim through his peanut experiments. Monroe N. Work edited the *Negro Year Book* and compiled the annual Tuskegee lynching report, both efforts to combat the images of blacks that whites held in the early 20th century. At the time of his death in 1915, Washington was the most influential American black and Tuskegee Institute the best-known black school in the country.

Robert R. Moton, the second principal, continued the accommodationist approach, though he was conciliatory to Washington's critics in the NAACP. He brought a veterans' hospital to Tuskegee in 1923 and stood firm against pressure for a white hospital staff, thus preserving the Tuskegee tradition of blacks controlling the institution. Recognizing that most Tuskegee graduates became teachers, professionals, and businessmen rather than farmers or tradesmen, Moton oversaw the development of a college department in 1927. Frederick D. Patterson succeeded Moton in 1935 and obtained substantial state support in the establishment of a graduate program (1943) and schools of veterinary medicine (1945) and nursing (1953). Patterson was also instrumental in establishing the Tuskegee Army Air Field in 1941 for the segregated training of black pilots for World War II, an action that brought him scorn from the NAACP.

Luther H. Foster followed Patterson in 1953 and steered the school through the civil rights movement, consistently supporting the voting rights efforts led by Charles G. Gomillion, a faculty member. In 1965 students vigorously protested segregation in the town and administration policies on campus, and students took members of the board of trustees hostage briefly in 1968. Benjamin F. Payton became president in 1981 and oversaw the change in the school's name to Tuskegee University in 1985, at which time its enrollment was approximately 3,500.

See also BLACK LIFE: / Washington, Booker T.; SCIENCE AND MEDICINE: / Carver, George Washington

Robert J. Norrell
University of Alabama

Pete Daniel, *Journal of Southern History* (August 1970); Louis R. Harlan, *Booker T. Washington: The Making of a Black Leader, 1856–1901* (1972), *Booker T. Washington: The Wizard of Tuskegee, 1901–1915* (1983); Linda O. McMurry, *George Washington Carver: Scientist and Symbol* (1981), *Recorder of the Black Experience: A Biography of Monroe Nathan Work* (1985); Robert J. Norrell, *Reaping the Whirlwind: The Civil Rights Movement in Tuskegee* (1985).

University of the South

The University of the South at Sewanee, Tenn., is the product of an educational thrust by 25 dioceses of the Episcopal church in 12 states south of Virginia. Its name connotes the intention of its founders in 1857 to provide a higher level of graduate education for the entire South, based on Oxford University as its model. Its site on nearly 10,000 acres at a height of 2,000 feet on the Cumberland Plateau was central to the South, healthful, and isolated enough for establishment of its own culture. War intervened before permanent buildings were erected or classes begun, and the principal founder, Bishop and Lt. Gen. Leonidas Polk, was killed in 1864 near Atlanta.

The university is a child of two eras—the prosperous pre–Civil War South and postwar Reconstruction. The donation of land by the Sewanee Mining Company in 1858 required opening the institution within 10 years. English churchmen contributed £2,500 to enable the school to open in September 1868 with nine students and four professors, a week before the deadline. The early faculty were of a caliber ordinarily unobtainable by a struggling college. Generals Josiah Gorgas, Francis A. Shoup, and Edmund Kirby Smith, other Confederate officers, bishops, and great ladies moved to the wilderness to provide a high standard of culture for students from all over the South.

Theology became a distinct department in 1878 and continues. Engineering degrees were awarded from 1875 to 1911. For nearly two decades (1892–1910) professional schools offered degrees in medicine (including dentistry and nursing) and law. Although most colleges abandoned preparatory education many years ago, the Sewanee Academy continued until 1981, when it was merged with St. Andrew's School nearby. Since 1892 the university has published in southern Appalachia, an area of low literacy, the *Sewanee Review*, now the oldest literary-critical quarterly in America, with international circulation and contributors. The School of Theology publishes the quarterly *St. Luke's Journal*.

The College of Arts and Sciences has an enrollment of 1,000 men and women (females were first admitted in 1969), with 75 students in the School of Theology. Total enrollment in the 1984–85 academic year was 1,158 students. Less than 25 percent of the college students come from Tennessee. A characteristic of the Sewanee student body is the kinship of present students to former ones. Fourth-generation students are now taking degrees, and a survey five years ago showed that 20 percent of the college students had been preceded, or were then accompanied, by one or more family members. Sewanee's 20 Rhodes Scholars are a per-capita-of-enrollment record in the region, with other national and regional records in the production of Fulbright and Woodrow Wilson scholars and NCAA scholar-athletes. In a region devoted to subsidized athletics, Sewanee took the lead in 1946 in abandoning athletic scholarships.

Special programs include Education for Ministry, in which 4,000 students here and abroad have enrolled for training of laity. A summer graduate program in theology awards the Doctor of Ministry degree in association with

Vanderbilt University. Two hundred students each summer attend the Sewanee Summer Music Center to play in three symphony orchestras. A medieval colloquium, an economics symposium, political science internships, and overseas study involve an area broader than the campus itself.

Owned and controlled by the Episcopal church, with All Saints' Chapel and its 56-bell carillon at the center of the domain, the university retains a character essentially unchanged since its conception. English influence continues in architecture, nomenclature, and academic gowns worn daily by students and professors. The English tutorial system never became the major model of instruction, but individual instruction is available. Latin and Greek are still studied, though no longer required for a degree. The Old South contributed a mixture of grace and gallantry and a dress code that survived the 1960s. Now absent from the campus is a military influence, which, though not a part of the founders' plans, persisted more than a century.

One hundred and twenty-five years after its founding, the University of the South has not reached the heights envisioned by its founders, but it has not lost their intention to serve an entire region.

See also RELIGION: / Protestant Episcopal Church; SCIENCE AND MEDICINE: / Gorgas, Josiah

Arthur Ben Chitty
University of the South

Donald S. Armentrout, *Quest for the Informed Priests: The Centennial History of the School of Theology of the University of the South* (1979); Arthur Ben Chitty, *Reconstruction at Sewanee: The Founding of the University of the South and Its First Administration, 1857–1872* (1954); Moultrie Guerry, with Arthur Ben Chitty and Elizabeth N. Chitty, *Men Who Made Sewanee* (1981).

Vance, Rupert B.

(1899–1975) Sociologist.

During his 40-year tenure as a scholar, author, and lecturer at the University of North Carolina at Chapel Hill (UNC), Rupert Bayless Vance sought to unravel the threads weaving the South's people and land into a tapestry of poverty, an effort that became a personal struggle both to understand his own ties to the South and to help break the vicious cycle of dependence and despair inherent in the South's cotton-based economy. With pioneer sociologist Howard W. Odum—founder of the Institute for Research in Social Science and of the department of sociology at UNC, the first sociology department created at a southern university—Vance developed the study of "regional sociology." His experience of living in the South shaped the forms of his scholarship and of his reform efforts.

Born at the turn of the century in Plummerville, Ark., Vance grew up in an area whose wounds from the Civil War had yet to be healed. His early life was filled with hardships. Contracting polio when he was three, Vance lost the use of both of his legs; through physical therapy at an orthopedic clinic in St. Louis, he eventually was able to walk with crutches and was able to enter elementary school when he was 10. In the depths of the 1920s agricultural depression Vance's father lost his farmland and went bankrupt. Vance later utilized the image of his father's failure to represent the general condition of the South. A love of reading, a bachelor's degree in English from Henderson Brown College in Arkadelphia, Ark., and contact with writers such as Edwin Mims and the Agrarians at Vanderbilt University, where he received his master's degree in economics, fostered the clear, descriptive, and humanistic style of his essays. The close relationship that developed between Vance and Howard Odum when Vance joined UNC's fledgling sociology department in 1926 encouraged the young sociologist to pursue his desire for social and economic reforms in the South.

Vance's studies of southern life were interdisciplinary, covering the topics of southern politics, culture, history, demographics, the transformation of the South from a rural area into an urban area, societal conflict, and cotton tenancy. In *Human Factors in Cotton Culture: A Study in the Social Geography of the American South* (1929), *Human Geography of the South: A Study in Regional Resources and Human Adequacy* (1932), the coauthored (with Nadia Danilevsky) *All These People: The Nation's Human Resources in the South* (1945), and in other studies Vance advocated the theory that the South's problems were man-made, that history—not geography—had arrested the South in a frontier stage of development. The social and economic patterns of the South had been shaped by the plantation. Locked into a rural economy based on the production of cotton while the North grew more urban and industrial, the South retained (until the mid-1940s) a colonial economy—an economy that necessitated the exploitation of natural resources and labor in order to afford goods manufactured in another region. Overpopulation, an unstable cotton market, Jim Crow laws, and parasitic diseases such as hookworm and malaria, Vance argued, had only worsened the South's problems.

As a scholar, government consultant, southerner, and as president or founder of several important sociology societies (including the Southern Sociological Society, the Population Association of America, and the American Sociological Association), Vance lobbied for social reforms such as the 1938 Bankhead-Jones Farm Tenant Bill and constructive urban and industrial planning in the South. Over a decade after his death in Chapel Hill in 1975, Vance's search for reform and his southern cultural studies remain relevant.

Elizabeth McGehee
Salem College

Rupert B. Vance, in *Regionalism and the South*, ed. John Shelton Reed and Daniel J. Singal (1982).

Vanderbilt University

Vanderbilt University in Nashville, Tenn., emerged after a protracted birth presided over by disparate midwives. These included Bishop Holland N. McTyeire of the Methodist Episcopal Church, South, and "Commodore" Cornelius Vanderbilt, the New York shipping and railroad baron. The early Vanderbilt blended denominational educational goals, northern hopes for sectional reconciliation, and southern needs for quality higher education in the post–Civil War years. Its founders conceived of Vanderbilt as a great university, a rival to such established northern private institutions as Harvard and Princeton. Yet, from the beginning, Vanderbilt was a captive to its geographic setting and the orthodoxy of its Methodist founders. Vanderbilt's story is one of growth from a Methodist to a southern and, finally, to a national university.

The Methodist Episcopal Church, South, granted a charter for the "Central University" in 1872, Cornelius Vanderbilt gave money for an endowment to it in 1873, and Vanderbilt University was dedicated in 1875. It remained a Methodist institution until an acrimonious separation from the church in 1914. While the majority of the first faculty and nearly all of the students were Methodists, Vanderbilt owed its existence to the financial largesse of the benefactor whose name it bore. In the beginning, Vanderbilt's endowment of $1 million made it southern Methodism's wealthiest institution, with greater financial resources than any other southern college except Johns Hopkins. Under Chancellor Landon C. Garland (1875–93), Vanderbilt faced the challenge of ministering to an educationally benighted South. Vanderbilt pioneered in establishing academic standards at the secondary level by way of entrance examinations held throughout the Southeast and a system of certifying the better preparatory and public high schools.

Under its second chancellor, James H. Kirkland (1893–1937), Vanderbilt grew further away from its Methodist origins. It gained a more cosmopolitan and less Methodist faculty and student body, and foundation money became more important to university budgets. Poised between the parochialism of its Methodist ties and a longing for national stature, Vanderbilt under Kirkland went through a severance of church ties and into an era of munificent gifts from the Carnegie Corporation and the Rockefeller-funded General Education Board. Such philanthropies funded a new Medical School and Nursing School, which, in the 1920s, rivaled the best in the nation. Vanderbilt's other claim to distinction rested on the intellectual flowering of the Fugitives and Agrarians.

From World War II to the present, through three successive chancellors, Vanderbilt has striven for national eminence; Vanderbilt saw its role as more than educational uplift to an impoverished South. Indeed, both the South and Vanderbilt benefited from the postwar economic boom. Vanderbilt's better-qualified students were recruited from a national pool, its faculty became more distinguished and pluralistic, and its graduate programs and research facilities greatly expanded. Yet accompanying Vanderbilt's emergence from a regional cocoon has been the need to comply with national norms.

The strains of modernity became acute after the mid-1950s. Chancellor Harvie Branscomb and President of the Board of Trustees Harold S. Vanderbilt, a major benefactor of the university, led Vanderbilt slowly to a policy of full racial integration in 1963. Branscomb's successor, Alexander Heard, faced the student turbulence of the 1960s and women's demands for equity beginning in the 1970s. Today, Vanderbilt functions in a national arena; it has grown outward from the confines of its Methodist and southern origins. The total enrollment in the 1984–85 academic year was 8,993.

See also MYTHIC SOUTH: / Agrarians, Vanderbilt; RELIGION: / Methodist Episcopal Church, South

Patricia Miletich
Vanderbilt University

Paul K. Conkin, *Gone with the Ivy: A Biography of Vanderbilt University* (1985); Edwin Mims, *Chancellor Kirkland of Vanderbilt* (1940), *History of Vanderbilt University* (1946).

Virginia, University of

Founded in Charlottesville by Thomas Jefferson, who designed its classically beautiful buildings, planned its trail-breaking curriculum, and recruited its mostly European faculty, the University of Virginia opened its doors in 1825.

The curriculum was divided into separate schools and offered courses in mathematics, the sciences, and modern languages. It included a novel elective system and rejected any organized religion or theological dogma. No honorary degrees have ever been conferred.

Established in 1842, the honor system is student operated and controlled. It has undergone modifications over the years, but the single sanction, under which lying, cheating, or stealing is punished by permanent expulsion, is still in full force by repeated vote of the students. The university in the 19th century gained its enduring renown as a center of upper-class southern gentility, a place to produce gentlemen.

Until the early 1900s the university never had a president, preferring to operate with a chairman of the faculty, a system instituted by Jefferson. Every other important university in the country had a chief executive officer, and the Board of Visitors finally decided to follow suit. In 1904 it elected Edwin Anderson Alderman, then president of Tulane University, to the presidency of the University of Virginia. Under him there were significant advances in curriculum, faculty, endowment, and enrollment.

Alderman was succeeded in 1933 by John Lloyd Newcomb, dean of the School of Engineering. It was the nadir of the Great Depression, but genuine progress was made. Upon Newcomb's retirement, Colgate W. Darden, Jr., former governor of Virginia, was elected, and served from 1947 to 1959. This was the beginning of the university's impressive forward surge, which has carried the institution to its highest levels of academic achievement and prestige. The impetus created by Darden was greatly enhanced by Edgar F. Shannon, Jr., a member of the English faculty and a Rhodes Scholar, who succeeded him. He served until 1974, when Frank L. Hereford, Jr., former vice president and provost, and an internationally known physicist, became president. Under Hereford the institution made further spectacular advances. A campaign for a $90,000,000 additional endowment had raised $145,900,000 by mid-1985. Hereford was succeeded in 1984 by Robert M. O'Neil, former president of the University of Wisconsin system.

With a fall 1985 enrollment of 17,417 full-time students, including hundreds of blacks and thousands of women, the University of Virginia has entered a new era. Nationally ranked academically, it is especially noteworthy for its Law School, Medical School, Graduate School of Business Administration, and several academic departments, especially English.

Famous alumni include Edgar Allan Poe; Woodrow Wilson; Walter Reed, the conqueror of yellow fever; Julien Green, the only non-Frenchman ever elected to the French Academy; and two judges of the Court of International Justice, John Bassett Moore and Hardy Cross Dillard.

See also HISTORY AND MANNERS: / Jefferson, Thomas; Wilson, Woodrow; LITERATURE: / Poe, Edgar Allan; SCIENCE AND MEDICINE: / Reed, Walter

Virginius Dabney
Richmond, Virginia

Thomas P. Abernethy, *Historical Sketch of the University of Virginia* (1948); Philip Alexander Bruce, *History of the University of Virginia, 1819–1919*, 5 vols. (1922); Virginius Dabney, *Mr. Jefferson's University: A History* (1981).

Virginia Military Institute

Since its founding in 1839 on the site of a state arsenal at Lexington, the Virginia Military Institute has held a unique position in the educational system of Virginia and the South. It was the nation's first state military college, and the success of VMI, which was patterned on the models of West Point and the École Polytechnique in France, influenced the establishment of military schools throughout the southern states in the 1800s.

VMI is a fully accredited, four-year, state-owned, undergraduate military college for men. It is a college dedicated to the total development of its students' academic excellence, military discipline, physical fitness, and high moral character, and to the founders' concept of educated and responsible citizen-soldiers, men prepared for chosen careers in civilian life but trained and ready for military leadership in time of national need.

While rigorous military training is required of every cadet, VMI's first emphasis has always been on the academic program. Civil engineering, a subject rarely taught in colleges before 1839, became the cornerstone of the academic program, which also offered, in 1846, the first industrial chemistry course in the South and, by 1868, modern courses in physics and meteorology. Today's approximately 1,300 cadets (1,338 in the 1984–85 academic year) pursue bachelor's degree programs in the general fields of engineering, science, and liberal arts, and all participate in Reserve Officer Training Corps (ROTC) programs leading to reserve or regular commissions in the nation's armed forces.

VMI's place in history was enhanced during the Civil War by the great number of its graduates and faculty, including Thomas "Stonewall" Jackson, who served in high command with the Confederacy, and by the Corps of Cadets, which at the 1864 Battle of New Market, Va., won lasting fame as the only college student body in the nation's history to fight as a unit in pitched battle. Notable among alumni of the institute is the late General of the Army George C. Marshall, a 1901 graduate who won the Nobel Prize for Peace in 1953 for the Marshall Plan.

Although VMI began as a military college for Virginians, cadets now come from states across the nation and several foreign countries, and all are part of an enduring "Brother Rat" fraternity that begins in the "rat" or freshman year. Cadets live by an honor code that is deeply rooted in their system of self-government, and the historic cadet barracks, which house the entire corps, are the landmark in VMI's designation as a National Historic District.

See also HISTORY AND MANNERS: / Jackson, Stonewall

Julia Martin
Virginia Military Institute

William Couper, *One Hundred Years at VMI*, 4 vols. (1939); Diane B. Jacob and Judith Morehead Arnold, *A Virginia Military Institute Album, 1839–1910* (1982); Henry A. Wise, *Drawing Out the Man: The VMI Story* (1978).

Washington and Lee University

Washington and Lee University traces its origins back to the mid-18th century when Scotch-Irish Presbyterian settlers in the valley of Virginia established a small classical academy. In 1776 another generation, fired by a zeal for independence and education, changed its name to Liberty Hall and began college-level studies based on John Witherspoon's Princeton curriculum. In 1782 the Commonwealth of Virginia chartered the school, which granted its first bachelor's degrees in 1785. In 1803 it moved to nearby Lexington. It was distinctive among southern colleges, having no official connection with either a church or state.

In 1796 the trustees convinced George Washington to endow the college with canal stock valued at $50,000.

The saving legacy still pays a part of each student's costs. In honor of Washington's gift the school became Washington Academy and later Washington College. Until the Civil War it remained a typical, southern classical college training lawyers, doctors, and preachers for regional leadership, particularly in newly opened lands in the South and West.

By 1865 the Civil War had deprived the college of students, decimated its alumni association, and depleted its endowment. Union raiders had wrecked the campus. That year the trustees offered General Robert E. Lee the presidency. He revitalized the place. He raised needed funds, recruited able teachers, and attracted talented students. Under Lee's leadership, the honor system began to take its modern form.

In 1860 all but 1 of 95 students had been Virginians. In 1869, a year before Lee's death, the student body numbered 400 strong from 20 states and one foreign country. Lee hoped to heal the nation's wounds by having boys from North and South studying together. Lee, the pragmatist, also strove to provide leaders in law, medicine, engineering, business, and journalism to rebuild a shattered South. Lee transformed the curriculum before his death in 1870. In 1871 the school, now Washington and Lee University, included a law school and pioneering collegiate courses in business instruction and journalism.

Washington and Lee struggled during the last two decades of the 19th century. During the 20th century, however, the school grew stronger with each generation. The School of Law, enrolling some 350 students, became coeducational in 1972. The first women undergraduates enrolled in September 1985.

Two undergraduate divisions, the College and the School of Commerce, Economics, and Politics, comprise some 1,400 students from throughout the nation and abroad, who choose from nearly 800 courses, 40 percent of which enroll fewer than 10 students. Since 1970 the college has averaged a Rhodes Scholar every third year. Freshmen, numbering about 350, are selected from more than 2,300 applicants.

John D. Wilson, Washington and Lee's president since 1983, guides a southern institution with a national mission, stressing academic excellence and leadership development in an atmosphere of courtesy, friendliness, student self-government, and honor, long the hallmarks of Washington and Lee. This small, independent school combines the intimacy of a college with the broad offerings of a university.

See also HISTORY AND MANNERS: / Lee, Robert E.; Washington, George

Taylor Sanders
Washington and Lee University

Ollinger Crenshaw, *General Lee's College: The Rise and Growth of Washington and Lee University* (1969); Charles Bracelen Flood, *Lee: The Last Years* (1981); William W. Pusey III, *The Interrupted Dream: The Educational Program at Washington College (Washington and Lee University), 1855–1880* (1976).

Weaver, Richard M.

(1910–1963) Intellectual.

Richard Malcolm Weaver, Jr., was born in Asheville, N.C., in a region first settled by his ancestors at the end of the 18th century. He was educated in the public schools of Asheville and Lexington, Ky., then attended the University of Kentucky, where he took the A.B. degree in 1932, and Vanderbilt University, where he finished his M.A. in English in 1934.

Weaver left Vanderbilt in 1936 without completing the terminal degree and took a teaching job in Texas. But the heady experience of studying in Nashville, at the time when activities of the Agrarians centered on the Vanderbilt campus, forever marked Weaver's intellectual development and compelled him to resume his studies at Louisiana State University, another institution under Agrarian influence during this period. Weaver's 1943 LSU dissertation, "The Confederate South, 1865–1910: A Study in the Survival of a Mind and a Culture," is at the heart of his intellectual development as a southern conservative and served as a grounding for his distinguished career as intellectual historian, rhetorician, and political philosopher.

Weaver's dissertation was finally published (posthumously) in 1968 under the title of *The Southern Tradition at Bay: A History of Postbellum Thought*. Before it appeared, he had issued the classic *Ideas Have Consequences* (1948), *The Ethics of Rhetoric* (1953), and *Visions of Order* (1964). Other posthumous collections include *Life without Prejudice and Other Essays* (1965) and *Language Is Sermonic* (1970). While producing this mass of scholarship, Weaver taught on the faculty of the University of Chicago and served as an editor for William F. Buckley's *National Review* and for *Modern Age*. Weaver brought to the revival of conservative intellectual thought an emphasis on traditional southern values and stress on the connection between language and ideology. He remains to this day an influence in rhetoric, history, and political philosophy. At the heart of his conviction was an unwavering devotion to the politics of principle and the tradition of limited government. At Chicago he spoke of himself as an "Agrarian in exile," but at the time of his death, he was preparing to return south (to Vanderbilt) in 1964.

See also MYTHIC SOUTH: / Agrarians, Vanderbilt

M. E. Bradford
University of Dallas

M. E. Bradford, *Modern Age* (Summer–Fall 1970); George H. Nash, *The Conservative Intellectual Movement in America since 1945* (1976).

Woodward, C. Vann

(b. 1908) Historian.

Born 13 November 1908 in Vanndale, Ark., to Hugh Allison and Bess Vann Woodward, Comer Vann Woodward has been the most influential historian of the modern South. Educated at Emory University (A.M., 1932), and the University of North Carolina (Ph.D., 1937), Woodward taught at the Georgia Institute of Technology, the University of Florida, Scripps College, Johns Hopkins University, and Yale University, where he is now Sterling Professor of History Emeritus.

Woodward has shown an unusual blend of activism and detachment, of aristocratic provenance and fascination with the masses, of great privilege conferred by family and friend and iconoclastic rebelliousness, of professional specialization and an eclectic training. Evoking irony in his writing, he has also lived a life of considerable irony, demonstrating what David Minter has called "deep reciprocities" between experiences of his personal life and the history he has written.

Growing up in Arkansas during a period of racial violence and of grinding regional poverty, Woodward was nurtured by a family of devout Methodists committed to moderate social reform. Forsaking this life, he left an Arkadelphia Methodist college for Emory University, studying philosophy there with LeRoy Loemker, who taught him German existentialism and demonstrated to him a life that successfully combined scholarly excellence with social activism. After brief "careers" teaching literature at the Georgia Institute of Technology and studying political science at Columbia University, Woodward entered the University of North Carolina, studying with Howard Kennedy Beale; there he developed a historical interpretation based on class analysis and economic determinism, writing a dissertation that became his first book and his only biography, a celebration of Georgia Populism entitled *Tom Watson: Agrarian Rebel* (1938). In subsequent years, during World War II, he began to integrate his understanding of literature with this economic history, producing his most enduring scholarship, *Origins of the New South, 1877–1913* (1951), and his most influential study, *The Strange Career of Jim Crow* (1955), which the Reverend Martin Luther King, Jr., called "the Bible of the civil rights movement."

After distinguishing himself as a professor at Johns Hopkins University and as a visiting professor at Oxford University, he became Sterling Professor at Yale University, where he directed excellent graduate students who have made their own impact on the study of southern history. At Yale he became an essayist and an editor, turning out the collections of poignant essays, *The Burden of Southern History* (1960) and *American Counterpoint: Slavery and Racism in the North-South Dialogue* (1971), while editing the Pulitzer Prize–winning *Mary Chesnut's Civil War* (1981). His work has also received the Bancroft and Sydnor awards; and he has served as president of the Southern Historical Association, the American Historical Association, and the Organization of American Historians. His interpretation of history, a subtle melding of lyric determinants, has been cricitized for underestimating the force of racism and the longevity of segregation; and many others have scorned him for overestimating the reformism inherent in agrarian movements at the turn of the century. He will be long recognized as the starting point for the major debates about the character of the New South.

John Herbert Roper
St. Andrews Presbyterian College

Sheldon Hackney, *Journal of Southern History* (May 1972); Michael O'Brien, *American Historical Review* (June 1973); David M. Potter, in *Pastmasters*, ed. Marcus Cunliffe and Robin Winks (1969).

Environment

MARTIN V. MELOSI
University of Houston
CONSULTANT

John Leon Moran, Natural Bridge, Virginia *(1885)*

Environment

In *The Colonial Search for a Southern Eden* (1953), historian Louis B. Wright noted, "The notion that the earthly paradise, similar to if not the veritable site of the Scriptural Eden, might be found in some southern region of the New World was widely held in the seventeenth and early eighteenth centuries." Some explorers claimed that God had placed Eden on the 35th parallel of north latitude, along a line from New Bern, N.C., to Memphis, Tenn. In more recent times, the idea of a southern Eden has faded, but the post–World War II "Sunbelt" phenomenon has restored a little piece of the myth and raised the esteem for the South as a land of opportunity.

Although the South may not represent a scriptural or a temporal Eden, its history has been influenced nonetheless by environmental factors. Indeed, a long-standing dispute over the relative importance of environment and culture permeates the study of the region. Some view geography as the key variable in its development. Others cite ideology and cultural factors. The issue of environment versus culture also has found its way into the debate over whether the South is best viewed as a "region" or as a "section." As a section, the South can be perceived as a cultural entity, a state of mind, an idea. This perspective is most useful for understanding the social, cultural, and political currents that run through southern history. Viewing the South as a region or a geographic area directs attention to the physical characteristics of the South and especially to its relationship to the rest of the nation.

Climate and the Sectional South. Environmental factors have frequently been used in a deterministic way to reinforce cultural stereotypes about the South as a region. No environmental issue was more influential than the notion of climate as a determining factor in southern culture.

Clarence Cason's *90° in the Shade* (1935) fused climate and culture into stereotypical clichés: "If snow falls infrequently on the southern land, the sun displays no such niggardly tendencies. In Mississippi there is justification for the old saying that only mules and black men can face the sun in July. Summer heat along the middle Atlantic coast and on the middle western plains causes more human prostrations than it does in the South. The difference lies partially in the regularity of high summer temperatures in the South but mainly in the way the southerner takes the heat." Much of the South surely suffers through oppressively hot and humid summers and enjoys mild winters, but to what degree has the climate actually influenced southern history? Historian Carl N. Degler has suggested that the climate has had "a passive, if not active, influence" in shaping the region's past. The commitment to agriculture, especially the opportunity to grow commercial crops such as cotton and tobacco, was made possible by a favorable climate. Cotton, for instance, requires a growing season of 200 frost-free days, a condition that can be duplicated in few regions outside the South. Rice and sugarcane also require long growing seasons. Degler asserts, "That the climate permitted the growth of these peculiarly southern crops goes a long way to explaining why the South is the only region of the United States that developed plantation agriculture. Certainly the plantation did not spread in the South because of the climate; but without a climate favorable to tobacco, cotton, sugar, and rice southern agriculture would probably have been like that of the North in both crops and organization."

Climate has been a controlling influence in the development of the southern economy and even in the South's social organization. But as a rationalization for such stereotypic traits as laziness, emotionalism, and volatility, climate can be a misleading explanation. As historian Jack Temple Kirby noted in *Media-Made Dixie: The South in the American Imagination* (1978), "southern laziness has long implied more than veranda-sitting (the gentry) and catfishing (blacks and white trash). It has meant the absence of thinking, too."

At its least appealing, climate has been used as a justification for slavery and the persistence of a social order associated with plantation life. The climatic theory of the plantation, in other words, was used to justify the resistance to social change in the South. According to sociologist Edgar T. Thompson, a critic of the climatic theory of the plantation, "a theory which makes the plantation depend upon something outside the processes of human interaction, that is, a theory which makes the plantation depend upon a fixed and static something like climate, is a theory which operates to justify an existing social order and the vested interests connected with that order. Under such a conception the problems of a plantation society can be looked upon as concerning only God who alone can control the climate, and the climatic theory turns out to be really a sort of divine-right theory of the plantation."

Relying on only one variable to evaluate the history of the South serves environmental history badly. However, discounting the importance of environment in understanding the regional and sectional Souths is equally limiting. To fully comprehend the impact of the physical environment on southerners requires an appreciation of the common physical characteristics, as well as the diversity, of the southern states and a comprehensive view of southern physiography, ecology, and the extent of human modification of natural patterns.

Physiography of the South. In popular usage, the Old South is often divided into a "Lower" South—the land of cotton and slavery, the heart of the Confederacy—and an "Upper" South—an area dominated by slaveless farmers with more ambiguous allegiances. Not only has there been an Old South, but a Deep South and several "New" Souths as well. All these designations, despite the imagery they evoke, are rather imprecise renderings of the physical South, because the region has never been a clearly defined geographical unit. This is a key to the difficulty of specifying the precise nature of the South along its borders—Delaware and Maryland to the east, West Virginia, Kentucky, and Missouri to the north,

Oklahoma and Texas to the west. However, two features dominate the physical South, whether the boundaries are drawn along the Coastal Plains or the Appalachian Mountains. These landscape features are also competing influences, which often have divided rather than unified the region.

The South's coast is its most dominant physical feature. Stretching more than 3,000 miles, it falls within the Atlantic and Gulf Coastal Plains. Most of the harbors are drowned river mouths that are shallow and subject to silting. The shore is composed of sandy beaches abutted in some cases by swamps, such as Dismal Swamp in Virginia and North Carolina. Along the Mississippi River run several muddy flats. The Coastal Plain, from the Potomac River to the Rio Grande, is an elevated sea bottom with low topographic relief and many marshy tracts. Therefore, coastal altitudes are mostly below 500 feet and more than half are below 100 feet. The Coastal Plains are widest at Texas—about 300 miles—and narrow to 100 miles as they wind eastward. They comprise about one-third of the South.

A major feature of the Coastal Plains is the Mississippi River Valley, which originates in the Central Lowlands of the United States and meanders to the sea. Traditionally the South's greatest "artery of commerce," the Mississippi continually changes the landscape along its route. Wide and marshy, with muddy and sandy banks, the Mississippi has long been an economic lifeline in the South, but it has also been a physical barrier and an environmental threat because of flooding.

Before reaching the higher elevation of the mountains, the Coastal Plains connect with the Piedmont Plateau. Extending from central Alabama northward, the Piedmont Plateau is really a plain of denudation with only a few hills rising about the gently rolling landscape. The western border of the Piedmont Plateau is formed by the Blue Ridge Mountains.

West and north of the Coastal Plains lies the Appalachian system, which begins in Newfoundland and extends to central Alabama. The southern section of the system is formed by two parallel belts and includes the Appalachian Mountains themselves. Historically, this range was the major barrier to east-west movement in what became the United States. The Cumberland Gap was one of very few routes through the mountains. The Appalachians gave the impression of a single geological system because of their formidable nature. In truth, the landscape varies considerably. For example, the southern Appalachians in western North Carolina and northern Georgia are various short ridges and isolated peaks separated by basins and valleys. In or near the Great Smoky Mountains and the Blue Ridge are the highest peaks of the system, including Mount Mitchell (6,684 feet), Cattail Peak (6,609 feet), Mount Guyot (6,620 feet), Mount Le Conte (6,593 feet), and Clingman's Dome (6,640 feet). Unlike the rugged and jagged Rockies, the Appalachians are rounder and substantially lower. Due in part to high humidity, weathering and erosion have shaped the Appalachian skyline. Winters are milder in the Appalachians than in the Rockies.

The northwestern and western reaches of the South—part of the Upper South and east Texas—fall within the Central Lowlands. The Central Lowlands are essentially a vast plain between the Appalachian Plateau and the

Flavius J. Fisher, Dismal Swamp *(1858)*

Rockies. At the eastern edge, where the Lowlands join the Appalachians, the elevation is about 1,000 feet, sloping westward to an altitude of about 500 feet along the Mississippi, then rising again westward. The most distinctive feature of the Lowlands within the South is the Ozark-Ouachita section. Sometimes referred to as the Interior Highlands, this group of low mountains interrupts the monotony of the Lowland landscape. The Ozark Mountains have a drainage pattern and landscape similar to the Appalachian Plateau. South of the Ozarks, beyond the Arkansas River, lie the Ouachita Mountains. The highest point is 2,700 feet, whereas the Ozarks' peak is about 2,000 feet.

An examination of the physiography of the South suggests its diversity and uniqueness. The contrast between the Coastal Plains and the Appalachian system helps explain many of the historical differences between the Upper and Lower South. And although three-fourths of the South has an elevation of less than 1,000 feet above sea level, barriers to east-west movement in the form of the Appalachians and the Mississippi have played an important role in determining regional settlement patterns. The South's geography, however, also demonstrates the important physical connection of the region to the rest of the nation. The Coastal Plains link the South with the Atlantic Seaboard, the Appalachians with the Northeast, and the Lowlands with the Midwest and Southwest. In no way has the South been geographically isolated from the other regions of the nation.

Ecology of the South. The great majority of the South lies within the Temperate Deciduous Forest Biome (natural community), which extends from the Great Lakes to the Gulf of Mexico. It also covers a large portion of the Florida peninsula and extends west to the Ozarks. Broadleaf trees dominate the biome, but evergreens are plentiful to the extreme southern reaches. The shedding of leaves by the deciduous trees in the autumn produces dramatic changes in light conditions and provides shelter for animals. The annual rainfall in the biome ranges from 28 to 60 inches, with the greatest amount near the Gulf.

The Temperate Deciduous Biome is composed of the oak-hickory region and the magnolia-maritime region. The oak-hickory region extends along a line from New Jersey to Alabama, westward into Arkansas and Texas, and then northward to central Illinois. The magnolia-maritime region begins in the southeastern corner of Virginia and extends southward to the magnolia forest near Charleston and then continues along the coast to Houston. A southeastern pine forest runs along the Coastal Plains from North Carolina to Texas. By contrast, the low, wet outer portion of the Coastal Plains is dominated by savannas, everglades, and flatwoods. Despite human modification of the southern forests over the years, forest cover is an important endowment of the South. It has approximately 40 percent of the nation's commercial forests, including the largest portion of its hardwood reserves.

Within or adjacent to the Temperate Deciduous forest are several other natural communities in the regional South. The Mississippi River floodplain sports light-colored cottonwoods along the riverbank. To the extreme west desert or mesquite grassland of a temperate grassland biome extend into the lowlands of west Texas. The southern boundary of the warm temperate magnolia forest is near Palm Beach on the Florida east coast. The vegetation of Florida is transitional between the tropics and the temperate regions with palms, mangroves, tall grass, sedge, rubber trees, hammocks, banyans, pine, and Spanish moss.

Southern soils reflect the significance of the forest cover. The region is blanketed largely by forest soils (podzols). Lime-rich brown soils are found in the bluegrass areas and the Great Valley of Virginia. In most other areas red and yellow soils are common. Along the coast are water podzols and marsh soils, and along the river valleys dark, fertile soils brought by floods are typical. Because the South escaped the last glaciation, southern soils lack the minerals ground by the ice. Heavy rains have leached the soil of its nutrients as well, leaving large deposits of clay throughout the South. Organic material is often vaporized by the heat, and the absence of sustained ground freezing traps nutrients above the ice. In large measure the South has medium- or low-grade soils, subject to erosion because of the considerable slope of the land. It is unlikely that most of the South ever had deep, fertile, heavy soils like those in the Midwest.

Despite its mediocre soils, the region possesses other important resources. Large quantities of bauxite are to be found in Arkansas; hematite iron ore near Birmingham; phosphate south of Nashville; titanium in Virginia; manganese, copper, and chromite in the mountains of eastern Tennessee and in the Carolinas. By far the most significant mineral resources are found along the fringes of the South: coal in the Appalachians and oil and natural gas in Texas, Oklahoma, and Louisiana. Sources of water have been crucial to the region. Blessed with several good waterways for inland navigation, fine ports from Houston-Galveston to the Chesapeake, and many lakes and streams, the South in recent times has faced diminishing surface-water supplies because of increased use, rapid economic growth, and pollution. The major rivers, especially the Mississippi and the Tennessee, are among the most significant natural forces for ongoing physical change in the region.

Although the climate and weather of the South vary more than popular lore would suggest, distinctive climatic features do exist. In general, the climate is rainy (except in the Southwest), the summers are hot, and the winters are mild. Compared to the rest of the nation, tornadoes, hurricanes, and fog are frequent.

East of the Rockies the climate of North America is the product of the interaction of two air masses—the continental air mass in the northern portions of Canada and the tropical maritime air mass in the Atlantic/Gulf of Mexico area. In the summer the latter is associated with high temperatures and especially high humidity. In the winter the tropical maritime air mass produces mild spells with rain and fog. Because of the interaction of these air masses, two of the three parts of North America with the most precipitation lie in the South—the southern Appalachians and the southeastern states. In the

Southeast and as far west as central Texas, humid subtropical or warm temperate weather is typical. Rainfall tends to be evenly distributed among the seasons. The South does not necessarily produce "hotter" highs than other portions of the nation, but the hot spells are of greater length. About three-fourths of the South has more than 30 inches of rainfall in an average year. The hottest section in the summer is the northern half of the Gulf Coast states. Although considerable variance occurs in the climate, especially between the Coastal Plains and the Appalachian system, no part of the South is subject to prolonged cold. That fact has been vital to its emergence in recent years as an important focus of human migration.

Human Modification of the Environment. Southerners have long exhibited a fierce pride in their section and its heritage. Indeed, this pride has some environmental roots. As writer James Seay noted, "The traditional concept of the southerner as one possessing a strong attachment to the land—and, by extension, a predilection for outdoor sports, especially hunting and fishing—has not diminished appreciably."

The South's agrarian tradition—at least in days past—has accounted for much of the southern affinity for the outdoors. Unintentionally or otherwise, however, human modification of the southern environment over the years has changed the South dramatically, and not always for the better. Human modification, as much as the natural heritage, has shaped the sectional and regional South. The exploitation of forests and the impact of the agricultural system, the Civil War, urbanization, and industrialization have had major roles in transforming a once unspoiled wilderness into a complex modern society. William Faulkner's image of a wilderness South in short stories like "The Bear" is more a literary convention than a reality in much of the South today. Contemporary writers, such as James Dickey in *Deliverance*, portray the modern southerner searching for a wilderness that has vanished.

Exploitation of Forests. As late as 1600 the forests of the south Atlantic and Gulf states were probably less modified than those of the Northeast, with the exception of Virginia where the Indian population was large. In the Lowland region Indians burned forests to facilitate hunting or to favor certain game. The burning produced savanna-type vegetation in the valleys.

Settlers in the southern colonies adopted Indian burning practices. Especially in the piney woods, remote hills, and in areas of sandy soils, where hunting and herding persisted, woodburning practices endured for many years. Woodburning was first practiced not for purposes of forestry, but for hunting, grazing, and the eradication of pests. According to historian Stephen J. Pyne, "fire practices were incorporated into the fabric of frontier existence. What made the South special, however, was the confluence of economic, social, and historical events that worked to sustain this pattern of frontier economy long after it disappeared elsewhere in the United States, a pattern that created a socioeconomic environment for the continuance of woodburning." Given the persistence of using fire for pasturage and game, efforts to stop or reduce burning were slow to develop in the South.

Firing of land was also extremely important in the development of southern agriculture. Here, too, Indian methods were adopted. Agricultural fires were used to prepare sites, to manage fallow fields, to eradicate pests, and to dispose of debris. And because plantation owners acquired the best agricultural lands, smaller farmers found themselves cultivating inferior sites, including piney woods, sandy barrens, and worn-out cotton fields, where annual firing kept the pines from overtaking them. An important result of firing for agricultural purposes was the replacement of many hardwood stands with pines.

Commercial logging did not spread through the South much before the 1880s. Some harvesting of pines and hardwoods had occurred in the antebellum South, but the Appalachian hardwood region generally remained inaccessible until railroad lines were extended into the region. Forests were also spared early commercial development because of the extensive cutting taking place in the Northeast, but after 1880 commercial logging grew by leaps and bounds. The national timber industry moved

Mississippi timber worker, Warren County, Miss., 1968

in, and logging in the southern Appalachians reached its peak. By 1920 the virgin pine forests were gone and little regeneration had occurred. Not until after 1930 did most southern states give any real attention to preserving the remaining virgin forests. As professional foresters entered the region to encourage the development of new crops of timber, they met resistance from the owners of rangelands. Southern forests were too intricately woven into the fabric of the southern economy to be easily protected by modern conservation laws and practices. Clear-cutting forestry methods have, since World War II, in fact, decimated the southern hardwood population, introducing a new southern monoculture—pine farms.

Wildlife was often a casualty of the use and abuse of southern forests. In the colonial South deer were hunted heavily as an essential source of meat. Numbers increased again after the several Indian expulsions and when cattle replaced deer in the leather trade. Hunting game for sale, however, persisted. White settlement also led to the extermination of bison east of the Mississippi. Among birds, turkey and quail were plentiful, but passenger pigeons were hunted eventually to extinction and parakeets were killed by farmers as pests or turned into pets. Predators such as wolves and black bear had bounties placed on them for threatening humans, livestock, or corn crops. Although the destruction of wildlife was not systematic, by the late 19th century many species were either declining rapidly or nearing extinction, namely the eastern elk, cougar, timber wolf, red wolf, bison, Labrador duck, Carolina parakeet, whooping crane, and ivory-billed woodpecker. However, as historian Albert E. Cowdrey has noted, "the destruction was much more than a regional phenomenon. These were, after all, the times when New Yorkers ate game shot in Minnesota, and when processing centers in Kansas City and Chicago received every week trainloads of 'ducks, geese, cranes, plovers, and prairie chickens'—a continental spoil." A revival of interest in wildlife conservation spread to the South in the 1870s, but was slow in developing over the years. When economic interests were threatened, as in the case of commercial fishing, state governments were quicker to act.

Agricultural System. Southern agriculture is generally thought of as a combination of monocultures. Although this is an overly simplistic view of a region that also practiced stockraising and mixed farming, the environmental implications of southern agriculture were most significant with respect to the staple-crop economies that emerged over the centuries. The long, hot summers in most of the South have made the growing of shallow-root crops difficult. Fodder crops, especially, have been hard to grow, limiting the effective combination of livestock and food crops that encouraged the profitability of small farms.

The notion that several staple crops—especially tobacco, sugar, rice, and cotton—were "ideal" for the southern clime ignores the pervasive problems, such as soil exhaustion and erosion, that resulted from the widespread development of these monocultures. Commercial dependence on these crops meant that immediate profit rather than long-term planning dominated the rise of the plantation system and its consequent dependence on slave labor. Commercial production of tobacco led to wasteful clearing of forests. Acreage of Tidewater plantations was increased in an attempt to counteract the low productivity of the poor soil. Exacerbating the problem of widespread and incessant planting was the draining of nitrogen and potassium. Planters were largely ignorant of the repercussions of their planting activity—and were unaware that the typical wooden plows did not cut deep enough to bring the necessary nutrients to the surface—or, at least, they exhibited little concern for their impact on the land because of the availability of new lands farther inland.

The use of fertilizers and the switch to other crops, such as wheat, eventually improved farming in Tidewater Virginia. But in the Atlantic Piedmont erosion was more likely in the weathered soil. Soil exhaustion was a chronic problem beyond the Piedmont—and not just from the planting of tobacco but also from the cultivation of corn. Overall, the South had the ignominious honor of sustaining the first large-scale soil erosion in the country, centered in the tobacco-growing regions of Virginia, Maryland, and North Carolina. The pattern continued as settlers moved west.

The cultivation of cotton and the emergence of the great cotton belt from the Carolinas to east Texas did little to reverse the pattern of soil erosion and soil exhaustion throughout the South. Over the years the cotton belt shifted, spreading westward in the 19th century as areas in the Southeast were infested with boll weevils or the soil was worn out by years of monoculture. After spreading into Texas the belt contracted again, and the western portion of cotton country was revitalized. The early cultivation of cotton in the Piedmont regions resulted in tens of thousands of gullies. Some of the gullies in Georgia were more than 150 feet deep. The long process of erosion in the Piedmont climaxed in 1920. In the years since the Civil War massive quantities of topsoil had disappeared, some estimates reaching as high as six cubic miles or more.

Both large and small landholders abused their soils, although smaller farmers may have done more damage because they had less land in reserve for rotation or lying fallow. Land policy was largely nonexistent. Nonetheless, until about 1945 cotton was still the agricultural byword in the South, and soil conservation was an unappreciated idea. Eventually extension workers, soil conservationists, and some private individuals began a slow process of educating southern farmers to terracing, contour plowing, and other techniques to avoid soil exhaustion and to improve yields.

In more recent times southern agriculture has changed dramatically. Cotton and corn areas contracted as new and localized special crops, such as soybeans and peanuts, appeared. The total area under cultivation declined as grazing returned to the South. Those staple crops that remained were grown under rotation systems as mechanization increased. Agricultural productivity returned to the South but often in new guises, such as in the fruit and truck belt of the Atlantic Coast and in the subtropical crop belt of the Gulf of Mexico. The memories of the old monocultures endure as a reminder of the hasty and shortsighted practices of the past.

Civil War. The environmental impact of war is often overlooked by scholars and other observers. It was difficult to forget that more than 600,000 people lost their lives in the Civil War, but memories soon faded about the physical devastation that the South suffered from 1861 to 1865. As John Brinckerhoff Jackson noted in his historical tour through the United States during its centennial years, the post–Civil War Reconstruction era required "the almost total reorganization of the Southern landscape—an undertaking scarcely less arduous than the creating of a brand-new landscape in the West."

The Civil War left southern cities in ruins, railroad lines ripped from the ground, plantations burned, factories and mills gutted, and it made itinerants of many southerners. Visitors were struck by the absence of fences—burned as firewood by raiding Yankees or trampled by Confederates searching for food. Other signs of human construction—bridges, trestles, even roads—were destroyed, creating an eerie sense of stillness and emptiness. Woodlands appeared in the deserted countryside where they had not existed for years; other forested areas were barren in the aftermath of battle. The urban South presented an equally depressing picture, be it the smoldering remains in Atlanta and Richmond or the deserted wharves of Charleston.

Recovery came more quickly in the major cities than in the countryside in the postwar South. In time, the physical scars of the war would disappear, but the ravages were a constant reminder that devastation need not come in the form of a hurricane, flood, or tornado. Of all human modifications on the physical environment, war was clearly the most frightening.

Industrialization and Urbanization. The slow transformation of the agrarian South into a region with a mixed economy and thriving cities may very well represent the most dramatic human modification of all. Until the 1870s southern industrialism was largely restricted to tobacco processing, textiles, and iron production. As late as World War I many southern cities had little more than regional influence. The "Sunbelt" phenomenon of the post–World War II era, however, dramatically points to the transformation made in the last 100 years.

In the New South era industrial growth was marked, especially after 1880, but it was not similar in kind or scale to what was taking place in the Northeast. The processing of agricultural goods, the manufacture of furniture, and the production of textiles were small, labor-intensive activities. Only in the manufacture of iron and steel and in the extracting of minerals did the South truly emulate northern industrial practices. Yet statistics bear out the change that was taking place in the postwar South. Even as early as the 1860s, industrial growth showed signs of change. The number of manufacturing enterprises increased 80 percent, the number of workers 30 percent, and the value of products 28 percent. Unfortunately capital investment (increase of 3 percent) and wages (up 8 percent) did not keep pace with this growth, but after the disruptions of Reconstruction had subsided, by the late 1870s, manufacturing again made an upturn.

Although this industrial growth was not impressive by the national standards of the time—in 1904 the South had about 15 percent of the nation's manufacturing establishments and 11 percent of capital invested in manufacturing—the activity could not help but provide a bridge between the monocultural activity of the past and the economic diversity of the present. In the Southeast in the 1960s, nonagricultural employment increased 45 percent, from 8.6 million jobs to 12.5 million. A good portion of this growth, however, did not come in manufacturing but in the professions, technical fields, and in the clerical area, suggesting the emergence of a vital white-collar sector in the economy. Also characteristic of nonagricultural economic growth was the dispersal rather than heavy concentration of industry. Few southern areas, therefore, physically resembled the industrial Northeast even after the infusion of an industrial capacity.

This is not to say that the physical South was little influenced by industrialization. The desire to improve inland navigation led to the transformation of the Mississippi River. The Tennessee Valley Authority virtually remade a gigantic portion of the Upper South. Greater exploitation of natural resources led to strip-mining, squandering of oil and gas resources, and all manner of pollution. Oil spills, effluents in major waterways, smoke, and smog were reminders of a newly emerging South. The creeks and rivers of much of the South were already polluted by cotton mill effluent in the 1920s and 1930s, before anyone talked of a "Sunbelt."

Urbanization of the South was probably the most dramatic aspect of the modernization and physical transformation of the region. Urban growth in most southern states outstripped the section's increase in general population between 1840 and 1860. Yet by 1900 southern states averaged only about 15 percent to 19 percent urban population. In striking contrast, by the 1970s the urban portion of the southern states averaged from 54 percent to 72 percent. The continuation of World War II prosperity into the postwar years played a large part in the emergence of the "Sunbelt" South as a vital economic, but also urban, force similar to the New West.

The environmental implications of southern urbanization are many. Certainly, technological innovations such as air-conditioning have encouraged the development of large cities and industries in a part of the country annually racked with long spells of heat and humidity. Urban sprawl, suburbanization, congestion, exploitation of available resources, and pollution are characteristic of both southern and northern cities. Competition for water resources has increased among cities and between rural and urban populations. Stream pollution, saltwater intrusion on the coast, and the reduction of water tables threaten a once abundant resource.

Industrialization and urbanization in the South in recent times point to a characteristic not associated with its antebellum past—constant change. The diversity of the southern environment imbedded in the contrast between the Coastal Plains and the Appalachian system has been magnified by the various forms of human modification over the years. In many ways these modifications have produced changes that link the South to the rest of the nation, undermining some of its unique physical characteristics. At the same time, the emergence of a "modern" South through the "Sunbelt" phenomenon suggests a region still in flux and likely to undergo a major physical transformation.

See also AGRICULTURE: Crops; Garden Patch; / Agricultural Extension Services; Boll Weevil; Fertilizer; Pest Control; ETHNIC LIFE: Indian Cultural Contributions; GEOGRAPHY articles; INDUSTRY: / Bulldozer Revolution; MYTHIC SOUTH: Garden Myth; RECREATION: Fishing; Hunting

Martin V. Melosi
University of Houston

Ralph H. Brown, *Historical Geography of the United States* (1948); Thomas D. Clark, *The Greening of the South: The Recovery of Land and Forest* (1984), *Three Paths to the Modern South: Education, Agriculture, and Conservation* (1965); James C. Cobb, *Industrialization and Southern Society, 1877–1984* (1984); Albert E. Cowdrey, *This Land, This South: An Environmental History* (1983); Carl N. Degler, *Place over Time: The Continuity of Southern Distinctiveness* (1977); Robin W. Doughty, *Feather Fashions and Bird Preservation: A Study in Nature Protection* (1975), *Wildlife and Man in Texas: Environmental Change and Conservation* (1984); Peter Farb, *Face of North America: The Natural History of a Continent* (1963); Gilbert C. Fite, *Cotton Fields No More: Southern Agriculture, 1865–1980* (1984); David R. Goldfield, *Cotton Fields and Skyscrapers: Southern City and Region, 1607–1980* (1982); Sam B. Hilliard, *Hog Meat and Hoecake: Food Supply in the Old South, 1840–1860* (1972); Charles B. Hunt, *Physiography of the United States* (1967); John Brinckerhoff Jackson, *American Space: The Centennial Years, 1865–1876* (1972); Peter Matthiessen, *Wildlife in America* (1959); Martin V. Melosi, *Coping with Abundance: Energy and Environment in Industrial America, 1820–1980* (1985); Howard W. Odum, *Southern Regions of the United States* (1936); Almon E. Parkins, *The South: Its Economic-Geographic Development* (1938); Stephen J. Pyne, *Fire in America: A Cultural History of Wildland and Rural Fire* (1982); James Seay, in *The American South: Portrait of a Culture*, ed. Louis D. Rubin, Jr. (1980); Victor E. Shelford, *The Ecology of North America* (1963); Edgar T. Thompson, *Agricultural History* (January 1941); Rupert B. Vance, *Human Geography of the South* (1932).

Air-Conditioning

"Let us begin by discussing the weather, for that has been the chief agency in making the South distinctive." This was the opening line of U. B. Phillips's 1929 classic, *Life and Labor in the Old South*. In Phillips's day, environmental determinism was a powerful force in American social science; it was the age of Ellsworth Huntington and Walter Prescott Webb, when the link between climate and culture was thought to be a simple relationship of cause and effect, when the southern climate in particular was credited with producing everything from plantation slavery to the southern drawl. Such determinist views are no longer fashionable, but the connection between regional culture and climate remains an intriguing subject, one that has taken on a new dimension since the advent of air-conditioning. Ask any southerner over 30 years of age to explain why the South has changed in recent decades, and he may begin with the civil rights movement or industrialization. But sooner or later he will come around to the subject of air-conditioning. For better or worse, the air conditioner has changed the nature of southern life.

The age of air-conditioning, in the broadest sense of the term, was initiated by Dr. John Gorrie, a Florida physician who began experimenting with mechanical cooling in the 1830s. In an attempt to lower the body temperatures of malaria and yellow fever victims, he blew forced air over buckets of ice suspended from a hospital ceiling. Gorrie eventually patented a primitive ice-making machine, but the world's first true air conditioner—a machine that simultaneously cools, circulates, dehumidifies, and cleanses the air—was not invented until 1902, when Willis Haviland Carrier installed an experimental system in a Brooklyn publishing company. Carrier's invention soon spread to the South, thanks to the efforts of two young southern engineers, Stuart Cramer and I. H. Hardeman. Cramer actually coined the term "air-conditioning" in 1906, and later the same year Hardeman helped Carrier design and install the region's first air-conditioning system, at the Chronicle Cotton Mills in Belmont, N.C. By 1920 the new technology was being used as a quality-control device in a number of southern cotton and rayon mills, paper mills, cigar factories, tobacco stemming rooms, breweries, and bakeries. Prior to the 1920s air-conditioning in the South was restricted almost entirely to industrial uses. The major exceptions were a Baltimore hotel and Montgomery's elegant Empire Theatre.

This situation began to change in 1923 when Carrier's invention of the centrifugal compressor ushered in the age of "comfort cooling." By the mid-1930s air-conditioned movie theaters and railway cars had become common. But the movement of air-conditioning into other areas of southern life was more gradual. Although a sprinkling of air-conditioned department stores, office buildings, homes, hospitals, drugstores, barber shops, and restaurants could be found across the region by the late 1930s, air-conditioning remained an oddity until after World War II. During the 1950s air-conditioning became an immutable part of southern life. After the air conditioner invaded the home (the inexpensive, efficient window unit appeared in 1951) and the automobile, there was no turning back. By the mid-1970s air-conditioning had made its way into more than 90 percent of the South's high-rise office buildings, banks, apartments, and railroad passenger coaches; more than 80 percent of its automobiles, government buildings, and hotels; approximately two-thirds of its homes, stores, trucks, and hospital rooms; roughly half of its classrooms; and at least a third of its tractors. The South of the 1970s could claim air-conditioned shopping malls, domed stadiums, greenhouses, grain elevators, chicken coops, aircraft hangars, crane cabs, offshore oil rigs, cattle barns, steel mills, and drive-in movies and restaurants. Even the Alamo had central air, and in Houston alone the cost of air-conditioning in 1980 exceeded the gross national product of several Third-World nations.

Not all southerners live in air-conditioned homes, ride in air-conditioned cars, or work in air-conditioned buildings. Among rural and working-class blacks, poor whites, migrant laborers, and mountaineers, air-conditioned living is not the norm. Nevertheless, in varying degrees virtually all southerners have been affected, directly or indirectly, by the technology of climate control. Air-conditioning has influenced everything from architecture to sleeping habits and has contributed to the erosion of several regional traditions, most notably cultural isolation, agrarianism, romanticism, poverty, neighborliness, a strong sense of place, and a relatively slow pace of life. The net result has been a dramatic decline in regional distinctiveness. In combination with other historical forces—the civil rights movement, advances in communication and transportation technology, and economic and political change—the air conditioner has greatly accelerated what John Egerton has called "the Americanization of Dixie."

To begin with, the air conditioner has helped to reverse an almost century-long southern tradition of net out-migration. It was more than a coincidence that in the 1950s, the decade when air-conditioning first engulfed the South, the region's net out-migration was much smaller than in previous decades; and that in the 1960s, for the first time since the Civil War, the South experienced more in-migration than out-migration. The 1970 census, according to the *New York Times*, was "The Air Conditioned Census." "The humble air conditioner," the *Times* concluded, "has been a powerful influence in circulating people as well as air in this country. . . . Its availability explains why increasing numbers of Americans find it comfortable to live year round in the semitropical heat." The 1960s was only the beginning; between 1970 and 1978, 7 million people migrated to the South, twice the number that left the region. By the end of the decade, the Sunbelt era was in full swing. Abetted by millions of tourists, northern migrants have brought new ideas and new lifestyles to the South, disrupting the region's long-standing cultural isolation. Thanks in part to air-conditioning, the southern population has become increasingly heterogeneous, and the concept of the Solid South—long a bulwark of regional mythology—has all but faded from view.

Air-conditioning has also played a key role in the industrialization of the modern South. In addition to bringing new factories and businesses to the region, it has helped to improve working conditions and increase productivity. Economic growth, partially induced by a better work environment, has led to a rising standard of living for many southern families; per capita income in the South has risen from 52 percent of the national average in 1930 to almost 90 percent today, and air-conditioning is one of the reasons why.

Air-conditioning has also fostered the urbanization of the South: by encouraging industrialization and population growth; by accelerating the development of large public institutions, such as universities, museums, hospitals, sports arenas, and military bases; by facilitating the efficient use of urban space and opening the city to vertical, high-rise development; and by influencing the development of distinctively urban forms of architecture. Without air-conditioning, skyscrapers and high-rise apartments would be less prevalent; urban populations would be smaller; cities would be more spread out; and the physical and architectural differences between inner cities and suburbs would be less striking. Although the region's agrarian legacy is still a force to be reckoned with, in the air-conditioned South the locus of power and activity has moved to Main Street.

In a related development, climate control has altered southern attitudes toward nature and technology. Air-conditioning has taken its toll on the traditional "folk culture," which, as David Potter once pointed out, "survived in the South long after it succumbed to the onslaught of urban-industrial culture elsewhere." The South has always been an elemental land of blood, sweat, and tears—a land where personalism and a curious mixture of romance and realism have prevailed. At the very least, climate control has taken the edge off this romantic element. As the southern climate has been artificially tamed, pastoralism has been replaced by technological determinism. Human interaction with the natural environment has decreased significantly since the advent of air-conditioning. To confirm this point, one has only to walk down almost any southern street on a hot summer afternoon, listen to the whir of compressors, and look in vain for open windows or front porch society.

In many cases, the porch is not simply empty, it is not even there. To the dismay of many southerners, air-conditioning has impinged upon a rich tradition of vernacular architecture. From the "dogtrot cabin" with its central breezeway, to the grand plantation with its wraparound porch, to the tin-roofed "cracker" house up on blocks, traditional southern architecture has been an ingenious conspiracy of passive cooling and cross-ventilation. The catalogue of structural techniques developed to tame the hot, humid southern climate is long and varied: high ceilings, thin walls, long breezeways, floors raised three or more feet off the ground, steeply pitched roofs vented from top to bottom, open porches with broad eaves that blocked the slanting sun, massive doors and windows, which sometimes stretched from floor to ceiling, louvered jalousies, transoms placed above bedroom doors, dormers, groves of shade trees blanketing the southern exposure, houses situated to capture prevailing breezes, and so on. Historically these techniques have been an important element of a distinctively southern aesthetic and social milieu. But with the proliferation of residential air-conditioning, vernacular architecture gave way to the modern tract house, with its low ceilings, small windows, and compact floor plan.

Residential air-conditioning has not only affected architectural form, it has also influenced the character of southern family life. As families have withdrawn into air-cooled private spaces, interaction with grandparents, aunts, uncles, cousins, not to mention friends and neighbors, has often suffered. As more than one observer has noted, the vaunted southern tradition of "visiting" has fallen on hard times in recent years.

The air conditioner has also had an impact on the basic rhythm of southern life. To a significant degree air-conditioning has modulated the daily and seasonal rhythms, which were once an inescapable part of southern culture. Thanks to air-conditioning, the "siesta mentality" has declined, and the summer sun is no longer the final arbiter of daily and yearly planning. In addition to these mundane changes, the declining importance of climatic and seasonal change may have profound long-term consequences, eventually dulling the southerner's sense of time and perhaps even his sense of history.

A more immediate threat is the air-conditioner's assault on the South's strong "sense of place." Southerners, more than most other Americans, have tied themselves to local geography. Their lives and identities have been rooted in a particular county, town, neighborhood, or homestead. Yet in recent years, thanks in part to air-conditioning, the southern landscape has been overwhelmed by an almost endless string of look-alike chain stores, tract houses, glassed-in high-rises, and, perhaps most importantly, enclosed shopping malls. The modern shopping mall is the cathedral of air-conditioned culture, and it symbolizes the placelessness of the New South.

See also FOLKLIFE: House Types; / Porches; HISTORY AND MANNERS: Manners

Raymond Arsenault
University of South Florida

Raymond Arsenault, *Journal of Southern History* (November 1984); Raymond B. Becker, *John Gorrie, M. D.: Father of Air Conditioning and Mechanical Refrigeration* (1972); Daniel Boorstin, *The Americans: The Democratic Experience* (1973); Robert Friedman, *American Heritage* (August–September 1984); Margaret Ingalls, *Willis Haviland Carrier: Father of Air Conditioning* (1952).

Animals

The woods and waters of the American South provide a rich habitat for the fauna of its lands, and this varied animal life has nourished the needs of peoples who have lived there. With its large populations of birds, mammals, fish, reptiles, and amphibians, the South was a bountiful wilderness of mixed forests, pine barrens, swamps, grasslands, and fish-bearing streams in the era before settlement. Its extensive coastline provided access to the marine wealth of the Atlantic Ocean and Gulf of Mexico. The growing presence of people in the South altered the biotic capabilities of the area to support wildlife. With Indians and white settlers utilizing the fauna of the region as a major source of food, the populations of specific animal species were subsequently reduced. In the South, as in the rest of the nation, the flora and fauna of an area were a larder of nondomestic foods upon which Indians and white settlers depended.

As white settlement increased its pace in southern states, the face of the land was noticeably altered. The development of agriculture in the South and the consequent clearing of land reduced the habitat for some animals and created new microhabitats for others. Civilization's incessant campaign against coyotes, wolves, bears, and cougars reduced their numbers and permitted the animals upon which they preyed to increase their populations. Deer, rabbit, and quail were frequently helped by the noncontiguous patterns of land clearing and the second growth vegetation that developed. While bears, wolves, and cougars found the presence of humans detrimental, deer found increased food, rabbits dined upon a variety of new crops, and the quail increased their numbers as they fed upon domestic grains. These animals, and others, learned to live with civilization and to be nourished by the fruits of newly planted fields.

Although the buffalo, the American bison, lived in historic times in all the southern states except Florida, by the early 18th century it was becoming rare in the southeastern states and was increasingly confined primarily to western lands. The buffalo did not play the crucial role in the evolution of the South that it played in the development of the trans-Mississippi West. The whitetail deer assumed the role of the buffalo in the South and became an antlered commissary for Indians and settlers. It provided them with meat for food; hides for shirts, moccasins, and gloves; and horns for implements and knife handles. In America from the 16th century to the present the whitetail deer has ranked only below cattle and sheep as an animal useful to humans. Its milk contains three times the protein and butterfat of a dairy cow's milk, and vain attempts were made to domesticate deer for milk production. During World War II, the nation consumed millions of pounds of deer meat as America stretched its limited meat rations.

Remarkably adept at increasing its numbers, the whitetail has been estimated to have once reached a population of 40 million throughout its natural ranges on this continent. When tobacco prices declined in the late 17th and early 18th centuries, the trade in deerskins increased, providing substantial economic activity for the developing region.

Trappers and traders in deerskins entered the Mississippi Valley and the lands along the Gulf Coast. From 1765 to 1773 Georgia exported 200,000 pounds of deerskins annually. As with the buffalo in the latter half of the 19th century, they were slain primarily for their hides with most of their meat left rotting upon the ground. Confronted by the reality of a declining resource, Virginia, North Carolina, and South Carolina in the 18th century passed legislation that limited unrestrained hunting. Seasons were closed, dog packs were not permitted, fire and night hunting were forbidden, and the meat of a deer could not be left upon the ground. By the 1770s every southern colony had passed laws protecting game, with deer receiving special attention. Writing of deer, John James Audubon remarked that the "tender, juicy, savoury, and above all digestible qualities of its flesh are well known and venison is held in highest esteem from the camp of the backwoodman to the luxurious tables of the opulent." In the South, the population of whitetail deer was probably more than 6 million in the years immediately prior to the Civil War. With its capacity to adapt itself to a variety of habitats and to increase its numbers through its remarkable fertility, the whitetail will maintain itself in the South as long as states preserve a balanced hunting season for this graceful species.

The capacity of deer populations to exceed the resources of their immediate habitat is well known. The mountain lion, or cougar, or puma, provided an ideal check on deer populations in the South until hunting reduced the numbers of this beautiful animal. Playful and secretive, it once was found in all the southern states. Today it is confined primarily to Florida. In spite of popular belief that it frequently preyed upon humans, its principal food has been deer. When settlers began to introduce pigs, sheep, calves, and horses into the South, those animals fell prey to the mountain lion. Presently an endangered species, this wild animal has an unsure future in the South.

Still common in the forests, swamps, and mountainous areas of all southern states, the black bear has been hunted since the colonial period. Omnivorous in its diet, it is a vegetarian throughout much of the year, although it is always willing to dine upon carrion or any animal it can catch. While agile, it does not usually possess the speed necessary to bring down a deer. Indians and settlers hunted the bear for its meat, oil, and hide. Its lengthy two-year breeding cycle usually produces two cubs, but its low reproductive rate makes it susceptible to overhunting.

Squirrels and rabbits historically have augmented the diets of Indians, blacks, and whites in the South, and in the 18th and 19th centuries they were important additions to southern meals. The gray squirrel with its characteristic white-bordered tail is a favorite target for southern hunters. Among the most agile of the tree squirrels, it prefers a habitat of hardwood forests where it feeds upon acorns and hickory nuts, usually foraging within 200 yards of its den or nest. Audubon observed that the gray squirrel's occasional nocturnal activities made it easy prey to the great horned owl.

The fox squirrel is also common in the South and often shares the same range as the gray squirrel. It is larger than the gray squirrel and varies in color from a reddish, yellowish rust to a gray shade. In the darker phases, it has a white nose the gray squirrel lacks. It is also characterized by its large head and is less graceful than other tree squirrels. Its preferred habitat is old growth forests of oak, longleaf pine, or the fringes of cypress swamps.

The most graceful squirrel of the southern states is the southern flying squirrel. Although it is the smallest and most carnivorous of the tree squirrels, these are not its only distinguishing characteristics. It is nocturnal and sometimes sleeps and eats while hanging by its claws upside down. Stretching the loose skin of its white stomach by extending its four feet, it can glide up to 150 feet. Intrigued by this small gentle animal, southerners have often kept them as pets.

Equally gentle in its habits is the cottontail rabbit. The most common rabbit in America, the Eastern Cottontail played a substantial role in the dietary history of the South. It is the most numerous of all southern game mammals. In the 19th century it was frequently trapped by slaves and became an important addition to their diet. Adapting well to a habitat altered by man, the cottontail continues to prosper in the South although most die before they are a year old.

The opossum, the only marsupial in North America, is an interesting and significant member of the fauna of the South. Living easily in the presence of civilization, it has an omnivorous diet that often includes dead animals and that allows it to maintain itself in various habitats. Seldom exceeding 12 pounds in weight, this nocturnal, gray, coarse-furred animal has a long, scaly, prehensile tail and is easily "treed" by hunters with dogs. When frightened, it feigns death, becomes rigid, and "plays possum." In the 19th and early 20th centuries, opossums were a favorite southern food. Easily captured, they were then caged and fed bread, sweet potatoes, or vegetables to improve their taste before they themselves became the meal.

Birds play an important role in the fauna of the South, gracing the region with the beauty of their songs, color, and activity. More species of birds can be found here than in any other region of the nation, and the South is privileged to bear witness yearly to the pageantry of migration. Numerous species breed regularly in southern states, including wrens, warblers, sparrows, vultures, hawks, owls, woodpeckers, tanagers, vireos, doves, turkeys, and quail. The mockingbird is closely identified with the human culture of the South. Some birds once common in the South, such as the passenger pigeon and Carolina parakeet, have become extinct. Other southern birds—the ivory-billed woodpecker, whooping crane, brown pelican, bald eagle, and Everglade kite—are endangered or threatened species.

The passenger pigeon once filled the skies of some southern states with numbers that defy description. The dedicated Scottish naturalist Alexander Wilson calculated that he saw a flock of passenger pigeons a mile in breadth and 240 miles in length. It took four hours for this great flock to pass before him. While passenger pigeons contributed significantly to the diet of the rural poor in the 18th and 19th centuries, their numbers were somewhat reduced in the Deep South. Pigeons were cooked in a variety of fashions and preserved in fat and by pickling and drying. Their fat was used for cooking and as a base for soap and their feathers were used for mattress ticking. Some pigeons were used as feed for hogs. This 16½-inch bird, which flew so gracefully through the skies, gained for itself the title of "blue meteor." Despite its speed and grace, it was easy prey for hunters. In 1914 the last of the species died. The cattle egret is a species that recently migrated to the South from Africa by way of South America. Each summer their flocks migrate north from Central America and nest in the Deep South. They are frequently seen devouring insects on the backs of cattle, and at times the white-plumed birds fill trees like blossoms.

Wild turkeys and quail are still important southern game birds. The turkey has been pursued for almost three centuries. Reaching a height of up to 40 inches, these gregarious birds roost in trees but nest and feed upon the ground. Early travelers commented upon the indifference these birds showed to human presence, but once they began to be hunted they became among the most wary animals of the South. Their eggs, flesh, and feathers were used by Indians and early settlers. By 1900 the turkey's numbers were quite small, but game management practices, which emphasized seasonal protection and maintenance of habitat, have allowed their numbers to increase in southern states.

Considerably more diminutive, but equally tasty, is the bobwhite quail. Less than 10½ inches in height, it is the smallest of the nation's quail. It often congregates in coveys of up to 30 birds, which explode with a characteristic burst of energy and frenetic fluttering when flushed. In the early 1930s, it has been estimated, 10 million bobwhites were taken each year. Today, they flourish in southern farmlands and scrub areas.

Southern lakes, rivers, bayous, and coastal waters nourish an abundance of marine and aquatic life. In freshwaters, bass, catfish, sunfish, and crappie are important sport fish; in the coastal waters, pompano, tarpon, snook, bonefish, snappers, bluefish, mackerel, shark, and sailfish attract anglers. Commercially, shrimp, oysters, and crabs are still significant products of the Gulf of Mexico.

Although Mark Twain's Huckleberry Finn caught a catfish that was as big as a man and "weighed over two hundred pounds," no documented southern catfish has yet attained this size. A blue cat caught at St. Louis weighed 150 pounds. Although 26 species of catfish may be found in the waters of the South, few reach the size of the blue catfish. Channel cats, bullheads, flatheads, and yellow cats are still pursued eagerly by southern anglers; and both commercially and as sport fish, catfish are important inhabitants of southern waters.

Praised repeatedly for its fighting abilities, the largemouth bass is the most popular freshwater gamefish in the nation. Found in lakes, bayous, and ponds, specimens of over 20 pounds are occasionally caught. Largemouth bass energetically strike artificial lures and are pursued diligently by southern anglers. Many bass tournaments are organized yearly to catch this exciting fish.

In the tropical saltwaters of the Gulf of Mexico, sport and commercial fish appear in large numbers. Great variety exists in the species that can be caught, and each year millions of anglers seek to harvest the products of this marine realm. The most exciting gamefish of the world's waters is the tarpon. Reaching lengths of up to eight feet and weights of over 300 pounds, this fish has long been praised for its strength, skill, agility, and fighting ability. From the west coast of Florida to the waters off south Texas, the explosive leaps of the silver king when hooked have captured the imagination of anglers.

The southern environment has sustained a variety of reptiles and amphibians. The American alligator is found exclusively within the South. It once was common along the Atlantic and Gulf coasts, from North Carolina south to Florida and west to Texas, but hunting for sport and commercial use of its hides has greatly reduced the alligator population. From early frontier days, gator killing was a popular sport. The alligator's large size and menacing shape seemed to make it fair game. The American crocodile has had a more limited range, mainly in south Florida, and was never large in numbers in the South. The Carolina anole is a slender bright green lizard known as the American chameleon because its coloring changes in different situations.

No family of North American salamanders is distinctively southern, yet many species can be found limited to specific regions of the South—the ringed salamander of the Ozark and Ouachita mountains, the flatwoods salamander of the Atlantic and Gulf coasts, and the hellbender of southern rivers. The largest toad in the South (*B. marinus*) is not native to the region but was introduced from South America to help control insects. Frogs found in the South include the leopard frog, the green frog, the eastern spadefoot frog, the carpenter frog, the pig frog, and the river frog. The best-known frog in the South may be the bullfrog since the distinctive call of the male punctuates the southern night. Its legs have been a prized food delicacy, leading to attempts at setting up frog farms. Turtles found in the South include the pond slider (the familiar dime-store turtle), the river cooter, and the common snapping turtle. The alligator snapping turtle is the largest freshwater turtle in the world; its languid movements allow green algae to grow on its shell. The gopher tortoise burrows underground along the southern coasts when temperatures become too high.

Four kinds of venomous snakes reside in the South—rattlesnakes, copperheads, cottonmouths, and coral snakes. Among rattlers, the eastern diamondback, which can reach a length of eight feet, and the canebreak rattler are found only in the South. The copperhead feeds on small animals and is rarely seen by humans, whom it avoids. The cottonmouth is also called the water moccasin. It is an aggressive reptile, found near swamps, rice fields, lakes, and rivers. Its bite is particularly dangerous, and it is fond of climbing trees and then dropping off the limbs when frightened. The eastern coral snake is found in the woods and grasses from the East Coast to Texas. It is among the most colorful of reptiles because of its ringed markings. Most southern snakes are nonvenomous and have been looked upon kindly by humans for keeping down the numbers of animal predators. The eastern indigo snake grows to eight feet in length and is the largest snake in North America. It is frequently seen at roadside snake farms in the Deep South, sometimes advertised as a cobra. The rainbow snake is found in swamps along the coast. Other snakes found in the South include the redbellied mud snake, the scarlet coral snake, racers, eastern worm snakes, rat snakes, king snakes, water snakes, milk snakes, and hognose snakes.

Since the time of early American Indian societies, animals have profoundly influenced human culture in the South. Animals, especially birds and reptiles, have long been dominant design motifs in Native American pottery in the region, reflecting the importance of serpent and bird symbolism in the Indian's belief system. Pottery effigies of the opossum, snake, deer, cougar, and assorted birds appeared in prehistoric Indian cultures in south Georgia, and examples have often been found at burial sites in the Gulf Coast area. Indian shell art in the Southeast included iconographic representations of such animals as rattlesnakes, woodpeckers, and spiders. Animals were central symbols of Indian religion, and objects such as eagle feathers and swan wings had ritual importance. Indian folklore included stories illustrating the personalities of various animals, such as the Choctaw tale "Why the Possum Grins."

Blacks and whites have similarly used animals in the culture they built in the South. Blacks brought to the New World an African tradition of animal tales about lions, elephants, and monkeys; those animals, as well as animals encountered by the slaves in the New World, appeared in black folktales. African omens and signs were altered to fit American fauna. Animals also played a role in black folk medicine. The plantation conjurer might wear a snake skin around his neck or carry a petrified frog in one pocket and a dead lizard in the other. A large body of black folklore related the stories of humanized animals such as Brer Rabbit and Brer Fox. African and American Indian prototypes for these trickster tales have been discovered, but, whatever their origins, most of these animal folktales suggested how clever slaves outsmarted their masters.

There is also a rich tradition among southern blacks, whites, and Indians of folk sayings and beliefs about animals. In Louisiana, for example, if a dog howls with his nose in the earth some people believe a fire will occur; if a rooster crows at the back door, it means death; if animals in the woods and swamps are unusually noisy, then it will rain soon. Black children have even incorporated the snake into a children's game ("Black snake, black snake, where are you hiding?").

In the folk arts and crafts of the whites of southern Appalachia animals emerge, as in Indian and black art, as a major design motif in wood carving, quilting, pottery, basketmaking, and toymaking. Animals are the central figures of Anglo-American folksongs such as "Froggie Went a Courtin'," "Raccoon," "Groundhog," "Little Sparrow," and "Bear Went over the Mountain." Again, as with Indians and blacks, animals fulfilled for mountain and rural whites in the South a variety of practical and symbolic functions. They served as a direct source of food and clothing, as an economic resource from trading in animal products, as an ingredient in the prevention and treatment of disease and illness, and as figures in folk art and lore. One group of Appalachian whites even made serpents the ritual center of a snake handler's religion.

Child and animal friend, Vicksburg, Miss., 1977

In the modern South animals have figured in the musical and literary traditions of the region. Blues singers, for example, apply animal comparisons to themselves through lyrics such as "the rattlesnakin' daddy who wants to rattle all the time," the "black wolf that hollers," or the "rootin' ground hog who roots both night and day." Southern writers generally see animals the same way rural people have over the years, as simply part of the land, beings encountered as part of normal living. Their portrayal of animals is rooted in familiarity. Marjorie Kinnan Rawlings raises her hat when she sees the water moccasin, which once refrained from biting her nervous horse. William Faulkner used an animal for what critics regard as one of his most profound tales, "The Bear." He conveyed an almost mystical awareness of the relationship between man and animal in the southern woods, an attitude rooted in American Indian belief. For Faulkner's southern hunters, there is great respect for the animals hunted, because they discover an identity between themselves and their prey. Harry Crews captures the drama of the rattlesnake roundup, a southern subcultural ritual, in his novel *A Feast of Snakes* (1976).

See also FOLKLIFE: Folk Medicine; RECREATION: Fishing; Hunting

Phillip Drennon Thomas
Wichita State University

Henry Hill Collins, *Complete Field Guide to American Wildlife* (1959); Albert E. Cowdrey, *This Land, This South: An Environmental History* (1983); Gilbert C. Fite, *Cotton Fields No More: Southern Agriculture, 1865–1980* (1984); Sam B. Hilliard, *Hog Meat and Hoecake: Food Supply in the Old South, 1840–1860* (1972); David Starr Jordan and Barton Warren Everman, *American Food and Game Fishes* (1902); Howard W. Odum, *Southern Regions of the United States* (1936); Olin Sewall Pettingill, Jr., *A Guide to Bird Finding East of the Mississippi* (1977); Arlie W. Schorger, *The Passenger Pigeon: Its Natural History and Extinction* (1955), *The Wild Turkey: Its History and Domestication* (1966); Walter P. Taylor, ed., *The Deer of North America: The White-Tailed Mule and Black-Tailed Deer, Genus "Odocoileus," Their History and Management* (1956).

Climate and Weather

Scholars and other observers have long seen the South's climate and weather as the key to understanding its people. James McBride Dabbs saw in the violence of southern thunderstorms a parallel for the violence of the region's people, nurturing the tension that demanded release. He called the weather a "demi-god." Wilbur J. Cash portrayed the southern climate creating "a cosmic conspiracy against reality in favor of romance." Clarence Cason, in *90° in the Shade* (1935), used the weather to explain the southerner's slow talk and movement. Sociologist Rupert B. Vance blamed the prevalence of hookworm in the South partly on the warm climate, which encouraged people to go shoeless and thus expose themselves to infection through the feet. He also argued that barns in the South were not as tightly constructed as those in New England because southerners did not have the incentive of the harsh northern winters. Certainly, the architecture of the South—with its use of high ceilings and tall windows, with its porches, galleries, verandas, and dogtrot breezeways, all to promote summer cooling—has testified to the southerner's awareness of the weather's importance in terms of daily living.

The warm, humid climate, long growing season, and abundant moisture of most of the South have indeed had a far-reaching impact on the region's economy and culture. Much of the South's early history involved the raising of agricultural products for export. Even in Texas, where the climate of the northern and western two-thirds of the state differs dramatically from the rest of the South, conditions proved ideal for large livestock operations. The southern climate has helped to make agricultural pursuits profitable. Southerners also have had to work to overcome the disadvantages imposed upon them by their climate. The hot and humid weather that produced unhealthy conditions took many an early southerner's life. Advances in medicine, architecture, and technology have curbed the outbreak of disease, permitted the construction of artificially cooled environments, and helped to create a healthy environment in which to live.

The South is divided into three large climate regions: the southern Plains and Lowlands, the Middle Atlantic Lowlands, and the Appalachian Mountains. The largest of these three is the southern Plains and Lowlands, a vast area including the states of Texas, Georgia, Florida, and South Carolina. The area inland from the Gulf and Atlantic coastlines has a continental climate featuring cold winters, warm to hot summers, and great extremes of temperature. Coastal regions are modified by the warm waters of the Gulf of Mexico and the Atlantic. Winters there are relatively humid and mild, summers very humid and warm. The southern portion of Florida has a special subtropical climate marked by dominating northwest tradewinds that differentiate it from the rest of the South.

As a whole the climate of the southern Plains and Lowlands is influenced by the interaction between strong, cold, and dry polar air masses from the interior and warm, moist maritime air masses from the Atlantic and, especially, from the Gulf. In winter the cold inland air is heavier and is drawn toward the warmer, lighter air over the water. This situation allows cold winter storms to penetrate, at times, as far as the coastal regions. When this occurs there can be freezes as far south as central Florida. In summer the inland air mass is warmer than the one over the ocean, and a reverse flow occurs that carries moist maritime air northward and provides a major source of precipitation for the interior. Along the Atlantic Coast precipitation is carried by southerly and easterly winds off the ocean. The intense summer heat of inland areas helps produce violent tornadoes and thunderstorms. Coastal areas are exposed to hurricanes with strong tides, considerable rain, and high winds.

With the exception of extreme southern Texas and Florida, temperatures in January range from a mean maximum of 70° to a mean minimum of 20° (in north Texas). In general there can be 0 to 30 days along the coast when temperatures fall below 32° and as many as 90 days in more northerly and westerly areas. In southern Texas and Florida temperatures range on average in January from 50° to 80° and days below 32° are very rare. July temperatures for this region range from 70° to 100° inland and from 70° to 90° on the immediate coast. The number of days with temperatures above 90° ranges from 60 to 120. Growing seasons for the most southerly parts of the region have a mean length of 330 days, though the most northern portions of Texas and Arkansas have growing seasons as short as 200 days.

Yearly snowfall accumulations decrease from north to south. In far northern regions three feet of snow is a normal yearly total while it rarely falls in coastal areas. With the exception of Atlantic coastal areas and Texas, yearly precipitation accumulations range from 48" to 64" and in scattered locations along the Gulf Coast may reach as high as 100". Along the Atlantic Coast there is less precipitation with yearly means of 32" to 48". In Texas the amount of yearly precipitation decreases from east to west with a high in eastern coastal areas of 56" and a low of 8" at El Paso.

Humidity levels are high for this entire region except in western Texas. Winter levels range from 60 to 85 percent and summer readings average over 90 percent. In more northern and western regions humidity levels are somewhat decreased, with El Paso having summer levels of only 60 to 70 percent.

The remaining two climate regions of the South are climatically connected to each other. The Middle Atlantic Lowlands comprise an approximately 200-mile-wide strip along the coastlines of North Carolina and Virginia. The Appalachian Mountain region is an upland area that extends northeastward from Georgia and includes eastern Tennessee and western North Carolina and Virginia. The mountain peaks, averaging from 2,000 to 4,000 feet above sea level, act as a partial barrier to air masses moving in from the west. Although some fronts cross the mountains and head to the coast, others are forced north and east away from the Middle Atlantic Lowlands. Other fronts are pushed south into South Carolina, Georgia, and Florida. When the latter occurs in winter, Atlantic coastal areas in the southern Plains and Lowlands climate region may be colder than coastal Virginia or North Carolina. As air masses approach the mountains from the west, they are forced to rise and often lose their moisture, producing considerable rain and snow for the western slopes. The Atlantic coastal region and the eastern slopes of the Appalachian chain receive their moisture from maritime air masses moving ashore from the Atlantic. Occasionally snow reaches these areas from air masses that pass over the mountain barrier. Coastal areas are exposed to sometimes destructive hurricanes.

Temperatures in these two regions range from annual mean minimums of 20° in winter to summer highs in the 90s. Along the coast there are from 30 to 90 days with temperatures below 32°, whereas in the mountains there may be as many as 150 days with below freezing temperatures. On the coast more humidity is typical (around 90 percent in summer). Humidity levels are relatively low in mountainous areas. Great extremes of both temperature and humidity occur as one moves from mountain valleys to higher elevations. Annual precipitation amounts range from 32″ to 48″ in coastal areas to as much as 64″ in some mountain locations.

Although numerous old weather records are available for the South, no climate reconstructions have been made. However, from studies conducted on other regions of North America, one can deduce the climatic changes that have taken place in the South. Considerable evidence suggests that a period of increased cold weather and variable temperatures and precipitation greeted the first Europeans to reach the American coast. Called the Little Ice Age, it lasted until the last third of the 19th century. In the South this period was probably marked by more outbreaks of cold, freezing weather in Gulf coastal regions and somewhat cooler temperatures in northern, western, and mountain areas. In this century there has been a gradual warming trend and a relative decrease in variable weather, until the late 1940s. Thereafter climatic conditions have remained fairly stable.

Talking about the weather has always been a favorite southern pastime. The region's folklore tradition contains a body of sayings on the weather, geared toward predicting it. The wider the stripes on a caterpillar's back, the colder the winter. A row of dark spots on a goose bone also means a harsh winter. Some of these sayings originated in Africa, some in Europe, and others with American Indians. The thicker an onion skin, the colder the winter is a Deep South regional saying found in Georgia, Mississippi, and Alabama, and similar proverbs about the weather can be found in other subregions of the South.

Southern writers have absorbed this interest in climate. Critic Malcolm Cowley has noted of William Faulkner that "no other American writer takes such delight in the weather," but Faulkner was merely typical of southern writers in this regard. "That's the one trouble with this country," says Dr. Peabody in *As I Lay Dying* (1930), "everything, weather, all hangs on too long." But it was not just southern writers who noted the weather's importance. Henry Adams wrote in *The Education of Henry Adams* (1907) of his visit to the South, whose people he portrayed negatively but whose climate left him enthralled. He viscerally recalled "the May sunshine and shadow," "the thickness of foliage and the heavy smells," "the sense of atmosphere," and "the brooding indolence of a warm climate and a negro population."

The changing South can be seen in the modern southern attitude toward weather. Historian Francis Butler Simkins once noted that a key change in the South had been "the disappearance of the fear of the hot climate inherited from European ancestors." Technology had much to do with this through the invention of artificial ice and refrigeration; air-conditioning has had a profound

A thermometer and a cola—southern icons, Reganton, Miss., 1975

role in freeing southerners of the climate's debilitating effects. Climate-related diseases such as malaria, yellow fever, and hookworm have been all but eliminated. Southerners, even more than other Americans, wear light and loose garments. "The South has learned to regard the sun as a beneficent god instead of a cruel tyrant," concluded Simkins. The southern attitude toward beauty and health now emphasizes that a brown skin is more attractive than a fair one. This is a true aesthetic revolution for a people as racially conscious as southern whites, but it also reflects a different attitude toward climate and weather than earlier in southern history.

William R. Baron
Northern Arizona University

John L. Baldwin, *Climates of the United States* (1973); Lorin Blodget, *Climatology of the United States* (1857); James C. Bonner, in *Writing Southern History: Essays in Historiography in Honor of Fletcher M. Green*, ed. Arthur S. Link and Rembert W. Patrick (1965); David Hackett Fischer, *Journal of Interdisciplinary History* (Spring 1980); Hubert H. Lamb, *Climate, History and the Modern World* (1982); W. J. Maunder, *The Value of the Weather* (1970); Edgar T. Thompson, *Agricultural History* (January 1941); U.S. Department of Agriculture, *Climate and Man* (1941).

Endangered Species

Through millions of millennia, the actions of climate, rainfall, and other agents of geological change have sculpted in the American South a rich and diverse topography. From the unique coral islands that form the Florida Keys to the expansive Delta of the Mississippi River with its wilderness of bayous to the great pine forests with their mixed stands of hardwoods, this area's distinctive habitat has nourished a rich and diverse flora and fauna. White settlement in the region led to a gradual but sustained alteration of the natural setting in which southern wildlife maintained itself. The rapid pace of industrialization in the South in the 20th century further altered the habitat. The reduction of virgin forests, alteration of waterways, introduction of domestic prey species, and consumption of land through urban development have encroached decade after decade upon the habitat of the South's wildlife. All of these developments have biologically impoverished the natural environment for every species but man and have demonstrated the fragility of ecosystems.

In every southern state wildlife is under pressure, with some species threatened, some endangered, and some extinct. "Endangered species" are those species in danger of becoming extinct in wild, natural environments. "Threatened species" are those species that will become endangered if present conditions are not altered. In the South, as in other regions of the nation, animal species became extinct or endangered through the alteration and destruction of habitat, competition with introduced species, predation, disease, or through the more direct pressure of unrestrained hunting. Although few animals in America have become extinct through the pressures of hunting alone, the demise of the passenger pigeon and the Carolina parakeet were substantially, if not decisively, aided by such activities, and the American alligator's future was threatened.

The passenger pigeon once ranged throughout most of the lands east of the Rocky Mountains and wintered in the southern states. Among the most numerous of all the world's birds, its population was greater than that of any other bird in North America. The noted early American naturalist, Alexander Wilson, recorded that in 1810 he had seen a flock of migrating passenger pigeons whose numbers he estimated at 2,230,272,000. In spite of such numbers, a century later the species was at the threshold of extinction because of a century of unrestricted hunting. In 1914 at the Cincinnati Zoological Garden, Martha, the last known passenger pigeon, died.

In the same year, the Carolina parakeet experienced a similar fate. North America's only parrot and a bird once numerous in the southern states, this aggressive yellow, green, and orange bird frequently devoured the fruits and nuts of orchards; consequently it had been hunted since colonial times. The bird's bright plumage attracted milliners and it subsequently fell subject to commercial utilization. Its pattern of behavior made it easy prey for bird catchers and market hunters. Since the death of a captive Carolina parakeet in 1914, no verified sightings of this colorful and active bird have been recorded. For the passenger pigeon and Carolina parakeet, the pressures of hunting, habitat destruction, and behavior patterns that limited their dispersal in times of danger led to their extinction.

Other birds have experienced the threat of extinction in the South, and the whooping crane, Mississippi sandhill crane, brown pelican, bald eagle, and Everglade kite are endangered or threatened in all southern states. The whooping crane is North America's tallest extant bird and a survivor from the Pleistocene era. Rare in historic times, it was by the end of the 19th century confined primarily to the region west of the Mississippi River. Hunted for sport, meat, and eggs and experiencing changes in its habitat as the result of agriculture, its numbers declined dramatically. Restricted to a population that numbers less than 75 today, this magnificent bird makes a 2,300 mile migration each spring from its wintering site at the Aransas Refuge in Texas to nesting sites in the Wood Buffalo Park in Canada. The whooping crane is protected by the governments of both the United States and Canada and the energetic advocacy of conservation groups who have made its plight well known. Attempts to improve its breeding cycle have met with some success, and determined efforts have been initiated to maintain this graceful but endangered species. Perhaps even more endangered than the whooping crane is its relative, the Mississippi sandhill crane, which has an even smaller population. This endangered species is now protected at the Mississippi Sandhill Crane Refuge.

Endangered in all southern states but Florida, where it is threatened, the brown pelican is an excellent example of an animal that can become suddenly devastated by the actions of pesticides on an avian species. Until the 1960s the brown pelican existed in abundant numbers, but the increased use of endrin to control the boll weevil, the bollworm, and the sugarcane borer in the Mississippi Delta led to the demise of brown pelicans by directly killing them, destroying their food supplies, and altering their physiological processes. Endrin was responsible for massive fish kills in the Mississippi River in the late 1950s and early 1960s. Brown pelicans have been transplanted from Florida, where the population is stable, to Louisiana to reestablish colonies of this once plentiful bird. In Texas, colonies are still limited with the population not yet considered viable.

Overspecialization in a species introduces an element of rigidity in that species' ability to adapt to changing environmental circumstances. America's largest woodpecker, the ivory-billed woodpecker, confronted a limited future because of its dependence upon virgin, old growth forests in the South with their characteristic dead and dying trees. Logging has so reduced its habitat that sightings have become limited and often unverified, and the species may be extinct.

Specialization has also limited the future of the Everglade kite. Until the second decade of this century, this strikingly beautiful hawk was frequently observed soaring above the freshwater marshes of Florida. Its principal food source was the large freshwater apple snail. Dependent upon this one snail, which in turn depended upon the standing water of a marsh for habitat, it had a fragile ecosystem. The progressive draining of wetlands in Florida for agriculture and urban development destroyed the populations of the apple snail and reduced the food supply of the Everglade kite. Today, its severely limited population is confined primarily to the southwestern reaches of Lake Okeechobee with a few small nesting sites at the Loxahatchee National Wildlife Refuge. This graceful and noble bird's future is now tied to the preservation of the apple snail's environment.

The federal government declared the piping plover, a once-common Atlantic and Gulf coastal shore bird, an endangered and threatened species in 1985. Scientists launched a major effort in the 1980s to save another bird, the dusky seaside sparrow, from extinction. The last known example of the species survives in a protected environment in Florida, as scientists continue cross-breeding experiments hoping to save the species.

Because of the habitat alteration and hunting pressures, the American alligator is an endangered species in Alabama, Arkansas, Georgia, Mississippi, North Carolina, South Carolina, and Texas. John Bartram could observe in the mid-18th century that alligators were so thick in Florida's St. Johns River that one could have walked across the river on their heads if they had been harmless; by the middle years of this century, hide hunters had severely reduced their numbers. Legislation that reduced the market for their skins and protected their habitat has permitted their numbers to increase in Florida and Louisiana, and they are no longer endangered in those states. Their situation is more precarious in other southern states.

A more timid and more nocturnal relative of the American alligator, the American crocodile, is also an endangered species in the South. Because of its limited range and specialized habitat, its prospects are less bright than those of the alligator. Confined primarily to the mangrove estuaries of southern Florida, the American crocodile is the only representative of this genera in North America, although its range includes the coastal littoral of Colombia and eastern Venezuela, the Caribbean and West Indies, the Pacific coasts of Ecuador and Colombia and most of the Pacific coast of Central America and Mexico. Protected today and watched carefully in the Everglades National Park and the lower Keys, it is no longer subjected to hide hunters, and habitat encroachment has now been restricted. There is hope that the declining numbers of this fierce-countenanced reptile have been stabilized and that a species that has existed for 140 million years will be able to maintain itself.

The crocodile's relatives, the sea turtles, are also endangered in the southern states. All five genera of sea turtles may be found in the Gulf of Mexico, and all once nested on the sun-caressed beaches of the southern states. Sea turtles are particularly vulnerable to predation and habitat alteration. After spending years at sea, they return to nest on the limited expanse of shore on which they were hatched. Once laid, their eggs are desired by man both as a source of protein and as an aphrodisiac that renews sexual vigor. Sea turtles are easily caught and drowned in trawlers' nets. The green turtle is among the most valuable of all reptiles and was once common to the majority of the world's oceans where temperatures did not drop below 68° F. Classified as an endangered species in the United States, it is still harvested outside of this nation because of the quality of its meat for soup, the skin of its forequarters for shoes, and its oil for cosmetics and soap. The Atlantic hawksbill turtle also serves the needs of fashion as a source for tortoiseshell. It is also harvested for its calipee, a cartilaginous material removed from the bones of the bottom shell, which is used in clear green turtle soup and for leather. Immature hawksbill turtles are often mounted for sale to tourists in Latin American countries.

In the warm waters of Florida and perhaps as far west as Texas in the Gulf of Mexico and as far north as southern Georgia, the docile, slow-breeding, marine herbivore the manatee is attempting to maintain its population against increasing habitat destruction and human intrusion into its domain. This imperfectly studied, large marine mammal, whose nearest relative is the elephant, can reach a length of 12 feet and a weight of 1,200 pounds. During the course of a day, it may consume up to 150 pounds of aquatic plants. It has no natural enemies, unless man is placed in this category, but it is among the most endangered of all marine mammals. Until the end of the 19th century, it was hunted by the Seminole Indians and early settlers because of the veal-like quality of its meat. Its hide made a strong, durable leather; its bones with their ivory appearance were often carved into small objects; and its fat was used for lubrication and light. Declining populations of this tranquil animal encouraged the Florida Legislature to pass in 1893 a bill to protect the manatee. In 1907 additional legislation imposed a $600 fine and a six-month prison term for killing a manatee. Part of a population that is probably less than 1,000, the manatee does not have a secure future. Even in protected waters, manatees are often injured by the propellers of motorboats. Development has restricted their access to warm springs. Highly susceptible to cold weather, they frequently become victims of harsh winters. Protected by state and federal legislation, their future depends upon the stability of their habitat.

Although the manatee is an elusive animal to investigate, even more secretive in its habits is the Florida panther, or eastern cougar. Historically, the cougar, or mountain lion or panther, had the greatest natural range of any terrestrial mammal in the New World, ranging from Tierra del Fuego at the tip of South America to southeastern Alaska in the north. The eastern cougar, or Florida panther, still maintains a limited presence in Florida and other southeastern states. While its present population is difficult to determine, its future is dependent upon the preservation of a protected habitat where it may range widely in pursuit of food. The Everglades National Park and other such large southern preserves may be ultimately the Florida panther's last refuge.

Florida is also the home for the endangered key deer, a small subspecies of the Virginia whitetail deer. With bucks ranging in weight from 60 to 110 pounds, with the does smaller, this dwarf deer of the Florida Keys was constantly hunted by the inhabitants of the area. Reduced in numbers during the 20th century, key deer were protected from hunters by a ban passed by the Florida Legislature in 1939. Poaching and the devastations of fire and hurricane continued to reduce their numbers, and by 1949 their population was estimated to be down to 30. After much political debate, conservationists secured the establishment in 1957 of the Key Deer National Wildlife Refuge. This 7,000 acre refuge, which embraces 16 keys, provides a sanctuary not only for the key deer but also for 11 other endangered or threatened species. The population has increased and presently numbers more than 400.

One of the tragedies of a species approaching the brink of extinction is that their population reaches such low numbers that it becomes very difficult to study the natural history of the animal. The southern red wolf faces such a predicament, and the study of the animal is confronted by countless difficulties. Early colonists in the South frequently confronted a distinctive native wolf population. Although called the red wolf, most members of this species had gray-brown, black, or tawny coats with only a few of them having the distinctive red coat. They were generally larger than a coyote but smaller than their relatives, the gray wolves. The red wolf was perhaps slightly less predatory than the gray wolf, but its natural history was quite similar. Civilization's constant war upon carnivores and increased patterns of settlement reduced the red wolves' range and their numbers. By the 1920s the red wolf had been eliminated from most regions east of the Mississippi River. Populations of red wolves still existed in the Coastal Prairie of Louisiana and Texas, in eastern Oklahoma, and in the Ozark-Ouachita Highlands of Arkansas. Among these animals, there was interbreeding with coyotes, and consequently the gene pool has been degraded by hybridization. In the mid-1960s the red wolf was placed on the rare and endangered species list. The future for this species lies in the protection of the limited number of nonhybridized members of this gene pool, which still reside in the upper Gulf Coast region of Texas.

See also RECREATION: Hunting

Phillip Drennon Thomas
Wichita State University

Albert E. Cowdrey, *This Land, This South: An Environmental History* (1983); Robin W. Doughty, *Wildlife and Man in Texas: Environmental Change and Conservation* (1983); Peter Matthiessen, *Wildlife in America* (1959); Arlie W. Schorger, *The Passenger Pigeon: Its Natural History and Extinction* (1973); Stanley A. Temple, ed., *Endangered Birds: Management Techniques for Preserving Threatened Species* (1978); James A. Tober, *Who Owns the Wildlife?: The Political Economy of Conservation in Nineteenth-Century America* (1981).

Energy Use and Development

The South is richly endowed with energy resources, but it exhibits a complex pattern in its production and use of particular fuels and power sources. The Atlantic coastal regions of the southern states, being energy importers, have committed themselves heavily to nuclear power. The southern Appalachian Mountains contain extensive seams of high quality coal, which has long been exported along the rivers, railroads, and highways that link mines to markets. Many of the rivers flowing out of the mountains have also been harnessed for hydroelectric power, most notably in the Tennessee Valley, and the great hardwood forests that clothe the hills they drain continue to provide fuel wood for domestic and local industrial heat. Petroleum and natural gas are the bonanza fuels of the southwestern states, especially Texas and Louisiana.

Although the South as a whole cannot be considered a cohesive energy region, southern culture, like that of other regions in the nation, has been profoundly affected by the historical experience of developing and utilizing energy resources. Before the 1820s, when new canals began carrying anthracite from northeastern Pennsylvania to the Tidewater ports of the East Coast, soft coal mines near Richmond, Va., served as one of America's few sources of commercial coal. In Alabama coal was shipped down the Coosa River as early as the 1830s and later fueled the ironworks that manufactured munitions for the Confederacy. Coal shipments out of western Virginia grew steadily after the Baltimore and Ohio rail line reached the Ohio River in the 1850s, and Tennessee coal, mined commercially from the 1830s, also gained access to growing markets when the Nashville & Chattanooga Railroad was completed in 1855.

Following the Civil War the South stepped up its laborious efforts to industrialize, a transformation that required much more intensive exploitation and utilization of energy resources. Water power was harnessed to drive machinery in fall line mills and factories at Richmond, Va., and at Augusta and Columbus, Ga. Railroad building also boomed after the war, creating both a demand for coal and iron and the means for satisfying it. The New River coalfield was opened in 1873 when the Chesapeake & Ohio Railroad pushed its lines through the rugged mountains of central West Virginia, and 10 years later the Norfolk & Western began shipping out high quality metallurgical coal from the Pocahontas field of southern West Virginia and southwestern Virginia. In the final decades of the 19th century the iron and steel industry was consolidated in great industrial cities such as Pittsburgh and Chicago; the South has its representative in Birmingham.

The 20th century brought new forms of industrial production and the discovery of new sources of energy. The oil industry, born in the Appalachian hills of western Pennsylvania and West Virginia, experienced explosive growth following the east Texas and Spindletop strikes. The chemical industry also expanded rapidly, especially in the Kanawha and Tennessee river valleys and, as petroleum feed stocks grew in importance, along the Gulf Coast of Texas. Cheap electrical power was used to produce chemical fertilizers, which, together with rural electrification and mechanization, became the mainstays of energy-intensive agriculture. This agricultural revolution in turn led to the great migration of population from the rural South during the middle decades of this century.

Taken as a whole, the South is comparatively rich in fossil fuels, but historically this has been a mixed blessing. Both the coal and the oil industries are unusually prone to cycles of boom and bust. Both industries include major corporations, which seek to reduce their vulnerability to cyclical shifts, and aggressive independent operators poised to reap high profits during times of rising demand. The hard-driving wildcatter depicted in the film *Giant* and the high-rolling strip miner are both southern types. Where the energy resources the independent operators exploit are utilized locally, as is the case in parts of Texas and Louisiana, they appear as marginal figures in a diversified economy. Where the fuels the independent operators mine are shipped out for use elsewhere, as is the case in the coal regions, they are dominant figures in local societies that are unbuffered against the dire consequences of the boom-bust cycle.

The migration of industries from older northern cities to the southern Sunbelt would not have been possible without the development of new types of energy utilization. Southern cities are just as dependent on air-conditioning and automobiles as are the older northern cities on central heating and urban rail systems. The South has used its energy resources shrewdly in the national competition for new industry. Whether southerners will be able to manage successfully the consequences of their energy decisions and how they will evaluate the long-term effects of these decisions on their regional culture remain open questions.

See also AGRICULTURE: / Rural Electrification; GEOGRAPHY: / Mills and Milling; HISTORY AND MANNERS: Railroads; INDUSTRY articles; SCIENCE AND MEDICINE: Technology; SOCIAL CLASS: Appalachia, Exploitation of

Arthur Donovan
Virginia Polytechnic Institute
and State University

Harry M. Caudill, *Night Comes to the Cumberlands* (1962); Louis C. Hunter, *Waterpower: A History of Industrial Power in the United States, 1780–1930* (1979); Ronald L. Lewis, *Coal, Iron, and Slaves: Industrial Slavery in Maryland and Virginia, 1715–1865* (1979); Martin V. Melosi, *Coping with Abundance: Energy and Environment in Industrial America, 1820–1980* (1985); Joseph A. Pratt, *The Growth of a Refining Region* (1980); John A. Williams, *West Virginia and the Captains of Industry* (1976).

Environmental Movements

The South followed, although sometimes tardily, the rest of the nation in its evolution from natural resource conservation to the environmentalism of the 1960s. Cooperative efforts often developed between federal and state governments, but at times various state governments followed federal guidelines only reluctantly. While the South faced conservation problems similar to those throughout the country, its geography, history, and economic and social conditions gave southern conservation activities their own regional characteristics. Just as the environmental movements began to develop in the 1960s, the southern economy lagged. The southern legacy of individualism and resentment of outside authority also affected southern attitudes toward conservation and environmental policy.

Although the Indians were not necessarily the natural ecologists they are often portrayed as being, they were the first humans to begin to change the environment of the South and to learn to live with its characteristics. Early European settlers, less inclined to adapt to the natural environment than the Indian, generally wanted to transform the landscape. England expected its American colonies to produce certain products. In addition to the native tobacco, Europeans introduced other crops such as wheat and rice, thus contributing new flora and fauna as well as new diseases to the southern environment.

Even before the American Revolution, soil exhaustion caused southern planters to become concerned with soil conservation. Both George Washington and Thomas Jefferson evidenced a concern for soil depletion and its consequences in the Tidewater region. While he advocated soil conservation methods, Jefferson realized that most people would solve their soil fertility problem by simply moving to cheaper lands farther west. In all probability the Moravians represented the first group to treat natural resources in a conservationist manner.

Colonials viewed forests ambivalently, as a nuisance

to agriculture to be removed as soon as possible and as a useful product for sale or building use. The English crown made some attempts to regulate cutting of the American forests, but most colonists resented such laws and contended that their freedom to cut forests was a right. In fact, it was a practical reality that conditioned future American attitudes toward use of forest resources. Much of the cut timber was wasted, often burned for clearing; thus by the time of the Revolution southern forests had been much modified.

Early European settlers found an abundance of wildlife in the South. Indians had already depleted some forms of wildlife by indiscriminate killing. The colonials killed either for food or to eliminate predators that interfered with agriculture. While they did not eliminate any species, the colonials' actions often created an ecological imbalance. In England, hunting rights had been considered a privilege of the upper class, and attempts to impose restrictions on the colonials created resentment. As with the cutting of trees, the settlers generally believed they had a right to hunt. Such attitudes have persisted, making the contemporary hunting laws in states such as Texas a patchwork of state and local control.

European settlers and travelers took an early interest in the exotic flora and fauna they found in the southern colonies. Planters like Jefferson and William Byrd II as well as other lesser-known settlers provided important accounts of colonial wildlife, laying the groundwork for further study. John Bartram, a Philadelphia botanist, and the English traveler Mark Catesby provided significant information concerning southern wildlife, although Catesby's writings provided misinformation as well.

Prior to the American Revolution both the crown and the colonial legislature passed conservation laws. Some colonial laws restricted the slaughter of deer while others controlled fishing activities. In practice colonials generally ignored conservation laws, but they established the principle, persisting into modern times, that the sovereign had the authority to control natural resources.

Between the American Revolution and the Civil War, movement of population across the Appalachian Mountains and into the Mississippi River Valley had a tremendous impact on southern soils, forests, rivers, and wildlife. Rapid expansion of cotton agriculture between 1790 and 1835 exhausted the soil in the more easterly parts of the South. By the 1830s much of the older South needed considerable fertilizer to maintain production, setting in motion a cycle that continued to characterize American agriculture. The use of fertilizer to maintain or increase production resulted in the demand for more, and increasingly expensive, fertilizers. Cutting of timber and the destruction of natural ground cover combined with the clean field and row crop cultivation of cotton, corn, and tobacco to accelerate soil erosion. A few advocates of agricultural reform, such as Edmund Ruffin, urged the use of contour plowing and cheaper natural fertilizers. With a seemingly endless abundance of cheap land farther west, few southern farmers heeded the advice of these prophets.

Both national and state governments attempted to control destruction of forests before 1860. The national government reserved certain trees for naval use, while most southern states prohibited burning of trees because of the danger to other property. Only the settlers' capacity to use and sell wood limited the continued exploitation of southern forest resources in the antebellum period.

In the postrevolutionary era, naturalists, particularly John James Audubon, focused attention on the South. Ignoring the development of conservation for aesthetic reasons, and often taking abundance for granted, they were extremely important in providing scientific understanding of southern flora and fauna. Also important to the use of southern resources in the postrevolutionary period was concern for improving navigation and controlling floods on the rivers of the South. Because most southern rivers provided an unreliable means of transportation, local, state, and national governments attempted to transform rivers to make them more navigable. The South's greatest river, the Mississippi, proved both a blessing and a threat. While providing fertile land and an avenue for much southern commerce, it often brought devastating floods. Settlers attempted to hold back the river's rampages with levees. Constriction of the river forced its flood waters to rise higher, requiring further heightening of the levees. Both federal and state governments attempted to improve navigation and to control floods on the Mississippi. Studies and recommendations made prior to the Civil War long influenced government policy toward the Mississippi and its tributaries.

So far as wetlands were concerned, neither antebellum southerners nor other Americans had any understanding of their ecological value, generally regarding them as a nuisance. In 1849 and 1850 the national government turned much of the wetlands over to state control for reclamation through drainage. Although exploitation characterized the general southern (and American) approach to resource use, a small population and limited industrial development moderated the degree of this exploitation prior to the Civil War.

After the Civil War the development of technology created an opportunity for almost unlimited exploitation of southern natural resources. Northern industrialists, Europeans, and some southerners saw in these resources opportunities for quick wealth. Both federal and state governments encouraged railroad construction through land grants. Much of the most valuable publicly owned timber and mineral lands in the South passed to private ownership between 1865 and 1900.

Although southerners played some role in calling for wiser use of natural resources, the impetus for conservation, like much of the force for exploitation, came from outside the South. In particular, government scientists occupied a prominent position in the early conservation movement. They helped establish national parks, forest reserves, and other important programs for natural resource management. Outside leadership focused on conservation of southern resources as part of a larger movement throughout the nation. While contributing some leaders in the struggle, the South more often provided the battleground for conservation controversies.

Agriculture and the extractive industries took the greatest toll on southern resources, ravaging soil, timber, and wildlife. Increased cotton production, fostered by the tenant system, encouraged a single crop economy greater in extent than prior to the Civil War. The use of fertilizers, promoted by agricultural reformers, helped maintain production in the face of a decline in natural soil fertility. A midwesterner who moved to Louisiana in the 1870s made one of the most significant contributions to southern agricultural reform. In 1903, at Terrell, Tex., Seaman A. Knapp introduced the demonstration farm as a means of agricultural education, a concept that became federal law with establishment of the Agricultural Extension Services. The spread of the boll weevil across the South demonstrated problems associated with a cotton monoculture, although little was effectively done about the threat prior to 1900.

The exploitation and conservation of southern forests during the Gilded Age followed an erratic course. Reconstruction government had restricted sale of public lands in the South. With Redemption, southern Democrats supported laws promoting the sale of such land, which included much forested land, although by 1889 southern members of Congress led a campaign to keep the few remaining areas under governmental control. During the period of sale large tracts of southern timber passed to speculators and lumbermen, especially non-southerners, most of whom considered timber a commodity and little understood its relationship to the rest of the environment. Although lumbermen attempted reforestation, in 1873 a committee established by the American Association for the Advancement of Science encouraged federal and state governments to pass laws protecting forests and promoting timber cultivation. Gradually, support grew for development of national and state forest reserves.

The development of scientific forestry began at Yale University, but the first practical demonstration of its principles occurred, serendipitously, in North Carolina. George W. Vanderbilt hired the young forester Gifford Pinchot to manage the forest reserves of his Biltmore estate. In 1898 the Biltmore Forest School opened. Although Pinchot's activities at Biltmore influenced other areas of the South, he was not alone in his concern for southern forest resources. The Mississippi politician L. Q. C. Lamar, in his position as secretary of the interior, supported President Cleveland's call for forest reserves. All these attempts to protect and manage southern forests, however, clashed with the strong American traditions of quick profits and individualism, as well as the southern suspicion of outside interference.

The commercial development of agriculture and forestry along with the fashion trade's desire for fur and feathers sped depletion of southern wildlife. The passenger pigeon disappeared completely while other species experienced rapid decline. State laws designed to protect favored species such as fish were spottily enforced, if at all. One historian claimed that the imposition of game and hunting laws in the South stemmed partially from southern white determination to maintain control of blacks after Reconstruction. Many blacks had supplied food for their families partly by hunting on unfenced public and private land, so hunting restrictions made the blacks more dependent on white landowners for their employment. Throughout the Gilded Age the American Ornithologists Union (AOU) joined with the Audubon Society to promote passage of model laws listing game birds and protecting nongame species. Although these attempts were often ineffective, their proposal represented a changing attitude among scientists and some sportsmen concerning feathered wildlife. Passage by Congress of the Lacey Act in 1900 spurred more effective state regulation of commercial hunting.

Water projects, both reclamation and flood control, became prominent during the Gilded Age. Southern interest in water projects centered generally on attempts to control floods on the Mississippi River or to improve navigation on southern streams. Responding to a proposal by Louisiana Congressman Randall L. Gibson, President Rutherford B. Hayes signed a bill establishing the Mississippi River Commission (MRC) in 1879—the first time the federal government had agreed to help control floods on an American river. Throughout the Gilded Age both the MRC and government policymakers debated the best technology for controlling floods on the mighty river, as well as the constitutionality of federal aid for flood control. Southern support helped establish the precedent for active federal participation in flood control activities. Ironically, by adopting a "levees only" approach the MRC actually aggravated flooding on the river. Levees constricted the river, forcing floods to rise higher and bringing extensive damage to property in the floodplain.

The period from 1900 to 1930 saw the development of embryonic conservation movements in the South that promised to halt the exploitation of southern resources. Many factors, ranging from the boll weevil pestilence to the influence of agricultural experiment stations, moved southern farmers toward more scientific and modern agricultural methods. In many ways the South responded positively to the Progressive conservation movement. Rational development of natural resources coincided with the New South emphasis on economic development, whether it be forest cultivation, river basin planning, or wildlife management. Following the lead of Theodore Roosevelt, many southern governments began to focus more attention on conservation matters, yet there was still much resistance to centralized control over resources whether from the state or national government. Forest conservation was most often embraced by larger corporations concerned with sustained yield. By the 1920s support for scientific forestry had become widespread throughout the South with establishment of several forestry programs in regional colleges and universities. Concern for wildlife conservation and management grew among certain groups in the South, often with guidance from the Audubon Society. Although more southern states passed game control laws after 1900, enforcement still proved difficult.

Economic developments of the 1920s both challenged and encouraged the southern conservation movements. Settlement in Florida during the 1920s led to attempts to drain swamps, including the Everglades. Looked upon as progressive, such drainage often created long-range problems similar to those associated with use of levees for flood control. Discovery of oil in Texas in 1901 ushered in a new era of opportunity and conservation problems; prior to World War II most efforts to conserve oil were prompted by wise use, rather than pollution concerns. Perhaps no idea so attracted those concerned with southern economic development as did river basin planning. By 1925 the principle of comprehensive river basin development had been embodied in federal law, as demands for new approaches to flood control on the Mississippi gained support. Senator George Norris attracted increased southern support for his plans to transform the Tennessee Valley through scientific planning.

The New Deal had a profound effect on southern conservation and development policy. This effect was nowhere more evident than in the implementation of water projects in the Mississippi and Tennessee valleys. The Corps of Engineers began the impressive Atchafalaya Floodway project to help relieve floods on the lower Mississippi. Engineers were soon to learn that nature had ways of pursuing its goals despite human activities. Some scientists predicted that despite human efforts the Mississippi would eventually change its main channel to the Atchafalaya, leaving New Orleans on a backwater tributary. In no way, however, did the New Deal touch southern resources and influence conservation ideas as it did with establishment of the Tennessee Valley Authority.

New Deal policies influenced southern policies concerning forest and wildlife conservation as well. Most noted of these influences were the reforestation programs carried out by the Civilian Conservation Corps. The federal practice of purchasing cutover and eroded land for development of parks and national forests was emulated by many states. The New Deal also focused attention on the need for soil conservation, important to a region that had some of the most exhausted and eroded soil in the nation. Above all, conservation activities during the New Deal created a greater understanding of the interrelated nature of natural resource use and preservation. The experiences of World War II altered the attitude of many southerners toward conservation. Private organizations, universities, and public bureaus cooperated to provide more effective development of southern resources. Tree farming combined with improved fire prevention methods laid the basis for a sustained yield of southern timber. Critics questioned the wisdom of a timber monoculture, and while cotton remained a significant part of farm production, a revolution occurred in southern agriculture. New crops such as soybeans, improved fertilizers and farming techniques, and the use of insecticides all profoundly affected the nature of southern farming. As with the changes in timber cultivation certain groups began to question whether these changes were all environmentally beneficial.

From 1960 to 1970 Roosevelt-Pinchot concepts of utilitarian conservation gave way to ideas stressing environmental quality. Again the South followed the national trends, not always enthusiastically. The National Environmental Protection Act (1969) was most important in promoting environmental activity at the state level both through its general philosophy and through its direct application in the South. Most southern states began to develop plans to protect public lands and supervise the use of natural resources, often consciously to avoid federal intervention. In addition, some of the first federal actions to enforce environmental protection laws were taken in the South. In 1971, under the Clean Air Act, the federal government obtained its first restraining order for environmental enforcement to control air pollution in Birmingham, Ala. Bringing about a complete, if temporary, stoppage of steel manufacturing in Birmingham, the national government demonstrated the potential power it could exercise to achieve environmental improvement.

Since 1960 local environmental groups in the South have independently or in cooperation with national organizations attempted to influence environmental policy within the southern states. Efforts were made to protect the biologically unique Big Thicket of Texas and to prevent development of expensive and environmentally questionable water projects.

While most southerners continue to consider economic growth more important than environmental protection, some groups increasingly insist that the South's water supply, air quality, coastal areas, and general environment have to be considered as part of the Sunbelt movement. Given the South's advantages for economic growth, such as labor and land costs, taxes, and climate, southerners need no longer fear that industry could be attracted only at the cost of a livable environment.

See also AGRICULTURE: Crops; Diversification; / Agricultural Extension Services; Knapp, Seaman A.; HISTORY AND MANNERS: Frontier Heritage; SCIENCE AND MEDICINE: Technology; / Ruffin, Edmund

J. B. Smallwood
North Texas State University

Nelson M. Blake, *Land into Water—Water into Land: A History of Water Management in Florida* (1980); Thomas D. Clark, *Mississippi Quarterly* (Spring 1972); Albert E. Cowdrey, *This Land, This South: An Environmental History* (1983); Gilbert C. Fite, *Agricultural History* (January 1979); Paul W. Gates, *Agricultural History* (January 1979); Martin Reuss, *Louisiana History* (Spring 1982); Stanley W. Trimble, *Man-induced Soil Erosion on the Southern Piedmont, 1700–1970* (1974).

Flood Control and Drainage

Although most sections of the United States have had to cope with floods, these problems have assumed extraordinary magnitude in two regions of the South—the lower Mississippi River Valley and the Florida peninsula.

The Mississippi River both blesses and curses lower valley residents. Bearing its tremendous burden of water, the river has built up a delta of rich alluvial soil ideal for agriculture, but at times it has also overflowed its banks and taken a tragic toll in lives, homes, and property. Recognizing its threat, the founders of New Orleans ordered a protective embankment to be built. As early as 1727 Governor Étienne de Perier reported construction of an earthen wall a mile long and 18 feet wide. Thus began the type of flood control on which valley residents would have to depend for the next 200 years. Appropriately, *levée*, the French word for such an earthen embankment, passed into the American language.

From 1718 to 1850 the burden of flood control was mostly carried by individual owners of riverfront property. The French government required each to build and maintain a levee as a condition of his grant; the government intervened only to enforce the requirement and occasionally to inspect the levees. The system established by the French continued after the United States purchased the territory. This early policy resulted in the extension of levees along both banks of the Mississippi as far as they were settled. But the levees provided a frail defense. With one man's levees poorly joined to the next and differing in size and condition, the raging river would frequently break through.

A great flood in 1844 strengthened a growing demand for federal help. Arguing that the destructive waters originated in remote parts of the Union, proponents urged Congress to appropriate funds for building levees just as it provided aid for oceanic commerce. Although strict constructionists opposed any such expenditure, Congress did find a way to provide indirect assistance. In 1849 it transferred to the state of Louisiana all unsold public swampland within its borders; in 1850 it made a similar grant to Arkansas on condition that the state apply the proceeds to reclaiming the land by means of levees and drains. The provisions of the 1850 act were extended to each state where swamp and overflowed land might be situated. Fifteen states received grants totaling almost 64 million acres. The South acquired almost two-thirds of this land: Florida, 20.2 million acres; Louisiana, 9.3 million acres; Arkansas, 7.6 million acres; Mississippi, 2.2 million acres; and Alabama, .4 million acres.

The swampland grants resulted in much state and local governmental activity. Florida's huge share encouraged schemes for draining the Everglades, but reversals of policy, diversions of land to the railroads, and the disruption caused by the Civil War delayed any effective reclamation. The lower Mississippi Valley states made a stronger effort to use the swamplands for the specified purpose. State and local agencies initiated works to prevent floods and provide drainage, but poor management, unsound projects, local jealousies, and fiscal chicanery handicapped the movement. Most of the new structures were swept away by floods in 1858 and 1859, and the whole levee system was devastated by military action and neglect during the Civil War.

A third period marked by renewed state activity and a cautious infusion of federal aid began in 1879 when Congress established the Mississippi River Commission to supervise all federal public works on the river. At first these projects were intended for the benefit of navigation, but the Army Corps of Engineers found indirect ways to help with the flood problem. As early as 1861 Captain Andrew Humphreys and Lieutenant Henry Abbot published an influential report, *Physics and Hydraulics of the Mississippi River*, which analyzed the inadequacies of existing levees. In planning later works for improving navigation, the Army Corps began to design levees that would also protect against floods. Local levee districts still bore the major burden, but the Commission served a vital coordinating function. By 1912 the combined efforts of state, local, and federal agencies had extended the levees along the Mississippi and its tributaries for 1,500 miles—the length of the Great Wall of China.

In Florida the ancient dream of draining the Everglades was revived by Hamilton Disston, heir to a Philadelphia toolmaker's fortune, who in 1881 contracted with the state to reclaim a vast area overflowed by Lake Okeechobee and nearby lakes and rivers. Disston was to receive one-half the drained land. Despite a major effort, the enterprise failed. In 1906 the state itself began to build a system of canals to lower the level of Lake Okeechobee and reclaim Everglades land. Modestly successful in opening up new regions for agriculture and residence, the program involved the state so deeply in debt that it had to be halted during the Great Depression.

The latest period of flood control began about 1928 with the federal government accepting major responsibility. Great floods in 1912, 1922, and 1927 demonstrated the inadequacy of the Mississippi levees. The 1927 flood, the most catastrophic of all, inundated 26,000 square miles of land, took 214 lives, drove 637,000 people from their homes, and ruined $236 million worth of property. Poet William Alexander Percy chronicled it in *Lanterns on the Levee* (1941). Events elsewhere emphasized that the problem had become a national one. In 1926 and 1928 hurricanes drove the waters of Lake Okeechobee through frail local levees and took more than 2,000 lives. California and New England both suffered serious floods, strengthening the call for federal government assistance.

At the request of Congress the Army Corps of Engineers began to study the flood problem on a national basis. In 1928 Lieutenant General Edgar Jadwin, chief of the Corps, laid out a $300 million program for the Mississippi and its tributaries. In addition to stronger levees, Jadwin advised deepening river channels, establishing floodways, and studying the feasibility of storage reservoirs. In the so-called 308 reports the Corps provided studies of over 200 other rivers, showing how they might be managed to serve multiple purposes—flood control, navigation, irrigation, and power generation.

Congress accepted the federal responsibility in a series of laws. The Reid-Jones Act of 1928 authorized the Corps to proceed with the Jadwin Plan. A 1930 law provided for the construction of Hoover Dike, an 85-mile long levee around Lake Okeechobee. In 1933 the Tennessee Valley Authority was established with a mandate to build multipurpose dams. The movement culminated in the Flood Control Act of 1936, affirming that flood control was "a proper activity of the Federal Government" and "in the interest of the general welfare." Some 2,111 projects spread over 31 states were approved.

These historic laws, extended by later ones, have resulted in a huge federal flood control program. The Mississippi levees have been strengthened with revetments of cement and steel. To speed the passage of the water, the channel has been deepened and made 152 miles shorter by cutoffs across the bends. Floodways have been provided to release surplus water in times of emergency.

Dams across the Yazoo River and other tributaries provide storage reservoirs. The federal government has also spent large sums in Florida. In 1948 Congress authorized the Central and Southern Florida Flood Control Project, a complex system of water management to benefit a large area both north and south of Lake Okeechobee.

Despite general acceptance of the value of flood control, this interference with nature often involved environmental damage. For example, canalizing the Kissimmee River, the principal source of Lake Okeechobee, has helped to create a serious pollution problem in the lake itself. In other places it might have been wiser to regulate development on the floodplain rather than to build dams or alter river courses. Federal budgetary problems may compel a more careful scrutiny of future proposals.

Pare Lorentz's 1937 film *The River*, which was made for the Farm Security Administration, was a striking visual portrait of the Mississippi River, its valleys and tributaries, its exploitation and pollution, and of flood control by levee building along its banks and through reforestation efforts. The vivid memory of southern flooding survives in music through blues songs such as Blind Lemon Jefferson's "Risin' High Water Blues" (1927), Sippie Wallace's "The Flood Blues" (1927), Joe Pullum's "Mississippi Heavy Water Blues" (1935), and Alabama Sam's "Red Cross Blues" (1933).

Nelson M. Blake
Syracuse University

Nelson M. Blake, *Land into Water—Water into Land: A History of Water Management in Florida* (1980); Hodding Carter, *Man and the River: The Mississippi* (1970); Pete Daniel, *Deep'n as It Come: The 1927 Mississippi River Flood* (1977); Robert W. Harrison, *Alluvial Empire: A Study of State and Local Efforts toward Land Development in the Alluvial Valley of the Lower Mississippi River* (1961); William G. Hoyt and Walter B. Langbein, *Floods* (1955); Luna B. Leopold and Thomas Maddock, Jr., *The Flood Control Controversy: Big Dams, Little Dams, and Land Management* (1954); Gary B. Mills, *Of Men and Rivers: The Story of the Vicksburg District* (1978); Dunbar Rowland, *History of Mississippi: The Heart of the South* (1925).

Forests

The Great American Forest is in good part southern. As of 1978 the estimated total commercial forest land in the South equaled 229 million acres, 40 percent of the national total. The South, moreover, contained nearly 60 percent of the nation's industrially owned timberlands. Most of the region is wooded, and virtually all of it can support forests. The southern forest consists of three general woodland types: hardwoods, pine, and various woody assemblages associated with swamps, pocosins (swamplands in an upland coastal region), and understories.

The hardwoods occupy much of the southern Appalachians, bottomlands and floodplains, and riverine environments throughout the Piedmont. Commercial hardwoods amount to about 143 million acres. More than 70 commercially important tree species make up the hardwood complex. In broad terms, the hardwoods divide into two groups—those in perennially wet bottomlands and those in Appalachian uplands. The gradation between hardwood types is subtle, and between hardwoods and pine quite variable, with each interpenetrating the other. Historically, some hardwoods were harvested for saw timber (especially oak for ships); much for furniture and charcoal; and much, in conjunction with drainage, for agricultural reclamation. Thanks to traditional logging practices and the use of fire in clearing land, most of the southern hardwood forest is of poor quality.

6773 I Pine for Thee at Gulfport, Miss.
looks as lonely as I
sometimes feel—

Pine trees, Mississippi coast, postcard, date unknown

The southern pines, however, are flourishing. Commercial pine forests cover some 100 million acres. Four pines are prominent: longleaf and slash along the Coastal Plain, and loblolly and shortleaf across the Piedmont and within interior highlands. The longleaf was the primary sawtimber species, the backbone of the southern lumber industry; the slash, along with the longleaf, was the source for naval stores; and loblolly and shortleaf were secondary sawtimber sources and, in more recent decades, the producers of pulp.

Pine and hardwoods compete for sites, and, without disturbances (principally fire) or deliberate cultivation, the pine will prevail over hardwoods. Fire was the great shaper of the southern forest: its realm was, in turn, dictated by the cultural practices and the geography of standing water. The relative distribution of pine and hardwoods still conforms to this pattern. Currently, hardwoods are being replaced by farms, especially along the Mississippi River floodplain; pocosins and coastal swamps are being transformed into pine plantations; and farm woodlots are being converted into pine, recreational woodlands, and fuelwood groves.

The present geography of the southern forest is the product of its human history. Among the American Indians, land was cleared for cultivation, then maintained as a prairie or a savanna by burning. Nearly everywhere, broadcast fire was used to control the tangle of hardwood saplings, shrubs, palmetto, and grass known as the "rough." If not burned frequently, this dense understory would supplant pine with hardwood. To perpetuate a desirable habitat and reduce fuels available for wildfire, to make travel possible, and to drive game, like deer, during hunting, nearly all naturally drained lands were fired. During droughts, even swamps burned.

Early southern settlers adopted and accelerated Indian practices. Slash and burn agriculture prepared sites for tobacco, corn, and cotton, but the soil was soon depleted of nutrients, and a pattern of shifting cultivation resulted. Agricultural land clearing across the Piedmont was completed during antebellum expansion, although pockets of forest remained in sandy areas, undrained sites, remote hills, and, where farms had been abandoned, in "old field" regeneration. The woods themselves, as long as the understory could be kept in grass, served for hunting and herding; the woods range was kept habitable by the liberal use of fire. Importing European techniques for the reclamation of wetlands, settlers drained low-lying bogs, exposing many sites to logging and fire that were not available to Indian use. They learned to tap resinous pines for sap, which could be processed into naval stores like turpentine. They cut timber for fuelwood and converted hardwoods into charcoal. Eventually, industrial logging moved into the region.

Between 1890 and 1920 the timber industry left the cutover pineries of the Great Lake states for the relatively virgin pineries of the South. Around 1909 national lumber production, concentrated in the southern yellow pine (longleaf), reached its all-time high. Even granted the extravagance of the process, however, the southern forest should have regenerated. That it did not was due, first, to the promiscuous use of fire ("woodsburning") and then, during the late 1920s, to an overly aggressive suppression of fire. Longleaf pine, in particular, shows peculiar adaptations to heat, and without fire it never recovered its former prominence. Fire practices, abandoned farmland (the result of a depressed farm economy and infestations by the boll weevil), and cutover forests made the South into a wasteland. In 1919 it was estimated that 92 million acres had been cut over and deserted.

Eventually, the forest reestablished itself. Industrial logging in the South coincided with the conservation reforms of the Progressive era and the coming of age of professional forestry. The nation's first forestry school was established at the Biltmore Estate in North Carolina. The U.S. Forest Service became active after the Weeks Act (1911) allowed for the acquisition of land for national forests; it greatly expanded its influence through cooperative programs with state forestry bureaus, themselves stimulated by the Clarke-McNary Act (1924), and quadrupled its holdings during the 1930s, as tax delinquent land accumulated and the Roosevelt Administration pushed major conservation programs. The Forest Service established two research stations, in Louisiana and North Carolina, and a forest fire laboratory in Georgia. Among private landholders, the experiment by Henry Hardtner in Louisiana—sustained production through regeneration—had national repercussions. The Great Southern Lumber Company of Louisiana and the Crosset Lumber Company of Arkansas were models for fire protection and management, and in 1941 the Forest Farmers Association was created as a southern counterpart to the Tree Farm movement of the Northwest. Professional foresters took the torch away from folk practitioners and developed the techniques of prescribed burning—one of the South's great gifts to land management in the United States.

But the crucial event was the development during the 1930s of a pulp industry based on the southern pines. Eventually, the southern forest would produce half the pulp and a third of the paper in this country. Pine plantations for pulp production, based on short rotations and genetically selected species, would become big business, though southern agrarianism resisted its encroachments as it did other forms of industrialization. Thus, industrial logging completed the destruction of the South's First (virgin) Forest; the commercialization of the southern pine for pulp led to the Second Forest; and the Third Forest is now undergoing harvesting and regeneration. The environmental potential of the southern forest is immense. Its limitations are socioeconomic, principally related to ownership patterns. By the 1970s about 10 percent of the southern forest was publicly owned and 20 percent was held by corporations; 70 percent remained in private hands, mostly under the care of farmers. Less than 1 percent of forest land was devoted to parks or wilderness.

See also AGRICULTURE: / Naval Stores; INDUSTRY: / Furniture Industry; Timber Industry; SOCIAL CLASS: / Timber Workers

Stephen J. Pyne
University of Iowa

John W. Barrett, ed., *Regional Silviculture of the United States* (2d ed., 1980); Thomas D. Clark, *The Greening of the South: The Recovery of Land and Forest* (1984); Henry Clepper, *Professional Forestry in the United States* (1971); Stephen J. Pyne, *Fire in America: A Cultural History of Wildland and Rural Fire* (1982); U.S. Forest Service, *Forest Statistics of the U.S.* (annual).

Gardens and Gardening

The South has long been noted for beautiful antebellum homes with lovely gardens, spacious lawns, beautiful large trees, and masses of flowering shrubs. With many beautiful native and introduced plants to use in landscaping and one or more botanical or public display gardens in nearly every southern state offering workshops, the southern gardening tradition continues.

A large proportion of the ornamental plants used throughout the southern states are broadleaf evergreens. These are far more predominant than the deciduous plants or the narrow-leaved evergreens such as junipers and dwarf hemlock pines. Once southern gardens consisted primarily of the magnolia (the handsome large evergreen southern magnolia), camellias, azaleas, boxwood, gardenias, groundcovers of English ivy, liriope, crape myrtle, and daylilies for summer color. This is now changing as gardeners use exciting deciduous and evergreen plants such as elaeagnus, hollies, hydrangeas, flowering quince, and viburnums. Interest in native plants such as native azaleas and many herbacious plants has also increased; some of these are grown by specialty nurseries.

The *Camellia japonica* was introduced to Europe from Asia in the 18th century. An old but popular variety, "Alba Plena," was displayed in Belgium in 1811 and arrived in the northeastern United States in 1880. Throughout the Northeast camellias were grown as tub plants for the greenhouse or conservatory and are still popular for this use. Large collections of camellias were a part of plantation life near port cities in South Carolina, Alabama, Louisiana, and Mississippi. In the late 1840s camellias were planted at Magnolia Gardens near Charleston, S.C. The first plants probably came from greenhouses in Philadelphia and other northern cities. Later they were imported directly from Europe. The glossy foliaged camellias range from large shrubs to small trees and are grown in shaded gardens from North Carolina southward to eastern Texas. The large flowers bloom from October to April and vary from white to pink to red or variegated. The American Camellia Society offices are surrounded by a large camellia garden and greenhouse near Marshallville, Ga. The *Camellia sasanqua*, which flowers in autumn, is also important to the landscape. Despite popular legend, the plant is not as cold hardy as *C. japonica* yet the colorful single to double flowers often suffer little if any fall damage, unlike some of the later flowering *C. japonica*.

Azalea gardens are a spectacular feature of the southern landscape. The large-flowered, evergreen Southern Indian Hybrid azaleas were first introduced from Europe to the United States as Belgian Indian Hybrids. The hybrids were developed in England and Belgium as greenhouse plants from several species native to Japan and China. Like camellias, they were used as tub plants in greenhouses and conservatories in the northeastern states before figuring as landscape plants in the South. In the 1840s they were introduced to Magnolia Gardens and proved to be hardy to the Deep South; they were soon popular throughout the Gulf Coast area. The hardier Belgian Indian Hybrids in the South became known as the Southern Indian Hybrids. The famous Fruitland Nursery in Augusta, Ga., played an important role in introducing azaleas, camellias, and many other ornamental plants to the South. A catalog of 1883 listed over 50 varieties of azaleas; unfortunately many of these old varieties are no longer available.

Southern cities such as Mobile, Savannah, and Charleston are famous for their azalea trails, roadside plantings, and special gardens lined with huge, colorful masses of such Southern Indian azaleas as the purplish-red Formosa, the Fielder's White, and the pink Pride of Mobile.

The small-flowering Kurume azaleas were known in Japan over 300 years ago and were introduced to the United States in 1915. These hardy plants survive in $-5°$ to $-10°$F, as far north as Kentucky and Maryland. Over 300 varieties of the Kurume azalea are still known in Japan and some gardens in the South have 50 or more named varieties. Over 20 Kurume azaleas are commonly grown in commercial specialty nurseries. Many of these plants were given English names after their introduction from Japan. Some of the favorites are Christmas Cheer (Imashojo), Hino (Hino de-giri), Pink Pearl (Asumakagami), Coral Bells (Kirins), Snow, and Salmon Beauty.

Other evergreen or persistent-leaved azaleas are noted in the South for flowering from early spring to May and June. These include the Glenn Dale hybrids (over 400 named varieties), the Back Acres hybrids (over 50 named varieties), and the late-flowering Satsuki hybrids, with over 600 varieties grown in the United States. The interest in growing and hybridizing new azaleas continues throughout the South, and seven chapters affiliated with the American Rhododendron Society and/or the Azalea Society of America exist in the southern states.

The South is also known for its attractive evergreen boxwood hedges and large, compact specimen plants. Two species are frequently discovered in southern gardens. *Boxus sempervirens*, the common box, was introduced from Europe and is especially popular in the South. There are many selected varieties, however. *Suffruticosa* is a popular dwarf plant known as the "true dwarf box" and is prominent in the gardens of Williamsburg and Mount Vernon. *Boxus microphylla*, from Japan, is much hardier and lower in growth, and is fond of the warmer areas of the Gulf states.

The large, handsome *Magnolia grandiflora*, southern magnolia, is typical of the South and native from North Carolina to Texas. A large tree (to 100 feet) with glossy evergreen leaves six to eight inches long, its large white flowers are borne in mid- to late spring and add a delicate fragrance to the garden.

Other broadleaf evergreens noted in southern gardens include the fragrant gardenia, tea olive, and *Elaeagnus*. Numerous hollies are used, such as the common American holly (*Ilex opaca*), the popular *Ilex cornuta* Burfordii holly, along with Japanese hollies (*Ilex crenata*). Other common broadleaf evergreens include mountain laurel, cherry laurel, leucothe, and osmanthus. Of the many deciduous ornamental plants in the South the crape myrtle is the best known. The crape myrtle (*Lagerstroemia indica*) is a large shrub or small tree known as the "lilac of the South." It is noted for its smooth, strong trunk formation and is frequently used as a street tree. The large pyramidal clusters of white, pink, red, or purple flowers appear in early to late summer. Many named varieties are available, and two favorites are Watermelon Red and Near East, a pale pink.

Other deciduous ornamental shrubs and small trees include the flowering quince or "japonica," *Chaenomeles speciosa* (lagenaria), pearl bush, *Exochorda racemosa*, hydrangeas, Bradford pear, redbud (*Cercis canadensis*), and the beautiful, native flowering dogwood (*Cornus florida*) and its many colorful varieties.

Two outstanding native shrubs are the oakleaf hydrangea and the many species of native azaleas often referred to as "wild honeysuckle." The fragrant native azaleas include the white to pink forms of rhododendron *R. canescens* (Piedmont azalea), *R. periclymenoides* [*nudiflorum*] (Pinxterbloom azalea), *R. alabamense* (Alabama azalea), the pink *R. vaseyi* (Pinkshell azalea), and the white *R. aborescens* (Sweet Azalea), *R. viscosum* (swamp azalea), and the yellow *R. austrinum* (Florida azalea).

The nonfragrant azaleas include the orange to red *R. flammeum* (*specosium*), Oconee azalea, the yellow to deep orange flame azalea (*R. Calendulaceum*), and the rare late-flowering plumleaf azalea (*R. prunifolium*).

The South has a tradition of public gardens, many of them associated with historic places such as Williamsburg, Mount Vernon, Monticello, Middleton, Hermitage, and numerous other plantation locales. Dumbarton Oaks, Biltmore, Bayou Bend, and the Elizabethan Garden represent spectacular gardens on private estates. Other well-known gardens include Callaway, Bellingrath, Cypress, Hodges, Magnolia, and Brookgreen. Botanical gardens at Fairchild in south Florida and the Plant Introduction Station at Savannah experiment with new plants to test their appropriateness to the southern environment.

Flower gardening, at a different level, has always had special meaning for the southern poor. Flowers offered an aesthetic dimension to the sometimes drab rural life, and women as far back as the 1600s set out ceramic flowerpots along porches or on steps in yards. One North Carolina mill town woman, Ida L. Moore, who was interviewed in the 1930s, was probably typical of many women in saying that "no place seems like home without a few flowers." Her husband made flower boxes out of old car gas tanks and painted them red. She grew petunias, phlox, and the simple but popular zinnias. "It's nice settin' on the porch when they's somethin' to look at besides a red, ugly hill," she said.

Writer Alice Walker has perhaps best captured the cultural importance of flower gardening for the poor, especially southern black women. She points out that, although circumscribed in much of what they could do in society, black women in the South expressed their artistic creativity, indeed their human spirituality, through such seemingly simple activities as gardening. In Walker's novel *The Third Life of Grange Copeland* (1970), the character Mem decorates with flowers the rundown houses she has to live in. Walker's own mother in Georgia did the same, ambitiously planting gardens of 50 or so varieties that would bloom from early March until November, bringing color to the lives of her family. "Because of her creativity with her flowers," writes Walker, "even my memories of poverty are seen through a screen of blooms—sunflowers, petunias, roses, dahlias, forsythia, spirea, delphiniums, verbena."

See also AGRICULTURE: Garden Patch

Fred C. Galle
Hamilton, Georgia

James C. Bonner, *Landscape* (Spring–Summer 1977); Ben A. Davis, *The Southern Garden: From the Potomac to the Rio Grande* (1971); Fred C. Galle, *Azaleas* (1974); Catherine Howell, *Landscape Journal* (Spring 1982); William L. Hunt, *Southern Gardens, Southern Gardening* (1982); Felder Rushing, *Gardening Southern Style* (1987); John Wedda, *Gardens of the American South* (1971); Brooks E. Wigginton, *Trees and Shrubs for the Southeast* (1963).

Indians and the Environment

The ecology of the South was well suited to Indian occupation, with large populations inhabiting the river valleys of the interior as well as the coastal plains at the time of white contact in the 16th century. These native people were highly successful at exploiting their ecosystem, drawing subsistence from a combination of hunting, farming, and gathering. When necessary, they purposely changed the environment, employing technologies that scholars only recently began to understand. Such economic diversity made Native American lives relatively secure. The southern Indians possessed an unusually sophisticated understanding of the environment, which provided virtually everything they needed for survival.

The largest concentration of Indian population in the western part of the South was in the Mississippi Delta and along the rivers east of it. Here the ancestors of the modern Choctaws and Chickasaws began building cities centuries before the voyage of Columbus. With the Spanish invasion, disease spread throughout the countryside killing at times 80 percent of the Indian occupants, leaving but a scattered remnant of people by 1600. To the west of the Mississippi River, Caddoan groups survived in well-protected villages, whereas on the river itself the Natchez were the dominant urban dwellers. To the east, Europeans found the Choctaws, living in towns along the Big Black, Pearl, Tombigbee, and Yazoo rivers. And to the north of the Choctaws lived their distant relatives, the Chickasaws. Hunters predominantly, the Chickasaws held the region from north-central Mississippi to the Ohio River, and eastward to the Tennessee and Cumberland rivers.

Farther east, the river valleys of Mississippi and Georgia were occupied by the Creek Nation, a loose confederacy with various subtribes including the Seminoles. The Creeks maintained some 50–60 towns after the initial decline in population brought about by European invasion. Related linguistically to the Chickasaws and Choctaws, the Creek populations were the largest in the eastern half of the South. The lands they occupied were part of an almost unbroken forest, with villages located generally along navigable streams such as the Alabama and Chattahoochee. The Cherokees lived north and east of the Creek towns in the more rugged landscapes of western Georgia, North and South Carolina, and eastern Tennessee. North and west of the Cherokees, in the Upper South, were the Shawnees, hunters of considerable skill, and eastward on the Atlantic Coast smaller tribal groups could be found such as the Virginia tribes, often called Powhatan's Confederacy, the Tuscarora, Catawba, Yamassee, Westos, and finally in Florida, the Timucua.

The forest environment of the South had an important impact on all the nations of the region, fostering unique skills needed for survival. Nearly every southern tribe turned to the hunt in November to begin the subsistence cycle, stalking the whitetail deer. The herds were approached by hunters during the rutting season when they were less inclined to run; hunters surrounded and killed the deer with bow and arrows. On occasions, thick underbrush and forest were set on fire to flush deer out, creating intermittent parklands across the South that allowed for better browsing. The winter hunt went into January, with large amounts of meat being smoked for later use. Some estimates suggest that deer provided upwards of 50 to 80 percent of the protein in the diet of southern Indians. Other game animals that contributed were bear and turkey.

The opening of farms followed the hunt in spring, with various varieties of corn, squash, and beans being planted on scattered fields, usually opened in the fertile floodplains of river valleys. Women took charge of the planting after men had cleared the wild cane and trees. This slash and burn agriculture left scars; large trees were seldom removed, but rather girted and left to die. The Indians planted their crops in hills, a practice that limited erosion. Planting sticks and shell hoes were used to break the ground. About half-a-dozen seeds were placed in each hill, necessitating some thinning when the seedlings came up. Although more food probably came from hunting and gathering, corn was a substantial part of the native diet, and all accounts suggest that yields were high. Because fertilizer was not used, however, towns had to move occasionally in order to find new land capable of sustaining crops.

Gathering provided the third means of subsistence. The list of edible foods found in the South was extraordinary, including nuts and seeds and many species of roots. Some wild plants such as sweet potatoes were semidomesticated, in that natives regularly burned off regions so that they might better compete with the surrounding fauna. Fishing was another form of gathering. Inland tribes depended less on fish for food than did coastal groups, but both stalked catfish, a southern delicacy. The fish were collected in V-shaped rock fishtraps, constructed at considerable effort, in fast-moving streams. The end of the V was pointed downstream so that the current forced fish into the enclosure. The Florida Indians were most adept at fishing and coastal food gathering. Sea life became a primary food source for them and they carried on the hunt for various edible sea creatures throughout the year. Everything from oysters to whales were taken, with men stalking the larger animals and women and children working primarily as gatherers. Even sharks were hunted, although the technique used to take them is still unclear. Apparently, they were clubbed while in shallow water.

The obvious diversity in subsistence forms of southern Indians led to a keen perception of nature and environment. Indian religion and social organization evolved around this economic relationship with nature. Cherokee hunters, for example, carefully disposed of the bones of animals they had taken, not wanting to offend their spirits. Florida tribes also treated with respect the remains of whales and fish. The planting of corn and the harvest were occasions for careful thought and celebration. Southern Indians manipulated the ecosystem to its fullest, changing the natural environment when necessary to suit needs, but living within its bounds more fully than most other civilizations in history.

See also ETHNIC LIFE: Indian Cultural Contributions; GEOGRAPHY: Indians and the Landscape

Gary Clayton Anderson
Texas A&M University

Robert S. Cotterill, *The Southern Indians: The Story of The Civilized Tribes before Removal* (1954); Frederick Hodge, ed., *Handbook of American Indians North of Mexico*, 2 vols. (1971); Charles Hudson, *The Southeastern Indians* (1976); Lewis H. Larson, *Aboriginal Subsistence Technology on the Southeastern Coastal Plain during the Late Prehistoric Period* (1980), Wilcomb E. Washburn, *The Indian in America* (1975); Richard White, *The Roots of Dependency: Subsistence, Environment, and Social Change among the Choctaws, Pawnees, and Navajos* (1983); J. Leitch Wright, Jr., *The Only Land They Knew: The Tragic Story of the American Indians in the Old South* (1981).

Insects

Imagine southerners living in a world without the flicker of the firefly, the chirp of a cricket, the buzz of the honeybee, or the flutter of a swallowtail butterfly. They would probably prefer to live in a world without the bite of a mosquito, the itch of a chigger, the sting of the wasp, or the invasion of cockroaches. Southerners cannot escape the influence of insects. As a group, insects comprise the largest and most diverse form of animal life on earth, a fact southerners can easily believe on summer nights.

Most people enjoy products like silk and honey that are made by insects. Southerners have been especially successful at the business of raising bees. They sell packaged bees—including a queen and her workers—to northerners, whose bees die during the cold winters if left outdoors. A common sight for travelers in the South is people by the side of the road selling jars of such local honey flavors as sourwood, tupelo, and orange blossom.

Shellac and carmine dyes are also products of insects, and many foods are available only because insects pollinate the plants from which they are produced. Although unknown perhaps to most people, significant benefits accrue from the lives of literally hundreds of insect species, which prey on other insects or parasitize other insects.

Throughout history insects have been well known for their ravages of humans and their domesticated animals, to crops and other material possessions. A negative image has resulted. One interested in learning more about how insects have influenced humans through the ages might begin with biblical accounts of swarms of flies or locust (grasshopper) plagues (Exodus 8:24, 10:4, and 10:13), and any text on the history of Europe will give a detailed account of the Black Plague.

American history is equally rich in its accounts of insect-human relationships. Indeed, settlement of many areas of the southern United States was greatly influenced by mosquitoes. Mosquitoes infested the early English colony at Jamestown and contributed to the diseases of the 1609 "starving time," which almost destroyed the colony. Later, southerner Walter Reed discovered that the mosquito (*Aedes aegypti*) transmits the yellow fever virus, and he helped to end a great plague in the region.

The fire ants (*Solenopsis invicta* and *Solenopsis richter*, the red and black imported fire ants) are pests common through the South. The red imported fire ant arrived from Brazil more than 60 years ago, apparently entering the South through wood off a freighter at Mobile. By 1985 these ants had caused nearly $59 million in damage to soybean crops, and one study by the Mississippi Cooperative Extension Service estimated that 744,000 people are stung annually in that state. The Mediterranean fruit fly has periodically endangered the South's citrus fruit industry, the screwworm has been costly for cattle growers to combat, the Texas cattle tick devastated cattle in years past, and the pine bark beetle is currently threatening the region's trees.

Perhaps no insect alien has gained greater notoriety than the boll weevil, originally a native of Mexico and Central America, because of its devastating effect on cotton culture during the early 1900s. In 1919, though, the citizens of Coffee County, Ala., erected a large monument to the boll weevil on the town square of Enterprise as acknowledgment of its influence on the economy of the region. The boll weevil was credited with causing farmers to pursue more profitable ventures like peanuts and livestock in the southern states.

Many insects that humans label as pests became pestiferous because of the alteration of environments to suit human needs. Southerners live in heated homes, thus creating a somewhat tropical habitat for formerly tropical creatures such as cockroaches; southerners drained floodplains and planted them with crops, creating vast "food tables" for literally hundreds of native and imported insect species; and, as Americans learned to travel by wheel, sea, and air, they ignored insect "hitchhikers" like the Hessian fly, the European corn borer, and the smaller European elm bark beetle.

Insects have been the subject matter for a variety of cultural expressions in the South. Insect life is portrayed through folk sayings such as the old rule for planting corn: "One for the cutworm, One for the crow, One to rot, and Two to grow." Because of the sheer numbers of places that insects inhabit, southern language is graced with such expressions as "finer than a gnat's eyeball!" and "snug as a bug in a rug." Vernacular names chosen for many common insects reveal that nonentomologists can be good observers of nature. Such names as devil's horse for the praying mantis, dung roller for the adult dung beetle, snake doctor for any of the numerous species of dragonflies, and chicken choker for the larva of the tiger beetle are not the common names accepted by professional entomologists, but they are accurate statements about each insect's behavior.

On the other hand, certain vernacular names such as waterbug for the Oriental cockroach and locust for the dog-day or 13- and 17-year cicadas have come about from observations, but convey misconceptions about the insect's ecology. Vernacular origins were likely for many of the accepted common names of insects including the tumblebug, hornworm, blisterbug or blister beetle, stink bug, water strider, cabbageworm, ladybug or lady beetle, plant louse, head louse, crab louse, bluebottle fly, house fly, stable fly, horse fly, deer fly, bedbug, mayfly or fishfly, May beetle, and June beetle.

Southern literature and music reflect the human-insect interaction. James Agee recalled in his short vignette, "Knoxville, Summer, 1915," lying in the yard of his family's house, after supper, listening to "the dry and exalted noise of the locusts," and that of the crickets, which was "of the great order of noises." Like many a southern child, he chased fireflies—or lightning bugs, as they are called in the vernacular. Preacher Will Campbell entitled his autobiographical memoir about growing up in Mississippi *Brother to a Dragonfly*, and used an image of that insect to convey his moving relationship with his brother. In a more humorous vein, Harper Lee made a rollicking scene in *To Kill a Mockingbird*, when Burris Ewell inadvertently disrupted the school classroom by carrying a head louse—a cootie—in his head to school.

"Just looking for a home, just looking for a home" is a verse from the boll weevil ballad, one of the most popular southern folksongs. Kokomo Arnold sang the "Bo-Weevil Blues." Bobbie Gentry's song "Bugs" is a veritable compendium of good-natured human annoyance with insects, evoking images of a "granddaddy long legs" creeping up a screen, boll weevils in the cotton, dirt daubers and red wasps swooping out of the sky, and yellow jackets buzzing around one's head; of shooing flies from the table and avoiding chiggers in the blackberry bushes.

Women in the South made spider leg quilts, in tribute to a close relative of insects; the pattern had 12 to 16 strips arranged like the limbs of a spider. Finally, one university, Georgia Tech, has made an ultimate modern southern tribute to an insect—the mascot for its football team is the Yellow Jacket.

See also AGRICULTURE: / Boll Weevil; Pest Control

T. J. Helms
Mississippi State University

W. J. Holland, *The Moth Book: A Popular Guide to a Knowledge of the Moths of North America* (1903); Maurice T. James and Robert F. Harwood, *Herm's Medical Entomology* (1969); Robert E. Pfadt, ed., *Fundamentals of Applied Entomology* (4th ed., 1985).

Land Use

Approximately 27 percent of the land area of Mississippi, Louisiana, and Arkansas, 26 percent of Texas and Oklahoma, and 16 percent of the Southeast as a whole is used for crops and pasture. These averages, varying from 36 percent in Oklahoma to 11 percent in Florida, place the South behind corn belt states and the northern plains' wheat belt, but ahead of the Northeast, mountain states, and the West as an agricultural region. Former Confederate states account for approximately 20 percent of the nation's cropland harvested.

The large arable area, in relation to its small population, has resulted in two centuries of widespread land exploitation. As historian Lewis C. Gray put it, "Planters bought land as they might buy a wagon—with the expectation of wearing it out"; the wave of farmers that swept from Virginia to Texas planting corn and cotton thus "passed like a devastating scourge." Poor husbandry, stemming from lack of motivation rather than ignorance about fertilizers or crop rotation, brought about soil exhaustion and erosion before the Civil War. In 1850 the South was basically a mixed farming region. Plantations, mostly cotton, represented 18 percent of holdings. The remainder took the form of farms whose size was greater than the national average; improved land was average, but value of holdings fell below the average. Livestock numbers were higher in the South, where 60 percent of U.S. swine, 90 percent of mules, about 50 percent of meat cattle, and a third of the country's sheep were run.

During Reconstruction the character of agriculture remained constant; after 1900, however, diversification and specialization and the shift away from cotton and corn began. Land planted in crops peaked in the 1920s, then declined. Texas, which had the largest harvested acreage, dropped from 30.6 million acres in 1930 to 22.2 million acres in 1960 and 19 million acres in 1970, a 35.5 percent decline. Farm numbers also tumbled 30 percent between 1950–60, and 9 percent in the 1970s to a total of 159,000, or 7 percent of the nation's total. Less cultivation, fewer farms, and more specialized crops have been the trend in many southern states.

Irrigation agriculture has boomed. In the mid-1970s almost one quarter of Texas's harvested cropland was irrigated. Six million acres under cotton and grains in the Panhandle and Coastal Plain represent a sevenfold increase in irrigation since 1939. Florida ranked eighth after Texas with 1.6 million acres irrigated, and Arkansas was 12th with 950,000 acres.

Rice requires heavy drafts of water and is concentrated in the South. Arkansas grows more than 1 million acres, Texas and Louisiana exceed 500,000 acres each, and Mississippi has 200,000 acres in long-grain rice.

Horticulture, drawing upon irrigaton, is pronounced. South Carolina ranks second in peaches, and Georgia is third. Florida excels in citrus. Just over 1 million acres nationwide are in grapefruit, oranges, lemons, and other citrus crops. Florida produced six times more than California and four times more than second-ranked Texas in 1978. Similarly, over 4 times more oranges come from Florida than California and 28 times more than from third-ranked Texas. Large-scale beekeeping to bolster pollination has a strong foothold with the growing season and varied subtropical and warm temperate produce. Florida has the most bee colonies (356 in 1978) after California (504), followed closely by North Carolina (190), Texas (150), and Tennessee (140).

Other specialized crops are tobacco, peanuts, and soybeans. Tobacco has had a southeastern focus where North Carolina's 399,000 acres (in 1978), 8 percent of cropland, were almost double Kentucky's acreage (195,000), followed by Virginia (73,000) and South Carolina (71,000). Yields have rocketed in North Carolina from 12 million pounds in 1850, triple that in 1900, 12.5 times that by 1950. The tobacco yield was 850 million pounds in 1978.

Georgia has 530,000 acres, 11 percent, of cropland in peanuts. Texas is second with 307,000 acres, followed by Alabama (216,000), North Carolina (169,000), and Oklahoma (123,000). Virtually all the 1.5 million acres in peanuts are in nine southern states.

Since 1950 soybean acreage has grown fourfold nationally, and soybeans are a major southern crop. Arkansas has about 4.7 million acres or 65 percent of the cropland. The Midwest dominates in acreage, but Mississippi (3.7 million acres), Louisiana (2.7), Tennessee (2.3), and Alabama (1.6) are important. These four states have a combined 75 percent of their croplands in soybeans.

Grassland pasture, covering 96 million acres or 57 percent of Texas, produced 6 million beef cattle in that state in 1979. Surprisingly, Arkansas, Kentucky, Tennessee, and Florida have over 1 million beef cattle each, or 12 percent of the U.S. total.

Two factors explain the decline in the use of land for agriculture in the 20th century. First, woodland is extensive, accounting for two-thirds of Alabama and Georgia, and over one-half of South Carolina, Florida, Mississippi, Arkansas, Louisiana, and Virginia. These states possess roughly 30 percent of forest area in the nation and have supplied 38 percent of the timber. Peak years of production were in 1916 and 1925, but output declined to a steady 20 percent, mostly softwood timber. Crop intensification, however, has released marginal lands back to native vegetation, and forest development, producing stands of even-age, quick-growing trees, has extended pinelands.

Second, one-third of the American population now resides in the 15 states termed the Sunbelt. Urban and other special use categories have increased to reflect the 22 percent population growth there in the 1970s. Florida and Texas are over 80 percent urban, and neighboring states have sizable urban populations. Over 14 percent of Florida falls into the urban industrial category. The Texas-Louisiana "oil patch," cities in Oklahoma, and the manufacturing belt in the Southeast are expressions of metropolitan land use in the region.

See also AGRICULTURE articles; GEOGRAPHY: Land Use; URBANIZATION: Urban Growth

Robin W. Doughty
University of Texas at Austin

Thomas D. Clark, *The Greening of the South: The Recovery of Land and Forest* (1984); Donald B. Dodd and Wynelle S. Dodd, *Historical Statistics of the South, 1790–1970* (1973); Lewis C. Gray, *History of Agriculture in the Southern United States to 1860*, 2 vols. (1932, 1941); Sam B. Hilliard, *Hog Meat and Hoecake: Food Supply in the Old South, 1840–1860* (1972); U.S. Department of Agriculture, *Agricultural Statistics: 1980* (1980); U.S. Department of Agriculture, Economic Service, *Major Uses of Land in the United States: Summary for 1969* (1969).

Natural Disasters

Natural disasters suddenly convey the vulnerability of human life and the fragility of civilization. They violently disrupt the fabric of society and create human misery as well as social dislocation. In the South most natural disasters are caused by weather-related phenomena—violent thunderstorms, tornadoes, floods, and hurricanes. The complex mechanics of warm, moisture-laden air from the Gulf of Mexico combining with the cool, drier air from the North spark violent thunderstorms that often engender short-lived tornadoes that tear unforgivingly across the landscape. Tropical weather patterns also spawn depressions that often evolve into hurricanes that threaten the Gulf and Atlantic coasts from June to November. Most of the South is also subject to heavy, anomalous rainfalls that push rivers beyond their banks, transforming towns and farms into a surreal watery landscape. The following cases illustrate the capricious forces of nature that often overwhelm the puny efforts of humankind to provide safe, comfortable habitats.

Thunderstorms are common natural occurrences of uncommon power and energy. A typical storm might be three miles across its base, tower 50,000 feet into the air, contain a half-million tons of condensed water, and release 10 times the energy of the atomic bomb dropped on Hiroshima. Tornadoes are the most devastating result of thunderstorms. Although they occur throughout the world, the American South and Midwest experience more tornadoes than anywhere else on earth. Southeastern tornadoes tend to be more deadly than those in the Great Plains and Midwest. Twisters in this region strike more often at night, are usually obscured in clouds and heavy rain, and are less prone to early detection than those that often are observed miles away on the plains. In fact, from 1916 to 1974 more tornado-related deaths occurred in Mississippi than in any other state—1,091.

Tornadoes sometimes break out in large patterns. In the so-called super outbreak of 2–3 April 1974, a record 148 tornadoes swept across the Upper South and Lower Midwest. Entire communities such as Xenia, Ohio; Brandenburg, Ky.; and Guin, Ala., were almost totally devastated. Losses totaled 315 dead, 6,142 injured, and $600 million in property damage. More than 9,600 homes were destroyed and 27,590 families suffered to some degree. The combined length of the tornadoes' paths was an incredible 2,598 miles.

A series of tornadoes also sliced through Mississippi and Georgia on 5–6 April 1936. At Tupelo, Miss., a huge tornado mangled the city's residences and business district, destroyed its municipal water reservoir, killed 216 persons, and injured 1,500. The next morning two tornadoes ripped through Gainesville, Ga., and ignited a large fire. Deaths totaled 203 and injuries from the funnels and fire reached 934. Gainesville, like other communities, suffered multiple tornado strikes. A 1903 twister claimed 28 lives and another in 1944 took 44.

Hurricanes develop over southern portions of the North Atlantic, as well as over the Gulf of Mexico and the Caribbean Sea, usually during the "season" that lasts from 1 June to 31 October. On average, 8 to 10 storms a year are large enough to be named by the U.S. Weather Service and carefully monitored as possible risks to mainland areas. The combination of great size (hurricanes average 100 miles in diameter) and long life compounds their destructive powers. They are the most damaging of all geophysical disasters because they produce heavy rainfall, high winds, and flash floods, as well as powerful storm surges and tides.

The first written account of a hurricane in the South recorded the destruction that occurred at Jamestown, Va., on 27 August 1667. The "dreadful Hurry Cane" produced "such violence that it overturned many houses, burying in the ruins much goods and many people . . . the sea swelled twelve foot above the normal height drowning the whole country before it."

Hurricanes occur along the Atlantic Coast, but the seaboard of the Gulf of Mexico is more prone to these violent attacks. Gulf Coast hurricanes usually follow a track toward the northeast and dump heavy precipitation across large areas of the South, causing widespread flash floods.

At the turn of the century, Galveston, Tex., was a thriving, prosperous community that boasted the fastest-growing port in the United States. Much of the city was built on a barrier island, with the highest point only 20 feet above sea level. When a hurricane struck the morning of 8 September 1900, a ship broke from its moorings and crashed through the three bridges to the mainland, cutting off any chance of escape. Tides soon rose 20 feet above normal, tearing apart homes and buildings and reshaping them into a two-story-high mass of debris that was driven inland by the storm surge. An estimated 6,000 of Galveston's 20,000 residents died, a weather catastrophe unequaled before or since. Because of the threat of disease, masses of bodies were piled into trenches and burned—an acrid postlude to the worst natural disaster in the nation's history.

As the Miami, Fla., area developed in the 1920s, the fertile muck lands surrounding Lake Okeechobee became a source of produce for Florida's urbanites. Hundreds of small shantytowns arose near the lakeshore to house fieldworkers, and long mud dikes were built to mitigate flooding. On 16 September 1928 a hurricane with winds estimated at 160 miles per hour drove the lake waters across the flat landscape, collapsing dikes and drowning hundreds of people. The final death toll was estimated between 1,800 and 2,500, the second worst hurricane disaster in American history. After the storm, the federal government funded a massive flood control program for some 12,000 square miles of the Lake Okeechobee Everglades area to prevent future disasters.

Hurricane Camille (14–22 August 1969) was by far the most powerful hurricane of recent times. It devastated the Louisiana, Mississippi, and Alabama Gulf Coast with winds over 170 miles per hour and gusts up to 200. Storm surges reached almost unbelievable proportions, including an estimated 25-foot height at Pass Christian, Miss. (The National Weather Service estimates that storm surges cause 9 of 10 hurricane-related fatalities.) Camille caused 152 deaths in Mississippi and Louisiana and, after passing over the Southeast, dumped unusually heavy rains on the Mid-Atlantic region. Some 21 inches of rain fell within 24 hours over parts of Virginia and West Virginia, causing serious flash floods.

Because of relatively heavy rainfalls, much of the South is prone to flash, general, and backwater flooding. The propensity of people to farm, build, and live upon former floodplains poses hazards to lives and property. Flood control measures such as levees, dams, pumping plants, and channel improvements have reduced these threats in many areas. For example, the Mississippi River and portions of its tributaries are now being controlled by the massive Mississippi River and Tributaries Project authorized by Congress in 1928 and still only 76 percent complete. The project was developed in response to the catastrophic 1927 flood that caused crevasses in levees and sometimes spread out nearly 100 miles. The statistical dimensions of the tragedy were nightmarish: 16.6 million acres flooded; 162,000 homes inundated; as many as 500 killed; and 325,500 people cared for in refugee camps. Then Secretary of Commerce Herbert Hoover headed a relief effort that included 31,000 volunteers.

Some parts of the South have also experienced major seismic activity. The most violent and prolonged series of earthquakes in U.S. history occurred in the supposedly seismically quiet Mississippi Valley, far from the great faults of the West. During the early morning of 16 December 1811, a series of tremors centered near New Madrid, Mo., literally tore apart the landscape. Cabins and houses creaked and groaned, huge waves capsized boats on the Mississippi, trees swayed and snapped, and huge fissures opened in the earth. The shocks were felt over two-thirds of the United States and continued intermittently until 7 February 1812. An estimated 150,000 acres of timberland were destroyed and new lakes were created in Arkansas (Lake Francis) and in Tennessee (Reelfoot Lake). In addition, thousands of acres of farmland were transformed into swamps through settling. So severe was the damage that in 1815 Congress passed the first national disaster relief act, which enabled owners of ruined property to obtain equal tracts of land elsewhere.

The South's other major seismic event occurred near Charleston, S.C., the evening of 31 August 1886. Felt as far away as Boston and Bermuda, the earthquake destroyed or badly damaged most of the city's major buildings, caused more than $5 million damage, and claimed some 111 lives.

In the past quarter century the life-threatening potential of some disasters has been reduced by improved weather forecasting, flood control, hurricane protection projects, and highly effective emergency management programs developed by federal, state, and local agencies. Nevertheless, property damage will probably escalate as the Sunbelt continues to grow.

Michael C. Robinson
U.S. Army Corps of Engineers
Lower Mississippi Valley Division
Vicksburg, Mississippi

Allen H. Barton, *Communities in Disaster: A Sociological Analysis of Collective Stress Situations* (1969); James Cornell, *The Great International Disaster Book* (1976); Gordon E. Dunn and Banner I. Miller, *Atlantic Hurricanes* (1960); Kendrick Frazier, *The Violent Face of Nature* (1979); Gary Jennings, *The Killer Storms: Hurricanes, Typhoons, and Tornadoes* (1970); David Ludlum, *Early American Hurricanes, 1492–1870* (1963); James Penick, Jr., *The New Madrid Earthquakes of 1811–1812* (1976).

Naturalists

Colonial Europeans were overwhelmed by the richness of the flora and fauna they found in the American wilderness. Until the middle of the 19th century and the development of specialization in science, those interested in examining the topography, geology, native peoples, and plant and animal life were amateurs—planters, ministers, teachers, mariners, and physicians—who had limited, if any, scientific training in a specific field of natural history. Most of them were self-taught. They generally focused their energies on the collection of data, the classification of that data into a systematic framework, and the development of a scientific nomenclature that would permit the integration of newly discovered scientific species and phenomena into a larger framework of knowledge. The knowledge they gained on the flora, fauna, peoples, and geography of this continent permitted the development of scientific specialization into distinct scientific disciplines. Although botany was the dominant interest among field naturalists in America until the middle of the 19th century, the most original contributions of Americans to science were in zoology and paleontology.

The American South lacked the libraries, gardens, and herbaria to permit the systematic study of natural history, but its varied topography and rich flora and fauna attracted many naturalists. As early as the 16th century, Thomas Harriot and John White chronicled and illustrated the plants, animals, and native peoples found near Sir Walter Raleigh's ill-fated Roanoke settlement. Harriot's *A briefe and true report of the new found land of Virginia* (London, 1588), which recorded his travels into the interior of Carolina, and possibly Virginia, distinguished between the geology of the Coastal Plain and the Piedmont, identified the mineral resources of the coastal region, commented upon the agricultural practices of the Indians, identified their crops, and recorded 28 species of mammals, 86 species of birds, and the presence of oak, elm, ash, walnut, fir, cedar, maple, witch hazel, willow, beech, and sassafras trees. His description of the American *Cervidae,* with its distinction between the deer of America and Europe, would not be surpassed for two centuries. Nevertheless, Harriot's scientific knowledge was limited, and his work provided generally accurate descriptions but little analysis. John White's delicate watercolors, housed in the British Museum, complemented Harriot's work and became the basis for the engravings that accompanied Harriot's published *Report,* the first work in English to describe the New World's natural history.

In the 17th century, individuals living in Virginia and other southern colonies served as correspondents for the Royal Society of London and provided Europeans with information ranging from the abundance of oyster shells in the soil to the proliferation of nettles, spinach, rattlesnakes, and turkey buzzards. As a result of such communications the *Philosophical Transactions* of the Royal Society began to publish accounts of New World phenomena. John Clayton and John Banister were particularly conscientious in providing English naturalists with field observations from America in the last decades of the 17th century.

John Lawson, surveyor-general for the Lords Proprietors of the province of North Carolina, traveled widely in North Carolina, and he published the results of his 1700–1701 reconnaissance as a *New Voyage to Carolina* (London, 1709). Two-thirds of this volume examined the natural history of the region and provided a description of 93 birds, 28 mammals, 70 fish, and 4 species of pine. Some of the information he provided was curious, for he classified tortoises, alligators, and snakes among insects, maintained that snakes charmed their victims and their bites could be cured by snake root, recorded that whales seldom washed ashore with their tongues intact, and noted that some American Indians hunted whales by climbing upon a whale's back and plugging up its spout. His ornithological observations and his comments upon Indian life in North Carolina were more carefully prepared and are important sources for that period. Lawson provided James Petiver, a fellow of the Royal Society and patron of John Banister, with information and specimens from North Carolina. Captured by Tuscarora Indians while on an expedition up the Neuse River, Lawson was slain on 22 September 1711.

Lawson's work was eclipsed by the endeavors of Mark Catesby. English by birth, Catesby had studied under the distinguished naturalist John Ray and became the most experienced naturalist to work in America up to that date. In 1712 he came to Virginia to live with his sister and her family to satisfy, as he notes in the preface to his major work, "a passionate Desire of viewing as well the Animal as Vegetable productions in their native countries; which are strangers in England." For seven years Catesby collected materials in Tidewater Virginia, made trips west into the Blue Ridge Mountains, and voyaged to Jamaica and the islands of Bermuda. He became an experienced field collector before returning to England in 1719. The variety of his collections and the knowledge he had gained of American flora and fauna won support in both England and America for his proposed study on American natural history. In 1722 he returned to America to conduct additional studies. For three more years he conducted field studies, made drawings, and collected specimens from North Carolina to Georgia and Florida and west into the Piedmont. Under conditions of poverty, Catesby labored to complete his work on American natural history. In 1731 his *Natural History of the Carolinas, Florida, and the Bahama Islands* began to appear in sections. The two volumes were completed in 1743. With their colored plates containing 220 illustrations, they became the most attractive works on American natural history published for the next century. Although Catesby's taxonomy was weak, Linnaeus utilized Catesby's work and frequently incorporated Catesby's descriptions and binomial names of birds, fishes, and plants in his work. Catesby's *Hortus Britanno-Americanus,* published in 1737, with its description of 85 southern trees and shrubs, was the first study in English dedicated to the trees of this continent.

As a descriptive ornithologist, Catesby surpassed the standards of his time and concerned himself with enduring problems that are still studied. Although the plates in his work have been criticized as being on occasion too brightly colored, he was a talented and influential scientific illustrator. Catesby developed the practice of portraying on one plate an ornithological, zoological, or botanical specimen in a balanced natural habitat with the appropriate ecological setting of trees, shrubs, grasses, or other animals. Alexander Wilson and John James Audubon followed Catesby's practice of including floral and faunal specimens on one plate. Through his correspondence, his collections, and his magnificent folio volumes, Catesby stimulated an interest in American natural history in America and England and on the continent.

Natural history in the South was further enhanced by the endeavors of the first native-born American naturalist, John Bartram. Praised by Linnaeus as one of the world's greatest natural botanists, this diligent and meticulous field naturalist made numerous expeditions to collect seeds and specimens for his English friend and patron, Peter Collinson. Always interested in the promotion of natural science in America, he established a major botanical garden on the banks of the Schuylkill River, corresponded with numerous European scientists and collectors, suggested to Benjamin Franklin the need for the exploration of the western reaches of the continent, contributed substantively to the understanding of southern flora and fauna, and was honored by King George III with appointment as "Botanist to the King."

With his son William, an able illustrator, naturalist, and author, he journeyed south in 1765 through Georgia and Florida with instructions from the English crown to find the sources of the St. Johns River. In the fall of 1765 they discovered along the banks of the Altamaha River a new species of small tea tree, which they named in honor of Benjamin Franklin, *Gordonia pubescens Franklinia*, today *Franklinia altamaha*. By the end of the 18th century this species was no longer seen in the wild state. The attractive specimens of this flowering tree, which can still be seen today in American gardens, are all descendants from specimens maintained by the Bartrams in their Pennsylvania garden. A new species of anise, *Ilicium parviflorum*, was also discovered on this expedition, and observations were made on soils, trees, fossils, and plants. With his vision declining, this was the 66-year-old Bartram's last expedition. Details of Bartram's experiences were published in 1767 in an *Account of East Florida*.

William Bartram maintained an interest in Florida and in 1773 embarked upon a five-year exploration of the natural history of Georgia, eastern Florida, the Carolinas, and Alabama. Named *Pucpuggy*, the "Flower Hunter," by Indians, he wandered patiently and alone through the southern wilderness studying and observing plants, animals, and Indians. Captivated by the richness and abundance of the area's natural history, he made the first detailed study of the American alligator and provided important early information on the reptiles, amphibians, birds, Indians, and plants of this region. His study contains many elements of a modern ecological survey. While Bartram's *Travels through North and South Carolina, Georgia, East and West Florida* (1791) contributes substantively to southern natural history, the wealth of romantic and exotic imagery in the *Travels* nourished the creative muses of Coleridge, Wordsworth, Chateaubriand, and other authors of the Romantic movement. "Kubla Khan" and "The Rime of the Ancient Mariner," as well as other works, bear the distinct intellectual imprint of the imagery of Bartram's *Travels*.

Science has traditionally developed in cities, and the lack of cities in the South impeded its development there. Charleston's momentary eminence in the development of southern natural history is related to its prominence as an urban area in the late 18th and early 19th centuries. Charleston physicians and planters nourished interest in natural history and provided an intellectual milieu attractive to visiting naturalists. Near Charleston in 1787, the French naturalists André and François Michaux established a nursery. André Michaux had been commissioned by the French monarch Louis XVI to ascertain which of America's trees, particularly the oaks, could be profitably grown in France. In 1801 he published the handsomely illustrated *Histoire des Chènes de l'Amérique*, the first major study of American oaks. From their base near Charleston, André and his son, François, collected specimens in the Carolina mountains, the southern Appalachians, Florida, and the Bahamas. André's posthumously published *Flora Boreali-Americana* (1803) was the first systematic study of North American flora and included valuable information about southern flora.

Thomas Jefferson's *Notes on the State of Virginia* (1785) presented a perceptive assessment of the resources and natural history of that state with clear descriptions of the Indians, animals, plants, minerals, climate, and topography found there. Jefferson took the opportunity to refute French naturalist Comte de Buffon's contention that the same species of animals and humans grew smaller in America than in Europe. Less disciplined than Jefferson in scientific interests, Constantine Rafinesque was as comprehensive as the Virginian in his activities. Born in Constantinople, he became an ardent, if occasionally unfocused, student of this nation's natural history. From 1819 to 1826 he collected specimens and studied plants, fishes, shells, fossils, and Indian mounds while a professor at Transylvania College in Lexington, Ky. Although he traveled widely and published profusely on these topics in a variety of journals, he failed to make a substantive contribution in any specific area.

John James Audubon also led a life of wide wanderings. Born in Santo Domingo, he traveled through many of the southern states in his quest to capture through his paintings the birds of America. Much of his life was characterized by economic failures and frustrations, but he labored almost without ceasing from 1827 to 1838 to complete his monumental *Birds of America*. To obtain specimens for study and to observe birds in their natural habitats, he traveled to South Carolina and Florida and to the Keys in 1831. Friends in Washington provided him with government schooners so that he could more comfortably conduct his studies on the St. Johns River and in the Keys. On this trip he made the sketches and studies for the Great White Heron and Brown Pelican, which appear in his *Birds of America*. In 1837 Audubon journeyed along the Gulf Coast to Galveston, Tex., but few significant studies resulted from this trip.

In the three decades immediately preceding the Civil War, science became more specialized. The economic advantages of natural resources began to be of concern to southern states, and in North Carolina, South Carolina, Tennessee, Virginia, Alabama, Mississippi, Texas, and Florida state geological surveys were established. The increasing pace of scientific advancement and the development of more sophisticated theoretical assumptions about the methodologies of a scientific discipline reduced in the last half of the 19th century the contributions that naturalists and natural historians could make to understanding the natural resources of the South. Although the age of naturalists was waning, the great variety of the South's flora and fauna would continue to attract the attention of scientists.

See also HISTORY AND MANNERS: / Jefferson, Thomas

Phillip Drennon Thomas
Wichita State University

Whitfield J. Bell, *Early American Science: Need and Opportunities for Study* (1955); Albert E. Cowdrey, *This Land, This South:*

An Environmental History (1983); Robert Elman, *First in the Field: America's Pioneering Naturalists* (1977); John C. Greene, *American Science in the Age of Jefferson* (1984); Kathryn Hall Proby, *Audubon in Florida, with Selections from the Writings of John James Audubon* (1974); Brooke Hindle, *The Pursuit of Science in Revolutionary America* (1956); William Martin Smallwood and Mabel Sarah Coon Smallwood, *Natural History and the American Mind* (1941); Henry Savage, Jr., *Discovering America, 1700–1875* (1979); Raymond Phineas Stearns, *Science in the British Colonies of America* (1970).

Natural Resources

Because gold and silver are not produced to any degree in the 11 states of the old Confederacy, there is a tendency to consider the South a region short of natural resources. Nothing could be further from the truth. If natural resources are defined as forms of wealth or potential wealth supplied by nature, then the South always has been blessed. Even though some of these treasures have been abused, they remain the region's greatest hope for a bright and prosperous future.

The South's most basic natural resources are high humidity and warm weather. From 45 to 70 inches of rain fall a year, and temperatures reach 90° more than 50 days annually. Most of the region enjoys a nine months' growing season.

In much of the South soils were originally rich and productive. The earliest white Virginians grew tobacco, followed by corn and wheat. South Carolina soil, in combination with large quantities of water, produced rice, and an excellent short-staple cotton was grown above tidewater in the Carolinas, in the Black Belt of Georgia and Alabama, and in the rich Mississippi Delta between the Mississippi and Yazoo rivers. The land was surely abused, leached, eroded, and often made sterile, but with conservation measures and intelligent husbandry, it can and, indeed, has come back. Whether one speaks of the Tidewater South along the Atlantic, the Piedmont above the fall line, the Appalachian Highlands, the Kentucky Bluegrass, the Gulf Coastal Plain, or the red clay hills of north Georgia and Alabama, the land has always borne foodstuffs in abundance.

The first white explorers initially exploited the most prevalent natural resource, the wild game. Deer, bear, buffalo, turkeys, passenger pigeons, bass, catfish, and other game, birds, and fish were killed in abundance. In the late 1600s more than 54,000 deerskins were shipped annually from Charleston, S.C. Even today sportsmen consider the South a paradise for hunters and fishermen.

When pioneer agriculturalists entered the South they exploited the game but also attacked another great natural resource—the great forest covering much of the land with both hardwoods and softer conifers. In the 19th and early 20th centuries much of the hardwood was cut. So favorable was the South to the growth of timber, however, that tree farming of soft woods, especially for papermaking, is today one of the region's major industries. Over 200 million acres are currently forested.

A consequence of the high rainfall is the veining of the southern countryside with deep, sluggish rivers. In the early days settlers were attracted to the river valleys because canebrakes filled them and stretched for hundreds of miles along the stream banks. Settlers' cattle could graze on the leaves of the corn-like stalks, and the destruction of the cane and replacement by fields of grain or cotton was easier than clearing the forest and preparing it for planting.

Rivers range from the Potomac and James in Virginia, the Savannah and Altamaha down the Atlantic, to the Suwannee, Apalachicola, Pearl, and Alabama along the Gulf and, in the Upper South, the Kentucky, Cumberland, and Tennessee. These rivers have always been, and remain, liquid highways of commerce; in the 20th century they have also furnished immense quantities of electric power. Greatest of all is, of course, the mighty Mississippi, immortalized by Samuel Clemens.

The rivers carry rich nutrients into the bays of the Atlantic and the Gulf of Mexico, feeding schools of edible fish and seafood including scallops, oysters, and shrimp. Apalachicola Bay off the north Florida coast is one of the world's richest bodies of water, providing fish and seafood for markets as far away as Japan.

Precious metals are rare in the South—although gold was discovered at Dahlonega, Ga., and in small quantities elsewhere—but other useful minerals have been found. Texas, Arkansas, Louisiana, and Mississippi are leading producers of petroleum and natural gas; some sulphur is also mined. Alabama, Tennessee, and Virginia (including West Virginia) produce bituminous coal. Within the South are found in quantities suitable for exploitation stone, cement, sand and gravel, and phosphates.

See also AGRICULTURE: Crops; INDUSTRY: / Mining; Oil Industry; Timber Industry; RECREATION: Fishing; Hunting

Richard A. Bartlett
Florida State University

Thomas D. Clark, *The Greening of the South: The Recovery of Land and Forest* (1984); Henry H. Collins, *Complete Field Guide to American Wildlife* (1959); Albert E. Cowdrey, *This Land, This South: An Environmental History* (1983); Gilbert C. Fite, *Cotton Fields No More: Southern Agriculture, 1865–1980* (1984); Charles B. Hunt, *Physiography of the United States* (1967); Howard W. Odum, *Southern Regions of the United States* (1936); Stephen J. Pyne, *Fire in America: A Cultural History of Wildland and Rural Fire* (1982).

Parks and Recreation Areas

Although parklands came late to the American South, the region today is renowned for its stunning variety of national, state, and local preserves. Paralleling the motivations for park establishment in the North, Middle West, and West, preservation in the South accelerated rapidly with the development of an urban population in the 20th century. Historically, after all, preservation had its roots in the city. As the noted environmental historian Roderick Nash has so eloquently written, "The literary gentleman wielding a pen, not the pioneer with his axe, made the first gestures of resistance against the strong currents of antipathy."

In this vein Thomas Jefferson was among the first to identify the natural world as a great source of national pride. In 1784, for example, writing his *Notes on the State of Virginia*, he challenged Europeans to concede the grandeur of Harpers Ferry and the Natural Bridge. "The passage of the Patowmac through the Blue ridge is perhaps one of the most stupendous scenes in nature," he wrote. "This scene is worth a voyage across the Atlantic." To the frontiersman, however, wilderness was an obstacle to settlement and commerce, an adversary to subdue rather than appreciate. It followed that most of the South throughout the 19th century was not receptive to the appreciation of the natural world visible in a Thomas Jefferson.

The gardens and common fields of Williamsburg, Va., underscored that appreciation was strongest where people of wealth, leisure, and culture prevailed. "A library, a Garden, a Grove, a Purling stream are the Innocent scenes that divert our Leisure," wrote Colonel William Byrd (1674–1744) of Westover speaking for the planter class. Byrd's emphasis on leisure—on recreation as opposed to the protection of nature for its own sake—was by far the most important catalyst leading to what might be considered the first parks in the South. To be sure, as early as 1832 the federal government set aside the Hot Springs Reservation in Arkansas; its purposes were strictly practical rather than aesthetic. Southerners concerned about their health looked to its waters for cures to common ailments; the preservation of the Hot Springs as a natural area was the last thing on most people's minds in 1832.

The first great scenic park in the United States was Yosemite, which became a state park in 1864 and then a national park in 1890. Yellowstone, the first national park, was established in Wyoming Territory in 1872. In contrast, few Americans recognized the South as naturally distinctive. Instead, adjectives such as "monotonous" and "commonplace" were often used to describe many southern landscapes. The obvious exceptions, such as the Great Smoky Mountains, were by and large outside the mainstream of national development. Equally significant, by the time Americans learned to appreciate the ecological if not the topographical distinctiveness of southern scenery, most areas worthy of park status had long ago passed out of the public domain and into private ownership.

These odds against preservation aside, southerners began making rapid strides in conservation shortly after the turn of the century. As early as 1899, for example, preservationists headquartered in Asheville, N.C., formed the Appalachian National Park Association (ANPA). In the words of the Association, time was running out for "the last of the Eastern wilderness." By "Eastern," of course, the ANPA meant the *southern* Appalachians. Areas of special concern included the Great Smoky Mountains, on the Tennessee-North Carolina border, and the Blue Ridge Mountains, running down the spine of north-central Virginia east of the Shenandoah Valley.

Congressional opposition to the creation of national parks from private lands, coupled with the claims of preservationists elsewhere in the nation that neither area possessed true national significance, frustrated the plans of the Appalachian National Park Association well into the 1920s. Finally, in 1926, Congress authorized both Great Smoky Mountains and Shenandoah national parks, provided that no federal funds would be used to make the actual purchases. Instead, acquisition was the sole responsibility of the states involved in the projects, specifically, Virginia, North Carolina, and Tennessee.

Even during the 1920s, when land values were relatively modest, none of these states had the wherewithal to complete a major undertaking such as the purchase of an entire national park. For this reason, private philanthropy became a crucial component in park acquisition in the South. Southerners were not alone in this effort. John D. Rockefeller, Jr., for example, donated nearly half the $12 million required to purchase Great Smoky Mountains National Park plus a more modest amount toward completion of the Shenandoah National Park.

Even more controversial was the establishment of Everglades National Park, located in the sawgrass and mangrove provinces at the tip of southern Florida. At least the Great Smokies and Blue Ridge Mountains had some topographical significance to link them with the common perception of national parks as scenic masterpieces; in the Everglades the elevation barely exceeded 17 feet above sea level. The Tropic Everglades National Park Association, formed in 1928 by the Miami activist Ernest F. Coe, retorted that the absence of geological uniqueness alone was no justification for denying the region national park status. The purposes of the Everglades were strictly biological: namely, the protection of vanishing forms of bird and animal life in the nation's only subtropical setting. The national parks "have much of interest in bold topography and other uniqueness," Dr. John K. Small of the New York Botanical Garden agreed. "Why not also have a unique area exhilarating by its lack of topography and charming by its matchless vegetation and animal life?"

Gradually, preservationists nationwide rallied to the argument, and in May 1934 Congress authorized Everglades National Park. Once again, however, the park faced crippling delays in the requirement that the state of Florida and private citizens must undertake the actual purchases. As a result, Everglades National Park was not formally dedicated until 1947; still another 10 years elapsed before all the critical parcels in the park had been acquired.

If the establishment of national parks came slowly and painfully, it is not surprising that state park systems in the South also lagged behind the rest of the nation. An important exception was Royal Palm State Park, established by Florida in 1916 at the urging of the Florida Federation of Women's Clubs. Originally only 1,920 acres, the tract later formed the nucleus of Everglades National Park. Another important milestone was achieved in 1924 with calls for the establishment of Cumberland Falls

State Park, Ky. In this instance the DuPont family donated $400,000 to make the purchase, thereby saving the area from a proposed hydroelectric project.

Spurred by government relief projects during the Depression, and followed by dramatic increases in population after World War II, state park systems throughout the South posted impressive gains. As late as 1933, for example, Virginia had only one state park; by 1962 her state park system included 20 separate areas totaling nearly 30,000 acres of land and water. Meanwhile, the federal government, shorn of its earlier prejudice against funding parklands from the national treasury, responded to the need for recreation areas through several agencies, especially the U.S. Forest Service, U.S. Army Corps of Engineers, and the Tennessee Valley Authority. The creation of TVA in 1933 not only led to an impressive chain of reservoirs throughout the Tennessee and Cumberland river valleys, but encouraged the use of those reservoirs—as well as tens of thousands of acres of lands bordering the manmade lakes—for a myriad of outdoor activities, including boating, fishing, waterskiing, swimming, hiking, and hunting. Undoubtedly the most impressive of these areas is the so-called Land Between the Lakes. Begun in January 1964 by the Tennessee Valley Authority, the 170,000-acre project lies in southwestern Kentucky and northwestern Tennessee, between Kentucky Lake, formed by the great dam just above the mouth of the Tennessee River, and Lake Barkley, created by a dam just above the confluence of the Cumberland and Ohio rivers.

Although such extensive disruptions of the environment have been controversial, preservation itself has made some important gains in the South during the past quarter century. As modern urbanites, more southerners of the 1960s and 1970s came to understand the concerns of Americans who confronted the disrupting influences of industrialization and urbanization a half century earlier. An outstanding example of the new ecological awareness in the South is Big Thicket National Preserve, Texas, authorized in 1974. In the spirit of Everglades National Park, the Big Thicket is purely biological in purpose, designed to protect the approximately 85,000 acres of the rare plant and animal associations once common in eastern Texas and neighboring Louisiana. Similarly, Big Cypress National Preserve, Florida, also authorized in 1974, will protect a critical aquifer northwest of Everglades National Park.

Southerners have taken further pride in their combination of recreational pursuits with preservation needs in the creation of the first national seashore at Cape Hatteras, North Carolina, in 1937. Not only has the idea caught on throughout the South, but along all the nation's coastline. In addition, the 1978 authorization of the Chattahoochee River National Recreation Area, in the heart of Atlanta, Ga., has proven a model for urban parklands across the United States.

Preservationists have not achieved everything they initially thought vital or desirable. They caution, for example, that achievements in recreation, especially recreation areas built around big dams and reservoirs, are not always in the best interest of ecological needs. Considering all the obstacles to preservation, however, especially the need to overcome widespread biases against landscapes lacking topographical distinction, such as those found in the West, environmental reform has indeed made impressive gains in the South during the past 75 years.

See also HISTORY AND MANNERS: / Jefferson, Thomas; RECREATION: Fishing; Hunting; / Colonial Williamsburg

Alfred Runte
University of Washington

North Callahan, *TVA: Bridge over Troubled Water* (1980); Carlos C. Campbell, *Birth of a National Park in the Great Smoky Mountains* (rev. ed., 1978); Hans Huth, *Nature and the American: Three Centuries of Changing Attitudes* (1957); John Ise, *Our National Park Policy: A Critical History* (1961); Roderick Nash, *Wilderness and the American Mind* (3d ed., 1982); Alfred Runte, *National Parks: The American Experience* (1979); Freeman Tilden, *The State Parks: Their Meaning in American Life* (1962).

Plants

To early colonial explorers and settlers accustomed to the relatively low plant diversity of Europe, the plants of the New World were one of its greatest wonders. The immense botanical diversity of the South has played, and continues to play, an important role in both the commerce and the culture of the region. Indeed, no other part of the country has such a strong association of its culture with plants. Native magnolias, Spanish moss, and longleaf pine and introduced plants such as indigo, rice, cotton, tobacco, peanuts, collards, okra, and kudzu elicit historical, political, economic, and culinary associations all of a regional nature.

Although the inland hardwood forests of the southern piedmont and mountains were generally similar in appearance to the deciduous forests of eastern North America and northern Europe, the first colonial settlements were in coastal areas that, in the South, are typified by forests of broad-leaved evergreens—magnolia, bay, live oak, and cherry laurel—which were quite unfamiliar. For the first two centuries after the discovery of America by the Europeans, these exotic evergreen trees, often shrouded in gray wisps of Spanish moss, typified the South. The associations remain even today a part of both actual and legendary southern culture.

Many of the early colonists truly had to "live off the land," and they depended upon the variety of native trees, shrubs, and herbs for basic needs of food, shelter, fuel, and medicine. Some southern plants that maintain a visible role in southern culture and commerce are the pecan (*Carya illinoensis*), persimmon (*Diospyros virginiana*), sassafras (*Sassafras albidum*), and muscadine grape (*Vitis rotundifolia*), all of which provide food and/or beverage; the various species of pine for pulp, timber, and solvents; the white oaks for timber and cooperage; and an array of other native hardwoods for furniture manufacture, paneling, and other specialized use. In addition, a number of native plants, such as magnolia, azalea, rhododendron, bayberry, and holly, are of horticultural value.

During the 18th century naturalists began to collect and describe the wealth of plants available in the South. Among these naturalists were John Clayton (1657–1725) of Virginia whose collections of native plants were carefully studied and published as *Flora Virginia* in 1739–43 by J. F. Gronovius of Holland; Mark Catesby (1682–1749), an English naturalist who spent the years from 1712 to 1726 in Virginia and the Bahamas and then returned to England to publish, in 1731 and 1743, his remarkably illustrated *Natural History of the Carolinas, Florida and the Bahama Islands*; André Michaux (1746–1802), a French botanist who established a garden at Charleston, S.C., and whose botanical explorations of much of eastern North America were the basis for his *Flora Boreali-Americana* published in 1817–19; the father and son naturalists, John (1699–1776) and William (1739–1823) Bartram of Pennsylvania, whose active botanical exploration, writing, and plant exchange program provided the strongest botanical link between Britain and America during the middle of the 18th century and led to the 1791 publication of William Bartram's classic *Travels through North and South Carolina, Georgia, East and West Florida*; and the English Thomas Walter (1740–88), who settled along the Santee River in South Carolina and from the surrounding area of 500 or so square miles collected the varied plants that formed the basis for his *Flora Caroliniana*, which was published in 1788.

Of special interest to the many professional and amateur European naturalists of the 18th century were the various species of insect-catching or "carnivorous" plants native to the moist, sandy, open Coastal Plain savannas of the South. Indeed, worldwide interest in these interesting and often colorful plants continues even today, and overexploration of the native populations has brought a number of these species to the verge of extinction. The greatest variety of insectivorous plants to be found in North America can still be observed, however, on protected lands in the vicinity of Wilmington, N.C. Here, with diligent searching in appropriate habitats one can find four species of pitcher plant (*Sarracenia* sp.), four species of sundew (*Drosera* sp.), nine species of bladderwort (*Utricularia* sp.), three species of butterwort (*Pinguicula* sp.), and the widely known Venus flytrap (*Dionaea muscipula*), which was first brought to the attention of botanists in 1759 by Governor Arthur Dobbs of North Carolina and which Charles Darwin called "the most wonderful plant in the world."

Wildflowers have long been a beloved part of the southern rural landscape. Tourists and natives alike have frequently commented on their growth along the roadside, in meadows, and in fields. They are hardy plants, adapting to a variety of climate and soil conditions. One sees buttercups in spring, Queen Anne's lace in summer, and goldenrod in fall. There are bloodroots, black-eyed susans, yellow lady's slipper orchids, bee balms, mayapples, atamasco lilies, bird's-foot violets, rue anemones, and jack-in-the-pulpits. In the modern South the natural heritage is reinforced through human efforts. Texas has launched a major program to promote wildflower growth, especially the state's floral emblem, the bluebonnet, making the state's highways more attractive. Regionally oriented magazines such as *Southern Living* and gardening books tell southerners how to cultivate wildflowers as parts of planned suburban gardens. Organizations such as the Plant Rescue Volunteers at the North Carolina Botanical Gardens in Chapel Hill collect endangered plants and grow plants from these specimens.

The southern states acknowledged the cultural significance of plants in the early 20th century when they adopted state flowers—goldenrod (Alabama, 1927, Kentucky, 1926, North Carolina, unofficial), apple blossom (Arkansas, 1901), orange blossom (Florida, 1909), Cherokee rose (Georgia, 1916), magnolia (Louisiana, 1900, Mississippi, 1900), yellow or Carolina jessamine (South Carolina, 1924), iris (Tennessee, 1933; earlier the passion flower or maypop), American dogwood (Virginia, 1918), and bluebonnet (Texas, 1901). Florida's nickname is the Flower State because of its abundant plant life.

During the past two centuries natural plant migrations and continued introductions by people have added many additional species to the varied flora of the South. In succession, corn, then cotton, and finally soybeans have been dominant cash crops in the region. Sugar in Louisiana, rice in low-lying terrains of the coast and river areas, tobacco in the Upper South, hemp in Kentucky—all represent cultivated plants of economic importance in specific regions within the South. The study of these native and naturalized plants is still of considerable scientific interest, and their role in commerce and recreation is of growing importance. The wise use and realistic conservation of the South's natural plant resources are issues that are also of growing relevance to the future of the region.

Plants not only add beauty to the environment and interest to a culture but are the world's only renewable resource that can reasonably be expected to supply the growing needs of humans for food, fuel, and fiber. Because the milder climate, longer growing season, and generally adequate rainfall characteristic of much of the South are often the primary factors in optimal plant growth, the plants of southern fields and forests will likely continue to play an important role in the economy, politics, and culture of the area for many years to come.

See also AGRICULTURE: Crops

C. Ritchie Bell
North Carolina Botanical Gardens
University of North Carolina
at Chapel Hill

William Bartram, *Travels of William Bartram*, ed. Francis Harper (1967); Ben A. Davis, *The Southern Garden: From the Potomac to the Rio Grande* (1971); Blanche E. Dean, Amy Mason, and Joab L. Thomas, *Wildflowers of Alabama and Adjoining States* (1973); Albert E. Radford, Harry E. Ahles, and C.

Ritchie Bell, *Manual of the Vascular Flora of the Carolinas* (1968); Harold W. Rickett, *Wildflowers of Southeastern States* (1967); J. K. Small, *Manual of the Southeastern Flora* (1933).

Plant Uses

In addition to making economic use of cultivated plants, southerners have long utilized wild plants in a variety of ways. The pattern was set long ago by southeastern Indians. Plants were an important part of their belief system. The Indians believed that humans, animals, and plants were interrelated and that a balance between these forms should exist to keep nature properly functioning. The boundary between the animal and plant realms was blurred by plants such as the Venus flytrap and the pitcher plant, which trapped and "ate" insects. This kind of anomaly was of particular interest to southerners and took on symbolic significance in their oral traditions, which attributed extraordinary powers to the roots of these plants.

Native Americans made plants part of their ritual life. The cedar, pine, spruce, holly, and laurel ranked at the top of the Cherokee belief system in terms of ritual purity. Tobacco smoking preceded council meetings of chiefs, and "black drink" was a ceremonial beverage regarded as essential for these occasions. The Indians in their own language called it "white drink," because it symbolized purity, happiness, and harmony. The Europeans labeled it "black drink" because of its color. Made from the leaves of a variety of holly (*Ilex vomitoria* Ait.), black drink was a tea with a bitter taste and high caffeine content. To make it, the Indians dried leaves and twigs and parched them over a fire to a deep brown color. The product of this process was then boiled in water, producing a dark brown liquid. It was a stimulant and a diuretic and the Indians also used it as an emetic. Early European colonists used black drink as a stimulant but gave it up after coffee and tea became more available in the later 1600s.

Wild vegetables were important as a food source for southeastern Indians. Women, the elderly, and children gathered vegetables, fruits, berries, seeds, and nuts, all of which were plentiful through much of the Southeast. Roots and tubers were the most valuable wild vegetables in the Indian diet. The big, tuberous roots that grow on various species of a green shrub called *Smilax* L., which twines itself around trees, were especially popular. The taproot of the "wild sweet potato," or wild morning glory (*Ipomoea pandurata* L.), can weigh as much as 20–30 pounds. "Swamp potatoes" were collected in low-lying marshlands from the root of arrowhead (*Sagittaria* L.). The crunchy roots of the Jerusalem artichoke were gathered in fall and winter. The southeastern Indians enjoyed the persimmon and collected muscadine grapes and scuppernongs. They also ate wild cherries, papaws, crab apples, and wild plums. The summer months saw them feasting on gathered blackberries, strawberries, gooseberries, and raspberries, and they picked from trees the huckleberries, black gum berries, mulberries, serviceberries, and palmetto berries. Nuts were especially important in the southeastern Indian diet. In autumn, they collected chestnuts, chinquapins (a small variety of chestnuts), pecans, hickory nuts, black walnuts, and the acorns of the live oak, white oak, chestnut oak, and others. They ground seeds from cockspurgrass (*Echinochloa Beau* V.), the nulumbo, and chenopodium (*Chenopodium ambrosioides* L.) to make meal to be used in cooking.

Herbs were crucial in the Indian medicinal system. The Creeks, for example, used "red root," made from the bark of the root of a willow tree, to treat rheumatism, nausea, fever, malaria, and other health problems. Creeks used "button snakeroot" to treat neuralgia, kidney troubles, snakebite, and as a spring tonic. The roots of ginseng (*Panex quinquefolium* L.) were boiled in water and used as a potion to help with shortness of breath, to heal a wound, and to keep ghosts away. Among the other main Creek herbs were angelica, wormseed, red cedar, spicebush, and horsemint—a typical list for other tribes as well.

The southeastern Indians had a multitude of other uses for wild plants: they made clothing from Spanish moss; used the bottle gourd (*Lagenaria siceraria*) for water vessels, dippers, ladles, cups, bowls, bird houses, rattles, and masks, among other things; and made baskets of bark, grass, and, especially, strips of the outer covering of cane.

Rural southern blacks and whites followed in the paths of the southeastern Indians and used wild plants as food, drink, cosmetics, and medicine, and in their arts and crafts. Much understanding of the uses of plants was also brought from Europe and Africa by early settlers. Medicine has made particular use of plants. Yellow root, tree bark, and sassafras have long been used by southern blacks as home remedies; traditional healers, or "root doctors," are still consulted to cure ailments such as headaches, loss of memory, itching, and exhaustion. Specialists are sought who deal with particular ailments. Among North Carolina root doctors, for example, mint tea is known as the treatment for hysteria, sassafras for stomach pains, and jimson tea for constipation. Allen Eaton, in a 1937 volume on the southern highlands, reported that one local root doctor in Tennessee had a list of 52 herbs that he used. The list included bloodroot, a spring tonic; blacksnake, to calm the stomach; blackberry root, for diarrhea; boneset, for colds; butterfly root, for female troubles; buckeye, for rheumatism; calamas, for an upset stomach; crab apple bark, for asthma; dandelion root, for the blood; heart leaf, good for "weak hearted persons"; larkspur tincture, for hair trouble; mullen for coughs; persimmon bark, a salve; pennyroyal, good for bed bugs and colds; redroot, to ease the bowels; stone root, good to ease kidney stone pain; slippery elm, to treat sore eyes; wild comfort, "a manhood medicine"; and redbud roots, to clean the teeth. In Louisiana sarsaparilla tea was drunk each spring in hopes of purifying the blood; a poultice of wild potato plant leaves was said to relieve boils and inflammation; copal moss, when soaked in hot water with whiskey, was an effective drink for general "miseries."

Rural whites and blacks used extracts from wild plants to color yarns, threads, baskets, and textiles. The most important colors used by Appalachian women were indigo and madder, which provided the blue and red colorings used in many blankets and quilts. Indigo comes from the plant *indigofera*; it produces yellow flowers in late summer and the boiled plant makes a blue dye, which was popular because it was a highly permanent natural dye and also subject to a variety of shades. Madder was both native and cultivated in the mountains, where pioneer women used the huge roots to produce a range of shades, from a deep red to a delicate pink, on both cotton and wool. Other natural vegetable dye colors used by southern blacks and whites included browns, blacks, and grays from walnuts; grays and tans from sumac berries; pinks and lavenders from pokeberries; yellows from hickory bark; yellow and orange from wild coreopsis; pink-yellow from sedge grass; and green from pine needles. The time of the year in which the roots, barks, hulls, fruits, nuts, leaves, seeds, stems, or whole plants are gathered can produce different shades.

During the Civil War, southerners relied on plants in various ways. They used caffeine-bearing holly berries to make tea, and they parched rye, acorns, beets, and sweet potatoes to make a coffee substitute. Chinaberries were used to make a shoe blacking paste, Spanish moss became an ingredient in rope, and cork was made from cypress "knees." Children were set to work puncturing poppies to obtain opium-bearing droplets for use as a medicine for the wounded.

Southerners used plants and their products in folk arts and crafts. Pine needles and straw, white oak strips, palmetto fronds, and other plant materials were essential ingredients in basketry. Mountain women gathered native barks, cones, grasses, seeds, leaves, pods, berries, and acorns to make home decorations for interiors or to sell to tourists and collectors. Gourds were used as sounding boxes for homemade fiddles and banjos, for decorative purposes, and for bird houses.

Southern writers and artists have frequently used plants to establish the sense of a distinctive place. Scholar Earl F. Bargainnier has noted that in literary portrayals of the myth of "moonlight and magnolias," "the aroma of magnolias—or honeysuckle, oleanders, or roses—is thick in the warm evening." William Faulkner entitled a short story "An Odor of Verbena" and described many plants, but his favorite must have been wistaria. "It was a summer of wistaria," says Quentin Compson in *Absalom, Absalom!* (1936). Quentin recalled the "sweet and oversweet" smell of "twice-bloomed wistaria" at Rosa Coldfield's house, and when he was a student at Harvard he still thought of the plant's "odor, the scent." Folk artist Theora Hamblett of Oxford, Miss., painted the calamus vine, recalling later that the morning after her stroke in 1964 she would close her eyes and see a vision of long vines and golden leaves. She had never actually seen a calamus, but she painted her vision and later discovered the actual plant it was. At a more popular level, southerners of all social classes and groups decorate their homes with paintings and ceramics of local flowers: magnolias in Mississippi, bluebonnets in Texas, and orange blossoms in Florida.

See also ETHNIC LIFE: Indian Cultural Contributions; FOLKLIFE: Folk Medicine; WOMEN'S LIFE: Healers, Women

Charles Reagan Wilson
University of Mississippi

Judith Bolyard, *Medicinal Plants and Home Remedies of Appalachia* (1981); Allen Eaton, *Handicrafts of the Southern Highlands* (1937); Wayland Hand, ed., *American Folk Medicine: A Symposium* (1976); Charles Hudson, *The Southeastern Indians* (1976); Clarence Meyer, *American Folk Medicine* (1973); Newbill Niles Puckett, *Folk Beliefs of The Southern Negro* (1926; reprint ed., 1969); Virgil Vogel, *American Indian Medicine* (1970); Eliot Wigginton, *The Foxfire Book* (1972).

Pollution

The southerner's attachment to the land has been a regional cultural axiom. Novelists, scholars, and journalists since early in this century observed an ambivalence, if not apathy, toward the region's natural environment, but poverty has encouraged industrial development irrespective of environmental consequences. Pollution, after all, was preferable to pellagra.

Even before the industrial development campaigns launched by southern states in the 1930s and 1940s, the region's natural resources proved attractive to firms more interested in extracting profits than in preserving the environment for future generations. Because local and state governments not only avoided placing legal obstacles in the path of exploiting companies, but actively supported their efforts, pollution intruded into primeval forests, fields, and cities.

The advancing petrochemical industry along the Texas (and later Louisiana) Gulf Coast during the first three decades of this century produced unparalleled water and air pollution, fouling beaches and rivers. Oil interests so controlled and influenced state government that, as late as the 1960s, the industry was self-policing. Also, the timber industry denuded wide swaths of virgin forest beginning in the late 19th century, causing soil erosion and excessive runoff.

The Nashville Agrarians were among the earliest southerners to point out the potential pollution hazards of industrialization, but such diverse writers as Howard W. Odum, William Faulkner, Robert Penn Warren, and Jonathan Daniels echoed similar themes in the 1930s. Faulkner and Warren noted the scars left by timber companies. Odum generalized from his discussion of the timber industry by observing that "the greater cultural tradition of the South has been one of exploitation of the land and its resources." Or, as Jonathan Daniels quoted a Knoxville newspaperman, "the trouble with the South was that southern people hated the land."

The post–World War II generation of southerners seemed intent on proving these characterizations true, as states offered low-cost labor, attractive financial schemes, and a moratorium on regulatory enforcement to prospective industrial investors. The results of this good business climate were predictable. The once-beautiful Savannah River was buffeted by daily discharges of sulfuric acid from an American Cyanimid plant, mercury from Augusta's Olin Corporation, and nuclear wastes from a DuPont factory. Paper mills have befouled the air and water along Georgia's coastline, in the North Carolina mountains, and in the countryside around Selma, Ala., where, by the late 1960s, according to Pat Watters, "the pall and stench of the mill were so heavy that one had to drive ten or twenty miles out of town to escape the low clouds of it." He added that "this is not an uncommon experience in the South."

Despite state and federal regulations, the petrochemical industry continues virtually unabated in its environmental negligence, infiltrating the water systems in Louisiana. One scientist warned in 1972 that the Gulf of Mexico "could become a dead sea," as a result of chemical effluvia. The national craving for fossil fuels has similarly enabled the coal regions of eastern Kentucky to bypass legal restraints. The situation is scarcely better in high consumption areas such as Houston where city highways now rival the ship channel in pollution.

The passage of the federal Clean Air Act of 1970 and the establishment of the Environmental Protection Agency that same year were significant landmarks for southern environmentalists. The federal legislation enabled Washington to intervene in especially egregious pollution cases (as in the Birmingham steel mills in 1971), and it inspired companion legislation throughout the South. More than that, by establishing uniform air and water quality standards, it removed the fear of environmentally minded states that unilateral pollution controls would frighten potential industrial investors away. Or, as journalist Joel Garreau colorfully put it, "The EPA's existence allows an Alabama mayor to say to a developer 'Now Fred, you know how much I'd like to let you dump your purple widget waste right into the drinking water here, and if it were up to me, Lord knows we could work something out, but it isn't. You know those damn boys in Washington would be all over me.'"

But "those damn boys in Washington" change with changing administrations. The historically lenient attitude of southern states toward potential polluters requires uniform and consistent enforcement of federal legislation. A vigorous Environmental Protection Agency inspired similar organizations and legislation in the South in the early 1970s, especially in Florida and Alabama, but a weak, inconsequential federal environmental presence would likely give succor to growth-at-any-cost enthusiasts, especially in the era of relatively high unemployment. If southerners were required to choose between jobs and clean air, polls indicate that a slight majority would opt for the former. Improved technology and uniform enforcement of existing legislation might render such choices unnecessary.

Increasing vigilance over environmental contamination will be necessary in the future as the toxicity of pollutants increases. The South, for example, is the region most dependent upon nuclear energy, and questions are arising about the disposal of nuclear wastes and about the safety of the nuclear plants themselves. There are some indications that carcinogenic substances from a Savannah River nuclear power plant may have seeped into the Tuscaloosa aquifer, a major southeastern water source. Moreover, cities are struggling against the costs and logistics of disposing of solid wastes, growing geometrically with population increases. Finally, an insidious visual pollution is creeping into the rural and suburban landscapes with billboards, fast-food emporia, and service stations dotting the once serene countryside. As Robert Penn Warren catalogued the lost landscape in his novel *Flood*, "the trouble was not so much what was not there. It was what was there."

There are some encouraging indications that the states are beginning to take the initiative in environmental protection as federal efforts lag. Florida has made belated attempts to protect its threatened natural water supply. Mississippi recently rescued a timber-company-threatened swamp that sustains natural life in the Pascagoula region. In the spring of 1983, in an unprecedented move, the state of South Carolina sued the federal government to clean up DuPont's Savannah River nuclear reactor, which has operated under federal contract since the 1950s. As South Carolina Attorney General Travis Medlock observed, "We sued 'em [the U.S. Energy Department] and they were shocked beyond belief. South Carolina has been very hospitable to these folks. But I think the hospitality had probably gone too far."

Indeed, the welcome mat is no longer automatic. Southern cities are appropriately shocked by the specter of the automobile-dependent, air-polluted Houston lurking in their midst and are promoting mass transit. Chambers of Commerce are discovering that clean environments are attractive to potential investors, tourists, and retirees, as that elusive "quality of life" becomes an increasingly important part of the lifestyle equation. Finally, if southerners have paid heed to environmental amenities—the carefully cultivated azaleas, the gracious and spacious parks, the proximity of the countryside, however eroded by suburban subdivision—the time is appropriate for that tradition to emerge from the shadows and replace environmental exploitation as a regional characteristic. Enough of the beauty and solace of the region's natural heritage remains to secure its enjoyment and protection for this and future generations.

See also INDUSTRY articles; MYTHIC SOUTH: / Agrarians, Vanderbilt

David R. Goldfield
University of North Carolina
at Charlotte

Nelson M. Blake, *Land into Water—Water into Land: A History of Water Management in Florida* (1980); James C. Cobb, *The Selling of the South: The Southern Crusade for Industrial Development, 1936–1980* (1982); Ray Jones, *Southern Living*

(January 1983); Linda L. Liston, *Industrial Development* (September–October 1971); Joseph A. Pratt, *Business History Review* (Spring 1978); William Reynolds, *Southern Exposure* (Winter 1979); Suzanne Rhodes, *Southern Exposure* (Winter 1979); Frank E. Smith, in *You Can't Eat Magnolias*, ed. H. Brandt Ayers and Thomas H. Naylor (1972).

Reclamation and Irrigation

Reclamation is a term more common to the West than the South. It usually denotes bringing former wastelands into production through the application of water. In the more humid South, the term has a broader usage. In most areas, settlement and expansion involved some major transformation of the land by clearing, providing drainage, and building flood control works. This process began with the first settlers of the Atlantic and Gulf coasts and continues to the present. Irrigation was first used extensively during the 17th century in Georgia and the Carolinas to support the production of rice. For over 200 years, from 1685 to 1890, rice production centered in the South Atlantic states. Then gradually a shift occurred, and by 1970 some 94 percent of the U.S. crop was produced in Arkansas, Louisiana, Texas, and California. The use of irrigation for other crops in the South, however, lagged until after World War II.

Unlike in the arid West, a chief problem of southern settlers was to keep water off rather than apply it to agricultural lands. This was especially true of the alluvial valley of the Mississippi River and its major tributaries—the focus of drainage, flood control, and other reclamation efforts since the early 18th century.

Land reclamation was largely in private hands until passage of the Swamp Lands Acts of 1849 and 1850, the first important federal legislation relating to land reclamation. Under their provisions, "swamp and overflowed" lands were given to the states on the condition that revenues from land sales be used to build levees and provide drainage. For the following 30 years, states undertook extensive flood control and drainage programs that were beset with failures, frauds, and scandals. Nevertheless, the experience gained from 1850 to 1880 contributed to later successful reclamation efforts by public and private interests.

The drainage programs launched in the late 19th and early 20th centuries were part of a nationwide reclamation and land-development movement. Following the end of the Civil War, most southern states created immigration agencies to attract settlers to undeveloped lands. After a boom in the timber industry from 1870 to 1890, large acreages of cutover lands were released by lumber companies, particularly in the Mississippi Valley. Consequently, the local economies based on lumber milling began to regress, and promoters came forth with schemes to transform barren areas as well as swamps and marshes into productive agricultural lands.

These efforts were, in part, a response to the closing of the western frontier. To many prospective farmers, the undeveloped wetlands of the South and the dry lands that required irrigation seemed the final opportunity to obtain productive farms. Many of these home seekers were recent immigrants and second-generation Americans who originally settled in the midwestern states. Their reputation for hard work and farming small acreages in an intensive manner attracted the attention of reclamation promoters. These boosters viewed the corn belt and Great Lake states as a key source for latter-day pioneers who would settle the reclaimed Everglades, the lower Louisiana marshes, and the swamps of Mississippi, Arkansas, and later Missouri. The hardscrabble hill farmers of Kentucky, Tennessee, Mississippi, and Arkansas were also viewed as prospective residents on reclaimed alluvial land in the lower Mississippi Valley. A vast pamphlet literature developed describing the ease of reclaiming southern land, the feasibility of harvesting two crops during the long growing season, and the comfort and attractiveness of the "good life" in the lower Mississippi Valley.

Lumber companies, with large, relatively worthless acreages of cutover lands, joined with the railroads in elaborate plans to provide transportation for potential buyers. Land offices were established in Chicago to advertise the fertility of Delta and coastal marsh soils. The companies advertised largely in the Midwest and obtained cooperation from city commercial interests in forming a regional promotional association. The land, offered in tracts of 40 acres or more, was touted as suitable for dairy farming as well as cotton and all staple crops grown in the corn belt. In some cases, groups of prospective purchasers were brought to reclamation projects where land auctions were held. Land selling for $8 to $10 per acre in the 1880s was selling for $75 to $100 by 1920. In southeastern Missouri, property within newly organized drainage districts was fetching $125 per acre prior to World War I.

Drainage districts played an important role in the development of southern agriculture. They were organized under a variety of laws and local customs, with the peak of activity from 1907 to 1927. The districts continued the prevailing concept of drainage as a local problem—jurisdiction remained with county or other units of local government and the projects were administered by local officials. State legislation relating to drainage and reclamation had three principal purposes: (1) to standardize cooperation among landowners; (2) to define methods of apportioning drainage costs among property owners; and (3) to authorize financing and payment for drainage improvements.

Despite the fact that reclamation is generally regarded as a phenomenon of the arid West, an extensive drainage program took place in the South concurrently under private auspices. The undertakings varied from marshland pump-reclamation projects requiring large capital investments to more common gravity-drainage projects of areas with higher elevations. The larger projects in Arkansas, Mississippi, Missouri, and the marshlands of Louisiana were organized to develop land that could be sold in small tracts to prospective farmers. However, most of the 400 to 500 gravity drainage districts developed in the Mississippi Valley were organized to improve the lands of existing owners.

The drainage movement was assisted by both state and federal agencies. The states promoted settlement and established the legal basis for special improvement districts. The federal government, especially the Department of Agriculture, conducted investigations of drainage problems and provided technical assistance in the planning of many projects. Federal funds were made available for reclamation of the arid lands of the West, and a strong desire existed throughout the South for federal support of the drainage movement. In the 1920s a strong effort was made to expand the Bureau of Reclamation's land development to the South and to regions of the country other than the West. A blue-ribbon panel of "Special Advisers on Reclamation and Rural Development" was created by Congress and issued a report in 1926 calling for a national effort to redeem southern agriculture. The group's views went unheeded.

With the onset of the Depression, drainage districts were hard hit and became heavily indebted. Tax delinquency became chronic in many areas, and farmers became disillusioned with many of the programs. Some relief was provided by the Reconstruction Finance Corporation and other New Deal programs. An important new element was added by the 1944 Flood Control Act, which, for the first time, enabled the U.S. Army Corps of Engineers to engage in drainage work not directly related to levee building and other flood control projects. With passage of the 1954 Watershed Protection and Flood Prevention Act, the drainage activities of the Department of Agriculture entered a new phase. It enabled the department to give technical and financial assistance in planning and conducting small watershed projects, in which drainage was a part. This landmark law bridged the gap between the work of the Soil Conservation Service on local farms and flood control, and major drainage projects carried out by the Corps of Engineers in cooperation with state and local interests.

Louisiana was the only state that inaugurated a large state-sponsored drainage program. In 1940 the state established a far-reaching program for rebuilding the existing drainage system and extending drainage to large undeveloped areas. The program served as a coordinating link between local organizations and the federal government.

Much of the reclamation effort undertaken after World War II has been land clearing by private farmers. This development has been prompted by growing demands for rice, soybeans, cotton, and livestock. Former timbered areas, in addition to swamplands, have been transformed into tillable acreages and pastures. For example, estimates are that large-scale agribusinesses rather than family farmers have cleared at least 70 percent of the land that has been cleared in the Mississippi Alluvial Valley since the close of World War II. The transformation of southern agriculture from tenancy and subsistence farming to increasingly larger operations also affected the development of irrigation. The postwar development of rice growing and the use of irrigation for crops such as soybeans have led to large amounts of land receiving supplemental water. In 1950 a total of 5,056 acres in Mississippi were irrigated; by 1982 the total had risen to 430,901 acres. Problems have arisen, however, with the drawdown of aquifers resulting from extensive pumping of groundwater. Thus, a new challenge has been added to the problems of flood control, drainage, and land clearing—the three additional elements in the reclamation of forested swamp and other so-called wastelands in the South.

See also INDUSTRY: / Timber Industry

Michael C. Robinson
U.S. Army Corps of Engineers
Lower Mississippi Valley Division
Vicksburg, Mississippi

Quincy C. Ayers and Daniels Scoates, *Land Drainage and Reclamation* (1939); Albert E. Cowdrey, *This Land, This South: An Environmental History* (1983); Robert W. Harrison, *Alluvial Empire* (1961); George W. Pickels, *Drainage and Flood-Control Engineering* (1941).

River Life

If southerners are "tied to the land," as many historians and cultural thinkers have argued, many are also tied to the water. One must not overlook the influence—occupational, economic, and environmental—that the freshwater streams and rivers have played and continue to play in southern life and culture. Just as many depend on the land as the prime sustainer and stabilizer of the traditional southern community, others choose a river way of life that offers occupational freedom and economic diversity. River culture here refers to the lives and methods of those who choose to work independently on the water—fishing, rafting logs, or musseling.

"Shantyboat" or houseboat life has all but died out as a widespread tradition on the navigable rivers of the region. Up until the 1950s one could find families living seminomadic lives on houseboats along the Mississippi, Tennessee, Cumberland, Yazoo, and other rivers and tributaries of the South. Often portrayed in the popular media as impoverished, lawless "water gypsies," these river folk made conscious choices to pursue lives of freedom and independence. In the Depression years the ranks of the water dwellers swelled as many southerners were forced through economic hardship to find alternative sources of survival.

Typically a houseboat family would tie up near fertile land, perhaps at the mouth of a small tributary, thus shielding themselves from disturbance by larger river traffic. A garden planted in the late spring provided summer food and vegetables to can for winter. Fish was the staple food, and catfish the most common. If the landing was suitable a family might stay for years; if not, perhaps only a few months, moving on with the aid of a small motorboat or simply drifting with the current.

More common today, however, are families who live on small pieces of land near the banks of freshwater streams or rivers. Commercial fishing, usually for catfish, buffalo, or spoonbill (sometimes called "shovelbill"), small farming, and hunting or logging form the economic base for a river family. In Tennessee, southern Kentucky, Arkansas, and Alabama river families also dig for mussel shells, a common occupation after German immigrants located pearl button factories on the Mississippi River in the late 1800s. Until the 1940s river men tied logs together to make log rafts and floated them down the river to a sawmill. Such work, generally done in the spring of the year, supplemented fishing, musseling, and farm income.

Commercial fishing is the center of the river economy. Commercial fishing families may at once be fisher folk, boat builders, net makers, bait-line box makers, small-engine repair specialists, trappers, and small farmers. Fishing tackle used in the South is largely built by hand within the community. Bait lines or trot lines are commonly set in the evening and checked each morning. Other common tackle includes hoop nets or barrel nets, snag lines, gill nets, trammel nets, and wooden and wire fish traps.

Musseling, today an important occupation on the rivers of the Upland South, has very early origins. Oral tradition in the lower Tennessee Valley suggests that musselers were active by the early 1900s. From Paducah, Ky., to Florence, Ala., there was musseling around 1910, and in 5 to 10 years an increasing number of men turned to shells for their income. Prior to 1900 there was a market for pearls, but very little demand for the shell itself, the "mother of pearl." With a growing pearl button industry in the United States, shells were in high demand.

Mussel shells are "dug" in a variety of ways. Toe digging, or feeling for the shells in shallow water with one's feet, is still a popular way to dig for shells. The most common historically, however, is brailing, a system of dragging a long wooden or steel pole (called a brail) on the bottom of the river. All along the brail, groups of mussel hooks are suspended from short pieces of string. When the brail gets heavy the musseler knows he has many shells and raises the brail. Brailing continues today, assisted since 1920 by gasoline-powered motors and winches.

Among younger river men, diving for mussels has become a popular occupation. An air compressor on an 18–24-foot boat provides the lifeline to divers as they work—sometimes as deep as 50 feet—with an air hose in their mouths, feeling for shells on the dark, muddy river bottom. A good day can bring as much as $300 when the price per pound is up. The freedom of the work hours, the independence from supervisors, and the possibility of earning the equivalent of a week's pay in one day lead many to take up mussel diving. Today, companies like the Tennessee Shell Company, located in Camden, Tenn., regularly buy shells to sell to Japanese companies in the cultured pearl industry.

Like rivers themselves, traditional river culture constantly evolves, adapting to changing environmental conditions, new laws, and new technologies. In parts of the South the farm-raised catfish industry threatens to destroy the independent commercial fisherman, and in others water pollution threatens the fish and mussel populations. These pressures will change the culture of the river family, but its reliance on the river, both spiritually and economically, will continue.

Tom Rankin
Southern Arts Federation

Ernest T. Hiller, *Houseboat and River-bottoms People* (1939); Harlan Hubbard, *Shantyboat: A River Way of Life* (1953).

Rivers and Lakes

From the Potomac to the Rio Grande, the South is blessed with rivers flowing, with few exceptions, to the Atlantic and Gulf coasts. Fed by an average annual rainfall of 40 to 50 inches, with even greater amounts in the Appalachians and along the Gulf Coast east of New Orleans, the rivers of the South have bountiful flows except in drier west Texas, and the warm southern climate keeps the streams free of ice during most of the year. Because the rains fall abundantly in the winter and spring, however, the rivers often flood during those seasons, and they sometimes dwindle to trickles during summer and autumn droughts. Although uneven flows have at times hampered their usefulness, rivers provide southerners, in varying regional proportions, with fertile floodplains for agriculture, convenient routes for trade and travel, power to turn mills and produce electricity, water to drink, and many fish and waterfowl for dietary variety. The history of southern rivers has been marked by cooperative efforts to make the rivers better serve those purposes, and it is in the field of water resource development that the South has most eagerly sought federal assistance.

Along the Atlantic Coast, Virginia has the Potomac, James, and Rappahannock rivers; North Carolina the Roanoke, Neuse, and Cape Fear; South Carolina the Pee Dee, Santee, and Edisto; Georgia the Savannah and Altamaha; and Florida the St. Johns River; all except the latter have sources in the mountainous western sections of the states. Estuarine near their mouths and easily navigated to the head of tidal influences, the rivers were ascended by explorers and colonists penetrating through the forests, into the interior. The earliest plantations and settlements were located along the lower reaches of the rivers where the colonists cooperated in the construction of wharves and later in port development to maintain trade and contact with their homelands by water. Port cities such as Charleston and Savannah arose there. At the fall line dividing the Atlantic Coastal Plain from the hilly piedmont and marking the head of navigation for larger vessels, water power for mills was available for manufacturing, and the transfer of commodities from small craft navigating the upper rivers to larger vessels was necessary. Cooperative efforts to develop that water power and to transfer the commodities from one vessel to another around the falls often contributed to the founding of cities at the fall line; Alexandria and Georgetown on the Potomac, Richmond on the James, and Augusta on the Savannah River are examples.

In the absence of railroads and highways, rivers became the southern arteries of travel and commerce, vital for the transport of bulky commodities—hogsheads of tobacco, sacks of rice and sugar, bales of cotton—to settlements at the falls and mouths of the rivers for use or for sale in foreign markets. Some of the earliest legislation enacted by colonial and state governments was therefore aimed at preventing the obstruction of navigable rivers and in some cases providing for cooperative efforts to remove those obstructions.

Pioneers pushing west from the coastal settlements also followed the rivers, ascending to their sources and crossing the Appalachians through water gaps to rivers leading farther west. In western Virginia the pioneers followed the Clinch and Holston and New rivers and in western North Carolina the French Broad and Little Tennessee. Those streams funneled the pioneer migration northwest into Tennessee, Kentucky, and the Ohio Valley, but not directly west into Alabama and Mississippi. This explains in part why Kentucky and Tennessee were settled earlier than Alabama and Mississippi, though factors such as Indian resistance were perhaps more significant.

A similar settlement pattern developed along the Gulf Coast, explored by the Spanish and French who planted their first settlements at Pensacola, Mobile, Biloxi, and New Orleans near the mouths of rivers flowing into the Gulf and then ascended the streams for exploration and Indian trade. In addition to the great Mississippi River in Louisiana, the major rivers emptying into the Gulf are the Suwannee, Apalachicola, Choctawhatchee, and Escambia in the Florida Panhandle, the Mobile and Alabama river system, the Pearl and Pascagoula rivers of Mississippi, and the Sabine, Nueces, Trinity, Brazos, and Rio Grande of Texas. Only Arkansas and Tennessee in the Old South had no direct outlet to the Gulf or Atlantic coasts, but they used the Cumberland and Tennessee rivers and the Arkansas, St. Francis, and White rivers flowing to the Mississippi as their outlets to markets.

Log rafting, Levisa Fork of the Big Sandy River, Johnson County, Ky., c. 1910

The Mississippi River, draining a 1,245,000-square-mile area covering all or parts of 31 states and two Canadian provinces, is the largest river in North America. Together with its tributaries, it funneled commercial navigation downstream to New Orleans from western New York state on the east to Montana on the west and Minnesota at the north. The lower Mississippi, the thousand miles of serpentine channel downstream of Cape Girardeau, Mo., was bordered by a 35,460-square-mile alluvial floodplain, initially settled by the French and Spanish at Natchez and New Orleans before Americans crossed the Appalachians into the central South. Called the "Father of Waters" by Indians, the Mississippi had a central role in the socioeconomic and cultural history of the South.

After settlements and plantations had been established in the fertile floodplains where ample water supply and fish and wildlife were available, southern pioneers built mills at falls on the streams for grinding grain, sawing lumber, and other manufacturing purposes. They marketed the products of those mills and the produce of the floodplains via the waterways, using unpowered craft at first and, after 1811, when the first steamboat reached New Orleans, adapting the steamboat to shallow river navigation. Able to rely chiefly on rivers for transport, southern states seldom undertook the elaborate canal and turnpike projects of the sort built in the North in the early 19th century, the significant exception being Virginia where the falls on the Potomac and James rivers were bypassed by canals extending upriver. More common were local cooperative projects to clear the rivers of snags and boulders and the organization of port authorities to dredge and improve harbors at such ports as Charleston, Mobile, and New Orleans.

The southern concern for waterways navigation was reflected in Congress. Although southern statesmen often questioned the propriety of federal funding for road and canal projects, they tended to support such aid for river and harbor improvements. During the presidential administrations of Andrew Jackson of Tennessee, John Tyler of Virginia, and Zachary Taylor of Kentucky and Louisiana, substantial federal appropriations were approved for clearing the channels of inland rivers, the Ohio and Mississippi especially, and for dredging the coastal entrances to the mouths of rivers. Southerners after the Civil War avidly sought federal waterways project funding; small indeed was the southern river that was not improved for navigation during the late 19th century.

Vigorous southern support for navigation projects continued in the 20th century. Both the Gulf and Atlantic coasts were lined with intracoastal waterways, and elaborate systems of locks and dams to provide navigation uninterrupted by droughts and low-water flows were built on many rivers, making possible navigation by powerful diesel towboats and barge tows. Locks and dams on the Arkansas and Red rivers, for instance, opened Arkansas and Louisiana to barge navigation into Oklahoma, and locks and dams on the Cumberland and Tennessee rivers supported barge traffic in northern Alabama and Tennessee to the western slope of the Appalachians. A canal for the movement of towboats and barges from the Tennessee River to Mobile, Ala., known as the Tennessee-Tombigbee Waterway and ranking in size with the Panama Canal, established a route other than the Mississippi River for shipment of commodities from the Upper South to the Gulf.

The pioneers settling in the floodplains also undertook cooperative efforts at an early date to protect their settlements and plantations from inundation by flooding, especially along the Mississippi River, where the first levee for flood protection was constructed by the French at New Orleans in 1727. Southerners organized local- and state-funded levee districts in the early 19th century and lined the Mississippi and other streams with earthen walls to hold out floods. Contending that flooding was a national problem because the Mississippi poured northern floodwater onto southern lands, southern statesmen ushered through Congress the 1850 Swamp Lands Act, used to assist levee construction, and the 1879 act establishing the Mississippi River Commission, which would assist local levee districts with levee construction. With vigorous southern support Congress enacted flood control legislation in 1917, 1928, and 1936, authorizing federal participation in an immense program for building levees and also for creating floodways and constructing multipurpose reservoirs for flood control, hydroelectric power generation, water supply, and recreation. That program converted the South into a land of lakes.

Because the South was unglaciated, it had far fewer natural freshwater lakes than the North and none comparing with the Great Lakes except Florida's Lake Okeechobee, a shallow lake in the Everglades covering 730 square miles and ranking second to Lake Michigan as the largest lake entirely within the borders of the United States. Lakes Pontchartrain and Borgne near New Orleans are brackish embayments of the Gulf rather than freshwater lakes. The other natural southern lakes are chiefly ponding areas in swamps, oxbows of abandoned river meanders, lakes in the Florida limestone region, and Reelfoot Lake in Tennessee created by the 1811 earthquake.

By the 1980s, however, cooperative water resource development along the South's rivers had dotted the map of the South with many lakes, some built by private power and utility companies for hydroelectric power production and water supply but most constructed by the Tennessee Valley Authority in the Tennessee River basin and by the U.S. Army Corps of Engineers throughout the remainder of the South. Those lakes harnessed rivers for many purposes, impounding flooding to protect downstream areas, furnishing pools for commercial navigation, producing economical hydroelectric power, supplying water for community and industrial uses, and offering recreational opportunities equal to those of the natural lakes of the North. Southern lakes, especially those built near the inland Atlanta, Nashville, and Dallas–Fort Worth urban areas, consistently ranked tops in the nation in terms of their use for recreation.

The Old South stereotypes in fiction and film portraying the plantation aristocracy and chattels greeting steamboats at the landings, or picturing heroic struggles to save mansions and cotton fields from crevasses in the levees, do not reflect the diversity of southern experience, yet they properly illustrate the paramount role of rivers in the history of the South. The relationship of rivers to exploration and settlement patterns and to the agricultural, urban, and industrial development of the South is noteworthy. Equally significant is the cooperative effort of southerners to improve and manage their rivers, for that effort belies the image of the South as the bastion of individualism and states' rights. At early dates, southerners cooperated to improve their rivers for navigation and to achieve a measure of flood protection, eagerly seeking federal assistance even before the Civil War and acquiring it in full measure during the Reconstruction years and afterwards. As a result, southern rivers have been developed to an extent exceeding that of any other section of the United States.

Leland R. Johnson
Hermitage, Tennessee

Stanley J. Folmsbee, *Sectionalism and Internal Improvements in Tennessee, 1796–1845* (1939); Robert H. Haveman, *Water Resource Investment and the Public Interest: An Analysis of Federal Expenditures in Ten Southern States* (1965); Institute for Water Resources, *National Waterways Roundtable: Proceedings, History, Regional Development, Technology, A Look Ahead* (1981); Leland R. Johnson, *Engineers on the Twin Rivers: A History of the U.S. Army Engineers, Nashville District* (1978); Charles L. White, Edwin J. Foscue, and Tom L. McKnight, *Regional Geography of Anglo-America* (1974).

Roads and Trails

From preindustrial times to the automobile age, elaborate networks of roads and trails have crisscrossed the South and made commerce, political activity, and cultural exchange possible. The locations of these routes were determined in many cases not entirely by men and women who built them, but by previous inhabitants who had already carved their own trails out of the landscape. These ancient trails served as a blueprint for later road-building efforts, and an unmistakable continuity exists between the trails established by early Native American residents of the South and the roads and highways built later by whites.

Long before humans inhabited the South, however, animals had worn a permanent system of trails to food supplies, watering holes, and all-important salt deposits. Salt licks like those in Mason and Boone counties, Ky., for example, attracted countless buffaloes and other animals, which, over thousands of years, tramped lasting routes to these locations. These particular trails served 18th-century white settlers who crossed the frontier south of the Ohio River to establish interior settlements in Kentucky. Animal trails were also a part of the elaborate arterial network of Indian traces throughout the South.

Indian trails paralleled water routes like the Alabama,

Altamaha, Apalachicola, Mississippi, Mobile, Pascagoula, Santee, Savannah, Tennessee, and Tombigbee rivers. Others avoided parts of the terrain that were either too rugged, dense with undergrowth, or swampy. These overland trails stretched across the South for hundreds of miles and made trade possible with Native American cultures in remote parts of the region, as well as other reaches of the country. The Natchez Trace, which ran from central Tennessee to Chickasaw towns in northern Mississippi, and the Great Indian Warpath, which began in the Creek country of Alabama and Georgia, traversed Cherokee settlements in eastern Tennessee, and, after dividing near Kingsport, Tenn., branched off to the northeast through Virginia and into Pennsylvania, were two of the more famous. Some Indian trails, notably the Natchez Trace in Tennessee and Mississippi and the famous Warriors' Path in Kentucky, served whites who used them for exploration, trade, and as military and wagon roads. Spaniards Navarez, De Vaca, De Soto, and De Luna explored parts of the 16th-century South over Indian trails. In his invasion of Creek territory in 1813, Andrew Jackson also made use of existing Indian trails, as did other American militiamen about that time, who constructed a series of outposts along the Georgia and Alabama frontiers to protect white settlers.

As white pioneers pushed into the South, both animal and Indian trails provided the beginnings for the construction of wagon roads, private turnpikes, post roads, and railroad rights-of-way. Although Daniel Boone built most of the historic Wilderness Road, which ran from Moccasin Gap in southwestern Virginia through the Appalachian Mountains to the fertile Bluegrass region of central Kentucky, portions of the route followed old Indian trails. Within the state of Kentucky, animal and Indian trails determined many lines of transportation and settlement patterns. In the construction of the Cincinnati, New Orleans & Texas Pacific Railway in Tennessee and southern Kentucky, the Tennessee Central Railroad from Rockwood to Cookeville, Tenn., as well as the Western & Atlantic Railroad from Chattanooga south to the Chattahoochee River, engineers followed parts of extant animal and Indian trails.

Post roads, which the federal government began constructing during the early 1800s, also facilitated the settlement of the South. After the United States acquired the Louisiana Territory, interest in opening a line of communication between the District of Columbia and New Orleans developed. A 1,500-mile circuitous route over the Appalachian and Blue Ridge mountains to Knoxville, Nashville, and on to New Orleans across the unsettled wilderness west of the Georgia frontier already existed. Congress decided to continue use of this route rather than build a shorter one, but not before Isaac Briggs, a government surveyor, had laid out a road to New Orleans through southern Alabama and Mississippi, which early 19th-century settlers used extensively. Despite Indian hostilities, post-road construction continued in the South until by 1823 a network of routes radiated from six mail distribution points located at Augusta, Ga; Savannah, Ga.; Creek Agency, Ga.; St. Stephens, Ala.; Huntsville, Ala.; and Natchez, Miss. And once mail service began over these and other post roads, the South became more attractive to settlers.

Aside from post roads, the federal government did not commit itself until 1921 to public road construction on a large scale within the United States. After the 1820s, southerners had adamantly opposed federal aid for internal improvements. Spokesmen for the South argued that Congress had no right of eminent domain or police powers necessary to build bridges, canals, or roads. They claimed that the Constitution specifically authorized only post-road construction and that any attempt on the part of Washington to engage in road building would violate the rights of individual states. This states' rights point of view prevailed throughout the 19th century, and, except for post roads built after 1896 in conjunction with the Rural Free Delivery program, the only roads constructed in the United States before 1921 were built either privately or by state and local governments.

Long-distance travel in the 19th-century South took place over post roads, privately built and maintained turnpikes, and stagecoach roads. By 1850, for example, there were approximately 180 turnpikes in Virginia, and a network of stagecoach roads, with Milledgeville as its hub, linked Georgia with neighboring states. These roads were good enough to accommodate Civil War cavalry and foot soldiers, but they proved completely inadequate for 20th-century automobile travel.

Poor roads were a nemesis to automobile travel in the South throughout much of the first half of the 20th century. Before the end of World War I, few automobilists braved the uncertainty of travel over the South's treacherous roads. R. H. Johnson, an Ohio automobile executive, was one of the earliest to do so. In 1908 Johnson blazed two motor routes over the largely unmapped and often impassable roads of the South. His first trek lasted 25 days and took him from Ohio south to Lexington, Louisville, Nashville, Huntsville, Chattanooga, Atlanta, and finally Savannah. To determine the correct directions between towns, Johnson relied on information he gleaned from Civil War documents. His second trip in 1908 opened an auto route that connected the cities of Savannah, Atlanta, Anderson, Spartanburg, Charlotte, Winston-Salem, Roanoke, Staunton, Philadelphia, and New York. Johnson mapped these routes and published them commercially as the first official automobile guides to the South.

As automobile ownership increased in the United States, more and more Americans chose to vacation in the "Sunny South." Southerners responded by developing a system of motor routes, which, like the ancient Indian trails, connected their region with the rest of the nation. By the early 1920s, 12 officially recognized automobile highways ran through the South to Florida from various parts of the country. They included the Dixie Highway, the (Robert E.) Lee Highway, the (Andrew) Jackson Highway, the Dixie Overland Highway, the Mississippi River Scenic Highway, and the Old Spanish Trail. When the federal government, as a result of the Federal Aid Highway Act of 1921, assumed the responsibility for building and maintaining a national network of highways, these roads lost much of their regional identity. The Dixie Highway, for example, which connected Sault

Sainte Marie, Mich., and Miami, Fla., became U.S. 41 and U.S. 441. The Bankhead Highway, named after the Alabama senator who had persistently advocated federalization of highways in the United States, became U.S. 29; and the old Capital Highway, the first north-south interstate route to be proposed that connected the national capital with the state capitals of Virginia, North Carolina, and South Carolina, received the distinction of becoming U.S. 1.

The construction of these first interstate automobile highways linked parts of post roads, county highways, and privately built turnpikes, which had comprised the 19th-century network of roads in the South. Some automobile highways, like much of the motor route from Augusta, Ga., to Petersburg, Va., were originally trails and roads used by Indians and early white settlers. During the automobile age, however, as road-building technology improved, construction engineers were able to ignore the established well-traveled routes of earlier generations. Speed of movement became the premium, and it was as technologically feasible to build a highway through a mountain as around one. Witness the modern four-lane superhighways that now shuttle travelers in and out of the South. In 1956 Congress set up the highway trust fund to pay for 90 percent of the interstate highway system, and today 97 percent of the 42,500-mile system is complete.

These modern interstate highways have erased the continuity that existed between generations of road builders in the South, and they have so homogenized travel that much of the uniqueness of the South has been exchanged for a uniformity manifest in motel accommodations and fast-food restaurants. Although earlier roads and trails in the South helped export southern culture to other parts of the nation, the modern superhighway has done much to destroy it. To be sure, some roads have enduring regional significance because national and regional culture celebrates them. Country music and trucking lore paint images of I-40 going into Nashville; labor union literature refers to I-85, or the "Textile Highway," in North Carolina; and blues singers and even Bob Dylan have celebrated Highway 61, which runs through the Mississippi Delta, north to Chicago. Nonetheless, perhaps more than any other medium, interstate-highway travel has eroded sectional differences and helped forever nationalize the South.

Highway 61 between Clarksdale and Tunica in the Mississippi Delta, 1968

See also AGRICULTURE: Good Roads Movement; / Rural Free Delivery; ETHNIC LIFE: Indian Cultural Contributions; GEOGRAPHY: Indians and the Landscape; HISTORY AND MANNERS: Automobiles; Railroads

Howard L. Preston
Spartanburg, South Carolina

Peter A. Brannon, *Alabama Highways* (April 1927); Robert F. Hunter, *Technology and Culture* (Spring 1963); Wheaton J. Lane, in *Highways in Our National Life: A Symposium*, ed. Jean Labatut and Wheaton J. Lane (1950); William E. Myer, "Indian Trails of the Southeast," *42nd Annual Report of the Bureau of American Ethnology, 1924–25* (1928); U. B. Phillips, *The History of Transportation in the Eastern Cotton Belt to 1860* (1908); Douglas L. Rights, *North Carolina Historical Review* (October 1931); Randle B. Truett, *Trade and Transportation around the Southern Appalachians before 1830* (1935).

Soil and Soil Conservation

Intertwined physical, climatic, economic, and cultural factors brought on severe soil erosion in the South. The Piedmont, the loessial bluff lands east of the Mississippi River, and the red clay hills of Alabama and Mississippi have been the areas of severest erosion. Farming steep slopes with cultivated row crops was the main cause, but soil characteristics also contributed to the erosiveness of these areas. Geologic processes washed the soil particles from the Piedmont uplands to form the Coastal Plain. The erosion plus the intense weathering process left the Piedmont with thin topsoils having little water-holding capacity. Impermeable clay-rich subsoils hastened erosion of topsoil.

The South has the highest annual precipitation in the United States, and the predominance of cultivated staple crops, especially tobacco and cotton, exposed the soil to intense summer thunderstorms. The use of close-growing grain crops, such as wheat and oats, and pasture and hay to support meat and dairying enterprises would have reduced erosion, but such crops held a minor place in southern agriculture. Availability of new lands to the west and south inhibited development of intensive agriculture employing fertilizers and conservation measures. An alternative to moving was to let fields rest for a few years and then extract the accumulated fertility in the organic matter. It was, and still is, a system prevalent in climates where high temperatures and rainfall accelerate leaching and decomposition of organic material, thus creating soils of low fertility and high erodibility.

In the 19th century southerners developed most of their means of contending with erosion. Thomas Jefferson observed horizontal plowing (contour farming) in France. He and his son-in-law Thomas Mann Randolph introduced the method in Virginia. A Jefferson correspondent, William Dunbar, popularized the method in the Natchez District of Mississippi. Another Mississippian, Joseph Gray, invented a level for precision layout of contour rows. By 1850 horizontal plowing was common in the South. In the two decades preceding the Civil War the hillside ditch—forerunner of the terrace—was widely used as an adjunct to horizontal plowing. Nicholas Sorsby devised the most elaborate of these systems and popularized his ideas through a series of publications on "Level Culture."

Several influential southerners, notably John Taylor and Edmund Ruffin, perceived conservation of the soil as necessary to the preservation of southern agrarian life. Ruffin, more than any predecessor, emphasized lime and drainage of level bottom lands. Adoption of Ruffin's teachings had an impact in the Tidewater of Virginia, where the use of green manures, fertilizers, and rotations restored depleted tobacco fields.

After the Civil War short-term sharecropping and rental arrangements aggravated the erosion problem. Piedmont farmers increasingly turned to commercial fertilizers as an alternative to resting fields. Structural measures of erosion control evolved into terracing. The Mangum Terrace, designed about 1885 by Priestly Mangum of Wake Forest, N.C., came into general use. Between 1880 and 1920 most farmers on steep lands in the Piedmont and upper Coastal Plain installed some type of terrace. Faulty design and construction as well as poor maintenance limited their value and occasionally created additional erosion problems.

The present programs of soil conservation began with the crusade of Hugh Hammond Bennett. A native of Anson County, N.C., Bennett proposed using vegetative controls and good land use, along with structural controls in a coordinated conservation plan designed specifically for each farm. Bennett became the first chief of the Soil Erosion Service (SES) in 1933. In 1934 the new agency conducted a reconnaissance erosion survey to ascertain the extent and conditions of soil erosion in Virginia, Tennessee, the Carolinas, Georgia, Florida, Alabama, Mississippi, Louisiana, and Arkansas. The results of the survey are shown in Table 1.

Table 1. *Conditions of Southern Soil Erosion, 1934*

Erosion condition	Acres	Percentage of total
Total area (exclusive of large cities and water)	300,967,150	100
Area with little or no erosion	147,256,748	48.9
Total area affected by sheet erosion	130,226,130	43.3
One-fourth to three-fourths of topsoil lost	94,415,128	31.4
Over three-fourths of topsoil lost	35,801,001	11.9
Total area affected by gullying	127,880,121	42.5
Occasional gullies	110,527,582	36.7
Severe gullies	16,073,713	5.3
Destroyed by gullies	1,548,826	.5

Source: Natural Resources Board, *Soil Erosion: A Critical Problem in American Agriculture* (1935).

The SES's successor, the Soil Conservation Service, moved from working on demonstration projects to cooperation with local conservation districts organized under state laws. The South became the national leader in organizing conservation districts. The obvious need for conservation and Bennett's evangelistic style and moral persuasion appealed to the farmers. District supervisors served without pay and set priorities for the conservationists supplied by SCS. The conservationist relied on an ever-expanding body of knowledge concerning structural design, the value of vegetation, and planting and tillage techniques to assist farmers.

In addition to improved technical expertise, the decline of cotton under the tenant system, mechanization of agriculture, and land use changes have influenced conservation since the 1930s. For example, tractors allowed frequent and deeper plowings that readied the soil for erosion, and large farm equipment was incompatible with the traditional serpentine terraces. As farmers eliminated these terraces, conservationists assisted farmers in installing parallel ones. Such land use changes in the last 50 years have both reshaped the southern landscape and benefited soil conservation.

Animal disease control, purebred cattle, and the introduction and spread of annual pasture grasses by SCS and other federal and state agencies expanded the cattle industry and brought pasture acreage from 19.5 million acres in 1929 to 44 million acres in 1977. High soybean and grain prices and a drop in cattle prices in the early 1970s reversed this trend, but livestock continues to be a major enterprise.

Pine tree occupancy of unprofitable hilly fields is no longer a nuisance to farmers, and expanded forest acreage results in part from developments in forest products technology and higher prices. Artificial regeneration through planting seedlings has replaced natural reforestation. Under one federal program, the Soil Bank (1956–64), landowners in South Carolina, Georgia, and Alabama planted 1,255,531 acres of the 2,154,428 acres of cropland reforested in the United States.

Cropland shrank from 65.5 million acres in 1929 to 53 million acres in 1977. Erosion-inducing row crops still predominate over close-growing crops, particularly because soybeans occupy much of the acreage formerly devoted to cotton. Regionally, farmers have shifted row crops to the gentler slopes of the lower Coastal Plain, deltas, and bottom lands. With the increase in fertilizer usage, the lower fertility of many Coastal Plain soils, compared to the Piedmont, is no longer a deterrent. Drainage systems, however, are necessary on many of the level fields. Southerners artificially drained 11.3 million acres by 1930 and 36.7 million acres by 1978. The rush to convert the fertile, easily farmed, bottom land hardwood areas to cropland is causing concern among some southerners who want to preserve portions of the area for its aesthetic, historical, recreational, and scientific value.

Along with farmers throughout the United States, southern farmers have increased acreage planted with conservation tillage systems that utilize herbicides to

Soil erosion, Natchitoches Parish, La., 1967

eliminate weed competition. In 1979 farmers used conservation tillage on 22 percent of the cropland, a figure that rose to 35 percent in 1981. In addition to retarding erosion and providing humus to the soil, the system permits double cropping in the southern climate. In traditional small farm areas of the South, where farmers rent widely scattered tracts of farm land, the time saved is a major inducement.

Southern farmers continue to cite soil erosion as their major resource problem. Twenty-two million of the 54 million cropland acres erode at a rate greater than soil formulation. The fertile, heavily farmed, loessial bluffs erode at four times that rate. But the 32 million acres of cropland on which soil erosion is negligible represent an evolution from an extractive, pioneering ethos to a permanent agriculture.

See also AGRICULTURE: Crops; Diversification; Garden Patch; / Agricultural Extension Services; HISTORY AND MANNERS: / Jefferson, Thomas; SCIENCE AND MEDICINE: / Ruffin, Edmund

Douglas Helms
Washington, D.C.

Arthur R. Hall, "Soil Erosion and Agriculture in the Southern Piedmont" (Ph.D. dissertation, Duke University, 1948); John Hebron Moore, *Agriculture in Ante-Bellum Mississippi* (1958); Arthur F. Raper, *Preface to Peasantry: A Tale of Two Black Belt Counties* (1936); *Soil Erosion: A Critical Problem in American Agriculture* (1935); U.S. Department of Agriculture, Soil Conservation Service, *Early American Soil Conservationists*, Misc. Pub. 449 (1941), *Soil, Water and Related Resources in the United States: Part I* (1981); Rupert B. Vance, *Human Geography of the South* (1932); Frank B. Vinson, "Conservation and the South" (Ph.D. dissertation, University of Georgia, 1971).

Streams and Steamboats

Waterways help explain much of the demographic, economic, and social history of the South. The Potomac, Ohio, and Missouri rivers formed a rough boundary for the slave states and the Confederacy. Seven thousand miles of the Mississippi River system with its tributaries from the Ohio and Tennessee southward to the Big Black and the Red rivers flow through the central agricultural region of the South. Smaller river systems from the Trinity at Galveston Bay, to the Alabama at Mobile Bay and the Suwannee in Florida drain the Gulf Coast states. On the Atlantic Seaboard, 20 river systems from the York and James to the Cape Fear, from the Pee Dee to the Broad, and from the Savannah to the St. Johns have offered transportation from fall line towns to tidewater ports. Few southerners in the past acknowledged that the Ashley and Cooper rivers joined at Charleston Harbor to form the Atlantic Ocean, but almost all farmers recognized the opportunities existing in fertile river valleys. *Niles Weekly Register* reported in 1818 that two thirds of South Carolina's farm exports were grown within five miles of a river and that all of the market crops were produced within 10 miles of navigable water.

More than 12,000 miles of navigable rivers flowed through the South. Henry Hall, reporting on American boat building in the *Tenth Census* (1880), noted that southern rivers were seldom closed by snow or ice, and that the "noble" Tennessee alone provided a transportation route of more than 800 miles. Although most southern rivers were "subject to variations in depth," Hall emphasized that they were "all good highways." He could have added that captains of small boats, boasting that their steamers could make way on a "heavy dew" or on the "foam from a barrel of beer," converted innumerable shallow streams into back roads, if not good highways.

Rafts, flatboats, and keelboats transported farm produce downstream from the early colonial period to the mid-19th century. Only an occasional keelboat on narrow rivers or a sailing vessel on broader sheets challenged the currents until the steamboat *New Orleans* reached her name city in 1811, and thereby inaugurated a new era in transportation. Steamboats, whether the grand floating palace or the meanest little workaday "trade boat" peddling notions and necessities along shallow rivers, served the South for more than 100 years. Regardless of size or opulence, steamers brought the sound of modernity to southerners along the meandering rivers. The loud puffing of the tall chimneys, the clanging bell, the steam whistle, and an occasional calliope interrupted the quiet farm life and transformed sleepy river towns and landings into centers of excitement and activity.

The commercial activity associated with steamboats in New Orleans is well known. But the same activity, although reduced in scale, occurred at thousands of landings. The antebellum cotton port of Apalachicola, Fla., is representative of the excitement. Sail and steam vessels brought cargoes to Apalachicola merchants in the late summer and early fall. As autumn changed into winter, the Apalachicola *Commercial Advertiser* (1844) dreamed of the "busy scenes which will ensue when the [steamboats] come booming down the river with their tall chimneys just peeping over the bales of cotton." When winter rains raised the Chattahoochee River, the newspaper announced that "*The river is riz*—the boat bells are ringing, ships are loading, draymen swearing, Negroes singing, clerks marking, captains busy, merchants selling, packages rolling, boxes tumbling, wares rumbling, and everybody appears up to his eyes in business." During the remainder of the cotton season, "steamboat follows steamboat—each wharf has its pile—every merchant his business—every clerk his duty—loafers are out of fashion." The "River News" column of newspapers throughout the South reported similar activity. Steamboats provided farms and plantations, river towns and rural hamlets, with news, gossip, and accommodations for travelers; boats came loaded with necessities, tools, and luxury goods and backed from the landing loaded with outgoing farm produce. The steamers provided a way to the outside world and brought the sights and sounds of the outside to the river valleys.

The everyday business of steamboating sometimes became dramatic. During the 1836 Creek Indian War, the little frontier settlement of Roanoke, a few miles south of Columbus, Ga., was attacked by Indians. The steamer *Georgian* touched at the landing, rescued the settlers, and escaped when the crew threw sides of bacon into the fires to get up steam and speed. During the 1848 Christmas season, William and Ellen Craft, making an exciting escape from slavery, traveled in disguise aboard steamboats from Savannah to Charleston and then to Wilmington, N.C., in their successful bid for freedom. During the Civil War, Robert Smalls, a slave pilot in Charleston Harbor, escaped to freedom by taking a Confederate steamer, the *Planter*, to the Union fleet standing offshore. During flood seasons throughout the South, steamers rescued stranded farmers from dangerous situations, and in a yellow fever epidemic along the Yazoo River steamboats brought medicine and supplies to ravaged towns and took panic-stricken citizens to safer ports. Steamboat fires and explosions saddened southerners when they lost relatives, friends, cargoes, or just a favorite boat. The worst steamboat disaster, the explosion of the *Sultana* in 1865 with more than 1,500 casualties, shocked the nation. Accidents and disasters only temporarily diminished southern reliance on, or affection for, the glamour and excitement of steamboats.

Many boats on southern rivers, especially steamers in the St. Louis to New Orleans trade, were floating palaces. Historian Louis C. Hunter described the elegance as "steamboat gothic" and regarded it as an "aesthetic experience" for many backwoods farmers. He noted that the *Eclipse* (363′ x 36′) was built for the lower Mississippi River in 1852, and offered an elegance surpassing "many of the best hotels in the country." By 1850 steamers had adopted a standard arrangement for passenger service. The main cabin of large steamers was 150 to 200 feet long, with staterooms of 50 to 100 square feet flanking each side. The ever present barroom, the boat's office, and the pantry were at the fore end, with the ladies' cabin aft. The main cabin was the showpiece. Often richly decorated with white paneling, gilded decorations, richly colored carpets, ornate chandeliers, stained glass skylights, polished furniture, gleaming tableware, and snow white linen, the saloon was the center of social activity, providing dining facilities for as many as 200 passengers. Smaller boats engaged in passenger service tried to offer a comparable degree of elegance, reduced only in scale.

The decade beginning in 1850 constituted the Golden Age of American steamboating, but the Golden Age for steamers in the southern passenger and cotton trade came after the Civil War. Some of the fastest, the most luxurious, and the largest boats steamed between New Orleans and St. Louis. The *R. E. Lee* raced the *Natchez* in 1870 with both boats making about 17 miles an hour on the lower Mississippi. Henry Hall reported on two "remarkably handsome vessels," which made their maiden trip to New Orleans in 1878. The *Ed. Richardson* (303′ x 48.5′) cost $125,000, while the *J. M. White*, (321′ x 48′) cost $220,000. The 233′ main cabin of the *J. M. White*, flanked by staterooms, with a polished bar forward, and the ladies' cabin overlooking the stern, could seat 250 guests for dinner. In addition to cabin passengers, this fine steamer could transport 2,600 tons of freight, or 10,000 bales of cotton. Everything about the boat seemed oversized: the magnificent bell weighed 2,500 pounds.

When such fine steamers as the *Natchez* or the *J. M. White*, and hundreds of smaller boats faced increased competition from southern railroads, steamboats changed to meet the challenge. The foredeck of steamers was first squared to accommodate barges; then the bow was further changed to handle larger tows. As tows increased, speed and passenger service diminished, and once steamboats completed the change to towboats, the magic was gone. In 1902 the giant *Sprague* (276′ x 61′), with a tow of 67,000 tons in 60 barges covering nearly seven acres, could not generate the excitement of the grand packets of the Golden Age of southern steamboats. Even before the Howard Boatyards at Madison, Ind., built their last steamboat in 1934, railroads, towboats, and the internal combustion engine ended the Age of Steamboats on southern rivers. Today only two steamboats—the *Delta Queen* and the *Mississippi Queen*—continue to travel the Mississippi.

See also RECREATION: / Showboats

Harry P. Owens
University of Mississippi

Charles P. Fishbaugh, *From Paddle Wheels to Propellers: The Howard Ship Yards of Jeffersonville in the Story of Steam Navi-*

gation on the Western Rivers (1970); Charles H. Fitch, "Report on Marine Engines and Steam Vessels in the United States Merchant Service," *Tenth Census of the United States* (1880); Henry Hall, "Report on the Ship-Building Industry of the United States," *Tenth Census of the United States* (1880); Forrest P. Holdcamper, ed., *Merchant Steam Vessels of the United States, 1807–1868* (1952); Louis C. Hunter, *Steamboats on the Western Rivers: An Economic and Technological History* (1949); T. C. Purdy, "Report on Steam Navigation in the United States," *Tenth Census of the United States* (1880); George Rogers Taylor, *The Transportation Revolution, 1815–1860* (1951).

Tennessee Valley Authority (TVA)

The 50th anniversary of the signing of the TVA Act by President Franklin D. Roosevelt was 18 May 1983. In that half century the Tennessee Valley Authority played a major role in transforming one of the most underdeveloped and poverty-stricken areas in the nation into one centrally involved with critical problems besetting the South, the nation, and the world in the waning years of the 20th century. Senator George Norris's vision of "taking the Tennessee River as a whole and developing it systematically, as one great enterprise, to bring about the maximum control of navigation, of flood control, and of the development of electricity" was realized along with other major environmental accomplishments before his death in 1944. And by the end of World War II the agency already was involved with matters that transcended the initial vision of its creators.

On 8 October 1945 President Harry Truman dedicated Kentucky Dam, the last of the on-river dams to be constructed and the 16th dam built by TVA within the seven states (Tennessee, Alabama, Georgia, Kentucky, Mississippi, North Carolina, and Virginia) encompassed by the drainage system of the Tennessee River, an area roughly the size of Scotland and England. The president in his remarks quoted those spoken by Roosevelt on 18 April 1933: "The usefulness of the entire Tennessee River . . . transcends mere power development; it enters the wide fields of flood control, soil erosion, reforestation, elimination from agricultural use of marginal lands, and distribution and diversification of industry." Truman then made the obvious point that Roosevelt's prophecy had been fulfilled, "for in the TVA the Congress has provided for a tying together of all things that go to make up a well-rounded economic development." With the goal of well-rounded economic development in mind, TVA in its first decade, through planned development, modified the environment in remarkable ways to achieve its mission.

In 1933 throughout the valley unemployment was endemic, mountains had been slashed and burned, a barter economy was widespread, and spring flooding was taken for granted. By constructing 16 dams within 12 years TVA put thousands of people to work and provided untold opportunities for the development of skills among a largely untutored rural work force. To further assist its work force, TVA encouraged the establishment of unions and collective bargaining with its employees. It also pursued a policy of working with landowners to increase the production and use of trees in ways that would assist in erosion control and watershed protection. And, as it generated electricity, rates came down so that electricity became easily available.

Through the Electric Home and Farm Authority, TVA facilitated the purchase of low-cost appliances. Before the advent of TVA 97 percent of the people had no electricity; within three decades thereafter it was universally available. In helping to ease the lives of an undernourished, deprived, rural population, TVA helped create opportunities for a better life that agency officials as well as many in government hoped could be emulated elsewhere.

TVA also pioneered in the development of rural regional libraries and helped to improve county school systems and to create parks throughout the region. Plans, ordinances, and codes developed in villages constructed by TVA at various dam sites were usually adopted by the councils of these communities as they were absorbed into the structure of county government. Many practices, notably TVA's emphasis on uniform accounting, were adopted by municipalities and other local and state government agencies.

One of the notable changes TVA accomplished, initially through the slight raising and lowering of water levels at various dams, was the eradication of malaria, previously considered endemic throughout a large portion of the valley. Before TVA came to the valley at least a third of the people there suffered from malaria. By making the river navigable, by providing a nine-foot channel from Knoxville to Paducah, where it entered the Ohio River, and by providing cheaper electricity, TVA helped to make cities and surrounding areas attractive to commercial and industrial ventures, furthering the economic development of the valley states. Moreover, research conducted at the TVA National Fertilizer Development Center at Muscle Shoals developed and encouraged the use of inexpensive phosphate fertilizers, thereby assisting farmers in the valley, throughout the nation, and in other countries as well to increase their yields and to combat erosion of their soils. TVA through various programs encouraged valley farmers in organizing cooperatives to bring electricity to their farms and in weaning them away from an agriculture largely based on cotton and corn.

The devastating flooding that occurred throughout the Ohio and Mississippi river valleys in 1937 brought to national attention the fact that flood control on the Tennessee River was already quite effective. At that time only three dams and reservoirs were in operation. By 1980 there were 9 dams on the Tennessee River itself, 5 major dams on headstreams, 12 smaller impoundments, 7 steam plants, and an equal number of nuclear plants in operation or in various stages of construction. The dams and impoundments provided the Tennessee River Valley with the nation's most effective flood control system. Moreover, the various TVA structures—dams, powerhouses, bridges, and generators—were widely proclaimed as magnificent functional structures. In most instances they blended harmoniously with the environment, imaginatively utilized building materials, and successfully coordinated the science of engineering with the art of architecture. They quickly gained national and worldwide attention as models of public architecture, a successful team effort in one of the largest construction projects in the world.

With the outbreak of World War II and America's participation in it, TVA put increased emphasis on the production of electricity to assist plants in the valley manufacturing aluminum for aircraft and for the installation at Oak Ridge utilizing uranium 235 to produce atomic weapons. The Muscle Shoals fertilizer program was set aside for the production of phosphates and nitrates for munitions. During these years the capacity of TVA's power system more than doubled from a little less than a million kilowatts in 1940 to more than 2.5 million in 1946. By 1980 TVA installations had a generating capacity of over 100 billion kilowatts.

The last figure indicates that TVA in the postwar years continued to play a leading role in the economic development and transformation of the valley. During these years TVA focused its attention on tributary area development and enhanced energy production, including nuclear energy. As a result, by 1980 Decatur, Ala., for example, had 20 Fortune 500 companies within the Tennessee River environs. Barges on the river were moving more than 30 million tons of freight. A more balanced economy, agricultural and urban, had been established in large part through the efforts of TVA. In a half-century the valley had been transformed from a deprived, eroded, flooded area where the per capita annual income was $168, to a modern region with an income nearly 80 percent of the national average. The towns of the region, in contrast to those of neighboring central Appalachia, had an air of solid brick-built prosperity.

All these changes did not come easily, and in the postwar years TVA was the butt of increasing criticism. At the outset blacks found much to complain about in the racism and discriminatory practices of the agency, some of which went beyond those prevailing in various parts of the valley. Black leaders noted that little rehabilitation for blacks was included in the programs and policies espoused by TVA. In addition, population removal was a serious problem as almost a million acres were flooded by TVA reservoirs. The agency, after several years, developed procedures to provide adequate compensation for displaced people. These became models for emulation in other parts of the country. Whenever possible TVA rebuilt or replaced roads, bridges, and other structures. It tried to move churches and cemeteries. But not everyone was satisfied. Farm families not owning the land on which they lived received no compensations and were placed in dire straits.

Moreover, TVA was never exempt from political pressures, legal challenges, and internal controversies. Investor-owned utilities at first challenged its constitutionality and later succeeded in preventing any expansion of the area TVA could serve. In the postwar years, as the institutional apparatus of the states and counties throughout the Tennessee Valley became more sophisticated, some resentment against TVA developed as various agencies of state and local government claimed that their prerogatives had been usurped or ignored.

In the late 1960s environmentalists in the valley and throughout the nation criticized various aspects of TVA's operations. They successfully challenged TVA's purchasing most of its coal for its 63 coal-burning steam-generating plants from strip-mine operators in eastern Kentucky. They correctly charged TVA with being one of the worst despoilers and polluters in the region and prompted the agency to mend its ways by installing scrubbers to reduce the emission of sulphur from its coal-fired plants as well as cooling towers to lower the temperature from its coal-fired and nuclear plants. Their interest in a then endangered species, the snail-darter, delayed the completion of Tellico Dam on the Little Tennessee River. By the next decade, however, TVA's concern for conservation had markedly improved.

As inflation and escalating interest rates became more evident and as energy costs increased in the 1970s (by 119 percent between 1973 and 1983), TVA raised its rates and many of the almost 3 million hard-pressed consumers throughout the valley became increasingly critical of the agency. Its attempts to produce nuclear energy and thereby lower utility rates have resulted in dismal failure and exacerbation of the situation. TVA planned to build 17 nuclear generating plants, but as of January 1986 the agency had abandoned eight of the projects and had halted work at the remaining nine because of construction or safety problems. In the face of Nuclear Regulatory Commission citations for over 1,000 violations plus legislative rumblings regarding restructuring of the agency, TVA has hired new top-level personnel to untangle managerial and operational problems with its nuclear projects. Current TVA chairman Charles Dean foresees gradual reopening and full operating of the existing reactors. Successful operation of the nuclear plants would enable TVA once again to provide cheap power, thus encouraging industry, especially the paper and aluminum companies, to remain in the valley. TVA has already made a tremendous impact on industrial growth. In the fiscal year 1982, in a recessionary economy, there were 273 announcements from industries planning to build new facilities or expand existing ones. Since 1933 the number of manufacturing plants in the region has increased by 400 percent.

See also AGRICULTURE: / Fertilizer; Rural Electrification; INDUSTRY: / Mining; Nuclear Industry

Richard Lowitt
Iowa State University

North Callahan, *TVA: Bridge over Troubled Waters* (1980); Wilmon H. Droze, *High Dams and Slack Waters: TVA Rebuilds a River* (1965); Erwin Hargrove and Paul Conkin, eds., *TVA: Fifty Years of Grassroots Bureaucracy* (1983); David E. Lilienthal, *TVA: Democracy on the March* (1944); Michael McDonald and John Muldowny, *TVA and the Dispossessed: The Resettlement of Population in the Norris Dam Area* (1982); R. C. Martin, ed., *TVA: The First Twenty Years* (1956); John Robert Moore, ed., *The Economic Impact of TVA* (1967); Martha E. Munzer, *Valley of Vision: The TVA Years* (1969); Philip Selznick, *TVA and the Grass Roots: A Study in the Sociology of Formal Organization* (1949); TVA, *Annual Reports* (1934–).

Trees

William Faulkner's story "Delta Autumn" talks of Mississippi Delta land that is an "impenetrable jungle of water-standing cane and cypress, gum and holly and oak and ash." Trees have been both a natural and a cultural resource for southerners. A great forest has covered much of the South since the region's human history began. Pine forests paralleled the Atlantic and Gulf coasts, hardwoods were found in the uplands, mixed pine-hardwood growth occurred in the low-lying swamps and river valleys, and the mountains produced appropriate high altitude hardwoods. The slopes of the Appalachian Mountains and the Ozarks have been especially rich with tree life.

Oaks found in the South include the chestnut oak (*Quercus acuminata*) in the Mississippi River Valley, the cinnamon oak from North Carolina to Texas, Durand's oak from Alabama to Texas, the laurel oak (*Q. laurifolia*) from Virginia to Florida, the swamp white oak along southern creeks and river banks, and the myrtle oak from South Carolina to Florida. Strips of white oak are used by Deep South basketmakers, and the bark from red oaks is commonly used by rural southerners to make a tea believed to cure backache, rheumatism, diarrhea, toothache, and chills and fever. The live oak, which figures prominently in southern literature and regional imagery, has been an important source for the American shipbuilding industry and is popular in landscape design throughout the region.

Evergreens are coniferous trees, with tough, needlelike leaves; they remain verdant throughout the winter months. The yellow or shortleaf pine (*Pinus echinata*) grows naturally in the Coastal Plain of the South, as does the longleaf, or Georgia, pine (*P. palustrisis*), which is hardy from Tampa Bay west to the Mississippi River and north to Virginia. The loblolly pine can grow to 170 feet in its native southern habitat, where it can adapt to either swampland or more barren highlands. The red spruce keeps to the uplands of the Carolinas and Georgia, whereas the white cedar (sometimes called a juniper) ranges along the Atlantic and Gulf coasts, growing up to 80 feet in height. One also sees the Carolina hemlock, the cherry laurel, and the evergreen magnolia. The Cherokee Indians regarded the red cedar, an aromatic wood resistant to the damp southeastern climate, as the most sacred of all trees. The litters on which their honored dead were carried were made from cedar wood. It also has been important to the regional furniture industry.

In 1936 Howard W. Odum pointed out that the South grew over a third of all the peach trees in the nation, a third of the orange trees, and four-fifths of the grapefruit trees. Today, delicious apples are abundantly grown in North Carolina and Virginia, the Japanese plum is found throughout the South, and the fig tree can be grown as far north as southern Virginia, with Florida, Georgia, South Carolina, Louisiana, Texas, and Mississippi among the largest producers of figs in the nation. The South grows a variety of pears as well. In terms of nut trees, the pecan is native throughout the Mississippi River Valley, but its special home is Texas, which adopted it as the state tree in 1927. The English walnut (*Juglans regia*) also thrives in the Southeast.

The southern Appalachians are noted for their hardwoods. The sweet gum (*Liquidamber styraciflua*), which is also called red gum in places, has massive branches, a light-gray bark, and is seen from the Upper South down to the Gulf of Mexico. In autumn, it is a glorious sight, with brilliant colors, described by one naturalist as running "the gamut in hues from kingly yellow, through bright orange and red, and on to a deep bronze." Hickories are abundant in the South, sturdy, tough trees, which gave a nickname to President Andrew Jackson, who lived among them in the uplands.

The South has always had a number of flowering trees that have captivated the southern imagination. In particular the dogwood (*Cornus florida*) is identified with the imagery of the region. In Atlanta a million dogwoods were once planted in a campaign to beautify the city. Red and white flowering dogwoods grow wild through most of the region and can reach 30 feet tall. They are slow growers, and their leaves are glossy, pointed, grayish-green in color, turning to a deep red in autumn. Dogwood festivals throughout the South attest to its popularity among southerners. Other flowering trees include the Texas ash and tulip trees.

Other trees in the South that are particularly associated with the region include the black willows, the red birch, the yellow birch, palm trees in Florida and along the Gulf Coast, and the blue ash (seen to best effect in the Great Smoky Mountains). The mimosa, or silk tree, is a somewhat fragile-looking tree that grows as far north as northern North Carolina. It has attractive colorings and delicate foliage. It belongs to the Mimosaceae family, is native to warm, tropical regions, and can grow to 40 feet. When flowering, it shows an array of whites, yellows, and reds. Chinaberry trees (*Melia azedarach*) are popular throughout much of the Deep South as flowering shade trees. They bear in the early spring, producing a pale-pink flower, slightly tinged with purple. Members of the Lester family in Erskine Caldwell's *Tobacco Road* were frequently lurking behind a chinaberry tree, and the tree crushed to death a character in Eudora Welty's "Curtain of Green."

See also INDUSTRY: / Timber Industry

Charles Reagan Wilson
University of Mississippi

William C. Coker, *Trees of the Southeastern States, including Virginia, North Carolina, South Carolina, Georgia, and Northern Florida* (1937); Charlotte H. Green, *Trees of the South* (1939); Ellwood S. Harrar and J. George Harrar, *Guide to Southern Trees* (1962); F. Schuyler Mathews, *Familiar Trees and*

Their Leaves (1903); Gary O. Robinette, *Trees of the South: Collected and Organized by Gary O. Robinette* (1985); John K. Small, *Florida Trees: A Handbook of the Native and Naturalized Trees of Florida* (1913).

Water Use

Stretching from the soggy Dismal Swamp of Virginia to the semiarid Llano Estacado of western Texas, the diverse southern geography and the associated climatic differences create the need for a variety of approaches to the utilization and management of southern water resources. Found in lakes, streams, and aquifers, these resources have both blessed and cursed the South. Watercourses provided the means by which early European settlers moved westward to settle the southern coastal plains and piedmont. Traversing the Appalachian Mountains, other pioneers sought the fertile valleys of the Tennessee and Cumberland rivers, and the access they gave to farther movement westward. Representing a temporary impediment to westward movement, the Mississippi River became the chief waterway to the southern states. Crossing the "Father of Waters," settlers moved up its lush and boggy tributaries until they reached the drier areas that foretold of the arid West.

As the settlers moved westward from the Atlantic Coast they discovered that southern rivers did not provide a reliable means of transportation. Periodic low water alternated with floods to make water transportation difficult, while rapids and other impediments added to the difficulty and danger of southern waterways. Early southerners focused on making southern streams more navigable. During the Monroe Administration, Secretary of War John C. Calhoun gave serious consideration to the Muscle Shoals rapids as an obstruction to navigation on the Tennessee River. After the administration of Andrew Jackson such projects were considered primarily state rather than federal responsibility.

Both the federal and state governments, however, struggled with improving navigation and controlling floods on the Mississippi River. In the antebellum era a government engineer, Charles Ellet, emphasized the need for scientific data on water flow and suggested that a relationship existed between stream flow and other conditions within a river's watershed. In suggesting the construction of tributary reservoirs to regulate the river's flow for navigation as well as to control floods, Ellet anticipated later engineering principles. The concepts of another pair of engineers, Andrew A. Humphreys and Henry L. Abbot, had a more immediate influence on attempts to control Mississippi waters by stressing the use of levees, outlets, and cutoffs.

As far as swamps and coastal wetlands were concerned, few people prior to the Civil War had much understanding of their value. In the Swamp Lands Acts of 1849 and 1850 the federal government ceded much of this area to the states to be reclaimed by drainage.

During the Gilded Age the attempts to reclaim wetland and to prevent flooding in the Mississippi basin continued as a practical matter. Only later in that period did such attempts merge as part of the conservationists' river basin development concept, with its implications for federal action on a regional basis. Responding to projects he had seen in Europe, Louisiana Congressman Randall L. Gibson proposed in 1876 to establish a commission for supervising developments on the Mississippi. When President Rutherford B. Hayes signed Gibson's bill in 1879 he implicitly committed the federal government for the first time to flood control on an American river.

In the following decades members of the Mississippi River Commission debated not only the best technology for controlling floods on the Mississippi but also the question of the constitutionality of federal aid for flood control. When the commission adopted a "levees only" policy as the primary solution for Mississippi flooding, the results often aggravated problems of control. The constriction caused by levees not only forced the river to rise higher during flood stage but levees encouraged expensive developments in the floodplain. Some scholars, particularly the geographer George P. Marsh, pointed to the dangers inherent in relying solely on levees for flood control. He considered headwater reservoirs of equal importance in solving the complicated problem of flooding.

During that same period both geographers and other social scientists developed the philosophy of approaching a river basin as an ecological unit for planning purposes. Advocates of this concept readily incorporated the idea of reservoir control as part of their philosophy. Among the promoters of the regional planning philosophy was the Scot, Patrick Geddes, whose ideas influenced American conservationists and politicians. John Wesley Powell and W. J. McGee of the Geological Survey promoted the principle of treating a river system as a unit, finding strong support for their ideas with politicians such as Gifford Pinchot and Theodore Roosevelt. Congressional approval of the Reclamation Act of 1902 reinforced the idea of multipurpose water developments under federal authority. In establishing the Inland Waterway Commission President Roosevelt instructed the group to consider a comprehensive plan for all the watersheds in the United States as well as the integration of varied water uses. Perhaps Roosevelt's most important single contribution to the future development of the nation's water resources was his resounding veto whenever Congress attempted to allow private development of water power sites without proper government supervision. His boldest statement of the government's duty to protect the public interest in power development came in the James River (Missouri) Dam veto of 1909, thus reserving a southern river for federally supervised development. Passage of the Weeks Act in 1911 recognized the association between forest conservation and watershed protection, an important element of river basin planning. The federal government took a major step toward acceptance of the idea of comprehensive watershed planning with passage of the Federal Water Power Act of 1920.

The first extensive proposal for multipurpose water planning within a river basin was made for a southern river, the Tennessee. Concerned primarily with establishing federal responsibility for water development and interested in public power development, Senator George Norris of Nebraska proposed that the government continue to develop the hydroelectric potential at Muscle Shoals, Ala., on the Tennessee River. Although government support for developing electric power at Muscle Shoals had been associated with the nation's war effort, Norris proclaimed that the government should retain the project to produce cheap electricity for the region and cheap fertilizer for the farmer. Eventually the senator incorporated into his proposal the multipurpose and river basin planning ideas that had already become current in some bureaucratic and academic circles. The noted North Carolina geologist and engineer Joseph H. Pratt recognized the need for an interchange system of electricity, and he also envisioned the possibilities for development that hydroelectric production offered the South. Beginning in 1917 George Norris consistently favored financing of reservoirs on the Missouri River, claiming they would contribute to flood control on the lower Mississippi, and would also provide irrigation water for parts of the arid West from whence the senator came. As early as 1913 he endorsed federal development of hydroelectric power on the Potomac River.

The congressional debates over Muscle Shoals continued throughout the 1920s. While Congress deliberated over government control of Muscle Shoals, it passed other legislation significant to water resource development. Significantly, the River and Harbors Bill passed by Congress in February 1925 embodied many of the principles of multiple use of water resources, which implied the need for integrated planning in developing each watershed.

The congressional debate about disposal of the Muscle Shoals property revealed that power production would be the project's primary importance. As this fact became more evident Norris gained greater support from southern congressional representatives. Progressive politicians from the arid West who supported government operation of the Boulder Dam project joined in support of government ownership of Muscle Shoals. Norris's campaign for multipurpose river development also gained support as a result of disastrous floods on the Mississippi River in the spring of 1927. Ironically, the Corps of Engineers' report a year earlier had ignored concepts of tributary control and had maintained that all was well with the levees and channel works on the lower reaches of the river.

The year 1928 proved to be a crucial one for advocates of water resource development. In May Congress passed a flood control act providing for a comprehensive study of water resources of the nation's major streams for purposes of flood control, irrigation, power, and navigation. The act included many of the ideas of comprehensive and integrated water resource management, although on the same day Congress approved a plan for flood prevention on the lower Mississippi which completely ignored tributary control.

In late May 1928 Congress passed Norris's bill calling for government ownership and operation of the Muscle Shoals property for purposes of improving navigation and controlling floods on the Tennessee as well as for producing electric power, but President Calvin Coolidge failed to sign the bill. By the beginning of the special session of Congress in the spring of 1929, many groups in the South more openly and firmly supported the comprehensive development of the Tennessee Valley by the central government as best for the economic and social well-being of the region. With a few minor changes, Norris reintroduced his bill for government ownership and distribution of power in May 1929. After intense debate in both houses of Congress and in conference committee, Congress approved a compromise version in February 1931. The bill allowed the president either to choose Norris's concept of government operation or to lease the property to a private chemical company. Southern congressmen and legislatures urged Hoover to sign the legislation. On 3 March the president issued a resounding veto of the bill, basing his rejection primarily on opposition to government distribution of power.

During the Muscle Shoals debate another controversy arose concerning a southern river that held great significance in settling the larger question of the government's right to promote comprehensive development of navigable streams and their tributaries. The issue arose when the Appalachian Electric Power Company asked for a "minor part" license to build a power dam on the New River, a tributary of the Kanawha, located in Virginia. Although Virginia granted permission the Federal Power Commission (FPC) refused to approve the request in 1927. The question arose as to whether the federal government had jurisdiction over a nonnavigable tributary of a navigable river located entirely within one state. In 1931 the courts upheld FPC jurisdiction over the New River under the Water Power Act. Eventually in the 1970s President Gerald Ford incorporated the New River as a part of the National Wild and Scenic Rivers System, ending a decades-long conflict between conservationists and development groups.

When the principles of planning and regionalism became more widely known and supported, the Muscle Shoals debate took on new vigor. Whereas previously it had been backed almost entirely by conservationists and public power advocates, by 1932 professional planners paid more attention to it as an opportunity for practical application of many of their theories. Franklin D. Roosevelt's nomination as the Democratic candidate for president in 1932 proved crucial to achieving Norris's goals for the Muscle Shoals project. An ardent conservationist, Roosevelt already understood the interrelationship of various conservation measures, such as reforestation, water control, and soil erosion.

The economic emergency of 1932 aided in creating a favorable atmosphere for the acceptance of Norris's proposal for integrated water resource development and Roosevelt's broader concepts of planning. During his campaign Roosevelt endorsed the Norris proposal for multipurpose development, declaring that conditions in the Tennessee Valley offered an opportunity to set an example of planning for the whole country. Roosevelt's election to the presidency resulted in the launching of an experiment in river basin planning as embodied in the Tennessee Valley Authority Act signed on 18 May 1933.

Most southern states established agencies to collect data concerning water resources but such agencies seldom had authority to develop or enforce water plans. By the end of the 1920s some southern states had begun to experiment with the river basin concept of water resource planning. In 1929 Texas established the Brazos River Conservancy and Reclamation District. The New Deal further spurred interest in water development and management throughout the South. With encouragement from the federal government some southern states developed river basin projects and established water planning agencies.

The Mississippi River continued to receive attention from both state and national governments during the 1930s and 1940s. The destructive flood of 1927 brought demands for action. The Corps of Engineers responded by deepening the Atchafalaya tributary, which left the main channel near its joining with the Red River. Acting as a safety valve for the Mississippi floods, the Atchafalaya channeled excess waters into the swamplands surrounding its course. In the process of deepening and straightening the Atchafalaya, the Corps blocked drainage into 22 tributary bayous, thus restricting the Atchafalaya's capacity to absorb Mississippi floodwaters. Eventually the Corps constructed an extensive, complicated levee system to hurry floodwaters through the Atchafalaya to the Gulf. This constriction of the floodwaters raised the ground level within the levees higher than that of the surrounding basin, reducing the capacity of the basin to absorb floods while creating a greater potential for disaster if the levees were ever breached. Controversy raged over this project, intensifying in the environmental debates of the 1970s and 1980s. Environmentalists not only questioned the effectiveness of the system as a flood control measure but condemned the ecological changes it wrought.

Pressure created by rapid expansion of water use during World War II highlighted the need for coherent water plans in the southern states. During the war both federal authorities and state governments attempted to develop desirable water policies in the South, but many southerners remained suspicious of federal efforts except when directly affected by floods or when water developments promised immediate economic benefits.

The period from the end of World War II until passage of the National Environmental Protection Act of 1969 represents a significant stage in the history of southern water development. As in other areas of the United States the 1950s and 1960s saw southerners evolve from the older conservation ethic to new principles of environmentalism, with their emphasis on quality of life as well as wise use of resources for development purposes. In the post–World War II period older concepts of water management were increasingly challenged by new environmental coalitions.

Like most other Americans, the majority of southerners tended to believe that there would always be an adequate supply of water. Throughout its history most water had been managed for developmental use. During the 1950s and 1960s, for the first time, conflict developed in many areas of the South over priority of water use, since the usable water supply was no longer adequate to accommodate all demands. Little thought was given to environmental protection until the 1970s, when it was supported by actions of the federal government such as passage of the National Environmental Protection Act and the Water Quality Act. As a result, many southern states established water development and water quality boards, but the thrust of their efforts has often been more toward development than protection. Some state boards, such as Georgia's, made serious efforts to protect water quality while others, such as the Texas Water Quality Board, did little that might retard economic growth. In 1973 one study indicated that at least 60 major industrial sources were contaminating the waters of the lower Mississippi with significant quantities of 89, often highly toxic, organic compounds.

Since 1969 environmental groups have challenged many of the traditional water projects in the South, especially the grandiose, very expensive ones funded by the federal government and enthusiastically supported by local development groups. Each region of the South had advocates of such projects. In the Arkansas Valley politicians and local support groups promoted development of a navigable waterway that would make Tulsa, Okla., a port city. Its critics called it wasteful and unprofitable. When Texans attempted to get the national government to fund channelization of the Trinity River for barge traffic to Dallas and Fort Worth, a decades-long controversy ensued. Local environmental groups combined with fiscal conservatives to defeat the project for ecological and financial reasons. In Mississippi and Alabama a similar controversy raged around the Tennessee-Tombigbee Waterway.

One of the most spectacular proposals that engendered intense support and opposition was the plan in Texas to pump water from the wet regions of the east to the arid regions of the west. Severe water depletion on the High Plains threatened the irrigated agriculture of that area. The plan recommended taking water from as far east as the Mississippi River and transferring it more than 1,000 miles westward. This suggestion not only encountered opposition from Louisiana and Arkansas but also from local environmentalists and fiscal conservatives, a combination that again stalled action on the plan. Even the Tennessee Valley Authority came under scrutiny by environmental groups.

The wetlands of the South, especially the coastal areas, have increasingly engaged the attention of environmentalists. Humans have made numerous demands on nature's resources in many of these areas. Traditionally, Americans viewed swampy and marshy lands as undesirable areas to be altered for the benefit of man. By the 1890s, scientists and others had become aware of the crucial nexus that this transitional area between land and sea represents. The federal government encouraged action in preserving the ecology of the South's coastal regions with passage in 1972 of the Federal Coastal Zone Management Act. With federal urging many southern states established coastal management programs.

The conditions in southern Florida represent the complexity of water resource management in the wetlands and coastal zones of the South. In 1971 21,000 acres of land south of Lake Okeechobee burned simultaneously. This situation resulted from decades of alteration by humans of the water conditions in southern Florida. The lake acted as a great reservoir for maintaining the marshes and swamps of the Everglades, essential to survival of the wildlife and the ecological balance of the region. Settlers in the area considered the wetland unproductive unless drained so that the fertile muck that remained could be cultivated. When dry, however, the muck was also flammable.

Canals were dug in the region to service the growing tourist centers of the east and west coasts of Florida, further altering the ecology of the wetlands. Some envisioned canals cutting across the state to shorten the barge route around the peninsula. In 1971 President Nixon halted construction by the Corps of Engineers on the Cross Florida Barge Canal project, the first time a president had ever stopped work on a public works project for environmental reasons. The state of Florida also turned away from its policy of encouraging drainage and canal building. With toughened laws the state inaugurated a program to protect and preserve its remaining wetlands.

The water problems of the Florida coast have parallels throughout the South: in South Carolina, where citizens prevented the construction of a chemical plant on their coast; in Savannah, Ga., where the people have demanded that polluting industries alter their practices; along the Texas coast where environmental groups insist on balancing clean water and air with industrial development. In 1982 the South still possessed more undeveloped islands and more productive wetlands than any region in the contiguous United States. The question for the future was how would resort and industrial developments affect the wildlife, commercial fishing industry, recreational opportunities, and the existing culture of these vital and attractive areas of the South.

J. B. Smallwood
North Texas State University

Nelson M. Blake, *Land into Water—Water into Land: A History of Water Management in Florida* (1980); Albert E. Cowdrey, *This Land, This South: An Environmental History* (1983); James M. Fallows et al., *The Water Lords: Ralph Nader's Study Group Report on Industry and Environmental Crisis in Savannah, Georgia* (1971); Donald E. Green, *Land of the Underground Rain: Irrigation on the Texas High Plains, 1910–1970* (1972); Martin Reuss, *Louisiana History* (Spring 1982); Thomas J. Schoenbaum, *The New River Controversy* (1979); *Southern Exposure* (May–June 1983).

Wetlands

Southern wetlands—those low-lying, swampy areas with high soil moisture—have played a role in the region's economy, recreation, and imaginative life. The vast expanses of wetlands inhibited extensive reclamation until this century, and the continued existence of Louisiana's bayous, Virginia's Dismal Swamp, Georgia's Okefenokee Swamp, and Florida's Everglades encouraged awareness of nature's intrinsic values. Southern seaboard districts are currently among the region's most densely populated and fastest growing areas. Once considered useless, disease-ridden wastes, wetlands there, especially southern estuarine marshes, have become the richest nurseries for commercial fisheries and wildlife, surpassing other ecosystems in productivity. The most recent 20-year survey of the U.S. Fish and Wildlife Service revealed, however, significant losses of wetlands in every southern coastal state except Virginia; Louisiana, Mississippi, Arkansas, Florida, the Carolinas, and Georgia led the nation in the destruction of the wetlands. Without wetlands to recharge underground aquifers with fresh water for cities, critical water shortages will become another burden for already polluted rivers and estuaries. By maintaining biologically healthy wetlands, the natural sanitizing function of rivers is enhanced, fisheries flourish, and wildlife thrives.

Reclamation, drainage, and dredging remain the primary strategies in conserving the resources of wetlands. Biologically productive wetlands are an essential facet, like rivers and aquifers, in the region's water supply, but no comprehensive program on the scale of the Tennessee Valley Authority (TVA) has emerged to wisely use, in perpetuity, the fisheries of the Atlantic and Gulf coasts. Southern oyster, shrimp, crab, and bass fisheries, so dependent on wetlands, water quality, and stream flow, employ over 10,000 fishermen in an industry annually worth more than $100 million.

The river valleys of the Atlantic and Gulf shores scour the Coastal Plain, carrying water, silt, and nutrients to many estuaries, which are bordered by numerous tidal marshes, sloughs, swamps, and overflowed woodlands or grasslands. Abundant wildlife thrives because of fecund soils, year-round plant growth, recycled nutrients, and plentiful water associated with both backcountry swamps and the marshes of the ocean shore.

Wetlands are transitional areas between deep-water habitats and dry uplands, and they are usually distinguished according to the causes, duration, and extent of submergence. Tidelands lying astride estuaries merge with swamplands that are inundated by seasonal river floods. Above the tide line inland swamps also nourish innumerable deer, turkey, turtle, and bear; rare, uncut hardwood forests; and endangered species including clapper rails, cranes, herons, and bald eagles. Wildlife managers have classified 17 varieties of wetlands according to soils, vegetation, and water conditions. Periodic inundation, sedimentation, and water chemistry can substantially influence the character of wetland soils and vegetation. Indigenous southern wetland habitats associated with freshwater cypress and saltwater mangrove forests and with alligators and manatees are particularly rare public interest lands of world significance requiring national protection.

The oldest economy sustained by southern wetlands derived from fishing and hunting. These activities encouraged dense Native American populations along coastal shores before prolonged European epidemics in the 15th and 16th centuries. Indigenous peoples relied on grasses for basketry, matting, and thatch; on clam and oyster shells for tools, ornaments, or building materials for mounds; and on hides, feathers, and trees for canoes. Pelts from muskrats, raccoons, rabbits, and otters were plentiful. For the peoples of the Powhatan Confederation, Chesapeake Bay linked and supported a diverse culture. The same was true of wetlands associated with Pamlico, Yamassee, Guale, Colusa, Chitimacha, and Natchez cultures indigenous to the coastal or river bottom lands of the Atlantic Seaboard and Gulf. Numerous remains of middens, mounds, and stilt villages still can be found along southern lake, river, and coastal shores.

Commerce among Native Americans thrived near the South's numerous estuaries or river mouths thanks to the back-and-forth tidal currents in protected bays. Countless broad rivers still meander down to the sea, depositing sediments behind coastal barrier islands, where productive wetlands once nourished indigenous cultures and fostered European imperial rivalry. After the initial Spanish missions, plantations and trade dominated the European uses of wetlands. Colonists relied on marshes and wetlands not only for fishing and hunting but also for cattle grazing, cultivating rice, and milling. Wetlands also supplied oyster shells for construction, marl for fertilizer, reeds for thatch, and mallow for confectionery. Sugar and rice plantations required the drainage and dredging of channels, while tobacco cultivation greatly added to erosion and consequent siltation of harbors.

The diversity, extent, and location of southern wetlands nourished original cultures while simultaneously tying a common regional culture to national and international events. Slave cultures on the plantations, including the Sea Island Gullah and Louisiana Creole peoples, survived amid coastal wetlands. Isolated wetlands became enclaves for runaway slaves, French Acadians, and Seminole peoples. At the same time burgeoning trade led people in the South's busiest ports of Baltimore, Charleston, and New Orleans to try to reclaim wetlands. Such reclamation efforts were bolstered by both religious faith in the human duty to steward God's creation and the advent of steam technology.

The modern uses of wetland resources evolved in three stages of landscape alteration, from preindustrial to agra-industrial to modern modifications. Shifting economic demands in each case required a resynthesis of laws, knowledge, and values from uncontrolled use, to picturesque admiration, and eventually to recreational and ecological protection. During each phase private-property rights, federalism, states' rights, and community interest underwent redefinition.

During the colonial, or preindustrial, era economic reliance on wetlands for subsistence made the mouths of rivers a nexus of southern plantation and maritime development. Maryland's extensive tobacco crops increased the siltation and obstruction of the northern Chesapeake Bay's navigation channels. However, Virginia's Tidewater tobacco farmers avoided wetland soils except for cattle grazing despite the House of Burgesses's encouragement of agricultural reclamation. Diked wetlands and salt marshes flooded for rice cultivation promoted the plague of malarial mosquitoes in South Carolina, while tidal energy ran gristmills throughout the seaboard region. Early investors, George Washington among them, unsuccessfully planned the drainage of the Dismal Swamp to connect Pamlico Sound and the Chesapeake Bay.

Colonial accounts of wildlife in wetlands by Robert Beverley and John and William Bartram provided the foundation for preservationist sentiments during the second, or agra-industrial, phase of wetlands alteration. Throughout the 19th century agriculturalists like Edmund Ruffin, engineers like Charles Ellet, poets like Sidney Lanier, and landscape architects like Frederick Law Olmsted fashioned a more sophisticated appreciation of wetlands' physical, scenic, and public aspects. Ruffin, a soil-conservation advocate, systematically described the North Carolina Outer Banks, recognized the increased incidence of malaria due to freshwater flooding of South Carolina rice fields, and inveighed against downstream flooding caused by upstream levees and drainage. Independent of Ruffin, Ellet, after surveying the Mississippi River Delta, criticized the Swamp Lands Acts (1849–50) as giveaways of wetlands to states. He believed that unplanned upstream reclamation was destroying valuable downstream farms in Louisiana. Ellet recommended a federal river conservation program to improve the navigability and regulate the flow of the Mississippi River, thereby avoiding damage to fisheries and commerce that might result from excessive flooding caused by disturbance of the river's natural floodplain.

With the Civil War and federal capture of southern rivers and coasts, the problems encountered by army engineers constructing canals, providing for sanitation, and housing homeless slaves encouraged national planning and experimentation. Georgia's Sea Islands, abandoned by loyal Confederate planters, were temporarily turned over to freedmen's families, who built their economy around the resources of the wetlands. Free blacks in the Upper South, often landless, had supported their families before the war by relying on wetland fishing and hunting.

Olmsted spoke favorably of health "resorts," which had emerged near wetlands in the Deep South before the war and afterward had grown in popularity because of improved transportation. Olmsted's landscape plans for urban parks also used wetlands and rivers as natural drainage basins. The picturesque qualities ascribed to the coast from Charleston to Saint Augustine by William Cullen Bryant were also reflected in Lanier's poem "The Marshes of Glynn." Despite the growing industrial and commercial demands for the reclamation of wetlands, southern tidal marshes became metaphors for the sublime and peaceful freedom embodied in wild landscapes.

Southern ambivalence about whether to convert wetlands to further farming and commerce or to preserve the marshland beauty through protected hunting, fishing, and recreation fostered conflicting national programs. The third phase of wetlands alteration—that of suburban modifications—began in the 20th century. Fisheries laboratories were constructed on the Carolina Outer Banks and Florida Keys, while Pelican Island, Fla., became the first National Wildlife Refuge in 1905 and Cape Hatteras the first National Seashore in 1937. Houston rose out of Buffalo Bayou and Miami Beach usurped Biscayne Bay's barrier islands, confirming the New South's ongoing reliance on wetland real estate. After World War II, suburban growth, automobile accessibility, and increasing per capita demands for resources jeopardized the uneasy balance between the use and preservation of wetlands.

The protection afforded wildlife and fisheries by the creation of the Everglades National Park in 1947 represented a departure from an older and narrower view of parks for recreation to an ecologically broader desire to protect the biological integrity of water, energy, and land. Studies of the Texas and Gulf shrimp fisheries by Gordon Gunther, and Eugene Odum's productivity experiments on Sapelo Island tidal marshes have challenged the utility versus beauty arguments for reclaiming wetlands. The accumulated ecological evidence now suggests that far from being disease-infested wastelands, wetlands are productive, transitional vegetation zones capable of sustaining fisheries, recharging groundwater supplies, protecting uplands from flooding, and decomposing biodegradable wastes. Ecologists have argued that merely preserving landscape is inadequate to protect the numerous public benefits provided by wild wetlands. Instead, the delicately functioning balances between growing plants, migratory wildlife, and impeccably high water quality must be surveyed, monitored, and guaranteed.

See also BLACK LIFE: / Sea Islands; ETHNIC LIFE: / Cajuns and Creoles; HISTORY AND MANNERS: / Beverley, Robert; LAW: River Law; RECREATION: Fishing; Hunting; SCIENCE AND MEDICINE: / Ruffin, Edmund

Joseph V. Siry
Solano Community College
Suisun, California

Nelson M. Blake, *Land into Water—Water into Land: A History of Water Management in Florida* (1980); Alexander C. Brown, *Dismal Swamp Canal* (1946); Archie Carr, *The Everglades* (1973); Malcolm L. Comeaux, *Atchafalaya Swamp Life: Settlement and Folk Occupations* (1972); Albert E. Cowdrey, *This Land, This South: An Environmental History* (1983); Cecile H. Matschat, *Suwannee River: Strange Green Land* (1938); Joseph V. Siry, *Marshes of the Ocean Shore: The Development of an Ecological Ethic* (1984).

Alligators and Crocodiles

The American alligator (*Alligator mississipiensis*), one of only two remaining species of alligator, inhabits the rivers, swamps, and marshes of the southeastern United States as far west as Texas. The name "alligator" is an Anglicization of the Spanish *el legarto*, "the lizard." The American crocodile (*Crocodylus acutus*), an extremely endangered species, is limited to the southern tip of Florida.

Eighteenth-century accounts and drawings by explorers and naturalists in the American South elevated the alligator to a symbol representing America in European cartography and art. William Bartram's *Travels through North and South Carolina, Georgia, East and West Florida* (1791) and his drawings of "the alegator of St. Johns" burned into both American and European imaginations the image of a fearsome, aggressive, bellowing man-eater.

E. W. Kemble drawing, "A Live Capture," in Harper's Weekly, *1890*

White southerners have alternately hunted and been hunted by the alligator. Up until the Civil War, alligator hunting was a sport common enough to decimate the alligator population in the lower Mississippi. The use of alligator hides for shoes, belts, and purses began in the 1850s and for the next century accelerated the hunt, as the value of the hides grew astronomically. In the 1940s the southern states outlawed the killing and trapping of alligators, and the 1970 U.S. Endangered Species Act banned the international sale of hides and products. Despite continued poaching, the protected alligator population had so replenished itself that in 1981 it became legal once more to sell the hides.

Stories of encounters with alligators, especially deadly attacks upon children and dogs, have been common throughout the South since the 18th century. The belief that alligators are especially prone to attack blacks began in early slave ship accounts and persists as a motif in white southern fiction and humor, and on postcards and souvenirs from the early decades of this century.

The attitudes of southern blacks and Native Americans toward alligators are quite mixed. Afro-American folktales portray the alligator as the victim of a trickster animal such as the rabbit with whom blacks identified. The Seminole Indians of Florida have had a relationship to alligators something like that of the Plains Indians to the bison. Alligator wrestling that has thrilled tourists since the 1920s at alligator farms and at dozens of smaller roadside attractions never was a Seminole native custom.

Blacks and Native Americans have incorporated the alligator into their foodways. Southern magical medicine employs alligator teeth and oil in treatments for pain, as antidotes for poison, and as charms against witches. A Cajun superstition alleges that an alligator crawling under one's house is a portent of death. Most southerners, it seems, attribute great power to the alligator.

Jay Mechling
University of California, Davis

Dick Bothwell, *The Great Outdoors Book of Alligators and Other Crocodilia* (n.d.); Sherman A. Minton, Jr., and Madge

Rutherford Minton, *Giant Reptiles* (1973); Wilfred T. Neill, *The Last of the Ruling Reptiles: Alligators, Crocodiles, and Their Kin* (1971).

Appalachian Coal Region

The Appalachian coalfields stretch from northern Pennsylvania to Alabama, with major southern sites in West Virginia, southwestern Virginia, western Kentucky and Tennessee, and northern Alabama. As a group, the Appalachian coal-producing areas comprise one of seven major coalfields in the United States. The mountainous topography and the industrial history of the Appalachian coalfields have uniquely shaped the inhabitants' lives, producing a sense of otherness within the fabric of southern culture.

The southern Appalachians were sparsely settled by self-sufficient mountain families before the coming of the railroad. The coal in their hills, however, was of great value to America's burgeoning industrial economy in the 19th century, so mining operations proliferated. Company towns were built, and mine workers were brought in from other states and many nations. Sharing more with the propertyless wage earners of the industrial cities of the North than with the sharecropping farmers of the South, the miners suffered through the ups and downs of an exceedingly unstable industry by clinging to visions of both militant unionism and individual success. Outsiders have found it easiest to attribute their stridency, pride, and recurring poverty to the fierce, if ignorant, independence of the mountaineer. This perception of the beliefs and problems of those who live in the coal regions turns a blind eye to the underlying industrial causes of Appalachian backwardness.

The development of the coalfields as an economic resource reflected technological and business innovation. Modern methods of exploiting fields of bituminous coal were applied to Appalachia beginning in the 1880s. Coal output rose from 6 million tons in 1880 to 26 million tons by 1890 and 52 million tons in 1900. Coal companies such as the Virginia Iron, Coal, and Coke Company, Western Kentucky Coal, and the Peabody Coal Company became giants of the American energy industry, controlling land and deposits of coal, limestone, oil, and gas.

Exploitation of the coalfields has left its mark on the Appalachian environment and on the region's inhabitants. The high sulfur content of coal has meant widespread pollution of air and a blackened landscape. Until the 1950s, miners worked primarily underground, gathering coal in deep-shaft mines. Mine explosions were common, and the death rate for miners was the highest in the industrial world. Strip mining became increasingly common after 1960, thanks to the development of huge new earth-moving machinery. "Big Muskie" is the world's largest piece of heavy machinery, broad as an eight-lane road, and it is used in Appalachian coalfields. Contour strip mining scars the region's hillsides, promoting erosion and flooding. Protest songs and folksongs—such as John Prine's "Paradise," which tells of the Peabody Coal Company in Muhlenberg County, Ky.—have chronicled the story of the Appalachian coalfields and the hardships of coal miners and their families, seldom the beneficiaries of the wealth they have helped reap.

See also INDUSTRY: / Mining; MYTHIC SOUTH: / Appalachian Myth; SOCIAL CLASS: / Coal Miners

Arthur Donovan
Virginia Polytechnic Institute
and State University

David A. Corbin, *Life, Work, and Rebellion in the Coal Fields: The Southern West Virginia Miners, 1880–1922* (1981); Ronald Eller, *Miners, Millhands, and Mountaineers: The Modernization of the Appalachian South, 1880–1930* (1981); Henry D. Shapiro, *Appalachia on Our Mind: The Southern Mountains and Mountaineers in the American Consciousness, 1870–1920* (1978); David E. Whisnant, *All That Is Native and Fine: The Politics of Culture in an American Region* (1983).

Appalachian Mountains

This extended mountain system stretches from the St. Lawrence Valley in Canada to central Alabama. It includes a series of ranges, and those in the South include the Allegheny Mountains, the Blue Ridge, the Black Mountains, the Great Smoky Mountains, and the Cumberland Plateau. Composed of sedimentary rock, the beds of insoluble material in the southern mountains have resisted erosion, resulting in the South's having the highest ranges of the series. Mount Mitchell (6,684 feet) in the Black Mountains is the highest peak in the Appalachians. The Blue Ridge Mountains run upward into Pennsylvania and represent the eastern escarpment of the southern Appalachians. They are a maze of coves, hills, and spurs, resulting from gradual erosion of a mound of irregular rock. The Appalachian Valley lies between the Blue Ridge Mountains on the east and the Great Smoky Mountains on the west. It is a series of river valleys, including the Coosa, Tennessee, Shenandoah, and Cumberland.

The Appalachian Mountains represented a barrier to the advance of the frontier in the colonial era, but were being crossed by the time of the American Revolution. Folksongs such as "The Cumberland Gap" and stories of Daniel Boone and other frontiersmen preserve the memory of this phase of southern history. Comparatively small and diffuse coves, gorges, basins, and hollows developed population centers that remained isolated until the late 19th century. The mountains were a source of Unionist sentiments in the South during the Civil War, and the Great Valley of Virginia was the scene of General Philip Sheridan's raids, one of the most dramatic chapters of the military struggle. In the late 19th century commercial interests began the exploitation of such mountain resources as coal, gas, petroleum, iron, and timber found abundantly in the mountains. The area has in the 20th century been the scene for some of the nation's worst poverty, with Lyndon B. Johnson's War on Poverty including special programs aimed at southern mountain economic and social development. The Appalachian Mountains' natural resources support tourism and recreational sports. Aaron Copland's "Appalachian Spring" conveys in music the beauties and mysteries of the mountains, and photographer Eliot Porter's *Appalachian Wilderness* (1973) captures their rhythms in visual images.

See also INDUSTRY: / Mining; MYTHIC SOUTH: / Appalachian Myth; SOCIAL CLASS: / Coal Miners

Charles Reagan Wilson
University of Mississippi

Thomas L. Connelly, *Discovering the Appalachians: What to Look for from the Past and in the Present along America's Eastern Frontier* (1968); Thomas R. Ford, ed., *The Southern Appalachian Region: A Survey* (1962); Karl B. Raitz and Richard Ulack, *Appalachia: A Regional Geography: Land, People, and Development* (1984); Charlotte T. Ross, ed., *Bibliography of Southern Appalachia* (1976).

Armadillo

The armadillo is an armored mammal about 30 inches long, including a tail of about 12 inches, usually weighing about 10 pounds. The body is enclosed by a three-sectioned shell. One section in the front protects the shoulders; another section in the rear protects the pelvic region. In the middle section between these two are a number of movable bands. The vulnerable underside is without armor, but it is protected by a tough skin covered with coarse hair.

Collectively, armadillos are distributed throughout South America and north to Texas and into the Deep South. Because the early explorers had not seen the animal before in Europe, it was natural for them to identify the "New Animal" with the "New World." Gradually this identification became so fixed that the armadillo took on the nature of a symbol. It was widely used in such symbolic contexts as decorative map frames in the 1500s and 1600s.

In 20th century America there has been special interest in a single species—the nine-banded armadillo, which is known formally as *Dasypus novemcinctus mexicanus*, or informally as the Texas Armadillo. In modern times the nine-banded armadillo has become identified with Texas just as strongly as the armadillo once was identified with America. This identification is somewhat emotional and symbolic because in fact the armadillo is not at all confined to present-day Texas. Indeed, there are large numbers of armadillos in Louisiana, Mississippi, and Florida.

The armadillo usually comes out only at night. It lives on insects and worms. The animal is basically harmless to people and does not put up a fight when captured. In fact, its peaceful nature invited its use by antiwar protestors as a symbol during the 1960s. In 1968 self-styled hippie artist Jim Franklin, asked to come up with a design for a poster for a free concert in a park in Austin, drew an armadillo smoking a marijuana cigarette, and after that the armadillo became the visual symbol of the Texas youth culture.

In the early 1970s a group of counterculture businessmen started an Austin music hall called the Armadillo World Headquarters in an abandoned armory. The music hall became the center of "redneck rock," a fusion of country and western with rock and roll.

The popularity of the new music catapulted the armadillo into high status at the University of Texas. The armadillo was soon rendered in orange and white, the university's colors. In 1971 the student senate voted to change the school's mascot from the longhorn to the armadillo, but the change was never made official.

The armadillo became familiar in Austin through the musical scene and was reinforced by posters and handbills, stories, and jokes. The connection between the armadillo and Texas youth culture may fade since the last concert at the Armadillo World Headquarters was on 31 December 1980. The building has since been torn down.

Angus K. Gillespie
Rutgers University

Larry L. Smith and Robin W. Doughty, *The Amazing Armadillo* (1984).

Atchafalaya Basin Swamp

The Atchafalaya Basin Swamp is a large swamp in south Louisiana located between the high natural levees of Bayou Teche on the west and south, and those of the Mississippi River and Bayou Lafourche on the east. This basin is about 100 miles long and 30 miles wide. It is a forested region laced with rivers, lakes, and bayous. The Atchafalaya River, a tributary of the Mississippi, traverses the swamp and brings high floods in late winter and early spring.

Early French settlers avoided swamps and settled rich agricultural lands along rivers. After the Louisiana Purchase southern plantation owners migrated to Louisiana and began acquiring the farms of the small French farmers, who then moved onto small ridges of high land in nearby swamps. Floods were not a problem in the Atchafalaya Swamp in the early 19th century, but by mid-century they had become severe, and all agriculture in the Atchafalaya Swamp ended by 1875.

A swamp culture slowly evolved as farmers adjusted to a new and alien way of life. Certain swamp products such as Spanish moss, cypress lumber, and various foodstuffs (crawfish and frogs) were always in demand by French speakers surrounding the swamp, and these exfarmers began to exploit the swamp, selling its products to surrounding peoples. English-speaking fishermen drifted into the Atchafalaya from the upper Mississippi River and introduced houseboats and new fishing gear. By 1900 the Atchafalaya Swamp had become the most productive swamp in the world, producing fish, crawfish, Spanish moss, alligators, frogs, turtles, game animals, crabs, pelts, lumber, and other swamp products (and today oil). It remains very productive.

All swamp dwellers are white. This is not unique, as there are few black commercial fishermen in the entire Mississippi River System. French- and English-speaking fishermen exchanged ideas about fishing and swamp life, but they occupied distinct portions of the Atchafalaya Swamp, and because of religious, linguistic, and cultural differences little mixing took place between them. Today, those who exploit the swamp live in small communities where they have access to the outside world, and they commute to their hunting, fishing, and trapping grounds by boat.

Malcolm L. Comeaux
Arizona State University

Malcolm L. Comeaux, *Atchafalaya Swamp Life: Settlement and Folk Occupations* (1972); Harold N. Fisk, *Geological Investigation of the Atchafalaya Basin and the Problem of Mississippi River Diversion* (1949); Charles Fryling, Jr., *Ozark Society Bulletin* (Autumn 1978).

Audubon, John James

(1785–1851) Naturalist and artist.

Although Audubon's observations of wildlife extended from Labrador to the Florida Keys and from New Jersey to the Missouri River country, his works are particularly rich in material gathered in Kentucky, Louisiana, Mississippi, and Florida. During the years when these southern frontiers abounded in birds, he was able to compile an extraordinary record in paintings and journals.

The illegitimate son of Captain Jean Audubon and Jeanne Rabine, a French servant, Audubon was born 26 April 1785 on his father's plantation in Aux Cayes, Santo Domingo. Brought up in Nice, France, as the adopted son of Captain Audubon and his legal wife, the boy received very little formal schooling, but did have some instruction in painting and music. In 1804 the 18-year-old Audubon came to America where he lived for a time on a Pennsylvania farm belonging to his father. From 1808 to 1819 he attempted to make a living as a frontier trader in Kentucky. He had some success operating a store and sawmill in Henderson, but had to declare himself bankrupt in 1819. After this failure he concentrated most of his energies on hunting and painting birds, activities in which he had spent his happiest hours since first coming to America. He occasionally earned a few dollars practicing taxidermy, painting portraits, and teaching drawing and music, but his remarkable wife, Lucy Bakewell, often had to support herself and their two sons by tutoring while Audubon was ranging the wilderness. He traveled extensively in the Mississippi Valley and lived briefly in New Orleans and West Feliciana Parish, La.

In 1826 Audubon's portfolios contained some 400 paintings of birds, done in watercolor and pastel. Unsuccessful in getting support for his work in America, Audubon carried his appeal to the British Isles where he managed to interest important savants and wealthy people. With this backing he was able to arrange for the reproduction of his paintings in color by Robert Havell, a skillful London engraver. Through persistent effort Audubon signed up enough subscribers for the publication of *The Birds of America* (1827–38) in four beautiful volumes, "double elephant" or 39½ by 29½ inches in size. No more than 200 complete sets were issued, and surviving copies now command very high prices in the rare book market.

Audubon's restless energy found many outlets. In 1831–32 he extended his knowledge of the South by hunting birds in the St. Augustine region and the Florida Keys. With the help of scientific collaborators and his own artist sons, John and Victor, he published *Ornithological Biography* (5 vols., 1831–39), a cheaper edition of *The Birds of America* (7 vols., 1840–44), and *The Vivaporous Quadrupeds of North America* (2 vols., 1845–46). He died 17 January 1851 at Minnie's Land, his estate on Manhattan Island near the Hudson River.

During his lifetime Audubon had to contend with the jealousy of other naturalists, and he defended himself vigorously against charges of plagiarism and mendacity. Modern critics have applauded the originality, general accuracy, and beauty of his work, including his documentation of an important phase of southern wildlife. Contemporary southern authors such as Eudora Welty and Robert Penn Warren have celebrated Audubon in their own works as a significant southern artist.

Nelson M. Blake
Syracuse University

Alice Ford, *John James Audubon* (1964); Kathryn Hall Proby, *Audubon in Florida, with Selections from the Writings of John James Audubon* (1974); Francis H. Herrick, *Audubon the Naturalist: A History of His Life and Time* (1938).

Azalea

This is the name for a group of colorful deciduous shrubs, now usually classified with their evergreen relatives in the genus *Rhododendron*. Although native primarily to the acid soils and more temperate climates of the southeastern United States and southeastern Asia, many of its botanical species and horticultural varieties are widely grown in other areas of the world that have comparable soils and climates. Indeed, although azaleas were among the first North American shrubs to be sent back to England in the early days of colonial exploration, their general association with the South stems primarily from the extensive plantings of horticultural forms in some of the major southern show gardens during the early to mid-20th century. Many of the varieties now grown in the South were introduced from Asia.

From the impact generated by colorful spring displays at such gardens as Bellingrath, near Mobile, Ala., Orton, near Wilmington, N.C., and the Magnolia and Middleton gardens near Charleston, S.C., azaleas have come to be associated with the South. The association is greatly strengthened by the brilliant spring display of the native flame azalea (*Rhododendron calendulaceum*) along the Blue Ridge Parkway in Virginia and North Carolina and by the intense, spicy fragrance of swamp honeysuckle (*R. viscosum*), another attractive native shrub, which grows in bogs and along stream margins over much of the South. The azalea has become a resource for luring tourists. Mobile annually sponsors its Azalea Trail; Lafayette, La., has an Azalea Tour; and Charleston greets spring with its Azalea Festival.

C. Ritchie Bell
North Carolina Botanical Gardens
University of North Carolina
at Chapel Hill

Charles Reagan Wilson
University of Mississippi

Ben A. Davis, *Azaleas, Camellias, Gardenias* (1950), *The Southern Garden: From the Potomac to the Rio Grande* (1971); Fred C. Galle, *Azaleas* (1974); William L. Hunt, *Southern Gardens, Southern Gardening* (1982).

Big Thicket

A biological and historical subregion of southeast Texas, the Big Thicket once covered approximately 3 million acres, from the Louisiana border across the lower Neches and Trinity river basins westward to the San Jacinto River and its tributaries. This dense wilderness is now reduced to approximately 300,000 acres, in Hardin and surrounding counties.

Biologically the Big Thicket is the southwesternmost extension of the Southern Evergreen Forest. Proximity to both the Gulf of Mexico and the dry Texas prairies accounts for the incursion of western and tropical species into its otherwise deep-southern ecology. Roadrunner and alligator, prickly pear cactus and water tupelo, sagebrush and subtropical orchids can be found there within sight of one another. Many of its rare, scarce, or endangered bird, plant, and animal species are now protected in the 84,550-acre Big Thicket (National) Preserve. Biologists have described the region as zoologically and botanically the most diverse area of its size in the Western Hemisphere.

Historically the Big Thicket has long been famous as a refuge. Early pioneers entering southeast Texas in the 1820s found their way blocked by dense vegetation along innumerable streams. They detoured around the area, which they termed the "Big Thicket." Though it was never an unbroken jungle, civilization tended to bypass the Thicket. During the Civil War deserters and conscientious objectors from Texas and nearby southern states hid there, pursued without success by conscription forces. During World Wars I and II descendants of some of these original fugitives hid there for the duration of the conflict. As late as the 1950s prisoners from nearby state prisons were said to have a good chance of escape if they could reach the Thicket ahead of their pursuers.

Pete A. Y. Gunter
North Texas State University

Geyata Ajilvsgi, *Wildflowers of the Big Thicket, East Texas, and Western Louisiana* (1979); Pete A. Y. Gunter, *The Big Thicket: A Challenge for Conservation* (1971); Campbell Loughmiller and Lynn Loughmiller, *Big Thicket Legacy* (1977).

Blue Ridge

The Blue Ridge is a long mountain barrier, a part of the Appalachians, running from southwestern North Carolina northeast some 1,400 miles to the vicinity of Gettysburg, Penn. The southern section is massive with peaks over 5,000 feet and a breadth of over 50 miles. North of Boone, N.C., the highlands become less broad and are interrupted by numerous gaps. The Indians called the mountain "the long divide," but early European colonists named it "blue" because of the blue haze hanging over it (the transpiration of water from the forest below the ridge creates the haze).

In colonial times the ridge became a temporary frontier between the plantation economies to the east and the Indians to the west. During the late 1700s English, German, and Celtic settlers moved into the area and intermingled. They formed a self-sufficient small farm society with almost no dependence on the African slave labor that dominated older southern societies.

During the 1930s a scenic highway (the Blue Ridge Parkway opened in 1933) was built along portions of the ridge. This highway now extends 470 miles from the Great Smoky Mountains to Front Royal, Va. The Appalachian Trail uses the ridge in its route from the Great Smokies to Maine. It attracts thousands of hikers every year.

The Blue Ridge thus serves as a prominent physical feature of the Appalachian region, a historical boundary between two major cultural hearths of the Americans, and a contemporary mecca for recreation.

Richard S. Little
West Virginia University

William A. Bake, *The Blue Ridge* (1977); Harley E. Jolley, *The Blue Ridge Parkway* (1960); Jean Thomas, *Blue Ridge Country*

(1942); Richard A. Williams, Jr., "The Regional Impact of the Blue Ridge Parkway in Virginia" (Ph.D. dissertation, Virginia Polytechnic Institute and State University, 1981).

Catfish

Southerners have never aligned themselves as closely with any cold-blooded creature as they have with the feline-looking catfish. Catfish are found elsewhere, to be sure. There are some 2,000 species throughout the world and more than two dozen in the United States alone. Southerners, though, have claimed the freshwater cat as their own. They have written the bewhiskered fish into their literature and sung songs and spun tales around it. And they have argued among themselves for years about which one tastes best and how it should be cooked.

The three major kinds, all of the family *Ictaluridae*, are the blue, the channel, and the flathead. Names change with locale, but none of the fish are particularly attractive. The flathead, in fact, looks like its head has been slammed in a car door. For long years, too, all three have suffered from the image of being a trash fish that would eat anything. Catfish were considered a lazy man's fish, a poor man's fish, a black man's fish. Still, the size and exploits of the catfish—and catfisherman—have become legend below the Mason-Dixon line, and their image is beginning to change.

Reports still exist from the 19th century of catfish weighing 150 to 200 pounds or more regularly surfacing at the major fishmarkets along the Mississippi River. It has been a century since Huck Finn and Jim pulled a catfish as big as a man out of the Mississippi. Roughly the same amount of time has passed since Mark Twain also reported that a gargantuan catfish bumped into Marquette's canoe, almost prompting the French explorer to believe what Indians had told him about the river's roaring demon.

Today's equivalent is the omnipresent tale about car-sized catfish lurking below the dams of the South's major rivers, but, like Twain's frequent references, facts of these sightings have never been verified. Still, the catfish's association with the South persists—enough so that catfish were the subject of one rollicking song from a 1982 Broadway musical, "Pump Boys and Dinettes," set somewhere near Frog Level, Ga.

Although sizes are not consistently documented, plenty of catfish are caught—and bragged about—yearly by southern anglers. In earlier times, dynamite was sometimes used to kill a mess of cats. So was "telephoning" or electric-shocking, but both these practices are strictly illegal. Big, old catfish, however, are still caught in a variety of ways in the South, many of them a legacy from the old days.

There are those who continue to work the banks with a cane pole, sinker, and handful of worms. A brave few carry on the practice of handgrabbing in the warmer, sluggish rivers of late spring or summer. Sometimes called grabbling or noodling, it consists of reaching into a submerged, hollow log, grabbing a resident blue or flathead by the lower jaw, and hauling it out by hand like a suitcase.

Many fishermen use trotlines to hook cats. "Jugging" is a mobile version of trotlining. Anglers simply take a piece of line, tie a jug on one end and a baited hook on the other, and then follow the jug as it bounces the bait along river's bottom. Snagging consists of just hooking the fish any way possible with bare treble hooks. It is not too sporting, admittedly, but it has brought in some flatheads weighing 130 pounds or more from Arkansas rivers.

The rod-and-reel fisherman in search of a good fight and a good meal began to modernize the image of the South's catfish. Casting with heavy rigs below the dams and using electronic equipment, southern fishermen are netting prize blues and flatheads of 38 to 55 pounds and more.

The channel catfish, too, has made another significant step toward revamping the tarnished image. Based in the South and Southwest, channel catfish farming is the nation's leading aquaculture industry. Since 1960 soybean and cotton fields in Mississippi, Alabama, Arkansas, and other southern states have been converted into catfish ponds. Fed on grain and carefully nurtured, the grown fish are trucked live from the ponds to processing plants, from which they are shipped out across the country. Supplying some 65 percent of the U.S. production, Mississippi currently leads the industry, which annually yields an estimated 200 million pounds of farm-raised catfish. Industry spokesmen swear that catfish is the best thing to hit the South since cotton.

Experts cite several reasons for the fish's growing popularity. Research is constantly improving the product, creating better strains of fish that are easier to raise. The channel cat's white, flaky-clean flesh is high in protein and low in fat and calories—a plus in an increasingly diet-conscious culture.

Recipes for dishes like soufflé-stuffed catfish, catfish amandine, and catfish kiev-style are appearing more and more often in magazines such as *Southern Living*, one of the South's self-proclaimed culinary bibles. A National Farm-Raised Catfish Cooking Contest, held in Mississippi, garners almost 1,000 recipe entries each year. One of the country's better-known fast-food chains, Church's Fried Chicken, has opted to add catfish to its standardized menu. When fried catfish was served to the world's leaders at the 1983 Williamsburg Summit Conference, not a single piece of the entree, according to observers, remained as leftovers. The South's lowly catfish has finally swum uptown.

New image and all, however, the catfish will probably never leave behind its down-home connections. Every southern state proclaims at least one "catfish capital of the world." To name but a few, Mississippi boasts Belzoni; Tennessee has Paris; and Arkansas declares Toad Suck as *the* spot for catfish. Most of these places and many more still hold annual festivals to celebrate their own hometown favorite—the catfish. They batter and fry huge amounts of the fish and serve it swimming in catsup on plates heaped high with hushpuppies, coleslaw, and french fries, usually all to the beat of local bluegrass or country music. Most of these are all-you-can-eat affairs, meant to be social occasions rather than gourmet experiences. Despite its changing image, the catfish's place as an excuse for a traditional southern celebration is not likely to change anytime soon.

Dianne Young
Southern Living

Kenneth D. Carlander, *Handbook of Freshwater Fishery Biology*, vols. 1 and 2 (1969, 1977); John Madson, *Smithsonian* (September 1984); Dianne Young, *Southern Living* (July 1984).

Chesapeake Bay

This is the largest estuary in North America, stretching 200 miles in length, from southern Virginia to northern Maryland, and ranging from 3 to 35 miles in width. The bay includes 4,300 square miles of water and covers 8,100 miles of shoreline. There are 170 miles of channel connecting the bay to the inland seaport of Baltimore. The area has historically nurtured a distinctive culture of the Upper South and today continues to provide an economic and environmental context for many southerners.

The Chesapeake Bay was the site of the first permanent English colony in North America and gave rise to a cohesive society in the colonial South. Jamestown was founded in 1607 on the lower bay, on the James River. Captain John Smith called it "a faire Bay." "Heaven and earth never agreed better to frame a place for man's habitation," he wrote. Some 200 Algonkian Indian villages were already in the area when the settlers arrived, and the Native American influence survives in the names of such rivers as the Potomac, Patuxent, Patapsco, Rappahannock, Nanticoke, and Wicomico. More than 10 major waterways feed into the bay, as well as 140 other rivers, creeks, and streams. The Susquehanna River is the bay's main artery.

Tobacco early became the dominant economic factor in the Chesapeake. The long shoreline and extensive system of navigable waterways encouraged the growing and exportation of staple crops, especially tobacco, for trade. In 1775 tobacco represented 75 percent of the total value of export from the Chesapeake area, was worth $4 million, and accounted for 60 percent of the colonies' total exports to England. Shipbuilding, another important economic activity dating back to the 1600s, reached a high point before the Civil War. The construction of canals in the 1820s and railroads in the 1830s and 1840s provided a foundation for the region's economic expansion during the 19th century. The Chesapeake became part of a Middle Atlantic industrial seaboard area, with its ports in Baltimore, Norfolk, and Hampton Roads serving as centers of international commerce.

The Chesapeake Bay has immense environmental importance. It gives life to 2,700 species of animals, especially fish and shellfish. Clams, crabs, eels, sea trout, flounder, bluefish, croakers, shad, and herring are found in the bay, which produces 33 percent of the United States oyster catch and 50 percent of its blue crabs. Crisfield, Md., the self-styled crab capital of the world, sponsors an end-of-summer hard crab derby and a Miss Crustacean Beauty Pageant. Geese, ducks, swans, and other waterfowl can be seen in the bay, as part of their winter migration from the North. Baltimore journalist H. L. Mencken called the bay "a great big protein factory" because of its animal resources. The environment there also supports recreational activities for sport fishermen and others from the surrounding areas.

The Chesapeake region has grown enormously in recent decades, now supporting almost 9 million people, with a 50 percent population increase from 1950 to 1984 in the bay's drainage area of six states (Virginia, Maryland, Pennsylvania, New York, Delaware, and West Virginia). This increased concentration of population, along with pollution from the factories and farms of the area, has brought a deteriorating environment and rising fear for its future. The Susquehanna empties chemical pollutants from Pennsylvania industries into the bay, the Patapsco in Maryland carries refinery contaminants, and the James River holds waste from Richmond and Norfolk. Fertilizer runoff from farms is considered perhaps an even greater threat than industrial pollution. A significant decline of sea life has resulted. In the mid-1970s the bay produced over 6 million pounds of striped bass yearly, but that had declined to 600,000 by the mid-1980s. The federal government and the Chesapeake states announced a major clean-up program in September of 1985.

See also LANGUAGE: / Chesapeake Bay Dialect

Charles Reagan Wilson
University of Mississippi

Carl Bridenbaugh, *Myths and Realities: Societies of the Colonial South* (1963); Ernest M. Eller, *Chesapeake Bay in the American Revolution* (1982); Carolyn Ellis, *Fisher Folk: Two Communities on the Chesapeake Bay* (1986); William C. McCloskey, *National Wildlife* (April–May 1984); Arthur P. Middleton, *Tobacco Coast: A Maritime History of Chesapeake Bay in the Colonial Era* (1984); Thad W. Tate and David L. Ammerman, eds., *The Chesapeake in the Seventeenth Century: Essays on Anglo-American Society* (1979); William W. Warner, *Beautiful Swimmers: Watermen, Crabs, and the Chesapeake Bay* (1976).

Collard Greens

Collard greens grow throughout the South and, probably more than any other food, delineate the boundaries of the Mason-Dixon line. Some claim greens kept Sherman's scorched-earth policy from totally starving the South into submission; many today are living testament to surviving Depression winters with greens, fatback, and corn bread. Southern childhood memories often focus on collard greens: either the pleasant, loving connection of grandma's iron pot and steaming pot likker, or the traumatizing effects engendered from the first whiff of the unmistakable odor for which greens are famous. Writing in the Charlotte, N.C., *Observer* in 1907, J. P. Caldwell explained, "The North Carolinian who is not familiar with pot likker has suffered in his early education and needs to go back and begin it over again." Particularly among rural and poor southerners, collard greens have endured as a dietary staple.

Sometimes defined as headless cabbages, collards are best when prepared just after the first frost, though they are eaten year round. They should always be harvested before the dew dries. First, they are "crapped," then "looked," then cooked; that is, cut at the base of a stalk, searched for worms, and then cooked "till tender" on a low boil, usually with fatback, or neck or backbone, added. The resultant "mess o' greens" topped with a generous helping of vinegar can easily make a meal in itself. If they are summer greens (and much tougher), the tenderizing could take two hours or more; after first frost, it may take less than an hour. A whole pecan in the pot should eliminate the pungent and earthy smell. Pot likker, the juice left in the pot after the greens are gone, is a southern version of nectar from the gods, and is valued both as a delicacy—particularly when sopped with corn bread—and for its alleged aphrodisiacal powers. Greens combine well with the black-eyed peas and hog jowl in the traditional New Year's Day meal. To ensure good fortune, one should either eat lots of greens, or tack them to the ceiling. In fact, a collard leaf left hanging over one's door can ward off evil spirits all year long.

Nutritionally, collards are good sources of vitamin A. They seem to have unique laxative qualities, though the resultant gas is often troublesome. Folk legends claim a fresh collard leaf placed on the forehead should cure a headache. The same remedy can be applied to nervous afflictions plaguing women, though it works best on such cases when the leaf is still wet with dew and the woman just rising. The roots bound on arthritic joints ease pain, and a poultice prepared from collard leaves has been recommended as a cure for cancers on the face, boils, and festering sores.

Though collard greens are grown throughout the South and Southwest (Indians call them "quelites"), they are most prevalent in the Deep South and the eastern plains of North and South Carolina. The exporting of collards to displaced southerners in the Northeast is big business for Texas and Arizona, but Georgia is easily the top exporter of whole, fresh greens. From the last week of October through May, seven firms around Cairo, Ga., ship 315 tons of collards a week to all the major northeastern metropolitan areas, though over half of that amount goes to New York City alone. The greens are cut and banded with rubber bands, then packed in bundles on ice, about 25 pounds per box.

Collards are usually grown for utilitarian purposes, but southerners have been known to decorate a particularly brilliant plant as a Christmas tree. Thelonious Monk, the jazz great born in Rocky Mount, N.C., wore a collard leaf in his lapel while playing New York club dates. Greens were first officially celebrated in 1950, when the North Carolina playwright Paul Green led a "Collards and Culture" symposium in Dunn, N.C. According to Sam Ragan, North Carolina's poet laureate, Green "urged us all to move out of the commonplace and bring a new dimension to our collard lives."

Flannery O'Connor's Ruby Hill, in "A Stroke of Good Fortune," takes a different view of greens. When her brother, home from the European Theater, asks her to cook him some, she complies grudgingly: "'Collard greens!' she said, spitting the word from her mouth as if it were a poisonous seed."

Collard greens are presently celebrated in two annual festivals—in Gaston, S.C., and in Ayden, N.C. In celebration of its 10th annual event, in 1984 the Ayden Collard Festival published the first volume of collard poetry, *Leaves of Greens: The Collard Poems*, and staged the first-ever collard poetry reading. Over 500 entries in the poetry contest were submitted from poets in 32 states and three European countries.

The world's record for eating collards was claimed at the 1984 Ayden festival when C. Mort Hurst ate 7½ pounds in 30 minutes, and kept them down just long enough to claim his prize.

Alex Albright
East Carolina University

Alex Albright and Luke Whisnant, eds., *Leaves of Greens: The Collard Poems* (1984); "Collard Files," Folklore Archives, English Department, East Carolina University, Greenville, N.C.; Greenville, N.C., *Daily Reflector* (9 September 1984); Flannery O'Connor, "A Stroke of Good Fortune," *The Complete Stories* (1971); Sam Ragan, "Southern Pines," *N.C. Pilot* (12 July 1984); *The State* (July 1984).

Cypress

Author Willie Morris, looking back on his childhood in the Mississippi Delta, recalled a vivid memory of the "cypresses, bent down like wise men trying to tell us something." The bald cypress (*Taxodium distichum R.*) is a common image in the literary and visual works of southerners who are well acquainted with the tree that grows in the Coastal Plain of the Gulf and Atlantic coasts, along inland swamps and rivers, and in pine-barren ponds. It is submerged during much of the year, often providing nearly total forest coverage of large wetland areas. Spanish moss is frequently seen draped over the cypress's heavy branches, and herons and water turkeys sometimes nest in its limbs.

Unlike most coniferous trees, the cypress sheds its foliage, leaving its gray trunk and its branches bare in winter months. This can create an eerie—and Gothic, in the mind of a romanticist—impression during the winter and early spring seasons. Known as the "wood eternal," it has survived since the ice age. The cypress can grow to be 100 feet high, but it grows slowly, typically expanding its radius by only one inch every 30 years. A stump of eight feet in diameter was once found 30 feet underground in

Florida. Such trees, which have been preserved in mud, are known as "Choctaw" cypress and are highly valued for their color and resistance to water. The cypress's distinctive "knees" are conical-shaped appendages rising into the air from the main roots; they help aerate the tree.

Cypress has played an important role in the economy of the Deep South. Its wood is highly durable and resists the humid climate of the Southeast. Builders value it for use as roof beams, flooring, and shingles. Southerners made cisterns, coopers' staves, and rail fences from it, and it was an essential material for the shipbuilding industry. As a result of the Swamp Lands Acts (1849–50), the region's best cypress lands near the Atchafalaya, Mississippi, and Red rivers ended up in the hands of lumbermen. They gained it through fraud involving surveyors and land agents and then proceeded to cut the land and to illegally clear nearby public land as well. After the Civil War, the cypress lands of the South were even more fully exploited, as the center of the nation's lumber industry moved south. Developers built railroads into swampy areas, giving access for sawmills and disturbing the entire ecology of areas. They produced "pecky" cypress, which is charred and brushed with acids to produce an antique effect, and it became popular for use as interior beams, paneling, and doors.

Charles Reagan Wilson
University of Mississippi

William C. Coker, *Trees of the Southeastern States, including Virginia, North Carolina, South Carolina, Georgia, and Northern Florida* (1937); E. S. Harrar and J. G. Harrar, *Guide to Southern Trees* (1962); Nollie Hickman, *Mississippi Harvest: Lumbering in the Longleaf Pine Belt, 1840–1915* (1962); John Hebron Moore, *Andrew Brown and Cypress Lumbering in the Old Southwest* (1968).

Everglades

The Everglades comprise a wilderness area in southern Florida, unique in the profusion and variety of vegetation and wildlife. Before 20th-century encroachments the Everglades extended from Lake Okeechobee to the tip of the Florida peninsula, a distance of 100 miles, and stretched halfway across the state, some 50 to 70 miles. This entire region, an ancient seabed, is almost flat. Most of it is covered with water, overflow from Lake Okeechobee and incremental rainfall, that moves sluggishly southward until it finally discharges into Florida Bay and the Gulf of Mexico. In this water, varying in depth with the seasons, tough sawgrass, sometimes growing to a height of 12 feet, stands waving in the breezes, dominating the landscape. Here and there so-called hammocks rise out of the water. On these islands trees, shrubbery, ferns, and flowering plants grow in profusion. The climate is subtropical, and much of the vegetation, particularly in the southern Everglades, is exotic. Indigenous to the West Indies, such species as royal palms, gumbo limbo and mahogany trees, and strangler figs may have sprung from seeds brought to the Florida wilderness by hurricanes or migrating birds.

In this unique and isolated terrain wildlife abounds. Where the water is not too deep, small brown deer and other common animals are found. Alligators multiply throughout the Everglades; rare American crocodiles and manatees still survive in the mangrove swamps and the coastal waters. The warm damp environment fosters the growth of snakes, turtles, and snails. Vultures, buzzards, and occasional bald eagles and kites soar over the sawgrass, and herons, cranes, egrets, and ibises wade through the waters. Also to be seen are such unusual birds as roseate spoonbills, wood storks, brown pelicans, and anhingas.

Twentieth-century development has reduced the Everglades to half their original size. Vast farms now grow sugarcane and winter vegetables south and east of Lake Okeechobee; housing developments and shopping malls stand on drained land once part of the eastern Everglades. Still more disruptive is the wholesale interference with the natural flow of the water, resulting from the construction of canals, levees, pumping stations, and conservation areas. Engineers now control the passage of the life-bearing stream.

Alarmed by the threat of encroaching development, nature lovers organized the campaign that led to the establishment of Everglades National Park in 1947. Located in the southern extremity of the state and containing almost 1.4 million acres, this is one of the largest national parks. Thousands of visitors annually walk its paths or boat upon its streams, marveling at the subtropical vegetation and the unusual birds and animals. But the park faces continual danger. Too much or too little water can destroy its fragile ecology, and the water must come from the northern Everglades. Accused of favoritism toward agriculture, the water managers at first appeared neglectful of the park, but the state is now committed to restoring a more natural flow. This is vital not only to protect the park, but to preserve the Biscayne Aquifer upon which the southeastern cities depend for their water supply.

Nelson M. Blake
Syracuse University

Archie Carr, *The Everglades* (1973); Patricia Caulfield, *Everglades: Selections from the Writings of Peter Matthiessen* (1970); Marjory Stoneman Douglas, *The Everglades: River of Grass* (1947).

Great Smoky Mountains

Located in the southeastern United States, near the junction of the Carolinas, Georgia, and Tennessee, the Great Smokies is a mountain range of some 80 peaks over 5,000 feet. Mount Mitchell (6,684 feet) is the highest peak in the eastern United States. The Smokies form an ellipse with the long axis running from southwest to northeast about 140 miles and the short axis about 70 miles. The name "Smoky Mountains" comes from the haze and clouds hanging over the peaks. Annual rainfall in this humid area is 83 inches.

Three distinct periods of human occupation have occurred in the mountains since the 1500s. Until the early 1800s Cherokee Indians occupied the surrounding region. They hunted in the mountains and considered them sacred. In 1980 Jackson and Swain counties, which include the Cherokee Reservation on the east side of the National Park, listed an Indian population of about 4,700. Most of the Indian population (over 35,000) in North Carolina is in Robeson County, south of Fayetteville on the Coastal Plain.

The appearance of Europeans represented the second stage of settlement. Spanish explorers, including possibly De Soto, came from the south in the 1540s. Some evidence suggests they conducted mining operations in the 1600s. French and English traders penetrated the region in the late 1600s. The third phase of development came when American colonists arrived in the 1770s. Indian culture was modified immensely during this time, changing from a relatively self-sufficient economy (with limited trade in seashells from the Gulf, copper from the Upper Great Lakes, and other high value goods) to a commercial gathering economy for the European fur markets. Deerskins from Cherokee traders were shipped to Charleston, S.C., by the tens of thousands in the colonial period.

The Great Smoky Mountains are a naturalist's delight. The first published reference to the mountains was by the French botanist, Michaux, in 1793. John Muir visited the area and wrote in the 1860s of the "cool, clear brooks" he saw every few miles. Botanists have identified between 1,500 and 2,000 specimens of plant life in the mountains. The azalea and laurel are in profusion in May and June, the rhododendron in June, and the wild tiger lilies on summits in August. Blazing autumn colors come from the extensive hardwood forest. Wildlife is also abundant. Bird aficionados, for example, have identified over 260 species from Knoxville east to the summits of the mountains. Over 50 mammals are indigenous to the area, including the giant black bear. The Appalachian Trail provides hiking across the crest of the mountains, and it is only the most famous of many paths. Geological interest in the region dates from Joseph Le Conte, the 19th-century Georgia botanist who traced the Smokies' geological history. The mountains were selected as the site for a national park in 1926, although it was not officially established until 1934.

In view of the dynamic changes in recent centuries, measuring the influence of the mountains on human cultural evolution is difficult. They have played a prominent part in regional literature, serving as a favorite setting for the local color writing of the late 19th century, and in song (the folksong "On Top of Old Smoky," for example). The American settlers tended to be people who sought isolation and often had a history of separation from the mainstreams of events. The people in the mountains were isolated until their "discovery" after the Civil War. Charles E. Craddock (Mary N. Murphree) was the first writer to portray the image of the mountaineer in the Smokies. The immense investment in transportation systems and the growth of major urban centers surrounding the mountains have transformed the area. The 1920s launched a new period of federal ownership of the region with a national park and national forests. Today, the permanent population is greatly augmented by seasonal influxes of tourists.

Richard S. Little
West Virginia University

Elizabeth Bowman, *Land of High Horizons* (1938); Alberta Brewer and Carson Brewer, *Valley so Wild: A Folk History* (1975); Carlos S. Campbell, *Birth of a National Park in the Great Smoky Mountains* (1978); Michael Frome, *Strangers in High Places: The Story of the Great Smoky Mountains* (1966); Roderick Peattie, *The Great Smokies and the Blue Ridge* (1943).

Homer, Winslow

(1836–1910) Painter.

Among the 19th century's most prominent artists, Winslow Homer has been praised for his engravings, genre paintings, and marine oils. Although the details of Homer's reclusive life and career are well known, his deep attachment to the South, its people, and its scenes is less frequently acknowledged. He was the quintessential New England Yankee, but his development as an artist was complemented by the incorporation of southern and tropical themes in his work. His bright, expressive, and energetic watercolors in particular reveal the impact of his southern experiences and differ substantively in color and mood from his famous marine paintings.

Homer's works began to appear in *Harper's Weekly* in the 1860s. One of his earliest engravings was of Abraham Lincoln shortly before his inauguration. With the outbreak of the Civil War, Homer became a special artist for *Harper's*, and for a brief period, he was with the Army of the Potomac during the early phases of the Peninsular campaign. Numerous sketches were made of the Union forces in the field with Homer frequently illustrating the monotony of military life. Essentially genre paintings of daily incidents in a soldier's camp life, the sketches and notes that he made of the early phases of the Civil War provided him with the themes for his first oil paintings. Of these 20 paintings, only one focused upon a battle. Homer exhibited selections of these early military paintings at the National Academy in 1863, 1864, 1865, and 1866. The most distinguished of these initial oils was Homer's *Prisoners from the Front*, which was exhibited at the Paris International Exposition of 1867 and later at Brussels and Antwerp.

During the Civil War, Homer became interested in blacks as a subject. He was one of the earliest American painters to portray blacks in a series of oil paintings. His

Upland Cotton, Sunday Morning in Virginia, and *Visit from the Old Mistress* demonstrate his skill in painting such subjects in a graceful, dignified, noncomic manner. His later watercolors from the Bahamas rejoiced in the physical abilities of the black fishermen of those waters and document his ability to define in art the human anatomy. In his most famous painting, *The Gulf Stream,* he captures the raw energy of human conflict with the sea as a black seaman drifts on a dismasted sloop circled by sharks.

Although his Florida watercolors are less graphic in the depiction of man confronting the elements, nature is still a fundamental theme. Homer traveled to Florida in the winters of 1885–86, 1890, 1903–4, and 1908. On each occasion he prepared watercolors of the area he visited, from the St. Johns River to the Homosassa River to Key West. The most striking and graceful of his Florida watercolors are those he painted at Key West. Key West was a favorite place for Homer to work, and his marine watercolors reveal his enthusiasm for this region. In his beautiful depiction of schooners and fishing boats at Key West, he demonstrated his mastery of the technical and pictorial skills appropriate to the medium and justified his recognition as one of the nation's premier watercolorists.

Phillip Drennon Thomas
Wichita State University

Philip C. Beam, *Winslow Homer* (1975), *Winslow Homer's Magazine Engravings* (1979); James Thomas Flexner, *The World of Winslow Homer, 1836 1910* (1966); Lloyd Goodrich, *Winslow Homer* (1944); Patti Hannaway, *Winslow Homer in the Tropics* (1973).

Kudzu

Kudzu is a weedy vine (*Pueraria lobata*) with often rampant invasive growth (a foot or more in a single day), which, if not controlled, soon covers anything in its path—shrubs, trees, automobiles, or even small buildings. A native of Asia, kudzu has been a useful plant to Orientals for 2,000 years. The Chinese made a medicinal tea from its roots and used it to treat dysentery and fever, and fibers from the vine were used to make cloth and paper. The Japanese as far back as the 1700s used starches from the plant's roots to make cakes. Kudzu powder is still used as a thickening ingredient in cooking and as a coating for fried foods. It is widely available in health food stores in the South.

Kudzu was introduced into this country at the Philadelphia Centennial Exposition of 1876, and it became known in the South through the Japanese pavilion at the New Orleans Exposition (1884–86). It was first used in the South as a shade plant on porches and arbors, but by the early 20th century some southern farmers were buying kudzu seeds and cuttings and planting them. Alabama Polytechnic Institute (Auburn University) led in the study of kudzu in this era. Florida farmer C. E. Pleas, beginning in 1902, devoted 50 years to singing kudzu's praises. He wrote a pamphlet, *Kudzu—Coming Forage of the South,* in 1925, and after his death a bronze plaque was erected near his agricultural center, announcing "Kudzu Was Developed Here."

The U.S. Department of Agriculture in the 1930s imported kudzu to help control erosion on bare banks and fallow fields throughout the South. The federal government paid as much as $8 per acre for farmers to plant kudzu, which became so popular during the ensuing years that kudzu festivals were held and kudzu beauty queens crowned. Georgia farmer Channing Cope, sometimes called the "father of kudzu," wrote about it in the Atlanta *Constitution* from 1939 on, formed the Atlanta-based Kudzu Club of America in 1943, and published the *Front Porch Farmer* in 1949, urging southern farmers to plant the crop. "Cotton isn't king here anymore," he once announced. "Kudzu is king!"

Because the plant is a member of the bean family (*Fabaceae*), the bacteria in the roots fix atmospheric nitrogen and thus help increase soil fertility. Although the vines are killed by frost, the deep roots easily survive the relatively mild winters of the South and produce a new and larger crop of vines each growing season. They bloom in late summer, but the clusters of purple or magenta wistaria-like flowers, which have the fragrance of grapes, are usually hidden beneath the large, three-lobed leaves. Kudzu is rich in protein and is sometimes used as fodder for livestock in times of drought. When animals graze on it regularly, though, they tend to kill it. Kudzu today has become a danger to timberland, because its vine will envelop a tree and eventually choke it to death by shutting out the sun. Kudzu is now categorized as a weed, and it covers 2 million acres of forestland in the South.

Whatever kudzu's current practical value to the South, it has assumed almost mythic cultural significance. James Dickey's poem "Kudzu" portrays it as a mysterious invader from the Orient, hinting at foreign domination, scientific misjudgment, and the ineptitude of a federal government that encouraged its use among unsuspecting southerners. The poem is filled with a sense of danger, as the vine he portrays kills hogs and cows, hides snakes, and threatens humans. "In Georgia, the legend says / That you must close your windows / At night to keep it out of the house. / The glass is tinged with green, even so. . . ." Marjie Short's 1976 film *Kudzu* is an informative and amusing documentary film, containing a scientific discussion of the weed by botanist Tetsuo Kyama, Dickey reading from his poem and referring to the plant as the "vegetable form of cancer," and interviews with Jimmy Carter about his memories of the vine in south Georgia, Atlanta resident James H. Jordan ("kudzu, city life, and mosketeers go hand in hand to make your life miserable"), and Athens, Ga., newspaper columnist Tifton Merritt, who suggests that the government may eventually subsidize kudzu and then pay farmers not to grow it. There is also a visit with the 1930s Kudzu Queen of Greensboro, Ala. (Martha Jane

Stuart Wilson), who said she was continuing the kudzu tradition "by spreading out in all directions."

There has been a southern rock band called Kudzu, a film entitled *Kurse of the Kudzu Kreature*, and an underground counterculture newspaper from Birmingham, Ala., named *Kudzu*. Finally, Doug Marlette chose Kudzu as the name for his comic strip dealing with the South.

C. Ritchie Bell
North Carolina Botanical Gardens
University of North Carolina
at Chapel Hill

Charles Reagan Wilson
University of Mississippi

William Shurtleff and Akiko Aoyagi, *The Book of Kudzu: A Culinary and Healing Guide* (1977); Larry Stevens, *Smithsonian* (December 1976); John J. Winberry and D. M. Jones, *Southeastern Geographer* (November 1973); Henry Woodhead, Atlanta *Journal and Constitution* (19 September 1976).

Lightwood

Pronounced "light'ood"—the *w*, particularly in the Deep South, having lost sound altogether—lightwood is the resin-saturated, naturally dried trunks, limbs, and knots of pine trees. It is important as a building and kindling material in areas of the South heavily forested with conifers. Not subject to replication by any known process, lightwood occurs only in nature. More often than not it begins with still-standing trunks of large trees killed by lightning strikes in the late spring, after sap has risen. Typically, an ensuing hot summer dries the moisture from the tree, leaving the resins free to permeate the wood before they solidify, a process that takes many years. The resulting material is extremely hard and brittle, practically impervious to bacterial rot or insect attacks, and readily ignitable, even when wet, by as little heat as that of a simple match. Similar in quality and color—dark red-black—to heart pine, lightwood differs from it in including the entire corpus of the tree, heart and pulp, all save the bark, thus providing much larger building members.

Found only rarely now, lightwood once served as a major product in the South. Trunks were used only whole or in short sections called "drums," for lightwood was too hard to rip lengthwise into boards or beams, though it can be cross-sawed. Lightwood drums, stood upright or laid on their sides (the preferred method, for in that position they were even less prone to deterioration), provided excellent, cheap, and convenient piers for log-and-frame structures, houses, and service buildings. Larger, finer houses in areas of the South where lightwood was easily available frequently had lightwood drums supporting the inner, unseen portions of the substructure, though they might have brick or stone piers on the periphery of the structure. Though whole lightwood tree trunks were sometimes used as sills for simple log houses and outbuildings, sills were usually hewn from the heartwood of new-felled trees. More often, whole lightwood trunks were stood upright in the ground to form tall pillars supporting whole structures, often quite large barns, storehouses, carriage houses, sheds, and shelters, as well as early "open-side" churches.

Lightwood as kindling was almost as important as its use in building. Limbs sawed into one-foot sections could, because of their brittle nature, be easily split into half-inch, square splinters. Lightwood splinters, tied in small 8- to 10-inch bundles, were long a standard commodity in southern grocery, hardware, and seed stores. Lightwood knots, cut out of limbs or found in the woods where they had fallen, were too hard to split—hence the expression "hard as a lightwood knot." The knots were left for the country poor—or in antebellum times, slaves, and later, tenants and sharecroppers—to pick up, cart, or carry into town and peddle to the urban poor for important extra cash.

Jerah Johnson
University of New Orleans

Nicholas Minov, *The Genus Pinus* (1967).

Live Oak

Few trees are as closely linked to southern culture as the live oak, or Virginia Live Oak (*Quercus virginiana*). This native tree grows along the Atlantic coastal area from southeast Virginia to south Florida and along the Gulf Coast from Florida to central Texas. A variety in central Texas and other southwestern locales called Texas Live Oak (var. *fusiformis*) has slightly different leaves and acorns. Called live oak because of its evergreen foliage, it is as tenacious as it is stately. It can be found growing in the driest sands of the Coastal Plain as a dwarf tree, or in the rich fertile soils of hardwood hammocks as a Spanish moss-ladened dominant tree.

Highly resistant to salt spray and hurricane force winds, the tree is ideally suited to the climate and geography of its range. The low-spreading tree rarely tops 50 feet in total height but can stretch 125 feet in crown spread. The trunk diameter can grow to eight feet.

The tree produces vast quantities of acorns that are highly desired by squirrels, turkeys, bears, and other animals. It is not uncommon for squirrels to bury the acorns, forget them, and thus plant future live oaks. This unique association helps both animal and tree.

Indians are said to have derived a sweet oil from the acorn and then used it to cook hominy, rice, and other foods. They would also roast the acorns in hot coals before eating them. It is also claimed that the Indians used the acorns to produce an imitation of cocoa.

Because of the live oak's great tensile strength, resistance to rot, tightly grained wood, and naturally curved branches, it became a highly prized timber for use in building this nation's early wooden sailing fleets. Shipwrights, called "live-oakers," would travel to the South each winter to cut and form live oak timber needed by the northern shipbuilding industry.

Heavy harvesting during this period forced the U.S. government to purchase over a quarter of a million acres of live oak forest preserves in Florida, Alabama, Mississippi, and Louisiana. Some of these acreages are still owned by the government. With the decline of the wooden shipbuilding industry, the live oak had no other commercial value. Its wood was not straight enough for lumber and was too hard to work.

Today, the live oak's main value is as an ornamental tree. In many of the South's coastal cities, long avenues of live oaks can be found planted along street rights-of-way, parks, and in homeowners' lawns. This relationship with the live oak has had a direct effect on the identity of many areas. There is a "Live Oak Street" in every southern coastal state. There is a city in Florida named Live Oak, while both Louisiana and Texas have towns named Live Oak. And the state tree of Georgia is the live oak.

W. Neil Letson
Montgomery, Alabama

Elbert L. Little, *The Audubon Society Field Guide to North American Trees, Eastern Region* (1980); William Trelease, *The American Oaks* (1924); William D. Weekes, *American Forests* (February 1979); Virginia S. Wood, *Live Oaking: Southern Timber for Tall Ships* (1981).

Magnolia

In an otherwise grim portrait of life in the segregated South of the early 20th century, Mississippian Richard Wright in *Black Boy* (1945) remembered from his youth "the drenching hospitality in the pervading smell of sweet magnolias." More than any other plant, the magnolia, a large tree with lustrous, dark green leaves and spectacular white, fragrant flowers, is associated with the South.

The southern magnolia (*Magnolia grandiflora*), sometimes also known as "bull bay," is native to the southern Coastal Plain from Virginia to Texas. Of somewhat wider, but still essentially coastal, distribution is the closely related sweet bay (*Magnolia virginia*), which is also an evergreen tree but has smaller leaves and flowers. Among other, and less known, native magnolias are three species with deciduous leaves: the umbrella tree (*M. macrophylla*), which has thin, pale green leaves up to three feet long and flowers over one foot in diameter; the cucumber tree (*M. acuminata*) with attractive yellow flowers; and the mountain or Fraser magnolia (*M. fraseri*). In addition, two very attractive horticultural species from Asia have been widely planted in the South. These shrubs or small trees are the star magnolia (*M. stellata*) and the Japanese magnolia (*M. X soulangeana*). The attractive and commercially valuable tulip poplar, or tulip tree (*Liriodendron tulipifera*), of southern forests is not a true poplar but is rather a member of the magnolia family.

The magnolia is one of the prime symbols for the romanticized South of the plantation. The phrase "moonlight and magnolias" describes one of the South's central myths—the story of the charmed and graceful society of the Old South. It is an image that appears frequently in literature and in visual portrayals of the region. It has come to suggest an unrealistic attitude toward life, of a people blinded by beauty. Paul Oliver, a blues scholar, has written that blues lyrics are unsentimental, and magnolias do not appear in them. A group of liberal southerners chose *You Can't Eat Magnolias* for the title of a book of 1971 essays urging reform in the region.

The magnolia image is frequently applied to southern women. Words typically used to describe the southern lady are those also applied to the magnolia—"beautiful and graceful," "delicate," "a fragrant beauty," "neatness, grace, and beauty," and "a showy flower." The sensual aspect of the magnolia is also sometimes noted and applied to the South and its women. A *Time* magazine article on the South in 1977 mentioned, for example, "the aphrodisiac-soporific magnolia, more potent by far in midnight bloom than overblown fiction can convey." The region's environment, then, nurtured its sensual women.

The magnolia is particularly associated with the Deep South. It was officially adopted as the state flower of Louisiana and Mississippi in 1900; in the latter, school children were allowed to determine the choice through a statewide vote (the magnolia won with 12,745 votes, to 4,171 for the cotton blossom, and 2,484 for the cape jasmine).

C. Ritchie Bell
North Carolina Botanical Gardens
University of North Carolina
at Chapel Hill

Charles Reagan Wilson
University of Mississippi

Pearl Cleage, *Southern Magazine* (June 1987); F. Schuyler Mathews, *Familiar Trees and Their Leaves* (1903); Brooks E. Wigginton, *Trees and Shrubs for the Southeast* (1963).

Mississippi River

The largest river in North America, the Mississippi River was named by Indians the "Father of Waters" and created the central South both literally and figuratively. The lower Mississippi over geologic eons built a fertile valley and delta to which it adds even now from a drainage area of 1,245,000 square miles including all or parts of 31 states and two Canadian provinces. The river system severed soil from the slopes of the Appalachians and Rockies, from prairies and plains, and carried it downstream eventually to become the croplands, forests, and swamps of an alluvial valley with a 35,460-square-mile area bordering the 1,000 miles of the Mississippi downstream of Cape Girardeau, Mo.

Celebrated in fiction, film, and music, the Mississippi was the setting for many Old South stereotypes: of crinolined belles and riverboat dandies, of cheerful roustabouts toting bales to steamboats at the levees, and of colonnaded mansions and cotton fields saved by heroic fights against floods. Steamboat transport, starting with the *New Orleans* in 1811, once was vital to the economy of the central South, and there were indeed belles, dandies, roustabouts, and mansions; yet, the stereotypes did not convey the richness of the cultures blended by the river—the Native American, the Spanish, French, British, and African threads that are part of the rococo fabric of the southern heritage.

The history of the river falls into two phases: efforts to secure strategic control of the stream and its hinterlands followed by efforts to control the river itself through engineering. In 1541 conquistador Hernando de Soto became the first European to see the Mississippi, and he later was buried in it; the French first settled the valley, building the first levee for protection against flooding in 1717. Through byzantine diplomacy and military raids, the Europeans wrested control of the river from the native tribes and from each other, the Spanish taking New Orleans and the British occupying Natchez after the French and Indian War in 1763. The Spanish and the Americans drove the British from its banks during the American Revolution, and the Americans purchased full control of the river from Napoleon in 1803, subsequently repulsing an effort by the British to retake it at New Orleans in 1815.

Through construction of levees, Americans then wrested croplands from the rich floodplain, establishing an agricultural system made possible not only by the soils brought south by the river, but also by flatboats crammed with midwestern foodstuffs and manufactures, barges of Pittsburgh coal for sugar refineries and steamship fuel, and thousands of steamboats funneling downriver the commerce of a network of waterways reaching as far north as St. Paul, Minn., as far west as Fort Benton, Mont., and as far east as Olean, N.Y.

The Mississippi also brought less welcome guests south: northern soldiers in ironclad steamboats breaking the chain the Confederacy placed across the river, scalawags and rascals, and the floodwater from its immense watershed. Southerners lost the fights against both the soldiers and the floods, but, through formation of the Mississippi River Commission in 1879, enlisted some of those soldiers in the efforts to control flooding and maintain navigation. Supplemented by floodways to sap the river's strength and by reservoirs to stop floods where they originated, the levee system was fortified after the 1927 flood. By 1972, 1,683.8 miles of the proposed 2,193.7 miles of levees had been completed, and they successfully withstood the record 1973 flooding.

Powerful diesel towboats pushing barges supplanted steamboats after 1930. The 1,832-mile navigation channel maintained between Baton Rouge and Minneapolis and the 12,350-mile network of connecting waterways bore a tonnage far larger than that carried by steamboats. The barges moved through the Illinois River to the Great Lakes and via the Gulf Intracoastal Waterway west to Houston and east to Tampa. The Tennessee-Tombigbee Waterway offers an alternative to the Mississippi for barge traffic, but it is not expected that tonnage moving on the Mississippi will significantly diminish.

Leland R. Johnson
Hermitage, Tennessee

Benjamin A. Botkin, *A Treasury of Mississippi River Folklore* (1955); Hodding Carter, *Lower Mississippi* (1942); Marquis William Childs, *Mighty Mississippi: Biography of a River* (1982); Pete Daniel, *Deep'n as It Come: The 1927 Mississippi River Flood* (1977); Normal R. Moore, *Improvement of the Lower Mississippi River and Tributaries, 1931–1972* (1972).

Mockingbird

Atticus Finch in *To Kill a Mockingbird* (1960) told his children "it's a sin to kill a mockingbird," because, as Miss Maudie explained to them, mockingbirds "don't do one thing but sing their hearts out for us." The mockingbird has been, indeed, particularly tied to the imagery of the South. It is as close to being an official southern bird as any; five southern states (Arkansas, Florida, Tennessee, Mississippi, and Texas) have adopted it as their state bird. The legislative resolution in Florida naming the mockingbird as the avian emblem of the state referred to it as a "bird of matchless charm." "Song of Louisiana," which was adopted as the official song of that state in 1932, speaks of the "singing of the mocking bird, and of the blossoms of the flowers" in describing the natural wonders found there.

The mockingbird, whose Latin name, *Mimus polyglottos*, means "many tongued," has been a prominent part of the environmental landscape of the South. Discovered over 250 years ago by naturalist Mark Catesby, who called it the "Mock-Bird of Carolina," it is now found from the eastern United States to California, but it is still particularly identified with the South. A noted songbird, the mockingbird is an unequaled mimic, noted, as an Audubon Society writer says, for "rapturous singing on moonlight nights among magnolias and moss-covered live oaks of the South." The male sings by day or night, repeating a phrase several times before striking a new one. Its "whisper song" is particularly soft and haunting, but its call notes tend to be harsh, grating noises. It can mimic 39 bird songs, 50 call notes, as well as the cackling of chickens, creaking of wheelbarrows, croaking of frogs, barking of dogs, and tinkling of a piano.

The appearance of the mockingbird is not particularly striking or colorful. Its predominant look is a dull gray, together with a faded white on its underside. It is slimmer than a robin and has long legs and a constantly twitching tail. It lives year-round in trees, shrubs, and on the edge of woods, pastures, rail fences, and farm hedges.

In the Southwest, it nests in sage and cactus. Found in both suburban and rural gardens, the mockingbird feeds on insects (especially grasshoppers and beetles), seeds, and wild and cultivated berries.

Mockingbirds are aggressive by nature. Males are belligerent and courageous, especially while courting. They tolerate no one intruding on their territory, and they quickly attack anyone or anything seen as a threat. Males challenge each other through a highly ritualized dance, squaring off and rapidly bouncing sideways like boxers sparring, with heads held high and wings arched defiantly.

Charles Reagan Wilson
University of Mississippi

Southern Living (September 1985); John K. Teres, *The Audubon Society Encyclopedia of North American Birds* (1980).

Natchez Trace

Originating as one of many narrow lanes beaten through the brush between the Great Lakes and the Gulf of Mexico, the Natchez Trace ran roughly north and south some 600 miles from the loess bluffs of the Natchez Indians into the game-filled hunting grounds of the Cumberland River Valley. As the native tribes that bordered the path settled and cultivated their land, the trace became an essential link in a network of commerce. When Europeans first forged their way into the tribal lands, they too used the well-worn path. Hernando de Soto traveled it on his way to the Mississippi River, while French explorers established trading posts at its extremities—Natchez and Nashville—in the early 18th century. During the American Revolution the road served as a path of freedom as colonists fled southwest.

The importance of the trace expanded with the new American Republic. White settlers who pushed past the Appalachian Mountains took their products downstream to market, sold their crude boats as lumber in New Orleans, and then proceeded back up the trace laden with gold. Poised to prey upon these hapless travelers were dense swamps, swirling rivers, and notorious highwaymen who lay in wait for the easy pickings on this thoroughfare of hunted and hunters.

Aside from rogues and plunderers, a motley array of other adventurers traversed the road: traders, medicine peddlers, pioneer mothers with their families, frontier tarts headed for Natchez-under-the-Hill, gentlemen and ladies from the East Coast, trains of slaves, circuit-riding evangelists, and fortune hunters—a diverse company of proud, predatory, courageous, land-hungry Americans.

The government also recognized the path's potential for public services. The trace was designated as a mail route in 1800 and then was cleared and widened to serve as a military road. Using the road in this capacity Major General Andrew Jackson earned for himself the nickname "Old Hickory" and marched up it victoriously after the battle of New Orleans.

The end of the short, rambunctious heyday of the trace was sounded with the whistle of the steamboat, which defied the Mississippi's current and thus eliminated the need for overland travel homeward. Gradually the road began to revert to nature, though it experienced a brief revival as a strategic artery during the Civil War.

Modern interest in the trace began in 1909 as the Daughters of the American Revolution initiated a program to mark the route of the Old Trace. Several years later a Natchez Trace Association was organized, but not until 1934 did the Department of the Interior, through the National Park Service, authorize a survey of the trace. It later initiated the construction of the Natchez Trace Parkway. Since that time three generations of local supporters have worked to generate interest and funding for the project, which, after 50 years, is nearing completion.

Lucie R. Bridgforth
Memphis State University

Patti Carr Black, *The Natchez Trace* (1985); Julian Bretz, *Mississippi Valley Historical Review* (June 1926); Jonathan Daniels, *The Devil's Backbone* (1962); L. M. Jamison, *Journal of Mississippi History* (April 1939); Dawson A. Phelps, *Journal of Mississippi History* (January 1949, July 1953), *Tennessee Historical Quarterly* (September 1954).

Nuclear Pollution

Attracted by the promise of money and jobs for the region, the South began actively courting the nuclear industry in the early 1950s. Soon the federal government responded to southern invitations and opened military-related facilities in the area, and southern utilities cooperated to exploit nuclear power for commercial uses. These developments led to the growth of the nuclear equipment industry in the South, which provides the necessary turbine generators, pressurizers, steam generators, and fabricated fuel for the nation's reactors.

In the 1960s the South also became the home for the radioactive waste generated by the nuclear industry. By 1980 well over one-half of the nation's commercial low-level nuclear wastes were stored in southern facilities, while approximately 30 percent of the nation's high-level military wastes and 40 percent of the low-level military wastes were also stored in the South. While recent disclosures about the potential dangers of stored waste due to leaks and inadequate plans for long-term storage have turned some southern policymakers against the continued growth of the region's reliance on and support of the nuclear industry, the promise of jobs and the threat of energy shortages have been enough to allow the industry to retain its hold on the region's economy.

The major nuclear waste storage facilities in the South are the Oak Ridge National Laboratory at Oak Ridge, Tenn., the Maxey Flats facility near Morehead, Ky., the

"SORRY, OPIE — THINGS JUST AIN'T BEEN THE SAME SINCE THAT NUCLEAR WASTE DUMP LOCATED OUTSIDE OF MAYBERRY!"

Doug Marlette editorial cartoon on nuclear pollution, 1986

Savannah River Plant near Aiken, S.C., and the Chem-Nuclear plant at Barnwell, S.C. In addition to the major facilities, smaller radioactive dumpsites are located in the South, including ones in Kentucky, Tennessee, Texas, and North Carolina. The Chem-Nuclear plant in South Carolina is the only currently operating low-level waste facility on the East Coast. The Chem-Nuclear plant alone now holds over one-half of the nation's existing commercial low-level waste, and each year it receives about 85 percent of all the low-level wastes commercially produced in the United States. Business at the Chem-Nuclear plant steadily increased in the late 1970s, as some other sites were either temporarily or permanently closed due to safety problems. South Carolina officials grew concerned about the increased number of shipments from outside the region and the possibility that the Barnwell facility would fill up quickly and be abandoned, creating a severe financial drain on the state for its perpetual maintenance. Concerned state officials proposed to reduce the flow of waste into Barnwell and help protect the state financially by raising the state's fees from Chem-Nuclear 600 percent.

High-level radioactive wastes are generated through the process of reprocessing spent fuel rods. In reprocessing, the still-usable uranium and plutonium are extracted, leaving only liquid high-level radioactive waste. Various options for the disposal of high-level waste have been investigated by the Department of Energy (DOE). Deep-earth burial has received the most attention, and one of the first federal attempts at implementing such a plan involved the Savannah River Plant in South Carolina between 1951 and 1972. According to the plans for this type of storage, the liquid waste is solidified and stored in double-walled steel tanks and then buried underground. The salt-dome formations in Louisiana, Texas, and Mississippi have been suggested as possible burial sites. Citizens in these areas have mobilized in opposition to locating a nuclear waste repository in their areas, and Louisiana has banned the disposal of radioactive waste in the state's salt mines. This opposition is leading the DOE to consider other possible sites; however, the federal government has the right to mandate the location of nuclear waste sites through the right of eminent domain regardless of state laws.

Other possible burial sites reportedly considered by the DOE include granite deposits, found in all the Appalachian mountain states, clay-based rocks found in the Piedmont region of the Carolinas and Virginia, and the sedimentary rocks in the Coastal Plain of the Carolinas. Until the DOE finalizes plans and activates a burial site, the majority of the high-level liquid waste will remain at the Savannah River Plant, which has already been rejected as a safe permanent depository, and in the temporary storage tanks of individual reactors.

One of the greatest concerns among southerners about nuclear waste is the transportation of radioactive materials through the region. Critics have said that the transport of irradiated fuel elements ("spent fuel") from nuclear reactors to storage sites is particularly dangerous. Furthermore, spent fuel from nuclear ships is carried from shipyards in Charleston, S.C., and Norfolk, Va., to reprocessing facilities in Idaho. Critics also complain that officials along the shipment routes have no prior notice as to when and where the shipments will take place and that vehicles carrying the hazardous materials are not marked with appropriate warnings. In response to what they see as limited safety efforts by the federal government, individual southern communities and environmental and pacifist groups have called for local and state regulation of the transport of radioactive materials. In 1978 the Louisiana Legislature passed a law banning the transport of high-level radioactive wastes through the state. Such measures have prompted the federal government to propose its own regulations of the transports which would preempt local authority, but which, some local officials charge, would not provide supervision equal to that demanded by local citizens.

See also INDUSTRY: / Nuclear Industry

Karen M. McDearman
University of Mississippi

Betty Brink, *Southern Exposure* (Fall 1981); Beth Damon Coonan, *Southern Exposure* (January–February 1985); Stephen Hoffius, *Southern Exposure* (March–April 1984); John W. Johnson, *Insuring against Disaster: The Nuclear Industry on Trial* (1986); *Southern Exposure* (Winter 1979); Joanne Thompson and Debra Castaldo, *Southern Changes* (April–May 1986).

Oil Pollution

The discovery of the Spindletop field on the Texas Gulf Coast in 1901 ushered in a new era for the American petroleum industry, characterized by the shift of major producing zones from the East to the Southwest and the emergence of giant firms such as Texaco and Gulf. It also introduced new threats to the southern environment. The "gusher" was the most visible ecological problem, as uncontrolled flush production led to massive drain-offs of crude that soaked the ground. The rapid removal of oil from subsurface strata resulted in the introduction of brine into the Gulf region's water system as well as into underground reservoirs of oil. Frequent oil spills at plants and terminals saw periodic floods wash much of this oil into rivers and streams. Oil particulates entered lakes and ultimately the Gulf of Mexico, joining oil spilled during the loading of tankers and the contaminated ballast those same vessels dumped at sea. Hydrocarbon vapors from poorly constructed transportation and storage equipment and sulphur fumes emitted from refineries also polluted the air.

The development of offshore drilling in the South, which increased dramatically after World War II, presented another environmental threat. In 1970, for example, the extinguishing by explosives of a fire on the Chevron Oil Company's platform-C, 12 miles off the Louisiana coast, resulted in a spreading oil slick that grew at a rate of 600–1,000 barrels a day.

As in earlier decades, oil spills are not limited to the ocean; pipelines break, refinery tanks rupture, and barges run into bridges. In January 1973 a barge struck a bridge pier over the Mississippi River near Helena, Ark., spilling 19,000 barrels of oil into the river. There have also existed instances of conscious polluting of rivers and groundwater by commercial firms, as in the case of the Union Camp Bag Company of Savannah, Ga., which was prosecuted in 1969 and 1970 for releasing oil into the Savannah River. In 89 documented cases of groundwater contamination before 1981 in South Carolina (a state that shares its main aquifer with Georgia and Florida), petroleum products were involved in the majority of the incidents.

A growing environmental consciousness in the South has tapped a historical tradition that is both sentimental about the natural ecology and wary of the exploitation of southern resources by outsiders. This was evidenced in the wake of the 1973 energy crisis when Louisiana openly criticized those northeastern states that blocked offshore drilling on their coasts for environmental reasons but that were all too willing to import natural gas produced off the coast of the Bayou state. There is clearly a trade-off between the search for new energy and protection of the environment, but the South in the latter 20th century is attempting to balance the two in a rational way.

See also INDUSTRY: / Oil Industry; SOCIAL CLASS: / Oil Workers

August W. Giebelhaus
Georgia Institute of Technology

John R. Holum, *Topics and Terms in Environmental Problems* (1977); Joseph A. Pratt, *The Growth of a Refining Region* (1980); Veronica I. Pye, Ruth Patrick, and John Quarles, *Groundwater Contamination in the United States* (1983).

Opossum ("Possum")

Over 70 species can be found in the opossum family, ranging from South America northward to Canada, but the Virginia opossum (*Didelphis virginia*) once resided only in the Southeast and is still identified closely with the region's culture. It is the only marsupial (a mammal that carries its newborn young in an abdominal pouch for weeks) found north of Mexico and the largest of the opossum family. It weighs from 4 to 15 pounds and is from 25 to 40 inches long. Captain John Smith, leader of the early Virginia settlement, described the female opossum in 1608: "An opossum hath a head like a Swine, and a taile like a Rat, and is of the bigness of a Cat. Under her belly she hath a bagge wherein she lodgeth, carrieth, and sucketh her young."

In the South opossums are brown and black. The head, face, and throat are whitish, and the dark ears have pinkish tips. They have short legs, an opposable thumblike toe on their back feet, and sharp claws on their forelegs. The opossum's tail is long (9 to 13 inches) and unadorned. Good tree climbers and mostly active at night, opossums are omnivorous, consuming insects, frogs, birds, eggs, snakes, earthworms, and small animals; they also eat grains, seeds, and fruits such as apples and persimmons. They are scavengers, eating any and everything including carrion. They live mostly in wooded areas, but are frequently seen in suburbs and have even been found in urban areas. Garbage dumps attract them, and farmers have charged them with invading chicken yards. Many are killed by automobiles, as the small creatures are attracted to other animals dead on the side of the road. When threatened, an opossum will roll over and play dead. It gives a convincing performance, as it goes semirigid, mouth open and drooling, tongue extended, and eyes open but glazed. Scientists have discovered that this is an actual catatonic state brought on by fear. The phrase "playing possum" has come, nonetheless, to mean feigning sleep or death.

The opossum is generally not considered the most intelligent of animals (25 small white beans would fit in the brain cavity of an adult male opossum's skull; 150 would be needed for the brain cavity of a raccoon of the same size). Its life expectancy is short, but it has shown what can be described as a Faulknerian sense of endurance, surviving since the age of dinosaurs. It has evolved numerous survival mechanisms. Feigning death is a device against danger. It spends most of its time lolling about in isolated, lazy seclusion in trees or in underground burrows, avoiding occasions for direct conflict with predators. It has a well-developed sense of smell that is useful for foraging, and its 50 small teeth—more than any other mammal in North America—provide protection. It is extremely fertile, with females in the South bringing forth two to three litters of 8 to 18 young ones in a year, with around 7 normally surviving the early phase of life in the pouch. The opossum has changed little since prehistoric times and now thrives in spite of evolving conditions.

The opossum has long figured prominently in human culture in the South. Stories of this critter's activities

Opossum, male and female, with their young

were told by Native Americans and blacks. The Choctaws' "Why the Possum Grins" was one such tale, and a Cherokee legend explains that the opossum's tail is naked because he burned it in a fire, trying to make his white tail black. A southern black version of this story has a ghost skinning all the hair off his tail when Possum, along with Fox and Rabbit, tries to steal corn from a graveyard. The Mississippi Delta has a story of the opossum that was killed and put in to cook, but ate all the sweet potatoes and gravy in the roasting pan, jumping out and escaping when the oven door was opened. Pottery effigies of the opossum from as far back as prehistoric times have been found in south Georgia burial sites, and poor southern blacks and whites have hunted the opossum for its fur and flesh. Roy Blount, Jr., after tasting the animal, wrote that "possum was sort of like dark meat of chicken, only stronger-tasting and looser on the bone, and stringy, like pork." It has also been described as somewhat greasy.

The opossum has been a prominent contemporary southerner. The Pogo comic strip featured the animal. Wausau, Fla., annually holds a Possum Festival in August, and a possum cult appeared in the South in the 1970s. The Possum Growers and Breeders Association of America, Incorporated, sponsored a national meeting in 1971 in Clanton, Ala., and from that beginning the group has expanded to include 40,000 members, who receive bumper stickers saying "Eat More Possum." It sponsors an annual gathering, including a Miss Possum pageant for female humans and an opossum judging contest, awarding the most worthy candidate of the latter the designation of "Beauregard." Frank Basil Clark, who manages the Clanton Drive-In Theatre and lives in a mobile home he calls the Big C Possum Ranch, was the guiding spirit behind the movement, and at one point he had plans to breed "superpossums" of giant size to provide protein for the world's hungry. Roy Blount, Jr., wrote an article on possums for *Sports Illustrated* (1 March 1976) and then featured the possum cult prominently in his *Crackers* (1980). *Possum Opossum* was an award-winning film by Greg Killmaster chronicling, with tongue firmly in cheek, the possum cult's activities.

Charles Reagan Wilson
University of Mississippi

Wayne King, *New York Times* (16 March 1975); Stanley Klein, *Encyclopedia of North American Wildlife* (1983).

Outer Banks

The Outer Banks are low, extremely narrow islands running from near Norfolk, Va., south for 175 miles to Cape Hatteras, N.C., and ending near Cape Lookout. They are separated from the mainland by the shallow Pamlico and Albemarle sounds. In 1524 Giovanni de Verrazzano landed on the Outer Banks and thought he was off the coast of China. The real history of the islands began, though, in 1584 when Sir Walter Raleigh chose Roanoke Island, which was between the Outer Banks and the North Carolina coast, as the site for the first attempted English colony in North America. A fort was built but the colony remained unstable, and its inhabitants had mysteriously disappeared by the time a supply ship arrived in 1590. The "Lost Colony" is the subject of Paul Green's outdoor dramatic presentation, which is staged each summer in Manteo, N.C., and the Fort Raleigh National Historic Site now includes a reconstruction of the early fort.

Captain Edward Teach—the infamous Blackbeard—was the most famous of a number of pirates who used the sounds and bays behind the Outer Banks as a hiding place in the 1700s. Most of the island inhabitants have been less exotic, though: mainly farmers, stockmen, fishermen, boatmen, marines, and pilots. Because of the relatively consistent winds in the area, Orville and Wilbur Wright picked a 100-foot-high hill near Kitty Hawk, N.C., as the locale for their first successful airplane flight in 1903. The Wright Brothers National Memorial was set up in 1927 and has become a center for a growing tourist industry on the islands. The Cape Hatteras National Seashore Recreation Area, established in 1937 as a public beach and campsite, provides access to the natural wonders of the Outer Banks.

The Outer Banks are an environmental treasure. Beach grass and sedges grow there, but sea oats is the most typical grass, growing in clumps and serving as an effective sand binder. Wax myrtle and yaupons (or Sea Island holly) are widespread, and one can find American holly, laurel oaks, and loblolly pines in the woods. Live oaks have been especially important to these islands. Near the shore of a sound, the wind makes them small and twisted, but several hundred yards away, they grow straight and tall and are hung with Spanish moss.

The Sea Island National Wildlife Refuge has almost 6,000 acres of beach, dunes, and marshes. Nearly 26,000 acres in the waters of Pamlico Sound are off limits to hunters. Estimates are that 265 species of birds visit or live at the refuge. One sees gulls and sandpipers, but migratory waterfowl are the most frequently sighted birds, with snow and Canadian geese common in the late fall. Brown pelicans can be seen in the summer, and peregrine falcons and other species live there year round.

At Cape Hatteras the cold waters from the north meet the warm currents from the Gulf Stream, making for turbulent navigation. The cape contains the tallest lighthouse in the United States—a 208-foot-high, black-and-white monument. The area's changing currents and dense fogs have resulted in more than 500 ships foundering near the cape, earning it the reputation of the "Graveyard of the Atlantic." The first lighthouse there was built in 1803, and the present landmark dates from 1870.

See also LANGUAGE: / Outer Banks Dialect

Charles Reagan Wilson
University of Mississippi

Charlton Ogburn, *The Winter Beach* (1971); Caleb Pirtle III, *Southern Living* (April 1975); John T. Starr, *American Forests* (April 1979).

Palm Trees

"Florida is the land of Palms," wrote horticulturist Henry Nehrling. "Avenues of Palms in our cities! Forests of Palms beside our streams and lakes! Thickets of Palms in our woods! Groves of Coconut Palms on the East Coast! Majestic Royal Palms in the south Everglades!" His enthusiasm was unbounded but appropriate because the palm has been one of the preeminent cultural-environmental symbols of the semitropical South, from the promotional advertising of Henry Flagler luring tourists south, to the contemporary lyrics of Jimmy Buffet songs and the visual images of television's *Miami Vice*.

The main physical feature of the palm is the cylindrical trunk, which supports a leaf-crown. Its drooping leaves can be 100 feet off the ground. The leaves are either plume-like (pinnate) or fan shaped (palmate). The South's native palmettos belong to the second group, whereas the royal, coconut, and date palms have plume-like leaves. About 14 species of palms are native to Florida and 2 or 3 can be found as far north as North Carolina. The palmetto is the official tree of South Carolina, where it is used by blacks to make distinctive Sea Islands baskets. Many imported tropical palms do well in south Florida, and subtropical varieties thrive along the beaches of the Gulf Coast down into the south Texas valley.

The cabbage palmetto (*Sabal palmetto*) is the most common palm in Florida and the one growing most frequently in other areas of the South. It is often found growing in groups with hundreds of plants standing close together. The early settlers named this tree the cabbage palmetto because of its heart, which they consumed like cabbage.

The coconut palm and the royal palm are conspicuously displayed, popular palms in Florida. One horticulturist called them "the exclamation points in the poetry of tropical landscape." The royal palm grows straight as a column, while the coconut will bend gracefully. The coconut palm grows in nearly all tropical coast regions of the world, but is never found growing naturally inland. The winter resort of Palm Beach gained its name from the stands of coconut trees growing there. When settlement in south Florida increased in the early 20th century, people planted inexpensive coconut palms in droves, further reinforcing the area's association with the plant. The royal palms are majestic looking in their hammocks, which are seen to best effect in the southern Everglades. Of the five species of its genus, one—the *Oreodoxa regia*—is native to south Florida. It is confined naturally to Biscayne Bay, the Keys, and several hammocks of south Florida. Royal Palm State Park (formerly Paradise Key) is in Dade County, with many trees there at least 100 feet tall.

Date palms also thrive in Florida, south Texas, and along the Gulf Coast. The genus *Phoenix* is Asian and African in origins. The date palms have pinnate leaves, which may be either soft and glossy or, in other species, hard. Many of these were introduced into the Southwest in the early 20th century. Other of the many palms found in Florida include the blue palmetto (*Rhapidophyllum hystrix*), the bamboo palm (*Rhapis flabelliformis*), and the silver palm (*Thrinax floridana*).

Charles Reagan Wilson
University of Mississippi

Henry Nehrling, *The Plant World in Florida*, ed. Alfred Kay and Elizabeth Kay (1933).

Red River Expedition

When the Louisiana Purchase was acquired by the United States in 1803, no true scientific surveys had been done in the West, and many geographical details were unclear. Thus President Thomas Jefferson conceived and put into the field two major exploring expeditions to examine Louisiana. That of Meriwether Lewis and William Clark into the northern Purchase was the most successful and is the best known. The second, intended to survey similarly the geography and natural history of the southern regions of the Purchase, only partially accomplished that task, because of Spanish opposition. On the expedition, however, was a young University of Pennsylvania naturalist named Peter Custis, the first American naturalist in the West. His reports are a principal source in determining the "virgin" conditions of the Red River Valley and parts of Louisiana, Arkansas, and Texas.

The plan for the exploration, formulated by Jefferson early in 1804, called for an ascent of the Red River "to the tops of the mountains" and a descent of the Arkansas. When at last attempted, in 1806, the 50-man expedition was terminated by a Spanish army after four months, at a location 615 miles above the mouth of the Red. The early termination (near today's Oklahoma border) prevented expedition leader/geographer Thomas Freeman from making many new geographical discoveries. His field courses were drawn into a definitive map of the lower Red River Valley by Nicholas King and appeared on Anthony Nau's 1807 map of the West based on American exploration. The map represents outstanding topographical features, game and trading paths, and Indian villages and sacred places.

The work done by naturalist Custis was of greater significance. He was the last-minute choice in a search that featured an offer of the position to the world-famous William Bartram and included applications by C. S. Rafinesque and Alexander Wilson. Custis's training under Benjamin Smith Barton was sound, but he was inexperienced and his small reference library was inadequate. He closely followed the directions of Jefferson and expedition supervisor William Dunbar. The result was a wide-ranging survey: he collected minerals and botanical specimens, kept a meteorological chart, and compiled natural history data on 80 birds and animals and nearly 190 plants. He offered eight new scientific names, three of which are currently recognized.

Jefferson's southern exploration failed in its larger objectives, but the data accumulated were important to environmental study. The explorers portrayed an organic environment in a state of change, a valley that European plants were already invading and whose waters were yearly modified by the growth of the immense logjam called the Great Raft. The prairies they saw and the relative absence of undergrowth in the towering virgin forest were, they believed, the result of Indian-set fires. Above all, they were most impressed with the beauty and richness of the river valley wilderness: "The Valley of the Red River is one of the richest and most beautiful imaginable," Freeman wrote in his journal, and Custis added that, "were the Rafts removed . . . this country would become the Paradise of America. . . . in point of beauty, fertility, and salubrity there is not its equal in America, nay in the world."

Daniel L. Flores
Texas Tech University

Daniel L. Flores, ed., *The Freeman & Custis Account of the Red River: The Chronicle of Jefferson's Southwestern Exploration* (1983); Donald Jackson, *Thomas Jefferson and the Stony Mountains: Exploring the West from Monticello* (1981); Conrad Morton, *Journal of the Arnold Arboretum* (1967).

Shellfish

The South has both recreational and industrial shellfish resources, all of which have been exploited as far back as the earliest aboriginal inhabitants. Shellfish may be categorized as mollusks or crustaceans found in either fresh or salt waters. Important mollusks include clams, mussels, oysters, scallops, and snails. Valuable crustaceans are crabs, freshwater crayfish, shrimps, and spiny lobsters.

Aboriginal settlements are often located by the presence of shell mounds, or middens, adjacent to inland rivers. Indians ate copious quantities of mussels and coveted those with pearls and lustrous mother-of-pearl inner shells for ornaments. European settlers ate few mussels but exploited them for the mother-of-pearl used in buttons. Even today, many tons of southern mussel shells are shipped to the Orient, where small pieces are used for nuclei of cultured pearls. In estuarine areas surrounding the South inhabitants have used clams and oysters as foodstuffs and their shells for building materials. Many mollusks, especially in Florida waters, are so beautiful that they are the subject of world-famous shell-collecting industries. Major offshore scallop resources have provided sustained yields of the sweet-meated bivalves. Mollusks are also valuable. In 1984 over 40 million pounds of oyster meats worth over $66 million were taken from southern waters, while scallop harvests accounted for at least 40 million pounds of meat worth in excess of $30 million.

Oysters deserve special attention. Most are cultivated in what represents the oldest form of American mariculture. Today's oysterman commonly relies on natural nursery beds where larval oysters settle. These so-called spat attach to old shells. Nursery beds are usually located in less productive, low salinity waters so that the spat must be moved to prime high-salinity growing beds. Low, squat white oyster boats are constantly relocating and/or harvesting oysters in Gulf coastal waters. In the Chesapeake Bay, sail-powered skijack oyster boats relocate and harvest oysters in waters where rival oystermen from Maryland and Virginia fought pitched sea battles over oyster grounds in the late 1800s. Fresh oysters are available in all months, but quality is somewhat poorer in warm months when they spawn. Oyster dishes vary from salted, raw, and live oysters on the half shell to savory stews and the always-popular fried oysters, including oysters en brochette (wrapped with bacon and fried). The New Orleans oyster "po-boy" sandwich on french bread is a favorite of oyster lovers who visit the Crescent City.

All southern coastal states have major shrimp and crab fisheries. White, brown, and pink shrimp spawn at sea, but larvae are nurtured in the fragile coastal wetlands before returning to sea to mature and spawn. Shrimp boats with high masts festooned with trawl nets are common sights along all coasts, and annual blessings of local fleets are gala festivities. Blue crabs generally remain in estuaries, growing, as do all crustaceans, by shedding their hard shells periodically. The crab boil is a southern coastal tradition, but soft-shelled crabs command the highest prices and are cultivated throughout the region. Spiny lobsters are a legacy of south Florida and are so valuable that the fishery is intensively regulated. Prawns, pandalid shrimps, are important as fish bait, especially the one- to two-inch grass, or glass, shrimp. Thriving fisheries once existed for the clawed, lobster-like langostino species in estuarine areas, but these have been largely displaced by pollution, habitat destruction, and man-made changes in hydrology. In fresh water, crayfish are the crustacean kings. Although exploited throughout the South by Indian communities, they became important food sources only in French Louisiana. There the inventive Acadians, or Cajuns, have even learned to cultivate the "écrevisse" in earthern ponds during the cool months, often in a unique rotation with rice, which is grown in the warm months.

In 1984 the marine shrimp harvest in south Atlantic waters was 19.2 million pounds worth $34 million, but this was dwarfed by a harvest of 254.3 million pounds in the Gulf of Mexico worth $439.2 million. The southern blue crab harvest in 1984 was 201.6 million pounds worth $56 million. While the spiny lobster catch was only 6.3 million pounds in 1984, it was worth $17.3 million. Southern crayfish production exceeded 70 million pounds in 1984 and was valued at more than $35 million.

Southern shellfish resources are threatened. Stream channelization, draining of wetlands, and pollution have destroyed many productive freshwater shellfish habitats. All southern coastal waters are polluted to some degree. Each state monitors edible mollusks for signs of sewage pollution to avoid health problems like hepatitis, which is contracted by eating raw, contaminated mollusks. Estuaries are especially hard-hit by all forms of water pollution because contaminants are dropped there when freshwater runoff reaches the sea. The problems of suffocating silt and toxic chemicals are obvious, but inorganic fertilizers and organic matter fuel microbial activity that strips bottom waters of oxygen and severely restricts habitat and productivity in once-fertile waters. Coastal development in the form of recreational centers and fossil-fuel exploitation has destroyed thousands of acres of productive marshes. Vigilance and environmental education are beginning to show significant and measurable improvement of conditions in southern waters and must continue to insure that future generations will share in the South's bountiful shellfish resources.

Jay V. Huner
Center for Small Farm Research
Southern University

R. Tucker Abbott, *Seashells of North America: A Guide to Field Identification* (1968); Jay V. Huner and E. Evan Brown, eds., *Crustacean and Mollusk Aquaculture in the United States* (1985); James A. Michener, *Chesapeake* (1979); Fred Ward, *National Geographic* (February 1985).

Shenandoah Valley

Located in northern Virginia, the Shenandoah Valley is approximately 6,500 square miles in area, 180 miles long, and 10 to 24 miles wide. It is drained by the Shenandoah River, which has played an important role in the valley's development as a rich agricultural area.

The Shenandoah Valley was settled in the early 1700s by Germans, Dutch, Scotch-Irish, and English. The valley was an important route for the westward pioneer movement in the early 19th century. Its population at the time of the Civil War was predominantly white and rural.

The valley was the site of an extraordinary Civil War battle in 1862. The residents' loyalties were divided between the Union and the Confederacy, and the area was strategically important to both sides. In an effort to divert Union General George B. McClellan's attack on the Confederate capital of Richmond, Confederate General Thomas J. "Stonewall" Jackson launched the successful "valley campaign" against the Union armies designated to join McClellan's. With an inferior number of troops, Jackson brilliantly used his interior lines of communication and tactics of strategic diversion to repel the Union forces.

Another successful defense of the valley came at the battle of New Market in 1864 under the command of General John C. Breckinridge. The battle, in which young cadets from the Virginia Military Institute fought, inspires one of the nation's largest Civil War reenactments each May at the site. The Union had its revenge for the losses, however, when General Philip Sheridan's army laid waste the region, wrecking railroad lines, burning factories, and destroying farms and supplies.

After Reconstruction the valley's economy was primarily agricultural, although many small manufacturing plants were established in the late 1800s. Resort spas and summer homes flourished after 1890, and the area became a popular tourist attraction. Today, the valley's rolling plains, stone farmhouses, quaint colonial inns, and a small-town southern lifestyle intrigue visitors from throughout the nation. Each May the valley is the site of festivals and historic commemorations such as the Shenandoah Apple Blossom Festival in Winchester, Va. A Museum of American Frontier Culture proposed for construction in Staunton, Va., in 1987 will feature 18th-century farm buildings from England, Northern Ireland, Germany, and Appalachia.

The Shenandoah National Park, established in 1935, encompasses over 195,000 acres with tree-covered mountains, trails, streams, waterfalls, and trout-filled pools. The Skyline Drive north-south highway extends for 105 miles through the park and offers an opportunity to view the scenic valley as well as the Blue Ridge Mountains, the Massanutten Mountain, and the Allegheny Mountains.

Some Shenandoah Valley residents are concerned that

the rural, small-town aspect of their region is disappearing. In 1985 the Adolph Coors Company began construction on a $70 million packaging and distribution center and announced plans for a brewery in the area by 1990. The valley's underground limestone aquifers will provide an excellent water source for the plant. Controversy surrounded the announcement of Coors's coming, and critics cited moral objections to alcoholic beverages and possible environmental problems. As early as the 1960s, concern over new developments spawned historic preservation societies in the area. These groups have been successful in restoring and improving over 100 buildings and residences.

Karen M. McDearman
University of Mississippi

William Couper, *History of the Shenandoah Valley* (1952); Julie Davis, *The Shenandoah* (1945); Gary D. Ford, *Southern Living* (May 1986).

Spanish Moss

Spanish moss is a soft, silver-gray, tropical herb (*Tillandsia usneoides*) with slender leaves and stems that grow on the branches of trees, often oak or other hardwoods, in the low woodlands and swamp forests of the southern Coastal Plain from Virginia to Texas. It is an epiphyte, using tree limbs for mechanical support, but drawing its nutrients from the air. Epiphytes never injure the host plant as do parasites. The long pendant strands may reach a length of 10 to 20 feet and sway with the slightest movement of the humid coastal air.

It is not a true moss but a member of the pineapple family, *Bromeliaceae*. The small, solitary, yellowish-green flowers and the brown, cylindrical, three-parted seed capsules that mark these as true flowering plants and not a moss are seldom noticed. However, a number of other species of epiphytic bromeliads, such as the quill-leaf (*Tillandsia fasciculata*) of peninsular Florida, have very colorful flower spikes. Spanish moss was a major fiber plant of the American Indians and was used to make skirts for Indian women, the French in south Louisiana once used it as a decoration at Christmas, and later it had limited commercial use as a packing and bedding material, but its primary cultural role has been as a botanical trademark for the Lowland South.

Spanish moss swaying in front of an old plantation home, south Louisiana, 1930s

Journalist James J. Kilpatrick sees Spanish moss as a metaphor for the South, "an indigenous, an indestructible part of the Southern character; it blurs, conceals, softens, wraps the hard limbs of hard times in a fringed shawl." It is particularly associated with Gothic imagery of the Deep South, suggesting romantic, mysterious, and sometimes menacing events.

C. Ritchie Bell
North Carolina Botanical Gardens
University of North Carolina
at Chapel Hill

Charles Reagan Wilson
University of Mississippi

Fred B. Kniffen and Malcolm L. Comeaux, *Melanges*, vol. 12 (1979).

Tennessee-Tombigbee Waterway

The Tennessee-Tombigbee Waterway, also known as "Tenn-Tom," is a man-made, 234-mile-long inland water route connecting the Gulf of Mexico with the Tennessee River in northeast Mississippi. This regionally significant and bold engineering project constructed by the U.S. Army Corps of Engineers links over 16,000 miles of inland navigable waterways, thus providing commercial users in at least 14 states an alternate route for shipping ores, chemicals, farm products, and many other commodities between ports along the Ohio River, the western tributaries of the upper Mississippi River, and the Gulf. By shortening distances that would ordinarily be traveled by water between the port of Mobile and such important commercial centers as Pittsburgh, Cincinnati, Louisville, Kansas City, and Chicago, the Tennessee-Tombigbee offers substantial savings in transportation costs. This benefit to commercial users has long been one of the most important justifications for its construction.

The idea of a navigable route connecting the Gulf and the Tennessee River is thought to have been originally proposed in the early 1700s by Jean-Baptiste Le Moyne, Sieur de Bienville (1680–1768). For nearly 250 years the idea surfaced and then faded in response to changes in American politics, economy, public opinion, and technological development. Finally, in July 1946, Congress passed legislation authorizing construction of the waterway. However, no funds were allocated directly for this purpose until October 1970, when President Richard

Nixon signed a bill authorizing expenditure of the first million dollars in construction costs. The project was controversial, with critics charging it was a political pork barrel measure to channel federal money to the Deep South. Environmental lawsuits also slowed development of the waterway. When the project finally was completed in December 1984, total costs reached approximately $1.992 billion.

The high total cost of the Tennessee-Tombigbee Waterway relates to many factors, including inflation, delays, legal expenses, environmental study expenses, and increased labor costs. It is also related to the complexity of its own engineering requirements, for the waterway truly is a unique hydraulic structure. The project makes use of the existing channel of the Tombigbee River in portions of Alabama and Mississippi, a man-made canal that parallels the river course in northeast Mississippi, and a "divide cut" through a high ridge of land in Mississippi's Tishomingo County. Throughout most of its length the waterway is maintained at 300 feet wide and 9 feet deep. There is also a drop of 341 feet in elevation between its northern and southern points, requiring the presence of five dams and 10 locks. Each lock along the route is 110 feet wide and 600 feet long and capable of accommodating a towboat and eight standard barges. These facilities are maintained year-round by the U.S. Army Corps of Engineers. In all, over 307 million cubic yards of earth were excavated when building Tenn-Tom—more material than was excavated during construction of the Panama Canal.

W. Lee Minnerly
Chicago, Illinois

James Williams Jones, "An Analytical History of the Tennessee-Tombigbee Waterway" (M.A. thesis, University of Mississippi, 1982); Tennessee-Tombigbee Waterway Development Authority, *The Tennessee-Tombigbee Waterway Story* (1969); U.S. Army Corps of Engineers, *Tennessee-Tombigbee Waterway, Alabama and Mississippi: Background and History* (1978); John P. Worsham, *The Tennessee-Tombigbee Waterway: A Chronological Bibliography in Report Form* (1976).

Ethnic Life

GEORGE E. POZZETTA
University of Florida
CONSULTANT

Tomochichi and his "nephew" Tooanahowi, from an untitled William Verelst portrait (1734)

Ethnic Life

Although the South received far less foreign immigration than other sections of the nation, the region throughout its history has contained a heterogeneous population by world standards. Too much has been made of the cultural homogeneity of the South. Not only did the region share in migrations that linked America with the rest of the world, it also assisted in shaping national attitudes that defined the role and place of ethnic and cultural minorities in American life.

The existence of ethnic and cultural minorities in the South occasioned two different but interrelated sets of adaptations. On the one hand, groups possessing distinctive customs and lifestyles helped to shape the general regional culture. On the other hand, the region profoundly influenced the internal cultural adjustments that newly arrived groups underwent as they dealt with the wider society. The relative balance of this give-and-take dialectic has varied over time and space, depending on a variety of factors including transportation networks, topographical conditions, agricultural possibilities, particular cultural preferences, and outside historical events. Significant variations also depended on whether groups settled in urban or rural locations. Additionally, it must be borne in mind that the South has seldom, if ever, possessed a single cultural unity. The region typically has been composed of a cluster of subregions, each with a distinctive cultural style, so every generalization made about the South must be qualified by a recognition of these realities.

Formative Ethnic Patterns. The colonial South received its initial cultural imprint from the settlers who first populated its lands. The majority of these people came from the British Isles, principally Scotland, Wales, Cornwall, and Ireland. These simple geographic designations, however, masked substantial diversity. Ireland sent Catholic immigrants from the south and Presbyterian Scotch-Irish from the north; Scotland contributed quite distinct Highlanders and Lowlanders.

Almost 75 percent of the colonial South's population was composed of these "Celtic" elements. Even though they initially possessed diverse cultural and religious characteristics, a set of shared cultural values came to predominate with time. According to historians Grady McWhiney and Forrest McDonald, the resulting regional lifestyle was characterized by "a pastoral economy based upon open range herding," an avoidance of sustained hard labor, belief in the traditional values of rural hospitality, and acceptance of personal violence. Furthermore, 16th- and 17th-century folk styles characterized the music and much of the craft of these people. In music, for example, they contributed to the development of a distinctive sound that became part of America's musical heritage through the "country and western" tradition. Remnants of Celtic culture, then, survived to influence the development of a southern culture.

Cultural adaptation of these settlers stemmed in part from early patterns of internal migration. As the 18th century advanced, the northern tier of the region received people from the Middle Atlantic zone (particularly from Pennsylvania and Maryland). Many of the Scotch-Irish settlers, for example, moved to the largely unpopulated middle and western portions of the Carolinas and Virginia in this manner. Wherever they settled, they farmed, fought Indians, and brought a rough "frontier culture" to the region. German settlers followed similar routes as they spilled down the Shenandoah Valley on the "Great Wagon Road." These newcomers generally engaged in more settled farming than their Celtic neighbors and exhibited a greater degree of cultural hegemony in their religions. Whether they were Mennonites, Moravians, Lutherans, or Reformed, church buildings quickly appeared. Their cultural and religious strength allowed such communities as Staunton, Bethania, Wachovia (Winston-Salem), and Salisbury to take root. These new towns often encouraged a further southward drift of population as the peopling of the region continued.

Port cities served some colonial settlers as entry points. Charleston, S.C., for example, set an early pattern that other coastal locations emulated. This bustling city not only served as a conduit for individuals bound inland but also attracted a heterogeneous population of its own. Charleston contained sizable numbers of black slaves and French Huguenots and smaller totals of Sephardic Jews, Germans, Spaniards, and Scotsmen. Such diversity set the pattern for similar developments later in Savannah, New Orleans, and Baltimore. In each case, the result was a cultural blend uncommon in more rural inland locations.

Occasional instances of direct group settlement also occurred in the colonial South. The German Moravians of Georgia and North Carolina established rural colonies, which, though short-lived, allowed for the creation of a cultural unity not possible in either more diverse urban settlements or more scattered farming areas. Small clusters of Swiss (Mennonites), Dutch, Swedish, and Spanish settlers briefly dotted the region as well, but were generally of less importance than the Germans.

Throughout the colonial period, and indeed beyond, white southerners were forced to deal with racial minorities in a more long-term and socially significant fashion than citizens of other regions. The presence of large numbers of Indians and blacks was, of course, of fundamental importance for the development of the region. These groups profoundly influenced the nature of southern customs, political institutions, racial beliefs, and cultural practices. Indeed, it is difficult to conceive of the South—even the contemporary South—without reference to them.

White southerners encountered Indians from the very earliest period of settlement. Unlike the coastal tribes of the North, southern groups were well organized and populous. Hence, they resisted encroachment more fiercely and persisted longer as a cultural presence. As a result, a long, intense period of contact, lasting until well into the 19th century, led to the partial "Indianization" of the region. Certain crops—corn, tobacco, and some herbs—trace their origins to Indian cultivation. In addition, various pottery and basket-weaving styles transferred to white society, where they still survive in certain locations, as do many Indian folktales and wildlife stories. Many southern place names (Chickamauga, Chattanooga, Alachua, Chattahoochee, etc.) are Indian in origin, and American English is sprinkled with many other linguistic carryovers. The physical presence of Indians themselves in areas of the South, of course, lends diversity to the human condition of the region. Vestiges of tribal cultures (dances, costumes, and rituals) are rare but can still be found in places such as the Seminole tribal areas of southern Florida and the Lumbee sections of North Carolina. Finally, the amount of intermarriage that has occurred between Indians (and blacks) and southern whites can never be known exactly, but undoubtedly such marriages have been considerable.

As important as Indians were, the antebellum South increasingly focused its attentions on blacks and the problems of slavery. Considerations involving immigration and ethnic group development slipped below the level of immediate public concern. Two exceptions bear mention. In major port cities such as New Orleans, ethnicity continued to exert an influence. New Orleans had been a distinctive southern city because for a century or so after its founding Anglo-Saxons (British Americans) were an ethnic minority within a predominantly French-Spanish culture. Many different cultural traditions and population strains enriched New Orleans during its antebellum history (French, Acadian, Spanish, African, Irish, etc.). A distinctive "Creole" culture evolved and persisted with remarkable strength into the 20th century. The city's vigorous blend of cultural patterns can still be seen in its architectural styles, linguistic adaptations, musical forms, food preferences, and religious observances. Even after the Civil War New Orleans continued to add to its population diversity. Sicilian laborers settled in substantial numbers, Jewish merchants peddled their wares, Chinese workmen operated small laundries, and Slavic immigrants staked out claims to the oyster industry. Each of these groups added new ingredients to the city's cultural mix.

Just as the South mirrored the nation in its ethnically diverse urban areas, so too did it participate in the periodic outbursts of nativism that swept America. Anti-immigrant sentiments intruded into the antebellum South, and on this level one finds the second exception to the region's seeming lack of public concern for ethnic issues. The most vivid political and social manifestation of this trend was the rise of the Know-Nothing party in the 1850s. Representing the culmination of two decades of growing anti-Catholic sentiment, the party appeared in various parts of the South. In Louisiana and Maryland anti-Catholic campaigns succeeded, and the Know-Nothings captured political office and established nativist newspapers and organizations. Election confrontations with Irish immigrants in Memphis, Louisville, and Baltimore also served to heighten tensions. Indeed, for a brief period after 1856 the Know-Nothing party became something of a southern institution. In that year the party's presidential candidate, Millard Fillmore, received his greatest support from the region. Concerns centered on foreign immigration, however, were soon erased by the mounting sectional crisis.

J. Grusset Saint Sauveur, Femme Acadienne *(1800)*

Recruitment of Immigrants. The return of peace after 1865 resulted in the creation of new contexts for the entry of various groups into the South. A regionwide effort to replace newly freed slaves with white European immigrants generated substantial organizational and promotional activity, though few actual results. Immigration enthusiasts succeeded in establishing a few colonies, and occasional work gangs of Irish, Italian, and Slavic immigrants crisscrossed the region. Some settlement "spin-off" resulted, as in the case of the Chinese areas of Texas and Mississippi, the Polish communities of Texas, and the Italian and Slavic enclaves of Birmingham, Ala., but no enduring transformations of the southern work force took place.

Nevertheless, the immigration campaign did solidify attitudes that defined the place of foreigners in southern society and assisted in determining the positions former slaves would occupy. Paradoxically, the campaign itself and its meager success led many potential immigrants to regard the South as undesirable. Because southerners recruited immigrants to replace blacks, they often relegated them to the same social and economic status as the freedmen. Hence, immigrants occasionally suffered social discrimination, vigilante violence, and even peonage. White foreigners quickly learned that to remain in the region and gain acceptance they must adopt local attitudes toward race. Immigrant leaders soon advised individuals to avoid the South.

Rebirth of Nativism. Even as the recruitment campaign failed, an upsurge in national nativist sentiment swung white southerners decisively to the side of the antiimmigrant cause. For their part, blacks had recognized from the beginning the threat foreign immigrants posed to their future and opposed further movement. Thus, by about 1910 both major elements of southern society shared the same negative attitudes toward immigration, although they had arrived at their positions by different paths.

The rekindling of nativism after 1890 had again forced southerners to confront directly questions dealing with foreign immigration. The pseudoscientific racialism (eugenics) that characterized this outburst of nativist activity merged neatly with southern cultural views on superior and subordinate racial structures. Sporadic outbreaks of violence against foreigners in the South made headlines. Italians and Jews were the most common targets, with the 1891 lynching of 11 Italians in New Orleans casily constituting the most dramatic episode. The region also resonated to the mounting tide of religious nativism that gained momentum after 1910. Located in rural, small-town America generally (and the South most particularly), this nativism coincided with the rise of religious fundamentalism.

By the second decade of the century, southern spokesmen, in Congress and elsewhere, were among the most articulate nativist advocates. Populist leader Tom Watson spread a message of papal intrigue and Jewish depravity, at first in his own publications and later in the U.S. Senate. Wilbur Franklin Phelp's virulently anti-Catholic *The Menace* reached a million circulation by 1914. The rebirth of the Ku Klux Klan after 1915 gave a vigorous institutional base to these attitudes. The Klan shaped the region's political culture by endorsing nativist platforms in various local, state, and national elections, sometimes with successful results. Although the hooded empire declined by the late 1920s, many of the anti-immigrant viewpoints it sponsored remained (albeit without a significant institutional foundation and often buried beneath other concerns). Disruptions to the region's equilibrium, however, have often served to bring these nativist assumptions to the surface of public attention. Hence, southern culture continues to be responsive to the presence of ethnic and minority groups.

Migrant Workers and Immigrant Communities. By the 20th century certain portions of the South could already look back to long traditions of migrant labor involving foreigners. Louisiana's experiment with Sicilian sugar harvesters, for example, fostered the spread of Italian cultural patterns in the state. Parts of Texas, Louisiana, and Mississippi had employed the services of Mexican agricultural workers for decades with similar results. Transient gangs of harvesters, pickers, and general field hands followed well-defined routes across the area, carrying with them a rough camp culture. Songs, tales, and poems emanating from this migrant life often endured for years, unwritten and passed from camp to camp by word of mouth. The transiency of the migrations, however, served to reduce their cultural impact on the region.

Southern Florida vibrated to different crosscurrents as migrants from the insular Caribbean probed the peninsula for economic opportunity. Farm workers and general laborers from Barbados, Jamaica, Trinidad, and Haiti made annual treks to engage in seasonal occupations, and they could regularly be found in dredging operations, canal building, railroad construction, and agricultural work. In some cases, handfuls of temporary workers remained behind and formed nuclei of settlement, which attracted permanent settlers later in the century.

Although the North has typically contained those areas of dense foreign settlement that so worried nativists, they were not completely absent from the South. Some urban locations attracted sufficient immigrants to create a "critical mass" of population, permitting different patterns of cultural adjustment. The case of New Orleans has already been mentioned, but it was not unique. In Tampa, Fla., for example, foreign population was concentrated enough to create a distinctive cultural unity. Cuban, Italian, and Spanish immigrants were able to erect complete institutional structures in their Tampa settlements, which included foreign language newspapers, mutual aid clubs, immigrant banks and stores, and churches. Such concentrations also nurtured the creation of elements of "high culture"—music, theater, reading and debating groups, literary clubs, etc.—which were typically not possible in more scattered locations. Finally, such large immigrant quarters allowed immigrant cultural expressions to spill over into the host society more easily and with greater permanence. This was particularly true of foods, linguistic adoptions, and musical styles. These patterns have continued to the present day and can be seen at work in the Cuban and Haitian sections of Miami, the Arabic quarters of Jacksonville, Fla., and in numerous Mexican *barrios* of Texas cities.

Although large-scale foreign settlement most commonly occurred along the coastal periphery of the region (especially since the 18th century), immigrants did not overlook interior locations entirely. Occasionally, an immigrant group existed in such settings in sufficient numbers to create a unique cultural landscape. The German sections of south-central Texas are a case in point. Arriving both before and after the Civil War, German immigrants moved vigorously into farming activities, often buying previously tilled lands. Because they were numerous and maintained their cultural bonds, they were able to exert an uncommon influence on the region. In terms of architectural styles, farming techniques, familial patterns, religious practices, and voting preferences, these locations still testify to the enduring impact of German settlers.

Various Gypsy groups have claimed the roads and fields of the South as their territories. Though relatively little is known about them, there appear to be four major groups—Continental European, English, and Scottish Gypsies, and the Irish Travelers (each with subgroups). The Travelers exhibited a typical pattern of development.

Arriving sometime in the 1850s from Ireland, where they had engaged in a number of itinerant occupations, Travelers moved south and specialized in horse and mule trading. Although they follow different trades today, they continue many old cultural practices, including a migratory lifestyle, seasonal occupational preferences, special language forms, and strong endogamous marriage patterns.

Similarly, a number of racial islands or "isolates" have added to the cultural diversity of the South. Often bearing pejorative local names such as Red Bones, Brass Ankles, or "Cajans" (as used in south Alabama), what most often characterizes these groups are allegations of racial crossovers (white with black or Indian or both) in their historical pasts. Ostracized by the dominant white society and occasionally by black society as well, these self-conscious groups have occupied a very marginal position in society. As a result they have developed distinctive cultural patterns, usually featuring a high degree of "clannishness," suspicion, and distrust toward outsiders. In these last characteristics they resemble the mountain people or "hillbillies" of Appalachia and the Ozarks.

Different dynamics explain the origins of ethnic pockets that were created by "target migrants," those who sought out a specific locale. Usually appearing along the coastal areas of the region, these settlements most often owed their beginnings to economic factors. The Greek community in Tarpon Springs, Fla., is an example. Begun in 1905, when an enterprising Greek sponge merchant discovered unusually rich areas of deep-water sponges, the settlement quickly attracted hundreds of experienced Greek divers and their families. Immigrants quickly outnumbered natives and soon thereafter a Greek Orthodox church appeared, along with Greek restaurants, groceries, clubs, and retail businesses. The cultural ambience of Tarpon Springs, with its Greek foods and colorful religious festivals, continues to attract visitors who find the old world style appealing. Smaller clusters of Portuguese, Filipinos, Dalmatian Yugoslavs, and, more recently, Vietnamese followed roughly similar patterns of settlement, adaptation, and cultural persistence in the South.

The passage of national restriction laws in the 1920s and the economic grip of the Great Depression drastically reduced the inflow of European immigrants and migrants from Mexico and the Caribbean. The movement of Mexicans into the South, however, revived after World War II and soon came to outstrip earlier totals. As a result, a vigorous Chicano culture evolved in the region. Though concentrated in Texas, Chicanos spread throughout the South, bringing with them distinctive styles of music, food preparation, and family practices. More recently, Chicanos have developed a political culture that has perhaps best been symbolized in the charismatic figures of union leader Cesar Chavez and San Antonio mayor Henry Cisneros.

Contemporary Patterns. Although the South failed to share heavily in the immediate post–World War II movement of displaced persons and refugees, the region has come to play an important role in immigration. Indeed, by the 1970s the South had become one of the principal immigrant receiving areas of the nation. Vietnamese exiles, Mexican migrant laborers, Cuban "boatlifters," Haitian refugees, and other Latin American immigrants have gravitated to the South in unusually heavy numbers, at times overtaxing the abilities of local areas to accommodate them. Accordingly, some areas of the region have shown renewed manifestations of antiimmigrant sentiment, much of it apparently economic in motivation.

At the same time, the South has received a large and still growing influx of second- and third-generation ethnics from northern locations seeking jobs or retirement homes. Coupled with the increased Asian and Latin American presence, this movement has redrawn the cultural map of many areas, especially the cities. Miami, Fla., for example, with its large Cuban sections, bordered by Haitian, Jamaican, and Afro-American quarters (which include thousands of other Central and South American peoples), and its populations of Jewish, Italian, and Slavic transplants from the North, resembles New York City of a century ago. In the future, therefore, ethnic and cultural minorities will play a greater rather than a lesser role in molding the cultural fabric of the region.

See also ART AND ARCHITECTURE: French Architecture; German Architecture; BLACK LIFE: African Influences; Appalachians, Black; Creolization; Immigrants and Blacks; Indians and Blacks; FOLKLIFE: / "Hillbilly" Image; GEOGRAPHY: Ethnic Geography; Indians and the Landscape; Ozarks; / Cherokee Settlement; Cuban Settlement; INDUSTRY: Industrialization in Appalachia; LANGUAGE: French Language; German Language; Indian Language; Mountain Language; Spanish Language / Conch; Indian Trade Languages; LITERATURE: Appalachian Literature; MUSIC: *Música Tejana*; / Balfa, Dewey; Jimenez, Flaco; MYTHIC SOUTH: Appalachian Culture; RELIGION: Appalachian Religion; Ethnic Protestantism; Jewish Religious Life; SOCIAL CLASS: Appalachia, Exploitation of; WOMEN'S LIFE: Appalachian Women; Indian Women; Mexican Women

George E. Pozzetta
University of Florida

Lucy M. Cohen, *Chinese in the Post–Civil War South* (1984); John Cooke and Mackie Blanton, *Publications of the Committee on Ethnicity in New Orleans*, 4 vols. (1978–); Leonard Dinnerstein and Mary Dale Palson, eds., *Jews in the South* (1969); Eli Evans, *The Provincials: A Personal History of Jews in the South* (1973); Russell L. Gerlach, *Immigrants in the Ozarks: A Study in Ethnic Geography* (1976); James Haskins, *The Creoles of Color in New Orleans* (1968); Charles Hudson, *The Southeastern Indians* (1976); Rosan A. Jordan, George F. Reinecke, Joseph V. Guillotte III, and H. F. Gregory, in *Louisiana Folklife: A Guide to the State*, ed. Nicholas R. Spitzer (1985); Terry G. Jordan, *German Seed in Texas Soil: Immigrant Farmers in Nineteenth-Century Texas* (1966); Lewis M. Killian, *White Southerners* (1970); James G. Leyburn, *The Scotch-Irish: A Social History* (1962); John Shelton Reed, *One South: An Ethnic Approach to Regional Culture* (1982); *Southern Exposure* (November–December 1985); Arnold Shankman, *Ambivalent Friends: Afro-Americans View the Immigrant* (1982); Henry D. Shapiro, *Appalachia on Our Mind: The Southern Mountains and Mountaineers in the American Consciousness, 1870–1920* (1978); Nicholas R. Spitzer, *Southern Exposure* (Summer–Fall

1977); Stephen Thernstrom, Ann Orlov, and Oscar Handlin, eds., *Harvard Encyclopedia of American Ethnic Groups* (1980); George B. Tindall, *The Ethnic Southerners* (1976); David E. Whisnant, *All That Is Native and Fine: The Politics of Culture in an American Region* (1983); Walter L. Williams, ed., *Southeastern Indians since the Removal Era* (1979); J. Leitch Wright, Jr., *The Only Land They Knew: The Tragic Story of the American Indians in the Old South* (1981); Klaus Wust, *The Virginia Germans* (1969).

Caribbean Influence

The culture of the southern coast, especially the Gulf Coast from Texas to Louisiana and down to south Florida, owes much to the African-Latin culture of the Caribbean. The Caribbean cultural area that has influenced the southern United States covers three island chains. The Bahamas includes about 3,000 mostly unoccupied islands stretching within 50 miles of the Florida coast and then southeast 760 miles to the Dominican Republic. The Greater Antilles includes Cuba, Puerto Rico, Hispanola (with Haiti on the western part of the island and the Dominican Republic toward the east), and Jamaica, a commonwealth nation in the United Kingdom. The Lesser Antilles lies to the east of Puerto Rico and includes the Virgin Islands, Leeward Islands, and Windward Islands; this archipelago ends northwest of Caracas, Venezuela, at the Netherlands Antilles. The Caribbean cultural zone also includes Costa Rica, Nicaragua, El Salvador, Belize, Guatemala, Panama, and Honduras—all of which touch the Caribbean and are united to the islands by ethnic composition, language, religious institutions, political instabilities, broad historical experiences, and economic problems.

Southern United States ties to this area have been historical, economic, ethnic, diplomatic, and military. The Gulf coastal areas of the American South and the islands share a semitropical physical environment and a history of colonial development. The North American Gulf Coast was first explored and settled by France and Spain as an offshoot of their exploration of the islands. Louisiana had sugar plantations resembling those on Santo Domingo (Hispaniola). Companies shipped bananas, coffee, and other products to the docks of New Orleans in the late 19th century, and today close economic ties remain as oil from refineries in Puerto Rico, bauxite from Jamaica, cocoa produced in the Dominican Republic, and illegal drugs from Colombia enter the United States through ports.

The Louisiana Gulf Coast was among the first areas of the South to experience Caribbean cultural influences. The *Islenos*—Spanish Canary Islanders—came to Louisiana from Cuba in 1777, introducing a long Spanish presence. They still fish and trap in Saint Bernard Parish, eat their distinctive foods such as *caldo*, and sing Spanish ballads. The Louisiana Purchase in 1803 led to the arrival of increased numbers of Americans, mostly from the Southeast, in Louisiana, but their influence on the area was diluted as a result of another population migration. Ten thousand French planters, their slaves, and free people of color fled Santo Domingo during and after the revolution that began with an uprising in 1791 and led to the establishment of a black republic, which was launched 1 January 1804 in what is now the nation of Haiti. This migration introduced many of the central cultural customs and institutions of southern Louisiana. Voodoo, gumbo, jambalaya, zydeco music, street dancing to Afro-Latin rhythms, shotgun houses, Creole cottages, the prevalence of festivals, and a Creole language (a language of French words within a system of African-derived grammar and pronunciation) have all been traced back to these early refugees.

The Louisiana Gulf Coast thus developed its abiding diversity of ethnic and cultural life partly because of the Caribbean influence. The Caribbean also played a part in the creation of a distinctive black southern folk culture. As far back as the 1700s blacks in the Low Country of Georgia and South Carolina, especially on the Sea Islands, created distinctive patterns that were African in background but that also reflected island ways. Scholars have shown Caribbean influences on southern basket styles, pottery, and music and dance. Zora Neale Hurston, who was from Florida, set out to study black folk culture in the 1930s, and her research led her first to the American South, then to Louisiana specifically (*Mules and Men*, 1935), and then to the Caribbean, where her fieldwork in Jamaica and Haiti resulted in *Tell My Horse* (1938).

The event that best symbolized the Caribbean's image for 19th-century southern blacks and whites was the Haitian Revolution that began in the late 18th century. The island had long been an important trading partner for the young American Republic, and some Americans, especially antislavery advocates, praised this uprising when it began in the early 1790s. But Americans, and southern whites particularly, became fearful as the rebellion against the French became increasingly bloody. It nurtured growing racial fears of southern slaveowners during the Jeffersonian era and was cited for decades afterwards as a terrible vision of a bloody postemancipation world in the South. Americans welcomed refugees from the island, but this was accompanied by a growing uneasiness among Virginians and South Carolinians. Charleston residents complained that the slaves brought by refugees from the island were insolent and potential carriers of rebellion. An era of increased slave unrest did occur after news arrived of the racial conflicts on the island, the most serious case being Gabriel Prosser's rebellion in the summer of 1800 in Richmond.

In the two decades before the Civil War some southern slaveowners looked upon the Caribbean as the potential locale for expansion. Stephen Vincent Benét called it the "purple dream" of a Caribbean empire. Americans of the time who considered the area were generally disturbed by the poverty, disease, political instability, and miscegenation they saw, but white Christian slaveowners—assuming the "white man's burden"—saw it as a challenge to bring "civilization" to the downtrodden while expanding slavery's influence within the United States. Cuba was to be the key to a tropical empire, based on either outright annexation of the Caribbean Islands or the creation of colonies managed by southern whites. This was regarded as progress for the unfortunate people of the islands and for the civilized world, which would then have plentiful and stable supplies of sugar, coffee, fruits, and rice. The U.S. government never supported the southern imperial idea. Charismatic Mississippian John Quitman advocated private military adventures in the area, but cautious moderate southern leaders disapproved. Filibusterer William Walker did gain control of Nicaragua in the mid-1850s, briefly introducing slavery there before his "reign" ended at the firing squad.

In the contemporary South the Caribbean cultural influence is seen most dramatically in Florida. The development of Florida dates back to the turn of the century. Henry M. Flagler had a vision of the state as a sunny playground for the leisured class, and his Florida East Coast Railroad promoted tourism and ties with the Caribbean Islands. Palm Beach grew around a resort hotel, the Breakers, and Flagler extended his railroad farther south to Miami and then in 1913 (at a cost of 700 dead workers on construction crews) to Key West. The importance of the Caribbean even at this early date was apparent when Flagler proposed building a railroad bridge to the Cuban capital, Havana.

The military played an important role in tying this southern subregion to the Caribbean. It was a point of departure for U.S. Army troops going to Cuba in the Spanish-American War in 1898, for Marines occupying Haiti in 1915, for airplanes taking part in the 1961 Bay of Pigs invasion of Cuba, and for American troops invading the Dominican Republic in 1967. The U.S. Navy has long sent its ships and personnel between Florida ports and the islands.

Up to the 1960s the development of southern Florida was culturally an Anglo vision of the good life in a semitropical world. Aristocratic yachtsmen, retired middle-class elderly from northern and midwestern cities, blacks and poor whites from the adjacent Deep South, violent mobsters, and well-off Jews from New York City dominated the culture. Jackie Gleason's television shows of the early 1960s were taped at Miami Beach, opening with shots of the city skyline while the announcer proclaimed the beach "the sun and fun capital of the world." Miami was throughout the 20th century the steppingstone to the Caribbean, but before the 1960s it clearly faced north, its development based on luring business and people south.

The post-1960 South in general has undergone dramatic and wrenching change, but south Florida has experienced a particularly traumatic change involving a geographical redirection in outlook. Its culture and business now face south. Jaime Raldos, for example, the former president of Ecuador, once called Miami "the capital of Latin America." The watershed event in this new Caribbean connection was the 1959 Fidel Castro revolution in Cuba. There had been earlier waves of Cuban immigration to Florida, particularly to Tampa, but the events of 1959 sent a distinctive group of generally well-educated, skilled, politically conservative, upper- and middle-class exiles to Florida. Some were obsessed with returning to their island homeland and became involved in a life of intrigue and conspiracy that began to cast dark shadows on the area's sunny image. Watergate burglars were Cubans from Florida. When despotic heads of state in Central America or the Caribbean were toppled, many headed for Miami. That city's banks have come to hold many fortunes of the wealthy to the south. Gun dealers are a prominent part of the Miami landscape (Gun City, Inc., is typical) and are suppliers to the Caribbean. Joel Garreau has surveyed south Florida's business life and characterizes the importation of illegal drugs as its number-one industry, with Colombia in particular sending marijuana, cocaine, and methaqualone. Violence from the "cocaine cowboys"—an affectionate name for Colombian drug dealers—periodically erupts on Miami streets. The new television image of south Florida is the violent, flashy *Miami Vice*.

The Caribbean connection has given Florida cities a new cultural vitality and diversity, but with an increasingly dominant Hispanic style. More than 40 percent of Dade County's population is Hispanic, and Miami has become a Spanish-speaking city. Its Little Havana, Calle Ocho Street, and festival Carnaval Miami each March are new symbols of Latin influence, as was Xavier Suarez's election in November 1985 as the first Miami mayor from its Cuban community.

The contemporary Caribbean influence on south Florida includes, however, more than its Cuban population. The first boatload of black boat people from Haiti arrived on American shores at Pompano Beach, Fla., 12 December 1972, and the island has sent over 50,000 refugees to those shores since then. These refugees are a national problem, but south Florida and other areas of the American South have experienced a particularly acute crisis with their arrival. These have been generally poor, desperate people, and their arrival has strained Florida's ability to deliver health care and social services. Many of them now work as low-paid migrant workers along the Atlantic Coast from Florida to Virginia. Their neighborhoods in Miami and elsewhere represent a different cultural landscape from native blacks and whites, or the Cubans from the last two decades. Voodoo, French-influenced Catholic rituals and images, foodways, and other aspects of Haiti's culture have again, as after the Santo Domingo revolution, become a part of a subregion of the South. The same racial fears directed against black-skinned people are also heard today as in that earlier period in the South.

Charles Reagan Wilson
University of Mississippi

William L. Barney, *The Road to Secession: A New Perspective on the Old South* (1972); Joel Garreau, *The Nine Nations of North America* (1981); Bob Hall and Jim Clark, *Southern Exposure* (May–June 1982); Winthrop D. Jordan, *White over Black: American Attitudes toward the Negro, 1550–1812* (1968); Lester D. Langles, *The Banana Wars: An Inner History of*

American Empire, 1900–1934 (1983), *The United States and the Caribbean, 1900–1970* (1980); Nicholas R. Spitzer, *Southern Exposure* (May–June 1982).

Indian Cultural Contributions

Indians seem to have affected southern culture little, but in fact the Native American legacy to the South is extensive. Narratives of 16th-century Spanish conquistadors describe populous Indian towns, powerful regional chiefdoms, copper ornaments and weapons, wooden carvings, hieroglyphics, picture writing, and large truncated temple mounds. Much of this was associated with the southeastern ceremonial complex, which was also known variously as the eagle, hawk, buzzard, or southern cult. It was part of the Mississippian cultural tradition. Flourishing in the centuries before Columbus's voyage, in what became the Cotton Kingdom in the early 19th century, Mississippian culture represented one of the most highly developed civilizations north of Mexico. This was the era of the mound builders, who constructed temple mounds up to 100 feet tall, with religious and political structures on their flat tops. Frequently there was not just a single isolated temple mound but several spread over acres in planned clusters. The organized labor necessary to construct these mounds implies a structured political organization. Coastal Indians, such as the Algonkians in Virginia and the Calusa in Florida, whom Ponce de León, Menéndez de Avilés, Sir Walter Raleigh's colonists at Roanoke, and John Smith encountered, were on the periphery of the maize-growing Mississippian heartland and the high culture there.

Much of this culture and many of the Indians themselves were destroyed before Englishmen ever made a permanent settlement at Jamestown in 1607. New diseases introduced by Europeans and Africans were the culprits. Pandemics wiped out entire tribes and linguistic families. Warfare and enslavement of Indians also took their toll. For several centuries between Ponce de León's 16th-century voyages and the early 19th-century removal of the southern Indians beyond the Mississippi River, the South was inhabited by three cultures—Indian, African, and European. These three peoples interacted with one another, modifying each other's culture. Despite prodigious population losses, during much of the period before western relocation the Indians were relatively numerous, and they had a considerable impact on whites and blacks.

Perhaps the most significant Indian contribution to the South—and the world—was in agriculture. Journeying through the South in George Washington's time, a traveler could notice fields of tobacco and corn, with pole beans climbing the stalks of the latter; these had long been familiar sights to the Indians. Plows might have turned the soil on large plantations, but plain white farmers often raised crops without a plow's benefit, using Indian methods. The Native American influence easily can be appreciated when considering maize (Indian corn). It is no accident that grits, hominy, hoecake, and corn bread are southern dishes typically consumed in areas where Mississippians formerly lived. Sweet potatoes,

Alfred Boisseau, Louisiana Indians Walking along a Bayou *(1847)*

squash, beans, and many other favorite items of the southern diet are Indian in origin. James B. Duke's 19th-century cigarette machines laid the basis for a major southern industry, but Indians had cultivated tobacco long before that. Tea, to take another example, was the most common nonalcoholic southern drink until the 19th century, and not all of it was imported from the Far East. Made from the southern holly (*ilex vomitoria*), yaupon tea was extensively consumed. Though eventually overshadowed by coffee and colas, the Indians' yaupon tea enjoyed a revival among southerners during periods of economic distress throughout the 19th century. This tea was the Mississippians' "black drink," their standard beverage in rituals and social gatherings. Europeans and Africans manifested keen interest in native medicines and cures, and a considerable portion of folk medicine in the South appears to be of aboriginal origin.

Indians made other major contributions to the material culture of the South. Recent archaeological discoveries permit a closer look at modifications in early white material culture, particularly its pottery. After European contact, Native Americans continued to produce large amounts of pottery in the usual fashion—coiled and hand-worked, shell-tempered, and stick- or pebble-burnished. This or similar pottery has come to be known as colono-Indian ware. Large amounts have been unearthed at sites throughout the South. Planters, wealthy merchants, and the governing elite dined and entertained on delft, majolica, and other imported china, but the middle and lower classes, including slaves, regularly used colono-Indian pottery. Mention should also be made of clay tobacco pipes. When George Washington and his circle called for their pipes, they were long-stemmed clay ones, modeled after those used by the Powhatans. Aboriginal baskets and mats appeared in colonial households, and are still prized by modern southerners. Colonists appropriated part of the Indians' dress as frontier clothing, used the dugout canoe for transportation, and even lived at times in Indian-style houses. Some scholars attribute a popular 20th-century, good-health institution—the sauna—to the hot houses and sweat houses of Mississippian times.

Indians also contributed to the oral lore of the South. They put such euphonious names as Rappahannock, Altamaha, Talladega, and Mississippi on the landscape. Settlers borrowed aboriginal words to describe unfamiliar objects. Early Jamestown residents borrowed from the Powhatans, for example, words such as moccasin, matchcoat, terrapin, opossum, raccoon, chinquapin, chum, hominy, pone, and tomahawk. Southern folklore has been enriched by the stories of Pocahontas's rescue of John Smith, Sequoyah's invention of a syllabary, William Weatherford (Red Eagle) and Andrew Jackson in combat during the 1813 Creek War, and the Cherokees on the Trail of Tears.

From the early colonial period onward the southern Indians interacted with black slaves. With mounting recent interest in the African heritage and pan-Indianism, scholars have shown little concern for the effects the two groups, living side by side in the South for centuries, had on one another. The evidence is overwhelming, though, that over the centuries Africans and Indians did not remain separate but for a long time associated and intermingled, in various ways influencing each other's development. Southern Indians were enslaved, especially in the 17th and 18th centuries, with males sometimes shipped to the West Indies and women and children left behind. In contrast, African slaves imported into the South in this early period had a higher ratio of males, and they often took Indian slave wives. Miscegenation led to the Native Americans' genetic contributions to the appearance of the new Afro-American in North America. There were other cultural ties. Though okra was an exception, much of modern soul food is Indian. Black English may owe a debt to remnants of Mississippian language. Assuredly this was true regarding black folktales: Mississippians had their own version of Brer Rabbit long before Africans arrived in the South.

The Indian influence has also survived among whites. Despite statements to the contrary early in southern history, extensive Indian-white miscegenation and intermarriage occurred. One can now find a governor of Virginia and a president of the United States proudly proclaiming descent from Pocahontas. Some Indians in the Old South were planters who modeled themselves on the white gentry. Some of Red Eagle's children, for example, were wealthy Alabama cotton planters who, like other southern Indians, lost their slaves and much more during the Civil War. Stand Watie led a brigade of Cherokee followers in the Confederate cause, participating in battles in the Indian Territory and at Pea Ridge in Arkansas. Watie became a brigadier general for the Lost Cause. As discussed earlier, southern material culture and oral lore, like southern history in general, would not have been distinctive without Native American influences.

In one fashion or another many people identifying themselves as Indian remained in the South after the removal of the major tribes to the Indian Territory in the 1830s. In recent times their presence has become more obvious. Cherokees, Choctaws, Seminoles, and Miccosukees have preserved their language and some aspects of their culture. Others, such as the Lumbees in North Carolina and the Creeks in the Florida Panhandle and southern Alabama, have lost all knowledge of their native tongues. The number of southerners who call themselves Indians seems, nonetheless, to be increasing, and in a variety of ways they are asserting their Indian identity. Moreover, consciously or not, southern whites and blacks perpetuate ancient Mississippian customs as they eat grits, smoke tobacco, read about Brer Rabbit, and possibly even sit in a sauna. One cannot escape the Indian legacy, which is far greater than suggested by the lonely temple mounds still dotting the South.

See also ENVIRONMENT: Plant Uses; FOLKLIFE: Basketmaking; Folk Medicine; / Brer Rabbit; Okra; HISTORY AND MANNERS: / Jamestown; Soul Food; Trail of Tears

J. Leitch Wright, Jr.
Florida State University

Maxine Alexander, ed., *Southern Exposure* (November 1985); Gary C. Goodwin, *Cherokees in Transition: A Study of a Changing Culture and Environment Prior to 1775* (1977); G. Melvin Herndon, *North Carolina Historical Review* (Summer 1967); Charles Hudson, *The Southeastern Indians* (1976); Winthrop D. Jordan, *White over Black: American Attitudes toward the Negro, 1550–1812* (1968); J. Anthony Paredes, in *Social and Cultural Identity: Problems of Persistence and Change*, ed. Thomas Fitzgerald (1974); John R. Swanton, Bureau of American Ethnology, *42d Annual Report* (1928), *The Indians of the Southeastern United States* (1946).

Indians before 1700

The first humans to inhabit the South were Paleo-Indians, who had spread over North America well before 10,000 B.C. Most archaeologists agree that the ancestors of these people migrated from Asia to America by way of a connecting land bridge between Siberia and Alaska between 10,000 and 30,000 years ago. During the Pleistocene "Ice Ages," when the climate was much colder, these wandering bands of big-game hunters traveled lightly with few possessions besides their basics for survival: fire-making tools, bone- or stone-tipped spears, and domesticated hunting dogs. They lived in extended family kin groups of about 20 to 40 people.

About 8000 B.C. a warming of the climate caused the extinction of many of the large mammals upon which the Paleo-Indians depended. As new environments began to form, the people living in them adapted in response to local conditions. The peoples of eastern North America, from the Great Lakes to Florida, evolved the Archaic culture, relying heavily on fishing, small-game hunting, and collecting shellfish and wild plants. They did not move often, and the Archaic Indians produced more material goods than their ancestors. About 2000 B.C. people of the coastal Georgia area independently invented pottery, which allowed for year-round storage of food. Pottery and other inventions led to the transformation of plant collecting into agriculture.

The Woodland period emerged in the Ohio River Valley about 1000 B.C. A new way of life began for most southeastern Native Americans and it lasted into the 19th century. Woodland Indians had a mixed economy of agriculture (corn, beans, squash, pumpkins, sunflower seeds, and other foods) and forest use (hunting, fishing, wild plants). Men hunted and women did the farming. Probably because their economic role was so important, women had high status, with kinship relations organized around extended-family matrilineages. Increased population and leisure time led men to develop craft specializations and religious ceremonies. The Woodland peoples paid particular attention to funeral rites, burying their dead in large earthen burial mounds. Bodies were carefully dressed and provided with food and tools to take with them into the afterlife. Objects of artistic and religious value were traded over an extensive territory, ranging from Florida to the Rocky Mountains and Great Lakes regions.

The next cultural explosion occurred in the lower Mississippi River Valley after about A.D. 700. This Mississippian period saw a further evolution of Woodland forms as well as a strong cultural influence from the Indians of Mexico. Through contact along the Gulf of Mexico, elements of the great civilizations of Meso-America reached the South. In fertile farmlands of large river valleys, the Mississippians developed towns around ceremonial centers consisting of huge mounds. Unlike the earlier Woodland burial mounds, these earth structures were built as high platforms for religious temples. Major temple mounds survive today, most notably at Etowah and Ocmulgee, Ga.; Moundville, Ala.; Emerald Mound, Miss.; and Spiro, Okla.

The various Mississippian city-states developed a high standard of living based upon intensive agriculture. Prosperity allowed the rise of an artistic class, as well as a high class of religious leaders. The growth of population meant that competition for the best valley farmlands increased to the point that organized warfare arose among the independent towns. Moats and palisades were built around the towns, and people lived in rectangular wood and plastered houses either inside or near the defenses. Mississippian tribes were stratified societies comparable to European city-states.

Mississippian culture, unique to the South, reached its height between A.D. 1200 and 1600, but several Indian states maintained this way of life into the early European era. French explorers wrote detailed descriptions of the Natchez Indians of Mississippi and Louisiana, who probably best exemplified the culture.

During the 1500s and 1600s the complex Mississippian societies declined drastically, due mainly to tremendous population decreases brought about by the introduction of Old World diseases. Europeans brought numerous foreign germs with them, left over from the plagues that earlier ravaged the Old World, and Indians had no immunity to them. Epidemics of smallpox, diphtheria, scarlet fever, measles, yellow fever, malaria, and other diseases rapidly killed from 50 to 90 percent of Native Americans. The successive waves of diseases, begun with the earliest explorers, helped destroy Mississippian culture.

As the large Mississippian towns declined, Indians living on the fringes reverted to Woodland ways of life. Native society now focused more on language-related ethnic or national groupings. The four main cultural subdivisions were: (1) Algonkians, probably the original settlers of the South, scattered down the Atlantic Coast from Canada to North Carolina; (2) Muskogeans, spread over a huge area of the central South from the Gulf Coast to Kentucky; (3) Iroquoians, who had migrated into the southern Appalachians and the Carolinas sometime between 100 B.C. and A.D. 1000; and (4) Siouans, scattered in pockets through different areas. Little is known about other language and cultural groupings, because they became extinct so early in the colonial era.

Depopulation produced a crisis among southern Indians that provoked a revolution in ethnic identity during the colonial era. As small bands were decimated, survivors joined a nearby larger group to form a new "tribe."

The larger groups were suffering their own population losses and thus welcomed additions. Where there was no predominant tribe, individuals from numerous bands tended to coalesce into small multitribal communities. These diverse groups sometimes adopted a European trade language as their only mutually understandable language and gradually absorbed more European and African culture, through contact with individual whites and escaping black slaves. This process accounts for the rise of numerous new "tri-racial isolates" in various areas of the South by the 18th century and also helps explain the fluidity of ethnic identity in the changing Indian "tribes."

Walter L. Williams
University of Cincinnati

Charles Hudson, *The Southeastern Indians* (1976); Wilbur R. Jacobs, *William and Mary Quarterly* (January 1974); Jesse Jennings, *Prehistory of North America* (1974); Wendell Oswalt, *This Land Was Theirs: A Study of the North American Indian* (1973).

Indians, 1700–1840

General Dance of the Natchez Indians, *from Le Page Du Pratz,* Histoire de La Louisiane *(1785)*

European contact with American Indians in the South over two centuries dramatically changed native societies. The first, most critical revolution in Indian life was due to disease. Though massive depopulation occurred in the 1500s and 1600s, severe epidemics continued to decimate Indian societies through the 18th century. Small tribes of the coastal areas were often completely wiped out by disease, warfare, and enslavement.

The larger native nations of the interior were protected from this onslaught by their greater population and their distance from white settlements. In fact, they began to prosper from European contact in terms of trading furs (especially deer) for manufactured goods (metal tools, firearms, cloth, alcohol). The Cherokees, Creeks, and Choctaws in particular drew on the resources of their own large territories and served as middlemen in the trade with Indians farther west. Because they were able to play off rival traders from the English coastal colonies, Spanish Florida, and French Louisiana, the interior southeastern Indians occupied an important economic and diplomatic position.

While the fur trade was revolutionizing Indian material culture and making hunting more important to native economics, warfare also became more important. Many coastal groups had earlier escaped white expansion by migrating west to join the interior nations or by leaving the area entirely (Tuscaroras to Pennsylvania and New York, Shawnees to Ohio, Yamassees and others to Florida). As various groups were pushed west, they clashed with previous native occupants. This, combined with competition over hunting territory and raiding for captives to sell to the English as slaves, vastly increased intertribal warfare in the colonial era. Europeans encouraged the use of native peoples to do their fighting for them, a tactic that reduced Indian population further. The Indian nations had become so dependent on European trade that they could not avoid involvement in European national rivalries in the Second Hundred Years' War. Yet they skillfully used their position in a complicated balance-of-power diplomacy.

Changes in the mid-18th century undermined these successful native adaptations based on trade and military alliances with the Europeans. First, as game declined, Indians had a diminishing product to trade for the European goods on which they had grown dependent. Second, by the Treaty of 1763 the French were forced to surrender their North American empire and Spain gave up Florida to the English. Indians no longer had the opportunity to exploit European rivalries. After the British evacuated the South in 1781, and other Europeans abandoned their claims to the new United States, Indians were left in a precarious situation. Their last attempt to use white rivalries was during the War of 1812, but the British abandonment of native interests left them without allies.

Though the new national government was weak and was forced to recognize Indian sovereignty in treaties, the white population was bent on expansion over native lands.

Despite their weakened economic and political situation, the interior Indian nations had managed to avoid cultural disintegration. Much of their 18th-century daily life continued to reflect aboriginal patterns. Communal agriculture, carried on by women, was still the basis of their food supply. Though stone tools and pottery were largely replaced by manufactured goods, and politically independent towns were unified under national governments, the basic cultural elements—language, matrilineal kinship, social patterns, and religions—remained primarily indigenous.

During the early 19th century even these cultural elements came under attack, primarily from missionaries, government agents, and "mixed bloods." Economic and political decline meant that some Indians were in a mood to listen when missionaries told them to save themselves from further decline due to "God's displeasure for following pagan lifestyles." Those Indians who already had white relatives, through intermarriage with frontier traders, were particularly susceptible to missionary propaganda. These "mixed bloods" (who were completely accepted as Indian because of matrilineal descent) were expected to deal effectively with whites, because of their familiarity with white ways. A new class of acculturated Indians, led by "mixed bloods" and mission converts, began adopting Western culture as part of a new peace policy of accommodation designed to gain American respect. By proving to whites that they had become "civilized," they hoped they would suffer no more land losses and could coexist in peace.

By the 1820s the Cherokees, Chickasaws, Choctaws, and Creeks were becoming known as the Civilized Tribes. They adopted Christianity, set up schools, and elected national governments at least outwardly modeled on the United States. Prosperous "mixed bloods" practiced cash-crop agriculture based on black slave labor. Slavery was seen as an indication that the Indians were "civilized." Much of the incentive for setting up centralized governments, other than the need to deal in a unified manner with the United States, was to enact laws enforcing slavery.

As the traditional communal-agricultural towns disintegrated and more Indians owned their own private family farms, they turned to the national councils rather than the old town councils. Society became disjointed and in flux. Missionaries led their converts not only to reject traditional ceremonials in favor of Christianity, but also to take English patriarchal family names, to use the English language, and to adopt white styles of clothing and housing. Even more importantly, European ideas of private property, inheritance, and wealth destroyed the old classless homogeneity. Classes of rich and poor emerged. Naturally, traditionalists—probably the majority—felt uncomfortable about this new departure, and each nation became factionalized. They all wanted to hold on to their remaining lands but were divided by repeated U.S. government pressures for land cessions.

Though the Supreme Court ruled in *Cherokee Nation v. Georgia* (1831) that the Indians were outside the control of state jurisdiction, Georgia and other states pressed for expansion over Indian lands. President Andrew Jackson pushed hard for Indian removal to the West. One group after another of eastern Indians was forced to sign removal treaties, exchanging their homelands for the promise of permanent self-government and possession of new lands in Indian Territory (Oklahoma). In vain the Indians pleaded for the United States to enforce its earlier treaty promises and Supreme Court decisions, but removal acts continued to be passed under Presidents Jackson and Van Buren. The removal of the Civilized Tribes proved that fears of "hostile savages" were not as important as white land hunger. In several of the removals, Indians were marched on winter "trails of tears," in which thousands died.

The last Indian holdouts in the South were the Seminoles. A group formed in the late 1700s from Creek, Yamassee, and other tribes who had fled to Spanish Florida to get away from white settlers, the Seminoles were united in their resistance to the United States. Southerners were not especially interested in Seminole lands, but they were threatened by the Seminoles' taking in runaway black slaves. Seminoles had resisted both acculturation and pressures for them to return their black allies. War broke out in 1835 and became one of the most costly and frustrating the United States ever fought. It did not end until 1842, after the United States commander captured Seminole leaders by violating a flag of truce. Once the national government promised to let the blacks accompany them to Indian Territory, the Seminoles agreed to remove. Though hundreds of Seminoles hid in the swamps and refused to leave (as occurred with other Indian tribes also), the completion of Indian removal allowed white southerners to expand into new lands and solidify their slave economy.

Walter L. Williams
University of Cincinnati

Robert Berkhofer, *Salvation and the Savage: An Analysis of Protestant Missions and American Indian Response, 1787–1862* (1965); Grant Foreman, *Indian Removal: The Emigration of the Five Civilized Tribes of Indians* (1953); Michael Green, *The Politics of Indian Removal: Creek Government and Society in Crisis* (1982); Charles Hudson, *The Southeastern Indians* (1976); Wilbur R. Jacobs, *Dispossessing the American Indian: Indians and Whites on the Colonial Frontier* (1972); Duane King, ed., *The Cherokee Indian Nation: A Troubled History* (1979); James O'Donnell, *Southern Indians in the American Revolution* (1973); J. Leitch Wright, Jr., *The Only Land They Knew: The Tragic Story of the American Indians in the Old South* (1981).

Indians since 1840

Because the majority of Native Americans were forcibly removed from the Southeast in the 1830s, southern Indians have been split geographically. The removal treaties set up Indian Territory (modern-day Oklahoma) as their permanent homeland, with federal guarantees of full ownership of lands and internal self-government. The Cherokees, Chickasaws, Choctaws, Creeks, and Seminoles were each granted a separate area. Though they were bitterly factionalized on the removal question (especially the Cherokees), the transplanted nations made remarkable progress in reestablishing themselves in the new lands during the 1840s and 1850s.

The Civil War tragically reopened factional disputes as those families who had cooperated with removal (led by "mixed blood" slaveowners) favored allying with the South. The withdrawal of U.S. troops, continual delays in federal treaty payments, and more favorable treaty terms from the Confederate government strengthened the pro-South Indians. Treaties of friendship were signed in 1861, and Confederate Indian regiments were organized. Along with Texas troops they terrorized pro-Union and neutral Indians, who fled to Kansas. Death and destruction occurred in the Indian Territory's severe guerrilla warfare, which laid waste to the countryside.

In 1865 the United States ignored the Unionist Indians, but imposed new treaties that punished southern Indians even more than the Confederates. Not only was slavery ended and blacks made citizens of the nations, but the Indians lost half their lands (the western half of Indian Territory was taken for settlement of Plains Indians) and the federal government imposed more restrictions on tribal governments. Indian governments were deeply divided because of wartime loyalties and new questions concerning white and black squatters on their remaining lands. These internal divisions weakened the Indian nations precisely at the time when the United States was putting most pressure on them. Congress and the courts set policies in the 1870s and 1880s that abrogated past treaty guarantees, forced the tribal governments to accept railroad landgrants, and transferred legal matters from native to federal courts.

By the 1890s Congress had abolished communal landholdings and substituted individual allotments, and then it abolished the tribal governments altogether. In 1907 Oklahoma was admited as a state. Although some acculturated Indians did well financially, many traditionalists lost control over their lands through legal proceedings declaring them "incompetent" or through illegal graft and intimidation. Traditional Indians isolated themselves in rural communities on economically marginal lands, while their government "guardians" or white settlers reaped bonanzas from oil discoveries. The 1936 Oklahoma Indian Welfare Act attempted to reestablish tribal governments, but with only mixed success. By the 1970s these governments had become more active in attempting to deal with continuing impoverishment among Oklahoma Indians.

Meanwhile, native peoples remaining in the Southeast suffered other problems. Some of these groups (North Carolina Cherokees, Florida Seminoles, Mississippi Choctaws, Alabama Creeks) represented only small portions of the removed nations who managed to escape removal by settling on isolated, economically marginal lands; others, who had never been pressured to remove, continued to reside in long-settled areas of Virginia (Chickahominy, Mattaponi, Pamunkey, Rappahannock), the Carolinas (Catawba, Lumbee, Haliwa, Coharie, Waccamaw), and Louisiana (Houma, Chitimacha, Tunica, Coushatta).

Whatever their origin, each native community isolated itself and survived by developing a localized subsistence economy. If whites became interested in Indian lands, they tried to dispossess the natives by lowering them to the status of landless blacks. This process culminated in guerrilla resistance during the 1860s by the Lumbees, the largest southeastern remnant. By the late 19th and early 20th centuries, as agriculture and timbering expanded in the South, more Indians lost their lands and were forced to become sharecroppers or wage laborers. Their local subsistence economies were destroyed, and their living standard declined as they entered the cash economy.

Up to this time southeastern Indians had continued to follow their traditional lifestyles, with many aboriginal activities predominating among the removal escapees and a mixed Indian-European-African folk culture among the nonremoved groups. Once they lost their independent economy, acculturation to modern white-dominated society occurred. Indians suddenly expressed great interest in Christianity and education, as they struggled to control their own institutions (mainly the church and

Deaconness Harriet M. Bedell with Seminole Doctor Tiger and a small boy, Florida, 1936

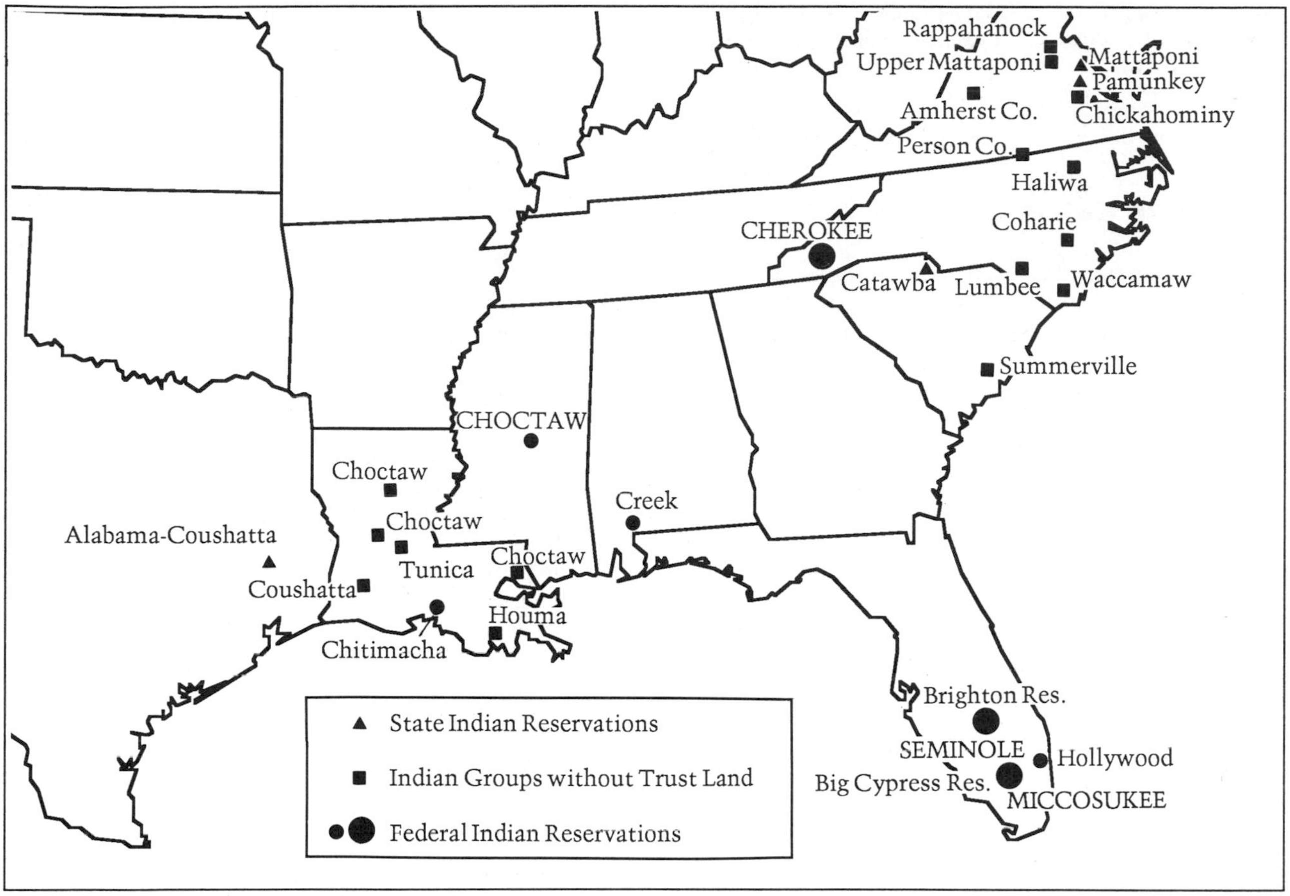

Southern Indian Reservations

Source: Charles Hudson, *The Southern Indians* (1976).

the school) as an ethnic group within the larger society. Several federally unrecognized groups attempted to gain treaty status as a means to protect their landholdings and legitimize their Indian status. Federal reservation Indians, especially the Cherokees, had to deal with a more diverse population because of white intermarriage and government-forced acculturation policies.

The 20th century has seen a steady increase in acculturation, due partly to intermarriage and government policy but more significantly because of outside employment. Especially since World War II more Indians have migrated to take jobs off the reservation, and some of them have abandoned a distinct tribal identity to merge into the larger urban society. Ease of automobile travel has encouraged this migration, as well as a reverse migration of white tourists to visit Indians. On the Cherokee and Seminole reservations in particular, much of the economy has become dependent on tourism. Television has also encouraged acculturation.

Yet even as Indians' lifestyles have become more like those of other southerners, their identity as Indians persists. The majority of them are not disappearing into the larger society as assimilated individuals. Instead, both reservation and unrecognized Indians are emphasizing their distinctiveness through revitalization of cultural traits (language, music, mythology, clothing, crafts) and a sense of a shared past in their kinship relations.

Better education has promoted more community organization and political-legal activism. This has also exposed southern Indians to other Indians outside the South and has promoted a Pan-Indian identity. By ending their isolation and attaching themselves to the larger Indian movement of the last two decades, they have preserved their Native American identity. If an Indian community has managed to retain at least some landholdings, and a sense of general community and kinship, its ethnic survival seems assured. The South will continue to be, as it has in the past, an area of three cultural and racial groups.

See also BLACK LIFE: Indians and Blacks; GEOGRAPHY: Indians and the Landscape; LANGUAGE: Indian Language; / Conch; Indian Trade Languages; WOMEN'S LIFE: Indian Women

Walter L. Williams
University of Cincinnati

Jesse Burt and Robert Ferguson, *Indians of the Southeast: Then and Now* (1973); Angie Debo, *And Still the Waters Run: The Betrayal of the Five Civilized Tribes* (1972); W. McKee Evans, *To Die Game: The Story of the Lowry Band, Indian Guerrillas of Reconstruction* (1971); H. Craig Miner, *The Corporation and the Indian: Tribal Sovereignty and Industrial Civilization in Indian Territory* (1976); Theda Perdue, ed., *Nations Remem-*

bered: An Oral History of the Five Civilized Tribes, 1865–1907 (1980); Walter L. Williams, ed., *Southeastern Indians since the Removal Era* (1979).

Mountain Culture

The inhabitants of the southern mountains do not refer to themselves as "hillbillies"—a pejorative that first appeared in print during the early 20th century. Nor do they call themselves "mountaineers" or, more politely, "highlanders." They simply refer to themselves as "just plain folks," which is precisely what they are—the descendants of the plain folk of the Old South.

Historian Frank Lawrence Owsley first drew attention to the mass of southern whites who lived outside the plantation economy and who composed the bulk of the antebellum southern free population. Dubbed the "plain folk" by Owsley, these agricultural masses included small slaveholding farmers, slaveless farmers, herders who ranged their livestock on the public domain, and the more substantial tenant farmers. Although some of these small-scale agriculturalists eventually joined the ranks of planters, most aspired "to acquire land and other property sufficient to give them and their children a sense of security and well-being." In addition, most plain folk practiced a "grazing and farm economy," meaning a "diversified self-sufficient type of agriculture, where the money crops were subordinated to food crops, and where the labor was performed by the family aided by a few slaves."

By 1860 these plain folk could be found throughout the Old South from Delaware to Texas, but they were especially prominent in the southern mountains—the Blue Ridge Mountains, the Cumberland-Allegheny plateaus, and the Ouachita ridges—where they composed the vast majority of the mountain inhabitants. Before the Civil War, these plain folk of the southern mountains attracted minimal attention. Their lives differed little from those of the plain folk who lived elsewhere in the Old South.

Antebellum plain folk were, above all, economic generalists. During the course of a single year, a family might engage in such varied activities as hunting, trapping, collecting, home manufacturing, livestock herding, subsistence farming, and growing cash crops. The key to their economic life was the herding of livestock on the unfenced range and the growing of corn on temporary fields claimed from forests. Free-range herding provided meat and surplus livestock for sale. Corn cultivation offered food for families, fodder for livestock, and cash, if the corn were distilled. Together livestock and corn furnished the subsistence base for a distinctive life and culture, the outline of which one finds in travelogues, reminiscences, and oral tradition. Plain folk lived in depressed rural neighborhoods, called "settlements," where many of their neighbors were also their kinsmen. They occupied houses built of horizontal logs cut from neighboring forests, and they usually fashioned their own agricultural implements, household furnishings, and even garments. They patronized mills, stores, and evangelical Protestant churches in crossroads hamlets. And they periodically visited the county seat towns to shop, trade, vote, and socialize.

The Civil War and the postwar cotton boom shattered this antebellum culture. Cotton plantations encroached on the unfenced rangelands. Planter-dominated state legislatures enacted laws forcing plain folk herders to fence in their livestock. The day of the free range having ended, plain folk in the cotton and plantation belt turned to cotton growing, borrowing money for seed and fertilizer as well as for food and clothing to last them until harvest and market. If cotton prices were high, they paid off their debts. If prices were low, they became debtors, often losing their farms in the process. Landless plain folk then joined the growing mass of tenant farmers and mill workers. Antebellum self-sufficiency and economic independence gave way to postbellum poverty and economic dependence.

In the southern mountains, however, the postbellum southern economy could not establish itself. Poor soils, rugged terrain, and unpredictable frosts hindered the spread of cotton culture. The mountains remained an isolated enclave of plain folk. But during the late 19th century, a series of family feuds, including the storied Hatfield-McCoy vendetta, focused national attention on the previously little-noticed southern mountain regions. The first "discoverers" were journalists, but they were soon followed by missionaries, educators, and a host of scholars. These outsiders found a world of log cabins, log barns, split-rail fences, ox-drawn plows, homemade furniture, and spinning wheels—all the familiar attributes of American pioneer life. Many of these observers reported that they had been carried back to the time of Daniel Boone, Davy Crockett, and Lincoln's boyhood. By the 1890s academic visitors were proclaiming the southern mountains to be a retarded frontier still bearing the stamp of 18th-century existence. By entering the southern mountains, one could hear archaic words, listen to traditional ballads, be regaled with folktales about the supernatural, and view the last frontiersmen plowing their corn and rounding up their razorback hogs.

The last frontiersman stereotype of the 1890s soon gave way to a more lasting hillbilly image. Following the defeat of Spain in 1898, the United States became a minor colonial power, shouldering the "white man's burden" in Puerto Rico and the Philippines. Concern for the primitive people of the world, however, was not confined to areas outside the continental United States. Some uplifters turned their attention to the mountain folk of the South, believing them to be as lost in ignorance and poverty as any foreign people of color. After all, they feuded with their neighbors, believed in witches, raised broods of children, practiced incest, and avoided work—except to distill illegal moonshine whiskey. In short, they were "hillbillies."

The term *hillbilly* first appeared in print in 1900 in the New York *Journal*. The word soon appeared in a spate of early 20th-century mass media articles and novels, purporting to describe the life patterns of the southern mountain people. The term even circulated among the mountain people themselves, serving as a jest or as an insult. For instance, a mountain string band, journeying to New York in 1925 to record dance tunes for Okeh records—a label that pioneered in recording white southern music—was asked by the record producer for the name of their group. Heretofore, producer Ralph Peer had simply termed the recordings of mountain music "Old Time Tunes." But in this instance, one band member facetiously replied, "We're nothing but a bunch of hillbillies from North Carolina and Virginia. Call us anything." Peer wrote down "Hill Billies" as the band's name.

On the group's return trip to New York, the members expressed second thoughts about their new title. As one musician later recalled, "Hillbilly was not only a funny word, it was a fighting word." The band's records, however, achieved such success that despite misgivings about the group's name, their music and the word *hillbilly* became inextricably linked. "Hillbilly music" remained a disquieting term, however, and no one proudly proclaimed himself to be a hillbilly.

Southern mountain people had been predominantly agricultural in the early 20th century. They grazed their livestock on the unfenced range and grew corn in fields claimed from wooded hillsides. Every range cow needed a minimum of 15 acres of woods pasture for a year's forage, and when a hillside field eroded, farmers would abandon the old field and clear new ground from the wooded slopes. Mountain agriculture thus required an abundance of forest land.

After 1900 forest lands were no longer abundant. Mountain families, with their high birthrates (children were needed to work on the farms), tended to produce more young farmers than the land could accommodate. As farms grew smaller because of population increase, productivity and average size of farms declined. And after 1900 extractive industries—mining and logging—began to compete with agriculture for the remaining lands. Timber and coal companies purchased entire valleys and mountain slopes. Lands that had once been grazed or farmed were left deforested and denuded.

Mountain agriculture could therefore no longer support the growing rural population. During the 1910s and 1920s many mountain families migrated westward to Texas and Oklahoma, hoping to continue their way of life as tenant farmers. Others abandoned farming altogether, settling in logging camps and coal towns. In the era of the Great Depression many migrants returned to the mountains they had left, surviving on tiny hillside farms. During and after World War II, out-migration accelerated as hundreds of thousands of mountain people sought jobs and homes in the industrial cities of the Midwest and South. In leaving the mountains these plain folk abandoned their traditional way of life based on livestock herding and corn cropping. They transferred aspects of the mountain culture, though, to northern cities such as Cincinnati, Detroit, and Chicago.

Today, the southern mountain region is primarily a land of government forests, cities, tourist centers, coal towns, and modern commercial farms. It scarcely resembles the rural, agricultural landscape of 1900. The world of plain folk, from which the hillbilly stereotype is conjured, has all but disappeared. Yet the pejorative and its demeaning images live on. Southern mountain people, in all their diversity, do continue to share one common attribute: they resent the "hillbilly" stereotype. They continue to regard themselves as "just plain folks."

See also BLACK LIFE: Appalachians, Black; FOLKLIFE: "Hillbilly" Image; GEOGRAPHY: Ozarks; / Northern Cities, Whites in; INDUSTRY: Industry in Appalachia; LANGUAGE: Mountain Language; LITERATURE: Appalachian Literature; MUSIC: Country Music; MYTHIC SOUTH: Appalachian Culture / Appalachian Myth; RELIGION: Appalachian Religion; SOCIAL CLASS: Appalachia, Exploitation of; WOMEN'S LIFE: Appalachian Women

Augustus Burns
John S. Otto
University of Florida

Harry M. Caudill, *Night Comes to the Cumberlands: A Biography of a Depressed Area* (1963); Archie Green, *Journal of American Folklore* (July–September 1965); James C. Klotter, *Journal of American History* (March 1980); Forrest McDonald and Grady McWhiney, *American Historical Review* (December 1980); John S. Otto and Augustus M. Burns, *Journal of American Folklore* (April–June 1981); Frank L. Owsley, in *The South: Old and New Frontiers*, ed. H. C. Owsley (1969); Henry D. Shapiro, *Appalachia on Our Mind: The Southern Mountains and Mountaineers in the American Consciousness, 1870–1920* (1978); David E. Whisnant, *All That Is Native and Fine: The Politics of Culture in an American Region* (1983).

Nativism

In the United States nativism—that is, hostility toward immigrants based on the belief that they threaten traditional American culture, institutions, and social order—has been rooted in racism, anti-Catholicism, antiradicalism, and anti-Semitism. Throughout the 19th century nativism flared in the North while it sputtered in the South, only to become a southern preoccupation in the 20th century as it abated in the North. Southern nativism, however, represented more than a response to immigration, for foreign immigration to the South was never sufficient to pose imminent danger to southern cultural norms or homogeneity. For southerners unsure of their place in a changing America, nativism provided a language of protest, a catch-all for deeper cultural and social fears regarding changes brought on by any external force. In the 20th century politicians and professional hate groups, especially the Ku Klux Klan, often used nativist rhetoric to capitalize on southern anxieties regarding modernization or federal interference in local ways, thereby sustaining nativist interest even in the absence of a significant foreign presence.

Political nativism in the form of the Know-Nothing movement in the 1850s made an appearance in the Old South, but, unlike nativism in the antebellum North, it did not fracture politics or influence social policy significantly. Old South Know-Nothingism lacked the ideological underpinnings of its northern counterpart, owing its existence largely to the demise of the two-party system during the slavery controversy. For former Whigs casting about for a means to oppose Democratic rivals, the Know-Nothing party fit nicely.

Anti-Catholicism, a staple of nativist thought in the North, appeared sporadically in the southern movement. Indeed, in the heavily Catholic sugar parishes of Louisiana, which were also former bastions of the Whig party, Know-Nothingism enjoyed its greatest strength. Catholic French Creoles of New Orleans embraced nativists as allies against the Irish newcomers who challenged their political and cultural power in both church and city. Here the Know-Nothing party ignored most traditional nativist appeals, focusing rather on local issues of law and order and economic development. After the party gained power in the late 1850s, it proved unable, and perhaps unwilling, to reform the city's morals and promoted railroad and street improvements instead. Likewise, in Baltimore the ascension of Know-Nothing candidates produced no changes in governmental controls over immigrants.

Know-Nothingism did attract individuals who feared immigrants, religious diversity, or any change in southern ways. Various editors who attacked immigrants and Catholics repeated old canards about popish plots and European corruption that were part of the republican heritage of America. Their impact, however, was confined to cities where immigrants competed with native-born southerners for social, economic, or political space. Louisville, Memphis, Baltimore, and New Orleans had sizable immigrant populations by the late antebellum period, and election disorders involving the Irish in these cities fueled nativism.

Nativism remained shallowly rooted in the Old South because immigrants were few outside of the cities and because the immigrants in the region soon adopted local norms on slavery and conservatism. Also, the politics of slavery intruded to push southerners away from nativist concerns. During the Civil War immigrant contributions to the Confederacy further discredited negative views of the foreign born, and after the war the whites' need to stand together on matters of race and home rule supplanted questions of ethnic or religious differences. For a time, nativism almost disappeared.

From 1865 to 1907 most southern state governments actively sought European immigration. Planters, eager to replace exslaves with supposedly more reliable, docile, and cheap laborers, became the principal immigration boosters. Chinese workers were brought to Mississippi and Louisiana cotton fields and southern Italians to Louisiana cane fields, but neither group proved any more tractable than the exslaves. Freedmen and their white Republican allies generally opposed efforts to pit immigrants against blacks, and nativism never prospered under black or Republican auspices in the South, diminishing even further after the return to "home rule." As late as the 1890s many southerners spurned nationally organized nativist groups, such as the American Protective Association, because they were identified with the Republican party. Immigration, not nativism, seemed the way to white rule.

By the first decade of the 20th century, however, official attitudes encouraging immigration for economic reasons masked a powerful nativist surge from below. Throughout the 1890s numerous incidents against immigrants revealed the deep-seated class and cultural tensions in southern society. Previously, nativist violence had been sporadic and confined to cities, but in the 1890s the attacks increased and spread across the rural South. In 1893, for example, night riders in Mississippi burned the property of Jewish landlords, and in Louisiana debt-ridden farmers wrecked the stores of Jewish merchants. In 1896 invaders twice burned the Catholic church in the Italian settlement at Tontitown, Ark. Several lynchings of Italian immigrants occurred in lower Louisiana. Most spectacularly, 11 Sicilians were lynched in New Orleans in 1891, following the mysterious death of the police chief. Although the hangings created an international furor, the local authorities and newspapers applauded the mob's action.

Regional nativism, as distinct from isolated local expressions, developed slowly, but by the early 20th century it had experienced revolutionary change and growth. Attacks on Jews and Italians pointed up the class basis of the new nativism, for Jewish merchants and landlords and Italian workers symbolized the altered economic and social order of the "New South." Nativism, like Populism, represented another response to industrialism. The Farmers' Union especially criticized the policy of importing Asian and southern European workers and demanded tight immigration restrictions. The black press in the South endorsed the argument for restriction. Significantly, almost every important southern politician who claimed a populist lineage and constituency converted to nativism. Cole Blease, "idol of the cotton mill operatives," made nativism a political shibboleth in South Carolina in 1908. Tom Watson, in 1912, helped to establish the Guardians of Liberty, a Protestant-nativist organization, and with his Jew baiting in 1915 contributed mightily to the lynching of Leo Frank, an Atlanta Jew who had been convicted of murdering a young woman in his pencil factory in 1913.

Racism went hand in hand with populist nativism. Until the 1890s southerners rarely invoked race in nativist arguments, except to insist on the unity of the white race. But the new immigrants, especially Jews and southern Italians, deviated too far from accepted norms. Italians caused particular concern because they worked alongside blacks in the fields, thus further demeaning their "white" status.

Racial nativism gained strength from a new concept of American nationalism based on pseudoscientific thinking that divided Europeans into different "races" rather than nationalities and, inevitably, encouraged the notion that one "race," the Anglo-Saxon, was superior. The South readily accepted the celebration of Anglo-Saxonism as the font of true Americanism. A nationalism so defined permitted the South to return fully to the nation it had once left, but on terms assuring its social prominence. Pseudoscientific racial arguments in the North blended with, indeed vindicated, southern arguments in defense of white rule over "colored people." Southern participation in the nation, then, was partly due to a nationalism of race.

The people's representatives in Congress echoed the racial theme. Led by Oscar Underwood of Alabama, they compared the "pure whiteness" of the older immigrants with the new immigrants' tainted mixture of "Asian and African blood." Armed with racism and the new nationalism, southern congressmen became ardent immigration restrictionists. The xenophobia of World War I and its aftermath reinforced the southern commitment to immigration restriction. During the 1920s southern congressmen played critical roles in the passage of restrictive legislation that for some 40 years thereafter effectively stemmed immigration from Europe and Asia. By the 1920s the South had become the most nativist region of the country, even as the small percentage of immigrants in the region continued to decline.

Religious nativism further propelled southern xenophobia. Born of the union between the rural, small-town revolt against modernism and the historic Protestant American distrust of Catholics and Jews, this was a nativism of faith and history rather than science. Wilbur Franklin Phelps of Aurora, Mo., galvanized religious nativism with his diatribes against alleged Catholic perversions and plots, which he exposed through his widely circulated weekly, *The Menace*. Other rustic publishers from such diverse places as Magnolia, Ark., and Moravian Falls, N.C., assisted. All bespoke the militant rural fundamentalism, the war against the moral laxity and secular liberalism of the cities, that marked religious nativism. The southern fundamentalists' failure to slow the spread of modernism and science only intensified their outlook.

The Ku Klux Klan played upon such frustrations with its anti-Catholic, anti-Semitic, antiimmigrant messages. The Klan's Bible thumping and patriotic breast-beating were exaggerated, if sometimes violent, expressions of what many southerners believed about the need to restore old-time religion and old-line groups to prominence. Several states responded to anti-Catholic pressures by considering official inspection of Catholic facilities, and Georgia actually enacted a law to supervise convents and monasteries. Sidney J. Catts rode anti-Catholicism into the governor's mansion in Florida in 1916, and Methodist bishop James Cannon, Jr., caused the first significant break in the Solid Democratic South when he mobilized fundamentalists against that party's wet, Catholic candidate, Al Smith, in 1928.

Religious nativism reached its peak in the 1928 election and ebbed slowly thereafter. By 1960, with southern voters helping the Catholic John F. Kennedy win the presidency, the political punch had gone out of anti-Catholicism. Among many factors, the narrowing of the European immigrant stream after the 1920s and the rising income and educational levels in the South made nativist fears seem superfluous, as did the post–World War II ecumenical movement and the conservative alliance of the Catholic church and southern evangelical churches on such social issues as family maintenance, abortion, and law and order in the South.

In the 1970s, however, the widening of the Asian and Latin American immigrant flow revived nativism in the South. Many Latin Americans remained in the region as migrant workers or laborers in low-wage jobs. Competing with white and black southerners for jobs and social services, they met increasing racial and religious nativism as, once again, the interests of southern economic boosters and lower-class southerners clashed. Compounding the new nativism was the post–World War II struggle of southerners against federal intervention in local affairs, a product of the civil rights movement. From the 1960s through 1980, federal policy advocated cultural pluralism and, consequently, encroached upon the local community's traditional monopoly over schools and other instruments of social control and cultural maintenance. Hostility toward new immigrants in many southern communities in the Gulf states, where Latin Americans and Asians congregated, derived from both the traditional taproots of southern nativism—racism, antimodernism, religious fundamentalism, and economic rivalry—and the resurgent antifederalism in the region. Thus, the federal government's programs for bilingual education or employment of immigrant refugees seemed to agitate both nativist and localist sentiments in the South. Further, the federal government's willingness to accept refugees from Asia and the Caribbean antagonized southern communities forced to receive them. The Cuban "Freedom Flotilla" of 1980 and the Haitian refugees who followed aroused fears of crime and disorder that subsequently spread from Florida across the Gulf states. The desperation of the refugees notwithstanding, they were unwelcome because many southerners were feeling the pinch of recession and the stresses of rapid social change.

Refugees from Asia also found their way to the South in the 1970s. They located in some odd places, broadening the immigration issue's geographic reach. Indochinese Hmong tribesmen, for example, clustered in Selma, Ala., and Memphis, Tenn., and Vietnamese peasants settled in Bucktown, La., and Seabrook, Tex., among other places. Hostility toward the Asians arose quickly. It was largely economic in tone, although racism and ethnocentrism also contributed. New Orleans's sizable Vietnamese community excited resistance from blacks who feared job competition, and violence erupted. Along the Gulf Coast and on Lake Pontchartrain in Louisiana struggling white shrimpers and fishermen resented competition from the Vietnamese, who were partly outfitted with government assistance and, perhaps worse, who worked too hard. In 1978, in Bucktown, La., and in Corpus Christi, Tex., whites attacked the Vietnamese fishermen and burned their boats. The Ku Klux Klan entered the fray, dusting off old racial and religious nativist arguments to remind southerners that the Vietnamese were colored and often Catholic.

A national debate emerged in the mid-1980s from the

"New Immigration." Congress debated but did not pass the Simpson-Mazzola bill, which proposed curbing the flow of illegal aliens by applying sanctions to employees hiring them but also granting amnesty to aliens in the United States before 1982. These most recent nativist rumblings lack force or direction in the South itself, though, and remain almost entirely peculiar to the Gulf area. The eagerness of hate groups such as the Ku Klux Klan to exploit nativist fears, however, bodes ill for the South's accommodation with immigration and social change, for large numbers of immigrants will continue to come, illegally or not, to the South because of its physical proximity to Mexico and the Caribbean. Whether the South will reemerge as the most nativist region in the country will depend on how much southerners choose to rise above their history.

See also BLACK LIFE: Immigrants and Blacks; Race Relations; LAW: Frank, Leo case; MYTHIC SOUTH: Racial Attitudes; SCIENCE AND MEDICINE: Racism, Scientific; VIOLENCE: / Ku Klux Klan, History of

Randall M. Miller
St. Joseph's University

Jean H. Baker, *Ambivalent Americans: The Know-Nothing Party in Maryland* (1977); Ray Allen Billington, *The Protestant Crusade, 1800–1860* (1938); John Higham, *Strangers in the Land: Patterns of American Nativism, 1860–1925* (1965); W. Darrell Overdyke, *The Know-Nothing Party in the South* (1950); Arnold Shankman, *Ambivalent Friends: Afro-Americans View the Immigrant* (1982).

Appalachians

The Appalachian Mountains range southward from Quebec and Newfoundland to Alabama. The central and southern highlands—consisting of the Blue Ridge and Smoky Mountain ranges, the Allegheny and Cumberland plateaus, and the Great Valley in between—are frequently conceived as a distinct sociocultural region known as "Appalachia." More than 10 million people live in the mountainous sections of Maryland, Virginia, West Virginia, Kentucky, Tennessee, North Carolina, and Georgia.

Appalachia is often portrayed as an arrested frontier, a geographically isolated subculture, and a reservoir of culturally homogeneous, white Anglo-Saxon southerners. Appalachians are commonly stereotyped, both favorably and unfavorably. Sometimes Appalachians are pictured as proud, fiercely independent, and God-fearing southerners. Conversely, they are portrayed as fighting and feuding, barefooted and backward, ignorant degenerates, downtrodden by centuries of isolation, inbreeding, and poverty.

The discovery of Appalachia as a distinctive cultural region was prompted in the mid-1870s by local color writers such as Mary Murfree and John Fox, Jr., who explored in fiction and travel sketches such mountain themes as conflicting Civil War loyalties, moonshining, and feuding. Later, educators and social reformers such as William G. Frost and John C. Campbell defined Appalachia as a social problem area deserving of uplift by church home missions and private philanthropy. Their depiction of Appalachia as a distinct cultural entity was subsequently reinforced by social scientists seeking to identify and catalog Appalachian subcultural traits. The idea that the region has a distinct identity was given further credibility by creation of a federal policymaking unit in the 1960s, the Appalachian Regional Commission. Actually, however, few people in the southern mountains identify themselves as Appalachians.

Appalachia is best viewed as a set of heterogeneous rural areas providing people and resources to eastern, midwestern, and southern cities. Though stereotyped as isolated and backward, many portions of Appalachia have been heavily industrialized since the late 19th century, providing lumber, coal, oil, gas, textile, and chemical products. Prior to industrialization subsistence agriculture supported rural communities that stressed personalistic, familial, puritanical, and democratic values. It is doubtful that rural mountain culture was distinguishable from that of the rest of the nonplantation South.

Appalachia was initially settled by English, Scotch-Irish, and German migrants. Few blacks were present prior to the Civil War. Despite claims of ethnic homogeneity, industrialization brought diverse ethnic populations into the mountains. One study reveals that more than half the new jobs in southern West Virginia coal mines between 1890 and 1910 were filled by southern and eastern European immigrants. Southern blacks augmented the labor force in the following two decades, and in southern West Virginia they comprised roughly one-fourth of its total workers. Although the Appalachian black population has been declining since World War II, it has been very significant in some localities.

See also EDUCATION: / Campbell, John C.; ENVIRONMENT: / Appalachian Mountains; MYTHIC SOUTH: / Appalachian Myth

Dwight B. Billings
University of Kentucky

Harry Schwarzweller, James Brown, and Joseph Mangalam, *Mountain Families in Transition* (1971); Henry D. Shapiro, *Appalachia on Our Mind: The Southern Mountains and Mountaineers in the American Consciousness, 1870–1920* (1978); David E. Whisnant, *All That Is Native and Fine: The Politics of Culture in an American Region* (1983).

Asian Groups

Asian Americans are rarely associated with the South. According to the 1980 census the South contained a third of the nation's total population (33.3 percent), more than half of its blacks (53 percent), nearly a third of its

Table 1. *Asian Southerners—1980 Census*

Census Div.	Total	Chinese	Filipino	Japanese	Asian Indian	Korean	Viet-namese	Hawaiian & Pacific Isl.
U.S.	3,500,636	806,027	774,640	700,747	361,544	354,529	261,714	241,435
South	469,762	90,616	82,596	44,636	83,586	70,375	80,240	17,713
% in South	13.4%	11.2%	10.7%	6.4%	23.1%	19.9%	30.7%	7.3%
Del.	4,132	1,004	813	426	1,075	495	205	114
Md.	64,276	14,485	10,965	4,805	13,705	15,087	4,131	1,098
D.C.	6,635	2,475	1,297	752	950	338	505	318
Va.	66,209	9,360	18,901	5,207	8,483	12,550	10,000	1,708
W.Va.	5,194	881	1,313	404	1,641	587	253	115
N.C.	21,168	3,170	2,542	3,186	4,718	3,581	2,391	1,580
S.C.	11,807	1,388	3,697	1,414	2,143	1,390	1,072	703
Ga.	24,461	4,324	2,792	3,370	4,347	5,970	2,294	1,364
Fla.	56,756	13,471	14,212	5,565	9,138	4,673	7,592	2,105
Ky.	9,971	1,318	1,443	1,056	2,226	2,102	1,090	736
Tenn.	13,963	2,909	1,901	1,657	3,195	2,237	1,391	673
Ala.	9,695	1,503	960	1,394	1,992	1,782	1,333	731
Miss.	7,412	1,835	1,442	687	1,163	576	1,281	428
Ark.	6,732	1,275	921	754	832	583	2,042	325
La.	23,771	3,298	2,614	1,482	2,873	1,729	10,877	898
Okla.	17,274	2,461	1,687	1,975	2,879	2,698	4,671	903
Tex.	120,306	25,459	15,096	10,502	22,226	13,997	29,112	3,914

Source: U.S. Dept. of Commerce, Bureau of the Census, *Race of the Population by States: 1980* (1981).

whites (31.3 percent), more than a quarter of its Amerindians (26.2 percent), and just over an eighth of its Asians, as shown in Table 1. Yet the nearly half-million Asians recorded by the census are many more than most Americans imagine. Most of these Asians are newcomers to the South, but significant numbers of Asians have been there since Reconstruction.

After the Civil War, amidst chimerical fears and hopes about the disappearance of black labor, many southerners talked about bringing in Chinese to replace the freedmen, and a few actually did so. The best-known example of such talk came at an 1869 Memphis convention that urged southerners to cooperate "with the apparent leanings of Providence" and import "pagans . . . of the Mongolian race" for work and "to bring to bear upon them the elevating and saving influence of our holy religion." The proposal was to import laborers from both California and the Caribbean (chiefly Cuba) at $100 per head with payment of $8 to $12 per month. A few thousand such laborers were brought to the South—chiefly to Alabama, Arkansas, Mississippi, and Louisiana—and employed in railroad construction, sugar refining, and the growing and processing of cotton. Some 200 Chinese were brought to work on the Houston and Texas Central Railroad and more than 900 on the Alabama and Chattanooga; 147 worked the Millaudon sugar plantation near New Orleans. In some instances wages were supplemented with opium. Chinese labor never became a significant factor in the regional economy, although newspapers frequently speculated about it. By 1880 the census found fewer than 1,000 Chinese in the whole South; in 1910 there were just over 3,000. Most of these had found their way into urban occupations, especially in laundries and restaurants, that were typical for Chinese of that era.

A different pattern developed among the several hundred Mississippi Chinese. With the decline of plantation agriculture, planters ceased to furnish staples to their black tenants on credit, and enough cash began to circulate that an opportunity for the independent merchant was created. Many Chinese in the Delta capitalized on this opportunity by opening small grocery and supply stores. Although providing goods and services to a largely black population, the Mississippi Chinese were careful to avoid identification with this socially inferior group. Three sets of public schools—white, black, and Chinese—were often set up, and a Chinese Baptist Church was established. Occupying a strategic position in a racially stratified society, Chinese throughout the Deep South have retained a cultural identity, absorbed by neither black nor white communities. Living in far-flung communities and cut off from the clans, *hui kuan* (secret societies), and temples characteristic of urban Chinatowns, they have relied on the nuclear family and the family-owned business to nurture and maintain this distinctiveness.

Although culturally intriguing the Chinese were not numerous in the South. In 1910, 3,299 Chinese lived in the southern states as a whole, and Mississippi's 257 made it the fifth most populous census division, after Texas (595), Louisiana, Maryland, and the District of Columbia. One further early increment of Chinese to the South occurred in 1917 when General John J. Pershing brought about 500 Chinese-Mexican refugees to San Antonio. By 1940 only about 5,000 Chinese were found in the South.

Japanese Americans entered the South in largest numbers during the World War II era. The 1940 census found just over 1,000 Japanese southerners, with a few hundred

Chinese grocery, Vicksburg, Miss., 1975

Texas rice farmers constituting the only significant community. Massive if largely temporary infusions of Japanese Americans occurred as a result of government actions during the war. Two of the 10 War Relocation Authority camps for the Japanese, Rohwer and Jerome, were on marginal land in Arkansas that had belonged to the Farm Security Administration. Almost 16,000 Japanese Americans from the West Coast were incarcerated there between 1942 and 1945. Starting in late 1942, more than 5,000 Japanese American recruits, many of them from Hawaii, were trained at Camp Shelby, outside of Hattiesburg, Miss., where they became the 442nd Regimental Combat Team. Again, educational arrangements were adjusted so that the few Japanese American children were educated separately from both whites and blacks. And, finally, several dozen Japanese American students were accepted by southern colleges and universities, largely in the Upper South. Few of these Japanese stayed in the South: the 1950 census found just over 3,000, whereas Chinese southerners numbered more than 10,000.

The increase in Asian groups since 1950 has been spectacular, with by far the greatest part of it coming in the 1970s. The 1970 census found 114,623 Asians in the South; a decade later the figure was 469,762, an increase of 310 percent. The reasons for the increase are threefold. First, many Asian American professionals have been drawn to the South, as other Americans have been, by the benign climate and the thriving economy. Second, the relaxation of immigration restrictions in 1965 has made it possible for relatively large numbers of Asians to come to the United States. And third, the continued involvement of the United States in Asian wars has increased the nation's Asian population in two ways. Since the mid-1940s servicemen, including many southerners, have been marrying Asian women and bringing them home, so that in some southern states adult Asian American women outnumber men by a substantial margin, reversing the previous sex ratio. In addition, American involvement overseas made the government receptive to Asian refugees, particularly from Southeast Asia.

Asian southerners today range from fourth- and fifth-generation Americans to persons newly arrived; from highly educated professionals and technicians to persons barely literate in their own language. The more recent immigrant groups, especially the Indochinese, have shown a greater propensity to come to the South than have the longer established Chinese, Filipinos, and Japanese.

Referring to the Southeast Asian peoples who were under French colonial rule from the late 19th century to the mid-20th, the term *Indochinese* includes the culturally and linguistically diverse Vietnamese, Cambodians, and Laotians. Before 1966 *Vietnamese* was not even a designation in immigration and naturalization statistics, suggesting the relatively low level of Indochinese immigration.

The fall of Saigon in the spring of 1975 dramatically changed the situation. Approximately 130,000 refugees from Vietnam, Cambodia, and Laos more than quadrupled the United States Indochinese population. Initially received at resettlement centers such as those at Fort Chaffee, Ark., and Eglin Air Force Base, Fla., they were eventually settled by church-affiliated or state sponsors. Fearing the social and economic consequences of massive concentrations in any one area of the country, the government favored diffusion. Some 9,000 were relocated in Texas, 5,000 in Florida, and 3,000 in Louisiana. Widely separated rural settlements, however, proved to be too isolated and within less than a year refugees began to move in significant numbers into adjacent cities, especially those with already established immigrant communities.

Given its Catholic-French heritage and waterland topography, the New Orleans metropolitan area, not surprisingly, attracted many recent arrivals. In 1980 Louisiana ranked behind only California and Texas as a haven for refugees, listing its Indochinese population at over 9,000. The Versailles community in east New Orleans, still possibly the largest concentration of Vietnamese in the United States, has become a socially stable community supporting traditional culture in the form of front-yard herb gardens, a Buddhist temple, and Vietnamese markets.

In other parts of the South tensions between local residents and Indochinese refugees have sometimes complicated resettlement. Often involving fishing rights, as in the Texas coastal community of Seadrift, these tensions have erupted into violence. The Indochinese continue to be a relatively mobile population with a preference for settlement in California and the southern states of Texas, Florida, and South Carolina.

Korean settlement in the United States has been concentrated on the West Coast and in Hawaii, but Koreans settled in New Orleans beginning in the early 1960s. Most of them were professionals, including university professors, architects, engineers, and musicians. The Korean community in New Orleans is served by a Korean American Friendship Association, two Korean restaurants, a supermarket, and a Korean Christian church. Little formal research has been done on Koreans in other areas of the South, although one dissertation has studied the acculturation process among Korean residents of Georgia.

Roger Daniels
University of Cincinnati

Russell Bearden, *Arkansas Historical Quarterly* (Winter 1982); Lucy M. Cohen, *Chinese in the Post–Civil War South* (1984); John Cooke, ed., *Perspectives on Ethnicity in New Orleans* (1979); Roger Daniels, *Comparative Studies in Society and History* (1983); Don Chang Lee, "Acculturation of Korean Residents in Georgia" (Ph.D. dissertation, University of Georgia, 1972); James W. Loewen, *The Mississippi Chinese: Between Black and White* (1971); *Mississippi Triangle* (film by Christine Choy, 1983); U.S. Department of Commerce, Bureau of the Census, *Race of the Population by States: 1980* (1981).

Cajuns and Creoles

The French founded Louisiana in 1699. At first, only a few forts perched precariously along the rivers of the frontier, but a society of French colonials eventually developed. Those born in the colony called themselves *Creoles*, a word meaning "home grown, not imported," to distinguish themselves from immigrants. Between 1765 and 1785 the Acadians arrived in south Louisiana. Exiled after French Acadia became English Nova Scotia, they isolated themselves to reestablish their society along the bayous and on the prairies. By the 19th century the varied French cultures, enriched by the Native American Indian tribes and immigrants from Germany, Spain, Italy, Ireland, England, and the new United States, created a people who came to be called *Cajun*. The descendants of African slaves added ingredients of their own and improvised a language, a culture, and an identity, which they called Creole.

In 1803, when Napoleon sold Louisiana to Thomas Jefferson, the territory, which stretched from the Gulf of Mexico to Canada, was divided. Artificial, arbitrary boundaries ignored cultural regions and historical settlement patterns. The new state of Louisiana included the piney hills of the north and east, populated by English-speaking farmers; the bayous and prairies of the south, where French-speaking Cajun and Creole farmers lived; the rich alluvial plains along the Red and Mississippi rivers, home of planters; and New Orleans with its multilingual, multicultural urbanites.

When the time came for statewide laws to be enacted, Louisiana's cultural and linguistic diversity strained the state's arbitrary borders. Early versions of the state constitution made valiant attempts to legitimize the French language. By the turn of the century, however, the battle cry of President Theodore Roosevelt, "one nation, one language!" thundered across the land. The approach of World War I induced a quest for national unity that suppressed regional diversity. Beginning in 1916, when mandatory English language education was imposed throughout the state, children were punished for speaking the language of their fathers and mothers in school. French was discouraged in campaigns against illiteracy. Over several generations Cajuns and Creoles were eventually convinced that speaking French was a sign of cultural illegitimacy. Those who aspired to the language of the future, of the marketplace, became more American than the Yankees. Western swing, for example, replaced Cajun music in the dance halls, while black Creoles, who had preserved their language and traditions largely in isolation, were increasingly diverted toward the national civil rights movement as their most pressing struggle. The discovery of oil fueled an economic boom, which brought both groups out of the 19th century just in time for the Great Depression. First shared by horse-drawn buggies and horseless carriages, Huey Long's new highways and bridges opened the countryside and linked the bayous and prairies of south Louisiana with the rest of America.

South Louisiana was humming down a newly paved road toward homogenization. But was this the right road? Stress cracks appeared on the social surface: alcoholism and suicide among musicians and artists; juvenile delinquency among children who could no longer speak for their grandparents because of the language difference and would no longer speak to their parents because of television; self-denigration among a people who now called themselves "coonasses."

Then, in the late 1940s, the tide seemed to turn, particularly, at first, among the Cajuns. Soldiers in France during World War II discovered that the language and culture they had been told to forget made them invaluable as interpreters and increased their chances for survival. After the war returning GIs, aching from foreign wars in faraway places, sank into the hot bath of their own culture. They drank and danced to forget. Dance halls throughout south Louisiana once again blared the familiar and comforting sounds of homemade music. The glowing embers of the Cajun cultural revival were fanned by political leaders like Dudley LeBlanc and Roy Theriot who used the 1955 bicentennial of the Acadian exile as a rallying point for the revitalization of ethnic pride (along with their own careers). The message of 1955 was that the Cajuns had survived the worst; their culture and language, though injured, were alive.

In 1968 the state of Louisiana officially fostered the movement with the creation of the Council for the Development of French in Louisiana (CODOFIL), designating former U.S. Congressman James Domengeaux its chairman. But the movement was not without problems. CODOFIL found itself faced with the monumental task of creating a quality French language education program. Older Cajuns who once wrote "I will not speak French on the schoolgrounds" a few thousand times learned the lesson well and avoided inflicting on their own children what was long considered a cultural and linguistic deficiency.

The mandate of CODOFIL, as a state agency, covered the entire state. CODOFIL was forced to press only for establishment of French as a second language in the elementary schools. A dearth of native-born French teachers compounded the problem, and CODOFIL opted to import teachers from France, Belgium, and Quebec as a stopgap. This, along with a broad program of cultural exchanges, brought the Louisiana French experiment to the attention of the Francophone world. Meanwhile, activists on the home front felt that the indigenous language and culture were once again being forced into the shadows as many Cajuns dutifully echoed past criticisms, apologizing that their language was "not the real French, just broken-down Cajun French."

The Cajuns were no longer alone. France, Belgium, and Quebec became interested in fanning the fires of self-preservation along the bayous. They invested millions of *francs* and *piastres* to create a life-support system in the hope that French culture and language might ultimately survive in south Louisiana. Along with money and teachers have come hordes of tourists eager to visit this long-lost, long-forgotten "exotic" place where, against all odds, French has somehow survived. This contact with outsiders has shown the Cajuns that, contrary to their childhood lessons, their French "works just fine" to communicate with folks who speak "real" French. And now that institutionalized segregation has diminished, black Creoles as well are increasingly interested in preserving the French parts of their culture.

Visitors to south Louisiana invariably bring their own cultural baggage. French Canadians, for instance, who seek in Cajuns a symbol of dogged linguistic survival in predominantly Anglo-Saxon North America, find virtually no Anglo-Franco confrontation and an absence of animosity in cultural politics. The French who seek vestiges of former colonials find instead French-speaking cowboys (and Indians) in pickup trucks. They are surprised that the Cajuns and Creoles love fried chicken and iced tea, forgetting this is the South; that they love hamburgers and Coke, forgetting this is the United States; that they love cayenne and cold beer, forgetting this is the northern top of the West Indies. American visitors usually skim along the surface, too, looking in vain for traces of Longfellow's Evangeline.

Black Creole culture involves more than the obvious confluence of African and French heritages. Before the Civil War, most black Creoles were slaves on French plantations, but others, called *gens de couleur libres*, held positions in the business and professional communities and sometimes owned their own plantations and slaves. Further, many generations of intermarriage by blacks with whites and Native Americans produced an intricate internal caste system within black Creole society based on skin tone, dialect, and family history.

The most consistent element in south Louisiana culture may well be an uncanny adaptability. Cajuns and Creoles have always been able to chew up change, swallow the palatable parts, and spit out the rest. This adaptability has become the principal issue of cultural survival in French Louisiana. Earlier, change had been slow, organic, and progressive. Now, much of it is imported at a dizzying pace. The fight to save the language looms large because many fear that if it is lost, the culture will go with it. Can the culture be translated into English without loss of cultural identity? To be sure, Cajuns and Creoles will eat gumbo and crawfish forever, but is "Jolie Blonde" sung in English still Cajun music?

Cajun accordionist Wayne Toups with his father, Emery Toups, Rayne, La., 1978

In the midst of this debate are signs of renewed vigor. Young parents are deliberately speaking French to their children. Authors choose to write in French. Louisiana teachers replace imported ones. Even a few movies have been produced locally in French. Cajun music, once dismissed as "nothing but chanky-chank," has infiltrated radio, television, and the classroom. Zydeco king Clifton Chenier, who recently brought home both a Grammy and a National Endowment for the Arts Heritage Award, has inspired a new army of black Creole musicians. With festivals and recording companies at the local and national levels, young musicians are not only preserving the music of their tradition but improvising to create new songs for that tradition. Contemporary musicians, however, would be less than honest if they pretended they never listened to the radio. They import the sounds of rock, country, and jazz today as they did blues and French *contredanses* earlier.

Cajuns and Creoles are constantly adapting their culture to survive in the modern world. Such change, however, is not necessarily a sign of decay, as was first thought; on the contrary, it is more likely a sign of vitality. Because the early effects of Americanization were too much too fast, the melting pot boiled over. But the cooks of south Louisiana culture have since regained control of their own kitchen and continue to simmer a gumbo of rich and diverse ingredients.

See also GEOGRAPHY: Ethnic Geography; Foodways, Geography of; LANGUAGE: French Language; MUSIC: Cajun Music; Zydeco; / Balfa, Dewey; Chenier, Clifton

Barry Jean Ancelot
University of Southwestern Louisiana

Barry Jean Ancelot, *The Makers of Cajun Music: Musiciens, Cadiens et Creoles* (1984), with Mathé Alain, *Southern Exposure* (Summer 1981); Glenn R. Conrad, ed., *The Cajuns: Essays on Their History and Culture* (1978); Jon L. Gibson and Steven Del Sesto, eds., *The Culture of Acadiana: Tradition and Change in South Louisiana* (1975); C. Paige Guittierrez, in *Ethnic and Regional Foodways in the United States*, ed. Linda Keller Brown and Kay Mussell (1984); William Faulkner Rushton, *The Cajuns: From Acadia to Louisiana* (1979); Nicholas R. Spitzer, *Southern Exposure* (Summer–Fall 1977).

Catawbas

The majority of the Catawba Indians live on a small state-owned reservation near Rock Hill, S.C. Others live in nearby towns, and some live elsewhere in the United States. The name *Cataba* is mentioned in the records of the Juan Pardo expedition of 1566–68, along with over two dozen other names of Indian groups who lived in upper South Carolina and western North Carolina. Present-day Catawbas are no doubt the genetic descendants of several of these groups, as well as of others, but why *Catawba* was the only one of these names to survive is unknown.

In the latter half of the 18th century, the Catawbas included people from several Indian societies that had been shattered by warfare and epidemic diseases. For a while they served as a buffer between the South Carolina colonists and the northern Indians. At the Indian Congress at Augusta in 1763, they were granted a reservation measuring 15 miles square (144,000 acres). However, by the time of the American Revolution, their population had dwindled to 300 or less, and they were unable to retain control of their reservation.

By 1852 the few Catawbas who survived were living on what is now called the "Old Reservation," some 630 acres of their original reservation, subsidized by a small pension from South Carolina. Most of them lived by sharecropping, as well as by making and selling Indian pottery. They used traditional materials and techniques, but the forms in which they made their pottery were designed to appeal to the tastes of tourists and curio hunters: pipes, animals, pitchers, vases, and toys. In the late 19th century a few Catawbas became Mormon converts, and as time went on more and more of them converted, so that today most Catawbas are Mormons.

Their most outstanding spokesman in this century was Samuel Blue (1873–1959), the last person who was fluent in the Catawba language. Wearing a Plains war bonnet, Chief Blue was a familiar sight in Rock Hill, and he periodically made appearances before the South Carolina legislature to plead for more assistance for his people. After Chief Blue died, the Catawbas appeared for a time to be on the verge of social dissolution. But this trend appeared to reverse itself in the late 1970s and early 1980s, when the Catawbas sought legal redress for the loss of their 144,000-acre reservation.

Charles Hudson
University of Georgia

Charles Hudson, *The Catawba Nation* (1970).

Cherokees

Of Iroquoian origins, the Cherokees migrated into the southern Appalachians over 2,000 years ago. Following a Woodland way of life, which was later influenced by the Mississippian culture, they depended on farming, hunting, and gathering wild plants. Cherokee society was practically a matriarchy, with women owning the property, leading family life, and doing the farming. Men spent much time away on the hunt, in warfare, and in dealing with outsiders. Each independent town had its own council, but the Cherokees were held together by the clan system's extended kinship ties.

Each town council was made up of a priest, who was a leader without any powers beyond his persuasive abilities, and seven elder men chosen by the women of each clan. The council operated by consensus, regulating relations with other towns and tribes, and organizing religious ceremonials. Cherokee religion did not emphasize the idea of a god, but instead focused on the spirituality of everything in existence. Spirits of animals, plants, water, earth, and sky were all equal to humanity. This view promoted respect for the ecosystem, which humans had no right to dominate or misuse.

The major annual religious event was the Green Corn Ceremony, held in thanksgiving to the corn spirit, at the first harvest of the major food crop of the Cherokees. The cornfields were owned communally, with each woman helping to grow the crops and everyone taking as much as they needed from the common store of grain. There was no private property nor hoarding of food. Cherokee values emphasized equality, generosity, and sharing. Private possessions were ritually destroyed each year and at the death of a person. These practices produced a society without class differences and with little need for formal laws. Social harmony was kept by social pressure and by negotiation between matrilineal clans.

By the late 1600s European influences heightened

men's importance, with the increase of the deerskin trade and accompanying warfare with other Indians competing for that trade. Cherokee diplomats dealt skillfully with English and French officials, alternately allying and trading with one side against the other. This role ended when France withdrew from America, and Indians were left with no one to play off against the British. In addition, the Cherokees were weakened by smallpox epidemics, which severely reduced their population in the late 1700s, precisely at the time that white settlers began moving into their lands. Several Cherokee towns, in reaction to the Americans' land hunger, allied with the British during the American Revolution. British defeat left them in an even weaker state.

The new United States signed several treaties in which the Cherokees gave up claims to parts of their homeland in exchange for promises of payment and guarantees of control over their remaining lands. With the end of warfare by the 1790s and under the influence of Christian missionaries and white traders who had married Cherokee women, more Indian men shifted to farming cash crops, sometimes using black slaves. In the early 1800s an acculturated minority emerged as leaders in establishing a national government. These "progressives" favored a white lifestyle, based on a plantation economy and adoption of European clothing, manufactured tools, and housing. They supported a newspaper and printing press, based on a syllabary invented by Sequoyah. By emphasizing their conversion to Christianity, "civilization," and pacifism, they hoped to retain their lands and coexist in peace with whites. This peace policy, however, was overcome by increasing white land hunger. President Andrew Jackson sponsored a removal treaty in 1835 that was renounced by most Cherokees, yet approved by Congress.

The removal of 16,000 Cherokees in 1838 was devastating, with 4,000 dying on the Trail of Tears. When the survivors reached Indian Territory, they received little assistance. Factionalism emerged during the Civil War as the slaveholding minority favored the Confederacy, and in 1865 the United States forced the war-ravaged Cherokees to cede half their lands and accept more federal control. By the late 1800s Congress had revoked earlier treaty promises, and in 1898 it abolished the Cherokee government altogether. Through intermarriage with whites, Cherokees in this century have merged into Oklahoma society, but traditionalists still isolate themselves in backwoods communities that have retained a strong Cherokee identity.

Meanwhile, in the North Carolina mountains, about 1,000 traditionalists on economically marginal lands managed to escape the 1838 removal. After 1870 the federal government gradually extended recognition to them. They are the largest federally recognized reservation in the South, with a growing population now over 8,000. Since the 1940s tourism has been an important, if undependable, part of their economy. Even as acculturation takes place, their Indian identity is growing, and traditionalists among both eastern and western Cherokees are becoming more influential in their tribal governments.

See also GEOGRAPHY: / Cherokee settlement; HISTORY AND MANNERS: / Trail of Tears

Walter L. Williams
University of Cincinnati

Charles Hudson, *The Southeastern Indians* (1976); Duane H. King, ed., *The Cherokee Indian Nation: A Troubled History* (1979); Theda Perdue, ed., *Nations Remembered: An Oral History of the Five Civilized Tribes, 1865–1907* (1980); Walter L. Williams, ed., *Southeastern Indians since the Removal Era* (1979).

Chickasaws

The Chickasaws in late pre-Columbian times numbered an estimated 4,000 and claimed a territory astride western Kentucky, Tennessee, northern Alabama, and Mississippi. Most Chickasaw lifeways resembled those of their neighbors—Choctaws, Creeks, Cherokees, and Natchez. Chickasaws are related to Choctaws; their language, the Muskogean, except for mild dialectal differences, is the same. Early European observers described these Indians as "tall, well-built people, with reddish skin, raven black hair, and large, dark eyes." They had a strong warrior tradition, and their incessant wars with neighboring tribes led them to replace losses in combat by adoption of captives and absorption of tribal remnants. Chickasaw men were hunters and warriors first and farmers only on occasion. Chickasaw women and Indian slaves performed the menial tasks of clearing land, caring for crops, and gathering firewood.

During the 18th century Spaniards, Frenchmen, and Britons vied for Chickasaw support in their drive for control of the lower Mississippi Valley. Traders from Charleston won the Chickasaws to a British alliance. Between 1720 and 1752 French armies from New Orleans invaded Chickasaw territory to force these tribesmen from the British orbit. Each invasion ended in French defeat. Chickasaws served with British armies in the lower Mississippi Valley during the Seven Years War. Chickasaws also supported the British during the American Revolution, fighting in Tory armies in the West against American insurgents.

Soon after 1800 Chickasaws came under the influence of missionaries and white neighbors settling on the margins of their territory. Indian youth attended mission schools, became literate, and eventually ascended to positions of tribal leadership. Several became slaveholders and developed productive plantations on tribal lands.

Through successive treaties with federal officials, Chickasaw leaders ceded tribal territory in western Tennessee and Kentucky so that all that remained by 1830 of their once vast domain was a residual area in northern Mississippi and a fragment in northern Alabama. By the Treaty of Pontotoc in 1832, and an amendatory treaty in 1834, the Chickasaws agreed to sell their eastern lands and remove to Indian Territory. In 1837 Chickasaw and Choctaw leaders signed the Treaty of Doaksville whereby the Chickasaws accepted a home in the Choctaw nation. In 1855 a treaty with the Choctaws permitted the Chickasaws to establish a separate union in south-central Indian Territory. They adopted a constitution providing for an elective council, a chief executive designated governor of the Chickasaw nation, a judiciary, and a public school system. In the antebellum period the Chickasaws sustained themselves by farming, stockraising, and frontier trade.

During 1861 the Chickasaw nation joined the Confederate States of America, and Chickasaw companies fought in several campaigns against Union troops in the Indian Territory. The Chickasaws were required to undergo Reconstruction, which included freeing their slaves and altering their constitution to provide equal civil and social status for freedmen.

Pressed by the Dawes Commission during the late 19th century to adopt allotment in severalty, Chickasaw and Choctaw leaders finally submitted by signing the Atoka Agreement in 1897. The following year the Curtis Act set forth the process for dissolving the Chickasaw nation, and in 1907 the Chickasaws were absorbed into the new state of Oklahoma.

Arrell Morgan Gibson
University of Oklahoma

Arrell Morgan Gibson, *The Chickasaws* (1971); John I. Griffen, ed., *The Chickasaw People* (1974); Daniel F. Littlefield, *The Chickasaw Freedmen: A People without a Country* (1980).

Choctaws

The Choctaws are today one of the largest tribes of Native Americans in the South. They speak the Muskogean language as do the Creeks and Chickasaws, whom they resemble. In historical times the Choctaws and related tribes occupied central and southern Mississippi. With the establishment of French settlements on the Gulf Coast in 1699, the Choctaws were rapidly plunged into a complicated colonial rivalry between European powers. They were generally allied with the French against the English and their allies, the Chickasaws. Although neutral during the American Revolution, the Choctaws, during the Creek War and the War of 1812, demonstrated their loyalty to the new American nation by fighting on the side of Andrew Jackson against the Creeks and the Spanish in Florida. In spite of this effort, they were the first major southern Indian tribe removed to Oklahoma.

Although the Treaty of Dancing Rabbit Creek in 1830 permitted individual Choctaws to remain in Mississippi, most were denied the land promised under the treaty. The Choctaws in Oklahoma and Mississippi fought on the side of the South in the Civil War and suffered from the impact of that conflict. The Mississippi Choctaws were finally legally recognized by the federal government as an Indian tribe in 1918. The Choctaw nation established in Oklahoma following removal came to an end with statehood in 1907, but a Choctaw tribal government still exists there.

Choctaw women, Mississippi, 1930s

Although outstanding agriculturalists, the Choctaws lacked distinguishing customs to excite the interest of travelers or scholars. They attained a degree of political centralization, but otherwise their activities were undramatic. As a result, they have received less scholarly or popular attention than other tribes. They were second only to the Cherokees in adopting European institutions, and early descriptions of their traditional culture are limited. They are best known for a detailed origin legend, their music and dance, and stickball. To a large extent they have continued to retain their language, dances, and ballgame and basketmaking skills. The Choctaws, and other southeastern tribes, contributed corn and hominy to the regional diet. The Choctaws probably contributed the use of sassafras in Louisiana French gumbo. Perhaps their most distinct characteristic has been an ability to adapt, yet remain distinctively Choctaw.

John Peterson
Mississippi State University

Angie Debo, *The Rise and Fall of the Choctaw Republic* (1934); John Peterson, in *The Southeastern Indians since the Removal*

Era, ed. Walter L. Williams (1979); John R. Swanton, *Source Material for the Social and Ceremonial Life of the Choctaw Indians* (1931).

Creeks

Historically, the Creek (Muskogee) Confederacy was the dominant American Indian political and military force in the present-day states of Alabama and Georgia. The native economy rested upon maize, beans, and squash cultivation and hunting and fishing. Politically the Confederacy consisted of several dozen autonomous chiefdoms, or towns, organized internally on the principle of matrilineal descent coupled with a prestige system based largely upon distinction in warfare. Religious life revolved around a ceremonial calendar culminating in the Busk, New Fire, or Green Corn Ceremony in late summer. Following sustained contact with whites in the late 17th century, the Creeks became increasingly dependent upon commercial hunting and trade, resulting ultimately in dependency, indebtedness, land cessions, and complicated entanglements with competing European powers in the Southeast. After the American Revolution the United States relentlessly pursued a "plan of civilization" for the Creeks that included greater centralization of authority in the "Creek Nation," precipitating internal divisions culminating in the Creek War of 1813–14 and the eventual subjugation and removal of most Creeks, then totaling about 20,000, to Indian Territory (Oklahoma) by 1840.

Despite the 1830s removal, a few Creek Indians managed to remain in the Southeast, particularly some of those who had remained friendly to the United States during the Creek War. Their descendants today number several thousand, and most are assimilated into the general population. Near modern-day Atmore, Ala., however, a sufficient concentration of unremoved Creeks remained to sustain a viable Indian community to the present. These Creeks, largely isolated and ignored by federal authorities throughout most of their history, have maintained a cohesive community through informal social and political mechanisms. Formally organized as the "Poarch Band of Creeks," the group actively pursues a program of community betterment, cultural enrichment, and political action.

This latter-day resurgence of the Poarch Creeks began in the 1940s and 1950s when Chief Clavin W. McGhee (1903–70) spearheaded a drive for improved educational opportunities for his people and directed a land-claim suit against the United States, efforts in which the Creeks eventually were successful. By 1984 there were approximately 1,300 enrolled members of the band headed by an elected Tribal Council. Many band members now live in cities, as do many other Indians, but over half the Poarch Creeks reside in the vicinity of the Tribal Center, near the sites of federal allotments received by "Friendly Creek" ancestors under terms of the 1815 Treaty of Fort Jackson, which concluded the Creek War.

Since the early 1800s the Poarch Creeks have become acculturated to white ways, yet some elements of native culture and language have survived. Once objects of discrimination, the Poarch Creeks lately have begun to transform their identity as Indians from a local stigma to a national asset. Since 1971 the Poarch Creeks have sponsored an annual Thanksgiving Day powwow at their community center attracting craftsmen, dancers, and others from tribes in Oklahoma, Mississippi, Florida, and North Carolina, as well as thousands of non-Indian spectators. Since 1977 the Poarch Band of Creeks has been a voting member of the National Congress of American Indians, and their tribal chairman, Eddie Tullis, was elected vice-president of the Congress in 1983. In August 1984, following a process begun in 1975, the Poarch Band of Creeks was officially acknowledged by the United States as an Indian tribe, historically related to but politically distinct from the modern Muskogee (Creek) nation of Oklahoma, and, thus, entitled to all the rights and privileges of other federally recognized Indian tribes under United States law.

J. Anthony Paredes
Florida State University

J. W. Fritz, *Federal Register* (Number 5, 1978); J. Anthony Paredes, in *Indians of the Lower South: Past and Present*, ed. John Mahon (1975), and in *The Versatility of Kinship*, ed. Linda S. Cordell and Stephen Beckerman (1980); Frank G. Speck, *American Indigena* (1947).

Creole

Few ethnic terms in North American society have been as controversial or as sensitive as the term *Creole*. Coined by the Spanish and Portuguese who ventured into the New World, the word originally denoted individuals born in the colonies of European parents. Under the restrictions of this connotation, the term should have fallen from disuse with the cessation of colonial immigration.

Within Louisiana, the disparities between the predominantly Latin culture of the original settlers and the predominantly Anglo-Celtic culture of the late 18th- and 19th-century newcomers served to encourage the perpetuation, evolution, and expansion of the term Creole. By the 19th century it had become synonymous with "native." In both the noun and adjective forms it embraced all objects indigenous to Louisiana, from cabbage to cotton, and all people, regardless of hue, whose families were native to the Louisiana colony. Its application to people appeared in one of three forms: Creole, Creole *de couleur* (which denoted Creoles with African or Indian admixtures), and Creole Negro (which denoted blacks of unmixed ancestry). By definition, the term was so inexclusive that it barred only those born outside of Louisiana.

Varied restrictions upon the usage of the term have

been attempted, within segments of Louisiana society, since at least the late 19th century, and a considerable degree of misunderstanding over the term has existed outside the state. The most commonly encountered circumscriptions suggest that a Creole *must* be of "pure" white ancestry, is necessarily wealthy and aristocratic, and is rooted in the Delta country of lower Louisiana. Travelogs of past generations, penned by those who sojourned chiefly among the upper classes of New Orleans and the sugar planters of the surrounding countryside, were perhaps initially responsible for this limited concept of the term. From their romanticized portrayal of Creole society, there has blossomed (in the words of one Louisiana historian) "a veritable cult of the Creole . . . for those who look so longingly to the past" in which "their kind . . . ruled . . . with a grace and charm long since lost to the modern world."

Simultaneously, the widely read works of the 19th-century Louisiana writer George Washington Cable, and those of a great number of his successors, have left much of Anglo-American society with the impression that Creoles are uniformly poor in worldly goods, quaint in customs, and mixed of blood. The latter misunderstanding has been propagated to a great degree in the 20th century by those of mixed racial heritage who seek to escape prejudicial injustices by identifying themselves as Creoles rather than by the term black, which is more commonly applied to their counterparts outside of Louisiana.

The only restriction that has been applied to the term *Creole* that has been customarily agreed upon by most segments of society is the exclusion of those individuals more commonly known as "Cajuns." Even this limitation, however, is arbitrary, in light of the degree to which the two groups have intermarried. In 20th-century America, Creoles with "Cajun" ancestry and "Cajuns" with Creole ancestry are probably more the rule than the exception.

In consideration of the ambiguity that surrounds what is principally a question of evolving semantics, the safest definition of the term may well be the classic Louisiana compromise: A Creole can be anyone who says he is one.

See also LITERATURE: / Cable, George Washington; URBANIZATION: / New Orleans

Gary B. Mills
University of Alabama

Elizabeth Shown Mills, *Louisiana Genealogical Register* (March 1977); William J. Thomas, *Wichita State University Bulletin* (February 1973); Joseph G. Tregle, Jr., *Journal of Southern History* (February 1952).

Cubans

Cubans constitute the largest Hispanic group in the southeastern United States. Although Mexicans are primarily concentrated in the Southwest and Puerto Ricans in the Northeast, Florida contains the nucleus of the Cuban community in this country. In 1980 more than half the 803,226 persons of Cuban origin in the United States resided in Miami's metropolitan area.

The concentration of Cubans in Florida has a long history. As early as 1831 Cuban cigarmakers were working in Key West, Florida's southernmost town, whose Cuban population increased throughout the 19th century. Starting in 1886, cigar manufacturers from Cuba, led by Vicente Martínez de Ybor, established factories on the outskirts of Tampa. The immigration of Cuban cigarmakers to the area increased dramatically during the height of the Tampa cigar industry (1886–1910), resulting in the founding of Ybor City, which survives to this day as a neighborhood within the metropolitan area of Tampa.

But by far the bulk of the current Cuban-origin population of the United States immigrated after 1959, the year in which the revolutionary government headed by Fidel Castro rose to power and began transforming the country's political, economic, and social institutions. Miami has been the principal destination of those postrevolutionary migrants, although important communities have also arisen in the New York City–New Jersey metropolitan area and in Los Angeles, Puerto Rico, Spain, and various Latin American countries. Miami bears the imprint of the large Cuban presence. The Cuban community has served as a magnet for other Latin American immigrants, so that in 1980 one of every two Miami residents was of Latin American origin.

The relatively high proportion of professionals and entrepreneurs among the Cuban immigrants has contributed to making Miami's Spanish-speaking population an institutionally complete ethnic community. Its members can work, shop, bank, dine, and be entertained in establishments in which Spanish is the principal language. This institutional completeness, coupled with the predominance of first-generation immigrants among Cuban Americans, has made possible the retention of many cultural traits from the country of origin. Evidence of this retention can be found, for example, in religious practices. Most Cubans in the United States are Roman Catholics, and others adhere to religious beliefs that have Afro-Cuban origins. Communitywide cultural events held by Miami's Cubans, such as Carnaval, art and music festivals, and the Three Kings' Parade, are all reminiscent of similar events once held in Cuba. The proliferation in Miami of grocery stores and restaurants that cater exclusively to Cuban dietary tastes is yet another example of the tendency to adhere to cultural traits of the country of origin. As expected, however, the younger generation, largely born in the United States, exhibits a substantial degree of assimilation to the cultural patterns of this country.

In 1980 the widely publicized Mariel sealift brought some 125,000 Cubans to the United States and dramatically increased the number and visibility of Cubans in this country, and especially in Florida. While Cuban immigration has slowed to a trickle since the termination of the sealift in September of 1980, the conditions that gave rise to it persist, and it is not unimaginable that the

Miami Cuban community will be replenished with new arrivals in the years ahead.

See also GEOGRAPHY: / Cuban Settlement; URBANIZATION: / Miami; Tampa

Lisandro Pérez
Louisiana State University

Thomas D. Boswell and James R. Curtis, *The Cuban-American Experience: Culture, Images and Perspectives* (1984); Richard R. Fagen, Richard A. Brody, and Thomas J. O'Leary, *Cubans in Exile: Disaffection and the Revolution* (1968); Lisandro Pérez, in *Harvard Encyclopedia of American Ethnic Groups*, ed. Stephen Thernstrom, Ann Orlov, and Oscar Handlin (1980); Eleanor Meyer Rogg, *The Assimilation of Cuban Exiles: The Role of Community and Class* (1974).

French

French presence in the South has been concentrated historically in two places, Charleston, S.C., and Louisiana. Beyond those two areas French influence has been so slight, insulated, or ephemeral as to be of negligible significance. The largest community was Henri Castro's settlement of several thousand Alsatians in Medina County in western Texas in 1844, but it left only a local imprint.

Even the celebrated South Carolina manifestation is little more than a historical memory. Beginning in the 1680s and continuing through most of the 18th century, a total of not more than 2,000 French Huguenots, fleeing persecution by Catholic authorities in France after Louis XIV's famous revocation of the Edict of Nantes that had protected French Protestants for nearly a century, took refuge in the recently founded English colony of South Carolina. Most of them settled in or around Charleston, where they quickly became the backbone of that important colonial city's business and financial class. With religion no bar and their language rapidly eroded, they were assimilated by the predominantly English population. Though they were of vital importance to the economic life of early South Carolina, they left no real ethnic legacy—nothing, for example, in the way of an architectural or linguistic heritage.

An important reminder of their presence is in the great number of Huguenot surnames found today throughout the South, carried there as the Huguenots' descendants joined other southerners in the classic migration to new territories that populated the Deep South. Another reminder is the Huguenot church they established in Charleston. After having its membership fall nearly to the point of extinction in the 1950s, the church is again viable today, its following enlarged as a result of renewed ethnic awareness during the 1960s and 1970s.

In Louisiana, on the other hand, 572,262 people in 1970 reported to the census takers that their mother tongue was French. An estimate of 450,000 Louisianians in 1980 had French as their mother tongue—slightly more than 1 out of every 10 people in the state. Of those, 291,137 still speak it, in one degree of fluency or another. That represents the largest concentration of French-speaking natives with an indigenous ethnic tradition in the United States.

All of them—save 5,000 or so foreign-born French-speaking immigrants of the recent past and their children—are the descendants of one or some combination of five French-speaking groups that largely made up Louisiana's colonial and antebellum population. The first group came from Canada or directly from France and settled in New Orleans, up to the Mississippi River, and along what are now the Mississippi and Alabama Gulf coasts. Toward the end of the 18th century that early population began to style themselves *l'ancienne population* in distinction to newcomers who were flooding into the colony. Some of the newcomers, or *les français étrangers*, emigrated directly from France, but great numbers, some of them free people of color, came from the French West Indies and Santo Domingo, particularly after revolutions there in 1791. The colonists also brought in many black African slaves who quickly learned French and became the third group. In the latter decades of the 18th century Acadians, or Cajuns as they came to call themselves, immigrated to Louisiana from Canada after the British conquest there and settled as small farmers and woodsmen in the swamps and along the bayous southwest of New Orleans. And throughout the 19th century continuing waves of emigrants from France, the fifth group, poured into Louisiana, and particularly into New Orleans, keeping it a predominantly French-speaking city until the Civil War and a largely French-speaking one until World War I.

Although reminders of historical French presence remain in some outlying areas of the great expanse of French territory that constituted the Louisiana Purchase—most notably at Saint Louis, Mo., Mobile, Ala., Biloxi and Natchez, Miss., and Natchitoches and Baton Rouge, La.—these are limited mostly to remnants of an architectural and town planning legacy, to a larger Catholic presence than normal for the South, and to numerous French family and place names.

In south Louisiana, however, a pronounced French influence continues. In addition to Catholicism and to French, which is spoken today by about 373,500 Cajuns as well as around 76,500 people in New Orleans, Cajuns maintain an architectural tradition, typically modern adaptations of a four-room, story-and-a-half, frame cottage with a narrow incorporated front porch; a rich folklore of sayings, superstitions, cures, songs, and tales; Sunday community dances called *fais-do-dos*; and a kind of poker called *bourré* in which even penny-ante stakes can suddenly rise to hundreds of dollars on the flash of a single card. They have also institutionalized and refined into a high athletic skill racing in pirogues, which are long, narrow dugout canoes. They have their own music, a unique French-folk-country-western-blues combination, and their own cuisine, hearty, highly spiced seafood, fish, crawfish, and game dishes that carry a distinctive French undertone and that have recently become increasingly popular across the nation.

In New Orleans the Creole tradition and the tradition

of "creolizing" natives of whatever background, and newcomers as well, also remains pronounced. New Orleans retains a viable local architectural tradition, the origins of which are French. And the city remains distinctly Catholic in tone, though now predominantly Protestant in numbers. New Orleans cooking, a rich, delicate cuisine that is essentially an adaptation, developed largely by black chefs, of traditional continental French dishes to local ingredients and seasonings supplied by the city's various 19th-century immigrant groups, is world famous. In addition, the city has developed a public culture, a way of life—best known but by no means limited to its expression in the celebration of Mardi Gras—that is also traceable to French colonial origins.

New Orleans's antebellum free black population, almost entirely French speaking, was not only the largest in the Deep South, but the only one anywhere in the South to develop a full-fledged high culture of its own. It included a coterie of poets, novelists, historians, and musicians and supported its own theater, newspapers, several schools, and a small symphony orchestra. That culture maintained continuing contact with France; Edmond Dédé, for example, served as conductor of the Bordeaux symphony for 25 years, and Victor Séjour had a number of his plays performed on the Paris stage. Moreover, the free black population and its descendants furnished most of the state's black leaders during Reconstruction and the latter 19th century, and in the course of the 20th century has exported such talent to the rest of the South, most recently in the examples of Atlanta mayors Maynard Jackson and Andrew Young, both of whose families have roots in New Orleans.

See also ART AND ARCHITECTURE: French Architecture; LANGUAGE: French Language; URBANIZATION: / Charleston; New Orleans

Jerah Johnson
University of New Orleans

Glenn R. Conrad, ed., *The Cajuns: Essays on Their History and Culture* (1978); Arthur Henry Hirsch, *The Huguenots of Colonial South Carolina* (1928); Jerah Johnson, *Contemporary French Civilization* (Fall 1976).

Germans

Although one of the largest "ethnic" components of the American population, Germans (that is, those emigrants from the area of Imperial Germany, the states forming Germany in 1871) as a group never assumed cultural importance for the entire southern region. German immigration to the South encompassed too broad a time span, was too irregular, and drew from too many diverse sources within "Germany" to impose a single cultural order anywhere. Still, large numbers of Germans settled in the southern region from the colonial period through the 19th century, and within their areas of concentration they built and maintained German subcultures that thrived into the modern era in several instances, at least in attenuated forms.

In the 18th century thousands of Germans moved along the great wagon road from Pennsylvania into the Virginia backcountry, the Carolinas, and even as far south as Georgia. German-speaking sectarian groups, such as the Salzburgers in Georgia, the Swiss Germans at Purrysburg in South Carolina, and the Moravians in North Carolina, augmented the "German" presence in the colonial period. German cultures proliferated in rural areas for more than a century, but they began to weaken in the 19th century because, after 1800, few immigrants arrived to renew them. Economic and social forces intruded on Germans' isolation or drew them into the larger commercial and social world of the antebellum South. Individual German groups, often religious in character and organized by colonizers seeking refuge and prosperity in America, continued to venture to the South in the 19th century, following the good reports of land and nature from such German promoters and travelers as Gottfried Duden, whose tract on Missouri stimulated a rush of Germans there.

Various German societies that formed after 1830 to colonize America looked to the South for land. Among them were the Auswanderungs Gesellschaft, which planned a settlement in Arkansas, and the Rhein-Bayerische Gesellschaft and the Mainzer Adelsverein, among several, which established German colonies along the Brazos River in Texas and elsewhere. These societies were particularly attracted to the southwestern region, but with the opening of western lands, the economic and social dislocations caused by the Civil War, and the shift in the sources of German immigrants generally by the 1870s, the South no longer appeared inviting to prospective agricultural colonies. Various entrepreneurs and southern state governments responded to pressure from planters who wanted to replace black workers with German and other immigrants after the Civil War, but few Germans responded to their appeals and those who did remained only briefly in the South. Except for a handful of successful experiments in recruiting, such as the work of John G. Cullman in bringing Germans to Cullman County, Ala., German farmers had ceased to enter the South by the late 19th century.

During the 19th century the character of German immigration changed significantly. Beginning with the great immigration waves to America in the 1840s, Germans came to the South through the port of New Orleans, often arriving on the cotton ships trading between New Orleans and Bremen. Many of the immigrants moved up the Mississippi River in search of jobs or land to settle in the Midwest, but many also remained in New Orleans or the river towns and cities to work on the levees, on railroads, on the docks, or as laborers and artisans in the towns. In cities such as Memphis and Louisville the German population swelled to more than 10 or 15 percent of the total city population in the 1850s. Meanwhile, other Germans left northern ports to seek work in Richmond's iron industry or went to other industrializing towns in the upper South. For a brief moment, German immigrants contributed to the "modernization" of southern urban life, adding cultural diversity, ethnic politics, Old World arts and crafts, and an infrastructure of social and cultural organizations to city life. The urban Germans developed a rich associational life throughout the South. In Richmond, for example, a German rifle club, *Turnverein*, Schiller society, benevolent society, drama club, choral group, and free thinkers' congregation brought German culture to the city. In Memphis, as late as the 1870s, the German population of no more than 4,000 persons then supported 18 benevolent and fraternal societies, a fire company, eight lodges, five militia companies, several theater groups, and a host of religious and social associations. Even a small German population, as in Mobile in the 1880s, could boast at least a German school, a charity organization, a choral society, a gymnasium, and a Lutheran church. German newspapers sprang up in every southern city, and German heroes and festivals were celebrated in print and parades as recently as the early 20th century in some places.

The strong associational life of the Germans reflected their numerical and cultural significance in the cities, but also their weakness. The diverse origins of the German population combined with class and religious differences to separate the Germans among themselves. So, too, did rivalries between old and new settlers, between the German "intelligentsia," who derived their identity from European liberalism, and the poorer, new immigrants, many of them Catholics, who showed greater respect for authority. These and other differences explain the proliferation of German associations, for each group inclined toward its own kind. No single German cultural imprint was possible under such conditions.

By World War I any viable German culture that remained was rooted in the southern countryside. In subtle ways the intensive agriculture of German farmers created a specific cultural landscape, particularly in the rural German enclaves of the Shenandoah Valley of Virginia, in scattered communities in the Carolina Piedmont, in Cullman County in Alabama, in south-central Tennessee, in the Arkansas Ozarks, along the Missouri River in Missouri, and in several pockets in eastern Texas. Because Germans viewed their farms as permanent homes rather than speculative investments, they have tended to farm them more intensively than non-Germans, with greater per-unit productivity and locational stability. In addition, they traditionally have exhibited relatively higher rates of landownership wherever they have clustered in numbers. German ethnic subcultures, with their high religiosity, family centeredness, and conservative values, grew in rural areas, nurtured by German agricultural societies, social clubs, fraternal and benefit associations, the local German churches, and, as late as the 1950s in a few instances, a German-language press. Rural isolation and German churches served as the twin pillars of German ethnicity for over a century or more, but since World War II mass communications, improved roads, changed market conditions, and consolidated school systems have combined to erode rural German distinctiveness.

Even those German cultural traits that have persisted did so only because they were modified somewhat to meet local conditions. Most German farmers have accommodated to local social, economic, and physical environments. Germans have followed southern practices both in the production of staple crops for the market economy and in the selection and treatment of livestock. They also abandoned their Old World village settlement patterns for the dispersed settlement habits of America.

Schmidt Brothers saloon, Fredericksburg, Tex., date unknown

German building and crafts further displayed the syncretic, dynamic qualities of German-American acculturation generally. In building large barns and substantial homes Germans adapted to local architectural styles and used available building materials. In the 19th century, for example, German settlers in Missouri and Texas first built with logs, which were both inexpensive and practical, and put up houses in the American style. In time, Germans constructed frame houses resembling those in the areas from which they had migrated. They also used stone widely, especially in Missouri. In cities with German craftsmen and German population concentrations distinctive brickwork traditions also developed, but by the early 20th century German urban design and construction had yielded to standardized American conventions and styles. In rural areas a Missouri-German, Texas-German, or Shenandoah-German vernacular style evolved, but everywhere the great diversity of German backgrounds among settlers and craftsmen produced much artistic and architectural variety within any given area. Little distinctive regional furniture or decorative art emanated from southern German settlements, as it did from Pennsylvania Germans, although sectarian groups such as the Moravians of North Carolina established their own folk expressions and, as in the Shenandoah Valley, rural isolation and German population density kept alive *fraktur* writing, basket weaving, and pottery making for several generations after immigration.

In rural areas German churches conducted services in the native tongue and ran schools that resisted the English monolinguistic culture. German publishing houses serving Lutherans particularly and the German language press proliferated throughout the 19th century, imposing a standard German idiom on German readers. Lack of funds, teachers, and readers, along with wider commercial contacts beyond German settlements, however, contributed to the weakening of German language institutions by the end of the century. Bilingualism entered the German churches via lay insistence, and English rapidly replaced standard German in the marketplace. Still, various spoken German dialects survived in isolated communities as the language of informal social intercourse.

In the cities the heterogeneity of backgrounds among Germans caused them to adopt the formal *Hochdeutsch*, used in churches and in the press and sprinkled with American usages, more readily than their rural counterparts. The urban Germans' more frequent and sustained contacts with non-Germans also rapidly forced them to become a bilingual people. Indeed, many German associations regularly conducted their affairs in both English and German by the late 19th century. Small numbers of German publicists and nationalists lobbied for German language maintenance, and educated, affluent urban Germans supported German-speaking theater and high culture in Richmond, Charleston, Memphis, Nashville, and New Orleans, among other places. But the bulk of the German population gravitated toward American entertainments and speech as the natural concomitant of their work and dispersed residence patterns within the cities.

Enough "German" restaurants, *Maifesten* and other festivals, folk art objects and architecture, and, especially, Lutheran and Reformed churches survive to recall a German contribution to southern life, but, save for the rural enclaves, German identity now exists largely, and then often dimly, too, in memory.

See also ART AND ARCHITECTURE: German Architecture; LANGUAGE: German Language

Randall M. Miller
St. Joseph's University

Kathleen Neils Conzen, in *Harvard Encyclopedia of American Ethnic Groups*, ed. Stephen Thernstrom, Ann Orlov, and Oscar Handlin (1980); Russell L. Gerlach, *Immigrants in the Ozarks: A Study in Ethnic Geography* (1976); Terry G. Jordan, *German Seed in Texas Soil: Immigrant Farmers in Nineteenth-Century Texas* (1966); John Nau, *The German People of New Orleans, 1850–1900* (1958); Charles van Ravenswaay, *The Arts and Architecture of German Settlements in Missouri* (1977); Klaus Wust, *The Virginia Germans* (1969).

Greeks

Although Greeks in the South are not numerous and comprise only about 10 percent of the total Greek American population, Greek southerners form a distinctive element in Greek American history. The first Greeks to settle in America—about 400 souls—were indentured servants brought over by a Scottish entrepreneur to New Smyrna, Fla., in 1768. The first Greek Orthodox church in the United States, Holy Trinity, was established in

A Greek American deep-sea sponge fisherman, Tarpon Springs, Fla., 1944

New Orleans in 1864. A Greek Orthodox religious commune—the Malbis Plantation—was founded in 1906 in Baldwin County, Ala. Tarpon Springs, Fla., underwent a metamorphosis in 1905 with the arrival of 500 Greek spongers. The Greek character of Tarpon Springs has been unique in America and remains well defined today. The American Hellenic Educational Progressive Association (AHEPA) was established in 1922 in Atlanta, Ga. The AHEPA became the leading Greek American fraternal organization.

The major wave of Greek immigration to the South—as elsewhere in the United States—occurred in the early decades of this century. Like their counterparts outside the South, the vast majority of these early Greek arrivals were males seeking their fortunes in America. Most came with the intention to return to the old country where they would lead lives of comfort from their American earnings. Because of their relative success, the Greek immigrants to the South, however, realized much earlier than their compatriots in other parts of the United States that America was to become their permanent home. This also meant that internecine political conflicts, which marred much of Greek immigrant life in this country, largely bypassed the Greeks of the South. To a degree even greater than their non-southern compatriots, Greeks in the South established small businesses, notably restaurants, and generally prospered. Greek emigrant women came over in substantial numbers after World War I. The children and grandchildren of those early emigrants have, in the main, moved into professional, white-collar, and upper-middle-class vocations.

Greeks in the South quickly established stable communities whose focal point was the Greek Orthodox church. By the mid-1980s there were 90 Greek Orthodox churches in the region. Some 100,000 persons of Greek birth or ancestry now live in the states of the old Confederacy. About half of these are "southern Greeks," descendants of the early immigrants. The others, especially in Texas, Florida, and northern Virginia, are migrants to the Sunbelt—part of the national pattern occurring since the 1950s.

An indigenous Greek American community, as opposed to a Greek immigrant colony, first developed in the South. The southern variant thus became the prototype of the Greek experience in America.

Charles C. Moskos
Northwestern University

Alexander Karanikas, *Hellenes and Hellions: Modern Greek Characters in American Literature* (1982); Charles C. Moskos, *Greek Americans: Struggle and Success* (1980); Theodore Saloutos, *The Greeks in the United States* (1964).

Gypsies

Well represented among southern ethnic minorities are the Romani people (*Rom*, or *Gypsies*), who maintain their distinctive language and way of life while remaining outside mainstream society. All Romani groups trace their ultimate heritage to 9th- or 10th-century India, but subsequent westward migration into Europe and thence to the Americas has scattered the original population, giving rise to a number of distinct ethnic subdivisions within the overall race. In the South, several of these subdivisions are represented, particularly the Romanichals, or Gypsies, who came from the British Isles, and the Vlax (*x* like *ch* in German *Achtung*), who arrived later from southeastern Europe.

The first Gypsies to reach the Americas came with Columbus on his third voyage in 1498 and were presumably from Spain. The first to reach North America were probably those banished to serve in the Virginia plantations by Cromwell in 1664. The transportation of British Gypsies to the American colonies continued sporadically until the mid-1800s, and the French began similar deportations to Louisiana after 1700. Spanish shipments to the same territory followed a proclamation issued in 1749; Gypsies came as redemptioners from Germany to Pennsylvania, New York, and New Jersey following the Thirty Years War, and some of them eventually made their way south. The Vlax Gypsies began coming to America in the middle of the 19th century when 500 years of Gypsy slavery in the Balkan states ended.

Romanichal Gypsies live throughout the South, probably numbering between 50,000 and 100,000. Particularly large communities are found in Texas, Arkansas, Georgia, Louisiana, Kentucky, and the Carolinas. Many are homesteaders who own much land and at the same time follow a variety of occupations such as horseraising, blacktopping, roofing, and paving. Others involved in these occupations follow an annual migratory business circuit and move from campground to campground living in motorized trailers. The Vlax Rom have little to do with the Romanichal population, whom they outnumber by perhaps five to one.

Romani culture, for both groups, requires that social contact with non-Gypsies, whom the Vlax Rom call *gadjé* (singular *gadjó*) and the Romanichals *gorjers*, be kept at a minimum. Gypsies avoid calling attention to ethnic identity and keep a low profile. Much of this reluctance is a reaction to the prejudice that operates against Gypsies at both the popular and administrative levels. Gypsies have not had the wherewithal to challenge the stereotype of Western tradition that portrays them in a generally negative light, and they have little motivation to draw attention to their ethnicity. One Mississippi law states that "gypsies . . . for each county . . . shall be jointly and severally liable with his or her associates (to a fine of) two thousand dollars"; another law in Georgia requires that "upon each company of gypsies engaged in trading or selling merchandise . . . $250 is to be collected." As a consequence, while Romani culture in the South is vigorous and in little danger of disappearing, the general public is hardly aware of it.

In recent years two independent movements, one sociopolitical and one evangelical, have begun to bring changes within the Romani population. The former has resulted in the creation in Florida of a national journal, *Romaníja*, the purpose of which is to bring news of national and international Gypsy-related matters to the Romani population. The evangelical movement has also led to the establishment of a newsletter, *Romany Fires of Revival*, which is sent out to some 600 families in Louisiana. Romani churches, both Vlax and Romanichal, are now found in many southern cities including Atlanta and Houston.

See also FOLKLIFE: / Traders

Ian Hancock
University of Texas at Austin

Irving Brown, *Gypsy Fires in America: A Narrative of Life among the Romanies of the United States and Canada* (1924); Ian Hancock, *American Speech* (Fall 1986), *The Pariah Syndrome* (1987); Andrew A. Marchbin, *A Critical History of the Origin and the Migration of the Gypsies* (Ph.D. dissertation, University of Pittsburgh, 1939); Anne Sutherland, *Gypsies: The Hidden Americans* (1986); John N. Wilford, *New York Times* (14 October 1986).

Haitians

Before the independence of Haiti in 1804, many emigrants from the island came to settle in the South. As early as 1526 slaves from Hispaniola were brought to South Carolina. In the first half of the 18th century, colonists and free people of color immigrated to Louisiana. Some of them, like the mulatto Stephen LaRue, remained in New Orleans; others, like Jean Baptiste Point Du Sable, moved to the Midwest or the East Coast.

In 1779 a battalion of 800 volunteers from Santo Domingo fought against the British troops at the battle of Savannah, Ga. These courageous men contributed in their own way to the strengthening of American independence. However, the first major wave of emigration from the island took place during the Haitian Revolution of 1791–1803. During this period more than 15,000 immigrants, including French planters, free people of color, and slaves, settled in Louisiana. A few thousand more went to Charleston, S.C. Some came to the United States after an interim stay in Cuba, Jamaica, or Trinidad. This explains why they were able to immigrate to the South even after the independence of Haiti. For the year 1809 alone, 2,731 whites, 3,102 free people of color, and 3,226 slaves—all former residents of Santo Domingo—came to New Orleans. The immigrants helped to restore the agricultural industry of Louisiana and made outstanding contributions in the arts and in New Orleans's cultural life. Writer Charles Gayarré wrote that "among the refugees who sought an asylum in New Orleans, was a company of comedians from Cape Français, who opened a theatre a short time after their arrival. From that circumstance dates the origin of regular dramatic exhibitions in New Orleans." They also played an important role at the elementary and secondary school levels. A few of them opened schools and others became school teachers, thus contributing to the maintenance of the French language in Louisiana.

The arrival of the slaves and free people of color contributed to the spread of the Creole language and voodoo practices in the South. Haitian Creole became part of the speech community in Louisiana and found its public expression through occasional voodoo dances and Mardi Gras songs. Marie Laveau, whose parents were emigrés from Santo Domingo and who married consecutively two Haitian immigrants, was known as the Voodoo Queen of New Orleans. In addition, slaves and free people of color brought with them the knowledge of traditional medicine, and they continued to participate in the activities of the Catholic church, thereby enlarging the population of black Catholics in Louisiana.

The early Haitian immigrants have left their mark on the military and architectural history of the South. For example, Joseph Savary headed the Second Battalion of Men of Color who fought in 1814–15 under the command of Andrew Jackson. Savary became the first black to hold the position of second major in the U.S. Army. In Old Charleston and in the French Quarter in New Orleans, the immigrants built French-style residences as well as shotgun houses.

During the 19th century and the first half of the 20th, Haitian immigrants came sporadically to the South, more particularly to Florida, almost every time a Haitian president was ousted from office. Because of the prevalent practice of racial discrimination in the South, however, they kept a low profile and their presence was not felt by the larger community.

The administrations of François "Papa Doc" Duvalier (1957–71) and Jean-Claude "Baby Doc" Duvalier (1971–86) resulted in the largest group of Haitian immigrants settling in the South, mostly in the state of Florida and more particularly in the Miami area. These new immigrants consisted mostly of individuals who came with a tourist visa and overstayed. Since 1972, however, numerous boatloads of refugees from Haiti and the Bahama Islands have arrived in Florida and requested political asylum. Many of these immigrants were placed in detention centers or refugee camps in or near Miami. Pending the clearance of their application for political asylum, most of them were released in 1982 to their sponsors after a long legal battle (*Haitian Refugee Center, Inc., et al.* v. *Immigration and Naturalization Service et al.*). In the meantime, the population of "Little Haiti," a Haitian enclave in Miami, has continued to grow. It remains the commercial, religious, and cultural center of the Haitian community in the South.

See also FOLKLIFE: / Shotgun House; LANGUAGE: Gullah; RECREATION: Mardi Gras; URBANIZATION: / Miami; New Orleans

Michel S. Laguerre
University of California at Berkeley

Rodolphe Lucien Desdunes, *Our People and Our History* (1973); Charles Gayarré, *History of Louisiana: The Spanish Domination* (1866); Michel S. Laguerre, *American Odyssey: Haitians in the United States* (1983).

Irish

The first important Irish migrations to the South came from Barbados to the Carolinas in the 1680s, Cromwell having sent many thousands of Irish to that island three decades earlier. During the next century many thousands made the move to the South directly from Ireland—some as self-financed emigrants, far more as indentured servants, and many who were transported for crimes or rebellious activity. Others went first to Philadelphia and migrated thence southwestward along the valleys. By 1790 people of Irish extraction, not counting the Scotch-Irish, constituted about one-eighth of the white population of the South.

The Irish were nominally Catholic, but in 17th- and 18th-century Ireland fewer than a third ever attended mass. The absence of Catholic churches in the South except in Maryland and in Charleston was thus of little consequence to them. Indeed, the Irish suffered little or no culture shock on being transplanted to the American frontier. For the most part they blended in with the Scotch-Irish and the Highland Scots—peoples with whom they had shared traditions and ways for centuries.

After the potato famine of the 1840s a new and larger wave of immigration to America began, and though most by far went to the North, as many as 100,000 may have gone to the South. In 1850 some 25,000 Irish lived in New Orleans alone, constituting a quarter of the city's population. The postfamine Irish had a considerably different experience in the South than had their colonial predecessors. Unlike the earlier Irish, they had been thoroughly reduced to the peasant class before they migrated; lacking money, they could not easily obtain land, and in the South of the 1850s there was but minimal demand for their labor. Nonetheless, they were enthusiastic supporters of the Confederacy, providing five general officers and Irish units for eight southern states. Not until after Reconstruction were they absorbed into the mainstream of southern life.

See also FOLKLIFE: / Traders; MYTHIC SOUTH: / Celtic South

Grady McWhiney
Texas Christian University

Forrest McDonald
University of Alabama

David Noel Doyle, *Ireland, Irishmen, and Revolutionary America, 1760–1820* (1981); Earl F. Niehaus, *The Irish in New Orleans, 1800–1860* (1965); Michael J. O'Brien, *Irish Settlers in America: A Consolidation of Articles from the Journal of the American Irish Historical Society*, 2 vols. (1979).

Italians

From the importation of Venetian glassblowers to Jamestown in 1622 to the Spoleto Festival in Charleston in the 1980s, Italians have added to the diversity and vitality of the South. Italians migrated to southern states in four distinct phases, reflecting American demands for labor, international labor patterns, and peninsular politics.

Between the age of exploration and the Civil War, Italians appeared prominently in southern history, but their notoriety derived from individual exploits rather than group endeavors. Giovanni Verrazzano charted the Atlantic Coast, and Henry di Tonti explored the southern interior. Italians helped explore and settle St. Augustine, San Antonio, and Savannah. William Paca of Maryland signed the Declaration of Independence, and Thomas Jefferson counted the intellectual Phillip Mazzei as a friend and teacher. Jefferson also persuaded a number of Italian sculptors and architects to help with the building of the Capitol. The New Smyrna experiment on the eastern coast of Florida offered the largest concentration of Italians in the South prior to the late 19th century. The experiment began in 1763 when an English physician, Andrew Turnbull, imported 1,500 Italians to labor on his plantation; the Minorcans and Italians soon rebelled, however, and the survivors scattered. On the eve of the Civil War, few southern states boasted many Italian residents; Louisiana numbered 915 and Mississippi 121, but all other states counted fewer than 100 Italians.

During the second stage, between the war and 1920, relatively few Italians migrated south, compared to the massive numbers concentrated in northern cities. A handful of Italian agricultural communities in the South, however, attracted much attention. The most noteworthy and successful of those rural experiments was in Arkansas. Between 1895 and 1897 about 1,200 Italians from northern Italy were recruited to replace black laborers in Sunnyside, Ark. The experiment failed almost immediately, but a faction, led by Father Bandini, resettled in what is today Tontitown. Other colonies claiming varying successes included Bryan, Tex., and Valdese, N.C.

Louisiana attracted more Italians than any other southern state in the early 20th century. Between 1880 and 1914 as many as 16,000 Sicilians migrated to the sugarcane fields and strawberry farms. New Orleans counted 5,866 Italians in the 1900 census. Sicilians there quickly dominated the fruit and vegetable markets—as they would in many cities. Italians thrived in the commercial and agricultural fields of Louisiana, in spite of vicious nativist violence, which took 19 lives in the decade of the 1890s.

Industrial enterprise characterized the third phase of Italian migration. Italians from Bisacquino, Sicily, sought their fortunes in the steel mills of Alabama. In 1890 Jefferson County included 130 Italians, a figure that increased to 2,160 by 1920. Italians constituted the largest ethnic group in Alabama, as in Louisiana. In Birmingham they labored as unskilled steelworkers, and, in typical fashion, they organized 13 mutual aid societies and branched into truck farming and small family enterprises.

Tampa, Fla., offered a unique setting for Italian immigrants—Ybor City. Founded in 1886 by the Spanish financier Vicente Martínez Ybor, Ybor City had evolved as the cigar capital of America by 1900, having over 100 cigar factories offering employment to 10,000 Cubans, Spaniards, and Italians. Several thousand Sicilians, after abandoning an ill-fated sugar colony at St. Cloud, Fla., arrived in Tampa between 1882 and 1920. In Ybor City they learned Spanish, rolled cigars, flirted with and embraced radical ideologies, organized unions, participated in a series of strikes, and eventually achieved an impressive amount of economic mobility as grocers, dairymen, and fruit vendors.

The second- and third-generation Italian Americans' migration to the Sunbelt, especially Florida, constitutes the fourth—and still active—phase. A number of salient trends appear in the developmental stage. Cities without historic Italian immigrant communities, such as Atlanta and Miami, have attracted thousands of Italian Americans in recent years. These midwestern and northeastern migrants have imported their social and cultural institutions, and today organizations such as the Sons of Italy and the National Italian American Foundation can be found throughout the South.

See also URBANIZATION: / New Orleans; Tampa

Gary R. Mormino
University of South Florida

Alexander De Conde, *Half Bitter, Half Sweet: An Excursion into Italian-American History* (1971); Jean Scarpaci, *Italian Immigrants in Louisiana's Sugar Parishes* (1981).

Jews

Southerners have often stereotyped Jews as "eternal aliens" who refuse to weave themselves into the fabric of southern culture. They largely have been ignored as newcomers who have not made any meaningful contribution to southern society.

Jews, however, are not new to the South. In 1800, for example, Charleston, S.C., had one of the largest Jewish populations in America; over 1,000 lived in South Carolina alone. For over 300 years Jews, individually and in small groups, have established themselves throughout the region in a myriad of cities, towns, and villages, some of which they helped to establish. Indeed, until the post–Civil War period, the centers of American Jewish life and the sources of many social, cultural, and religious institutional changes shaping the character of all American Jewry were found in Charleston and in Savannah, Ga., which had gathered a Jewish community as early as 1733. Not only did Jews living in the South set the course for American Jewish tradition by leading the Jewish Reform Movement, they helped mold southern traditions as well.

Though Jews never comprised more than 1 percent of the South's population, few phases of the southern experience and few places in the South escaped their influence. Individuals such as Mordecai Sheftall of Savannah and Francis Salvador of Charleston stood among the southern leadership during the American Revolution. After the Revolution, Jews such as Abraham Mordecai, who is credited with founding Montgomery, Ala., moved westward, occasionally joining other Jews who had been living along the Mississippi since the early 18th century. David Yulee of Florida and Judah P. Benjamin of Louisiana were instrumental in bringing their territories into the Union and later were no less influential in taking their states out of it.

Having crossed vast chasms of culture, Jews adopted not only southern folkways, but the full range of political opinions and passions of their Gentile neighbors as well. Jews such as Rabbi Maximillian Michelbacher of Richmond could be counted among the defenders of all southern institutions including slavery. Not only did Jews fight in the Confederate regiments, they assumed positions within the Confederate military and political

A rabbi, Alamo, Ga., c. 1854

leadership, including the offices of surgeon general, judge advocate, quartermaster general, and secretary of state.

After the Civil War, Jews contributed significantly to the recovery of the South. They started as peddlers and shopkeepers, and many rose to the ranks of the most prominent and influential businessmen. Outstanding examples were the Rich brothers in Georgia, the Sanger brothers as well as Neiman and Marcus in Texas, Godchaux in Louisiana, Psitz in Alabama, the Maas brothers in Florida, and the Levine brothers in North Carolina. Jews assumed an active role in their communities' social and civic life, thereby continuing a tradition begun by Mordecai Sheftall when he helped to establish Savannah's Union Society, one of the first charitable and interfaith ventures in the United States. As leaders, Jews became involved in all branches of government at the local, state, and national level. Adolph Ochs, who was from Chattanooga, developed the *New York Times* into the great American newspaper; his mother, Bertha, was a charter member of Chattanooga's United Daughters of the Confederacy.

To be sure, the anti-Semitism that southerners inherited as part of Christian culture appeared sporadically in the form of quotas, social restrictions, and strong words. Exclusion could be found from the Mardi Gras in New Orleans to the local country clubs. Nevertheless, the active involvement of Jews, past and present, in southern culture shows that the South has not been a monocultural society, existing apart from the American melting pot. Nor, with a very few notable exceptions such as the Leo Frank case in Georgia, has it been an altogether violent, savage place in which minorities live fearfully at the mercy of drunken white bigots. In South Carolina, for example, Jews experienced real freedom after over a millennium of religious, civil, and political persecution. Georgia can boast of having elected David Emanuel in 1801 as the country's first Jewish state governor, and Florida sent David Yulee to Congress as the country's first Jewish senator. Some Jews even saw the South as a possible homeland for their people. The "Galveston Project" in the early 20th century helped send more than 10,000 eastern European immigrants into the region as a base for future growth, and earlier, in the 1880s, a much smaller group tried to establish a Jewish communal colony in Sicily Island, La. Jews in the South, in short, have reflected, and added to, the region's overall complexities.

See also LAW: / Frank, Leo, Case; URBANIZATION: / Charleston; Savannah

Louis E. Schmier
Valdosta State College

Leonard Dinnerstein and Mary Dale Palson, eds., *Jews in the South* (1973); Eli Evans, *The Provincials: A Personal History of the Jews in the South* (1974); Nathan Kagnoff and Melvin Urofsky, eds., *"Turn to the South": Essays on Southern Jewry* (1979); Carolyn Lipson-Walker, "Shalom Y'all: The Folklore and Folk Traditions of Southern Jews" (Ph.D. dissertation, Indiana University, 1986); Louis E. Schmier, ed., *Reflections of Southern Jewry: The Letters of Charles Wessolowsky, 1878–1879* (1982).

Lumbees

Lumbee Indians are the largest tribe east of the Mississippi River; they are also the largest federally unrecognized tribe in the United States. More than 40,000 Lumbee live in Robeson and adjoining counties in southeastern North Carolina.

The origin of the Lumbee people is cloaked in mystery, but some scholars trace the Lumbee ancestry to the Cherokee, the Tuscarora, and the eastern Sioux. Many historians support the "Lost Colony Theory." According to this view, the Lumbee are descendants of John White's Lost Colony who left Roanoke Island between 1587 and 1590. These people probably mixed with the Hatteras Indians who lived near Roanoke. Historian Samuel Eliot Morison believed that the dangers and difficulties on Roanoke Island led the Lost Colony settlers to move among the friendly natives of Croatan, near Cape Hatteras. They probably found few supplies on the Outer Banks, and around 1650 the Croatan tribe likely migrated to southeastern North Carolina. Scotsmen began to arrive in 1730 in what is presently Robeson County, where they found a mixed Indian-white group living like Europeans.

The Lumbee, a nonreservation people, were free prior to 1835, when the revised North Carolina constitution disfranchised free Negroes and mulattoes. The Lumbee were also deprived of their political and civil rights because they were not white and were regarded as dangerous. A number of Lumbees served in the Continental army during the Revolutionary War and fought in the War of 1812, but during the Civil War the Lumbee were denied the right to fight as soldiers. Many were taken, however, to Fort Fisher, N.C., where they worked as forced laborers. Knowing working conditions there were intolerable, some Lumbee refused to leave their homes for the infested swamps at the fort. At the beginning of the war the Indians of Robeson County favored the Confederacy, but by the end of 1863 they had come to view the government as oppressive. Allen Lowrie, a Lumbee, had 10 sons and all refused to serve the Confederacy as laborers at Fort Fisher, although, if given the opportunity, they would have been willing to serve as soldiers. On 3 March 1865 Allen Lowrie and his son William were shot by soldiers. According to Lumbee legend, they were forced to dig their own graves. Allen Lowrie's 18-year-old son, Henry Berry, witnessed the killing of his father and brother. Seeking justice, he imposed a reign of terror on the whites of Robeson County that continued for the next 10 years. The Lowrie War had its impact for decades to come. Today an outdoor drama, "Strike at the Wind," portrays the folk hero Henry Berry Lowrie.

In 1885 the General Assembly of North Carolina passed an act to provide for separate schools for the Croatan Indians of Robeson County. The segregated school system continued until the 1960s. As a result of the law, Croatan Indian Normal School was established in 1887, the forerunner of Pembroke State University. Today it has an enrollment of more than 2,000 students with 65 percent white, 20 percent Indian, and 15 percent black.

In the 1880s the Lumbees also formally organized churches, although they had been following Christian teachings for over a century. The Burnt Swamp Baptist Association became the chief church group among members of the tribe; in the 1980s Methodist, Holiness, Assembly of God, and other churches are also found.

From the 1880s to World War I, Lumbees from Robeson County went to Georgia to work in the turpentine industry, but by 1917 most had returned to North Carolina. Lumbees served in the armed services during World War I, but they returned home to farm cotton, corn, or tobacco. During the Great Depression most Lumbees were tenant farmers, day laborers, Works Progress Administration workers, or landlords renting out their own land. The migration to cities like Baltimore and Detroit that had begun earlier increased during World War II. Those who remained in North Carolina faced intimidation in the 1950s from the Ku Klux Klan, although Lumbee protesters broke up a Klan demonstration in 1958 and showed increasing assertiveness of their rights thereafter.

Today, most Lumbees in North Carolina are farmers,

with flue-cured tobacco the chief money crop. Increasing interest in Indian heritage is seen in Pembroke's "Indian Day" homecoming on 4 July.

Adolph L. Dial
Pembroke State College

Adolph L. Dial and David Elidades, *The Only Land I Know: A History of the Lumbee Indians* (1975), and in *Indians of the Lower South: Past and Present*, ed. John Mahon (1975); W. McKee Evans, *To Die Game: The Story of the Lowry Band, Indian Guerrillas of Reconstruction* (1971).

Mexicans

Mexican Americans (Chicanos) live in every southern state. However, their greatest impact on the South has been in Texas, where they number over 3 million, make up more than 20 percent of the state's population, and comprise some 30 percent of the national Mexican-descent population. More than half the residents of such Texas cities as Brownsville, El Paso, Laredo, and San Antonio are Mexican Americans, who are also growing in number throughout the entire South.

The average Mexican American is young, Roman Catholic, bilingual in English and Spanish, and native born in the United States to parents themselves born in this country. Chicanos are about seven years younger than the national average, and approximately 90 percent belong to the Catholic church. English is the primary language of Chicanos, but an estimated 75 percent speak (but do not necessarily read) Spanish, and about half use Spanish at home.

Mexican Americans entered southern life in two ways—through annexation and through immigration. They first became part of the South via the emergence of the Republic of Texas. In 1822 Americans, mainly southerners, began to settle in the northeastern corner of Mexico, which had just won its independence from Spain. Mexico hoped these immigrants would become a loyal, integral part of Mexican society. However, in 1835, supported by some native Mexicans who also opposed the central government, the settlers revolted and in 1836 established the independent Lone Star Republic. When the Republic joined the United States as the state of Texas in 1845, the 5,000 Mexicans in Texas became the South's and the nation's first large group of Mexican Americans.

Although Mexicans first entered the South through annexation, their ranks have expanded both through relatively high birth rates, compared to other Americans, and through continuous immigration. In contrast to most other immigrants into the United States, Mexicans have not had to cross an ocean. The 2,000-mile Mexican border with the United States has generally functioned more as an avenue than as an obstacle, with people constantly flowing back and forth across the frontier, including the long, winding Rio Grande River, which forms the Mexico-Texas border.

Mexican immigration during the second half of the 19th century was relatively modest. However, that immigration trickle turned into a flood as a result of the 1910 Mexican Revolution, which drove thousands of Mexicans north for sanctuary in the United States. At the same time, growing economic opportunities in this country, including Texas, attracted Mexicans. Immigration increased through World War I and the 1920s. The coming of the Great Depression and the drastically reduced job market in this country sharply curtailed Mexican immigration and led to the Repatriation Program, through which some 500,000 persons of Mexican descent were voluntarily or involuntarily shuttled to Mexico. The end of the Great Depression and the start of World War II brought another migration reversal, establishing a pattern of major Mexican immigration into the United States that continues to the present.

Within the Mexican American experience, Texas has held a special place. On the negative side, Mexican-Americans in Texas have traditionally had some of the lowest indices among Mexican Americans nationally, in such areas as jobs, income, poverty, and educational attainment. Moreover, discrimination against Mexican Americans has taken harsher and more virulent tones in Texas than in most other parts of the country, partly as a result of the strife-ridden beginnings of the state's Anglo-Mexican relations during the Texas war for independence.

On the positive side, Texas Mexican Americans have taken a strong leadership role within the Chicano community nationally. For example, such major national Chicano organizations as the League of United Latin American Citizens and the American G.I. Forum began in Texas, as did the Partido de la Raza Unida (PRU—United People's Party), formed in Crystal City, Tex., by José Angel Gutiérrez. *La Prensa* of San Antonio, founded in 1913, is the oldest Chicano newspaper still operating.

Texas has also been a launching pad for Mexican Americans who work in the agricultural migrant stream, which stretches into the Midwest and the Pacific Northwest. Spreading throughout the nation in this way, tens of thousands of Texas Chicanos have settled around the country. There they have formed *barrios* (communities or neighborhoods) of transplanted Texas Chicano society and culture.

The core of Chicano society is the *familia* (extended family). Mexican Americans generally have a strong sense of familial, rather than merely individual, identity, and individuals feel a deep sense of family obligation. Moreover, particularly in traditional Chicano families, the roles of the father, mother, children, grandparents, and other relatives are more sharply defined than is the norm in the contemporary United States. One special feature of Chicano family life is the practice of *compadrazgo* (godparentage), which involves the assumption of serious obligations toward godchildren.

Chicanos have contributed to southern culture in many ways, ranging from tacos to *teatro* (theater). Texas Mexican Americans have been in the forefront of the development of Chicano literature and visual arts. San Antonio has been the site of the annual national Chicano Film Festival. In a more popular vein, Mexican food—especially such popular dishes as tacos, tostadas, enchiladas, carnitas, and tamales—has increasingly become a feature of southern life.

The many varieties of Chicano music include that unique southern form, the Tex-Mex music of south Texas (also known as *conjunto* or *música norteña*). An outgrowth of early 20th-century Chicano contact with the music of German Americans, particularly in New Braunfels, Tex., Tex-Mex music has evolved over the years as Chicanos have added their own instrumentation and musical variations to the basic German polka rhythm. Traditional Tex-Mex *polkeros* still feature the accordion and bass. However, more contemporary Tex-Mex groups use horns, drums, and electric instruments, integrate jazz, rock, and country-and-western elements, and sometimes use lyrics to portray and comment on the Chicano experience.

Chicanos are becoming an increasingly visible, vocal, and significant part of the South, as well as of the United States as a whole. Possibly the best symbol of the growing importance of Chicanos is the 1981 election of Henry Cisneros as mayor of San Antonio—the largest city ever to be led by a Mexican American.

See also MUSIC: *Música Tejana*; / Jimenez, Flaco; URBANIZATION: / San Antonio; VIOLENCE: / Cortez, Gregorio

Carlos E. Cortés
University of California at Riverside

Rodolfo Acuña, *Occupied America: A History of Chicanos* (1981); Leo Grebler, Joan W. Moore, and Ralph C. Guzmán, *The Mexican-American People: The Nation's Second Largest Minority* (1970); Joan W. Moore with Harry Pachón, *Mexican Americans* (1976).

Mulatto

The term *mulatto* is the most commonly used and the most ambiguous of all the racial designations that have evolved in the Americas. In current usage and in that of certain societies of the past, it broadly denotes anyone with a visible physical mixture of light and dark ancestry. Historically, it was but one of a multiplicity of terms coined to describe almost every conceivable mixture that resulted from the introduction of Europeans and Africans into the Western Hemisphere.

The principal terms that have been used, and their most common definitions, are

MULATTO	½ white	½ black
QUADROON	¾ white	¼ black
OCTOROON	⅞ white	⅛ black
SAMBO	¼ white	¾ black
SACATRA	⅛ white	⅞ black
MESTIZO	½ white	½ Indian

Even in Catholic New World societies, where infant baptismal registrations have been customary for centuries, the application of racial terms has been exceedingly imprecise. Exact genetic mixtures have often been difficult to identify, and popular confusion has existed over the meaning of many of the terms. Mulatto, as previously indicated, was corrupted to include sundry mixtures of black and white as well as, on occasion, those of mixed Indian-white ancestry.

Synonymous with the word *octoroon* there developed *sang-melée*, which literally translates as "mixed blood"; both were convenient terms to denote individuals whose darker color was but barely visible. *Mestizo* evolved into *mustée*, which in early Anglo-America was popularly used to denote a mixture of black and Indian. Yet another term, *griffe*, was variously used as a synonym for *sambo* or—like mustée—applied to those of mixed Indian-black heritage. In popular usage within historical documents, such terms as mulatto are frequently followed by the phrase "in color," indicating that appearance rather than precise genetic mixture was the criteria for racial designation.

Application of the term *mulatto* to individuals or families of African ancestry has traditionally continued as long as a visible mixture remains. The application of special racial designations to those of Native American descent has been less rigorous; individuals of less than one-half Indian blood have more commonly been identified with the color of the society in which they mingled, and the term *mulatto* is seldom applied to them in current usage.

Gary B. Mills
University of Alabama

Gary B. Mills, *The Forgotten People: Cane River's Creoles of Color* (1977); D. Jose F. Pujol, *Guia del Propietario de Terrenos, Poseedores y Denunciantes de Baldios* (1879); Joel Williamson, *New People: Miscegenation and Mulattoes in the United States* (1980).

Okies

Throughout the 20th century the migration of white southerners to the industrial regions of the North and West has served to highlight cultural distinctions between the South and the rest of the United States. The experience of southerners who settled in the Great Lakes industrial belt and formed quasi-ethnic "hillbilly" enclaves there is well known. Less well understood is the parallel experience of white southerners who moved westward to California during the 1930s and 1940s.

The so-called Dust Bowl migration of Okies and Arkies to California during the Great Depression marked the first large-scale introduction of southern whites into that state. Drawn by attractive images of life in California, and fleeing economic hardship in the cities and farms of the western South, more than 400,000 people left their homes in Oklahoma, Texas, Arkansas, and Missouri during the 1930s and headed west. They were followed during the subsequent decade by at least 600,000 more migrants. But it was the initial Dust Bowl migration that proved decisive. Arriving in California at a time of severe economic and political crisis, the first wave of migrants triggered a reaction that set the stage for the emergence of a distinct Okie subculture in California.

Californians responded with unexpected hostility to the Dust Bowl migrants. Their central concern was economic: the newcomers seemed to pose a threat to scarce jobs and resources. But the intensity of the Californians' response showed that the migrants were also perceived as culturally alien. Their southern accents, their style of dress, and their extreme poverty set them visibly apart from the native population, who treated them as an inferior ethnic group. Disregarding the diversity of their origins, Californians labeled all the newcomers Okies and heaped upon them the kind of abuse and prejudice normally reserved for non-whites and foreign immigrants.

That prejudice provided the context for a separate Okie social life in California. Drawing together defensively, many of the migrants settled in separate neighborhoods called "little Oklahomas," where they set up their own Southern Baptist and Pentecostal churches, listened to "hillbilly music," and remained for the most part alienated from the larger population. In that way an Okie subculture based on values and institutions brought from the western South gradually took shape in California. In time, the term *Okie* took on a new and more positive significance as former migrants learned to embrace their separate status and express an aggressive sense of pride in their southern heritage. Today, nearly a half century later, most of the differences between Okies and natives have disappeared, but evidence of a separate subculture survives. In certain California communities the children and even grandchildren of former migrants still speak with distinctly southern accents and talk proudly of what it means to be an Okie.

James N. Gregory
University of California, Berkeley

James N. Gregory, "The South Moves West: The Dust Bowl Migration and the Emergence of an Okie Subculture in California" (Ph.D. dissertation, University of California, Berkeley, 1983); Walter J. Stein, *California and the Dust Bowl Migration* (1973); John Steinbeck, *The Grapes of Wrath* (1939).

Scotch-Irish

The Scotch-Irish are usually thought of as descendants of Lowland Presbyterians who settled on the "Plantations" established in the north Ireland province of Ulster by James I in 1609. Actually, Scots from the Hebrides had been in Ulster for many centuries before that; they constituted a Celtic subculture that was neither quite Irish nor Scottish. By the early 19th century they had become the industrious and frugal Presbyterians of the stereotype, but their massive migrations to America had taken place earlier. Scotch-Irish filled the southern backcountry from the late 17th century until the Revolution, and there they were able to retain many of their ancient ways. As much as any group, they stamped the South with its enduring traits. They have been characterized as a leisurely folk who preferred herding to tillage, telling tall tales to accomplishing, talking and listening to reading and writing; they have been seen as improvident and disdainful of accumulating worldly goods; they were said to be violent and tending toward extremes of apathy or enthusiasm in politics as in religion; they appeared at once clannish and hospitable, oriented toward the extended family rather than toward an abstract community.

Upwards of 250,000 Scotch-Irish migrated to America before the Revolution. Many went to the Carolinas and some went to upper New England, but most landed in Philadelphia, whence they moved southwestward in a steady stream. From 1776 until the end of the 19th century they comprised the largest single ethnic group in the white population of the southern interior. During the Revolution they were fiercely anti-English, as they had always been, and they provided a disproportionate share of the soldiers in the Continental army—as they would do in all America's wars during the 19th century. They had the reputation of being fearless, impetuous, and undisciplined soldiers. In politics, never having acquired the English habit of obedience to central authority, they were intensely local-minded. Most therefore opposed ratification of the federal Constitution, and they formed the backbone of the Jeffersonian Republican party and, later, the Jacksonian Democratic party.

See also MYTHIC SOUTH: / Celtic South

Grady McWhiney
Texas Christian University

Forrest McDonald
University of Alabama

R. J. Dickson, *Ulster Emigration to Colonial America, 1719–1775* (1966); James G. Leyburn, *The Scotch-Irish: A Social History* (1962).

Scots, Highland

The first appreciable settlement of Highland Scots in the South began in North Carolina in 1732. During the next three decades they trickled in; after 1763 the flow became a great wave. Between then and 1775 probably 20,000 (of a total of 25,000 coming to America) settled in the South, half or more in North Carolina. At first the Highlanders lived in compact areas isolated from others, and they preserved their accustomed ways. During the American Revolution they were Loyalists almost to a man; in Virginia, Loyalists were referred to as "the Scotch party." After the war many left for Florida, the West Indies, or Nova Scotia, but they were more than replaced by a new wave of immigrants: perhaps another 25,000 Highlanders migrated to the South between 1783 and 1789. In 1790 Scots constituted a fifth to a third of the white population in the southern states, though most of these were doubtless Scotch-Irish. One more wave was yet to come: during the five years after the Napoleonic Wars, between 5,000 and 10,000 Highlanders settled in northwestern Alabama and northeastern Mississippi.

Historically, western Highlanders had moved back and forth between the Hebrides and Ulster, north Ireland, home of the "Scotch-Irish," and culturally the two were virtually indistinguishable. In the American South both continued to live much as they had in the Old World, preserving a leisurely lifestyle based on open-range animal husbandry and a minimum of crop raising. As the population moved westward, they usually led the way, with the result that perhaps half the people in the trans-Appalachian and Gulf Coast South were of Highland Scots or Scotch-Irish extraction.

Scottish influence remains in the modern South through family names, remnants of the language, a few folk festivals celebrating customs, such as The Highland Games and Gathering of Scottish Clans at Grandfather Mountain, N.C., and a simple consciousness in some people of the ethnic identity.

Grady McWhiney
Texas Christian University

Forrest McDonald
University of Alabama

Ian C. C. Graham, *Colonists from Scotland: Emigration to North America, 1707–1783* (1956); John P. MacLean, *A Historical Account of the Settlements of Scotch Highlanders in America Prior to the Peace of 1783* (1978); Duane Meyer, *The Highland Scots of North Carolina* (1961).

Seminoles

The Seminole Indians of Florida have historically presented a unique enclave of tribal-traditional culture within the broader context of southern society. Yet these seemingly changeless people have proven highly successful in modifying aspects of their lifestyle to accommodate major shifts in the milieu.

The Seminoles were originally constituent elements of the Creek nation who had migrated southward to Spanish Florida during the early 18th century. The tribal name is derived from the Creek term *simano-li* (after the Spanish *cimarrones*) meaning "wild, runaway" as applied to plants or animals. It was extended to identify those Indians who went to live in the wild country or frontier. The Seminole towns, actually independently governed kinship units, moved primarily to escape political domination by the Creeks, as well as to avoid the encroachment by white settlers from the seaboard. In Florida they developed a prosperous lifestyle based on their Creek cultural origins. They retained a highly developed town life and distinctive sociopolitical organization, augmented their basic agriculture with extensive cattle herds, and perpetuated traditional ceremonies such as the Green Corn Dance as a source of spiritual values and social cohesiveness.

The Seminoles also evolved new cultural patterns that set them apart from other tribes—and often placed them at odds with southern whites. In Spanish Florida they were virtually free of the pressures for land, trade, and religious conversion that most southern tribes experienced. This limited culture contact left the Seminoles to develop as a fiercely independent people. During the British period (1763–83) in Florida the Seminoles developed close trade and political ties to the English and supported them in both the Revolutionary War and the War of 1812. The Seminole towns also became havens for runaway slaves from southern plantations. Blacks became fighting allies as well as a source of technological innovation in Seminole life; blacks also incurred the enmity of southern whites who harbored a long-standing fear of an Indian-black alliance.

When Florida became a U.S. territory in 1821, missionary groups did not rush to proselytize the Seminoles in the same manner as they had attempted to transform the Cherokees. Perhaps the Florida tribesmen were perceived as too incorrigibly pro-British, pro-black, and anti-American to live with in peace, or more likely were dismissed as "savages" who were totally unreceptive to "civilizing and Christianizing" influences. In either case, the Seminoles were not afforded an opportunity to assimilate in peace. Caught up in the maelstrom of Jacksonian removal policy, they were forced to choose between fight or flight. Led by Osceola, most Seminoles opted to defend their homeland in a guerrilla war from 1835 to 1842. Another Seminole war occurred from 1855 to 1858, but the U.S. Army gradually captured most of the members of the tribe.

The remaining Seminoles settled in the forbidding swamp and sawgrass region of south Florida known as the Everglades. There they lived in secluded island camps, cultivated subsistence plots, and supplemented this by hunting, fishing, and gathering. In the last quarter of the 19th century, white traders moved to the periphery of the Everglades and carried on a thriving business with the Indians. Moreover, Seminoles were easily accepted

George Catlin, Osceola, the Black Drink, a Warrior of Great Distinction *(1838)*

in the egalitarian frontier communities that grew up around trading posts at Miami, Fort Lauderdale, and similar locations.

By World War I the social and economic status of the Seminoles had drastically declined. Drainage projects in the Everglades seriously depleted animal life, and the market for pelts and hides collapsed at home and abroad. The arrival of railroads in the 1890s brought waves of settlers who took up lands formerly occupied by Indians. The Seminoles soon became a poverty-stricken, landless minority.

The Great Depression affected the Seminoles as severely as any minority in the South. Fortunately, a federal reservation, which had been opened in 1926, became the locus of relief, employment, and health and education programs for many Indians. By the late 1930s two rural reservations were also opened and became the hub of a Seminole cattle enterprise. These reservations afforded safe havens for the renaissance of tribal life.

The modern era of the Seminole tribe began in the 1950s, when a federal charter was issued allowing them to elect officers and conduct business affairs with government supervision. Today the tribe is virtually self-regulating. Such business enterprises as tax-free cigarette sales and high-stakes bingo games on the reservations have brought negative reaction from many quarters, yet federal courts have upheld the legality of these Seminole ventures. Moreover, as Indian leaders point out, traditional tourist attractions are no longer economically viable in a period of shrinking federal assistance to the tribe. Thus, Seminoles are undergoing yet another transformation as they seek their niche in the modern South.

Harry A. Kersey, Jr.
Florida Atlantic University

Harry A. Kersey, Jr., *Pelts, Plumes and Hides: White Traders among the Seminole Indians, 1870–1930* (1975); John Mahon, *History of the Second Seminole War, 1835–1842* (1967); Walter L. Williams, ed., *Southeastern Indians since the Removal Era* (1979).

Spanish

Spain was the first European power to establish and impose a culture upon the aboriginal inhabitants of the American South. Ponce de León's discovery of La Florida in 1513 encouraged the Spanish crown to explore the mainland. Expeditions by *conquistadores*, most notably Narváez and De Soto, ended in tragedy. Spain failed to establish a permanent colony until the founding of St. Augustine in 1565.

Spanish explorers reached as far north as Virginia, and the Spanish presence contributed to the founding of Pensacola, Mobile, and New Orleans. A vigorous Franciscan missionary system across the South added to the Spanish influence. Spain was ultimately unsuccessful in maintaining its empire, ceding Louisiana (which it gained in 1763) to France in 1800 and Florida to the United States in 1821. Another area of the modern South, Texas, remained a part of the Spanish borderlands until Mexican independence in 1821.

Despite the inability to sustain settlements in the United States, Spanish culture infused the South with a distinctive spirit. Spanish ways influenced the legal systems, land-use patterns, traditions of self-government, and economic affairs of states like Louisiana, Texas, and Florida, which were once under Spanish control. Spain's Roman Catholicism provided the first European religious influence on the southern landscape. New Orleans, after the fire of 1788, was rebuilt in the Spanish design, characterized by wrought-iron grillwork, shaded patios, arcades, and fountains. The Spanish also added to the cosmopolitan nature of Louisiana, most notably in the Delta, where Isleños from the Canary Islands farmed in settlements such as New Iberia. Today the Spanish language in Louisiana survives only on the Delacroix Islands.

Spanish settlements were rare on the eve of the Civil War; only Louisiana claimed more than 1,000 Spanish immigrants. Beginning in the 1850s, the pace of Spanish emigration quickened due to economic, political, and diplomatic tensions, as Spain wished to increase its loyalist population abroad. Key West emerged as a significant refuge during the Ten Years War in Cuba, 1868–78. A number of Spanish cigar manufacturers relocated their beleaguered factories in Key West, creating a thriving

American institution with the skills imported from Cuba and Spain.

Later, during the mass influx of "new" immigrants, 1890–1921, relatively few Spaniards entered the United States, and even fewer migrated to the South. Spain encouraged emigration to its own colonies, especially Cuba, and Florida became a safety valve for Hispanics on that island. Tampa, Fla., evolved into the greatest Spanish-American enclave outside New York City. In 1885 Vicente Martínez Ybor and Ignacio Haya, after considering offers from Galveston, Mobile, and Pensacola, chose Tampa as the new center for their cigar industry. Ybor City, organized as a company town in 1886 and soon incorporated into Tampa, attracted thousands of Latin *taba-queros* (Spanish, Cubans, and Italians). By 1900 over 1,000 Spanish workers had settled in Tampa, providing the organizing genius for the city's 100 cigar factories. In contrast, the next largest Spanish center in the South was New Orleans, with 493 Spaniards. By 1920 almost 4,000 Spaniards (and 5,000 Cubans) had created a cohesive Latin culture in Tampa.

Spaniards transplanted to Tampa their traditions from the homeland. In 1887 Spanish doctors organized *La Iguala*, the first of many medical cooperatives in Tampa; these group enterprises aroused antipathy from the American medical establishment. Spaniards also erected magnificent clubhouses to house their mutual aid societies, Centro Español and Centro Asturiano. These societies provided complete medical care with the erection of modern hospitals amid a thriving cultural milieu. During the Spanish-American War in 1898, the U.S. Army took over Centro Español. During the New Deal, the only Spanish-language theater sponsored by the WPA was in Ybor City. The stringent immigration quotas imposed in 1924 severely curtailed the Spanish population flow to America, an act especially injurious to the Spanish because of the imbalance of men over women.

A small but forceful group of Spanish anarchists coalesced in Ybor City between the 1890s and 1920s, serving as social critics and intellectual leaders. They supplied a class ideology that helped shape a labor consciousness of lasting power. Moreover, through their clubs, newspapers, educational work, and debating forums, they articulated a leftist orientation to the social problems of the day. By the 1920s the radical edge of the Ybor City labor movement had dulled. The labor wars of attrition had taken their toll, as had vigilante police tactics, especially evident during the long strikes of 1901, 1910, and 1920 and the Red Scare, 1918–19.

See also URBANIZATION: / Tampa

Gary R. Mormino
University of South Florida

R. A. Gomez, *The Americas* (July 1962); *Southern Folklore Quarterly* (1937–41) for articles pertaining to Spanish folkways in Tampa; Glenn Westfall, "Don Vicente Martínez Ybor, the Man and His Empire: The Development of the Clear Havan Industry in Cuba and Florida" (Ph.D. dissertation, University of Florida, 1977).

Syrians and Lebanese

Ninety percent of the population of Syrians and Lebanese in the South is Christian and 10 percent Muslim. The Christian sects include the Maronites, the Melktines, and the Chaldean Catholics (affiliated with Rome) as well as the Eastern Orthodox and numerous Protestant groups. Most of the original Arab immigrants, who arrived between 1878 and 1948, were from the Syrian Province of the Ottoman Empire, which included the Mt. Lebanon district. They called themselves Syrians, identifying more specifically in terms of their region of origin, native village, or religious sect. The term *Lebanese* was not used until the independent republic of Lebanon was created in 1946.

Among the earliest immigrants to the United States from Syria were those who escorted a shipment of camels purchased by the federal government to help facilitate travel in the undeveloped Southwest. On 14 May 1856 a cargo ship, the *Supply*, brought the first 33 camels to Indianola, Tex. The camels adjusted to the varying climatic conditions and continued to be used in the Southwest until 1875.

The Arbeely family, who became known as the first family to immigrate to this country from Syria, arrived in 1878 and spent the next three years in the South. Two sons remained in Austin, Tex., when the rest of the family moved to New York. Two of Dr. Arbeely's sons later founded the first Arabic language newspaper in the United States called *Kowbab Amerika* (The Star of America).

Most Syrian and Lebanese immigrants were unskilled laborers and farmers. They came hoping to earn money quickly and then return home. Some returned to Lebanon or Syria temporarily but most remained in this country. A network was quickly established that attracted relatives and others from a native village to a particular city here.

The concentrations of Syrians and Lebanese in the South developed slowly but otherwise followed the general patterns of American settlement. Early settlers tended to gather temporarily in colonies, with sizable communities existing only in cities. Significant concentrations remain in Atlanta, Ga.; Birmingham, Ala.; Miami, Fla.; and New Orleans and Shreveport, La. One reason the South did not attract many Syrians or Lebanese at first was the lack of industrialization. Those who did not establish businesses of their own sought employment in the factory centers of the Northeast and Midwest. During the Depression, because of the lack of business opportunities throughout the United States, almost 50 percent of the Syrian and Lebanese immigrants went to the southern states, where many were able to find farm work.

The Syrian and Lebanese immigrants to the South did not consistently follow the usual economic pattern of initially earning a living by peddling. New Orleans in 1920, for example, had 20 Lebanese peddlers but 15 well-established merchants. Many families operated their own businesses, most of which were economically successful.

Today the Syrians and Lebanese in the South are well integrated into larger communities, although they are generally quite proud of their Syrian and Lebanese backgrounds. Ethnic culture is preserved through clubs and churches. Festivals and holiday celebrations focus on ethnic food and folk music. The most popular foods include *kibbee, tabouli, humous, baba ganouj, baklawa,* and *kahwee.* Two musical instruments used by the Syrian and Lebanese Americans are the *oud,* a stringed instrument related to the lute, and the *dulbeky,* a small drum. Two styles of dancing that have been retained are the *debke* (a line dance) and belly dancing.

Noted Syrian or Lebanese southerners include Dr. Michael DeBakey, Houston heart surgeon; Dr. Adel Yunis, professor of medicine at the University of Miami; U.S. Congressman Abraham Kazen from Texas; Florida State Senator James R. Deeb; and Alan Jabbour, director of the Library of Congress American Folklife Center.

See also SCIENCE AND MEDICINE: / DeBakey, Michael

Dena Shenk
St. Cloud State University

Louise Seymour Houghton, *The Survey* (July–October 1911); Philip M. Kayal and Joseph M. Kayal, *The Syrian-Lebanese in America* (1975), Alix Naff, in *Harvard Encyclopedia of American Ethnic Groups,* ed. Stephen Thernstrom, Ann Orlov, and Oscar Handlin (1980); Afif I. Tannous, *American Sociological Review* (June 1943).

Travelers

Often referred to as "gypsies," the population calling itself the Travelers has quite separate origins from the true Gypsies, the Romani people, yet shares a number of characteristics with them. Living in settlements from Texas to Florida, the Travelers are descendants of Irish and Scottish Traveler families who began to arrive in the South during the 19th century, probably with the influx of Irish forced to leave their land because of famine. Records are scant, but some Irish, and particularly Scottish, Travelers may have arrived even earlier as indentured laborers to the plantations. Each Traveler community, numbering together perhaps 20,000, interacts with others—and with the Romanichal population to some extent—but each staunchly maintains its distinctiveness. Like the Romanichals, Travelers have their own ethnic language and have traditionally engaged in horse trading, paving, and other specific occupations. There are frequent references to the "Irish Travelers" in the southern press, but the most complete studies are those of Jared Harper.

See also FOLKLIFE: / Traders

Ian Hancock
University of Texas at Austin

Ian Hancock, *American Speech* (Fall 1986); Jared Harper, "The Irish Travelers of Georgia" (Ph.D. dissertation, University of Georgia, 1977), *Proceedings of the Southern Anthropological Society* (1972); Edwin Muller, *Reader's Digest* (July 1941); George Ryan, *Ave Maria* (18 March 1967).

Virginia Indians

Virginia's surviving Indians fall into two categories: communities (about 1,200 people) descended from the Powhatan tribes on the Coastal Plain, and scattered mountain populations (size uncertain) whose diverse tribal origins are now lost. All of these groups lack federal recognition as Indians.

The Powhatan Indians encountered large numbers of European settlers earlier than any other North American Indians except the southwestern Pueblos. They have been culturally adjusting since 1607, so their present state may show what the future of other tribes will be.

By 1700 the Powhatan tribes had lost nearly all their land to Europeans. Today, there are only two reservations left in Virginia, with about 125 persons in residence and land totaling some 1,000 acres. However, treaties and reservations are not outdated relics of the past to Virginia's Indians. The Pamunkey and Mattaponi are intensely proud of their treaty of 1677 with Virginia, and they are deeply attached to their communally owned land, even though most of them must commute to work off-reservation and some of them own nearby land privately. These tribesmen are equally at home with private and communal ownership. More importantly, the reservation land has never been owned by non-Indians, so it is "home" in every sense of the word. The nonreservation Indians have continued to live near one another, keeping their sense of community alive. Some of them have occasionally tried to reestablish their lost reservations and treaty rights.

By 1800 all Indian groups in Virginia outwardly resembled their non-Indian neighbors, except for their physical appearance. They farmed, hunted, and fished as they had always done, but now they lived in log cabins or frame houses, spoke only English, and attended the Baptist church. They had adopted these customs gradually, without pressure from government or missionaries. Their apparent assimilation, together with their near-landlessness, protected them from any attempt at removal to Oklahoma, but ever since 1800 they have had to face charges that they are not "real Indians" anymore.

Rumor, in the absence of reliable documents, classed them as Afro-Americans.

Virginia was like the rest of the nation in her attitudes toward non-whites and like the rest of the South in her willingness to translate these attitudes into law. Virginia's Indian-descended people had to defend their civil rights by fighting against the "free black" label before the Civil War and against the "colored" label afterward. For nearly a century after the war, Virginia society became increasingly segregated and polarized, and the Indians struggled to establish themselves as a third race. The coastal groups set up their own tribal churches and schools. After 1900 the nonreservation groups formally organized as tribes with state Corporation Commission charters: the Chickahominy (now split into Eastern and Western Bands), the Upper Mattaponi, and the Rappahannock. But credibility remained poor even for the reservation people. The civil rights movement ended much of the harassment, but it also took away those hard-won tribal schools. Recent access to federal ethnic-heritage funding has helped to restore that essential part of the modern "Indian" identity.

Today's Virginia Indians are moderately prosperous country—and now city—folk who remain unique in the state because of their long perspective on American history and their feelings of kinship with Indian people nationwide.

Helen C. Rountree
Old Dominion University

Helen C. Rountree, *The Chesopiean* (June 1972), *Journal of Ethnic Studies* (Fall 1975), in *Southeastern Indians since the Removal Era*, ed. Walter L. Williams (1979).

West Indians

The assimilation of black emigrants from the British West Indies has been complicated by the need to adapt to patterns of racial stratification. Nowhere has this condition been more pronounced than in the southern states. Nevertheless, thousands of West Indian immigrants established homes and found new opportunities in the postbellum South. The flow of West Indians became regular after the Civil War and was directed primarily toward Florida, where 2,189 foreign-born blacks lived in 1880. They formed one stream in a growing migration from the British West Indies that carried newcomers to Michigan, New York, and Massachusetts. Because of its proximity to the island homelands, Florida was a major point of entry from which West Indians fanned out to settle in neighboring states. By 1900 over 7,500 black immigrants, 37 percent of the foreign-born black population, lived in the South Atlantic and South Central states. As the influx continued, the West Indian population in the South Atlantic states alone grew to nearly 13,000 by 1930.

A sizable proportion of the newcomers were skilled workers and most had sufficient schooling to read and write English. Other young adult males came to take jobs in agriculture and construction during the labor shortages of World War I. Over 3,200 laborers from the Bahamas arrived to work on government construction projects in Charleston, S.C., and on the truck farms of Florida's east coast.

Although the West Indian population in the South grew substantially in the early 20th century, West Indians were migrating in greater numbers to the cities of northeastern states such as Massachusetts and New York. Industrial and commercial jobs were more available there than in the South, where the proportion of West Indians employed in rural jobs was 10 times higher than in the Northeast. Because of the structure of a labor market with rigid racial barriers, the South could not attract as many West Indians as the Northeast. Thus, the share of black immigrants who lived in the southern states shrank from 37 percent in 1900 to 15 percent by 1930.

The group life of West Indians in the South was profoundly affected by proximity to the home islands. The West Indian community of Florida provides a valuable case study. The relative ease of going home from the peninsula produced a high rate of return migration. A third of all departing black aliens in the 1920s left from Florida.

The migratory flow between the West Indies and Florida kept alive attachments to home-island traditions. Many West Indians worshipped as Episcopalians and revered the British royal family. A study of West Indian immigrant life indicated that the cultural forms persisting strongly after migration were customs relating to death and burial, courtship and marriage, spiritualism, folk narratives, and a semitropical diet. The West Indians stressed and displayed proudly their English traditions, partly to differentiate themselves from native southern blacks and to impress whites with their cultural sophistication. Unwilling to exchange an identity as a British subject for American citizenship under Jim Crow law, West Indians in Florida became naturalized at one-half the rate at which West Indians in New York were becoming citizens.

Even during the post–World War II economic expansion and lessening of racial discrimination, West Indian immigrants avoided permanent settlement in the South. The West Indian population in the South grew only 8 percent from 1960 to 1970, while in the Northeast it more than doubled in size. Unlike the communities of the Northeast, those in the South contained a much higher proportion of transient males, which produced a gender imbalance that limited endogamous family formation. In 1960, while the sex ratio was nearly even among West Indians in the Northeast, West Indian males in the South outnumbered females by three to one. The difficulties of maintaining permanent employment and finding marriage partners may have discouraged newcomers from flocking to the South. Also, West Indian immigrants may have wanted to avoid the pressure of merging with the southern black community, and so chose to settle in Boston or New York City where they could be identified as another immigrant group. Still, by 1970 over 17,000 West Indians had made their homes in the South, and in the subsequent decade newcomers arrived on the currents of legal and illegal migration from the Caribbean. They and their forebears who had settled in the South added to the region a distinctive pattern of racial assimilation in which the conditions of immigration superseded the heritage of slavery as a factor shaping the process of adjustment.

Reed Ueda
Tufts University

Ira Reid, *The Negro Immigrant* (1939); Thomas Sowell, *Race and Economics* (1975); Reed Ueda, in *Harvard Encyclopedia of American Ethnic Groups*, ed. Stephen Thernstrom, Ann Orlov, and Oscar Handlin (1980).

Folklife

WILLIAM FERRIS
University of Mississippi
CONSULTANT

Doris Ulmann photograph of a weaver, Shooting Creek, N.C., 1930s

Folklife

Southern folklife is the heart of southern culture, and its traditions are intimately tied to the region. Southern communities and states define themselves through folklife as do the region's racial and ethnic groups. As southerners increasingly acknowledge their folk roots, they link formal learning at the university with traditions learned in the home. They join the South's written and oral heritage to create a more complete portrait of her culture.

Southern folklife includes music, narrative, and material culture traditions that are passed on orally from generation to generation. These traditions have diverse roots in Anglo-American, Afro-American, ethnic, and Native American cultures. Interest in southern folklife has grown rapidly since the 1940s, when Benjamin A. Botkin's *A Treasury of Southern Folklore* and several other ground-breaking folklife studies were published. Sociologists at the University of North Carolina's Institute for Research in the Social Sciences in the 1930s and 1940s produced pioneering regional studies materials, including such massive works as Howard W. Odum's *Southern Regions of the United States* (1936), which incorporated aspects of southern folklife into a general portrait of the region. Scholarly journals like the *Journal of American Folklore*, which began at the turn of the century, intermittently included articles on southern folklife, and in 1937 the *Southern Folklore Quarterly* provided an important outlet for information on the South and paved the way for later periodicals such as *Mid-South Folklore*, which began in 1973.

During the 1970s the Library of Congress American Folklife Center was launched and sent a team of folklorists to develop a project in Georgia. The National Endowment for the Arts Folk Arts Panel and the National Endowment for the Humanities Special Projects Division provide significant support for folk musicians, festivals, and scholarship in the South, and state folklorists have developed valuable research throughout the region. Also during the 1970s three important folklife projects developed in the South. Foxfire in Rabun Gap, Ga., Appalshop in Whitesburg, Ky., and the Center for Southern Folklore in Memphis, Tenn., did significant work in north Georgia, Kentucky, and Mississippi, respectively. Their films, records, and books have been widely used in the study of southern folklife. In addition, graduate programs in folklife now exist at the University of North Carolina at Chapel Hill, the University of Texas at Austin, and Western Kentucky University at Bowling Green.

Contributions to Southern Folklife. The origins of southern folklife and the cultural contributions of blacks and other racial and ethnic minorities have increasingly been recognized. British-derived contributions to southern folklife have been clear, but the African roots of black folklife were questioned by scholars earlier in this century. In response, Melville Herskovits clearly documented the survival of African folk roots in his classic study, *The Myth of the Negro Past*, which was published in 1942. Since that time extensive research on black music, tales, and folk art and crafts has shown their relationship to Africa; and the study of black folklore has focused predominantly on the South. For example, the 1978 bibliography entitled *Afro-American Folk Culture* lists 1,428 articles and books focusing on the South, as opposed to 375 focusing on non-southern communities. This growing body of research balances the view of the respective contributions Africa and Europe have made to southern folklife. African and European folklife were both reshaped in the South, and the interaction of these black and white traditions created important new styles of music, tales, and art. Blues and country music, for example, influenced each other as black and white musicians shared musical ideas. Scholars are also exploring the contributions of Native Americans to southern culture and their legacy to black and white southerners.

Southern folklife is also the legacy of the southern working class. Poor white and black sharecroppers and factory workers expressed themselves through music, tales, and folk art distinctively different from the music, literature, and art embraced by wealthy black and white classes in the South. Ballads and blues, folktales, and quilts are closely associated with poor whites and blacks, whose cultures are symbolized by the dogtrot and shotgun house, respectively. By contrast, classical music, the novel, and portraiture are associated with wealthy whites and blacks, whose culture is symbolized by the columned Georgian mansion. Though separated in many areas by caste and class, southerners nonetheless established significant cultural exchanges across these lines. Formally taught writers and artists were drawn to and inspired by folk artists and performers whose skills they admired. The result was a merging of southern folk and academic cultures from diverse backgrounds that in time produced extraordinary literary, musical, and artistic achievements in the 20th century.

Understanding how Old World cultures, the American South, and individual artists shape folklife contributes to an appreciation of their diverse influences on southern folk traditions. Many of these traditions are defined through occupational lore. Truckers, railroad engineers, miners, sailors, and cowboys as well as doctors, lawyers, and students all have important folklife traditions. Each group has folksongs, tales, and superstitions that reflect its identity. Sailors' superstitions focus on the weather, while students' superstitions deal with final exams and term papers. Both groups use folk belief to control events that directly affect their lives.

Age is also a major influence on folk tradition. Children, adolescents, adults, and old people develop different bodies of lore based on their stage of life. Children's games are an example of a folklife genre identified with two age groups. In communities where old people have contact with children such games are shared between the old and the young. A grandmother, for example, may recall games she played as a child and teach them to her grandchildren. Ghost stories and lullabies are other forms of folklore that older people use to entertain children. Elders also pass on countless rituals and traditions associated with marriages, births, funerals, holiday celebrations, manners, and social relations. Family photos, diaries, oral histories, and genealogies help preserve families' folkways and strengthen intergenerational ties.

Gender also shapes folklife in significant ways. Quilts are closely associated with the lives of women who make them, and the women's movement has repeatedly acknowledged the contributions—often anonymous—that quilt makers made through their needlework. The folksongs, tales, and crafts of women express a feminine perspective. Female blues singers, for example, complain about their men as predictably as bluesmen sing of their problems with women. Southern women's folklore often derives from the traditional home-centered roles that long defined women's sphere of activity. Folk beliefs about choosing a spouse, bearing children, and maintaining a home have certainly changed in the last several decades, but southern women continue to incorporate elements of folk wisdom even as they forge new family and work patterns.

Oral Lore. The storyteller is a familiar figure in southern culture. Every community has its "crackerbox philosopher" who entertains and teaches through folktales. These folktales are an important part of southern literary and folk heritage. The folk sermon is a narrative form central to the Protestant religious service. Black and white preachers trained "by the spirit" rather than "by the book" lead congregations in both rural and urban communities. They frequently use chanted verse forms to heighten the emotional intensity of their performance. Anointing with oil, faith healing, snake handling, speaking in tongues, and baptism by immersion are at times included in these services. Preachers draw on a rich array of biblical stories and images to illustrate their sermons. Belief in voodoo, which originated in West Africa, has at times influenced black religion and its lore. African belief systems were overlaid with Christian tradition beginning in the early 1800s with the Great Awakening.

Folktales. Folktales tell a fascinating story of southern culture. In trickster tales a small trickster outwits a larger person or animal. Joel Chandler Harris popularized Brer Rabbit, the best-known black trickster, in his *Uncle Remus Tales*. These animal tales evolved from Africa and are still told today. Black tricksters frequently outwit whites in protest tales. The signifying monkey and Stagolee are contemporary black tricksters who appear in long epic poems called toasts. The toast is a highly obscene form popular in prisons and urban black neighborhoods. Both tricksters and the tales in which they appear have been popularized on records by comedian Ruby Ray Moore and in songs such as "King Heroin" by James Brown. Interestingly, Anansi, the spider trickster who is a favorite in African and Caribbean cultures, did not survive in the United States.

The tall tale is a narrative form often associated with Texas and the frontier in which events appear larger than life. In southern tall tales men outrun deer and wrestle alligators and wildcats in displays of uncommon strength and power. A well-known Appalachian cycle of tall tales is known as the Jack tales. In these tales the protagonist, Jack, defeats giants and outwits the Devil. The tales are derived from Europe and offer an interesting comparison to Afro-American tales.

Folktales are a key to understanding southern humor, and popular comedians have developed comic styles based on folk narrative forms. Dick Gregory builds performances using Afro-American trickster tales, while Jerry Clower uses tall tales drawn from his rural white Mississippi roots. Each develops popular humor based on folktales from black and white southern cultures. Their performances demonstrate the humorous appeal of southern folktales to the American public.

Music. Music is the best-known area of southern folklife. Its links to European and African Old World roots and its impact on contemporary music are both important. Musical forms such as the Anglo-American ballad and the Afro-American blues are shaped by Old World traditions, by southern cities and rural communities, and by individual artists who perform them. Anglo-American ballads brought to this country by British colonists have been widely collected in Appalachia and the Deep South. British ballads like "The Unfortunate Rake" reemerged in the South as "St. James Infirmary." The ballad's narrative verse form evolved in country music, which was first recorded on 78 rpm "hillbilly" records by performers like Jimmie Rodgers, who is regarded as the "Father of Country Music." Later Hank Williams, Johnny Cash, Loretta Lynn, and many other country singers popularized country music through their recordings and performances on WSM's Grand Ole Opry in Nashville, Tenn. Hank Williams's songs celebrated the small nightclub, or honky-tonk, as the symbol of a faster urban life and often expressed longing for the simpler ways of the rural South.

Bluegrass is a recent white music sound that develops complicated fingerpicking styles on guitar, mandolin, and banjo. Bill Monroe and the Bluegrass Boys and Lester Flatt and Earl Scruggs have been among the most popular bluegrass performers. Their musical "breakdowns" introduce high-speed runs on instruments in pieces like "Cannonball Special," which is a standard at concerts.

Afro-American blues has an equally rich heritage. With roots in spirituals and work chants, the blues lyric verse form emerged after the Civil War and was first recorded in the 1920s on 78 rpm "race" records. These early country blues recordings featured artists such as Blind Lemon Jefferson and Charley Patton, who performed with acoustic guitars. As blacks from the Mississippi Delta and other areas in the South moved north to Memphis, St. Louis, and Chicago in the 1930s and 1940s, B. B. King, Muddy Waters, Howlin' Wolf, and other artists developed an urban blues with faster rhythms and amplified instruments. B. B. King epitomizes a performance style that individualizes the music's sound. King's blues evolved from African musical roots shaped in the Mississippi Delta where he grew up, and to this tradition King adds his personal style as a blues artist using the distinctive voice of his guitar, Lucille. Both rural and urban blues artists sing of lost love and of racial suffering.

Their music began as one of the few escapes blacks found from their hard labor in the fields and factories of our nation. Like his ancestor the African griot, the bluesman became—and remains—a spokesman for the suffering and the aspirations of his people. Blues reached a large white and black audience in the South in the 1950s through Nashville radio station WLAC, which featured disc jockeys "John R." Richbourg and William T. "Hoss" Allen.

Although jazz has long outgrown its folk roots and modern progressive jazz has become America's most sophisticated popular music, Dixieland jazz is still heard widely. Dixieland is associated with New Orleans, and some of its original performers can still be heard at the city's Preservation Hall nightclub. Jazz funerals are a familiar tradition in New Orleans. When a musician dies, a jazz band plays a slow dirge as mourners march to the cemetery. After the burial the band leaves the cemetery playing fast-tempo pieces, recalling the dying musician's request in the "St. James Infirmary": "Put a jazz band on my tailgate, and let's raise hell as we travel along."

Black and white sacred music evolved from roots in the Great Awakening, when itinerant preachers brought religious music to the South. Four-part, shape-note singing of traditional hymns that were "lined out" was common in black and white congregations. Shaped notes in the form of rectangles, triangles, diamonds, and circles proved a simpler system of reading music and were widely used by singing teachers. These teachers "lined out," or read each line before the group sang it. The shape-note hymns of four-part sacred harp singing are still performed in the Deep South and are being revived in New England, where their roots date back to the revolutionary period.

At the turn of this century a faster paced gospel music emerged and has steadily grown in popularity. Gospel music is often performed by white and black family groups such as the Blackwood Brothers and the Staple Singers. White and black sacred music, like country music and blues, was first recorded on 78 rpm hillbilly and race labels. Today southern gospel music has an enormous appeal and can be heard throughout the nation.

Ethnic folk music reflects the rich diversity of southern cultures. Cajun music of Louisiana and norteño music of Texas are two major southern ethnic musics, and both were performed on 78 rpm records sold to ethnic audiences. These early performances have been reissued by the Library of Congress and commercial record companies on long-playing albums as part of the growing interest in southern ethnic music. Contrary to the melting-pot theory, these recordings clearly show how southern folk music is preserved in the region's ethnic neighborhoods and communities. Contemporary performers such as Dewey Balfa and Flaco Jimenez have brought renewed popularity to these ethnic musical forms.

Southern folk performers thus reshaped their musical heritage from Africa and Europe and created new sounds of country, blues, gospel, and ethnic folk music. Each of these folk musics in turn has had an enormous influence on contemporary American music. Popular traditions of early rock and roll, folk, and rock are heavily influenced by blues and country music. Elvis Presley, Bob Dylan, and the Rolling Stones "covered" pieces by black blues artists that became hit tunes on the popular charts. Michael Jackson's fame is built on his early Motown performances with the Jackson Five, performances heavily influenced by urban blues rhythms and dance styles. Even classical composers such as Aaron Copland and William Grant Still have developed techniques and tunes from southern folk music.

The role of southern places in shaping folk music is particularly interesting. Harlan County, Ky., is famed for its white ballad singers and the South Carolina Sea Islands for their black Gullah culture, while the Mississippi Delta produces an unending stream of blues artists. These areas and, more broadly, the Upland and Lowland South, define culture zones in which black and white folklife varies in distinctive ways. White singers in the Deep South such as Jimmie Rodgers, Hank Williams, and Johnny Cash are heavily influenced by blues because they grew up among, and often learned music from, black people. Their Upland South counterparts such as the Carter Family and Lester Flatt and Earl Scruggs were part of an Upland South region with a smaller black population and a greater British-derived cultural influence than the Deep South.

As performers moved from rural to urban areas, important musical associations with cities developed. Nashville is known for the Grand Ole Opry and its "Nashville sound," while Chicago, the "windy city," is celebrated by urban black singers. Detroit is the home of the Motown sound, and Memphis produced the first rock-and-roll recordings of Elvis Presley on its Sun Record label and important rhythm-and-blues and soul artists on Stax Records. As white and black southerners moved to urban industrial centers beyond the South, they carried country and blues musical traditions with them. Their neighborhoods in Chicago, Cincinnati, and other cities represent a southern diaspora in which the region's music continued to thrive. The Chicago urban blues, for example, is closely tied to the Mississippi Delta, where many of its musicians were born.

Since the 1950s, organizers of folk music festivals throughout the South have rediscovered older performers and have encouraged young artists to continue their musical traditions. Many southern musicians were first recorded by folklife field-workers such as John A. and Alan Lomax, who traveled in the South and gathered large folksong collections, which are deposited in the Library of Congress Archive of Folk Song. Since its establishment in 1928 distinguished scholars have directed the Archive's efforts to collect and study folksong. Through their efforts, the Archive has produced over 60 long-playing records, many of which feature Native American, Afro-American, Anglo-American, and ethnic music from the American South.

While field-workers like the Lomaxes gathered and studied folksongs, the record industry issued thousands of commercial folk recordings dating from the 1920s. Afro-American "race," white "hillbilly," and ethnic commercial records are a significant complement to folksong archives. Commercial issues were often recorded by field units of companies like RCA that traveled to remote southern areas in search of undiscovered performers.

An important tie developed between southern folk music and southern social change as labor and civil rights leaders repeatedly used southern folk music to support their causes. In the 1940s folksingers like Leadbelly and Aunt Molly Jackson drew widespread support through their music and influenced young white musicians such as Pete Seeger and Bess Lomax Hawes, who sang with the Weavers and the Almanac Singers. This music was chronicled by *Sing Out!* magazine and appeared on the Folkways label issued by Moses Asch. During the 1960s the civil rights movement mobilized popular support with the folksong "We Shall Overcome," and gifted black vocalists such as Bernice Johnson Reagon organized the Student Nonviolent Coordinating Committee's Freedom Singers in support of the movement. The folk music revival of the 1960s also established a national audience for southern protest songs popularized by Joan Baez and Bob Dylan. As Americans turned to their musical roots, southern performers at the Newport Jazz and Smithsonian Folklife festivals grew in popularity. These and small regional festivals in the South continue to be an important public platform for southern folk music.

Because of recent discographies, studies of the recording industry, and large record collections, commercial recordings now are a major resource for study of southern folksong. Important archives of these recordings can be found in the South at the Country Music Foundation in Nashville, the Blues Archive at the University of Mississippi in Oxford, the Tulane Jazz Archives in New Orleans, and the John Edwards Memorial Foundation at the University of North Carolina at Chapel Hill.

A distinguished body of international research on southern music has encouraged further folk-music scholarship, the development of institutional archives, and federal support for both scholarly study and performances. A jazz appreciation movement began in Europe shortly after World War I, and for several decades the systematic collection of jazz records and the publication of works and periodicals devoted to the music took place almost exclusively in Europe. While Alfons Dauer in Austria analyzed African polyphony and rhythm in jazz in his *Der Jazz* (1958), Paul Oliver in England expanded blues scholarship through *Blues Fell This Morning* (1960), *Screening the Blues* (1968), and *The Story of the Blues* (1969). The Institut für Jazzforschung in Graz, Austria, and the *Folk Music Year Book* in England reflect the continuing European interest in southern folk music.

Material Culture. Southern houses, barns, folk art, and crafts—known as material culture—have been increasingly studied by folklorists over the past three decades. Much of this work is based on models developed by European folklife scholars whose extensive study of material culture is developed in open-air museums. Building on this European research, scholars study house types such as the dogtrot and shotgun and their respective roots in Europe and Africa. By measuring and photographing structures and their locations across the southern landscape, one learns how architecture is influenced by and in turn defines the American South. The cabin, for example, may be built with stones or logs depending on its location.

Rural barn, Hickory Flat, Miss., 1968

Folk crafts such as basketmaking also vary in pattern and material as the location and ethnic culture of their makers change. White-oak baskets made by whites in Appalachia, pine needle baskets made by blacks in the Georgia Sea Islands, and cane baskets made by Choctaws in Mississippi demonstrate how patterns and materials can vary.

Craftspeople learn their skills through apprenticeship with older members of their community. Their traditions are often maintained within families through father-son or mother-daughter relationships, which quilter Pecolia Warner describes as "fireplace training." Recycling of used materials is common in folk crafts as old clothing is reused to make quilts and automobile tires are transformed into planters for flowers in the yard. Both function and aesthetic change when such materials are recycled by the folk artist.

Stoneware pottery has often been produced in southern communities by the same families for generations. Potters' kilns and wares were once familiar throughout the region, and many potters are now reviving the tradition. "Face jugs" made by the Meaders family in north Georgia have been a favorite topic for folklife scholars and filmmakers. These face jugs and other southern stoneware pottery are now prominently displayed in folk art collections throughout the nation.

Quilts are the most colorful example of southern folk crafts. Quilts made by southern whites present a more controlled design than the asymmetrical Afro-American "crazy" quilts with their juxtaposition of bright primary colors such as red and yellow. In each tradition the quilter uses stitched bits and pieces of cloth to evoke colorful images. Events from both biblical and community history are often included in quilts, and quilted blocks at times present a narrative sequence of events that range from literal to abstract images.

Afro-American paintings, clay sculpture, and carved walking canes frequently use the snake motif, which is known in West Africa as Damballah, the snake god of the vodun religion. Images of other animals familiar in West African and southern black animal tales also appear in Afro-American folk art. African conjure canes are clear prototypes for Afro-American walking canes with carved faces at their top. These visual connections between African and Afro-American folk art parallel similar Old and New World links in black music and folktale traditions. The work of contemporary black artists like Romare Bearden has a striking similarity to the collages of folk painters. Bearden works with narrative themes in his paintings and acknowledges the influence of folk forms such as quilts on his work.

A strong sense of place influences southern folk artists. Their work reflects memory, imagination, and visions that shape an internal place as a balance to the literal rendering of landscape into art. These artists often stand apart as children and observe others their age, and childhood memories of landscape, homes, and family provide a foundation for later work. There is an urgency in the folk artist's work, as each artist freezes this memory of life before it changed. Theora Hamblett remembered the old hickory trees her father planted, and she painted them as they stood before they were "slain." "I don't go back out there. I don't want to see that. My favorite trees are all gone," she said. But the trees stand remembered and preserved in their full beauty on Hamblett's canvases. By depicting memories through art, the artist frames his or her culture into recognizable units. Pecolia Warner's quilts stretched across her bed and Theora Hamblett's paintings on her walls preserve the memories of their makers and enable the viewer to see life through the artist's eyes.

The internal sense of place recalled in the artists' memories is expanded and enriched by their imagination. Images are rendered greater than life and give the art suggestive rather than literal power. Literal and imaginary worlds merge as imaginings become part of art. The more interesting level of the artist's internal place involves dreams and visions. This level appears during sleep or in semiconscious states, and its revelation haunts the artist until released through art.

In developing folk art, repetition, balance, and superimposition of materials are particularly important. When artists repeat the same visual idea, repetition is never exact. Rather, variations are shaped on the same theme. Artists thus develop incremental repetition in their work as they unveil variations with each piece. Balance and symmetry are important in quilts, needlework, and painting—all of which often focus the eye on the central image. Theora Hamblett's paintings of her dogtrot home, the structure she knew as a child, focus the viewer's eye through a central hall with two rooms on either side to the seed house beyond. Superimposition of materials is basic to mediums such as painting, needlework, and quilting, where oil paint, stitches, and cloth pieces, respectively, are attached to a primary surface. Through superimposition of materials folk artists increase texture and three-dimensionality. Each animates his or her work with bursts of color and shapes that draw the viewer's eye to unexpected, sometimes frightening images.

At times folk artists insert themselves more literally into their work through self-portraits or signatures. They take the license of introducing the audience to the art's creator. Artists' homes are filled with their work, and a visitor moving through each room feels watched by their work. Within this world the artist locates a space where at certain times he or she works. Artists find their spot and from it produce objects that soon decorate their homes and those of their friends. Their art draws the community together as people gather and comment on new pieces by the artist. An important affinity is felt for animals and the natural world. The artist's eye wanders from barnyard animals to creatures such as crawfish, alligators, and bullfrogs. Artists are curious about animal life and sometimes imagine themselves as the animals they portray.

Old photographs are another important resource for folk artists. Photographs offer a glimpse of ancestral faces and establish the expression of a person posing. The frozen, wide-eyed stare familiar in old photographs is at times recaptured by artists in a literal rendition of a photograph.

Folk artists and their images unveil a moving portrait of the South and suggest how landscape and season inspire artists to share real and imagined worlds with their neighbors. Their art is a special gift offered to friends, to those who know, who will understand. It leads into a sacred place where one sees and marvels at familiar, everyday beauty transformed by the artist's hand. Like Pecolia Warner's quilt on a cold night, folk art offers beauty and shelter.

Folk Medicine. American folk medicine traditions have been particularly strong in the South, where such practices still thrive, though perhaps less so than in pre–World War II eras. Among mountaineers of Appalachia and the Ozarks, Native Americans, and rural blacks of the South, folk medicine practices have flourished only partly because of lack of access to modern medical care. Folk healers embody and act on their communities' concepts of life and death, health and illness. Thus, they act as trusted confidants within a system of beliefs, a system that may clash with that of the white medical establishment. For example, many types of African healing practices were used among slaves in the South, and some masters designated certain slave women to be plantation nurses. Vestiges of these practices still influence black folk healers. Folk medicine practices of many rural black southerners also remain strongly rooted in voodoo, an amalgam of African beliefs and French Catholicism brought to the United States by Haitian blacks in the 1700s. Likewise, the conjurer-curer role that is still important among Cherokee Indians in the Southeast reflects adherence to a variety of rich—and non-Anglo—traditions.

Practices of folk healers in the Ozarks and Appalachia have foundations in fundamentalist Protestant beliefs, with much reliance on scriptures as an integral part of cures. Unfortunately, many studies of folk medicine overlook religious or spiritual components and merely list remedies, plant sources for concoctions, and "superstitions" about illness. Folk healers and their patients also have received relatively little attention, but the *Foxfire* books and some recent academic investigations have provided fresh insights. Increasingly, the wide range of southern folk healers has been recognized, ranging from herbalists, bone setters, and granny women (midwives) to faith healers, psychic healers, spiritualists, root doctors, and conjurers, among others. Only recently, too, scholars have noted the crucial roles women have played in the South as folk healers and as teachers of traditional folk medicine practices. Urbanization and modernization have diluted the importance of folk healing in many southern locales, yet many practices still flourish. For example, one Alabama herbalist was in such demand that he drew the attention of *Wall Street Journal* reporters (8 July 1985), and many drugstores in the Lowland South have special sections stocked with ingredients for conjure bags and other voodoo components. For many poorer southerners, especially, folk medicine practices—and the beliefs they represent—remain important adjuncts to health care.

Traditional Customs. Folk customs and rituals helped to structure living in the South. The rural cycle of life so pervasive until recent times developed pronounced seasonal rhythms for people on the region's farms and rural areas. Spring planting and fall harvesting, corn shucking and hog killing were only a few of the occasions with ritual meaning. Southerners have valued family and kin, and the family reunion remains a popular regional custom. Families often develop their own unique traditions, sometimes drawing on regional foodways, recreational activities, and religious commitments.

Traditional customs are often associated with rites of passage, the special events of childbirth, marriage, and death. Rituals such as the shivaree, honoring the newly married couple, and the "sitting up," a modified wake honoring the dead, once were popular in the South, although they can be traced back to Old World traditions. Calendar customs are holidays celebrating annual events. Christmas has been traditionally an especially important holiday in the South, evoking some true folk traditions within families and local communities, whereas Thanksgiving was associated more with New England. Southern blacks had distinctive folk celebrations for Emancipation Day and Juneteenth, the day on which the end of slavery was celebrated in Texas.

Festivals are communitywide celebrations of annual events. Many festivals are not true folk events. The Mardi Gras in New Orleans, for example, has become a commercial enterprise, yet it had folk origins, and rural Cajuns in southern Louisiana continue traditional celebrations of the carnival spirit. In the modern South the term *folk festival* is widely used to describe the numerous annual occasions for performances of folk music and dancing and for the display of folk art and crafts.

Religion has long been a major source of custom and ritual in the South. Frontier camp meetings emerged after the Cane Ridge meeting in Kentucky in the late 1790s, and afterwards revival meetings, river baptisms, brush arbor encampments, sacred harp and gospel singings, dinners on the church grounds, and church homecomings were common occurrences for southerners, black and white. Civil rights protest marches and meetings had pronounced aspects of folk ritual drawn from the southern black church.

Food has been a significant yet often overlooked aspect of southern folklife. The region's people have an enduring attachment to certain foods, such as country ham, fried chicken, biscuits, and corn bread, and to ways of food preparation, especially frying. The consumption of black-eyed peas on New Year's Day is a common custom of southern blacks and whites, both of whom, in fact, share an appreciation of regional cuisine. Subregions within the South develop their distinctive foodways, such as the Cajuns with their crawfish dishes and southwesterners with their beef and Mexican dishes.

Folklife and Literature. The emergence of southern folklife closely parallels the birth of southern literature. Europeans traveling in the South, like Tocqueville, noted the rugged beauty of the southern landscape and were equally fascinated by local inhabitants whose language and colorful folkways reflected this landscape. As the region developed, its identity was influenced by places such as the Mississippi River, where folk heroes like Mike Fink inspired a rich body of river lore.

Mark Twain built on this lore and consciously integrated southern dialect, superstition, and folktales in *The Adventures of Huckleberry Finn*. Twain listened carefully before writing, and his love for the folktale and southern humor is evident in the novel's accurate description of the river's inhabitants and their folkways. Through the life of Jim and Huck on their raft, he also explores the relationship of white and black culture, an ever-present theme in southern folklore and literature. Twain saw the art of storytelling as central to his fiction.

Twentieth-century southern writers such as William Faulkner also pay close attention to regional culture and its folk roots. Faulkner portrayed his "little postage stamp of native soil" in a series of novels that create a mythic Yoknapatawpha County. Within this county he presents a southern *comedie humaine* through the voices of white, black, and Native American characters whose lives span over a century in their small Mississippi community. Pat Stamper, a horse trader in *The Hamlet*, is modeled on horse and mule traders whose wit and storytelling skills attracted Faulkner. Like these traders, Faulkner admired the mule, who, he wrote, would "work for you ten years for the chance to kick you once."

Ralph Ellison taps the rich vein of southern black folklore in *The Invisible Man*. As he shifts the novel from the rural South to Harlem, he effectively shows the spectrum of southern rural and northern urban black folk experience. Ellison stresses that blacks are a people "of the word" and argues that any study of black culture must begin with black folklore. He uses folktales, the sermon, and blues to structure his novel, and like Twain and Faulkner he focuses on the white-black issue as the central theme of his fiction.

Alice Walker is a part of a new generation of southern

writers who base their fiction on folk traditions. Walker greatly admires Zora Neale Hurston, the black folklorist and novelist whose *Mules and Men* is a classic portrait of black folktales and voodoo. Walker draws on folk roots as she presents blues singers, voodoo doctors, and quiltmakers through her poetry, short stories, and novels. Her most recent novel, *The Color Purple*, features a female blues singer, Shug Avery, in a moving description of black culture and its folk roots.

Southern folklife offers a rich, complex vision of the region as seen through its music, tales, and material culture. Southern places and their inhabitants are defined and shaped by this folklife. The appreciation of contemporary southern art, music, and literature is also enriched by study of folk traditions that influence them.

See also BLACK LIFE: Preacher, Black; / Hurston, Zora Neale; GEOGRAPHY: Foodways, Geography of; Log Housing; HISTORY AND MANNERS: Foodways; LITERATURE: / Ellison, Ralph; Faulkner, William; Harris, Joel Chandler; MUSIC articles; RELIGION: Folk Religion; Preacher, White; SOCIAL CLASS: Poverty; WOMEN'S LIFE: Children's Games; Healers, Women

William Ferris
University of Mississippi

Barry Ancelet, *Musiciens, Canadiens et Créoles/ The Makers of Cajun Music* (1984); John Beardsley and Jane Livingston, *Black Folk Art in America, 1930–1980* (1982); Benjamin A. Botkin, *A Treasury of Southern Folklore* (1949); Simon J. Bronner, *Grasping Things: Folk Material Culture and Mass Society in America* (1986); Jan Harold Brunvand, *The Study of American Folklore: An Introduction* (2d ed., 1978); John Burrison, *Brothers in Clay: The Story of Georgia Folk Pottery* (1983); Richard M. Dorson, *American Folklore* (rev. ed., 1977), *American Negro Folktales* (1967), *Buying the Wind: Regional Folklore in the United States* (1964), ed., *Handbook of American Folklore* (1983); Alan Dundes, *Mother Wit from the Laughing Barrel: Readings in the Interpretation of Afro-American Folklore* (1973); Dena J. Epstein, *Sinful Tunes and Spirituals: Black Folk Music to the Civil War* (1977); David Evans, *Big Road Blues: Tradition and Creativity in the Folk Blues* (1982); William Ferris, ed., *Afro-American Folk Art and Crafts* (1983), *Blues from the Delta* (1979), with Mary L. Hart, *Folk Music and Modern Sound* (1982), *Local Color: A Sense of Place in Folk Art* (1982); Henry Glassie, *Pattern in the Material Folk Culture of the Eastern United States* (1968); Daniel Hoffman, *Form and Fable in American Fiction* (1961); Bruce Jackson, *Get Your Ass in the Water and Swim Like Me: Narrative Poetry from Black Oral Tradition* (1974), *The Negro and His Folklore in Nineteenth Century Periodicals* (1967); Alan Lomax, *The Folk Songs of North America* (1960); Bill C. Malone, *Country Music U.S.A.* (1968), *Southern Music—American Music* (1979); William Lynwood Montell, *The Saga of Coe Ridge: A Study in Oral History* (1970); Américo Paredes, *A Texas-Mexican Cancionero: Folksongs of the Lower Border* (1976); Vance Randolph, *Ozark Magic and Folklore* (1964), *Pissing in the Snow and other Ozark Folktales* (1976); Sharon A. Sharp, *Women's Studies International Forum* (October 1986); Nicholas R. Spitzer, *Louisiana Folklife: A Guide to the State* (1985); John F. Szwed and Roger D. Abrahams, *Afro-American Folk Culture: An Annotated Bibliography of Materials from North, Central and South America and the West Indies*, 2 vols. (1978); Jeff Todd Titon, *Early Down Home Blues: A Musical and Cultural Analysis* (1977); John Michael Vlach, *The Afro-American Tradition in Decorative Arts* (1978); Wilbur Watson, ed., *Black Folk Medicine: The Therapeutic Significance of Faith and Trust* (1984); Eliot Wigginton, ed., *The Foxfire Book* (1972), ed., *Foxfire 2* (1973).

Aesthetic, Afro-American

This tradition is an open-ended one that favors extensive experimentation in a search for novelty. This is an aesthetic of freewheeling improvisation and innovation, and the art works it generates and the cultural contexts in which it operates are marked by a distinctive dynamism that can be regarded as indicative of black cultural values. This dynamism stems from an ever-present delight in the surprise value of new, not completely anticipated discovery.

When commenting about his elaborate ornamental ironwork designs, Philip Simmons, one of the foremost Afro-American blacksmiths still practicing his craft, noted: "It isn't always a thing gonna be set in your mind and when just half way you can see you ain't gonna like it. . . . You think you like it to start, [but] it isn't always you like something that you can visualize. . . . I may not like these scroll[s] when I start but still I see it that way after puttin' it in and I see where I can improve it." These words about composing a piece of wrought iron art give a glimpse of a crucially important aspect of black culture, for they reveal how its traditional art forms are enacted. What Simmons says about ironwork other black artists have said about music, dance, and many other expressive forms: namely, that the preferred shape of a specific work will only be known when it is completed.

As Simmons indicates, the black folk artist himself may at midpoint sense that something is amiss in his performance, but, rather than starting over completely, he will work with what he has until a satisfying pattern emerges. The artist is then doubly rewarded for his effort in that both his product and his creative process are enjoyable. In the end, he has a beautiful item and has solved his problem of composition by playing with it.

The Afro-American aesthetic encourages the exploration of new possibilities such as unlikely blendings of motifs, inversions of common patterns, and the layering of embellishments on standard forms. Black quilters can make quilt tops that have much in common with Anglo-American patterns, but when they enact their most distinctive artistic codes their bed covers can be spectacularly different after only a minor adjustment of a "normal" quilt motif. Consider, for example, the commonplace log cabin quilt square, a block composed of small, concentrically arranged strips that are usually no larger than one foot on a side. Many of these blocks will be set into a grid to form a quilt top. Black quilters employ this particular motif in an ordered and precisely geometric manner, but they can also make the log cabin so big that one block alone will constitute the entire quilt top. They may also skew the center of the block to one side and select high effect colors that are rarely employed by Anglo-American quilters. Such a quilt when viewed from the perspective of the Anglo-American aesthetic would seem strange or flawed or even so lacking in aesthetic quality that it could only be referred to as "crazy." Closer consideration, however, reveals that such a quilt, which seems random, misshapen, and crazed, does in fact have an order, albeit not an order marked by the same meticulous, geometric precision employed by white quilters. The black quilt, when harshly evaluated, might be read as a distorted white pattern, but when viewed from the perspective of the Afro-American aesthetic its randomness, its off-balance composition, and its deviance from the "norm" should be read as playfulness, as willingness to test the norm, as a strong desire to find novelty within the familiar.

Such quilts manifest the same spirit of innovation and improvisation that is encountered in Philip Simmons's ironwork. In the midst of composition and performance the artist gathers new insights about previously unconsidered possibilities. If judged as positive, these possibilities become "improvements," and they are used to convert the usual quilt or ironwork or song or dance step into something unusual. Thus, Afro-American works have an emergent quality to complement the open-endedness of their design. Improvisations, testings, or improvements are compiled to produce an additively composed artwork. Because this additive approach is incremental, even piecemeal, the final goal is not often seen from the outset of the creative process. Later, at some critical, even magical point, when an acceptable shape begins to emerge, it may seem that the work almost creates itself. In an instant, seemingly random elements come together and appear as powerful, evocative, or beautiful.

It is not surprising, then, that many black folk artists speak of a visionary episode as the source of their work. The plans for their creativity, they say, come in dreams, mysterious voices, prophecies, or spiritual visitations: that is, from some external force over which they have no control. Clay sculptor and bluesman James "Son" Thomas reports: "The dreams just come to me. If I'm working with clay, you have that on your mind when you lay down. You dream some. Then you get up and try." Leon Rucker, a carver of fancy walking sticks, explains his ideas in the following manner: "The idea came with the voice of the man. Now who was the man, I don't know but I say he must have been a god 'cause man couldn't do a thing like that just by himself." Gravestone maker William Edmondson while lying in bed received a command to carve from his "Heavenly Daddy." Soon after that communication he experienced another extraordinary event: "I looked up in the sky and right there in the noon day light He hung a tombstone out for me to make." Beneath such diverse statements is the Afro-American aesthetic that encourages its proponents to experiment spontaneously and somewhat randomly until they seize upon an order that suits them. That order will seem marvelously self-generated even though it is the artists who are actually responsible.

Improvisation is sometimes perceived as a symptom of the decline of tradition; it is thought to signal the demise of historically sanctioned standards. When a form changes constantly, it is assumed that its traditional base must be unstable and its aesthetic impact must be weakening. This is not the case in Afro-American culture where novelty is expected as the norm, where the rules of artistic composition are loosely rather than rigidly enforced, where the creator is expected to stand out from his community. There is thus a strong sense of individuality in black folk expression. Cultural license exists for black artists to do whatever they do in their own way. Blues singers today often refer to standard numbers by famous traditional celebrities such as Robert Johnson or Charley Patton as "my own" even though the original authorship is well-known to all. They are expected to remake the tradition and in fact they do transform old favorites with the addition of their own new elements. Sonny Matthews explains: "I will sing their songs, but I will put the words my way. If he have a word do one way, I'll change it and put it another. That's the way I do most of my singing." Philip Simmons in like manner claims: "I like doing *my own* work." A strong sense of self, then, enters black folk art and is responsible not for the demise of tradition but for its perpetuation. The aesthetic of improvisation promotes a freedom to explore the limits of one's imagination, encouraging each would-be artist to examine fully the creative formats of his or her community. Such freedom could lead to chaos and confusion, but this is not the case, for most artists exercise their options for self-expression conservatively and modestly, observing that the past is a valuable and useful resource. They negotiate between their sense of self and their sense of society. Their creativity involves a measure of compromise between what they think is good and what their audience will accept as good. Because the shape of these negotiations is similar to the testings and probings required for the composition and performance of black expressive culture, the Afro-American aesthetic seems to consist not simply of the rules for creativity but also of the rules for living.

See also ART AND ARCHITECTURE: Sculpture; MUSIC: Blues

John Michael Vlach
George Washington University

Ralph Ellison, *Shadow and Act* (1972); William Ferris, ed., *Afro-American Folk Art and Crafts* (1983), *Blues from the Delta* (1979); Leroi Jones, *Blues People: Negro Music in White America* (1963); Linn Shapiro, ed., *Black People and Their Culture: Selected Writings from the African Diaspora* (1976); John Michael Vlach, *The Afro-American Tradition in Decorative Arts* (1978), *Charleston Blacksmith: The Work of Philip Simmons* (1981).

Aesthetic, Anglo-American

A shared aesthetic dictated much of the look of the South's man-made landscape. White British settlers brought with them guiding principles of order, balance, and proportion. The Anglo standard for good proportion—apparently intuitive but actually acquired by traditional learning—was the "Golden" or "Greek" oblong. It measured two units on the short side to three on the long side. According to one aesthetic primer, this perfect rectangle "is more beautiful than a very long, narrow oblong, in which the breadth and length vary so greatly that they do not seem to be related." This folk aesthetic of what constitutes proper order and proportion is represented in the basic southern folk house—the single pen, usually a rectangular unit (with roots in West Britain). Variations on this unit, like the double pen, dogtrot house, and I house, extend the rectangular image. Indeed, at the earliest settlement of Jamestown the most efficient housing would have been large multifamily dwellings, but instead the settlers insisted on small, single-family rectangular houses. The predominance of the rectangle as a basic constructional concept, in fact, extended also to dining and art, for the table was typically rectangular and so was the frame for paintings.

The ideal three units of the oblong's long side is manifested in a preference for two identical design elements flanking a different central one. The windows of the typical folk house are symmetrically placed around a central door. The southern mountain cabin typically has the fireplace in the center of the far wall, rather than in the corner where the Scandinavians preferred it. The Anglo preference for the bilaterally symmetrical pattern is indeed a contrast to African, Gothic, and Italianate architectural styles. Beyond architecture, the American design of gravestones and dress, even the arrangement of food (meat, potatoes, vegetables) on the dinner plate, follows the bilaterally symmetrical pattern as well. In the English language sentences are rectilinear, reflecting symmetry and a design of threes: beginning, middle, and end; subject, object, and verb; past, present, and future.

The symmetrical aesthetic stems from a geometric projection of the human body as an ideal form; faces and bodies are designed symmetrically. The regularity expressed helped nurture within southern culture a sense of order, balance, and harmony. Anglo-rooted and southern-based country music, for example, is noted by its rhythmic regularity and evenness; it also represents politically a conservative attitude. The so-called English barn is another example of the Anglo geometric aesthetic: it contains two bays around a centrally placed passage. The entrance is on the nongable end to emphasize the ordered rectangular facade.

The rectangle is the key form in the Anglo-American aesthetic, reflecting the opposition of two equal pairs. Even the Stars and Bars consists of two crossed rectilinear bars that form a field of solid colored pairs. The double-doored double pen, a pair of rectangular units, is the limit of folk architectural extension; a triple pen is not found in the Anglo folk repertoire. The house might be extended by placing a double pen over the first pair, thus forming the so-called I house, or an L or T extension can be put on the back to preserve the binary facade. The special case is the addition of a central door and hallway that projects an image of bilateral symmetry. Inside a rear door is typically paired in line with the front door, and, even in a single pen, a light partition often divides the cabin into two rooms. The basic Anglo-American house consists of a Golden Oblong with central front and rear door and symmetrically placed windows.

Again, there is geometric projection of the human body in the binary aesthetic—paired arms, eyes, and legs. In fact, in language people use this reference when saying "on the one hand, on the other." Binary thinking goes further, from artifact to worldview. The classic binary oppositions of North and South, upland and lowland, and black and white show the place of aesthetic not as ornament but as a central, socially important idea. Indeed, "separate but equal," a common guiding doctrine of an earlier South, was an aesthetic principle as much as a social one.

In addition to a concern for shape, the southern Anglo-American aesthetic stresses a natural look. The pronounced image of an agrarian South finds characterization in the country-gentleman ideal borrowed from the English. The folk painters and tale tellers of the South have shared a long tradition of celebrating its rusticity. This means more than depicting the adored everyday activities of the country church and farm; it reflects an overarching aesthetic stressing man's close ties to nature. The emphasis may be partly explained by southern settlers' need to adapt to a geography and climate most unlike their point of British origin. The look of the folk-built landscape thus more often blends into the environment than clashes with it.

Natural materials add to the appeal of artistic products. Wood is especially favored for its look and feel. Whittlers refuse to paint their wooden chains to make them more realistic; the natural wood, they will tell you, *should* be shown. Baskets, houses, and pottery commonly display soft, natural colors. Figures made from corn husks, bedcovers in a honeycomb pattern, and instruments made from skins or gourds are among the mainstays, for instance, of a 1937 survey of southern handicrafts by Allen Eaton.

Pieced quilt showing Anglo-American aesthetic form, Oxford, Miss., 1973

The pride expressed by southerners in the naturalistic appearance of their objects is coupled with an aesthetic preference for objects shaped or controlled by hand. The title of a recent Mississippi folk art exhibition was, in fact, *Made by Hand*. The persistence of handicrafts such as chairmaking, whittling, and quilting, even in the face of factory goods, makes an aesthetic statement in favor of handmade quality. Although some observers associate this predilection with southern cultural conservatism, another more plausible interpretation relates the value seen in handwork to the connections—both to nature and to other people—provided by the aesthetic control and emotional compassion of human touch. Like the symbol of ample "time on your hands" reflected by traditional southern storytelling, handworked items represent for southerners the value of close attention to the object and a sense of leisureliness.

Although the form and feeling of southern material folk culture are varied, the major British inheritance did find prominent expression. A set of coherent aesthetic principles emerged in the southern experience. They were not identical with, or exclusive to, the Anglo antecedent but drew inspiration from general principles of proper order, balance, and proportion. Yet scholars disagree over how many of those principles were imposed on non-white or non-Anglo southerners. Some, like folklorist John Michael Vlach, see a major African presence on the landscape, whereas others, like folklorist Richard M. Dorson, argue that the European culture in America transformed or eliminated most of the cultural traditions of blacks and Indians. Identifying distinctive, multiple aesthetic systems of ethnic origin, however, does not contradict the existence of a dominant southern aesthetic. Despite different, frequently overlapping, identities expressed aesthetically, a predominant influence on southern folk design has been those aesthetic principles based on a combination of an Anglo-Celtic heritage and new demands of the American scene.

Simon J. Bronner
Pennsylvania State University
Capitol Campus

Simon J. Bronner, *Grasping Things: Folk Material Culture and Mass Society in America* (1986); Richard M. Dorson, in *American Folklore in the New World*, ed. Daniel Crowley (1977); Allen H. Eaton, *Handicrafts of the Southern Highlands* (1937; reprint, 1973); William Ferris, *Local Color: A Sense of Place in Folk Art* (1982); Henry Glassie, in *The Study of American Folklore: An Introduction*, ed. Jan Harold Brunvand (2d ed., 1978), in *Folklore and Folklife: An Introduction*, ed. Richard M. Dorson (1972), and *Folk Housing in Middle Virginia: A Structural Analysis of Historic Artifacts* (1975); Warren Roberts, "Folk Architecture," in *Folklore and Folklife: An Introduction*, ed. Richard M. Dorson (1972); John Michael Vlach, *The Afro-American Tradition in Decorative Arts* (1978).

Arts and Crafts

Southerners have produced a wide variety of arts and crafts. Men and women, blacks and whites, Native Americans and ethnic groups have all contributed to the region's traditions. The Appalachian white, rural Afro-American, Native American, and Moravian ethnic traditions are among the best documented in the region.

Folk painting includes works sometimes called primitive or naive, such as the work of Clementine Hunter in Louisiana, Nellie Mae Rowe in Georgia, Theora Hamblett and Luster Willis in Mississippi, and Minnie Evans and Minnie Reinhardt in North Carolina. Distinctive pottery traditions can be found in North Carolina, Georgia, and east Texas. Among the South's most famous potters are Lanier Meaders of north Georgia and Burlon Craig of North Carolina.

Carving of stone and of wood has been a frequently practiced craft and includes the documented stone carvings of animals and angels by Tennessean William Edmondson, the sculpted clay skulls of James "Son" Thomas of the Mississippi Delta, and the wooden walking sticks of Victor "Hickory Stick Vic" Bobb in Mississippi. Ironworking has included utilitarian products with aesthetic dimensions. Philip Simmons of Charleston is the best-documented among many examples of black craftsmen who have used iron to make art.

Basketmaking provides a good example of the existence of the three ethnic-artistic folk art and craft perspectives in the South—Native American, Afro-American, and Euro-American. Each used somewhat different materials and designs. The Mississippi Choctaw baskets, the Afro-American Sea Islands baskets from South Carolina and Georgia, and the baskets from Appalachian rural areas are well known to collectors and scholars. Other craftsmen in the South have specialized in creating musical instruments, including Louis Dotson (guitar) of Mississippi and Homer Ledford (dulcimer) of Kentucky. Women have produced distinctive and distinguished textiles, including quilts (Pecolia Warner of Mississippi and Harriet Powers of Georgia) and needlework (Ethel Mohamed of Mississippi). "Sewing" encompasses many specific techniques. The regional arts and crafts tradition would also include chairmaking and furniture making, weaving and spinning, Indian beadwork, jewelry in general, rug making, leather work, glass work, toy and doll making, and countless other activities.

Like those found in other regions, folk arts and crafts in the South are rooted in the traditional values of communities and families. Embedded within folk objects, made with skill and designed for beauty, is a conservative desire to preserve the ways of an honorable past, believed still to have worth in the present. What southerners are saying in a material mode when they fashion quilts or baskets or churns is that the people from whom they learned their craft were good, decent, and intelligent folk worthy of imitation. Thus, contemporary artisans turn their talents to making objects whose designs may be a century old. They repeat again, rather than create anew, so that tradition will survive, so that their sense of group is more pronounced than their sense of self. These patterns, which are seen in all folk societies, are repeated in folk society in the South.

From the colonial period until the first decade of the 19th century, most American artifacts were made by traditionally trained artisans. But throughout the 19th century these same goods came to be made more often in factories by large numbers of workers using machines. Industrialization and the factory system took hold first in New England, however, and did not reach the South in any appreciable manner until after World War I. Hence, in the 20th century the number of folk artisans in the South is significantly larger than in other regions. Consequently southern folk arts and crafts today enjoy relatively high visibility and homemade items are often presented as emblematic of the region. What one really sees in coverlets and carvings is a national pattern that has simply survived longer in the South than elsewhere.

Although the various genres of traditional art and craft are found all over the country, southern examples have some distinctive features. Southern stoneware vessels, for example, are sealed with a wood-ash or alkaline glaze not found in other regional pottery-producing areas. Its characteristic runny finish, variously called "Shanghai" or "tobacco spit" and found from North Carolina to Texas, but nowhere else, can be used to distinguish a Deep South style of ceramics. Other glazes and glazing techniques have been carried into the South, but the alkaline glaze has remained exclusively in its original territory.

In patchwork quilting many block patterns such as "log cabin," "double wedding ring," "drunkard's path," or the ubiquitous "nine patch" are shared across regional boundaries. However, southern blacks, in addition to using block patterns, have also composed quilt tops with strip units. As a consequence of this ethnic tradition, southern quilting as a whole is quite different from quilting done in other regions; it includes an Afro-American as well as an Anglo-American approach to quilt composition and design.

Until the 19th century the slat-back chair was a piece of sitting furniture common in all parts of the eastern United States. At that point other chair types became popular in the North while the slat back remained the most typical southern "settin'" chair. Subsequently, it underwent a number of modifications: most notably its rear posts were curved backwards and their front surfaces were shaved flat, producing the so-called mule-ear motif. Southern furniture making thus evolved a distinctive chair type at roughly the same time its earlier form was nationally distributed. To identify the "southernness" of southern folk art and craft, then, one must be aware not only of national patterns but also of very minute and specific attributes of an item's materials, techniques, and social history. What is uniquely southern about an item may consist of a minor detail, important mainly to the maker of the object.

A folk society is often, although not necessarily, a rural society. Because the South has only recently been open to major industrial development, farming remains quite prominent and rural agrarian values are widespread. Life on a farm is, above all, marked by making do with whatever is at hand, and craftsmanship of either the production or repair variety is part of the daily routine as handwork helps supplement the marginal finances of a small, family-owned farm. The economic benefits of traditional know-how mean that craft activities are not archaic, quaint survivals. Rather, they are necessary, useful, and practical ways to live, independent of urban control, and they make one proud of inherited skills. The decorative touches that grace rural homes and yards in the South likewise manifest a spirit of independence. Quilts and bottle trees and tractor-tire planters and whirligigs and walls covered with newspaper and magazine cutouts all convey the message that life can be brightened with means that are close to home. Homegrown art, it is asserted, is as good as any other.

Visitors to the South in recent years, imagining the place to be peopled with exotic "hillbilly and cracker" personalities, have expected southern folk art to be extraordinarily deviant. Indeed, one can find southern artists without conventional studio credentials who have created highly innovative works. Walter Flax of Yorktown, Va., has his fleet of almost 150 battleships and cruisers; Charlie Field near Lebanon, Va., decorated a whole house, inside and out, with polka dots; and Eddie Owen Martin of Buena Vista, Ga., made a stepped Aztec pyramid in his backyard. But these people, though they are southern and artists and possibly members of folk communities, are not southern folk artists. Their efforts reflect private visions and fantasies rather than a shared folk heritage. In looking for folk art, one looks not for spectacular expressions but for the regular and commonplace, confirming the ordinary rather than celebrating the novel. A culture is kept vital by the mutual agreement of the members of a group, not by the efforts of a lone individual. In communities and families folk art and craft are perpetuated in the South.

See also ART AND ARCHITECTURE: Sculpture; ETHNIC LIFE: Indian Cultural Contributions; Mountain Culture; RELIGION: / Moravians

John Michael Vlach
George Washington University

Carl Bridenbaugh, *The Colonial Craftsman* (1950); John A. Burrison, *Southern Folklore Quarterly* (December 1975); William Ferris, *Local Color: A Sense of Place in Folk Art* (1982); Henry Glassie, *Pattern in the Material Folk Culture of the Eastern United States* (1968); John Michael Vlach, *The Afro-American Tradition in Decorative Arts* (1978).

Basketmaking

Basketmaking is a dynamic craft with ancient roots. More than one basketmaker has proclaimed that baskets trace their origin back to Moses in the bullrushes, and, indeed, woven baskets of various fibers are an essential cross-cultural craft known in practically every civilization from antiquity to the modern day. The craft has retained a position in the constellation of cultural traditions in communities and families through lean times and good in every part of the South. Basketmaking is well-embedded in the distinct yet related traditions of southerners of Native American, European, African, Caribbean, and Asian descent.

There are three major traditions of southern basketmaking: Native American, Afro-American, and Anglo-American. Of these, the black basketmakers in the Georgia and South Carolina Sea Islands have long been admired for the beauty and quality of their coiled grass baskets, whereas less attention by scholars or the public has been paid to Native American baskets (arguably the most intricate and finely made by any civilization) and to those in the white traditions. Even less attention has been paid to Asian basketmaking traditions in the South.

The various culturally determined forms, materials, and modes of construction (essentially a process of weaving, plaiting, or coiling) indicate a rich exchange between peoples over the generations, but distinctive characteristics remain within each group. Indian peoples favor split reed, willow, and grasses, as do black craftsmen, but incorporate colorings and special designs in the woven container. Certain baskets made by black makers are not known among Indians or whites and may echo West African or Caribbean traditions. Anglo-Americans have always favored straight-grained hardwood stock for baskets, chiefly white oak and hickory. Pure function and physical rigidity mark the work of culturally conservative white craftspeople, while playful ornamentation in color scheme often highlights the work of Indian and black American builders. White-oak basketmaking of the Anglo southerners is similar from the Virginia Piedmont across the mountains into Missouri, Arkansas, and Texas, while the work of Native Americans differs from the coastal areas of the South to the western edge of the region (where some of the tribes lived separately for countless centuries).

Craftsman making a white-oak basket, Sharon, Miss., 1972

The purposes to which baskets are put are as numerous as the chores of daily life. Baskets take whatever shape is necessary for their function. All are artifacts of flexible woven material and are used to gather, hold, measure, transport, store, and sort everything from eggs and seeds to babies and firewood. Southern baskets are created from every kind of useful plant and wood: from cornshucks, straw, grasses, branches, stalks, cane, bark, vines, pine needles, hickory, ash, willow, and oak.

Among the regional types are cotton baskets made and used by both black and white people in southern agriculture, fish traps for mountain streams, Choctaw corn sieves, and Sea Island Afro-American flower baskets. Some basket types—such as the Choctaw basket of split dyed cane, black South Carolina coiled grass basket, and white riven and ribbed oak egg basket—require great labor and intricate skill. Others are easily made from gatherings of vines, grasses, or branches.

Craft revivals have played an important role in southern basketmaking. Movements of the 1920s and 1930s were fostered by various foundations, craft guilds, and New Deal agencies that sought to document and interpret southern life and work. From the 1960s to the present, basketmaking has been nourished by the folklife studies movement, folksong revivals, back-to-the-land enthusiasts, the *Roots* phenomenon, tourism, Foxfire-like projects, and a return to the craft by older artisans in retirement.

The interest in country things and "primitive" artifacts at rural auctions and art galleries reflects the growth of outside markets for traditional baskets that, in spite of philosophical misgivings of some scholars, has encouraged the continuation and occasional rebirth of authentic basketry. Adult craft classes and recreational programs also foster basketmaking in the modern South, allowing one to learn to produce a basket under proper tutelage.

Modern machines cannot produce a satisfactory "traditional" basket. Despite 19th-century attempts, the failure of technology to create good, inexpensive baskets in factory settings helped generate demand for the development of other cheaper containers, from paper sacks to plastic bags and glass jars. The domination of cheap sacks and bags has encouraged the decline of basketmaking, a craft that flourished when baskets were genuinely needed in society and that still can flourish among a small group of knowledgeable workers.

The process of craftsmanship is a fluid, dynamic one of

constant if unnoticed inspiration, innovation, and alteration as builders encounter inviting technologies, new outlets, and new ideas in aesthetics, design, decoration, and function. If the basket made by Earl Westfall in Howard County, Mo., in 1969 holds magazines in a parlor rather than kindling by the hearth, the artifact remains a vivid and stable testament to a rich legacy, and it remains a traditional basket no matter what its present function. While one may mourn the loss of the old-timers, theirs is a craft of life, not death, and baskets will continue to be produced in response to the vicissitudes of cultural expression.

Basketmaking is well suited to the workshop or spare room and is a convenient way to supplement income from other jobs. Other factors, however, such as the difficulty in obtaining suitable wood or fiber or even high-quality tools, have inhibited the growth of the craft in some areas. Without a proper market outlet or the patrimony of the museum, there would be little incentive to retain the old skills so laboriously learned and manifested in basketmaking, nor would conservative, unassertive craftspeople come to the attention of researchers, collectors, nontraditional imitators, and businessmen. Some, like the late Jim Nicholson of northern Virginia (coming from a long line of basketmakers), continued making white-oak baskets and selling them from the hood of his car on the highway shoulder.

Basketmaking has always been central to the life of all economic classes and groups of people in the South. Baskets today are considered art or handsome functional artifacts. Some basketmakers continue production in traditional contexts for traditional purposes. Although there are few "traditional" makers at work today, the craft continues, ever changing but still a characteristic feature of the cultural landscape of the South.

See also ENVIRONMENT: Plant Uses; ETHNIC LIFE: Caribbean Influence; Indian Cultural Contributions

Howard W. Marshall
Missouri Cultural Heritage Center
University of Missouri at Columbia

Gerald L. Davis, in *Afro-American Folk Art and Crafts*, ed., William Ferris (1983); Allen H. Eaton, *Handicrafts of the Southern Highlands* (1937; reprint 1973); Howard W. Marshall, in *Readings in American Folklore*, ed. Jan Harold Brunvand (1978); Otis T. Mason, *Aboriginal American Basketry: Studies in a Textile Art without Machinery* (1904); Sue Stephenson, *Basketry in the Southern Appalachian Mountains* (1977); Mary Twining, in *Afro-American Folk Art and Crafts*, ed. William Ferris (1983).

Cemeteries

The South has two major distinct cemetery types, urban and rural. Urban cemeteries are less regionally distinctive because they exhibit a greater degree of cross-cultural exchange. National trends in sepulchral art, cemetery design, and botanical landscaping are more obvious in the burying grounds of Savannah, Charleston, Atlanta, and New Orleans than in the small graveyards of the more prevalent rural communities. Moreover, the rate of innovation is more rapid in the urban context, often creating cemeteries that represent an eclecticism difficult to classify into meaningful types. The rural burial grounds, however, more aptly express the region's peculiar attitude toward the proper disposal and veneration of its deceased.

Southern rural cemeteries are modest in size, averaging between two and five acres. The rural South had two general graveyard categories until recent times—the family cemetery and the loosely identified community cemetery, with or without the association of a church structure. The family cemetery is not uniquely southern; however, it is found more frequently in the South than in other regions of the United States. The distinctiveness of the plantation as a southern land-use phenomenon certainly fostered the use of private burial plots. The lag in urban development also promoted the regional predisposition toward family cemeteries.

By far the most common southern cemetery is the public graveyard associated with the hamlets and crossroad settlements that pepper the landscape. The cemetery may or may not be adjacent to a church; indications are that some of the older, more established burial grounds preceded any church association by many years. These southern graveyards had common traits. Excluding for the moment any urban innovations or ethnic peculiarities, several definitive characteristics lend a distinctive regional stamp to southern rural cemeteries: (a) decided preferences for location of the cemetery site, (b) preferred species of vegetation, (c) axial grave alignments, (d) diverse innovations in decoration, and (e) cults of piety.

One term suggested for this distinctive regional burial ground is the Upland South folk cemetery. Widely associated with the uplands found throughout the South, it is found scattered across the South from central Texas to the Atlantic Piedmont and from the Ohio Valley to the Gulf fringe. A number of its characteristics have been shared by rural blacks as well as whites; a major distinction between the two is that the black cemeteries tend to be less well cared for than those of the whites.

Rural folk graveyards show a marked tendency for hilltop location. Wherever feasible, these cemeteries will be perched on the very summit, or, if not on the summit, on the crest of a ridge or well up the side of any slope or inclined plane. The sacredness of hilltops is recognized as being of great antiquity, but locals rationalize cemetery location in terms of drainage.

Certain species of vegetation have evolved by long use as "cemetery" plants. Evergreens are a particularly obvious example, with dominant species being the eastern red cedar, various pines, or oaks. Evergreens are symbolic of immortality. In addition, a wide variety of shrubs, perennials, and annuals are also common. Arbor vitae, roses, azalea, spirea, and various lilies abound. Species of vegetation will, of course, vary somewhat with environmental differences across the South.

Graves in southern rural cemeteries are almost always aligned along an east-west axis with the head toward the west and the feet to the east. Sacredness associated with direction is another Old World trait of great antiquity. The alignment of graves is not always cardinally accurate, though. Rather, the graves are placed in what is perceived to be an east-west direction; actually, it is more southeastward than eastward. The orientation of graves has a strong religious component, rationalized as proper so that the faithful will rise to face the risen Christ on Judgment Day. Jerusalem lying to the east is also of some significance.

Innovativeness of decoration in southern rural cemeteries covers a broad spectrum of traits. In general, there is a well-established tradition of "making do." Grave mounds are covered with shells, dishes, personal artifacts (such as favorite mugs, eyeglasses, medicine bottles, and the like), or other paraphernalia. Coffee cans or fruit jars covered with foil make suitable flower containers. A particularly eye-catching, homemade container is made by cutting an aqua, or white, gallon detergent bottle in half. A hole is cut in the bottom center, the neck of the top half is inserted, and the cap screwed on. The resulting container has a broad enough base to resist easy toppling and will hold an abundant array of flowers. Children's graves display a phenomenal array of personal items. Favored toys, marbles, animal or diverse-shaped figurines, or stuffed animals may be encountered. There appears to be less difference among graves of black and white children than among those of adults. Dishes, for example, are seldom broken on white adults' graves, whereas some scholars hold that the African trait of breaking pottery is especially evident on black adults' graves. Evidence of the latter is, however, very restricted and may prove less characteristic with continued research.

Other grave artifacts are symbolic of occupation or of the tragedy responsible for death. The use of a toy log truck on the grave of a young adult was the family's way of respecting his love of trucking, even though the young man died as a result of a freak trucking accident.

Shells used for grave decoration have a wide global distribution and date from the far past. Originally associated with pagan fertility symbolism and rites, the shell appears to have been absorbed into Judeo-Christian symbolism through the Romans. It is widespread throughout rural southern cemeteries as a decoration. Most often the shells are freshwater varieties of clams or mussels. Where available, they include various whelks and conchs. Shells are placed along the crest of the grave mound, randomly spotted or sometimes totally blanketing the grave; other times a single conch or large whelk may be placed near the head. There are pagan overtones, even psychological ones, but the southerner is seldom, if ever, cognizant of why shells are used, recognizing only that they are attractive.

Other decorative practices include the use of white sand for grave plots or even for covering entire graveyards. Various tombstone styles are represented as well, although the introduction of commercial stones has not been uniform across space or time. The grave shelter is an unusual decorative form. The typical shelter is a rectangular structure with open sides, picket fencing, gable roof, and with gables at the head and foot of the grave. This practice is not found among blacks, and its prevalence among whites remains inexplicable. It has experienced a morphological evolution and appears to be a matter of preference; distribution is widespread across the South.

Cults of piety express veneration of deceased family members. One of the most widespread of these cults is graveyard workday, once again a phenomenon more prevalent among whites than blacks. Graveyard workday is an annual event where all people with relatives in a particular cemetery gather to clean the cemetery. Activities include scraping all grass from the cemetery (creating a stark visual contrast with surrounding woodland or field), mounding all graves, raking or sweeping all debris from the grounds, righting fallen tombstones (when present), and mending fences to keep animals out. Associated with this daylong event is "dinner on the grounds," light courting, business dealing, and general renewing of family bonds and friendships. Thus, graveyard workday serves multiple functions within the community, much the same way that southern funerals are family-strengthening affairs.

The traditional southern rural cemetery described still exists, although decreasingly so. As the South has urbanized and become more accessible via the automobile and blacktop road, ideas and attitudes concerning proper disposal and care of the dead have changed. Within towns especially the traditional cemetery landscape has given way to the memorial garden concept conceived in California and diffused eastward across the United States. The graveshed has all but disappeared, graveyard workday has been supplanted by perpetual care, decoration is relegated primarily to the artificial flower, and the naked graveyard with its mounds of earth has been replaced by parklike expanses of grass. Yet some locales doggedly adhere to traditional folkways, and cemeteries there are a curious blend of elements from both ends of the spectrum. Large, sweeping expanses marked by family plots, some of which are still scraped and have mounded graves, remind one that the landscape of the dead is not as static as one might initially perceive.

Thus, the South has one of the most varied cemetery landscapes found anywhere in the United States. There are still pristine examples of the folk graveyard; there are black cemeteries embodying a number of the same cultural traits found in white graveyards; examples of aesthetically appealing memorial gardens can be found in nearly all modest-sized southern towns and certainly in the cities. Across this range of sacred space one finds evidence of pagan ritual and symbolism, traits having greater geographic distribution than the South, a strong Old World influence (probably more European than any other), and more unanswered questions than definitive conclusions. For all this, however, the southern cemetery remains an important element of the cultural landscape. It remains a barometer of the economic and social viability of a community and a looking glass into the southerner's innermost feelings about proper burial and veneration of the dead.

See also BLACK LIFE: Funerary Customs, Black

D. Gregory Jeane
Auburn University

D. Gregory Jeane, *Journal of Popular Culture* (Spring 1978); Terry Jordan, *Texas Graveyards: A Cultural Legacy* (1982), *Southwestern Historical Quarterly* (Janurary 1980); Fred Kniffen, *Geographical Review* (October 1967); Fred A. Tarpley, *Southern Folklore Quarterly* (December 1963); Robert Farris Thompson, *Flash of the Spirit: African and Afro-American Art and Philosophy* (1983); John Vlach, *The Afro-American Tradition in Decorative Arts* (1978).

Childbirth

The first stage in the cycle of human life, childbirth, is universally recognized as a period of crisis. Until recently, the distressingly high mortality rate of both mothers and babies at childbirth and the lack of professional health care resulted in the universal usage of traditional strategies and behaviors to prophesy and protect mothers and babies. In the South, folk beliefs, customs, and medicine associated with childbirth derived from more diverse sources, developed more fully, and endured longer than in any other region of the United States.

The 18th and 19th centuries saw the amalgamation of Native American, Afro-American, and Euro-American folk remedies and beliefs in the South. Although the spread of black medical knowledge was limited somewhat by harsh laws in the antebellum South, on many large farms and plantations black midwives played a significant role, even when white men and women were officially in charge of plantation health. Before the advent of modern hospitals, medical doctors, and adequate transportation, trained and untrained white and black midwives, granny women, or female neighbors assisted during home births. Prenatal care was almost nonexistent. Even when doctors and hospitals were available, many women in the rural South preferred to give birth at home with the help of midwives.

In each phase of the birth process—conception, gestation, delivery, and postpartum—southern families sought to insure the health and intelligence of babies and the safety of mothers through prophecy, strict control of environment, and principles of homeopathic medicine ("like cures like"). Many southerners believed that it was possible to determine or control the sex of an infant at conception. Some southerners believed that a baby boy was assured if the father kept a leather string in his pocket during conception; the side to which the female turned following intercourse (to the left for girls and the right for boys) was also believed to be effective in determining the sex of an infant. Other folk beliefs surround the gestation period of pregnancy, such as the notion that the pregnant female who crosses a threshold or begins to climb stairs using her left foot will have a girl, but if she does so with her right foot, it will be a boy.

One of the oldest beliefs about childbirth is based on the concept that the events occurring while a woman carries her baby have a direct effect on the fetus. Southerners believed and continue to believe in prenatal influences. It is thought that a pregnant mother's experiences—of fright, deprivation, contact, or craving—may be manifested in her child's habits or physical marks. In the past, mothers-to-be were warned to look only on beautiful things during pregnancy. If a pregnant woman was frightened by a snake, her baby would weave when he or she walked. If she saw her husband bleeding a mule, her baby would be marked with a blood-red birthmark. A birthmark on an infant also was attributed to a mother's unfulfilled craving for a particular food or overeating of a particular food during pregnancy. Often dietary allergies, aversions, or preferences in a child were and still are credited to a mother's prenatal behavior. A child's disposition could be affected positively or negatively prior to its birth by the mother's own disposition and aspirations for the child; if a pregnant woman was ill-natured during pregnancy, her baby would share her mean-spiritedness. Some believed that if a pregnant woman looked at a dead baby or spoke the name she intended to give her baby before its birth, it would be stillborn. Names were carefully chosen because it was believed the baby would have characteristics similar to his or her namesake.

To hasten labor, herbal teas were offered to the woman or pepper was blown in the mother-to-be's face. The most difficult and dangerous phase of childbirth, delivery, and the concerns about this process provoked many protective and divinatory practices. An almost universal technique used during labor consisted of placing a sharp instrument—a knife, scissors, an axe—on or under the pillow or bed of the laboring woman "to cut the pain." This was the most prevalent method for alleviating the pain of labor among southerners, although the ingestion of certain herbs or of that most popular of southern soft drinks, Coca-Cola, was believed to be efficacious in the relief of labor pain. Southerners believed it was inappropriate and a bad omen for the father to be present at the birth, although in some areas of the South the presence of the father or some article of his clothing was often utilized to transmit male strength to the female in labor. In rare instances, the southern man followed the primitive custom of the "couvade"—taking to bed as if bearing the child himself.

One of the most persistent and widespread beliefs about childbirth, which still endures among some southern black people, concerns the psychic powers of babies born with faces covered with a veil or caul, the membrane of the amniotic sac. The belief prevails that these babies will possess the power to foresee the future and to see and hear ghosts. In the case of excessive bleeding during and after delivery, several common verbal formulas, including a section from the book of Ezekiel, were recited. The delivery phase of the birth process ended with the careful and traditional disposal through burning or burial of the placenta, membranes, and cord. These disposal methods were believed necessary for the future well-being of infant and mother.

The less medical science knows about a condition, the more likely traditional medical beliefs are to survive. In recent decades in the South childbirth has evolved into a highly institutionalized, bureaucratized, and safe procedure. This evolution in modern medical practice has replaced, for the most part, the alternative traditions of folk medicine. Today, by and large, the southern way of birth is the American way of birth. The bearing of a child is circumscribed by how-to books and classes, hospital deliveries, and modern medical practice. Yet even now the medical practices of childbirth, woven from the knowledge of Europeans, Africans, and Native Americans, are not entirely dead, particularly among working-class families in the South.

See also SCIENCE AND MEDICINE: Health, Public; Health, Rural; WOMEN'S LIFE: Healers, Women

Carolyn Lipson-Walker
Bloomington, Indiana

Marie Campbell, *Folks Do Get Born* (1946); Karen Cox, in *Foxfire 2*, ed. Eliot Wigginton (1973); Josephine B. Currie, *Mississippi Folklore Register* (Spring 1978); Ronald G. Killion and Charles T. Waller, *A Treasury of Georgia Folklore* (1972); Harry Law, *Tennessee Folklore Society Bulletin* (December 1952); Alice H. Murphree, in *Southern Anthropological Society Proceedings, No. 1: Essays on Medical Anthropology*, ed. Thomas Weaver (1968); J. Hampden Porter, *Journal of American Folklore* (April–June 1894); Vance Randolph, *Ozark Superstitions* (1947); Carroll Y. Rich, *Journal of American Folklore* (July–September 1976); Lawrence S. Thompson, *Kentucky Folklore Record* (January–March 1959); Newman I. White, ed., *Frank C. Brown Collection of North Carolina Folklore*, vol. 6 (1964); Gordon Wilson, *Tennessee Folklore Society Bulletin* (June 1965); Peter H. Wood, *Southern Exposure* (Summer 1978).

Clothing

Don Yoder specifies four characteristics of folk clothing: it is immediately identifiable and distinct; it identifies the wearer to the outside world as well as to the community; it is prescribed by the community; and its forms are dictated by the community's traditions. For these reasons, folk clothing has always served as a potent symbol of the South.

In the southern United States clothing styles fall along an elite-popular-folk continuum. Elite clothing includes the one-of-a-kind creations of haute couture. Popular clothing includes both mass-produced and homemade garments designed with an eye to current fashion. Folk clothing, whether purchased from catalogs, small-town stores, or made at home, is not seen as subject to the whims of fashion. Early journals and diaries, magazine pictures, and photographs document traditional clothing in the South. By and large, the dress of southern subsistence farmers, tenant farmers, and Appalachians did not differ notably from the dress of rural people of other parts of the United States, especially of the Midwest and Great Plains. The Wisconsin clothes in the photography of Charles Van Schaick are not notably different from the clothing worn in Kentucky and Arkansas photos from the same period. The Walker Evans Farm Security Administration photographs of Alabama and Mississippi farmers reveal the same sort of clothes as the Dorothea Lange and Russell Lee photographs from Oklahoma, Ohio, Idaho, and California. Even the warmer climate of the South did not necessarily dictate lighter clothing in summer, though it did create less demand for warm clothing in winter.

Nevertheless, some distinctive styles and garments have developed in the South. Joseph Doddridge, in describing the mode of dress he saw on the Appalachian frontier in the revolutionary period, speaks of "the hunting shirt . . . a kind of loose frock reaching half way down the thighs, with large sleeves open before, and so wide as to lap over a foot or more when belted. . . . The bosom of this served as a wallet to hold a chunk of bread cake, jerk, tow for wiping the barrel of the rifle, or any other necessity for the hunter or warrior. The belt . . . was always tied behind." The hunting shirt, which seems to have been a civilian adaptation of the military coat, was usually made of cloth rather than of deerskin, because wet leather is clammy and cold. It was worn over another shirt, also long, but opened only at the neck. This inner shirt was the ancestor of the modern "soft-collar" shirt and also of the night shirt.

Through much of the 19th century, work clothing for rural men consisted of trousers, high boots, a soft shirt, a vest, and a broad-brimmed hat. For women it consisted of a long full dress, an apron, ladies' boots, a bonnet, and perhaps a fichu (a light triangular scarf draped over the shoulder). Black women favored a turban or bandana. In New Orleans this took the form of a *tignon*, an elaborately folded madras square worn around the head, reminiscent of African women's head coverings.

Between the Civil War and World War I there was a shift to bib overalls for men and to prints and shorter skirts for women. Mills in the Upland South provided inexpensive ready-made clothing, but shirts and dresses were frequently made at home from the white or print cotton sacks that staples such as rice and flour were packaged in. Women often wore men's shoes.

Specific occupations often necessitated special clothing. Tanners, cobblers, carpenters, tailors, and smiths in the South, as in other parts of the country, wore distinctive aprons. Street vendors often wore unconventional clothing, such as smocks, sashes, or sailor's jumpers, to distinguish themselves. Of all occupations, however, the cowboy produced the most colorful American folk costume. The cowboy early adopted the choke-barreled, copper-riveted blue canvas pants manufactured in San Francisco by Levi Strauss and the broad-brimmed hat by J. B. Stetson of Philadelphia. The rest of the cowboy's working outfit consisted of a collarless shirt, a bandana for a collar, high-heeled riding boots, and perhaps a vest and chaps. Cut like Indian leggings, chaps were leather for protection in cactus country and were fur or hair in rainy or snow country.

Florida cowboys were slow to adopt the full southwestern regalia. Early photographs show broad hats and jeans but also regular soft-collared shirts and laced boots or wellingtons. Perhaps more dress conscious than most occupational groups, cowboys developed clothing-related customs and superstitions, such as avoiding yellow shirts, setting the hat down brim-side up "to hold in the luck," and avoiding placing the hat on a bed.

Much folk clothing is sewn, but stockings, mittens, gloves, scarves, and caps are often knitted or crocheted, as are a wide variety of garments for infants. In addition, knit or crocheted lace was long used to decorate women's undergarments.

Even garments of popular manufacture may be worn in a distinctive folk way. The man who wishes to identify himself with the folk end of the clothing continuum, for instance, will wear the appropriate head covering, whether a broad-brimmed hat, as in the 1850s, or a baseball cap, frequently called a "gimme cap" and decorated with different sayings or business names. Folk custom at different times has decreed that jeans be worn cuffless or with deep cuffs. Bandanas too have been used over the years as scarves, collars, halter tops, headbands, turbans, and belts. Cherokee lacrosse players have even worn them as breech cloths.

In the South both sectarian and ethnic groups have at times set themselves off from the larger community by wearing distinctive dress in their everyday lives. By the end of the 18th century the plain style had emerged among the Quakers, Methodists, and Baptists. A southern variation of this style was worn by the white Quakers of the Maryland Eastern Shore and the Piedmont.

The most distinctively southern sectarian dress emerged among the Holiness churches in the 20th century. These churches prescribe rules of modesty for women, forbidding slacks or trousers and requiring long sleeves, high necks, lower hemlines, and uncut hair. Women in these churches, like Quaker women before them, frequently found in the styles of an earlier period a way to meet their religious obligations. In the 1980s Holiness women frequently wear the shirtwaist dress that was an item of popular culture in the 1950s, and on dress occasions put up their long hair in a style suggestive of the bouffant hairdos of that same period.

Mennonite women in the South, cut off from the center of Mennonite culture in Pennsylvania, frequently wear a "plain" style that is much like that of Holiness women. They retain the Mennonite cap or "prayer covering," however, and their hairstyle is more severe. Old Regular Baptists likewise favor conservative dress. In this sect, as in some Mennonite groups, men do not wear neckties. Afro-American churches frequently have distinctive clothing for choirs, nurselike white uniforms for deaconesses, and white gowns for baptisms.

One of the most distinctive ethnic folk clothing traditions in the United States is found among the Five Civilized Tribes of the Southeast (Creek, Cherokee, Choctaw, Chickasaw, Seminole). These tribesmen very early abandoned aboriginal dress and made a distinctive adaptation of European dress. They took the hunting shirt, added to it the lace collar from the inner shirt, belted it with a colored sash, and wore it over leggings or trousers and moccasins or boots. Formal headgear was a turban, an item 18th-century gentlemen wore in place of a wig at home. Beads and gorgets (pieces of armor protecting the throat) completed the costume. This costume survives, much altered, especially among the Seminoles. Up until World War II Seminole men often wore brightly colored hunting shirts as their sole garment. The shirts are now made in two parts, a full top and a gathered skirt.

The Seminole women also developed a distinctive version of southern dress. They came to prefer a blouse with a long ruffle all around the yoke. In time this ruffle was lengthened to waist length, and the remainder of the blouse was no longer necessary, the upper garment becoming a full chiffon cape dropping to the waist and worn over a full skirt made of horizontal bands of materials. Patchwork began to show up early, and the treadle sewing machine, introduced to the Seminoles about 1890, made possible the elaborate patchwork bands out of which traditional Seminole garments are composed today.

After World War II most Seminole men exchanged the skirts of their shirts for jeans, but they still favored the patchwork tops. By the 1970s these tops were frequently worn as windbreaker jackets. Because construction of traditional patchwork garments is time consuming, Seminoles since World War II have tended to wear them only on dress occasions or when dealing with the public.

Dress for self-presentation on public occasions is another type of folk costume. Country music groups have frequently chosen cowboy clothes. Some, like the Coon Creek Girls, wore stylized versions of turn-of-the-century clothing, and some comic groups chose the hayseed or "hillbilly" image—bib overalls, plaid shirt, straw hat, and bandana handkerchief. The western image has faded from popularity among female singers, and many male singers now don sequined tuxedos along with stetsons and boots. Gospel groups, black and white, sometimes dress like country groups, sometimes wear choir robes, and sometimes dress in formal attire.

At festivals and craft fairs the presenters, especially women, often dress to suggest heritage. The typical costume for women is a long-sleeved blouse, long gathered skirt, apron, and sunbonnet. The "southern belle" outfit may also qualify as a folk costume, since it represents not a historical picture of antebellum women's clothing, but a folk sense of the period. Even unbecoming stereotypes provide inspiration in costuming for self-presentation. The Appalachian county seat that is celebrating Hillbilly Days will be full of solid citizens wearing variations of the hayseed costume and drawing on corncob pipes or whiskey demijohns.

Mumming, or the wearing of a costume for disguise as part of a celebration or ritual, seems not to be widespread in the South. Costuming is a more recent development in the celebration of Halloween in this part of the country. But folk costume has long been a part of the Mardi Gras celebration all along the Gulf Coast from Mobile to southwest Louisiana. In New Orleans folk costume can be quite elaborate, especially in the feathered creations of the black "Mardi Gras Indians." East and west of New Orleans, the folk costumes tend to be more informal. On the Mardi Gras ride in Mamou, La., anything that will disguise or conceal the wearer can be worn. Similar informal costumes were also worn in the Christmas mumming known as Dry Setting once practiced in Alabama.

Disguises of the Ku Klux Klan are more serious. The typical costume is a long white robe and a tall pointed hood that conceals the face. But red and black are also used, and the robes are sometimes elaborately decorated with Klan symbols.

As elsewhere in the country, costumes are worn at Christmas, Easter, and Purim; for parties, plays, and pageants. In New Orleans, children dressed as Mary and Joseph or as angels have a role in the 19 March Saint Joseph's Day celebration. On this day, too, the Mardi Gras Indians don their costumes for a final march before destroying the finery so that it cannot be used the following year.

Folk clothing continues to mark the distinctiveness of subgroups. As not only functional objects but expressive ones, items of clothing highlight religious, family, social class, and community values and heritages throughout the South.

See also BLACK LIFE: / Mardi Gras Indians; ETHNIC LIFE: Indians

Bill McCarthy
College of the Ozarks

John Blay, *After the Civil War: A Pictorial Profile of America from 1865 to 1900* (1960); Joseph Doddridge, *Notes on the Settlement and Indian Wars of the Western Parts of Virginia and Pennsylvania from 1763 to 1783, Inclusive, Together with a Review of the State of Society and Manners of the First Settlers of the Western Country* (1824); Ralph Henry Gabriel et al., eds., *The Pageant of America: A Pictorial History of the United States*, 15 vols. (1925–29); Leon H. Grandjean, *New Orleans Characters* (1949); Margaret Wood, *Native American Fashion: Modern Adaptations of Traditional Designs* (1981); Don Yoder, in *Folklore and Folklife: An Introduction*, ed. Richard M. Dorson (1972), in *Forms upon the Frontier: Folklife and Folk Arts in the United States*, ed. Austin Fife, Alta Fife, and Henry Glassie (1969).

Collectors

When folklorists organized the American Folklore Society in the late 19th century, they intended to use the society to record and preserve the old ballads, songs, and beliefs that members thought would disappear in the face of rapid modernization. Among the subjects they felt should be preserved were "relics of old English folk lore" and "lore of negroes in the Southern states." Both subjects attracted numerous collectors who scoured the South for material. Many collectors romantically viewed the isolation of the mountain and river people of the South as nurturing folklore that had died in other areas. In the mountains, song collectors found a homogenous population of English descendants; along the rivers they found tightly knit communities resisting change; in the lowlands they looked for segregated black communities preserving vestiges of African and plantation lore. Although modern folklorists do not generally share the antiquarian outlook of the past, they are still drawn to the South as a particularly fertile ground for folklore collection.

J. Frank Dobie, Texas folklore scholar, c. 1940s

The first collection of black folksongs, *Slave Songs of the United States*, was published in 1867 by a trio of non-southerners (William F. Allen, Charles P. Ware, and Lucy M. Garrison) collecting in the South. Following their work was the collection of black folktales by Joel Chandler Harris in the 1880s. He rewrote the texts and published them in a successful series of Uncle Remus books. His books sparked new interest in the folktales of the South. The *Journal of American Folklore*, for instance, founded in 1888, published over a hundred articles and notes on black folklore, most of them coming from the South. The zeal for collecting such material could still be felt generations later in the publication of *American Negro Folktales* (1967) by the dean of modern American folklorists, Richard M. Dorson (1916–81). His book was based largely on his work in the 1950s among Mississippi and Arkansas blacks.

Major collectors also staked their reputations on gathering relics of old English folklore, and especially folksong, in the South. Standing out was Cecil J. Sharp (1859–1924). Sharp was well known in the early years of the century for collecting folksongs in England. Traveling to America to assist with the staging of a New York play, he was visited by Olive Dame Campbell, the wife of John C. Campbell, the director of the Russell Sage Foundation's Southern Highland Division. She showed him songs she had collected from Appalachian residents. He recognized remnants of English folksongs and was determined to pursue the lead. In the summer of 1916 he traveled with a former student, Maud Karpeles (1886–1976), hunting folksongs. They returned for two more extended trips before 1918. Their pioneering efforts resulted in the publication of the monumental *English Folk Songs from the Southern Appalachians* in two volumes. The first edition appeared in 1917 and was revised in 1932 and 1952.

Several southerners distinguished themselves with extensive collections of folksongs. Josiah H. Combs (1886–1960), for example, published his collection of southern folksongs in Paris, and in 1967 the collection was published as *Folk-Songs of the Southern United States* by the American Folklore Society. Combs hailed from Hazard, Ky. He came under the influence of another great collector of southern folksongs, John Harrington Cox (1863–1945) of West Virginia University, who published his *Folk-Songs of the South* in 1925 and *Traditional Ballads, Mainly from West Virginia* in 1939. Cox was a student of the famous ballad scholar George Lyman Kittredge (1860–1941) of Harvard. In Virginia, Arthur Kyle Davis, Jr. (1897–1972), a professor of English at the University of Virginia, compiled the influential *Traditional Ballads of Virginia* in 1929. Mississippi native Arthur Palmer Hudson (1892–1978) added to the hefty bookshelf of southern folksong collections in 1936 with his well-received *Folksongs of Mississippi and Their Background.* Another Mississippi-born collector, John A. Lomax, had completed his comprehensive *Cowboy Songs and Other Frontier Ballads* by 1910, and he went on to gather and publish a wide range of American folksongs. His son, Alan Lomax, and daughter, Bess Lomax Hawes, continued the tradition. The efforts of these collectors and others resulted in the founding of the two longest-running regional folklore journals in America, *Southern Folklore Quarterly* (established 1937) and *Tennessee Folklore Society Bulletin* (established 1934).

The South also provided the setting for landmark collections of folk belief. Harry Middleton Hyatt (1896–1978) and Newbell Niles Puckett (1898–1967) independently put together volumes of material taken primarily from southern blacks. After compiling the folklore of Adams County, Ill., in the 1930s Harry Hyatt left his native Illinois for field trips up and down the southern coast and inland to New Orleans. Hyatt, an Episcopal minister, had a natural interest in religious and magical practices. He meticulously recorded encounters with root doctors, conjurers, and hoodoo men. Eventually his notes filled five volumes of *Hoodoo-Conjuration-Witchcraft-Rootwork* published from 1970 to 1978.

Newbell Niles Puckett was born in Columbus, Miss., and went on to teach sociology at Western Reserve University in Cleveland. His magnum opus was *Folk Beliefs of the Southern Negro* brought out by the University of North Carolina Press in 1926. To get his collection, he interviewed over 400 informants mostly from Mississippi, Alabama, and Georgia. Puckett took great pains to compare what he collected to other finds from around the world. He added photographs that documented the believers and their surroundings.

Frank C. Brown (1870–1943), a colorful teacher and administrator at Duke University, was an avid collector of North Carolina folklore who received most of his recognition after his death. He sought to record the range of folklore from games to songs, beliefs to legends, and proverbs to tales. After his death leading folklorists edited his collection into seven weighty volumes entitled the *Frank C. Brown Collection of North Carolina Folklore* (1952–64). The work is now a standard reference of folklore.

Perhaps the most indefatigable folklore collector in the South was writer Vance Randolph (1892–1980). Although originally from Kansas, he spent most of his years collecting and writing in the Ozarks. He marveled at the lively oral tradition he found there, and he devoted his career to reporting it. He began publishing articles on folk beliefs he found in the late 1920s. His first two books, *The Ozarks: An American Survival of Primitive Society* (1931) and *Ozark Mountain Folks* (1932), were general descriptions of Ozark mountain life, which included chapters on dialect, folksong, folk belief, and magic. Beginning in the 1940s, Randolph increased his folklore collecting and publishing. Among his notable contributions were *Ozark Folksongs* (4 vols., 1946–50), *Ozark Superstitions* (1947), *We Always Lie to Strangers: Tall Tales from the Ozarks* (1951), *Who Blowed Up the Church House? and Other Ozark Folk Tales* (1952), *Down in the Holler: A Gallery of Ozark Folk Speech* (1953), *The Devil's Pretty Daughter* (1955), *Hot Springs and Hell, and Other Folk Jests and Anecdotes from the Ozarks* (1965), *Ozark Folklore: A Bibliography* (1972), and *Pissing in the Snow, and Other Ozark Folktales* (1976).

Collectors were also drawn to the distinctive handicrafts and housing of the South. A major work that brought attention to this trove was Allen Eaton's *Handicrafts of the Southern Highlands* (1937). Eaton (1878–1962) had erected craft exhibitions at major expositions and lectured on art appreciation in the North. The same Olive Dame Campbell who influenced Cecil J. Sharp invited Eaton to the Appalachians. Eaton then helped organize the Southern Highland Handicraft Guild and collected examples of native craftsworkers and their arts and architecture. In his book he chronicled the efforts to organize southern craftsworkers, and he carefully documented a wide range of artisanship from spinning to whittling, house construction to furniture making, and pottery to basketmaking. His book thus was partly a valuable record of Appalachian material folk culture and also a proposal for reviving and protecting the crafts economy.

Although today's motivation for collecting is different from that of the past, the fervor for collecting southern material remains strong among folklorists. Native southerners such as William Ferris of Mississippi, William Lynwood Montell of Kentucky, and Daniel Patterson of North Carolina have used their southern university bases to collect tales, songs, and material culture in their native states. In Tennessee, David Evans and Charles Wolfe are deeply involved in the collection of blues and old-time music, respectively. John Michael Vlach with his book *Charleston Blacksmith* (1981), about a black craftsman from South Carolina, and Michael Owen Jones with his *The Hand Made Object and Its Maker* (1975), about Chester Cornett, a Kentucky chair maker, have added greatly to the knowledge of personalities behind the folklore usually collected. Also concerned with material culture, Henry Glassie scrupulously documented southern folk architecture in "The Types of the Southern Mountain Cabin" (appearing in Jan Harold Brunvand's *The Study of American Folklore*, 1968) and *Folk Housing in Middle Virginia* (1975). In Kentucky and Georgia, Thomas A. Adler collects and studies regional foodways and music, and in Missouri Howard Wight Marshall reveals the southern influences on foodways and folk architecture in publications including *Folk Architecture in Little Dixie* (1981). Picking up from where Vance Randolph left off, W. K. McNeil, equally indefatigable, has continued collecting folklore in Arkansas and Missouri.

In addition to this mere sample of folklorists independently working in the South, centers of southern folklore collection and study encourage and carry out collecting at the University of Texas, Western Kentucky University, University of Kentucky, University of Alabama, University of North Carolina at Chapel Hill, University of South Carolina, Center for Southern Folklore in Memphis, and Center for the Study of Southern Culture at the University of Mississippi. Appalshop in Whitesburg, Ky., produces films and records about Appalachia, and Eliot Wigginton's Foxfire project in north Georgia collects and publishes Appalachian folklife materials. Journals featuring collections of southern folklore are published by state and regional folklore societies in North Carolina, Virginia, Mississippi, Tennessee, Kentucky, Arkansas, Missouri, and Florida. An Association of Folklorists in the South produces a newsletter to reach the many professional collectors and scholars working in the South. They are building on the proud legacy of earlier collectors, who often worked without the benefit of academic credentials or outside funding. They saw in the South a large and distinctive crop of folklore, and they harvested a copious amount of material for future generations to appreciate and study.

See also BLACK LIFE: Folklore, Black; EDUCATION: / Campbell, John C.; *Foxfire*; LANGUAGE: / Randolph, Vance; LITERATURE: / Harris, Joel Chandler

Simon J. Bronner
Pennsylvania State University
Capitol Campus

W. Amos Abrams, *North Carolina Folklore* (1964); Simon J. Bronner, *American Folklore Studies: An Intellectual History* (1986); Bertrand H. Bronson, *Journal of American Folklore* (October–December 1977); Jan Harold Brunvand, *The Study of American Folklore: An Introduction* (2d ed., 1978); Richard M. Dorson, *American Folklore* (rev. ed., 1977), *Buying the Wind: Regional Folklore in the United States* (1964); Susan Dwyer-Shick, "The American Folklore Society and Folklore Research in America, 1888–1940" (Ph.D. dissertation, University of Pennsylvania, 1979); Herbert Halpert, *Journal of American Folklore* (July–September 1981); Ed Kahn, *Kentucky Folklore Record* (October–December 1960); W. K. McNeil, "A History of American Folklore Scholarship before 1908" (Ph.D. dissertation, Indiana University, 1980); D. K. Wilgus, *Anglo-American Folksong Scholarship since 1898* (1959).

Family Folklore

Family folklore grows out of the shared experiences of family members and their shared view of a common past. These experiences are often given creative expression in such forms as stories, songs, sayings, pastimes, names, customs, photographs, and memorabilia. Often traditions are passed down through several generations of a family; other times they are created anew, shaped to meet the demands of the present. Quite often a successful party becomes an annual family event or a word mispronounced becomes a private family expression. Families frequently develop their own calendar of pastimes and celebrations, their own repertoire of stories and expressions, their own version of the family's past.

Southerners have long maintained a strong sense of the importance of family, not only the nuclear group but a broad family network that includes several branches, distant cousins, and persons who may not be blood kin. This is partly because many southern families have lived in the same area for several generations, developing strong ties with their relatives and their communities. Although many nuclear family groups also have a wealth of family traditions, families who have maintained continuity with relatives and community for generations often develop an especially rich store of folklore. Sociologists James Bossard and Eleanor Boll, who define family rituals as the "ceremonial use of leisure," found in their study of American families that the "larger the family the more numerous and rich the rituals." This may be explained in part because the more time family members spend with their relatives, the more experiences they have to draw on in their folklore; and the more continuity there is between generations, the more likely it is that traditions will survive over time.

In large, extended family groups, traditions often serve an important role in defining family membership and in keeping separate the different branches of the family. Which relatives are invited to traditional family events and, of those invited, which ones regularly participate, can be a telling indication of who is a member. In communities with several large, interrelated families, an invitation to an annual picnic may be a more important sign of family membership than the same last name. Family membership and a sense of family identity may derive from shared traditions as much as from blood ties.

The South has often been called a region of storytellers, and quite often stories are a major genre of southern family folklore. Remarkable similarities show up in family stories throughout the United States. Studies suggest that American families tend to tell stories about major transitions, such as births, courtships, and migrations, and about the personalities of family members. These broad themes appear in southern family stories, shaped by the southern experience.

Historical events and periods, such as the Civil War and the Great Depression, which had a tremendous effect on southerners, provide material for many family stories. Legends of Civil War heroes and rogues, tragedies and triumphs, have kept that event alive for many families. A common American story-type first described by Stanley Brandes is the "lost fortune story." In it, a family describes how an ancestor lost what would have been a fortune for them through foolishness or a lack of entrepreneurial spirit. In the South this theme often appears in stories of a family member burying the family silver to prevent Yankee troops from finding it and then forgetting where it was buried or dying without telling relatives the location. In black families, stories are often told about the capture of ancestors by slave traders in Africa, the indignities of slavery, and ancestors who rebelled against their slavemasters.

Bossard and Boll, in their study of American families, argue that leisure is the key to family rituals, that the more time allowed for leisure in a family, the more rituals it will develop. In an area where leisure has long been held up as one of the virtues of the southern way of life, family pastimes not only become important in themselves but provide the shared experiences that give rise to other forms of folklore; they also provide the setting for sharing them. Stories are often told, as well as set, at family picnics, parties, vacations, and other leisure events.

Family relationships and the traits and personalities of family members are also dominant topics of southern family folklore. The legends that grow out of long-standing family feuds, especially common in the southern Appalachians but found in other parts of the South as well, tell of the violence and bitterness that sometimes erupt between, and within, clannish southern families. More often, however, family folklore celebrates the ties that bind. In communities with several large interrelated families, the relationships among kin become complex, and family members can use their folklore to reaffirm kinship connections that might otherwise be forgotten. Drawing on characteristic traits associated with family names, stories often connect a relative with different branches of the family by showing how he or she exhibits family traits. Such stories may begin with a statement such as, "You know how stubborn the Hardens are," and then follow with an example of how Amy Johnson, whose grandmother was a Harden, refused to change her position in a family argument. The folklore of family traits may be seen as part of a larger preoccupation in the South with genealogy and with "placing" persons in terms of their family background, social class, race, and geographical location.

Southern family stories and expressions also dwell frequently on the idiosyncracies of relatives, the traits that distinguish them from other members of the family. The eccentric uncle, the flamboyant aunt, the relative who is "set in his ways" are central figures in much family folklore and often are given a special status as "family characters." The folklore surrounding these "characters" may be one way in which large, closely knit family groups accept nonconformity among their relatives and thus maintain family harmony.

The emphasis on leisure time, the strong continuity between generations of many families, the interest in family background and genealogy, and the love of storytelling have contributed to a rich folklore among southern families.

See also BLACK LIFE: Family, Black; Genealogy, Black; MYTHIC SOUTH: Family; WOMEN'S LIFE: Genealogy; Maiden Aunt; / Family Reunion

Amanda Dargan
Queens Council on the Arts
New York, New York

Mody Boatright et al., *The Family Saga and Other Phases of American Folklore* (1958); James Bossard and Eleanor Boll, *Ritual in Family Living: A Contemporary Study* (1950); Stanley H. Brandes, *Journal of the Folklore Institute* (No. 1, 1975); Deirdre LaPin, *Hogs in the Bottom: Family Folklore in Arkansas* (1982); Kathryn Morgan, *Children of Strangers: Stories of a Black Family* (1980); Steven J. Zeitlin et al., *A Celebration of American Family Folklore: Tales and Traditions from the Smithsonian Collection* (1982).

Folk Medicine

Folk medicine can be defined as a cultural system using herbs, roots, over-the-counter drugs, and folk specialists to achieve health. It is based on the integration of scientific medicine with traditional knowledge. Although exact statistics on the distribution and frequency of folk medicine are unavailable, the practice has been, and remains, widespread, particularly among the poor in both rural and urban southern areas.

Folk medicine has been utilized for chronic health problems more frequently than acute ones, by both blacks and whites and by men and women. Women are most often sought out for help. Men, however, are also often folk healers. Blacks will use white healers and whites will use black ones. Hazel Weidman (1978) reports that in choosing a healer the power of the healer is more important than ethnic background to the client.

Illnesses treated through this system generally exhibit familiar symptoms that do not seriously incapacitate the victim. Most home remedies are easily available animal products (i.e., milk, fat, bones), chemical or mineral substances (i.e., sulphur, ashes, vinegar, sugar, turpentine), and plants (i.e., yellow root, tree bark, sassafras). A variety of these substances is kept in the home for use in treating colds, indigestion, burns, sores, sore throats, fevers, headaches, and general aches and pains. Plants are administered in the form of teas. Knowledge of these folk remedies is widespread, and although substances may change for particular health problems, confidence in them remains. Many substances used in the home are "over-the-counter" medicines and the repertoire keeps changing. There has been an increasing reliance on medicines advertised in the media. Some of them have been used for years but new ones advertised by drug companies continue to be incorporated into health beliefs and behaviors. Folk healers will often combine new remedies with more traditional roots or herbs in their treatment of illness. For example, a root doctor in North Carolina prescribes Pepto-Bismol mixed with whiskey for the "shakes."

Several types of traditional healers can be found in the rural and urban South. They are referred to by a variety of names such as hoodoo doctor, voodoo doctor, herb doctor, root doctor, and conjurer. The practice of voodoo medicine is concentrated on the coast of Georgia and South Carolina and in southern Louisiana, although its influence has survived in other areas with large numbers of blacks. Voodoo specialists have reputations that span several hundred miles, and people will travel considerable distances to see them for healing purposes.

Among many blacks in the South illnesses from natural causes are organized into a belief system based on the need to balance the blood in the body. Blood can become unbalanced by being either too sweet ("high blood") or too bitter ("low blood"). Imbalance can result from an improper diet (too many sweet or bitter foods), a lack of proper rest, or too much worry. The treatment involves diet modification, family counseling to deal with stress, and herbal remedies. Furthermore, when blood is not balanced, other bodily fluids also may be out of balance, resulting in an individual becoming more susceptible to illnesses. Thus, the individual must keep a balance between the good and evil forces.

Some healers are believed to be particularly competent to treat specific problems. There are specialists who "talk the fire out of burns," "stop bleeding," "cure the thrash," and "conjure warts." Root doctors are often used for "high blood" or "low blood" and for other ailments such as headaches, tiredness, or itching. They may heal either with herbal remedies (a natural condition) or with "rootworks" (an unnatural condition). They are frequently consulted by people who also participate in the scientific medical system. Others have the knowledge and ability to rid the body of general aches and pains and mental stress.

People use these specialists for symptoms such as headaches, backaches, occasional loss of memory, tiredness, thinking about a particular subject or person too much, and sexual impotency. The folk healer will diagnose such cases as overwork, "nerves," or worry. They generally do not compartmentalize the problems of their clients into mental and physical problems. Healers seek knowledge of the social and religious lives of their clients before making a diagnosis and recommending treatment. Clients are consequently treated on physical, psychological, and social levels simultaneously. Through the ritual use of roots and herbs, diets, popular medical cures, passages read from the Bible, and counseling, the healer attempts to restore a balance in the patient's life.

Health is seen as maintaining a balance between the good and bad forces in the universe. These forces are believed to be ever present and the individual is continually caught between them. The individual must maintain harmony with these forces through his or her own behavior. Illnesses are classified according to natural or unnatural causes. For example, a study of root doctors in North Carolina found that they determine whether an illness is the result of unnatural causes, such as spells, which are treated by counter rootwork, or natural causes generally treated by herbal or medicinal remedies. Furthermore, the root doctors decide if the illness is predominantly a problem of the body or of the mind. Most illnesses, though, are classified as both (such as nerves and hysterics) and the proper treatment prescribed. Indeed, in folk medicine the cause of the illness is more relevant than symptoms in diagnosis and treatment.

Southern folk beliefs about health are widely shared by people who practice folk medicine. Obviously, their concepts of disease and illness involve a broader conceptual framework than those of scientific medicine. It combines elements of African culture, European culture, Greek classical medicine, American Indian medicine, scientific medicine, and voodoo religion. These elements are synthesized within the framework of fundamentalist Christianity and provide the participants in the folk medical system with a broad belief system allowing them to explain illness and misfortunes.

See also ENVIRONMENT: Plant Uses; SCIENCE AND MEDICINE: Self-dosage; WOMEN'S LIFE: Healers, Women

Carole E. Hill
Georgia State University

Wayland Hand, ed., *American Folk Medicine* (1976), *Magical Medicine: The Folkloric Component of Medicine in the Folk Belief, Custom, and Ritual of the Peoples of Europe and America* (1980); Carole E. Hill, *Southern Medicine* (1976), *Journal of Popular Culture* (Spring 1973), with Holly Mathews, in *Perspectives on the American South*, vol. 1, ed. Merle Black and John Shelton Reed (1981); Harry Middleton Hyatt, *Hoodoo-Conjuration-Witchcraft-Rootwork*, 5 vols. (1970–78); Alice H. Murphree, *The Health of a Rural County: Perspectives and Problems* (1976); Newbell Niles Puckett, *Folk Beliefs of the Southern Negro* (1926; reprint ed., 1968).

Folk Painting

Southern folk painting cannot be understood apart from American folk art in general. Scholars, folk art collectors, museum curators, and others have hotly debated the nature of American folk painting, describing it with terms such as *primitive*, *visionary*, *popular*, *provincial*, *amateur*, *schoolgirl*, *crude*, *naive*, *unsophisticated*, *grass roots*, *outsider*, *innocent*, *homemade*, or *nonacademic*.

Art historians often view folk painting within the context of academic styles and movements, but some art historians argue that true folk painters derive their creative inspiration from isolation. Curators and collectors sometimes see these paintings as quaint artifacts of rural, preindustrial life. Folklorists view the folk painter within the context of the traditional ideas in a particular folk culture. They point out that folk paintings, like all folk artifacts, have utilitarian functions, are not limited to one historical era, and are not inevitably rural. Folklorists shy away from an all-inclusive definition of folk art that takes in all times and places, preferring to concentrate on the life history and biographical case study of a particular folk artist.

Popular interest in folk art began with 19th-century romantic nationalism, and efforts of American scholars and collectors to study folk painting increased in the 1930s. The egalitarian spirit of that decade promoted an interest in the art of the common people, expressed in Thomas Hart Benton's studies of folklife and in New Deal murals. Holger Cahill, art historian and museum director, assembled a pioneering folk painting exhibition at the Museum of Modern Art in 1932, and the catalog, *The Art of the Common Man in America, 1750–1900*, appeared the same year. Well-illustrated volumes from the 1940s to the 1970s portrayed folk painting as consisting mostly of 19th-century portraits, genre paintings, landscapes, seascapes, town views, house and farm views, historical scenes, religious images, patriotic images, *fraktur*, and still lives. Portraiture, often executed by itinerant painters, has been seen as the major category of southern folk painting before the Civil War. Irish-born Virginia artist John Toole, for example, was perhaps the most prominent early 19th-century itinerant painter, traveling the Piedmont and Tidewater areas of Virginia and painting over 300 still-extant works. Joshua Johnston is the best-known black folk painter of the early 1800s. Southern women artists produced a large number of watercolors at female seminaries and elsewhere, and these are viewed as folk paintings by art historians. Many of these same works, styles, and artists also figure, however, in discussions of early American academic art.

The regional aspect of American folk painting has long been a category used by scholars and collectors, but until recently they have downplayed the importance of the South. Nina Fletcher Little, an early historian of folk art, wrote in 1957 that "New England was the richest center of folk art because it was richest in craftsmen," but "in the South there is less evidence of folk art." In fact, collections of American folk art have often included a disproportionately large number of works by southerners without acknowledging the region's dominance. The flowering of scholarship on black folk art since the 1960s has shown that most Afro-American folk painting is southern in origin.

Memory is at the core of the work of many southern folk painters. Older contemporary southerners have witnessed the change from preindustrial life to the space age. Folk painters in the region often reflect on what one of them calls "that long time behind and that short time ahead." Respect for elders is a constant theme among these folk artists. They regard the past with reverence and acknowledge older masters from whom they learned skills. Many self-taught folk artists learned their skills at an early age but did not become active artists until late in life. North Carolina's Minnie Reinhardt liked to draw during her school years, but most of her life was spent engaged in, as she says, "more practical" tasks. Not until she was 77 years of age did she begin to chronicle from memory the folklife of the North Carolina Piedmont. Similarly, Queena Stovall of Virginia painted no pictures until she was 62, Jessie DuBose Rhoads of Alabama did not paint seriously until after an illness and her husband's retirement, and Theora Hamblett of Mississippi began her visionary works only after her mother's death.

Folk painters are conscious of the place and season in which they work. Theora Hamblett drew places from memory, and her paintings recapture the landscape, buildings, and family that shaped her childhood in Paris, Miss. Sam Doyle portrays local characters such as Dr. Buz, the voodoo doctor, from his home on Saint Helena Island in South Carolina. Clementine Hunter's scenes of everyday life are usually set at the Melrose plantation near Natchitoches, La., where she has long resided. Texas artist Fannie Lou Spelce painted works with evocative titles of rural life such as *Peach Season*, *County Memorial Fair*, *Roadside Fruit Stand*, and *Bennett's General Store*. Minnie Reinhardt similarly chronicles the everyday life of her "place" in North Carolina. Charles G. Zug III noted that she painted a dozen or so basic scenes, including homeplaces, the Hog Hill School, Possum John Rudisill's cabin, Wade Smith's pottery, plowing, the wheat harvest, cornhusking, cotton picking, molasses-making, and flowers. A male artist such as Bill Traylor might paint scenes of coon hunting and drinking matches as well as of the routines of farm life.

Southern folk art often shows an affinity for animals and the natural world. The painter's eye portrays barnyard animals with affection or annoyance and wanders also to creatures such as crawfish, alligators, raccoons, bullfrogs, opossums, and snakes. Artists are curious about animal life and sometimes imagine themselves as the animals they portray.

Dream vision painting, in which literal and imaginary worlds often merge, is another major category of southern folk art. Revelations often appear while the artist is asleep or in a semiconscious state, haunting the painter until they are released through artistic creation. Theora Hamblett felt that her gift for visions was inherited from her grandmother who frequently dreamed of supernatural events. Hamblett had only to close her eyes to see visions. Literal and imaginary worlds often merge. Another Mississippian, Luster Willis, discovers characters as they run through his mind, and he puts these "made-up" people in his paintings. Minnie Evans of North Carolina portrays Oriental images, exotic floral patterns, and baroque designs with multiple sets of eyes.

Folk painters in the South draw heavily on religion as a source of images. Their works are filled with biblical characters, stories, and themes. Luster Willis illustrates parables such as the story of Lazarus. Minnie Reinhardt painted a dinner-on-the-grounds series to preserve the memory of the yearly homecoming ritual at her neighborhood's Corinth Baptist Church each August. Other folk artists have painted camp meetings and revivals,

Velox Ward, Sunday Afternoon *(1966)*

baptizings, Sacred Harp singings, funerals, and decoration days at church graveyards.

Southerners are also fond of painting apocalyptic visions. Sister Gertrude Morgan of New Orleans did a series of New Jerusalem paintings, and Minnie Evans was inspired by the book of Revelation to portray fantastic scenes, although her images are more gentle than biblical accounts. The Reverend Howard Finster's work portrays a vision of apocalypse that combines Old Testament prophecies, scenes from Revelation, and modern images of nuclear war. Finster's *Crossing Jordan* (1971) fills the canvas not only with visual images but with words as well. The river Jordan runs with biblical and biblical-sounding sayings: "The Lord Will Deliver His People across Jordan," "Enemies Wish to Destroy Me. They Despise My Prayers, and My Works," "My Only Escape Is Hope." The South's oral folk culture and its Bible Belt religion are appropriately transposed to a visual image in which prominently displayed words reflect a revelation rooted in evangelical religion.

Repetition, balance, and superimposition of materials and perspectives are characteristic features of southern folk painting. When artists repeat a visual idea, the repetitions are never precise, but all are variations on a general theme. Balance and symmetry cause the eye to focus on a central image. When materials are superimposed, the surface textures can affect responses from the viewer. Combining oil paint, stitches, cloth pieces, and other items on a primary surface deepens texture and creates a three-dimensional look. Savannah, Ga., native Ulysses Davis's *Farmhouse with Airplane* (1943) and Mississippi-born Elijah Pierce's *Monday Morning Gossip* (1935) employ both paint and carving on a wood surface.

Contemporary folk art often combines painting with other media to create distinctive environmental art. Georgia artist Nellie Mae Rowe covered her walls with photographs, her crayon drawings, gifts from friends, and plastic flowers. The Temple Compound of Saint Eom—an acronym for artist Eddie Owens Martin—in Buena Vista, Ga., features painted scenes with images from world religions, along with carved walls, dance platforms, totems, gods, and shiny tin roofs. In such creations the lines between painting and a broader conception of folk art as environment are blurred.

Film and video resources on southern folk painting include: *Fannie Lou Spelce: Folk Artist*, Sandra Mentz and Larry Cormier, producers, Institute for Texan Cultures, 1978; *Folk Artist of the Blue Ridge*, Colonial Williamsburg Foundation, producer and distributor, 1963; *Four Women Artists*, William Ferris, producer, Center for Southern Folklore, 1977; *Missing Pieces: Contemporary Georgia Folk Art*, Steve Heiser, producer, Georgia Council for the Arts, 1976; *Queena Stovall: Life's Narrow Space*, Jack Ofield, producer, Bowling Green Films, 1980; *Reverend Howard Finster: Man of Visions*, John F. Turner, producer and distributor, 1981; *Made in Missis-*

sippi: Black Folk Art and Crafts, William Ferris, producer, Center for the Study of Southern Culture, 1975.

Charles Reagan Wilson
University of Mississippi

William Ferris
University of Mississippi

Jan Arnow, *By Southern Hands: A Celebration of Craft Traditions in the South* (1987); Robert Bishop, *Folk Painters of America* (1979); Patti C. Black, ed., *Made by Hand: Mississippi Folk Art* (1980); David C. Driskell, *Two Centuries of Black American Art* (1976); William Ferris, ed., *Afro-American Folk Art and Crafts* (1983), *Local Color: A Sense of Place in Folk Art* (1982); Herbert W. Hemphill, Jr., and Julia Weissman, *Twentieth Century American Folk Art and Artists* (1974); Elinor Lander Horwitz, *Contemporary American Folk Artists* (1975); Sidney Janis, *They Taught Themselves: American Primitive Painters of the Twentieth Century* (1942); Jean Lipman, *American Primitive Paintings* (1942), with Alice Winchester, *The Flowering of American Folk Art, 1776–1876* (1974); Jane Livingston and John Beardsley, *Black Folk Art in America, 1930–1980* (1982); Cynthia E. Rubin, ed., *Southern Folk Art* (1985); Cecilia Steinfeldt, *Texas Folk Art: One Hundred Fifty Years of the Southwestern Tradition* (1981); John Michael Vlach and Simon J. Bronner, eds., *Folk Art and Art Worlds* (1986); Anna Wadsworth, ed., *Missing Pieces: Georgia Folk Art, 1770–1976* (1976); Charles G. Zug III, in *Five North Carolina Folk Artists*, ed. Charles G. Zug III, with Quincy Scarborough, Mary Anne McDonald, and W. Neal Conoley, Jr. (1986).

Folk Sculpture

See ART AND ARCHITECTURE: Sculpture

Folksongs

A folksong is a song without an identifiable composer that survives in a community through oral tradition. Isolated, agrarian southern communities have fostered the survival of folksong traditions. Genres as diverse as Native American ballads, coal-mining songs, mountain love songs, Delta blues, coastal fishing songs, and camp-meeting spirituals, produced and perpetuated by traditional communities, form the core of the southern folksong repertoire.

Southern folksong developed largely from the musical resources of Great Britain and Africa. Both areas made important contributions to southern music, and aspects of those traditions became components of new forms created by southerners, particularly during the 19th century, a period of great innovation and synthesis. Unfortunately, attention to the many varieties of folksong inspired by these two great traditions has been uneven, and knowledge of the development of southern folksong has gaps. Especially prized in the 19th century and early 20th century were the venerable British ballads, and many American versions were collected and published, albeit collected at times from less accurate secondary sources and published without tunes. The most thorough early collecting effort was that of English folklorist Cecil J. Sharp, who embarked on a series of song-hunting trips in the southern highlands beginning in 1916 and uncovered firsthand the richness of southern balladry. The songs Sharp collected (published as *English Folk Songs from the Southern Appalachians*, 1932) echoed vividly their British origins but also displayed remarkable adaptations to the American context, as evidenced by altered place names, modified references, and the replacement of plain-spoken British bawdiness with a characteristically American sense of decorum and moral reserve.

Also common in the South were versions of songs of more recent British origin, including such broadside ballads as "Jackie Munroe" and "The Butcher Boy." There were also songs British in style but American in origin, among them ballads on various subjects of local and regional interest, modeled after not only the British ballads themselves but also the ballad-meter English hymns found everywhere in southern hymnbooks. Popular ones were the railroad ballad "The Wreck of the Old 97," the cowboy ballad "The Streets of Laredo," and numerous murder ballads such as "Poor Omie" and "On the Banks of the Ohio." Other songs in the British mold included widely known lyric songs such as "Drowsy Sleeper," "The Cuckoo," and "The Wagoner's Lad."

A great many Anglo-American folksongs from the South are religious, and although they were not as widely noticed by early collectors, their influence has been considerable. The oldest were unharmonized hymns based on British models, sung to traditional tunes and often lined out. Traces of that tradition still survive among the more conservative of the Primitive Baptists and some black congregations. Surviving folk hymns in the old style include the tune "New Britain," usually sung today with John Newton's text "Amazing grace, how sweet the sound." The spirituals, unlike the hymns, were American creations, arising in the wake of religious revivals taking place on the 19th-century frontier. The great camp meetings of the Second Great Awakening, beginning in Kentucky around 1800, produced hundreds of these easily learned songs, which were based loosely on elements from British hymns in combination with local musical elements. Some of them, including "Wondrous Love" and "Pisgah," were harmonized and found their way into shape-note songbooks compiled by and for southerners in the 19th century and still in use today in the Deep South and parts of the highlands. The first gospel hymns arose after the Civil War. Based in part on the old hymns and spirituals and blending traditional and popular musical elements, gospel singing has proved remarkably adaptable and has grown into a thriving commercial industry, national in scope but strongest in the southern states that have been its creative center.

While the sacred folksongs of white southerners tended at first to be underdocumented, the religious songs of southern blacks were among the first Afro-American songs to attract attention. A by-product of the abolitionist movement in the 19th century was the great interest in black spirituals as symbols of the noble aspirations of the slave population. The first published collection of southern black folksong was William Francis Allen's *Slave Songs of the United States* (1867), which contained mostly sacred and a few secular songs. Numerous other collections of black spirituals followed. Many of the anthologies of black music that came to public attention, however, failed to reveal the energy and essence of the black musical tradition, both by ignoring secular song and by reshaping songs to fit European performance style. Black singing, nevertheless, has been an enormously creative force, ranging from game songs ("Little Sally Walker"), work songs ("Long John"), and field hollers, to later forms including the blues and black gospel, both of which were among the primary components of rhythm and blues and, later, rock and roll.

Although scholars have disagreed, occasionally acrimoniously, as to the relative dominance of black and white sources in southern folksong, the most accurate view seems to be that the two traditions have not been separate and parallel musical streams, but interlocked components of a single tradition. Only in a few regions, where the population was predominantly white (the southern uplands), or predominantly black (the Sea Islands of Georgia and South Carolina), did song traditions remain relatively close to British or African sources. In most of the South the creative exchange between black and white singing gave southern folksong its identity and strength. Because blacks and whites often worked side by side and participated in the same social events, there was ample opportunity for musical exchange. Black singers learned European instruments and adapted them to a black aesthetic, while white singers absorbed these products of the black synthesis. Blacks attended church with whites and learned the same hymns, while white singers used black musicians to entertain at social gatherings. The ballad was a European song form, but some of the best-known American ballads began in the black community, including "John Henry" and "Frankie and Johnnie." The spirituals represented a joint effort, bringing together the structure and rhythm of African music and the melodic and textual elements of British song. The banjo, best known as a staple of the white folk tradition since the late 19th century, was an African import, and blacks as well as whites contributed to the songs and performance style associated with it. The obvious differences between black and white folksong style have served to obscure this cultural interdependence.

Afro-American and Anglo-American sources are by far the dominant influences on southern folksong, but several smaller, more localized traditions have also survived. One of the best-known regional traditions is represented by the Cajun and Creole songs of southern Louisiana, the most culturally complex region in the South, bringing together elements of African, British, Spanish, and French traditions. Cajun music, the songs of the French-speaking Acadians, whose ancestors came to Louisiana from Nova Scotia in the 18th century, includes songs of 17th- and 18th-century France as well as Cajun versions of familiar southern songs. Creole music contains both African and French elements and includes counterparts of black songs from other regions of the South, songs with strong African or Afro-Caribbean elements, and versions of Cajun songs. The Spanish-language songs of the Texas-Mexican border, particularly the balladlike *corrido*, have been well documented by collectors and on older commercial recordings. A number of smaller and more isolated song traditions in the South are associated with religious communities and include the hymns of the Dunkards (or German Baptist Brethren) of Virginia and Cherokee-language versions of Protestant hymns in western North Carolina.

Southern folksongs are more than the fossilized remnants of archaic art forms. In the lively American context, adapting to changing conditions has been as much a part of the folk process for local communities as passing along the old songs. Neighboring ethnic traditions, local songwriters, and even commercial popular culture have contributed new songs that have taken their place in the oral tradition alongside older ones. "Frog Went A-courtin'" is a folksong, but so, in a broader sense, are "Weave Room Blues," written and recorded by Dorsey Dixon, a member of a South Carolina textile mill community, and Louisville journalist William Shakespeare Hays's sentimental song "Little Old Log Cabin in the Lane." Since the advent of the commercial recording of traditional music in the 1920s, local artists have served not only to steer the course of local tradition but also to channel traditional songs into popular culture. The list of southern singers with traditional roots whose influence has spread well beyond their communities includes Tennessee's Uncle Dave Macon, for many years a performer on the Grand Ole Opry; Mississippi-born Jimmie Rodgers, an innovative blender of black and white traditions and a pivotal figure in the foundation of country music; and singer/guitarist Huddie Ledbetter, known as Leadbelly, who absorbed a large and varied repertoire of folk material and later in his life came to represent the southern black tradition for urban audiences who had no other access to the genre.

The richness and vitality of southern traditional song are due to no particular group or locality but to a creative exchange of musical ideas over 150 years. Southern music is a continuum, and there is no clear point at which southern folksong becomes southern song or American song. As traditional spirituals are arranged for choir and set down in denominational hymnbooks, as blues becomes rhythm and blues, as old-time mountain music is incorporated by bluegrass and country and western music, new kinds of songs arise, expressing changes in southern communities, yet without severing their nourishing traditional roots. Thus, age-old links between communities and their folksongs survive even as new musical forms evolve.

See also BLACK LIFE: Music, Black; MUSIC articles

Brett Sutton
Carrboro, North Carolina

Josiah H. Combs, *Folk-Songs of the Southern United States* (1967), ed. D. K. Wilgus; William Ferris and Mary L. Hart, eds., *Folk Music and Modern Sound* (1981); Henry Glassie, Edward D. Ives, and John F. Szwed, eds., *Folksongs and Their Makers* (1970); Charles Joyner, *Folk Song in South Carolina* (1971); Alan Lomax, *Folk Songs of North America* (1975); Newman I. White, ed., *Frank C. Brown Collection of North Carolina Folklore*, vols. 2–5 (1952); D. K. Wilgus, *Anglo-American Folksong Scholarship since 1898* (1959).

Folktales

Southern folktales existed long before the transatlantic migration of Europeans and Africans to the New World. The Cherokees, the Creeks, the Choctaws, and other Native American groups told stories of origins—of how the Great Sun, the earth, the clans, corn, bears, and fire came to be—as well as lighter etiological tales explaining such things as "Why the Possum Grins" and stories about the adventures of the fabulous rabbit trickster. Such narratives were common across the Southeast.

Beginning in the 16th century, the Spanish became the first to import European folktales into the South. Planting colonies in what is now South Carolina, Florida, and Louisiana, and exploring from Texas to California, the Spanish left a strong cultural imprint on these areas. Following the Spanish, French settlers in South Carolina and especially in Louisiana brought zestful versions of such Gallic narratives as "Beauty and the Beast." The English at the dawn of the 17th century settled the coastline between the Chesapeake Bay and Spanish Florida, accompanied by their storehouse of such folktales as "Jack the Giant Killer." The British folktale repertoire was enhanced in the 18th century with the coming of large numbers of Scotch-Irish, who pushed down from Pennsylvania into the backcountry and highlands of the South.

But Europeans were not the only transatlantic settlers of the South. From Senegal and Gambia, from Guinea and Angola came shiploads of enslaved African men, women, and children. They brought with them shared traditions of storytelling and a host of animal trickster tales.

In the crucible of a new physical, social, and cultural environment, the folk narrative traditions of all southerners—Native Americans, Euro-Americans, and Afro-Americans—were modified by one another. Tales of European origin have been collected from black southerners; tales of African origin have been collected from white southerners; and both African and European tales have been collected among the Natchez, the Creeks, and the Seminoles. Old World tales entered Native American tradition through both Euro-Americans and Afro-Americans. Although there has been considerable interchange among the folktales of black, white, and Indian southerners, there has been less syncretism of the narratives of such Asian southerners as the Mississippi Chinese, who came to the South in the 19th century.

The most characteristic Afro-American tales in the South are animal trickster tales, and the most characteristic Euro-American tales are narratives that are often called "fairy tales," such as "Cinderella," "Jack the Giant Killer," and "Rumpelstiltskin." Folktale scholars call them *Märchen* after the usage of the Brothers Grimm.

There are European animal tales told in the South (such as the widespread "Three Little Pigs"), but the Afro-American animal tales are preeminently stories of the fabulous trickster Brer Rabbit. Although these tales are widely published in authentic field-collected versions, they are best known in Joel Chandler Harris's Uncle Remus books. Numerous tale types in the Uncle Remus canon, once thought to be of European origin, are now confirmed as African.

Southern Indians also have a tradition of animal trickster stories, but the Afro-American rabbit trickster differs from the Native American rabbit trickster in important ways. Although he sometimes fails (and may be repaid for his trickery in kind), Brer Rabbit is neither a clown nor a self-devourer, as is the Indian trickster figure. The main attribute of the Brer Rabbit stories is their focus on small but sly animals who gain the advantage over more powerful adversaries by using their brains rather than their muscles. The central theme of these tales is the struggle for mastery between the trickster Rabbit and his adversaries—Brer Bear, Brer Fox, Brer Gator, and Brer Wolf. Other animal tales were told by black southerners, including their own versions of such tales as "The Tail Fisher," a humorous explanation of why Rabbit's tail is short and his ears are long.

There was also a cycle of human trickster tales among black southerners. On the slave plantations the trickster was usually called John, and he was a real slave, not a surrogate like Brer Rabbit. The continuing battle of wits as the master sought to avoid being duped by John's mischief and guile paralleled the central struggle of the Brer Rabbit tales. The slave trickster tales have had their post-Emancipation counterparts in similar tales of High John, John the Conqueror, John Henry, John Hardy, Railroad Bill, Stagolee, Dupree, Brady, Daddy Mention, and Crooked-Foot John.

In the South, as in Europe, white folktales exhibit formulaic beginnings and endings ("Once upon a time . . ." and "They all lived happily ever after"); remote settings; casts including royalty, giants, dragons, and helpful animals; and triepisodic plots with such motifs as transformations and magical objects. The protagonist is typically a poor stepchild who gains wealth and power through pluck, luck, and supernatural assistance.

Southern white folktales derive largely from British tradition, but distinctive versions of some of them have developed in the South. One of the most famous stories, best known as "Cinderella," has been found in several forms in southern tradition. A story found in most European collections, called by the Grimms "Hansel and Gretel," survives in a traditional North Carolina version entitled "Mutsmag." Another story known throughout Europe as "Beauty and the Beast" still lives in Arkansas, North Carolina, and Virginia, as well as in a Kentucky version known as "The Girl Who Married the Flop-eared

Hound Dog." Distinctive southern versions of "The Taming of the Shrew" have been collected in Virginia, Kentucky, Arkansas, and Texas. An Afro-American version of "Rumpelstiltskin" has been recorded in North Carolina, and an entire cycle of "Jack Tales" has been collected in the southern Appalachians.

Another characteristic form of southern folktale is the tall tale. It was developed for European audiences using the exaggerations of explorers' adventures in the New World as early as Peter Martyr's accounts of the Spanish exploration of Chicora on the South Carolina coast in the 1520s. These accounts pandered to their readers' desire for strange and wondrous descriptions of savages and wild beasts in an exotic environment. One of the Chicora Indians, baptized Francisco when he was taken to Spain, regaled the royal court with his stories of Datha, the king who was born of normal size but was stretched to gigantic proportions during his childhood, and of a race of highly intelligent humans with long, inflexible tails who inhabited the South Carolina coast.

By the 19th century similar tall tales were told throughout the backwoods South, especially in Georgia, Alabama, and Mississippi—the Old Southwest. They were often told in competitive liars' contests in which frontier narrators outdid one another in spinning tales about "The Split Dog," "The Snakebit Hoehandle," mythical beasts, crops that grew overnight, and impossible weather.

Many of these tall tales—including fabulous narratives of Davy Crockett, the Tennessee congressman who was both storyteller and subject of tall tales—are known to posterity by having been printed in the newspapers and in a series of antebellum almanacs. Drawing their style and characters from such tall tales, a new kind of fiction known as Southwest humor emerged in Augustus Baldwin Longstreet's *Georgia Scenes* (1835), Johnson J. Hooper's *Adventures of Simon Suggs* (1845), Joseph Baldwin's *Flush Times in Alabama and Mississippi* (1853), and George W. Harris's *Sut Lovingood's Yarns* (1867). Southwest humor influenced the writings of Mark Twain, and it survives in the work of William Faulkner and Guy Owen.

Many examples of European *jestes* have also been collected in the South, such as versions of "The Deaf Peasant" in the Carolinas. The Texas version of "The Hat That Pays for Everything" and the South Carolina Sea Island version of "Clever Elsie" are examples of what folktale scholars call *Numskull Stories*, a subdivision of *jestes*. Stories about preachers—such as "Counting Souls," the Mississippi version of an English tale known as "The Sexton Carries the Parson"—are another subdivision, as are such stories about married couples as the "step-husband tales" of the southern Appalachians. There is even a South Carolina version of the famous European "shaggy dog" story, "The Farmer and His Ox."

Two kinds of formula tales remain widespread in southern oral tradition, the cumulative tale and the cante-fable. The cumulative "Yay! Boo!" cycle not only survives in tradition but has passed into popular culture. The cumulative tale known among folktale scholars as "The Troll Who Was Cut Open" survives in numerous versions in the southern Appalachians. Cante-fables (folktales in which songs are an integral part) have been collected across the South, including an Appalachian version of "Jack and the Beanstalk," the South Carolina Sea Island "Barney McCabe," and North Carolina, Kentucky, and Tennessee versions of "The Robber Bridegroom," or "Mr. Fox's Courtship."

These and other forms of folktales have been narrated in the South for centuries, enriching the lives of generations of southerners, whether their ancestors came from Europe or from Africa—or were already here.

See also BLACK LIFE: Folklore, Black; / Sea Islands; ETHNIC LIFE: Indian Cultural Contributions; HISTORY AND MANNERS: / Crockett, Davy; LITERATURE: Folklore in Literature; / Clemens, Samuel; Faulkner, William; Harris, George W.; Harris, Joel Chandler; Longstreet, Augustus Baldwin

Charles Joyner
University of South Carolina
Coastal Campus

J. Mason Brewer, *Worser Days and Better Times: The Folklore of the North Carolina Negro* (1965); Marie Campbell, *Tales from the Cloud-Walking Country* (1958); Richard Chase, *The Jack Tales* (1943), *The Grandfather Tales: American English Folk Tales* (1948); Richard M. Dorson, *American Negro Folk Tales* (1967); Joel Chandler Harris, *Uncle Remus* (1881); Charles Joyner, *Down by the Riverside: A South Carolina Slave Community* (1984); Elsie C. Parsons, *Folk-Lore of the Sea Islands* (1923); Vance Randolph, *The Devil's Pretty Daughter, and other Ozark Folktales* (1955), *Pissing in the Snow and other Ozark Folktales* (1976), *Who Blowed Up the Church House, and other Ozark Folktales* (1952); Leonard Roberts, *South from Hell-fer-Sartin: Kentucky Mountain Folk Tales* (1955); South Carolina Writers' Program, *South Carolina Folk Tales: Stories of Animals and Supernatural Beings* (1941); William O. Tuggle, *Shem, Ham, and Japeth: The Papers of W. O. Tuggle* (1973); Newman I. White, ed., *Frank C. Brown Collection of North Carolina Folklore*, vol. 1 (1952).

Foodways

See HISTORY AND MANNERS: Foodways

Funerals

Southern funerals have served sacred and social functions. As far back as the colonial era, a funeral was the occasion for the display of both grief and hospitality. Although the early Puritans in the North held simple funerals, Virginians made their death ceremonies into elaborate events. Southern settlement patterns made for rural isolation, but the funeral was a recognized time to overcome the separation. Mourners shared with the bereaved family the loss of a community member, as well as the need ritually to overcome it. The firing of guns, the consumption of liquor, and the funeral feast tradition brought from England were all characteristic of public funerals.

In the early 19th century southern funerals in general did not differ markedly from those in the rest of the country. Plantation funerals, however, were distinctive occasions. Slaves and slaveowning families shared the same burial grounds. When a slave died, the plantation community responded with an immediate burial and, later, an elaborate memorial service, usually on Sunday, the day of rest. When a slaveowner died, activity on the plantation stopped and a grand public funeral resulted, complete with both real and feigned grief among the planter's chattels.

In the late 19th and early 20th centuries, southern funerals came to differ from those in the rest of the nation. Funerals for public figures like Robert E. Lee and Jefferson Davis were true ceremonies of the southern identity. Symbols of Dixie were prominently displayed, while eulogies explained the contribution of the deceased to the South as a region. Funerals of the average person reinforced social and cultural characteristics associated with the South. They were among the region's chief ceremonies. Neighbors and friends played a major role in them, thus strengthening the bonds of community. Funerals nurtured also the sense of family. Death resulted typically in a homecoming and a gathering of the extended kin.

Funerals reflected caste and class arrangements so important in the region. Whites and blacks at times attended funerals together, but they behaved in highly patterned ways reflecting racial segregation. Blacks at white funerals sat or stood in the back of the room, but whites at black funerals sat on the front row and viewed the body before others attending did so.

For the southern poor, death was an event to be dealt with in a memorable way. A proper funeral was deemed necessary by people who had so little in life. If he had no other recourse, the poor rural tenant farmer so common in the South might borrow money from the landowner or merchant, driving the tenant deeper into debt. Burial societies became especially prominent in the South as a cooperative way to set aside money for funerals.

The funeral industry transformed the way Americans handled death in the late 1800s, but southerners persisted in old-fashioned ways. The American way of death as it emerged in the Northeast and the Midwest included the embalming process, elaborate caskets, funeral homes, and a secular funeral service. Professional funeral directors set the tone for the funeral, and they tended to discourage emotional expressions. The development of the funeral industry lagged in the South because of the poverty, rurality, and religious outlook of southerners. Southern funerals have remained distinctive because of the level of their emotional displays of grief. Southerners in general have been more outgoing in their grief than northerners, with Pentecostal services, black funerals, and the death ceremonies of the rural poor the most visibly grief-ridden and emotional. While the American way of death downplayed such emotional grief, sentimental southerners typically nurtured it.

The traditional southern funeral went through a series of stages. It was a community affair throughout, with family, neighbors, and friends directing each stage, including laying out the body, constructing a coffin, visiting at the deceased's home, and shoveling dirt into the grave. A distinctive regional custom was the "sitting up" ceremony, between the death and the burial. Family and friends stayed with the body, even through the night, in a modified wake. A sad, solemn occasion for the bereaved family, it was a social event as well. Distinctive regional food and drink were usually in abundance during the wake. The funeral service was held at home or in church. A church funeral and the presence of a minister were especially important for a proper funeral. The most trying time was likely at the burial itself, as everyone stayed until neighbors, friends, and family had shoveled the last spade of dirt into the grave. Hysterical behavior was not uncommon at this point.

The southern funeral was shaped by the predominant evangelical, fundamentalist religious style and outlook. A central focus of the funeral was the evangelical sermon, which used the death to remind mourners of their own mortality and of the need to get right with God. Funeral hymns and prayers portrayed the peace of heaven, but they also kept southerners aware of the inevitability of death.

Southern funerals in the contemporary era increasingly reflect the standardization and secularization of death. Funeral directors now arrange the process, resulting in less community and family involvement. Regional customs such as the sitting up ceremony and the open-casket funeral are on the decline, although they remain a common occurrence. Attitudes toward death and funerals show even greater continuity with the past. Religion and the churches continue to be so central to southern life that religious beliefs shape the predominant view of death. The churches continue to be popular locations for funerals, ministers are still regarded as necessary for proper services, and emotionalism is probably more common than elsewhere. Finally, the funeral remains a prime ceremonial occasion for eating southern food, hearing southern music, and nurturing the region's renowned sense of family and community.

See also BLACK LIFE: Funerary Customs, Black

Charles Reagan Wilson
University of Mississippi

Christopher Crocker, in *The Not So Solid South: Anthropological Studies in a Regional Subculture*, ed. J. Kenneth Morland (1971); James J. Farrell, *Inventing the American Way of Death, 1830–1920* (1980); Charles O. Jackson, *Passing: The American Vision of Death* (1977); William Lynwood Montell, *Ghosts along the Cumberlands: Deathlore in the Kentucky Foothills* (1975); James I. Robertson, Jr., *Georgia Review* (Spring 1959); Charles Reagan Wilson, *Georgia Historical Quarterly* (Spring 1983).

Grave Markers

The southern grave markers most distinctive to the region are normally the work of vernacular craftsmen. Most monuments currently made in the South follow nationally popular design patterns, and their makers employ standard industrial tools and techniques. Even for most of the 19th century, when the local hand-cutting of stones remained a vigorous occupation, most carvers followed national fashions in their choice of stone, profile, lettering, and design motifs. Work peculiar to the South is the output of earlier stonecutters or of craftsmen working in geographic or ethnic or economic isolation from American popular culture. Their products are in fact "southern" chiefly in their extreme localism and diversity.

The earliest monuments erected were either locally carved wooden headboards and footboards (long since decayed) or stones imported from the British Isles and, in particular, from the northern colonies. The sandy Tidewater South provided no supply of stone and hence failed to support a stonecutting tradition among 17th- and 18th-century English settlers. The cemeteries of a Charleston or a Wilmington are therefore museums of early New England stone carving.

The rocky uplands, however, offered the German and Scotch-Irish immigrants of the 18th century a wide choice of workable material: sandstone, limestone, slate, granite, and especially soapstone. Their output is scattered in two kinds of sites—the churchyard and the family plot—marking the two institutions of greatest importance in the lives of the settlers. The churchyard stones have had the better chance of survival to the 20th century.

Many 18th-century churchyards show a few examples of early local amateur carving. Any significant output, however, is usually the work of a settler who arrived with prior training as a stone-cutter. Because few localities had the density of population or wealth to support a full-time monument business, most such craftsmen cut stones as a sideline to farming and other activities. Like other master artisans settling in the southern backwoods, the stonecutter typically became a jack-of-all-trades.

A major exception was the Scotch-Irish workshop of the Bigham family—Samuel, Sr., his sons Samuel and William, and at least two others probably trained by them. Carvers from this workshop tradition had been active from about 1740 in Lancaster and Adams counties, Penn., and in the 1760s they made their way to Mecklenburg County, N.C., where they settled near two major transportation arteries—the Great Wagon Road from Philadelphia to Charleston and the Catawba River. They were patronized by the wealthier Scotch-Irish settlers, and some 850 of their skillfully carved soapstone markers survive in early Presbyterian churchyards scattered across seven counties of North and South Carolina, the earliest artwork demonstrably the product of this Piedmont region. The Bigham stones illustrate clearly the transformation of the immigrant ethnic settler into the American patriot. The designs on the earliest stones were Scottish motifs (the thistle) or Scotch-Irish emblems (most typically, a sprig-bearing dove) or family armorial bearings. Across the decades the animal motifs of the coats of arms (lions, stags, horses, falcons, fish, two-headed eagles) came to be used as independent decorations. At the time of the Revolution the Bighams began to reinterpret the coat of arms as a national emblem, filling the shield with 13 stars, selecting eagles for the supporters, topping the design with a fist and sword, and for the motto choosing "Virtue, Liberty, Independence." The spread eagle became another of their favorite nationalistic designs. After the revolutionary era, they further filled the coat-of-arms form with symbols drawn from the Masonic repertory, showing another identity that their patrons were assuming. Late Bigham stones also show rear-face decoration and motifs such as the swastika, both traits suggestive of influence from neighboring German settlers.

Although no direct German-American models for these Bigham stones have as yet been located, several major German workshops did exist in the southern uplands. One active between 1800 and the 1840s in Davidson County, N.C., produced remarkable pierced or "open-work" soapstone markers with such symbols of resurrection as swastikas and trees of life. In their profiles and their use of molding, the stones also betray their cutters' knowledge of woodworking and cabinetry. Another major German workshop was that of Laurence Crone, who left work in Wythe, Roanoke, and Pulaski counties, Va., between 1815 and 1836. His large, handsome sandstone markers typically bear a rear-face carving of a heart rising from the earth and flowering into roses.

The early southern stonecutting traditions normally ended abruptly in an area with the death of the carver (such as Laurence Crone or the South Carolina stonecutter Hugh Kelsey) or his westward migration (as in the case of Samuel Bigham, Jr., and his brother William, who moved to Tennessee, or the Davidson County carvers, some of whom left for Indiana, or Samuel Watson, who removed from South Carolina to Missouri). They were succeeded by carvers who simply followed national tastes, decorating white marble slabs with weeping willows, urns, figures in togas, and fat cherubs.

For both economic and cultural reasons many grave markers made by post–Civil War and 20th-century blacks are exceptions to the dominance of popular culture. Older black burial sites show graves decorated with seashells or household objects—practices interpreted as a survival of West African traditions. Beginning in the 1920s, Afro-Americans working in building trades that trained them in the use of concrete started to cast grave markers of that material, incising or painting them with designs, or decorating them with shells or pebbles or colored glass marbles. An occasional gifted craftsman like William Edmondson of Nashville, Tenn., worked in stone, impelled by religious inspiration to become a stonecutter and guided by it to his characteristic sculptural forms: doves, lambs, and angels. In the absence of any strong persisting vernacular tradition or any compelling economic necessity, only such a religious imperative is likely in the foreseeable future to inspire black or white craftsmen and their patrons to ignore popular commercial products that embody popularly accepted standards of taste and symbolize affluence attained. Only a religious vision is likely to cause them to dignify the resting places of their dead with monuments made locally to express the values of a local subculture shaped by the South.

See also ART AND ARCHITECTURE: Sculpture; BLACK LIFE: Funerary Customs, Black; ETHNIC LIFE: / Germans; Scotch-Irish

Daniel Patterson
University of North Carolina
at Chapel Hill

Ruth Little-Stokes, *Newsletter of the Association of Gravestone Studies* (Summer 1982); Bradford L. Rauschenberg, *Journal of Early Southern Decorative Arts* (November 1977); Klaus Wust, *Folk Art in Stone, Southwest Virginia* (1970).

House Types

The initial spread of house types characteristic of the South was brief and decisive. It manifested aspects of the frontier experience that were less obvious in other dimensions of southern history and geography. Three major phases occurred in the diffusion of the typical folk and vernacular houses of the South—colonial (1604 to 1775), frontier (1775 to 1850), and modern (1880 to 1940). Each phase revealed distinct aspects of the southern experience.

Understanding southern house types requires knowing the people who immigrated to and migrated across the South, as well as the changing, shifting conditions that made possible expression of the ideals, preferences, and tastes of southerners. During the first century of colonial settlement, the houses built in the South reflected, in simplified rendering, the homes that had been built in Britain. In Virginia and the Carolinas, common houses had plans based upon the British bay, or pen, an oblong unit with a gable roof, a chimney on one gable end, and doors on the two eave sides. Commonly made of one or two such units, the earliest versions lacked the broad porches and the pier foundations so typical of later models. All along the Tidewater and into the valley of Virginia, these basically British houses of brick, half-timber, and lumber sheltered the small class of white commoners. Somewhat later, and mainly through Charleston, new traits arrived from the Caribbean; these included galleries, external stairs, and pier foundations.

After about 1725 new settlers, arriving from northern Ireland and Rhineland Germany, settled lands in the backcountry in the western parts of Pennsylvania, Virginia, and the Carolinas. They entered the colonies principally through Philadelphia and Charleston, moving north and south along the then main road of the colonies, running between Philadelphia and Charleston by way of Roanoke. Commercial traffic, repeated moves, and flights from Indian attacks promoted a common awareness of a variety of building traits from both British and German sources. Gradually, during the span from 1725 to 1775, shared experience produced a frontier solution to building a house; that packet of ideas spread westward during the next two generations to nearly all places in the wooded eastern United States, south of the Great Lakes drainage. The very suddenness of the diffusion showed that the novel solution was destined to enter the new settlement zones of the Old West.

In the frontier South the British pen and German log-notching provided the basic plan and the most distinctive building techniques, although the record clearly shows that many of the earliest houses in any area were built of, in addition to logs, timber framing, lumber, brick, and even stone. The very first cabins in an area normally had dirt floors, crude log walls, and roofs of split boards held down by poles or stones. Such cabins were, however, universally regarded as temporary. The permanent structure was a house, a well-made, reasonably stylish home with a proper floor and a foundation of piers. Its walls were formed of shaped and dressed logs or of such materials as sawn lumber, brick, or stone. In any case, the house of the frontier, rather than being a crude invention fathered by necessity, was an expression of current fashion worked in available material. The main significance of notched logs lay in the southern acceptance of them as suitable for permanent houses and in the advantage that they gave southerners relative to others competing for the wooded eastern United States.

The theme of ethnic origins showed in the persistence of the dogtrot, double-pen, saddlebag, and I plans among the houses built by southerners in the frontier context and on into the 20th century. These two-room-wide models were worked in the available materials and adorned in the contemporary fashion. The dogtrot had an open central hall between two pens, whereas the saddlebag had a central chimney in that location. The double pen lacked both the hall and the central chimney. Chimneys normally, except for the saddlebag, appeared on the exterior ends of the houses. The I house is a two-story version of the other three, most typically, a two-story dogtrot or central-hall house.

Fashion, whether stylistic or technical, can gain dominance in the landscape only during periods of local prosperity. Periods of prosperity, such as the first and the last thirds of the 19th century, made possible the adoption of innovations in houses no less than in industry. The commercial dominance of contemporary fashion introduced the third phase in the spread of southern house types. Modernity in houses was a departure from the ethnic models, characterized by the acceptance of nationally distributed, expertly created, commercial models. Especially significant for the South was the California bungalow style of architecture. This once new-fangled, exotic fashion gained such wide acceptance during the flush times of the early southern lumber boom that it now, incorrectly, seems to be a southern creation.

From about 1900, then, such national styles as the bungalow increasingly displaced the old folk models of the frontier phase. By World War II the southern types had largely ceased to be built, and by the 1950s nearly all southern construction involved national models.

See also ART AND ARCHITECTURE: Vernacular Architecture

M. B. Newton, Jr.
Louisiana State University

Fred B. Kniffen, *Annals of the Association of American Geographers* (December 1965); Fred Kniffen and Henry Glassie, *Geographical Review* (January 1966); Dell Upton and John Michael Vlach, *Common Places: Readings in American Vernacular Architecture* (1986); H. J. Walker and W. G. Haag, *Geoscience and Man*, vol. 5 (1974).

Legends

No more fertile ground for legends exists than the South. The terrain, the climate, and the inhabitants have shaped unique legends, many of which are nationally known. Many folklorists define legends only in terms of oral lore, but legends are also part of the historiography of any region. Although the body of oral legends reflects the heritage of diverse subcultures in the South, the southern legends popular in literature and movies, like American legends in general, focus more on males than females, more on whites than nonwhites, and more on Protestants than non-Protestants.

Anglo-American southerners have worked diligently to keep the nation mindful of their roots in the region. Legends abound, for example, about the mysterious lost colony of Roanoke, site of the first attempted English colony in the New World and birthplace of Virginia Dare, the first English child born in this land. Paul Green's outdoor drama, *The Lost Colony*, has celebrated the tale for countless visitors to North Carolina.

Jamestown, Va., site of the first permanent English settlement in America and capital of colonial Virginia from 1607 to 1699, lives in legend partly because of Captain John Smith's purported rescue from execution by the Powhatan Indian princess Pocahontas. Romantic tales about the pair flourished in the mid-19th century, and the legend was immortalized through a bronze sculpture and a painting in the Capitol rotunda in Washington. When writers in the late 1800s tried to debunk the legend, southern authors leapt to its defense.

Southerners strove, too, to shape the legends surrounding Virginian George Washington, revered as the nation's quintessential statesman and public servant. Parson Mason Weems, a Maryland minister and author, concocted the most famous Washington stories such as the cherry tree tale. A more scholarly effort was Chief Justice John Marshall's five-volume official biography of Washington. The state of Virginia in 1784 commissioned the French sculptor Antoine Houdon to create a bust of Washington, and the U.S. government eventually distributed plaster copies to public schools nationwide. A reflection of the white upper-class South's high esteem for Washington was the Confederates' selection of the general to appear on their great seal.

Virginians further nurtured the traditions of the antebellum planter class through special reverence for Thomas Jefferson, the South's and the nation's legendary Renaissance man. Up to the Civil War, however, it was not Jefferson but Francis Marion, dubbed "the Swamp Fox," who "ranked next to Washington as the idol of the South," according to Dixon Wecter. Marion's brilliant guerilla tactics against the British in the 1780s gave rise to biographies (Parson Weems produced one), folklore, paintings, and poems.

Other legendary southerners of the late 1700s and the early 1800s embodied a bold, adventuresome nature. The South could not lay full claim to Daniel Boone, a native of Pennsylvania who moved to Virginia at age 15. However, Boone's exploits throughout the Kentucky territory and his establishment of Fort Boonesborough garnered him a special place in southern folklore. The entire nation enjoyed and participated in the South's creation of its own outrageous, comic version of the frontiersman by weaving tall tales about Tennessean Davy Crockett. Dying in a blaze of glory at the Alamo, Crockett became a symbol of the country's bold expansionist goals. Legends of rough-hewn, firebrand southerners developed, too, around the exploits of General Andrew Jackson, who led his Tennessee troops against the British in the Battle of New Orleans during the War of 1812. Known as "Old Hickory" or simply "the Hero," Jackson, a native of South Carolina and later a Tennessee resident, was once called "the most roaring, rollicking, game-cocking, horse-racing, card-playing, mischievous fellow that ever lived in Salisbury [N.C.]." The South's raw edge had begun to take shape in legend.

Southerners' brilliance, tenacity, and fearlessness in war certainly were central to legends of the Lost Cause. Legends of Confederate heroes and of pivotal battles carry in them a southern apologia, white southerners' answer to the question of whether one could be both a good Confederate and a good American. Cavalry expert J. E. B. "Jeb" Stuart with a bold stroke disarmed the federal army of the Potomac in 1862; Nathan Bedford "First with the Most" Forrest repeatedly disrupted federal campaigns with daring cavalry raids; and William C. Quantrill's raiders made a bloody, infamous raid on free-state guerillas in 1863. During the war Stonewall Jackson reigned as the Confederates' supreme hero. Belle Boyd, daughter of a prominent planter, disrupted numerous Union plans and gained notoriety as a spy.

After the war, however, the South's most revered warrior was Robert E. Lee, described by Marshall Fishwick as "the archetypal cavalier." The legends of Lee's military abilities, devotion to duty, nobility, deep religious faith, integrity, charity, self-denial, and wisdom abound. Says Dixon Wecter, Lee "reclaimed her [the antebellum South's] chivalry from bombast, and made into poetry the fact of her defeat. The South lost the war, but she still had Robert E. Lee." White southerners launched innumerable efforts after Lee's death to immortalize him, and until the beginning of the 20th century, the Lee cult flourished almost exclusively in the South. Over time, though, the Lost Cause's saint has gained acceptance in national legends as the exemplar of grace in defeat.

The Civil War brought to a head the conflicting legends of black and white southerners. While whites exalted Lee, southern blacks—and Union supporters in general—heralded Kentucky-born Abraham Lincoln as the Great Emancipator. Eventually, southern whites who had offered Lee as an example to the nation came to accept Lincoln as legendary too. But black southerners' legends, shaped by the experience of slavery, had a long and rich history apart from the legends that grew in white culture.

Based on a rich oral tradition, black creation legends and trickster tales had clear roots in African culture. Lawrence W. Levine notes that "African trickster figures were more obsessed with manipulating the strong and reversing the normal structure of power and prestige." This emphasis on overcoming powerful forces through shrewdness persisted until well after emancipation, and only after that time did tales of grandiose individual exploits become common among blacks.

Among the individuals who became legendary among blacks were the conjurer Old Julie and voodoo queen Marie Laveau. Legendary slave insurrectionists included Denmark Vesey and his chief lieutenant, Gullah Jack (Jack Pritchard); Nat Turner, leader of the Southampton insurrection; and Bras Coupé, leader of a group of runaway slaves in New Orleans in 1830. Revered, too, was Harriet Tubman, a Maryland-born abolitionist and former slave who aided Union troops in South Carolina and led more than 300 slaves to freedom through the Underground Railroad.

Minority ethnic groups' legends have also flourished. Cajuns warned of the *loup-garous*, or werewolves, and preserved the tragic tale of Emmaline Labiche, or Evangeline, whom Henry Wadsworth Longfellow immortalized. American Indians emphasized legends of the mystery and power of nature, and the communal relationships between humans and nature. Through a strong oral tradition, American Indian tribes in the South passed on a variety of creation legends, such as the Cherokee's tales of the sun as a life-giving female. Legends from non-white cultures have had little place in white culture, although Anglo-Americans have lauded legendary Indians, such as Pocahontas and Sequoyah, who lived peaceably with whites.

After emancipation many of the best-known legendary figures were workers, and southerners celebrated their amazing occupational feats. Legendary figures immortalized in song include John Henry, the black railroad worker who died after outperforming a steam drill, and Casey Jones, the white railroad engineer who lost his life in a train crash. Tall-tale characters include Annie Christmas, a huge black female longshoreman who could outdrink, outwrestle, and outlift any man; riverboatmen and gamblers James Girty and George Devol; and riverboatman Mike Fink, so-called king of the keelboatmen, who was known for his skills on the river and his sadistic pranks. Some heroes worked outside the law, and few can rival in notoriety the pirates Blackbeard, Gasparilla, and Jean Lafitte, who patroled the southern coastline.

Women have seldom been the subject of southern legends, although they have been among the most ardent hero worshipers in the region. The characteristics most exalted in American legendary figures—tenacity, drive, independence, and bravery—have been culturally defined as antithetical to femininity. In the South the most concerted efforts to create heroines have centered around the mothers or wives of famous men. One notable exception is Helen Keller, who overcame limitations of deafness and blindness through the devotion of her teacher, Anne Sullivan.

Southern legends deal not only with illustrious individuals but with star-crossed lovers (the lovers of Dismal Swamp in Virginia), disastrous feuds (the Hatfields and McCoys), haunted locales (Metairie Cemetery in New Orleans), and buried treasures (Jean Lafitte's booty). Although many such legends grow out of superstition, a love of exaggeration, or a sense of fun, southerners also transmit legends to preserve traditions, solidify cultural images, and express beliefs.

Sharon A. Sharp
University of Mississippi

Benjamin A. Botkin, ed., *A Treasury of American Folklore* (1944), *A Treasury of Southern Folklore* (1949); Marshall Fishwick, *American Heroes: Myth and Reality* (1954), *The Hero, American Style* (1969); Zora Neale Hurston, *Mules and Men* (1935); Lawrence W. Levine, *Black Culture and Black Consciousness: Afro-American Folk Thought from Slavery to Freedom* (1977); *The Life Treasury of American Folklore* (1961); Lyle Saxon, Robert Tallant, and Edward Dreyer, *Gumbo Ya-Ya: A Collection of Louisiana Folk Tales* (1945); Dixon Wecter, *The Hero in America: A Chronicle of Hero-Worship* (1941); Gary Wills, *American Heritage* (February–March 1981).

Personal Experience Narratives

First-person stories are based on whatever an individual considers important or entertaining enough to relate. Southern regional identity will partially determine the aspects of a person's life that are worth telling stories about, but these narratives also relate to American culture and to universal human concerns.

Southern personal experience narratives reflect specific southern customs and patterns of behavior; for instance, courtship stories clearly indicate courtship and marriage traditions for the time and place in which they are set. Elderly couples in the Blue Ridge Mountains of Virginia and North Carolina tell personal narratives about their courting days, which show that 50 to 60 years ago courting took place in community and family contexts, at church socials and in homes. An idealized view of love relates the stories to the tradition of medieval courtly love; the woman is presented as an untouchable object of desire to be pursued from a distance until her heart has been won and the marriage takes place. Traditional sex roles are fulfilled; the man is the active pursuer and the woman is a passive object. Dual narration often occurs in which the husband and wife interrupt and correct each other; the mode of narrating is a model for the marriage itself in that there are disagreements but cooperation overcomes these so that the relationship continues.

Personal experience narratives can occur in families or in larger contexts such as occupational groups. Commercial fishermen along southern coastlines tell stories about personal disasters or narrow escapes while at sea. Some of these have to do with men injured at sea who almost bleed to death before they make it back to land; others deal with men, often brothers or other close relatives, swept overboard during storms. The survivors recount these disasters as reminders to others about the dangers of their occupation, one of the most hazardous in the United States. These narratives are an important indication of the physical risk and uncertainty of their occupational environment; anxiety is a part of their work. This in turn helps to explain the dependency of commercial fishermen on magic and superstition. Their superstitious behavior is an attempt to get control of their environment, thus relieving some of the anxiety. Other hazardous occupations in the South, such as coal mining, also have traditions of personal disaster stories.

Another area of experience that is traditionally the subject of stories in the South is personal contact with local characters, individuals whose eccentric behavior is often noted in comic ways. Stories are still being told about two brothers who lived along the Gulf Coast of Texas in the 1930s and 1940s. People who knew them remember incidents of their abnormal behavior: they never took baths, they lived in a shack with a pack of dogs, and they never worked at regular jobs. They broke many of the norms of the society, such as personal hygiene, but they also had a freedom from societal restraint that was admired by other men in the community. Several of the stories are about outsiders, especially from the North, who were brought into contact with the brothers as a prank. The people in the community knew that outsiders would be offended, thereby establishing boundaries between themselves and outsiders and also projecting a community identity that allows a wide range of acceptable behavior. The outdoorsmen of the Gulf Coast see these brothers as perennial Huck Finns who have permanently lit out for the territory and rejected societal restraints, especially those associated with women.

The great range of personal experience narrative is apparent when viewing the mundane comic antics of local characters on one side and the sacred spiritual quality of personal conversion stories on the other. The emphasis in southern Protestant fundamentalism on personal revelation, on being born again through a transcendant experience, results in a large body of traditional stories existing within this religious context. The stories are based on individual mystical experience, but they reflect traditional and communal patterns. Often people speak of visions and voices, of being in contact with angels, Christ, or God, of being outside of ordinary reality. These traits suggest a ritual process that is cross-cultural; there is a separation from everyday existence, an entering into a mystical state in which the person experiences oneness with God and all humanity, and then a return to structured society. The personal experience narrative acts as a means of reincorporating the mystical event into everyday reality, a structuring of an unstructured incident so that it can be shared with and perhaps inspire, others.

See also WOMEN'S LIFE: Marriage and Courtship

Patrick B. Mullen
Ohio State University

Roger D. Abrahams, in *Folklore Genres*, ed. Dan Ben-Amos (1976); Patrick B. Mullen, *Folklore and Folklife in Virginia* (1980–81), *I Heard the Old Fishermen Say: Folklore of the Texas Gulf Coast* (1978); John Robinson, *Journal of American Folklore* (January–March 1981).

Pottery

Pottery vessels for storing, processing, and handling food and drink were indispensable in American life before the availability of inexpensive glass, metal, and plastic containers. This was especially true for the South, where the mild climate made food preservation even more critical. Most colonial pottery was earthenware, composed of a reddish-brown clay and glazed with lead in the British and German manner. However, by the time the interior of the South was becoming extensively settled in the early 19th century, stoneware—a harder, more durable product made from a purer, higher-firing clay—emerged as the dominant medium for traditional utilitarian ceramics.

Throughout the North and Upper South, stoneware was glazed in the European way by throwing salt in the kiln at the height of firing to form a transparent coating of glass over the gray or tan clay, and it was decorated with cobalt-oxide paint that produced a deep blue color when fired. Salt-glazed stoneware was made sporadically in the Deep South, but rarely was it cobalt decorated. Instead it often displayed unintentional surface irregularities (brick drippings, melted fly ash blown from the fuel, puddled salt deposits, and fire-flashing) resulting largely from the regional rectangular kilns.

A second type of stoneware glaze, applied as a solution before firing, was unknown in the North but was widely used—especially in the second and third quarters of the 19th century—from the western Carolinas to east Texas. Using slaked wood ashes or lime to help melt the other ingredients (normally clay and sand), it produced colors in the green or brown range and sometimes a drippy texture. These distinctly regional alkaline glazes may have been developed in Edgefield District, S.C., about the second decade of the 19th century, possibly inspired by a published account of similar glazes in the Far East (the only other part of the world where they are well known).

Some Edgefield potters in the 1840s and 1850s decorated their alkaline-glazed stoneware with white and dark brown slips (liquid clays), a technique adapted from European earthenware.

A characteristic southern vessel type is the large, two-handled syrup jug, whose prevalence is linked to the importance of molasses as a liquid sweetening in the regional diet. Novelty jugs with stylized or grotesque human faces, although occasionally made elsewhere, are concentrated in the Southeast, where they are still produced by folk potters. Ceramic grave markers, wheel-turned or molded to serve as headstones or planters, although scattered through the Midwest, are more focused in the region bounded by southwestern Pennsylvania and east Texas, where they date mainly from the 1870s through the 1920s.

Certain aspects of the production technology are specific to the South. The most significant is the wood-burning rectangular kiln with its arched ceiling, firebox at one end, and chimney at the other. It sometimes was surrounded by earth, giving rise to the term *groundhog kiln*. Northern kilns, by contrast, were round. Rectangular kilns were used to fire stoneware in Germany and France, and, although rare, a 17th-century example is known for England. The earliest discovered in the South at Yorktown, Va., dates from the 1720s.

The frequency of the place name "Jugtown" testifies to the tendency of southeastern potters to cluster in communities, most of which are located in the Piedmont plateau near suitable clay. Georgia's folk potters (who typically were also farmers) were concentrated in eight centers, the most extensive being Mossy Creek in White County where over 70 have worked. These pottery centers were dominated by key families who shaped localized ceramic styles. The Browns, who trace their ancestry to an English immigrant potter, have been potting in the South for more than eight generations. Individuals not born into pottery families often became potters after marrying into them, and members of different "clay clans" tended to marry one another, thus consolidating the pottery dynasties. With some notable exceptions, access to the craft was limited to white males. This family control and transmission of the craft (as opposed to the formal apprenticeship more common elsewhere) may be tied to the centrality of the kin group, dispersed settlement, and agrarian life characteristic of the region.

Prohibition and the shift away from self-sufficiency lowered demand for folk pottery and led to its decline in the 20th century. Rather than abandon clay work, some traditionally trained potters changed to the production of unglazed flowerpots and other "garden" pottery or colorful artistic and table wares oriented to a more affluent urban market. A fair number of these transitional potters or their offspring continue to make a good living at the trade today. A smaller number of potters, including Georgia's Lanier Meaders, North Carolina's Burlon Craig, Alabama's Norman Smith, and Mississippi's Gerald Stewart, remain faithful to the older tradition, carrying on an essentially 19th-century approach to pottery making. As the last stronghold of American folk pottery, as in other realms of culture, the South can be seen as a region of survivals where old ways die hard.

See also ART AND ARCHITECTURE: Decorative Arts

John A. Burrison
Georgia State University

John A. Burrison, *Brothers in Clay: The Story of Georgia Folk Pottery* (1983), *Southern Folklore Quarterly* (December 1975); Stephen T. Ferrell and T. M. Ferrell, *Early Decorated Stoneware of the Edgefield District, South Carolina* (catalog, 1976); Georgeanna H. Greer, *Antiques* (April 1977), *Northeast Historical Archaeology* (Spring 1977); Ralph Rinzler and Robert Sayers, *The Meaders Family: North Georgia Potters* (1980); Nancy Sweezy, *Raised in Clay: The Southern Pottery Tradition* (1984); John Michael Vlach, *Ceramics Monthly* (September 1978).

Pottery, North Carolina

North Carolina is the only state in the nation that possesses a balanced folk ceramic heritage of lead-glazed earthenware, salt-glazed stoneware, and alkaline-glazed stoneware. This unique combination of the three major types of traditional pottery results from North Carolina's position as a "border state" between the North and the South. From Virginia up into New England, earthenware and salt-glazed stoneware predominated: the former was produced in small, family-run shops; the latter, particularly after the mid-19th century, in very standardized, cobalt-decorated forms, most often in large factories. To the south and west of North Carolina, however, the picture was very different. Almost no earthenware existed, and the salt-glazed stoneware was normally unembellished and made in modest quantities in scattered communities. What best characterizes this southern region is the alkaline-glazed stoneware that was "turned" and "burned" by many generations of potters from North Carolina south to Florida and west into Texas.

The first pottery produced in North Carolina was lead-glazed earthenware. Although the earliest permanent settlement occurred in the 1650s in the Albemarle region in the northeast corner of the state, potters did not appear for another 100 years. The Coastal Plain lacks first-rate clays; more important, the early plantation economy and active commerce with England, the West Indies, and the Northeast seem to have discouraged potters from setting up shop. Thus, the bulk of the pottery was produced in the Piedmont, largely by British and German immigrants who began to flood the midsection of the state in the middle of the 18th century. Here an abundance of readily accessible sedimentary clays, a rapidly swelling population, an economy characterized by small, independent farms, and a relative isolation from outside markets all combined to create ideal conditions for the folk potter.

From the 1750s to about 1825 the most prominent craftsmen were the Moravians, who in 1753 commenced building a palisaded settlement called Bethabara on the north side of what is now Winston-Salem, in Forsyth County. For such a frontier community, their pottery was highly varied, and included "bottles, jugs, jars, drinking vessels, bowls, pans, pots, plates, lighting devices, miscellaneous forms, and pressed ware." No less remarkable was their emphasis on decoration—they "considered slip-decorated ware a standard item in their everyday production." Under German-born masters like Gottfried Aust and Rudolf Christ, the potters concentrated on lead-glazed earthenwares, but they also experimented with English creamware, stoneware, and even faience. Through the first quarter of the 19th century these potters worked within a small, closely controlled craft community in which the pottery was owned by the congregation, the potter was a full-time craftsman, and the craft was perpetuated by the guild system with its ranks of apprentice, journeyman, and master.

The thoroughly documented achievements of the Moravians tend to obscure the work of a far larger body of potters who were simultaneously producing earthenwares across the Piedmont from Orange County in the east to Lincoln in the west. Few of their wares were signed or decorated; thus, it is extremely difficult to attribute them to a particular potter, date, or place. The most common surviving forms are jars, dishes, bowls, jugs, and, less commonly, kegs, chamberpots, colanders, and grease lamps. Unlike the Moravian shops, these were family businesses run by farmer-potters, men who worked at the craft as a sideline in order to generate the cash or barter to acquire the goods they could not make for themselves.

Salt-glazed stoneware jug, Randolph County, N.C., c. 1850

At some point during the first quarter of the 19th century, the potters began converting to stoneware, and by 1850 two highly concentrated centers of production had emerged. The larger one was located on the adjacent borders of Randolph, Chatham, and Moore counties in the eastern Piedmont, where at least 200 potters, most of British stock, made salt-glazed jars, jugs, milk crocks, churns, and pitchers. The gray-green jug in the accompanying photograph well illustrates their achievement. A sturdy, utilitarian container for molasses, vinegar, or "medicinal" liquors, it also exhibits a striking bulbous form, bold opposed handles, and a rich texture of brown spotting from the fly ash blowing through the kiln. Other than the incised rings and "sine waves" on the jug's shoulder, North Carolina pottery was rarely decorated in any self-conscious sense. The blue cobalt oxide so common on northern stoneware was expensive and hard to obtain; at best, it was used to delineate the gallon capacity (as shown here), accent the handle terminals, or provide a bit of colorful trim. Pictorial designs such as trees, birds, and Masonic emblems are only rarely encountered. To the local potter this entailed extra time and labor and made the pot no more "useful." And, ultimately, his competition did not warrant such extra flourishes.

Although the salt glaze prevailed in the east, the alkaline glaze was used throughout the western Piedmont and also in the relatively small number of shops in the mountain region. The major concentration of potters occurred along the western border between Lincoln and Catawba counties; in a compact area once called "Jugtown," 150 potters, most of German descent, turned out thick, flowing alkaline glazes. The term *alkaline* designates the flux used to lower the melting temperature of this glaze. In North Carolina this was almost always wood ashes, which contain varying amounts of such alkaline substances as calcium, sodium, and potassium. Moreover, the potters designated two major glaze subtypes, based on the silica source: the typically brown and runny "cinder glaze," made from the slag collected from early iron furnaces in Lincoln County, and the smooth, greenish "glass glaze," which employed instead crushed glass from windowpanes and bottles. In all, the heavy use of the alkaline glaze—combined with the highly variable, unembellished forms in the salt glaze—firmly sets North Carolina in the southern ceramic tradition.

Because of a complex mix of social and economic forces, the folk tradition terminated in the eastern Piedmont about the time of World War I but continued in the west and the mountains until World War II. Many descendants of the old turners still flourish by selling a new line of domestic, artistic, and horticultural wares to a middle-class clientele, but today only a single folk potter remains at work. In Lincoln County Burlon Craig still digs his own clay out of the local river, "kicks" his treadle wheel, grinds his alkaline glazes by hand in a stone mill, and burns his wood-fired groundhog kiln half a dozen times a year. Behind him lies a tradition extending over two centuries and comprising 700 to 800 potters, who worked efficiently—and sometimes with stunning aesthetic force—to supply the essential needs of a rural, self-sufficient people.

Charles G. Zug III
University of North Carolina
at Chapel Hill

Dorothy Cole Auman and Charles G. Zug III, *Southern Exposure* (Summer–Fall 1977); John Bivins, Jr., *The Moravian Potters in North Carolina* (1972); Daisy Wade Bridges, ed., *Potters of the Catawba Valley, North Carolina* (1980); Jean Crawford, *Jugtown Pottery: History and Design* (1964); Stuart C. Schwartz, *North Carolina Pottery: A Bibliography* (1978); Charles G. Zug III, *Pioneer America Society Transactions* (1980), *The Traditional Pottery of North Carolina* (1981), *Turners and Burners: The Folk Potters of North Carolina* (1986).

Pottery, Texas

Pottery in the Southwest is a distinctive variant of the southern ceramics tradition. The area known as Texas entered the scene of American crafts at a late date, after the establishment of the Republic of Texas in 1835. During the 17th and 18th centuries, and the first quarter of the 19th, this area was governed by Spain and then Mexico. Even after Texas became a part of the Union in 1846, Native American and Spanish-influenced crafts were manufactured in the southern and western areas of the state, which had not yet become "Americanized."

The U.S. Census Population Schedule for 1860 listed five women in the Isleta township of El Paso County as "Potteress." Presumably, these were women producing traditional coil-formed American Indian pots for their local area. Cameron County population schedules for that same year list Severino Najare, born in Mexico, as an earthenware manufacturer. He was undoubtedly manufacturing simple, lead-glazed earthenwares based on the Spanish tradition. Ware of this same type has been used continually until the present day by Mexican Americans in the preparation of their traditional foods, but there is little evidence of manufacture here. Such earthenwares are freely available along the Mexican border and imported locally in most areas predominantly Mexican in population.

The population of Texas by emigrants from the United States took place very rapidly after the war with Mexico ended in 1848. Farmers, craftsmen of all types, and professional men poured in through the northeastern, eastern, and Gulf of Mexico entrances to the state. During the 19th century pioneering craftsmen were involved in farming and settling land as well as the pursuance of their craft. When they arrived in Texas, they followed this established pattern. Most potters farmed a crop, potting at intervals in that work.

Coarse earthenwares were produced in Texas in very small amounts. The persistent manufacture of traditional American Indian vessels occurred in the western part of the state, and traditional Spanish earthenwares were noted along the Rio Grande in 1860. One pottery is known to have produced common earthenwares of the Anglo-American type near the city of Houston in 1847. There were possibly one or two other very early small earthenware potteries in that area. A pottery operating in Jackson County in 1860 was found to have been producing poor-quality salt-glazed stoneware and numerous lead-glazed earthenware milk bowls.

The stoneware produced by the majority of the potters in Texas during the second half of the 19th century was of the utilitarian or folk type. Most of the vessels were formed by wheel throwing and fired in simple updraft or rectangular groundhog kilns. The common stoneware glazes of the period were employed for the single firing process used by these potters. Salt glazes applied during firing by the vapor method, southern alkaline glazes prepared mainly from wood ash and clay, and slip glazes prepared from natural clays were all used. After 1875 the Albany and other commercially dug slip clay glazes of that type became available. During the last two decades of the 19th century, slip glazing of both the interior and exterior of pots became popular.

The vessel forms most commonly manufactured were large storage jars (3- to 10-gallon capacities), preserving jars (¼ to 2 gallons), churns (3 to 6 gallons), jugs (½ to 5 gallons), and milk pans (½ to 2 gallons). Pitchers of various sizes, chamber pots, spittoons, and serving bowls were made in smaller numbers. The pots were almost entirely undecorated and frequently unmarked. Decoration with trailed cobalt slip before 1900 was limited to a few pieces made in Denton County and having cobalt calligraphic design and numbers. A small amount of underglaze combing was done by J. C. Rushton in Rusk County, and mugs combed and decorated to resemble tree bark were popular in Bexar County around 1900. Ceramic tombstones or cemetery markers occur only in one small area in east Texas. Toys, whimseys, or other decorated pieces are exceedingly rare, and no anthropomorphic or grotesque jugs have so far been found that were made in Texas.

Potters of the southern tradition entered the state directly from the east and began to manufacture their traditional alkaline-glazed pots before 1850. Texas also received emigrant potters from the midwestern states and from foreign countries over the next several decades. The 1850 Census Population Schedules show that seven potters working in Texas were from families associated with the southern alkaline-glaze tradition, which moved westward out of South Carolina through Georgia, Alabama, and Mississippi into Texas. The eighth potter in that census was German born and undoubtedly used the salt glaze.

After the Civil War there was a continued influx of potters from other parts of the United States, England, and Germany. The majority of the shops were then located along outcroppings of the Wilcox geological formation that occur along a line diagonally from Texarkana in the northeast to near San Antonio in the southwest. This formation still supplies clays for the brick and tile industry.

By 1900 larger shops, semiindustrialized potteries, had

developed and were beginning to produce large amounts of stoneware covered with a white Bristol form of glaze. A number of these shops continued to operate through the first quarter, and well into the second, of the 20th century. Today only the Marshall Pottery at Marshall in Harrison County continues to produce wheel-thrown ordinary stoneware pitchers, jars, churns, and water coolers. These represent only a small part of their output, the majority being pressed red clay flower pots.

Georgeanna H. Greer
San Antonio, Texas

Georgeanna H. Greer, *American Stonewares: The Art and Craft of Utilitarian Potters* (1981), with Harding Black, *The Meyer Family, Master Potters in Texas* (1971); Sherry B. Humphreys and Johnell H. Schmidt, *Texas Pottery, Caddo Indian to Contemporary* (1976); Cecelia Steinfeldt and Donald Stover, *Early Texas Furniture and Decorative Arts* (1973); U.S. Bureau of the Census, *Industry and Manufacture for Texas* (1850, 1860, 1870, 1880); U.S. Bureau of the Census, *Population Schedules for Texas* (1850, 1860, 1870, 1880).

Storytelling

A robust and vital storytelling tradition is part and parcel of the South's persona. "A storied region," folklorist Benjamin A. Botkin aptly called the South. Indeed, southern narrators boast extensive repertoires of folktales, legends, jests, and anecdotes. Attracted by the lure of this trove, early folklore collectors flocked to isolated pockets of the Appalachians, Ozarks, and bayous to find centuries-old tales of international circulation. But the romantic draw of pristine backsections aside, storytelling holds social significance throughout the South.

Verbal artistry dramatizes and gives meaning to mores, locales, and events. Even though communities acknowledge a particularly adept storyteller, each person knows narratives that he or she can occasionally relate. Nonetheless, of significance to many communities is how people cherish the styles and stories of that favorite yarnspinner. They easily remember those particular settings for the good story—the store, the porch, the courthouse, and the city street.

Despite the misleading homey image of southern storytelling as a quaint form of peripheral entertainment, narration continues to touch on central social roles in modern settings. The tale teaches values, develops communicative skills, binds people together, and imbues life with art. Storytelling can be described in terms of the narrator and the content, social context, and style of the expression.

Content. Although remnants of the European fairy tale (or *Märchen*) tradition seemed not to survive the growth of the new American nation, folklorists found in the South versions of numerous such tales, canonized in *The Types of the Folk-Tale* (1964) by Antti Aarne and Stith Thompson. The title story of Vance Randolph's collection *The Devil's Pretty Daughter and Other Ozark Folk Tales* (1955), for example, was proudly described as a version of Type 313, "The Girl as Helper in the Hero's Flight." The narrator had localized the text by an unusual introduction of folk beliefs to reinforce obstacles in the hero's flight. To give credence to the South's claim for the highest order of preserving old traditions, Randolph reported variants collected in Virginia, South Carolina, Louisiana, Texas, and Missouri.

Many of the distinctive qualities of such Old-World folktales have also been uncovered in Kentucky by folklorists Kenneth and Mary Clarke. They report tales having familiar motifs of remarkable adventures or quests, magical objects or incantations, and giants or other fearsome creatures. Yet the variants found by collector Leonard Roberts of "Jack and the Beanstalk," "Jack the Giant Killer," and "The Devil's Pretty Daughter" have a decidedly Kentucky flavor to them. For the most part, the European *Märchen* types popularized by the Brothers Grimm lose their supernatural and fantastic elements in America. The tales reportedly become shorter; often the actions or characters are made humorous.

Although the early folklorists spotlighted the New World *Märchen*, this genre actually constituted a minor part of most narrators' repertoires. Vance Randolph, in fact, redressed his own preoccupation with reaping *Märchen* by publishing *Hot Springs and Hell* (1965), a collection of traditional jokes and anecdotes. Put down on paper, many of the local jests lose the cutting edge of humor. Still, doing so points out the abundance of comical situations made for the storyteller's interpretation. Take the story collected by Randolph and called "Fit to Sleep with the Hogs":

> There was a fellow named Howard that had a pretty wife, but somebody says that Howard's wife ain't fit to sleep with the hogs. Howard got pretty mad when he heard that, and he says "She is too!" So then everybody laughed.

The themes of language misunderstood or maimed, marital relations ridiculed, and the fool made foolish give this story a familiar ring.

Folk humor frequently revolves around stereotypical, comical characters or "folktypes." Typically, southerners have sheafs of stories using either the mountaineer (or "hillbilly"), the poor white, the black, the preacher, or the city slicker as the butts of humor. Using the veil of laughter, the jests deal with the concerns and tensions of southern society. There is the caution against hypocrisy in fundamentalist southern religion and the fallibility of the clergy underlying the popular series of preacher jokes, for example. Racial tensions and rural-urban conflicts of values also find expression in the South's folk humor. The characters themselves establish categories in the minds of people, often based on the exaggeration of one or two traits, for people to confront the diversity of regional, occupational, and ethnic groups within the unity of the South.

Perhaps the most celebrated genre in the narrator's repertoire is the tall tale, also called "windies," "whoppers," or simply "lies." The tales can be brief exclamations, such as the following boast collected in Mississippi: "You think your tomatoes are big? Well, I had a tomato so big the picture of it weighed five pounds!" Typically though, tall tales are extended narratives, as in common stories like "The Lucky Shot" collected by folklorist Richard M. Dorson from Mississippi-raised J. D. Suggs:

> Fellow went out hunting. He didn't have but one shell. And he happened to look up, and first thing he seed was ten ducks sitting on one limb. He looked over to one side before he shot, and saw a panther standing there. He looked over on his left—there was a big buck standing there. He looked behind, and there was a covey of partridge right behind him. He didn't know which one to shoot at. He looked straight in front of him and he seed a big bear coming towards him. He knowed he had to shoot the bear, for the bear would kill him—he knowed that. So he cocked both muzzles of a double-barreled muzzle loader, pulled both triggers the same time. The shot killed the bear. The ramrod shot out and hit the limb and caught the ducks' toes before they could fly away. And the hammer on the left, it flew off and killed the deer. The right hammer, it flew off and killed the panther. He kicked his overcoat off, and smothered the covey of partridges.

This tall tale, Type 1890 in Aarne and Thompson, is widely reported in the South, having been collected by Zora Neale Hurston from Florida's Larkins White and by Arthur Huff Fauset in Alabama—to name just two notable southern folklore collectors.

Another form of the tall tale is the embellished personal experience story. Folklorist Kay L. Cothran found many such stories in the Okefenokee Swamp Rim of Georgia, where narrators delighted in relating remarkable hunting and fishing exploits. The success of the tall tale, according to folklorist Jan Harold Brunvand, "does not depend on belief in the details of the story, but rather on a willingness to lie and be lied to while keeping a straight face. The humor of these tales consists of telling an outrageous falsehood in the sober accents of a truthful story." Depending therefore on common situations and themes, the storyteller creatively weaves his characters and remarkable exploits together and then stretches the tale to the tallest limits his audience will tolerate.

The South's particular folk heroes have a strong part to play in story and ballad. Yet the lines between folk and popular tradition often become blurred in accounts of Davy Crockett, Stonewall Jackson, Jesse James, and others. More common in today's oral tradition are local characters given notoriety by storytellers. In the Mississippi Delta, for instance, a local outlaw, "Bad Man Monroe," is the subject of many narratives told about his remarkable deeds, extraordinary size and strength, and difficult capture. Also in the Delta, moonshiner, outlaw, or lawman (depending on who you listen to) Perry Martin remains an important folk hero to the river people. In southern Kentucky, the guerilla actions of Beanie Short during the Civil War for the Confederate cause, or, some say, for his own gain, still circulate. Like other legendary figures, they give rise to not one but a series of stories. Beanie Short's legend includes accounts of buried treasure, ruthless activity, and tragic death. In the communities of the South, these legends compose the rich folk history of the locality and help give residents a sense of past and place.

Context. The occasion and the setting for people gathering influence the types of stories told. Folklorist Patrick Mullen, for example, contrasted the fishing spots, feed stores, and public festivals at which Texas storyteller Ed Bell performs. Mullen found that Ed told personal experience narratives at the feed store but related tall tales to festival audiences. In the studies of folklorists William Ferris and Kay Cothran, setting also played a crucial role, for storytelling was generally found to be dominated by men and thus recurred in sexually segregated activities like hunting or music making. In a Mississippi storytelling session documented for *Folklore Forum*, the men involved entertained themselves trading stories in a gamelike atmosphere. The presence of two recognized storytellers led to a competitive spirit in the session. At one point, though, a woman entered and disrupted the session. It became inappropriate to continue, because the context had changed.

Storytelling often occurs in "sessions." In social centers people gather to hear and tell stories. The session provides entertainment and passes time, but by drawing people together, it also reinforces shared values and binds a group together. In the Okefenokee Swamp, for example, the storytelling custom of "talking trash," says Kay Cothran, "comes from a time when men did not work by the time clock but by cycles of nature. Talking trash today is an act of identification with that older way of life, and whether one does it as a matter of course or as something of a rebellion, talking trash is a sneer at middle-class subservience to continuous gray work and a denial of that class's identification of the materially unproductive with the counterproductive." In other areas, the "liar's bench" at the courthouse, the hunting camp, or the general store may also serve as appropriate places for the activity. But storytelling sessions are not limited to rural areas, for city and industrial hangouts nurture narrative exchange also.

In encounters outside storytelling sessions, people use stories in bartering and conversation to make a rhetorical point. The context of dog and horse trading is a prime example. Folklorist Richard Bauman found hunters and traders using stories in the process of negotiating for a purchase or trade:

> Byers too has been taken in a trade. He comes back with his account of having traded once for two dogs that were supposed to be good fox dogs and then discovering that the "sumbitches wouldn't run a *rabbit*." This story establishes that he has already been victimized at least once in a trade and, by implication, that he does not intend to let it happen again.

William Ferris found similar interaction with Mississippi horse trader Ray Lum, and also reported that, indeed, Lum's popular reputation was based in part on his stature as a renowned storyteller.

The ages of participants are also contextual factors. Although the popular image exists of the grandfather warmly relating a tale to a child on his knee, storytelling occurs from early childhood on. In early years, fantasy and fictional narratives dominate; in adolescence, legends and jokes about matters close to teenage concerns of sex, driving, morality, and education hold center stage. Later, personal experience narratives become prevalent parts of conversation and entertainment. The ages of the storyteller's listeners and of the storyteller frequently dictate the type of material related. In fact, development of narrative skills is part of the aging process, for in early years formulaic tales, rhymes, and patterned narratives prevail, whereas later, when cognitive and social skills increase, more creative experiential narratives take precedence. Of course, other factors, like primary social contacts, also affect content. In Mississippi, William Ferris found ghost stories limited largely to the repertoires of children and old people, whereas protest tales were found primarily among black adolescents and adult informants who encountered racial tension daily in their work.

Storytelling is a way of communicating ideas and concerns that may not be effectively articulated or desired in conversation. Often, putting feelings and ideas on the fictive plane of a story helps to clarify or act out personal and social concerns. Further, storytelling changes according to the needs and demands of the situation in which it occurs. The function of storytelling—be it entertainment, education, or social maintenance—depends on the intent of the narrator and the composition of the audience, as well as the place in which they interact and the nature of the material presented. As there are many contexts for people to gather, so there are many contexts for storytelling. Vance Randolph thought that the isolation of places like the Ozarks and the ample time on the hands of its residents explained the vitality of the region's storytelling, but the existence of storytelling in new urban and suburban areas and in other modern contexts challenges that notion. Given the proper time and setting wherever people interact, people need and demand the good story told well.

Style. A common hunting-camp story is told about an old hunter who would entertain his comrades by exclaiming "number three!" Sure enough, the fellas would respond with laughter. A novice hunter hearing this decided to try his hand by interjecting "number four." But to him they gave a harsh silence. Puzzled, he asked why he failed. One of the hunters came over, put his hand on the youngster's shoulder, and explained, "*Well, some can tell 'em and some can't.*" What often distinguishes the storyteller and gives depth and meaning to texts, the youngster learned, are expressive qualities arranged and repeated as a *style*. In storytelling, style especially comes into play when presenting and delivering narratives.

Observers of southern styles usually note the relaxed, casual verbal performance, paced, Botkin claimed, "to the relaxed tempo of Southern living." Dorson agreed and also commented on the distinctive chants, mimicry, whiny dialogue, rhymes, and bits of song that punctuated narratives he collected from southern blacks. Imitations of animal sounds and even the preacher's rhythms mark many a tale's telling. Altering one's voice to identify different characters or to emphasize an action is another common stylistic technique. Of course, narrators try to distinguish themselves by adopting a personal style, but reports of southern storytelling refer often to the shared qualities of understatement and casualness.

Although formula openings and closings are not as common in southern storytelling as elsewhere, certain qualities still stand out. Zesty phrases and localized vocabularies spice up the content of stories. "He was busier than a one-armed paper hanger," Kentuckian Steve Poyser said during one story, and topped even that with "and making more noise than two skeletons in armor making love on a tin roof—with brass bras on!" One can also hear "lit out" for "left" or "lickety-split" for "at high speed." To the question "What are you doing?" Vance Randolph's informants would whimsically reply "fattenin' frogs for snakes," "makin' kitten-britches for tomcats," and "punchin' peth out of elders." According to Dorson, "All these piquancies of speech do not constitute a primitive dialect, but a vivid and racy handling of the common tongue."

Southern storytellers share with other narrators general attributes of folk composition. The tale is given symmetry and order by use of *threes*, for example. One finds the recurrence of three episodes, three tasks, or three characters to structure the tale. The narrator also often uses oppositions like good and evil, north and south, city and country to underline that structure. Plots in folk narrative tend to be unified and single stranded; they typically begin calmly, work toward a climax, and close calmly. No more than two characters usually appear in a scene, and when they do, they commonly are stark contrasts to each other. Description and reflection take distant back seats to action. Dialogue commonly carries the action.

The cultivation of stylistic technique in oral deliveries is apparent when someone offers you the smooth flow of a "good one," or just slips it into conversation. Symbolizing this pride in vocal ability is Andy Griffith's gleeful comment in the play *No Time for Sergeants*. When asked if he could do Hamlet, he replied, "No, but I *tell it*." Indeed, the power of style is evidenced by humorist Jerry Clower's remark, "I don't tell funny stories, I tell stories funny."

Whereas manipulating the voice to produce a captivating, melodic tone is important to any sense of style, developing expressive gestures and motions is also crucial. Among many southern storytellers, the hands are powerful tools of persuasion. They express emotions, point out directions, and give dimensions in the tale. The hands work with the pliable face to give full expression to the narrator's words. Style, then, helps give the story form and feeling, and insures that listeners will remember the narrator, too.

Narrators. Even before recording equipment was available, writers used storytelling characters to give novels and short stories the ring of vernacular authenticity. Perhaps best known was Joel Chandler Harris's Uncle Remus, set in Georgia. Writing in the late 19th century, Harris inserted folktales into his literature by letting the story apparently develop from Remus's lips rather than from the author's pen. Similarly, Carolina-raised Charles Chesnutt introduced Uncle Julius; Tennessean George Washington Harris had Sut Lovingood; Kentuckian Jesse Stuart used Uncle Op Akers and Grandpa Tussie. Despite literary embellishment, the authors commonly base such characters on real people and thus give a glimpse of storytelling that otherwise would go unwitnessed.

Sometimes, storytellers gain renown through circulation of their stories in almanacs, pamphlets, and other forms of popular literature. Free use of dialect and vernacular mark these stories as oral narrative adapted to print. Davy Crockett's tall tale account of "Bear Hunting in Tennessee" is one widely circulated example; another is Colonel Charles Noland as "Pete Whetstone of Devil's Fork." Writing from his Arkansas home for the weekly *Spirit of the Times*, he re-created numerous tall tales, including the favorite "Bear Hunt."

With the introduction of cylinder recording the public could actually hear the tale being told whenever they wanted. The telling of "The Arkansas Traveler" was released by Edison at least three times prior to 1920. Rural-styled entertainers like Arthur Collins and Cal Stewart (popularly known as Uncle Josh) captured on disc numerous folk narratives, often in the guise of "rube sketches." The record, though, placed limitations on the storyteller's performance. The story had to conform to a certain time limit, and the teller had to strain to get a clear reproduction of his voice. More often the trained voice, rather than the authentic, relaxed raconteur, found its way onto the early recordings.

Radio shows, however, like the Grand Ole Opry, gave many genuine southern folk humorists a chance to ply their craft effectively before a wide listening audience. Benjamin Francis (Whitey) Ford, popularly known as the Duke of Paducah, and Archie Campbell are Opry humorists who combine theatrics and traditional texts in their performances. Campbell is especially adept at a tongue-twisting form of storytelling—the spoonerism. He builds stories on the interchange of word sounds, such as "Rittle Led Riding Rood."

Television spread southern storytelling further. *Hee Haw*, for instance, regularly features genial John Henry Faulk storytelling against the backdrop of a country store and Archie Campbell holding court in a barber shop. Out on a porch another of the show's amiable raconteurs, the Reverend Grady Nutt, specializes in anecdotes and preacher jests.

Hosting his own show is Mississippi's ebullient Jerry Clower. He developed his narrating skill regaling customers with stories while working for a fertilizer company in Yazoo City. Clower has achieved national popularity, but many storytellers are recognized and occasionally celebrated only in their home localities. Near Banner Elk, N.C., Marshall Ward and Ray Hicks perform Jack tales that have attracted folklore collectors. Solsberry in southern Indiana annually holds a liar's contest featuring the Ray brothers, specialists in tall tales, from whom folklorist Brunhilde Biebuyck collected 200 tales. Some local storytellers, like Ed Bell of Luling, Tex., have gone beyond their hometowns to present personal experience stories and tall tales at an occasional regional or national folklife festival.

Despite the spotlights placed on the aforementioned storytellers, American folklorists have generally given more attention to the narrator's texts than to the narrator. Recently, though, some folklorists have explored the biography, repertoire, and creativity of several outstanding southern narrators.

James Douglas Suggs, for example, gave folklorist Richard M. Dorson almost 200 folktales. Born in Kosciusko, Miss., in 1887, the black Suggs worked the famed Rabbit Foot Minstrel Show throughout the South in 1907. He sang and played guitar, danced, and told jokes. The years after found him working as a professional baseball player, railroad brakeman, and cook. With his wife and many children he eventually settled in Calvin, Mich., an area populated largely by southern blacks. He absorbed many narratives in his various occupations and travels, recounting them to the workers at the next job and to friends at the tavern. In 1952, while searching for storytellers in the field, Dorson was directed by a local barkeep to Suggs, whom she knew as a "good talker." In Suggs's repertoire animal stories predominated, followed by equivalent numbers of ghost and hoodoo stories, tall tales, preacher jests, and Ol' Marster tales. Dorson's visit was opportune, for Suggs died two years later. Suggs's life and narratives compose a major portion of Dorson's classic study *American Negro Folktales* (1967).

Eugene Powell is a comparable figure among Mississippi black narrators. Born in 1908, Powell was raised amidst song and story in the Mississippi Delta. After sharecropping for a time, he turned to operating a roadhouse and music making for a livelihood. Powell expanded his narrative repertoire and honed his storytelling ability in frequent sessions that took place at the roadhouse. When Powell moved to Greenville, he gave up the roadhouse but still hosted many a storytelling session among friends at his house. Powell had a remarkable memory for folk narratives and songs. He knew scores of animal stories, preacher jokes, and John and Ol' Marster tales—many of which he passed on to his storytelling son Ernest. In addition, Powell related a host of local historical legends and personal experience narratives.

Another notable narrator is Ray Lum, loquacious mule trader of Vicksburg, Miss. Lum's rapid-fire delivery unveils a quick wit and an impressive verbal ability, which serves to relax people in trades. Indeed, the trader as clever trickster and affable talker runs throughout Lum's many tales.

Storytellers do not hang out shingles or announce their wares. Storytelling is rather an informal part of their jobs or social life. In a traditional anecdote attributed to many raconteurs, the renowned Texas *Munchausen*, Gib Morgan, when asked for a good "lie" by fellow oilworkers, would tell them that he was too busy to lie right then, for his brother lay sick and Gib had to leave. Later the workers discovered that indeed they were told a good lie. Such informal, impromptu exchanges recur often today at work and at play. Less easily spotted than the European wonder-tale-telling counterpart, the American storyteller nonetheless thrives on informal opportunities for a joke or anecdote. The South's sociable, leisurely image and its strong oral tradition help foster the association of the region with storytelling.

See also BLACK LIFE: / Chesnutt, Charles; Hurston, Zora Neale; HISTORY AND MANNERS: / Crockett, Davy; Jackson, Stonewall; LITERATURE: Humor; / Harris, George Washington; Harris, Joel Chandler; MUSIC: / Grand Ole Opry; RECREATION: Roadhouses; VIOLENCE: Outlaw Heroes; / James Brothers

Simon J. Bronner
Pennsylvania State University
Capitol Campus

Richard Bauman and Roger D. Abrahams, eds., *And Other Neighborly Names: Social Process and Cultural Image in Texas Folklore* (1981); Benjamin A. Botkin, *A Treasury of Southern Folklore* (1949); Simon J. Bronner, *Folklore Forum* (Fall 1981), *Mid-South Folklore* (Summer 1977); Richard Chase, ed., *The Grandfather Tales: American-English Folk Tales* (1948); Kenneth Clarke and Mary Clarke, *The Harvest and the Reapers: Oral Traditions of Kentucky* (1974); Hennig Cohen and William B. Dillingham, eds., *Humor of the Old Southwest* (1964); Kay L. Cothran, in *Readings in American Folklore*, ed. Jan Harold Brunvand (1979); Richard M. Dorson, *American Negro Folktales* (1967); Arthur Huff Fauset, *Journal of American Folklore* (July–September 1927); William Ferris, *Journal of American Folklore* (April–June 1972), *Ray Lum: Mule Trader* (1977); Zora Neale Hurston, *Mules and Men* (1935); *North Carolina Folklore Journal* (September 1978).

Voodoo

For the average American, the term *voodoo* suggests vague notions of black magic and practices found in isolated Caribbean Islands. In reality voodoo is an underground American religious sect that has often merged with or borrowed from Christianity in its use of the crucifix and saints as religious symbols. The religion is widespread in many areas of the United States and is by no means limited to blacks in its belief and practice.

Voodoo is also called "vodun" and "hoodoo" and derives from the religion of Dahomey in West Africa, where the term *vodu* designates gods worshiped by Dahomeans. The cult first entered the United States in the latter part of the 18th century when the French brought slaves from Haiti to Louisiana. Through strong leaders such as Sanite Dede and the two Marie Laveaus (mother and daughter), voodoo influenced New Orleans's black and white communities. Voodoo is still openly practiced in Haiti and has deep roots in New Orleans and southern Louisiana.

Though extensive research on voodoo by Zora Neale Hurston and Newbell Niles Puckett focuses on the New Orleans area, voodoo cults exist throughout the United States. Stores in Philadelphia, Penn., New Haven, Conn., and New York City specialize in the sale of candles, charms, and ointments used either to hex or to remove hexes. Urban "doctors" and "healers" solicit business through leaflets and are more open in their practice than are rural practitioners.

In the rural South those who have intimate knowledge of voodoo are called "doctors" and often combine voodoo spells and herbal remedies in their practice. Voodoo doctors have power of life and death over people regardless of whether they believe in voodoo. The "mojo" reaches the lives of all—white or black, believer or nonbeliever—and can curse or heal depending on the doctor's will.

The vehicle through which a spell is placed or removed is usually a "mojo hand," or in abbreviated form, a "hand" or "mojo." The mojo hand is a small cloth sack that is carried in a wallet or purse and may contain parts of dead insects, animals (especially lizards), birds, and items that have had intimate contact with the person being hexed (underclothing, feces, fingernails, and hair). Through "sympathetic" magic, objects closely associated with the person to be "hoodooed" are doctored to produce the desired effects, which range from influencing their love to death.

Hoodoo doctors are often older men or women who have apprenticed under earlier practitioners. Their skills are passed on orally, and there is an unspoken taboo against writing verbal wisdom on paper that might fall into the wrong hands. The hoodoo doctor is often marked from birth as exceptional and is likely to develop hoodoo skills. One born with a veil (with the placenta) over his face or the seventh son of a seventh son will have special powers.

Medical doctors are often unable to diagnose illnesses that are imposed through hoodoos because no physical signs of sickness exist. The medical doctor will find his patient in good health except for fatigue and depression. To the hoodoo doctor, however, these signs are clear evidence of a "jinx," and cures must be worked immediately to counteract a spell that might prove to be fatal to the patient.

The pervasiveness of voodoo, among blacks especially, is seen through its role in music. Blues recordings often speak of hoodoo and its importance in love. A classic blues verse on hoodoo says, "Going down to Louisiana, get me a mojo hand. / Gonner show all you womens how to love a good man."

Blues musicians have special power over women through their music, which is associated with the Devil. At times, they call on hoodoo doctors to enforce this power. In 1932 "Jelly Jaw" Short from Port Gibson, Miss., recorded the "Snake Doctor Blues":

> I am a snake doctor man, gang of womens
> everywhere I go.
> I am a snake doctor man, gang of womens
> everywhere I go.

And when I get to flying, sometimes I can see
a gang of womens standing out in the door.

The hoodoo doctor, as the verse suggests, has the power to fly through space.

The snake, or "Damballah," is the chief god in Dahomean vodun cults and also plays a major role in hoodoo work. As a symbol of hoodoo, the snake assumes sexual meaning when used in the blues such as "Crawling King Snake Blues" by John Lee Hooker.

In 1953 Walter Davis of Grenada, Miss., recorded the "Root Doctor Blues" with the verses:

The root that I'm selling, from it you can get
a lot of juice.
The root that I'm selling, from it you can get
a lot of juice.
And when I'm giving it to you, Momma, you
don't want to turn it loose.
I was doctoring a woman, she said I can't see
how it can be.
I was doctoring a woman, she said I can't see
how it can be.
She say go way from here, doctor, you got too
much root for me.

The most popular root used in hoodoo is "John the Conqueror root," the most potent root used to conjure. It is also called "High John the Conqueror," and those who understand hoodoo tremble at the sight of its presence in the hands of others. The root is mentioned in several blues tunes, including "I'm a Man" by Bo Diddley. It is best known through the 1954 recording of "Hootchie Kootchie Man" by Muddy Waters:

I got a black cat bone. I got a mojo too.
I got the John the Conqueror Root. I'm gonner
mess with you.
I'm gonner make you girls lead me by the hand.
Then the world will know the Hootchie Kootchie
Man.

Voodoo clearly evolved from West African culture, but knowledge of it in the United States is by no means limited to blacks. Wherever the hoodoo doctor practices his mojo, both white and black follow him. Zora Neale Hurston worked with a Doctor Jenkins in New Orleans and commented that "most of his clients are white and upper-class people at that." And in *After Freedom*, a sociological study of Indianola, Miss., Hortense Powdermaker found one hoodoo doctor had 1,422 white clients, roughly one-third of his total. Both male and female white clients consulted him regularly.

Southern writers have been drawn to voodoo. Charles Chesnutt's *The Conjure Woman*, George Washington Cable's *The Grandissimes*, Ernest Gaines's *Bloodline*, and Alice Walker's *The Third Life of George Copeland* all devote major sections to voodoo. Southern schools of medicine and psychiatry are increasingly interested in the study of voodoo as a valid part of medical practice. The University of Mississippi Medical School has worked with voodoo doctors to heal patients who in traditional diagnoses would be considered paranoid schizophrenics. Although African in origin, voodoo has affected the lives of white and black southerners in many ways. Their religious beliefs, music, literature, and even medicine attest to the old and continuing influence of voodoo on the American South.

See also ENVIRONMENT: Plant Uses; ETHNIC LIFE: Caribbean Influence; WOMEN'S LIFE: Healers, Women

William Ferris
University of Mississippi

Wayland D. Hand, ed., *American Folk Medicine* (1976); Zora Neale Hurston, *Mules and Men* (1970); Harry Middleton Hyatt, *Hoodoo-Conjuration-Witchcraft-Rootwork*, 5 vols. (1970–78); Newbell Niles Puckett, *Folk Beliefs of the Southern Negro* (1926; reprint ed., 1968); Robert Tallant, *Voodoo in New Orleans* (1967).

Weddings

Throughout the world, weddings are momentous events. In the South wedding ceremonies and celebrations have been shaped by traditional beliefs and practices that affirm marriage as an occasion for familial and communal celebration.

Weddings in the 18th- and 19th-century South were typically brief and plain. They were held in the home rather than a church (even in Catholic southern Louisiana), though they were presided over by a minister or priest. The courtship and nuptials of slaves constituted the simplest of southern wedding ceremonies, often being arranged by a master with a view toward an increased slave population. Slaves often had no ceremony at all, merely getting or being given a master's permission to move into a cabin together. Some slaves and poorer whites were pronounced husband and wife after "jumping the broomstick"—hopping over a broomstick together and afterward being feted at a gathering with food and drink. Most southern marriages, black and white, occurred in the morning or at noon to allow family and community to gather at the bride's house after the wedding for a meal and often dancing, music, and games.

"Racing for the bottle," the shivaree, the infare, and a pounding—18th- and 19th-century southern pre- and postnuptial traditions—were common marriage rituals extant throughout preindustrial, rural America. Occasionally, on the wedding morning the groom's friends would gather at his home as an escort and would ride on horseback to the bride's house or the scene of the ceremony, "racing for the bottle." The prize would be shared by the victor. More often the infare, pounding, and shivaree were postnuptial rituals, because most southern newlyweds, not enjoying the 20th-century opportunity for travel and thus for honeymoons, immediately joined a community. In some areas of the South a bride and groom's association with a community was recognized with a celebration a few days after a wedding to help newlyweds set up housekeeping. The "pounding" was a gathering where furniture and food were brought to the new home by neighbors and family. The whole community was generally invited to the "infare" or "infaire"—a dinner at the bridegroom's parents' house held the day after the wedding or occasionally immediately following the wedding.

Particularly in the Upper South, newlyweds came to expect, even anticipate, a "shivaree" (derived from the Old World custom and word *charivari*). Friends of the bridal couple would surround their home, awakening them with rough music, shouting, and pestering until the couple invited them inside for refreshments. If the new couple failed to be hosts, the groom was "taken for a ride on a rail" or thrown into the nearest creek or pond regardless of the weather. In Kentucky and Tennessee it was traditional to kidnap the bride and groom on their wedding night until the abducted offered food, drink, or even money to their abductors. Although some couples looked forward to the test of the shivaree as proof that they were well liked in the community, the shivaree became less and less prevalent because of occasional violent and tragic results. In the South today the only remnants of the mischievous shivaree tradition are more harmless practical jokes and noisemaking—tying noisemakers to the getaway car or sabotaging the newlyweds' luggage.

In the South a rich corpus of folk beliefs and practices is associated with love, courtship, and marriage. The hoped-for future of many southern women was marriage and children; the supreme apprehension was spinsterhood. Because of the frequently passive role of southern women in mate selection, love potions, charms, divinations, and signs and practices to predict spouse selection or insure marital happiness were women's special prerogative. Certain signs foreboded a solitary life—falling up steps, taking the last piece of food on a serving dish, sitting on a table, or sneezing three times in a row. Omens promised or predicted marriage—if a grasshopper spit on you, you would marry within the year; if you caught a bridal bouquet, you would be the next female to marry. Love charms and potions having European and African parallels (a 10-fingered plant, a lodestone, sassafras, cherry pits, or soapstones worn secretly about the neck, or possession of some of one's lover's hair), often predicated on the principles of similarity or contact, were used to manipulate the future.

Signs of love were numerous—dropping a dishcloth, unintentionally making a rhyme, or having an untied shoelace. If you threw a love vine on a bush and it grew, your sweetheart loved you; if you could blow all the down from a thistle in one breath, your love was returned. Southern women made use of a number of methods to determine the character, fortunes, and physical characteristics of their future husbands. It was believed a girl could prophesy the precise identity of her mate by looking in pools of water on her birthday or May Day. Some southerners believed that to insure that the course of true love would run smoothly, the bride-to-be should walk backwards downstairs the first morning after she was engaged.

The precarious status of the bride reinforced many protective beliefs, customs, and taboos: the bride risked her happiness if she made her own wedding dress, tried on her complete bridal array prior to the wedding, or was seen in public between the time the wedding invitations were issued and the ceremony occurred. Auguries of the future included the bride's clothes: for luck the bride must wear something old, new, borrowed, and blue, and to insure financial success she should have an old coin in her shoe. Weather was also important. In the Ozarks and other parts of the South it was unlucky to marry when it was snowing or raining; in other locations a snowy wedding day assured great happiness. Special precautions were taken at the ceremony. Some couples were careful to stand so that the floor planks ran straight from the minister to the couple. Contemporary southern brides and grooms and their families still observe some of these practices that are believed to insure the success and happiness of their marriages.

Although distinctive and regulated by a conception of southern tradition, the structure and rituals of prenuptial and postnuptial southern wedding ceremonies and festivities today reflect many national trends. For example, in the South as elsewhere, there has been a return in the last several years to expensive, traditional wedding ceremonies. Many contemporary southern weddings are notable for their distinctive style, although the style of wedding ceremonies and receptions varies to some extent according to personal preferences and economic, social, religious, and ethnic considerations. Southern weddings tend to be preceded by prenuptial showers, teas, and dinners. Registering for gift preferences at local stores is prevalent, as are church weddings with large numbers of guests. Many stores in larger cities target brides and grooms from wealthy "old" southern families, and in some weddings magnolias and antebellum-style dresses are used to evoke an Old South atmosphere. In most cases, though, southern traditions are incorporated into weddings in more modest ways. A bride may wear a brooch that her grandmother wore on her wedding day, or a groom may carry his great-grandfather's watch, for instance.

Southern individuality is proclaimed in wedding festivities more than in the celebration of any other rite of passage. Contemporary weddings in the South still clearly reflect a romanticization of womanhood. At its core, a southern wedding pays homage to the bride. It is usually the bride's picture alone that appears in the announcements of engagement and marriage; it is her dress, veil, and flowers that are described in detail in these announcements; it is she who is the center of attention. In addition to the emphasis on the bride, southern weddings reveal southerners' strongly developed sense of community and family and their commitment to hospitality. Some southerners strive in weddings to emulate a genteel image of the region, and some see the wedding as a commitment to religious ideas of marriage.

See also WOMEN'S LIFE: Marriage and Courtship

Carolyn Lipson-Walker
Bloomington, Indiana

Frances Boshears, *Tennessee Folklore Society Bulletin* (September 1953); Jan Harold Brunvand, *The Study of American Folklore: An Introduction* (2d ed., 1978); Philip W. Conn, in *Glimpses of Southern Appalachian Folk Culture: Papers in Memory of Norbert F. Riedl*, ed. Charles H. Faulkner and Carol K. Buckles, Tennessee Anthropological Association, Miscellaneous Paper No. 3 (1978); Amanda Dargan, *Center for Southern Folklore Magazine* (Summer 1981); J. Hampden Porter, *Journal of American Folklore* (April–June 1894); Newbell Niles Puckett, *Folk Beliefs of the Southern Negro* (1926; reprint ed., 1968); Vance Randolph, *Ozark Superstitions* (1947); Joe Gray Taylor, *Eating, Drinking, and Visiting in the South: An Informal History* (1982); Newman I. White, ed., *Frank C. Brown Collection of North Carolina Folklore*, vol. 1 (1952); Henry Wiltse, *Journal of American Folklore* (July–September 1901).

"Arkansas Traveler"

A classic, humorous dialogue, a tune, a play, and a patchwork quilt pattern are all known by the title "Arkansas Traveler." Most of the printed references to the "Arkansas Traveler" deal with the history of the dialogue, which is one of the most pervasive folk stories in the southern storytelling tradition. The basic story tells of a traveler on horseback who has become lost and confused and who approaches the log cabin of a fiddling squatter. The traveler ends up as a "straight man" in a comic contest of wits in which the squatter evades or pretends to misunderstand his questions. Finally, though, the traveler offers to play the balance or "turn of the tune" the squatter is playing on his fiddle, and in this manner he breaks down the other man's resistance and is heartily welcomed.

Such whimsical dialogues between a traveler and a local person are relatively common in the literature of the British Isles and frontier America, but none achieved the fame of the "Arkansas Traveler." A melody of the time, "Arkansas Traveler," originated sometime prior to the mid-1840s, but the first known printing occurred in 1847, when an arrangement by William Cumming was published at Louisville and Cincinnati as "The Arkansas Traveller and Rackinsac Waltz." The tune was certainly popular before the first printing of the dialogue and apparently predates it. Although three individuals are commonly cited as the composer, they most likely appropriated a melody that was thriving in oral tradition. By 1850 both the melody and the name had achieved widespread popularity.

The earliest known commercial recording of the "Arkansas Traveller" was by Len Spencer, a blackface minstrel popular during the first two decades of the 20th century. Certainly the most widely distributed recent recording is by the Stanley Brothers. The piece has been a very popular number for recording artists and, in fact, was one of the first two tunes put on record by country musicians. In June of 1922, Eck Robertson and Henry Gilliland, two old-time fiddlers, recorded "Sally Goodin" and "The Arkansas Traveller" for Victor Records. Fittingly, Robertson was a native of Arkansas.

During the late 19th century a five-act melodrama entitled *Kit, the Arkansas Traveler* (originally known as *Down the Mississippi*) was extremely popular, going through hundreds of performances between 1869 and 1899. Certainly the magazine the *Arkansas Traveler*, established in Little Rock in 1883 by humorists Opie Read and P. D. Benham, was inspired by the dialogue, and Texas composer David Guion's symphonic composition was based on the tune. The dialogue and tune also influenced the Arkansas Traveler patchwork quilt pattern, which apparently does not predate the 1850s. The design is of large squares consisting of four smaller squares pieced from seven still smaller scraps. Every unit is of a simple, straight-edged, geometrical shape allowing for the most economical use of various scraps of material. Similar designs were relatively common in frontier homes.

W. K. McNeil
Ozark Folk Center
Mountain View, Arkansas

Fred W. Allsopp, *Folklore of Romantic Arkansas* (1931).

Bottle Trees

Bottle trees are a product of southern black culture with roots in the animistic spiritualism and totemism of several African tribal cultures. Glassblowing and bottlemaking existed as far back as the ninth century in Africa, and the practice of hanging found objects from trees or huts as talismans to ward off evil spirits also existed. The bottle tree was a Kongo-derived tradition that conveyed deep religious symbolism.

The bottle tree was once common throughout the rural Southeast. Trees were made by stripping the foliage from a living tree, with upward-pointing branches left intact. Bottles were then slipped over these branch ends. Cedars were a preferred species, because they were common, resisted decay, and were well-shaped with all branches pointing upward.

Folk custom dictated that spirits would enter the bottle because of the bright colors and become trapped. When the wind blew and shook the tree, the spirits would be heard moaning inside the bottles. In some cases, paint was poured into the bottles before hanging them on the trees. This was done ostensibly to help trap "spirits," but the addition of color to clear bottles may have been the true motivation.

Today bottle trees are scarce. Those that exist in northeast Mississippi, for example, are produced by rural whites as often as blacks. Like the hex signs of Pennsylvania Dutch barns, they are a vestige of the past, produced more for the sake of art than for protection from the supernatural. They can be beautiful and even the worst examples are still curiosities.

Southern authors, notably Eudora Welty, have commented on bottle trees, perhaps because they have a primal fascination. Sunlight on and through colored glass has charmed people for centuries; the bottle tree can be considered the poor person's stained glass window.

See also LITERATURE: / Welty, Eudora

Jim Martin
Yazoo City, Mississippi

Robert Farris Thompson, *Flash of the Spirit: African and Afro-American Art and Philosophy* (1983); John Michael Vlach, *The Afro-American Tradition in Decorative Arts* (1978); Eudora Welty, "Livvie" in *The Wide Net* (1943), *One Time, One Place* (1971).

Brer Rabbit

The most widely known trickster figure associated with Afro-American folklore is Brer Rabbit (the word *Brer*, of course, is a contraction of *Brother*). The rabbit trickster was commonly known in those areas of Africa from which slaves came to America. Although several folktale collectors have recorded Brer Rabbit texts, the tales are best known to the general public through their presentation in several volumes by Joel Chandler Harris (1848–1908), beginning with *Nights with Uncle Remus* (c. 1881). Harris's versions are edited and are closer to literature than folklore. The Georgian proclaimed himself both an accidental author and an unintentional folklorist. Harris was dogmatic on the matter of origins, proclaiming that the narratives were certainly of "remote African origin." Others, most notably folklorist Richard M. Dorson, have been less convinced, arguing that the Brer Rabbit and other animal narratives in the Afro-American repertoire came from a number of dispersal points including Europe.

In the 19th century there was also debate about the Afro-American–Native American exchange of rabbit trickster tales. Bureau of American Ethnology scholars like John Wesley Powell and James Mooney espoused the view that the Indian would be less likely to borrow black tales than the black would be to take over Indian narratives. Harris, of course, held the opposite view of an issue that has been debated off and on to the present. Folklorists Stith Thompson and Alan Dundes inclined toward Harris's view, whereas such books as Mary Alicia Owen's *Voodoo Tales* (1893) provide evidence for the Powell-Mooney view.

Most authorities have interpreted the Afro-American rabbit trickster hero narratives as protest tales in disguise. Thus, when the rabbit triumphed over a stronger animal because of his superior wits, it was really a tale of black slaves triumphing over their white oppressors. Certainly, such an interpretation is consistent with rabbit trickster tales, but those who insist that blacks totally identify with the rabbit trickster hero may be overstating their case.

See also LITERATURE: / Harris, Joel Chandler

W. K. McNeil
Ozark Folk Center
Mountain View, Arkansas

Richard M. Dorson, *American Negro Folktales* (1967); Alan Dundes, *Southern Folklore Quarterly* (September 1965); Maria Leach, ed., *Funk & Wagnalls Standard Dictionary of Folklore, Mythology, and Legend* (1949–50); Lawrence W. Levine, *Black Culture and Black Consciousness: Afro-American Folk Thought from Slavery to Freedom* (1977).

Bungalow House

An enigmatic type of common house in the South, the bungalow played a minor role in the cultural landscape until the late 19th century. The word *bungalow* comes from a Hindustani word *Bangla*, meaning a low house with surrounding porches. An international house type, its antecedents include adobe dwellings in the Southwest, Japanese houses, the raised Creole cottages of Louisiana, the Swiss chalet, and barn and log cabin buildings. The plan of the bungalow is two rooms wide and three or more rooms long. Normally built of lumber, it has a foundation of piers and a gable roof with eaves to the sides (causing some confusion with the shotgun type). It often has a porch across the front and additional rooms on the rear or side. In some urban settings, it has been divided down the middle to form two apartments, giving rise to the mistaken notion that the form is usually a duplex.

The bungalow was normally the home owned by an independent family. During the early 20th century it became in many areas the standard tract house, filling in large areas of the early suburban cityscape. The California bungalow gained nearly complete dominance of southern domestic construction in the 1890–1920 period. As a consequence, many—perhaps most—southern bungalows also sport at least some elements of the California bungalow style.

In both rural and urban contexts, the flurry of bungalow building in the early 20th century reflected the increased prosperity of middle-income southerners. Brick bungalows proliferated after World War I, one of the first times brick was used extensively in popular domestic architecture. After World War II, however, the bungalow type ceased to be built, giving way to national styles and to mobile homes. The bungalow served as the transition from traditional to modern housing throughout the South.

M. B. Newton, Jr.
Louisiana State University

Anthony D. King, *The Bungalow: The Production of a Global Culture* (1984); Clay Lancaster, *The American Bungalow, 1880–1930* (1985); Leila Wilburn, *Southern Homes and Bungalows: A Collection of Choice Designs* (1914).

Clower, Jerry

(b. 1926) Entertainer.

Clower is a modern humorist who uses the rustic settings of the South and the animated styles of the southern storyteller to entertain concert audiences across the country. He has recorded many albums that have reached the national charts; he appears on the renowned Grand Ole Opry; and he hosts a nationally syndicated television show. His stories have been published in two best-selling books, *Ain't God Good!* (1977) and *Let the Hammer Down!* (1978), and in a series of long-playing record albums.

His success as an entertainer sprang from his many years as a fertilizer salesman for the Mississippi Chemical Company in Yazoo City, Miss. In the best tradition of the salesman-talker, he accompanied his sales with humor grown from the homespun life of the Deep South. Born in Liberty, Miss. (on a dirt road, he reports) in 1926, he knew the land and its characters well. He drew laughter of affection and nostalgia for the region and its values.

Clower rose within the company and became a sought-after banquet speaker. At the urging of a friend, he recorded his banquet stories for a local label in 1971. "A Coon-Hunting Story," which used traditional tall-tale storytelling techniques spiced with Clower's distinctive style, caught the southern public by storm. Acclaim for the sincerity and directness of Clower brought him offers to record and perform nationally. Stories such as "Bully Has Done Flung a Cravin' on Me," "The Chauffeur and the Professor," "Sittin' Up with the Dead," "A New Bull," "Bird Huntin' at Uncle Versies," and "Marcel's Talkin' Chain Saw" have become nationally famous.

Clower's boisterous vocal delivery and exaggerated southern speech and gestures (saying "what" for "that," framing superlatives like "most hugestest rat," letting go whoops and hollers, and embellishing phrases with favored adjectives like "cottonpickin'") raise the effect of his down-home humor. His colorful cast of characters, including Marcel, New-Gene, Aunt Pet, and Uncle Versie Ledbetter, endure, thanks to his yarnspinning, as favorite comic figures of the South. Yet Clower is serious about his storytelling and the cultural heritage, and Christian conviction, from which he springs. Clower continues to regale audiences outside the South, gaining fame as he does, but in performances he makes sure to show great pride in the life and people of the South. His stories serve to bring laughter and to preserve the color and spirit of the region.

Simon J. Bronner
Pennsylvania State University
Capitol Campus

Tom Chaffin, *Southern Exposure* (September–October 1983).

Cobb, Ned (Nate Shaw)

(1885–1973) Sharecropper.

Ned Cobb (alias Nate Shaw in Theodore Rosengarten's *All God's Dangers: The Life of Nate Shaw* [1974]), was a cotton farmer from Tallapoosa County, in east-central Alabama—gentle hill country, once extensively cultivated, now in pine woods and pastures. Cobb was born in 1885, the oldest son of Liza and Brown Cobb, former slaves and poor tenant farmers. He went to school for a total of two weeks, spending most of his childhood farming for his father and working for white people. At 21 he married Viola Bentley, an educated young woman whose parents owned land and were able to help the couple buy a mule and get a start. The Cobbs progressed rapidly from sharecropping to tenant farming; in the late 1920s, by which time nine children had arrived, they began buying a farm. In spite of the depression that struck agriculture right after World War I, the Cobbs prospered. But as cotton prices fell to six cents a pound, they, too, were pressed to meet their debts. When landlords and merchants cut off credit in their neighborhood in 1931, Cobb sought and received federal loans to buy fertilizer and see his family through the harvest.

In late fall 1932 the Sharecroppers Union, a voluntary organization of farmers founded the year before to defend the rights and interests of its members, formed a local near Reeltown. Ned Cobb was one of the first to join, moved by the idea of collective resistance to economic and social injustice. In December he assembled with other union men at the home of a neighbor to stop the sheriff from foreclosing on the man's livestock. A shootout ensued and several union men were killed or wounded. Cobb was shot in the back, but he managed to get away and evade arrest for one day. (The episode is the subject of John Beecher's epic poem *In Egypt Land.*) Along with a handful of other survivors, he was tried for attempted murder, convicted, and sent to prison for 12 years. Several times he refused a parole conditional on his never returning to Tallapoosa County. In 1945, at age 59, he went home and resumed farming. But he was a mule farmer in a tractor world, and he lacked the education and capital a man needed to get ahead. Toward the end of his life, he worked on shares with his son Wilbur, a successful cotton grower who had held the family together in his absence. Ned Cobb sold his last mule in 1970 and lived quietly, making white-oak baskets for which he was renowned, until his death in 1974, just before his 88th birthday.

See also SOCIAL CLASS: / Sharecroppers Union

Theodore Rosengarten
McClellanville, South Carolina

Cornett, Chester

(1912–1981) Chairmaker.

Chester Cornett was an eastern Kentucky craftsman who embodied in both his life and his work the tradition of folk craftsmanship. Born on King's Creek, Letcher County, Cornett learned the traditional design and construction of chairs from his maternal uncle, grandfather, and great uncle. Though he worked briefly in a commercial carpentry shop before his induction into the army in World War II, Cornett never owned or used power tools as an independent chairmaker until 1967, and even after that date he preferred to work "by hand."

A trying early life left its mark on Cornett. He was rejected and deserted by his parents, a girl he intended to marry, and his first and second wives. He emerged from his two years of military service in the Aleutian Islands with "a nervous condition," a skin disease, bad teeth, and eye troubles. He could not or would not tolerate the marginal life he lived in Hazard, Ky., where he worked as a handyman, stacked cases of Coca-Cola, and briefly worked in a coal mine. About 1947 he moved to the vicinity of Dwarf, Ky. In a secluded hollow on Main Lotts Creek he resumed making chairs, though against his wife's wishes, for his low income from the only work that gave him personal satisfaction insured their continued poverty. By 1950 he abandoned the use even of his foot-powered lathe and began to build his chairs with eight-sided pieces produced with axe and drawknife.

In 1953 Cornett built his first eight-legged chair, inspired in part by the geometric possibilities inherent in octagonal legs and posts, and in part by his belief that a novel design would enhance his ability to sell or barter his chairs. Over the next 15 years he developed a remarkable set of stylistic trademarks that blended novel and "antique" elements. The innovative design features, which began with octagonal rather than turned pieces, continued with Cornett's increasing emphasis on very large chairs with many deeply curved slats, his exaggerated use of pegs as decorative elements, his development of many variations in bark widths and weaving patterns used in chair seats, and his employment of contrasting species of wood. Though all his later, larger, chairs suggest a sense of protective enclosure that is lacking in traditional models, and though some of his chairs were, by his own designation, "strange," Cornett felt that most of the trademark elements he employed were antique features. The antique hallmarks of Cornett's work include emphatically decorative pegs, the large "knobs" (finials) of slat-back chairs, and the pronounced outward and backward bend on the rear posts of "mule-eared settin' chairs"; in Cornett's view, these features distinguished his "handmade" chairs from the "homemade" chairs of other eastern Kentucky chairmakers, as well as from "factory chairs" made with power tools and kiln-dried lumber.

Cornett became the subject of scholarly attention in 1965 when folklorist Michael Owen Jones met him and began to study his work, along with that of other traditional chairmakers from southeastern Kentucky. He received increased popular attention after April 1965, when Kentucky writer Gurney Norman published an article on him in the *Hazard Herald*. Subsequent articles in state, regional, and national periodicals brought Cornett orders for chairs from far beyond his locale. In 1981 he became the subject of a film entitled *Hand Carved*, in which he makes a chair of a type he had invented 20 years before, the eight-legged "two-in-one" rocker; he also describes the advantages and disadvantages of making chairs by hand for a living. Chester Cornett died in a Veterans' Administration nursing home in Ft. Thomas, Ky., soon after the film's release.

Thomas A. Adler
University of Kentucky

Hand Carved (Herb E. Smith and Elizabeth Barret, directors, Appalshop Films, Whitesburg, Ky., 1981); Michael Owen Jones, "Chairmaking in Appalachia: A Study in Style and Creative Imagination in American Folk Art" (Ph.D. dissertation, Indiana University, 1969), *The Hand Made Object and Its Maker* (1975); *The Mountain Eagle* (18 June 1981).

Dogtrot House

A house with an open hallway separating two rooms under a roof that has its gables to the sides is a dogtrot house. Such a house may have been built of log, lumber, heavy timber, or other materials. In the popular mind, however, the dogtrot house is made of logs, and that manner of building seems to have been one of the determinants of the form.

Although there were European antecedents, with open passages between two rooms under the same roof, the American dogtrot drew only peripherally from that Old World tradition. At least as likely a source for the house was the Georgian Revival, which emphasized bilateral symmetry: two sides of the facade mirroring each other across the midline. When early settlers were entering the backcountry and preparing for the great sweep westward across the South, the Georgian style dominated.

The pioneers set about building British bay, or pen, houses, using German log-working methods, and in the

Dogtrot house, Hickory Flat, Miss., 1968

Georgian style. The resulting ideas on enlarging a log house to embrace two rooms included, among others, the dogtrot plan. Two log pens, say 20 feet across the front and 18 feet from front to back, were built side by side and surmounted by a common roof. Under Georgian rules, they had to have like facades, placed so as to share a common hall. The result was a dogtrot (also known by many folk names: hallway house, possum trot, two pens and a passage). Limited by log construction, the building of a two-pen house with a central hall made the enclosing of that hall a special problem. When it was enclosed, it was with other material and usually at a later date.

Whatever the origin of the dogtrot in the eastern part of the South, it spread over the region from the Appalachians to the edge of the Great Plains and from just north of the Ohio to near the Gulf shores during the brief span from 1775 to 1835. In this diffusion, the dogtrot was one of the steady hallmarks of the Upland (as opposed to the Lowland or Tidewater) South.

The dogtrot has been a frequent image in southern literature. William Faulkner uses the dogtrot as home to both poor white and black families in his fictional Yoknapatawpha County. Examples in *The Reivers, The Mansion, Go Down, Moses,* and *As I Lay Dying* range from the classic dogtrot with its open hallway to those with enclosed hallways and second floors added. As dwellers become more affluent, they make predictable changes in their houses. In Eudora Welty's *Losing Battles* Granny Renfro and her dogtrot home are a link with life "a long time ago." Although times have changed, Granny Renfro has neither painted her dogtrot nor "to this day closed in" its central hallway.

Photographers who worked with the Farm Security Administration, including Eudora Welty, Dorothea Lange, Arthur Rothstein, and Russell Lee, documented dogtrot homes in the 1930s South. In *Let Us Now Praise Famous Men,* Walker Evans and James Agee explored the dogtrot with painstaking detail through Evans's photographs and Agee's text. William Christenberry, who grew up in Hale County, Ala., the locale for the Agee and Evans book, now photographs dogtrots in his home county and has re-created a dogtrot house in his studio in Washington, D.C.

The dogtrot house has inspired folk artists in the South with its distinctive shape. Mississippi's Theora Hamblett, for example, painted the home she knew as a child, focusing the viewer's eye through its central hall. Architects such as Arnold Aho and William Turnball have been inspired by the aesthetic and functional aspects of this traditional southern home, and Aho has even designed a passive solar "neo-dogtrot" house utilizing cross ventilation.

M. B. Newton, Jr.
Baton Rouge, Louisiana

Walker Evans and James Agee, *Let Us Now Praise Famous Men* (1941); William Ferris, ed., *Afro-American Folk Art and Crafts* (1983); Richard H. Hulan and Douglas K. Meyer, *Pioneer America* (July 1975); Terry G. Jordan, *Texas Log Buildings: A Folk Architecture* (1978); Dianne Tebbetts, *Pioneer America* (June 1978); Eugene M. Wilson, *Pioneer America* (July 1971).

First Monday Trades Day

Known in most southern states, but most notably Texas and Alabama, the First Monday Trades Day harks back to an earlier, more neighborly time. On a regular basis, usually the first Monday of each month, the people of some southern counties held an open market for traders, commonly on the street surrounding the courthouse. During the monthly session of the county court, the town and country folk gathered to trade by cash or by barter all manner of goods: dogs, canned goods, horses, used tools, stitchery, notions, fresh produce, and indeed nearly anything of value. Itinerant peddlers often joined the trading, and impromptu fiddling, picking, storytelling, and gossiping added a carnival tone to the monthly gathering.

Among the best-known trades days are those at Scottsboro, Ala., and Canton, Tex. Even before the recent rise in popularity of "flea markets," these two had acquired wide repute and attendance numbering in the thousands. On Labor Day, the greatest First Monday of the year, Canton drew tens of thousands of visitors, all determined to enjoy bartering, food, yarns, friends, and animals. Where several nearby counties held trades days, some had to content themselves with second, third, or fourth Monday as their regular time for the event; such was the case in much of east Texas. Once the flea-market mania gained hold of the South, some of the First Mondays had to be moved to the outskirts of the county seats. Despite the "Monday" name, trading often began on the Saturday before the first Monday, resuming late Sunday and continuing until sundown Monday.

The origin of First Monday is ascribed to "hard times when folks had no money and had to barter." The question arises, however, as to why the same solution appeared—presumably spontaneously—at so many places across the South, why it is always associated with the sessions of the county court, and why it focused so much on dogs and horses. The practice seems more likely to have been an element of backcountry commerce carried westward with the frontier. Similar trades days are common in Ireland and Great Britain and suggest a historical reason for the tradition.

Names for the event differ somewhat. At Abingdon, Va., it is "Jockey Day," referring to the trading and racing of horses that accompany the trading. At several places, it is called "Court Day," referring to the concurrent county business. In most places, however, "First Monday" is the preferred term.

M. B. Newton, Jr.
Baton Rouge, Louisiana

Fraktur

The art of *fraktur*—illuminated manuscripts—was a German tradition brought to this country by emigrants coming from the Rhineland in the late 17th and 18th centuries. The art form entered the South as these Germans, who had settled primarily in Pennsylvania, began migrating down the wagon road into and through the Shenandoah Valley. As a result, pockets of Germanic settlement appeared in Maryland, Virginia, North Carolina, and South Carolina. From these regions, especially Virginia, numerous examples of *fraktur* have survived.

The German word *fraktur* referred originally to a 16th-century German typeface, which resembled the calligraphic script often used on medieval documents. Birth and baptismal certificates, *taufshein*, and other family documents and texts were lettered with this script and decorated with watercolor illustrations. Decorative writings, called *zierschrift*, were a type of *fraktur* common to Mennonites of Swiss ancestry who moved from Lancaster County, Penn., to the Shenandoah Valley in Virginia.

Fraktur produced in the South, where artists used both English and German script, was much the same as that drawn by northern artists. The watercolor embellishments were usually colorful borders incorporating stylized and symbolic figures. Popular motifs, such as hearts, tulips, and birds, were painted in bright reds, blues, greens, yellows, and oranges, and sometimes outlined in black ink.

Because producing *fraktur* required reading and writing skills, ministers and schoolmasters were the predominant *fraktur* artists. At different times a post rider, a cobbler, and a schoolmaster, Peter Bernhart sold *fraktur* forms prepared by a Pennsylvania artist before he began producing his own in Rockingham County, Va. Dated examples exist from the period 1789–1819. The 40 known works by the "Stony Creek" artist date from 1805 to 1824, with over half having been prepared for members of the Stony Creek Lutheran and Reformed Zion Congregation in Shenandoah County (now Page County), Va. Jacob Strickler, born in Shenandoah County in 1770, may have been a Mennonite preacher. Ten of his works have been identified and date from 1787 to 1815. Also from Shenandoah County was Barbara Becker Hamman (1774–1850), who produced *fraktur* as early as 1786. She developed her calligraphic skill through training at a German school in Strasburg, Va.

At least 28 works by the "*Ehre Vater*" artist, who produced *fraktur* in western North Carolina and South Carolina (as well as in Pennsylvania), are known. The "*Ehre Vater und Mutter*" (Honor Father and Mother) appears on much of the work by this artist, probably an itinerant schoolmaster in Lutheran or Reformed schools. There were other southern *fraktur* artists, many unidentified. Together, they continued a tradition begun by their European forebears, thus adding to the artistic culture of the South.

Jessica Foy
Cooperstown Graduate Programs
Cooperstown, New York

John Bivins, *Journal of Early Southern Decorative Arts* (November 1975); Nancy Goyne Evans, *Antiques* (February 1973); Cynthia Elyce Rubin, ed., *Southern Folk Art* (1985); Klaus Wust, *Virginia Fraktur: Penmanship as Folk Art* (1972).

Furniture Making

In the 18th- and 19th-century South, furniture was made in both small towns and isolated farming communities.

Craftsmen in both places used the same woods—oak, maple, ash, and hickory (rather than the mahogany popular in the fancy furniture of the city). The closer the craftsman lived to town the more tools he used, the more aware he and his clients were of fashion, and the more he mixed styles and used ornamentation to please his clients. The town craftsman was influenced by city styles and derived his status from his craft. The more isolated the craftsman, the fewer tools he used. A chairmaker used only a draw knife, pen knife, froe, axe, and pole lathe for a slat-back chair compared to the 75 to 100 tools the town craftsman employed for a chest. The rural craftsman worked at his craft only part-time, farming the remainder; although aware of style, he usually produced less ornamented furniture for a clientele who saw an object's principal attribute as its utility. His status was not dependent on the use and acceptance of popular fashion; rather, the rural craftsman maintained his reputation through his quiet skill.

In the late 19th century mass-produced urban furniture shipped by rail from centers like High Point, N.C., displaced the work of the town craftsman. In rural locales, though, cheap, handmade furniture—bedsteads, chests, cabinets, and chairs—continued to find a narrow market until mass merchandizing arrived there also.

At this point southern furniture became synonymous with concepts of folk "simplicity." The birth of southern handicraft publicized southern crafts nationwide and allowed the rural craftsman to continue his work within the furniture industry. His new customer base required that an object simply appear rustic and handmade.

Although the craftsman fashioned essentially the same types of furnishings as his urban counterpart, his awareness of the outsider's romantic conceptualization of "folk" and "natural" increased. The rustic object, once thought of negatively, became, within this century, positive. The rural southern furniture maker carefully began to preserve the appearance of country, while creating a technology that allowed him to increase his output. Rather than limit production to suit his neighbors' needs, he produced as much as his skills and resources would allow for an ever-widening market. Rather than building by hand and relying on notching and the calculated shrinkage of wood to hold his furniture together, he adopted more modern technology. Nails and power tools, for example, quickly achieved the same end. Rather than minimizing fashion's impact, he studied furniture catalogs for ideas that would fit the "country" image of his crafts.

Southern traditional furniture has evolved into a furniture produced for a mass audience frequently using modern techniques, and it owes much of its continuing existence to America's changing attitudes toward things country.

See also INDUSTRY: / Furniture Industry

Charles E. Martin
Alice Lloyd College

Antiques (March 1968); Michael Owen Jones, *The Hand Made Object and Its Maker* (1975); Charles E. Martin, *Appalachian Journal* (Fall 1981); Christine Ritter, *Early American Life* (December 1977); Warren E. Roberts, *Midwestern Journal of Language and Folklore* (Fall 1981).

"Get Right with God"

Often done in a rough, hand-lettered style, numerous signs greet the traveler of southern back roads. They proclaim abrupt and straightforward messages of salvation: "Christ Is the Answer," "Jesus Saves," "Get Right with God." These terse testimonies set forth the central tenet of fundamentalist Christianity, which is that, above all, good Christians must believe in God. From this belief flows the strict moral order that determines the proper conduct of a righteous life. Simple and direct, these signs allow no leeway in interpretation. Just as their message is uncompromisingly to-the-point, so too one's faith should be firm and unshakable.

Sophisticated observers smirk at the homemade plywood placard that, in dripping left-over paint, says: "Christ Died for Your Sins." The sophisticate does not share the painter's emotion and believes that surely such matters as religion, morality, and the afterlife are not to be summed up in four or five words. Given the aesthetic

Roadside sign, Mississippi Delta, 1975

of southern Christianity, the roadside signs should not be so easily targeted for derision. Folk hymns have high, tight, restricted harmonies. Sunday meeting is a demanding all-day affair allowing little time for secular diversions. Country churches have almost no ornamentation and are noted for their stark, solitary settings where their white clapboarded facades dominate the landscape. In this context a terse proclamation that "Jesus Saves" is not only consistent but appropriate. To say more would suggest a degree of uncertainty rarely encountered among devout believers. A roadside sign, although a minimal statement, is densely packed with significance. It is an icon of faith, a modest but meaningful symbol conveying the truths upon which a stable, reasonable life can be built.

John Michael Vlach
George Washington University

Samuel S. Hill, ed., *Encyclopedia of Religion in the South* (1984); *Southern Exposure* (Fall 1976).

Ghost Stories

The word *ghost* seems to be a straightforward term. Traditionally many terms—*ghost*, *revenant*, *wraith*, *specter*, *apparition*, and *spirit*, to name the most popular—have been used for essentially the same phenomenon. Complicating the matter of definition, the returning dead supposedly come back in several forms. First, they may come back in the same body they had while alive; second, they may appear in some sort of spectral form; third, they may be invisible and known only by their deeds, noises, or mischief. For simplicity's sake a ghost can be defined as a being returned from the dead in human or animal form or having some features of humans or animals.

The best bearers of ghost lore—or any type of folklore—are sometimes stereotyped as rustic illiterates. Like most stereotypes this one has an element of truth but is also misleading. Certainly unschooled rural people know and tell such stories, but by no means do they have an exclusive hold on them. Indeed, ghost narratives flourish as well if not better in cities because more people can hear and tell them. Suffice it to say that most southerners—in fact, most Americans—know or know of such tales, which they have heard related by friends and acquaintances, sometimes as firsthand experiences but more often as something that happened to a friend of a friend.

When one speaks of ghost stories, many people think of an old abandoned house with loose, banging shutters and doors that seem to be closed by some unseen hand. Such a thought is logical, for houses are the favorite hangouts of ghosts; but ghosts are also commonly found in battlefields, mines, highways, boats, graveyards, gallows, and wells. Most ghosts are bound to a single place, but some carry their haunting farther afield. Usually the wraiths move about by horseback or automobile rather than by supernatural means. This activity has a lengthy tradition throughout Russia and much of Europe. As early as the 1660s people were telling stories about these traveling ghosts, and they were undoubtedly being discussed prior to that time.

Most ghosts return for a specific reason, one of the most popular in the South, indeed in the United States, being to reveal the whereabouts of hidden treasure. Other reasons for ghostly hauntings include unjust execution, suicide, a restless soul, a need to complete business left unfinished at the time of death, and attempts to find some forgotten possession. Many ghosts are harmless to anyone with a clear conscience, but some are vengeful and malevolent and return to torture their victims eternally. Often the ghosts of dead lovers or husbands and wives return to haunt their faithless sweetheart or spouse. Sometimes a parent comes back to make life unpleasant for his or her children; on other occasions the ghost returns to slay a wicked person or take revenge on the person who murdered, injured, or cheated him or her. Frequently, the dead return to punish a person who has stolen part of the corpse or who has in some way disturbed the grave; at other times they punish someone who is mistreating a relative. A few southern ghosts have no specific motivation for their return, but these purposeless wraiths are rare.

W. K. McNeil
Ozark Folk Center
Mountain View, Arkansas

W. K. McNeil, ed., *Ghost Stories from the American South* (1985); Flo Hampton Scott, *Ghosts with Southern Accents and Evidence of Extra-Sensory Perception* (1969); Fred Siemon, *Ghost Story Index* (1967); Jack Solomon and Olivia Solomon, eds., *Ghosts and Goosebumps: Supernatural Tales from Alabama* (1981); Dean Faulkner Wells, ed., *The Ghosts of Rowan Oak: William Faulkner's Ghost Stories for Children* (1980); Kathryn Tucker Windham, *Thirteen Georgia Ghosts and Jeffrey* (1973).

Gumbo

The heady, aromatic soup that goes by the name of gumbo is the product of varied cultures that produced this hybrid of southern cuisine. From Africa comes its name—*ngombo*, the Bantu word for okra. The herbs, spices, the carefully chopped and sautéed seasoning vegetables, the seafoods, meat, fowl, and the rice with which it is always served come together in a nourishing and enticing amalgam that is unique to the region.

In Louisiana, gumbo has several classifications. First, there is *Creole*. The word began as a description of offspring of European settlers (in Spanish, *criollo*) and then evolved into meaning homegrown (as in "Creole" tomatoes). Creole cooking, as a style, refers to that practiced in the areas in and around New Orleans by European and African immigrants and their descendants. Then there is *Cajun*: a shortening of the word *Acadian*, which refers to French settlers of the Nova Scotia region displaced by the English who finally settled in the Louisiana Southwest in the late 18th century.

As in any kitchen dispute, there are as many theories as there are cooks, but the usual difference between a Cajun and a Creole gumbo lies in the "roux." Browning flour in fat (slowly, slowly, stirring all the while) creates a roux and in Cajun gumbos this is a necessary thickener. Creole gumbos rely mainly on vegetable aids for thickening, with a much thinner roux if one is used. Cajun gumbos have more pepper and other spices.

In both Creole and Cajun gumbos one finds two families—okra and filé. Okra, when slowly sautéed over a low flame (not in a cast iron pot that would blacken it), loses its ropey consistency and forms a smooth thickening agent. Filé (powdered dry sassafras leaves) gets its name from the French because when improperly used it makes threads (*filé*), and green gummy blobs appear. Properly used (never added to a boiling liquid) it gives a lightly gelatinous texture to liquids. Filé, in the 19th century, was chiefly manufactured by the Choctaw Indians on the north shore of Lake Pontchartrain. They came to the French Market, by the Mississippi River at the French Quarter, and sold their product to generations of New Orleans housewives.

Gumbo always begins with what some chefs call the "holy trinity" of vegetables—onion, celery, and bell pepper. These are seasoned and sautéed, and seasonings might include salt, black pepper, cayenne pepper, thyme, garlic, green onions, parsley, bay leaves, and basil. In okra gumbo, tomatoes are added. A typical filé gumbo contains the above seasonings, plus chicken or other fowl and its stock, oysters and oyster water, and a seasoning pork—ham, andouille sausage, a smoked sausage, or tasso (dried and smoked meat, in this case, pork). A seafood gumbo contains okra, tomatoes, all the above seasonings, possibly a flavoring pork, and shrimp (with stock from boiling their shells) and hard shelled crabs (also with stock). Crabmeat may be added.

Any variations on the two above recipes are possible: some people use both filé and okra. Rice always accompanies the dish, and some cooks sprinkle filé over each bowl rather than add it to the pot. Chefs have been known to add a serving of potato salad on top, but this is not recommended for novices.

Two other gumbo families exist. One uses meats, either beef or game, and this is usually an okra gumbo. The other is gumbo z'herbes, which is very similar to what is called greens and pot liquor in other southern kitchens. When seasoning meat is left out, gumbo z'herbes becomes an ideal Lenten soup, and the number of greens in a Good Friday gumbo z'herbes can correspond to the number of apostles.

Gumbo does have other meanings. Gumbo mud is black, sticky, and is best created by the Mississippi River. Gumbo or "Gombo" French is a patois of French and African languages once spoken by New Orleans blacks. Gumbo, meaning a mixture of many ingredients, also is used in a Cajun saying: "Gumbo ya-ya," roughly translated as "Everybody talks at once."

Carolyn Kolb
New Orleans, Louisiana

Howard Mitcham, *Creole Gumbo and All That Jazz: A New Orleans Seafood Cookbook* (1978); *The Original Picayune Creole Cook Book* (1966); Paul Prudhomme, *Chef Paul Prudhomme's Louisiana Kitchen* (1984); Lyle Saxon, ed., *Gumbo Ya-Ya: A Collection of Louisiana Folk Tales* (1945).

Hamblett, Theora

(1895–1977) Painter.

Theora Hamblett was born 15 January 1895 in the small community of Paris, Miss. Hamblett lived the first half of her life on her family's modest farm in Paris. Her experience as a white woman growing up and living in the impoverished rural South was typical of her times, with the exception that she never married or had children. From 1915 to 1936 Hamblett taught school intermittently in the counties near her family home. In 1939 she moved to the nearby town of Oxford, where she sup-

Theora Hamblett, painter, Oxford, Miss., 1973

ported herself as a professional seamstress and converted her home into a boardinghouse.

Hamblett began painting in the early 1950s, fulfilling an interest in art that had begun in her youth. Although she enrolled in several informal art classes and a correspondence course during her later life, Hamblett was largely self-taught. Her first paintings depicted memories of her childhood, and she painted scenes of southern country life for the next two decades, culminating in a series of paintings about children's games. Hamblett's most unusual works are the over 300 religious paintings representing biblical subjects and Hamblett's own dreams and visions. These paintings began in 1954 with *The Golden Gate*, later renamed *The Vision*. Today, this first painting is owned by the Museum of Modern Art in New York; most of Hamblett's religious paintings and many memory paintings were never available for sale, and were bequeathed by the artist to the University Museums in Oxford, Miss.

Hamblett's religious paintings and interpretations of her dreams and visions were firmly rooted in her personal religious history. The popular, transdenominational southern Protestantism practiced in the churches, revival meetings, and hymn sings Hamblett attended in and around Paris, Miss., all emphasized the possibility of unmediated encounters between God and communicants, usually taking the form of visionary or dreamlike experiences. Church services were often structured around testimonies in which the worshipers described these experiences, and hymn lyrics regularly referred to them. Hamblett's vision and dream paintings bear structural similarities to traditional testimonies, and many of her paintings employ images from the popular southern hymnody.

Hamblett's aesthetics and working methods were also largely products of her background. The needlework skills she learned as a southern rural woman, and with which she occasionally supported herself, are evident in her art. Hamblett's characteristic tiny brushstrokes of unmixed color resemble embroidery stitches, and many of her images suggest lacework and tatting. Hamblett's interest in painting was not unusual, but the dedication with which she pursued that interest and the role it played in her life were exceptional. The record her work provides of a vanishing regional history and the complex associations of her religious paintings raise Hamblett from the status of an amateur to that of a significant artist of popular southern traditions.

Ella King Torrey
Philadelphia, Pennsylvania

William Ferris, *Local Color: A Sense of Place in Folk Art* (1983); *Four Women Artists* (William Ferris, director, Center for Southern Folklore, Memphis, Tenn., 1977); Theora Hamblett, in collaboration with Ed Meek and William S. Haynie, *Theora Hamblett Paintings* (1975); Ella King Torrey, "The Religious Art of Theora Hamblett, Sources of Attitude and Imagery" (M.A. thesis, University of Mississippi, 1984).

Henry, John

The legend of John Henry, the "steel-driving man," had its beginnings in the building of the Chesapeake & Ohio Railroad in West Virginia in the early 1870s. Construction of tracks for the C & O line through the mountainous terrain required a series of tunnels, the most important of which was the 1¼-mile-long Big Bend Tunnel, which was completed in 1872. According to tradition, John Henry worked on the construction of this tunnel, which at the time was the longest in the United States. Although the song about John Henry is popular with both blacks and whites, he is generally thought of as an Afro-American folk hero, an example of the black hero who defeats white society on its own territory and by its own rules. He is also seen as a symbol of human strength prevailing over machines, an appropriate theme for southerners faced with industrialization of their region.

The first published report of a John Henry ballad was in a brief note in a 1909 issue of the *Journal of American Folklore*. The most extensive studies of the traditions came over two decades later with the publication of books by Guy B. Johnson and Louis W. Chappell. Johnson's *John Henry: Tracking Down a Negro Legend* (1929) and Chappell's *John Henry: A Folk-Lore Study* (1933) resolved the questions of John Henry's relationship to John Hardy, another black West Virginia hero, and the factual basis for the steam-drilling contest in which John Henry lost his life. The books, however, did not stop popular interest in the black hero, who appeared as a figure in a play, a popular book, and several children's books; in addition, there are now over 65 recordings of the ballad. The ballad has also been anthologized in numerous folksong collections.

W. K. McNeil
Ozark Folk Center
Mountain View, Arkansas

Louis W. Chappell, *John Henry: A Folk-Lore Study* (1933); Guy Johnson, *John Henry: Tracking Down a Negro Legend* (1929); Lawrence W. Levine, *Black Culture and Black Consciousness: Afro-American Folk Thought from Slavery to Freedom* (1977); Alan Lomax, *The Folk Songs of North America* (1960).

"Hillbilly" Image

Although the word *hillbilly* probably predates the 20th century, no known record of the word appeared in print until 23 April 1900. On that day the *New York Journal* referred to a hillbilly as "a free and untrammelled white citizen of Alabama, who lives in the hills, has no means to speak of, dresses as he can, talks as he pleases, drinks whiskey when he gets it, and fires off his revolver as the fancy takes him." Except that he is confined to Alabama, this is an accurate description of the major stereotypes of the hillbilly, who is now thought of as being any resident of the southern mountains.

The stereotyped hillbilly made his first widespread appearance in the comic dialogue-song the "Arkansas Traveler," first published in the 1840s. Although he was not specifically identified as a mountain resident, it was generally assumed that the Arkansan who supplied humorous retorts to the eastern traveler's questions was a mountaineer. The hillbilly was poverty stricken and apparently unconcerned with improving his lot in life, but those faults were somewhat compensated for by his wit and love of music. This figure was a far different personality from those mountain men encountered in Hot Springs, Ark., by the protagonist of the song "The State of Arkansaw." These hillmen had "misery depicted in their melancholy faces," and were lantern jawed with stringy, unkempt hair that hung in rattails down their faces. Without redeeming qualities, these personalities were akin to the hillbilly of 20th-century popular imagery, a stereotype that was spread by various forms of mass media as well as by scholarly sources.

Popular literature was one of the forces perpetrating and propagating the hillbilly image. In Charles S. Hibbler's *Down in Arkansas* (1902) the hillbilly is depicted as a conservative, almost regressive being, who "is proud in his poverty, contented with his environment, happy in his seclusion." Thomas W. Jackson's *On a Slow Train through Arkansaw* (1903) provided a more graphic account of the hillbilly, not so much in the text but in the illustrations accompanying the volume. Here the mountaineer was presented in the classic pose, as a person who is obviously stupid, uncouth, unkempt, and no stranger to poverty. This concept reappeared in a large number of later books such as Marion Hughes's *Three Years in Arkansaw* (1908). Other works of fiction, such as Mary N. Murfree's *In the Tennessee Mountains* (1884) and John Fox's *Trail of the Lonesome Pine* (1908), although not specifically negative, pictured the mountaineer as a person in conflict with the forces of the modern industrial age. In so doing they contributed to the common belief that the hillbilly was really a living anachronism, a contemporary but one who temperamentally and intellectually belonged to an earlier era.

Movies also helped keep the hillbilly image alive. The so-called hick flicks such as the low-budget films of the Weaver Brothers and Elviry, Ma and Pa Kettle, and others presented a corny, hard-working, decent, poor but honest, uneducated hillbilly who was often unintentionally funny. In the 1960s this hillbilly was transferred to television most notably in the form of *The Beverly Hillbillies*, whose humor, like that of the earlier rural films, largely revolved around the conflict between the hillbilly's manners and philosophy of life and those of city folks. The characters in this and similar series had little touch with reality or modern civilization.

In 1934 two comic-strip figures who have had far-reaching effect in keeping the popular concept of the hillbilly alive first appeared. L'il Abner was, throughout the comic strip's long run, a noble and naive character possessed of little education, intelligence, pretension, or ambition, blissfully happy in his ignorance and poverty. The other figure, Snuffy Smith, eventually became the main character in the comic strip *Barney Google*, which ultimately was retitled to include both names. At first Snuffy was somewhat rambunctious and obnoxious but he later became a milder personality temperamentally akin to L'il Abner. Older than Abner, Snuffy was equally lazy, unambitious, uneducated, poverty stricken, and unfamiliar with modern conveniences. Unlike Abner, Smith was inclined to feuding and drinking moonshine. These were two of the most popular comic-strip heroes that kept a certain stereotyped view of the hillbilly before the American public, but there were others, such as Ozark Ike, a tall, thin, bumbling, and ignorant ball player, who helped perpetuate the image.

These various views of the hillbilly were not confined to mass media but also permeated scholarly thought and writing on the southern mountaineer. The popular writer John Fiske, in *Old Virginia and Her Neighbors* (1897), stated as fact something that, at best, can only be speculation when he declared that the southern mountaineer was descended from criminals and "degraded white humanity." Fiske observed, though, that the hill residents of his day were noted more for shiftlessness than for criminality. William Goodell Frost, long-time president of Berea College, thought of the mountaineer as a living anachronism, a "contemporary ancestor." The eminent British historian Arnold Toynbee found him little more than a barbarian. Harry M. Caudill, a mountain native, averred in *Night Comes to the Cumberlands* (1963) that Fiske's account of the mountaineer's origin was accurate, and that these people were shiftless and lazy, unskilled and illiterate, and had degenerated into wild and cruel beings. James Dickey's novel *Deliverance* (1970) offered a contemporary version of the cruel, forbidding hillbilly, an image of the "redneck."

Even those who were kindly disposed to the mountaineer and his problems often accepted the image as reality. Thus, organizations such as the Tennessee Valley Authority, the Office of Economic Opportunity, Council of the Southern Mountains, the Appalachian Regional Commission, and others generally failed in their expressed goals of improving the lot of the southern mountaineer, in part because they assumed unrealistically that he represented a "deviant subculture" whose problems were primarily due to physical isolation, depleted gene pools, pathological inbreeding, feuding, moonshining, and welfarism. These groups carefully avoided the word *hillbilly*, but they accepted the stereotype conjured up by the term.

MYTHIC SOUTH: / "Crackers"; Rednecks

W. K. McNeil
Ozark Folk Center
Mountain View, Arkansas

John C. Campbell, *The Southern Highlander and His Homeland* (1921; reprint 1969); Harry M. Caudill, *Night Comes to the Cumberlands: The Biography of a Depressed Area* (1963); James Masterson, *Tall Tales of Arkansaw* (1943; reprinted as *Arkansas Folklore*, 1974); Mitford Mathews, *A Dictionary of Americanisms on Historical Principles* (1951); Henry D. Shapiro, *Appalachia on Our Mind: The Southern Mountains and Moun-*

taineers in the American Consciousness, 1870–1920 (1978); *Strangers and Kin: A History of the Hillbilly Image* (Herb E. Smith, director, Appalshop Films, Whitesburg, Ky., 1984); David E. Whisnant, *All That Is Native and Fine: The Politics of Culture in an American Region* (1983), *Modernizing the Mountaineer: People, Power, and Planning in Appalachia* (1979).

Hunter, Clementine

(1882–1988) Painter.

Born Clementine Rubin, the granddaughter of slaves, in 1882 at Hidden Hill Plantation, south of Natchitoches, La., Clementine Hunter late in life became a renowned primitive painter sometimes called "the black Grandma Moses."

At age 15 Hunter moved to Melrose Plantation, where she worked as a field hand picking cotton, gave birth to seven children, married twice, tended a garden, and became a cook and maid. Melrose was founded in the 1740s but was a 20th-century colony for artists, writers, photographers, and scholars. An artist left tubes of paint at the plantation house in 1940, and Hunter, who was nearing 60 then, discovered them in cleaning. When she expressed interest in painting, author François Mignon, who was also staying at Melrose, encouraged her, providing brushes, turpentine, and a window shade for a canvas. At first she sold her paintings along with watermelons in her front yard to help pay hospital bills for her husband Emmanuel (who died in 1942). Famous visitors to Melrose championed Hunter and promoted her popularity. She received a Rosenwald Foundation grant in the late 1940s, and *Look* magazine did a feature on her work. The New Orleans Museum of Art honored her with its first one-person exhibition of a black artist's work. The Smithsonian Institution in Washington, D.C., and the American Museum of Folk Art in New York City have also given major exhibitions of her work.

Clementine Hunter's first painting was of a baptism, and her more than 5,000 oil paintings in general closely reflect southern life. She records the rituals of daily living, painting weddings, funerals, laundry days, Saturday afternoons in town and Saturday nights in juke joints, Sunday dinners, and children decorating Christmas trees and hunting for Easter eggs. Her works feature farm animals and colorful flowers. Religious images are frequent, including angels in flight, a black Jesus on the cross, and nativity scenes with the manger set in a cotton field. Hunter's creativity was also expressed in baskets she wove, dolls she made, and colorful quilts she crafted.

Charles Reagan Wilson
University of Mississippi

Herbert W. Hemphill, Jr., and Julia Weissman, *Twentieth-Century American Folk Art and Artists* (1974); Jackson *Clarion-Ledger* (24 August 1986); Jay Johnson and William C. Ketchum, Jr., *American Folk Art of the Twentieth Century* (1983).

I House

Whenever and wherever southerners prospered during the late 18th and the 19th centuries, they built bigger, more commodious, stylish houses. The concept that governed their choice of a plan remained nameless throughout the time of its popularity. Later academic practice called the form the "I house." The reasons for the name lie in the vagaries of a gradually awakening scholarly awareness, inspired by the efforts of Fred B. Kniffen to make sense of the houses that he was seeing in Indiana, Illinois, and Iowa (hence, the *I*). Further study showed that the form was the most widespread customary type of house in the United States.

The minimum criterion of the I-house form was a plan two rooms wide, one room deep, and two rooms tall. This plan has been dubbed "two over two." The whole was surmounted by a gable roof with eaves to the front and rear. The house might have had a gallery on the front, shed (or pent-roofed) rooms on the rear, and pavilion rooms on the sides. The I house might have had chimneys on the ends, in the center, or even on the rear of the main rooms (pens). It might have had a central hall or even an open passage (dogtrot) on one or both stories. Earlier versions often had blind (windowless) end walls. I houses were built of log, timber, lumber, brick, and stone. All these elements are independent variables; they do not alter the basic classification.

Through the northern part of the South, the I house was usually of a plainer, leaner variety. Farther South, however, exterior chimneys, broad galleries, and central halls stressed horizontals for a feeling of repose. In one distinct version, the Carolina I house, these feelings are still more accentuated. In the Carolina I house, which appeared in the country back of Charleston and is everywhere connected with migrants from that region, the basic two-over-two plan had two standard additions: a one-story gallery, added to the front, and a one-story shed added to the rear.

Although not uniquely southern, the I houses of the South contributed to popular imagery of the region and illustrated the South's conversion of an architectural form to its own tastes.

M. B. Newton, Jr.
Baton Rouge, Louisiana

Fred Kniffen, *Annals of the Association of American Geographers* (December 1965); Fred Kniffen and Henry Glassie, *Geographical Review* (January 1966).

Jack Tales

Jack tales are long, episodic, oral prose narratives that chronicle the fictional adventures of a poor, teenaged Appalachian farm boy named Jack as he journeys from his home on an eventually successful quest to eliminate poverty from his and his family's lives. As C. Paige Gutierrez has shown, Jack's success is usually due to the nature of his character: a clever, quick-thinking trickster, basically virtuous and kind (but capable of cruelty, violence, and deceit), who regularly displays skill, courage, industry, perseverance, imagination, independence, and a propensity for attracting good luck and supranormal assistance. The consistency and frequency of the association of these traits with Jack essentially define the subgenre.

Jack tales are derived ultimately from an international and widely distributed fund of traditional tale types and motifs, but correspond most closely to European (especially British) *Märchen* and African trickster stories. Appalachian storytellers have combined these inherited narrative elements with their creative imaginations and regional ethos into verbal art that both reflects and informs the Appalachian worldview. Although Jack tales have been collected throughout central Appalachia (the region to which the subgenre belongs)—eastern Kentucky, eastern Tennessee, southwestern Virginia—the center of Jack tale activity seems to be the Beech Mountain area of northwestern North Carolina, in which numerous storytellers such as Ray Hicks, Stanley Hicks, and Frank Proffitt, Jr., continue to keep the tradition alive.

The standard collection of Jack tales is Richard Chase's *The Jack Tales* (1943), which includes 18 texts that Chase recovered largely on or near Beech Mountain. Unfortunately, Chase printed composite texts that were pieced together from several different performances. A valuable feature of the book is folklorist Herbert Halpert's "Appendix," in which he discusses qualities of the tales and provides copious notes on their sources and parallels.

An indispensable work of scholarship on the subject is the "Jack Tales" issue of the *North Carolina Folklore Journal* (September 1978), in which editor Thomas McGowan has assembled transcriptions of four field-collected texts and essays by C. Paige Gutierrez, W. H. Ward, and Charles T. Davis that analyze the stories in terms of distinguishing characteristics, context, setting, narrative style, literary unity, and archetypal patterns.

Storyteller Ray Hicks may be heard and seen performing Jack tales on *Ray Hicks of Beech Mountain, North Carolina, Telling Four Traditional "Jack Tales"* (Folk-Legacy Records FTA-14) and in the Appalshop film *Fixin' to Tell about Jack*. Stanley Hicks tells a fine "Jack and the Giants" on *It Still Lives* (Foxfire Records 001). Several recordings of authentic performances are housed in both the Appalachian State University Oral History Collection and the East Tennessee State University Burton-Manning Folklore Collection.

William E. Lightfoot
Appalachian State University

Richard Chase, *The Jack Tales* (1943); *North Carolina Folklore Journal* (September 1978).

John and Old Marster

John and Old Marster stories represent, along with animal trickster tales, the best-known cycle of Afro-American folk narratives. Joel Chandler Harris included one such story in his various publications but apparently was unaware that it was part of an independent cycle of tales. A direct expression of the plantation black character, John is a generic figure representing the antebellum slave who enjoyed some measure of favoritism and familiarity with his owner. The slave is always called John, and the white owner is known as Old Marster or Old Boss.

The John and Old Marster narratives are concerned with the physical circumstances of slave life and reflect the various ways in which slaves regarded those who held them in bondage. Both John and Old Marster know each other well and in many tales in the cycle engage in a good-humored battle in which John's petty thefts and duplicities are exposed. In others John outwits Old Marster. In several of the John–Old Marster narratives the slave-owner prizes his favorite hand's cunning and boasts about it to other planters. This bragging usually leads to a contest that John must win to avoid losing favor. The slave always wins, either by a ruse or luck. Some John–Old Marster texts suggest the brutal side of slavery and the harsh conflict that often existed between slaves and masters.

W. K. McNeil
Ozark Folk Center
Mountain View, Arkansas

John Q. Anderson, *Southern Folklore Quarterly* (September 1961); Richard M. Dorson, *American Negro Folktales* (1967); Lawrence W. Levine, *Black Culture and Black Consciousness: Afro-American Folk Thought from Slavery to Freedom* (1977).

John the Conqueror Root

Centuries of superstitions surround John the Conqueror root, or High John the Conqueror, popular names for St. John's wort, a family of plants containing about 8 genera and 400 species. Considered one of the most potent herbs for warding off evil spirits and insuring good luck, the plant figures prominently in southern folk beliefs. *Hypericum perforatum*, the species on which European myths have been based, is not common in the southeastern United States, but the name John the Conqueror root has been loosely applied to the whole family. Species such as *H. punctatum* grow in fields, woods, and ditches throughout the Southeast.

In most species the leaves, and often the yellow petals, contain oil- and pigment-filled glands that appear as translucent reddish spots when held up to the light. These spots, according to legend, are the blood of the beheaded John the Baptist, and the herb's potency can supposedly be increased through rituals surrounding St. John's birthday, 24 June.

Voodoo conjurers and other folk medicine practitioners revere the herb, which may be used in root form, as an infusion from the leaves or stems, as an oil, or as a ground-up mixture one chews or mixes with other ingredients that go into a small pouch worn around the neck. Mail-order suppliers and drugstores that stock voodoo potions carry a range of John the Conqueror products. St. John's wort, which affects the central nervous system, has been used to treat everything from dysentery to pulmonary ailments. It is best known, however, for its supernatural applications.

Voodoo conjurers evoke awe and fear when they prescribe "John de Conker." Some practitioners distinguish varieties: for example, Low John de Conker to drive away evil spirits; High, or Big, John de Conker to insure good luck; White Man de Conker to insure that a black man will get a job from a potential employer who is white; Little John de Conker to insure gambling wins. In folklore the herb can also insure a favorable outcome in court, bring bad luck to one's enemies, and ward off ghosts, witches, and nightmares.

The plant's imagery figures prominently in many aspects of Afro-American folklore. Blues masters such as Muddy Waters sing of enticing women through voodoo conjuring with John the Conqueror root, and Zora Neale Hurston's folktales celebrate the exploits of the larger-than-life hero High John de Conquer, or in some stories Big John the Conqueror. The root's mystique is directly reflected, too, in the folktale character of Old John, described by B. A. Botkin as "the wizard and 'hope-bringer' of slave days." John the Conqueror root, says Botkin, is "a fitting symbol for a slave hero as the protector, healer, and prophetic eye of his people."

Sharon A. Sharp
University of Mississippi

Benjamin A. Botkin, ed., *A Treasury of Southern Folklore* (1949); David Conway, *The Magic of Herbs* (1973); William A. Emboden, *Bizarre Plants: Magical, Monstrous, Mythical* (1974); William Ferris, *Blues from the Delta* (1979); Zora Neale Hurston, *Mules and Men* (1935); Harry Middleton Hyatt, *Hoodoo-Conjuration-Witchcraft-Rootwork*, vol. 1 (1970); William Niering and Nancy Olmstead, *The Audubon Society Field Guide to North American Wildflowers: Eastern Region* (1979); Newbell Niles Puckett, *Folk Beliefs of the Southern Negro* (1926; reprint ed., 1968); Harold W. Rickett, *Wild Flowers of the United States: The Southeastern States*, vol. 2 (1967).

Jones, Casey

(1863–1900) Railroad engineer.

That John Luther "Casey" Jones lived at all surprises many people. Legend and song have embellished the life of this American folk hero, the railroad's version of a Davy Crockett or an Annie Oakley.

Born 14 March in the Missouri backwoods, Jones grew up in an age when railroads captured America's imagination. When Jones was a teenager, his family moved across the Mississippi River and into the tiny Kentucky town of Cayce. There, Jones watched steam locomotives draw water from tanks alongside the Mobile & Ohio tracks. The oldest of Frank and Ann Jones's five children, Casey Jones went into railroading, as did his three brothers. His boyhood home inspired the nickname "Casey" when he went to work for the Mobile & Ohio. When Jones told his mother of the newly invented, air-hose brakes for trains, she quoted him in her journal, saying that "riding on the train will be as safe as attending church."

In 1886 Jones married Jane Brady, the daughter of a boardinghouse proprietor in Jackson, Tenn., and there they made their home and brought up three children. By the time Jones was in his mid-20s, he worked for the Illinois Central, which promoted him to engineer. As he barreled through the countryside and cities along a line that ran through 13 states, his reputation grew as a man who liked to run his trains fast. Those who lived near the tracks knew when Jones passed by: the whistle sounded like a whippoorwill call in the night.

Just before midnight on 29 April 1900, Jones pulled his train into Memphis. He had come from Canton, Miss., to the south and was told he would have to return to Canton with the Cannonball Express, a six-car train with passengers. The engineer scheduled to make the run was sick.

You could set your watch by Jones's trains. Considered the Illinois Central's fastest, the Cannonball on this night was 95 minutes behind schedule. Jones and his fireman, Sim T. Webb, worked hard to speed the 188 miles to Canton. In the foggy darkness at Vaughan, 12 miles north of Canton, Jones spotted the caboose lights of a train ahead. Jones told Webb to jump and he did. Jones stayed with the train. The Cannonball rammed into four cars of a freight laden with hay, corn, and lumber. The rest of the freight, stalled due to a broken air hose, was on a side track. Reports later said Jones perhaps did not see warning signals.

Jones was killed. He was the only fatality in an accident not noteworthy at a time of spectacular train wrecks. But a song, written by Wallace Saunders, soon made the crash the most celebrated of train wrecks. Saunders, a black railroad worker, was a friend and coworker of Jones, who was white.

In 1909, long after Jones was buried in Mt. Calvary Cemetery at Jackson, Tenn., the vaudeville team of T. Laurence Seibert and Eddie Newton revised Saunders's ballad. They set their story in the western United States, and it served as the basis for some 200 other versions, evoking train whistles and rumbling locomotives. Mississippi John Hurt, the blues singer; the Grateful Dead, a rock group; and even a Boy Scout songbook commemorate Casey Jones. Yet most of these songs only remotely record what really happened in the early morning of 30 April 1900, on the edge of the Mississippi Delta.

Berkley Hudson
Providence, Rhode Island

Benjamin A. Botkin and Alvin F. Harlow, eds., *A Treasury of Railroad Folklore: The Stories, Tall Tales, Ballads, and Songs of the American Railroad Man* (1953); G. Malcolm Laws, *Native American Balladry* (rev. ed., 1964); Fred J. Lee, *Casey Jones* (1939).

Lum, Ray

(1891–1976) Mule trader.

Lum was born on 25 June 1891 in Rocky Springs, Miss., a rural community of about 75 people located on the Natchez Trace. His grandmother reared him, and during childhood he milked cows, herded cattle and goats, and trained horses. At the age of 12 he moved to Vicksburg and was a delivery boy for two years in local stores. His trading career began at 14, when he bought a horse for $12.50 and sold it for $25.00. This trade launched him on a long and varied life during which he bought and sold livestock in every area of the United States. His base of operations was Vicksburg, where at one time he owned five stables and hundreds of horses and mules.

As a young man, Ray Lum traded with gypsies who were said to "hoodoo" horses because of their ability to make a plug look like a fine animal. From Vicksburg he traveled up the Sunflower River into the Mississippi Delta, where he sold horses and mules to farmers. Shortly thereafter he began regular trips to Texas to acquire the trainloads of stock that he auctioned at his three barns in Vicksburg.

Lum moved to Texas in 1922 and established a central sale barn in Fort Worth that was managed by his partner and ring man, Harry Barnett. Lum then set up throughout west Texas local sales run by "six Mississippians and thirty Texans." He shipped stock to every barn in the region and personally auctioned the animals on a partnership basis with his local managers. During this time he introduced night sales, where both buyers and stock could escape the Texas heat. After fifteen years of auctioning in Texas, Lum returned to live in Vicksburg. At this time (1937) he introduced registered Hereford cattle into the Deep South to upgrade the quality of beef.

Ray Lum, quintessential trader, Vicksburg, Miss., 1973

As late as 1967 he auctioned uninterrupted for hours at large sales in Atlanta and Birmingham. Failing eyesight eventually forced him to withdraw from the extended auctions of his earlier years because he could no longer see bids. As recently as 1976, Lum traveled each week to sales in Mississippi at Lorman, Vicksburg, Port Gibson, Natchez, and Hazlehurst. He drove a large car filled with "everything pertaining to a horse." Bridles, bits, and curry combs were piled on the dashboard; boxes of hats and boots covered the back seat; saddles filled the trunk; and cans of ribbon cane syrup lined the back floor.

As a trader, Lum was adept at both humor and deception. At times he offered the customer veiled truth that only seasoned traders would understand. Ray Lum began as an "angel" (inexperienced buyer) when as a child he sold his wagon and team of goats in Port Gibson, Miss., for $20 after being promised $25. "That was one of the best lessons I ever got. That was the best five dollars ever I earned." He was beaten in this trade but afterwards was "awake." He learned from his mistakes and quickly became a shrewd judge of animals and people.

Ray Lum defined a trader as "a man that trades in everything. A real trader don't never find nothing that he can't use. If he is a trader—and you're looking at one right now—he will trade you for anything you have got. If he can't use it, he'll find someone else that can. There is lots of people that can take a pocket knife and run it into a barrel of money, and there are a lot of people that you can give a barrel of money and won't be long until they won't even have the pocket knife. It's all in who it is trading. Yes sir, I think traders are born." Ray Lum preserved his world through tales of men and animals he knew: "When you get 85 years old, you outlive all your friends. That's the bad part of being old; you can't find nobody to talk to about things that happened back there. They're all gone. You live and learn. And then you die and forget it all."

William Ferris
University of Mississippi

William Ferris, *Ray Lum: Mule Trader* (1976); Ben Green, *Some More Horse Tradin'* (1972); Edward Mayhew, *Illustrated Horse Management, Containing Descriptive Remarks upon Anatomy, Medicine, Shoeing, Teeth, Food, Vices, Stables* (1864).

Meaders, Lanier

(b. 1917) Potter.

Quillian Lanier Meaders of Cleveland, White County, Ga., is identified with a domestic ceramics industry that flourished in parts of the rural South through the first quarter of the present century. Loosely organized in cottage-industry fashion, southern potters settled around their clay sources, combining craft work with farming. Technical skills were transferred rather informally through the male line, resulting in the formation of potter dynasties spanning several generations.

The Meaders family came to pottery making during the winter months of late 1892 through early 1893. Lanier's grandfather, John Milton Meaders (1850–1942), had earlier freighted ceramic ware, along with farm produce, for several artisans in clay-rich White County and evidently saw financial benefit in the work. He therefore directed his six sons (Wiley, Caulder, Cleater, Casey, Lewis Quillian, and Cheever) to build a ware shop and kiln on the family property where, with assistance from their neighbors, they commenced manufacturing stoneware preserve jars, dairy crocks, and sorghum syrup or whiskey jugs. A distinctive feature of the local product, one confined in the main to ware made in Georgia and contiguous parts of the Carolinas and Alabama, was the application of lime and wood-ash (alkaline) glazes. The family's "face jugs"—sometimes grotesque—are striking examples of how a simple jug can be molded to resemble a human face.

Though demand for ceramic vessels subsided after 1910, as glass and metal containers penetrated into local farm kitchens, the Meaders family sustained a limited market for their ware. Their persistence in this regard was first noted in Allen H. Eaton's *Handicrafts of the Southern Highlands* (1937). For three more decades, Cheever Meaders (1887–1967), the youngest of the original Meaders potters, derived a marginal livelihood from the production of alkaline-glazed stoneware, which he sold to local customers and to tourists.

Lanier Meaders, Cheever's bachelor son, continues today to manufacture the same traditional ware, employing a similar repertoire of tools and techniques as his forebears. His preservation efforts have won for him not only a devoted following of folk art collectors and crafts enthusiasts, but have encouraged a brother, Edwin, and a cousin, Cleater, Jr., to resume the work as well. In recognition of such efforts and the assistance he has provided folklife researchers in their attempts to reconstruct the history of southern industry, Lanier Meaders in 1983 was awarded a National Heritage Fellowship.

Robert Sayers
California Academy of Sciences

John A. Burrison, *Brothers in Clay: The Story of Georgia Folk Pottery* (1983); Ralph Rinzler and Robert Sayers, *The Meaders Family: North Georgia Potters*, Smithsonian Folklife Studies No. 1 (1980); Nancy Sweezy, *Raised in Clay: The Southern Pottery Tradition* (1984).

Mobile Homes

Variously disparaged as tramps, Okies, and tin-can tourists, over 40,000 people took part in the Dust Bowl migration of the 1930s. Integral to their trek south and west was something akin to the ancient Hudson described in Steinbeck's *Grapes of Wrath*. "Half passenger car and half truck, high-sided and clumsy," it was the home-grown equivalent to the compact manufactured trailer first built in 1929 by the Covered Wagon Company of Detroit. Nine by six feet, complete with folding bunks and a coal-burning stove, early mobile homes met the need for mobility and inexpensive shelter for itinerant job seekers and tourists alike. By 1936 the industry was one of the fastest growing in the nation.

Table 1. *Top 10 States in Manufactured Home Shipments in 1984*

State	Number of Homes
Texas	37,462
Florida	30,990
North Carolina	24,637
Georgia	17,879
South Carolina	15,074
Louisiana	11,432
Alabama	11,318
California	10,425
Tennessee	6,834
Arizona	6,694

Source: Manufactured Housing Institute.

At first used interchangeably, the terms *trailer* and *mobile home* soon became distinct. World War II demonstrated the usefulness of mobile homes as low-cost housing on job sites. They became larger (10 feet wide was standard by 1955; 12 to 14 feet wide by the 1960s) and increasingly less mobile. In the rural South they often took the place of traditional folk or vernacular housing.

Like the tenant farmhouse of Alabama, described by James Agee as "an enlarged crate or box, scarcely modified to human use," the flat-roofed, metal-sided mobile home was basic, economical shelter, unconcerned with fashionable design or detail. Like the traditional shotgun house, it was linear in design—one room wide and two rooms deep—and could be placed short end to the road where lots were narrow or land expensive. A trailer often substituted for the small house out back or the additional rooms customarily added onto the family home when children married and families grew.

Mobile homes have increased dramatically in size; 16-foot-wide versions are now manufactured in Texas and multiple-section double wides are popular. Often "skirted" in sheet metal, brick, or wood to disguise wheels, with foundations, pitched and shingled roofs, cathedral ceilings, and "tip-outs" or bay window alcoves, many are all but indistinguishable from conventional site-built homes. Although still taxed as motor vehicles in some states, mobile homes gained a greater recognition as real estate through 1984 federal legislation allowing Veterans' Administration mortgage financing on the same basis as that provided for conventional housing. The relative immobility and appearance of permanence in modern mobile homes also improved the low-rent image of mobile homes and the transient stereotype of the people who live in them. In 1976 the industry officially adopted the term *manufactured housing*.

About 54 percent of today's manufactured homes are placed on individually owned property in rural or small-town locations. The majority of these homes end up in the South. Of the top 10 states in manufactured home shipments in 1984, 8 were southern, with the high growth states of Texas and Florida in the lead. Whether as unpretentious low-income rural housing, a temporary outbuilding, or part of a lushly landscaped retirement community, the mobile home has altered the topography of the southern landscape.

Elizabeth M. Makowski
University of Mississippi

Jean Hess Bergmark, *Kentucky Folklore Record* (January–December 1981); *Builder* (March 1984); Margaret J. Drury, *Mobile Homes: The Unrecognized Revolution in American Housing* (1972); John Brinckerhoff Jackson, *Discovering the Vernacular Landscape* (1984); Virginia McAlester and Lee McAlester, *A Field Guide to American Houses* (1984); *Manufactured Housing Quarterly* (Fall 1984); Charles W. Moore et al., eds., *Home Sweet Home: American Domestic Architecture* (1983); *New York Times* (20 April 1985); Michael Aaron Rockland, *Homes on Wheels* (1980).

Mules

The South developed a regional culture of "mules and men" that spanned 200 years. The mule is a hybrid, born of a horse and an ass, and unable to reproduce. Southerners fervently endorsed the mule in preference to the horse, and defenders of the mule ranged from George Washington to thousands of small farmers throughout the South. The father of our country has also been called the "father" of American mule breeding, for Washington praised the animal and commented on the "great strength of mules, on their longevity, hardiness, and cheap support which gives them a preference over horses that is scarcely to be imagined." Washington bred mules on his farm, and when he died his will listed 57 mules. Other prominent mule owners in his period included Thomas Jefferson and John Skinner, editor of *American Farmer*.

Robert Lamb outlines three periods in which mules were widely used throughout the South: (1) antebellum (1850–60); (2) Civil War and westward expansion (1860–1900); and (3) southern rural economy (1900–25). As tractors were introduced (1925–50), mules declined in importance.

Travelers in the antebellum South often commented on the strength of mules and the diverse labors they performed. In Virginia, Frederick Law Olmsted noted, "Immense wagons drawn by six mules each, the teamster always riding on the back of the rear wheeler, are a characteristic feature of the streets." Olmsted marveled that mules that were roughly treated, poorly fed, and overworked continued to perform in good health. The animals pulled deep-running plows during both seeding and cultivation, and because of their speed and strength they were preferred to oxen.

In every period of southern history the roles of the mule and of black people were intimately linked. As

Plowing mule, Picayune, Miss., 1967

slaves before the Civil War and as tenant farmers afterward, blacks worked with mules and both were essential to the southern economy. In 1925, for example, 84 percent of the mule farmers in the Mississippi Valley were black. During that period in Anderson, S.C., the money spent on mules each day exceeded the daily wages of blacks. The mule cost an average of $1.32 per day to work and blacks were paid $1.25 per day. Blues singer Huddie "Leadbelly" Ledbetter sang a mule-skinner blues with the verse:

> Honey, I'm down in the bottom, skinnin' for Johnny Ryan. Putting my initials, honey, on the mule's behind. With my line baby, with my line babe, with my line babe.

Blacks knew their mules so well that whites often felt they had a special gift to read the mule's thoughts.

Some white writers argued that only mules could endure the rough treatment accorded by black workers. This may sometimes have been the case during slavery, but accounts by blacks who owned their stock show that great care and love was shown for the animals. Nate Shaw (Ned Cobb), an Alabama sharecropper, stressed "my mules was more than slaves to me. . . . She'd make you a living if you plowed her right . . . you had to be careful with her." Shaw took such care of his mules that a neighbor once accused him of worshipping them. Shaw's mules worked to his voice commands. After picking up the lines and calling "All right, babies, let's get to it," says Shaw, "you'd see them big heifers fall out then. Oh, my mules just granted me all the pleasure I needed, to see what I had and how they moved." Shaw's mules were probably raised outside the South and shipped to his county by traders.

Most mules were raised in the border states and shipped to the "southern market." The prosperity of mule farms in the border states was directly proportional to that of southern farmers. When cotton and tobacco prices boomed, the mule business prospered. One of the biggest mule markets was Columbia, Tenn., where thousands of animals were raised and sold each year. Will Rogers called it "the biggest street mule market in the world. What the thoroughfare of Wall Street will do to you if you don't know what a stock is, Columbia will do to you if you don't know a mule. Maiden Lane, New York City, for diamonds, but Mule Street in Columbia for Mules." Mules were classed according to size and were sold for a wide variety of uses. Their major classes were (1) sugar mules (for southern sugar plantations), (2) rice and cotton mules, (3) levee mules (for Mississippi River levee work), (4) mine mules, (5) railroad mules, and (6) mountaineer pack mules. In addition to meeting these needs, Columbia supplied 5,000 mules purchased by the British army in 1916.

Mules reached their ascendancy in southern history during the first 25 years of this century. Their number doubled from 2½ million in 1900 to 4½ million in 1925, when almost four-fifths of the mules in the United States were in the South. During this period extensive research was done on the feeding and housing of mules and the relative merit of mules versus tractors, and as tractors began to replace them in 1931, writers argued that both were necessary for the successful farmer.

The number of horses and mules in the country peaked at almost 26 million in 1920 and declined to less than 4 million in 1958. As their numbers declined, those who remained were concentrated in the South. When tractors displaced horses and mules in the West, traders bought the animals and shipped them to southern farmers. During the period from 1937 to 1946 prices for horses and mules declined in every area of the country except in the South.

When southern farmers bought tractors this last mule market disappeared and the animals were slaughtered for animal food. During the 1950s half the horses and mules sold by farmers each year—more than 357,000 animals—were converted into cat and dog food. Their death signaled the end of an era; and one trader reflected, "I lived in a day when a man and a mule worked together. Now they've pensioned the man and eaten the mule."

In *The Reivers* (1962) William Faulkner wrote this eloquent tribute to the animal:

> [A] mule is far too intelligent to break its heart for glory running around the rim of a mile-long saucer. In fact, I rate mules second only to rats in intelligence . . . assuming of course that you accept my definition of intelligence: which is the ability to cope with environment; which means to accept environment yet still retain at least something of personal liberty. . . . [The mule] will work for you patiently for ten years for the chance to kick you once. In a word, free of the obligations of ancestry and the responsibilities of posterity, he has conquered not only life but death too and hence is immortal; were he to vanish from the earth today, the same chanceful biological combination which produced him yesterday would produce him a thousand years hence, unaltered, unchanged, incorrigible still within the limitations which he himself had proved and tested; still free, still coping.

William Ferris
University of Mississippi

William Ferris, *North Carolina Folklore Journal* (September 1973); Robert Byron Lamb, *The Mule in Southern Agriculture* (1963); Frederick Law Olmsted, *A Journey in the Seaboard Slave States in the Years 1853–1854, with Remarks on Their Economy* (1904); U. B. Phillips, *Life and Labor in the Old South* (1957); B. D. Raskopf and M. T. Danner, *Public Horse and Mule Market at Nashville, Tennessee* (1947); Theodore Rosengarten, *All God's Dangers: The Life of Nate Shaw* (1974); James Westfall Thompson, *A History of Livestock Raising in the United States* (1942).

Murder Legends

Legends are oral prose narratives about extraordinary persons, places, and events that are usually told in a conversational style. Acts of murder are, of course, unusual, and as they explode the most fundamental rule of social order, stories about them understandably persist in oral tradition.

Stories about murders are in all likelihood universal, and though they have a tendency to become localized, some become widely known through the media and the composition of narrative folksongs. In fact, most of the following murder legends also exist in ballad form.

Many prominent southern murder legends center upon the murderers, but in others the victims are dominant. Examples of the former include stories about such men and women as Alabama's Morris "Railroad Bill" Slater; Talt Hall, Doc "Red Rox" Taylor, and the Harpe brothers in Kentucky; Mississippi's Kinnie Wagner; Frankie Silvers and Tom Dula in North Carolina; Claude Allen of Virginia; and John Hardy in West Virginia. Legends in which the victims are central are those concerning Georgia's Mary Phagan; Kentucky's Pearl Bryan, Lulu Voyers, and Sammie Adams; Naomi Wise and Ella May Wiggins in North Carolina; South Carolina's Theodosia Burr Alston; and the Mormons killed at Cane Creek, Tenn. In legends about feuds (e.g., Kentucky's Jones-Wright, Martin-Tolliver, Hatfield-McCoy; Tennessee's Kelly-Turney), it is difficult to distinguish the aggressors from the victims.

A number of southern murder legends (like ones involving death by conjuring or voodoo, death by witchcraft as in Tennessee's "Bell Witch" stories, the ineradicable bloodstain, the corpse rising to accuse its murderer) contain supranormal themes that set them apart from the "historical" legends just cited.

See also VIOLENCE: / Hatfields and McCoys

William E. Lightfoot
Appalachian State University

Olive Wooley Burt, *American Murder Ballads and Their Stories* (1958); Richard M. Dorson, *America in Legend: Folklore from the Colonial Period to the Present* (1973).

Needlework

Through the years, women in the North and the South have created and produced needlework in many forms. Samplers, needlepoint (known as canvas work in the 18th century and as Berlin work in the 19th), crewelwork, drawnwork, beadwork, and lacework are examples of a craft practiced widely in the South. As early as 1766 a teacher in Virginia advertised instruction in "Petit Point in Flowers, Fruit, Landscape, . . . Embroidery in silk, Gold, Silver, Pearls or embossed, . . . Dresden Point Work, Lace." Of course, southern women have in the past been proficient also in sewing, usually providing clothing and other sewn items for their households.

Although often learning needlework skills from family members, many women learned the craft at female academies. There were several such institutions in the South, one of the best known being the Salem Female Academy, founded and operated by the Moravian community at Salem, N.C. Recognized for their needlework skills, the Pennsylvania Moravians were the first to teach silk embroidery in this country. The close interaction between the two groups of Moravians allowed the transfer of skills, techniques, and designs. One common motif frequently seen on Salem samplers, for example, is the covered well. The Moravian community produced many of the extant examples of early southern needlework and influenced its development and style throughout the South.

Though usually not easily distinguished from northern work, southern needlework can sometimes be identified by the prolonged presence of early designs and motifs. Southern samplers do not exist as abundantly as do northern ones. Early examples exist, however, such as the one made by Elizabeth Hext in 1743 in Charleston, S.C. She embroidered on her sampler "Elizabeth Hext is My Name Carolina is My Nation / Charles Town is My Dwelling Place and Christ is My / Salvation." Two samplers dated around 1865 carry distinctly southern scenes that depict the joy of freed slaves. Below four dancing blacks on a piece worked by Elizabeth Jane Hawkes in Salem, N.C., are the words "Hurrah Hurrah Hurrah / We come from Carolina and are all free now."

Southern scenes are found on needlework by other

Ethel Mohamed, needlework artist, Belzoni, Miss., 1976

southern artists as well. On her needlework pictures, Ethel Wright Mohamed (b. 1907) of Belzoni, Miss., embroiders scenes recalled from her own past. Sacred harp singing, other folk traditions, and experiences from her life and her family's life in Mississippi provide illustrations of a place and of a way of life. Thus, her work is uniquely southern. Other southern needleworkers have created motifs, scenes, and pieces that may not always be so readily identified with the South, but they have in great numbers participated in a craft, utilitarian and decorative, that has been widely popular and practiced throughout the region since its earliest years of settlement. The Mung people who have recently moved from Cambodia to Memphis have introduced detailed, colorful needlework, which they sell to supplement family income. Their designs are abstract and provide an interesting contrast to traditional southern examples.

See also RELIGION: / Moravians

Jessica Foy
Cooperstown Graduate Programs
Cooperstown, New York

Elizabeth Donaghy Garret, *Antiques* (September 1978); Robert Morton, *Southern Antiques and Folk Art* (1976); Betty Ring,

Antiques (October 1971, September 1974); Cynthia Elyce Rubin, ed., *Southern Folk Art* (1985).

Okra

If a southerner with a predilection for both ancestor worship and cooking decided to form a First Families of Vegetables society, okra would be a charter member. Thomas Jefferson recorded planting it and reported its cultivation in Virginia before 1781. It had reached Louisiana shortly after 1700.

Okra (*Hibiscus esculentus*) is a member of the mallow family (*Malvaceae*) as are cotton, hibiscus, and hollyhocks. The okra pod is a tapering, five-sided capsule containing numerous round seeds, and its best-known quality is its gummy, mucilaginous juice.

The word *okra* is *nkru* in the Ashanti language of West Africa; Accra, the name of the capital of Ghana, comes from the same root word. In Bantu, the language family of southern Africa, it is called *ngombo*, from which our word *gumbo* comes; *gumbo* and *okra* have been used interchangeably to refer to the vegetable.

Probably okra was first cultivated in Africa, and from there it spread to India (where it is called "lady fingers"). It was recorded in Egypt in the 13th century. Okra could have come to the South with Africans, either directly or via the West Indies, or it could have been brought in by European colonists who knew that it would grow in a warm climate. It is planted in early spring and matures in about eight weeks. Southern agricultural specialists tried to breed out okra's prickly outer surface with the Clemson Spineless variety.

Okra has vitamins A and C and a 3.5-ounce serving has about 29 calories. This, of course, does not apply to that favorite southern dish, fried okra, in which the cornmeal-salt-pepper coating and the bacon drippings in the frying pan add to the calorie count. Okra can be pickled, stewed with tomatoes, or—best of all—used as the thickening base for gumbo, a rich stew of seafood or meat.

Okra, like the peanut, has a myriad of uses: southerners have used it to staunch bleeding, substitute for plasma, make a coarse cloth or paper, adorn dried flower arrangements, produce seed necklaces, clean metal, unstop drains, increase milk yield of cows, and provide a poor coffee substitute from roasted and ground seeds. Raw okra will also adhere to the nose and forehead for a speedy Halloween mask.

Carolyn Kolb
New Orleans, Louisiana

Alphonse Pyramus de Candolle, *Origin of Cultivated Plants* (1884); Carroll Lane Fenton and Herminie B. Kitchen, *Plants We Live On: The Story of Grains and Vegetables* (1971); Thomas Jefferson, *Thomas Jefferson's Garden Book, 1766–1824* (1944); Sonia L. Nazario, *Wall Street Journal* (21 January 1983); Eileen Tighe, *Woman's Day Encyclopedia of Cookery* (1966).

Play-Party

The play-party is a ritual event in which people gather to play singing games that feature dance movements; it is also a game played at such parties. These gatherings were known in other parts of the United States as "evening party," "flang party," "fuss," "frolic," "gin-around," "bounce around," and "bounce-about." Generally, the play-party is considered an activity for young people in rural settings, an assumption that is not altogether correct. Adults also attended play-parties and at one time they were common in urban as well as country surroundings. Religious prejudice against dancing was one reason for the popularity of play-parties, in contrast to true dances. Equally important was the flexible nature of the play-party, which required no musicians and thus could be arranged on short notice. It was not unique to the South but was popular there longer than elsewhere.

Typically, the play-party was organized by one or two young men looking for diversion and entertainment. In many rural communities homes were small, with rough native lumber floors and, more often than not, a bed in the front room that had to be removed to make space for the games. In good weather the play-party was held in the front yard. The games consisted of players swinging one another by the hand instead of by the waist, to the accompaniment of their own singing. Such devices as chasing and kissing as a means of choosing or stealing a partner were popular. Some games featured swinging or marching movements. "Skip to My Lou," which is derived from "Bull in the Park," was a popular accompaniment for these movements. Much of the song repertoire was borrowed from popular song ("Buffalo Gals," "Captain Jenks," "Old Dan Tucker") or, less often, religious song ("I Want To Be an Angel").

The activity itself is much older than the term *play-party*, which apparently came into widespread use only in the early years of the 20th century. A reference to the play-party in a 1902 Houston, Mo., newspaper is the earliest known printed use of the term. This traditional activity remained a vital form of amusement in the South until just prior to World War II when it went into decline, in large part because of the availability of other forms of inexpensive mass entertainment. Play-parties are seldom performed now, except by revival groups, but the songs are still remembered and sung.

W. K. McNeil
Ozark Folk Center
Mountain View, Arkansas

Benjamin A. Botkin, *The American Play-Party Song; with a Collection of Oklahoma Texts and Tunes* (1937); David S. McIntosh, *Folk Songs and Singing Games of the Illinois Ozarks* (1974); William A. Owens, *Swing and Turn: Texas Play-Party Games* (1936); Vance Randolph, *Journal of American Folklore* (July–September 1929).

Porches

The distinction between southern porches and American porches is one both of kind and of degree. Although black and white southerners have traditionally used a variety of porch types in a variety of locations, the important "porch" for the student of southern culture is the public/private space across the front of a building.

Until the mid-19th century, only in the South were dwellings—"big houses" on the great plantations, slave cabins, and everything in between—routinely equipped with sitting porches, and since the decline of the bungalow, only in the South are new houses still equipped with front porches. The style of the porch and its supports has signaled the social status of those who use it. For example, two-story porches graced with Doric columns traditionally mean wealth and power; today imitations of such porches appear on banks, motels, and other establishments that wish to attract the would-be wealthy or powerful. Porches supported with incompletely trimmed posts, on the other hand, suggest working-class inhabitants.

These status delineations owe something to the history of the southern porch. While Thomas Jefferson, George Washington, and their contemporaries were searching for a truly American architecture, African slaves and less prominent white emigrants from the West Indies were adapting the architecture of their homelands to the American milieu. The porches on classic southern buildings may have borrowed from ancient Greek porticos, but the front porch as extended living space almost surely owes a great debt to the experience in dealing with an inhospitably hot and humid climate, experience that Africans and West Indians brought with them to the American South. Early aristocratic southern architecture (in Charleston, S.C., for instance), hid side galleries behind traditional European flush fronts; only after slaves and small farmers had demonstrated its usefulness for decades did influential southerners adopt the wide, columned-front porch. The development of screen porches, a bridge perhaps between the openness of the traditional front porch and the confinement of today's air-conditioned South, is unclear, but wire mesh itself can be traced to the looms of early 19th-century Shakers. Although southerners did adapt screen to their own needs for protection from insects and for increased privacy, the move indoors occasioned by widespread air-conditioning meant that the screen porch would remain, in modern times, more prevalent in non-southern America than in the South.

Southern porches have traditionally been transitional spaces between indoors and out where marginally welcomed guests could be entertained without violating the sanctity of the home. The races could comingle when necessary or desirable, and visitors on business could escape the elements while plying their trade. Much of the southern reputation for hospitality must emanate from the ubiquitous porch. Even though pervasive air-conditioning makes the porch almost unnecessary today, new middle-class homes continue to sport vestigial porches with skinny imitations of grand columns, perhaps still to suggest affluence and power. And they continue to be furnished—albeit with antique wooden and wrought-iron benches useless for sitting but redolent of ancestry and hospitality. Spacious porches of older middle-class homes are also furnished—often with an abundance of rockers, gliders, and swings whose careful arrangement and spotless white paint imply that the furniture is for show rather than for sitting. These porches indicate not only concern with appearances but an unwillingness to relinquish bygone graciousness.

Southern porches have been used to entertain, to prepare food, to wash clothes and bodies, and to provide sheltered play space for children, but their most important ongoing use is to transmit folklore. Children continue to invent games designed around the architecture of a particular porch style, and fabled southern storytellers gather with family and friends on porches to benefit from any possible breeze and to regale each other with tales. Today's older southerners, unwilling to adjust to ubiquitous air-conditioning, pass family lore to children and grandchildren on ancestral porches, and folklorists as far back as Zora Neale Hurston in the 1930s have gathered the lore of the South on the porches of southerners.

Sue Bridwell Beckham
University of Wisconsin–Stout

Barrie B. Greenbie, *Spaces: Dimensions of the Human Landscape* (1981); Richard L. Perry, *Journal of American Culture* (Summer 1985); Davida Rochlin, *Home Sweet Home: American Domestic Architecture*, ed. Charles W. Moore et al. (1983); Ovid Vickers, *Mississippi Folklore Register* (Fall 1978); John Michael Vlach, *The Afro-American Tradition in Decorative Arts* (1978).

Powers, Harriet

(1837–1911) Quilter.

Two quilts, beautifully crafted and historically significant, are the legacy of Harriet Powers, who was born a slave in Georgia on 29 October 1837. These quilts, classic examples of the appliqué technique, are also of interest because of Harriet Powers's use of the narrative folk tradition. One of the quilts, owned by the Smithsonian Institution, illustrates biblical stories; the second, at the Museum of Fine Arts in Boston, depicts biblical tales as well as local legends and astronomical occurrences. Stories of the hog named Betts, who ran from Georgia to Virginia, and the man frozen at his jug of liquor are two of the illustrations in the Boston Powers quilt. The stories appear to be local, but each is actually the plot of a traditional folk narrative, which has been recorded in several versions. Legendary accounts of actual phenomena (eclipses, meteors, and comets) were intermingled with traditional motifs by Powers.

Central to Powers's religious symbols are the legends of biblical heroes such as Noah, Moses, Jonah, and Job, all of whom struggled successfully against overwhelming odds. The serpent of the Garden of Eden is portrayed with feet before it suffered God's curse; Adam's rib, from which Eve was made, is prominently featured. Harriet Powers's fascination with biblical animals and characters stemmed from her attendance at southern churches where vivid sermons, which she committed to memory, were the order of the day, according to Jennie Smith, a white woman who purchased the first Powers quilt.

Although narrative quilts are a distinctly American art form, the appliqué technique evident in Powers's quilts is traceable to Eastern and Middle Eastern civilizations with discernible roots in African culture. Harriet Powers's quilts form a link to the tapestries traditionally made by the Fon people of Abomey, the ancient capital of Dahomey in West Africa. Fon people brought to the South their knowledge of appliqué, which had been executed by men in Dahomey but was perpetuated by slave women in America.

Gladys-Marie Fry
University of Maryland

Marie J. Adams, in *Afro-American Folk Art and Crafts*, ed. William Ferris (1983); Gladys-Marie Fry, *Missing Pieces: Georgia Folk Art* (1976).

Proverbs

As metaphors of collective experience, southern proverbs embody the emphasis of the folk on generalized wisdom. The southern proverb repertoire seems to serve some southerners as a set of universal laws against which individual experience is measured. With their characteristic use of metaphor and their perceptions of similarity and difference, southern proverbs remain close to both poetry and philosophy. Proverbs have served several generations of southerners as guides to appropriate behavior and as informal channels of education. They are still in widespread use today.

Southern proverbs have their roots in the Old World, especially in Europe and Africa. Europeans and Africans alike adapted their traditions of proverb usage to a new natural and social environment in the South. The African preference for indirect and highly ambiguous speech, both as an aesthetic variation on drab everyday discourse and as a means of avoiding the sometimes painful effects and insults of direct commentary, had a counterpart in the South in the European proverb tradition. That tradition included British proverbs stretching from the 16th century's "Beggars cannot be choosers" and the 15th century's "Eat us out of house and home" to the 14th century's "Look before you leap" and the 12th century's "You can lead a horse to water, but you can't make him drink." That tradition also included such literary proverbs as St. Augustine's "When in Rome, do as the Romans do" and the classical Greek proverb "A rolling stone gathers no moss." Biblical proverbs, such as "Cast your bread upon the waters," "Pride goeth before a fall," and "Money is the root of all evil" were particularly widespread in the South. In the colonial period southern folk tradition also absorbed proverbs from Benjamin Franklin's *Poor Richard's Almanac*, such as "A word to the wise is sufficient" and "Early to bed and early to rise makes a man healthy, wealthy, and wise." Such proverbs are still used across the South.

Like all forms of folklore, proverb wording is subject to variation, but structural patterns of proverbs are relatively fixed. The most common structural forms in southern proverbs are simple positive or negative propositions, such as "Beauty is in the eye of the beholder" or "Nobody's perfect." But double propositions ("Everybody talks about the weather, but nobody does anything about it" or "Young folks, listen to what old folks say, when danger is near keep out of the way") are common in southern tradition, and triple propositions ("So I totes my powder and sulphur and I carries my stick in my hand and I puts my trust in God") are not unknown. Multiple propositions provide an apt structure for making invidious distinctions, as in the biblical "Man proposes, but God disposes."

In their proverbs, southerners make distinctions by comparison and contrast. They emphasize the equivalence of things ("Seeing is believing") or they deny it ("All that glitters is not gold"). Or they emphasize that one thing is bigger, or of greater value than another, as in "His eyes are bigger than his belly," "A bird in the hand is worth two in the bush," and "Half a loaf is better than none." Proverbs purport to explain how things come about ("Politics makes strange bedfellows" and "New brooms sweep clean") or to deny causation ("Barking dogs don't bite" and "Two wrongs don't make a right").

An important attribute of southern proverbs is their sense of authority, deriving partly from their detachment from common speech and partly from their allusive poetic nature. They are set off from ordinary discourse by such poetic devices as alliteration ("The proof of the pudding is in the eating" and "A miss is as good as a mile"), rhyme ("A friend in need is a friend indeed" and "Haste makes waste"), repetition ("All's well that ends well" and "No news is good news"), meter ("Nothing ventured, nothing gained" and "A word to the wise is sufficient"), and parallelism ("Like father, like son" and "The more he has, the more he wants").

Because of their poetic qualities (their allusiveness and ambiguity), proverbs may be cited with equal authority in a broad range of situations. Their flexibility has sometimes made proverbs seem contradictory to modern readers. Are two heads better than one, or do too many cooks spoil the broth? Some proverbs used by southerners tout the virtues of cautious conservatism ("Look before you leap," "Rome wasn't built in a day," and "Haste makes waste"), whereas others, equally authentic, urge hearers to "Strike while the iron is hot" (similarly, "Time and tide wait for no man," "He who hesitates is lost"). But proverbs are not really contradictory. Just as a language gives its speakers words with which to praise or to criticize as necessary, the southern proverb repertoire enables southerners to offer whatever advice seems appropriate to a particular situation, to advise either action or inaction, and to do so through heightened poetic language.

In offering advice, a southern proverb might pursue either of two strategies. It might recommend acceptance of the situation or it might recommend action to relieve the situation. "Put up or shut up" and "Nothing ventured, nothing gained" are examples of the *action* strategy. Some proverbs counsel defensive action, such as "A stitch in time saves nine" and "An apple a day keeps the doctor away." Some *acceptance* strategy proverbs suggest that the situation is normal ("Accidents will happen" and "Boys will be boys"); thus, no action is called for. Some urge their hearers not to overreact ("Look before you leap" and "Barking dogs don't bite"). Others counsel patience, for troubles come and troubles go ("March comes in like a lion, but goes out like a lamb"). Some even suggest that the hearer is responsible for the situation and must accept the consequences ("You've made your bed, now you have to lie in it"). Yet other proverbs maintain that, no matter how hard the misfortune may seem, it can be borne ("Every back is fitted to the burden").

Though relatively simple in form, proverbs are perhaps the most complex of all folklore genres in their extreme sensitivity to context. The meaning and distinctiveness of the southern proverb does not lie in its form or content, but in the context of its use. And those contexts range as widely and deeply as southern life itself.

Charles Joyner
University of South Carolina
Coastal Campus

F. A. DeCaro and W. K. McNeil, *American Proverb Literature* (1970); Alan Dundes, *Analytic Essays in Folklore* (1975); Charles Joyner, *Down by the Riverside: A South Carolina Slave Community* (1984); P. Seitel, *Genre* (1969); Archer Taylor, *The Proverb* (1931); Archer Taylor and Bartlett J. Whiting, compilers, *A Dictionary of American Proverbs and Proverbial Phrases, 1820–1880* (1958); Newman I. White, ed., *Frank C. Brown Collection of North Carolina Folklore*, vol. 1 (1952).

Pyramidal House

Because of its popularity among upper-middle-class southerners, the pyramidal house symbolized economic security. Its distinctive feature is its high pyramidal roof, usually with two chimneys flanking its short ridge. Having two rooms on each side of a wide central hallway, the dwelling could house two families and was sometimes built in lumber-mill settlements to accommodate workers. The form evolved from early gable-roofed, Georgian-style houses along the Carolina-Georgia coast. It was confined largely to the towns and rural areas of the Lowland South and was built from the mid-19th century to the early 20th century.

Jessica Foy
Cooperstown Graduate Programs
Cooperstown, New York

Henry Glassie, *Pattern in the Material Folk Culture of the Eastern United States* (1968); D. Gregory Jeane, ed., *The Architectural Legacy of the Lower Chattahoochee Valley in Alabama and Georgia* (1978).

Quilting, Afro-American

Afro-American quilts are characterized by strips, bright colors, large designs, multiple patterns, asymmetry, and improvisation, all design principles with roots in African textile techniques and cultural traditions. The antecedents of contemporary African textiles and Afro-American quilts developed in Africa over 1,000 years ago. The actual links between African and Afro-American textile traditions occurred from 1650 to 1850 when Africans were brought to the United States from areas that are now Senegal, Mali, Ivory Coast, Ghana, Republic of Benin Nigeria, Cameroon, Zaire, and Angola. When they came to the New World, African women combined their own textile traditions with American quilting traditions, creating a unique, creolized art—the Afro-American quilt. Their combined ideas were passed down from generation to generation, thus preserving many African textile traditions.

Like Anglo-American quilt tops, Afro-American quilt tops are made either by sewing pieces of cloth together (piecing) or by sewing cutout shapes onto a larger fabric (appliqué). Quilt tops are sewn to an inner padding and a bottom cloth (quilting). All these techniques (piecing, appliqué, and quilting) were known in Africa, Europe, and the United States, yet Afro-American quilts are profoundly different from European or Anglo-American quilts.

In West African textiles and in Afro-American quilts, strips are a dominant design element as well as a chief construction technique. For centuries in West Africa, most cloth has been constructed from strips woven on small, portable looms. Long narrow strips are sewn together into larger fabrics worn as clothing or displayed as wall hangings and banners. Strips are sometimes used in Euro-American quilts, but as only one of many geometric patterns.

The bold colors and large designs of the Afro-American textile aesthetic derive from the communicative function of textiles in Africa, where they are worn and displayed as an indicator of social status, wealth, occupation, and history. The strong contrasting colors characteristic of African textiles are necessary to insure a cloth's readability at a distance, in strong sunlight. Maintaining that aesthetic beyond its original function, Afro-

American quilters think not in terms of pastel or coordinating colors, but speak of "colors hitting each other right." Their quilts are best seen from a distance, in contrast to New England quilts, which should be inspected in intimate settings.

Multiple patterning is another characteristic shared by African textiles and Afro-American quilts. Multiple patterns are important in African royal and priestly fabrics, for the number and complexity of patterns decorating a fabric increase in accordance with the owner's status. A cloth woven for a king or priest may include up to 30 patterns. Multiple-patterned cloth communicates the prestige, power, and wealth of the wearer. Contemporary Afro-American quilts do not communicate an owner's status, but they do retain this preference for mixing patterns as an aesthetic tradition.

In West Africa, when woven strips with many patterns are sewn together to make a larger fabric, the resulting cloth has asymmetrical and unpredictable designs. These characteristics are retained in Afro-American quilts, for lines, designs, and colors do not match up but vary with a persistence that goes beyond a possible lack of cloth in any color or pattern. Afro-American quilters have taken this tradition one step further, introducing improvisation. Black quilters often adapt traditional Euro-American quilt patterns and "Afro-Americanize" them by establishing a pattern in one square and varying it in successive squares. Typical Afro-American quilt squares do not repeat but change in size, arrangement, and color. Although ostensibly reproducing Euro-American patterns, Afro-American quilters maintain through improvisation African principles of multiple patterning, asymmetry, and unpredictable rhythms and tensions similar to those found in other Afro-American arts, such as jazz, black English, and dance.

Whereas Euro-American appliquéd quilts are primarily decorative, Afro-American appliquéd quilts often tell stories and express ideas in the same manner as African appliquéd textiles. With bold appliquéd shapes, African cultures record court histories, religious values, and personal histories of famous individuals, using designs symbolizing power, skill, leadership, wisdom, courage, balance, composure, and other personal qualities. In contrast, with iconography drawn from their imaginations, from southern black rural culture, and from American popular culture (magazines, television, and cereal boxes), Afro-American appliquéd quilts mirror the diverse influences that shape the lives of black women in the southern United States.

Afro-American quilt making is inextricably linked to the thrift and industry that characterize rural black southern life, for Afro-American quilters grew up in a time when there was no social security and to survive was to keep constantly busy. Afro-American quilt making is unique in America, fusing two alternative textile traditions—the African and the Euro-American—to produce a third. Afro-American quilters maintaining this hybrid aesthetic demonstrate the strength of African cultural traditions in contemporary American society, affirming the extraordinary tenacity of African ideas over hundreds of years in the face of major historical obstacles. Practiced today mainly in the southern United States, this vital aspect of our nation's artistic and cultural heritage must be recognized and celebrated now so that it can be promoted and preserved in the future.

Maude Southwell Wahlman
Ella King Torrey
University of Mississippi

Jill Salmons, *Textile History* (No. 2, 1980); Robert Farris Thompson, in *Black Studies in the University: A Symposium*, ed. A. Robinson (1969), *Flash of the Spirit: African and Afro-American Art and Philosophy* (1983); John Michael Vlach, *The Afro-American Tradition in Decorative Arts* (1978); Maude Southwell Wahlman, *Contemporary African Arts* (1974), with Ella King Torrey, *Ten Afro-American Quilters* (1983).

Quilting, Anglo-American

Having a long history in Great Britain, quilted items such as bed coverings, curtains, and clothing came to America with the colonists. Quilting skills and a variety of patchwork patterns that flourished and changed with time were brought to the southern United States through the migration of settlers.

The typical quilt, constructed with three bound layers, including a top of appliquéd or pieced patchwork, a cotton or wool batting, and a lining, offered good insulation against the cold, damp winters of the South. Quilt types have varied with the socioeconomic status and aesthetic standards of the makers and the intended use of the quilt. With cotton for batting plentiful in the South, even on small subsistence farms, but fabric scarce and expensive, simple "everyday" quilts were common. However, more decorative "fancy" quilts with elaborate color-coordinated patterns and intricate quilting were also made, frequently by members of the wealthier classes, who often had slave help until the Civil War, and also in fewer numbers by members of the lower classes.

Although quilters have bought at least some of their fabric, quilt making has been mainly a salvage craft, employing in its early years homespun, worn clothing, muslin flour and sugar sacks, cotton print feed sacks, as well as sewing remnants collected from the home, family, friends, and neighbors, and, more recently, from garage sales and clothing and fabric factories. Today synthetic fabrics, polyester batting, and machine piecing are often accepted by traditional quilters, although some quilters, more affected by the popular quilt revival, buy only cottons or cotton blends in coordinated colors and insist on hand sewing.

Traditional quilters, who learn their craft informally from family or neighbors rather than from books and formal classes as the revivalists do, pass along community standards and preferences. Traditional southern Anglo-American quilts, often with bright or pastel printed fabrics and intricate patchwork patterns, contrast sharply with the bold dark solids and simple large scale patterns of the Amish quilts and the bright solid colors of the Pennsylvania German quilts. Although the southern quilters do strive for their ideal of precise piecing of complex patterns such as the "Double Wedding Ring" or "Flower Garden" and tiny close quilting stitches, they do not often employ the elaborate hearts, plumes, and floral quilting motifs so common in the Pennsylvania German quilts. Today, southern Anglo-American quilts are typically quilted in wooden frames suspended from the ceiling or placed on chairs or "horses." Quilting is generally done "by the piece," with stitching about one-fourth inch from the edge of each patchwork seam. Early quilts may have more quilting often done in "shells," or concentric half circles.

As in the past, quilts are still made as heirlooms or gifts to mark occasions such as weddings and baby showers. Traditional quilters usually work alone; however, in urban areas senior citizens centers and women's groups are reviving the once-popular quilting bee. These groups, as well as many individual quilters, also quilt "for the public" to earn extra income and to keep busy. The survival of the quilting tradition may be attributed not only to the prevalent Protestant work ethic, which abhors waste of materials and time, but also to the social and symbolic functions of quilting in maintaining community, family, and personal creativity.

Susan Roach
Ruston, Louisiana

Ruth E. Finley, *Old Patchwork Quilts and the Women Who Made Them* (1929); Jonathan Holstein, *American Pieced Quilts* (1972); Susan Roach and Lorre Weidlich, *Folklore Women's Communication* (Spring 1974).

Saddlebag House

The saddlebag house has a rectangular shape, a central chimney, two front doors, and is one room deep. As a popular means of enlarging a single pen structure, a second room was added to the chimney end of the original, thus forming the saddlebag house. Originally an English and then a Pennsylvania house type, it became common in areas of the South, where it was usually of frame rather than log construction. This vernacular house form did not appear frequently in the South until the 19th century, and its use there extended from Kentucky to North Carolina to the eastern Gulf Coast region.

Jessica Foy
Cooperstown Graduate Programs
Cooperstown, New York

Henry Glassie, *Pattern in the Material Folk Culture of the Eastern United States* (1968); Dell Upton and John Michael Vlach, eds., *Common Places: Readings in American Vernacular Architecture* (1986).

Shine

Shine is the hero of a series of Afro-American toasts, which are epic narrative poems involving an extended battle between protagonists. A trickster, Shine is said to be the only survivor of the 1912 *Titanic* disaster. As a black stoker aboard the ship, he frequently warns the captain of impending danger only to find his warnings ignored because he is black. Then, heedless of a number of temptations and threats, he jumps overboard and with superhuman skill swims to shore, thereby becoming the only survivor. As the ship finally sinks, he is drinking toasts at a bar in Philadelphia. In reality, of course, there were many survivors of the tragedy.

Shine survives and triumphs over his enemies by actual deeds and in doing so provides an explicit black rejection of white middle-class values such as respect for the law, romantic love, pity and gratitude, chivalry, and special consideration for women. Shine is, in short, a hero but not a gentleman. He is an epic figure whose exploits are performed in the name of his race. He breaks precedents and stereotypes; against all odds he defies white society and triumphs. His name is a generic one derived from the term *shine*, a slang word used by both blacks and whites to describe a very dark-skinned person. The name possibly comes from the idea of a person being so black that he shines. Stories about Shine were first collected in Louisiana and Mississippi in the late 1930s and early 1940s, but, considering Shine's association with the *Titanic*, they are probably at least two decades older.

W. K. McNeil
Ozark Folk Center
Mountain View, Arkansas

Langston Hughes, *The Book of Negro Humor* (1966); Bruce Jackson, *Get Your Ass in the Water and Swim Like Me: Narrative Poetry from Black Oral Tradition* (1974); Lawrence W. Levine, *Black Culture and Black Consciousness: Afro-American Folk Thought from Slavery to Freedom* (1977).

Shotgun House

The shotgun house is distinctive to the land along waterways and to plantations, mill towns, and poorer urban neighborhoods of the Deep South. One room wide and three rooms long, under a gable roof, with eaves to the sides, almost all surviving examples have walls of sawn lumber and pier foundations. Extra rooms and porches may have been added to the ends, and, in some areas, long galleries appear along the sides and T or L additions across one end, usually the rear. In rare cases, a second row of rooms was added to one side, producing a double shotgun, a form often confused with the bungalow.

In New Orleans, the shotgun appeared about 1800, and excellent, comfortable, stylish examples there date from the 19th and early 20th centuries. Elsewhere, however, the type occurred in lower social contexts, such as rental tracts, plantation quarters, company housing, and stream-front "camps" (temporary homes for holiday diversion or for seasonal fishing and trapping). Adding complexity to the story, lumber companies in the late 19th century began offering shotguns on a commercial basis. The shotgun house has generally been a house for dependent people and not privately owned.

The most striking aspect of the shotgun house (and the bungalow) is its roof, oriented in a direction opposite to those of nearly all other historic southern houses. Whereas the other southern folk and vernacular houses had their gables to the sides, the shotgun had them to the front and rear.

Theories, each having respectable advocates, variously envision the shotgun house originating with marsh dwellers or American Indians, with the rise of the Greek Revival style, with the arrival of black Creoles from the Caribbean (who brought African-derived influences), with the beginning of prefabricated housing, or even as an adaptation to narrow city lots. Of these, the last explanation is the most easily criticized because the shotgun house was a common, and perhaps the oldest, rural form. Even so, the existence of narrow lots in urban areas, combined with the other factors mentioned, may account for the popularity of these houses today.

M. B. Newton, Jr.
Baton Rouge, Louisiana

William Ferris, *Blues from the Delta* (1984); Henry Glassie, *Pattern in the Material Folk Culture of the Eastern United States* (1968); M. B. Newton, Jr., *Melanges* (No. 2, 1971); John Michael Vlach, *Pioneer America* (January 1976).

Simmons, Philip

(b. 1912) Blacksmith.

Born on Daniel Island, S.C., Philip Simmons has become one of the South's most distinguished artisans. He first came to Charleston in 1919 and began blacksmithing as a 13-year-old apprentice in 1925. He took over the blacksmith shop around 1931 and completed his first decorative piece about 1939. By the mid-1960s, when he was commissioned to build his masterpiece, Simmons had already acquired almost 40 years of experience. He was a general blacksmith and thus understood the work of the wheelwright and wagon builder, a horseshoer, a tool maker, and an ornamental ironworker.

"That snake taught me a lesson," recounted Philip Simmons during an evening of reminiscence. But what did he mean? What connection could there be between a reptile and the dean of the Charleston blacksmiths? The snake to which Simmons referred is a fearsome rattler that he fashioned and perched in the driveway gates of the Gadsden house in Charleston, S.C. Although Simmons has designed many gates—well over 200 in the Charleston area—the "snake gate" is the one of which he is most proud. It is his masterpiece. The labor, both physical and mental, that this gate demanded turned out to be a rite of passage. When that ritual was completed, Simmons's sense of his work was forever changed.

After several attempts at shaping the snake, he had found that the animal just did not seem right. He recalled, "You just see something that looked like a dead snake." But after continually shifting the eye in its head, Simmons made the snake come to life. Simmons claims that it seemed suddenly to look back at him. He was then satisfied with his sculpture, as was his client.

He had brought vitality to metal by applying extra effort to the task before him. That was the lesson of the snake—diligent effort yields excellence. The experience of making the snake gate showed Simmons that perseverance allows a special quality of vigor to emerge from raw material. In subsequent commissions that featured either animals or elements of nature, he again struggled to make them appear natural and lifelike. To Simmons they are alive like the snake; like the snake they represent his best effort.

Philip Simmons was a competent artist decades before he made the snake gate. He proudly carried on a profession that had been practiced in Charleston since 1739 and for which he can trace a personal genealogy of blacksmiths back to the 18th century. But despite the comforting influence of a praiseworthy history and his own energetic displays of skill, Simmons felt that he had not fully matured as a blacksmith. His own creative talents were not crucially tested until the snake-gate commission, for only then did he have the opportunity to make a unique contribution to the decorative ironwork of Charleston with the first wrought-iron animal sculpture to be seen in that city. Once the gate was completed, he could add to the confidence that comes from a noble past a confidence that comes from within: a confidence based on his own imagination and creative power.

John Michael Vlach
George Washington University

John Michael Vlach, *Charleston Blacksmith: The Work of Philip Simmons* (1981).

Smokehouse

Because southerners for at least two centuries have not been willing to live without pork, their farms commonly have included smokehouses. Although any kind of meat could be dried and smoked, it was the butchering of hogs that truly necessitated the construction of this particular outbuilding. Mid-19th-century reports on southern pork consumption indicate that a male field hand was fed between two and five pounds of hog meat per week. Each year between 1840 and 1860 no less than 2.2 hogs were raised for every man, woman, and child in the South.

This pork craving gave rise to a problem in meat preservation that the smokehouse solved.

Because the meat-packing industry was not well developed in the southern states, every farmer was left to fend for himself. Thus, in a spirit of self-sufficiency and independence, southern farmers made the smokehouse a central artifact in the conduct of the annual agricultural round. Hogs slaughtered late in the fall, after they were well fattened from foraging on the mast that they found in the woodlands, could be kept after they were smoked until the following year's butchering. Once the carcasses were cut into manageable sections, each piece was packed in salt for about six weeks. The pieces of meat were then washed and hung in the smokehouse to acquire the distinctive flavor of the slow-drying fire. In the popular mind, hickory is considered the universal fuel, but many different woods were used. In fact, some farmers in "Little Dixie" Missouri preferred fresh corn cobs, what they still call "meat cobs." The quantity and kind of smoke varied considerably from locale to locale and from person to person, as the main arbiter in these matters was one's own taste buds.

There has also been considerable variation in the kinds of structures used as smokehouses. Large plantations used sizable buildings constructed to the same dimensions as dwelling houses, say 18 feet by 26 feet. In colonial Virginia the smokehouse could have a tall pyramidal roof. Along the shores of the Chesapeake a small brick house with diamond-shaped ventilators in the gables served as the meathouse, whereas in the Alabama highlands the smokehouse might feature a gable-end doorway with a roof cantilevered several feet over one end to protect the entrance. Some Missouri smokehouses are two-story affairs with a smoking chamber below and a meat preparation area above. Taken collectively, the look of these various buildings might suggest a lack of cultural coherency. The behavior enacted in all these structures is, however, consistent. Whatever their particular form, the cultural statement made is clear—"we will take care of our needs, we will have ham and bacon when we want it."

John Michael Vlach
George Washington University

Henry Chandlee Forman, *Tidewater Maryland Architecture and Gardens* (1956); Sam B. Hilliard, *Hog Meat and Hoecake: Food Supply in the Old South, 1840–1860* (1972); Howard Wight Marshall, *Journal of American Folklore* (October–December 1979).

T House

One of the first styles of popular domestic architecture to become widespread in the South was the one-story T house, sometimes called a "cross-plan" or "gable-front-and-wing" house. The style, although not uncommon to the rest of the United States, was widely adopted in the South for historical, aesthetic, climatic, and cultural reasons. Built primarily between 1880 and 1910, the T house is significant as a "hybrid" house type that reflects the confluence of architectural styles prevalent in the last part of the 19th century. It also reflects changes that took place during the New South period. The T house met an urgent need for inexpensive housing to shelter the burgeoning working- and middle-class population in small towns that proliferated around cotton-processing centers throughout the South. Built for a rapidly advancing white working class, the T house may also be seen as a reflection of the Jim Crow years.

The basic T house was almost always frame and consisted of a gable or projecting wing two rooms deep, one behind the other, straddled by a side wing one room deep. Usually there were three or four rooms, but T houses were frequently altered and augmented so that they appeared to be much larger and the T configuration was disguised. Often there was a central hall between the two wings. Rooms were nearly always close to square and similar in size, with high ceilings and internal chimneys.

The southerner's pervasive concern with managing oppressive climatic conditions is expressed quite clearly in the T house, which incorporated a number of structural elements enabling its inhabitants to defend themselves against intense summer heat and seasonal wetness. T houses were commonly built on pillars about two feet off the ground, with roofs that were rather steeply pitched. High ceilings, front porches, and the dogtrot-style alignment of front door with back door or window permitted maximum air circulation and cooling.

Three distinct architectural influences are evident in the T house: the folk tradition, the classical or formal tradition, and the popular building fashions of the day. By featuring a projecting gable in the Gothic Revival cottage style popularized by A. J. Downing and A. J. Davis, the T house abandoned traditional symmetry and "frontality" in its facade but retained spatial configurations and elements that were common to both southern high-style and folk houses: square, almost cubic rooms to each side of a central passage, and front porches. The T house provided southerners with the traditional living spaces to which they were accustomed but at the same time afforded them a means of "modernizing" their houses and expressing individual taste with the profusion of mass-produced Victorian millwork embellishments that became easily accessible in the late 19th century.

Cultural messages were strong in the T house. The projecting gable wing protected the porch and entrance from the view of other houses built in a row, very close together. An elevated porch and a central hall created transitional buffer zones to provide the family with more protection and privacy—modern concerns in an increasingly "urban" environment. The hall and boxlike rooms provided more private spaces away not only from outsiders but from other family members. An indication of the success of the T house as a southern domestic structure is that not only were many built in the New South, but many still survive. They survive as ubiquitous features of the southern landscape and as living examples of a very popular style, which was so pleasing and flexible to southerners that they still enjoy inhabiting T houses a century later.

Lisa N. Howorth
University of Mississippi

Lisa N. Howorth, "Popular Vernacular: The One-Story T House in the South" (M.A. thesis, University of Mississippi, 1984); Paula Jane Johnson, "T House in Texas: Suiting Plain People's Needs" (M.A. thesis, University of Texas at Austin, 1981); Virginia McAlester and Lee McAlester, *A Field Guide to American Houses* (1984).

Thomas, James

(b. 1926) Blues musician and sculptor.

James "Son Ford" Thomas was born 14 October 1926 on a farm near Eden in Yazoo County, Miss. His life embodies a spectrum of black folklife including blues music, clay sculpture, and storytelling, all of which are rooted in Mississippi Delta cultural traditions.

James Thomas learned to play the guitar by watching his uncle play, after which he imitated the chords in his own tunes. As a teenager Thomas moved to Leland, Miss., where he began playing blues on weekends. He played juke joints and barrelhouses around Leland and Greenville, Miss., through the 1960s. Since the early 1970s he has performed at folk music and blues concerts for colleges and universities, including Jackson State University (1971–72), the University of Maine (1972), Tougaloo College (1973), and Yale University (1973–76). He has participated in the Smithsonian Festival of American Folklife and in festivals in Norway and Germany. He has made records produced in the United States, Holland, West Germany, and Italy.

James Thomas is also a sculptor. His sculpture is largely self-taught rather than being derived from other artists. As a child he began making clay imitations of animals, patterning his first work after similar figures made by his uncle. He later made clay models of Ford tractors and was nicknamed "Son Ford." Apart from his uncle, Thomas had no continuing contact with artists who work with clay. His work has been highly personal, and perhaps the most unusual figures in his repertoire are heads and skulls, which often have openings in their tops and serve as containers or ashtrays. Animals, water, and death are recurring motifs. His clay faces present an image of the black man as poised and proud.

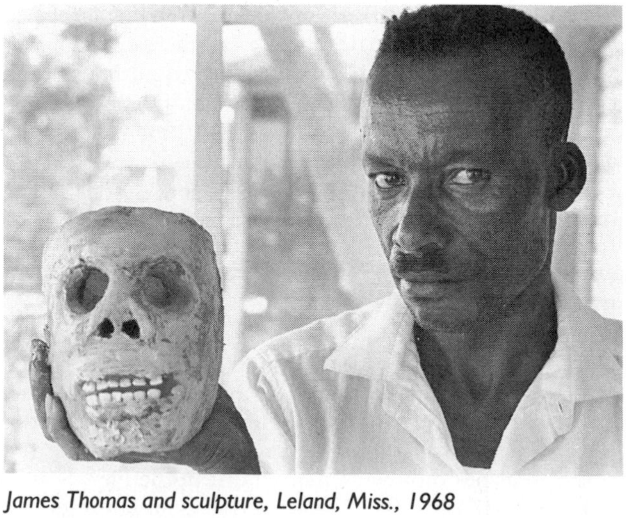

James Thomas and sculpture, Leland, Miss., 1968

Son Thomas's sculpture attracted national attention at the opening of the exhibition *Black Folk Art* at the Corcoran Gallery in Washington, D.C. Thomas has been featured in three films: *James "Son Ford" Thomas: Delta Blues Singer* (1970), *Mississippi Delta Blues* (1974), and *Give My Poor Heart Ease: Mississippi Delta Bluesmen* (1975).

William Ferris
University of Mississippi

William Ferris, ed., *Afro-American Folk Art and Crafts* (1983), *Blues from the Delta* (1984); *Highway 61 Blues: James "Son" Thomas*, Southern Culture Records, SC 1701 (1983).

Toasts and Dozens

In Greenville, Atlanta, Memphis, or other towns and cities in the South, you might hear preadolescent, lower-class black boys playfully hurling rhymed insults at each other. The language is rough and the themes are risqué, but the composition is creative. They are playing the "dozens," as they often call it. "I fucked your momma on the levee," a Greenville, Miss., youth told his playmate while others looked on. "She said, 'get up baby, your dick's getting too heavy.'" The onlookers roared with delight. After shouts of encouragement to the butt of the insult, he replied "I fucked your momma in New Orleans, her pussy started poppin' like a sewing machine." The challenge was put to the first boy to top the retort. He came back strongly with "I fucked your momma on a fence, selling her pussy for 15 cents; a bee come along and stung her on the ass, started selling her pussy for a dollar and a half."

The dozens are social entertainment, a game to be played, but they have also sparked considerable socio-psychological comment. Folklorist Roger D. Abrahams observed, for example, that the dozens represent a striving for masculine identity by black boys. They try symbolically to cast off the woman's world, indeed the black world they see as run by the mother of the family, in favor of the gang existence of the black man's world. In dozens playing, the black boy is honing the verbal and social skills he will need as an adult male. A form of dozens playing, usually called "ranking," has also been collected among white boys, but most collections have stressed the black dozens, also called "woofing," "sounding," and "joning."

Although Roger Abrahams did his classic study of black verbal contests and creativity in Philadelphia, his informants had deep roots in the South. Other southern connections to the dozens are found in a spate of southern blues songs popular from the 1920s on. "The Dirty Dozen" was first recorded by Georgia's Rufus Perryman, known as Speckled Red, in 1929. Other versions quickly followed by southern artists including Tampa Red, Little Hat Jones, Ben Curry, Lonnie Johnson, and Kokomo Arnold. The content of the dozens was apparently in circulation even prior to these recordings; folksong collectors Howard W. Odum and Newman I. White found references in the field to the dozens before World War I. Alan Dundes and Donald C. Simmons have suggested an older existence of the dozens in Africa.

Also collected from lower-class blacks has been a form of narrative poetry called by their reciters "toasts." Toasts use many of the rhyming and rhythmic schemes and the rough imagery of the dozens, but are performed by young men as extended poetic recitations rather than ritualized insult. Indeed, Abrahams called toasts the "greatest flowering of Negro verbal talent" (although similar recitations are also known among whites).

The performance of toasts is intended to be dramatic. The settings are placed in barrooms and jungles; the characters are badmen, pimps, and street people; and the props are often drugs, strong drink, and guns. Here is an excerpt, for example, from a common toast, "The Signifying Monkey."

> Down in the jungle near a dried-up creek,
> The signifying monkey hadn't slept for a week
> Remembering the ass-kicking he had got in the past
> He had to find somebody to kick the lion's ass.
> Said the signifying monkey to the lion that very same day,
> "There's a bad motherfucker heading your way.
> The way he talks about you it can't be right,
> And I know when you two meet there going to be a fight.
> He said he fucked your cousin, your brother, and your niece,
> And he had the nerve enough to ask your grandmom for a piece."
> The lion said, "Mr. Monkey, if what you say isn't true about me,
> Bitch, I'll run your ass up the highest tree."
> The monkey said, "Now look, if you don't believe what I say,
> Go ask the elephant. He's resting down the way."

Other popular toasts in oral tradition include "Stackolee," "The Titanic," "Joe the Grinder," and "The Freaks (or Junkers) Ball."

The origin of the term and the tradition of toasts is uncertain. Bruce Jackson suggested roots in prison and hobo life. Roger Abrahams looked to the influence of recitations common on the blackface minstrel stage and in subliterary comic forms. The name *toasts* may be derived from once-popular books of after-dinner speeches, jokes, and drinking toasts, or from underworld slang.

Several collections of toasts come from the South. In the North most texts come from the cities. Although some southern examples are reported in cities like New Orleans and Austin, southern texts often come from the rural and small-town South. In Mississippi, David Evans, William Ferris, and Simon J. Bronner collected them in small towns. Bruce Jackson's book on toasts, *Get Your Ass in the Water and Swim Like Me* (1974), had texts primarily collected from prisons in Texas and Missouri. The connection to southern life is usually passed up by interpreters of toasts in favor of links to the life of the underworld and the urban ghetto. Relations exist, however, between the themes and heroes of the toasts and those of southern black folksongs, including "Stackolee" and "The Titanic." The blues also are influenced by the erotic and violent verses of the toasts. Other connections are found between southern black animal folktales featuring the monkey and the toast "Signifying Monkey." Indeed, Richard M. Dorson reported prose versions of "Signifying Monkey" in his classic collection *American Negro Folktales* (1967) taken from southern-born blacks.

Dozens and toasts stand out because they are framed as play or performance, and they contain strong themes and sounds. Dozens and toasts creatively manipulate imagery and metaphor to bring drama to words. The boy telling dozens may eventually tackle the more sophisticated toasts. Mastering the techniques in these traditional performances gives the teller an important sense of prestige and power that is reserved for the man of words in black society. Their dozens and toasts entertain friends and pass the time; they communicate values and feelings. The tellers of dozens and toasts are narrators of imagined scenes and cultural critics for the audiences to which they perform. The tellers also draw attention because they are themselves characters in the social drama of communication through folklore.

Simon J. Bronner
Pennsylvania State University
Capitol Campus

Roger D. Abrahams, *Deep Down in the Jungle: Negro Narrative Folklore from the Streets of Philadelphia* (1970), *Positively Black* (1970); Simon J. Bronner, *Western Folklore* (April 1978); Richard M. Dorson, *American Negro Folktales* (1967); William Ferris, *Jazzforschung* (1974/75); Bruce Jackson, *Get Your Ass in the Water and Swim Like Me: Narrative Poetry from Black Oral Tradition* (1974); William Labov, Paul Cohen, Clarence Robins, and John Lewis, in *Mother Wit from the Laughing Barrel: Readings in the Interpretation of Afro-American Folklore*, ed. Alan Dundes (1973); Lawrence W. Levine, *Black Culture and Black Consciousness: Afro-American Folk Thought from Slavery to Freedom* (1977); Paul Oliver, *Aspects of the Blues Tradition* (1970); Dennis Wepman, Ronald B. Newman, and Murray B. Binderman, *Journal of American Folklore* (July–September 1974).

Toys

Handmade folk toys now seen as oddities at crafts fairs once served as principal playthings for children throughout the South. Especially in poorer, rural regions, adults fashioned toys from such native materials as wood, corn shucks, cane, vines, apples, and gourds. Native Americans shared techniques for making corn-shuck dolls with white and black settlers and made miniatures of their own weapons and implements. Many settlers brought or recreated toys from Europe, among them the cup-and-ball game based on the French bilboquet. Minstrel shows provided the idea for the limber jack, a marionette-type doll also called dancin' man and stomper doll. Children spent hours rubbing their notched, propeller-ended whimmydiddle sticks—also called whammydiddle sticks, hooey sticks, or gee-haw whimmydiddles. Miniature furniture, puzzles, and carved figures abounded. Many ingenious, carved action toys depicted everyday activities; for example, two men take turns chopping wood or chickens peck for corn.

Poppets, dolls made of buckeye wood, and other dolls with heads of dried apples or painted hickory nuts and stuffed cloth bodies enthralled youngsters. Children endlessly shot peas or rocks at targets with homemade flips and slingshots. Other favorites were the noisemakers such as "the buzz saw" and "the bull." On Sundays in many communities children could play only with biblically based toys such as the puzzles Pillars of Solomon and Jacob's Ladder. Today craftspeople often sell such folk toys through crafts fairs or small local shops and occasionally contract with large department stores like Bloomingdale's.

Residents of Appalachia and the Ozarks continued using homemade toys long after others in the country had shifted to store-bought toys. Although toy manufacturers in the northeastern and northcentral states long dominated the markets, some southern toys, such as the dolls of Wolf Fletcher and Philip Goldsmith in Covington, Ky., in 1875, had a wide appeal. No other southern toy, though, has ever rocked the nation like the Cabbage Patch Kids. In 1977 Georgia artist Xavier Roberts began producing handmade cloth dolls, "delivering" them at Babyland General Hospital in Cleveland, Ga. Roberts negotiated a licensing agreement with Coleco Industries, whose mass-produced versions became *the* toy craze from 1982 to 1984 and garnered unprecedented media attention. Although a renewed appreciation for southern folk toys is growing, today's southern children, tantalized by television ads, clamor for the latest crazes—not flips or whimmydiddles.

Sharon A. Sharp
University of Mississippi

Allen H. Eaton, *Handicrafts of the Southern Highlands* (1937; reprint 1973); *Foxfire Book of Toys and Games* (1985); Inez McClintock and Marshall McClintock, *Toys in America* (1961); *Newsweek* (12 December 1983); *Southern Living* (December 1983); *Time* (12 December 1983).

Traders

Whereas England has been described as a nation of horsemen, the South is a land of horse traders. Southerners are attracted to the trade more than to the animal, and Joseph Baldwin argued that in the South "nearly every man was a speculator; at any rate, a trader."

Mules and horses were raised in the cooler climate of border states by "graziers." During "court days" in states like Kentucky, streets were filled with stock and traders who bought and shipped their animals to livery stables in the Deep South to supply local farmers. The animals arrived in the late winter and early spring, and farmers would visit the barns to look them over. Customers quickly learned the relative merits of each animal and began to visit the trader and discuss terms. For the next two or three months the horse and mule barn was a center of business and social activity, and the trader the most important man in town. Mules were usually sold on credit with nothing down and one year to pay. These terms suited the dealer because he sold unbroken three- and four-year-olds, and if farmers broke them and kept them in good shape they would be worth $50 to $100 more the next year.

The southern trader usually left school and began trading at an early age. A seasoned trader often traveled with a "hossler," who was a black assistant, and the two were a skillful team. Manuel Allen was a black trader in Mississippi who always "traded slow." Allen's philosophy was "never to seem anxious to sell or trade if I wanted to make a good deal." He was awake to tricks of the profession, and once, when a man said his wife wanted to keep a mare for her buggy horse, Allen recalled, "Right then I knew he was baiting me and wanted me to take the mare."

Both trader and customer knew their "limits" and presented their cases with courtroom seriousness. Both remembered their trades and, more importantly, were judged for them by the community for years to come. The southern trade was a pact among men, and one emerged with honor or ridicule depending on his judgment.

The southern trader is known for his wit and is a shrewd judge of both animals and men. He weaves humorous tales and anecdotes into his work with special skill. Deception in folk humor reaches its most eloquent form among southern traders who argue that they never lie to a customer. All agree with Mississippi mule trader Ray Lum that "the truth always fits in better." Rather than lie to a customer, traders tell a veiled or embroidered truth, using word play and double entendre in describing an animal. For example, Lum recalls an animal sold to a hunter who was told he could "shoot off him." When he fired his gun, the mule bucked and he literally "shot off him." Southern traders like Ray Lum also developed a "singing" style in both auctioneering and trading using phrases such as "broke to a queen's taste," "kept like a hat in a band box," and "If a fly lit on her he would slip off and break his neck."

The southern trader dressed well to impress customers with the professional quality of his work. An important part of his dress was the western hat, a trademark of the profession. He carried a whip or cane and skillfully used it to assure that animals moved with spirit before a customer. The trader's eloquence and graceful manners set the customer at ease and guided his imagination, if not his eyes, in the trade.

Of all traders, gypsies are said to have the greatest knowledge of horses, and in the South it is said they "hoodoo" horses with their powers. Gypsies sometimes love a horse so much that they will buy the animal back at a loss rather than lose it. Such affection for an animal is a clear exception to the practice of other traders, who always love the trade more than the horse. Gypsies also practice ritual burial of horses and strictly forbid the eating of their flesh. Ironically, gypsies, like other traders, are usually very poor horsemen and use horses either as draft animals or for barter.

Gypsy men taught their sons how to bring out a horse's good points and disguise his weak ones. They were not content simply to buy and resell animals, for their greatest art lay in "putting right" a horse's defects. An old horse became a spirited animal through "gingering," the insertion of a piece of ginger into its anus.

Both Ray Lum and Ben Green, author of *Hoss Trades*, described Irish traders as even more formidable than gypsies. Irish tinkers immigrated to the United States in the early 1800s, and in Washington they established a communal livery stable. After the Civil War their leader, Pat O'Hara, led the group south to Atlanta. From this center, groups settled in Nashville and Fort Worth and began trading with farmers.

Irish traders traveled in two-family convoys consisting of three cars, each drawing a trailer bearing living equipment, and three trucks for the stock. Often four generations traveled together and camped in tents with two large carpeted rooms. As soon as the presence of the traders was known in a community, local farmers brought their worn-out mules to the camp to trade for young five-year-olds. The farmer always paid "boot" to cover the difference between the two animals. The old field mules could still be used for light hauling in cities, and one of the trucks shuttled between stockyards and the camp to supply fresh stock and haul the old mules back. While the men traded mules, their wives often sold hand-sewn lace to the women of the community.

During their trades the Irish protected themselves with a secret language, or cant, which was used to conceal their conversations from outsiders. Their language was derived from the Gaelic language of ancient Ireland, "Bearlangair na Saer." Once a high-caste language, it declined as the status of wandering smiths declined and became no more than an argot among tinkers. Its speakers today refer to their speech with phrases such as "Shelta," "Bog Latin," "Tinkers' Cant," and "The Ould Thing," whereas for outsiders it is "the gibberish of tinkers." Cant is passed on from generation to generation and effectively protects the Irish trader from outsiders.

William Faulkner was attracted to traders whose narrative skills in many ways paralleled his own as a writer. In *The Hamlet* he developed Pat Stamper, a trader who "played horses against horses as a gambler plays cards against cards, for the pleasure of beating a worthy opponent as much as for gain."

Traders prospered throughout the South until about 1955 when tractors replaced the mule. Many traders then became used-car dealers where they adapted their talents to new forms of transportation and "horsepower."

See also ETHNIC LIFE: / Gypsies; Travelers

William Ferris
University of Mississippi

Jean-Paul Clébert, *The Gypsies* (1969); J. Frank Dobie, *Guide to the Life and Literature of the Southwest* (1969); William Ferris, *Mississippi Folklore Register* (Spring 1978), *North Carolina Folklore Journal* (September 1973); Ben Green, *Horse Conformation and Hoss Traders of Yesteryear* (1963); T. V. Harper, "Irish Traveler Cant: An Historical, Structural, and Sociolinguistic Study of an Argot" (M.A. thesis, University of Georgia, 1969); Robert Byron Lamb, *The Mule in Southern Agriculture* (1963); Albert Thomas Sinclair, *American Gypsies* (1917); S. G. Thigpen, *A Boy in Rural Mississippi* (1966).

Wagner, Kinnie

(1903–1958) Outlaw.

Kinnie Wagner was a particularly good candidate for popular acclamation as an outlaw hero. During his lifetime he ran whiskey, robbed from the needy, killed at least five people (including three lawmen), and escaped four times from jail or prison; he also won the admiration of a grass-roots constituency that made him its champion. While critics attacked him, his supporters sang ballads about him and retold for generations legendary yarns about his marksmanship, cunning, and bravery. Indeed, Kinnie Wagner is one of the modern South's most controversial outlaws.

William Kenneth Wagner was born 18 February 1903 on a farm outside Gate City, Va. He spent most of his youth in the region, but in 1919 he left home and joined the Richard Brothers Wild West and Concert Show, working as a roustabout. During a swing through the piney forests of southeastern Mississippi, Kinnie left the circus and found work in lumber camps as a mule skinner. In the circus, Kinnie had taken to wearing western attire, and he passed himself off to local folks as a Texan. He started wearing sidearms that on some occasions he brandished, demonstrating that he was a skilled marksman.

Logging did not long appeal to Kinnie, and he started running whiskey from Mobile and Gulfport to customers as far north as Meridian and Jackson. In the summer of 1924 Wagner robbed a poor box and stole a gold watch from a mill guard in George County. Sheriff McLeod arrested him, and shortly he was sentenced to four months in the Lucedale jail. On 11 November Wagner escaped in a daring daytime breakout. A month later the authorities located Wagner living in a cabin outside McLain, Greene County. When a posse tried to recapture the fugitive, on 24 December, a gunfight erupted and Wagner shot to death Deputy Sheriff McIntosh before making his escape.

On 13 April 1925 he again eluded capture, this time leaving two Kingsport, Tenn., officers dead and one seriously wounded. The following day, however, Kinnie surrendered, and in less than two weeks he was tried, convicted, and sentenced to death. While awaiting a retrial, he escaped and fled to Mexico.

Wagner was back in the headlines on 19 August 1926. This time he surrendered to Sheriff Lillian Barber in Texarkana, Ark., after he had killed two men in a fight. He was returned to Mississippi to stand trial for the McIntosh slaying, for which Kinnie was convicted on 30 October. The Meridian jury, unable to agree on a death penalty, granted a life sentence. Wagner accepted the sentence and was moved to the Parchman State Prison Farm. He tried to escape the following year, but failed.

Wagner escaped from Parchman in 1940 and was retaken in 1943 by the FBI. Wagner had spent most of his time hiding out in the hills of northeastern Mississippi and Alabama, running whiskey. Back again in Parchman, Wagner became a model prisoner and received Christmas furloughs. But these rewards were not enough, and on 15 March 1948 he walked again from prison while on trusty duty. This time the fugitive eluded the law until 30 January 1956, when a contingent of Highway Patrol officers, state identification experts, and local officials in true Hollywood style captured the now-ailing Wagner near Shuqualak, Miss.

He was sent to Parchman with Mississippi's Governor Coleman saying that this prisoner would receive no special treatment. Wagner's health grew worse, and on 9 March 1958 he suffered a fatal heart attack. His body was returned home for burial, where according to an Associated Press account, over 10,000 persons turned out to view the famous gunman.

Richard Sweterlitsch
University of Vermont

Claude Gentry, *The Guns of Kinnie Wagner* (1969); Richard Sweterlitsch, *Mississippi Folklore Register* (Spring 1978).

Warner, Pecolia

(1901–1983) Quilter.

Born 9 March 1901 near Bentonia, Miss., raised on plantations in the Mississippi Delta, and educated in Yazoo City, Pecolia Leola Deborah Jackson Warner was taught to sew at the age of seven by her mother, Katherine Brant Jackson. One of seven children, Pecolia Warner learned from her schoolteacher mother to cook, clean, wash and iron, sew, and make quilts. Her first quilt was made from little "strings" of rectangular cloth, sewn into long strips alternately pieced with solid strips to fashion a top quilt. The pattern, called Spider Leg by Pecolia Warner's mother, is the oldest one known for Afro-American quilters. It is similar to African textiles made by sewing woven strips together, and it is the one most often first taught to young children.

Pecolia Warner, quilter, Yazoo City, Miss., 1976

Warner considered her quilt-making skills a gift from God. Although inspired by memories of her mother's quilts, by dreams, by quilt-pattern books, by household objects, and by farming artifacts, Warner's quilts are in the mainstream of Afro-American textile traditions. Pecolia Warner was as articulate verbally as she was visually, and interviews with her clarified those features that distinguished Afro-American quilts from Euro-American textile traditions: organizational strips; bold, contrasting colors; large designs; asymmetrical arrangements; multiple patterns, and improvisation. Warner often commented on how important it was for colors to "hit each other right," how "stripping" a quilt brought out the designs, and how varying parts of a pattern made quilt designs more interesting.

Pecolia Warner lived in New Orleans, Washington, D.C., and Chicago, working as a domestic servant for whites. She first received attention as a folk artist in 1977 when she was "discovered" by folklorist William Ferris and featured in his film, *Four Women Artists*. Her quilts were featured in "Folk Art and Craft: The Deep South," a traveling exhibition organized by the Center for Southern Folklore for the Smithsonian Institution Traveling Exhibition Service, as well as numerous other exhibitions. She was a featured artist at folklife festivals in the late 1970s, but her health became progressively worse in 1982. She suffered a series of small strokes and died at age 82 in March 1983.

Maude Southwell Wahlman
University of Mississippi

Patti Carr Black, ed., *Made by Hand: Mississippi Folk Art* (1980); William Ferris, ed., *Afro-American Folk Art and Crafts* (1983); Robert Farris Thompson, *Flash of the Spirit: African and Afro-American Art and Philosophy* (1983); John Michael Vlach, *The Afro-American Tradition in Decorative Arts* (1978); Maude Southwell Wahlman, in *Something to Keep You Warm*, ed. Patti Carr Black (1981), with John Scully, in *Afro-American Folk Art and Crafts*, ed. William Ferris (1983), with Ella King Torrey, *Ten Afro-American Quilters* (1983).

Geography

RICHARD PILLSBURY
Georgia State University
CONSULTANT

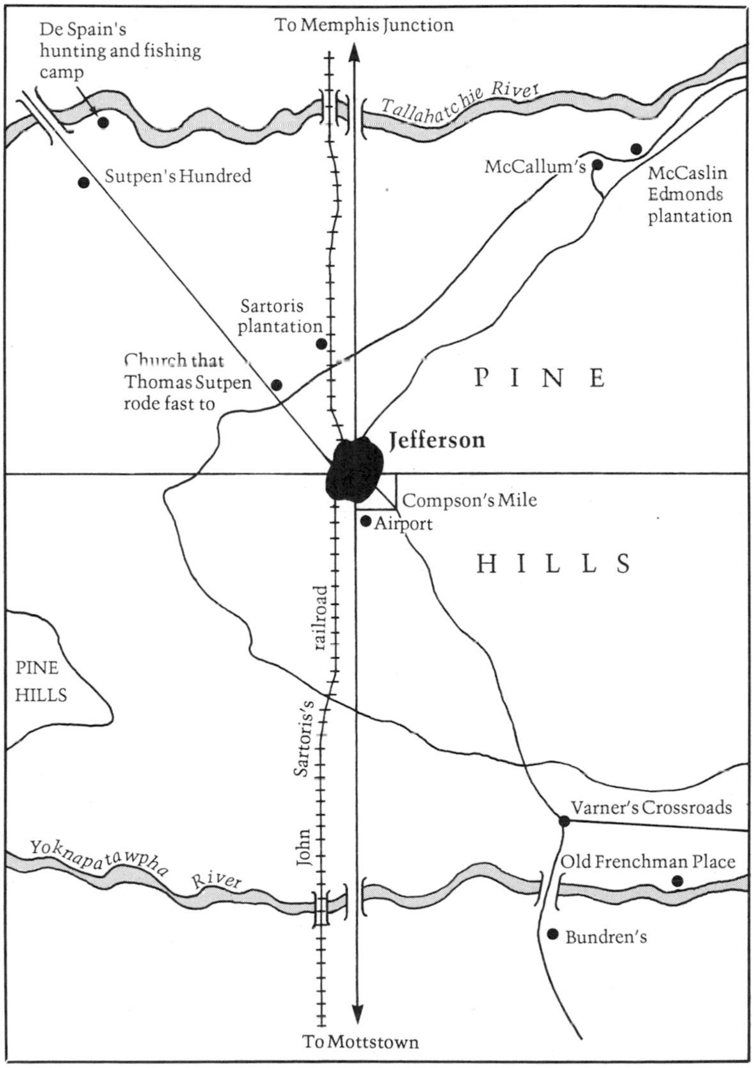

Yoknapatawpha County, Mississippi

Source: Charles S. Aiken, "Faulkner's Yoknapatawpha County: Geographical Fact into Fiction," *Geographical Review* (1977).

Landscape, Cultural

The South is at once both the most visible and most ambiguous of all American cultural landscapes. The region's visibility stems largely from its strong sense of regional identity, its ambiguity from its lack of a definable geographic core. The vision of a unified southern cultural landscape is thus more myth than reality. A portrait of the region's landscape is possible only with the understanding that it is selective and synthetic.

Traditionally the South has been considered to extend northward from the Gulf of Mexico to the Potomac and Ohio rivers and westward from the Atlantic to eastern Texas. Transition zones, or spheres of influence, are found along the northern border, where the region intermixes with the Midwest, and on the western margins, where it mingles with the Hispanic Southwest. The western limits of the region are the most poorly defined today because of the recent explosive growth of eastern Texas. Dallas and Houston once were strongly influenced by southern themes and values, but today these roots are obscured.

Britain provided the basic cultural stamp of the human landscape throughout the colonial period, in spite of Spanish settlements in Florida and Texas and French settlement of southern Louisiana and the surrounding environs. The abiding significance of the initial Anglo role in the South is made clear by the Doctrine of First Effective Settlement, which suggests that new immigrants in previously settled areas live in houses already built and farm fields already cleared. The early settlers of the South may have initially desired houses like those of the old country, but local builders were unfamiliar with those designs and special materials were not available. Some New England–style houses were located in coastal South Carolina and Georgia and German houses near Winston-Salem, N.C., but these stand as anomalies in a greater landscape fabric.

The region's mixed racial heritage is only partially reflected in the visual cultural landscape of the contemporary South. Recognized black contributions to traditional southern landscape have been limited. Both the shotgun house form and swept-yard landscaping have African roots, but the racial origins of these elements were forgotten as they were amalgamated into the culture as a whole. Other landscape elements of black origin, such as the distinctive use of broken pottery in cemeteries, have continued to exist but mainly among blacks in isolated areas.

Maize and tobacco cultivation were the two most important aboriginal contributions to the regional landscape, but they are also largely unrecognized by the dominant culture. Other notable Indian contributions to the landscape were the raised-square corncrib, the use of multicropping techniques in house gardens, and the preference for small separated fields in the Upland and Gulf Coastal southern areas.

Defining the Traditional Southern Landscape. The South is the least urbanized culture area in the nation. Cities over a million in population are rare, and small towns are more common than the national standards. The county seat is the single most important type of community settlement in the region. The earliest county seats in Virginia were founded as linear collections of building lots mandated by the House of Burgesses. An enlarged central lot was designated as a courthouse square. Many of these and other southern county seats have never grown beyond a handful of buildings clustered around an isolated courthouse.

A typical mid-19th-century county seat was a planned community named for a prominent state or national figure, or the hometown of one of the development committee members. It was located on the highest vantage point near the geographic center of the county. The unpaved rectilinear streets gave form to about 25 building blocks with 80 to 100 one-quarter- to one-half-acre residential building lots, 30 or more narrow frontage commercial lots facing the square, and 20 or so larger commercial lots at the rear of the small commercial lots. The proceeds of the sale of these lots were used to pay for the development of the town and the construction of public buildings.

The central courthouse square was the focal point of the county seat. Early courthouses were of log or frame, but by the late 19th century most were two-story brick structures with a distinctive cross-hallway pattern. The courthouse was the most important building in town. Its rooms, halls, and steps were the stage for trials, sheriffs' sales, tax and permit payments, and gossip for the entire county. The jail occupied a separate building behind the courthouse, although many towns preferred to have it in a less conspicuous place. Town wells for public use and fire protection were located at one or more corners of the square. Confederate war memorial statues of a soldier in battle dress began to appear after about 1890. Many early towns allowed lawyers to have offices on the square.

The square, the courthouse, and the facing businesses formed the core of the town. The largest and most prestigious businesses included the hotel, four or five large general merchandise stores, a ladies' apparel shop or two, the bank, and a drugstore. Doctors', lawyers', and insurance offices were located on the second floors of these solid brick buildings. The post office, telegraph office, and livery and artisan shops were on the side streets. Churches were located off the square on a corner of a block touching the square.

Large residential building lots in southern towns encouraged the use of tall oaks, hickories, and magnolias to shade white painted houses. Large backyards and gardens furthered this bucolic look. The practice of utilizing widely differing sizes of lots in preplanned rectilinear towns is not found elsewhere in the nation.

Dispersed communities actually were the most common type of urban settlement in the region. These dispersed communities are not towns in the true sense of the word, but have the name, identity, and activities of such. They only lack traditional population density. Many are dying as rural out-migration continues and

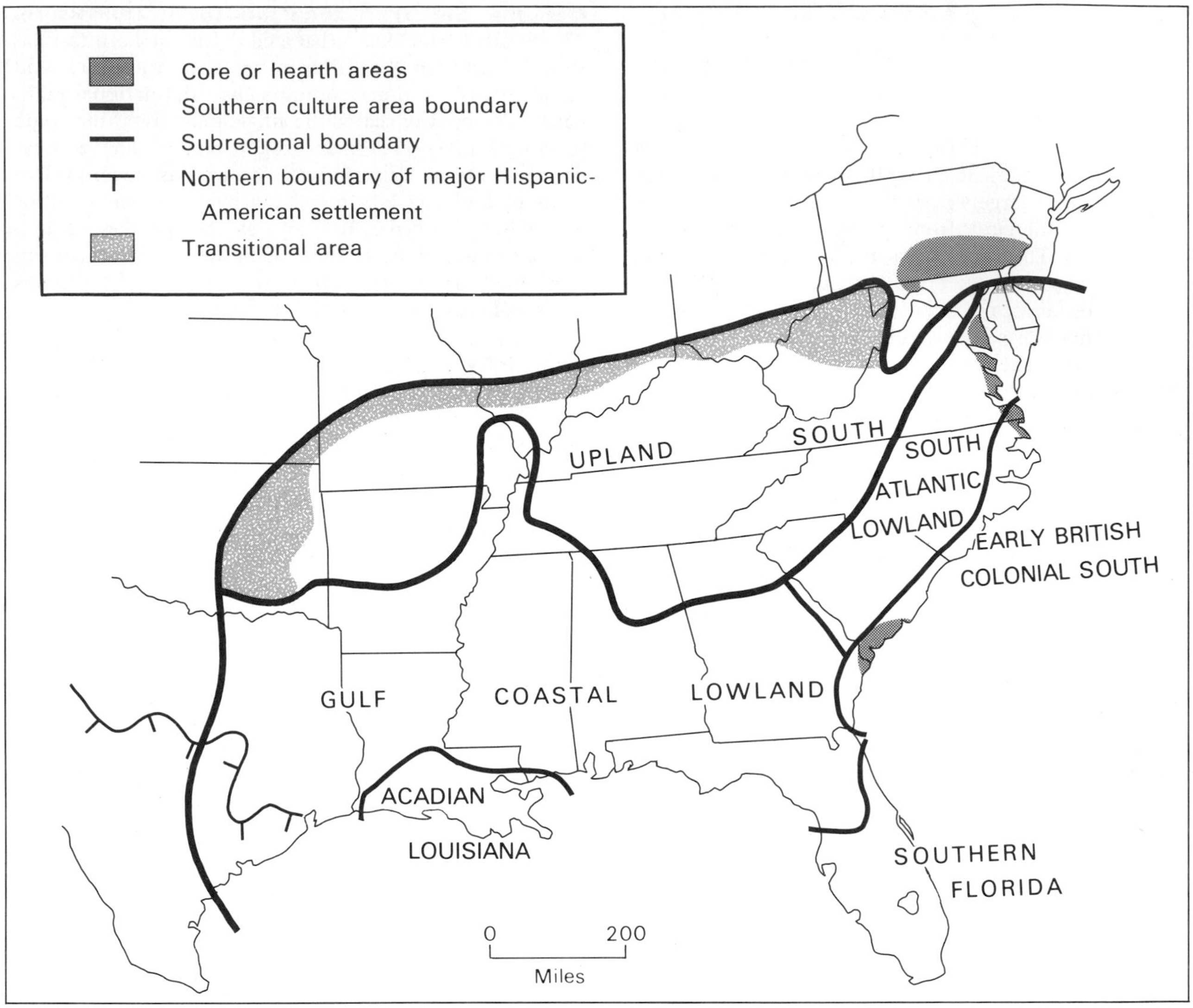

Southern Culture Regions

Map by Richard Pillsbury

roads to larger communities with more comprehensive services improve. The church and the crossroads store often are the only functioning remnants today.

Land abandonment and piney woods are the overriding rural images for much of the region. Large commercial farms have replaced traditional farming in some areas, but these are mere pockets in the greater fabric of a rolling wooded landscape. Vast acreages of the Gulf Coastal Plains and Upland South are planted in tree farms of loblolly, slash, and other pines, or have been allowed to become wooded through land abandonment. Part of this wooded image, however, is illusory. The separation of fields by forest buffer zones creates impressions of wooded acreages that do not exist. These impressions are intensified for the casual traveler by the interstate highway system that frequently bypasses farmed areas in small towns.

Five diagnostic features of the South are particularly valuable in charting the cultural landscape of the region: vernacular house form, religion, individualistic attitudes, diet, and music. Vernacular house form is one of the clearest ways of determining the extent and subregionalization of a cultural landscape. Conceptually, house form refers to the arrangement, relative size, and function of a structure's rooms combined with its facade characteristics. These apparently superficial elements have proven to be amazingly effective indicators of cultural origins because they represent measures of a society's attitudes about family life and interaction within the home.

Residential construction preferences aid in the identification of regional forms. The classic southern vernacular house was raised 18 or more inches off the ground, rarely had a basement, had outside end chimneys, was of frame construction sheathed with clapboard, and usually possessed a porch or piazza stretching across the facade and possibly sides. Exterior walls of many rural houses appeared to be well aged, as paint has only recently been applied regularly. Fireplace chimneys are located inside the endwalls in several sections of Virginia. They disappeared altogether after the adoption of stoves for cooking and heating in the late 19th century. Stone construction was virtually unknown outside of the northern transitional zone. In scattered areas in Virginia and the Kentucky Bluegrass traditional houses were constructed of brick. Porches were least common in the Virginia Tidewater and northern transition zones.

Many southern vernacular house forms have existed, but only the southern hall-and-parlor house and the I house are found throughout the region. The hall-and-parlor house originated in Britain, and versions of it are found throughout the original colonies. It is a one-and-a-half story, one-room-deep house with two rooms across the facade. The southern hall-and-parlor house is found both with and without a central hallway separating the first-floor rooms. The I house developed as a two-story version of the earlier hall and parlor. It could be ornamented with elaborate piazzas, wings, and stylistic ornamentation, allowing its use both as a middle-class dwelling and as an elaborate plantation residence.

Religion is another factor that reveals the nature of the cultural landscape. Southern religion is distinguished by its conservative fundamentalist orientation, not its denominations. The Southern Baptist Convention is the largest single denominational body, and its distribution is often considered characteristic of the region. Church attendance and activities play a far more significant role in family and community life than in other parts of the United States.

A strong belief in the rights of the individual and the localization of political power is reflected in the South's political attitudes about local options, states' rights, and other manifestations of localized decision making. There are more counties, and each county is smaller and has more administrative duties than in any other region in America. The consolidation of school districts has been slower; state police units have less authority. These beliefs are also reflected in the region's violent-crime rate. Many southerners believe that it is the individual's right and duty to resolve conflict personally.

If regional attitudes can reveal southern distinctiveness, so can the distribution of regional and subregional foodways. The classic southern diet is distinguished by its wide use of quick breads (muffins and biscuits), corn products, grits, sweetened iced tea, and carbonated drinks. There is also greater dependence upon pork and chicken products for meat. Biscuits are so important to the southern breakfast that even McDonald's and Burger King have added biscuits to their breakfast menus. The consumption of grits is less evident than in the past but continues to be widespread. Consumption of carbonated drinks, especially colas, generally exceeds national averages. Fried foods and the overcooking (as judged by national tastes) of vegetables are two significant local preparation preferences.

Country music has long been recognized as a southern phenomenon but recently has lost much of its regional identity. Gospel music is less well known but is possibly more useful as a regional factor today. Thousands of gospel groups constantly perform throughout the South at revivals, churches, and concerts.

The Evolution of Subregions. The southern landscape began as a series of isolated settlement nodes along the Atlantic Coastal Plain that evolved independently throughout the 18th century. Three variables favored this situation: (1) the planters' desire to sell their products directly to British customers, rather than utilize American distribution centers; (2) the wide Atlantic Coastal Plain that allowed the unchallenged agricultural expansion into new lands; and (3) the presence of the Blue Ridge on the western frontier, which halted expansion of the agricultural frontier about the time that settlement overlap would have taken place.

The South thus has never possessed a homogeneous cultural landscape. The Atlantic Lowland is characterized by internal heterogeneity, which stems from its development prior to the Americanization of the landscape. The Gulf Coastal landscape primarily evolved from landscape features originating on the Atlantic Coast, with interregional differences stemming from its later development and the presence of large numbers of Upland South migrants and Caribbean immigrants. These two subregions form the Lowland South, but it is an uncomfortable unity. The Upland South developed more independently. Its original Pennsylvania culture was molded by a demanding physical environment and finally modified by transfusions of traditions from the Carolinas and Virginia. Some authorities consider the Upland South a separate region.

The Lowland South: The Atlantic Lowland. The Atlantic Lowland was the first landscape created in the South and has the most internal variation. At least six subareas may be identified within its extent, as well as numerous pockets of two or three counties with less distinctive differences.

The urban landscape has the least consistency of character. A typical early Virginia Tidewater county seat has about 20 building lots on a single street. The two-story brick courthouse fronted by its aged Confederate war memorial and newer eternal flame is set on a central enlarged courthouse-square lot under a grove of sheltering oaks. A store covered with soft-drink signs faces it across the road; a nearby house or two completes the scene. In contrast, the later 19th-century county seats and rail centers were planned communities of substantial buildings looking much like those found throughout the remainder of the region.

The most important vernacular structures of the Atlantic Lowland are the southern hall-and-parlor house (Tidewater), the porched Tidewater house, the I house, and some special-function barns. Early regional houses were duplications of British houses with initial modifications, such as raised foundations for mildew control, primarily made to meet environmental problems. Houses were raised even higher in the Carolinas and southward to combat miasma. Kitchens were placed in a separate building to reduce house temperatures in summer.

Southern hall-and-parlor houses were built throughout

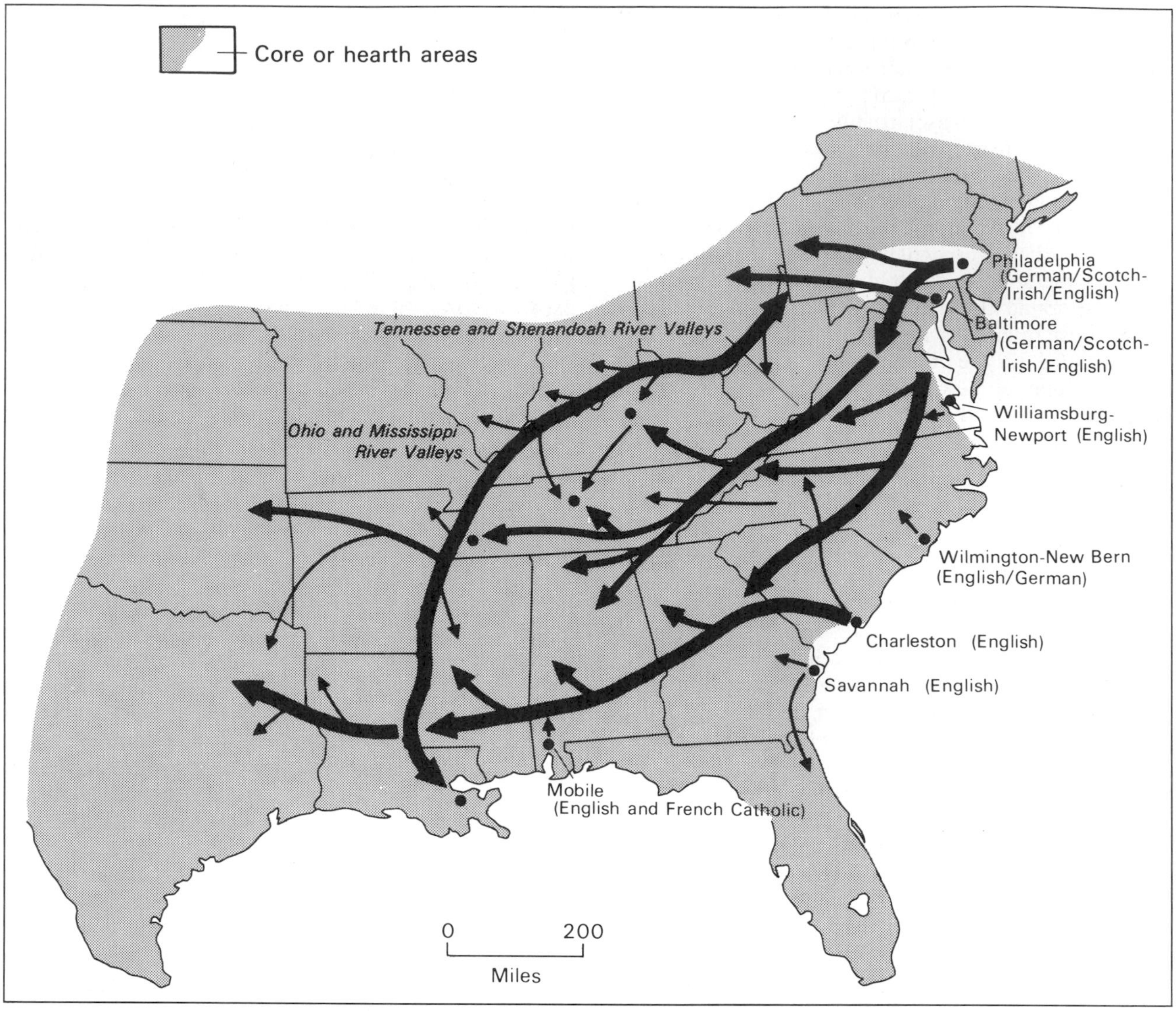

Diffusion Routes of Cultural Patterns

Map by Richard Pillsbury

the Atlantic Lowland, especially in Tidewater Virginia. The porched Tidewater is made distinctive with an incised front porch and frequent use of the catslide, or rear shed, kitchen. It was most common on the northern Piedmont and is found in scattered pockets in the Tidewater zone. Transitional versions of the house with attached porches are found in coastal Carolina and Georgia.

There is no standard I house in the Atlantic Lowland, although several distinct subtypes exist. Many early Chesapeake Bay examples are of brick, often with decorative glazed diaper brickwork. The later Piedmont Virginian version is a smaller frame three-bay structure with end chimneys. The typical Piedmont North Carolina version is squarer than those of Virginia, often with the chimneys placed inside the endwalls. A South Carolina Tidewater and Savannah River version is larger and thinner and is distinguished by the centering of the fireplaces on the rear walls of the rooms.

Three distinctive barns are found in the region: the Chesapeake air-cured tobacco barn, the Carolina flue-cured tobacco barn, and the Carolina gable-opening barn. The Chesapeake air-cured tobacco barn is found on the western shore of Virginia and Maryland, in Lancaster County, Pa., and in the Bluegrass of Kentucky. It is an adaptation of the English flat barn modified for tobacco curing by placing the entries at the gable ends, adding racks for hanging the curing tobacco, and attaching movable siding to increase air flow through the structure.

Flue-cured tobacco barns are found in central North Carolina and in southeastern Georgia and adjacent Florida. The earliest Carolina flue-cured tobacco barns were saddle-notched log cubes with a small door in one side. Granny's apron porches wrap around two or more of the sides to shelter workers tying tobacco hands. Newer examples are of frame and clapboard construction. The entire structure is being phased out today by aluminum and galvanized metal garagelike buildings that can accommodate the tobacco wagons.

The Carolina gable-opening barn is found on the central Carolina Piedmont and environs with no obvious precursors. It is a large two-story structure with the upper floor used as a hay loft. The half-open center first floor may have been a threshing and unloading area for hay wagons. Two side aisles lead to a series of stalls for horses and cattle. This barn is related to the transverse crib barn of the southern Appalachians.

The cultural landscape has been shaped by many other factors as well. Baptist and Methodist denominations in the Atlantic Lowlands account for only 60 percent of the region's church membership. The Presbyterian Church of the United States, the Church of God, Disciples of Christ, the Pentecostal Holiness, and the Protestant Episcopal churches follow in order of importance. These denominations are found throughout the region as a whole, but several islands of atypical groups are also present. Central North Carolina, with its large population of the Society of Friends, Moravian, and United Church of Christ members, is the best known of these. Others are remnants of early settlements that have maintained their religious identities.

Regional dietary preferences reflect the Atlantic Lowland's prototypical relationship to the remainder of the South. Recipes for Brunswick stew, barbecue, and other regional favorites reflect these dishes at the earliest stages of their development. The standard regional menu also exhibits greater diversity than generally found farther west.

The Lowland South: The Gulf Coastal Lowland. The Gulf Coastal landscape begins near the Savannah River and extends westward into eastern Texas. The Federal Road, connecting Charleston, S.C., with Augusta, Ga., and thence along the fall line to Macon and Columbus, Ga., and Montgomery, Ala., and beyond, served as the single most important route for new settlers into the region. The Upper Federal Road connecting the Carolina and Virginia Piedmont with the Gulf Coast was nearly as significant. Moderate numbers of settlers from the Caribbean entered the region through Savannah, Mobile, and New Orleans. The northern section was strongly influenced by Appalachian settlers migrating through the valleys of the Tennessee River into northern Alabama and Mississippi.

Urban patterns in the region are essentially refinements of those established earlier on the Atlantic Seaboard. County-seat planners almost universally adopted the rectilinear street plan, the central courthouse square, large residential building lots, and standardized street names. The dispersed community continued to be the most common urban type, although railroad builders established hundreds of cotton gin and warehouse centers during the 19th century. Morphologically these towns follow national models: rectilinear street pattern; main business district facing the depot; relatively smaller residential lots; and streets numbered in one direction and in the other direction either lettered or named after plants, animals, or important people.

The rural scene is also an extension of the Atlantic Lowland landscape. Wooded sections are more frequent, and forest buffers between fields are more common. Southernmost areas are composed of seemingly endless tree farms, which often obscure the presence of the traditional agrarian landscape. The Gulf Coastal Lowland was once known as the cotton belt, but the boll weevil, competing agricultural areas, and polyester have changed that. Large acreages have reverted to forest, others have been converted to pasture, and the remainder have been used primarily for corn and soybeans. Cultivation of agricultural products including strawberries, pecans, peanuts, table vegetables, and catfish adds variety to the landscape.

The classic image of a Gulf Coastal tenant farm is of a small two-room frame hall-and-parlor house with rusting galvanized metal roof and unpainted clapboard walls. Two or three chairs sit on a drooping, attached porch that stretches across the front. The house stands in the midst of a hard-packed swept yard in the shade of a huge chinaberry tree. The attached rear kitchen is connected to the house with a wrap-around porch on the inside of the "L." A frame single-crib barn with shed addition on one side sits behind the large family garden. Dried gourds for purple martin houses hang from a line stretching from a pole in the garden to the barn. The small, raised, square, log corncrib and smokehouse to one side are shaded by giant oaks. Three small cornfields behind the barn can barely be seen through the hazy white heat of summer.

Gulf Coastal vernacular houses have lower-pitched rooflines than those of the Atlantic Lowland because of the popularity of the Greek Revival in the early 19th century, when most were built. Summer heat also made the lofts difficult to use. Central hallways were often widened into breezeways to promote cross-ventilation. The dogtrot hall—meaning here a central hallway extending the length of the house—was used on all house forms in the region. True dogtrot houses—those with a covered, open-ended hallway between two wings of the house—were common as well. Gulf Coastal houses had taller foundation pillars than were found to the east. The detached kitchen was moved closer to the house so that only a few feet separated the two buildings, with an inside "L" rear porch tying them together.

The most important vernacular house forms during the early period were two versions of the hall-and-parlor house, the I house, and the dogtrot house; the southern pyramidal, shotgun, and frame saddlebag house types were popular in later periods. The southern (Louisiana) bungalow was widely used after World War I. National styles dominated the scene after 1930.

Tenant and small farmers were the most frequent occupants of the smaller hall-and-parlor house described previously. The larger hall-and-parlor house often served as the main house of small plantations. It was modified with a flattish roofline and enlarged returns on the eaves. A stylish Greek Revival portico stretched across the center third of the facade to give the house greater presence. The kitchen was a catslide (shed) extension across the rear of the house.

Gulf Coastal I houses tended to be larger and somewhat more pretentious than those of the Atlantic Lowland. The central hall was wider, often with double front doors; the rooms were larger; and the facade was built with five bays. It was a favorite house form to be modified for use as a plantation house with splashes of exterior ornamentation such as columns, porticos, friezes, and/or brackets.

Dogtrot houses began as two single-pen log units tied together with a floored breezeway, porch, and common roof. The origin of the house is unknown. Isolated examples may be found as far north as Maryland, although the upper Tennessee River basin was apparently the earliest center for their widespread use. Log versions of the houses are found on the northern Gulf Coastal Plain, but it is more widely seen as a frame-and-clapboard house in the southern half of the region.

The shotgun house originated in Africa, matured in the Caribbean, and first appeared in America in New Orleans and in other Caribbean settlement areas. Most Gulf Coastal shotgun houses probably were not an expression of the region's vernacular tradition. Thousands were sold in the late 19th and early 20th centuries as tenant and worker housing by lumber companies specializing in precut and prefabricated houses. Most are in the mill and lumber towns of the Mississippi drainage basin, where their narrow frontage was in demand.

Saddlebag houses were used as tenant and worker houses during this period in the eastern Gulf Coast. They are frame, central-chimney, two-front-door, two-room houses, which were occasionally used to shelter two families. A two-room, rear-kitchen-shed addition is typical. The form originated in Britain and was adapted for log construction in Pennsylvania. The frame version was developed by Appalachian settlers in the 19th century. Most were built after the Civil War from precut or prefabricated house kits.

The southern pyramidal probably evolved during the mid-19th century from an earlier straight gable house in the Savannah River area of Georgia. The oldest version of this house has four rooms with a wide central hall. A high-peaked pyramidal roof with two chimneys placed a few feet on either side of its short roofridge distinguishes the house. This was a favorite town home of the upper middle class from Reconstruction to the Depression, although it is found in smaller numbers in rural areas as well. Prefabricated housing companies also marketed several other versions of this house for management and worker housing in company towns.

Frame single-crib barns with side-shed additions are the most visible outbuildings of the Gulf Coast. These structures evolved from the single-crib log barns of the Upland South. Some double-crib log barns are also found along the northern margins of the region, but they are not common. Several types of corncribs are found, although the most distinctive is of Cherokee (possibly Creek) origin and is a squarish log (or frame) crib raised a few feet off the ground.

Religious patterns helped to distinguish this subregion, as with other areas in the South. The Southern Baptist and United Methodist churches claim more than 80 percent of all church membership on the Gulf Coast. In some areas as much as 90 percent of the population tabulated by the United Council of Churches in a 1971 survey claimed membership in these two bodies. The region's dietary patterns are also a simplified version of those found on the Atlantic Coastal Plain. The dominance in foodways of pork, chicken, and corn products is almost complete, although yams are also popular. The high consumption of colas, sweetened iced tea, buttermilk, catfish, hush puppies, greens, and peas is also significant.

The Upland South. The evolution of the Upland South began with the southward migration of Pennsylvanian settlers along the limestone valleys of the Ridge and Valley physiographic province. They mixed with Piedmont Virginians moving up the Potomac and James rivers and Carolinian elements entering by way of the Wilderness Road and the Little Tennessee River. A cultural milieu soon evolved that was strikingly different from that of either hearth region. Complexity was added by the Cherokee nation, which stopped significant European expansion into their section of the southern Appalachians through 1838 and contributed many cultural elements to this milieu. The Mississippi and Ohio rivers and the Natchez Trace were significant commercial arteries serving the region, but they had little impact on the evolution of the cultural landscape.

Urban landscapes in the Upland South are dominated by three types of centers: industrial cities, county seats, and coal camps. The Industrial Revolution left its mark on the region's larger cities: grimy brick buildings, thriving chemical plants, abandoned factories, tortuous streets bent to match sites never meant for urban living, and aged housing. In contrast, the region's county seats are marked by their formal designs and relative cleanliness, as are those of the Gulf Coast.

Traditional coal and agrarian landscapes have always maintained an uneasy coexistence in the Upland South, each almost unaware of the other. Miners rarely strayed from their camps, perched precariously overlooking the mine apparatus or squatting in a straggling line of matchbox houses along a narrow hollow leading to the overshadowing mine, tipple, and slag piles. There has always been a sense of impermanence about these places, although most are more than 50 years old. The recent rise of strip mining and decline of the fixed-site mining operations have spelled doom for many.

Land abandonment is the most pervasive phenomenon in the rural Upland South. Despite a widely scattered population, few people make their living from the land. The sense of having a homeplace and of being connected with distant forefathers is, nonetheless, strong here. Appalachia has the highest percentage of rural nonfarm population in the nation. Many have left, only to discover the depth of their attachment to home. It has taken more than 30 years of living and working in Pittsburgh, Detroit, and other industrial cities for many of the post–World War II expatriates to finally begin to set roots in their new homes.

The terrain of the Upland South favors the creation of many distinctive landscapes. A typical traditional farmstead of central West Virginia consists of a log saddlebag

Cabin in eastern Kentucky mountains, 1940

or small-frame I house, a single-crib log barn, a small house garden, a springhouse, a smokehouse, and several fields of corn or hay, all clustered in a small hollow. The hay is piled on poled haystacks in the fields, the fences are made of split rail, and the plowing is done with a horse—or more recently with a large rototiller. Transverse crib barns, double-crib log barns, log dogtrot houses, fewer outbuildings, and larger fields are more common in southern Appalachia.

Larger houses, mechanization, and commercial agriculture appear where the land is better—in the Ridge and Valley province, the Nashville Basin, and elsewhere. The rolling limestone pastures, thoroughbreds lolling behind their wooden fences, and mansions of the Kentucky Bluegrass certainly form yet another landscape. So, too, do the estates, orchards, and poultry farms of the Shenandoah Valley, the dairy farms of the Ridge and Valley province, and the horse farms of central Tennessee.

Log houses are still widespread in the region. Early builders favored central-European log construction featuring hewn logs, half dovetail corner timbering in the earlier and "V" corner notching in the later structures, and boards to cover the eaves. Group house raisings were one of the most important forces in the early evolution of standardized construction and housing styles. Construction techniques became simplified through time. Logs continued to be used in the house and outbuilding construction until the 1930s, and isolated examples were built as late as the 1970s.

Log single-pen houses, log and frame saddlebag houses, I houses, and single- and double-crib barns are the most common traditional structures in the region. Dogtrot houses frequently appear in southern Appalachia. Four- and six-crib transverse barns possibly originated in the southeastern section. Coal mining introduced company towns and several new house forms to the region: gable-facing I houses, a saltbox duplex, and a simple southern pyramidal house. The gable-facing I house is a common Industrial Age company house in America, created by turning a standard I house 90 degrees on its axis to reduce street frontage. Two-story duplexes with rear shed sections, much like the New England saltbox, were popular in the northern coal camps. The pyramidal house was most common in the South. It has four interconnected rooms and stove heating.

In regard to the other diagnostic features of southern regionalism, literal interpretation of the Bible is the most identifiable feature of the religion of the Upland South. The Baptist and Methodist churches dominate numerically, but the region's religious character stems from its unaffiliated churches and small denominations that stress fundamentalism. Most are untabulated in church membership surveys, but the larger denominations include the Church of God, Disciples of Christ, Assemblies of God, the Churches of Christ, and the Pentecostal and Holiness sects. The Presbyterian church is strong in many areas because of the numerous early Scotch-Irish settlers.

Country music has recently undergone a dramatic nationalization making it less clearly than before tied to the South. However, recording continues to be concentrated in Nashville, and performers continue to be predominantly southern in origin. Gospel music and general religious programming in the electronic media are far more distinctive to this area today than is country music.

Other Cultural Landscapes: Acadian Louisiana. The South also encompasses areas that are not a part of the mainstream regional landscape including Acadian Louisiana and, increasingly, southern Florida. Transition zones often become distinctive in their look as well. Acadia began to develop in southern Louisiana after the arrival of French settlers from maritime Canada in the 18th century. These Acadians, or Cajuns, formed a coherent community along the waterways of southern Louisiana and adjacent areas. Their isolation continued until the discovery of oil in the early 20th century brought outsiders, roads, a new Cajun self-awareness, and money. Recently, too, tourism has increased.

Acadian Louisiana illustrates well the role of culture in determining the look of a place. Inheritance laws required the equal division of estates among the children, so land lots are fairly uniform in size. The importance of water access for transportation and commerce, coupled with the character of the natural levee lands that the Acadians traditionally settled, virtually forced the division of the lands into narrow farms radiating away from the streams. Strassendorfs, or street villages, developed as landowners built their homes along the lot frontages. Today most commercial activities, and the Catholic churches, are located in the formal towns.

The Acadian house is a one-and-a-half-story, four-room house with an incised front porch. The rooms may be separated by a central hall. Fireplaces are located between the two rooms on each side of the hall. The rear kitchen addition looks like a smaller mirror image of the main house. Drainpipe systems and cisterns once collected rainwater for household use in low-lying areas. Houses with partial Acadian features are found, as well as greatly enlarged "plantation" houses.

Other significant elements of the Acadian cultural landscape include Roman Catholicism, place names, a variety of unique dietary preferences, and some retention of the French language. Almost 88 percent of the entire population of St. Martin Parish and more than 80 percent of all church adherents in Acadia belong to the Roman Catholic church. French alliterations and terminology, especially the names of saints, dominate the region's place names. The term *bayou* is commonly used and is believed to be French in origin, although, in fact, it is from the Choctaw word *bayuk*. The most striking dietary preferences include dark-roast and chicory coffee, rice, and seafood. Crawfish have almost become a fetish in recent years. The Cajun French language is rarely heard on the street today but is still used in the home by older citizens. Most residents have a distinct regional accent.

Other Cultural Landscapes: Southern Florida. Southern Florida was only sparsely settled prior to the 20th century, and little traditional cultural landscape remains. Population growth began with the construction of railroads in the 1890s and dramatically increased after World War II. This unfettered development created a unique melange of early tourist kitsch and 20th-century fads beneath a garish, land-promoter facade.

Most of Florida was originally subdivided by the township-and-range land-division system. The straight lines and square properties are often only obvious in the many straight segments of the secondary road system. This unique 20th-century landscape is dominated by the familiar. Most older towns have rigidly numbered street grids with endless modern, curved-street subdivisions. The 1920s are early history here, and the architectural styles and structures of that period, especially the Spanish stucco rococo, dominate the older sections of many towns. The 1950s brought the legitimization and widespread use of stucco-faced concrete block construction; brick is less common.

Florida's late-developing towns in many ways epitomize strip-development America. Strong central business districts are rare, as the commercial landscape is dominated by chaotic strips of white concrete suburban shopping centers, with pale yellow and green galvanized facades above plate-glass windows, interspersed among fast-food stores and motels at the edge of town. Endless walls of high-rise condominiums now separate the beaches from the public along the Florida coastlines.

The arrival of thousands of Cuban and other Caribbean immigrants since the late 1950s has had a revolutionary impact on the landscape. The addition of over 100,000 Cuban immigrants in the early 1980s further intensified the Cubanization of the Miami and southern Florida cultural milieu. Currently, over 40 percent of metropolitan Miami is of Hispanic descent, whereas only 6 percent of the state's overall population has a similar origin. Language and other cultural differences have tended to accentuate the Cuban presence, much as they did that of the Italian, Polish, and Czech immigrants in the Northeast. The Cubans have built few distinctive edifices, but the rise of Cuban food specialties, the increase in the number of signs in Spanish, and the use of more vibrant colors have made the Hispanic residents a visible part of the landscape.

The greatest changes in Florida's landscape in recent years stem from the state's rapid industrialization. Small factories are springing up throughout the state as it is becoming an electronics, consumer-goods, and apparel-manufacturing center. Miami is replacing New Orleans as the gateway to the Caribbean and South America. Melbourne and Orlando have become major electronics centers. The last remnants of the regional landscape are disappearing as rapid growth covers the poorly preserved past.

Other Cultural Areas: Transition Zones. Transition zones between two dynamic areas are typified by cultural tension as residents adapt their lifestyles to fit the changing milieu. The term *Little Dixie* has been applied to a variety of southern border areas in Arkansas, Missouri, Oklahoma, and Illinois. These places are characterized by a mixture of the traits of the South and adjacent regions. Surviving southern traits generally include accent, the importance of the Baptist denomination, and the retention of some food preferences.

New Directions. Change is sweeping the traditional South and creating a new landscape. Saddlebag houses lie abandoned in overgrown fields, camp-meeting grounds are deserted, and boarded cotton-gin towns stand beside their railroad tracks. Landscapes are never static, but the nationalization of the southern landscape has been exceptionally rapid. The new era began with the exposure of thousands of young American soldiers to Europe and the migration of southerners to the labor-short northern factories during World War I. World War II sent another generation of young men away but also introduced many northern soldiers to snowless winters. The postwar period saw the death of traditional tenant farming and the virtual emptying by out-migration of vast sections of the agricultural South. These shifts in the region's population set the stage for the massive changes in culture and landscape that were to follow.

Television and the national print media have long been considered two of the most potent forces underlying the homogenization of contemporary American culture. They brought national fads, accents, and trends into southern living rooms. The impact of national retailers and franchisers has been recognized less frequently, but their insensitivity to regional tastes and their reliance on homogenized menus, central purchasing, and standardized inventories have been equally destructive of regional personality. There is little room here for men in overalls sitting at country stores, drinking R. C. Colas and eating Moon Pies.

The southern landscape has not been altered uniformly. Change has been most rapid in the cities, least rapid in rural areas. Traditional cuisine, regional vernacular housing, and southern values are increasingly difficult to find in Atlanta. The skylines and street scenes of Atlanta, Dallas, and Houston look much the same as those in other 20th-century American cities. Their landscapes are dominated by department stores, restaurants, specialty retailers, malls, and fast-food chains that strive for national identities. Even southern and non-southern street signs are alike.

Simultaneously, small towns with such names as Union Point, Jackson, Haralson, and Magnolia are enduring slow deaths as stores close, buildings crumble, and weeds find their way through the cracks in the streets. Thousands of small towns are passing from the landscape because they no longer seem to have a role in modern society; paved roads, automobiles, and increased ties to national culture have seen to that. There has been some return to the small town, but mainly as a residential retreat within urban commuter zones.

Industry is thriving in the South. North Carolina has the third highest percentage of industrial workers in the nation. Small, labor-intensive factories increasingly are coming to the region's towns in search of cheap labor. These towns are transformed, too, as traditional courthouse-square business districts are bypassed by national retail and food chains that prefer suburban, automobile-oriented commercial strips. New subdivisions and houses fashioned from images in *House Beautiful* and *Family Circle* spring up helter-skelter around the towns' edges.

The rural scene has undergone even more radical change. Dispersed communities focused on country stores are changing as the rural residents increasingly seek nonfarm occupations and commute to jobs in town. Traditional housing is rapidly giving way to the new southern "vernacular" architecture of Jim Walters and mobile homes.

The South's contemporary experience is a reminder that landscapes are composed of overlays of new fashions and technologies, and the cultural elements of each new era compete with those of earlier times. The new thus pushes aside the old and continually creates a new landscape.

See also ART AND ARCHITECTURE: Farm Buildings; Vernacular Architecture (Lowland South); Vernacular Architecture (Upland South); ENVIRONMENT articles; ETHNIC LIFE: Caribbean Influence; Indian Cultural Contributions; Mountain Culture; / Cajuns; Cubans; FOLKLIFE: House Types; / Dogtrot; I House; Pyramidal House; Saddlebag House; Shotgun House; HISTORY AND MANNERS: Foodways; / Beverages; LANGUAGE: Names, Place; MUSIC: Country Music; Gospel Music, Black; Gospel Music, White

Richard Pillsbury
Georgia State University

Thomas R. Ford, ed., *The Southern Appalachian Region: A Survey* (1962); Raymond D. Gastil, *Cultural Regions of the United States* (1975); Henry Glassie, *Pattern in the Material Folk Culture of the Eastern United States* (1968); J. Fraser Hart, *The Southeastern United States* (1967); Sam B. Hilliard, *Hog Meat and Hoecake: Food Supply in the Old South, 1840–1860* (1972); John Brinckerhoff Jackson, *American Space: The Centennial Years, 1865–1876* (1972), *The Southern Landscape Tradition in Texas* (1980); Terry G. Jordan, *Annals of the Association of American Geographers* (No. 4, 1967), *Texas Graveyards* (1982); D. W. Meinig, *The Shaping of America: A Geographical Perspective on 500 Years of History: Atlantic America, 1492–1800*, vol. 1 (1986); Howard W. Odum, *Southern Regions of the United States* (1936); James R. Shortridge, *Journal for the Scientific Study of Religion* (June 1977); John R. Stilgoe, *Common Landscape of America, 1580–1845* (1984); Rupert B. Vance, *Human Geography of the South: A Study of Regional Resources and Human Adequacy* (1932); Wilbur Zelinsky, *The Cultural Geography of the United States* (1973), *Social Forces* (December 1951).

Appalachia

See ETHNIC LIFE: Mountain Culture

Ethnic Geography

Many of the social systems and distinctive elements of culture that vary within the South and that collectively help distinguish the region can be explained on the basis of ethnicity. Ethnic geography explores the spatial aspects of ethnicity. Place is an important component of ethnicity, and ethnic groups exhibit territorial patterns of organization by clustering in defined areas. Ethnic groups in the South are distributed in spatial units that range from a few relatively large regional concentrations, including Mexican Americans along the borderlands of Texas, Cubans in south Florida, and Cajuns in southern Louisiana, to numerous small rural and urban enclaves scattered throughout the region.

The impact of ethnicity on the culture and landscape of the South, vis-à-vis other large regions of the country, depends to some extent upon the operational definition of *ethnic group*. Traditionally, ethnic groups have been defined strictly on the basis of common ancestry, national origins, and associated cultural traits. By this standard the South is comparatively lacking in ethnic diversity, considering that the region has attracted proportionately few foreign immigrants, especially foreign-born Caucasians, since the mid-19th century.

Many groups in the South, however, can best be characterized by traits that are essentially ethnic in nature. One of the most significant identifying elements of an ethnic group is an internalized sense of distinctiveness and an external perception of that distinctiveness. Ethnic identity is not ascriptive; it is a matter of individual and group choice. The recognition of minority status tends to foster among members of an ethnic group an intense feeling of belonging to a community.

Examples of ethnic indicators might include race, religious affiliation, ancestral or mother language, common settlement and employment patterns, political philosophy, shared literature, folklore and music, cuisine preferences, and migratory status. By these indicators blacks, American Indian tribes, mixed-blood groups, various religious sects and groups, and perhaps even selected occupational enclaves in the South may be considered—and are most likely to consider themselves—ethnic groups.

The South has been called the most "native" region of the country because most southerners trace their ancestry in the United States back to settlers who arrived before 1850, and in many cases before 1800. The South's share of the nearly 50 million immigrants who have settled in America since the beginning of the 19th century is disproportionately small. The region's inability to attract foreign immigrants has been due to limited economic opportunities, a social climate many of them found unacceptable, and a xenophobia on the part of southerners. Although ostensibly more ethnically diverse through recent immigration, the South in 1980 had fewer than 5 million first- and second-generation Americans. Moreover, well over half of these were either of Mexican or Cuban descent and resided on the geographical fringes of the region.

The relative lack of foreign immigration is coupled with the fact that the Anglo population of the South is derived overwhelmingly from one source area—northwest Europe, especially the British Isles. The black population, too, though diverse in its African ethnic origins, was rather quickly homogenized into an Afro-American mold.

The consequences of this pattern of settlement were profound, particularly in terms of the relatively uniform cultural milieu that evolved. The narrowed range of religions, for example, resulted in the South's becoming the most Protestant region of the country. This lack of ethnic diversity greatly influenced the shaping of the southern identity and southern attitudes toward both the region itself and the rest of the world. The relative cultural and social homogeneity of the South has even led some scholars to suggest that white and black southerners should be considered ethnic groups in their own right.

The lack of diversity has served to heighten ethnic groups' awareness of their minority status. This has encouraged such groups to settle in well-defined, often small-scale concentrations, thereby increasing their external visibility. Residential segregation likewise tends to increase social interaction and reinforces institutional differences between the group and the larger society, thus perpetuating distinctive ethnic identities. Although ethnic exclusiveness is a source of mutual support and cultural security, it may also lead to conflict through clannish suspicion and distrust of outsiders.

Ethnic groups are the keepers of distinctive cultural traditions. From the Germans of the Ozarks and the hill country of Texas to the Hungarians in Tangipahoa Parish, La., to the mixed-blood Lumbees of North Carolina, ethnic groups foster the continuity of culture and of social systems. These traditions are reinforced through friendships, family ties, business contacts, church affiliations, and social activities. Periodic celebrations and festivals, both secular and religious, also strengthen these ties.

The nonmaterial elements of culture, including language, religion, music, symbols, beliefs and values, along with cuisine preferences, are generally retained longer than most material elements of culture. Yet land-survey systems, settlement patterns, agricultural practices, and architectural preferences, among other material elements, may persist indefinitely among certain groups; they provide graphic imprints of an ethnic group's tenure in an area.

While ethnic groups persist in the South, they also change through the process of acculturation. The Scotch-Irish, for example, have been completely assimilated, existing only in the memories of their descendants. As migration continues to add new ethnic groups to the South, ethnicity continues to enrich the life and landscape of the region.

See also BLACK LIFE: Immigrants and Blacks; ETHNIC LIFE articles; RELIGION: Ethnic Protestantism

James R. Curtis
University of Miami

Russel L. Gerlach, *Immigrants in the Ozarks: A Study in Ethnic Geography* (1976); Terry G. Jordan, *German Seed in Texas Soil: Immigrant Farmers in Nineteenth-Century Texas* (1966); William Lynwood Montell, *Saga of Coe Ridge: A Study in Oral History* (1970); Lauren C. Post, *Cajun Sketches: From the Prairies of Southwest Louisiana* (1962); George B. Tindall, *The Ethnic Southerners* (1976); Wilbur Zelinsky, *The Cultural Geography of the United States* (1973).

Expatriates and Exiles

Basil Ransome, a character in Henry James's *The Bostonians* (1886), left his native South after the Civil War and headed for New York City "with fifty dollars in his pocket and a gnawing hunger in his heart." He exemplified what Thomas Wolfe described as the southerner consumed by an "eternal wandering, moving, questing, loneliness, homesickness." The uprooted southerner, Wolfe's Ishmael, has been a culturally important figure since the Civil War. Despite the notable southern attachment to localism, mobility has also been a characteristic of 20th-century southerners, but perhaps because of the power of memory and of place, emigrant southerners have continued to ponder the region and its meaning.

"Exile" is used here in the *Webster's* definition of "voluntary absence from one's country or home." Many of the thousands of Confederates who left the region after the Civil War did so for political reasons, as did many blacks at that same time and since, who left to escape the South's racial system. These were political emigrés, of a sort, but they were part of the broader phenomenon of individuals who left the region for economic, intellectual, or social reasons, as well as political ones, and yet took their southern identity and customs with them. White working-class emigrants and black emigrants established communities in northern cities, but the focus here is on business leaders, professionals, writers, scholars, teachers, painters, sculptors, and other intellectual and gifted southerners who left the region, causing a "brain drain" of talent out of the South.

In the aftermath of the Civil War, prominent former

Confederates headed in all directions, to all parts of the United States and to other areas of the world. Unhappy with postwar conditions and fearful of the Reconstruction future, they left the South seeking better opportunities for financial, social, and artistic success. Confederate cabinet member Judah P. Benjamin went to England and had a successful legal career there. Diplomat John Slidell moved to Paris and was in England when he died. Former vice president John C. Breckinridge and Confederate general Jubal Early moved to Canada. Three Confederate generals (C. W. Field, William C. Loring, and Henry W. Sibley) went to Egypt to help train that country's army, and a few Lost Cause refugees wound up in Japan and Australia.

Between 4,000 and 6,000 Confederates immigrated to Central America, with Mexico attracting the largest number. Several thousand southerners set up colonies in Mexico, mostly at Carlota and Cordova, between Mexico City and Vera Cruz. Matthew Fontaine Maury, Confederate admiral and an oceanographer, served as commissioner of immigration to Mexican Emperor Maximilian's government and helped to launch a group exodus from the South. At least 17 Confederate generals were part of this migration, including Edmund Kirby-Smith, Thomas C. Hindman, Sterling Price, and John B. Magruder. Other Confederates sought refuge in Honduras and on Caribbean islands such as Jamaica and Cuba.

Between 2,500 and 4,000 southerners reached South America, most of them before 1870 and most in Brazilian agricultural colonies. The Brazilian government, like that of Mexico, encouraged the immigration, offering cheap land, advertising in southern periodicals, and providing agents to promote and facilitate the migration. The Reverend Ballard S. Dunn of New Orleans proved to be an especially effective lobbyist for migration, with his book *Brazil, The Home for Southerners* (1866). Four areas of Brazil attracted southerners: Santeram, on the Amazon River; Rio Doce; Iguape, or "Lizzieland," as Ballard Dunn named it in honor of a daughter; and a cluster of three colonies (Campo, Retiro, and Villa America) in the São Paulo region.

Most of the immigrants to Latin America had returned to the United States by the 1870s, but about 20 percent of southern emigrants to Brazil settled there permanently, a greater percentage than in other areas of Latin America. Many descendants of Confederate immigrants to Brazil have lost any sense of their southern ancestry, but some still retain southern identity. Americana, Brazil, has 400 or so surviving descendants, and 440 tombstones, marked with English inscriptions, which mark the graves of ex-Confederates. A Fraternity of American Descendants meets quarterly in the cemetery and holds a potluck dinner. The menu in 1984 included such down-home fare as fried chicken, biscuits, corn bread, pecan pie, watermelon, and soda pop. As well as speaking Portuguese, many of these Confederate descendants can still speak the southern English dialect of their ancestors. Their association sells Confederate-flag decals to raise money.

A larger number of southern Confederates went north and west within the United States, but until recently scholars have been less interested in studying their lives than those of the more exotic migrants to foreign lands. "Texas fever" hit the South in the 1870s, and thousands of freedmen and whites went there seeking anonymity and a fresh start. Many became cowboys and participated in the postwar cattle industry. California also proved a popular spot for southern emigrants, but northern cities such as New York City, Philadelphia, and Boston attracted even more southerners. Most of these migrants were young—mostly under 35 years of age—and well educated. Many had lived in the North at times before the war or had been frequent visitors there. The key years for emigration were 1865–68, with a sharp drop after 1871. According to the leading scholar of this movement, Daniel E. Sutherland, 57 percent of a group of 298 subjects who have left detailed records remained in the North after going there.

Southern landowners who had fallen on hard times went north, as did professional and business people who hoped to find a better market than the postwar South for goods and services. Fear of the future motivated many of them. Northern schools, especially medical colleges, attracted those wanting to further their education. War widows were frequent visitors, sometimes for extended periods. Painters, sculptors, and architects sought training and patrons. Some young southerners, like other restless rural Americans, went north to seek excitement in the region's bustling cities. Sutherland noted, however, that these emigrants "remained southern in mind and heart."

New York City held the greatest attraction of all northern cities for these southerners. It was traditionally a gathering spot for southern financiers and vacationers and a hotbed of pro-southern sentiment during the war. As a result of earlier contacts, friends, relatives, and business acquaintances in the city provided assistance to postwar exiles such as Thomas F. Ryan and John H. Inman, who became financial magnates, and Charles B. Rouss, a former Confederate private who by the 1880s had become a leading wholesale and retail merchant. Roger A. Pryor in law, John A. Wyeth in medicine, William R. O'Donovan in art, and George C. Eggleston in literature were all former Confederates who made their reputations in the North.

Southerners in the North were a self-conscious group. They associated with each other, organized societies, went to church together, and assisted each other in time of need. Proud of their heritage, they donated money to the construction of universities, churches, and public buildings in the South. Many expatriates were sensitive to northern slights and scornful of Yankees. Though some were eager to exploit northerners, they nonetheless played a role in sectional reconciliation. Northerners generally accepted southerners in their midst, and personal contact mitigated political prejudices. Northern businessmen also used southerners with old names and admirable war records as liaisons to win back the southern market for their products.

The New York Southern Society, founded in 1886 by southerners who had succeeded in the North, preserved relics of the Old South, worked toward sectional reconciliation, and helped normalize business relations between the regions. The society welcomed New Yorkers of southern birth or heritage. Southern businessmen were allowed to enjoy the benefits of the club while in town. The society was more a New South organization than an unreconstructed Old South group. It canonized Washington and Jefferson more than Lee and Davis. It typically commemorated Washington's birthday, for example, in a gaudy manner, appropriate to the era. Banjo players provided music, members dined on dishes including Old Dominion Fried Hominy, and they toasted sectional harmony with large amounts of Magnolia Punch.

Black southerners are another, larger group that has frequently been in exile from its land of birth. Black migration out of the South in the early 20th century had important meaning for the emergence of a mature and distinct black artistic and intellectual tradition. Writers such as Richard Wright (Mississippi), Zora Neale Hurston (Florida), and James Weldon Johnson (Florida); scholars such as Arna Bontemps (Louisiana) and Carter Woodson (Virginia); performers such as Ma Rainey (Georgia), Bessie Smith (Tennessee), Leontyne Price (Mississippi), Roland Hayes (Georgia), Fletcher Henderson (Georgia), and later, Dizzy Gillespie (South Carolina), Lester Young (Louisiana), and Thelonious Monk (North Carolina)—all were southern born yet made their cultural contributions outside the region. Each took advantage of opportunities in the North that were denied under the South's repressive racial system. Also, the South's paucity of cultural and intellectual resources did not provide support for many kinds of cultural achievements for either race.

The Harlem Renaissance of the 1920s was an outpouring of energy in black literature, music, dance, and entertainment. It followed the great wave of black migration to the North during and after World War I, and many of the leaders of this renaissance were southern born and utilized southern settings and themes. Sterling Brown's collection of poems was called *Southern Road* (1932); Arna Bontemps's *Black Thunder* (1936) was based on Gabriel Prosser's 1821 slave revolt in South Carolina; Zora Neale Hurston's play *Color Struck* (1925) was set in a segregated railroad coach in the South; and Jean Toomer's *Cane* (1923), a series of poems, short stories, and vignettes, captured the life of black people in Georgia lumber camps of the 1890s.

It was natural that black intellectuals, many of whom were born in the South, would turn to the region for material. Exile from the region gave them both perspective and the freedom to work realistically with this material. Earlier black writers, though, had employed genteel literary traditions, frequently writing stories of well-off northern blacks. In the aftermath of the wave of black migration during and after World War I, intellectuals "discovered" the culture of southern black folk. Ohio-born Langston Hughes recalled that his view of black culture was shaped by seeing migrants from the South coming into and through Ohio. Southern blacks in exile, then, gained an opportunity for cultural achievement, using as their raw material their own personal and group experiences from the South.

The maturation of 20th-century southern intellectual life in general has depended on the exile experience. Critic Louis D. Rubin, Jr., argues that the writers of the Southern Literary Renaissance were alienated from their communities, partly because of time spent out of the South. All of the contributors to *I'll Take My Stand* (1930), the preeminent statement of southern Agrarianism, had spent time out of the South; Robert Penn Warren's essay for that volume was written while he was in England. Their perspective gained on the region came from leaving it. Future novelists and poets grew up in the traditional South of the 1900s and 1910s, went off to college, but did not return home after graduation. Education and living away from their communities distanced them from their origins. Some left the country. William Faulkner took a walking tour through France and Italy in the summer of 1925. Katherine Anne Porter worked for the revolutionary government in Mexico in that decade. Thomas Wolfe traveled extensively in Europe, and especially Germany. These southern writers were not, however, a part of the lost-generation exile experience, which centered in France and rejected tradition and the general idea of regionalism.

More important than European exile, almost all the South's major writers in this period went north at some point. Thomas Wolfe, growing up in Asheville, N.C., dreamed of "the golden vision of the city," as he says in *The Web and the Rock* (1939). The city was a place of escape and of fulfillment. Southern literature is filled with descriptions of youthful southerners loose without moorings in the big city: Peyton Loftis in Styron's *Lie Down in Darkness*; Eugene McLain wandering through San Francisco in Welty's *The Golden Apples*; and Quentin Compson in Faulkner's *The Sound and the Fury*, who wanders to and eventually commits suicide in far-off Cambridge, Mass. All are southerners far from home, estranged from their region, and yet also alienated from the city. Most of these southern writers, however, did not remain in northern cities. Only Wolfe, the great American poet of exile, remained away. But those who returned south did not return to their hometowns. They went to university towns or metropolitan areas. Those few who did return to their home communities, like Faulkner and Welty, were only physically there; they were spiritual exiles, living in what Rubin calls "the faraway country," the South of their imaginations.

Allen Tate stayed in the South in the 1930s, convinced that southerners who left the South "sacrifice some great part of their deepest heritage." Nevertheless, many of his Agrarian colleagues, those seemingly most convinced of the need to preserve the South as a bastion against modernism, did eventually leave the region and move north. Writing in 1950, Richard M. Weaver admitted "a fairly general exodus of Southern Agrarians to the North," to the big cities and the renowned universities. "The truth about the Agrarians is that they were becoming homeless," he said. "The South no longer had a place for them." A long process of alienation was completed with the move north. Intellectuals who moved north could at least pursue their work in freedom. As Weaver noted, they were "regional expatriates," but in their new home "their ideas are negotiable" and "their convictions did not clash with local immaturities." The Agrarians were engaged in a worldwide battle between humanism and materialism. Instead of a flight of Agrarians, it was a "strategic withdrawal." Weaver betrayed a certain bitterness because the South had been lost. He applied to the region Stephen Dedalus's phrase about Ireland—"an old sow that eats her farrow."

Willie Morris, who is Thomas Wolfe's successor as poet of the southern exile experience, testified to the existence of an "exile" mentality in more recent southerners living outside the South. He wrote in his 1967 memoir *North Toward Home* of "New York's burgeoning and implacable Southern expatriate community," and he suggested that Mississippi and a few other southern states were the only states in the nation that "had produced a genuine set of exiles, almost in the European sense: alienated from home yet forever drawn back to it." Morris recalled the importance of the exile experience to a growing understanding of a common background and interest with black southerners.

Sociologist John Shelton Reed has argued for the importance of exile in nurturing cultural nationalism among southerners. By standing at a distance from a culture, one achieves perspective on it. The experience of the provincial youth in the city reminds those away from their homeland that they are from a culture viewed as inferior. Cultural nationalists engage in "the politicization of homesickness," nurturing their memory of the homeland and forgetting the divisions and disagreements back home. Being aware of people with different ways makes one, at times, appreciate the ways left behind. Southerners have been frequently reminded of being southern. The accent has marked one as identifiably southern, and non-southerners reacted accordingly by treating those with an accent as different. Many southern whites have been assumed to be racially bigoted. Those non-southerners who themselves are prejudiced may treat all white southerners as kindred spirits, while northern liberals may force white southerners to assume the personal burden for all the sins of the region. Southern black intellectuals living in the North have complained of being treated as "rubes" by northern blacks and of hypocritical whites who spoke of equality but distanced themselves from personal relations with blacks. Looking back on his own education in Cambridge, Mass., in the 1960s, Reed has written that northerners "would apparently believe anything at all about the South, provided only that it was weird." The result was that southerners "almost had to think about the South." Many southerners apparently have discovered or intensified their regional identity while living away from the region.

Educated, exiled southerners outside the region frequently, when meeting, discuss where they are from and whether they have common friends or even family. They may complain about the coldness of the North, and of northerners, and exaggerate the legendary southern hospitality. The ritual of food has always been important as a token of retaining and renewing the southern identity in exile. Morris has recalled gathering with two southern black couples, the Ralph Ellisons and Albert Murrays, for a traditional southern New Year's Day dinner in 1967 in Murray's Harlem apartment, feasting on bourbon, collard greens, black-eyed peas, hamhocks, and corn bread. Morris, like other southerners, discovered the importance of food as a shared ritual of a common regional identity with blacks. He observed within New York that only in Harlem could a "southern white boy greet the New Year with the good-luck food he had had as a child."

The South's economic backwardness has had a discernible effect on the intellectual life of the region by promoting the exile of its intellectuals and artists. The loss of scholars, artists, entertainers, and others with special talents has been an enormous "brain drain" from the region. A study of the 1932–33 edition of *Who's Who in America* showed that of the 6,015 persons listed there as born in the South, 2,229 were living in other sections. The depletion was largest among editors, authors, educators, lawyers, judges, businessmen, religious workers, medical doctors, politicians, diplomats, army and navy officers, and actors and actresses. The superior opportunities for employment outside the region were singled out as the main reason for the loss of talented personnel. Another study in 1949 found similar findings but concluded that the South was retaining more of its talented offspring. The categories of loss have remained the same over the years, although with improved graduate and professional education in the region, the number of those remaining has increased.

Charles Reagan Wilson
University of Mississippi

Wilson Gee, *Social Forces* (March 1937); Eugene C. Harter, *The Lost Colony of the Confederacy* (1985); Lewis M. Killian, *White Southerners* (1970); Willie Morris, *North Toward Home* (1967); John Shelton Reed, *One South: An Ethnic Approach to Regional Culture* (1982); Daniel E. Sutherland, *Journal of Southern History* (August 1981); Richard M. Weaver, *Sewanee Review* (Autumn 1950).

Foodways, Geography of

The mechanisms of the natural environment and the historical processes of culture link food to place. Together, ecology and culture account for the diversity of foodways in the South. Early settlers carried with them knowledge, practice, and predisposition concerning food. Those traditions were usually derived from Europe, but they were also filtered through other parts of the New World such as Acadian Canada. Native Americans provided new culinary inspiration and strategies. Afro-Americans, in slavery and freedom, blended African food preferences, techniques, and even vocabulary with those of the predominantly European agricultural and urban populations.

For settlers, the South's natural habitats, whether coastal or interior, mountain, piedmont, or delta, established certain ground rules of availability and feasibility that tempered food traditions. Virtually everywhere, for instance, seemed appropriate for raising hogs and corn, two common features of agriculture and diet throughout the South. On the other hand, certain foods are closely tied to particular parts of the South because of ecological factors unique to those areas. Conch salad and conch chowder are known only in south Florida precisely for that reason. In comparatively recent times, agribusiness, contemporary food-marketing techniques, and the general blurring of regional boundaries—which is sometimes counterbalanced by the rise of regional self-consciousness—have all had their effects on the southern geography of food.

Corn and pork, two staples of the southern diet, illustrate the ways in which food varies with locality. Ground into meal, corn is the source of a variety of breads. Spoonbread, a puddinglike corn bread, is common in Tidewater Virginia and not unknown in Kentucky, at least in the Bluegrass. In south central Kentucky and parts of Tennessee, cornmeal is mixed in a batter and fried on a griddle, where it becomes corncakes, hoecakes, or just plain corn bread, depending on whom you ask. Mixed with onion and other seasonings and fried, cornmeal is the main component of hush puppies, a ubiquitous accompaniment for fried fish, especially catfish, a creature whose culinary acceptance appears to be spreading steadily northward from its original Deep South base. Bourbon is, of course, a corn-based distillation. Only Kentucky produces whiskey by that name, although other well-known brands of corn-based sour-mash whiskeys are produced in Tennessee. Bourbon is most popular in the Upper South, although it is also the most commonly consumed hard liquor in virtually the entire South.

The preparation of pork, particularly hams and barbecue, is clearly related to place. If in the process of curing, hams are hung from six months to two or more years, the resulting country ham is likely to come from either the vicinity of Smithfield, Va., or central Kentucky. Barbecue, which refers both to cooking techniques and to ways of serving the result, is so closely tied to place that for many it seems to serve as an emblem of home. Wherever it is found, barbecue is generally meat cooked slowly over embers and basted with a sauce. In North Carolina it must be cooked so long that it falls apart, and it is supposed to be served in shreds in a sandwich on a hamburger bun. Many North Carolinians add coleslaw to the sandwich as a topping for the meat, illustrating that food traditions may also involve "grammars" or rules concerning appropriate food combinations. In south central Kentucky, barbecue may be slices of pork shoulder, bones-in, dipped in a peppery sauce and served on slices of white bread. In parts of Texas, sausage links are barbecued. And, of course, there are parts of the South in which barbecue is not pork. Texans eat barbecued beef brisket; in western Kentucky, mutton is the preferred meat. The International Barbecue Festival, in Owensboro, Ky., features mutton and chicken.

The potent combination of ecology and culture has yielded a number of very distinctive regional cuisines in the South. The best known of these, and perhaps the most distinctive of all, is that of the southwest Louisiana Cajuns. Journalist Calvin Trillin, the chronicler of regional American food traditions, has written a number of essays on Cajun foodways covering the local crawfish festivals, the liberal use of various sorts of peppers, and the now celebrated and generally familiar repertoire of Cajun food traditions.

In south Florida, Cuban immigrants have created another strongly distinctive set of food traditions, a more contemporary example of the same sorts of historical circumstances and cultural processes that underlie Cajun food traditions. Cuban sandwiches—long, narrow loaves of bread stuffed with roast pork, pickles, and other ingredients—are commonly available in south Florida, as is thick, rich Cuban coffee and the black bean soup that merits those same adjectives. And one should also note the Tex-Mex cooking of south Texas, another Spanish-speaking cuisine with a distinct southern accent. In these parts of the South, food is clearly emblematic of the region's plural cultures.

Even when recipes remain the same from place to place, vocabulary may vary. In the Deep South, the term *battercakes* refers to what in the Upper South is generally called pancakes. Reportedly, *flitters* are pancakes in southern Kentucky. Vocabulary may reflect settlement patterns. The distribution of the terms *smearcase* and *kochcase* in Texas provide a link to the history of German settlements in Texas. Elsewhere in Texas the term *cottage cheese* suffices.

Some southern foods have spread far beyond their original localities. If the "grits belt" was once thought to have covered roughly the same southern territory as the Bible Belt, President Jimmy Carter from Plains, Ga., helped nationalize that southern breakfast food, at least temporarily. A number of fast-food chains have recently begun serving biscuits for breakfast, first in the South where the practice is well known, and now through much of the country. Population shifts have also helped bring southern food traditions to much of the nation. The large out-migration of Afro-Americans to the North and Midwest brought soul food, a combination of distinctly African-American and regional southern culinary practices and preferences, to most of the cities of the Snowbelt. The geography of southern cooking, then, extends far beyond the South.

See also ENVIRONMENT: / Catfish; Collards; Shellfish; FOLKLIFE: / Gumbo; Okra; HISTORY AND MANNERS: Cookbooks; Foodways; / Barbecue; Beverages; Chitlins; Country Ham; Fried Chicken; Goo Goo Clusters; Grits; Mint Julep; Moon Pies; Moonshine and Moonshining; Soul Food; Whiskey

Burt Feintuch
Western Kentucky University

Linda Keller Brown and Kay Mussell, eds., *Ethnic and Regional Foodways in the United States* (1984); Charles Camp, *American Quarterly* (No. 3, 1982), *Journal of American Culture* (Fall 1979); Floyd M. Henderson, in *This Remarkable Continent: An Atlas of United States and Canadian Society and Cultures*, ed. John F. Rooney, Jr., et al. (1982); Sam B. Hilliard, *Hog Meat and Hoecake: Food Supply in the Old South, 1840–1860* (1972);

Calvin Trillin, *American Fried: Adventures of a Happy Eater* (1974); Eugene Walter, *American Cooking: Southern Style* (1971).

Indians and the Landscape

The southern American Indians at the time of the Europeans' arrival represented a population of about 1 million. These Indians spoke distinct languages of the Algonkian, Iroquoian, Siouan, Yuchean, Muskogean, Tunican, and Caddoan stocks. A short list of the better documented tribes speaking those languages includes the Powhatan, Shawnee, Tuscarora, Cherokee, Catawba, Yuchi, Choctaw, Seminole, Natchez, Tunica, Chitimacha, and the Natchitoches. After decimation by European diseases and forced movement west by secretly arranged treaties and violent expulsions, the Indian population in most of the South vanished. Although today their numbers in the region have grown to almost 195,000, this is a mere shadow of their historic presence. Indeed, that number is but a small percentage of the modern southern population. More salient than their numbers has been the sustaining cultural impact upon the Europeans who settled in the South. Indian trails became traces and eventually highways, their wild and domesticated foods became staples in the southerner's diet, their place names enhanced the southern landscape, and their ancient earthen monuments are now preserved as parks. Rarely, if ever, has one race intruded into the kingdom of another without drawing upon a share of the native culture, and European settlers in the South were no exception.

Even if most non-Indian southerners do not personally encounter their Indian compatriots in daily activities, they do constantly hear Indian words. A number of characteristically southern words are, in reality, of Indian origin. A few of the more familiar examples would include the words *bayou, hammock, hominy, opossum,* and *persimmon.* The very names of half the southern states are of Indian derivation: Alabama, Arkansas, Kentucky, Mississippi, Tennessee, and Texas. The same is true of the names of countless cities and towns (e.g., Chattanooga and Tupelo), mountains (e.g., Appalachian), valleys (e.g., Shenandoah), rivers (e.g., Monongahela, Atchafalaya), lakes (e.g., Okeechobee), swamps (e.g., Okeefenokee), islands (e.g., Assateague), and bays (e.g., Chesapeake). Indian place names are of value for their characteristic euphony, and they lie at the root of much historic research. In innumerable instances the native place names are the most valuable descriptors of locations and landmarks as they existed before European settlers altered geographical characteristics. For example, few people think of the city name *Chattanooga* as meaning "a rock rising to a point," yet this Indian name clearly applies to Lookout Mountain nearby.

The attraction to nature is another intangible Indian contribution to southern culture. The traditional southern affection for the pleasures, adventures, and freedom of the outdoors or backwoods was learned from Native Americans. This was not a trait brought from Europe by the majority of the peasants who settled in the South in the 17th and 18th centuries. In fact, few of them could have experienced such freedom under the authoritative oligarchies that prevailed in their native countries. Southerners' love of the outdoors might well be seen as a legacy of the Indian prowess that the colonists learned from and developed. It is ironic that this legacy is so prominent in the South, a region that exerted much energy to rid itself of its Indian habitants.

In the realm of tangible items the innumerable wild and domesticated food plants known to the Indians aided the European explorers and settlers and then became staples in the diets of populations worldwide. Cardinal among the food plants was the Native American cultigen maize, or corn, which has proved to be the favorite food for both man and animal in the South and the most notable staple in the southern diet. While other regions of the nation consumed wheat bread, the mainstay of the southern diet was corn bread. Corn, ground into meal, is not only used to make bread; it is concocted into a myriad of recipes and served as pone, muffins, biscuits, corn dodgers, hoecake, hush puppies, mush, sourings, griddle cakes, and waffles. Corn is also converted to hominy and grits. Nor can one forget to honor the contribution of corn to the manufacture of two particularly southern beverages, sour-mash whiskey and "moonshine."

The traditional beliefs, languages, crafts, and lifeways of the South's Native Americans have broadly influenced and immeasurably enriched the culture of the South.

See also BLACK LIFE: Indians and Blacks; ETHNIC LIFE: Indian Cultural Contributions; HISTORY AND MANNERS: Foodways; LANGUAGE: Names, Place

Robert W. Neuman
Louisiana State University

Alexander P. Chamberlain, *Proceedings of the American Antiquarian Society* (1905); Felix S. Cohen, *The American Scholar* (Spring 1952); Sam B. Hilliard, *Hog Meat and Hoecake: Food Supply in the Old South, 1840–1860* (1972); George R. Steward, *Names on the Land* (1945).

Land Division

A number of different survey systems were used in the American South, including the "metes and bounds" system, the "state rectangular" systems, the "French long lot" system, and the "U.S. township and range" system. Each of these helped shape the distinctive physical and cultural landscape of the South.

The metes and bounds survey system was introduced from Europe. It utilized natural boundary markers such as trees, streams, rocks, and other features. Very few of the areas where it was employed were surveyed before settlement. It created a series of very irregular and unsystematic landholding patterns. Surveyors made every effort to lay out these lots in rectangular shapes, but these patterns generally failed to survive through time. The sizes of the holdings were heterogeneous on the landscape but were usually between 200 and 1,000 acres. The metes and bounds survey system was indiscriminate at best. The system created incalculable lawsuits and challenges concerning property boundaries as well as actual land ownership. This unsystematic survey was employed in the southern Atlantic Seaboard colonies as far south as Georgia, where massive land frauds occurred.

The metes and bounds survey system extended westward in Georgia to the Oconee River. It was also utilized in some river valleys of the lower Gulf South, notably in the alluvial Mississippi Valley as well as in east Texas. Other vestiges of this survey system can be found scattered throughout the region. The states of Tennessee and Kentucky also employed the metes and bounds survey system.

One of the most spectacular and successful state-controlled rectangular survey systems employed in the American South was implemented in the early 19th century. Between 1805 and 1832 a state-controlled land-lottery system was established in Georgia, and a series of six lotteries was held. By this method the western two-thirds of Georgia was made available to the public at little or no expense to settlers. Each of the lotteries consisted of land districts containing rectangular lots that were surveyed before settlement and then offered to the citizens by public lottery. Several town sites were selected and surveyed at strategic locations, and town lots offered at public auctions. The individual land-lot sizes varied in different lotteries, but an effort was made to maintain rectangular land districts and land lots. The land-lot sizes in Georgia included lots of 40, 160, 202½, 250 and 490 acres. The land district lines in Georgia were primarily surveyed north-south and east-west. A similar state rectangular survey system was later used in portions of central and west Texas as well.

An unusual and not so well known survey system found essentially in the Gulf South and concentrated in the state of Louisiana is the French long lot system. There is evidence, however, of the utilization of long lot surveys in Tennessee, North Carolina, and Texas. The major concentrations of long lots in Louisiana are found in the Mississippi alluvial valley and related bayous, the Atchafalaya basin, and the Red River Valley. The long lot survey lines were laid out perpendicular to stream channels and roads; in southern Louisiana most were surveyed perpendicular to water courses. Usually the depth of the lot was three or four times greater than the width. Most of the lots were roughly rectangular in shape; a few were true rectangles. By surveying at right angles to stream courses, landowners were given access to a variety of environmental zones. They had access to the water courses, the well-drained lands along the levee, pasture lands, and woodland swamp areas.

The fourth major survey system used in the South was the U.S. township and range survey, which was initiated in the later 18th century in northeastern Ohio. The basic unit of measurement was a township or an area of 36 square miles. The survey began with a zero base line and a zero north-south coordinate; principal meridian units six miles in distance were then measured north and south of the base line and east and west of the principal meridian. These units were then designated Township one north (T1N) and Township one south (T1S) from the zero baseline. Ranges were designated Range one east (R1E) and Range one west (R1W) of the principal meridian. Each of these townships was then subdivided into 36 sections of 640 acres each. These sections were numbered 1 through 36. Section number 1 was always located in the northeast corner of the township and section 36 in the southeast corner of the township.

Because the range lines were in fact meridians that converge as they extend northward, adjustments were made to prevent reduction in township widths. There was a total of four base lines and seven principal meridians used in the South. This survey system was superimposed on earlier surveys in the states of Florida, Alabama, Mississippi, Louisiana, and Arkansas. However, in many instances prior survey lines were honored and maintained. This was especially true in the long lot regions of Louisiana. Essentially, the major advantages of the township and range survey system were that land records were more nearly correct and more easily accessible to the public.

Gerald L. Holder
Sam Houston State University

Vernon Carstensen, ed., *The Public Lands: Studies in the History of the Public Domain* (1963); Everett Dick, *The Dixie Frontier: A Social History of the Southern Frontier from the First Transmontane Beginnings to the Civil War* (1948); Edward M. Douglas, *Boundaries, Areas, Geographic Centers, and Altitudes of the United States and the Several States*, Geological Survey Bulletin 817 (1930); Sam B. Hilliard, *Geographical Review* (October 1982), *Studies in the Social Sciences*, vol. 12, (1973); Gerald L. Holder, *Pioneer America* (September 1982); Hildegard Binder Johnston, *Order upon the Land* (1976); Roy M. Robbins, *Our Landed Heritage, The Public Domain, 1776–1970* (2d ed., 1976); Norman J. G. Thrower, *Original Survey and Land Subdivision* (1966); Payson J. Treat, *The National Land System, 1785–1820* (1910).

Land Use

In its most general form, land use in the South may be viewed from the perspective of an Upland South and a Lowland South. The Upland South includes much of the Appalachian Highland and the Ozark-Ouachita Highland. These hilly to mountainous areas with steep slopes and poor soils have rarely supported an intensive and profitable agriculture. The predominant land-use pattern has been that of small, independently owned and operated farms on which woodlands and pastures served as low-quality grazing space for small livestock herds. Such limited farming enterprises, even with their provisional crops, have provided a meager living. Often the owners of such farms have had to seek supplemental work in forestry, mining, or manufacturing firms.

The Lower South includes the Atlantic and Gulf

Coastal Plain and the outer Piedmont. It possesses the best of the southern agricultural resources—especially on the inner Coastal Plain from southern Virginia to southeastern Alabama and Mississippi, the Tennessee Valley of northern Alabama, the Mississippi Delta, the black prairies of Texas, and the Gulf Coastal prairies of Louisiana and Texas. These regions have provided the resources for the traditional cotton and tobacco crops, and, to a lesser extent, the sugar and rice crops. Currently they support such diverse crops as corn, soybeans, peanuts, cotton, tobacco, and rice, and they provide excellent pastures.

Land-use patterns emerge from the interactions of a given culture system with a physical habitat. Changes in the physical-cultural milieu within which these interactions occur induce change in the organization and structuring of land use. Such has certainly been the case in the American South, where for the past half century changes in land-use patterns have reflected the economic, social, and technological changes that have engulfed the region. Two broad and encompassing events provide a perspective for understanding recent developments in southern land use.

The first is an agricultural revolution originating in the early decades of this century. Developments such as the boll weevil infestation; agricultural depressions; erosion problems; competition for labor; rising expectations; genetic, chemical, and mechanical advances in agricultural technology; federal agricultural programs; and market forces, all in their own persistent manner, have changed land-use patterns. The imprint of this revolution on the landscape was widely evident by the post–World War II years.

Substantial areas within the South have experienced declining use of agricultural land, particularly cleared land on farms. The entire Piedmont and adjacent segments of the Coastal Plain, the Appalachian Highland of eastern Kentucky, and the interior highlands of Arkansas and northern Louisiana all experienced this loss. The cropland losses can be attributed to modest physical resources, federal programs, and the loss of competitive ability with respect to particular crops. Where agriculture has retained vitality the cropland has often been converted to the production of alternate crops, such as soybeans, corn, peanuts, and winter wheat. Agriculture has become decidedly more diversified. Other cropland has given way to forest or pasture—with terraces the only visible evidence of former cropland use. Indeed, forestry has become the single most common component of southern land-use patterns.

Sixty-two percent of all land area in the South is forested. Nearly 75 percent of this land is privately owned as woodland on farms or simply forested tracts. Nineteen percent of the forest land is owned by the forest industry and the remainder by national and state agencies. Though large forested tracts are owned by private corporations and the federal government, most forest land remains under the control and ownership of small holders; the average parcel is 66 acres. The quality of forest land is highly variable because of differences in management practices. Paradoxically, however, even though vast areas are forested and have experienced woodland expansion, other areas such as the lower Mississippi Valley and southwest Georgia have witnessed forest clearing for expansion of agriculture. Adaptation of modern irrigation technology has made some southern lands more valuable for agriculture.

A second major influence on land-use change has been urbanization. The peripheries of most southern cities have experienced a shift from nonurban to urban land use. The "growth zone" surrounding the city shows a curious juxtaposition of old and new patterns of land use. The edges of southern cities now extend far into the countryside—blurring the once-distinct rural-urban boundary and rendering the terms virtually obsolete. Some southerners have chosen to retain a rural environment for residence, and this has increased not only the rural nonfarm population but also the growth of retailing and services in response to that market. Many nonmetropolitan residents commute to metropolitan work sites. This pattern is an outgrowth of new settlement patterns and modern transportation, and it has become extensive throughout the South, reflecting and reinforcing the continued change in nonmetropolitan land use.

The use of land for nonagricultural and nonforestry purposes increasingly extends beyond the metropolitan areas. The economic revolution has focused upon small cities and towns throughout the South—in fact the nonmetropolitan location of much of southern manufacturing growth has been one of the notable features of the regional experience. Numerous towns and small cities have gained new employment opportunities as a result of major American firms locating branch plants nearby. These local employment opportunities have reversed a longstanding population loss in towns and cities where surrounding peripheries, 20 to 30 miles in extent, realize residential expansion and the growth of retailing and services.

Any attempt to envision the patterns of southern land use in the future must recognize the following forces: (1) the rate of population increase in the South will exceed the national average for the foreseeable future; (2) contemporary patterns of settlement, including urbanization and the spread of urban and quasi-urban land uses into the nonmetropolitan periphery, will continue; (3) the demand for recreational space will increase; (4) the economic growth of the past two decades will continue as part of national decentralization and southern regional development; (5) the demand for prime agricultural land will increase; and (6) the forest industry of the United States, indeed of the world, will increasingly look to the American South. The result of the foregoing can only be increased competition for use of the best southern land.

See also AGRICULTURE articles; ENVIRONMENT: Forests; Land Use; URBANIZATION: Urban Growth

James S. Fisher
University of Georgia

J. Fraser Hart, *Annals of the Association of American Geographers* (December 1978, December 1980), with Ennis L. Chestang, *Geographical Review* (October 1978); Robert G. Healy and James L. Short, *The Market for Rural Land: Trends, Issues, Poli-*

cies (1981); Merle C. Prunty and Charles S. Aiken, *Annals of the Association of American Geographers* (September 1968, June 1972).

Log Housing

Until the arrival in the backcountry South of central Europeans after 1723, notched-log construction was not popular in the region. A few log houses may have survived from the Swedish settlement in the Delaware Valley, but the distinctive traits of that area did not become those of the southern log-building tradition. The log buildings of the South were of either British or central European plan and were executed with central European techniques.

Pioneer German and Scotch-Irish settlers in the backcountry built houses much like those in the Old World. Even today, a few directly transplanted German log houses dot the Virginia Valley and the Piedmont (for example, at Winston-Salem). By the eve of the American Revolution, however, a small set of distinctively New World models had emerged. These forms became characteristic of the broad expanse of the South, spreading out to cover a million square miles between 1775 and 1835.

The forms that spread so suddenly and so extensively were six variant arrangements of a British pen, or bay, made using German methods. The basic unit was the single-pen house, an oblong, one-room house having its gables to the side, its doors on the eave front and rear, its chimney against the outside of one gable end, a wooden floor, and a foundation of piers. If built to stand alone, such a house would have measured from 16 by 20 feet to 20 by 26 feet.

Two versions of this basic pen spread, in succession, across the South. The earlier one, built of logs joined by half-dovetail notches, usually had a loft supported by joists that had been let through the front and rear walls by means of mortises. At the same tier or the next up, wall logs extended about 12 feet to the front and rear as cantilevers that supported the roof. The extension of the continuous-pitch roof permitted the plan to include a gallery in front and a room in back, both half the depth of the pen. The facade of the oldest of these had only a door, centered on the wall.

Porch on dogtrot house, Hickory Flat, Miss., 1968

The second version, which followed the first by about a generation, had walls formed by V-notched logs. Its loft, if present, was supported by joists that had merely been sharpened and wedged between logs at the front and rear. Any porch or rear room added to the V-notched pen was usually a lean-to addition, rather than space lying under a cantilever-supported roof. The front facade commonly had a single door off center, plus one window between the door and the end having the chimney.

In time these two forms blended so that later, and especially more western, versions were likely to have traits of each. The half-dovetail forms of the northern South often lacked galleries, whereas those emanating from the backcountry west of Charleston, the entry point of Caribbean immigrants, almost always had broad galleries.

To form larger houses, two pens were joined in one of three set ways. The most favored enlarged house, the dogtrot, was formed by setting two pens together along a common, central, open hallway. The other two plans involved separating the two pens either by a chimney (saddlebag) or a common wall (double pen). Any of these three types of houses may have had a gallery, loft, shed rooms, separate kitchen, dormers, or any of a host of architectural additions.

Where the owner was more successful, these two-room plans may also have been built in two stories. Such houses, known academically as "I houses," may have had one or both stories built of logs. I houses existed both with and without open dogtrots, central halls, and central chimneys.

Log construction extended also to the outbuildings. Log barns were built of various arrangements of units, known in this case as "cribs." The single-crib barn was an ancient, central European form. Its gable roof extended out over the area in front, sheltering the step to the door. The single-crib barn usually held corn still on the cob; consequently, the structure was set upon piers made of rocks or blocks of wood. The walls were formed of horizontal logs notched at their ends to join the tiers. Although all kinds of notches were used in barns, the saddle and V notches were the most common. Crib sizes differed widely, ranging from 8 by 10 feet to 20 by 30 feet, the length lying along the ridge.

The single-crib barn was put to many uses and served many functions. Many had dirt floors and shed-roofed areas on one or more sides. In some, a crib and a dirt-floored side room shared the same roof. Single-crib forms also served as smokehouses, well houses, and root houses. Single cribs were also combined to form larger structures. Two cribs set facing each other across a common drive-through space formed a double-crib barn. Four cribs under a common roof and sharing two crossing driveways formed a four-crib barn. Two sets of three facing a common driveway formed a transverse-crib barn. Some double-crib specimens had large, cantilever-supported lofts.

The making of log walls required shaping the log, forming the notches, and finishing the walls. Traditionally, the logs were split to form one face, the other being hewed to a line with a broadaxe; otherwise, both faces would be shaped by the broadaxe or sawed into the shape required. During the heyday of the log house, notches were formed on logs that had been raised to the top of the finished part of the crib; axemen standing atop the walls cut the bottoms of notches as needed. Once notched, the logs were rocked into place and the tops of their notches cut to receive the next logs. The most common notches for houses were half-dovetail and square (for one variety); V and saddle (for the other). Log walls were finished either by chinking between the logs with wood or stone chips and mud or mortar or by "sealing" the inside with sawn lumber. Cribs generally lacked any finish siding, the cracks aiding in the drying of the corn.

Notched-log construction is a technique, not a type or a style. Nearly any kind of building made of logs also appears in other material. Southern log work is central European in origin; the buildings are mostly British New World in form. That American log construction is basically southern is seen in the near uniformity of frontier log buildings, their specific forms having developed in the backcountry between Lancaster and Augusta.

See also ART AND ARCHITECTURE: Vernacular Architecture (Upland South); FOLKLIFE: House Types; / Dogtrot; I House; Saddlebag House

M. B. Newton, Jr.
Baton Rouge, Louisiana

Terry G. Jordan, *American Log Buildings: An Old World Heritage* (1985), *Texas Log Buildings: A Folk Architecture* (1978); Fred Kniffen, *Pioneer America* (No. 1, 1969); M. B. Newton, Jr., *Geoscience and Man*, vol. 5 (1974); Eugene Murphy Wilson, "Folk Houses of Northern Alabama" (Ph.D. dissertation, Louisiana State University, 1935).

Migration Patterns

The historical and geographical dimensions of southern culture are partly the product of human migration. Migration streams have brought to the South a mix of peoples, spawning a unique cultural milieu. The variation of culture within the region is the product of an intricate pattern of migration streams within its boundaries. Migration has also influenced the diffusion of many aspects of southern culture to other parts of the United States.

By 1700 the most populous of the European settlements along the Atlantic shore of North America were in the Chesapeake region. During the next century additional footholds gained prominence, especially Charleston, and the English and black-slave populations were supplemented by a variety of other ethnic enclaves. In the mid-18th century, 200,000 Germans and 250,000 Scotch-Irish migrated to the colonies and spearheaded a movement from the Philadelphia area down the Great Valley of Virginia, then ultimately westward across the mountains. That new immigration wave, plus various changes in agricultural systems, eventually led to a multitude of additional migration pathways, which carried persons of European origin westward within the South.

Migration forced upon a group or impelled by circumstances also played an important role in the South. After 1750, Cajuns began arriving in Louisiana as refugees from Acadia. Their imprint on the cultural landscape of Louisiana remains today. European settlements encroached on American Indians, forcing them to relocate, and mass expulsion of Indians to the Indian Territory occurred between 1820 and 1840. At least 50,000 Cherokee, Chickasaw, Choctaw, Creek, and Seminole were driven from their home areas in several southern states. The mass exodus, with its resultant high mortality rate as the Indians journeyed from northern Georgia through Tennessee, western Kentucky, southern Illinois, and southern Missouri, became known as the Trail of Tears.

Numerically, the most significant forced migration affecting the South was one having worldwide impact—the importation of slaves from Africa and the West Indies. This resulted in what has been perhaps the most important juxtaposition within one location of large and nearly equal numbers of people of European and African descent anywhere in the world. In 1750 there were more than 200,000 slaves in the colonies, and from 1750 to 1800 as many as 1 million additional slaves were imported. Changes in agriculture on the Atlantic Coastal Plain led to a variety of internal slave trade routes that shifted the center of the black population from Virginia in the 18th century to northern Georgia in the 19th century.

During the 19th century a number of important new black migration streams developed: migration to the Liberian colony, which involved 15,000 emigrés; the underground railroad routes carrying about 90,000 blacks into the North before the Civil War; a postwar movement of thousands to Kansas, resulting in a series of all-black towns in that state; and steady post–Civil War migration streams to northern cities.

The truly great mass exodus of blacks from the South, however, occurred in the World War I era. Both the "pushes" by agricultural labor surpluses and heightened social conflicts and the "pulls" of industrial jobs in northern and western cities are well documented. The net migration of blacks out of the South totaled about 3 million between 1910 and 1960.

A parallel movement of whites from the Upland South sent hundreds of thousands of people to northern cities, especially in the 1940s and 1950s. In both black and white movements the dependence upon friends and relatives as sources of information, advice, and comfort led to "channelized" streams of migration that connected migrants from the South with acquaintances in northern cities and even particular neighborhoods within those cities. These channelized flows initially followed rail lines and created regional connections such as northern Louisiana to Los Angeles; Mississippi to Chicago; the

Carolinas to New York City; eastern Kentucky to Hamilton, Ohio; and southern West Virginia to Cleveland. Today, the nonmetropolitan South can still be divided into a complex mosaic of small subregions that traditionally depended upon different cities in the North and West as migration destinations, such as St. Louis, Mo.; Gary and Muncie, Ind.; Youngstown, Ohio; and Wilmington, Del.

Two other major migration patterns of the post–World War II era had earlier roots. The first was the rapid population growth in southern regional centers such as Charlotte, Atlanta, Jackson, Memphis, and Houston. Each gradually exerted a powerful draw on surrounding nonmetropolitan populations. The second was the rapid growth of Florida, which continues unabated today. Florida attracted migrants via mechanisms such as land developments and promotion, and it rapidly became the most important destination for elderly interstate migrants in the United States. The elderly, plus significant numbers of other migrants, streamed from the Midwest to the Gulf shore of Florida and from the Northeast (New Yorkers who moved to Miami and Miami Beach) to the east coast of Florida.

Beginning in the late 1960s, two new major population redistribution patterns affected the nation as a whole, and especially the South. First, the South became a part of a broad population growth area, the "Sunbelt." Decentralization of employment from the traditional northeastern "core," plus the emergence of a great variety of new amenity growth regions, including the Arkansas Ozarks and extensive areas in the southern Appalachians, fueled the broad Sunbelt migration movement. The balance of migration toward the Sunbelt was significant, because for every migrant headed for the "Frostbelt," two were directed toward the Sunbelt. Also, many fewer persons moved from the rural South to cities outside of the region in the 1960s and 1970s, contributing to this migration pattern. Because for many years people in their twenties had moved outside the South, and birthrates had fallen, there were simply fewer people prone to move away from the rural South by the 1960s. By 1970 the South was attracting overall net in-migration from the Midwest and Northeast but was still losing migrants to the West, a region that had a considerable pull on southern out-migrants in the 1940s, 1950s, and 1960s. By the end of the period 1975–80, the South had a net gain of 800,000 from the Northeast, 700,000 from the Midwest, and 160,000 from the West. Blacks, lagging behind the population as a whole in these migration trends, left the South for all regions through migration in 1965–70; yet by 1975–80 the South was gaining black migrants from each of the three other regions.

A second recent trend was more abrupt than the broadening of the Sunbelt migration. A nonmetropolitan population turnaround occurred, whereby for the first time in memory more people were moving away from metropolitan areas than toward them. This pattern has been seen both within the South and in the nation as a whole. However, compared to the North, a large number of metropolitan areas in the South are still growing rapidly, primarily because of the Sunbelt migration streams.

Migration made another contribution to southern culture in the 1970s. In the 19th and early 20th centuries the South was not a major destination for European or Asian immigrants (as were the West and the North), but in the 1970s immigration became much more important to the region. Primary examples include an expansion of the traditional Mexican immigration into Texas, significant additional numbers of Cuban refugees settling in south Florida, large numbers of Haitians moving to Miami, and a pattern of settlement of southeast Asian refugees in Houston and other cities, including some "remigration" from the Frostbelt. Partly as a result of these recent migration streams, the cultural mosaic of the South continues to change.

According to census data, between 1980 and 1984 the South's population grew by 7 percent, increasing from 74,139,633 in 1980 to an estimated 79,340,321 as of 1 July 1984 (these figures include the 11 Confederate states plus Kentucky, Missouri, Maryland, and Oklahoma). Florida's population grew by 12.6 percent, the most marked growth in the region. Texas followed, with an increase of 12.4 percent in its population. The growing population and increasing cultural diversity will affect many elements of lifestyles in the South.

See also BLACK LIFE: Migration, Black; Northern Cities, Blacks in; ETHNIC LIFE: Caribbean Influence; / Appalachians; Cajuns; Cherokees; Chickasaws; Choctaws; Creeks; Cubans; Haitians; Mexicans; Okies; Scotch-Irish; Seminoles; HISTORY AND MANNERS: / Trail of Tears; INDUSTRY: Sunbelt South; MYTHIC SOUTH: New South Myth; URBANIZATION: / Atlanta; Charlotte; Houston; Memphis

Curtis C. Roseman
University of Illinois

George A. Davis and O. Fred Donaldson, *Blacks in the United States: A Geographic Perspective* (1975); Martin Gilbert, *American History Atlas* (1968); Daniel M. Johnson and Rex R. Campbell, *Black Migration in America: A Social Demographic History* (1981); M. B. Newton, Jr., *Geoscience and Man*, vol. 5 (1974).

Ozarks

The Ozark region is perceived as a remote backwoods area, a trans-Mississippi Appalachia devoted primarily to general or subsistence farming, where traditional lifestyles and technologies persist. However, rapid economic and social changes in the region over the past half century have rendered this broadly held view less valid.

The Ozarks, together with the Ouachita Mountains just to the south, comprise the only extensive elevations between the Appalachians and the Rocky Mountains. The region extends over 50,000 square miles, including all or part of a total of 93 counties in Missouri, Arkansas, Oklahoma, and Kansas. Several geographical features distinguish the region. The boundaries are marked in a general way by major rivers: the Mississippi on the east, the Missouri on the north, and the Arkansas on the south. These rivers and their tributaries have defined and shaped the Ozark region and its people. People first came via the rivers, and many stayed because of the access to those rivers and to large man-made lakes.

The natural and aesthetic qualities of Ozark streams are at the center of a rich ecological system. The Current, Jacks Fork, Eleven Point, and Buffalo are prorivers. Several rivers sustain stocked trout. The surrounding oak-hickory-pine woodlands support squirrel, rabbit, quail, wild turkey, and deer. A large fur harvest is sustained by mink, otter, raccoon, beaver, and coyote.

Dolomite, a calcium magnesium limestone, and chert (flint) are abundant. The resistant chert, when weathered from the dolomite in which it is imbedded, accumulates at the surface and must be cleared from the fields. Streambeds are filled with chert gravel washed from steep hillsides, and the dark red upland soils are often choked with residual chert. There is an abundance of karst landforms, including such spectacular features as Grand Gulf, a massive collapsed cavern near Koshkonong, Mo., and Big Spring, near Van Buren, Mo., the largest single-opening spring in the United States. There are hundreds of caves, some of which, like Meramec Caverns and Blanchard Springs Cavern, are quite large.

Culturally, the Ozark region is more difficult to define. First, the region is rural. Rural suggests open country and an agricultural lifestyle that contrasts with city life. To some it implies rudeness and lack of polish; to others, idealized simplicity, solitude, and independence. All these things may be found in the Ozarks. Although urban centers like St. Louis, Springfield, and Joplin in Missouri and Fayetteville-Springdale in Arkansas exert a strong cultural influence on the Ozarks in many ways, the general character of day-to-day living is rural.

Second, the Ozark heritage stems from the Upper South hill country of Tennessee and Kentucky. The population of the Ozark region is 98 percent white, native-born American, and Protestant. The paucity of agricultural resources discouraged settlement by the southern planter class with slaves, so there is none of the black legacy one finds in the Deep South.

Third, the region is something of an arrested frontier distinguished by traditional lifestyles, a slowness to accept change, and a distinctive cultural landscape that retains much of the past. The rural nature of the Ozarks, its frontierlike character, its Upper South hill-country heritage, its history of poverty, and a wealth of tourist advertisements combine to produce the popular imagery of the Ozark hillbilly, with all his cultural idiosyncrasies.

Ozarkers have an uncommon sense of place. Moreover, this sense of place transcends state boundaries. The word *Ozark* appears everywhere and in various forms. Schools, churches, planning agencies, clubs, and businesses carry the name. The 1983 Springfield, Mo., telephone directory listed more than 100 names containing "Ozark." Rural-come-to-town people freely identify themselves as Ozarkers, and, only half-jestingly, they refer to nonresidents as "outsiders." Rural-on-the-farm people tend to identify more closely with specific valleys, rivers, or towns, identities historically derived from the time when a trip to another valley or town was a trip to another world, another culture.

The Ozarks were settled in three phases: the old Ozarks frontier, the "New South" Ozarks, and the cosmopolitan Ozarks. The old Ozarks frontier progressed from the eastern border to the lead mines in the eastern interior and finally, by 1860, spread over the whole region. Ozark pioneers were a diverse population. French fur traders, miners, and farmers settled in the environs of Ste. Genevieve and the Old Lead Belt beginning about 1735. Scotch-Irish settlers, mainly from Tennessee and Kentucky penetrated the interior by way of small streams and old Osage Indian trails even before the Louisiana Purchase of 1803. Cherokees, driven from their southern Appalachian home, migrated to the Oklahoma Ozarks over the Trail of Tears in the winter of 1838–39. German immigrants settled on the eastern and northern Ozark borders, forming a cultural enclave called the Missouri Rhineland. Later, when railroads were built, Germans, Italians, and other immigrant groups added their ethnic legacies.

The Reconstruction period and the so-called New South brought railroads and the spread of modern civilization to the Ozarks. Corporate mining replaced the "poor man's operations" in the Old Lead Belt in the eastern Ozarks and in the Tri-State Lead-Zinc Mining District of Missouri, Kansas, and Oklahoma. Company towns were founded, and deep ore deposits were exploited. Today closely spaced towns, mountains of waste rock, and ruins of mills and smelters identify these two defunct mineral districts. Railroads were built to open up lead and iron mines, pine forests, and hardwood timber tracts. Farms producing fruit, grain, livestock, and dairy products were laid out along the railroads, forming corridors of the New South development cutting into and finally surrounding the old Ozarks frontier. Many of the new immigrants who were attracted by the rapid economic development were progressive, liberal, capitalistic, educated, and bourgeois in culture.

Large lumber companies established company towns and became the largest property owners and the chief employers in many interior Ozark counties. In two generations the lumber companies had cut out the timber, leaving behind a depleted resource base, eroded soils, gravel-choked streams, tax-delinquent lands, and a few ramshackle lumber towns destined to fall into decay. During this same era resorts were established near some of the larger springs that were served by railroads, and the Ozarks became a vacation spot. New wealth in midwestern cities and a yellow fever epidemic in the Mississippi Valley contributed to the growth of a score of health resorts.

The third settlement phase, the cosmopolitan Ozarks, began with events connected with World War I and continues to the present. The initial stimulus for change during World War I stemmed from factors such as the military draft, high agricultural prices, loans that brought marginal land into production, pay sent home by soldiers, and new war-stimulated industries.

In three more wars (World War II and the Korean and Vietnam wars) the same shock waves washed over the

Ozarks, each time reaching farther onto ridgetops and back into isolated valleys, carried by the new power generated in the internal-combustion engine. During the Great Depression the New Deal agencies discovered the region's poverty, and through political propaganda the national stereotype of the Ozarks was born. Ozarkers received "relief commodities," discovered such new foods as grapefruit and oranges, and became familiar with the label "poor." The Works Progress Administration (WPA), Civilian Conservation Corps (CCC), and a host of other social agencies provided work, training, education, and sustenance beginning in the 1930s. National forests were established in the same decade. Fort Leonard Wood, Fort Chaffee, and Camp Crowder came later, as did the Corps of Engineers and its dozen reservoirs. Tourism, second-home development, skyrocketing land prices, and the population explosion of the 1960s, 1970s, and 1980s are all part of the settlement phase known as the cosmopolitan Ozarks.

Evidence of all three of these development phases persists not only in human attitudes, beliefs, and daily activities but also in the landscape of the region, its buildings, farms, and technologies.

Events that have shaped the Ozarks since World War II, particularly in the last two decades, include the following: (1) the shift from agriculture and extractive industries (mining and lumbering) to secondary and tertiary activities (manufacturing and services); (2) large investments in public and social services and delivery systems such as highways and rural electrification; (3) significant increases in transfer payments, including social security payments, survivors' benefits, veterans' benefits, relief and welfare payments, unemployment benefits, and food stamps; and (4) population growth.

There has been a striking shift from general farming to livestock and dairying. Mining has been rejuvenated by the discovery of a new lead belt in Iron and Reynolds counties, Missouri. Lumbering and wood-products manufacturing have declined from former years, but the number employed in lumbering has stabilized. Manufacturing has increased substantially, and tourism is now a booming industry.

Since about 1965 population has grown rapidly. While the largest increases have occurred in towns, the most rapid rates of growth are in counties around large reservoirs. New Ozarks migrants fall into three categories: returnees, escapists, and opportunity seekers. Included in these categories are the back-to-the-land people, retirees, those who have local family ties, those escaping the real and imagined ills of big-city life, and those who are simply looking for employment and a place to live.

Ozarkers are concerned about the effects of this new population growth. There is concern about the loss of the small family farm, which inevitably leads to the disintegration of the native culture. Small farms are being purchased by absentee owners and by newcomers who have no intention of wresting a living from the land. There is particular concern about the crowds of people who camp and float on Ozark rivers and the rapid growth of tourist attractions and second-home developments near the large lakes. Although the economy is supported by tourism and agriculture, zoning, subdivision ordinances, and enforced septic controls are lacking. The conflict between the region's traditional rugged individualism and the encroaching signs of the tourist industry—flashing signs, A-frames intruding on ridge and valley alike, curio shops—is especially perplexing to residents around the Lake of the Ozarks and Table Rock Lake.

For many years the Ozarks was a backwater area affected only marginally by growth and development in the rest of the country. Just as the hilly terrain once diverted glaciers on its northern border, the poverty of the region halted settlers from the North and the East. Today, as a more affluent and mobile population is attracted to regions possessing scenery, water, and recreational potential, the Ozarks is experiencing rapid growth and development.

See also ETHNIC LIFE: / Germans; Scotch-Irish; INDUSTRY: / Mining; Timber Industry; RECREATION: Tourism

Milton D. Rafferty
Southwest Missouri State University

Russel L. Gerlach, *Immigrants in the Ozarks: A Study in Ethnic Geography* (1976); Milton D. Rafferty, *Missouri: A Geography* (1983), *The Ozarks: Land and Life* (1980); Carl O. Sauer, *The Geography of the Ozark Highland of Missouri*, Geographical Society of Chicago Bulletin No. 7 (1920).

Plantation Morphology

The southern plantation symbolizes large-scale agricultural operations and landscapes and contrasts with the smaller family farm in the South. Whether the sites of sugarcane, cotton, rice, indigo, or tobacco production, southern plantations inscribed distinctive traits into the landscape.

For nearly two centuries traditional plantations included large level fields extending over hundreds, even thousands, of acres. They were located primarily in the flat terrain of the Atlantic and Gulf coasts and Mississippi floodplains or in the rolling fields in the Upland South. A latticework of ditches, canals, and field roads were etched into the landscape. Centrally located outbuilding complexes consisted of sugarhouses, cotton gins, rice mills, mule barns, tractor and implement sheds, storage tanks and sheds, blacksmith and mechanical repair shops, stores, and churches. Laborers' quarters of simple houses formed characteristic patterns. And at a distant site, set amid moss-draped oaks or in the shade of magnolias and pines, stood the plantation mansion—a symbol of power, opulence, and cultural achievement.

The architecture of plantation mansions reflected the ethnic traditions of their builders. Creole plantation mansions on sugar plantations in southern Louisiana showed the taste of French Creole planters. Anglo plantation mansions are associated with Anglo-American planters who used architects from the Tidewater region of the Atlantic Coast, from Virginia to Georgia. Furthermore, Anglo plantation mansions with Upland traits largely reflect the tastes of Anglo-American planters from western Virginia, Kentucky, Tennessee, the Carolinas, Georgia, Alabama, Mississippi, and northern Louisiana.

Creole plantation mansions are characterized by (1) interior central chimneys at the center of the roof line; never exterior chimneys on the outside gabled ends of the house; (2) multiple front doors that allow all front rooms to open onto the gallery or front porch; (3) floor plans several rooms wide and one or two rooms deep, without a central hall; (4) all stairs on the exterior; (5) hip roof; (6) galleries, a wide front porch, and often wide porches on all sides of the house; (7) one-and-a-half- to two-story height; and (8) half-timbered wall or all-wood construction.

The traits of Anglo-American plantation mansions include (1) exterior chimneys; (2) a single front door; (3) floor plans usually one to two rooms deep and no more than two rooms wide; (4) inside stairs; (5) a central hall or passage extending from front door to back; and (6) construction materials of all wood, brick, and plaster but never half-timbered construction.

Anglo houses of Tidewater origin further display a front-facing gable, two full stories, pediments, porticos, large white pillars, end chimneys (outside end or inside end), a single front door and hallway, and, in some cases, side pavilions or wings, common to the Georgian style. Other modest Anglo plantation structures of the Upland South have traits of the southern pen tradition—one to two rooms wide, deep, and tall; single front door; central hall; and exterior brick chimneys.

Settlement patterns based on the arrangement of quarter houses within the plantation complex also have distinctive traits. On modern sugar plantations in Louisiana, the quarters—a villagelike settlement that once housed slaves—contain the dwellings of field laborers, tractor operators, sugar mill workers, field overseers, and mill foremen. The arrangement of dwellings follows traditional 18th- and 19th-century linear settlement patterns marked by parallel rows of quarter houses divided by a road that bisects the long axis of the plantation landholding. Traditional land surveys from the French long lot system created long, narrow landholdings, which dictated the arrangement of structures into a linear settlement pattern that is characteristic of early French plantations.

On other present-day Louisiana sugar plantations, on early cotton, rice, indigo, and tobacco plantations of the Tidewater, and on cotton plantations of the Upland South distinctive block-shaped or gridded quarters are associated with Anglo-American plantation origins.

Elsewhere on southern cotton plantations, the antebellum quarters disappeared in the post–Civil War era, to be replaced later by individual sharecropper and tenant houses widely scattered among cotton fields. Blacks often insisted that quarter houses near the plantation mansion be relocated as a symbol of their new status. Such a dispersed pattern remained until the 1940s, when agglomerated plantation settlements reappeared on cotton enterprises in the lower Mississippi Valley and other parts of the South.

See also AGRICULTURE: Plantations; MYTHIC SOUTH: Plantation Myth

John B. Rehder
University of Tennessee

Lewis C. Gray, *History of Agriculture in the Southern United States to 1860*, 2 vols. (1933); Merle C. Prunty, *Geographical Review* (45, 1955); Roger L. Ransom and E. Richard Sutch, *One Kind of Freedom: The Economic Consequences of Emancipation* (1978); John B. Rehder, *Geoscience and Man*, vol. 19 (1978), "Sugar Plantations in Southern Louisiana: A Cultural Geography" (Ph.D. dissertation, Louisiana State University, 1971); Edgar T. Thompson, *Plantation: A Bibliography* (1957).

Population

In 1980, 61,287,000 persons lived in the 11 states of the old Confederacy, as shown in Table 1. This number is almost double that of 1940, when 31,832,000 people lived in the region, and a more than 40-fold increase from the 1,454,000 enumerated in the nation's first census in 1790. Despite this growth, the South's share of the nation's population has, until recently, steadily declined from the 37 percent of 1790. A low 23 percent was recorded in 1930; the current share is 27 percent.

After initial settlement, the South became less a destination than a point of origin for migrants. In the 100 years following the Civil War, Alabama, Georgia, Mississippi, North Carolina, and Tennessee each recorded over a million more out-migrants than in-migrants. Only Florida (4.3 million) and Texas (1.5 million) consistently gained population from migration over this period. By

Table 1. *Population of the South, by State, 1790–1980*

	1790	1860	1900	1940	1980
			Population in Thousands		
Alabama	—	964	1,829	2,833	3,894
Arkansas	—	435	1,312	1,949	2,286
Florida	—	140	529	1,897	9,746
Georgia	83	1,057	2,216	3,124	5,463
Louisiana	—	708	1,382	2,364	4,206
Mississippi	—	791	1,551	2,184	2,521
North Carolina	394	993	1,894	3,572	5,882
South Carolina	249	704	1,340	1,900	3,122
Tennessee	36	1,110	2,021	2,916	4,591
Texas	—	604	3,049	6,415	14,229
Virginia	692	1,220	1,854	2,678	5,347
TOTAL	1,454	8,726	18,977	31,832	61,287

Source: U.S. Bureau of the Census, *Population Reports* (1790, 1860, 1900, 1940, 1980).

the late 1960s the general pattern of net out-migration had begun to reverse. For the period 1975 to 1980, *all* southern states had population gains from migration.

For 1970–80 the South grew by 22.5 percent, almost double the nation's growth rate of 11.4 percent. Increased migration to the South is primarily responsible for the region's dramatic growth in recent years, although a high birthrate also has contributed. The South has long had a birthrate above the national rate; even when out-migration was high in the 1940s and 1950s, large numbers of births enabled the South to grow. In 1960 the South recorded 25.0 births per 1,000 population, while the nation's rate was 23.7 per 1,000. Both rates declined over the next 20 years, so that by 1980 the South remained marginally higher: 16.5 as compared to 15.9 for the entire United States. Of the 10 states with the highest birthrates, three are in the South: Louisiana (sixth nationally with 19.5 births per 1,000 population); Texas (seventh; 19.2); and Mississippi (ninth; 19.0). Utah led all states at 28.6.

The population of the South is younger than the nation as a whole. The median age in 1980 was 29.1 years, compared to the country's 30.0 years. This gap would have been even greater were it not for Florida; deleting that state with its median age of 34.7 years results in a median age for the remaining 10 states of 28.3 years. The proportion of southerners who are aged 65 and over is exactly the same as for the entire country, 11.3 percent. In Florida one in six residents is at least 65 years old, the highest proportion in the country. Excluding Florida, the remaining 10 southern states have a combined proportion 65 and over of 10.2 percent. More women (31.5 million) than men (29.7 million) live in the South, resulting in a sex ratio of 94.4 men per 100 women. This ratio is almost identical to that for the entire country, 94.5.

In 1980 the South's net death rate was 8.70 deaths per 1,000 population, lower than the 8.80 per 1,000 recorded for the entire nation. This lower rate is misleading, however; because the South has a younger population than the nation as a whole, it has relatively more of its population at those ages where the fewest deaths occur. When rates are adjusted for age, mortality in the South is slightly higher than that for all of the United States, a pattern that has held since adequate death statistics became available in the 1930s. Life expectancy figures for the 1979–81 period confirm this higher mortality. Nationally, newborns could expect to live 73.9 years on average, but this figure was surpassed in only one southern state, Florida, at 74.0 years. The four states with the lowest life expectancies were all in the South: Georgia (72.2 years), Mississippi (72.0), South Carolina (71.8), and Louisiana (71.7). (The District of Columbia had the nation's lowest life expectancy—69.2 years.) Infant mortality has been relatively high in the South; in 1980 there were 13.6 deaths in the first year of life per 1,000 births, compared to the national rate of 12.5 such deaths per 1,000 births. Among individual states, the four with the highest rates were in the South: Mississippi (15.9 infant deaths per 1,000 births); Louisiana (15.4); South Carolina (15.4); and Alabama (15.1).

The South has a smaller proportion of its population in rural areas (67.5 percent) than the country as a whole (73.7 percent). While a majority of southerners now reside in places of at least 2,500 population, this level of urban residence is a new phenomenon: as recently as 1950, over half of all southerners lived in rural areas. Two states, Mississippi and North Carolina, remain predominantly rural, and only two states—Florida and Texas—have proportionately fewer residents in rural areas than the nation as a whole.

Similarly, the South has proportionately fewer metropolitan residents (67.6 percent) than the entire United States (74.8 percent). Arkansas and Mississippi have fewer than 40 percent of their residents living in metropolitan areas, whereas Texas and Florida both exceed 80 percent. A total of 12 of the 50 largest metropolitan areas in the country are in the South: three in Texas (Dallas–Fort Worth; Houston; San Antonio) and three in Florida (Fort Lauderdale; Miami; Tampa–Saint Petersburg). Dallas–Fort Worth (3.0 million; ninth largest nationally) and Houston (2.9 million; 10th nationally) are the region's largest metropolitan areas. Washington, D.C., the nation's eighth largest metropolitan area (3.1 million), is partly located in the South, occupying part of Virginia.

The South's population is concentrated in two states, Texas (14.2 million inhabitants) and Florida (9.7 million). Combined they contain just under 40 percent of the region's population. All southern states have at least 2 million residents; Arkansas (2.3 million) and Mississippi (2.5 million) have the fewest residents.

The population of the South is largely of African and European stock. In 1980 just under one in five southerners was black. These 12 million blacks comprised over 45 percent of the total black population in the United States. As recently as 1960, more than half the nation's black population lived in the 11 old Confederacy states, and until the early 1900s over 80 percent of all blacks lived in the South. Mississippi (35.2 percent) and South Carolina (30.4 percent) have the largest relative black populations, although in absolute numbers Texas (1.7 million) and Georgia (1.5 million) have the largest black populations. All 11 southern states have a higher proportion of blacks than the nation's 11.7 percent.

Over one-quarter of all southerners indicate English ancestry. Other northern and western European groups are well represented: Irish, 16 percent; German, 13 percent; Scottish, 5 percent. (Some persons claimed more than one ancestry group.) Almost one-third of all persons claiming English ancestry live in the South, as do 30 percent of those claiming Scottish ancestry. Southern and eastern European immigrant groups are underrepresented in the South; only 1.9 percent of southerners indicate any Italian ancestry and only 1.1 percent have Polish ancestry. Other ethnic groups, uncommon in much of the South, are locally concentrated. Over a fifth of all Louisianans claim French ancestry, for example, and over half of all United States residents who claim Cuban ancestry live in Florida. Persons of Spanish origin, principally of Mexican descent, constitute 21 percent of Texas's population; in 1980, 2.7 million Texans claimed Mexican ancestry.

The South's population has the lowest educational attainment of any region in the country. In 1980 just under 60 percent of southerners aged 25 and over had completed at least four years of high school; the national proportion is 66.4 percent. Only one southern state, Florida, exceeds the national share; its figure is 67.2 percent. Of the 10 states with the lowest educational attainment, 8 are in the South: Alabama, Arkansas, Georgia, Louisiana, Mississippi, North Carolina, South Carolina, and Tennessee; the two remaining states, Kentucky and West Virginia, border the old Confederacy. Kentucky has the lowest proportion of its population aged 25 and over with at least four years of high school, 51.9 percent; the Deep South state with the lowest proportion is South Carolina (54.0 percent).

The two poorest states in the nation are in the South—Mississippi (per capita money income, 1979, of $5,327) and Arkansas ($5,467). Only Florida ($7,593) and Virginia ($7,549) exceed the national average ($7,313). The South has a disproportionate share of its population living in poverty, 15.2 percent, compared to the nation's 12.5 percent. Mississippi has the nation's greatest proportion, 24.5 percent; no other state is above 20 percent. Only Virginia (11.5 percent) of the southern states has a proportion in poverty below the national share. A total of 8 of the 10 poorest counties in the nation are in the South: Greene, Lowndes, and Wilcox in Alabama; Lee in Arkansas; Holmes, Humphreys, and Tunica in Mississippi; and Starr in Texas.

The rapid growth in the South since the late 1960s is likely to continue in the near future, particularly in Florida and Texas. From 1980 to 1983, Census Bureau estimates indicate that Texas grew by 1.5 million inhabitants, Florida by over 900,000. Together, these two states accounted for almost two-thirds of the South's population growth since 1980. Still, all southern states grew from 1980 to 1983, and all except four (Alabama, Arkansas, Mississippi, and Tennessee) exceeded the national rate of 3.3 percent.

See also BLACK LIFE: Migration, Black; SOCIAL CLASS: Poverty

John P. Marcum
Max W. Williams
University of Mississippi

Estimates of the Population of States: 1970 to 1983, Current Population Reports, Series P-25, No. 957 (1984); *Historical Statistics of the United States, Colonial Times to 1970*, Bicentennial Edition (1975); National Center for Health Statistics, *U.S. Decennial Life Tables for 1979–81*, vol. 2 (1985); Harry M. Rosenberg and Drusilla Burnham, in *The Population of the South: Structure and Change in Social Demographic Context*, ed. Dudley L. Poston, Jr., and Robert H. Weller (1981); David F. Sly, in *The Population of the South: Structure and Change in Social Demographic Context*, ed. Dudley L. Poston, Jr., and Robert H. Weller (1981); *State and Metropolitan Area Data Book, 1982* (1982); U.S. Department of Commerce, *Statistical Abstract of the United States: 1983* (1984).

Religious Regions

Viewed from a national perspective the South is remarkably homogeneous in its religion. Protestantism predominates and, in the majority of counties, Baptists and Methodists together account for nearly all church affiliation. The South is further distinguished by high rates of church membership in comparison with other regions of the country. Within the general uniformity of southern religion, however, a degree of diversity exists that is worthy of attention.

The dominance of Baptist groups is perhaps the most striking feature of southern religion. They predominate in most counties, reaching maximum strength along a corridor extending from southern Appalachia through Georgia, Alabama, and Mississippi and into northern Louisiana and Texas and southern Arkansas and Oklahoma. Baptists came to the South during the Great Awakening in the mid-18th century. They were extremely successful evangelists, in part because of a reliance on farmer-preachers who settled among the people they served.

Methodists were the chief rivals of Baptists within the southern missionary field. The two groups grew at similar rates throughout the 19th century, but they employed differing strategies. Methodist expansion emphasized a well-organized system of circuit riders and regular camp meetings. In the last half century the growth of Methodists has lagged behind that of Baptists, possibly because of the latter's strong regional ties through the Southern Baptist Convention. Methodism remains tremendously important, however. Large Methodist minorities exist in most counties, and majorities are found frequently in the Carolinas, the Virginias, Maryland, and Tennessee.

Baptists and Methodists together constitute the core of southern conservative Protestantism. Other groups of similar orientation include Disciples of Christ, Presbyterians, and the larger Pentecostal and Holiness denominations. These denominations are widespread throughout the region but have special concentration in the Upper South, where several of them originated, and in the Carolinas.

Concentrations of Catholics form the most significant exceptions to the Baptist-Methodist domination of the South. Some Catholic groups existed in the region before the growth of evangelical Protestantism; others are relatively recent immigrants. Catholics frequently represent not only religious diversity in the South but ethnic diversity as well, and locations where they are concentrated are major cultural "islands" in the region.

Southern Catholicism is most firmly established in southern Louisiana and southern Texas. The Catholic presence in Louisiana dates from the early 18th century,

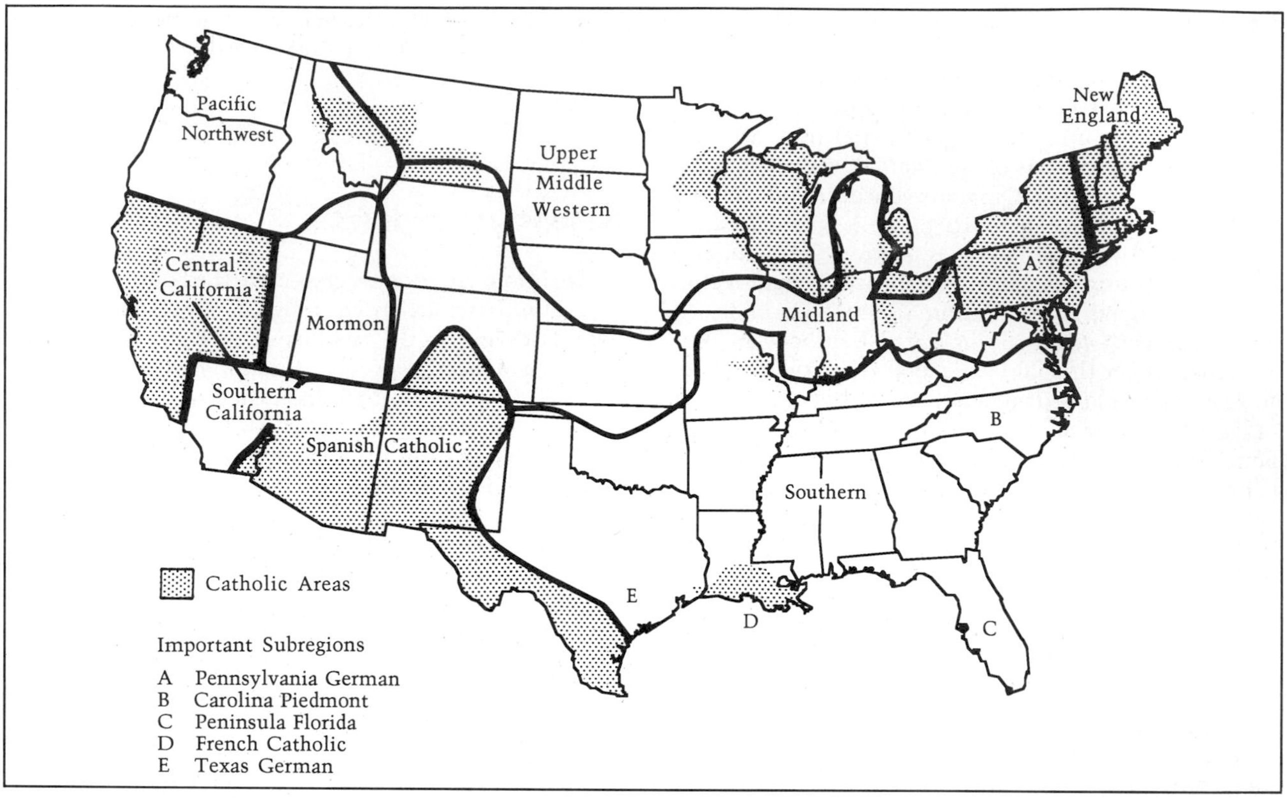

Religious Regions

Source: Raymond Gastil, *Cultural Regions of the United States* (1975); modified from Wilbur Zelinsky, "An Approach to the Religious Geography of the United States," *Annals of the Association of American Geographers* (1961).

and it became firmly established in the middle of that century when French-speaking Catholics deported from Nova Scotia arrived in large numbers. Catholicism in Texas is even older, beginning with Spanish missions in the late 17th century. Catholics now constitute nearly three-fifths of the total church membership in Louisiana and nearly one-third in Texas. The cultural identities of both Cajuns and Mexican Americans are strongly intertwined with their faiths.

Smaller regions of Catholic influence occur along the northern border of the South. The oldest of these has its core in Maryland, a colonial center of Catholicism and of general religious tolerance under Lord Baltimore. Immigration of Marylanders to north-central Kentucky created another Catholic concentration. Farther west, along the Ohio River in Illinois and Indiana and along the Missouri and Mississippi rivers in east central Missouri, Catholic clusters occurred through the migration of German and Swiss settlers. Recent migration is responsible for Catholicism in southern Florida—primarily the flow of retirees and other northerners. Cubans, Haitians, and other emigrants from the Caribbean region constitute another component of Florida Catholicism.

Subtle variations within Protestantism provide a second departure from the norm of southern religious geography. Areas best described as pluralistic, places where Baptist and Methodist strength is somewhat diluted, although rarely replaced, have a cultural or historical background different from the mainstream and are among the most religiously diverse places in the South.

Peninsular Florida has become a major area of pluralism during this century. The amenities of the Sunbelt have attracted Protestants of various persuasions, Jews, and Catholics alike. Episcopalians, Lutherans, the Reformed churches, and the United Church of Christ, as well as Disciples and Presbyterians, are all found in greater proportion here than throughout most of the region.

Another distinctively pluralistic religious subregion is the Carolina Piedmont, where Friends, Lutherans, Moravians, Presbyterians, and the United Church of Christ are all well represented. North Carolina's lack of restrictions on nonconformists attracted these groups to the area as early as the late 17th century, but the major immigration came during the 18th century. A scarcity of available good land in Pennsylvania prompted many people of varied religious backgrounds to migrate southeastward along the Appalachian front into the Carolinas. The Christian Church, now part of the United Church of Christ, was founded in North Carolina and Virginia.

German, Scandinavian, and eastern European immigration to the hill country of central Texas during the mid-19th century created a distinctive religious and ethnic complex. Lutherans remain the most numerous group there, but Evangelical and Reformed adherents (now part of the United Church of Christ), Moravians, and Catholics are also important components of the hill-country religion.

Appalachia should also be considered a religious subregion within the South. Its distinctiveness came not from immigration but from the local emergence of numerous strongly fundamentalist denominations, mainly Pentecostal or Holiness in belief but sectarian in orientation. Religion here reflects the individualism, traditionalism, and localism of Appalachian society generally. In many ways this religion is a relic of the emotional, evangelical faith that characterized the interior South during the 19th-century frontier period.

A final zone of religious diversity lies along the northern border of the South, an area where northern and southern denominations intermix. Catholic concentrations here have already been noted, but one also finds Lutherans, Episcopalians, United Church of Christ congregations, Presbyterians, and other Protestant groups in occasional concentrations.

See also RELIGION articles

James R. Shortridge
University of Kansas

Roger W. Stump
State University of New York at Albany

Sydney E. Ahlstrom, *A Religious History of the American People* (1972); Jackson W. Carroll, Douglas W. Johnson, and Martin E. Marty, *Religion in America: 1950 to the Present* (1979); Edwin Gaustad, *Historical Atlas of Religion in America* (rev. ed., 1976); Charles Heatwole, *Southeastern Geographer* (May 1986); Samuel S. Hill, ed., *Religion and the Solid South* (1972); Douglas W. Johnson, Paul R. Picard, and Bernard Quinn, *Churches and Church Membership in the United States: An Enumeration by Region, State, and County, 1971* (1974); James R. Shortridge, *Geographical Review* (October 1976); Wilbur Zelinsky, *Annals of the Association of American Geographers* (June 1961).

Roadside

Donald Davidson wrote in *The Attack on Leviathan* (1938) that southern cities reflecting "the finest flavor of the old regime" could not be reached except by passing "over brand-new roads where billboards, tourist camps, filling stations and factories broke out in a modernistic rash among the water oaks and Spanish moss." Davidson saw the roadside in the South as a prime symbol of the evils of modernization, which were destroying the best of the region's agrarian tradition.

The automobile has indeed reshaped the southern roadside in the 20th century, promoting Americanization and standardization through billboards, service stations, fast-food restaurants, trailer camps, motels, and other aspects of the car culture. But for travelers in motor vehicles the roadside also reflects and reinforces an awareness of southern history and culture and promotes the consciousness of being in a landscape different from that elsewhere. It has thereby promoted regional self-consciousness.

Historic sites, for example, especially Civil War battlefields, have become modern locales for pilgrimage. The war marked the southern roadside for generations. Most of the fighting during the conflict was on southern soil, and the countryside long after the war held tangible memories of the past. As Mary Winn, a traveler in the region, wrote in 1931, "At intervals on the road one passes a group of magnificent live-oaks, in the middle of which rises a tall chimney, all that is left of the 'great house' that was once the center of a feudal property." Virginia pioneered in erecting historical markers by the side of the road, and now the history of every state in the region is revealed in concise statements on signs, markers, and monuments on the roadside. Historian Thomas D. Clark suggested in 1961 that traffic congestion from automobile tourists made it more dangerous to pull off the road "to take a leisurely look at the scene of a Civil War battlefield than it was to have engaged in the battle itself."

Natural attractions have been roadside lures in the South. "See Rock City" and "Ruby Falls" were the most pervasive of signs painted on the side of southern barns, nailed to a tree as placards, or displayed on standard billboards. But there were also signs for Silver Springs, Natural Bridge, or even Dog Patch. "The southern landscape has been sacrificed in many places to this mad campaign to snatch the tourist dollar," wrote historian Clark. "Scarcely a roadside post, tree, fence, or barn has escaped the signmaker. On some of the main highways there is hardly a quarter of a mile left undefiled."

Engineers in the South, as elsewhere, generally adopted the utilitarian approach to the countryside in roadbuilding, with aesthetics having little role. Wildflowers and trees, for example, were discouraged. Southern roadsides were, however, so naturally luxuriant, especially in the warm humid areas, that they could not be kept down, and the simple attraction of the region's plant life has always added a distinctive look to the roadside, one noted by outsiders looking for regional differences. In a 1938 book, native southerner Jonathan Daniels recalled the road north of Greenville, S.C., where "the dogwood, the mountain magnolia, the azalea and tiny nameless wild flowers bloomed in profusion on the May highway."

Tourist traps also grew up to give a distinctive ambience to the southern roadside. Billboards and handmade signs for miles announced what were sometimes rip-off businesses. "Pet baby alligators" would be a typical come-on. Reptile farms, bears on display, shetland ponies to ride—all were designed to lure tourists off the road and out of their cars to buy souvenirs, gasoline, or food. South of the Border, located on Interstate 95 near the North Carolina–South Carolina border, has a 220-foot-high Mexican sombrero, an artifact that automatically earns attention. Billboards from Virginia to Georgia announce its importance. Started in 1949, it has a gas station, campground, and volunteer fire department. Sometimes the artifacts at such places are a kind of folk-

Roadside store, near Savannah, c. 1940

pop art. Mammy's Cupboard is at the top of a hill near Natchez, Miss. A 28-foot-tall black woman stands atop the rise, embodying the "mammy" image, down to her apron. Her "cupboard" lies beneath her crinoline skirt, which covers a 20-foot area. It was built in 1940, and its owners serve southern plate lunches inside and gasoline outside. The king of the southern roadside businesses is Stuckey's, whose spread nationwide represents an example of the "southernization of America." Gaudy red-and-yellow billboards dot the countryside advertising the place to buy pecans, candy, gifts and souvenirs, gasoline, and fast food. William Sylvester Stuckey from Eastman, Ga., founded his roadside business in 1932, in the middle of the Great Depression, with only a few sacks of peanuts and a $35 loan. He sold pecans to tourists passing through Eastman headed from New York to Florida, supplied candy to the military during World War II, and then expanded his roadside service nationwide after the war.

Souvenirs, artifacts of perceived "southernness," are part of the roadside in the South. They are localized, suggesting place. T-shirts, clothing, and ashtrays are common everywhere, but are marked with local references. There are country music references in Tennessee (hairbrushes in the form of guitars, Dolly Parton dolls); Confederate flags and miniature cotton bales are sold in Mississippi; moccasins and other Indian goods are in North Carolina Cherokee country and in Florida Seminole land; hillbilly characters, outhouses, and scatological artifacts can be purchased on Appalachian roadsides; seashells and seashell art are common along the coasts. Natural products of the region are also popular souvenirs giving a sense of place—a packaged sack of oranges in Florida, grapefruit in south Texas, peaches in Georgia, boiled peanuts in south Alabama, and fresh honey all around. Folk and pop art, whether quilts, velvet paintings of Elvis, or ceramic animals for the yard, are common beside the road. Fireworks stands are pervasive in certain areas and increase before holidays. They sell Chinese fireworks that are repackaged to strike regional themes (as in the Robert E. Lee collection of firecrackers seen in one Kentucky stand).

Religious folk art has flourished on the southern roadside, especially in the Appalachians, Ozarks, and in rural areas. Both handmade primitive signs and mass-produced ones are found. These provide among the most distinctive of regional touches to the roadside, because their messages are evangelistic, reflecting the region's predominant religious outlook and style. Statements include "Get Right With God," "Prepare To Meet Thy God," "Where Will You Spend Eternity," "Jesus Is The Answer," or simply "Jesus Saves." Scholar Samuel S. Hill has speculated they are most common in areas undergoing the trauma of modernization; they are most likely associated with Protestant sectarians. One rough drawing on wood in North Carolina had a stark picture of a hand with a nail through it, and blood spurting forth. "He Loved You So Much It Hurt," said the words under the drawing. Such signs are folk art reflecting the intense, passionate southern faith. Appropriately, Flannery O'Connor refers to them in *Wise Blood.* While driving along the road, Hazel Motes sees a gray boulder, emblazoned with white letters that say, "WOE TO THE BLASPHEMER AND THE WHOREMONGER! WILL HELL SWALLOW YOU UP?"

In the contemporary era the roadside along southern interstate highways is becoming more bland, although southerners in cities, in small towns, and on smaller roads maintain in places the colorful man-made landscape. The use of portable signs—the small, metal-framed and illuminated signs on wheels—is especially popular in the South. *New York Times* reporter William E. Schmidt noted in 1984 that they "seem to be crouched everywhere beside highways across the South these days." Since the mid-1970s over 100,000 of them have appeared throughout the nation, providing a useful message board to the small businesses who use them. They are most typically found along suburban commercial strips. Their garish flashing lights and arrows effectively catch the eye of the motorist; and garages, service stations, barber and beauty shops, bakeries, and nightclubs all use them. Marietta, Ga., attempted to restrict their use, but the Supreme Court ruled in 1984 that restrictions were unconstitutional limitations on businesses' First Amendment rights of expression. Churches have adopted them widely, delivering for the motorist not only evangelistic messages but also general moral precepts and homely proverbs.

See also ENVIRONMENT: Parks and Recreation Areas; FOLKLIFE: / "Get Right With God"; HISTORY AND MANNERS: Automobile; Historic Sites; RECREATION: Tourism, Automobile

Charles Reagan Wilson
University of Mississippi

John Baeder, *Gas, Food, and Lodging: A Postcard Odyssey through the Great American Roadside* (1982); Warren J. Belasco, *Americans on the Road: From Autocamps to Motel, 1910–1945* (1975); Thomas D. Clark, *The Emerging South* (1961); John Brinckerhoff Jackson, *The Southern Landscape Tradition in Texas* (1980); John A. Jakle, *The Tourist: Travel in Twentieth-Century North America* (1985); Chester H. Liebs, *Main Street to Miracle Mile: American Roadside Architecture* (1986); William E. Schmidt, *New York Times* (19 October 1984).

Southwest

The term *Southwest* has long been used popularly and by scholars to refer to a major subregion of the South. The Old Southwest of the early 19th century included lands recently opened to white settlement—Alabama, Mississippi, Tennessee, Kentucky, Arkansas, and Louisiana. By the 1840s the Southwest included Texas. With the acquisition and settlement of land reaching to southern California, the "Southwest" grew to the west, but the relationship of this land to the South was increasingly unclear.

The problems in defining the Southwest are important ones in understanding the complexities of southern culture and its cultural boundaries. Until recently, scholarly attempts to define regions have reflected physical and economic patterns rather than broader cultural ones. Some scholars have seen the American Southwest as a distinct region, altogether separate from the South. Sociologist Howard W. Odum in *Southern Regions of the United States* (1936) wrote that Texas, Oklahoma, New Mexico, and Arizona were the Southwest, one of six major American regions. Using over 200 indices of specific sociocultural characteristics, Odum concluded that "Texas and Oklahoma qualify as 'southern' in less than a third of the indices selected." He insisted that placing the Southwest with the Southeast was inaccurate and "detrimental to genuine regional analysis and planning." Ruth F. Hale identified the same four states as the Southwest in a more recently developed "Map of Vernacular Regions," based on a mail sample of people's identification with region. Cultural geographer D. W. Meinig identifies New Mexico and Arizona as the main focus of the Southwest, exploring the cultural contributions of Anglos, Indians, and Hispanics to its distinctiveness. Although not a part of the "South," Meinig's Southwest was formed partly through contributions of southern whites, particularly Texans, who, he wrote, were "a special regional type, differentiated by political and racial attitudes, religion, and social mores."

Political scientist Daniel Elazar in *Cities of the Prairies* (1970) defines the Southwest to include Louisiana, Arkansas, Missouri, Oklahoma, Texas, and New Mexico (with half of Texas and Oklahoma in what he calls the Greater South and half in the Greater West). Elazar's definition is based on "the expression of social, economic and political differences along geographic lines." Cultural geographer Wilbur Zelinsky divides the United States into five regions with Texas divided between the South and the West. In creating his division, Zelinsky uses such indicators as food habits, religion, language, and self-conscious identification with region.

Most of these definitions of the Southwest come from broader attempts to chart the nation's overall regional boundaries. From the viewpoint of southern history and culture, questions about the nature of a western *part* of the South center on Texas and Oklahoma. In one of the most recent efforts at defining regions, Raymond D. Gastil has placed most of Texas and Oklahoma in a "western" subregion of the South, based on secondary cultural factors "induced by differences in the origin of the people, the requirements of particular geographical situations, or subsequent creativity." Joel Garreau in *The Nine Nations of North America* (1981) does not use traditional regional terminology but carves up Texas and Oklahoma, placing the eastern portions of each in "Dixie" and the western parts in the "Breadbasket" (with southern and far western Texas in "MexAmerica").

The Southwest is clearly, then, a borderland area of the South, but it offers the opportunity to observe the cultural configuration of a subregion of Dixie, one that has a distinctive history and identity that is, nonetheless, closely related to that of other areas of the South. Texas is the core area of the South's Southwest, the centerpiece for any attempt to understand the line dividing the Southwest into "southern" and "western" spheres. Writer Willie Morris recalls the Texan who insisted the dividing line was Conroe, Tex., because west of there bar fights occur indoors and to the east they are outdoors. The "bar fight" line has never been formally charted, but environmental, demographic, historical, and cultural factors suggest an answer. For a study of the South, the Southwest is a most significant area for the clash of cultures, where a southern white-black tradition came into contact with a more pluralistic Hispanic-Indian-frontier culture.

Environmental and climatic factors suggest that much of Texas is southern. A fault line, the Balcones Escarpment, is a geological dividing line, marking in solid rock a physical separation between east Texas—the center of southern influences—and west Texas. In the middle of the state the land changes from piney woods in the east to grassy prairies to the west, with increasingly barren-looking plains and desert even farther west. Markedly decreased rainfall in west Texas reinforces the sense of a western physical landscape, nurturing different forms of animal and plant life. These physical differences were matched by differing settlement populations as well—blacks form a major population group in east Texas, gradually diminishing in numbers to the west, where Hispanics increase in numbers and cultural influence. Texas in general has been more ethnically diverse than the rest of the South, with Indians, Hispanics, Germans, Czechs, Danes, Swedes, and, more recently, Vietnamese significant populations in different areas of the state. The dividing line between southern and western parts of Texas based on these environmental and demographic facts, in any event, seems to be somewhere between the 98th meridian and the 103rd meridian. Walter Prescott Webb's *The Great Plains* (1931) was a landmark exploration of the response of frontier settlers to the challenges of a new environment in the West. Webb argued that the West began near the 98th meridian—or at that point where water becomes scarce.

In addition to environmental and demographic factors,

Wheaton, A Texas Rancher *(date unknown)*

history made Texas partly southern and partly western. The Anglo founder of Texas, Stephen Austin, was born in Virginia, and most early Anglo settlers were southern whites who brought their black slaves with them when they immigrated to Mexican soil. Cotton grew well in east Texas, and historian Frank Vandiver has noted that early Texans saw wealth in southern terms as "land, cotton, and slaves." The Republic of Texas (1836–45) was surely the creation of aggressive southern white Americans, symbolized by leaders such as Sam Houston, born in Virginia, and Davy Crockett, from Tennessee. The evangelical churches that dominated the rest of the antebellum South also dominated in Texas, among both whites and blacks, a situation that remains true in east and central Texas. Texas was a Confederate state, and with defeat in the Civil War Texans claimed the Lost Cause. The erection of Confederate monuments all the way west to El Paso established a southern landscape.

East and north Texas were dominated by sharecropping after the Civil War, with George Sessions Perry's *Hold Autumn in Your Hand* (1941) a major novel of southern social life under crop lien. These areas were among the centers of Populist agrarian discontent in the 1880s and 1890s, befitting their location between other areas of unrest in the Deep South and on the Great Plains. V. O. Key, Jr., discussed Texas as a southern state in *Southern Politics* (1949), showing that the state produced the kind of early 20th-century rural demagogues (James Ferguson, W. Lee "Pappy" O'Daniel) found elsewhere in the South, but they did not exploit the race issue to the same degree as elsewhere. Key noted that Texas was less concerned with race than "about money and how to make it."

The post–Civil War period had seen increasing southwestern divergence from southern patterns. The range cattle industry seemed by the end of the 1860s to be an economic substitute for the cotton economy. Cattle culture generated capital but, perhaps more importantly, a new mythology for the Southwest, one not shared with the rest of the South. The rancher became a southwestern hero and the longhorn a near mythic animal, but the prime new legendary figure was the cowboy, a symbol of western freedom. The cowboy, to be sure, had southern roots. Owen Wister's *The Virginian* created the model, a romantic figure who had much of the honorable cavalier in him. Black and white southerners after the war did go west seeking opportunity and some became cowboys, but they were seeking to escape the South. The cowboy's real life of hard work and loneliness made him more a working-class frontiersman than a cavalier. The cowboy has shown an enduring appeal for 20th-century Texans and other southerners, especially country music entertainers from Jimmie Rodgers to Charlie Daniels who have nurtured the cowboy legend. Cowboy hats and boots spread eastward to become common southern rural working-class badges of identification with the Southwest.

Discovery of oil at Spindletop near Beaumont on 10 January 1901 further differentiated the Texas economy from the southern, and oil and natural gas would provide a southwestern economic bond between Texas, Oklahoma, and Louisiana. Petroleum lore created another new mythology for the Southwest, as colorful wildcatters such as Dad Joiner became Texas legends. The massive amounts of money generated by petroleum would enable Texas culture and society to escape much of the enervating southern culture of poverty.

Twentieth-century southwestern culture has continued to reflect both southern and western influences. Before the 1920s, for example, Texas Anglo music came out of a southern heritage. Rural Texans played the same instruments and sang the same kinds of songs found elsewhere in the South. Western swing emerged in Texas and Oklahoma in the 1930s, showing the influence of ethnically diverse Texas and becoming a major genre of country music. Its creators, including Bob Wills and His Texas Playboys, dressed in western costume but played music drawing on blues and jazz as well as southern white fiddle music. The first country star, Jimmie Rodgers, lived his last few years in Texas and promoted a western, "singing cowboy" image. Later Texas country music performers such as Ernest Tubb and Gene Autry made "western" music a southwestern contribution to "southern" country music. Lightnin' Hopkins was similarly a major figure in a southwestern blues tradition centered in east and central Texas. Contemporary Tex-Mex music represents a blending of Mexican, German, and southern musical styles.

Southwestern writers have been, until recently, preoccupied with the frontier, which has been a source of the region's enduring mythology. Southwestern literature was traditionally peopled principally by hardy frontiersmen, gruff ranchers, romantic cowboys, and always-just Texas Rangers. The greatest literary achievements until the 1950s were in nonfiction. Folklorist-biographer J. Frank Dobie, historian Walter Prescott Webb, and naturalist Roy Bedichek were dominant forces. Novelist Larry McMurtry has noted that the "Big Three," as he calls them, "revered Nature, studied Nature, and hued to Nature." It was a literature celebrating western triumph rather than exploring the complex, tragic themes of modern southern literature. Since the 1950s writers such as William Humphrey, William Goyen, Bill Brammer, John Graves, and Larry King have created a southwestern fiction tradition that draws on themes earlier articulated by Faulkner and other southern writers. Larry McMurtry is perhaps the most accomplished and successful novelist, telling the story of the movement of Texans off the land and into a new urban Southwest.

Southwestern cooking illustrates the meeting of southern, western, and Mexican cultures. Southern dishes such as grits, biscuits, corn bread, turnip greens, fried chicken, country ham with redeye gravy, and pork sausage are all popular in Texas. Texan Elmore Tora was founder of the National Blackeyed Pea Association and marketed the pea in Asia. The chicken-fried steak is particularly popular fare in Texas truck stops and cafes; it applies a southern style of cooking to a piece of beef—battering and frying like cooking fried chicken. A cream gravy is the essential accompanying sauce. Larry McMurtry insists that "only a rank degenerate would drive 1,500 miles across Texas without eating a chicken-fried steak." Barbecue is the object of cult-like obsession, although southwestern barbecue is beef, not the pork found in the Deep South. Tex-Mex cooking is a particularly revealing product of a cultural borderland, combining ingredients and styles of cooking from Mexican, Indian, and Anglo traditions. Texas produces about 10 percent of the world's jalapeño pepper supply for its cuisine. Texans in 1951 formed the Chili Appreciation Society International in Dallas, launching a crusade for chili that has brought increasingly passionate identification of chili with the state. South, west, and central Texas are the centers of Tex-Mex cooking, but on the cultural borderland its popularity has spilled over into east Texas, Louisiana, and other parts of the South.

The 1970s saw the emergence of an energetic southwestern culture in central Texas. It was a youth culture, the southwestern version of the counterculture. Drinking beer (preferably the regional Lone Star Longnecks), smoking marijuana, listening to "progressive country" music (especially Willie Nelson), eating Tex-Mex food, admiring armadillos—all were rituals of a lifestyle that self-consciously identified with the region. Periodicals such as the *Texas Monthly* (begun in 1973), the *Texas Observer* (a reform journal that began publishing in 1954 and calls itself "a window on the South"), and the *Southwestern Historical Quarterly* explore the cultural dimensions of the Southwest, including its southern ties. In a January 1977 feature entitled "How To Be Southern," for example, *Texas Monthly* noted that through the years "we Texans have been the perfect fair-weather friends of the South." Texans had "the credentials to be Southern when we wanted," but in trying times "we've been able to step neatly aside into our Southwestern identities." With Jimmy Carter's inauguration the Southwest seemed to reclaim a part of its southern heritage. By the late 1970s, though, the symbols and rituals of Texas culture had come to predominate over either the western or the southern identity.

See also ENVIRONMENT: / Armadillo; ETHNIC LIFE: / Mexicans; FOLKLIFE: Pottery, Texas; INDUSTRY: / Oil Industry; LAW: / Foreman, Percy; MUSIC: *Música Tejana*; Western Swing; SOCIAL CLASS: / Oil Workers; URBANIZATION: / Dallas; Houston; VIOLENCE: Southwestern Violence

Charles Reagan Wilson
University of Mississippi

J. Frank Dobie, *A Guide to the Life and Literature of the Southwest* (1943), *Some Part of Myself* (1967); T. R. Fehrenbach, *Lone Star: A History of Texas and the Texans* (1983); Lawrence Goodwyn, *Texas Observer* (27 December 1974); Ruth F. Hale, "A Map of Vernacular Regions in America" (Ph.D. dissertation, University of Minnesota, 1971); Jon Holmes, *Texas: A Self-Portrait* (1983); Paul Horgan, *Southwest Review* (Summer 1933); Terry G. Jordan, *Annals of the Association of American Geographers* (December 1967, September 1970); Joseph Leach, *The Typical Texan* (1952); Larry McMurtry, *In a Narrow Grave: Essays on Texas* (1968); D. W. Meinig, *Imperial Texas: An Interpretive Essay in Cultural Geography* (1969); Ben Proctor and Archie P. McDonald, eds., *The Texas Heritage* (1980); Frank

Vandiver, *The Southwest: South or West* (1975); Walter Prescott Webb, ed., *Handbook of Texas*, 2 vols. (1952).

Sports, Geography of

A trilogy of national games clearly dominates the South. Football is the premier sport, though baseball and basketball are played, enjoyed, and in some places avidly followed.

The best gauges of a sport's grip on an area are per capita involvement and the number of high quality performers originating from the place. The per capita production of major college and professional football (NFL) players has been calculated for the period 1968–80 so as to identify regional differences. The geographical origins of major league baseball players and collegiate basketball players have been charted for the same period.

The relative importance of baseball, football, and basketball varies across the South, as seen in Table 2. A value of 1.00 in the table indicates that a state's per capita talent output is equal to the national average. Values in excess of 1.00 indicate that a state produces more players than would be expected, and values of less than 1.00 suggest that the state is placing less emphasis on the sport than the nation as a whole. The majority of southern states are near or above the national norm for America's three major sports. Among southern states Louisiana, Mississippi, and Texas stand out as producers of football talent; Kentucky and Tennessee are the basketball leaders; Florida is the dominant baseball producer. The majority of the southern states (unlike most northern ones) are above the national football norm.

Table 2. *Southern Emphasis on Football, Basketball, and Baseball as Measured by per Capita Production of Players*

State	Football: Collegiate	Football: Professional	Basketball	Baseball
Alabama	1.03	2.19	1.09	1.07
Arkansas	1.13	1.69	0.75	0.37
Florida	1.22	1.31	0.81	1.55
Georgia	1.21	1.92	0.80	0.73
Kentucky	0.88	0.57	1.37	0.60
Louisiana	2.20	2.26	1.19	0.87
Mississippi	1.63	3.40	0.81	0.71
North Carolina	1.00	1.43	0.88	0.69
South Carolina	0.83	1.43	0.70	0.95
Tennessee	0.99	1.15	1.46	0.54
Texas	1.60	2.18	0.73	0.97
Virginia	1.16	0.75	1.15	0.83

Source: John F. Rooney, Jr., *American Demographics* (September 1986).
Note: A value of 1.00 indicates that a state's per capita talent output is equal to the national average.

Though football is a national game, the ability to play it well is inordinately concentrated in the South. As the

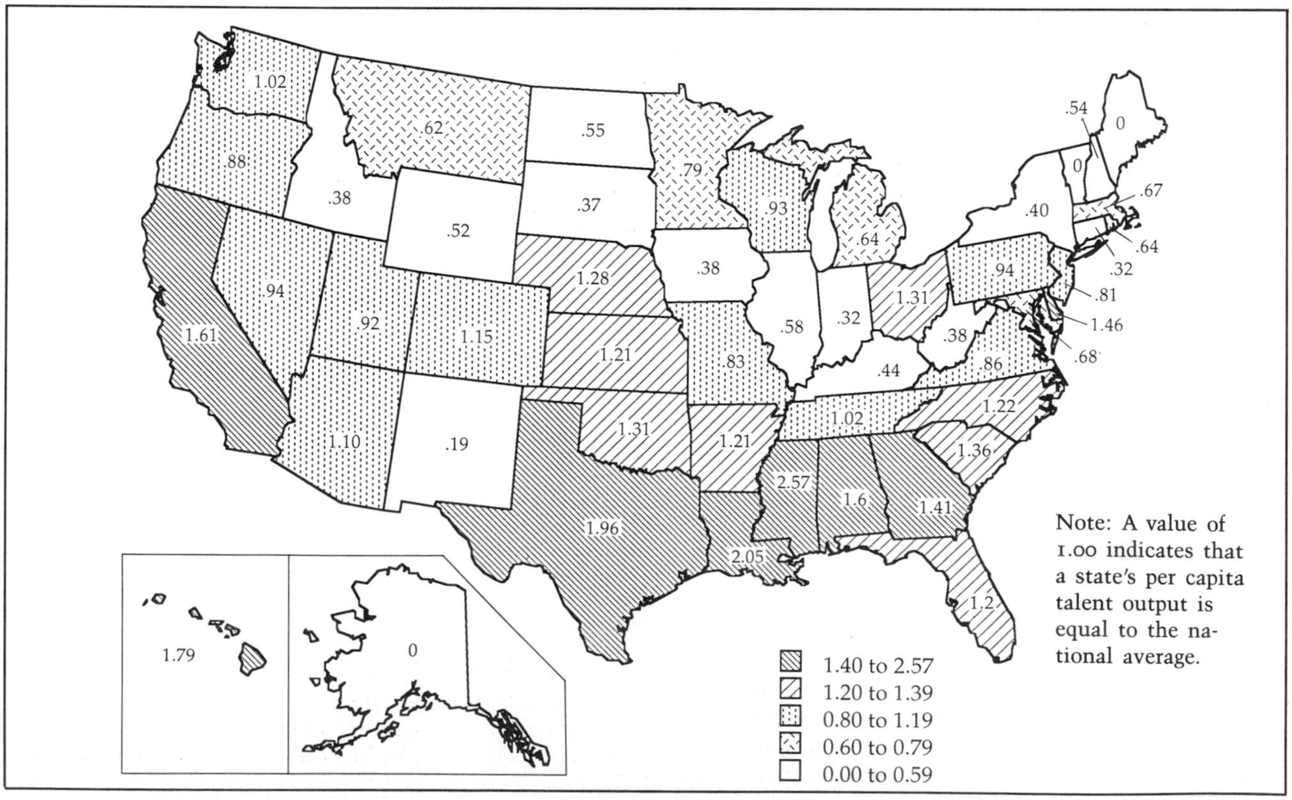

Index of Professional Football Players Produced by State, 1981

Source: John F. Rooney, Jr., "The Pigskin Cult and Other Sunbelt Sports," *American Demographics* (September 1986).

Table 3. *Leading Metropolitan Areas in Production of Major College Football Talent, 1968–1980*

Metropolitan Area	Total Players	Per Capita Rate
1. Lake Charles, La.	125	5.20
2. Monroe, La.	91	4.55
3. Beaumont–Port Arthur, Tex.	214	3.81
4. Shreveport, La.	184	3.34
5. Midland-Odessa, Tex.	88	3.24
6. Longview, Tex.	62	3.06
7. Youngstown-Warren, Ohio	238	2.85
8. Boise, Idaho	59	2.62
9. Biloxi-Gulfport, Miss.	116	2.61
10. Baton Rouge, La.	175	2.60
11. Jackson, Miss.	117	2.56
12. Tallahassee, Fla.	49	2.29
13. Great Falls, Mont.	29	2.23
14. Tyler, Tex.	38	2.21
15. Gainesville, Fla.	39	1.99

Source: John F. Rooney, Jr., *American Demographics* (September 1986).
Note: A value of 1.00 indicates that a metropolitan area's per capita talent output is equal to the national average.

Table 4. *Leading Nonmetropolitan Counties in Production of Major College Football Talent, 1968–1980*

County	Total Players	Per Capita Rate
1. St. James, La.	20	6.66
2. Warren, Miss.	38	4.93
3. Wharton, Tex.	24	4.17
4. Natchitoches, La.	23	4.07
5. Acadia, La.	33	3.94
6. Lincoln, La.	21	3.67
7. St. Martin, La.	19	3.50
8. Iberia, La.	30	3.05
9. Clarke, Ga.	33	3.03
10. Washington, La.	19	2.89

Source: John R. Rooney, Jr., *American Demographics* (September 1986).
Note: A value of 1.00 indicates that a county's per capita talent output is equal to the national average.

figures in Tables 3 and 4 reveal, southern cities and rural areas lead the nation in producing football players on the major college level. The South adopted a northern game, absorbed it fully into its culture, and gradually outdid the innovators. Based on the basketball evidence for the period 1970 to the present, the same pattern has been repeated with that sport. Football mania peaks each autumn in towns like Knoxville, Tuscaloosa, Auburn, Oxford, Gainesville, Baton Rouge, Grambling, Athens, Clemson, and Columbia. In February the recruiting saga now overshadows basketball and other ongoing sporting activities. In high schools the level of community pride associated with football is unparalleled.

Football mania is still intensifying throughout the South. Young players with football promise are frequently held back, "redshirted in the eighth grade," so that they will be physically capable of meeting the challenges of high school and college ball. Blacks now have access to the southern university of their choice, and they select big-name football schools with increasing regularity. In fact, much of the growth in southern player production can be attributed to the rise of the black athlete.

As a result of the emphasis on football, most high school sports programs in the South are lacking in breadth. High school boys throughout the region have very limited access to competitive swimming, gymnastics, wrestling, and soccer. Georgia and Florida are the only states above the national norm in soccer participation. Track-and-field and cross-country programs are relatively scarce, and Texas is the lone state above the national average. Golf and tennis are absent from a sizable portion of the high schools.

Women's sports receive little support in the South. Federal legislation requiring equal opportunity for women in sport has thus far failed to bring the South up to national standards. Texas and Oklahoma, possessing long-term basketball traditions, are exceptions to the southern void.

The South is heavily involved in a variety of other sports. Stock car racing is indigenous to the region, and even today the majority of the great drivers are of southern origin. Thoroughbred racing and breeding are concentrated in Kentucky and Virginia. Fox hunting and horse shows are common throughout the Upland South. Tennessee walkers are a distinct southern breed, and the quarter horse continues to grow in popularity throughout the Southwest. Florida is the shuffleboard capital of the world.

Though most southern states are below the national average in number of golf courses per capita, new course construction is proceeding at a rapid pace. Golf-oriented communities and golf resorts are highly concentrated within the region, creating the ultimate in luxury sports landscapes. Despite its lack of facilities, the South leads the nation in the output of professional golfers.

Lacrosse, rugby, and crew are largely absent from the southern sports scene, and for obvious reasons most activities requiring ice and snow are poorly developed.

See also BLACK LIFE: Sports, Blacks in; RECREATION articles

John F. Rooney, Jr.
Oklahoma State University

John F. Rooney, Jr., *American Demographics* (September 1986), *Geography of American Sport* (1974), *Geographical Review* (October 1969).

Towns and Villages

Early urban communities in the South were not founded by investors or entrepreneurs as they had been in New England and New York, nor were they created by government-subsidized railroads as in much of the Midwest and West. Rather, towns and villages that formed across much of the frontier South as service centers for a primarily agrarian clientele evolved out of transplanted European tradition and law. The plantations of the Tidewater colonies produced cotton, tobacco, and other commodities on a commercial scale, but their proprietors preferred to trade directly with Caribbean or European markets. Consequently, the market town did not develop early in eastern Virginia or the Carolinas as it did in the North, where farmers sold their surplus produce in village markets. Inland from the coast, the first hamlets were established by English, Scotch-Irish, and German settlers moving south from Pennsylvania along the Great Valley and Piedmont. At mill sites or where open country roads met, a farmstead or two, a church, school, and store would eventually coalesce into a loosely ordered crossroads hamlet.

The tradition of English law as established in the South was administered through a system of counties. County government was conducted at the county seat, usually the largest and often the only real town in the county. Government attracted professionals who served it and were served by it, and the county seat became the home of politicians, lawyers, bankers, enforcement officers, surveyors and engineers, and merchants—in short, the economic and social elite of the county. Their offices often faced a central town square on which stood the courthouse and jail, a county seat pattern that has diffused widely through the South from its origin in Pennsylvania. Few farmers lived in the county seat. If they lived in an urban place at all, it would be the crossroads hamlet. As the South grew, towns built around the central square appeared in adjacent territory and newly formed counties.

Variations on this urban scheme appeared as early as the 1760s when French Acadian migrants from Nova Scotia moved into Louisiana's Mississippi River Delta marshlands. There they built small line villages atop the natural levees of major streams according to a system of community organization and land division that had begun to mature in French Canada.

Before the Civil War, the economy of the South remained largely agricultural, and its urban settlements were small and parochial. The largest towns were coastal cotton shipping ports: Galveston, New Orleans, Mobile, Charleston, and Savannah. Inland, a string of river or fall line towns grew up at mill sites and navigational breaks: Richmond, Petersburg, Raleigh, Columbia, Augusta, and Macon.

After the Civil War, fundamental changes in regional and national culture and economy began to lay a foundation for dramatic alteration of the urban system. Freed slaves created a new type of settlement in some areas. Freedmen on many cotton plantations settled on dispersed parcels of plantation land in an initial stage of the sharecropping system. On sugar plantations in Louisiana and the livestock estates of the Kentucky Bluegrass, a somewhat different pattern of black resettlement occurred. In Louisiana, sugar plantations had large labor requirements during harvesting and refining. Consequently, freedmen working on plantations were housed in small linear hamlets, often located near sugar mills. In Kentucky, large Bluegrass estates required workers to handle livestock and produce hemp and tobacco cash crops. Slave quarters were eliminated and freedmen were given, or were allowed to rent or buy, housing in small hamlets, which were often subdivided out of a portion of estate property.

The end of the Civil War marked the rebuilding and extension of the southern rail system and the establishment of reliable trade links with the North. Rail lines focused at coastal harbors, river bridging points, and mountain gaps; when a new rail line was built into an existing town there was often a small boom in development as local entrepreneurs built lumberyards, tanneries, furniture plants, textile mills, and cotton gins. Towns on the Piedmont near streams that could provide small-scale hydroelectric power, or those near the hardwood stands of the Appalachian uplands, tended to benefit most from this transportation revolution. In peninsular Florida the effect of rail building was substantially different. Inhospitable marshlands became accessible for the first time, allowing rail companies to establish a number of new towns and resorts along the coasts.

The extension of railroads into the South also brought entrepreneurs seeking resources to fuel northern industry. Pennsylvania coal, for example, was used in local iron furnaces until high-strength steel rails and rolling stock made mining in the central Appalachians a profitable alternative. After 1870 northern industrialists sent representatives into the southern mountains to buy mineral rights over broad areas. As coal mines were established in eastern Kentucky, Tennessee, western Virginia, and West Virginia, company towns were built to house the men that the companies hoped to employ. Some towns, constructed by poorly financed companies, were small and pitifully built. Others, such as Lynch and Wheelwright, Ky., were extensive, planned communities housing populations of a thousand or more within a year of completion. Southern blacks, European immigrants, and local hill farmers were hired to mine coal and were settled in socially stratified towns. Small miners' houses were often crowded together in a valley bottom. More substantial mine managers' homes were usually placed upslope, away from dust, noise, and the miners. About 1870 several small company towns grew amidst the ridges and hardscrabble farms of north-central Alabama where local coal, iron ore, and limestone were used to produce iron. Gradually, the town of Birmingham grew from several such towns.

By the 1880s and 1890s the textile milling industry, so strongly entrenched in New England before 1860, was beginning to migrate to the Carolina and Georgia Piedmont. Mill owners, as they had done in England a century before and in New England after about 1790, built small towns at their mill sites to house workers. Many Piedmont farmers, burdened by debt and constrained by poor farming practices that produced little more than eroded fields, sent their wives and children to work in nearby mills. Mill homes clustered around a central company store, where workers purchased food and dry goods or used the post office or barber shops. Pay was often in scrip negotiable only at the company businesses.

Recreational towns began to appear at Virginia's thermal springs in the ridge and valley country west of Roanoke by the turn of the 19th century. Their growth was paralleled by high-altitude resort towns in the southern Blue Ridge Mountains such as Asheville and Highlands, N.C., which attracted wealthy Coastal Plain planters and merchants seeking relief from oppressive summer heat and miasma.

The broad pattern of small market towns interspersed with large numbers of crossroads hamlets and clusters of specialized company towns changed little until about 1930 when improved roads and automobiles allowed greater residential flexibility. Since World War II the population of many small towns has stagnated or even declined, and a new urban form, the linear roadside housing strip, has evolved. People purchase road-front lots from farmers, build homes, and commute to work in nearby towns. Consequently, town population may not change noticeably, but rural nonfarm density increases substantially. This process is especially evident in the Carolina Piedmont.

See also BLACK LIFE: Towns, Black; INDUSTRY: Industrialization in Appalachia; Industrialization in Piedmont; SOCIAL CLASS: / Company Towns; URBANIZATION articles

Karl B. Raitz
University of Kentucky

Conrad M. Arensberg, *American Anthropologist* (December 1955); Dwight B. Billings, *Planters and the Making of a "New South": Class, Politics, and Development in North Carolina, 1865–1900* (1979); John C. Campbell, *The Southern Highlander and His Homeland* (1921); Robert D. Mitchell, *Commercialism and Frontier: Perspectives on the Early Shenandoah Valley* (1977); M. B. Newton, Jr., *Geoscience and Man*, vol. 5 (1974); Peter Smith and Karl Raitz, *Geographical Review* (April 1974).

Black Belt

The Black Belt region, also called the Black Prairie, extends 300 miles across central Alabama and northeast Mississippi and into Tennessee. It is flat land, 20 to 25 miles wide, and lies from 200 to 300 feet below the uplands that are north and south of the region. The dark soil for which the Black Belt was named was once famous for its richness and the abundant cotton produced in it. Cotton was, in fact, the main cash crop from the 1820s until early in the 20th century, when losses from the boll weevil forced agricultural diversification. Some geographers speculate that the region, drained by the Alabama and Tombigbee river systems, was originally a grassland.

Social scientists sometimes use the term *black belt* to refer to that part of the South dominated by cotton plantations and having a high proportion of blacks in the population. Howard W. Odum, for example, in *Southern Regions of the United States* (1936), defined the Black Belt as extending into Georgia, the Carolinas, and western Mississippi. The culture of the poor who live in these areas has been the topic of several major studies, beginning with Odum's and including Charles S. Johnson's *Growing Up in the Black Belt* (1941) and Arthur F. Raper's *Tenants of the Almighty* (1943). These accounts give an insight into the lives of tenant-farm families and portray the changes that they experienced as tenancy collapsed. Johnson's description of the lives of rural black youths in several southern counties, based largely on interviews, gives details of their home life, education, aspirations, and attitudes toward whites. The Black Belt has been the incubator for much black culture, probably because of the concentration of population. Raper's study of Greene County, Ga., examines the benefits brought to the area by New Deal programs designed to alleviate the poverty of tenancy and to improve living conditions in the area. Other observers have noted the insularity of the region.

The region's white tenant-farm families were the subjects of James Agee and Walker Evans's *Let Us Now Praise Famous Men* (1936). Their blend of compassion and objectivity in photographs and text gives an intimate portrait of the lives of poor whites in Hale County, Ala., and includes vivid details of clothing, education, housing, and work. The book inspired William Christenberry, a Hale County native, to photograph the rural southern landscape, preserving the icons of that culture. Christenberry's artwork has attracted further attention to the unique Black Belt area and its people. The Black Belt Folk Roots Festival in Eutaw, Ala., celebrates the culture of western Alabama and eastern Mississippi each August.

Karen M. McDearman
University of Mississippi

William Christenberry, *Southern Photographs* (1983); Nevin M. Fenneman, *Physiography of Eastern United States* (1938); William D. Thornbury, *Regional Geomorphology of the United States* (1965).

Cherokee Settlement

The Cherokee nation, located in eastern Tennessee, the western Carolinas, northeastern Alabama, and northern Georgia, was one of the last important American Indian strongholds in the eastern United States in the early 19th century. The direct impact of their historical presence is confined to a few historic sites and buildings scattered throughout their home region and the small Qualla Reservation in North Carolina. Their influence on contemporary rural Appalachian settlement landscape, however, continues. Cherokee settlement patterns represent a case study of Indian influence on the South.

The Cherokee were divided into four culturally distinct communities on both sides of the Great Smoky

Mountains at the time of European contact in the 18th century: the Valley, Overhill, Middle, and Lower Towns. The core of Cherokee settlement was in the Middle Towns along the upper reaches of the Little Tennessee River in the western Carolinas. This period's settlement landscape featured large palisaded villages of 350 to 600 persons located in the major stream valleys of the region.

On his visit to the Cherokee country during the 1770s, William Bartram found clustered villages focusing upon roundish council houses located on an artificial hill or rise, as well as some scattered dwellings. The palisades around the villages disappeared during the relatively peaceful mid-18th century, and a more dispersed settlement pattern soon followed.

The four most common Cherokee building types during the 18th century were the council house, the summer and winter residential houses, and storage buildings. The council house was a large domed post-and-beam structure designed so that each of the Cherokee clans present in the village would have equal access to the center during community meetings. Its size varied depending upon the population of the village. The summer house was a three-roomed, raised, rectangular, post-and-beam house with woven reed or wicker walls. A long porch was built across the facade for use during the muggy summers. The adjacent winter house was often occupied by more than one family. It was built of poles in a domed shape with heavy walls, no windows, a small door, and an upper air hole for a chimney. A fire burned continually during the winter. Beds were located around the sides of the single room. The corn storage sheds were small post-and-beam structures raised four to five feet off the ground.

The Cherokee settlement landscape was massively altered after the incursion of white influences in the region. Population pressures and conflict along the eastern and northern borders moved the focal point of power from the western Carolinas first to Tennessee and later to northern Georgia. The Cherokee settlement pattern at the time of removal was also almost totally transformed. Clustered village settlements were replaced by isolated farmsteads. The traditional domed council house vanished. The summer and winter houses were replaced by small, single-pen, hewn-log, one-story, puncheon-floored, wooden-end chimney cottages. These log houses were occasionally enlarged to dogtrot, saddlebag, and I-house forms, but more often a second or third structure was built when additional space was needed. The outbuildings were also patterned on the white frontiersman's buildings and included, in declining order of frequency, corncribs, smokehouses, potato houses, and stables. The remainder of the farmstead consisted of a small truck garden near the house and one or more 5- to 20-acre cornfields.

The impact of Cherokee settlement upon both initial white settlement and the current landscape has been greater than generally believed. The Cherokee were removed from their traditional lands in the 1830s, and the vacated areas were distributed among white settlers. White settlement of the region, therefore, was essentially a continuation of the previous Indian patterns of field- and house-site selections. The recently vacated Cherokee housing generally was occupied by new white owners; many such houses are still used today. Indian agricultural methods, especially in the house gardens, crop complexes, and philosophies of field selection, also continued to be important in the white landscape. Indian paths and roads became white wagon roads and were eventually preserved in the state and county highway systems.

The principal differences between the two landscapes have been in the growth of towns. There were no true European-style Cherokee towns in northern Georgia at the time of removal. The Cherokee capital of New Echota, for example, never had more than a handful of houses occupied at one time, most of those by whites. At the time of removal, Cherokee towns were social and economic communities, whose residents were widely dispersed. Thus, at the time of removal the Indian "town" of Hightower had more than 100 residents scattered along 30 miles of the Ellijay River Valley, whereas the white town of Ellijay founded in the same location had only about 50 residents clustered around the courthouse within three years of its occupation.

See also ETHNIC LIFE: / Cherokees

Richard Pillsbury
Georgia State University

Gary C. Goodwin, *Cherokees in Transition: A Study of Changing Culture and Environment prior to 1775* (1977); Henry T. Malone, *Cherokees of the Old South* (1956); Richard Pillsbury, *Geoscience and Man*, vol. 23 (1983).

Cotton Gins

Cotton gins once were common features on the landscape across much of the Lowland South. The demise of cotton in areas where it was king and the replacement of many small gin plants by a few large ones in areas where cotton continues to be an important crop have resulted in the dramatic decrease in the number of cotton gins in the South. The number declined from 30,000 in 1900 to less than 10,000 in 1945. In 1981 only 1,819 active cotton gins remained in the southern states. However, the average number of bales processed per cotton gin increased from less than 500 in 1900 to more than 5,000 in 1981.

During the early part of the 20th century larger, centrally located plants employing what was termed a "ginning system" replaced small, labor-intensive antebellum-type ginning facilities. The type of ginning facility that developed prior to the Civil War consisted of a ginhouse in which the removal of seed from the lint, or ginning, took place. In the ginhouse the seed cotton was fed into a gin stand powered by horses or mules. The lint cotton was carried in baskets from the ginhouse to a horse- or

Cotton gin, Mississippi, no date

mule-powered press. Most of the cotton plantations had such a facility, and it could process three or four bales of cotton in a day.

The ginning system was developed during the 1880s. A steam-powered plant integrated the ginning with the baling and automated the movement of cotton through the facility. A ginning system contained several gin stands and could process three or four bales of cotton per hour. The term *cotton gin* came to refer to such plants, whereas in its original usage the term had referred to just the gin stand.

The introduction of mechanical harvesters following World War II initiated another period of dramatic change in cotton ginning. Because mechanically harvested cotton contains more trash and moisture than cotton picked by hand, seed-cotton dryers and lint-cleaning devices had to be added to gin plants, and whereas hand picking commenced in late summer and frequently continued into December, mechanical pickers compressed the harvest season into a period of approximately six weeks. High-capacity gin plants with larger gin stands were introduced to handle the increased flow of cotton from the fields. Recent innovations include module storage of cotton prior to ginning and the use of universal density presses that produce bales ready for shipment to distant markets without further compressing.

A modern cotton gin represents a substantial capital investment and is capable of ginning 10 or more bales of machine-harvested cotton per hour. Antebellum-type ginning facilities were within 2 to 4 miles of one another, and plants employing ginning systems were 3 to 12 miles apart. Modern cotton gins may draw cotton from a 30-mile radius.

See also AGRICULTURE: / Cotton Culture

Charles S. Aiken
University of Tennessee

Charles S. Aiken, *Geographical Review* (April 1973); Charles A. Bennett, *Cotton Ginning Systems in the United States and Auxiliary Development* (1962), *Saw and Toothed Ginning Developments* (1960).

Courthouse Square

The county seat was the South's most traditional urban form. The courthouse and its square were the scene of the vital governmental activities, as well as the focal point of the town's commercial life. Four basic courthouse-square designs have been found in the South. The oldest is the widened-street design dating from 17th-century Virginia. It consists of an enlarged courthouse lot on one side of the main street. The plan is most common in Tidewater Virginia, although examples are occasionally found in earlier settled areas throughout the South. The widened street, an extension of the medieval European market-street concept modified to meet the needs of a courthouse site, is rarely found outside of Virginia.

The second design, called the secant square, is a subform of the widened-street plan. It was created by cutting back the four corners of the main intersection to leave an open square in the street. In America the design was first used in 1681 to create space for the Philadelphia city hall. This geometric adaptation of the widened street plan was most common in county seats founded after 1790 in the Upland South, especially in the southern Appalachians.

The third design, the central square, is considered to be the regional archetype. It consists of a full-city-block square at the intersection of the two main through roads. This is the most common courthouse square pattern in county seats founded after 1800, and its distribution parallels the founding of new counties in the South after that date.

A fourth design is the off-set central-square subform created when the courthouse block is astride the main through road. This design, with obvious ancillary antecedents in the secanted design, has the advantage of placing the courthouse in a position of physical, visual, and psychological dominance within the town plan. Used primarily after 1800, the off-set square design appeared occasionally in the later settled South.

The courthouse square is significant because of its centralizing influence within a community. The square was for decades the center of governmental, economic, and social life in the surrounding area. Nineteenth-century county courthouses almost always were located on the square. Other typical structures on the early-19th-century square included wells, cisterns, and occasionally the jail and lawyers' offices. County officials in later periods tended to move the jail off the square to a less prominent location.

Examples from Georgia illustrate the range of activities common on late-19th-century courthouse squares. The most common retail activities on the blocks facing

Courthouse in Monticello, Fla., 1939

the square in Georgia county seats at this time, in declining order of frequency, were general-merchandise stores, offices, grocery stores, dry-goods stores, millineries, drugstores, hotels, lodge halls, and saloons. The second most common land use on the blocks facing the square was residential: typically about 20 percent of this space was devoted to dwellings located along one side and at the back of other blocks.

The courthouse square of the late 20th century has undergone a metamorphosis since the halcyon days of a century before. The original courthouse has frequently been replaced with a new building on a different site. The automobile has often forced competitive retailers to new locations on the commercial strip at the edge of towns. The remaining commercial establishments often have a sagging air of knowing that their time has passed. The smallest of the county seats have lost their viable commercial functions to larger towns. A few attempts at historic preservation and downtown revival impede this process, but even these activities often do little more than highlight the decline of this urban form.

Nonetheless, the courthouse has long been identified as the geographical center of southern communities. In *Requiem for a Nun*, William Faulkner wrote of Jefferson, Miss.: "But above all, the courthouse: the center, the focus, the hub . . . looming in the center of the county's circumference . . . laying its vast shadow to the uttermost rim of the horizon . . . ; dominating all: protector of the weak, judicate and curb of the passions and lust. . . ."

Richard Pillsbury
Suzanne Andres
Georgia State University

Richard Francaviglia, *The Geographical Survey* (1973); Richard Pillsbury, *Southeastern Geographer*, vol. 18 (1978); Edward T. Price, *Geographical Review* (January 1968).

Cuban Settlement

Cuban Americans represent the third largest group of Latin American origin living in the United States, being exceeded in number only by Mexican Americans and Puerto Ricans. Currently, about 1 million Cubans live in the United States, approximately 70 percent of whom are in the state of Florida. Very few Cubans live in other southern states (even in Florida they account for only about 6 percent of the state's population), but their importance is magnified because they are heavily concentrated in the metropolitan area of Miami, where over 600,000 persons of Cuban descent live. They have made a distinctive mark on a southern subregion. In Dade County (Metropolitan Miami) about 41 percent of the population consists of persons of Hispanic origin, and about 80 percent of these people are either first- or second-generation Cubans. The Cubans have had a major impact on the cultural landscape and economy of Miami, so much so that their major area of concentration is called "Little Havana."

Cubans came as permanent settlers to Key West as far back as 1831. Immigration to Florida, and especially to Tampa, increased in the 1870s. These early Cuban Americans came to the United States for a variety of reasons; many were simply unemployed or looking for better jobs, while others in the 20th century were politically alienated from right-wing Cuban regimes. The number of emigrants from Cuba rose sharply after the 1959 Castro Revolution. The Cubans who have moved to the United States have not, until recently, been representative of the population left behind in Cuba. The earliest significant wave of immigrants after 1959 was especially selective of professionals and entrepreneurs and thus created a serious "brain drain" in Cuba. As a result of this selection, a social and economic base was established in Miami that would help ease the adjustments of future immigrants. Today, Cuban Americans generally enjoy high levels of socioeconomic status compared to most other groups of Latin American descent.

Without warning, in April 1980, Fidel Castro suddenly allowed a massive exodus to the United States through the Cuban port of Mariel. Over the next six months approximately 125,000 Cubans immigrated to this country, with about 80 percent settling in south Florida. The "Marielitos" come closest as a group to representing the population in Cuba. Although the Cuban government included in their number about 5,000 prisoners from Cuban jails and patients from mental institutions, the vast majority (perhaps 95 percent) were not criminals or misfits. The collective wisdom of most who have studied them is that the Mariel immigrants will quickly and effectively accommodate themselves to life in the United States.

Cuban Americans attempted to preserve parts of their island culture after moving to Florida. The refugees from the 1959 revolution especially worked at this goal. The widespread use in south Florida of Spanish in shops, restaurants, banks, churches, and government offices is the most visible evidence of their success in maintaining cultural forms. Spanish-language bookstores stock writings of Cuban expatriates, Cuban-born artists perform in ethnic theater and dance groups, and neighborhood grocery stores in Miami stock fruits and vegetables traditional to the Cuban diet. Spanish-language television and radio stations broadcast programs for Cuban Americans, and a daily newspaper—owned, like the broadcast facilities, by Cuban Americans—publishes stories of interest to the community. Latin rhythms are heard in the nightclubs in Little Havana.

See also ETHNIC LIFE: / Cubans

Thomas D. Boswell
University of Miami

Thomas D. Boswell, in *Ethnic Minorities in the United States*, ed. Jesse O. McKee (1983), with James R. Curtis, *The Cuban-American Experience: Culture, Images, and Perspectives* (1983); Sergio Diza-Briquets and Lisandro Perez, *Cuba: The Demography of Revolution*, Population Reference Bureau, vol. 36, no. 1 (April 1981).

Delta

The Yazoo-Mississippi Delta is not the true delta of the Mississippi River, but the fertile alluvial plain shared by the Mississippi and Yazoo rivers. One hundred sixty miles long and 50 miles wide at its widest point, the Delta encompasses all of 10 Mississippi counties and parts of 8 more. Distinguished by its flatness and its fertility, the Delta was even better defined by its late-developing plantation economy and the distinctive society that economy nurtured.

Destined to become the richest agricultural region in the South, the Delta was only sparsely settled in 1860 and still not far removed from the frontier in 1880. During the next two decades a new network of levees and a modern railway system opened the plantation South's last frontier for full-scale settlement and development.

The fertile Delta drew not only ambitious whites, but blacks who saw it as the best place to test their newly won freedom and climb the agricultural ladder to become independent landowners. For many whites the Delta became a land of wildest fantasies fulfilled, but for thousands of blacks the Delta that had promised them the rural South's best chance for upward mobility became the burial ground for hopes and dreams. In reality the Delta proved to be little more than a stopover for many southern blacks on their way (via the conveniently located Illinois Central Railroad that bisected the area) to the North. The Delta experienced a massive out-migration of blacks in the years after World War I. During the same period the region was emerging as a spawning ground for the blues. This new musical idiom explored the shared experiences of southern blacks who had tested the economic, social, and political parameters of their freedom, as defined by a rigidly enforced system of caste, and discovered that, for them, the American Dream was little more than a cruel myth.

Meanwhile, despite their constant fears over labor shortages, Delta planters thrived on the annual gamble on the price of cotton, living lavishly and laughing at debts. Even the onslaught of the boll weevil did the Delta relatively little harm. Meanwhile, the Agricultural Adjustment Administration (AAA) confirmed the dominance of the large landholder in the region by channeling all of its acreage reduction and related payments through planters and looking the other way as these same planters illegally evicted now-superfluous sharecroppers. In 1934, 44 percent of all AAA payments in excess of $10,000 nationwide went to 10 counties in the Delta. This largesse facilitated the mechanization and consolidation of agriculture, and as federal farm programs continued, the money kept rolling in. In 1967 Delta planter and U.S. senator James Eastland received $167,000 in federal payments. The Delta's poor blacks were not nearly so fortunate, as a power structure dominated by lavishly subsidized planters declared war on the War on Poverty.

Many Delta planters finally met their day of reckoning in the farm crisis of the 1980s and, although the Delta was the birthplace of the Citizens' Council and a citadel of white resistance to racial equality, the black-majority area finally elected a black congressman, Mike Espy, in 1986. The region's history had been one of tension and struggle—between the races, against the poorer hill counties, against the impenetrable swampy wilderness and the ravages of flood, pestilence, and disease, and, finally, against the intrusions of civil rights activists and federal civil rights policies.

Out of this tangle of tension and paradox came a remarkable outpouring of creativity, one that made the Delta's artistic climate arguably as rich as its agricultural one. Greenville alone produced writers William Alexander Percy, Walker Percy, Shelby Foote, Ellen Douglas, Hodding Carter II, Hodding Carter III, David Cohn, and Beverly Lowry. Classical composer Kenneth Haxton is from the Greenville area, as are sculptor Leon Koury and artist Valerie Jaudon. The Delta has produced a host of entertainers including Jim Henson, creator of the Muppets, country singers Charley Pride and Conway Twitty, and an especially large number of blues singers past and present, from the legendary Charley Patton to contemporary artists like B. B. King and James "Son" Thomas. Sometimes appalling, always fascinating, the Delta's historical and cultural experience often seemed that of an entire region in microcosm. It richly deserved the title accorded it by writer Richard Ford, "the South's South."

See also BLACK LIFE: / Citizens' Council; FOLKLIFE: / Thomas, James; LITERATURE: / Foote, Shelby; Percy, Walker; MEDIA: / Carter, Hodding; MUSIC: / King, B. B.

James C. Cobb
University of Alabama

Robert L. Brandfon, *Cotton Kingdom of the New South: A History of the Yazoo Mississippi Delta from Reconstruction to the Twentieth Century* (1967); David L. Cohn, *Where I Was Born and Raised* (1967).

Faulkner's Geography

Most of William Faulkner's works are set in Yoknapatawpha County. Yoknapatawpha is a fictional place inhabited by fictional persons, but Faulkner integrated it into a geographical setting that included prominent actual places. Yoknapatawpha County is in north central Mississippi, 70 miles south of Memphis, Tenn. Faulkner thought of Yoknapatawpha as having the same geographical position as the real Lafayette County, Miss., and the geography of the fictional place is based heavily on the geography of that county. Like Lafayette, Yoknapatawpha County is drained in the north by the Tallahatchie River and in the south by the Yoknapatawpha, the fictional name of the Yocona River. Jefferson, the political seat of Yoknapatawpha County, has many geographical similarities to Oxford, the political seat of Lafayette County.

Despite similarities between Yoknapatawpha County and Lafayette County, many differences exist. Faulkner created Yoknapatawpha by combining the real, the modified, and the imaginary. The geography of Lafayette County and Oxford were changed in four principal ways—locations were shifted, place names were changed, components were omitted, and reality was blended with fabrication. Shifts in locations of objects, places, and events were sometimes intercounty and involved temporal as well as geographical changes. In addition to Lafayette County, Faulkner also drew from Marshall, Tippah, and Panola counties, Miss., in creating Yoknapatawpha.

In developing his model for Yoknapatawpha County, Faulkner intended it neither as Lafayette County thinly disguised nor, at the other extreme, as the entire South in microcosm. Rather he viewed it as a place that, though located in the South, was one in which he could describe the universal experience of humankind.

See also LITERATURE: / Faulkner, William; MYTHIC SOUTH: / Yoknapatawpha County

Charles S. Aiken
University of Tennessee

Charles S. Aiken, *Geographical Review* (January 1977, July 1979); Calvin S. Brown, *A Glossary of Faulkner's South* (1976).

Georgia Land Lottery

The land-lottery system used to distribute Georgia public lands to citizens of the state after 1803 was unique, and, although little known outside the state, it brought about a considerable change in the method of land occupation and settlement. Instead of pioneers moving into former Indian territories and claiming vacant land almost at random, orderly land acquisition was achieved after 1803. The new lands were systematically surveyed and mapped by the state prior to their occupation by settlers.

The Headright Land Act of 1783 proved to be a reasonable method of dispensing public lands to Georgia's citizens until 1789. From 1789 to 1802, however, the state became entangled in a series of land frauds concerning land within the present state limits as well as a vast territory extending west from the Chattahoochee River to the Mississippi River.

The radical new system of distribution adopted in response to this situation was a public land lottery controlled and conducted by state officials. Six lotteries were held between 1805 and 1836. Each area of the public land to be opened for settlement was created as a county unit and then divided by survey into large numbered land districts. Each district was then subdivided into numbered land lots. The size and area of both land districts and individual land lots in each lottery were determined by the specific legislative acts authorizing each of the six lotteries. Land-district and land-lot lines were generally aligned with the four principal compass points—north, south, east, and west—with the exception of the lotteries of 1805 and 1807 and a portion of the 1820 lottery. Fragments of land lots in the various lotteries were retained by the state and, after each lottery, sold at public auction.

After the lottery was authorized, qualified citizens of the state registered for it in their respective counties. The list of registrants was then sent to the capital, where each name was placed on an individual lottery ticket and put in a drum. Each land lot offered in the lottery was identified by county, land district, and land-lot number on another ticket (for example, "District 2, Lot 27, Baldwin County"), and each of these was placed in a second drum. Winners were required to pay a small grant fee. Upon payment the land won became theirs. Lots that were not claimed reverted to the state and were sold later. Once a person received land by lottery draw, there were no requirements for improvements or even residence on the land in order to maintain possession. Essentially, all of the territory west of the Oconee and Altamaha rivers was distributed by means of public lottery.

Gerald L. Holder
Sam Houston State University

James E. Callaway, *The Early Settlement of Georgia* (1948); Georgia Secretary of State, Surveyor General Department, *Land Lotteries* (1966); S. G. McLendon, *History of the Public Domain of Georgia* (1924).

Little Dixie

The establishment of "dixies" beyond the boundaries of the Confederacy itself in the 19th century was a phenomenon rich with meaning. The idea of a "Little Dixie" located outside the geophysical South echoes important themes in cultural history. Although there are "dixies" in Utah, Wyoming, Oklahoma, southern Illinois and Indiana, and probably elsewhere, the best-known of these islands of southern culture is Missouri's "Little Dixie" folk region.

Little Dixie is a cultural region in northern Missouri (significantly not in the widely publicized Ozarks of the southern part of the state) composed of eight counties and a vague zone of transition in surrounding counties. The principal counties are Howard, Boone, Callaway, Audrain, Randolph, Monroe, Pike, and Ralls. The main towns are Fayette, Keytesville, Salisbury, Marshall, Columbia, Fulton, Mexico, Huntsville, Moberly, Paris, Monroe City, Bowling Green, New London, Hannibal, and Palmyra. The region was settled in the early 19th century by emigrants from the Tidewater and Piedmont areas of Virginia, Maryland, the Carolinas, Kentucky, and Tennessee, with Virginia and Kentucky the most important sources. The settlers were largely of British Protestant stock and transplanted their cultural traditions alongside their valuable crops of burley tobacco and hemp. These pioneers were well suited to the new environment, and many chose this area because it so closely resembled their home territories.

The region, which comprises forest, prairie, and rich bottomland, is bounded by major rivers—the Missouri on the south and the Mississippi on the east. The northern border of Little Dixie coincides with later settlement by northerners and easterners, while the western border is vague and lingers along the Missouri River toward Kansas City. The region lies culturally and physiographically between the Ozark Highlands and the corn belt.

Upland southern traditions of fiddle playing, social dance, basketmaking, the preservation of meat, religious practices, dialect and speech, attitudes toward social organization, and most eloquently, perhaps, architectural patterns and political behavior demonstrate the linkages between the people of Little Dixie and the home regions of the Piedmont, the Tidewater, and the Bluegrass. The "old southern mansions" that mark the rural landscape and the persistent devotion to "the Democratic party" are reminders of a way of life now nearly lost because of the Civil War (and particularly the memory of Reconstruction), settlement by "Yankees," and simply the passage of time. Material culture—architecture, diet, farmstead site arrangement, craft traditions, agricultural economic practices—can still, however, provide a tangible nexus for regional feeling. The region's most famous son, Samuel Langhorne Clemens (Mark Twain), born to a slaveholding family in Monroe County, first learned about life and human behavior at his Uncle John Quarles's farm in Missouri's Little Dixie.

Disenfranchised by Reconstruction "carpetbag" administrators and left with a meager remnant of the prewar way of life, white southerners after the Civil War began to create a psychological space for themselves, a region thought of as Little Dixie, in which old ways and old things retained meaning in the face of change and loss. For older white southerners, the postwar events that upset the economy and altered hierarchical social patterns, and the coming of northerners and Germans able to purchase the lands of the impoverished settlers, represented the close of an era that would later be thought of as a golden age of prewar Missouri.

The idea of Little Dixie evolved in the 1870s and 1880s in response to the malaise and loss experienced by those who had originally created much of Missouri society. A feeling of continuity and order was achieved through evolution of a memory culture that respected and lauded past ways of life and work. The vision of Little Dixie's residents is largely based on a "southern" past (which some call "the old slave days") of log houses, tobacco fields, country hams, fox hunts, rail fences, and what they imagine to have been a more genteel lifestyle, and on the dominance of the Democratic party in political life.

Today media attention keeps the vision of Little Dixie alive in Missouri and in other areas. Such visions operate with the tacit approval of the local population who created a microregion and a safe harbor beyond the geographic South.

Howard W. Marshall
Missouri Cultural Heritage Center
University of Missouri at Columbia

Robert M. Crisler, *Journal of Geography* (November 1950), *Missouri Historical Review* (October 1947, July 1948); Howard W. Marshall, *Folk Architecture in Little Dixie: A Regional Culture in Missouri* (1981), *Journal of American Folklore* (October–December 1979), in *Readings in American Folklore*, ed. Jan Harold Brunvand (1979).

Mason-Dixon Line

"An artificial line . . . and yet more unalterable than if nature had made it for it limits the sovereignty of four states, each of whom is tenacious of its particular systems of law as of its soil. It is the boundary of empire."

Writing his history of the Mason-Dixon line in 1857, James Veech reflected the well-founded anxieties of the day: the fear that the horizontal fault between slave and free territory was about to become an open breach. Although the Mason-Dixon line was long associated with the division between free and slave states, slavery existed on both its sides when it was first drawn. To settle a long-standing boundary dispute arising from ambiguous colonial charters, the Calvert and Penn families chose English astronomers Charles Mason and Jeremiah Dixon to survey the territory. After four years of work (1763–67) they fixed the common boundaries of Maryland and Pennsylvania at 39°43′17.6″ north latitude, marking their line at every fifth mile with stones bearing the arms of the Penn family on one side and the Calvert crest on the other. Mason and Dixon were halted in their westward survey by the presence of hostile Indians, but their work was concluded in 1784 by a new team that included David Rittenhouse, Andrew Ellicott, and Benjamin Banneker.

In 1820 the Missouri Compromise temporarily readjusted the fragile tacit balance between slave and free territory and extended the Mason-Dixon line to include the 36th parallel. By that date, all states north of the line had abolished slavery, and the acceptance of the line as the symbolic division both politically and socially between North and South was firmly established.

The Mason-Dixon line has been a source of many idiomatic expressions and popular images. Slogans ("Hang your wash to dry on the Mason-Dixon line") originated with early antislavery agitation; variations on the theme (Smith and Wesson line) and novel applications (the logo for a cross-country trucking firm) are contemporary phenomena. A popular shorthand for a sometimes mythic, sometimes very real regional distinction, the term *Mason-Dixon line* continues to be used and its meaning is immediately comprehended.

Elizabeth M. Makowski
University of Mississippi

Journals of Charles Mason and Jeremiah Dixon (1969); John H. B. Latrobe, *History of Mason and Dixon's Line* (1855); James Veech, ed., *Mason and Dixon's Line: A History* (1857).

Mills and Milling

Southern gristmills were generally small, custom-grinding operations that were scattered profusely across the landscape. Their service area was small, and frequently they were built where water could power a waterwheel.

The southern mill (as distinct from that of the Mid-Atlantic, Midwest, or New England) was usually a frame structure of one or two stories. The earliest mills were occasionally log and closely resembled the Norse mill of central and northern Europe. Water was directed against the vanes of a horizontal wheel attached to a vertical shaft. The shaft passed through a stationary bedder stone and balanced a runner stone that turned at the same speed as the wheel. Found mostly in mountainous areas of the South, this horizontal mill quickly gave way to the vertical mill.

Grist mill, on the way to Skyline Drive, Virginia, 1938

Southern mills were neither as sophisticated nor as structurally well built as those encountered in the North or in Europe. They also differed as a regional feature in that they persisted in the use of vertical waterwheels long after the turbine was commonly accepted in other parts of the eastern United States. Rather than changing from waterwheels to turbines as rapidly as possible for the sake of efficiency, the change and requisite regearing occurred when the old wooden or iron wheels required replacement. As a result, larger northern mills modernized more rapidly and outstripped southern grinding capacity.

In addition, southern gristmills focused almost exclusively upon the production of cornmeal. Wheat was a secondary crop, especially in the Deep South, and other cereals were even more rare. Wheat milling, or merchant milling, was restricted to urban areas, where there was a demand for sifted flour and where capitalization for the necessary additional equipment was more readily available. Thus, the smaller frame mill served primarily for private use by local farmers.

Milling was one of the earliest economic activities in the South. Although European, technological antecedents are undisputed, the southern miller and millwright were quite flexible in adapting mills to meet local demands. No evidence exists to support the generally held view that mills acted as magnets drawing settlers to the frontier, either within or without the South, nor did mill sites often serve as centers for town development. Merchant milling, changes in dietary preference, and the blacktop road and automobile all had an impact on the decline of milling in the South. This decline was evident in the 1930s and accelerated by the end of World War II to the point that southern gristmilling ceased to be a viable economic activity. *Waterground* (Appalshop Film, Frances Morton, director, 1977) is a film study of one of the last water-powered gristmills.

D. Gregory Jeane
Auburn University

Charles Howell and Allan Keller, *The Mill of Philipsburg Manor, Upper Mills and a Brief History of Milling* (1977); Charles Bryon Kuhlman, *The Development of the Flour-Milling Industry in the United States* (1929); John Storck and Walter Dorwin Teague, *Flour for Man's Bread* (1952).

Northern Cities, Whites in

The most visible southern culture found in northern cities is black culture, but millions of white southerners have also migrated, taking their southern culture with them. Like most migrants they have been a varied lot, including professional people, artists, and intellectuals. The largest segment has been poor people seeking work. They have concentrated in low-rent areas accessible to factories or transportation lines, developing neighborhood institutions and informal networks.

In these places both "southern culture" and stereotypes of southerners as "hillbillies," "rednecks," or "crackers" have been most evident. Clannishness, a proclivity to violence, love of hillbilly music, and low standards of sexual morality, household cleanliness, and personal hygiene have been part of the stereotype. White southerners have also been accused of diffusing attitudes of white supremacy to other regions.

Although appearing to be ethnically distinct because of differences in language, music, and food preferences, such culture is ethnic only by coincidence. The overlay of southern ethnic features on working-class culture is seen most clearly in the "hillbilly taverns" found in sections of some northern cities. The language is English, but it is spoken with a southern accent. The music is country or western, the ambience small-town.

The distinctive accent and regional food preferences constitute enduring traits of southern culture. The most pervasive and persistent feature of regional culture retained by these southerners living outside the South is religion, evangelical Protestant Christianity. Storefront churches of southern Pentecostal sects are most noticeable, but Baptist, Methodist, and Presbyterian churches have found their customs influenced by the presence of southerners.

Lewis M. Killian
University of Massachusetts
at Amherst

Lewis M. Killian, *Social Forces* (October 1953), *White Southerners* (1970); William W. Philliber, *Appalachian Migrants in Urban America: Cultural Conflict or Ethnic Group Formation?* (1981).

Piedmont

The Piedmont region extends from the Hudson River to central Alabama, bordering on the Blue Ridge and Appalachian mountains, and ranges from 10 to 125 miles in width. While it is part of the Appalachian highlands, the Piedmont landscape is not mountainous but rolling. Its relatively infertile soil discouraged settlers until the late 18th and early 19th centuries. The region has been known predominantly as an agricultural region, although it developed industries such as textiles and furniture making in the 19th century. The development of the southern Piedmont (extending to Birmingham, Ala.) has been shaped by the iron and coal industries.

The term *Piedmont* refers to the Piedmont "crescent" of North and South Carolina, continuing into parts of Georgia and Alabama. The Carolina Piedmont has been characterized in the mid- to late-20th century by urban growth. Its cities are headquarters for various large business enterprises, including R. J. Reynolds tobacco company in Winston-Salem, N.C., and Burlington Industries in Greensboro, N.C.

The textile industry was the first industry to develop in the Piedmont. Numerous small streams attracted power spinning (built on waterwheels) as early as 1790 in several South Carolina communities. The first mill was built in North Carolina in 1813, and, after the Civil War and Reconstruction, abundant cheap labor gave the area's textile industry an enormous boost. The low humidity of the region was originally thought to be an obstacle to the operation of the mills, but artificial humidity was developed to create the necessary atmosphere.

Tobacco is one of the most important crops in the northern Piedmont area. The attendant tobacco industry, the manufacture of cigarettes and chewing and smoking tobacco, is concentrated in a few centers in Virginia, Kentucky, and Tennessee, but is centered in North Carolina. James B. Duke's use of the first cigarette-rolling machine in the 1880s catapulted the region into its prominent (and, at one point, dominant) role in the industry.

The Piedmont region has been the source of and the setting for some important southern literature. *The Mind of the South* (1941) was written by W. J. Cash from Gaffney, S.C., whose father was an employee of a textile mill. His interpretation of the nature of southerners rests largely on his treatment of his native Carolina Piedmont region. Cash focused much of his study on the rise of the upland cotton planter in the early 19th century and the later growth of the textile mill and mill village. The fiction of Reynolds Price, from Macon, N.C., is set in the rural Piedmont South. His works, such as *A Long and Happy Life*, his first novel, and *The Names and Faces of Heroes*, a collection of stories, use regional syntax and colorful description to evoke an understanding of the setting. Other writers who were influenced by their roots and study in the Piedmont region are Thomas Wolfe, born in Asheville, N.C., and Erskine Caldwell, whose *Tobacco Road* (1932) is set in Wrens County, Ga.

Karen M. McDearman
University of Mississippi

Neal R. Peirce and Jerry Hagstrom, *The Book of America: Inside 50 States Today* (1983); Louis D. Rubin, Jr., *William Elliott Shoots a Bear: Essays on the Southern Literary Imagination* (1975); Anthony M. Tang, *Economic Development in the Southern Piedmont, 1860–1950: Its Impact on Agriculture* (1958); William D. Thornbury, *Regional Geomorphology of the United States* (1965); Rupert B. Vance, *Human Geography of the South: A Study in Regional Resources and Human Adequacy* (1932).

Piney Woods

The piney woods, or pine belt, of the Southeast is a vast region of forestland stretching through nine southern states from the Carolinas through Georgia and into Texas. The land of the "pine barrens" is not particularly well suited for agriculture, but the heavy rainfall and long, warm, sunny summers provide ideal conditions for the rapid growth of pines. The most important species of pine found in the region are the shortleaf, longleaf, loblolly, and slash pine. The heaviest and strongest of these, the southern longleaf yellow pine, is the most popular among timber growers.

The piney woods has been the victim of human settlement and exploitation. Pioneers used burning techniques they learned from the Indians to clear the land for cultivation and building. Industries later developed markets for pine products and methods for extracting resins and producing turpentine. Beginning in the 20th century, pine was used for a variety of timber products including pulpwood for paper. The free grazing of livestock also took its toll on the piney woods region.

During the antebellum period the national government first attempted to preserve and protect forests. At the turn of the century the government began the development of policies that recognized that forests are not only commodities to be exploited but are renewable resources. During the New Deal era, state and national conservation efforts were given a boost by the Civilian Conservation Corps, which planted acres of worn-out farmland with trees.

Geographers and historians have studied the way people have adapted to the southern forests. The region has been characterized by poverty and relatively sparse population because of the dense woods. Frank L. Owsley showed in the early 1950s that classification of antebellum pine-belt inhabitants as agricultural poor whites was misleading. Actually, the primary occupation of the people of the piney woods was grazing cattle and hogs. They also hunted and trapped for food—true to their character as frontiersmen, according to Owsley.

Developments in the south Mississippi area drained by the Pearl River are indicative of 20th-century trends in the piney woods region. The Pearl River, positioned halfway between the Mississippi River and the Alabama and Tombigbee river systems, runs through the heart of the pine belt. The Pearl River bottomlands were uncharacteristically fertile for the pine lands, and some cotton plantations were developed there. Migrants eventually set up communities along the river and cleared the land, using the river to transport pine and cypress logs to the sawmills downriver. Railroads eventually changed the landscape further, and the timber industry flourished. By the 1930s, however, the pine supply had been devastated and the cutover soil depleted of nutrients, forcing the region to turn to alternate sources of income. Initially the lower Pearl River residents planted the Chinese tung tree for its nuts, from which oils were extracted for sale to varnish and paint companies. Hurricane Camille in 1969 destroyed the troubled tung industry. At the same time, a National Aeronautics and Space Administration (NASA) rocket test facility in the area also gave economic hope to the piney-woods people, but the NASA program fell short of expectations and once again the region was left in poverty.

Karen M. McDearman
University of Mississippi

John Hawkins Napier III, *Lower Pearl River's Piney Woods* (1986); Howard W. Odum, *Southern Regions of the United States* (1936); Frank L. Owsley, *Plain Folk of the Old South* (1949); Rupert B. Vance, *Human Geography of the South: A Study in Regional Resources and Human Adequacy* (1932).

Primogeniture

Legally defined, *primogeniture* is the right of the eldest son to inherit to the exclusion of younger sons the estate of his family because of his seniority of birth. In Europe the practice was long included in so-called entail laws, which limit the inheritance of property. These ancient European practices had virtually no impact on the landholding patterns that emerged in the South. Although southern colonial history dates back to Jamestown, the medieval concept of one great landed aristocracy in the southern colonies passing down vast domains to their eldest sons is false. In fact, ambitious sons interested in land, agriculture, and profit moved south into the Carolinas and Georgia and later westward as far as coastal Texas. These locations offered an abundance of land superior in quality to much of that found in Tidewater Virginia.

Primogeniture had a formidable and unrelenting foe in the person of Thomas Jefferson of Virginia. For him these practices represented an evil that must not be allowed to exist in the American colonies. Through the efforts of Jefferson and many other southern patriots, primogeniture was abolished and legally prohibited throughout the South by 1791.

Therefore, if primogeniture was ever important in the South, it was short-lived and was implemented in a rather restricted geographical region. Although the concept appeared in regional folklore and in earlier historical accounts, in fact the law did not shape the landholding systems of the early South.

Gerald L. Holder
Sam Houston State University

John R. Alden, *The South in the Revolution, 1763–1789* (1957); Julian P. Boyd, *William and Mary Quarterly* (October 1955); Walter Clark, ed., *The State Records of North Carolina* (1895–1905); Thomas Jefferson, *Notes on the State of Virginia*, ed. William Peden (1955); C. Ray Keim, "Primogeniture and Entail" (Ph.D. dissertation, University of Chicago, 1926), *William and Mary Quarterly* (October 1968); Richard B. Morris, *Columbia Law Review* (1927).

Sugar Plantations

Sugar plantations are traditionally large agricultural enterprises with landholdings ranging from 200 to 8,000 acres. Primary functions of a sugar plantation are planting, cultivation, and harvesting of sugarcane and processing of cane juice into brown sugar and molasses.

Sugar plantations have been a distinctive part of the southern landscape since the mid-18th century. They originated in New Orleans, La., in 1742. By 1806, 75 enterprises were dispersed along the Mississippi River to Baton Rouge. By 1844 some 464 French- and Anglo-American-owned sugar plantations of 200 acres or more each had made their appearance along the Mississippi River and westward into south central Louisiana along the alluvial natural levees of Bayou Lafourche, Bayou Teche, and the bayous of Terebonne Parish.

Although sugar mills numbered 1,240 in 1845, their zenith was reached in 1849 with 1,536 sugar mills on the Louisiana landscape. The Civil War, cane diseases, and the incorporation and consolidation of enterprises brought the number of mills to 50 on 190 plantations by 1970. Recently, depressed sugar prices, rising fuel and machinery costs, environmental regulations, and the urbanization and industrialization of cane lands have reduced the Louisiana sugar industry to 21 mills.

Elsewhere in the South, small numbers of antebellum sugar plantations once occupied parts of coastal South Carolina, Georgia, Florida, and southeastern Texas. Louisiana, however, dominated the sugar industry with 95 percent of the total antebellum production and continued to hold dominion over the southern sugar industry until 1973. Today a modern sugar industry in Florida leads the South with 54 percent of the cane acreage and 65 percent of production from seven high-capacity mills. By comparison, Louisiana now has 39 percent of the acreage and 29 percent of the production from 21 mills. In the lower Rio Grande Valley of Texas, a single new mill accounts for the remaining 6 percent of the southern sugar crop.

Eighteenth- and 19th-century source areas for sugar plantation traits in Louisiana were principally the French Caribbean and Anglo-American areas of the Upland and Tidewater South. The French Caribbean contributed (1) the initial sugarcane plants and cultivation techniques of Jesuits in 1742 from Santo Domingo (Haiti); (2) an early but specialized sugar technology brought by skilled Caribbean sugar makers; (3) a cultural mix of French Caribbean settlers, planters, and slaves; (4) architectural traits, most notably the hip roof and *galeries* (wide porches) for plantation mansions, half-timbered construction (a trait also directly from France), and quite possibly the shotgun house type initially used for slave quarters. Furthermore, from France, the arpent survey system of linear measure (192 feet per arpent) produced long, narrow landholdings 40 arpents deep, which led to linear settlement patterns among French plantations.

The Anglo-American source areas of the Upland South and the Atlantic Tidewater region supplied the sugar plantation system with: (1) landscape traits of block-shaped or gridded settlement patterns; (2) Tidewater architectural traits in plantation mansions with front-facing gables, porticos, pediments, and Georgian symmetry in floor plans; (3) architectural traits from the Upland South's houses of the pen tradition with paired rooms, central hallways, and exterior chimneys; and (4) a significant cultural mix of culture-bearing planters and settlers from the English-speaking South.

See also AGRICULTURE: / Sugar Industry; FOLKLIFE: / Shotgun House

John B. Rehder
University of Tennessee

Bob Angers, *Acadian Profile* (April 1982); John B. Rehder, "Sugar Plantations in Southern Louisiana: A Cultural Geography" (Ph.D. dissertation, Louisiana State University, 1971); J. Carlyle Sitterson, *Sugar Country* (1953); U.S. Department of Agriculture, *Sugar and Sweetener Report*, vol. 5 (February 1980).

Tidewater

The Tidewater coastal region extends from Delaware to northeastern Florida and from northwestern Florida to the Mississippi Delta. It is a low, flat, sandy or swampy area that enjoys abundant rainfall and a long, warm growing season. The Tidewater is known particularly for its agriculture, forest industries, commercial fishing and oystering, and military installations. It is also attractive to millions of tourists. The Outer Banks, a chain of islands off the North Carolina coast, is the site of a rapidly developing tourist industry that features the Wright Brothers National Memorial and many public recreational areas.

The term *Tidewater* is often used to refer only to the coastal area of Virginia, stretching some 100 miles inland from the sea and southward to the North Carolina border. Tidewater Virginia has been called "a blend of romance and fact." It is in the Virginia area that historic preservation efforts have successfully restored and promoted the region's history as tourist attractions. Beachfront tourist sites and recreational facilities have been developed, and each year thousands of people visit the Tidewater's historic areas, including Jamestown, Williamsburg, and the Yorktown battlefield. The popular Assateague Island nature preserve and the seashore town at Chincoteague testify to the natural beauty of the region. The southern Tidewater in Virginia contains the important seaport of Hampton Roads and the center of the region's sea industry. The densely populated area is the headquarters for the U.S. Navy's Atlantic fleet, as well as one of the biggest shipyards in the world. Norfolk, Va., the largest city in this branch of the Tidewater, was renewed during the mid-20th century and today boasts new downtown and waterfront developments, as well as a convention center and the Eastern Virginia Medical School.

Some of the swampy areas of the Tidewater have recently been drained in an effort to reclaim the rich soil for agriculture. New crops, such as soybeans, have proved successful on some of this reclaimed land. Two of the area's famed swamps are protected as wildlife refuges and state park areas. Okefenokee Swamp, which lies mostly in Georgia, is the third largest swamp in the South. Legendary Dismal Swamp in Virginia is the home of a variety of unique wildlife and species of plants, and since the 1960s it has been the focus of concerted preservation efforts.

Karen M. McDearman
University of Mississippi

Neal R. Peirce and Jerry Hagstrom, *The Book of America: Inside 50 States Today* (1983); Paul Wilstach, *Tidewater Virginia* (1929).

History and Manners

CHARLES REAGAN WILSON
University of Mississippi
CONSULTANT

Ruins of Windsor, antebellum mansion, in Mississippi

History

Anthropologist Clifford Geertz argues that culture is a "historically transmitted" pattern of meaning, suggesting the central importance of historical experience and the collective memory of it in providing a sense of identity and purpose to a culture. Two points are central in exploring the relationship between southern history and culture. The first is the connection between history and the sense of identity among southerners as a distinct people. The southern people have had characteristic assumptions, values, and attitudes apart from other Americans. When did that identity arise and how was it transmitted to future generations? How did historical events and forces create a sense of common purpose among people in the South and how was that purpose passed on from generation to generation, adapting to new circumstances? How did a sense of history in itself contribute to the identity? The second broad point to explore is the way of life at the heart of southern culture, the complex pattern of institutions, rituals, myths, material objects, and other aspects of a functioning culture. This pattern reveals how the region differed from other areas of the United States in behavior as well as attitude. It also shows the degree to which cultural integration occurred over time, despite formal attempts to maintain racial separation between whites, blacks, and Native Americans.

Origins. The English first attempted a colony in North America in 1587 when settlers arrived in Roanoke Island off the coast of present-day North Carolina, but Jamestown in Virginia was the first successful English colony, established in 1607. Other southern colonies would follow, but they had separate identities, leading historian Wesley Frank Craven to note that historians of the colonial South have "to write about the South when there was no South." When southern self-consciousness emerged, it grew out of concrete differences in institutions and attitudes that had appeared earlier.

The early South differed from the northern colonies in physical environment and motives for settlement. The first settlers in Virginia were charmed by the sights and smells of the new land. Observers focused on the climate as a key factor in the region. The climate favored a long growing season, which promoted an agricultural economy based on tobacco, rice, and indigo, and later cotton and sugar. The climate and environment affected architecture, clothing, and seemingly even the very pace of life and speech. Geography, however, unified neither the early nor later South. The region is divided by mountain ranges and rivers, and its plains and valleys run north and south, connecting with land in other regions. Partly because of geography different societies developed in the colonial South: an aristocratic society along the Chesapeake Bay; a second elite-dominated society in the Carolina Low Country; a frontier land to the west of the Tidewater; and perhaps another, loosely formed society in central North Carolina.

The motives of early Virginia settlers and of later southern colonists differed significantly from those of the North. Although both groups were predominantly middle-class English, the southern colonists came primarily for economic reasons, seeking opportunities not available in England. If the Puritans established New England to be a City on a Hill, the early southerners portrayed their area as a new Garden of Eden. The first signs of an emerging southern self-consciousness appeared couched in this mythic outlook. But ease of environment seemed to promote a decline in the moral character of the people. Residents south of Chesapeake Bay compared themselves with northern settlers, sometimes to their own disadvantage. William Byrd II, for example, saw New Englanders as "Frugal and Industrious," whereas those in the southern colonies had "very loose and Profligate Morals." Blessed with a beneficent land, southerners seemed to give in to the environment, and failed to live up to another part of their cultural legacy—the demands of a Christianity heavily tinged with Calvinism.

The colonial South had already begun to develop in distinctive ways. New England made a partial commitment to public education as early as the 1640s, but the South did so only much later. Eight colleges existed in the North by 1776, compared to only one (the College of William and Mary) in the South. The colonial South lacked not only schools and colleges, but libraries, books, and periodicals as well. Religion was also institutionally weak, lacking the intensity, idealism, and organization of that in the North.

At the top of the social structure was a small class of large planters who dominated society through control of land, wealth, and political power. Prominent southern colonial planter families included the Byrds, Randolphs, Carters, Burwells, Pages, Beverleys, Lees, Masons, Fitzhughs, and Wormsleys in Virginia, and the Rutledges, Pringles, and Draytons in South Carolina. Their names have reappeared throughout the ages of southern history as symbols of social prestige, southern style. The life of the English country gentry was their model, and their mansions are symbolic of southern gentility. The planters dominated the imagination of the region, symbolizing social success.

Members of the middle class were sometimes related by blood or marriage to the wealthiest planters. They enjoyed a degree of social mobility themselves and aspired to be seen as gentry. Beneath the middle class were the poorer whites. This group included landless farmers, farm workers, unskilled laborers, indentured servants (who agreed to work a period of time for a colonial employer in exchange for passage to America), and craftsmen who were not self-supporting. A separate, peculiar group known already in the 1700s as the "poor whites" also existed. They appear in colonial writings as a defeated people, subject to disease, beset by illiteracy, given to laziness (in middle-class eyes), and living in physical isolation on the worst lands.

Afro-southerners were at the bottom of the social structure. A system of white racial dominance developed as soon as Europeans, Indians, and blacks encountered each other in the early days of Virginia. A Dutch ship

Artist unknown, The Plantation *(c. 1825)*

brought 20 Africans to Jamestown in 1619, the same year that Virginia established the House of Burgesses, embodying the hope of political liberty. The slave population expanded throughout the late 1600s and early 1700s, creating economic prosperity but fueling whites' fear of blacks. Southern whites saw slavery as a method of racial control as well as an economic system. Although powerless, blacks became one of the central factors in early southern society, both passively and actively.

Scholars have only recently begun a serious study of the cultural integration that began in the South in the colonial era. The history of the South begins, in fact, with the role of the American Indians as pioneers of cultural patterns in the southern part of North America, although until recently histories of the American South hardly mentioned the Indians and studies of Indian history ignored the relationship between early Indian history and later southern developments. Anthropologists such as Charles Hudson, historians such as J. Leitch Wright, and archaeologists have recently shown, though, that early Indian cultures established many of the patterns involving use of natural resources and location of settlements and transportation routes that Europeans later exploited. Indians introduced Europeans and Africans to New World ways of living, and many white and black southerners have Indian ancestry. The Indians named rivers and states. They influenced the agricultural and dietary habits of later southerners, and folk medicine used by southerners consists of Indian herbal knowledge mixed with European and African elements. Many of the folk tales in southern oral tradition are influenced by Native American lore.

English colonists adapted their institutions and customs to the American environment and combined them with native ways. British social hierarchy, European musical and literary forms, Christian institutional forms and worldview, European agricultural methods—all of these became a part of early southern culture. Upper-class, elite culture from the colonial period to contemporary times has been based on values and behavior of the English gentry. In exploring the cultural contributions of previously overlooked groups in the South, recent scholars have shown little interest in English cultural contributions, but these contributions were surely crucial. Later generations of influential southerners often acted as though English culture was the South's culture.

By the beginning of the 18th century African slaves mediated between Indian and European cultures. West Africans and Indians, who were more familiar with the South's kind of environment than the English, shared a similar body of customs and knowledge. As Indians declined in power and numbers, blacks helped preserve traditional Indian lore and passed it on to Europeans. Africans also brought useful knowledge with them from their homelands. They were familiar with techniques of herding livestock and cultivating rice and indigo, which became key crops in the early Carolina Low Country. Some crops may even have been introduced from Africa and plants such as okra surely were. Europeans realized the economic advantages of slaves with such knowledge and made use of them. Despite the rigid legal boundaries of an emerging caste system, cultural integration was beginning through the transfer of knowledge, customs, and ways of separate peoples.

While cultural integration of a sort was occurring among white Europeans, African blacks, and Native Americans, a distinctive Afro-southern culture was also appearing. Before 1700, black cultural life was restricted by the relatively small numbers of slaves in North America and by their wide geographical distribution. The 18th century saw the forging of a rigid racial caste system and the creation of a separate black culture by slaves. South Carolina was the center of this emerging black culture because it contained a critical mass of Africans concentrated in a relatively narrow, coastal, rice-growing area.

About 60 percent of all slaves brought to what would be the United States came between 1720 and 1780, and these years represent the cultural watershed for black southerners. Africans from different areas and tribal backgrounds learned in the New World to communicate through pidgin languages and found a common identity in the South. The common factor brought from Africa was an intellectual outlook, a worldview, with definite attitudes about the deity, time, social relations, and rituals of life. Slaves preserved African notions about kinship, the individual's place in the cosmos, musical forms, and concrete skills such as metalworking and wood carving, herding, boat making and navigation, and rice cultivation. Where slaves were concentrated in significant numbers, blacks created distinctive southern cultural traditions involving everything from music and dance to customs of child raising, crafting, and even speaking. The planter's mansion was recognized from the colonial era on as a symbol for one aspect of southern culture; the slave quarters deserve recognition as the hearthstone for another central aspect of that culture.

The frontier experience was also crucial to the formation of a southern character. In the late 1600s and early 1700s settlers flocked west, and sectional tensions appeared between Tidewater aristocrats and backcountry farmers. These were class conflicts, reflecting the social divisions between frontier and Tidewater. The upcountry Piedmont frontier was the scene of Bacon's Rebellion in Virginia in 1676 and the Regulator movement in western North Carolina in 1766–71 on the eve of revolution.

Some disputes on the frontier were also ethnic conflicts. Land-hungry Scotch-Irish and German settlers migrated from western Pennsylvania into the Piedmont and later crossed the Appalachian Mountains. The Scotch-Irish represented the other large ethnic tradition introduced into southern life in the colonial era, one that became closely associated with the frontier. If the Tidewater aristocracy was English in style and outlook, the frontier was predominantly Scotch-Irish. Like the Africans, this group brought distinctive institutions and customs, which were Celtic in origin, reflecting long-held attitudes about kinship, work, religion, music, and herding and farming skills. By the end of the colonial era, the Scotch-Irish had established communities in what would become Tennessee and Kentucky. This was the "dark and bloody ground" of legend, with brutal warfare between white settlers and Indians and a struggle for survival in the lush wilderness of the Great Meadow. Daniel Boone was the romantic symbol of this phase of southern life.

The frontier experience promoted both individualism and communal neighborliness, impatience with formal institutions, and allegiance to family; it encouraged hard work; it promoted violence, and yet evangelical religion flourished there. Most southerners lived in frontier conditions up to the time of the Civil War. Recent migrants to the areas they lived in, they engaged in subsistence or small-scale commodity farming, used rivers and streams for transportation, and vividly remembered the Indian wars that preceded settlement. They lived in simple log cabins, which became another major symbol of southern culture. Many of the traits now called "southern" were nurtured in these isolated outposts. The frontier experience was common in America, but perhaps nowhere else in the nation did frontier attitudes and ways persist over so many generations through the preservation of a rural folk culture permeated by the effects of the frontier.

Historians do not agree as to when a self-conscious southern identity appeared. The American revolutionary era (1775–89) was, though, one landmark in its definition. John Alden referred to it as the time of the "First South," which was at that time geographically defined toward the west by the Mississippi River with major settlements along the Atlantic Coast. The phrase "southern states" was frequently used in those years. At the beginning of the period, though, the term *southern* was used to describe all the colonies except those in New England, from New York to Georgia. When Charles Mason and Jeremiah Dixon drew a surveyor's line between Pennsylvania and Maryland in the 1760s to settle a boundary disagreement, there was no understanding that a "North" and a "South" were being divided. But *southern* soon acquired a more restrictive meaning, as *middle states* was increasingly used to describe New York, New Jersey, Pennsylvania, and Delaware. There was the abiding problem of definition, with some observers including Maryland as southern and others excluding it. By the end of the Revolution the common view was that the northern boundary of the South was the Ohio River and the Mason-Dixon line. The southern population in the first census of 1790 showed approximately 1.9 million people (over a third of whom were black) below that line and 2 million above it.

The Revolutionary War gave the colonists a common enemy and served to draw northern and southern colonists together. Many unifying forces existed: a common language, a predominantly British and Western European background among colonists (except for the politically powerless slaves), a clear cultural and political heritage, and transportation, communication, and trade ties among the colonies. The term *American* was increasingly used both in the colonies and outside of them to describe the residents of the 13 colonies.

Nationalism surely triumphed in the revolutionary era. White southerners played a crucial role in events from the First Continental Congress in 1774 to George

Washington's Administration as president in the 1790s. Yet nationalism was a necessary precondition for the appearance of sectionalist concerns. The Revolution, for example, created heroes who were national but also local and regional. Disagreements between the North and South appeared as early as the conflict over the embargo sponsored by the First Continental Congress, and as John Alden has written, "that body during the years 1781–1787 was often rived by strife between South and North. Southern fears of Northern domination appeared in the Philadelphia Convention of 1787, and were frequently and forcefully asserted in the contests over ratification of the Constitution which took place below the Mason-Dixon line."

Economic conflicts emerged over regional interests, especially those related to trade and to the protection of slavery. The revolutionary ideology expressed in words such as *liberty* and *equality*, in documents such as the Declaration of Independence, and in emerging antislavery sentiment made southerners aware of their dilemma as slaveowners in a democratic republic and thereby helped to promote regional self-consciousness. Events that dramatized the South's racial situation included the debate over slavery during the Philadelphia Convention in 1787, the slave uprising in Santo Domingo in the early 1790s, and Gabriel Prosser's slave conspiracy near Richmond in 1800. These events connected southern identity to peculiar racial concerns and promoted racial fears. They helped to crystallize the South's commitment to slavery as a system of race control. By 1800 southerners felt threatened by outsiders, generating the siege mentality that would later characterize the evolving southern identity.

Thomas Jefferson, with his party and supporters, was the central political and intellectual force in the South during the years from the Revolution to the 1820s, and he is crucial to understanding southern developments. The South in this era, according to Clement Eaton and others, appeared to be a liberal, humane society. Southern leaders such as Jefferson and Madison reflected the intellectual influence of the Enlightenment, expressing belief in the natural rights of human beings and confidence in human reason. Freedom of thought and expression was respected, and the rhetoric of liberty and equality was articulated not only by Jefferson but by many other southerners.

Racial fears did not disappear, though, nor did the commitment to the maintenance of white supremacy. Slavery was not dying out, contrary to the hopes of some earlier southern leaders. Most southerners saw it as a profitable system when well managed; the planter's lifestyle depended upon it; social success—the southern version of the American dream—was defined within its parameters; and the fear of black equality without slavery remained. Racism was the dark underside of the luminous Jeffersonian dream of a chosen agrarian people.

The Jeffersonian era experienced an economic transformation that contributed to southern identity. The invention of the cotton gin in 1793, the emergence of sugar growing in Louisiana in the mid-1790s, and the rising prices for frontier lands in the early 1800s brought an increased commitment to an agriculture of staple crops. Outlandish profits could be made by a few people, further strengthening the power of the elite planters. Cotton became the prime symbol of the South's expansive development into the Old Southwest in this era. Like Faulkner's Thomas Sutpen in *Absalom, Absalom!*, the pioneer planters of the Deep South carved slave plantations out of frontier forests. The mentality of the planter was thus transferred to the frontier; in the Southwest a rough-hewn character such as Andrew Jackson could become a self-made man and take on the trappings of an elite planter. The raw materialism of the frontier challenged the paternalism of the Tidewater planters as a cultural ideal.

Old South to New South. The Civil War has generally been seen as the crucial watershed in southern history. For the cultural historian, though, the period from 1830 to 1910 is a single era. After 1830 the self-conscious identification with "the South" notably increased, and a distinctive pattern of institutions, values, myths, and rituals took shape, reflecting a southern worldview that developed but never fully matured before the Civil War. The war and Reconstruction stand as the crystallizing events that promoted the postbellum development of a peculiar regional culture.

The years 1830 to 1832 were particularly important in the growth of a southern regional consciousness. Sectionalism dramatically appeared in politics during the preceding decade with the Missouri Compromise of 1819–20. After a bitter debate, Congress admitted Missouri as a slave state and Maine as a free state, and drew a 36° 30′ line of latitude, prohibiting slavery above the line. The Missouri Controversy awakened southern fears over the region's position as a minority section in the Union and pointed the way to an emerging regional consciousness that took form after 1830.

A minority psychology developed as the northern population outgrew that of the South. North-South conflict developed over control of the national government and the direction of national policy. A southern states' rights philosophy and the fears underlying it were seen in the nullification crisis of the late 1820s and early 1830s. South Carolina challenged the national government, specifically over the issue of the national government's power to pass a tariff, but more generally over the rights of the majority to legislate over a minority—defined as a regional population. John C. Calhoun emerged as the premier figure of antebellum southern politics, a defender of southern rights, one of the nation's greatest political philosophers, and a symbol of the southern consciousness.

The driving force propelling southern identity was racial fear. Rumors of slave unrest periodically appeared, reinforcing white uneasiness. The Nat Turner rebellion in 1831, a slave uprising led by a visionary slave preacher, killed 60 whites in Southampton County, Va., and became a symbol thereafter for the potential of slave rebellion. It solidified white fears and led to new restrictions on the activities of slaves and free blacks. William Lloyd Garrison, one of the chief Devil figures to southern whites, also stirred racial fears in 1832 when he began publishing the *Liberator*, a Boston antislavery newspaper that called for immediate, uncompensated emancipation of the slaves. He led a strident new antislavery movement that stressed the immorality of slavery. The southern reaction was an equally strident intellectual defense of the "peculiar institution"—a proslavery argument that justified the institution as a positive good, using religious, scientific, and historical arguments.

By the 1840s southern attitudes toward history were beginning to change with the growing sense of regional self-consciousness. More and more southerners after 1830 began questioning the national republican tradition as the proper framework for telling the regional story. The conflict with the North caused southern whites to stress their belief in a common historical experience and to play down differences within the South. The Virginia Historical Society appeared in 1831, the first such organization in the South, and other historical societies proliferated in the region during the next two decades of growing North-South tensions. By the 1850s southern histories had shifted from focusing on the national contributions of southern states to documenting the differences in the historical experiences of the South and the North. Southerners believed, moreover, that only they could be trusted to write their history. Dates of historic events in the South were ritually honored with celebration that praised the South's noble history. National revolutionary heroes such as Patrick Henry and Francis Marion were seen after 1830 as state or regional heroes. The refocusing of American history into southern history was a factor in forging a self-conscious regional identity.

The 1830s also witnessed the emergence of a new mythic center for the southern identity: the Cavalier image, which embodied the belief that southerners were descendants of aristocratic Royalist exiles from Cromwell's England in the 1600s. Northern colonists, according to the legend, were Puritans by origin. Many Americans came to believe that these two "types" generated northerners and southerners with differing temperaments, psychologies, and concerns.

John Pendleton Kennedy's *Swallow Barn* appeared in 1832 and became a prototype for the romantic plantation legend. Kennedy and other writers portrayed the southern plantation as an orderly, feudal world of harmonious, static, hierarchical relationships between master and slave. The southern planter was a noble, honorable figure, and the southern lady, a vital part of the myth, was chaste, saintly, sacrificial, and spiritual. Slaves were childlike and loyal. The contrast between the Cavalier planter and the grasping Yankee was popular among conservative northerners and had remarkable power among southern whites.

Northerners and southerners still shared much in this era, but belief in the differences between northerners and southerners had some basis in reality. The slave-based plantation system was uniquely southern, and its crops were distinctive to the region. The nature of the southern population was different from that elsewhere, with English, African, and Scotch-Irish elements remaining dominant at a time when the northern population was being transformed through immigration. Southerners remained rural, while industry, immigration, urbanization, and reform were changing the North.

The southern way of life reflected not only the region's central theme of racial obsession, but positive features as well. There was a strong attachment to local communities and to the family, which offered both blacks and whites a refuge, a measure of security and warmth. Both races shared an intense religious faith that promised ultimate salvation after time served in this vale of tears. For whites the rural, daily monotony was broken by rituals such as visiting neighbors and relatives, attending political gatherings and camp meetings, observing the activities of county court days, participating in community militia days, and wagering on sports such as horse racing and cockfighting. These events provided entertainment and pageantry, but they also displayed the symbols of power in this society and reinforced the hierarchical social structure and the paternalistic bonds between wealthy and plain folk.

This southern social structure was the background against which a distinctive culture appeared. Planter hegemony over society was based partly on control of the South's wealth. Wealthy planters owned the best farming land, and the productivity of these lands was greater than that of smaller farms. The planter elite included two groups: those traditional southern families whose wealth extended back several generations or more, taking on the refinements and prestige of "old money," and a larger group of self-made men, humble in origins, who had seized opportunities and luck to amass fortunes from cotton. Eugene D. Genovese has portrayed the planter elite as paternalist and precapitalist, but other historians point out their essentially bourgeois outlook. Their cultural significance was in their control of cultural and social values in the South. The "big house" was the tangible symbol of their power over the southern imagination.

The yeoman farmer, the independent landowner, was the Jeffersonian ideal and W. J. Cash's "man at the center." Historians overlooked the importance of the "plain folk" until Frank L. Owsley in the 1930s showed they were the largest class in the Old South. White racism brought a shared racial solidarity between the wealthy planters and the yeoman farmers. The commitment of the South was to both slavery and democracy. The term *herrenvolk democracy* describes the southern system of democracy for the master class and repression for a subordinate group. The region's political rhetoric said that all white men were created equal with inalienable rights, which depended, though, on black subjugation. Seeing slaves around them led whites to value their own freedom and to celebrate their bond with whites in other classes. This ideal triumphed in the period of Jacksonian democracy in the 1830s and promoted a sense of internal southern white solidarity in facing the North.

North-South tensions became an urgent national issue during the 1850s. The debate over slavery in the western territories, which were gained as a result of the Mexican War, stirred sectionalism to a new pitch in the late 1840s. The Nashville Convention, an expression of southern consciousness during this debate, met in 1850, but moderates controlled it, and the situation was diffused by the Compromise of 1850. A litany of laws and events polarized the nation throughout the decade: the publication of *Uncle Tom's Cabin* (1851), the Kansas-Nebraska Act (1854), the civil war in Kansas (late 1850s), South Carolina Congressman Preston Brooks's beating of Massachusetts Senator Charles Sumner in Congress (1856), the death of the Whig party and emergence of a northern-based Republican party, the Supreme Court's Dred Scott decision (1857), John Brown's raid on Harpers Ferry, Va. (1859), and the election of Abraham Lincoln (1860).

The Civil War was the crucial event cementing the southern white identity. The experience of fighting and losing a war would isolate the region's people. As C. Vann Woodward has written, losing the Civil War became a central burden of southern history.

The Confederate States of America stands as the supreme statement of the southern desire for self-determination. The Confederacy aimed at preserving a traditional life that seemed threatened by outside intervention. It did not attempt any utopian transformation for the future but represented instead a conservative political revolution aimed at preventing social and economic changes in its fundamental institutions. White southerners did not simply justify the war as a crusade for slavery. Orators emphasized not race but the issues of self-determination, localism, righteous holiness, and constitutional rights. Nonetheless, there is no escaping the racial dimension of a war fought by a slave society; the conflict was a logical culmination of the proslavery argument.

Historians generally agree that southerners during the Civil War developed only a limited sense of political nationalism and that a romantic cultural nationalism may have been more a product of the war than a cause for it. As David M. Potter noted in *The Impending Crisis, 1848–1861* (1976), "The Civil War did far more to produce a southern nationalism which flourished in the cult of the Lost Cause than southern nationalism did to produce the war." Novelist Robert Penn Warren has written in *The Legacy of the Civil War: Meditations on the Centennial* (1961) that the Confederacy became immortal, a "City of the Soul," when it expired, and the memory of it has had a tenacious hold on the southern imagination. No southern *War and Peace*, *Guernica*, or "Gettysburg Address" came out of it. Its tragedy, however, surely shaped postwar southern life. Southerners learned the lessons of defeat, the lessons of human limitation and mortality, and the virtues of upholding the basic human values of family, community, and economic survival. The war was a tremendous bonding experience for southern whites who had tried and failed at independence; that separate history would forever differentiate the region from others in the nation.

Confederate soldiers from Georgia

The economic base of southern culture had been transformed by the end of the war. A $2 billion investment in land had been destroyed, a $3 million cotton crop confiscated, factories dismantled, banks closed, public buildings damaged, and cities leveled. The physical landscape had changed. Throughout the South there were damaged bridges, roads, railroad tracks, and burned cotton gins, factories, fences, and barns. Chimneys stood without houses. Few horses, mules, sheep, cattle, or hogs could be found. Items necessary for daily living had vanished, and no replacements could be found. Lack of tools, livestock, and seed made even good land useless.

The human toll was even more awesome. There were 258,000 dead and 150,000 disabled. Every third household saw one of its members dead, a rate that was four times that of the North. Lingering wounds and illnesses plagued the surviving soldiers; the number of widows and orphaned children was uncounted. A spiritual depression settled on the region, as its people tried to understand how they could lose a war they had been told was a holy one. The South was cast back into subsistence living, into frontier life, "the frontier the Yankee made," said W. J. Cash. The North moved into a new modern era after the war while the South reverted to a primitive, violent, individualistic, provincial life. A culture of poverty appeared that would haunt the region.

The Reconstruction era from 1865 to 1877 was nearly equal to the Civil War in forging a self-conscious white southern identity. It marked white southerners against northerners on the one hand and against southern blacks on the other. Fear, grievance, defensiveness, and the memory of hardship and bitterness—all were central to cementing this identity. The southern white view of Reconstruction was preserved and passed on for generations by the South's official history books, by literature such as Thomas Dixon's *The Clansman* (1905), and by family stories told generation after generation. Eventually the southern white legend of Reconstruction was nationally reinforced by D. W. Griffith's film *Birth of a Nation* and academic histories produced by William A. Dunning and his students at Columbia University.

Journalist Hodding Carter called Reconstruction "the angry scar," and it was a major setback for black-white cultural integration in the South. Under slavery there had been much social interaction because of the intimate role blacks played in the lives of southern whites. Blacks helped in the birthing, nursing, and raising of white children; they tended to white men and women throughout their lives and were there at high moments of marrying and dying. Blacks continued that intimate role, but under very different circumstances. There was less paternalism and less institutional, public contact.

Developments in religion were revealing. Blacks had once worshiped as members of the same churches as whites. To be sure, slaves had their "invisible institution," the religion they practiced in their slave quarters, outside the bounds of Christian institutions. Nonetheless, their Christian worship was a shared communion, where baptism, the ritual of church worship, and the ecstasy of revivalism were shared with whites. During Reconstruction blacks withdrew from white churches and set up independent congregations. They joined the northern-based African Methodist Episcopal church or the African Methodist Episcopal Zion church in large numbers. Others joined the Colored Methodist Episcopal church, an organization created with the assistance of southern white Methodists. Thousands of independent black Baptist churches emerged logically from the Baptist heritage of local church autonomy. These churches were often established with the encouragement and active support of white congregations, and fraternal ties remained. This development was one of the most significant results of Reconstruction and was vital for the emergence of a distinct black culture. It was a peaceable separation; the violence seen in politics was not reproduced here. But in terms of a culturally integrated southern life, it was a setback. Ironically, white and black southerners shared many beliefs, but the region's spiritual life was now segregated.

The southern legend of Reconstruction drove a psychological wedge between blacks and whites. Southern black legends of nightriders reflected the opposite side of a Reconstruction myth, also centered on fear, but fear of the awesome brutality southern whites would tolerate to preserve their racial purity. The memory of Reconstruction's failure and of an era of violent racial conflict was, thus, the same for both races, although the substance of the fears and the meaning of the failure differed in each case.

The mind of the white South after the Civil War was dominated by myths—the romantic legend of the Old South, the tragic Lost Cause, and the pragmatic creed of a New South. The myth of the "moonlight-and-magnolias" Old South originated in the antebellum era, but the idealization of the plantation world received its most influential expression in the 1880s and after in the local color stories of Thomas Nelson Page and others. The myth of the Lost Cause described heroic men from plantations and farms crusading for the Confederacy against invading forces of evil. Ministers and religious groups created a civil religion that tied regional patriotism and religion together so that the remembered Confederate cause took on spiritual significance.

After the Civil War southerners worked hard to preserve the memory of their regional historical experience. The sense of history was given a tangible meaning through memorial celebrations, the erection of monuments, and the expansion of historical societies. Paintings of Robert E. Lee and Jefferson Davis were hung in schoolrooms across the region. Folk ballads, poems, and storytelling by the old passed on to the young the region's memory of the Civil War. Patriotic societies such as the United Confederate Veterans and the United Daughters of the Confederacy campaigned for the teaching of southern history in schools and for the preservation of historical records. The Southern Historical Society was organized in 1873 and soon accumulated an archive of Confederate history. Southerners complained of the bias against the South in textbooks written by northerners and began writing their own histories and lobbying for southern school boards to adopt them. In all these efforts white southerners wanted to explain their view of the past, especially the Confederate and antebellum eras, confident of their ultimate vindication. "Lest ye forget," which appeared on countless Confederate monuments, was an apt motto for southerners of that era. The intense cultivation of an interest in history surely helped preserve the self-conscious southern identity. The history was more a cultivation of myth than a critical examination of the past. The historical record, though, became a prime foundation for the preservation of southern ways.

If the myth and history of the Lost Cause looked to the past, the story of the New South embodied the hope of change. The key word was progress. The central historiographical issue of the period was continuity versus change. C. Vann Woodward in *The Origins of the New South, 1877–1914* (1951) made the case for the significance of the Civil War as a profound break in southern history; Carl N. Degler in *Place over Time: The Continuity of Southern Distinctiveness* (1977) made the case for continuity. Recent historians focus on the planter and the sharecropper as the main symbols for the issue. Agriculture after the Civil War seemed very different from before, but new institutions simply emerged to accomplish aims similar to those before the war. The plantation survived, albeit transformed, and blacks were held in near peonage as sharecroppers. During Reconstruction the crop-lien system emerged, providing a way for landowners with little cash or credit and laborers without land or money to restart the economy. Sharecroppers and tenants made the crop and shared the harvest with the landowner. Credit for food, tools, livestock, seed, and living necessities was based on the tenant's mortgaging a crop that had not yet been planted. This credit system involved great risk for all concerned and it opened the way for severe exploitation of the poor.

The postwar planter remained a crucial southern character, and recent studies by Dwight B. Billings, Jonathan Wiener, and others suggest the antebellum planter class continued to exercise considerable power in the New South. But other cultural figures also emerged. The planter himself had to rely frequently on the storekeeper. Thomas A. Stribling wrote of the merchant in *The Store* (1932), and William Faulkner created a portrait of a mercenary family of merchants in his Snopes trilogy. Newspaper editors such as Henry W. Grady of the Atlanta *Constitution*, Henry Watterson of the Louisville *Courier-Journal*, Richard H. Edmonds of the *Manufacturer's Record* in Baltimore, and Francis W. Dawson of the Charleston *News and Courier* became especially prominent supporters of a New South. The businessman as hero became a new part of the folklore of the South in this era. Businessmen were typically self-made men from the middle class. The lumber, tobacco, textile, furniture, iron and steel, and mining industries expanded in the 1880s, generating wealth and a new privileged class. Lawyer-politicians were powerful figures in the New South, dominating courthouse rings, monopolizing public offices, and supervising public expenditures.

If the nature of the New South can be conveyed through these social types, its meaning can also be seen through the appearance of newly important institutions on the landscape. Textile mills had existed before the Civil War, but in the 1880s southerners went on a veritable crusade for industry, which focused mainly on the mills. W. J. Cash called it "a mighty folk movement," the "dream of virtually the whole southern people." The cotton mills were to be the salvation for the South's poor whites, providing employment opportunities for them but not for blacks. By 1915 the South produced more textiles than the rest of the nation combined, but this production was achieved at a great cost in human misery, in the form of desperately low wages, 72-hour work weeks, and the exploitation of women and children. The mills exacerbated the culture of poverty rather than ending it.

Railroads became as important a symbol in the southern psyche as they had been in the North generations earlier. They nurtured ties with the regional past by hiring Confederate generals such as Jubal Early as representatives. In fact, though, northerners controlled the South's expanding rail system after the Civil War, with southerners usually involved only in support positions. Ambitious young southerners were now allied with Yankee businessmen, not fighting them as their fathers had. Railroads helped bring the development of cities such as Atlanta, Birmingham, and Durham, which emerged as New South industrial and commercial centers.

Despite these changes, race in the late 19th century was still the central theme of southern identity. The New South was achieved at the expense of blacks. Life for southern blacks reached its lowest point between the end of Reconstruction and the beginning of World War I. Economically, they were prisoners of a sharecropping system that kept them in near bondage to the land. They lost political power as disfranchisement was achieved through poll taxes, residency requirements, literacy tests, "understanding the Constitution" tests, grandfather clauses basing the right to vote on ancestors having voted, and whites-only primaries. Segregation of the races became an accepted part of New South life. In the decades after the Civil War a period of experimentation in race relations had occurred. Although custom had prevented extensive social mixing between the races, both blacks and whites had commonly used the same public facilities. This changed in the 1890s; Jim Crow laws sought to establish a rigid caste system. A torrent of legislation was passed in the 1890s, setting up a comprehensive legal framework for a biracial society. Unwritten customs of racial etiquette also hardened. The economy segregated black jobs and white jobs. The Supreme Court case of *Plessy* v. *Ferguson* (1896) gave federal approval to southern actions by declaring "separate-but-equal" facilities to be legal. Railroads, schools, theaters, hotels, restaurants, rest rooms, water fountains, parks, public offices, and even cemeteries were segregated by the early 20th century. The landscape itself reflected this aspect of the New South—"colored" and "white" signs were soon pervasive. In spite of this terrible setback for black-white cultural interaction, daily occasions often arose for contact between blacks and whites, especially in the region's small towns and rural communities.

The late 19th century was perhaps the age of the most cohesive regional culture and an identifiable, distinctive southern way of life. In addition to the peculiar racial system, a host of customs and cultural ways were associated with southern blacks and whites. Poverty and rural isolation promoted the persistence of attitudes and customs. Blacks and whites placed a high value on family and kinship. People dined, entertained, lived, and visited, all within the boundaries of the family. The family sheltered maiden aunts, distant cousins, and respected grandparents. Household matters were central concerns. Distinctive culinary styles of the typical family were noted by southerners and others as well. On a less positive note, violence was common in the South, which had a high homicide rate, lynchings, public executions, and in general a visible culture of accepted violent behavior.

Churches became even more important institutions in southern culture after the war. Whites joined evangelical churches, and separate black churches emerged. Religious institutions were racially segregated, yet black and white worshipers shared a Protestant, predominantly Baptist and Methodist, orientation. Southern Baptists, Methodists, and Presbyterians did not reunite with their northern brethren after the Civil War but instead worshiped in regionally organized churches. Southern whites remained evangelical and fundamentalist at a time when northern religion was becoming pluralistic in denominations and liberal in theology. Churches extended a pervasive moralism into southern culture through crusades for prohibition of alcohol, for blue laws honoring the Sabbath, and for restrictions on gambling.

Southern culture was also transmitted through distinctive regional rituals such as Confederate Memorial Day, Sunday dinners on the church grounds, political campaign barbecues celebrating the Democratic party, religious camp meetings, and revivals. On such ritual occasions one heard storytelling and swapping of folk sayings, proverbs, and superstitions; ballad singings; and the formal oratory of the political rabble-rouser and the fiery itinerant evangelist. Sports were a central part of living for southerners. Hunting and fishing had long been regional favorites and remained so for a people who were predominantly rural.

The emergence of agrarian political and economic protest in the 1890s marked the beginning of nearly 30 years of efforts at reform and represented the most serious challenge to southern orthodoxy. Efforts for change began in the Grange, and then the Farmers' Alliance spread over the South, gaining 3 million white members by 1890–91 with over a million more in the Colored Alliance. The Alliance was significant in southern history in trying to forge a class coalition by overcoming racial divisions. Its reformers called for structural changes in the economy to give the federal government a greater role in regulating and controlling an economy increasingly dominated by corporate power. Agrarian protesters attempted to substitute economic issues for racial issues as the dominant concerns in public policy. Historian Lawrence Goodwyn in *Democratic Promise: The Populist Moment in America* (1976) argues that the agrarian movement represented the last chance for true structural reform in American society. It was a direct class appeal to the poor, articulating the profound grievances of farmers and forging a democratic political culture. Other historians see the movement as backward looking, parochial, and conspiratorial. They think agrarian reformers sought a black-white coalition out of convenience, not principle, and only a minority of reformers used a rhetoric of class appeal across racial lines. In their view, agrarian radicals were not entirely alienated, in other words, from the southern way of life. Radicals accepted the color line, used the words and teachings of evangelical Protestantism in demanding reform, and did not challenge the sharecropping system.

The existence of agrarian protest suggests also that the southern way of life was not monolithically conservative. Southern reformers developed a political culture that reflected the abiding democratic and religious style of the South. Southern culture has periodically produced charismatic spokesmen demanding reform for an oppressed people. Rural protesters such as Pitchfork Ben Tillman in South Carolina and James H. "Cyclone" Davis and H. S. P. "Stump" Ashby in Texas used the incendiary language of itinerant democratic ministers and politicians. With the failure of serious reform by the turn of the 20th century, racial extremism appeared. Political demagogues blamed blacks for the failure and exploited the emotions of poor whites.

The Progressive era presented a social type seldom seen in the earlier South—the middle-class, liberal reformer. Like Progressives in other regions, southern Progressives favored reform to deal with political corruption and irregularities, to rationalize society along more businesslike and scientific lines, to limit business monopoly and the abuse of society, and to restore traditional moral values. They accepted racial segregation and disfranchisement, regarding them as forms peculiar to the South. Southern Progressives thus attempted to achieve reform at the expense of blacks. Lynchings and race riots were ironically at a peak in this era of reform. The appearance of biracial groups such as the National Association for the Advancement of Colored People and the Commission on Interracial Cooperation did lay the basis for future change.

Black cultural attitudes in this period were symbolized by two leaders—Booker T. Washington and W. E. B. Du Bois. Born a slave, educated at Hampton Institute in Virginia, and appointed director of Tuskegee Institute in Alabama in 1881, Washington expressed the predominant black view favoring economic self-help. Rather than directly challenge segregation, Washington proposed that blacks work toward building community strength. Washington was one of the most influential southerners in the nation. He communicated with blacks and whites, northerners and southerners, and advocated postponement of political and civil rights and concentration on individual self-improvement. Washington secretly challenged features of the southern system, but publicly he strongly supported black economic development through jobs, landownership, training in business leadership, and vocational skills. Du Bois came to maturity in the early 20th century and reflected the outlook of the Progressive era. He helped found the NAACP and urged concentration of black efforts on gaining political and civil rights. His book *The Souls of Black Folk* (1903) was an evocative description of turn-of-the-century black southern life.

Americanization. The major theme of the years from 1910 to 1985 was the Americanization of the South. Woodrow Wilson was a southerner by heritage and training, and his election as president in 1912 (along with the election of a Democratic party-controlled Congress) marked the reappearance of southern political influence on the national scene.

While Wilson was president, World War I promoted patriotic nationalism in the South. The Spanish-American War (1898–99) had been an earlier landmark reincorporating southerners into the nation, and by 1917 memories of the Lost Cause and Reconstruction had diminished enough to make southerners enthusiastic about the nation at war. Soon southerners were honoring fallen warriors for the nation rather than the region.

The outbreak of war in 1914 led to economic advancement for the South, because of a rising demand for agricultural goods. The employment picture in the region improved and cash incomes rose. The war-related changes also promoted mobility. Southerners had been a relatively static people in the late 19th century, but they now flocked to southern and northern cities seeking jobs. The South was the setting for the training of American troops after the United States entered the war in 1917. Northerners came south, and almost a million southerners served in the army and naval forces, helping to diminish the isolation characteristic for generations of southern life. Blacks in particular began leaving the plantations to seek work elsewhere.

Change in the post–World War I South became apparent with the decline in the price of cotton in 1921. On top of that, the boll weevil entered the southern landscape and psyche, devastating cotton in the 1920s and thereafter. The specter of starvation was especially significant in further spurring black migration from the land to northern cities. The southern economy, in general, made some improvement in the 1920s, with an increase in the number of textile mills, a growing chemical industry that had been stimulated during the war, expansion of coal and iron production, and advancement of hydroelectric power. Nonetheless, the southern economy as a whole was in decline well before the stock-market crash of 1929 set off the Great Depression.

The Depression was more devastating to the South than to any other region. A federal government report referred to the region as "the Nation's no. 1 economic problem." Franklin D. Roosevelt's New Deal directed a disproportionate share of programs to the region, as symbolized best perhaps by the TVA, relief and public-works projects, and farm and crop-control efforts. The southern populace generally supported the New Deal, although many regional political leaders became critical of it as an experiment in socialism. They especially feared the effects of social experimentation on the region's racial caste system. Overall, New Deal farm programs and farm mechanization combined to promote a revolutionary exodus of sharecroppers and tenants from the land.

The Americanization of the South brought a crisis in the southern identity. The years from 1920 to 1945 were creative ones for southern culture, but the creativity came out of a period of transition. The identity crisis especially affected the region's intellectuals and artists who felt the impact of the region's transition from a traditional society to a modern one. What did the regional identity—being southern—mean in the context of world wars and international, modernist intellectual currents? During the 1920s the region appeared to the nation as, in George B. Tindall's phrase, the "Benighted South," symbolized by the Ku Klux Klan, hookworm and pellagra, chain gangs, lynchings, the Scopes Trial, and the Fundamentalist movement in religion. The leadership of the South was in the hands of those of the booster mentality. Intellectuals realized they could no longer take the southern identity for granted. Literary critic Louis D. Rubin, Jr., called the 1930 Agrarian manifesto *I'll Take My Stand* "an assertion of identity." The South to the Agrarians represented the last hope of the Western world to tame industrialization and the forces of modernization and dehumanization. Generations of material deprivation had given a spiritual strength that should be used. Intellectuals began questioning and rejecting the romantic and sentimental view of southern culture.

From this period of transition came the Southern Literary Renaissance and a flowering of studies in the social sciences. Journalism, literary criticism, history, fiction, and poetry were all affected by the new spirit of self-criticism, which set the stage for changes after World War II in the southern identity and way of life. Daniel J. Singal, Michael O'Brien, and others have analyzed this watershed southern intellectual period from 1920 to 1945. Scholars are just beginning to place southern achievements in music, art, architecture, and other fields into this framework.

These changes also affected the South's folk culture. Small-town, rural folk culture had survived longer in the South than in other regions of the nation. It nurtured distinctive musical, painting, and craft traditions. In the years from 1920 to 1945 the folk culture provided materials for the expansive achievements in popular culture that would flourish in the era after World War II. Authentic, traditional folklife has survived in the South despite the commercialization of mass culture. That the folk culture combined black and white contributions became increasingly clear after World War II. Southern ideology had never sanctioned such cultural miscegenation, yet two races living for 300 years on the same soil, often isolated in rural areas from outsiders, had exchanged much specific knowledge and skill and had developed shared attitudes on such matters as religion, the family, recreation, and the importance of land and community.

The South since World War II has experienced a revolution. World War II itself was central to change in the region; it may prove to be even more significant for the region than the Civil War. The pace of economic development stepped up as the federal government poured defense-related investment into the South. The region's lingering isolation was broken as the war encouraged mobility. Many blacks and whites left the South to serve in the military, and civilian workers left rural areas to work in southern cities or left the region to work in northern and western defense industries. Millions of nonsoutherners came into the region, exposing southerners to new influences. The war turned the South's interests outward.

The war laid the basis for postwar economic development and the emergence of the Sunbelt. The decade of the 1960s was the key period, an era of extraordinary growth. Incomes and the standard of living rose. There was still a gap with the rest of the nation, but the once-pervasive poverty was broken. Agriculture was transformed. There has been a drastic decline in the number of farms and the farm population. Cotton no longer is king. Mechanization has helped to displace rural tenant farmers and sharecroppers. Farming has become agribusiness, a commercial enterprise, not the activity promoting the agrarian life urged by the contributors to *I'll Take My Stand*. The southern economy has diversified, and industry is now more economically important than agriculture, even in the most predominantly rural state, Mississippi. To be sure, problems remain. Southern economic development has been based on exploiting extractive resources, such as coal or oil, or on low-wage industries such as textiles. Tax and wage policies have left fewer economic benefits than advocates of those policies earlier claimed. Much of the growth has been through branch plants controlled by national firms. Moreover, the growth has been uneven, with Texas, Florida, Georgia, and North Carolina the major beneficiaries. Pockets of poverty remain in states such as Mississippi, Alabama, and Arkansas, and among Appalachians and rural blacks. The Sunbelt image of regional prosperity has become, though, a new myth of southern success.

The southern landscape has changed as a result of the dramatic economic developments. Gangs of cotton pickers are gone, and tenant shacks are torn down or covered with kudzu. In the 1980s soybeans and peanuts, as well as cotton, grow in southern fields, and rural homes have television satellite dishes. Southern cities look much like those elsewhere, and the modern highway strip, mobile home parks, and shopping malls are more typical of the region's urban areas than the once powerful symbol of the county courthouse. The nation's communications and transportation systems have drawn the South in and ended its isolation. If one had to pick a symbol of the modern South, it might be the sight of the bulldozer on a construction crew where once the mule or later the tractor worked.

The average contemporary southerner has more money, lives in a larger urban area, goes to better schools, and goes to church in bigger buildings than his or her ancestors. Sunbelt wealth has dramatically affected traditional southern culture. Material advances have promoted cultural achievements—more art galleries, symphonies, universities, and libraries. But the evolving southern culture shows continuities with the past as well. In religion, for example, many southerners use their newfound incomes to contribute to their denominations, which build bigger church centers. The church remains a dominant symbol on the southern landscape. Sports have become a new secular religion, combining recreational, military, and religious features of the traditional South.

Another major development since World War II is the decline of race as the central theme—and obsession—of the South. In the 1950s black activists entered a new stage of the struggle to end the region's caste system. The NAACP's traditional strategy of working through the judicial system led to a legal victory over segregation in *Brown* v. *Board of Education* (1954), which overturned the *Plessy* decision of the 1890s legalizing racial segregation. Southern white conservatives responded with a strategy of massive resistance, and legalists such as journalist James J. Kilpatrick revived interposition theories from the 19th century. The 1950s witnessed a resurrection of Confederate symbolism and die-hard racism. Groups such as the Ku Klux Klan and the White Citizens' Councils led the opposition to change. They proposed once again associating southern identity with race alone. Moderate whites stood on the sideline and offered little constructive leadership, with a few notable, brave exceptions.

Black civil rights activists, led by the eloquent Martin Luther King, Jr., took the offensive, with a campaign of nonviolent resistance based partly in regional religious tradition. Civil rights leaders faced economic and physical intimidation, mean spiritedness, and outright violence. The height of violence was 1963–68, when 97 people were killed in racial conflict in the South, according to figures compiled by the Southern Regional Council. Through television the world witnessed sit-ins, freedom rides, boycotts, marches, and freedom summers. Little Rock, Selma, Oxford, Montgomery, Birmingham, Neshoba County, and Greensboro may one day rank as great battlefields in the southern imagination, along with Shiloh, Manassas, Antietam, and Gettysburg. The Southern Christian Leadership Conference may take its place beside the Army of Northern Virginia in the southern mind.

External pressure from the federal government, along with the internal pressure of civil rights reformers, led to the passage of the Civil Rights Acts of 1964 and 1965 and the Voting Rights Act of 1965. These laws destroyed the legal basis of caste, overturning the segregation laws and promoting the return of blacks to southern politics. Belief in white supremacy was surely not destroyed, but the South's racial picture by the 1980s resembled the nation's pattern more than its own once-distinctive system. An emerging myth of the Redemptive Biracial South even suggested the region would achieve true integration before the rest of the nation.

The modern South has experienced dramatic change—the end of the one-crop cotton economy, the growth of industrialization and the end of its culture of poverty, the rise of the Republican party and the end of the one-party Solid South, the draining of the rural countryside and the growth of cities, the end of isolation and the incorporation of the region's peoples into the national culture, and the end of the peculiar racial caste system embodied in Jim Crow laws. Despite the changes, a degree of continuity with the region's past remains—religion, as distinct as ever, is expressed in the overwhelming dominance of evangelical Protestant denominations; regional traditions in literature, music, sports, eating, and the appreciation of leisure time, outdoor life, family activities, and community life remain vital; and the willingness to use violence and force in certain situations is still a regional trait. Studies by sociologist John Shelton Reed suggest that a profile of the future southerner has already appeared—he or she is well educated, well traveled, middle class, attuned to the nation's communications systems, lives in a suburb, and has the strongest sense of regional identity of anyone living in the South. The locus of southern identity has thus shifted from the rural plantation and small farm of a century ago to the most modern form of residential living, the suburb.

Despite these changes in the contemporary South, the sense of history thrives and continues to provide a foundation for the idea of southern distinctiveness. C. Vann Woodward's seminal volume *The Burden of Southern History* (1961) argues that the South's military defeat, poverty, guilt over slavery, and strong attachment to localism were distinctive experiences in U.S. history and would continue to nourish a sense of southern identity. Woodward's argument was an outgrowth of the stress on research and published scholarship in the increasingly sophisticated field of southern history after World War II. The founding of the Southern Historical Association in 1934 and the publication of the *Journal of Southern History* the following year were turning points in the emergence of a critical view of the southern past that finally replaced the mythic view. Revisionist views of slavery, the Civil War, and Reconstruction, along with the growth of black history in the 1960s, offered southerners a revolutionary new vision of their past.

Interest in the South's history was also seen in improvements in university, state, and local libraries. Historical societies took on new life, and institutions such as the Institute for Early American History and Culture at Williamsburg and the American Association for State and Local History in Nashville appeared. Southern university presses came to specialize, in many cases, in publishing regional history. The publication of the collaborative 10-volume *History of the South* by the Louisiana

State University Press and the Littlefield Fund for Southern History at the University of Texas introduced important new scholarship on the region.

Southern interest in history transcended the academic context as genealogical and patriotic societies and museum and archaeological collections thrived. History was learned from parents and grandparents, school teachers, local storytellers in small towns, from letters, diaries, journals, photographs, and other family artifacts. Historic preservation groups maintained the image of the past through restoration of mansions and older public buildings. The South is full of Civil War battlefields, which continue to fascinate and instill a sense of history. Modern southerners in the short stories of Bobbie Ann Mason may watch television and frequent the shopping malls, but they also still visit Shiloh.

In the 1974 Jefferson Lecture in the Humanities, Robert Penn Warren said that "a society with no sense of the past, with no sense of the human role as significant not merely in experiencing history, but in creating it can have no sense of destiny." The South's destiny is now an American destiny, but its historical experience provides a distinctive perspective to draw on in charting the future.

Charles Reagan Wilson
University of Mississippi

Thomas P. Abernathy, *The South in the New Nation, 1789–1819* (1961); John Alden, *The First South* (1961), *The South in the Revolution, 1763–1789* (1957); Kenneth K. Bailey, *Southern White Protestantism in the Twentieth Century* (1964); Numan Bartley, *The Rise of Massive Resistance: Race and Politics in the South during the 1950s* (1969); Ray Allen Billington, *Westward Expansion: A History of the American Frontier* (1949); John W. Blassingame, *The Slave Community: Plantation Life in the Antebellum South* (1972); John B. Boles, *Black Southerners, 1619–1869* (1983), *The Great Revival, 1787–1805: The Origins of the Southern Evangelical Mind* (1972); Carl Bridenbaugh, *Myths and Realities of the Colonial South* (1952); Edward D. C. Campbell, Jr., *Celluloid South: Hollywood and the Southern Myth* (1981); Clayborne Carson, *In Struggle: SNCC and the Black Awakening of the 1960s* (1981); W. J. Cash, *The Mind of the South* (1941); William H. Chafe, *Civilities and Civil Rights: Greensboro, North Carolina, and the Black Struggle for Freedom* (1980); Thomas D. Clark, *The Emerging South* (1961), with Albert D. Billington, *American South: A Brief History* (1971); James C. Cobb, *Industrialization and Southern Society, 1877–1984* (1984), with Michael V. Namorato, eds., *New Deal and the South* (1984), *The Selling of the South: The Southern Crusade for Industrial Development, 1936–1980* (1982); Wesley F. Craven, *The Southern Colonies in the Seventeenth Century, 1607–1689* (1949); James McBride Dabbs, *Who Speaks for the South?* (1964); Pete Daniel, *Breaking the Land: The Transformation of Cotton, Tobacco, and Rice Cultures since 1880* (1985), *Standing at the Crossroads: Southern Life in the Twentieth Century* (1986); F. Garvin Davenport, Jr., *The Myth of Southern History: Historical Consciousness in Twentieth-Century Southern Literature* (1967); Richard Beale Davis, *Intellectual Life in Jefferson's Virginia, 1790–1830* (1964); Carl N. Degler, in *The Development of an American Culture*, ed. Stanley Coben and Lorman Ratner (1983), *The Other South: Southern Dissenters in the Nineteenth Century* (1974), *Place over Time: The Continuity of Southern Distinctiveness* (1977); Clement Eaton, *Growth of a Southern Civilization, 1790–1860* (1960), *The Waning of the Old South Civilization, 1860–1880s* (1968); John S. Ezell, *The South since 1865* (1963); Gilbert C. Fite, *Cotton Fields No More: Southern Agriculture, 1865–1980* (1984); J. Wayne Flynt, *Dixie's Forgotten People: The South's Poor Whites* (1979); Paul M. Gaston, *New South Creed: A Study in Southern Mythmaking* (1970); Eugene D. Genovese, *The Political Economy of Slavery: Studies in Economy and Society of the Slave South* (1966), *Roll, Jordan, Roll: The World the Slaves Made* (1972); Patrick Gerster and Nicholas Cords, eds., *Myth and Southern History* (1974); Henry Glassie, *Pattern in the Material Folk Culture of the Eastern United States* (1968); David R. Goldfield, *Cotton Fields and Skyscrapers: Southern City and Region, 1607–1980* (1982), *Promised Land: The South since 1945* (1987); Dewey W. Grantham, *Southern Progressivism: The Reconciliation of Progress and Tradition* (1983); Joanne V. Hawks and Sheila Skemp, eds., *Sex, Race, and the Role of Women in the South* (1983); William R. Hesseltine and David L. Smiley, *The South in American History* (2d ed., 1960); Samuel S. Hill, ed., *Encyclopedia of Religion in the South* (1984), *Southern Churches in Crisis* (1966); Fred Hobson, *Tell about the South: The Southern Rage to Explain* (1983); C. Hugh Holman, *The Immoderate Past: The Southern Writer and History* (1977); Arthur Palmer Hudson, *Folklore Keeps the Past Alive* (1962); Charles Hudson, *Southeastern Indians* (1976); Rhys Isaac, *The Transformation of Virginia, 1740–1790* (1982); Winthrop D. Jordan, *White over Black: American Attitudes toward the Negro, 1530–1812* (1968); Charles Joyner, *Down by the Riverside: A South Carolina Slave Community* (1984); Benjamin B. Kendrick and Alex M. Arnett, *The South Looks at Its Past* (1935); V. O. Key, Jr., *Southern Politics in State and Nation* (1949); Jack Temple Kirby, *Media-Made Dixie: The South in the American Imagination* (1978), *Rural Worlds Lost: The American South, 1920–1980* (1987); Lawrence W. Levine, *Black Culture and Black Consciousness: Afro-American Folk Thought from Slavery to Freedom* (1977); Leon F. Litwack, *Been in the Storm So Long: The Aftermath of Slavery* (1979); Bill C. Malone, *Southern Music / American Music* (1979); John McCardell, *Idea of a Southern Nation: Southern Nationalists and Southern Nationalism, 1830–1860* (1979); Forrest McDonald and Grady McWhiney, *American Historical Review* (December 1980); D. W. Meinig, *The Shaping of America: A Geographical Perspective on 500 Years of History: Atlantic America, 1492–1800*, vol. 1 (1986); Edmund S. Morgan, *American Slavery, American Freedom: The Ordeal of Colonial Virginia* (1975); George Mowry, *Another Look at the Twentieth-Century South* (1973); I. A. Newby, *The South: A History* (1978); Michael O'Brien, *Idea of the American South, 1920–1941* (1979); Howard W. Odum, *The Way of the South* (1947); Frank L. Owsley, *Plain Folk of the Old South* (1949); U. B. Phillips, *Life and Labor in the Old South* (1929); David M. Potter, *The Impending Crisis, 1848–1861* (1976), *The South and the Sectional Conflict* (1968); Albert J. Raboteau, *Slave Religion: The "Invisible Institution" in the Antebellum South* (1978); James G. Randall and David Donald, *The Civil War and Reconstruction* (1969); Charles P. Roland, *The Improbable Era: The South since 1945* (1976); Louis D. Rubin, Jr., et al., *The History of Southern Literature* (1986); Henry Savage, Jr., *Seeds of Time: The Background of Southern Thinking* (1959); Anne Firor Scott, *The Southern Lady: From Pedestal to Politics, 1830–1930* (1970); Charles G. Sellers, Jr., ed., *The Southerner as American* (1960); Henry D. Shapiro, *Appalachia on our Mind: The Southern Mountains and Mountaineers in the American Consciousness, 1890–1920* (1978); Frances Butler Simkins, *The Everlasting South* (1963), with Charles P. Roland, *A History of the South* (1972); Daniel J. Singal, *The War Within: From Victorian to Modernist Thought in the South, 1919–1945* (1984); Charles S. Sydnor, *The Development of Southern Sectionalism, 1819–1848* (1948); William R. Taylor, *Cavalier and*

Yankee: The Old South and American National Character (1961); Emory Thomas, *The Confederate Nation, 1861–1865* (1979); George Tindall, *Emergence of the New South, 1913–1945* (1967), *Ethnic Southerners* (1977); Kerry Trask, *Southern Studies* (Summer 1983); Joel Williamson, *Crucible of Race: Black-White Relations in the American South since Emancipation* (1984); Peter H. Wood, *Black Majority: Negroes in Colonial South Carolina from 1670 through the Stono Rebellion* (1973); C. Vann Woodward, *The Burden of Southern History* (1960), *Origins of the New South, 1877–1913* (1951), *Strange Career of Jim Crow* (1955); J. Leitch Wright, Jr., *The Only Land They Knew: The Tragic Story of the American Indians in the Old South* (1981).

Anglo-American Antebellum Culture

The Old South's high culture was marked by two strong currents: it began and remained an Anglo-American culture in its tastes and loyalties, and it was sustained by an agrarian economic system partially supported by black slave labor. The first was seen in a strong taste for goods from abroad, and the second created tensions and anxieties about man's relation to man.

White colonial settlers in the South were northern European, predominantly from the British Isles, who were not always seeking the same religious and political freedoms as their Puritan contemporaries in the North. The cultural evolution of the Old South proceeded as a logical extension of the English squirearchy, the Whig mentality wherein communal political authority was held in less regard than the customs of the local aristocracy. This aristocracy respected men of ability who became men of means, the type of "natural aristocrat" Thomas Jefferson espoused. Save in Virginia, the most English of the southern states, a hereditary aristocracy did not develop. Indeed, as Clement Eaton has written, "With few exceptions, the ruling families were developed on the native soil from middle class origins."

Affiliation with the Church of England through the colonial period in the South resulted in a consensus code of behavior. Abstract codes of honor and decency coalesced into an Anglo-Saxon common law of human behavior. Unlike the Puritans who felt they were living in a time of declension from the virtues of a distant past, southern whites, according to Bertram Wyatt-Brown, "believed that they had made peace with God's natural order." By and large southern culture was at odds with the national culture and was inclined to regard property and local option as the most important aspects of a democratic society and disinclined to respect external elective authority. These attitudes led inevitably to theories of nullification, actual secession, and war.

The southern antebellum economy was agrarian, stratified into large and small farms, many of which were called, in the archaic fashion of the 17th century, *plantations*. One lingering colonial trait within the culture was a factor system of exchanging agricultural produce for manufactured commodities from abroad or the North. This exchange system had a significant effect upon the market for local commodities and may have retarded the growth of the southern plastic arts.

Any understanding of southern plastic arts prior to 1861 must involve the integration of architecture, furnishings, and the exotic within the home. Coastal colonial architecture was by and large built of brick in the English manner of the 18th century, broadly fenestrated and preferring rear or side galleries to frontal porticoes. As the South moved west, builders used timber available from the virgin forests being cleared for farm lands and developed the first high-style frame architecture in the West. The rage for Greek Revival architecture, which seized most of the Western world in the first 50 years of the 19th century, was especially strong in the South.

The English gentry were fascinated with the classical age, as were southerners of a comparable class. Southern states were also dotted with towns named Troy, Athens, and Rome, and southern children were called Lucius, Cassius, Marcus—even Valerius Publicola in several Tennessee families. Collegiate education emphasized classical studies, not mechanical arts. Clearly, in the midst of an awesome controversy over slavery and its moral ramifications, some southerners thought of themselves as living in an ancient agrarian utopia, enshrined in white-columned temples.

Initially excellent and recently neglected traditions emerged in the plastic arts of the South. Superior cabinetmaking developed in the Coastal Plains, especially in Baltimore and Charleston. Baltimore remained through the period an important source for crafted and imported goods, though later in the period rivaled by New Orleans in influence and significance as a source for manufactured goods. Equally strong rural cabinetmaking traditions emerged in North Carolina and Kentucky, using cherry and hickory woods. Southern cabinetmakers tended to favor existing English styles, notably those to be seen in the pattern books of Thomas Sheraton, Thomas Shearer, and George Hepplewhite. An exception to the English taste was found in New Orleans, which introduced the French Empire and Rococo Revival styles to the Lower South.

Silversmiths excelled in the South, especially Samuel Kirk & Sons in Baltimore, Frederick Marquand in Savannah, James Conning in Mobile, and the Hyde and Goodrich firm of New Orleans. Many local craftsmen rendered silver coins into a variety of cups, pitchers, and spoons, but the works of Kentucky silversmiths, such as Asa Blanchard, were particularly prized.

In keeping with the tastes of England, portraiture was more esteemed than landscape painting, although a few painters, such as Granville Perkins (1830–95) and George Cooke (1793–1846), attempted to depict the scenic splendors of the region. George Caleb Bingham's (1811–79) river and political paintings are vivid documents of southern life and work.

Much of the portraiture of the Old South was rendered by itinerants, who established seasonal studios in favored urban areas like Natchez or Richmond. Some traveled from plantation house to plantation house, entertaining and depicting several members of a family at once. Under the influence of Gilbert Stuart (1755–1828) and Thomas Sully (1783–1872), a strong neoclassical portrait tradition emerged in Lexington, Ky., represented by William Edward West (1788–1857), Matthew Harris Jouett (1788–1827), Joseph Henry Bush (1794–1865), and Oliver Frazer (1808–64). New Orleans was a major center for portrait activity, especially by French academicians working there between 1820 and 1850. These artists, including Jean Joseph Vaudechamp (1790–1866) and Jacques Amans (1801–88), influenced several generations of southern itinerant painters, most notably C. R. Parker, who painted in Alabama, Mississippi, Georgia, and Louisiana.

Oratory was esteemed and well attended, favorites being the fire-eating secessionist speeches of William Lowndes Yancey (1814–63) and Robert Barnwell Rhett (1800–76). Chautauquas were held on the subjects of natural science, historical curiosities, and female education. "Camp meetings" by religious fundamentalists were particularly popular in the Upper South and were attended by as many as 15 to 20 thousand people at a time. Although a certain amount of speaking in tongues and writhing in the Holy Ghost took place at these gatherings, Clement Eaton felt that "beneath the tumult and excitement of the camp meetings can be discerned the craving of lonely frontier people for human companionship."

The literary tastes of affluent southerners mingled English influences with more homespun products. Romances of the medieval period, especially those of Sir Walter Scott, were wildly popular. So too were the humorous sketches of frontier southern life written by Augustus Baldwin Longstreet (1790–1870) and William Tappan Thompson (1812–82). Historical fiction by William Gilmore Simms (1806–70) assuaged the southern desire for a cavalier past, while the morbid Gothic musings of Edgar Allan Poe made little impact. Literary journals, such as *De Bow's Review* and the *Southern Literary Messenger*, combined humor, political speculations, and natural history articles.

The 40 years following the Missouri Compromise of 1820 saw the southern mind become increasingly paranoid, hysterical, and preoccupied with the slavery issue. Paternalism "accepted by both masters and slaves," says historian Eugene D. Genovese, "afforded a fragile bridge across the intolerable contradictions inherent in a society based on racism." Southern culture was conservative and deeply suspicious of the Industrial Revolution, an attitude it shared with the English intelligentsia of the same period, several of whom, including Thomas Carlyle and Charles Darwin, supported the South in secession.

The material culture that evolved from English influences on the antebellum South reflected the tastes of local aristocrats. The ruling families, most of whom came from middle-class backgrounds, sought tangible expressions of their good fortune and their aspirations. A strong cultural belief in the sanctity of private property prevailed, obscuring for many southerners the moral issue of keeping other human beings in bondage.

See also ART AND ARCHITECTURE: Decorative Arts; Greek Revival Architecture; Painting and Painters; Sculpture; BLACK LIFE: Slave Culture; EDUCATION: Classical Tradition; FOLKLIFE: Aesthetics, Anglo-American; LANGUAGE: Conversation; Oratory; MYTHIC SOUTH: Romanticism; / Anglo-Saxon South; Cavalier Myth; Celtic South; SOCIAL CLASS: Aristocracy

Estill Curtis Pennington
Lauren Rogers Museum of Art

Frances Gaither Blake, ed., *Mary Savage Conner of Adams County, Mississippi: A Young Girl's Journal, 1839* (1982); Clement Eaton, *The Freedom of Thought Struggle in the Old South* (1964), *A History of the Old South* (1964); Eugene D. Genovese, *Roll, Jordan, Roll: The World the Slaves Made* (1974); Robert Manson Myers, ed., *The Children of Pride: A True Story of Georgia and the Civil War* (1972); Estill Curtis Pennington, *Southern Quarterly* (Fall 1985); Jessie Poesch, *The Art of the Old South: Painting, Sculpture, Architecture and the Products of Craftsmen, 1560–1860* (1983); William R. Taylor, *Cavalier and Yankee: The Old South and American National Character* (1961); Bertram Wyatt-Brown, *Southern Honor: Ethics and Behavior in the Old South* (1982).

Automobile

"Nobody with a good car needs to be justified," said Hazel Motes in Flannery O'Connor's *Wise Blood*. She was satirizing the idea, but the suggestion that the automobile can be the source of salvation has not been far off for many southerners in the 20th century. The automobile has had a profound impact on changing the region. It has affected class relationships, economic development, geographical mobility, and physical and psychological landscapes. "Such names as Ford, Chrysler, Olds, Willis, Nash, Shakespeare, Reo, Studebaker, and Dodge had more long-range economic meaning for the South than all the Civil War generals combined," writes historian Thomas D. Clark. "The established way of life in the South was shaken to its very foundation by this new Yankee machine."

The South was the scene of occasional early automotive activity. In 1906, for example, at a mile run at Ormond Beach, Fla., a Stanley Steamer averaged the unheard-of speed of 127.66 miles per hour. Long-distance road races stressing speed were started in the late 1890s, and many were held over closed routes on southern public highways. The American Automotive Association sponsored the Vanderbilt Cup races in Georgia and Florida, the nationwide Glidden tours came into the South for the first time in 1910 and 1911, and the National Association of Automobile Manufacturers held the first official showing of 1910 model cars in Atlanta, the first time the show had been held outside of New York or Chicago. All this promoted a new attitude toward the South in the industry.

Despite such activity, motor vehicles at first made less impact in the South than elsewhere. The region's poverty made the automobile a luxury for most, and its dispersed rural population meant no concentrated urban market. In 1910 statistics on the ratio of automobiles registered to persons aged 18 or over showed the highest-ranking southern state to be Louisiana, but it ranked only 33d.

All the southern states were well below the national average. In the geographic distribution of registered automobiles by state, Texas was the highest ranking of the former Confederate states in 1900 at 12th, with only 180 cars. But change was coming. "Southerners have finally awakened to the importance of the automobile," said a writer in *Motor* magazine in 1909.

The key decade of the automobile's introduction into the region was the 1920s. Historian Blaine A. Brownell has argued that the southern attitude toward the automobile in that decade was one of "ambiguity and uncertainty" that "cut across class and racial lines." People in the region bought cars and adopted the car culture, but this involved dramatic changes, which were part of the general rural-urban conflict of the times. Newspapers promoted the automobile through special advertising and travel sections. Annual automobile shows promoted awareness of the car, and roads improved dramatically. In 1921 a writer in *Motor* praised "the tendency of the automobile to bring into intimate and helpful contact sections of our population which normally would never meet." Automobile outings and vacations became national institutions in the 1920s, as the car became a middle-class possession, and it fostered a new mobility of the labor force as well. Buses soon crisscrossed the region, facilitating the movement of people and freight. A few motor-vehicle assembly plants were brought to such southern states as Georgia, and raw materials needed for automobile manufacturing were processed in the South. The development of wholesale and retail businesses related to some aspect of the car was especially significant in the regional economy. In a typical case car dealerships represented 14.4 percent of Birmingham's 1929 retail trade, and businesses listed in the U.S. census as automobile related accounted for 20.5 percent of retail trade that year in Nashville and 16.5 percent in Atlanta.

Although southerners adopted the automobile, some of them criticized its effect on living patterns. Jonathan Daniels referred to the salesmen of Chevrolets as the "most profoundly disturbing agitators" in the region. Ministers blamed the automobile for leading to a decline in sexual morality by loosening courtship habits, and they said it nurtured crime, desecrated the Sabbath, hurt family bonds, and reinforced materialistic instincts. One of the most frequent complaints was of traffic congestion. As Faulkner noted in his 1927 novel *Mosquitoes*, traffic in New Orleans "inched forward, stopped, inched forward again." The lack of parking space was a continual concern of businesses seeking customers downtown. The rising number of deaths and injuries from automobile accidents also was a concern. The country music song "Wreck on the Highway," with its graphic images of shattered glass, screams, and whiskey and blood running together, conveyed the negative side of the automobile's impact in the region.

The automobile led to the reshaping of the southern land through road building. Organized southern efforts toward good roads began in the 1890s. By the second decade of the 20th century, writes historian Thomas D. Clark, "surfaced roads were still so much a novelty that pictures of them appeared in southern elementary textbooks as modern wonders." By this time, though, "the southern campaign for good roads had almost achieved the fervor of a religious revival." By 1920 all the southern states had established state highway commissions, which acquired tremendous amounts of money and power. In 1918 North Carolina voters, for example, approved a $50 million bond issue to build improved road systems, and in 1956 they took on $76 million in debt for 1,771 miles of new roads. Governors and county public officials have found this a major source of patronage.

The automobile helped to revolutionize the southern relationship to the federal government. The passage of the Federal Highway Act of 1921 led to a massive involvement of the federal government in the southern states. It has pumped billions of dollars into the region for road building, and the Federal Bureau of Highways has standardized requirements for bridges, roadbeds, and road markings and has employed inspectors to administer the guidelines. Despite recurrent talk of states' rights by southern congressmen, they have not opposed federal support for interstate highways.

Southerners are supposedly not attuned to technology, but this has not been so with automobiles. In Faulkner's *The Reivers*, a character has a vision of the nation's future "in which the basic unit of its economy and prosperity would be a small mass-produced cubicle containing four wheels and an engine." Despite this fear, the image of the mechanic as a rather romantic working-class hero has been common, "the romance of the backyard mechanic with grease up to his elbows," says Sylvia Wilkinson. The good old boy image is closely tied to the automobile. Like the cowboy and his horse, the good old boy needs his car. A good man knows cars and takes care of them.

The current image of the automobile man in the South is the clean professionalism of a stock-car driver and crew. To be sure, the driver may have wild tales to tell of his youth. Robert Mitchum symbolized this as a moonshine runner in the film *Thunder Road*, and Burt Reynolds's series of *Smokey and the Bandit* movies has taken it to its extremes. It is a male world in its imagery; women are not allowed in the pits and are considered to be bad luck. It is a sometimes violent world, where violence is direct and graphic. Junior Johnson recalled that in his early days driving on dirt tracks in the South the drivers "liked to fight about as good as race." He remembered arming himself with a cola bottle for a fight with a competitor on the infield. The "rambling man" is another romantic southern figure associated with the automobile. He is a common figure in country music as far back as Jimmie Rodgers. Merle Haggard's 1977 song "Rambling Fever" expressed this theme, as did Kris Kristofferson's "Me and Bobby McGee." Even the automobile factory worker has made it into regional folklore. A Johnny Cash song tells of an assembly-line automobile worker who sneaks car parts out of the factory, one piece at a time, until he has a new automobile at home. The plight of southerners working in northern automobile plants is poignantly explored in "Detroit City." A great number of blues and rock-and-roll songs—such as "Mabelline"—celebrate the automobile.

The automobile has affected modern southern recreation. Hank Williams wrote that "a hot-rod Ford and a two dollar bill" was all that was required in the 1950s for a southern good time, while Lefty Frizzel in "If You've Got the Money, I've Got the Time" sang of good times in Cadillacs. In stock car racing, the South produces the majority of the tracks, races, and participants, as well as a massive turnout of spectators. Dirt-track racing is an important participant form of southern sport in local communities throughout the region. Recreational vehicles are pressed into service on weekends for camping, promoting the traditional southern pastimes of fishing and hunting.

One should not forget the recreational significance of the drive-in movie, a good example of a new recreational institution based on the automobile. The first drive-in opened on 6 June 1933 in Camden, N.J. It helped to structure recreation for a generation of Americans. The drive-in was at its peak in the 1950s, serving as a source of family entertainment and a central locale for teenage courtship. The number of drive-ins was greatest in 1958, when 4,000 were in operation. The "passion pits" have continued that role, although the number is on the decline, with 3,178 drive-ins nationwide in September of 1982. Most now are located in suburban areas, on the edge of cities, or in rural areas and small towns. Drive-in movies were surely not uniquely southern, yet the southern climate and the pervasiveness of small towns and rural communities have given them special recreational significance in the region. They are open later in the year than elsewhere and are a larger component of entertainment in small towns and rural communities.

The automobile had a particularly important effect on the southern poor. Mobility liberated impoverished sharecroppers from their chains to the land. In their automobiles they found "both dignity and independence," says historian Thomas D. Clark. Rich and poor, black and white, all rode in the same kind of vehicle, which proved to be a leveling device. W. J. Cash pointed out that the mill worker as well gained status from the car.

Young people and the automobile, Florida, 1930s

Mobility and speed were the keys to understanding the special appeal of the automobile to a southern populace suffering geographic and social stagnation. In Flannery O'Connor's short story "The Life You Save May Be Your Own," Mr. Shiflet notes that "the body, lady, is like a house: it don't go anywhere: but the spirit, lady, is like a automobile: always on the move, always." "Sugar-Boy couldn't talk," said Jack Burden while riding with Willie Stark's driver in Robert Penn Warren's *All the King's Men*, "but he could express himself when he got his foot on the accelerator." The automobile meant escape from the farm or the mill village. It was a way out of poverty. It represented an escape from the negative side of the strong southern sense of place, the static rootedness. Thanks to the car, says the hitchhiker in Warren's novel, "a man could just get up and git, if'n a notion came on him."

Some scholars argue that southerners have shaped the very character of the car culture. Landscape historian John Brinckerhoff Jackson has written that "the rest of the United States sees the highway and car culture as essentially a Southern phenomenon." He outlines the southern roots of the contemporary car culture:

> Our interstate highways are extensions of the Southern landscape: truck stops as far west as Utah or Colorado provide Southern breakfasts and Southern music on the jukeboxes, Southern banter with the waitresses. Small (and I must say) uninviting roadside nightclubs advertise the music of young Southerners with names like Clyde and Jesse and Leroy and Floyd. The Southern accent is widely adopted by used car salesmen all over America.

Other scholars, however, would see some of his examples as more national than regional.

The contemporary era has seen the increasing impact of motor vehicles on southern cities, furthering suburban growth, close rural-urban ties, and interregional connections. The problems of the automobile have been recognized in the South, as in the nation. The sheer number of cars is a key concern, especially because of air pollution. Heavy traffic leads to congestion equal to that of the California freeways on streets sometimes not even built for automobiles. The lack of planning and zoning has created a cluttered jungle of businesses serving the automobile and its inhabitants. Moreover, automobiles are violent killers in the South. As historian Clark has written, "They take an annual toll of life that approaches that of the old regional diseases." The poverty of the South's people has made the accident and death problems worse, because poor tires and poorly maintained cars hamper safety.

See also AGRICULTURE: Good Roads Movement; MYTHIC SOUTH: / Good Old Boys and Girls; RECREATION: Stock Car Racing; URBANIZATION: Urban Transportation

Charles Reagan Wilson
University of Mississippi

Blaine A. Brownell, *American Quarterly* (March 1972); Thomas D. Clark, *The Emerging South* (1961); Cynthia G. Dettlebach, *In the Driver's Seat: The Automobile in American Literature and Popular Culture* (1976); William E. Geist, *New York Times* (7 June 1983); John Brinckerhoff Jackson, *The Southern Landscape Tradition in Texas* (1980); Howard L. Preston, *Automobile Age Atlanta: The Making of a Southern Metropolis, 1900–1935* (1979); Sylvia Wilkinson, in *The American South: Portrait of a Culture*, ed. Louis D. Rubin, Jr. (1980).

Battlefields

Southerners honored those who fought in the Civil War, but they had a markedly different response to hallowing the fields on which nearly 1 in every 19 white southern males died. A monument erected in the county seat or state capital was an immediate and local recognition of "our heroes," a very personal expression of the community's grief and affection. Battlefields were another story. They had been all too infrequently the sites of southern victories, and for the vast majority of southerners major battlefields were remote places. The courthouse monument or local marker gave southerners the opportunity to honor the men and women of the Confederacy and their cause at home.

The earliest battlefield parks set aside—Gettysburg and Shiloh—began as adjuncts to national military cemeteries. Their supporters, like the memorial associations, wished to honor those brave men who had fallen in battle. All six of the major battle sites that became military shrines in the 19th century became so because of Union veterans' initiatives, congressional action, or both. Two of these sites, Gettysburg and Antietam, were outside the boundaries of the Confederacy. Founded on 30 April 1864, the Gettysburg Battlefield Memorial Association was the first organization of its type—North or South. The association maintained the site until 1895, when it deeded some 600 acres to the federal government. This land was the nucleus of the battlefield park that today contains more than 3,400 acres. Dotted with state and unit monuments, Gettysburg is one of the most heavily visited Civil War battlefields in the country.

While Union groups were actively working at Gettysburg, Kennesaw Mountain, and other battlefields, southerners were noticeably inactive. Historic preservation really came into its own in the South during this period, but preservation focused on buildings and, for the most part, the 18th century.

Southerners did not create battlefield shrines until after World War I. Appropriately, Manassas was one of the first sites set aside. In 1922 the Manassas Battlefield Confederate Park, Inc., and the Sons of Confederate Veterans purchased the 128-acre Henry Farm. In 1938 they deeded the land to the federal government as an "everlasting memorial to the soldiers of the Blue and Gray." Significant additions were made to the original property during the 1940s so that today both the Stone House and Dogan House are within the nearly 3,000 acres of Manassas National Battlefield Park.

The nation's military showed considerable interest in Civil War sites. In 1920 the Historic Section of the U.S. Army War College conducted a historical survey of battlefields in the United States. The War Department operated all national military cemeteries, parks, and sites until 1933 when President Franklin Roosevelt ordered them placed under the Department of the Interior.

Shiloh, Vicksburg, Antietam, Petersburg, Gettysburg, Manassas, and Chickamauga and Chattanooga are among those currently operated by the Department of the Interior as military or battlefield parks. In addition to these, important fortifications such as Fort Sumter in Charleston are national monuments.

Southern state governments have created a number of Civil War battlefield parks. Some are of peculiarly local interest, such as Rivers Bridge (near Ehrhardt, S.C.), Natural Bridge (near Woodville, Fla.), and Poison Spring (Ark.). Others, such as Fort Morgan (Ala.), Fort Pickens (Pensacola, Fla.), and Bennett Place (Durham, N.C.), are of regional or national interest.

The creation of Rivers' Bridge State Park in South Carolina displayed the typical evolution from cemetery to battlefield park that occurred elsewhere in the South. In the spring of 1876 men of the Rivers' Bridge community gathered the remains of Confederate soldiers who had been killed during Sherman's advance into South Carolina and reinterred them at Rivers' Bridge. A monument and a pavilion were erected, and the site became the location of an annual Confederate Memorial Association observance. In 1938 the Rivers' Bridge Memorial Association was given 90 acres, which included the breastworks thrown up in a vain attempt to halt the Union advance into the state. The association, in turn, deeded the site to the state. Rivers' Bridge State Park is the *only* state park in South Carolina honoring the Confederacy.

In southern state parks history certainly takes a back seat to fishing, boating, hiking, or just about anything else. The parks are there and the Civil War themes are loudly proclaimed, but for the most part there does not seem to be a great deal of interest in preserving Civil War battle sites. There is far more interest in creating antebellum plantation parks.

A visit to some state parks will confirm this not-so-benign neglect. Fort Gaines, at the entrance to Mobile Bay, scene of one of the more important naval/land battles of the war, is in a sad state of disrepair. Those tourists bored with history can view a live alligator in a tank created out of a Spanish-American War powder magazine! The significance of the site would suggest a better fate, but at least it survives.

Given the importance of the Civil War in southern history, the relatively small number of state parks identified with Civil War battles is surprising. The colonial, frontier, and antebellum eras have far more attraction as themes than does the war itself. One obvious reason for this is that the battlefields often were the scenes of Confederate defeats. This was particularly true in the coastal areas of the lower South. No amount of promotional literature can erase the cold facts of history. It is no wonder that the initial efforts to preserve Civil War battlefields as battlefields per se came from the victors.

Walter Edgar
University of South Carolina

Charles B. Hosmer, Jr., *Presence of the Past: A History of the Preservation Movement in the United States before Williamsburg* (1965), *Preservation Comes of Age: From Williamsburg to the National Trust, 1926–1949,* 2 vols. (1981); Emory Thomas, *Travels to Hallowed Ground: A Historian's Journey to the American Civil War* (1987).

Beauty, Cult of

"The modern Southern belle has, of course, long been the Pageant ideal," writes Frank Deford of the Miss America contest, "so that—even in those years when a Southerner does not win—the likely winner is still probably patterned after that type." The "fundamental Southern-belle personality" that has become the nation's beauty ideal is "vivacious, sparkle-eyed, full of fun, capable of laughing at herself, and incapable of speaking either (a) briefly, or (b) without using the hands to illustrate all points." She has poise and personality beneath the outward physical attractiveness.

Beauty pageants such as the Miss America competition suggest the influence of southern ideas in shaping national ideals of beauty. Within the specifically southern context, beauty pageants are part of a cult of beauty, with certain definite ideas on what beauty is and why it is significant to be beautiful. The South's cult of beauty reflects southern attitudes on race, social class, and especially gender and sexuality, and these attitudes have changed significantly over time.

Beauty has long been related in the South to color. English colonists in North America brought European concepts of beauty, which became a factor justifying the enslavement of black Africans. Historian Winthrop D. Jordan has noted that "the English discovery of black Africa came at a time when the accepted standard of ideal beauty was a fair complexion of rose and white. Negroes not only failed to fit this ideal but seemed the very picture of perverse negation." Judged on this standard, blacks were seen as "pronouncedly less beautiful than whites." In his age, Thomas Jefferson asked whether skin color is not "the foundation of a greater or less share of beauty in the two races?" He insisted that "the fine mixtures of red and white" were "preferable to that eternal monotony" of black skin. Jefferson's concept of beauty included "flowing hair" and an "elegant symmetry of form," both of which he attributed to whites more than to other races. "The circumstance of superior beauty," he wrote, "is thought worthy of attention in the propagation of our horses, dogs, and other domestic animals; why not in that of man?" The idea of beauty was tied in for southern whites with ideas of sexuality and morality. Southern whites used the dark skin color of slaves as an outward indicator of the immorality of blacks, attributing to them impurities, lasciviousness, and evil.

The myth of the Old South included a prominent role for the beautiful white lady. Indeed, as W. J. Cash noted in *The Mind of the South* (1941), she became identified "with the very notion of the South itself." Physical beauty was a part of the definition of southern womanhood. The 19th-century conception of woman's appearance emphasized her fragility, purity, and spirituality, rather than her physical nature. The southern lady, according to Anne Firor Scott, was to be "timid and modest, beautiful and graceful." Anne Goodwin Jones has pointed out that white women in the Old South "became not only the perfect embodiments of beauty" but also "the appropriate vehicles for the expression of beauty in language." Beauty itself, like the lovely woman who best represented that quality, "was fragile and ethereal, or sensuous and pleasurable, but it was finally irrelevant to the serious business of life." Beauty was a culturally admired trait, but it was also a limiting one for women.

The identification of whiteness and women with beauty has survived in the 20th century. Cash wrote that the southern woman was "the South's Palladium," "the shield-bearing Athena gleaming whitely in the clouds," "the lily-pure maid of Astolat." Carl Carmer wrote in *Stars Fell on Alabama* (1934) of the University of Alabama fraternity dance that included a toast: "To Woman, lovely woman of the Southland, as pure and chaste as this sparkling water, as cold as this gleaming ice, we lift this cup, and we pledge our hearts and our lives to the protection of her virtue and chastity."

The southern ideal of the beautiful woman has evolved, though, in this century. The Scarlett O'Hara type, who is associated with the Old South, is beautiful but somewhat artificial. Sexuality is much more openly associated with beautiful women in the modern South. Victoria O'Donnell's typology of images of southern women in film points out that one dominant type is the "Sexual Woman": "She is beautiful, voluptuous, only partially clothed, and openly erotic. She is able to give sexual fulfillment, but she does so in order to impart strength to her man." Sometimes the beautiful southern woman becomes the "Rich, Spoiled Woman," who has "beauty, money, men, and friends" but is "spoiled and wild." Another film image of the modern southern woman portrays her as "earthier, gaudier" than women of the past, embodying open "carnal qualities, for she has lost her purity and chastity and is glad of it." The "Unfulfilled Sexual Woman" wants to be sexually appealing, but she is frustrated because "she has little to offer in terms of physical beauty." For all of these social types in the southern imagination, beauty remains an important ingredient of culturally determined happiness, which now includes sexual satisfaction.

Changing attitudes toward the sun have affected the southern ideal of beauty. In Western civilization white, pallid skin was traditionally a sign of upper-class status, and such makeup as face powder and rouge highlighted whiteness. With industrialization, upper-class Europeans and white Americans, including eventually southerners, developed an interest in outdoor life. The laboring class now worked indoors so the upper class sought suntans and outdoor recreation as an indicator of social-class status. "The lithe, sun-tanned, tennis-playing, outdoor woman," writes Marvin Harris, "became a respectable alternative to the cloistered, snow-and-alabaster ideal of the old regimes." Soon the middle class adopted this ideal of a physically healthy, athletic, sun-tanned woman.

This cultural change had special significance in the South, where the sun is intensely felt and "whiteness" has its most deeply rooted racial-cultural meaning. The sun has long helped determine southern social status—rednecks were laborers, and their women were said to be less beautiful because they were less pallidly white than the plantation wife. By the 1920s the South, according to historians Francis Butler Simkins and Charles Roland, had "learned to regard its very hot and very bright sun as a beneficent friend instead of as a cruel tyrant." Sunbonnets and long, tight-fitting clothes were abandoned for lighter garments, and the sun was soon regarded as a source of health. Sun bathing gradually became common, and "the acme of Southern comeliness became blue eyes, blond hair, and brown skin."

Black attitudes toward beauty have gone through their own changes. Illustrations of Afro-Americans up to the 1880s show a predominance of natural hair and little cosmetic beautification of the face. By the turn of the 20th century, though, black males were beginning to use hot combs to straighten hair, while black women used oils and pomades. Evidence suggests that many blacks internalized white ideals of beauty. They used cosmetics to lighten the skin color and hair straighteners to "conk" the hair in attempting to approach the white ideal. This probably reached a peak during the 1940s. Beauty parlors became important institutions of the black community, and cosmetic manufacturers were among the wealthiest of black Americans.

Skin color has been a symbol of social class status *within* the black community. John Dollard noted in *Caste and Class in a Southern Town*, his 1937 study of Indianola, Miss., that "consciousness of color and accurate discrimination between shades is a well-developed caste mark in Southerntown; whites, of course, are not nearly so skilful [*sic*] in distinguishing and naming various shades." Toni Morrison's *The Bluest Eye* (1970) portrays the tragic results of a black family's self-hatred because of a "white skin" ideal of beauty. Lawrence Levine cautions, however, against overemphasizing the effect of a cultural ideal of white beauty on blacks. For many blacks a light skin did not suggest social status within the black community, but rather a corruption of the race. If some black people have admired white skin, others have viewed black skin as natural, and many cosmetics have existed not to cloak that color but to highlight it. Moreover, when color preference has been seen in black cultural expressions such as blues lyrics, it has most often been brown, rather than either black or white-yellow. Paul Oliver's study of blues lyrics, *Blues Fell This Morning: The Meaning of the Blues* (1960), found that rural folk expressed an ideal of beauty somewhat different from the urban black and white ideal of "the streamlined woman." Bluesmen admired the "big, fat woman with the meat shaking on her bone." They also celebrated certain physical features, such as teeth that "shine like pearls" as a natural and attractive contrast with dark skin.

The civil rights movement of the 1950s and 1960s surely strengthened pride in a black ideal of beauty. "Black Is Beautiful" reflected a new appreciation of dark skin specifically as well as a more general pride in black culture. Magazines such as *Beauty Trade* and *Essence* are now published by blacks outside of the South, but their ideas influence the southern beauty industry and black ideals of beauty. Black beauty pageants have become a fixture on black campuses and in black communities across the South.

The beauty pageant is the ritual event that best displays modern national and regional attitudes about beauty. Predecessors of American beauty pageants were European festivals that crowned queens. European May Day activities have included selection of beautiful women as symbols of fertility. In the colonial era this custom took root more in the South than among the Puritans. Schools for young southern white women throughout the 19th century included contests for selection of attractive, popular queens. Southern romanticism expressed itself in antebellum tournaments, re-creating medieval pageants, and these festive occasions included queens selected for their beauty. Postbellum festivals also included selection of beauties. Mardi Gras chose its first queen in 1871, de-

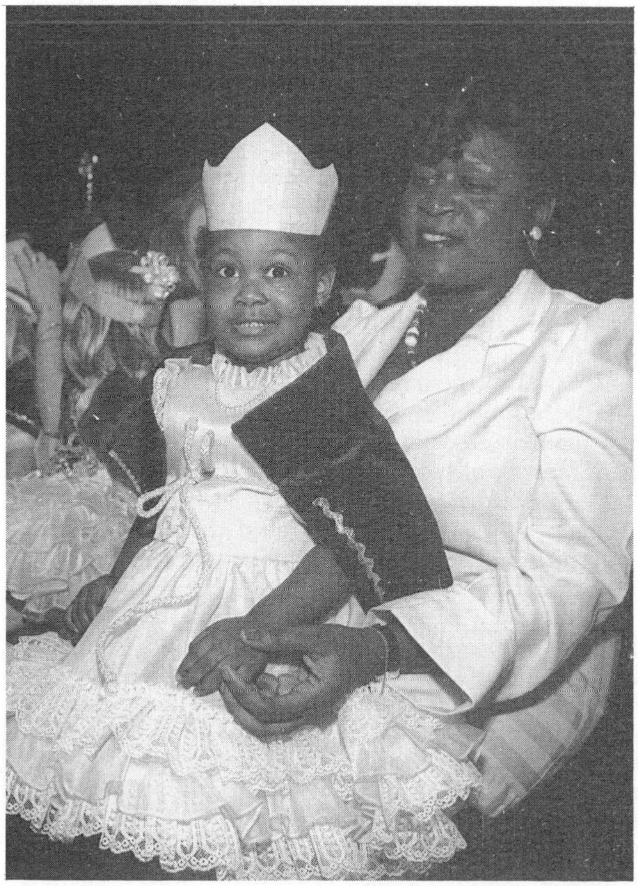

Young competitor in a children's beauty pageant, Atlanta, 1986

spite the protest of some moralists who objected to any public display of women. These May Day, tournament, and festival queens were upper-class figures, and these contests reinforced, as historian Lois Banner has written, "the centrality of physical beauty in women's lives and made of beauty a matter of competition and elitism and not of democratic cooperation among women."

Commercial beauty pageants appeared first in the late 19th century. P. T. Barnum sponsored a female beauty pageant in 1854, but it involved only the display of daguerreotypes of women, with observers voting on winners. Carnivals in the South, often attached to agricultural fairs, helped pave the way for beauty contests displaying beautiful women in native costumes from around the world. The Atlanta International Cotton Exposition of 1895 had a beauty show on its midway, and this part of the exposition was described as "the Mecca of the show." By 1900 chambers of commerce and fraternal groups in the South sponsored carnival beauty shows at fairs, but it was still not considered appropriate for middle-class women to be on display in competitive contests. The first true competitive beauty contest was the Miss United States contest at Rehobeth Beach, Dela., in 1880, but the South's beach resorts did not follow suit generally until after the turn of the century.

The Miss America pageant began in 1921, but the judges did not select a southerner until Texan Jo-Carrol Dennison was chosen in 1942. With the Americanization of the South—and the southernization of the United States—in recent decades, southerners have become identified with love of beauty pageants. *Newsweek* magazine (17 September 1984) estimated that 750,000 beauty contests are held each year in the United States, ranging from pageants for school homecoming queens, county- and state-fair queens, and festival representatives to the Miss America contest. "The phenomenon is strongly regional," said *Newsweek*. "The 'Pageant belt' stretches from Texas (where there are men who will date only titleholders) throughout the South, overlapping the Bible belt with odd precision."

Beauty pageants in the South are part of a regional cult of beauty. Young southern white ladies have long been encouraged in the feminine arts, and aspects of beauty have been taught in female academies, charm schools, and modern modeling salons. Cosmetologists, beauticians, and hairdressers are well-known figures in small and large southern towns, where concern for "looks" is endemic. Eudora Welty reproduced the ambience and conversational sound of the southern beauty parlor in her short story "Petrified Man."

Cosmetics were slow to take root in the poor rural South of the early 20th century. Even today, some Pentecostal-Holiness groups stress an ascetic ideal of outward plainness and inner beauty. Nevertheless, most women in small southern towns and cities have long accepted national views on cosmetics. Mary Kay Ash, founder of the successful Mary Kay Cosmetics, is from Texas; a key figure in the black cosmetic industry in this century, Madame C. J. Walker, came from Louisiana. Changes in contemporary southern religion's attitude toward beauty are evinced by Tammy Faye Bakker, the television celebrity formerly on the Pentecostal-oriented show, the *PTL Club*. Bakker flaunted her makeup by using a great deal of it. She even launched her own line of cosmetics.

Beauty pageants are central to small-town, middle-class life in the South and the nation. In 1970, for example, only 8 of 50 contestants in the Miss America pageant were from the nation's 25 largest cities. Few large urban areas sponsor contests, and even statewide beauty pageants tend to take place in smaller cities and towns. James Rucker, a former executive director of the Miss Mississippi contest, notes that whereas big-city northern girls enter the contest for the scholarship money or a chance at show-business success, "in Mississippi, it's tradition for the best girls to come out for the Pageant. In Mississippi, the best girls just want to be Miss America."

Beauty contests are community events in towns and small cities. Beauty-contest winners are contemporary regional celebrities—the female equivalents of football stars. Beauty queens, whether Miss America or Miss Gum Spirits (representing the southern timber industry), make personal appearances, travel extensively, earn scholarship money, and have their photos on calendars. Meridian, Miss., rewarded Susan Akin, Miss America in 1985, with an enthusiastic hometown parade. She rode through town before a cheering crowd that included young girls who had won their own honors as Deep South Beauty Queen, Cameo Girl, Mini Queen, and Miss Cinderella Queen. This ritual event showed an intense American middle-class patriotism. The band played "This Is My Country" and "God Bless America." State representative Sonny Meredith was there to praise her, and Meridian's mayor named the day in her honor. Religion was a central feature. The pastor of the First Baptist Church gave an invocation, thanking God for "letting us live in a country where a neighborhood girl could be selected Miss America." The Baptist kindergarten students had penned portraits of the queen. A friend from childhood told the crowd that Susan Akin was "the one of us who earned immortality."

Florida bathing beauties, 1920s

Participants in the Miss America pageant and those who have studied it believe that southerners who compete have an advantage. After Tennessee's Kellye Cash won in 1986, another contestant claimed that Cash had won because judges desired a "sweet kind of non-aggressive Southern belle." Cash revealed her regional consciousness, when she said she was "basically a conservative Southern gal." The contestant representing Mississippi that year insisted southerners had no special advantage, except that "they just work harder." Eight of the 10 finalists, in any event, were from former Confederate states. Miss Montana, Kamala Compton, gave no evidence of knowing about John C. Calhoun's concept of the concurrent majority, which proposed presidents from the North and the South, but she suggested a variation of it. Southerners were "just a lot more prepared than us Western girls who try once for a title," she told a reporter. "I mean, they should have a Southern Miss America and a Western Miss America."

Southerners clearly devote considerable time and resources to doing well in the Miss America pageant. University of Southern Mississippi sociologists Don Smith, Jim Trent, and Gary Hansen have theorized in unpublished research reported in the Jackson, Miss., *Clarion-Ledger* (15 October 1986) that southern contestants likely do better in the national contest because of three factors: (1) pageant officials, judges, and contestants assume, based on past experience, that southerners will do well; (2) the southern states encourage beauty contestants; (3) and southern states have strong pageant systems. Twenty-five states have never won the contest, whereas Texas, Alabama, and Arkansas have won twice, and Mississippi has won four times. Texas spends on contestants' clothes more than twice as much as Vermont spends for its entire pageant. Vermont has never placed a contestant in the top 10 at Miss America, but Texas obviously values its success. From 1945 to 1970 California led the nation in scholarship prize money ($47,300) awarded to contestants. Mississippi was second ($43,000), but Mississippi's commitment was much greater, given that the state had a tenth of California's population. Four of the top seven states in awarding scholarship money up to 1970 were Arkansas, Alabama, South Carolina, and Mississippi.

The Miss America contest and beauty pageants in general earn the condemnation of many men and women. "The whole gimmick is one commercial shell game to sell the sponsors' products," said critic Robin Morgan in 1968. "Where else could one find such a perfect combination of American values? Racism, militarism, and capitalism—all packaged in one 'ideal' symbol: *a woman.*" Spokesmen for the Miss America pageant defend it, noting it is the largest provider of scholarships for women in the United States. Women themselves are, of course, actively involved as participants and, behind the scenes, as trainers and managers, but men run the Miss America contest and other beauty contests. In September 1986, for example, no women served on the 12-member commission that represented the state pageants. The Jaycees are sponsors of most local Miss America contests, and men's service clubs are involved in other beauty contests. Pageants are hobbies for many men, a time for having fun and for theatrical displays. The head of the Miss Arkansas contest wears a hog suit and cheers for his choice each year; the state chairman in Mississippi dresses in a tuxedo made from Confederate flags. Miss America pageant director Albert Marks, Jr., notes that "watching pretty girls" is "the greatest spectator sport in America." Southerners have been unusually involved in this sport as both participants and spectators.

Charles Reagan Wilson
University of Mississippi

Lois Banner, *American Beauty* (1983); Frank Deford, *There She Is: The Life and Times of Miss America* (1971); Lisa DePaulo, *TV Guide* (6 September 1986); *Ebony* (May 1983); Marvin Harris, *Natural History* (August–September 1973); Shelby Hearon, *Texas Monthly* (October 1974); Anne Goodwyn Jones, *Tomorrow Is Another Day: The Woman Writer in the South, 1859–1936* (1981); Winthrop D. Jordan, *White over Black: American Attitudes toward the Negro, 1550–1812* (1968); Robin T. Lakoff and Raquel L. Scherr, *Face Value: The Politics of Beauty* (1984); Lawrence W. Levine, *Black Culture and Black Consciousness: Afro-American Folk Thought from Slavery to Freedom* (1977); Victoria O'Donnell, in *The South and Film*, ed. Warren French (1981); Kathrin Perutz, *Beyond the Looking Glass: America's Beauty Culture* (1970); Anne Firor Scott, *The Southern Lady: From Pedestal to Politics, 1830–1930* (1970); Francis Butler Simkins and Charles P. Roland, *A History of the South* (1972).

Civil War

The South was once a small corner of an American Indian civilization that covered two continents. Then the South was in the middle of the western fringe of the British Empire. Next the South was one section within a union of former colonies. In that union the South became a self-conscious minority section, later a collection of "conquered provinces," and still later "Uncle Sam's other province." Whether the site of "the Nation's No. 1 economic problem" or the potential recipient of Sunbelt prosperity, the South has been a peculiar region within the American nation. And southerners have defined themselves within the context of a civilization, empire, union, or nation in which they have been a minority. The single exception to this was that four-year "moment" during which the South was itself a de facto nation, the Confederate States of America.

In theory, Confederate southerners should have been able to shape their corporate identity and define themselves as a separate people. In fact, a war for their survival as people and nation severely circumscribed the inclinations and efforts of southerners to create a recognizable Confederate culture. Some historians have even contended that the Confederate South never quite became a nation and thus never developed a national life worthy of the name. To be sure, the Confederacy lived only briefly, and then only in the midst of a devastating, modern war. But within limits, the Confederate experience led (and drove) southerners into novel cultural expressions and relationships, some of which outlived the abortive southern nation.

Discovering Confederate southern culture is a challenge. Examinations of some traditional forms of cultural expression—art, music, literature, and the like—are disappointing. During the war southerners sang and listened to music that was all but identical to that of their enemies. Both northern and southern armies marched to the strains of "Dixie," and soldiers on both sides sang romantic ballads like "Lorena." Paintings, such as William D. Washington's *The Burial of Latané*, enjoyed brief fame but have since served as examples of "sentimentalism," "exaggeration," and "historical anecdote" in 19th-century art. Confederate southerners produced little in the realm of belles lettres and less of any lasting value. And the trench networks at Vicksburg, Petersburg, and elsewhere were but sad architectural expressions that fortunately did not endure in southern life. None of this should be very surprising; wartime is seldom conducive to contemplative pursuits, especially when the war is going badly. Southerners, like most people at war, preferred escape and diversion to challenge and creativity in their theater, books, and songs.

Nevertheless, Confederates did make significant contributions to southern culture; the challenge in discovering these contributions lies in knowing where to look for them. Augusta Jane Evans's *Macaria or Altars of Sacrifice*, which was the most popular novel produced in the Confederacy, was not the best example of southern literature during the war. Southerners who responded immediately and directly to wartime experience in letters, diaries, magazines, and newspapers did, however, generate a body of literature that was lively and lasting. John M. Daniel and Edward A. Pollard in the Richmond *Examiner*, to cite only one newspaper, offered vigorous (often vicious) editorials as well as vivid coverage from the South's battlefields. The family papers of the Fleets in Virginia and the Joneses in Georgia have become classics a century after their composition, as *Greenmount, a Virginia Plantation Family during the Civil War* and *The Children of Pride: A True Story of Georgia and the Civil War*. Likewise, the diaries of Mary Chesnut and Phoebe Pember continue, with reason, to charm readers. Confederate southerners generated a "literature of immediacy," which generally surpassed the leisured efforts of southern writers in the rest of the 19th century.

The Confederate experience affected southerners in myriad ways; the creation of an informal wartime literature is only one example. "Rebel ingenuity" is another. The agricultural southern people involved in an industrial war developed a remarkable resourcefulness. Esteemed oceanographer Matthew Fontaine Maury developed "torpedoes" (mines) for the Confederate navy, and officers in the niter and mining bureau learned how to use urine in the manufacture of gunpowder. On the homefront southerners experimented with substitutes for coffee and adjusted to the scarcity of imported items.

Among Confederate institutions the church proved to be the most steadfastly patriotic. Most southerners recognized the authority of some Protestant evangelical denomination, whether or not they took an active part in organized religion, and southern churches were overwhelmingly supporters of the Cause. Quakers, Universalists, and the like who did not share the enthusiasm of their fellow Protestants were few in number compared to the evangelical majority, and other southern religious minorities, Jews and Roman Catholics, actively backed the Confederacy. In the early months of the war, sermons likened southerners to God's chosen people and northerners to Philistines. Later, when southern armies seemed to be losing, the church offered an explanation: God was testing and chastening the southern people; in renewed righteousness lay God's favor and victory. Churches not only preached national salvation, they sent chaplains, and countless tracts, into Confederate camps for the sake of individual souls. Revivals swept through the ranks of the Confederate armies, especially during 1864, and religion offered spiritual comfort to many in the midst of death and defeat. Southern churches, too, developed a stronger social consciousness in response to wartime. Congregations donated their bells to be recast as cannon, offered their buildings as hospitals, and organized knitting and sewing sessions to fashion items of clothing for the troops. As the Confederacy collapsed, southern churches offered the consolation that religion transcends temporal circumstance and that righteousness would ultimately prevail.

Certainly the Civil War contributed to the southern "cult of the soldier"—the conviction that the military was an ultimate expression of manhood. Even when the dirt, disease, and death of war's reality contradicted this conviction, many southerners clung to the fantasy. For families of those who died in camp and combat and for thousands of wounded men, the association of military service with manhood somehow justified the sacrifice.

That the administration of Jefferson Davis and the Confederate Congress should have authorized the participation of black southerners in the "cult of the soldier" is some index of the war's impact upon the South. In 1861 Confederate Vice President Alexander H. Stephens proclaimed slavery to be the "cornerstone" of the southern nation. By 1864 the southern government was advocating the use of black troops in the war, and Robert E. Lee went on record as welcoming black men into his armies. When the Congress finally acted to arm the slaves, the Davis Administration made sure that black soldiers would serve as free men. These efforts occurred too late to save the Cause, but their very occurrence is significant.

The idea of woman as southern belle, ornament and object, did not fare well in wartime. Women often became heads of households when men went off to fight. Confederate women also became nurses, refugees, and factory workers. The variety of experience was novel, and to the degree that it became more than an emergency irregularity in the lives of southern women, it revised roles and expectations among these women.

However much wartime influenced southern life, the most profound effect of the Civil War upon southern culture occurred only after the war was lost. It is supreme irony that southern culture since 1865 has been more the product of Lost Cause mythology than Confederate realities. The southern response to defeat, reunion, and Reconstruction inspired a myth-history that ennobled the destruction of the southern nation. The Lost Cause mythology held that the southern cause was not only undefiled by defeat but that the bloodbath of war actually sanctified the values and mores of the Old South. High priests of this message were beaten warriors. Southerners enshrined the politicians and especially those military officers who had presided over failure and defeat. The influence of the unreconstructed proved to be pervasive.

The Lost Cause inspired a romantic literature perhaps best exemplified by Margaret Mitchell's *Gone with the Wind*. If literary critics are correct, the myth helped to spawn the Southern Literary Renaissance and fueled the intellectual movement known as the Nashville Agrarians. Indeed, the Lost Cause became a civil religion south of the Potomac, and it continues in various ways and degrees to influence southern thought and action.

The Civil War offered southerners the opportunity to win their independence and mold for themselves a national, as opposed to sectional, culture. As Confederates, southerners did respond creatively to the stress of wartime. But the most significant impact of the Civil War upon southern culture lay not in its reality but in its memory. The memory may have been myth; but for many southerners the Lost Cause has been myth believed and acted upon.

See also LITERATURE: Civil War in Literature; MYTHIC SOUTH: / Lost Cause Myth

Emory Thomas
University of Georgia

Henry Putney Beers, *Guide to the Archives of the Government of the Confederate States of America* (1968); Clement Eaton, *A History of the Southern Confederacy* (1954); Shelby Foote, *The Civil War: A Narrative*, 3 vols. (1958–75); Douglas Southall Freeman, *The South to Posterity: An Introduction to the Writings of Confederate History* (1939); Clarence L. Mohr, *On the Threshold of Freedom: Masters and Slaves in Civil War Georgia* (1985); Allan Nevins, James I. Robertson, Jr., and Bell I. Wiley, eds., *Civil War Books: A Critical Bibliography* (1967); James G. Randall and David Donald, *The Civil War and Reconstruction* (2d rev. ed., 1969); Charles P. Roland, *The Confederacy* (1960); James W. Silver, *Confederate Morale and Church Propaganda* (1957); Emory Thomas, *Confederacy as a Revolutionary Experience* (1971), *The Confederate Nation, 1861–1865* (1979); Frank E. Vandiver, *Their Tattered Flags: The Epic of the Confederacy* (1970); Bell I. Wiley, *Confederate Women* (1975), *The Plain People of the Confederacy* (1943).

Colonial Heritage

Judged by a conception of culture as the pursuit and patronage of arts and letters, the early South has conventionally been found wanting. No more in the North than in the South, however, did early American poets, painters, or philosophers achieve a golden age of the mind, the spirit, or the imagination. No more in Boston or Philadelphia than in Williamsburg or Charleston did drama or divinity, song, story, or scholarship rise above provincial consequence.

By another standard, the planters of the southern colonies were, in fact, highly significant. On the ethnographic level—culture as the integrated lifeways of an entire people—students of the outposts south of the Delaware need not be defensive at all. The southern provinces prefigured the American way of life more clearly than even the Middle Atlantic did. From the sunrise of settlement, at Roanoke and Jamestown, southern colonists manifested the norms and values that ultimately mastered the continent.

The colonial South was quintessentially American. Colonists were settled on the Chesapeake for almost a quarter of a century before the *Arbella* eased into Massachusetts Bay, and the priority of the plantations of the South was more than merely chronological. The men who established England's first successful stronghold in the New World were engaged in such decidedly American enterprises as racial exploitation, representative self-government, and market-oriented economic endeavor for a decade and more before the Puritans dreamed of departing their mother country. The men and women who succeeded them consolidated their initiatives and fused them into a coherent course of life.

That course appalled the few who clung to conventional European categories. Would-be reformers condemned again and again the immoderate acquisitiveness that dispersed southerners over the countryside and the importunate self-interest that left them indifferent to the common good. But the criticisms fell on deaf ears. Planters set out from the first to advance their own affairs. At Roanoke they abandoned the fort for their farms. From Jamestown they fanned out along the river rather than remain in the town. And ever after, they continued heedless of calls to congregate for the sake of religion, the common defense, or civility itself.

Southerners simply would not subordinate their unruly ambition to any public concern or sense of social responsibility. In the words of the 18th-century planter Robert Beverley, "the chief design of all . . . was to fetch away the treasure . . . aiming more at sudden gain than to form a regular colony." Exactly on account of such worldly priorities, southern colonial social institutions were always unable to control southern settlers.

Virginians and Carolinians, Marylanders and Georgians alike had crossed the ocean as adventurers and evolved virtues appropriate to their situation. They esteemed independence and prized personal liberty. They resented discipline, spurned spirituality, and often indulged themselves with hedonistic abandon. They cultivated a taste for proud display. As they did, they disdained civic consciousness and forfeited social cohesion. They committed little to the community. They valued their own private pursuits above all, and they measured them primarily by criteria of material accumulation.

None of this inattention to the common good was unique to the South or in any way exceptional in a wider prospect of English outposts in the New World. If there was a peculiar institution in early America, it was not southern slavery and the extravagant avarice it embodied. It was the New England town and the anachronistic restraint of greed it attempted. If southern ways were distinctive at all, they were distinctive only in their intensity. Lust for the good life—a heedless, headlong scramble after personal gratification—was already at the center of an emerging American dream. Such lust was simply less impeded in the southern provinces.

In their pell-mell pursuit of that dream southerners developed a recognizably American readiness for slavery, refusal of deference to their designated superiors, and attachment to a rough-hewn democracy of hustlers, speculators, and salesmen. In their devotion to the subtropical monocultures that afforded them their opportunities for aggrandizement, southerners enmeshed themselves more elaborately than any other mainland Americans in market relations and market values. And in doing so, southerners immediately encountered the enduring American dilemmas of labor and laziness.

When southern pioneers and publicists extolled their region, they exalted above all the indolent ease that the land allowed. In their New World as in Adam's, "everything seemed to come up by nature." Husbandmen lived "almost void of care and free from . . . fatigues." By the bounty of a benign providence, the earth brought forth "all things in abundance, as in the first creation, without toil or labor."

In every precinct colonists were content to "sponge upon the blessings of a warm sun and a fruitful soil." Domestic stock cost them "nothing to keep or feed" because animals grazed freely in winter as well as summer, sparing settlers the drudgery of fencing and the tedium of foddering. Cattle, swine, and sheep could all be left to themselves to feed on the rich and self-renewing grasses of the new continent. Fish and fowl too presented themselves for the settlers' effortless enjoyment. Marylanders met "rich bosoms" of marine creatures in their bays, all "easily taken." Carolinians could "easily gather" more oysters in a day than they could "well eat in a year." And all the planters encountered birds "so numerous . . . that you might see millions in a flock."

Everywhere men echoed the enthusiasm of the initial English endeavor in the New World, that the land lavished its largesse upon them without their exertion. The husbandman as much as the herder and the hunter lived on the "benevolent breast" of nature. Crops that others elsewhere had to cultivate with unremitting diligence simply "thrust . . . forth" in the South "as easily as the weeds." American grains were "so grateful to the planter" that they returned him "his entrusted seed" with a treble growth; and they were "so facilely planted that one man in 48 hours may prepare as much ground and set such a quantity of corn that he may be secure from want of bread all the year following." Men managed "very easily" though unwilling to work "above two or three hours a day" or more than "three days in seven." Indeed, under such circumstances, it was difficult to distinguish work from leisure. Planting presented itself as a pastime of "pleasure," hunting as an "exercise" of "delight," and fishing as a "pretty sport" for profit, in a land in which everything grew plentifully "to supply the wants or wantonness of man."

Payne Limner, Alexander Spotswood Payne and His Brother, John Robert Dandridge Payne, with Their Nurse *(c. 1790–1800)*

Yet such celebration of hedonic ease was a perilous ploy. Even as it stimulated real estate sales, it stirred specters of corruption, inciting castigation of the colonists as degenerate outcasts of the Old World. The exaggeration of effortlessness that enticed also offended. The emphasis on immunity from harsh labor that enthralled also appalled. Southerners uncertain of their own civility were sensitive to suggestions that they might be overwhelmed by the wilderness and lapse into self-indulgence.

Virginians therefore feared the felicity they flaunted, that so "little labor" was "required to fill their bellies." Carolinians bemoaned the blessing they boasted, that their paradise was "apt to make people incline to sloth." And Georgians trembled that their prolific province might be "deformed by its own fertility." The same settlers who proclaimed their tracts gardens of earthly delight insisted that they would not welcome people who wished to live there in a "state of idleness and dependence." They declared that men "were appointed to cultivate the earth," not to bask in its bounty.

Exactly as they careened from one extreme to the other, colonial southerners enunciated the dilemma in economic ethics that would occupy the nation ever after. Just as they gloated over their effortless indolence in one breath and gloried in their exemplary industry in the next, so they anticipated the tension between the imperative to work and the compulsion to consume that would set the shape of aspiration for centuries in America.

Suspended between those demands for exertion and those dark desires for exemption from exertion, the planters of the southern provinces were also driven to develop an incipiently American temporal horizon. Because they disdained methodical economic endeavor yet sought the splendid display that rewarded such steadiness, they could only envision attainment of their ends by sudden strokes of fortune. Because they scorned unremitting application to a calling, they could only imagine success by slipping the constraints of history itself.

The past, then, held little fascination for southerners of the 17th and 18th centuries. It provided them no notable local heroes, memorialized for them no vivifying regional myths, and engendered in them no discernible curiosity. It certainly entailed no burdens. Indeed, it was rarely invoked even to validate prevailing social arrangements or to legitimate specific institutional establishments.

Early southerners simply ceded their patrimonies. The fragility of their attachment to traditions was evident in the unraveling of the religious and familial threads that webbed men and women in the mother country. The permanence of their ties to the land on which they lived was legible in the flimsy houses in which they encamped upon the country, far into the 18th century. And the transiency of their interests was apparent in the ease with which they departed their estates and operations for others elsewhere. As George Washington noted, the great fortunes of the Tidewater were not made by a steadfast cultivation of the southern staples. They were the result of shrewd speculation in frontier lands, and they reflected the readiness of the planters to relinquish established assets for the sake of visionary futures.

Colonial New Englanders might revere ancestors and look to the past for legitimate authority. Colonial southerners were impatient of inheritance and eager for futurity. Thomas Jefferson declared their sense of time in his insistence that "the earth belongs in usufruct to the living." He articulated the logic of their lives in affirming that he liked "dreams of the future better than the history of the past." And increasingly his countrymen, north as well as south, came to concur. That early southern sensibility came to color a national culture sublimely indifferent to history and uncommonly attracted to New Freedoms, New Deals, and New Frontiers.

Ironically, as the nation came to the colonial South's sense of time, the South itself came to take history seriously. First in the declining economies of the Tidewater, then across a region ravaged by civil war, southerners created legends of cavaliers and cherished memories of gallant warriors and galling defeat. But in their initial period of settlement their experiences embodied a quite different heritage.

Michael Zuckerman
University of Pennsylvania

David Bertelson, *The Lazy South* (1967); Timothy H. Breen, *Puritans and Adventurers: Change and Persistence in Early America* (1980); Carl Bridenbaugh, *Myths and Realities: Societies of the Colonial South* (1952); Richard Beale Davis, *Intellectual Life in the Colonial South, 1585–1763* (1978); Rhys Isaac, *The Transformation of Virginia, 1740–1790* (1982); Edmund S. Morgan, *American Slavery, American Freedom: The Ordeal of Colonial Virginia* (1975); Bertram Wyatt-Brown, *Southern Honor: Ethics and Behavior in the Old South* (1982).

Confederate States of America

After Abraham Lincoln's election in November 1860, South Carolina called a convention, which unanimously adopted the Ordinance of Secession on 20 December 1860. A Declaration of the Immediate Causes of Secession justified the action, and the convention urged other southern states to follow this lead. Six other states promptly responded in early 1861: Mississippi, 9 January; Florida, 10 January; Alabama, 11 January; Georgia, 19 January; Louisiana, 26 January; and Texas, 1 February. There was considerable opposition to secession in many of these states. Georgia, a geographically crucial state for any southern resistance, seceded 4 March. The four border states were slow and cautious in approving secession, but after the Confederate attack on Fort Sumter, S.C., in April of 1861, Virginia (17 April), Arkansas (6 May), North Carolina (20 May), and Tennessee (8 June) left the Union. The slave states of Missouri, Kentucky, and Maryland remained in the Union, and the western counties of Virginia formed a new state, West Virginia. Divided in sentiment, the people in the border South were the source of the most frequent brother-against-brother warfare. The border South had economic and patriotic ties to the North, but slavery and social customs made it a southern area, too. Missouri was the scene of bloody fighting during the war, and 30,000 in that Unionist state fought for the Confederacy.

Delegates from the seceding states met at Montgomery, Ala., 4 February 1861 to organize a provisional government for the Confederate States of America. The delegates saw themselves following in the steps of the American revolutionaries fighting for self-determination against a distant, oppressive government. The Confederate Constitution was modeled on the federal document and contained few innovations. It did recognize and guarantee slavery in all territory belonging to the new government, and it prohibited protective tariffs, appropriations for internal improvements, and the payment of bounties. It overtly asked for the "favor and guidance of Almighty God." The new constitution was officially adopted 11 March 1861. Jefferson Davis of Mississippi was chosen president of the new government, and Alexander H. Stephens became vice president. The Stars and Bars became the official flag.

In proclaiming their political independence, southern leaders seemed willing to compromise on earlier principles. Delegates to the convention created a stronger central government than secession rhetoric seemed to support. The concept of states' rights was not explicitly affirmed in the document. Leaders of the new government were generally moderates and conservatives, not the fire-eating revolutionary secessionists. The tension between centralization and localism would be a continual headache for those leaders.

At the start of the war, a serious discrepancy existed in the resources of the two combatants. The Union had a population of 22.7 million, compared to the 9 million (including 3.5 million slaves) in the Confederate states. In addition to its growing industrial capacity and an extended rail system for transportation, the Union had an

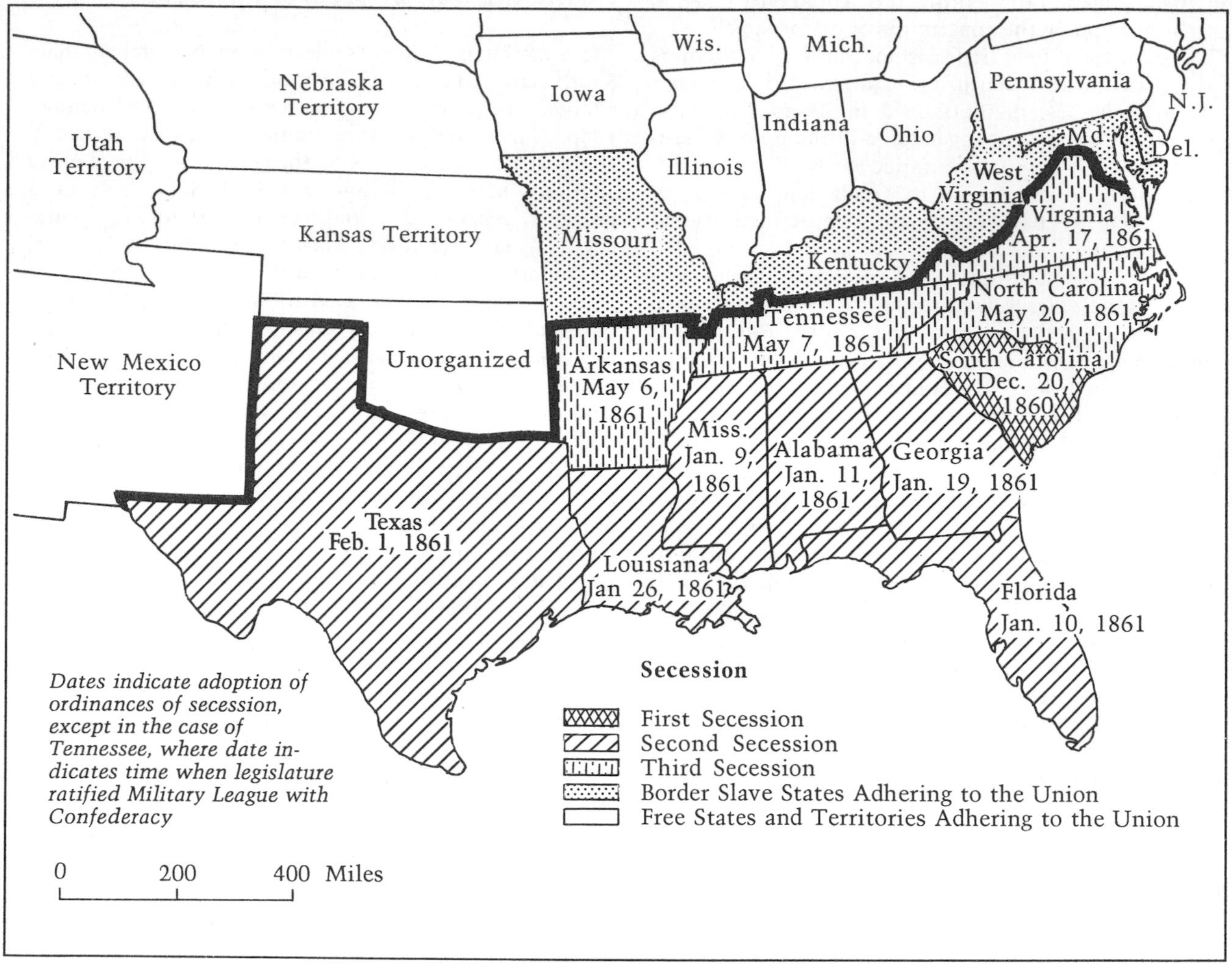

Secession

Source: Bernard Bailyn et al., *The Great Republic*, 3d ed. (1985).

established national government, navy, and regular army of 12,000. The Union strategy was a naval blockade of the southern coast and an invasion of the region from the North and Midwest. When Lincoln issued the Emancipation Proclamation on 23 September 1862 and declared slaves under Confederate control to be free after 1 January 1863, the goals of the Union war effort became not only nationalism but also human liberty. The North thus attempted to isolate the South economically, politically, and morally.

Southerners made war with great hopes of victory. The Confederacy raised and equipped a formidable fighting force. Josiah Gorgas, the chief of ordnance for the Confederate forces, resourcefully supplied the armies with needed weapons and munitions, and the Tredegar Iron Works produced innovative weaponry in the form of torpedoes, submarines, and plates for ironclads. Southerners had the enthusiasm of fighting for a cause, for tribal defense, and what seemed like basic human concerns—freedom, home, family, the land, and racial solidarity. They feared fundamental change in their way of life.

As the war progressed, though, divisions appeared in the social solidarity and cultural unity. Banking resources were inadequate, inflation rose, citizens refused to submit willingly to heavy taxes, and food shortages and protests about them occurred. Conscription became necessary, and desertion became a major problem for the military. Social-class conflicts appeared, as the burdens seemed to grow heavier for the humble as time went on, while some plantation families not near the fighting managed to do well and speculators clearly profited. Jefferson Davis proved to be an uninspiring leader and could not make an eloquent case for national unity. Advocates of states' rights, such as Governor Joseph E. Brown of Georgia and Zebulon B. Vance of North Carolina, hounded him, and by war's end Davis was unpopular.

Southern institutions and people in them generally rallied around the Confederacy, and they felt the disruptions of war. Churches, schools, colleges and universities, businesses, social groups, ethnic groups—all were affected by war. Colleges contributed soldiers and civilian leaders, while businesses reoriented their facilities to war work. Religion was particularly important in supporting political and military activities. Southern ministers and religious organizations supported the Confederacy and proved to be essential in maintaining morale. Leading ministers such as James Henley Thornwell and Stephen Elliot preached on the home front that the Confederacy was a holy crusade against the atheistic North, and revivals occurred periodically within the ranks of the Confederate armies. Episcopal Bishop Leonidas Polk and Baptist minister Mark P. Lowrey were only two of the many ministers who became Confederate generals.

The myth of the southern lady had appeared in the antebellum era, but the war challenged the image. Women were left to run the plantations and to raise the crops on small farms. They cared for the wounded under deplorable hospital conditions and found and shipped necessary supplies to men at the battlefront. The South's women experienced physical deprivation and the psychological trauma of the absence of loved ones and grief over the dead. The Confederate experience surely provided the context for new roles and expectations for women in southern culture and perhaps represented one stage in their liberation from gender stereotyping.

War also led to the more dramatic emancipation of southern slaves from the peculiar institution. Although the Emancipation Proclamation issued in 1862 did not immediately free slaves in the Confederate-controlled areas, it was a symbolic landmark for southern blacks—the Day of Jubilee. The Thirteenth Amendment to the federal Constitution became law on 18 December 1865, providing a constitutional prohibition against slavery. Most slaves stayed on the plantations during the Civil War, but evidence of slave conspiracies and plots in Virginia, Alabama, and Arkansas has been discovered. Thousands of blacks fought for the Union against slavery. The legend of the faithful wartime slave became, nonetheless, a key part of a romanticized myth of the Old South plantation.

Despite defeat in the war, the southern military made its greatest impact on the southern imagination while fighting for the Confederacy. Confederate military leaders were the true cultural heroes of the period—Robert E. Lee was the Virginia cavalier, Thomas J. "Stonewall" Jackson the holy warrior, Jeb Stuart the gallant horseman, P. G. T. Beauregard the hot-tempered Louisiana Creole, and Nathan Bedford Forrest the Tennessee guerrilla fighter. The names of battles had a lyrical, biblical ring to them: Manassas (Bull Run) in July 1861; Shiloh in April 1862; Antietam in September 1862 (the bloodiest day of the war); and the crucial Confederate defeat at Gettysburg in July 1863. There was Chancellorsville in Virginia, where Lee lost Stonewall Jackson, victim of a bullet from one of his own soldiers; Vicksburg, where the Confederates lost the West; Chickamauga and Chattanooga, which had been the key to the Confederate heartland; the fiery battle of Atlanta; Sherman's march to the sea; and the melancholic Appomattox, where Lee surrendered his 26,000 troops and refused to approve a guerrilla war against the North.

Each battle contained its own folklore and legends, gave birth to its songs, jokes, stories, heroes. Writers, singers, painters, sculptors, storytellers, and others have attested to the Confederacy's continuing cultural appeal by producing artifacts that explore the war's memory. "For every Southern boy fourteen years old," wrote William Faulkner of the memory of the decisive Gettysburg in *Intruder in the Dust* (1948), "not once but whenever he wants it, there is the instant when it's still not yet two o'clock on that July afternoon in 1863, the brigades are in position behind the rail fence, the guns are laid and ready in the woods . . . and Pickett himself with . . . his hat in one hand . . . and his sword in the other looking up the hill waiting for Longstreet to give the word and it's all in the balance, it hasn't happened yet, it hasn't even begun yet, it not only hasn't begun yet but there is still time for it not to begin."

Charles Reagan Wilson
University of Mississippi

E. Merton Coulter, *The Confederate States of America, 1861–1865* (1950); Clifford Dowdey, *The Land They Fought For: The Story of the South as the Confederacy, 1832–1865* (1955); Clement Eaton, *A History of the Southern Confederacy* (1954); Paul Escott, *After Secession: Jefferson Davis and the Failure of Confederate Nationalism* (1978); Douglas Southall Freeman, *The South to Posterity: An Introduction to the Writing of Confederate History* (1939); Charles P. Roland, *The Confederacy* (1960); Emory Thomas, *Confederacy as a Revolutionary Experience* (1971), *The Confederate Nation, 1861–1865* (1975); Frank E. Vandiver, *Their Tattered Flags: The Epic of the Confederacy* (1970); Bell I. Wiley, *Plain People of the Confederacy* (1943), *The Road to Appomattox* (1956).

Cookbooks

The first cookbooks in the South were brought from England by the early colonists. Until near the end of the 18th century cookbooks in the United States were simply manuscript collections or printed editions of English recipes. The first cookbook published in the colonies appears to have been *The Compleat Housewife; or, Accomplish'd Gentlewoman's Companion* (1742), by E. (Eliza) Smith, printed in Williamsburg. Hannah Glasse's *The Art of Cookery, Made Plain and Easy* (1747) was the most popular volume in Virginia, but others, such as *The English Huswife* (1623), by Gervase Markham, also were found throughout the South.

Virginia Housewife (1824), by Mary Randolph, has been called by Karen Hess "the most influential American cookbook of the nineteenth century." Randolph was a member of a prominent family, and her cookbook reflected a knowledge of regional produce, cooking practices, and overall social context. In addition to showing the dominant English influence, Randolph's cookbook reflected Indian contributions to southern food, through recipes that included Native American foods such as maize, sweet potatoes, squash, beans, fruits, and nuts. An African influence came through recipes learned from servants who prepared food using such ingredients as field peas, eggplant, yams, and tomatoes (which possibly were of African background). Randolph's recipes used 40 vegetables and 17 herbs, but did not specify the extended cooking for meats and vegetables that later became a trademark of southern cooking.

The ritual of setting a good table has been a veritable religion in the South since Mary Randolph's time. Cookbooks have been guides to southern ways of eating and have reinforced the southerner's belief that the food eaten and the manner of eating it have social significance. In antebellum times the great distance between homes (especially plantations) meant that any social gathering was a real occasion. The food was the entertainment. The Civil War had a profound effect on the way southerners were able to carry out this ritual of eating. Polly Alice Masten Körner (Mrs. Jule Gilmer Körner) wrote in her memoirs as recorded in the *Körner's Folly Cookbook* of the "troublous times toward the end of the War and for some time thereafter" when her father buried things of value, including her mother's "brown flowered china and tea set to protect them from the Yankee soldiers." Emma S. Layton in *I Remember When* recalled that "during the Civil War the Yankees came through taking everything they could get." Her grandmother "hid a peck of meal in the cradle with the baby" and had one of her boys "hide a ham in a big oak tree. . . . Grandmother hid her silver in a barrel of hog-feed."

Display of canned food, Greene County, Ga., 1941

Setting a good table began with the table covering. The standard "snow-white cover, damask or home-made" reflected the character of the housewife as well as her table, according to *Mrs. Elliot's Housewife* by Sarah A. Elliot (1870). Elliot admonished her housewife to keep "her castors bright and well-filled."

The food available in the South prior to the modern supermarket was primarily grown "on the place." Spring or young chickens were available only in the spring; new potatoes were the first potatoes to mature; and green peas (called English peas) were fresh from the vines for only a few days each year.

Before World War II most recipes, called receipts, were not written down. They were instead carried around in the cook's head. Some of these cooks, possessed of great intuitive skill, still exist and will explain in detail the art of preparing pinto beans or stewed potatoes. What they cannot explain is the special knack they bring to any cooking enterprise, which makes such a difference in the finished product.

Often when a recipe was recorded, it was preserved simply as a list of ingredients on a piece of paper. There were no accompanying directions. It was assumed that once the cook knew the ingredients and their amounts, she could figure out the rest for herself. The following recipe by Mrs. Jed Giddings of Maryland was contributed to S. R. Rhodes's *The Economy Administration Cook Book* (1913):

> Two Pound Cake by Measure
>
> The whites of twenty-four eggs, seven teacups of flour, four and one-half teacups of granulated sugar, two teacups of butter, one of sweet milk, a heaping teaspoon of cream of tartar. Have the pan warm and bake as quickly as possible.

When bound cookbooks started to appear in great numbers, they were put out by people like Henrietta Stanley Dull. She edited the weekly food page in the Atlanta *Journal*, which appeared under the slogan "It covers Dixie like the dew." Dull's name was a household word when her book *Southern Cooking* was published in 1928.

Another popular compilation of recipes in booklet form was by Sara Spano, food editor in Columbus, Ga. Her recipe for deep chocolate cake called for eight plain 5-cent chocolate bars and two 10-cent cans of chocolate—an indication of staple grocery prices in the 1920s and 1930s.

An early example of the many popular cookbooks put out by food companies is *The Rumford Complete Cookbook* by Lily Haxworth Wallace, published in 1934. Cookbooks published by churches, clubs, schools, and Junior Leagues also began to appear, bearing a wealth of excellent recipes. One of the most successful of these was *River Road Recipes* published by the Junior League of Baton Rouge, La. Its first printing was in 1959. By the 25th printing in 1971 at least 310,000 copies were in circulation.

Afro-American cooking styles and recipes are rooted in the South, and they are preserved in Sue Bailey Thurman, *Historical Cookbook of the American Negro* (1958), Jim Harwood and Ed Callahan, *Soul Food Cookbook* (1969), and Bob Jeffries, *Soul Food Cookbook* (1970). Norma Jean and Carole Darden assembled *Spoonbread and Strawberry Wine* (1978) through visiting relatives in Alabama, North Carolina, Virginia, and Ohio. Included are recipes for sweet potato biscuits, Cousin Johnnie K's macaroni and shrimp salad, Aunt Marjorie Palmer's every-kind-of-cookie-dough, and syllabub (a drink made from cream, sugar, nutmeg, and rum or brandy). Ernest M. Mickler's *White Trash Cooking* (1986) offers recipes from the southern rural poor. Like many recent cookbooks, *White Trash Cooking* contains numerous anecdotes and stories as well as 240 recipes stressing the use of salt meat, corn meal, and molasses.

Chef Paul Prudhomme's *Louisiana Kitchen* (1984) helped usher in a national fad for a southern subregional type of cooking. Another volume, Marjorie Kinnan Rawlings's *Cross Creek Cookery* (1942), assembled recipes from rural north-central Florida. Eudora Welty wrote the introduction to the Jackson Symphony League's *Jackson Cookbook* (1971), which includes a recipe for squash Eudora. The recipes of other southern writers appear in Dean Faulkner Wells's *Great American Writers' Cookbook*, published by Mississippi's Yoknapatawpha Press in 1981. It includes Harry Crews's snake steak, Roy Blount, Jr.'s garlic grits (and an "ode to grits"), and Willie Morris's John Birch Society beans (which cause a violent internal reaction).

Of course, southern cookbooks have their idiosyncracies. In 1969, when Albert Brewer was governor of Alabama, his wife, Martha Farmer Brewer, helped produce the *Alabama First Lady's Cookbook* as part of the celebration of the 150th birthday of the state. The book offered 41 recipes for preparing chicken, but not one for preparing fried chicken. The assumption was that everyone already knew how to fry chicken.

Among many things, the 1960s brought popular cooking programs on television, hundreds of new cookbooks, and a magazine named *Southern Living* based in Birmingham, Ala. A 23 November 1981 *Wall Street Journal* article described the magazine's formula for success as simply giving the readers what they wanted to read. The article mentioned a recipe for a nutmeg feather cake, which had appeared in an issue of the magazine, and predicted that "it would be safe to wager that nutmeg feather cakes will shortly appear on tables from Biloxi to Kannapolis."

In 1970 a cookbook named *Our Best Recipes* was published by *Southern Living*—the beginning of a series of cookbooks that is still tremendously popular. Their annual cookbook sells in excess of one and one-half million copies. In February 1985 Ann H. Harvey, managing editor of Oxmoor House, *Southern Living*'s book division, said that the division has approximately 35 titles. It began publishing an Antique American Cookbooks series in the 1980s, including historic southern volumes.

The library at the University of North Carolina in Greensboro, N.C., has an extensive collection of southern cookbooks. James H. Thompson, director of the library, describes it as one of the "strongest collections in the state and the South." Southern cookbooks reinforce a regional appreciation for tradition and encourage southerners to continue to enjoy the old favorites. People may not live by squash casseroles alone, but a southern cookbook without a recipe for at least one is rare.

Beth Tartan
Kernersville, North Carolina

Alabama First Lady's Cook Book (1969); John Egerton, *Southern Food: At Home, on the Road, in History* (1987); Sarah A. Elliott, *Mrs. Elliott's Housewife* (1870); Margaret Husted, *Virginia Cavalcade* (Autumn 1980); Mary Randolph, *The Virginia House-wife* (1984 facsimile of 1824); Blanche S. Rhett, *Two Hundred Years of Charleston Cooking* (1984); Sarah Rutledge, *The Carolinian Housewife* (1984 facsimile of 1847); Lena E. Sturges, *Southern Living: Our Best Recipes* (1970); Beth Tartan, *Körner's Folly Cookbook* (1977); Hazel Valentine, ed., *I Remember When* (1978); Lily Haxworth Wallace, *The Rumford Complete Cook Book* (1908); Eugene Walter, *American Cooking, Southern Style* (1971).

Debutantes

The social institution known as the debutante season is certainly not a peculiarly southern (nor even American) phenomenon, but in the face of the turbulent 1960s and 1970s, it has exhibited more tenacity and vitality in Dixie than elsewhere in the United States or in Great Britain, where the custom began. A number of factors help explain the custom's popularity: the South's pride in its womanhood, a tendency to keep women on a pedestal, a conservative clinging to venerable institutions, social distinctions by status, and belief in a cavalier heritage.

Although many societies, both primitive and advanced, have had their own rituals to signal the coming of age of men and women, England's Queen Elizabeth I supposedly began the custom of formal presentations of eligible young women at court. However, nearly three centuries later, Great Britain's young Queen Victoria, shortly after she married Prince Albert, gave the ritual much of its present form, when the daughters of the rising *haute bourgeoisie* of the Industrial Revolution began to be included in court presentations, along with those of nobility and gentry. A century later, yet another British queen, Elizabeth II, ended such events after the last presentations in March of 1958.

The custom of debutante presentations spread across the Atlantic when America began to prosper during the late 19th-century Gilded Age. In New York, according to social historian Cleveland Amory, public presentations began in 1870 at Delmonico's. Dixon Wecter wrote 50 years ago how the costly rituals of debutante presentations symbolized the wealth of fathers. On the other hand, in the impoverished postwar South the custom displayed another dimension—emphasizing who had been well born before all was "gone with the wind." The criterion was necessarily not that of wealth but of the family's antebellum status and lineage.

At the turn of the 20th century the most exclusive of the southern debutante seasons was held in Charleston. The St. Cecilia Society began in 1737 as America's first concert society but abandoned that function by 1822 and became a purely social organization. This elite all-male society began to sponsor what has been termed "the ultimate debutante presentation in the South, if not the whole United States." It is so proper and exclusive that any local publicity about either the society or its ball is taboo.

In Montgomery, Ala., Lila Matthews was presented to society with a dance and collation at her parents' house in 1884. The 1900 *Social Directory of Montgomery, Alabama* listed 33 debutantes, and the Montgomery Debutante Club began in the depths of the Depression in 1931. Today, young women of Montgomery society are presented at junior, senior, and debutante assemblies and at mystic society balls. Most notable of these are the New Year's Eve Ball given by the men of the Mystic Order of Revelry , the Mardi Gras Ball of the male Krewe of the Phantom Host and the ball of the female Mystic Order of Minerva, where debutantes are presented in pastel Victorian court dress with plumes, trains, 18-button gloves, and fan bouquets. There are also presentations of military officers' daughters at Maxwell Air Force Base, and since 1970 Montgomery's black debutantes have been sponsored by the local chapter of the national black teachers' sorority of Phi Delta Kappa, founded in 1923.

In Mobile, where mystic societies in America began, the season's leading debutante is queen of Mardi Gras, and she and King Felix III salute merrymakers from the Athelstan Club. Each season's debutantes are presented first at the Camellia Ball at Thanksgiving time. In New Orleans, which is synonymous with Mardi Gras, debutantes reign over the predominantly all-male Krewe festivities and are presented at the Debutante Club and Les Débuts des Jeunes Filles de la Nouvelle Orléans and many private debut parties.

Space permits only a limited listing of the debutante balls in other southern cities. Moving down the Atlantic Seaboard, Baltimore has its Bachelors' Cotillion; Washington, D.C., has its Debutante Cotillion and Thanksgiving Ball; Richmond has the Bal du Bois in June at the Country Club of Virginia; and the all-male Norfolk German Society selects those who will come out in that city. Raleigh's Terpsichorean Club stages the North Carolina Debutante Cotillion, Savannah features the Cotillion and Parents' Debutante Ball, Atlanta has its Halloween Ball at the Piedmont Driving Club, and Jacksonville has its Presentation Ball at the Florida Yacht Club.

In Birmingham the Redstone Club Christmas Ball is at the Birmingham Country Club and the Beaux Arts Ball at the Mountain Brook Club. The Mississippi Debutante Ball is in Jackson, while the Delta Debutante Ball is at the Greenville Country Club. In Memphis the Queen of Cotton Carnival reigns, and there is the ball at the Hunt and Polo Club. West of the Mississippi River at Texarkana there is the Cotillion Club Ball, at San Antonio the German Club Ball, and at Austin the Bachelors Cotillion. Dallas has its Idlewild Ball, where debutantes bow to the floor in all white at the beginning of the season and make their final bow at the Terpsichorean Ball in pastels.

See also RECREATION: Mardi Gras; / St. Cecilia Ball

Cameron Freeman Napier
Montgomery, Alabama

D. Susan Barron, *Sunday New York Times Magazine* (15 January 1984); Stephen Birmingham, *The Right People: A Portrait of the American Social Establishment* (1968); Lisa Birnbach, ed., *The Official Preppy Handbook* (1980); Bethany Bultman, *Town and Country* (November 1977); *Montgomery Advertiser* (6 February 1884, 4 November 1931, 15 April 1984); Mary Ann Neeley, *Alabama Review* (April 1979); *New York Times* (19 March 1958, 21 March 1958); Dixon Wecter, *The Saga of American Society: A Record of Social Aspiration, 1607–1937* (1937).

Fashion

Fashion in the South, as in the rest of the nation, serves a variety of functions. People pursue fashion because they seek meaning in their existence or a sense of personal identity. They may use fashion to enhance their social status or to demonstrate their affluence. Fashion also expresses the nature of society—its ideas, values, and roles. In a rapidly changing society, fashion is a form of control, offering people a particular direction out of the myriad possibilities. Fashion can also be used by people to facilitate change, as when women adopt a style that clearly rejects a traditional female role.

During much of the 18th and 19th centuries, fashion both reflected and helped maintain the white southern way of life with its dominant planter class and its dependence upon England. The lavish, extravagant fashions of the upper class, in contrast to the homespun apparel of slaves and the white lower classes, reinforced the stratification of society. Inventories of clothing from the period reveal costly wardrobes of silk, satins, and laces for both males and females. Clothing and materials were imported from England and followed the latest London fashions. Most of the fashions, particularly those of women, were impractical, nonfunctional, and mainly decorative—the ideal apparel of an upper class that wanted to display its wealth and secure its status. For example, the 18th century hoopskirts of upper-class women reached as much as six feet in diameter. They were both inconvenient and costly, requiring yards of material. Shoes, available in bright colors and rich materials, were also useless for work or exercise. Perhaps the greatest impracticality and frivolousness was the fashion in hairstyles. The tower or commode arrangement had the hair piled high in rigid curls and puffs on a wire frame. The whole was intertwined with various ornaments. The elaborate hairstyles required a professional hairdresser and consumed extensive amounts of time. Consequently, arrangements were often made to last for weeks or even months, an unsanitary condition to say the least.

In the antebellum years fashion became an even greater factor in maintaining southern society. In response to rapid change, fragmentation, and challenge, the white South clung tenaciously to what it saw as the essence of its society—the planter's cavalier tradition with its emphasis on aristocracy, stability, gentility, and honor. Women played a central role in this tradition. The southern woman, viewed as inferior by nature and thus subject to the domination of her husband, was nonetheless idealized as the possessor of higher morals and purity. As she kept her place and her purity, she played an important stabilizing force in a threatened society. And her fashions provided guidelines for what was acceptable behavior. The restricted functions and ornamental nature of upper-class women were accentuated: waistlines became smaller as corsets became tighter, petticoats became heavier, and skirts became longer and more cumbersome. Indeed, the symbol of the cavalier tradition and southern chivalry was the pure, white female with her ever-present parasol to protect her pale complexion from the hot sun.

The decades following the Civil War witnessed a growing democratization in southern fashion. The hardships of war, to be sure, contributed to this. One traveler noted the decline in fashions and said that South Carolina was an excellent place to live for one forced to wear old clothes. The war also militated against the presumed uniqueness of the southern way of life and with it the system of rigid stratification. The realities of war, the impact of industrialization, the increased availability of ready-mades, sewing machines, inexpensive patterns, and dry goods, all combined to eradicate the sharp class distinctions in fashion.

In the final decades of the 19th century and increasingly throughout the 20th century, the South has experienced trends in fashion that have characterized the entire nation. Hemlines have risen and fallen; waistlines have shifted, disappeared, and reappeared; areas of focus in women's fahions have moved from head to bosom to leg and back again; the modal type has moved from the "Gibson girl" to the "flapper" to the "New Look" and, ultimately, the "American Look." The American Look is characterized by egalitarianism, freedom, comfort, casualness, and action. These varied fashion trends have reflected and facilitated change toward an increasingly homogenized national lifestyle.

Although the American Look reigns supreme, local and sectional variations still exist. In part, variations are a practical response to differences in climate (differences that central heating and air-conditioning have minimized though not eliminated). The clothing needs, and hence the fashion choices, of a Georgia farmer's wife are very different from those of a female lawyer in Atlanta. But a good part of the variation arises from the more conservative traditions of the South.

Southern blacks have their own fashion traditions, based in a visual style emphasizing bright colors and sometimes bold designs. Although often poor, black people tried to dress well for Sunday church services and for special occasions. Urban clothing stores such as Lansky's in Memphis catered to distinctive black fashion tastes. Zoot suits in the 1940s and dashikis in the 1960s did not originate in the South, but many southern blacks adapted the styles. Black southern women helped make such African-derived ceremonial items as capes, turbans, caftans, and braided hair into modern fashion wear.

The 19th-century view of woman and her role lingers on. Consequently, many of the more radical fashion changes, which seem to threaten the virtue and place of women, have met with resistance. Religious leaders, newspaper editors, and public officials have openly denounced radical fashions, whether the slit skirt of 1913 or the miniskirt of the 1960s. Fashions of this sort have been more slowly, and sometimes less widely, adopted in the South. The conservative tradition means that styles that are perfectly acceptable in most other parts of the nation may not be acceptable in areas of the South. For example, in some small-town and rural areas neither the local minister nor his wife may appear publicly in shorts with impunity. Nevertheless, with the exception of some women's fashions, and with due consideration for climatic differences and local moral codes, department stores in the South, especially the urban South, offer customers the same styles available in stores throughout the rest of the nation. Fashion serves the same functions for southerners as for the rest of Americans. For that reason, southerners are as fashion conscious as other Americans, though they are more cautious and a bit more discriminating.

See also FOLKLIFE: Clothing

Jeanette C. Lauer
Robert H. Lauer
U.S. International University
San Diego, California

Michael Batterberry and Ariane Batterberry, *Mirror, Mirror: A Social History of Fashion: 1900 to the Present* (1977); Ernestine Carter, *The Changing World of Fashion* (1977); Clement Eaton, *The Growth of Southern Civilization, 1790–1860* (1961); Prudence Glynn, *In Fashion: Dress in the Twentieth Century* (1978); Jeanette C. Lauer and Robert H. Lauer, *Fashion Power: The Meaning of Fashion in American Society* (1981); Naomi Sims, *All about Health and Beauty for the Black Woman* (1976); Julia Cherry Spruill, *Women's Life and Work in the Southern Colonies* (1938).

Foodways

The first white men to come into the South ate what the American Indians ate. From the southern Indians the Europeans had much to learn about cultivated plants, wild fruits and nuts, the animals of the forest, and the fish in ocean, rivers, and lakes. They had to learn these lessons to survive and later push their way westward.

The Indian diet included much game, and Indians near

the coast ate large quantities of fish and shellfish. In their fields they grew corn, beans, squash, and other vegetables. They harvested wild plums, hickory nuts, chestnuts, blackberries, and other forest foods. Indians elsewhere on the continent domesticated the turkey and had developed the potato, tomatoes, eggplant, all peppers except black pepper, probably sweet potatoes, and possibly cowpeas. Both the Indians and the European settlers drew from other cultures, too. Originating in Brazil, the peanut was carried to Africa and later, bearing the African name "goober," was brought to Virginia aboard the slave ships.

As settlers reached the frontier, they planted corn and other food plants as soon as possible but relied at first on game or fish, although fish played a large role only along the coasts of the Atlantic and the Gulf of Mexico. The pioneer in the interior was happy to have a catfish, especially a large one, but he trusted his rifle more than his rod, net, or fish trap.

Buffalo provided the best meat, but they were quickly exterminated east of the Mississippi River. The pioneer also relished the meat of the black bear; he even salted it and cured it like pork. If killed in the autumn, the bear provided fat for shortening or other uses. Some southerners ate bear more or less regularly throughout the 19th century, but in most areas the animal disappeared as settlers multiplied. That left as big game the white-tailed deer, and venison was a frequent dish on southern tables until, and in some areas long after, the Civil War. Wild turkey were astonishingly abundant and unbelievably unwary in the pioneer South, and they played a large role in the pioneer diet. So did smaller game, especially rabbits, squirrels, raccoons, and opossums.

One should not think of the pioneer as baking a bear ham, roasting an opossum, or turning a haunch of venison on a spit. As often as not the southern frontiersman had only one cooking pot, and whatever was available went into that pot to mix with the previous day's leftovers.

The Indians lived in a feast-or-famine condition much of the year, and when food was abundant, they stuffed themselves. In the England that the earliest settlers called home, a host took as much pride in the quantity of the food he served his guests as in its quality. This background, combined with the abundance of food in the South as compared to the diets of German, English, Scotch, or Scotch-Irish peasants in the Old World, carried the concept of "big eating" over to the southern frontier and from the frontier forward to the Old South and eventually to the modern South.

As soon as he could, the pioneer farmer planted corn and established a herd of swine. Thus, the primary items in the diet of most southerners when the frontier had passed were corn bread and pork. Wild hogs were already in the forests, and those that the settlers brought with them were little tamer than their wild kinsmen. High in the shoulder, low in the rear, thin, with a long head and snout, and very swift of foot, they were often killed in the woods. More often, however, the owner carried out a "roundup" each fall, castrated excess boars, marked the ears of pigs born since the last roundup, and took those destined for killing home to be fattened on corn. Gradually, better-quality boars were brought in, and the quality of southern swine improved.

Hog killing usually took place during the first spell of cold weather that seemed likely to last for several days. Chitterlings (small intestines), livers, knuckles (ankles), brains, and other edible parts that could not be preserved had to be eaten quickly, and an orgy of pork eating followed hog-killing day. During those hectic days the fat was boiled in a large pot and rendered into lard. Cracklings, the crisp remnant of this process, were delicious baked into a pone of corn bread, called cracklin' bread. Scraps of leaner meat were pounded or ground into sausage.

Hams, shoulders, jowls, and sides of bacon could be cured to last indefinitely. After being trimmed, these pieces were buried in salt for four to six weeks. Then in the smokehouse they were smoked, preferably with smoke from hickory wood. Farmers differed as to the use of sugar, spices, and the like to flavor hams and shoulders, but almost all rubbed red pepper into exposed areas to prevent contamination by skipper flies, whose larvae would burrow through the meat.

So long as he had pork, the southerner ate it every day and at nearly every meal. Fried ham, shoulder, bacon, or sausage was almost an essential part of breakfast. The main meal, in the middle of the day, usually included pork, and unless it was Sunday or some special occasion, fried pork. Vegetables were normally either fried or, most often, boiled with a piece of fat-cured pork. A dish of green beans, for example, was not good unless it had enough grease in it to "wink back" when one lifted the lid and looked at it. This is the way vegetables were cooked in most southern households well into this century.

Southerners did eat meat other than fish, game, and pork from time to time. Once the frontier stage had passed and predatory animals had begun to follow the Indians into oblivion, it was possible to raise poultry; and chicken, duck, goose, and turkey became fare for Sundays and holidays. Fried chicken became the delicacy that it has remained ever since, and hen eggs and, occasionally, duck eggs became table items. Southerners sometimes ate beef, but it appeared on the table far more often in Texas and on the prairies of Louisiana than elsewhere in the South. Technically, what southerners ate was not really beef but veal, or "baby beef." Animals that had reached maturity were too tough for chewing.

Milk cows, on the other hand, were prized possessions. Compared to the dairy cows of today, they were inferior creatures that produced little milk, an important food for the antebellum southern family as well as for families in later eras. In general, mutton was not a favorite southern meat, but Virginians seem to have been fond of it, and it was certainly not unknown in Tennessee, Kentucky, and Louisiana.

Corn bread was the primary bread of nearly all antebellum southerners. Most southern mills ground corn well but could not handle glutinous wheat, though there were flour mills in the Upper South. Moreover, rust reduced the yield of wheat in most of the South. The more prosperous did eat yeast bread; beaten biscuits were a common item on plantation tables, but this was not true of the ordinary farmer's or townsman's table.

Corn bread took many forms, from the elementary hoecake baked on a hoe blade or board in front of the fireplace to various sophisticated mixtures of cornmeal with milk, buttermilk, eggs, shortening, and even sometimes flour or sugar. Cracklin' bread has already been noted. Hushpuppies were balls of corn bread and additives, such as onion, fried in the grease where fish were, or had been, frying. Corn bread did not keep well, and this led to the expectation of hot bread with meals, a fact that delayed and infuriated many a Yankee or foreign traveler.

Corn itself was an important vegetable, and for breakfast or supper many a living southerner has eaten cornmeal mush, which in modern parlance is a cereal. Green corn, "roasting ears," could be roasted in the shuck, boiled as corn on the cob, or sliced off the ear and cooked in various ways. Ripe corn, treated with lye obtained from an ash hopper, became hominy; and hominy, dried and broken into small bits, became hominy grits. Hominy grits, next to corn bread, was the most nearly universal southern food. It was, and still is, delightfully good served with butter or gravy—or even solidified, sliced, and fried.

In one or another part of the South almost all vegetables eaten anywhere else were served. Southerners were especially fond of green beans, butter beans (a variety of lima bean), okra, eggplant, red beans, and white or navy beans. Carrots, parsnips, squash, cabbage, and even green peas (usually called English peas) were eaten, but with less enthusiasm. Southerners enjoyed Irish potatoes, but they could not be kept over the winter for seed, and the necessity for imported seed limited their popularity.

The great triumvirate of southern vegetables was made up of turnips, cowpeas, and sweet potatoes, and it would be difficult to say that one was more important than the others. Turnips were often planted in an open space near a pioneer's house site before he had built the house, because they could be planted in late summer and would produce turnips and greens before a freeze ruined them. The greens were more valued than the turnips themselves, and in the spring they met the residents' almost desperate need for a green vegetable.

Cowpeas were of many varieties. Today, black-eyed peas, crowder peas, and "blue hulled peas" are almost the only variations known, but many others have flourished, including whippoorwills, britches and jackets, cuckold's increase, and tiny lady peas. Better green but good dry, peas were boiled with a piece of fat salt pork. With corn bread they provided enough calories and enough protein to sustain a hard day's work, and that was what the southern farmer needed. The liquid in which any vegetable had been cooked—the "pot liquor"—could be eaten with corn bread, but the pot liquor of cowpeas was especially delicious. Local custom and preference determined whether the corn bread was dunked or crumbled.

It would be difficult to exaggerate the role of the sweet potato. From the harvest in late summer until as long as they lasted into the winter, sweet potatoes were a major item in the antebellum southern diet. Like the turnip, they could be preserved in a "hill" of earth and decaying vegetable matter, but some farmers had a "potato house," partly or wholly underground, in which the potatoes were stored for protection. Sweet potatoes could be boiled, baked, candied, fried, or made into pudding or pie. Most often they were baked in the coals of the fireplace, and a hot sweet potato with butter was an especially delectable dish.

On the great plantations the food in the mansion's dining room was far more elaborate and abundant than in the house of the ordinary southerner. Travelers and Yankee tutors have left accounts of gargantuan meals. Turtle, venison, ham, turkey, and chicken might grace the same meal, with fruits and vegetables in equal abundance. These plantation meals were often accompanied by good wines, whereas in the farmhouse or the townsman's home, milk, coffee, or whiskey was more likely to serve as the drink. Indeed, once the Scotch-Irish had learned to make whiskey from corn, tremendous quantities of that beverage were drunk on the frontier and in the antebellum South.

The food of the slaves, though sufficient, was as modest as the food of the great planter was abundant. In most of the South the basic slave ration was two to three pounds of cured pork and a peck of cornmeal a week per adult. In coastal areas fish might be substituted for pork much of the time, and in southwest Louisiana and Texas slaves got much beef, but these were exceptions. The basic ration was supplemented by vegetables in season, and especially by turnip greens, cowpeas, and sweet potatoes. On large plantations the slaves' meals might be prepared in a common kitchen, but in most instances they were cooked in the cabin. This meant primarily in a pot in the fireplace, and southern blacks became accustomed to boiled foods; until recently, and probably to this day, black people of the South tend to eat more boiled foods than do southern whites.

The Civil War left the South impoverished, and the lowest economic classes of society bore the hardest burden. The vast majority of former slaves became sharecroppers, and they were soon joined by millions of southern whites. Sharecroppers got their food and other necessities from a plantation commissary or from a general store. It was still cornmeal and pork, but the cornmeal now came from the corn belt, and in the milling much of the nutrition had been removed. The pork was no longer homegrown and killed on the plantation; it too came from the Middle West, but rather than bacon it was fatback, the layer of meat between the skin and the ribs, containing little protein. The basic diet of corn bread and fatback was not supplemented by fruits and vegetables nearly to the extent of antebellum days. Diseases associated with malnutrition, especially pellagra, which had seldom been observed before the Civil War, began to take a heavy annual toll. Nor was malnutrition confined to sharecroppers; cotton-mill workers, poor townsmen, and the slum dwellers of the developing southern cities also suffered.

Some of the poorer yeoman farmers who managed to hold on to their land were malnourished also. In general, however, they ate pork that they had raised and killed

Dinner after the corn shucking, Granville County, N.C., 1939

themselves, and they took their own corn to the mill. They may have had to buy fatback from the general store part of the year, but most had milk from a scrub cow or two. Also, they planted a vegetable garden, and the old triad of turnips, cowpeas, and sweet potatoes helped them survive. Yeoman farmers were much more likely than tenants to have a fruit orchard.

Two very significant changes, one in food itself and the other in preparing food, took place during the later 19th century. As the result of increased wheat production and new milling methods, the great flour mills of the Middle West brought the price of flour down so low that even relatively poor southerners could afford it. Even the comparatively prosperous farmer or townsman had seldom eaten wheat bread before the Civil War, but by 1900 wheat-flour biscuits had become as common as corn bread. People ate huge quantities of biscuits. Many farmers bought one or more barrels of flour before the winter almost isolated them from the store. The smallest amount available for sale was twenty-four pounds in a cloth sack.

Food patterns formed on the southern frontier persisted well into the 20th century, until after World War II in many small-town and rural areas. Canned goods, commercial bread, and the refrigerator joined the cook stove and cheap flour in making a difference, albeit a small one. However, urbanization, the dislocation and travel brought on by two world wars, the ease of travel in the age of automobiles and interstate highways, and the homogenizing effect of radio and television eventually brought major changes in southern eating habits.

Probably the most basic change was the growth in "eating out," a trend spurred by the availability of reasonably good restaurants in the cities (superb ones in some cities) and, especially, by the advent of so-called fast foods. The hamburger emporium, the fried-catfish stand, and the fried-chicken establishment provide meals for a tremendous number of southerners every day. It is noteworthy that two of these foods, chicken and catfish, have been a part of the southern diet for two hundred years. Furthermore, they are still fried!

See also AGRICULTURE: Garden Patch; Livestock; Poultry; ENVIRONMENT: Plant Life; Plant Uses; / Catfish; Collards; ETHNIC LIFE: Indian Cultural Contributions; FOLKLIFE: / Gumbo; Okra; GEOGRAPHY: Foodways, Geography of; MYTHIC SOUTH: / Watermelon; RECREATION: Fishing; Hunting

Joe Gray Taylor
McNeese State University

John Egerton, *Southern Food: At Home, on the Road, in History* (1987); Sam B. Hilliard, *Hog Meat and Hoecake: Food Supply in the Old South* (1972); "Our Food, Our Common Ground," *Southern Exposure* (November–December 1983); Stephen A. Smith, in *American Material Culture*, ed. Edith Mayo (1985); Joe Gray Taylor, *Eating, Drinking, and Visiting in the South: An Informal History* (1982); Gertrude I. Thomas, *Foods of Our Forefathers* (1941); Rupert B. Vance, *Human Geography of the South: A Study of Regional Resources and Human Adequacy* (1935); Eugene Walter, *American Cooking, Southern Style* (1971).

Foreign Policy

The southern experience in world affairs reflects variations on a set of ideas common to much of the American experience, indeed of Western civilization. At certain points in the 20th century, southerners have exhibited an intense belief in internationalism: belief in multilateral organizations, especially for European matters and Anglo-American cooperation. On several occasions since the Civil War, southerners also have shown signs of isolationism: a "nonentangling" outlook usually aimed at Europe and Britain but sometimes at Latin America, Africa, or the Pacific. Finally, a strong strain of expansionism persisted through much of the South's antebellum as well as postbellum experience. This belief in the justice of southerners' increasing their influence over foreign places has often appeared in conjunction with territorial growth and colonialism but, in other instances, it has surfaced in a nonterritorial form—expansion for trade and investment as well as for religious reasons. A review of the major episodes of the South's history in world affairs reveals internationalism, isolationism, and expansionism at work in particularly southern ways and places the South's experience in world affairs within the broader context of ideals and self-interest in American history.

Like most American viewpoints, southern ideas about the world began with the activism and assertiveness spawned by the Renaissance, Reformation, and Enlightenment. With these movements Western people increasingly perceived the improvement of their condition on earth as a matter of religious mandate. This concept of progress is a well-established part of New England's history, but the people of the southern colonies had much the same cultural background and reflected a similar optimism and fervor. Abundant natural resources, removal from the "decadent" Old World, a Puritan zeal even in the predominant Anglican churches, a liberal belief that "property" was a matter of "right" and the key to "individual freedom"—here were cornerstones of a powerful sense of Manifest Destiny and progressive idealism in the developing culture of the colonial South. Southern colonials also were subject to less idealistic forces. An unending frontier and brutal Indian fighting, plus more fighting and diplomatic intrigue against Spanish and French colonials, were all part of the unavoidable realities of living in a Western society and competing for empire in the new world. Because of these experiences, Anglos in the southern colonies developed a high tolerance for violence (though they rarely enjoyed, much less excelled at, soldiering) and became effective users of economic and political self-interest. By the end of the colonial era, two key ingredients of the South's future foreign policy outlook had begun to surface: a faith in its mission (idealism) and a pursuit of realpolitik (materialism and self-interest).

During the American Revolution and the early national period, most views articulated in the South reflected these two strains of expansionism in equal, balanced proportions. A powerful array of southern expansionists—George Washington, Thomas Jefferson, James Madison, James Monroe, and Henry Clay—helped guide the nation through the first and second wars with Britain and onto a course of continental and foreign expansionism seen in the acquisition of Louisiana, Florida, and Missouri and also in the development of the Monroe Doctrine. The vast majority of southerners thrived in the mainstream of Jeffersonian expansionism. Sensitive to what soon would jell as "the Southern interests," that is, slavery and export economics, a subsidiary group of southern congressmen dissented, however, from the goal of a neighborly reciprocity with Latin America. This sectional self-interest would soon broaden and carry considerable weight.

Indeed, the transition from the Jeffersonian to the Jacksonian era brought major changes. Those southerners uninvolved with slavery continued to reflect the old balance of ideals and self-interest. Some slaveowners did, too, but for other Jacksonian planters, ideals quickly became subordinate to self-interest as abolitionists began to attack their "peculiar" labor institution. When the West realigned with the Northeast on the tariff issue, the already defensive planters became even more fearful. A new congressional alliance might ban slavery from the territories and weaken the South's role in national affairs. Thus, in the three decades before the Civil War many planters who feared social and economic ruin showed little enthusiasm for the altruistic mission of expansionism. With a steely, defensive tone, they advocated territorial growth for their own sectional self-interest. If President James K. Polk was chiefly a commercialist with national goals, he still made good use of the South's practical and materialistic political focus—as well as the missionary idealism among other elements of the South—as he maneuvered the nation through its final transcontinental thrust to the Pacific. Ironically, the planters' realpolitik was a far less effective force in policy when it was channeled by its own sectional leaders. The southern dream of a Caribbean empire remained just that—a dream. And when secession and war finally came, the southern strategy of a supposedly hardnosed realpolitik lacked the deft diplomacy to translate this approach into the foreign negotiations essential to a Confederate victory.

After the war many white southerners became so embittered that they rejected the expansionist ideology of the conquering Yankees. Southern views of the late 19th century reflected misgivings about American expansion into Hawaii, Cuba, Puerto Rico, and the Philippines. Most southerners ultimately surrendered, though, to the patriotism generated by the 1898 action against Spain, showing cautious interest in the anticipated opening of Caribbean and Pacific markets. Yet they still talked incessantly about the pain and dislocation a similar surge of Yankee imperialism had brought to their own region just half a century earlier and characterized that type of expansionism as contrary to key American principles of self-determination. They also focused on contemporary problems spawned by the new foreign expansionism: the annexation of nonwhites could cause further conflict in their already strained race relations. More than half the southern senators voted with the antiimperialist opposition to the treaty of Paris. In short, more than party politics was involved. Isolationism—generated out of anti-imperialist principles and racism—grew to consensual proportions in the postbellum period. Such a tormented reversal made many southerners appear ambivalent, and many downright insular, as they reacted to America's rise to world power.

A small, vocal, and powerful group within the emerging middle class showed signs of being anything but isolationists. To publicists such as Alabama politicians John Tyler Morgan and Joseph H. Wheeler, both highly acclaimed veterans of the Confederacy, the American mission of the late 19th century remained as justified as it had been in the days of Jefferson, and the national mission could hardly hinder the blueprint for a revived, industrial South. On racial objections to world power they blithely responded that the problem could be solved with segregation. With ideals and self-interest harmonized in classic Gilded Age liberalism, these "new southerners" would simply export the emerging institutions of their own region.

In the 20th century Morgan's form of expansionism, an outlook intensely ethnocentric but nevertheless balanced in terms of mission and realpolitik, gradually prevailed as the dominant view in the South. The ascendancy of Woodrow Wilson spurred southern expansionism to rapid and full recovery. Most white southerners, even some of the lower classes, perceived President Wilson's crusade for a moral and legal world order receptive to American influence as clear indication of "the return of the South" to international prominence. In fact, with the exception of a few isolated cases like Mississippi's James K. Vardaman, southerners worshiped Wilson's notion of international order as something brought back to life from the presidency of another great southerner, Thomas Jefferson. That historical connection had serious flaws. Although born a southerner, Wilson derived his internationalism primarily from experiences with highly idealistic liberals of the Northeast, some with abolitionist roots and most with far less pragmatism than the sage of Monticello. Yet as Civil War memories dimmed and sectional reconciliation offered industry and profits as well as psychological security, southerners grasped at Wilsonian internationalism as "a Southern idea" reunited with American patriotism. Southern Wilsonians actually were motivated as much by the practicalities of New South economics and politics as by a renewed enthusiasm for the American mission. Still, they followed Wilson straight through the crusade of World War I and then down the unpragmatic road of the League of Nations.

This ironic and contradictory outlook—balanced, Jeffersonian expansionism advanced through the medium of relatively strong idealism—did not die with Wilson. During the 1920s and 1930s the League of Nations Association and the Carnegie Endowment for International Peace, two organizational bridges between the Wilsonianism of World Wars I and II, recruited far more effectively in the South than in any areas beyond a few urban centers in the Northeast where they were based. Indeed, between the wars southern voices dissenting from Wilson's internationalism were uniquely few. And when war reopened in Europe in 1939, a regional arm of the Carnegie Endowment, the Southern Council on International Relations, worked to convert this regional sentiment into political support for President Franklin D. Roosevelt's developing war policies. As might be expected, when the war ended Southern Council members and other southerners urged the second chance at realizing the dream of Wilsonian internationalism—the United Nations. Nevertheless, in the early 1950s, shortly after the creation of the UN, most southerners turned against the organization because it seemed ineffective in achieving the Wilsonian goal of blocking the growth of socialist and communist power. They also feared Joseph McCarthy's attacks on supporters of organized internationalism. Such a waning interest in internationalism did not place southern leaders at odds with others associated with the general goals of Wilsonianism; on the contrary, it brought them closer together. The Cold War caused most Americans once committed to internationalism to move to the right and to espouse American rescue of the world through collective security agreements, economic expansionism, and interventionism. Considering this trend, the South's interventionist sentiment in the Korean War and in the initial stages of the Vietnam War appeared synchronized to late 20th-century American expansionism.

Other than a few antiexpansionist mavericks like Florida's Claude Pepper, there have been only two major exceptions in this recent harmony between southern and national attitudes. In the 1950s and 1960s Richard B. Russell of Georgia and many other southern leaders balked at sending economic aid to the nonwhites of Africa, Latin America, and the Mideast, whereas many expansionists and the few enduring internationalists from other sections generally supported these measures. Southerners feared that competing low-technology products might be developed in these lands with the assistance of American funds. More important, southerners exhibited a racial reaction to nonwhites that was triggered by the civil rights movement at home. In some ways this attitude resembled the isolationism reflected by southerners in the years following the Civil War. On the other hand, just as stabilization of southern internal affairs gradually eased southern insecurities after the turn of the century and resulted in a new interest in expansionism, so did the slackening of the civil rights movement a century later contribute to increased southern political support for numerous foreign aid projects.

At roughly the same time, the late 1960s and early 1970s, another peculiarly southern attitude emerged. At this time most southerners in Washington—and their constituencies—followed Mississippi's James Eastland in opposing withdrawal of American troops from Vietnam long after most other Americans had accepted the limits of interventionism. At least as early as World War I, southerners had seemed excited about formal military activity abroad because of investments and jobs it provided within the generally poor southern population: economic opportunities in home-front war industries and military bases, plus "jobs" abroad through actual military service. These same considerations, coupled no doubt with the southerners' relatively high tolerance for violence, encouraged what was characterized as a prolonged southern militarism in the Vietnam episode. In time this attitude too gave way to internal forces.

As increased black voting power raised issues of human rights in southern politics and elevated Andrew Young and other advocates of economic aid to national prominence, the interventionist strain of southern expansionism lost out. Simultaneously, the economic development of the Sunbelt created more jobs and a slightly larger middle class of whites and blacks. These upwardly mobile businessmen and professionals lived off corporate profits and often looked to reports from the local chapter of the Council on Foreign Relations for appropriate responses to world problems. They advocated whatever moderation in American policy was necessary for American capitalism to reverse its energy shortages and trade imbalances and to establish more influential relations with developing nations.

Finally, out of this moderated expansionist consensus, in which ideals were increasingly harmonized with self-interest, there emerged Georgia's Jimmy Carter. President Carter's approach to foreign policy has been criticized for its lack of cohesiveness and its ineffectiveness. His approach to foreign policy included commitment to expanding American trade—a crusade foreshadowed by New South booster trips to Latin America while he was still a governor—complemented by an equal emphasis on human rights, reduction of nuclear arms, and other progressive internationalist goals. Indeed, despite occasional overzealous rhetoric, he usually advanced the human rights program with a policy well attuned—though not always effectively—to the influence the United States might expect to have in a given area of the world. Hence the Carter years suggest the possibilities of an ironic trend. In the minds of most educated Americans, and certainly many historians, Woodrow Wilson provided the ideological foundation for the predominant foreign policy sentiment of the 20th-century South. Yet the viewpoint that helped recent southerners reclaim some of their once-powerful role in world affairs and find new economic growth was not so much Wilsonian idealistic internationalism but the formula that had given the South its first period of prominence. It was the more basic Jeffersonian approach—minus the agrarian rhetoric—that harnessed ideals and self-interest to the cause of pragmatic influence abroad and assisted the emergence of a less distinctive but increasingly confident southern culture in the late 20th century.

Tennant S. McWilliams
University of Alabama at Birmingham

Henry Blumenthal, *Journal of Southern History* (May 1966); Wayne S. Cole, *An Interpretive History of American Foreign Relations* (1974); Alexander DeConde, *Journal of Southern History* (August 1958); George L. Grassmuck, *Sectional Biases in Congress on Foreign Policy* (1951); Alfred O. Hero, Jr., *The Southerner and World Affairs* (1965); Marian Irish, *Journal of Politics* (May 1948); Warren F. Kuehl, *Seeking World Order: The United States and International Organization to 1920* (1969); Charles O. Lerche, Jr., *The Uncertain South: Its Changing Patterns of Politics in Foreign Policy* (1964); James M. McPherson, *Civil War History* (1983); Tennant S. McWilliams, *The New South Faces the World: Foreign Affairs and the Southern Sense of Self, 1877–1950* (1988); Frederick Merk, *The Monroe Doctrine and Expansionism, 1843–1849* (1966); Robert E. Osgood, *Ideals and Self-Interest in American Foreign Relations* (1953); Paul Seabury, *The Waning of Southern "Internationalism"* (1957).

Fraternal Groups

Fraternal organizations have long been an important part of the social life of southern communities large and small. Beginning with the introduction of Freemasonry in the colonial era, the spirit of fraternalism grew after the Civil War to support the Sons of Temperance, Good Templars, Red Men, Woodmen of the World, Knights of Pythias, Odd Fellows, Grangers, Masons, and others. Blacks in the region had separate, distinctive fraternal groups that were nonetheless closely related to white groups in style and significance. Patriotic societies such as the United Daughters of the Confederacy, the United Confederate Veterans, the Sons and Daughters of the American Revolution, and others were based on race and ancestry and thrived in the tradition-oriented South. The region had fewer immigrant societies, such as the Ancient Order of Hibernians and Sons of Italy, because of the proportionately smaller number of immigrants in the region. The Knights of Columbus was popular among southern Catholics. The Ku Klux Klan represented many things, and narrowly defined secretive fraternalism was one of them. "The elaborate ceremonies and rituals, colorful costumes, and mysterious titles helped members escape the humdrum aspects of their daily lives," concluded historian John S. Ezell. In the 20th century, service organizations such as the Kiwanis, Rotary, Lions, and Service International clubs emerged as middle-class, business-oriented versions of fraternalism.

The Masonic order is the oldest and most extensive fraternal society in the Western world. Coming mainly from Britain and to a lesser degree from France, Freemasonry makes use of symbols and allegories derived from the craft guilds of the Middle Ages. It preaches the universal virtues of friendship, morality, truth, charity, and prudence. It does not permit discussions of religion and politics within its temples. Consequently it has surmounted many difficulties associated with those topics, even during the period of American fratricidal strife in the 1860s.

The Masonic order has two rites, commonly called York and Scottish, which allow for advancement in their particular teachings. The individual local lodge is governed by a Grand Lodge, which generally follows state lines and is sovereign within its jurisdiction. Although the two rites are international, they remain subordinate to their respective Grand Lodges. Masonry is secret only in certain salutations and dramatic rituals. Otherwise its membership, times and places of meeting, and organization are well known. As an organization, the Masonic order seldom, however, appears in public, except at the laying of the cornerstone of a building or at graveside ceremonies for its deceased members.

Attached to the lodge and its rites are bodies like the Shrine, Order of the Demolay (for boys), Order of the Rainbow (for girls), and the Order of the Eastern Star (largely female). An adopted southerner, Rob Morris, originally from Massachusetts, founded the Eastern Star in the 1850s at the "Little Red Schoolhouse"—now known around the world as a sacred spot to members of the group—at Richland in Holmes County, Miss. He wrote many of the manuals and originated the rituals still in use in the group.

In most states the Masonic lodges maintain homes for care of orphans, the aged, and the infirm. The Shrine has hospitals that specialize in treatment of crippled children and burn victims. Knights Templar, the peak of the York Rite, offers funds for treatment of correctable eye maladies; the Scottish Rite provides funds for the treatment of aphasia and also scholarships for students of political science.

The term *lodge* is also applied to the structure where Masons meet. Often in the past such a building was owned jointly by the Masons and a church, a school, or a business firm. More recently, however, the building typically is owned and used only by the order. The architecture varies from a simple, unobtrusive frame or brick structure to a pretentious edifice adorned with columns and exotic representations. But regardless of size or ornamentation, the lodge has been a center of unity for vast segments of the southern male population, Jew and Gentile alike.

The Masonic order that came to the South during the colonial era was derived mostly from the York Rite. Operating in the three basic degrees of "Blue Lodge" Masonry, these early York Rite lodges received their charters mainly from the Grand Lodges of either England or Scotland. The other primary Masonic movement in the colonial South was the Scottish Rite, which was introduced from either France or the West Indies.

Among the first of the early colonial lodges comprising the Provincial Grand Lodge of Virginia (where Masonry was introduced as early as 1729) were the Royal Exchange Lodge 172, established at Norfolk under an English charter in 1733, and Kilwinning Port Royal Cross Lodge, formed under a Scottish Charter in 1730. Elsewhere in the colonial South, first lodges were chartered in North Carolina at Wilmington (1755), in South Carolina at Charleston (1760), and in Georgia (through Solomons Lodge, organized by the founder of Georgia, James Oglethorpe, under an English Charter in 1734 and now the oldest of the English lodges in the United States).

After the Revolutionary War, the Provincial Grand Lodges became independent from their mother lodges in England and Scotland, and enunciated the doctrine of "exclusive jurisdiction"—only the Grand Lodge of any state had authority over the lodges within that state's borders. However, in the newly created states to the west of the Atlantic seaboard, the several Grand Lodges were free to charter and establish daughter lodges. In that way, the Grand Lodges of Virginia, North Carolina, South Carolina, and Georgia were largely responsible for the spread and diffusion of Freemasonry across the South. By 1800 Kentucky, Tennessee, and Louisiana had new York Rite lodges as well as those derived from the colonial period. By 1820 additional Grand Lodges had been established in Alabama, Mississippi, and Louisiana. The next three decades added Arkansas, Texas, and Florida. In the case of Florida, Freemasonry had been introduced during the British colonial period in the form of military lodges chartered in Scotland. The story of Louisiana Freemasonry was a particularly complex one of struggle between French and Spanish colonists and their descendants, the early York and Scottish rites, and American and Spanish authorities in West Florida. In 1812, 12 Masonic lodges were chartered in Louisiana. From the five French-speaking lodges, the Grand Lodge of Louisiana was formed in 1812; 14 years later they were joined by the English-speaking York Rite lodges.

Masonry spread widely after the American Revolution and was a conspicuous feature of southern life. Virginian George Washington used a Masonic Bible during his first inauguration and a Masonic trowel in ceremonies laying the cornerstone for the Capitol building in Washington, giving the Masonic order new prominence. This prominence eventually resulted in suspicions of the secret order and a wave of anti-Masonic hysteria that affected the South, as well as the rest of the nation, in the late 1820s and 1830s. This was one of the few periods of Masonic involvement in national affairs.

Prominent southern Masons from the 19th century included U.S. Supreme Court Chief Justice John Marshall (Virginia), Senator John C. Breckinridge (Kentucky), John Blair (Virginia), Confederate General Albert Sidney Johnston (Texas), and Governor Robert Toombs (Georgia). Former Confederate General Albert Pike from Arkansas edited and rewrote the rituals of the Scottish Rite in the late 19th century.

Masonry is typical of other fraternal groups in being far more than a strictly regional association, yet it has been an important institution for southerners and has taken on peculiar features at times in adapting to the regional context. In the 1890s, for example, a controversy appeared in Freemasonry over whether it should go beyond its traditions and become more explicitly religious, specifically acknowledging Christianity. Southerners and midwesterners, according to historian Lynn Dumenil, tended to link the health of Masonry to orthodox interpretation of the Bible. They were especially prone to "Masonic Biblicism." A few trials were even held in the South with the purpose of expelling nonbelieving Masons. At times, also, southerners showed a greater interest than other Masons in becoming involved in politics. The Southern Jurisdiction of Scottish Rite Masons, for example, enthusiastically supported political involvement in the 1920s. Leaders of Masonry in the region did, however, speak out against any Ku Klux Klan–Masonry connection in that period. Masonic magazines have supported good citizenship, public education, and "True Americanism," the latter a favorite phrase.

See also BLACK LIFE: Fraternal Orders, Black

Allen Cabaniss
University of Mississippi

Ernest S. Easterly III
Baton Rouge, Louisiana

Allen Cabaniss, *Freemasonry in Mississippi* (1976); George B. Clark, *From Whence Came We: Masonic Ancestry and Antecedents of the Grand Lodges of the United States* (1953); Henry W. Coil, *Freemasonry through Six Centuries*, 2 vols. (1967); Lynn Dumenil, *Freemasonry and American Culture, 1880–1930* (1984); Glen L. Greene, *Masonry in Louisiana* (1962); Ray B. Harris, *Eleven Gentlemen of Charleston: Founders of the Supreme Council, Mother Council of the World* (1959); William J. Hughan, G. P. Jones, and Ray B. Harris, *Freemasonry* (1958).

Frontier Heritage

In 1893 a Wisconsin-born historian, Frederick Jackson Turner, read a paper entitled "The Significance of the Frontier in American History" at the annual meeting of the American Historical Association. He launched a new hypothesis in which the American frontier was viewed as the dominant factor in the development of American civilization. "The existence of an area of free land, its continuous recession, and the advance of American settlement westward," he stated in his first paragraph, "explain American development."

Even today, more than 90 years after Turner read his paper, historians cannot ignore his thesis. A generation of graduate students at Wisconsin and later at Harvard studied under him. In time they wrote hundreds of monographs with Turner's thesis as their basic premise. Many of his students went on to become successful history professors. They in turn passed Turner's ideas on to more historians; they also produced a number of American history texts from elementary to college level. All of them were imbued with Turnerian ideas even if Turner was not mentioned by name. Although the frontier hypothesis has suffered considerably in the past 50 years, it must still bear consideration when American history is being interpreted.

In his essay Turner gave proper attention to the southern frontier. Land hunger, he noted, drove the Scotch-Irish, Germans, and many other colonials into the transmontane South. Discovery of salt springs along the Kanawha, Holston, and Kentucky rivers freed them from dependence for that commodity on the Atlantic Coast. These men of Kentucky and Tennessee were so fiercely independent that the new nation almost lost them. They demanded free navigation of the Mississippi and initially profited most from the Louisiana Purchase. As for the institution of slavery, Turner did not consider it of prime importance in the history of American development.

Finally, for all the American people, Turner found in the frontier experience "intellectual traits of profound importance." He perceived a "coarseness and strength combined with acuteness and inquisitiveness: that masterful grasp of material things, lacking in the artistic but powerful to effect great ends; that restless, nervous energy; that dominant individualism, working for good and for evil, and withal that buoyancy and exuberance which comes with freedom."

Davy Crockett, a southerner born along the Nolichucky River in east Tennessee in 1786, exemplifies just such a man. Restless yet ambitious, he moved first to middle Tennessee, served in military campaigns against the Creek Indians, and next settled for several years in west Tennessee. From there he was elected to the state legislature and later to Congress, where he served three terms. Still restless and not yet 50, he headed for Texas and achieved immortality by dying at the Alamo. Another exemplar was Sam Houston who possessed those same traits of intelligence, restlessness, a practical turn of mind, a dominant individualism, and an ability to effect great ends that Turner identified as frontier attributes.

Certainly the most successful southern frontiersman was Andrew Jackson. He was a leader of the rough-and-tumble society that constituted the businessmen's and planters' world of the Tennessee frontier. He had fought duels, lost and won horse races, speculated in land, purchased slaves, married a beautiful frontier woman, and entered into the turbulent politics of his adopted state. A natural leader of men, he climbed the frontier political ladder as the representative of a people who possessed a fierce belief in a rustic democracy that left no place for Indians and accepted the institution of slavery. The spirit of the frontier spoke through him when Jackson stated in his bank veto message that the benefits of government should, "as Heaven does its rains, shower its favors alike on the high and the low, the rich and the poor."

Turner's great essay embraced all frontiers, north and south (but always west), and a chronology from colonial times until the end of the frontier as defined by the Bureau of the Census in 1890. He did not differentiate regional frontiers.

Subsequent critics did, pointing out certain frontier characteristics that were not so admirable. The frontier, they said, demonstrably fostered violence, lawbreaking, discrimination against minorities, antiintellectualism, and individualism so fierce that it worked against the common good. Such unpleasant characteristics were self-evident in the lives of southern frontiersmen like Crockett, Houston, and Jackson.

The word *frontier* does not appear in the indexes of several of the principal texts and surveys of southern history. Emphasis has instead been placed on the antebellum South as a *rural* area—a dynamic but raw agrarian society advancing into a wilderness that indeed was the southern frontier, but which in the South was not always looked upon as such. A description of a southern frontier heritage may sound to some like an essay on the rural aspects of the South.

The southern frontier began with Jamestown and the beginnings of Virginia and spread northward into Maryland and southward along the coast eventually to embrace North and South Carolina, Georgia, and north Florida. Pioneers from the southern coastal colonies spilled over the Appalachians into Tennessee and Kentucky. After the War of 1812, the practical application of the cotton gin, and the rapid elimination of the Five Civilized Tribes, the Old Southwest filled in. This included the Black Belt, so named for its deep, black loam, which, with the warm, humid climate, made the cultivation of short-staple cotton economically profitable. Besides Georgia (1788) and Louisiana (1812), Alabama (1819) and Mississippi (1817) had achieved statehood by 1819. Within another generation Arkansas (1836) and Texas (1845) were added as states with a southern outlook. Florida, very much a frontier although south, not west, of the other states, entered the Union in 1845. W. J. Cash in *The Mind of the South* (1941) emphasized the persistence of frontier conditions in the South: "It is impossible to conceive the Great South as being, on the whole, more than a few steps removed from the frontier stage at the beginning of the Civil War."

In every sense the South's progression was along an advancing frontier. Crushing the Indians, buying the land, breaking it to the plow, and building cabins, outbuildings, and fences were common tasks. Roads had to be constructed leading to new villages where trade, religion, education, business, litigation, and government flourished. The steamboat, a practical conveyance by the 1820s, made water highways of the sluggish southern rivers. As with other frontiers, the southern one produced a raw, heavy-drinking, vulgar, speculative, turbulent society. Augustus Baldwin Longstreet in *Georgia Scenes* (1835) and Joseph Glover Baldwin in *Flush Times of Alabama and Mississippi* (1853) well portrayed the southern frontier society at the time of land booms and rapid settlement. In addition, there was the southern cattlemen's frontier. It included the red-clay hill regions of northern Georgia and Alabama, the pine barrens of the Carolinas, and central Florida's prairies; to a degree, the cattle industry thrived in every southern state in the antebellum period. However, the barefooted, floppy-hatted "cracker" with his long whip never struck the romantic vein of the national psyche as did his later counterpart, mounted and gazing out over the Great Plains.

All of this was a part of the frontier experience and was

similar to the societies of the same period in the Old Northwest and trans-Mississippi West. Yet the South's frontier experience differed from the common frontier experience in a number of ways. One-crop agriculture, especially the raising of tobacco and cotton, both of which enervated the soil, made it absolutely necessary for southerners to advance to new lands. Soil depletion forced Virginians and Carolinians to pack up and leave their old fields for the Black Belt. Once there, they again depleted the soil. They practiced the negative frontier characteristic of waste. The land was abused because of the belief that more free land always lay to the west—even as far west as Texas's Brazos River bottoms. So too were the pine and live oak forests logged and left as wasteland to catch on fire or become a malarial morass. Such practices occurred on other frontiers, but in the South the damage was greater. This was not because the southern frontiersman was any more rapacious of the land than his northern or western fellow pioneers, but because the single-crop system, the southern climate with heavy rainfall, and the nature of the southern soil resulted in greater, longer-lasting damage. Soil erosion was an early problem resulting in the end of one frontier and the beginning of another.

These differences also created or made more inevitable a social system that is usually considered harmful to southern progress. Some have called the southern social system, based upon one-crop agriculture, which was callous to the maintenance of good soil and extremely detrimental to all but the most successful of southern planter-businessmen, a "hot-house" society. A yeomanry existed that was more likely to lapse downward into "po' white" status than rise to plantation aristocracy, and once the social status was set, it was very difficult for a white person to rise out of it. Beyond attaining manumission, blacks were relegated to lowest status, of course, as slaves. This social stratification was notably a southern frontier characteristic, not a national one. Yet the system was unstable, and southern literature is filled with narrations of aristocratic families who fell upon hard times and tried desperately to retain their status. William Faulkner's fictitious Yoknapatawpha County, with its Compson family, is of this genre. Eudora Welty's stories of southern families in rustic settings likewise harken back to frontier times.

Individualism, a trait common to all frontiers, was a fine-tuned tradition on the southern frontier. It manifested itself in a dislike of government—any government—that proposed to control a man's life—how he ran his plantation or his business, how he managed his slaves, or where he fired the woods or chose to go hunting. To the proud white southern agrarian, the Bill of Rights was the most important part of the Constitution.

This individualism did not extend to religion or political opinions. The frontier South worshiped God through many sects, but nearly all were fundamentalist and emotional in their attraction. Their religious spectrum did not include atheists, Deists, Unitarians, or other groups who questioned in any way the accepted emotional, fundamental appeal of religion by Bible, and Bible alone.

Slavery, as the solution to racial problems, broached no opposition, and although Turner was not bothered by slavery on the frontier, certainly it contributed to the South's distinctiveness. Similarly, on matters of the tariff, internal improvements, and interpretation of the Constitution, the white southern frontiersman accepted a common attitude and stuck to it. He was not, as men were on other frontiers, an equalitarian. He accepted the concept of class, beginning with the black slave, working upward past the free black, the poor white, the yeoman farmer, and the plantation owner; in towns, the merchant, banker, and gin operator (often one and the same person) adhered to many of the same ideas, though for a few years prior to the Civil War he may have voted Whig instead of Democratic.

The southern rural frontier allowed a white man to carry a gun, use profanity, break the Sabbath, participate in a lynching, drink heavily, or fight a duel, and have it all considered normal. Such a person, if he was capable of accepting discipline, made an excellent soldier. He served well in all the nation's wars (although he was on the Confederate side in the 1860s).

The southern frontier heritage, then, includes fundamentalist religion, perhaps the strongest rugged individualism in the modern nation, and a love of the outdoors stemming from frontier ruralism including hunting and fishing. A strain of violence may still be discerned. For many decades into the 20th century, to be a white southerner was also to be a Democrat, for the society demanded that everyone adhere to the majority political opinion. Loyalty to family, honor, love of the land, and devotion to country, all inherited from the frontier-rural traditions of their pioneering past, remain strong among southern whites today.

See also ENVIRONMENT: Indians and the Environment; RELIGION: Frontier Religion

Richard A. Bartlett
Florida State University

Ray Allen Billington, *America's Frontier Heritage* (1966); Thomas D. Clark, *The Rampaging Frontier: Manners and Humors of Pioneer Days in the Southern Middle West* (1939); Avery O. Craven, *Journal of Southern History* (August 1939); Gene M. Gressley, *Agricultural History* (October 1958); Todd M. Lieber, *Mississippi Quarterly* (Fall 1969); Frank L. Owsley, *Journal of Southern History* (May 1945); Malcolm J. Rohrbough, *The Trans-Appalachian Frontier: People, Societies, and Institutions, 1775–1850* (1978).

Great Depression

The Great Depression began with the collapse of the stock market in late 1929, and it devastated the American South more than any other region during the 1930s. The calamity's paralyzing severity and dismaying persistence enveloped the whole republic: nationwide statistics reveal fully a third of the work force unemployed, and by 1933 the nation's business activity had plunged to half that of 1929. But the American South suffered even greater harm as yearly per capita income plummeted from a national low of $372 in 1929 to just $203 in 1932.

Southern agriculture, in decline since the end of World War I and scarred by tenancy, sank deeper into stagnation; even nature seemed hostile as the 1930–31 drought, the most severe on record, staggered the failing southern farm economy. Southern industry, still in its infancy, with only 15 percent of the nation's factory workers, fell even farther behind that of the North. Partners in misfortune, both rural and urban southerners shared the bitter trials of the times as the Depression exacerbated long-standing problems of poverty, race, and class.

Some starved to death in the depths of the Depression; thousands scavenged through garbage dumps; many of the homeless took refuge in city parks; evicted families lived in packing crates, junked automobiles, or anything else that might provide shelter. Because a physician's fee was an easily cut expense, illnesses went untreated in a society hesitant to ask charity from physicians sometimes reluctant to give it. Fear and insecurity overwhelmed some, but for most there was an implacable determination to survive.

Southern Americans, dazed by the hard times, initially received little aid from government. The Depression's unprecedented demands quickly exhausted private charity sources, and welfare apparatuses of local and state governments collapsed almost as rapidly. The multiplying poor could turn only to their national government.

The baffled and lethargic Hoover Administration tried to stabilize agricultural prices by limiting foreign imports (Hawley-Smoot tariff, 1930) and offered limited federal aid for relief (Reconstruction Finance Corporation, 1932), but its actions were ineffective. The New Deal of Franklin D. Roosevelt took shape early in 1933 with times at their worst. Responding to a people now willing to accept unique solutions, FDR's government was well intentioned but never adequately funded. In spite of such imaginative programs as the Tennessee Valley Authority (1933) and the Rural Electrification Administration (1935), the New Deal remained an essentially conservative reaction to the nation's ills. Government aid, when it was sent, came in smaller quantities to the South; with some 28 percent of the nation's population, the South received only 15.4 percent of the aid disbursed by the federal government in a typical Depression year such as 1937.

Most blacks lived in the South, and the racist policies of all levels of government meant that southern blacks fared worst of all. The meager government subsidies directed south invariably ended in white hands for distribution. Following the inviolable patterns of a systematically segregated society, southern bureaucrats did not ignore all blacks' needs, but inevitably gave whites' problems first attention. And in some instances welfare agents simply refused to accept blacks' applications for aid. Washington made no serious efforts at correction; blacks had perhaps even fewer friends in the capital than at home.

Factory hands fared as badly as farmers. As a primarily agricultural region, in 1929 the South had employed only 1,338,000 workers in industrial production. This newness to industry had produced 72-hour weeks, and wages lagged 40 percent behind those of the rest of the nation even before the Depression struck. The textile industry was the dominant industrial competitor. Virtually all factory workers were white, with blacks denied access to fledgling southern industry except in the most menial capacities.

The basic skills required in the textile mills meant that easily replaced workers enjoyed little success in organizing to improve wages, hours, and working conditions. And the industry's evolution had produced the company town where management owned or controlled housing, schools, churches, and government. Management generally responded to the Depression with wage reductions, increases in production quotas, and work stretch-outs. Workers' resistance to these cruel measures provoked immediate discharge underscored by institutionalized violence.

Resignation born of stunted expectations typified the industrial South. Even the company town's selective paternalism furnished support only so long as the worker kept his peace—and his job. Religion, family, or the close-knit society of a southern mill town provided what little enduring comfort employees gained. For the southern industrial worker the Depression was thus a lost decade; not until 1939 would the number of industrial jobs regain the 1929 level.

Southern farmers faced even worse circumstances. In the South's distinctive agricultural system, tenancy had replaced slavery as the "peculiar institution" after the Civil War. Most southern farmers were tenants; over 60 percent plowed land they did not own in the cotton states of Arkansas, Louisiana, Mississippi, Alabama, and Georgia. For blacks the figure ballooned to over 80 percent.

Cotton served as tenancy's dynamic. Half of all southern farms raised cotton, and tenants worked three-quarters of these; production had totaled 14,096,000 bales in 1929. The owner demanded cotton, for which a market always existed, but the Depression drove cotton prices to a record low of 4.6¢ per pound and production to only 10,613,000 bales. In addition, cotton neatly fitted a stringent pattern of controls over the life of the southern sharecropper, strictures the landowner tightened during the Depression.

Essential to the pattern was the country store, often owned by the landholder. Since the tenant usually began the crop year without cash, the owner guaranteed his credit at the nearby store where he was obligated to buy—at inflated prices and exorbitant interest rates. Attempting to insure steady purchases during the Depression, some landowners even forbade tenants to plant gardens or keep food animals. Although some did manage to flee to such comparative havens as Cleveland, Detroit, or California, many sharecroppers, black and white, lived in a state of outright peonage, ensnared by the South's skewed legal system.

The domination of the whole of southern society by the landowning class made all this possible. Political control insured complaisant lawmakers and enforcers who cowed the tenants. Denied access to public education, tenants had little comprehension of alternatives to their pattern of life. In the religious South even churches served planter interests by preaching to tenants the need for hard work and debt payment and neglecting to urge upon landowners biblical injunctions concerning masters' duties to laborers. By 1935, in the peasant society that was the South, 1,831,475 farms were tenant operated.

In the cotton country of northeastern Arkansas, hard-pressed sharecroppers sought relief by forming the Southern Tenant Farmers' Union (STFU). The nonviolent and racially integrated STFU called for nothing more radical than fair treatment and adherence to established laws. But a planter-led reign of terror smashed this stirring of tenant assertiveness with shootings, beatings, kidnappings, and kangaroo justice.

Black and white alike bore the weight of this malignant system, which extracted from them the last measure of both labor and dignity, but the realities of a rigidly segregated society handicapped blacks even further. The most remarkable aspect of southern tenancy during the Depression is the striking triumph of human spirit over the inhumane environment. Caught in an economic and cultural trap in some respects fiercer than slavery, tenants displayed a luminous courage and an inexorable determination.

Only sweeping changes could restructure southern society after the Depression. The coming of World War II, with its military draft and insatiable demands for war-industry workers, drew the next generation of potential sharecroppers from the farm; seeing a better world, they would never return.

Many landowners, envisioning greater profits in operating mechanized and larger single units with governmental subsidies, had begun to encourage an exodus of sharecroppers as the Depression lingered. The New Deal's Agricultural Adjustment Administration (1933) paid landowners, not the tenants who did the work, 50 percent more for plowing under cotton than for producing it. At the same time, improved farm machinery and the availability of capital helped make mechanization more attractive; in 1930 southern farmers used only 134,000 tractors; this number climbed to 255,000 in 1940 and to 468,000 in 1945. These factors helped speed tenancy's demise, as the number of white tenants declined a remarkable 25 percent during World War II.

The South's Depression story is not, however, one of unrelieved misery. Normal work persisted to a degree; while perhaps a third of the labor force sat idle, the remainder still held jobs and often shared their meager bounty with impoverished friends, as traditional southern neighborliness proved more compassionate than Washington's geographically and racially distorted policies. Many crafts workers, although finding fewer tasks, did remain relatively busy. A favorably located merchant with a long-established clientele often maintained an acceptable trade. Not surprisingly, professionals in the legal and health fields, the planters' close allies, suffered perhaps least of all. Depression then, as always, was a matter of relative decline.

Most southerners, however, struggled through these years with wounds healed only slightly by a government more interested in relief and recovery than in real reform. The impersonal numbers on unemployment lists and graphs of falling income meant empty stomachs, sinking spirits, and desolate confusion. Although despair existed, the survival of an open-hearted and optimistic spirit may be the most remarkable legacy of these impoverished southerners.

See also AGRICULTURE: Country Store; Sharecropping and Tenancy; / Cotton Culture; Rural Electrification Administration; ENVIRONMENT: Tennessee Valley Authority; INDUSTRY: / Textile Industry; SOCIAL CLASS: Politics and Social Class; Poverty; / Company Town; Southern Tenant Farmers' Union; Textile Workers

John L. Robinson
Abilene Christian University

James C. Cobb and Michael V. Namorato, eds., *The New Deal and the South* (1984); David E. Conrad, *The Forgotten Farmers: The Story of Sharecroppers in the New Deal* (1965); Pete Daniel, *The Shadow of Slavery: Peonage in the South, 1901–1969* (1972); Federal Writers' Project, *These Are Our Lives* (1939); Donald H. Grubbs, *Cry from the Cotton: The Southern Tenant Farmers' Union and the New Deal* (1971); Robert S. McElvaine, *The Great Depression, 1929–1941* (1984); Arthur F. Raper, *Preface to Peasantry: A Tale of Two Black Belt Counties* (1936); Roger W. Shugg, *Origins of Class Struggle in Louisiana: A Social History of White Farmers and Laborers during Slavery and after, 1840–1875* (1939); Gavin Wright, *The Political Economy of the Cotton South* (1978).

Historians

The oldest tradition of historical literature in the South is that of state descriptions and history. This tradition began before the settlement of Virginia with the pamphlets and books that promoted and inflated the virtues of colonization. It continued through the studies of Robert Beverley (*History and Present State of Virginia*, 1705), William Stith (*History of the First Discovery and Settlement of Virginia*, 1747), and Thomas Jefferson (*Notes on the State of Virginia*, 1785). By the 19th century a considerable body of such writings existed, among them, David Ramsay's *History of South Carolina* (1808), which celebrated the American Revolution; Charles Gayarré's *Histoire de la Louisiane* (1846), which domesticated European historicism; and William Gilmore Simms's *History of South Carolina* (1840), which anticipated the Confederacy.

Such history was an amateur and gentlemanly undertaking, local in focus and patriotic in tone, though later useful for the gathering of documents and the establishment of state historical societies. Before 1861 such societies existed in 10 southern states: Virginia (1831), North Carolina (1833), Louisiana (1836), Kentucky (1838),

Georgia (1839), Tennessee (1849), Alabama (1850), South Carolina (1855), Florida (1856), and Mississippi (1858).

Notable before the Civil War, however, was an absence of regional historiography, which had to wait until the late 19th century brought a generation of southerners schooled in sectional thought by the experiences of war and Reconstruction. The first regional historical organization was the Southern Historical Society, founded in New Orleans in 1869 by ex-Confederates and dedicated to the vindication of the Lost Cause. Its successor, the Southern History Association founded in Washington in 1896, was both more New South in persuasion and less bitter in tone; its *Publications* appeared between 1896 and 1907. Insofar as professional historiography is an offshoot of industrialization, it is no surprise that the southern historical and educational industry should have commenced outside and on the borders of the South before moving into the region in the 1920s.

The earliest centers of academic southern history were the Johns Hopkins University, where Herbert Baxter Adams taught Woodrow Wilson and William P. Trent; Columbia University, where William A. Dunning instructed students of Reconstruction such as Walter L. Fleming and J. G. de Roulhac Hamilton; and the University of Chicago, where William Dodd directed Frank L. Owsley's studies. The first course in southern history was taught by James C. Ballagh at Johns Hopkins in 1896 and the first within the South by William K. Boyd at Trinity College (later Duke University) in 1907.

Usually under the direction of northern graduates born in the South, an infrastructure of graduate programs, journals, archives, presses, and professional organizations was fashioned indigenously after 1920. About a hundred doctorates in history were granted by southern universities between the world wars, mostly on southern topics. In 1930 the Southern Historical Collection, the largest archive of regional documents, was founded at Chapel Hill. In 1934 the Southern Historical Association was organized, and publication of its *Journal of Southern History* commenced in 1935. In the 1920s the University of North Carolina Press began to publish books on regional history and culture, and in 1937 the Louisiana State University press began a multivolume *History of the South*.

Southern history, as both a professional and an amateur pursuit, is largely written in the South by southerners for southerners and is published by southern journals and presses; occasionally non-southern publishers issue works on southern history, but these are usually by nonsoutherners or southerners living outside the region. The study of southern history thus forms an important subculture in American social discourse, possessed of many private symbols and rituals. There is a healthy amateur industry, flourishing as tourism, cheerfully anecdotal political journalism, and military and genealogical antiquarianism; all are characterized by a warmth of nostalgia: hooped skirts, Earl Long's penchant for striptease artists, grandfather's exploits at Shiloh.

Professional historians in the South are notable for being an accepted part of their society, often partisan toward the South, formerly bitter against the North but recently—as a function of growing relative affluence—more amiable. Their specialities are social history (particularly of slavery and race relations), biography, and political history. Military history, once popular as a function of bitterness, is now in decline. Economic history has been a weaker tradition, and intellectual history, save as literary history, has been almost nonexistent. Southern historians divide by social persuasion (usually conservative, often liberal, rarely radical), by place of birth (Virginians, Tennesseans), and by ancestry (yeoman, planter, Tidewater, Piedmont), rather than by theoretical persuasion (Marxist, Hegelian, structuralist). However, the youngest generation of southern historians shows a growing interest in social theory.

Southern history is implicitly comparative history, because scholars of southern history assume a distinction from "northern" culture and occasionally offer comparisons with non-American cultures, as in the writings of Eugene D. Genovese (Japan and Sicily), Forrest McDonald and Grady McWhiney (the Celtic fringe), Carl N. Degler (Brazil), or C. Vann Woodward (Europe). More usually—and this is necessary to its function as social discourse—southern history is inward looking. The old tradition of state history continues and constitutes the bulk of southern historical literature, chiefly because archives and higher education are organized largely by states. Because the region is not merely a collection of states but a gestalt, however, the subject matter of a broad regional history is unclear. At present southern history thus tends to be either the aggregate of state histories or an impressionistic synthesis of unevenly gathered particularities, in which a specific state or social group is made to do service for the whole.

There is no known analysis of the social origins, recruitment patterns, or social habits of southern historians. As a category within the broad scheme of Western historical literature, southern history is an optional, rather than an inevitable, classification, imposed by author or reader, and strongest as social discourse when imposed by both.

See also MYTHIC SOUTH: History, Central Themes

Michael O'Brien
University of Arkansas

George H. Calcott, *History in the United States, 1800–1860* (1970); E. Merton Coulter, *Journal of Southern History* (February 1936); Arthur S. Link and Rembert W. Patrick, eds., *Writing Southern History: Essays in Historiography in Honor of Fletcher M. Green* (1965); Wendell H. Stephenson, *The South Lives in History: Southern Historians and Their Legacy* (1955), *Southern History in the Making: Pioneer Historians of the South* (1964); George B. Tindall, ed., *The Pursuit of Southern History: Presidential Addresses of the Southern Historical Association, 1935–1963* (1964).

Historic Preservation

In the South, the past is more than learned; it is remembered. It is an integral part of present lives and gives meaning and character to future prospects. As William Faulkner wrote in *Intruder in the Dust* (1948), in the South "yesterday today and tomorrow are Is: Indivisible: One." So historic preservation in the region is more than merely a movement to preserve old structures; it seeks to preserve a part of the southern people as well. For the structures themselves are more than brick and mortar replications of a past style or fashion; they are the stories of the communities and generations that have resided there. So the historic preservation movement in the South, primarily a phenomenon of the last half century, was not so much a sudden awakening to a historical heritage, as a formal, organized response to a feeling and a culture most southerners had internalized.

Actually, organized historic preservation in the South predates this century. Since the 1850s the work of the Mount Vernon Ladies' Association in restoring and maintaining the home of the nation's first president has served as a model of privately funded preservation. But the major efforts in the region have occurred since the 1920s when Williamsburg, Va., Charleston's historic district, and the Vieux Carré in New Orleans received their initial support. The appearance and acceleration of historic preservation efforts in the 1920s resulted from the modest prosperity experienced by cities in the region at the time. Poverty and stagnation had been excellent natural preservers. Relieved of the pressures of growth, ancient districts and structures survived in the twilight of indifference, secure that no wrecker's ball would penetrate their murky confines. As the booster mentality conquered southern cities, however, the prospect, if not fact, of growth became a great obsession. Thomas Wolfe lamented of his native Asheville that "a spirit of drunken waste and wild destructiveness was everywhere apparent. The fairest places in town were being mutilated at untold cost."

A survey of residential buildings conducted in Charleston in 1917 concluded, "May it . . . be hoped that what has accidentally been preserved may be long retained." The survey surprised Charlestonians by documenting an extensive collection of historic structures, many of which were suffering from neglect. When, a few years later, the Manigault house, constructed in 1790, was threatened with demolition, the women who had commissioned the survey sprang into action and organized a permanent watchdog committee, the Society for the Preservation of Old Dwellings, which effectively lobbied for a comprehensive Historic District Zoning Law that passed in 1931. City planner Charles Henry Cheney termed the ordinance "one of the most forward advances in city planning work and architectural control that we have ever yet had in the country." Six years later in New Orleans after a similar lobbying effort to save the historic Vieux Carré, the Louisiana Legislature established a commission, the first such publicly supported body in the United States, with broad powers ranging from the protection of structures within the French Quarter to the exempting of historic properties from local taxation.

These projects, together with the Rockefeller-funded Williamsburg restoration and the Natchez Garden Club, which in 1931 began using the techniques of annual pilgrimages to stimulate interest in preserving Natchez's unique collection of antebellum homes, thrust the South into the lead of a nascent national historic preservation movement. After World War II the movement regained and surpassed its prewar level, most dramatically in Savannah but also in the less notable towns and cities throughout the region, encompassing not only dwellings and public buildings but shops and factories as well. Most significantly, there was a drawing together of two former antagonists—the boosters and the preservationists—as the latter demonstrated that history was good business. In Savannah, for example, the preservation movement was largely responsible for developing a tourist industry that generated $60 million in revenue for the city by 1980. Also, by the 1960s there was increased participation by the federal government, and, especially after the 1974 Community Development Act, even those structures and districts not so obviously "historical" received funding support. "History" now inhabited not only the structures of the famous but the quarters of everyman as well.

By the 1970s, however, two clouds appeared on the otherwise-clear horizon of historic preservation. First, there was the question of equity. Southern cities and towns have not, historically, been particularly solicitous of their black residents, and the individuals attracted by the preservation movement—overwhelmingly white, typically professional, and often with family connections—have generally ignored the social consequences of the preservation movement, which have included the gentrification of neighborhoods and displacement of people, the difficulties of relocation, and the burdens of higher taxes for those remaining. Preservation and social equity can, of course, coexist nicely, as Lee Adler has demonstrated with his Savannah Landmark group, a project that has successfully preserved the city's Victorian District, by purchasing homes in the district and leasing them back at reasonable rents to the black tenants who have resided in the neighborhood for decades.

Second, there is a growing concern that historic preservation may be too successful in the region; that vast areas of towns and cities may become untouchable museums for the wealthy and the tourists. The depredations of developers notwithstanding, each generation, according to this view, should be allowed to add its own legacy to the rich historical traditions of the South. A fixed backward gaze could only degenerate into a self-centered antiquarianism that would belie the dynamic and comprehensive quality of historic structures and districts in the region.

The search for new methods and flexibility in interpreting and preserving historic structures to make them more usable for more of the people will likely continue: adaptive reuse of old textile mills into condominiums as in Greensboro, N.C., or the transformation of a graceful turn-of-the-century mansion in uptown New Orleans into a public library are increasingly seen not as desecrations of the past, but rather as paeans to that heritage, reinforcing that resilience and relevance of southern history and culture for all.

See also ENVIRONMENT: Gardens and Gardening; RECREATION: Tourism; / Colonial Williamsburg; URBANIZATION: / Charleston; Savannah

David R. Goldfield
University of North Carolina
at Charlotte

James Deetz, *In Small Things Forgotten: The Archaeology of Early American Life* (1977); Frank Gilbert, ed., *Readings in Historic Preservation* (1983); Charles B. Hosmer, Jr., *Preservation Comes of Age: From Williamsburg to the National Trust, 1926–1949*, 2 vols. (1981); David Kyvig and Myron Marty, *Nearby History: Exploring the Past Around You* (1983); Kevin Lynch, *What Time Is This Place?* (1972); Nathan Weinberg, *Preservation in American Towns and Cities* (1979).

Historic Sites

With the founding of the Mount Vernon Ladies' Association of the Union in 1856, the South became an early leader in the historic preservation movement in the United States. The association, chartered by the Commonwealth of Virginia, was organized with the sole purpose of purchasing and preserving George Washington's home and its surrounding grounds. Also in 1856, Tennessee provided funds to purchase and preserve Andrew Jackson's estate, the Hermitage. Like so many early preservation efforts, these mansions were selected for restoration and perpetual care largely because of their association with important figures in American history. A few other sites and structures were saved because of their role in significant events.

The Civil War interrupted historic preservation efforts throughout the South and also provided scores of potential sites with which to memorialize the Lost Cause. By the end of the century several Civil War battlefields had been set aside as national military parks. Tennessee's Chickamauga and Chattanooga park, formed in 1890, was one of the first. By the early 1900s the South seemed intent on preserving almost any Civil War site of even moderate significance. Although the region was often forced to rely on federal aid to finance these preservation efforts, state and local activities continued. The Association for the Preservation of Virginia Antiquities, a private organization founded in 1888, concentrated its early efforts on preserving colonial sites in the Jamestown area. Other state and local organizations gradually emerged to tackle specific preservation projects. In Virginia, for example, Richmond's Confederate Literary Society was founded in 1890 to preserve the Confederate White House, and the Thomas Jefferson Memorial Foundation purchased Monticello in 1923. Both were typical of the local organizations that collectively have played a crucial and continuing role in southern preservation efforts.

During the 1920s John D. Rockefeller became interested in preserving and restoring Williamsburg, Va., and his interest and financial assistance in the project demonstrated the potential of private preservation efforts. Several other communities, including Charleston, S.C., and St. Augustine, Fla., drew on the experience, techniques, and spirit of the Colonial Williamsburg project to develop historic districts of their own. For the first time historic preservation in the South began to reflect larger cultural and historic concerns. While Williamsburg and similar sites were usually related to major historic events and personalities, the preservationists and historians associated with these projects also attempted to interpret patterns of everyday life. As the 1900s wore on, this impulse became ever more significant, but the portrayal of southern society at historic sites has nevertheless largely focused on the white elite.

Several major federal initiatives had enormous impact on the development of southern sites. The establishment of the National Park Service to administer federally funded sites (1916) and the Historic Preservation Act of 1935, which finally provided focus to the national preservation movement, were especially noteworthy. Although state and local organizations would continue to preserve and interpret the past throughout the region, southern reliance on federal leadership and funding for major projects, particularly in the area of military sites and parks, became increasingly important. At Civil War parks the significance of this national support has been seen in the tendency of federally funded areas to play down the Lost Cause myth in favor of a more straightforward interpretation of events. Still, southern organizations have often been able to contribute monuments and exhibits to national battlefield parks, which continue to emphasize, however subtly, the romance and glamor of the Confederacy. At other sites, particularly those related to the colonial period, federal leadership has tended to favor a portrayal of colonial life that emphasizes an emerging *national* character, whereas those colonial sites administered by southern organizations often seek to demonstrate the uniqueness of the southern identity.

A number of culturally significant patterns emerge from an examination of the South's preservation activities. First, the sheer number of such areas in the South suggests that the region indeed *does* tend to be more enamored with its history than other portions of the United States. The 11 states of the Confederacy together with Maryland, Kentucky, and Missouri account for 45 percent of eastern historic sites listed in the *National Register of Historic Places* and over 36 percent of *all* listings. State and local sites, which sometimes are not included in the *Register*, are also a bit more common in the South than in other areas. Southern preservationists have the advantage, particularly in the Atlantic Seaboard areas, of an unusually lengthy history. Moreover, much of the Revolutionary War and virtually all of the Civil War were fought on southern battlefields. Nevertheless, the region's early leadership of the preservation movement and the continued high level of state, local, and individual enthusiasm for preserving the past have enabled the South to outstrip the level of commitment in most other regions.

The nature of the sites preserved and exhibited is also revealing. One important theme in the southern preservation movement always has been the memorializing of southern leadership during the colonial and revolutionary periods. Numerous sites, from the reconstructed House of Burgesses at Williamsburg, to the homes of Washington and Jefferson, through the Yorktown and Jamestown areas, demonstrate the crucial role played by southerners in shaping the early history of the United States. Although Virginia tends to dominate in this category, North Carolina, South Carolina, and Georgia have also preserved significant sites.

The southern insistence on its own uniqueness of identity and aristocratic origins is suggested by the dominance of plantation architecture among historic restorations. The life of the colonial and antebellum white elite is interpreted at literally scores of sites, and from George Mason's Gunston Hall in Virginia southward to Louisiana's Oak Alley the South seems to be one great plantation. The romance of the antebellum years and the heroic struggle for the Lost Cause are clearly central themes in historic preservation in the South. This was especially true of work carried out during the period from 1890 to 1930, but even in more recent periods this impulse has carried considerable weight.

Perhaps the best example of this movement to memorialize the plantation South is found at Stone Mountain Park near Atlanta, Ga. This state-owned recreation area includes the "Ante-Bellum Plantation" exhibit, a romantic reconstruction of a "typical" 1850s plantation. This plantation never existed, however, but has been assembled on the spot from period buildings that were moved to Stone Mountain from throughout the state. That the scene is drastically glamorized is confirmed by the use of the Kingston House to represent the home of the overseer and his family, for the structure was actually the *main* house at Allen Plantation near Kingston, Ga. Such portrayals, even those that are not so exaggerated, have played a significant role in shaping popular conceptions of southern history.

Other segments of southern society often have been slighted by this emphasis on the plantation South. Indeed, it might be argued that those elements that are missing from historic sites are as significant as those that are present. For example, many plantations have been preserved with little or no reference to slave life and culture. Although some sites have begun to exhibit slave quarters (Gunston Hall and the Stone Mountain Plantation, for example), many others have none at all. Some slave quarters that *are* preserved or reconstructed—for example, those at Mount Vernon—are not typical and are sometimes far more commodious and well furnished than would have been the case. The southern middle class, the southern merchant, and the southern poor white are similarly slighted, at least in terms of the number of sites preserved. Even when merchants and artisans are represented, as at Williamsburg, the overall effect often suggests that this portion of society merely provided support and service for the more important planter class. Another curious weakness in the portrayal of the region's history is found in the comparatively limited number of sites related to Native Americans. In terms of numbers of sites, only in Mississippi does the interpretation of the Native American impact on the South approach realistic proportions. Native Americans in Mississippi have pressed for recognition of their forebears' contributions, and one result has been a change in many historic plaques.

The record of southern history as preserved in historic sites is, then, both an illustration of the South's desire to maintain a sense of identity and a reinforcement of popular images of the region held generally throughout the nation. That the historic South as it is preserved never existed is not the point. The preserved past is a record of regional pride and identity that seeks to highlight and help preserve southern distinctiveness in the face of forces that would "Americanize" the region. As many scholars have suggested, the use of the past, particularly the preserved past, is an ideological exercise. Nowhere is this more clear than in the South.

See also MYTHIC SOUTH: / Lost Cause Myth; RECREATION: / Colonial Williamsburg

Christopher D. Geist
Bowling Green State University

Edward D. C. Campbell, Jr., *Journal of Regional Cultures* (Fall–Winter 1982); Alvar W. Carlson, *Journal of American Culture* (Summer 1980); Beverley Da Costa, *Historic Houses of America Open to the Public* (1971); Larry Ford, *Growth and Change* (April 1974); Christopher D. Geist, in *Icons of America*, ed. Ray B. Browne and Marshall Fishwick (1978); Charles B. Hosmer, Jr., *Presence of the Past: A History of the Preservation Movement in the United States before Williamsburg* (1965); U.S. Department of the Interior, National Park Service, *The National Register of Historic Places* (1974); Walter Muir Whitehill, *Interdependent Historical Societies* (1962).

Holidays

Sunday has been the most frequently commemorated holiday in the South. Originally kept with some solemnity, it has now become largely a celebration of the cessation of work, although it is still a *dies non* in law. Once there was also a weekly half holiday, usually Wednesday or Thursday, but a tendency to slacken work on Saturday has recently appeared. Banks have generally transferred most of their holidays to a Monday.

The only total holiday is Christmas and perhaps the day following. New Year's Day shares in some of the Christmas festivities, but it has become mainly an occasion for viewing football bowl games. The popular meaning of Memorial Day is that it is the beginning of summer and vacation season. Early in the 20th century the South observed it as a memorial to veterans of the Spanish-American War. In many southern states 26 April is the special Confederate Memorial Day; in others it is 3 June; still others combine it with the national Memorial Day. The Fourth of July Independence Day was observed by southern blacks, but whites mainly viewed it as a nonworking day or picnic day. The 1976 bicentennial commemoration revived its significance, and it has grown in popularity. Labor Day used to be marked by a parade and baseball game, but now it generally marks the end of summer and vacation time. Thanksgiving in the South never had quite the importance it held outside the region. It is a time of hunting and feasting, and also the date for special football games.

The preceding holidays are of primary regional importance, but southerners, like other Americans, celebrate a variety of additional special occasions as well. St. Valentine's Day (14 February) is an occasion promoted by gift and stationery shops. The George Washington observance is a bank and post office holiday. Mardi Gras (Shrove Tuesday) is a major festival in New Orleans, Mobile, and Pensacola, the culmination of a season of Carnival preceding Lent. St. Patrick's Day (17 March) has grown from an ethnic Irish commemoration to a more extensive observance, once again promoted by gift and stationery shops. Easter Sunday is a high religious festival but, being a Sunday, is somewhat less commercialized than Christmas. Both Easter and Christmas celebrations tend to be only day-long rather than season-long events. The Jewish days of Rosh Hashanah, Yom Kippur, and Hanukkah are quietly recognized by the news media and stationery shops. Halloween (31 October), especially the night, is a party festival and a time of pranks by children and some adults.

A third group of holidays are, as yet, minor days to be noted. The birthdays of Robert E. Lee (21 January), Stonewall Jackson (22 January), and Matthew Fontaine Maury (24 January) are observed by organizations of descendants of Confederate veterans. Groundhog Day (2 February) is noted by news media and schools. St. Joseph Day (19 March) attracts major attention in New Orleans and some other Roman Catholic communities, and Good Friday is a legal holiday in Louisiana. May Day evokes some school attention. Flag Day (14 June) is a legal holiday. The days of St. John (the baptizer, 24 June, and the evangelist, 27 December) are occasions for Masonic lodges (picnics in summer, banquets in winter). There is a sentimental Francophile notice of Bastille Day (14 July) and a school recognition of Columbus Day. All Saints' Day (1 November) is a legal holiday in Louisiana. In nearby states it is an occasion for decorating cemeteries, although the latter practice belongs more aptly to the following day, All Souls' Day. Armistice Day (11 November) used to be a widespread observance, but under the designation of Veterans' Day it has become a day noted by veterans' organizations of all wars from World War II onward.

Four holidays—Christmas, New Year's, the Fourth of July, and Thanksgiving—are times when most institutions of a community are closed. Memorial Day and Labor Day are also nonworkdays for many; they serve to signal the opening and closing, respectively, of resort areas and vacation spots. Other holidays attract less attention (except for Easter), but they are nonetheless generally commemorated. The Jewish high holy days have gradually become more significant, especially because of the prominence of Jewish merchants and Jewish academics, many of whom celebrate Rosh Hashanah and Yom Kippur.

Among blacks there used to be extensive, if informal, commemoration of Emancipation Day (variously 8 May, 19 June, and perhaps others); businesses did not close, but blacks frequently did not report for work. Blacks in Texas celebrated the distinctive Juneteenth holiday. More recently other events, as, for instance, those of the civil rights activities of the 1960s, as well as disillusionment with the progress of emancipation, have pushed it into the background. The late Martin Luther King, Jr.'s birthday (15 January) won approval in 1983 as a federal holiday.

See also BLACK LIFE: / Juneteenth

Allen Cabaniss
University of Mississippi

Hennig Cohen and Tristram P. Coffin, eds., *The Folklore of American Holidays* (1987); Jane M. Hatch, *The American Book of Days* (3d ed., 1978); Robert Lee, *National Forum* (Summer 1982); Robert J. Myers, *Celebrations: The Complete Book of American Holidays* (1972); William E. Woodward, *The Way Our People Lived: An Intimate American History* (1944).

Jacksonian Democracy

The source of the political division of antebellum America into Jacksonian and Whig parties lay in the expansion of the market economy in the years between the War of 1812 and the Civil War. Acceptance of the values of the marketplace and resistance to those values each implied a conception of the meaning of freedom. For Jacksonians—dedicated to defending the ideal of economic and social self-sufficiency and fearful of being exploited by centers of power in the society—freedom was something the citizenry had by right, although evil, antidemocratic forces were attempting to take it away. A man was free when he was dependent on no one else for his livelihood and welfare. Movements and institutions whose succcss would diminish the existing autonomy of the individual were thus by definition aristocratic and inimical to the American experiment. For Whigs freedom was not something Americans already had but something for which they perpetually strived. A man became free by fulfilling his potential, by becoming all that he could be. The shackles of ignorance and poverty were his greatest enemies; the expansion of knowledge and opportunity was his principal security. Morality and justice required that citizens cooperate in order to build a better social order for all.

These differing definitions of freedom carried with them differing notions of the proper role of government. Whigs sought the enactment of programs intended to break the bonds that they felt held the mass of Americans in economic, social, or moral bondage: governmental aid for the construction of railroads, roads, and canals; protective tariffs; central regulation of the currency supply and the banking system; the establishment of public schools; the prohibition of the sale of liquor; and the creation of hospitals to cure the insane, institutions to train the deaf and blind, and penitentiaries to redeem criminals. Jacksonians generally regarded all such programs as the products of paternalistic elitism. They thought it intolerable that the ordinary citizen should be taxed to benefit railroads, factories, and banks; that his private conduct should be regulated; that his children should be forcibly indoctrinated with alien, urban ideals.

The Jacksonians campaigned for the abolition of all property qualifications for voting and officeholding, hoping that a broadened electorate could use the government not to assist the growth of corporations but to restrict and ultimately to destroy them. But beyond such activities, which they considered defensive, Jacksonians sought limited government, states' rights, and strict construction of federal and state constitutions. They viewed their political party as a trade union of the electorate through which ordinary citizens, individually weak, could band together and use their numbers to counterbalance the power of the wealthy. Whigs, on the other hand, were often doubtful that poverty-stricken, ill-educated citizens were capable of appreciating what was actually in their own best interest. Whigs conceived of their party as a sort of religious denomination, an organization of believers seeking to convert and to save the society at large. Though practical political considerations quickly led Whig politicians to abandon their early defense of restrictions on voting and officeholding, the Whigs continued to insist upon examinations for admission to such professions as law and medicine—examinations that Jacksonians frequently opposed.

In the Lower South the origins of Whiggery lay in the use of nullificationist doctrines to insist upon the right of each state to expel the Indians within its boundaries. The ease with which these nullifiers embraced the broad-constructionist program of the national Whig party in the later 1830s is an index of the degree to which ideology in the region was an extension of interest. Those merchants and planters who had eagerly sought the opening of Indian lands for speculation and commercial exploitation also eagerly awaited roads, railroads, and the easy credit promised by a national banking system. Although the majority of planters supported the Whigs, planters were not the cutting edge of the party; the intellectual leaders of Whiggery were the urban merchants and factors, whom the planters envied and emulated. The strength of the Jacksonians, in contrast, was usually to be found concentrated in those areas of the region most isolated from large-scale market agriculture.

In the Jacksonian period the attitudes and programs at issue between the parties in the South were essentially the same as those at issue throughout the nation. The expansion of the market economy and its values was a national phenomenon, and the response to it was national, embodying fears and hopes as real in the South as in the North. However, states' views toward one institution—slavery—differed. Slavery was an integral assumption in the ideology of each party. Jacksonians conceived of it protecting communities of self-reliant small farmers from the marketplace; as they saw it, with slaves to supply plantation labor, the white, independent yeomanry could not be converted into a proletariat, subservient to planters and capitalists. Whigs thought slavery a mechanism of social mobility, another of the many happy institutions facilitating the efforts of the industrious to achieve economic success. Both regarded it as essentially American, a bulwark of the freedom and democracy that were the Republic's distinguishing characteristics. Therefore, when proposals to exclude slavery from the western territories gained popularity in the North, both Jacksonians and Whigs in the South concluded that the absence of slavery from the territories would lead to the establishment in them of a hierarchical, un-American society, on the northern model.

Just before the advent of the party period in the early 1830s, Lower South factions that would become Jacksonians and Whigs were united in desiring the expulsion of the Indians—the Jacksonians so that settlers could establish independent farms on the Indians' lands and the Whigs so that the territory could be brought into the expanding American economy. The end of the party period in the mid-1850s found Jacksonians and Whigs throughout most of the region equally united in desiring slavery in the West—the Jacksonians because it would permit the yeomanry to be secure from the exploitation of the rich and the Whigs because it would promote the settlers' material advancement. In the intervening decades, however, the issues dominant on the national scene—banking, tariffs, and aid to internal improvements—revealed the sharply differing conceptions of freedom held by the more upwardly mobile and by those less willing to take risks in both the South and the nation at large. The salience for a time of this set of issues permitted the definition of the two parties in the southern states.

With the collapse of the Whig party in the 1850s the Democrats lost their social and ideological coherence. A group of ambitious younger Democratic politicians, who generally accepted the label "Young America," began to use aspects of Jacksonianism, especially its devotion to laissez-faire and strict-constructionist doctrines, in ways that defended rather than attacked commercial and industrial interests. Adopted in most instances as well by the leaders of the Republican party during the 1850s, these ideas became the ideology of American's dominant culture after the Civil War; they have often been called, though misleadingly, "social Darwinism."

Reconstruction in the southern states led to virtually all whites in the region becoming Democrats and had the effect in the later 19th century of depriving the yeoman constituencies—to which southern Jacksonianism had most strongly appealed—of a political party dedicated to defending them from rival sectors of society. And the heretical "social Darwinist" formulation of the Jacksonian creed deprived them, in some measure, of their familiar ideology upon which to ground a protest against their evident marginalization, in the South as elsewhere. The elimination of the public domain, and with it the squatter who had lived upon it, as well as the end of the open range for the grazing of livestock with the passage of fencing laws, left the yeomanry's economic and social position increasingly precarious. Yet important elements of the Jacksonian tradition persisted, particularly in the most isolated, small-farming areas of the South. Its influence is to be seen in the Independent movement of the late 1870s, in the Farmers' Alliance of the 1880s, in the Populist movement of the early and mid-1890s, and, indeed, in the appeals of popular political leaders well into the 20th century.

J. Mills Thornton III
University of Michigan, Ann Arbor

Lacy K. Ford, Jr., "Social Origins of a New South Carolina: The Upcountry in the Nineteenth Century" (Ph.D. dissertation, University of South Carolina, 1983); Steven Hahn, *The Roots of Southern Populism: Yeoman Farmers and the Transformation of the Georgia Upcountry, 1850–1890* (1983); Lawrence F. Kohl, "The Politics of Individualism: Social Character and Political Parties in the Age of Jackson" (Ph.D. dissertation, University of Michigan, 1980); J. Mills Thornton III, *Politics and Power in a Slave Society: Alabama, 1800–1860* (1978); Harry L. Watson, *Jacksonian Politics and Community Conflict: The Emergence of the Second American Party System in Cumberland County, North Carolina* (1981); Rush Welter, *The Mind of America, 1820–1860* (1975).

Jeffersonian Tradition

Thomas Jefferson is invariably linked in the American mind with such concepts as liberty, freedom, and democracy. Indeed, the Jeffersonian tradition, as a general pattern of recognizable beliefs and behavior, provides much of the basis for America's liberal tradition. Through Jefferson, Charles M. Wiltse writes in *The Jeffersonian Tradition in American Democracy* (1960), "the political liberalism of accumulated centuries passed into the

Monticello, Thomas Jefferson's home

American democratic tradition, where it helped to mold the American way of life." To basic liberal tenets Jefferson added his own strain of agrarian thought, which praised the superiority of a self-sufficient, agricultural lifestyle. The independent yeoman farmer became a symbol for American democracy, and the image persisted, particularly in the South, into the 20th century.

Southerners have invoked Jefferson's precepts on numerous occasions in the 160 years since his death. For much of America's history the South has served as "a kind of sanctuary of the American democratic tradition," according to David M. Potter. Until comparatively recently the region was still a bastion of Jeffersonian ideals, at least for liberal critics of American society. There, Jefferson's agrarian descendants carried on resistance to the crass commercialism and capitalism of the Northeast and Midwest.

Following themes elaborated by Frederick Jackson Turner in the late 19th century, Americans easily linked the frontier with the development of democratic institutions and economic opportunity. Turner's "frontier thesis" exalted the role of the West, yet agrarian democracy and frontier democracy share obvious similarities, as William E. Dodd later noted in *Statesmen of the Old South* (1911). One of the first historians to realize the implications of agrarian democracy, Dodd asserted that the "real South" was precisely the South of Thomas Jefferson. Any conservative, hierarchical developments, as opposed to progress along democratic, equalitarian lines, were mere aberrations from true southernism. Dodd subjected his thesis to little critical evaluation, and later writers have disputed his findings. But his version was not entirely lacking in historical foundation. Jefferson and the Jeffersonian tradition originated in the South, and for much of American political history the region has supported men who shared such ideas.

Southerners have invoked, in addition to Jefferson's agrarian philosophy, a number of other principles that can be traced to the intellectual and political heritage of the third president. His name is often associated with arguments sustaining states' rights, and southerners cite his authorship of the Kentucky Resolution of 1799 as evidence of his opposition to the extension of federal power. Inhabitants of the region recall his arguments against Alexander Hamilton's plans for industrialization, national banks, and tariffs, and much of America's antiurban tradition can be traced to Jeffersonian origins as well. Ironically, for all his praise of yeoman farmers as God's "Chosen People," Jefferson eventually admitted the need for commerce and manufacturing, and his immediate successors in the White House acquiesced in the chartering of a Second Bank of the United States and the development of a tariff policy. Slavery also received considerable attention in Jefferson's writings, but his recommendations for abolition did not endear him in the South. Few southerners would admit that such ideas represented Jefferson's settled policy.

Jefferson's commitment to liberalism, grounded in the 18th century Enlightenment, provided the intellectual foundation for his writings on agrarianism, states' rights, and restricted governmental power, as well as his opposition to slavery. The most widely known examples of his ideas on liberal political theory appear in the Declaration of Independence and in other sources, including his *Notes on the State of Virginia*. His liberalism contributed to the practical reforms that connected his administration with those of Andrew Jackson, Woodrow Wilson, and Franklin D. Roosevelt. Both Jeffersonian agrarianism and idealism surfaced in the programs advocated by the Populists in the 1890s and in the writings of the Nashville Agrarians in the 1930s.

Jefferson's influence in the South remains difficult to assess precisely. The region unquestionably cherished his agrarianism and his defense of states' rights, but his more liberal, equalitarian doctrines languished there in the years after independence. By the "era of good feelings" Jefferson was viewed as the defender of states' rights in his native Virginia, where his principles coincided with powerful economic and political interests. The nullification movement in South Carolina contributed to the transformation of his image in the South. The patriot who was eulogized in 1826 as the "Apostle of Liberty" became the "Father of States' Rights."

Jefferson's Kentucky Resolution enhanced his position among nullifiers, because his words in that document implied that nullification of an unconstitutional federal law was a legitimate procedure. Nullification, Merrill D. Peterson asserts in *The Jefferson Image in the American Mind* (1960), "was the pivot upon which many states' rights Jeffersonians swung toward the policies of sectionalism, slavery, and secession." At the very least, the Jeffersonian tradition was linked to the South's cause, and the episode also demonstrated that Jefferson's ideas could be appropriated for purposes alien to the original intent.

The nullifiers were not the only faction in Jacksonian society to rely on the Jeffersonian tradition. Jacksonian democracy itself revived essential Jeffersonian themes that were modified and strengthened by new influences in the 1830s and 1840s. In the *Age of Jackson* (1945) Arthur M. Schlesinger, Jr., defines Jacksonian democracy as a "more hard-headed and determined version of Jeffersonian democracy," adding that democrats had to accept that new era's industrialism, factories, mills, labor, banks, and capital—all distasteful to orthodox Jeffersonians. The latter's view of independent yeomen as the nation's unique class of producers had to be enlarged to accommodate urban wage earners.

In the meantime, defenders of slavery still invoked Jefferson, noting that the Virginian had owned extensive property in slaves throughout his life. At the same time, the Wilmot Proviso linked the Jeffersonian heritage with the growing opposition to the extension of slavery into the western territories. The proviso revived the language and intent of the old Northwest Ordinance of 1787, which banned slavery in the states of the Old Northwest. Jefferson made no contribution to that legislation, although he had proposed a similar ban on slavery in congress's 1784 land ordinance. Congress had rejected that restriction, only to add its own to the Northwest Ordinance. Southerners viewed Jefferson's alleged authorship of the antislavery provision as one of his "fatal legacies," but most doubted that he ever favored outright abolition. Later, southerners advocated the concept of popular sovereignty in Jefferson's name, for it implied frontier individualism, self-government, and local control. Even Stephen A. Douglas described his brainchild, popular sovereignty, as "the Jeffersonian plan for government in the territories."

As the South's leaders gradually retreated from the democratic idealism of the Jeffersonian tradition, the Democratic party lost a degree of its identity, and its spokesmen seemed opposed to the doctrines that many Americans typically defined as being Jeffersonian or liberal. In the 1850s the new Republican party easily incorporated the Jeffersonian commitment to human rights, antislavery, and agrarian democracy. The powerful rhetoric of free men and free soil composed an idealistic image for the new Republican party. And in the political upheaval that flowed logically from the compromises of 1850, the Republican platform corresponded to what most Americans imagined to be Jeffersonian and "in essentials," Merrill D. Peterson adds, "with what had in fact been Jeffersonian."

After the Civil War, Democratic leaders called for a return to Jeffersonian principles, but Jefferson's influence in the party remained limited until the 1880s and 1890s. Only in 1892, for example, did the party's platform openly reaffirm allegiance to the principles formulated by the third president. As for the New South of the postwar era, its dynamic leaders preached industry, business, and progress. By the 1880s such tendencies in the region stimulated the rise of a vocal group of Jeffersonian critics. The oratory of such men as Robert L. Dabney and Charles C. Jones conjured up the polemics of John Taylor of Caroline and reflected more clearly the influence of Thomas Jefferson than Jefferson Davis. These critics saw the growing cities of the South much as Jefferson and John Taylor had earlier described urban centers—"sores on the body politic."

By the 1890s some southern Jeffersonians had drifted toward the Populist party, and in that era of agrarian revolt they emphasized the radical side of the Jeffersonian tradition. Although men like George G. Vest of Missouri and John Sharp Williams of Mississippi remained within the Democratic party, Tom Watson's disillusionment led him to the Populist party where he worked to revive the agrarian alliance of earlier years. The Populist-Democratic fusion and the ensuing defeat of William Jennings Bryan in 1896 destroyed Watson's hopes and those of most agrarians in the South.

When Populists invoked Jefferson's philosophy in the 1890s, they harked back to the lost world of independent cultivators, doing so at a time when the South yearned to advertise its new, modern outlook. At the same time, agriculture had become more of a business and less of a way of life. Still, Populists evaded their critics by appealing to the body of native southern tradition and doctrine that dated back to the writings of the revolutionary period. Moreover, southerners recalled the ideas upon which their ancestors relied when they provided the leadership against Hamilton's Federalists and later against the Whigs. The Texas Populist "Cyclone" Davis campaigned with volumes of Jefferson's collected works tucked under his arm, and in response to questions responded: "We will now look through the volumes of Jefferson's works and see what Mr. Jefferson said on this matter." Professor Dodd is likely correct in his contention that Jefferson would have been a Populist in 1892.

With the Populist defeat the Jeffersonian tradition entered a period of quiescence, although Woodrow Wilson invoked his name and praised his philosophy in the years before World War I. By the 1920s the Jeffersonian tradition was of limited value in America; clearly its agrarianism was of little worth in the Jazz Age, and liberal reform found few successful advocates. Yet in the next decade, Franklin D. Roosevelt's Administration was keenly aware of its intellectual and political roots in the liberal tradition of Jefferson, and such measures as the Civilian Conservation Corps reflected the president's personal commitment to the land. Roosevelt, too, shared a Jeffersonian suspicion of the crowded atmosphere of large cities and feared their detrimental impact on people. As a result of the New Deal's response to the Great Depression, the Democratic party of Thomas Jefferson became the Democratic party of Franklin D. Roosevelt.

Jeffersonian ideals flourished in the 1930s, according to a newspaper columnist who declared, "Everyone has a kind word for him. Nearly everyone writes a book about him." Jeffersonian agrarianism enjoyed a special resurgence in some parts of the South, following publication of *I'll Take My Stand: The South and the Agrarian Tradition* (1930). The essays by the Twelve Southerners, or Nashville Agrarians, praised the agrarian way of life while damning the modern, industrial New South. The book stimulated a vigorous debate in southern intellectual circles, but this last agrarian revival ran its course before the end of the decade. Still, the movement testified to the tenacity and vitality of the Jeffersonian tradition. For southerners, Jefferson's writings served as a bulwark against unwanted change and as a defense for the southern way of life. If the Jeffersonian heritage could not exclude the forces of progress or defuse the power of an ever-expanding federal government, those concepts always offered a calm, self-sufficient alternative to the exigencies of modern life.

George M. Lubick
Northern Arizona University

Daniel J. Boorstin, *The Lost World of Thomas Jefferson* (1948); Merrill D. Peterson, *The Jefferson Image in the American Mind* (1960), ed., *Thomas Jefferson: A Profile* (1968); David M. Potter, in *Myth and Southern History*, ed. Patrick Gerster and Nicholas Cords (1974); Twelve Southerners, *I'll Take My Stand: The South and the Agrarian Tradition* (1930); Charles M. Wiltse, *The Jeffersonian Tradition in American Democracy* (1960); C. Vann Woodward, *Origins of the New South, 1877–1913* (1951).

Korean War

Historians have found few distinctively regional aspects to the Korean War. In fact, neither southern historians nor American military historians have even sought systematically to explore either the role the South played in the war or the role the war played in the South.

The economic effect of the Korean War was similar in the South and the rest of the nation. Inflation appeared in 1950, leading to rising prices, including the historic end of the nickel Coca-Cola. The position of the region's farmers did not improve, despite the rising demand for food; costs of production rose to offset rising farm prices. The federal government's freeze on wages and prices in January 1951 helped control inflation in the South, and increased prosperity and lowered unemployment marked the final two years of the war. Defense spending for the Cold War as well as the Korean War was especially important in promoting southern economic improvement in the early 1950s. As in World War II, southern bases were key mobilization points for American soldiers.

A few prominent southerners symbolized various aspects of southern attitudes toward the war. Georgian Dean Rusk was one of Secretary of State Dean Acheson's closest advisors; Senator Tom Connally of Texas, chairman of the Senate Foreign Relations Committee, was an unquestioning supporter of President Harry Truman's policies; Congressman L. Mendel Rivers of South Carolina endorsed Douglas MacArthur's request to use atomic weapons during the war against North Korea and China; Lieutenant General Walton H. Walker of Texas, Commander of the Eighth Army, was a high ranking military figure; Virginia Durr opposed the war and her husband, Clifford, lost his job with the Farmers Union after she signed a petition opposing American involvement. The Korean War was the first occasion testing Truman's policy, established by executive order in July 1948, of desegregating the military.

Southern public opinion generally supported the Korean War enthusiastically. Americans were convinced the conflict was a just one, caused at the height of the Cold War by communist aggression. When Herbert Hoover suggested in December 1950 a new isolationist policy and abandonment of Korea, Ralph McGill of the Atlanta *Constitution* wrote that this would be national suicide, and he seemed to reflect regional attitudes. Conservative southerners were uncomfortable with a national policy aimed not at total military victory, but limited war for strategic purposes.

Charles Reagan Wilson
University of Mississippi

Bernard C. Nalty, *Strength for the Fight: A History of Black Americans in the Military* (1986); John Edward Wiltz, in *The Korean War: A Twenty-five Year Perspective* (1977).

Manners

Manners are a formal code of proper behavior. The South has stressed etiquette and has attributed much significance to the form of verbal expression and behavior in a group. Stark Young wrote in *I'll Take My Stand* (1930) that "manners are the mask of decency that we employ at need, the currency of fair communication," and William Alexander Percy insisted in his memoir *Lanterns on the Levee* (1941) that "manners are essential and are essentially morals." Southerners have, in fact, traditionally equated manners—the appropriate, customary, or proper way of doing things—with morals, so that unmannerly behavior has been viewed as immoral behavior. Thus, in the South moral codes, laws, and manners have been intertwined, with the aim of curbing individual aggressiveness and maintaining social order through a combination of external community pressures and internalized individual motivation.

"He did everything correctly, but with the faintest smile, as though to say he knew what he was doing and could do it another way if necessary," wrote James McBride Dabbs in *The Southern Heritage* (1958) about his bachelor uncle who embodied the ideal of manners many southern mothers taught their children. "He was a balance of reserve and openness, of formality and informality, which the South aimed at but often failed to attain." Southerners such as Dabbs who have written about manners mention words such as polite, courteous, kind, gentle, hospitable, friendly yet dignified. Rigidity in following the rules is not prized as much as the flexibility and resiliency that enable the well mannered to handle any situation graciously. There are, to be sure, rules: one must respect one's parents ("Yes, sir," "No, ma'am"), honor obligations to kin, welcome neighbors, and protect the weak and helpless; a gentleman must open doors for a woman and stand when she enters a room; one must not dive into the food before grace is said and everyone served. In the colonial era, particularly, manners were of a prescriptive nature, defining for the upper classes the standards for behavior indicative of refinement, good breeding, and sophistication. Among the wealthy, manners served in general as parameters for social class relations.

The concern for manners goes far back in southern history. The ideal of the English country gentleman provided the basis for proper manners among the colonial planters. European, particularly English, books on manners were commonly found in plantation libraries: Richard Brathwaite's *The English Gentleman*, Harry Peacham's *The Compleat Gentleman*, Count Baldesar Castiglione's *The Book of the Courtier*, and the most influential of all for the southern elite—*The Whole Duty of Man* (usually attributed to Richard Allestree), one of the first books printed in Virginia and the popular source for guidelines on behavior until the mid-19th century. Estates with English names, such as Drayton, Berkeley Hundred, and Exeter Lodge, became famous centers of the best formal colonial manners. William Byrd II chronicled in his diary the etiquette of the people in that society, suggesting their power, the respect they received when displaying their manners, and their aspirations to noblesse oblige. A code of honor appeared that provided strict rules for proper conduct in all situations.

The frontier was a very different force that affected the development of manners among early southerners. Observers characterized plain folk on the frontier and in settled areas as generous, hospitable, and polite. Everyone also agreed their behavior was deplorably crude. Travelers from abroad saw little refinement or sophistication among them and were sometimes dismayed at southerners' disregard for the proper rules of behavior. The formal manners of the Virginia and Carolina Tidewater, to be sure, were transferred to the southwestern frontier. Andrew Jackson was a frontiersman, but in social circles he displayed the courteous manners expected of the planter he became. On the frontier, manners could help an ambitious person create a persona with a well-bred background. Manners among the nouveau planters were, nonetheless, simpler and less formal than among the Tidewater elite. The veneer came off easily on the frontier. Disagreements were often settled with an angrily drawn pistol instead of through the honorable code duello. W. J. Cash insisted, though, that an enduring and basically admirable ideal of manners developed among the antebellum frontier plain folk, an ideal that promoted, he wrote, "a kindly courtesy, a level-eyed pride, an easy quietness, a barely perceptible flourish of bearing."

Between 1830 and 1850 the southern cult of chivalry became a major expression of southern romanticism, and the cult had significance for manners. Southern whites believed they were descended from aristocratic English noblemen, from Cavaliers, who were the ultimate embodiment of proper manners. The key was in ritual. After a trip to Richmond in 1853, Frederick Law Olmsted noted that "more ceremony and form is sustained" among southerners than "well-bred people commonly use at the North." A regional fondness for the splendid gesture, theatrical behavior, and extravagant pageantry had appeared.

Women in the antebellum era were central to the southern code of manners. The cult of chivalry taught that the mythic lady was the essence of manners. A white woman's social role was highly restricted by "proper" conduct, and the men around her had to be on their best behavior as well. The myth of the lady was not unique to the South, but, as Anne Firor Scott stresses in *The Southern Lady* (1970), southern regional culture was distinctive in the intensity and tenacity of the ideal. Southern courtship and marriage had clear expectations of correct behavior stressing male aggressiveness and female coyness. This romanticized ideal of mannerly behavior between the sexes was reinforced in the late 19th and early 20th centuries by Victorian sentimentalism and Protestant moralism. Those attitudes are no longer predominant in the late 20th-century South, but the code of southern courtship manners retains vestiges from the past. Florence King's *Southern Ladies and Gentlemen* (1975) is a near-definitive account of southern sexual manners practiced by regional types such as the Self-Rejuvenating Virgin, Dear Old Thing, Good Old Boy, Bad Good Old Boy, and Gay Confederate. She explores such central southern concepts as "trashy" behavior, "passing the time of day," the "freeze" (a blood-curdling look of disapproval), the "pert plague" among women, and the "deliverance syndrome" among men.

Southern culture has much lore on the effort to teach manners to the young. Manners have been encouraged by schools and churches and sometimes by the legal systems. Folklore from the region's blacks and whites tries to link crude manners with unpleasant results. Singing while eating will bring bad luck, taking the last bit of bread on a plate means a young man will never find a wife, and eating too rapidly leads to marriage before one is ready. Such sayings are apparently intended to scare the young into respectability.

Accounts of teaching manners in the South frequently focus on meals. In *Black Boy* (1945) Richard Wright told of the preacher coming to Sunday dinner, finishing his soup early, and then eating piece after piece of fried chicken before young Wright could even finish his soup. He finally stood up and said, "that preacher's going to eat *all* the chicken!" His mother, he wrote, gave him "no dinner because of my bad manners." In *To Kill a Mockingbird* (1960) young Scout is reprimanded when she comments on her classmate Walter's habit of putting syrup on all his food. The young man had come to lunch, and Scout's father had made him feel at home until her breach of manners. Her father pours syrup on his own bread to put the guest at ease—another gesture of good manners. The black housekeeper Calpurnia lectures Scout for poor behavior. All of these examples suggest the crucial role of women, black and white, in nurturing southern manners. Sometimes manners are enforced with the harsh discipline of Calvinistic patriarchs, but more commonly women teach proper behavior.

An emphasis on manners reflects the South's stress on community. As Stark Young wrote in *I'll Take My Stand*, manners are only understood in regard to "a state of society that assumes a group welfare and point of view." Southerners have valued their individualism, but their regard for manners has been the counterbalance to individualism. In the large industrial cities of the North from the 19th century on, people have moved among strangers, creating little pressure for observing the niceties of behavior in a pressurized world. In contrast, in the South's characteristic smaller communities and rural areas one conducted business and daily living among people one saw all too frequently. "Manners are to be seen," wrote James McBride Dabbs, suggesting that manners are a public matter of image among a group of people well known to each other. The upper-class elite, in particular, set the tone for etiquette in society. "The aristocrat was to reveal," observed Dabbs, "to make public, what life could, and should, be."

Southern manners were not only a community binding force, an agreed upon code for groups to aspire to; they were also divisive, separating those with manners from those without. The Tidewater planter looked down on the manners of the backcountry folk. Virginians looked down on the manners of those in early North Carolina (William Byrd II referred to them as lazy, ignorant, and filthy). Southerners by the antebellum era looked down on northern manners. South Carolina Congressman Preston Brooks cane-whipped Massachusetts Senator Charles Sumner in 1854 over alleged poor manners, an insult to honor, contained in a Sumner speech. Such violence has often been ascribed to violations of the code of honor, and mannerly behavior has cloaked violent instincts. A southerner is courteous and friendly, goes an old saying, until he is mad enough to kill. Southerners ironically viewed manners and decorum as so vital to the maintenance of social order that defense of such codes warranted violence.

This double-edged emphasis on manners has been apparent in other ways, too. In many cases manners have been a veneer that masked social inequities while institutionalizing them. Manners have been seen as one aspect of upper-class ideology and power. The southern elite used manners to soften tendencies toward social class conflict. At public gatherings, wrote W. J. Cash of a typical plain farmer, "there would nearly always be a fine gentleman to lay a familiar hand on his shoulders, to inquire by name after the members of his family, maybe to buy him a drink." The result was to patronize the yeoman farmer, but in such a smooth way that he went home "not sullen and vindictive" at all over the planter's wealth and prestige. Manners were an aspect of a paternalistic style. The personal kindness and thoughtfulness of the landowner and later the millowner, moreover, bound whites together. Mannerly behavior between whites of different social groups helped cement Cash's "Proto-Dorian" bond.

A deeply rooted code of etiquette is found among black families in the South. Frederick Douglass suggested black etiquette derived from similar African codes and noted, "there is not to be found, among any people, a more rigid enforcement of the law of respect to elders, than they maintain. . . . There is no better material in the world for making a gentleman, than is furnished in the African."

Melville Herskovits in *The Myth of the Negro Past* (1942) argued that "outstanding among the intangible values of Negro life in the United States is strict adherence to codes of polite behavior." Newbell Niles Puckett in *Folk Beliefs of the Southern Negro* (1926) also stressed the importance of etiquette in black life, which links "unpleasant results with uncouth manners in an attempt to frighten the young into a quicker acquisition of American good-breeding." Herskovits noted a number of practices of etiquette that have important African roots. Respect for elders among southern blacks can be also found among Africans who feel that "old folks" are "almost ghosts." An ancestral cult thus developed with the understanding that ancestors have the power to help or harm their descendants.

Herskovits also observed African etiquette in "the matter of turning the head when laughing (sometimes with the hand over the mouth), or in speaking to elders or other respected persons of averting the eyes and perhaps the face." In the *Etiquette of Race Relations* (1939) Bertram Doyle showed how such politeness was adopted in dealing with whites. Gestures of respect reserved in Africa for elders were a defense against white aggression in the South. Black writers such as Ralph Ellison have preserved this racial etiquette in their fiction. Ellison's protagonist in *The Invisible Man* remembers his father's advice: to survive in the white man's world, you must "yes'em to death." Politeness is the ultimate weapon the old man bestowed on his son.

Black etiquette is thus a double-edged tradition. Its African roots, like those of whites in Europe, were formed in Old World cultures to regulate relationships within families and communities. Faced with slavery and later with segregation, southern blacks adopted etiquette as a means of survival. They developed a racial etiquette as a foil to the racism of southern whites.

Racial etiquette also revealed a southern stress on personal relationships. Post–Civil War southerners developed a complex and elaborate ritual to govern interracial behavior. William Alexander Percy argued that only their good manners enabled the two different races to live together in an orderly, single way of life: "The Southern Negro has the most beautiful manners in the world, and the Southern white, learning from him, I suspect, is a close second." But, in addition to this, a distinctive caste etiquette worked to maintain racial separation. The etiquette required whites to behave in certain ways toward blacks, ways seemingly at odds with their normal code of good manners. One should use first names, not "Mr." or "Mrs.," in addressing blacks; one did not shake hands with a black person or tip a hat. Blacks should address all whites with respect, should not crowd whites on sidewalks, should enter the home of a white person through the back door, should sit at the back of a bus, and should stand or wait at the end of a line for service until all whites had been served. Segregation laws enforced some racial behavior, but "manners" were enforced by individual and collective white intimidation of blacks. "Uppity" blacks were a constant worry of southern whites. A breech of racial manners by a black man could lead to a tongue-lashing, humiliation, and sometimes violence. When black teenager Emmett Till violated ultimate sexual-racial manners in Mississippi in the 1950s by whistling at a white woman, he was lynched.

Racial manners were justified by the "best" people as a way to maintain social distance between the races and thus prevent overt aggression. Interracial etiquette did at times ease tensions between blacks and whites. Kindly manners between persons who happened to be of different races helped to soften the rigidity of the segregated society. Many southern whites treated blacks with respect and were concerned not to hurt their feelings. Kindly manners did not, however, ease the injustice of that society, but rather nurtured a ritualized, daily sense of inferiority among blacks. Outsiders were expected to follow southern racial manners, and there are legendary stories of northerners moving south and adopting them more enthusiastically than southern whites. The requirements of racial manners in the South meant that blacks lived in an atmosphere of daily intimidation and frequent anxiety. Blacks were polite because they were dealing with a life-and-death matter—an ultimate expression of southern regard for manners.

With the end of racial segregation laws in the 1960s an accompanying change in southern racial manners has taken place. The decline in the formal code of polite and honorable behavior that both black and white southerners have proclaimed seems to be a by-product of long-term social changes in the region. W. J. Cash saw a decline in southern manners dating back to the New South era of the late 19th century. A grafting of northern back-slapping heartiness onto southern geniality, he wrote, created "the Rotary ideal," which represented "an unfortunate decline in the dignity of the southern manner." The Agrarians of *I'll Take My Stand* saw threats to the survival of formal manners in any industrial, business-oriented society. Robert B. Heilman, in an essay entitled "The Southern Temper," warned of a decline of manners in the contemporary South because southern whites had "popularized and made the object of public self-congratulation" their tradition of manners. "Promotional facsimilies" of manners, involving the exploitation of hoop-skirted ladies dressed for tourists, marks, he said, a decline in the real thing.

Sociologist John Shelton Reed's studies of contemporary North-South attitudes have shown that both northerners and southerners continue to see southerners as more mannerly than persons from north of the Mason-Dixon line. Respondents to a North Carolina opinion poll in the early 1970s described southerners by using words such as *considerate*, *polite*, *friendly*, *courteous*, *hospitable*, *genteel*, *cordial*, and *nice*—terms synonymous with the manners that southern mothers, black and white, have tried to teach their children.

Southerners have not written any widely known etiquette books despite the continued fascination of the gentry and the upwardly mobile with manners. One theory for this is that southerners prefer to learn proper behavior from mothers rather than from books. Southerners are rarely mentioned in etiquette books nowadays. Judith Martin, better known as Miss Manners, has chastized southerners for wearing white shoes after Easter rather than at the proper time, after Memorial Day. The often-hot southern spring is perhaps responsible for this abiding regional faux pas, but her criticism is a reminder that northerners, not those from the South, have traditionally set national standards of manners.

The southern fascination with manners, though, has been expressed in literature. Peter Taylor's short stories, Reynolds Price's and Hamilton Basso's novels, and all of Eudora Welty's works are among the most subtle explorations of southern manners. Three of Welty's best-known works show how the southerner's sense of ritual led to an appreciation of form: *Delta Wedding* explores a happy ceremony of marriage, *Optimist's Daughter* a sad one of death, and *Losing Battles* a joyous yet melancholy family reunion. Southern concern with family and kin, the proper clothing, food, courtesy in daily living, talking and visiting—all are expressed in the region's best writing.

See also BLACK LIFE: Race Relations; LANGUAGE: Conversation; MYTHIC SOUTH: Racial Attitudes; / Hospitality; WOMEN'S LIFE: Child-raising Customs

Charles Reagan Wilson
University of Mississippi

W. J. Cash, *The Mind of the South* (1941); Thomas D. Clark, *The Rampaging Frontier: Manners and Humors of Pioneer Days in the Southern Middle West* (1939), *Travelers in the New South*, 2 vols. (1962), *Travelers in the Old South*, 2 vols. (1959); James McBride Dabbs, *The Southern Heritage* (1958), *Who Speaks for the South?* (1964); John Dollard, *Caste and Class in a Southern Town* (1937); Bertram Doyle, *The Etiquette of Race Relations in the South* (1937); Clement Eaton, *The Mind of the Old South* (1967); Melville Herskovits, *The Myth of the Negro Past* (1941); Florence King, *Southern Ladies and Gentlemen* (1975); Rollin G. Osterweis, *Romanticism and Nationalism in the Old South* (1949); Newbell Niles Puckett, *Folk Beliefs of the Southern Negro* (1926; reprint ed. 1969); John Shelton Reed, *The Enduring South: Subcultural Persistence in Mass Society* (1972), *Southerners: The Social Psychology of Sectionalism* (1983); Anne Firor Scott, *The Southern Lady: From Pedestal to Politics, 1830–1930* (1970); Bertram Wyatt-Brown, *Southern Honor: Ethics and Behavior in the Old South* (1982).

Maritime Tradition

American experience began on the water and steadily moved inland. The various peoples who discovered, explored, and settled this country depended on bodies and arteries of water. Of necessity they were conscious of matters marine and riverine. The writings of the colonists who settled along the Atlantic Seaboard, the Gulf region, and even the interior abound with references to the importance of the waters and their existence. This was equally true of both southerners and those who lived north of the Chesapeake Bay. Yet few historians, including southerners, recognize that the southern states have a maritime heritage. For example, in 1954 Clement Eaton characterized southerners as "agricultural and unskilled in the ways of ships."

This was certainly not true in the colonial period. In 1769 exports from the southern colonies to Great Britain were four times more valuable than the products sent there from the colonies above Chesapeake Bay. In the English colonies, Norfolk and Savannah, along with a number of small ports such as Edenton and New Bern, N.C., and Georgetown, S.C., were established by the crown as official ports. Charles Town (Charleston) was the most important port of the colonial South. In 1769 two hundred vessels carried Charleston's exports to market in Europe, the West Indies, and the other American colonies. In that year more ships entered Virginia and Maryland ports than those of all other colonies combined.

The majority of ships engaged in maritime trade with the southern colonies were built outside of those provinces. Nevertheless, a substantial shipbuilding industry did develop in the South. This was inevitable considering the section's dependence upon water transportation as well as the availability of abundant timber. Between 1740 and 1773 there were at least five shipyards in South Carolina that built a total of 24 square-rigged ships as well as a large number of sloops and schooners. During the decades preceding the Revolutionary War, nearly a hundred ships engaged in the coastal and foreign trade were built in North Carolina.

Fishing was primarily for subsistence in the colonial period. Salted fish in barrels were sold to ships trading with the southern colonies, and occasional cargoes were carried to the West Indies. Weirs and fishpots were employed, and large seines were introduced in the 1760s. Fishing was not done in the ocean but rather in the rivers and sounds.

The American Revolutionary War was as much a maritime as a land war in the southern colonies. The British blockade extended as far south as Savannah, and privateers from Charleston, New Bern, Norfolk, and other ports along the South Atlantic Seaboard ranged as far as the West Indies seeking prizes. Lord Cornwallis's surrender at Yorktown in October 1781 was at least partially a result of naval action in the Chesapeake Bay and the subsequent siege of British forces on land and water.

The War of 1812 was primarily a maritime war in the southern states, occasioned by blockade and privateering, and concluded by the British combined attack against New Orleans in January 1815.

The early decades of the 19th century witnessed the expansion of the United States to include the Gulf region from Florida to Texas. The rapid growth of sugar and cotton production along with exports from the Midwest made New Orleans by 1820 the second most important port in the country. New Orleans had been founded as a port by the French early in the 18th century, but it was the development of steam transportation on the Mississippi River and its tributaries that crystalized the port's rapid rise in importance. Mobile, another Gulf port with French origins, also developed rapidly and by the Civil War was the third largest exporting city in the country.

The first half of the 19th century saw the appearance of dozens of small ports throughout the region. The expansion of steam navigation on inland waters along the seaboard and the interior states was a major factor in the development of the southern economy. Steamboats became feeders, carrying cargoes to coastal ports and later to rail centers.

Shipbuilding expanded as shipping expanded. In the United States as a whole, over 8,000 vessels of wood or iron were constructed between 1849 and 1858. Of this number, southern shipyards built approximately 1,600. One writer in 1850 estimated that the South, including Maryland and Kentucky, had 145 shipyards.

In the middle of the 19th century, commercial fishing began to emerge as an industry of importance in the South. This was partly a result of improved transportation, which enabled fish and shellfish to reach inland markets, and partly the result of seasonal trips to southern waters by New England fishermen. In the 1830s Connecticut fishermen were using gill nets off Savannah, and smack fishermen were reaching as far south as Florida. By 1860 North Carolina had 33 commercial fisheries, and its herring fishery concentrated in the Albemarle Sound area was among the largest in the world.

The Civil War was devastating to southern fishermen, as it was to others engaged in maritime activities. The Union blockade, although never totally effective, was tight enough severely to limit maritime trade. Union combined operations gradually gained control of the navigable waters in the Confederacy. Maritime activities in the southern states, however, achieved some success.

Several hundred vessels ran the blockade, bringing into southern ports badly needed supplies and other goods. An impressive number of warships, including more than 20 armored vessels, were built for the Confederate navy. Many of these ships contributed to the defense of southern ports, including Mobile, Savannah, Charleston, and Richmond.

The postwar years saw a revival and expansion of maritime activities in the South. Shipping along the coast, linking the Gulf and South Atlantic ports with the Northeast, revived but with some important changes. Wooden schooners continued to carry certain low-grade cargoes, particularly lumber and naval stores. With the expansion of railroads into coastal areas, steamship traffic declined. Local river steamers prospered, however, carrying passengers and cargo to railheads.

While the construction of wooden vessels declined nationwide after the Civil War, it gradually revived in the South late in the 19th century. Nearly 3,000 wooden vessels were built in the southern states in the period between 1865 and 1900. Various factors contributed to this: local needs, the development of a wooden barge–building industry for inland waterways, and the rapidly expanding commercial fishing industry in the South.

Improved rail transportation resulted in the introduction of the iced-fish trade in the mid-1870s. First introduced in North Carolina, it spread farther south in the 1880s. By 1880 Charleston had an important offshore fishery with the catch of blackfish, flounder, and red snapper being shipped to northern markets. Of the 17 schooners and 49 sloops built in Charleston from 1870 to 1880, two-thirds were engaged in commercial fishing. In the 1880s the oyster industry became important in the North Carolina sounds, but it was not until the 20th century that shrimp would become commercially important.

Although the fishing industry would continue to expand in the 20th century, only in the shellfisheries (oyster, crab, shrimp), particularly shrimp, did the southern states gain a position of prominence. Louisiana would take the lead in shrimp harvesting, followed by Texas and Florida. The introduction of the outboard motor and the otter trawl early in the century, the development of refrigeration in the 1920s, and the continued improvement in transportation in the coastal areas were the major factors that stimulated the shrimp industry. By the middle of the century, southern shrimping had overtaken in value all rival shrimp or shellfish catches from Maine to Alaska. In 1956 the national shrimp catch (more than 90% from southern waters) paid fishermen $70 million, followed in order by salmon ($46 million), tuna ($43 million), and oysters ($30 million). In 1950, the New England states had approximately 10,500 fishermen while the southern states claimed more than 23,000. Today nearly 38 percent of the total poundage of fish and shellfish caught in the United States comes from the southern states.

The shipping industry in the southern states went through a transition in the latter years of the 19th and early years of the 20th centuries. Developments in road and rail transportation resulted in a significant decline in river and coastwise traffic. This in turn gradually ended the maritime commerce for most of the small southern ports. Only the ports with deep-water harbors capable of holding the large ocean-going vessels survived and actually expanded. New Orleans continued to lead southern ports and today is the third largest port in the United States. The Hampton Roads area, comprising the ports of Norfolk, Newport News, and Hampton, Va., grew into the largest exporter (in volume) in the country and today handles 90 percent of coal exports. Charleston is 13th, and Houston and Galveston, Tex., Wilmington, N.C., Savannah, Ga., and Tampa and Jacksonville, Fla., also rank among the country's important ports.

Shipbuilding has also gone through a transition. The decline in inland and coastwise shipping resulted in a parallel decline in shipbuilding in the southern states. At the turn of the century only a few southern yards had built iron or steel ships; the overwhelming majority concentrated on wooden ship construction. Only Newport News Shipyard in Virginia was building metal vessels on a large scale. World War I witnessed a revival of the shipbuilding industry in the South with the construction of steel, concrete, and wooden vessels. This boom ended shortly after the war was over. The pattern recurred in World War II. Today a large number of shipyards in addition to Newport News build steel merchant and naval vessels in the South.

Wooden vessels continued to be built in southern yards, but by the second decade of the 20th century nearly all of them were small fishing vessels. In the last two decades, steel and fiberglass fishing vessels have challenged the wooden boat-building industry.

Finally, the U.S. Navy has long been a major presence in the coastal South. Southern naval bases have been the training and embarkation points for soldiers and sailors in overseas conflicts since the Spanish-American War. Pensacola's Naval Air Station has been the home of the navy's air training program since 1914. Bases such as the Norfolk Navy Yard and the Charleston Navy Yard are major economic forces in their communities and beyond. Charleston, for example, has a Polaris submarine base, a Sixth Fleet supply and ammunition depot, and a mine warfare program, as well as nearby Air Force and Marine facilities. Maritime activities of many sorts, then, continue to be important in the region's economic life.

See also ENVIRONMENT: / Chesapeake Bay; Shellfish; RECREATION: Fishing; URBANIZATION: / Charleston; Houston; Mobile; New Orleans; Savannah; Tampa

William N. Still, Jr.
East Carolina University

Charles C. Crittenden, *The Commerce of North Carolina, 1763–1789* (1936); Rusty Fleetwood, *Tidecraft: The Boats of Lower South Carolina and Georgia* (1982); Joseph A. Goldenberg, *Shipbuilding in Colonial America* (1976); Herbert Ryals Padgett, "The Marine Shellfisheries of Louisiana" (Ph.D. dissertation, Louisiana State University, 1960); William N. Still, Jr., *Confederate Shipbuilding* (1969); George Rogers Taylor, *The Transportation Revolution, 1815–1860* (1951); Emory Thomas, *Georgia Historical Quarterly* (Summer 1983).

Mexican War

The War with Mexico (1846–48) was a significant episode in the cultural life of mid-19th-century America. Widely perceived as the country's first foreign war, the conflict embodied many elements of romanticism. Fought in a strange and exotic land against an unfamiliar foe at a time when Americans were reaching out to distant places, the war provided a window on a civilization and a people that differed markedly from their own. At the same time, it assumed all the rhetorical trappings of a romantic nationalism that preached a unique mission and destiny for the Republic. The war was viewed as an opportunity to recall Americans to the idealism of the American Revolution at a time when the revolutionary generation was passing from the scene and to advance the republican form of government the Revolution had sired. Stung by the taunts of Europeans against their "experiment in democracy," many Americans saw the war as a test of republican vitality. In fighting against a country dominated by military leadership, Americans regarded the war as a measure of the ability of a republic, lacking a strong professional military force and relying on untrained citizen-soldiers, to fight a successful foreign conflict. The Mexican War was an exercise in national self-identity, as Americans looked more closely at themselves and their place in the sweep of history.

Although the imaginative response of the South to the war did not differ significantly from the national norm in its general manifestation, southerners did perhaps react to the war with greater homogeneity and less equivocation. The tension between republican simplicity and the rise of what was called the "commercial spirit," with which northerners were grappling, was largely absent in the agrarian South. The elements of romanticism, fostered by a concern for the past, a reverence for heroes, and an allegiance to a code that emphasized honor, had a stronger grip on the southern than on the northern mind. Opposition to the war, seated in the North in such reform activities as the abolition and peace movements as well as in certain constituencies of the Whig party, was less evident in the southern states. And finally, the militant tradition, so widely identified with the South, made southerners more receptive to the romance of the war. There is, however, danger in exaggerating the difference between the South and the rest of the United States, for Americans in all parts of the nation shared essentially the same imaginative outlook.

When President James K. Polk issued his first call for volunteers following the outbreak of the war, southerners were among the first to enlist. In some states, like Tennessee, the numbers so far exceeded the quotas levied by the president that large numbers had to be turned away. Many of the volunteers were motivated by a spirit of adventure and a curiosity to visit a land they had only read about in storybooks. Mexico, with its ruins of a destroyed civilization and its stirring tales of the heroic struggle between Montezuma and Cortez, held the aura of romance for which so many Americans yearned. To a generation nurtured on Sir Walter Scott, the Mexican War seemed to be a step into a romantic past. Volunteers were likened to young knights, and there was much talk of chivalry. Many were the soldiers who fancied themselves marching off to meet the foe on some medieval field. The mountains and villages of Mexico and the Mexican soldiers themselves, especially the colorful, armor-clad mounted lancers, seemed straight out of the books. According to a writer in the *Southern Quarterly Review*, an "age of chivalry" had returned, every soldier fighting "as if he were striving to pluck from the 'dangerous precipice,' the glittering flowers of immortality."

Because of its geographic proximity to the Mexican battlefields, the South played an important part in the logistics of the war. New Orleans became the principal supply depot and embarkation point for the army in Mexico. Volunteers from the western states traveled down the Ohio and Mississippi rivers to a staging area on the site of Jackson's triumph over the British south of the city. New Orleans newspapers dispatched the first war correspondents to the scenes of action; their reports, first printed in the New Orleans press, were speeded to newspapers throughout the country. The first perceptions of the conflict to be circulated were those of southern newspapermen. When the volunteers returned to the United States, they sailed to New Orleans (and to a lesser extent, Mobile), where they were accorded their first triumphant homecoming celebrations. Southern orators, poets, and politicians vied with one another in their colorful rhetoric as they welcomed the returning heroes. The veterans were compared with the "sainted fathers of our land," carrying on the analogy between the Mexican War and the American Revolution that was so large a part of the imaginative response. Lighting anew the "fires of freedom," they had unfurled the "standard of the stars above those lofty palaces where once floated the golden gonfalon of Cortez." Jefferson Davis's Mississippi Rifles, fresh from their triumph on the field at Buena Vista, were received with a wild enthusiasm; their feats, it was said, would live on in the "enduring records" of the Republic. Future Civil War heroes such as Davis and Robert E. Lee first made their military reputations in Mexico.

The war penetrated the American (and hence, the southern) imagination in many different ways, in literature, poetry, art, music, and drama. Soldiers kept diaries and journals and published accounts of their campaigns soon after their return home. Historians began writing histories of the war almost as soon as the war began. New Orleans newspaperman Thomas Bangs Thorpe, with a reputation already established as a writer of southwestern humor, not only followed the army as a correspondent but wrote the first accounts of the campaigns on the Rio Grande and against Monterrey. Albert Pike, an Arkansas volunteer, wrote a poetic description of the Battle of Buena Vista on the field before the guns had hardly cooled, and his work was widely reprinted throughout the country. In South Carolina, Marcus Claudius Marcellus Hammond, younger brother of the prominent planter-politician, penned the first complete analysis of the war's military operations, serialized in the *Southern Quarterly Review.*

In a class by himself was William C. Falkner, of Ripley, Miss., great-grandfather of the 20th-century novelist, who was turned back at the first call for volunteers. He later served in Mississippi's Second Regiment but to his disappointment was too late to take part in any of the fighting. Nonetheless, Falkner commemorated his service in a 493-stanza, 4,000-line poem, *The Siege of Monterrey*, in which he portrayed the war's leaders as Homeric heroes. Undaunted by the failure of his poem, Falkner turned to fiction in *The Spanish Heroine: A Tale of War and Love*, a stock romance dealing in part with the battle of Buena Vista.

The South's greatest antebellum literary figure, William Gilmore Simms of South Carolina, was among those American writers who helped create the mood in which the war was viewed. From his early poem *The Vision of Cortes* (1829) to his biography of the Chevalier Bayard, published during the war, Simms wove a romantic net that captured the southern responses to the conflict. His work on Bayard held up to the wartime generation the ideal of a soldier in whom heroic valor was blended with the gentle virtues of knightly honor and chivalry. When South Carolina's Palmetto Regiment returned home after winning distinction in the battles around Mexico City, Simms celebrated the event with a collection of verses, *Lays of the Palmetto: A Tribute to the South Carolina Regiment, in the War with Mexico*, the "outpourings of a full heart, exulting in the valor and worth, and lamenting the misfortunes and losses, of the gallant regiment."

The Mexican War was marked by bitter conflict between North and South over the explosive question of the expansion of slavery into the western territories. The clash of northern and southern interests seemed to polarize popular sentiment. At the same time, however, there were those in the South who perceived the war as a force for national unity, symbolized by the volunteers from both North and South who marched, camped, and fought side by side. It was symbolic, for example, that a New York Regiment and South Carolina's Palmetto Regiment fought together in the Valley of Mexico in a brigade commanded by an Illinoisan.

Southerners (and northerners) saw something in the war that transcended sectional conflict. It was put into words by President James K. Polk, North Carolina born and Tennessee reared. The war gave meaning to the American Republic. "Who can calculate the value of our glorious Union?" Polk asked. "It is a model and example of free government to all the world, and is the star of hope and haven of rest to the oppressed of every clime." The war, in the imaginations of countless Americans, had demonstrated the strength of the Republic and had legitimized its mission. "We may congratulate ourselves," said Polk, "that we are the most favored people on the face of the earth."

See also MYTHIC SOUTH: Militant South; Romanticism

Robert W. Johannsen
University of Illinois

Marcus Cunliffe, *Soldiers and Civilians: The Martial Spirit in America, 1775–1865* (1973); Clement Eaton, *The Mind of the Old South* (rev. ed., 1967); Robert W. Johannsen, *To the Halls of the Montezumas: The Mexican War in the American Imagination* (1985); Ernest M. Lander, Jr., *Reluctant Imperialists: Calhoun, the South Carolinians, and the Mexican War* (1980); Rollin G. Osterweis, *Romanticism and Nationalism in the Old South* (1949); Fred Somkin, *Unquiet Eagle: Memory and Desire in the Idea of American Freedom, 1815–1860* (1967); Ronnie C. Tyler, *The Mexican War: A Lithographic Record* (1973).

Military Bases

Observers of the southern scene have long remarked upon Dixie's distinctively martial spirit. One highly visible evidence of this is the presence of so many military, naval, and air installations in the South. They range in time from the Castillo de San Marcos in the South's oldest city, St. Augustine, to the futuristic George C. Marshall Space Flight Center in Huntsville, Ala. They range in size from Williamsburg's restored Powder Magazine, which supplied Virginia Frontier Rangers, to the 465,000 acres of sprawling Eglin Air Force Base in Florida, where both the Tokyo raiders of 1942 and the Son Tay raiders of 1970 secretly trained. They range in climate and terrain from the green live oaks and manicured lawns of Fort Myer in humid Tidewater Virginia to the sunbaked parade-ground plaza of Fort Bliss in the desert of El Paso, Tex.

During the colonial wars three European powers—Spain, France, and England—established forts in the South. Spanish soldiers and monks were probing northwards from Spanish Florida, cavaliers and *voyageurs* established French Louisiana on the Gulf Coast and were moving up the Alabama River, while English traders and trappers were pressing inland from Charles Towne in Carolina down around the tag end of the Appalachians. There were military posts at Saint Elena, on the site of today's Parris Island Marine Corps Base; at Fort Frederica, near the present Glynco Naval Air Station near Brunswick, Ga.; and at Fort Maurepas on Biloxi Bay, close to the modern Keesler Air Force Base. Within 80 miles of the site of Montgomery, later to be the Cradle of the Confederacy, were the short-lived Spanish Fort Apalachicola on the Chattahoochee, the French Fort Toulouse commanding the Alabama, and the British post at Okfuski on the Tallapoosa. The key to the strategy of all the contenders was control of southern coasts and rivers.

The British eventually won the prize of North American hegemony, only to be displaced in turn by their American colonial cousins in the War for Independence, the outcome of which was finally decided at the fortifications around Yorktown, Va. Then the infant United States had to fortify its seaboard against foreign invasion and to garrison inland posts against the perceived threats posed by American Indians, the British still in Canada, and the Spanish still in the Floridas. One southern stronghold gave us our national anthem—Fort McHenry in Baltimore Harbor during the War of 1812. Defense of two other forts created rallying cries for war—the Alamo in

1836 in the Texas War for Independence and Fort Sumter in 1861, site of the opening battle of the Civil War.

As the United States became a world power in the 20th century, climate influenced the choice of the South for military installations. To raise mass armies to fight abroad in two world wars, America needed good weather to train its forces, especially its new air arm. In World War I, 13 out of the total of 16 National Guard cantonments were in the South, as were 6 of the 15 national army camps. There arose camps (later forts) Lee, Gordon, and Benning, not to mention the inappropriately named camps McClellan and Sheridan in Alabama, while aviation cadets learned to fly at Langley, Carlstrom, Brooks, and Kelly fields.

Surviving military posts represent a history of military architecture. There are the wooden stockades from the colonial wars, restored at James Towne and Fort Toulouse. Brick coastal defense forts built after the British seaboard invasions during the War of 1812 are strung around the southeastern littoral. Among these are Fortress Monroe, Va., where Confederate President Jefferson Davis was later held by Union authorities, and Fort Massachusetts on Ship Island in Mississippi Sound, site of "Beast" Butler's advance in occupying New Orleans. Rifled artillery rendered all these masonry forts obsolete before they were finished. Some of these forts were overlaid with the low-level concrete-and-steel coast artillery batteries of the Spanish-American War period, batteries that never fired a shot in anger, much like those twin forts Washington and Hunt guarding the Potomac River approach to Washington, D.C., and forts Morgan and Gaines protecting Mobile Bay, past which, earlier in 1864, Admiral Farragut had damned the torpedoes and ordered full speed ahead.

After World War I some of the sprawling temporary cantonments were kept. Tar-paper and fiberboard huts were replaced by brick, stucco, and tile barracks, many of Spanish-inspired architecture, at such bases as Quantico, Pensacola, Maxwell, and Randolph fields, and forts Knox and Sam Houston. Then during World War II they were swamped with inducted men and women. "Tent cities" mushroomed alongside well-groomed peacetime garrisons. New temporary installations arose, only to be activated again for the Korean War, made permanent in the Cold War, and used again to train men for the Vietnam War. The first special warfare groups to go to Vietnam in 1961 were the army's Green Berets from Fort Bragg, the navy's SEAL Teams from Little Creek, Va., and the Air Commandos from Hurlburt Field, Fla.

Local citizens were both attracted to and repulsed by military bases. On the one hand, they appreciated the dollars the bases brought to local economies, not just as extra monies during wartime booms but as cushions against depressions and recessions. On the other hand, the honky-tonk atmosphere surrounding many bases repelled local citizens—never mind that local businessmen often foisted land "on the wrong side of town" on the services. One recalls Jacksonville, N.C., in 1944. Southern townspeople often disliked northern servicemen, whom they viewed as loud-talking Yankees with brusque manners; some northern servicemen felt a reciprocal dislike. Nevertheless, many non-southerners fell in love with the South, met and married southern women, and stayed. Many non-southern servicemen who experienced the discomforts of preparing for war at camps Lejeune, Blanding, Shelby, or Polk were glad to get home to Waukegan or Walla Walla. If the servicemen were black, and especially if they were from the North, assignment to a post in the still rigidly segregated South was painful. There was racial trouble, for instance, at Camp Van Dorn, Miss. At Tuskegee Army Air Field, however, black men proved they could fly and became combat pilots over Europe in the thrice-decorated 99th Fighter Squadron.

Military bases are the centers for a distinctive sense of community among active and former service personnel. Today, retired military officers and noncommissioned officers congregate in Norfolk, Charleston, Southern Pines, Montgomery, and San Antonio. Military amenities abound because such senior southern congressmen as Georgia's Carl Vinson, South Carolina's L. Mendel Rivers, and Mississippi's John Stennis have so packed military installations into their districts that they have been accused of sinking their states under the weight.

The military tradition continues to attract southerners. Sociologist Morris Janowitz found in 1950 and 1971 that officers with southern affiliations of birth, schooling, or marriage continued to be represented disproportionately in America's military. During the Vietnam War, when there was a national backlash against the military, ROTC continued to thrive on southern college campuses, and the Virginia Military Institute and South Carolina's Citadel maintained their traditions of military service. Currently, the 101st Airborne Division easily meets its recruiting quotas in the area around its Kentucky home, Alabama's National Guard is the largest in the nation, and southern small-town armories and American Legion posts remain social clubs for good old boys.

See also EDUCATION: Military Schools; INDUSTRY: Military and Economy; MYTHIC SOUTH: Fighting South

John Hawkins Napier III
Montgomery, Alabama

Army-Navy-Air Force Times Magazine (28 June 1978); Irvin Hass, *Citadels, Ramparts and Stockades: America's Historic Forts* (1979); Morris Janowitz, *The Professional Soldier* (1960, 1971); Theo Lippmann, Jr., Baltimore *Sun* (20 April 1969); David McFarland, *Montgomery Advertiser and Alabama Journal* (20 June 1982); John Hawkins Napier III, *Alabama Review* (October 1980); Duncan Spencer, Washington *Star-News* (1 May 1974).

Military Tradition

For a century and a half commentators have written about the bellicosity and martial spirit of the southerner. Other observers have analyzed Dixie's military proclivities to determine the reasons for their enduring tenacity.

More recently, some writers have sought to deny the existence of a peculiarly southern military tradition.

Back in 1835 Alexis de Tocqueville reported that the white southerner was "passionately fond of hunting and war." During World War II D. W. Brogan, in explaining to his fellow Britishers their wartime American Allies, stated that "in the South, the heroes were nearly all soldiers." In 1943 Alabama editor John Temple Graves II devoted a book to *The Fighting South*. Later the distinguished black historian John Hope Franklin examined the antebellum South and saw there a distinctive military spirit, as did fellow historian Avery O. Craven and political scientist Samuel P. Huntington.

However, the British historian Marcus Cunliffe has denied that before the Civil War the South was any more martial than was the North. He held that Dixie's martial prowess was a post-Appomattox myth fostered for the benefit of northerners to rationalize why it took them four bloody years to win the Civil War, despite the overwhelming odds in their favor, and as solace to southerners for their crushing defeat. The South's earlier enthusiasm for fighting the War of 1812 and the Mexican War, in contrast to northern tepidity and even civil disobedience in both conflicts, has been explained away as a drive to extend chattel slavery into new lands. Yet the South *did* rally behind the national war effort in 1812 and 1846 and went down fighting to the last in 1865.

Some writers think that the South's enthusiasm for the military ethos was even more marked after Appomattox than before Fort Sumter, and much evidence supports this idea. Military schools and colleges continued to attract public support and students. After Reconstruction volunteer military companies proliferated in the South. For instance, in 1885 Montgomery, with a population of less than 25,000, had five military companies, and later a black unit appeared. W. J. Cash noted in *The Mind of the South* (1941) that in 1898 young southerners rushed to don *blue* uniforms for the Spanish-American War. They had also been drawn back to West Point and Annapolis, so that by 1910, 93 percent of U.S. Army general officers had southern affiliations—by birth, family, residence, schooling, or marriage. In World War I two of the three top commanders in the American Expeditionary Force (AEF) in France were General John J. Pershing from the border state of Missouri and Lieutenant General Robert E. Lee Bullard from Alabama. All four commanders of the first outfit to fight on the Western Front, the 1st Division ("The Big Red One"), were southerners.

Before Pearl Harbor, Texans bragged that the federal government introduced the draft to keep them from filling up the ranks of the armed forces. Professor Brogan explained that southerners early favored American intervention on the Allied side in World War II more than other citizens because from experience they "knew that war could settle a lot." When the Korean War broke out, 46 percent of the American military elite still had southern affiliations, although the South's population was then only 27 percent of the country's total. When the U.S. armed forces intervened actively in Vietnam the top army and air force commanders were southerners, and later antiwar activism was almost nonexistent on the campuses of Dixie.

More recently, indications are that southern overrepresentation in the officer corps may have ended, perhaps because of declining southern distinctiveness along with increasing urbanization and affluence. Other factors may include changes in the military profession itself, with the military manager nearly replacing the heroic warrior, and a lingering racist perception that the services are filling up with blacks. The democratization of the career military force has resulted in a decline in participation by the southern upper and upper-middle classes, following the pattern set earlier by their northern peers.

Various explanations have been offered for the traditional military bent of the white southerner. One was southern upper-class affinity for the ideal of the English country gentleman, with its concept of *noblesse oblige* and the pattern of the oldest son's farming and the others' choosing the church, the law, and the army. More recently F. N. Boney has denied the reality of this ideal and asserted that the plain folk, the "rednecks," were the uniquely belligerent warriors of the South. However, he also denies the reality of a distinctive planter elite, holding that most of them were "at heart rednecks on the make." Grady McWhiney and Forrest McDonald claim, despite the demographic evidence to the contrary, that southerners were of Celtic descent and more ferocious than northerners who, they argue, were all "Anglo-Saxon."

Contradictory explanations would have it that Johnny Reb was particularly amenable to hierarchy and discipline coming as he did from a deferential society, or on

Texan Audie Murphy, World War II battlefield hero and movie star, a modern embodiment of the military tradition

the contrary that he was an unregenerate individualist standing up for his rights. A favorite explanation is that he was rural, an outdoorsman expert at camp life, hunting, and shooting, but today's largely urbanized South still provides more than its share of recruits for the forces. Preoccupation with honor supposedly predisposed the young of the past to the profession of arms, but that concept is virtually extinct today with the "me generation" and probably was 30 years ago with the "silent generation." Yet another construal is that the southerner is militant because he is a violent white racist, Cash's "proto-Dorian," who just lives to shoot "gooks," but the southern black man also has made a fine soldier. During the Civil War 186,000 blacks served in the Union army and 29,000 were in the Union navy. The Department of War created four Afro-American units after the war, and many black southerners served in them in the western Indian Wars. Blacks fought in World Wars I and II, although in segregated outfits. President Harry Truman opened new opportunities for black southerners in 1948 when his executive order ended military segregation.

A mystique of the southern martial spirit and tradition does remain, however, curiously immune to analysis or debunking. The southern military tradition may have become self-reinforcing, as with other elements of southern distinctiveness, persisting in an age that threatens to smother and level differences. The South struggles to maintain its own *Gemeinschaft* against homogenization, and the rest of the nation will not allow the idea of the South to perish. "The consensus remains that a separate quality of myth, tradition, and values characterizes the South despite the compelling forces of modernization," write Thomas L. Connelly and Barbara L. Bellows. A key element of this lingering regional quality is the tradition of "the Fighting South."

John Hawkins Napier III
Montgomery, Alabama

F. N. Boney, *Midwest Quarterly* (1980), *Southerners All* (1984); D. W. Brogan, *The American Character* (1944); Thomas L. Connelly and Barbara L. Bellows, *God and General Longstreet: The Lost Cause and the Southern Mind* (1982); Avery O. Craven, *The Growth of Southern Nationalism, 1848–1861* (1953); Marcus Cunliffe, *Soldiers and Civilians: The Martial Spirit in America, 1775–1865* (1968); John Hope Franklin, *The Militant South, 1800–1861* (1956); John Temple Graves II, *The Fighting South* (1943); Samuel P. Huntington, *The Soldier and the State: The Theory and Politics of Civil–Military Relations* (1957); Morris Janowitz, *The Professional Soldier* (1960, 1971); Grady McWhiney and Forrest McDonald, *American Historical Review* (December 1980); John Hawkins Napier III, *Alabama Review* (October 1980); Bertram Wyatt-Brown, *Southern Honor: Ethics and Behavior in the Old South* (1982).

Modernism

To the popular mind "modern" is simply that which is up to the moment, but modernism was a specific cultural movement that was both reactionary and radical, conservative and revolutionary, packaging its puritanism in the latest fashions. The modernists were simultaneously the avant-garde and the guards of the derriere. The modern movement was part of a conservative effort that used revolutionary techniques. Everything about the movement implied tension, mediation, paradox. To many observers, modernism was mainly a matter of technique: new styles and structures; new and startling juxtapositions of language; new strategies of form in painting, sculpture, poetry, and fiction; fresh use of mythology and ritual in providing a literary framework; new stress upon personality and motivation in characterization and a new vocabulary to express the workings of the mind; new applications of time and memory. These techniques represented a new view of existence, a view corroborated by the sciences. By the early 20th century science had begun to uncover the discontinuities and uncertainties that existed beneath the surface of commonsense reality. Daniel Singal summarized the movement as an attempt "to reintegrate the human consciousness and thus to liberate man from the restrictive culture of enforced innocence with which the century began."

Scholars disagree as to the precise years of the modernist movement. Monroe Spears, in *Dionysus and the City* (1970), a study of modernism in poetry, suggests 1870 as a rough beginning for "modernism as an epoch in the cultural history of the West." Evidence of early modernism included the work of the French and Russian novelists, symbolist poets, and impressionist painters, plus a range of other styles and attitudes that appeared before, during, and after the fin de siècle. Spears chooses 1909 as "the beginning of modernism as a specific movement in the arts," as seen in the beginnings of cubist painting and sculpture; the emergence of Schönberg and Stravinsky's music; Hulme, Pound, and Eliot's poetry, Stein and Joyce's fiction; and the increasing popularization of Freud's psychology, Frazer's mythology, and Bergson's philosophy. Walker Percy argues that the age that began three centuries ago with the dawn of science came to an end with modernism in the early 20th century and along with it the lessons science offered for human self-understanding. Those who realized this and took it seriously suffered the symptoms of alienation, either wordlessly because they did not know the cause of their problem or, like Percy, by looking for new meanings. The modernist generation felt these discontinuities and was engaged in a search for new meaning.

The Southern Literary Renaissance of the 20th century has usually been seen as the prime expression of modernism in the South. Some scholars see the Renaissance as unique, because the region's writers did not, as Richard James Calhoun has written, fully feel "the historical and metaphysical discontinuities of the most modern writers." They were not "completely modern." But the southern movement, according to another critic, Lewis Simpson, was "fully joined in the wider literary and artistic opposition to *modernity*." Southern experience during the years in question was similar to that of the rest of the Western world, and the Renaissance should, therefore, not be seen as a unique regional experience but as part of modernism. Louis D. Rubin, Jr., has observed that this was the first generation of southerners since the antebellum era to confront directly "the vanguard of the most advanced thought and feeling of their times," but nevertheless they were part of a national literary generation, all of whom had grown up under certain cultural and familial pieties, whether they were raised in Oak Park, St. Paul, Reading, Cambridge, or a southern community. They were all part of what Simpson called a general "culture of alienation."

The attempt to isolate the so-called Southern Literary Renaissance from the modernist movement has given a false sense of distinctly regional achievement to southern writing. To be sure, the regional historical experience has provided the southern writer with paradoxical advantages in exploring the uncertainties that modernism has typically been interested in. The southern modernists were preoccupied with the myth of the fall of traditional southern society, an excellent regional metaphor for a world condition. The serpent was not only in the southern garden; he whispered his knowledge of the discontinuities all around.

Harry Levin has identified the experience of expatriation as one of the chief preconditions of becoming a modernist. The most acclaimed southern literary figures—Glasgow, Welty, Faulkner, Warren—traveled widely outside the South, thus experiencing changes that were transforming the traditional world of their childhood into the modern world of their maturity. But they returned to be "underfoot locally," having seen that the country of the mind is a far country indeed, to most people, and one might as well live where one finds the material. Indeed, by staying at home, engaging in an "inner expatriation," one is perhaps in a better position to monitor the discontinuities of the modern age.

The study of modernism's influence in the South has mainly focused on literary concerns. Recently, however, scholars have suggested broadening the scope of the inquiry to include music and painting. Musical contributions have been among the South's most important in the 20th century. Jazz, in particular, bears on the issue of modernism. Jazz was southern by origin, and regional expatriates have been its prime practitioners. It represents an authentically new form of music, and its existential qualities and its stress on the individual, on spontaneity, and on the present moment seem appropriate modernist concerns. However, much work remains to be done exploring the relationship of music, and particularly jazz, to the broader cultural context within the South.

The idea of a Southern Renaissance should also be applied to 20th-century painting in the region. "For painting in the South," writes art historian Rick Stewart, "the period between the two world wars was marked by the problematical relationship between a romantic sectionalism and a modernist internationalism." To be sure, southern painters generally followed Thomas Hart Benton's direction in combining modernist forms with the idea that art had a moral obligation to instruct. But Black Mountain College in North Carolina was the institutional center of more experimental modernist painting in the region, especially through the influence of Charles Olson and Josef Albers. One can date the beginnings of modernist painting in the region from 1933, when Albers came to Black Mountain. However, the full impact of the movement was not felt until the 1960s. George Bireline's painting *Malcolm's Last Address*, for example, was an influential abstract painting exhibited in 1965. It seriously challenged the dominance of realism in regional work and has led to the increased prominence of abstract forms. By 1976 critic Elizabeth C. Baker could write that contemporary southern art "bespeaks an almost universal acceptance of the modern vernacular."

The failure to relate modernism adequately to 20th-century southern cultural development, and especially to the Southern Literary Renaissance, has fostered the belief that the Renaissance is over. Postwar southern writing can be characterized as postmodern, but that should not imply a radical break with what went before. The gnosticism that is supposed to characterize postmodernism existed in the work of Eliot and Faulkner from the beginning, and it existed in the writing of Melville, Hawthorne, and Poe much earlier. Modernism found deep significance in the real, linked the contradictions, fused the ambiguities, made the mirror and the lamp into a single tool, mediated between past and present, and tried to bridge the supposed chasm between reason and intuition. This modernist impulse is still present in the Western world—including the South. The literary, musical, and artistic achievements of the South will likely continue to exist because the South will continue to "go modern"—that is, it will still be forced to confront the discontinuities of life and be able to name them.

See also ART AND ARCHITECTURE: Painting and Painters; BLACK LIFE: Art, Black; GEOGRAPHY: Expatriates and Exiles

Thomas L. McHaney
Georgia State University

Richard H. King, *A Southern Renaissance: The Cultural Awakening of the American South, 1930–1955* (1980); Thomas L. McHaney, in *Southern Culture in Transition: Heritage and Promise*, ed. Philip Castile and William Osborne (1983), *William Faulkner: Materials, Studies and Criticism*, vol. 3 (1980); Michael O'Brien, *The Idea of the American South, 1920–1941* (1979), *Perspectives on the American South*, vol. 4, ed. James C. Cobb and Charles Reagan Wilson (1986); Darden Asbury Pyron, *Perspectives on the America South*, vol. 2, ed. Merle Black and John Shelton Reed (1984); Lewis Simpson, in *Southern Literary Study: Problems and Possibilities*, ed. Louis D. Rubin, Jr., and C. Hugh Holman (1975); Daniel J. Singal, *The War Within: From Victorian to Modernist Thought in the South, 1919–1945* (1982); Rick Stewart, in *Painting in the South, 1564–1980*, Virginia Museum of Fine Arts (1984).

Monuments

Before 1860 Americans, including southerners, erected very few monuments other than grave markers. Some, like the statue of George III in Charleston, S.C., were holdovers from the colonial period; others, such as the Baron de Kalb Monument in Camden, S.C., honored heroes who had fallen fighting for American independence. The still-young country had not yet acquired a pantheon of gods to be immortalized in stone and bronze. The American Civil War, however, provided ample subject matter, North and South, for sculptors and memorial committees.

It is not unusual to honor those who fought for a victorious cause, but it is unusual to memorialize those who supported a lost cause. In remembering its military men, the South stood apart from the rest of the triumphant United States. In 1865 there were no victory parades, no laurel wreaths, no congratulatory speeches for a job well done. The shock of the collapse of the Confederacy precluded such a homecoming, but the South did remember her heroes and within a few decades inscribed their names and faces in stone on monuments throughout the region.

In 1866 Henry Timrod composed a stirring "Ode" that was "sung on the occasion of decorating the graves of the Confederate Dead, at Magnolia Cemetery, Charleston, S.C." Given what transpired during the next 50 years, Timrod's words were prophetic. The ravages of war and economic dislocation had left precious little money available for permanent markers. The scene in Charleston could have been repeated in scores of cemeteries across the South:

> Sleep sweetly in your humble graves,
> Sleep, martyrs of a fallen cause!—
> Though yet no marble column craves
> The pilgrim here to pause.

Southerners, particularly southern women, mourned their lost menfolk. "Humble graves" would simply not do. In town after town, memorial associations sprang up. At first, they busied themselves with decorating graves on Confederate Memorial Day; then they turned to working for suitable monuments honoring the men who had fought for the Lost Cause. One of the earliest markers was a simple marble shaft erected at Fort Gordon, Ga., in 1866.

The earlier monuments tended to be shafts or obelisks. Their designs were similar to cemetery markers of the day, but also bore a striking resemblance to the triumphant monuments designed decades earlier by Robert Mills.

Reconstruction and occupation did nothing to stimulate economic growth. And, in some states, it was not politically expedient to publicly espouse much enthusiasm for the Confederacy. It is estimated that only 5 percent of the Confederate monuments standing today were dedicated prior to the end of Reconstruction in 1877.

Although the end of Reconstruction did not bring prosperity, it restored the old elites that had led the South into war. The changed political climate and the mythology of the Lost Cause led to public veneration of the men who had participated in the war. This veneration took many turns: pensions, Confederate homes, and monuments.

In state capitals, county seats, and towns, committees organized for the sole purpose of raising funds to construct Confederate monuments. Public as well as private funds were used, and women usually took the initiative. In the half century after the Civil War, 60 percent of the existing monuments were dedicated.

These monuments appeared in a variety of forms. The shaft was still popular, but in larger towns it tended to be truncated and topped with a life-sized stone likeness of a Confederate soldier. The figure, in virtually all cases, was "at ease," not on the attack. Inscriptions on the base usually included some statement about the cause. These words from the monument in Manning, S.C., were typical: "Hope like the eastern sun rose bright in the heart of the Southerner for home, covenant and the Confederate States of America. Contending against armies overwhelming in numbers and with resources inexhaustible he fought with patriotism undaunted, and love of country unexcelled in history. Unawed by fear of defeat, he defended the sacredness of home and the sovereignty of his state."

The phrase "OUR HEROES" or "OUR CONFEDERATE SOLDIERS" generally appeared in outsized lettering. Occasionally, there was a list of the men from the locality who made the supreme sacrifice.

Toward the end of the century, the sacrifices of southern womanhood began to be recognized with monuments. Sometimes female figures were included in larger monuments along with soldiers' memorials and at other times southern womanhood was honored by a monument of its own. The sacrifices of the home front became as much a part of southern lore as those of the battlefield.

The various organizations responsible for honoring the Confederacy were local in nature and sprang up spontaneously in communities all across the South. News of their activities was reported in the pages of the *Confederate Veteran* and other publications such as those of the United Daughters of the Confederacy and the Confederated Memorial Associations of the South.

By the 1930s the war was not even a memory for most

Albert Sydney Johnston monument, Vicksburg, Miss., battlefield

southerners, yet monuments continued to rise. The Civil War Centennial in the 1960s saw a number dedicated, particularly on battlefields. Even with the onset of the civil rights movement and a downplaying of the Confederacy by public officials, groups of determined southerners have seen to it that no spot has gone unmarked.

The largest monument of all, at Stone Mountain, Ga., was finally completed in the 1970s. Its larger-than-life-sized carved figures of Davis, Jackson, and Lee dominate the north Georgia plain. Two allegorical monuments unveiled at Stone Mountain in 1978 continue the main themes appearing in southern monuments for over a century. "Valor" is depicted by a youth with upraised arms; he clasps in his right hand a sword broken off just above the hilt. "Sacrifice" is a tribute to southern womanhood and shows a female figure carrying an infant on her shoulder.

Defeated Valor and Noble Sacrifice, the twin themes that run through the creed of the Lost Cause, are evident in monument after monument across the South, in metropolis and in rural crossroads: in Mobile, New Orleans, Nashville, Charleston, and Richmond; and in Camden, Ala.; Tallulah, La.; Lebanon, Tenn.; Cheraw, S.C.; and Dinwiddie, Va. The size of the community might dictate the intricacy of the monument, but not the decision to erect one. Fading memories have not stopped the process. Since the Civil War Centennial, at least three dozen more have been added to the lists.

Other public monuments in the South honor local citizens, veterans of later wars, and industry and agriculture, but these are not uniquely southern. Anytown, U.S.A., could have a Doughboy Monument for World War I or a statue of the local boy who became governor. Only southern towns have monuments commemorating a Lost Cause and honoring the men who fought it and the women who supported them.

In 1866 Timrod wrote:

> In seeds of laurel in the earth
> The garlands of your fame are sown;
> And, somewhere, waiting for its birth,
> The shaft is in the stone.

Over the years, the poet was proven a prophet.

See also ART AND ARCHITECTURE: Sculpture

Walter Edgar
University of South Carolina

Confederated Southern Memorial Association, *History of the Confederated Memorial Associations of the South* (1904); Stephen Davis, *Journal of Popular Culture* (Winter 1982); Mrs. B. A. C. Emerson, compiler, *Historic Southern Monuments: Representative Memorials of the Heroic Dead of the Southern Confederacy* (1911); W. Stuart Towns, *Florida Historical Quarterly* (October 1978); Charles Reagan Wilson, *Baptized in Blood: The Religion of the Lost Cause, 1865–1920* (1980).

Museums

The South's approximately 1,500 museums represent almost 25 percent of the 6,000-plus institutions recognized by the American Association of Museums. By the AAM definition a museum is "an organized and permanent non-profit institution, essentially educational or aesthetic in purpose, with professional staff, which owns and utilizes tangible objects, cares for them, and exhibits them to the public on some regular schedule." The AAM recognizes 13 major categories of museums: art, children's and junior, college and university, company, general, history, science, and specialized museums; exhibit areas; libraries with collections in additions to books; national and state agencies, councils, and commissions; nature centers; and park museums and visitor centers. Within these categories are such diverse settings as archaeological sites, zoos, planetariums, and wildlife refuges. Many museums span several classifications, and certain museum types predominate in the South, as is true in other regions. The tremendous variation in museums is well represented in the South.

The growth of all types of museums in the South accelerated in the 20th century, although more slowly in the Deep South than in states such as Virginia, Maryland, and the Carolinas, all of which stand out in the history of American museums. The Charleston Museum, founded in 1772, was the first permanent museum in the American English colonies and began as a natural history museum containing such objects as an Indian hatchet, human skeletal remains, and minerals. One of the nation's oldest and most renowned historic house museums is Mount Vernon, George Washington's Virginia plantation. Ann Pamela Cunningham of South Carolina spearheaded the campaign to restore Mount Vernon, and she ranks as one of the country's first and most noted historic preservationists. Arlington, home of Robert E. and Mary Ann Custis Lee, became the first federally owned historic home following a 21-year controversy. Federal troops occupied the house in 1861, and the federal government auctioned off and illegally bought Arlington and established a national cemetery on its grounds in 1864. In 1882, however, George W. C. Lee, Robert and Mary's son, won his case before the U.S. Supreme Court regarding ownership of the estate but stuck by an earlier offer to convey the property to Congress in return for a fair monetary settlement.

The South has led the way in other aspects of museum history. Colonial Williamsburg, the beautifully restored capital of 18th-century Virginia, opened in 1926 as the nation's first major outdoor museum and is still considered by many to be second to none. Preservation of historic districts began in the South: Charleston, S.C., and New Orleans, La., both of which were developed in the 1930s, were the first such projects in the United States. In historic districts selected buildings are designated as museums, but the architecture serves as the setting for modern-day activities. Outdoor museums of other sorts also have roots in the South. The zoos in St. Louis, Mo. (1913), and Fort Worth, Tex. (1923), were two of the first major zoos in the United States; and the nation's first safari zoo, Lion Country Safari, opened near West Palm Beach, Fla., in 1966.

Other landmarks in the nation's museum history exist in the South. Two of the country's battle galleries, a museum type uncommon in the United States, are in the South. In Battle Abbey of the Virginia Historical Society, Richmond, Va., stand four large murals of Confederate heroes and battles painted by Charles Hoffbauer; and at Stone Mountain, Ga., loom Gutzon Borglum's gigantic sculptures of the Confederate leaders Lee, Davis, and Jackson. Somewhat similar in concept and popular in the 1800s were panoramas, or cycloramas, which surrounded the viewer with a huge circular painting of a battle or other scene. One of only two panoramas of the 1880s still being shown in the United States is the *Battle of Atlanta* at the Cyclorama in Atlanta. The battle galleries and panoramas effectively represent the post–Civil War South's penchant for memorializing Confederate heroes and their war efforts.

History museums are the most prevalent museum type in the South and include, among other things, historic structures and sites, preservation projects, and military museums, many of which are overseen by national and state agencies, councils, and commissions. Many of the South's historic museums grew from the burgeoning efforts in the 1890s and early 1900s to establish memorials, museums, and monuments and to preserve historic buildings associated with the Civil War. Economic difficulties of the Reconstruction period severely limited efforts at historic preservation in the South, but in the 1890s countless preservation organizations—primarily women's societies—were created. Monuments were erected in courthouse squares throughout the South, and numerous local museums preserving Civil War relics were established. The preservation societies' efforts drew much popular support, even though funds garnered from the scattered, rural, largely poor populace of the South were often limited. In undertaking large-scale restoration projects southern preservationists usually relied heavily on state or federal monies and fundraising activities rather than on the support of wealthy individuals. Such was true, for instance, of the Ladies' Hermitage Association's efforts to preserve Andrew Jackson's home in Nashville. For many years the preservation of buildings and relics associated with the Civil War far outstripped museum efforts of other types in the South. The South's homage to military sacrifice is further seen not only in the battlefields of the Civil War, such as Shiloh National Military Park and Cemetery, Shiloh, Tenn., but also in battlefields of the American Revolution, such as Cowpens National Battlefield, Chesnee, S.C., and in battleship museums commemorating World War II combat, such as the USS *Alabama* at Mobile, Ala.

The heritage of the South is evident in a wide variety of other historic museums. The struggles and triumphs of the South's Afro-American citizens are commemorated in such institutions as the Old Slave Market Museum and the Avery Institute of Afro-American History and Culture, both in Charleston, S.C. Numerous sites and museums preserve the heritage of the South's Native Americans. Examples include the Natchez, Miss., Grand Village of the Natchez Indians, site of the capital village of the Natchez Indians from 1700 to 1730; New Echota, Calhoun, Ga., where the Cherokee Indians constructed a capital in 1825; Marksville State Commemorative Area, Marksville, La., site of a prehistoric Indian ceremonial center from A.D. 1 to 400; and the Native American Museum at Pembroke State University, Pembroke, N.C., an institution preserving relics and images of tribes throughout the South. Ethnic diversity of the region is further celebrated in museums ranging from the Bayou Folk Museum in Cloutierville, La., and the Acadian House Museum in St. Martinsville, La., to the Mexican American Cultural Heritage Center in Dallas, Tex.

The South's religious background is evident in numerous historic churches, religious museums, and settlements established by religious groups. Examples include not only the World Methodist Building at Lake Junaluska, N.C., and the Baptist Museum of the Southern Baptist Historical Commission at Nashville, Tenn., but also the Archives Museum, Temple Mickve Israel at Savannah, Ga., and the Immaculate Conception Catholic Church, Natchitoches, La. Other fascinating examples of the South's religious heritage include Old Salem in Winston-Salem, N.C., and Shakertown at Pleasant Hill, Ky. Old Salem, a town founded in 1766 by Moravian settlers from Pennsylvania, has well-restored homes, shops, taverns, and a church plus the Museum of Early Southern Decorative Arts. At Shakertown the restored buildings and exhibits of tools, weaving looms, and other implements reflect the lifestyle of the Shakers, a religious group whose adherents lived communally at the site from 1805 to 1910.

Homes or birthplaces of countless famous individuals have been preserved in the South. Some statesmen whose homes or birthplaces have become museums include John C. Calhoun, Henry Clay, Jefferson Davis, Andrew Jackson, Thomas Jefferson, Abraham Lincoln, James K. Polk, and George Washington. Numerous writers with southern links have been commemorated, including Pearl S. Buck, William Faulkner, Ernest Hemmingway, O. Henry, Edgar Allan Poe, Marjorie Rawlings, Carl Sandburg, Mark Twain, and Thomas Wolfe. In addition to female writers, several other famous southern women honored by historic sites include Clara Barton, Helen Keller, Mary Todd Lincoln, Annie Riggs, and Lurleen Wallace. Booker T. Washington and Martin Luther King, Jr., two of the nation's most prominent black leaders, have been recognized through southern museums. Commemorated, too, have been scientists such as George Washington Carver and John James Audubon, military leaders such as Francis Marion and Douglas MacArthur, and musicians such as W. C. Handy, Stephen Foster, and Elvis Presley.

Vestiges of the antebellum South are preserved at numerous plantations and historic homes, ranging from Boone Hall Plantation, Mount Pleasant, S.C. (one setting for the movie *Gone with the Wind*) to Madewood in Napoleonville, La., and Melrose in Natchez, Miss. The plantation homes represent many architectural styles, and numerous historic home museums and other historic buildings interest both the general public and preservationists primarily because of their design. For example, the Sarasota, Fla., residence of circus owner John Ringling represents the ornate architecture of the Gilded Age. Palatial Biltmore House in Asheville, N.C., designed for George Vanderbilt, dazzles visitors with its opulent French Renaissance features. The elaborate, eclectic Victorian-style Bishop's Palace, Galveston, Tex., has been cited by the American Institute of Architects as one of the most outstanding buildings in the United States. These are but a few of the historic home museums in the South that represent architectural trends and reflect lifestyles of earlier eras.

An overview of other museum types in the South provides a picture of the region's diverse institutions. Art museums include such long-standing institutions as the Telfair Academy in Savannah and the Gibbes in Charleston plus city-owned art museums in most major southern cities. Various museums, libraries, monuments, and historic sites are classified as libraries with collections in addition to books. A historical focus is important in these and many other southern museums, although there is increasing emphasis on experiential learning in museum settings. Children explore the collections of such institutions as the Cobb County Youth Museum in Marietta, Ga., the Estelle Carmack Bandy Children's Museum in Kingsport, Tenn., the Junior Museum of Bay County in Panama City, Fla., and the Youth Cultural Center of Waco, Tex. Many southern college and university museums exhibit outstanding art collections. Other college and university collections take the form of planetariums, arboretums, historical exhibits, herbariums, marine science exhibits, and even zoos. The George Washington Carver Museum at Tuskegee Institute and the Tuskegee Institute National Historic Site are examples of college-based museums honoring renowned southerners, in this case both Carver and Booker T. Washington. Obviously, southern college and university collections are not restricted to large institutions. The Berea College Museums at Berea, Ky., are an excellent example of small museums that effectively display the region's culture. Three museums at Berea College focus on the folk culture of the southern Appalachian highlands through exhibits of native arts and crafts, demonstrations by craftsmen, photographs, and oral history tapes.

Other examples of museums exhibiting southern folkways are the Blue Ridge Institute, Ferrum, Va.; the Mississippi Crafts Center, Ridgeland, Miss; the Museum of Appalachia, Norris, Tenn.; the Ozark Folk Life Center, Mountain View, Ark.; and the Rural Life Museum, Baton Rouge, La. On display at these museums are such items as folk artwork, crafts, farm tools, and household furnishings and implements. Several notable folk art museums focus on musical and literary contributions, such as the Stephen Foster State Folk Culture Center, White Springs, Fla., and Wren's Nest, the Joel Chandler Harris Memorial, Atlanta, Ga.

The South has a limited number of company museums, but two related to textiles are located in North Carolina: Biltmore Industries' Biltmore Homespun Shops in Asheville and the Cannon Mills Company's Cannon Visitor Center in Kannapolis. Other company museums include the U.S. Tobacco Company's Museum of Tobacco Art and History in Nashville, Tenn., and the Coca-Cola Company's Schmidt Museum of Coca-Cola Memorabilia in Elizabethtown, Ky. Other museums commemorate particular industries; for example, the Fort Worth, Tex., Western Company Museum, which highlights the history of the petroleum industry, and the McCalla, Ala., Iron & Steel Museum of Alabama at Tannehill Historical State Park.

Exhibit areas vary widely and include such examples as the Branchville Railroad Shrine and Museum, Inc., Branchville, S.C.; the Morehead Planetarium at Chapel Hill, N.C.; and the Barnwell Garden and Art Center at Shreveport, La. At Dry Tortugas Island off of Key West, Fla., visitors to the Fort Jefferson National Monument examine the largest masonry fort in the United States and see Brown Noddies and frigate birds in their natural habitat. Similar sights exist at such nature centers as the Seashore State Park Natural Area Visitor Center, Virginia Beach, Va.; the Audubon Park and Zoological Garden, New Orleans, La.; and the Big Bend National Park, Big Bend, Tex. Many nature areas are also classified as park museums, a designation that applies as well to many historical sites.

In the category of general museums are institutions such as the Kiah Museum, Savannah, Ga., which exhibits African, folk, 15th-century, and contemporary art, among other things. The Cottonlandia Museum in Greenwood, Miss., and the Daughters of the Republic of Texas Museum in Austin, Tex., are but two of the many other general museums. The former exhibits regional agricultural implements and household furnishings plus artifacts of the Mississippian-period Indians. The latter, housed in an 1857 land-office building, contains Indian artifacts, archives, and objects relating to early Texas history, coins, stamps, and artwork.

Southern science museums encompass varied collections, including the following: the Huntsville, Ala., Alabama Space and Rocket Center; the Salisbury, N.C., Catawba Museum of Anthropology; the Winter Park, Fla., Beal-Maltbie Shell Museum; the Dallas, Tex., Dallas Arboretum and Botanical Garden and the Dallas Zoo; the Birmingham, Ala., Red Mountain Museum; the Murrells Inlet, S.C., Brookgreen Gardens, a society for southeastern flora and fauna; the Asheville, N.C., Colburn Memorial Mineral Museum; the Bailey, N.C., Country Doctor Museum; the Charleston, S.C., Macauley Museum of Dental History; and the Memphis, Tenn., Mississippi River Museum at Mud Island. Specialized museums include such sites as the Tifton, Ga., Georgia Agrirama, the State Museum of Agriculture; the Fort Smith, Ark., Patent Model Museum; the Pine Ridge, Ark., Lum and Abner Museum and Jot 'em Down Store; the Nashville, Tenn., Country Music Hall of Fame and Museum; the Front Royal, Va., Warren Rifles Confederate Museum; the Louisville, Ky., Kentucky Derby Museum; and the Murray, Ky., National Museum of the Boy Scouts of America.

Clearly, the South's museums preserve and promote countless national, regional, and local treasures, and the growth of museums in the South parallels a national trend toward heightened appreciation for such institutions.

See also ART AND ARCHITECTURE: / Art Museums; RECREATION: / Colonial Williamsburg; SCIENCE AND MEDICINE: / Charleston Museum

Sharon A. Sharp
University of Mississippi

Edward P. Alexander, *Museums in Motion* (1979); American Association of Museums, *The Official Museum Directory, 1984* (1983); American Heritage Publishing Co., *Historic Houses of America* (1980); Edward D. C. Campbell, Jr., *Journal of Regional Cultures* (Fall–Winter 1981); Charles B. Hosmer, Jr., *Presence of the Past: A History of the Preservation Movement in the United States before Williamsburg* (1965); Reader's Digest Association, *Treasures of America* (1974).

New Deal

Agriculture in the 1930s was the South's major economic activity; and New Deal farm programs—such as the Agricultural Adjustment Act (1933), the Resettlement Administration (1935), and the Bankhead-Jones Farm Tenancy Act (1937)—by cutting production, raising farm income, and pushing southerners from farm poverty to southern and non-southern cities created the basis for the sweeping change soon to come to the largely rural South. Along with the agricultural revolution the New Deal infusion of federal money disrupted the cycle of poverty, and the region's economy began to merge with that of the nation. New Deal labor legislation such as the National Labor Relations Act (1933), the Social Security Act (1935), and the Fair Labor Standards Act (1938) helped to spur the first significant unionization of the country (one of every four workers by the end of the 1940s). The South, with its major industry, textiles, overwhelmingly nonunionized, was the most underunionized region of the country, with all the attendant cultural and economic impact of nonunionization. In the nation's poorest region, the Federal Emergency Relief Administration provided limited but badly needed amounts of money to fund welfare programs; and the Public Works Administration (1933), Civilian Conservation Corps (1933), and the Works Progress Administration (1935) offered public service work to the unemployed.

At first the personal popularity of Franklin D. Roosevelt and his Depression-fighting New Deal programs meant rocklike support among southern politicians and southern voters. But New Deal politics and programs threatened white supremacy and lessened the power of local oligarchies. The centralizing tendencies of the New Deal menaced the basic institutions of southern life. The subsequent slow defection of southern Democrats from the New Deal created a new conservative southern political culture.

The role of the New Deal in creating the modern political economy of southern society remains controversial. Statistical study indicates that the Dixie economic miracle dates from the 1940s. Ambiguity surrounds the New Deal years in the South. In many ways the New Deal nationalized southern culture, and the South became by the 1940s not the nation's number one economic problem but its ever-growing, ever-Americanizing region. The persistence, however, of such cultural patterns as racial segregation, dire poverty, and rural and small-town control kept the South looking more old than new. The New Deal, with its host of centralizing agencies and its nationalized political ideology, changed the Old South but did not destroy it. Only the war years, the racial revolution of the 1950s and 1960s, emigration, and the postwar prosperity of industrialization and urbanization would do that.

See also ENVIRONMENT: Tennessee Valley Authority; INDUSTRY: / Textile Industry; POLITICS: National Politics; SOCIAL CLASS: Politics and Social Class; Poverty

James A. Hodges
College of Wooster

James C. Cobb and Michael V. Namorato, eds., *The New Deal and the South* (1984); Pete Daniel, *Agricultural History* (July 1981), *Breaking the Land: The Transformation of Cotton, Tobacco, and Rice Cultures since 1880* (1985); Gary Fink and Merl Reed, eds., *Essays in Southern Labor History: Selected Papers, Southern Labor History Conference, 1976* (1976); Frank Freidel, *FDR and the South* (1965); Donald H. Grubbs, *Cry from the Cotton: The Southern Tenant Farmers' Union and the New Deal* (1971); Michael Holmes, *The New Deal in Georgia: An Administrative History* (1975); John B. Kirby, *Black Americans in the Roosevelt Era: Liberalism and Race* (1980); Robert S. McElvaine, *The Great Depression, 1929–1941* (1984); Paul E. Mertz, *New Deal Policy and Southern Rural Poverty* (1978); John Dean Minton, *The New Deal in Tennessee, 1932–38* (1959); Harvard Sitkoff, *A New Deal for Blacks: The Emergence of Civil Rights as a National Issue*, vol. 1 (1978); George B. Tindall, *The Emergence of the New South, 1913–1945* (1967).

New Deal Cultural Programs

The Great Depression had a substantial impact on many parts of southern life. The region's economy, its relationship with the federal government and the Democratic party, and social relations between the races were all profoundly and lastingly changed by the New Deal. Franklin D. Roosevelt's policies also had repercussions on the culture of the South. The New Deal legacy may be less apparent here than in other areas, but that legacy continues to have perceptible consequences for modern southern culture.

FDR and his relief administrator, Harry Hopkins, shared a desire to use the opportunity provided by the Depression to begin an experiment in federal patronage of the arts. Attempts were made to give "appropriate" employment to writers and artists during the short-lived Civil Works Administration in the winter of 1933 to 1934, and the Treasury Department's Section of Painting and Sculpture began commissioning works of art (usually murals) for public buildings (most often post offices) in 1934. The principal effort of the New Deal to encourage culture through providing suitable work relief for people involved in the arts began with the launching of the Works Progress Administration in 1935.

Included under WPA Federal Project One were the Federal Writers' Project, Federal Music Project, Federal Theater Project, Federal Art Project, and the Historical Records Survey. The dream behind the WPA arts projects was nothing less than the democratization of American culture. Stimulated by the Depression era's revival of interest in uncovering and building a distinctively American culture, the Federal One projects set out with great expectations. One of the basic problems that they confronted from the start was that the national culture they sought to shape had distinctive demarcations. Regionalism was a major movement in the 1930s, and it was strongest in the South, where it was inspired by such intellectuals as the Nashville Agrarians who published *I'll Take My Stand* in 1930 and, in a quite different way, by University of North Carolina sociologist Howard W. Odum. The regional traits peculiar to the South led to the development of unique characteristics in the New Deal arts projects in that region. At the same time the federal supervision of its projects carried forward a slow process of homogenization of the South with the rest of the nation.

The Federal Writers' Project had a greater impact upon the South than did any of the other WPA arts projects. The FWP's most publicized accomplishment was the publication of a guidebook for each state. Their quality varied, of course, but on the whole they were a remarkable achievement. The compilers of guides in the southern states faced considerable difficulty in their treatment of blacks. Many of the white writers employed by the FWP shared the white South's stereotypical perceptions of blacks and wrote those views into the state guides. The Louisiana guide portrayed "the Negro" as "imitative." FWP editors strove to reduce such references, but sometimes they failed. They did manage to delete from the Mississippi guide the statement that "the passing of public hanging was, in the eyes of the Negro, a sad mistake," but the published version took what has been described as a tone of "amused condescension" toward blacks. For example, the authors claimed that "the Mississippi folk Negro" is "credulous," yet "he has never been known to take anyone's advice about anything."

One of the Writers' Project's most important contributions was the conducting of more than 2,000 interviews with former slaves. These slave narratives constitute an invaluable historical resource, although most of the interviewers were white and thus may have elicited less than complete candor on the part of some of the former slaves. FWP writers employed these slave narratives in writing the path-breaking *The Negro in Virginia*, published in 1940. This book and the treatment of blacks in several other FWP publications played a small role in the building of a more realistic picture of black life, history, and values. Accordingly, the FWP was one of the New Deal agencies that helped sow the seeds for the later civil rights movement.

Another important FWP contribution to southern culture was the collection of "life histories" of southern workers and farmers. These interviews, some of which were edited by W. T. Couch and published in 1939 under the title *These Are Our Lives*, marked a truly pioneering effort in social history at the same time that they turned the stories of "ordinary" people into a genuine literature. Under the direction of Benjamin F. Botkin, the FWP also collected folklore in the South. Many of these tales reached print under such names as *Bundle of Troubles, and Other Tales, God Bless the Devil! Liar's Bench Tales*, and *Gumbo Ya-ya: A Collection of Louisiana Folk Tales*.

The Federal Writers' Project's single most significant contribution to modern southern culture was the nurturing of several leading writers in the region whose talents might never have been developed had it not been for their FWP employment. Notable among these was Richard Wright, who won a $500 prize for four stories he wrote in 1939 while employed on the project. They were published as *Uncle Tom's Children*, and Wright applied the prize money toward completion of his masterpiece, *Native Son*. Eudora Welty traveled and wrote for the project in Mississippi. Her photographs are included in the Mississippi guidebook.

The Federal Music Project sought to bring first-class orchestral music to a wider audience while providing work for unemployed musicians. Its major impact on the culture of the South, however, fell into a quite different realm. It was a collaborative effort by Charles Seeger of the FMP and Alan Lomax of the FWP to collect the region's folksongs. This effort made a lasting contribution by helping to preserve a most important aspect of regional life.

The Federal Theater Project was the largest and most controversial of the WPA arts projects, but its activities in the South were not as extensive as they were in some other parts of the nation. The FTP did have some notable success stories in the region, particularly in North Carolina, where its actors put on the historical pageant *The Lost Colony*. Also, FTP directors assisted amateur groups throughout North Carolina and in Jacksonville, Fla., which became the center of a small drama revival in northern Florida.

The Theater Project in the South was not free from the political controversy that swirled about it elsewhere. FTP companies in Birmingham, Tampa, and Miami were among 22 nationwide that produced Sinclair Lewis's *It Can't Happen Here* in the fall of 1936, but officials in Louisiana refused to allow the play about the potential for dictatorship in America to be performed in New Orleans a year after the assassination of Huey Long. Thomas Hall-Rogers's *Altars of Steel*, which portrayed labor-management strife in the southern steel industry, set off an uproar when it premiered in Atlanta.

The FTP's success in bringing live theater and new ideas to the South was limited. Black FTP units were set up in Atlanta and Birmingham. The latter produced *Great Day*, a musical depicting early African history. Traveling companies existed briefly in the region, but by the fall of 1937 the FTP was operational in only three states in the South.

The contribution of the Federal Art Project in the South was principally through its sponsorship in six states of Community Art Centers, some of which became permanent museums, as in Mobile in conjunction with its art education programs. More persuasive were the murals of the Treasury Department's Section of Painting and Sculpture. This was not a relief program but one with the sole aim of public beautification. Post office murals were painted in many cities and towns across the region. They offer a revealing view of southern culture in the 1930s and early 1940s, because the artists were, at least in theory, required to consult local public opinion in determining what to paint. Most southern communities seemed to prefer historical themes—themes that provided a sense of stability in the midst of the uncertainty of the Depression.

One other aspect of the New Deal played an important part in southern culture. The photography project begun under the Resettlement Administration and carried forward by the Farm Security Administration brought together many of the nation's leading photographers. Most of them spent some time working in the South. The FSA photographers, especially Walker Evans, left indelible images of southern life in the Depression years.

See also MYTHIC SOUTH: Regionalism; / Agrarians, Nashville

Robert S. McElvaine
Millsaps College

F. Jack Hurley, *Portrait of a Decade: Roy Stryker and the Development of Documentary Photography in the Thirties* (1972); Alan Lomax, Woody Guthrie, and Pete Seeger, eds., *Hard-Hitting Songs for Hard-Hit People* (1967); Robert S. McElvaine, *The Great Depression, 1929–1941* (1984); Richard D. McKinzie, *The New Deal for Artists* (1973); Jerre Mangione, *The Dream and the Deal: The Federal Writers' Project, 1935–1943* (1972); Karal Ann Marling, *Wall-to-Wall America: A Cultural History of Post-Office Murals in the Great Depression* (1982); Jane DeHart Mathews, *The Federal Theatre, 1935–1939* (1967); Monty Noam Penkower, *The Federal Writers' Project: A Study in Government Patronage of the Arts* (1977); William Stott, *Documentary Expression and Thirties America* (1973).

Philanthropy, Northern

Northern philanthropy emerged as a significant social, economic, and political force in the South following the Civil War. At a time when the region was suffering from the effects of defeat, desolation, and social confusion, northerners, as individuals and through corporate bodies, sought by means of philanthropic gifts to influence the current and future direction of southern life. Generally, the philanthropists were attempting in a variety of ways to assist in "bringing racial order, political stability, and material prosperity to the American South." These goals were perceived as supportive of two crucial ends: insuring that the South's restoration enhanced rather than weakened the United States and promoting the "reformation and elevation" of the southern people, their institutions, and their politics by bringing them into greater conformity with the North.

Between the closing years of the Civil War and the middle decades of the 20th century, northerners of means invested millions of philanthropic dollars in the South. Although this giving had several phases, most donations fell into a number of clearly identifiable categories: (1) support of segregated public and private education for southern blacks and whites; (2) aid to individuals, programs, and governmental agencies endeavoring to increase the skills and productivity of southern farmers; (3) creation and support of programs designed to raise the quality of southern rural life through educational and medical programs to eliminate social diseases, increase public knowledge in regard to hygiene and health, and provide adequate medical services; (4) direct grants and matching funds to southern schools, colleges, and universities to build endowments, raise salaries, and erect new buildings; (5) studies and grants to assess and upgrade medical education, and incorporate it into the major universities of the region; (6) improvement of library services and the erection of new libraries; and (7) aid to theological education.

Beginning in the 1920s some philanthropic agencies also began to support programs designed to facilitate the exchange of ideas and information between black and white leaders of the South. Although all of these programs made contributions to southern life, some had a widespread positive effect throughout the region, particularly those that sought to develop an adequate system of public and private education for whites; to increase southern farmers' productivity and improve the quality of rural life; and to professionalize and elevate the quality of medical education.

The earliest group of northern philanthropists to have an impact on the South was the Protestant missionary societies, which began during the Civil War to send money and workers into the region. Although a significant number of large and small church-related organizations engaged in this activity, the most important, in terms of money expended, schools and other institutions established, as well as constancy of interest, were the American Missionary Association (nominally nonsectarian, but primarily Congregational), the Freedmen's Aid Society of the Methodist Episcopal Church, the American Baptist Home Missionary Society, and the Presbyterian Church's Board of Missions for the Freedmen. Fueled by missionary energy and the abolitionist desire to uplift the freedmen, these organizations increased their efforts after the Civil War and, in conjunction with the federal government's Bureau of Refugees, Freedmen, and Abandoned Lands, became the major forces for "uplift" and education among blacks.

When the Freedmen's Bureau went out of existence in 1870, these organizations remained actively involved in this work, becoming even more important to blacks and more controversial among southern whites. Whites accurately perceived them as subverters of traditional southern racial mores because of their support of black education based on northern models, espousal of character reform that sought to transform Afro-Americans into black Yankees, and support of black political rights. The northern missionary societies strengthened the hostility of white southerners by an almost exclusive interest in the southern black community and its welfare. From the post–Civil War period to the first decade of the 20th century, the northern church agencies, as the largest contributors to black education, were a major philanthropic force in the South. Although the denominations that supported these groups would maintain an interest in southern blacks throughout the first half of the 20th century, after 1900 the secular philanthropic agencies began to make a greater impact.

Between 1867 and 1902 a small number of secular philanthropic foundations established by wealthy white northerners joined the missionary societies in the work of reforming and elevating the South. By 1910 these foundations, because of their focused goals and numerous connections with white business and political leaders in both the North and the South, were more visible and influential than the missionary societies. The most important of the foundations active in the South were the General Education Board of the Rockefeller Foundation, the Southern Education Board, the Julius Rosenwald Fund, the Phelps-Stokes Fund, and the Carnegie Foundation. All these agencies were established between 1866 and 1918 in direct response to two parallel developments in United States history—the growth of large personal fortunes derived from business and the presence of a powerful movement to promote more efficient philanthropy through organization.

The intersection of these two movements with the interest of secular philanthropists in the South is reflected in the individual histories of these foundations. Often considered the first modern American foundation, the Peabody Fund was established in 1867 by George Peabody, a wealthy banker who lived in England. This fund, using its $2 million endowment, promoted public and private black and white education in the South until the fund was liquidated in 1914. In 1881 a Connecticut merchant named John F. Slater, impelled by his belief that the education of the former slaves would promote black welfare and ensure "the safety of our common country," placed $1 million in the hands of a board of trustees for this purpose.

John D. Rockefeller's lifelong concern to distribute a portion of his earnings to charity led to the creation of the General Education Board in 1902. Because of its immense resources, creative programs, and capable administrators and trustees, it would become the most important of the foundations involved in southern life. Organized as a discretionary perpetuity with an endowment of over $153 million, it sought, according to its stated goals, to promote "education within the United States, without discrimination of race, sex, or creed."

Between 1885 and 1920 public concern about America's educational, medical, and social problems increased. The South, burdened with poverty, low standards of public education, health problems, and peculiar racial problems, was a special focus of these concerns. The philanthropic possibilities created by the multiplication of great private fortunes and by Andrew Carnegie's influential argument that the rich were obligated to serve others increased public esteem for the agencies established by Peabody, Slater, and Rockefeller. At the same time, they caused many wealthy Americans to view the foundation as an excellent means for stimulating efforts to solve a wide variety of problems. This belief was reflected in the increasing rate with which foundations were established after 1900. To the Progressive era, such organizations seemed the embodiment of the new "scientific philanthropy," which sought not simply to concern itself with the symptoms of social disorder but, through research and careful application of insights, to eliminate the root causes of social problems.

During the second decade of the 20th century the Phelps-Stokes Fund and the Julius Rosenwald Fund were established. Before her death in 1910, Caroline Phelps-Stokes of New York City made provision in her will for a charitable endowment to support the efforts of black Americans to improve their conditions, especially through education. Accordingly, a foundation bearing her name was established and incorporated in 1911. This fund provided occasional direct grants to individual black schools and colleges, but its major support of black education was through a series of surveys and studies for which it provided money and other forms of assistance.

As early as 1910 Julius Rosenwald had begun a regular program of gifts to support educational and social-service institutions in the South and to provide direct aid to "talented individuals." In all instances, southern blacks were beneficiaries of his largesse. After 1917 Rosenwald's giving was institutionalized in the Julius Rosenwald Fund. Disliking the restrictive nature of perpetual endowments, Rosenwald included provisions for the termination of the fund within 25 years of his death. Sixteen years after his death in 1932 it was liquidated, having provided roughly $63 million to improve rural education, racial relations, and black health education.

The wealth of these northern philanthropic agencies gave them the power to influence greatly the lives and futures of black and white southerners. In their dealings with whites the agencies pursued specific goals but in most cases exercised a cautious and diplomatic approach designed to secure the cooperation and support of white southern leaders. By 1910 this had produced strong and, in some quarters, enthusiastic white southern endorsement of the foundations as "friends."

Initially, though, white southerners greeted the secular philanthropic agencies with the same suspicion and distrust the missionary societies received. Their public and financial support of black education and character reform at first seemed another variant on the familiar Yankee reformer, plotting to elevate blacks at the expense of southern whites. However, after 1902, as the General Education Board began to dominate the field of southern philanthropy, directly influencing the work of most other northern secular philanthropies and much of what was done by the missionary societies, the policies and programs of the secular philanthropic agencies began to convince white southerners that their welfare was uppermost in the minds of the individuals directing these organizations. This was an accurate assessment, because from 1902 to the early 1920s the major programs of the secular northern philanthropists included (1) the development of a comprehensive educational system for southern whites justified by the belief that the southern white community would neither tolerate nor fund a comprehensive educational system for blacks until they first had a good system of public and private schools for themselves; (2) a commitment to the development and maintenance of a working relationship between northern philanthropy and the dominant forces in southern society; and (3) a strong espousal of industrial rather than collegiate and professional training for blacks, based on the judgment that they needed basic skills and training that inculcated the dignity and worth of labor.

To promote racial order, political stability, and material prosperity in the South, the secular philanthropic agencies, the most important forces in northern philanthropy, accepted and made their peace with white supremacy in the South. Consequently, from 1902 to 1960, when the General Education Board exhausted its funds, the bulk of the monies expended by northern secular agencies in the South went for programs that benefited southern whites solely. Frequently, the relations of the philanthropic agencies with blacks contrasted sharply with the treatment accorded their white counterparts. With blacks, these organizations were often more directive and far less flexible in pursuing policies and programs they saw as suitable. At times, some foundation officials deemed it part of their work to directly influence the conduct of black institutions, in some instances effecting removal of persons heading them and the selection of others considered more suitable.

From the mid-1920s until the U.S. Supreme Court's 1954 decision in *Brown* v. *Board of Education* outlawing segregation, the major northern philanthropic agencies manifested a growing concern over the weakness of black institutions and a disenchantment with industrial education as the major tool for black development. This led to an increase in the number and amount of their grants to southern black institutions of higher education, efforts to make southern governments less discriminatory towards blacks in their distribution of public funds, and support of interracial conferences. Little was done directly, however, to attack or publicize black poverty, segregation, and political powerlessness—the root causes of the problems that plagued the southern black community. Instead, northern philanthropic agencies sought to aid blacks primarily by grants and programs designed to create a strong separate southern black community, an impossible goal given the foundations' limited resources, the size of the black community, the impact of black poverty, and the scant interest of powerful southern whites in supporting such a goal. After 1954, with the emergence of the civil rights movement, northern philanthropists began to reevaluate their programs and goals. However, the increased involvement of the federal government in all aspects of southern life steadily reduced the importance of these organizations.

Although southern blacks were the major direct beneficiaries of the northern missionary societies, the investments and programs of these groups, by providing blacks with skills and education, as well as by strengthening their will to work for a genuinely democratic and biracial society, benefited all southerners. In contrast, the second phase of northern philanthropic activity in the South, signaled by the dominance of the secular philanthropic agencies, was more conservative. These organizations gave lip service to the missionary societies' goals with regard to black education, development, and political rights, but the chief beneficiaries of their money and programs were southern whites, with whom they collaborated until 1954 in the subordination and segregation of the southern black community.

See also BLACK LIFE: Education, Black; EDUCATION: / General Education Board

Alfred Moss
University of Maryland
College Park

Henry A. Bullock, *A History of Negro Education in the South: From 1619 to the Present* (1967); Edwin R. Embree and Julian Waxman, *Investment in the People: The Story of the Julius Rosenwald Fund* (1949); Abraham Flexner, *Funds and Foundations: Their Policies, Past and Present* (1952); Louis R. Harlan, *Separate and Unequal: Public School Campaigns and Racism in the Southern Seaboard States, 1901–1915* (1968); Elizabeth Jacoway, *Yankee Missionaries in the South: The Penn School Experiment* (1980); Jacqueline Jones, *Soldiers of Light and Love: Northern Teachers and Georgia Blacks, 1865–1873* (1980); Ullin Whitney Leavell, *Philanthropy in Negro Education* (1930); James M. McPherson, *The Abolitionist Legacy: From Reconstruction to the NAACP* (1976); Joe M. Richardson, *Christian Reconstruction: The American Missionary Association and Southern Blacks, 1861–1890* (1985); Morris R. Werner, *Julius Rosenwald: The Life of a Practical Humanitarian* (1939).

Populism

Adherents of the People's party, launched formally in 1892, were commonly known as Populists. The nucleus of the third party was the combined strength of the southern and northern branches of the Farmers' Alliance, which had grown from a local organization of Texas cattlemen and farmers in the 1880s into a formidable national body. Local, county, state, and national alliances developed coordinated programs designed to achieve economic reform and benefit the agricultural classes. Southern Alliance warehouses, exchanges, and stores engaged in numerous ventures in cooperative buying and selling. Even as its lecturers and newspapers denounced the impoverished condition of the agrarians, the Farmers' Alliance promoted social and educational activities for farmers and their families.

The South produced a number of Alliance leaders, such as Leonidas L. Polk of North Carolina. Dr. Charles W. Macune, an itinerant reformer, edited the *National Economist* from the Alliance's headquarters in Washington, D.C. Macune championed the subtreasury plan, which would have enabled farmers to store perishable products in local warehouses and receive loans on their goods while waiting for better prices. The subtreasury plan became the basic economic demand of the Southern Alliance. It was denounced as socialistic heresy by the ruling Democrats, a group of conservative politicians often called Bourbons. The alliance was both specific and general in its program that decried the results of one-crop agriculture and tenant farming: soil depletion, rising costs and falling prices, and the loss of a sense of worth and dignity.

In the South members of the Farmers' Alliance backed Bourbon Democrats who pledged themselves to enact the subtreasury plan and other measures (fertilizer inspection laws, railroad regulation, reform of the tax laws on land). The alliance leaders' plan was to gain control of the Democratic party and pursue their program from within the power structure. It went awry when the Bourbons reneged on campaign promises. It seemed logical that southern alliancemen, like their counterparts in the Midwest, would break away and form a third party. Yet a similar defection in the South was more difficult. There the Democrats had gained control of state government at the end of Reconstruction. Since the mid-1870s the region had been controlled by the Bourbons, who pledged themselves to honesty in government, fiscal conservatism, and, most importantly, white supremacy. Any divisive issue that threatened a return to Reconstruction and Republican rule was stifled. Reconstruction was blown out of proportion as an era of corrupt dominance by dishonest carpetbaggers, traitorous scalawags, and ignorant blacks.

Most white southerners wanted to maintain white supremacy and looked to the Democratic party as the sacrosanct instrument of that preservation. Yet as the alliance program faltered, desperate white farmers turned to the People's party. Their sense of solidarity led them to abandon the "party of the fathers," which was no longer sensitive to their needs.

Populism had many facets, but when viewed as the sum of its parts, it was a class movement. The southern experience was distinct and unique. Southern Populism drew its foot soldiers from the ranks of the farmers, many of whom were bedrock alliancemen. This was so even though some Alliance leaders (for example, Benjamin R. Tillman in South Carolina and James S. Hogg in Texas) refused to leave the Democrats and branded the Populists dangerous radicals.

Realizing the need for additional support, southern agrarians broadened their party's appeal. The Populists favored direct election of U.S. senators and other plans to secure political democracy. They sought the regulation of monopolies and carriers and a revision of the nation's monetary policy. Campaigning in urban areas, the Populists depicted the Bourbons as a selfish elite opposed to the common people whether they lived in the city or the countryside.

Workers in textile mills and mines were outside the mainstream of southern life. The embryonic labor movement had different goals from those of Populism, but workers and farmers had many miseries in common. Although national labor unions remained neutral, in Alabama union leaders supported reform, and a majority of the coal miners marked their ballots for Populist candidates.

Populist tenets and those of the Republicans were widely dissimilar. Yet the two parties "fused" in some elections, particularly in North Carolina, and achieved victory. The fusion occurred because of their mutual antipathy to the Democrats who controlled the election machinery, manipulated the votes of blacks, and defied legal attempts to challenge their tactics. Whatever the differences between Republicans and Populists, political cooperation was a small price to pay to unseat the Democrats.

Blacks continued to vote after Reconstruction, and their votes were crucial in the 1890s. Large landholders in cotton-producing counties, in the area known as the Black Belt because of the large black population and the color of the soil, held economic mastery over the sharecroppers. They also controlled the blacks politically. The conservative planters aligned with the industrialists in the cities to dominate various states.

Challenging this arrangement, Populists openly sought black support. If their appeals fell short of promoting social equality, such a program was not credible in the 1890s. Even so, numerous Populists declared that skin color bore no relation to political freedom and economic opportunity. If part of the Populists' courtship was based on political expediency, their commitment to improved race relations was greater than that of the Democrats. The brief political alliance between whites and blacks was aborted when Democrats resorted to flagrant election abuses. This fleeting racial liaison was shattered by the Populist defeat in 1896 and destroyed in the decades of racism that followed. Yet the interlude was a significant phenomenon.

Various Populists were middle-class farmers and businessmen who simply opposed Bourbon arrogance and self-aggrandizement. Yet impassioned leaders—Hardy Brian in Louisiana, Thomas E. Watson in Georgia, and Joseph C. Manning in Alabama—were philosophers as well as politicians, theorists as well as power seekers. They viewed Populism as a movement, an upheaval spawned by the lower classes and directed against their self-proclaimed betters. Theirs was a native radicalism that wished not to destroy democracy but to reform it so that the poor could share in its promise.

See also RELIGION: Politics and Religion; SOCIAL CLASS: Politics and Social Class; Religion and Social Class; / Bourbon / Redeemer South; Farmers' Alliance

William Warren Rogers
Florida State University

Robert F. Durden, *The Climax of Populism: The Election of 1896* (1965); Helen G. Edmonds, *The Negro and Fusion Politics in North Carolina, 1894–1901* (1951); Lawrence Goodwyn, *Democratic Promise: The Populist Moment in America* (1976); Sheldon Hackney, *Populism to Progressivism in Alabama* (1969); William I. Hair, *Bourbonism and Agrarian Protest: Louisiana Politics, 1877–1900* (1969); Robert L. Hart, *Redeemers,*

Bourbons, & Populists: Tennessee, 1870–1896 (1975); Robert C. McMath, *Populist Vanguard: A History of the Southern Farmers' Alliance* (1975); Theodore Saloutos, *Farmer Movements in the South, 1865–1933* (1960); C. Vann Woodward, *Tom Watson: Agrarian Rebel* (1938).

Progressivism

During the early years of the 20th century the South experienced an extraordinary wave of political and social reform. Unlike Radical Reconstruction, this reform was largely an indigenous phenomenon, and, in contrast to the Populist movement, it was both less disruptive and more successful in achieving its objectives. Progressivism embodied a series of movements for public education, railroad regulation, more efficient agricultural methods, and a more nearly adequate welfare system. Although the South's distinctive institutions, one-party politics, and perennial concern with the "race question" no doubt shaped its social reforms, the region shared in the national progressive ethos and interacted with other parts of the country in developing its own brand of progressivism.

Southern progressivism was a wide-ranging but loosely coordinated attempt to modernize the South and to humanize its institutions without abandoning its most prized values and traditions. Its origins can be found in a confluence of internal and external developments in the late 19th century: the growth in industry, urbanization, and the importance of business and professional classes; the restructuring of southern politics in the 1890s and early 1900s; the emergence of a stronger and more pervasive sense of social needs; and the belief in southern progress, an idea encouraged not only by the concept of economic development but also by a group of critics who wanted to reform various institutions and practices in the South. Improving economic prospects, the easing of political turmoil in the late 1890s, the apparent success of the new racial settlement, and the intersectional harmony displayed in the patriotic response to the Spanish-American War combined to provide a favorable setting for southern progressivism. Although rural influences were important in many of the reform movements, southern progressives were, characteristically, middle-class men and women, inhabitants of the urban South, and representatives of the new commercial and professional groups. They were moderate, eclectic, and resourceful in their approach to social problems. In general they sought to impose a greater measure of social order, to foster economic opportunity and efficiency, and to promote the well-being and morality of children, women, and other dependent persons.

One group of reforms was primarily concerned with establishing social controls and state regulation in troublesome areas such as race relations. The white consensus on race that evolved during this period reflected a widespread conviction that disfranchisement, segregation, and black proscription constituted a workable system of racial control and that these measures promised less corruption in politics, more consideration of "real" political issues, and a greater degree of social stability and public calm. Another example of the regulatory impulse was the movement to control railroads, insurance companies, and other large corporations. Given impetus by insurgent factions in the Democratic party, "reform governors," and coalition campaigns involving freight bureaus, farm organizations, and other interests, the effort to restrict the corporation induced most southern states to reorganize and strengthen their railroad commissions, to enact laws against corrupt practices and lobbying, and to try in various ways to protect consumers and to make government honest, efficient, and publicly responsive. State legislatures passed pure food and drug legislation, conservation measures, penal reforms, and other regulatory statutes. Almost all the southern states eventually adopted statewide laws prohibiting the manufacture and sale of alcoholic beverages.

A second significant class of reforms revolved around the theme of social justice. Social reforms of this kind included the movement to curb child labor, a series of spirited campaigns to establish public schools in the southern states, and an organized charity movement. Efforts to promote social justice in the South were closely related to the woman's movement, which emerged more distinctly in the region early in the 20th century. As time passed, this feminist reformism tended to find greater focus in the drive for suffrage. There was also an embryonic movement, spearheaded by black leaders and black organizations, to provide public services for Afro-Americans and to strengthen the black community.

Social efficiency, especially as it applied to economic development, was a discernible motif in another category of progressive endeavors. Among these concerns were a multifaceted attack on the ills of southern agriculture, a succession of civic improvements and municipal reforms, and an array of laws pertaining to railroad employees and other industrial workers. Efficiency was also an objective in the movements for public education, good roads, and public health. The success of these campaigns demonstrated that the state had become the source of vital new services.

By the time Woodrow Wilson assumed the presidency in March 1913, a new stage had arrived in the evolution of southern progressivism. Reform movements in the southern states, as in other sections, were increasingly influenced by national organizations, standards, and solutions. This tendency was evident in the formation of the Southern Sociological Congress, a regional civic association established in 1912; in the antitrust movement and the prohibition crusade; and in the South's greater involvement in the debate over national issues and elections. The region took a long step during the Wilson years in the direction of a more positive role in national politics. World War I also enlarged the presence of the federal government in the South and provided additional opportunities for the mobilization of the section's resources for social improvement as well as for military preparedness. Although the end of the war and the collapse of the Wilson administration in 1919 and 1920 weakened southern progressivism and disrupted its unity, reform continued to manifest itself in the form of "business progressivism" at the state level, in the work of the Commission on Interracial Cooperation, and in the struggle to preserve traditional morality.

Southern progressives espoused a complex of ideas that included material progress, efficiency, ethical standards, social order, a more vigorous regulatory state, social justice, public services, and especially the vision of a revitalized regional community. Even though the social balance they had nourished lost much of its vitality in the 1920s, the synthesis that resulted from their efforts to reconcile progress and tradition survived for half a century as an important influence in the politics and social thought of the South.

See also POLITICS articles

Dewey W. Grantham
Vanderbilt University

Hugh C. Bailey, *Liberalism in the New South: Southern Social Reformers and the Progressive Movement* (1969); Dewey W. Grantham, *Southern Progressivism: The Reconciliation of Progress and Tradition* (1983); Sheldon Hackney, *Populism to Progressivism in Alabama* (1969); Jack Temple Kirby, *Darkness at the Dawning: Race and Reform in the Progressive South* (1972); Raymond H. Pulley, *Old Virginia Restored: An Interpretation of the Progressive Impulse, 1870–1930* (1968); George B. Tindall, *The Emergence of the New South, 1913–1945* (1967); C. Vann Woodward, *Origins of the New South, 1877–1913* (1951).

Railroads

Even before the steam engine arrived in America, southerners considered the possibility of rail travel. In the late 1820s the Charleston & Hamburg tried sail-cars (which overturned or knocked the passengers out of their seats as the winds shifted) and cars drawn by a brace of dogs. For all their deficiencies—the sparks they showered on passengers, the jolting ride given by the stagecoaches used as cars, the high rate of accidents—the early steam engines worked much better. By 1830 the Baltimore & Ohio had introduced steam power to the South. That same year, Kentucky chartered the Lexington & Ohio, and Louisiana approved the Pontchartrain line from New Orleans to its nearby lake. As late as 1840 Georgia had only 185 miles of track, South Carolina 137—and they were better provided than most other southern states.

But in the next two decades railroads spread. During the 1850s mileage increased 244 percent in Virginia, 158 percent in North Carolina, and 1,062 percent in Mississippi. Visionaries of the Confederacy could not have wished them to grow faster. Until the late 1850s New Orleans had no rail link to Richmond; on the eve of the Civil War Arkansas had a mere 38 miles of track. During the conflict the North could depend on railroads to bring in supplies far more than could the South; and while the former expanded its network in wartime, the latter diminished it. War brought havoc, worst of all in South Carolina, where Union troops lifted rails from the roadbed, heated them, and twisted them around trees as "Sherman's hairpins." With American military aid in 1865 and public aid thereafter, a new railroad boom began. By 1900, 10 southern states had some 35,000 miles of track and Arkansas over 3,000.

Not all southerners appreciated railroads. Many suspected them as an alien invader of the plantation world they cherished. Thus, in eastern Kentucky the Louisville & Nashville found locals so unhelpful where one station was being planned that it finally named the place Uz, after the land in which Job had suffered. Two generations earlier, the same railroad's president was so offended by rudeness and squalor in Danville, Ky., that he ordered surveyors to build the track beyond earshot of the town; from then on, townsfolk could catch the train only by chartering taxis for a three-mile trip outside the city limits. In the 1830s a leading Barnwell landholder forced a projected railroad to pass through a town 10 miles distant by refusing a right-of-way across his land. To such folk, the railroad was, as a farmer once called it, "hell in harness."

But to most southerners railroads were welcome. Believers in a New South in the 1870s saw the lines as an essential beginning: without them, no immigrants could be brought in, mineral resources exploited, or factories built. Atlanta owed its growth to railroads, just as Milledgeville owed its decline and the loss of the state capital to its refusal to fund lines in the 1850s. Where Birmingham stood in 1900 there had been only farms in 1865; the crossing of two railroads had made a city known for its coal and steel production. Those who wanted a South economically independent of the North pressed for a transcontinental line from the Gulf to southern California and sought federal subsidies for it; so eager were they that a few Republican politicians in 1877 hoped to resolve the disputed presidential election by promises of aid. Southern Democrats denounced national aid to railroads, but they backed bills helping southern railroads, took land grants for the Mobile & Ohio and the Cairo & Fulton, and used state legislatures to provide still more aid.

Few doubted that railroads would make any town prosper. In the 1890s the Missouri & Northern Arkansas showed its influence, as construction created 33 new towns. The line fostered zinc mining and turned Harrison into a major Ozark trading center whose population increased by 117 percent in the second decade of the 20th century. Bypassing Carrollton, Duff, and Old Mount Pisgah, the road doomed them all. But for this reason, competition for railroads set southern state against state, town against town, as each tried to obtain special connections and prevent any rival from sharing in the benefits. Irritated by the lack of rail connections, Florida's panhandle threatened secession; annoyed by central Alabama's relationship with Pensacola, Mobile merchants hinted that they would join their city to Mississippi unless railroad aid was forthcoming. Louisville directors dreamed of an empire reaching the Gulf; Gilded Age Atlanta businessmen strove to dominate the Atlantic Seaboard and vied with Richmond interlopers. Often, fights dubbed "the Railroads against the People" turned out to be no more than the fight of one southern railroad's backers against another. Thus, the South became less united through railroad quarrels.

It also became less southern. From 1870 on, northern capital was crucial to southern lines, and with it northern control intruded. Of 311 directors on southern major roads (those with 100 or more miles of track) in 1900, 193 were northerners, including 121 New Yorkers. Northern railroads, eager to exploit Appalachian coal and timber, set the pace of development there, denuded the hillsides, and left slag and stumps where forests had been. Nor did railroads end the cash-crop economy. Rather, railroads opened new lands to cotton growers. Thus, Raymond, Miss., shipped 1,100 bales in 1851 and 7,000 bales in 1853.

Even so, railroads were welcomed with subsidies, land grants, and liberal charters. A line's completion became a holiday. When the Baltimore & Ohio commenced building, its ceremonies featured national politicians, Baltimore's mayor and city council, and surviving veterans of the American Revolution. To break ground, the company chose Charles Carroll of Carrollton, the last surviving signer of the Declaration of Independence. In 1896 the railroad even made a catastrophe an occasion by inviting visitors to Crush, Tex., to watch a railroad collision—which, when a boiler exploded, killed two onlookers and injured several more.

Louisville & Nashville railroad in mountains

The railroads also took on a special, if dubious, mystique in popular culture. They became a part of the landscape, described by such writers as William Faulkner, Eudora Welty, and Thomas Wolfe. They symbolized mobility, escape from the confinements of rural life. Southern musicians frequently sang of the rails, partly because so many of them had personal connections to railroad life. Bluesman Sleepy John Estes was a caller on track gangs in west Tennessee; Jimmie Rodgers ("the Singing Brakeman") grew up the son of a section foreman for the Gulf, Mobile & Ohio Railroad; A. P. Carter worked on a railroad crew; and Peg Leg Sam lost a leg while riding a freight train.

Two of the most popular railroad songs enshrined southern figures. As an engineer on the Illinois Central, Casey Jones saved his passengers at the cost of his own life in 1900; in 1950 the postal service issued a special stamp with the Missourian's likeness on it. John Henry, the black steel driver, who probably worked on the Big Bend Tunnel in West Virginia around 1870, actually did challenge the steam drill and win, and he may actually have driven a 14-foot hole when his rival could only do a 9-foot one. Other southern railroad ballads have a tragic flavor: classics like "The Wreck of Old 97," based on a 1903 Virginia smash-up, and "The Wreck of the C & O," based on a catastrophe some years later. Other blues and country songs take a melancholy tone from their recollection of that "lonesome whistle" sound.

Other expressions of popular culture humorously noted the inefficiency of southern lines. Playing on initials, observers christened the Georgia & Florida the God-Forgotten; the Carolina & Northwestern was the Can't and Never-Will; and the Houston, East & West Texas was the Hell Either Way You Take It. In 1903 Thomas W. Jackson published a best-selling joke book, *On a Slow Train through Arkansas*, mocking that state's transportation. One story told how a train halted. "There are some cattle on the track," the conductor explained. Soon the train was moving again, but not for long. "We have caught up with those cattle again," passengers were told. The lines' unprofitability may even have made the roads safer from robbery, though in the 1880s Rube Barrow robbed at least seven trains in the Old Southwest and even held up the same train three days apart, once on the northbound and once on the southbound journey. After the Civil War a bandit stopped the Cotton Belt, and the company president got off to chide him. "Aren't you ashamed of yourself to . . . try to rob a road as poor as this one?" he is said to have complained. "Why don't you go over and hold up the Iron Mountain?" The bandit slunk away—and took the advice.

But such joking never concealed the real need the railroads answered, nor the petty favors they could do. Southbound trains entering Florida would toot to warn farmers of a coming freeze; the branch line into Lebanon, Tenn., would blast its whistle to announce an important news story or spread the fire alarm. In Kentucky a thoughtful engineer reportedly broke into church services to play "Oh, How I Love Jesus" on his whistle, but he blasted his reputation with the ministers the next week by playing "How Dry I Am." In the early 1900s railroads ran special trains to bring city folks to lynchings in outlying counties. More substantially, the Illinois Central encouraged Mississippians to go into commercial vegetable farming by sponsoring practical demonstrations of new methods and carrying in agricultural exhibits. Thanks to railroad encouragement, Lebanon, Tenn., cedar served in the building of Pittsburgh and adorned the lounge of Chicago's Palmer House.

Southern railroads continued to grow until the 1920s. Then, under increasing competition with automobiles and trucks, the rail lines cut back service, merged, or closed down operations altogether. Between 1916 and 1960 mileage fell over 20 percent in Arkansas, Louisiana, and North Carolina. After the Depression the roads never fully recovered. The Pontchartrain was sold, and its roadbed became a boulevard, Elysian Fields Avenue. The Middle Tennessee & Alabama shared a similar ignominious fate. With the railroads' decline the towns that had been built around them either adapted to highways or died out. As engines switched to diesel power, towns that had provided coal, wood, and water vanished as quickly as they had come. Today most southern towns have at best a boarded-up depot, a mute monument to the New South that was.

See also FOLKLIFE: / Jones, Casey; Henry, John; INDUSTRY: / Railroad Industry; MYTHIC SOUTH: New South Myth; SOCIAL CLASS: / Railroad Workers

Mark W. Summers
University of Kentucky

Eugene Alvarez, *Travel on Southern Antebellum Railroads, 1828–1860* (1974); Benjamin F. Botkin and Alvin F. Harlow, eds., *A Treasury of Railroad Folklore: The Stories, Tall Tales, Traditions, Ballads and Songs of the American Railroad Man* (1953); Norm Cohen, *Long Steel Rail: The Railroad in American Folksong* (1980); Lee A. Dew, *Arkansas Historical Quarterly* (November 1970); Lawrence R. Handley, *Arkansas Historical Quarterly* (Winter 1974); Steve Hoffus, *Southern Exposure* (Spring 1977); Richard D. Lawlor, *Tennessee Historical Quarterly* (Winter 1972); James L. McCorkle, Jr., *Journal of Mississippi History* (May 1977); John Hebron Moore, *Journal of Mississippi History* (February 1979); John F. Stover, *The Railroads of the South, 1865–1900: A Study of Finance and Control* (1955); Mark W. Summers, *Railroads, Reconstruction, and the Gospel of Prosperity: Aid under the Radical Republicans, 1865–1877* (1984).

Reconstruction

Reconstruction was the period from 1865 to 1877, when national efforts were concentrated after the Civil War on incorporating the South back into the Union. The period involved important constitutional and political issues, but from the viewpoint of cultural history Reconstruction's underlying significance was its effort to remake southern culture. Neither before nor since have northerners had the opportunity to refashion a peculiar region. Some northerners approached this in a spirit of vengeance, seeking to punish southerners for the war; others had political motives for wanting to reduce southern influence and insure Republican party dominance and patronage for themselves; others were adventurers out to earn their fortune; still others were idealistic reformers hoping to aid freedmen adjust to their new status. Organizations such as the Freedmen's Bureau, the American Missionary Association, the northern Protestant denominations, the Republican party, and the Union League represented the forces of the North. The image of the Yankee schoolmarm in the South was a prime example of this effort at cultural transformation. The Union soldier was another symbol of the effort: under the Reconstruction Act of 1867 the South was divided into five military districts and troops enforced government decisions. The cast of characters also included rapacious carpetbaggers, traitorous native scalawags, and ignorant freedmen.

This at least was the mythic view of Reconstruction. According to the myth of Reconstruction, for a decade after 1867 carpetbaggers, scalawags, and freedmen ran the governments of the southern states, looting their financial resources, passing high taxes, denying whites a role in government, and spreading terror throughout the region. Only with the withdrawal of federal troops in 1877 did the terror end. Claude Bowers spoke for a generation of historians when he called Reconstruction "the tragic era."

Beginning in the 1950s modern historians such as Kenneth Stampp, C. Vann Woodward, and others challenged and revised this mythic view. Reconstruction, for example, did not last as long in most states as the myth suggests. Southern conservative, white-dominated governments took power in Virginia and North Carolina in 1870, in Georgia in 1871, in Arkansas, Texas, and Alabama in 1874, and in Mississippi in 1876. Federal troops were not withdrawn in South Carolina, Louisiana, and Florida until 1877. Moreover, actual military rule ended in 1868 in all the states except Virginia, Mississippi, and Texas, where in each case it ended in either 1869 or 1870. Civil state governments were in charge after that, except for brief periods of reliance on the militia or federal troops. No more than 20,000 federal troops were involved in the process.

Fraud surely occurred in elections, but the same was true of elections elsewhere in that period and under the conservative regimes that followed the Reconstruction governments. Only 150,000 whites were disfranchised under the initial military phase of Reconstruction, out of an 1868 white registration of approximately 630,000. Few whites voted and many blacks did, and more than disfranchisement, this explains the character of the participants in the governments. Blacks held offices during Reconstruction, mostly at the local level, but only in South Carolina was there a black on the Supreme Court and only the South Carolina and Louisiana legislatures had a majority of blacks. And no black served as a southern governor.

"The tragedy of Reconstruction is that it failed," wrote Carl N. Degler in *Out of Our Past: Forces That Made Modern America* (1970). Degler points out that modern historical scholarship rejects the idea of Reconstruction as a unique period of bad government and oppression, but one should remember that generations of southerners believed the myth, which nurtured in them the belief in regional differences and a consciousness of past abuse at the hands of northerners and their own former slaves. At the end of the war southern whites had accepted the end of slavery, but Reconstruction showed their real commitment to a racial color line. This, not slavery, was a life-and-death matter. The thought of black social and political equality was unacceptable to whites. Southern whites united in the 1870s in resisting northern-imposed radical change designed to end white supremacy. After the war, in fact, the defense of white supremacy became more clearly a southern position than before. In the proslavery argument the defense of white supremacy was couched in the broader defense of slavery, but race itself became the key issue in the postbellum era.

Reconstruction was a struggle fought on many fronts. The same conflicts and issues seen in political life were also present in other areas of the culture. The Protestant denominations, for example, experienced troubles between blacks and whites, northerners and southerners. The spirit of Christian brotherhood did temper religious disputes more often than political conflicts. The northern missionary was an important symbol of Reconstruction. Missionaries came south to convert the freedmen and succeeded as blacks joined several northern-based, predominantly black denominations. They also came expecting that southern whites would reunite with the northern churches, but southern whites exercised their spiritual self-determination during Reconstruction by preserving their regionally organized churches—the Southern Baptist Convention, the Methodist Episcopal Church, South, and the Presbyterian Church in the United States of America.

Education also reflected issues of Reconstruction. Northern teachers believed education would end the ignorance and brutality that abolitionists said existed in the South. Schools would promote democracy and class equality in good American idealistic fashion. Blacks responded enthusiastically to the opportunities, but faced the opposition of southern whites, who ostracized the northern teachers. Sometimes blacks also faced condescension of northern teachers who had their own racist preconceptions about southern blacks. Ultimately, though, the Radical Reconstruction program for public education was accepted. The southern white-controlled governments that came after Reconstruction did not reject black education, although insisting on racially segregated systems of instruction.

In the development of southern black culture, the Reconstruction period should not be seen as a failure. Much progress occurred in the development of vital institutions: in education and landowning, in particular, and in community development. New leadership was tested for the future. Scholars have shown that the family survived slavery and in Reconstruction became a typically southern focus for individual endeavors. There was, to be sure, a debate on approaches toward the future. Was the best strategy racial self-help or interracial cooperation? Some black leaders worked for civil and political rights, while others—and probably the majority of the freedmen themselves—favored land and education.

Efforts by southern whites to end Reconstruction began almost as soon as the radical state governments took power. Not until northern weariness with enforcing Reconstruction took hold could much be done. Virginia was the first state "redeemed," a term southern whites used. Redemption was the process of replacing the radical governments with conservative southern white governments. It was a well-organized political effort that also involved economic intimidation, community ostracism, political fraud, and violence. The Ku Klux Klan was the most common group involved in the violence. The Klan was a terrorist group that used violence against blacks and white Republicans in the name of preserving the morality and virtue of white civilization. Conservative whites eventually favored disbanding the Klan, which Nathan Bedford Forrest, its grand wizard, did in 1869, charging that outlaws had diverted it from its once high mission. Groups such as the Knights of the White Camellia and the White Brotherhood carried on the Klan's tradition, and Congress passed three Enforcement Acts in 1870–71 to deal with their violence. Nonetheless, the use of violence and other tactics led to the election of white southern conservatives, who maintained power thereafter, ending the threat to white supremacy. These methods of regaining power were called the Mississippi plan, because they were perfected in that state in 1875–76. The Compromise of 1877, an informal, extralegal arrangement between southern Democrats and northern Republicans, brought the removal of federal troops from the South and the official end of Reconstruction.

Reconstruction had a positive legacy for the South. New state constitutions were written, many of which are still in effect as the basic documents of the states. It brought reforms in judicial systems, in codes of government procedure, in operation of county governments, in procedures for taxation, and in methods of electing governmental officials. Education was advanced, laying the basis for free public education. And constitutional amendments passed in that era supported the 20th-century civil rights movement's use of federal force to change the South's system of legal segregation.

See also MYTHIC SOUTH: Reconstruction Myth

Charles Reagan Wilson
University of Mississippi

Dan T. Carter, *When the War Was Over: The Failure of Self-Reconstruction in the South, 1865–67* (1984); LaWanda Cox and J. H. Cox, *Reconstruction, the Negro, and the New South* (1973); Avery O. Craven, *Reconstruction: The Ending of the Civil War* (1969); Robert Cruden, *The Negro in Reconstruction* (1969); John Hope Franklin, *Reconstruction: After the Civil War* (1961); Michael Perman, *The Road to Redemption: Southern Politics, 1869–1879* (1984); Howard N. Rabinowitz, ed., *Southern Black Leaders of the Reconstruction Era* (1982); George C. Rable, *The Role of Violence in the Politics of Reconstruction* (1984); James G. Randall and David Donald, *The Civil War and Reconstruction* (1961); Kenneth M. Stampp, *Era of Re-*

construction, 1865–1877 (1965); Mark W. Summers, *Railroads, Reconstruction, and the Gospel of Prosperity: Aid under the Radical Republicans, 1865–1877* (1984); C. Vann Woodward, *Reunion and Reaction: The Compromise of 1877 and the End of Reconstruction* (1951).

Revolutionary Era

The revolutionary era did not create the southern states, but it did help to create the South as a section. The efforts of national leaders during the period failed to bring the region fully and comfortably into the new national framework at the same time that events turned the South into a more distinct, uniform region. The resulting conflicts marked and marred the antebellum period and ultimately led to civil war.

Prior to 1774 southerners unquestionably thought of themselves as distinct from "eastern" or northern residents, but they thought in provincial rather than in sectional terms. When Patrick Henry in 1774 told the members of the First Continental Congress that he was "not a Virginian, but an American," the alternatives he chose were state and nation, not North and South. Fifteen years later he had changed both his outlook and his choice of terms. Fighting adoption of the Constitution, he was to argue that "southern" interests would be overpowered by the demands of "northern" states.

This is not, of course, to suggest that there was no thought of regional characteristics before the American Revolution. George Washington, arriving in Boston to take command of the Continental army, found New Englanders impossibly democratic. Abigail Adams blamed the institution of slavery for the cruelty and selfishness she found in southerners. Thomas Jefferson had clearly given some thought to sectional characteristics long before 1785, when he reported to the Marquis de Chastellux that northerners were hypocritical in religion, cool, sober, independent, and conniving, while southerners were fiery, voluptuary, indolent, generous, candid, and unsteady. Even after the adoption of the Constitution some South Carolina leaders found New York City a more acceptable location for the national capital than Annapolis because the former was more accessible.

At the beginning of the revolutionary era at least three distinct regions existed within the South. The Chesapeake, with its tobacco culture, differed significantly from the South Carolina Low Country with its rice, indigo, and majority-slave population. Even more distinct was a third region, the vast southern upcountry, which stretched from Virginia into Georgia and was characterized by the absence of a full-scale slavery system, smaller land holdings, and a significant population of Native Americans. The revolutionary era helped to erase many of the distinctions between these regions and contributed to a sense of sectional solidarity.

The South was ultimately defined, though, by slavery and the plantation system. The rise of the great planter families, the reduced flow of emigration from Europe, the fear of slave revolts, the desperate efforts to replicate English society, and the failure to develop a strong commercial or industrial economy were all tied to the institution of slavery. Edmund S. Morgan has suggested that even the commitment of Virginians to freedom during the Revolution was made possible by the establishment of an enslaved, and therefore powerless, working class.

The Revolution and the creation of a new nation intensified the distinction between North and South. At first the contradiction between fighting for freedom and holding slaves bothered many prominent southerners, just as it did leaders in the northern states. Pauline Maier, in a provocative essay on Richard Henry Lee, has argued that for at least one prominent Virginian, slavery was only one in a series of problems that made the South feel inferior, at least in theory, to New England. Virginia's colonial government had been inferior, the College of William and Mary was unsuitable, the economy was backward, and the climate was unhealthy. It seems unlikely that many prominent southerners gazed enviously at the "New England Way," but certainly many considered the effects of slavery unhealthy for both the enslaved and the enslavers.

With the formation of the new nation and the elimination of slavery in the colonies north of Maryland, the sense of southern isolation intensified. The Constitution marked the effort of a group of major leaders from Virginia and South Carolina to bring their states fully into the new national framework on acceptable terms. Compromises on slavery and restrictions on regulating trade marked that effort. Both northerners and southerners gave ground in a sincere attempt, temporarily successful, to bring the diverse interests of the two sections into harmony. In the long run this effort would fail, in large part because slavery became more firmly entrenched in the South.

The development of political parties in the new nation illustrates the growing sense of common economic and political interests among the southern states. James Madison's unsuccessful attempt to remain supportive of the emerging Federalist party is illustrative. Men like Madison and Jefferson opposed the Federalists not simply because the Washington Administration was increasing the power of the new central government but, more importantly, because they feared the influences that seemed to dominate the policies of the Federalists. Alexander Hamilton's financial plans regarding the nation's and the states' debts and the Bank of the United States seemed to favor commercial interests, and the South appeared destined to remain agricultural and rural. The French Revolution and the ensuing conflict between England and France further divided the nation along sectional lines. The importance of trade brought the northern states to the support of England, while southerners were moved by the struggle of the French revolutionaries. Along with this hardening of sectional lines, the development of the cotton gin in 1791 was to reduce further the differences between the coastal areas and the upcountry, as the extension of slaveholding and the rise of an upcountry planter class in South Carolina would illustrate.

By the time John Adams took office, the so-called Virginia-Massachusetts alliance, which had so often dominated the revolutionary movement, was clearly broken, and at least some Federalists seemed determined to crush the southern dissidents once and for all. The Alien and Sedition Acts and the machinations of Alexander Hamilton drove the new nation close to disruption, and the refusal of Adams and Jefferson to communicate for years after the election of 1800 further illustrates the divisions between the two sections.

The Virginia presidents after 1800 seemed to unite the nation again and bring the South not only back into the mainstream but into a position of dominance. Benjamin W. Labaree, among others, has noted that it was the merchants of the North who screamed for disunion by the second decade of the 19th century. Below the surface, however, the peculiar needs of the South, which had presumably been guaranteed by constitutional compromises—the three-fifths clause, the prohibition of export duties, the limits on restricting the slave trade—were still at odds with the rest of the nation. The tendency of southerners to look to England and Europe for culture was to continue, and regional dialects flourished.

Although it is important to remember that the South was not monolithic—the area that produced John C. Calhoun also brought forth Andrew Jackson—the dominant influences binding the South made it distinct from the North and, ultimately, from the West. South Carolinians from the Charleston area who for a time supported the Federalist party and even the protective tariff were to be disappointed in their hopes of creating a commercial center. In the end they would lead the movement to secession and become the most rabid southerners of all.

Many contradictions existed in the revolutionary South. Those who accused New Englanders of being levelers became the firm supporters of the French Revolution; southerners who cherished their English heritage gave up their established church, while New Englanders clung to theirs; plantation owners who condemned slavery and constantly worried over the issue in their private correspondence refused to free their own slaves. Southerners were open, hospitable advocates of the ideals of freedom and virtue, fiercely loyal to their region, and confused by the seemingly insoluble problems of slavery.

The enthusiasms of the revolutionary movement of 1774 to 1776, which bound the colonists together and brought Patrick Henry to declare himself "an American," soon faded as a variety of sections—and individuals—began to pursue their own interests. The South was different, and that difference could not be masked. In agriculture, in political institutions, in culture, and—most importantly—in the development of slavery and the plantation system, there were differences that set the region solidly apart from the rest of the nation. The Revolution did not create those differences and, for a time, the development of a new nation seemed to reduce their importance. But for good or for bad the South was a distinct region in 1776 and despite many variations on the theme has remained so.

David Ammerman
Florida State University

John R. Alden, *The First South* (1961), *The South in the Revolution, 1763–1789* (1957); Carl Bridenbaugh, *Myths and Realities: Societies of the Colonial South* (1952); Jack P. Greene, *The Quest for Power: The Lower Houses of Assembly in the Southern Royal Colonies, 1689–1776* (1963); Rhys Isaac, *The Transformation of Virginia, 1740–1790* (1982); Benjamin W. Labaree, *Patriots and Partisans: The Merchants of Newburyport, 1764–1815* (1975); Pauline Maier, *The Old Revolutionaries: Political Lives in the Age of Samuel Adams* (1980); Edmund S. Morgan, *American Slavery, American Freedom: The Ordeal of Colonial Virginia* (1975); Charles Royster, *A Revolutionary People at War: The Continental Army and American Character, 1775–1783* (1979); Robert M. Weir, *"The Last of American Freemen": Studies in the Political Culture of the Colonial and Revolutionary South* (1986).

Sexuality

The South is often portrayed as a subculture obsessed with sexual repression yet charged with undercurrents of sexual tension. Little concrete evidence exists, however, for evaluating the uniqueness of sexual attitudes and behaviors among southerners, despite widespread attention to the study of human sexuality in the 20th century. Many social-science researchers either do not control for or do not consider regional differences in analyzing their data. In addition to the limited data from social science, however, many insights about southerners and sexuality can be found in the region's literature, music, and oral folklore.

Probably the best-known images of southern sexual relations are the portrayals of steamy antebellum-era trysts in the vein of Kyle Onstott's *Mandingo*, emphasizing miscegenation and brutal control and use of sexuality. Historians generally agree that certain codes of behavior did in fact dominate the antebellum South: white men had the greatest latitude in fulfilling their sexual desires; black women were expected to be sexually accessible and more sexually expressive than white women; black men's sexuality was viewed as threatening and was tightly controlled; and white women were expected not to have sexual desires and to stand as asexual paragons of virtue. Sociological studies such as John Dollard's *Caste and Class in a Southern Town* (1937) confirmed the persistence of some of these attitudinal and behavioral patterns during the early 20th century.

Aspects of the striking gender- and race-based double standards were not endemic to the South but represented national trends as well. Nineteenth-century physicians, moralists, and social commentators were obsessed with appropriate channeling of men's sexual urges and with suppression of women's sexuality. Physicians writing in the *New Orleans Medical and Surgical Journal* in the mid-1850s, for example, recognized men's strong sex drives but warned against masturbation because it drained men of the will for self-sufficiency. Women were exhorted to be virtuous, chaste, and pious—to keep their minds above sexuality. Married women, though, were also duty-bound to be available sexually to their husbands. Historian Barbara Welter refers to this view as "the cult of true womanhood," which flourished nationwide between 1820 and 1860. Although historian Carl N. Degler and others question the extent of actual acceptance of such exhortations, a strong double standard prevailed and was probably intensified by the chivalric code in the South.

Some examples of brutal repression of sexuality in the South exist. During the 18th and 19th centuries the nationwide trend was toward disapproval of the use of castration as a legal punishment. However, notes Eugene D. Genovese, "scattered evidence suggests that some masters continued to apply it [castration] especially to slaves who had become their rivals for coveted black women." Female castration became common throughout the country after 1872, when Georgia physician Robert Battey developed the surgical techniques for "normal ovariotomy," a procedure he enthusiastically endorsed for "problems" ranging from "erotic tendencies" to "troublesomeness." As G. J. Barker-Benfield notes, this technique remained popular until about 1921, and numerous female circumcisions and clitoridectomies were also performed.

Scientific studies of sexual behaviors and attitudes began in the late 1800s. Unfortunately, no regionally specific data are available from such early studies as those of Dr. Clelia Mosher and Katherine Davis. Even Alfred Kinsey and associates employed no regional identifiers in analysis of the data from their landmark 1948 study, *Sexual Behavior in the Human Male*. Other demographic variables such as religion, education, and urban-rural residence that are confounded with region of residence were the primary bases for analyses. According to Kinsey and associates' *Sexual Behavior in the Human Female* (1953), approximately 3,600 of their total male and female samples of 16,392 cases were southerners. Nevertheless, the researchers commented in the 1953 volume that despite widespread assumptions about regional differences in sexual behavior, "we have an impression, as yet unsubstantiated by specific calculations, that there are actually few differences in sex patterns between similar communities in different portions of the United States." This impression seems to have guided much subsequent research.

As the so-called sexual revolution gained momentum, interest grew in the changing rates of premarital intercourse, and regional comparisons became more common. One important early investigation was Winston Ehrmann's 1959 study of premarital sexuality among students at the University of Florida. Sixty-five percent of the 576 males and 13 percent of the 265 females in the sample reported having had premarital intercourse. In a major 1964 study, Ira Reiss concluded that there was a nationwide trend toward acceptance of premarital intercourse on the basis of affection but not necessarily commitment to marriage, though in behavior the double standard still prevailed. Sixteen percent of the high-school and college students in Reiss's Virginia sample accepted the "permissiveness with affection" standard compared to 72 percent of the respondents in New York.

Attention to regional differences heightened with publication in 1968 of Vance Packard's *The Sexual Wilderness*. Packard reported results of a study of college juniors and seniors nationwide, with a total of 185 respondents from 3 southern institutions represented. Among the southern respondents about 69 percent of the males and 32 percent of the females reported having had premarital intercourse. This rate for males was the highest in the country; the rate for southern females was next to the lowest. Furthermore, southern males were the most likely to have taken part in a one-night affair with someone they never dated again. "The South has the nation's strongest reputation for a double standard in regard to sexual behavior," said Packard. "That reputation receives support in the survey results." Regarding attitudes, Packard found the strongest support of the double standard among females from the South and the Midwest. Commented Packard, "A major surprise (to us) was that next to the Easterners the males most untroubled by the idea of courting a nonvirginal girl were the Southerners (36 percent responding 'no')." More recent investigations have shown that southerners are now following the trend toward "permissiveness with affection." For example, researchers who compared data from 1965, 1970, and 1975 samples of students at one major state university in the South found trends congruent with national ones, particularly in the "dramatic liberalization in both premarital sexual behavior and attitudes for college females."

Beyond the information on premarital sexual standards, especially among the college educated, however, little reliable information exists about regional variations in sexual behavior and attitude, whether normative (e.g., sexual relations among married couples) or nonnormative (e.g., extramarital sexual relations, homosexual or lesbian relations). Most recent large-scale studies of sexuality have not dealt with regional patterns. Laws in the South regarding sexual activities, however, provide valuable insights about the mixture of attitudes regarding sexuality.

For a brief period during the Civil War, Nashville registered and periodically inspected prostitutes, the first such system in the nation. As of 1885 Louisiana, Arkansas, and New Mexico were the only three states in which "red light" districts for prostitution were legal. New Orleans's notorious district, Storyville, was such an accepted institution in the late 1800s that guide books were distributed at restaurants, taverns, and other tourist attractions. As of 1975 Mississippi was the only state that allowed conjugal visits for married prisoners and provided cottages for such meetings. When the streaking craze hit the country and many locales prosecuted the participants for indecent exposure, the Louisiana Legislature "excluded from prosecution streakers who did not attempt to arouse the sexual desires of their viewers." Also, southern states legalized use of birth control by married couples and interracial marriage before some other states.

On the other hand, although many states in the 1960s and 1970s revised their penal codes to allow adults to engage in any sexual acts in private, Georgia doubled its penalties for consensual sodomy. Georgia, Kentucky, South Carolina, and Wisconsin stood out for years as the few states specifically penalizing both female and male homosexual practices (most states overlooked lesbian activities). In 1986 national attention focused on the Georgia sodomy statutes when the U.S. Supreme Court heard the case of a homosexual man from Georgia and upheld the state's right to define sodomy (oral or anal sex) as a felony punishable by 20 years in prison. As of 1986, 12 of the 24 states that had criminal penalties for sodomy were southern, with maximum penalties in the South ranging from a $200 fine in Texas to Georgia's 20-year term. Southern laws gained further attention in 1986 when a federal appeals court panel upheld Virginia's laws against fornication and cohabitation, enacted in 1829 and 1860 respectively.

Impressionistic information about southern sexuality abounds in anecdotal accounts, literary images, and representations in television, movies, and popular music. According to historian Thomas L. Connelly, southern folklore contains a variety of sexual stereotypes, such as "the high school bad girl," who dresses provocatively and undulates rather than walks, and the "good old boy tribal shouter," who hangs out of his pickup truck to "deliver ancient Celtic tribal shouts such as 'who-oo-wee'" when an attractive girl passes by. Southerners have not been reticent about examining sexuality's role in their lives. Writers such as Florence King, author of *Southern Ladies and Gentlemen* (1976), and Rayna Green, a contributor to *Speaking for Ourselves: Women of the South* (1984), provide lively personal observations on southern morals, sex roles, and sexual behaviors. For decades southern poets and novelists have grappled with "sin, sex, and segregation," according to Richard H. King, and examples of southern writers' struggles with the theme of sexuality are innumerable. Southern newspaper columnists write openly about sex and social relationships in the region; country music and blues lyricists incorporate many frank sexual themes; "common folk" readily swap sexual tales and advice; and such "sex symbols" as Burt Reynolds, Cybill Shepherd, George Hamilton, and Lauren Hutton cast images of southern sexuality. Nevertheless, strong community, family, and religious norms remain important influences on southerners' views about sexuality; and a majority of southerners maintain that these influences are the keys to addressing such problems as the region's alarmingly high teenage pregnancy rates. Much remains to be discovered about sexual behaviors and attitudes in the South and their integral ties to religion, race relations, social class, and gender stratification.

Sharon A. Sharp
University of Mississippi

Edward G. Armstrong, *Journal of Sex Research* (August 1986); G. J. Barker-Benfield, in *The American Family in Social-Historical Perspective*, ed. Michael Gordon (2d ed., 1978); Thomas L. Connelly, *Columbia Record* (30 August 1985); Carl N. Degler, in *The American Family in Socio-Historical Perspective*, ed. Michael Gordon (2d ed., 1978); John R. Earle and Philip J. Perricone, *Journal of Sex Research* (August 1986); Winston Ehrmann, *Premarital Dating Behavior* (1959); Paul H. Gebhard, *Sexual Behavior in the Human Female* (1953); Eugene D. Genovese, *Roll, Jordan, Roll: The World the Slaves Made* (1972); Rayna Green, in *Speaking for Ourselves: Women of the South*, ed. Maxine Alexander (1984); Herant A. Katchadourian and Donald T. Lunde, *Fundamentals of Human Sexuality* (2d ed., 1975); Karl King, Jack O. Balswick, and Ira E. Robinson, *Journal of Marriage and the Family* (August 1977); Richard H. King, *A Southern Renaissance: The Cultural Awakening of the American South, 1930–1955* (1980); Alfred C. Kinsey, Wardell B. Pomeroy, and Clyde E. Martin, *Sexual Behavior in the Human Male* (1948); *Newsweek* (14 July 1986); Vance Packard, *The Sexual Wilderness* (1968); Ira L. Reiss, *Journal of Marriage and the Family* (May 1964), *The Social Context of Premarital Sexual Permissiveness* (1967); Bradley Smith, *The American Way of Sex* (1978); Barbara Welter, in *The American Family in Socio-Historical Perspective*, ed. Michael Gordon (2d ed., 1978); John Wheeler and Peter Kilman, *Archives of Sexual Behavior* (June 1983).

Spanish-American War

Congress declared war against Spain on 11 April 1898. The conflict grew out of the general imperialist sentiment of the age, the desire of the American business community for overseas trade, the frustrations accompanying economic depression in the early 1890s, the growth in American military power, and humanitarian interest in the supposed Spanish repression of the Cuban people. The war was short and decisive, lasting 113 days, costing 5,500 American lives (most of those died from disease or accident rather than in battle), and resulting in American control of Cuba, Puerto Rico, Guam, and the Philippines.

Southerners supported the war enthusiastically, reflecting longtime regional interests in the Caribbean. Southerners had dreamed of controlling Cuba—the "Pearl of the Antilles"—before the Civil War. Mississippian John Quitman had helped plan a filibustering expedition to seize the island in the mid-1850s. Southerners saw Cuba as the target for sectional Manifest Destiny, which would extend plantation slavery to Cuba and promote southern political strength. This hope for a southern empire in the Caribbean was the "purple dream" immortalized by Stephen Vincent Benét in *John Brown's Body*.

In the 1890s the Spanish-American War brought prosperity to parts of the South. New South boosters saw the war as a boon to regional economic growth. Chickamauga, Tenn., Mobile, Ala., and New Orleans were assembly points for American troops, while Tampa, Fla., was the chief training and embarkation site for the invasion of Cuba. South Florida had become before the war the center of Cuban settlement in the United States, as refugees from the island worked in cigar factories and planned the overthrow of Spanish rule. José Martí, the chief Cuban revolutionary figure, had visited in Tampa in 1891.

Racial attitudes were important in creating southern reactions to the war. The nation had accepted the "white man's burden" in this era of Anglo-Saxon racism. Southerners saw this national attitude as a confirmation of regional segregation. Over 10,000 black troops—known as "smoked Yankees"—served in the volunteer army that waged war. The four regular-army regiments of black troops, who had served in Indian campaigns in the West, moved to the South in preparation for a Cuban invasion. They endured segregated restaurants, hotels, waiting rooms, saloons, and other public facilities, and violence resulted. About 4,000 black soldiers were stationed in Tampa and Lakeland, Fla., and tensions there led to rioting between white and black soldiers and civilians. Shortly after this, black troops played a key role in the Cuban invasion, especially at San Juan Hill.

The Spanish-American War was a landmark of North-South, post–Civil War reconciliation. Young men from Dixie eagerly volunteered for the fighting. Methodist Bishop Warren Candler spoke for many other southerners when he said that the military tradition, the memory of the Confederate past, and belief in fighting for principle had inspired the patriotism of 1898 in the South. "Visions of heroic sires inflamed the courage of gallant sons," he said in a speech. Southern newspapers pronounced the Spanish-American War the real end of the Civil War. Some of the unreconstructed, to be sure, proposed that southern troops be allowed to wear gray uniforms while fighting for the Union, but that was not taken seriously. Two veterans of the Confederate cause, Fitzhugh Lee and "Fighting Joe" Wheeler, were appointed as major generals, and Wheeler was credited with the best line of the war. As the Spaniards retreated during the battle, Wheeler yelled, "We've got the damn Yankees on the run." The saying was widely retold, and the humorous appreciation of it by all sides contributed to the feeling of reconciliation. The spilling of northern and southern blood in a common cause, fighting for liberty, represented a new national bond. Southerners now honored young heroes of nationalism. "These dead, at least, belong to us all," said a Confederate veteran's meeting in 1899. President William McKinley promoted this spirit, pledging in Atlanta in 1898 that the national government would now care for Confederate graves. The memory of the Spanish-American War was preserved in the stories of, and tributes to, the veterans of the struggle and by such regional folksongs as "Manila Bay."

Charles Reagan Wilson
University of Mississippi

Paul Buck, *The Road to Reunion, 1865–1900* (1938); Frank Freidel, *The Splendid Little War* (1958); Willard B. Gatewood, Jr., *"Smoked Yankees" and the Struggle for Empire: Letters from Negro Soldiers, 1898–1902* (1971); Gerald Linderman, *The Mirror of War: American Society and the Spanish-American War* (1974); H. Wayne Morgan, *America's Road to Empire: The War with Spain and Overseas Expansion* (1965); David F. Trask, *The War with Spain in 1898* (1981).

Stoicism

Stoicism entered the South through the influence of the Enlightenment, when there was renewed appreciation of the classical tradition. Cosmopolitan southerners of the revolutionary era were familiar with Greek and Roman writings. One of the most influential of southerners, Thomas Jefferson, read avidly at an early age the classical moral philosophers, although no comprehensive philosophy emerged from his study and he was never a true disciple of them. Jefferson was attracted to both stoicism, with its emotional restraint, and epicureanism, with its hedonistic ethics. He saw moral advantages in each position and tried to hold them in balance. Stoicism seemed especially strong in his youth. In one of Jefferson's earliest letters he wrote that human beings must "consider that whatever does happen, must happen," and they must "bear up with a tolerable degree of patience under this burden of life." Jefferson surely admired the discipline of the will he saw in stoicism. Like many Enlightenment thinkers, Jefferson saw both stoicism and epicureanism as systems of practical morality, separate from any church or governmental connection. He used the classical Stoics to prove that an adequate moral philosophy could exist without any supernatural justification. In general, for Jefferson and early southern students of classical thought, epicureanism provided the goal of a good life, and stoicism, with its control of the will, offered the means of attaining it.

A few intellectuals like Jefferson had been attracted to stoicism in the 18th century, but the philosophy took on a broader social significance in the antebellum period of the 19th century. The southern cult of honor became deeply rooted in the region under the influence of Enlightenment rationalism. The southern model of honorable behavior conformed to the classical heritage. One had to face public examination for a moral failure rather than experience private alienation from God. James McBride Dabbs once wrote that the "basic flaw at the heart of the South" was "the unresolved conflict between Christianity and Stoicism." Walker Percy, another analyst of regional stoicism, has agreed, arguing that the South was always more stoic than Christian. When a southerner named a city Corinth, Percy wrote, "he did not mean Paul's community." Whatever degree of nobility and graciousness has existed in the South, according to Percy, "was the nobility and graciousness of the Old Stoa."

Stoicism took root in the Old South partly because of its stress on individualism, which seemed to suit the planter elite. Human freedom was all important to the early Stoics, and living surrounded by slaves apparently made the same concern a central one of southern planters. But freedom was not unrestrained. In its social role stoicism in the South was based on paternalism, reflecting a hierarchical social structure, as had the earlier Greek version. It taught the southern elite to behave with noblesse oblige. Not to behave honorably would be, again in Percy's words, "to defile the inner fortress which was oneself."

From another direction, a pronounced moralistic tendency among some southerners also provided fertile ground for stoic thought. Religious moralism set forth clear guidelines for life, and southern Protestants could use stoic moralism to reinforce their views. The religion of the Old South was predominantly evangelical, concerned primarily with individual sin, guilt, and private redemption. Evangelical Protestantism, with Calvinistic theology one of its sources, promoted a fatalistic view of the world, an outlook that fit comfortably with practical stoicism. Dabbs claimed that stoicism enabled southerners to be both Cavaliers and Puritans, nurturing both a romantic outlook toward the social world and a moralistic outlook toward individual religious experience, combining outward grace and inner sternness.

The Civil War provided a crucial stage in the development of stoicism in the South. Rather than destroying the philosophy of the prewar elite, the conflict and its aftermath confirmed a fatalistic, even tragic outlook on life. The collapse of the outer world confirmed the southern stoic's original decision to invest everything in the sanctity of the inner self. Just as evangelical Christianity took stronger hold of the South as a result of defeat, so did stoicism. Stoicism has generally been most influential in societies undergoing social decay and collapse, and this seems true of the postbellum South. Robert E. Lee exemplifies this postwar stoicism. An admirer of Marcus Aurelius, a fanatic in his dedication to such stoic virtues as duty, honor, patriotism, loyalty, and humility, Lee combined with these qualities the moralism and Christian piety that in the South could even rub off on an Episcopalian. Lee was notably ambivalent—confident in the material world, yet brooding and guilt ridden in his religious outlook. Lee embodied the southern tendency toward stoic reserve. Honor, which in many times and places has been related to pride, in Lee was tied in with humility. He was the supreme example of the South's attempt to balance Stoic and Christian virtues. Dabbs saw two religions in the late-19th-century South—"the social religion of this world and the individualistic religion of another." The result of the first, which was a reflection of stoic influences, was to equate God with the southern way of life and to provide a philosophical basis for what would emerge after the war as a southern civil religion.

Stoicism in the late 19th century became tied in with, and hard to separate from, Victorianism. James Branch Cabell, Ellen Glasgow, and other transitional writers of the turn-of-the-century South were skeptics. They saw decline in the region and tried to face it with the dignity and courage that Victorians valued. Sometimes, to be sure, they seemed detached from their society and from pondering man's fate, but at other times they preached of enduring the tragedies of life with fortitude. Glasgow, who came from a Presbyterian background, wrote of the "vein of iron" that was necessary for survival in her era. She came to believe that the universe was governed by blind chance and her society was coming apart. Renewed moral fiber was the only hope. Her novel *Barren Ground*, with its good stoic title, came out of her inner turmoil. The central character, Dorinda Oakley, learns to live a joyless existence and to suppress her natural instincts. As Daniel J. Singal argues, *Barren Ground* illustrates "nineteenth century theology got up in stoic dress." However, southern stoicism was not complete in Glasgow; Dorinda cannot stop longing for something more than the "agnostic realism" that seemed to be Glasgow's position. Her stoicism was different in origins, then, from that of earlier southerners. Hers was an attempt to reconcile her Calvinistic legacy with the realities of late-19th-century naturalistic science, with its belief in the evolution of an unstable universe. The result was what can be called her "stoic realism," a position that saw little meaning in human events.

The Agrarian writers of the 1920s and 1930s also reflected stoic influences. John Crowe Ransom, for example, struck a pose of stoic detachment in dealing with conflicts in his own mind between the modern demands of balancing rationality and spontaneity. He hid his inner conflicts behind a front of stoic reserve—self-control, mannerly behavior, and ironic humor. Ransom believed that artists should tap and express their emotions but his stoicism made this difficult for him to do in practice. William Alexander Percy shared many of the literary concerns of the Agrarians, and he achieved perhaps the South's greatest literary expression of the stoic philosophy. *Lanterns on the Levee* (1940) reflected a profound debt to the *Meditations of Marcus Aurelius* in both the form of the work and its content. Percy, the descendant of a distinguished family and himself both a planter and a poet, believed that the good do not triumph, and he chronicled the decline of the southern elite, as seen in his own history and that of his family. The Agrarians believed the old order could be restored, but Percy did not. He strove in his personal life and his writing to embody the stoic virtue of graceful acceptance of defeat. As Richard King says, "he was the melancholy Roman to the end" and found only temporary relief from his prophecies of southern decline. He did affirm the ability of the individual to effect at least limited change through individual actions in a limited area. Percy was a respected leader of his local community (Greenville, Miss.), and he believed that in such a place a person could do good. In any event, the important point was individual integrity and courage in making the effort. No one better exemplified what Walker Percy calls the spirit of "a poetic pessimism" at the heart of modern southern stoicism.

William Faulkner portrayed southern stoicism through numerous characters. Quentin Compson's father speaks of "fate, destiny, retribution, irony" and of the "stage manager" behind it all. Rosa Coldfield calls her region a "land primed for fatality" and "cursed with it." But stoicism by Faulkner's time was difficult to separate from a generalized Calvinism, a predestinarian, mechanistic philosophy that was also a 20th-century southern legacy. Faulkner did not draw directly on the ancient or modern Stoic philosophers. Cleanth Brooks suggests that Faulkner's stoicism cannot be understood apart from its close connection with Christianity, in both of which the essence of human living is freedom. The Christian concept that God grants freedom through grace, though, is weak in Faulkner, who seems closer to Epictitus's belief that man achieves freedom through self-discipline.

Faulkner, then, saw the human problem in Christian terms—the world is a fallen world—yet he did not advocate the Christian solution of redemption through God's grace. He was willing to rely on individual virtue, as embodied by a Sartoris during the Civil War, to gain a modicum of dignity, if not redemption. Man must rescue himself through stoic virtues such as courage, honor, justice, duty, endurance, and reason. Stoicism was transmuted in Faulkner into the generalized trait of endurance. Dilsey in *The Sound and the Fury* and other black literary characters in the modern South embody the ancient wisdom best of all. Theirs is no grim stoicism but a cheerful one of overcoming. As Isaac McCaslin says of blacks in "The Bear," "they will endure. They will outlast us." Poor whites also are blessed with endurance, for example, in *The Mansion*, where Mink Snopes waits 40 years to carry out an act of vengeance. Faulkner's appreciation of endurance reflects the stoic attitude toward time. The Stoics believed one could transcend time through detachment and patience. Characters such as Quentin Compson and Gail Hightower in *Light in August* seem almost primitive in their belief in re-creating the past, so that the normal historical boundaries are overcome.

Writing in the 1950s in the midst of the conflicts over racial desegregation, Walker Percy argued that the South could no longer afford stoicism alongside Christianity. In a democratic society, he said, stoicism cannot exist as the social philosophy of any social class. "What the Stoic sees as the insolence of his former charge—and this is what he can't tolerate, the Negro's demanding his rights instead of being thankful for the squire's generosity—is in the Christian scheme the sacred right which must be accorded the individual, whether deemed insolent or not."

Stoicism, then, since the early 19th century has been a philosophy of the educated southern elite, held alongside of and sometimes in contradiction to evangelical Protestantism. The philosophy has been less influential on society as a whole in the 20th century, but is probably still held by some southerners as a guide to individual behavior.

See also MYTHIC SOUTH: / Agrarians, Vanderbilt; RELIGION: / Fatalism

Charles Reagan Wilson
University of Mississippi

Cleanth Brooks, *William Faulkner: The Yoknapatawpha Country* (1963); James McBride Dabbs, *Who Speaks for the South?* (1964); Richard H. King, *A Southern Renaissance: The Cultural Awakening of the American South, 1930–1955* (1980); Adrienne Koch, *The Philosophy of Thomas Jefferson* (1943); Walker Percy, *Commonweal* (6 July 1956); Daniel J. Singal, *The War Within: From Victorian to Modernist Thought in the South, 1919–1945* (1982); Bertram Wyatt-Brown, *Southern Honor: Ethics and Behavior in the Old South* (1982).

Tobacco

Tobacco was the most important herb among the American Indians and later became closely associated with the South. The Indians used it as snuff, chewed it, smoked it as cigars, smoked it as cigarettes wrapped in corn husks, and made poultices of snake fat wrapped in tobacco leaves. They sometimes also swallowed tobacco pellets as a tranquilizer. But pipe smoking was the near universal method of use in North America. Tobacco in the sacred calumet was the ritual way to seal peace. American Indians smoked "ancient tobacco" (*Nicotiana rustica*), which dated to pre-Columbian times. They used it in medicine and religion, two realms that were believed to be connected. Sickness was believed to stem from spiritual imbalance, and Native Americans used tobacco to nurture their spirituality before sacred rituals.

European colonists in the South thought of tobacco mainly in medical terms and discounted its religious significance. It was seen as a panacea that would cure cancer, asthma, headaches, coughs, cramps, gout, worms, female troubles, and any other ailment. Physicians supported this belief, disagreeing only on the best way to use the weed. The medieval theory of the humors—which taught that sickness came from an imbalance in the body's four humors (blood, yellow bile, black bile, and phlegm)—still had its adherents, who saw tobacco consumption as a way to keep balance in the body and thus maintain good health. In early America, including the South, tobacco was used to cure respiratory, head, internal, and skin diseases.

Tobacco growing and its use became the bases for early Virginia's prosperity. North American Indians had long smoked *Nicotiana rustica*, but it proved too bitter for many European colonists. John Rolfe in 1612 introduced into Virginia a sweet-scented tobacco developed by the Spanish in the West Indies. Sir Walter Raleigh is credited with making tobacco use a fad among the elite in London. The tobacco market expanded, and soon the people of Jamestown were growing it in the streets. By 1624 the Jamestown colony was exporting 60,000 pounds of tobacco a year, and in the colonial era it also became the major crop in Maryland and North Carolina. The English Navigation Acts of the 1660s made tobacco one of the "enumerated goods" that were regulated by shipment from the colonies through English ports.

The dominant form of tobacco consumption in the colonial era was pipe smoking. Snuffing became popular, though, among the colonial elite by the mid-1700s. They used the snuffbox and its required gestures, a ritual that came from France, through London, to the colonies. In the second third of the 19th century the way of using snuff changed: instead of sniffing it through the nose, people began dipping it, placing a pinch in the mouth.

In the first half of the 19th century chewing became the main method of consumption. It was popular after the American Revolution and was seen as an American way to use tobacco, a variation from the European styles. Appropriately, the use of chewing tobacco seems to have peaked in the Jacksonian era, the age of the common man. The frontier now seemed to be setting the tone for society. English traveler Charles Mackay thought the national symbol for the United States should not be the eagle but the spittoon.

From the Civil War to World War I the annual consumption of tobacco in the United States rose dramatically. The cigar became something of a fad in the South after the Mexican War and was certainly popular among, and associated with, the upper classes in the Gilded Age. In fact, the cigar has been an accessory of power for important southern politicos throughout the 20th century as well.

A sudden shift to smoking tobacco occurred during and after the Civil War. This was the era of cigarettes, both hand rolled and machine made. Bright-leaf tobacco was developed beginning in the 1850s in North Carolina, and by 1880 it was grown from Virginia south to Georgia. In this age of the New South the tobacco industry grew and expanded. Durham and Winston-Salem, N.C., Louisville, Ky., and Richmond, Va., became the centers of the cigarette industry, bringing economic prosperity to North Carolina, Virginia, and Kentucky, in particular, and promoting the use and consumption of the weed by southerners. A southerner, James A. Bonsack of Virginia, invented the cigarette-rolling machine in 1880, and this led to a steady increase in demand. Annual national per capita consumption rose from 1.5 pounds in 1860 to 5.5 pounds in 1900, a 267 percent rise. The Duke and Reynolds families became new power brokers in the South and symbols of success. The landscape reflected the new importance of tobacco. Tobacco barns became pervasive, and by the 1880s the towering, stolid tobacco factories producing cigarettes were new symbols on the landscape. In 1929 the South produced 60 percent of all tobacco in the United States and 84 percent of the cigarettes.

This success story has a dark side, though. Opposition to tobacco use goes back to the colonial era. By the late 1600s debunkers of tobacco smoking were dismissing it as a nasty, ungodly, dangerous habit. King James I opposed smoking tobacco, calling it a "stinking weed." It was, he said, "a custome Lothsome to the eye, hatefull to the Nose, harmfull to the braine, dangerous to the Lungs, and in the blacke stinking fume thereof, nearest resembling the horrible Stigian smoke of the pit that is bottomeless." Others charged that smoking actually upset the balance of the body instead of maintaining it. The American Anti-Tobacco League led opposition to tobacco in the 19th century. The antitobacco crusade of 1830–60 was led by northerners, but Virginian John Hartwell Cocke was one southerner actively involved in the movement. Cole Blease of South Carolina and Dr. Alton Ochsner of New Orleans later were prominent southern opponents of "Demon Nicotine." Religious groups, even in North Carolina, have periodically been vocal in opposition to the sinfulness of tobacco use.

Tobacco advertising has long enlivened the southern countryside and provided some of the region's most notable material artifacts. James B. Duke used promotion of his tobacco products as one way to consolidate his dominance of the tobacco industry. Tobacco vendors used wooden Indians in front of shops selling cigars and tobacco goods. A landmark of advertising was when John Ruffin Green adopted the symbol of the bull after the revival of the tobacco business in Durham at the end of the Civil War. He saw a bull's head on a jar of Colman's mustard, which came from Durham, England. A neighbor had a breeding bull, which became the model for the trademark Durham Bull. It caught the imagination of rural southerners and others as well. His company later fought hard in courts and elsewhere for control of the bull as a trademark and won. The company blanketed the southern rural countryside with testimonials from prominent people, including ministers. The greatest sign painter of the bull symbol was J. Gilmer Koerner, who was known as Reuben Rink.

By the 1890s the industry was more sophisticated in marketing, and more artifacts began to appear. Chewing plugs now had tin or paper tags with the name of the maker and the brand name of the product. Colorful lithographs were pasted on wooden boxes of chewing tobacco. This was a regionally produced and identified pop art that used a variety of images: flowers, historical events and people, animals; nude girls sometimes appeared. The sides of barns became the canvas for painters such as Koerner. Whereas the cigar salesman and advertising, with strong ethnic overtones, had become identified with the North's urban areas by the early 20th century, advertising for smoking and chewing tobacco stressed rural themes appropriate to the South.

In the 20th century several tobacco products have been especially identified with the South. Snuff is one. Margaret J. Hagood reported in 1939 that half of the North Carolina Piedmont tenant women she studied used snuff. In Erskine Caldwell's *Tobacco Road* the Lester family's landlord, Captain John, stops giving rations and snuff at the store, and the grandmother in the story is desperate for restoration of her snuff. "There were times when she would have been willing to die, if she could only have for once all the snuff she wanted." Even after World War II sales of snuff in the region did not drastically decline. Black women, farm women, and mountain women all had reputations as snuff dippers.

The South is also still identified as the home of tobacco chewing. In 1947, 100 million pounds of chewing tobacco were still produced, most being consumed in the rural South, and cuspidors were common until the 1950s. Texas author John Graves has written of the virtues of chewing tobacco, which he calls "a great solacer." Unlike the "fury of a tense cigarette smoker's puffing," chewing is a laid-back method of use that calms and offers perspective.

Chewing tobacco has made a comeback in the 1970s and 1980s, appealing now to the young and the middle class, as well as to blue-collar and farm workers, who never abandoned it. Chewing tobacco now takes three forms. The first is the *plug,* which is a compressed brick of tobacco wrapped in a light brown leaf. A variation of the plug is the "twist," which has become rare except in rural parts of the South. A second form of chewing tobacco used to be called "scrape." It is coarse, sweet shreds, packed in foil pouches. Legendary brand names include Beech Nut, Red Man, and Mail Pouch. The third form of chewing tobacco in the modern South is "smokeless tobacco," or "snoose" as it is known in the Midwest (that name probably comes from *snus*, the Swedish-Danish name for snuff). Smokeless tobacco is a wet, grainy tobacco, flavored with mint, wintergreen, and the unlikely raspberry packed in cylindrical boxes with tin lids. It has brand names such as Skoal, Copenhagen, and Levi Garrett. A communal symbol of the regional importance of chewing tobacco is the tobacco spitting contest, which has become a staple of several southern communities. Jeff Barber won the National Tobacco Spitting Contest in Raleigh, Miss., in 1981 with a heave of 33 feet, 7½ inches, a record that the *Guinness Book of World Records* has noted as a landmark.

See also INDUSTRY: / Tobacco Industry; SOCIAL CLASS: / Tobacco Workers

Charles Reagan Wilson
University of Mississippi

John Graves, *Texas Monthly* (November 1978); Charles Hudson, *The Southeastern Indians* (1976); Katherine T. Kell, *Journal of American Folklore* (April–June 1965); Joseph C. Robert, *The Story of Tobacco in America* (1949); Robert Sobel, *They Satisfy: The Cigarette in American Life* (1978).

Victorianism

When in 1953 the Armstrong Browning Library at Baylor University acquired a first edition of Robert Browning's *Pauline*, its collection of the poet's first editions was complete. Housed in a magnificent building of Texas stone, Italian marble, bronze doors, and stained-glass windows, this library today is a surprising conglomeration of memorabilia, first editions, manuscripts, and scholarly works dealing with the Brownings and their Victorian world. In Browning's day scholars and critics of the poet would not have imagined traveling to Waco, in the central plains of Texas, to pursue their research. This splendid collection of Victoriana in a seemingly unlikely place is partly the result of Texas wealth, regional pride, and especially the indefatigable work of A. Joseph Armstrong at Baylor. But the Browning Library is also a reflection of the profound and persisting influence of Victorian ideas, ideals, and personalities on the culture of the South, even as it extends itself westward into Texas.

In the imagination of the southerner, Browning epitomizes many of the Victorian qualities particularly appealing to a people whose lives and history bristled with losses, spiritual and material. In his robust optimism, Browning represents the profound belief that, despite the disillusionment of lost causes, the law of history is one of development and progress. One who "marched breast forward," and "never doubted clouds would break," incarnated in his person and his work an optimism that refused in a benighted world of crass materialism to give up the notion that human beings are more than biological organisms or economic animals devoid of a higher destiny and significance. His influence in the South was assured by hundreds of Browning Societies that developed in communities throughout the region in the 20th century. And Pippa Passes, Ky., was named for one of his more sentimental poems.

In good Victorian fashion the South has always been given to heroes and hero worship. "You can know a man by his heroes" has the force of a southern proverb. For southerners, as for Matthew Arnold, the ancient heroes were Hellenic and Hebraic, captured in the personalities of Socrates and Jesus and in the ideas and myths associated with these seminal figures. In a narrower vein, the South idealized with great imaginative power the Founding Fathers, particularly Jefferson and Washington. After the tragedy of the Civil War, southern healing was promoted by the nostalgic romanticization of Robert E. Lee, who became an incarnation of the Victorian ideal of the complete gentleman: patriot and statesman, military genius, scholar, educator, philanthropist, and Christian family man. Only slowly, through several decades, did Lincoln take his place in the pantheon of southern heroes. Even Texas's own particular frontier heroes, Houston, Travis, and Crockett, became Victorian heroes.

To such heroic status southern imagination also elevated the eminent Victorian literary geniuses: Arnold, Carlyle, Tennyson, Sir Walter Scott, and Browning. But the typically Victorian anti-Catholic feeling in the South made John Henry Newman suspect despite his literary and religious genius. Southerners, like their English counterparts, could never fully forgive a man of Newman's brilliance and stature for having given up his Oxford heritage to join forces with that most un-English of traditions, the church of Rome. On the other hand, despite his secular humanist assumptions, John Stuart Mill has enjoyed heroic status among that intellectual elite in the South who are jealous of individual liberty. In declaring "eternal freedom from the dual tyranny of priest and sword," early Texas heroes, for example, sought to establish constitutionally the personal freedoms that later found classic formulation in Mill's *On Liberty*.

But among the eminent Victorians, Browning seems most to have epitomized the southern ideal of the heroic. Himself a commoner, he nevertheless enjoyed status and favor with the nobility, including Queen Victoria herself. Not personally identified with the ancient centers of learning and authority at Oxford and Cambridge, he yet was acclaimed a poet of the intellect. Many southern intellectuals could admire that. Without allegiance to any particular dogma or institutional tradition, Browning was still deeply religious—a classic example of that muscular Christianity fully at home in the world, a temporal existence ennobled and idealized by the confident assumption that "God's in his heaven, all's right with the world." Like Matthew Arnold, Browning represented and espoused that sweetness and light which combined the humane intelligence of Socrates with the reverence for life and passion for social justice of Jesus.

The higher criticism of the Bible emanating from the German universities touched Christianity in the South even less than it affected the Christianity of Victorian England. Southerners were, like their English ancestors, a people of the book—and that book was the Bible. Despite isolated struggles over the implications of Darwin and the new geology—and some momentary debates dealing with Strauss and the historical Jesus—popular biblicism in the South went fundamentally unchallenged well into the middle of the 20th century.

As in Victorian England, a hallmark of southern culture has been its profound commitment to Protestant Christianity. Puritan influences, also at work in Victorian England, have left their indelible mark, not only on the role of the Bible in popular culture but also on the most basic human institutions and daily activities: the understanding of family life and sexuality; attitudes toward work and leisure; the significance of education and learning; and ultimately the very meaning of human life.

Southern life has been dominated by the Victorian notion of the primacy of the patriarchal family, centered around a deference to the father and idealization of the mother, extended in concern and caring to children, cousins, and other kin. This family ideal captures that most basic of southern convictions, biblical in origin, that human beings are above all relational creatures. Rooted in an unacknowledged sexism, the cultural ideal of the family elevated women to a special status and role. Women represented the altruistic virtues of nurturing, compassion, morality, and religious piety. Their place was in running the home, in educating the young, and in caring for the sick. They were far removed from the areas of finance and commerce, the manufacture and distribution of goods, the military service, the law, or politics and public policy. Men were, therefore, in the ideal, thrust into positions and roles of power and responsibility for the common good. Such roles demanded knowledge, a high level of intelligence and rationality, emotional toughness, and a sense of justice. Not surprisingly, higher education in the South, as in Victorian England, was therefore dominated by classic Christian models designed for a male intellectual elite.

Southern sexual attitudes and mores reflected the deep ambivalence also found in English Victorian responses to sexuality. Tenaciously holding to the biblical and Christian view that all God's creation is essentially good, southern culture managed to affirm sexuality as a part of God's good intention. Hence celibacy was strongly suspect, both as a religious ideal and as a personal way of life. Unmarried males were peculiarly problematical, smacking of the unnatural. Although, like the "other Victorians" among their English counterparts, southerners allowed a certain unspoken sexual license in private, the cultural norm has always been an idealized version of erotic love, buttressed by the Christian notions of monogamy and lifelong fidelity. This made it possible to glorify the virtue and purity of wives and mothers while allowing certain concessions to the animal nature of males. Sexual expression before and outside of marriage for males, although never fully accepted as a norm, was nonetheless tacitly tolerated.

It is impossible to understand the sexual values of the South without recognizing their deep, indeed symbiotic, relationship to the racial values. Here again, English Victorian notions gave southerners categories of thought that explained existing social arrangements and sensibilities. Victorian England often justified to its Christian conscience its expansive colonialism and imperialism as a way of bringing civilization to the heathen. "Darkest Africa" symbolized the aboriginal savages' life before the impact of the humanizing influences of Christianity and culture. Much of this Victorian attitude is found in southern conceptions of blacks after emancipation. Blacks at best were children, to be tolerated and patronized; at their worst they were savages, to be controlled and kept in their place. Never fully citizens nor quite finally human, blacks evoked a complex set of symbols in the white southern imagination. It is no surprise that such elemental racist symbols should form a symbiosis with elemental sexist symbols to produce cultural mores and sensibilities defying rational explanation or rational redress. In this sense, southern racism has been and is deeply sexual in nature and origin.

In its grand outlines southern culture has been formed and informed by staple Victorian certainties: an idealized anthropology; a confidence that history reveals an inevitable progress in human affairs; the conviction that the universe is ordered and its laws are discoverable by human reason. Such confident views of epistemology and morality were grounded in a nondogmatic, personalistic biblical Christianity. Darwin, Freud, and Marx were long ignored or resisted by southerners, who viewed humankind as rational, free, and responsible. The nether regions of the psyche, the animalistic dimensions of the self, fundamental economic instincts and interests—all these were covered up or ignored by the emphasis on freedom and dignity of man. History, in its inevitable progress, reflects the rationality of humankind and the order of the cosmos, energized and directed ultimately by the providential intentionality of God.

Hence the moral certainty. Hence the anxiety before change, and the emphasis upon personal, social, and political peace and equanimity. Hence the genteel insistence upon courtesy and propriety of conduct, and the disfavor toward critical temperaments and unconventional ideas and behaviors. Above all, uncertainty, open conflict, and overt criticism are to be kept in check and resisted. Victorian cultural traits represented a restraint on contrary, paradoxical southern tendencies toward extreme individualism and brutal violence. When Victorian restraints dropped, the result was what W. J. Cash called the "savage ideal." Only in the 20th century has a fusion of ideological elements been forced to yield to modern circumstances and intellectual categories. And even in the New South the forces of Victorianism have not been fully spent.

W. D. White
St. Andrews Presbyterian College

William L. Burn, *The Age of Equipoise: A Study of the Mid-Victorian Generation* (1964); Walter E. Houghton, *The Victorian Frame of Mind* (1957); Gertrude Himmelfarb, *Ideas and Beliefs of the Victorians: An Historic Revaluation of the Victorian Age* (1966); Richard H. King, *A Southern Renaissance: The Cultural Awakening of the American South, 1930–1955*

(1980); Richard A. Levine, ed., *Backgrounds to Victorian Literature* (1967); Daniel J. Singal, *The War Within: From Victorian to Modernist Thought in the South, 1919–1945* (1982).

Vietnam War

The American South, whose people were the only group of Americans to suffer a military defeat prior to the Vietnam conflict, assumed an important role in leading the United States out of the malaise that followed the collapse of American efforts in South Vietnam. The southern way of handling defeat has been to persist in the idea that the cause is never lost, that defeat is beyond belief, so deeply are the roots of honor sunk into a land dearly loved.

The key to understanding the South's regional contribution to the Vietnam War is its rhetoric of belligerence, rhetoric backed by action—out of necessity—to serve a cause with honor. To a southerner, all of this follows naturally from an ingrained sense of duty. As the Vietnam War ground to its perplexing conclusion, people in many parts of the nation wavered in their sense of purpose, but the South's fundamental conservatism held fast. Every president since Richard Nixon has needed a "southern" strategy, and the core of that strategy rests in an appeal to patriotism—to a reverence for American ideals, which for southerners includes a readiness to defend democracy aggressively and the essential right of self-determination, no matter how cloudy and uncertain the specific case may be.

Texan Lyndon Johnson believed in the power of this rhetoric, but he lost faith in it with the sweep of nightmarish television images and week-by-week statistics of American casualities, which led to his surrender of the presidency. Beginning with the 1968 election and continuing through the 1970s, George C. Wallace—operating sometimes as a candidate of the American Independent party and sometimes as a Democratic party nominee—championed the rhetoric of belligerence, thus giving Richard Nixon, Jimmy Carter, and Ronald Reagan a clear signal on how to win the heart of the South in the post-Vietnam era. Ironically, the southerner Carter did not catch the signal; he became the next president after Johnson to see his ambitions fall to ruin in the wake of perceived American military weakness during the Iranian hostage crisis. Carter's pardon of Vietnam draft resisters—his first major act as president—had led southerners much earlier to conclude that he was not zealous enough on the matter of patriotism.

During the major escalation of an American military presence in Vietnam, the war had distinctly southern overtones. A Texan's administration sent the marines ashore. Bill Moyers, another Texan, had to field the early hard questions about combat activity involving U.S. troops, although when the questions loomed larger than the answers, Moyers departed, a foreshadowing of what would happen later to his president.

For Dean Rusk, a native of Cherokee County, Ga., Vietnam became the dark center of his tenure as secretary of state. And heading the order of battle in Vietnam was William C. Westmoreland, of Beaufort County, S.C. When Westmoreland first left the South for West Point at the outset of his military career, he was reminded by his great-uncle (a veteran of Gettysburg who had also been with Lee at Appomattox) that Lee and Jackson, not just Grant and Sherman, had gone off to the academy in their time. Westmoreland brought to the Vietnam War a clear image of the honorable warrior, an image inherited directly from Robert E. Lee. The image, of course, was not sufficient to win the war.

The southern quality of the war reached far beyond Westmoreland himself. In the early 1970s, four out of five army generals were from southern towns. The disproportionate overrepresentation of southerners in the army and marines reached all the way down to the lowest ranks; many southern blacks were brought into the army through Robert McNamara's three-year Project 100,000. This infamous scheme opened up military service to "marginally qualified" youths as an escape from impoverished backgrounds. All too frequently, however, the exit led only to Vietnam—or to desertion. Largely because of the southerners placed in the service through Project 100,000 (which eventually involved more than 240,000 men), the South is overrepresented in the cases of military desertion.

Another blemish on the honor of southerners came through the court-martial of William Calley, a Floridian. Nevertheless, many southerners were quick to defend Calley, angrily denouncing the hypocrisy of those who would punish Calley while at the same time forgiving draft resisters. Senator Strom Thurmond of South Carolina made this point frequently, though he was hard-pressed to reconcile his harsh views on Vietnam protesters with the historical precedent in the pardon extended to southerners in the aftermath of the Civil War.

The South had only 22 percent of the nation's population, but it produced 29 percent of the Medal of Honor recipients for Vietnam service, reaffirming its claim to honor. These figures confirm the enduring nature of an outlandish rage to valor in the region, sometimes manifesting itself in nonsensical ways, which have been well documented in war scenes from William Faulkner's fiction of an earlier time. Moreover, on the home front the protest movement against the war never reached the cataclysmic proportions in the South that it did in the North and far West. Despite a few major incidents on southern campuses—particularly the shooting death of two blacks by policemen during the 1970 confrontation at Jackson State—and student-led marches and demonstrations throughout the South, protest activities tended to be more moderate there than elsewhere.

Nevertheless, some voices of protest sounded. An important protest movement within the military developed at Fort Bliss in El Paso, Tex., where the GI's for Peace staged public rallies and published a newsletter, *Gigline*. Also, at the University of North Carolina at Chapel Hill, after a series of student-administration standoffs in the late 1960s, the war resistance movement evolved to a weekly silent vigil in front of the post office on East

Franklin Street. Yet even as quiet as this protest was, it drew the ire and contempt of Jesse Helms, then a radio commentator for WRAL in Raleigh. At one point, when the North Carolina Legislature was considering creation of a state zoo, Helms responded that there was no need to create a zoo—all the legislators needed to do was put a fence around the university in Chapel Hill. Such a response typified the stance taken by southern practitioners of the rhetoric of belligerence. L. Mendel Rivers of South Carolina, chairman of the Armed Services Committee, asserted during the war that Americans protesting the government's war policy were "filthy buzzards and vermin," a viewpoint more recently revived by Senator Helms of North Carolina to fit anyone who questions the use of American military capabilities wherever and whenever the need arises.

Backing for such a determined position on the American role in Vietnam came readily and regularly from the churches in the South, particularly those represented at the Southern Baptist General Convention. The military itself had a formidable presence in the South as well. In 1967, a typical war year, 42 percent of the stateside payroll for military personnel went to the 11 states of the Confederacy. Two outcomes merit special attention. First, this particular infusion of federal dollars resulted in dependence on the military by an extended network of people and proliferation of sprawling ghettos of seamy nightclubs and other clip joints around military bases. These situations continued after the Vietnam conflict ended; thus, the South's economic status was tied closely to war. Second, large numbers of soldiers who went to Vietnam passed through training at southern bases: Fort Benning and Fort Gordon in Georgia; Fort Bragg in North Carolina; Parris Island in South Carolina; and Fort Polk in Louisiana.

Many southern bases built mock Vietnamese bases for training soldiers in the ways of war, Vietnam style. In this endeavor the climate of the South contributed significantly, giving trainees a feel for the heat, humidity, and other discomforts to be encountered in combat. Anyone entering the main gate at Fort Polk, La., was greeted by an unabashed declaration of southern pride in preparing soldiers for battle in Vietnam: "Welcome to Ft. Polk, Birthplace of Combat Infantrymen for Vietnam."

Occasionally, people of southern origin found themselves at odds with the American role in Vietnam—and hence at odds with their own background. Two such southerners, Dan Rather of Texas and Tom Wicker of North Carolina, often seemed to be in the vanguard of critics of the war in the national press; Wicker eventually landed on President Nixon's "enemies list" for his denunciation of several military strategies in Vietnam. Rather and Wicker had both left the South, and perhaps this distance, coupled with their journalistic preoccupation with facts instead of rhetoric, contributed to their individual variation from the southern norm.

The case of the southern veteran after the war also shows some cracks in the rhetoric of belligerence. The proportion of Vietnam veterans to total population in the 1980 census is the same for the South as for the nation generally, about 22 percent. The South was disproportionately represented in enlistees, so it appears that many southern soldiers chose to remain in the military rather than return to civilian life. For the veterans who returned ravaged by the horrors of their combat experience, coping with the mood at home has not always been easy. Southern veterans interviewed in Myra McPherson's *Long Time Passing: Vietnam and the Haunted Generation* reflect some of the same sense of dislocation suffered by veterans across the nation. As elsewhere, veterans in the South suffer quietly.

One exception to this pattern is James Webb, a decorated marine veteran and author of *Fields of Fire*, perhaps the most widely read novel of the Vietnam War, with over a million copies in print. Webb's southern heritage is reflected in one of the novel's main characters, a lieutenant named Robert E. Lee Hodges. Three members of the Hodges family died at Gettysburg, all full of the glory of fields of fire; his grandfather died in battle under Pershing; and his father fell in the Battle of the Bulge. Hodges himself dies in Vietnam, yet the express purpose of Webb's fiction is to reassert the honor of fighting for one's country.

Thus do fiction and fact converge, with the South seemingly less traumatized than other regions and undaunted by the failure to preserve some semblance of democracy in Southeast Asia. In an ironic twist of fate, the Vietnamese refugees who have found Gulf Coast weather to their liking are living proof of an American military defeat. Still, the South seems to repeat the rhetoric of belligerence. After sending the 82nd Airborne from Fort Bragg, N.C., to the tiny island of Grenada, Ronald Reagan gained a good measure of southern allegiance in his 1984 reelection campaign. An understanding of presidential politics in the 1970s and 1980s must thus include recognition of the South's steadfast role in the Vietnam War.

Owen W. Gilman, Jr.
St. Joseph's University

Kent B. Blevins, *Foundations* (July–September 1980); Marion A. Bressler and Leo A. Bressler, *Country, Conscience, and Conscription: Can They Be Reconciled?* (1970); G. David Curry, *Sunshine Patriots: Punishment and the Vietnam Offender* (1985); Melton A. McLaurin, in *Perspectives on the American South*, vol. 3, ed. James C. Cobb and Charles Reagan Wilson (1985); Myra McPherson, *Long Time Passing: Vietnam and the Haunted Generation* (1984); James Reston, Jr., *Sherman's March and Vietnam* (1985); Charles P. Roland, *The Improbable Era: The South since World War II* (1976); James Webb, *Fields of Fire* (1978); William C. Westmoreland, *A Soldier Reports* (1976).

War of 1812

The people in the southern states generally supported the War of 1812, reflecting the strong spirit of American nationalism in the region in that era. Southern presidents Jefferson and Madison steered the nation's course in the events leading to war, and southern congressmen endorsed efforts to gain respect for American neutral rights—the main cause of war. A majority of congressmen representing the farming areas of the South and West voted for war, whereas the members from the maritime regions of the Northeast voted against the declaration of war. British interference with American trade had damaged southern farm exports in cotton and tobacco, hurting the region economically and making it eager to stand up to the British.

In addition, Americans on the frontier, in both the South and the Northwest, saw war with the British as a way to end Indian attacks on pioneer settlers and gain land in Canada and Florida. The "War Hawks" were congressmen eager for war, and many of them were southerners—Henry Clay from Kentucky, John C. Calhoun and William Lowndes from South Carolina, and Felix Grundy from Tennessee. Virginian John Randolph tagged them "War Hawks" because of their belligerent nationalism that sought a fight.

The nation was unprepared for war, though, when it came. The earliest fighting in the South included a Native American uprising on the frontier. The Creeks won a victory at Fort Mims, north of Mobile, in August 1813, but Andrew Jackson then led a volunteer militia campaign that crushed Indian resistance. The key battle was at Horseshoe Bend, on the Tallapoosa River, in March 1814. The Creeks surrendered about 60 percent of their territory as a result of the Treaty of Fort Jackson in August of that year. The British campaign in the South concentrated on blockading the coastline and raiding coastal settlements. The Chesapeake Bay area was especially hard hit, including the invasion of Washington, D.C., on 24 August 1814. The British moved on to Baltimore but did not launch a major attack on the well-fortified U.S. forces.

The battle of New Orleans was the culminating event of the War of 1812 and a major contribution to both the national and regional imaginations. The British hoped to seize the port city and gain control of the Mississippi River. Andrew Jackson organized efforts to strengthen the Gulf Coast defenses in the fall of 1814 and led an unauthorized raid into Pensacola, in Spanish Florida, where the British had been planning attacks. In November, Americans put up new fortifications on various approaches to New Orleans. The Treaty of Ghent was signed in Europe on 24 December 1814, officially ending the war, but this news did not reach the combatants in North America until after the battle of New Orleans. On 8 January 1815 British commander Sir Edwin Pakenham, who was contemptuous of the Americans, launched a frontal attack on Jackson's forces, who included an eclectic combination of frontier riflemen, upper-class Creole volunteers, free blacks, and pirates. Pakenham and about 2,000 British died in the assault.

The peace treaty ending the war settled few of the trade problems that had led to war, but the conflict itself became a major symbol of early American nationalism. The South was particularly proud of the victory over the British at New Orleans. The republican form of government now seemed safer than before. After the war, southern congressmen such as John C. Calhoun, who later would be the greatest sectionally oriented politician in the South, supported nationalistic legislation.

The legend of the battle of New Orleans was an especially important cultural legacy. From it General Jackson augmented his enormous popularity on the southern frontier and gained a reputation as one of the great national heroes. Folksongs about "The Hunters of Kentucky" and their sharpshooting communicated pride in southern fighting abilities and popularized the phrase "half horse, half alligator" as a description of the bigger-than-life frontiersmen in the region. (The free blacks, pirates, Creoles, and other defenders did not, however, receive similar cultural immortality for their roles in the battle.) In the 1950s the popular tune "The Battle of New Orleans," by country singer Johnny Horton, reminded listeners of this heroic event in the southern past.

Charles Reagan Wilson
University of Mississippi

Roger H. Brown, *The Republic in Peril: 1812* (1964); Gilbert Byron, *The War of 1812 on the Chesapeake Bay* (1964); Reginald Horsman, *The War of 1812* (1969); John K. Mahon, *The War of 1812* (1972); Bradford Perkins, *Prologue of War: England and the United States, 1805–1812* (1961); Robert Remini, *Andrew Jackson and the Course of American Empire, 1767–1821* (1977); John William Ward, *Andrew Jackson: Symbol for an Age* (1955).

World War I

The onset of a seemingly remote war in Europe set in motion forces that would have great consequences for southern life. The most immediate impact was a sharp economic downturn caused when the British blockade of the Central Powers denied cotton producers access to the continental market. Abruptly punctuating a period of modest prosperity for southern agriculture, the collapse initially stirred considerable hostility toward the Allies. Even as the United States moved closer to its own declaration of war, many prominent southerners urged President Woodrow Wilson to maintain American neutrality. This attitude stemmed partly from parochialism as well as economic concerns, but southern opposition also drew on the region's strong anticorporate impulse. Spokesmen such as Congressman Claude Kitchin and Senator James Vardaman believed that business interests were eager to turn a profit on a war the United States did not need to enter. Several southern legislators opposed the president's preparedness program, and a few even voted against his declaration of war. Senator Vardaman's criticism of the war ultimately cost him his political career.

Skeptical though southerners might have been of a foreign conflict, the region nevertheless threw itself into the war effort. Both culturally and ethnically the white South had strong ties to Great Britain, a link the British shrewdly stressed by purchasing huge amounts of cotton. Moreover, the military tradition has always been strong in the South, and the patriotic call to arms in 1917 stirred a tide of popular sentiment. Perhaps typical of the attitudes of his fellow southerners was Tennessee draftee Alvin C. York, who initially requested deferment on religious grounds but later became America's most decorated combat soldier.

Although individual southerners were eager to seize arms, the region's traditional distrust of centralized federal power and the economic giantism of major corporations sparked opposition to many aspects of the political economy of the war years. Led by Kitchin, southern legislators worked for a revenue policy that fell most heavily on upper-income groups. Others such as Secretary of the Navy Josephus Daniels criticized the growing partnership between big business and big government and alleged that industry was exploiting the crisis to enhance its profits. Whatever their criticisms of the corporate state, however, southern leaders were determined to see that their region got a substantial share of wartime profits. The army placed a majority of its training camps in southern states, and naval contracts stirred new life in the shipbuilding industry. At a time when the government was imposing price controls on many commodities, southern political clout exempted cotton from this list, allowing its price to soar, thereby fueling a burst of regional prosperity.

The war also accelerated important changes in the structure of the southern economy. The federal government began construction of explosives and wood chemical plants, which helped to spur the growth of hydroelectric power and chemical manufacturing after the war. Most important was the nitrate plant and dam at Muscle Shoals, Ala., which represented the idea of cheap, federally sponsored power and later served as the model for the Tennessee Valley Authority projects of the 1930s. Moreover, the war years saw a general rise in regional prosperity, a prosperity that bred optimism about the future for a section long marked as the poorest in the nation.

World War I had enormous human consequences for the South as well. Military service diminished the region's provincialism as thousands of native southerners left Dixie for assignments elsewhere while thousands of non-southerners came to the area for training. These masses of people in transit created considerable stress, especially in race relations. The number of lynchings increased markedly during the war years, and blacks occasionally retaliated in kind, as in Houston, Tex., where a black army unit responded to racial harassment by killing 17 civilians. Simultaneously, the war years saw the beginning of the Great Migration, the massive shift of blacks from the rural South to the urban North. With immigration disrupted and the draft under way, industry needed a source of cheap labor, and by 1920 roughly a million blacks had moved north, the beginning of one of the most important demographic shifts in American history. Southern women also saw important changes in their lives as the women's suffrage amendment moved closer to ratification, although only a few state legislatures in the South supported the proposal. Another longtime political goal of many southern women, prohibition, also won ratification shortly after the war.

The Great War left the South an important cultural legacy. The years after the Armistice saw a great flowering of letters known as the Southern Renaissance. "With the war of 1914–1918," Allen Tate wrote in 1945, "the South re-entered the world—but gave a backward glance as it stepped over the border: that backward glance gave us the Southern renascence, a literature conscious of the past in the present." Led by William Faulkner, Thomas Wolfe, the Nashville Agrarians, and many others, for the next two decades the South stood at the forefront of American literature. Indeed the sense of a changing perspective was a hallmark of southern life during the Great War. After a half century of material poverty and political impotence, the South returned to influence in Washington and embraced some of the idealism and internationalism of its native son, Woodrow Wilson, by supporting both his great crusade and his League of Nations.

See also BLACK LIFE: Migration, Black; GEOGRAPHY: Migration Patterns

David D. Lee
Western Kentucky University

Richard M. Abrams, *Journal of Southern History* (November 1956); Howard Allen, *Journal of Southern History* (May 1961); Dewey W. Grantham, *North Carolina Historical Review* (April 1949), *Southern Progressivism: The Reconciliation of Progress and Tradition* (1983); Arthur S. Link, *American Scholar* (Summer 1951), in *Studies in Southern History in Memory of Albert Ray Newsome, 1894–1951*, ed. J. Carlyle Sitterson (1957), *Wilson*, 5 vols. (1947–1965); George B. Tindall, *The Emergence of the New South, 1913–1945* (1967); Richard Watson, *Journal of Southern History* (February 1978).

World War II

The South has probably undergone more change since World War II than at any other time in its history. Given the Civil War, this claim may seem astounding; yet the region in 1940 was more like the antebellum South than like the South of today. Nowhere is the discrepancy more apparent than in the realm of economic development. In 1938 President Franklin D. Roosevelt characterized the South as "the Nation's No. 1 economic problem." In 1980, on the other hand, one of President Jimmy Carter's commissions classified the South as part of the booming "Sunbelt" in contrast to the economically declining "Frostbelt" of the North.

Although the change occurred over several decades, World War II brought a decisive shift away from the South's economic backwardness, its distinctive rural life, and its poverty. For better or worse, it finally started becoming more like other sections, with roughly the same standard of living. Some agrarians bemoaned this transition, but the great majority of southern whites and blacks have, with good reason, welcomed it.

To appreciate the impact that wartime spending had on the South, one has to keep in mind that World War II produced the biggest boom in American economic history. The figures are startling. Between 1940 and 1944 the 10 largest recipients of government war contracts alone received about the same amount of money as the federal government spent on *everything* from 1932 to 1939. During the war the volume of American industrial output increased at an average rate of 15 percent a year; the average rate of increase for the period 1896 to 1939 had been 4 percent. By 1945 the direct investment by the government in new plants and equipment had increased the productive capacity of the economy by about 50 percent.

With the South receiving its full share of this spending, the regional impact was immediate. Between 1939 and 1943 approximately 1.2 million new industrial jobs were created. "For the first time since the War between the States," according to *Fortune* magazine, "almost any native of the Deep South who wants a job can get one." The combination of military installations and defense plants altered the lives of southerners in ways that would have been inconceivable only a few years earlier. Economically marginal persons, displaced since the 1920s by the collapse of the South's traditional cotton economy, now had an alternative to leaving the South. Many found employment in the booming shipyards along the Atlantic and Gulf coasts, others in the aircraft, metals, machinery, petroleum, and chemical industries that began to dot the region. Relatively minor regional cities, such as Houston and Tampa, began a process of growth that would eventually make them national urban centers.

Persons caught up in these changes found them profound. Some complained that only old men, women, and children were left in the countryside. "Them that ain't gone in the army," one Alabamian told a visiting reporter, "have gone to the shipyards." Not all who moved necessarily wanted to abandon rural life, but the economic incentive to do so was irresistible. Migrants to rapidly urbanizing areas found them dirty, overcrowded, and unpleasant, but wages of a hundred dollars or more per week represented small fortunes to people accustomed to hardscrabble lives.

The South was, in fact, booming. According to the U.S. Bureau of the Census, Mobile County, Ala., was the fastest-growing metropolitan area of the entire country. The bureau estimated that during the war more than 15 million persons (i.e., 12 percent of the entire U.S. population) moved to counties different from those in which they had been living at the time of Pearl Harbor. Along with West Coast cities, those in the South were the biggest gainers. Together with Mobile, the Norfolk, Va., and Charleston, S.C., areas comprised three of the four fastest growing areas of the nation. Like Mobile, Norfolk attracted thousands to its shipyards. In the case of Charleston, its busy industries and proximity to Fort Benning, Ga., the army's largest basic training center, prompted the following advice to prospective travelers: "You'll drive blocks looking for a place to park, and just about the time you begin wondering where all the people came from you bump into a new housing development, or run into a squadron of navy uniforms, or if the wind is right, get a whiff of Charleston's pulp mill."

Soldier home on furlough with his family outside a service station in Brown Summit, N.C., 1944

Not all parts of the South would be affected so dramatically, but repercussions were nonetheless widespread. When compared to the sharecropper's endless cycle of indebtedness or the meager wages of the typical prewar southern textile worker, war-related jobs represented a step forward for large numbers of southerners. These jobs not only gave them their first taste of prosperity but began to tear apart the paternalistic patterns to which many southern whites as well as the great majority of blacks had been subjected. All the highly publicized talk among middle- and upper-class southerners about "how difficult it was to get good help any more" reflected not only their racism and paternalism but also the economic transformation that was taking place. Most of its beneficiaries were white, but the overall rise in the South's economic situation was such that some blacks were also included. Perhaps the most telling trend was that the South's industrial growth was slowest in what up to World War II had been its most important industry, textiles. In effect, a structural transformation was occurring in the very nature of southern industry.

Both the intensification of southern economic change and its implications for the future were exemplified by the region's most famous wartime industrialist, Andrew Jackson Higgins. In 1939 Higgins Industries in New Orleans consisted of one plant, which employed about 400 workers manufacturing shallow-draught boats for use in the swampy bayous of southern Louisiana and Mississippi. Higgins's gross sales amounted to $850,000, and rumor had it that his best customers were bootleggers. In 1941, however, his designs for landing craft and patrol torpedo boats were accepted by the U.S. Navy, and Higgins's prominence skyrocketed. By 1944 his operations in New Orleans consisted of eight plants that employed over 20,000 workers; his gross sales were estimated at $120 million. Higgins became a local folk hero who disregarded many southern traditions. He was willing to work with labor unions and also willing, indeed eager, to hire blacks and pay them on the same basis as whites. To be sure, he maintained segregation, but his shipyards were relatively free of the racial tensions that periodically erupted into violence elsewhere, most notably in 1943 at the Alabama Drydock Company in Mobile.

Although the impact of the war on southern agriculture was less dramatic, the developments were hardly insignificant. The prices of traditional commodities such as cotton and tobacco rose sharply, as did the production of new ones like peanuts and livestock. Booming war plants and military mobilization led to severe labor shortages—a sharp reversal of what until recently had been a longstanding problem of surplus agricultural labor. Increasingly, the region's planters and commercial farmers resorted to mechanization or to novel solutions such as importing migrant laborers from Mexico and the West Indies, or, more novel still, leasing Axis prisoners of war to do fieldwork. (Over 400,000 enemy prisoners were interned in the United States during the war, most of them in the South.) Occasionally, planters even resorted to paying native workers reasonable wages and providing them with better living conditions.

The very nature of American mobilization during the war altered what C. Vann Woodward has called the "counterpoint" of "North-South dialogue." Twelve million Americans entered the armed services during the year, and at least half of them spent some time at southern military bases, which accounted for more than half the nation's military installations. A substantial number of outsiders experienced their first direct contact with the region during the war, and the impressions and attitudes that they carried away with them had an indelible impact upon postwar sectional issues, particularly civil rights. However much these northern GIs may have been impervious to racial injustices in their own areas, or were themselves prejudiced against blacks, given the time and place, not to mention the circumstances of war, most did not find the white South's highly visible efforts to enforce segregation compatible with the democratic ideals they were ostensibly defending.

At the same time that large numbers of northerners were discovering the South, southern whites and blacks were also exposed to new locales, ideas, and influences outside the region. The impact of wartime experience on southern blacks is significant. Over 1 million saw military service, which for many was a prelude to subsequent civil rights involvements. Medgar Evers of Decatur, Miss., served with U.S. Army forces in Normandy and received his college education on the GI Bill; Harry Briggs, the plaintiff in the 1949 Clarendon County, S.C., case that launched into the courts the issue of public school desegregation, had spent all of his 34 years in the county, except for the three he spent in the South Pacific with the navy; and Oliver Brown of Topeka, Kan., whose daughter was the focus of the suit that led to the *Brown* v. *Board of Education* decision, was a veteran. During the war black Americans argued that the discrepancy between the democratic values for which the United States was fighting overseas and the realities of racially discriminatory practices at home had become intolerable. This attitude particularly affected blacks who experienced these discriminations firsthand while in their country's uniform.

The war disturbed the South's economic, social, and moral isolation and had a demonstrable impact on one of the region's greatest natural resources—its literary imagination. Flannery O'Connor's masterful story "The Displaced Person" conveyed the full sense of World War II's impact on the South. In it, O'Connor evoked a powerful image of the traditional world of the rural South—a world of white landowners and their poor white and black tenants—about to be torn asunder by the arrival of a Displaced Person, literally a DP, a refugee from Poland who with his family had somehow managed to survive Hitler's death camps and who had come to the South to work as a hired farmhand. To the farm's white tenants the displaced person, whose name is Guizac, brings home all the recent horrors of Europe—"the devil's experiment station"—of which they had been only dimly aware. Guizac is most efficient, a much better farmer than the resident white and black tenants, who fear that his industriousness makes them expendable. With his lack of understanding of the social conventions of the Jim Crow South, though, Guizac might as well have been from Mars. His ultimate transgression is to promise in marriage to one of the farm's black males his 16-year-old female cousin, whom Guizac wanted to bring to the United States from Poland. This is too much for the social world of a southern tenant farm, and the story ends with Guizac's being crushed to death by a runaway tractor as the landlady and her tenants, who could have warned the Pole to move out of the way, stand by mutely. Guizac's death, however, only hastens the breakdown of the farm, which is sold at a loss while its inhabitants disperse—an appropriate ending for a story conveying the social, economic, and moral impact of World War II on the South.

William Faulkner, the South's foremost literary chronicler, captured the totality of the changes in the region. In his first postwar novel, *Intruder in the Dust* (1948), Faulkner vividly portrayed the economic transformation reaching into Jefferson, the seat of his mythic Yoknapatawpha County. He contrasted Jefferson's "old big decaying wooden houses," which had known several generations of the town's residents and the South's anguished history, with the decidedly Sunbeltish image of "neat, small, new, one story houses designed in Florida and California set with matching garages in their neat plots of clipped grass and tedious flowerbeds, three and four of them now, a subdivision now in what twenty-five years ago had been considered a little small for one decent front lawn, where the prosperous young married couples live with two children each and (as soon as they could afford it) an automobile each and memberships in the country club and the bridge clubs." For Faulkner, tawdriness was a by-product of the South's new prosperity. Yet few, including Faulkner, mourned the passing of the endemic poverty that had shackled the region for so long.

Morton Sosna
Stanford University

Carl Abbott, *The New Urban America: Growth and Politics in Sunbelt Cities* (1981); James C. Cobb, *The Selling of the South: The Southern Crusade for Industrial Development, 1936–1980* (1982); Pete Daniel, *Breaking the Land: The Transformation of Cotton, Tobacco, and Rice Cultures since 1880* (1985), *Standing at the Crossroads: Southern Life in the Twentieth Century* (1986); William Faulkner, *The Mansion* (1955), *Requiem for a Nun* (1950); David R. Goldfield, *Cottonfields and Skyscrapers: Southern City and Region, 1607–1980* (1982); Calvin B. Hoover and B. U. Ratchford, *Economic Resources and Policies of the South* (1951); Bernice Reagon, *Southern Exposure* (Nos. 3 and 4, 1974); George B. Tindall, *The Emergence of the New South, 1913–1945* (1967).

Barbecue

Three topics upon which southerners never agree are religion, politics, and barbecue. Depending upon where they live, from the coast of the Carolinas to the plains of Texas, southerners will argue that barbecue is beef or pork, mutton or goat, ribs or chicken, or even link sausage. Universally loved in the South, barbecue is a menu of meats, sauces, and side dishes that changes from state to state, and even from one town to the next. And in each locale, residents claim their style of barbecue is the best.

Barbecue begins in the eastern Carolinas either as a whole hog or shoulders cooked over hardwood coals. The meat is then chopped finely, sprinkled with a sauce of apple-cider vinegar, salt, and pepper, and usually served with cole slaw, hush puppies, and Brunswick stew.

As one moves westward through the Deep South, sauces thicken and turn redder from a tomato or catsup base. West of the Mississippi River, beef and pork share the bill of fare in Louisiana, Arkansas, and Oklahoma, but Texans normally acknowledge barbecue only in the form of beef, usually a four- to eight-pound slab of boneless brisket. Traditionally, beef was wrapped in burlap and smoked underground, but it is now usually cooked in pits over hickory, oak, or mesquite wood. It is served with potato salad, baked beans, cole slaw, and two slices of white loaf bread, with spareribs as a side delicacy. The sauce is a dark-brown brew, consisting of butter, catsup, Worcestershire sauce, chili powder, vinegar, lemon juice, salt, pepper, and sugar.

Other meats that dominate certain locales include goat in south and west Texas; link sausage in central Texas; mutton in Owensboro, Ky.; and ribs in Memphis, Tenn.

Once, barbecue was prepared primarily for special occasions; in the antebellum South, many of the cooks who prepared it were black. When numerous barbecue restaurants opened in the middle of the 20th century, many were black establishments, to which whites, in a strange reversal of Jim Crow traditions, made stealthy excursions for take-out orders. Now, whites sit down for service in such black businesses as Cromwell's Barbecue in Phenix City, Ala., Archibald's Drive-In in Northport, Ala., and The Spare Rib in Greeneville, Tex.

Buildings that house barbecue restaurants fall mainly into two architectural classifications. One might be called barbecue primitive style—the older, usually rural eateries, identified by torn screen doors, fire-sale furniture, jukeboxes, cough-syrup calendars, and always the counter and stools, all producing an ambience strikingly similar to a county-line beer joint. Establishments in more urban areas decorate with old tin signs and farm equipment and dress their help in cute calicos and denims, all in an attempt to look country. These facilities can be categorized as the neoprimitive revival barbecue style.

The barbecue "addict" who is also a seasoned traveler looks only at the parking lot to prejudge a restaurant's product. If he notices pickup trucks parked next to expensive imports, he knows the barbecue is good because everyone in town eats there. More than any other cuisine, barbecue draws the whole of southern society, from down the street and from miles around. Many will drive miles to a revered barbecue shrine that serves what its customers claim as the best barbecue in the world.

Gary D. Ford
Southern Living

John Egerton, *Southern Food: At Home, on the Road, in History* (1987); Gary D. Ford, *Southern Living* (May 1982); John Marshall, "Barbecue in Western Kentucky: An Ethnographic Study" (M.A. thesis, Western Kentucky University, 1981); Jerry Simpson, *Southern World* (May–June 1980); Stephen A. Smith, *Studies in Popular Culture* (No. 1, 1985); Kathleen Zobel, *Southern Exposure* (1977).

Beverages

The first mechanical refrigeration plant for the manufacture of ice was built in New Orleans in 1865, but long before that inventive southerners found ways to slake the thirst of long hot summers in the region. In springhouses, cellars, and underground icehouses, 19th-century housekeepers cooled sweet milk, buttermilk, cider, and other liquids. Using winter ice insulated with straw, they made special-occasion pitchers of lemonade and iced tea. In winter they drank hot coffee, tea, and cocoa, imported beverages used widely in the South before the Civil War. Later, orange juice and other juices from Florida-grown citrus fruits became universally popular. Mineral water from the hot springs of Arkansas was first bottled in 1871.

Southerners also drank homemade beer, wine, and whiskey. In the late 1700s Kentucky became a mecca for whiskey makers, and the sour-mash bourbon that originated there is now world renowned; in fact almost all the whiskey made from corn and limestone water comes from Kentucky and Tennessee.

Besides the generic liquids just mentioned, a number of brand-name beverages originated in the South and now enjoy wide popularity. Ten of the better-known drinks, listed in the order of their origination, are as follows: (1) Dr Pepper, created in 1885 by Charles Alderton in Waco, Tex., and named for Dr. Charles K. Pepper of Rural Retreat, Va., in 1885; (2) Coca-Cola, created by John S. Pemberton, a pharmacist in Atlanta, Ga., in 1886; (3) Maxwell House coffee, roasted and blended by Joel O. Cheek in Nashville, Tenn., about 1880; (4) Pepsi-Cola, created in 1896 by Caleb D. Bradham, a pharmacist in New Bern, N.C.; (5) Barq's root beer, developed by Edward A. Barq in Biloxi, Miss., in 1898; (6) Buffalo Rock ginger ale, developed by Sidney Lee of Birmingham, Ala., about 1901; (7) Blenheim ginger ale, created by Dr. John May of Blenheim, S.C., in 1904; (8) Dixie beer, brewed in 1907 by Valentine Merz in New Orleans, La.; (9) RC Cola, developed in Columbus, Ga., in 1933 by successors to Claud A. Hatcher, a pharmacist whose first commercial soft drink in about 1902 was a ginger ale he called Royal Crown; and (10) Gatorade, developed by Dr. Robert Cade, a University of Florida kidney specialist, at Gainesville, Fla., in 1965.

John Egerton
Nashville, Tennessee

Harry E. Ellis, *Dr Pepper: King of Beverages* (1979); Sam B. Hilliard, *Hog Meat and Hoecake: Food Supply in the Old South* (1972); E. J. Kahn, Jr., *The Big Drink: The Story of Coca-Cola* (1950); Martha McCulloch-Williams, *Dishes and Beverages of the Old South* (1913); John J. Riley, *A History of the American Soft Drink Industry: Bottled Carbonated Beverages, 1807–1957* (1958); Joe Gray Taylor, *Eating, Drinking, and Visiting in the South: An Informal History* (1982); Rupert B. Vance, *Human Geography of the South: A Study in Regional Resources and Human Adequacy* (1935).

Beverley, Robert

(c. 1673–1722) Virginia gentleman and planter.

Beverley was the first native-born American to write a history of the Virginia colony—*The History and Present State of Virginia* (1705). Educated in England, he returned to Virginia at 19 when he inherited from his father a large estate. In 1697 he married Ursula Byrd, the 16-year-old daughter of Colonel William Byrd I. She died less than a year later in childbirth, and Beverley never remarried. He held various governmental clerkships and was elected to the House of Burgesses in 1699, but his political career ended about 1703 after he criticized Governor Nicholson and his administration for subverting the rights of Virginians. Settled at Beverley Park in King and Queen County, he pursued his studies and speculated in land. He identified strongly with the New World, proclaiming "I am an Indian," and in spite of his great wealth lived a deliberately simple life, using furniture made on his own plantation and producing wine from his own grapes. He went on Colonel Alexander Spotswood's 1716 expedition over the Blue Ridge Mountains with the group later known as the "Knights of the Golden Horseshoe." Shortly before his death, he prepared a revised version of the *History* (1722) and *An Abridgement of the Public Laws of Virginia*.

His history was characteristically colonial southern in its approach. Although Puritan histories explained events in terms of divine providence, Beverley's was secular and rationalistic; the nearest he came to any supernatural wonders was in a story of Indian rainmaking, which he handled with the skeptical amusement of later front-porch, rocking-chair tellers of folktales. Nature he viewed not as a wilderness but as a paradise of natural abundance; his descriptions ranged from scientific observation to rhapsodic wonder. He gave extended, sympathetic treatment of Native Americans and indicted white society for the tragic injustice it inflicted on them. Ironically, however, he referred to black slavery in the briefest terms, merely remarking that slaves generally were not overworked. Demonstrating pride in being an American, he was sharply critical of oppressive English economic policies and of mismanagement by royal governors. But he also lamented the indolence and luxury of the colonists themselves and urged them to work to improve the natural garden of Virginia, to diversify their agriculture and develop manufactures, and to live moderately. He thus held forth a pastoral ideal for the American South.

Judy Jo Small
University of North Carolina
at Chapel Hill

Robert D. Arner, *Southern Literary Journal* (Spring 1976); Robert Beverley, *The History and Present State of Virginia*, ed. Louis B. Wright (1947); Judy Jo Small, *American Literature* (December 1983).

Boone, Daniel

(1734–1820) Frontiersman.

The idea of the frontier serves as one of the main themes in the American and southern self-images, and it is impossible to discuss the frontier without discussing Daniel Boone. In fact and in myth perhaps no single individual is more central to the frontier experience.

Nearly 70 of his 86 years were involved with the exploration and settlement of the frontier. On 2 November 1734 Boone was born on the western perimeter of European settlement in Berks County, Penn. At the age of 31 he ventured as far south as Pensacola, Fla., in search of a new home. Four years later, on 7 June 1769, after a 37-day trek that he called "a long and fatiguing journey through a mountainous wilderness," he first "saw with pleasure the beautiful level of Kentucke." When he died on 26 September 1820, he was living on the western boundary of frontier settlement in St. Charles County, Mo., one of the outposts for fitting out expeditions to explore the Rocky Mountains. Boone constantly placed himself upon the advancing edge of settlement and did so with evident relish.

In the popular imagination Daniel Boone is the prototype of the frontier hero. His life formed a general pattern that was reenacted with certain variations by the next three major heroes of the westward frontier of the 19th century—Davy Crockett, Kit Carson (a distant relative of Boone), and Buffalo Bill Cody—and as well as by Natty Bumppo, the protagonist in James Fenimore Cooper's *Leatherstocking Tales*. Boone and Crockett most clearly symbolize the southern phase of the frontier. Like the physical frontier, Boone progressively moved to the west. Indeed, he and others like him were largely responsible for the retreat of the frontier toward the setting sun. Like the frontier, he remained an invaluable spiritual constant. Daniel Boone exemplified both the American way of life and the ideals of frontier independence and virtue, which were embodied in the expanding 19th-century South of yeoman farmers. In a country whose history has been dominated by continuing migration, the majority of early Americans believed themselves to be pioneers to some extent and, as such, identified with Boone as their hero.

Boone also mirrored the conflict between civilization and the wilderness: which was the ideal state? Boone was the pioneer, a man happy to do his part to help civilize the frontier and to praise these improvements; but, equally the hunter and man of nature, he was appalled at the encroachments of civilization and retreated before its corrupting influence to insure his own happiness. His achievements and fame live on for Americans in this dual role of pioneer and preserver because this is the dual role—imagined, desired, or enacted—of the American people, as well.

Significantly, Boone still functions as a model worthy of emulation. Dan Beard, the founder of the Boy Scouts of America, a group that influences the lives of millions of young Americans, based his conception of this organization upon the following premise: "A society of scouts to be identified with the greatest of all Scouts, Daniel Boone, and to be known as the Sons of Daniel Boone."

Michael A. Lofaro
University of Tennessee

John E. Bakeless, *Daniel Boone: Master of the Wilderness* (1939; 1965); Michael A. Lofaro, *The Life and Adventures of Daniel Boone* (1978); Richard Slotkin, *Regeneration through Violence: The Mythology of the American Frontier, 1600–1860* (1973).

Burma Shave Signs

In 1930 travelers on southern roads joined in a rapidly spreading national pastime—reading Burma Shave signs. Set 100 paces apart along the roadside, a series of six signs contained a catchy jingle promoting Burma Shave, a new brushless shaving cream. A typical gem was the jingle "Water Heater/ Out of Kilter/ Try the Brushless/ Whisker/ Wilter/ Burma Shave." The humorous, often public-spirited advertising tickled the nation's fancy for almost 40 years, providing a focal point for travelers throughout the country.

In Minneapolis in 1925 Clinton Odell and his sons, Allan and Leonard, introduced Burma Shave, the key product of their Burma-Vita Company. A year later Allan proposed the use of sets of roadside signs with catchy jingles to plug the new product. The soaring popularity of the signs was matched by impressive sales records throughout the Midwest in 1926 and 1927, on the Pacific and Atlantic coasts in 1929, and in the South and New England in 1930.

Though lacking the population density—and therefore the potential market—of more urbanized regions, the South offered many locations suitable for the Burma Shave signs. Having found a good spot, the company agent contacted the owner of the land and offered him a jar of Burma Shave and a small fee for a year's lease of the site. Many of the farmers purportedly became very attached to the signs, repairing them when damaged and willingly renewing the leases. This facet of the automobile age changed southern landscapes, and a new product became part of changing lifestyles.

None of the 600 jingles used between 1926 and 1963 had a specifically regional theme, but one jingle referred to a southern locale: "From Saskatoon/ to Alabam'/ You Hear Men Praise/ The Shave/ What Am/ Burma Shave." Regional marketing campaigns and contests for new jingles were used, and the contests sparked a tremendous response. One Alabama woman, for example, contributed the safe-driving jingle, "A Girl/ Should Hold On/ To Her Youth/ But Not/ When He's Driving." Another example is the 1952 series used in the South, "Missin'/ Kissin'?/ Perhaps Your Thrush/ Can't Get Thru/ The Underbrush—Try/ Burma Shave."

By the mid-1950s the Burma-Vita Company faced decline, and in 1963 Philip Morris, Inc., bought the company and abandoned the signs. The demise of Burma Shave signs caught the public's attention, and one set of signs was eventually placed in the Smithsonian Institution. A national marketing phenomenon had incorporated the South and tapped the rich folk humor of the nation. The television show *Hee Haw* used the signs in the 1970s in evoking its image of the South.

Sharon A. Sharp
University of Mississippi

Frank Rowsome, Jr., *The Verse by the Side of the Road* (1965).

Byrd, William, II

(1674–1744) Virginia aristocrat, lawyer, politician, planter, writer, and amateur scientist.

Born 28 March 1674, Byrd inherited a large plantation on the James River and the family home, called Westover, from his father, Colonel William Byrd I (1652–1704). Son of a London goldsmith, Colonel Byrd had risen to prominence by inheriting the estate from his uncle and acquiring vast wealth through land speculation, fur trading, and importation of indentured servants and black slaves. Like other wealthy southern colonials, the young Byrd was educated in England, where he developed many of his talents and tastes. He went to grammar school in Essex, studied law at the Middle Temple, was elected to the Royal Society, attended the theater frequently, and moved in London's elite social and literary circles. He lived in England in the years 1681 to 1696, 1697 to 1705, and 1715 to 1726. He married Lucy Parke in 1706, and after her death in 1716 he courted several wealthy women and carried on intrigues with various others before finally marrying Maria Taylor in 1724.

In Virginia, Byrd devoted his time to managing his plantations. He enlarged Westover into a splendid Palladian mansion with luxurious furnishings, improved its gardens, and entertained friends with generous hospitality. He collected one of the best and largest libraries in colonial America and read nearly every day in Latin, Greek, or Hebrew as well as in modern literature. He also took an active role in public affairs, as a man of his station was expected to, serving in the House of Burgesses briefly and in the Executive Council from 1708 until his death. He was the chief member of the joint commission that traveled in 1728 from the coast to the mountains surveying the disputed boundary line between Virginia and North Carolina. The manner of his life was in some ways modeled after the ideal of the English country gentleman, and the cosmopolitan Byrd sometimes described his world in pastoral terms. In continually buying and selling land, though, he represented a new southern type divergent from the English. Though he was a slaveholder, Byrd disapproved of the institution of slavery because of its inhumanity and its fostering of severity in slaveholders, laziness among whites, and the danger of bloody insurrections. His attitude toward New England Puritans blended admiration for their industriousness with contempt for their hypocritical traffic in rum and slaves.

Byrd's writings, marked by urbane good humor, were diverse. He was author of a scientific treatise for the Royal Society, gallant and witty verses, and *A Discourse Concerning the Plague* (1721), an anonymous pamphlet recommending tobacco as a preventive for plague. He seems to have written part of *The Careless Husband*, a play he also directed at a private house in Virginia, and he contributed to a promotional tract in German, *Newgefundenes Eden* (1737). His letters and three portions of his shorthand diaries have been found and published. Most important are the accounts of his travels—*A Progress to the Mines* (1841), *A Journey to the Land of Eden* (1928), and two versions of the dividing-line expedition. Of these, *The Secret History of the Dividing Line*, a travel journal circulated privately among friends and not published until 1929, is rich in racy humor and satirical caricatures of the commissioners; the much longer *History of the Dividing Line* (1866), evidently intended for London publication, diminishes the personal elements and includes political and natural history. Both versions, from the vantage point of a Tidewater Virginian, ridicule the vulgarities of shiftless backwoods Carolinians. Byrd thus inaugurated the southern tradition of literary humor dealing with poor whites.

Judy Jo Small
University of North Carolina
at Chapel Hill

Richard Beale Davis, in *Major Writers of Early American Literature*, ed. Everett Emerson (1972); Pierre Marambaud, *William Byrd of Westover, 1674–1744* (1971); Louis B. Wright, ed., *The Prose Works of William Byrd of Westover* (1966).

Chitterlings

Many aspects of Afro-American and southern white cuisine have their roots in the eating habits of the Old South. Many of the principal foods and dishes use pork products. These dishes include fatback, pigs' ears, pigs' feet, pork chops, and chitterlings. Chitterlings, or chitlins, are the small intestines of hogs, cooked in batter. Studies of early Afro-American eating habits suggest that such foods as chitlins came into the "soul food" diet because of the necessity for rural, poverty-ridden southerners to use every bit of food available. When a hog was slaughtered, no edible part was wasted.

To prevent spoilage, chitlins were prepared and eaten soon after the hog was killed. The common method of preparation was to clean the intestines carefully, soak them in water for a day, parboil them, and only then to fry them in batter. Viscera have been part of the staple diets of other cultures, including the Eskimos and people in Central Europe and the Balkans. They have been found to be nutritious and a good source of iron.

Southerners have disdained the eating of viscera at times, and those eating chitlins attempted to hide them behind names such as "Kentucky oysters." Not all southerners are ashamed of the uncommon food, however. Each fall in Salley, S.C., as many as 20,000 people gather to celebrate chitlins at the Chitlin' Strut festival. The one-day event features the crowning of Miss Chitlin' Strut, the frying and eating of 5 tons of chitlins, and the Chitlin' Strut contest itself. The "Chitlin' Strut" is a dance with twisting gyrations reflecting, some participants say, "the way chitlins make you feel."

Karen M. McDearman
University of Mississippi

William Price Fox, *Chitlin Strut and Other Madrigals* (1983); Bob Jeffries, *Soul Food Cookbook* (1970); Julian H. Lewis, *Negro Digest* (April 1950); *Southern Living* (November 1979).

Christmas

The first celebration of Christmas in North America was likely by the Spanish in the 1500s, and it certainly took place in the South, although whether in Florida or the Southwest is unknown. The first recorded commemoration of Christmas in the British colonies on the mainland was in Jamestown, Va., in 1607. About 40 of the original 100 colonists, unsure of their survival, gathered in a primitive wooden chapel for a somber day. Until well into the 19th century, the Protestants of New England looked with suspicion upon Christmas as a "popish" day, but southerners generally encouraged a joyous celebration.

Gentleman-farmers, in particular, regarded the day more as a time of relaxation and social activity than as a religious holiday. They preserved such European customs as caroling, burning the Yule log, and decorating with greenery. But the environment worked to make a distinctive festival. Native seafood and turkey replaced the traditional European dishes of beef and goose. Southerners added regional touches such as eating fried oysters, drinking eggnog with rum, and going on a Christmas-morning hunt for foxes or other small game. Pines replaced European firs and cedars for the Christmas tree, and Spanish moss was used as a primitive "angel hair" for decorating in the Deep South. The poinsettia became a custom in 1825 when a Charleston man with that name brought a red flower back from Mexico as a gift, and others were soon decorating with poinsettias.

The French in Louisiana introduced the tradition of Christmas fireworks, setting off firecrackers and firing rifles. Until the World War I era southerners rarely used fireworks on the Fourth of July but did punctuate the Christmas holiday with them. A long-standing Cajun custom is the Christmas Eve bonfires, known as *feux de joie* (fires of joy), burning all night along the Mississippi River from Baton Rouge to New Orleans.

Three southern states were the first in the nation to make Christmas a legal holiday—Louisiana and Arkansas in 1831 and Alabama in 1836. The plantation was the center for the most elaborate and distinctive antebellum southern celebration of Christmas. In back-country rural areas plantation houses became the scene of sometimes extravagant Christmas partying, eating, and playing, including the morning hunt. For slaves, Christmas had special meaning. December was a slow work month on the typical plantation, and it became the social season for them. The slaves' holiday lasted until the Yule log burned, which sometimes took over a week. The setting off of fireworks became a noted custom among the slaves as well as the whites.

Christmas as currently celebrated, in broad outline, was an invention of the 19th-century Victorians, who sentimentalized the day and made it the focus for new traditions. By the 1930s the celebration of Christmas had become even more secular than before, with the exchange of gifts for adults and Santa Claus for children. The religious aspects of Christmas were played down by the Victorians, but in the mid-20th century this dimension has become stronger. Some Protestant churches even imitate, in modified manner, the Catholic midnight Eucharist. In Jewish communities the festival of Hanukkah has expanded and absorbed many of the characteristics of Christmas.

Christmas has become the holiday par excellence in the South as elsewhere in the United States. Merchants begin to prepare for it and to advertise their offerings long before Halloween. The Santa Claus parades come early in December, if not sooner, and parties are given throughout the month. Fireworks, the antebellum custom, are still seen. Christmas trees adorn the streets, and one southern state, North Carolina, is the nation's largest producer of Christmas trees. Christmas programs and music are the fare on television and radio. Cards and presents flood the post offices. Charities set up stalls on street corners and with ringing of bells summon passersby to make contributions. Churches, of course, have special services. A few southern families make some effort to celebrate the 12 days culminating on 6 January, a day sometimes called "Old Christmas" (which is perhaps a faint recollection of when Britain adopted the Gregorian calendar in 1752, changing the celebration of Christmas from the 6 January date on the Julian calendar). In New Orleans the season of Carnival officially begins with Twelfth Night parties on the eve of Old Christmas. Many communities now sponsor candlelight tours of historic places at Christmas, reinforcing the holiday's ties to the idea of tradition itself.

Allen Cabaniss
University of Mississippi

William M. Auld, *Christmas Traditions* (1968); John E. Baur, *Christmas on the American Frontier* (1961); Harnett T. Kane, *The Southern Christmas Book: The Full Story from the Earliest Times to the Present: People, Customs, Conviviality, Carols, Cooking* (1958); Joanne B. Young, *Christmas in Williamsburg* (1970).

Claiborne, Craig

(b. 1920) Food critic.

Born in Sunflower, Miss. (population 500), Craig Claiborne cherishes childhood memories of beaten biscuits, churn clabber, hot corn bread, and chicken barbecues tended by his father. Another memory, that of his mother's monogrammed silver spoon, used to stir so many sauces that "the lip once a perfect oval [was] worn down by an inch," had special significance. Forced by financial setbacks to move to Indianola and open a boardinghouse in 1924, his mother used her ability to "divine" ingredients, reproducing countless dishes from Creole snapper to Brunswick stew, to keep the family solvent and make "Miss Kathleen's" one of the most "genteel" and well-regarded establishments in the Mississippi Delta.

John Dollard rented a room in her home while researching his classic study of southern race relations, *Caste and Class in a Southern Town*.

Shortly after graduating from the University of Missouri in journalism (June 1942), Claiborne enlisted in the navy, having "never sampled a glass of wine" nor eaten anything more exotic than jellied consommé. By the end of his tour of duty, however, he had tasted Moroccan lamb couscous and French pastries in Casablanca and had visited cafés and bistros throughout Europe. Following a brief stint in advertising and publicity in Chicago, another year in Europe and reenlistment in the navy at the outbreak of the Korean War, he finally decided to fuse his interests in food and writing and enrolled in the Lausanne Professional School of the Swiss Hotel Keepers Association.

Claiborne settled in Manhattan and after a series of part-time jobs, including freelance work for *Gourmet* magazine and bartending in upstate New York, met and was interviewed by Jane Nickerson of the *New York Times*; upon her resignation in 1957 he became the paper's food editor, a job he has held with only brief interruption for more than 25 years.

Shortly before the publication of his now-classic *New York Times Cook Book* in 1961, Claiborne began to test and prepare recipes with Pierre Franey, former chef of Manhattan's *Le Pavillon* restaurant. Working together in Claiborne's East Hampton home, the two concocted recipes that enriched the food pages of the *Times* and served as the basis for a series of cookbooks.

In addition to his regular column, cookbooks, and a dining guide to Manhattan, Claiborne has published *A Feast Made for Laughter* (1983), a memoir complete with 100 favorite recipes. Listed next to the *oeufs á la chimay* is, of course, a recipe for cheese grits.

Elizabeth M. Makowski
University of Mississippi

Confederate Memorial Day

Honoring the graves of warriors is an ancient custom, and southern whites after the Civil War made the custom a central ritual of southern life. Vicksburg, Miss., Petersburg, Va., Columbus, Miss., Charleston, S.C., and Columbus, Ga., have all claimed the first observance honoring the Confederate dead after the war. The early observances were spontaneous efforts by individuals or small groups.

Southern states could not agree among themselves which day would serve as the official Memorial Day, but by 1916, 10 states had designated 3 June, Jefferson Davis's birthdate. Other dates set aside have included the fourth Monday in April (Alabama and Mississippi); 10 May, the date of the capture by Union troops of Jefferson Davis in 1865 (North Carolina and South Carolina); and 26 April, the anniversary of the final surrender in 1865 of Confederate General Joseph E. Johnston in Durham, N.C., (Florida and Georgia). The choice of a date has sometimes been tied to an event of local importance, such as the death of a Confederate leader or anniversary of a nearby battle.

Whenever celebrated, Confederate Memorial Day was a time of solemn ritual. There were speeches, sermons, prayers, the decoration of graves with flowers and Confederate flags, the singing of religious and wartime anthems like "Dixie," and the playing of Taps. A military honor guard usually fired a salute to end the ceremonies. The day's rhetoric reminded southerners of their regional identity, based on the Confederate experience. Women played a key role in this ritual, with the United Daughters of the Confederacy particularly prominent in organizing activities. Groups like the United Confederate Veterans, the Sons of Confederate Veterans, and the Children of the Confederacy also assisted. Various states—Georgia, Florida, Arkansas, Alabama, and Mississippi—soon adopted state flags based partially or fully on the design of Confederate banners. They also proclaimed state holidays commemorating Robert E. Lee's birthday (19 January), Jefferson Davis's birthday, or a separate Confederate Memorial Day. Ministers were actively involved in this holy day. As one would expect, black southerners were not prominently involved in the day's events, although former slaves regarded as "loyal" occasionally were encouraged to speak. After World War II, Confederate Memorial Day declined as a vital holiday in the South. In states where it still exists, Confederate Memorial Day is observed on Mondays to give state employees long weekends. Many small towns continue to have popular ceremonies, but even in these places the Fourth of July has emerged as a more notable community event.

Charles Reagan Wilson
University of Mississippi

Wallace Evan Davies, *Patriotism on Parade: The Story of Veterans' and Hereditary Organizations in America, 1783–1900* (1955); Lucille C. Lowry, *Origin of Memorial Day in Dixie* (1937); Charles Reagan Wilson, *Baptized in Blood: The Religion of the Lost Cause, 1865–1920* (1980).

Confederate Veterans

To the white southerners who fought it, the Civil War remained forever poignant; and even after many years had passed, it dominated their thinking. To be sure, a few veterans regarded the war and all its trappings as having been too horrible; their greatest desire was to forget. But for most of them the memory refused to fade.

Reverence for the Lost Cause, it has been argued, grew into a new civil religion after the war. As long as any of them remained, the actual veterans were that religion's

Aged Confederate veterans, at Soldiers' Home in Richmond, 1930s

living apostles. And, just as is the case with a religion, the veterans tended to nurture their identity institutionally through various organizations—especially the United Confederate Veterans (UCV).

Initially, Confederate veterans, impelled by emotional pressures of living with defeat, associated informally. The basic psychological impetus was an intense belief that the world misunderstood both the history and the people of the South. As time passed, the relationships and organizations they engendered grew more symbolically meaningful. The great episode had "sanctified" its participants, and that sanctification spilled into the UCV's ancillary groups—the United Daughters of the Confederacy, the Sons of Veterans, the Children of the Confederacy, the Confederated Southern Memorial Association, the Order of the Stars and Bars, and the Confederate Choirs of America.

The UCV officially prohibited "the discussion of political or religious subjects" at meetings and forbade taking "any political action." What they meant to avoid was internal controversy. Their activities had considerable religious aspects: prayers, inspirational lectures, memorial ceremonies, even a special funeral service. Although they showed certain clear and strong political preferences, they rationalized such attitudes as not actually being political: any Confederate veteran obviously was more qualified for public office than a nonveteran; and benefits such as state pensions, soldiers' homes, and relief for needy veterans or their families, as well as the financing of hundreds of Civil War monuments, were humanitarian issues transcending politics.

The Confederate veteran wanted his name mentioned in historical writings, and he desired vindication as well as status and deference within his own society. He certainly managed to get all of that; it might well have come to him even without his efforts. During his more contemplative moments he wished for a "just treatment" in historical interpretation of himself and of his region. He was a powerful force, both a subject of, and a contributor to, the Lost Cause.

See also MYTHIC SOUTH: / Lost Cause Myth; Reb, Johnny

Herman Hattaway
University of Missouri
Kansas City

Herman Hattaway, *Louisiana History* (Summer 1971; Winter 1975); William W. White, *The Confederate Veteran* (1962); Charles Reagan Wilson, *Baptized in Blood: The Religion of the Lost Cause, 1865–1920* (1980).

Country Ham

Country ham is a 19th-century southern term for a pork delicacy that has been known and loved in Asia and Europe for more than 2,000 years. It is the hind quarter of a hog that has been cured with salt, colored and flavored with wood smoke, and hung up to age through a summer or longer.

The first British colonists who came to Virginia brought pigs with them, and they also brought a knowledge of the ancient technique of preserving meat by covering it with salt. The necessary combination of winter cold for slaughtering and summer heat for curing was ideally found in the colonies of Virginia, Maryland, and North Carolina, and ever since, country hams have remained popular in those states and their westward extensions, particularly Kentucky and Tennessee. Virginia's renowned Smithfield hams and the prime products of western Kentucky and other places in the region are unsurpassed by the best that France, Italy, and other nations have to offer.

Modern food technology has developed short-cut methods of duplicating the appearance of genuine country ham, but not its taste. As a result, most commercial "country" hams on the market today have been artificially cured, smoked, and aged and do not have the rich aroma and flavor of hams produced by traditional processes. Diligent inquiries in rural areas of the Upper South can still turn up hams that are in every way equal to those that came from the smokehouses of the region more than 300 years ago.

Ideal country hams are produced from year-old hogs that weigh at least 300 pounds and have been fattened on corn or peanuts. Such hams will weigh 20 to 25 pounds when properly cured and aged. As soon as a hog has been butchered in cold weather, the hams are rubbed down with a dry mixture of salt and other additives, usually sugar and saltpeter. Next, they are completely covered for four to six weeks in a bed of salt, then washed off and trimmed, and finally hung by their hocks in a dark smokehouse, there to take on a deep nut-brown appearance and a distinctive flavor from the enveloping hickory smoke. The hams must remain suspended to sweat through the hot summer months. A bare minimum of nine months is needed to complete the entire curing, smoking, and aging process; a full year, or even two years, is considered more nearly ideal.

Many variations on this basic method are favored from one ham maker to the next. Some mix a large amount of sugar with the salt and call their hams "sugar cured" (though sugar is not a preservative); some make smoke with oak or sassafras; some skip the smoking stage altogether, claiming it has no effect on flavor. But for salt and the summer sweats, there are no substitutes and no alternatives, modern technology notwithstanding.

When a ham is ready to eat, it may be baked in the oven, boiled on top of the stove, or sliced and fried. The latter method yields a rich bonus in the form of red-eye gravy, produced by adding a little water to the frying skillet. In whatever form it is prepared, country ham is as old as the South itself.

John Egerton
Nashville, Tennessee

John Egerton, *Southern Food: At Home, on the Road, in History* (1987); Sam B. Hilliard, *Hog Meat and Hoecake: Food Supply in the Old South* (1972); Stephen A. Smith, in *American Material Culture*, ed. Edith Mayo (1985).

Crockett, Davy

(1786–1836) Frontiersman, politician, humorist.

The life of the historical David Crockett is interesting but in no way as remarkable as the legendary lives of *Davy* Crockett. Born on 17 August 1786 in Greene County, Tenn., Crockett was a first-rate but relatively obscure backwoods hunter and Indian fighter with a knack for storytelling. He parlayed his local reputation into a state, and then national, political career. He was elected to the Tennessee Legislature in 1821 and 1823 and won congressional elections in 1827, 1829, and 1833. In Congress he promoted sale of public land at low prices but was frequently at odds with President Andrew Jackson. Crockett became perhaps the representative symbol of both the noble and savage aspects of frontier life in Jacksonian America. His death at the Alamo on 6 March 1836 assured him a prominent place in the history of the South and the nation and, more importantly, opened the cultural floodgates to the boundless expansion of his legendary image in the popular media of his day and ours.

Crockett promoted himself as a simple, down-home country boy whose extraordinary marksmanship was a metaphor for his character: he was a straight shooter. By the early 1830s his image had achieved a life of its own, so much so that in 1834 he published his autobiography (*A Narrative of the Life of David Crockett*) to counteract the compilation of tall tales printed under his name a year earlier by Matthew St. Clair Clarke as the *Sketches and Eccentricities of Col. Crockett.*

Davy Crockett, frontier humorist and politician

David was becoming Davy, the screamer and "ring-tailed roarer" who could "run faster, jump higher, squat lower, dive deeper, stay under longer, and come out drier, than any man in the whole country." Davy was not the first to give vent to the backwoods brag, but in the hands of the Boston literary hacks who produced the tall tales for the *Crockett Almanacs* (1835–56), he became its finest practitioner. This fictional Davy was both the Promethean figure who saved the earth by unfreezing the sun from its axis and the "humanitarian" who killed and boiled an Indian to help cure his pet bear's stomach disorder. He was also an ardent advocate of expansionism, with Mexico and Oregon but two of his targets.

The violent, racist, and jingoistic Davy of the almanacs competed with and was eventually subsumed by over 150 years of romantic melodrama. From Nimrod Wilfire, James Kirke Paulding's Crockettesque character in his play *The Lion of the West* (1831), to the Davys played by Fess Parker and John Wayne, 19th-century drama and 20th-century film always presented the hero in the kindest light. Courageous, dashing, and true blue, this nature's nobleman protected his country and those who were helpless with equal fervor.

Both the outrageous and the idealized Davy were firmly grounded in a southern sense of place. Whether as the purveyor of southern or southwestern humor over the full spectrum of good and bad taste or as the gallant southern gentleman, the knight errant of the backwoods, Davy reflected the range of the region whose hero he became and, in the larger context, the diversity and individuality of the entire nation.

Michael A. Lofaro
University of Tennessee

Richard Boyd Hauck, *Crockett: A Bio-Bibliography* (1982); Michael A. Lofaro, ed., *Davy Crockett: The Man, the Legend, the Legacy, 1786–1986* (1985); James A. Shackford, *David Crockett: The Man and the Legend* (1956).

Davis, Jefferson

(1808–1889) Politician.

"The man and the hour have met," a distinguished secessionist proclaimed when Jefferson Davis became president of the Confederate States of America. In most ways Davis seemed ideally suited to directing the South's struggle for independence. Born in Fairview, Ky., in 1808, Davis moved with his family to Wilkinson County, Miss., when he was still a boy. Experienced in warfare and politics, he had attended the U.S. Military Academy (graduating in 1828), participated in the Black Hawk War, commanded a regiment of Mississippi volunteers and been wounded in the Mexican War, served as President Franklin Pierce's secretary of war, and headed the U.S. Senate's Military Affairs Committee. A brave, bold, erudite agrarian who believed in slavery and the right of secession, Davis worked tirelessly for the Confederacy. Against the localism of certain governors and congressmen, he advocated measures for the Confederacy such as a military draft, conscription of blacks into the army, impressment of private property, government management of railroads and blockade runners, and an income tax.

But his inability to maintain the support of the Confederate Congress and his unwillingness to delegate authority except in certain areas created problems; so did his direction of military strategy and tactics. Ironically, it may have been in military affairs, where so much was expected of him, that Davis failed. He picked only one outstanding army commander, Robert E. Lee; other commanders proved to be unsuccessful, distrusted by Davis, or both. Squabbles among generals and over military politics hampered the Confederate war effort, and, as Union armies advanced, Confederate morale deteriorated. Davis hoped that his defensive-offensive strategy would save the South, but in practice it became little more than a series of courageous but costly attacks on

Jefferson Davis, Confederate president, 1861–65

enemy forces until dwindling manpower forced the Confederates on the defensive after 1863.

Davis may have been "perverse and obstinate" and "an indifferent judge of men," as his critics claimed, but he maintained during the last months of the war an unfailing will to win and even tried to continue the war as the Confederacy collapsed. Captured in May 1865 and imprisoned for two years without a trial, he became in the North the symbol of the South's treasonable sins. In the *Rise and Fall of the Confederate Government*, which he wrote after release from prison, Davis shared much of the blame for Confederate defeat with others. Throughout the remainder of his life he neither repented nor asked forgiveness for himself or for the cause he led.

Grady McWhiney
Texas Christian University

James T. McIntosh, ed., *The Papers of Jefferson Davis* (1971–); Dunbar Rowland, ed., *Jefferson Davis* (10 vols., 1923); Allen Tate, *Jefferson Davis* (1929); Robert Penn Warren, *Jefferson Davis Gets His Citizenship Back* (1980).

Flag, Rebel

The so-called rebel flag is a well-known *oblong* red banner on which is a blue cross of St. Andrew (saltire) edged with white and bearing 13 white five-pointed stars. It is a modification of the Confederate battle-flag, which was *square*, reputedly designed by General P. G. T. Beauregard, and erroneously, but popularly, called "the Stars and Bars." The battle-flag, however, was never adopted by the Confederate Congress and never officially flew over government offices of the Confederate states. It was not employed officially by Confederate veterans organizations and seldom by any of the later societies of descendants of Confederate veterans.

Yet out of that limbo emerged the modern imitation generally called a "rebel flag." This imitative innovation owed its origin to the simplicity of the battle flag's design as well as to ignorance about authorized flags of the Confederacy. It did not reach its great popularity until the 1950s, possibly owing to widespread southern white dissatisfaction with the federal government during that period. Several extremist groups, such as the Ku Klux Klan, have made notorious use of the *oblong* cloth. It has now more or less been confined in conventional use to sporting events in the South, especially football games. Black students at the University of Mississippi protested the school's use of the flag in 1983 and forced the administration to discourage use of the flag as an official symbol. Predictably, emotions associated with the flag run deep among both white and black southerners.

Allen Cabaniss
University of Mississippi

Whitney Smith, *The Great Flags of America* (1974).

Forrest, Nathan Bedford

(1821–1877) Confederate general.

A man of little formal education and no prior military experience, Nathan Bedford Forrest became one of three Confederate soldiers with no military training to rise to the rank of lieutenant general. Born in Bedford County, Tenn., Forrest struggled from poverty to a position of considerable wealth as a planter and slave dealer. Soon after the outbreak of the Civil War he raised and equipped a battalion of cavalry, of which he was elected lieutenant colonel. Forrest performed brilliantly at the battles of Fort Donelson and Shiloh and as an independent cavalry commander behind enemy lines through the summer of 1863, rising to the rank of brigadier general.

In command of the cavalry on the right wing of General Braxton Bragg's Army of Tennessee during the battle of Chickamauga, Forrest led his troops, fighting as mounted infantry, through some of the most severe fighting of the war. Afterward he quarreled bitterly with Bragg, was relieved of his corps, but was granted an independent command in west Tennessee and north Mississippi and promoted to major general.

Nathan Bedford Forrest, Confederate hero

Operating out of northern Mississippi, Forrest staged several intrepid and damaging raids against federal supply links and depots in Tennessee while successfully defending his base against numerous incursions by greatly superior Union forces. Forrest was reassigned to the Army of Tennessee as commander of all cavalry during John Bell Hood's abortive Tennessee campaign, and only his bold and skillful rear-guard actions saved that army from utter annihilation following the Confederate disasters at Franklin and Nashville. Although elevated to the rank of lieutenant general for his heroic efforts on the retreat from Nashville, Forrest was at last overwhelmed by vastly superior federal numbers at Selma, Ala., in April 1865.

Following the collapse of the Confederacy, Forrest served for some years as president of the Selma, Marion, & Memphis Railroad and was reportedly the principal organizer and first Imperial Wizard of the Ku Klux Klan. To many military historians, though, Nathan Bedford Forrest remains significant as the preeminent American cavalry leader.

Because he was the only unvaryingly successful Confederate commander in the western theater and because of the relative poverty of his origins, Forrest quickly became the darling of the plain people of the Old Southwest. Unlike the Virginia aristocrats, Lee and Stuart, or the Louisiana Creole, Beauregard, Forrest was a product of the South's hardscrabble frontier and an archetypal example of Jefferson's yeoman class. Writers in the 20th-century South, most notably William Faulkner and the

Nashville Agrarians, seized upon Forrest as a symbol of the best that the South's frontier culture produced. Andrew Lytle's biography, *Bedford Forrest and His Critter Company* (1931), Caroline Gordon's novel *None Shall Look Back* (1937), and Jesse Hill Ford's *The Raider* (1975) are full-length interpretations of Forrest's character and military career, and the Confederate "Wizard of the Saddle" also provided material for George Washington Cable, who served under him in the war's final year; Stark Young, whose father rode with Forrest; Robert Penn Warren, whose grandfather was one of his captains; and Donald Davidson, who attempted but failed to complete an epic poem based on the great cavalryman's campaigns. To each of these writers Forrest represents the highest emanation of Anglo-Saxon, agrarian democracy on the Old Southwest frontier, an unlettered man of the soil hurling back in confusion the minions of modern industrial, materialistic society. Of the legend of Forrest and his men, William Faulkner wrote that "even seventy-five years afterwards, [it was] still powerful, still dangerous, still coming!"

Thomas W. Cutrer
Texas State Historical
Association

R. S. Henry, *"First with the Most" Forrest* (1944); James H. Mathes, *General Forrest* (1902); John A. Wyeth, *That Devil Forrest* (1959).

Fried Chicken

Columbus brought chickens to America in 1493, and they have graced American tables—particularly in the South—ever since. Southern fried chicken is probably the single most popular and universally consumed food ever to come from this region of the country. It appeared in the earliest cookbooks; Mary Randolph's *Virginia Housewife* (1824) recommended a method strikingly similar to that commonly used today: cut-up pieces of chicken dredged in flour, sprinkled with salt and pepper, and fried in hot fat.

There are, of course, numerous variations on the basic technique. Some cooks insist on frying chicken in lard, but others prefer vegetable oil; some say pan frying in an inch or so of fat is best, and others choose deep frying instead; some use flour alone as the dusting substance, but others add cornmeal or milk or egg; some restrict seasoning to salt and pepper, while others go for spicier or more pungent tastes, such as hot sauce, garlic, red pepper, or lemon; some seek a dry, crisp, crunchy exterior, and others pour gravy or cream sauce over the finished product.

Virtually the only aspect of southern fried chicken that no one debates is the best way to eat it: with the fingers, the only practical means of separating the crisp skin and tender meat from the bone. "Finger lickin' good" became a motto of Colonel Harland Sanders's Kentucky Fried Chicken when the Corbin, Ky., entrepreneur launched a fast-food chicken business in 1956.

With Kentucky Fried Chicken still in the lead, numerous fast-food franchise outlets now dispense the popular finger food in cities and towns throughout the nation and the world. The volume of fried chicken sales is such that the raising of chickens has become a major agricultural industry in the South. Purists note that mass production yields an inferior fowl, one that lacks the leanness, tenderness, and taste that young pullets had when they scratched in southern yards and received ample rations of cracked corn as they approached frying size. Nonetheless, southern fried chicken has truly become a universal food, even as the delectable taste of lean and tender young pullets has faded into memory.

Chicken gravy remains one of the classic examples of southern food, its qualities undiminished by changes in the chickens themselves. Gravy is made from the dregs in the frying skillet, supplemented by a mixture of flour and either milk or water and seasoned with salt and pepper. Spooned onto potatoes or rice or biscuits, chicken gravy offers a savory flavor that southerners have known and loved for generations.

See also INDUSTRY: / Sanders, Colonel Harland

John Egerton
Nashville, Tennessee

John Egerton, *Southern Food: At Home, on the Road, in History* (1987); Page Smith and Charles Daniel, *The Chicken Book* (1975); Stephen A. Smith, in *American Material Culture*, ed. Edith Mayo (1975); *Southern Living* (July 1982).

Gardner, Dave

(1926–1983) Entertainer.

Gardner, stand-up entertainer, comedy recording star, and shrewd observer of southern manners in the 1950s and 1960s, was born in Jackson, Tenn., on 11 June 1926. Christened David Milburn Gardner, he grew up in and near Jackson, where he attended junior high school—the last he would see of school until his brief enrollment in a Baptist college. His brother, Kent, recalls that "Dave was always a quiet kid, rather puny, and never much of an outgoing person. His comedy did not show up until he was in his twenties, and then it evolved as an off-the-top-of-his-head thing. He never had writers."

In fact, Gardner, who was playing the drums professionally when he was 13, began his career in the late 1940s as a drummer and singer. Then he struck out on his own as a comedian. It was 1957 before opportunity knocked, and he made the first of a number of appearances on NBC-TV's *Tonight Show*, then hosted by Jack Paar. Almost overnight "Brother Dave," as he liked to be called, found himself with a national following; but nowhere was he more warmly received than on the college campuses of the South where, cigarette in one hand, microphone in the other, he ad-libbed his way through performances.

Brother Dave's routines were a crazy mixture of one-liners, stories that enabled him to make use of his amazing ear for regional speech, jive talk, and sly profundity. He picked no particular target but poked fun at them all: black civil rights leaders, bikers, good old boys, preachers, presidents. "Dear hearts," he would say in the midst of the protest of the 1960s, "I'm for the minorities—the Armed Forces and the Po-leece." Though he was accused by some of racism, he may have been closer to the truth when he told one interviewer toward the end of his life, "I was *left* when the world was *right*."

At the peak of his success he made several comedy albums for RCA and later for Capitol. His popularity faded in the social and political turmoil of the Vietnam years, but after a writer for the Atlanta *Constitution* found him living in obscurity in Dallas in 1981 and wrote a Sunday magazine article about him, Gardner made a comeback in Atlanta. While doing a film in 1983, he suffered a heart attack and died in Myrtle Beach, S.C.

Charles East
Baton Rouge, Louisiana

Larry L. King, *Harper's* (September 1970); Robert Lamb, *Atlanta Weekly* (22 November 1981).

Gays

Poverty and religion, both so prevalent in southern life, have molded homosexuality and society's reaction to it. The sexual attitudes of the poorer classes result both in widespread bisexual experimentation and in a violent reaction against such behavior. Often nominally justified by religion, this reaction is actually based on paranoia over the threat that effeminacy poses to the masculinity cult of the poorer classes. Thus, in the South some teenage boys go through a phase as amateur prostitutes with homosexual customers, yet the region has had more than its share of witch-hunts against homosexuals. Florida's homosexual witch-hunts since 1945 include the notable Anita Bryant "crusade" of 1977.

Religion, however, has been a comfort to southern homosexuals, who originated the "gay church" movement. The concept of homosexuality as a "sexual orientation" or a "sickness" tends to be replaced in the South by an attitude that the basic division is not between homosexuals and heterosexuals but between those who are active/masculine and those who are passive/effeminate (an idea widespread among the poorer classes throughout the world, whereas "sexual orientation" tends to be a middle-class concept). The southern attitude is that homosexuality is not a condition or a sickness but a sin of which (according to evangelical doctrine) anyone is capable. The idea of orientation suggests that homosexuality is limited to a small group of unusual people, but if it is seen (as it is in the South) as a sin, it will be seen more as habit than as condition, and by no means limited to a small in-group. The evangelical idea that "all men are sinners" can be used to suggest that all men are able to practice homosexuality. Universal sin is translated into universal bisexuality.

Half of the 24 states that have not decriminalized sodomy are in the South. The sodomy laws in Arkansas and Texas apply to homosexuals only, and the laws in the remaining southern states apply to both homosexuals and heterosexuals. Sodomy is a misdemeanor in Florida, Texas, and Arkansas, but is a felony in nine other southern states. Lesbian acts are specifically included as a felony in Georgia. In the South the punishment for sodomy ranges from a $200 fine in Texas or a maximum 60-day jail term in Florida to a maximum 15-year jail term in Tennessee or a 20-year term in Georgia. In July 1986 the Georgia sodomy law came to national attention when it was upheld by the U.S. Supreme Court in a case involving homosexual partners. Although the Georgia statute applies to any sodomy, the court's majority opinion addressed only the state's right to prohibit homosexual acts, a move seen as a direct threat by gay rights activists.

Many homosexual men move from small towns to cities, such as Atlanta, New Orleans, and Key West, which have large homosexual subcultures. However, many small towns have a "town queer" who is the focus of the covert bisexuality of the local youths. Many of these youths know only the word *queer* without ever having heard the words *gay* or *homosexual*. On the other hand, the homosexual subculture is so developed in the cities, especially in New Orleans, that homosexuality tends to be associated with the artistic and literary elements in the South more than in other sections. There is a long tradition of homosexual transvestism associated with Mardi Gras. But even middle-sized towns such as Pensacola, Fla., and Jackson, Miss., have well-organized homosexual subcultures. When interracial homosexual relations have taken place, it has been traditional for the black partner to play the active/masculine role and the white partner to play the passive/effeminate role. This role-playing derives from social class, as well as racial factors. American concepts of masculinity are associated with the proletariat, and most concepts of effeminacy are associated with the middle classes. Sexual role-playing involves imitating the behavior of one class or the other, so that it is really class role-playing rather than anything sexual, and yet is linked with sexual relationships.

The literature on homosexuality in the South is rather meager. Negative views include the interviews with policemen in *The Puritan Jungle: America's Sexual Underground* by Sara Harris (1969), and the official pamphlet *Homosexuality and Citizenship in Florida* (1964). Sociologists can read *Sex in Prison: The Mississippi Experiment with Conjugal Visiting* by Columbus B. Hopper (1969), *Scottsboro Boy* by Haywood Patterson and Earl Conrad (1950), and "The Social Integration of Peers and Queers" by Albert J. Reiss in Hendrik Ruitenbeek's *The Problem of Homosexuality in Modern Society* (1963).

James Kirkwood's *American Grotesque: An Account of the Clay Shaw-Jim Garrison Affair in the City of New*

Orleans (1970) deals with political persecution of homosexuals, while Mississippi writer Jere Real's cover article, "Gay Rights and Conservative Politics" (*National Review*, 17 March 1978) urged political restraint on sexual issues. Southern writers such as Tennessee Williams (in *Cat on a Hot Tin Roof*; *Suddenly Last Summer*; and *Small Craft Warnings*), Truman Capote (in *Other Voices, Other Rooms*), Carson McCullers (in *Reflections in a Golden Eye* and *Ballad of the Sad Café*), Charles Henri Ford, and Erskine Lane have discussed homosexuality, as have some biographies and autobiographies (Craig Claiborne's autobiography *Feast Made for Laughter* is one such work). Mississippi playwright Mart Crowley studies a homosexual Mississippian living in Manhattan in his drama *The Boys in the Band* (1968) and that same character's adolescence in his later *Breeze from the Gulf* (1973) and in his *Remote Asylum* (1970). Edward Swift's 1978 novel, *Splendora*, is a comic tale of sexual confusion in a small Texas town. Florence King's *Southern Ladies and Gentlemen* (1975) has a satiric chapter on southern homosexuals. The national gay news magazine *Advocate* has done extensive reportorial accounts of gay life in various southern cities and states.

Stephen Wayne Foster
Coral Gables, Florida

Jonathan Katz, *Gay American History: Lesbians and Gay Men in the U.S.A.: A Documentary Anthology* (1976); *Newsweek* (14 July 1986); William Parker, *Homosexuality: A Selective Bibliography of over 3,000 Items* (1971), *Homosexuality Bibliography: Supplement, 1970–1975* (1977); Troy Perry, *The Lord Is My Shepherd and He Knows I'm Gay* (1972); *Southern Exposure* (September–October 1985).

Goo Goo Clusters

"A Good Ole Southern Treat," announces the six-pack box of Standard Candy Company's Goo Goo Clusters. Often advertised as "the South's favorite candy" and "the Goodest Bar in town," the Goo Goo Cluster has been a candy staple in the Nashville, Tenn., area and throughout the South for over 70 years.

First created by William H. Campbell in Nashville in 1912, the Goo Goo Cluster is a combination of caramel, marshmallow, peanuts, and pure milk chocolate. (Recently the company has been making Goo Goo Supremes, which substitute pecans for peanuts.) Though the packaging and distribution techniques have changed with modernization and company expansion, the ingredients, cooking methods, and essential southern identity have remained the same.

The Goo Goo Cluster has been a curiosity since its origin. One account says that Campbell settled on the name because his son, only a few months old at the time, uttered those words when first introduced to the new candy. Another version suggests that Campbell was struck with his son's first utterance and decided it was an appropriate name. Whatever the true version, Standard Candy Company has contended for years that a Goo Goo is the first thing a southern baby requests.

Along with the Goo Goo, the company, founded in 1901, produces the ever-popular King Leo stick candy, a staple in many southern homes and a common Christmas treat and gift. Since 1968 the Grand Ole Opry has been singing the praises of the Goo Goo, sharing the wise culinary advice with those in attendance and reaching thousands more over WSM radio. So closely associated is the candy with the Opry, some have suggested that "Goo" stands for Grand Ole Opry. Grant Turner continues to let listeners know how to order the candy by mail, encouraging them further with the familiar slogan: "Go Get a Goo Goo. . . . It's Good."

Tom Rankin
Southern Arts Federation
Atlanta, Georgia

Margaret Loelo, *Wall Street Journal* (8 December 1982); John F. Persinos, *Inc.* (May 1984).

Grits

Grits are—or is, as the case may be—a by-product of corn kernels. Dried, hulled corn kernels are commonly called hominy; grits are made of finely ground hominy. Old-fashioned grits may also be produced from hard corn kernels that are coarsely ground and bolted (sifted) to remove the hulls.

Writing in the *New York Times* on 31 January 1982, Turner Catledge of New Orleans provided a succinct history of grits in the South:

> Grits is the first truly American food. On a day in the spring of 1607 when sea-weary members of the London Company came ashore at Jamestown, Va., they were greeted by a band of friendly Indians offering bowls of a steaming hot substance consisting of softened maize seasoned with salt and some kind of animal fat, probably bear grease. The welcomers called it "rockahominie."
>
> The settlers liked it so much they adopted it as part of their own diet. They anglicized the name to "hominy" and set about devising a milling process by which the large corn grains could be ground into smaller particles without losing any nutriments. The experiment was a success, and grits became a gastronomic mainstay of the South and symbol of Southern culinary pride.

Thus, throughout its history, and in pre-Columbian times as well, the South has relished grits and made them a symbol of its diet, its customs, its humor, and its good-spirited hospitality. From Captain John Smith to General Andrew Jackson to President Jimmy Carter, southerners rich and poor, young and old, black and white have eaten grits regularly. So common has the food been that it has been called a universal staple, a household companion, even an institution.

Grits cooked into a thick porridge are so common in some parts of the South that they are routinely served for breakfast, whether asked for or not. They are often flavored with butter or gravy, served with sausage or ham, accompanied by bacon and eggs, baked with cheese, or sliced cold and fried in bacon grease. Mississippi-born Craig Claiborne loves grits and has published elegant recipes for their preparation.

Some historians assert that neither hominy nor grits was universally eaten in the South prior to the Civil War, but most food scholars conclude that Indian corn in all its myriad forms—grits, hominy, roasting ears, succotash (usually a combination of corn kernels and lima beans), and various kinds of corn bread—sustained the pioneers and their succeeding generations from the beginning of European settlement on the Virginia coast.

Curiously, grits have seldom caught on in the North or spread to other countries, although expatriate southerners do often eat them and serve them to company. Stan Woodward's film *It's Grits* (Weston Woods, 1978) chronicled national and regional attitudes toward the dish. Grits enjoyed a surge of popularity during the early part of the Carter Administration but have since returned to their status as a distinctly regional food. One noted foreign visitor who took a liking to grits was the Marquis de Lafayette, hero of the American Revolution. So much did he enjoy eating the dish during his return visit to the United States in 1824 to 1825 that he took a substantial supply back to France for himself and his friends.

John Egerton
Nashville, Tennessee

Arkansas Gazette (14 August 1983); Gorham Kindem, *Southern Quarterly* (Spring–Summer 1981); Stephen A. Smith, in *American Material Culture*, ed. Edith Mayo (1985).

Hammond, James Henry

(1807–1864) Planter and politician.

Hammond was born in 1807 in upcountry South Carolina. Son of an impecunious schoolmaster who had moved South at the turn of the century, young Hammond graduated from South Carolina College in 1825. After several years of teaching while he prepared for the bar, he began the practice of law in Columbia. The excitement of the nullification controversy gave Hammond his initial prominence as a strongly sectionalist newspaper editor. After a fortunate marriage to a Charleston heiress, Hammond left public life to manage the Savannah River plantation and 147 slaves he had acquired as a result of the union. Elected to Congress, Hammond moved to Washington in 1835, but after a dramatic debut attacking the reception of abolition petitions by the House of Representatives, he was stricken with a nervous ailment and resigned his seat in Congress to travel in Europe.

In 1842 Hammond reentered politics as governor of his native state and gained attention during the next few years with an extreme sectionalist position more radical than that of John C. Calhoun. At the end of his term a scandal over charges of improprieties in his relationship with his four nieces, the daughters of the powerful Wade Hampton II, returned Hammond once again to his plantation, where he continued to write on agricultural and political topics and to experiment with agricultural innovations until he was chosen for the U.S. Senate in 1857. More sanguine about the possibilities for the South in the Union than at any previous time of his life, Hammond had profound doubts about its readiness for secession. Upon Lincoln's election, he resigned and privately differed sharply and vociferously with the Davis Administration on Confederate policy. His health declined throughout the war years, and he died in November of 1864, just before Sherman began his march through South Carolina.

One of the South's leading intellects, Hammond is perhaps best remembered for his widely distributed tracts defending slavery as a positive good, *Two Letters on Slavery in the United States, Addressed to Thomas Clarkson, Esq.* (1845) and *Letter of His Excellency Governor Hammond to the Free Church of Glasgow on the Subject of Slavery* (1844), as well as for his oft-quoted proslavery "mud-sill" speech to the U.S. Senate in 1858. His extraordinarily rich personal, political, and plantation papers have been extensively used by 20th-century historians of slavery and the South.

Drew Gilpin Faust
University of Pennsylvania

Carol K. Bleser, ed., *The Hammonds of Radcliffe* (1981); Drew Gilpin Faust, *James Henry Hammond and the Old South: A Design for Mastery* (1982); James Henry Hammond Papers, Library of Congress; James Henry Hammond Papers, South Caroliniana Library, University of South Carolina, Columbia.

Jack Daniel Distillery

Lynchburg, Tenn. (pop. 361), the seat of a dry (Moore) county in the Cumberland foothills, is the home of the nation's oldest registered distillery.

In the 1860s, Jack Newton Daniel chose Lynchburg's Cave Spring Hollow as the site for his whiskey-making business. Using cold spring water stabilized at a year-round 56 degrees and all but free of iron and other trace minerals, a "yeasting back" process (retaining some of the mash from previous runs to use as a starter), charcoal leaching, and oaken-cask warehousing, Daniel produced a distinctive Tennessee whiskey that by the turn of the century was winning international acclaim.

Inheriting the business from his uncle in 1907, Lem Motlow was forced to turn to the mule and harness trade (he opened Lynchburg Hardware in 1912) during Prohibition, but he resumed distillery operations soon after re-

The "Black Jack" bottle—a southern icon

peal. When Motlow died in 1947, the prosperous distillery passed on to his four sons.

Continuity, an unshakable commitment to traditional brewing standards and methods, marks the history of Jack Daniel Distillery. In 1946, when the war-effort ban on whiskey production was lifted on condition that processors use inferior grades of grain, Daniel's preferred to reopen a year later rather than compromise quality. Today, burning rick yards producing the hard sugar-maple charcoal through which the whiskey is slowly mellowed still dot the hollow; white oak barrels continue to be used for aging. Although twist caps have replaced cork stoppers, the "square shooter" bottle chosen by Jack Daniel in 1895 continues to be the company trademark.

Owned now by Brown-Forman, Inc., the Jack Daniel Distillery avoids a corporate image and stresses in its advertising the timeless character of its small-town operations. Ad copy has immortalized the Lynchburg General Store (where Coke still costs a dime), Miss Mary Bobo's Boarding House (where Mr. Jack took his noonday meals), and the Moore County Court House, built in 1884.

Although consumer profiles note that the average Jack Daniel drinker is an upwardly mobile, college-educated, urban male, it is clear that he still finds a place in his heart for a little southern town that has not changed much and for a whiskey that "hasn't changed at all."

See also INDUSTRY: / Liquor Industry

Elizabeth M. Makowski
University of Mississippi

Jeannie R. Bigger, *Tennessee Historical Quarterly* (Spring 1972); Ben A. Green, *Jack Daniel's Legacy* (1967).

Jackson, Stonewall

(1824–1863) Confederate general.

Born in far western Virginia, at Clarksburg, on 21 January 1824, Thomas Jonathan "Stonewall" Jackson was raised by an uncle after his parents died when he was a child. He graduated from the U.S. Military Academy in 1846, gained renown in the Mexican War, and in 1851 accepted a professional appointment at Virginia Military Institute. He commanded his institution's cadet corps, which was involved in the public hanging of John Brown on 2 December 1859. He served as a field officer in the Confederate army, first as colonel and then, on 17 July 1861, as brigadier general. As commander of a brigade at the first battle of Bull Run (21 July 1861), he and his troops earned everlasting fame when Confederate General Barnard E. Bee praised them for standing "like a stone wall" in battle.

Promoted to major general on 7 October 1861, Jackson assumed command in the Shenandoah Valley on 5 November and led the Shenandoah Valley Campaign from March to June 1862. One of the most praised and studied of all American military displays of tactics and strategy, the Valley Campaign showed Jackson's ability to use speed, mobility, secrecy, and sheer willpower to distract a larger force. With fewer than 20,000 soldiers, Lieutenant General and Corps Commander Jackson frustrated the movements of over 125,000 Union troops. Jackson was less successful in the Seven Days Campaign, but he regained his dominance of northern commanders at Harpers Ferry (15 September 1862), Antietam (17 September 1862), Fredericksburg (13 December 1862), and Chancellorsville (1–2 May 1863). During the night of the Chancellorsville victory, Jackson was wounded by one of his own troops, and he died of pneumonia on 10 May. He was only 39 years old, but Jackson, a lieutenant general when he died, had already become Robert E. Lee's most trusted subordinate.

Jackson was an eccentric personality. Untidy in appearance, rigidly moral and devoutly religious, shy and quiet, Jackson nonetheless was a charismatic figure to the Virginia soldiers he drove relentlessly. His success in the Shenandoah Valley made Jackson's name well known to southerners, most of whom apparently regarded him less as Lee's subordinate than as a coinstrument with Lee of God's destiny for the South.

Jackson was a military genius. English biographer George F. R. Henderson claimed in his 1898 study that Jackson's few written maxims "are almost a complete summary of the art of war." But Jackson's importance to southern culture transcended his military significance. He was a stern Calvinist, a spiritual descendant of Cromwell. Southern ministers during and after the war pointed to Jackson as a prophet-warrior on the Old Testament model. They admired his unbending righteousness. The moralistic, hardscrabble South identified with Jackson, the puritanical teetotaler. Henry A. White even included Jackson as an exemplar of his denomination's faith in *Southern Presbyterian Leaders* (1911). Allen Tate's search for the southern heritage in the 1920s led him to write a narrative biography of Jackson, published in 1928. More recently, Bob McDill's country-western song "Good Old Boys" refers to the songwriter's childhood, when a picture of Stonewall Jackson hung on the wall, quietly teaching southern lessons.

Jackson was, along with Lee and Jefferson Davis, one of the Confederate trinity of saints. A group of English admirers raised the money to erect a statue of him in Richmond in October of 1875, and another one was later dedicated on that city's Monument Boulevard. A bronze monument marks his grave in Lexington, Va., and a statue by Moses Ezekiel guards the parade grounds at the Virginia Military Institute. VMI's Preston Library displays items from Jackson's life. Elected to the Hall of Fame for Great Americans in 1955, Jackson now has a monument in New York City as well. His image has been carved into the Stone Mountain Memorial in Georgia. The third Monday in January is a Virginia holiday honoring Jackson and Lee.

Charles Reagan Wilson
University of Mississippi

Robert Lewis Dabney, *Life and Campaigns of Lieut.-General Thomas J. Jackson* (1866); Allen Tate, *Stonewall Jackson: The Good Soldier* (1928); Frank E. Vandiver, *Mighty Stonewall* (1957).

Jamestown

The founders of Jamestown, Va., had an unrealistic vision of the South's promise. They imagined a lush, naturally abundant, semitropical paradise replete with exotic fruits ripe for the picking, peopled by friendly natives who would shower them with precious jewels and metals. They hoped to find, as well, the illusory Passage to India, which continued to draw scores of Europeans to America's shores.

By the 19th century generations of Americans had devised their own myths about the first English settlement to survive in the New World. Some talked of a race of noble Englishmen who carried Christianity and civilization to America and, with the creation of the hallowed House of Burgesses in 1619, provided the country with democratic self-government. Others, not so generous, noted that the first slave ship also arrived on Virginia's shores in 1619, creating an institution that would tear the nation apart in less than two centuries. Finally, everyone loved the romantic tale of Pocahontas, the Indian princess who fell in love with Captain John Smith, saving him from certain death at the hands of Chief Powhatan and fostering an era of friendly relations between Native Americans and the European interlopers.

The actual story of Jamestown's settlement was neither romantic nor inspiring. Financed as a short-term joint stock company under the auspices of Sir Thomas Smith's Virginia Company, the odd mix of gentlemen, servants, and ne'er-do-wells who sailed into Chesapeake Bay in the spring of 1607 were looking for profit for the company and reward and adventure for themselves. They would work for the company seven years. Then, their obligations at an end, they would be free to make their own fortunes in a bountiful new land.

But no one got rich in Virginia. The company did not send adequate supplies to its New World servants, and the men living in America either would not or could not procure sufficient food for themselves. Consequently, they suffered a "starving time." Well over half the population died the first year, and by 1611 only 60 of the 500 adventurers who came to America were still alive.

Successive charters in 1609, 1612, and 1619, authorized by Sir Edwin Sandys, introduced two important innovations—the headright system and the House of Burgesses. The headright system gave the settlers a stake in the country by promising land to anyone who came to America on his own or who paid for someone else's transportation. The House of Burgesses had very limited powers. Its laws, mere recommendations, became valid only when approved by the company in London. Never particularly democratic, it quickly became a means by which the most ambitious and ruthless adventurers could exploit their less fortunate counterparts. Still, it was the first representative legislative assembly in English America.

In 1619 the first slave ship arrived in Jamestown. Slavery did not take root in Virginia, though, until the end of the century. The mortality rate for new settlers was so high that white servants, often provided gratis by the company, were more economical than chattel slaves.

With the introduction of tobacco into the colony, Virginia found itself a money-making crop. But though the "noxious weed" brought riches to a few, it caused the development of what Edmund Morgan has described as "boom town" mentality in Jamestown and its environs. Settlers refused to grow anything but tobacco. Sharp dealing and outright thievery abounded; the streets were filled with men who whored, drank, and gambled away their fortunes in a single night. While some Americans became rich in Jamestown, the company's English investors failed to realize any profits on their investments. Lack of communication, loss of control over its servants, and the self-interest of its settlers combined to destroy the Virginia Company. An Indian massacre in 1622 demolished any remaining hopes for success that the company's investors may have harbored. In 1624 the crown assumed control of the settlement, and Virginia became the first royal colony in America.

A short-term company designed for quick profit had evolved into a permanent society. It was not a society characterized by the close-knit communities that dominated New England. Rather it was highly individualistic, some would say almost anarchistic. It had few churches and fewer cities; its members lived on widely dispersed farms and consequently developed a distrust of outsiders that would to some extent translate to hostility toward royal interference in the next century. A disappointment to its founders, it nevertheless successfully survived penury, greed, and mismanagement to become England's oldest enduring New World possession.

Sheila Skemp
University of Mississippi

Philip L. Barbour, *Pocahontas and Her World: A Chronicle of America's First Settlement in Which is Related the Story of the Indians and the Englishmen, Particularly Captain John Smith, Captain Samuel Argall, and Major John Rolfe* (1969), *The Three Worlds of Captain John Smith* (1964); Carl Bridenbaugh, *Jamestown, 1544–1699* (1980); Edmund S. Morgan, *American Slavery, American Freedom: The Ordeal of Colonial Virginia* (1975); Alden T. Vaughan, *American Genesis: Captain John Smith and the Founding of Virginia* (1975).

Jefferson, Thomas

(1743–1826) Politician, writer, planter, scientist, architect.

Rembrandt Peale, Thomas Jefferson *(1805)*

Thomas Jefferson was born 17 April 1743 on the edge of the frontier in colonial Virginia. He went on to acquire as fine an education as America offered, graduating from the College of William and Mary in 1762. He studied law under George Wythe and practiced at the bar until the Revolution. He was elected to the Virginia House of Burgesses in 1769. Already the inheritor of large landholdings, he increased his property greatly through the dowry of his wife, Martha Wayles Skelton, whom he married in 1772. They had two daughters who survived to maturity.

In 1774 Jefferson drew political attention with his pamphlet *A Summary View of the Rights of British America*, the best remonstrance against the king and defense of colonial rights that had yet been seen. He carefully controlled his writing style so that any literate reader might follow his argument. Then, in 1776, Jefferson—now a member of the Continental Congress—was chosen to write the Declaration of Independence. It is his masterpiece and America's fundamental political document. In succeeding years he was elected governor of the state of Virginia and member of Congress and was appointed minister to France. From 1790 to 1793 he served under Washington as the first secretary of state.

Jefferson's only book, *Notes on the State of Virginia*, was published in 1785. In it he recorded the milieu of early America. Jefferson was an advocate of the scientific method, and his book included efforts to classify botanical, geological, and paleontological specimens. He showed the confident Enlightenment belief that science could promote progress. His collection and classification of items reflected the practical need of a farmer to know the environment, as well as simply the desire to satisfy his curiosity. He agonized over the question of slavery (he held many slaves), echoing most of the persistent stereotyping of blacks so noticeably American. Yet he was a true Enlightenment man, also voicing—as in the Declaration—the finest of ideals concerning justice, religious freedom, and equality.

He was paternalistic, not only at home but in his attitudes toward Indians, blacks, women, and commoners. Thus, his long political service was noblesse oblige. He was elected third president of the United States in 1801 (a second term followed). While president he arranged the Louisiana Purchase (1803), doubling the size of the nation.

Always busy, he designed his mansion, Monticello, the Virginia capitol at Richmond, and, late in life, the University of Virginia. He designed an Episcopal chapel in Charlottesville, dozens of Virginia country homes, simple and functional courthouses, and even jails in Cumberland and Nelson counties. He accumulated an architectural library of 50 titles in French, Italian, German, and English. His architectural achievement was to adapt classical forms to Virginian and southern needs.

Jefferson personified character, vision, grace, scholarship, and leadership—the qualities of the early southern gentleman that are part of his legacy. Students of southern culture look to him as the exemplar of major themes, ideals, and achievements of the region as well as the nation.

William K. Bottorff
University of Toledo

Julian P. Boyd et al., eds., *The Papers of Thomas Jefferson* (1950-); Fiske Kimball, ed., *Thomas Jefferson, Architect: Original Designs in the Coolidge Collection of the Massachusetts Historical Society, with an Essay and Notes* (1968); Dumas Malone, *Jefferson and His Time*, 6 vols. (1948–81).

Lee, Robert E.

(1797–1870) Confederate general.

Robert Edward Lee was born at Stratford, Va., the son of Revolutionary War hero "Light Horse Harry" Lee and Anne Hill Carter. He graduated from West Point in 1829, became an officer in the engineer corps, served with distinction in the Mexican War, was appointed superintendent of West Point in 1852, commanded the marines who captured John Brown in 1859, and became one of the South's preeminent military figures during the Civil War and its most famous hero afterwards.

Lee's hero status benefited from the adulation of three seemingly disparate groups: Virginians, other southerners, and other Americans. Each group lauded and idealized many of the same features when viewing Lee. The devoted son of an ailing mother, Lee was a young man of abstemious habits and a model student at West Point. He was the loving, devoted husband of ailing Mary Custis, the "child of Arlington." In his life before the Civil War and thereafter, Lee displayed elements of a gentlemanly, Christian character shared by few others. His life was the epitome of humility, self-sacrifice, and reserve. Even Robert E. Lee's involvement in the Civil War was viewed as different. Lee was the reluctant rebel who disliked slavery and secession, one whose love for the Union transcended that of other southern officers in 1860 and 1861.

After the Civil War, Lee the Confederate became Lee the American. He refused to prolong conflict by guerrilla warfare; Lee declined as well to flee the South or to keep alive the embers of sectional bitterness. Instead, the Virginian shunned lucrative business offers and accepted the modest post as president of Washington College. There he counseled moderation and acceptance of defeat. By his postwar example, Robert E. Lee thus helped to restore the Union. The consistent repetition of these images is evident first in southern writings and then in general American literature from 1865 until World War I.

The rapid development of the Lee mystique is one of the most remarkable developments in the genre of American

Robert E. Lee, April 1865

heroic symbolism. Evidence from contemporary accounts indicates that Lee's status as a hero did not evolve until after his death in 1870. In wartime he shared popularity with such Confederate notables as generals Thomas "Stonewall" Jackson, Joseph E. Johnston, and P. G. T. Beauregard. A number of writers criticized Lee's military leadership, particularly his direction of the Gettysburg campaign.

By the 1870s, after the general's death, the tone of Lee historiography changed markedly. A high degree of organization was evident in the commemoration of Lee's exploits, as groups such as the Lee Memorial Association, Lee Monument Association, and Ladies' Lee Monument Association labored to improve his image. They were aided by the Southern Historical Society, whose *Papers* became the most respected southern outlet of Civil War history in the late 19th century. The society and its *Papers* were dominated totally by Lee devotees such as former generals Jubal Early and Fitzhugh Lee and exrebel chaplain John William Jones. For them and scores of others, mainly Virginians, the depiction of the stainless Robert E. Lee became a crusade for the Lost Cause.

The literary dominance of Virginia authors continued in a second generation of writers whose main literary impact was felt in the period between the 1880s and World War I. Although the postwar generation had written mainly for a southern audience, the new authors wrote for the northern public. Virginia authors seemed to dominate the topic of the Civil War in both fiction and nonfiction. For several decades, beginning in the 1880s, the national reading public was fed a version of the war by Virginia writers such as Thomas Nelson Page, Francis Hopkinson Smith, Constance Cary Harrison, Robert Stiles, Philip A. Bruce, Robert E. Lee, Jr., Sara Pryor, and many others.

The new generation was attuned to new ideas in American thought, such as social Darwinism and the influence of environmental forces in shaping social values. The environmental argument was a keystone of late 19th-century southern authors. For them the South possessed a two-edged sword of triumph and tragedy. For apologists Lee was the supreme example of the alchemy of the noble and tragic. He was the man of superior virtues entrapped in a civilization beset by environmental faults such as human bondage.

The second generation of southern apologists stressed the postwar Lee—an emphasis that meshed well with the elements of both social Darwinism and New South imagery. Lee the war chieftain was now Lee the nationalist, who stressed reunion, shunned the old issues, and emphasized practical mechanical skills for Washington College students.

Lee, then, was the central focus of two generations of southern authors who used his heroic status for different reasons. The earlier generation coped with a theological dilemma. Defeat had gone against the Calvinistic ideal that success is a sign of God's grace. To replace this, the Lost Cause artists fashioned a complicated image whereby the southern cause became a knightly quest in which the righteous may lose but ultimately endure. Lee, the supreme image of this argument, became almost a Christ symbol, evidence that good men do not always prevail at first.

Henceforth the Lee image would change little, except to be altered in succeeding generations as the national mood demanded. In the 1930s an America faced with economic defeat in the Depression era identified with the imagery of Lee and the defeated South. Later, in the 1950s a nation approaching the Civil War Centennial and reflecting a new post–World War II nationalism would concentrate more upon the qualities of the post–Civil War Lee.

Thomas L. Connelly
University of South Carolina

Thomas L. Connelly, *The Marble Man: Robert E. Lee and His Image in American Society* (1977), *Civil War History* (March 1973), with Barbara L. Bellows, *God and General Longstreet: The Lost Cause and the Southern Mind* (1982); Marshall Fishwick, *Lee after the War* (1963); Douglas Southall Freeman, *R. E. Lee*, 4 vols. (1934–35); Dixon Wecter, *The Hero in America: A Chronicle of Hero-Worship* (1941).

L. Q. C. Lamar Society

Founded in 1969 outside Durham, N.C., the Lamar Society brought together middle- and upper-middle-class professionals to share information and ideas about the future of the South. The group named itself after L. Q. C. Lamar, an ardent Mississippi secessionist in the 1860s who became a champion of conciliation after the Civil War.

From the states of the old Confederacy plus Kentucky the Lamar Society accepted members who shared the vision of a South that preserves its regional distinctiveness while overcoming its perennial problems of racism and poverty. The members were particularly concerned with how the South and its way of life would fare in a rapidly growing technological and industrial society. They hoped to point the way for the South to avoid some of the problems that plagued the North after rapid urbanization, such as decay of the cities, destruction of the land, and a government removed from the people.

While the Lamar Society has been compared with the Nashville Agrarians of the 1930s because of the similar structure of the two groups and because each offered a vision of a future South, the agendas of the two are very different. H. Brandt Ayers, one of the Lamar Society's founders, wrote that although this comparison would inevitably be made, the Lamar Society would provide "a new definition of the South, by a new generation of southerners, just as deeply devoted to their region as the Agrarians but more democratic and realistic." The Agrarians felt that the traditional southern culture they applauded was threatened by a modernizing, urbanizing society and called for a return to the values of the agrarian, preindustrial South. The Lamar Society, on the other hand, sought to stress the advantage of a modernizing South in alleviating poverty and overcoming backwardness. Rather than attempting to retard urbanization, the members of the group called for new ideas to help the southern leaders create a "humane urban civilization." This concept involved retaining what the members saw as the best of traditional small-town southern life and incorporating these characteristics (such as responsive, direct-participation government) into new cities.

In 1972 the Lamar Society published a volume of essays called *You Can't Eat Magnolias*, which presented their vision of the South in much the same way as did the Agrarians' *I'll Take My Stand* (1930). During the 1970s the society issued the *Southern Journal*, which served as a forum for the ideas of its members. Inspired by the activities of the Lamar Society, the Southern Growth Policies Board was formed in late 1971 to coordinate regional growth strategies. Now located in Washington, D.C., the Lamar Society has focused on the desegregation of school systems. The society's leadership in defining the southern challenge of adapting regional myths in an urban setting has been successful in its aim of provoking discussion throughout the region.

Karen M. McDearman
University of Mississippi

H. Brandt Ayers and Thomas H. Naylor, eds., *You Can't Eat Magnolias* (1972); Stephen A. Smith, *Myth, Media, and the Southern Mind* (1985).

Madison, James

(1751–1836) Politician and political philosopher.

Madison defended the interests of Virginia and the South within the framework of the federal government that he helped create. Educated by private tutors at plantation schools in Orange County, Va., and at the College of New Jersey (now Princeton University), he became an effective spokesman for his state and region. In the Continental Congress, 1780–83 and 1787–88, he worked to ensure Virginia's cession of western lands to the Confederation government on conditions favorable to his state. He urged that the United States secure navigation rights to the Mississippi River—then controlled by Spain—which he recognized as crucial for the South's economic development.

At the 1787 Constitutional Convention Madison urged that the federal government be strengthened with delegated powers while the states retained reserved powers. As a congressman he worked to establish the new government while opposing efforts by the Federalist administration for further consolidation of national powers. His 1798 Virginia Resolutions defended civil liberties and asserted the right of states to interpose their authority to declare unconstitutional the Federalist-sponsored Alien and Sedition Acts. Those resolutions became the foundation of states' rights doctrine for early 19th-century Republicans.

James Madison, fourth president of the United States

Sectional divisions and his own Republican scruples over legislative supremacy impeded Madison as fourth president of the United States, 1809 to 1817. Longstanding disputes with Great Britain finally erupted in the War of 1812, which was supported in the South but unpopular in the North. In retirement, Madison was embarrassed when—during the 1828–33 South Carolina nullification controversy—states' righters invoked his Virginia Resolutions. He objected that his proposals for interposition meant only cooperation among the states to repeal federal laws or amend the Constitution. He advised President Andrew Jackson and cabinet officers on responding to the nullifiers.

Madison deplored slavery but remained economically dependent on the slave labor of his plantation. He was a founder and president of the American Colonization Society, which worked to return free blacks to Africa. His interests ranged beyond political theory and practice to architecture, the visual arts, and education. Madison supervised additions to Montpelier, his Orange County house, which he filled with his collection of books and paintings. He worked with his lifelong friend and political confidant, Thomas Jefferson, to establish the University of Virginia, which he served as visitor and second rector. Throughout an extraordinarily long career, Madison advanced the political and cultural life of his state, region, and nation.

Thomas A. Mason
University of Virginia

Irving Brant, *James Madison*, 6 vols. (1941–61); William T. Hutchinson et al., eds., *The Papers of James Madison*, 16 vols. (1962–); Ralph Ketcham, *James Madison: A Biography* (1971).

Mint Julep

The mint julep, along with white columns, moonlight, jasmine, and magnolias, is of the very fabric of the southern myth. The only volume devoted solely to its history asserts: "Wherever there is a mint julep, there is a bit of the Old South. For the julep is part ceremony, tradition, and regional nostalgia; and only by definition liquor, simple syrup, mint, and ice. It is all delight. It is nectar to the Virginian, mother's milk to the Kentuckian, and ambrosia to southerners anywhere."

The origin of the South's most famous drink—excepting only Coca-Cola—has as many claimants as Homer's birthplace: Virginia, Maryland, New England, Georgia, Kentucky, and Louisiana. It may be all of these locales, for wherever whiskey was drunk in the Federal period (and it was drunk enthusiastically almost everywhere), it was natural that it should be drunk with the local plant that imparted a most delectable flavor to the rough distillation of those days.

Actually, credit for the julep belongs to Virginia. Its first recorded use was there. In 1797 the *American Museum* described the Virginian who upon rising "drinks a julep made of rum, water, and sugar, but very strong." The mint was added a few years later. Describing life on a James River plantation in his *Travels in the United States* (1803), John Davis noted the early morning mint julep.

Mint was as widespread as alcohol in America, and the drink spread to Maryland (made, as in Virginia, with rye whiskey), to New England (made with rum), to Kentucky (made with the corn whiskey that was ancestor to bourbon), to New York (made with anything, even gin), and to Louisiana (made with brandy). Recipes for the drink were wildly varied, sometimes full of fruit to the point of resembling a salad, often with rum ladled on top of other liquors, sometimes with bourbon lending additional flavor to apricot or peach brandy.

As tastes changed in post-Prohibition America the drink became simpler but no less ceremonial. It has been praised by historians—C. J. Latrobe, Frederick Marryatt, and W. H. Russell—and used for atmosphere by O. Henry, Margaret Mitchell, and a thousand other writers of fiction. It has truly passed into the realm of cliché, but this concoction of bourbon whiskey, sugar, mint, and ice retains both its charm and its good taste.

Richard B. Harwell
Athens, Georgia

Richard B. Harwell, *The Mint Julep* (1975); Soule Smith, *The Mint Julep: The Very Dream of Drinks* (1949); Jerry Thomas, *How To Mix Drinks* (1862).

Moon Pies

The Moon Pie, long marketed as "the original marshmallow sandwich," had humble beginnings at the Chattanooga Bakery in Chattanooga, Tenn. Although its precise origin is not known, the Moon Pie is believed to have been created in 1918 or 1919. Legend has it that a traveling salesman stopped by the bakery and suggested that a snack consisting of two cookies with marshmallow in between and covered with chocolate would sell. At that time, reports one version, the bakery produced over 200 different items; so successful was this one suggestion that it now is the only snack produced by the company.

Since their invention Moon Pies have had broad appeal throughout the South and have been a favorite snack food for both children and adults. Consisting of one quarter inch of marshmallow sandwiched between two cookies about four inches in diameter, Moon Pies have been coated with chocolate, banana, coconut, or vanilla frosting. Many companies have attempted to imitate the Moon Pie and capitalize on the snack's popularity, but any discerning southern palate can distinguish the real taste.

In 1969 the bakery introduced a "Double Decker" pie, featuring two layers of marshmallow sandwiched between three cookies and then covered with flavored frosting. This version can be found primarily in convenience stores. With increased interest and new distribution techniques, the Moon Pie has moved beyond its traditional southern territory and is now available in nearly all parts of the country. The Moon Pie Cultural Club is a Charlotte, N.C., group dedicated to spreading "the story of the Moon Pie" and establishing "club chapters throughout the civilized world."

Tom Rankin
Southern Arts Federation
Atlanta, Georgia

Ron Dickson, *Moon Pie Handbook* (1985); William E. Schmidt, *New York Times* (30 April 1986).

Moonshine and Moonshining

Blockade whiskey, corn liquor, corn "squeezins," panther's breath, rotgut, ruckus juice, tiger's sweat, and white lightning are all names for moonshine. Comic-strip character Snuffy Smith, a Kentucky moonshiner, is one of its most ardent defenders, sometimes outwitting the "revenooers," but not always. The same is true for many actual moonshiners in the rural South, where the illegal making of corn whiskey has been carried on since the 18th century.

Moonshine looks clear, tastes raw, and sells fast. It usually runs close to 100 proof or more. To make it, sugar, water, yeast, cornmeal, and malt (cornmeal made from sprouted kernels) are variously combined and processed in three stages: fermentation, distillation, and condensation. Bootleggers today, frequently unconcerned about quality, have been known to add such substances as lye and embalming fluid to the product to give it a sharper flavor.

The moonshining factory is the still. There are several types, but the most prevalent is the simple pot still. It consists of an airtight kettle with a "worm," or copper coil, running from its cap through a barrel filled with cool water. Hiding the stills is essential, and methods of concealment range from bending saplings over them to setting them up in dug-out underground rooms. Nighttime is the safest time for working a still, with the moon providing enough light by which to see—hence, the name moonshine.

Many Scotch-Irish immigrants settled in the southern Appalachian mountains, bringing with them the practice of making whiskey. The beginnings of moonshining can be traced back to 1791 when the government, trying to pay Revolutionary War debts, imposed an excise tax on whiskey. Unwilling to pay the tax, distillers operated secretly. Illicit distilling persisted and flourished in the

Revenue agents with captured still, Kentucky, date unknown

South largely for economic reasons: corn liquor brought higher prices than did the unprocessed vegetable; it was readily marketable; it assured a steady income in the poorly developed, economically unstable region; and, because of the bad road conditions, it could more easily and efficiently be transported to the distant marketplaces than could bulky bushels of corn.

Moonshining is a tax violation, so tax agents and other law enforcement officers seek offenders. Garland Bunting, an Alcoholic Beverage Control officer in Halifax County, N.C., has seized and destroyed hundreds of stills and is the subject of Alec Wilkinson's *Moonshine: A Life in Pursuit of White Liquor* (1985). Selling fish and preaching sermons are two of the many, diverse tactics he has used to accomplish his purpose. There are moonshiners enough in his territory to keep him busy, and they still operate in large numbers elsewhere in the South—carefully selling their goods.

Corn is a major southern cash crop. The production of "corn juice" has proved economically advantageous to many a southerner. Land has represented the basis of a way of life for many mountain people. Moonshine has also been a popular beverage. During the Depression, consumers bought it when they could buy no other alcoholic beverage. Through the years, moonshine has become significant in the popular culture of the region, frequently appearing in literature and in country songs like George Jones's "White Lightnin'." *Raw Mash* (Blaine Dunlap and Sol Korine, directors; Center for Southern Folklore, 1978) and *Tradition* (Bill Hatton and Anthony Slone, directors; Appalshop, 1973) chronicle aspects of mountain moonshining.

See also INDUSTRY: / Liquor Industry

Jessica Foy
Cooperstown Graduate Programs
Cooperstown, New York

John C. Campbell, *The Southern Highlander and His Homeland* (1921); Esther Kellner, *Moonshine: Its History and Folklore* (1971); Horace Kephart, *Our Southern Highlanders* (1913); Robert A. Pace and Jeffrey W. Gardner, *Tennessee Anthropologist* (Spring 1985); Eliot Wigginton, ed., *The Foxfire Book* (1972).

Olmsted, Frederick Law

(1822–1903) Travel writer and architect.

Olmsted, born in Hartford, Conn., was nurtured by a tolerant father who encouraged him to explore his various talents, a background that prepared him to be a cultural observer. Like many of his New England generation, Olmsted sought to assist his fellowman, and his opportunity to write about the South proved to be beneficial for his subsequent work. Olmsted left farming to make a tour of England, a trip that became the basis for his book *Walks and Talks of an American Farmer in England* (1852) and the paradigm for much of his travel and cultural observation. Because of that book's success Olmsted was asked to tour the South and do a series of articles for the New York *Daily Times*, a project that began modestly but led to many articles, three books, and the 1861 compilation, *Journeys and Explorations in the Cotton Kingdom*, an abridgment of his books about the South.

The process of the development of Olmsted's writings from newspaper accounts to books and rearrangement into *The Cotton Kingdom* is a complicated textual story. It reveals much about the era when Olmsted sought to become a member of what he described as "the republic of letters." In 1855 he purchased an interest in the company that published his first southern book, *Journey in the Seaboard Slave States* (1856); yet its financial collapse and the sudden death of his brother, John (who had written a considerable portion of Frederick's *A Journey through Texas* [1857] from Olmsted's notes), complicated his life sufficiently to make desirable a shift in 1857 toward landscape architecture.

The urgency of abolition and his free-state interests were reflected in Olmsted's writing. An apparent sympathy for slaveholding dwindled as his articles were rewritten for books, then abridged. He gradually became convinced that a slave economy could not be profitable. Even though predisposed to find the South backward, one of his valuable accomplishments was to reveal that southern states were remarkably more complex than might have been assumed in the North. A desire for objectivity allowed him to provide a documentation of antebellum conditions that present-day historians corroborate.

Olmsted sought to be factual. His two long trips (from 1852 to the spring of 1854) yielded a cumulative record of farms and villages, a way of life that did not support stereotyped views. He showed the real South as culturally diverse; in the German settlements of Texas, for example, he reported the good results of democracy, freedom, and efficiency. *A Journey in the Back Country* (1860) documented many types of living conditions. The artistic design of Olmsted's writing should also be noted.

His southern writings have proven beneficial for over a century. As source material for various studies, as demonstrated in *Olmsted South* (1979), his writings remain valuable. As a landscape architect Olmsted returned South in the 1890s and imprinted his vision at places as diverse as Biltmore, the Vanderbilt estate, near Asheville, N.C., and the Druid Hills area of Atlanta, which together are his most important living southern legacies.

Victor A. Kramer
Georgia State University

Albert Fein, *Frederick Law Olmsted and the American Environmental Tradition* (1972); Victor A. Kramer and Dana F. White, eds., *Olmsted South: Old South Critic, New South Planner* (1979); Elizabeth Stevenson, *Park Maker: A Life of Frederick Law Olmsted* (1977).

Patriotic Societies

Southern reporter Pat Watters once wrote about "all the complex stratifications (clubs and circles and hierarchies of elitism) of high society that the South continued to take more seriously than the rest of the country." He had in mind that web of clubs of all kinds—town, country, yacht, debutante, literary, garden, bridge, luncheon and service, junior leagues and auxiliaries, ball societies, fraternities and sororities, and, not least, hereditary patriotic societies, all of them with their own pecking orders. Patriotic societies, based upon descent from an ancestor's services to colony or nation, received their greatest impetus in the Northeast during the wave of late 19th-century immigration. Nonetheless, they also had southern roots and particularly southern flavors.

The first society in the 13 colonies, named for Scotland's patron saint, was the St. Andrew's Society of Charleston, S.C., founded in 1729 and followed there in 1733 by the St. George's Society. The Society of the Cincinnati, composed of Continental army officers and their eldest male descendants, was founded 10 May 1783, with Virginian George Washington as its first president general. The Society of the War of 1812 was founded in 1814 by the defenders of Fort McHenry after the British withdrawal, and its first commander was Maryland's Revolutionary War hero, Major General Samuel Smith of Baltimore, who had led the defense. In Mexico City on 13 October 1847 U.S. military officers organized the Aztec Club on primogenitive lines, and its first president was John A. Quitman of Mississippi, who had led the successful attack upon "the Halls of Montezuma." However, the greatest impetus to the organization of patriotic societies in the South came after the Civil War and during Reconstruction, with southern women in the lead.

One year to the day after General Joseph E. Johnston surrendered the last large Confederate field army, southern women began organizing to care for Confederate soldiers' graves, and April 26, "the South's All Souls' Day," became the most popular Confederate Memorial Day. Ladies' Memorial Associations appeared across Dixie, with Columbus, Ga., and Columbus and Jackson, Miss., each claiming the "first." Later, as the South revived in its fortunes and as urbanization increased, came formation of the United Confederate Veterans in New Orleans in June 1889, the United Daughters of the Confederacy in Nashville in September 1894, the Sons of Confederate Veterans in Richmond on 1 July 1896, and the Children of the Confederacy under UDC auspices in Alexandria, Va., also in 1896. Much later came the Military Order of the Stars and Bars for the male descendants of Confederate officers, in July 1938 in Columbia, S.C. Robert E. Lee's and Jefferson Davis's birthdays, January 19 and June 3, also became southern holidays.

Meanwhile, spurred by the centennial celebration of the American Revolution and in reaction to emigration from outside northern Europe, hereditary societies arose to memorialize the Revolutionary War: the Sons of the Revolution in 1883, the rival Sons of the American Revolution in 1889 (both organized in New York City), and the Daughters of the American Revolution in 1890 in Washington, D.C. Two of the founders of these three groups were southern women. Others reached farther back in time to found the rival Societies of Colonial Dames in 1890 and 1891 and their male counterpart, the Society of Colonial Wars, in 1893. As a rule of thumb, except for the sui generis Cincinnati, the more remote the ancestor, the greater is the society's exclusiveness and prestige and the higher its members' social status. As one Alabama matron put it, "Heaven on earth in the Black Belt is to be a Kappa Delta, a Colonial Dame and an Episcopalian." By the time of the Spanish-American War, these colonial and revolutionary hereditary organizations were established in the Deep South.

Also concerned with remembrance of the past, but not organized on hereditary lines, were the societies founded to save historic houses. First came the Mount Vernon Ladies' Association, which Charlestonian Ann Pamela Cunningham organized in 1853 to rescue George Washington's home. Others of note were the Ladies' Hermitage Association, founded in Nashville in 1889 to preserve Andrew Jackson's mansion, the Confederate Memorial Literary Society in Richmond in 1890 to maintain the second White House of the Confederacy there, and the White House Association of Alabama in Montgomery in 1900 to enshrine the First White House of the Confederacy.

More recent arrivals on the southern scene are such state- or family-oriented organizations as the Daughters (1891) and Sons (1893) of the Republic of Texas, Maryland's Society of the Ark and Dove (1910), Louisiana Colonials (1917), Jamestown Society (1936), National Huguenot Society (1951), Southern Dames of America (1962), Order of First Families of Mississippi (1967), Society of the Lees of Virginia (1921), Washington Family Descendants (1954), and the Davis Family Association (1973). Standing at the head of these is that apotheosis of the FFV, the Order of First Families of Virginia (1912).

Each of these organizations has its place in the social scheme of things for certain southerners. The gentlemen's hereditary societies seem to be important status indicators in the more mobile societies of the New South, in newer industrial cities such as Birmingham, rather than in Old South cities such as Montgomery, where primacy goes to the local Society of Pioneers of Montgomery (1955), the membership of which is limited to 100 gentlemen with ancestors living there before 1855. Historian Francis Butler Simkins once admitted that, "in the aristocratic aspiration of Southerners are elements of snobbery" but he added that "ancestor hunting is an important activity" because a "consciousness of illustrious forebears gives satisfactions not unlike those of religion to old people without material assets."

John Hawkins Napier III
Montgomery, Alabama

Cleveland Amory, *Who Killed Society?* (1960); Jerome Francis Beattie, ed., *The Hereditary Register of the United States of America* (1978); Bethany Bultman, *Town and Country* (November 1977); Sophy Burnham, *The Landed Gentry* (1978); Wallace Evan Davies, *Patriotism on Parade: The Story of Veterans' and Hereditary Organizations in America, 1783–1900* (1955); Lucy Kavaler, *The Private World of High Society* (1960); Marie Bankhead Owen, *The Blue Book, Montgomery, Alabama, 1909–1910* (1909).

Pickup Truck

The pickup truck in the South has a variety of uses, most of which do not involve hauling cargo. In fact, the pickup is next to worthless for anything but light hauling on paved roads. Being front-end heavy, it bogs down on wet grass, spins out in its own shadow, and can even flip on a straight, dry stretch of roadway. The cab offers little storage space, and anything carried in the bed is open to theft.

Beginning in the second decade of this century the pickup (essentially a car with the back seat and trunk removed and replaced with a wooden or metal platform) proliferated on farms. In the last 30 years, despite its limited hauling potential, the pickup's popularity has grown. About half the new vehicles sold in the South are pickups. Often constituting a second family vehicle, the pickup has become a status symbol for many. In a historical and literary context, a "good old boy" without a pickup is like a cowboy without a horse. "Work" (or "rat" or "bad") trucks, battered and rimmed with rust from long-standing farm or construction work, carry lock boxes full of tools and materials of the owners' trades.

In a more modern vein, the rising number of fancy pickups, the "showboats," in suburban driveways represents a curious phenomenon in America's love affair with motorized vehicles. New models, unburdened with dents and scratches, offer the means of escape for the suburban family. Various attachments (from simple bed covers to fancy camper tops) allow the entire family to go "camping" on the weekends. Whether for work or for pleasure, the pickup truck represents ties to the bygone rural aspects of American life. And, because of its rural ties, the pickup is associated with the South.

More particularly, the pickup is associated with the male southerner. Usually the second vehicle in a family, the pickup most often is the man's to drive and to care for. Men drive them to work, whether that work occurs in a factory, medical center, or courtroom. For the younger man not tied to a family, the pickup becomes his chariot, in which he cruises around looking for women. Apparently, the higher riding the pickup (jacked up with large frame-extending shock absorbers and bouyant on oversized mud tires), the more likely the southern boy will land a date with a cheerleader. Of course, the ever-present gun rack (with rifle or shotgun prominently displayed, or, in more urban settings, simply an umbrella) reflects ties to the rural mystique of southern culture.

Underscoring both its lack of utility and its importance as a status symbol, the pickup has changed drastically in the last 30 years. In 1950 Ford introduced a handsome pickup with styling of its own, the F-100. Ford still uses the F-series designation on trucks, but the company turned pickup sales around with the slogan "Where men are men, trucks are Ford V8s." Ford dominated pickup sales for several decades until Chevrolet countered with its "built tough" trucks with cowboy names. The Scottsdale, Silverado, Bonanza, and GMC confirmed their position, as did the Sierra Classic. Styling and male imagery are key appeals; Power Wagon brought Dodge trucks out of the doldrums, and Ram Chargers and The Little Red Express keep them out.

Trucks imported from Europe never caught on in America. The Volkswagon suffers from having the truck bed preloaded with its own engine and transmission. The British Morris Minor was good, but faded over 25 years ago. There was country-boy resistance to the first small trucks from Japan. Chevrolet called one Luv, and Ford's was the Courier, avoiding Oriental-sounding names. But as American pickups grew larger and more expensive, Toyota, Datsun-Nissan, Mazda, and Isuzu earned respect with their pickups, as they had with their cars. To counter this market invasion Ford introduced the smaller Ranger, Dodge a smaller Ram, and Chevrolet the S-10, all of which are slightly larger than Japanese trucks and increasingly popular.

From the basic platform wagon on four wheels the pickup now embraces a multitude of styles and options. Deluxe models (with more chrome trim than found on 1950s automobiles) include passenger seats in the rear of an extended cab, long wheel bases, dual rear wheels, four-wheel drive, magnesium wheels, long-range fuel tanks, and lights similar to those found on the 18 wheelers, not to mention quadraphonic stereos and elegant CBs. Such extraneous options, again, reflect southern values, especially that of individuality. An owner reveals his character with his choice of options.

If the pickup reflects southern culture, its very popularity may tend to whittle away at the "southernness" of its heritage. As with the trucking culture in general, the pickup truck is becoming subsumed in a more general American culture, becoming a common sight in urban areas far removed from the South.

Gordon Baxter
Car and Driver

Floyd Clymer, *Henry's Wonderful Model T* (1955).

Pilgrimage

In the spring of 1931 the Mississippi State Federation of Garden Clubs held its annual meeting in Natchez, Miss. For a combination of reasons, including a blighting freeze in late spring and the depressing state of the economy, the ordinarily ornate gardens of Natchez were not in peak condition. As an alternative to garden tours, the Garden Club of Natchez prevailed upon the owners of the city's antebellum mansions to open their homes for two daily tours during the two-day convention. The response to the mansion tours was so enthusiastic that Mrs. J. Balfour Miller organized another tour of Natchez antebellum homes the next year. She publicized the week-long pilgrimage throughout the South and in other parts of the country where she had friends or connections with the media.

The response to the first Natchez Pilgrimage in 1932 exceeded all Miller's expectations, and, following her slide presentation explaining the pilgrimage to the National Convention of Garden Clubs in 1933, the movement spread quickly throughout the South. In many southern towns these annual pilgrimages now provide a significant boost to the community's economy. Most southern pilgrimages are accompanied by Confederate pageants or balls commemorating life in the Old South, and southern belles who show the visitors through the mansions are dressed in Old South styles, which include long, swaying hoop skirts, layers of petticoats, and bonnets. In recent years some southern communities have deemphasized the Confederate connection and have restyled such a tour, calling it a "Parade of Homes." The new designation allows other homes in the community that are not antebellum to be included on the tours.

See also URBANIZATION: / Natchez

David Sansing
University of Mississippi

James T. Black, *Southern Living* (March 1983); Les Thomas, *Southern Living* (March 1978).

Randolph, John

(1773–1833) Politician.

John Randolph of Roanoke represented the interests of traditional slaveholding Virginians in Congress and expressed the aristocratic style of the Virginia past in

Elms, Natchez, Miss., one of the South's most visited homes

American public life from the early Republic through the Jacksonian period. Randolph entered public life as part of the Jeffersonian opposition to the Adams Administration and was a prominent member of the congressional leadership in Jefferson's first administration. He broke with Jefferson and, along with purist Republicans, formed an extreme group called the "tertium quids" within the party.

Beginning with an uncompromising assertion of states' rights, in time they became suspicious of democracy as well as American nationalism, detecting in the growth of the federal government an ultimate threat to slavery and the plantation way of life. Randolph's career was largely one of opposition, although he sometimes found allies on particular issues. He was probably the first important American statesman to stake out the positions that came to characterize the secessionist southern view of the Union. Although he dismissed Calhoun's metaphysics, he influenced the South Carolinian's development as a sectional leader.

Randolph's notorious, exciting, and eccentric public persona, his witticisms and verbal challenges, and his stinging contempt for the barbarities of American democratic public life contributed to the mythology of southern bluebloods and hot bloods. Randolph seized the American imagination, North and South, in a pattern that would come to characterize the southern hold on the American imagination.

In his antidemocratic and anticommercial conservatism, his states' rights consistency and republican purity, and his prophetic sense of where southern slaveholding interests must lie, Randolph earned his place in the pantheon of southern activists. In his extravagant and dramatic eccentricity, his keen eye for the appetites of the democratic electorate, and his attempt to embody the Virginia heritage, Randolph earned a lasting place as a mythic southerner.

Robert Dawidoff
Claremont Graduate School
Claremont, California

William Cabell Bruce, *Randolph of Roanoke: A Biography Based Largely on New Material*, 2 vols. (1922); Robert Dawidoff, *The Education of John Randolph* (1979); William R. Taylor, *Cavalier and Yankee: The Old South and American National Character* (1961).

Soul Food

Popularized in the 1960s, the term *soul food* refers to a distinctive, traditional southern style of cooking. Use of the term implies that this cuisine is limited in popularity to blacks, but it is in fact the native fare of both black and white southerners of all economic and social strata.

The distinctive ingredients of southern cuisine, as well as the distinctive styles of cooking them, have been common for centuries in Africa but not in Europe. Sweet potatoes, okra, chicken and fish rolled in meal or batter and deep fried, greens and cowpeas boiled with pork and served with pot liquor, and corn bread in many varieties form the basis of a regional cuisine whose roots may be more African than European. Maize and sweet potatoes were taken from America to Africa by Portuguese traders in the 16th century, and peas of the black-eyed type have been eaten in Africa for some 400 years. Even specialized local cuisines with identifiable European roots, such as French cooking in Louisiana, have been heavily influenced by Afro-American taste in such things as the heavy use of red pepper and the creation of dishes like gumbo based on ingredients, such as okra, that came from Africa. In fact, the black presence may explain why foods like maize and cowpeas, which will grow anywhere in America and were eaten in other parts of the country while the frontiers lasted, remain staple foods only in the South, aside from those areas of the Southwest where they were staple foods of Native Americans. Some scholars see Native American influences on soul food as well.

Margaret Jones Bolsterli
University of Arkansas

Eugene D. Genovese, *Roll, Jordan, Roll: The World the Slaves Made* (1976); Bob Jeffries, *Soul Food Cookbook* (1970); Bruce F. Johnston, *The Staple Food Economies of Western Tropical Africa* (1958); Helen Mendes, *The African Heritage Cookbook* (1971).

Southern Historical Association

In November 1934, 18 historians from throughout the South met in Atlanta to form the Southern Historical Association, a group focusing on "the promotion of interest and research in southern history, the collection and preservation of the South's historical records, and the encouragement of state and local historical societies in that section to vigorous activity." To address this objective, the founders launched the *Journal of Southern History*, a quarterly publication. Historians from the South, such as Charles Knapp of the University of Kentucky, Philip Hamer of the University of Tennessee, Thomas Abernethy of the University of Virginia, and Benjamin Kendrick of the Women's College of the University of North Carolina, led the group's early efforts but encouraged participation by historians throughout the country.

Changes over the years in leadership and focus in the association reflect in large part the fluctuations in parochialism and sectionalist fervor among historians throughout the South. E. Merton Coulter, the association's first president, avoided controversial sectional sentiment, but Frank L. Owsley in a 1940 presidential address indicted the North for an egocentric sectionalism, which he viewed as a principal cause of the Civil War.

A South-versus-North focus, rooted partly, too, in disagreements with President Franklin Roosevelt's policies, flourished for several years in the association. Historian Robert Durden notes that "[Albert B.] Moore's diatribe of 1942 signalled the high-water mark of polemical bitterness in the presidential addresses . . . and such sectionalist sentiments virtually disappeared from the succeeding addresses."

Among the other outstanding historians who have headed the group are Fletcher M. Green, who in 1945 delivered an influential address on political democracy in the Old South; Ella Lonn, the first female president, who in 1946 examined 20th-century reconciliation between the North and South; C. Vann Woodward, who in 1952 delivered a widely respected address entitled "The Irony of Southern History"; Francis Butler Simkins, who "in 1954 sounded what may have been the last bugle call . . . for the old-time sectional verities and attitudes" with his address entitled "Tolerating the South's Past"; James W. Silver, who in his 1963 address on "Mississippi: The Closed Society" scrutinized the South's white-supremacist policies; Robert Durden, who examined "A Half Century of Change in Southern History" during the association's 50th annual meeting in November 1984; and Carl N. Degler, who in 1986 dialectically assessed the evolving relationship of the South, the North, and the nation. The various leaders have not only mirrored prevailing sentiments of their times regarding sectionalism but also shaped new frameworks for gaining perspective on southern history.

Articles in the *Journal of Southern History* pinpoint the South, but the association's annual meeting includes sessions on American, European, and Latin American history as well as special-interest sessions. The organization gives various awards for outstanding books and articles on southern history, and it maintains an editorial office at Rice University and administrative offices at the University of Georgia.

Sharon A. Sharp
University of Mississippi

Robert F. Durden, *Journal of Southern History* (February 1985); Arthur S. Link and Rembert W. Patrick, eds., *Writing Southern History: Essays in Historiography in Honor of Fletcher M. Green* (1965); George B. Tindall, ed., *The Pursuit of Southern History: Presidential Addresses of the Southern Historical Association, 1935–1963* (1964).

Southern Historical Society

In May 1869 a group of Confederate veterans met in New Orleans to establish an organization to collect, preserve, and publish records of the Confederacy. General Braxton Bragg chaired the newly formed group, which planned to establish an affiliate in every southern state. The new group floundered in its first few years, but supporters convened in August 1873 at White Sulphur Springs in West Virginia to reorganize the Southern Historical Society. Headquarters for the group were moved from New Orleans to Richmond, Va., where an archive of Civil War documents was established at the state capitol.

General Jubal A. Early, first president of the reorganized society, served with a group of vice-presidents, one from each southern state. Historian E. Merton Coulter noted that the group might well have been called the Confederate Historical Society, because the leaders were "erstwhile warriors turned historians and conservers of history," determined to garner evidence for the tribunal of history. Racing to collect Confederate materials before the federal government completed its congressionally mandated gathering and publication of official records of the Civil War, the Southern Historical Society members rekindled the flames of Confederate patriotism by exhorting good southerners to contribute to their cause—the assembly of the archives of the covenant. Materials collected included wartime correspondence, memoirs, unit rosters, books, newspaper articles, manuscripts, military reports, maps, charts, speeches, ballads, and poetry. Initially the society published materials regularly in the *Southern Magazine* of Baltimore. In 1875 the Reverend J. William Jones, who had been the society's temporary secretary, became the permanent secretary-treasurer and served until 1887. Jones, described by historian Charles Reagan Wilson as "the most influential and well-known clergyman in the cult of the Lost Cause," shaped what became the preeminent publication institutionalizing the preservation of Confederate history, the *Southern Historical Society Papers*. Launched in 1876 as a monthly publication, the papers were published quarterly from 1880 until 1888, when they became annual volumes, then occasional publications until 1959. Jones edited 14 of the total 52 volumes of the *Southern Historical Society Papers*, and in so doing shaped and disseminated one of the most valuable and complete bodies of information available on Confederate military history—and its interpretation from a Confederate viewpoint. Some of the state organizations, such as North Carolina's and Kentucky's, separately published materials, too.

After 1900 membership in the society waned, and only a few members in the Richmond area remained by the 1950s. Among the last members was noted journalist and historian Douglas Southall Freeman, whose death in 1953 marked the demise of the society. In its heyday, however, the Southern Historical Society had organized the documentation and galvanized the core of ideas upon which the vision of the South as a defeated "redeemer nation" flourished for decades.

Sharon A. Sharp
University of Mississippi

E. Merton Coulter, *Journal of Southern History* (February 1936); Gaines Foster, *Ghosts of the Confederacy: Defeat, the Lost Cause, and the Emergence of the New South, 1865–1913* (1987); Arthur S. Link and Rembert W. Patrick, eds., *Writing Southern History: Essays in Historiography in Honor of Fletcher M. Green* (1965).

Stone Mountain

Stone Mountain is a natural landmark, a historic site, and a recreational area located 16 miles east of Atlanta, Ga. The world's largest mass of exposed granite, the 825-foot dome rises 1,683 feet above sea level on a path once used by Creek Indians. The mountain is 285 to 294 million years old. Carved on its side is the world's largest piece of sculpture, a memorial to the Confederacy composed of the mounted figures of Robert E. Lee, Jefferson Davis, and Thomas J. "Stonewall" Jackson. The United Daughters of the Confederacy (UDC) leased the land in 1915 and commissioned Gutzon Borglum, an Idaho sculptor who would later carve Mount Rushmore, to design and execute a carving of Lee. Borglum conceived a grandiose plan—a gigantic model of Confederate leaders riding around the mountain. Little progress on the memorial occurred before the end of World War I. In November of 1915 Colonel William Simmons, a former Methodist circuit rider and salesman, used Stone Mountain as the location for a fiery ritual resurrecting the Ku Klux Klan. The locale thereafter was periodically the scene of Klan rallies.

In May of 1916, with a huge Confederate flag, 30 by 50 feet, draped across the face of the cliff, southerners dedicated the unfinished Stone Mountain as a memorial to the Lost Cause. Still in need of financing though, Borglum traveled throughout the South promoting the project. In 1923 Atlanta businessmen took charge of the project, forming the Stone Mountain Monumental Association. Borglum began work on the carving in June of 1923 and unveiled the partially carved head of Lee on 19 January 1924, the general's birthday, before an estimated crowd of 20,000. After a rift developed between Borglum and the UDC, Augustus Lukeman began work on the project but was unable to finish the carving before the UDC lease ran out in 1928.

For more than 30 years the memorial remained unfinished, with the property owned by the Venable family. In 1958 the state of Georgia decided to develop Stone Mountain as a tourist attraction. The state commissioned Walter Hancock to complete the memorial and to develop the park around it. George Weiblin was hired to direct completion of the carving, with Roy Faulkner as chief carver. Using a thermo-jet torch and working at times in the face of 70-mile-per-hour winds on the side of the mountain, the crew finished the project between 1964 and 1970, when the memorial was dedicated.

The carving, which is 90 feet high by 190 feet wide, in a frame 360 feet square, depicts Lee, Davis, and Jackson—the Lost Cause trinity—on horseback; Lee's horse, Traveller, stretches across 145 feet. Stone Mountain became a major tourist attraction at the heart of a 3,200-acre park. More than 5 million people a year come to the park, which is geared, according to promoters, to family recreation. The park features a 90-room inn and a 500-site campground. Inside the park, visitors can see a 19th-century plantation and a gristmill, drive across a covered bridge, fish, circle the mountain on a train or scale it on a skylift, ride the side-wheeler riverboat the *Scarlett O'Hara*, play tennis or golf, or stroll through the grounds, which contain flowers such as the now-rare Confederate daisy (*viguiera porteri*). Guides costumed in hoop skirts or Confederate army uniforms provide assistance. In Confederate Hall a light-and-sound performance shows Sherman's "March to the Sea." The Georgia Heritage Museum contains artifacts and documents from the state's history. An Antique Auto and Music Museum contains antique toys, cars, trains, musical instruments, gas pumps, and other items. Indigenous animals roam the 60-acre Stone Mountain Animal Forest.

In the summer, tourists now come to see "A Night on Stone Mountain," which is said to be the world's largest outdoor laser show. Laser beams flash onto the carving such images as spiders, spaceships, and animals, accompanied by fireworks. In the finale, the Confederate heroes gallop off the mountain, courtesy of the laser lighting, all to the familiar tune of "Dixie."

Charles Reagan Wilson
University of Mississippi

Robert J. Casey and Mary Borglum, *Give the Man Room: The Story of Gutzon Borglum* (1952); Gerald W. Johnson, *The Undefeated* (1927); Bari R. Love, *Southern Living* (June 1984).

Stuart, Jeb

(1833–1864) Confederate general.

During his short life, James Ewell Brown "Jeb" Stuart accomplished much. Born in Patrick County, Va., in 1833, "Jeb" Stuart graduated from West Point (1854) and served on the western frontier in the U.S. Army until 1861. He resigned to serve Virginia and the Confederacy as commander of a regiment of cavalry. Stuart was conspicuous at First Manassas (Bull Run) and tireless in his employment of mounted troops as scouts and pickets between rival armies. Promoted to brigadier general in September 1861, Stuart expanded his command and his fame. In June 1862 Stuart rode completely around George B. McClellan's Union army and was able to supply Robert E. Lee with the intelligence upon which Lee based his Seven Days Campaign. In July 1862 Stuart became a major general and assumed command of the cavalry component of the Army of Northern Virginia. He led other cavalry raids—Catlett's Station in August 1862, Chambersburg in October 1862, and Dumfries in December 1862—which embarrassed his enemies and enhanced his fame. At Chancellorsville (May 1863) Stuart succeeded Stonewall Jackson in command of an infantry corps and played a key role in the Confederate victory.

The cavalry battle at Brandy Station (June 1863) opened Stuart to criticism because he allowed the federals to surprise him. His protracted raid during the Gettysburg campaign deprived Lee of his "eyes and ears" and contributed to the Confederate defeat. But when Stuart suffered a mortal wound at Yellow Tavern in May of 1864, he died a southern hero. He had worn a plume in his hat, collected a retinue that included a banjo player, and flirted with women wherever he went. He had sung and danced and laughed; but he had avoided alcohol, remained faithful to his wife, and set an example of Christian piety.

Stuart made himself a legend while he lived, and later his legend grew larger than life. Stuart has stood for southerner as cavalier and knight in the American mind. As symbol he is eternally dashing, romantic, and gallant. Stuart's life may have been brief, but his legacy yet lives.

Emory Thomas
University of Georgia

Burke Davis, *Jeb Stuart: The Last Cavalier* (1957); Henry Brainerd McClellan, *I Rode with Jeb Stuart: The Life and Campaigns of Major General J. E. B. Stuart* (1885, 1958); Emory Thomas, *Bold Dragoon: The Life of J. E. B. Stuart* (1986).

Taylor, John

(1753–1824) Political philosopher.

Taylor, born in December 1753 in Caroline County, Va., is referred to as "John Taylor of Caroline"; he was one of the fathers of southern politics. He was more famous in his own time than later; his prestige was such that he was several times elected U.S. senator from what was then the most powerful state in the Union without campaigning and against his wishes. He was a soldier in the American Revolution who died regretting that the Revolution had ended in the construction of a federal government more dangerous to the colonies than that of Great Britain. He retired from a lucrative law practice to become not only a highly successful planter and agricultural reformer but the foremost political defender and philosopher that American agriculture ever had. He was an eloquent advocate of economic, political, and religious freedom for the citizen, and an unbending defender of slavery.

Taylor may even be said to have been a pioneer figure in southern literature. His books and pamphlets are not only full of keen political and economic analysis but are written in a colloquial style—full of satire, hyperbole, and front-porch digressions—highly suggestive of the oral tradition evident in later southern writers.

Taylor embodied many persistent and recurrent tendencies and themes of southern politics. He represented both a conservative allegiance to local community and inherited ways and a radical-populist suspicion of capitalism, "progress," government, and routine logrolling politics. He was at the same time more radical and more conservative than his friend, admirer, and fellow Virginia planter Thomas Jefferson. Taylor was Jefferson's down-home side—exactly what Jefferson would have been had he been less cosmopolitan and less of a practical politician. In many respects Taylor was a more authentic voice of Jeffersonianism than was Jefferson himself. Taylor's Old Republican defense of states' rights, strict construction, and intelligent farming and his opposition to federal power, judicial oligarchy, paper money, stock jobbing, taxation, and expenditure were reflexive, reluctant defenses of native soil and were based upon the unyielding conviction that an unoppressed and predominantly agricultural population was the only possible basis for free government.

At the core of Taylor's thinking was a belief that the world is divided between producers and parasites. The producers are decent folk who labor in the earth for their daily bread and produce everything of real economic and moral value in society. They are subject to endless depredations from those that Taylor referred to as "aristocrats." By "aristocrats" he meant not people of good birth but people, mostly northerners, whose main business was manipulating the government for artificial advantages for themselves. This view of the world, as much a folk attitude as a philosophical position, is a recurrent theme in much southern behavior.

Taylor's more important works are *Definition of Parties, or the Political Effects of the Paper System* (1794); *An Enquiry into the Principles and Tendency of Certain Public Measures* (1794); *A Defense of the Measures of the Administration of Thomas Jefferson* (1804); *Arator, Being a Series of Agricultural Essays, Practical and Political: In Sixty-Four Numbers* (1814); *An Inquiry into the Principles and Policy of the Government of the United States* (1814); *Construction Construed, and Constitutions Vindicated* (1820); *Tyranny Unmasked* (1822); and *New Views of the Constitution of the United States* (1823).

Clyde N. Wilson
University of South Carolina

M. E. Bradford, introduction to John Taylor, *Arator* (1977 reprint); Eugene T. Mudge, *The Social Philosophy of John Taylor of Caroline* (1939); Robert E. Shalhope, *John Taylor of Caroline: Pastoral Republican* (1980).

Trail of Tears

In 1838 the U.S. government uprooted some 13,000 Cherokee Indians from their land east of the Mississippi River and forced them westward into the Oklahoma territory. The 1,000-mile route they took to Oklahoma is called the Trail of Tears because of the hardships of weather, disease, and starvation that accompanied the Native Americans.

The forced migration along the Trail of Tears was a dismal journey, much of which took place in the middle of a harsh winter. Eyewitness accounts by missionaries, soldiers, government officials, and the uprooted Indians themselves describe how natives marched and suffered for hundreds of miles before reaching Oklahoma. Thousands of Native Americans died on the trip, which took them from north Georgia through middle Tennessee, southern Kentucky, and Missouri, and into present-day Oklahoma. The trip itself was only part of the harrowing experience the Indians endured in this stage of the removal. Federal troops held as many as 15,000 Cherokees in detention camps prior to the trip. Many of the detainees died of starvation or disease while in the camps.

The Trail of Tears has become a symbol for the historic oppression of Native Americans by whites, of which the forced removal of Indians to the west between 1820 and 1840 is only a part. Many southern Indians were tricked with unfamiliar legal practices or intimidated into giving up their land. The federal government demoralized the Native Americans by reducing the supply of game and negotiating separate treaties with certain tribesmen who were willing to accept white civilization. The Removal Acts of 1830 proposed the "final solution"—the exile of the southeastern Indians to the territories west of the Mississippi. At the time of the Indian removal, some Cherokees, like John Ross, advocated the move as the natives' only hope of survival; others, like John Ridge, argued for remaining in the Southeast and preserving traditional ways.

Today, the Trail of Tears has become a historic route developed by the Tennessee Department of Conservation in conjunction with the Department of Tourist Development. Along the route the tourist can see the final capitol of the Cherokee nation near Cleveland, Tenn., the only remaining stockade where the Indians were imprisoned before removal, and Andrew Jackson's home outside Nashville. The inclusion of Jackson's home, the Hermitage, is ironic because as president, Jackson was a staunch advocate of many of the brutal policies against the Indians, and he was instrumental in implementing the forced migration policy. Sixty thousand Indians were relocated west of the Mississippi under Jackson's direction.

Karen M. McDearman
University of Mississippi

Gloria Jahoda, *The Trail of Tears: The Story of the Indian Removal, 1813–1850* (1975); *Southern Exposure* (November–December 1985).

Trucking

Trucking culture materialized as the business of trucking transformed the way that goods were transported in the United States. Trucking as a business began in the 1920s, after World War I had proven the commercial value of the new motorized wagons. Veterans of the European conflict and farm boys familiar with steam machinery entered the new business of trucking. Lured by travel to exotic places such as New York City, enticed by the money to be made, and drawn by the opportunity to escape the routine of farm life, many midwestern and southern young men became truckers. Although trucking as a business appeared first in the Midwest and East, trucking as a culture quickly took on southern elements, particularly in language, food, music, and religion.

The essential loneliness of trucking—one man, one truck; driving many hours at night—kept the culture out

The Confederate flag—an icon of the trucking culture

of view of mainstream America until the popularization of the Citizens Band (CB) radio during the oil embargo of 1974. National news personalities featured the cowboy loneliness and the rich, unique language of the truckers on strike. Whether from Montana or Maine, Oregon or Ohio, truckers talked to one another with southern inflections and syntax. Accurately described as a cross between an Arkansas and a west Texas dialect, this "good old boy" style captured the faddish fancy of the American public. Millions of nontruckers purchased a CB and joined in the southern subculture that promoted evasion of highway patrol radar, as well as simple camaraderie during long and lonely drives along the nation's highways. Truckers and automobile drivers alike became "good buddies," many of them attempting to copy the southern dialects. Thus, in the 1970s the American public discovered a distinctly southern subculture that had been in the making since the 1920s.

Trucking culture reflected not only southern language but also other attributes that tended to rest on a peculiarly southern base. Southern fried food appeared in truck stops across the nation. Country songs climbed the popular music charts, and Hollywood movies drew in customers as the mass media exploited the emerging southern image of trucking. New lyrics (set to old cowboy and blues melodies) extolled the virtues of truckers, while detailing the evils and stupidity of governmental regulations and the state and local police who enforced them. Movies featured good old boys breaking speed laws and easily evading potbellied, cigar-chomping southern sheriffs.

Meanwhile, another aspect of southern culture, religion, influenced trucking. Evangelical ministers, such as the Reverend Jimmy Snow, son of country-and-western singer Hank Snow, used the CB to reach lonely drivers on the road. Other ministers established mobile churches and traveled from truck stop to truck stop looking for converts.

The very media that exposed the southern influence in

the trucking culture, alas, have also led to a dilution of that regional influence. Certainly truckers continue to wear traditional western clothes (jeans, cowboy boots and hats, and western shirts) and many continue to operate their rigs just the other side of the law (much as southern moonshiners have done). Yet organization of trucking associations, more efficient trucks, and massive truck stops catering to the entire traveling public have muted the rebellious and unique spirit of trucking and, by extension, the southern culture supporting it.

See also INDUSTRY: / Trucking Industry

James H. Thomas
Wichita State University

Frederick E. Danker, *Journal of Country Music* (January 1978); Jane Stern and Michael Stern, *Trucker: Portrait of the Last American Cowboy* (1975); James H. Thomas, *The Long Haul: Truckers, Truck Stops, and Trucking* (1979); D. Daryl Wyckoff, *Truck Drivers in America* (1979).

United Daughters of the Confederacy (UDC)

Southern fiction frequently portrays indomitable southern women in the Civil War. Given the late 19th century's predilection for organizations, it was perhaps inevitable that real-life die-hard women who saw themselves as guardians of the Lost Cause would create the United Daughters of the Confederacy (UDC) in Nashville in September 1894. The roots of the UDC may be traced back to the wartime Ladies' Aid Societies that sprang up spontaneously throughout the South in 1861 to assist Confederate soldiers. Perhaps the earliest organized voluntarism among Victorian southern women, these societies began as sewing groups, many of them in the churches, to prepare socks, mufflers, gloves, balaclava helmets, uniforms, and blankets for Confederate soldiers. As war took its human toll, some societies changed into Women's Hospital Associations, which set up hospitals and convalescent homes for Confederate sick and wounded soldiers.

During the spring of 1866 many of these organizations reorganized as Ladies' Memorial Associations to insure proper interments for hastily buried Confederate dead, to honor their graves on 26 April (Confederate Memorial Day), and then to raise funds for monuments and statues commemorating the Lost Cause in settings ranging from courthouse squares to battlefields.

Many members of the Ladies' Memorial Associations joined the UDC when it was organized, with its founders' declared goal of obtaining an accurate history of the Confederacy. The UDC was and is a social, literary, historical, monumental, and benevolent association made up of widows, wives, mothers, sisters, and other lineal descendants of men who rendered military, civil, or other personal service to the Confederate cause.

Organized 10 September 1894, the UDC was incorporated in the District of Columbia on 18 July 1919. It has erected numerous memorials, it presents Crosses of Military Service to lineal Confederate descendants who themselves have served in later American wars, and it presents awards to outstanding service academy cadets and midshipmen. At its height in the early 20th century, the UDC totaled some 100,000 members and was a political force to be reckoned with. As the years took their toll and memories faded, its membership dwindled to about 20,000 in the 1950s; but since the Civil War Centennial a quarter of a century ago, interest has revived. Today there are about 27,000 members, including those in chapters in northern and western states, as well as in Paris and Mexico City. Associated organizations include the Sons of Confederate Veterans (SCV), founded in 1896; the Children of the Confederacy, organized in 1899; and the Military Order of the Stars and Bars, (MOSB), begun in 1938 and made up of male descendants of Confederate officers.

Cameron Freeman Napier
Montgomery, Alabama

Jerome Francis Beattie, ed., *The Hereditary Register of the United States of America* (1972); Wallace Evan Davies, *Patriotism on Parade: The Story of Veterans' and Hereditary Organizations in America, 1783–1900* (1955); Mary B. Poppenheim et al., *The History of the United Daughters of the Confederacy* (1925; reprint 1956).

Washington, George

(1732–1799) U.S. president.

Washington was born into a well-established and prosperous Virginia family in 1732. By his own efforts and by his marriage to Martha Dandridge Custis he entered the ranks of the First Families of Virginia. In youth his loyalties were to Virginia and the British empire. Convinced that it was wrong for one people to have power to tax and to dominate another, he came to the forefront of the Virginia patriots.

As commander in chief of the Continental army he was one of the first to indicate that he desired independence from Britain. In the fall of 1775 he referred to America as "my country" and "my bleeding country." He gave utter allegiance thereafter to the American Republic. In the 1780s he referred to Virginia as a "middle" state rather than a southern one. He condemned the Articles of Confederation because they gave the central government insufficient power, and he was the most influential champion of the Constitution. As president he steadily and effectively toiled to assure the safety and growth of the nation. He denounced sectionalism of every sort, in particular condemning all efforts to set the emerging sections, North and South, against each other. It is fair to say that he was an ardent Federalist in his last years.

Washington was a land speculator and a farmer rather than a planter, for he turned away well before 1775 from emphasis upon tobacco growing to general husbandry. With the years he became increasingly hostile to black slavery. He declared that it ought gradually to be abolished, said that he would vote for emancipation, and arranged in his will to free his slaves and those of his wife.

John R. Alden
Duke University

John R. Alden, *George Washington: A Biography* (1984); James Thomas Flexner, *George Washington*, 4 vols. (1965–72); Douglas Southall Freeman, John A. Carroll, and Mary W. Ashworth, *George Washington: A Biography*, 7 vols. (1948–57).

Whiskey

From the throat-searing drop of moonshine fresh from the copper worm of a still to the dark amber waves of Kentucky's mellow bourbon in a silver julep cup, the quencher for a southern thirst through the years has been whiskey.

The first southern whiskey produced from corn was probably made on the James River in Virginia in a still run by Captain George Thorpe, who was killed by Indians 27 March 1622. Later Scotch-Irish settlers brought with them pot stills. Those who practiced their trade using such devices in early Pennsylvania revolted at the institution of excise taxes on their product. The crushing of the Whiskey Rebellion in 1794 proved the strength of the new government, but some hardy souls intent on the least possible government interference in their trade removed themselves to the lands that would become Kentucky and Tennessee. The rye they had used in Pennsylvania was in large part replaced by corn. And, taxed or not, the whiskey flowed. Already Kentucky had seen nearly a generation of whiskey makers.

The process of whiskey making was simple enough for an energetic small farmer. It would also bring him greater economic yield per bushel of corn than other uses, perhaps a 300 percent price increase. Besides, whiskey was easier to get to market, and age improved it.

Whiskey fueled the riverboat men, gave courage to pioneers going over the Appalachians, provided the perfect repentable sin for saved souls in the Great Awakening—in short, whiskey, its making and its drinking, its rampant enjoyment and its aftermath of misery, seemed particularly suited to the complex southern temperament from an early point. With that peculiarly southern trait of both embracing and rejecting at one time, the South both intemperately imbibed and then as vigorously espoused temperance.

Early southern seaboard residents were at first accustomed to rum or peach brandy as their hard liquor of

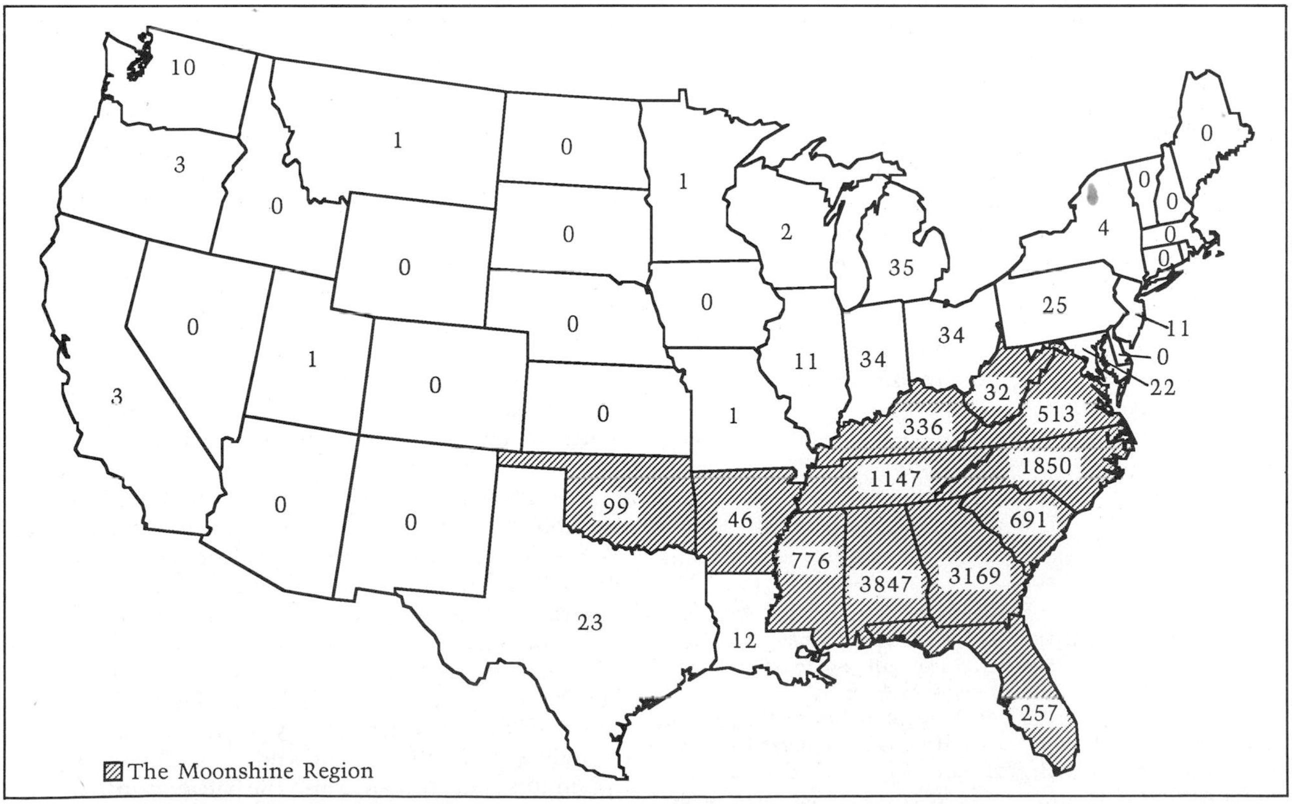

Number of Illegal Stills Seized, 1968

Source: Licensed Beverage Industries, Inc., *Moonshine: The Poison Business* (1971). Reprinted with permission of Distilled Spirits Council of the U.S.

choice. Whiskey changed this, being readily available, less expensive, and producing like results. "You see no persons besotting themselves with imported spirits, wines, liquors, cordials, &c. Whisky claims to itself alone the exclusive office of sot-making," wrote Thomas Jefferson in 1823.

Nineteenth-century southerners drank enormous quantities of whiskey, both homemade and store-bought. Journal writers bragged on their capacity. Malcolm Bedford in Stark Young's Civil War novel *So Red the Rose* (1934) sips his toddy while he composes florid obituaries for his still-living friends. Other southerners seemed to reflect the dictum expressed well by singer Willie Nelson. "Whiskey," observed Willie, "makes you want to fight." Whiskey is the topic of countless popular songs in the South, such as "Whiskey River," "Whiskey and Gin Blues," "Rye Whiskey, Rye Whiskey," and "Whiskey Heaven," where "Jack Daniel's falls like rain."

It also made others wish to stop all drinking. The South experienced early periodic local temperance crusades, but it was after the Civil War (when the stigma of the organized temperance movement's ties to abolitionism was removed) that the effort began in earnest. Part of this could have been the middle-class wish to impose higher standards on those they saw as less fortunate. There was also genuine religious fervor as the Baptists, Methodists, and other evangelical sects came out strongly against drink. The result was not only the passage of the Eighteenth Amendment but years of skirmishes both before and after repeal. Will Rogers once said that Mississippians will "vote dry as long as they can stagger to the polls." All southern legislatures regularly faced the "wet or dry" issue, producing a mass of conflicting, confusing, and still-changing laws. One result was the flourishing of an illegal liquor industry that exists today: the making and distributing of whiskey without government taxation.

Whiskey, to the South, is more than a drink. It is at once the problem and the solution. It adds fire not only to the orator who imbibes but also to the preacher who inveighs against it. Its production and consumption—legal or not—provide an income to thousands. It is the topic of countless songs, from hymns to ballads to country music's latest hits.

See also INDUSTRY: / Liquor Industry

Carolyn Goldsby Kolb
New Orleans, Louisiana

Gerald Carson, *The Social History of Bourbon: An Unhurried Account of Our Star-Spangled American Drink* (1963); Kim Chapin, *Fast as White Lightning: The Story of Stock Car Racing* (1981); J. C. Furnas, *The Americans: A Social History of the United States, 1587–1914* (1969); Joseph R. Gusfield, *Symbolic Crusade: Status Politics and the American Temperance Movement* (1963); Harry Kroll, *Bluegrass, Belles and Bourbon: A Pictorial History of Whisky in Kentucky* (1967); Joe Gray Taylor, *Eating, Drinking, and Visiting in the South: An Informal History* (1982).

Wilson, Woodrow

(1856–1924) U.S. president.

Born in Virginia and raised in Georgia, South Carolina, and North Carolina, Woodrow Wilson was one of the South's most influential leaders in American history. His first memories, he once said, were of the news of Lincoln's election and the outbreak of the Civil War. The most important influence on his early life was his father, Joseph R. Wilson, a prominent Presbyterian minister who helped form the Presbyterian Church in the United States and ardently defended slavery. Woodrow Wilson later declared that "the only place in the country, the only place in the world, where nothing has to be explained to me is the South."

He began his education at Davidson College in North Carolina, completed his undergraduate work at Princeton, and pursued his legal training at the University of Virginia under John B. Minor. For a brief time in Atlanta he practiced law, which he found at odds with his primary interests—history and literature. During this period he met his first wife, Ellen Axson Wilson, herself the daughter of a distinguished family of southern Presbyterian ministers. He left Atlanta to do doctoral work at the Johns Hopkins University, where he received his Ph.D. for his work *Congressional Government*.

Southern observers watched with pride as Wilson steadily achieved fame and influence as an educator, historian, man of letters, and political commentator, and Wilson's successful campaign for the White House in 1912 was due in great measure to his ability to portray himself paradoxically as both a southerner and a national figure.

In fact, he was both. He retained southern attitudes toward women throughout his life but insisted on a college education for his own daughters. He shared the racist values of American society of his day and as president (1913–21) presided over the segregation of federal agencies yet never trafficked in blatant racism. In his historical writing he lauded the South for its adherence to principle in fighting the Civil War but described both the institution of slavery and the South's understanding of the Constitution as doomed by the progressive forces of history. He disciplined himself and his wife to drop their southern accents, although his southern political alliances brought him to national power.

Wilson's political achievements include breaking the Republican hold on the White House in the post–Civil War period and bringing the South into national politics. But perhaps the greatest irony is that this son of a region known for its parochialism should have laid the foundations for America's self-understanding in world affairs. Ellen Axson Wilson praised him for being "an infinitely better, more helpful son to her [the South] than any of those who cling so desperately to the past and the old prejudices." "I believe," she said, "you are her *greatest* son in this generation and also the one who will have the greatest claim on her gratitude."

John M. Mulder
Louisville Presbyterian
Theological Seminary

Arthur S. Link, *Journal of Southern History* (February 1970), *Wilson: The Road to the White House* (1947); John M. Mulder, *Woodrow Wilson: The Years of Preparation* (1978).

York, Alvin C.

(1887–1964) Soldier.

In the last days of World War I, Alvin C. York came marching out of the Argonne Forest with 132 German prisoners and a tale of individual daring unsurpassed in the nation's military annals. One of the least likely heroes in history, the Tennessee-born York was initially a conscientious objector who was drafted only after his pleas for a deferment on religious grounds were rejected. However, his army superiors persuaded him that America was fighting God's battle in the war, an argument that transformed the pacifist from the Appalachian Mountains into a veritable soldier of the Lord.

During the final Allied offensive of the conflict, York single-handedly outshot an entire German machine-gun battalion, killing 25 men in the process. His explanation that God had been with him during the fight meshed neatly with the popular attitude that American involvement in the war was truly a holy crusade, and he returned to the United States in the spring of 1919 amid a tumultuous public welcome and a flood of business offers from people eager to capitalize on the soldier's reputation. In spite of these lucrative opportunities, York decided to return to his native hamlet of Pall Mall, where he spent the rest of his life working to bring schools and other public services to his mountain neighbors.

York's Appalachian heritage was central to his popularity, because the media portrayed him as the archetypal mountain man. At a time of domestic upheaval and international uncertainty, York's pioneer-like skill with a rifle, his homespun manner, and his fundamentalist piety endeared him to millions of Americans as a kind of "contemporary ancestor" fresh from the backwoods of the southern mountains. As such, he seemed to affirm that the traditional virtues of agrarian America still had meaning in the new era. In short, York represented not what Americans were but what they wanted to think they were. He lived in one of the most rural parts of the country at a time when a majority of Americans lived in cities; he rejected riches at a time when the tenor of the nation was crassly commercial; he was pious at a time when secularism was on the rise.

For millions of people, York was the incarnation of their romanticized understanding of the nation's past when men and women supposedly lived plainer, sterner, and more virtuous lives. Ironically, although York endured as a symbol of an older America, he spent most of his adult life working to bring roads, schools, and industrial development to the mountains, changes that irrevocably altered the society he had come to represent.

David D. Lee
Western Kentucky University

Samuel K. Cowen, *Sergeant York and His People* (1922); David D. Lee, *Sergeant York: An American Hero* (1985); Thomas Skeyhill, ed., *Sergeant York: His Own Life Story and War Diary* (1928), *Sergeant York: Last of the Long Hunters* (1930).

Industry

JAMES C. COBB
University of Alabama
CONSULTANT

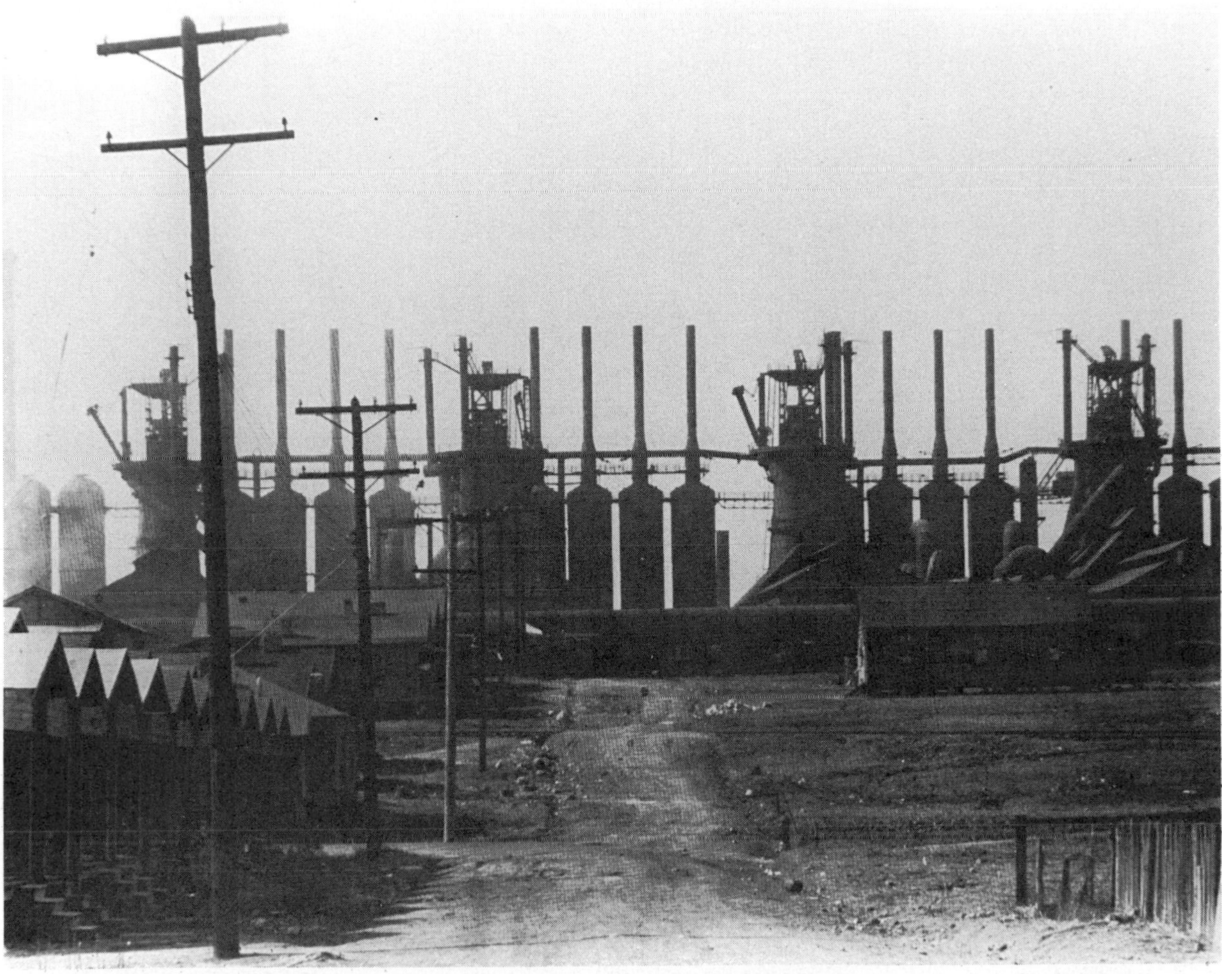

Birmingham steel mill and workers' houses, 1930s

Industry and Commerce

The perception of the antebellum South as a plantation society and southerners as "an agricultural people" is rooted in both myth and reality. The belief that a large number of southerners were "agrarians" who shunned all industrial investments and commercial pursuits is largely rooted in myth. Prominent southerners have voiced their fears or their disdain of industrialization, but the primary influences that held back southern commerce and industry were economic, rather than cultural or political.

The traditional wisdom has been that slavery stunted the South's economy, particularly its commercial and industrial growth, by tying up the region's already scarce capital and discouraging immigration by free labor, all the while stigmatizing labor as an activity unbefitting a white person, regardless of social status. The result was a society obsessed with land and slaves and lacking in the labor, markets, money, and human energy needed to stimulate industry and commerce.

In recent years economic historians have questioned this theory. They have shown that cotton planting was a reasonably profitable endeavor. If only whites are considered, on the eve of the Civil War average wealth was almost twice as great among southerners as among their northern counterparts. Moreover, despite the planter's dominant position in the socioeconomic and political hierarchy, overall distribution of the wealth was not significantly more unbalanced south than north of the Mason-Dixon line.

Antebellum Industrialization. The antebellum South was capable of supporting considerably more industrial and commercial activity than it ever generated. In fact, annual returns from investments in southern manufacturing were often higher than the national average and as much as twice as high as those from investments in planting. Such evidence suggests either that southerners were too naive to realize they were missing a good bet by not investing in a mill or a business or that they simply succumbed to social pressures by pursuing wealth in cotton and slaves rather than in textiles, lumber, or general merchandise. Certainly, planters had no desire to surrender even a particle of their preeminence to industrialists, and they seldom forfeited an opportunity to lionize themselves as the noblest of southerners and their profession as the highest calling known to man. They were obviously nervous about a challenge to their social or political status from members of the industrial or commercial classes. Such a challenge, after all, might divide southern society and undermine the institution of slavery.

State and local policymakers rarely translated their anxieties into legislation that forbade or hindered the expansion of industry and commerce. Consequently, there were few legal impediments to the growth of the nonagricultural sector in the antebellum South's economy. Did most southerners simply fail to recognize the opportunities for profit they were forfeiting by clinging to agriculture? If not, why did they settle for returns so much lower than those they might have gained from investing in industry? The answer lies not in ignorance but in conservative investment behavior premised on the notion that the more dependable profits (in the neighborhood of 10 percent) offered by planting involved considerably less risk than the much higher profits possible in a still-uncertain manufacturing sector. Such behavior was certainly cautious but hardly irrational or abnormal.

It is unlikely that the antebellum South would ever have been industrialized on a scale comparable to the North even if its investors had been more venturesome. Climate, topography, and the slave-labor system gave the region a comparative advantage in agriculture that shaped its economic destiny. In the antebellum era most southern industry involved the processing of agricultural products and raw materials. Flour and corn milling accounted for much of this processing activity across the South, and the tobacco industry was crucial to the industrial economy of Virginia and the Carolinas. Cotton mills took advantage of the South's abundant cotton, water power, and cheap labor. Richmond's Tredegar Iron Works was the major heavy industry in a region whose entire industrial output was less than that of Pennsylvania in 1860.

So long as cotton prices were good, the South was in a position to overindulge its advantage in agriculture, but the end of the antebellum cotton boom and the slowing of the rate of growth in demand for cotton after the Civil War put the southern states well behind the vibrant northeastern and central states, which were experiencing an economic revolution in the late 19th century. With technology, labor, capital, and resources all in their favor, the northern states attracted the overwhelming majority of investments in the dynamic industries and businesses needed to sustain rapid economic growth in that period. The South, on the other hand, had little to offer industries but abundant labor, certain raw materials (particularly cotton and wood), and a fervent desire for industry.

A New South. The postbellum South's most prominent advocate of industrialization was Henry W. Grady, an Atlanta newspaperman who became famous as the orator of the New South movement. Grady preached industrialism and economic independence and stressed sectional reconciliation as a means of creating a happy marriage of northern capital with southern labor and raw materials. Although Grady promised a "New" South, he also took great pains to assuage the concerns of southern planters that industrial development would not drain off the cheap, controllable labor that was essential to the preservation of the plantation system of agriculture. Critics charged Grady with "selling out" to the planters as well as to the northern investors who sought to perpetuate an exploitive colonial relationship with the South. Although Grady and his disciples could not be exonerated on this count, he and his followers had few options. Planters remained influential enough to block or severely impede the industrial development effort if it promised to reduce their supply of cheap labor or undermine their dominance of the South's socioeconomic hierarchy. As for facilitating the further "colonization" of the South's economy, New South leaders may have had little choice given the region's resemblance to other underdeveloped regions of the world that have experienced economic growth only by offering their labor and raw materials to absentee investors at bargain rates. The South's economic destiny was less in the hands of its own leaders than at the mercy of the external resource, labor, and market factors that were at the heart of national and international growth patterns in the late 19th century.

The structure and the administration of the South's railroad system helped to shape its economic development. With nearly all the region's railroad mileage controlled by northerners by the turn of the century, highly discriminatory freight rates were the rule when shipping goods within the South. It was much cheaper, for example, to ship Arkansas cotton to Massachusetts than to South Carolina. Also, as the railroads penetrated the countryside, small crossroads towns sprang up as mercantile, processing, and marketing centers. With such excellent connections outside the region, the products of these towns of approximately 10,000 people went directly to northern cities without passing through major southern cities (with the probable exception of the regional hub city of Atlanta). As a result, the configuration of the South's railroads played a major role in retarding urban growth in the region. Meanwhile, the country store and small-town merchant occupied the pivotal position in a capital-scarce economy where cotton often served as currency. Prosperous merchants supplied everything from farm implements to face powder and often provided banking, postal, and other services, all the while serving, as David R. Goldfield noted, "as the middleman in the link between plantation and northern market."

In the South of 1900 only 18 percent of the work force was employed in pursuits unrelated to agriculture, and per capita income stood at 51 percent of the national average, exactly where it had been 20 years earlier. Industry remained largely confined to the extraction of raw materials and the elementary processing of agricultural products. Absentee owners drew away much of the income from these activities, and wages were meager. In 1910 the manufacturing payroll for the entire state of Georgia was smaller than that for the city of Cincinnati. Moreover, much of the South's nonagricultural economy was devoted to commerce rather than manufacturing. Even in a relatively industrialized city like Memphis the value of annual trade in 1900 was 10 times that for manufacturing.

The structure of the post-Reconstruction South's economy was directly related to its ultraconservative social and political climate. The region's commitment to low-wage, labor- and resource-exploitive industries required a parallel commitment to maintaining social and political stability and an austere, rigidly conservative government disinclined to regulate or tax too heavily or to see any side but management's in a labor-management dispute.

Late-19th- and early-20th-century economic development helped to shape southern society and culture. The commercial classes dominated policymaking in southern cities, and their ties to the agricultural and processing activities of the countryside made them wary of any alterations of the status quo likely to create instability in an economy based on labor control, low taxes, and minimal government interference. Tensions were always present, but during the late 19th and much of the 20th century the urban South accommodated itself to the politics of the countryside.

Atop the South's agriculturally oriented system of commerce sat a sinister nabob described by Ralph McGill as the "small town rich man" who, "according to his geographic location," owned the gin, the cotton warehouse, the tobacco warehouse, or the turpentine works. He also owned the town's largest store, selling feeds, fertilizer, and other farm supplies. Often, he served as a director of the local bank. He controlled local credit and was on a first-name basis with his governor, his legislator, his senators, and his congressman. Paranoid about maintaining a large pool of cheap labor loyal only to him, he hated New Deal relief programs and union organizers with equal passion. Because he dominated the South's rurally biased state political systems, the small-town rich man was an agent of inertia representing a large segment of the region's business and industrial capitalists.

The Crusade for Economic Development. Despite the region's social and political stagnation, the South's efforts to industrialize continued unabated as the 20th century unfolded. The almost religious fervor of the crusade for economic growth revealed itself in the "Atlanta Spirit," an urban booster ethos that rallied the leaders of southern cities to intense, competitive crusading for growth during the 1920s. Commercial and civic leaders, black spokesmen, and even the Ku Klux Klan joined the hunt for more smokestacks. Any industry was better than no industry to these zealots, but not so to the Vanderbilt Agrarians, a group of 12 conservative writers whose views were published in 1930 in *I'll Take My Stand*, a spirited critique of industrialism typified by John Crowe Ransom's assertion that "the dignity of personality is gone as soon as the man from the farm enters the factory door." The Agrarians offered a Depression-ridden South a stout defense of southern traditionalism but no real alternative to the impoverished, benighted society that dependence on agriculture had bequeathed to the region. Most southerners who knew about the Agrarians at all probably would have, for once, agreed with H. L. Mencken, who ridiculed them for "spinning lavender fancies under a fig tree."

The Depression era saw the campaign for growth intensify and expand. The Atlanta Spirit spread from the cities to the small towns in response to a series of shocks beginning with the boll weevil invasion of the 1920s. Plummeting cotton yields drove both landowners and sharecroppers from the land and posed a serious threat to the agriculturally oriented commerce and industry that was the mainstay of the southern economy. As Georgia's cotton belt played unhappy host to the boll weevil at its hungriest, the state amended its constitution to allow tax exemptions for new industries. Coming on the heels of the boll weevil, the Depression intensified the insect's impact, forcing both planter and sharecropper off the land. Ironically, the New Deal's Agricultural Adjustment Act, which paid farmers to produce less, further reinforced the trend toward farm consolidation and reduced farm labor requirements. The dwindling farm population posed a serious threat to the merchants, lawyers, bankers, and other professionals who comprised the small-town middle class because demand for goods and services was certain to shrink proportionally. Out-migration of displaced farm labor might lead ultimately to a similar fate for many members of the small-town middle class if a means could not be found to provide alternative employment (and income) to a burgeoning surplus labor force. Industrialization seemed the most likely solution to the problem, especially since concerns over any potential shortage of agricultural labor had been greatly reduced.

In its zeal for payrolls the small-town South prostrated itself at the feet of any and all industrialists who looked its way. The enterprising employer who required no more than a building and a work force could usually get the former for nothing and the latter for not much more. Subsidies for buildings were raised by public subscription or mandatory deductions from already meager employee paychecks. Tax exemptions, legal or not, were seldom difficult to secure, and local law enforcement officials were prepared to discourage any union organizers who might come to town. Not surprisingly, some companies exploited an already advantageous situation by hiring unpaid or barely paid trainees, or moving almost overnight to any industry-hungry community ready to raise the ante. Out of this chaotic scramble for payrolls came more organized, state-sanctioned programs to attract industry, most notably Mississippi's "Balance Agriculture with Industry" (BAWI) program (1936–58), which used tax-free municipal bonds to finance plant construction, and Louisiana's organized tax-exemption plan for new industries. Both approaches spread across the South and ultimately much of the nation. Although designed to make southern communities more attractive to industry, subsidy programs only confirmed the existing pattern of industrial development based on low-wage industries because such operations, attracted to the South initially by their need to save on labor costs, were also the ones most likely to be swayed by an opportunity to save on construction and tax costs. Although the old agricultural system was yielding to mechanization and consolidation, the traditional pattern of industrial development remained fundamentally unchanged.

The concentration of southern manufacturing in small-town and rural locations helped to minimize the cultural and demographic impact of industrialization in the region. As Dixie's most industrialized state, North Carolina showed a population in 1900 that was less than 10 percent urban. As technological advances slowed, the southern textile industry became less likely to spawn the rapid urbanization that had accompanied industrialization in the North. Moreover, after 1900 the proliferation of electric power and the automobile allowed even greater dispersal of manufacturing facilities. Industrialists chose locations where they could draw on a large-scale surplus of underemployed agricultural workers eager to work for steady, if meager, wages. Such workers were also prepared to commute long distances in order to continue to work their farms. Because they were not forced to relocate in industrial communities, they could maintain the cultural ties and lifestyles associated with life on the farm.

Inside a Cherryville, N.C., textile mill, 1908

Worker-farmers sacrificed much of the independence and periodic leisure they had known when they were only farmers. Many of them took night-shift jobs so that their days would be free to work their fields, the result being that they actually held two jobs. Ironically, employers justified the substandard wages they paid such workers on the ground that these employees were supplementing their paychecks with their farm incomes and therefore needed less than their counterparts elsewhere in the country. The same was true for farm wives who were actively recruited for work in small "sewing" (apparel) plants. Not only did they live on a farm that supplied much of their food, but they were merely working to supplement their husband's farm, or farm and industrial, income and should be willing to accept even lower wages than those paid farm-based male workers. At the same time she was being underpaid, the wage-earning farm wife was being overworked. She not only performed her eight-hour job at "the plant" but kept up with her cooking, cleaning, and canning just as she had when she was "only" a farm wife. As the profitability of farming declined and government subsidies of the New Deal and post–New Deal era encouraged farmers to farm less, or not at all, the former head of the household was often reduced to the status of "a go-getter" whose principal duty each day was to take his wife to work and "go get 'er."

Effects of World War II. Although much of the South's new industry continued to choose rural and small-town locations, World War II did more to alter the course and pace of southern economic development than any other event since the Civil War. The war's greatest contribution consisted of a large helping of federal money for a traditionally capital-starved region. More than $4 billion went into military facilities and perhaps as much as $5 billion into defense plants. The result was a 40 percent increase in the South's industrial capacity. Per capita income tripled during the 1940s, leaving southerners with enough disposable income to make them attractive potential consumers for a number of market-oriented industries that had previously found the South's consuming capacity too puny to justify the location of a production or distribution facility in the region. Automobile assembly and parts plants, for example, began to spring up in the Atlanta vicinity as executives realized the growing potential of the southeastern market.

With its rapidly mechanizing agricultural sector and its consumer markets expanded by World War II, the South became a region even more firmly committed to industry. The terrible memories of the 1930s spurred a renewed commitment to industrialization and a determination not to surrender wartime gains. All the southern states strengthened and extended their development programs, and more state and local leaders became involved. The governor became the state's supersalesman, and no gubernatorial aspirant dared to neglect economic development as a campaign pledge. Growth indicators suggested that this vigorous development effort was paying off, but the more rapid expansion of the post–World War II era was primarily the result of basic economic considerations related to costs, markets, and demographic shifts.

The stunted neocolonial economy of the South had preserved lower labor and general operating costs even as the war-born boom stimulated consumer buying power. Meanwhile, the traditional pattern of out-migration gradually reversed itself in the 1950s, augmenting the South's traditionally high birthrate and enhancing the region's market attraction.

As the South was experiencing its long-awaited economic boom, the industrial North was beginning to show definite signs of decay. Mounting labor and tax costs, technological obsolescence, labor agitation, rising crime, and an increased government regulatory role were among the considerations that led industrialists to forego expansion or new investments in the North in favor of a new plant in the South. As investment capital moved out, so did a number of residents, many of whom found new homes and jobs below the Mason-Dixon line.

By 1960 the trends set in motion by World War II were readily apparent. Between 1940 and 1960 the South's population had shifted from 65 percent rural to 58 percent urban. In the latter year only 10 percent of the population still worked in agriculture, while 21 percent worked in manufacturing. Average per capita income stood at 76 percent of the national average.

The Sunbelt Era. Although World War II marked the beginning of the South's economic takeoff, not until the end of the 1960s did the region begin to bask in the glow of "Sunbelt" prosperity. Between 1970 and 1976 the South enjoyed a net population gain of nearly 3 million. In contrast to the past, by the mid-1970s those moving into the region were significantly younger and better educated than the national average. The South's climate and relatively uncomplicated lifestyle were also pulling in retirees whose fixed incomes made lower living costs important. The South finally had its all-important nucleus of middle-class consumers. Industrial output and employment skyrocketed. Houston alone accounted for 79,000 new jobs in 1979. Much of Houston's growth was energy related, but the bulk of the region's expansion in the 1970s came in services such as retail trade, real estate, and banking.

Much of the industrial and commercial capital invested in the South had traditionally come from outside the region, and in the Sunbelt era an increasing amount came from outside the nation as well. Foreign investors moved in to take advantage of expanded markets and all of the region's traditional enticements—cheap, nonunion labor; low taxes; cooperative government; and a generally lower cost of living. By the end of the decade, the Carolina Piedmont was spotted with plants from Germany, France, and Japan, to name but a few. The Nissan truck plant at Smyrna, Tenn., attracted considerable attention as a prime example of the way in which Japanese management styles could be transferred to an American plant. Ironically, the "one big happy family" approach used by the Japanese bore a striking resemblance to the paternalism practiced in the cotton mills of the late-19th- and early-20th-century South.

Like many of their domestic predecessors, the foreign employers hoped to avoid unionization of their workers, and toward that end they provided wages and benefits that were better than the local and regional average, although generally still below national norms. The foreign executive and managerial personnel who moved into southern communities often regarded the local populace with curiosity and friendly amusement, but the culture gap appeared to narrow quickly as the loyalty of the work force and the hospitality of the community turned "foreigners" into southerners whose accents simply happened to be more distinctive than those of the natives. The Spartanburg, S.C., area attracted such a diverse mixture of foreign plants that Swiss rolls with Viennese jam soon became as much of a local delicacy as biscuits and redeye gravy.

The Sunbelt, however, was not always aglow. The Sunbelt could be more accurately described as an area splotched by "sun spots" with large areas of shade in between. High unemployment remained the rule in states like Mississippi with large concentrations of rural blacks. Such areas had little attraction for many industries, which appeared to shun locations with significant black populations.

Meanwhile, even in fast-growing areas, Sunbelt growth left many of the region's old problems unsolved. In cities like Atlanta, skyscrapers and an intimidating futuristic airport created the impression of prosperity, but the developed downtown had little to offer low-income blacks except custodial employment. In the meantime, rapid commercial growth and the mania for taller, more ostentatious buildings left no room for an adequate supply of low-cost housing in the downtown area. Although blacks shared but little in the expansion of Atlanta's commerce, by 1980 the city's population was two-thirds black.

Across the South, cities continued to attract blacks who opted for a disproportionately small share of the urban boom rather than struggle for subsistence in rural areas where the boom had yet to be felt.

Meanwhile, middle-class whites continued to flee the urban South, leaving the unemployed and underemployed of both races to inhabit cities that were commercial meccas during the day and hotbeds of crime at night. Houston, the acknowledged growth leader, was also the Sunbelt's homicide capital, and Atlanta became known as a wonderful place to visit if one could do so without having to venture out onto the streets.

Economic Development and Southern Culture. In 1973 country songwriter Bobby Braddock proudly reported his observations of "wooded parks and big skyscrapers where once stood red clay hills and cotton fields" and "sons and daughters of sharecroppers drinking scotch and making business deals." Not everyone shared Braddock's enthusiasm for a "risen" South. Along with the concern of some southerners that Sunbelt progress had not touched many areas sufficiently to solve their problems came the fear that this progress was creating cultural problems of its own. Many of those who were once critical of the South for its backwardness now lamented its rapid growth, expressing the belief that a more prosperous South would soon cease to be the South at all. Marshall Frady feared a "cultural lobotomy" as fast-food restaurants, discount stores, and industrial parks spread over the landscape.

Frady's concern was, of course, not a new one. The Agrarians had already expressed the same fear by the end of the 1920s. Post-Reconstruction literature had celebrated the South's "pastoral" tradition, as opposed to the New South creed espoused by Henry W. Grady and others. In the face of the boosterism that enveloped the South after World War I, writers like Thomas Wolfe and William Faulkner decried the materialism of the booster ethos and expressed particular regret at the conquest of the South's wilderness areas. Erskine Caldwell had the lowly Jeeter Lester in *Tobacco Road* express his preference for farming, even sharecropping, over work in a cotton mill. After World War II had accelerated the South's economic growth and spurred industrialization and the mechanization of agriculture, Flannery O'Connor wrote a short story about a "displaced person" who brings mechanical, but impersonal, Yankee-like precision and skill to a rundown Georgia farm only to have his contribution rejected by the inhabitants, who allow him to be flattened by a runaway tractor.

The same concern was reflected in country music, where examples of a fear and loathing of the alien, "northernizing" influences of the city and the factory and a preference for the idyllic agrarian lifestyle abounded. Songs like "Cotton Mill Colic" and "Weave Room Blues" depicted the dreariness of industrial life, while "Detroit City" and "Streets of Baltimore" presented the northern city as a heartless and foreboding place.

The proliferation of shopping centers and chain stores had a homogenizing effect on the small-town South, where restaurant cuisine soon featured corn dogs and tacos instead of corn bread and turnip greens. Unknown and impersonal salesclerks and two pieces of identification to pay by check were other seemingly inevitable concomitants to progress. Many observers insisted that southerners had managed to some extent to humanize the technological and commercial advances that had bred anonymity and alienation elsewhere, but such contentions were usually more impressionistic than objective. It was difficult to identify what part, if any, of the region's response to economic modernization was clearly southern instead of the predictable reaction of any traditional rural and small-town society to dramatic changes in its means of production and exchange.

On the other hand, opinion surveys of better-educated, more affluent southerners showed economic progress was finally eroding the racism, traditionalism, and authoritarianism that constituted some of the darker elements of the South's traditional value structure. Still, the young beneficiaries of the region's economic progress were the most likely of all southerners to prize their identities as southerners and to express a preference for foods, friends, and an overall lifestyle identifiable as southern. Paradoxically, while economic progress appeared to be undermining certain traditional values, it was also reinforcing the southernness of those whose imminent baptism in the economic mainstream posed the threat of a rootless, anonymous existence.

Although it was clearly true that in fast-growing areas young southerners were being drawn into mainstream mass culture and even their parents and grandparents were being affected to a lesser extent, the notion that factories, skyscrapers, and interstate highways had "northernized" the South rested on the assumption that there were distinct value differences between industrial and agrarian societies and that, as industrialization proceeded, industrial values were bound to triumph.

For many years liberal social scientists and journalists had seen agrarian traditionalism and economic progress as arch enemies, the former being the villain in the ongoing saga of southern backwardness, with the latter cast in the role of oft-thwarted would-be savior. In the widely accepted scenario, if southern traditionalism could be weakened sufficiently to allow economic modernization to gain a foothold, its benevolent and progressive influences would then overwhelm the vestiges of racism and reactionary politics and transform Dixie into an enlightened liberal society like the industrial Northeast. Ironically, however, the South's economic emergence not only failed to follow this widely accepted model, it practically turned it on its head. The "favorable business climate" so vital to the Sunbelt South's fabled economic success story was actually rooted in the historically conservative social and political atmosphere long condemned as the nemesis of southern progress. Cheap, intimidated labor, low taxes, and a cooperative rather than meddlesome government—all of these were both trademarks of the traditionalist, plantation South and keys to the Sunbelt South's appeal to business and industrial investors. The South's belated economic emergence demonstrated that the "value gap" between agrarian and industrial-commercial societies had been greatly exaggerated. The experience of the Sunbelt South also had profound implications for those who prescribed economic modernization as a panacea for the problems of underdeveloped nations, particularly those who continued to expect American investors to sponsor progressive reform and the overall democratization of these societies.

Businessmen and industrialists fleeing northern locations were actually running away from labor activism, government supervision, and mounting tax and living costs. They were, therefore, generally opposed to any changes likely to introduce such conditions in their new southern locations. But what of the long-awaited middle class swelled by the migration of executives and managers? Would not this new "white-collar" class become a force for innovation and improvement in government and public services and facilities?

In the post–World War II years the South's business and professional middle class, fed by more rapid commercial and industrial expansion, played an increasingly active role in promoting social and political change in the region. Immediately after the war, young veterans returning to the South's business and professional ranks led a series of "GI Revolts" that overthrew local political rings in urban areas and small towns across the South. These political uprisings represented the first wave of a long-awaited assault on a political structure built around an agricultural system rooted in the rural, small-town South and presided over by the small-town rich man.

Urban businessmen pushed for slum clearance, mass transit, and expansion of public facilities and services. In cities like Atlanta, Dallas, and Charlotte, business leaders became the reluctant advocates of racial moderation, and although their efforts seldom extended beyond the promotion of tokenism, the importance of their intervention was underscored by the ugly events in the 1950s and 1960s in Birmingham and New Orleans where the business elite failed to act vigorously enough, soon enough. The growth of the business and professional classes also paralleled the emergence of a viable Republican political alternative in the traditionally Democratic South.

Middle-class expansion clearly did bring some major changes to the South in the post–World War II period, but the impact of this expansion was not as far-reaching as had once been predicted. Business-inspired political reforms tried to create conditions favorable to efficient operation and rapid expansion of industrial and commercial enterprises. Government became more efficient and generally less corrupt but remained fiscally conservative and especially frugal in the social welfare arena. In Atlanta and elsewhere business boosters patted themselves on the back for urban renewal, freeway, and mass-transit projects, but their enthusiasm for low-cost public housing was lukewarm at best. Tax structures remained quite favorable to business and industry. The effective business tax rate stood below 60 percent of the national average, while the regressive sales tax was grossly overworked. The underutilization of tax potential left high-growth areas facing the dilemma of keeping taxes low enough to please business and industry without sacrificing the expanded services that a burgeoning population and revived economy seemed to demand.

The rise of two-party politics had been seen as a genuine plus for southern blacks because they seemed likely to represent the balance of power between the Democratic and Republican camps. As it emerged in the wake of the Goldwater campaign of 1964, however, southern Republicanism fused a business-oriented fiscal conservatism with an appeal to discontented white Democrats based on opposition to social programs and government intervention in behalf of blacks. The result was a virtual write-off of black voters by the GOP in the South and a reciprocal response that compelled southern blacks to work within a Democratic party whose white leaders regarded them with unease and whose white voters declined to support them when they appeared on the ballot. With the white middle class flocking to the GOP banner and working-class whites still unenthusiastic about a biracial political coalition, blacks failed to reap the anticipated benefits of two-party politics in the South.

In sum, the expansion of the business and commercial middle class fed many of the changes that marked the post–World War II years, but the growth of the middle class failed to spark the rapid social and political transformation many had predicted. The failure of the southern bourgeoisie to sponsor more dramatic change was due in large part to the region's lack of a unified, upwardly mobile working class capable of forcing the middle class to support more far-reaching reforms in the interest of maintaining overall stability in southern society. The South's working class remained largely unorganized and hesitant about class-oriented political action. Significant intergenerational progress left southern workers reluctant to challenge a system that they seemed to feel had rewarded them reasonably well. In the absence of pressure from below, the South's middle class was left to use its influence to create and maintain the economic and living conditions it preferred. Many social scientists had predicted that a bona fide middle class would demand drastic improvement in education and other public services, but white-collar southerners declined to sponsor such improvements, opting instead for the short-run enjoyment of the lighter demands placed on them by the South's conservative tax climate and minimal service and social welfare commitments.

The story of the development of commerce and industry in the South suggests the difficulty of predicting the outcome of one society's economic development on the basis of another's. For many years the Marxian perspective drew on the experience of Western Europe to identify certain inevitable social, cultural, and political concomitants of economic progress. American scholars buttressed this notion with the experience of the industrial Northeast, which they viewed as the epitome of the modern, enlightened liberal capitalist society.

Fascinated with the North's "success story," many American scholars underestimated the technological, demographic, and resource factors that accounted for the economic, social, and cultural differences that separated the North and the South. The South's persistence as a distinctive region was surprising largely because so many scholars and other observers had assumed that economic modernization had certain universal results. In reality, the South's experience with economic transformation, though distinctive, was hardly remarkable. No society has ever modernized economically in precisely the same fashion as another because the same set of social, cultural, historical, and economic circumstances is never in place in two truly distinct societies. The South of industrial parks, skyscrapers, and fast-food emporiums bore scant resemblance to the South of planters, slaves, or sharecroppers, but its elusive identity still reflected the influences of an intense and complex history and a cultural heritage that had not only withstood but had shaped its economic development.

See also AGRICULTURE: Country Store; / Boll Weevil; BLACK LIFE: Migration, Black; Workers, Black; HISTORY AND MANNERS: Great Depression; New Deal; World War II; LITERATURE: Agrarianism in Literature; / Caldwell, Erskine; Faulkner, William; O'Connor, Flannery; Wolfe, Thomas; MYTHIC SOUTH: New South Myth; / Agrarians, Vanderbilt; Mencken's South; POLITICS: County Politics; Ideology, Political; Partisan Politics; Taxing and Spending; RECREATION: Tourism; SCIENCE AND MEDICINE: Aerospace; URBANIZATION articles; WOMEN'S LIFE: Workers' Wives; Working Women

James C. Cobb
University of Alabama

Fred Bateman and Thomas Weiss, *A Deplorable Scarcity: The Failure of Industrialization in the Slave Economy* (1981); Reinhard Bendix, *Comparative Studies in Society and History* (April 1967); Dwight B. Billings, *Planters and the Making of a "New South": Class, Politics, and Development in North Carolina, 1865–1900* (1979); James C. Cobb, *Industrialization and Southern Society, 1877–1984* (1984), *The Selling of the South: The Southern Crusade for Industrial Development, 1936–1980* (1982); Pete Daniel, *Agricultural History* (July 1981), *Standing at the Crossroads: Southern Life in the Twentieth Century* (1986); Ronald D. Eller, *Miners, Millhands, and Mountaineers: The Modernization of the Appalachian South* (1982); Paul M. Gaston, *The New South Creed: A Study in Southern Mythmaking* (1970); David R. Goldfield, *Cotton Fields and Skyscrapers: Southern City and Region, 1607–1980* (1982); Emory Q. Hawk, *Economic History of the South* (1934); Broadus Mitchell and George S. Mitchell, *The Industrial Revolution in the New South* (1930); Wayne Mixon, *Southern Writers and the New South Movement, 1865–1913* (1980); Gerald D. Nash, *Journal of Southern History* (August 1966); William H. Nicholls, *Southern Tradition and Regional Progress* (1960); William N. Parker, *Southern Economic Journal* (April 1980); Roger L. Ransom and Richard Sutch, *One Kind of Freedom: The Economic Consequences of Emancipation (1977)*; Robert S. Starobin, *Industrial Slavery in the Old South* (1970); Jonathan M. Wiener, *American Historical Review* (October 1979), *Social Origins of the New South: Alabama, 1860–1885* (1978).

Antebellum Industry

The distinctive qualities of business and industry in the Old South have been obscured by the pervasive shadow of the plantation. The roar of a blast furnace or the din of a cotton factory were more likely to jar the southern imagination than to capture it, given the South's traditional idealization of itself as a pastoral paradise. Much less specialized than their northern peers, southern factory owners often blended their careers with those of planter and politician. Because they owned a disproportionate share of the region's surplus wealth, planters who themselves did not become businessmen often invested capital in the industrial expansion that did occur. If planters and businessmen managed and financed this expansion, the established social and economic imperatives predetermined that slaves would turn the wheels of industry just as surely as they picked the South's cotton. In fact, the use of slave labor was the most distinctive characteristic of southern industry.

Tobacco factories relied on slave labor almost exclusively. Two centers of production dominated the market, the eastern district of Virginia and North Carolina and the western district of Kentucky. In the eastern district many tobacco-factory slaves were hired hands; however, the employers also owned a sizable proportion of their workers. The number of slave workers—either owned or hired—at tobacco factories in the district was always large, totaling 12,843 by 1860.

Hemp production represented another leading industry of the Old South. During the 18th century Virginia hemp became a major staple from which osnaburg, linsey woolsey, linen, rope, and sail were manufactured. Many Virginia planters, such as Robert Carter of Nomini Hall, erected small establishments for the commercial production of cloth and, even in these first small transitionary shops between the homespun and the factory stages, slaves spun and wove the finished products. During the Revolutionary War numerous slaves worked at Virginia's public ropewalk and similar establishments. By the turn of the 19th century, however, the center of the American hemp industry had shifted westward to Kentucky, where the fiber became a staple of major importance. In fact, without hemp slavery might not have flourished in Kentucky. By the Civil War nearly 200 Kentucky hemp factories utilized 5,000 bondsmen. At the same time, another 2,500 slave operatives toiled in the hemp factories of Missouri.

Southern salt production was centered primarily in the Kanawha River Valley of western Virginia. The constant demand for this vital food preservative led to a steadily increasing capital investment in its manufacture. Between 1810 and 1850 the industry grew dramatically; and as production increased, the slave population grew to 3,140 in 1850. Because so few bondsmen resided in the district, surplus hands from eastern Virginia and Kentucky formed the backbone of the labor force at the Kanawha saltworks.

The South possessed an abundance of forest resources. Out of the Mississippi and Louisiana swamps black bondsmen chopped, trimmed, and rafted cypress to New

Orleans and Natchez, where still other slaves operated the steam-powered sawmills that could be found in most southern cities. These mills became sizable operations, frequently employing more than 100 slaves. Many black slaves disappeared into southern swamps for months at a time to cut wooden shingles and barrel staves. On the eve of the Civil War most of the 16,000 men who labored in the region's lumbering operations were slaves. Similarly, the naval-stores industry relied on blacks almost entirely. The industry was centered in the Carolinas, an area that produced over 90 percent of the nation's tar and turpentine in 1850. Large turpentiners such as Daniel W. Jordan of North Carolina utilized slave work forces totaling 200 or more in 1850. By 1860 the South's turpentiners worked 15,000 bondsmen.

Southern fisheries yielded a very important protein supplement to the diet of slaves and masters alike, and exports of the product reached significant, if yet undetermined, proportions. The famous traveler Frederick Law Olmsted observed that the fishing industry constituted a "source of considerable wealth." Like most industries, fisheries also employed "mainly negroes, slave and free." By 1861 upwards of 20,000 slaves operated fisheries in the region.

Although the South lagged far behind the North in internal improvements, the region's turnpikes, bridges, canals, levees, railroads, city sewers, and waterlines were all built by slave labor. Probably a total of 20,000 slaves toiled on the southern railroads during the antebellum period. Blacks also frequently worked in shipyards (Frederick Douglass being the most famous) and labored by the hundreds in southern brickyards and by the thousands in the small local gristmills that ground flour throughout the South. Commercial mills, such as the Gallego and Haxall mills (the world's largest) of Richmond, Va., operated with slave manpower. Throughout the South Carolina and Georgia Tidewater, hundreds of slaves toiled at the rice mills concentrated in that area. Likewise, Louisiana and Texas sugar mills worked bonded labor exclusively.

Few nonagricultural occupations in the Old South utilized slaves so universally and over such an extended period of time as the production of iron and the mining of coal. For a half century prior to the American Revolution, Maryland and Virginia iron dominated the colonial export market. Although the Chesapeake region lost its national preeminence after the Revolution, within the South it remained the most important single center for the production of iron. At least 65 Maryland and Virginia ironworks during the colonial era and about 80 during the antebellum period utilized thousands of slave laborers. Similarly, the eastern Virginia coalfield yielded the major supply of coal for homes and industries along the Atlantic Coast, from the development of the first commercial mine in the 1760s until the 1840s, when railroads made it economically feasible to develop the enormous reserves of bituminous coal in western Virginia and Pennsylvania. Until the late 1850s, however, when the Alabama and Tennessee fields assumed a minor importance, commercial coal mining in the South was confined almost exclusively to Virginia. A minimum of 40 coal companies in the Richmond Coal Basin employed several thousand slave workers.

With the growth of southern industry, slaveowners found themselves caught on the horns of a dilemma: which was the best form of labor, black slave or free white? More than simply a question of labor allocation, the ensuing debate reflected a mixture of economic, political, and social anxieties about the nature of southern society. Extensive industrialization threatened the planters' way of life. There was a relative loss of control over blacks in the more fluid industrial setting, but planters had even less control over a free white industrial proletariat. In practice, however, the perennial labor shortage forced southern manufacturers to employ any kind of available labor, and frequently that meant a "mixed" labor force of free whites, slaves, and free blacks.

See also AGRICULTURE: / Naval Stores; Tobacco Culture; SOCIAL CLASS: / Coal Miners; Timber Workers; Tobacco Workers

Ronald L. Lewis
University of Delaware

Ronald L. Lewis, *Coal, Iron, and Slaves: Industrial Slavery in Maryland and Virginia, 1715–1865* (1979); James E. Newton and Ronald L. Lewis, eds., *The Other Slaves: Mechanics, Artisans, and Craftsmen* (1978); Frederick Law Olmsted, *A Journey in the Seaboard Slave States, with Remarks on Their Economy* (1859); Robert S. Starobin, *Industrial Slavery in the Old South* (1970).

Black Business

See BLACK LIFE: Business, Black

Civil Rights and Business

The civil rights movement of the 1950s and 1960s represented a major departure in southern history. In accommodating itself to that movement's assaults on white supremacy, the South took a giant step toward moving into the mainstream of American society and culture. That step was possible because of an erosion in traditional values that had been under way in the South for three-quarters of a century.

Out of the trauma of defeat in the Civil War, southern businessmen and publicists forged a new ideology to guide the South in its quest to rejoin the national family. Promising to build a New South from the ashes of defeat, the sponsors of this program proposed an end to southern hostility toward the North, antipathy to industrialization, and the more virulent expressions of racism in the region. Although by no means a dominant mode of thought at the time of its formulation in the 1870s and 1880s, the New South ethic steadily gained adherents in succeeding decades. It blossomed into the business progressivism of the 1920–50 period, laying a foundation for the triumph of commercial and industrial values that was a major by-product of the civil rights movement.

W. J. Cash argued eloquently in *The Mind of the South* in 1941 that the Old South did not die with the Civil War; indeed, Old South values were strengthened and confirmed by that most tragic of American conflicts. Nor did these values succumb under the concerted assaults of the New South prophets, or even at the hands of those prophets' heirs, the business progressives. When Harry Ashmore proclaimed their demise in 1958 with his *Epitaph for Dixie*, many skeptics took a quick look across the South and declared it was not true.

The civil rights movement heralded the triumph of a new set of values in the South, values that had been stirring beneath the surface and growing imperceptibly for years, values that finally emerged dominant—to the surprise of many southerners—in the heat of the civil rights struggle. Simply stated, the desire for white supremacy at last yielded primacy in southern thought to the desire for progress.

The South's cities were the battlegrounds for most of the region's civil rights struggles, and the cities were dominated, as always, by small groups of economic or business elites. The degree to which these elites had accepted commercial and industrial values, or, in other words, the degree to which they were willing to place the goal of economic progress above the goal of maintaining white supremacy, determined the nature of their cities' responses to the civil rights assault on traditional southern race relations. From the quintessential New South city of Atlanta—the city that was "too busy to hate"—to the fine old southern community of St. Augustine—where violence and extremism abounded—the South's cities ranged across the spectrum from progressive to traditional. In most of these cities, after the dust had settled from the initial shock of disbelief and the occasional abdication of power to the extremists, the businessmen regained control of their communities and worked with varying degrees of enthusiasm to preserve their cities' progressive images. In city after city, from Norfolk to Tampa to Birmingham to Dallas, as the economic impact of yielding to extremism and violence in Little Rock and New Orleans became clear, the business elites threw their influence behind the desegregation efforts in an attempt to shield their cities from this very real threat to economic growth and progress. This is not to say that the businessmen became advocates of the civil rights cause or champions of racial equality; in most cases, in fact, the businessmen worked to yield a minimum of change and to maintain control in their own hands. They did, however, become public advocates of the dreaded changes in southern race relations, and they used their influence to guarantee acceptance of the changes in their communities.

Social scientists often note that the city has traditionally functioned as an agent of change and as a catalyst for reform, and the South's cities clearly performed these functions for the region in the 1950s and 1960s. Social scientists also argue that change must always be preceded by establishing the respectability of the proposed new ideas, and this was the function of the South's businessmen; in becoming reluctant advocates of the fundamental alteration of southern racial patterns that the civil rights movement demanded, the southern business elites led the way toward acceptance of a new pattern of thought in the South. Southern leaders would never have capitulated to such fundamental changes in their "way of life" if they had not believed—because of unremitting federal and activist pressures—that the changes were inevitable.

For a brief time, southern business leaders allowed themselves to believe they could maintain the traditional pattern of the South's race relations at the same time they pursued industrialization and progress; the civil rights movement made them realize they had to choose. In choosing, they consciously accepted a new ordering of their values and priorities, placing economic imperatives above racial ones. At last, the "common resolve indomitably maintained" that the South should preserve white supremacy yielded to a new resolve to share in the nation's prosperity. In short, the civil rights movement brought to fruition a revolution in the southern businessman's values.

See also BLACK LIFE: Freedom Movement, Black; LAW: Civil Rights Movement; MEDIA: Civil Rights and Media; URBANIZATION articles on cities

Elizabeth Jacoway
University of Arkansas at Little Rock

Harry Ashmore, *Epitaph for Dixie* (1958); Numan Bartley, *The Rise of Massive Resistance: Race and Politics in the South during the 1950s* (1969); Blaine A. Brownell and David R. Goldfield, *The City in Southern History: The Growth of Urban Civilization in the South* (1977); William Chafe, *Civilities and Civil Rights: Greensboro, North Carolina, and the Black Struggle for Freedom* (1980); Paul M. Gaston, *The New South Creed: A Study in Southern Mythmaking* (1970); Elizabeth Jacoway and David R. Colburn, eds., *Southern Businessmen and Desegregation* (1982).

"Colony," South as

From Jamestown to Fort Sumter there was a three-way conflict over exactly who would control the output of southern labor, white and black. The British crown attempted, sporadically, to gain control of the southern surplus of goods for itself or at least for its merchant friends. The commercial interests of the northern colonies, later states, wanted to control the surplus, whereas the southern planters thought it would be appropriate to keep it close to home. As long as the institution of slavery existed, the southern planters could explore strategies to maintain high prices partly through low labor costs. Once slavery and its political power were destroyed, it was hardly to be expected that a new system of high wages would replace it.

In this view, then, the colonial position of the South was first defined in the explicit establishment of the slave system. As in many "settler colonies" the planters of the South attempted to avoid the losses of unequal exchange with other areas and to keep the surplus of produced goods at home. In these efforts the planters were extremely sensitive to the pitfalls of a colonial status, they advanced the cause of the American Revolution, and they subsequently propounded an ideology of southern nationalism. Their ultimate failure left the South in the late 19th and early 20th centuries in its most clearly colonial situation.

The treatment thus far of the South as a colony helps to reconcile conflicting views of the colonial status of the region. On the one hand, those historians who have tended to label the South a colony have emphasized the striking sensitivity of southern leadership to symptoms of colonial status, e.g., low levels of urbanization, specialization in agriculture, and a poor system of transportation. On the other hand, those who have denied the colonial position of the South have pointed to the high levels of productivity and per capita income achieved in the mid-19th century. In the present approach to defining a colony, the relatively high per capita income of the South represented the remarkable success of the planter class in injecting itself between slave and market. The sensitivity of that class to symptoms of dependency underscored their awareness of the precarious role they were playing. Surely the most dramatic change in the distribution of the national income in the United States occurred between 1860 and 1880. The planters' success in the antebellum period represented a prodigious juggling act, and the Civil War seemed to expose their weakness.

It would be surprising if the southern worldview did not reflect the region's experience with colonial status. Indeed, some would argue that white southerners are far too engrossed in the colonial analogy. At least in part this is the result of the white southerner's direct observation of slavery. The awareness of slave dependency gave a uniquely southern meaning first to the revolutionary protest and subsequently to a broad spectrum of political-economic initiatives. The assertion of the South's colonial status explained, even if it did not justify, the origin and persistence of slavery for many southerners. At the same time, the denunciation of the colonial status created a way for white southerners to prove that they, unlike the slaves around them, would not tolerate a condition of dependency. In the late 19th century and the early 20th these themes, only slightly modified, became stock components of southern politics. As a result, even those most closely allied to northern interests were likely to use the colonial analogy. And, of course, this analogy lies behind the entire history of the states' rights debate, both its serious content and its cliché rhetoric. The idea of economic and political dependency has been continually present in both the formal and popular thought of the South.

In the 20th century the South has experienced a strong and surprisingly steady economic growth. This record has often been used to question the colonial designation. But the issue is not so much whether the South was dependent on the North circa 1900, which would be difficult to deny, but rather why its subsequent development was so different from a colonial area such as Latin America. Quite simply, some colonies are more favored than others. The South, because of location, political security, and political integration, was a logical first choice for capital seeking low wages. The process was anything but speedy. Nevertheless, it did occur, and the post–World War II economic development has resulted in a substantial rise in southern wages. Indeed, the difference in development between the now-advanced southern United States and the Third World economies of Mexico or Argentina tends to reveal just how essential geographic, political, and other noneconomic factors are in making the classical convergence of labor and capital to build a growing economy work.

For years the colonial analogy cited by southerners has been sustained by an awareness of their differentness from other Americans and a sense of being abused. With the ongoing homogenization of the regions of the United States, there is the temptation to consider this matter closed. But southern writers who have considered the South's role in the nation have always insisted that the desirable alternative to overly specialized regional economies is not a characterless collection of interchangeable parts. For all of their reactionary leanings and racist psychology, intellectuals like George Fitzhugh in the 19th century and the Vanderbilt Agrarians in the 20th century understood that parity in income between the regions is not the same as self-determination for all of them in the national context. Although unequal wages between North and South may have long been the cause of the colonial condition, equal wages now still may not establish full southern economic independence. The degree of independence possible in the modern technocratic society remains in question.

Joseph Persky
University of Illinois at Chicago

David Bertelson, *The Lazy South* (1967); Clarence Danhof, in *Essays in Southern Economic Development*, ed. Melvin Greenhut and W. Tate Whitman (1964); Arghiri Emmanuel, *Unequal Exchange: A Study of the Imperialism of Trade* (1972); George Fitzhugh, *Sociology for the South* (1854); John McCardell, *The Idea of a Southern Nation: Southern Nationalists and Southern Nationalism, 1830–1860* (1979).

Industrialization, Resistance to

In the South before the Civil War the prevailing philosophy held that a culture rooted in an agricultural economy and agrarian values was superior to any other. Although manufacturing, largely of the household variety, existed in the region on a level comparable to that of New England early in the 19th century, sectional differences soon began to emerge. Aided by the disruption of overseas commerce surrounding the War of 1812, the factory system began to expand in the North. By mid-century, northerners who 50 years before had harbored grave doubts about extensive industrialization viewed it as a positive good.

By and large, southerners underwent no such conversion. Here and there, a manufacturer such as William Gregg or an editor such as J. D. B. De Bow heralded the benefits of industrial progress. Yet economic factors seemed to offer no compelling reason to promote industrialization. If one might earn a high return on an investment in manufacturing, it was also possible to make good money in the more customary manner of investing in land and slaves. To many cautious and conservative southerners the proper study was still the improvement of agriculture.

Broad social concerns were more important than narrow economic considerations in the antebellum South's resistance to industrialization: the popular belief that a factory system might rely on the labor of black slaves and the accompanying fear that discipline would be diminished and the chance of rebellion enhanced; the suspicion that if white people were employed, their attachment to slavery might be weakened by adopting an industrial outlook; the conviction that industrial labor robbed a person of humanity and rendered him or her a wage slave of little social worth.

In the good society that antebellum southerners believed was theirs, the planter was the beau ideal. Rare indeed was the plantation master who left the land to become an industrialist. Among the plain folk, or yeomen, there were many who believed with Thomas Jefferson that "those who labour in the earth are the chosen people of God . . . his peculiar deposit for substantial and genuine virtue."

The Civil War worked a fundamental change in the attitude of many southerners. One of the region's most notable casualties was the agrarian ideal, severely wounded in the conflict. Union armies had hardly sealed the fate of the Old South before southerners began proclaiming a New South. For many of its leaders a New South meant above all else an industrialized South with an economy modeled on that of the victorious North.

As the ranks of industrial promoters swelled, recruited largely by urban editors such as Henry W. Grady, Henry Watterson, and Richard H. Edmonds, those southerners who resisted industrialization increasingly found themselves a besieged garrison, heavily outnumbered. Still, they fought hard, from the end of the war to the end of the century. Whether opposing industrialization in general as contrary to the best in southern tradition or denouncing the form of regional industrialization as wantonly exploitative, the critics often upheld the ideal of the South as an Arcadian alternative to a materialistic national culture. Yet, despite the best efforts of an orator such as Charles C. Jones, Jr., of editors such as Albert T. Bledsoe and D. H. Hill, of churchmen like Robert L. Dabney, J. C. C. Newton, and Benjamin M. Palmer, and of writers like Sidney Lanier, Mark Twain, George W. Cable, and Joel Chandler Harris, those who resisted industrialization were seldom able to effect action. Even the Populists of the 1890s, the strongest challengers of Gilded Age capitalism, could not reverse those policies of the New South establishment that encouraged reckless industrialism from which, the Populists argued, most southerners received little benefit.

As of 1900 the New South movement toward industrialization had failed to change the South's economic position relative to that of other parts of the nation. Notwithstanding a considerable increase in the number of factories, the South remained predominantly agricultural, with only a little more than 6 percent of its labor force working in manufacturing.

Undaunted, southern leaders early in the 20th century continued to pursue industry. Convinced that poverty, illiteracy, and disease were the result in great measure of the region's agricultural economy, many southern Progressives believed that industrialization would deliver the region from those evils.

A few southerners were not so sure. Here and there, voices were raised in dissent. In the pages of *Uncle Remus's Magazine* Joel Chandler Harris warned that the liabilities of industrialization might overbalance the assets. The historian William E. Dodd wondered what effect the educational philanthropy of northern industrialists would have upon the independence of southern academicians. The Reverend Alexander J. McKelway, a leader in the movement to prohibit labor by children in southern factories, became disgusted with what he called the mercenary New South.

The objections of the skeptics notwithstanding, the industrial tide continued to roll in, cresting in the boosterism of the 1920s. During the "dollar decade" resistance again came largely from bookish people whom practical men either ridiculed or ignored, although the work of some of those intellectuals would provide a telling critique of industrialism.

Many of the 12 men who contributed essays to *I'll Take My Stand: The South and the Agrarian Tradition* (1930) celebrated the yeoman ideal; all of them lamented the coming of an industrial society that massed individuals physically as it atomized them spiritually, reducing them to pawns of the marketplace. In more than 200 essays written throughout the 1930s, some of these Vanderbilt Agrarians continued to defend the South's agricultural society, charging that large-scale industrialization, by allowing too few people to own too much wealth and by creating a large, insecure proletariat, would rend the social fabric and encourage a politics dominated by either plutocrats or socialists. The Agrarians proposed that the pernicious influence of industrialism be contained by distributing land widely among the American people, by encouraging subsistence farming, and by establishing regional governments to insure that the South remain free of northern domination.

For a brief season in the 1930s some of the Agrarians' proposals received a hearing from public officials, but glimmerings of economic recovery rekindled the desire of southerners for more industry. Even before the Great Depression had ended, the booster spirit of the 1920s had reappeared in full force.

Propelled by World War II, manufacturing accelerated

throughout the South. The region was becoming more industrial than agricultural, with only one-third of its population still on the farm in 1945. After the war the attempts of promoters to "sell" the advantages of the South to industrialists elsewhere reached unprecedented proportions. Public efforts to attract industry were many and varied: local governments financed plant construction, sometimes in violation of state constitutions; tax levies were either abnormally low or nonexistent; advertising expenditures far exceeded the rest of the nation's; labor was kept cheap, docile, and unorganized; and state governments implemented "start-up" programs for new businesses. By 1960 southern cultural thought had come full circle. What distinguished the South from the rest of the nation was not the fervor of the region's resistance to industrialization but rather the intensity of its yearning for more of it. And the desire grew ever more ardent, as many southerners felt that, at long last, it was their turn to enjoy a fair share of American affluence.

Opposition either to the idea of further industrialization or to the form that it took in the South came largely from literary men, a tradition that had emerged with Lanier and Harris, continued through the Agrarians, Thomas Wolfe, and William Faulkner, and found contemporary expression in writers such as Wendell Berry, Harry M. Caudill, and James Dickey. Opposition came occasionally from scholars: a distinguished southern historian warned that if the region's past were any guide, the South would fail to profit from mistakes made by the North during the course of its industrialization and would suffer many of the same problems. Organized opposition also came from those directly victimized by the excesses of industrialism: residents of Appalachia and other parts of the South suffering displacement by the strip mining of coal; miners suffering from black lung; textile workers suffering from brown lung. Southerners generally became aware of a major cost of extensive industrialization—pollution. As industrial waste fouled the streams, coastline, and air of the South, state governments responded by creating agencies to control that refuse; each southern state had such a body by 1971. Moreover, chambers of commerce and development boards sometimes recruited industries more selectively. Occasionally, industrial projects were abandoned because it was feared that they would irreparably damage an area's ecology.

Critics of industrialization charged that all too often the regulators failed to enforce the inadequate restrictions that did exist, particularly against powerful offenders, and that a clean environment took second place to economic growth in the South's scale of values. Critics contended that the spillover from urban sprawl caused by industrialization was resulting in the overdevelopment of areas of great natural beauty such as the southern mountains. They questioned the promoters' claims that higher incomes and an unprecedented abundance of material goods meant perforce that life was better for most southerners. They pointed to data that suggested that the quality of life in the South had not been improved at all by industrialization and to other data that showed that for all the impressive gains the South had made, it remained, even in strictly economic terms, at the bottom of the nation, despite a hundred years of industrial promotion. Critics feared that if industrialization continued apace, the atomistic mass culture that characterized much of the rest of the country would overwhelm the organic folk culture that had long distinguished the South. Nevertheless, as the region entered the 1980s, those articulate southerners who resisted industrialization appeared to be the distinct minority.

See also HISTORY AND MANNERS: Jeffersonian Tradition; Populism; Progressivism; World War II; LITERATURE: Agrarianism in Literature; / Cable, George W.; Clemens, Samuel; Dickey, James; Faulkner, William; Harris, Joel Chandler; Wolfe, Thomas; MYTHIC SOUTH: New South Myth; / Agrarians, Vanderbilt

Wayne Mixon
Mercer University

Fred Bateman and Thomas Weiss, *A Deplorable Scarcity: The Failure of Industrialization in the Slave Economy* (1981); James C. Cobb, *The Selling of the South: The Southern Crusade for Industrial Development, 1936–1980* (1982); Paul M. Gaston, *The New South Creed: A Study in Southern Mythmaking* (1970); Wayne Mixon, *Southern Writers and the New South Movement, 1865–1913* (1980); Norris W. Preyer, *Georgia Historical Quarterly* (Fall 1971); Twelve Southerners, *I'll Take My Stand: The South and the Agrarian Tradition* (1930); Mary Ann Wimsatt, *Mississippi Quarterly* (Fall 1980).

Industrialization and Change

It is a persistent myth, running through popular and academic writing, that industry in the South is of recent origin. Some views attribute the birth of industrialism to the New South movement at the end of the 19th century, others to the notable rise of the Sunbelt South since World War II. Such truncated accounts of economic modernization ignore the deep roots and persistent patterns of southern industrial development. For at least 100 years, from the antebellum origins of the factory system to the collapse of the plantation system during the Great Depression, the shape and pace of industrial growth and social change in the region developed in relation to southern agriculture.

Slaveholding and the plantation system set limits on industrial and urban growth in the antebellum South. Antebellum cities developed as marketing and transportation centers for plantation products. Slaveholding inhibited the growth of domestic markets for manufactured goods, although some mass-produced items such as cheap clothing and farm implements were in demand. A limited number of antebellum industrial establishments developed in response to this market. Also, a significant number of factories, especially in the cotton textile industry beginning in the 1830s, were established to process plantation products. Many early factories were built by planters, some experimenting with the use of slave labor in manufacturing. In general, however, southern planters feared all-out industrialization, arguing that industry would compete with the labor needs of agriculture and threaten social control. Prior to the Civil War most agricultural profits were reinvested in land and slaves.

Perhaps the most rapid phase of industrial expansion in the South occurred from 1860 to 1864. Southern planters sponsored a thoroughgoing, nondemocratic, and state-controlled form of industrialization through confiscation and government investment in order to build a war machine. Under the auspices of the Confederate States of America, the South rapidly built ironworks, shipyards, textile mills, coal and iron mines, machine shops, clothing and food-processing plants, and munitions factories. The South lost the war but acquired significant industrial experience.

The extent and rapidity of industrial expansion after the Civil War, especially in the Piedmont states, led many observers to view the New South in an entirely different way. Despite stress on the demise of the planter class and the plantation system that characterized New South promotional literature, recent studies show that planters remained economically and politically dominant in many southern states at the end of the 19th century. Former slaveholders retained their land and reasserted labor control through sharecropping and the debt peonage system that effectively bound tenants to the soil. A culture of paternalism persisted well into the 20th century, influencing industrial patterns. In the Deep South, where cotton growing remained profitable and white labor was relatively scarce, planters continued to oppose all but minimal industrial growth. In contrast, planter-industrialists in the Upper South, who were faced with declining agricultural returns and drew on labor reserves of impoverished white farmers, accommodated industry to the postbellum agrarian social order.

Traditionally, the most important sector of southern industry has been cotton textile manufacturing. Here the influence of plantation agriculture was greatest as the ethos of the cotton plantation was extended into rural mill villages. The South's forced labor system of plantation agriculture was transferred to the industrial-capitalist sector at first primarily through all-white wage labor in the textile mills, but this was done with great strain, requiring immense measures of social control. The old culture of paternalism and the new logic of capitalist industrialism were tensely interwoven. Despite industrial expansion, individual textile plants remained small and personal. Southern workers were far more dependent on mill-village services than were northern workers. Mechanization permitted heavy reliance on unskilled labor, including children; isolation, paternalism, and racial exclusivity blunted occupational militancy. Low wages and long workdays enabled southern mill-owners to compete with northern manufacturers and eventually to draw northern textile firms and capital into the region.

The textile industry set the pattern for southern industrial culture, though work relations outside the planter-dominated textile industry developed contrasting characteristics. This was most notably true in tobacco manufacturing and coal mining. As proclaimed for the whole of postbellum industry, the tobacco industry was built by "new men" in North Carolina after the Civil War. By 1900 the Dukes and their associates in Durham had transformed a small craft industry into the South's largest industrial enterprise, the American Tobacco Company. Outside the sphere of planter interests, tobacco manufacturers employed large numbers of black workers. Realizing greater profits than the textile industry, they paid significantly higher wages and accepted unionization. The coal industry in Alabama and the southern Appalachians also employed black workers and, faced with an extraordinarily militant work force, was forced to accept unionization. Some of America's bloodiest labor struggles occurred in the mining communities of the southern highlands where, unlike the textile villages, corporate paternalism and wage pressures did not accord with the mountain heritage of agricultural self-sufficiency and with underground worker autonomy.

By the time of the New Deal, the plantation system was giving way in southern cotton fields to crop subsidies, mechanization, and federal welfare payments just sufficient to keep an unemployed labor supply on the land. Southern agriculture became increasingly capital intensive. Institutionalized paternalism lingered in the textile industry; but consolidation, rationalization, and, more rarely, industrial conflict became the rule. Demise of the nonwage system in agriculture intensified the drive for further industrialization. Southern towns competed to lure industrial plants to their localities by offering tax incentives, subsidies, and nonunion labor to corporate employers.

Since 1950 the South's rate of economic expansion has been greater than the national average. New growth sectors include agribusiness, defense industries, energy resources (oil and nuclear as well as coal, gas, and water), and "high-tech" research and development complexes such as North Carolina's Research Triangle Park. Educational and public services, along with race relations, have improved dramatically; but much industrial expansion is still dependent on a repressive, nonunion labor environment. (Research complexes such as North Carolina's Research Triangle Park encourage highly paid managerial and research personnel to migrate south without their unionized blue-collar work forces.) Average industrial wages in the region remain substandard. North Carolina and South Carolina, in the heart of the textile industry, rank as the two most heavily industrialized states in the United States. At the same time, however, they rank 49th and 50th in wage and unionization levels. Both the accomplishments and the failures of southern industrialization are evident in such statistics.

See also AGRICULTURE: Plantations; BLACK LIFE: Workers, Black; HISTORY AND MANNERS: Confederate States of America; MYTHIC SOUTH: New South Myth; SOCIAL CLASS: / Coal Miners; Company Towns; Textile Workers; Tobacco Workers

Dwight B. Billings
University of Kentucky

Dwight B. Billings, *Planters and the Making of a "New South": Class, Politics, and Development in North Carolina, 1865–*

1900 (1979); James C. Cobb, *The Selling of the South: The Southern Crusade for Industrial Development, 1936–1980* (1982); Ronald D. Eller, *Miners, Millhands, and Mountaineers: The Modernization of the Appalachian South* (1982); Eugene D. Genovese, *The Political Economy of Slavery: Studies in Economy and Society of the Slave South* (1967); Jay Mandle, *The Roots of Black Poverty: The Southern Plantation Economy after the Civil War* (1978); Jonathan M. Wiener, *Social Origins of the New South: Alabama, 1860–1885* (1978); C. Vann Woodward, *Origins of the New South, 1877–1913* (1951).

Industrialization in Appalachia

Although the southern mountain region has sometimes been said to be predominantly agricultural in its economy and rural in its culture, industrial development occurred there much as it did elsewhere in the United States and at the same times. During the antebellum period extractive and manufacturing activities developed as decentralized, locally capitalized, and locally managed enterprises, serving a local or regional market. During the late 1860s, in Appalachia as elsewhere in the nation, these same activities became increasingly centralized through the emergence of large-scale enterprises serving a national or international market and developed with nonlocal capital by nonlocal entrepreneurs. The impact of these changes on all aspects of American life was substantial, not least because they completed the transformation, begun by the transportation revolution of the 1820s, of the mixed American landscape into the characteristic American cityscape of our own time.

As early as the 1840s visitors to the southern mountains had noted the region's untapped resources in minerals, timber, and waterpower; its human resources of a hardworking, healthy population free of the taint of slavocracy and its ideology of leisure; the potential of its rivers to serve as arteries of commerce; and a landscape and climate conducive to the development of tourism. During the 1860s the list of apparent economic advantages of Appalachia came to include the availability of a rail system and the proximity of the region to major national markets. The list has remained intact, except that concrete roads and air transportation have been added. The persistence of these factors has made Appalachia seem an underdeveloped region of the nation even at times when economic development was most vigorous and the resources of the region—both natural and human—were being depleted most rapidly.

During the 1870s the first systematic cutting of the Appalachian hardwood forests was begun under the same impulse that spurred timbering in Wisconsin and Minnesota and then along the Pacific Coast when the eastern forests were exhausted. During the 1880s the first systematic extraction of Appalachian coal, iron, and nonferrous metals was begun under the same impetus that promoted the growth of mining in Pennsylvania, Minnesota, and the Rocky Mountain states. Beginning in the late 1880s a variety of manufacturing centers was established in Appalachia through the same drive that yielded the great industrial cities on the Great Lakes from Buffalo to Duluth. These manufacturing activities included steel production in Birmingham and Bessemer, Ala., and Middlesboro, Ky.; wood finishing and furniture production, most notably around Asheville, N.C.; glass production at several sites in West Virginia; and textile milling throughout the Piedmont.

Lumber mill, Tappahannock, Va., 1941

These developments in Appalachian timbering, mining, and manufacturing during the late 19th and early 20th centuries replicated the general pattern already evident in the American economy of a movement from small-unit production and local capitalization and control toward large-unit production and external capitalization and control. In these "new" industries, however, the conventional growth pattern with its normal impact on society and culture was compressed into a decade or less rather than spread over half a century or more. The social dislocations consequent to these developments in Appalachia, moreover, seem to have been more severe than the analogous dislocations felt in similar growth sites elsewhere in the nation.

Western timbering, for example, occurred largely on land acquired as part of the public domain. Much of the Appalachian timberland was owned, or at least claimed, by individuals who used portions of their holdings for agriculture. Many of these persons were displaced by the large timber companies, especially after the beginning of the 20th century, when large-scale forest preserves were established to ensure the profitability of future operations. Much of Pennsylvania coal mining, like most of western mining of all sorts, required deep-shaft mining and therefore yielded the establishment of permanent facilities for the industry and its workers, and a more or less permanent work force at a particular site. Most of the Appalachian coal mining around the turn of the century could be carried on as surface mining or by tunneling in short-term operations. When the mine played out, equipment, and often the buildings of a company town, were loaded on flat cars and moved to a new site. Appalachian coal mining thus tended to be a transient industry, worked by transients, many of whom had themselves been displaced by timber- or coal-company land purchases, who followed the job from place to place. The emergence of large-scale timbering and coal mining displaced those persons who had engaged in the same industries on a small scale, either by squeezing them out of the market or by denying them access to the natural resources they had previously exploited for their own profit, frequently as a complement to farming or some other activity. With no other source of income, these persons either were forced into subsistence farming or entered the labor market as transients.

With the notable exception of such "model" town developments as Pullman, Ill., most of the Great Lakes manufacturing of the late 19th century occurred in or near already established population centers. By contrast, almost all large-scale manufacturing in Appalachia developed on new sites and required a skilled labor force of in-migrants to the site, if not to the region. Although the real impact of massive immigration on the character of the Great Lakes cities cannot be denied, in Appalachia the development of manufacturing affected the rapid urbanization of a "rural" area previously dominated by small towns rather than cities, without displacing the system of social and political elites that dominated in courthouse and statehouse. At the same time, it brought to the region hundreds of thousands of new workers who were outsiders to the structure of local politics and society and who rapidly became either its victims, its rebels, or its exiles. That most of the manufacturing centers in Appalachia, as well as the short-lived timber towns and almost all the coal towns, were company owned and controlled exacerbated this situation by making impossible the local mediation of labor and social conflict that occurred in other urban areas during the Progressive era.

Turn-of-the-century tendencies toward vertical consolidation within industries, exemplified by the establishment of the Standard Oil Company, were extended horizontally across industries in Appalachia, yielding a pattern in which single corporations routinely controlled several industries at once—land development, timber and coal operations, transportation and marketing, and frequently all services needed to support the several sectors of their economic activity as well as those needed by their workers. Finally, although industrial development elsewhere in the nation generally has enriched all strata of the local economies by generating markets for additional goods and services, industrial development in Appalachia has often enriched only the local elites and has left the local economies highly vulnerable to the vagaries of market conditions.

See also BLACK LIFE: Appalachians, Black; ENVIRONMENT: / Appalachian Coal Region; Appalachian Mountains; ETHNIC LIFE: Mountain Culture; / Appalachians; FOLKLIFE: "Hillbilly" Image; MYTHIC SOUTH: Appalachian Culture; / Appalachian Myth; SOCIAL CLASS: Appalachia, Exploitation of; / Coal Miners; Company Towns; URBANIZATION: / Birmingham

Henry D. Shapiro
University of Cincinnati

Harry Caudill, *Night Comes to the Cumberlands: A Biography of a Depressed Area* (1962); Ronald D. Eller, *Miners, Millhands, and Mountaineers: The Modernization of the Appalachian South* (1982); Helen Lewis et al., *Colonialism in Modern America: The Appalachian Case* (1978); Gordon B. McKinney, *Southern Mountain Republicans, 1865–1900: Politics and the Appalachian Community* (1978); Henry D. Shapiro, *Appalachia on Our Mind: The Southern Mountains and Mountaineers in the American Consciousness, 1870–1920* (1978); David E. Whisnant, *Modernizing the Mountaineer: People, Power and Planning in Appalachia* (1979); John Alexander Williams, *West Virginia and the Captains of Industry* (1976).

Industrialization in Piedmont

Before 1830 the Piedmont region had a small but relatively diverse manufacturing sector, including woolen mills, foundries, and nail and rifle plants. But such promising industry dwindled with the expansion of the slave economy and concentration on the lucrative cash crop, cotton. By 1860 significant production was limited to a small number of cotton textile mills in towns such as Graniteville, S.C. The Civil War destroyed most of these modest gains, and manufacturing did not demonstrate any real momentum until the 1880s. But from that time forward cotton textile expansion and Piedmont industrialization became virtually synonymous. By the 1950s regional control of the textile industry had been wrested from New England and has continued since, with three-fourths of current output produced in the Piedmont states. Although northern competition was met successfully, that from foreign producers, especially Japan, growing since before World War II, has presented an increasingly serious challenge to Piedmont mills.

One interesting difference between Piedmont and New England textile development is the wholehearted community support that marked early southern efforts to establish local industry. Religious leaders as well as state and local officials joined farm populations in what has been termed a "crusade" in the 1880s to urge entrepreneurs to open mills. The collective hope was that heavy investment in cotton textiles would not only provide desperately needed jobs for local workers and effectively use the region's main crop, but would also draw producers in related manufacturing and service industries to locate in the region. In turn, rapid urbanization would create demand for locally made goods as well as for meat, dairy, and other food items, leading to a healthier local agriculture, less dependent on the fortunes of the cotton crop.

By the time investment in Piedmont manufacturing began on a broad scale, machinery, power, and transport technologies were far more advanced than they had been at the inception of northern and midwestern industrialization earlier in the 19th century. Of particular importance was the critical impetus given Piedmont progress by the widespread availability of cheap hydroelectric power after 1900. Investment by power companies in the region was stimulated initially by demand from cotton mills, but other labor-intensive light industry located there in part to benefit from its prevalence. Textile-finishing plants; wood, paper, and furniture factories; knit-goods, apparel, and later synthetic-fiber factories all became numerous.

Even the presence of excellent water and wood supplies, however, could not compensate for a relative regional scarcity of heavy mineral deposits such as coal and iron, which laid the foundation for investment in capital-intensive industry elsewhere. Although the chemical industry is strongly represented through artificial-textile production, the location of this component of the industry in the Piedmont may be viewed as a function of the ease with which cotton mills and equipment could be converted for artificial-fiber manufacture. Its introduction into the Piedmont was thus linked more to the presence of the older cotton manufacture than to the region's supply of skilled labor and natural resources. Traditionally, the region has not attracted heavy industry, although textile- and electrical-machinery producers have long clustered near cotton-mill centers. Nontextile manufacture has tended to resemble cotton manufacturing in demanding a large supply of cheap unskilled labor and by having few economies of scale in production.

The social environment of the rural Piedmont contributed also to the distinctive character of its industrialization experience. Because mills were constructed in rural areas, housing had to be provided for workers and their families. In early New England textile towns, company-owned boardinghouses served an unmarried female work force but disappeared with the advent of immigrant labor. The concentration of New England mills in a few locations contributed to the growth of large cities. Piedmont mill villages did not undergo such an evolution for the most part. The agrarian tradition so often noted by students of southern culture was reflected in mill dispersion over a wide geographical area. The relative isolation of mills strengthened a comprehensive paternalism on the part of owners that, in contrast to New England, persisted, assisting owners in effectively thwarting unionization efforts by keeping workers dependent and suspicious of outside organizers. In addition, a perennial threat facing white workers in this labor-surplus agricultural region was that black labor, heretofore excluded from cotton mills, would be hired to replace union sympathizers. Thus, mill villagers remained remarkably homogeneous in cultural and religious heritage, race, and ethnic origin. Although they have been described as a transient group, they usually migrated only to another mill village, similar to the last in social structure and economic opportunity. One outcome of textile dominance in Piedmont industrialization has been that alternatives to farm work for the large black population of the region have historically been few. Only in recent years have cotton mills opened all job categories to blacks.

By the time of Piedmont industrial expansion, textile technology, particularly in spinning, allowed extensive use of child labor. This practice characterized Piedmont mills long after it had been eliminated in New England. When states introduced age-and-hour legislation more widely after 1912, Piedmont standards were distinguished by their inadequacy. The laws were rarely enforced, so the employment of entire families continued, entrenching the mill villages in the southern landscape and delaying the development of a skilled and literate nonfarm labor force, an essential resource for the attraction of high-wage, capital-intensive industry.

Although the very rapid rate of growth of Piedmont cotton mills was a critical feature of its industrialization, it should not obscure the enduring rural character of the region. For example, although South Carolina was the preeminent southern textile state in 1900, fewer than 4 percent of its people were employed in manufacturing industry of any kind. The Piedmont's industrial pattern incorporated features of its rural heritage, and in this it contrasts with other regions where urbanization occurred relatively quickly as manufacturing expanded. Urban development in the Piedmont, on the other hand, has been more typically expressed through the rise of small towns than the growth of large cities. Scholars sometimes emphasize a tension between the agricultural and manufacturing sectors because the progress of one could threaten the labor supply of the other. But the development of Piedmont industry was accomplished by recruiting unemployed and underemployed white labor from local farms. The farm population increased for many decades at a rate more than sufficient to meet the demands of both farms and mills, so industrialization had a positive effect on the productivity of local farm labor.

As truck and automobile transportation became accessible in the 1920s, many Piedmont workers commuted to factories from farms. Such retention of a predominantly agricultural character in the long run helps to explain the slow progress of the Piedmont toward industrial diversification. The lack of skilled labor continued to dictate the type of manufacture located in the region. When considered with the related absence of essential large-scale economies, one can understand more fully the persistence of the region's low per capita income relative to other sections of the United States.

While certain distinguishing marks continue to characterize the industrial organization of the Piedmont today, there have been important economic changes in the region. World wars, larger and more sophisticated markets for southern goods, and foreign competition have lured more complex industry and have evoked a broader social and political awareness in the region. In small towns as well as in more urban areas, a middle class has developed with ambitions and lifestyles more American than regional. The peculiar industrialization experience of the Piedmont has had, nevertheless, a lasting impact on the cultural path of its society. The region's industrial structure has been molded not only by circumstances of time, technology, and resource utilization, but also by the character and social values of its populace.

See also SOCIAL CLASS: / Company Towns; Textile Workers

Mary J. Oates
Regis College

Fred Bateman and Thomas Weiss, *A Deplorable Scarcity: The Failure of Industrialization in the Slave Economy* (1981); Victor S. Clark, *History of Manufactures in the United States*, vols. 2 and 3 (1929); Victor R. Fuchs, *Changes in the Location of Manufacturing in the United States since 1929* (1962); Patrick J. Hearden, *Independence and Empire: The New South's Cotton Mill Campaign, 1865–1901* (1982); William N. Parker, *Southern Economic Journal* (April 1980); Anthony M. Tang, *Economic Development in the Southern Piedmont, 1860–1950* (1958); George B. Tindall, *Emergence of the New South, 1913–1945* (1967).

Military and Economy

Since the Civil War, and especially following World War II, the South has become the most powerful base of support for the continued American military buildup that has resulted in the rise of the *Military-Industrial Complex*, a term coined by Malcolm Moss and popularized by Dwight D. Eisenhower. More accurately, the complex should be styled the Military-Industrial-Technological-Labor-Academic-Managerial-Political Complex (MITLAMP). All sectors of modern technological society are involved in its functioning. Within the MITLAMP Complex are military and industrial beneficiaries, technical specialists, labor recipients of defense funds, academic elites, managerial elements, and political opportunists. These groups, especially in the South and in California, are reaping financial rewards and causing, particularly in the South, extraordinary cultural changes because of their continued support for the complex.

The origins of this regional military-economic relationship can be traced far back in southern history. Antebellum southern life and culture were conducive in many ways to an excessive spirit of militancy and extreme martial behavior. As the frontier moved westward in the 18th and early 19th centuries, southerners, like the frontiersmen of the Midwest, felt vulnerable to Indian uprisings. More importantly, as a slaveholding population, southern whites lived in constant fear of slave revolts, so the constabulary forces they organized patrolled the rural roads nightly. Many southerners, weaned on the novels of Sir Walter Scott, were obsessed with a sense of honor. John Hope Franklin, W. J. Cash, and others have suggested this martial spirit of the South helped it face the consequences of secession with confidence, if not eagerness.

Following the Civil War southern males were even more obsessed with proving their manhood and, above all, regaining their lost sense of honor. Combine this fact with the existence of poverty and extreme racism in the region and it is small wonder that southerners, white and black, have been attracted in large numbers to the military establishment, in times of both peace and war. The South has more enlistees serving in the armed forces than any other region. No other section of the country has a greater percentage of personnel in the armed forces on a per capita basis. The report of the Secretary of Defense for Manpower Reserve Affairs and Logistics (1981) showed that in 1980, 35.7 percent of the enlistees in the professional armed forces were natives of the South, while southerners constituted 33.7 percent of the nation's population.

The subsequent economic benefits for the region are obvious. Southerners in the armed forces throughout the world are fueling the southern economy with allotment checks deposited in local banks. Moreover, although military personnel serve in many places during their careers, seldom do they escape service at some southern camp or station. This is especially true in the case of the army. Twenty-four of 46 major posts are located in the South. In 1980, 48 percent of all service people were located in southern states and the District of Columbia. Moreover, colonies of military retirees exist along the Florida coastline and in San Antonio and El Paso, Tex.

The impact of military expenditures on the southern economy is immense. A total of 39.5 percent of all Department of Defense dollars ($50,091,677,000 of a total budget of $127,135,626,000) was spent in the South in fiscal year 1980. The one-party system combined with the rule of seniority enabled southerners to dominate the House and Senate Armed Services Committees and direct this heavy expenditure of defense funds to the South.

In addition, of the $10,696,556,000 allocated to the Department of Energy, $554,350,000 was expended in the South in conducting nuclear weapons activities for the Department of Defense. Further, National Aeronautics and Space Agency funds, closely linked to defense needs, are primarily allocated to southern states and the Dis-

World War II naval vessel, the USS Charleston

trict of Columbia. The total NASA budget in 1980 was $5,365,761,000; $2,169,012,000 of this was spent in the South. Finally, Veterans Administration expenditures in the South amounted to $8,635,108,000 of an agency total of $22,106,822,000. Thus, the entire amount of military money spent in southern states and the District of Columbia in 1980 was $61,450,147,000. If one employs a conservative multiplier effect in order to determine the number of *real* dollars spent in the South by the military in 1980, the amount equals $122,999,822,000.

The vast wealth of the MITLAMP Complex is a significant, if not the significant, factor in explaining the economic boom that has taken place in the South since the 1950s. Military money constitutes close to 10 percent of the total income of the South ($667,400,000,000) and 33 percent of all federal expenditures in the South ($183,000,000,000). However, the money is not equitably distributed. While $2,752,509,000 is spent in Alabama and $12,066,000,000 is prorated to Texas, only $500,116,000 is expended in West Virginia, the least rewarded of the southern states.

Cultural changes are wrought by such vast military expenditures. In cities and towns where industries and military installations traditionally reflected racist views, employment and personnel policies have become more equitable. The white South has been forced to reconsider its racial attitudes as a consequence of the Supreme Court decisions and the civil rights legislation of the 1950s and 1960s enforcing equal employment opportunities for blacks in southern industries under contract to the federal government.

In addition, many northerners, including unskilled workers and skilled managers, technologists, engineers, and scientists, have moved South in search of the economic opportunities provided in the Sunbelt, further changing the character of life, especially in cities like Dallas and Houston. Thus, large military expenditures, producing social as well as economic results, must be considered important factors in the recent growth and development of the South.

See also HISTORY AND MANNERS: Military Bases; Military Tradition; MYTHIC SOUTH: Militant South; SCIENCE AND MEDICINE: Aerospace; VIOLENCE: Honor

Alvin R. Sunseri
University of Northern Iowa

W. J. Cash, *The Mind of the South* (1941); John Hope Franklin, *The Militant South* (1956); *Geographical Distribution of Federal Funds in Summary, Fiscal Year, 1980*; Alvin R. Sunseri, in *War, Business and American Society: Historical Perspectives on the Military-Industrial Complex*, ed. Benjamin Franklin Cooling (1977); U.S. Department of Commerce, *Statistical Abstract of the United States: 1981* (1982); *U.S. Government Selected Manpower Statistics, Fiscal Year 1981*.

New South

See MYTHIC SOUTH: New South Myth

Sunbelt South

"Sunbelt South" and, more generally, the "American Sunbelt" are media creations designed to give coherence and meaning to the dramatic population growth and political upheavals that have occurred in the South and Southwest since 1940. Coined by political analyst Kevin P. Phillips in his book *The Emerging Republican Majority* (1969), the concept of "Sun Belt" (or "Sunbelt") lay dormant and ill-defined until the mid-1970s, when a combination of census reports on migration, the growing Republican potential in the South and West, and the presidential candidacy of Georgian Jimmy Carter brought the lower tier of states to public attention. Although he did not use the term *Sunbelt*, journalist Kirkpatrick Sale, in *Power Shift: The Rise of the Southern Rim and Its Challenge to the Eastern Establishment* (1975), alerted northern intellectuals to the emergence of the nation's "Southern Rim" as a new center of power. Soon the *New York Times*, the *Wall Street Journal*, *Fortune*, and news weeklies discovered the region. *Time*, prompted by Carter's nomination, devoted a special issue (27 September 1976) to "The South Today." Yet definitions remained unclear. Nearly all observers included in the Sunbelt the area below the 37th parallel, along the northern borders of North Carolina, Tennessee, Arkansas, Oklahoma, New Mexico, and Arizona and that in California below Fresno. Some added Virginia, Kentucky, southern Nevada, and northern California, while others cautiously included the slow-growing Mississippi Delta. All agreed, however, on the general concept of an expanding southern and southwestern region with a casual and inviting lifestyle, a favorable business climate, and conservative politics increasingly inclined to Republicanism.

For roughly five years the press showered the nation with promotional reports of "the good life" in the Sunbelt that was seemingly unattainable elsewhere. By the early 1980s, however, the northern-based national media became less enchanted and focused reports on crime in Miami, the lack of services in Houston, and the high cost of living in southern California. By 1982 *Newsweek* saw a "Dark Side of the Sunbelt," and the *New York Times* began a follow-up on its glowing 1976 series under the headline: "Sun Belt Having Difficulty Living Up to Its Promise." As a media creation, the concept of the Sunbelt faced severe editing.

If the Sunbelt South was partly a mythic image, it did reflect real demographic and economic trends. Between 1940 and 1980 the number of Americans living below the 37th parallel increased by 112 percent, whereas the combined populations of the Northeast and Midwest rose by only 42 percent. Southern California, Florida, and Texas each gained over 7.5 million new residents. By 1980 the populations of the Los Angeles–Long Beach, Dallas–Fort

Worth, Houston, and Atlanta metropolitan areas had grown to more than 2 million each, and 18 Sunbelt metropolises (including 11 from the former Confederate states) had joined the nation's 50 most populous metro regions. This growth was especially strong during World War II, the 1960s, and the early 1970s.

Most commentators attributed this increase to economic development fostered by federal and state aid to business, and to changing American lifestyles. Beginning with World War II, Washington poured enormous sums into the South and West for the construction and maintenance of military installations and the production of modern weaponry. From Miami to Mobile to Monterey, these defense bases and plants lured wartime migrants who came and stayed. Cold War and Vietnam expenditures, protected by powerful congressional leaders such as L. Mendel Rivers (S.C.), John Stennis (Miss.), Edward Hebert (La.), and John Tower (Tex.), have guaranteed millions of Sunbelt jobs. Nondefense spending, shared more equally with the other states, also boosted Sunbelt growth through funding for items ranging from construction projects to transfer payments. State governments scrambled for these federal dollars but also for new industries and their private payrolls. Beginning with Mississippi's plan to "Balance Agriculture with Industry" (1936), southern and southwestern government and civil officials attracted branch plants and encouraged new operations with promises of low costs for land, buildings, equipment, labor, and taxes, plus expanding markets. Packaged as, in the Texas vernacular, a "good bidness climate," these appeals emphasized tax concessions and weak labor unions—by-products of southern prejudice and right-to-work laws. "Business Loves the Sunbelt (and Vice Versa)," proclaimed a 1977 *Fortune* article.

A warm and inviting climate encouraged this mutual attraction and convinced many businessmen to move South. Winter temperatures in the 60s and 250 to 350 days of sunshine annually made for an informal, outdoor-oriented lifestyle, equally appealing to retirees in Fort Lauderdale, top executives in Atlanta, and oil-field workers in western Oklahoma. Postwar affluence gave many northerners the wherewithal to relocate, and many moved to improve their quality of life.

This mighty demographic shift has triggered significant economic and political realignments. Economic power is drifting south and west, where Miami, New Orleans, Houston, and Los Angeles are now international trade centers, and Atlanta and Dallas service substantial regional markets. The Sunbelt is becoming dominant in energy development, technical innovation, tourism, and many categories of agribusiness. In national politics the region is already flexing its new muscles. The 1970 census was the first to give the South and West a majority in the electoral college, but every elected president since 1964 has come from the southern rim. In 1964 and 1980 voters chose among or between Sunbelt candidates. In 1940 only 121 congressmen came from below the 37th parallel, but the 1980 census awarded the region 145 seats, a gain of 12 since 1970. Drawing support from newcomers and old-line Democrats upset over civil rights and federal spending priorities, Republicans won many of the seats. Some were conservative ideologues, but most were pragmatic business types. Republicans swept west to east, from coastal areas to the inland and into the suburbs to win national and statewide offices barred to them a generation earlier. Blacks and Hispanics, encouraged by the civil rights movement and federal support, integrated the Democratic party and won local races. In the cities, once-entrenched commercial elites began to share power with young business promoters, suburbanites, and neighborhood and minority groups. The degree of sharing has varied, from almost none in Dallas–Fort Worth to an almost total power shift in Atlanta, where a black majority now rules.

The probusiness, laissez-faire attitude of the region has allowed problems, especially those related to density, to multiply unchecked; but so far crime, poor schools and services, and low wages have not destroyed the Sunbelt's appeal. Eventually, Sunbelt governments will have to expand their activities, but their constituents are in no hurry. As one observer claimed of archetypical Houston, it has a 19th-century outlook with 20th-century technology. In the meantime, migrants continue to stamp their approval on the region, for although lessening economic advantages and higher relocation costs have slowed Sunbelt growth in the early 1980s, the march is still southward.

See also HISTORY AND MANNERS: Military Bases; Military Tradition; MYTHIC SOUTH: New South Myth; POLITICS: National Politics; URBANIZATION: Urban Growth; / Atlanta; Dallas; Houston; Miami; New Orleans

Richard M. Bernard
Marquette University

Carl Abbott, *The New Urban America: Growth and Politics in Sunbelt Cities* (1981); Richard M. Bernard and Bradley R. Rice, eds., *Sunbelt Cities: Politics and Growth since World War II* (1983); James C. Cobb, *The Selling of the South: The Southern Crusade for Industrial Development, 1936–1980* (1982); David C. Perry and Alfred J. Watkins, eds., *The Rise of the Sunbelt Cities* (1977); Kevin P. Phillips, *The Emerging Republican Majority* (1969); Kirkpatrick Sale, *Power Shift: The Rise of the Southern Rim and Its Challenge to the Eastern Establishment* (1975); Bernard L. Weinstein and Robert E. Firestone, *Regional Growth and Decline in the United States: The Rise of the Sunbelt and the Decline of the Northeast* (1978).

Atlanta as Commercial Center

Atlanta's role as the commercial center of the Southeast began in the late 1830s when the Georgia Legislature decided to build a railroad from the Chattahoochee River northwesterly to Chattanooga, Tenn. Atlanta grew around the terminus of this Western & Atlantic line. By the mid-1840s two private lines had arrived, and Atlanta had connections to Augusta and Savannah. Eventually, 15 rail lines would converge on the "Gate City" as she far surpassed her state rivals.

During the Civil War Atlanta served as a major manufacturing and supply point for Confederate forces until General William Sherman's troops destroyed it in 1864. Atlanta's location, railroads, and spirit guaranteed its phoenix-like revival from the ashes of war. In 1869 the city became the state capital, and in 1871 the chamber of commerce was formed. Boosters organized international trade expositions in 1881, 1887, and 1895. The Cotton States and International Exposition of 1895 drew 800,000 visitors to the ambitious city of 75,000. Atlanta had become the principal distribution center for the country-store economy of the South.

The city passed the 100,000 threshold shortly after the turn of the century. In the 1920s the chamber of commerce sponsored the "Forward Atlanta" movement, which attracted nearly 800 new businesses with over 20,000 employees. This was also the take-off decade for Coca-Cola, Atlanta's most famous business. Although the city had some important factories, manufacturing always lagged behind the trade and services sectors in a diversified employment picture.

As World War II began, Atlanta fell behind New Orleans and ranked close to Memphis and Birmingham in size. By 1980, however, metropolitan Atlanta had 2 million residents and far outstripped these regional competitors. The prewar base had been built on railroads, distribution, and state government. In the postwar era, Atlanta built on that foundation and became the preeminent southeastern center for air transportation, trucking, corporate offices, and federal government activities. The local power structure believed that a moderate approach to race relations would be good for the business climate, and Atlanta forged its image as the "City Too Busy To Hate." In the 1960s boosters launched another "Forward Atlanta" campaign. This one brought urban renewal, a gleaming skyline, and the Southeast's first major-league sports team, the Braves in baseball. Georgia could not match the phenomenal population growth of Florida, but none of the Florida cities could challenge Atlanta's commercial dominance of the eastern third of the Sunbelt. As the executive secretary of the chamber of commerce noted in 1976, "We found out that while Atlanta was trying to be a regional city, it had become one of a handful of national cities."

See also URBANIZATION: / Atlanta

Bradley R. Rice
Clayton Junior College

Franklin Garrett, *Atlanta and Environs: A Chronicle of Its People and Events* (1969); Truman A. Hartshorn, *Metropolis in Georgia: Atlanta's Rise as a Major Transaction Center* (1976).

Banking

During the colonial period banking and financial intermediaries, except for general fire and life insurance companies, were almost nonexistent. By 1781 the situation was beginning to change with the establishment by Robert Morris of the Bank of North America and the later creation of the First Bank of the United States.

Under Alexander Hamilton's guidance, Congress chartered the First Bank of the United States (1791–1811) to provide a uniform currency and enhance the stability of the economy. Although the First Bank was not completely successful in achieving these objectives, it did provide financial services to the South through its branches in Baltimore, Charleston, New Orleans, Norfolk, Savannah, and Washington, D.C. In 1811, with political opposition growing, Congress refused to renew the bank's charter. The financial difficulties that resulted from the War of 1812 convinced Congress, however, to create another central bank, the Second Bank of the United States (1816–36). Under the leadership of Nicholas Biddle, the Second Bank operated more consciously as a central bank in its attempts to provide for economic stability and as a way of controlling state banks. However, the Second Bank also encountered opposition, especially from President Andrew Jackson, who convinced Congress not to renew the bank's charter.

Centralized banking was a highly important, if short-lived, development for the growing American economy. Another state-supported form of banking developed thereafter. With the demise of the Bank of North America in 1784, both New York and Massachusetts incorporated banks, thereby setting a precedent other states followed.

In the South the development of banking largely paralleled the financial development of the North. Southern states chartered a large number of private commercial banks and a smaller number of state banks. However, there were differences. Savings banks did not become important in the South because the region did not possess the large middle class that provided the necessary funds for such banks in the East. In the South "property banks" were unique in that their purpose was to attract foreign capital for agriculture and internal improvements, using real estate as collateral for notes. The liquidity of southern banks was low and bank runs were disastrous, causing southern state legislatures to be the mainstay of these banks.

The 1830s was a critical decade for southern banking. President Jackson's attack on the Second Bank in the early 1830s reduced its influence over other financial institutions, leading to a rapid expansion of banks throughout the nation. However, the southern agricultural depression from 1837 to 1843 retarded this growth and even forced many southern banks to close.

In the aftermath of these financial failures most states adopted regulations, especially stricter reserve requirements, to promote sounder banking practices. The most famous such action was Louisiana's Bank Act of 1842 providing for a specie-backed currency. By providing specie reserves as a percentage of bank notes issued and thereby limiting the amount of notes, Louisiana successfully stabilized its banking system. Several other southern states during the 1840s and 1850s adopted the free-banking system outlined in the Free Banking Act of New York. In some cases, like Louisiana, the free-banking system worked well.

The turbulence of the 1830s and the political hostility toward banks in the 1840s were replaced by cautious expansion of southern banking in the 1850s. Reflecting the growth of the southern economy, a period of sustained prosperity appeared imminent, until the outbreak of the Civil War. In 1861 many southern banks began to suspend the convertibility of their notes into gold. In the same year, southern banks subscribed heavily to the first Confederate loan, thereby losing much of their specie. During the Civil War the specie that the Confederate States of America was able to obtain came largely from Britain and the continent. With limited ability to tax and to borrow, the CSA used the printing presses to pay for the war effort.

Between January 1861 and January 1864 the South's money supply increased over 11 times. Bank notes and deposits increased less than threefold, because southern commercial banks drastically raised their reserve ratios in anticipation of mass withdrawals triggered by the approach of Union troops. Although this behavior moderated the increase of the money supply somewhat and provided some protection for individual banks, many southern banks did not survive the Civil War. And the aftermath of the war was even worse.

The major feature of the years 1865 to 1913 was the South's financial underdevelopment; banking services were severely limited relative to those in other regions. The South, in fact, was the last region to be integrated into a national capital market. Most economic historians attribute this situation to the banking structure that resulted from the National Banking Acts of the Civil War years. This legislation limited national banks in the South by restricting agricultural loans and imposing relatively large capital requirements. Its tax on state bank notes, moreover, hindered the development of state banks. The result was that many banks operated in a noncompetitive market, a situation that limited the amount of bank credit available and raised interest rates. Because of local bank monopolies, country stores began channeling credit to borrowers, with serious long-run ramifications for the structure of southern agriculture.

After 1880 interest-rate differentials declined as such institutional changes as the spread of commercial paper and a reduction of the money power of local banks took place. Local monopoly power of southern banks declined, in part because of the 1900 Gold Standard Act, which formally put the nation on a gold standard and reduced minimum capital requirements for national banks, thereby making it easier for small banks to become national banks.

The next major change in the nation's banking system was the establishment of the Federal Reserve System (FRS) in 1913. The FRS was designed to prevent financial panics by acting as a lender of last resort or, in other words, by operating as a central bank. However, the original legislation also attempted to diffuse power geographically by establishing 12 regional or district banks, which were to play a role in formation of monetary policy. Federal Reserve Banks in the South were located in Atlanta, Dallas, and Richmond. The framers of the legislation hoped that the regional banks would be more aware of and concerned with the problems of banks within their region than would one central bank in New York or Washington, D.C.

The establishment of the Federal Reserve System did not solve southern banking problems, as witnessed by the difficult experiences of southern banks in the 1920s. Indeed, the Roaring Twenties saw the South experience a disproportionate number of bank failures when measured either by the number of bank closings or by deposits. The high rate of bank failure was probably caused by the long agricultural depression beginning in the early 1920s, the large number of small state banks, lax supervision, and incompetent management.

The Depression of the 1930s was extremely traumatic for the southern banking industry, as it was for the nation's banking industry generally. From 1929 to 1934 assets of southern banks fell from $7 billion to $4.7 billion, a decline of about 33 percent, compared with 21 percent in the rest of the country. Southern assets reached the 1929 levels only a decade later.

Although after World War II the South's banking structure grew to more closely resemble the national system, a larger percentage of southern banks were, in 1945, still small, nonmember state banks. They were also nonpar, not paying the full value of checks but deducting a service charge from the face value of each check. More importantly, southern banks still held large net deposits in banks outside the region. After 1945 the substantial economic growth that the South experienced caused rapid expansion in southern banking as well.

During the 1950s all southern states except the unit bank states experienced a reduction in the number of banks and a rapid expansion of branch banks. This was due to the increased urbanization of the South and the concurrent growth of suburbs. In the 1960s and 1970s bank expansion was fostered in such states as Georgia, Texas, and Virginia through the device of bank holding companies. Major financial centers developed in Atlanta, Dallas, Houston, and Miami, while North Carolina National Bank Corporation and Wachovia Corporation became important regional banks.

During the 1960s the major southern banks rapidly expanded by following the national trend of increased utilization of liability management techniques. Rather than only managing assets within a given liability structure, southern banks began aggressively to pursue additional deposits in order to obtain a target asset growth. The period of rapid and often reckless expansion ended abruptly in 1974 when the real estate market collapsed. Because so much construction was going on in the South, southern banks were more affected by this collapse than were northern banks. Banks such as North Carolina National, Atlanta's Citizen and Southern, and Florida's Flagship Banks wrote off millions of dollars of bad loans. Since then, cautious growth on the long-term pattern of Wachovia has been the dominant trend. Although such stringent credit practices curtail asset growth, they do provide banks with an increased ability to survive economic difficulties.

Not all modern southern bankers are cautious, however. Bert Lance was forced to resign as President Jimmy Carter's budget director because of repercussions from his loose, small-town Georgia credit practices. Tennessee banking magnate Jake Butcher, a Democratic candidate for governor in 1978 and the driving force behind the 1982 Knoxville World's Fair, used to claim that he rose from southern rural poverty to financial and political power the honest way—by borrowing. In 1983, however, his financial empire began to unravel when the Tennessee Banking Commission shut down Butcher's flagship, the United American Bank of Knoxville, a $760 million institution. This fourth largest U.S. commercial bank failure since the 1930s resulted from what the commission cited as "large and unusual loan losses," many of them to Democratic politicians and the bank's directors.

The emphasis on international banking will likely continue in the near future, and the specter of interstate banking looms over all banks. Some southern bankers are urging an interim step of regional banking in order to allow southern banks to acquire the time and resources needed before having to compete with external money-center banks. Although this proposal has not yet been enacted and implemented, it does indicate the desire of southerners to avoid increased control by nonsouthern banks. No matter what the outcome of these structural changes, the 1980s will not be a decade in which a lack of financial resources will hinder economic development. Instead, southern financial institutions have progressed to the point where they can now provide the funds necessary for further economic expansion.

Michael V. Namorato
University of Mississippi

R. Stanley Herren
North Dakota State University

Lance E. Davis, *Journal of Economic History* (September 1965); Thomas P. Gavan, *Banking and the Credit System in Georgia, 1810–1860* (1978); George D. Green, *Finance and Economic Development in the Old South: Louisiana Banking, 1804–1861* (1972); Bray Hammond, *Banks and Politics in America: From the Revolution to the Civil War* (1957); Emory Q. Hawk, *Economic History of the South* (1934); Calvin B. Hoover and B. U. Ratchford, *Economic Resources and Policies of the South* (1951); John A. James, *Journal of Interdisciplinary History* (Winter 1981); George Macesich, *Commercial Banking and Regional Development in the United States, 1950–1960* (1965); Fritz Redlich, *The Molding of American Banking: Men and Ideas* (1951); Richard Sylla, *Journal of Economic History* (December 1969); Elmus Wicker, *Journal of Economic History* (September 1980).

Bulldozer Revolution

Historian C. Vann Woodward has suggested that the most apt "symbol of innovation" in the modern South is the bulldozer. "The roar and groan and dust of it greet one on the outskirts of every Southern city," he wrote in a 1958 essay on "The Search for Southern Identity." The mule had been the popular symbol of the South's traditional agricultural economy, but the giant earthmoving machine in the post–World War II period had become central to the industrial revolution in the region. The bulldozer symbolized the revolution "in its favorite area of operation, the area where city meets country; in its relentless speed; in its supreme disregard for obstacles, its heedless methods; in what it demolishes and in what it moves."

The bulldozer made possible the rapid and concentrated urbanization of the South in the 1940s and 1950s, and it facilitated the clearing of land for suburban development in the same period. Southerners and others traveling through the region became familiar with the giant machine on the landscape. It made possible the transforming work of the Tennessee Valley Authority, the Corps of Engineers, and the construction crews building interstate highways. The bulldozer swept away sharecroppers' shacks to make way for Sunbelt shopping malls.

Robert G. LeTourneau was perhaps the most notable bulldozer businessman in the South. Born in Vermont and raised in Minnesota, LeTourneau spent his young adulthood in California, working as an automobile repairman. A natural inventor, he developed tools for sale to contractors and opened a small factory in Stockton, Calif., in 1935 and another one later in Peoria, Ill. His southern operations were at Toccoa, Ga., Longview, Tex., and Vicksburg, Miss. In the latter case, the Warren County Chamber of Commerce purchased much of the land LeTourneau needed in order to encourage him to come to the site eight miles south of Vicksburg. LeTourneau's factories made much of the earthmoving equipment used by the armed services during World War II. By 1952 the Mississippi plant alone produced 22 types of heavy machinery used in 44 states and many foreign nations.

LeTourneau sold his earthmoving business in 1953 for $31 million to Westinghouse Air Brake Company. He retained, however, his factories in the South and converted them to the production of offshore oil rigs and missile-loading transport machinery. LeTourneau reentered the bulldozer business in 1958. Born out of the region, LeTourneau came to live in the South and "adopted" it. He was an evangelical who found the region a congenial spot. Known as "God's businessman," he once observed that his life had "three planks—speed, the welding torch, and the Bible." This southern earthmover provided financial support for the Billy Graham revivals in the early 1950s, and Graham helped dedicate and bless LeTourneau's work.

Charles Reagan Wilson
University of Mississippi

Longview, Tex., *News-Journal* (1 January 1953); Vicksburg, Miss., *Evening Post* (26 November 1942); *Wall Street Journal* (28 January 1957); C. Vann Woodward, *The Burden of Southern History* (1960).

Chain and Specialty Stores

After the Civil War the rural South witnessed the development of country or general stores. Mail-order houses such as Sears, Roebuck and Company caused socioeconomic rumblings, but the real merchandising revolution was the advent of specialty stores—which sold one product (such as shoes) rather than a variety of products—and their spread as chains under common ownership. These new stores grew in number during the early 20th century until by the 1920s they held a sufficiently large share of the market to feed the growing cult of consumerism through the promise of standardized goods and lower prices made possible by economies of scale. But if there was the prospect of a better standard of living, there was also the threat—or so it seemed to some—of the destruction of local proprietorship and community involvement in stores held by absentee owners from the North. The issue of regional versus national culture was expressed in populist rhetoric in the context of an urban-industrial progressive spirit.

By the 1930s—in the face of the Great Depression—numerous attempts were made across the nation to regulate chain stores by means of municipal and state taxation and fair-trade laws. Many of these measures originated in the South, and some of the most significant Supreme Court cases concerning chain-store regulation involved southern states (*Stewart Dry Goods* v. *Lewis* [Kentucky]; *Liggett* v. *Lee* [Florida]; *A&P* v. *Grosjean* [Louisiana]). Among the more prominent antichain figures were southerners such as Congressman Wright Patman of Texas—who sought national chain-store regulation—and W. K. "Old Man" Henderson, who broadcast nationwide tirades against the chains over radio station KWKH, Shreveport.

Even in the face of such opposition chain stores prospered as the South's urban areas joined in the creation of innovative merchandising. Clarence Saunders of Memphis pioneered many self-service techniques in his Piggly Wiggly stores; the Florida-based Winn-Dixie stores became leaders in the food field. The growth of national and regional chains within the South reflected its increasing urbanization and transformation from a region characterized by Franklin D. Roosevelt as "the Nation's No. 1 economic problem" to a part of the developing Sunbelt. As it changed from exploited to exploiter, the South altered its characteristic forms of marketing. In a nation where merchandising is a key to culture, the results have been startling.

Carl Ryant
University of Louisville

Thomas D. Clark, *Pills, Petticoats and Plows: The Southern Country Store* (1944); Godfrey M. Lebhar, *Chain Stores in America*, 1859–1959 (3d ed., 1963); Carl Ryant, *Journal of Southern History* (May 1973).

Coca-Cola

William Allen White once called it "the sublimated essence of all that America stands for," and an anonymous but no less fervent admirer called it "the holy water of the American South." The "it," as the latest in a long line of slogans proclaims, is, of course, Coca-Cola.

John S. Pemberton, known as "Doc" like most pharmacists of his era, concocted Coca-Cola in 1886 primarily as a hangover cure. It has subsequently been many things to many people—to Robert Winship Woodruff, its high priest for nearly 60 years, "a religion as well as a business." Pemberton first made Coke, its nickname from early on, in Atlanta, and Coca-Cola men have bestrode that city ever since. Pemberton was pleased soon after his invention to sell the rights to it for $1,750 to another Atlanta pharmacist, Asa Candler. Candler was even more pleased in 1919 to sell the Coca-Cola Company for $25 million. It was the biggest financial deal, until then, in the history of the American South. (Candler sold only part of his bounty; earlier, in 1899, thinking that consumption of the drink would be limited largely to soda fountains, he had disposed of practically all the bottling rights to it for one dollar. The drink had first been bottled back in 1894 by Joseph Biedenharn in Vicksburg, Miss.) The prime mover in the 1919 transaction was the banker Ernest Woodruff. His son Robert (1889–1985) took over the company in 1923. "Asa Candler put us on our feet," one Coca-Cola executive would say years afterward, "and Bob Woodruff gave us wings."

Dwight D. Eisenhower once speculated that his good friend Bob Woodruff might be the richest man in the United States. Atlanta's Emory University, on whose predecessor campus Woodruff had spent less than a year as an undergraduate before being invited to leave, would over the ensuing years be endowed, by him and his family, with some $150 million of Coca-Cola largess.

Until World War II, when the Coca-Cola Company construed it to be its patriotic duty to get Coke to every thirsty American serviceman abroad, the drink was chiefly marketed in the United States. Soon it was universal. Asa Candler briefly flirted with the idea of Coca-Cola cigars and Coca-Cola chewing gum at the turn of the century, but until the 1950s the company was strictly a one-product enterprise. Then it began to diversify. Orange juice, other soft drinks, eventually even wines, and most recently films (Columbia Pictures) were merchandised around the world. The placid liquid that Doc Pemberton had first mixed in a backyard, three-legged iron pot (stirring it with an oar) had become the foundation of a multibillion-dollar industry.

In 1985 Coca-Cola chairman Roberto Guizueta announced that, for the first time in 99 years, the drink's taste formula would be changed, leading to much hoopla and to criticism from some for yet another change in a southern tradition. The company relented in the face of public pressure and continued marketing "classic" Coke.

See also HISTORY AND MANNERS: / Beverages

E. J. Kahn, Jr.
The New Yorker

Bob Hall, *Southern Exposure* (Fall 1976); E. J. Kahn, Jr., *The Big Drink: The Story of Coca-Cola* (1951).

De Bow's Review

Established in New Orleans in 1846 by James Dunwoody Brownson De Bow, *De Bow's Review* was the preeminent southern antebellum journal of business, economics, and public opinion. Modeled on *Hunt's Merchant's Magazine* of New York, the *Commercial Review*, as it was often called, was initially devoted to "the diversities and ramifications of commercial action." Always a partisan of the South, De Bow increasingly advocated southern nationalism and the defense of slavery after 1850, and he opened the journal's pages to supporters of secession, including Edmund Ruffin and George Fitzhugh.

Despite the *Review*'s importance, De Bow always had difficulty keeping the journal in print. Southerners refused to subscribe in sufficient numbers, and De Bow was forced to suspend publication in 1847 and 1849. Circulation never exceeded 5,000. Slow to realize the possibility of revenue from advertising, De Bow on the eve of the Civil War found the advertisements of northern firms to be his best source of income. He was also forced, after repeated failures with southern printers, to have the *Review* printed in the North, a fact he kept hidden from his readers. De Bow managed to keep the publication alive during the Civil War until April 1862, when financial problems, scarcities of printing supplies, and the fall of New Orleans forced suspension. One issue was published in 1864; the journal then lay dormant until war's end. De Bow resumed publication in January 1866 with the *Review* now devoted to the restoration of national unity and the development of the nation's wealth and resources. Some of the familiar contributors returned, for instance George Fitzhugh; but De Bow was unable to restore the magazine to its prewar eminence. De Bow's death in February 1867 brought a quick end to his journal. Sold in March 1868, the *Review* soon ceased publication.

Influential beyond its limited circulation, *De Bow's Review* reflected both southern opinion and the somewhat idiosyncratic views of its editor. Always advocating southern interests, De Bow's contributors ardently defended slavery, argued the superiority of southern civilization, promoted the improvement of southern agriculture, and after 1850 championed southern nationalism. De Bow, however, also firmly believed in promoting southern commercial, mercantile, and industrial interests. His frank advocacy of the urgent need to achieve commercial and industrial independence for the coming contest with the North set De Bow apart from the reigning planter ethos and probably limited the *Review*'s appeal to the planter elite. De Bow astutely recognized the economic and industrial weaknesses of the South, yet his untiring campaign to build a solid commercial and industrial economy failed. Not wholly typical of antebellum southern thinking, then, *De Bow's Review* still provides a superb window into the southern mind during the 15 years before secession and civil war.

See also MYTHIC SOUTH: / Fitzhugh, George; SCIENCE AND MEDICINE: / Ruffin, Edmund

Daniel J. Wilson
Muhlenberg College

De Bow's Review, vols. 1–34 (1846–64), After the War Series, vols. 1–8 (1866–70), New Series, After the War Series, vol. 1 (1879–80); Paul F. Paskoff and Daniel J. Wilson, *The Cause of the South: Selections from De Bow's Review, 1846–1867* (1982); Ottis Clark Skipper, *J. D. B. De Bow: Magazinist of the Old South* (1958); Diffee William Standard, "*De Bow's Review*, 1846–1880: A Magazine of Southern Opinion" (Ph.D. dissertation, University of North Carolina, 1970).

Delta Airlines

Beginning in 1924 as Huff Daland Dusters and specializing primarily in crop spraying in the southern United States and Latin America, Delta adopted its enduring name in 1928 from the Mississippi Delta region. Guided by Collett Everman ("C. E.") Woolman, a former county agricultural agent who ultimately became its patriarch and longtime chief executive, it began passenger operations in 1929 from its Monroe, La., base on a route eventually extending from Fort Worth to Atlanta. Forced to abandon this service in 1930 when it failed to win an essential federal government airmail contract, it survived precariously on meager earnings from crop dusting and fixed-base activities.

In 1934 congressional probing of irregularities in the

Delta Airlines stewardess with portable Coca-Cola cooler, c. 1945

awarding of previous airmail contracts led to cancellation of most existing contracts and fresh opportunity for Delta, which in June of that year won an airmail route from Fort Worth to Charleston via Atlanta and other cities. Resuming airline operations, the company became a vigorous regional carrier. Increasing capital requirements, partly connected with acquisition of Douglas DC-2 and DC-3 aircraft, led in 1941 to a transfer of Delta's headquarters to Atlanta.

Delta's intensive use of a restricted fleet in World War II produced earnings that, coupled with a Chicago-to-Miami route award granted by the Civil Aeronautics Board (CAB) in 1945, laid the basis for postwar expansion. Inflation, mounting costs, and other industrywide problems produced spotty earnings in the late 1940s; but thereafter Delta enjoyed steady profits, enlarging its system by absorbing another regional carrier, Chicago and Southern, in a 1953 merger and winning a route the following year from Atlanta to Washington and New York.

Delta was a pioneer of the jet age, the first line to inaugurate DC-8, DC-9, and Convair 880 service. It also won new routes to such key destinations as Los Angeles and in 1971 absorbed Northeast Airlines in another merger. Woolman's ability to project the company as a southern-style extended family promoted loyalty among Delta's mainly nonunion employees. After his death in 1966 a management team trained under his tutelage continued to emphasize this "family feeling" and retained his conservative financial policies. Such strategies, coupled with rigorous fleet standardization and new routes to such places as London, made Delta the most consistently profitable firm in the airline industry, a position it continued to hold in the 1970s and early 1980s despite rising fuel costs, periodic recessions, and the onset of federal deregulation.

W. David Lewis
Wesley P. Newton
Auburn University

W. David Lewis and Wesley P. Newton, *Delta: The History of an Airline* (1979).

Duke, James B.

(1856–1925) Businessman and philanthropist.

Youngest of three children of Washington Duke and Artelia Roney Duke, James Buchanan Duke was born in what was then Orange (now Durham) County, N.C., on 23 December 1856. Although his mother died in 1858 and his father was later drafted into Confederate service, "Buck" Duke, as he was known in the family, spent most of his childhood on his father's modest farm about three miles from the new village of Durham. He received some schooling at an academy in Durham and, after a brief stay at New Garden School (later Guilford College), attended the Eastman Business College in Poughkeepsie, N.Y.

Washington Duke began the home manufacture of brightleaf smoking tobacco after the Civil War, and

James B. Duke, North Carolina businessman, c. 1900

James B. Duke grew up with a first-hand knowledge of every phase of the tobacco business. In 1874 Washington Duke sold his farm and moved his family into Durham to launch a more ambitious manufacturing operation. Displaying a rare talent for business and an appetite for hard work, James B. Duke became a full partner in W. Duke Sons and Company when it was incorporated in 1878. Though the company prospered, it was overshadowed by the older, larger W. T. Blackwell Company, which produced the famed Bull Durham brand of tobacco. After bringing in handrollers from New York to produce the newfangled cigarette, the Dukes, apparently inspired largely by James B. Duke, gambled in the mid-1880s on a machine-made cigarette and entered into an important, secret contract for the machine invented by James A. Bonsack of Virginia.

The gamble paid off handsomely, for by 1890 W. Duke Sons and Company was the leading manufacturer of cigarettes in the nation, and James B. Duke, who moved permanently to New York in 1884 to manage the branch factory there, had played a key role in organizing the leading cigarette manufacturers into a combination or "trust," the American Tobacco Company. Within a decade, that company, with Duke as its president, controlled the major portion of the nation's entire tobacco industry—save for cigars—and with operations in Britain, Japan, and elsewhere in the world became a pioneer multinational corporation.

Even before the U.S. Supreme Court called for the dissolution of the American Tobacco Company in 1911, James B. Duke, along with his older brother Benjamin N. Duke and others, had invested heavily in textile manufacturing in Durham and elsewhere in North Carolina. Partly as a result of that activity, the Dukes early became interested in the new electric-power industry and specifically in hydroelectric power. In 1905 they launched the Southern Power Company with headquarters in Charlotte, N.C., and, largely under the leadership of James B. Duke and a brilliant engineer with whom Duke worked closely, William S. Lee, the business eventually grew into the giant Duke Power Company serving the Piedmont regions of North and South Carolina.

Starting in the late 19th century, Washington Duke and his family began regularly to give substantial support to various philanthropic causes, especially, but not exclusively, Methodist-related ones. The Dukes were instrumental in bringing the Methodist-sponsored Trinity College to Durham in 1892, and Benjamin N. Duke became the family's main link with the college as well as its chief patron. In December 1924 James B. Duke, after several years of careful planning, established the Duke Endowment as a perpetual trust for certain philanthropic purposes in the Carolinas. Systematizing on a perpetual basis a long-standing pattern of family giving, James B. Duke specified that a prime beneficiary of the endowment was to be a new university organized around Trinity College, which, at the suggestion of Trinity's president William P. Few, was to be named Duke University. Annual support from the endowment went also to nonprofit hospitals for both races in the Carolinas, three other colleges (Davidson, Furman, and Johnson C. Smith), child-care institutions in the Carolinas for blacks and whites, and rural Methodist churches and retired Methodist preachers in North Carolina.

After a first marriage that ended in a much-publicized divorce in 1906, James B. Duke in 1907 married a Georgia-born widow, Mrs. Walker P. Inman (née Nanaline Holt); and in 1912 a daughter, Doris Duke, was born to the couple. James B. Duke died in his mansion on New York's Fifth Avenue on 10 October 1925 and is buried alongside Washington and Benjamin N. Duke in the Memorial Chapel on the campus of Duke University.

See also EDUCATION: / Duke University

Robert F. Durden
Duke University

Robert F. Durden, *The Dukes of Durham, 1865–1929* (1975); John K. Winkler, *Tobacco Tycoon: The Story of James B. Duke* (1942).

Flagler, Henry

(1830–1913) Businessman and promoter.

From the beginning of his Florida enterprises in 1885 until his death in 1913, Henry Morrison Flagler led the development of the east coast of Florida. Starting with the luxury resort hotel Ponce de Leon in St. Augustine, he opened a chain of hotels that stretched from Jacksonville Beach to Key West and across the Gulf Stream to Nassau. His Florida East Coast Railroad linked Jacksonville and Miami and ultimately extended over the sea to Key West. The Model Land Company constituted the third division of Flagler's empire in Florida.

Born into modest circumstances in rural western New York in 1830, Flagler rose in the business world through force of will, tireless work, and entrepreneurial skill. He became one of the original partners with John D. Rockefeller in the Standard Oil Corporation and was a multimillionaire when he arrived in Florida at the age of 55 to begin a second career as the builder of the Florida east coast. During his years in Florida he was praised for opening the frontier to settlement and providing employment through his enterprises, as well as for his philanthropic contributions to local communities. He was also condemned by populist-spirited individuals who opposed the plutocratic economic and political power he personified.

Florida's character was altered by the activities of men like Flagler and his west-coast Florida contemporary Henry B. Plant, the developer of Tampa. Departing from the typical Deep South cotton-state mold, Florida began to assume a new character based on tourism, citrus, and specialized agriculture. This was most true in the lower east coast area, which had been only very sparsely populated prior to the time when Flagler's railroad made it possible to transport northern tourists in and winter vegetables out. While panhandle and north Florida retained much of the ambiance of neighboring Alabama and Georgia, the newly settled parts of the peninsula showed the influence of large-scale immigration from northern states. Palm Beach, West Palm Beach, and Miami owe their existence to Flagler.

A small tourist industry had existed since early in the century based on the infirm and the aged who sought relief from the northern winter. This changed in Flagler's day. The completion of the national rail network made it possible for larger numbers of tourists to come to Florida, and the tubercular invalid was displaced as the typical visitor by the pleasure-seeking, newly affluent class created by the urban-industrial revolution.

Flagler's use of Spanish Renaissance architecture in his St. Augustine hotels (but not elsewhere) foreshadowed the extensive employment of Mediterranean styles in the state in the present century.

Henry M. Flagler epitomizes such features of Florida's culture as the spirit of "development," the prominent role of the wealthy in society, and the injection of external influences, which have made Florida different from other Deep South states.

Thomas Graham
Flagler College

David L. Chandler, *Henry Flagler: The Astonishing Life and Times of the Visionary Robber Baron Who Founded Florida* (1986); Sidney Walter Martin, *Florida's Flagler* (1949).

Foreign Industry

Foreign industry, or commercial enterprises owned by residents outside the United States, has been a part of America and the South from the beginning of American history. Food, tobacco, and forest-products industries were among the first sectors of foreign investments, followed by textiles and numerous other industries. Much of the early railroad and canal construction in the United States was also done or financed by foreign investors. However, the major influx of foreign industry occurred during the 20th century and became particularly significant for the South as late as the 1960s and 1970s. For example, only 10 percent of the foreign industry in South Carolina existing in 1983 was established before 1970. Much of the increase in foreign investments in the South during the 1970s can be attributed an increased awareness of foreign investors about the South—in both cultural and economic terms—caused in large part by the worldwide media coverage of the presidential campaign and subsequent presidency of Jimmy Carter.

While the South is not the dominant region of foreign investment in the United States, it does have a disproportionately high percentage of foreign industry, based on comparative population and industrialization. Since 1970 it has been the fastest-growing region in terms of attracting foreign investment. In several southern states, such as South Carolina, foreign investment accounts for more than 25 percent of all new manufacturing investments. In addition, southern employment in foreign industry is at levels generally four to five times higher than the national average.

The Dutch, English, Germans, French, and Canadians are the primary investors in the South, but Japanese investments have also become significant. In addition, more than a dozen other nations have invested in the region. Although the textile industry brought many early foreign investors to the South, other industries now attract more foreign backing, including rubber and plastics, petrochemicals, electronics, chemicals and pharmaceuticals, metalworking, machinery, scientific equipment, and stone, clay, glass, and cement. Still other foreign investments have occurred in retailing, commercial real estate, agriculture, and banking. In short, as the South's economy has diversified, so too has its foreign industry. In fact, much of the South's diversification occurred as a result of foreign investment.

No two states have equal amounts or varieties of foreign industry, making generalizations difficult. In value terms, South Carolina is the leader, but in employment North Carolina is the leader. Georgia is the leader in terms of Japanese investments, South Carolina in terms of German ones. Foreign industry in Florida is concentrated in banking and real estate; but in Louisiana it is in petrochemicals, in South Carolina in chemicals and tires, and in Georgia in sales offices and warehousing/distribution. In the Mississippi Delta a large tract of land is owned by the Queen of England.

Major similarities in all these include the motivations of the investors and the high degree of state promotional activity and investment incentives. Overall, the major investor attractions of the South appear to be labor, land, and lifestyle considerations. Labor is still relatively abundant, inexpensive, and nonunionized, and the labor force has an excellent track record of high productivity, low absenteeism, and stability of employment. Land is also comparatively abundant, inexpensive, and generally well connected through transportation to other areas of the nation and the world. The lifestyle of the South is perhaps the most similar of all American regions to that of Europe and Japan—more tradition- and family-oriented and more hospitable, with numerous recreational opportunities.

Virtually all the southern states have become active and aggressive in state investment promotion activities and incentives. Numerous trade and investment missions are conducted to promote the states to foreign business interests, and packages of free worker training, site selection, tax credits, and industrial revenue bonds are also offered to potential investors. Numerous southern governors have played active roles in these promotional activities, underscoring the states' interest in and commitment to foreign investment in the minds of potential foreign investors.

Foreign industry has had an increasing impact on the South, economically and socially. The development of new industries, the expansion and modernization of existing industries, the upgrading of worker skills and wages, and the broadening of tax bases are only a few of the direct economic impacts. In turn, income generated directly by foreign investments creates additional income for suppliers, retailers, and other parts of the community. Foreign industry also has brought foreign people to the South, largely management and technical employees and their families, resulting in an internationalization of the communities in which they locate.

Neither the social impact of foreign industry nor its economic impact can yet be determined precisely, and some effects on existing firms have been negative. In both economic and cultural terms, foreign investments are still too new and, as a percentage of all activity, too small to have had any major impact. However, foreign industry will likely play a larger role in the future economic development of the South and, in the process, begin to have a larger impact on the culture of the South.

Jeffrey S. Arpan
University of South Carolina

Jeffrey S. Arpan and David Ricks, *Directory of Foreign Manufacturers in the United States* (1975); Jeffrey S. Arpan, Edmond Flowers, and David Ricks, *Journal of International Business Studies* (Summer 1981); Cedric Suzman, ed., *The Costs and Benefits of Foreign Direct Investments from a State Perspective* (1982); U.S. Department of Commerce, *Foreign Direct Investment in the United States*, vols. 1–9 (1976); Mira Wilkins, ed., *Foreign Investment in the United States* (1977), *Foreign Enterprise in Florida: The Impact of Non-United States Direct Investment* (1979), *New Foreign Enterprise in Florida* (1980).

Furniture Industry

Most of the fine furniture used in the South during the colonial period was imported from England. As towns and cities grew in size and wealth, however, skilled craftsmen from England, Scotland, Ireland, Germany, and France and from northern cities in America made their way in increasing numbers into lucrative southern markets such as Williamsburg, Charleston, New Bern, and Savannah. Some of the early craftsmen were itinerants, some were employed on large plantations, and some established shops in the larger towns and cities. The common folk made most of their own furniture or used the products of local carpenters.

Woods used by early southern furniture makers were largely walnut, cherry, and pine. Mahogany became increasingly popular after 1750, but pine, oak, and poplar continued to be used for framing and as the base for mahogany veneers. Maple and birch were not used extensively until 1800.

Although a few small factories had been established in Nashville, Tenn., and Danville, Va., somewhat earlier, the South's entrance into modern furniture manufacturing occurred in 1888 when local businessmen built a factory in High Point, N.C. The abundance and low cost of both wood and labor gave High Point a cost advantage over northern competition, and the industry spread from there into nearby centers in North Carolina and Virginia. As worker skills improved, so did the quality of High Point furniture. The industry grew rapidly after World War I, and following World War II North Carolina moved ahead of New York to become the leading furniture-manufacturing state. By that time High Point and southwestern Virginia had established reputations for producing furniture of high quality, with cheaper grades coming from newer centers to the south and west. Besides North Carolina and Virginia, important centers of furniture manufacturing are found in Tennessee, Texas, Arkansas, Georgia, and Mississippi.

The southern furniture industry began, and remains, a largely craft-oriented, family-owned business. During recent years a number of small companies have been purchased by larger competitors, and other corporate structures have shown increasing interest in the high return on capital investments that has characterized the southern furniture industry. Whatever ownership structure may develop in the future, however, the South's abundant wood supplies and high-quality labor should continue to provide the competitive edges needed for substantial growth.

See also FOLKLIFE: / Furniture Making

Sidney R. Jumper
University of Tennessee

Paul H. Burroughs, *Southern Antiques* (1931); B. F. Lemert, *Economic Geography* (April 1934); *New York Times* (25 October 1984); Lonn Taylor and David B. Warren, *Texas Furniture: The Cabinetmakers and Their Work, 1840–1880* (1975); U.S. Department of Commerce, Bureau of the Census, *Census of Manufacturers: 1958* (1961).

Grady, Henry W.

(1850–1889) Newspaper editor.

Born 24 May 1850, in Athens, Ga., to William Sammons and Ann Gartrell Grady, Henry Woodfin Grady enjoyed a comfortable upbringing. The wise management of his father, a substantial merchant who died in 1864 from wounds received serving in the Confederate army, enabled Henry to enroll at the University of Georgia in 1866. Following graduation in 1868, he attended the University of Virginia for a year, excelling in oratory and displaying journalistic talent as a contributor to the Atlanta *Constitution*. Returning to Georgia in 1869, Grady located in Rome, edited various newspapers there, and married Julia King, his childhood sweetheart, in 1871. The next year, he purchased an interest in the Atlanta *Daily Herald* and moved to that bustling city to join the *Herald*'s editorial staff. When the *Herald* ceased publication in 1876, Grady, while serving as special correspondent to a number of papers outside of Georgia, joined the staff of the *Constitution*, the journal with which he would be associated until his death on 23 December 1889.

Part owner and managing editor after 1880, Grady helped build the *Constitution* into the region's most popular newspaper as he himself emerged as the leading spokesman of the New South movement, the attempt to revive the region largely through industrialization. For economic progress to occur, he said, the South must cultivate the goodwill of northern investors. Reconciliation between the sections depended, he believed, upon the social stability that would result from an amicable resolution of the race issue in the South. Given northern restraint and trust, white southerners would respect the civil and political rights conferred upon black southerners during Reconstruction but would maintain white supremacy and segregation—an arrangement, he argued, that merely reflected the instinct of both races.

Not only in the pages of the *Constitution* but before audiences from Boston to Dallas, Grady spread the gospel of southern progress. In his celebrated "New South" address of 1886, he assured New York's New England Society that southerners, while cherishing the memory of the Old South and the Confederacy, had accepted the verdict of war and bore the North no ill will. Hard at work rebuilding, the South, he contended, treated blacks equitably, desired intersectional harmony, and wished to promote further economic development.

Grady's vision of a South of "sunshine everywhere and all the time" gave hope to many of his contemporaries, yet at his death it remained still a vision.

See also MEDIA: / Atlanta *Constitution*

Wayne Mixon
Mercer University

Paul M. Gaston, *The New South Creed: A Study in Southern Mythmaking* (1970); Mills Lane, *The New South: Writings and Speeches of Henry Grady* (1971); Raymond B. Nixon, *Henry W. Grady: Spokesman of the New South* (1943).

Gregg, William

(1800–1867) Businessman.

Gregg was born 2 February 1800 in Monongalia County, [West] Va., and died 13 September 1867 in Graniteville, S.C. His outspoken advocacy of manufacturing and his entrepreneurship of the Graniteville Manufacturing Company (1846–67) fixed his reputation as "the father" of the southern textile industry, an image enhanced by Broadus Mitchell's laudatory biography (1928). Initially, Gregg amassed a fortune as a jeweler and silversmith in Columbia (1824) and Charleston (1838). Introduced to cotton manufacturing at his uncle's small mill (circa 1810) near Madison, Ga., Gregg in 1837 purchased stock in the Vaucluse Mill (1833) in the Horse Creek Valley of Edgefield District, S.C.

In 1844 he retired as a merchant and devoted his energies and financial resources to industrialization. After touring New England mills, Gregg authored a series of newspaper articles, later published as *Essays on Domestic Industry* (1845), admonishing southerners to build more textile factories. By the late 1840s most South Carolina newspaper editors supported Gregg's crusade. In 1846 Gregg launched his own mill at Graniteville in the Horse Creek Valley. For the next 20 years he planned and directed every detail of the large-scale (initially 9,245 spindles and 500 looms), two-story granite factory and its surrounding village. Although only one of several pioneer southern entrepreneurs, Gregg was the region's best-known industrial publicist. In a cultural context his ideas and policies at Graniteville played a major role in creating the stereotypical image of the rural, paternalistic southern mill village. Antiurban in his writings, Gregg refused to invest in the nearby Augusta mills being erected during the 1840s. He advocated the model of an isolated, self-contained community. His company controlled the lives of the rural poor white families who moved into his picturesque wooden cottages. Such control over white operatives was possible in the South, Gregg suggested, because of the presence of potential black workers. His rhetoric punctuated the central tenet of the South's cotton-mill ideology: social as well as economic dividends flowed from industrialization. Mill villages would "uplift" the poor whites. Although his social ideas persisted and his mill paid reasonable dividends, the antebellum South, in general, failed to adopt Gregg's industrial philosophy.

See also SOCIAL CLASS: / Company Towns

John S. Lupold
Columbus College

Ernest M. Lander, Jr., *The Textile Industry in Antebellum South Carolina* (1969); Thomas P. Martin, *Journal of Southern History* (August 1945); Broadus Mitchell, *William Gregg: Factory Master of the Old South* (1928); Tom E. Terrill, *Journal of Economic History* (March 1976).

Insurance

The persistence of deep-rooted facets of southern socioeconomic life and culture—limited financial assets, African-bred burial practices, rural lifestyles long retained by urban dwellers, insecurities derived in the painful adjustment from plantation paternalism to semifreedom—go far to explain the seeming paradox of the region's high personal-security consciousness linked with its below-average insurance coverage. In 1982 southern states accounted for 9 of the top 17 states in the number of life insurance policies in force, but only 5 states were above the national average in per family life insurance in force. No southern-headquartered insurer ranked among the top 30 in terms of assets.

In the antebellum period limited southern commercial expansion failed to lure scarce capital into the casualty business. The region also failed to share in the northern surge of life insurance activities induced by the extensive breakdown of rural-bred kinship ties. High mortality rates for poor white southern males discouraged sales, although plantation owners paid high premiums to northern insurers on the lives of their skilled slaves, especially those hired out for railroad construction and industrial work. As early as the 1790s free southern blacks organized mutual benefit societies to fulfill their obligations to the deceased in the "sweet sorrow" of passage to the netherworld, as well as to assure their own avoidance of a pauper's burial or, worse, disposal of their body to a medical school.

In the postbellum era southern white mortality rates improved, enhancing the market for large northern-based insurers, whereas black death rates rose dramatically, especially in the urban South. Black churches and lodges established a plethora of benevolent, often secret and ritualistic self-help societies. Over time, poor business practices and occasional peculation led to rising contempt for "coffin clubs." Between 1890 and 1910, as discriminatory hiring practices eroded employment opportunities for black males and denied them the franchise in state after state, black-owned-and-managed health and life insurance companies were organized, primarily to provide sickness and burial insurance coverage to all family members. The small weekly premiums were paid primarily by black women, who had an employment rate more than double that of white women.

Joining altruism with capitalistic incentives and motivated by black pride, such black entrepreneurs as Alonzo Herndon and John Merrick—both barbers with white clienteles—created well-managed companies that provided employment opportunities for college-educated black youth faced with restricted regional opportunities. (Thus, Walter White agonized over the decision to give up his job with Standard Life of Atlanta in 1917 in order to accept an administrative post in New York City with the National Association for the Advancement of Colored People.) Over the years successful black insurance companies, often associated with funeral homes and banks to which they channeled premium income, emerged as one of the most significant sources of wealth and high status in the southern black community.

Although they viewed the southern black population

as their legitimate preserve, black insurers faced vigorous competition from white-owned regional stock companies offering the same coverage, usually at similar rates. Both white- and black-managed insurance enterprises in many instances achieved excellent records for solidity and financial reliability, provided mortgages for home buyers, and generated funds that flowed into regional utilities and state and municipal bonds. The failure rate for smaller and weaker insurers, however, was considerable, and when so dynamic and hitherto successful an enterprise as black-owned Standard Life collapsed in the mid-1920s, even a stalwart exponent of racial self-help like policyholder W. E. B. Du Bois was plunged into despair. Convinced that white-managed firms were safer institutions and that holding one of their contracts conveyed a measure of prestige, blacks in large numbers continued to favor white insurers. Successful white-owned enterprises provided a powerful vehicle for wealth accumulation in the region, and they afforded extensive employment to a legion of high-school-educated home service agents. Increasingly, large home-office operations stimulated the growth of Richmond, Nashville, Jacksonville, Atlanta, and Dallas as regional financial centers.

The burgeoning southern economy of the post–World War II period, with its expanding white middle class, led many larger insurers to phase out home service to the lower-income groups. A proliferation of small concerns, primarily white-owned, were organized to serve the still-large traditional market. A number of region-based, white-owned firms attempted to cultivate the biracial market, with its wide income disparities. They relied for a time on "sociological underwriting" to justify rate differentials between black and white policyholders.

With the passage of civil rights legislation in the mid-1960s, the top management of white-owned insurers began to take steps to integrate their sales and home-office staffs. The pace of compliance varied widely as many insurers experienced difficulty in overcoming the opposition of white employees and decentralized sales staffs. The conventional belief was that black agents could not possibly sell white prospects, and widespread apprehension appeared regarding the ramifications of integrated staffs at social functions and company conventions. Nonetheless, a Wharton study in 1970 found that some southern white-owned insurers exhibited a greater willingness than those elsewhere to actively pursue nondiscriminatory hiring practices. By the early 1980s black-owned insurers found themselves outbid for black sales and technical specialists. Complaints of a "black brain drain" were voiced and stress was placed on the necessity for cooperative training programs and shared infrastructure in order to compete effectively.

During the 1970s a major merger-and-acquisition movement took place among white-owned insurers in the region, altering the structure of the industry. In the acquisition of Nashville-based National Life and Accident Insurance Company by American General Life Insurance Company of Houston, Tex., competition was considerably reduced. In 1979 Nationale-Nederlanden NV, the Netherlands' largest insurance company, acquired the Life Insurance Company of Georgia (organized in 1891 with negligible funds) for $360 million. The declining role of small and medium-sized regional insurers and the probable impact of this change upon the socioeconomic and cultural life of the South has thus far aroused little interest.

See also URBANIZATION: / Atlanta; Dallas; Nashville; Richmond

Jack Blicksilver
Georgia State University

Charles S. Johnson, *The Negro in American Civilization* (1930); Armand J. Thieblot, Jr., and Linda P. Fletcher, *Negro Employment in Finance: A Study of Racial Policies in Banking and Insurance*, vol. 2, *Studies in Negro Employment* (1970); Walter B. Weare, *Black Business in the New South: A Social History of the North Carolina Mutual Life Insurance Company* (1973); Viviana A. Rotman Zelizer, *Morals and Markets: The Development of Life Insurance in the United States* (1979).

Liquor Industry

The distillation of southern liquor dates from the early colonial period. Efforts to reproduce European wines and beers generally failed, but colonists quickly learned to distill local fruits and grains. They made corn whiskey in Jamestown, for example, while Georgians distilled peach brandy. By the late 1600s cheaply imported rum had further confirmed colonial preferences for hard liquor, and Scotch-Irish immigration in the mid-1700s widely popularized whiskey making, particularly on the frontiers. Rye and barley distilling consequently flourished in Maryland and parts of Virginia, where even George Washington made rye liquor.

Whiskey production soared after the Revolution (which had disrupted the rum trade) as new western harvests increased grain supplies. Farmers routinely distilled surpluses, as whiskey kept better and brought higher prices than grains. By 1810 good water and abundant corn centered American distilling in Kentucky, where 2,000 stills annually produced over 2 million gallons of liquor. Some of these early Kentucky ventures became companies of considerable reputation (e.g., the James Beam Distilling Company), and important enterprises also grew in Tennessee, Virginia, Maryland, and North Carolina. By midcentury, liquor was one of the South's most important products and had a firm place in sectional heritage. Southern producers, however, competed among themselves and with northern distillers, and by 1850 overproduction and falling prices increasingly forced them to view their operations in a national perspective.

Commercial whiskeys were chiefly corn blended with varied amounts of rye and other grains. Bourbon, aged in charred oak barrels, was the most distinctive. First distilled in Kentucky as early as 1789, production centered in Bourbon County until the 1840s and then spread regionally. Bourbon won national acclaim, while other blends, such as Tennessee Whiskey, were also popular. Rye remained important in Maryland. The industry standardized most blends by the turn of the 20th century, a process formalized in federal regulations by the 1930s.

By 1900 large distilling concerns (e.g., the Kentucky Distilleries and Warehouse Company) emerged as smaller producers merged in the face of competition and temperance agitation. National prohibition accelerated this trend as investors, anticipating repeal, acquired many southern distilleries. Thus, with exceptions such as Jack Daniel and Beam, many brand names steeped in southern tradition are now products of a few national beverage corporations.

Moonshining, never exclusively southern, also secured an important place in sectional history. As early as 1794, the Whiskey Rebellion, although centered in western Pennsylvania, engendered considerable sympathy in the South, where many distillers ignored federal excises on their product. Over time, Kentucky probably was the largest single source of illegal whiskey, although Georgia, the Carolinas, Virginia, and sections of other states also boasted significant production, and moonshiners often enjoyed considerable local prestige. Moonshine was essentially corn and frequently was of higher proof than legal whiskeys. Production peaked in the 1950s but then dropped off as quality fell, law enforcement suffered, and drinking preferences shifted away from distilled beverages.

Despite the prominence of southern distilling, beer and wine did maintain a regional presence. Early attempts to establish European grapes, including efforts by Washington and Jefferson, failed as commercial ventures, but some small southern vineyards survived generally using local vines. The most important of these was the Catawba grape, native to North Carolina, which became the basis of a viticulture that spread beyond the South. Commercial brewing—never a significant part of the antebellum South—expanded with growing southern urban populations around the turn of the 20th century. Northern capital helped establish such regional companies as Lone Star Brewing (San Antonio) as early as 1883; and as the century advanced, Anheuser-Busch, Carling, Schaefer, and other national concerns opened brewing and distribution facilities in many southern cities. (Richmond, for instance, saw the nation's first sales of canned beer in the early 1930s.) The border South was the center of regional beer production, notably in St. Louis and Louisville. New Orleans's Dixie Brewing Corporation has utilized regional imagery in marketing. Compared to distilling—legal and illegal—however, brewing and viticulture remain lesser aspects of southern tradition.

See also HISTORY AND MANNERS: / Jack Daniel Distillery; Moonshine and Moonshining; Whiskey

Mark Edward Lender
Kean College of New Jersey

Stanley Baron, *Brewed in America: A History of Beer and Ale in the United States* (1962); Gerald Carson, *The Social History of Bourbon: An Unhurried Account of Our Star-Spangled American Drink* (1963); William L. Downard, *Dictionary of the History of the American Brewing and Distilling Industries* (1980); Mark Edward Lender and James Kirby Martin, *Drinking in America: A History* (1982).

Mining

Although coal was discovered in Virginia in the early 1700s, southern coal mining remained a small-scale enterprise until the late 19th century because of the lack of transportation. Following the Civil War the increased demand for coal as a fuel for the Industrial Revolution, the development of the steam-driven plow, which tunneled out the Appalachian Mountains, and the appearance of railroads in the mountains promoted the emergence of coal as a significant southern product.

The rise of the coal industry consumed farm land and life, as well as mountain culture, as the industrial transformation tied the previously rural, isolated regions to the international economy. In 1890 McDowell County, W.Va., produced 245,000 tons of coal a year; two decades later it was producing 13 million tons annually. In 1910 Harlan County, Ky., did not produce a single ton of coal; by 1926 the county yielded over 13 million tons of coal annually. By 1940 southern coalfields produced over 40 percent of the coal mined in the United States, and over half the nation's coal by 1960. West Virginia and Kentucky in that year accounted for 80 percent of southern coal production.

To house, feed, and shelter a work force in the isolated coalfields the coal companies established company towns in which the company built and retained control over every aspect of community life including houses, stores, churches, and schools. Miners in the northern coalfields struggled to unionize for higher wages, but southern miners sought to unionize for social, political, and economic reasons. To preserve their feudalistic controls and capitalistic profits the coal companies fought back tenaciously. The result was bitter and bloody labor-management conflicts; the "Armed March on Logan," the Mingo County Strike of the 1920s, and the Harlan County strikes of the 1930s are extreme, but good, examples of how far each side would go in pursuit of its objectives.

The southern coalfields were unionized in the 1930s, a combined accomplishment of John L. Lewis, the legendary chief of the United Mine Workers of America, President Franklin Roosevelt and his New Deal, and, most importantly, a massive uprising of miners. The union, however, failed as a counterbalance to the power of the coal companies as it became bogged down in internal corruption and autocracy. The coal companies established cultural and political hegemonies over the states of West Virginia and Kentucky and continued to exercise considerable political clout in other southern coal-producing states.

Mine disasters, labor-management strife, slag dams

(such as the one that killed 175 people in February 1972 at Buffalo Creek, W.Va.), and strip mining (in 1970 strip mining accounted for about 35 percent of southern coal mining) have been the coal industry's legacy to southern culture.

By their control of the land, the coal companies have prevented the economic diversification of the coal regions. Underdeveloped and bound to a single industry, the economies of the southern coalfield regions fluctuate with the boom-and-bust cycle of the coal industry. A protracted and disastrous bust began in the 1920s with the rise of competing fuels, mainly oil and gas, and an overabundance of coal mines. In the late 1940s the southern coal industry mechanized, mainly in the form of the Continuous Miner, a machine that did the work of many miners. Automation may have saved the southern coal industry, but it prompted massive unemployment and poverty throughout the coal regions and resulted in thousands of miners migrating to the midwestern urban-industrial areas in search of employment.

The energy crisis and oil embargo of the 1970s produced another boom in the industry as the nation, especially under President Jimmy Carter's Administration, turned to coal as the means of achieving national energy security. The 111-day 1977–78 coal strike, a worldwide oil glut, and Reaganomics, which wiped out federal energy programs, led the nation away from coal and produced another bust in the southern coalfields.

In the 1960s oil companies began purchasing the southern coal companies. Occidental bought Island Creek, Continental Oil took over Consolidation Coal, and more were to come. The impact of these takeovers remains to be seen, but with more capital and a greater emphasis on technology, especially strip mining, the oil companies' takeover of the southern coal industry does not promise a bright future for the land or the people.

See also ENVIRONMENT: / Appalachian Coal Region; SOCIAL CLASS: / Coal Miners; Company Towns; VIOLENCE: Harlan County, Kentucky

David A. Corbin
Arlington, Virginia

Appalachian Land Owner Task Force, *Who Owns Appalachia?: Landownership and Its Impact* (1983); David A. Corbin, *Life, Work, and Rebellion in the Coal Fields: Southern West Virginia Coal Miners, 1880–1922* (1981); Ronald D. Eller, *Miners, Millhands, and Mountaineers: The Modernization of the Appalachian South* (1982); William Graebner, *Coal-Mining Safety in the Progressive Period* (1976).

Music Industry

The development of commercial popular music in the South has paralleled trends in other industries. The region has served as a source of musical raw materials—styles, performers, and creative talents—for the nation as a whole. Until World War II, however, non-southerners controlled most of the institutions vital to marketing popular music, including publishing houses, recording companies, and theater chains. Professional musicians in the South pursued the American goal of material advancement, but profits tended to flow toward New York, Chicago, or Hollywood, the three major music centers of the United States before World War II. Of course, there were exceptions to this generalization, chiefly in the form of southern publishers who were beginning to tap a market for spiritual music by the mid-19th century. Between the Civil War and World War I minstrelsy and ragtime music offered opportunities for both black and white southern musicians.

Northern executives also held sway in the pop market, the mainstream of American commercial music centering on Broadway shows, New York's "Tin Pan Alley" music-publishing district, and, later, Hollywood film musicals. This pattern continued as the music industry turned to country music (then called "hillbilly") and jazz in the 1920s. Both genres were southern based, but their markets were not strictly regional. In that decade the phenomenal growth of commercial radio frightened many recording executives, who saw radio as a competing source of popular entertainment. Northern record companies, eager to reach new markets, had ready access to the southern-born jazz musicians of both races who had left their native region for the thriving jazz centers of Chicago and New York. Record firms also brought white hillbilly singers north, or sent agents to Atlanta, New Orleans, Memphis, Charlotte, and other southern cities to record dozens of local musicians in the hillbilly and jazz fields. These musicians frequently received only flat fees (as opposed to long-term royalties) for their work. Northern businessmen and their southern allies (typically retailers in some other line who carried recordings as an adjunct product) often secured control of musical copyrights or stole them outright from relatively unsophisticated performers.

Some southerners were more industry wise, and they began to sell their own songbooks. A handful moved north and set up publishing houses. The most successful southern entrepreneurs in music-related endeavors prior to World War II were those who organized radio stations, in many cases companion operations to insurance companies, newspapers, or retail stores. Stations like Nashville's WSM originated programs for network broadcast and served as proving grounds for pop singers and big bands.

The modern southern music industry took shape during the two decades after 1940. Prosperity revived popular music markets that had been blighted by a decade of economic depression. Urbanization and interregional migration advanced the nationalization of country music, rhythm and blues, and rock and roll, all styles with solid southern foundations. The formation of the performance-rights society Broadcast Music, Incorporated (BMI) in 1940 paved the way for a decentralization of music institutions. Set up by radio networks to rival the older, exclusive, and pop-oriented American Society of Composers, Authors, and Publishers (ASCAP), BMI allowed songwriters and publishers in all fields to join, and it monitored local as well as network programming. By collecting and distributing performance royalties on a wide range of music, it assisted fledgling publishing operations that sprang up across the South and Midwest, including firms that soon captured significant shares of the pop, country, and rhythm-and-blues markets. After 1945 record manufacturers and recording studios complemented broadcasting and publishing in emerging music centers like Nashville, Atlanta, and Dallas. Southern music entrepreneurs extended a long tradition of urban boosterism through shrewd promotion and publicity, formed national trade organizations like the Country Music Association, and enhanced urban growth by investing in banking, real estate, and other ventures. Southern businessmen now sit on the boards of most national music organizations.

In the processes of commercialization and nationalization, southern music entrepreneurs have helped to transform the social settings that originally spawned folk-derived styles like country music and jazz and to dilute these music forms to the point that they have lost many of their qualities as southern-based idioms. To be sure, southern executives, after the fashion of their northern counterparts, have helped to perpetuate images of the region as a land of folksy and sometimes backwards characters, such as the unlettered white hillbilly or the exotic, sensual black. More often, southern businessmen have prompted the adoption of the cowboy or western image, a non-southern image more palatable to a national audience. All of these images have furthered the purposes of southern entrepreneurs and musicians, who have increasingly asserted their own interests within the world of commercial music.

See also MUSIC articles; URBANIZATION: / Nashville

John W. Rumble
Nashville, Tennessee

Bill C. Malone, *Southern Music/American Music* (1979); John W. Rumble, "Fred Rose and the Development of the Nashville Music Industry, 1942–1954" (Ph.D. dissertation, Vanderbilt University, 1980); D. K. Wilgus, *Journal of American Folklore* (April–June 1970).

Nuclear Industry

During the 1950s and early 1960s the development of nuclear energy for peaceful purposes was widely regarded as a glamorous technological breakthrough that could offer dramatic benefits in industry, agriculture, medicine, and the generation of electrical power. The southern states acted with particular enthusiasm to promote the use of nuclear energy as a part of their effort to encourage economic growth. They also played a leading role in increasing the authority of state governments to safeguard public health and safety from radiation hazards, a reflection of their determination to protect traditional state responsibilities from federal infringement.

When Congress passed the Atomic Energy Act of 1954, it ended exclusive government control over nuclear technology and opened it to commercial enterprise for civilian applications. The South moved promptly to investigate the opportunities the measure presented. Responding to the appeals of Florida Governor LeRoy Collins, who argued that "nuclear energy for the South can mean economic emancipation," the Southern Governors' Conference sponsored a series of studies and meetings on the advantages that the technology could provide for the region. In February 1957, after concluding that exploitation of atomic energy promised substantial economic benefits, the governors created the Regional Advisory Council on Nuclear Energy. The council embarked on an ambitious program to foster the growth of atomic technology in the South, not only through construction of nuclear power reactors but also through expansion in the use of radioactive isotopes and increased private investment in atomic energy–related industries.

At the same time, the advisory council and other southern spokesmen were lobbying to extend to the states regulatory authority over atomic energy, which had been largely delegated to the U.S. Atomic Energy Commission (AEC) by the 1954 act. Many state leaders protested federal "usurpation" of the states' traditionally dominant role in public health and safety. The South played an important part in persuading Congress in 1959 to amend the 1954 act to explicitly acknowledge state authority to regulate radiation hazards arising from certain atomic energy operations, not including those from power reactors. Under the amendment, a state with demonstrated technical competence could sign an agreement with the AEC to assume specified functions.

The Regional Advisory Council on Nuclear Energy achieved another of its major goals in 1962 by the creation of a regional compact for nuclear energy, administered by the Southern Interstate Nuclear Board. The board boasted the same year that "the states of the South have achieved a national lead in preparing for the nuclear age" and cited several significant "firsts" for the region: the first regional compact for nuclear energy, the first state to assume atomic regulatory duties formerly exercised by the federal government (Kentucky), the first state nuclear-development program (Texas), and the first college reactor (North Carolina State University). The board also expressed pride that regional efforts since 1955 had made nuclear energy "a substantial factor in the South's total economy."

In the early period of peaceful atomic development, the promotional and regulatory activities of the South were not unique. Other states also acted to obtain economic benefits by encouraging atomic growth and state participation in regulating against the hazards of atomic energy. Yet southern efforts were exceptional in degree, if not in manner and motivation. As a region, the South established broader programs more promptly than other sections and most individual states. The South's economic status relative to other parts of the country made atomic technology especially appealing and gave southerners greater incentive to move quickly. Southern leaders heeded LeRoy Collins's 1955 warning that unless they took immediate measures, "nuclear energy for industrial use will gravitate to the existing industrial areas, mostly in the North." The South's particular sensitivity on the matter of states' rights, especially at a time when the growing civil rights struggle made the issue increasingly controversial, intensified its commitment to preventing exclusive federal authority over nuclear regulation. Sooner and in greater numbers than states in other sections, southern states signed agreements with the AEC to undertake the regulatory responsibilities permitted them. In these respects, the response of the South to the opening of atomic technology to private enterprise was distinctive.

In the last decade the nation's nuclear industry has faced increasing challenge, especially after the dramatic 1979 accident at the Three Mile Island plant in Pennsylvania. Plants have been abandoned in the South as elsewhere, with the Clinch River Breeder Reactor in Tennessee being one of the most famous. Several southern states were considered as possible locations for the storage of nuclear waste, although none had been so designated by mid-1985.

See also ENVIRONMENT: / Nuclear Pollution; POLITICS: / Southern Governors' Association

J. Samuel Walker
United States Nuclear
Regulatory Commission

Redding S. Sugg, Jr., ed., *Nuclear Energy in the South* (1957); J. Samuel Walker, *Prologue* (Fall 1981).

Oil Industry

Within a year after E. L. Drake brought in the nation's first oil well outside Titusville, Penn., the South entered the petroleum picture. In the spring of 1860 a well in Wirt County, Va. (about 12 miles southeast of Parkersburg), began producing 37 to 50 barrels per day. After the creation of West Virginia, all the oil activity was in the new state. As important as oil was in West Virginia (well into the 20th century), significant numbers of West Virginia and Pennsylvania oil field workers migrated to the nascent Texas industry. The 1894 discovery in Corsicana signaled the beginning of commercial production in Texas, but the strike at Spindletop, near Beaumont, on 10 January 1901 immediately made the South a major force in the industry. The Texas Gulf Coast fields in the next few years produced quantities of oil that transformed the national, as well as the regional, economy. This new industry attracted much northern capital, mainly from Pennsylvania, and it created thousands of jobs to which farm boys flocked, thus beginning to shift the balance from a rural to an industrial economy. Once farmers went into the oil field, they usually stayed, following the booms from one new field to another.

Although Spindletop caught the national spotlight, other southern states quickly contributed significant quantities of oil. Louisiana's first important field, just outside Jennings, opened in September 1901, to be followed by the Caddo field in 1906 and Haynesville in 1921. Since World War II southern Louisiana has continued prolific production. Arkansas had two banner fields in the early 1920s—El Dorado (where H. L. Hunt entered the business) and Smackover. Oil wrought tremendous changes in the lives of farm folk in Texas, Louisiana, and Arkansas, but it had much more impact on the Indians of Oklahoma. Even before statehood in 1907, Oklahoma had experienced several notable strikes—at Bartlesville (1897), Red Fork (1901), Cleveland (1904), and Glenn Pool (1905). The last occurred on Creek land south of Tulsa, making the Creeks wealthy and Tulsa the "Oil Capital of the World." The Burbank field (1920) tapped the Osage pool, and members of that tribe experienced far more affluence than most could prudently manage. Developing that field was E. W. Marland, who in 1935 became governor of Oklahoma. That oilmen were influential in politics was also attested to when Ross Sterling, onetime president of Humble, was elected governor of Texas in 1930.

Workers at a Queen of Waco Oil Company derrick, Wortham, Tex., c. 1925

Refineries have been important, along with oil fields, in the urbanization and industrialization of the South. The region's first sizable refinery, the Standard Oil (now Exxon) plant in Baton Rouge, opened in 1909. From the 1920s onward, the Texas Gulf Coast has boasted such giants as the Magnolia (now Mobil) in Beaumont, the Gulf and Texaco in Port Arthur, and the Humble (now Exxon) in Baytown. Offshore drilling symbolizes the technological sophistication of the 1980s, but the South's first wells in water were in the Goose Creek, Tex., field in

1908. Subsequent drilling in the Red River between Texas and Oklahoma helped develop the techniques that now enable behemoth rigs to drill in the deep Gulf waters off Texas and Louisiana.

See also SOCIAL CLASS: / Oil Workers

Walter Rundell, Jr.
University of Maryland

Kenny A. Franks, *The Oklahoma Petroleum Industry* (1980); Carl C. Rister, *Oil! Titan of the Southwest* (1949); Walter Rundell, Jr., *Early Texas Oil: A Photographic History, 1866–1936* (1977).

Railroad Industry

Even though the South possessed many navigable rivers and had basically an agricultural rather than an industrial economy, it was active in the promotion of railroads in the early 19th century. Baltimore businessmen obtained a charter for the Baltimore & Ohio in 1827, and Charleston interests built a 136-mile railroad to Hamburg, S.C., between 1830 and 1833. In 1860 the 15 slave states had more than 10,000 miles of railway, or about one-third of the national total. Virginia, Georgia, and Tennessee led the South in rail mileage. On the eve of the Civil War southern railroads lagged well behind northern lines in the quality of original construction, equipment, the number of employees, traffic volume, and maintenance facilities. Long before Appomattox the southern lines were suffering from a growing deterioration of service due to general neglect, poor track repair, lack of equipment, and the war itself. By early 1865 Confederate railways were in a crippled condition.

In the late 1860s and early 1870s the South suffered from railroad carpetbaggers, men more interested in personal profit than in building new railroads. The greatest corruption was in North Carolina, South Carolina, Georgia, and Alabama. After the Panic of 1873 nearly half of the southern lines faced the sequence of default, receivership, and foreclosure. Southern rail mileage expanded with the appearance of the New South, though, and by 1900 the former slave states possessed a network of about 60,000 miles, nearly a third of the national total. In the last years of the 19th century many southern lines were merged into larger systems, consolidations generally dominated by northern men and money.

By the turn of the century the major lines serving the South included the Baltimore & Ohio, Chesapeake & Ohio, Norfolk & Western, Southern, Atlantic Coast Line, Seaboard Air Line, Louisville & Nashville, Mobile & Ohio, Illinois Central, Southern Pacific, and Missouri Pacific railroads. Both in World War I and World War II the contributions to victory made by southern railroads were unique because so many military installations were located in the South. By the 1920s southern railroads, like those of the entire nation, were being hurt by the growing competition from highways, airlines, pipelines, and improved river and canal barge service. During World War II southern railroads prospered even more than northern or western lines. This prosperity continued after the war as southern rail freight expanded with the economic surge toward the Sunbelt. By the 1980s such giant rail networks as the Family Lines, CSX, and Norfolk Southern were among the most prosperous and efficient of American railroads.

John F. Stover
Purdue University

Robert C. Black III, *The Railroads of the Confederacy* (1952); U. B. Phillips, *A History of Transportation in the Eastern Cotton Belt to 1860* (1908); John F. Stover, *The Life and Decline of the American Railroad* (1970).

Research Triangle Park

Research Triangle Park is a planned industrial research park in the Raleigh-Durham area of North Carolina including more than 5,000 acres near three research universities: Duke University, North Carolina State University, and the University of North Carolina at Chapel Hill. Developed by the nonprofit Research Triangle Foundation, it includes 40 research organizations with 20,000 employees, an annual payroll of $400 million, and an investment of $1.6 billion in construction and equipment.

The park contains industrial laboratories and trade associations, federal and state government laboratories, nonprofit research institutes, and university-related research activities. Areas of concentration include environmental sciences, pharmaceuticals and agricultural chemicals, microelectronics, and computer technology.

Governor Luther Hodges initiated the program in 1955 with the appointment of the Governor's Research Triangle Committee of corporate and university leaders. With private funding, the Governor's Committee was incorporated in 1956, and sociologist George Lee Simpson, Jr., from the Chapel Hill faculty, was appointed director. The plan was to promote the region for industrial research, and faculty members were employed initially to promote the idea. The objectives were to improve the state's low per-capita income by attracting industrial laboratories and high-technology industry to North Carolina; to diversify the industrial base from the traditional tobacco, textiles, and furniture; to reverse outmigration of North Carolina youth trained in science and engineering; and to help the universities attract and retain science and engineering faculty members by expanded consulting opportunities.

In 1957 private venture capital, with public stock offerings, was invested in 4,000 acres of scrub pinelands as "Pinelands, Inc.," but by fall 1958, the committee recognized the advantages of nonprofit ownership of the research park. With the theme of "an investment in North Carolina," banker Archie K. Davis raised $1.5 million in gifts from corporations and citizens of North Carolina to purchase Pinelands. In December the Committee became the Research Triangle Foundation, Inc., and the Research Triangle Institute was established. The institute has a staff of 1,000 with research contracts exceeding $40 million annually.

Educational support activities in the park include the North Carolina Board of Science and Technology, the Triangle Universities Computation Center, and the Triangle Universities Center for Advanced Studies, Inc. (TUCASI), which holds 120 acres in the park for joint activities of the three universities. On the campus of TUCASI are the National Humanities Center and the Microelectronics Center of North Carolina.

Although the park was developed without state appropriations, the state provided leadership, cooperation, and the support of its educational base. The success of the Triangle is a notable example of effective cooperation among state government, higher education, and the corporate community.

See also EDUCATION: / Duke University; North Carolina, University of; National Humanities Center

William F. Little
University of North Carolina
at Chapel Hill

Victor J. Danilov, *Industrial Research* (May 1971); W. B. Hamilton, *South Atlantic Quarterly* (Spring 1966); Luther H. Hodges, *Businessman in the Statehouse* (1962); Ruth Walker, *Christian Science Monitor* (15 June 1982); Louis Round Wilson, *Louis Round Wilson's Historical Sketches* (1976).

Sanders, Colonel Harland

(1890–1980) Businessman.

To people all over the world the words "It's finger lickin' good" evoke the image of a quintessential southerner, the Kentucky colonel, personified by Harland David Sanders. Neither a native southerner nor an army colonel, Sanders built a chicken franchise empire that began in the back room of a filling station in Corbin, Ky., and grew to revenues totaling $3.5 billion by 1986, with 6,500 stores in 56 countries.

Harland David Sanders was born 9 September 1890 in Henryville, Ind., to Wilbert D. and Margaret Ann Sanders. Wilbert D. Sanders died when his son was young, and Sanders left home when he was only 12. He enlisted in the army at 16; then worked on the railroad; and after taking correspondence courses in law, began representing clients in court. What by some accounts was a promising legal career ended with a courtroom incident in which Sanders was charged with assault and battery by his own client.

Sanders began selling—first insurance, then Michelin tires. Realizing that he had a knack for business, Sanders in 1930 bought a Shell Oil service station in Corbin, Ky., on old U.S. Route 25, which went south to Atlanta and east to Asheville. At the foot of the eastern Kentucky mountains, Corbin lay in an area known locally as "Hell's Half Acre." Sanders soon moved his dining-room table and six chairs into a storage room and began cooking and serving boardinghouse-style meals for truckers and travelers. He then expanded his operation from Sanders Cafe to Sanders Court, a motel with seven rooms, and began experimenting with pressure cookers and a fried chicken recipe given to him by a neighbor.

By 1949 Sanders had received from Governor Lawrence Wetherby his second Kentucky colonel's commission, an honor typically bestowed for outstanding community service or as a political favor. Although Sanders himself said "It don't mean a daggone thing" when he received the first commission from Governor Ruby Laffoon in 1935, he apparently took the second commission more seriously. He began signing his name "Colonel Harland Sanders," grew a moustache and a goatee, and allowed his nearly white hair to lengthen. Later he added the white suit and string tie to complete the Kentucky colonel image traditionally caricatured in popular films and literature: an aristocratic and chivalrous Dixie gentleman with a fondness for good horses and good bourbon. (The Colonel, though, never touched a drop.)

By 1950 the Colonel had settled on the cooking method and the 11 herbs and spices that would make his chicken world famous. In 1953 the first franchised Colonel Sanders' Kentucky Fried Chicken was sold at the Dew Drop Inn in Salt Lake City, Utah. To accommodate his daughter's distaste for dishwashing in her Florida restaurant, the Colonel came up with the notion of a "take-home" store. The prototype KFC franchise was erected in Jacksonville, Fla., and the fast-food industry was revolutionized.

By 1960 there were more than 200 franchises in the United States and Canada. The Colonel sold KFC, Inc., to John Y. Brown, Jr., and Nashville entrepreneur Jack Massey for $2 million. The Colonel was to continue in the services of the corporation as a goodwill ambassador. At times, he was more of an embarrassment than an asset, commenting publicly that the gravy he had worked so hard to perfect "tasted like wallpaper paste."

In 1971 KFC Corporation merged with Heublein, Inc., in a $288 million deal. The tireless Colonel, now in his 80s and in failing health, continued his promotional work for charities and KFC, and he attended the dedication of the Colonel Sanders Museum in Louisville in 1978. In 1980 he was hospitalized with pneumonia and died on 16 December. Colonel Harland D. Sanders, the man who personified an American dream and a southern myth, lay in state in both the Kentucky capitol and the corporate offices of KFC before interment in Louisville's Cave Hill Cemetery. Governor John Y. Brown, Jr., eulogized the Colonel, quoting from *Hamlet*: "He was a man. Take him for all and all. We shall not look upon his like again."

In 1982 R. J. Reynolds (now RJR Nabisco, Inc.) acquired

KFC, and in July 1986, Pepsico, Inc., agreed to buy the company for a book value of $850 million.

Lisa Howorth
University of Mississippi

John Pearce, ed., *The Colonel: The Captivating Biography of the Dynamic Founder of a Fast-food Empire* (1982); Harland D. Sanders, *Life as I Have Known It Has Been Finger Lickin' Good* (1974); Lawrence S. Thompson, *Georgia Review* (Spring 1953).

Southern Growth Policies Board

The Southern Growth Policies Board was established through an interstate compact in December 1971 by nine southern governors who saw that the region was undergoing rapid growth in its population and economy. Terry Sanford, former governor of North Carolina and president of Duke University, proposed the idea for a regional planning agency in a speech to a reform group, the L. Q. C. Lamar Society. Sanford suggested that interstate planning and cooperation would be the keys to helping the South "win the awesome race with time to save the cities and preserve the countryside. Now is the time, and the South can lead the way."

The member states now include Alabama, Arkansas, Florida, Georgia, Kentucky, Louisiana, Mississippi, North Carolina, Oklahoma, South Carolina, Tennessee, and Virginia, as well as the Commonwealth of Puerto Rico. Texas, Maryland, West Virginia, Missouri, Delaware, and the Virgin Islands are also eligible to join.

The agreement specifies that the board shall consist of five members from each participating state—the governor, a state senator, and a state representative appointed by their respective presiding officers, and two leading citizens appointed by the governor. A governor serves as chairman of the board for a one-year term. The work of the staff is reviewed quarterly by an executive committee of approximately 15 board members, and the staff is headed by an executive director.

Article III of the Interstate Agreement directs the board to prepare and maintain a "Statement of Regional Objectives," including recommended approaches to regional problems. The statement may also identify projects deemed to be of regional significance. It is amended or revised at least once every six years.

The first "Statement of Regional Objectives" was prepared in 1974 by a distinguished panel of civic leaders appointed by the governors. The mission of this panel, known as the Commission on the Future of the South, was to recommend policies to foster continued economic growth, while at the same time mitigating adverse sociological and environmental effects. The commissioners concluded that a policy of "no growth" for the South was neither feasible nor desirable and suggested that the staff consider policies to influence the distribution of growth in the region.

Within this framework the board strengthened its research and information capabilities, emphasizing regionwide economic-development activities. The board also developed a significant role in representing the interests of the southern states in Washington in the so-called Sunbelt-Frostbelt conflict. As the board became more deeply involved in federal issues, a second office was staffed in Washington in 1977 to monitor federal actions that could result in negative consequences for the region.

In 1980 the second Commission on the Future of the South framed a new report to guide the board's program activities. Their recommendations focused on four areas of regional development: the economy, cities, children, and energy. Utilizing this basic planning document, the board began to assess and redefine its mission.

In 1982 the board relinquished its Washington office, maintaining a reduced presence in a new office to be supported by the Southern Governors' Association. At its Tenth Anniversary Conference, the board rededicated itself to regional economic development—specifically, "to provide an early alert system for our states as to intermediate-range policy options of regional importance which will maximize opportunities for and minimize impediments to economic growth and development."

The board today represents a unique vehicle for regional coordination and public-private cooperation. The availability of opportunities in the region, the positive attitudes regarding future growth potential, and the healthy confluence of business and government interests provide a strong framework for future progress.

See also HISTORY AND MANNERS: / L. Q. C. Lamar Society; POLITICS: / Southern Governors' Association

William Winter
David Crews
Jackson, Mississippi

James C. Cobb, *The Selling of the South: The Southern Crusade for Industrial Development, 1936–1980* (1982); *New York Times* (9 January 1977); Southern Growth Policies Board, *Annual Report* (1977).

Stevens, J. P., and Company

J. P. Stevens and Company traces its beginnings to a Massachusetts woolen mill founded in 1813 by Nathaniel Stevens. In 1899 John P. Stevens, Nathaniel's grandson, established the New York commission house from which the present firm takes its name. Stevens came to serve as selling agent for a number of southern cotton textile firms, eight of which merged with the Stevens family interests in 1946 to form the modern corporation. In succeeding years, Stevens transferred its woolen operations to the South, in part to counter unionization efforts. It also expanded its holdings of southern mills, becoming the second largest publicly held American textile corporation.

In 1963 the Textile Workers' Union of America (TWUA) launched a campaign to organize Stevens's southern plants. Company management, notably Board Chairman James D. Finley, a native Georgian, responded aggressively, being found guilty repeatedly of illegal harassment of organizers and prounion workers. The TWUA was unable to win a representation election at any Stevens mill until workers at the firm's Roanoke Rapids, N.C., plants gave the union a small majority in August 1974. Despite its victory, however, the union was unable to negotiate a contract. Complaining of company delaying tactics, the newly created Amalgamated Clothing and Textile Workers' Union (ACTWU) launched a boycott in June 1976 against Stevens products. The boycott proved ineffective, but it successfully focused national attention on Stevens as a symbol of southern antiunion obduracy. Numerous church groups endorsed the boycott, and demonstrators besieged stockholders' meetings; the Roanoke Rapids saga became the basis for a critically acclaimed motion picture, *Norma Rae* (1978).

More telling than the boycott was ACTWU's innovative "corporate campaign," which mobilized the investment power of unions and their sympathizers to press Stevens's lenders and "outside" directors to sever their links to the company. Pressure of this sort, along with growing internal problems, began to sap the company's strength, while the retirement of Finley in January 1980 permitted it to take a more flexible stance. In October 1980 Stevens and ACTWU reached an accord, the company agreeing to contracts at unionized mills, the union to calling off its anti-Stevens campaign. Although unionization has made little progress at Stevens since 1980, contests have been largely free of irregularities, and collective bargaining has proceeded routinely. All outstanding legal disputes between the company and the union were settled in October 1983.

See also SOCIAL CLASS: / Textile Workers

David L. Carlton
Vanderbilt University

Mimi Conway, *Rise Gonna Rise: A Portrait of Southern Textile Workers* (1979); Lloyd C. Ferguson, *From Family Firm to Corporate Giant: J. P. Stevens and Company, 1813–1963* (1970); Jim Overton et al., *Southern Exposure* (Spring 1978).

Textile Industry

Small-scale textile mills could be found in the South as far back as the American Revolution, and the textile industry gained a firm foothold in the Piedmont area of Virginia, North Carolina, South Carolina, and Georgia during the antebellum era. By 1850 more than 200 textile mills operated in the South. Leaders of the industry included William Gregg and Daniel Pratt, both of South Carolina. The textile mill has made its greatest impact on the region in the past hundred years. Developing rapidly after 1880, the industry soon rivaled the enormous New England center in plants, equipment, and personnel. The number of spindles in operation more than doubled in the 1890s, and the amount of capital invested in the southern textile industry rose from $22.8 million in 1880 to $132.4 million in 1900. It remains today the region's major industrial employer.

The pattern of mill expansion in the South differed in important ways from that which marked the older textile region chiefly because of distinctive physical and labor conditions of the area. Hydroelectric power, developed extensively because of the geographic advantages of the Piedmont, enabled mill entrepreneurs to locate their factories in rural areas where labor was relatively more plentiful. Textile technology required comparatively large numbers of unskilled workers. Cheap labor was to be found in the Southeast and this, more than any other single factor, stimulated indigenous textile expansion and, in time, lured northern capital to the region.

Although the pool of surplus white farm labor in the Piedmont has varied over time with changing agricultural and industrial conditions, it has generally been large. Unlike those in other southern industries, textile-mill jobs were long reserved for these white workers. The virtual certainty of widespread social protest long discouraged mill managers from employing black operatives. Only in recent years have black workers been welcomed in the mills, where they now account for approximately one-fourth of southern textile employees.

Remote mill sites encouraged the construction of owner-controlled mill villages to house workers and their families. The pattern developed in the antebellum era from the factory and mill village built by William Gregg at Graniteville, S.C. Mill villages traditionally contained housing for workers, as well as schools, general stores, churches, and sometimes medical centers and recreational areas, all owned and operated by the manufacturing company. Although mill housing has been worker owned since the 1950s, this strong community orientation continues to distinguish the industry in the South. The Southeast remains a region with good transportation facilities and few large cities. Its rate of urbanization has been slower than that of other industrial centers, a fact related to its established dependence on the textile industry. The organizational structure adopted by the industry in the South was dictated by unique qualities in the factors of production in the region. In turn, the textile industry has powerfully influenced the culture and socioeconomic position of the modern South.

See also SOCIAL CLASS: / Company Towns; Textile Workers

Mary J. Oates
Regis College

Jack Blicksilver, *Cotton Manufacturing in the Southeast: An Historical Analysis* (1959); Glenn Gilman, *Human Relations in the Industrial Southeast: A Study of the Textile Industry* (1956); Broadus Mitchell, *The Rise of Cotton Mills in the South* (1921).

Timber Industry

Beginning with a concentration on naval stores (turpentine and pitch), the southern timber industry has come to include a diversity of products related primarily to southern yellow pine but including cypress and other hardwoods as well. The 17th- and 18th-century timber industry was located in the Carolinas and characterized by small, low-capital establishments with low annual production. Sawmills and distilleries for turpentine were located in the woods. Those industries used slave labor organized on a task system. The smaller, less-developed but still-important business of searching for live oak timbers used in shipbuilding often involved migrant crews who searched the coastal islands for appropriate timber.

By the middle of the 19th century the entire industry was both shifting its location and broadening its scope. During the years immediately after the Civil War, naval stores and sawmilling operations moved into Georgia, Florida, and the Gulf Coast South. In the 1880s Georgia led the South in naval stores and timber production, and in the 20th century Florida and Gulf Coast states have come to dominate. That shift was accompanied by the increasing use of southern pine not only for naval stores but also for other timber products including crossties, building materials, and, increasingly, pulpwood for paper manufacturing.

Changing labor patterns accompanied expansion. Slave labor gave way to free labor at the end of the Civil War. Many of the early postwar laborers were migrants from the Carolinas who followed the timber industry into other states. Later timber workers included both contract migrant workers and seasonal workers who retained ties to the agricultural economies of the Southeast. In some areas of the timber belt, labor came from the often-harsh convict lease system. Lumber camps and lumber towns similar to textile towns appeared throughout the South and particularly the Gulf Coast South as the industry expanded. Regardless of the source of the labor, the laborers were a colorful but transient population. Not as radical as their Pacific Northwest counterparts, southern timber workers nevertheless participated in the activities of the Knights of Labor and the Industrial Workers of the World.

Lumbering in western North Carolina, postcard, early 20th century

In the 20th century small-scale industries gave way to large concerns owning substantial tracts of land throughout the South. Although originally exploitive and unscientific, southern timber companies have built on the turpentine and conservation experiments of Charles Holmes Herty to provide an important example of scientifically inspired diversity of products and management of renewable resources. Led by trade associations such as the Southern Pine Association, timber operators have standardized the product and often controlled the price. A diverse product line, large-scale operations, and the control of land continue to make the timber industry an important part of the southern economic landscape. For many southern laborers and cities such operations are crucial to survival.

See also AGRICULTURE: / Naval Stores; ENVIRONMENT: Trees; / Cypress; SCIENCE AND MEDICINE: / Herty, Charles Holmes; SOCIAL CLASS: / Timber Workers

Thomas F. Armstrong
Georgia College

Thomas D. Clark, *The Greening of the South: The Recovery of Land and Forest* (1984), *Mississippi Quarterly* (Spring 1972); James Defebaugh, *History of the Lumber Industry of America* (1906); Percival Perry, "The Naval Stores Industry in the Ante-Bellum South" (Ph.D. dissertation, Duke University, 1947).

Tobacco Industry

Tobacco is the fifth most important cash crop in the United States. It has occupied an important position among crops grown in the southeastern United States since the days of Sir Walter Raleigh. North Carolina and Kentucky are the principal tobacco-producing states in the country, but Virginia, South Carolina, Georgia, Tennessee, and Florida all contain significant areas where tobacco is grown. In recent years tobacco has meant $1 billion annually for the farmers of North Carolina and approximately half that amount for their counterparts in Kentucky. All five major tobacco regions of the United States are in the South: the Burley Belt, the Old Belt, the New Bright Belt, the Border Belt, and the Georgia-Florida Belt.

Towns in tobacco regions are dotted with large warehouses, some as big as a football field, where the crop is sold at auction. From 2 to 12 such structures may be concentrated in a single town, giving it a distinctive character. A typical tobacco town of 40,000 people has, for example, 3,000,000 square feet of floor space under the roofs of specialized structures designed for selling tobacco, a process that lasts for only three and a half months.

The processing of tobacco (redrying, cleaning, and stemming) is carried on in the same towns where the sales warehouses are located; thus, the processing normally takes place within the borders of producing re-

Scene at a Kentucky tobacco auction, c. 1960

gions. Tobacco products, such as cigarettes, pipe and chewing tobacco, and snuff, are manufactured in large cities—near, but not necessarily in, the areas where the crop is grown. Notable among tobacco-manufacturing centers are Richmond, Va.; Durham and Winston-Salem, N.C.; and Louisville, Ky. Partially processed tobacco and tobacco products are important American agricultural exports. The two outstanding tobacco ports of the United States are Norfolk, Va., and Wilmington, N.C.

Tobacco was the last important cash crop in the United States to be mechanized. Within the past quarter century that process has replaced thousands of workers in all the flue-cured tobacco producing areas. The shift to machinery has freed a large labor force from agriculture. Unlike the mechanization of other cash crops, tobacco mechanization has not resulted in massive out-migration of recently emancipated farm workers; they have remained at home and become a powerful force in attracting many new factories into the old tobacco districts. In fact, the "eastern" or "New Bright Belt" of North Carolina has shifted from a predominantly rural economy to a mixed economy in a single generation.

One of the oldest agricultural products of the United States, and an indigenous crop, tobacco is still a cornerstone of the agricultural economy of no less than five southern states. It is a controlled substance in the sense that growth of the crop is strictly regulated by an elaborate federal acreage-poundage crop-allotment and price-support system. As a revenue source, tobacco is a crop of national significance. When additional money is needed, tobacco products are always on the list for a tax increase. Though a warning from the surgeon general about cigarette smoking being dangerous to one's health appears on every cigarette pack, and religious groups, including the Southern Baptist Convention, have discouraged use of tobacco, the multibillion-dollar tobacco industry appears to be alive, well, and growing.

See also AGRICULTURE: / Tobacco Culture; SOCIAL CLASS: / Tobacco Workers

Ennis L. Chestang
East Carolina University

W. W. Garner, E. G. Moss et al., U. S. Department of Agriculture, *Yearbook of Agriculture* (1922); J. Fraser Hart and Ennis L. Chestang, *Geographical Review* (October 1978); Tobacco Institute, *Tobacco Industry Profile* (1982); U.S. Department of Commerce Bureau of the Census, *Census of Agriculture* (1978).

Trucking Industry

Though trucking appeared in the Northeast and Midwest soon after World War I, the industry's southern beginnings were slow. Initially, trucks connected rural locales and serviced metropolitan areas, but no large cities on the scale of those in the North existed in the South of the 1920s. Early southern trucking, moreover, met with hostile actions from its natural competitor, the railroads. Suffering revenue losses, particularly to cotton-hauling trucks, rail executives pressured legislators in Texas, Louisiana, Kentucky, and Tennessee to enact restrictive motor-carrier laws in the late 1920s and early 1930s. Ad hoc truck associations challenged these laws, but Texas successfully defended its statutes before the U.S. Supreme Court in 1932. The state's right to protect and conserve its highways emerged as the controlling issue in these cases.

Southern truckers remained undeterred, however, and, in a somewhat un-southern manner, joined forces with executives from other sections of the country in the fall of 1933 and established the American Trucking Association, Inc. (ATA). As part of the National Recovery Administration of the New Deal, southern officials in the ATA offices in Washington, D.C., and in the state associations worked hard to stabilize the disparate industry. In a few instances intimidation forced white and black truckers alike to join the state organizations and to register their vehicles with the federal agency. The subject of regional wage scales elicited some concern for the welfare of black truckers. One business manager urged the North Carolina Truck Owners Association to keep "the wage scale sufficiently low," for "[w]ith conditions being the same the great majority of employers of labor will hire white men to the total exclusion of negro men." With the advent of federal regulation in 1935, the trucking industry nationwide began a protected existence under which it has since flourished.

The growth of trucking in the South paralleled the rise of the Sunbelt phenomenon. By the 1970s every southern

Trucking on U.S. Route 29 in Georgia, 1943

state except Arkansas, Mississippi, and South Carolina received over $1 billion in salaries from the industry each year (Texas received over $5 billion). In fact, the South as a region leads the nation in trucking salaries. Further, if pickups and vans are included, the South contains over one-third of all trucks registered in the United States. From a slow beginning, trucking has become an integral aspect of the southern economy.

See also HISTORY AND MANNERS: Automobile; / Pickup Truck

William R. Childs
Ohio State University

William R. Childs, *Trucking and the Public Interest: The Emergence of Federal Regulation, 1914–1940* (1985); Milton S. Heath, *Southern Economics Journal* (August 1934); Motor Vehicle Manufacturers Association of the United States, Inc., *Motor Truck Facts* (1974).

Walton, Sam

(b. 1918) Businessman.

U.S. News & World Report magazine in 1986 proclaimed Sam Moore Walton of Bentonville in northeastern Arkansas the wealthiest man in the United States. He had, at that point, made $4.3 billion from his 900 Wal-Mart discount stores that operated in 22 states, mainly in the South and Southwest. Walton and his family own 39 percent of Wal-Mart, which had fiscal 1985 sales of $6.5 billion.

Walton began in retailing working for J. C. Penney, and then in 1945 he and his brother J. L. raised $25,000 to open a variety store in Newport, Ark., and later bought a five-and-dime store on the town square. By 1962 the Waltons operated 15 dime stores, and the number had grown to 30 by 1970, when the business went public. Walton targets small towns especially for his stores, and they have been vital economic forces in many southern states. Walton, through Wal-Mart and a new business, Sam's Wholesale Club, created more employment in Mississippi in the 1980s than any other person.

Sam Walton, founder of Wal-Mart Stores, Inc., 1980s

Despite his success Walton remains an almost stereotypical traditional southerner in many ways. He continues to live in a modest house on a shady street in his small hometown in Arkansas; he drives a 1979 Ford pickup truck, hunts quail, and has his hair cut at a traditional, three-chair, no-waiting barbershop. He encourages a family feeling among his Wal-Mart employees, and his store openings are southern theater—combining the emotionalism of revivalism, fiddling contests, and school pep rallies.

Charles Reagan Wilson
University of Mississippi

Forbes (28 October 1985); *U. S. News & World Report* (21 July 1986).

Language

MICHAEL MONTGOMERY
University of South Carolina
CONSULTANT

Sequoyah, inventor of the Cherokee alphabet

English Language

Few traits identify southerners as readily as their speech. For better or for worse, the way that southerners use the language is often noticed first by non-southerners and draws the most comment from them. When Lyndon Johnson and Jimmy Carter ran for president, the country and the media gave extraordinary attention to their accents. Frequently the way southerners talk also draws admiration. When Sam Ervin chaired the Watergate hearings, the nation was spellbound by this North Carolinian's adroit manipulation of the English language. Southerners are well known for their ability to stump, to preach, and to tell stories.

For many southerners, speech is a badge that signifies much about them: their upbringing, their loyalties, their education, and their roots. Speech is as much a part of their heritage as grits, football, and barbecue. Speech is inseparable from local and regional pride and cultural traditions. Yet southerners are acutely aware of how conspicuous their speech is to non-southerners (Tennessee Williams was given his nickname by his fraternity brothers in the Midwest because of his thick southern accent) and that their speech is often caricatured elsewhere in the country. They are thus often schizophrenic about their speech, unsure whether they want to be set off from the rest of the country. This makes some southerners insecure, and over the past two generations many middle-class southern parents have tried to eradicate the more distinctive regional features of their children's speech.

Most southerners, however, defy the notion that they have any reason to change the way they talk. A typical way for a southerner to put his feelings is "I don't want my speech to be viewed as nonstandard, but I don't want to change my speech, either." When an urban university in the South recently offered a course for southerners wanting to change their accents, particularly those aspiring to traffic with non-southerners, the instructor of the course was publicly vilified and harassed.

Although the South is the most distinctive speech region in the United States, it is hardly more uniform than the nation as a whole. Most discussions have obscured the diversity within the region by unfortunately contrasting a generalized "southern English" with "General American English" or "Standard English," the latter two being abstract, even mythical entities never described and certainly not uniform. Neither the Mason-Dixon line nor any other demarcation has ever set the region off from the rest of the country by its speech. Early immigrants to the South were as heterogeneous as those in any other region, and the South was no more isolated as a whole than other regions. Yet all Americans, southerners and non-southerners alike, tend to perceive the South as a speech region. Linguistic research cannot, however, identify any common denominator that can safely be termed a "southern accent" or a "southern dialect."

Explaining the discrepancy between linguistic facts and folk perceptions and beliefs is not easy. Take the putative "southern drawl," for instance. Linguists have hardly begun to describe it and are now relying on spectrographic analyses to do so; to them *drawl* refers to the lengthening and raising of accented vowels, normally accompanied by a change in voice pitch. It involves the addition of a second or even a third vowel but does not necessarily entail a slower overall speech tempo. What nonlinguists mean when they say "drawl," however, is different. To the general public a drawl is a very broad and inclusive term for the speech cadence, voice quality, and general language patterns most often associated with southerners. These speech qualities (rhythm, cadence, intonation, and vowel qualities) are noticed by non-southerners, and this is why the term *drawl* is so widely and loosely applied.

The persistent folk notions alleging a distinctive speech in the region usually refer to a "drawl" and mention the influence of the hot climate and the slow pace of life. The heart of why the region's speech is distinctive, though, lies in the mundane realms of demography and social factors on the one hand and, on the other, in the realm of psychology, in the consciousness of the region's people.

The South is more diverse in speech than any other region of the country, with the most distinctive varieties of southern speech found in isolated areas such as the mountains and the coastal areas of the Outer Banks, the Chesapeake Islands, and the Sea Islands. Speech patterns vary immensely within the region, so that even the well-worn stereotypes (e.g., the lack of *r* after a vowel, or the use of *y'all*) do not characterize speakers throughout the territory. Moreover, nearly all features usually ascribed to the South can be found, usually among old-fashioned speakers, elsewhere in the country. The usual admonitions against stereotypes apply here not only because of the vast range of speakers within the region, but also because many linguistic features considered southern often differentiate citizens within the region sociologically. One can see, for example, several features that characterize most speakers of the region and that also characterize most black speakers outside the South, whose language is a "transported English" one or two generations removed from the rural South.

Among the representative grammatical features that are southern, some of which do not have exact equivalents in other varieties of American English, are the following: (1) *y'all* and *you all* (the second being the somewhat more formal variant) as second-person plural pronouns; (2) "double-modal" or "multiple-modal" constructions such as *might could*, *may can*, and *might should*; (3) "perfective" *done* used for emphasis, as in *I done told you that*; (4) *liked to*, meaning "almost," as in *I liked to died*; (5) frequent use of the *a-* prefix with verbs ending in *-ing*, as *a-walking* and *a-talking*.

Among representative phonological features of southern English are the following: (1) the tendency to pronounce as a diphthong [ai] the monothong [i] in words like *tide* and *time*; (2) *r*-lessness, for blacks, upper-class whites, and many middle-class whites, in words like *beer* and *bear*; (3) drawling of vowels (discussed previously), especially common in the Lower South, in words like *bid*, *bed*, and *bad*; (4) "breaking" of some vowels, especially common in the Upper South, so that *steel* is pronounced like *stale,* and *stale* like *stile;* (5) similar pronunciation of front vowels before nasal consonants, so that pairs of words like *pen* and *pin* and *ten* and *tin* are pronounced alike; and (6) nasalization of vowels, as in words like *pumpkin.*

If no unique linguistic features distinguish the South as a speech region, then on what basis do linguists identify it as a speech region? Three characteristics differentiate the region linguistically: (1) a unique combination of linguistic features; (2) the use of these linguistic features more often and by a wider range of the population than in other regions of the country; and (3) the consciousness of the people in the South that they form a region with characteristic southern speech. These three qualities are clearly interrelated; a person's use of "southern features" can best be correlated with his or her attachment to the region. Because the South is so large and diverse and because linguistic research is so painstaking, only a few comprehensive descriptions of the speech of the region exist, among these being Gordon Wood's *Vocabulary Change* (1971) and the *Linguistic Atlas* volumes on the South Atlantic states (Kurath, 1949, and Kurath and McDavid, 1961) completed by material on the remaining southern states (Pederson et al., 1981 and Pederson et al., 1986).

From the beginning, scholarly study and popular curiosity have focused on two general issues: (1) When and how did the distinctiveness of southern speech develop? What is its extent? How distinctive is it, and how is it changing? and (2) What is the relationship between white speech and black speech in the South? In exploring its distinctiveness one must detail the history of southern speech and its geographical dimensions by outlining the principal speech areas within the region. The history of the study of southern English is another aspect of the story, as is the consciousness of the speakers of the region. Finally, one must outline the relevant issues surrounding the question of how white speech and black speech are related. There is not yet a consensus on these general issues, but present-day linguistic research in the South is very active and promises to bring a fuller understanding.

The subregional designations based primarily on Linguistic Atlas research will be used here. These are, namely, the Coastal Southern (also known as Lower Southern or Lowland Southern, covering the Atlantic Coastal Plain from Virginia to Texas), and the South Midland (sometimes known as Upland Southern or Upper Southern, covering the Piedmont and the southern Appalachians from Virginia through South Carolina and the hill areas above the Piedmont in Georgia and Alabama).

Historical Derivation. What historical factors account for the development of a distinctive southern speech? Several have been proposed. Theories about the impact of climate and personality are widely adhered to, but they must be dismissed as invalid.

1. Climate and pace of life. The notion that weather is responsible for habits of southern speech is widely prevalent but easily refuted. The nasality of South Midland speech is often attributed to rainfall and humidity, and the "drawl" of the Coastal and Lower South to the long, hot summers, which supposedly retard the pace of life and consequently the pace of speech. Put forth by several early social scientists and journalists (such as Clarence Cason in his *90° in the Shade*) and still widely believed by the general public, this theory is clearly inaccurate. Natives of Charleston and the South Carolina Low Country, among the hottest areas of the region, normally speak with abbreviated vowels rather than the elongated ones of the "drawl"; besides, southerners are not known to talk more rapidly in the winter.

2. Personality of the people. The notion that southerners and their speech are distinctive out of politeness and gentility is a sentimental folk notion. While such qualities may be encoded in speech (such as in the traditional use of *ma'am* and *sir* as modes of address in the South) and in other social behavior, the case for any close connection between southern hospitality and typical language behavior can hardly be carried far.

3. Demographic factors. These are the most valid suggestions, particularly regarding original settlement patterns, migration, and the influence of topography.

A firm understanding of the exact area(s) of the British Isles from which the speech of the South's early settlers derives continues to be an elusive quest because of three factors: the diversity of the early settlers; the uncertain social dynamics of the 17th, 18th, and 19th centuries; and the intrinsic problems of "proving" dissemination of a linguistic feature. Even though a majority of the early white settlers in the Lower South, for instance, were from London and the southern counties of Britain, scholars know little about their speech patterns of more than 200 years ago. No doubt the competition of languages and dialects in the early days of settlement in the South involved a leveling and an amalgamation, producing a sort of middle ground between dialects; this differed from region to region of the country. The speech of the coastal areas of the South seems to resemble the speech of the eastern counties of Britain, the speech of the Lower South in general resembles that of London and the southern counties of Britain in many respects, and the speech of the southern hill country is akin to the speech of the north of Britain, of Scotland and Northern Ireland.

Such gross connections with British speech patterns can be made because far fewer non-English-speaking immigrants from continental Europe settled in the South than in the northern colonies. But the influx of millions of Africans, speaking many dozens of languages and brought against their will, has multiplied the complexity of the situation manyfold, and their social disparity with the white population compounds it as well. The cauldron of competing speech varieties and languages brought by different speakers was the norm throughout the region, even in remote locations. But widely encountered statements about isolated areas of the South—whether the Outer Banks, the Chesapeake Islands, or the southern Appalachian Mountains—preserving "pure Scotch-Irish" or "pure Elizabethan" are exaggerations, however powerful or appealing these myths may be and however ardently they may be held by the local population or by the early linguistic literature on the region.

South Midland speech derives ultimately from the colonial settlements in the Delaware Valley of Pennsylvania. It was carried southwestward down into Virginia and North Carolina and then in the 19th century across the northern parts of Georgia, Alabama, and Mississippi and also across Tennessee, Kentucky, Arkansas, and into east Texas. Coastal Southern speech was also carried southwestward from the colonial settlements in Virginia and the Carolinas into southern Georgia, Alabama, and Mississippi and then northward into Arkansas, western Tennessee, and Kentucky, into Louisiana and east Texas, and into Florida. Crossing migration patterns have blended these two general varieties of speech in the interior South, so that the more clear-cut distinctions found in the Atlantic states diminish. Language contact with non-English speakers—French, Mexican, American Indian—also distinguishes the English one finds in the interior South.

When the speech of the South became distinctive is unclear, although the first half of the 19th century, the period when the region achieved its fullest expression of regional consciousness, would make the most sense. Brief statements of Noah Webster and the Reverend John Witherspoon in the late 18th century noted (and condemned) characteristic southern usages as contrary to the national ideal. In the early 19th century one can find extended published comments about speech in the South, such as Fanny Kemble's comments (see Mathews, 1931).

Although the vocabulary of American English began to differ from that of British English almost immediately, because of borrowing from the American Indians and from African and continental European settlers, the grammar and the pronunciation throughout the colonies remained close to the mother country until their separation; a large proportion of colonists were either born in Britain or were one generation removed. The comments of British travelers and journalists both before and after the American Revolution focused on a few peculiarities of American speech (usually to condemn them, even though they were with rare exception terms derived from regional British speech), but more often they expressed wonder at the relative uniformity of American dialects, even those of the backwoods. After the Revolution all aspects of American English increasingly diverged from British English, either by diminishing contact or by deliberate choice (e.g., spellings and pronunciations attributed to Noah Webster's Anglophobia). (This does not mean, however, that American English was usually the innovator; American English, especially in the South, exhibits a kind of colonial lag in retaining many words and pronunciations prevalent in Britain in the 17th and 18th centuries.)

Just as the South has been conservative in its cultural institutions and agrarian habits, so too southern speech in general (not just the isolated relic areas) has been more conservative than other regional varieties of American English, preserving many usages common to 19th-century British speech that today are rarely found either in Great Britain or in any other area of the United States. Most of the salient older forms preserved in southern speech are lexical (e.g., *poke, tote,* these features usually being considered "quaint"), and grammatical (e.g., the past tense verb forms *holp, clum, knowed*), but several of the region's distinctive pronunciations are in fact preserved from the 18th century. The pronunciation of *get* as *git*, the alveolar pronunciation of the suffix *-ing* as *in* in words like *singing* and *dancing*, and the absence of *r* after vowels were all fashionable British usage 200 years ago, for example, even though many such pronunciations today are ignorantly stigmatized as "nonstandard" and discouraged in the 20th-century schoolroom. Cleanth Brooks (1937) claims these pronunciations survived in southern English, as opposed to New England speech, because of a strong oral tradition that has resisted admonitions of schoolteachers to pronounce words as they are spelled. Thus, if they wish, southerners can with some justice claim that their speech is closer to the "King's English" than that of most other Americans, although it is certainly not "Elizabethan."

The southern interest in determining roots applies to language no less than to bloodlines, so efforts to establish cross-Atlantic ties continue to be undertaken by both linguists and nonlinguists. Hans Kurath, the founder and longtime director of the Linguistic Atlas project, designed the Atlas questionnaire to collect linguistic items that could be compared to regional British dialects, and several scholars have made comparisons of this kind. The odds against establishing clear relationships are staggering, but the quest continues. The matter of time span is not as problematic as the means of establishing proof. Cleanth Brooks has contended for over 50 years that southern speech, including such general features as the drawl and specific archaic pronunciations such as *gyarden* (for *garden*) and *bile* (for *boil*), derives primarily from the southwestern counties of Britain. In his efforts to hear the rhythm and record the echoes of the southern idiom in the old country, Brooks tried to compare the intonation of British speech with that of southern speech, a quest far more elusive than pinning down individual words.

For over a century researchers in the South, often nonlinguists, have published studies detailing analogs of southern features in British English. Most often these have been lists comparing words in the speech of relic groups such as mountaineers, blacks, islanders, or southerners in general to forms found in Chaucer, Shakespeare, and even Old English. A combination of regional and local pride and defensiveness about southern English has motivated such efforts.

Change in Southern Speech. Southern speech has undergone major changes in the latter half of the 20th century, as have all regional varieties of English in our highly mobile and increasingly urbanized and industrialized society. Yet this does not mean, as linguistic research reveals, that southern English is necessarily converging with other varieties of American English or losing its distinctiveness. Changes in vocabulary are the most dramatic and are primarily in the direction of homogeneity with the rest of the country, but grammar and especially phonology, while evolving, are by no means moving in the direction of the rest of the country. One recent study has shown, for instance, that young men in a small Alabama city use the "drawl" more than older women, an important indication of the desire of southerners to preserve their speech, since grammar and pronunciation carry more social weight and tend to be stigmatized more than vocabulary.

The sentimental often bewail linguistic change, especially in vocabulary, as the demise of a language that had more color, expressiveness, and charm. Their assumption is that the standardized, nondescript speech of the national media, and of newscasters in particular, is responsible for homogenizing Americans' speech in our television-addicted society. This assumption has little foundation in empirical evidence, and it presupposes conditions unlikely to be true for most individuals: that the newscasters themselves possess sufficient prestige to be mimicked and that Americans talk back to their televisions and radios (linguists believe people usually pattern their speech after real-life models). Television is not standardizing American speech, nor is homogeneity developing.

The principal forces of change in contemporary American English are social ones—mobility (especially the upward kind), mass education, and urbanization (the massive shift of the population to urban areas since World War II). In the South these forces have blurred the traditional distinctions in speech lingering from the days of greater social stratification. The speech, even of natives, in the urban South of Atlanta or Memphis today is very different from that of a generation ago. The speech of successive generations just down the road in the small-town South of Milledgeville, Ga., or Henning, Tenn., is not nearly so divergent. Today young, middle-class speakers of the urban and suburban South are often closer to their counterparts in the urban North and West than to their peers in the rural South living just a county or two away. One doubts that urbanites watch more television than their country cousins. The extent to which the speech of modern-day, middle-class citizens in the urban and suburban South, and in a few respects the speech throughout the country, is converging reflects common social forces, not the influence of television.

The influence of these social forces has meant two things: (1) the variety of regional dialects in the South is being replaced by social dialects, and (2) regional dialect boundaries are shifting in the South, as the South Midland region expands at the expense of the Lower Southern region. Whereas urban centers such as Charleston, Savannah, and Richmond exercised prestige in the days of the colonies, the newer metropolises in the Upper South, such as Charlotte, Nashville, and Atlanta, are now the dynamic centers for linguistic change and development of regional standards of speech.

McDavid (1957) claims the older type of "elegant" Lower Southern speech found in the former plantation belt, from Virginia southward and then westward to west Texas and northward into Kentucky and dominated by such focal areas as Charleston and Richmond, has been losing its prestige. The influence of Charleston is also receding, even though it was still strong and spreading in the 1920s (see McDavid, 1948). McDavid attributes this not to the influence of a national standard but rather to the increasing dominance of both the Upper Southern speakers and the former lower- and middle-class speakers who have ascended the social ladder. Other studies, in Georgia and Alabama, confirm the expansion of the Upper South or South Midland dialect's influence at the expense of the Lower South.

There is, however, scant evidence that the recent settlement of northern migrants and retirees in the region is making southerners speak more like these new arrivals. Most southerners are rather strongly attached to their way of talking, and one of the last things they would want is to talk "like a Yankee." Recent research suggests that the accents of some younger southerners are becoming more distinctive and less like those of either their parents or non-southerners.

The Scholarly Study of Southern Speech. There is more commentary on the speech of the American South (including the southern Appalachian areas) than on that of any other region of the country. Much of this has been written by nonacademics, suggesting that the people of the region are curious about and proud of their own speech. Their work is motivated by a fascination with local language patterns and an antiquarian interest in exotic and picturesque localisms found in such isolated relic areas as southern Appalachia, the Outer Banks, and the Sea Islands. Localisms are used most often by older, less-educated, and less-traveled speakers. The frequent discussion of such expressions has in some respects exaggerated the exoticism of the region's speech, particularly the speech of blacks in the South.

The South is the only region to have a book-length bibliography devoted to its speech. The *Annotated Bibliography of Southern American English* (1971) has been recently updated to include over 3,000 items. The early literature on southern speech, until roughly 1930, was predominantly word lists, collections of picturesque and unusual localisms. These collections, rarely rigorous or based on surveys of any kind, dealt mostly with vocabulary but occasionally commented on phonology and grammar. With few exceptions, they discussed speech impressionistically, without relating the use of language to social variables such as age, social status, education, occupation, or gender. Neglecting these variables has led to a presentation of southern speech as more uniform and more different from the rest of the country than has ever been the case.

The collection of phonological information on southern English from local surveys, especially in Louisiana, predominated through the 1930s and 1940s. The systematic study of language patterns in the region began in earnest with the completion of fieldwork for the *Linguistic Atlas of the Middle and South Atlantic States* (LAMSAS) in the late 1930s. Details on the age, education, occupation, and social habits and contacts of each informant for the project were noted. Summary volumes covering this territory, which includes Maryland, Virginia, North Carolina, South Carolina, eastern Georgia, and the north-

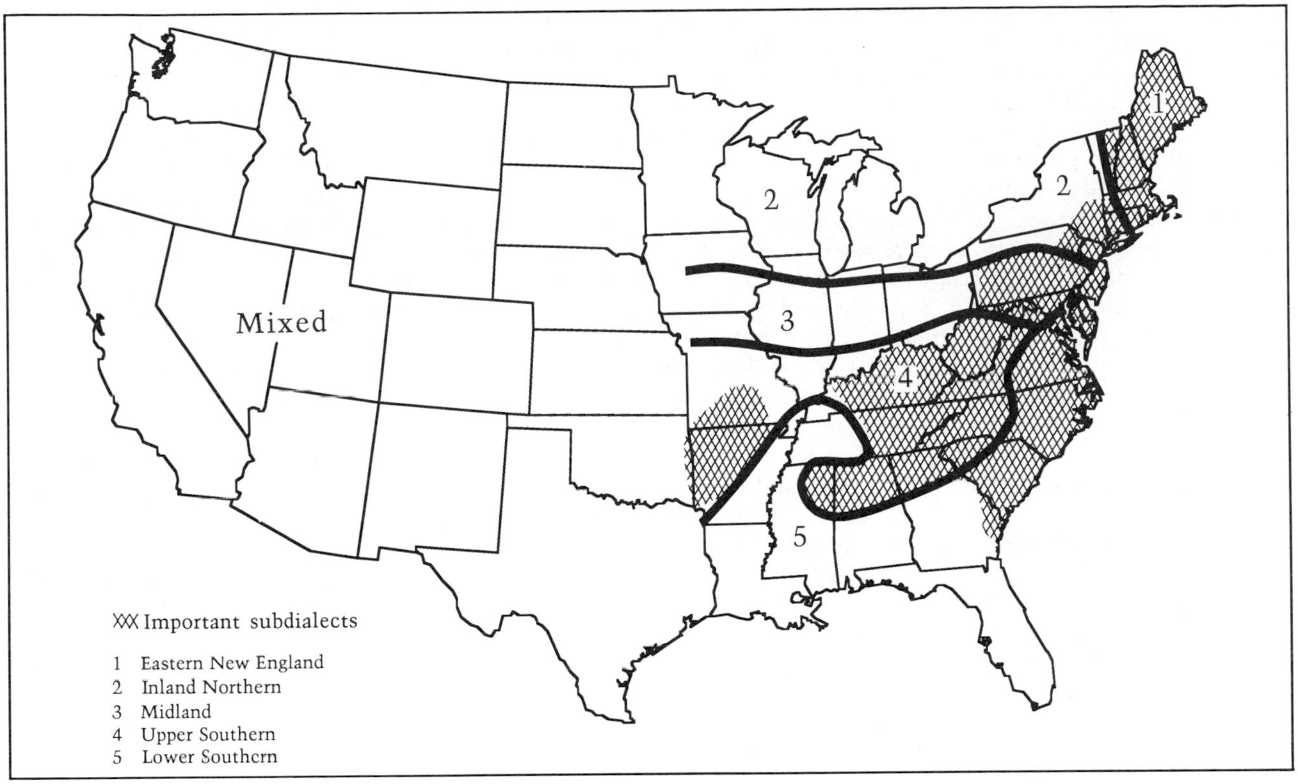

Dialects

Source: Raymond Gastil, *Cultural Regions of the United States* (1975); modified from Jean Malmstrom and Annabel Ashley, *Dialects-USA* (1963), and other sources.

ernmost part of Georgia, are by Kurath (1949), Atwood (1953), and Kurath and McDavid (1961). The data from well over 2,000 informants reported in the LAMSAS and the *Linguistic Atlas of the Gulf States* (LAGS) (begun in 1968 and published in microtext in 1981) roughly equal the data from all the individual studies that have been conducted. Atlas methodology, investigating hundreds of specific items using a standardized questionnaire for features of grammar as well as vocabulary and phonetics, has been highly influential in the region and has spawned a number of small-scale studies.

Central to the Linguistic Atlas and other regionwide projects has been determining the number and the designation of subregions of southern English. This major effort has generated considerable controversy over methodology and the designations of specific speech areas. The lines for dialect areas are drawn closer to principal migration routes than to topographical features, but the lines are hardly exact and can vary according to the supporting data one adduces. They also become less and less clear as one moves west across the region.

Early subjective studies divided American speech into three areas—New England, Southern, and General American (Western)—but it was Hans Kurath in 1949 who first made the systematic case, on the basis of vocabulary, that the eastern states have three general dialect areas—Northern, Midland, and Southern. In dividing the Midland area into two subareas, the North Midland (from Pennsylvania southwestward into West Virginia) and the South Midland (extending southward into South Carolina, Georgia, and Alabama), Kurath made the proposal that the speech of the southern mountains and hills had more affinities to Pennsylvania speech than to that of the Lower South.

Also using vocabulary, Wood (1971) identified three principal subregions, the first two of which correspond generally to Kurath's major division: Coastal Southern, extending from southern Maryland through the Atlantic states south to Florida; Mid-Southern, extending from West Virginia south through the hill country of Alabama and Georgia and, in another belt, from southern Missouri southwesterly through Arkansas and Oklahoma into Texas; and Gulf Southern, a region of mixed vocabulary extending from the Alabama-Georgia border west along the Gulf states and northward through the Mississippi Valley.

In a 1986 formulation based on grammar and pronunciation as well as vocabulary, Pederson and associates identified at least 11 major subregional dialects of southern speech and as many as 14 urban dialects.

The Consciousness of Southern Speakers. The regional consciousness of southerners accounts in part for the region's distinctive speech patterns. One's speech, as well as much of the rest of one's social behavior, expresses one's identity—local, regional, and national—and indicates the speakers with whom one prefers to be identified. The attachments of most southerners to their home, community, and region tend to be strong and are expressed through choice of speech features. These attachments are perhaps the strongest buffer against the disappearance of southern English; as long as there is regional consciousness in the South, a discernible variety of speech will likely express and embody it.

The native southern dialect usually commands regional, but rarely national, prestige, and this often means that southerners acquire one or more varieties of speech in addition to the one they already have and thus develop a repertoire of two or more different styles of speaking (depending on the audience or situation). Many southerners have long had this ability to shift styles. A Tennesseean who has moved to New York City may alter his speech for New Yorkers, but with other Tennesseans who have migrated to the city, he will shift his speech quickly and naturally. Because of the class and ethnic structure of the region, many southerners command more than one variety of southern English; this ability to shift language styles makes it more difficult to identify their typical speech.

The self-consciousness that southerners have about their speech is perhaps most acute when a southern politician is in the national limelight or when they hear southern speech in the movies and on television shows such as *The Beverly Hillbillies*, the *Dukes of Hazzard*, or *Hee Haw*. Southerners are embarrassed by the stereotypes of mountain people, hayseed bumpkins, and stock car addicts, even though such programs frequently portray southerners using their country wisdom to thoroughly outwit their city counterparts. Southern speech and behavior are often caricatured in a fashion consistent with northern stereotypes of southern speakers. Southerners frequently find themselves striving to overcome these stereotypes. This does not mean, however, that southerners are slow to capitalize on them. The tourist-shop exaggerations of southern speech in popular booklets found throughout the region are vastly overpriced but sell well, expressing pride in the local speech and profiting from Yankees at the same time.

The national media's consuming attention to southern speech whenever a southern politician gets his due alternately pleases and pains southerners. Jimmy Carter's presidential campaign in 1976 sparked countless newspaper stories by Washington feature writers who feared they would have to learn a second dialect and also produced a rash of cocktail-circuit primers on the region's speech. In 1984 the populace was presented with such a caricature of the speech of South Carolina's Ernest Hollings during the presidential campaign that few knew his positions on any issue or took him seriously as a candidate (one national columnist claimed that Hollings's "lockjaw Southern drawl is almost unintelligible"). Southern politicos are also often recognized as having superior linguistic and rhetorical skills. Sam Ervin of North Carolina captured the imagination of the country with his down-home quips and anecdotes when chairing the special Watergate investigating committee in 1973. And Jesse Jackson of South Carolina thoroughly enlivened the Democratic presidential primaries with his powerful rhetoric in 1984.

The Speech of Whites and Blacks. The question of how speech differs between blacks and whites in the South is as sensitive as the general issue of the social relations between the races. It is a question that has inspired countless researchers and commentators, many of them antiquarians trying to record unusual speech forms before they disappear, to offer their evidence and proposals. Popular notions on the subjects of the extent and origin of differences between white and black speech lack all perspective, but scholarly views have and still do run the entire gamut and have rarely been dispassionate. Uninitiated readers of the principal commentators on the issue are easily confused by the attendant politics of the various scholarly camps—linguistic geographers, sociolinguists, and creolists—and there is little, if anything, on which the specialists agree. (For a survey of recent research and an attempt at an evenhanded explication of the scholarly issues, see Montgomery and Bailey [1986].)

The question of how the speech of blacks and whites differs has two principal subquestions—one historical, the other pedagogical. Most research on and discussion of black-white speech differences has centered on the pedagogical issue: How teachers can handle a diversity of dialects in the teaching of literacy skills? The answer to this question, however, inevitably hinges on the answer to the historical question: What are the origins of speech patterns and the relative influences of African, Caribbean, and British Isles linguistic heritages?

Here the views run the gamut. At one extreme is the view that the speech of blacks (except for Gullah, the creole language spoken on the offshore Sea Islands of South Carolina and Georgia) retains only a small handful of nouns (e.g., *goober*, *gumbo*, *juke*, *zombie*) and names from African languages and that the otherwise distinctive features of black speech derive from older (17th- and 18th-century) or regional British speech, these features having been acquired from whites on plantations and perpetuated by segregation.

At the other extreme is the view that present-day black speech represents a superficial English derivative of a plantation creole language (one similar to present-day Gullah or Sea Island creole). This plantation creole is said to have been heavily influenced, lexically and to

Language and humor among friends in Franklin, Ga., 1941

some extent grammatically, by African languages and Caribbean creoles and was ultimately derived from a pidgin language spoken in West Africa.

The charged social tensions and the close connection that speech has with racial identity have made both blacks and whites reluctant to discuss the connection between black speech and white speech and to give any credence to the notion that there is such a thing as "black English." Whites have historically been uneasy about inferences that their speech resembles that of black southerners, resisting the notion that their speech has been influenced by the speech of blacks. White scholars have tried to trace southern English (both white speech and black speech) to regional British dialects in part in an effort to show that white speech does not derive from black speech. Whites are upset when northerners say they sound like blacks and when, as has often happened, non-southern linguists label features found in speech throughout the South as features of black speech. Blacks are aware of how frequently the differences between white speech and black speech have been exaggerated and that their distinctive speech patterns have often been isolated and exploited to brand them easy targets for discrimination. Thus, they usually minimize the differences (and insist, often correctly, that the differences are merely older white English) and are often suspicious that modern-day descriptions of "black English" are disguised paternalism.

In point of fact, the case for "racial dialects" is far more difficult to substantiate in the South than in the urban North. Social differences are often more significant than racial ones, and a key problem with much of the research comparing white and black speech is that whites and blacks of comparable education and social status have not been contrasted. Few, if any, specific linguistic forms are now used exclusively by either blacks or whites. The differences that do exist are probably greatest in intonation and rhythm, the parts of language structure most difficult to describe and to generalize about.

See also BLACK LIFE: Creolization; Preacher, Black; Speech, Black; / Jackson, Jesse; FOLKLIFE: Storytelling; GEOGRAPHY: Expatriates and Exiles; LAW: / Ervin, Sam; LITERATURE: / Brooks, Cleanth; MYTHIC SOUTH: Stereotypes; / Carter Era

Michael Montgomery
University of South Carolina

E. Bagby Atwood, *A Survey of Verb Forms in the Eastern States* (1953); Cleanth Brooks, in *A Southern Treasury of Life and Literature*, ed. Stark Young (1937), *The Language of the American South* (1985); William A. Kretzschmar, Jr., ed., *Dialects in Culture: Essays in General Dialectology by Raven I. McDavid, Jr.* (1979); Hans Kurath, *Word Geography of the Eastern United States* (1949), with Raven I. McDavid, Jr., *Pronunciation of English in the Atlantic States* (1961); Raven I. McDavid, Jr., *American Speech* (April 1948), in *The Structure of American English*, by Winthrop Nelson Francis (1957); James B. McMillan, ed., *Annotated Bibliography of Southern American English* (1971), with Michael Montgomery, eds., *Annotated Bibliography of Southern American English* (2d ed., 1986); Mitford M. Mathews, ed., *The Beginnings of American English* (1931); Michael Montgomery and Guy Bailey, eds., *Language Variety in the South: Perspectives in Black and White* (1986); Lee A. Pederson et al., eds., *LAGS: The Basic Materials* (1981) et al., eds., *Handbook of the Linguistic Atlas of the Gulf States* (1986); Gordon R. Wood, *Vocabulary Change: A Study of Variation in Regional Words in Eight of the Southern States* (1971).

Black Language

See BLACK LIFE: Speech, Black

Conversation

Sometimes referred to as talking, chatting, visiting, jawing, small talk, or repartee, conversation involves the oral exchange of ideas, opinions, and sentiments. Unstructured, it flows along according to whims and inclinations with little purpose beyond visiting or "passing the time of day." Allen Tate, in an essay entitled "A Southern Mode of the Imagination," argued that northern conversation is about ideas, whereas "the typical southern conversation is not going anywhere; it is not about anything. *It is about the people who are talking*." An aspect of regional manners, Tate wrote, southern conversation is a way "to make everybody happy." Ellen Glasgow, in *The Woman Within* (1954), insisted that in the South "conversation, not literature, is the pursuit of all classes."

In the frontier South with dwellings miles apart and life lonely and often harsh, lengthy visits were common, and hospitality was extended even to strangers. Church meetings, court days, political rallies, funerals, and even hangings became occasions to socialize, to hear the news, and to discuss mutual concerns. At the country store loafers congregated, and in cold weather they clustered around the warm stove to play checkers or cards and swap yarns.

Southerners took pride in being, and listening to, great talkers, making folk heroes of preachers, lawyers, politicians, and storytellers. Whether conversing in a lowly cabin, a white framed house, or a mansion, they reveled in loquaciousness. Young ladies mastered the art of "small talk"; matrons loved to gossip about household matters, child rearing, and sensational happenings. Thomas Nelson Page commends "the master of the plantation" as a "wonderful talker" who "discoursed of philosophy, politics, and religion." When discussing hospitality Page reports, "The conversation was surprising: it was of crops, the roads, politics, mutual friends, including the entire field of neighborhood matters, related not as gossip, but as affairs of common interest which everyone knew or was expected and entitled to know."

In Charleston, New Orleans, Natchez, and other cities,

Swapping stories, Vicksburg, Miss., 1974

planters and professionals met in their social and literary clubs, welcomed distinguished guests, and engaged in enlightened repartee, sometimes over dinner or while sipping old wines.

Blacks, meanwhile, developed distinctive conversational skills. Zora Neale Hurston, in *Mules and Men* (1935), recalled from her childhood in Eatonville, Fla., the men who gathered at the country store or on the front porch to exchange tales, and her works are filled with examples of black conversation, including the "lying" sessions when stories were swapped. Writers such as Ralph Ellison and Alice Walker structure their works around conversational lore.

In more recent times the front porch (the "gallerie" to Cajuns) attracted the family and their friends. Shaded perhaps by tall trees and equipped with rocking chairs and sometimes palm-leaf fans or ceiling fans, it was a place to relax, to watch passersby, and to welcome relatives, neighbors, the postman, a salesman, the minister, whoever happened to stop and "sit a spell." In French Louisiana the visitor might be offered dark-roast coffee, in other areas iced tea or lemonade; the mint julep sometimes encouraged joviality on plantation verandas. With the advent of radio, television, and air-conditioning, the front porches were enclosed or gave way to cooler interiors out of the heat and dust, and no longer were people as likely to pass the time with simple conversation. Nonetheless, Hobson Pittman's late 1940s painting *The Conversation* conveys the traditional importance of conversation in the South, portraying a dreamlike setting of two women talking while sitting in chairs, both dwarfed by a high-ceilinged interior—a remembered scene from the artist's childhood.

See also BLACK LIFE: Folklore, Black; HISTORY AND MANNERS: Manners

Waldo W. Braden
Louisiana State University

Roger D. Abrahams, *Southern Folklore Quarterly* (March 1968); Waldo W. Braden, *The Oral Tradition in the South* (1983); Merrill G. Christophersen, *Southern Speech Journal* (Winter 1954); Everett Dick, *The Dixie Frontier: A Comprehensive Picture of Southern Frontier Life before the Civil War* (1948); Frank L. Owsley, *Plain Folk of the Old South* (1949); Allen Tate, *Essays of Four Decades* (1968).

Folk Speech

Southern folk speech refers to the variations in speech from the standard, formal language taught in the schools. It is a simple form of verbal folklore—the expressions, place names, and ways of speaking commonly accepted by people in the South. Most southerners value their region's folk speech highly because it preserves and keeps alive a wealth of traditions, sometimes through slang, proverbs, and euphemisms. The southern dialect, in general, includes variations in grammar, pronunciation, and vocabulary. There is often, for example, the use of the past tense of verbs ("I seen him"). Linguistic atlases profusely document the differences in pronunciation of words in different American regions ("greasy" or "greazy"). Linguists verify the popular perception as well that southerners' vocabulary often differs from that of other Americans. The southerner's use of "y'all" is perhaps the best example of folk speech in the region.

The American Dialect Society, which started in 1889, is an institutional focus for the study of southern folk speech, and its journal, *American Speech*, published since 1925, is a chief organ for publication in the field. The study of folk speech in the region has often focused on the legacy of, or deviations from, British speech patterns in Appalachian or rural southern areas. The nature of black English, the influence of other languages, and the relationship between speech and social class have also been central concerns. A variety of linguistic atlas projects—including Frederic G. Cassidy's *Dictionary of American Regional English* (1985–), Hans Kurath and associates' *Linguistic Atlas of the Middle and South Atlantic States*, and Lee A. Pederson's *Linguistic Atlas of the Gulf States*—precisely shows the distribution of speechways across the region.

Folk speech uses language that calls attention to itself. *Raining like an old cow pissing on a flat rock in Arkansas* gets much more immediate notice than *It's pouring rain*. This immediacy of reaction is precisely what allows southern folk speech to make its double contribution. Hans Kurath, director of the Linguistic Atlas project, used the label "folk-speech" to identify nonurban, uneducated performance in American dialects, and folklorists incorporated this definition into their work. But a community's folk speech is better defined not in terms of its users but of its uses, its style, and its saliency. When speech is based in and uniquely valued by its own community, it is *internal* folk speech; when it is everyday talk found anywhere, it is not folk speech. A southerner who says *He's so high he couldn't hit the floor with his hat* ("drunk") will be understood by his or her own community as using folk speech; one who says *I'll carry you to Greenville* ("give you a lift"), will not. Non-southerners overlook such distinctions and tend to see any talk by southerners as folk speech.

A review of southern speech sources would duplicate the region's settlement history, and the relations of groups to specific items would be speculative. A better approach is an admittedly cross-classifiable taxonomy of types and an indication of how they have fared in past scholarship.

Below the word. Folk noises and morphemes have hardly been studied, though chants, calls, and imitations have figured in a few works, and the "rebel yell" is a famous folk cry.

The word. The numerous publications of the *American Dialect Society, Dialect Notes, American Speech,* and regional publications might have contributed to a regional slang dictionary, but they rarely distinguish between words that are limited socially and geographically and those that are especially valued and recur throughout the region—folk speech. Regional words that may qualify have been extensively collected and appear in dictionaries of slang and of American language usage.

Phrases. In the area of phrases and proverbial sentences southern folk speech (and the study of it) shines. Proverbial comparisons are the subject of much study. *As X as a Y* (or *X-er than a Y* and other obviously related forms) is the target of Preston (1975)—*busy as a one-armed paperhanger. So X that Y* is studied by Halpert (1951)—*so tight* [that] *he wouldn't give a dime to see the Statue of Liberty piss across New York Bay.* Most collections combine the grammatical forms cited above with the others—*X enough to Y* and *too X to Y* (both related to *so X that Y*); *to X like a Y* (often interchangeable with some forms of *as X as a Y*); and other minor comparative forms. Boshears (1954) is the largest individual collection—*look like a sheep-killing dog, run around like a chicken with its head cut off, make more noise than 99 cows and a bob-tailed bull.*

Though comparisons dominate, a few other forms based on nouns (*the straw that broke the camel's back*), verbs (*come a cropper*), and prepositional phrases (*in hot water*) are included in most studies along with other expressions not so easily classified grammatically. Some might be identified as threats (*I'm going to jerk a knot in your tail*), wisecracks and comebacks (*your feet don't fit no limb*—said to one who asks *who?*), exclamations and warnings (*Katy bar the door!*), insults (somebody doesn't *amount to a hill of beans*), taunts (*redhead, cabbagehead, 10 cents a pound* directed to a redheaded person), boasts (*Hooo-eee! I'm half horse and half alligator!*), and miscellaneous sentential items (*hope in one hand and shit in the other and see which fills up first*), though such a classification is practical rather than theoretically exhaustive.

Randolph and Wilson (1953) and Whiting (1952) are noteworthy collections. Taylor and Whiting (1958), although not exclusively concerned with southern speech, provide important references as do the dictionaries and periodicals already mentioned. Proverbs, mentioned in many of these collections, are excluded from folk speech, although borderline examples of items that may be fully integrated in conversations exist.

Beyond the sentence. Least studied are aspects of folk speech having to do with so-called stylistic tendencies. For example, the classical tradition in southern education left behind names and references. This, combined with a traditional knowledge of the Bible, produced a genre known as "fancy talk" in black speech and influenced southern pulpit styles in general. Rosenberg (1970) and Kochman (1972) have studied these and other aspects, though the focus has been primarily on black genres.

McMillan (1971) shows that local language has always been an important aspect of southern culture. Though every American reader will sense the "southernness" of these contributions, comparable studies from the North are sparse, and comparisons are limited (but see Preston, 1975). Although content analyses of southern folk speech reveal preoccupation with rural, traditional matters, newer items display changing attitudes and concerns. Growing evidence suggests that southerners more than any other Americans may assign particular importance to folk speech. Such speech is important to the region, has a distinct local flavor, and will likely be around as long as the culture exists.

See also BLACK LIFE: Speech, Black

Dennis R. Preston
State University of New York
at Fredonia

Lester V. Berrey and Melvin Van den Bark, *The American Thesaurus of Slang, with Supplement: A Complete Reference Book of Colloquial Speech* (1947); Frederic G. Cassidy, *Dictionary of American Regional English* (1985); Sir William A. Craigie and James R. Hulbert, *A Dictionary of American English on Historical Principles* (1938–44); Herbert Halpert, *Midwest Folklore* (1975); Thomas Kochman, *Rappin' and Stylin' Out: Communication in Urban Black America* (1972); James B. McMillan, *Annotated Bibliography of Southern American English* (1971); Mitford M. Mathews, ed., *Dictionary of Americanisms on Historical Principles* (1951); Dennis R. Preston, *Orbis* (1975); Vance Randolph and George P. Wilson, *Down in the Holler: A Gallery of Ozark Folk Speech* (1953); Bruce A. Rosenberg, *The Art of the American Folk Preacher* (1970); Archer Taylor and Bartlett J. Whiting, *A Dictionary of American Proverbs and Proverbial Phrases, 1820–1880* (1958); Richard H. Thornton, *An American Glossary: Being an Attempt to Illustrate Certain Americanisms upon Historical Principles* (1962); Harold Wentworth and Stuart Berg Flexner, eds., *Dictionary of American Slang* (1958); Norman I. White, ed., *The Frank C. Brown Collection of North Carolina Folklore* (1952).

French Language

There was a time when the French language could have been heard throughout the vast area of the North American continent west of the Appalachian divide. Along the Mississippi River, place names from Baton Rouge to St. Louis recall the French presence, and the pronunciation of Indian names such as Arkansas (note the silent final consonant) indicates that they were transmitted to English through French. But the early French speakers were explorers and traders, and permanent settlements were few. Except for a small enclave at Old Mines, near Ste. Genevieve, Mo., where the oldest people still remember the language, French survives today only in southern Louisiana and adjacent parts of Texas.

Groups of Huguenots (French Protestant refugees) settled in some of the eastern colonies, especially South Carolina, where the French language was used in church services until the mid-18th century. This group appears, in the main, to have been linguistically assimilated by the time of the Revolution. An enclave of Provençal-speaking Waldensians is found in the town of Valdese, N.C.

Three varieties of French were formerly spoken in Louisiana. Colonial French, the language of the Creoles (here meaning white settlers coming directly from Europe and their descendants—of German and Spanish origin as well as French), was close to standard (educated) French. Many Creole children received a good education; some went to school in Europe. Obviously, spoken usage differed from that of France, particularly in the vocabulary for local customs, fauna, flora, and foods. The pronunciation had a regional flavor, but the grammar was basically standard.

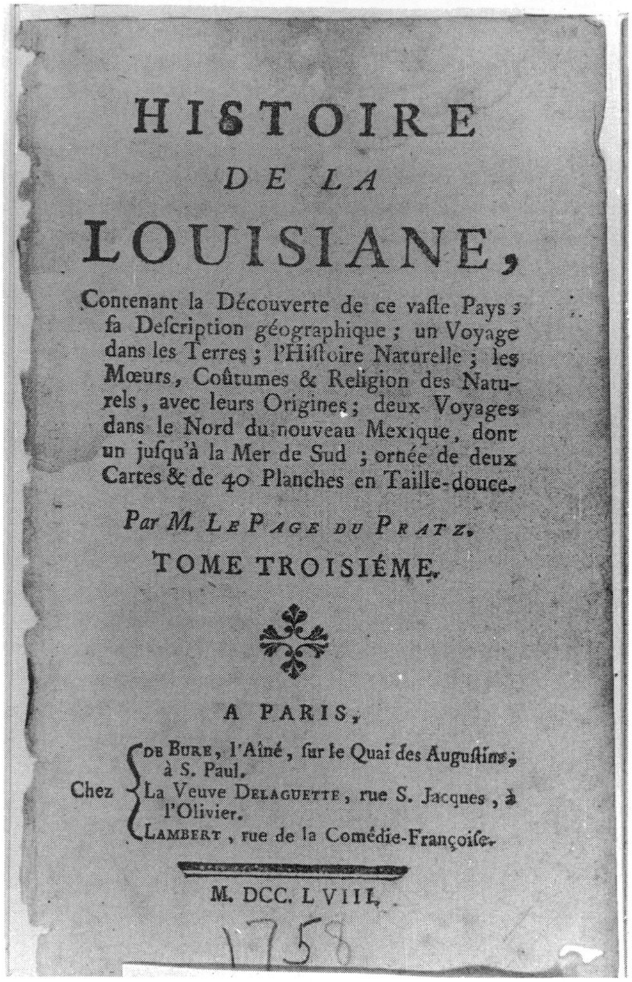
HISTOIRE
DE LA
LOUISIANE,
Contenant la Découverte de ce vaste Pays; sa Description géographique; un Voyage dans les Terres; l'Histoire Naturelle; les Mœurs, Coûtumes & Religion des Naturels, avec leurs Origines; deux Voyages dans le Nord du nouveau Mexique, dont un jusqu'à la Mer de Sud; ornée de deux Cartes & de 40 Planches en Taille-douce.
Par M. LE PAGE DU PRATZ.
TOME TROISIÉME.
A PARIS,
Chez DE BURE, l'Aîné, sur le Quai des Augustins, à S. Paul.
La Veuve DELAGUETTE, rue S. Jacques, à l'Olivier.
LAMBERT, rue de la Comédie-Françoise.
M. DCC. LVIII.
1758

French book circulated in Louisiana

The second type of French was brought to the southern and southwestern parishes of Louisiana by the Acadian, or Cajun, refugees from the Atlantic provinces of Canada. Deported by the British from a place where, after over 100 years, they had created a unique culture and way of life, these people spoke a type of French whose roots lay in 17th-century western France, particularly the provinces of Poitou and Aunis. It differed from standard French in its preservation of archaic and regional vocabulary, pronunciation, and grammar. For some time after its introduction into Louisiana in the mid-18th century, it maintained its special characteristics through relative isolation.

Finally, most black people spoke what linguists call Louisiana Creole—the word Creole used here in a technical linguistic sense, meaning a language with a largely French-derived stock of words, but restructured in grammar, pronunciation, and semantics. So, for example, the definite article follows the noun instead of preceding it: "the book" is *liv-la*, not *le livre*. Verbs are conjugated by prefixed participles instead of endings: "I shall see" is *mo va oua* or *m'a oua*, not *je verrai*.

Much controversy surrounds the origin of Creole, of which several types are found in the Caribbean and the Indian Ocean. Current research suggests that it resulted in part from a deliberate policy among slave traders and plantation owners of teaching their African captives a simplified version of French or English, for which a precedent existed in the Portuguese-derived trading jargon of the West African Coast. Another factor was the social isolation and incomplete acculturation of the plantation slaves, who had no single African language to use as a common tongue and so had to create an emergency communication device from whatever bits and pieces of French they had learned. Inevitably, some African ways of saying things were included in the new language, although it continued to contain few specific words of African origin (and these have often spread to white dialects, and even English: e.g., *gombo*, "gumbo"). In any case, Louisiana Creole is too similar to other forms of Caribbean Creole to be altogether independent of them. By the time the first slaves arrived in Louisiana about 1719, planters and traders must have had some knowledge of existing Creole dialects, and they tried to teach them to newly arrived Africans. Later, emigration from Santo Domingo (Haiti), following the slave revolts at the end of the 18th century, left its imprint on the language through Haitian imports (although there are certain fundamental differences: e.g., "his book" is *so live*, instead of the Haitian *liv-li*—literally, "book him").

Today, the boundaries between the three varieties of

Louisiana French have been blurred. Many descendants of Creoles now speak only English. In the rural areas Cajun has survived but has lost some of its uniqueness. Louisiana Creole, mixed with Cajun, is still spoken in some black families, particularly in St. Martin Parish, and by many whites (an inheritance from the days when white children learned their first language as much from their black servants as from their parents). Louisiana French today, then, is a blend, showing much variation in vocabulary, grammar, and pronunciation. English borrowings and expressions are pervasive.

A whole generation of children received no education in French and were discouraged from speaking it. Recent attempts to revive the use of French by teaching it in the schools have encountered a dilemma: should the standard language or the local dialect(s) be used? For many, there can be no question: only standard French is worth teaching, because the ultimate goal must be to give young Louisianans a useful second language. This approach, sponsored by CODOFIL (the Council for the Development of French in Louisiana), has been challenged by Cajuns who point out that children of French-speaking families often find their grandparents cannot understand the words they are learning in school. Recently, a textbook was created to teach Cajun French in an English-based spelling system easier to learn than the irrational standard French orthography. This would give Cajun children a pride in their heritage but would make it more difficult for them to continue with French later if they wished. The future of French in Louisiana, already endangered, will depend on finding a solution to this problem.

See also BLACK LIFE: African Influences; Creolization; Speech, Black; ETHNIC LIFE: Caribbean Influence; / Cajuns; Creoles; French

Alexander Hull
Duke University

James F. Broussard, *Louisiana Creole Dialect* (1942); James Donald Faulk, *Cajun French I* (1977); John Francis McDermott, *A Glossary of Mississippi Valley French, 1673–1850* (1941); Raleigh Morgan, Jr., in *Texas Studies in Bilingualism*, ed. Glenn G. Gilbert (1970); Larbi Oukada, *Louisiana French: An Annotated Linguistic Bibliography* (1979); William A. Read, *Louisiana French* (1931; rev. ed., 1963); Dorice Tentchoff, in *The Culture of Acadiana: Tradition and Change in South Louisiana*, ed. Steven L. Del Sesto and Jon L. Gibson (1975).

German Language

German immigrants arrived in America as early as 1683. They formed self-sufficient farm communities and small rural towns, where they maintained their German language and customs. In the South, varieties of German survive in two areas: (1) Virginia, in the western parts of Shenandoah County (Jerome) and Rockingham County (Criders and Dayton) and in neighboring Pendleton County, W.Va. (Sugar Grove and Propst Gap); and (2) Texas, in the city triangle San Antonio-Austin-Houston, particularly in the counties of Gillespie, Kendall, Comal, Guadalupe, Lee, Washington, Austin, Fayette, DeWitt, and Medina. The German immigrants did not speak a single, homogeneous variety of German, and the German dialects still spoken in Virginia and Texas differ from each other and from Pennsylvania German, with which they are often compared.

The Germans began to settle Virginia in the 18th century via Pennsylvania, but they were, for the most part, native Germans or their children, who had come from Switzerland, Alsace, and the Palatinate. The Dayton area of Rockingham County became a stronghold of the plain sects, especially of Mennonites, who are known for their German-language loyalty, which helps them maintain their isolation from mainstream American society. In addition to specific lexical items and phonological features that are peculiar to Virginia German varieties, such as the loss of *r* and word-initial *sch*, Dayton German retains the front rounded (or umlauted) vowels of standard German. (These vowels are not found in dialects of Pennsylvania German.) Virginia German is not one single dialect but a cluster of similar dialects, each one exhibiting independent developments.

German settlements in Texas were first established in 1831, and, as in Virginia, Texas German developed independently of other varieties of German in the United States. The German settlers in Texas came predominantly from north and middle Germany, and linguistic studies of Texas German reveal a loss of southern German dialect features found in Pennsylvania and Virginia. Texas German is a dialect more closely approaching the middle-northern-based standard German. However, the influence of English has been pervasive. The German of Fredericksburg in Gillespie County, for example, shows a loss of front rounded vowels and the adoption of the American English vowel sound found in *cat*. American English influence on Texas German is also found in the pronunciation of *l* and *r* and in the merger of the German dative and accusative noun cases.

In spite of the great numbers of German immigrants who settled in America, the language never achieved an official status. Its communicative functions are being increasingly fulfilled by English, and German as a spoken language in Virginia and Texas may be expected to die out within the next two generations.

See also ETHNIC LIFE: / Germans

Marion Lois Huffines
Bucknell University

Glenn G. Gilbert, *Texas Studies in Bilingualism* (1970), *The German Language in America: A Symposium* (1971); Elmer Lewis Smith, John G. Stewart, and M. Ellsworth Kyger, *The Pennsylvania Germans of the Shenandoah Valley* (1964).

Gullah

Gullah is the most conservative form of "black English" spoken in the United States today. It preserves features of vocabulary, grammar, and idiom that other kinds of black English have lost, or never had. It is a true "creole" language, the only creole English still alive in the United States and a close cousin to the flourishing creoles of the Caribbean: Jamaican, Guyanese, Trinidadian, Barbadian, and others. Like these, Gullah preserves features of African languages brought in by plantation slaves as far back as 300 years ago.

Gullah is spoken chiefly on the coastal islands—the so-called rice islands—that stretch for 160 miles along the seaboard of South Carolina and Georgia, but it is also heard on parts of the adjacent mainland. Until recent years these settlements were isolated, as some still are, so that the black inhabitants, who worked in rice fields, had little contact with the English of the white and black communities ashore. Gullah was thus sheltered from the process of "decreolization," by which creole speech gradually changes under the influence of the prevailing language. Gullah, with its mixture of English and African features, is quite adequate for the daily life of its speakers. But outsiders do not readily understand it, and as the Gullah communities become less isolated, linguistic features differing most from the surrounding American English are bound to yield.

The word *Gullah* may come from *Gola*, the name of a people from Liberia and Sierra Leone (West Africa), whence some slaves were brought to the Carolina colony. This group, however, was relatively small, whereas a very large number of slaves were brought earlier and over a longer period from Angola. The latter, therefore, seems the more plausible source for the word. The Gullah people and their language, however, are far more mixed, as both the history of slave importations and the surviving African language features show.

The Charleston colony, founded in 1670, is the geographical center of Gullah. Planters from Barbados started it, bringing their slaves who in the early years were from the Gold Coast (now Ghana) and Nigeria. Others came later from the entire coast of West Africa which stretches over 3,000 miles from Senegal to Angola, bringing various languages and dialects. Thus, the creole English of these first slaves was constantly affected by new importations. The African features that have survived best in Gullah must have arrived early and have been reinforced by the continuing influx of Africans. Creole blacks—those born in America—looked down on the African-born as savages and made little or no attempt to keep African languages alive. But it is striking that a large number of African features in Gullah are like those flourishing in the Caribbean today, in French-, Dutch-, and Spanish-based, as well as English-based, creoles. This implies either a similar origin or else convergence so that for linguistic or other reasons the same basic features emerged as the dominant ones. These and other possibilities are now being debated by scholars in the field. In many fundamental ways at least, Gullah is strikingly like its Caribbean cousins already mentioned.

The main features that set Gullah apart from the rest of American English, black or white, are sound, word form, and syntax. Vocabulary, being a superficial feature (words come and go more easily than any other part of language), will be treated briefly. In records made about 1940, Lorenzo Turner, the first linguist to study Gullah closely, found African words and phrases still in use or at least remembered, though in many cases they were being replaced by English words. Such foodstuff names as *okra*, *yam*, *benne*, *cush*, *goober*, and *cala* were at least locally known; others included *buckra*, "white man," *hoodoo*, "sorcery," and *cooter*, "tortoise or turtle." Turner also collected hundreds of the personal names that the Gullah give their children at birth—all of African derivation. Though the meaning and origin of these names are forgotten, the names continue to be used out of tradition.

More significant, however, are features of syntax, such as the plural pronoun *una* meaning *you all*, which is prevalent in southern speech. *Una*, however, is not a translation of *you all*; it comes from one or more West African languages, and its cognates are widespread in the Caribbean, from the Bahamas to Jamaica, Belize, Tobago, the Nicaraguan shore, and Guyana. Similarly, the little word *da* (or *duh*) is used to indicate continuing verbal action. *We go* does not specify the time or status of the action, but *we da go* or *we da goin* shows progressive action. The latter is a feature of several West African languages, which survives also in the creole speech of the Caribbean colonies. Apart from use of *-ing*, verbs have a single form, usually taken from the English infinitive or else from the past: *mek* and *tek* (make, take), in common with most other English-based creoles, betray north-of-England origin. One other such feature is the use of *dem* (and them) added to a noun, especially a person's name, to mean that person and those associated with him or her (usually family members). This explains a Gullah expression such as *Sancho dem*, "Sancho and his bunch," as reported by Ambrose E. Gonzales. This Gullah feature was also reported from white speech in Memphis, Tenn., in the 1920s.

The greatest number of Gullah words are not African but English, though many are disguised by phonetic changes, most of which are, or were, also found in general black speech: the lack of *th-* sounds, so that *this* is *dis* and *through* is *tru*; use of *b* for English *v*, so that *very* is *bery* and *vexed* is *bexed*; and the loss of final consonants especially from clusters, so that *past*, *wasp*, *blind*, and *salt* become, respectively, *pas*, *wass*, *bline*, and *saal*. Gullah has special pronunciations of its own, however: *put* is regularly *pit*, *see'em* is *shum*, *ain't it* becomes *enti*, and *young* is *nyoung*. Sometimes, under influence of African word endings, a vowel is added in Gullah: *wikiti*, "wicked"; *nekiti*, "naked." And a goodly number of African turns of speech are translated in Gullah: *hard-ears*, "stubborn," *peel-head*, "bald," and so on.

The famous Uncle Remus stories of Brer Rabbit (Joel Chandler Harris) are told in the language of middle Georgia, not Gullah. But the corresponding tales in Gullah may be found in two good sources, *Negro Myths from the Georgia Coast* (1888), by Charles Colcock Jones, and *The Black Border* (1922), by Ambrose Gonzales. In *Africanisms* (1949) Lorenzo Dow Turner included phonetic transcriptions and translations into standard English of 14 texts that he had recorded on phonograph records. Much study has been done since, but little of it has been published. Gullah especially interests scholars of creole languages because it is the most distinctive and archaic type of American black English. But the attention is almost too late, for with the exploitation of the rice islands for tourist development the process of decreolization has accelerated. Gullah, especially in its more traditional form kept alive by isolation, is now fading fast. Dialects, however, are surprisingly vital; Gullah may survive as the intimate, home talk of rice island natives for generations.

See also BLACK LIFE: African Influences; Creolization; Speech, Black; ETHNIC LIFE: Caribbean Influence; FOLKLIFE: / Brer Rabbit; LITERATURE: / Harris, Joel Chandler

Frederic G. Cassidy
University of Wisconsin

Ambrose E. Gonzales, *The Black Border: Gullah Stories of the Carolina Coast* (with a glossary) (1922), *With Aesop along the Black Border* (1924, 1969); Guy B. Johnson, *Folk Culture on St. Helena Island, South Carolina* (1930); Raven I. McDavid, Jr., and Virginia G. McDavid, *American Speech* (1951); Julia Peterkin, *Scarlet Sister Mary* (1928); John E. Reinecke et al., *A Bibliography of Pidgin and Creole Languages* (1975); Lorenzo Dow Turner, *Africanisms in the Gullah Dialect* (1949, 1968); Norman E. Whitten, Jr., and John Szwed, *Trans-Action* (1968).

Indian Languages

Like the more familiar languages of Europe, the aboriginal languages of the Americas fall into families, all traceable to a single parent or protolanguage in the past, much the way the modern Romance languages are traceable to, and descended from, Latin. Of the 11 or so major linguistic families or stocks of North America, seven were represented in the South. There were also numerous language isolates whose affiliations cannot be determined. All told, probably upwards of 75 different Indian languages were once spoken in the South.

Languages of the Algonkian family were spoken primarily in the North and Northeast, but there were intrusions into the Southeast, notably the Pamlicos of North Carolina, the Powhatans of Virginia, and the widely traveled Shawnees. Most of the tribes of coastal Virginia were Algonkian speaking, but their languages became extinct at an early date. Shawnee is still spoken by some tribal members (those over 40 years of age) in Oklahoma.

Iroquoian languages are also spoken primarily in the Northeast. Southern offshoots fall into two groups: (1) Meherrin and Nottoway in Virginia and Tuscarora in North Carolina, and (2) Cherokee, still spoken by approximately 10,000 Cherokees whose families were deported to Oklahoma in the 1830s and 1,000 or so who remain in North Carolina. Sequoyah developed the justly famous Cherokee Table of Syllables in the early 1800s. The system served the tribe well for many decades, and for a period of time there was considerable publication in the language. Many Cherokees still learn the syllabic writing, although several recent grammars and dictionaries have added or substituted a romanized script.

In historical times most of the languages of the Siouan family were found spread across the prairies and plains from Missouri to Alberta, but there were pockets of Siouan speakers in the Southeast as well, and it is still unclear whether these represent an intrusion or a remnant. The Ofo and Biloxi tribes of Mississippi spoke Siouan languages, as did the Tutelos, Occaneechis, and Saponis of Virginia. All of these languages are apparently now extinct. Also Siouan speaking were the Quapaws of Arkansas and the Osages and Missourias of Missouri, all of whom were closely affiliated with the more westerly Siouan groups. Of their languages only Osage is still spoken.

The Catawbas and Woccons of the Carolina Coastal Plain and Piedmont spoke languages that were apparently distantly related to the Siouan. Both were documented but are now extinct. A number of other tribes are mentioned on early maps of the Carolinas and are assumed to have spoken languages related to Catawba, although these were never recorded. This group included the Cheraw, Eno, Congaree, Pedee, Santee, Sewee, Wateree, Waxhaw, Yadkin, and other tribes.

Yuchi (or Uchee) was spoken by the tribe of the same name in Georgia and adjacent portions of Tennessee and Alabama. It may be distantly related to the Siouan and Catawban language families. Yuchi is still spoken by about 30 people in the Sapulpa, Okla., area.

Two major areas of the South were inhabited by tribes that spoke languages of unknown affiliation—the Florida peninsula before the arrival of the Muskogean-speaking Seminoles and the lower Mississippi Valley and adjacent areas of eastern Texas. The Florida languages included Timucua, Calusa, and Tawasa, all now extinct. In Mississippi, Louisiana, and Texas the isolates included Chitimacha, Atakapa and Akokisa, Tonkawa, Karankawa, Tunica, and Natchez. The last two may be distantly related to Muskogean. Again, all are now extinct.

Arkansas, Louisiana, and eastern Texas were probably the original home of the Caddoan-speaking peoples. The Caddo language proper is well documented in the historical period and is still spoken in Caddo County, Okla. The related tribes, the Wichitas, Pawnees, and Arikaras, migrated northward, some all the way to North Dakota.

Although the South has become home to a number of tribes speaking languages of diverse affiliations, only the languages of the Muskogean family were spoken entirely within the confines of the area at the time of first contact with Europeans. Those Muskogean-speaking tribes were the politically and socially dominant groups, and their languages have been selected to illustrate grammatical structure.

The Muskogean family consists of four separate languages, each with two mutually intelligible dialects corresponding to tribal groupings. All except Hitchiti are still spoken in Oklahoma (Choctaw, Chickasaw, Creek, and Seminole), in Florida (Miccosukee, Seminole), in Mississippi (Choctaw), in Louisiana (Choctaw, Coushatta), and in Texas (Alabama, Coushatta). Choctaw-Chickasaw represents the western branch of the family, and the other languages the eastern branch. The speech sounds of the Muskogean languages are relatively simple, containing few of the "exotic" sounds found in some Indian tongues. Each language contains certain linguistic features such as the plosives *p, t, ch, k,* and all but Creek-Seminole have an asymmetrical *b*. Fricatives include a voiceless *l* (written *thl* here) along with *f, s,* and *h*; Choctaw-Chickasaw has an *sh* in addition. Resonants *m, n, l, y, w*; three vowels—*i, a, o*—with contrasting length; and a pitch or tonal accent complete the system.

Grammatically, the Muskogean languages share certain characteristic features. In all, the subject (S) precedes the object (O), and the verb (V) comes at the end of the sentence. The Miccosukee equivalent of the English sentence "The girl drinks water" is *Taykot okon iskom*, literally, "Girl water drinks." Although nouns do not normally distinguish singulars from plurals, many verbs signal the number of their accompanying nouns. Totally different verb roots are used for a single concept depending on whether the subject (for intransitive verbs) or the object (for transitive verbs) is singular, dual, or plural. Thus, there are three different Creek roots for "run" to agree with the number of the implied subject: *Litkáhaanís*, "He's going to run," *Tokothlkáhaanís*, "They (two) are going to run," *Pifaatkáhaanís*, "They (three or more) are going to run." A transitive verb like "take" has two distinct forms to agree with the number of the implied direct object: *Isáhaanís*, "He's going to take it (one)," *Chawáhaanís*, "He's going to take them (two or more)."

Although the Cherokee, Creek, and Choctaw nations adopted written words in the 19th century, most of the other indigenous languages of the South remained unwritten. Each tribe has a rich oral literature consisting of folktales passed from generation to generation. Some myths explain the existence of natural phenomena or recount the exploits of native folk heroes, but the vast majority of the traditional tales deal with encounters among animals, with Rabbit playing the role of trickster. Many of the Uncle Remus stories have parallels in the Indian tradition.

Since the 1960s there has been renewed interest among Indians in their native languages, and many Indian schools and colleges in communities where Choctaw, Creek, Seminole, Miccosukee, or Cherokee is spoken now offer course work aimed at teaching reading, writing, and fluency in the spoken languages.

See also ETHNIC LIFE: Indian Cultural Contributions; FOLKLIFE: / Brer Rabbit; GEOGRAPHY: Indians and the Landscape

Karen M. Booker
Robert L. Rankin
University of Kansas

Lyle Campbell and Marianne Mithun, *The Languages of Native America: Historical and Comparative Assessment* (1979); Wallace Chafe, *International Journal of American Linguistics* (1962); James M. Crawford, in *Studies in Southeastern Indian Languages*, ed. James M. Crawford (1975); Mary R. Haas, *The Prehistory of Languages* (1969); T. Dale Nicklas, "The Elements of Choctaw" (Ph.D. dissertation, University of Michigan, 1974); John R. Swanton, *The Indians of the Southeastern United States* (1946).

Linguists

A southern "school" of linguists has never been formed, but southerners have pioneered in language study, ranging widely and energetically over the discipline. Perhaps because of the diversity of the region, southerners usually understand variation as a fundamental linguistic fact, and they seldom conceive of language in monolithic terms. For this reason, southerners tend to view language as a changing cultural artifact rather than an innate, quasi-mathematical product of mechanically operating grammatical rules. Furthermore, many southern linguists react negatively to academic orthodoxy, a fact that helps explain their theoretical and methodological innovations.

Thomas Pyles is characteristic. Through 17 years of teaching at the University of Florida, Pyles led a generation of educated Americans to see language in evolutionary perspective. In *The Origins and Development of the English Language*, Pyles assembled an opulent collection of facts, invited the reader to form opinions, and demonstrated sound methods of critical evaluation. Instead of teaching a narrow doctrine, *Origins* continues to show us how "our language is inextricably bound up with our humanity." It also helps us to see that to understand ourselves, "the best place to start . . . is with our own language, the one that has nurtured our minds and formed our view of the world."

And more than other Americans, southerners have assiduously studied their own speech. James B. McMillan's *Annotated Bibliography of Southern American English* lists literally hundreds who have given some part of their lives to this task. A short list of worthies, concentrated in the first part of this century but extending back well into the last, might include Cleanth Brooks, Robley Dunglison, Norman Eliason, Bennett Wood Green, Archibald A. Hill, Atcheson L. Hench, Sumner Ives, Vance Randolph, Maximilian von Schele de Vere, Edward A. Stephenson, James Sledd, William R. Van Riper, Floyd C. Watkins, Gordon Wilson, and Gordon R. Wood.

This random selection could be updated and expanded indefinitely, but the acknowledged dean of the congregation since the 1940s has been Raven I. McDavid, Jr. McDavid's abridged version of H. L. Mencken's *The American Language* summarized two centuries of scholarship in a bold, readable idiom, and, with Hans Kurath, McDavid wrote the first full-dress treatment of English below the Potomac. In dozens of original studies that clarify the relations between southern language and culture, McDavid characteristically focused on the impact of postwar industrialization, urbanization, and mass education while reveling in "the flux, the competing forms and styles, the endless possibilities for innovation that a language must possess if it is to be alive."

In spite of McDavid's preeminence, if a school of southern linguists were to form today, it would necessarily gather around the *Linguistic Atlas of the Gulf States*, the work of McDavid's student Lee A. Pederson, of Emory University. The LAGS project, in 5,000 tape-recorded hours, exhibits the southern tongue from the Savannah River to the Rio Grande and from the TVA lakes to Key West. It surpasses even its great European and American models in scope, methodological innovation, and usefulness for orienting further work. Properly interpreted, LAGS and its parent, the Linguistic Atlas of the Middle and South Atlantic States project, will yield new insight into southern American English and, in turn, into southern population movements, the development of trade areas and transportation systems, the growth of cultural centers and institutions, and the stratification of society.

By applying traditional methods of linguistic analysis to southern cultural institutions and freely inventing or adapting new techniques as needed, southern linguists have generated other remarkable innovations. David W. Maurer, for example, used scholarly, lexicological methods to study criminal argots, for which Louisville, Ky., provided a unique laboratory. Robert A. Hall, Jr., pioneered in the study of creole languages. E. Bagby Atwood was the first linguist to use data-processing equipment to attempt a comprehensive description of American morphology and syntax and to study the effects of urbanization over a wide area.

Meanwhile, the impact of African language contact, apparent in loans like *juke* and *goober*, has been carefully studied by Lorenzo Dow Turner and Juanita V. Williamson. Linguists elsewhere concentrated on syntactic patterns in the speech of isolated black groups, but Williamson succeeded in a thorough phonological and grammatical analysis of an adequately representative sample, and thus uncovered the profound structural identity of black and white speech.

Southern linguists enjoy the support of a half-dozen forums for the exchange of ideas, where lively discussions range over the topics that interest linguists everywhere, not excluding Japanese syntax and the verb forms of Old Church Slavonic. But the title of a recent collection edited by David L. Shores and Carole P. Hines, *Papers in Language Variation*, reveals an enduring concern. When in 1829 Robley Dunglison noticed that "the population of our country is of a motley character" and its language is therefore "modified by admixture," he expressed the common southern view. So perhaps what appears to *auslander* as fiercely independent thought is, to the thinkers themselves, just obvious common sense. If so, it is common sense laced with creative scholarship.

See also BLACK LIFE: Speech, Black

Michael I. Miller
Virginia Commonwealth University

E. Bagby Atwood, *A Survey of Verb Forms in the Eastern United States* (1953), *The Regional Vocabulary of Texas* (1963); Cleanth Brooks, *The Language of the American South* (1985); William A. Kretzschmar, ed., *Dialects in Culture: Essays in General Dialectology by Raven I. McDavid* (1979); Hans Kurath, *A Word Geography of the Eastern United States* (1949), with Raven I. McDavid, Jr., *The Pronunciation of English in the Atlantic States* (1961); David W. Maurer, *Language of the Underworld* (1981); Raven I. McDavid, Jr., *Varieties of American English* (1980), with Raymond K. O'Cain and George T. Dorrill, eds., *Linguistic Atlas of the Middle and South Atlantic States* (1979, volumes forthcoming); James B. McMillan, *Annotated Bibliography of Southern American English* (1971); H. L. Mencken, *The American Language: The Fourth Edition and the Two Supplements*, ed. Raven I. McDavid, Jr. (1963); Lee A. Pederson et al., eds., *LAGS: The Basic Materials*, part 4 (1981); Thomas Pyles and John Algeo, *The Origins and Development of the English Language* (3d ed., 1982); David L. Shores and Carole P. Hines, eds., *Papers in Language Variation: Samla-Ads Collection* (1977); Juanita V. Williamson, "A Phonological and Morphological Study of the Speech of the Negro of Memphis, Tennessee" (Ph.D. dissertation, University of Michigan, 1961).

Literary Dialect

The South has produced a large number of writers sufficiently interested in regional language variations to render many of them in literature. Among the earliest examples are the works of the mid–19th-century frontier humorists like George Washington Harris of Tennessee, creator of the comic character Sut Lovingood. But in a sentence like the following, from "Sut Lovingood's Daddy, Acting Horse" (1854), the language variation is more apparent than real: "Look out, mam, . . . better sen' fur sum strong man body tu keep him frum huggin' yu tu deth." Words like *fur* "for," *tu* "to," *frum* "from," and *deth* "death" are simply examples of the convention of "eye dialect," or nonstandard spellings that represent perfectly standard pronunciations. The aim is not to convey exact regional or social variation but to give a broad comic impression. Yet such eye dialect should not be scorned; for its purpose, it is an effective device.

In general, however, those who are considered genuine practitioners of literary dialect are writers like Joel Chandler Harris, who, while occasionally using eye dialect, go beyond it and attempt to represent precise regional and/or social departures from a standard, not only in pronunciation but in grammar and vocabulary as well. And though there were early exemplars of literary dialect like William Gilmore Simms of South Carolina, whose novel *The Yemassee* appeared in 1835, the heyday of the art in southern literature, and in American literature in general, is usually conceded to be the latter part of the century—especially the 1870s and 1880s. In addition to Joel Chandler Harris in Georgia, the roster for these two decades would include at least George Washington Cable in Louisiana, Mary Noailles Murphree—alias Charles Egbert Craddock—in Tennessee, Thomas Nelson Page in Virginia, and Irwin Russell in Mississippi. For the last decade of the century, Ruth McEnery Stuart in Arkansas and Louisiana and Charles W. Chesnutt in North Carolina would probably be added.

Moreover, literary dialect is not confined to minor writers but appears also in works of major authors like Mark Twain in Missouri and Edgar Allan Poe in Virginia. Nor is literary dialect just a curious artifact from the last century. Its use continues in works of major contemporary authors like William Faulkner in Mississippi, Flannery O'Connor in Georgia, and Jesse Stuart in Kentucky and Tennessee, as well as in the writings of non-southerners like Marjorie Kinnan Rawlings, who lived in and wrote about Florida, and children's writer Lois Lenski, who has captured dialects in Texas, South Louisiana, North Carolina, and Florida with the sure touch of a native.

The most widely known literary dialect is probably that of Joel Chandler Harris's Uncle Remus stories, exemplified in the following passage from *Uncle Remus: His Songs and Sayings* (1880):

> "Atter Brer Fox hear 'bout how Brer Rabbit done Brer Wolf," said Uncle Remus, scratching his head with the point of his awl, "he 'low, he did, dat he better not be so brash, en he sorter let Brer Rabbit 'lone. Dey wuz all time seein' one nudder, en 'bunnunce er times Brer Fox could er nab Brer Rabbit, but eve'y time he got de chance, his mine 'ud sorter rezume 'bout Brer Wolf, en he let Brer Rabbit 'lone."

The Uncle Remus stories were not written primarily as children's books. With their unique blend of black folklore and folk speech, they have—like most good children's books—an appeal that is well-nigh universal.

A lesser known, yet equally perceptive, dialect writer who worked at the same time as Joel Chandler Harris but with a quite different kind of literary dialect was George Washington Cable. His special combination of French and English, the speech of the fashionable, French-speaking upper-class society in and around New Orleans, is reflected in this passage from his best-known novel, *The Grandissimes* (1880):

> "Doze Creole' is lezzy," said Aurora. . . . "'Sieur Frowenfel,'" said Aurora, leaning her head on one side, "some pipple thing it is doze climade; 'ow you lag doze climade? . . . I thing Louisiana is a paradize—me! . . . W'ere you goin' fin' sudge a h-air?" She respired a sample of it. "W'ere you goin' fin' sudge a so rich groun'? De weed' in my bag yard is twenny-five feet 'igh . . . twenty-six! . . . W'ere you fin' sudge a reever lag dad Mississippi?"

In spite of the enthusiastic reactions of writers like Mark Twain, the appeal of this dialect has been something less than universal. Yet the speech of Aurora is as probable as that of Uncle Remus; and both would pose few problems of comprehension if read aloud—particularly by a speaker from the same area. This was dramatically demonstrated by the warm reception Cable received when reading his dialect works on the lecture circuit with Mark Twain.

Implicit in this audience reaction are two points of some importance about literary dialects. The first is that there is a significant difference between a spoken dialect—standard, as well as nonstandard—and a written one. The quasi-phonetic spelling and the grammatical restructuring that the dialect writer may be obliged to adopt often make the dialect look more exotic, and thus more difficult to decipher, than it really is. Harris works primarily with sound in the Uncle Remus passage, changing consonants, as in *dat* "that," and especially omitting initial and final elements, as in *'ud* "would," *'bout* "about," and *en* "and"—the latter a frequent characteristic of relaxed speech.

The Cable passage, however, seems more difficult because Cable alters not only consonants, as in *sudge* "such," but also vowels, as in *pipple* "people" and *reever* "river," and transforms the grammar as well—often by deletion—as in *W'ere you goin' fin' sudge a h-air?* "Where are you going to find such air?" Considering the obvious influence of French, the variation here is real, but much of the difficulty is only apparent and can be largely eliminated by reading the passage aloud.

The second thing to remember about literary dialect is that it is useful—at times crucial—to know something about the speech of the writer and the area. For example, in the Georgia speech of Uncle Remus, a form like *sorter* "sort of" is not meant to rhyme with the word *porter*, as pronounced by most non-southerners, but rather with a word like *aorta*. In other words, both Uncle Remus and his creator, lacking a final *r* sound like so many other southern speakers, would have said what many dialect writers would spell *sorta*. But Harris, quite naturally taking his own usage as a norm, wrote *sorter* since a final *-er* spelling represented for him the same sound as a final *-a*. The question lurking behind all this, of course, is how far to go in accuracy of detail without losing the reader. This is the dialect writer's perpetual dilemma.

One thing is clear, however: A reader of literary dialect in the 1980s has a distinct advantage over a reader of the 1880s, for a great deal—and not just in reference to *r* sounds—has been recorded about southern dialects in the ensuing century. In a wide variety of dialect studies—many of them part of the Linguistic Atlas of the United States project—readers near and far now have extensive resources for understanding a literary dialect and for gauging a writer's accuracy. As a number of language/literature scholars have shown, some writers—Joel Chandler Harris, for instance—are very accurate indeed, while still maintaining a balance between linguistic authenticity and literary artistry.

At its best, southern literary dialect—like the southern local color writing that it so often helps to enhance—transcends its local origins and becomes an invaluable part of the cultural heritage of the South and of the English-speaking world.

See also FOLKLIFE: / Brer Rabbit; LITERATURE: Folklore in Literature; / Cable, George Washington; Harris, Joel Chandler

William W. Evans
Louisiana State University

Harold B. Allen and Gary N. Underwood, eds., *Readings in American Dialectology* (1971); William W. Evans, *American Speech* (Fall–Winter 1971); Charles W. Foster, "The Representation of Negro Dialect in Charles W. Chesnutt's *The Conjure Woman*" (Ph.D. dissertation, University of Alabama, 1968);

James B. McMillan, *Annotated Bibliography of Southern American English* (1971); Lee A. Pederson et al., eds., *LAGS: The Basic Materials*, part 4 (1981); Juanita V. Williamson and Virginia M. Burke, eds., *A Various Language: Perspectives on American Dialects* (1971).

Mountain Language

Mountain English is a broad term covering the varieties of English spoken in two geographically separate mountainous areas of the United States—the Ozark region of northwestern Arkansas and southern Missouri, and the southern Appalachian Mountains of eastern Kentucky and Tennessee, mid-to-southern West Virginia, western Virginia and North Carolina, and northern Georgia. The separate terms *Ozark English* and *Appalachian English* denote the language of the two regions.

Mountain English has long been the object of much curiosity. Outsiders often comment on its old-fashioned flavor and its colorful figures of speech. Early study of it was limited to the search for relic usages and pronunciations. Mountain speech has often been romanticized and stereotyped as *Elizabethan* or *Shakespearean*, terms that connote a language frozen in time from the late 17th and early 18th centuries, when emigrants from the British Isles first settled in southern Appalachia.

Some speakers of Mountain English still use the pronouns *hit* and *we'uns*. But Mountain English is, in fact, no more frozen than any other variety of American English; all varieties retain archaisms, as well as exhibit features in various stages of change. Speakers of Mountain English tend to use certain linguistic features—some archaic and some innovative—to provide social and regional identity and the cultural cohesion to bind them as a group. This is the way dialects work. The specific features are not absolute; it is their frequency of use that characterizes the group. In other words, an old-time resident of Hazard, Ky., may not use the archaic form *done* to emphasize a completed action every time it might "fit" into her speech, but she probably says *They done got married* or *He done made me forget*, or some such phrase, more often than a native-born resident of, say, New Harmony, Ind. The higher frequency of use of features like *done* distinguishes Mountain English from other varieties of American English.

Another archaism that occurs with a degree of regularity in Mountain English is the *a-* prefix, which intensifies a continuous action, as in *He was a-tellin' the truth.* Both the *a-* prefix and completive *done* were used in the early history of English and still survive in mountain speech. Interestingly, both forms seem to be dying out in the Ozarks, with little evidence of their use by younger generations. The *a-* prefix occurs with less frequency among younger speakers of Appalachian English as well, but completive *done* is holding its own.

Innovation, or language change, seems to be occurring in two specific grammatical areas of Mountain English: subject-verb concord and the marking of principal parts of verbs. Whereas American English in general distinguishes between *was* and *were* for grammatically singular and plural subjects (having historically lost this distinction with all other past tense verbs), Mountain English speakers often eliminate the distinction, using *was* with plural or singular subjects. In both Appalachian English and Ozark English, the change is almost complete in constructions with the expletive *there*, as in *There was many flowers on the grave.* The same type of grammatical simplification is evident in the use of *don't* with third-person singular subjects, as in *She don't know the truth.* In present tense affirmative constructions, however, there is less evidence of simplification, with utterances like *I have a teacher that explain things* occurring rarely. This low frequency of *-s* deletion marks Ozark English and Appalachian English as distinct from other nonmainstream varieties of English that are otherwise much like them in their simplified use of *was* and *don't*.

Mountain English speakers tend to regularize the principal parts of verbs that other American speakers of English keep irregular. (Irregular verbs are those like *grow [grew/grown]* as distinct from those like *own [owned/owned]* that form the past forms with *-ed*.) In Mountain English, some regularized forms, such as *knowed*, are used for both the past tense and past participle; some irregular past tenses are also used for the past participle, as in *go (went/went)*; and some bare root forms are generalized to both the past tense and past participle, as in *give (give/give)*. Although other varieties of American English also show wide variation in their verb principal parts, the combination of linguistic forms within patterns of variation—forms like completive *done*, *a-* prefix, simplified subject-verb concord, and regularized verbs—work together to characterize Mountain English.

Before recent studies (such as Christian et al., 1984) documented the similarities between language patterns of the Ozarks and southern Appalachians, a sameness of language and culture was assumed. Although geographically separate, the two regions share, after all, a common cultural heritage. Many of the descendants of the Scotch-Irish who settled in southern Appalachia in the 1700s moved on to northwestern Arkansas in the 1800s, when incentives in the form of free or cheap land were offered by the state to those who would homestead it. Characterized by a strong sense of place, their rural isolation, a stable social system bordering on clannishness, and a common heritage, the people of the Ozarks and southern Appalachia have maintained a singular ethnic and linguistic identity.

See also ETHNIC LIFE: Mountain Culture; / Appalachians; GEOGRAPHY: Ozarks

Linda Blanton
University of New Orleans

Lester V. Berrey, *American Speech* (February 1940); Linda Blanton, in *Toward a Social History of American English*, ed. J. L. Dillard (1985); Donna Christian, Walter Wolfram, and J. Duke, *Variation and Change in Geographically Isolated Communities: Appalachian English and Ozark English* (Final Report to the National Science Foundation, Grant No. BNS 8208916, 1984); Walter Wolfram and Donna Christian, *Appalachian Speech* (1976), *Sociolinguistic Variables in Appalachian Dialects* (Final Report to the National Institute of Education, Grant No. NIE-G-740026, 1975).

Names, Personal

Personal names can document the settlement history of the South. The names of the English and the Celts (the most numerous colonists), the Spanish, French, Germans, Sephardic Jews, and others are linked to the cities or states they built. But names do more than substantiate historical facts; they convey the southern ethos.

Commemorative given names have been popular in the South. Surnames of the first families of the South—Byrd, Carroll, Clay, Jefferson, Pinckney, Taylor, and Washington—are bestowed on yeoman and patrician alike, as witnessed by any southern telephone book. In particular, the first and third presidents have had great influence on names. George Washington Cable was the novelist of the Creoles, and George Washington Carver was an accomplished black botanist and inventor. (The surname was adopted by many blacks after emancipation.) Jefferson Davis, the president of the Confederate States of America, was named for the famous Virginia president, as was Thomas Jefferson Wertenbacker, the historian.

The South has consistently honored military heroes. Andrew Jackson Hamilton was a governor of Texas and Andrew Jackson Montague a governor of Virginia. Francis Marion Cockrell, a Confederate general and Missouri governor, pays tribute to the Swamp Fox. Robert E. Lee's name is perpetuated by many southern lads with the surname Lee. (Robert E. Lee Prewitt, the protagonist of James Jones's *From Here to Eternity*, possessed the heroism if not the gallantry of his namesake.) French and Hispanic heroes are also honored. The names of Florida governor Napoleon Bonaparte Broward and the distinguished Confederate hero Simon Bolivar Buckner illustrate the process.

Some southern magnificoes have been remembered ironically. The Gowrie twins—Bilbo and Vardaman—in Faulkner's *Intruder in the Dust* are shiftless and nocturnal and satirize the two Mississippi politicians for whom the boys are named. The most common type of commemorative naming, however, does not invoke the heroic or illustrious. Rather, it passes on a family name, like an heirloom, from generation to generation. Often a surname is given as a first or middle name, e.g., Davis Smith, Bobby Brown Travis, or James Strom Thurmond, the Dixiecrat-turned-Republican, who is called by his mother's maiden name.

In naming, as in southern architecture, the classics have been influential. Many southerners bear a first or middle name of Greco-Roman origin, Augustus being among the most popular. This naming practice reveals the South's respect for antiquity as well as its hope that Herculean feats would be replicated in Dixie. Without rival, onomastically speaking, was Lucius Quintus Cincinnatus Lamar, the South's "Redeemer Politician" and later Supreme Court justice. Although abating in the last 50 years, the custom has flourished for centuries. Caesar Rodney represented Delaware in the Continental Congress; Cadmus Marcellus Wilcox distinguished himself on the battlefields of Virginia; Cassius Marcellus Clay, like the pugilist now known as Muhammad Ali, was a famous Kentuckian; Augustus Baldwin Longstreet portrayed the South movingly in fiction; Virginius Dabney is an award-winning journalist; Cleanth Brooks is a respected literary critic; and Thomas Dionysus Clark an eminent historian. In southern literature, characters with classical names perpetuate a noble tradition (Atticus Finch in Harper Lee's *To Kill a Mockingbird*) or suggest mythic models (Phoenix Jackson in Eudora Welty's "A Worn Path"). In the popular arts, Homer and his biblically christened partner, Jethro, offered bardic entertainment, mountain style.

Although known as the Bible Belt, the South does not surpass the North in using biblical first names. Still, the practice is strong. Biblical names are borne by distinguished senators from North Carolina (Jesse Helms), Alabama (Jeremiah Denton), and Tennessee (James Sasser), among others. Some southerners have been named for religious figures. Texas outlaw John Wesley Hardin carried the name of the early Methodist leader; his father was a circuit-riding preacher in that church. Martin Luther King, Jr., was named for the Protestant reformer, and other young southerners later carried King's name.

If southern names reflect the grandeur and formality of tradition, they also embody the folksy congeniality cherished by the region. More than in other parts of the nation, names in the South are diminutives, ending in *y* or *ie*, making them friendlier and less pretentious. The Carter brothers Jimmy and Billy typify in name and character an affection for this sentiment. Other similarly named southern dignitaries in the U.S. House of Representatives as of 1984 included Ronnie Flippo (Alabama); Andy Ireland (Florida); Larry Hopkins (Kentucky); Lindy Boggs, Billy Tauzin, Jerry Huckaby, and Cathy Long (Louisiana); and Jamie Whitten (Mississippi). Few in America would recognize William Franklin Graham, although Billy Graham is a household name. Nor are these folksy names considered inappropriate for someone of status. Diminutives such as Bubba (which approximates a young southerner's pronunciation of "brother"), Buddy, Lonnie, Sissy, Sonny, and Stoney are recorded legal names.

Many southerners have a double given name, one or both parts often a diminutive or shortened form. Such names suggest the southern ideals of youthful vigor and inviting informality. Among males, characteristic doublets are Billy Bob, Danny Lee, Eddie Ray, and Larry Gene. For belles, popular names are Bonnie Jean, Connie Ann, Ellie Mae (Jed Clampett's daughter in *The Beverly Hillbillies*), Suzy Kay, or Tammy Jo. A subpattern for females combines a male and a female name—Billy Sue, Johnnie Mae, Tommy Ruth, Willie Jean. By a reverse process, some men in the South have female names, thus making the popular song "A Boy Named Sue" less bizarre. Beryl, Doris, Emma Gene, Lynn, and Zelma Kay are given to southern men *and* women. The explanation for these bisexual names may be in commemorative patterns (boys named for mothers or aunts) or simply idiosyncratic independence. The gender of the tragic lovers implied in the song title "Frankie and Johnnie" is less disconcerting below than above the Mason-Dixon line.

An extreme example of unpretentious names is the use of initials in place of first names in the South. Sometimes these initials stand for first names (J. R. of *Dallas* fame), but the initials are also given as legal first names—B. J., B. W., J. T., and T. W. Initial names discomfit the U.S. government, especially the military, which adds "only" after such initial first names for easier processing of recruits.

Perhaps more than any other section of the country, the South is distinguished by picturesque names, including nicknames. From politics come William "Fishbait" Miller, the longtime doorkeeper of the House of Representatives; Goat Harris, an official in Durham, N.C.; Foxy Robinson, the water commissioner of Laurel, Miss.; and Shag Pyron, a former Mississippi football star and highway commissioner. The world of sports, too, glitters with the names of southern luminaries—Bear Bryant, Dizzy Dean, Mudcat Grant, Catfish Hunter, Bum Phillips, Vinegar Bend Mizell, and Oil Can Boyd.

Philip C. Kolin
University of Southern Mississippi

Adele Algeo and John Algeo, *Names* (June 1983); Philip C. Kolin, *Names* (September 1977); Forrest McDonald and Ellen Shapiro McDonald, *William and Mary Quarterly* (April 1980); Grady McWhiney and Forrest McDonald, *Names* (June 1983); Thomas Pyles, *American Speech* (December 1947), *Names* (June 1959).

Names, Place

Place-names in the South, as elsewhere, reflect the concerns and interests of the early inhabitants of the region. Not all of the most informative ones have yet been collected and explained, however. Although book-length studies of the best-known names in 9 of the 11 states of the Confederacy have been made, only those appearing on maps have been included because of space and time limitations. William S. Powell's *The North Carolina Gazetteer: A Dictionary of Tar Heel Places* and Bertha E. Bloodworth and Alton C. Morris's *Places in the Sun: The History and Romance of Florida Place-Names* are among the best of this kind of study, but each book contains only a few thousand of an estimated 50,000 or more names per state.

As Raven I. McDavid, Jr., says in his article "Names *Not* on the Map," the Place Name Survey of the United States, now under way, should include not only the kinds of names in the books already published but also those of features too small to be on maps and the informal designations used by the local residents for the well-known places. A large number of names not on maps have been collected by the field workers for the *Linguistic Atlas of the Middle and South Atlantic States* (fascicles 1 and 2, 1980) and the *Linguistic Atlas of the Gulf States* (1986), whose data are also on microfilm, but much work remains to be done to identify and explain many of them. Meanwhile, it is possible, by consulting the best of the state and national studies and those dealing with the periods and processes of place naming like George R. Stewart's *Names on the Land* and Mary R. Miller's "Place-Names of the Northern Neck of Virginia: A Proposal for a Theory of Place-Naming," to discover some of the main characteristics of southern geographical names.

The first inhabitants of the region, the Indians, gave names like *Sooktaloosa*, "black bluff," for a prominent landmark; *Cotahaga*, "locust-tree-there-standing," for a noticeable plant or animal of the area; or *Quilby*, "panther-there-killed," for an event occurring at the place. Because the Indians had little use for mountains, they rarely gave them distinct names. Often the mountains simply acquired the one already given to a certain area. *Appalachian*, recorded in 1528 as *Apalachen*, the Indian name of a province, was applied by the English to the southern part of the mountain system included in this area.

When settlers from Europe arrived, they retained a number of the Indian names for places and gave others to some of the settlements they founded. For example, *Tallahassee* and *Miami* both are Creek names, the former meaning "old town" and the latter, first applied to the river, then to the settlement, meaning "very large." Sometimes in attempting to pronounce and spell these names, the European settlers changed the form, as with the Choctaw term *bok*, "creek," which the French made *bayou*, and with *Arkansea*, the name of a tribe and village, which the French changed to *Arkansas*. At other places, they translated the Indian names. *Baton Rouge* is the French translation of the Indian term for a red stick or post used to mark the boundary between the hunting grounds of two tribes. The many *Cedar* and *Bear* creeks are likely examples of translations made by the English settlers. Not only did the English translate many of the Indian names, but they also sometimes translated the names earlier given by the French. *Little Rock* is a translation of *Petite Roche*, a designation used to distinguish this location from a larger area farther upstream on the Arkansas River, which the French had called *Grande Roche*.

In the South the English established tobacco and rice plantations rather than towns, as the settlers of New England did, and gave many of them and the colonies where they were located names in honor of their kings or queens, such as *Virginia*, a designation for Elizabeth I; *Carolina* for Charles I; and *Georgia* for George II. A number of plantations, which grew into towns, and counties were given names borrowed from England. Richmond on the James River, which honored James I, was named in 1733 for the town in Surrey located on the Thames River; the seaport of Norfolk in 1691 received the same designation as the Virginia county, which earlier had been named for the county in England; and Birmingham, Ala., because of its steel industry was named in 1871 for the city in Warwickshire famed for its manufacturing of steel. The English settlers also remembered the early explorers and colonizers of their new land. For example, the names of Columbia, S.C., and Raleigh, N.C., honored, respectively, Christopher Columbus in 1786 and Sir Walter Raleigh in 1792.

The French, like the English, named places for their kings or members of their nobility. Louisiana honored Louis XIV in 1681, and La Nouvelle (New) Orleans was named in 1718 for the regent of France, the Duc d'Orleans. The Spaniards, on the other hand, frequently chose the names of saints for their settlements. *St. Augustine* was the one given in 1665 to the fort founded in Florida (whose Spanish name means "flowerlike") because land was sighted on that saint's day; and *San Antonio*, the Spanish form of the name of the saint who helps persons find lost articles, was given first to the small river, then the mission, and finally the city in Texas, the territory whose name was derived from an Indian term meaning "friends."

Sometimes the settlers gave regions, particularly Mississippi, Alabama, and Tennessee, the name of an important river. *Mississippi* is Algonquian for "great water," and *Alabama* is "river of the Alibamons" (the Choctaw name, meaning "thicket clearers," for an Upper Creek people). *Tennessee* was named for the Tennessee River, which got its name from that of an ancient Cherokee town, recorded by the Spanish in 1567 as *Tanasqui* and by the English in 1707 as *Tinnase*, no longer having any literal meaning.

After the Revolution few names were borrowed from England. New settlements and counties honored national heroes, statesmen, and events. Greene County in Alabama, Mississippi, Georgia, Tennessee, and Virginia, and Greenville in North Carolina, South Carolina, Georgia, and Mississippi were all named for Nathanael Greene, a general of the Revolution. Knoxville and Nashville, Tenn., honored two other generals of the Revolution, Henry Knox and Francis Nash. Eutaw, Ala., commemorated a battle of that war occurring at Eutaw Springs in South Carolina. Austin and Houston, Tex., honored two of that territory's important early settlers and statesmen, Stephen F. Austin and Samuel Houston.

As the growing of cotton became important in the early 1800s, many new plantations came into being. By this time the planters' wives were doing some of the naming. Having through their study of music become familiar with Italian, they recommended such designations as *Belmonte*, "beautiful mountain," and *Monte Sano*, "healthful mountain." They also liked names containing "hall," such as *Stanton Hall*, because of the associations this word had with English country life. Literature provided plantation or town names like *Melrose* (mentioned in Scott's novels) and *Auburn* (in Goldsmith's poem "The Deserted Village"). During this period, exotic names like *Memphis* for the city in Egypt and *Carthage* for the ancient city in northern Africa were also popular. A few years later, in 1845, because what were thought to be feminine forms were considered appropriate for city names, *Atlanta* was derived from *Atlantic*.

Few names in the South are directly related to the days of slavery. Cities with "quarters" may reveal some trace of this period, and an all-black community with a name like *Freedman's Village* commemorates the emancipation of the slaves. The name *Pinder*, a town in South Carolina, comes from an African word for the peanut. The name was probably given by the white residents after this word had attained general currency in the region.

See also ETHNIC LIFE: Indian Cultural Contributions

Virginia Foscue
University of Alabama

Bertha E. Bloodworth and Alton C. Morris, *Places in the Sun: The History and Romance of Florida Place-Names* (1978); Kelsie B. Harder, ed., *Illustrated Dictionary of Place Names, United States and Canada* (1976); Raven I. McDavid, Jr., et al., *Names* (December 1985); H. L. Mencken, *The American Language: The Fourth Edition and the Two Supplements*, ed. Raven I. McDavid, Jr. (1963); William S. Powell, *The North Carolina Gazetteer: A Dictionary of Tar Heel Places* (1968); George R. Stewart, *American Place Names: A Concise and Selective Dictionary for the Continental United States of America* (1970), *Names on the Land* (3d ed., 1967); Fred A. Tarpley, *From Blinky to Blue-John: A Word Atlas of Northeast Texas* (1970), *1001 Texas Place Names* (1980).

New Orleans English

Greater metropolitan New Orleans—where precincts, wards, major streets, levees, bridges, and bayous are natural boundaries linguistically dividing a populace—includes seven parishes: Orleans, Jefferson, St. Bernard, Plaquemines, St. Tammany, St. Charles, and St. John the Baptist. The terms *city* and *country*, in the greater metropolitan area, no longer conveniently describe the geographic or demographic landscape or lifestyle of the parishes.

It is imprecise to speak of "white" or "black" English as discrete varieties of American English in the South, and the lack of precise rubrics is even more noticeable in referring to the English of the New Orleans areas. For example, in rural New Orleans and outside of Orleans Parish there are black speakers of Louisiana Creole and white speakers of Louisiana Cajun as well as whites who know Creole and blacks who perceive themselves as being culturally more Cajun than Creole. These groups are also native speakers of English. Commingling has always been the key to the cultural and linguistic development of New Orleans. In southern Louisiana spoken English has been greatly enriched by the penetration of vernacular French. Many ethnic groups, in fact, have created the public culture of New Orleans—not only the Europeans from Ireland, Germany, Yugoslavia, Hungary, Italy, France, and Spain, but also blacks from West Africa, Haiti, Belize, Virginia, and South Carolina. The creation continues today in the city's Honduran restaurants, Vietnamese restaurants and shops, Greek festivals, Filipino social organizations, and spiritualist churches of Mississippi blacks.

Though there are linguistic differences among speakers of New Orleans English, common elements do exist. Certain idiomatic expressions, for example, are characteristic. Idioms with *make* abound: *make groceries* "shop for groceries," *make menage* "clean house," *make dodo* "take a nap." The term *save* also appears as a frequent verb form, meaning "to put away," as in *save the groceries, save the dishes, save the clothes, save the jewelry*. Just as *ya' hear* can be used in many varieties of southern English as a tag at the end of a sentence, the terms *hear, yeah,* and *no* or an objective pronoun are often used as sentence tags in New Orleans English, as in *I'm gonna have another cup of coffee, hear?*, or *I don't like that, no,* or *She's smart, her*.

Some phrases in the English of New Orleanians show a division in usage according to gender. Some terms are known by both male and female but are more often used by males because they describe activities in which men more frequently participate—for example, *to shine*, meaning "to hunt with lanterns at night" during duck season, or *chunk*, meaning "to throw a ball extremely hard."

A double subject is frequently encountered in southern speech, as in *My brother, he went to the store*; however, among speakers of New Orleans English one will hear, for emphasis, a triple subject with three pronouns, as, for instance, in *Me myself I don't like to drive over that bridge*. Also, in a double-subject form characteristic of New Orleans speakers, where another person can be the second subject named, the pronoun precedes the second subject (*Me and my daddy*, or *Myself and Mr. Frank*, or *I and Helen*). Doublets also occur in expressions such as *Yet and still* for "however" or *feel to believe* for "I believe beyond all doubt," as in *I feel to believe that she'll get better*.

Various semantic changes seem to be taking place in New Orleans English. For example, *still* has taken on the implied meaning of "all the same" or "nonetheless," as in *I thought I was picking up the white wine instead of this red. It's still good (though)*. As for verb forms, *had* + the past participle of a verb is replacing the simple past tense form. Teachers not originally from New Orleans report its frequent appearance in the essays of university students. Thus, the following kind of narrative is not uncommon: *Yesterday afternoon I had run into Sylvia. I had told her we're thinking about going to Dauphin Island for the weekend. And she had said that she'd get in touch with us tonight*. One way to interpret this usage is to say that *had* + the past participle conveys a notion of past + present (i.e., when the speaker is narrating the events). In these and other ways the rich heritage of New Orleans English continues to evolve.

Mackie J V Blanton
University of New Orleans

Madeline Aubert-Gex, "A Lexical Study of the English of New Orleans Creoles" (M.A. thesis, University of New Orleans, 1983); Mackie J V Blanton and John Cooke, eds., *Perspectives on Ethnicity in New Orleans* (1981); Joseph Logsdon, in *Perspectives on Ethnicity in New Orleans*, ed. John Cooke (1979); Margaret M. Marshall, *Anthropological Linguistics* (Winter 1982); Dorice Tentchoff, *The Culture of Acadiana: Tradition and Change in South Louisiana*, ed. Steven L. Del Sesto and Jon L. Gibson (1975).

Oratory

The mythical southern orator is a white male said to possess qualities that distinguish him from speakers heard in other regions. This regional persona speaks emotionally, in ornate symbolic language with expansive gestures and a thunderous voice, about sacred themes. General John B. Gordon speaking against Reconstruction policies embodied this mythical presence. Exhibiting a "rare physical vigor," this scar-faced Confederate veteran dramatically trumpeted "Dixie," "our soil," "sacrifice," "our fathers," and the "spirit of Lee." Prideful public performance became the hallmark of the southern orator, no matter that John C. Calhoun talked "impersonally" with "few gestures" and that Joseph Brown rejected "sickly sentimentality" for unadorned speech about financial prosperity.

Conceived in Old South culture and created in suffering and defeat, this ostentatious persona helped shield the region from federal encroachment, economic exploitation, social change, and outside criticism, while maintaining traditional thought and policies at home. Even as veterans of the Confederacy died and their children and grandchildren forgot the war, this fictive image of the raging public warrior persisted, providing speakers with stock rhetorical forms of delivery, argument, and language as well as topics for their oratory.

A second type of southern oratory consists of the real-life performances of whites, blacks, males, and females of different postures and persuasions from the 1800s to the 1980s. White males held communicative dominance in the region, developing the authoritative strategies of white superiority, southern manhood, and southern ladyhood. Some women spoke effectively in public, but always in a manner considered suitable to their low social status. More recently, although women had won the vote and a wider voice in society, defeat of the Equal Rights Amendment in the South demonstrated that many persons still preferred traditional social and rhetorical roles for women and men in the region.

Until the 1960s black men and women experienced few safe and meaningful opportunities to speak in the general cultural institutions. As slaves, blacks confronted coercive sanctions with both a defensive posture of accommodation and an aggressive assertion of exploitation. Former slaves from the South did become influential orators in the northern antislavery movement. Drawing on their southern experiences, they offered dramatic testimonials about slavery. Frederick Douglass, a former slave from Maryland, became one of the 19th century's greatest orators. With the physical gifts of a great orator—tall in stature, melodious in voice—Douglass won converts to abolition throughout the North and in England. During Reconstruction some blacks spoke a new rhetoric that rejected racist stereotypes and called for equal opportunities. The black church became the most significant forum for black public speaking, although the style was more one of folk speech than oratory. Audience interaction with the preacher and the use of biblical language, musical rhythms, and sometimes even chanted sermons—all in a passionate religious setting—characterized speaking in the black church. After the judicial and legislative decisions of the 1950s and 1960s, blacks had increased opportunities for open communication. They marched in streets and talked in churches, on campuses, and over television of constitutional rights, basic freedoms, human dignity, economic opportunities, and cruel discrimination.

Prior to the Civil War, white leaders saw the threat to their slave society and responded with a "rhetoric of desperation." They differed on the nature and future of the Union, and a new sectional awareness emerged. Confronting social and economic change, orators perfected defensive rhetorical forms dealing with the recurring themes of constitutionality, states' rights, regional pride, Old South culture, white superiority, agrarianism, and God. Equally important was the omission from public discourse of the topic of civil rights for blacks.

During Reconstruction most white speakers supported the restoration of white rule in state government. Initially, some leaders refused to participate in Reconstruction politics and thereby legitimize the political role of former slaves. A few whites called for submission to northern conquerors as a means of reclaiming economic security and political control and, as a consequence, were ostracized from public office for a number of years. To resist Reconstruction laws and to restore white authority, the majority of white orators constructed regionally appealing arguments from mythic themes of the Old South, white superiority, threats to southern womanhood, regional pride, states' rights, constitutional claims, violence, economic prosperity, and regional security. Supplementing these stock southern appeals were emotional references to God, sacred principles, and past loyalties, as well as to Civil War experiences, including heroic acts by soldiers, sacrifices of women left behind, regional suffering, and economic ruin.

From 1800 to 1954 whites relied on racial authority, hoping to hold blacks in their rhetorically impotent status as obedient listeners. At the same time, to communicate with northerners, white orators practiced a "rhetoric of accommodation," a stance opposite to their Reconstruction discourse of resistance. This conciliatory posture combined a regional loyalty oath with an emphasis on sectional prosperity. Listeners heard the same orators talk of Old South themes of "southern honor" and New South appeals of "practical progress" for the "new age." Between 1880 and 1946 a number of southern demagogues, noted for their fiery delivery, belligerence, magnetism, assumed infallibility, and monopolizing strategies, governed the region. During the 1940s, when courts ruled that blacks could participate in white primaries, these demagogues and other less dogmatic whites began a new round of intimidating bribes and threats.

The most dramatic change in southern oratory occurred from 1954 to the 1980s, when the Supreme Court ruled against racially segregated public schools and the Congress passed civil rights legislation. Blacks challenged the dominant rhetorical status of whites. A pluralistic public speaking emerged, with a variety of views being stated on questions of race, economy, political parties, crime, national defense, ecology, industry, and education. Blacks were able publicly to communicate feelings, convictions, and aspirations previously kept private. Blacks and some whites directly confronted the morality, expediency, economy, and legality of racial discrimination. Many blacks abandoned their former accommodating posture and developed more candid and assertive language, strategies, topics, and arguments appropriate for newly won freedom.

Martin Luther King, Jr., used oratory as a key weapon in the civil rights movement. He drew from the communications style of the black folk church and combined biblical themes with national egalitarian ideals. His "I Have a Dream" speech at the 1963 March on Washington echoed Lincoln's language in the Gettysburg Address, portraying the South as the locale of a hoped-for racial reconciliation.

To oppose social changes resulting from legal and judicial decisions, many whites escalated their defensive rhetoric of white superiority, black inferiority, constitutional interpretations, states' rights, God, free enterprise, and racial segregation. Increasingly, however, whites were forced to share the public forum with blacks. As more blacks registered to vote and campaigned for office, whites for the first time since Reconstruction were required to communicate directly and respectfully with the new minority audience. Although awkward initially, white orators experimented with rhetoric appropriate to their new, less-powerful status. In the 1970s a few governors actually called for an end to racial discrimination. Some writers have called this new white male speech an "oratory of optimism," but a more accurate characterization would be a public admission of the expediency of social change and shared authority.

See also BLACK LIFE: Preacher, Black; / Douglass, Frederick; King, Martin Luther, Jr.; POLITICS: Demagogues

Cal M. Logue
University of Georgia

Waldo W. Braden, ed., *Oratory in the Old South, 1828–1860* (1970), *Oratory in the New South* (1979), *Southern Speech Journal* (Summer 1964); Kevin E. Kearney, *Southern Speech Journal* (Fall 1966); Cal M. Logue, *Quarterly Journal of Speech* (February 1981); Cal M. Logue and Howard Dorgan, eds., *The Oratory of Southern Demagogues* (1981); John D. Saxon, *Southern Speech Communication Journal* (Spring 1975).

Spanish Language

Ethnic Hispanics who habitually speak Spanish are rare or almost nonexistent throughout much of the South.

Yet in three southern states—Louisiana, Texas, and Florida—the Hispanic presence historically antedates English settlement and incorporation into the United States. And in two of those states (Texas and Florida), the 1970s and 1980s have witnessed dramatic increases in foreign-born Spanish speakers. Thus, Spanish in the American South is widespread in a few states but almost totally absent in others.

Although New Orleans and its suburbs are not without a certain Hispanic presence, chiefly the product of contemporary immigration, only in the eastern reaches of St. Bernard Parish (lying southeast of New Orleans between the Mississippi and Lake Borgne) does one find a concentrated Hispanic population historically linked with pre-American Louisiana and the Spanish language. They are the *isleños*, "islanders," so named after their 18th-century place of origin, Spain's Canary Islands. The *isleños'* ancestors were brought to Louisiana from 1778 through the 1790s by Bernardo de Gálvez, governor of the province. Settling in small communities (today Shell Beach, Yscloskey, Delacroix, and Reggio), the *isleños* led a largely isolated fishing-trapping-farming existence throughout the 19th century and into the 20th, thereby retaining Spanish in the face of only moderate pressures to acquire French and later English.

Isleño Spanish was spoken by the several thousand *isleños* in the 1940s, when it was investigated by Raymond R. MacCurdy, but that is no longer the case. At present, only the oldest residents are Spanish-dominant and use the language regularly. Middle-aged *isleños* typically understand it well but speak it haltingly, and the younger generations range from poor speaking ability and middling comprehension to no knowledge of Spanish at all. (Reputedly, however, there are differences between the two main settlements: Shell Beach/Hopedale, where Spanish loss is most advanced, and Delacroix, where Spanish retention is somewhat higher.) Language loss can be attributed to the usual factors: longer attendance at consolidated schools where English is the sole medium of instruction, improved transportation, expanded contacts with the outside world, marriages outside the group, and increased economic opportunities. Today, while *isleño* culture and sense of Hispanic identity are undergoing a revival, local Spanish is effectively moribund.

The Spanish spoken by *isleños* is Canary Island dialect with numerous lexical borrowings from French and to a lesser extent English. Linguistically, the Canary Islands have always formed a bridge between the Andalucía region of southern Spain and the New World. Andalusian Spanish (together with Canary Island, Caribbean, and, in general, "coastal" Spanish throughout much of the Western Hemisphere) can be characterized by weakened, altered, or eliminated consonants at the ends of syllables or words, by occasionally nasalized vowels (as in French), by a rather lax manner of producing voiced consonants, and, of course, by the absence of the Castilian voiceless "th" sound. The overall acoustic effect of *isleño* Spanish is not unlike that of the rural dialects of Cuba and the Dominican Republic.

In recent years, Dallas and especially Houston have become home to increasing numbers of Central and South Americans, but when Hispanics in Texas come to mind, one first thinks of Mexicans. This is inevitable, given the status of Mexican Americans as Texas's largest minority group (22 percent of the state's population of more than 12 million).

Whereas small though significant numbers of Spanish-speaking families have lived in what is now Texas from the 17th through the 19th centuries, the majority of Mexican Americans/Chicanos in the state today are descendants of 20th-century immigrants or are immigrants themselves. According to figures from the 1980 U.S. census, 29 of Texas's 254 counties now have Mexican-American majorities, in several cases well in excess of 66.7 percent. Mexican Americans form the majority population in two of Texas's five biggest cities—San Antonio and El Paso. Mexican-American settlement patterns reveal, however, an uneven distribution throughout the state, with the greatest numbers concentrated in a 150- to 200-mile-wide strip along the international border. Save for the Dallas and Houston areas, north and east Texas are home to relatively few Mexican Americans.

In Texas, is "Mexican American" coextensive with "Spanish speaking"? According to a study by Calvin J. Veltman, based on the 1976 National Survey of Income and Education, Hispanic Americans in general are more conservative of their ethnic language than are other major American ethnolinguistic groups. For example, although slightly over 60 percent of Americans of Italian descent born in the United States switch over to English monolingualism, only about 30 percent of Hispanics do so. However, the rate of Hispanic linguistic anglicization varies from region to region, with the highest Spanish loss being found in the Rocky Mountain states and the lowest in Texas. So the report provides some statistical confirmation of what the unaided ear can hear: that a lot of Spanish is spoken in Texas. Yet the size and great diversity of Texas almost guarantee that for Spanish, degrees of usage and levels of proficiency will vary widely too. Socioeconomic standing, place of residence, generation of removal from Mexico, sex, profession, family ties, education, degrees of local Anglo/Chicano ethnic tension, sociopolitical attitudes, and many other factors influence how much Spanish one speaks, to whom and how well one speaks it, what type(s) of Spanish one uses, and whether one will pass Spanish on to the next generation. For example, it is popularly known that a larger number of Mexican Americans speak Spanish more often and with greater proficiency in border cities like El Paso, Laredo, and Brownsville than in Fort Worth, Lubbock, or Port Arthur. But even on the border, variability takes its toll (though in cities like El Paso it is almost impossible to find a native Mexican American who does not at least *comprehend* Spanish).

In Texas the Spanish of Mexican Americans is the Spanish that they or their ancestors brought north and altered through increased contact with English and decreased contact with a society that is exclusively Spanish speaking. Allowing for the impossibility of generalizing about *the* language and language behavior of a population as diverse as are the Mexican Americans of Texas, it is still useful to describe the Spanish of a hypothetically typical speaker with the following composite picture. As compared to an *isleño* or a Cuban American, his consonant system is strong. His grammar is probably that of the rural Mexican with the concomitant regularizations, archaisms, hypercorrections, and forms of respect. The years in Texas will have brought about a diminution in the use of the subjunctive mood and an expansion of English-parallel patterns such as the present progressive tense. His lexicon will show on the one hand an increasing adaptation of English words and phrases and on the other hand a decrease in learned Spanish terminology, especially of the technical sort.

There are certain historical parallels between Texas and Florida, but not many. Thus, while Florida was steadily claimed by the Spanish crown from 1513 until 1763, colonization was not extensive, and nearly all Spanish subjects abandoned San Agustín (the only settlement of any substance) in 1764 with the onset of British occupation. Twenty years later, Spain again took formal possession of the peninsula, but the period between then and 1819 (when the United States added Florida to its domains) was chaotic, unstable, and unmarked by any serious success in Hispanicization. Ironically, the only Hispanic or, more properly, Iberian settlers' group to survive the English-speaking onslaught well into the 19th century were the descendants of the 1,100 Minorcans who were brought to what is now the New Smyrna Beach area in 1768 by Andrew Turnbull during the two-decade period of British colonization. In 1777 Turnbull's plantation venture collapsed, and the Minorcans migrated northward to settle in San Agustín (modern-day St. Augustine). Although half the Minorcans departed Florida in 1784, the remainder stayed on. The language indigenous to the Mediterranean island of Minorca is a dialect of Catalan, not Spanish, and it is thus not possible to speak of the Minorcan's permanence as representing a Spanish-speaking presence in Florida. It is probable that Spanish (and English) were added to their linguistic repertoire during the first five decades of their settlement in Florida. In any event, studies such as that by Rasico (1983) point to a growing loss of the Minorcan language by the end of the 1800s save for several dozen words and expressions retained by some of the settlers' descendants well into the 20th century.

With the exception of the famous 1868 migration of large numbers of Cuban cigar makers to Key West, and a similar movement in 1886 to the Ybor City neighborhood of Tampa, the bulk of Florida developed into a southern state not unlike the others until 1 January 1959, a date that marked the beginning of the Cuban exodus from the regime of Fidel Castro. Since then, well over 1,000,000 Cubans have left Cuba, with the majority of them settling in southeastern Florida. At present, Dade County's population of 1,750,000 contains around 450,000 persons of Cuban descent, who, together with smaller colonies of Puerto Ricans, Central Americans, and others, constitute between 55 and 60 percent of the population of the city of Miami proper.

Periodically, Cuban mass arrivals make international headlines, and these "wave" immigrants give rise to local Anglo fears of inundation. These fears culminated in 1981 in the passage of a law voiding a generalized 1973 proclamation of official bilingualism. In light of this, it may be surprising (and to nervous Anglos, reassuring) to learn from Carlos A. Solé, a professor at the University of Texas, that "language shift [to English] seems to have already begun among young Cuban-Americans in spite of the recency of the Cuban arrival and settlement." But for an unpredictable number of years to come, Miami will continue to impress the visitor as "Spanish speaking," given the steady stream of new arrivals from the Caribbean basin and beyond.

For the moment, though, the Spanish of the Miami area can still be equated with Cuban, so to describe Cuban Spanish is to describe the varieties of Dade County: weak consonants, vowel nasalization, and an intonation rhythm that gives out a somewhat machine-gun effect. Inevitably, English borrowings will enter Miami Spanish as they have the Spanish of Texas, though perhaps not to the same degree, because the average Cuban political exile typically enjoyed a level of education that the average Mexican economic refugee did not.

See also ETHNIC LIFE: / Cubans; Mexicans; Spanish; URBANIZATION: / Dallas; Houston; Miami; New Orleans; Tampa

Richard V. Teschner
University of Texas at El Paso

Raymond R. MacCurdy, *The Spanish Dialect in St. Bernard Parish, Louisiana* (1950); Philip D. Rasico, *El Escribano* (1983); Carlos A. Solé, *A Festschrift for Jacob Ornstein: Studies in General Linguistics and Sociolinguistics*, ed. Edward L. Blansitt, Jr., and Richard V. Teschner (1980); Calvin J. Veltman, *The Assimilation of American Language Minorities: Structure, Pace and Extent* (1979); U.S. Bureau of Census, *Population and Housing; Advance Reports, Texas, Final Population and Housing Counts* (1981).

Urban Speech

The Linguistic Atlas of the Gulf States project consists of interviews with informants in eight southern states (Tennessee, Georgia, Florida, Alabama, Mississippi, Arkansas, Louisiana, and Texas), with a lexical Urban Supplement added to the basic work sheets of 164 of the 1,121 interviews. These 164 urban records cover the speech patterns of 100 white and 64 black informants, 79 of whom were age 30 or younger. The majority of the records represent natives of the larger cities in the area—Knoxville, Chattanooga, Atlanta, Jacksonville, Tampa, Miami, Nashville, Birmingham, Montgomery, Mobile, Memphis, Jackson, New Orleans, Shreveport, Little Rock, Dallas, Houston, and San Antonio. The remainder report the speech of primarily younger informants from smaller cities and towns, included for comparison with their urban counterparts.

LAGS evidence shows that urban speech in the South retains distinct regional characteristics, particularly among older and more insular informants. For example, although *dragonfly* is preferred by a large majority of urban informants, the South Midland form *snake doctor* is strong in Tennessee, Arkansas, and the upper portions of Georgia, Alabama, and Mississippi; and among residents of the lower South *mosquito hawk* prevails in Florida, Louisiana, Gulf Alabama, Gulf Mississippi, and the lower portion of Georgia. Likewise, *chigger* is the dominant term among informants in Tennessee, Arkansas, and upper Georgia, while *red bug* occurs more frequently elsewhere in the territory.

Younger urban informants, however, preserve fewer of the regionalisms usually noted in dialect surveys. Most of these southerners, for instance, offer no variant for *peanuts*, though some recognize *goobers* as an old-fashioned or rural form. Such choices as *ground peas*, *goober peas*, and *pinders* are rare. To many urban informants, there are no valid distinctions among types of peaches: *cling* is recognized only as a descriptor on the label of a can. Thus, such regional patterns as *press* versus *plum peach* are lost in the cities.

In some sections of the urban South, regionalisms have developed for items covered in the Urban Supplement. A coin-operated self-service laundry, known by the trade name *laundromat* in most places, tends to be a *washateria* in east Texas, a *washhouse* in Miami, and a *wishy-washy* in Nashville. A *hero sandwich* is usually a *submarine* in the eastern and east-central zones of the LAGS territory and a *poor boy* in the west-central and western zones, probably reflecting the influence of the New Orleans focal area where the *poor boy* was reputedly invented. Exceptions occur in Florida, where *Cuban* is common, and in the east-central zone, from middle Tennessee to Gulf Alabama, where the sandwich is often called a *Dagwood*, after the comic-strip character.

Other items investigated by the Urban Supplement show no such regional variation. *Water fountain* prevails over *drinking fountain* throughout the LAGS territory, and an informal room in the house is usually a *den* everywhere, with *family room* a distant second. In Florida, it may be called a *Florida room*, but even there, *den* occurs more often. The speech of urban informants, particularly the younger and more sophisticated, contains a variety of synonyms for the LAGS words associated with crime, street life, and illegal activities, among them synonyms for marijuana and other drugs, colloquial names for money such as *bread* and *cabbage*, and derogatory names for policemen.

Urban speech in the South, while retaining some of the old regionalisms, has developed various new regionalisms, while other items evoke a common response from city to city. Regional distinctions are more likely to appear in the speech of southerners over age 30. Younger urban southerners, both black and white, are more likely to share the vocabularies of their peers in other parts of the country.

Susan Leas McDaniel
Emory University

Charles E. Billiard, Susan E. Leas, and Marvin W. Bassett, eds., *A Manual for Dialect Research in the Southern States*, 3d ed., *The Protocols. LAGS: The Basic Materials*, part 1 (1981); Charles E. Billiard and Lee A. Pederson, *Orbis* (1979); Susan E. Leas, LAGS Working Papers (First Series), no. 7 (1981); Lee A. Pederson, *American Speech* (Spring–Summer 1971, Fall 1980).

Chesapeake Bay Dialect

The South is more diversified in speech than other major geographical areas of the United States. In such coastal regions as the Chesapeake area, one finds particularly pronounced language differences. The most linguistic diversity in the Chesapeake is found among those who live in the southern island communities (Tilghman, Deal, and Smith in Maryland; Saxis, Chincoteague, and Tangier in Virginia) and make their living by fishing, crabbing, clamming, and oystering.

At times, outsiders, especially journalists, grossly exaggerate the speech they hear in these areas as "pure dialect," "fossilized language," and "Elizabethan English"—labels that are nonsense but hard to dispel. All American English derived, of course, from 17th-century British English, which at the time was itself quite diverse. What one finds throughout the United States—especially on the Atlantic Seaboard, the region of original settlement—are survivals of British English. The dialects of the islands (relic areas, to dialectologists), however, seem quite different, and they are; but to look at them as old-fashioned and preservers of Chaucerian and Elizabethan speech is incorrect.

Nevertheless, the islanders and their language are very special. Tangier Island, which is the best known and has received the most attention, is 3.5 miles long and 1.5 miles wide and is roughly at sea level. It lies in the middle of the Chesapeake Bay, a part of Accomac County on the Eastern Shore of Virginia. The closest neighbors are on Smith Island, just across the Virginia line in Maryland. Tangiermen think that their own language is different from the Smith Islanders'. Except for daily necessities, the islanders have relatively little contact with the mainland. The approximately 800 residents, persuaded by the authority of a national historical marker and some imaginative brochures and newspaper stories, believe that their history goes back to 1686, the year a certain John Crockett settled the island, although "facts" have not been substantiated by the records. A more likely date for settlement would be somewhere around 1790 to 1800.

A homogeneous community of working-class whites of English descent (called watermen), Tangier reflects very few social differences. Lives are simple and hard, and inhabitants are independent, deeply religious, and patriotic. Tangiermen are essentially single-style speakers, but when encountering strangers, they occasionally correct toward what they believe to be standard speech. Their speech is distinctive in grammar, word forms, and vocabulary, but most striking are the unusual tenseness and emphasis that characterize pronunciation. These traits, plus the Tangierman's curious mixture of double negatives, stated opposites, clipped phrases, nicknames, and nautical terms can be both amusing and baffling to an outsider.

The Tangier dialect does not share the commonly cited distinctive features of eastern Virginia speech still heard in the Piedmont and Tidewater areas: the broad *a* of *aunt*; the loss of *r* in words like *car, corn, year,* and *dinner*; or the pronunciation of *afraid* and *naked* as *afred* and *neked*. Some of the rustic pronunciations heard along the coastal localities of the Chesapeake are not heard on Tangier; for example, *can't* with the vowel of *paint, push* with the vowel of *pooh, dog* with the vowel of *hoe, fish* with the vowel of *fee,* and *poor* with the vowel of *Poe*. The Islanders do not distinguish *hoarse* and *horse, mourning* and *morning,* and *poor* and *pour,* as many southerners do. *Mary* and *merry* are pronounced as many pronounce *Murray*. They pronounce *tire, tired, wire,* and *fire* with the vowel of *lard*. *Chair, care,* and *scared* are pronounced with the vowel of *curd*, as are *year, hear, here,* and *ear*. *Paul* and *ball* are pronounced like *pull*. All words that rhyme with *trash* invariably have the vowel of *bay*. *Creek* has the Pennsylvanian sound, that of the vowel of *tick*. *Bomb* and *bum* are pronounced the same. *Calm*, in reference to slatelike water, is *cam*. *Zinc* is used for *sink* (kitchen), and *spider* and *frying pan* are used interchangeably, but at times show age distribution. *Coal oil* is more prevalent than *kerosene, curtains* is used for *roller shades*, and *bateau* is the common term for *small boat*.

The most prominent aspect of Tangier speech is the phonetic diversity of the vowels, which are pronounced in such a way that one seems to be hearing several vowels in a continuum and Cockney-like drawling and whining. Tangier speech then seems to be a mixture, sharing features with the speech of the Middle Atlantic states to the north, the southern mountain area, the southern Coastal Plain, and the outermost Atlantic communities.

See also ENVIRONMENT: / Chesapeake Bay

David L. Shores
Old Dominion University

William Cabell Greet, *American Speech* (December 1933); David L. Shores, *Journal of English Linguistics* (1984); William W. Warner, *Beautiful Swimmers: Watermen, Crabs, and the Chesapeake Bay* (1976).

Conch

The term *Conch* refers both to a subset of the population of the Florida Keys and to the distinctive speech of this group. Unlike many other groups in the United States, the Conchs are characterized not by ethnicity or the use of a non-English language, but by settlement history and regional and social insularity. The Conchs originated with the formation in 1649 of a company of Cockney Englishmen, the Eleuthian Adventurers, who migrated to Bermuda seeking religious and political freedom. During the next century the group migrated again, this time to the Bahamas. From there, many of them settled in Key West after its acquisition by the United States from Spain in 1819, and by the middle of the century they had moved into the upper Keys as well. The absence of direct transportation routes and the economic activities of the Conchs served to isolate them from the United States mainland and to favor continued cultural and commercial relations with the Bahamas, which provided a steady stream of new settlers, and later with Cuba. Initially, their economic activity revolved around the ocean, with salvaging, sponging, and fishing (the conch was a major source of food as well as the source of the name for the people) the primary commercial activities.

During the last quarter of the 19th century, however, Key West became the world's most important center for manufacturing cigars. In spite of the infusion of new people from the United States mainland and Cuba, the Conchs associated primarily with their own people and often educated their children separately. The demise of the cigar industry and subsequent decline in population after 1910 reinforced their isolation. Although tourism and military installations brought a new flow of people from the mainland after World War II, the Conchs continue to maintain a strong sense of their distinctiveness as a group.

The linguistic consequence of their history is a dialect that is clearly different from any other spoken on the U.S. mainland. To outsiders it sounds much like the speech of the Bahamas, and as linguist Frank K. LeBan shows, it shares some features with British English. Although the Conch vocabulary includes a number of unique words, such as *locker* for *closet, grits box* for *stove,* and *natural sponge* for *dishcloth*, the dialect is more remarkable for its distinct pronunciation. Like British and southern American speech, Conch speakers do not pronounce the *r* after vowels. More importantly, the vowels in words like *coat* and *hot* are closer to the British than the American pronunciation. The combination of these features, along with others, provides a speech that is unique, as is the social history of the Conchs.

Guy Bailey
Texas A&M University

Frank K. LeBan, in *A Various Language: Perspectives on American Dialects*, ed. Juanita V. Williamson and Virginia M. Burke (1971), "A Phonological Study of the Speech of Conchs, Early Inhabitants of the Florida Keys, at Three Age Levels" (Ph.D. dissertation, Louisiana State University, 1965); Lee A. Pederson et al., eds., *LAGS: The Basic Materials*, (1981).

Drawl

The southern drawl is a slow speech heard in the South and distinguished in part from the more general American drawl. Myth associates the southern drawl with the prestige of first families whose ancestors owned antebellum plantations. Observation shows that among the best families there are those who drawl and those who do not, and within the same family a grandmother may drawl markedly while her grandsons may not do so at all. Furthermore, the poor white cousins living on farms and in mill towns probably have entirely different characteristic speech patterns. The range and complexity of black southern speech have yet to be explored systematically throughout the entire South.

If the southern drawl has identified speakers as socially prominent, it has also served as a vehicle for public amusement in the way that any regional speech amuses. The Missourian Mark Twain regularly entertained his audiences by reading from Joel Chandler Harris's Tar Baby story; its black dialect let Twain give a virtuoso display of the range of his southern drawl.

The American drawl has often been noted as a defect—witness Noah Webster's *Dissertations* (1798), which urged New England workers to correct their "drawling, nasal manner of speaking." The southern drawl cannot be traced to the influence of personal laziness, a hot climate, or the presence of a black mammy rearing planters' children during infancy. (How any given mammy spoke, incidentally, is lost in the past. Using diaries and similar evidence, Norman Eliason stated in *Tar Heel Talk* (1956) that in North Carolina slaves learned to speak English from "largely illiterate or semi-literate overseers." Little other evidence on the point has been assembled.)

A distinguishing feature of the southern drawl is that it differs from the southern mountaineer's pronunciation of *thing* as *thaing*, notably by using an added *y* sound and by losing an *r* in particular settings: *dyuty*, *tyube*, and for some Virginians *cyah*, and *gyahden* sound more drawn out than do *duty*, *tube*, *car*, and *garden*. These pronunciations arose among 18th-century British aristocrats and were adopted by well-to-do southern colonial planters and their social equals. The effect of the lost *r* on the pronunciation of preceding stressed vowels or diphthongs is shown in the graphic tables of Kurath and McDavid, *The Pronunciation of English in the Atlantic States* (1961); no comparable graphs exist for the states formed after the American Revolution.

See also BLACK LIFE: Speech, Black

Gordon R. Wood
Southern Illinois University

James B. McMillan, *Annotated Bibliography of Southern American English* (1971); Thomas Pyles, *Words and Ways of American English* (1952).

Indian Trade Languages

Because the North American Indians spoke a great variety of languages, they developed several ways of communicating among themselves or with the European settlers regarding preparations for travel or war, peacemaking, and, chiefly, trade. Though the sign language of the Plains Indians is well known, Native Americans generally used second verbal languages, like the Chinook jargon of the Northwest. A number of such jargons, lingua francas, or trade languages developed in the Southeast.

Robert Beverley, at the beginning of the 18th century, cited Ocaneeche (perhaps actually Tutelo) of eastern Virginia as a trade language. John Lawson, writing at the beginning of the 1700s, found Tuscarora, the language of the Iroquois tribe of the same name, widely used by smaller tribes in eastern North Carolina. Not long after Lawson's publication, the Tuscaroras went to war with the settlers, and, after being defeated, slowly migrated to New York and Ontario, thus ending use of their tongue as a trade language. According to James Adair (1775), the Catawba language was used in South Carolina much as was the Tuscarora farther north. Francis Le Jau in 1706 remarked that, according to hearsay, the Savanna (Shawnee) language was similarly in use in Georgia. Evidence exists that the Shawnee used Muskogee (Creek) as a trade language, so Le Jau was likely making a first reference to Creek as a lingua franca.

The Muskogee spoken by the Creeks of Alabama and Georgia was closely allied to the languages spoken by the Chickasaws and Choctaws and by several smaller southeastern tribes. The Creek political confederacy included the Alabama, Chickasaw, Koasati, Hitchiti, Natchez, Shawnee, and Yuchi tribes, all of whom probably spoke Muskogee (Creek) until about 1840, when the last of the southeastern Indians were forcibly moved west. Some scholars suggest, however, that the common language was, in fact, Mobilian, and clear evidence exists that the Alabamas, Chickasaws, Natchez, and Koasati did use Mobilian.

Mobilian, doubtless the most widespread and long-lasting of the southeastern intertribal languages, was also at first called the Chickasaw trade language. The term *Mobilian* was first used by the French founders of Louisiana, who encountered it among Indians in the vicinity of their original Gulf settlements near Mobile, Ala. Other French travelers in the lower Mississippi Valley first encountered it among the Chickasaws in present-day Tennessee. Le Page du Pratz (1758) states that "Tchicacha" and "Langue Mobilienne" were the same and comprised a jargon used by tribes of both Muskogean and non-Muskogean linguistic stocks to communicate with the French. Le Page du Pratz spoke of Mobilian as "a corrupted Chickasaw," meaning that it had pidgin qualities—lexical, grammatical, or both. The Indian agent John Sibley, writing in the period just after the Louisiana Purchase, stated that the Biloxi, Alabama, Taensa, and Pascagoula (all by then in central Louisiana) were among the dozen tribes still relying on Mobilian. Some black and white inhabitants knew it as well. Caddoan, according to Sibley, was used by a number of northwest Louisiana tribes.

In the 1960s Mary R. Haas learned that Mobilian speakers could still be found among the remnants of Kosati and Alabama bands in western Louisiana and central Texas, and in 1970 James Crawford undertook their scientific study. Crawford published his data chiefly in

The Mobilian Trade Language (1978), which provided a substantial glossary, with comparisons to Choctaw and Alabama usages. Unlike most of his predecessors, Crawford thought Mobilian developed as a result of French settlement. Emanuel Drechsel, whose dissertation followed Crawford's book, did further fieldwork and archival research and increased the glossary to more than 1,000 words. He rejected Crawford's theory of the origins of Mobilian as a reaction to European presence. As a whole, the research of Haas, Crawford, and Drechsel has provided invaluable insights about the complexities and extensive usage of the primary southeastern intertribal language.

Viron L. Barnhill
George F. Reinecke
University of New Orleans

James M. Crawford, in *Studies in Southeastern Indian Languages*, ed. James M. Crawford (1975), *The Mobilian Trade Language* (1978); Emanuel Johannes Drechsel, "Mobilian Jargon: Linguistic, Sociocultural and Historical Aspects of an American Indian Lingua Franca" (Ph.D. dissertation, University of Wisconsin, 1979), *Ethnohistory* (Summer 1983); Mary R. Haas, in *Studies in Southeastern Indian Languages*, ed. James M. Crawford (1975); John Lawson, *A New Voyage to Carolina*, ed. Hugh Talmage Lefler (1967); John Sibley, *American State Papers*, Class II, Indian Affairs, vol. 1 (1805).

Linguistic Atlas of the Gulf States Project

Directed by Lee A. Pederson of Emory University, the Linguistic Atlas of the Gulf States (LAGS) project is an extensive survey of regional and social dialects in eight southern states: Tennessee, Georgia, Florida, Alabama, Mississippi, Louisiana, Arkansas, and Texas (as far west as the Balcones Escarpment). As the largest and most inclusive research project on southern speech, LAGS provides basic texts for the study of speech in the region and a description of the sociohistorical and sociolinguistic contexts necessary for their interpretation. Ultimately, the project seeks to achieve four additional, interrelated goals: (1) an inventory of the dominant and recessive patterns of usage in the Gulf states; (2) a global description of regional and social varieties of southern speech; (3) an abstract of regional phonology, grammar, and lexicon; and (4) an identification of areas of linguistic complexity that require further study.

From its inception in 1968, LAGS has been an extension of the direct method of dialect geography initiated by Gilliéron in France and refined by Kurath in the United States. These methods involve the following: selection of a network of communities, including focal, relic, and transitional communities, on the basis of the social history of the region; conversational interviews with natives of these communities conducted with a questionnaire of selected items; and recording of the responses in finely graded phonetics. LAGS regards the county or parish as the community. The LAGS territory includes 665 of these, but they are grouped into a grid of 168 units on the basis of their social history. Although only one county in each grid is an obligatory target, the sample includes interviews with 1,118 informants in 451 counties. The informants are of three types: Type I, folk informants with a grade school education or less (40 percent); Type II, common informants with a high school education (35 percent); and Type III, cultivated informants with a college education (25 percent). Blacks comprise 22 percent of the sample, which also contains a number of informants whose first language is Spanish, French, or German. Both the questionnaire and the system of phonetic notation are adaptations of those used by Kurath.

The LAGS corpus includes two basic components, with three projected interpretive components. The primary corpus, the field records, consists of some 5,300 hours of tape-recorded speech stored at Emory University. The protocols are the principal analogues of these field records. They contain phonetic transcriptions of questionnaire items and of other phonological, grammatical, and lexical data and serve as guides to the field records. The 1,118 protocols, along with the questionnaire and a guide to phonetics and protocol composition, were published in microtext by University Microfilms in 1981. A concordance to the protocols is forthcoming. The three interpretive components will include a handbook, summarizing LAGS methodology and the social history of the region, to be published by the University of Georgia Press; a series of maps, summarizing the distribution of data; and a legendry, providing descriptions of the data on maps.

Guy Bailey
Texas A&M University

Lee A. Pederson, *American Speech* (Winter 1981), *Papers in Language Variation*, ed. David L. Shores and Carole P. Hines (1977), et al., eds., *LAGS: The Basic Materials* (1981).

Linguistic Atlas of the Middle and South Atlantic States

The *Linguistic Atlas of the Middle and South Atlantic States* (*LAMSAS*), together with the *Linguistic Atlas of New England* (*LANE*), is the record of a dialect survey of the area of American colonial settlement. This survey was proposed in 1929 by Hans Kurath. Fieldwork in New England was carried out from 1931 to 1933 under Kurath's direction and *LANE* was published in three two-part volumes from 1939 to 1943. Meanwhile, a preliminary survey of the South Atlantic states was carried out by the principal field-worker of *LANE*, Guy Lowman, during 1933 and 1934. Lowman completed 68 interviews, primarily in the states of Maryland, Virginia, North Carolina, South Carolina, and Georgia, using a modified version of the New England questionnaire with about 700 items designed to elicit variations in pronunciation, usage, and vocabulary.

In 1935 Lowman began a systematic survey of the South Atlantic states. He had completed the fieldwork in Maryland, Virginia, and North Carolina and the survey of the Middle Atlantic states except for upper New York state by the time of his death in 1941. Kurath hired Raven I. McDavid, Jr., to complete the fieldwork, but McDavid was able to complete only a few field records in South Carolina before World War II interrupted the survey. After the war, McDavid resumed fieldwork and completed the survey in New York, South Carolina, and Georgia by 1949.

Publishing the findings of the two surveys (now combined into LAMSAS) was not possible; rather, Kurath published an important analysis of the data, *The Word Geography of the Eastern United States*, in 1949. Two other summary volumes followed—E. Bagby Atwood's *A Survey of Verb Forms in the Eastern United States* (1953) and Kurath and McDavid's *The Pronunciation of English in the Atlantic States* (1961). Upon Kurath's retirement in 1964, McDavid became editor-in-chief of LAMSAS and continued editorial work on it, hoping eventually to achieve full publication. At the time of his death in 1984, two fascicles of a proposed 60 of LAMSAS had been published by the University of Chicago Press (1980), and nearly all the basic materials were available on microfilm from the Regenstein Library of the University of Chicago. William A. Kretzschmar, Jr., succeeded McDavid as editor-in-chief, and the atlas materials are now on deposit at the University of Georgia.

LAMSAS is an invaluable repository of cultural and linguistic information on the vocabulary of a rural society that is in the process of disappearing. The study of the language of a community can provide an important means of interpreting the culture of that community.

George T. Dorrill
University of South Carolina

William A. Kretzschmar, Jr., ed., *Dialects in Culture: Essays in General Dialectology by Raven I. McDavid, Jr.* (1979); Raven I. McDavid, Jr., *Orbis*, vol. 5 (1956); Michael Montgomery and Guy Bailey, eds., *Language Variety in the South: Perspectives in Black and White* (1986).

McDavid, Raven I., Jr.

(1911–1984) Linguist.

Raven Ioor McDavid, Jr., was born and raised in Greenville, S.C. He graduated from Furman University in 1931 and received his Ph.D. in English in 1935 from Duke University, with a dissertation on the political thought of John Milton. In 1937 he attended a summer linguistic institute at the urging of his commandant at The Citadel (his first teaching position), who wanted McDavid to get remedial training in elocution. He was selected as a model informant for a dialectology class at the institute, was intrigued with what he heard there, and proceeded to become the foremost student of southern speech—and of American English more generally—of his time.

McDavid entered the field of linguistics just at the point of its rapid development as a modern academic discipline. After his initial spark and further institute training, he embarked on a survey of South Carolina for Hans Kurath's American Linguistic Atlas project. World War II intervened, but after working in the Army Language Section during the war, McDavid became Kurath's chief fieldworker. During the next 15 years he spent a great deal of his time in the field with informants from Ontario south to Florida; he eventually completed over 500 interviews (averaging six to eight hours each), a record unmatched by any other American dialectologist. At the same time McDavid wrote prolifically, including landmark articles, his abridgement of H. L. Mencken's *The American Language* (1963), and, with Hans Kurath, a volume that still serves as a standard reference, *The Pronunciation of English in the Atlantic States* (1961). His first major academic appointment was at Case Western Reserve University in 1952. In 1957 he moved to the University of Chicago, the institution with which he was most closely identified. In 1964 McDavid succeeded Kurath as editor-in-chief of the *Linguistic Atlas of the Middle and South Atlantic States* (McDavid et al., fascicles 1 and 2, 1980, 1982), and in 1975 accepted responsibility for the *Linguistic Atlas of the North-Central States* (McDavid et al., 1976–80). He directed editorial work on both projects until his death. Recognition came late for McDavid, but in time he won major funding for his atlas projects from the National Endowment for the Humanities and received honorary degrees from Furman, Duke, and the Sorbonne. The *Linguistic Atlas of the Middle and South Atlantic States* began appearing in print in 1980 from the University of Chicago Press. The university's Joseph Regenstein Library contains microfilm copies of the *Basic Materials* volumes from the two atlas projects.

McDavid's experience in the field shaped his thought: he always insisted on the importance for linguistics of primary data, of real speech by real people, as opposed to rarified theory. He believed that contemporary speech was a product of the cultural circumstances of its speakers, of their social and economic life, and of the historical development of that life, and that an accurate understanding of our speechways could have a positive effect on the well-being of all members of society.

These ideas made McDavid a primary force in the development of sociolinguistics. His first landmark article, "Postvocalic /-r/ in South Carolina: A Social Analysis" (1948), shows a mature handling of the complex correlations between South Carolina culture and speakers' pronunciation of *r* after vowels. Another benchmark, "The Relationship of the Speech of American Negroes to the Speech of Whites" (1951, written with Virginia G. McDavid), provided a corrective to common misapprehensions about the speech of blacks long before black English became a sociolinguistic industry. McDavid was in the vanguard of those examining the effects of population movements and urbanization upon our speech, and, in an effort to carry benefits from dialectology to a wide audience, McDavid also promoted applications of his research, especially for the schools. McDavid studied the speech of all regions of the United States but never forgot his roots in the South: his extensive bibliography is studded with both technical and popular essays such as "The Position of the Charleston Dialect" (1955), "Changing Patterns of Southern Dialects" (1970), and "Prejudice and Pride: Linguistic Acceptability in South Carolina" (1977, written with Raymond K. O'Cain).

William A. Kretzschmar, Jr.
University of Wisconsin—Whitewater

McDavid's articles cited above are reprinted in one or both of two collections of his essays: William A. Kretzschmar, Jr., ed., *Dialects in Culture: Essays in General Dialectology by Raven I. McDavid, Jr.* (1979); and Anwar Dil, ed., with a bibliography by William A. Kretzschmar, Jr., *Varieties of American English: Essays by Raven I. McDavid, Jr.* (1980).

Outer Banks Dialect

Early settlement, separation from the mainland, and cultural isolation shaped the distinctive speech patterns of the Outer Banks in North Carolina. The relic dialect spoken by Outer Banks residents has, through cultural and geographic isolation, preserved some archaisms and linguistic divergences.

Settlement of the Outer Banks started in the first quarter of the 18th century and was relatively complete by mid-century. Most of the settlers were originally of English descent and came to the Outer Banks from Tidewater Virginia and the Albemarle Sound region and from other settlements to the south and west. Until the introduction of highways, vehicles, mailboats, ferries, and modern conveniences such as improved fishing rigs and refrigeration, the people had little to do with outsiders, or "strangers," as they tended to call them. Just when others began to think of them—or they, of themselves—as "Bankers" or "different" is hard to tell, but their cultural habits and speechways probably began to take on a distinctive color early in the 19th century. Even though Outer Banks residents live in an area stretching over 150 miles along the Carolina coastline, they are somewhat homogeneous socially; whether their language is homogeneous is a different matter. Exact statements about the diversity of speech among the villagers need more detailed study.

The distinctiveness of Outer Banks speech has been long recognized by laymen and specialists alike. Lay observers mislead others when they characterize the Outer Banks speech as Old English or Elizabethan English. They notice the unfamiliar, but the tenacious use of *pint* for *point*, *bile* for *boil*, *holp* for *help*, *tard* for *tired*, *cam* for *calm*, and *hit* for *it* makes no particular claim for antiquity or distinctiveness. Outer Banks speech is not, therefore, Elizabethan—or, for that matter, 18th-century English—but clearly it is different and may be accurately called a "relic dialect." As a rule, the speech follows that of the coastal South, but it differs significantly in some respects. The dialect of the Bankers derived from 17th-century British English, which at the time reflected much regional and social diversity, but since then it has taken on a character that deserves such labels as "Outer Banks speech" or the "Outer Banks brogue."

Like other relic dialects, the Outer Banks dialect is most distinctive in pronunciation, not in word forms, grammar, and vocabulary. In vocabulary, as one would expect, the Outer Banks is southern and eastern, but not exclusively so. With reference to the hour, *quarter to*, a southern expression, stands alongside *quarter of* and *quarter till*, northern and midland expressions respectively. Outer Banks residents use *breezing up*, *squall*, *gutters*, and *kerosene*, the last of which shows some influence from the North. *Coal oil*, a midland term used frequently by Chesapeake Bay fishermen, rarely, if ever, occurs on the Outer Banks. *Spider*, a New England feature, is heard, but *skillet*, primarily a midland term, is the normal word. *Armful* (of wood), distinctively a midland term, is used over *turn-of-wood*, the usual southern form. *Lightwood* and *curtains*, basically southern forms, are heard in some villages rather than *kindling* and *window shades*. Sometimes *coal hod* and *corn husks*, typically northern forms, are found beside *coal skuttle* and *corn shucks*. *Comforter*, the northern form, is more common than the usual southern form, *comfort*. *Throw-up* is used more than *vomiting*, but *spew* and *puke* are also heard. A local word rarely heard elsewhere is *mammock*, "tear in shreds," which some dictionaries list as obsolete or "dialectal."

As they do among fishermen everywhere along the coast, certain nautical terms persist. Among them are *nor'east* or *no'theast*, *sou'west*, *windward*, and *leeward* (the last two respectively pronounced as "win'erd" and "loo'erd"), and for rising and falling tides, *flood tide* and *ebb tide*. For a grove of trees on certain parts of the islands *hammock* is used; and for menhaden, the oily fish used for fertilizer and cosmetics, *fatback*, which seems to be limited to the Outer Banks. Two other interesting usages are *abreast*, "across from," and *to* as in "he's to the marina."

There are few, if any, words and expressions that are exclusively and characteristically Banker ones. But what is important is that the language of Outer Banks residents, like that common to the islanders of the Chesapeake, shows northern and midland, as well as southern, influences.

Their pronunciation is quite another thing, often described as a "strange accent" or "brogue." But even in pronunciation, the language poses few problems once an outsider gets attuned to the intonation patterns. There is a strong pronunciation of *r* after vowels and in the final position of words in examples like *farm*, *thirty*, *door*, *car*, and *dinner*. This feature stands against the mixed pattern of *r*-lessness historically found on the coastal mainland of the Atlantic Seaboard. The most distinctive feature is the quality of the vowel in words like *eyes*, *tie*, *tide*, *light*, and *time*, which many journalists and other visitors erroneously report as rhyming with *toy*. They, for example, distort the Bankers' pronunciation of *high tide* as "hoy toyde." The sound is highly recognizable and clearly identified, but its precise quality cannot accurately be indicated without phonetic notation.

Another feature long recognized by mainland North Carolinians, but also difficult to describe, is what linguists refer to as the centralization of onsets of the vowels in words like *east*, *beach*, and *three* and in *great*, *age*, and *eight*. In these words the vowels have the "uh" sound as if the first syllable of "about" occurs before them, giving the impression of hearing several vowels. Moreover, the vowels in some words are fronted, for example: *musty* and *rusty* are pronounced with the vowel sound of "rest," and *boat* with the vowel sound of "boot." Words like *dish*, *fish*, and *wish* have their vowels fronted and raised to the vowel sound in "be." One also hears *year*, *hear*, and *ear* pronounced with the vowel sound in "fur." These features are benchmarks of a single dialect, even though they crop up in widely separated areas. They represent important linguistic traditions associated with the Outer Banks.

See also ENVIRONMENT: / Outer Banks

David L. Shores
Old Dominion University

Robert Howren, *American Speech* (October 1962); Hilda Jaffee, *Publication of the American Dialect Society* (November 1973); David Stick, *The Outer Banks of North Carolina* (1958).

Randolph, Vance

(1892–1980) Folklorist.

Vance Randolph, linguist and folklorist, 1930s

Vance Randolph's academic training was in psychology (M.A., Clark University, 1915), and Randolph described himself most often as a "hack writer." The shelf of books resulting from his long lifetime's work in the Arkansas and Missouri Ozarks, however, is responsible for Vance Randolph's continuing reputation as one of the nation's premier regional folklorists.

Randolph was born in Pittsburg, Kan., just west of the Ozarks, but he lived his adult life in small Missouri (Pineville, Galena) and Arkansas (Eureka Springs, Fayetteville) towns, where he assiduously sought out and perpetuated in print and on recordings the sayings, doings, singings, and believings of his Ozark neighbors. His first books, *The Ozarks* (1931) and *Ozark Mountain Folks* (1932), are long out of print but remain notable as excellent examples of what later were called folklife studies. Randolph's methods and definitions were often in advance of their time; he included, for example, discographical references to "hillbilly" records in his four-volume folksong collection *Ozark Folksongs* (1946–50) at a time when many scholars found such recordings unworthy of notice. As early as 1956 he was urging the notion of folklife museums upon Arkansans, suggesting that they "imitate, in a small way, the work of the State Historical Association at Cooperstown, New York."

Randolph first achieved renown as a student of dialect when his article-length studies were lavishly praised by H. L. Mencken. His major work in this area, *Down in the Holler: A Gallery of Ozark Folk Speech*, did not appear until 1953. Along with his massive folksong collection, the 1940s saw the publication of Randolph's major study of folk belief, *Ozark Superstitions*, in 1947. In the 1950s Randolph published five volumes of folktales, including *We Always Lie to Strangers: Tall Tales from the Ozarks*. A collection of jokes, *Hot Springs and Hell*, appeared in 1965, and Randolph's huge bibliographic work, *Ozark Folklore: A Bibliography*, was published in 1972. His classic collection of bawdy humor, *Pissing in the Snow*, was finally published in 1976. Taken together, Randolph's many books provide a detailed and sympathetic portrait of Ozark traditional life. Academic folklorists honored Randolph in 1978 by electing him a Fellow of the American Folklore Society.

Robert Cochran
University of Arkansas

Robert Cochran, *Vance Randolph: An Ozark Life* (1985).

Schele de Vere, Maximilian von

(1820–1898) Linguist.

Schele was Professor of Modern Languages at the University of Virginia from 1844 to 1895. He taught French, Spanish, German, Anglo-Saxon, Latin, and modern history and participated actively in university governance. His publications include *Stray Leaves from the Book of Nature* (1855), *Studies in English* (1867), and *The Great Empress* (1870), a novel. Schele (pronounced shay-lee) also translated German romances, wrote grammars of Spanish and French (which Robert E. Lee thought too complicated), and contributed to periodicals like *Harper's New Monthly Magazine*.

A native Swede, Schele had studied at Bonn, Berlin (Ph.D., 1841), and Greifswald and had served in the Prussian army—a family tradition—before immigrating to Boston in 1843 and then to Virginia. During the Civil War of 1861–65, he functioned as drillmaster to the university's faculty defense squad, and in 1863 he prepared for a secret diplomatic mission to Napoleon III. But he never saw action or left Virginia during the war.

Students liked Schele, and William Dwight Whitney recognized his *Outlines of Comparative Philology* (1853) as a groundbreaking popularization. However, Schele's ignorance of articulatory phonetics encouraged absurd etymologizing, as, for example, that English *more* and *most* derived from *to mow* because "what was mown made a little heap." Schele's acquaintance with Bopp, Humboldt, and Grimm nevertheless placed him one step ahead of Noah Webster. And in spite of phonological innocence, Schele was the first Virginia professor, perhaps the first in the United States, to teach spoken along with written language, a revolutionary feature of Jefferson's original plan. Working at a leading southern university, Schele frequently studied southern words and became, in effect, an early student of language in the region as well as the nation.

Schele considered language "a faculty, planted in the inmost nature of man," but his professorship required him to teach both language and the ethnological history of modern Europe, a circumstance that led to repeated theorizing about the bonds between language and culture. In this field, his most enduring work was *Americanisms: The English of the New World* (1871), a precursor of Mencken's *The American Language*. *Americanisms* achieved a novel effect by discussing American English topically (e.g., the influence of the Indian, the railroad, cant, and slang) rather than in dictionary form. And 50 years after its publication, Sir William Craigie still considered *Americanisms* "a treasure trove."

The *Dictionary of American English* credits Schele with having discovered the earliest uses of *bob*, "sled," *bound*, "resolved," *hike up*, "rise," among others. Furthermore, he contributed useful material on *benzene*, *buckra*, *yam*, *tar heel*, *lynch*, *saloon*, *bar-tender*, *sleeper*, *derail*, *ditch* (verb), *be* (as finite verb), *hired man*, *casket*, *pew*, and many others. On the negative side, Schele was capable of explaining *papoose* as a corruption of *babies*. Such nonsense aside, his generous enthusiasm for everything American added new illustrative material, new definitions, and even a few successful etymologies to the record. *Americanisms* remains, moreover, an entertaining treatment of how "we still speak English, but we talk American."

Michael I. Miller
Virginia Commonwealth University

Michael Crowell, "The Lexicography of Americanisms to 1900" (Ph.D. dissertation, Northwestern University, 1966); Atcheson L. Hench, *Publication of the American Dialect Society* (1966); David W. Maurer and Atcheson L. Hench, *Studies in Linguistics in Honor of Raven I. McDavid, Jr.* (1972).

Law

MAXWELL BLOOMFIELD
The Catholic University of America
CONSULTANT

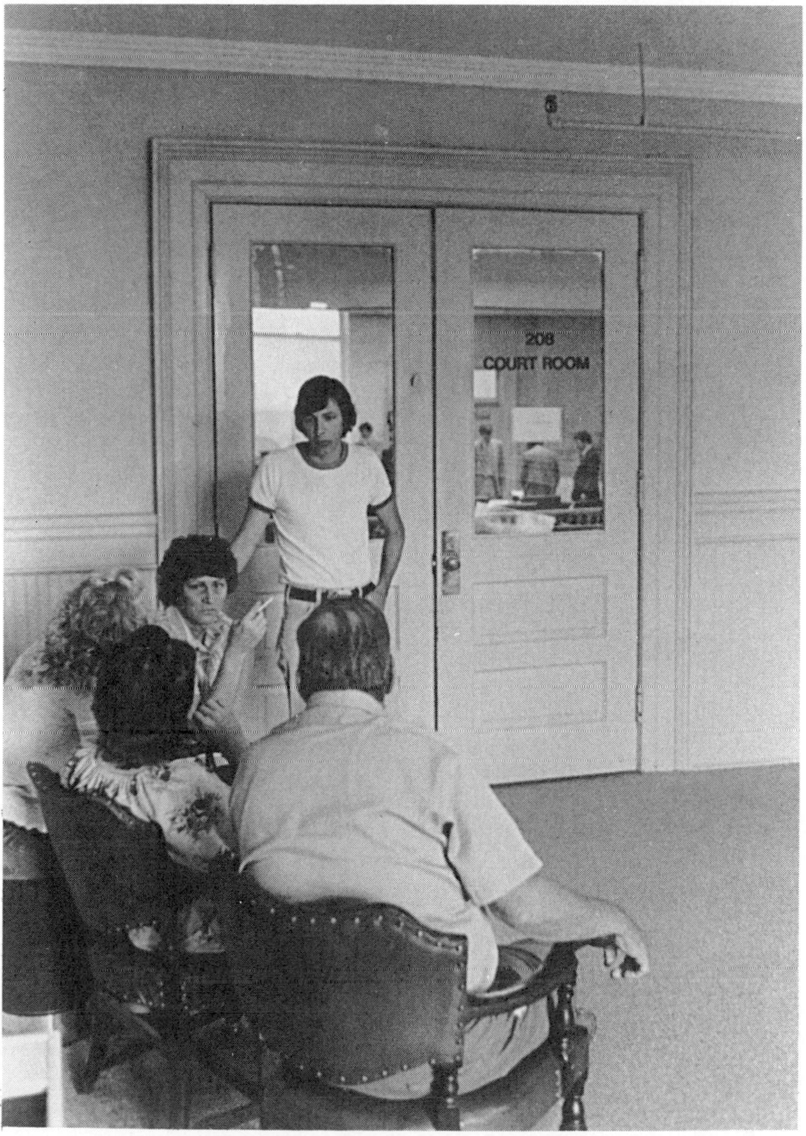

Outside a courtroom, Decatur County, Ga.

Law and Southern Society

The legal history of the South, apart from the topic of slavery, has not yet been explored in a systematic way, although pioneering essays and monographs on specialized subjects have begun to appear in recent years. Until scholars know more about regional patterns of legislative and judicial policy-making—the selective borrowing of one state's institutions by another—they can only sketch the possible contours of a distinctively southern legal culture. At the outset, moreover, it must be emphasized that southern lawyers and statesmen have always shared the core values of the Anglo-American legal tradition and have never tried to create an alternative system, even in antebellum times. Although Louisiana did adopt the civil law of France as the basis of its legal system, it modified the Napoleonic Code in many ways to reflect the more liberal mores of a republican society. The revised constitutions adopted by the South Atlantic states before the Civil War displayed the same democratizing trends in voting and officeholding requirements that characterized the constitutions of northern and midwestern states. Southerners who framed the Confederate Constitution included specific guarantees for the protection of slavery, but otherwise carried over verbatim most of the provisions of the U.S. Constitution.

Antebellum South. The peculiar legal needs of a developing plantation economy caused the jurisprudence of the Old South to diverge from national norms in some major ways. Historians have described antebellum southern society as patriarchal and particularistic, rooted in a class structure and in the traditional folkways of a scattered rural population. Unlike the modernizing commercial and industrial elites of the North, southern planters favored a nonbureaucratic legal system that left important public powers in the hands of private individuals. A personal and discretionary approach to the settlement of disputes suited the temper of the English and Scotch-Irish settlers who predominated throughout the South. Preindustrial attitudes and behavior—clan loyalties, submission to community standards, an unwritten code of masculine honor—remained strong in the Cotton Kingdom long after they had been displaced elsewhere by the more impersonal mores of a market-centered legal order. Without the presence of slavery, however, these factors would have produced only minor legal differences between the South and the rest of the nation. Every state, after all, possessed some idiosyncratic laws and institutions that grew out of diverse settlement patterns, geographic conditions, and socioeconomic needs. Slavery alone unified the South and shaped a unique regional mentality that found expression in every aspect of antebellum southern culture, including the law.

The slave codes established an oppressive system of social control that denied basic common-law and republican values. Common-law doctrines protected a person's natural rights of life, liberty, and property; republican ideology encouraged enterprising individuals to share in the risks and profits of a developing capitalist economy. But market individualism and personal autonomy had no place in slave law. The master-slave relation, unlike the employer-employee relation, rested not upon voluntary agreement, but upon force. Confronted with the impossible task of reconciling two antithetical labor systems within a single body of law, southern lawmakers tried to create a separate category of paternalistic regulations that defied the laissez-faire thrust of modern property law. Slave issues could not be completely divorced from the rest of American law, however, nor could masters always claim exclusive control over their slaves. Personal injuries, contracts, and crimes often involved nonslaveholding whites, and southern judges in such situations looked for guidance to the leading decisions of northern jurists. As the Civil War approached, capitalistic values made increasing inroads into the law of slavery and threatened to undermine even the status slaves had as "chattels personal."

In mortgage cases involving slaves, for example, some southern courts at first fashioned equitable remedies to preserve slave families and to give hard-pressed masters additional time to redeem their slaves. By the 1850s, however, judges had become more responsive to the legal claims of creditors and tended to treat slaves no differently than other forms of property subject to forced sale. (Harriet Beecher Stowe did not exaggerate the cruelty of slave auctions in her classic *Uncle Tom's Cabin*.) The treatment of slave victims and defendants in criminal cases followed a similar pattern. Although a few judges made common-law protections available to slaves through statutory construction, most agreed that slaves had no enforceable legal rights. The slave codes did prohibit the worst kinds of white abuse, such as maiming and killing, but penalties varied greatly, depending on whether the offender was a master, a lessee, an overseer, or a total stranger. Such a classification scheme strongly resembled that used to compensate any property owner for the loss or impairment of a valuable commodity.

Did a paternalistic or anticommercial ethic significantly influence other areas of law in the antebellum South? Preliminary inquiries by historians indicate that southern lawmakers espoused some policies that may actually have impeded the region's economic development. Despite the emergence elsewhere of a modern contract law based upon objective market values, southern judges adhered for decades to the older standard of a "just price" and protected individuals from the consequences of one-sided bargains. In insolvency cases, courts displayed unusual sympathy for debtors, and attachment laws exempted from seizure much property that would have been available to creditors in many northern states. Although legislatures throughout the South chartered banks, railroads, and other corporations, judges often resisted the principle of limited liability for stockholders and refused to apply other procorporate doctrines, such as the fellow servant rule, that had become standard in the industrial Northeast. The pervasive localism of the Old South further insured that small railroads, built to serve the limited needs of inland farmers and merchants, would not be consolidated into efficient trunk lines.

For the enforcement of their laws and customs, southerners relied much more than other Americans upon informal agencies of social control. In every southern state, the judicial and police systems were rudimentary and weak, compared to the bureaucratic structures that existed in the North, and southerners sought extralegal solutions to many problems that would have been resolved elsewhere through litigation. The gentlemanly elite—large planters, merchants, and professionals—demanded reparation for personal insults on the dueling ground; slaveholders dispensed discretionary justice on their plantations, which resembled slave prisons in some ways, and convened special courts to settle neighborhood slave disputes; and slave patrols, made up in large part of nonslaveholders, served as a private police force to apprehend runaway slaves and prevent insurrections. As the antislavery movement intensified after 1830, local vigilance committees incited mobs to assault (and sometimes kill) abolitionist critics, while other vigilante groups meted out summary punishment to those who violated a community's moral standards, such as gamblers and prostitutes.

States' Rights. To defend their slave society against political interference from the more numerous free states of the Union, southern theorists developed a states' rights argument based upon a compact model of constitutionalism. In the Virginia and Kentucky resolutions of 1798 and 1799, Thomas Jefferson and James Madison contended that the states had delegated only limited powers to the national government and could interpose their authority to prevent the implementation of unwarranted federal policies within their borders. Antebellum law students, most of whom were self-taught, learned strict constructionist and states' rights principles from the appendix to St. George Tucker's edition of *Blackstone's Commentaries* (1803), the most widely read legal text in the nation prior to 1852. Southern law schools, such as the University of Virginia Law School, combined Tucker's *Blackstone's Commentaries* with later states' rights commentaries on the Constitution to train generations of elite practitioners and judges in the ways of "true republicanism." The proslavery argument culminated in the *Dred Scott* decision of 1857, in which Chief Justice Roger B. Taney held that Congress had an affirmative duty under the Fifth Amendment to protect slave property in all federal territories. When antislavery forces captured the presidency in the election of 1860, 11 southern states declared the constitutional compact broken and seceded from the Union to form a new government, the Confederate States of America.

Although founded as the expression of a distinct regional subculture, the Confederacy had little time to establish its separatist claims. Four years of bloody fighting and military defeat left the South devastated, slavery abolished, and the national government in apparently firm control of the reconstruction process. Legal differences between the South and other regions thereafter diminished perceptibly, as improved transportation and communication networks brought southerners into ever-closer contact with modern corporate America. The transition from patriarchy to mass society was slow and painful, however, and antebellum folkways continued to influence the developing law of labor relations, family relations, and civil rights.

The Law and Postwar Economic Adjustment. Since emancipation made the law of master and slave irrelevant, southern planters sought new legal means to control a work force of "free" blacks. At first they insisted that the freedmen sign long-term written contracts that tied them to the land for a full year in return for share wages. Military commanders and officials of the Freedmen's Bureau approved such arrangements, which promised to stabilize agricultural production and enable landless exslaves to become property owners in time. But the planters and their legal allies soon managed to circumvent the rights of tenants under existing law by constructing a novel system of sharecropping that was peculiar to the South. The cropper, unlike the tenant, had no possessory rights in the land he farmed but was merely a wage worker, subject in practice to whatever conditions his employer imposed. Farm credit legislation further contributed to a vicious debt cycle that impoverished many white yeoman farmers and brought croppers and tenants alike under the permanent control of a new business class of landlords and merchants.

The Redeemer legislatures of the post-Reconstruction 1870s enacted crop-lien laws that greatly increased the power of rural creditors. Landlord-tenant law had long recognized a landlord's right to seize the crop of a tenant who had not paid his rent; the new legislation extended the rental lien to cover all advances made by a landlord or merchant and exempted little or none of a debtor's personal property from attachment. If the sale of a particular crop did not repay all advances, southern courts ruled that the remaining indebtedness would operate as a preferred lien on future crops. The only way a poor farmer could escape from a mounting burden of debt was to move away and find a new landlord, but lawmakers foreclosed this possibility by using the criminal law to enforce contractual duties. Antienticement statutes made it a criminal offense for anyone to hire a laborer already under contract; other laws imposed criminal penalties upon those who failed to fulfill a contract after receiving money or other advances from an employer. Despite the doubtful constitutionality of such measures, they remained in effect in many southern states well into the 20th century.

Black tenant farmers and sharecroppers suffered most from the neopaternalism of postwar labor relations. Just as the black codes of 1865–66 had attempted to compel freedmen to work, the contract-labor laws and analogous vagrancy statutes established a modern system of peonage in the South. A defaulting black farm worker might be arrested and returned to his workplace; an unemployed stranger in town might be charged with vagrancy and put to work on a road gang or sent to a backwoods plantation until he earned enough money to pay his fine. Although the Thirteenth Amendment clearly prohibited

A jury section in a courtroom, Franklin, Ga., 1941

such "involuntary servitude," peonage persisted in some southern areas for decades and may not be completely eradicated today. By appealing to customary bonds of deference and personal loyalty as well as to comprehensive laws, southern landlords achieved a degree of control over their work force unmatched by employers elsewhere in the nation. Local power structures did not begin to collapse until the emergence of New Deal farm policies in the 1930s. As federal agencies, such as the Agricultural Adjustment Administration and the Farm Security Administration, set production quotas and regulated farm credit, southern agriculture lost its distinctive legal characteristics and entered the age of mechanization and standardization in earnest.

Did regional values play as important a role in shaping the industrial policies of the New South? On the basis of available historical research, it seems doubtful that they did. From the beginning of industrialization in the late 19th century, southern workers engaged in proportionally as many strikes as their northern counterparts and maintained a consistently high level of union organizing activity. Although southern millowners and manufacturers treated their employees in a paternalistic and arbitrary fashion, northern industrialists, such as George Pullman and Henry Ford, behaved in much the same way.

Southern legislatures were slow to enact workmen's compensation statutes—Mississippi, the last holdout in the nation, capitulated only in 1948—while right-to-work laws and other union-busting measures proliferated. Without comparative studies of regional labor practices, however, the distinctiveness of the southern experience remains unclear. The changes in class relations introduced by the factory system may well have evoked similar responses from employers and lawmakers everywhere. By the 1930s, in any event, the passage of the National Labor Relations Act, the Fair Labor Standards Act, and other congressional measures effectively ended any lingering claims of regional autonomy, as the federal government began to regulate labor conditions throughout the country.

Family and Religion. Ongoing research in family law suggests that the late 19th century also witnessed the reconstruction of domestic relations in the South. Prior to the Civil War, southern judges tended to uphold patriarchal authority in the household and seldom intervened in family matters except to protect wives and children from physical abuse. Although Mississippi inaugurated a nationwide movement toward married women's property acts in 1839, such laws gave wives only limited control of their separate estates. Rather, they served, especially in the South, to protect a woman's blood relatives by shielding family assets from the creditors of an improvident husband. Liberalized divorce laws, which opened the courts to women of the middle and lower classes in the North, received restrictive interpretations from many southern jurists and benefited primarily the wives of the propertied elite. In child custody cases, southern appellate judges lagged behind their northern counterparts in acknowledging the separate interests of wives and children and almost invariably denied challenges to parental authority from relatives or other third parties.

The defeat of the Confederacy marked the end of a patriarchal slaveholding society and left many southern widows in charge of one-parent households. Courts responded to these realities by playing a more active supervisory role in family disputes and by scrutinizing more rigorously the behavior of husbands and fathers. In an increasing number of cases judges awarded custody rights to mothers and third parties, while narrowing the scope of other common-law doctrines of paternal power. Although patriarchal values continued to influence many areas of jurisprudence (as they did, to a lesser extent, in other regions), the modernization of southern family law was virtually complete by the turn of the century. Jurists now embraced a more psychological and contractual view of domestic relations and used their power to reshape conditions within the home. Instead of relying on a network of patriarchs to preserve social order, they linked family members directly to the state through new forms of public control. By doing so, they entered the mainstream of American legal history.

Law and religion have long influenced each other in the South. The fundamentalist outlook so noticeable in the region's spiritual life has also been present in attitudes toward the law. Southerners have had great respect for the U.S. Constitution of 1787, for example, as shown in a literal-minded adherence to its supposed original meaning. They made few changes in the federal Constitution in adapting it as the Constitution of the Confederate States of America. Before and after the Civil War the South has reiterated the belief in the supremacy of an unchanging, literally interpreted constitution and has looked upon itself, in historian Charles S. Sydnor's words, "as the special custodian and defender" of this near sacred legal document.

Southerners have often used the legal system to maintain the moral code of the Protestant churches. To be sure, the Baptist tradition includes belief in the separation of church and state, and the southern Presbyterian doctrine of "the spirituality of the church" taught that the church was a strictly religious, not secular, institution. Southerner Thomas Jefferson's "Bill for Establishing Religious Freedom" in 1786 disestablished religion in Virginia and contributed to the federal government's guarantees of religious freedom as expressed in the First Amendment.

Most religious southerners have, nevertheless, seen strict obedience to the moral law as prime evidence of a Christian society and have suppressed doubts they might have had about using the legal system to achieve that society. Gerald Johnson saw southerners committing "the heresy that equates legality with morality." When antislavery advocates attacked slavery, the southern defense was a typical one, citing chapter and verse of a literal reading of selected biblical passages suggesting God's sanctioning of the institution. Before the Civil War southern believers, moreover, campaigned for strict enforcement of blue laws promoting Sabbath observance and, after 1839, for state legislation enforcing prohibition in the sale of alcoholic beverages. The Methodists and Presbyterians led the antebellum temperance campaign, but southern reformers were less successful than those in the North. After Reconstruction, the southern temperance movement gained strength, as Methodists and Baptists, the relative latecomers to the issue, led the call for nationwide prohibition. Religious leaders and institutions crusaded also for still stricter enforcement of Sabbath observance, control of gambling, and the limitation or prohibition of dancing, card playing, and professional sports activities. The churches favored rigorous enforcement of the Eighteenth Amendment when it established national prohibition and, after repeal of the amendment in 1933, they continued to support legal prohibition at state and local levels.

The late 1970s and 1980s have witnessed a resurgence of conservative legal moralism in the South, as in the nation. The Moral Majority, a Virginia-based organization associated with Jerry Falwell, has established a *legal* agenda, especially centering on the constitutional amendment, as a way of achieving such moral goals as opposition to abortion and the promotion of school prayer.

Civil Rights. In the field of civil rights law southern resistance to change was particularly intense and unyielding. Although Congress intended to place the civil rights of freedmen and other Americans under comprehensive federal protection through the Thirteenth, Fourteenth, and Fifteenth Amendments, the U.S. Supreme Court blocked the nationalizing potential of these measures by construing their provisions narrowly. In the *Civil Rights Cases* (1883), for example, the Court ruled that the Fourteenth Amendment prohibited only state violations of individual rights; acts of private discrimination remained subject to state, not federal, control.

Encouraged by judicial adherence to antebellum principles of federalism, southern states proceeded to construct an elaborate caste system that prescribed racial segregation in restaurants, schools, housing, theaters, public conveyances, and other facilities. The Supreme Court approved such Jim Crow laws as reasonable exercise of a state's police power in *Plessy* v. *Ferguson* (1896). Reflecting the social Darwinist temper of the time, Justice Henry Billings Brown noted: "In determining the question of reasonableness [a state legislature] is at liberty to act with reference to the established usages, customs, and traditions of the people, and with a view to the promotion of their comfort, and the preservation of the public peace and good order." Customary racial practices in the South thus gained new legitimacy at the hands of the nation's highest court. With the further imposition of poll taxes, literacy tests, and other electoral "reforms" in the 1890s, southern lawmakers completed a modern structure of racial suppression. Its victims—the mass of poor southern blacks as well as poor whites—found themselves effectively disfranchised and unable even to protest their degradation through normal political channels.

As in antebellum days, a mix of public and private law enforcement agencies policed the social order and used terror as a major weapon against blacks and other suspect groups. Professional police forces, whose capabilities varied greatly from place to place, tended on the whole to be politicized and often corrupt. Nor could black defendants in criminal cases expect impartial treatment from southern trial judges, who usually shared the racial outlook of their local white electorates. At times, indeed, the official system of criminal justice openly flouted the requirements of due process. In the notorious Scottsboro case of the 1930s, successive all-white juries found a group of young blacks guilty on rape charges, despite the absence of any meaningful evidence against them. Such flagrant miscarriages of justice were uncommon, however. With all their faults, southern courts and other public agencies at least professed respect for individual rights and operated according to fixed procedures. The same could not be said of vigilantes, who also flourished in the New South as the self-appointed defenders of a crumbling agrarian culture.

The Ku Klux Klan, the most celebrated vigilante organization, arose during Reconstruction to preserve white supremacy by intimidating black voters and their Republican allies. In the 1920s and the 1950s a revived Klan resorted to further acts of violence and terrorism in defense of white Anglo-Saxon Protestant hegemony and the folkways of a vanishing rural society. Such planned violence formed part of a larger pattern of regional lawlessness that included an alarming increase in lynchings between the 1880s and World War II. Most lynch victims in the South were blacks and most lynchings went unpunished because of the obvious collusion that existed between law officers and local mobs. Antilynching organizations, including the Atlanta-based Commission on Interracial Cooperation and its affiliate, the Association of Southern Women for the Prevention of Lynching, called repeatedly for strong federal legislation to remedy the problem. But southern senators filibustered all proposed antilynching bills to death, invoking states' rights and racist arguments that might have been lifted from the congressional slavery debates of the 1850s. Like their antebellum counterparts, the statesmen of the New South took an inflexible stand on racial issues and refused to bow to changing circumstances.

Civil libertarians, on the other hand, had never accepted the caste laws of the late 19th century. From the beginning many black communities, often inspired by charismatic black ministers, engaged in economic boycotts and other forms of protest against local segregationist measures. The pioneer black lawyers of Galveston, Tex., sought to mobilize black voters by establishing a Poll Tax Club and also challenged Jim Crow laws in the local courts. Some of their arguments anticipated those found in successful Supreme Court briefs of the 1930s. Further research in the records of southern trial courts—a source hitherto neglected by most historians—should uncover other patterns of early civil rights litigation.

With the founding of the National Association for the Advancement of Colored People (NAACP) in 1909, civil rights strategy began to be formulated on an interstate basis. By the 1930s black NAACP attorneys launched a carefully orchestrated legal campaign that culminated in *Brown* v. *Board of Education* (1954). The *Brown* decision—handed down by a unanimous Warren Court—rejected *Plessy* v. *Ferguson* and held that segregated schools violated the equal protection clause of the Fourteenth Amendment. Because of the long-standing and complex nature of the segregation issue, however, the Court granted state school boards a reasonable time in which to submit desegregation plans to federal district judges for their approval.

Southern authorities responded to *Brown* by vowing noncompliance. White Citizens' Councils called for a return to antebellum policies of interposition and nullification; police assaulted peaceful black demonstrators; and some state legislatures replaced their public schools with "private" institutions. Despite the rise of "massive resistance," however, southern whites remained deeply divided over civil rights. The economic boom that accompanied World War II had accelerated the urban and industrial development of the South and created a large middle class of businessmen, professionals, and white-collar employees. These groups feared economic instability more than integration and helped to mediate tense racial confrontations, as in the Little Rock crisis of 1957. The Warren Court's reapportionment decisions strengthened urban liberalism by curbing the power of entrenched rural white minorities; both *Baker* v. *Carr* (1962) and *Reynolds* v. *Sims* (1964) struck down unrepresentative political structures in southern states. Yet the Second Reconstruction stalled until Congress belatedly passed a comprehensive Civil Rights Act in 1964 and the supplementary Voting Rights Act the following year. Vigorous federal enforcement of these measures brought a recalcitrant South under control at last. By the early 1970s every southern state had made substantial progress toward the integration of public facilities.

Southern legal culture today displays no striking deviations from national norms. Even professional training has become standardized and homogenized through the accreditation requirements imposed upon law schools across the country. The legal props supporting white hegemony could not survive the collapse of the traditional rural society that had fostered their development. In the fast-paced and ultracompetitive world of the contemporary Sunbelt, the idea of a hierarchical and paternalistic legal order evokes only smiles—nostalgic in some cases, derisive or incredulous in others.

See also AGRICULTURE: Sharecropping and Tenancy; BLACK LIFE: Commission on Interracial Cooperation; POLITICS: Ideology, Political; Segregation, Defense of; RELIGION: Fundamentalism; VIOLENCE: Crime, Attitudes toward; Honor; / Ku Klux Klan, Culture of; Ku Klux Klan, History of; Mob Violence; Peonage

Maxwell Bloomfield
The Catholic University of America

Elizabeth K. Bauer, *Commentaries on the Constitution, 1790–1860* (1952); Maxwell Bloomfield, *American Lawyers in a Changing Society, 1776–1876* (1980), *Vanderbilt Law Review* (January 1979); David J. Bodenhamer and James W. Ely, Jr., eds., *Ambivalent Legacy: A Legal History of the South* (1984); W. Hamilton Bryson, ed., *Legal Education in Virginia, 1779–1979: A Biographical Approach* (1982); Harvey C. Couch, *A History of the Fifth Circuit, 1891–1981* (1984); Pete Daniel, *The Shadow of Slavery: Peonage in the South, 1901–1969* (1972); George Dargo, *Jefferson's Louisiana: Politics and the Clash of Legal Traditions* (1975); Fletcher M. Green, *Constitutional Development in the South Atlantic States, 1776–1860: A Study in the Evolution of Democracy* (1930); Steven Hahn, *Radical History Review* (September 1982); A. Leon Higginbotham, *In the Matter of Color: Race and the American Legal Process: The Colonial Period* (1978); Michael S. Hindus, *Prison and Plantation: Crime, Justice, and Authority in Massachusetts and South Carolina, 1767–1878* (1980); Herbert A. Johnson, ed., *South Carolina Legal History* (1980); Richard Kluger, *Simple Justice: The History of Brown v. Board of Education and Black America's Struggle for Equality* (1976); Steven F. Lawson, *Black Ballots: Voting Rights in the South, 1944–1969* (1976); Suzanne D. Lebsock, *Journal of Southern History* (May 1977); Gail W. O'Brien, *The Legal Fraternity and the Making of a New South Community, 1848–1882* (1986); William M. Robinson, Jr., *Justice in Grey: A History of the Judicial System of the Confederate States of America* (1941); A. G. Roeber, *Faithful Magistrates and Republican Lawyers: Creators of Virginia Legal Culture, 1680–1810* (1981); Charles S. Sydnor, *Journal of Southern History* (February 1940); "Symposium on the Legal History of the South," *Vanderbilt Law Review* (January 1979); Mark V. Tushnet, *The American Law of Slavery, 1810–1860: Considerations of Humanity and Interest* (1981); Harold D. Woodman, *Agricultural History* (January 1979).

Civil Rights Movement

After the Civil War many black leaders worked for equal status between blacks and whites. The most prominent spokesman for this aspiration in the early 20th century was W. E. B. Du Bois. The National Association for the Advancement of Colored People was founded in 1909, and a year later the National Urban League was organized. Nonetheless, the nation made little progress in the field of civil rights until the end of World War II.

The emergence of New Deal social programs and the

egalitarian rhetoric of World War II produced a change in American thought and helped to undermine the intellectual justification for racial segregation in the South. In turn, this development produced a gradual but significant shift in the role of the federal government. President Harry S. Truman identified his administration with the movement for equal rights. In 1948 Truman issued an executive order eliminating segregation in the armed forces. He also called for a Fair Employment Practices Commission and a ban on poll taxes. Although Congress rejected Truman's legislative program, he established civil rights as a national issue. Moreover, the federal courts began to adopt a broader reading of the equal protection clause of the Fourteenth Amendment. During the late 1940s several Supreme Court decisions outlawed segregation in interstate transportation and higher education. This trend culminated with the historic 1954 decision in *Brown* v. *Board of Education*, which proscribed compulsory segregation in public schools as a violation of the equal protection clause.

Important new developments also took place at the state level and in the private sector. Several northern states passed laws against racial discrimination. In 1946 Jackie Robinson became the first black to play major league baseball. Four years later diplomat Ralph Bunche became the first black to win the Nobel Peace Prize.

The NAACP led the legal battle against segregation, working for civil rights legislation and instituting litigation to compel desegregation of public schools in the South. Despite the *Brown* ruling and pressure from the NAACP, only a limited amount of racial integration occurred in southern schools between 1954 and 1964. Most southern states rallied to the banner of "massive resistance" and sought to obstruct implementation of racial desegregation. President Dwight D. Eisenhower did not envision an active role for the federal government in promoting school desegregation. Nonetheless, he did send federal troops to Little Rock in 1957 when state authorities attempted to block implementation of a court-ordered desegregation plan.

Other organizations also struggled for equal rights. Foremost among these was the Southern Christian Leadership Conference, headed by Dr. Martin Luther King, Jr. Late in 1955 blacks in Montgomery, Ala., under King's guidance, began nonviolent protest by instituting a successful boycott of the city's segregated bus system.

During the early 1960s the civil rights movement underwent several important changes. After a period of hesitation, President John F. Kennedy placed the executive branch of the federal government squarely behind desegregation efforts. In 1963 Kennedy endorsed a broad civil rights proposal to outlaw segregation in public accommodations. At the same time, many blacks grew impatient with the slow progress in achieving desegregation. Blacks increasingly resorted to direct forms of protest. There were sit-ins at segregated lunch counters and Freedom Rides that challenged segregation in transportation facilities. Defenders of segregation often employed violence against blacks or civil right workers in an attempt to halt their activities.

The civil rights movement may have reached its climax in August of 1963 when more than 200,000 persons took part in the March on Washington. King, who had emerged as the leading spokesman for the civil rights movement, delivered an impassioned plea for racial equality. President Lyndon B. Johnson responded to this initiative by calling upon Congress to enact sweeping civil rights legislation. The resulting Civil Rights Act of 1964 required equal access to public accommodations and outlawed discrimination in employment. The Voting Rights Act of 1965 suspended literacy tests in several states and strengthened federal protection of the right to vote. The Twenty-fourth Amendment, ratified in 1964, barred poll tax requirements for participation in federal elections. Subsequently the Supreme Court declared unconstitutional the poll tax in state elections. Thus, by the mid-1960s the civil rights movement had attained most of its original objectives, which concerned conditions in the South.

The late 1960s saw a marked shift in the goals of civil rights leaders. The large-scale migration of blacks to northern cities, which had begun by World War I, produced recurrent ethnic conflict in urban neighborhoods. Accordingly, the movement increasingly focused upon racial discrimination in the North. In particular, black leaders challenged residential segregation, poor schooling, high unemployment among members of racial minorities, and alleged police brutality. Given the heavy concentration of impoverished blacks in the inner-city areas, resolution of these problems proved extremely difficult. Indeed, civil rights gains hardly affected the living conditions of many northern blacks. A wave of urban riots across the North highlighted racial tensions and also served to alienate white opinion.

In addition, by promoting new remedies for discrimination, civil rights activists moved well beyond the national consensus in favor of equality. The busing of pupils from one neighborhood to another in an effort to integrate schools, although endorsed by the Supreme Court in 1971, threatened traditional neighborhood schools and was opposed by the vast majority of whites. Congress debated numerous proposals to restrict this practice. In 1974 the Supreme Court ruled against busing across school district lines to achieve integration between suburban areas and the inner city. Affirmative action policies in employment and university admissions were widely perceived as favoritism to members of minority groups. In 1978 the Supreme Court outlawed the use of quotas to aid racial minorities in the university admissions process.

As a consequence of these trends during the 1970s the civil rights movement became increasingly fragmented and isolated from the opinions of a majority of whites. Civil rights supporters did win an extension of the Voting Rights Act in 1982.

See also BLACK LIFE: Freedom Movement, Black; / King, Martin Luther, Jr.; National Association for the Advancement of Colored People; Southern Christian Leadership Conference; MEDIA: Civil Rights and Media

James W. Ely, Jr.
Vanderbilt University

James W. Ely, Jr., *The Crisis of Conservative Virginia: The Byrd Organization and the Politics of Massive Resistance* (1976); Richard Kluger, *Simple Justice: The History of Brown v. Board of Education and Black America's Struggle for Equality* (1976); Anthony Lewis and the *New York Times, Portrait of a Decade: The Second American Revolution* (1964); Harvard Sitkoff, *A New Deal For Blacks: The Emergence of Civil Rights as a National Issue* (1978); J. Harvie Wilkinson III, *From Brown to Bakke: The Supreme Court and School Integration, 1954–1978* (1979).

Common Law

The reception of English common law by the American colonies along the southern Atlantic Seaboard was largely a consequence of the shared cultural heritage of the dominant English-speaking folk. The continued growth and development of the common law in the South, however, was principally determined by external influences: (1) availability of case reports and law treatises, (2) legal training of the bar, and (3) a common English language. These factors not only resulted in the preservation of the common-law inheritance of the settlers but promoted resistance to Benthamite codification efforts surfacing in New England. These influences also encouraged the transplanting of the English-based common law to the South's western frontier.

To the colonists, legal tradition was embodied in the common law, which was in essence a set of personal rights in the form of procedures that governed and restricted the exercise of sovereign power. The view of common law as tradition and custom, the inherent birthright of the English settlers, became preserved in the form of judicial decisions and statutes. This enshrinement of the common-law heritage would have perhaps succumbed to external political movements favoring codification, however, but for the conservative influences of the entrenched professional bar of the South and a body of legal literature that enunciated the common-law tradition.

Early colonial America had no regular school of law. Unless American lawyers were so fortunate as to study in England with its Inns of Court, professors of law at Oxford and Cambridge, and learned judges, they entered practice with little formal law education, i.e., they only "read" law. For their instruction, postrevolutionary lawyers depended upon such literary sources as William Blackstone's *Commentaries on the Laws of England*. One cannot overestimate the influence of Blackstone's *Commentaries* on the early bar of the American South. From this work, American lawyers acquired knowledge of natural law, common law, equity, and "the charter rights of Englishmen." Indeed, the *Commentaries* were probably more influential in the American South than in the British Isles. Blackstone's treatises remained the standard manual for the South's lawyers until the publication in 1826 to 1830 of Chancellor James Kent's *Commentaries on American Law*. These early sources of case law and commentary were at once highly traditional, grounded in precedents of actual experience, and capable of growth and adaptation. Thus, no perceived need existed for a comprehensive written code. Even though there were repeated attempts at codification in New England, all failed in the southern states (except, of course, in Louisiana, where a previous legal heritage prevailed before the entry of the common law).

Interior of law library, City Hall, Memphis, Tenn., date unknown

As Americans settled west of the original 13 states of the young Republic, not only did they carry with them the common law, but often they found that it preceded their arrival. The governor and the judges of the Northwest Territory, for example, adopted the Virginia Act of Ratification (1788), which put into force in the area the common law of England and all English statutes of general application. Similarly, when the Mississippi Territory was established in 1798, its law embraced most of the provisions of the Northwest Ordinance and Virginia Act of Ratification as regarded the common law.

Generally being bookish people, the early frontier lawyers and judges brought the common law with them rather than making their own law, especially in the Old Southwest. As Judge Thomas Rodney of the Mississippi Territory wrote: "Special Pleading is adhered to in our Courts with as much strictness, elegance and propriety as many of the States, so that even the young lawyers are obliged to read their books and be very attentive to their business or want bread."

In addition to the treatises and doctrinal writings of Blackstone, Kent, and Joseph Story, frontier lawyers had access to an abundance of both English and American case reports, evident in their frequent citation of English and early American case precedents. In that way, the English common law was transmitted westward across the American South.

Ernest S. Easterly III
Baton Rouge, Louisiana

William Blackstone, *Commentaries on the Laws of England* (1765); Melvin E. Bradford, *A Better Guide Than Reason: Studies in the American Revolution* (1979); René David and J. E. C. Brierley, *Major Legal Systems of the World Today: An Introduction to the Comparative Study of Law* (1978); Ernest S. Easterly III, *Geojurisprudence: Studies in Law, Liberty and Landscapes* (1980); W. B. Hamilton, *South Atlantic Quarterly* (Spring 1968); Russell Kirk, *The Roots of American Order* (1974); A.

Kocourek, *American Bar Association Journal* (October 1932); Roscoe Pound, *The Spirit of Common Law* (1921).

Criminal Justice

The South has a long-standing reputation for violence and criminal disorder. It also has an image as a region where violent white men went unpunished and where, until recently, citizens frequently resorted to vigilantism to maintain order. Recent scholars have blamed the region's poverty, its racism, its pessimistic view of human nature, and even its debatable Celtic heritage for this crime and violence. Historians have suggested that an ineffective legal system intensified the combativeness of southern society.

Two themes from the Old South—frontier individualism and the plantation system—have served most frequently to explain the legal system's inability to deal with crime. No one has advanced these ideas with more assurance than W. J. Cash in his book *The Mind of the South* (1941). To Cash, an intense individualism, buttressed by a belief in white supremacy, blunted the development of law and government, while the growth of the plantation system kept the police power decentralized. An effective legal system was neither expected nor desired.

Historians have done little to rebut Cash's interpretation. Charles S. Sydnor, for example, declared that just as geographical distance isolated the westerner from legal restraints, so "the social order diminished the force of law in the South." For other scholars the private discipline enforced by masters over their slaves found its counterpart in extralegal or illegal means of resolving disputes between whites.

Although an ineffective legal response to crime may be yet another burden of southern history, there are reasons to doubt traditional interpretations of its causes. Students of the westward movement are no longer so certain that the frontier experience was abnormally violent or excessively individualistic. Much of the frontier, including the South, was a peaceful place where settlers tried to maintain order and re-create community. The urban disorder of the 19th and 20th centuries, especially in the North, also makes it difficult to conclude that lawlessness was uniquely western or southern. Moreover, the idea that informal punishment of slaves diminished respect for legal process finds little support in recent scholarship. Several studies reveal a surprisingly high regard for due process in slave trials in the lower courts and upon appellate review. Thus, slavery may not have dulled the region's legal sensibilities, as many scholars have supposed.

Two other problems remain with older interpretations of southern criminal justice. Historians have rarely compared the southern experience with that of other states, even though such comparisons are essential to the argument that an inefficient criminal process was peculiarly southern. A more fundamental weakness is that the literature on southern justice often has not examined the best evidence of the region's legal behavior, local court records.

Recent efforts to gauge the response of local courts to crime suggest the need to revise significantly—but not to abandon completely—standard themes advanced by historians, especially as they apply to the colonial and antebellum South. There is considerable evidence, for example, of the inability of local southern courts to complete prosecution in a large percentage of criminal cases. An examination of colonial courts in North Carolina found that only half of all bills of indictment brought before the General Court reached trial; almost one criminal action in three simply disappeared from the system. More dismal figures surfaced in a study of four counties in antebellum Georgia, where just one case in four reached a decision on the merits of the accusation. But in neither instance was the southern experience unique. Comparisons with local courts in colonial New York and antebellum Indiana revealed strikingly similar patterns of ineffective prosecution. Southern law enforcement, in other words, was not atypical in its inability to secure judgments in criminal cases; the problem was endemic to rural, prebureaucratic communities in both the North and the South.

Many of the patterns of prosecution in southern jurisdictions parallel those found elsewhere. Most criminal actions involved petty offenses, although prosecutions for felonies consumed much of the time courts devoted to criminal matters. Of the more serious crimes, theft and other property offenses appeared regularly on criminal dockets, with urbanizing areas devoting considerable prosecutorial energy to these cases. The available data suggest, moreover, that southern grand juries and prosecutors, like their northern counterparts, identified those without property as offenders in such cases.

Crimes against morality also occupied the attention of local authorities. Although the incidence of prosecution was less than in the colonies and states of Puritan New England, gaming, liquor-related offenses, and sexual immorality were frequent crimes before southern trial courts. These findings not only suggest a modification in traditional interpretations that emphasize southern laxity in crimes against morality but also in recent arguments that 19th- and 20th-century criminal process ignored such crimes in its attempt to protect the economic order. Perhaps crime as theft replaced crime as sin in the criminal codes of other states, but southern courts continued the effort to maintain a common morality.

Of course, violent crime rather than theft or moral disorder gave the South its image as a lawless region. Tales of duels, murder, and assault were stock items in scores of travel accounts, newspaper stories, and grand jury presentments. Historians also have credited southerners with a readiness to settle private disputes with fists, dirks, or pistols. Examinations of felony indictments appear to confirm this conclusion. Crimes against persons were constant items on court dockets; some studies have discovered that almost 4 of every 10 indictments involved either petty or serious acts of personal violence. This circumstance, present in the earliest records, continues to exist. In the mid-1970s the southern states led the nation in these crimes. Forty-two percent of all murders in 1975 were committed in the South, and the region's fastest-growing urban area, Houston, had earned the name "Murder City" for its large number of capital crimes.

While the rate of indictments for violent behavior surpasses the standards for other regions, it is inaccurate to claim that grand juries and circuit solicitors ignored violent crime or treated it casually. Instead, the figures suggest that prosecution of violent crime was a central concern of the legal system. In cases tried to a verdict, moreover, the violent offender stood little chance of acquittal, especially in jurisdictions with urbanizing areas. The degree of success enjoyed by courts in securing convictions in cases of violent crime underscores the social agreement that law and not private vengeance provided the most acceptable method of resolving personal conflicts. For most southerners, criminal justice remained a matter for the courts.

See also VIOLENCE: Crime, Attitudes toward

David J. Bodenhamer
University of Southern Mississippi

Edward L. Ayers, *Vengeance and Justice: Crime and Punishment in the 19th Century South* (1984); David J. Bodenhamer, *Criminal Justice History* (1983); Bradley Chapin, *Criminal Justice in Colonial America, 1606–1660* (1983); Daniel Flanigan, *Journal of Southern History* (November 1974); Michael S. Hindus, *Prison and Plantation: Crime, Justice, and Authority in Massachusetts and South Carolina, 1767–1878* (1980); Kathryn Preyer, *Law and History Review* (Spring 1983); Philip J. Schwarz, *Ambivalent Legacy: A Legal History of the South*, ed. David J. Bodenhamer and James W. Ely, Jr. (1984); Donna J. Spindel and Stuart W. Thomas, Jr., *Journal of Southern History* (May 1983).

Criminal Law

Criminal law outlines standards of conduct for every member of the community and sets the punishment for violation of those rules. Its substance proscribes behavior that might variously be described as immoral, violent, disruptive of public order, or destructive of property rights and relationships. Its procedures seek to ensure that accused persons receive a fair hearing on the merits of charges against them. Yet, as sociologists, criminologists, and legal scholars have demonstrated in numerous studies, the law in operation at times bears little resemblance to its formal codes, maintaining a close, supportive relationship to the dominant class in society.

Historians have generally failed to study the South's criminal process. Nowhere is this neglect more pronounced than in the written and common law that defined criminal behavior. Available scholarship, however, tends to refute the traditional view of the South as a region with primitive, unenlightened penal codes. From the colonial period to the Civil War, southern legislators and jurists joined with reformers elsewhere to rid the law of the vast number of crimes and harsh punishments of 16th- and 17th-century England. Although the South moved to prescriptive or legislative law somewhat later than did New England, criminal law in the colonial South relied more heavily on English precedent. It was strongly affected by local interpretation and less reliant on biblical injunction than was true in the northern, especially Puritan, colonies.

The tenets of revolutionary republicanism demanded a limitation on the power of the state, thus stimulating reform of the criminal law throughout the new nation, including the South. Heavily influenced by 18th-century rationalism, the writings of Montesquieu and Cesare Beccaria, and the codification efforts of Edward Livingston, southern legislators by the 1820s had drafted criminal codes that rivaled those of northern jurisdictions. In fact, some scholars have labeled Georgia's code of 1816 the first successful codification of criminal law in the new Republic. Reforms included a sharp reduction in the number of statutory crimes and in the punishments prescribed for their commission. Capital crimes for whites were limited to treason (rarely enforced), murder, arson, and rape of a minor; and imprisonment in a state penitentiary—originally created as a place for the reformation of the individual miscreant—became the norm for most other serious crimes. Criminal procedures conformed closely to the due process requirements of state and federal bills of rights, at least as interpreted by 19th-century judges and commentators. Recent studies of local trial courts, moreover, reveal that patterns of prosecution, conviction, and sentencing paralleled those found in non-southern jurisdictions with similar demographic and economic characteristics.

These reforms in the written criminal law did not, however, apply to slaves, and in practice their application to free blacks was uncertain and idiosyncratic. Separate laws for slaves, often called black codes, prescribed different courts, fewer procedural safeguards for defendants, and harsher punishment upon conviction. In addition, enforcement of punishment for misdemeanors and even some felonies was often left to owners or overseers.

It would not be accurate to claim that trial and punishment of criminal slaves fell outside the legal system or that their treatment was totally at the whim of the master. Undoubtedly, justice at the local level varied widely, depending upon the locale, the ratio of blacks to whites, and the nature of the crime. But historians have probably overestimated the degree of discretionary justice attendant upon slave trials. Several studies reveal a surprisingly high regard for due process in the lower courts and upon appellate review. This result should not suggest that the white South was wedded to the concept of equal rights before the law for slaves, but rather that the application of due process in these cases satisfied the formal requirements of a legal culture without jeopardizing white control over blacks. Procedural safeguards for slaves and free blacks were, for example, at risk whenever black violence threatened the status quo.

In one area of criminal law, namely, statutory prohibitions of immorality, the South differed from the North.

Laws against crimes such as adultery, fornication, intemperance, and gambling remained prominent in southern codes long after northern legislatures had shifted attention to property and economic crimes. Crime as theft may have replaced crime as sin elsewhere, but official regulation of immoral conduct continued to be a feature of the criminal law in southern states. It was no accident that prohibition and other moral crusades found ready reception in the South; the region's legal system had a long history of attempting to regulate morality.

The abolition of slavery and an increased level of violence that followed the Civil War caused dramatic changes in southern criminal law. Separate courts and codes for blacks disappeared, but the law did not suddenly become color-blind. A breakdown of the traditions that, together with the plantation system, had kept the races separate led to late 19th-century revisions in criminal law designed to punish violations of racial separation, although most of the infractions were properly classed as misdemeanors rather than felonies. Extralegal actions, especially lynching and vigilante actions, were used for more serious violations of racial and moral order.

Except for the area of race, southern criminal laws in the 20th century resembled those in other regions of the country. Codes became more complex and defined more possible criminal actions as the South became more urban and industrial. But there remained some differences between South and North. Although details are sketchy, southern lawmakers and prosecutors appeared less willing to use criminal statutes to prosecute corporate offenders but did increase considerably the severity of punishment for individuals convicted of economic crimes, especially those involving racial violence. For example, some southern states by the 1930s had enacted laws that allowed the death sentence for convictions of armed robbery, a clear reversal of a two-centuries-long trend to limit the number of capital crimes.

Criminal law in the modern South is virtually indistinguishable from codes elsewhere. At least three reasons account for this: pressures from the federal judiciary and the U.S. Justice Department, especially in the area of civil rights; the growth of a professional bar in the southern states; and the incorporation of southern states into a national economy. In the interpretation and enforcement of these laws, however, regional differences remain because of the force of precedent in the Anglo-American legal tradition and because of the unique influence each community exercises in decisions to prosecute criminal violations and, through the jury, in decisions on individuals charged with crimes.

See also VIOLENCE: Crime, Attitudes toward

David J. Bodenhamer
University of Southern Mississippi

Edward L. Ayers, *Vengeance and Justice: Crime and Punishment in the 19th Century South* (1984); Bradley Chapin, *Criminal Justice in Colonial America, 1606–1660* (1983); Daniel Flanigan, *Journal of Southern History* (November 1974); Michael S. Hindus, *Prison and Plantation: Crime, Justice, and Authority in Massachusetts and South Carolina, 1767–1878* (1980); A. E. Nash, *Virginia Law Review* (February 1970); Kathryn Preyer, *Law and History Review* (Spring 1983); Charles S. Sydnor, *Journal of Southern History* (February 1940).

Family Law

The rules of family law have varied significantly from one southern state to another since the 17th century. From the beginning of English colonization of the southern area of North America, the family law that prevailed there was *English* in the sense that marriage was monogamous and indissoluble, and rules of succession were similar to prevailing English rules. Few disputes, however, turned on familial status, and, unlike in England, no system of ecclesiastical courts adjudicated them. Significant French and Spanish colonization in the southwestern region did not occur until the 18th century. In the Spanish settlements the law of Castile prevailed along with special rules promulgated for the Indies, and these principles replaced the custom of Paris in the formerly French territory of Louisiana in 1769. For a decade in the mid-18th century a Spanish auxiliary bishop resided in Florida, and from the end of the 18th century a Roman Catholic bishop was in New Orleans. But episcopal jurisdiction was never exerted in a way that had any permanent effect on the development of familial legal institutions.

Marriage. In Virginia until 1794 marriages were by law performed by an Anglican clergyman, but thereafter civil marriages by a magistrate were allowed. Elsewhere in the English South, civil marriage and marriage by the rules of various nonconformist sects had been tolerated from the 17th century. The governor's license to marry could generally be substituted for the premarital ecclesiastical publication of banns throughout the English South.

In the Spanish region marriages were entered into in accordance with the formalities required by the Roman Catholic church. In the absence of a priest, the Spanish military commandant acted as a notary with two witnesses and supervised written contracts to marry, contracts that were solemnized by a priest at the first opportunity. In the case of unions of non-Roman Catholics this formality was frequently not followed by a later religious ceremony.

As a consequence of the early lack of available religious officiants, in some areas during the 18th century informal (or common-law) marriage defined by agreement, cohabitation, and public notoriety was recognized or went uncontested. In the 19th century this institution was particularly well rooted in the Lower South and Texas. Elsewhere in the South other legal doctrines accomplished the same results as the informal marriage, though without giving the marriage validity for all purposes. Today 4 of the 13 states recognizing informal marriages include Georgia, Alabama, South Carolina, and Texas; and where entered into by citizens of those states, the marriage can be dissolved only by divorce and not by agreement.

Some legal requirements for marriage, such as waiting periods before marriage, vary widely nationwide as well as within the South. Other requirements, such as the age for marriage without consent of a parent or guardian and/or the court, are fairly uniform nationwide. Only four states' minimum ages for marriage without consent vary from 18 for both parties; two of the four exceptions are in the South. In Mississippi both parties must be 21, and in Louisiana the minimum age is 16 for the woman and 18 for the man. The requirements for marriage with consent, however, vary widely regionally and nationally. Kentucky, like three non-southern states, requires parental and/or court consent for either party if under 18, but specifies no minimum age. The age for marriage with consent is 14 in Alabama and Texas for both males and females and in South Carolina for females (16 for males). These are the lowest specified ages in the South, though not in the nation.

Marital Property. As under Spanish law, equal sharing of the gains of marriage (community property) between spouses continued to prevail in Louisiana and Texas and is still maintained there. In other former dominions of Spain, the English law of marital property quickly supplanted the Spanish law as those territories were incorporated into the United States. Whereas under Spanish law the personality of both spouses was distinctly recognized in law, under English law the married woman's legal capacity was largely merged into that of her husband. All of her movable property became her husband's on marriage, he had the power of management of her lands, and he owned the income derived from them.

The married woman was given significant control over her lands and slaves first in Mississippi in 1839 and later elsewhere (Alabama, in 1848; North Carolina, in 1849; Tennessee, in 1850). In Alabama a judicial means was provided as early as 1872 for a married woman to have her disabilities removed so that she might enter into business transactions. Similar legislation was enacted elsewhere. But unless complying with such requirements, married women in most of the South lacked general contractual power. Spanish principles that recognized a married woman's capacity to enter into contracts survived only in Louisiana. In order to protect the creditors who supplied a married woman with goods necessary for her subsistence and that of her children, the law generally recognized the wife as her husband's *agent of necessity*, so that he was liable on such contracts that she made. Married women did not acquire full contractual capacity throughout the South until the mid-20th century.

Though all the southern states protected such necessary movable property as household furniture and tools of trade from the claims of creditors, Texas extended this protection to the family home in 1839. The concept of the homestead was rapidly adopted throughout the Lower South but not in Virginia or the Carolinas until the late 1860s. From the early 19th century a number of states also gave the surviving spouse occupancy of the homestead during widowhood.

Children. In the social and economic conventions of the 17th through the 19th centuries, the husband-father was the head of the family and was responsible for its support. All family members, including the wife, were identified by his surname. This legal requirement no longer exists, although the practice is still widespread. Though the law traditionally has not imposed a duty on children to support needy parents, such support generally has been provided.

Divorce. As in the states to the North, legislative divorce had been available in some southern states from the late 18th century (in Virginia and North Carolina as early as 1789 and 1794, respectively), and some legislative divorces were granted in almost every southern state. For a time Georgia, Mississippi, Alabama, and Louisiana required a prior judicial divorce before a legislative divorce could be granted, but during the first half of the 19th century over 300 legislative divorces were, nevertheless, granted in Georgia alone. From the mid-19th century onward, legislative divorce disappeared in the South, as elsewhere in the United States.

Although judicial marital dissolution for a cause arising during marriage was introduced in Connecticut in 1667 and some other northern states followed this example, it was not available in the South until Tennessee so provided in 1798. Judicial divorce followed rapidly in the Mississippi Territory, Louisiana, Georgia, and the Missouri Territory. In the Upper South it was somewhat delayed (North Carolina, 1827; Virginia, 1850), and divorce was finally provided in South Carolina in 1872. But almost as soon as it was adopted in South Carolina, judicial divorce was abolished there, and it was not reinstituted until 1949. A single act of adultery of the wife and persistent adultery of the husband were generally recognized as grounds for divorce, and North Carolina and Virginia recognized no other grounds than marital infidelity until the early 20th century. Elsewhere cruel treatment and incompatibility of disposition were recognized as additional grounds and, where recognized, these causes were relied on in most cases.

When faced with the need to provide for the wife on divorce, the laws of most southern states restored her lands to her and ordered the exhusband to pay her support (alimony) until her remarriage or death, rather than making a division of property (which usually meant the husband's property). Louisiana and Texas divided the community property on divorce, and in Louisiana, but not in Texas, alimony might also be granted. From 1872 alimony after divorce was not available in North Carolina but it was restored to a limited extent in 1919. As a substitute for granting support to an exspouse, by the late 20th century all southern states had shifted to allowing a division of property associated with the marriage.

Divorce occurred infrequently in the 19th century, but

there was no question that the father had a continuing liability for the support of his minor children after a divorce. Though many statutes of southern states spoke in terms of "nullification" of a marriage by divorce, they specifically provided that the children of the marriage were nonetheless legitimate. There seem to be few disputes as to parental fitness for custody of children, and on the divorce of their parents children of tender years were typically put in the custody of their mothers as a matter of course.

Existing patterns of family law remained largely intact in the South until after World War II. In the 1940s divorce became more widely sought, but local standards were strictly maintained in some states, as in Virginia and North Carolina, or divorces were simply not made available, as in South Carolina. For some years Alabama courts tended to open their doors to outsiders by applying very lax standards of proving local residence, and some southerners also sought divorces in non-southern locations with lax residence standards. By 1985 divorce for marital incompatibility or breakdown of the marriage, so-called no-fault grounds, was possible in Alabama, Florida, Georgia, Kentucky, Mississippi, Tennessee, Texas, and West Virginia. Arkansas, Louisiana, North Carolina, South Carolina, and Virginia were among the 12 states nationwide that did not have no-fault or modified no-fault grounds for divorce. By the mid-1980s the custody of minor children was commonly awarded to fathers as well as to mothers. Mothers as well as fathers were also required to support minor children after divorce. Although reciprocal legislation was passed as interstate compacts to achieve enforcement of postdivorce support of exspouses and minor children, the system was too cumbersome to have much practical effect, and with greater population mobility, support orders became increasingly difficult to enforce.

During the 1970s and 1980s the states have enacted uniform laws to govern jurisdiction in the modification of child-custody orders when parents and children move from one state to another. At the same time the federal government has attempted to assist in the enforcement of child-support orders and to prevent abduction of minor children contrary to child-custody decrees. But the success of these efforts is, thus far, difficult to measure.

Legitimation and Adoption. Where English legal traditions were maintained, a child's rights of intestate inheritance rested on its being the legitimate offspring of its parents. Most southern states followed the model of the Virginia succession statute of 1785 in making children born out of wedlock legitimate as to their mothers, and legitimate as to both parents if they later married. Legitimacy as to the father who did not marry the mother required legitimation on the part of the father by administrative or legislative act.

In the legislative records of southern states from about 1810 there are increasing instances of changes of children's names. Many name changes are unrelated to legitimation, but some clearly have intestate succession as their object. In the early 19th century, however, many legislative acts for legitimation began to be identified as such, and some legislative acts mix the terminology of legitimation and adoption. Most southern states also provided for bastardy proceedings by which a father was required to support his illegitimate minor offspring; these proceedings, however, did not legitimate the children.

As a further consequence of concern for illegitimate birth and orphanage of minor children, instances of *legislative* adoption in the South increased after 1820. First in Mississippi (1846) a *judicial* means of adoption was also provided, while Texas (1850) and Alabama (1851) provided for adoption by formal, administrative process. Both of these patterns were followed in other states and became the standard modes of adoption after the new state constitutions of the 1860s and 1870s made private legislative acts of adoption unavailable. Virginia, however, did not provide for judicial adoption until 1892.

Succession. By the end of the 18th century the rule of intestate succession in the English South in favor of the eldest male had been everywhere replaced by intestate inheritance in favor of all children equally, and parents were forbidden to create entails. Apart from the right of the surviving widow, however, a married man had the right to dispose of his property as he pleased and to disinherit children with or without cause, except in Louisiana and Texas. In 1856 forced inheritance of children was abandoned in Texas, but the right of descendants to inherit a portion of a parent's estate has been maintained in Louisiana except for certain specified reasons for which they may be disinherited. Until 1981 only Louisiana also assured ancestors a share of a child's estate, though the ancestor could have been disinherited for certain specified causes.

In most of the South married women were not allowed to make an effective will as long as their husbands lived. But the law was otherwise in the former Spanish provinces and has so remained in Louisiana, Florida, and Texas. Married women did not obtain the power to make wills elsewhere in the South until the late 19th century. Because in most of the South so much of a wife's property and its control passed to her husband at marriage, the married woman was provided (as under English law) with a dower interest in one-third of her husband's land if she survived him. During the late 19th century this principle was expanded in most of the South to a statutory right in both lands and movable property in favor of either spouse in the property of the other, in spite of any provisions made by will. In Louisiana and Texas, however, the surviving spouse was entitled to his or her half-share of the community property as well as a share of the separate property of the deceased spouse.

In this century no significant changes have been made in the law of succession except with respect to illegitimates who have attained the right of intestate inheritance in Louisiana and have been accorded the status of legitimation when paternity is proved during the father's lifetime in Texas.

Slave Families. In the era prior to the end of the Civil War a sizable part of the population—the black slaves—was outside the legal scheme of familial relations, and that fact had a significant impact on social mores and legal institutions of the region for some time to come. In the subculture of slavery, which prevailed in all of the South until the fall of the Confederate government, the family was not a recognized legal entity. Marriage between free whites and blacks (free or slave) was generally prohibited (as it was in many other states at that time), and criminal sanctions were provided for breach of the rule. Legitimization of illegitimate children of color was also generally forbidden. After the Civil War former slave unions were recognized as marriages, but legislation prohibiting and punishing interracial marriages persisted in most areas of the South well into the 20th century. With the repeal of antimiscegenation laws, interracial marriages are now permitted, and the prohibition of them in the Mississippi Constitution until 1987 was a relic of past times.

See also BLACK LIFE: Family, Black; Miscegenation; Slave Culture; HISTORY AND MANNERS: Sexuality; MYTHIC SOUTH: Family; Fatherhood; Motherhood; WOMEN'S LIFE: Childraising Customs; Elderly; Family, Modernization of; Marriage and Divorce Laws

Joseph W. McKnight
Southern Methodist University

Jane T. Censer, *American Journal of Legal History* (January 1981); Carl N. Degler, *At Odds: Women and the Family in America from the Revolution to the Present* (1980); Joseph W. McKnight, *Southwestern Historical Quarterly* (January 1983).

Labor Relations and Law

No other area in the United States has been so affected by labor shortages as the South, and problems stemming from this situation have been reflected in southern law. The early European colonists in the New World discovered the need for labor, a need partially satisfied through Indian acculturation, Indian slavery, European indentured servitude, and finally African slavery. Contact between Europeans and Indians resulted in cultural interaction, but it did not solve the labor shortage problems of the white settlers. By the end of the 17th century British traders in the Carolinas had resorted to an extensive Indian slave trade, particularly in the deerskin trade network, but wars and diseases would terminate this experiment with forced Indian labor.

Indentured servitude was legally sanctioned, and it enjoyed longer existence. Indentured servants were at least declared "persons" within the meaning of the law, but the right to their labor was distinctly the property of their masters. Indentured servants did have the right to contract, and this contract was negotiated to secure passage to the New World and to work to pay out this debt. The labor contract could be modified once the servant arrived in the colonies. Conflicts soon arose between free whites, indentured whites, and slaves; the poor whites had only their labor to sell, and blacks in slavery eventually precluded this sale in the South. This led to the appearance of rudimentary guilds and unions, whose members adamantly refused to train either slaves or, often, free blacks.

In North America slavery was centered in the South. Some scholars believe that the southern plantation had labor needs that could not have been met in any other way. These economic needs spawned legislation designed to augment and preserve the labor system that evolved. Other historians posit that the structure of law did not reflect the evolution of slavery but promoted it, aiming at industry and production. They contend that slavery could not have existed but for "positive legislation."

Laws, however, were not designed to guide the system, but to correct it. Regulation was not imposed until problems had already become evident. Much of the early legislation was directly borrowed from Barbados, where the English had vast legal experience in the control and marketing of slaves. South Carolina adopted the 1688 Barbados Slave Code in 1712; Georgia, which originally forbade slavery, followed, and Florida adopted the Georgia Code in 1822. Most of the laws were not aimed at particulars of slave existence but at the preservation of the institution itself.

By 1755 most of the southern colonies had adopted slave codes that included under their jurisdiction most blacks and persons of mixed blood, excluding most Indians. The lineage of a black was also a factor because the child's status followed that of the mother. Any free black who remained in slave territory for 12 months or more might be enslaved and a freedman could be reenslaved. A free black in the South was merely a paroled inmate. In fact, Georgia and Florida required all free blacks to have a guardian appointed; there were criminal sanctions for an omission.

Still there were few actual *labor* laws in the colonial South. Not until after the colonial period did extensive labor legislation and litigation occur. The masters seemed to make up the rules as they went along, and only changes in the economy and political pressures eventually forced sophisticated labor legislation.

Labor legislation in the South after the American Revolution began to reflect more clearly certain applicable concepts of property. The ownership of a slave was the ownership of equipment capable of labor. Most of the laws governing slaves and slave trade came to be based upon existing principles of property and, later, tort law. Most labor law was enforced on the plantation itself or in a local municipal court. Often punishments for slaves were quite harsh. Particularly stringent punishments such as lashings or mutilations were imposed for brawling and drinking. As the black population grew, southern states required identification papers and travel cards for slaves leaving their master's land for any reason.

Because the slave was property (as later defined in *Dred Scott* v. *Sanford*), the masters were taxed accordingly. Some states required an importation tax and also a yearly tax for keeping slaves. The use and sale of slaves became an important business; labor brokers were jealously protected. The slave trade was second only to the production of cotton as a mainstay of the southern economy; labor was big business. Importation costs were great for slave traders, and they preferred a domestic trade. Hence, the market was reduced by forbidding the importation of new slaves. This stabilized the market and kept the demand for labor high. Statutes were passed making it illegal to buy, use, possess, or sell any illegally imported slaves.

With the taxation of slaves and the reduction of the importation of slaves, a new business arose to meet the labor demand: slave renting. Most renting contracts were for 50 weeks with two weeks off near the Christmas holidays. The lessor held title to the slave, but the lessee assumed all responsibility for the slave. If the slave ran away, the lessee paid; if the slave committed a crime or tort, the lessee had the responsibility for making it right. The lessee was also responsible for food, clothing, and medical care of the slave as well as paying the annual taxes for "owning" a slave.

Southern courts heard a number of contract disputes concerning the rights of lessees and lessors in slave-rental relationships. The Georgia Supreme Court ruled, for example, in *Latimer* v. *Alexander* (1853) that the lessee of a slave was to be held responsible for reasonable medical costs, adding that any other ruling would undermine the labor system.

Clearly any master could hire out a slave for any period of time, but a slave or former slave was not allowed to offer his own services for hire. If the temporary master allowed any harm to befall a slave, the lessor could demand compensation for loss of value. Sometimes the lessee found it easier and cheaper to purchase the slave rather than pay compensation. In later years slave insurance became available and many rental masters required the lessee to purchase a policy before allowing the slave to leave.

The actual regulation of labor was left to the plantation owner, slaveowner, or overseer. Any law enforcement was carried out as a private matter upon private land. Almost every aspect of the slave's life was dependent upon the needs or the whims of the master. Few laws existed to control the time or type of his labor. Slaves were not allowed to work for themselves or on Sundays, and they were not to be kept in the fields more than 14 to 16 hours per day. Certainly by the advent of the Civil War, the master could determine with minimal interference the kind, degree, and time of labor to which the slave was subjected. Such was the state of southern labor law.

Immediately after the Civil War, most white southerners still thought of "labor" as black. Widespread fears were that labor would leave the South or that it would be unstable. This prompted efforts to restrain the newly freed blacks in their exercise of what are generally perceived as traditional rights of labor. A highly restrictive crop-lien system, which led to pervasive sharecropping, was devised that featured exorbitant rents and one-sided contracts. When blacks tried to leave the South, white southerners reacted by imprisoning the "exodusters" for debt or by using violence. Black codes were passed by southern legislatures, forcing many blacks to labor against their wishes. These took the form of work contracts, peonage, convict labor, and surety agreements.

During the late 19th century economic developments placed even greater stress upon a labor-short southern society. The Industrial Revolution spread to the South, and it was particularly evident in the southeastern states with their abundant water. The industrialization of the Piedmont occurred with labor that was white and youthful. Much of the labor demand was for work in cotton, textile, tobacco, or lumber mills.

Child labor was especially prominent in southern manufacturing, in part because poorer whites and blacks stayed on the farm, sending their children to work in the plants. By 1889 Louisiana was the only southern state to limit child labor in manufacturing to certain ages (between 12 and 14, depending upon the industry), and by 1900 only Tennessee had any further age restriction.

The end of the 19th century brought with it a young, exuberant breed of politicians who wanted to fight the nation's social problems. They wanted to use law to reform society, and in the South this fervor took the form of fighting for child-labor legislation. North Carolina was a leader in southern progressivism, beginning with the election of Governor Charles Brantley Aycock in 1900. In 1903, during Aycock's term, the first child-labor law in North Carolina was passed. This culminated a campaign begun by southern ministers such as Alexander J. McKelway and by northern textile manufacturers. Many ministers reflected the public indignation at the maiming of young children by machinery. The states of the Northeast had enacted child labor laws, and manufacturers there saw the South as operating at an unfair advantage, particularly in textiles.

North Carolina industrialists fought the child-labor laws with vigor. The first major child-labor court test came one year before the North Carolina Legislature acted. In *Fitzgerald* v. *Alma Furniture* (1902) the North Carolina Supreme Court ruled in favor of a nine-year-old boy who had suffered a smashed hand while working. The case sent a message to the North Carolina Legislature, which adopted child-labor legislation the next year. That legislation would be tested and upheld in North Carolina's courts in *Rolins* v. *R. J. Reynolds Tobacco Co.* (1906) and *Gaines Leathers* v. *Blackwell Durham Tobacco Company* (1907). By 1909 all the southern states had adopted child-labor laws.

The federal government also passed child-labor legislation. In 1916 Congress approved, and President Woodrow Wilson signed into law, the Owen-Keating Act, which prohibited passage in interstate commerce of any goods produced by child labor. This all-encompassing legislation was strongly opposed by southern industrialists who supported a test case in the U.S. Supreme Court. In *Hammer* v. *Dagenhart* (1918) the Court held the Owen-Keating Act to be unconstitutional because it exceeded the commerce powers of Congress and preempted powers reserved to the states. The Charlotte, N.C., cotton mill involved in the case could continue to hire children and to have its products shipped interstate. The states were now left to regulate the age at which minors could work, and for the South it remained at 12 to 14.

Eventually the *Hammer* precedent was struck down. Under the New Deal, the Fair Labor Standards Act of 1938 incorporated virtually the same language as the

Owen-Keating Act. This was tested in 1941 in *United States* v. *Darby*. Although Darby violated portions of the Fair Labor Standards Act that did not apply to child labor, the full act was held as constitutional. The fight for child-labor regulation at the national level was over, and southern employers, such as Darby of Georgia, had to adjust accordingly.

The shortage of labor and the attitude toward labor relations as a private rather than public affair created in the 20th-century South a climate hostile to unionization. Membership in unions was protected by the Erdman Act, enacted in 1898 in the aftermath of a national railroad strike. Section 10 of that act prohibited any employer from requiring an employee not to become a member of a labor organization. The prohibition of "yellow dog" contracts was challenged by the Louisville and Nashville Railroad when it fired William Adair, a master mechanic, because he had joined a union. The U.S. Supreme Court decision in *Adair* v. *United States* (1908) validated "yellow dog" contracts. Conditions of employment were not deemed the proper sphere of national regulation, and the Erdman Act became illegal.

The *Adair* case and a particularly vicious longshoreman's strike in Galveston, Tex., in 1920 encouraged southern states to pass antistrike legislation, termed right-to-work laws. Texas implemented five right-to-work laws. The first was instituted by Governor W. Lee O'Daniel. The O'Daniel Act made violence in the course of a labor dispute a penal offense. In 1943 the Manford Act was passed regulating unions. A 1947 law contained three sections that gave all workers the right to bargain individually without discrimination, and it outlawed contract clauses providing for union security. The Parkhouse Act of 1951 placed contracts containing union-security clauses under the antitrust laws of the state of Texas, and an act of 1955 made it illegal to strike or picket in order to force an employer to bargain with any except a majority union. By 1947 every southern state except Alabama and Louisiana had right-to-work laws, and in 1954 Alabama adopted one. Today only Louisiana is without right-to-work legislation in manufacturing.

Challenges to southern right-to-work legislation by labor have been fruitless. Exemplary was the Tennessee case of Joe Mascari, who questioned a union contract providing for a closed shop. In *Mascari et al.* v. *International Brotherhood of Teamsters et al.* (1948) the Tennessee Supreme Court upheld the Tennessee Open Shop Law and, furthermore, made the act retroactive to those contracts of a closed-shop nature signed prior to the act.

See also AGRICULTURE: Sharecropping and Tenancy; SOCIAL CLASS: Labor, Organized; Tenant Farmers

John R. Wunder
Clemson University

David Brion Davis, *The Problem of Slavery in Western Culture* (1966); J. R. Dempsey, *The Operation of the Right-to-Work Laws* (1961); Eugene D. Genovese, *From Rebellion to Revolution: Afro-American Slave Revolts in the Making of the Modern World* (1979); Herbert Gutman, *The Black Family in Slavery and Freedom, 1750–1925* (1976); Sarah S. Hughes, *William and Mary Quarterly* (April 1978); Gary B. Nash, *Red, White, and Black: The Peoples of Early America* (1974); William F. Ogburn, *Progress and Uniformity in Child-Labor Legislation* (1968); Nell Irvin Painter, *Exodusters: Black Migration to Kansas after Reconstruction* (1976); William M. Wieck, *William and Mary Quarterly* (April 1977); Peter H. Wood, *Black Majority: Negroes in Colonial South Carolina from 1670 through the Stono Rebellion* (1974).

Law Schools

For most of the 19th century studying in a law school was not the predominant method of preparing for admission to the bar in this country. Although law schools had existed in the South since the founding of William and Mary Law School in 1779, most candidates for admission to the bar prepared by studying in a law office as required in many states by the rules of the local courts. If no such preparation was required, then self-study was the usual method. Study in a law school, however, conferred prestige and added to the credentials of the lawyers who attended. Not until the middle of this century did law schools provide the only means of preparing for a career as a lawyer.

The introduction of lectures on law at the College of William and Mary in 1779 was the result of the efforts of Thomas Jefferson who, as governor of Virginia, suggested the establishment of a professorship of law and police. "Police" referred not to law enforcement but to government. George Wythe, a judge in the court of chancery in Virginia, was appointed law professor. His course of study was limited to one year and consisted of lectures with frequent moot courts. In 1824 the college began conferring degrees. The law school suspended operation during the Civil War and did not become permanent until 1922. Many of the leaders of the postrevolutionary bar of Virginia, including John Marshall, attended the lectures by George Wythe or his successor, St. George Tucker.

The second law school established in the Southeast was at the University of Transylvania at Lexington, Ky. The law department was established in 1799 and continued until it was interrupted by the Civil War. It affected the legal profession in several respects. It was the first to seek out and collect a law library, which was supported by fees from auctioneers in Lexington. The library was one of the largest antebellum law collections in the country. Many leaders of the American bar in the central area of the nation attended the school. The course of study was typical of the period, consisting of lectures and moot court arguments.

Many of the law schools established in the antebellum South began as private endeavors of lawyers or judges and later were incorporated into a college or university. Joseph Henry Lumpkin apparently had established such a "law school" in Athens, Ga., around 1843; the school was incorporated into the University of Georgia in 1859. Lawyers and judges found it profitable to teach students in their offices, but if these endeavors can be called "schools," it is difficult to establish their identities or determine the precise number that existed at any particular period. This continued to be true in states where unapproved law schools were permitted.

If these proprietary schools are disregarded, approximately seven other law schools were established in the Southeast during the period prior to the Civil War. Generally, the courses consisted of a one-year program made up of lectures and moot court participation. Although this education may be considered primitive by today's standards, it was generally of higher quality than many of the lawyers received through training in law offices or self-study. The justification for the schools was to promote a more thorough and systematic study of the law. This was not a barren period in the annals of legal education, for many of the founders of these law schools were intellectuals who experimented with various techniques of teaching.

Law schools continued to be founded at a slow rate in the Southeast after the Civil War, but events in another part of the country were shaping legal education and laying the foundation for law schools to become the only means of preparation for the legal profession. In 1870 Christopher Columbus Langdell introduced at the Harvard University Law School the case method system of teaching law. This system consisted of reading cases to extract "principles or doctrines" in a scientific manner to arrive at the fundamental legal doctrines. However, southern schools were reluctant to embrace this method of teaching and most held out for the lecture method into the next century.

Meanwhile, the American Bar Association was responsible for founding the Section on Legal Education, and later the same organization was instrumental in establishing the Association of American Law Schools in 1900. These organizations began to agitate for a three-year program of study and the attendance at law schools as a method of professional preparation. The University of Tennessee Law School was the only southern chartered member of the Association of American Law Schools, which indicates that school's early acceptance of the standards prescribed by these accrediting agencies. After 1910 such law schools as Texas, Kentucky, Tulane, Vanderbilt, and Virginia became members. At the beginning of this century many of the better law schools began to hire academic law teachers rather than rely upon practicing attorneys as professors; this strengthened the methods of teaching. During the decade of the 1920s other southern law schools became members of the Association of American Law Schools and began to meet the standards prescribed by the association.

These organizations did not have a significant impact on legal education until the 1940s when statistics were collected and inspections of the programs at each individual school began. ABA approval was made a necessity as more states adopted a statute requiring graduation from an accredited law school as a prerequisite for admission to the practice of law. Most of the standards were objective rather than qualitative, based on the theory that better teaching methods would be the result of better libraries and facilities. After World War II the number of law schools increased significantly as the demand for legal education mushroomed.

Unapproved law schools exist in the South only in Georgia and Alabama. Though unsupervised, these institutions continue to graduate a sizable number of lawyers.

Acting under the doctrine of separate-but-equal education, three southern states founded all-black law schools—at North Carolina Central in 1939, at Southern University in Louisiana in 1947, and Texas Southern University Thurgood Marshall School of Law (which began in 1947 and moved to new quarters named for Justice Marshall in 1976). The faculties of the state university law schools were often used as the faculty at these black law schools. Desegregation has had little impact on these schools, which have kept their identities and, generally, their limited student body. The Supreme Court case of *Sweatt* v. *Painter* (1950), which mandated the desegregation of the University of Texas Law School, was a landmark in overturning legal support for racial segregation.

By the beginning of this century women had won the right to become members of the bar, but their numbers were small, usually limited to under 5 percent of the student body. In the 1960s this changed drastically as women came to constitute as much as 40 percent of the total student body.

See also EDUCATION: / College of William and Mary; Georgia, University of; Kentucky, University of; Texas, University of; Tulane University; Vanderbilt University; Virginia, University of

Erwin Surrency
University of Georgia

David John Mays, *The Pursuit of Excellence: A History of the University of Richmond Law School* (1970); Alfred Z. Reed, *Training for the Public Profession of the Law* (1921); John Richie, *The First Hundred Years: A Short History of the School of Law of the University of Virginia* (1978); Robert Stevens, *Law School: Legal Education in America from the 1850s to the 1980s* (1983).

Lawyer, Image of

Two types of lawyers have traditionally appeared in American fiction—conscientious, elite practitioners and predatory shysters. Although southern legal characters tend to conform to these basic stereotypes, they also embody distinctive regional values that set them apart from Yankee and western lawyers.

The typical antebellum practitioner, such as Philpot Wart in John Pendleton Kennedy's plantation novel *Swallow Barn* (1832), is a transplanted English gentleman. Warmhearted, courtly, and a bit eccentric, he can quote passages from the Greek and Latin classics as readily as citations from Coke and Blackstone. With ties of kinship and professional service to the planter class, he also shares the patriarchal ideology of slaveowners. A staunch defender of slavery and states' rights, he recognizes the importance of unwritten law—local custom and community opinion—in regulating the behavior of white southerners.

Even extralegal violence, including dueling and vigilantism, may seem at times an appropriate means of settling personal disputes, and the lawyer is generally as willing to seek personal retribution in affairs of honor as the most thin-skinned of his clients. Judge York Leicester Driscoll in Mark Twain's *Pudd'nhead Wilson* (1894) thus reacts in characteristic fashion to the news that his nephew has taken an assailant to court: "You cur! You scum! You vermin! Do you mean to tell me that blood of my race has suffered a blow and crawled to a court of law about it?"

As a practitioner the antebellum attorney takes a special interest in the plight of the legally disadvantaged, including women, paupers, and slaves. Ishmael Worth, the lawyer-hero of Emma Dorothy Eliza Nevitte (E.D.E.N.) Southworth's *Ishmael*; or, *In the Depths* (1863), wins fame by vindicating the legal rights of women before all-male juries; Edward Clayton in Harriet Beecher Stowe's *Dred: A Tale of the Great Dismal Swamp* (1856) argues unsuccessfully for extending to slaves the legal protection granted as a matter of course to children and other dependents.

More paternalistic and emotionally involved in his client's affairs than his counterparts in other regions, the southern lawyer prizes equity above black-letter rules in all cases. Although he is quite familiar with abstract legal terminology and doctrine, he prefers to appeal directly to the feelings of jurors through spellbinding courtroom oratory in the manner of Patrick Henry. The image of the antebellum practitioner as a wise and chivalrous community leader has persisted in popular fiction, and it figured prominently in Hollywood's sentimental recreation of the Old South in the movies of the 1930s and 1940s.

There was, however, a darker side to antebellum lawyering that found expression in fictional accounts of the frontier bar. Joseph G. Baldwin's humorous classic, *The Flush Times of Alabama and Mississippi* (1853), introduced a variety of lower-class backwoods attorneys who used their minimal legal skills to exploit a gullible public. Typical of the breed was Simon Suggs, Jr., who won his law license in a card game. Although the village pettifogger appeared in much northern fiction as well, he represented for southerners a peculiarly dangerous and subversive force. In a plantation society that cherished personal honor and customary practices, Suggs and his kind threatened to establish a new system of pecuniary values that had no place for patriarchal mores. As quintessential economic men, they repudiated all obligations except those dictated by self-interest. A clear line of descent links them to William Faulkner's unsavory Snopes clan in the 20th century.

The archetypal imagery of a divided profession—patricians versus rednecks—reappeared in Thomas Nelson Page's *Red Rock* (1898), Thomas Dixon's *The Clansman* (1905), and other Reconstruction novels. The legal villains in these works tend to be poor white carpetbaggers and scalawags who are explicitly allied with Yankee businessmen in a conspiracy to "mongrelize" and industrialize southern society. Leading in a grass-roots resistance movement against these alien forces is a younger generation of elite attorneys, who preserve the paternalistic outlook of their elders. Schooled in the racist tenets of social Darwinism, they equate southern "civilization" with white supremacy and invoke higher-law sanctions to justify disfranchisement and other assaults upon the legal rights of blacks. "We will take from an unprofitable servant the ballot he has abused," declares Charles Gaston, the hero of Dixon's *The Leopard's Spots* (1902). "It is the law of nature. It is the law of God." Dixon's ideas, dramatized in D. W. Griffith's powerful film, *Birth of a Nation* (1915), reached mass audiences around the world.

Until the Warren Court precipitated a "Second Reconstruction" of the South by holding segregated schools unconstitutional in *Brown* v. *Board of Education* (1954), fictional lawyers continued to support the racist institutions they had helped create. The self-righteousness of Dixon and Page diminished perceptibly, however, in works that dealt with race relations from World War I to mid-century. Here the typical lawyer was a troubled liberal, who acknowledged the injustice of segregation and risked community censure by defending individual blacks who had been falsely accused of crimes. Yet he never attacked the system directly, because he believed that fundamental changes must await the erosion of custom and the growth of a more enlightened public opinion. Such ambivalence characterized the actions of Gavin Stevens in William Faulkner's *Intruder in the Dust* (1948), Atticus Finch in Harper Lee's *To Kill a Mockingbird* (1960), and Mary Winston—one of the few female attorneys in southern fiction—in Robert Rylee's *Deep Dark River* (1935).

As the civil rights movement intensified in the South during the early 1960s, the image of the tradition-conscious practitioner underwent a striking reevaluation. No reputable novelist of the Second Reconstruction had a kind word for diehard segregationists. In sharp contrast to the literary stereotypes of the late 19th century, legal characters who defended southern autonomy and customary racial practices were now perceived as villains, while NAACP attorneys and other latter-day carpetbaggers received praise for forcing state and local officials to comply with national civil rights laws. The pattern is clearly discernible in Jesse Hill Ford's *The Liberation of Lord Byron Jones* (1965), in which the mindless traditionalism of an aging small-town lawyer serves to radicalize his young partner, Steve Mundine, who resolves: "Never again will I stand aside, defer to age and bigotry. We'll take it [the civil rights struggle] into the streets."

Female and black lawyers did not appear regularly in southern fiction until the 1960s. In scattered earlier works they were often treated with humorous condescension, and for black practitioners the transition from clown to hero was especially marked. Illustrative of popular attitudes in the 1920s were the *Amos 'n' Andy*-type sketches of black professionals in Birmingham, Ala., that Octavius Roy Cohen wrote for the *Saturday*

Evening Post. From their comical antics it is a long step to the civil rights activism of David Champlin, the hero of Ann Fairbairn's *Five Smooth Stones* (1966). Champlin is as idealized a legal character as the virtuous Anglo-Saxons of Page and Dixon, whom he resembles in many ways. Like them, he uses his professional skills to liberate a worthy and long-suffering people.

With the nationalization of civil rights and the reemergence of two-party politics in the South, little remains of the shared values and siege mentality that once gave the region a sense of unique identity. Depictions of contemporary professional life reveal a notable absence of issues or practices that might be labeled distinctively southern. The television series *Hawkins* (1973–74), which starred James Stewart as a West Virginia attorney, contained no identifiably southern themes; and William Harrington's novel *Partners* (1980), which examines the careers of three women lawyers in Houston, Tex., might have been set as easily in any large city. Here, as in other respects, art mirrors the reality of changing political and cultural conditions.

See also EDUCATION: Classical Tradition

Maxwell Bloomfield
The Catholic University
of America

Maxwell Bloomfield, in *Law and American Literature: A Collection of Essays*, ed. Carl S. Smith, John P. McWilliams, Jr., and Maxwell Bloomfield (1983); James McBride Dabbs, *Civil Rights in Recent Southern Fiction* (1969); Floyd G. Watkins, *The Death of Art: Black and White in the Recent Southern Novel* (1970).

Police Forces

Police forces in the South increasingly resemble their counterparts in other regions of the country. The civil rights movement of the 1960s and the influence of national standards of professionalism in law enforcement in the late 1960s and 1970s combined to eliminate the distinctive features of southern law enforcement. With respect to role, organizational structure, personnel practices, operational procedures, and community relations, police forces in all regions of the United States share a high degree of similarity.

Prior to the civil rights movement of the 1960s, law enforcement agencies in the South were primary instruments in the maintenance of the racial caste system. Racial discrimination existed in both personnel practices and law enforcement policies. The civil rights movement swept away the more blatant forms of discrimination, and the increasing acceptance of professionalism in law enforcement supported the ideal of equality under the law. Racial problems persist today, but they are largely indistinguishable from similar problems faced by law enforcement agencies in other regions.

The primary responsibility for law enforcement in the United States is borne by the 3,300 county sheriffs' departments and over 13,500 municipal and township police agencies. Size rather than region accounts for the principal variations among these institutions. The Atlanta Police Department with 1,100 sworn officers, for example, has more in common with other big-city police departments across the country than with the small-town departments in neighboring parts of Georgia. By the same token, the two- or three-officer police department in Georgia is very similar to the small-town police departments in other parts of the country.

Atlanta best exemplifies the impact of national influences on southern law enforcement. In the late 1970s the city of Atlanta hired Lee Brown as police commissioner. Not only was he black but he held a doctorate in criminology and had been the director of justice services (i.e., sheriff) in Multnomah County (Portland), Ore. The fact that he was from outside the South and had academic credentials was almost as significant as his race. By the early 1980s the Atlanta Police Department was one of the three in the entire country (Detroit and the District of Columbia were the other two) that had made substantial progress in the recruitment of black officers.

The county sheriff occupies a unique role in American law enforcement. The oldest law enforcement agency, with roots going back to the earliest English settlements, it has responsibility for all three branches of the criminal justice system. The sheriff polices rural areas, serves as an officer of the court, and maintains the jail. In addition, sheriffs in many states have important civil duties such as tax collection. An elected official, the sheriff has traditionally been one of the most important political figures in county politics. While the role of the sheriff has been greatly diminished in cities, where it is overshadowed by the municipal police, the office continues to be extremely important in rural areas.

The southern sheriff is a stock character in the entertainment and advertising media. The stereotype portrays a fat, uneducated, ill-trained person who is either a comic buffoon or a vicious racist. In fact, southern sheriffs are no worse than their counterparts elsewhere in terms of physical condition, education, training, attitudes, or performance. Regardless of region, larger agencies tend to have higher standards than the very small rural agencies.

Municipal police departments fall into two general categories—big city and small town. Big-city departments are large and complex bureaucratic structures dominated by a military-style command. Civil service systems and collective bargaining agreements impose a high degree of rigidity on all personnel decisions. Southern police departments are somewhat less likely to have collective bargaining agreements between officers and their employers than are departments in other regions. This reflects the general weakness of organized labor in the South.

Big-city police departments have the most complex role of all law enforcement agencies. In addition to enforcing the criminal law, urban police spend most of their time as "peacekeepers." Officers are confronted with all of the social problems found in the urban context: crime, delinquency, family disputes, alcoholism, drug abuse, mental illness, and other problems arising from poverty and racial discrimination. In addition, the crowded urban environment generates conflicts over different standards of moral behavior.

The convergence of poverty and racial discrimination produces the most difficult problems for police. As the real and symbolic manifestations of the established legal order, police are inevitably in conflict with powerless groups. This problem, generally labeled "police-community relations," is found in all urban communities. As a result of the civil rights movement and the drive to make law enforcement more professional, the police-community relations problem in southern cities is little different from that in other American cities.

Small-town police departments in the South, like their counterparts elsewhere, have a much less complex role. Even though the South as a region has a higher rate of criminal violence, particularly in terms of homicide, small towns have comparatively few serious crimes. Peacekeeping in small towns is primarily a matter of coping with minor acts of juvenile vandalism. Small-town police departments have an average of five or six officers. Professional standards, particularly in terms of personnel, are less stringent in small-town police departments than in big-city police agencies.

Samuel Walker
University of Nebraska

John F. Heaphy, ed., *Police Practices: The General Administrative Survey* (1978); National Sheriffs Association, *County Law Enforcement* (n.d.); Elliott M. Rudwick, *Journal of Criminal Law, Criminology, and Police Science* (July–August 1960); Southern Regional Council, *Southern Justice: An Indictment* (1965); U.S. Department of Justice, *Sourcebook of Criminal Justice Statistics* (annual); U.S. Department of Justice, Federal Bureau of Investigation, *Crime in the United States* (annual); Samuel Walker, *The Police in America: An Introduction* (1982), *Popular Justice: A History of American Criminal Justice* (1980).

River Law

River law deals with rights of seamen, harbor workers, shippers, adjoining landowners, and various states where the river constitutes a boundary. Because of the tremendous volume of the waters of the Mississippi River and the relatively soft alluvial floodplain through which it courses, the southern states lying within the lower Mississippi Valley account for a large portion of this body of law. No distinctive "southern" law exists in this field, but the laws of southern states do differ from those elsewhere.

One of the most important property rights is that of the riparian owner—the person living adjacent to a waterway. The value of land bordering on a navigable stream far exceeds that of a parcel located away from the waters. It is access by commerce to the waters that gives the riparian land its value. As Justice Holmes noted, "A river is more than just an amenity, it is a treasure."

Most of the states of the Union follow the common law of England regarding land titles, but in determining the locus of state boundaries marked by navigable streams, the courts have looked to international law for guidance. International law and European custom suggest that when a navigable river constitutes the boundary between two independent states, the line defining this boundary is the middle of the main channel of the stream. However, the courts of the various states in early decisions reached differing conclusions as to what constituted the middle of the channel of a stream, some holding it to be a line equidistant from the banks at ordinary low water and others holding that it was a line marking the deepest water in the channel. The controversy was laid to rest in the case of *State of Iowa* v. *State of Illinois* (1892), wherein Justice Field, writing for the U.S. Supreme Court, concluded that the boundary should be "the middle of the main channel of the stream." This line has also been defined as the deepest channel, the principal channel, the track of navigation, and the thalweg.

As the bed of the river changes because of the gradual caving away of its banks and the concomitant building up of the opposite shore by the deposition of alluvion—a process called accretion—the boundary follows the migration of the river. However, during periods of great floods the river sometimes leaves its old channel by cutting a new channel across the narrow neck of an elongated "point," followed in time by the adoption of the new channel by navigation.

Numerous disputes have arisen as to the apportionment of alluvion that has built up against a river bank resulting in the creation of an elongated body of land called a "point" or "point bar." While all courts hold that this alluvion belongs to the owners of the banks to which it is attached, they are not at all in agreement as to how it is to be divided between coterminous owners of the banks. Generally, they all seek an equitable apportionment. The rule most often followed is that of allotting to each landowner as much of the new bank as would be in proportion to his ownership of the original bank. Thus, if A owned 500 feet and B owned 1,000 feet of old bankline and the new point bar measured 1,300 feet, A would be given 600 feet along the new bank and B would be allotted 1,200 feet with the boundary connecting the old point of division with the new point of division by a straight line.

There is no uniformity among the states regarding the ownership of the beds of rivers, and each state determines its own laws. Thus, Mississippi holds that the riparian owner holds title out to the "thread" or "thalweg" of the stream, while in Louisiana, Arkansas, and Tennessee title is vested in the states. Again, there is no uniformity as to whether the "bed" stops at the low-water mark or high-water mark on the bank.

If an island forms on the bed of the stream by the deposition of alluvion, it becomes the property of the owner of the bed. However, if an island builds downstream to such an extent that it crosses the boundary of a downstream owner, the owner of the downstream bed gets title to as much of the island as is located on his portion of the riverbed.

All private rights in the bed and bank of a stream are subject to the superior right of navigation by the public. Therefore, the government can dredge or construct dikes in the interest of navigation. Structures that might cause an obstruction to navigation, such as piers and wharves, must first be authorized by public authorities.

See also ENVIRONMENT: River Life; Rivers and Lakes; / Mississippi River

M. Emmett Ward
Vicksburg, Mississippi

States' Rights Constitutionalism

States' rights constitutionalism holds that in the federal system the states retain certain rights and powers that cannot be taken from them. The doctrine has never been a whole cloth; generations of southerners have tailored their constitutional views to fit changing social and economic realities.

Diversity characterized southern attitudes in 1787 toward relations between state and nation. Led by James Madison of Virginia, southern Federalists wanted a strong central government of enumerated powers that was also responsive to local self-interests. Ardent states' rights proponents, such as Patrick Henry of Virginia, denounced the new Constitution because it left unclear the balance between state and national powers. They also rebelled at Madison's successful effort in 1789 in preventing the insertion of the word "expressly" in the Tenth Amendment as a limit on national powers. Southern Federalists won important concessions for the peculiar institution of slavery in return for their support of the national Constitution.

States' rights constitutionalism after 1787 evolved from a passive doctrine of resistance to national authority based on strict construction to an aggressive theory of state sovereignty. Southern proponents of the Constitution, like Madison and Thomas Jefferson, believed that the national government should remain sensitive to local self-interest and agrarian values. Thus, they resisted northern Federalist attempts to consolidate national power. Madison and Jefferson in 1798 most fully argued their position when they denounced the Alien and Sedition Acts. Their famous Virginia and Kentucky resolutions insisted on strict construction of the delegated powers of the national government and set forth the theory that a state might interpose itself between the citizenry and the national government in order to nullify a federal law. Few southerners supported the broad implications of the resolutions, and both Jefferson and Madison in the White House frequently adopted an expansive view of federal powers.

Economic depression and the large slave population in the Southeast during the 1820s radicalized states' rights constitutionalism. John C. Calhoun of South Carolina linked federal tariff policies to the region's economic woes. He pushed beyond the strict constructionism of Madison and Jefferson by asserting that the states could not only interpose their authority to nullify a federal law but also break from the Union altogether. During the nullification controversy of 1832 South Carolina's attempt to put Calhoun's theory into action faltered before Unionist sentiment in the Palmetto State, the leadership of Andrew Jackson, and the refusal of other southern states to lend support.

Under the pressure of the slavery expansion issue, states' rights constitutionalism emerged during the 1850s as a doctrine of power and not of right. Jefferson Davis of Mississippi replaced Calhoun as the South's most radical proponent of this view of states' rights. Confronted with a hostile antislavery movement in the North and declining power in Congress, Davis claimed that the federal judiciary was responsible for sustaining slaveholders' property rights in the new territories. Because the states were sovereign entities, Davis argued, the national government had a constitutional responsibility to protect slaveholders' rights aggressively. Ironically, northern antislavery forces resorted to the traditional Jeffersonian notion of states' rights as a passive restraint on the national government to justify their attempts to frustrate enforcement of the Fugitive Slave Act of 1850. The Supreme Court in *Dred Scott* v. *Sanford* in 1857 confirmed Davis's arguments, but it was a Pyrrhic victory; the social calculus of the peculiar institution and the election of Abraham Lincoln in 1860 culminated in the most extreme form of states' rights—secession. The ideals of local self-government and strict construction did retain vitality, however; the Confederate wartime effort, under Davis's leadership, suffered because authorities in the southern states refused to cooperate fully with the Confederate government in Richmond.

Confederate defeat marked the end of exaggerated claims for states' rights constitutionalism. Southern Democratic leaders in the post-Reconstruction era reaffirmed the traditional passive meaning of the doctrine in their successful efforts to deny free blacks the national protection of the Fourteenth and Fifteenth Amendments. The Supreme Court abetted this process in a series of decisions that culminated in the 1896 case of *Plessy* v. *Ferguson*. The justices sustained segregation by race in public places as long as the states provided equal facilities.

Events inside and outside the South during the 20th century undermined this coupling of states' rights and a dual system of race relations. The Supreme Court beginning in the mid-1930s broadened the interpretation of the commerce and other "elastic" clauses of the Constitution and accepted limited incorporation of the Bill of Rights into the Fourteenth Amendment. The justices enhanced the powers of the national government at the expense of the states. Moreover, the moral legitimacy of states' rights ebbed as a result of southern resistance to ending de jure racial segregation. Following the Supreme Court's decision in *Brown* v. *Board of Education* in

1954, southern Democratic politicians orchestrated a strategy of massive resistance in order to prevent integration of public facilities. Governors Orval Faubus of Arkansas and George C. Wallace of Alabama resorted to Calhoun's exploded theories in futile attempts to block integration of public schools and universities. States' rights appeared in the South to be little more than a code word for racism.

The principle that the states retain certain distinct powers remains constitutionally alive within the American federal system. But the absorption of the South into the mainstream of American culture and the demise of the section's legally mandated dual system of race relations have made the South more like the rest of the nation and, therefore, less dependent on states' rights constitutionalism.

See also HISTORY AND MANNERS: / Davis, Jefferson; Jefferson, Thomas; POLITICS: / Calhoun, John C.; Faubus, Orval; Wallace, George C.

Kermit L. Hall
University of Florida

William Anderson, *The Nation and the States, Rivals or Partners?* (1955); Numan Bartley, *The Rise of Massive Resistance: Race and Politics in the South during the 1950s* (1969); Arthur Bestor, Jr., *Journal of the Illinois State Historical Society* (Summer 1961); Daniel Elazar, *American Federalism: A View from the States* (1972); William W. Freehling, *Prelude to Civil War: The Nullification Controversy in South Carolina, 1816–1836* (1966); James J. Kilpatrick, *The Sovereign States: Notes of a Citizen of Virginia* (1957); Alpheus T. Mason, ed., *The States Rights Debate: Antifederalism and the Constitution* (1972); Frank L. Owsley, *States' Rights in the Confederacy* (1925).

Supreme Court

Writing more than a half-century ago, Charles S. Sydnor observed that the two traditional sources of authority in the South were the Bible and the Constitution. Relying on the Constitution, the region's leaders developed a cultural constitutionalism intended to protect regional values and institutions from external forces. At the heart of cultural constitutionalism lay the political theory of states' rights, which preserved the powers of the states from any encroachment by the national government. The Supreme Court's interpretation of the Constitution remained compatible for a century and a half with the region's dominant values. But during the last half-century the Supreme Court has played a major role in reshaping the institutional structure of the region and forcing changes in the South's public values. As a result, Supreme Court decisions have become the focal point of many of the region's modern controversies.

By far the most significant subject of judicial interpretation has been the Supreme Court's definition of the constitutional terms of race relations. During the course of a century, the Supreme Court sanctioned slavery, legitimized segregation, and ordered integration of public institutions. Through the antebellum period, a series of Supreme Court opinions sustained the institution of slavery. These cases culminated in 1857 with the Dred Scott case. In that case, the Court decisively confronted the conflicting values that circumscribed the slaveowners' approach to the institution of slavery—the dilemma over whether slaves would be treated as property or as human beings. Dred Scott was a black slave who had been the property of an army surgeon. Scott had been taken by his owner into Illinois and into Wisconsin Territory, which was free territory under the Missouri Compromise. Scott eventually returned to Missouri with his owner. The surgeon died and title to Scott passed to a New York resident named John F. A. Sanford. In 1846 Scott brought suit in the Missouri courts to obtain his freedom. He claimed that he had become a free person because he had been taken into free territory. The Missouri courts rejected Scott's plea, and his attorneys initiated a new suit in federal courts. After years of litigation, the Supreme Court held on 6 March 1857 that Scott could not sue for his freedom and that he was still a slave. Chief Justice Roger B. Taney argued that Scott could not sue because he was not a citizen. He was not a citizen because he was black and a slave. In effect, Scott had no rights under the Constitution.

The abolition of slavery in the aftermath of the Civil War placed race relations in a state of flux. By the early 1890s an increasingly rigid system of legal racial separation was in place throughout the region. The Supreme Court was unwilling to challenge the new system. In 1896, in the celebrated case of *Plessy* v. *Ferguson*, the Court gave constitutional legitimacy to the so-called separate-but-equal principle. The opinion feigned a commitment to the concept of equality but consigned black southerners to a status little removed from slavery.

During the next half-century, carefully drawn constitutional challenges gradually chipped away at legal segregation by means of a slow and tortuous strategy. The Supreme Court did not abandon generations of inaction and aggressively assert the basic political and civil rights of all citizens until 1954. In *Brown* v. *Board of Education* the Court attacked the separate-but-equal principle by concluding that in public education separate facilities were "inherently unequal." Thus the segregated educational systems of the southern states violated the equal protection clause of the Fourteenth Amendment to the Constitution. Opponents of the *Brown* decision throughout the South placed blame not on the Constitution, but on the Supreme Court's interpretation of the Constitution. In 1957 resistance to *Brown* was encouraged by 101 southern congressmen who signed the "Southern Manifesto," whereby they pledged to "use all lawful means to bring about a reversal of this decision which is contrary to the Constitution and to prevent the use of force in its implementation." Eventually, force was used and the Supreme Court's interpretation of the Constitution prevailed. The Court's attack on segregated educational institutions proved to be merely the first step in a long struggle against all forms of racial discrimination in the public life of the South.

The South's system of race relations was not the only element of the traditional southern value system to come under Supreme Court review. Agrarianism, however defined, has been an essential element of the distinctive regional culture for the last 200 years. A major source of continuing agrarian dominance in southern public life has been rural control over state legislative politics. By the 1950s, burgeoning urban areas in the region were severely underrepresented in state legislatures, while the rural areas and adjacent small towns enjoyed representation far in excess of what their declining populations would warrant.

In the 1962 case of *Baker* v. *Carr* the Supreme Court abandoned its long-standing decision not to intervene in legislative reapportionment matters. *Baker* v. *Carr* challenged the 1901 Tennessee statute that had provided the method of periodically reapportioning the state legislature. Provisions of the law assured continued rural dominance of the legislature at the expense of the urban areas. The decision held that it was permissible to challenge the statute as a violation of the equal protection clause of the Fourteenth Amendment but provided little in the way of a remedy. Two years later the Supreme Court embarked on a course of simple majoritarianism in reapportionment matters. In *Reynolds* v. *Sims* the Court struck down a complex Alabama reapportionment plan and ordered the implementation of a reapportionment plan based on the principle of one person, one vote. The consequence of these decisions has been gradually to shift the locus of political power in the states from the rural areas to the cities. One other likely consequence may well be the gradual erosion of agrarianism as a dominant value in the culture of the region.

The third major element of the region's culture that has come under Supreme Court scrutiny has been religious fundamentalism. The flash points of the conflict between regional cultural values and the Supreme Court have been the issue of school prayer and the teaching of evolution in the public schools. In each case religious conservatives have been especially forceful in pressing their case in favor of school prayer and against the teaching of evolution. In like manner, Supreme Court opinions have stood as the major bulwark against the widespread adoption of both these practices in the public school systems throughout the region. Rulings in these cases have raised opposition to the Supreme Court opinions that was surpassed only by the desegregation cases. Unlike the desegregation and reapportionment cases, however, the school prayer and evolution cases seem unlikely to alter the South's tradition of religious conservatism. If anything, the zealous defense of religious values may strengthen their place in the pantheon of southern life.

Robert Haws
University of Mississippi

Richard Cortner, *The Apportionment Cases* (1970); Don E. Fehrenbacher, *The Dred Scott Case: Its Significance in American Law and Politics* (1978); Richard Kluger, *Simple Justice: The History of Brown v. Board of Education and Black America's Struggle for Equality* (1976); Charles Lofgren, *The Plessy Case: A Legal-Historical Approach* (1987).

Black, Hugo

(1886–1971) U.S. senator, Supreme Court justice.

Through intelligence, grit, determination, and temporary alliance with the Ku Klux Klan, Hugo Lafayette Black rose from simple origins in the Alabama hills to the U.S. Senate (1927–37) and the Supreme Court (1937–71). During 34 years as an associate justice, Black, whose only prior judicial experience had been as judge of Birmingham's police court, forged a reputation as an eloquent defender of First Amendment freedoms. The seeming paradox of a former Klansman evolving into an ardent civil libertarian remains an intriguing episode in Supreme Court annals.

Son of a small-town merchant, Black was born 27 February 1886 in Clay County, Ala. He completed his formal education in the two-year law school of the University of Alabama, Tuscaloosa, in 1906. By the early 1920s he was a highly successful damage-suit lawyer, suspected by Birmingham's establishment of being a "Bolshevik" because of his ties to organized labor. Black joined the Klan in 1923 by swearing allegiance to its principles, including white supremacy and anti-Catholicism. Thereby he allied himself with a large, highly disciplined organization soon to dominate state politics. The Alabama Klan of the 1920s reflected not only the prejudices, ignorance, and inherent violence of numerous poor, white Protestants but also their desire for a share in political and economic power from which they had long been virtually excluded. Undoubtedly, Black knew of the Klan's excesses against individuals; evidently, his personal ambition persuaded him to believe that, over the long run, the Klan's democratizing impact could prove beneficial to these less-privileged and underrepresented white Alabamians. With the crucial aid of Klan-controlled votes, Black achieved in 1926 the otherwise unattainable office of U.S. senator. Although he had resigned from the Klan for appearance's sake at the start of his campaign, he remained politically indebted to the Invisible Empire until the early 1930s, by which time most Alabamians had become temporarily satiated with violence and appeals to prejudice.

Senator Black proved an ardent New Dealer, even alarming Franklin Roosevelt by advocating a 30-hour work week. As a Senate investigator he dramatically demonstrated his hostility to special privilege and entrenched interests. Black's progressive record, coupled with the Senate's tradition of confirming its members nominated to high office, led Roosevelt to make him the first appointee in an ultimately successful endeavor to reshape the Supreme Court in favor of federal activism in economic, political, and social spheres. Despite the initial skepticism of some of his judicial colleagues and a nationwide outburst over his former Klan membership, Black became a major intellectual force on the high

Hugo Black, U.S. Supreme Court justice, 1926

court, pressing his fundamental concept that the guarantees of the Bill of Rights are absolute and should bind states as well as the nation. To the acute dismay of many fellow southerners, Justice Black sided with the Court majority to strike down legal segregation in schools and public facilities; to advance the principle of one man, one vote; and to outlaw reading of official prayers in public schools. Through the unlikely instrument of the Klan, the Senate and the Supreme Court gained the services of a type of southerner rarely chosen for public office in the 20th century—a latter-day disciple of Jeffersonian and Jacksonian democracy.

Virginia Van der Veer Hamilton
University of Alabama
at Birmingham

Howard Ball, *The Vision and the Dream of Hugo L. Black: An Examination of a Judicial Philosophy* (1975); Hugo Black, Jr., *My Father: A Remembrance* (1975); Gerald T. Dunne, *Hugo Black and the Judicial Revolution* (1977); Virginia Van der Veer Hamilton, *Hugo Black: The Alabama Years* (1972); Virginia Van der Veer Hamilton, ed., *Hugo Black and the Bill of Rights: Proceedings of the First Hugo Black Symposium in American History on the Bill of Rights and American Democracy* (1978).

Black Codes

One legal response of southern white governments to the end of the Civil War and the passage of the Thirteenth Amendment was the adoption of laws purporting to bestow upon the newly freed men and women certain civil rights. Mississippi passed the first of these codes in 1865. They granted rights of blacks to hold personal property, intermarry, sue in state courts, swear out criminal warrants, and testify against whites under certain conditions. The right to vote, however, was not given to blacks under these codes.

Black codes were primarily promulgated to control a newly fluid black labor force. For example, Section 1 of the Mississippi Black Code allowed blacks to sue and be sued and to acquire and dispose of personal property, but limited their property owning to incorporated towns or cities and severely hampered individual rural agricultural pursuits. Involuntary labor was authorized by statutes concerning vagrancy, peonage, work contracts, enticement, convict labor, surety, and emigrant agency. Law and terror were successfully combined to enforce what those who opposed black codes called a "new slavery."

Congressional Reconstruction required temporary abandonment of many of the black codes. After Reconstruction most states reconstituted the involuntary labor sections. These vestiges of the original black codes remained a part of southern social and economic life until the civil rights movement of the 1950s and 1960s.

See also VIOLENCE: / Peonage

John R. Wunder
Clemson University

William Cohen, *Journal of Southern History* (February 1976); Theodore B. Wilson, *The Black Codes of the South* (1965).

Brown v. *Board of Education*

On 17 May 1954 the U.S. Supreme Court ruled in *Brown* v. *Board of Education* that separate educational facilities for blacks and whites "are inherently unequal." With that decision the Court overturned the precedent of "separate but equal" set by the 1896 *Plessy* v. *Ferguson* case and set the stage for the civil rights movement of the 1960s.

The National Association for the Advancement of Colored People (NAACP) played a major role in the instigation of the case, which centered around Linda Brown, a black child denied admission to a Topeka, Kan., elementary school because of her race. *Brown* brought together five related cases from South Carolina, Delaware, Virginia, Kansas, and the District of Columbia, all of which challenged racial segregation as a violation of the equal protection clause of the Fourteenth Amendment. The arguments heard by the Court centered on the intentions of the framers and ratifiers of that amendment.

In the brief, unanimous opinion delivered by Chief Justice Earl Warren, the Court ruled that the separate-but-equal doctrine, which held that racial segregation was permissible as long as equal facilities were provided for both races, was in violation of the equal-protection clause. The justices wrote that the segregation of white and black children in public education "generates a feeling of inferiority" among the black children that could have an irreversible detrimental effect on the rest of their lives. In the spring of 1955 the Court heard arguments about how their *Brown* decision might be implemented. At the end of these arguments the Court remanded the four cases back to the district courts with the order to take whatever steps were necessary to "admit to public schools on a racially nondiscriminatory basis with all deliberate speed the parties in these cases."

The *Brown* decision and the Court's demand for swift integration did not bring about the immediate desegregation of public schools. The only school boards legally bound by the *Brown* decision were those named directly in the cases on which the Court ruled, and the only laws held unconstitutional were those specific laws cited by the plaintiffs. Ordinarily, rules of constitutional law decided by the Supreme Court are universally accepted and implemented where they apply. Technically, however, compliance is voluntary, and there was intense resistance to implementation of the controversial *Brown* decision. The political branches of government were employed to speed integration. The threat by the Department of Health, Education, and Welfare (HEW) under the Civil Rights Act of 1964 to withhold federal education funds from school districts that persisted in segregation policies was one such way of encouraging integration. Many school districts began busing students from one neighborhood to another in an effort to achieve integration. Many southern states sought to obstruct integration through "massive resistance," and in 1965 less than 10 percent of the South's black students were in integrated public schools.

The *Brown* doctrine, which said that segregated schools are illegal, was extended to apply to other public facilities through separate court cases involving, for instance, the segregation of beaches (in Maryland), golf courses (in Atlanta), and recreation facilities (in Memphis). Probably the most famous case ever decided by the Supreme Court, *Brown* v. *Board of Education* was the first step in major reform of not only public education but also race laws and policies in almost all aspects of American life.

Karen M. McDearman
University of Mississippi

Robert Cushman, *Cases in Constitutional Law* (1975); Richard Kluger, *Simple Justice: The History of Brown v. Board of Education and Black America's Struggle for Equality* (1976); J. Harvie Wilkinson III, *From Brown to Bakke: The Supreme Court and School Integration, 1954–1978* (1979).

Ervin, Sam, Jr.

(1896–1985) Lawyer and U.S. senator.

Samuel James Ervin, Jr., graduated at age 26 from Harvard Law School in 1922. He subsequently practiced law with his father in Morganton, N.C., held various local and state offices, and from 1954 to 1974 served in the U.S. Senate.

Ervin's Senate career spanned a tumultuous era in the history of the South and the nation. Ervin viewed the South's dual system of race relations as a social reality that only the individual states could change. In the wake of the Supreme Court's 1954 decision in *Brown* v. *Board of Education*, he joined other southern members of Congress in signing the 1956 Southern Manifesto that denounced court-ordered integration. Ervin in 1960 filibustered the Eisenhower Administration's civil rights proposals. He also opposed the civil rights acts of 1964, 1965, and 1968. Yet Ervin was neither an apostle of massive resistance nor a racist. He rejected radical states' rights ideas of nullification and interposition. Moreover, on questions of civil liberties, where the racial issue did not threaten his political base in North Carolina, Ervin was liberal. He supported the 1966 Bail Reform Act and the 1968 Indian Bill of Rights.

Sam Ervin, North Carolina country lawyer and U.S. senator, 1970s

Late in his Senate career Ervin emerged as a significant voice in constitutional matters. In 1971 he orchestrated the Senate attack on spying by army intelligence on civilians. More dramatically, as chairperson of the Select Committee on Presidential Campaign Activities in 1973, Ervin treated the American public to a lesson in constitutional government. His homespun stories, biblical quotations, and pointed questions captured the imagination of a national television audience. The commonsense wisdom of this southern country lawyer was more than a match for the Watergate conspirators.

Ervin believed that persons were only truly free when they accepted responsibility for their own lives. This notion paled before the historical realities of southern race relations, but it was an otherwise fundamentally correct insight into the nature of southern character. Sam Ervin the southerner, moreover, in his confrontation with Richard Nixon's White House, reaffirmed for all Americans the connection between this ideal and the value of limited constitutional government.

Kermit L. Hall
University of Florida

Paul L. Clancy, *Just a Country Lawyer: A Biography of Senator Sam Ervin* (1974); Dick Dabney, *A Good Man: The Life of Sam J. Ervin* (1976).

Fifth Circuit Court of Appeals

Spanning the Lower South from Florida to Texas, the Fifth Circuit Court of Appeals was one of the regional federal circuit courts created in 1891. Following the 1954 decision of the U.S. Supreme Court in *Brown* v. *Board of Education*, the Fifth Circuit was called upon to supervise the dismantling of separate schools and the elimination of racial discrimination in the region. Dominated by several prominent liberal judges, notably Elbert P. Tuttle and John Minor Wisdom, the court repeatedly insisted upon compliance with desegregation despite widespread public hostility. Indeed, the Fifth Circuit has been described as "the nation's greatest civil rights tribunal." This court took the lead in fashioning new remedies for school segregation and devising streamlined procedures to expedite discrimination cases. One of the most celebrated matters handled by this court was the admission of James Meredith to the University of Mississippi.

The judges who constituted the circuit bench held widely differing opinions on many issues. The tribunal was racked by a bitter schism over the handling of contempt proceedings against Governor Ross Barnett and by the allegations of Judge Ben F. Cameron that the Fifth Circuit's three-judge panels were being stacked in favor of liberals.

In addition to difficult racial cases, the Fifth Circuit was required to handle an extremely heavy volume of general litigation. In fact, the docket of the Fifth Circuit was dominated by cases involving economic issues such as labor law and taxation. Proposals to divide the Fifth Circuit were blocked by desegregation proponents who feared that the resulting new circuits might prove to be more conservative. Instead, Congress repeatedly enlarged the size of the tribunal until it reached the unwieldy number of 26 judges. This was by far the largest circuit court in the federal system. Finally, despite lingering opposition from civil rights activists, Congress voted to split the Fifth Circuit effective in October of 1981. Alabama, Georgia, and Florida were placed in the newly created Eleventh Circuit Court of Appeals.

James W. Ely, Jr.
Vanderbilt University

Jack Bass, *Unlikely Heroes* (1981); J. Woodford Howard, Jr., *Courts of Appeals in the Federal Judicial System: A Study of the Second, Fifth, and District of Columbia Circuits* (1981); Frank T. Read and Lucy S. McGough, *Let Them Be Judged: The Judicial Integration of the Deep South* (1978).

Finch, Atticus

A major character in Harper Lee's novel, *To Kill a Mockingbird* (1960), Atticus Finch represents the conscience of the white South in the years before the advent of the Warren Court and the civil rights revolution. As a descendant of local slaveowners, he well understands the deep-rooted racial prejudices that continue to exist in

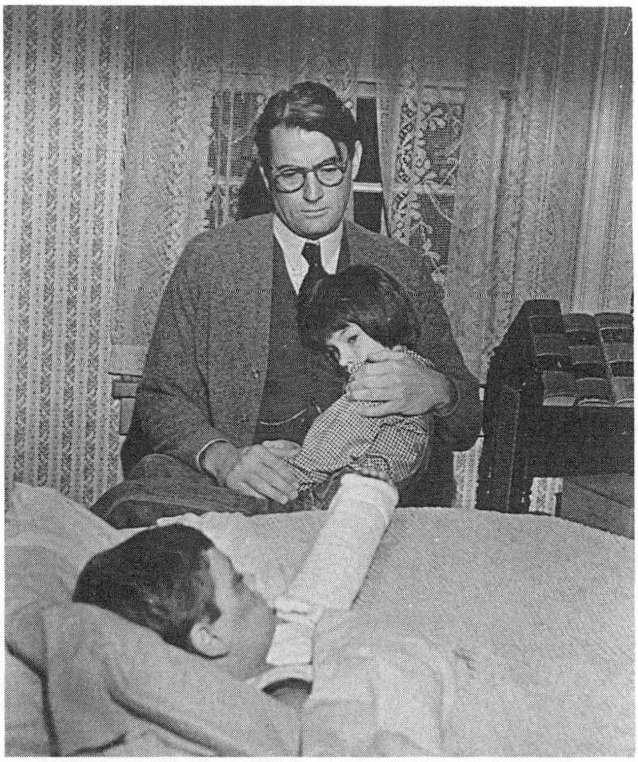

Gregory Peck as Atticus Finch in the film made from Harper Lee's Pulitzer Prize–winning novel To Kill a Mockingbird *(1963)*

Maycomb, the small Alabama town in which he practices law during the Depression. Mild-mannered and scholarly, he is a stubborn idealist who believes in equality before the law for everyone, regardless of color or class. When Tom Robinson, a black man, is accused of raping the daughter of a poor white ne'er-do-well, Atticus is appointed by the court to defend him. Convinced of his client's innocence, he makes a determined effort to save his life, despite the growing opposition of the white community. His neighbors denounce him as a "nigger-lover," his children suffer insult and ridicule at school, and a mob threatens his life on the eve of the trial.

In the courtroom Atticus destroys the credibility of the prosecution's witnesses through skillful cross-examination. There is no proof that a rape occurred, he demonstrates, and strong circumstantial evidence suggests that the complainant, a lonely girl, was savagely beaten by her own father because she had made sexual advances to a black man. Reminding the white male jurors that "in our courts all men are created equal," Atticus pleads with them to abandon racial stereotyping and to decide the case on its merits.

After deliberating for several hours, the jury returns with a verdict of guilty, and Robinson is sentenced to death. The time has not yet come when southern juries will accept the word of a black man against that of any white man, Atticus explains to his children. Yet there are some indications that the grip of custom may be loosening. As a neighbor observes, only Atticus could have kept a jury out so long in a rape case. Through his gentlemanly appeals to shared southern values of honor and paternalism, he gradually persuades other white southerners to reexamine their inherited racial attitudes.

To Kill a Mockingbird received the Pulitzer Prize for fiction in 1961, and Gregory Peck won an Oscar for his portrayal of Atticus Finch in the movie version in 1962.

Maxwell Bloomfield
The Catholic University of America

Foreman, Percy

(b. 1902) Lawyer.

As a defense lawyer, Percy Eugene Foreman combined his knowledge of law, his courtroom prowess, and his thirst for wealth to achieve legendary status in his native Texas and throughout the nation's legal community. His own celebrity status has attracted celebrated defendants and, in turn, been enhanced by his association with them.

Born in Polk County, Tex., in a backwoods area known as the Big Thicket, Foreman is the son of a former county jailer and sheriff. At eight years of age, he began earning money by shining shoes. He soon bought out his sole competitor in the town of Livingston and added a delivery business to his growing empire. By age 11 he was making as much money as most adults in the impoverished east Texas community. His next enterprise was loading cotton onto trains. While his bid of 25 cents per bale was low, he hired laborers at 8 cents per bale to do the actual loading. At 15 he quit school and at age 16, having saved $6,500, he moved to Houston. Subsequently he briefly attended Staunton Military Academy in Virginia before joining a chautauqua company as an advance man. He delivered his first public oration as an 18-year-old with the company in Burnside, Ky.

Returning to his native state, Foreman enrolled at the University of Texas. He attended classes part of each year but continued to tour with the chautauqua company as a circuit manager and lecturer. At age 25 Foreman completed law school, having served as president of the student body during his senior year.

In December 1927 Foreman formed a partnership with J. W. Lockett with offices across from the Rice Hotel in Houston. The Rice remained a favorite Foreman hangout through much of his career. A few months after forming the partnership, he went to work for the district attorney in Houston. In 1929 he returned to private practice when his boss failed to win reelection. In 1933 Foreman became an assistant district attorney with a special interest in keeping gamblers from nearby Galveston out of Houston. In 1935 he again left the district attorney's office for private practice. His 1940 bid for election as district attorney failed.

Foreman's legendary status owes much to his record in capital punishment cases. By the late 1960s he had represented over 1,000 defendants in such cases, only one of whom had been executed; only 55 had even served time in prison. His most celebrated defendants include Jack Ruby, James Earl Ray, General Edwin Walker, and Candy Mossler.

Although part of his celebrity status stems from his successful record and the clients attracted by it, some of it derives from Foreman's being a member of that small fraternity of lawyers who have become wealthy doing criminal defense work. He received both his Houston home and a New York City co-op apartment as fees. His obvious early interest in making money has not abated over the years.

Foreman is the most famous of a special breed of southern attorney; Richard "Racehorse" Haynes and Warren Burnett are other examples. Although Foreman has tried cases across the country, he has the physical stature—at 6′4″—and the down-home manner that make him the literal embodiment of that dominating courtroom presence, the Texas trial lawyer.

C. Martin Wilson III
Austin, Texas

Michael Dorman, *King of the Courtroom: Percy Foreman for the Defense* (1969).

Frank, Leo, Case

Described by Leonard Dinnerstein as "one of the most infamous outbursts of anti-Semitic feeling in the [history of] the United States," the Leo Frank case inspired formation of both the second Ku Klux Klan and the Anti-Defamation League of B'nai B'rith. The case began on Confederate Memorial Day in 1913 with the murder and mutilation of Mary Phagan, a 13-year-old employee of an Atlanta pencil factory. The mayor and an anxious populace, aroused by yellow journalism, demanded that the police find her killer quickly. They responded by arresting the victim's boss, Leo Frank. A Jew from New York, Frank rapidly became a focal point for the resentment toward factories and outsiders that rapid industrialization had ignited in southern traditionalists.

Frank's Atlanta trial took place in an atmosphere of public hysteria and amidst threats of mob violence. The prosecution, led by Solicitor Hugh Dorsey (who rode the publicity he gained from this case into the governorship), portrayed Frank as a lecherous employer who preyed on young factory girls. The state relied heavily on the testimony of Jim Conley, a black janitor with a criminal record, who claimed to have been asked by Frank to help him hide a body and to write two notes found next to Phagan's remains. Evidence available to police and prosecutors strongly suggested that he, not Frank, was the killer. Nevertheless, the jury convicted the Jewish factory manager. Although he believed Frank was innocent, Judge Leonard Roane denied his motion for a new trial and sentenced him to death.

A good deal of new evidence soon surfaced, which raised further doubt about Frank's guilt. Efforts to secure a new trial failed, however, despite an appeal carried to the U.S. Supreme Court. The Court also spurned a petition seeking Frank's release on a writ of habeas corpus. He gained a temporary reprieve when Governor John Slaton sacrificed a promising political career by commuting his sentence to life in prison. Then, on 16 August 1915, a group of respectable citizens from Mary Phagan's hometown, Marietta, Ga., abducted Frank from the state prison farm at Milledgeville and hanged him.

Frank's death and the events preceding it aroused intense interest throughout the country. Governors, state legislators, and members of Congress joined more than 100,000 other Americans in efforts to save Frank's life. This outpouring of public sentiment and the nationwide press coverage of the case owed much to the efforts of Jewish leaders, who viewed this incident as a threatening manifestation of anti-Semitism, comparable to France's infamous Dreyfus affair.

Concerned Jewish groups persisted in trying to clear Frank's name, and evidence continued to surface. In 1982 a former office boy at Frank's factory, Alonzo Mann, came forward and said that he had seen another man carrying Mary Phagan's slain body. As of 1983 Governor Joe Frank Harris publicly supported a posthumous pardon of Leo Frank, but the Georgia Board of Pardons and Paroles refused to take such action. The Anti-Defamation League, the American Jewish Committee, and the Atlanta Jewish Federation submitted another petition focusing on the denial of justice to Frank, and the Board of Pardons and Paroles reversed itself and granted the pardon in March 1986, 71 years after the lynching of Leo Frank.

See also ETHNIC LIFE: / Jews

Michael R. Belknap
University of Georgia

Leonard Dinnerstein, *The Leo Frank Case* (1968).

Greensboro Sit-in

The sit-in demonstrations in Greensboro, N.C., marked an important turning point in the history of the civil rights movement. In February of 1960 four black college students sat down at a Woolworth's lunch counter and demanded service. Woolworth's, like other chain stores in the South, sold merchandise to all customers but denied black patrons the use of its lunch counters. The demonstrations rapidly grew in intensity. More black students participated and occupied the lunch-counter seats. White counterdemonstrators soon appeared. The incidents captured national headlines and within a week sit-ins had spread to Winston-Salem, Durham, and other cities across the South. There was supportive picketing in the North against local branches of chain stores that denied service to blacks in the South.

At the end of February the students agreed to suspend their sit-ins while negotiations were in progress. When discussions failed to produce any resolution, direct action was resumed. Woolworth's then closed its lunch-counter operation. The students successfully mobilized the entire black community in support of their cause. Local blacks participated in an economic boycott and refused to patronize stores that would not serve them food. In the face of mounting business losses, Woolworth's quietly opened its food service in July to all persons.

Sit-in at Woolworth's store, Greensboro, N.C., February 1960

It was ironic that Greensboro was the site for such a watershed in race relations. The home of five colleges, Greensboro had long enjoyed a reputation for moderation on the racial issue. City leaders had early announced that they would comply with the school desegregation requirements of *Brown*. Blacks, nonetheless, shared a sense of continuous frustration in achieving equal rights. Only minimal school integration had occurred by 1960 and other institutions remained racially separate.

This spontaneous action by Greensboro students provided a catalyst for a decade of direct, active protests. The Greensboro sit-ins altered the nature of the civil rights movement in two important respects. First, the sit-ins suggested new and more dynamic methods by which protests could be expressed. Shortly thereafter the Freedom Rides began to challenge racial segregation in bus facilities. No longer were blacks content to await the often slow and elusive results of court decrees. Second, blacks were no longer willing to permit moderate whites to define civil rights objectives. Blacks were increasingly willing to jeopardize the goodwill of white moderates and liberals in order to follow their own agendas for social reform, which would culminate in the black-power demands of the late 1960s.

James W. Ely, Jr.
Vanderbilt University

William H. Chafe, *Civilities and Civil Rights: Greensboro, North Carolina, and the Black Struggle for Freedom* (1980); Miles Wolff, *Lunch at the Five and Ten: The Greensboro Sit-Ins* (1970).

Herndon, Angelo, Case

The most famous civil liberties and civil rights case in Georgia during the 1930s centered around Angelo Herndon, a young black Communist. A native of Ohio, Herndon moved to the Deep South in the early Depression years in search of work and traded his fundamentalist Christianity for communism in 1930 while living in Birmingham, Ala. Assigned by the Communist party to Atlanta, the 19-year-old Herndon organized a large interracial demonstration in June 1932, protesting the suspension of public relief. As a result, Atlanta police eventually arrested Herndon and charged him with attempting "to incite insurrection" against the state of Georgia, a capital offense. In his January 1933 trial, Herndon was represented by black attorneys Benjamin J. Davis, Jr., and John Geer, who boldly challenged the exclusion of blacks from local juries, while the prosecuting attorneys responded with an emotional condemnation of communism. An all-white jury quickly found Herndon guilty and sentenced him to 18 to 20 years in prison.

The seeming injustice of Herndon's conviction helped stimulate greater solidarity among Atlanta blacks and prompted a somewhat more assertive stance toward racial discrimination. Through vigorous publicity efforts the International Labor Defense, a Communist-influenced legal defense organization, eventually turned the affair into a national cause célèbre. A team of prominent attorneys headed by Whitney North Seymour of New York City twice appealed the conviction to the U.S. Supreme Court, which in *Herndon* v. *Lowry* (1937) declared the Georgia insurrection law to be unconstitutional. After his release from prison, Herndon moved to New York City, where he remained active in radical causes and later helped to edit a literary magazine. Toward the end of World War II he left the Communist party and eventually moved to Chicago, where he pursued a career in business.

Along with the more famous Scottsboro case in Alabama, the Angelo Herndon case symbolized the use of political justice to maintain racial subordination in the Deep South. Unlike Scottsboro, however, Herndon's prosecution under the insurrection law also raised a serious challenge to free speech and helped rally many civil libertarians to his cause. Although the Supreme Court eventually freed Herndon after nearly five years of proceedings, dramatic improvement in the status of blacks within the southern legal system had to await the advent of the civil rights movement in the mid-1950s.

Charles H. Martin
University of Texas at El Paso

Angelo Herndon, *Let Me Live* (1937); Charles H. Martin, *The Angelo Herndon Case and Southern Justice* (1976).

Jaworski, Leon

(1905–1982) Lawyer.

Jaworski, who became nationally recognized as the special prosecutor of the Watergate affair, was born in Waco, Tex., on 19 September 1905. He was the son of the Reverend Joseph Jaworski, a Protestant minister of Polish birth, and Marie Jaworski, who was born in Vienna.

After deciding to devote his life to a career as a trial lawyer, Jaworski attended law school at Baylor University, receiving his LL.B. in 1925; he then spent a year at the George Washington University School of Law and was granted the LL.M. in 1926. Returning to Waco to begin practice as a trial attorney, he was immediately successful, and he soon moved to Houston. His reputation spread rapidly, and in 1931, at age 26, he was asked to join one of the leading firms in that city, Fulbright, Crooker and Freeman. He remained with this firm, becoming a senior partner in 1951. Fulbright and Jaworski became one of the largest and best-respected firms in Texas.

During World War II, Jaworski served in the Judge Advocate General's Corps, attaining the rank of colonel. He conducted the prosecution of Nazi prisoners of war in this country and then became the chief of the United States War Crimes Trial Section in the European Theatre in our zone of occupation, with headquarters at Wiesbaden. He personally prosecuted the first war crimes trials in Germany. In 1946 he returned to his law practice in Houston. His reputation continued to grow, and he became increasingly involved in civic and social affairs. He was president of the American College of Trial Lawyers in 1961, president of the State Bar of Texas the next year, and president of the American Bar Association in 1971. He received numerous awards, including 15 honorary degrees, and was an elder in the Presbyterian church.

Jaworski's significant accomplishment was the successful prosecution of the Watergate crimes. He served as director of the special prosecution team in 1973 and 1974; his expertise as a trial lawyer and his professional, dispassionate conduct exposed the burglary and obstruction of justice by President Nixon and his close associates. Jaworski died 9 December 1982 in Wimberley, Tex. His four books of memoirs are *After Fifteen Years* (1961), *The Right and the Power: The Prosecution of Watergate* (1976), *Confession and Avoidance: A Memoir* (1979) [with M. Herskowitz], and *Crossroads* (1981) [with D. Schneider].

W. Hamilton Bryson
University of Richmond

James Doyle, *Not above the Law: The Battles of Watergate Prosecutors Cox and Jaworski* (1977).

Johnson, Frank M., Jr.

(b. 1918) Federal judge.

Frank M. Johnson, Jr., U.S. circuit judge, 1980s

Frank Minis Johnson, Jr., was born on 30 October 1918 in rural Winston County, Ala. During the Civil War, Winston and other northwest Alabama hill counties with few slaves had little sympathy for the Confederate cause. After the war, Winston became a lone Republican stronghold in Democratic Alabama. Frank Johnson's father was active in GOP politics and was elected probate judge and a member of the Alabama Legislature on the Republican ticket. Following law school at the University of Alabama and military service in Europe during World War II, Frank Johnson, Jr., practiced law in Jasper, Ala., and, like his father, also became active in GOP politics. His services on behalf of Dwight Eisenhower's 1952 presidential campaign led to his appointment, in 1953, as U.S. attorney in Birmingham. In 1955 Eisenhower appointed him to the U.S. District Court for the Middle District of Alabama in Montgomery, where he served until his appointment to a federal appeals court in 1979.

While a U.S. attorney, Johnson successfully prosecuted members of a prominent Sumter County plantation family on peonage and slavery charges, though such convictions had been rare since Reconstruction. As a district judge, he quickly gained a reputation as a vigorous defender of civil rights. During his first year on the federal bench, he helped to form a majority outlawing segregation on Montgomery's city buses. In the years that followed he issued numerous decisions on voting rights and became the first judge to order the names of qualified blacks added to county voting rolls. He also outlawed discrimination in Alabama's transportation facilities, libraries, agricultural extension service, and political parties; wrote the first statewide school segregation decree; and placed numerous state agencies under permanent federal court order.

Judge Johnson's opinions on civil rights perplexed and angered his fellow white Alabamians, making him a convenient scapegoat for George C. Wallace and other race-baiting politicians. During his 1962 gubernatorial campaign, Wallace—Johnson's law school classmate and an associate of more than passing acquaintance—condemned "lying, scalawagging" federal judges, with Johnson his principal target. Court baiting remained a familiar Wallace tactic for years after the 1962 election, and on at least one occasion, a Wallace aide urged Alabamians to ostracize federal judges, their wives, and children. Judge Johnson had become a pariah in his native state, however, even before the Wallace era in Alabama politics. Intermittently for 18 years, a dusk-to-dawn guard maintained a vigil at his home. His mother's home was bombed, crosses were burned on his lawn, and hate mail was directed to him. In 1975 his adopted son committed suicide. His son's emotional problems, some suggested, had their origins partly in the pressures to which his family had been subjected.

With increased black voter registration and the subsiding of race as *the* issue in Alabama politics, the attitudes of white Alabamians and the state's officialdom mellowed somewhat toward Judge Johnson. In the 1970s his landmark decisions mandating reform of Alabama's mental institutions and prisons prompted challenge from other quarters—critics who contended that Johnson and other activist judges were confusing their own social preferences with constitutional commands and encroaching unduly on legislative and administrative domains. Combined with his record on civil rights, however, such decisions served largely to enhance rather than damage his judicial reputation. His name was invariably mentioned when Supreme Court vacancies arose. In 1977 President Carter selected him to head the Federal Bureau of Investigation, but Johnson ultimately withdrew his name from nomination for medical reasons. In 1979 President Carter appointed Judge Johnson to the Court of Appeals for the Fifth Circuit. In 1981 the Fifth Circuit was split into two courts, and Judge Johnson became a member of the new Court of Appeals for the Eleventh Circuit, with jurisdiction over Alabama, Georgia, and Florida.

Tinsley E. Yarbrough
East Carolina University

Robert F. Kennedy, Jr., *Judge Frank M. Johnson, Jr.: A Biography* (1978); Tinsley E. Yarbrough, *Judge Frank Johnson and Human Rights in Alabama* (1981).

Little Rock Crisis

White southerners invoked the doctrines of states' rights and interposition to counter the NAACP's post–World War II campaign against de jure segregation. A few places in the Upper South immediately complied with the Supreme Court's decision in the 1954 case of *Brown* v. *Board of Education*, which overturned the doctrine of separate but equal, but throughout states of the old Confederacy governments embraced a strategy of "massive resistance." The first major constitutional test of this strategy grew out of efforts to integrate the Little Rock, Ark., public schools.

The NAACP in 1956 brought one of its more than 50 post-*Brown* desegregation suits against the Little Rock Board of Education. Under federal court order the board in September of 1957 proposed to admit a small number of blacks to formerly all-white Little Rock Central High School. Governor Orval Faubus invoked states' rights and interposition as constitutional grounds to block the plan. Acting on the governor's orders, the Arkansas National Guard, accompanied by a jeering white mob, rebuffed black students. Faubus denounced as unconstitutional federal court orders directing compliance.

Republican President Dwight D. Eisenhower responded to this attack on federal judicial authority by asserting the supremacy of the national government. He directed the attorney general to obtain an injunction against Faubus, who in turn withdrew the national guard. The president on 25 September 1957 dispatched troops from the 101st Airborne Division to restore order and to force the admission of black students.

The tug-of-war between state and federal authorities continued until late 1959. The Supreme Court, in *Cooper* v. *Aaron* in September 1958, unanimously reasserted the supremacy of the federal government, denounced interposition, and reaffirmed the federal judicial power. Governor Faubus then implemented two statutes that authorized him to close the Little Rock schools. The Court in the 1959 case of *Faubus* v. *Aaron* unanimously declared these statutes in violation of the due process and equal protection clauses of the Fourteenth Amendment.

Little Rock Central High School reopened quietly in September 1959. Events of the preceding two years discredited die-hard segregationists' arguments that states' rights and interposition could thwart the massive social changes sweeping the South.

See also URBANIZATION: / Little Rock

Kermit L. Hall
University of Florida

Numan Bartley, *The Rise of Massive Resistance: Race and Politics in the South during the 1950s* (1969); Daisy Bates, *The Long Shadow of Little Rock: A Memoir* (1962); Benjamin Muse, *Ten Years of Prelude: The Story of Integration since the Supreme Court's 1954 Decision* (1964).

Marshall, John

(1755–1835) U.S. Supreme Court chief justice.

Born in Fauquier County, Va., Marshall was a prominent member of the Richmond legal profession before he accepted federal office, first as a minister to France during the X.Y.Z. Mission (1797–98), then as a member of the House of Representatives (1799–1800), and as secretary of state (1800–1801). Appointed chief justice of the United States in January 1801, he served for the remaining 34 years of his life during a period of unprecedented institutional change in the Court and unparalleled constitutional growth in American law. He is best remembered for his articulation of the doctrine of judicial review (*Marbury* v. *Madison*, 1803), the use of the contract clause to defend private property against legislative seizures (*Fletcher* v. *Peck*, 1810; *Dartmouth College* v. *Woodward*, 1819), and his classic expositions and constructions of the interstate commerce power (*Gibbons* v. *Ogden*, 1824) and the necessary and proper clause (*McCullough* v. *Maryland*, 1819). A former officer in the Virginia Continental Line during the American Revolution and a close friend of President George Washington, Marshall displayed in his jurisprudence an affection for a strong federal government and a desire to perpetuate the moderate Federalist concern for sustained economic growth and political cohesion among the various states.

Despite growing isolation from both his pro-Jeffersonian Virginia contemporaries and the "high Federalist" branch of his own party, Marshall remained a political power in his native state. This was due in no small measure to his personality and mannerisms, which won him friends and supporters. The simplicity of his behavior and carelessness of his dress have become legendary. Even in the last decades of his life he welcomed the opportunity to toss horseshoes with friends at a local Richmond tavern. His "lawyers' dinners" were famous throughout the Old Dominion, and he persisted in that hospitable practice even after his entertainment of Aaron Burr during Burr's treason trial had generated public criticism. Charming, chivalrous, and, in later years, flirtatious with women, the chief justice remained devoted to the ailing wife he had married in 1783, mother of their 10 children. Gifted with a self-deprecatory sense of humor, Marshall was liked by virtually every Virginian of note in his generation. He in turn treasured his association with other Virginians, missing their unadorned hospitality while he was living in Paris and seeking their company when compelled by judicial duties to reside in Philadelphia or Washington. Next to Virginia society Marshall loved the landscape of his native state, particularly the mountain region of his birth; in the months immediately preceding his sudden death he was planning his retirement to the Fauquier homestead he had retained throughout his active career.

A veteran of Virginia local politics, John Marshall may well have derived his sense of federal balance from the example of Virginia state government. In Virginia substantial local autonomy in the county courts was balanced by extensive legislative power in the general assembly and general judicial authority in the general court, which exercised appellate review over county courts and broad original jurisdiction. Marshall was not a nationalist but rather an advocate of a federal government adequate to perform the necessary functions of a national state.

Like his Virginia contemporaries the chief justice preferred an agrarian way of life, and hence an agricultural economy for the United States. But unlike them he foresaw the inevitability of economic diversification. Recognizing the potential evils of commercial development and industrial growth, he sought means by which government might encourage the accumulation of national wealth and soften the impact of such development upon the people. A contemplative and compassionate man, the chief justice brought to the national scene all that was exemplary in the Virginia of his day.

Herbert A. Johnson
University of South Carolina

Leonard Baker, *John Marshall: A Life in Law* (1974); Albert J. Beveridge, *The Life of John Marshall*, 4 vols. (1916–19); Robert K. Faulkner, *The Jurisprudence of John Marshall* (1968).

Morgan, Charles, Jr.

(b. 1930) Civil rights attorney.

Born in Cincinnati, Ohio, in 1930, Morgan was reared in Kentucky and at age 15 moved with his parents to Birmingham, Ala. He graduated from the University of Alabama and received his law degree from the same institution. Morgan first achieved national prominence when he denounced the September 1963 Birmingham church bombing and blamed community attitudes for the tragedy. In the resulting furor Morgan left Birmingham. A year later he became the regional director for the American Civil Liberties Union in Atlanta.

Throughout the 1960s Morgan was involved in much of the litigation that altered political and social life in the region. He was instrumental in handling lawsuits challenging racial segregation in jury selection, state prisons, and the choice of delegations to political conventions. Perhaps Morgan's most significant impact came as a result of *Reynolds* v. *Sims* (1964), in which the Supreme Court mandated equal population districts for legislative bodies. Morgan was one of the plaintiffs and successfully argued the case before the Court. Subsequent litigation by Morgan forced a reapportionment of the Alabama Legislature.

Morgan has also demonstrated a commitment to civil liberties. He defended Captain Howard Levy at his court martial for refusing to teach dermatology to Green Beret medics. Morgan also represented Julian Bond in the early stages of his challenge to the 1967 action of the Georgia Legislature denying Bond his seat because of his antiwar political views. He appeared on behalf of Muhammad Ali, a conscientious objector, in his prolonged fight against conviction for draft evasion.

In 1972 Morgan moved to Washington and became head of the ACLU's national office. He was one of the first persons to call for the impeachment of President Richard M. Nixon over the Watergate scandal, and he persuaded the ACLU Board to adopt this position in September of 1973. Morgan resigned from his ACLU post in 1976 when he was criticized for publicly supporting fellow southerner Jimmy Carter's presidential bid. Always the maverick, Morgan then organized his own law firm and began defending corporations from assaults on their rights. In 1979 he instituted a lawsuit on behalf of Sears, Roebuck, and Co., which attacked affirmative action employment efforts. A skillful and dedicated advocate, Morgan once declared that "you don't hire a lawyer to lose."

James W. Ely, Jr.
Vanderbilt University

Philip Kopper, Washington *Post Potomac* (7 October 1973); Charles Morgan, Jr., *A Time to Speak* (1964), *One Man, One Voice* (1979).

Napoleonic Code

To prevent the complete adoption of the Anglo-American common law after the Louisiana Purchase (1803), the largely French and Spanish residents of Louisiana sought to preserve their Latin legal tradition by the reception and enactment of a civil code modeled after the *projet* of the *Code Napoleon*. On 31 March 1808 the territorial legislature of Orleans adopted a "code" drafted by Louis Moreau-Lislet and James Brown, the *Digest of Civil Laws Now in Force in the Territory of Orleans*. Printed in both English and French, and patterned after the Napoleonic Code of France, this was indeed a digest, i.e., a compilation of existing law, rather than a definitive and final statement of the law, a true code. Unlike the French code upon which it was based, the Digest of 1808 was not enacted in revolutionary times, nor was it intended to effect a national legal unification or extensive social transformations through legislation. It was not a break with the past, it did not abrogate the preceding law, and many of the radical ends that the authors of the French code championed were the very things Louisiana's inhabitants sought to avoid. This precursor of the modern civil codes of Louisiana was mainly the result of a confrontation between competing cultures rather than a true codification effort.

The legislative act promulgating the Digest of 1808 stipulated that "whatever in the ancient civil laws of this territory . . . is contrary to the dispositions contained in the said digest, or irreconcilable with them, is hereby abrogated." In this clause, the earlier law was not necessarily abrogated. As the Superior Court of Louisiana observed in 1812, "what we call the Civil code, is but a digest of the civil law which regulated this country under the French and Spanish Monarchs." Moreover, unlike the products of legislative positivism associated with civilian codification movements at the time, the Louisiana "code" gave legal effect to custom. Spanish law, therefore, survived in Louisiana as an authoritative source of law as custom. The two major sources of Spanish law in Louisiana had been the *Recopilacion de Indias* and *Las Siete Partidas*. Indeed, because the Spanish had previously abrogated much of the former French law, the Digest of 1808 was largely a digest of Spanish law.

The Digest of 1808 did serve the purpose of preventing the erosion of the Roman civil law during the early high tide of the common law in Louisiana. It remained for Edward Livingston, sometimes called the "Bentham of American Jurisprudence," to awaken in Louisiana a zeal for true codification. Livingston, with Moreau-Lislet and Pierre Derbigny, drafted the Louisiana Civil Code of 1825, which repealed all previous civil laws and which was enacted by the state legislature. The authors asserted that "in the Napoleonic code we have a system approaching nearer than any to perfection." Although modified after the Civil War to reflect the abolition of slavery and reenacted as the Louisiana Civil Code of 1870, the version of the Napoleonic Code received by Louisiana in 1825 remains the fundamental basis of the state's system of private law. Thus, the Roman civil law has been preserved in Louisiana as a mixed jurisdiction in the midst of a basically American-style judiciary and in the face of general reception of the Anglo-American public law such as prevailed elsewhere throughout the South.

Ernest S. Easterly III
Baton Rouge, Louisiana

R. Batiza, *Tulane Law Review* (April 1971); George Dargo, *Jefferson's Louisiana: Politics and the Clash of Legal Traditions* (1975); Ernest Easterly III, *Geojurisprudence: Studies in Law, Liberty and Landscapes* (1980); Robert A. Pascal, *Louisiana Law Review* (December 1965).

Plessy v. *Ferguson*

In *Plessy* v. *Ferguson* (1896) the U.S. Supreme Court ruled in favor of the "separate but equal" principle in public transportation facilities for whites and blacks. In doing so it affirmed the role of states in controlling social discrimination, and, many argue, the decision actually promoted enforced segregation. The number of Jim Crow laws increased rapidly during the following years.

The case originated in Louisiana, which had a statute requiring separate-but-equal accommodations for whites and blacks on railroad cars. In 1892 Homer Adolph Plessy purchased a train ticket from New Orleans to Covington, La. Plessy, seven-eighths white and one-eighth black, sat in a "whites only" car and refused to move to a "colored" section. He was arrested for violating the "Jim Crow Car Act of 1890." The "Citizens Committee to Test the Constitutionality of the Separate Car Law," a group of 18 blacks, had instigated the incident, choosing Plessy as the example and making sure train officials knew his racial status. Their attorney was Albion Winegar Tourgee, a carpetbagger during Reconstruction and author of the Reconstruction novel *A Fool's Errand*.

Four years later, the Supreme Court heard the case and voted seven to one (Justice David Brewer did not participate) against Plessy. In the majority opinion Justice Henry B. Brown wrote: "We consider the underlying fallacy of the plaintiff's argument to consist in the underlying assumption that the enforced separation of the two races stamps the colored race with a badge of inferiority. If this be so, it is not by reason of anything found in the act, but solely because the colored race chooses to put that construction on it." Furthermore, he wrote, "The argument also assumes that social prejudices may be overcome by legislation, and that equal rights cannot be secured to the negro except by an enforced comingling of the two races. We cannot accept this proposition. If the two races are to meet upon terms of social equality, it must be the result of natural affinities, a mutual appreciation of each other's merits and a voluntary consent of individuals."

Ironically, the only southerner then serving on the Court, Justice John Marshall Harlan, cast the sole vote against the final decision. In the minority opinion he asserted the equality of all men with regard to the civil rights "as guaranteed by the supreme law of the land." He stated, "Our Constitution is colorblind, and neither knows nor tolerates classes among citizens. In respect of civil rights, all citizens are equal before the law."

Not until the 1950s did Supreme Court decisions, most notably in *Brown* v. *Board of Education* (1954), begin to dissolve the Court's sanction of the concept of separate but equal. For more than a half century, the principle had dictated the social treatment of blacks, with "equal" facilities providing the legal rationale for segregation. Finally, though, what had been the minority opinion in *Plessy* became that of the majority, a belated response to Justice Harlan's statement that "the thin disguise of 'equal' accommodations for passengers in railroad coaches will not mislead any one, nor atone for the wrong this day done."

Jessica Foy
Cooperstown Graduate Programs
Cooperstown, New York

Henry J. Abraham, *Freedom and the Court: Civil Rights and Liberties in the United States* (1982); Catherine A. Barnes, *Journey from Jim Crow: The Desegregation of Southern Transit* (1983); John C. Livingston, *Fair Game?: Inequality and Affirmative Action* (1979); Frank T. Read and Lucy S. McGough, *Let Them Be Judged: The Integration of the Deep South* (1978).

Lewis Powell, U.S. Supreme Court justice, 1980s

Powell, Lewis F.

(b. 1907) U.S. Supreme Court justice.

A private lawyer possessing no elective or judicial experience is seldom appointed to the U.S. Supreme Court. Lewis Powell, nominated to the Court in 1971 by Richard Nixon, is an exception.

A lifelong Virginian, Powell was born 19 September 1907 in Suffolk, Va. He received his law degree in 1931 from Washington and Lee University. From 1937 to 1971 Powell was a member of a large, prestigious Richmond law firm. During this period he quietly established a reputation as one of the South's leading corporation lawyers, earned a handsome income, served as a director of 11 major companies, and was elected president of the American Bar Association and the American College of Trial Lawyers. During the 1950s he served as the chairman of the Richmond School Board, steering a moderate course in the slow-paced desegregation of the public schools.

Powell's nomination met with less resistance from liberals than did several of Nixon's other choices for the Supreme Court seats: unlike Harold Carswell, Powell was judged to be highly competent; unlike Clement Haynesworth, Powell was seen as a racial moderate; and unlike William Rehnquist, Powell was not regarded as an uncompromising ideologue. In Powell, Nixon found the highly qualified southern jurist that he so desperately wanted to appoint to the Court.

As a justice, Lewis Powell has not assumed a self-consciously "southern" stance. A regional orientation has not emerged in his opinions—even those touching federalism or race. Favoring a "balancing approach" in constitutional adjudication similar to that of his avowed idols, Felix Frankfurter and John Marshall Harlan, Powell has proven to be the swing vote in several close cases and the author of some of the Burger Court's most carefully wrought opinions. In 1972 he wrote a thoughtful majority opinion reaffirming the position that a wiretap is a search or seizure within the meaning of the Fourth Amendment. In his opinions on equal protection, Powell has resisted the expansion of "suspect classifications."

Only in his opinions involving big business—perhaps because of his long service to large corporations—has Powell been unable to maintain a stance of moderation. His aggressive support of big business is characteristic of the New South—a South no longer consumed by virulent racism but now willing to adopt strategies pioneered by northern corporation lawyers in the service of improved quarterly reports.

Powell's most famous opinion, *Regents* v. *Bakke* (1978), is characteristic of his balanced, trenchant, perceptive, and articulate legal analyses. In this landmark case that divided the Court and the country, Powell presented a lucid argument that invalidated racial quotas but upheld the concept of "affirmative action."

One scholar described Powell's work habits and temperament as being distinguished by "conscientiousness, thoroughness, craftsmanship, and sheer capacity for hard work." Powell is already being spoken of as a particularly distinguished "lawyer's judge" among the Supreme Court justices.

John W. Johnson
Clemson University

Leonard W. Levy, *Against the Law: The Nixon Court and Criminal Justice* (1974); Burt Neuborne, *The Justices of the United States Supreme Court* (1978); *Richmond Law Review* (1977).

Robinson, Spottswood W., III

(b. 1916) Jurist and civil rights lawyer.

Robinson is one of the most prominent black jurists in the United States. Born in 1916 in Richmond, Va., he was graduated from Virginia Union University and then studied at Howard Law School, where he earned the highest scholastic average ever achieved at that institution. Robinson remained at Howard in a part-time faculty position for several years, dividing his time between teaching and the private practice of law in Richmond. His legal career was interrupted by military service during World War II. Robinson subsequently left Howard and devoted his energies to real-estate law in Richmond and civil rights litigation for the NAACP. In the late 1940s he filed numerous lawsuits seeking equalization of facilities and teacher salaries between white and black schools in Virginia.

Throughout the 1950s Robinson served as Southeast regional counsel for the NAACP. Noted for his clarity of expression and scrupulousness in handling details, Robinson played a major role in preparing and arguing *Brown* v. *Board of Education* (1954) before the Supreme Court. Following the decision in *Brown* he pushed actively for school desegregation across Virginia. From 1960 to 1963 Robinson was dean of Howard Law School. In 1961 President John F. Kennedy named him to the Civil Rights Commission. In October of 1963 he was nominated by President Kennedy as the first black judge of the Federal District Court for the District of Columbia. Three years later President Lyndon Johnson appointed Robinson as the first black judge on the U.S. Court of Appeals for the District of Columbia.

Robinson wrote more than 300 opinions while serving on the appellate court. He usually voted with the liberal wing of judges on this court, which has often been polarized along philosophical lines. In *Nixon* v. *Sirica* (1973) Robinson joined the majority opinion holding that the courts and not the president must determine the extent of executive privilege. He became chief judge of the D.C. Court of Appeals in 1981, only the second black to head one of the federal circuits. As chief judge, Robinson has handled the administrative duties of the court.

James W. Ely, Jr.
Vanderbilt University

Howard Law Review (No. 1, 1977); Richard Kluger, *Simple Justice: The History of Brown v. Board of Education and Black America's Struggle for Equality* (1976); *Washington Post* (27 May 1981).

Scopes Trial

See SCIENCE AND MEDICINE: / Scopes Trial

Scott, Dred

(c. 1795–1858) Slave.

Captain John Emerson of Missouri in 1833 purchased Dred Scott, an illiterate slave born in Virginia. Emerson took Scott to Illinois, to that portion of Wisconsin territory embraced in the Missouri Compromise, and then back to Missouri. When Emerson died in 1843, putative ownership of Scott passed to John F. A. Sanford, Emerson's brother-in-law and executor. Three years later Scott sued in the lower courts of Missouri claiming that his sojourn in free territory had made him a free man.

Scott's litigation consumed more than a decade. The Missouri Supreme Court in 1848 held that the laws of Illinois and Wisconsin territory had no extraterritorial status in Missouri. Scott in 1854 filed suit in the U.S. Circuit Court for Missouri against John Sanford, who had moved to New York. Judge Robert Wells rejected Scott's substantive claim, but he left open the question of the slave's citizenship. Scott appealed this issue to the U.S. Supreme Court.

The Court on 6 March 1857 issued its opinion in *Dred Scott* v. *Sanford*. A proslavery, southern majority, led by Chief Justice Roger B. Taney, rejected Scott's claims. Taney struck down the Missouri Compromise, denied the power of Congress to abridge slaveholders' property rights, and held that a black person could not be a citizen of the United States within the meaning of the Constitution.

Taney's invocation of judicial authority complemented postnullification southern attitudes toward relations between state and nation. Southern leaders believed that declining influence over the political branches of the national government dictated a greater reliance on the federal judiciary to protect slaveholders' interests. Yet the cost of obeisance to the Court in *Scott* was further division of the northern and southern wings of the Democratic party and potential destruction of the Union.

Irony and tragedy have plagued the South's efforts to harmonize states' rights, the rule of law, and a dual system of race relations. Although freed by a new owner following the Court's decision, Scott died of consumption on 17 September 1858. The postwar freedom of other blacks, to which Scott's case contributed, also proved ephemeral. After Reconstruction the South, with the blessing of the Supreme Court, reasserted the concept of states' rights to foster white supremacy, a concept that reigned until the civil rights changes of the 1960s.

Kermit L. Hall
University of Florida

Don E. Fehrenbacher, *The Dred Scott Case: Its Significance in American Law and Politics* (1978).

Scottsboro Case

The "Scottsboro case" was the cause célèbre of American race relations in the 1930s. Touching on both the North's outrage at southern racism and the South's defensiveness about northern claims of moral superiority, this trial of nine black youths for rape in Scottsboro, Ala., reminded the nation of its failure to reconcile its image as the world's leader of democracy with the squalid reality of bigotry and repression daily faced by its black citizens.

On 25 March 1931 the deputy sheriff of Jackson County, Ala., reacting to reports of a fight among "hobos" on a Southern Railway freight bound for Memphis, stopped the train at Paint Rock, Ala., and arrested nine black youths, jailing them at the county seat of Scottsboro. The deputy also removed several white hobos from the train, including two white women. Minutes later, the women accused the blacks of rape, and only courageous action by the Jackson County sheriff saved the blacks from a lynching. The first rape trial took place in Scottsboro just three weeks later, and despite the trumped-up nature of the charges, the jury convicted eight of the nine and sentenced them to death.

The severity of the youths' sentences galvanized public opinion throughout America. When an appellate court overturned the verdicts, the state of Alabama immediately launched a second prosecution of the "Scottsboro boys" in 1933. During the second trial the International Labor Defense, an organization closely aligned with the Communist party, defended the youths, and the case became front-page news. Five years of legal maneuvering followed in both the state and federal courts. In 1937 defense attorneys and the prosecution finally reached a compromise, which freed four of the defendants while sentencing the others to long prison terms. Not until 1950 did the last of the Scottsboro boys emerge from the Alabama prisons. For many southerners, the Scottsboro case marked a low point in 20th-century race relations because it starkly revealed white southerners' oppression of blacks.

Carroll Van West
Center for Historic Preservation
Middle Tennessee State University

Dan T. Carter, *Scottsboro: A Tragedy of the American South* (1969).

Slave Codes

The first statute reflecting slavery in the South was adopted by colonial Virginia in 1660. That law recognized a class of blacks as life servants, and it established as a punishment for white servants who ran away with black life servants the service time the black servant would have been required to render. This rather brief and simple act gave way within a generation to a complex code of laws concerning slavery in Virginia, which was a pioneer in this effort. In 1705 the Virginia Legislature passed a slave code, one of the first such codifications in the South.

The Virginia Slave Code of 1705 clearly established two themes that would remain a part of the slave codes in every southern colony and state. Slaves were defined by race, and this meant black persons; and slavery was associated primarily with a plantation economy. Provisions of the early Virginia slave code included sections concerning the torture and murder of slaves, the legal status of children whose fathers and mothers were slaves, penalties for failure to obey commands of a master, and restrictions on nonslave fraternization with slaves. For example, Chapter 49, Section 37, of the 1705 Virginia slave code provided that "any slaves, against whom proclamation hath been thus issued, and once published at any church or chapel, stay out, and do not immediately return home, it shall be lawful for any person or persons whatsoever, to kill and destroy such slaves by such ways and means as he, she, or they shall think fit, without accusation or impeachment of any crime for the same." The section further allowed dismemberment of any slave caught and returned alive.

The first codes and all subsequent codes encompassed three elements. First, the slave status was defined; second, the slave was regulated as a form of real property; and third, codes delineated slaves' social behavior and provided legal forms for social control of slaves. This latter element reflected the southern fixation on slave insurrections. As the Civil War approached, slave codes added further restrictions on personal freedoms of slaves, including the virtual abolition of manumission. By the 1850s slave codes in most southern states provided procedures for the expulsion of free blacks or their reinslavement with a master of their choice.

John R. Wunder
Clemson University

Eugene D. Genovese, *Roll, Jordan, Roll: The World the Slaves Made* (1972); Kenneth M. Stampp, *The Peculiar Institution: Slavery in the Ante-Bellum South* (1956).

Tucker Family

Over several generations the Tuckers of Virginia produced a number of eminent attorneys, jurists, politicians, and authors. From the early postrevolutionary years the family name was bound inextricably to the legal and political culture of the Old Dominion and of the South. St. George Tucker (1752–1827), progenitor of the main Tucker line in the Commonwealth, pursued a lengthy career as a state and federal judge, poet and political essayist, and successor to George Wythe as law professor at the College of William and Mary. On the bench, Tucker's able decisions set important precedents during the formative years of Virginia jurisprudence. His opinion in *Kamper* v. *Hawkins* (1793), for instance, forcibly stated the doctrine of judicial review by holding the state constitution to be the supreme act of a sovereign people with which all subsequent legislation had to conform.

Tucker's lengthy series of notes and annotations derived from his experience as a law teacher prompted him to prepare a five-volume American edition of *Blackstone's Commentaries* (1803). In appendices designed to identify and explain areas of American practice that had diverged from English substantive and procedural law, Tucker expressed admiration for the profound American innovations in constitutional government that had occurred during his lifetime. He took occasion, too, as he had done in student lectures, to assert his strong objections to the institution of slavery and his hope for its gradual elimination. Though keyed largely to Virginia's law and practice, Tucker's edition of *Blackstone's Commentaries* rapidly emerged as an essential reference tool for student and practitioner alike and found a receptive and loyal audience throughout the South until superseded by later editions at mid-century. But beyond its practical value, Tucker's work served as an important early exposition of Jeffersonian concepts of democratic government.

A distant Bermuda kinsman of St. George Tucker, George Tucker (1775–1861) acquired less fame as a lawyer than as an author and political economist. Written on the eve of Virginia's troubled constitutional debates, *The Valley of Shenandoah* (1824), his best-known work, castigates the financially irresponsible Tidewater aristocracy, frets about the cultural and political alienation of the western portions of the Commonwealth, and berates the legal profession. Most importantly, however, Tucker's book marks the first significant use of the plantation setting and the stereotyped southern slave in fiction. His later works on political economy, some written while Tucker was professor of moral philosophy at the University of Virginia, saw his strident opposition to slavery somewhat muted as his main focus turned to a deep concern for public prosperity and a growing anxiety over the economic future of his section.

Henry St. George Tucker (1780–1848), son of St. George Tucker, made his greatest contribution as the state's highest judicial officer and as a legal writer. Thoroughly skilled in the application of complex principles of equity, he led the Virginia bench in quest of justice over legal technicality and, unlike many of his contemporaries, refused to be hampered by precedent. With this enlightened approach he exerted further influence on the legal culture of the Old Dominion by training a remarkable generation of attorneys drawn from throughout the South at his own private law school in Winchester and later at the University of Virginia. From his lecture notes he prepared in 1831 the two-volume *Commentaries on the Laws of Virginia*. This encyclopedic work became a handbook for Virginia practitioners and students, as well as a valued legal text across the South.

The most prolific of the Tuckers, Nathaniel Beverley Tucker (1784–1851), parted from his father and brother to espouse extreme states' rights and proslavery positions in numerous essays and contributions to Virginia newspapers and southern periodicals. Eventually assuming his father's old post as law professor at the College of William and Mary, he imbued a restless generation of aspiring southern attorneys with his own fiery brand of southern nationalism and secessionist rhetoric. His anxiety over northern domination of the South led to the prophetic *Partisan Leader* (1836), a novel that perhaps most effectively captured the spirit of states' rights proponents who foresaw clearly the coming conflict. But Tucker also took the training of law students as competent advocates seriously. His broad approach to legal education blended the practical with the theoretical, stressing the importance of the *Principles of Pleading* (1846) as firmly as did his *Lectures on the Science of Government* (1848).

After the Civil War, John Randolph Tucker (1823–97) assumed the family mantle of leadership in Virginia jurisprudence. Son of Henry St. George Tucker, this Winchester attorney served as Virginia's wartime attorney general and later became dean of the law school at Washington and Lee University and an influential Virginia congressman. Conservative southern Democrat and strict constructionist, Tucker mirrored the temper of his times in Virginia. Yet, at the same time, he led his southern contemporaries in renewing their devotion to the federal Constitution and understanding its usefulness to their section. He represented a group of Chicago anarchists before the U.S. Supreme Court in the case *Spies* v. *Illinois* (1887), which first contended that the Fourteenth Amendment incorporates the Bill of Rights. He explained his action by stating, "I do not defend anarchy, I defend the Constitution." One of the first southerners elected to the presidency of the American Bar Association (1892–93), Tucker wrote frequently on topics of concern to practitioners in the South. In a last great attempt to withstand the rising influence of Harvard and the developing case method of instruction, Dean Tucker stood as one of the leading opponents of such innovation in southern legal education. He continued to proclaim throughout the last years of his life the virtues of those attorneys who were formally educated but ultimately self-trained.

E. Lee Shepard
Virginia Historical Society

W. Hamilton Bryson, *Legal Education in Virginia, 1779–1979: A Biographical Approach* (1982); William R. Taylor, *Cavalier and Yankee: The Old South and American National Character* (1961); J. Randolph Tucker, *Virginia Law Register* (March 1896).

Tuttle, Elbert P.

(b. 1897) Federal judge.

As chief judge of the Fifth Circuit Court of Appeals throughout the 1960s, Elbert Parr Tuttle provided leadership in the development of civil rights law comparable to that of Earl Warren on the Supreme Court. In a 1967 tribute to him Chief Justice Warren praised Tuttle for combining "administrative talents with great personal courage and wisdom to assure justice of the highest quality without delays which might have thrown the Fifth Circuit into chaos." Tuttle and three other judges—John Minor Wisdom of New Orleans, Richard T. Rives of Montgomery, and John R. Brown of Houston—were disparagingly labeled "The Four" by an outraged fellow judge, who saw them as destroyers of the Old South he cherished.

Tuttle, Wisdom, Brown, and Rives shared a quiet passion that reacted to injustice and translated the Supreme Court's basic school desegregation decision into a broad mandate for racial justice and equality under law. They battled to make the law work during a period of social upheaval. They not only accepted the constitutional philosophy that extended downward from the Warren Court but also reinforced it upward and outward, stretching and expanding the law to protect rights and liberties granted by the Constitution. They proved that change can come from below, provided there is an accepting climate in the structure above.

Born in California on 17 July 1897, Tuttle grew up in Hawaii, attending multiracial schools. He settled in Atlanta in 1923 after graduation from Cornell University Law School. In Atlanta he opened a law practice with his wife Sara's brother, William Sutherland, who had grown up in Jacksonville, Fla., and had clerked for Justice Brandeis. As a lawyer, Tuttle won a landmark case before the Supreme Court, establishing an indigent's right to counsel.

A World War II battlefield hero who became a brigadier general in the army reserve, Tuttle led a floor fight that seated the contested Georgia delegation that supported Dwight Eisenhower at the Republican National Convention in 1952. Following Eisenhower's election, Tuttle served as general counsel to the Treasury Department until 1954, when the president appointed him to the Fifth Circuit Court of Appeals. In his first 29 years on the federal bench, Tuttle wrote 1,225 opinions, reputed to be more than any federal judge in history, including 94 dissents.

Based on his belief in the theory of common law development, Tuttle believed that "the law develops to meet changing needs . . . according to changes in our moral precepts." In civil rights cases that broke new legal ground, Tuttle explained, "I never had any doubt that what I was doing would be affirmed by the Supreme Court. It was the easiest field of the law I could write in. . . . The truth is, the black person in the litigation I sat in on was entitled to the result he got, under what the Constitution required."

In 1965 Harvard University awarded Judge Tuttle an honorary Doctor of Laws degree, stating, "The mind and heart of this dauntless judge enhance the great tradition of the federal judiciary."

Jack Bass
University of South Carolina

Jack Bass, *Unlikely Heroes* (1981); Howell Raines, *My Soul Is Rested* (1977); Earl Warren, *Georgia Law Review* (Fall 1967).

White, Edward Douglas

(1845–1921) U.S. Supreme Court justice.

The first sitting Supreme Court justice promoted to the chief justiceship, Edward Douglas White was a jurist who carved a place for himself in legal history because of strong personality and longevity rather than legal brilliance.

The son and grandson of Irish Catholic judges, White was born in 1845 in Louisiana on his father's 1,600-acre sugar beet plantation. The young White was educated almost entirely in Jesuit institutions. After a brief, frustrating service as an aide-de-camp in the Confederate army, White apprenticed himself to a distinguished New Orleans lawyer and in 1868 was admitted to the Louisiana bar. White's affiliation with influential New Orleans law firms, coupled with the income from his Thibodaux plantation, provided him with the financial security to enter politics. His fortuitous association with the Redeemer governor Francis Nicholls ultimately won him the state legislature's selection to the U.S. Senate.

As a senator, White conformed to the dominant laissez-faire spirit of turn-of-the-century America except for a self-serving defense of the high protective tariff on imported sugar. In 1894 he was nominated for the Supreme Court by President (and fellow Democrat) Grover Cleveland. The choice of White to fill a Supreme Court vacancy in the midst of the Populist upheaval of the 1890s was intended by Cleveland as a device to bolster the southern wing of the Democratic party.

On the Supreme Court, White used his hearty friendliness and access to the best parties in Washington to create a place for himself as one of the Court's social leaders. Although not characterized by a rigorous legal mind, White was a hard worker and possessed an absorbent memory that allowed him, upon occasion, to deliver his opinions without notes.

In 1910 President William Howard Taft nominated White for the chief justiceship. Apparently Taft wished to place someone in the Court's center seat sufficiently advanced in age (White was 64 at that time) to allow the position to become vacant again in a few years so that Taft himself could be appointed to head the Court. Although Taft eventually obtained his coveted judicial position, he had to wait until White's death, 11 years later, in 1921.

The traditional southern states' rights doctrines that White articulated as a senator from Louisiana were occasionally enunciated in his Supreme Court opinions. However, his judicial orientation was not self-consciously southern. White's status as a Confederate veteran did not keep him from developing a close personal friendship with Justice Oliver Wendell Holmes, a Boston Brahmin and Union veteran.

One biographer has referred to White's opinions as following a "jagged pattern," the product of "judicial whimsey." White's positions on such dominant legal concerns of the time as substantive due process and federal regulatory activity showed little consistency. In the *Insular Cases* White introduced the novel but slippery doctrine that the Constitution followed the flag only for those overseas possessions properly "incorporated" by Congress. White's most famous contribution to public law was the creation of the "rule of reason" as a test for alleged restraints of trade: only those business combinations that were deemed "unreasonable," White argued, should be dismantled pursuant to the Sherman Antitrust Act. What White and his like-minded brethren meant by "unreasonable" was never articulated. This crude, pragmatic concept was White's principal doctrinal legacy.

John W. Johnson
Clemson University

Robert B. Highsaw, *Edward Douglas White: Defender of the Conservative Faith* (1981); John Semonche, *Charting the Future: The Supreme Court Responds to a Changing Society, 1890–1920* (1978); James F. Watts, Jr., *The Justices of the United States Supreme Court*, ed. Leon Friedman and Fred I. Israel (1969).

Wisdom, John Minor

(b. 1905) Federal judge.

The "scholar" on the Fifth Circuit Court of Appeals during the turbulent battle over civil rights in the 1960s, Judge John Minor Wisdom "transformed the face of school desegregation law" in the absence of Supreme Court leadership. Born 17 May 1905 in New Orleans, Wisdom received a B.A. degree from Washington and Lee and a LL.B. from Tulane. As a young man the New Orleans aristocrat became one of a handful of Republicans in Louisiana who openly argued that Huey Long's dictatorial control threatened democratic principles in the state. In 1952 Wisdom served as chairman of the 15-member Southern Conference for Eisenhower, which helped draft the former general to run for president. Wisdom played a significant role in the nominating convention, arguing successfully before the Credentials Committee for the seating of the contested Eisenhower delegation from Louisiana. President Eisenhower appointed Wisdom to the Fifth Circuit Court of Appeals in 1957.

In *U.S.* v. *Jefferson* (1967) Wisdom declared that school boards had "the affirmative duty under the Fourteenth Amendment to bring about an integrated, unitary school system in which there are no Negro schools and no white schools—just schools." The doctrine of affirmative duties developed by the Fifth Circuit shifted the burden from black plaintiffs to school boards and other public officials to end discrimination. It also helped lead to affirmative action programs to overcome the effects of past discrimination. "The Constitution is both color blind and color conscious," Wisdom wrote in *Jefferson*; "the Constitution is color conscious to prevent discrimination being perpetuated and to undo the effects of past discrimination. The criterion is the relevancy of color to a legitimate government purpose."

In his opinions in civil rights cases Wisdom combined literary flair with a scholarly depth that left a major imprint on constitutional law. In *Jefferson*, he placed school desegregation in a larger historical and philosophical framework. "*Brown*'s broad meaning, its important meaning," Wisdom asserted of the landmark 1954 Supreme Court decision, "is its revitalization of the national constitutional right the Thirteenth, Fourteenth, and Fifteenth Amendments created in favor of Negroes. This is the right of Negroes to *national* citizenship; their right as a class to share the privileges and immunities only white citizens had enjoyed as a class. *Brown* erased *Dred Scott*, used the Fourteenth Amendment to breathe life into the Thirteenth, and wrote the Declaration of Independence into the Constitution. Freedmen are free men."

Wisdom also wrote landmark opinions in cases that involved jury discrimination, voting rights, and affirmative action in employment, as well as in fields of law besides civil rights.

Jack Bass
University of South Carolina

Jack Bass, *Unlikely Heroes* (1981); J. Harvie Wilkinson III, *From Brown to Bakke: The Supreme Court and School Integration, 1954–1978* (1979).

Literature

M. THOMAS INGE

Randolph-Macon College

CONSULTANT

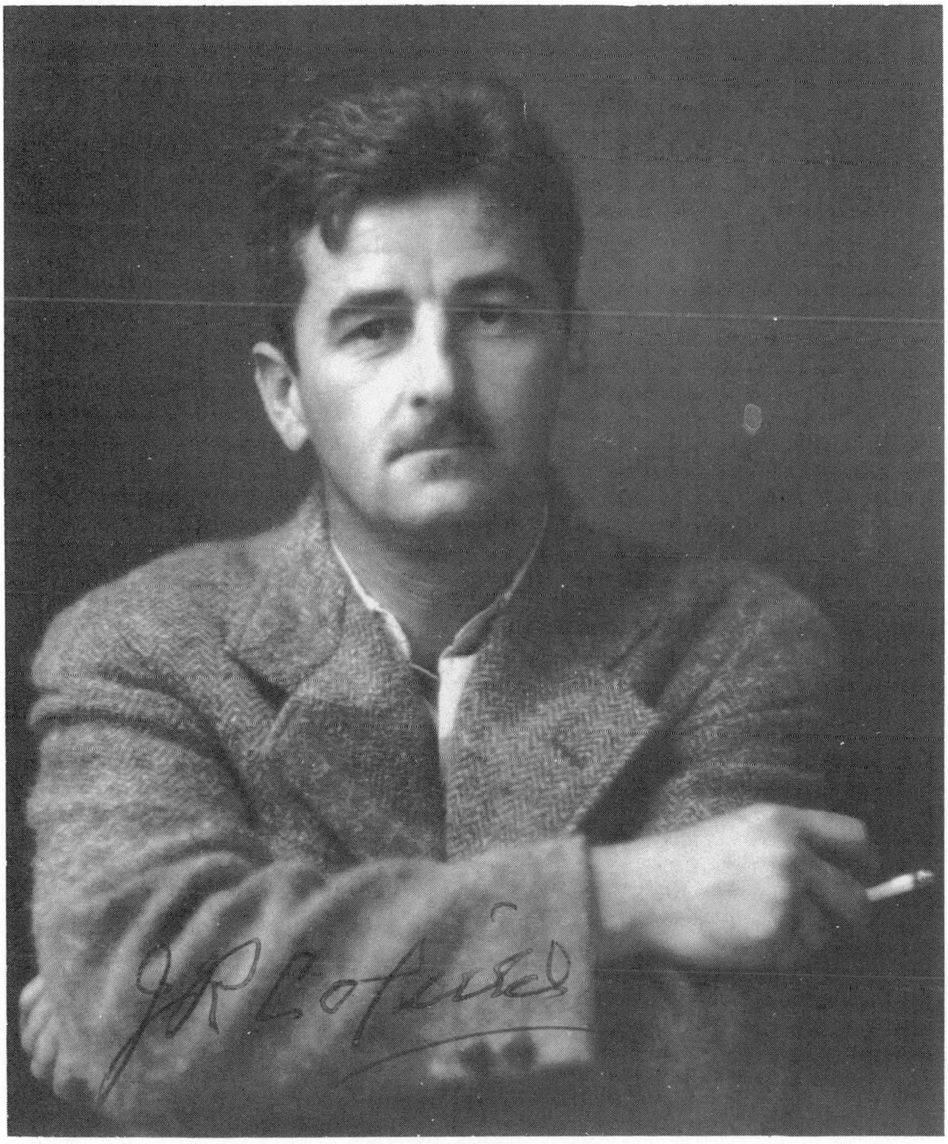

William Faulkner, c. 1930

Literature

One could argue that literature in the American South began as early as 1608 when the explorer and adventurer Captain John Smith published his promotional pamphlet *A True Relation of Occurrences and Accidents in Virginia*, the first of a series of accounts, each of which became more embellished, to include finally the story of his rescue by Pocahontas. Or, to move ahead a hundred years, perhaps southern letters began with the secret diaries, character sketches, poems, and satiric prose of the true Renaissance gentleman in residence at Westover, William Byrd II. But because America as an independent nation did not exist until 1776 and neither Smith nor Byrd considered himself other than a British citizen, the most one can say is that they established the traditions of exaggeration, irony, wit, stylistic versatility, and experimentation with form that would characterize southern literature.

Despite general impressions to the contrary, the intellectual life of the colonists in what would become the southern states was rich and varied. In the political and cultural center of Williamsburg citizens attended the theater, gave concerts for each other, built well-designed houses with beautifully patterned gardens, collected selective but impressive libraries, wrote articulate and well-argued letters to friends at home and abroad, read classical authors in the original Greek and Latin, and engaged in political and religious debate. Colonial authors expressed themselves in poetry and prose, satire and invective, essays and pamphlets. Noteworthy published works of the period include the translation into heroic couplets of Ovid's *Metamorphoses* (1626) by George Sandys, Jamestown treasurer and director of industry and agriculture; a humorous prose account of colonial life interspersed with lively poetry, *A Character of the Province of Maryland* (1966), by indentured servant George Alsop; the engaging first history of Virginia, *The History and Present State of Virginia* (1705), written by a plantation owner and member of the House of Burgesses, Robert Beverley; *The Sot-Weed Factor* (1708), a verse satire by poet laureate of early Maryland, Ebenezer Cooke whose point of view and low-life subject matter were precursors of the southern humor tradition; the two very early novels written by the master of grammar school and professor at the College of William and Mary, Arthur Blackamore, *The Religious Triumverate* (1720) and *Luck at Last; or, The Happy Unfortunate* (1723); and the works of New Light Presbyterian minister and later president of Princeton University, Samuel Davies, who composed hymns, elegies, sermons, and poems, many of the last of which were collected in *Miscellaneous Poems, Chiefly on Divine Subjects* (1752).

During the revolutionary period lawyer, architect, educator, scientist, philosopher, governor of Virginia, secretary of state, vice president, and president of the United States, Thomas Jefferson served as the intellectual center of a burst of rational and enlightened thought about the American political state, the foundations of society, and the nature of man. The creative energy of Jefferson and such colleagues as Richard Bland, Patrick Henry, James Madison, and John Taylor was invested in political treatises, pamphlets, oratory, and cogent essays rather than belles lettres. Although he wrote only one full-length book, *Notes on the State of Virginia* (1785), perhaps the most significant political and scientific work of its time, it was through his composition of the text of the Declaration of Independence (1776) that Jefferson had a lasting and profound impact on the subsequent history of the political, social, and cultural life of the South and the nation. It is, then, a literary document of the first order. Jefferson continues to arrest our attention as a man of great creative intellect through biographies, histories, plays, poems, and novels about his life and relationships.

Antebellum Era. Political and economic leadership in the South by the end of the 18th century had moved from Virginia to South Carolina, especially Charleston, when it became clear that raw cotton was to be that state's and the region's essential product and that slavery was therefore necessary to the future. For the first 50 years the southernmost outpost of the British empire in America, Charleston became a major commercial center and supported the development of a wealthy merchant and planter class, which in turn encouraged a lively cultural life including one of two newspapers published in the South, a library society, and bookstores. It was at one of these, Russell's Bookstore, that the members of the "Charleston School" gathered under the leadership of statesman and critic Hugh Swinton Legaré, editor and contributor to the *Southern Review* (1828–32). The group included among its membership romantic poet Paul Hamilton Hayne, editor of *Russell's* magazine (1857–60), and other lyrical sentimental poets of the pro-Confederacy school such as Henry Timrod, "Laureate of the Confederacy."

The most influential member of the group, and probably in his time the best-known southern writer, was William Gilmore Simms, editor during his career of 10 periodicals and author of over 80 volumes of history, poetry, criticism, biography, drama, essays, stories, and novels, including a series of nationally popular border romances about life on the frontier and historical romances about the American Revolution. He was one of the first to make a profession of writing. Simms's only serious rival as a writer in the South was Baltimore politician John Pendleton Kennedy, whose informal fictional sketches in *Swallow Barn* (1832) helped establish the plantation novel, which in its depiction of a mythic genteel past and an ideal social structure has found hundreds of imitators in American romance fiction.

Less-accomplished but talented fiction writers of the time, all of whom wrote historical romances heavily under the influence of Scott, Cooper, and Irving, and all Virginia born, were Nathaniel Beverley Tucker, William Alexander Caruthers, and John Esten Cooke. Two extremely popular southern sentimental novelists of the time were Augusta Jane Evans Wilson and Caroline Lee

Hentz, both of whom succeeded where many men had failed—achieving financial independence as professional writers.

A southern-born slave, William Wells Brown, wrote the first novel by an American black, *Clotel; or, The President's Daughter* (1853), based on the rumor that Thomas Jefferson had fathered a daughter with one of his slaves. In writing what was, in essence, a novel of social protest, Brown established the mainstream tradition for black fiction in this country. Another important work of black protest was the *Narrative of the Life of Frederick Douglass* (1845), the work of a former slave who was America's leading abolitionist organizer, orator, newspaper editor, and political figure. The first book published by a black in the South was *The Hope of Liberty* (1829), which contained poems decrying the slaves' condition, by George Moses Horton of North Carolina.

The only writer of this period who, with the passage of time, was to rise to a level of national and international prominence was Edgar Allan Poe, whose relationship to his southern heritage may indirectly be seen in his work. Although he was raised in Richmond, attended the University of Virginia, and edited the *Southern Literary Messenger* (1834–64) in Richmond from 1835 to 1837, he turned away from regional materials for the most part in his poetry, fiction, and criticism to devote himself to a form of literary expression that aspired to universality in style and structure. His poetry in which sound and sensuality superseded sense, his fiction in which meaning or message was secondary to emotional impact, and his criticism in which independently and objectively derived standards are used in the evaluation of artistic success, would help shape, first in Europe and then in this country, the modern literary sensibility. Creative writing throughout the world was never the same after Poe.

So dazzling was the achievement of Poe from the modern point of view that the work of numerous contemporary southern poets pales in comparison. This includes the sentimental, romantic, lyric poetry of Irish-born Richard Henry Wilde of Georgia, Thomas Holley Chivers also of Georgia, British-born Edward Coote Pinkney of Maryland, Philip Pendleton Cooke of Virginia, Theodore O'Hara of Kentucky, and James Matthewes Legaré of South Carolina.

Outside of Poe, the most influential writing produced by the antebellum South was the work of a group of humorists who had no literary pretensions and therefore were free of the prevailing influences of the literary marketplace. They were lawyers, doctors, editors, politicians, and professional men who set down for the amusement of newspaper readers stories and tales they heard as they traveled through the frontier territories of Georgia, Alabama, Mississippi, Tennessee, or Louisiana—what was then called the Old Southwest. The sketches and fictional pieces they wrote were realistic, bawdy, vulgar, and often brutal, but they were written in a language and style close to the southern idiom and the point of view of everyday people. No one was more surprised than they when their sketches were collected between hard covers and soon constituted an impressive bookshelf of what would prove to be classics of southern humor: Augustus Baldwin Longstreet's *Georgia Scenes* (1835); William Tappan Thompson's *Major Jones's Courtship* (1843); Johnson Jones Hooper's *Some Adventures of Captain Simon Suggs* (1845); Thomas Bangs Thorpe's edition of *The Big Bear of Arkansas* (1845), which included his famous title story originally published in an 1841 issue of the *Spirit of the Times*, where much of this humor first appeared; Henry Clay Lewis's *Odd Leaves from the Life of a Louisiana Swamp Doctor* (1850); Joseph Glover Baldwin's *The Flush Times of Alabama and Mississippi* (1853); and Charles Henry Smith's *Bill Arp, So Called* (1866). Related to this tradition in its uses of comic exaggeration and oral folklore was *A Narrative of the Life of David Crockett* (1834) in which the part Crockett played as an author is uncertain.

The most accomplished of the humorists of the Old Southwest was Tennessean George Washington Harris, creator of the irascible Sut Lovingood, the liveliest comic figure to emerge from American literature before Huckleberry Finn. His first sketches were contributed to the New York *Spirit of the Times* and to Tennessee newspapers in the 1840s; however, the Lovingood stories were not collected until after the Civil War as *Sut Lovingood, Yarns Spun by a "Nat'ral Born Durn'd Fool"* (1867). In masterful use of dialect, striking control of metaphor and imagery, and kinetic creation of explosive action, Harris was to have no match until Mark Twain and William Faulkner, both of whom read Harris with appreciation.

Through studying Harris and the other southern humorists, Samuel Clemens, or Mark Twain, learned his trade, and his first published sketches, such as "Jim Smiley and His Jumping Frog" (1865), belong to this school of humor. Born of southern parents in Missouri, and raised in the slaveholding community of Hannibal on the Mississippi River, employed as a steamboat pilot on the great river from St. Louis and Cairo down to New Orleans from 1857 to 1861, and enlisted briefly in the Confederate army before deserting to go with his brother to Nevada, Clemens and his formative experiences were more southern than western. His masterwork, *The Adventures of Huckleberry Finn* (1885), is the most incisive satire ever written of southern attitudes, customs, and mores, aside from its central importance as a pivotal work of American literature. In Clemens, frontier humor was brought to a high level of literary artistry and through Clemens was transmitted to the majority of subsequent practicing humorists. Modern southern writers who have maintained this tradition include Guy Owen of North Carolina; William Price Fox, Jr., and Mark Steadman, Jr., of South Carolina; Robert Y. Drake, Jr., of Tennessee; and Roy Blount, Jr., of Georgia.

Local Color Era. If frankness and realism were dominant characteristics of frontier humor, the movement that superseded it was devoted to delicacy and romanticism. The development of a number of large-circulation, well-paying magazines in New York after the Civil War and an intense interest in things regional encouraged the local color movement, which Bret Harte's California stories instigated. Peculiarities of speech, quaint local customs, distinctive modes of thought, and stories about human nature became the primary subject matter of this fictional movement, and because the South had an abundance of all these qualities in the popular American mind, southern authors flourished. Unlike the frontier humorists, these were conscious craftsmen producing a marketable commodity; thus the finished product says more about popular misconceptions of the South in many cases than it says about the reality, and nothing that might upset the sensibilities of a young maiden, to use William Dean Howells's criterion, was allowed to see print. Although once thought to be early realists, many of the local color writers described a quaint and curious world that may never have existed.

In any case, they came from all parts of the South to vie for space in the popular magazines and described in their fiction the worlds they inhabited—George Washington Cable, Kate Chopin, Grace King, and Ruth McEnery Stuart from Louisiana; Thomas Nelson Page and John Esten Cooke (in his postwar fiction) from Virginia; Richard Malcolm Johnston, Harry Stillwell Edwards, and Will N. Harben from Georgia; James Lane Allen from Kentucky; Sherwood Bonner from Mississippi; and Mary Noailles Murfree from Tennessee. The aesthetic sensibilities of such writers as Cable, Chopin, and Murfree allowed them to achieve a level of psychological sophistication in their characters and a stylistic skill unusual for their times.

Joel Chandler Harris's popularity was also fed by the same interests that fostered the local color writers, but his was a special achievement. Although the exterior settings and scenes for his stories of Uncle Remus were directly out of a romantic world of a Thomas Nelson Page, the stories themselves are remarkable renderings of Afro-American folktales, in which Brer Rabbit serves as an exemplum for black survival in an Anglo-American world. Harris greatly improved, then, on the legacy of happy darky stereotypes that Page and the Mississippi dialect poet Irwin Russell had left. One black writer who spoke for his own race in local color fiction was Charles Waddell Chesnutt, raised in North Carolina, but he had to begin his literary career by disguising his racial identity because of the prejudice that only whites could understand and explain blacks.

The American reading audience seemed to glory in the tales of southern times "befo' de wah," but some southern writers and leaders began a movement to reject that heritage for a concept of a New South that would be industrialized, modernized, and adapted to the larger pattern of American economic and social development. George Washington Cable and Joel Chandler Harris were supporters of this movement, but the intellectual leaders were journalists Walter Hines Page and Henry W. Grady, and Booker T. Washington in the black community.

Their sentiments were shared by the best postwar poet in the South, Sidney Lanier of Georgia, whose poetry aimed for a musical and tonal beauty that stressed sound over content and whose literary criticism attempted to establish a basis for versification in the principles of music. Less-accomplished poets publishing at the end of the 19th century and the beginning of the 20th were John Bannister Tabb of Virginia; former slave Albery Allson Whitman, Madison Cawein, Cale Young Rice, and Olive Tilford Dargan, all of Kentucky; Lizette Woodworth Reese of Maryland; William Alexander Percy of Mississippi; and John Gould Fletcher of Arkansas, at first a member of the Imagist school of poets in London and later a member of the Fugitive poets, but overshadowed by more talented writers of both groups.

At the turn of the century, southern literature was dominated by several writers residing in Richmond, Va. Mary Johnston produced a series of popular historical romances set in Virginia, while her friend Ellen Glasgow, much more the insightful and talented artist, wrote a series of distinctive and well-crafted novels designed to constitute a social history of the state. Her critical realism was counterbalanced by the medieval romanticism and fantasy of James Branch Cabell, whose epic biography of Manuel set in Poictesme turns out to be, after all, an ironic, disguised commentary on the manners and mores of his real world. The following generation of writers in Richmond proved to be eminent journalists and historians—Douglas Southall Freeman, who finally left newspaper work after 34 years to complete his distinguished biography of Robert E. Lee; Clifford Dowdey, who had equal success in magazine editing, publishing historical novels, and writing Civil War histories; and Virginius Dabney, who paralleled a career in journalism with that of a liberal commentator on history, politics, and social change in the South.

Southern Literary Renaissance. In a November 1917 issue of the New York *Evening Mail* Baltimore journalist H. L. Mencken published his notorious essay, "The Sahara of the Bozart," in which he excoriated the South as being culturally backwards and "almost as sterile, artistically, intellectually, culturally, as the Sahara Desert." In his usual fashion, Mencken was, of course, exaggerating, but almost as if in response the next two decades witnessed an overwhelming production of literature by southern authors, called the "Southern Literary Renaissance." Some literary historians have not been happy with the term, given the quantity of writing in the South up to that time, but if the term is also used to mean a "flowering," then it is clearly appropriate.

Mencken's attack, of course, had nothing to do with initiating the Renaissance, which was the culmination of a number of historic and cultural forces at work in southern society. The region had experienced a military defeat on its own soil and the trying Reconstruction era, which brought about a period of self-analysis and reflection on the values it had fought to preserve and in some cases a reaffirmation of those values. Some white southerners assumed a burden of guilt with regard to the treatment of blacks, but nonetheless maintained a belief in white superiority. Resistance to cultural reconstruction intensified the traditional regional sense of identity and distinctiveness in which some took pleasure and from which others felt the need to escape. These tensions stirred the creative sensibilities of writers, who were instructed well by southern history in mortality and the inevitability of death—concerns that would bring their themes to a level of universal relevance.

These matters were treated in the grand and eloquent style of William Faulkner, the major writer to emerge from the Renaissance and the greatest American writer of the 20th century. Using local, family, and Mississippi history, Faulkner constructed a fictional world populated by southern figures of tragedy and comedy who acted out his major theme of the human heart in conflict with itself. His stylistic innovations under the influence of James Joyce, his mastery of external and internal landscape, the incredible range of characterization in his fiction, and the affirmative spirit that provides a philosophic base for his work—all these promise to make him a writer for the ages, a Shakespeare in southern homespun.

Major writers contemporary with Faulkner were Thomas Wolfe, who attempted a herculean transformation of his personal dislocation as a southerner into fiction of bardic proportions; Richard Wright, who achieved a disturbing, razor-sharp portrayal of what growing up black in the South and America meant and forced whites to pay attention; and Robert Penn Warren, whose fiction constitutes a lifelong philosophic discourse on the meaning of history, the nature of man, and the compromises necessary in building a workable political and social system. Though overshadowed by Faulkner's achievement, all three achieve distinctive voices in fiction.

Others worked in Faulkner's shadow but followed their own separate sensibilities with notable results, as evidenced by the stylistically perfect stories of Katherine Anne Porter, the keen sensitivity to adolescence in the fiction of Carson McCullers and James Agee, and the richly textured re-creations in the southern vernacular of myth and metaphor in Eudora Welty's stories and novels. Except for their lack of artistic discipline and willingness to publish too much too fast, Erskine Caldwell and Jesse Stuart might have entered this golden circle; as it is, they remain of interest because of the philosophically opposite variations they offer on some of the same material handled by Faulkner. The single writer who reached more readers than all these major writers put together and has probably done more to shape the larger public's attitude toward the South was Margaret Mitchell. With more enthusiasm than artistry and less skill than imagination, she wrote one novel, *Gone with the Wind* (1936), which remains an enigma but must be counted a significant event of the Renaissance.

A host of other fiction writers should be accounted for in any survey of the Renaissance, including Harriette Simpson Arnow, Hamilton Basso, Roark Bradford, Brainard Cheney, Alfred Leland Crabbe, Caroline Gordon, Dubose Heyward, Zora Neale Hurston, Andrew Lytle, William March, Julia Peterkin, Josephine Pinckney, Marjorie Kinnan Rawlings, Elizabeth Madox Roberts, Lyle Saxon, Evelyn Scott, Lillian Smith, James Still, T. S. Stribling, Jean Toomer, and Stark Young.

Although drama was never to be a major mode for southern writers, Paul Green began in the 1920s a 50-year career as the successful author of folk plays and historic symphonic dramas; Lawrence Stallings had a notable success in collaboration with Maxwell Anderson, *What Price Glory?* (1924); Lillian Hellman, beginning with the popular reception of *The Little Foxes* (1939), wrote a series of sensitive treatments of life in southern settings; and Tennessee Williams began in the 1940s a singularly distinctive career as the author of numerous plays that examined in depth and detail southern elements of life and character and gained for himself a reputation as one of America's three most accomplished playwrights (along with Eugene O'Neill and Arthur Miller).

A formidable body of poetry emerged during the Renaissance beginning with the publication in 1922 of the first issue of the *Fugitive*, a little magazine edited by a group of young faculty members and students at Vanderbilt University in Nashville. Many would mark the event as the official beginning of the Southern Literary Renaissance. Although they were for the moment in agreement that modern poetry must escape the conventionalism of the past, the major figures were to follow different patterns of development—John Crowe Ransom finding in irony and paradox the tension necessary to good poetry, Allen Tate turning to abstract methods as more suitable for treating the dislocations in modern society evident to the traditional sensibility, Robert Penn Warren preferring narrative forms deeply philosophical in their import, and Donald Davidson finding more compatible folk narratives incorporating history and the lives of influential southern figures. Merrill Moore, John Gould Fletcher, and, for a brief time, Laura Riding were associated with the Fugitive poets. A young Randall Jarrell would come to Vanderbilt in the early 1930s to study under Ransom, Davidson, and Warren and under their influence to begin writing poetry striking in its combination of the erudite with the ordinary and its contrast of desperate violence with the seemingly peaceful surface of daily life. Two black poetic voices of the period who used their southern experiences in ethnically sensitive verse were James Weldon Johnson and Arna Bontemps, the former best known for his political activities with the NAACP and

Reunion in 1956 of the Fugitive poets (left to right, front row) Allen Tate, Merrill Moore, John Crowe Ransom, Donald Davidson, and (back row) Robert Penn Warren

the latter as the author of the lyrics for the musical *St. Louis Woman*.

After the *Fugitive* ceased publication in 1925, the four major forces—Ransom, Davidson, Tate, and Warren—began discussions about the state of the South in political and economic terms and found themselves in agreement that only by resisting modern progress and technology could the region maintain a hold on the virtues of its traditional agrarian past. Joining forces with eight other southern intellectuals, including writers Stark Young, John Gould Fletcher, Andrew Lytle, and John Donald Wade, they published the Agrarian manifesto *I'll Take My Stand* (1930), a major document in the debate between science and humanism in the 20th century. The only other prose volume to generate more controversy during the Renaissance was W. J. Cash's effort to interpret *The Mind of the South* (1941), which has proven to be more valuable as a study of the mind of *a* southerner—Cash himself.

In the exciting intellectual milieu of the Fugitive and Agrarian movements, modern southern literary criticism had its birth. Ransom, Tate, and Warren had already been practicing criticism early on, but Ransom in particular began to encourage the development of a formalist approach called the New Criticism, which assessed a work of art on its own terms apart from its relation to the life of the artist or the times in which it was written. One of Ransom's best students at Vanderbilt, Cleanth Brooks, would develop the system more fully, incorporating it in two highly influential textbooks written in collaboration with Robert Penn Warren, *Understanding Poetry* (1938) and *Understanding Fiction* (1943). The adherents to this critical approach became more single-minded in its application than either Ransom or Brooks ever intended, as demonstrated by the fine biographical and historical criticism practiced by Brooks in his important studies of William Faulkner.

Ransom, Davidson, Tate, Warren, and Brooks also provided another service in establishing a role model for the modern man of letters as teacher, all serving throughout their literary careers as lecturers in American universities and becoming, in effect, some of the first writers in residence. A number of university teachers achieved national distinction as practicing critics, scholars, and historians of southern culture, including Edwin Mims and Richmond Croom Beatty at Vanderbilt; Jay B. Hubbell at Duke; Benjamin Brawley at Morehouse and Howard; Floyd Stovall at the University of Virginia; Randall Stewart at Brown and Vanderbilt; Lewis Leary at Duke and Columbia; Edd Winfield Parks at Georgia; Sterling A. Brown, Saunders Redding, and Arthur P. Davis at Howard; Richard Beale Davis at Tennessee; and C. Vann Woodward at Johns Hopkins and Yale University.

As if the first generation had not been sufficient to leave an indelible mark on American letters, a second generation of Renaissance writers flooded the bookstores with their works following World War II. Flannery O'Connor arrested the attention of everyone by producing stories and novels shocking in their use of perversely exaggerated southern characters but orthodox in the Catholicism that informs their meaning. William Styron moved away from the stylistic influence of Faulkner and his early novels to achieve a major mode of fiction based on history and personal experience. Truman Capote published stories of impeccable style, while developing what he would call the "nonfiction novel," and his childhood friend Harper Lee wrote a single novel, *To Kill a Mockingbird* (1960), which remains a classic for its sensitive treatment of adolescence and racism in an Alabama town. Another one-novel writer, Ralph Ellison, captured history, folklore, music, and the political significance of the black man in America in *Invisible Man* (1952), which was as much concerned with the existential fate of modern man as with the black experience. Walker Percy's interests in Christian existentialism provided a foundation for his increasingly conservative novels, and John Barth brilliantly played with and reworked all the traditional forms and points of view developed in the entire history of fiction.

A beginning list of other significant practitioners of short fiction and the novel among the second generation Renaissance writers should include Doris Betts, Fred Chappell, Ellen Douglas, Shelby Foote, Jesse Hill Ford, Ernest J. Gaines, George Garrett, William Goyen, Shirley Ann Grau, Chester Himes, Madison Jones, John Oliver Killens, David Madden, Cormac McCarthy, Marion Montgomery, Reynolds Price, Mary Lee Settle, Elizabeth Spencer, Peter Taylor, Margaret Walker, John A. Williams, Calder Willingham, and Frank Yerby.

The leading poet to emerge in the postwar period was James Dickey, trained at Vanderbilt and devoted to the achievement of a careful balance between the formal and the emotional within an intricate poetic structure, and raising the ordinary experience to the level of epiphany. His novel *Deliverance* (1970) is a metaphoric study of man's potential for violence and salvation. Other poets to attract critical praise include A. R. Ammons, Wendell Berry, John William Corrington, Julia Fields, Dabney Stuart, and Miller Williams.

A second generation of university teachers continued the earlier critical explorations of southern literature and scholarship; many of them were trained by members of the first generation: C. Hugh Holman at North Carolina; Arlin Turner at Louisiana State University and Duke; Richard Weaver at Chicago; Lewis Simpson at LSU; Ruel Foster at West Virginia; Thomas Daniel Young and Walter Sullivan at Vanderbilt; Floyd Watkins at Emory; Louis D. Rubin, Jr., at Hollins and North Carolina; and Louise Cowan at the University of Dallas. Southern journalists who established a tradition for crusading liberal journalism in the 1950s were Ralph McGill, Hodding Carter, Harry Ashmore, and Willie Morris, but in a class by himself was Tom Wolfe, a founder of the free-wheeling, personal, stylistically fluid school of New Journalism.

Contemporary Era. Some scholars argue that the Renaissance is over, that contemporary writers share too little in the sense of southern tradition and are swept up in faddish social causes and personal crises, but a third generation of considerable promise has emerged. Although they both came to fiction late in their lives, black novelists Robert Dean Pharr and Alex Haley attracted attention in the 1970s, Haley in particular for his recreation of the history of his family in America, *Roots* (1976). Other writers producing fiction and poetry of note are Lisa Alther, Maya Angelou, Pat Conroy, Nikki Giovanni, Gail Godwin, Barry Hannah, Beverly Lowry, James Alan McPherson, Bobbie Ann Mason, Lee Smith, Anne Tyler, Alice Walker, and Sylvia Wilkinson. Many of them are black and female, perhaps a sign of racial and feminine liberation at work in the South.

Whatever the future may hold for literature in the South, the social changes and the cultural challenges at work in the rapidly changing cities of Atlanta, Charlotte, Birmingham, Nashville, and Richmond, as well as the suburbs and the countryside along interstate routes 95 and 85, create the kinds of intellectual conflict that often stir the imagination and stimulate creative writing. Whether in the form of fiction, poetry, or play; memoir, history, or journalism; docudrama, screenplay, or criticism, in all likelihood, the last distinctively southern writer, like the last southern gentleman, has not yet been seen.

See also BLACK LIFE: Literature, Black; / Bontemps, Arna; Chesnutt, Charles W.; Douglass, Frederick; Free Southern Theater; Gaines, Ernest J.; Haley, Alex; Hurston, Zora Neale; Johnson, James Weldon; Murray, Pauli; Toomer, Jean; Walker, Margaret; HISTORY AND MANNERS: / Byrd, William, II; Jefferson, Thomas; MEDIA articles; MYTHIC SOUTH: / Agrarians, Vanderbilt; Mitchell, Margaret; Yerby, Frank; RELIGION: Literature and Religion; SOCIAL CLASS: Lower Class, Literary; WOMEN'S LIFE: Writers; / Chesnut, Mary Boykin; Chopin, Kate; Peterkin, Julia Mood

M. Thomas Inge
Randolph-Macon College

Robert Bain, *Southern Writers: A Biographical Dictionary* (1979); Richmond Croom Beatty, Floyd C. Watkins, and Thomas Daniel Young, eds., *The Literature of the South* (1952; rev. ed., 1968); John M. Bradbury, *Renaissance in the South: A Critical History of the Literature, 1920–1960* (1963); Louise Cowan, *The Fugitive Group: A Literary History* (1959); Donald Davidson, *Southern Writers in the Modern World* (1958); Richard Beale Davis, *Intellectual Life in the Colonial South, 1565–1763* (1978); Richard Gray, *The Literature of Memory: Modern Writers of the American South* (1977); C. Hugh Holman, *Three Modes of Southern Fiction* (1966); Jay B. Hubbell, *The South in American Literature* (1954); Anne Goodwyn Jones, *Tomorrow Is Another Day: The Woman Writer in the South, 1859–1936* (1981); Richard H. King, *A Southern Renaissance: The Cultural Awakening of the American South, 1930–1955* (1980); Michael O'Brien, *The Idea of the American South, 1920–1941* (1979); Ladell Payne, *Black Novelists and the Southern Literary Tradition* (1981); Joseph V. Ridgely, *Nineteenth-Century Southern Literature* (1980); Louis D. Rubin, Jr., ed., *The American South: Portrait of a Culture* (1980), *The Wary Fugitives: Four Poets and the South* (1978), with Robert D. Jacobs, eds., *South: Modern Southern Literature in Its Cultural Setting* (1961), with others, *A History of Southern Literature* (1985); Lewis P. Simpson, *The Dispossessed Garden: Pastoral and History in Southern Fiction* (1975); Edmund Wilson, *Patriotic Gore: Studies in the Literature of the Civil War* (1962); Thomas Daniel Young, *The Past in the Present: A Thematic Study of Modern Southern Fiction* (1981).

Agrarianism in Literature

The ideas associated with agrarianism in this century may be stated as an interrelated set of beliefs:

1. The cultivation of the soil is an occupation singularly blessed by God that provides benefits from direct contact with physical nature. It is the mother of all the arts and instills in the cultivator such spiritual and social virtues as honor, courage, self-reliance, integrity, and hospitality.

2. The standard by which an economic system is judged is not the amount of prosperity it produces but the degree to which it encourages independence and morality. Because the farmer's basic needs of food and shelter are always met through a cooperative relationship with nature, only farming offers complete self-sufficiency regardless of the state of the national economy.

3. The life of the farmer is harmonious, orderly, and whole, and it counteracts the tendencies toward abstraction, fragmentation, and alienation that have come with modern urban existence. The farmer belongs to a specific family, place, and region; participates in a historic and religious tradition; and has, in other words, a sense of identity that is psychologically and culturally beneficial.

4. Since nature is the primary source of inspiration, all the arts, music, literature, and other forms of creativity are better fostered and sustained in an agrarian society. The mass-produced culture of the industrial society lacks the individuality, humanity, and simple beauty of folk culture.

5. The thriving cities created by industry, technology, and capitalism are destructive of independence and dignity and encourage crime and corruption. The agricultural community, on the other hand, which depends on friendly cooperation and neighborliness, provides a possible model for an ideal social order.

These ideas are the culmination of a philosophical development that is a part of the mainstream of Western civilization. In classical literature, Hesiod, Aristotle, Cicero, Vergil, and Horace are among those who reiterated the advantages of country life and husbandry over the other modes of existence and occupations. From the Middle Ages through the Renaissance and down to the 18th century, most major and minor writers praised the pastoral and rural life over city life and cursed the materialism and decadence fostered by the new spirits of commercialism and progress. When the European settlers arrived in North America, they brought with them these ideas as a part of their cultural heritage.

The land of the New Englanders was hard and stony and poorly suited to farming. The fertile soil and amenable climate of the South, however, naturally encouraged agriculture as the primary economic pursuit of the entire region. Among his contemporaries, Virginian Thomas Jefferson did more to advance experimentation and technique in agriculture than anyone else by introducing his own innovations and inventions and including agricultural science in the curriculum of the University of Virginia. Of greater importance to southern thought was his early formulation of the agrarian ideal in query 19 of his *Notes on the State of Virginia* (1785), where he states, "Those who labour in the earth are the chosen people of

God, if he ever had a chosen people, whose breasts he has made his peculiar deposit for substantial and genuine virtue." Jefferson's concise statement of fewer than 400 words has inspired almost two centuries of literary, social, and political debate.

The place of agriculture in the wealth of the new nation was contested in the early party battle between the Federalist and Republican forces led respectively by Alexander Hamilton and Jefferson. The Federalists favored a centralized federal government, controlled by a propertied few, supported by commercial and industrial expansion. The Republicans, however, favored reliance on local government, under the leadership of a natural aristocracy of talent and virtue, with a primarily agrarian national economy based in independent farmers and landholders. The tensions of this debate were to reverberate down to and beyond the Civil War, which some have contended was basically a struggle between the two competing economies. While Jefferson's democratic theories largely prevailed in politics, Hamilton's industrial program prevailed in the economic sphere as America realized the extent of its natural resources and looked to capitalism to exploit them.

Southern literature offers a wide variety of novels, poems, and stories that deal in imaginative ways with the theories and realities of agrarianism. The virtues of agrarian life were celebrated in the 19th century in the works of John Esten Cooke, Joel Chandler Harris, Richard Malcolm Johnston, John Pendleton Kennedy, Sidney Lanier, Mary Noailles Murfree, Thomas Nelson Page, William Gilmore Simms, Henry Timrod, and Mark Twain. In 1930 agrarianism was the unifying force for a group of writers led by John Crowe Ransom, Donald Davidson, Allen Tate, and Robert Penn Warren of Vanderbilt University in Nashville, which resulted in the publication of a symposium *I'll Take My Stand: The South and the Agrarian Tradition*. To one degree or another, these ideas were to remain the subject matter of much of their later poetry, fiction, and criticism, especially in Davidson's work.

Along with the portraits of the husbandman as an honest champion of individualism, southern literature also contains obverse portraits of poor white farmers as lazy, shiftless, uncouth members of a mongrel race. William Byrd II of Westover initiated this brutish characterization with his colonial sketches of the idle lubberlanders observed in North Carolina during his survey of the boundary line between that state and Virginia. Reacting partly out of his upper-class sensitivities and partly out of the tradition that North Carolina was a refuge for criminals and malcontents, Byrd fathered a long-continuing series of descriptions of poor white degenerates, extending through 19th-century southern writing, the humor of the Old Southwest, and local color fiction, down to Erskine Caldwell's lustful and depraved sharecroppers. H. L. Mencken also had little sympathy for the romance of agrarianism and called the farmer "a tedious brand of ignoramus, a cheap rogue and hypocrite, the eternal Jack of the human pack."

In this century, the writers whose fiction and poetry are reflective of agrarian problems and principles include Ransom, Davidson, Tate, Warren, Ellen Glasgow, Caroline Gordon, Andrew Lytle, Margaret Mitchell, Flannery O'Connor, Elizabeth Madox Roberts, Mary Lee Settle, Jesse Stuart, Alice Walker, Eudora Welty, Thomas Wolfe, and Stark Young.

Agrarian themes are particularly important in William Faulkner's fictional saga of Yoknapatawpha County. The passing away of the wilderness in the face of industrialism and commercialism is the theme of his story "The Bear," and in the Snopes trilogy (*The Hamlet*, *The Town*, and *The Mansion*) Faulkner projected on a broad canvas the conflict between agrarianism and materialism, the principles of the first embodied in the defeated chivalry of the Sartoris family, and the valueless animalism of the second embodied in the successful Snopes breed. The independent, small-farm families, such as the McCallums and the McCaslins, are always favorably treated. Faulkner was concerned in much of his work with the transformation of the idyllic agrarian society into the modern urban industrial world. Popeye of *Sanctuary*, described as a mechanical creature with a face of stamped tin, grows hysterical at the sight of fields and trees, and thus stands as Faulkner's ultimate symbol of the machine and its effects on society.

Many southern writers continue to hold onto the humanism inherent in agrarianism, and some of its concerns have found a voice in the modern ecology, environmental, and back-to-the-land movements. However, as farming ceases to be a way of life in the South and elsewhere, the coherent philosophy it once represented will likely lose much of its impact or find a new mode of expression.

See also HISTORY AND MANNERS: / Byrd, William, II; Jefferson, Thomas; MYTHIC SOUTH: / Agrarians, Vanderbilt; Mencken's South

M. Thomas Inge
Randolph-Macon College

M. Thomas Inge, ed., *Agrarianism in American Literature* (1969); Leo Marx, *The Machine in the Garden: Technology and the Pastoral Ideal in America* (1964); Henry Bamford Parkes, *The American Experience* (1947); Twelve Southerners, *I'll Take My Stand: The South and the Agrarian Tradition* (1930).

Appalachian Literature

The literature of Appalachia has coincided with distinct historical developments: the early exploration by Indians, hunters, trappers, and adventurers; the pioneer period characterized by scattered settlement and an agrarian lifestyle (barely interrupted by the Civil War); and the exploitation of coal and wood during the turn of the century, spawning mass migration. Cratis Williams, in a classic dissertation on Appalachian literature, divided the literary-historical periods into three: (1) early exploration to 1880, (2) 1880–1930, (3) 1930–present. Called "pioneer," the first period included writers who sought a distinct James Fenimore Cooper-like flavor. Writers such as Mary Noailles Murfree, who wrote about real Appalachian characters and situations set in the Great Smoky Mountains, typify the second era. The last period began shortly after the Great Depression and saw the emergence of literary figures who carved a place in American letters for Appalachian themes and characters. In the mid-1980s this group is passing that torch to a younger set of regional writers such as Wilma Dykeman, Harry Caudill, Jim Wayne Miller, Lillie D. Chaffin, Earl Hamner, Jr., Jane Stuart, Loyal Jones, and Jack Weller.

Among the notable members of the post-1930 group were Jesse Stuart, with his more than 40 books covering biography, autobiography, novel, short story, poetry, essay, and journalism; Harriette Simpson Arnow, with her powerful novel *The Dollmaker* (1954); James Still, with his highly respected attention to art and craft in fiction, short story, and poetry in *River of Earth* (1940), *On Troublesome Creek* (1941), and *Hounds on the Mountain* (1937); and Thomas Wolfe, the famed author of *Look Homeward, Angel* (1929) and *The Hills Beyond* (1935).

The themes of Appalachian literature have followed historical developments closely. The early writing consisted mainly of diary or journal accounts of travel through the region when trappers and traders first began to form their impressions. Higgs and Manning in their 1975 anthology include works from John Lederer, who began to write about the region in 1669; John Fontaine, whose journal published in 1838 included accounts of his travels into the Blue Ridge and the Shenandoah Valley; Timothy Flint, whose *Biographical Memoir of Daniel Boone* (1833) was perhaps the most widely read biography of the early 19th century; James Kirke Paulding, whose *Letters from the South* (1816) demonstrated the captivating qualities of the Appalachian Mountains; and Anne Newport Royall, called America's first hitchhiker, who wrote of the unspoiled region in her *Sketches of History, Life, and Manners in the United States* (1826).

Immediately following this period a group of writers emerged who exploited the stereotypes and romantic notions associated with the region. Although the mountaineers were not specifically the object of their writing, they emerged from a larger pool of "southern characters" whose adventures, romances, brave feats, and foolish ways were chronicled in such works as those by Mark Twain, George Washington Harris, and David (Davy) Crockett. Tall tales, backwoods humor, and romanticism were major thematic elements of this literary era "in which men were more than a match for the wilderness that surrounded them."

The next period was dominated by native writers such as John Fox, Jr. (*Trail of the Lonesome Pine* [1931] and *The Little Shepherd of Kingdom Come* [1931]), Mary Noailles Murfree (*In the Tennessee Mountains* [1884] and 25 other works, mostly fiction set in the southern mountain area), and Elizabeth Madox Roberts (*The Time of Man* [1926], *The Great Meadow* [1930], and hundreds of poems published in national magazines). Their works were largely romantic and were often written in dialect. Sentimentality and a neoromanticism merged with Appalachian stereotypes and motifs to set the tone until the 1930s. Feuding, the Civil War in Appalachia, moonshining, and historical romance became common topics.

The 1930s were characterized by native writers who developed local material into larger, more universal themes. This period was dominated by Jesse Stuart, James Still, Harriette Simpson Arnow, James Agee, and Thomas Wolfe. Their writing is highly conscious of custom and tradition as it forms the total consciousness of America. If Appalachia was exemplary of America's pioneer past, then their duty, as these writers saw it, was to find meaning in, and to come to grips with, the passing of the folkways that had so tightly bound the isolated Appalachia to that past. They would be compelled to announce the significance of that passing to the "modern world," which might not have otherwise paused to learn of it. Many of these writers simply ignored the stereotypes and transcended the local color stories by developing more universal themes.

The final period began in the 1950s. Younger, better-educated, and more socially conscious writers began to develop a literature examining the region through its social consciousness, political issues, historical significance, religious disposition, and economic impact. Most notable among these books are Harry Caudill's *Night Comes to the Cumberlands* (1962), *Watches of the Night* (1976), *Theirs Be the Power* (1983), and a half-dozen other documentary and fiction pieces; Jack Weller's *Yesterday's People* (1965), which is probably one of the most widely discussed books ever written on southern Appalachia; Ron Eller's scholarly study *Miners, Millhands, and Mountaineers: The Modernization of the Appalachian South, 1880–1930* (1981), which traces the history of the industrial movement in Appalachia and its impact upon this once-pristine region; John C. Campbell's *The Southern Highlander and His Homeland*, the classic 1921 study, which details the history and lifestyle of the southern Appalachians; Henry David Shapiro's *Appalachia on Our Mind: The Southern Mountains and Mountaineers in the American Consciousness, 1870–1920* (1978), which does much to help identify the role of the Appalachian people in the larger American culture; Horace Kephart's *Our Southern Highlanders* (1913), a social history of the Appalachian region; John Gaventa's *Power and Powerlessness: Quiescence and Rebellion in an Appalachian Valley* (1980), a work of Appalachian political theory and a history of the mine wars in the 1930s; and David E. Whisnant's *All That Is Native and Fine: The Politics of Culture in an American Region* (1983), a study of cultural intervention by outsiders in Appalachia.

Others who frequently write about the region include Fred Chappell (poetry and short stories), Jeff Daniel Marion (poetry), James B. Goode (poetry and essays), Lee Pennington (poetry, short stories, criticism, and drama), Billy Edd Wheeler (poetry, song lyrics, and music), Jean Ritchie (poetry, song lyrics, and music), George Scarbrough (poetry), John Rice Irwin (histories and documentaries), Loyal Jones (histories, essays, and documentaries), and Gurney Norman (novels, short stories, and poetry).

Several current periodicals have consistently published Appalachian literary criticism, poetry, short fiction, and topical essays. Among the notable ones are *Appalachian Journal: A Regional Studies Review*, *Appalachian Heritage: A Magazine of Southern Appalachian Life and Cul-*

ture, Foxfire, Mountain Life and Work: The Magazine of the Appalachian South, Appalachian Notes, and *The Plow: The Monthly Magazine for Mountain People.*

Substantial anthologies on the region are rare but a few good ones exist: Ambrose Manning and Robert J. Higgs's *Voices from the Hills*, Cecille Haddix's *Who Speaks for Appalachia?*, Joy Pennington's *Selected Kentucky Literature*, and Ruel Foster's *Appalachian Literature: Critical Essays*. There are also several good bibliographies. The most complete one is Charlotte T. Ross's *Bibliography of Southern Appalachia*. Others include Louise Boger's *The Southern Mountaineer in Literature* (1976), Robert Munn's *Appalachian Bibliography* (1968), and Appendices A-G "A Guide to Appalachian Studies" (Autumn 1977 issue of *Appalachian Journal*). A few shelf lists are also helpful: the fiction and poetry list of the Berea College Weatherford-Hammond Mountain Collection, the Council of Southern Mountains' *Bibliography of the Appalachian South*, *Appalachian Outlook* (a cumulative listing of periodical literature issued by the University of West Virginia Library), and the Appalachian Book and Record Shop's *Appalachian Literature and Music: A Comprehensive Catalogue* (which is arranged by 11 topics, is fully indexed, and contains approximately 635 entries).

Appalachian literary history includes a variety of writing, which adds to the evolving body of American letters. A part of that literature unmistakably has kinship with the South. The rural agrarian mind-set, the mass immigration from nearby southern states, the fierce independence as evidenced by the bloody union movements (which may parallel the ideas reflected in the Civil War), the emphasis upon folk tradition and culture, the history of oral tradition, and the inclination to use literature to express sociological or anthropological concerns are all characteristics that prove the link. But many other aspects of the literature make it a legitimate entity apart from the southern literary experience. A frequent theme in Appalachian literature, for example, has been the struggle by Appalachians to bridge the gulf between traditional Appalachian culture and contemporary America. Appalachian writing remains an independent body of letters struggling for a place in American, including southern, literature.

See also EDUCATION: / Campbell, John C.; ETHNIC LIFE: Mountain Culture; / Appalachians; FOLKLIFE: / "Hillbilly" Image; INDUSTRY: Industrialization in Appalachia; LANGUAGE: Mountain Language; MYTHIC SOUTH: Appalachian Culture; RELIGION: Appalachian Religion; SOCIAL CLASS: Appalachia, Exploitation of; WOMEN'S LIFE: Writers, Women

James B. Goode
University of Kentucky
Southeast Community College

George Brosi, ed., *Appalachian Literature and Music: A Comprehensive Catalogue* (1981); James B. Goode, *Temporary Finding Guide: Southeast Community College Oral History Project, 1978–1983* (1984); Cecille Haddix, ed., *Who Speaks for Appalachia?: Prose, Poetry, and Songs from the Mountain Heritage* (1975); Robert J. Higgs and Ambrose Manning, eds., *Voices from the Hills* (1975); Jim Wayne Miller, *Appalachian Journal* (Autumn 1977); Cratis Williams, "The Southern Mountaineer in Fact and Fiction" (Ph.D. dissertation, New York University, 1961).

Autobiography

Southern autobiographers exhibit a historical consciousness typical of southern literature. They value religious or moral interpretations of the world, are loyal to family, friends, and community, and unavoidably confront a heritage of slavery and racial struggle. Largely because of the irony and tragedy of southern history, the regional autobiographers are conscious of human imperfection, social injustice, and the existence of evil in the world. At the same time, they are storytellers who in a casual, literary way reveal the individual context of regional history and the distinctiveness of southern culture while preserving and continuing the dialogue between region and nation.

Until the 19th century, southern autobiography could not be distinguished from the established form of English spiritual autobiography. Southern autobiographers, including Thomas Jefferson, were prominent public officials who equated their professions with their identity and function in *American* history. As sectional conflict became more pronounced and serious, autobiography became more popular, and ordinary southerners more frequently wrote their autobiographies. Antebellum plantation mistresses silently recorded their life stories in their diaries, and escaped slaves wrote narratives detailing their journeys from South to North. Among antebellum diaries, *Mary Chesnut's Civil War* (edited by C. Vann Woodward, 1982) most elaborately details antebellum southern cultural life, landscape, social events, political controversy, and domestic relations. It is, as well, a moral critique by a southern aristocrat experiencing the social tumult and disruption of civil war. The diary exemplifies the cultural ambivalance of a South in crisis, a questioning of traditional social and moral behavior, of patriarchy and the slave system, and of the ever-apparent disparities between the myth of the leisured southern lady and the reality of her everyday life.

Chesnut's portrait of the antebellum South is enhanced by a reading of the hundreds of slave narratives that established the literary form for black autobiography in America. Most significant among them are the narratives of William Wells Brown (1847), Henry Bibb (1849), James W. C. Pennington (1849), Sojourner Truth (1850), Solomon Northup (1853), Samuel Ringgold Ward (1855), Booker T. Washington (1911), and the three-volume autobiography of Frederick Douglass (1845, 1855, 1881). The cultural foundation for the narratives was laid within the slave community, where the religion of the quarters provided a moral framework for criticizing the slave system. Each author condemns the institution of slavery for its inherent evil nature and its racism. At the same time, the narratives portray the heroic struggle of black families who battled forced separation, sale, and migration to maintain strong kinship networks. Committed to the betterment of the South and the advancement of their race, slave narrators present the evils of the slave system, not of its perpetrators. The slaves' unique heritage, their existence in bondage, their fusion of African and evangelical religion, and the strength of the slave community represent their vital contribution to southern autobiography.

More recent southern autobiographers are guided by a historical consciousness that fuses identity and community. They are acutely conscious of southern cultural distinctiveness, as created and maintained through individual lives. Five autobiographical masterworks exemplify the character of modern southern autobiography: Richard Wright's *Black Boy* (1945), William Alexander Percy's *Lanterns on the Levee* (1941), Katherine Du Pre Lumpkin's *The Making of a Southerner* (1946), Willie Morris's *North Toward Home* (1967), and Will Campbell's *Brother to a Dragonfly* (1977).

Richard Wright's autobiography condemns racism while describing the author's quest for human dignity and achievement as a writer. Family history and racial struggle provide the foundation for Wright's rebellious spirit, his distrust of authority, tradition, and the white world. Like antebellum slave narrators, Wright found it necessary to gain an education and then leave the South in order to escape danger and achieve his goals. He nevertheless retains a loyalty to the South and a sense of place that guide the development of his life. Nostalgically, he recalls the Mississippi landscape, the "yellow, dreaming waters of the Mississippi River and the verdant bluffs of Natchez," "the drenching hospitality in the pervading smell of sweet magnolias," and "the aura of limitless freedom distilled from the rolling sweep of tall, green grass swaying and glinting in the summer sun." Wright left the South in order to understand it more clearly; and he wrote *Black Boy* so that others would join him in the struggle against racism.

William Alexander Percy and Katherine Du Pre Lumpkin, both of whom are descendants of slaveholders, wrestle with the assumptions behind racial inequality and sectional conflict, while placing their life histories within the context of southern history. Born in 1885 and 1897, respectively, each inherited some of the values and lifestyles that characterized the Old South. Both define their lives by describing a shared heritage: the settlement of the South, the importation of slaves, Reconstruction, the development and demise of the sharecropping system, the Depression, World War I, and the civil rights movement that emerged at the turn of the century. Percy's *Lanterns on the Levee* is the sensitive exposition of a southern aristocrat who feared the rule of the masses and was determined to confront the criticism of northern liberals in order to defend the cultural traditions of the Old South. Writing during a time when the nation viewed the South as poor, backward, and disease ridden, Percy describes an idyllic southern childhood, including his early exposure to religion, turtle soup, and crawfishing along the Mississippi River. Impressionistically, he outlines his life with Delta landscapes and history, friends and relations, cultural traditions, and his favorite stories. He discusses his confrontations with northern liberals when he attended Harvard, when he served in the army during World War I, and when northern journalists criticized as racist his decisions as chairman of the Greenville, Miss., Flood Relief Committee, after the disastrous flood of 1927. Thoughtfully and carefully, he rationalizes and attempts to justify white supremacy, manifesting a patience and tolerance for slow change that is absent from more recent southern autobiography.

Unlike Percy, Katherine Du Pre Lumpkin altered her racial attitudes as southern society changed and the incongruities of the old life, particularly between racism and Christian doctrine, became apparent to her. Her vivid descriptions of family and community portray southern culture in its most basic sense: a living record of voices and lives. Lumpkin struggles to overcome her bondage to slavery, transmitted to her through several generations of relatives and through acquaintances who taught her to accept the inequality between white and black. She represents well a changing South, and ultimately rejects racial inequality and discrimination, as well as "the entire peculiar set of ways which it allegedly justified."

Willie Morris's autobiography, *North Toward Home*, best illustrates how 20th-century southerners become acutely conscious of regional identity and southern ethnicity when they travel to the North. A Mississippi childhood shapes and informs the autobiography, as Morris describes his travels from Mississippi to Texas to New York. In New York he is stereotyped by northerners, black and white, who assume that he is backward, uneducated, unsophisticated, and racist. Thrust back upon himself and his past, he befriends other southerners up North: Richard Wright, Ralph Ellison, and William Styron. His conversations with them enable him to define his cultural identity and to formulate a clear definition of southern temperament, intellect, and imagination:

> . . . easygoing conversation; the casual talk and the telling of stories, in the Southern verbal jam-session way; the sense of family and the past and people out of the past; the congenial social manner and mischievous laughter; the fondness of especial *detail* and the suspicion of more grandiose generalizations about human existence; the love of the American language in its accuracy and vividness and simplicity; the obsession with the sensual experience of America in all its extravagance and diversity; the love of animals and sports, of the outdoors and sour mash; the distrust in the face of provocation of certain manifestations of Eastern intellectualism . . . and a pointed tension just below the surface of things, usually controlled but always there.

Morris's autobiography provides evidence for the persistence of southern regional distinctiveness and the sense of place that defines southern lives.

Will Campbell's *Brother to a Dragonfly* exemplifies the interconnectedness a southerner perceives between self, family, morality, and community. Like Lillian Hellman's outstanding autobiography, *Pentimento* (1973), Campbell's autobiography views the author through a portrait of another. The lives of Will and Joe Campbell intertwine within the context of Mississippi social history. In the Campbell family, each brother's identity is assigned and unquestioned. Joe is the worker; Will is the preacher. Through tales of mischief, Will recalls their childhood: his nearly burning down an outhouse or fooling the WPA when they tested southern schoolchildren for hookworm. As youngsters, the brothers are intimate friends, but their lives diverge during adulthood after Will attends Yale and receives what Joe calls his "bachelor's of sophistication." When desegregation and civil rights become Will's mission during the 1950s, the brothers find themselves on opposite sides of racial issues. Joe increasingly adopts the role of the dragonfly—grasping for stability and security where there is none, becoming addicted to sedatives and amphetamines, and finally committing suicide. *Brother to a Dragonfly* describes two responses to the historical changes that affected 20th-century southern life: the Depression, World War II, integration, and the civil rights movement. Will and Joe Campbell's lives are "bound inextricably together . . . sometimes in a nearness approaching, surpassing illness. And sometimes so far apart that neither could hear the cry of the other."

Regardless of their race or social class, southern autobiographers define their lives within the shared context of southern history and culture. They present a realistic portrait of the South, while assessing and interpreting their relationship to the region, constructing a meaning through autobiography. One of the best-known recent autobiographies, Theodore Rosengarten's *All God's Dangers: The Life of Nate Shaw* (1974), was a landmark in using oral history to tell the life story of Alabama sharecropper Ned Cobb; it conveyed the experience of one who lived through the dramatic changes of the 20th-century South yet would not have written a traditional autobiography. Despite their individual diversity, the authors of autobiographies portray a shared regional identity and cultural past, which have created the rich southern literary imagination. They indicate that South and North differ, in their landscapes, interaction patterns, traditions, and social conventions. Southern autobiographers differ from American autobiographers in general because of their historical consciousness. They stress the importance of family and community to identity and art, combining introspection, parable, and social critique to convey the cultural history of the South.

See also FOLKLIFE: / Cobb, Ned (Nate Shaw); MEDIA: / Morris, Willie; RELIGION: / Campbell, Will; WOMEN'S LIFE: / Chesnut, Mary Boykin

Ruth A. Banes
University of South Florida

Ruth A. Banes, in *Perspectives on the American South*, vol. 3, ed. James C. Cobb and Charles Reagan Wilson (1985); Cleanth Brooks, *Journal of Southern History* (February 1960); Will Campbell, *Brother to a Dragonfly* (1977); Harry Crews, *A Childhood: Biography of a Place* (1978); Frederick Douglass, *Life of an American Slave* (1845); Ellen Glasgow, *The Woman Within* (1954); Lillian Hellman, *Three* (1979); Zora Neale Hurston, *Dust Tracks on a Road* (1942); Katherine Du Pre Lumpkin, *The Making of a Southerner* (1946); Willie Morris, *North Toward Home* (1967); William Alexander Percy, *Lanterns on the Levee* (1941); John Shelton Reed, *One South: An Ethnic Approach to Regional Culture* (1982); Charles P. Roland, *Journal of Southern History* (February 1982); Lillian Smith, *Killers of the Dream* (1949); C. Vann Woodward, *The Burden of Southern History* (1960), ed., *Mary Chesnut's Civil War* (1981); Richard Wright, *Black Boy* (1937).

Biography

Almost 40 years ago, in his own study of Leonardo da Vinci, Sigmund Freud warned that biographers, for personal reasons, often choose heroes for their subjects. Out of their own "special affection," Freud wrote, "they then devote themselves to a work of idealization." Intolerant of anything in their subject's inner or outer life that smacks of human weakness or imperfection, biographers "then give us a cold, strange, ideal form instead of a man to whom we could feel distinctly related." Freud might have added that because the majority of biographers have been white men, so are the subjects of most biographies, South and North.

Two of the best examples of this kind of deification in southern biography are Thomas Jefferson and Robert E. Lee, both of whom have been the subjects of numerous biographies. The "Sage of Monticello" was truly an eloquent, erudite scholar and a brilliant statesman, but his chief biographers—James Parton, Douglas Southall Freeman, Merrill Peterson, and Dumas Malone—have glorified his accomplishments, minimized or denied his flaws, and canonized his name so that a demigod, not a man, emerges from the pages of their biographies. Not until 1974 and the appearance of Fawn Brodie's eye-opening psychobiography, *Thomas Jefferson: An Intimate History* (1974), did someone finally put flesh and bone on Jefferson. Brodie's Jefferson was ambivalent about love and power, slavery and revolution. Brodie's Jefferson was extremely virile and passionate and at the same time compulsively controlled. Most controversial of all, Brodie insisted that rumors of Jefferson's longtime love affair with Sally Hemmings, one of his slaves, were indeed true. The vehemence with which Jefferson's white male biographers, particularly Peterson and Malone, have leaped to their subject's defense in this sensitive matter is evidence of a continued refusal to admit that Jefferson had even a particle of human frailty.

Jefferson's sanctified image has been matched only by that of Robert E. Lee. Of the two Virginians, Lee is the one who, for most southerners, evokes the lump in the throat, the tearful faraway gaze. This is partly because Lee's biographers have purposely created and perpetuated the Lee myth: the man of flawless character; the perfect son, husband, and father; the noble officer torn between love for Union and loyalty to Virginia; the gallant general and brilliant militarist defeated only by overwhelming odds. He exemplified all that was best in the Old South, in the vanquished Confederacy. For the white South, Lee was a saint.

Thomas Connelly, in *The Marble Man: Robert E. Lee and His Image in American Society* (1977), traces the fascinating history behind the creation of the Lee legend. During and immediately after the Civil War, Lee was only one of several celebrated Confederate military leaders. Others, like Thomas "Stonewall" Jackson, Joe Johnston, and Pierre T. Beauregard, were rivals for southern popularity. Lee even received criticism from his earliest biographers for his alleged mistakes at Gettysburg. But in the mid-1870s, shortly after Lee died, a group of Virginians led by General Jubal Early, one of Lee's corps commanders, took control of the Southern Historical Society and its influential papers. For personal reasons, their image of the Civil War centered upon Lee and the Virginia military theater. So they decided to raise Lee far above the other war heroes, silence any critics, and downplay or discredit the exploits of other Confederate generals. Connelly shows how every subsequent biography of Lee, including Douglas Southall Freeman's prizewinning four-volume work, has taken its cues from these far-from-disinterested Virginia men.

Connelly suggests that none of Lee's biographers tells much about the inner man or the drives that shaped his life. Like Freeman, they paint a superficial portrait of Lee, leaving out his humanity, giving readers a man more marble than flesh. The real Lee, the essential Lee, says Connelly, has been buried under the hero symbol. And though his own book is a history of Lee biographies, not a biography of Lee, Connelly's "Epilogue" raises the kind of questions about Lee—his troubled marriage, his ambivalence over slavery and secession, his morbidity and haunting sense of failure, his parochial vision of war—that should provide the meat for a new biography.

Jefferson was a statesman, Lee a military leader; politics and the military were traditional avenues to male power. Not surprisingly then, much of southern biography focuses on politicians and generals. Southerners, active in the American Revolution, dominated presidential politics for the first quarter of a century of the new nation and dominated federal politics until secession in 1861. So there has been no dearth of biographies about southern statesmen like George Washington, Jefferson, James Madison, James Monroe—all from Virginia—John C. Calhoun, and Andrew Jackson. Civil War leaders Jefferson Davis and Alexander Stephens have also had their biographers, although in the case of these two political foes, early biographies were acts of justification with the biographers carrying old fights into print. Southern fire-eaters like Robert Barnwell Rhett, William Lowndes Yancey, Edmund Ruffin, and James Henry Hammond have received less attention, although several new biographies have appeared, among them Drew Gilpin Faust's *James Henry Hammond and the Old South* (1982) and Betty L. Mitchell's *Edmund Ruffin: A Biography* (1981). And, of course, Robert E. Lee's comrades in arms—Longstreet, Jackson, Jeb Stuart, Beauregard, Johnston—have all been the subjects of essentially military biographies.

The usual subjects for southern biography have been white and male, and they have come, almost exclusively, from the upper classes. Those men not blessed with wealth and/or family position at birth, like Washington, Lee, and Hammond, had the good sense to marry wives who had been. But politics sometimes makes for strange bedfellows, so biographers have studied the lives of important rednecks like populist rebel Tom Watson, "Kingfish" Huey Long (who liked to masquerade as a redneck despite his respectable yeoman background), and rock-and-roll sensation Elvis Presley. C. Vann Woodward's *Tom Watson: Agrarian Rebel* (1938) and T. Harry Williams's Pulitzer Prize-winning *Huey Long* (1969) are fine examples of this kind of southern biography.

Whether biographers are discussing Jefferson's paradoxical feelings about slavery, Ruffin's unapologetic defense of the peculiar institution, or Watson's vicious race baiting, race itself has been a constant theme in southern biography. But distressingly few biographies have been written about blacks. Those that do exist have usually treated men working in one way or another toward black liberation and racial justice. Thus, in Stephen B. Oates's *The Fires of Jubilee: Nat Turner's Fierce Rebellion* (1935), readers witness the re-creation of the dramatic but short life of a black revolutionary, a slave convinced he is God's violent instrument for the salvation of his people. Benjamin Quarles and Nathan Huggins, biographers of runaway slave and abolitionist Frederick Douglass, reveal a man just as dedicated to black freedom but convinced, at first, that this freedom could be won through nonviolence. Booker T. Washington's biographers, Louis Harlan and Bernard Weisberger, demonstrated his commitment to racial self-improvement through accommodation to segregation. And finally, Oates's recent *Let the Trumpet Sound: The Life of Martin Luther King, Jr.* (1982) vividly connects the line of history that exists among these four black leaders. Like Turner, King was nurtured by his family and encouraged to feel he was somebody special, a Moses for his people. Like Washington, he was committed to improvement for his race, but unlike the great founder of Tuskegee, he was not satisfied with segregated "racial uplift" programs. With Douglass, he believed in peaceful means to conquer racism and thus embraced Gandhian techniques of nonviolent resistance in order to combat racial oppression and social injustice.

If few biographies exist on southern black men, there are fewer still on black women. Southern white women have fared better with the recent emphasis on women's history, but not much. Biographies of southern white women, like those of white men, usually deal with the concept of honor, because, as historian Bertram Wyatt-Brown argues in *Southern Honor: Ethics and Behavior in the Old South* (1982), honor was the psychological and social linchpin of the antebellum South. For southern white men, honor required "both riches and a body of menials"; for white women, honor required sexual innocence and a childlike meekness. This "cult of true womanhood" touched women North and South, but southern men made a fetish out of extolling the purity and excellence of southern womanhood and, by extension, southern civilization. Biographers of southern women have shown how their subjects accept, reject, or modify this feminine domestic ideal.

Gerda Lerner's *The Grimké Sisters from South Carolina* (1970) recounts the lives of Sarah and Angelina Grimké, daughters of a South Carolina planter, who refused to accept meekly the South's peculiar institution of slavery and moved to the North to become the first salaried female abolitionists and the first American women to speak in public. These two women, who were the epitome of piety and purity—both were Quakers—violated the sacred canons of southern honor to perform what they believed was God's own work.

Elizabeth Muhlenfeld's portrait of Mary Boykin Chesnut reveals a South Carolina woman much like the Grimké sisters in class background and wealth. She, too, hated slavery, calling it a "monstrous institution," not out of any sympathy for the slaves, but because of the plight of white women whose honor depended on ignoring evidence of miscegenation in their own families. Unlike the Grimké sisters, Chesnut never left the South, and she became an ardent Confederate. Yet she, too, spurned the southern feminine ideal. In antebellum days this educated, intelligent, but childless woman often felt like a useless ornament; in the postwar period, she took charge of the family plantation.

Nancy Milford's biography *Zelda* (1970), the tragic story of Zelda Sayre Fitzgerald, gives the reader a 20th-century twist on the 19th-century feminine ideal of southern white womanhood. Zelda Sayre, a Montgomery, Ala., belle who lived life in the fast lane, rejected the innocent passivity of the "true woman" to boldly embrace the modern "New Woman": the flapper who used her good looks and sexual allure to get what she wanted from men. But this new brand of femininity was equally perverse, even schizophrenic, and Zelda finally succumbed.

Hero worship—or heroine worship—may be a kind of secular religion in America, South and North. Individuals like Washington, Jefferson, and Lee have taken on an almost Christlike aura, and to suggest that such men, such symbols of sectional and national righteousness, had blemishes and complex motivations like other human beings frequently raises more than a few hackles. But to deify human beings, no matter how accomplished and worthy, sacrifices truth to illusion in biography. To limit southern biography to great white men would sacrifice the richness, variety, and wholeness of southern history. Fortunately the many fine, probing biographies of southerners, male and female, black and white, that have appeared in recent times promise to make Freud's warnings increasingly unnecessary by giving readers life-size, not larger-than-life, subjects to whom they can feel more than "distantly related."

See also BLACK LIFE: / Douglass, Frederick; King, Martin Luther, Jr.; Turner, Nat; Washington, Booker T.; HISTORY AND MANNERS: / Davis, Jefferson; Hammond, James Henry; Jackson, Stonewall; Jefferson, Thomas; Lee, Robert E.; Madison, James; Stuart, Jeb; MEDIA: / Freeman, Douglas Southall, MUSIC: / Presley, Elvis; POLITICS: / Calhoun, John C.; Jackson, Andrew; Long, Huey; Watson, Thomas; SCIENCE AND MEDICINE: / Ruffin, Edmund; WOMEN'S LIFE: / Chesnut, Mary Boykin

Betty L. Mitchell
Southeastern Massachusetts University

Black Literature

See BLACK LIFE: Literature, Black

Civil War in Literature

One of the anomalies of the American literary imagination has been its inability—in spite of the vast amount of ink consumed in the effort—to derive a major poem, novel, or play from the central crisis in the national existence. This failure seems even more curious because one of the prominent characteristics of the southern literary mind, at least of the white literary mind, has been the compulsive remembrance of the Civil War. But the southern writer—and this would appear to be a primary reason for the want of a southern *War and Peace*—has been less concerned to reconstruct the actual time of the struggle than to recount the consequent loss of the antebellum southern culture and, in the response to this loss, the creation of a postbellum culture of survival. Reaching its first full-fledged expression in *Marse Chan: A Tale of Old Virginia* (1884) by Thomas Nelson Page and its most profound and complex expression in *The Sound and the Fury* (1929) and *Absalom, Absalom!* (1936) by William Faulkner, the enactment of this drama has found a continuing, significant, if attenuated, expression in novels as recent as those of Walker Percy, especially *The Moviegoer* (1961) and *The Last Gentleman* (1966), and of William Styron, notably *Sophie's Choice* (1979).

Even the earliest southern writing about the Civil War, in the period from the firing on Fort Sumter to the final surrender, produced no treatment of the war comparable to Walt Whitman's *Drum-Taps* (1865) or Herman Melville's *Battle-Pieces and Aspects of the War* (1866). In contrast to these limited but distinctive representations of marching and fighting, the best southern poet of the time, Henry Timrod, wrote celebratory poems about the birth and mission of the Confederacy—"Ethnogenesis," "The Cotton Bowl," "Carolina," "A Cry to Arms"—and reached his highest poetic achievement with the exquisite classical "Ode," written to be sung at a memorial service in Charleston's Magnolia Cemetery for the dead of a lost war. On a clearly lesser level of literary achievement, the years of the Confederacy found their voice in "Maryland, My Maryland" by James Ryder Randall; "Music in Camp," "Burial of Latané," and "Lee to the Rear" by John R. Thompson, editor of the *Southern Literary Messenger* from 1847 to 1860; and "Little Giffen," a popular sentimental ballad about a Confederate soldier by Francis Orray Ticknor. In the immediate aftermath of the war Father Abram Joseph Ryan became the poetic spokesman of the Lost Cause in such banal yet influential effusions as "The Conquered Banner" and "The Sword of Robert Lee."

The most effective literature of the Confederacy remained largely unknown for a generation or longer in journals, diaries, and letters. Among the most valuable of the contemporary records are those by Sarah Morgan Dawson (1842–99), Kate Stone (1841–1907), and Mary

Boykin Chesnut (1823–86). Published in 1913 under the title *A Confederate Girl's Diary*, Dawson's account of the war years as she witnessed them in Louisiana's capital city of Baton Rouge and in New Orleans is informed by a perceptive eye for detail and a lively intelligence; brought out in 1955 under the title *Brokenburn: The Journal of Kate Stone*, Stone's record of life on a northern Louisiana plantation and later, after the flight of her family from federal invaders, in the east Texas town of Tyler, is also marked by a penchant for realistic detail.

The Dawson and Stone works are surpassed in both literary and historical importance by the account of the Charleston aristocracy during the Confederate period by Mary Boykin Chesnut. First published in 1905 and again in 1949 as *A Diary from Dixie*, Chesnut's work took on a new significance when C. Vann Woodward, after careful study of the manuscripts, concluded that the diary was written not in the 1860s but between 1881 and 1884, its basis being a journal Chesnut had kept intermittently in the era of the Confederacy. Published in 1981 as *Mary Chesnut's Civil War*, Woodward's edition of the presumed diary shows that it is essentially an incipient novel. Yet while the motive to make her journal into a work of art reduces Chesnut's reliability as a factual witness, Woodward observes, it enhances her depiction of "the chaos and complexity of a society at war" and endows individual lives across the whole Confederate social spectrum with dramatic reality. A similar power to invest the age of the Civil War with graphic reality emanates from the extensive correspondence of the Jones family of Liberty County, Ga. As collected and edited by Robert Manson Myers in *The Children of Pride: A True Story of Georgia and the Civil War* (1972), the Jones family documents constitute the most remarkable epistolary record yet discovered of a southern family in the years immediately before, during, and after the Civil War. Possessing a literary quality conferred both by well-educated minds and by a deep feeling for the drama of life, the Jones letters belong on the shelf of the best southern writing.

In some cases the southern experience of the Civil War as recorded in memoirs by Confederate army officers also deserves a place on the literary shelf, for example, *Destruction and Reconstruction: Personal Experiences of the Late War* (1879) by Richard "Dick" Taylor, *War Reminiscences and Stuart Cavalry Campaigns* (1887) by John Singleton Mosby, and "Lee in Pennsylvania" (in *Annals of the War Written by Leading Participants*, 1879) by James Longstreet. Of greater significance, however, is "The History of a Campaign That Failed" (*Century Magazine*, 1885), a quasi-fictional memoir in which Mark Twain, a private in a hastily organized volunteer Confederate unit in Missouri, describes his enlistment, brief service, and desertion. By implication a profound questioning of the meaning of war as a social institution, "The History of a Campaign That Failed" is unique in southern writing about the Civil War.

Except insofar as *A Connecticut Yankee in King Arthur's Court* (1889) can be interpreted as a reflection on the Civil War, Mark Twain did not use the war as a subject for his stories and novels. In fact, although Sidney Lanier in his hastily composed *Tiger-Lilies* (1867) attempted to use his war experiences as the basis of a novel critical of war, southern postbellum fiction largely followed the romantic pattern established by John Esten Cooke in *Surry of Eagle's Nest* (1866) and *Mohun* (1869). Persisting well into the 20th century in numerous, now-forgotten popular novels, the romantic mode is illustrated in *The Cavalier* (1901) and *Kincaid's Battery* (1908) by George Washington Cable; by the early 20th century Cable had fallen away from the realism of his first Civil War novel, *Dr. Sevier* (1884), in which he had announced his sympathy with the antislavery motive and provoked the criticism that eventually drove him from the South. Cable's early realism was in a sense picked up by Ellen Glasgow in *The Battle-Ground* (1902), one of the novels that would eventually comprise a "social history" of Virginia, in which she hoped to rectify a failing of the southern literary imagination that Chesnut had felt but had lacked the literary sophistication to define, namely a "deficiency in blood and irony."

The rectifying irony in Glasgow's attitude toward the Confederacy pales in comparison with the ironic scope of the southern literary vision in the decade following World War I. At the end of the decade a southern woman writer, Evelyn Scott, published a large, panoramic novel, boldly experimental in technique, entitled *The Wave* (1929). Intended by Scott to be a "progression" toward her final design, the writing of "a comédie humaine of America," this novel, now unjustly neglected, may be the most ambitious attempt to embrace the Civil War in its totality. For most readers the image of the war is more convincingly presented in a still-famous novel that, in its mingling of southern piety and irony, is probably a better novel than serious literary critics have generally said, *Gone with the Wind* (1936) by Margaret Mitchell. From the standpoint of literary art the Civil War is more enduringly presented in Faulkner's only novel that focuses on the war years, *The Unvanquished* (1938). This work employs a family and community situation as a microcosm of the conflict, as do *The Forge* (1931) by T. S. Stribling, *None Shall Look Back* (1937) by Caroline Gordon, and *The Fathers* (1938) by Allen Tate. *Shiloh* (1952), by Shelby Foote, strikingly presents the war through a few selected participants in one battle. But Foote's achievement in *Shiloh* is minor compared with his success in his massive three-volume *The Civil War: A Narrative History* (1958, 1963, 1974). A masterpiece of the art of narrative, this work has been compared in its sustained narrative skill and power to the writings of Thucydides, Gibbon, Clarendon, and Henry Adams. Walker Percy has called it the "American Iliad." Foote's triumph in historical narrative underlines the fact that no southern writer has written a battlefield story possessing the classic quality of Stephen Crane's *The Red Badge of Courage* (1895). The southern novelist has been better at creating plot situations and characters that embody the long, haunted aftermath of the Civil War, as in Faulkner's *The Sound and the Fury* and *Absalom, Absalom!*

The direct use of the Civil War as setting and theme in southern poetry has never been more pronounced than it was in the time of Timrod and Ryan. One of the most noted poems of the 20th-century Southern Literary Renaissance, "Ode to the Confederate Dead" (the first version of this appeared in 1926), by Allen Tate, employs the dead soldiers of the South not primarily as defenders of a historical society but as symbols of a capacity for chivalric action that has been lost in the fragmented, narcissistic society of the present century. Critical of Tate for using the Confederate dead merely as symbolic, Donald Davidson composed "The Army of Tennessee," a poem in the conventional heroic manner, but he never published it. His finest Civil War poem, "Lee in the Mountains"—a long meditation by the defeated general projected through a modified stream-of-consciousness technique—is a part of the literature associated with the southern culture of survival.

See also BLACK LIFE: Literature, Black; HISTORY AND MANNERS: Civil War; MYTHIC SOUTH: / Mitchell, Margaret; WOMEN'S LIFE: / Chesnut, Mary Boykin

Lewis P. Simpson
Louisiana State University

Daniel Aaron, *The Unwritten War: American Writers and the Civil War* (1962); Robert A. Lively, *Fiction Fights the Civil War* (1957); Edmund Wilson, *Patriotic Gore: Studies in the Literature of the American Civil War* (1962).

Folklore in Literature

With the exception of Native American lore, folklore, like language and literature, came to this country as part of the cultural baggage of the various waves of its settlers. In the South its sources were mainly British, African, and French, with important admixtures of Spanish and German, and touches of almost everything else.

From the beginning, new experiences and a new environment eroded this imported lore and reshaped it to new purposes. Erosion and adaptation may be rapid, but the emergence of a new folklore, like the development of a distinctive and significant literature, is always slow. It was slowed further in the United States by increasing literacy, mobility, urbanization, homogenization, and the influence of the mass media. Forces at work in the South, however, and not alone its geography and history, reduced the effect of such inhibiting factors while encouraging the evolution of a southern folklore and easing its incorporation into its literature. The result was to enhance the regional flavor of southern letters.

If the Puritans of New England were a people of the book, then southerners harkened enthusiastically to pentecostal tongues—and to the silvery words of their politicians at the hustings, the tall tales of their hunters and riverboatmen, the animal stories of their slaves, the brags, songs, and sayings that were part of the life of what came to be folk communities. Mark Twain charmed audiences all over the world because he knew from his memories of folklife that the way the tale is told is as important as the tale itself. Style, the manner in which things are said and done, was prized, whether on a bear hunt in the backwoods or at a Mardi Gras ball. In short, the living word and the performance, the marrow of folklore, were likewise the marrow of southern culture.

The most obvious feature distinguishing the South from the rest of the United States was its racial composition and the resulting historical developments provoked by profound sectional difference. Like others who crossed the Atlantic, Africans brought with them their myths and their music, their beliefs and their words. Folklore travels in the heart of humankind and therefore had the power to survive even the horrors of the middle passage and the merciless process of annihilation of African traditions that took place upon arrival. The archsurvivor, Brer Rabbit, was born in Africa.

People forget their victories and virtues but never their defeats and sins. Thus, southerners were hypersensitive to the past, for it included racial repression and the loss, on their own precious soil, of the bloodiest war in American history, followed by a decade of military occupation. Original sins and lost causes can be the cement of a culture and the germ of its folklore and literature.

As the North raced into the Industrial Age, the South seemed to stand still. Its folk traditions remained in place. Such southern writers as George Washington Cable, Joel Chandler Harris, Mary Noailles Murfree, and Charles Chesnutt—local colorists for whom folklore was a vital element—won national recognition. From the viewpoint of the Gilded Age, the postbellum South was backward. It valued old ways more than new dollars. The South's literary success may be attributed to its reluctance to deny its past. It refused to run away from its history, traditions, and reverence for form.

Folklore in literature is not folklore in the raw. Certainly a folktale told in its natural habitat is art of its own kind, but literary art is another kind of performance. The explorer John Lawson, who included folk materials in his descriptions of the interior of Carolina, was a sophisticated writer using what he found to render his account vivid or incorporating what he saw and heard because it was too good to pass up. The contributors of frontier sketches to the *Spirit of the Times*, a popular sportsman's journal in the antebellum period, were mostly lettered men—doctors, lawyers, college presidents, army officers—with a taste for the earthiness and oddities of folklore, and a talent, not untrained, for storytelling. Professional writers who employed folklore, such as William Gilmore Simms, bent it to an immediate purpose. Even such classic American writers as Edgar Allan Poe, Mark Twain, and William Faulkner were less concerned with folklore as such than with the ways it could serve their art.

John Lawson's *New Voyage to Carolina* (1709) exemplifies one of the earliest genres of southern literature, the travel account. He describes a thousand-mile journey from Charleston to the foothills of the Blue Ridge Mountains with a ready eye for the inhabitants' customs and lore, which he sets down with gusto and exploits with literary skill. Thus, he provides a lively description of Indian deer hunters who disguise themselves so perfectly with antlers and skins that they sometimes shoot each other. Lawson's method here is to record a curious hunting practice and then dramatize it with a folk story. Or, he brings a gritty account of starved and abused Indian dogs to a climax with a literary application of a folk remedy: "It is an infalliable Cure for Sore Eyes, even to see an *Indian's* Dog fat." Or, he illustrates the prodigious power of rattlesnakes by citing their ability "to charm Squirrels . . . in such a way that they run directly into their Mouths." Lawson also contributes to the emergence of indigenous southern legend as he moves from an authentic history of the Lost Colony and speculation about its fate to a local folktale: "I cannot forbear inserting here a pleasant story that passes for an uncontested Truth among the Inhabitants of this Place; which is, that the Ship, which brought the first colonies, does often appear among them, under sail, which they call Sir Walter Raleigh's Ship." Paul Green, whose plays drew upon southern lore and legend, would use this material for his historical drama *The Lost Colony* (1937).

Edgar Allan Poe and William Gilmore Simms, the major professional writers of the antebellum period, each used folklore in a different, though characteristic, way. Poe saw himself as an alienated poet, ideally the resident of a dreamland "Out of space—Out of time," and his settings and sources are usually consistent with this vision. "The Gold Bug" is a notable exception. His source is the folk motif of the buried treasure, particularized in the widespread legends of Captain Kidd. His locale is Sullivan's Island, which he knew well from his military service at Fort Moultrie on the South Carolina coast. His characters, if not southern folk types, are southern stereotypes—William Legrand, the withdrawn, decayed aristocrat, and Jupiter, the faithful, comic, superstitious black servant. Even his narrator is familiar, a rational man doubting the sanity of the friend whose summons he answers. (There is much here reminiscent of the timeless "The Fall of the House of Usher." Is this, too, within the context of southern folklore?) For the black servant, the gold bug that he and his master find is an object of superstitious dread, and Poe uses it for minstrel-show effects. "I'm berry sartain dat Massa Will bin bit somewhere about de head by dat goole-bug," Jupiter tells the narrator. The rational faculties of Legrand, an amateur scientist, have been superseded by his fancies—his mind, as the narrator comes to believe, "infected with some of the innumerable Southern superstitions about money buried." These "Southern superstitions" are validated by the recovery of the pirate treasure. Poe's concern is the balance between rational method, epitomized in Legrand's solution of a cryptogram, and the irrational, here represented by a romantic legend and the inexplicable force of superstition. In "The Gold Bug" folklore is associated with poetry and revery and is a way of knowing what surpasses rational methodologies and precedes their application.

In *The Yemassee* (1835), one of his romances of the southern frontier, William Gilmore Simms expands Lawson's account of the rattlesnake's fabulous powers into a flamboyant set piece. The heroine, a "peerless forest flower," goes into the wilderness to meet her lover, an English officer. Entranced by the beauties of nature, she is captivated "by a star-like shining glance—a subtle ray, that shot out from the circle of green leaves." She is dazzled by its "dreadful beauty" and then transfixed with terror when she realizes that what she sees is the "fascinating gleam" in the eyes of a rattlesnake. As the snake slithers toward her and coils to strike, it is shot through the head by the arrow of her lover's Indian ally. Simms, in a footnote, doubts the rattler's "power over persons" but claims to have heard of "numberless instances," a sufficient number, in any case, "for the romancer." Not given to subtleties, the sexual implications of his serpent in Eden would have surely surprised him. Simms's end was melodrama, and a folk belief was his means.

In 1870, the year he died, Simms wrote a North Carolina mountain sketch for *Harper's*, "How Sharp Snaffles Got his Wife and His Capital." It is essentially a tall tale, told at a hunting camp by a backwoods trickster whose nickname, "Big Lie," indicates his qualities as a hunter, sharp operator, and storyteller. His performance, much appreciated by his backwoods peers and the gentleman hunters who comprise his audience, is presented within a descriptive frame by one of the latter. Such separation between the genteel observer who transcribes the tale and the folk artist who tells it may be a way of maintaining a distance of generation, caste, race, or political persuasion, but always a factor for the southern writer is the art of the performance itself. This was not entirely an aesthetic matter. In southern culture, the way a thing is done is significant. Simms himself, in this story, was reaching back to the frontier humor of the Old Southwest, with its folkloric situations, in order to recover his own literary capital, the northern readership he had lost during the sectional conflict; and he reached forward toward the emerging local color movement, likewise seamed with folklore.

In Mark Twain's *The Adventures of Huckleberry Finn* (1885) identifiable elements of folklore give this masterpiece its flavor as they serve complex purposes, and the folklife of the Mississippi Valley, broadly speaking, provides physical and moral texture. The role of the runaway slave, Jim, is evidence of this. Poe's Jupiter, with his superstitious gibberish about the gold bug, is little more than a comic stereotype. But Mark Twain's Jim, a comparable character at the outset, becomes in the end not simply a rounded character, a stereotype humanized, but the spiritual center of the book. To accomplish this transformation (as well as to move his plot, enhance verisimilitude, and add humorous touches), Mark Twain uses superstition.

Superstitions, by definition, are the supernatural beliefs that some disdain but others accept. At the beginning of the novel, Tom Sawyer and Huck to amuse themselves play upon Jim's belief in witches. Jim also believes in ghosts, weather signs, omens, and dreams. On the river with Huck, he becomes a free and living man, and when he puts his superstitions to work, they become effectual. This natural world has a place for the supernatural, and Jim's superstitions save his own life and Huck's and ultimately make possible Huck's spiritual salvation as well. In two other great books, *Adventures of Tom Sawyer* (1876) and *Life on the Mississippi* (1883), southern folk-

Scene from The Reivers, *the 1969 film made from William Faulkner's novel*

life also functions memorably. Seeking a cure for warts in a graveyard at midnight, as the folk remedy requires, is the occasion that initiates the plot of *Tom Sawyer. Life on the Mississippi* contains the classic description of the folklife of raftsmen, including their songs and dances, brags and fights, beliefs and stories. It is a genre painting, both realistic and idealized.

Like Mark Twain, William Faulkner embodied within his southern particularity a moral depth and artistry that brought him the acclaim of the world. Faulkner's novella *The Bear* (1942) is a capstone to a series of earlier, major works that emerged from his response to the southern cultural experience. Its motif, a ceremonial hunt of a totemic animal, is universal, but the version he adopts derives from American Indian lore and, more immediately, from countless stories of bear hunts in backwoods oral tradition. Stories of this kind had already made their way into antebellum popular culture through the media of the Davy Crockett almanacs and the sporting journals. Thomas Bangs Thorpe's "The Big Bear of Arkansas" (1841), a case in point, is essentially a literary creation originating in southern hunting lore. So is *The Bear*.

The Bear, like *Huckleberry Finn*, is an initiation story in a pristine natural setting. Sam Fathers, "son of a negro slave and a Chickasaw chief," is teacher and surrogate parent of young Ike McCaslin, in an analogue to the relationship of Huck and Jim. His knowledge of woodcraft, which he imparts to Ike, has moral validity, like Jim's old beliefs. In the end Ike learns how to hunt Old Ben, the legendary bear, and how to "relinquish" his quarry and his heritage. Though it contains specific folk elements (e.g., the hunt motif), *The Bear* transcends them and emphasizes folklife, the totality of the culture, rather than its details. This transcendence and extension, even as they detach *The Bear* from its folkloric detail, bring folklore and literature into closer proximity and make their southernness universal.

Faulkner moved beyond folklore at a pivotal time for both folklore and southern tradition generally. There are southern-style ironies in this movement to a broader context: the irony of lost causes won and regrets for the loss of old ways assuaged. Ironically, southern literature has attained its greatest eminence at a time when the South becomes more and more like the rest of the country, and its folklore, a prime source of its distinction, withers under the increasing pressure of literacy. Ultimately, at its best, literature absorbs folklore, and in this way assures its survival.

See also FOLKLORE articles

Hennig Cohen
University of Pennsylvania

Gene Bluestein, *The Voice of the Folk: Folklore and American Literary Theory* (1972); Daniel Hoffman, *Form and Fable in American Fiction* (1965); Bruce A. Rosenberg, in *Interrelations of Literature*, ed. Jean-Pierre Barricelli and Joseph Gibaldi (1982); Constance Rourke, *American Humor: A Study of the National Character* (1931).

Humor

Southern humor, like much of the best southern writing in general, has been boisterous and physical, often grotesque, and generally realistic. On the whole, it has no doubt been better received and more appreciated outside the region than in it. Mark Twain, a frontier writer in essence but joyfully proclaimed as southern these days, was recognized and lionized first by the Brahmins of Boston and the London literary establishment. And William Faulkner was certainly a puzzle to the people of Oxford in his time. Writing has never been a particularly admired occupation in the South, and its comic writers, as well as the most perceptive serious writers, have singled out aspects of southern culture that many southerners would sooner forget. This combination has produced what many southern readers would no doubt characterize as a literature of betrayal. But adversity can be beneficial to an artist, furnishing the stone of resistance against which his or her talent may be honed. A hostile climate is frequently the best one a writer could ask for—especially a comic writer.

Southern humor fits fairly well into the chronological framework of four periods usually applied to American humor generally: (1) 1830 to 1860, (2) 1860 to 1925, (3) 1925 to 1945, and (4) 1945 to the present.

1830 to 1860. This was the most energetic and inventive period for purely comic writing in the history of southern letters, if not the most respectable. It saw the establishment of the major comic stereotypes that would, it seems, serve southern humor more or less forever. The dominant figure was the frontiersman, and he is the literary ancestor of the redneck-hillbilly who is still around. In this period the black minstrel also appeared. Of the writers who can be classified as primarily comic (the southwestern yarnspinners), the best were

Augustus Baldwin Longstreet (*Georgia Scenes*), William Tappan Thompson (the Major Jones character), Thomas Bangs Thorpe (*The Big Bear of Arkansas*), Johnson J. Hooper (the Simon Suggs character), and George Washington Harris (the Sut Lovingood character). All these writers were regarded as subliterary (by themselves as well as by others), and most were published outside the South, many in Porter's *Spirit of the Times*—a New York periodical. Generally these writers carefully separated themselves from the disreputable characters of their sketches by using an "envelope" structure, in which a literate narrator introduced the illiterate character who told the story. Hooper and Harris stand a bit closer to their characters than discretion would seem to dictate—a fact that Hooper, at least, later regretted. But there was always a certain amount of ambivalence in the attitude of these writers toward their disreputable "Suts" and "Simons," and at times the characters undoubtedly function as alter egos for the proper men who undertook to describe their antics. In any event, Harris was an authentic comic genius—recognized in his own day by Edgar Allan Poe and imitated later by an appreciative William Faulkner.

1860 to 1925. Mark Twain, though more western than southern, was the foremost figure of this period. In his own day he was classified as a literary comedian and local colorist, very closely related to such writers as Artemus Ward and Bret Harte, and it took time for the genius of his combination of humor and local color to be recognized as serious literature—which it was. Of the pure literary comedians—"phunny phellows"—Bill Arp is probably the outstanding southern example, but for the most part these comic writers tended to be western and midwestern. After the Civil War, the general taste of the region ran strongly to plantation memories of moonlight and magnolias, and the writer who could combine a reverence for the good old days with chaste and genial humor was absolutely assured of success. That was the formula developed to such good effect by Joel Chandler Harris in his Uncle Remus stories.

1920 to 1945. This was the golden age of southern writing, the time of the Southern Renaissance. The best southern writers began to combine serious literary purpose with profoundly comic elements. Southern humor—at least that written by southerners—would henceforth be a leaven in the hard brown bread of literature. William Faulkner and Erskine Caldwell were among the best practitioners of art, but an intrinsic comic element can be found in the work of nearly all southern writers of the first rank. There were many purely comic artists in the years between the wars, for this was also a golden age for American comedy—in magazines, in films, and on the radio. But the dominant influence on written humor was the *New Yorker* magazine, and although not many of its writers were New Yorkers, none of them were southern. In motion pictures and on the radio, southern characters did appear, but as often as not they were little more than parodies of existing southern types.

1945 to the Present. Flannery O'Connor, Eudora Welty, and Walker Percy are among the premier writers of the South in this period, and they are all writers with a highly developed comic talent. All of them are much more than comic, but comedy is, again, an intrinsic element in their writing. In popular works by comic southern writers, such as William Price Fox's *Southern Fried*, Guy Owen's *The Ballad of the Flim-Flam Man*, and Mac Hyman's *No Time for Sergeants*, the humorous stereotypes continue to be what they had been before—poor whites (hillbilly, redneck, and rural) and blacks. On television, *The Real McCoys*, *The Andy Griffith Show*, and *The Beverly Hillbillies* have enjoyed considerable success.

It is something of a truism that the American South is a unique region in America. Visitors remark that it is more like a foreign country than any other area contained within the national boundaries. And while American writers are still producing plenty of comedy tied to ethnic minority groups, the South remains the only *region* that still has identifiable comic types associated with it—Texans and hillbillies are notable in this respect, and the "grits" jokes of Carter's presidency are proof that the rural South still has a strong identity. The South seems to be the only section of the country that outsiders still consider fair game for comic jibes—a fact noted by Roy Blount, Jr., in *Crackers*.

But the uniqueness of the region is giving way to the inexorable leveling process of the culture. And comedians like Jerry Clower, television programs like *Hee Haw*, and the moonshine-car-smashing films of Burt Reynolds constitute something like a self-parody of former southern comic types. Russell Baker, Terry Southern, Tom Wolfe, and Hunter S. Thompson are all southern by birth, but their writing, like the fiction of John Barth, Donald Barthelme, and Barry Hannah, transcends regional boundaries. The best comic writing is being done by southern writers who cannot be identified as southern in any superficial way. It would be premature, if not witless, to predict the demise of southern humor. But that it seems to be in a period of transition—like every other aspect of the culture—seems undeniable.

See also FOLKLIFE: Storytelling; / Clower, Jerry; HISTORY AND MANNERS: / Gardner, Dave; MEDIA: Comic Strips; / *Andy Griffith Show*; *Beverly Hillbillies*; Grizzard, Lewis; Reynolds, Burt

Mark Steadman
Clemson University

Jesse Bier, *The Rise and Fall of American Humor* (1968); Walter Blair, *Native American Humor* (1960); Sarah Blancher Cohen, ed., *Comic Relief: Humor in Contemporary American Literature* (1978); Wade Hall, *The Smiling Phoenix: Southern Humor from 1865 to 1914* (1965); M. Thomas Inge, *The Frontier Humorists: Critical Views* (1975); Raven I. McDavid, Jr., and Walter Blair, eds., *The Mirth of a Nation: America's Great Dialect Humor* (1983); Constance Rourke, *American Humor: A Study of National Character* (1931); Louis D. Rubin, Jr., *The Comic Imagination in American Literature* (1973).

New Critics

John Crowe Ransom long ago complained that no one had defined what the critic's responsibilities were. Criticism, he said in 1937, was in the hands of amateurs who had insufficient instruction to prepare them to perform the important function for which they were responsible. The 20th century, Ransom believed, had produced some of the most important poetry in the history of English literature, but it was difficult verse and no one made it available to the general reader. The poets and the philosophers should be culture's critics, but the modern poet's understanding of his craft was "intuitive rather than dialectical" and the philosopher's "theory is very general and his acquaintance with the particular work of art is not persistent and intimate." Only the college teachers of literature were left, and "they are learned but not critical men." They "spend a lifetime compiling the data of literature" and yet rarely "commit themselves" to a literary judgment. Criticism, Ransom concluded, must be precise and systematic; it must be "the collective and sustained effort of learned persons"; adequately trained persons in the universities should do it.

Almost as if on cue, the year following Ransom's challenge two of his former students, Cleanth Brooks and Robert Penn Warren, who had become university teachers of literature, published a new approach to the teaching and reading of poetry, one that they had been using in mimeograph form in their classes. It was *Understanding Poetry* (1938), which in the subsequent 20 years went through four editions and left a lasting impression on the way poetry is taught and read. Rather than disseminating facts of the authors' lives or historical and cultural information about the times in which they lived, it demonstrated that if a poem is to reveal its unique quality, it must be read purely as poetry and not as history, biography, philosophy, or anything else. Rather than dealing with the kind of questions that lead to vague, impressionistic interpretations of a poem—the kind included in most textbooks of the time—*Understanding Poetry* offered concrete, inductive analyses of some 200 poems, demonstrations of how poems should be read, and questions that stated explicitly and exactly the "approach" to literature upon which the book was based. This approach is explained in a lengthy and detailed "Letter to the Teacher": "(1) Emphasis should be focused on the poem as poem; (2) Discussion of all poems should be specific, concrete and inductive; (3) A poem, if it is to be fully understood, must always be treated as an organic system of relationships and never thought to be included in one or more isolated lines or parts."

This book, followed by *Understanding Fiction*, also by Brooks and Warren (1943), and *Understanding Drama*, by Brooks and Robert B. Heilman (1945), surely contributed to the improved audiences for creative writers to which Ransom referred. The critical principles in these books came from the theoretical criticism of Ransom, as well as from that of his friends, associates, and former students. "Poetry," Ransom explained in *The World's Body* (1938), "is the kind of knowledge by which we must know that which we cannot know otherwise." Its intent is not to "idealize" the world, but to help its readers to "realize" it, to know its "common actuals," its "concrete particularities" (what he calls "the world's body"), which science, social science, and philosophy have attempted to reduce to abstract principles. The world that poetry reveals is not one of absolute innocence, one in which a reader should expect "to receive the fragrance of the roses on the world's first morning." The poetic world is a postscientific world, one that is revealed through both intellect and emotion. Only poetry can show the "body and solid substance of the world, that which has retired into the fullness of memory." With a combination, however, of image and idea, figure and statement, the poet can "construct the fullness of poetry, which is counterpart to the world's fullness."

In *The New Critics* (1941), the book that gave the movement under discussion its name, Ransom sought to identify the cognitive function of poetry by examining the way in which it differs from prose discourse. Allen Tate, like Ransom, was concerned with the unique nature of poetic discourse and the specific order of knowledge it contains. He agreed with Ransom that the poet attempts to reconstitute reality, not to make some comment about it. One of the first betrayers of literature, Tate said, was Matthew Arnold, who "extended the hand of fellowship to the scientist" and tried to make literature and religion synonymous. I. A. Richards followed Arnold's lead by suggesting that the significance of poetry resides in a "mere readiness for action." He could not find in poetic thought "action" itself. Readers of poetry are, therefore, merely passive recipients; they do not expect poetry to move them to significant action or reveal to them a fundamental truth.

In their attempt to restore literature to its rightful place in the center of human life, Ransom and Tate were joined by Cleanth Brooks and Robert Penn Warren. Soon after *The World's Body* (1938) appeared, Brooks published *Modern Poetry and the Tradition* (1939), in which he hoped to assist those readers—whose "conception of poetry is . . . primarily defined . . . by the achievements of the Romantic poets"—to appreciate the poetry of their own age. One must go back beyond the 18th century, Ransom and Brooks both insist, to find poets who do not attempt to oversimplify human experience by removing all discordant elements from it.

Although Warren is well known for the essays in which he introduced readers to important modern writers—William Faulkner, Peter Taylor, Katherine Anne Porter, Eudora Welty, John Crowe Ransom, and many others—he did write at least one basically theoretical essay. In "Pure and Impure Poetry" he argues that one finds in poetry many points of resistance: there is tension between the rhythm of the poem and the rhythm of speech; between the formality of the rhythm and the informality of the language; between the general and the abstract; between the beautiful and the ugly. This statement of tension among the various elements of a poem is very similar to Ransom's theory of the discord between its structure and texture. Both critics believed the poem is achieved through this tension.

The southerners who developed the New Criticism

Robert Penn Warren, American man of letters, 1979

did so as a collective effort. Two earlier movements served as background for this collective literary endeavor. The Fugitives of the 1920s, including Ransom, were interested in a new poetry that would depart from traditional romantic, sentimental, southern verse. The Nashville Agrarians, including Ransom, Tate, Brooks, and Warren, were social critics, concerned with social and economic ideas; their ideas appeared in the symposia *I'll Take My Stand* (1930) and *Who Owns America?* (1936). As an organized movement, Agrarianism was over by 1937, though, and New Criticism had already begun to assume central importance. The New Critics made a number of periodicals into organs for disseminating their views. Brooks and Warren edited *Southern Review* from 1935 to 1942, Ransom founded the *Kenyon Review* in 1940 and remained its editor for over two decades, and Tate made the venerable *Sewanee Review* into a quarterly for literary and critical studies reflecting his theories. In addition to their textbooks and quarterlies, the influence of the New Critics was also felt through teaching, as they shaped a generation of students at Vanderbilt, Louisiana State University, Kenyon College, the University of Minnesota, Bread Loaf, and Yale. One can chart the changing geography of New Criticism, as its leaders moved from Nashville to Baton Rouge to Gambier, Ohio, and finally to New Haven, Conn. The peak of the New Criticism was in the 1940s and 1950s, but its influence continues to be felt.

The effect of the New Critics upon the understanding of what a poem is and how it works has been profound. One of their most enduring achievements is to make available the material essential to exploring the cognitive function of literature. Surely every student who has had an introductory course in literature in this country since World War II has been affected by the concerns of Ransom, Tate, Brooks, and Warren, even in the unlikely event that he has never heard the name of any one of them.

Thomas Daniel Young
Vanderbilt University

Louise Cowan, *The Southern Critics* (1972); Richard Foster, *The New Romantics: A Reappraisal of the New Criticism* (1962); William J. Handy, *Kant and the Southern New Critics* (1963); Murray Krieger, *The New Apologists for Poetry* (1968); Robert Wooster Stallman, in *A Southern Vanguard*, ed. Allen Tate (1947); Walter Sutton, *Modern American Criticism* (1963); Thomas Daniel Young, ed., *The New Criticism and After* (1976).

North in Literature

Flannery O'Connor's first published story, "The Geranium," opens with an old man, come up from the South to stay with his daughter in New York, looking "out the window fifteen feet away into another window framed by blackened red brick." He is waiting for the people across the way to put a potted geranium on the sill, even though "those people across the alley had no business with one. They set it out and let the hot sun bake it all day and they put it so near the ledge the wind could almost knock it over. They had no business with it, no business with it." In "Judgement Day," her final story and retelling of the matter of "The Geranium," O'Connor's displaced old southerner stares through a window looking "out a brick wall and down into an alley full of New York air, the kind fit for cats and garbage. A few snowflakes drifted past the window but they were too thin and scattered for his failing vision." "The Geranium" ends with a man across the alley telling the old southerner to mind his own business; "Judgement Day" ends with old Tanner grotesquely dead, his feet dangling over the apartment house stairwell "like those of a man in the stocks."

O'Connor's images of New York as a sterile desert and New York as a freezing prison almost too neatly epitomize the North as it figures in southern literature. Sometimes it is a wasteland awaiting apocalypse, even at times an infernal region of horror. In Alice Walker's *Meridian*, "The subway train rushed through the tunnel screeching and sending out sparks like a meteor. . . . Ninety-sixth street flashed by, then 125th, then there was a screaming halt, a jolt as the car resisted the sudden stop, and the doors slid back with a rubbery thump. The graffiti, streaked on the walls in glowing reds and yellows, did not brighten at all the dark damp cavern of the station." Sometimes the North as viewed by southerners is a region of freezing cold, lacking in human warmth and community. The hero of Robert Penn Warren's *A Place to Come To*, a southern-bred academic who spends most of his life in Chicago, a city he thinks of as a "benign and *fourmillante* hive of de-selfedness," toward the end of the novel goes walking along the shore of Lake Michigan, "watching the sparse flakes ride in over the darkening water, out of the infiniteness of the north," toying with the idea he is "some lost man with nothing before him but the snow-blind lake and nothing behind but the tundra, and only one obligation, or doom—that of survival."

The image of the North as a dark region of cold finds its classic expression in the closing words of William Faulkner's *Absalom, Absalom!*, when Shreve McCannon, the Canadian, asks Quentin Compson, the Mississippian who soon afterward kills himself in Cambridge, Mass.: "'Why do you hate the South?'" Quentin's reply, "quickly, at once, immediately," is: "'I dont hate it, . . . I dont,' he said. *I dont hate it* he thought, panting in the cold air, the iron New England dark; *I dont. I dont! I dont hate it! I dont hate it!*" Faulkner's New England is a region of cold, iron, darkness; it is not a good place. And such is the case with the North as depicted in southern literature in general, particularly in southern literature of the 20th century.

Such was not always the case, however. As John Hope Franklin has pointed out, southerners who traveled to and wrote about the North in the early decades of the 19th century found the region "invariably interesting and frequently attractive and admirable." In 1836 John H. Hammond wrote from Philadelphia to his wife in South Carolina: "I never was in so delightful a city. Chestnut Street is worth all I ever saw before in the way of commercial elegance. You must see it." Two years earlier, William Carruthers, in the novel *The Kentuckian in New-York*, had advised: "Every southerner should visit New York. It would allay provincial prejudices, and calm his excitement against his northern countrymen. The people here are warm-hearted, generous, and enthusiastic, in a degree scarcely inferior to our own southerners." Even while Carruthers was testifying to the warmth and generosity of the "northerns," however, the southern penchant for looking favorably, even enviously, upon the North was weakening, and the land of the Yankees was increasingly viewed as a spawning ground of evil and corruption. A negative view of the North was prompted in part by the South's growing defensiveness with regard to the matter of slavery, its sense of being beleaguered in the expanding American union. It may also have been part of the South's emerging sense of itself as, in Lewis P. Simpson's words, "a special redemptive community fulfilling a divinely appointed role in the drama of history." Perhaps more importantly, the unfavorable view of the North taking shape in southern literature was congruent with criticisms of northern society being formulated by northerners themselves.

William R. Taylor's *Cavalier and Yankee: The Old South and American National Character* notes that early in the 19th century Americans of the North and the South began to worry about the direction their democracy seemed to be taking, "about the kind of aggressive, mercenary self-made man who was making his way in their society. . . . In the face of the threat posed by this new man, Americans—genteel and would-be genteel—began to develop pronounced longings for some form of aristocracy. . . . They sought, they would frankly have conceded, for something a little old-fashioned." The democratic-egalitarian, commercial-industrial North was not a region in which such a fantasy could take root, but the agrarian-hierarchical South did lend itself to such mythologizing. By the 1930s, Taylor points out, the "legendary Southern planter, despite reservations of one kind or another, began to seem almost perfectly suited to fill the need" for a hero who could be invested with admirably aristocratic virtues. Concomitantly, "the acquisitive man, the man on the make, became inseparably associated with the North." In elaborating the myth of Cavalier and Yankee, northern writers such as Sarah Hale, James K. Paulding, and Harriet Beecher Stowe, were probably more influential than writers from the South.

The image of the North in southern literature is, then, to some extent, a curious legacy *from* the North. That image, at any rate, which has persisted since before the Civil War, unmodified except during those years when evangelists for the New South were wooing northern capital and good feeling, is not very different from the harshly critical portrait of the urban and industrial North to be found in northern writers. O'Connor's brick walls are not as frighteningly alienating as those confronting Melville's Bartleby; Faulkner's Cambridge is almost idyllic if compared to the muddy suburb of James's *The Bostonians*.

It is no surprise, then, that images of the North provided by black southerners such as Walker and Ellison and Wright, agree with those projected by white southerners. Blyden Jackson has argued that "all negro fiction tends to conceive of its physical world as a sharp dichotomy, with the ghetto as its central figure and its symbolic truth," but such a vision—of the North as a confining and dehumanizing prison—is not alien to the imagination of white southerners (at the beginning of *Sophie's Choice*, William Styron's narrator describes himself, "self-exiled to Flatbush," as "another lean and lonesome young Southerner wandering amid the Kingdom of the Jews"). Faulkner would have felt himself in sympathy with the words that begin Richard Wright's *American Hunger*, the account, published in 1977, of what happened to "black boy" after he had escaped from the South: "My first glimpse of the flat black stretches of Chicago seemed an unreal city whose mythical houses were built of slabs of black coal wreathed in palls of gray smoke." And Faulkner would have sympathized with the ending of his fellow southerner's account of his sojourn in the North. Sitting alone in his narrow room, "watching the sun sink slowly in the chilly May sky," he is nevertheless determined to "hurl words into this darkness and wait for an echo." Alone in the cold dark of the North, he is yet determined "to tell, to march, to fight, to create a sense of the hunger for the life that gnaws in us all, to keep alive in our hearts a sense of the inexpressibly human."

Robert White
York University
Ontario, Canada

John Hope Franklin, *A Southern Odyssey: Travelers in the Antebellum North* (1976); Jay B. Hubbell, *The South in American Literature, 1607–1900* (1954); Blyden Jackson, *The Waiting Years: Essays on American Negro Literature* (1976); Lewis P. Simpson, *The Man of Letters in New England and the South: Essays on the History of the Literary Vocation in America* (1973); Robert B. Stepto, *From Behind the Veil: A Study of Afro-American Narrative* (1979); William R. Taylor, *Cavalier and Yankee: The Old South and American National Character* (1961).

Periodicals

The southern periodicals of paramount cultural importance have been the literary magazines, the most impressive of which were the antebellum *Southern Review* [Charleston] (1828–32), the *Southern Literary Messenger* (1834–64), the *Southern Quarterly Review* (1842–57), and the *Magnolia* (1840–43). Twentieth-century titles of note include the *Sewanee Review* (1892–), the *Southern Review* [Baton Rouge] (1935–42, *n.s.* 1965–), the *South Atlantic Quarterly* (1902–), and the *Virginia Quarterly Review* (1925–). The problems that beset the antebellum editor were given a definitive summary in two letters from William Gilmore Simms, printed January and February of 1841 in the *Magnolia*, which Simms, against his better judgment, would soon edit. Literary magazines were begun with "confident hope and bold assurance" but ended in "early abandonment" because two essentials were lacking in the South—contributors who possessed literary talent and subscribers who could pay when promised. The task of the 20th-century southern editor has been easier because he often has the support of a college or university as well as having contributors with literary talent.

Although most literary magazines in the 19th century floundered and failed, agricultural magazines such as the *American Farmer* (1819–97) and the *Southern Planter* (1841–1973) survived and even prospered modestly by reaching the planter class, from whom the literary magazines could never entice much-needed subscriptions. Religious magazines also outlived literary magazines; but their flowering was not until the 1850s, after southern churches had broken away from the North and were providing financial support for their own magazines. At least two political and economic magazines, *Niles' Weekly Register* (1811–49) and *De Bow's Review* (1847–61), persisted and apparently thrived for a reason Simms knew too well: the real passion of the southern male reader was for politics. It was, therefore, essential that historical and political articles have a prominent place in each issue of a literary magazine. A strictly belles-lettres magazine had no chance of survival in the South. The *Orion* (1842–44) was founded by William Richards, a scholarly minister, and his artist brother, Thomas Addison Richards, with the intention of publishing southern literature and featuring etchings of southern scenes. Political articles were added too late. The *Orion* was the handsomest antebellum magazine, but it perished in less than two years.

Although the *South Carolina Weekly Museum* (1797–98) is credited as being the pioneer southern magazine, the first with tangible influence on the character of subsequent magazines was the *Southern Review*, edited in Charleston by William and Stephen Elliott and the scholarly lawyer Hugh Swinton Legaré. Legaré, with his impressive classical learning, his devotion to neoclassical tenets, his rational political conservatism, and his judicial fairness as critic, contributed notably to the self-image of southern editors. Southern magazines have been edited, usually briefly, by men of letters (Poe, Simms, Hayne, Tate); but most of the work has been done by professionals like Legaré, Daniel K. Whitaker, and John Reuben Thompson, all of whom had a strong ulterior motive of promoting a southern literature to rival the best efforts in the North.

These editors of antebellum southern literary magazines were consistently conservative in their political and social views and in their literary tastes. New ideas (such as transcendentalism, positivism, and unitarianism) and new literary movements (including Romanticism, and, later, naturalism) were regarded with suspicion. The editors were professedly traditional in their views of what should be said about literature. Henry Timrod, writing in *Russell's* in 1857, complained of the lingering influence of the Scottish rhetoricians. Lord Kames was still the model for a literary critic in Charleston, and Hugh Blair was the author of what continued to be the most widely used rhetoric in the South. Until Timrod and Paul Hamilton Hayne started writing for *Russell's*, there was little interest in sympathetic or reproductive criticism, advocated for indigenous American works in the North as early as the 1830s and 1840s. Southern editors were apparently convinced that they were judicious in contrast to many northern editors, who were seen as unfair to southern writers and as advocates of northern writers. But by the 1850s sectional tensions had made it almost impossible for editors like Thompson of the *Southern Literary Messenger* and Paul Hamilton Hayne of *Russell's Magazine* to maintain any pretense of objectivity about northern literature and magazines.

There was an attempt to revive southern magazines immediately after the Civil War and to continue the traditions of maintaining critical standards against the intrusions of popular taste and of promoting a proper southern literature. Editors of the new magazines of the 1860s, *Southern Opinion*, *Southern Magazine*, and the *Land We Love*, tended to be "unreconstructed," idealizing the Old South and showing less sympathy toward new trends in literature than the antebellum editors had. New writers, including Sidney Lanier and Thomas Nelson Page, were introduced; but southern magazines still faced the old problem of few contributors and subscribers. There was a new problem as well: southern magazines lacked the resources to compete with a new type of periodical, the pictorial magazine, most successfully exemplified by *Harper's Weekly*. The best literary magazine before the 1890s was the *Southern Bivouac* (1882–87), which published some of the best work of Paul Hamilton Hayne.

The renaissance of southern magazines began in the 1890s with the *Sewanee Review* in 1892, published by the University of the South, and the *South Atlantic Quarterly*, started 10 years later in 1902 at Trinity College, now Duke University. The *Sewanee Review* continued the tradition of promoting southern literature without being provincial; the *South Atlantic Quarterly*, founded by historian John Spencer Bassett, began with an emphasis on social and political issues, earning a reputation for controversy, and gradually became more literary. By the time these two magazines were joined in 1925 by the *Virginia Quarterly Review* and in 1935 by a new *Southern Review*, the dream of the antebellum editors was being realized. The Southern Literary Renaissance sparked by the writings of William Faulkner, Robert Penn Warren, Katherine Anne Porter, John Crowe Ransom, Allen Tate, Thomas Wolfe, and others, was well under way.

Twentieth-century southern magazines had two important advantages over their predecessors—the flowering of southern literature and, in some cases, a dependable means of financial support, the southern college or university. Editors could at long last pay contributors and more nearly compete with northern magazines. Southern magazines could retain their southern identity but become truly national and even international. Modernism in literature and in literary criticism could be supported. The avant-garde, however, was not pushed. With few exceptions—the *Fugitive* (1922–25) in Nashville and the *Double Dealer* (1921–26) in New Orleans—the South did not develop the true home of the avant-garde, the little magazines, and those that did appear were not experimental. Conservatism and traditionalism still prevailed. There were conservative social and political essays. The criticism of industrialization and of positivism in philosophy begun by George Fitzhugh in *De Bow's Review* in the 1850s and 1860s was renewed in the Agrarian essays of Donald Davidson, Allen Tate, John Crowe Ransom, and other contributors to the 1930 Agrarian manifesto *I'll Take My Stand*. Literary criticism and formalist analysis were practiced in the *Southern Review* in the 1930s under Robert Penn Warren and Cleanth Brooks, in southern critic John Crowe Ransom's *Kenyon Review*, a bastion of the New Criticism, and in the *Sewanee Review* under Allen Tate in the 1940s.

The day of the southern literary magazine had come. Some magazines were as influential as northern magazines. Circulation of the *Sewanee Review* and the *Southern Review* even exceeded 3,000. And yet a proper perspective on these literary magazines must be maintained. As far as a mass southern audience is concerned, the situation has not changed greatly. In 1860 *Southern Field and Fireside* (1859–65) could afford the luxury of hiring the discouraged John Reuben Thompson away from the *Southern Literary Messenger* for the handsome salary of $2,000 a year. Today's *Field and Fireside* equivalent, *Southern Living*, (1966–), is in the 1980s the most widely read southern magazine, with an estimated circulation of 2 million.

See also INDUSTRY: / *De Bow's Review*; MEDIA: Magazines; / *Southern Exposure*; *Southern Living*

Richard J. Calhoun
Clemson University

Richard J. Calhoun, *Southern Literary Journal* (Fall 1970); John C. Guilds, *Southern Literary Journal* (Spring 1972); Jay B. Hubbell, in *Culture in the South*, ed. W. T. Couch (1934), *The South in American Literature* (1954); Robert D. Jacobs, *Southern Literary Journal* (Fall 1969); Frank L. Mott, *A History of American Magazines*, 5 vols. (1930–68); John R. Welsh, *Southern Literary Journal* (April 1971).

Popular Literature

The romantic South has been a mainstay of popular fiction in the United States from the beginning of mass market publishing. John Pendleton Kennedy, the first major novelist to set fiction on southern plantations, achieved early popularity with *Swallow Barn, or A Sojourn in the Old Dominion* (1832) and *Horse-Shoe Robinson* (1835). These novels were patterned after the works of Sir Walter Scott and painted a picture of the Virginia gentry and romantic plantation life that would become typical in popular fiction during the next decades. Almost immediately, southern settings became the symbol for romance, aristocracy, gallant chivalry, grandeur, and a lifestyle of elegant leisure.

By the 1850s the "plantation romance" had become moderately successful. Eliza Ann Dupuy set her 1857 novel, *The Planter's Daughter: A Tale of Louisiana*, in Louisiana, and Mary J. Holmes, who published *Meadow Brook* that same year, wrote of plantation life in Kentucky. In general, these works portrayed the South as a region containing only plantations, genteel planters, delicate and beautiful women, and contented slaves.

None of the antebellum novelists portraying southern life and culture was, however, the equal of Emma Dorothy Eliza Nevitte (E.D.E.N.) Southworth. One of the most prolific and popular American novelists of all time, Southworth used plantation settings in her romantic novels. Among her many best-selling works were *Shannondale* (1850) and *Virginia and Magdalene* (1852). Like all of her books, Southworth's novels of the South were contemporary "domestic romances," a form that dominated American best-sellers until late in the century. Typically, Southworth's tales offered no truly distinctive southern themes, but they did contribute greatly to popular imagery of the plantation South. Southworth and her contemporaries filled their novels with palatial homes, endless social gaiety, princely and gallant aristocrats, and sentimental belles.

Harriet Beecher Stowe's *Uncle Tom's Cabin* (1852), essentially a domestic novel, not only caused a stir over the slavery issue, but also spawned numerous novels in imitation and elicited a healthy number of proslavery novels. In spite of Stowe's didactic, antislavery tone, *Uncle Tom's Cabin* tended to reinforce the image of romance and aristocracy associated with the South. In fact, the true villain of the novel, Simon Legree, was a northerner. Although Stowe's book was intended to condemn and vilify the institution of slavery, the work also contributed to the popular image of the South as a romantic region, an image that has dominated popular fiction since the antebellum era.

The Civil War and the end of the slave system did not weaken the impulse of popular authors to glorify the plantation South. Quite the contrary, the antebellum South took on new romance as a "lost civilization," and popular writers celebrated the Old South with nostalgia. Joel Chandler Harris offered his *Uncle Remus* tales from 1888 through 1906. These "folktales" reflected a world of racial harmony on the South's plantations. Similarly, F. Hopkinson Smith's popular novelette of 1891, *Colonel Carter of Cartersville*, delineated a world of contented servants and genteel masters.

The works of Harris and Smith were typical and widely popular, but their impact was not nearly so great as that of Thomas Nelson Page. More than any other postbellum writer, Page codified the popular image of the Old South, rounding out the traditional stereotypes of the beautiful young belle, her chivalrous beau, and the faithful slave. Like almost all of his works, *In Ole Virginia, or Marse Chan, and Other Stories* (1887) was a collection of short stories, which centered on romance among the southern aristocracy. Narrated by elderly freedmen, the stories recalled the glory and tranquility of the perfect social order that, in Page's view, prevailed before the war. Most significantly, they depicted loyal and totally devoted slaves who believed that their own happiness was tied to that of their masters.

Later in his career Page became disillusioned with the state of race relations in the post–Civil War South. In *Red Rock: A Chronicle of Reconstruction* (1898) and *The Red Riders* (1924) Page developed more sinister characterizations of black people. Along with Thomas Dixon, Jr., who published *The Clansman: An American Drama* in 1905, Page blamed the South's difficulties, particularly racial and economic problems, on the freedmen and northern interventionists. Implicit in the Page and Dixon novels of the Reconstruction South was the glorification of the Old South as an idyllic Garden of Eden.

From about 1890 and continuing into the 1930s the historical novel was a dominant genre of popular fiction in the United States, and novels of the antebellum South assumed a central position. Most of the Old South bestsellers that emerged were of the "moonlight-and-magnolias" variety. Mary Johnston, who wrote more than 20 historical novels, penned significant portrayals of both the antebellum and postbellum South. Her *Miss Delicia Allen* (1933) was a classic story of aristocratic grace and romance on a Virginia plantation, and *The Long Roll* (1911) remains one of the best popular treatments of the impact of the Civil War. Stark Young's widely successful *So Red the Rose* (1934) explored life on a Mississippi plantation. Young continued the tradition developed by Page, and he seemed to argue that the Old South was a highly admirable society and that its demise after the Civil War was a crushing blow to civilization itself. Ellen Glasgow was not only popular, but talented as well. Her novel *The Battle-Ground* (1902) demonstrated that the South could be portrayed as a many-faceted society with flaws as well as strengths. Although Glasgow portrayed the southern elite in rather grand and romantic fashion, she also recognized the importance of the yeoman farmer and the poor white in the southern social structure.

By the mid-1930s popular writers, following Glasgow's lead, seemed to be on the verge of offering a more accurate and realistic treatment of the Old South. But a single event, the publication in 1936 of *Gone with the Wind*, brought popular fiction squarely back into the romantic and sentimental portrayal that had flourished for so long. Margaret Mitchell's incredibly successful novel relied on stock settings and stereotypes to mythologize the Old South more effectively and more popularly than any other book before or since. Moreover, the sections of *Gone with the Wind* that deal with the Reconstruction South clearly portray the antebellum era as a lost and glamorous period of aristocratic gentility and high romance.

Mitchell's immediate successor was Frank Yerby, a black writer whose short fiction exploring racial issues had won literary acclaim. Yerby turned to historical fiction in 1946 with the publication of *The Foxes of Harrow*. He eventually became one of the most popular novelists of all time. Although he worked within a "potboiler" formula, Yerby was always careful to research the historical background of his tales in meticulous detail. His works continued the romantic tradition established by Margaret Mitchell, but Yerby was also careful to include details of life in the slave quarters. Additionally, Yerby's portrayal of sexuality among the planter elite was more explicit than earlier writers'.

Yerby's popularity undoubtedly piqued the public's interest in romantic fiction set in the Old South. Kyle Onstott cashed in on the trend with *Mandingo* in 1957, the same year that Yerby issued *Fairoaks*. But the novels were quite different. Yerby's novel provided a wealth of accurate information related to slave life and culture, including a sensitive and painfully detailed passage on the slave trade. On the other hand, *Mandingo* can make no claim to historic accuracy. Onstott's novel and its several sequels are still in print, and total sales for the series are around 30 million copies.

The world of *Mandingo* is a miasmic wasteland of slavebreeding plantations, populated by vicious masters, their drunken wives, generously endowed "breeding studs," and eager and wanton "breeding wenches." *Mandingo* might be passed off as a prurient example of the worst tendencies in popular fiction were it not for its impact on the publishing industry. Onstott's success was so great that hundreds of imitations, mostly paperback originals, were published over the next quarter of a century. All of them relied on sensational portrayals of interracial sexuality, degenerate aristocrats, and black people who found it impossible to control their libidinous desires. The widespread popularity of the post-Onstott "plantation novel" attests to his importance in developing popular imagery of the Old South as a land of "lust in the dust."

Onstott's successors in this genre included Norman Daniels, the author of skillful paperback originals in several genres, who created the "Wyndward Plantation" series (1969 and after), and Raymond Giles, who wrote the "Sabrehill" saga (1970–75). Marie de Jourlet offered several novels in the "Windhaven" series beginning in 1978, and Richard Tresillian initiated his "Bondmaster" series in 1977, with each novel enjoying an initial print run of roughly 700,000 copies. Although Tresillian's series is set in the West Indies, the novels are clearly modeled on Onstott's work, and the books often use details and portrayals based on United States settings. Finally, Lonnie Coleman's hardback best-seller *Beulah Land* (1973) evolved into an influential series, which was eventually adapted as a controversial television miniseries. Coleman's history was somewhat more accurate than that of the other popular novelists, but his concentration on themes of miscegenation, degenerate gentry, and "women on the pedestal" clearly indicated his debt to Onstott's work.

Although the so-called poor white generally has been neglected in popular fiction set in the South, the paperback reprinting of Erskine Caldwell's *Tobacco Road* (1947; hardcover edition 1932) spawned an impressive trend in "backwoods" novels that extended throughout the 1950s and maintained moderate success in the 1960s. *Tobacco Road* was a racy tale of poor sharecroppers and seemed to strike a responsive chord among readers who had tired of the "moonlight-and-magnolias" imagery. The paperback sales of the work far outstripped the publisher's expectations, and soon dozens of authors were rushing to cash in on the trend. Indeed, the paperback publishing revolution seemed to provide the perfect outlet for Caldwell's many imitators. In the words of one publisher, the "backwoods" novels centered on the "earthy humor, the primitive passions and quaint ways of Southern hill folk." These "folk" were libidinous, raucous, and illiterate, and the stories involved cockfighting, moonshining, prostitution, gambling, and general depravity.

Other notable "backwoods" authors included John Faulkner (William's brother), whose *Cabin Road* (1951) was reprinted at least six times, Jack Boone, who offered *Dossie Bell Is Dead* in 1951, and Charles Williams, who published a series of novels using variations on a single theme. Under titles such as *Hill Girl* (1951), *River Girl* (1951), and *Girl Out Back* (1958), Williams penned stories in which a dishonest and somewhat brutish "po' white" meets his match in a tough and ruthless backwoods siren with whom he falls in love. Williams was imitated by many, including Cord Wainer (pseudonym of Thomas B. Dewey) with *Mountain Girl* (1952), Allen O'Quinn with *Swamp Brat* (1953), and Jack Woodford and John B. Thompson with *Swamp Hoyden* (no date).

Cover from 1956 paperback edition of Erskine Caldwell's best-seller

Although dozens of additional authors might be mentioned, none was able to capture the spirit of the "backwoods" formula and play to the demands of the audience quite so well as Harry Whittington, who also wrote under the pseudonyms of Hallam Whitney and Whit Harrison. His works included *Backwoods Hussy* (1952), *Shack Road* (1953), *Cracker Girl* (1953), *Shanty Road* (1954), and *Backwoods Tramp* (1959). His "backwoods" tales were enormously popular and eventually gave the formula its name. Later in his career Whittington helped to complete the "Falconhurst Series" begun by Kyle Onstott, and he created the popular "Blackoaks" series of plantation novels which were published under his Ashley Carter pseudonym.

Even after the rise of Kyle Onstott and the backwoods formula, both considered male genres, there remained a market for less violent and less racist versions of romantic fiction set in the antebellum South. This genre continued to maintain substantial popularity into the 1980s. Mainly targeted at women, historic romances in an Old South setting were very similar to the traditional historical romance set in *any* period. By the 1970s the form was referred to as the "bodice ripper" by critics. In these tales the principal focus was on the romantic involvement of the heroine and a rough but handsome hero, a macho figure who often nearly raped the heroine in their first sexual encounter, an act that only served to heighten her desire for him. The setting was essentially a mere backdrop for the romance, but the overall portrayal served to extend and popularize the "moonlight-and-magnolias" image of the Old South, albeit in somewhat unsavory fashion.

Many authors wrote popular novels of this sort, and recent representative titles include *Wild Honey* (1982) by Fern Michaels, Julia Grice's *Emerald Fire* (1978), and *Texas Temptress* (1985) by Jean Haught. Other novelists adapted the Old South setting to closely related genres in the general field of romantic fiction. For example, Jane Aiken Hodge's *Savannah Purchase* (1970) is little more than the traditional "gothic romance" set in the Old South. Even major figures in feminine romantic fiction, such as Kathleen Woodiwiss, could not resist the temptation to set their sentimental and always passionate tales in the antebellum South. Woodiwiss's romantic *Ashes in the Wind* (1979) is typical of the feminine fiction set in the Old South during the past decades. It recounts the tale of "an impudent, plantation bred beauty" with "reckless bravado" who falls in love with a "ramrod straight Yankee" who renders her "incapable of reason." Such paperback romances, coupled with occasional bestselling historical fiction such as John Jakes's *North and South* (1982), have helped to maintain the popular romantic image of the "lost civilization" of the antebellum South.

Popular fiction set in the South has provided a consistent and rather limited perspective on the region since the rise of mass fiction during the two decades prior to the Civil War. Geographically the region has been depicted either as one great plantation or as an impoverished wasteland of "hill folk" and backwoods hamlets. Only two levels of society have been portrayed, the elite planter class (including their slaves) and the extremely poor white class. In the former case novelists have either presented a highly idealized and romantic image or have depicted a depraved and sadistic society that glorifies violence and justifies racism. In portraying poor whites writers have contented themselves with simplistic images of illiterate and sexually active bumpkins. Black southerners have most often appeared in fiction set in the antebellum era and have been relegated to one of two categories—wanton, sex-starved slaves or contented, childlike slaves intent on making their masters happy. Popular fictional portrayals of the South, however inaccurate, have had an enormous impact upon public perceptions of the region and its people.

See also MEDIA: / *Mandingo*; MYTHIC SOUTH: Plantation Myth; / Mitchell, Margaret; "Moonlight-and-Magnolias" Myth; *Uncle Tom's Cabin* (book); Yerby, Frank

Christopher D. Geist
Bowling Green State University

Earl F. Bargainnier, *Journal of Popular Culture* (Fall 1976); Bill Crider, *Journal of Popular Culture* (Winter 1982); F. Garvin Davenport, Jr., *The Myth of Southern History: Historical Consciousness in Twentieth-Century Southern Literature* (1967); Robert B. Downs, *Books That Changed the South* (1977); Francis Pendleton Gaines, *The Southern Plantation: A Study in the Development and the Accuracy of a Tradition* (1925); Christopher D. Geist, *Southern Quarterly* (Spring 1980); Jack Temple Kirby, *Media-Made Dixie: The South in the American Imagination* (1978); James M. Mellard, *Journal of Popular Culture* (Summer 1971); C. Michael Smith, *Journal of Popular Culture* (Winter 1982); Alice K. Turner, *New York* (magazine) (13 February 1978).

Publishing

Although the migration of big business to the South and the decay of northern urban centers are undisputed, there have been no major book publication centers in the South, with the exception of university presses. In 1981, of the 1,200 publishers in the country issuing five or more titles annually, 83 were located in the South. Of the annual national production of 66,000 titles, southern presses issued 2,200 titles, one-fourth of which bore the imprints of university presses. The South, with over one-fourth of the nation's population, published only 3 percent of its book titles. Why did southern printshops and booksellers not develop into publishing houses prior to 1830, the period of greatest growth in the publishing industry? Why did the balance of activity in publishing shift from localized presses in the late 18th century to centers like New York and Philadelphia at the beginning of the 19th century rather than to Charleston or Richmond? The answers reside in the very nature of the region.

Historically, the establishment of those primal founts of heresy and rebellion, printing presses, was inhibited in the South by royal governors; geographically, the South had only limited access to distribution routes that would enable it to claim interior markets; demographically, the South never developed those large population centers necessary to support major publishing houses; culturally, the South remained dependent on the North and England for too long—moving to create its first publishing centers several decades after the northern publishing houses had established their fortunes by issuing cheap reprint editions of English works; and, traditionally, the southern ideal of cultural isolation created an insular society that, until tensions began to arise between the North and the South prior to the Civil War, felt no need for active regional publishing. By the 1850s when the southern press first called for a regional publishing center, New York and Philadelphia already dominated the American publishing industry, and whatever hopes the South might have had of creating a parallel publishing center in the wake of the regional sentiment that preceded the Civil War were dashed with those of the southern cause during that conflict.

For all this, southern university presses have recorded notable achievements in the 20th century. The titles published by these presses reflect a close identification with their region. The story of publishing in the South falls into five stages: (1) the establishment of the printing industry in the colonial South, (2) the effort to establish a southern publishing center in the antebellum South, (3) the expansion of that industry during the Civil War, (4) the production of southern titles during Reconstruction, and (5) the formation of southern university presses in the 1920s and 1930s.

The desire to establish a press in the South preceded its establishment by close to half a century. The earliest southern printers combined the functions of printer and publisher in their shops. They served at the discretion of royal governors who, like their English monarch, perceived the printer to be promulgator of disobedience and heresy. Thus, in 1682, when William Nuthead attempted to establish the first southern press in Jamestown, the Virginia Council banned printing of any kind in the colony, and Nuthead moved his press to Maryland. Only in 1730, nearly a century after the establishment of the first press in New England, did the Virginia Assembly reconsider its act and, succumbing to a need for a public printer, lure William Parks to Williamsburg. Within succeeding decades presses were established in Charleston, S.C. (1731), New Bern, N.C. (1749), and Savannah, Ga. (1762), at the behest of colonial assemblies, which, like Virginia's, found the dangers of insurrection posed by the free printer to be less threatening than the need for someone to make clear the confused manuscript copies of the acts of the assembly.

More than one-half of all titles produced in the South during this period were legal (assembly proceedings, executive utterances, and statutes), whereas the titles of New England presses were 46 percent theological and only 17 percent legal. The figures have been misread to imply that southern colonial interests were legal rather than theological. In fact, the number of government publications issued in both regions was about the same. What the figures suggest is that the South never developed interests—beyond those of governmental procedure—that required active regional publication. Whatever regional controversies took place in the South, like the smallpox inoculation controversy of 1738–39 chronicled by Lewis Timothy's Charleston press, were amply treated in pamphlets. The population density of the New England area, its cultural diversity, its trumpeting of rights and launching of crusades—all these resulted in the kind of polemics that supported a functioning regional press; the scattered nature of the southern population, its cultural homogeneity (only 12,320 unnaturalized foreigners were counted in the South in 1820 in contrast to 41,335 in the rest of the nation), its insular nature, and its confidence in traditional values required no such outlet.

Until the end of the 18th century the book publisher in America was a tradesman, either a bookseller who printed editions for his own shop or a printer who sold the products of his press in a back room. By 1830 this structure had become outmoded. In the publishing centers of New York and Philadelphia, craft and trade functions were abandoned by the publisher who turned his attention to selecting books to be printed and marketed on the basis of popular appeal and potential profits. In the 1830s, for instance, the Philadelphia firm of Carey & Hart boldly purchased all the seats in a mail stage to ship Bulwer Lytton's *Rienzi* (1836) to New York, beating the New York firm of Harpers in their own market. In contrast, John Russell of Charleston chose William Gilmore Simms's *Areytos* (1846) as his firm's first imprint, basing his decision not on the profit motive but on an idealistic desire to serve the literary needs of his region. Russell's firm (with a stock valued at $20,000) was essentially a bookstore, not a publishing house. In the North publishing had become a competitive business in and of itself—in the South it remained the avocation of printers and booksellers.

The American copyright act of 1790, which provided that the works of English authors could be reprinted in America without payment of royalties, had a great part in encouraging the growth of the northern publishing houses. New York became a trade center after the War of 1812 by developing a triangular trade that carried cotton from the South to England, manufactured goods from England to New York, and northern and foreign goods from New York to the cotton ports. The preference of the average American reader prior to 1840 for English authors was reflected in the publishing industry (only 30 percent of the titles published at this time were written by American authors), so that the publishing industry was largely an import industry. This fact not only contributed to the growth of the New York firms—ideally situated at the center of the American import system—but paradoxically created the very situation in which the early domination of the publishing trade by northern houses would appear least threatening to southern audiences. Literature imported into the South, whether channeled through northern or southern shops, reflected English values rather than the values of either region. Although some important titles were reprinted in the South during this period, the favorite publishers of southern readers were northern houses that "puffed" and promoted their wares. Works published in the South, though technically comparable to their northern counterparts, were simply not promoted. A book published in the North would receive national distribution, but southern-issued books were rarely even read in neighboring states.

By 1840, when approximately half the books printed in the United States were written by American authors, the North with its Protestant work ethic and business acumen had acquired a virtual monopoly on book publishing. Not until the middle of that decade did southern authors, who perceived the increased interest in publishing among their northern counterparts, feel themselves uncomfortable with northern publishing houses; and not until the northern publishing houses began exporting to the South books and texts espousing northern rather than English ideals did the South feel sufficiently besieged by northern culture and propaganda to establish its own publishing houses.

As tensions increased between the North and the South prior to the Civil War, the South came to resent keenly its literary vassalage to the North. One writer complained of textbooks, which were prepared by northern men unfamiliar with the South, that devoted 2 pages to Connecticut onions and broomcorn and only 10 lines to Louisiana and sugar. Charges of moral laxity made by the abolitionists angered southerners who, because of the limited number of publishing houses established in their region, saw no means of promoting their side of the issue. Southern authors, like William Gilmore Simms, who sought a national audience found that the novels they published in the South sold far less than those that came out of the North. Although a substantial number of Simms's titles were printed by southern presses, of the major works only *The Sword and the Distaff* (published in 1852 by Walker, Richards of Charleston) was of southern issue. By 1858 Simms, who had extensive experience with both northern and southern publishers, could remark that there was "not in all the Southern States a single publisher." Less prestigious writers found themselves in the dilemma of either subsidizing their own works in southern houses that lacked the capital of the northern operations or seeking publication in the North where southern writers were widely considered to be inferior.

Prior to the Civil War only three publishing houses of any consequence, Randolph & English and West & Johnston in Richmond and Sigismund H. Goetzel in Mobile, existed in the South. Richmond, New Orleans, and Charleston were the printing centers. The desire for reading matter did not cease with the Civil War, however, although blockades cut off northern book sources. Much that he produced during the war was ephemeral, but the southern publisher, his competition to the North removed, flourished.

Of the 105 book titles published in the Confederacy between 1861 and 1865, nearly one-third were published in Richmond and most of these were by West & Johnston. In the early days of the war southern publishing houses issued the essential field manuals and military handbooks, but by 1862 the South was forced, in a way that it had never been, to turn to itself for books and authors. West & Johnston, in searching for regional talent, unearthed Augusta Jane Evans [Wilson] whose novel *Macaria* (1864) outsold any other edition in the South. The Richmond firm also issued the Confederacy's first original drama, James Dabney McCabe's *The Guerillas* (1863). In all, the Confederacy produced 49 works of fiction, 29 volumes of verse, 15 songsters, and 5 dramas among other miscellaneous publications.

Had Reconstruction been less agonizing, the Confederate presses might well have developed into a publishing center of some kind. But with the end of the war, the hopes of southern publishers were vanquished. The products of the few Reconstruction presses, most notably Clark & Hofeline of New Orleans, were devoted to embittered defenses of the South and to angry denunciations of the North. Among Clark & Hofeline's imprints were Randell Hunt's *Appeal in Behalf of Louisiana, to the Senate of the United States for the fulfillment of the constitutional guaranty to her of a republican form of government as a state in the union* (1874) and James Dugan's satirical depiction of postwar Louisiana, *Doctor Dispachemquic; A Story of the Great Southern Plague of 1878* (1878). But for all his bravado, the southern publisher working in the Reconstruction era found himself enduring a period of emotional and financial bankruptcy. When in 1922 the first state university press was established at the University of North Carolina, it was the only professionally staffed, continually publishing book publisher in all the states that once composed the Confederacy.

The university presses, which have flourished in the South during the 20th century, have filled a need for serious scholarly southern study that was, prior to their inception, both ignored and misunderstood by northern publishing houses. Most of these presses (Duke University Press, the University of North Carolina Press, the University of Georgia Press, the University of South Carolina Press, the Louisiana State University Press, the Southern Methodist University Press, the University of Tennessee Press, and the University Presses of Florida) were established in the 1920s, 1930s, and 1940s—when their treatment of the social and economic ills of the region was often controversial. Others (the University Press of Mississippi, the University of Texas Press, and the University Press of Virginia) have been established only in the past few decades.

W. T. Couch, who became assistant director of the University of North Carolina Press in 1925 and its director in 1932, sought the kind of regional studies, books on the South written by southerners, that would shake the region out of its complacency. Under his direction the press produced a number of important regional studies, like Howard W. Odum's *Southern Regions of the United States* (1936) and Stella Gentry Sharpe's *Tobe* (1939), as well as critical studies of textile unions, mill villages, child labor, lynching, and race relations. Couch's aggressive attitude toward regional studies filled a vacuum left by northern houses and provided the South with a publishing center, which, as an organ of the region it served, offered a means of defining and molding a "New South" during the days of the New Deal. His leadership set the tone for other southern university presses.

The representation of the southern university presses among the nation's university presses is more indicative of the intellectual health of the region than are the figures relating to publishing as a whole. Of the 2,300 titles published by the nation's university presses in 1981, close to 500 were issued by southern university presses. Yet the impact of the university press on the South, especially in the 1920s and 1930s when a modern South was in its early stage of self-definition, has been out of proportion to its productivity. For the first time in their history, southerners read analyses of their region written by southerners and selected for publication by southerners. The impact was enormous.

The number of presses the South should have 100 years from now will depend on how the needs of the industry are met by the region. On 11 February 1982 Harcourt Brace Jovanovich, Inc., a major New York publishing house since 1919, announced its decision to move its operations from New York to centers in Florida and California. Although a single move of this kind does not suggest a trend, William Jovanovich's announcement did express a genuine dissatisfaction with New York as a publishing center, and in the future other major publishers may also head South.

See also EDUCATION: / Couch, W. T.

Carol Johnston
Clemson University

Book Forum, vol. 3 (No. 2, 1977); Richard Barksdale Harwell, *Confederate Belles-Lettres* (1941); Jay B. Hubbell, in *American Studies in Honor of William Kenneth Boyd*, ed. David Kelly Jackson (1940); Hellmut Lehmann-Haupt, *The Book in America: A History of the Making and Selling of Books in the United States* (1951); *Literary Market Place with Names and Numbers: The Directory of American Book Publishing* (1982); Madeleine B. Stern, *Imprints on History: Book Publishers and American Frontiers* (1956); John Tebbel, ed., *A History of Book Publishing in the United States*, 4 vols. (1972–81).

Regionalism and Local Color

Although the terms *regionalism* and *local color* are sometimes used interchangeably, regionalism generally has broader connotations. Whereas local color is often applied to a specific literary mode that flourished in the late 19th century, regionalism implies a recognition from the colonial period to the present of differences among specific areas of the country. Additionally, regionalism refers to an intellectual movement encompassing regional consciousness beginning in the 1930s.

Even though there is evidence of regional awareness in early southern writing—William Byrd's *History of the Dividing Line*, for example, points out southern characteristics—not until well into the 19th century did regional considerations begin to overshadow national ones. In the South the regional concern became more and more evident in essays and fiction exploring and often defending the southern way of life. John Pendleton Kennedy's fictional sketches in *Swallow Barn*, for example, examined southern plantation life at length.

The South played a major role in the local color movement that followed the Civil War. Although the beginning of the movement is usually dated from the first publication in the *Overland Monthly* in 1868 of Bret Harte's stories of California mining camps, a disproportionate number of contributors of local color stories to national magazines were southerners. The genesis of the local color movement was not surprising. The outcome of the Civil War signified the victory of nationalism over regional interests. With the increasing move toward urbanization and industrialization following the war and the concurrent diminishing of regional differences, it is not surprising that there was a developing nostalgia for remaining regional differences. Local color writing, which was regionally, and often rurally, based and usually took the form of short stories intended for mass consumption, met a need for stories about simpler times and faraway places.

Although local color writing encompassed a number of regions, including New England and the Midwest, southern local color had about it a special quality—the mystique of the Lost Cause. In many stories written about life in the antebellum South there was an idealization of the way things were before the war; the South was often pictured in these stories not as it actually had been but as it "might have been." Representative of this writing is the fiction of Thomas Nelson Page, whose tales of Virginia plantation life in such stories as "Marse Chan" pictured beautiful southern maidens, noble and brave slaveowners, and happy, contented slaves. Although not all southern local color writing depicted the South in such romanticized terms, the exotic and quaint characteristics of this region were dominant motifs.

Southern writers after the Civil War wrote about a variety of places and people, providing a sense of the diversity of the South. Sidney Lanier's poems ("The Marshes of Glynn," 1878, "Sunrise," 1887) offered images from the marshes of south Georgia; Richard Malcolm Johnston's *Georgia Sketches* (1864) and *Dukesboro Tales* (1871) presented stories of the "cracker"; Mississippian Irwin Russell's sketches and *Collected Poems* (1888) popularized the use of black dialect in literature; and Sherwood Bonner's *Dialect Tales* (1884) and her accounts of Tennessee mountain life dealt with the everyday life of plain folk.

Other writers achieved more national fame and literary success in portraying aspects of southern life. George Washington Cable immortalized the Creoles of south Louisiana in the pages of *Scribner's Monthly* and then in such books as *Old Creole Days* (1879) and *The Grandissimes* (1884); Mary Noailles Murfree spent her summers in the Cumberland Mountains of Tennessee and then wrote about the mountaineers, using pen names such as Charles Egbert Craddock and E. Emmett Dembry, in the *Atlantic Monthly* and in a book of stories, *In the Tennessee Mountains* (1884); James Lane Allen created initial literary images of Kentucky life and people with stories in *Harper's Magazine* (April 1885) and in such books as *Flute and Violin, and Other Kentucky Tales and Romances* (1891) and *Kentucky Cardinal* (1894); and Joel Chandler Harris used folklore in his *Uncle Remus: His Songs and Sayings* (1880), which created enduring portraits—some say stereotypes—of black southerners. Other local colorists included Kate Chopin, Ruth McEnery Stuart, Charles E. A. Gayarré, and Grace E. King (Louisiana); Margaret Junkin Preston and Mary Johnston (Virginia); John Fox, Jr. (Appalachia); and Lafcadio Hearn (New Orleans).

As a genre southern local color writing flourished through the 1890s, after which this genteel mode of writing lost popularity. At the turn of the century regional writing in the South was still evident, as in the Virginia-based novels of Ellen Glasgow, whose work attempted a more realistic depiction of the strength and weaknesses of the South. By the 1930s there was a resurgence of interest in regionalism, this time as an intellectual movement. Writers sought to treat each of the regions of the country as discrete geographical, cultural, and economic entities. Again the South played a major role in the regional movement. In fact, a cornerstone of the movement was the manifesto *I'll Take My Stand: The South and the Agrarian Tradition* by Twelve Southerners, published in 1930. The authors of this work, among them John Crowe Ransom, Donald Davidson, Allen Tate, and Robert Penn Warren, argued that the South, having held on to its agrarian culture longer than the rest of the country, could serve as a model for a society in which man rather than the machine was dominant. Citing the dehumanization brought about by industrialization and the assembly line, the authors posited that, although the South would not remain entirely agriculturally based, the southern way of life was more conducive to a full relationship between man and his surroundings.

Although the regional, agrarian philosophy set forth in *I'll Take My Stand* was to a great degree sociological in its thrust, as was much writing about regionalism at this time, there was in the South a corresponding literary movement, known as the Southern Literary Renaissance, which, although not always parallel to the regional movement in its philosophic principles, also emphasized the importance of regional setting and tradition to individuals' lives. Notable writers of this period who explored the importance of their southern heritage and environment included William Faulkner, Robert Penn Warren, and Thomas Wolfe. Although it may be argued, and rightly so, that their works are universal in their implications, each writer's work is firmly rooted in the southern region.

In the decades since the 1930s literature and the other arts that grew out of southern culture have flourished. Such writers as Flannery O'Connor, Carson McCullers, and, more recently, Eudora Welty and Walker Percy, have continued to place characters and action in the South. Although their work is regional, it is universal as well. Each writer, through the exploration of specific characters and places, seeks answers to the questions of life and death that concern all men and women. One can conclude of the work of these contemporary southern writers that all art must find its roots in a specific place or region. The best art is not *of* a region but *transcends* region.

In the last quarter of the 20th century, the South seems to have retained many regional distinctions. Although the region has not lived up to its position as the agrarian model so bravely postulated in *I'll Take My Stand*, it has not succumbed entirely to the homogeneous tendencies resulting from mass media and the shift in population toward the Sunbelt. The South continues to assert in its art its distinctive regional qualities.

See also MYTHIC SOUTH: Regionalism; / Agrarians, Vanderbilt; WOMEN'S LIFE: / Chopin, Kate

Anne E. Rowe
Florida State University

George Core, ed., *Regionalism and Beyond: Essays of Randal Stewart* (1968); Donald Davidson, *The Attack on Leviathan: Regionalism and Nationalism in the United States* (1938); Merrill Jensen, ed., *Regionalism in America* (1951); Claude M. Simpson, ed., *The Local Colorists: American Short Stories, 1857–1900* (1960); Robert E. Spiller et al., eds., *Literary History of the United States* (1963).

Sex Roles in Literature

The heritage of a strong class and caste system in the South narrows the range of roles for men and women in southern literature. Within that range the most prominent writers of the modern South—Ellen Glasgow, William Faulkner, Robert Penn Warren, and Eudora Welty—explore the depths of a variety of individual characters. In southern fiction, as in most American writing, a confused identity is often attributed to failure to deal with sexuality directly and responsibly, whereas healthy sexuality becomes the basis for self-awareness.

The southern white male appears in fiction most frequently as either the gentleman-father or his cavalier son. The prototype of the gentleman-father appears in John Pendleton Kennedy's *Swallow Barn* (1832). Frank Meriwether has dominion over all, white and black; his wife's control of daily plantation life frees him for leisure and contemplation. Meriwether's fictional descendants include the ineffectual Gerald O'Hara in Margaret Mitchell's *Gone with the Wind* (1936) and Battle Fairchild, continuing Meriwether's life into the 1920s in Welty's *Delta Wedding* (1946). Faulkner shows the deterioration of the southern aristocrat in alcoholic Mr. Compson in *The Sound and the Fury* (1929), portrays Sutpen ironically attempting to become a gentleman and found a dynasty in *Absalom, Absalom!* (1936), and further mocks the tradition in Flem Snopes's journey to his mansion-mausoleum. Warren satirizes the figure of the southern gentleman in Bogan Murdock, with his bogus sense of honor, in *At Heaven's Gate* (1943) and even has Jed Tewksbury, a redneck-scholar in *A Place to Come To* (1977), jokingly refuse to become an "S. G."

The fictional cavalier frequently dies young; if not, he may become a gentleman-father, a rake (like Rhett Butler), or a true southern bachelor. Thomas Nelson Page's hero in "Marse Chan" (1885), the ideal cavalier, dies in the war. Faulkner's cavaliers, often confused about sexual roles, are likely to destroy themselves early, like young Bayard in *Sartoris* (1929) and Quentin Compson. In *All the King's Men* (1946) Warren details Jack Burden's rebellion against his aristocratic heritage in his long journey toward becoming a true gentleman. Will Barrett, Walker Percy's protagonist in *The Last Gentleman* (1966), is haunted by his past, particularly his gentleman-father's suicide. In *The Second Coming* (1980) Will finally frees himself from the past and achieves a sensitive relationship with a sexually free younger woman. Faulkner excels in his depictions of true southern bachelors, especially Ike McCaslin, whose obsession with the past destroys his marriage.

The prevailing roles in fiction for the southern white female are the lady-mother and the belle. Kennedy's Lucretia Meriwether, controlling domestic life in spite of her physical weakness, is followed by fictional lady-mothers like Ellen O'Hara and Ellen Fairchild. Augusta Jane Evans [Wilson] gives characters like Edna Earl in *St. Elmo* (1866) the education and opportunity to choose nontraditional roles, but they usually marry gentleman-fathers. In *The Awakening* (1900) Kate Chopin focuses on the unfolding sexual identity of Edna Pontellier, who marries and bears children, then realizes she is unsuited for the role of "mother-woman" in her Creole society. Glasgow's protagonist in *Virginia* (1913) rigidly follows the pattern of her lady-mother's life but loses her husband to an unconventional New York actress. Faulkner's Granny Millard in *The Unvanquished* (1938) is strong, but she relies on the conventions of society to the point of destruction; Mrs. Compson is lady-mother evolved into controlling matriarch.

The life of a fictional belle is short; for she is most often portrayed as moving toward the goal of marrying a cavalier, as Kennedy's Bel Tracy does, and settling down as a lady-mother. The refusal to play the role of belle can have grave consequences, as seen in Faulkner's Drusilla Hawk and Caddy Compson. Katherine Anne Porter's Miranda, in "The Old Order" and other stories, must reject the legacy of the belle with her destructive sexuality before she can live as an independent woman. Glasgow's incisive portrait of Eva Birdsong in *The Sheltered Life* (1932) shows that marriage does not always offer the belle a new role; Scarlett O'Hara, rebelling at the prospect of becoming a lady-mother, finds new options in the chaos of the Reconstruction. However, in *The Moviegoer* (1961) Percy gives hope for stability in the comfortable role of the southern lady, while her cousin-husband Binx Bolling assumes the role of gentleman-father. The fictional South of the 1920s produces a variation on the role of belle with the flapper, most notably Temple Drake in *Sanctuary* (1931) and Sue Murdock in *At Heaven's Gate*, both of whom illustrate the dangers of irresponsible sexual freedom.

Although the fictional southern woman's sexuality may destroy her or imprison her in a prescribed role, it may also free her from tradition. Glasgow's lower-class rural protagonist in *Barren Ground* (1925) is saved from the entrapment of an illegitimate pregnancy by miscarrying. Faulkner's mythic Eula Varner Snopes is imprisoned by her sexuality, but Lena Grove in *Light in August* (1932) placidly bears her illegitimate child. In *The Reivers* (1962) Corrie rejects her life as a prostitute and is rewarded with an optimistic future with Boon Hogganbeck. Welty's Gloria in *Losing Battles* (1970) rejects the opportunity for freedom through education but gains a strong sexual identity in her relationship with Jack Renfro; and Laurel McKelva Hand in *The Optimist's Daughter* (1972) finds hope for an independent future in understanding her parents' marriage and her own. Doris Betts portrays, in *The River to Pickle Beach* (1972), the healthy sexuality and strong marriage of Bebe and Jack Sellars, contrasted with the destructive perversion of Mickey McCane. Betts also confronts the complexity of woman's struggle for independence through librarian Nancy Finch in *Heading West* (1981). Percy's Allison is freed from a conventional role in society by mental illness, which allows her to find a positive relationship with Will Barrett.

Demeaning roles for black men and women, especially as the child and the brute, haunt the pages of southern fiction from *Swallow Barn* through *Gone with the Wind* and after. Less demeaning but still lacking individuality and dignity are the tragic mulatto, male or female, and the faithful uncle or mammy. However, a few black characters, mostly in recent fiction, are freed from these roles and given autonomy as human beings. In *Clotel* (1853) William Wells Brown traces the suffering of three generations of mulatto women under the domination of insensitive southern gentlemen who perceive them as the lowest of human beings—black and female. George Washington Cable focuses on the Creole society of Louisiana for his moving story of Honoré Grandissime, a free man of color in *The Grandissimes* (1880). In *The House Behind the Cedars* (1900) Charles W. Chesnutt allows Rena Walden to question her role in society as a black woman who appears white; her brother John can live with dignity only by assuming the identity of a southern cavalier. Faulkner portrays mulatto characters, especially Joe Christmas and Charles Bon, as individuals in their quests for identity; likewise, Warren's Amantha Starr in *Band of Angels* (1955) and Margaret Walker's Vyry in *Jubilee* (1966) transcend the limitations of stereotyping.

The stereotype of the black uncle, such as the narrator of "Marse Chan," has occasionally been displaced by the role of the autonomous black male. In spite of the ending of *The Adventures of Huckleberry Finn* (1885) Mark Twain gives the character of Jim dignity and wisdom in his quest for identity as a free man. Tea Cake, in Zora Neale Hurston's *Their Eyes Were Watching God* (1937), is an independent man who is strong enough to think of Janie's happiness as well as his own. Faulkner gives Rider in "Pantaloon in Black" (1940) the sensitivity to be destroyed by the real human emotion of grief. Through the struggles of Bigger Thomas in *Native Son* (1940) Richard Wright emphasizes the significance of race and sex in attaining self-identity, even in defeat. Black leaders Ned and Jimmy, although destroyed by the white society in Ernest J. Gaines's *The Autobiography of Miss Jane Pittman* (1971), are autonomous.

The fictional black mammy, often seen in contrast to the aloof white lady, may have originated in the local color fiction of Sherwood Bonner; Mitchell and others strengthened the stereotype. Occasional black women characters are more complex, like Twain's Roxy in *Pudd'nhead Wilson* (1894), strong and passionate, or like Faulkner's Dilsey, superior to the white Compsons in her patience, her love, her wisdom, her endurance. Rather than portraying Janie in *Their Eyes Were Watching God* as a tragic mulatto or turning her into a mammy, Hurston develops her as an independent woman with love for and commitment to a strong black man. Gaines's Miss Jane, old and wise, is in no sense a stereotyped mammy; in fact, like Janie, she is not even a biological mother. Rather, Gaines gives her identity as a strong, brave, loving, free black woman.

See also BLACK LIFE: Literary Portrayals of Blacks; Literature, Black; HISTORY AND MANNERS: Sexuality; / Gays; MYTHIC SOUTH: / Cavalier Myth; Good Old Boys and Girls; "Mammy"; WOMEN'S LIFE: Belles and Ladies

Martha E. Cook
Longwood College

Francis Pendleton Gaines, *The Southern Plantation: A Study in the Development and the Accuracy of a Tradition* (1924); Anne Goodwyn Jones, *Tomorrow Is Another Day: The Woman Writer in the South, 1859–1936* (1981); Richard H. King, *A Southern*

Renaissance: The Cultural Awakening of the American South, 1930–1955 (1980); Anne Firor Scott, *The Southern Lady: From Pedestal to Politics, 1830–1930* (1970); William R. Taylor, *Cavalier and Yankee: The Old South and American National Character* (1961).

Theater, Contemporary

The Barter Theater, one of the oldest professional regional theaters in the nation, was a unique product of the Depression-era economy. Founded in 1932 by Virginia-born actor Robert Porterfield and located in the Town-Hall Opera House of Abingdon, the company in its first season made a profit consisting of $4.30 plus three barrels of jams and jellies and assorted surplus foods, some of which were canned and stored and used to "pay" playwright royalties. Growing slowly but steadily, in 1945 it became the official state theater of Virginia.

The Barter Theater holds a distinctive place in the annals of regional theater, which has generally had a shaky history. At the turn of the century hundreds of legitimate professional theaters could be found throughout the United States, but in the decades before World War II the Barter was one of less than a dozen outside New York City.

Although the Little Theater movement of the 1920s, the Federal Theater Project (founded in 1935 as part of the Works Progress Administration), and the American National Theater and Academy (1935) had sought to counter the influences of motion pictures and the radio and had expressed a commitment to audiences throughout the country, the situation for regional theater remained bleak. Professional theater activity had once been supported even in remote locales, but outside of New York it had all but ceased by 1940.

Not surprisingly, the postwar modern regional theater movement first bore fruit away from the East Coast. A principal concern of those active in it was decentralization, so cities closer to Broadway, despite their artistic traditions, received less initial attention. Modern American regional theater *began* in the Southwest, however, largely because of one dynamic personality, Margo Jones.

In June of 1947 Jones, a native Texan, a teacher, and a director, opened Theater '47 (the date changed annually) in Dallas. Conscious of the need for innovation yet responsive to public taste, she helped develop new talents and popularize important playwrights such as William Inge and Tennessee Williams. Inge's *Farther Off From Heaven*, retitled *Dark at the Top of the Stairs*, was the theater's initial production. Both Williams's production of *Summer and Smoke* and Jerome Lawrence and Robert E. Lee's *Inherit the Wind* debuted in Dallas before moving to Broadway.

In the same year, 1947, another "southern belle with a will of iron," Nina Vance, established the Alley Theater of Houston. Recruiting local support through a postcard campaign (the cards bore two words: "Why Not!"), Vance fostered what has been called the most regional of regional theaters.

A fully professional company by the mid-1950s, the Alley was one of the first professional resident theaters to receive major financial support from the Ford Foundation. From its quarters in an abandoned fan factory (225 seats), the theater moved into Houston's spacious $3.5 million playhouse in 1968. Among the Alley's most notable productions was Paul Zindel's Pulitzer Prize-winning *The Effect of Gamma Rays on Man-in-the Moon Marigolds*, which premiered in 1965.

In 1955 a Richmond theater became the first in the nation to be located in a fine arts museum. With its stable physical setting (audience capacity of 500) and consistent community support, Virginia's Museum Theater was able to develop into a full equity company before the start of its 1972–73 season.

Two years later actor-producer George Touliatos began his work with an amateur group that performed in the basement of the King Cotton Hotel, and he went on to found The Front Street Theater of Memphis. By 1959 the company moved to a refurnished movie house. Front Street Theater performed a broad range of plays, from *Othello* to *Guys and Dolls*, until financial burdens forced it to close in the late 1960s. More recent Memphis productions have been developed by black playwright Levi Frazier.

A similarly significant if short-lived regional experiment, Repertory Theater of New Orleans, opened in the fall of 1966 under the direction of Stuart Vaughan. From the onset, the federally funded company faced strong competition from the very popular Le Petit Theater de Vieux Carré. Failing to establish itself as an integral part of the local scene, the theater closed its doors after the 1971–72 season.

Established in Jackson, Miss., in 1963, Free Southern Theater was an outgrowth of civil rights activism, especially that of the Student Nonviolent Coordinating Committee. Dedicated to presenting nonstereotypic views of southern blacks, the company had relocated in New Orleans by 1964, alternating tours of rural areas in the South with resident seasonal productions.

Actors Theater of Louisville, founded in 1964 by Richard Black, presented bills featuring the classics, but leavened its fare with bold, often controversial productions such as *End Game* and *Slow Dance on the Killing Ground*. Continuing the theater's tradition of responsiveness to new talent, *Crimes of the Heart* by Beth Henley (1979) and *Getting Out* by Marsha Norman (1979) made their pre-Broadway premieres on its stage.

In 1968 the $13 million Atlanta Memorial Cultural Center opened to house symphony, ballet, and also resident drama produced by Atlanta's Repertory Theater. Reorganized as the Alliance Theater in 1969, it supplemented offerings by that city's already active and innovative Pocket Theater.

Professional resident companies now exist throughout the South, but they are not the only sources of serious, quality drama. Adding to the diverse dramatic scene are community and educational theaters and university-affiliated companies, such as the illustrious Carolina Playmakers; festival theaters such as the High Point, N.C., and Anniston, Ala., Shakespeare festivals; and the Festival of Southern Theater at the University of Mississippi. Lighter fare is offered by ever-popular dinner theaters like Sebastiáns in Orlando, Fla., while annual outdoor dramas, staged in unique open air settings like that of the 2,900-seat Mountainside Theater in Cherokee, N.C., continue to attract regional and national interest.

See also BLACK LIFE: Theater, Black

Elizabeth M. Makowski
University of Mississippi

Robert Gard et al., *Theatre in America* (1968); Sandra Schmidt, *Southern Theatre* (1971–); *Tulane Drama Review* (Summer 1963); Joseph Wesley, *Regional Theatre* (1973).

Theater, Early

A long period of vitality, from the colonial era to the Civil War, marked theater in the South. Virginia, the only colony other than Maryland not to pass legislation against the theater, was a center of American theatrical life during the colonial period. The first known play to be acted in America, *Ye Bare and Ye Cubb*, was performed at Cowle's Tavern, in Accomac County, in 1665, and in the next century the first theater was erected there, at Williamsburg.

Charleston, S.C., was, however, the South's theatrical center for 100 years. The first dramatic season opened in 1735 with Thomas Otway's *The Orphan* performed in the city's courtroom; in a prologue, the actors ridiculed the theatrical censorship of New England. The following year plays were staged at the city's new Dock Street Theater.

In 1790 two pioneers in the Georgia backcountry opened Augusta's first theater. Professional actresses from Baltimore, Ann Robinson and Susannah Wall, established themselves in a converted schoolroom, where they staged performances of *The Beaux Stratagem*, *Douglas*, and a variety of simplified 18th-century dramas. The final performance of the group coincided with George Washington's postelection trip to Augusta, with a banquet honoring the president held in the makeshift theater.

Touring companies provided audiences in the colonial South with the chance to see many of the best works of English drama. London's Lewis Hallam began his American tour in 1752 at Williamsburg with *The Merchant of Venice*. David Douglass's American Company visited Virginia theaters from 1758 to 1761. Douglass's 1773–74 season in Charleston, according to one chronicler, "the most brilliant" of colonial America, included 58 plays, 20 of which were musicals. Shakespeare, however, was the favorite dramatist, with *Richard III* and *Romeo and Juliet* his most popular works.

Postrevolution conditions helped to encourage the production of native dramatic writing in the South. From 1793 in Charleston, for example, there were strong resident companies, managers who encouraged native playwrights, newspaper critics, and the Federalist-Republican controversy, which often turned the stage into a political platform.

William Ioor (1780–1850), a country doctor living near Charleston and a fervent Jeffersonian, wrote his first play, *Independence* (1805), to praise the small farmer and country life. Although its setting was England, *Independence* dramatized Jefferson's agrarian philosophy. Ioor's *Battle of Eutaw Springs* (1807) commemorated the last Revolutionary War battle in South Carolina and indirectly condemned contemporary impressment by Great Britain. A prototype of the southern gentleman appeared as a humorous, hospitable farmer named Jonathan Slyboots.

John Blake White, also from Charleston, wrote plays advocating American social reform. His *Modern Honor*, presented in 1812, was the first antidueling play given in America. After 1825 novelist William Gilmore Simms continued the tradition of dramatic writing with *Michael Bonham, or the Fall of Bexar* (written 1844; produced 1852), favoring the annexation of Texas, and *Norman Maurice, or The Man of the People* (published 1851), a proslavery play set in Missouri.

In Virginia, dramatist Robert Munford (1737–83), a planter and a member of the House of Burgesses, wrote *The Candidates* (published in 1798), which satirized corruption in electioneering, and *The Patriots* (published in 1798), which ridiculed intolerant Tories and Whigs. George Washington Parke Custis (1781–1851) wrote several patriotic plays including *The Indian Prophecy* (1827) and *Pocohontas* (1836). The fascination with history, state pride, and an agrarian bias—themes that emerge in some of these early regional plays—would continue to be distinctive hallmarks of southern drama.

In the 19th century, architecture testified to the popularity both of serious drama and extravaganza. At the turn of that century even minor southern towns had their sometimes opulent theaters.

In Richmond, the Marshall Theater (1838), remodeled and named in honor of Chief Justice John Marshall in 1838, was said to rival, in its "pure classical character," with its burnished gold, crimson, and damask, the celebrated New Orleans Caldwell. Destroyed by fire in 1862, the theater was rebuilt in the midst of the Civil War by determined Richmonders.

The elegant North Broadway Opera House, which opened in 1887 in Lexington, Ky., made that already performance-conscious city even more theater oriented. With a seating capacity of 596, illumination provided by 250 gaslights, and a stage large enough to be adapted for the chariot race in the 1904 production of *Ben Hur*, the Opera House attracted touring companies and talents like Lillian Russell, the Barrymores (John, Ethel, and Lionel), Sarah Bernhardt, James O'Neill, and Helen Hayes.

Mobile's splendid Saenger Theater, built at a cost of $750,000 in 1927, was the capstone of a chain of playhouses located throughout the South. The Springer Opera House (1871), of Columbus, Ga., booking such notables as Mme. Modyeska, Irene Dunne, and Edwin Booth, continued as a legitimate theater well into the Depression.

Whether performing in opera houses or in rented halls, professional stock and touring companies, vaudeville acts, and minstrel shows enlivened the southern theater scene into the 20th century. Not until the second decade of the century, when live performances were forced to compete with "talkies" and with the radio at home, did the era of decentralized professional theater in the South, and in the nation at large, decline. It would not be revitalized until the modern regional theater movement of the late 1940s and early 1950s.

A new movement in drama did begin, though, at the University of North Carolina in the 20th century with the folk plays of the Carolina Playmakers and later the outdoor dramas of Paul Green. This close associate of the Playmakers started his career with folk plays like *In Abraham's Bosom* (1926), about a black educator in the New South, for which he received the Pulitzer Prize. Disenchanted with the commercial theater of New York, Green advocated taking drama to the people and exploiting regional material. Under the influence of Bertolt Brecht's epic theater, Green began his series of symphonic dramas in 1937 with *The Lost Colony*, celebrating the 350th anniversary of Virginia Dare's birth. It was performed on the historical site, Roanoke Island, N.C., and has been repeated almost every summer since. By "symphonic" Green meant the blending of all the stage arts in one production, including spectacle, music, and acting.

Green's dramas, almost all produced in the South, commemorate historic events of the region. The first category deals with the early explorers' transmission of their culture to a new land. *The Lost Colony* was in this category as were *The Founders* (1957, featuring John Rolfe and Pocohontas of the Jamestown settlement, performed at Williamsburg) and *Cross and Sword* (1965, at St. Augustine, Fla.). The second category, the making of America, includes *The Common Glory*, Green's second most popular production. This play about Jefferson and the Revolution exemplifies the glory of democracy through Cephus Sicklemore, a propertyless but patriotic humorist; expresses Jefferson's philosophy of the individual's importance in forming the corporate personality; and presents the battle of Yorktown. It opened in 1947 at the Lake Matoaka Amphitheater, Williamsburg. Among Green's colleagues with productions in the South and elsewhere, Kermit Hunter dramatized Indian history in *Unto These Hills* (published in 1950 and performed at Cherokee, N.C.).

Significant links exist between early and modern drama in the South. The first native plays and outdoor dramas reflect the fascination with history, state pride, and the sense of place found in the region. These affirmative plays reveal also such distinctive southern qualities as an agrarian, antiurban bias and a liking for outdoor, spectacular entertainment. As a balance to urbane plays, epitomized by those of Tennessee Williams, which have also attained wide popularity in the South, the historical dramas have given expression to deep-seated feelings of the people.

See also BLACK LIFE: Theater, Black; RECREATION: Traveling Shows

Charles S. Watson
University of Alabama

Rodney M. Baine, *Robert Munford: America's First Comic Dramatist* (1967); James H. Dormon, Jr., *Theater in the Ante-Bellum South, 1815–1861* (1967); Clarence Gohdes, *Literature and Theater of the States and Regions of the U.S.A.: An Historical Bibliography* (1967); Vincent S. Kenny, *Paul Green* (1971); Hugh S. Rankin, *The Theater in Colonial America* (1965); Charles S. Watson, *Antebellum Charleston Dramatists* (1976).

Travel Writing

Between 1948 and 1962 the University of Oklahoma Press published six bulky volumes devoted to description of and comment upon travel books about the South: E. Merton Coulter's bibliography of travels in the Confederate South and five other volumes, under the general editorship of Thomas D. Clark, dealing with books published between 1527 and 1955. All told, these six bibliographical volumes take into account 2,703 titles. Although they include many books that are perhaps only marginally travel accounts (memoirs, for example, written long after journeys undertaken, or accounts of military campaigns and experiences), the editors are under no illusion that they have ferreted out all the travel books that explore or venture into the South. In the decades since 1955 many more travel books about the South have appeared.

Categorizing and evaluating this welter of writing is difficult. Even if one puts aside the obviously superficial and leaves out of the reckoning all those books that are more strictly "guides-to" than "reports-upon" (guidebooks to southern cities and regions began to circulate prior to the Civil War), and even if it were possible to assess the biases and prejudices all travelers to the South carry in their carpetbags, this most troublesome question would still remain: In "travel writing," is the "travel" of more importance than the "writing"? Does one read a travel book primarily as a more or less reliable *record* of things seen and persons encountered? Or does one read a travel book primarily for the *recording* of the traveler's experiences? Some travel books, of course, inform the historical sense while at the same time appealing to an aesthetic bent, but such books are exceptional. A literary critic can term Henry James's *The American Scene* (1904) "one of the great American documents," but a historian is apt to complain that James, in writing of Charleston, gives "the impression of having visited a state of mind rather than a city." And a historian might find vexing what other readers might find entertaining in the earliest English-language travel writing about the South—John Smith's "unusually vivid imagination."

Smith, whose *True Relation of . . . Virginia* was printed in 1609, was, in his active, roving life if not in his tendency to embroider fact with fiction, a typical early traveler. Of the more than 100 travel books by observers from the British Isles or by English colonials written between 1600 and 1750, 40 were by preachers and missionaries, 30 by government officials, 12 by merchants and fur traders, 10 by doctors and scientists, and others by ship captains, land speculators, and surveyors. Indians and natural history, and the unpleasantness and difficulty of travel, were major concerns of these writers. Perhaps most entertaining among these early writings are William Byrd's 1728 *History of the Dividing Line*, with its Virginian put-down of North Carolina and its inhabitants, and Ebenezer Cooke's *The Sot-Weed Factor* (1708), a virulent verse diatribe against Maryland and its settlers.

The second half of the 18th century in the South was a time of war, new nationhood, and expansion westward across the Appalachians, as well as a period in which slavery and the condition of blacks began to claim the attention of travelers. Most reliable among these reporters were those whose business and professional concerns had prompted their travels, men such as Thomas Jefferson, whose *Notes on the State of Virginia* appeared in 1785; William Bartram, whose *Travels through North Carolina* (1791) recounts his pioneering botanical expeditions; and Philip Vickers Fithian, whose journals deal with his employment as a tutor in the Tidewater and his work as a frontier missionary.

By the turn of the century the corps of travelers in the South had been swelled by numerous Europeans, who came to America sometimes on professional errands but more frequently as observers of the American experiment in democracy. They were drawn to the South by Washington's Mt. Vernon, a mecca for travelers, but they also wished to investigate plantation society and to inquire about the growth and expansion of slavery. Increasingly, the South was viewed as a region distinct from the rest of the new United States, almost as another country. Access to this South was primarily by water—along the coastal shipping lanes and into the interior by way of the Ohio and Mississippi. Notable among travel accounts of the first decades of the 19th century are Thomas Ashe's *Travels in America* (1808), John Melish's *Travels through the United States of America* (1812), J. K. Paulding's *Letters from the South* (1817), and Timothy Flint's *Recollections of the Last Ten Years* (1826).

As the American nation lurched toward civil war in the middle decades of the century, more and more travelers visited the South; Thomas D. Clark observes that never again would there be so many "in so short a time." By the 1830s most travelers moved along segments of what had become an established "Grand Tour" in America: along the seaboard to Georgia, across Alabama to Mobile and New Orleans, then up the Mississippi and Ohio, with dips into the interiors of Tennessee and Kentucky. Many of the travelers were distinguished Europeans (Charles Dickens, Harriet Martineau, Charles Lyell, Fredrika Bremer, Alexis de Tocqueville, Frederick Maryatt), but the most important travel writing of the antebellum years (Tocqueville's *Democracy in America* is not really a travel book) was the work of a young New Englander, Frederick Law Olmsted, who published three books detailing his travels through the South, with *A Journey in the Seaboard Slave States* (1856) being perhaps the most readable. After the war, which occasioned a good bit of fortuitous travel, travelers from abroad tended to bypass the South in their eagerness to board transcontinental trains headed west, but Americans, particularly American journalists, flocked to the South to see and report on postwar conditions and Reconstruction efforts. In addition, "promotional" travel writing extolling the attractions of a "New South" began to appear. The booster literature may not have advanced southern prosperity, but books such as Whitelaw Reid's *After the War: A Southern Tour* (1866) may have furthered the efforts of Radical Republican legislators; later, James Pike's *The Prostrate State: South Carolina under Negro Government* (1874) and Edward King's *The Great South* (1875) undoubtedly helped into being a climate of opinion that welcomed the end of Reconstruction efforts. The last decades of the century were notable for several quirky individualistic classics of southern travel writing: Mark Twain's *Life on the Mississippi* (1883); Charles Dudley Warner's *On Horseback* (1888), about a trip into some of the more rugged sections of Appalachia; and Nathaniel Bishop's two books about his small-craft voyages along the seaboard and down the Mississippi—*Voyage of the Paper Canoe* (1878) and *Four Months in a Sneak-Box* (1879).

In the 20th century the South again figured in the "grand tour" of visitors from abroad, and after World War I the automobile and better highways made the region more accessible to visitors of all sorts, who came in search of health, for economic advantage, and out of curiosity about southern social conditions—with race relations the topic of most concern. Attempting to "get at the facts" about black-white relations was the motive for Ray Stannard Baker's *Following the Color Line* (1908); Jay Saunders Redding's *No Day of Triumph* (1942) is about an auto trip undertaken to obtain insight into the lives of southern blacks; and the issue of race is ever present in Jonathan Daniels's *A Southerner Discovers the South* (1938), which Rupert B. Vance characterizes as "the definitive travel account of the South in the depression." Other striking books from the Great Depression era are Erskine Caldwell and Margaret Bourke-White's *You Have Seen Their Faces* (1937) and James Agee and Walker Evans's *Let Us Now Praise Famous Men* (1941), two books that wed prose and photography. Photographs began to be incorporated in southern travel books as early as the first decade of this century, being essential and integral parts of Clifton Johnson's explorations of southern rural life, *Highways and Byways of the South* (1904) and *Highways and Byways of the Mississippi Valley* (1906). Today, the camera—still, motion picture, video—is as ubiquitous an instrument of southern travel "writing" as the word processor.

Since World War II, when technological change and new wealth set in accelerated motion forces that would forever alter the old agrarian order, and since the Supreme Court's *Brown* v. *Board of Education* decision of 1954, which marked a drastic unsettling of the "color line" in the South, there has been no abatement of the fascination with, and concern about, the land below the Mason-Dixon line. Books continue to appear that undertake to explore and explain what Jonathan Daniels termed the South's "warm dark." Among all these books, among all this travel writing about the contemporary South, three in particular stand out: John Howard Griffin's *Black Like Me* (1961), about the southern encounters of a white man who chemically darkens his skin; Albert Murray's account of his tentative return to the land of his birth and youth, *South to a Very Old Place* (1971); and perhaps the finest of all the reports on voyages in the wake of Huck and Jim's archetypal trip down the Mississippi, the Britisher Jonathan Raban's *Old Glory* (1981).

See also ART AND ARCHITECTURE: Photography; HISTORY AND MANNERS: / Byrd, William, II; Jefferson, Thomas; Olmsted, Frederick Law; MEDIA: / Daniels, Jonathan

Robert White
York University

Thomas D. Clark, ed., *Travels in the Old South: A Bibliography*, 3 vols. (1956), *Travels in the New South: A Bibliography*, 2 vols. (1962); E. Merton Coulter, *Travels in the Confederate States: A Bibliography* (1948); Eugene Schwaab and Jacqueline Bull, eds., *Travels in the Old South, Selected from Periodicals of the Times* (1973).

Women's Literature

See WOMEN'S LIFE articles

Agee, James

(1909–1955) Writer.

James Agee, Tennessee poet, novelist, and critic, 1930s

Born in Knoxville, Tenn., in 1909, James Agee was to remain a dedicated southerner until his death in New York City in 1955. His childhood in Knoxville and his adolescence at St. Andrew's School, later evoked in two of his novels, *A Death in the Family* (1957), which won the Pulitzer Prize in 1958, and *The Morning Watch* (1950), shaped his sensibility and his imagination and provided him with crucial and contradictory experiences—that of happiness and bereavement (after his father's death), that of community and solitude (in the religious atmosphere of the school). Leaving the South to study at Exeter and Harvard, and later becoming the most gifted and versatile writer in the Henry Luce empire, Agee nevertheless liked to think of himself as a sort of hillbilly stranded in the sophisticated world of academia.

When asked by *Fortune* to write an article on sharecroppers, with photographer Walker Evans, he welcomed this opportunity of going back to his roots, "all the way home." This assignment also awakened his sympathy for, and sense of commitment to, the southern poor and led to his most striking work, *Let Us Now Praise Famous Men* (1941), which became a book on three tenant farmer families in the 1930s. It contains some of Agee's best writing: as a poet alive to the "cruel radiance of what is," as an ethnographer respectful of "the other," and as an impassioned humanist angry with injustice and pretense.

Wavering between his attraction to worldly intellectuals and his longing for a humbler, more authentic life in the South, he also vacillated between experimental and realistic writing. Intent on improving his art, he was no less concerned for people, and for the events that shook his times—the Depression, the rise of fascism, the war. As an artist he was extremely curious about all aesthetic forms: poetry (*Permit Me Voyage*, 1974), photography, journalism, and movie making. His passion for the cinema, born in his early childhood in Knoxville, drove him to become one of the most attentive and witty film critics and a versatile screenwriter, who went to Hollywood and worked with such directors as Charles Laughton (*The Night of the Hunter*) and John Huston (*The African Queen*). As a journalist, he contributed many articles for *Time* and *Fortune*, and Paul Ashdown has collected the best of Agee's articles from those magazines in *James Agee: Selected Journalism* (1985).

Concerned to avoid involvement in any movement, whether literary or ideological, Agee stands as an isolated, original artist who voyaged far but who never forgot his dedication to his real homeland, the South.

Geneviève Fabre
University of Paris

Alfred Baxson, *A Way of Seeing: A Critical Study of James Agee* (1972); Laurence Bergreen, *James Agee* (1984); Mark R. Boty, *Tell Me Who I Am: James Agee's Search for Selfhood* (1981); Peter H. Ohlin, *Agee* (1966); Kenneth Seib, *James Agee: Promise and Fulfillment* (1968).

Brooks, Cleanth

(b. 1906) Critic.

The son of a Methodist minister, Cleanth Brooks was born in Murray, Ky., and grew up in the villages and small towns of that state and of west Tennessee in which his father served as pastor. After graduating from the McTyeire School in McKenzie, Tenn. (1920–24), he attended Vanderbilt University, from which he received a bachelor's degree in 1928. The following year he earned a master of arts degree from Tulane University and enrolled as a Rhodes Scholar in Exeter College, Oxford University, from which he earned a B.A. (Honors) in 1931 and a B.A. Litt. the following year.

After leaving Oxford he accepted a position in the English department of Louisiana State University. On 12 September 1934 he married Edith Ann Blanchard. The following year he and Robert Penn Warren, who had recently joined the faculty, and a small group of scholars and critics from the university founded the *Southern Review*, which before it ceased publication in 1942 was one of the most distinguished literary quarterlies ever published in America. Many of the writers later called the "New Critics" were regular contributors.

Brooks's reputation as one of the most respected modern American critics is based primarily on three books: *Modern Poetry and the Tradition* (1939), *The Well Wrought Urn: Studies in the Structure of Poetry* (1947), and *William Faulkner: The Yoknapatawpha Country* (1963). Some of the other books he has written are *Literary Criticism: A Short History*, with W. K. Wimsatt (1957); *The Hidden Gods: Studies in Hemingway, Faulkner, Yeats, Eliot, and Warren* (1963); *American Literature: A Mirror, Lens, or Prism?* (1967); *A Shaping Joy: Studies in the Writer's Craft* (1971); and *William Faulkner: Toward Yoknapatawpha and Beyond* (1978).

In addition to the influential books of criticism he has written, Brooks coedited four textbooks that brought the principles of the New Criticism into the classroom and virtually revolutionized the way literature is taught and read: *An Approach to Literature*, with John T. Purser and Robert Penn Warren (1936, 1939, 1952, 1964, 1975); *Understanding Poetry*, with Robert Penn Warren (1938, 1950, 1956, 1960); *Understanding Fiction*, with Robert Penn Warren (1943, 1959); and *Understanding Drama*, with Robert B. Heilman (1945).

Thomas Daniel Young
Vanderbilt University

John Edward Hardy, in *Southern Renascence: The Literature of the Modern South*, ed. Louis D. Rubin, Jr., et al. (1953); Lewis P. Simpson, ed., *The Possibilities of Order: Cleanth Brooks and His Work* (1976); Thomas Daniel Young, *Tennessee Writers* (1981).

Cable, George Washington

(1844–1925) Writer and critic.

During the local color era Cable wrote of Creole New Orleans, and he has been called the most important southern artist working in the late 19th century, as well as the first modern southern writer. He is praised both for his courageous essays on civil rights, such as *The Silent South* (1885) and *The Negro Question* (1890), and for his early fiction about New Orleans, especially *Old Creole Days* (1879), *The Grandissimes* (1880), and *Madame Delphine* (1881). Cable was not a Creole himself, but he had deep roots in New Orleans. He was born and grew up there, and, after service as a Confederate soldier, he returned to live and work in the city until 1885, when he moved to Massachusetts.

Cable's study of the colonial history of Louisiana while writing sketches for the *Picayune* revealed "the decline of an aristocracy under the pressure of circumstances," as well as the "length and blackness" of the shadow in the southern garden. In his essay "My Politics" Cable tells how his reading of the *Code Noir* caused him such "sheer indignation" that he wrote the brutal story of Bras-Coupé, incorporated later as the foundation of *The Grandissimes*. Cable connected the decline of the Creoles to their self-destructive racial pride, and his best work, *The Grandissimes*, makes clear that such racial arrogance has direct application to broader problems of southern history, especially the black-white conflict after 1865. Like the best stories of *Old Creole Days*, *The Grandissimes* balances sympathy for and judgment of New Orleans and the South, but it is stronger because it "contained as plain a protest against the times in which

George Washington Cable, late 19th-century critic of southern society

it was written as against the earlier times in which its scenes were set."

Cable continued to write about New Orleans and Louisiana throughout his long career, most notably in *Dr. Sevier* (1884), *The Creoles of Louisiana* (1884), and the Acadian pastoral *Bonaventure* (1888). In all, he published 14 novels and collections of short fiction, with his last novel, *Lovers of Louisiana*, appearing in 1918, just seven years before his death. In his career after *The Grandissimes* Cable was unable to reconcile his love for the South with his abhorrence of slavery and racism. The result was a split in his career—the polemical essays embody the spirit of reform and the New South, while the romances, beginning with *The Cavalier* (1901), attempt to retrieve an idyllic past, devoid of the problems of racism.

See also ETHNIC LIFE: / Cajuns and Creoles; Creole

Thomas J. Richardson
University of Southern Mississippi

Cable's diary, cited in Newton Arvin, "Introduction" to *The Grandissimes* (1957); Shirley Ann Grau, "Foreword" to *Old Creole Days* (1961); Thomas J. Richardson, ed., *The Grandissimes: Centennial Essays* (1981); Louis D. Rubin, Jr., *George W. Cable: The Life and Times of a Southern Heretic* (1969); Merrill Skaggs, *The Folk of Southern Fiction* (1972); Arlin Turner, *George W. Cable: A Biography* (1956).

Caldwell, Erskine

(1903–1987) Writer.

The son of an itinerant preacher, Erskine Caldwell was born in Coweta County, Ga., in 1903. After an education that included four semesters at the University of Virginia, Caldwell began to write short fiction, taking a series of odd jobs to support himself until he arrived in New York in the spring of 1930. Shortly thereafter he began to publish the novels of southern life for which he is most famous. In *Tobacco Road* (1932), *God's Little Acre* (1933), and *Trouble in July* (1940), among others, Caldwell wrote with a strong sense of moral outrage at the grotesque dehumanization of the tenant farmer, who had been reduced to grinding poverty by the social and economic system.

Caldwell was sensitive as well to the effects of racial injustice and wrote of it powerfully both in his novels and in such notable collections of short fiction as *Kneel to the Rising Sun* (1935). His strong sense of social consciousness spilled over from his fiction into compelling documentaries. Some, such as *Some American People* (1935), were written alone; others, among them *You Have Seen Their Faces* (1937) and *Say! Is This the U.S.A.?* (1941), were collaborations with his second wife, the photographer Margaret Bourke-White.

Along with William Faulkner, Caldwell helped to establish a dominant southern literary stereotype of the Depression, creating characters who were amoral, shrewd, venal, and gullible, reflecting primarily the basic human impulses of lust and the urge for propagation, but who nonetheless displayed an almost mystical connection with the land. Caldwell's indictment of society, however, lacked Faulkner's nostalgic fondness for a redemptive if quixotic historical ideal. Mixing the southern traditions of comic exaggeration and an often sadistic violence, Caldwell evolved a gothic humor that emerged in what may arguably be regarded as comic masterpieces—*Journeyman* (1935) and *Georgia Boy* (1943). More subtle is the mixture of fact and exaggeration that informs the supposedly autobiographical *Call It Experience* (1951).

Throughout his career, Caldwell had to defend himself against charges of pornography that stemmed from his treatment of both sexuality and hysteria in southern revivalism and that led to the widespread banning of his books. Caldwell did not think of himself as exclusively a regional writer, insisting that "I'm not exactly a Southerner or I'm not a Floridian; I'm not a Georgian; I'm not anything you can name or pin down because I have lived everywhere and I like everywhere I've lived." Nonetheless, his work is unmistakably rooted in a sense of place. "I think regional writing is more important than trying to be universal," he acknowledged.

Caldwell has yet to achieve significant critical recognition, nor will his writing likely ever again enjoy the popularity that saw his work translated into 27 languages and made him one of the most widely read novelists in the world. In both his journalism and his fiction, however, the "cycloramic depiction of Southern life," as he called it, reveals a portrait that is at once historical and outside of history, an unflinching documentary and part of the ongoing development of southern myth. He died 12 April 1987.

See also MEDIA: / Caldwell, Erskine, and Film

Stanley Trachtenberg
Texas Christian University

James Korges, *Erskine Caldwell* (1969); Scott MacDonald, *Critical Essays on Erskine Caldwell* (1981); Guy Owen, *Southern Literary Journal* (Fall 1979).

Capote, Truman

(1924–1984) Writer.

Truman Capote, who was born Truman Streckfus Persons in New Orleans on 30 September 1924, the son of J. A. (Arch) Persons, later took the name of his stepfather. Capote early determined to be a writer and spent much of his childhood in the lonely pursuit of putting stories down on paper. Following the divorce of his parents, he made his home with relatives in Monroeville, Ala., but in the 1930s went to live with his mother in New York City and later in Connecticut, where he attended high school. Although his formal education ended there, he found a substitute in his reading. After his mother and his stepfather moved back into New York City in the 1940s, Capote took a job as an office boy at the *New Yorker*, the magazine that would eventually publish many of his stories and nonfiction pieces.

Truman Capote achieved overnight fame at the age of 23 with the publication of *Other Voices, Other Rooms* (1948), his first novel. He had already dazzled the New York literary world with his prizewinning stories. A gifted prose stylist—"a fanatic on rhythm and language," as he told one interviewer—he never quite fulfilled his great promise as a writer, though he published a second novel (*The Grass Harp*, 1951) that he later rewrote for the stage, as well as several volumes of short fiction and collections of essays, memoirs, and travel pieces. His early short stories were collected in *A Tree of Night and Other Stories* (1949) and *Breakfast at Tiffany's* (1958), whose centerpiece was the novella that gave the book its title.

Capote's tour de force was *In Cold Blood*, first published serially in the *New Yorker* in 1965 and then as a book; he described it as a new form—the nonfiction novel. A gripping account of the mass murder of a Kansas farm family, it follows the two young killers from the murder scene to their eventual execution five and one-half years later. *In Cold Blood* was enormously successful and was followed by an equally successful motion picture.

Though his roots were in the South, Truman Capote lived most of his life in New York City. A celebrity himself and a man who cherished the art of conversation, he cultivated the rich and famous of the world and was a frequent guest on network television talk shows. When he died in 1984 during a visit to California, he had still not published his much-talked-about novel *Answered Prayers*.

Charles East
Baton Rouge, Louisiana

James Dickey, *Paris Review* (Fall 1985); Lawrence Grobel, *Conversations with Capote* (1985); Kenneth T. Reed, *Truman Capote* (1981); "Truman Capote," *Writers at Work: The Paris Review Interviews*, ed. Malcolm Cowley (1958); "Truman Capote," *Current Biography Yearbook 1968*.

Clemens, Samuel Langhorne ("Mark Twain")

(1835–1910) Writer.

Although Samuel Clemens initially tasted fame and employed his pen name in Nevada and California, he traced his "Mark Twain" pseudonym to his pilot days on the Mississippi River, and many features of his writings can also be attributed to that southern background. Clemens was born 30 November 1835 in the border state of Missouri and grew up in Hannibal, but his father was a Virginian and his mother was from a Kentucky family. Sam Clemens became a printer, working in New York, Pennsylvania, Ohio, Illinois, and Missouri before becoming a steamboat pilot. As a pilot posted at the river ports of St. Louis and New Orleans from 1857 until 1861, Clemens glided regularly through the Deep South sugarcane fields of Louisiana and Mississippi.

The South's watershed year of 1861 was momentous for Clemens, who accompanied his brother Orion to the Far West. Subsequently, Clemens moved east to Buffalo and then settled in the New England climate of Nook Farm in Hartford, Conn. His family, too, moved northward—to Fredonia, N.Y., and to Keokuk, Iowa. These shifts resulted in a hybridization, reflected in his literature, of the traditions and atmosphere of the South, the extravagance and energies of the West, the taboos and commerce of the East. But Louis D. Rubin, Jr., has argued persuasively that "the southern experience of Samuel L. Clemens is so thoroughly and deeply imaged in his life and work that one may scarcely read a chapter of any of his books without encountering it," and that in *A Connecticut Yankee* (1889) "the whole ambivalent love-hate relationship of Sam Clemens with the South is dramatized" to indicate "the South's similarity to feudal England."

Mark Twain objected to the South's pretensions. Remembering the grand, absurd village names of his youth, he chose "St. Petersburg" as the name for his fictional river town, trying to catch and satirize those grandiose dreams of splendor. After the Civil War, Twain would

Samuel Clemens (Mark Twain), one of the nation's best-known novelists, c. 1905

blame the historical novels of Sir Walter Scott for the "romantic juvenilities" and "inflated language and other windy humbuggeries" that still bedeviled the South. Returning to the river for a nostalgic visit in 1882, Clemens was aghast to learn that duels were still being fought by prominent citizens of New Orleans. However, as his steamboat drew into the Louisiana reaches of the Mississippi, he found himself admiring the "greenhouse" lawns and "dense rich foliage and huge, snow-ball blossoms" of the magnolia trees that, along with a "tropical swelter in the air," announced that he was "in the absolute South, now—no modifications, no compromises." On the streets of New Orleans, too, he "found the half-forgotten Southern intonations and elisions as pleasing to my ear as they had formerly been. A Southerner talks music."

This homeland had been a place of grief and disappointment for Twain. In Memphis he had knelt helpless and agonized while his brother Henry died from scalding burns suffered when the steamboat *Pennsylvania* blew up in 1858. Twain also knew firsthand the uncouth, ruffian character of river-town idlers; he portrayed their cruelties in a backward Arkansas town in *The Adventures of Huckleberry Finn*.

Like most southern authors of his generation, Twain felt obliged to explain why he had lived in a land that countenanced human slavery. "In my schoolboy days I had no aversion to slavery," he testified. "I was not aware that there was anything wrong about it. No one arraigned it in my hearing; the local papers said nothing against it; the local pulpit taught us that God approved it." Ultimately, Twain became a great American writer in part because his family *had* owned slaves, so that he felt a lifelong involvement in that system of bondage. His finest novel, *The Adventures of Huckleberry Finn* (1885), like Faulkner's *Absalom, Absalom!*, addresses the volatile racial issue that has periodically threatened the unity of a nation. Twain's entrée to the pages of the high-brow *Atlantic Monthly* was a poignant story inspired by a black woman cook he met at Quarry Farm near Elmira, New York. An angry essay of 1901, "The United States of Lyncherdom," castigated Missouri for joining the southern states in resorting to mob violence against accused blacks, though Twain conceded that "the people in the South are made like the people in the North—a vast majority of whom are right-hearted and compassionate."

Twain could also portray an idealized South. One commentator, Arthur Pettit, has observed that in *The Adventures of Tom Sawyer* (1876), Mark Twain transformed antebellum Hannibal "into a Golden Age of prelapsarian innocence and charm." The image of this dozing village rose before Twain's eyes again and again, although *The Tragedy of Pudd'nhead Wilson* (1894) discloses lurking secrets behind the "whitewashed exteriors" of a similar town, Dawson's Landing. Twain's benign movie-reel depiction of the typical downtown district appeared in "Old Times on the Mississippi" (1875), a passage later subsumed in *Life on the Mississippi* (1883); the stir and bustle on Water Street when a black drayman called out "S-t-e-a-m-boat a-comin'!" and the boat came into sight on "the great Mississippi, the majestic, the magnificent Mississippi, rolling its mile-wide tide along, shining in the sun," vividly evoked this scene even for readers who had seen neither that river nor any states bordering it.

Always he acknowledged sincere admiration for amenities of life taken for granted in the South. He lauded its gastronomic delights in *A Tramp Abroad* (1880), listing and praising 20 southern dishes such as "fried chicken, Southern style," "black bass from the Mississippi," "hot corn-pone, with chitlings," "hot hoe-cake," hominy, butter beans, and apple puffs. His mental map of the Quarles farm where he spent his boyhood summers—the main log house, the smokehouse, the slave quarters, the orchard, the tobacco field, the schoolhouse—was recreated for his autobiographical recollections.

Although Twain had a broader and more venturesome approach to fiction than his contemporaries George Washington Cable, Joel Chandler Harris, and Thomas Nelson Page, he is equally indebted with them to the shaping forces of southern culture. His experiments in reproducing black dialect, such as "A True Story," compare favorably with the studied idiom in Harris's *Uncle Remus* (1880) and Page's "Marse Chan" (1884); Jim's patois and Huck's vernacular in *Huckleberry Finn* enriched the form of the American novel forever. In language and in delineation of character, setting, and society, his sketches, short stories, and novels have influenced writers as diverse as Thomas Wolfe, Erskine Caldwell, and William Faulkner. The beneficiary of a tradition of southern frontier humor, Mark Twain multiplied their notable achievements into the richer legacy he bequeathed to modern southern authors.

Alan Gribben
University of Texas at Austin

Justin Kaplan, *Mr. Clemens and Mark Twain* (1974); Lewis G. Leary, *Southern Excursions: Essays on Mark Twain and Others* (1971); Arthur G. Pettit, *Mark Twain and the South* (1974); Louis D. Rubin, Jr., *The Writer in the South* (1972); Thomas A. Tenney, *Mark Twain: A Reference Guide* (1977).

Davidson, Donald

(1893–1968) Writer and critic.

Of the 12 writers who, in 1930, published *I'll Take My Stand: The South and the Agrarian Tradition*, Donald Grady Davidson remained the most firmly committed to "the cause of agrarianism versus industrialism." Not a farmer's but a schoolteacher's son, he was born on 18 August 1893, in the village of Campbellsville, Tenn., near the Alabama border, but spent most of his mature life in Nashville, studying at Vanderbilt University before World War I and returning there after the war to teach and to write, until his death on 25 April 1968. For a half century he worked as a cultivator in the field of letters, contributing to the Southern Literary Renaissance through his poetry, his criticism, and his active encouragement of talent. He was one of the founders of the *Fugitive* magazine, which in the early 1920s published poetry of such high quality that it quickly gained an international reputation, despite its regional character. As Davidson observed in the final issue of the *Fugitive* in 1925, "the strangest thing in contemporary poetry is that innovation and conservatism exist side by side"; his own poetry reflected his consciousness of the paradox that the traditional culture of the South was in the process of disappearing at the very moment when its highest artistic expression was being achieved.

Like most educated southerners of his generation (and like Thomas Jefferson before them), Davidson was as much a classicist as an agrarian, viewing Greek and Latin as fundamental to civilization, but looking skeptically "On a Replica of the Parthenon" built in a city park in Nashville, amid the noise and smoke of motors, and asking: "What do they seek, / Who build, but never read, their Greek?" He favored a native southern idealism, of the sort mirrored in such memorable poems as "Sanctuary" and "Hermitage," where he re-created imaginatively the pioneer family farm of his ancestors, and in "Meditation on Literary Fame," where he declared:

> Happy the land where men hold dear
> Myth which is truest memory,
> Prophecy which is poetry.

Davidson was the heir not only of southern agrarianism and classicism, but of southern puritanism (his father came from Blue Stocking Hollow, Tenn.), and he sometimes sounded like a Hebrew prophet in his denunciation of material progress (which he believed to be detrimental to a truly humane culture) and in his praise for the relative poverty and simplicity, even the backwardness, of the South as a region. The latter qualities allowed the oral tradition of storytelling and ballad singing to flourish, laying the basis for literary art to develop naturally (to him, it was no accident that Mississippi was one of the lowest states in the nation in per capita income and one of the richest in talented writers). For Davidson, a strong regional loyalty was essential to a writer's integrity, as he argued persuasively in his essay "Still Rebels, Still Yankees," and he admired those modern writers outside the South who kept a definite identification with their place, such as Robert Frost, William Butler Yeats, and Thomas Hardy. Davidson's own loyalty to the South may have limited his appeal and his reputation outside it, but the genuineness of his convictions was evident in everything he wrote and gave fervor and keenness to both his poetry and his prose. His style was intellectually rigorous and spare, and if his weakness was for didacticism, he was above all a teacher, and in his generation, a great one. A fine poet, an exacting critic, and an able editor, in addition to being an inspiring teacher, Davidson exerted a powerful influence in the creation of a rich modern literature for the South.

First to be mentioned among his many books are *Poems, 1922–1961* (1966); *Still Rebels, Still Yankees and Other Essays* (1957); and *Southern Writers in the Modern World* (1958).

William Pratt
Miami University (Ohio)

John Fair and Thomas Daniel Young, eds., *The Literary Correspondence of Donald Davidson and Allen Tate* (1974); Thomas Daniel Young and M. Thomas Inge, *Donald Davidson* (1971), *Donald Davidson: An Essay and a Bibliography* (1965).

Donald Davidson, Vanderbilt Agrarian, late 1940s

Dickey, James

(b. 1923) Writer.

A native of Atlanta, Ga., James Lafayette Dickey was born 2 February 1923. A football player in high school and college and an air force combat veteran of World War II, Dickey in his life and his art exhibits a physically aggressive quality matched by few significant poets. He received a bachelor's degree (1949) and a master of arts degree (1950) from Vanderbilt University, where he was influenced by Monroe K. Spears and was surrounded by the Fugitive-Agrarian literary tradition of Donald Davidson, John Crowe Ransom, and Allen Tate. He taught at Rice Institute in Houston and at the University of Florida, served in the Air Force again during the Korean War, and traveled afterward in Europe. Dickey broke out of academia in 1956 and into the world of advertising, where he was successful in both New York City and Atlanta.

James Dickey, South Carolina poet and novelist, 1980s

By the end of the decade, however, Dickey grew weary of "selling [his] soul to the devil during the day and buying it back at night." Three national poetry prizes from 1958 to 1959 and a Guggenheim Fellowship in 1961 confirmed his decision to leave advertising and go again to Europe, basing himself in Positina, Italy, from 1962 to 1963. From 1960 to 1964 he published three books of poems: *Into the Stone, Drowning with Others*, and *Helmets*. When *Buckdancer's Choice* appeared in 1965, Dickey garnered the National Book Award and enormous public notice for being what *Life* magazine called "The Unlikeliest Poet." Dickey was appointed Consultant in Poetry for the Library of Congress, 1966 to 1968, recognition of a firm national reputation.

By 1969 Dickey had published two books of criticism—*The Suspect in Poetry* and *Babel to Byzantium*—and moved to Columbia, S.C., to teach at the University of South Carolina. The 1970s saw the publication of Dickey's best-selling and increasingly well regarded novel, *Deliverance*; four books of poetry—*The Zodiac*; *Tucky the Hunter* (a children's book); *The Strength of Fields*; and *The Eye-Eaters, Blood, Victory, Madness, Buckhead, and Mercy*; four books of belles lettres—*Self-Interviews, Sorties, Jericho: The South Beheld*, and *God's Images*; two screenplays—*Deliverance* and *The Call of the Wild*; and several limited-edition shorter works.

Dickey's southernness is inescapable. He relies frequently on storytelling, often with a typically southern version of exuberance and broad humor, as in "Cherrylog Road" and "The Shark's Parlor." His sense of southern place is strong in poems like "Going Home" and "Hunting Civil War Relics at Nimblewill Creek" and in prose works like *Deliverance, Jericho*, and the work-in-progress, *Wilderness of Heaven*, with artist Hubert Shuptrine. Family is important, both immediate, as in "The Celebration," "The String," and "Messages," and ancestral, as in "The Escape" and "Dover: Believing in Kings." Racial issues arise rarely in Dickey's work, with "Slave Quarters" the conspicuous exception. Whatever guilt appears in Dickey's poems is most often attached to war, as in "The Firebombing," or to a mysterious, ghostly dread regarding one's sheer existence, as in "The Other," "The String," and perhaps *The Zodiac*. Religion appears as a curious amalgam of southern fundamentalism and animistic neoromanticism, as in "May Day Sermon," "Approaching Prayer," and "The Heaven of Animals."

More conventionally, Dickey embraces bluegrass music (he plays 6- and 12-string guitars quite well), espouses athletics as personal and community rituals of a peculiarly southern mystique, and keeps to the middle ground in southern politics and economics. Dickey's works show no deep longing for a return of the Old South; rather, he appears comfortable between city and country. Content in the New South suburbs, he calls Columbia "a mixture of university town, southern political capital, and military base." The natural scene is important, of course, "the way it balances Appalachia and the Atlantic," but the clichés of southern living are always modified in Dickey's works—and apparently in his life.

Robert W. Hill
Clemson University

Richard J. Calhoun, ed., *James Dickey: The Expansive Imagination* (1973); Jim Elledge, *James Dickey: A Bibliography* (1979); Stuart Wright, *James Dickey: A Descriptive Bibliography of First Printings of His Works* (1982).

Dixon, Thomas, Jr.

(1864–1946) Writer.

Born in the rural North Carolina Piedmont a year before the Civil War ended, Thomas Dixon lived to see the atomic bombing of Hiroshima and the end of World War II. Between 1902 and 1939 he published 22 novels, as well as numerous plays, screenplays, books of sermons, and miscellaneous nonfiction. Educated at Wake Forest and Johns Hopkins, Dixon was a lawyer, state legislator, preacher, novelist, playwright, actor, lecturer, real-estate speculator, and movie producer. Familiar to three presidents and such notables as John D. Rockefeller, he made and lost millions, ending up an invalid court clerk in Raleigh, N.C.

Paradoxically, Dixon is among the most dated and most contemporary of southern writers. In genre an early 19th-century romancer, thematically Dixon argued for three interrelated beliefs still current in southern life: the need for racial purity, the sanctity of the family centered on a traditional wife and mother, and the evil of socialism.

In the Klan trilogy—*The Leopard's Spots* (1902), *The Clansman* (1905), *The Traitor* (1907)—and in *The Sins of the Fathers* (1912), Dixon presents racial conflict as an epic struggle, with the future of civilization at stake. Although Dixon personally condemned slavery and Klan activities after Reconstruction ended, he argued that blacks must be denied political equality because that leads to social equality and miscegenation, thus to the destruction of both family and civilized society. Throughout his work, white southern women are the pillars of family and society, the repositories of all human idealism. *The Foolish Virgin* (1915) and *The Way of a Man* (1919) attack women's suffrage because women outside the home become corrupted; with the sacred vessels shattered, social morality is lost. In his trilogy on socialism—*The One Woman* (1903), *Comrades* (1909), *The Root of Evil* (1911)—he attacks populist socialism expressed in such works as Edward Bellamy's *Looking Backward*, arguing that it is impossible for all classes to be equal in a society. Dixon's last novel, *The Flaming Sword* (1939), written just before he suffered a crippling cerebral hemorrhage, combines the threats of socialism and racial equality, presenting blacks as communist dupes attempting the overthrow of the United States. Through all his work runs an impassioned defense of conservative religious values.

Young Dixon's religious and political beliefs were melded in a crucible shaped by his region's military defeat and economic depression and by the fiercely independent, Scotch-Irish Presbyterian faith of the North Carolina highlands. As a student reading Darwin, Huxley, and Spencer, he suffered a brief period of religious doubt. But his faith rebounded stronger than ever, and Dixon sought the grandest pulpit he could find. He abandoned a successful Baptist ministry in New York for the larger nondenominational audience he could reach as a lecturer and, after the success of *The Leopard's Spots*, as a novelist and playwright. With the movie *Birth of a Nation* (based on *The Clansman*), Dixon believed he had found the ideal medium to educate the masses, to bring them to political and religious salvation. Although his work is seldom read today, both in his themes and as a political preacher seeking a national congregation through mass media, Thomas Dixon clearly foreshadowed the politicized television evangelists of the modern South.

See also MEDIA: / Dixon and Film

James Kinney
Virginia Commonwealth University

Raymond A. Cook, *Fire from the Flint: The Amazing Careers of Thomas Dixon* (1968), *Thomas Dixon* (1974); F. Garvin Davenport, *Journal of Southern History* (August 1970).

Ellison, Ralph

(b. 1914) Writer.

Born on 1 March 1914, in Oklahoma City, Okla., Ralph Waldo Ellison grew up in the black communities of the city's East Side. His father, Lewis Alfred Ellison, died when Ralph was three, leaving his wife, Ida Millsap Ellison, with the arduous task of supporting Ralph and her younger son, Herbert, on the meager wages she earned as a service worker. Ellison left Oklahoma City when he was 19 and left the South when he was 22. Although he has lived practically all of his adult life in New York City, the lasting influence of his immersion in southern black folk life and culture is readily evident in the contents of his essays and in both the form and meaning of his fiction.

Between the two world wars, Oklahoma City was one of the South's strongholds for black blues and jazz. From his early childhood through his young adulthood, Ellison was absorbed with blues and jazz and knew several of the city's musicians. He balanced his strong affinity for blues and jazz with his interest and training in classical music. Music was his first love, but his mother provided him with an environment rich also in the other arts. Even as a child he was an avid reader of imaginative literature, and during his school years he excelled as a student, musician, and athlete.

When he graduated from Douglass High School in 1931, he could not afford to attend college. He worked at odd jobs during the next two years, and in 1933, with a music scholarship, he entered Tuskegee Institute in Alabama as a major in classical music. At Tuskegee he sustained his interest in blues and jazz and continued to read widely in various disciplines, especially literature. His chance reading of T. S. Eliot's *The Waste Land* during his sophomore year marked the beginning of his desire to become a professional writer rather than a professional musician.

In the summer of 1936 he went to New York City with the intent of saving enough money by the fall to complete his education at Tuskegee. Failing to do so, he remained in New York, where he studied music and sculpture and the craft of various literary artists. In New York he met Langston Hughes, Richard Wright, and other black writers who encouraged his ambition to become a writer. His job as a researcher for the New York Federal Writers' Project from 1938 to 1942 provided him with his first steady employment since coming to New York.

With experience as editor of *Negro Quarterly*, with a few short publications behind him, and with a Rosenwald Fellowship, in 1944 he concentrated on writing a novel. His first attempt was unsuccessful, and in 1945 he began work on another novel, *Invisible Man*. Except for time he devoted to his wife Fannie McConnell (he married in 1946), his life from 1945 to the publication of *Invisible Man* in 1952 was spent in polishing his novel, whose content and sophisticated artistry were derived primarily from Ellison's knowledge of music, southern black folklife, American culture, and literature.

Invisible Man was greeted with high critical acclaim. In 1953 it won the National Book Award and the Russwurm Award. By the mid-1960s it had been accepted as an American classic and Ellison as a first-rate American novelist. In 1965 a poll of prominent authors, critics, and editors declared *Invisible Man* to be the most distinguished work of American fiction published since 1945. The publication of his collection of essays, *Shadow and Act* (1964), revealed that he also was an astute essayist and a perceptive critic of literature and music and of southern and American culture in general.

Since the 1960s he has been a favorite speaker on the lecture circuit, has taught at the University of Chicago, Rutgers, and other institutions, has received numerous honorary degrees and awards (including France's Chevalier de l'Ordre des Artes et Lettres and America's Medal of Freedom), and has been a favored subject among literary critics and literary and cultural historians in the United States and abroad. Since his retirement in 1980 from New York University after 10 years as a chaired professor in the humanities, Ellison has worked on his long-awaited second novel.

J. Lee Greene
University of North Carolina
at Chapel Hill

John Hersey, ed., *Ralph Ellison: A Collection of Critical Essays* (1974); R. S. Lillard, *American Book Collector* (November 1968); James A. McPherson, *Atlantic Monthly* (December 1970); Carol Polsgrove, *American Book Collector* (November–December 1969).

Faulkner, William

(1897–1962) Writer.

William Cuthbert Faulkner was born on 25 September 1897, in New Albany, Miss. The great-grandson of William Clark Falkner, a southern novelist and Confederate officer, Faulkner was responsible for adding the *u* to his family name—just as he was responsible for transmogrifying his native South into a universal place of the imagination in brilliant novels and stories that have put him first among 20th-century American writers of prose fiction.

Cover from William Faulkner's 1947 novel

Faulkner came to maturity at a time when Mississippi and the South were changing. He grew up a part of post–Civil War southern culture, which was dominated by memories of the Old South and the war, and yet he experienced also the modernizing forces of the early 20th century in the region. He had romantic instincts, expressed in his early poetry and prose and in his enlistment in the Royal Canadian Air Force in 1918, hoping to be a gallant fighter pilot. He went back to Oxford, Miss., in that same year, though, and pursued work as a writer. Lawyer Phil Stone encouraged him, financially and intellectually, introducing him to the work of modernists such as T. S. Eliot.

Faulkner spent several months in New Orleans in 1925, becoming friends with Sherwood Anderson and other creative talents there, and in July of that year embarked on a walking tour through parts of Europe. With the exception of stints working as a screenwriter in California, he mostly lived thereafter in Mississippi. His first novel, *Soldiers' Pay*, appeared in 1926, followed by *Mosquitoes* in 1927.

All of Faulkner's major novels reflect his southern rootedness. Beginning with *Flags in the Dust* (published as *Sartoris* in 1929), he creates a mythical Mississippi county, Yoknapatawpha, in which his main characters and their families confront not only specifically southern subjects—such as a native Indian population, the Civil War, plantation life, and race relations—but also themes that transcend a regional focus. *Absalom, Absalom!* (1936), perhaps Faulkner's greatest achievement, explicitly conjoins his southernness and his universality in the partnership of the southerner, Quentin Compson, and the Canadian, Shreve McCannon, Harvard roommates, whose exploration of the southern past provokes questions about the meaning of history itself.

In *The Sound and the Fury* (1929), his first great novel, Faulkner depicts several generations of a southern family, the Compsons, with a sophisticated handling of point of view and human voice that is equal to the greatest work of his European contemporaries. In *As I Lay Dying* (1930), *Light in August* (1932), *The Hamlet* (1940), and *Go Down, Moses* (1942), Faulkner portrays many different kinds and classes of southerners exemplified by the Bundrens, the Snopeses, and the McCaslins; he also conveys penetrating insights into southern Protestantism, miscegenation, and discrimination that again point beyond themselves—especially in the figure of Joe Christmas—to fundamental concerns about the nature of human identity and how it is shaped.

Other leading Faulkner novels include *Pylon* (1935), *The Unvanquished* (1938), *The Wild Palms* (1939), *A Fable* (1954), and his last major work, *The Reivers* (1962). *Sanctuary* (1931) was one of the few Faulkner novels to sell well, and he had abiding financial problems that led to his work in films and as a short story writer for popular magazines. His accomplished short fiction appears in *Collected Stories* (1950) and *Uncollected Stories* (1979). Despite his critical success, especially in Europe, all of Faulkner's novels were out of print when Malcolm Cowley's edited *Portable Faulkner* appeared in 1946 and led to a steadily rising appreciation, and sale, of his work.

In the latter part of his career Faulkner became increasingly aware that he had established his apocryphal county as a counterweight to the actual South, where he had spent most of his life. In *Requiem for a Nun* (1951), he juxtaposed the development of Yoknapatawpha and its town, Jefferson, with the history of Mississippi and its capital, Jackson. In this underrated experimental drama, as well as in his later Snopes novels *The Town* (1957) and *The Mansion* (1959), he directly addressed the issue of the South's changing culture and political structure in the context of world history and national events—as he did at the same time in numerous public letters, speeches, and interviews, especially after receiving the Nobel Prize in 1950. He died in Oxford, Miss., on 6 July 1962.

See also GEOGRAPHY: / Faulkner's Geography; MEDIA: / Faulkner and Film; MYTHIC SOUTH: / Yoknapatawpha County

Carl E. Rollyson, Jr.
Wayne State University

John E. Bassett, *William Faulkner: An Annotated Checklist of Criticism* (1972), *William Faulkner: An Annotated Checklist of Recent Criticism* (1983); Joseph Blotner, *William Faulkner: A Biography*, 2 vols. (1974); Louis Daniel Brodsky and Robert W. Hamblin, eds., *Faulkner: A Comprehensive Guide to the Brodsky Collection*, 2 vols. (1982–84); Cleanth Brooks, *William Faulkner: The Yoknapatawpha Country* (1963), *William Faulkner: Toward Yoknapatawpha and Beyond* (1978); Thomas L. McHaney, *William Faulkner: A Reference Guide* (1976); Michael Millgate, *The Achievement of William Faulkner* (1965).

Foote, Shelby

(b. 1916) Writer.

Shelby Foote, author of six novels and a three-volume narrative history of the Civil War, was born 17 November 1916 and raised in Greenville, Miss. Among the early influences on his writing career was William Alexander Percy, an uncle of Foote's lifelong friend, novelist Walker Percy.

After attending the University of North Carolina, Foote returned to Greenville in 1939 and enlisted in the Mississippi National Guard. While waiting for his unit to be called to active duty, Foote wrote his first novel, *Tournament*, set in the fictional town of Bristol in the also fictional Jordan County. This Delta locale is the setting for four of Foote's six novels.

The publication of *Tournament* was delayed until 1949 by Foote's World War II service as an artillery captain in Europe. After the war, Foote settled in Greenville and resumed his writing career. In the four years following the publication of *Tournament*, he wrote and published four novels: *Follow Me Down* (1950), the story of a tenant farmer/evangelist who commits a murder; *Love in a Dry Season* (1951), which he considers his only comedy; *Shiloh* (1952), a fictional re-creation of the Civil War battle told through a series of first-person monologues; and *Jordan County* (1954), a collection of seven short works detailing the history of Foote's fictional county in reverse chronological order.

With five novels completed and a solid critical reputation established, Foote moved to Memphis in 1953. There he began work on *The Civil War: A Narrative* (3 vols.), an endeavor that required 20 years to complete. It contains more than 1,650,000 words and is an account of the events, sights, sounds, and feel of the Civil War. *Volume One: Fort Sumter to Perryville* was published in 1958, *Volume Two: Fredericksburg to Meridian* in 1963, and *Volume Three: Red River to Appomattox* in 1974. Historian T. Harry Williams described *The Civil War: A Narrative* as "one of the historical and literary achievements of our time."

After completing his Civil War history, Foote returned to writing novels. In 1978 he published *September, September*, the tale of the kidnapping of a black child in Memphis, where Foote continues to live.

David Dawson
Memphis, Tennessee

George Garrett, *Mississippi Quarterly* (Winter 1974–75); *Mississippi Quarterly* (special issue on Foote, Fall 1971); Louis D. Rubin, Jr., *Prospects*, vol. 1 (1974); Helen White and Redding S. Sugg, *Shelby Foote* (1982).

Glasgow, Ellen

(1873–1945) Writer.

Ellen Anderson Gholson Glasgow, born in Richmond, Va., on 22 April 1873, published her first novel, *The Descendant*, in 1897, when she was 24 years old. With this novel Glasgow began a literary career encompassing four and a half decades and comprising 20 novels, a collection of poems, one of stories, and a book of literary criticism. Her autobiography, *A Woman Within*, was published posthumously in 1954.

Born into an aristocratic Virginia family, the young Glasgow rebelled against the conventional modes of feminine conduct and thought approved by her caste. Educated at home and through her own energetic readings in philosophy, social and political theory, and European and British literature, she developed a mind with enough strength and resilience to confront the truths of human experience without the sheltering illusions carefully nurtured by the dying southern aristocratic order she saw about her.

Glasgow's strong intellect led her to a conscious channeling of her creative energies toward the making of a substantial body of fiction. The framework of these works was to be, as she stated in 1898, at age 25, "a series of sketches dealing with life in Virginia." As she matured artistically, this early half-formed intention realized itself in a series of novels that constitutes a social history of her native Virginia. The great organizing ideas of her fiction are the conflicts between tradition and change, matter and spirit, the individual and society. The natural bent of her mind taught her that realism and irony were the best tools with which to fashion a new southern fiction to take the place of the sentimental stories of a glorified aristocratic past that dominated the regional fiction of her day. Through her poor white heroes and heroines, she introduced democratic values seldom found in the works of other southern writers outside Mark Twain. From the very beginning of her intellectual and creative life, she rejected Victorian definitions of femininity dominating the social attitudes of her day.

Glasgow produced seven novels of enduring literary merit. *The Deliverance* (1904), the best of her early novels, offers a naturalistic treatment of the class conflicts emerging after the Civil War. Its evocation of the Virginia landscape and tobacco farming invites comparison with Hardy's epics of the soil. In her women's trilogy—*Virginia* (1913), *Life and Gabriella* (1916), and *Barren Ground* (1925)—Glasgow assigns each of her Virginia heroines a fate determined by her response to the patriarchal code of feminine behavior that had formed her, a code that, as Glasgow shows so well in *Barren Ground*, always pitted women against their own biological natures. After *Barren Ground*, which marked her arrival at artistic maturity, Glasgow produced three sparkling comedies of manners—*The Romantic Comedians* (1926), *They Stooped to Folly* (1929), and *The Sheltered Life* (1932), the last the author's finest work. In these novels of urban Virginian life depicting the clash of generations, she again shows her women characters reacting to patriarchal stereotypes limiting their individuality and growth, while at the same time exposing either with comic or with satiric irony the limitations these views of women place on the male characters who hold them.

Ellen Glasgow, Virginia author, 1922

A popular writer, Glasgow was on the best-seller lists five times. In 1942 she received the Pulitzer Prize for her last published novel, *In This Our Life*, though by this time her powers had declined. Her artistic recognition had reached its height in 1931, when, as the acknowledged doyenne of southern letters, she presided over the Southern Writers Conference at the University of Virginia. For many years the victim of heart disease, she died in her sleep at home in Richmond on 21 November 1945.

Tonette Bond Inge
Randolph-Macon College

C. Hugh Holman, *Three Modes of Southern Fiction: Ellen Glasgow, William Faulkner, Thomas Wolfe* (1966); M. Thomas Inge, ed., *Ellen Glasgow: Centennial Essays* (1976); Julius Rowan Raper, *From the Sunken Garden: The Fiction of Ellen Glasgow, 1916–1945* (1980), *Without Shelter: The Early Career of Ellen Glasgow* (1971).

Green, Paul

(1894–1981) Playwright.

Paul Green was born 17 March 1894 on a farm in Harnett County, near Lillington, N.C. He worked side by side with the black tenants and hired hands, whom he regarded as part of his larger family. He dramatized this background in his poems, stories, novels, and plays.

In the early 1920s he wrote one-act folk dramas as a student at the University of North Carolina at Chapel Hill. *The No 'Count Boy*, first published in 1924 in *Theatre Arts Magazine*, gave Green his first recognition beyond the South. In 1925 *The No 'Count Boy* won the Belasco Cup competition in New York City. In *The Hawthorn Tree* (1943) Green elaborated on his imaginative concept of the "folk," referring to "the people whose manners, ethics, religious and philosophical ideals are more nearly derived from and controlled by the ways of the outside physical world . . . than by the ways and institutions of men in a specialized society." The success of *The No 'Count Boy* led to the publication of two collections of Paul Green's plays in 1925 and 1926. A longer version of one of these plays, *In Abraham's Bosom*, was awarded a Pulitzer Prize in May 1927. Other Broadway plays were *The Field God* and *The House of Connelly*, subtitled *A Drama of the Old South and the New*. These plays helped establish Paul Green's place among America's leading playwrights.

Instead of writing for what he termed the commercial theater of New York, however, he decided to produce his plays outdoors, amalgamating pageant, music, dance, and poetry into a theater he created and named "symphonic drama." Celebrating events and characters in history as well as nationalistic myths, Green defined symphonic drama in his 1948 "Author's Note" to *The Common Glory* as "that type of drama in which all elements of theatre art are used to sound together—one for all and all for one, a true democracy. The theatre of such a drama is sensitized and charged with a fierce potential of evocation and expressiveness for any moment." The most famous of these symphonic dramas is *The Lost Colony* (1937), the story of Sir Walter Raleigh's dream of settling America in the late 16th century. The play is produced each summer for thousands of visitors to North Carolina.

Paul Green recognized early the dramatic richness of his native South, championing always human rights and his thought that "the greatest sin society can commit is to cause a man to miss his own life."

Shelby Stephenson
Pembroke State University

Vincent Kenny, *Paul Green* (1971); Walter S. Lazenby, Jr., *Paul Green* (1970); William S. Powell, ed., *Dictionary of North Carolina Biography*, vol. 2 (1986).

Harris, George Washington

(1814–1869) Writer.

Harris was born in Allegheny City, Pa., but his parents were probably North Carolinians. At five he was taken to Knoxville, Tenn., by his married half brother, Samuel Bell, who opened a metalworking shop. Harris received little formal education, was early apprenticed, and by his late teens had served as captain for a Tennessee River steamboat. In 1835 he married Mary Emiline Nance, tried large-scale farming in Blount County, Tenn., and lost his land, a slave, and even household goods. By 1843 he was back in Knoxville operating a metalworking and jewelry shop.

While living on his farm Harris had already begun to contribute to local newspapers, and during the next decade he practiced a variety of literary forms and published in the internationally circulated sporting magazine, the New York *Spirit of the Times*. During 1843 Harris published, under the pen name "Mr. Free," four formal letters describing rural customs, sports, and hunts. Presented from a gentlemanly perspective, the Tennessee backwoods is evoked in versions of pastoral. In 1845, in "The Knob Dance," Harris created a fictional account of a ritual frolic presented in the comic dialect of a narrator whose extravagance and sense of community are richly expressive of deep patterns of the folk culture. Action and language celebrate freedom, intensity, and the joys of the body.

In 1854, again in the *Spirit*, Harris expanded his comic depiction of southern backwoods life with the creation of his vital, intense, "nat'ral born durn'd fool," Sut Lovingood, a Tennessee youth who declares his brains are "mos' ove the time onhook'd," recounting his family background in a comic, grotesque fable of conflict with his father and flight from home. Throughout the 1850s Harris created a variety of adventures for his character, many revised and included in *Sut Lovingood's Yarns* in 1867.

Although Harris's achievement is complex, two areas stand out. Harris peoples his backwoods with self-assertive characters and develops Sut as an arresting seer. Sut's folk speech, metaphorically rich and presented in painstakingly detailed dialect, is an unsurpassed creative distillation of the American comic vernacular. Inseparable from this aesthetic achievement and embodied in it is a set of unique, uninhibited southern social and political ideas.

Harris's topics cluster around the prankster's search for excitement, the family and community, the reduction of authority figures—sheriffs, judges, preachers, and fathers—and the complexities of relations between the sexes. Some episodes convey the responses of the insular community to outsiders, such as blacks, Jews, Catholics, Mormons, and Yankees. Harris's first political targets were Tennesseans, but later he treated many national figures, including James Buchanan, John C. Frémont, Abraham Lincoln, and numerous abolitionists. Other targets were "strong minded women," philosophers, and utopian theorizers. His reductive satires express dramatically the narrowest fears and hatreds of his community.

Writers such as Mark Twain, William Faulkner, and Flannery O'Connor have praised Harris's characterization and language. Critics' responses have been from "Rabelaisian" to "repellent." Clearly, Harris's range extends from vituperative satire to the ambiguities of grotesque realism and, finally, to the celebratory mode of folk humor.

Milton Rickels
University of Southwestern Louisiana

George Washington Harris, *High Times and Hard Times*, ed. M. Thomas Inge (1967), *Sut Lovingood: Yarns Spun by a "Nat'ral Born Durn'd Fool"* (1867); Milton Rickels, *George Washington Harris* (1965).

Harris, Joel Chandler

(1848–1908) Writer.

Harris, the illegitimate son of Mary Harris and an Irish laborer, was born on 9 December 1848, near Eatonton, Ga. His death from nephritis came in Atlanta on 3 July 1908.

Harris's formal schooling was spotty, but he read widely in world, English, and American literature, with Goldsmith's *The Vicar of Wakefield* being his favorite book.

His major training came at the hands of Joseph Addison Turner, who edited *The Countryman*, a weekly newspaper published at the middle Georgia plantation Turnwold. From 1862 to 1866 young Harris worked on the paper, read from Turner's library, and listened to the speech and tales of the plantation blacks. It was his beginning as a writer.

Harris worked for several other newspapers before joining the staff of the Atlanta *Constitution* in 1876 as associate editor. Here he began publishing his famous Uncle Remus stories, using the black dialect he had heard on the plantation. His fame soon spread nationally because of the Uncle Remus tales, and three major Remus books followed: *Uncle Remus: His Songs and His Sayings* (1880), *Nights with Uncle Remus* (1883), and *Uncle Remus and His Friends* (1892). Numerous other volumes of the tales were published both during his lifetime and posthumously.

Diverse in taste and talents, Harris also wrote six children's books, all set on a Georgia plantation, and several novelettes and novels—most importantly, *Sister Jane: Her Friends and Acquaintances* (1896), a novel that depicts antebellum Georgia, and *Gabriel Tolliver: A Story of Reconstruction* (1902), his major long work. Other ventures into long narrative include an autobiographical novel, *On the Plantation* (1892), the setting of which is Turnwold. Adept at the short story, Harris produced five collections, the main ones being *Mingo, and Other Sketches in Black and White* (1884) and *Free Joe and Other Georgia Sketches* (1887). And with his son Julian he established *Uncle Remus's Magazine* in 1907.

Although Harris disavowed regionalism in art ("My idea is that truth is more important than sectionalism, and that literature that can be labeled Northern, Southern, Western, or Eastern, is not worth labeling at all"), his writings are unsurpassed in reflecting the southern environment. His short stories are born of the Georgia soil, his novels echo the strains of the Civil War South, his editorials for the *Constitution* deal with southern social and political issues, and, of course, his famed Uncle Remus tales capture the diction and dialect of the plantation blacks while presenting genuine folk legends. Enlivened with gentle humor and irony, Harris's portraits of the Georgia Negro and his faithful handling of the folk tales constitute his major contributions to southern and American literature. His was a southern voice with a national range.

See also FOLKLIFE: / Brer Rabbit

David B. Kesterson
North Texas State University

R. Bruce Bickley, Jr., *Joel Chandler Harris* (1978), with Karen L. Bickley and Thomas H. English, *Joel Chandler Harris: A Reference Guide* (1978); Arthur Hobson Quinn, *American Fiction: An Historical and Critical Survey* (1936); Bernard Wolfe, *Commentary* (July 1949).

Hellman, Lillian

(1905–1984) Writer.

Lillian Florence Hellman was born of Jewish heritage in New Orleans, La., on 20 June 1905, the only child of Julia Newhouse and Max Bernard Hellman. During childhood, she divided her time between New York, where her father's job took him when she was quite young, and New Orleans, attending schools in both cities. Between 1922 and 1924 she attended New York University but left before her senior year to work as a manuscript reader for publisher Horace Liveright. On 31 December 1925 she married Arthur Kober, a theatrical press agent, and spent the ensuing four years reading scripts for New York producers, writing book reviews for the New York *Herald Tribune*, and traveling. In the fall of 1930 she and Kober moved to Hollywood, where he worked as a scriptwriter for Paramount and she as a manuscript reader for Metro-Goldwyn-Mayer and where, in November 1930, she met Dashiell Hammett, a successful and popular writer. In March 1931 Hellman moved back to New York and shortly thereafter divorced Arthur Kober and began her 30-year relationship with Hammett.

After writing a few short stories and discovering that was not to be her literary mode, Hellman collaborated with critic Louis Kronenberger on a play, *Dear Queen*, which was completed in 1932 but never produced. In November 1934 *The Children's Hour* opened on Broadway and was both a hit and a sensation, at least partially because it introduced the topic of lesbianism to the American stage. Its success sent its author back to Hollywood, where she adapted *Dark Angel* from a novel by Guy Bolton and did a sanitized film version of *The Children's Hour* entitled *These Three*. For the next 30 years she continued to write for both the stage and screen, doing movie versions of Sidney Kingsley's *Dead End* (1937) and of Horton Foote's novel *The Chase* (1966), as well as of her own plays *The Little Foxes* (1941) and *The Searching Wind* (1944), in addition to a documentary, *North Star* (1943).

Her other plays included *Another Part of the Forest* (1946), *The Autumn Garden* (1951), and *Toys in the Attic* (1960). The last play and *Watch on the Rhine* (1941) each won a New York Drama Critics' Circle Award for best American play of the year. Hellman also adapted a number of works for the Broadway stage.

Having grown disillusioned with Broadway, Hellman turned in the 1960s from writing plays and began a series of autobiographical memoirs, which included *An Unfinished Woman* (1969), *Pentimento* (1973), and *Scoundrel Time* (1976), the last her account of the McCarthy years after World War II, her blacklisting in Hollywood, and her appearance before the House Un-American Activities Committee.

Although only four of Hellman's plays—*The Little Foxes*, *Another Part of the Forest*, *Autumn Garden*, and *Toys in the Attic*—have southern settings and southern characters (some based on her family), they are among her best writing. In a 1939 interview about *The Little Foxes*, probably her most enduring work, she indicated that she chose the South as a setting "because it fitted the period I wanted for dramatic purposes and because it is a part of the world whose atmosphere I personally am familiar with as a Southerner. I also wanted a certain naive or innocent quality in some of my characters which I could find in the South but which would have been quite out of place in any other American setting." And late in her life, when she had lived in the Northeast for some 55 years, she admitted that she still considered herself a southerner, despite the fact that at age 11 she had moved North: "I came from a family of Southerners. It wasn't simply that I was brought up and down from the South. I came from a family, on both sides, who had been Southerners for a great many generations."

Jackson R. Bryer
University of Maryland

Mark W. Estrin, *Lillian Hellman: Plays, Films, Memoirs: A Reference Guide* (1980); Doris V. Falk, *Lillian Hellman* (1978); Katherine Lederer, *Lillian Hellman* (1979); Richard Moody, *Lillian Hellman: Playwright* (1972).

Heyward, DuBose

(1885–1940) Writer.

Edwin DuBose Heyward, the son of aristocratic white parents, was among those who protested Mencken's indictment of the South as the "Sahara of the Bozart." Although Heyward deserves credit for calling attention to the folklore and legends of Low Country South Carolina and the mountains of North Carolina, his greatest achievement was his creation of black characters, especially the lame beggar Porgy. And though the name of their creator is often forgotten, his Porgy and Bess have taken their places among the legendary characters of the American imagination.

That achievement is the result of a series of fortunate collaborations. The germ of Heyward's novel *Porgy* (1925) was a newspaper article on a crippled beggar, but Heyward, who had spent a year working for a steamship company on a Charleston waterfront, had developed a keen ear for black speech and a sensitivity to the black community. The novel was a popular success, widely praised. His wife, Dorothy Hartzell Kuhns, a dramatist, recognized the dramatic potential of the novel, and the couple collaborated on the play *Porgy*, which opened in New York in 1927 to resounding acclaim. It was counted a part of the Harlem Renaissance and was certainly an important event for black performers, who had previously found limited opportunities for serious drama. The play was later the inspiration for George Gershwin's opera *Porgy and Bess* (1935). Heyward wrote the libretto and, assisted by Ira Gershwin, most of the lyrics. George Gershwin had insisted that the work be an opera, not a musical, which it would have become if Heyward had had his way. Since Heyward's death, most Americans know Porgy and Bess only through the opera.

Brass Ankle (1931), the only play Heyward wrote alone, is a study of miscegenation. It is the only Heyward play in which white characters dominate, but its success was limited. With his wife, he collaborated on *Mamba's Daughter* (1939). The play, written for Ethel Waters, who played Hagar, was the first serious Broadway play to make a star of a black woman. Heyward had plans to make into an opera *Star Spangled Version* (1939), his novel based on the effect of the New Deal on blacks in the Virgin Islands, but his early death prevented that.

In his novel *Peter Ashley* (1932), Heyward looked at his native Charleston through the eyes of history. Peter, a young aristocrat who has been educated in Oxford, knows that the course of the Confederacy is wrong, but his heart finally leads him to that side. In the 1920s Heyward made his commitment to the cause of southern art and its future by founding, with Hervey Allen and John Bennett, the Poetry Society of South Carolina. He lectured throughout the state and read his poems. His *Carolina Chansons: Legends of the Low Country*, with Allen, appeared in 1922. His other verse collections were *Skylines and Horizons* (1924) and *Jasbo Brown and Selected Poems* (1931). Important as these works were to the Southern Literary Renaissance, calling attention to the region and its folklore, they helped train Heyward for his more powerful explorations of black experience, especially of the black lovers Porgy and Bess.

Joseph M. Flora
University of North Carolina at Chapel Hill

Hervey Allen, *DuBose Heyward: A Critical and Biographical Sketch* (1927); Frank Durham, *DuBose Heyward: The Man Who Wrote Porgy* (1954), *DuBose Heyward's Use of Folklore in His Negro Fiction* (1961).

Kennedy, John Pendleton

(1795–1870) Writer.

Descendant of a Tidewater Virginia clan, Kennedy was born in Baltimore, Md. He studied law with an uncle after receiving his formal education at a local academy and at Baltimore College. Following his admission to the bar in 1816, he practiced law rather aimlessly while writing essays and satirical pieces. In 1820 he began a political career as a member of the Maryland House of Delegates. Returning to creative writing, Kennedy published *Swallow Barn* (1832), a pioneer contribution to plantation literature that enjoyed moderate success. Capitalizing on a genre made popular by James Fenimore Cooper, Kennedy published his best work, *Horse-Shoe Robinson*, in 1835. An American historical romance, it was an early contribution to the legend of the southern role in the Revolution. Appearing in 1838, Kennedy's *Rob of the Bowl* was a tale of religious and political rivalries in 17th-century Maryland. His budding career as a romancer ended with his election to the U.S. House of Representatives in 1838. Kennedy subordinated his creative work to his political and business interests for the remainder of his life. His last major literary work was *Memoirs of the Life of William Wirt* (1849).

As Kennedy grew to manhood during the early years of the 19th century, he saw his native Baltimore change from village to thriving commercial town—its atmosphere becoming distinctly less southern. Such changes wrought their effect upon Kennedy. His ties to the South were strong, but his commitments to the border state he lived in led him to fear the rise of southern sectionalism and to embrace a nationalistic point of view.

Kennedy's place in southern letters rests on *Swallow Barn*, *Horse-Shoe Robinson*, and *Rob of the Bowl*. Of the three romances, *Swallow Barn* proved to be the most important in reflecting an image of a self-conscious South. Though the book cataloged all that seemed good in the plantation world, it also satirized the provinciality of a closed Virginia society. Despite his somewhat sympathetic depiction of slavery in *Swallow Barn*, Kennedy was convinced that the institution kept Virginia and the rest of the South from enjoying the benefits of commercial and industrial expansion. He portrayed Virginians after the Revolution living in a dream world that slavery and sectionalism would turn into a nightmare.

L. Moody Simms, Jr.
Illinois State University

Charles H. Bohner, *John Pendleton Kennedy: Gentleman from Baltimore* (1961); Jay B. Hubbell, *The South in American Literature, 1607–1900* (1954); Joseph V. Ridgely, *John Pendleton Kennedy* (1966).

Longstreet, Augustus Baldwin

(1790–1870) Writer.

Longstreet is remembered today for his collection of humorous stories, *Georgia Scenes* (1835). A native of Augusta, Ga., he earned a degree from Yale University in 1813, studied law in Litchfield, Conn., and returned to his home state. He later attained professional success as a lawyer, a superior court judge, a proprietor and editor of a newspaper (the *State Rights Sentinel*, which he used as a forum for his political views, especially for a defense of slavery and nullification), a Methodist minister, and president of four institutions of higher learning (Emory College in Georgia, Centenary College in Louisiana, the University of Mississippi, and the University of South Carolina).

His experiences as a lawyer and judge in Georgia furnished Longstreet with an opportunity to observe southerners of every social class, and he made use of these people as characters for *Georgia Scenes*. Ostensibly related by two refined narrators—Hall, a country gentleman, and Baldwin, an urbane judge—the 19 sketches are populated by crackers, dirt eaters, crafty horse traders, and other indigenous southern types. The clash of the narrators' values and highly literate writing styles with the values and vernacular speech of the rural people that Hall and Baldwin encounter is the basis for much of the humor of the volume.

Walter Blair called *Georgia Scenes* "the first and most influential book of Southwestern humor." Longstreet's themes and techniques foreshadowed those in the works of such antebellum humorists as Johnson Jones Hooper and George Washington Harris, who followed in this tradition, a tradition that attracted Mark Twain during his writing career. In his use of the South and its people to create a sense of place in fiction, Longstreet opened new territory later traveled by such local colorists of the postbellum period as Richard Malcolm Johnston and Thomas Nelson Page and by writers of the 20th century, from William Faulkner to Eudora Welty.

Georgia Scenes is also important as social history. In it Longstreet wished to depict representative "Characters, Incidents . . . in the First Half Century of the Republic" in his state because he realized that complex social and economic forces had already begun altering the mores and daily activities there. In the book, for example, the narrator Hall described in detail a no-holds-barred Georgia fight, a backwoods shooting match, and the brutal sport of gander pulling; the narrator Baldwin contrasted the attitudes and popular tastes of the time with those of his youth. For the most part, Longstreet projected an optimistic view of the narrowing of the gulf between wealthy planters and poor whites, but he recognized that both classes would lose something of their unique lifestyles in the process. Perhaps the most notable aspect of *Georgia Scenes* is Longstreet's generally objective portrayal of southern poor whites, a group frequently viewed with complete disdain by other antebellum writers.

Mark A. Keller
Middle Georgia College

Kimball King, *Augustus Baldwin Longstreet* (1984); James B. Meriwether, *Mississippi Quarterly* (Fall 1982); John Donald Wade, *Augustus Baldwin Longstreet: A Study in the Development of Culture in the South* (1924, new ed. 1969).

Lytle, Andrew

(b. 1902) Writer.

Born in Murfreesboro, Tenn., Andrew Lytle graduated from Vanderbilt University, where he met the Fugitive poets and was a minor contributor to the *Fugitive* magazine. His essay "The Hind Tit" in *I'll Take My Stand* (1930) establishes the philosophical basis for Lytle's agrarianism: humankind must understand "nature's invincible and inscrutable ways" in order to prevent people from brutalizing either nature or one another. A defense of the yeoman farmer and a critique of industrialism, this essay reveals the milieu for much of Lytle's fiction, not the plantation economy of the Lower South but the disappearing folk culture of the upcountry farms of middle Tennessee. Lytle's first book, *Bedford Forrest and His Critter Company* (1931), is a biography of the Tennessee Civil War hero that examines strategic weaknesses within the Confederate high command, especially the inept leadership of General Braxton Bragg, and "the one great mistake" of Jefferson Davis: to rest the foundation of the Confederacy on cotton and not "the plain folk" like those who fought under Forrest. As a historian and writer of cultural essays, many of which were collected in *The Hero with the Private Parts* (1966), Lytle has continued to examine the South's legacy of defeat, but unlike many of his contemporaries he does not accept the legacy of guilt. Influenced by Spengler, Lytle associated the decline of southern tradition with the decline of the West, "the gradual fall from a belief in a divine order of the universe into a belief in history, that is man judging man as the final authority of meaning in life."

As a writer of dramatic, not didactic, fiction, Lytle has been careful to distinguish between the voice of the artist and that of the cultural critic. In *The Long Night* (1936), a boy's private need to avenge his father's murder is finally dissolved in the public violence of the Civil War. Through its examination of pride and the often violent code of the Scotch-Irish clan, this novel presents both the light and dark sides of southern tradition. *At the Moon's Inn* (1941), the story of Hernando de Soto's unsuccessful effort to conquer the wilderness of Spanish Florida, places Lytle's agrarian beliefs within the context of Western civilization, not just American history. *A Name for Evil* (1947) clearly reveals that a literal regeneration of the southern past is not possible.

Rejecting the outer world of political, social, and religious restraints, Lytle's alienated characters either turn inward toward the self or outward toward the only remaining institution, the isolated family, and this, Lytle says, "require(s) of the family more meaning than it can sustain." The result—as in the fiction of Poe and Faulkner—is physical and spiritual incest, which leaves both family and community severely diminished but not entirely broken in Lytle's masterpiece, *The Velvet Horn* (1957). His most recent book, *A Wake for the Living* (1975), is a family and social memoir that celebrates traditional southern life and mores in the face of death.

Thomas M. Carlson
University of the South

M. E. Bradford, ed., *The Form Discovered: Essays on the Achievement of Andrew Lytle* (1973); Victor A. Kramer et al., *Andrew Lytle, Walker Percy, Peter Taylor* (1983); Stuart Wright, *Andrew Nelson Lytle: A Bibliography, 1920–1982* (1982).

McCullers, Carson

(1917–1967) Writer.

Born and raised in Columbus, Ga., Carson McCullers published her first novel in 1940, following the most important decade in the history of southern letters. She extended the tradition of the Southern Literary Renaissance by employing the modern South as a symbolic setting in all of her major fiction. More importantly, her work uses the harsh symbolism of southern life to re-create the universal failures and anxieties of modern America.

In *The Heart Is a Lonely Hunter* (1940) her allegorical structure—the complex solar system of grotesque "lonely-hearts" in complementary orbits—is perfectly balanced by an intensely realistic documentation of the social conditions discovered in a southern mill city during the Depression. It remains her finest effort. *Reflections in a Golden Eye* (1941), her second novel, is an example of the modern Gothic; McCullers's tale of bizarre sexuality on a peacetime army base demonstrates considerable versatility and artistic daring. *The Ballad of the Sad Café* (1941, 1951) is a more traditional work in the Gothic mode. The distancing effect of the balladeer-narrator allows the bizarre characters and strange events to be unified in one of the most intriguing novellas in modern southern fiction.

After a long silence caused by physical and psychological problems during the war, McCullers re-created some of the literary and popular success of her first novel in *The Member of the Wedding* (1946). This smaller portrait of the mill city again probes social relationships and individual feelings through the symbolic use of the alienated adolescent. It is a narrower achievement, though one that was more accessible for a popular audience in the stage (1951) and screen (1952) versions that made the author famous and financially secure.

McCullers worked for over a decade on *Clock without Hands* (1961), her last novel. Unfortunately, her long and debilitating illness made the successful completion of the book impossible. The novel's weak characterization and stereotyped action cannot create a structure strong enough to make order of the complicated changes transforming the South in the days of integration.

Like many southern writers, Carson McCullers developed an ambivalent attitude toward her native land; in her northern expatriation she cut herself off from the southern roots of her vision, yet she never developed others to replace them. Her achievement was still a considerable contribution to the fiction of the Southern Literary Renaissance.

Joseph R. Millichap
Western Kentucky University

Virginia Spencer Carr and Joseph R. Millichap, in *American Women Writers: Bibliographical Essays* (1983); Virginia Spencer Carr, *The Lonely Hunter: A Biography of Carson McCullers* (1975).

Mencken, H. L.

(1880–1956) Editor, essayist, and critic.

Henry Louis Mencken was a writer of enormous national influence who also played a leading role in southern intellectual life of the 1920s. A native of Baltimore, he became a contributor to the *Smart Set* and the *American Mercury*. As such, he was, Walter Lippmann wrote, "the most powerful personal influence on this whole generation of educated people." In particular, he conducted a crusade against American provincialism, puritanism, and prudery—all of which he believed he found, to a degree larger than elsewhere, in the states below the Potomac and Ohio. Mencken shocked southerners when he published a severe indictment of southern culture, "The Sahara of the Bozart," which first appeared in 1917 in the New York *Evening Mail* and was reprinted in his book, *Prejudices, Second Series* (1920). In his essay he charged that the South was "almost as sterile, artistically, intellectually, culturally, as the Sahara Desert." "In all that gargantuan paradise of the fourth-rate," he contended, "there is not a single picture gallery worth going into, or a single orchestra capable of playing the nine symphonies of Beethoven, or a single opera-house, or a single theater devoted to decent plays." Most southern poetry and prose was drivel, he charged, and "when you come to critics, musical composers, painters, sculptors, architects and the like, you will have to give it up, for there is not even a bad one between the Potomac mud-flats and the Gulf." Nor, Mencken added, a historian, sociologist, philosopher, theologian, or scientist.

The essay, written in characteristic Menckenian hyperbole, suggested that the condition of the modern South was especially lamentable because the antebellum South, particularly Virginia, had been the seat of American civilization. Mencken attributed the decline of southern culture to the "poor whites" who, he charged, had seized control of the South after the Civil War. Particularly to blame were the preachers and the politicians. What the South needed, he maintained, was a return to influence of a remnant of the old aristocracy.

Mencken's "Sahara" and other essays on the "godawful South" attracted widespread attention in Dixie in the decade that followed. Traditional southerners denounced him as a "modern Attila," a "miserable and uninformed wretch," a "bitter, prejudiced and ignorant critic of a great people." But other southerners such as James Branch Cabell, Howard W. Odum, Gerald W. Johnson, Paul Green, Thomas Wolfe, and Wilbur J. Cash declared their agreement with the substance of the indictment.

The Southern Literary Renaissance followed Mencken's "Sahara," and literary historians have suggested that Mencken shocked young southern writers into an awareness of southern literary poverty and thus played a seminal role in the revival of southern letters. But as important as Mencken's effect on southern literature was his effect on the general intellectual climate of the "progressive" South. Menckenism became, as the 1920s progressed, a cultural force, a school of thought for iconoclastic southerners. Not all young southerners accepted him: Donald Davidson, Allen Tate, and other southern Agrarians challenged him with particular vigor. In the mid-1930s Mencken lost interest in the South, as the South lost interest in him. Nevertheless, his impact on southern letters, even if indirect, was felt for many years.

See also MYTHIC SOUTH: / Mencken's South

Fred Hobson
University of Alabama

Carl Bode, *Mencken* (1969); Fred Hobson, *Serpent in Eden: H. L. Mencken and the South* (1974); William H. Nolte, *H. L. Mencken, Literary Critic* (1966).

O'Connor, Flannery

(1925–1964) Writer.

Flannery O'Connor was born a Roman Catholic in Savannah, Ga., on 25 March 1925. She attended parochial school there until 1938, when her father's disseminated lupus was diagnosed and the family moved to Milledgeville, Ga., the home of the author's maternal grandparents. O'Connor attended high school in Milledgeville and went on to that town's Georgia State College for Women as a major in English and social science. Her father died in 1941. Upon her graduation from college in 1945 she received a Rinehart Fellowship to the Writers' Workshop of the University of Iowa. She received an M.F.A. from Iowa in 1947, a year after her first story had appeared in *Accent*. From Iowa she went to Yaddo, where she started her first novel, *Wise Blood*. She met Robert and Sally Fitzgerald while in New York and moved in with them in Ridgefield, Conn., in 1949.

In 1950 her own disseminated lupus was diagnosed, and she moved to her mother's farm, Andalusia, just outside Milledgeville. She finished *Wise Blood* there and published the book with Harcourt, Brace in 1952. Her collection of short stories, *A Good Man Is Hard to Find*, came out in 1955; her second novel, *The Violent Bear It Away*, in 1960. She died on 3 August 1964, a year before her last collection of stories, *Everything That Rises Must Converge*, appeared. Her other posthumous publications are *Mystery and Manners* (1969), *The Complete Stories* (1971), and *The Habit of Being: Letters of Flannery O'Connor* (1979).

O'Connor worked with the traditional themes and characters of the South. But because of her specifically religious view, she seemed to find new meaning in them as she focused on postlapsarian existence. Her grotesques usually reflect some spiritual shortcoming with their physical handicaps. Her southern children are as deeply into sin as her adults; her adults are as helpless in this life as her children. And the vanity of aristocratic backgrounds is a trap for the sinner. To her the land, traditionally a symbol of well-being in southern literature, is one more sign of the foolish accumulation of earthly stores that gets no one into heaven. The industrialization of the South that Faulkner symbolized so well with the car of *The Reivers* came to be just another sign of human vanity as Hazel Motes of *Wise Blood* established "The Church Without Christ" in a broken-down Essex, a vehicle that ends up in the kudzu of a Georgia pasture. O'Connor even discovered religious implications in polite southern conversation. Her rednecks and aristocrats alike point inadvertently to a godless world as they make casual statements such as "a good man is hard to find" or "the life you save may be your own."

Religion, of course, has long been a concern of southern writers; but probably no successful writer of the region has treated it as specifically and as thoroughly as O'Connor. Her considerable talent lay in rendering scenes with vivid accuracy, allowing them to reflect, almost invariably, the emptiness of existence in worlds—southern and otherwise—without Christ.

See also RELIGION: / O'Connor and Religion

G. W. Koon
Clemson University

Kathleen Feeley, *Flannery O'Connor* (1972); Sally Fitzgerald, ed., *The Habit of Being: Letters of Flannery O'Connor* (1979); Melvin J. Friedman and Lewis Lawson, eds., *The Added Dimension: The Art and Mind of Flannery O'Connor* (1966); Josephine Hendin, *The World of Flannery O'Connor* (1970); Miles Orvell, *Invisible Parade: The Fiction of Flannery O'Connor* (1973).

Page, Thomas Nelson

(1853–1922) Writer.

Thomas Nelson Page, author of short stories, novels, essays, and poetry, is best known for his role as literary spokesman for the glories of the Old South. Born in 1853 and only 12 years old when the Civil War ended, Page, writing in the plantation genre of John Pendleton Kennedy and others, created of the antebellum South a mythical, would-be land of noble gentlemen and ladies, of contented slaves, a society ordered by the laws of chivalry.

A descendant of the prominent but no longer wealthy Nelson and Page families, and a native of Virginia, Page attended Washington College and later studied at the University of Virginia for a legal career. Page married in 1886, and his wife died two years later. He practiced law in Richmond from 1876 until 1893, when he moved with his second wife, the former Florence Lathrop Field, to Washington. Although Page became active in the social life of the capital and later served six years as ambassador to Italy under Woodrow Wilson, he continued in his writing to depict Virginia and the passing of the old order there. His works, set for the most part in the South, comprised 18 volumes when they were published in a collected edition in 1912.

In Ole Virginia (1887) was Page's first collection of short stories treating the antebellum South. Other works dealt with later periods in southern history. For example, *Red Rock* (1898) was a sympathetic portrait of the South during Reconstruction, and *John Marvel, Assistant* (1909) depicted the New South of the early 20th century. Page was consistently a proponent of the southern way of life, and in such stories as "Marse Chan" in *In Ole Virginia* his finest sketches were realized. In this story, told by a faithful exslave, of a young southerner who died for the southern cause and who placed duty and honor above all personal gain, Page postulates a kind of heroism that seemed to be missing from modern life. Page's South, of course, was finer than any real place could ever be, but he satisfied the nostalgia of his readers for what might have been—a place where heroic men and women adhered to a code of perfect honor. Only in the 20th century would Ellen Glasgow and, later, the writers of the Southern Literary Renaissance dispel the romantic image of the Old South so carefully fashioned by Thomas Nelson Page.

See also MYTHIC SOUTH: / "Moonlight-and-Magnolias" Myth

Anne E. Rowe
Florida State University

Theodore Gross, *Thomas Nelson Page* (1967); Kimball King, "Introduction" to Thomas Nelson Page, *In Ole Virginia or Marse Chan and Other Stories* (1969).

Percy, Walker

(b. 1916) Writer.

Percy is a novelist and lay philosopher whose important and popular writings embody his vision of a sadly dualistic existence. Percy himself was raised first in Birmingham, Ala., and then, after his parents' deaths, in Greenville, Miss., by his father's cousin William Alexander Percy (author of *Lanterns on the Levee*). He took a bachelor of science degree in chemistry from the University of North Carolina at Chapel Hill and an M.D. from Columbia's College of Physicians and Surgeons in 1941. Working as a pathologist at Bellevue Hospital in New York, Percy contracted tuberculosis. While recuperating he began to read such existentialist writers as Dostoevsky, Camus, Sartre, Marcel, Heidegger, and Kierkegaard. Convinced by them of the inadequacy of scientific methods that "cannot utter a single word about an individual as individual," Percy determined to be a novelist. He did not practice medicine again.

Percy returned south, married Mary (or "Bunt") Townsend, whom he had met in Greenville, moved with his bride to Covington, La., and became a Roman Catholic. For the next 15 years he published philosophical essays in scholarly quarterlies and learned to be a novelist. His first novel, *The Moviegoer*, was published in 1961 and won the National Book Award. Since then he has published five more novels—*The Last Gentleman* (1966), *Love in the Ruins: The Adventures of a Bad Catholic at a Time Near the End of the World* (1971), *Lancelot* (1977), *The Second Coming* (1980), and *The Thanatos Syndrome* (1987)—a collection of essays, *The Message in*

Walker Percy, Louisiana novelist, 1983

the Bottle: How Queer Man Is, How Queer Language Is, and What One Has to Do with the Other (1975), and a nonfiction volume entitled *Lost in the Cosmos: The Last Self-Help Book* (1983).

Percy's novels are distinctly southern because they are set almost exclusively in the South and because their protagonists are all southern men. The novels are clearly placed; streets and homes in New Orleans, antebellum homes along the River Road, a country club in Birmingham, a hotel in Asheville—all are clearly recognizable. But if Percy is southern in his sensuous apprehension of place, he is southern also in his concern with the ideal. The southern patrician outlook taught him by William Alexander Percy brought meaning to terms like "honor" and "gentlemen"; these are meanings whose limits Percy exposes but whose values he never abandons. Perhaps the wry satire of his novels owes more to a Roman Catholic sense of man's fallibility and an aristocratic southern sense of right (and hence of the absurdity of departures from the right) than to Percy's readings in absurdist literature. Mid-20th century problems such as the civil rights struggle and the Kennedy assassination are alluded to in Percy's fiction, but the central focus is always upon the dilemma of being at once alive *in* this world and alive *to* it. Percy's nonfiction is principally concerned with the ways in which language impedes or enhances the business of being alive to this world and the next. It is southern only in the remarkable particularity of some of the images Percy uses.

Panthea Reid Broughton
Louisiana State University

Panthea Reid Broughton, ed., *The Art of Walker Percy: Stratagems for Being* (1979); Robert Coles, *Walker Percy: An American Search* (1978); Martin Luschei, *Walker Percy: The Sovereign Wayfarer* (1972); *Southern Quarterly* (Walker Percy issue, Summer 1982); J. O. Tate, in *Perspectives on the American South*, vol. 3, ed. James C. Cobb and Charles Reagan Wilson (1985).

Poe, Edgar Allan

(1809–1849) Writer.

The South's most renowned literary artist of the 19th century spent most of his productive years as a struggling journalist in large northern cities. Born on 19 January 1809, in Boston, Mass., Poe was the second child of David and Elizabeth Arnold Poe, both active theatrical performers on the East Coast of the United States. His father mysteriously disappeared in 1810, and after his mother's subsequent death, in December 1811, he became the foster son of John Allan, a prominent Richmond, Va., tobacco merchant who gave Poe many childhood advantages. In 1826 he attended the University of Virginia, leaving after only a few months to join the United States Army. His first volume of poems, entitled *Tamerlane and Other Poems*, was privately published in 1827; a second volume, *Al Aaraaf, Tamerlane, and Minor Poems*, appeared in 1829, shortly after he was honorably discharged from the army. Aided by his foster father, he entered West Point in 1830 as a cadet but was soon discharged for failing to heed regulations. Beginning in 1829, influential writers and journalists like John Neal and John P. Kennedy began to support his efforts to attain literary prominence. *Poems*, a third volume of poetry, was published in 1831.

Thoroughly trained in the classics and in the rhetoric and aesthetics of the Scottish common-sense school of philosophers, Poe was, according to the critic Robert D. Jacobs, indeed a southerner by temperament and inclination. Many of his formative years were spent in the southern cities of Richmond and Baltimore, the latter being the home of his blood relatives. Choosing a literary career after the death of his foster father, Poe began to contribute critical reviews to the Richmond *Southern Literary Messenger* in 1835 and later became its editor for two years. He married Virginia Clemm, his cousin who was less than 14 years old, in 1836. Until his death in 1849, Poe worked tirelessly as an editor and a reviewer, composing at the same time poetry, fiction, reviews, and essays of the highest literary excellence. He contributed to several noted American periodicals and newspapers; and in October 1845 he edited and briefly owned his own magazine, *Broadway Journal*.

Poe published his only major long piece, *The Narrative of A. Gordon Pym*, in 1838 and a short story collection, *Tales of the Grotesque and Arabesque*, in 1839. His poem "The Raven," printed in the New York *Evening Mirror* on 29 January 1845, brought him considerable recognition. *Tales*, a second collection of short stories, and a third volume of poems, *The Raven and Other Poems*, appeared in 1845. After the death of his wife in January

1847, he continued to write and to pursue his ambition of owning his own magazine. In early October of 1849, while traveling to New York to marry Sarah Royster Shelton, a widowed former sweetheart, Poe stopped in Baltimore, where he was later found ill on a city street. He died in a Baltimore hospital on 7 October 1849. His unexpected death was noted by nearly every significant newspaper and magazine in the eastern United States.

A controversial figure, Poe has been the subject of much speculative analysis. Generally, his biographers conclude that his instability as a person was in part due to the pressure of being a journalist. Although periodically he experienced poverty and the ill effects of poor health, Poe managed to perfect a variety of literary forms. He absorbed the current wave of romantic thought, which in his day brought significant changes in literary theory and practice. His classical bent, along with his background in Scottish philosophy and aesthetics, contributed to his theory of unity of effect and to his ideas about the short poem. He and Nathaniel Hawthorne introduced the ambiguities of symbolism in their Gothic tales, and Poe is credited with defining the short story as a distinct literary form. His attempts to formulate an objective method for writing poetry had some impact upon the French Symbolist poets of the later decades of the 19th century. In the area of popular literature, he is said to have fathered the modern detective story and some forms of science fiction.

Poe believed his art—all art—should be evaluated by international, rather than national or regional, standards, but he was, nonetheless, frequently identified at the time with the South. He did not defend his region's politics or social customs, like other antebellum southern writers, but his lyricism was common to southern poets. Raised a Virginian, Poe sometimes posed as the southern gentleman, even if transcending regionalism in his work.

J. Lasley Dameron
Memphis State University

James A. Harrison, ed., *The Complete Works of Edgar Allan Poe* (1902); Robert D. Jacobs, *Poe: Journalist and Critic* (1969); Arthur H. Quinn, *Edgar Allan Poe: A Critical Biography* (1941).

Porter, Katherine Anne

(1890–1980) Writer.

Porter was born in Indian Creek, Tex., on 15 May 1890, the fourth of five children born to Harrison Boone and Mary Alice Porter. Her mother's death before she was two and her father's ineffectuality as a provider led to her being brought up in poverty by her severely puritanical grandmother. Porter was so deeply affected by these events—the deprivation, the social embarrassment of being perceived, she thought, as "poor white trash," her father's emotional unreliability, and her grandmother's relentless prohibitions on her behavior—that throughout her life she reacted against or simply denied this early unhappiness.

Porter early began to rely on a vivid imagination to create a life—and soon a past—more palatable to her than that she experienced. She fabricated so many stories about herself, and was so persuasive in doing so, that biographers endlessly recorded "facts" that had never been true. Porter's imagination also contributed significantly to the richness of her finest stories, in which (through protagonists who were personae for herself) she described her family as once aristocratic, living in a plantation home with still-loyal former slaves, longing for more prosperous days. In writing such stories as "Old Mortality" and "The Old Order," Porter was like other southern writers who found the imagined past much more congenial than the troubled present. In a recurring character such as Miranda, Porter conveyed her sense of herself as a child of the "lost (Civil) War" and explored the historical, familial matrix out of which she had emerged.

Although Porter's stories are sometimes set in the South and the pasts remembered are often linked to southern history, Porter's larger themes are not uniquely southern. She was concerned with the universal issue of how human beings create myths about themselves that keep them from recognizing and responding to one another's needs, with how, indeed, the immersion in myth can lead human beings, through blindness, to be accomplices in evil. The children in her stories gradually learn the falsehood of adult myths and in doing so find their own loneliness confirmed. Porter's personal ambivalence toward these matters—her oscillation between human involvements as crippling and isolation as a kind of death—suggests the remarkable candor of her stories, whose power often resides precisely in their delineation of human failures.

In later years, public recognition of Porter's achievements included honorary degrees, Guggenheim Fellowships, Fulbright and Ford Foundation grants, the O. Henry Memorial Award, and the Pulitzer Prize. Although her only novel, *Ship of Fools* (1962), was considered a failure because of its heavy-handed ironies, Porter's place in American fiction was already secure. In the subtlety, precision, and insight of her best work, she had proven herself a genius of the short story.

Porter's major works include *Flowering Judas and Other Stories* (1930), *Pale Horse, Pale Rider: Three Short Novels* (1939), *The Leaning Tower and Other Stories* (1944), *The Old Order: Stories of the South* (1944), *The Days Before* (1952), *A Defense of Circe* (1955), *Ship of Fools* (1962), *Holiday* (1962), *The Collected Stories of Katherine Anne Porter* (1965), and *The Collected Essays and Occasional Writings of Katherine Anne Porter* (1970).

Gail L. Mortimer
University of Texas at El Paso

Jane Krause DeMouy, *Katherine Anne Porter's Women: The Eye of Her Fiction* (1983); Joan Givner, *Katherine Anne Porter: A Life* (1982); Myron M. Liberman, *Katherine Anne Porter's Fiction* (1971); William L. Nance, *Katherine Anne Porter and the Art of Rejection* (1964).

Ransom, John Crowe

(1888–1974) Writer and critic.

John Crowe Ransom was born 30 April 1888 in Pulaski, Tenn., the third of five children of Methodist minister John James Ransom and his wife Ella Crowe Ransom. John Crowe attended the Bowen preparatory school in Nashville, completing a rigorous program in classical languages, English, history, mathematics, and German. Entering Vanderbilt University at 15, he continued his classical studies. He was a Rhodes Scholar at University College, Oxford, from 1910 to 1912, reading widely in classics and philosophy. In 1914 Ransom accepted an instructorship in English at Vanderbilt, where he immediately began the method of teaching that, through texts written in the late 1930s and early 1940s by his former students Cleanth Brooks and Robert Penn Warren (the "New Critics"), was to dominate the teaching of literature in American colleges and universities for nearly 30 years: close analysis of individual texts with emphasis on the uses of language.

Except for army service during World War I, followed by a term at the University of Grenoble, Ransom remained in the English department at Vanderbilt until 1937 (teaching many summer sessions in other colleges and programs). His first volume of poetry, *Poems about God*, appeared in 1919.

In the fall of 1919 Ransom began meeting with the group that would, in 1922, begin to publish the *Fugitive*, a magazine whose name signified flight from "the high-caste Brahmins of the Old South" (according to Ransom's foreword). Ransom, an already-published poet and a respected teacher, was sought out for advice and judgment by such younger members of the group as Donald Davidson and Allen Tate (and later Warren, Andrew Lytle, Jesse Wills, and others). The *Fugitive*, which lasted 19 issues, from 1922 to 1925, and expired not for lack of funds but for want of an editor, published the bulk of Ransom's mature poetry, collected in the volumes *Grace after Meat* (1924) and *Chills and Fever* (1924). In 1927 *Two Gentlemen in Bonds* was published, containing some of Ransom's best poems: "Dead Boy," "Blue Girls," "Janet Waking," "Vision by Sweetwater," "Antique Harvesters," and "The Equilibrists."

John Crowe Ransom, Vanderbilt Agrarian, 1927

In *God without Thunder* (1930) Ransom proposed that new rationalistic theologies were destructive of the religious sense, for they destroyed a person's respect for the mysterious universe and elevated "science," which analyzes and uses "nature" rather than fearing and loving it. Ransom's religious ideas were coordinate with his defense of the South in "Reconstructed but Unregenerate," his essay for *I'll Take My Stand* (1930), and other essays about the South in contemporary society, such as "The South Defends Its Heritage" and "The South—Old or New?" For the former Fugitives and others who published *I'll Take My Stand*, the respect and love for nature associated with farming, especially family subsistence farming, were intimately bound up with the best social values of the culture—filial piety, kindliness, good manners, respect for the past, contemplativeness, and appreciation not only of the natural world but of art.

The publicity focused upon *I'll Take My Stand* and a series of debates related to it made the agrarian position a focal point for discussion of broad cultural values of American society. In an essay for a 1936 collection, *Who Owns America?: A New Declaration of Independence* (edited by Herbert Agar and Allen Tate), Ransom retreated from the extreme agrarian position, acknowledging that the South must accept industrialization in order to preserve economic autonomy. By 1940 Ransom had called the agrarian ideal a "fantasy" in the *Kenyon Review*, thus making public and final his defection from the economic position he had defended a decade before. The espousal of humane values—including respect for the mysteries—was not recanted but became the center of Ransom's poetic theory in *The World's Body* (1938), *The New Criticism* (1941), and later essays.

Ransom accepted a teaching position at Kenyon College in Gambier, Ohio, in 1937 and founded the *Kenyon Review* two years later. During Ransom's editorship of the *Kenyon Review* (1939–59), he published important works by such southern writers as Andrew Lytle, Randall Jarrell, Caroline Gordon, and Flannery O'Connor. Although Ransom had left the South and had abandoned the agrarian program, he remained a staunch spokesman for the aesthetic and ethical values formulated in the essays and poems of his Vanderbilt period. He died 2 July 1974, in Gambier, Ohio.

Suzanne Ferguson
Ohio State University

Louis D. Rubin., Jr., in *The New Criticism and After*, ed. Thomas Daniel Young (1976); John L. Stewart, *John Crowe Ransom* (1962); Thomas Daniel Young, *Gentleman in a Dustcoat: A Biography of John Crowe Ransom* (1976).

Simms, William Gilmore

(1806–1870) Writer.

Simms was born in Charleston, S.C., and lived much of his life in or near it, making frequent visits to northern publishing centers and to the Gulf Coast and the southern mountains. His extensive knowledge of southern regions influenced novels and tales set in the Low Country, such as *The Yemassee* (1835), *The Partisan* (1835), and *The Golden Christmas* (1852), which trace the development of the region from the colonial era through the Revolution and into the antebellum period. Simms also published border and mountain romances like *Richard Hurdis* (1838) and *Voltmeier* (1869), set in the antebellum backwoods South.

To a greater extent, perhaps, than any other 19th-century southern author, he gave a comprehensive picture of his region in its historical and cultural diversity—of the Low Country with its class hierarchy, its agrarian economy, its increasingly conservative politics, and its keen sectional self-consciousness; of the Gulf South, both civilized and violent, part plantation, part frontier; and of the Appalachian Mountain South in its pioneer phase. His writing exhibits qualities that mark southern literature from its beginnings: a sense of time and history, a love of southern landscape, a respect for southern social institutions, and a firm belief in class stratification and enlightened upper-class rule. In addition to fiction, poetry, drama, orations, and literary criticism, he wrote a history and a geography of South Carolina and biographies of Francis Marion, Captain John Smith, the Chevalier Bayard, and Nathanael Greene. At the beginning and near the end of his career, he edited several South Carolina newspapers, and in the 1840s and 1850s he served as editor of important southern journals, among them the *Magnolia*, the *Southern and Western*, and the proslavery *Southern Quarterly Review*, which gave voice to sectional issues.

The embodiment of southern letters, Simms was also an influential spokesman for what he saw as the region's social and political concerns. A unionist in the 1832 nullification controversy, in the 1840s he supported the intensely nationalistic Young America group, which pushed for American freedom from British literary models. Active in politics, he served in the South Carolina Legislature from 1844 to 1846, conferred with prominent planters like James Henry Hammond about southern agricultural policies, conducted a copious correspondence with fire-eating Beverley Tucker of Virginia about slavery and secession, and helped develop the proslavery argument. As his southern nationalism mounted in the 1840s and 1850s, he supported the annexation of Texas and advocated the creation of a southern empire in the Caribbean. When the Civil War broke out, he served as advisor to several southern politicians and made elaborate proposals for Confederate military defenses. During the war he wrote little of literary importance save the lively backwoods novel *Paddy McGann* (1863); after it, he ruined his health by the incessant writing and editing chores he took on to support his impoverished family. Energetic and often humorous, his work is important for its sweeping picture of the colonial and antebellum South in its regional diversity and also for its representation of continuing southern literary and intellectual issues.

Mary Ann Wimsatt
Southwest Texas State University

C. Hugh Holman, *The Roots of Southern Writing: Essays on the Literature of the American South* (1972); James E. Kibler, Jr., *The Poetry of William Gilmore Simms: An Introduction and Bibliography* (1978), with Keen Butterworth, *William Gilmore Simms: A Reference Guide* (1980); Mary C. Simms Oliphant et al., eds., *The Letters of William Gilmore Simms* (1952–56).

Stuart, Jesse

(1906–1984) Writer.

One of seven children, Stuart was born 8 August 1907 in a log cabin in W-Hollow near Greenup in the northeast corner of Kentucky. After attending Plum Grove school and completing high school in Greenup, Stuart graduated from Lincoln Memorial University (B.A., 1929) in Harrogate, Tenn., and did graduate work at Vanderbilt (1931–32) and George Peabody College in Nashville, Tenn. Stuart led a busy and productive life, writing nearly 50 books, serving as a teacher and administrator in local schools, and farming in his beloved W-Hollow. He died on 17 February 1984 and was buried in Plum Grove Cemetery near W-Hollow, his lifelong home.

Stuart spent over 50 years exploring his native locale and making good use of local characters and incidents. One of Appalachia's most prolific writers, Stuart portrayed southern mountain and hill people to a reading audience that was becoming interested in Appalachians as distinct cultural types. His W-Hollow stories, published in collections from *Head O' W-Hollow* (1936) and *Men of the Mountains* (1941) to *Thirty-Two Votes before Breakfast* (1974), depict elemental experiences of life—births, deaths, funerals, weddings, elections, marital and intergenerational relationships. His poetry, collected in several volumes from *Man with a Bull-Tongue Plow* (1934) to *Hold April* (1962), also celebrates the youth, men, and women of W-Hollow.

Many of Stuart's novels mirror a youth's (usually a narrator's) growing awareness of himself, an awareness shaped by the conflicting demands of a small nuclear family and the larger society that surrounds it. In *Trees of Heaven* (1940) young Tarvin Bushman sees the virtues of both the town and the hill way of life and is prepared at the end of the novel to try to merge the best qualities of the two. The young boy Sid, the outsider in the Tussie clan in *Taps for Private Tussie* (1943), gains knowledge of the Tussies and appreciation for "book-learning" and formal education. David Stoneking, in *Daughter of the Legend* (1965), has been part of the Melungeon culture and will presumably carry that culture beyond the setting of Sanctuary Mountain.

Stuart's own struggles in growing up and coming to a broader and deeper view of life are recorded in *Beyond Dark Hills* (1938). His efforts to educate youth are told in *The Thread that Runs So True* (1949) and *To Teach, To Love* (1970). His recuperation from a nearly fatal heart attack is described in *The Year of My Rebirth* (1956).

Stuart's last book, *The Kingdom Within* (1979), recounts an out-of-body experience in which Shan Powderjay, Stuart's fictional alter ego, attends his own funeral along with all of Stuart's "head children"—the fictional characters he created.

Donald H. Cunningham
Texas Tech University

J. R. LeMaster and Mary Washington Clarke, eds., *Jesse Stuart: Essays on His Work* (1977); H. Edward Richardson, *Jesse: The Biography of an American Writer—Jesse Hilton Stuart* (1984).

William Styron, Virginia author, 1982

Styron, William

(b. 1925) Writer.

Born and raised in Newport News, Va., William Styron received his preparatory education at Christchurch School, in rural Tidewater, and his college education in North Carolina, first at Davidson College and then at Duke. His earliest work was written at Duke under the tutelage of William Blackburn. After graduation in 1947 Styron left the South, and he has subsequently pursued his career in Europe and New York.

Styron's decision to live and to write outside the South has perhaps fueled critical disagreement over how closely his fiction should be linked to a regional context. With the publication of *Lie Down in Darkness* in 1951, some critics have noted a strong thematic, technical, and stylistic indebtedness to southern writers, especially William Faulkner and Robert Penn Warren. The dominant thrust of Styron criticism has been to weigh lightly these regional influences, concentrating instead on the universal dimensions of his themes and identifying broader contemporary ideas, from existentialism to the French *nouveau roman*.

Few who have read the entire corpus of Styron's work, however, would deny that important southern perspectives exist in his fiction. Much of the power of *Lie Down in Darkness* derives from the novel's highly evocative rendering of its suburban Tidewater country club setting, and Styron's strongly delineated characters are grotesque distortions of the conventional character stereotypes of southern gentleman, southern lady, and southern belle. Though Styron consciously moved his setting from Virginia to Europe in *Set This House on Fire* (1960), the novel's primary characters remain southerners, and they re-create the tragic narrative, sitting in a boat on the Ashley River a few miles from one of the South's oldest and most legendary cities. Styron returned triumphantly to his Virginia fictional terrain in *The Confessions of Nat Turner* (1967), a narrative of the infamous and bloody slave uprising, which enlists the Old Dominion's hallowed plantation tradition as part of a provocative and unflinching analysis of black rage. In Styron's most recent novel, *Sophie's Choice* (1979), the horrors of Auschwitz and of a fatally destructive relationship between a Polish concentration camp survivor and her brilliant but insane Jewish lover are filtered, much like the action of *Set This House on Fire*, through a point of view that is both intensely personal and southern.

William Styron does not share the historical perspective of an earlier generation of southern writers in which individual failure is inextricably linked to the failure of community or culture. It would be a mistake, however, to underestimate the importance of the South, and particularly of his native state, in his novels. Though he deftly inverts their romantic associations, the traditional staples of the southern novel—the plantation, the cavalier figure, and the idea of gentility—occupy an important place in Styron's fiction.

See also BLACK LIFE: / Turner, Nat

Ritchie D. Watson
Randolph-Macon College

Philip W. Leon, *William Styron: An Annotated Bibliography of Criticism* (1978); Robert K. Morris and Irving Malin, *The Achievement of William Styron* (1981); Marc L. Ratner, *William Styron* (1972).

Tate, Allen

(1899–1979) Writer and critic.

The most cosmopolitan of major modern southern writers, [John Orley] Allen Tate was a prime exemplar of his own theory that the highest artistic achievements come from a combination of native and foreign influences. He was born on 10 November 1899, in Winchester, Ky., a town in the heart of the Bluegrass country. Family loyalty first led him away from home, for he followed his elder brothers to Vanderbilt University in Nashville and there encountered the writers who were to determine the course of his life. John Crowe Ransom and Donald Davidson were his teachers, Robert Penn Warren was a younger fellow student, and all became colleagues in the *Fugitive* magazine, which began appearing in 1922 while Tate was still an undergraduate.

Allen Tate, Tennessee poet, early 1920s

By 1930 Tate had produced the centerpiece of modern southern poetry, the "Ode to the Confederate Dead," using techniques of imagery and deliberate fragmentation learned from foreign poetry to portray the experience of a native southerner who felt cut off from the traditional society he wished to memorialize. His theme in this masterful poem, as in the equally masterful literary essays he wrote and in his only novel, *The Fathers* (1938), was the decline, not simply of southern tradition but of the whole tradition of Western civilization, which he came to see as the result of the loss of religious faith. "Modern man suffering from unbelief," he wrote near the end of his illustrious career, was what all his writing was about.

Tate was by education and conviction a Renaissance man, a Classical Christian humanist, but by force of circumstance he became a modernist, trapped unwillingly in what he called "the squirrel cage of modern sensibility," a "provincialism of time" (more constrictive than the old provincialism of place) where solipsism, or uniquely personal intuition, was the sole alternative to scientific determinism, or positivism, as the measure of truth and value. His theory was that traditional society, where people were bound into community by ties of family, locale, and religion, had been replaced by industrial society, in which the only ties were economic and political; the southern writer's vantage point, living in a place where the agrarian community was still alive, if rapidly vanishing, made him an eyewitness to the change from traditional to industrial society, which in other places was already an accomplished fact.

Tate's definition of the Fugitive was "quite simply a Poet: the Wanderer, or even the Wandering Jew, the man who carries the secret wisdom about the world." He lived out this definition himself, as he went from Nashville to New York, where he became part of another group of writers, less regionally aligned, that included Hart Crane, Malcolm Cowley, and E. E. Cummings, then to Paris on a Guggenheim Fellowship, where he spent some time in the circle of Gertrude Stein, with Ernest Hemingway, Scott Fitzgerald, and Archibald MacLeish, then back to Southwestern College in Memphis, where he taught, to Princeton University, to the Library of Congress, as its first Consultant in Poetry, to the University of the South, where he edited the *Sewanee Review* for a few distinguished years, and finally to the University of Minnesota, where he became Regents Professor of English. His career had taken him far away from the South and earned him an international reputation and many honors, including the Bollingen Prize for Poetry and the presidency of the National Institute of Arts and Letters, but he had always remained a southerner as well as a Fugitive. At the end of his life he returned to Tennessee, where he died, in Nashville, on 9 February 1979.

Southerner, American, and internationalist in turn, Tate retained his regional identity all his life, nowhere more convincingly than in his late poem, "The Swimmers," where he recalled his Kentucky boyhood in an elegant series of *terza rima* stanzas that are a triumphant blend of the local and the universal. He wrote and edited many notable books; much of his best work can be found in *Collected Poems, 1919–1976* (1977); *Essays of Four Decades* (1968); and *Memories and Opinions, 1926–1974* (1975).

William Pratt
Miami University (Ohio)

Ferman Bishop, *Allen Tate* (1967); George Hemphill, *Allen Tate* (1964); Radcliffe Squires, ed., *Allen Tate and His Work: Critical Evaluations* (1972); Thomas Daniel Young and John Hindle, eds., *The Republic of Letters in America: The Correspondence of John Peale Bishop and Allen Tate* (1981).

Walker, Alice

(b. 1944) Writer.

Alice Walker's *The Color Purple* is saturated with the atmosphere of the South, the rural Georgia farmland of her childhood. Walker, who has written more than 10 books of poetry, fiction, biography, and essays, finds strength and inspiration in the land and the people: "You look at old photographs of Southern blacks and you see it—a fearlessness, a real determination and proof of a moral center that is absolutely bedrock to the land. I think there's hope in the South, not in the North," she says.

Alice Walker was born in 1944 in Eatonton, Ga., the youngest of eight children. Her parents were poor sharecroppers. As a child, she read what books she could get, kept notebooks, and listened to the stories her relatives told. She attended Spelman College in Atlanta and graduated from Sarah Lawrence College in Bronxville, N.Y., where her writing was discovered by her teacher Muriel Rukeyser, who admired the manuscript that Alice had slipped under her door. Rukeyser sent the poems to her own editor at Harcourt Brace, and this first collection of Walker's poetry, *Once*, was published in 1965. From 1966 through 1974 Walker lived in Georgia and Mississippi and devoted herself to voter registration, Project Head Start, and writing. She married Mel Leventhal, a Brooklyn attorney who shared her dedication to civil rights in his work on school desegregation cases. Their daughter Rebecca was born in 1970. After they left the South, Walker and Leventhal lived for a while in a Brooklyn brownstone, then separated. Alice Walker now lives in rural northern California, which she chose primarily for the silence that would allow her to "hear" her fictional characters.

Alice Walker, author of The Color Purple, *1976*

Alice Walker is the literary heir of Zora Neale Hurston and Flannery O'Connor. Walker has visited O'Connor's home in Milledgeville, Ga., and Hurston's grave in Eatonville, Fla., to pay homage. Walker's novels *The Third Life of Grange Copeland* (1977), *Meridian* (1976), and *The Color Purple* (1982) and short stories *In Love and Trouble* (1973) and *You Can't Keep a Good Woman Down* (1980) capture and explore her experiences of the South. She draws on her memories and her family's tales of Georgia ancestors in creating the portraits of rural black women in *The Color Purple*. Their speech is pure dialect—colloquial, poetic, and moving. Walker's poems too are filled with the rich landscape and atmosphere of the South.

Consciousness of the South has always been central to Alice Walker. The flowers and fruits in her California garden recall her mother's garden back in Georgia, a place so important to Walker that it became the inspiration for her collection of essays entitled *In Search of Our Mother's Gardens: Womanist Prose* (1983). Her mother's creativity was a compelling example to Alice Walker as well as a constant source of beauty amid the poverty of rural Georgia.

Among her many accomplishments and honors, Alice Walker has been Fannie Hurst Professor of Literature at Brandeis University and a contributing editor to *Ms.* magazine. In her writing and teaching she continually stresses the importance of black women writers. She edited a Zora Neale Hurston reader and a biography of Langston Hughes for children. Her literary awards include the Rosenthal Award of the National Institute of Arts and Letters, the Lillian Smith Award for her second book of poems, *Revolutionary Petunias* (1972), and the American Book Award and the Pulitzer Prize for fiction for *The Color Purple*.

Elizabeth Gaffney
Baruch College
City University of New York

David Bradley, *New York Times Magazine* (January 1984); Robert Towers, *New York Review of Books* (12 August 1982); Alice Walker, Atlanta *Constitution* (19 April 1983).

Warren, Robert Penn

(b. 1905) Writer.

Described by Allen Tate as the most gifted person he had ever known, Robert Penn Warren has excelled in every area in which his literary interest has taken him. Pulitzer Prize-winning novelist and poet, literary critic, social historian, biographer, editor and essayist, creator of plays and short stories, insightful co-writer of pedagogical guides to understanding literature and rhetoric, Warren has created a large body of work that reflects the major themes and concerns of the southern writer.

Born in 1905 in Guthrie, Ky., Warren entered Vanderbilt University at 16 in 1921. By 1923 he was a member of the Nashville Fugitive group, and in 1930 he contributed to that group's Agrarian manifesto, *I'll Take My Stand.* During the interim he had graduated summa cum laude from Vanderbilt, earned a master of arts degree in English at the University of California at Berkeley, and spent two years as a Rhodes Scholar at Oxford.

Warren's first published book, *John Brown: The Making of a Martyr* (1929), reflected his early interest in history, especially the tragic social and historic events that produced the 20th-century South. During the 1930s he taught at both Vanderbilt and Louisiana State University, collaborated on *An Approach to Literature* (with Cleanth Brooks and John T. Purser), wrote *Thirty-six Poems,* helped found the *Southern Review,* collaborated again with Brooks on *Understanding Poetry,* and published his first novel, *Night Rider.*

Warren's early work typifies the range of his interest in poetry, fiction, and criticism. The intelligence he and Brooks brought to bear on textual analysis in *Understanding Poetry* and its sequels shows through precept and example the major tenets of the New Criticism that had such a formative influence on American letters during the middle of this century.

The 1940s saw Warren move from Louisiana State University to the University of Minnesota and publish more poetry, criticism, novels, and short fiction. The most critically acclaimed of these was the Pulitzer Prize-winning *All the King's Men* (1946), a novel that is almost a case study in characteristic southern literary concerns. Based on the career of Huey P. Long, it considers such themes as man and change in history, the difficulty of self-knowledge, human responsibility, free will, problems of ends justifying means, and the southern social condition. It also demonstrates the southerner's characteristic concern with time and its meaning, his fascination with the power of rhetoric, and his propensity toward violence. His other major fiction includes *At Heaven's Gate* (1943), *World Enough and Time* (1950), *Band of Angels* (1955), *The Cave* (1959), *Wilderness* (1961), *Flood* (1964), *Meet Me in the Green Glen* (1971), and *A Place to Come To* (1977).

In 1950 Warren accepted a professorship at Yale, where he served until retirement. He became the only person ever to receive a Pulitzer Prize for both fiction and poetry when he received the award again in 1957 for *Promises: Poems 1954–1956.* In this and his subsequent poetry Warren treats personally the same themes of original sin, self-knowledge, love, and human possibilities he presents more objectively in his fiction. His meditations on history—*Brother to Dragons* (1953), *The Legacy of the Civil War* (1961), and *Jefferson Davis Gets His Citizenship Back* (1980)—deal with the same philosophical concerns.

Warren's creative energies have continued to sustain him. He has also continued to garner honors—a National Book Award, two Guggenheim awards, a MacArthur Foundation Fellowship, the Bollinger Prize for poetry, the National Medal for Literature, and even, for *Now and Then* (1978), a third Pulitzer Prize. In 1986 he was named the nation's first poet laureate.

Ladell Payne
Randolph-Macon College

Leonard Casper, *Robert Penn Warren: The Dark and Bloody Ground* (1960); Neil Nakadate, *Robert Penn Warren: A Reference Guide* (1977), *Robert Penn Warren: Critical Perspectives* (1981); Marshall Walker, *Robert Penn Warren: A Vision Earned* (1979).

Welty, Eudora

(b. 1909) Writer.

Born in Jackson, Miss., Eudora Welty attended Mississippi State College for Women and graduated from the University of Wisconsin. After attending Columbia University School of Business, Welty moved back to her home in Jackson, worked for the Works Progress Administration as a junior publicity agent, and began seriously to pursue a career as a writer. She has continued to live in Jackson and has received both the Pulitzer Prize and the American Book Award for fiction.

Welty has never belonged to a southern school of writers such as the Agrarians. Her fiction seldom deals with southern history, but the southern milieu informs her writing, perhaps most obviously in her depiction of family life. Welty's earliest stories tend to focus upon individuals unable to overcome a crippling isolation, and her subsequent fiction deals with complex family relationships. Only child Laurel McKelva Hand in *The Optimist's Daughter* (1972) learns to know herself by coming to understand the web of love and separateness that was her parents' marriage. On a larger scale, the extended southern families in *Delta Wedding* (1946) and *Losing Battles* (1970), whether they consist of prosperous Delta gentry or impoverished hill folk, know both the triumphs and the tragedies of their individual members. Though Welty does not portray family in the simplistic fashion that southern romances have made a cliché, she does share the South's preeminent concern with family life.

The oft-discussed southern sense of place also characterizes Welty's fiction, as she herself has noted. Southern writers, Welty has written, feel "passionately about Place. Not simply in the historical or philosophical connotation of the word, but in the sensory thing, the expe-

Eudora Welty, 1977

rienced world of sight and sound and smell, in its earth and water and sky and in its seasons." And certainly the "experienced world of sight and sound and smell" establishes a credible backdrop for all of Welty's stories, even those that rely upon fantasy or dream such as *The Robber Bridegroom* (1942) and *The Wide Net* (1943). But place in Welty's fiction also serves as an emblem of values or of their absence. The isolation of Tom Harris in "The Hitch-Hikers," Phoenix Jackson's harmony with nature and with man in "A Worn Path," the willful ignorance that typifies Morgana, Miss., in *The Golden Apples* (1949), the destructive incursions of modern society into this same community—all are inextricably tied to Welty's various uses of setting. The literary sense of place is mirrored in Welty's collection of Depression-era photographs, *One Time, One Place* (1971).

Throughout her stories, which were brought together and published in 1980 as *The Collected Stories of Eudora Welty*, Welty displays an acute ear for southern speech and storytelling. Tall-tale narration is seen in *The Ponder Heart* (1954). But nowhere is speech more vividly rendered than in *Losing Battles* (1970). This novel about a family reunion consists almost wholly of stories told by family members. The Vaughns and Beechams and Renfros retell old stories, they add new stories that will be retold at future reunions, and everyone participates in the telling—Percy with his "thready" voice, Etoyle who "embroiders," Aunt Beck with her "mourning dove's" voice, everyone. The sound of these voices draws the reader into *Losing Battles* and makes him part of the family reunion. The oral tradition of the South seems to live in the written word.

Finally, Welty's concern with time, with the overwhelming importance of the past, with human mortality is a concern that has always been central to great writers, with southerners notably among them. Welty has written, "We are mortal: this is time's deepest meaning in the novel as it is to us alive. Fiction shows us the past as well as the present moment in mortal light; it is an art served by the indelibility of our memory, and one empowered by a sharp and prophetic awareness of what is ephemeral. It is by the ephemeral that our feeling is so strongly aroused for what endures, or strives to endure." Such an awareness of mortality and of its implications for their lives proves crucial to Welty's progatonists—to Audubon in "A Still Moment," to Virgie Rainey in *The Golden Apples*, to Jack Renfro in *Losing Battles*. Indeed, it is a sense of human transience that permits Laurel McKelva Hand to realize more fully than any of Welty's other characters that life is "nothing but the continuity of its love."

In *One Writer's Beginnings* (1984) Welty explores, in three autobiographical essays, the experiences of her early life in Mississippi. In describing how she became a writer, she reveals the same sense of family, place, and time that informs all of her fiction. The book deals only briefly with the plots and characters in Welty's fiction, but it tells much about the concepts and values that make that fiction so profoundly significant and that make Eudora Welty one of the 20th century's most important writers.

Warren Akin IV
and Robert J. Linn
Floyd Junior College

Suzanne Marrs
State University of New York
at Oswego

Michael Kreyling, *Eudora Welty's Achievement of Order* (1980); Peggy Whitman Prenshaw, ed., *Conversations with Eudora Welty* (1984), *Eudora Welty: Critical Essays* (1979); Ruth M. Vande Kieft, *Eudora Welty* (1962); Robert Penn Warren, *Kenyon Review* (Spring 1944).

Williams, Tennessee

(1911–1983) Dramatist.

Tennessee [Thomas Lanier] Williams was born in Columbus, Miss., in 1911. His mother was the daughter of an Episcopal minister. His father, from Tennessee, had among his ancestors Sidney Lanier and Tennessee's first governor and first senator. A traveling salesman, he was home very little; and his wife and children, Williams and his older sister Rose, lived with his wife's parents. In about 1919 Williams's father moved his family to St. Louis, thus taking his children out of a traditional southern environment to a big-city life, in which at least part of the time they lived in apartments in relatively poor neighborhoods.

The nostalgia for a southern past reflected in plays such as his first two successes, *The Glass Menagerie* (1945) and *A Streetcar Named Desire* (1947), is in part clearly a product of Williams's bitter dislike of the new environment and his fond memories, perhaps exaggerated, of the old. Williams himself is reflected in Tom Wingfield in *Menagerie*, who, like Williams, became a wanderer because of his unhappiness with his home environment, and in Blanche DuBois in *Streetcar*, who, like Williams, bitterly misses her gracious past and finds the modern world alien and forbidding. *Streetcar* and a later play, *Cat on a Hot Tin Roof* (1955), won the Pulitzer Prize. After *The Night of the Iguana* (1962) his plays failed to be popular successes, but he continued to write and be produced. All his major plays are set in the South and concern southerners, except *Iguana* (Mexico) and the expressionistic *Camino Real* (1953; set in Central America).

His southerners represent a wide variety: most importantly, Tom's mother Amanda in *Menagerie*, a genteel southerner displaced in St. Louis; Blanche and her sister Stella, fallen aristocrats in lower-class New Orleans; Stella's husband Stanley Kowalski and his friends, born to the neighborhood; an upper-class New Orleans family in *Suddenly Last Summer* (1956); transplanted Sicilians in a Gulf Coast town in *The Rose Tattoo* (1951); middle-class small-town southerners and Latin American "invaders" in the early 20th century in *Summer and Smoke* (1948); a corrupt southern politician in *Sweet Bird of Youth* (1959); and poor white southerners risen to money and power in *Cat on a Hot Tin Roof*. Oddly, however, his plays include almost no blacks and none prominently.

The most important dramatist to come out of the South, Williams provided innumerable insights into southern life and character, conveying authenticity to southerner and non-southerner alike. Like Chekhov, his dramatic master, Williams's best plays go beyond the world of their origin to achieve portraits of human nature and human situations that are of universal interest and validity.

Despite a nervous collapse, alcoholism, drug dependence, and scant critical acclaim, Williams continued to write in his Key West, Fla., home until his death, at 71, in a New York hotel room. Ironically, and against his stated wishes, he was buried in Calvary Cemetery, in the city he claimed to despise. "He came into the theater bringing his poetry," dramatist Arthur Miller said in his final tribute, "his hardened edge of romantic adoration of the lost and the beautiful."

Jacob Adler
Purdue University

Esther Jackson, *The Broken World of Tennessee Williams* (1965); Jac Tharpe, ed., *Tennessee Williams: A Tribute* (1977); Nancy Tischler, *Tennessee Williams: Rebellious Puritan* (1961).

Wolfe, Thomas

(1900–1938) Writer.

His parentage and the time and place of Thomas Wolfe's birth created the cultural tug and pull underlying most of his writing. His father's Pennsylvania roots and his mother's close ties to the southern highlands were the first of many opposing forces that shaped Wolfe and were to be the subject matter of his plays and novels.

Thomas Wolfe and his mother at her boarding house, My Old Kentucky Home, Asheville, N.C., 1937

Born in a place (Asheville, N.C.) still suffering from the ravages of the Civil War and Reconstruction, Wolfe not only sensed the brighter prospects of the North but felt the clash of power and ideas that kept largely pro-Union western North Carolina and pro-Confederacy eastern North Carolina from solving scores of problems facing the state. "The Men of Old Catawba" explores some of the cultural differences dividing his native state.

Much of western North Carolina remained poverty stricken long after other areas of the state had begun to recover from the war. Yet amidst the poverty still evident in Asheville were signs of fabulous wealth, such as the building of the Biltmore House. Thousands of tourists crowding into such expensive quarters as Grove Park Inn began to vie with one another for choice lots in Asheville and surrounding towns. A boom in building seemed to point the way out of poverty and toward power for Ashevillians and their mountain neighbors. Wolfe's mother lodged many of the tourists in her boarding house, My Old Kentucky Home, and bought, swapped, and sold lots with such zeal and success that she became one of Asheville's wealthiest women. Asheville was thus aswirl with diverse groups of people and ideas when Wolfe was growing up there.

Beginning with *Welcome to Our City*, a play Wolfe wrote while at Harvard (1920–23), and continuing with *Look Homeward, Angel* (1929) and parts of *You Can't Go Home Again* (1940), Wolfe chronicled Asheville's hectic rush toward becoming a tourist mecca, and he reached back in *The Mountains* (1970), *The Hills Beyond* (1941), and *The Web and the Rock* (1939) to trace the patterns of migration, religious beliefs, political notions, and educational values linked to Asheville's southern highlands heritage, which was largely Scotch-Irish with an admixture of German, English, African, and Indian stock.

The time and place of Wolfe's collegiate education also helped to shape him and to provide materials for his plays and novels. When Wolfe attended the University of North Carolina, champions of the ideas and goals of the New South held important posts and were working to solve the economic, educational, and health problems of the state and region. Progressive teaching was in the air, but Wolfe still clung to many of the agrarian values of his maternal forebears, a position made clear in his sympathetic portrayal of Nebraska Crane in *You Can't Go Home Again*.

Still another shaping experience at Chapel Hill was his study of Hegelian philosophy under Horace Williams, who reinforced Wolfe's tendency to see opposite positions. As the late C. Hugh Holman showed many years ago, this philosophic training informs the picture Wolfe painted of the South and North and provides vital clues to understanding Wolfe and his surrogate protagonists, Eugene Gant and George Webber.

His graduate studies at Harvard, his subsequent teaching and writing career in New York City, and his European travels led Wolfe to see the provincialism of his youth, but at the same time the golden visions of the North inspired by his father's stories were growing tarnished. Wolfe's tumultuous affair with wealthy stage designer Aline Bernstein began in 1925 but ended in 1930 with his increasing resentment of her involvement in the sophisticated New York literary and theatrical scene. During the years following the 1929 stock market crash, Wolfe saw both human suffering and the heroic will to endure and thus turned from his Joycean dream of winning love, fortune, and fame to work toward achieving a dream of America he had had in France.

He would celebrate America, become her bard, speak as her prophet, embrace both the South and the North, and assume the mantle of Whitman. But Wolfe came to this bardic role with some limitations: he had not lost the mountaineer's penchant for deflating the social claims of plantation aristocrats, he excessively despised the money-grubbing proclivities of Snopesian people escaping from hard times, he too eagerly defined and described his world in Hegelian terms, and he had not overcome racial prejudice. Still, his achievement as a writer was enormous: one of his contemporaries, William Faulkner, ranked Wolfe as one of the nation's greatest writers.

John L. Idol, Jr.
Clemson University

David Donald, *Look Homeward: A Life of Thomas Wolfe* (1987); Leslie A. Field, comp., *Thomas Wolfe: Three Decades of Criticism* (1968); C. Hugh Holman, in *South: Modern Southern Literature in Its Cultural Setting*, ed. Louis D. Rubin, Jr., and Robert Jacobs (1961); Louis D. Rubin, Jr., *Thomas Wolfe: The Weather of His Youth* (1955); Floyd C. Watkins, *Thomas Wolfe's Characters: Portraits from Life* (1957).

Wright, Richard

(1908–1960) Writer.

Born near Natchez, Miss., on 4 September 1908, Richard Wright, like the famous protagonist of his first novel, was a native son. The child of a sharecropper who deserted the family in 1914, young Richard moved with his mother during his early years from one to another of the extended family's homes in Arkansas and Jackson, Miss., living in Memphis after he completed the ninth grade. Poverty and the fear and hate typifying post-Reconstruction racial relations in the Lower South, more than the sustaining power of black culture or education in segregated schools, prepared him to be an author. If he omitted from his autobiographical record his experience with middle-class values in his mother's family, or the effect of the motions and rituals of the black world, there was psychological truth in his record of nativity as written in *Black Boy* (1945). He was surely a product of the older South and of the great black migration to the cities; his distinction lay in his refusal to be simply a product.

In "The Ethics of Living Jim Crow," published in a WPA writer's anthology, *American Stuff* (1937), which first appeared in the year he moved from Chicago to New York City, Wright revealed the dynamics of his life's work as an author. Caste, he says, prescribed his public behavior; but though he knew its requirements, he would not accede. Terror could not induce him to adopt the pretense that he knew his place. Conflict was unavoidable and its only resolution was violence.

Uncle Tom's Children (1938, and expanded 1940), the collection of novellas with which Wright won his first literary success, indicates by an irony of its title the goal southern whites had for southern blacks. The stories are united by the theme of collective response to racist terror, as the children of Uncle Tom refuse to accept the popular stereotype.

Lawd Today was the first example of Richard Wright's extension of southern learning to life in the migrant black communities of the North, but this apprentice novel was not published until 1963. *Native Son* (1940) first carried his insights to a large and appreciative audience. A Guggenheim Fellowship to complete the novel, its selection by the Book-of-the-Month Club, and its arrival within weeks at the top of the best-seller list attested to the appearance of a major American author. In the compelling character of Bigger Thomas, Wright creates a complex symbol of a rising awareness that no risk is too great in order to become master of one's own life. Through creating sympathy for Bigger's violent actions, Wright carries the tradition of protest to new lengths.

Richard Wright, Mississippi-born writer who became an expatriate in France, c. 1940

His insider's view of Jim Crow earned Wright acclaim for his use of literary naturalism. His projection of violence and rebellion against social conditions led to his emergence as a major literary voice of black America.

Wright's next book, *12 Million Black Voices* (1941), presents a folk history extending from slavery's middle passage through the development of an Afro-American culture in the South and the hope of a black nation as a result of migration north. On the other hand, *Black Boy*, an ostensible autobiography representing the birth of the artist, necessarily suppresses the importance of group experience in order to focus on the power of the individual sensibility. Wright forged his identity among his people on southern ground but sought room to write by passage into modern life, symbolized by northern cities. This strategy becomes even clearer in the second part of the autobiography, published as *American Hunger* in 1977.

In time Wright found that Jim Crow knew no regional boundaries. Chicago and then New York constrained him as much as had Mississippi. So in 1946 he moved with his wife, Ellen Poplar, whom he had married in 1941, and their daughter to Paris. Suggestions have been made that the self-imposed exile, which was to last until Wright's death in 1960, sapped his creativity. To be sure, distance prevented intimate knowledge of contemporary changes in his native region and the black migrant communities; yet he created two novels concerning American racial relations and politics even after his exile. *The Outsider*, presenting an existentialist antihero living in Chicago and New York, appeared in 1953, and *The Long Dream*, a comprehensive reimagining of coming-of-age in Mississippi, appeared in 1958. Other fiction from the exile years includes *Savage Holiday* (1954), an experiment in raceless fiction, and the collection of stories, old and new, posthumously published as *Eight Men* (1961). This record of production hardly suggests flagging creativity.

Even more important to Wright's career, however, was the energy he found in exile to undertake four studies on a global scale. *Black Power* (1954) relates observations on his travels in the Gold Coast shortly before it became the nation of Ghana; *The Color Curtain* (1956) reports on the anticolonial positions developed at the conference in Bandung; *Pagan Spain* (1957) records a trip into a culture Wright viewed as a survival of premodern Europe; and *White Man Listen!* (1957) collects essays on race in America and the European colonies.

Despite the apparent departure from the experience of the American South in these later works, continuity exists between the original treatments of Jim Crow and the commentary on historical change in Africa and Asia. The prevailing subject remains race relations between whites and blacks, but beyond that is the more profound connection Wright saw in the special history of "colored" peoples. To be black in America, he believed, was to be marched forcibly into the pain of the modern world that even powerful white society could not fully comprehend. As a representative black American Wright already had lived the historical experience that awaited the Third World. By the power of literary imagination, Wright with matchless skill drew forth the significance of his southern education for world citizenship.

John M. Reilly
State University of New York
at Albany

Charles T. Davis and Michel Fabre, *Richard Wright: A Primary Bibliography* (1982); Michel Fabre, *The Unfinished Quest of Richard Wright* (1973); John M. Reilly, in *Black American Writers: Bibliographical Essays*, ed. M. Thomas Inge and Maurice Duke (1978).

Young, Stark

(1881–1963) Writer and critic.

Born in Como, Miss., 11 October 1881, Stark Young, a versatile figure in the Southern Literary Renaissance, devoted his life entirely to the arts and achieved widespread recognition for his contributions as teacher, poet, playwright, director, drama critic, fiction writer, essayist, translator, and painter. His parents were both descended from distinguished families who emigrated from the British Isles in the 17th and early 18th centuries.

Young's feelings and attitudes were powerfully influenced by the southern ways of living in Como and Oxford, Miss., to which his father moved after his second marriage. Young attended elementary school in Como and received his baccalaureate from the University of Mississippi. In 1902 he was awarded the master of arts degree from Columbia University. He taught English at the University of Mississippi, the University of Texas, and Amherst College, and began publishing poetry, plays, and aesthetic criticism.

After moving to New York in 1921, Young entered a period of intense activity in the theater. He became drama critic for the *New Republic* and a member of its editorial board as well as that of *Theatre Arts*. Soon he was recognized as the leading New York critic. He associated himself with the Provincetown Players and the Theatre Guild. His own plays, *The Colonnade* (1924) and *The Saint* (1925), both dealing with southern themes and reflecting Young's southern values, were produced with success. As early as 1923 he began to assemble from his drama criticism several volumes treating virtually every aspect of the theater: *The Flower in Drama* (1923), *Glamour* (1925), *Theatre Practice* (1926), and *The Theater* (1927).

While still involved in drama criticism, Young turned to fiction. He published *Heaven Trees* (1926), *The Torches Flare* (1928), and *River House* (1929). In 1930 he wrote the concluding essay, "Not in Defense, but in Memoriam," for *I'll Take My Stand*, supporting the manifesto of the Nashville Agrarians. In all of these works, as in others like *The Three Fountains* (1924), *Encaustics* (1926), *The Street of the Islands* (1930), and *Feliciana* (1935), Young's object was to identify those elements of life in the Old South that should be preserved in subsequent generations. His final novel, *So Red the Rose* (1934), was the most complete and powerful statement of his position. Although critical of the urban, industrial, highly competitive life in the North, Young had no desire to resurrect the southern civilization that had perished in the Civil War. Consistently, he defended the traditional values of the individual, the family, and the community, values that ultimately derived from classical humanism and the art of Western society.

By 1940 Young believed that the New York theater had declined notably from the promise and achievements of the 1920s and early 1930s. When changes at the *New Republic* rendered his position there less congenial, he began to think of retirement; and in 1947, after writing more than a thousand essays during the previous 40 years, he resigned. In 1959 he suffered a stroke from which he never fully recovered. He died 6 January 1963.

John Pilkington
University of Mississippi

Thomas L. Connelly, *Tennessee Historical Quarterly* (March 1963); John Pilkington, *Stark Young* (1985), ed., *Stark Young, A Life in the Arts: Letters 1900–1962* (1975).

Media

EDWARD D. C. CAMPBELL, JR.

Virginia State Library

CONSULTANT

Tennessee Ernie Ford as an announcer for WOPI *radio, Bristol, Tenn., 1939*

Media

In the late 1920s radio listeners in the South, and even nationwide, could tune in to KWKH in Shreveport and hear the exuberant W. K. Henderson sign on with "Hello, world, doggone you!" Each day, "talkin' to you," Henderson cajoled, attacked, and generally stirred up emotions. His program was in exaggerated form the embodiment of the mass media: communication to inform, to entertain, to influence, and to make money. He was also distinctly southern. Broadcasting from "Lou-ee-siana," he was representative of a print and broadcast media that traditionally had had regional characteristics.

By the mid-19th century the South had begun to stamp its identity on the region's early forms of media. *Southern Field and Fireside*, the *Southern Literary Messenger*, *Magnolia*, and the *Southern Planter* by title alone denoted periodicals attuned to a sectional readership. Little changed with the post–Civil War magazines; *Southern Opinion*, *The Land We Love*, *Southern Bivouac*, and especially *Confederate Veteran* left little doubt that a large part of the South was staunchly unchanged and a land apart.

After Reconstruction the other print medium—newspapers—helped bolster change and initiate a "New South." Francis Dawson's Charleston *News and Courier* in the 1880s pitted itself against the politics of "Pitchfork Ben" Tillman; Henry W. Grady of the Atlanta *Constitution* and Henry Watterson of the Louisville *Courier-Journal* stressed the region's need for new industry, refined agricultural techniques, and general social and economic progress. In many respects, southern print media were part of a national, and not just a southern, progressive trend. They reflected national patterns in growth as well. Taking newspapers as an example, by 1890 the number of weeklies had tripled nationally in just two decades. Correspondingly, in the South there were over 1,800 weeklies in 1890; just 20 years before, barely 500 existed.

But despite following broad trends in growth, business practices, journalistic techniques, and even slanting editorials in support of "progress," print media nonetheless remained very much a regional product. Local issues continued to dominate the news—in the South that often meant fashioning overblown claims of economic success and racial harmony.

By the first decades of the 1900s the region's magazines and journals reflected a healthy renewal. The new growth began with the University of the South's *Sewanee Review* in 1892. Although it first stressed southern literature, the later *South Atlantic Quarterly* printed essays on social and political topics. The *Virginia Quarterly Review* in 1925 and a new *Southern Review* in 1935 joined the renaissance of southern periodicals. Often affiliated with universities, the publications not only reflected the newest literature and most penetrating thinking of their region but with their academic associations and interests also spoke to a national audience on far broader issues of criticism, art, and social philosophy. Like the newspapers, however, they were still southern in outlook. Amidst examples of the New Criticism, there were, for instance, essays by John Crowe Ransom, Donald Davidson, and other so-called Agrarians warning against the headlong rush to modernization at the expense of the South's character.

But while the Charlotte *Observer* or Nashville's short-lived, innovative *Fugitive* magazine fulfilled media's functions to inform and influence, they had a relatively small audience. A new, burgeoning southern broadcast industry—whose primary functions were to entertain and to make money—garnered a far more enthusiastic following and, more important, a far broader one.

Within the first quarter of 1922, 11 radio stations received broadcast licenses, including WWL in New Orleans and Atlanta's WSB. During the 1930s growth slowed greatly, and the South could claim less than 12 percent of the country's radio listeners. Not until the late 1940s did the number of stations significantly expand.

The critical need for programming, though, created an outlet for the region's talent. The resulting impetus to showcase local country music performers led to a distinct southern radio format, Nashville's WSM being the most famous of numerous examples. In November 1925 the station began broadcasting the "WSM Barn Dance"; a year later the enormously popular show was renamed the "Grand Ole Opry," the regional counterpart to the "Grand Opera" network programs.

Spurred on by the popularity of turn-of-the-century nostalgic southern writers, theatrical and musical representations of the region's antebellum history, and even the attraction of the South to artists and lithographers, the infant film industry in the early 1900s turned to the region as a proven and easily recognizable topic for commercial motion pictures. The productions by their very number and success did as much to form southerners' views of themselves as they did to form the impressions of non-southerners.

To be sure, some productions were directed by native southerners—D. W. Griffith or King Vidor for instance—but primarily the complimentary media image of the South so prevalent between 1900 and 1945 was a product of outside forces. Some films, such as *Cabin in the Cotton* (1932) or *In This Our Life* (1942), were not by any means positive media views of the South's poor or privileged. But the vast majority, and there were hundreds of films on the Civil War alone, presented a genial, pleasurable land in musicals such as *Dixiana* (1930), light dramas such as *Virginia* (1941), and even comedies like *Steamboat 'Round the Bend* (1935).

Stereotypes of the region and its pace of life were widespread and popular in other media, too. For example, the nation's newspaper comic pages presented delighted readers with a range of humorous, likable characters. Most successful were William Morgan De Beck's 1934 creation *Barney Google and Snuffy Smith*; Al Capp's *Li'l Abner*, first introduced the same year; and Walt Kelly's *Pogo*, syndicated in 1948.

After 1945 the South continued to be a source of media material. Different times, though, influenced the media to develop a different product and view. In the motion picture industry demands for new story lines, more contemporary attitudes, and even more excitement influenced Hollywood, for instance, to increase greatly its film adaptations of the works of William Faulkner, Tennessee Williams, Robert Penn Warren, Ellen Glasgow, Carson McCullers, Erskine Caldwell, and Lillian Hellman. The South was hardly the same; from a film image represented by, say, *Jezebel* in 1938, the South by the 1960s was instead best symbolized in film by *Cat on a Hot Tin Roof* (1958).

Besides the popular, national media, the media within the region after World War II also reexamined old assumptions. Newspapers in particular once again scrutinized the South. Newspapermen such as George Fort Milton of the Chattanooga *News*, Jonathan Daniels of the Raleigh *News and Observer*, and Mark Ethridge of the Macon *Telegraph and News* and later the Louisville *Courier-Journal* all represented the increasingly liberal attitude among the region's editorial writers. Virginius Dabney of the Richmond *Times-Dispatch* attacked a range of regional ills: religious fundamentalism, the poll tax, and segregation. The Atlanta *Constitution*'s Ralph McGill labeled the separate-but-equal doctrine "undemocratic" and won a Pulitzer Prize in 1959 for a series on racial terrorists.

The preoccupation with matters southern was not so nearly duplicated in the region's post-1945 magazines, however. The number of magazines edited and printed in the South continued to grow, but new probing publications such as *Southern Exposure* became fewer; even the South's periodicals of primarily a regional orientation declined. Magazines such as *Southern Living*, with a 1.9 million circulation, or *Southern Interiors* were outdone by, for example, *Boys' Life*, with 1.5 million subscribers, and *Mother Earth News* with 1 million readers.

The newest southern broadcast industry, television, reflected the same trends since 1945: sustained growth in southern outlets matched by declining attention paid the region itself. Television, like radio 25 years earlier, grew slowly at first and then steadily. Richmond's WTVR secured the South's first license in 1948, but it was not until 1953 that each southern state could claim a station. As with radio, initially the local stations filled airtime with local talent and religious programming. But by 1980 the southern television industry included 350 stations, 32 percent of the national total; by then, many of the stations were no longer particularly southern, but were parts of broadcast groups, such as LIN Broadcasting headquartered in Cincinnati with stations in Tennessee and Virginia. Atlanta's Cable News Network and WTBS, like their smaller counterparts, were not even intended to reflect a regional reference point.

However, if the South's commercial stations had forsaken regional themes, the commercial networks did not. Network television, like film, sustained an interest in portraying the South. From *The Andy Griffith Show* to *The Beverly Hillbillies* and *Carter Country*, to *The Waltons* and the *Dukes of Hazzard*, the region's rural scene has still proved popular and profitable. More serious programming—*Roots* or *The Autobiography of Miss Jane Pittman*—has proved probing material can succeed as well.

Programming reflective of the stations' locale, therefore, has increasingly become the preserve of the South's noncommercial, educational television stations. For instance, SCETV in Columbia, S.C., the University of North Carolina's educational station, and both Alabama's and Kentucky's statewide ETV systems have produced popular and news programs on Afro-American history, state politics, and adaptations of regional literature.

Southern media—in the form of newspapers, magazines, journals, and more recently radio and television—has evolved from a means of communication often logically enmeshed in regional concerns and interests to institutions intent on presenting the South's diversity and sometimes exposing its admitted shortcomings.

See also BLACK LIFE: Film Images, Black; Press, Black; INDUSTRY: / Grady, Henry W.; LITERATURE: Agrarianism in Literature; New Critics; Periodicals; / Davidson, Donald; Ransom, John Crowe; MUSIC: / Grand Ole Opry; MYTHIC SOUTH: / Agrarians, Vanderbilt

Edward D. C. Campbell, Jr.
Virginia State Library

Erik Barnouw, *Tube of Plenty: The Evolution of American Television* (1975); *Broadcasting-Cablecasting Yearbook: 1985* (1985); Edward D. C. Campbell, Jr., *The Celluloid South: Hollywood and the Southern Myth* (1981); Thomas D. Clark, *The Southern Country Editor* (1948); Thomas J. Cripps, *Slow Fade to Black: The Negro in American Film, 1900–1942* (1977); Warren French, ed., *The South and Film* (1981); William C. Havard, *Virginia Quarterly Review* (Winter 1983); M. Thomas Inge, ed., *Handbook of American Popular Culture* (1978–81); Jack Temple Kirby, *Media-Made Dixie: The South in the American Imagination* (1978); J. Fred MacDonald, *Blacks and White TV: Afro-Americans in Television since 1948* (1983), *Don't Touch That Dial: Radio Programming in American Life, 1920–1960* (1979); Horace Newcomb, *Appalachian Journal* (Autumn–Winter 1979–80); Sam G. Riley, *Magazines of the American South* (1986); Peter A. Soderbergh, *Mississippi Quarterly* (Winter 1965–1966); Morton Sosna, *In Search of the Silent South: Southern Liberals and the Race Issue* (1977); *Southern Exposure* (Winter 1975); George B. Tindall, *The Emergence of the New South, 1913–1945* (1967).

Actors and Actresses

Actors are trained to depict fictitious characters who have no relation to the actor's personal life. There is no reason, therefore, why any capable actor cannot play a southerner on the stage or in a movie, or why a southern actor cannot assume the roles of non-southern characters. Indeed, many of the most famous southern characters in movies have been played by actors born outside the South. Clark Gable (Rhett Butler) was born in Cadiz, Ohio, and Vivien Leigh (Scarlett O'Hara and Blanche DuBois) was a British citizen born in India. Bette Davis, remembered for several southern roles, most notably in *Jezebel* (1938) and *The Little Foxes* (1941), was born in Massachusetts. Gregory Peck, from La Jolla, Calif., played the model southern liberal in *To Kill a Mockingbird* (1963); and Broderick Crawford, from Philadelphia, played the demagogue Willie Stark in *All the King's Men* (1949). And, of course, actors born and reared in the South have often made their reputations in roles that had nothing to do with their southern background.

The South has, in any event, produced some of the best actors to grace the silver screen. From bit players to important stars, actors from the South have become an integral part of the American myth of Hollywood. Perhaps one facet of southern life that has influenced youth in the region toward acting is the southern penchant for storytelling. Most southerners, however, have had to leave the state of their birth in order to pursue their careers, and only a few, such as Burt Reynolds, have consistently returned to the South to make movies.

No list with limited space can catalog all southern actors, but what follows is a sketch of some actors who were born in the South, with an emphasis on their southern roles, if any. As with many entertainers, the dates and places of birth are often questionable, as records are sometimes contradictory, but care has been taken to use data from reliable sources. The actors are here arranged geographically.

Virginia. Bill Robinson (born in Richmond in 1878, died in 1949) made his fame as Bojangles, the tap dancer with Shirley Temple. In both *The Little Colonel* (1935) and *The Littlest Rebel* (1935) he played the faithful family servant and accompanied Temple in some of her best-remembered dance routines. In *So Red the Rose* (1935) Randolph Scott (Orange County, 1903) played Duncan Bedford, son of the Old South during the Civil War. He also carried his southern demeanor into numerous westerns, such as *The Texans* (1938) and *Fort Worth* (1951). Joseph Cotten (Petersburg, 1905) played the good Texan in *Duel in the Sun* (1946) as well as the family physician in *Hush . . . Hush, Sweet Charlotte* (1964). Margaret Sullavan (Norfolk, 1911–60) was Valette Bedford, the young belle of the southern household in *So Red the Rose.* Sister and brother Shirley MacLaine (Richmond, 1934) and Warren Beatty (Richmond, 1937) heard family stories of the South from their father. She played the daughter in a southern family full of conflict in *Hot Spell* (1958), and he achieved fame as Clyde Barrow racing across Texas and Oklahoma with Bonnie Parker in *Bonnie and Clyde* (1967). Other Virginia actors and examples of their films with southern settings include Richard Arlen, Lynn Bari (*Man from Texas*), James Bell (*Streets of Laredo*), Jack Holt (*The Littlest Rebel*), Mae Murray (*To Have and to Hold*), John Payne (*El Paso*), and George C. Scott.

North Carolina. Sidney Blackmer (Salisbury, 1896–1973) had small roles in *The Little Colonel* and *Duel in the Sun*, and then played an aging author living in a southern town in *The View from Pompey's Head* (1955). Ava Gardner (Smithfield, 1922) sang her way through the part of Julie Laverne in *Show Boat* (1951) and also sang in *Lone Star* (1952), a historical drama set in the early days of Texas. Kathryn Grayson (Winston-Salem, 1923) was also both singer and actress. She sang in *The Toast of New Orleans* (1950) and *Show Boat* (1951). In *The Vanishing Virginian* (1942) she had played Rebecca Yancey of Virginia in a sentimental account of the Old South. Andy Griffith (Mount Airy, 1926) created the role of Will Stockdale, the hayseed who enjoys the army in *No Time for Sergeants* (1958). He also played Lonesome Rhodes, a country boy in Arkansas who gains fame and power, in *A Face in the Crowd* (1957).

South Carolina. This state has produced few who followed the actor's trade. Nina Mae McKinney (Lancaster, 1913–67) was selected by King Vidor to play Chick, the female temptress, in *Hallelujah* (1929), his all-black musical.

Georgia. Charles Coburn (Savannah, 1877–1961) had the title role in *Colonel Effingham's Raid* (1945), in which he played a retired Confederate officer who sets life straight in a Georgia town. Generally known for his suave, sophisticated roles, Melvyn Douglas (Macon, 1901–81) had a different role in *Hud* (1963), in which he played the head of a tough modern Texas family. He returned to his more accustomed roles in *Hotel* (1967) where, as the cultured owner of a hotel in New Orleans, he tried to preserve the hotel's aging charm. Joanne Woodward (Thomasville, 1930) achieved fame playing a Georgia woman with three personalities in *The Three Faces of Eve* (1957). She went on to depict Faulkner women in *The Long Hot Summer* (1958) and *The Sound and the Fury* (1959). Burt Reynolds (Waycross, 1936) is the prototype of the southern "good old boy," a persona he created as Gator McKlusky in *White Lightning* (1973) and *Gator* (1976) and as the Bandit in *Smokey and the Bandit* (1977). In his more serious roles Reynolds can project another side of southern character, as he did in *Deliverance* (1972). Other Georgia actors have included Claude Akins (*The Defiant Ones* and *Inherit the Wind*), May Allison, Edward Andrews, Oliver Hardy (*The Fighting Kentuckian*), Miriam Hopkins, Louise Huff, Stacy Keach (*The Heart Is a Lonely Hunter*), Lee Tracy, and Jane Withers.

Florida. Prissy in *Gone with the Wind* (1939) was played by Thelma "Butterfly" McQueen (Tampa, 1911). She also had a role in *Cabin in the Sky* (1943). Even though Sidney Poitier was born in Miami almost by accident (his Bahamian parents were there on business), he later moved there and grew up in that southern city. In *The Defiant Ones* (1958) he played Noah Cullen chained to Tony Curtis on a southern chain gang. In *In the Heat of the Night* (1967) he was Virgil Tibbs, a Philadelphia detective visiting his mother in a small southern town; and he had the lead role in *Porgy and Bess* (1959), George Gershwin's musical set in Charleston, S.C. Faye Dunaway (Bascom, 1941) was the Texas country girl Bonnie Parker, looking for a way out of her small hometown in *Bonnie and Clyde.* She also played a member of a gang kidnapping an old man in Miami in *The Happening* (1967). Other Florida actors include Elizabeth Ashley, Judy Canova (*Louisiana Hayride, Carolina Cannonball*), Pat Boone (*Mardi Gras*), Wanda Hendrix, Frances Langford (*Mississippi Gambler, Dixie Jamboree*), Lincoln Perry (Stepin' Fetchit), and Ben Vereen (*Roots*).

Alabama. Ben Cameron, the Little Colonel, perhaps one of the best examples of mythical southerners from *Birth of a Nation* (1915), was played by Henry B. Walthall (Shelby County, 1878–1936). The film had been directed by the most southern of directors, D. W. Griffith, from Kentucky, who had begun his career as an actor. Walthall had acted in *In Old Kentucky* (1909) and later was to play southern roles in a remake of *Tol'able David* (1930) and in *Cabin in the Cotton* (1932). Other actors from Alabama include Mary Anderson, Tallulah Bankhead, Gertrude Michael (*Flamingo Road*), and Gail Patrick (*Mississippi*).

Tennessee. Of all southern actresses, perhaps Elizabeth Patterson (Savannah, 1874–1966) played the most roles with southern connections. In addition to numerous minor roles as a southern woman, she played the grandmother in *The Vanishing Virginian*, the lady who stands up against a lynch mob in *Intruder in the Dust* (1949), and the prim old wife in *Tobacco Road* (1941). George Hamilton (Memphis, 1939) played the son in a Texas family in *Home from the Hill* (1960) and Hank Williams in the movie biography of the country singer, *Your Cheatin' Heart* (1965). Other Tennessee actors include singer Dolly Parton and Marjorie Weaver (*Kentucky Moonshine*).

Kentucky. Patricia Neal (Packard, 1926) has played contrasting southern roles. In *Bright Leaf* (1950) she was a rich girl, but in *Hud* she was the hard-bitten housekeeper for the Bannon men. Warren Oates (Depoy, 1928) made his reputation playing tough characters in numerous westerns. In *In the Heat of the Night* he depicted the local deputy in the Mississippi town visited by Virgil Tibbs. Other Kentucky actors include William Conrad (*Lone Star*), Irene Dunne (*Show Boat*), Henry Hull (*El Paso*), Arthur Lake, Victor Mature, and Una Merkel (*Comin' Round the Mountain* and *The Kentuckian*).

Mississippi. Dana Andrews (Collins, 1909) had two important southern roles in the same year. He was Dr. Tim in John Ford's version of Erskine Caldwell's novel *Tobacco Road*, and he was also featured in Jean Renoir's film set in Georgia, *Swamp Water* (1941). Elvis Presley (Tupelo, 1935–77) began his movie career with several southern films—*Love Me Tender* (1956), *Loving You* (1957), and *King Creole* (1958). His persona was usually some variation of the poor boy singer who overcomes obstacles to make good and win the girl. Other Mississippi actors include Roscoe Ates, James Earl Jones (*The Great White Hope*), Larry Semon, and Stella Stevens.

Louisiana. Dorothy Lamour (New Orleans, 1914), best remembered for her "Road" films with Bob Hope and Bing Crosby, made a film with Crosby called *Dixie* (1943). In it she played the girlfriend of Dan Emmett, the author of the song "Dixie." Jeffrey Hunter (New Orleans, 1926–69) played in many westerns, some of which were set in Texas, such as *Three Young Texans* (1954) and *The Man from Galveston* (1964). In the Walt Disney version of *The Great Train Robbery* (1956) he had the role of the Confederate conductor who leads the chase to recover the stolen train. Other Louisiana actors include Mary Alden (*Birth of a Nation*), Louis Armstrong (*New Orleans*—playing himself), Ben Turpin (*Uncle Tom without the Cabin*), Kitty Carlisle, and Paul Burke.

Texas. In *Flamingo Road* (1949) Joan Crawford (San Antonio, 1908–77) had the role of a carnival girl who retired to a crude southern town. In this role she was courted, then given up, by another Texan, Zachary Scott (Austin, 1914–65), who also starred in another Renoir film set in the rural South, *The Southerner* (1945). Audie Murphy played himself as war hero in *To Hell and Back* (1955) and Billy the Kid in *The Kid from Texas* (1950). Biography also was well suited to Sissy Spacek (Quitman, 1949). In *Coal Miner's Daughter* (1980) she portrayed singer Loretta Lynn, who is from Butcher Holler, Ky. Other Texans in the movies include John Arledge (*Gone with the Wind*), Gene Autry (*Texans Never Cry*), Joe Don Baker (*Walking Tall*), Florence Bates (*San Antonio*), John Boles (*The Littlest Rebel*), Carol Burnett, Vikki Carr, Bebe Daniels (*Dixiana*), Linda Darnell, Sandy Duncan, Shelly Duvall (*Nashville*), Dale Evans (*The Yellow Rose of Texas*), Corinne Griffith, Hope Hampton, Ann Harding, Martha Hyer, Carolyn Jones (*King Creole*), Evelyn Keyes (*Gone with the Wind*), Guy Kibbee, Bessie Love, George McFarland (Spanky in *The Little Rascals*), Fess Parker (*Davy Crockett*), Valerie Perrine (*The Last American Hero*), Paula Prentiss, Debbie Reynolds, Ann Sheridan, and Rip Torn (*Sweet Bird of Youth*).

Robert A. Armour
Virginia Commonwealth University

Ephraim Katz, *The Film Encyclopedia* (1979); *The New York Times Film Review, 1913–1968* (1970); David Thomson, *A Biographical Dictionary of the Cinema* (1975); *The World Almanac and Book of Facts, 1987* (1986).

Civil Rights and Media

Both print journalism and electronic journalism nurtured dramatic images of the South during the civil rights movement, and both changed as a result of it. The early years of the movement in the South from 1954 to 1965 came at a time of tremendous technological advancement in the media. The rise of national network-news reporting in the United States coincided with the first years of the civil rights movement. The relationship between the two is complex because television news developed into a national medium partly through its experiences in the South during the civil rights struggle, and civil rights organizers and activists learned to use the emerging electronic press as a means of advancing their agenda.

A national press, and especially a visually oriented media, made the sweeping changes in the South not only possible but imperative by propelling the civil rights struggle into the homes of Americans across the country and even into the White House. At the same time, journalists themselves recognize that the civil rights movement helped to shape the operation of television and radio network journalism for the future. Such veteran reporters and photographers of the civil rights story as John Chancellor, Harry Reasoner, Dan Rather, Chuck Quinn, Herbert Kaplow, Robert Schakne, Jack Nelson, Haynes Johnson, and David Halberstam are among today's best-known journalists.

One of the earliest uses of media in civil rights was a documentary produced by Howard University School of Law professor Charles Houston. In 1930 Houston traveled to South Carolina to record for the National Association for the Advancement of Colored People the disparity between black schools and white schools. He used a 16mm camera to produce *Examples of Educational Discrimination among Negroes in South Carolina*, a documentary film showing graphically the reality of racial discrimination among schoolchildren.

The 1955 trial in Mississippi of two white men, Roy Bryant and J. W. Milam, accused of murdering 14-year-old Emmett Till from Chicago, became one of the first media events of the modern civil rights movement. Both the white and black national press arrived in Money, Miss., to report on the trial. The Emmett Till case provides an example of the patterns of media coverage that would continue for most of the civil rights era. Local law enforcement officials developed a siege mentality once the national press became involved. They quickly moved from a vigorous prosecution of the two accused of killing Till to a refusal to even acknowledge that it was Till's body that was found. The local press became defenders of the prevailing southern white attitudes in racial conflicts.

The members of the press themselves were segregated. White journalists from around the country and from the state were seated near the front of the courtroom, while black journalists were seated in the back of the room at a card table. Besides *Jet* magazine, reporters and correspondents came from *Ebony* magazine, the Chicago *Defender*, the Pittsburgh *Courier*, the Baltimore *Afro-American*, the *Amsterdam News*, and the National Negro Press Association. Seated with them were Till's mother and a black member of Congress. *Jet* magazine's publication of the mutilated face of the corpse signaled one of the most important roles the media played in reporting the civil rights story. The *Jet* photograph was responsible for outrage across the nation and a mobilization of the black community.

Throughout the years of the civil rights movement, reporters and photographers from both the electronic media and the print media shaped the image of the South in the nation and the world. White community leaders tried to use the news media to gain support among white Americans for "our way of life," while black leaders used the media to show the inhuman and un-American treatment of blacks in the South. Community leaders became concerned about the future of economic development in the South as the violence and racial strife were broadcast across the country.

Civil rights leaders such as the Reverend Martin Luther King, Jr., soon realized the impact that the presence of the national media could have on the success or failure of a project. Civil rights strategists began to plan events that would attract the attention of the national press, especially television crews. When the media arrived, the chances of success for the movement improved. The national media became the ally of civil rights leaders in presenting their case to an American public.

The presence of the national press did not guarantee success. The Albany, Ga., campaign (November 1961–August 1962) by King is one example of a civil rights protest that failed even with the presence of the national press. The Albany campaign saw mass arrests, including that of King, but the deft handling of the situation by Sheriff Laurie Pritchett and other local white leaders prevented the campaign from winning its civil rights goals.

Few civil rights protests were as well contained by white leaders as those at Albany. Southern white intransigence at King's next campaign, in Birmingham during April and May of 1963, resulted in televison and newspaper accounts of police dogs attacking demonstrators and firehoses spraying black children. Police commissioner Theophilus Eugene "Bull" Connor emerged from the ugly violence as a major symbol of racial conflict. The emotional responses these scenes evoked shook the nation and forced Birmingham leaders to deal with civil rights leaders. In March 1965 the American Broadcasting Company interrupted its regularly scheduled programming to broadcast the graphic images of people being trampled by police horses at the Edmund Pettus Bridge in Selma, Ala. Those scenes of "bloody Sunday" brought thousands of people to Alabama to make the march to Montgomery from Selma. President Lyndon B. Johnson announced the introduction of voting rights legislation within days of the broadcast of the scenes from Selma.

Technology had made possible live addresses from the White House and Congress, and Presidents Dwight Eisenhower, John F. Kennedy, and Johnson used this means to communicate national government expectations to southern leaders. Perhaps the most ironic use of the live televised address was the appeal by President Kennedy for a peaceful solution to the threat of violence at the University of Mississippi on the Sunday that James Meredith arrived on campus. Kennedy's words to the state were echoing through televison sets across the nation as rifle fire and tear gas bursts were resounding on the campus.

The president's power to command media attention was once used to circumvent a civil rights activist's access to the national media. President Johnson envisioned the 1964 Democratic Convention as a harmonious meeting to confirm his leadership of the party and nominate him for the presidency. Mississippian Fannie Lou Hamer's testimony before the Credentials Committee was carried live by the television networks, and her story of the beatings she suffered in Mississippi was so dramatic that it threatened to disrupt the convention. This so angered President Johnson that he ordered his aide to announce an immediate presidential press conference. Johnson's strategy kept Hamer off the air temporarily, but her testimony was given extensive coverage during the evening news.

Southerners who became journalists in the civil rights era were frequently from rural backgrounds where segregation was not challenged. Often their experiences in reporting changed their beliefs about race relations in the South. Many of these reporters came to recognize that the southern system of segregation was morally and legally wrong. Other southern white journalists and white-owned newspapers as well as broadcast stations continued to uphold racial segregation.

Black and white journalists often were in physical danger. White journalists in some cases were especially vulnerable because they were visible outsiders in the midst of predominantly black activists or protesters; segregationists accused the journalists of provoking racial troubles. Throughout the civil rights struggle, journalists and photographers were targets for segregationist violence. Several were beaten, including National Broadcasting Company reporter Richard Valeriani. One journalist, French reporter Paul Guihard, was killed during the riot on the University of Mississippi campus in 1962.

In 1987 the Public Broadcasting System aired the six-part series, *Eyes on the Prize*, produced by Blackside Productions. The series told the story of the civil rights movement in the South through news and television footage and with interviews with civil rights participants and reporters. This compilation of photographs and film footage proved that media coverage of the civil rights movement has left an enduring visual and aural image of a crucial period in southern history. The University of Mississippi sponsored a 1987 symposium on civil rights and the media and has recorded videotaped oral history interviews with journalists who covered the story.

See also BLACK LIFE: Freedom Movement, Black; LAW: Civil Rights Movement

Marie Antoon
University of Mississippi

Jack Bass and Jack Nelson, *The Orangeburg Massacre* (1970; rev. ed., 1984); Clayborne Carson, *In Struggle: SNCC and the Black Awakening of the 1960s* (1981); *Covering the South: A National Symposium on the Media and the Civil Rights Movement* (videotapes, Center for the Study of Southern Culture, University of Mississippi, 1987); David J. Garrow, *Protest at Selma: Martin Luther King, Jr., and the Voting Rights Act of 1965* (1979); Howell Raines, *My Soul Is Rested: The Story of the Civil Rights Movement in the Deep South—Told by the Men and Women Who Made It Happen* (1977); Juan Williams, *Eyes on the Prize: America's Civil Rights Years, 1954–1965* (1987).

Comic Strips

For almost 40 years, except for an occasional appearance or incidental use as background, the South did not feature in the American comic strip. In 1934, however, two cartoonists turned to southern materials and produced characters that were to influence the way the larger population has viewed southerners.

A young artist from Connecticut named Alfred Gerald Caplin, or Al Capp, first discovered the charm of the South while ghosting some comic-strip sequences about hillbilly characters for Ham Fisher's *Joe Palooka* in 1933. On 20 August 1934 the world saw the debut of his own creation, *Li'l Abner*, which eventually would reach approximately 60 million readers in 900 American newspapers and 100 foreign papers in 28 countries.

The central character, Abner Yokum, was a large, handsome, and hopelessly naive young man who, along with his parents, Mammy and Pappy Yokum, his girlfriend, and later wife, Daisy Mae, and the other residents of Dogpatch, represented for Capp a kind of innocence that he described in this way: "This innocence of theirs is indestructible so that while they possess all the homely virtues in which we profess to believe, they seem ingenuous because the world around them is irritated by them, cheats them, kicks them around. They are trusting, kind, loyal, generous and patriotic."

Although originally set somewhere in the mountains of Kentucky, Dogpatch soon took on a fantasy identity of its own, which had a good deal in common with the Lubberland described by William Byrd II in his 18th-century histories of the dividing line between Virginia and North Carolina. Dogpatch corresponded to the actual South in only a few ways: in its emphasis on kinship and the family unit, an acceptance of the individual and the grotesque, a reliance on violence when the social order is disrupted, and a depleted agrarian economy that annually brings starvation when the turnip crop is destroyed by insects. Southern religion, race, literature, and culture were never allowed in Dogpatch, where the satire was directed at the national scene rather than the local and at man's inhumanity to man rather than at regional mores. However, like the humorists of the Old Southwest, Capp relied heavily for his humor on dialect, exaggeration, the grotesque, and lively narrative action. There are many similarities, for example, between the riots instigated by Sut Lovingood in the yarns of George Washington Harris and Marryin' Sam's five-dollar wedding special.

In the same year that Capp began *Li'l Abner*, another major southern character appeared in an already widely popular strip about the sporting life. William Morgan De Beck, or Billy De Beck, of Chicago, had begun *Barney Google* on 17 June 1919. Barney and his racehorse, Spark Plug, took the nation by storm and generated millions of dollars worth of merchandise, a popular song, and three stage musicals that toured the country. In 1934 Barney became the manager for a wrestler named Sully, and to escape some trouble they headed into the Kentucky hills and met a bootlegger named Snuffy Smith and his wife Loweezy. Snuffy and his mountaineer friends stole the spotlight and slowly dominated the strip until, after De Beck's death in 1942, his assistant, Fred Lasswell, took the strip entirely into the fictional Appalachian community.

This was no incidental excursion into an exotic environment on the part of De Beck but the result of a personal fascination with the life and culture of the mountaineer. De Beck read deeply in the literature of Appalachia and in particular was intrigued by the Tennessee writers George Washington Harris and Mary Noailles Murfree and by the Ozark folklore collections of Vance Randolph. He traveled into the mountains of Virginia and Kentucky, talked with the natives, and made numerous sketches of people and places. Under his hand, the comic strip reflected a brilliant use of Appalachian language, folklore, customs, motifs, themes, and stories inspired by his reading and experience.

The Snuffy Smith drawn over the last 40 years by Fred Lasswell has obscured the work of De Beck. Both Lasswell's Snuffy and Capp's Li'l Abner have been charged with encouraging Americans to consider southern mountaineers as backward, lazy, dumb, and unable to cope with the modern world. Neither has presented a very flattering portrait (though neither made a claim to realism or accuracy), but De Beck's original Snuffy may be considered a legitimate addition to modern art and literature about Appalachia, free of the charge of defamation.

Two strips inspired by the success of *Li'l Abner* were *Ozark Ike* in 1945 and *Long Sam* in 1954. Basically a sports strip, Ray Gotto's *Ozark Ike* brought an ignorant and inept baseball player and his blond girlfriend Diana out of the hills and onto the bush-league playing fields. Though the art was distinctive, the continuity was weak, and the strip was only a moderate success. *Long Sam*, created by Al Capp, written by his brother Elliott Caplin, and drawn by Bob Lubbers, involved a beautiful hillbilly girl whose mama never allowed her to see a man. Although the art was striking, the plot device wore thin and it became a routine strip. For both these strips, the use of southern backgrounds was merely incidental and served only to maintain the Capp stereotypes.

In 1943 a former Disney animator from Connecticut, Walt Kelly, created a comic-book series about a black boy named Bumbazine and his pet alligator Albert in the Okefenokee swamp. This was the genesis of his 1946 strip *Pogo*. Kelly had studied Georgia dialect while working for the army's language section during the war, and, although there is no certain evidence, he must have encountered the Uncle Remus tales of Joel Chandler Harris. Like the stories of Uncle Remus, *Pogo* was an animal fable, told in dialect, about the techniques of survival in a largely hostile world. The innocent Pogo Possum, the vain Albert Alligator, the cynical Porky Porcupine, and other denizens of the swamp acted out morality plays in the style of the drama of the absurd with multilayered social, political, and philosophic meanings. The southern setting and pseudodialect, however, were merely a means to achieve Kelly's larger artistic concerns in one of the most brilliant comic strips of our time. As a teller of moral fables in an original idiom, Kelly belongs in the company of Mark Twain and William Faulkner.

One might make a case for Jeff MacNelly's 1978 *Shoe* as a southern comic strip, but the birds that populate its world are representative of broad types of human behavior, and there is little in it of a distinctive southern flavor. As an adopted Virginian, however, MacNelly has absorbed much of his southern environment in his fine sense of the grotesque and appreciation for hyperbole.

Entirely southern in content is *Kudzu* by Doug Marlette, a native of Greensboro, N.C. Introduced in 1981 while Marlette was working for the Charlotte *Observer*, *Kudzu* details the life and hard times of an adolescent of the same name, beset by an itch to write like Thomas Wolfe; beleaguered by his dominating mother, his redneck Uncle Dub, an ineffective preacher named Will B. Dunn, and a sarcastic parrot named Doris; befriended by Maurice, a black who aspires to be a great blues singer without undergoing any hardships; and hopelessly in love with Veranda, an indifferent southern belle who finds it difficult to choose between baton twirling and cheerleading as a career. Set in Bypass, N.C. (based partly on Laurel, Miss., Sanford, Fla., and other towns where Marlette lived), the widely popular *Kudzu* is the first genuinely southern comic strip by a southern artist that gently but incisively satirizes the culture and mystique of the South.

See also ENVIRONMENT: / Kudzu; ETHNIC LIFE: Mountain Culture; FOLKLIFE: / Brer Rabbit; "Hillbilly" Image; HISTORY AND MANNERS: / Byrd, William, II; LANGUAGE: / Randolph, Vance; LITERATURE: / Harris, George Washington; Harris, Joel Chandler; Wolfe, Thomas; MYTHIC SOUTH: Appalachian Culture

M. Thomas Inge
Randolph-Macon College

Al Capp, *The World of Li'l Abner* (1953); Maurice Horn, *The World Encyclopedia of Comics* (1976); M. Thomas Inge, *Appalachian Journal* (Winter 1977); Jerry Robinson, *The Comic: An Illustrated History of Comic Strip Art* (1974).

Film, Blaxploitation

The term *blaxploitation film* is a euphemism for a genre of tightly budgeted, poorly scripted and acted, and highly stereotypical films starring black performers and more often than not treating subjects related to black life and culture. The films were a commercial response to the heightened sense of black awareness spawned by the civil rights and black power movements of the 1960s and 1970s. In still another sense they were a handy, short-term, and specifically targeted solution to a general decline in moviegoing, and the films' themes and characters were designed to attract inner-city audiences back to theaters.

Many of the films in question were set in northern urban ghettos and centered on the exploits of various pimps, prostitutes, hustlers, drug dealers, hit men, super spades, crime fighters, and buffoons. A representative sampling would include *Superfly*, *Shaft*, *Coffy*, *Cleopatra Jones*, *The Mack*, *Trick Baby*, *Hit Man*, *Foxy*

Brown, Willie Dynamite, Sweet Sweetback's Badass Song, Truck Turner, Legend of Nigger Charley, Black Belt Jones, and *Trouble Man.* Other films—not of the blaxploitation genre—that appeared during the period and won critical acclaim include *Sounder, Claudine, A Warm December, Save the Children, Uptown Saturday Night, Five on the Black Hand Side,* and *Lady Sings the Blues.*

When the South was the setting for films of the blaxploitation genre, it was often in a rural locale where racial passions were stirred and a very complex social and political situation was reduced to gross stereotypes. Southern blacks were more important as consumers than as subjects in blaxploitation films, but some films did represent a new view of the antebellum South. Films such as *Slaves* (1969), *The Quadroon* (1971), *Mandingo* (1975) and its sequel *Drum* (1976), and *Passion Plantation* (1978) had as central characters blacks who were angry foes of a brutal slave system. Dino De Laurentis, executive producer of *Mandingo,* argued that his movie, for example, meant to go "beyond the sentimentalized South of other films" and show "the true brutalizing nature of slavery." Even these films, however, used sensationalized advertising and exploited nudity, multiracial sex, and violence, undermining pretentions to present a serious new view of history.

Although highly successful financially, the blaxploitation films were the objects of intense criticism. Blacks did not reap financial benefits from most of the films because the directors, producers, and distributors were predominantly white. Black performers, who were generally starving for parts, were presented with weak scripts that required them to play one-dimensional characters. Blacks did not serve as writers, technicians, or directors or have other important behind-the-scenes roles.

The films were also thought to present a one-sided image of black life, one in which certain negative lifestyles and practices were presented to the exclusion of more favorable images and diversity. Blaxploitation films were also troubling because they tended to transmit undesirable values to adolescents and young adults. Crass materialism, drug use, inhumane male/female relationships, social degradation, violence, and a general glorification of nonproductive lifestyles were major concerns of critics. The movies were said to undermine the work ethic because many of the characters were dropouts from the regular economy, choosing instead to live by their wits. The level of violence in the movies was also singled out for special concern. The impression given was that black lives were very expendable and violence was a legitimate means of resolving disputes. The violence against women, the degraded and dependent image of women, and the glorification of casual and irresponsible sex were particularly intense and enduring concerns of black feminists.

See also BLACK LIFE: Film Images, Black

Earl Picard
Atlanta University

Francis W. Alexander, *Black Scholar* (May 1976); Donald Bogle, *Toms, Coons, Mulattoes, Mammies, and Bucks: An Interpretive History of Blacks in American Film* (1973); Thomas J. Cripps, *Black Film as Genre* (1978); Daniel Leab, *From Sambo to Superspade: The Black Experience in Motion Pictures* (1976); Richard A. Maynard, ed., *The Black Man on Film: Racial Stereotyping* (1974); Webster L. Wallace, "Attitudes of Black College Freshmen Students toward Contemporary 'Controversial' Films" (Ph.D. dissertation, Georgia State University, 1975); Renee Ward, *Black Scholar* (May 1976).

Film, Contemporary

Following a spate of Old South plantation romances and similar Civil War epics in the late 1930s (films such as *So Red the Rose* and *Gone with the Wind*), Hollywood motion pictures about the South changed to more contemporary, realistic treatments in the years following World War II.

Among the first such motion pictures were several drawn from best-selling novels, specifically Robert Penn Warren's *All the King's Men* and William Faulkner's *Intruder in the Dust.* Like the novels, the film adaptations dealt with topics of concern not only in the South but throughout the nation in the 1940s: the rise of a dictatorial political boss in Robert Rossen's 1949 film version of *All the King's Men* and race relations in the MGM film *Intruder in the Dust,* directed by Clarence Brown (also 1949). The Faulkner adaptation—filmed on location in Oxford, Miss., Faulkner's hometown—explored the reaction of a southern town to a black falsely accused of murdering a white.

Race relations played a part in several Faulkner adaptations (*The Sound and the Fury,* Martin Ritt, 1959, and *Sanctuary,* Tony Richardson, 1961), but the film adaptation of Harper Lee's best-selling novel, *To Kill a Mockingbird* (Robert Mulligan, 1963), provided one of the more dramatic presentations of the conflict within a small southern town, as did the later *In the Heat of the Night* (Norman Jewison, 1967). The film of Carson McCullers's *Member of the Wedding* (Fred Zinneman, 1952) gave full expression to the personal relationships between white families and their black servants.

Political themes were the focus of *All the King's Men* and *A Lion Is in the Streets* (Raoul Walsh, 1953), both of which dealt with fictional characters based on Louisiana's political "Kingfish," Huey Long. Perhaps the most impressive political film about the South in recent years has been Robert Altman's epic-length *Nashville* (1975). *Nashville* brought together strands of patriotism in the South with country music, mysterious political candidates, and political assassination to give a chillingly prophetic view of contemporary trends in the South and nation. (*Nashville*'s prediction of a southern political "unknown" becoming president anticipated the candidacy of Georgia's Jimmy Carter in 1976.)

Robert Altman's *Thieves Like Us* (1974) was an interesting nostalgic sociological study of Mississippi during the Depression era of the 1930s. Filmed on location in

Mississippi (Jackson, Parchman penitentiary, Canton, and other locales), it carefully created a portrait of young people casually drawn into a life of crime in filmic parallel to Bonnie and Clyde. Another nostalgic picture of an era—the 1950s—was seen in the Max Baer film *Ode to Billy Joe* (1976), which was an original screenplay based on the popular song by Mississippi singer Bobbie Gentry. That film explores sexual confusion—that of Billy Joe McCallister in recognizing his budding homosexuality—in the less sophisticated and more sexually repressive 1950s.

These post–World War II films dealt with realistic topics such as politics, race relations, and explicit sexual matters; they also achieved realism by being filmed on location in southern small towns to render an accurate physical environment. Oxford, Miss., has been used for several films (*Intruder in the Dust* and *Home from the Hill*); Louisiana for Faulkner's *The Long Hot Summer*; north Mississippi for *Ode to Billy Joe*; Selma, Ala., for *The Heart Is a Lonely Hunter*; and Nashville for the film of the same name. In the 1980s, Texas provided locales for films like *Tender Mercies*; *Paris, Texas*; *Places in the Heart*; and Horton Foote's *1918*, while Tennessee became the backdrop for 1984's *The River*.

Jere Real
Lynchburg College

Edward D. C. Campbell, Jr., *The Celluloid South: Hollywood and the Southern Myth* (1981); Fred Chappell, *Southern Humanities Review* (Fall 1978); Jack Temple Kirby, *Media-Made Dixie: The South in the American Imagination* (1978).

Film, Decadent South

Drawing heavily upon the work of southern Gothic writers such as Tennessee Williams, Carson McCullers, Truman Capote, and William Faulkner, a genre of films dealing with the South as a region of decadence and depravity emerged in the years following World War II. In these films, the South was often portrayed as dark, exotic, morbidly gloomy, violent, and both sexually repressed—generally because of religion—and sexually obsessed.

Like the literary works that often spawned these motion pictures, such films contained elements of Gothic romanticism found in the psychological insights of Freud and Jung. Once, in attempting to define and explain the southern Gothic, Tennessee Williams termed it a literary style that sought to capture "an intuition, of an underlying dreadfulness in modern experience," thus frequently making use of violent and grotesque external symbols.

A Gothic sensibility is easily discerned in such works of William Faulkner as *As I Lay Dying*, *Sanctuary*, *The Sound and the Fury*, *Light in August*, and, notably, in his famous short story "A Rose for Emily." Similarly, it is found in such Williams plays as *A Streetcar Named Desire* (which deals with madness and rape), *Sweet Bird of Youth* (rape and castration), *Cat on a Hot Tin Roof* (homosexuality and nymphomania), and *Suddenly Last Summer* (adultery, madness, homosexuality, Oedipal love between mother and son, and, ultimately, cannibalism).

All the above-cited Williams plays were adapted for films by Hollywood in the 1950s and 1960s, as were several of the William Faulkner titles. Additionally, some of Faulkner's short stories were filmed as decadent plantation melodrama—most notably *The Long Hot Summer* (directed by Martin Ritt, 1958)—as was Williams's play set in an abandoned plantation house in the Mississippi Delta, *The Seven Descents of Myrtle*, filmed as *The Last of the Mobile Hot Shots* (1969).

While Tennessee Williams's *A Streetcar Named Desire* (filmed in 1951 by Elia Kazan) offered Vivien Leigh as Blanche DuBois, a kind of fallen Scarlett O'Hara, in gentle but devastating conflict with the brutish Stanley Kowalski (Marlon Brando), that film's decadent air resulted primarily from its New Orleans French Quarter setting rather than from the inherent plot devices or characterization. Yet, its ominous brooding quality of impending madness and possible violence was a forerunner of more explicitly developed decadent themes in such films of Williams as *Suddenly Last Summer* (directed by Joseph Mankiewicz, 1959) and in his only script written exclusively for film, the 1956 Elia Kazan film, *Baby Doll*.

In *Suddenly Last Summer*, Katharine Hepburn is Violet Venable, a wealthy New Orleans matron who plots the forced lobotomy of her niece, Catherine Holly (Elizabeth Taylor), simply to save the reputation of her poet-son, Sebastian Venable, a homosexual with ravenous sexual appetites; Sebastian eventually is devoured alive by a band of boys in a Spanish village.

As Williams had used the grotesque to sensational and morbid effect in *Suddenly Last Summer*, so he did it again in his film *Baby Doll*, set in the Mississippi Delta,

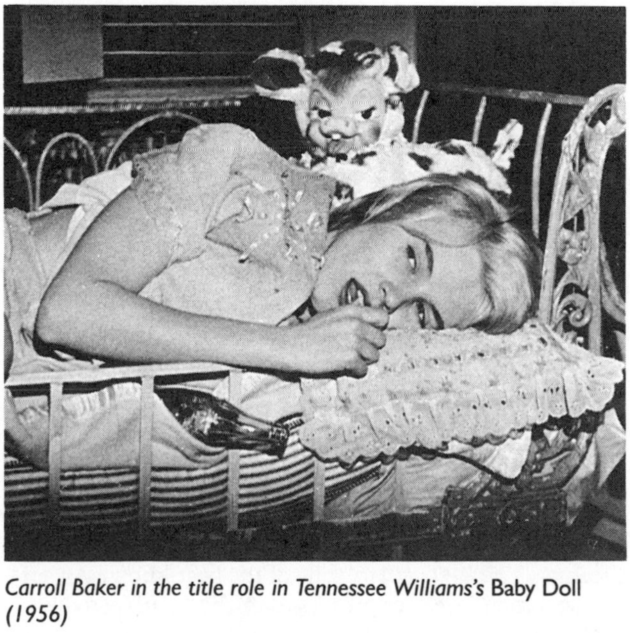

Carroll Baker in the title role in Tennessee Williams's Baby Doll *(1956)*

with a similarly grotesque situation used to comic effect. There Silva Vaccarro, the owner of a cotton gin burned to the ground by Archie Lee Meehan, resolves to get vengeance by seducing Archie Lee's child bride, Baby Doll, before Archie Lee can ever consummate his marriage to her. As played by Eli Wallach, Carroll Baker, and Karl Malden, the film approached the comic grotesquerie of Faulkner's funeral scene in *Sanctuary*.

A similar mood is found in film versions of Carson McCullers's novels: first in *Member of the Wedding* (1957, Fred Zinneman); most flamboyantly in the John Huston film *Reflections in a Golden Eye* (1967); and in *The Heart Is a Lonely Hunter* (filmed in 1968 by Thomas Ryan), in which a young girl desperately tries to establish contact with a deaf-mute jeweler. *Reflections* brought the repressed sexuality theme of much southern Gothic fiction to the setting of a Georgia army post where a closeted homosexual captain pursued an unyielding and disinterested young soldier, while the soldier, taught by fundamentalist religion to view sex as sinful, is fulfilled by riding nude on horseback. The film also offered Julie Harris as a frustrated army wife who resorts to self-mutilation prior to going mad.

Most decadent South films portrayed the region as a land of much-violated sexual taboos and eccentric behavior by impoverished aristocrats. Many were adaptations of outstanding southern writers, but a few other Hollywood productions played on the same elements manipulated less effectively by lesser talents. A typical example is Otto Preminger's 1967 film, *Hurry Sundown* (with Michael Caine and Jane Fonda as unconvincing southerners), which merged some of the Gothic elements with a civil rights sociology.

See also HISTORY AND MANNERS: Sexuality; LITERATURE: Sex Roles in Literature; / Capote, Truman; Faulkner, William; McCullers, Carson; Williams, Tennessee

Jere Real
Lynchburg College

Edward D. C. Campbell, Jr., *The Celluloid South: Hollywood and the Southern Myth* (1981); Warren French, ed., *The South and Film* (1981); Jack Temple Kirby, *Media-Made Dixie: The South in the American Imagination* (1978).

Film, Documentary

The South has made a unique contribution to the documentary film. It has been both the subject and setting of artistically significant documentary films and more recently the home and support of documentary filmmakers and filmmaking units who have advanced the art of the documentary form and used film to record and preserve important aspects of southern culture.

Among the classic southern documentaries is Pare Lorentz's *The River* (1937), one of the best-known American documentaries set primarily in the South. Produced by the U.S. Farm Security Administration, this film considered the effects of deforestation and silt erosion on the Mississippi River and its tributaries. After depicting a tragic history of misuse and abuse, the documentary concludes optimistically by promoting the Tennessee Valley Authority as a model of river and flood control and an effective means of generating power and stimulating positive social change. The film was also an artistic success, combining powerful images of devastation with Virgil Thomson's intense musical score and Thomas Chalmers's somewhat didactic, if poetic, free-verse commentary. *The River* engendered interest in an important regional problem and suggested some possible solutions at the same time that it advanced the art of the American social documentary.

Another documentary classic set in the South is Robert Flaherty's *Louisiana Story* (1948). With major financial backing from the Standard Oil Company, Flaherty produced a poetic, semidocumentary story about oil exploration in southern Louisiana from the point of view of a native Cajun boy and his family. The film suggested that traditional aspects of southern culture could coexist with modern technology and the exploitation of natural energy resources. The pastoral beauty of Richard Leacock's photography and the serenity of Virgil Thomson's score help to smooth over and reshelve, cinematically, the many problems and contradictions inherent in technological changes that have affected traditional southern values and lifestyles.

In 1952 George Stoney produced an important documentary film about black midwives in Georgia titled *All My Babies*. This film focuses on the high infant mortality rate in the South at that time and suggests that careful preparation both physically (in terms of cleanliness) and psychologically (in terms of developing positive attitudes toward prenatal and postnatal care) could improve the situation. Stoney combines starkly realistic and direct images of midwifery and actual childbirth with spiritual music and a soft but effective narration by one of the midwives. The simplicity and directness of this film make it a classic exploration of southern social and public health problems.

The tradition of southern social documentary form has been continued more recently by several southern filmmakers who explore serious social problems within contemporary southern society. Elizabeth Barrett's *Coal Mining Woman* (1978) was made by Appalshop films, which began in 1969 as a community film workshop in Kentucky and developed into a vital center for the cinematic preservation of Appalachian folk culture. Barrett's *Coal Mining Woman* examines some of the physical and emotional hazards in the working conditions of women coal miners and the attempts of women to achieve a better working environment. Exploring a similar problem from a broader perspective, Barbara Kopple's *Harlan County, Kentucky* (1976) has achieved international acclaim and stimulated world interest in the plight of coal miners and coal-mining unions in Kentucky. Kopple's film rebuilds a powerfully dramatic confrontation between unionized and nonunionized working groups. Another important, if somewhat more notorious, social problem in the South is scrutinized by James Reston, Jr., and the University of North Carolina Television's *Ku Klux Klan* (1982). This public television documentary film provides a chilling behind-the-scenes look at a group devoted to extremist politics and the perpetuation of racial prejudice in the South. The specific events investigated by Reston are those that led to the shooting deaths of several members of the Communist Worker's party in Greensboro, N.C. Bill Vanderkloot's *Iron Horse* (1982) focuses upon the subtle but pervasive problem of southern intolerance toward the free expression of ideas and artistic impulses, especially during the 1950s. Vanderkloot deploys a unique blend of documentary footage, interviews, and re-creations and reconstructions of historical events to depict the violent response of students at the University of Georgia to an abstract sculpture of a horse constructed on campus by sculptor Abbot Pattison.

Not all documentaries about the South have centered on social problems, however. Many recent documentary films have introduced audiences to the unique personalities of men and women who live and work south of the Mason-Dixon line. In 1978 and 1979 Ross McElwee, a native of North Carolina and an MIT-trained documentary filmmaker who is currently an artist in residence at Harvard University, created two cinema verité portraits of native southerners. *Charleen* is an intense, revealing film about Charleen Swansea, a "poetry-in-the-schools" teacher in Charlotte, N.C. The daughter of a false-teeth manufacturer and friend and correspondent of great poets like Ezra Pound and e. e. cummings, Charleen engages her students, audiences, and friends with her impassioned appreciation of life and art. McElwee's film is an unrelenting, penetrating, yet compassionate exploration of the public and private life of a vivacious, intelligent southern woman. His next film, *Space Coast*, assesses the impact of the decline of the space program at Cape Canaveral, Fla., upon the private lives of several admittedly bizarre residents of a typical southern community. These real-life "characters" include a woman newspaper reporter who has covered over 1,600 consecutive space launches and still struggles for new clichés to describe these events, a Bible-toting motorcycle gang leader who lost his job as a maintenance man at the space center, and an abusive owner of a small construction company who doubles as the host of a children's television program while building low-cost housing for the retirees who have replaced the departing engineers. There is something pathetic about these people, despite McElwee's best efforts to treat them as sympathetic but tragic figures caught in the middle of profound social, economic, and cultural changes.

Another probing examination of personalities in a Florida town is Errol Morris's *Vernon Florida* (1980). Morris's film is less an investigation of the social contexts and cultural changes that affect personalities and daily lives than it is a questioning of what it means to be human in an absurd world. Morris focuses on the personal obsessions of a preacher who earnestly delivers a sermon on the meaning of the word "therefore" in Paul's Epistles, a turkey hunter who talks about his "big game" with all the dramatic angst of an existentialist facing death, and a small-town policeman who sits and waits for something, anything, to happen, like one of the characters in Samuel Beckett's *Waiting for Godot*. Like McElwee's *Space Coast*, Morris's *Vernon Florida* hovers between an appreciation of unusual southern characters and an unflattering depiction of bizarre behavior and skewed personalities that borders on the satirical.

Southern documentary does not, however, exclusively focus on southern eccentrics. *Lila* (1980), by Fran Furst-Terranella and Cheryl Gosa, is a gentle portrait of Atlanta's Lila Bonner-Miller, a great-grandmother, a doctor and psychiatrist, an artist, and a community leader at the age of 80. *Lila* almost reverently documents the life of a woman who insists that she's "not gonna talk about senility, because I'm not gonna fool with it." *Lila* is not quite a didactic treatise against stereotypical representations of the elderly, but the film does insist that, although Dr. Bonner-Miller may be "extraordinary," older people can, and do, lead rich, productive existences.

Some southern documentaries assume the form of cinematic essays on aspects of southern culture. Marjie Short's *Kudzu* (1976) is a humorous essay about the uses and abuses of a prolific southern plant. Kudzu, Short explains through various interviews, was imported from Japan in the 1930s as a means of combating soil erosion in the South. This documentary, which Short made while at Boston University, won an Academy Award; it effectively blends contrasting opinions and information about the ubiquitous plant in an amusing and enlightening way, although emphasizing the former. Usually sympathetic to her interviewees, Short sometimes seems to approach her subject from the outside and evokes humor at both the behest and the expense of her southern subjects.

This point of sympathy versus ridicule and "inside" versus "outside" perspectives on the South separates native from nonnative documentary filmmakers and filmmaking units. Stan Woodward's *It's Grits* (1981) is quite similar to *Kudzu* in form and subject matter but it also typifies the native southerner's somewhat more understanding treatment of southern culture, customs, and personalities. Although *It's Grits* is a humorous essay about a popular ethnic food, it rarely elicits amusement at the expense of southerners, although it sometimes enthusiastically exposes the naïveté of northerners, sufficiently gullible to be persuaded that tobacco plants are "grits bushes." Even the most unsophisticated or idiosyncratic southern personalities, such as a woman who eats grits with "coon and possum" and a man who freezes "gritsicles," are treated with warmth and respect rather than derision.

Tom Davenport's *Thoughts on Fox Hunting* (1979) explores and questions the place of traditional English fox hunting in a Virginia context. In part the film is structured around Lord Peter Beckford's classic 1781 book of the same title. Davenport uses subjective camera techniques and skillful editing to involve the spectator in the fox's point of view and to intensify the inherently dramatic action of the chase. Working in cooperation with the Curriculum in Folklore at the University of North Carolina, Davenport also created a richly sympathetic portrait of a master North Carolina tale-teller, John E. "Frail" Joines, in *Being a Joines* (1982). This film studies the changes that have swept the life of one rural North Carolina family and powerfully documents important aspects of southern folk culture.

Uniquely southern literary and musical arts and artists have been preserved on film by many southern filmmakers and filmmaking units. Ross Spears's James Agee Film Project produced a feature-length documentary entitled *Agee* (1980) about the life and literary work of James Agee, a well-known poet, film critic, and author. This lyrical film combines contemporary interviews with dramatic reconstructions of events in Agee's life that had a significant impact on his creative expression. William Ferris, Les Blank, and Bryan Elsom have all explored southern blues and jazz music with sensitivity and deep understanding. Ferris's film *Give My Poor Heart Ease* (1973) focuses on a Mississippi Delta bluesman who sings in a barbershop about the loss of his woman and his money. Filmmakers Les Blank and Bryan Elsom go beyond recording performances for posterity and future study. They use cinematic techniques that capture the spirit and sense of the music and the sensibility of musicians through camera placement, shot selection, and editing rhythms. Their films paint inner portraits of artists and their working methods, as in Elsom's *A Night in Tunisia: A Musical Portrait of Dizzy Gillespie* (1980), which combines an instructional film about jazz with an intense, affectionate, and evocative portrait of a major jazz artist. Elsom's careful lighting and compositions are as aesthetically eloquent as Gillespie's music. The film won the Best Film award at the London Film Festival in 1981.

Les Blank is a prolific documentarian whose films, many of which explore traditional southern and southwestern music and culture, have achieved international recognition. *The Blues Accordin' to Lightnin' Hopkins* casually, yet acutely, searches through the social milieu from which blues music emerged and documents an ethnic lifestyle and social context as it penetrates beneath the surface of the blues and the personality of a unique artist, Lightnin' Hopkins. Blank's films, amicable, warm, deeply felt, and insightful, have examined a number of ethnic and traditional subjects, most notably music and cultural rituals celebrated in the Mardi Gras in *Always for Pleasure*, Cajun life in *Spend It All*, and Cajun food and zydeco music in *Dry Wood and Hot Pepper*.

Within the context of a rich and active film culture that documents traditional southern passions, problems, and personalities, some southern filmmakers have produced films that extend the normal limits of the documentary itself as an art form. Bryan Elsom's *Alabama Departure* (1979) is an experimental documentary and a poetic journey through southern Alabama, in which images gliding through an abandoned resort town covered with Spanish moss are blended with an almost magical combination of natural and artificial sounds. Like *Alabama Departure*, Jan Millsapps's *Folly Beach Journal* (1981) experiments with the conventional boundaries of the documentary. A cinematic journal of the filmmaker's self-reflections through her episodic encounters with the environment of a South Carolina beach, the film compiles live action and animation into a visual autobiographical record that is also a compelling depiction of the fluid, cyclical rhythms of the site where ocean and land meet.

See also ENVIRONMENT: / Kudzu; HISTORY AND MANNERS: / Grits; LITERATURE: / Agee, James; MUSIC: / Hopkins, Lightnin'; SOCIAL CLASS: / Coal Mining; VIOLENCE: Harlan County, Ky.; / Ku Klux Klan

Gorham Kindem
Laurie Schulze
University of North Carolina
at Chapel Hill

Linda Dubler, *American Film* (April 1986); Lewis Jacobs, *The Documentary Tradition* (1971); Gorham Kindem, *Southern Quarterly* (Spring–Summer 1981).

Film, "Hick Flick"

The forces of the law and its relationship—sometimes favorable, sometimes malign—with working-class white southerners constitute one of the basic elements in what has been termed in recent years the "hick flick." This film genre has been extremely popular throughout the South, creating its initial "cult" audience through limited drive-in theater showings, later moving into more widespread commercial theater distribution, and eventually achieving mass commercial and entertainment appeal and major "star" actors' appearances.

The precedent for such formula films might be the 1958 Arthur Ripley film, *Thunder Road*, in which a youthful Robert Mitchum foiled the constant attempts of law enforcement officials to stop his illegal moonshine whiskey operations. That film, like so many that followed and expanded on its basic conflict, was notable for its high-speed automobile chase sequences, now a staple of the genre. Indeed, the popular *Dukes of Hazzard* television series utilized many salient aspects of the "hick flick" as the basis for its rural situation comedy.

In the motion pictures, however, the conflicts involving the southern working-class white hero (and sometimes heroine, though the genre largely is devoted to both the adventurous and sexual exploits of a macho male hero) have taken both comic and serious directions. In the comic version the southern lawman (often a small-town police chief or a county sheriff) becomes an exaggerated buffoon who is regularly outwitted by the working-class protagonist, who is involved in illegal, but generally victimless, activities. In a sense, the comic southern law figure may be seen as the modern equivalent of the *miles gloriosus* (the braggart soldier) of Roman comedy. This kind of comic law figure was seen in the series of Burt Reynolds films that began with the highly successful *Smokey and the Bandit* and was carried through several sequels with Jackie Gleason as Sheriff Buford T. Justice.

As in *Thunder Road*, the "illegality" was the transport of alcoholic beverages, but in the *Smokey* films the beverage was a particular brand of beer. These films—together with Reynolds's earlier *Gator* films—are marked by a glib southern hero who combines his rebellious attitude and contempt for organized authority, especially that of the local lawman, with a kind of Robin Hood–Don Juan adventurism.

In a more serious vein, the law achieves an authoritarian upper hand, either by misuse of legal authority (in such films as *Mason County Line*, *Jackson County Jail*, and the 1984 film *Tank*) or through simple force of a sadistic will. This same sadistic law enforcement figure appears in a related type of film where the working-class hero actually is imprisoned—the Paul Newman film *Cool Hand Luke*, the Burt Reynolds film *The Longest Yard*, or the more recent John Schneider film, *Eddie Macon's Run*. In each case, the protagonist is accused of only a minor crime and, while in jail, continues his conflict with a sadistic prison system and administrative law figure. (A more dramatic version of this theme is developed in the true-story film adaptation *Brubaker*, which featured Robert Redford as a well-meaning warden trying to clear up the corruption of an Arkansas prison system.) Occasionally, the serious "hick flick" combines the defiant aspects of the working-class hero with those of an honest lawman trying to overcome massive corruption in the society of which he is a small part; that kind of confrontation marked the various *Walking Tall* films.

Both serious and comic, the basic appeal of the genre lies in the depiction of an average man overcoming, outmaneuvering, or facing down an opponent who represents unfair, authoritarian power—even that of the legal system itself. The "hick flick" provides an interesting parallel with "blaxploitation films," which focus on underworld black heroes and their conflict with southern white society.

See also LAW: Police Forces; MYTHIC SOUTH: / Rednecks

Jere Real
Lynchburg College

Edward D. C. Campbell, Jr., *The Celluloid South: Hollywood and the Southern Myth* (1981); Jack Temple Kirby, *Media-Made Dixie: The South in the American Imagination* (1978).

Film, Musical

The South emerged as a setting for song-and-dance films partly because of the enormous Broadway success of the stage adaptation of Edna Ferber's novel *Show Boat* in 1928, with Jerome Kern and Oscar Hammerstein II's memorable score, just as talking pictures were beginning to revolutionize the industry. Universal rushed a "part-talking" version starring Laura LaPlante into production for 1929 release. It has disappeared, with most of its generally unsatisfactory hybrids; but it launched a vogue for the riverboat musical films, which included Buddy Rogers's *River of Romance* (1929) and Bing Crosby's *Mississippi* (1935), two versions of the same fable, as well as Crosby's *Rhythm on the River* (1940) and *Dixie* (1943), and a spectacular remake of *Show Boat* itself with Helen Morgan, Paul Robeson, and other members of the original Broadway cast (1936). After World War II a third *Show Boat* (1951) was followed by Elvis Presley's *Frankie and Johnny* (1966), but these failed to match the success of the earlier films.

Two other southern musical subgenres that were established in the late 1920s also appear to have run their course. An early start was made toward establishing a tradition of all-black musicals, emphasizing talented black song-and-dance performers. The happy life of the slaves on the old plantation was exploited in early two-reel short subjects like *Slave Days* (1929) and *Night in Dixie* (c. 1930), while the feature-length *Hearts in Dixie* (1929) made the New South look like the Old. All-black casts were subsequently featured in *The Green Pastures* (1936), which, although set in Heaven, featured the Hall Johnson choir's rendition of spirituals in a Dixie-like setting, and *Cabin in the Sky* (1943), which provided the best filmed record of Ethel Waters's remarkable voice. (On the other hand, the only filmed Bessie Smith performance was her rendition of "St. Louis Blues" for a 20-minute program filler.)

Romantic New Orleans was also quickly appropriated as a setting for screen musicals. Casting about for a follow-up to Bebe Daniels's enormously successful *Rio Rita* (1929), RKO hit upon the idea of commissioning the screen's first original musical score for *Dixiana* (1930), which also boasted the talents of black tap dancer Bill "Bojangles" Robinson. Since then most major musical stars have graced extravaganzas set in the Crescent City: Mae West's *Belle of the Nineties* (1934), Bing Crosby's *Birth of the Blues* and Marlene Dietrich's *The Flame of New Orleans* (both 1941), Bob Hope's *Louisiana Purchase* (1942), Mario Lanza's *The Toast of New Orleans* (1950), and Pat Boone's *Mardi Gras* (1958). The great black jazz singer Billie Holiday had her only major screen role in *New Orleans* (1947); but this series seems to have ended with the film that made best use of the setting, Elvis Presley's *King Creole* (1958).

During the 1930s the southern musical also became a special preserve of popular child entertainers. Bill "Bojangles" Robinson enjoyed the best of his scandalously few film opportunities dancing with Shirley Temple in *The Little Colonel* (1935) and *The Littlest Rebel* (1935); Miss Temple's archrival at 20th Century Fox, Jane Withers, made *Can This Be Dixie?* in 1936; and their male rival at Universal, Bobby Breen, made *Rainbow on the River* (1936) and *Way Down South* (1939). These were succeeded by such "hillbilly" musicals as Bob Burns's *Mountain Music* (1937) and *The Arkansas Traveler* (1938), the Weaver Brothers and Elviry's misleadingly titled *Grand Ole Opry* (1940), and Judy Canova's long series for Republic from *Sis Hopkins* (1941) to *Lay that Rifle Down* (1955). *The Singing Brakeman* (1929) was a short film featuring country singer Jimmie Rodgers. An elaborate grotesquerie related to this subgenre was an adaptation of the stage play *Li'l Abner* (1959), with live actors prancing around as Al Capp's comic-strip characters.

The 1930s was also the decade of biographical films, and the South's beloved Stephen Foster came in for his share with *Harmony Lane* (1935), starring Don Ameche, who also had portrayed Alexander Graham Bell and other notables, and *Swanee River* (1939), Al Jolson's last attempt to recover his earlier film popularity. Foster's music was also featured in *My Old Kentucky Home* (1938), another vehicle for the popular black Hall Johnson choir.

The Old South has not fared well in musical films. Walt Disney's attempt to reinvigorate the plantation myth in *Song of the South* (1946), though popular with the public, was criticized by blacks and ridiculed by reviewers. Although the South produced in Elvis Presley the most durable star for modest musicals since Bing Crosby, only a few of Elvis's films (besides the aforementioned *Frankie and Johnny* and *King Creole*) were set in the South. His first film, *Love Me Tender* (1956), was set in Texas after the Civil War, but only *Loving You* (1957), *Wild in the Country* (1961), and *Kissin' Cousins* (1964) were set in the rural southern regions where Presley had grown up. After these films he was packed off to Hawaii, Acapulco, Las Vegas, the Seattle World's Fair, and other fantasylands far from Mississippi.

The enormously popular *Reader's Digest*, seeking new fields to conquer, made a spectacular entry into film production in 1973–74 with musical versions of Mark Twain's *Tom Sawyer* and *Huckleberry Finn*, both with southern settings. Although *Tom Sawyer* was well received and did well at the box office, *Huckleberry Finn* was a disaster with both reviewers and the public. The magazine has not continued its project of revamping American classics, and other producers have shied away from such ventures.

James Baskett and Bobby Driscoll as Uncle Remus and Johnny in Walt Disney's Song of the South *(1946)*

Especially in view of the continuing success of the television program *Hee Haw* and Opryland's popularity as a tourist attraction, the best prospects for future musical South films appear to be films employing country music stars. Except for *Coal Miner's Daughter* (1980), based on the life of singer Loretta Lynn, such films have been few and not particularly successful. Robert Altman's *Nashville* (1975) was viciously critical of the city and its music industry and was shunned by established troupers for the Grand Ole Opry. Willie Nelson made something of a hit with *Honeysuckle Rose* (1981, retitled *On the Road Again* for television), but his *Barbarosa* (1982) quickly disappeared. *The Best Little Whorehouse in Texas* (1982) showcased Dolly Parton as well as Burt Reynolds. Kenny Rogers's only production, *Six Pack* (1982), was popular in small towns and at drive-ins, and he appears to offer the only current possibility for restoring the Bing Crosby/Elvis Presley tradition of small-scale, tuneful films. With few musical extravaganzas being produced at all, the days of the riverboat romances seem over.

See also BLACK LIFE: Film Images, Black; MUSIC: / Foster, Stephen; Presley, Elvis; Smith, Bessie; RECREATION: / Showboats; URBANIZATION: / New Orleans

Warren French
Indiana University

Andrew Bergman, *We're in the Money: Depression America and Its Films* (1971); Edward D. C. Campbell, Jr., *The Celluloid South: Hollywood and the Southern Myth* (1981); Thomas J. Cripps, *Slow Fade to Black: The Negro in American Film, 1900–1942* (1977); Jane Feuer, *The Hollywood Musical* (1982); John Russell Taylor and Arthur Jackson, *The Hollywood Musical* (1971).

Film, Plantation

From just off screen a small, wooden model of a Mississippi steamboat was pushed across what was obviously just a tub of water. To the back of the tub was attached a simple drawing of vast cotton fields and a porticoed mansion. Though technically crude, that 1903 silent film adaptation of *Uncle Tom's Cabin* first presented on film what quickly became the cinematic mythology of a grand Old South.

In the first years after 1865 a general interest in descriptive, regional color developed, focusing on dialect and folktales, descriptions of the antebellum social scene, and characterizations of the planter class. It was not long before southern writers such as Thomas Nelson Page and George Cary Eggleston were regular contributors to such leading northeastern periodicals as *Atlantic Monthly*, *Lippincott's*, and *Scribner's Magazine*.

Matters southern were not just for periodicals, though. Sometimes lavish, sometimes simple, presentations of plantation stereotypes—large homes, prim belles, imposing colonels, and contented slaves—were standard fare for stage productions as, for example, with the popular Lew Johnson's Plantation Minstrels. Artwork such as Eastman Johnson's, nostalgic prints by Currier & Ives, songs by Stephen Foster—all contributed further to a mystique of plantation culture.

The earliest silent films were therefore quick to adopt what had become an established, familiar setting. As the early, predominantly urban motion picture theaters attracted ticket buyers eager for excitement, the romantic plantation image was perfect for the new medium: in very brief films the stories furnished escape with by-then instantly recognizable characters and settings.

Silent film productions such as *The Planter's Wife* (1909), *In Slavery Days* (1913), or *Colonel Carter of Cartersville* (1915) presented a gentle, pastoral South dominated by wealth and tended by large numbers of slaves. One reviewer, after seeing *The Confederate Spy* (1910), commented that such films were important, because "in that way a better understanding of the Southern people can be disseminated." So dominant did the image become that even *Uncle Tom's Cabin* was reworked so as to change completely its liberal slant. Southerner Harry Pollard, directing *Uncle Tom's Cabin* for Universal Studios in 1927, remarked that the story actually provided a chance to comment on "the gallantry, charm, hospitality, and gentility of the antebellum days."

No one, however, created a stronger statement of that than D. W. Griffith, also a southerner (ironically, few from the region directed or produced tales of the plantation). Griffith regarded *Birth of a Nation* (1915) as an accurate portrayal of the South. Taking his story from Thomas Dixon, Jr.'s novel *The Clansman*, Griffith indeed found the attractive plantation lifestyle so prevalent that the home of his fictionalized well-to-do South Carolina family was described as "a more representative reproduction than any that has yet appeared on the screen of the typical dwelling place."

The commercial viability of sound films after 1927, the onset of the Depression with its accompanying heightened need for entertaining motion pictures, and even the attraction of a predominantly agrarian South as counterpoint to a devastated industrial economy all made the plantation theme more attractive, exaggerated, and profitable during the 1930s. An initial wave of tentative sound shorts—*Dixie Days* (1928) and *Slave Days* (1929), for example—followed by the feature-length *Hearts in Dixie* (1929) centered the story around singing and dancing blacks. But once the general formula was proven popular in sound productions, a steady stream of musicals, comedies, and dramas emerged with the planter's family as focus and the slave as foil or comic relief.

RKO's *Dixiana* (1930) included the first original music commissioned for a film. Bill "Bojangles" Robinson danced through *The Littlest Rebel* (1935) with Shirley Temple. *Can This Be Dixie?* (1936) and *Way Down South* (1939) also featured child stars. Paramount Pictures paired W. C. Fields and Bing Crosby in *Mississippi* in 1935; the same year the studio released *So Red the Rose*. The latter served as an example of the extremes to which the film industry had taken the plantation story line. Posters drew audiences to "see the Old South ride again," while press releases claimed that star Margaret Sullavan personally made the Confederate flag used in the picture.

David O. Selznick's *Gone with the Wind* (1939), however, was the capstone to Hollywood's fictionalization of the South in the 1930s. Having purchased the film rights to Margaret Mitchell's 1936 best-seller for $50,000, Selznick devoted himself to making his film even better than Warner Brothers's *Jezebel*. Rushed into production in 1938 to upstage Selznick International's projected epic, *Jezebel* had been almost an inventory of familiar antebellum clichés. In response, Selznick meticulously fashioned his image of the plantation lifestyle; impressed critics and audiences alike proclaimed the atmosphere "faithful."

The coming of World War II quickly brought changes to Hollywood. The films produced in such profusion before were now strongly discouraged by the Office of War Information's Motion Picture Section. Fighting a war for the free world and democracy, the government could hardly condone repeated celebrations of the plantation.

Bette Davis in the title role in Jezebel *(1938)*

The change was soon obvious, as in the 1943 musical *Dixie*, in which characterizations of the slaves and scenes of plantation life were essentially omitted in favor of southern urban settings.

By the late 1940s even more pressure was brought to bear. Various court decisions and Truman's integration of the armed services, in addition to the first federal laws aimed at ending discrimination, all signaled Hollywood that the Old South stories would have to adapt to the times. Change was soon evident. By 1947, in *The Foxes of Harrow*, a slave kills her child and herself rather than submit to further life on the plantation; in *The Mississippi Gambler* (1953) and *The Gambler from Natchez* (1954) images of slavery were few. And by 1957, in both *Raintree County* and especially *Band of Angels*, the antebellum South's mythical lifestyle and system of labor were objects of considerable reinterpretation if not derision.

By the late 1960s television was accelerating the decline of the traditional Hollywood studio system, as well as drawing people away from the old downtown theaters. Freed from the usual commercial constraints, a number of filmmakers found in the theme of the plantation, especially slavery, an appropriate framework for analyzing contemporary society. Racial violence, the debate over civil rights, and black separatist movements all contributed to productions such as *Slaves* (1969), *The Quadroon* (1971), *Mandingo* (1975) and its sequel *Drum* (1976), as well as *Passion Plantation* (1978). All reversed previous formulas by making the slave the central figure.

But as the political climate cooled so too did the productions. Just as *Gone with the Wind* and *Slaves* reflected their respective periods, recent films such as *Roots* (1977, 1979) have pointed to a more balanced assessment of the plantation in film, seen from the perspective of both the mansion and the slave quarters.

See also MUSIC: / Foster, Stephen; MYTHIC SOUTH: Plantation Myth; / *Uncle Tom's Cabin*

Edward D. C. Campbell, Jr.
Virginia State Library

Edward D. C. Campbell, Jr., *The Celluloid South: Hollywood and the Southern Myth* (1981); Thomas J. Cripps, *Slow Fade to Black: The Negro in American Film, 1900–1942* (1977); Jack Temple Kirby, *Media-Made Dixie: The South in the American Imagination* (1978); Peter A. Soderbergh, *Mississippi Quarterly* (Winter 1965–66).

Film, Southern

Although two of the most popular and historically important American films—director-producer D. W. Griffith's *Birth of a Nation* (1915) and producer David O. Selznick's *Gone with the Wind* (1939)—are archetypal southern classics, the "southern" as a distinctive film genre has not flourished as did the "western." To be sure, most of the techniques that accounted for the success of *Birth of a Nation* (as a suspense film, not an ideological drama) became the basic conventions of horse operas. The "southern" itself, though, evolved through markedly different stages, reaching its greatest popularity in the 1930s, the 1950s, and the late 1970s.

Before the spectacular success of his epic feature, Griffith, a native Kentuckian, set in the South a number of the several hundred one-reel narratives he ground out for Biograph between 1908 and 1914 (*In Old Kentucky, The House with Closed Shutters*). His first film that extended nickelodeon features to two reels was finally released in two parts as *His Trust* and *His Trust Fulfilled* (1911), the story of an exslave's devotion to the daughter of his master, who was killed in the war. After the introduction of feature films around 1915, however, Griffith returned to a southern setting only for *A Romance of Happy Valley* (1919), his most nearly autobiographical film about growing up in rural Kentucky, but one that exercised little influence on future films.

Indeed, from the 1920s only Buster Keaton's unique *The General* (1926), a Civil War farce about a stolen locomotive, has established itself as a southern classic. The South, however, attracted the critical eyes of filmmakers during the first years of talking pictures before the Hays Office production code (1934) drastically changed the tone of American film fare. *I Am a Fugitive from a Chain Gang* (1932), *The Story of Temple Drake* (1933, from William Faulkner's *Sanctuary*), and *Wild Boys of the Road* (1933) were bitter attacks on decadent racial and prison policies and on the wealthy families that controlled the South.

The advent of the Motion Picture Producers Code precluded such offerings and saw them replaced by sentimental tales that developed a myth of old Dixie, like Shirley Temple's *The Little Colonel* (1935) and *The Littlest Rebel* (1935), W. C. Fields's *Mississippi* (1935), and Will Rogers's posthumous *Steamboat 'Round the Bend* and *In Old Kentucky* (1935). This trend culminated in the grandest of several film versions of *Show Boat* (1936), one of the greatest examples of the musical South film.

A more somber tone colored those films dealing with the threat of rebellion hanging over the antebellum South, including *So Red the Rose* (1935, from Stark Young's novel) and *Jezebel* (1938), both of which foreshadowed *Gone with the Wind*, only recently voted the all-time favorite of American filmgoers. Cecil B. DeMille attempted to continue the epic tradition with *Reap the Wild Wind* (1942), but shortages of color film and a pronounced interest in current events during World War II shortened the life of a promising genre.

The Old South occasionally reappeared in films like *The Foxes of Harrow* (1947) and *Band of Angels* (1957), a watered-down version of Robert Penn Warren's tale of miscegenation, but these traditional deglamorizing films failed to distract audiences from searching new looks at the modern South. A frightening antilynching film, *They Won't Forget*, aroused so much controversy in 1937 that filmmakers did not go so far in portraying cynical southern politicians again before World War II, but the film versions of Lillian Hellman's play *The Little Foxes* and Erskine Caldwell's novel *Tobacco Road* (both 1941) left distinctly unfavorable impressions of the region.

From such beginnings would emerge after the war the largest coherent body of films so far made about the South, the "southern Gothics," based often upon the writings of William Faulkner and Tennessee Williams or derived from them. Efforts were made at the end of the war to present more endearing pictures of the South in Jean Renoir's *The Southerner* (1945) and Walt Disney's *Song of the South* (1946), a mixture of animation and live action based on Joel Chandler Harris's Uncle Remus stories, but audiences found Renoir's tribute "arty," and critics found Disney's popular musical saccharine.

The South especially took a beating in 1949 with the film versions of Robert Penn Warren's *All the King's Men* and Faulkner's *Intruder in the Dust*, which appeared along with Elia Kazan's overt attack on racism in *Pinky*. The new trend was really given impetus by the film versions of Tennessee Williams's successful plays *The Glass Menagerie* (1950) and *A Streetcar Named Desire* (1951), which whetted the appetite for more of Williams's shockers—*The Rose Tattoo* (1954), *Baby Doll* (1956), *The Fugitive Kind* (1960), and *Suddenly Last Summer* (1959), which still stands unchallenged as the climactic revelation of aristocratic decadence. However, botched versions of Faulkner's *The Sound and the Fury* (1959), *The Long Hot Summer* (1958), and *Sanctuary* (1961) proved no match for these, and the Gothic genre trailed off into titillating horror shows like *Hush . . . Hush, Sweet Charlotte* (1964).

Excellent films treating racial problems more realistically than in earlier years began to appear—*The Intruder* (1962), *To Kill a Mockingbird* (1963), *Nothing But a Man* (1964), *In the Heat of the Night* (1967), and *Sounder* (1972)—but they established no formula. More important from the viewpoint of establishing a genre have been *Deliverance* (1972, from James Dickey's novel) and the *Walking Tall* series, which began in 1973 and portrayed the South as a still violent frontier prone to vigilante action. The 1970s also saw a brief flourishing of films like *Mandingo* (1975) and *Passion Plantation* (1978), which turned the plantation legend upside down by celebrating the uprisings of defiant blacks against decadent masters. Attacks on continuing labor problems in the modern South, like *Harlan County, Kentucky* (1976) and *Norma Rae* (1979), were more positively received.

The best possibilities for the development of a continuing popular southern genre, however, seem likely to be in the use of country music materials. Although Robert Altman's *Nashville* (1975) was shunned by the Grand Ole Opry's faithful, films like *Coal Miner's Daughter* (1980), the story of singer Loretta Lynn; Willie Nelson's *Honeysuckle Rose* (1982); and especially Burt Reynolds's *Smokey and the Bandit* films (1977, 1980), which employ the same kind of rural characters and humor as television programs like *Hee Haw* and the *Dukes of Hazzard*, have proved particularly popular with Sunbelt drive-in crowds.

Warren French
Indiana University

Edward D. C. Campbell, Jr., *The Celluloid South: Hollywood and the Southern Myth* (1981); Fred Chappell, *Southern Humanities Review* (Fall 1978); Warren French, ed., *The South and Film* (1981); Jack Temple Kirby, *Media-Made Dixie: The South in the American Imagination* (1978); Andrew Sarris, *The American Cinema: Directors and Directions, 1929–1968* (1968); Peter A. Soderbergh, *Mississippi Quarterly* (Winter 1965–66).

Film Images

Hollywood has presented the South as a corrupted Eden, dwelling first on an idyllic image and later on a harsher ("realistic") vision. Throughout, the treatment of the South centers upon the tension between a mythic ideal and a severely flawed reality. Perhaps because the industry knew it was dealing with a national myth, the most important film representations of the South have been adaptations of literary works.

The idyllic South image was fully represented by two early masters of the silent cinema, D. W. Griffith and Buster Keaton. Their artistry and the fullness of their vision assured the South of complex representation in American cinema.

With *Birth of a Nation* (1915) Griffith introduced the epic feature film using innumerable technical and narrative innovations. Himself a Kentuckian, Griffith presented the South as an elegant, idealistic, humane civilization ruined by the ravages of the Civil War and the intrusive politics of its aftermath. Justifiably charged with perpetuating racist stereotypes, the film can with equal fairness be read as an earnest idealist's view of a lost social harmony. The unprecedented scope of Griffith's spectacle established the tradition of the southern epic. It implied that this historic territory required a large canvas and a flamboyant style to cover its tumultuous events and the sweeping emotions of its characters, a tradition amply sustained by *Gone with the Wind* (1939) and *Raintree County* (1957).

Buster Keaton's representation of the South was rooted in the comic artist's pathos more than in spectacle. He opens *Our Hospitality* (1923), his second feature, with a noncomic presentation of hero Willie McKay's slow train trip home to the Shenandoah Valley, where he has inherited both a family estate and a family feud with the Canfields. Keaton lovingly re-creates the period detail, atmosphere, and especially the courtly code of conduct that restrains even the most violent of passions in the South. In *The General* (1926) Keaton played Johnnie Gray, the quintessential southern soldier, in a comic version of the famous railway robbery by James J. Andrews at Big Shanty, Ga., in 1862 (recounted in William Pittenger's book *Daring and Suffering: A History of the Great Rail-*

road Adventure, 1863). Although Keaton had to do his filming in Cottage Grove, Ore., because Tennessee patriots objected to a comedy being made about that heroic escapade, the result was a stirring demonstration of the modest hero's integration of both his patriotic and romantic duties, with an incidental line of solid, inventive comedy.

Keaton's *Steamboat Bill Jr.* (1928) concludes what is, in effect, if not in intention, an Old South trilogy. Here he plays an eastern college boy who joins his father on a Mississippi riverboat, emblematically named *The Stonewall Jackson*. Through pluck and romance he ends the feud between his traditionalist father and a new-style industrialist. In all three films the humorous pathos and the romantic interest gloss a common concern with ending violent social divisions. The first deals with the tension between personal ambition and the social code in the prewar South, the second with the same conflict during the war, and the third with the need for postwar reconciliations. The trilogy covers the traumatic history of the South and its reconciliation of opposing forces, first within itself, then with the North, and finally with the emerging new economic and social structure. Through all adversity, Keaton embodies the doomed but undaunted spirit of the South: even when he tries to protect himself under a broken dam—with an umbrella!

Keaton's kind of modest social history by analogue proved more fertile ground for subsequent filmmakers than the epic vision (and expense) of Griffith. During the 1930s the bleak life of southern sharecroppers provided the most dramatic image of the whole country's suffering during the Depression. The familiar rural tragedies—erosion, flood, drought, dust storms, and disintegrating relationships—expressed a sense of man as victim of both social and natural disasters. In this regard, Michael Curtiz's *Cabin in the Cotton* (1932) was an important film despite its saccharine ending, a fantasy of implausible reconciliation between the classes. The classics in this vein are King Vidor's *Our Daily Bread* (1934), John Ford's *The Grapes of Wrath* (1940), and Ford's follow-up, *Tobacco Road* (1941), with the latter turning Erskine Caldwell's novel into a populist critique of the sharecropper's life, alternating passages of fine, lyrical observation with broadened comedy. Whereas Caldwell blamed the South's antiquated social system for the people's poverty and their inescapable debt to the banks, the film blamed the banks for the new farming system. That is, the film seemed to endorse the tenant-farming system that the novel attacked! A more clear-headed and moving portrayal of the tenant farmer's hardship can be found in Jean Renoir's *The Southerner* (1945). As the producer of *Cabin in the Cotton*, *The Grapes of Wrath*, and *Tobacco Road*, Darryl F. Zanuck must be acknowledged as an important impetus toward social realism in Hollywood.

Social realism as a genre was sadly susceptible to sensationalism, as in *White Bondage* (1937) and *John Meade's Woman* (1937), where social critique gave way to a hackneyed image of corrupt villains. Unfortunately, this cynicism dominated post–World War II Hollywood visions of the South. Anthony Mann's *God's Little Acre* (1958) broadened even further the comedy and the bawdry of *Tobacco Road*. Another minor tradition details the region's corrupt power structure. Examples include the Huey Long surrogate of *All the King's Men* (1949); the corrupt citizen-bosses in Tony Richardson's *Sanctuary* (1961), a violation of Faulkner's *The Sound and the Fury* (arguably the most unjust classic adaptation ever filmed), Vincent Minnelli's *Home from the Hill* (1960); and two Tennessee Williams adaptations, *The Fugitive Kind* (1960) and *Sweet Bird of Youth* (1962).

The device of concentrating evil in a single villain turns to caricature and cliché in the recent tradition of the redneck sheriff, which Rod Steiger began innocently enough in Norman Jewison's *In the Heat of the Night* (1967) but which was ballooned and repeated in countless television commercials and in the *Smokey and the Bandit* film series. Other films have blamed southern corruption upon an entire community. In contrast to these many B films stand a few thoughtful, responsible works, most notably Clarence Brown's *Intruder in the Dust* (1949), *Inherit the Wind* (1960), and *To Kill a Mockingbird* (1963). Here the tradition of a tight, enclosed community in the South provides a critique of prejudice, the mob mind, and reactionary conservatism.

Even the seamiest social realism draws upon the idyllic vision, however. Implicit in every lynching scene set in the South is the audience's memory of the nobility in the Griffith and Keaton visions. The mythic and the realistic treatments converge in the most successful film ever made about the South, *Gone with the Wind*. The spectacle and the sweep of this epic seem antithetical to the grainy, close focus of *The Grapes of Wrath*, which appeared within a few months, but both are documents of periods of economic depression. Both show survivors of financial ruin and social upheaval longing to return to a lost agrarian simplicity. Tom Joad's resolution—"Can't nobody lick us. We'll go on forever, Pa. We're the people."—is memorable though it pales beside the indomitable Scarlett O'Hara's unsentimental resolve: "As God is my witness . . . I'll never be hungry again."

Scarlett (Vivien Leigh) again makes the South stand for the whole nation. She continues and deepens her girlish revolt against stifling traditions to become a strong and practical, though ever-selfish, character. When Rhett Butler (Clark Gable) returns to the past gentility of Charleston, Scarlett prefers to recover her roots in the soil of Tara. But it fails to nourish her in the new times. She vomits the turnip begrudgingly yielded by the scorched red earth. Under the pathetic illusion that she can somehow recover her lost past, she throws herself into the new industrialization. The adaptability that fulfilled the hero in the Keaton trilogy dooms the heroine to a soul-destroying progress in this more modern South.

As America sees itself in both the mythic and the realistic depictions of the South, something of an unarticulated guilt often emerges through these chronicles of lost innocence. At its source, Griffith and Keaton aimed to recreate the past in the documentary style of Matthew Brady and the history texts, as if recovering the bygone images could erase the intervening loss. The more modern reflex is to expose the seaminess of the present. Martin Ritt's *Sounder* (1972), for example, a return to 1930s social realism, offsets his more conventional exploitation of the southern-boss myth in *The Long Hot Summer* (1958).

Guilt is most explicit in the films that present the South in terms of steamy sexuality. In some instances there is a political implication. When Temple Drake is raped in *Sanctuary*, the South is violated. The coarsening of Scarlett O'Hara is the South's coarsening under pressure, so too the rape and maddening of Blanche DuBois in *A Streetcar Named Desire* (1951). Indeed, most of the Tennessee Williams adaptations can be read as a psychodrama about the South, with solitary suppression and forced sexual conformity the traumas of a culture torn between futilely trying to sustain its character and the temptation to sell itself to the new order.

In John Huston's innovative adaptation of Carson McCullers's *Reflections in a Golden Eye* (1967), the shallow sensibility of northern order is undermined by southern deviance in all its kinky and glorious vitality. In the prints as originally released (but later withdrawn and replaced by more conventional ones), Huston drained the image of all color but a pale, glowing amber until the murder at the end brought a full burst of technicolor. The effect was the viewer's tremulous involvement in the characters' withdrawal from reality into their own private natures, private eroticism, private harmonies and heats, until the repressive public world imposed an illusion of order.

In all these films, the public history replays and amplifies private tensions. Even in Walt Disney's *Song of the South* (1946) there is a strain between the fantasy animation of the Uncle Remus stories and the traumatic world in which the live-action character (James Baskett) operates as guide, pal, and sentimental surrogate for a fatherless boy (Bobby Driscoll). In Hollywood's persistent vision the South represents both a lost, ideal past and a corrupt, hypocritical, and repressive present. The cool, perfect mansions and their reeking ruins, the brightest and the most brutish, stand balanced together. The two visions are inseparable and contiguous: when Bette Davis plays a southern belle (*Hush . . . Hush, Sweet Charlotte*, 1964), cleared of 37 years of guilt for a murder she did not commit, there is a belated justice for her antebellum *Jezebel* (1938). Vivien Leigh's Blanche DuBois draws upon the same actress's Scarlett, as she cowers behind whimsical, longing illusions to escape the vicious reality that shattered her beautiful dream of the South.

As anthropologist Claude Lévi-Strauss suggests, a myth functions to provide a logical model, overcoming a contradiction not by explaining anything, but by displacing mythic difficulties with those it raises itself. When America sees itself in Hollywood's South, the flawed present harkens back to another Eden, fragile and spent. Hollywood's South stands as one of the nation's key cultural myths.

See also MYTHIC SOUTH articles

Maurice Yacowar
Brock University

Edward D. C. Campbell, Jr., *The Celluloid South: Hollywood and the Southern Myth* (1981); Fred Chappell, *Southern Humanities Review* (Fall 1978); Jack Temple Kirby, *Media-Made Dixie: The South in the American Imagination* (1978); Peter A. Soderbergh, *Mississippi Quarterly* (Winter 1965–66).

Film Production

Moviemaking in the South dates back to the 19th century when travelogs and early precursors to the newsreel such as *U.S. Cavalry Supplies Unloading at Tampa, Florida* and *Transport Ships at Port Tampa* (both 1898) were shot as part of the coverage of the Spanish-American War.

But despite the emergence of New South Sunbelt politics and the important continuing role southerners play in American cultural life, the region still suffers from antebellum stereotypes dating back more than a century. Thus, one should make a distinction between film and television productions actually made in the South and films made about the South. In the often-mythic southern film genre, much as in the western, the movie industry for decades artificially romanticized the South or portrayed the dark side of race relations by falsely picturing a world of sentimentality and salaciousness unrepresentative of Dixie as a whole.

A local production base (which existed during the silent era and once again is being reestablished throughout the South) may well result in a more realistic, prosouthern image than that of a Hollywood art director creating "Tara" on a California backlot. Indeed, the stereotypical "moonlight-and-magnolias" screen image of the South is an unfortunate by-product of the consolidation of American motion picture production in greater Los Angeles.

During the pioneering years of the industry hundreds of films were shot in authentic locales by movie companies operating semipermanently in a number of southern states. Even after Hollywood's opulent rise during World War I to its position as the world's preeminent movie mecca, many films and television episodes continued to be shot on location regionally. These precedents have today helped spur a burgeoning local media industry of increasing importance and sophistication.

Pointing to the development of the South as a major "Third Coast" film and video center, regional production in the mid-1980s has an economic impact estimated at up to $3 billion annually. Even conservative motion picture and television statistical projections expect the South to maintain its impressive media industry growth through the rest of the decade. This is particularly true when taking into account not only highly touted feature-film releases and broadcast television programs but also television commercials, business training and public relations films, documentaries, and other specialized productions.

Early moviemakers such as D. W. Griffith were first attracted to the South by its warm climate, scenic beauty, relative proximity to New York, historic setting, and civic hospitality. These positive lures have been augmented over the years by other developments that further encourage expanded utilization of southern settings:

1. Cheaper production costs (averaging 10 to 40 percent below California) because of right-to-work wage-union conditions;
2. Locally experienced crews, extras, and support personnel for needs ranging from laboratories to catering services;
3. Ready availability of nearly a dozen large new studio soundstages ranging from the $30 million Las Colinas Dallas Communications Complex (*Streamers*, *Silkwood*) in Texas to the $17 million, 32-acre Wilmington Center in North Carolina (*Year of the Dragon*, Stephen King's *Cat's Eye*);
4. Aggressive marketing by state and city film and television commissions providing valuable assistance from red-tape cutting clearances to location-scouting services;
5. Successful track records and positive cooperation from many independent producers working in the South;
6. Increasing availability of local financing;
7. The demise of the old studio system; and
8. The conveniences afforded by rented, mobile technology.

Historically, the most serious regional challenge to the dominance of "West Coast Filmland" occurred in Florida, which for a brief period from 1908 to 1917 seemed destined to become *the* major producing center in the country. As late as 1914 so many movie troupes were attracted to the north Florida city of Jacksonville that the metropolis was widely heralded as "The World's Winter Film Capital." The end of the motion picture Patents Trust and defeat of a Jacksonville mayor popular with industry figures contributed to the exodus to California. But Florida never entirely severed its film and television connections (*Flipper* and *Miami Vice* are examples) and today vies with Texas as the number-three production site in the United States after California and New York.

Texas is particularly well situated to take advantage of the continuing need for entertainment and information programming. Between 1923 and 1980 more than 140 feature films, made-for-television movies, and television series pilots were shot on location in Texas; nearly as many major projects (108) with gross budgets in excess of $375 million were completed in the four years 1981 through 1984. Among the more notable recent releases are multi-Oscar winner *Terms of Endearment*, Tri-Star Pictures' *Places in the Heart* starring Sally Field, and Wim Wenders's *Paris, Texas*, which received the prestigious Golden Palm Award at the 1984 Cannes Film Festival.

Other southern states and cities also have long filmic histories and are now emerging from their cameo role in the industry. Louisiana, for example, hosted several dozen studio ventures during the silent years. These ranged from the prolific Selig Company, famous for its animal menagerie, and the National Film Corporation, maker of the earliest *Tarzan* releases, to less reputable stock promotions pushed by shady motion picture salesmen. Since the end of World War II, Louisiana has experienced a renaissance with more than 100 productions shot at in-state locations, including *Easy Rider*, *Sounder*, and *The Autobiography of Miss Jane Pittman*.

Because of its position as the South's leading motion picture equipment distribution center and major supplier of theater equipment and supplies along the East Coast, North Carolina already has a sizable investment in the film industry. Asheville's mountains and famed Biltmore estate (used most prominently for the Academy Award–winning *Being There*) have attracted a number of film companies over the years. Although the North Carolina Film Office has been particularly active since its formation in 1980, many observers credit Shelby, N.C., businessman-actor Earl Owensby with spurring banking interest in locally based productions. Specializing since the early 1970s in low-budget, profitable, regional "backwoods" and exploitational screen stories typified by *Chain Gang* and *Tales of the Third Dimension*, Owensby's Shelby studio now encompasses six soundstages. He plans to expand in Myrtle Beach, S.C., during the mid-1980s by opening a new $200 million studio project complete with theme park, airport, and 10 soundstages employing 1,200 people.

Georgia's film office, created under then-Governor Jimmy Carter, also actively boosts its cinematic possibilities by working closely with major Hollywood personalities such as Burt Reynolds in making pictures like *The Longest Yard* and *Sharkey's Machine*. Alabama, Kentucky, Mississippi, South Carolina, and most other states now have similar governmental departments advertising to promote film and television production. These agencies also generally offer a videotape or slide location library, publish directories of technicians and additional guides, catalog climatological information, host conferences, and provide other useful services. Current developments can be followed by reading trade press coverage in *Back Stage*, *Daily Variety*, *Florida Golden Pages*, *Hollywood Reporter*, *Millimeter*, *On Location*, and *Shooting Commercials*, as well as official state publications such as *Film Texas*.

Richard Alan Nelson
University of Houston

George Adcock, *The South Magazine* (November–December 1977); Paul W. Beutel, "Development of the Feature Film Industry in Texas, 1955–1965" (M.A. thesis, University of Texas at Austin, 1979); James R. Buchanan, *Texas Business Review* (January 1972); Warren French, ed., *The South and Film* (1981); Gene Gautier, *Woman's Home Companion* (November 1928–March 1929); Gulf State Research Institute, *Development of the Motion Picture Industry in Louisiana* (May 1971); Kalton C. Lahue, ed., *Motion Picture Pioneer: The Selig Polyscope Company* (1973); Todd E. Lindley, "Major Developments in the American Cinema 1908–1913 as Reflected by the Film Industry in New Orleans" (M.A. thesis, University of New Orleans, 1973); Richard Alan Nelson, *Florida and the American Motion Picture Industry, 1898–1980*, 2 vols. (1983); Don Umphrey,

"The Economic Impact of the 1980 Film/Tape Industry in Texas" (Texas Film Commission, January 1982); *U.S. News & World Report* (19 November 1984).

Journalists, Modern South

As the American liberal creed spread to the South in the 20th century, its converts included a small but influential number of southern newspapermen, who, beginning in the 1930s, helped to revive the idea of a New South of economic, educational, and racial progress. A decidedly Yankee notion, progress had not historically won much applause in Dixie, but during the disastrous Great Depression even southerners recognized that change might mean escape from poverty and starvation. In such recognition dwelt at least the half-hearted acceptance of another long-standing Yankee notion: the South as a problem to be solved. To this end, the journalists of the Modern South focused a critical yet affectionate eye on their native region. From the gloomy 1930s to the tumultuous 1960s and beyond, their central message was that the South, if not too firmly pressed by neoabolitionists, might finally emerge from its colonial status to rejoin the Union.

Modern South journalists brought to their work an abiding attachment to most southern traditions, but what set them apart was their avowal that "ancestor whooping" had become a hindrance. The author of that sprightly phrase, Jonathan Daniels of the Raleigh *News and Observer*, forthrightly established the stance of the new breed of southern journalists in the World War II and *Brown* v. *Board of Education* era when he noted that even if "one Reb can beat ten Yankees, it is irrelevant." Above all, these men (among others, Virginius Dabney in Richmond, W. J. Cash in Charlotte, Mark Ethridge in Louisville, John Temple Graves in Birmingham, Hodding Carter in Greenville, Miss., Ralph McGill in Atlanta, and Harry Ashmore in Little Rock) thought themselves realists. No longer could they accept the moonlight-and-magnolias mythology of southern life. At the same time they disdained to consort too closely with what they called "liberals" (i.e., northerners) or with neo-Gradyite chamber of commerce boosters. Rather, they wrote balanced commentaries that noted southern flaws but cautioned about the difficulties attending their correction. Daniels, Dabney, and their successors counseled a middle-path road to progress via civility, reasonable compromise, and gradual reform.

Liberal newspapermen of the Modern South set forth an agenda for gradual change on the eve of World War II. Although they wrote a good deal about poverty and the South's dismal educational record, their version of the mind of the Modern South was, as ever, preoccupied with race. Lynchings and poll taxes must go. Lest they be convicted, however, of preaching Yankee doctrine (which, of course, they were), progressive journalists at first advocated state rather than federal solutions to such evils; moreover, they emphasized that it was in the interest of whites to help lift up blacks, because no human resource could be wasted in the struggle to rid the South of poverty and ignorance. In league with other southern liberals, the leading journalists of the late 1930s undertook an editorial campaign for racial moderation.

Ironically, however, the War against Aryan Supremacy interrupted the nascent southern effort at racial reform. Chaos and disorder abroad were paralleled by a kind of disorder at home that blasted the hopes of Virginius Dabney and others to effect gradual, peaceful change in the southern racial ethos. Down home the war brought enormous social disruption in the form of firm black insistence, seconded by the ever-present northern "agitators" (i.e., liberals), not only that lynching be ended but that Jim Crow segregation be dismantled. When Mark Ethridge of the Louisville *Courier-Journal* assured southern whites that segregation would not be undone by the war-born Committee on Fair Employment Practices, northern liberals railed at the hypocrisy of their distant cousins in the South. Southern liberals such as Dabney and John Temple Graves, so optimistic in 1940, by 1943 ered aloud whether northerners understood that racial discrimination could never be ended forcibly. Only by "gradual evolutionary development," necessarily suspended for the duration of the war against Hitler and the Japanese, would the South ever consent to anything like equal opportunity for blacks. Irked at agitators, Graves spoke for southern liberals: "The friendship of the white liberal Southerner is the Negro's basic hope there."

This kind of not-so-hidden warning spoke more to the concerns of southern liberals than to the hopes of black people. Its intended audience, however, was moving rapidly beyond earshot. The war years worked a profound change among many blacks in the North and South, among northern white liberals, and in turn among southern white liberals, who were thrown off balance by the assertiveness of the "New Negro." Heretofore relatively quiet, these blacks and their white allies used the war (almost traitorously, in the view of southern liberals) to present their own program of reform, the blueprint for which bespoke neither moderation nor gradualism nor acceptance of leadership by southern liberals. From the mid-1940s to the late 1960s, therefore, journalistic proponents of a Modern South found themselves not so much leading a reform movement as tagging along in hopes of making such a movement palatable to moderates in Dixie. Harry Ashmore later described their task as "trying to preserve order at an incipient riot."

Recognizing that the war had loosed forces of radical change, and, more to the point, recognizing the obvious thrust of a series of Supreme Court decisions in the 1940s and early 1950s against Jim Crow education, journalists such as Virginius Dabney, Jonathan Daniels, and Hodding Carter adopted for a brief time what might be called the doctrine of "separate-but-this-time-truly-equal." This attempt to introduce fair treatment for blacks within the parameters of segregation was a classic example of the progressive road to a Modern South: good-hearted, fair-minded, but unenlightened southerners must be ever so gently coaxed to do right, both because it was right and because the courts were going to force the issue anyway. The *Brown* v. *Board of Education* decision in 1954 asserted a principle ("Separate educational facilities are inherently unequal") that, when implemented by federal district judges, undercut the ameliorative strategy of southern liberals. The phrase "with all deliberate speed" turned out to be not a gentle breeze of gradualism but a false calm before the storm.

These liberal journalists loved the South and believed in reason and in law and order. Although they feared that the courts might force too rapid a pace in the black's stride toward freedom, they did their best to convince readers that law must triumph over emotion, that black and white could live (i.e., go to school) together in harmony, and that the South would be the better for the change, however disagreeable and confusing things might be in the short run. Progressive editors after *Brown* v. *Board of Education* appealed to moderates in the South, who, precisely because they loved their native region, must obey the new law of the land. Frequently the McGills and the Ashmores were disappointed, of course, because on more than one occasion from *Brown* v. *Board of Education* to Selma (1965) the "respectable people" in the South stayed home and allowed what Ashmore called "the thin-lipped men" literally to dynamite the path to racial progress.

The path to the Modern South, therefore, was considerably more wrenching than that envisioned in the optimistic scenarios of the earliest liberal journalists. In the first place, none of them had predicted the role assumed by southern blacks in the civil rights revolution after World War II. Nor did they particularly applaud it at first; they were accustomed to leading, not following, and were thus dismayed and offended by the activism of the New Negro. In time most of the liberal newspapermen overcame the paternalism they shared with so many white southerners (and not a few white northerners) and accepted the assertiveness and admired the courage of southern blacks who struck on their own for a New South.

More difficult to accept was the failure of their beloved South to live up to its own best traditions except under the outside pressure of Yankee law and guns. By the late 1950s it was clear that the South, if left alone, might *not* do right. Ralph McGill angrily charged in 1964 that the "practicing moderates contributed largely to the undoing of a fine, honorable word. . . . There is nowhere on record a single constructive plan or action proposed by so-called moderates."

The years after the *Brown* decision left liberal editors profoundly shaken, though by no means utterly destroyed. If leadership had passed from them in significant measure, important work remained to be done. Without their editorials condemning violence, the acceptance of the law among their constituents, the decent folk of Dixie, might have been even more belated than it was. Ralph McGill in Atlanta, Hodding Carter in Greenville, Harry Ashmore in Little Rock, and many others expressed a Modern South conviction that to love the South was to insist that its people examine their society and change its worst aspects. The cumulative effect of several decades of such conviction and criticism by insiders who so clearly wanted the best for and from their region at least established the context within which "massive resistance" might ultimately be overcome. A new kind of racial accommodation did seem to exist in many parts of the South by the 1970s. Perhaps Ashmore's famous "epitaph for Dixie"—the title of his 1958 book—was only a bit premature.

The role of journalists in achieving that accommodation and in writing that epitaph by modernizing the southern consciousness required them both to display their southernness and partially to overcome it. Twentieth-century southern journalists, for instance, have surely lived by SPT—Southern People's Time. "More time" from the mouths of reactionaries meant "never," but southern liberals expressed the more common connotation: "Very slowly, we will reach our destination, and you Yankees make a mistake to try to hurry us, because life's not like that down here."

In striking fashion southern journalists have carried the burden of an ancient love-hate relationship with Yankeedom; southernness is symbiotically entwined with Yankeeness. The very idea of a New South (the Modern is the Newest South—there may be others to come) is an attempt to Yankeeize the South, to achieve the American creed of racial equal opportunity, to become prosperous, to triumph over adversity. But southerners, forward-looking editors no exception, have preferred to approach these goals gingerly, without prodding from Yankee missionaries, improvers, and South-baiters. For it is bad enough to become abolitionists and businessmen; outside pressure in that direction is insufferable. Put another way, the southern search for respectability in the modern world has necessitated Yankee imitation. This has been since the 1930s a very painful process psychologically, involving as it has the partial adoption of the ways of the archenemy.

For all their modernity, southern progressive journalists have been Lost Causers of a (mild) sort, too. Paternalistic, defensive, past-haunted in spite of themselves (as Hodding Carter once noted), they have been enthralled by the southern consciousness and its traditionalism. As liberals, they distanced themselves just enough from the southern way of life to see its weaknesses, its excesses, in some cases, indeed, its horrors. As natives who remained steadfastly loyal to their region while imploring it to join the modern world, liberal editors in the last half-century collectively delivered a running commentary on the demise of the Lost Cause and on its replacement by the Modern South. By the 1970s and 1980s southerners had become prominent in the national news media (Dan Rather, Hodding Carter III, Bill Moyers, Charles Kuralt, and Tom Wicker come to mind), and the subjects of their reporting and commentary were no longer primarily southern. Irony of ironies, when the South in the late 20th century became chic, southern journalists were no longer thought of particularly as southerners. The Modern South had arrived. In the 1980s journalists who had cogently commented on the latter stages of its journey were asking, along with their academic cousins, whether this Newest South meant no more South.

See also MYTHIC SOUTH: / Cash, W. J.

Gary L. Williams
Rollins College

Harry Ashmore, *An Epitaph for Dixie* (1958), *Hearts and Minds: The Anatomy of Racism from Roosevelt to Reagan* (1982); Hodding Carter, *Southern Legacy* (1950); Virginius Dabney, *Atlantic Monthly* (January 1943); Jonathan Daniels, *A Southerner Discovers the South* (1938); Charles W. Eagles, *Jonathan Daniels and Race Relations: The Evolution of a Southern Liberal* (1982); John T. Kneebone, *Southern Liberal Journalists and the Issue of Race, 1920–1944* (1985); Morton Sosna, *In Search of the Silent South: Southern Liberals and the Race Issue* (1977).

Journalists, New South

The idea of a New South, born after the Confederate defeat, was rhetorically transformed by journalists into a palpable reality during the 1880s. All histories of the New South movement list newspaper editors as prime movers, and chief among them were Henry W. Grady of the Atlanta *Constitution*, Francis W. Dawson of the Charleston *News and Courier*, Henry Watterson of the Louisville *Courier-Journal*, Richard Hathaway Edmonds of the *Manufacturers' Record* in Baltimore, and Daniel Augustus Tompkins who, as an industrialist, bought three newspapers, including the Charlotte *Observer*, to proclaim his gospel of work. These men argued for industrialization, enlightened agricultural practices, racial harmony, and national reconciliation, and if their vision of progress exceeded social and economic reality, they closed the gap by proclaiming a triumphant South. Their names, rather than those of politicians, attracted national attention and drew invitations to speak on behalf of the region, and, in the cases of Grady and Dawson, they were dominant influences in state politics.

The importance of the journalists can be accounted for in two ways. First, the persistence of relative economic privation and a sense of second-class citizenship within the nation created a demand in the South for publicists who could transform the region's promise into claims of actual accomplishment. Though rightly charged with fabricating myths of southern success, abundance, and racial goodwill, the images they fashioned were enduring and served to balance the region's deeper sense of frustration and failure. Second, New South journalists were part of a larger trend toward preeminence of both the news and newspapers in national life. Between 1870 and 1900 the number of daily newspapers in the United States quadrupled, from 489 to 1,967, and the number of copies increased six times, from 2.6 million to 15 million. The number of weekly papers tripled in the same period, rising from 4,000 to more than 12,000 by the end of the century. Proportionately, the South experienced the same growth. At war's end 182 weeklies were available, three years later the number swelled to 499, and within 20 years 1,827 weeklies were serving a largely rural audience.

Henry Watterson, editor of the Louisville Courier-Journal, *c. 1910*

Accompanying the explosion in readership came the ascendance of news over editorial opinion, especially in the dailies. The reporter upstaged the editor because telegraphy had dissociated communication from transportation, thereby enabling news to be, in fact, new. No longer was the newspaper simply an editorial digest, concocted by editors for partisan ends. Moreover, new printing technologies made for rapid dissemination of the news, and large evening editions began to appear in urban areas. Southern journalism, however, was not in lockstep with national trends. For one thing, the southern experience with democracy and literacy was different from that of the rest of the nation; it came late and, in part, by force. Responding to the New South, southern editors found themselves in a position not unlike that experienced by northern journalists 50 years earlier. The "penny press" that sprang up to serve Jacksonian democracy encouraged an editorial style called "personal journalism." Editors were also owners, and they used their position—indeed they believed it their duty—to shape public opinion. Such became the calling of New South editors, most of whom obtained a small amount of capital, usually from a northern investor, acquired controlling interest in a struggling newspaper, and then built circulation by determined advocacy.

Francis W. Dawson's career was typical of the pattern. At the age of 20 he changed his name from Austin John Reeks and left his native England to fight for the Confederacy. At war's end he moved to Charleston, where, with aid from friends, he acquired the Charleston *News* for $6,000 in cash and the Charleston *Courier* for $7,100. Dawson showed an independent streak by opposing the Straightout movement, which was designed to restore white supremacy, and later by showing occasional irreverence for the state's military and political hero, Wade Hampton. Still, the *News and Courier* became the dominant voice in the Palmetto State. When "Pitchfork Ben" Tillman sought power after 1885, he did so by attacking Dawson, not the elected leadership. Dawson did not shy away from editorial controversy and in that respect was more like Horace Greeley before the war than like Joseph Pulitzer, who was famed for ushering in the "new journalism" of the 1880s. Dawson believed that an editor must "write for or against something; for or against an idea; for or against a party," but as his son later put it, he also knew "that a newspaper while assuming the leadership of public opinion could not and must not fight against the unanimous will of the community which it represented."

Thus, no matter how crusading the editor or how personal the journalism, newspapers in the South were constrained to reflect the sentiment of the dominant whites in their respective communities. Failing to be representative or even arousing personal antagonism could mean the start of a rival newspaper, as when Patrick Walsh of the Augusta *Chronicle* had to fight off the upstart *Gazette* in 1887; and rival newspapers, no matter how faltering, threatened circulation and profits. The leading New South editors not only represented their metropolitan constituencies, they also influenced their country cousins. Even before the 1880s these weeklies had set up a chorus for industrialization and railroads, but increasingly they took their cues, if not their lines, from Grady, Dawson, Watterson, and Edmonds. When Dawson and Grady came to their untimely deaths in 1889, it occasioned great mourning and public grief throughout the rural South.

New South journalists offered their readers more than promises of prosperity. They provided respectable connections with a national community of opinion leaders. The rise of the fourth estate in the last half of the 19th century spawned a group of journalists who spurned traditional party allegiance, in part out of a felt need to maintain the independence of their class. In so doing, they fashioned a national fraternity that housed Liberal Republicans and New South Democrats. They united on civil service reform, free trade, and a view that only the "best men" should rule (by which they meant not black, not immigrant, not subscribing to an "ism," and not politicians pandering to these groups). The most famous journalists of the day belonged to the fraternity, including E. L. Godkin, Carl Schurz, George William Curtis, Samuel Bowles III, and Charles Dana, the man who pinned the label Mugwump on this group when they bolted the Republican party in 1884. Through these men, New South editors talked to the nation in ways the region's political leaders could not.

Finally, New South editors were good journalists. The larger dailies assembled excellent staffs, kept up with advances in technology, and produced newspapers that were aesthetically pleasing for the day and interesting to read. Henry Grady advanced the art of interviewing to the point that imitators made it a staple of reportorial practice. His invitation to address the New England Society of New York on the subject of the New South was the direct outgrowth of his interviews and reports on the Charleston earthquake of 1886. Adolph Ochs of the Chattanooga *Times* proved that good management could turn a profit and later applied the same principles in rescuing the *New York Times* from ruin (he would not be the last southerner to make his mark on that distinguished newspaper). And, as with all good newspapers, the New South journals mirrored their times. Not that out-groups such as blacks or opposition political movements received fair play, but they did get covered, even though the coverage itself was biased and often vicious. The net result has been that critical readings of these journals provide an excellent introduction to the multidimensional New South.

See also INDUSTRY: / Grady, Henry W.; MYTHIC SOUTH: New South Myth

E. Culpepper Clark
University of Alabama
at Birmingham

E. Culpepper Clark, *Francis Warrington Dawson and the Politics of Restoration: South Carolina, 1874–1889* (1980); Thomas D. Clark, *The Southern Country Editor* (1948); Edwin Emery and Michael Emery, *The Press and America: An Interpretive History of the Mass Media* (5th ed., 1984); Paul M. Gaston, *The New South Creed: A Study in Southern Mythmaking* (1970); Raymond B. Nixon, *Henry W. Grady: Spokesman of the New South* (1943); Joseph F. Wall, *Henry Watterson: Reconstructed Rebel* (1956); C. Vann Woodward, *Origins of the New South, 1877–1913* (1951).

Magazines

The new Sunbelt prosperity in recent decades has been mirrored by substantial growth in southern magazine publishing. The 1982 *Ayer Directory of Publications* lists 1,486 nonnewspaper periodicals published in the 11 states that made up the Confederacy, plus Kentucky.

Since World War II the number of southern periodicals has more than doubled, and the growth rate of magazines in this region has outstripped that of the nation as a whole. Texas, with 342 nonnewspaper periodicals, ranks first in the South, followed by Virginia (259), Florida (212), Tennessee (150), Georgia (130), North Carolina (111), Kentucky (80), South Carolina (68), Alabama (62), Louisiana (55), Mississippi (29), and Arkansas (26).

Only four southern periodicals have circulations of 1 million or above: *Upper Room*, a religious periodical printed in 40 languages, 2.1 million; *Southern Living*, the South's premier regional magazine, 1.9 million; *Boys' Life*, a nationally distributed youth magazine, 1.5 million; and *Mother Earth News*, an energy-ecology magazine, 1 million. Six more have circulations in excess of 500,000, and an additional 41 have circulations of at least 100,000.

Of these 51 high-circulation periodicals, 7 are devoted

to outdoor/sports/wildlife interests, 6 are airline inflight magazines, 5 are agricultural periodicals, 5 are motor club/motoring periodicals, 5 are religious in focus, 5 are youth magazines, 5 are rural electric periodicals, 4 are house and garden/decorating/antiques magazines, 3 are published for persons in the military, 2 are regional magazines aimed at a general audience, and 4 are classified here as miscellaneous. Of an additional 32 southern periodicals in the 50,000–100,000 circulation category, the largest group, 8, are regional and city magazines and the next largest category, 7, are outdoor/sports/wildlife magazines.

Something of southern culture can be deduced from these figures. To be successful in the South, a magazine needs focus. Few homegrown general-interest magazines have been taken to the South's bosom; in fact, the South historically has been known as a magazine graveyard. Most of the region's larger magazines are aimed at a specialized audience of persons having a strong interest in outdoor recreation, agriculture, homes, and antiques—each a deeply engrained part of the southern mystique. The South, for example, has long been regarded as the heart of the Bible Belt. Southerners also regard themselves as "closer to the soil" than the average American; agriculture, though losing ground to urban development, is still a vital southern industry. Finally, the southerner has not completely lost his feelings for the "old home place," even in today's increasingly mobile southern culture.

Most of the remaining 1,403 periodicals are relatively small but range widely in circulation and serve a bewildering array of interests, from *Cats Magazine*, circulation 81,000, a pet-lover's periodical in Port Orange, Fla.; to Dallas's *Black Tennis Magazine* (5,000); to Houston's *Ultra Magazine* (75,000) for the society-minded; to Chattanooga's *Glider Rider* (13,200) for hang-glider enthusiasts; to *Chase Magazine* (3,200), a Lexington, Ky., offering for fox hunters; to *American Atheist* (15,800) in Austin, Tex.

The South's growing technological base is reflected in the *Journal of Petroleum Technology* (40,000) in Dallas, and its more traditional industries can be seen in Memphis's *Cotton Farming* (42,679) and *Cotton Grower* (39,829) and in *America's Textiles* (30,881) in Greenville, S.C.

The South's interest in the past has its reflection in a number of successful magazines of recent vintage: *Antique Monthly* in Tuscaloosa, founded in 1967, with a 1980 circulation of 87,000, and two Kermit, Tex., magazines—*American Collector* (1969; 152,000) and *Antiques USA* (1980; 110,000).

Southern preoccupation with sports has made possible Waco's *Texas Football* (1960; 205,000), San Antonio's *Skeet Shooting Review* (1946; 18,500); Houston's *Horseman* (1956; 125,265); the Woodbridge, Va., *Running Times* (1977; 51,000); and Miami's *Florida Sportsman* (1969; 81,200).

Leading outdoors/conservation magazines are *Southern Outdoors* (1953; 177,054) in Montgomery, Ala.; Raleigh's *Wildlife in North Carolina* (1947; 47,000); Houston's *Texas Outdoor Guide Magazine* (1968; 102,000); *Outdoor America* (1922; 48,500) from Arlington, Va.; and Richmond's *Virginia Wildlife* (1937; 113,000).

Some scholars say the South's first magazine was *North Carolina Magazine; or, The Universal Intelligencer* (1764–65?); others classify this periodical as a newspaper and cite *South Carolina Weekly Museum* (1797–98) in Charleston as the first true magazine south of Baltimore.

Many of the best-remembered titles from the South's magazine past were literary magazines that functioned as mouthpieces for southern high culture. Prominent among these were the *Southern Literary Messenger*, edited in Richmond from 1835 to 1837 by Edgar Allan Poe, and the *Southern Review* (1828–32) in Charleston, edited by the Stephen Elliotts, father and son. Today's southern literary magazines are university-based. Notable among them are the venerable *Sewanee Review* at the University of the South, *Carolina Quarterly* at the University of North Carolina, *Shenandoah* at Washington and Lee, and the *Southern Review* at Louisiana State University.

Publishing just after the Civil War was difficult because of materials shortages and the population's impoverishment. Some leaders in this period were *De Bow's Commercial Review of the South and West* (1848–80) in New Orleans, *Scott's Monthly* (1865–69) in Atlanta, and *Southern Bivouac, A Monthly Literary and Historical Magazine* (1882–87) in Louisville. The only southern magazines to reach 100,000 circulation by 1885 were Atlanta's *Sunny South* (1875–1907) and Louisville's *Home and Farm* (1876–1918). A later favorite of the South was *Uncle Remus's Magazine* in Atlanta (1907–13), edited by Joel Chandler Harris; its circulation had reached 200,000 by Harris's death. The *Progressive Farmer* first appeared in 1886 but did not achieve its great influence until the early 20th century.

In the 1960s and 1970s the biggest growth category in southern magazine publishing was city and regional magazines, which contained articles on a wide range of topics, focused on geography. Many have been born and many have died since 1960. The 1960s mainly saw the creation of city magazines, and in the 1970s southern publishers turned to founding new regional magazines that covered an area larger than a city—part of a state, an entire state, parts of several states, or even the South in general.

Prominent city magazines include *New Orleans*, *D* in Dallas, *Houston City Magazine*, *Houston Monthly*, *Atlanta*, and *Memphis Magazine*; regionals include the undoubted leader, *Southern Living*, plus *Texas Monthly*, *Brown's Guide to Georgia*, *Country Magazine*, *Shenandoah Valley Magazine*, *Tar Heel: The Magazine of North Carolina*, and *Sandlapper*.

Even more recently, a number of southern magazines that specialize both by geography and by topic are meeting success. Examples are *Southern Accents*, an Atlanta house and garden magazine featuring ultra-exclusive southern homes; *Houston Home and Garden*; *Texas Homes Magazine*; and Arkansas's *Southern* magazine, which began in 1986 and focuses on the region's cultural distinctiveness. In the South, a region of relatively small cities, the key to substantial circulations appears to be a practical and well-thought-out focus or specialization.

See also AGRICULTURE: / *Progressive Farmer*; INDUSTRY: / *De Bow's Review*; LITERATURE: Periodicals

Sam G. Riley
Virginia Polytechnic Institute

Ben Moon, *Journalism Quarterly* (Winter 1970); Frank Luther Mott, *History of American Magazines*, 5 vols. (1938–68); Theodore Peterson, *Magazines in the Twentieth Century* (1972); Lyon Richardson, *A History of Early American Magazines, 1741–1789* (1931); Sam G. Riley, *Index to Southern Periodicals* (1986), *Journalism Quarterly* (Autumn 1982), *Magazines of the American South* (1986); John Tebbel, *The American Magazine: A Compact History* (1969); Roland E. Wolseley, *The Changing Magazine: Trends in Readership and Management* (1973).

Newspapers

In appearance, depth of coverage, and content, southern papers differ little from newspapers in the rest of the nation. Their strengths are essentially the same, as are their several shortcomings. This lack of marked regional distinctiveness is possibly a result of the changes industrialization brought to the region.

Today's South—defined here as the 11 states of the Confederacy plus Kentucky—is home to 28 percent (483) of the nation's dailies and 23 percent (1,778) of all weeklies in the United States. In like proportion, 24 percent of the 100 top-circulation papers in America are located in southern cities. Largest of these are the Miami *Herald* (483,095), the Houston *Chronicle* (384,305), the Houston *Post* (348,571), the New Orleans *Times-Picayune/States-Item* (275,376), and the Dallas *Times Herald* (245,325).

Size, of course, is no measure of quality. The Pulitzer Prize, given for reporting, editorial writing, and public service, is one of the best measures of journalistic performance. The southern paper that shines brightest is the Louisville *Courier-Journal*, with six Pulitzer awards; the *Courier-Journal* was also the first southern paper to win a Pulitzer (1918). Other standout papers are the Atlanta *Constitution*, with four Pulitzers in the three categories; the Miami *Herald* and the *Miami News*, with three each; and the Montgomery (Ala.) *Advertiser*, the Norfolk *Virginian-Pilot*, the *Arkansas Gazette* in Little Rock, the St. Petersburg *Times*, and the Gainesville (Fla.) *Sun*, with two each. Gene Miller of the Miami *Herald* is the only writer on a southern paper to have won two Pulitzers, and Hazel Brannon Smith of the Lexington (Miss.) *Advertiser* was the only southern woman to receive a Pulitzer (1964) until 1980, when Bette Swenson Orsini of the St. Petersburg *Times* was corecipient of the prize for national reporting. In the early years Pulitzers often went to southern papers for courageous stands against lynching, the Ku Klux Klan, and other manifestations of prejudice. Recent prizes have less frequently involved stories on racial issues.

Most lists of "best newspapers" include only the large metropolitan dailies. This article will mention some of the newspaper leaders in each southern state in three categories: metro dailies, smaller dailies, and weeklies.

The best of Alabama's metropolitan papers is the Birmingham *News*, known as a "writer's paper," and possibly the strongest link in the Newhouse chain. Outstanding smaller dailies are the Decatur *Daily* and the Anniston *Star*; a standout among weeklies is the Monroe *Journal*.

Of Arkansas city newspapers, the *Arkansas Gazette* is the clear choice. The Pine Bluff *Commercial* is a fine smaller daily with an outstanding editorial writer, Paul Greenberg; and the North Little Rock *Times* is consistently the best weekly.

The Miami *Herald* with its large editorial staff is Florida's best daily, followed by the St. Petersburg *Times* and the Orlando *Sentinel*. Among smaller dailies, Lakeland's *Ledger*, Fort Myers's *News-Press*, and Cocoa's *Today* stand out. Better weeklies are the Melbourne *Times*, *Gadsden County Times* (Quincy), and Titusville *Star Advocate*.

Atlanta's *Constitution* and *Journal*, followed by Macon's *News* and *Telegraph*, are the leading Georgia metros; the Griffin *News* is well known in the smaller daily category; and among weeklies, the Dawsonville *County Advertiser and News* and the Swainsboro *Forest-Blade* are of fine quality. The Augusta *Chronicle*, established in 1785, is the South's oldest surviving paper.

Clearly, the Louisville *Courier-Journal* is Kentucky's finest metro; most respected among smaller dailies is the Paducah *Sun*. An extraordinary weekly is the crusading *Mountain Eagle* ("It Screams!") of Whitesburg.

Though its reputation has slipped in recent years, the New Orleans *Times-Picayune/States-Item* is Louisiana's premier daily. Gannett's Shreveport *Times* and the independent Baton Rouge *Advocate* are quality small dailies, and the innovative *Greater Plaquemines Post* is a frequent award winner among weeklies.

Jackson's *Clarion-Ledger* is Mississippi's best daily. Smaller dailies of note are the Greenwood *Commonwealth* and Biloxi-Gulfport *Daily Herald*. Quality weeklies include the Tylertown *Times*, *Lawrence County Press* (Monticello), and Kosciusko *Star-Herald*.

North Carolina choices in each category are the Charlotte *Observer*, the Morganton *News Herald*, and the Smithfield *Herald*; South Carolina's are the Greenville *News*, the Myrtle Beach *Sun-News*, and the Hilton Head Island *Island Packet*; Tennessee's are the Memphis *Commercial Appeal*, the Jackson *Sun*, and the Clinton *Courier-News*.

Texas's best metros are in Dallas, where the Times-Mirror group's *Times Herald* and Belo Corporation's *News* provide an example of competition breeding excellence. Good smaller dailies are the Corpus Christi *Caller* and the Lufkin *News*, and quality weeklies are the Marble Falls *Highlander* and Fort Stockton *Pioneer*.

Virginia selections are the Richmond *Times-Dispatch*,

the only statewide metro; the Fredericksburg *Free Lance-Star*; and the *Coalfield Progress* in Norton.

Today's South has no southern "newspaper of record" in the sense that the Richmond *Enquirer* filled that role in the Old South of the early 1800s when it was edited by the elegant and influential Thomas Ritchie.

Most of the South's earliest newspapers employed the designation "Gazette" in their mastheads, as in the earliest, the *South Carolina Gazette* (Charleston, founded in 1732). Gazettes appeared as the first newspapers in the following states: Virginia (Williamsburg, 1736), North Carolina (New Bern, 1751), Georgia (Savannah, 1763), Florida (*East-Florida Gazette*, St. Augustine, 1783), Kentucky (Lexington, 1787), Tennessee (the *Knoxville Gazette*, 1791), Mississippi (Natchez, 1799), and Arkansas (Port of Arkansas, 1819). Alabama's first paper was the *Mobile Centinel* (1811) and Texas's was the *Texas Republican* (Nacogdoches, 1819). Louisiana's first was published in French—the *Moniteur de la Louisiane* (New Orleans, 1794).

In the revolutionary era some of the earliest southern newspapers, such as the *South Carolina Gazette*, one of the papers in Benjamin Franklin's "chain," were staunchly behind the patriot cause. Others steered a less certain course. The *Georgia Gazette* became the *Royal Georgia Gazette* during the British occupation of Savannah, and the *South-Carolina and American General Gazette* of Charleston, originally a patriot organ, became the *Royal Gazette* when founder Robert Wells turned it over to son John. A second *Virginia Gazette*, this one in Norfolk, was removed to a British ship in 1775 and was published briefly from that unsteady location.

The nine dailies of New Orleans in the 1840s, most especially the *Picayune*, *Delta*, *Crescent*, *Tropic*, and *Bee*, enjoyed a period of prominence during the Mexican War. Outstanding among the special correspondents they dispatched to cover the action were George W. Kendall, cofounder of the *Picayune*, and James "Mustang" Freaner of the *Delta*.

During the Civil War southern papers suffered severe shortages of newsprint, ink, and labor, and they were subject to stiffer military censorship than their northern counterparts. When Associated Press copy was cut off, the Press Association of the Confederate States of America, or P.A., was founded to provide wire copy, operating during 1863 and 1864. The Memphis *Appeal* abandoned its physical plant just before the capture of that city in 1862 and set up on a flatcar. The "Moving Appeal" continued to publish in four states.

Important postwar journalists were Henry W. Grady of the Atlanta *Constitution* and Henry Watterson of the Louisville *Courier-Journal*, both leading spokesmen for the "New South."

The coming of chain ownership to the South began in earnest in the 1920s with E. W. Scripps's son Robert, who purchased or founded in that decade the Norfolk *Post*, Birmingham *Post*, Ft. Worth *Press*, Knoxville *News*, El Paso *Post*, Memphis *News-Scimitar*, and Knoxville *Sentinel*. Since that time the independent newspaper owners of the South have seized the tax advantages offered by chain purchase with an avidity that has matched publishers in other parts of the nation.

Certainly, southern journalism has seen its share of colorful individuals: "Parson" William Brownlow, the picturesque mountaineer who edited and published the Knoxville *Whig*, last of the Union holdouts in the Civil War period; Cassius M. Clay of Kentucky, founder of the antislavery *True American* in Lexington, who armed his paper's offices with rifles and a cannon; Opie Read of the *Arkansas Traveler* in Little Rock, which built a large circulation based on Read's humorous sketches of rural life; and W. B. Townsend, who founded Georgia's *Dahlonega Nugget* in 1892 and composed his stories while setting them in type. The Atlanta *Journal* alone can boast having employed humorist Don Marquis; Erskine Caldwell, chronicler of red-clay poverty; Margaret Mitchell, author of *Gone with the Wind*; and Grantland Rice, the first American newspaperman to gain fame writing about sports.

Of the 205 foreign-language newspapers currently published in the United States, only 12 are located in the largely homogenized South; all 12 are in Florida and Texas. Eight are Spanish-language papers, the best known of which are probably Miami's daily *Diario Las Americas* and the Dallas weekly *El Sol De Texas*. The Miami *Herald*'s all-Spanish edition, *El Miami Herald*, has also been a successful response to the tremendous influx of Hispanics that has altered that city's cultural makeup. The remaining four are two Czech weeklies in Granger and West, Tex.; an Italian weekly in Tampa, Fla.; and a Swedish weekly in Austin, Tex.

The South makes a stronger showing in black newspapers. Of the 210 being published nationwide, 86 (41 percent) are in the South. The greatest number are in Florida (18), Texas (16), and Georgia (13). Atlanta has five black papers; Dallas, Houston, and Fort Worth have four each; and Miami three. Of the 86, the sole daily is the *Atlanta Daily World*. Largest of the weeklies are Houston's *Forward Times* and Little Rock's *Southern Mediator*. Few southern whites are aware of these papers, which is evidence of the persistence of two cultures in the South despite the great strides that have been made toward racial harmony. The first American Indian newspaper, the *Cherokee Phoenix*, was published in New Echota, Ga., from 1828 to 1834.

Because an area's newspapers generally reflect the population they serve, a paper's failings tend to be those of its readers. Particular problems for southern papers are shortsightedness, a reluctance to look farther than one's own borders; triteness, most especially in the community correspondents' columns of small-town weeklies; and a failure to lead in redressing social ills.

The latter problem is mainly a failure of the editorial page, where far too many southern papers resort to bland "canned copy" rather than producing incisive opinions written locally. In so doing, these papers serve as lapdogs to vested interests rather than as watchdogs for their readers. How many of today's southern editors and columnists will enjoy the reputation for courage earned by yesterday's Douglas Southall Freeman and Virginius

Dabney of Virginia, Nell Battle Lewis of North Carolina, Henry Watterson of Kentucky, John Temple Graves of Alabama, Hodding Carter of Mississippi, or Julian Harris and Henry W. Grady of Georgia?

See also BLACK LIFE: Press, Black; INDUSTRY: / Grady, Henry W.; LITERATURE: / Caldwell, Erskine; MYTHIC SOUTH: / Mitchell, Margaret

Sam G. Riley
Virginia Polytechnic Institute

John D. Allen, in *Culture in the South*, ed. W. T. Couch (1934); Thomas D. Clark and Albert D. Kirwan, *The South since Appomattox: A Century of Regional Change* (1967); Robert Spencer Cotterill, *The Old South: The Geographic, Economic, Social, Political, and Cultural Expansion, Institutions, and Nationalism of the Ante-Bellum South* (1936); Edwin Emery and Michael Emery, *The Press and America: An Interpretive History of the Mass Media* (1978); Frank Luther Mott, *American Journalism: A History, 1690–1960* (1962); Francis Butler Simkins, *The South, Old and New: A History, 1820–1947* (1947).

Newspapers, Country

The Civil War all but decimated southern country newspapers. Only 182 weeklies, nearly all of them short-staffed and many published with substitute paper and inks on worn-out equipment, survived after Appomattox. Yet the southern country press reemerged to serve its region as a unifying element and a catalyst for change. To an extent seldom found elsewhere in the world, country newspapers in the postwar American South reflected an intimacy with their readers and a profound identification with the region's culture. A Henry Watterson of the Louisville *Courier-Journal* or a Henry W. Grady of the Atlanta *Constitution* commanded—and deserved—national attention; but it was in the town halls and country courthouses that the real New South took shape and the soul of southern journalism grew.

The community press generally existed to report local items that would appear in no other newspaper and to recognize and encourage local progress. Post–Civil War southern country papers, however, were additionally characterized by the problems that a one-party political system and a one-crop agricultural economy posed. Most debilitating of all was the difficulty of publishing a balanced community newspaper in a multiracial environment where old prejudices died hard. Many southern editors simply ignored news of the black community. As late as 1960 a leading black spokesman declared, "If you read the white press, Negroes are never born, never finish school, never marry, never have children, and never win any honors." Papers that did report on the black community were apt to segregate such news well inside the paper under such headings as "News of Colored." Often a thin line replaced the heading; news of the black community appeared below the line. No other label was necessary.

Southern black leaders attempted, with only limited success, to develop newspapers of their own. The first, *L'Union*, published half in French and half in English, appeared in New Orleans in 1862; the *Colored American* of Augusta, Ga., began in 1865. Both represented attempts to explain to blacks their new constitutional rights.

The white press, meanwhile, grew rapidly; 20 years after the end of the Civil War, southern newspapers had increased tenfold, to 1,827. Most were modest-sized county seat weeklies, their thin economic base bolstered by income from legal advertising and county job printing contracts. The editors extolled the virtues of the small family farm and of shopping with hometown merchants, while simultaneously promoting their communities as sites for urgently needed industrial development. Attention in the news columns focused overwhelmingly on local matters. "If it doesn't happen here, as far as my paper is concerned, it doesn't happen at all," a North Carolina editor said, and many of his fellow southern editors would have agreed with him.

The editorial columns of southern country newspapers reflected, and often gave direction to, the conservatism of their audiences. But the region also produced an astonishing number of spirited editors who have spoken out, often explosively, against the prevailing climate of opinion. The South's first commercial printers, John Buckner and William Nuthead, for example, were shut down by royal authorities soon after they set up shop in Gloucester County, Va., in 1682; they were chastised for presuming to publish without an official license. Nuthead resurfaced three years later in St. Mary's, Md., where, under a different jurisdiction, he established the South's first ongoing commercial press.

After licensing and other forms of prior restraint began to disappear, crusading southern editors often faced another, and potentially even more sinister, kind of repression—the hard disapproval of their fellow citizens. In Lexington, Ky., for example, when Cassius M. Clay launched an abolitionist newspaper, the *True American*, he and his small staff endured hatred from throughout the community. Undaunted, Clay lined the outside door with sheet iron, then "purchased two brass four-pounder cannon at Cincinnati and placed them, loaded with shot and nails, on a table breast high; had folding doors secured with a chain, which could open upon the move and give play to my cannon. I furnished my office with Mexican lances, and a limited number of guns. There were six or eight persons who stood ready to defend me. If defeated, they were to escape by a trap-door in the roof; and I had placed a keg of powder, with a match, which I could set off and blow up the office and all my invaders; and this I should most certainly have done." Proslavery forces gave Clay a wide berth for several weeks, but then, when the nervy publisher was recovering at his home from typhoid fever, they broke into his newspaper office, neatly packed up his type cases and his press, and shipped everything to Cincinnati.

The literature of southern journalism is filled with

colorful, sometimes shocking, stories of country editors who risked life and property by attacking racism in all its manifestations. Several of these individuals—Hodding Carter and Hazel Brannon Smith of Mississippi, among other southern country editors—received Pulitzer Prizes for courage and excellence in editorial writing. P. D. East established the *Petal Paper* (1953) in Petal, Miss., and made it into an institution of small-town racial liberalism. His memoir *The Magnolia Jungle* (1960) chronicled his conflicts. Editors and reporters thrived on politics and parlayed their early journalistic experience on southern country newspapers into positions of national prominence. Turner Catledge began his newspaper career on the Neshoba, Miss., *Democrat* and ended it as the distinguished editor of the *New York Times*, where the chief political columnist was Arthur Krock, formerly of Glasgow, Ky., who became the only journalist ever to be honored with four Pulitzer Prizes. Some southern editors made news as well as reported it; more than a few were elected to legislative seats, and several country editors—W. D. Jelks of Alabama, James K. Vardaman of Mississippi, Keen Johnson of Kentucky, James Stephen Hogg of Texas, and Robert Taylor of Tennessee among them—were elected governors. Also, network television news teams and national newspaper and newsmagazine staff rosters currently contain the names of many correspondents who earned their spurs covering political rallies in the South.

In addition to political matters, the southern country editor typically devotes a great deal of space to local history. While many community editors everywhere feel a strong sense of tradition, southern country editors often write about local pioneers in tones approaching reverence. As one result, regional historians—and the South has had superb ones—can find in the files of the country press an uncommonly rich vein of authoritative source material, nostalgic though it may be.

Historically, though, sentimentalism has not characterized other aspects of country newspapers' operations, and modern equipment has been eagerly embraced. Since the Civil War, when the loss of slave help signaled an end to cheap labor, southern editors have been national leaders in developing improved production facilities and in adopting labor-saving methods and equipment. Southern weeklies were trailblazers in the adoption of offset lithography, which ushered in a dramatic new era in printing technology; and in 1939 the Opelousas, La., *Daily World* attracted wide attention by becoming the first daily newspaper to publish exclusively by this process. Since that time nearly all the country's community papers and most of the metropolitan dailies have adopted the offset system.

Editorial and advertising staffs remain overwhelmingly white, despite a number of vigorous efforts to hire, retain, and promote minority employees. Studies indicate that some 2,700 black newspapers have been founded in the United States, 70 percent of them in the South. Relatively few have lasted more than a year. Many southern publishers strive to meet the American Society of Newspaper Editors' goal of developing in their newsrooms by the year 2000 the same racial percentages as in the society as a whole but face such problems as a shortage of trained minority applicants.

See also BLACK LIFE: Press, Black; INDUSTRY: / Grady, Henry W.

Ronald Truman Farrar
University of Kentucky

Thomas D. Clark, *The Southern Country Editor* (1948); Cassius M. Clay, *The Life of Cassius Marcellus Clay* (1886); William C. Havard, *Virginia Quarterly Review* (Winter 1983); Douglas C. McMurtrie, *History of Printing in the United States: The Story of the Introduction of the Press and of Its History and Influence during the Pioneer Period in Each State of the Union*, vol. 2 (1936); Frank Luther Mott, *American Journalism: A History, 1690–1960* (1962); William Howard Taft, *American Journalism History: An Outline* (1968).

Radio Industry

Radio communication designed for reception by the general public is known as broadcasting. The origins of southern broadcasting are indistinct. Clearly, southerners engaged in wireless telegraphy and telephony before the advent of formal broadcasting. As early as 1892 Nathan B. Stubblefield, a melon farmer, transmitted speech successfully from a small shack near his farmhouse in Murray, Ky., but he hardly intended to reach the general public. Nevertheless, a historical marker on the outskirts of Murray announces to all that the site is "The Birthplace of Radio."

Beginning in 1912, federal regulation required every wireless transmitter operator to secure a license from the Department of Commerce's Radio Service Section. The Radio Act of 1912 made amateur operators aware that a significant number of them were scattered across the country. Under the law, "call letters" were assigned to each licensee, and a list of the radio stations so licensed was published. Radio clubs sprang into existence for the exchange of information, and the contact between them tended to reinforce the enthusiasm of their members. From such organizations came many of the early broadcasters of the 1920s.

The first licenses issued in the South under the specific classification of broadcasting were granted in February 1922 to two utility companies, one in Alabama and the second in Arkansas. Montgomery Light & Water Power Company of Montgomery, Ala., received the call letters WGH, and the Pine Bluff Company, a division of Arkansas Light and Power, was given WOK. As with many early stations, though, the realities of broadcasting quickly overcame the glowing visions of the initial moments on the air. The result was that both soon vanished from the roster of operational stations.

Within a month the pace had quickened. During March 1922 nine more southern stations were licensed, including two destined to be mainstays among the region's broadcasters—WWL in New Orleans, licensed to Loyola University, and WSB, operated by the Atlanta *Journal*. But the southern states were slower to develop substantial radio facilities than the nation as a whole. Indeed, a continuing complaint of Dixie politicians during the middle 1920s was the supposed discrimination being suffered by a South saddled with inadequate radio service.

The 1928 Annual Report of the Federal Radio Commission, created by Congress in 1927 to bring some order out of the chaos of broadcasting's first decade, revealed that the 11 former Confederate states (excluding the border states of Missouri, Kentucky, and Maryland) could boast only 77 operating stations, slightly more than the state of Illinois alone and just 11.6 percent of the nation's total. Further, per capita incomes that trailed badly behind national figures prevented the number of "radio families" in the South from approaching the totals for the United States as a whole. While the South's share of American families was 28.9 percent in 1930, its percentage of radio families was a scant 11.9 percent. Northern radio families at the same time exceeded 76 percent.

Despite the relatively slow overall development, some individual broadcasters made their impact felt. One of the most flamboyant and controversial was William Kennon Henderson, whose unvarying formula—"Hello, world, doggone you! This is KWKH in Shreveport, Lou-EE-siana, and it's W. K. Henderson talkin' to you"—introduced him to a daily radio audience that stretched across the bulk of the United States. He continually exceeded his authorized power and usurped frequencies not assigned him. A New Orleans newspaper referred to Henderson as the "Bolshevik of radio," but admitted that "nearly every home in the South where there's a radio set has listened to him."

In 1929 Henderson embarked upon his most famous crusade; he declared war on the nation's retail chain stores. He castigated them on the air as "dirty, low down, daylight burglars" and as "damnable thieves from Wall Street." Moreover, Henderson established a nationwide organization, ostensibly to assist him in the chain-store struggle. Naming it the "Merchant Minute Men," he bragged that it numbered 35,000 independent merchants in 4,000 towns throughout the country by 1931. The deepening depression, however, mired Henderson in debt, and increasing pressure from creditors forced him to acquiesce in the sale of the station to new owners in 1933.

From its earliest days southern broadcasting developed a close association with country music. With the coming of radio, southern folksingers found an important new outlet for their talents. Probably the first station to feature country music was WSB in Atlanta. Within a few months after going on the air in 1922, WSB was presenting several folk performers including the Reverend Andrew Jenkins, a blind gospel singer, and Fiddlin' John Carson. With WSB leading the way, radio stations all over the South and the Midwest, as well, began offering country musicians and singers.

No discussion of southern country music and its relation to radio would be complete without recognizing the impact of Nashville's Grand Ole Opry. The vehicle by which it gained attention was WSM, a station owned by the National Life and Accident Insurance Company. In November 1925, just a month after WSM first went on the air, it broadcast a program initially known as the WSM Barn Dance. A year later the country music show acquired the new name of Grand Ole Opry (to contrast it with the Grand Opera concerts being broadcast by the networks). Agents of National Life often took advantage of the connection by introducing themselves to potential clients as being from the Grand Ole Opry Insurance Company. By World War II the program had become the most important country music show on the air, especially after 1939, when the National Broadcasting Company began carrying a 30-minute segment on the network every Saturday night.

Stations such as Memphis's WDIA and Nashville's WLAC were key institutions in the spread of black music in the 1940s and 1950s. WDIA popularized the blues of the Mississippi Delta and Beale Street. WLAC was typical of other stations in broadcasting news and popular music during the days but switching to blues, gospel, and rhythm and blues at night. The station's 50,000-watt signal reached 20 states, and its format made celebrities of disc jockeys such as William T. "Hoss" Allen and John R. (Richbourg).

The immediate postwar years saw a broadcasting explosion. In October 1945 there were some 900 commercial AM stations in the United States, but soon that situation was dramatically changed. By June 1948 over 2,000 AM broadcasters were on the air, plus something new—about 1,000 FM licensees and 109 television stations, the latter representing the wave of the future. Translated into community terms, the number of towns and cities with stations grew from 566 on V-J Day to 1,063 in early 1947. The growth was greatest in the smaller hamlets, which lacked radio facilities before the war. In Louisiana, for example, there were just 13 operating stations in seven cities in 1941, but 10 years later there were 45 stations and local service had finally come to the rural areas of the state.

Although the best-known programs deserted radio for the new medium of television, radio was still regarded as a successful business opportunity. The number of AM and FM licensees continued to grow to the point that virtually every American town of respectable size now has its own station or stations. As for the larger cities, to cite just three southern examples, Atlanta today has a choice of 12 AM and 10 FM stations; Houston has 11 AM and 15 FM; and New Orleans 11 AM and 12 FM stations.

Outstanding among stations based in the larger metropolitan areas are those broadcasting on clear channel frequencies with 50,000 watts of power, making them regional or even interregional rather than just local operations. Among this group are such longtime southern broadcasting leaders as WSB (Atlanta), WHAS (Louisville), WWL (New Orleans), WOAI (San Antonio), WSM (Nashville), and WRVA (Richmond). All date from the

1920s and thus can cite over a half century of broadcast experience.

See also MUSIC: / Grand Ole Opry

C. Joseph Pusateri
University of San Diego

John H. De Witt, Jr., *Tennessee Historical Quarterly* (Summer 1971); C. Joseph Pusateri, *Enterprise in Radio: WWL and the Business of Broadcasting in America* (1980); Reginald Stuart, *New York Times* (12 July 1982); Barnwell R. Turnipseed, "The Development of Broadcasting in Georgia" (M.A. thesis, University of Georgia, 1950); Wesley H. Wallace, "The Development of Broadcasting in North Carolina, 1922–1948" (Ph.D. dissertation, Duke University, 1962).

Television Industry

New York's television station WNBT inaugurated the first commercial telecasts on 1 July 1941. But it was not until 22 April 1948 that Richmond's WTVR began broadcasting; it has ever since billed itself as "the South's first television station." That fall stations opened in Atlanta, Fort Worth, Louisville, Memphis, and New Orleans. The next year, 1949, Miami and Charlotte stations went on the air. Not until 1953, after a temporary Federal Communications Commission (FCC) moratorium on new licenses, were stations sanctioned in Mobile, Charleston, Jackson, and Little Rock.

Those first licenses awarded between 1948 and 1953 permitted at least one station in each of 12 southern states. The region's television broadcast industry since then has sustained considerable growth relative to its population and market share. For example, during the late 1940s the FCC granted licenses to only 16 southern stations, but during the 1950s it licensed 145, followed by 97 in the 1960s (many were for PBS or state education system channels), and another 92 since 1970.

Thus, by 1980 the region had approximately 350 stations, or 32 percent of the nation's total. That year Texas led all southern states with 72 stations, followed by Florida with 45. Arkansas had the least, 14, with Mississippi's 18 next. During the initial development of the southern television broadcasting industry, stations were overwhelmingly affiliated with one of the three major commercial networks. However, by the early 1960s many more of the region's new stations chose to be independent commercial enterprises or were intended as nonprofit educational broadcast facilities. As of 1980 network-affiliated stations accounted for 58 percent of the South's total, and independent and nonprofit channels for 42 percent.

Many of the region's commercial stations were originally closely held organizations, perhaps the most famous being KTBC in Austin, Tex., owned by Lady Bird Johnson. KTBC-TV received one of the first licenses awarded in 1952 after the FCC's four-year freeze. More importantly, it was the only VHF channel assigned to the market, providing the station with a monopoly against UHF competition. It illustrated a station's potential impact upon its viewing area.

Upon occasion the stations, particularly those locally owned, could offend elements of their white viewing audience simply by offering network programming. In 1952 Georgia's Governor Herman Talmadge spoke for many when he attacked network television for racially integrated programming, which he believed would lead to a "complete abolition of segregation customs." Later when the networks in 1957 announced a censorship of racially objectionable words such as "massa" and "old black Joe" from the songs of Stephen Foster, some southern white viewers reacted with considerable anger.

A decade later it was local programming that came under attack for perpetuating just what the networks had been accused of ending. For instance, liberal public protest in 1969 prevented a license renewal for WLBT in Jackson, Miss. Then owned by the Lamar Life Insurance Company, the station fought charges that it utilized its air time to promote segregation and in general denied use of its airwaves to blacks and civil rights proponents. A U.S. federal court found WLBT in violation of its license obligation to serve the Jackson community, 40 percent of which was black. It was the first time a television license was lost on substantive grounds.

In a similar but far broader action, the FCC in 1975 denied the renewal of eight licenses held by the Alabama Educational Television Commission, a state agency. The federal government determined that the eight stations were racially discriminatory in overall programming and were guilty of "pervasive neglect" of the state's black population. A considerable improvement in the stations' operations led eventually to a restoration of broadcast rights.

As was true of the industry as a whole, however, stations increasingly began to serve a broader community and at the same time to represent a wider ownership. KWTX Broadcasting Co., for example, by 1980 included stations in Waco and Bryan, Tex., as well as affiliates in Louisiana and Oklahoma. Many of the corporations are not even southern: the LIN Broadcasting Company, headquartered in New York, and the Scripps-Howard Broadcasting Company in Cincinnati manage stations in Florida, Tennessee, Texas, and Virginia as well as Illinois, Ohio, and Oklahoma.

In recent years southern television has demonstrated considerable business acumen and innovative promise. The Turner Broadcasting System's Atlanta-based "superstation" WTBS and Cable News Network (CNN) are but the most familiar examples of regional production for a national audience. Numerous other local stations have begun to contribute original programming; Miami PBS station WPBT in 1982 produced *A House Divided: Denmark Vesey's Rebellion*, one of many productions originating from public televison stations in particular. Especially well known in the ETV industry is the Southern Educâtional Communications Association (SECA), both a production center and regional network. Based in Columbia, it is usually referred to as "the South Carolina Network." Among its productions have been William F. Buckley's *Firing Line* and *Lowell Thomas Remembers* as well as a series of regional theater and dramatized short stories. SECA serves 87 public television stations in 16 states with both instructional and general programming.

Edward D. C. Campbell, Jr.
Virginia State Library

Erik Barnouw, *Tube of Plenty: The Evolution of American Television* (1975); *Broadcasting-Cable Yearbook: 1980* (1980); Les Brown, *Encyclopedia of Television* (1982), *The New York Times Encyclopedia of Television* (1977); J. Fred MacDonald, *Blacks and White TV: Afro-Americans in Television since 1948* (1983); *Southern Exposure* (Winter 1975).

Television Movies

Over eight nights in January 1977 approximately 130 million Americans watched all or part of the television miniseries *Roots*. The eighth segment of *Roots* averaged 51 percent of the possible television audience and 71 percent of the actual audience, a record at that time. *Roots* broke the previous record set by the first broadcast of the 1939 classic *Gone with the Wind* in November 1976, which attracted 47 percent and 65 percent shares of the respective audiences. These figures not only document the immense popularity of media depictions of Dixie, but also demonstrate the complications inherent in differentiating among media forms.

Neither *Gone with the Wind* nor *Roots* is, strictly speaking, a television movie. *Gone with the Wind*, of course, was created as a theatrical film, and its drawing power in 1976 can be attributed precisely to its earlier exclusion from the smaller screen. *Roots* was originally planned as an eight-week miniseries; ironically enough, Fred Silverman's decision to present it on eight consecutive nights was motivated by his fear of a flop. By stricter definition, television movies are dramatizations using video technology intended entirely for home viewing at a single sitting. In any case, television "movies" concerned with the South, like other media depictions of the region, use the symbols provided by its history to dramatize the contradictions of larger American myths. Although the television movie has a relatively short history—the first three were made in 1964—over the past two decades the form has grown to be a staple of television programming. Each of the three major networks makes dozens each year, while educational networks, cable television companies, and independent producers provide even more. In general, the television movie was developed in response to changes in the feature-film industry. The breakup of the big studios and the fragmentation of the mass audience meant that Hollywood was producing fewer pictures suitable for televising. To satisfy their omnivorous appetite for film, the networks soon were making their own movies. NBC began its *World Premieres* in 1966, ABC launched its *Movie of the Week* in 1968, and CBS followed suit with its *Friday Night Movies* in 1971. Essentially, the television movies are the "B" pictures of the contemporary era. Like the traditional program fillers of the past, they are low-budget, topical, melodramatic, genre pieces.

The predominant television image of the South depicts rural innocence, whether at home in Mayberry or expatriated to Beverly Hills. These mindless series portraits reflect the "hick flicks" of the past that presented Will Rogers, Bob Burns, Lum and Abner, and others at home and abroad. The present-day "gasoline operas" starring good old boys like Burt Reynolds inspired the antics of the *Dukes of Hazzard* characters. Television movies presented minor variations in dozens of yokel epics and open-road sagas. Most of these efforts are immediately forgettable except in terms of confirming the American predilection for innocence triumphant and pretension-leveling comedy, which can be traced back as far as the 19th-century stage and the humor of the Old Southwest.

A more serious version of rural innocence was the phenomenon of the Waltons. "Serious" television writer Earl Hamner, Jr., re-created his memories of Appalachian family life during the 1930s for a Christmas movie, *The Homecoming*, which proved a surprisingly strong draw in 1971. It inspired a very successful series, *The Waltons* (1972–81), and several other special movies, such as *A Wedding on Walton's Mountain* (1982). Production values were excellent, striking a fine balance of realism and sentiment. The social importance of *The Waltons* existed in its affirmation of simple, agrarian, and familial values in fictional form during a decade when America veered sharply away from them in reality.

The plantation South, probably because of production costs, was less often seen on television. This situation changed in the 1970s when the ongoing American reconsideration of its racial myths elicited several important works. The first was the adaptation in 1974 of black author Ernest J. Gaines's harshly realistic novel, *The Autobiography of Miss Jane Pittman*. Cicely Tyson projected the personality of a slave girl who lived long enough to participate in the civil rights demonstrations with such power that many viewers thought her a historical figure. Indeed, New York Governor Hugh Carey listed Jane Pittman in a speech honoring actual black heroes and heroines. Cicely Tyson also re-created Harriet Tubman, the black emancipationist, in *A Woman Called Moses* (1978), from a script by black writer Lonnie Elder III. Some of the scenes in this television movie, including one in which the young slave woman is harnessed to pull a farm wagon, are among the most powerful and moving depictions in any art form of the American national sin of slavery.

The most important, if not the most artistically successful, of television's plantation images exists in *Roots*. For all of its limitations, the made-for-television miniseries must rank with *Uncle Tom's Cabin*, *Birth of a Nation*, and *Gone with the Wind* as popular dramatizations of America's complex racial myths. In fact, *Roots* might be viewed as a contemporary *Uncle Tom's Cabin*, a work that simply upends the stereotypes of *Birth of a Nation* and *Gone with the Wind*. In Dixon's or Mitchell's novels blacks are either docile or demented; in Alex Haley's novelized family memoir, whites are either evil or weak, or both. Such stereotyping does not make for subtle art, but it does create exciting entertainment. *Roots* was all of that on television, mixing the traditional sensationalism of floggings and miscegenation with a cathartic wallow in collective guilt.

Roots spawned sequels, of course, and as they became better they suffered in popularity. *Roots: The Next Generations* (1979) proved much stronger if less popular television, and *Palmerstown, U.S.A.* (1980), an irregular series based on Haley's youth in Henning, Tenn., lasted just a season. These later works demonstrate some interesting connections with *The Waltons* and other family fare. Perhaps *Roots*'s ultimate success was in its combination of a nightmare past with the dream of the nuclear family reunited in the future.

Since *Roots*, television movies about the South have covered all the genres. The plantation South has appeared once more in *Freedom Road* (1979), a reprise of *Roots* characterized by Muhammad Ali's inept acting, and *Beulah Land* (1980), a *Gone with the Wind* ripoff presenting the moonlight-and-magnolias mythology intact. The Civil War received extensive treatment from both northern and southern viewpoints in *The Blue and the Gray* (1982). The docudrama, an important variant of contemporary television movies, was represented well in *King* (1978), a thoughtful biography of the martyred civil rights leader ably portrayed by Paul Winfield. The country music film, a big screen subgenre in recent years, had small-screen exposure in *Stand by Your Man* (1982), the story of often-married country star Tammy Wynette.

A woman who does stand by her man, Gertie Nevels, is at the center of *The Dollmaker* (1984), perhaps the finest television movie about a southern character ever made. Jane Fonda played a beleaguered mountain woman transplanted to Detroit by the migrations to the defense plants of World War II. The television version proved a literate adaptation of Harriett Arnow's neglected classic novel.

The Dollmaker represents the literary adaptations that, like their sources, remain the most complete and complex visions of the South. Some were done by the commercial networks, such as ABC's recent remake of *A Streetcar Named Desire* (1983), which presented Ann-Margret grappling with the grand role of Blanche DuBois. Cable networks like HBO, as well as PBS, have also remade Tennessee Williams's plays; Showtime presented a memorable *Cat on a Hot Tin Roof* in 1984 with Jessica Lange and Tommie Lee Jones. PBS underwrote the *American Short Story* (1977–80), with fine short versions of works by William Faulkner, Richard Wright, Mark Twain, Katherine Anne Porter, Flannery O'Connor, and Ernest J. Gaines.

None of these literate works captured the audience ratings of *Roots* or *Gone with the Wind* or the *Dukes of Hazzard*, precisely because they pictured the lights and shadows of southern life. Through the southern genre's simplified stereotypes, television movies both reflect and reinforce the generic patterns found in other popular media; therefore, television movies not only form an important piece in the mosaic of the southern experience, but also finally tell us a good deal about the national use of the symbols provided by southern history.

See also MYTHIC SOUTH articles

Joseph R. Millichap
Western Kentucky University

Tim Brooks and Earle Marsh, *The Complete Directory to Prime Time Network TV Shows, 1946–Present* (1979); Jack Temple Kirby, *Media-Made Dixie: The South in the American Imagination* (1978); Marsha McGee, *Journal of American Culture* (No. 3, 1983); Horace Newcomb, *Appalachian Journal* (Autumn–Winter 1979–80); Eric Peter Verschuure, *Journal of Popular Culture* (Winter 1982).

Television Series

With the exception of the "Old West," no region of the United States has been subjected to such frequent treatment on network series television as has the South. Networks occasionally featured southern themes and settings in separate episodes of dramatic anthology series throughout the 1950s, but the earliest southern presence in series television was in the country music/variety format. ABC's *Hayloft Hoedown* (1948) was short-lived, but its energetic assortment of country music, square dancing, and rural comedy hinted at things to come. As with other series such as *Kobb's Korner* (a 1948–49 CBS entry ostensibly set in Shufflebottom's General Store, U.S.A.) and the popular *Midwestern Hayride* (syndicated 1947–67, NBC/ABC, 1951–59), *Hayloft Hoedown* was not directly linked to the South. Nevertheless, performers and audience alike understood that the humor, music (including yodeling), dress (overalls and flannel shirts were ubiquitous), and general demeanor of the artists were somehow linked to life and culture south of the Ohio River. *Midwestern Hayride* regulars included "The County Briar Hoppers" and the "Pine Mountain Boys," groups whose names were clearly intended to evoke the rural South. Although not nearly so fast paced nor so finely produced, these early series contained all the elements that would make the more self-consciously southern *Hee Haw* a success in the 1970s.

The Real McCoys (ABC 1957–62, CBS 1962–63) was the first major fictional television series featuring southerners. This situation comedy with dramatic overtones was set on a small California ranch, but the central characters were a family of West Virginians who had migrated west in search of a better life. The McCoy family consisted of Amos, his grandson and his wife, Luke and Kate, and Luke's younger brother and sister, Little Luke and Hassie. This extended, nearly impoverished, but always resilient farm family relied heavily upon its southern heritage to weather hard times. Themes of pride, religious values, determination, willingness to work hard, and, perhaps most of all, the preeminence of the family dominated episodes, and this portrayal set the tone for many series to follow. *The Real McCoys* was quite successful, once having risen to fifth place in the year-end Nielsen ratings, and probably influenced CBS to try in 1960 *The Andy Griffith Show*, the success of which is often credited with the rise of the southern/rural situation comedy as a dominant form of television in the 1960s.

Both series had demonstrated that situation comedies in southern settings (or at least those featuring southern characters) could draw respectable audiences. The series *were* more popular in the South and in rural areas in general, but their national and urban appeal was strong enough to entice advertisers. In 1962 James T. Aubrey, president of CBS, sensed a trend, and he played a key role in the introduction of *The Beverly Hillbillies* (1962–71), which was instantly and overwhelmingly popular.

By 1965 CBS offered three additional situation comedies set in the South: *Petticoat Junction*, *Green Acres*, and *Gomer Pyle, U.S.M.C.* In 1968 Andy Griffith left his series and it became *Mayberry, R.F.D. Hee Haw*, a country music/variety show, found a place in the CBS schedule the following year. Such successes at CBS inspired ABC to offer southern series. The network included the animated *Calvin and the Colonel* in the 1961–62 schedule and in 1965–66 offered *Tammy*, a situation comedy set in a Louisiana bayou, and *The Long Hot Summer*, a dramatic series based on William Faulkner's short novel, *The Hamlet*, but none of these ventures had lasting impact.

By 1970 advertisers had begun the demographic study of television audiences, and, although the CBS series were still successful, the network decided to eliminate the southern programs from its 1971–72 schedule. These shows drew too heavily on rural, southern, and small-town portions of the populace to satisfy Madison Avenue. Nevertheless, all the CBS comedies remained popular in syndication into the 1980s, and their impact on the image of the South and of southerners has been enormous. Moreover, *Hee Haw*'s producers simply refused to allow the show to die. The series continued in first-run production for syndication, and, as of the 1983–84 season, seemed as healthy as ever in scores of local markets throughout the nation. NBC later attempted to resurrect the country music format with *The Nashville Palace*, but the 1981 series was a dismal failure.

After a one-year hiatus the South rose again in network prime-time programming, and once again CBS led the way. After surprisingly high ratings were achieved by *The Homecoming*, a 1971 Christmas special, in 1972 the network decided to develop a series around the Depression-era struggles of the Walton family from the Blue Ridge Mountains of Jefferson County, Va. Although *The Waltons* had a rocky beginning, the series built a loyal following and was one of the more positive portrayals of the South in series television. The tradition of *The Waltons* was extended by *Palmerstown, U.S.A.* in 1980, which depicted race relations in Henning, Tenn., in the 1930s and 1940s. Launched as a seven-episode miniseries in the spring, *Palmerstown, U.S.A.* was successful enough to be returned as a regular series the next season. Alex Haley, the author of *Roots*, and Norman Lear were the series's creators.

Other series of the 1970s and early 1980s were often less than positive in their portrayals of the South and its people. *The Texas Wheelers* began its brief ABC run in 1974. The Wheelers were poor, rural Texans (a lazy, scheming, and cantankerous widower and his four children), and the series exploited the "poor white trash" stereotype. In 1977 ABC launched *Carter Country*, a situation comedy set in a tiny village in rural Georgia. Also in 1977, NBC offered *The Kallikaks*, the story of a poor Appalachian family that moved to California to run a service station. The *Dukes of Hazzard* (CBS) and *The Misadventures of Sheriff Lobo* (NBC) appeared in 1979. The former was a mixture of comedy, adventure, hot cars, and "good old boy" escapades, while the latter featured the antics of a slightly corrupt law officer. These series portrayed the South as a raucous, backward, and largely rural region populated by stereotypical redneck white people and dishonest public officials.

Recent series have portrayed the New South, including *Dallas*, the saga of the oil-rich Ewing family, and *Flamingo Road*, a racy nighttime soap opera set in Florida. Only *Dallas*, which began its CBS run in 1978, has enjoyed lengthy popularity. *Flamingo Road* ran on NBC from 1980 to 1982 and was set in a "small Southern town" run by Sheriff Titus Semple, a small-time political boss. Both series featured the unsavory antics of wealthy southerners, but in some respects the characterizations and plots were not distinctively southern. With minor alterations these dramatizations, especially *Dallas*, might easily be set in other regions. Nevertheless, popular images of the South as a land of corruption and avarice among the well-to-do were undoubtedly affirmed.

Matt Houston opened on ABC in 1982. The program, which features a Texan who solves crimes while in California, simply provided an attractive backdrop for run-of-the-mill detective yarns. Early in 1983 CBS launched *The Mississippi* as a midyear replacement. The series concerned Ben Walker, a lawyer who traveled the river in search of adventure. Along the way he defended a series of desperate clients who could not afford to pay for legal services. In many instances the stories centered on distinctly southern themes and issues, including sensitive episodes on racism and bigotry in the region.

The fall of 1983 brought five new series, none overly successful. CBS offered *Cutter to Houston*, which was the story of three doctors working in comparatively primitive conditions in Cutter, Tex., a small town of "rednecks and cowgirls." NBC's *The Yellow Rose* was set on a sprawling ranch in west Texas and was as much a contemporary western as a southern series. *Boone*, on NBC, told the story of a 1950s Tennessee youth who wanted to become a Grand Ole Opry star—his family wanted him to sing in the church choir. Two continuing dramas were set on southern military bases—*For Love and Honor* on NBC and *Emerald Point N.A.S.* on CBS. Both extended the popular association of the South with military life.

With a few exceptions, television series have depicted

the South as a backward, somewhat uncivilized, largely rural, simple, and rather monolithic region. Geographic variations seemingly do not exist in television's Dixieland—Hooterville (*Petticoat Junction* and *Green Acres*), Mayberry (*The Andy Griffith Show* and *Mayberry, R.F.D.*), Frenchman's Bend (*The Long Hot Summer*), and even Walton's Mountain (*The Waltons*) are curiously similar. *Hee Haw*'s "Cornfield County" setting exploits every conventional stereotype of the rural, small-town South, from the ubiquitous general store to the ramshackle cabins of the small farmer. Fictional Hazzard County, the setting of the enormously successful *Dukes of Hazzard* series, is a land of swamps (complete with alligators!), fertile valleys, pine barrens, and mountains; in short, the fictional county's geography is that of the South as a whole.

Moreover, the geographically indiscriminate television South is populated by characters who are often far easier to deal with in terms of stereotypes than as individuals. Several clusters of characters are easily identified. First are the young, buxom country belles who, as often as not, romp through the countryside in cut-off jeans and panty hose, including Daisy of the *Dukes of Hazzard*, Elly May of *The Beverly Hillbillies*, and the three daughters of *Petticoat Junction*'s lead character. Pathetically inept bumpkins who frequently are unable to function competently in their occupational roles comprise a second group. A few examples include the title character in *Gomer Pyle, U.S.M.C.*, Deputy Barney Fife of *The Andy Griffith Show*, Jethro of *The Beverly Hillbillies*, Sheriff Roscoe P. Coltrane of the *Dukes of Hazzard*, and, from the same series, the naive Deputy Enos Straight, a character who was spun off in the short-lived *Enos* series.

Experienced, somewhat timeworn, but always witty bearers of southern folk wisdom form another major group of characters, with Jed Clampett of *The Beverly Hillbillies* being one of the finest examples. Three others worthy of mention, all dressed in the familiar bib overalls so often associated with this stereotype, are Grandpa Amos of *The Real McCoys*, Grandpa Zeb Walton, and the *Dukes of Hazzard*'s Uncle Jesse. The unscrupulous and corrupt southern "boss" stereotype is best represented by Jefferson Davis Hogg of the *Dukes of Hazzard* and *The Long Hot Summer*'s Will Varner. Even J. R. Ewing of *Dallas* can be forced into this mold. Shiftless, "no account" southerners, video versions of "poor white trash," appear in such creations as Zack Wheeler of *The Texas Wheelers* and Uncle Joe Carson of *Petticoat Junction*. Expectedly, "good old boys" abound in the television series South, with Bo and Luke Duke, who careen through Hazzard County in their hot car, "General Lee," providing the purest examples.

Although these stereotypes are the most common, nearly all of the stereotypes traditionally associated with the South have been portrayed in television series. The only major exception has been the traditional negative black stereotypes, which rarely appear on network television. Indeed, the opposite has sometimes been the case, as in *Carter Country*. This series featured policeman Curtis Baker, a talented black man from the North, who worked for a "lovable redneck sheriff." Baker was surrounded by bumbling white southerners, from the overweight major to Deputy Harley Puckett, good old boy *par excellence*.

The closest network television has come to presenting negative stereotypes of southern blacks in a regular, continuing series format was probably the 1961–62 animated series, *Calvin and the Colonel*. However, ABC was fairly cautious, for the civil rights movement was gaining momentum. The series was clearly derived from the *Amos 'n' Andy* series, which had been presented nearly a decade earlier, but *Calvin and the Colonel* featured the antics of a community of animals from the Deep South. Although this tactic served to quiet potential critics, there really was little question that the series was centered on black stereotypes: the voices of the colonel, a devious fox, and Calvin, a dimwitted bear, were supplied by Freeman Gosden and Charles Correll, the white actors who had performed *Amos 'n' Andy* on radio. Later series, primarily *Palmerstown* and *The Waltons*, also relied to a certain degree on black stereotypical characters in minor roles. However, these series regularly featured both black and white characters who were *not* stereotypes but who represented fully developed and individualized southerners.

Overall, television's portrayal of the South is a mixed bag of negative and positive images. Often seen as a region where family and community ties are strong and vital, a recurring theme nevertheless suggests that many southerners in positions of power take advantage of those virtues. Although some southerners are characterized as wise and witty, more are depicted as crude and insensitive bumpkins. Except for the comic-book violence of the *Dukes of Hazzard* and similar series, the image of the South as a violent region has not played a significant part in television's portrayal. Yet few series have grappled with the region's many difficulties in such important areas as race relations and economic structures, preferring instead to highlight superficial conflicts in their stories. An entire segment of the southern population, the middle class, is rarely treated in the television South. Instead, writers and producers offer stereotypical images of the very wealthy (*Dallas*) and the rural poor (*The Waltons* and *The Texas Wheelers*). While there have been some attempts to deal with the South and southern topics in dramatic series, the most common type of television series to portray the South has been the

Southfork Ranch, home of the television series Dallas

situation comedy. The television South has been a land of fantasy, redneck humor, adventure, and family drama, and as such has played an important role in the formation of popular images and attitudes toward the South, both within the region and in the nation at large.

See also BLACK LIFE: / Haley, Alex; MYTHIC SOUTH articles

Christopher D. Geist
Bowling Green State University

Roy Blount, Jr., *TV Guide* (2 February 1980); Tim Brooks and Earle Marsh, *The Complete Directory to Prime Time Network TV Shows, 1946–Present* (1979); Larry J. Gianakos, *Television Drama Series Programming: A Comprehensive Chronicle, 1947–80*, 3 vols. (1978); Jack Temple Kirby, *Media-Made Dixie: The South in the American Imagination* (1978); Marsha McGee, *Journal of American Culture* (No. 3, 1983); Horace Newcomb, *Appalachian Journal* (Autumn–Winter 1979–80); Eric Peter Verschuure, *Journal of Popular Culture* (Winter 1982).

Altman, Robert

(b. 1925) Film director.

The South represents a cross section of American attitudes and lifestyles in the films of Robert Altman. His southerners embody some of the best and worst traits of the American public. They are typically proud, resilient, and forceful, but they are also prone to racial and regional biases, to stubbornness and greed. Complacency appears to be the dominant trait of the southerner. In this quality the southerner most resembles the majority of the population of the United States—a population that, according to Altman, implicitly accepts corrupt political and economic institutions as natural parts of the American way of life. The South is depicted as a locus of conservatism in the United States. Altman seems to argue that the tendency to ignore or reject platforms for social change often results in the denial of individual freedom. This perspective is clearly suggested in Altman's films with southern characters or settings, such as the early films *M*A*S*H** (1969) and *Brewster McCloud* (1970), and is more fully developed in the later films *Thieves Like Us* (1974), *Nashville* (1975), and *Health* (1980).

In *M*A*S*H**, Captain Duke Forrest (Tom Skerritt) voices a set of racial prejudices that unfortunately have always been a part of the American national character. In *Brewster McCloud*, Houston is the perfect setting for a satiric attack on the dreams, ambitions, and foibles of middle America in general and the South in particular. *Thieves Like Us* is the director's first serious investigation of life in the South itself. The film depicts a claustrophobic and actively hostile environment for three convicts on the run, and from this landscape Altman draws some bleak generalizations about southern culture. The complacent acceptance of violence in *Nashville* also provides a striking index of the decadence of society within this large southern city. The songs in the film repeatedly describe a potentially strong and uncompromising American who has capitulated to superior and corrupt forces, basing that surrender on terms that enhance his material surroundings. *Health* is a similar, perhaps more cynical, essay on political institutions that have run out of control.

In these films Altman, who is a midwesterner born in Kansas City, Mo., uses settings, characters, and interactions based in the urban and rural South to present a composite picture of America—his sobering vision of complacency and hypocrisy in American life. He indicates the possibly deadly effects of racism, unrestrained regional ethnocentrism, and apathy toward reform. He argues that these corrupt social, political, and economic forces may lead to the loss of freedom in this country, unless they are first recognized as abusive conditions and then corrected.

Gerard Plecki
Chicago, Illinois

Gerard Plecki, in *The South and Film*, ed. Warren French (1981).

The Andy Griffith Show

The Andy Griffith Show, first televised by CBS on 3 October 1960, was one of the most enduring and influential of the television series set in the South. The series, which was inspired in part by the earlier success of *The Real McCoys* (ABC 1957–62, CBS 1962–63), starred Griffith as Sheriff Andy Taylor of Mayberry, a fictional North Carolina hamlet. Taylor, a widower raising his young son Opie (Ronny Howard), lived with Bee Taylor (Frances Bavier), his aunt. Other characters populating Mayberry over the years included Deputy Barney Fife (Don Knotts in a role that earned him five Emmy Awards), gas station attendants Gomer and Goober Pyle (Jim Nabors and George Lindsey), town drunk Otis Campbell (Hal Smith), barber Floyd Lawson (Howard McNear), and two of Andy's sweethearts, drugstore clerk Ellie Walker (Elinor Donahue) and the woman he eventually married, teacher Helen Crump (Anita Corsaut). These recurring supporting characters, along with several others, helped add a remarkable air of verisimilitude to the series, and viewers came to know and understand their distinctively individualized personalities far better than they did those of most series characters of the era.

Mayberry, and by extension the small-town, rural South it represented, was a bucolic haven in which nothing ever happened. Most of the individual episodes centered on the difficulties and misunderstandings that arose among the friends and neighbors in the community. Andy used his considerable charm and homespun wisdom to settle these disputes and to return Mayberry to a state of peacefulness and order at the conclusion of each tale. Occasional outsiders, including relatively few criminals, considering Andy Taylor's occupation, would

Andy Griffith and Frances Bavier as Andy Taylor and Aunt Bee in The Andy Griffith Show

disrupt the everyday rhythms of Mayberry until Andy's timely intercession. Other stories revolved around Andy's domestic life; he constantly worked to build Opie's character and to reassure Aunt Bee of her value to both the community and the Taylor household. Many episodes involved Andy's tact in dealing with Barney's eccentricities. Deputy Fife was so incompetent that Andy allowed him only a single bullet, which he had to carry in his pocket rather than in his gun. In numerous episodes Andy's major aim was to prevent Barney from getting into serious trouble and to keep the sensitive Fife from discovering just how gullible and inept he was. Andy Taylor was the quintessential and ever-present wise southerner (later manifestations included Grandpa Zeb in *The Waltons* and Jock Ewing in *Dallas*), and Barney Fife was the stereotypical "hickish" buffoon (Sheriff Rosco P. Coltrane of the *Dukes of Hazzard* continued the type), two character models that have become so common in television's Southland as to be almost obligatory.

In addition to delineating lasting themes and stereotypes, *The Andy Griffith Show* had an even more significant role in Dixie's television history. The series was an instant and enduring success in the ratings. In its initial season A. C. Nielsen listed the show fourth in overall popularity and first among situation comedies; by its final season (1967–68) the series was number one in the overall ratings. It never dipped below seventh place during its entire run. Inevitably such success in television spawns imitations and spin-offs. Soon CBS entered its "rural comedy" (most of these programs were, in fact, *southern* comedies) era, and the airwaves became cluttered with series of such varied quality as *The Beverly Hillbillies*, *Green Acres*, *Petticoat Junction*, and *Gomer Pyle, U.S.M.C.*, in which Jim Nabors reprised his Mayberry creation. When Andy Griffith left his series in 1968, new lead characters moved to town, and *Mayberry, R.F.D.* continued successfully until 1971 when, in search of younger and more urban audiences, CBS dropped all its southern-oriented series.

In 1986 NBC aired *Return to Mayberry*, a nostalgic television movie that reunited most of the original cast of *The Andy Griffith Show*, with the notable exceptions of Frances Bavier, who was ill, and Howard McNear, who died in 1969. In the story Andy returned to Mayberry after 18 years in Ohio; Andy and Barney both ran for sheriff, with Andy getting the position; Barney and his longtime sweetheart, Thelma Lou, reunited and married; and Opie and his wife had their first child and planned a job-related move from Mayberry. The characters' slow-paced, laid-back lives had changed, but warmth and humor still pervaded the fictional southern town.

Christopher D. Geist
Bowling Green State University

Tim Brooks and Earle Marsh, *The Complete Directory to Prime Time Network TV Shows, 1946–Present* (1979); Richard Kelly, *The Andy Griffith Show* (1981).

Appalshop

Appalshop is a rural arts and education center in Whitesburg, Letcher County, Ky. Founded in 1969 in one of the poorest and most rural areas in the nation, Appalshop produces and distributes creative materials relating to southern mountain culture.

Appalshop began as the Community Film Workshop of Appalachia, training poor and minority youth in film and television production. Artists at the workshop soon formed a nonprofit media center, and since then Appalshop's purposes have been to document Appalachian life, produce educational materials, nurture indigenous culture, destroy stereotypes of Appalachians, encourage community discussion, and relate the region and its people to other people and places.

Appalshop sponsors numerous specific programs. Roadside Theater develops and presents original theatrical work. It began in 1974 as an itinerant troupe trying to perform in a way appropriate to the region's theatrical heritage, which was found less in traditional separate theater than in church worship, storytelling sessions, and musical performances. In 1986 the ensemble performers gave 126 shows in 50 communities, over half of which were rural. Roadside Theater sponsored arts programs in schools and colleges, appeared nationally through the National Performance Network and regional tours, and performed at a Scandinavian festival.

June Appal Recordings features traditional and contemporary mountain music. The record label distributes over 40 albums in bluegrass, gospel, folk, blues, and old-time music. Appalshop schedules 112 hours a week of programming on WMMT-FM, its noncommercial radio station, develops and distributes other regionally oriented work, and provides free training for local volunteers. WMMT began operations in 1985.

Appalshop's television unit is Headwaters, which annually produces seven half-hour programs. The Kentucky Educational network broadcasts these productions, as do public stations in Virginia, West Virginia, and Tennessee. Mountain Photography is another division of Appalshop. It assembles, exhibits, and publishes books, including Wendy Ewald, ed., *Portraits and Dreams* (1985) and Loyal Jones, *Appalachia: A Self-Portrait*.

Appalshop films are among the best-known documentaries of southern life. They deal with political, economic, social, and cultural topics. Recent films include *Buffalo Creek Revisited* (Mimi Pickering, director, 1984), *Sunny Side of Life* (Scott Faulkner, Anthony Stone, and Jack Wright, directors, 1985), *Strangers and Kin: A History of the Hillbilly Image* (Herb E. Smith, director, 1984), and *Coal Mining Women* (Elizabeth Barrett, director, 1982). Other Appalshop films have dealt with chairmaker Chester Cornett (*Hand Carved*, Herb E. Smith, director, 1981), home medical remedies (*Nature's Way*, John Lang and Elizabeth Barrett, directors, 1973), the Old Regular Baptist Church (*In the Good Old Fashioned Way*, Herb E. Smith, director, 1973), dulcimers (*Sourwood Mountain Dulcimers*, Gene DuBey, director, 1976), and strip mining (*Strip Mining: Energy, Environment and Economics*, Frances Morton and Gene DuBey, directors, 1979).

Charles Reagan Wilson
University of Mississippi

Leslie Bennetts, *New York Times* (1 December 1984); Jack Fincher, *Smithsonian* (December 1981); Sharon Hatfield, *Southern Changes* (June–July 1984); Kathleen Hulser, *Independent* (October 1983).

Atlanta *Constitution*

The Atlanta *Constitution* was first published by Carey W. Styles in July 1868 as a response to Reconstruction radicalism. Styles subsequently sold the paper to William A. Hemphill, and in 1876 reporter and then city editor of the Atlanta *Intelligencer* Evan Park Howell purchased a half interest in the enterprise, thus beginning a long-term family involvement. *Herald* correspondent Henry W. Grady and Joel Chandler Harris soon joined Howell's staff, and the *Constitution* began to build its national reputation.

Part owner and managing editor after 1880, Grady successfully employed correspondents, new technology, and innovative journalistic techniques such as the interview to increase weekly circulation from 10,000 to 140,000, making the *Constitution* the most widely circulated paper of its kind in America. Convinced that the region was "heartily sick of sectionalism" and in desperate need of northern capital to support industrialization, Grady championed his New South creed in the pages of the *Constitution* and from speakers' platforms in Boston and New York.

Clark Howell succeeded Grady and became editor-in-chief in 1897. Under his management the newspaper supported civic improvement, engaged in a caustic political debate with the rival Atlanta *Journal*, frequently gave way to sensationalism, and won its first Pulitzer Prize for investigative reporting in 1931.

On questions of race Howell, like Grady, supported the separate-but-equal myth—a conciliatory stance not altered until liberal journalist Ralph McGill assumed editorship in 1938. Awarded the Pulitzer in 1959 for "long, courageous, and effective editorial leadership," McGill opposed racial terrorism, Klan activities, and, ultimately, segregation, placing the *Constitution* in the vanguard of New South journalism.

Merged with the Atlanta *Journal* since 1950, the *Constitution* continues to be a separate daily. It is owned by Cox enterprises and has a Sunday circulation exceeding 540,000.

See also INDUSTRY: / Grady, Henry W.; LITERATURE: / Harris, Joel Chandler; URBANIZATION: / Atlanta

Elizabeth M. Makowski
University of Mississippi

Wallace B. Eberhard, *Journalism Quarterly* (Spring 1983); Sidney Kobre, *Development of American Journalism* (1969); *Newspaper Directory* (1985); Raymond Nixon, *Henry W. Grady: Spokesman of the New South* (1943).

The Beverly Hillbillies

Universally despised by critics and totally neglected in Emmy Award considerations, *The Beverly Hillbillies* nevertheless stands as one of the most popular television series to feature southerners and to represent to the general public lifestyles that are supposedly southern. The Columbia Broadcasting System series premiered in September 1962 and according to A. C. Nielsen was the highest-rated series by the end of the 1962–63 season, with an estimated audience of about 60 million. The series maintained its popularity for several years and was rated no lower than 12 through the 1968–69 season.

Jed Clampett, the family's patriarch, discovered oil while hunting on his impoverished Ozark farmstead, became fabulously wealthy, and, to use the words of the series's hit theme song, "moved to Beverly—Hills, that is—swimming pools and movie stars." He was accompanied into this strange and materialistic new world by his cantankerous but lovable mother-in-law, Granny

Daisy Moses, and his naive daughter and bumbling nephew, Elly May Clampett and Jethro Bodine. These characterizations were performed, in order, by Buddy Ebsen, Irene Ryan, Donna Douglas, and Max Baer, Jr. Other characters included the Clampetts' slightly dishonest California banker, Milburn Drysdale (Raymond Bailey); Jane Hathaway (Nancy Kulp), who was Drysdale's love-starved, wallflower secretary; and a wacky assortment of Ozark visitors and Beverly Hills socialites. Lester Flatt and Earl Scruggs, who wrote and performed the theme, sometimes appeared as themselves.

As might be expected, the plots revolved around the Clampetts' inability to cope with their new surroundings. Audiences laughed at Jethro's attempts to understand "courting" in Beverly Hills, or at Elly May's adjustment to modern fashion—she believed a brassiere to be a "double-barreled sling shot." Granny thought the billiard table was a "fancy eatin' table" and Jed thought "golfs" were animals to be clubbed to death with an elaborate collection of woods, irons, and a putter. The Clampetts continued to eat squirrel and opossum, practiced folk medicine, and always dressed in worn homespun. Many episodes depicted Drysdale's attempts to take advantage of the Clampetts and to use their fortune for his own benefit. Inevitably, the innocence and basic goodness of the Clampetts triumph over Beverly Hills characters who value money and material possessions more than honesty and integrity. And, throughout all their trials and tribulations, the Clampett clan exhibits a strong sense of family loyalty, a trait almost universally associated with the portrayal of southerners in television series.

Although ratings had slipped by 1970, the series was still a respectable success when it was cancelled after the 1970–71 season. Network officials had determined that the audience was too heavily rural to attract major advertisers. *The Beverly Hillbillies* remains significant for several reasons other than its phenomenal ratings successes. First, although "corny" (the series was often sponsored by Kellogg's), the series was totally without violence in an era when television fare was severely criticized as overly violent. The series also led to an impressive array of spinoffs and imitations, including *Green Acres* and *Petticoat Junction*, causing the decade of the 1960s to be labeled the heyday of southern sitcoms. It also led indirectly to a host of other comedy series based on outlandish situations, not all of which included southerners. Finally, its emphasis on the stereotype of the backward, poor southern hillbilly did much to fix the image in popular consciousness. The series remains widely available and popular in local syndication and on cable systems through the 1980s.

See also FOLKLIFE: / "Hillbilly" Image

Christopher D. Geist
Bowling Green State University

Tim Brooks and Earle Marsh, *The Complete Directory to Prime Time Network TV Shows, 1946–Present* (1979); Arthur Hough, *Understanding Television: Essays on Television as a Social and Cultural Force*, ed. Richard P. Adler (1981); Alex McNeil, *Total Television: A Comprehensive Guide to Programming from 1948 to the Present* (1980); Horace Newcomb, *TV: The Most Popular Art* (1974).

Birth of a Nation

D. W. Griffith's film *Birth of a Nation* (Epoch, 1915) celebrates the Ku Klux Klan. This organization, according to the film's subtitles, saved the South from the anarchy of black rule by reuniting former wartime enemies "in defense of their Aryan birthright." Griffith based his film on two novels by the Reverend Thomas Dixon, Jr., *The Leopard's Spots* (1902) and *The Clansman* (1905).

One of the most controversial and profitable films ever made, the movie set many precedents. It was the first film to cost over $100,000 and exact a $2 admission, the first to have a full-scale premiere, and the first to be shown at the White House. President Woodrow Wilson reportedly declared, "It's like writing history with lightning. My only regret is that it is all so terribly true."

Originally called *The Clansman* when it opened in Los Angeles 8 February 1915, it was retitled *Birth of a Nation* just prior to its Broadway showing in March. Fully exploiting the motion picture as a propaganda vehicle, Griffith used every device he had developed in his years at Biograph studio—long shot, closeup, flashback, montage —to create excitement and tension. Provocative subtitles heightened his messages, and southern audiences acclaimed the film enthusiastically; horsemen in Klan costumes often rode through towns prior to the film's showing to promote box-office receipts. In cities like New York, Chicago, and Boston, however, the film was greeted with pickets, demonstrations, and lawsuits.

For a time, Newark and Atlantic City, N.J., banned the film, as did St. Louis, Mo., and the states of Kansas, West Virginia, and Ohio. (In the 1950s Atlanta banned the film, fearing that the violence of some scenes might provoke audience emulation.) As a result of the widespread interest in *Birth of a Nation*, newspapers began to review new films regularly, and motion picture advertising began to appear in the press. This film helped make moviegoing a middle-class activity, and its success led to the erection of ornate movie palaces in fashionable districts.

The two-part film centered on two families, the Camerons of South Carolina and the Stonemans of Pennsylvania, who are eventually joined by marriage. An idyllic, gracious, carefree antebellum South, based on the labor of happy slaves, is shattered by bloody battles and the devastation and defeat of the Confederacy. With the assassination of Lincoln, the South appears to be doomed to black control. Part two concerns the Reconstruction period and focuses on the Little Colonel, Ben Cameron (Henry B. Walthall), who is in love with Elsie Stoneman (Lillian Gish), daughter of a Negrophile congressman and his black mistress. One of the key scenes shows the Little Colonel's sister (Mae Marsh) hurling herself off a cliff, terrified by the black renegade Gus's lustful pursuit. "For her who had learned the stern lesson of honor we should not grieve that she found sweeter the opal gates of death," reads the subtitle.

Two kinds of blacks appear in the film: the sober, industrious slaves inspired by Uncle Tom who stay on as loyal servants after the war and the freedmen, portrayed as arrogant, lecherous, and bestial. Instead of working in the cotton fields, the former slaves make a mockery of legislative government, spend time carousing in saloons, lust after white women, and demand "equal rights, equal politics, equal marriage." The rise of the Ku Klux Klan led by the Little Colonel promises to restore the social order, disenfranchise the blacks, protect southern womanhood, and reunite the nation.

The film is said to have inspired the revival of the Klan in November 1915 and to have promoted the passage of the prohibition amendment. Generally regarded as a masterpiece and the greatest American silent film, *Birth of a Nation* has never, because of its overt racism, received unequivocal praise.

See also LITERATURE: / Dixon, Thomas, Jr.; VIOLENCE: / Ku Klux Klan

Joan L. Silverman
New York University

Roy E. Aitken, *The Birth of a Nation Story* (1965); Fred Silva, ed., *Focus on The Birth of a Nation* (1971); Edward Wagenknecht and Anthony Slide, *The Films of D. W. Griffith* (1975).

Caldwell, Erskine, and Film

The works of Erskine Caldwell have achieved enormous popularity. *Tobacco Road* has sold well over 3.5 million copies; *God's Little Acre* has reached sales considerably over 8 million, more than even *Gone with the Wind*. It is no surprise, then, that Hollywood has taken note of the enormously popular stories of Caldwell's rural and poverty-stricken South.

Films of the contemporary South produced during the same period as the novels were predominantly in a lighter vein, such as *Carolina* (1934) or *Virginia* (1941). Warner Brothers's exposé *I Am a Fugitive from a Chain Gang* (1932) and *Cabin in the Cotton* (1932), from Harry Kroll's novel of class conflict, were exceptions, but Caldwell presented the film industry with more than just a stock exception to the usual. Called a southern "hovelist" by some, Caldwell mercilessly struck at the controversial, powerful, titillating, and depressing aspects of a steamy and backward South. Despite huge book sales, the writer's themes required careful handling by Hollywood.

Not until 1941, nine years after its publication, did a studio take a chance on filming *Tobacco Road*. Though based on Jack Kirkland's extremely successful theater version of the novel and with a cast that included Dana Andrews, Ward Bond, and Gene Tierney, the story was vastly changed from a shocking novel to an almost farcical film for 20th Century Fox. In order to capture Caldwell's tale accurately, director John Ford and scriptwriter Nunnally Johnson would have faced enormous censorship problems in the early 1940s, and hence they developed instead a story line of rustic humor and glamorized southern poor folk, all enhanced by slick studio techniques.

Another attempt to adapt Caldwell's work to the screen was not made until 1958. Surely, many reasoned, the times were better for more forthright productions. By the 1950s, Hollywood had purchased the screen rights to works by William Faulkner, Tennessee Williams, Robert Penn Warren, and Lillian Hellman. *God's Little Acre* was released by Security Pictures/United Artists and featured Robert Ryan as Ty Ty Walden. Although this adaptation captured the realism that *Tobacco Road* missed, critics believed that it still lacked the sociological significance that Caldwell's novels provided.

In 1961 Warner Brothers touted *Claudelle Inglish* as, at last, authentically depicting Caldwell's settings, characters, and native region. Taken from the writer's 1958 story, the movie featured Diane McBain as the daughter of a tenant farmer (Arthur Kennedy) and the object of a rich man's (Claude Akins) affections. A critic for *Time* summarized the story succinctly as merely another exploration of the "Deep (read shallow) South."

For all the success and impact of Caldwell's considerable literary effort, Hollywood appeared each time unable to translate the novels to the screen as anything more than rural humor or salacious drama.

See also LITERATURE: / Caldwell, Erskine

Edward D. C. Campbell, Jr.
Virginia State Library

Erskine Caldwell, *Call It Experience* (1951); Edward D. C. Campbell, Jr., *The Celluloid South: Hollywood and the Southern Myth* (1981); James D. Devlin, *Erskine Caldwell* (1984); Warren French, ed., *The South and Film* (1981).

Carter, Hodding

(1907–1972) Newspaper editor.

William Hodding Carter, as editor of the Greenville, Miss., *Delta Democrat-Times* from 1938 until a short time before his death in 1972, was a major advocate of racial tolerance and an ardent opponent of the system of state-supported racial segregation in the South, particularly in his own state of Mississippi. His battle against racism and other forms of intolerance was a consistent theme in the editorial writing of his own newspaper, in his magazine articles, and in his novel, *The Winds of Fear* (1944).

In that novel, a young journalist, Alan Mabry, tried to bring racial tolerance to the troubled town of Carvell City, a town caught "in this tragic predicament of race." But, as Carter wrote, the racial hatred in his novel "could have happened in almost any of the small towns of the South," and "it might also be happening today in any other section of the country." At the conclusion of *The Winds of Fear*, Alan Mabry sums up his own resistance to racial hatred: "At least, he had confronted the Thing, and the Thing had been for the moment beaten. If you stood against the Thing, then people would eventually listen."

Hodding Carter's writing career was a clear example of one man's stand against the "Thing" of racial bigotry, an attitude shaped in him in childhood. As *Time* magazine once reported, Carter lived with two childhood memories: first, seeing as a six-year-old a gang of white boys chasing a black, and, later, coming across the slain black victim of a lynching.

A Louisianian by birth, he was educated at Bowdoin College in Maine (B.A., 1927) and studied journalism at Columbia University (B.A. Litt., 1928). Carter joined the staff of the New Orleans *Item-Tribune* in 1929 and later became night manager for the United Press in New Orleans. He next served with the Associated Press in Jackson, Miss., as bureau manager, but was dismissed in early 1932 for "insubordination." Carter had married Betty Brunhilde Werlein in October 1931, and they moved to Carter's hometown of Hammond, La., where they launched the *Daily Courier* newspaper.

During the 1932–35 period, one of Carter's chief targets was Louisiana political boss and U.S. Senator Huey Long. After Long's assassination in 1935, Carter moved to Greenville, Miss., where he first established the *Delta Star* newspaper, later merged it with a competitive paper, and became publisher-editor of the *Delta Democrat-Times*.

During World War II, Carter served in the Army Bureau of Public Relations, later helped begin the Middle East editions of *Yank* and *Stars and Stripes*, and also served in intelligence activities.

Returning to Mississippi at age 38, Carter then took up the antibigotry editorial stance that resulted in a 1946 Pulitzer Prize for editorials against racial intolerance. The award specifically cited his pleas for fairness for returning nisei veterans of World War II. In that editorial he had urged his readers to "shoot the works in a fight for tolerance" and suggested that bigotry was always possible, even in a democracy, when "an active minority can have its way against an apathetic majority." Carter remained active as editor until just a few years before his death, when his son, Hodding Carter III, assumed the editorship. Hodding Carter III became widely known in the late 1970s as the State Department spokesman for the administration of President Jimmy Carter.

Hodding Carter's writing includes articles for *American Magazine*, *The New Republic*, *The Nation*, *The Saturday Evening Post*, and the *New York Times Magazine*; among his books are *First Person Rural* (1963); *Where Main Street Meets the River* (1953); *The Winds of Fear* (1944); *Southern Legacy* (1950); *The Angry Scar* (1959); and one volume of verse.

Jere Real
Lynchburg, Virginia

John T. Kneebone, *Southern Liberal Journalists and the Issue of Race, 1920–1944* (1985); Donald Paneth, *The Encyclopedia of American Journalism* (1983); James E. Robinson, "Hodding Carter: Southern Liberal, 1907–1972" (M.A. thesis, Mississippi State University, 1974).

The Color Purple

In December 1985 Warner Brothers released the movie version of the novel *The Color Purple* by Georgia native Alice Walker. Produced with a $14 million budget and directed by Steven Spielberg, the film grossed almost $29 million during the first month of its release. Its popularity made it one of the most influential visual portrayals of southern black life.

The novel, for which the author won a Pulitzer Prize and an American Book Award, portrays impoverished southern blacks. Its setting is an imaginary rural Georgia town during the first four decades of the 20th century. The focus is the abuse, struggle, and self-discovery of Celie, a black woman whose letters to God and to and from her sister Nettie comprise the narrative. The strength of relationships between women and the oppression of black women are central themes.

Although the movie brought increased attention to controversial elements in the novel, its own treatment of the story stimulated additional dispute. Critics claimed, for example, that the movie was simplistic and romanticized, distorting the intense and somber tone of Walker's novel. Advertisements for the movie said, "It's about life. It's about love. It's about us. . . . Share the joy." Spielberg's neglect of the novel's lesbian theme caused further complaint, even though the explicitness of the relationship between Celie and blues singer Shug Avery had been partly responsible for criticism of the novel.

Most public controversy, however, focused upon Spielberg's depiction of black men. Many blacks were outraged by the portrayal of black men as violent, abusive, and cowardly. The picketers who marched outside a Los Angeles theater where the movie was premiering were only one group of many (including the National Association for the Advancement of Colored People and the Coalition Against Black Exploitation) that publicly expressed objections. A commonly held view was that the considerations of commercial moviemaking had taken precedence over the sensitive presentation of racial issues in the novel.

On the other hand, supporters heralded the movie as an important milestone for blacks in the film industry. In her contract with the filmmakers, Walker had required that no less than half the cast and crew be women, blacks, or other "Third World" people. Celie's husband, Mr. ———, was played by black actor Danny Glover, who had received acclaim for his work in several other recent movies. The four main women characters were played by Whoopie Goldberg (Celie), Akosua Busia (Nettie), Margaret Avery (Shug), and Oprah Winfrey (Sofia). Goldberg, whose role in the movie marked her screen debut, had initially wanted the part of Sofia, Celie's spirited stepdaughter-in-law. Winfrey was born in Koscuisko, Miss., and is the only one of the four who is actually a native of the South. She, along with Goldberg and Avery, was nominated for an Academy Award, but neither they nor any of the other eight *Color Purple* nominees won.

Contemporary black composer Quincy Jones was one of the film's coproducers and, along with several other songwriters, composed the musical score, which included blues, jazz, African, and gospel music. The score ignited further controversy as parts were said to be suspiciously similar to music written by Frenchman Georges Delerue for a British film, *Our Mother's House*, made almost 20 years earlier.

Despite the controversy surrounding its production and adaptation of Walker's novel, *The Color Purple* was a successful movie. Filmed in North Carolina, Africa, and Hollywood, it received widespread publicity. The product pleased even the story's author, who described it as "a beautiful child of the book."

See also LITERATURE: / Walker, Alice

Jessica Foy
Cooperstown Graduate Programs
Cooperstown, New York

Lisa Belkin, *New York Times* (26 January 1986); Susan Dworkin, *Ms.* (December 1985); Mona Gable, *Wall Street Journal* (19 December 1985); Nan Robertson, *New York Times* (13 February 1986); E. R. Shipp, *New York Times* (27 January 1986); Marie Saxon Silverman, *Variety* (12 March 1986).

Crews, Harry

(b. 1935) Writer.

A son of tenant farmers, Harry Edward Crews was born 6 June 1935 in Bacon County, Ga. Between his life on the subsistence farm and his full professorship in the University of Florida English Department that had denied him admission as a graduate student, he served in the Marine Corps; attended the University of Florida (B.A., 1960; M.S.Ed., 1962); knocked around the country for 18 months on a motorcycle; taught in a junior high school and a junior college; wrote five-minute daily inspirational stories of achievement for Nelson Boswell, a Florida radio commentator; and passed through the academic ranks at Florida. In 1972 Crews received the Arts and Letters Award from the American Academy and Institute of Arts and Letters.

Harry Crews claims to have written his first novel, a detective story, when he was 13. His first published story, "The Unattached Smile," appeared in 1963; his most recent work, a novel entitled *All We Need of Hell*, was published in 1987. In the intervening years he produced 11 books—8 novels, an autobiography, and 2 collections of essays and stories. Many of his stories first appeared in national magazines, notably *Esquire* and *Playboy*, and he is an example of the prominent place southern writers have long had in those magazines. His stories are rooted in the intersection of biography and history; the biography is poor white, the history is southern. His characters are engaged in a futile struggle to balance the achievement ethic and marketing ethos of modern society against traditional cultural values.

Each of his novels, from *The Gospel Singer* (1968) through *All We Need of Hell*, has received mixed reviews. Critics and reviewers seem unable to agree on either the content or significance of Crews's books. Most, however, react strongly to them. He is in the southern Gothic tradition, and each of his novels has been identified by various critics as his best. Crews's comments on his own work suggest that he regards *Naked in Garden Hills* (1969), *The Gypsy's Curse* (1974), and *A Childhood: The Biography of a Place* (1978) as among his best.

A Childhood is a superb ethnography of a rural subsistence community from the perspective of Crews's people. It details the first five years of his life and traces the consequences of the transition from subsistence farming to a one-crop agricultural and industrial economy. The autobiography shows that Crews's fiction follows the survivors of that culture, whose hermetic seal was broken by the intrusion of the outside world or, more commonly, the outmigration of its inhabitants. *A Childhood* and *A Feast of Snakes* (1976), two of his most widely acclaimed works, may be the best examples of the literary and analytic talents of Harry Crews.

His works illuminate both an internal struggle—heart versus mind—and an eternal struggle—man versus society and culture. His characters, often "freaks," come to appear less unusual as their struggles with each other, place, time, and culture create the story. Crews's work provides important insights into the Americanization of the South and the southernization of America.

Harry Crews's other books are *This Thing Don't Lead to Heaven* (1970), *Karate Is a Thing of the Spirit* (1971), *Car* (1972), *The Hawk Is Dying* (1973), *Blood and Grits* (1979), and *Florida Frenzy* (1982).

Larry W. DeBord
University of Mississippi

Larry W. DeBord and Gary L. Long, *Southern Quarterly* (Spring 1982); David K. Jeffrey and Donald R. Noble, *Southern Quarterly* (Winter 1981); Gary L. Long and Larry W. DeBord, *Texas Review* (Fall–Winter 1983).

Curtiz, Michael

(1888–1962) Film director.

Ironically, this director, who ranks with D. W. Griffith and King Vidor in shaping the celluloid image of the South, was neither born nor raised in America, let alone in the South. Born in Budapest in 1888, Michael Curtiz (née Mihaly Kertesz) was one of the film world's most prolific and versatile directors. The peripatetic Hungarian directed more than three dozen films in seven European countries before Warner Brothers brought him to Hollywood in 1926, where he completed well over 100 more films of extraordinary variety. While working within the Warners' studio system, he gained a reputation as a harsh taskmaster on the set, often barking out orders in his celebrated fractured English. Among the many westerns, swashbucklers, social dramas, musical comedies, and romantic adventures directed by the colorful Curtiz were several that dealt with expressly southern themes.

The first to appear was *Cabin in the Cotton* (1932), a melodrama featuring Bette Davis and Richard Barthelmess in the midst of bitter struggles between sharecroppers and landowners in the cotton-growing South. Lynchings and child marriages were among the topics of Curtiz's 1937 *Mountain Justice*, which told the story of a young nurse (Josephine Hutchinson) who helped a doctor set up a clinic in the Tennessee mountains, much to the outrage of her Bible-thumping father. Three years later, Curtiz directed a "southern-western" entitled *Virginia City*, which starred Miriam Hopkins as a Confederate spy seeking to transfer $5 million of Nevada gold to CSA coffers. She was helped by fellow Confederate spy Randolph Scott, but hindered (and inevitably romanced) by dashing Yankee Errol Flynn.

Curtiz continued to explore southern themes following World War II with *Flamingo Road* (1949), which traced the fortunes of a tough young woman (Joan Crawford) from her job as a carnival dancer through her romance with a deputy sheriff (Zachary Scott) to her eventual marriage to a prominent southern politician. *Bright Leaf* followed two years later, focusing on the rise and fall of a vengeful North Carolina tobacco magnate (Gary Cooper) at the turn of the century. As a publicity tactic, Warner Brothers held the film's world premiere in Raleigh, N.C.

Curtiz left Warner Brothers during the 1950s to direct for other American film companies, but the resulting films were generally inferior to his cinematic output of the 1930s and 1940s. Among these films was *The Proud Rebel* (1958), about the efforts of a Confederate veteran (Alan Ladd) to help his young son who had been struck dumb on seeing his mother killed by Sherman's troops. The same year saw the creation of *King Creole*, an adaptation of Harold Robbins's *A Stone for Danny Fisher*. Set in New Orleans, the film centered on a young Bourbon Street nightclub performer (Elvis Presley) and his conflicts with his father and a gangster. The seaminess of the novel was toned down considerably for this early Presley vehicle. Two years later, Curtiz directed a remake of *The Adventures of Huckleberry Finn*, starring Eddie Hodges in a wholesome portrayal of the title character and boxing champion Archie Moore in a remarkable performance as Jim. Curtiz's last film was *The Comancheros* (1961), a strictly standard western featuring John Wayne battling renegades in Texas. Curtiz died in 1962.

Martin F. Norden
University of Massachusetts
at Amherst

Kingsley Canham, *The Hollywood Professionals* (1973); Martin F. Norden, *Southern Quarterly* (Spring–Summer 1981).

Dabney, Virginius

(b. 1901) Journalist and author.

Born and raised in Charlottesville, Va., Virginius Dabney completed a bachelor's and a master's degree and graduated Phi Beta Kappa from the University of Virginia, where his father was a professor of history. After graduation Dabney began his journalism career in 1922 as a reporter for the Richmond *News-Leader*. Six years later he became an editor for the Richmond *Times-Dispatch* and in 1936 assumed the position of editor-in-chief. Dabney edited the Richmond *Times-Dispatch* between 1936 and 1969, winning the Pulitzer Prize in 1948 and other awards for his editorials. In *Liberalism in the South* (1932), Dabney chronicled a southern liberal tradition that embraced Thomas Jefferson as its leader and defended civil liberties and intellectual freedom. Through the 1930s Dabney's editorials expanded upon these values, defending the right of labor to organize, aid to distressed sharecroppers, elimination of the poll tax, and legislation to prevent lynchings.

His *Below the Potomac* (1942) reported optimistically on the state of the region but also evidenced his early recognition of potentially powerful challenges to racial segregation. Like most white southern liberals, Dabney believed that racial justice could be achieved without abandoning segregation. Black protest against Jim Crow during World War II disturbed him, and he warned the nation of an impending racial crisis. His editorial proposal to abolish segregation on public transportation in Richmond (1943) and his part in the founding of the Southern Regional Council (1944) reflected these fears, and he tried but failed to defuse black militance through demonstrations of white goodwill. His conviction that growing pressure on an unwilling South for racial reform portended disaster contributed to his postwar shift toward conservatism.

When the U.S. Supreme Court outlawed school segregation in 1954, Dabney acknowledged that the South must comply with the decision and endorsed local option as the best means to slow the change. Advocates of massive resistance to desegregation, however, insisted upon total white solidarity, and Dabney reluctantly acquiesced. After the courts rejected Virginia's massive resistance, Dabney returned to his persistent editorial theme of gradualism in reform as preferable to protest and conflict. By the time of his retirement, few recalled his onetime reputation as a leading southern liberal. Since retirement Dabney has written several popular books on Virginia's history. These works display a mix of decency and defensiveness characteristic of southern liberalism before the civil rights movement. Dabney's career reflects the prominent role journalists played in 20th-century southern liberalism and also reveals how swiftly southern race relations have changed since World War II.

See also SOCIAL CLASS: / Southern Regional Council

John T. Kneebone
Virginia State Library

Virginius Dabney, *Across the Years: Memories of a Virginian* (1978); John T. Kneebone, *Southern Liberal Journalists and the Issue of Race, 1920–1944* (1985); Morton Sosna, *In Search of the Silent South: Southern Liberals and the Race Issue* (1977).

Jonathan Daniels, editor of the Raleigh News and Observer, *c. 1950*

Daniels, Jonathan

(1902–1981) Journalist and author.

Jonathan Worth Daniels was born 26 April 1902, the son of Josephus Daniels, owner and editor of the Raleigh (N.C.) *News and Observer*. He grew up in Raleigh and in Washington, where his father served as secretary of the navy. After receiving B.A. and M.A. degrees in English from the University of North Carolina, he studied law briefly at Columbia University before entering journalism. He wrote for the Louisville (Ky.) *Times*, the *News and Observer*, and *Fortune* magazine in the 1920s, and in 1933 became the editor of the Raleigh daily. During World War II he served as an administrative assistant to the president; he resumed the editorship of the family paper after his father's death in 1948 and relinquished it only in the late 1960s.

From an early age Daniels dissented from southern cultural norms regarding religion, sex, liquor, gambling, and race. His 1921 college yearbook described him as "very impressionable to anything that smacks of innovation just so it threatens some old, traditional customs; therefore, he is of that coterie styled as the left wing of Carolina thinkers." In 1930, for example, his novel *Clash of Angels* satirized conventional religious dogma. The editor earned a reputation in the 1930s as a southern liberal because of his ardent support for the New Deal, his defense of organized labor, and his proposals for equal treatment of blacks. W. J. Cash even described Daniels in 1941 as "sometimes waxing almost too uncritical in his eagerness to champion the underdog." After World War II, Daniels allied with the state's two leading liberal politicians, Frank P. Graham and Kerr W. Scott. More important, he endorsed the *Brown* v. *Board of Education* decision and led the opposition in North Carolina to massive resistance to school desegregation.

Daniels expressed his liberal views on the *News and Observer*'s editorial page and in dozens of essays and more than a score of books. His popular *A Southerner Discovers the South* (1938) explored the changes occurring in race relations, agriculture, and industry and recounted stories about southerners in the Depression. Three years later *Tar Heels* provided a more detailed portrait of his native state. His understanding of southern history influenced much of Daniels's work. In 1938, for instance, he saw the South's faults but claimed that the Civil War had only "served as an alibi—a magnificent alibi—for them all"; instead of excuses Daniels wanted change. In the tumultuous 1950s Daniels saw parallels with Reconstruction and acknowledged that in neither period was any side faultless. His constant attention to southern themes revealed Daniels's affection for his region at the same time he implored it to change. The Charlotte *Observer* hailed Daniels as "a graceful writer and tart social critic" and "a force for progress in North Carolina" and the South.

See also EDUCATION: / Graham, Frank P.; LAW: / *Brown* v. *Board of Education*

Charles W. Eagles
University of Mississippi

Charlotte *Observer* (10 November 1981); Jonathan Worth Daniels Papers, Southern Historical Collection, University of North Carolina; Charles W. Eagles, *Jonathan Daniels and Race Relations: The Evolution of a Southern Liberal* (1982).

Davis, Bette

(b. 1908) Actress.

Born in Lowell, Mass., in 1908, Bette (Ruth Elizabeth) Davis made her stage debut in 1928, but fame came from her long film career, which began in 1931. Bette Davis has played a variety of roles—the good sister, the supportive wife, the career woman, and the courageous martyr. Nevertheless, she gained notoriety for a specific type of character, "the bitch," which was introduced in her first portrayal of a southern woman. Madge Norwood, the blond, rich seductress of a bewildered sharecropper, evoked both sensuality and aloofness in *Cabin in the Cotton* (1932). Although Bette Davis went on to play unpleasant women who were not southerners, some of her most notable characters were belles whose behavior tended both to symbolize and to indict southern culture.

Davis's characterizations were always more or less femmes fatales. A repertoire of mannerisms—darting eyes that signify duplicity, gestures verging on the hyperkinetic, and a strutting, confident walk convey both toughness and vulnerability. These gestures helped to define the film image of the high-strung southern belle. Davis's bad women sought liberation from social and cultural definitions of women's roles, but their transgressions were always contained within those very definitions—hence, the power and pathos of many of her performances. They encouraged audiences to scrutinize not only the sinning woman but the culture that judged her. Davis's wicked southern women of the late 1930s and early 1940s anticipated the degenerate belles of post–World War II motion pictures.

In *Jezebel* (1938) Julie Marsden's defiance of the rules of behavior imposed by antebellum New Orleans society was connected with the decadence of that society. The plague that permitted Julie to sacrifice herself to achieve redemption also pointed to the South's failure to confront its own backwardness. Regina Giddens and her brothers, in *The Little Foxes* (1941), represented the capitalist New South—greedy exploiters who cared little for their community and upstarts who lacked the charm and sensibilities of the Old South. Yet Regina's viciousness derived, in part, from impotent rejection of the stultifying systems, old or new, which permitted no outlet for the satisfaction of her desires. Desire impelled Stanley Timberlake in the adaptation of Ellen Glasgow's *In This Our Life* (1942) to destroy one man and nearly destroy another—a black prelaw student who was accused of the hit-and-run murder that she committed. Selfish and unrepentant to her death, Stanley represented the unchecked darker side of a contemporary South split between the declining genteel traditions, which are associated with progressive reformism, and the advancing forces of avarice.

Davis's Maggie in *The Great Lie* (1941) was a mature, stable southern woman who represented simplicity and traditional values. When Maggie prevails over a selfish, urban northerner in a love triangle, the country of Maryland's landed gentry and loyal retainers is the victor in a dramatic opposition frequently employed in American media. And there is Charlotte in *Hush . . . Hush, Sweet Charlotte* (1964), a mixture of southern Gothic and horror film. Maligned by the community for a murder she did not commit, the repellent, childlike recluse is, in a narrative reversal, victimized by her charming Yankee cousin.

Ida Jeter
St. Mary's College
Moraga, California

Bette Davis, *The Lonely Life: An Autobiography* (1962); Whitney Stine with Bette Davis, *Mother Goddam* (1975).

Dixon, Thomas, Jr., and Film

Thomas Dixon, Jr.'s Klan novels became the literary source for *Birth of a Nation* (1915), one of the most historically important and financially successful movies in the early American film industry. The film, one of the first feature-length motion pictures, is remembered for its technical innovations, its romantic depiction of the South, and its racial views.

D. W. Griffith and his company purchased the rights from Dixon to make a film based on *The Clansman* for a large percentage of the profits from the movie. Griffith, the most prominent filmmaker of his day and himself a southerner, was willing to pay dearly for the rights because the topic of a southerner returning home after the Civil War to a changed society appealed to him and provided him with a vehicle for telling the southern version of the war and Reconstruction.

The plot of the film remained basically that of *The Clansman*, with significant additions drawn from Dixon's stage plays of *The Clansman* and *The Leopard's Spots*. Griffith did, however, make important shifts in tone: he made the novel's racism less inflammatory, all but eliminated Dixon's view of a commercialized South, and deemphasized the novel's detailed history of the Ku Klux Klan.

Dixon claimed that up to the time of the New York screening of the film it had retained the title of the novel, but he became so carried away with the film's drama during this screening he cried out that it should be given the grander title, *Birth of a Nation*. The story is doubted by later scholars but has become part of the myth surrounding the film.

Dixon's success with *Birth of a Nation* led him to other film projects. He established the Dixon Studios, and from 1916 to 1923 he produced five additional films, including one entitled *The Fall of a Nation* (1916), which expressed fear that America's early pacifism during World War I would lead to its destruction. The other films were based on Dixon's writings and promoted his social and economic theories, but none brought the financial success or critical acclaim of the first film with which he was associated.

See also LITERATURE: / Dixon, Thomas, Jr.; VIOLENCE: / Ku Klux Klan

Robert A. Armour
Virginia Commonwealth University

Robert M. Henderson, *D. W. Griffith: His Life and Work* (1972); Russell Merritt, *Cinema Journal* (1972).

Dukes of Hazzard

The mass media's fascination with southern idiosyncracies has contributed to television's celebration of the South's alleged differences from the rest of the nation. Whereas television's main characters, both fictional and real, have traditionally been intelligent, well educated, successful, affluent, and middle class, this is not so if the characters are southerners. The highly rated *Dukes of Hazzard* provided a 1980s view of a southern extended family (Uncle Jesse and cousins Bo, Luke, and Daisy Duke) in weekly episodes in which they fought for "truth, justice and wild driving." Perhaps the real star of the show was the boys' souped-up Dodge Charger, appropriately named "General Lee." This car served as the show's tribute to southern stock car racing and was regularly wrecked several times during each show. Most critics bombed the *Dukes*, but viewers, particularly in the South, loved it and kept it in the top 10 in the Nielsen ratings for several seasons.

Plots on *Dukes* revolved around the Duke clan and their run-ins with the Hazzard mayor, Boss J. D. Hogg, and his sidekick, Sheriff Roscoe P. Coltrane, or various outsiders who came into town and stirred up trouble in Hazzard County. As has often been the media stereotype, southern politicians and law enforcement officers were caricatured as zany, ignorant incompetents. The good old Duke boys were handsome; Uncle Jesse was wise and unflappable; and cousin Daisy was usually portrayed as a scantily clad, ultrafeminine tomboy. The show's theme song, sung by the outlaw country singer Waylon Jennings, set the stage for the action. Bo and Luke Duke were just good old boys who never meant any harm, but they had been in trouble with the law since they were born. This stereotype of rowdy boys and corrupt politicians and law enforcers has regularly been applied to southerners by the media.

The stereotypes included in *Dukes of Hazzard* fostered the viewers' image of the South as a wild and crazy place where most people were basically simple and good, but a few were merely simple. Middle-class morality and cleanliness were linked to southern rural poverty and good times in themes rich with the adolescent fantasy of outwitting the law. The portrayal of the South as a frontierland populated by independent souls in charge of their own destinies undoubtedly led to some of the show's popularity among southerners. This theme of individual rights also reflected American ideals and drew a large following from the rest of the nation as well. In some ways the South was portrayed as a land of opportunity. According to *Dukes*, if you have enough gumption and a good heart, all your dreams can come true. *Dukes* considered the South to be a land of freedom, escape, laughter, traditional moral values, and simple people. Good and evil were easily defined, and the good guys always won.

Marsha McGee
Northeast Louisiana University

David Johnston, *TV Guide* (12 July 1980); Horace Newcomb, ed., *Television, the Critical View* (1979).

Dunaway, Faye

(b. 1941) Actress.

Faye Dunaway was born 14 January 1941, in Bascom, Fla., the daughter of a career army officer. She distinguished herself as a member of the University of Florida's student acting company, and after further training, she joined the new Lincoln Center Repertory Company in New York in 1962. After a succession of roles on and off Broadway, her performance in *Hogan's Goat* led to her film debut in *The Happening* (1967). She quickly established herself as a major star only a few months later with her performance as the ill-fated Bonnie Parker in Arthur Penn's *Bonnie and Clyde*, one of the films that marked the turn from western to southern settings in popular adventure dramas.

Although this performance earned her an Academy Award nomination, she has not since been typecast in southern roles. Rather, selecting her relatively infrequent performances with great care, she has played demanding roles in films with varied international settings. She was nominated for a second Academy Award for her performance in Roman Polanski's *Chinatown* (1974), and she was at last honored as best actress for her portrayal of a tough television executive in *Network* (1976).

See also VIOLENCE: / "Bonnie and Clyde"

Warren French
Indiana University

Amy Gross, *Vogue* (March 1979); Jack Hamilton, *Look* (13 December 1966); Charles Moritz, ed., *Current Biography* (1973).

Faulkner, William, and Film

William Faulkner wrote screenplays for most of his adult life. Although he considered fiction his primary interest and achievement and often denigrated his screenwriting and many studio practices, he indicated admiration for such films as *Citizen Kane*, *The Magnificent Ambersons*, and *High Noon* and satisfaction with his own work for directors Howard Hawks and Jean Renoir. His friendship and collaboration with Hawks led to the films *Today We Live* (1933, Faulkner's first screen credit, from his story "Turn About"), *The Road to Glory* (1936), *To Have and Have Not* (1944), *The Big Sleep* (1946), and *Land of the Pharaohs* (1955, Faulkner's last screen credit). Faulkner contributed significantly to these films and also wrote for Hawks some scenes for *Air Force* (1943) and several unproduced scripts, including *War Birds* (1933), *Sutter's Gold* (1934), *Dreadful Hollow* (1943), and *Battle Cry* (1943). For Renoir he wrote much of *The Southerner* (1945).

Faulkner went to Hollywood in 1932, perhaps with the intention of writing a vehicle for Tallulah Bankhead, which may have been *The College Widow*. He worked at MGM for one year, although much of his work was done at his home in Oxford, Miss., and mailed to the studio. Early scripts were often closely related to the themes of his fiction. His first treatment, *Manservant* (1932), was an adaptation of his story "Love"; *The College Widow* (1932) was often reminiscent of *Sanctuary*; *Turn About*, released as *Today We Live*, included some interesting twists on *The Sound and the Fury*; *War Birds* concerned the wartime experiences of John and Bayard Sartoris and was a significant link between *Flags in the Dust* and *The Unvanquished*; and the *Mythical Latin-American Kingdom Story* (1933) reflected an active interest in the Conrad of *Nostromo*. Like most of the scripts he produced at this time, the treatments *Absolution* (1932) and *Flying the Mail* (1932) were centrally concerned with aviation and possibly reflected his disappointment at not having flown in combat during World War I. Of all these, only *Turn About* was filmed and released. His work on the film *Lazy River* (1934) was not used.

Faulkner later worked at 20th-Century Fox, receiving screen credit on *The Road to Glory* and *Slave Ship* (1937) and doing uncredited work on *Banjo on My Knee* (1936), *Four Men and a Prayer* (1936), *Submarine Patrol* (1938), and *Drums along the Mohawk* (1939). Other work at this time included material for *Gunga Din* (RKO, 1939) and *Dance Hall* (Fox, 1941). (The dates given refer to the release date of each produced film; Faulkner was at Fox from 1935 to 1937.) Of this group, only *The Road to Glory* and an unpublished screenplay for *Drums along the Mohawk* can be considered significant work.

Faulkner was at Warner Brothers on a ruinous seven-year contract that began in 1942, but he did no work for them after 1945. He worked on many unproduced films during this period or provided interesting scripts that were not used on produced films. The best unproduced scripts were *The De Gaulle Story* (1942), *Country Lawyer* (1943), and *Fog over London* (1944). The best screenplays that were rejected were for the produced films *Mildred Pierce* (1945) and *Stallion Road* (1947). He made recognizable contributions to the produced films *Deep Valley* (1947) and *The Adventures of Don Juan* (1945) and also worked on such films as *Northern Pursuit* (1943), *God Is My Co-Pilot* (1945), and *Escape in the Desert* (1945). A 1943 story conference on *Who?*, a film about the unknown soldier, gave him the basic idea for his novel *A Fable*. During this period he wrote several independent scripts of special interest: *Dreadful Hollow* (c. 1943, for Hawks, about vampires), *Revolt in the Earth* (1942, loosely adapted from *Absalom, Absalom!*), and *Barn Burning* (1945, from his story of the same name). His best work from this period includes the shooting script for *To Have and Have Not*, the first draft of *The Big Sleep* (coauthored with Leigh Brackett), contributions to *The Southerner* (which have not yet been precisely identified; Renoir and Faulkner each claimed to have written the script), and *Dreadful Hollow*.

After his term at Warner Brothers, Faulkner wrote several teleplays, including an adaptation of his novella *Old Man* (1953); CBS produced his teleplays *The Brooch* (1953), *Shall Not Perish* (1954), and *The Graduation Dress* (1960). He performed minor revisions on the script for MGM's film *Intruder in the Dust* (1949, directed by Clarence Brown and shot in Oxford) and went to Egypt with Hawks to work on *Land of the Pharaohs*.

Of the many Faulkner novels adapted for the screen by others by far the worst is *The Sound and the Fury* (1959, directed by Martin Ritt). Others include *The Story of Temple Drake* (1933, from *Sanctuary*, directed by Stephen Roberts; a relatively scandalous film that contributed to the demand for a production code); *Intruder in the Dust*, generally regarded as a classic; *The Tarnished Angels* (1957, from *Pylon*, stylishly directed by Douglas Sirk); *The Long Hot Summer* (1958, from *The Hamlet*, directed by Martin Ritt); *Sanctuary* (1961, from *Sanctuary* and *Requiem for a Nun*, directed by Tony Richardson); and *The Reivers* (1969, directed by Mark Rydell). A recent adaptation is Faulkner's story "Tomorrow" in a fine film distinguished by an excellent script by Horton Foote (*Tomorrow*, 1971, directed by Joseph Anthony). Faulkner short stories were filmed in the 1980s as *A Rose for Emily*, *Two Soldiers*, *The Bear*, and *Barn Burning*.

The South was a significant presence in Faulkner's film writing. Southern characters or locations are important aspects of *The College Widow*, *Absolution*, *War Birds* (alternate title, *A Ghost Story*), *Louisiana Lou* (*Lazy River*), *Banjo on My Knee*, *Revolt in the Earth*, *Deep Valley*, *Country Lawyer* (one of his best), *Battle Cry*, and of course *The Southerner*.

See also LITERATURE: / Faulkner, William

Bruce F. Kawin
University of Colorado
at Boulder

Regina L. Fadiman, *Faulkner's Intruder in the Dust: Novel into Film* (1977); Evans Harrington and Ann J. Abadie, eds., *Faulkner, Modernism, and Film: Faulkner and Yoknapatawpha, 1978*

(1979); Bruce F. Kawin, *Faulkner and Film* (1977), *Faulkner's MGM Screenplays* (1982), with Tino Balio, eds., *To Have and Have Not* (1980); George Sidney, "Faulkner in Hollywood: A Study of His Career as a Scenarist" (Ph.D. dissertation, University of New Mexico, 1959).

Foote, Horton

(b. 1916) Writer.

Horton Foote, playwright and award-winning television and motion picture writer, was born in Wharton, Tex., and began his career as an actor. From 1933 to 1935 he studied at the Pasadena Playhouse Theatre and from 1937 to 1939 at an acting school in New York City. He appeared in several Broadway plays in the late 1930s and early 1940s and from 1942 to 1945 managed a production company in Washington, D.C., where he also taught playwriting.

Foote's first play to be produced professionally was *Texas Town*, which opened at the Provincetown Playhouse in New York in 1942. A number of his plays were produced on Broadway, among them *Only the Heart* (1944), *The Chase* (1952), *The Trip to Bountiful* (1953), and *The Traveling Lady* (1954). Much of Foote's best work has been done in television, a medium that he entered when he wrote a teleplay for *The Kraft Television Theatre* in 1947. His work was frequently seen on *Playhouse 90*, *DuPont Show of the Week*, and other important dramatic series during the so-called Golden Age of Television in the 1950s. His adaptation of Harper Lee's *To Kill a Mockingbird* (1962) earned him an Academy Award for best screenplay based on material from another source.

Foote's other film credits include *Baby, the Rain Must Fall* (1965); *Tender Mercies* (1983), for which Robert Duvall received an Academy Award for best actor; *The Trip to Bountiful* (1985), for which Geraldine Page received an Academy Award for best actress; and *1918* (1985), which starred the writer's daughter, Hallie Foote. He has also done adaptations of stories by southern writers such as Flannery O'Connor (*The Displaced Person*) and William Faulkner (*Old Man*, *Barn Burning*, *Tomorrow*).

Most of Horton Foote's plays and films have been set in the fictional town of Harrison, Tex. Foote's strength, as more than one writer has noted, has been his ear for the speech of his part of the country.

Charles East
Baton Rouge, Louisiana

Samuel G. Freedman, *New York Times Magazine* (9 February 1986); Joseph R. Millichap, in *American Screenwriters: Dictionary of Literary Biography*, vol. 26, ed. Robert E. Morsberger, Stephen O. Lesser, and Randall Clark (1984); *Who's Who in the Theatre: A Biographical Record of the Contemporary Stage*, vol. 1: Biographies (1981).

Ford, John

(1895–1973) Film director.

One of America's most famous filmmakers, John Ford was also one of the foremost interpreters of its land and legends. Born Sean O'Feeney to Irish immigrant parents in Cape Elizabeth, Me., he followed his brother Francis to Hollywood, where he directed his first movie in 1917. From that time his name became almost synonymous with the western genre; in fact, the look of the West was, for most moviegoers, established by Ford's many films using Monument Valley in Utah as a backdrop. Interspersed among his numerous westerns, however, is a large body of films devoted to the South and its lifestyles. Approximately 11 works, including films like *Steamboat 'Round the Bend* (1935), *Tobacco Road* (1941), *The Sun Shines Bright* (1954), and *The Horse Soldiers* (1959), focus on the region's distinctive people and places.

Because he did not have a personal familiarity with the South to draw on, Ford often turned to the widespread myths and stereotypes of popular literature, which account for both the strengths and weaknesses of his films. Three works, for instance, were based on the local color writings of Irvin S. Cobb, and they carry over some of the racial stereotypes and cultural beliefs of that source. Because his was essentially a South of the imagination, though, Ford placed far less weight on the distinctive look of the region than was the case in his westerns. Instead, he grounded these films in character, especially focusing on figures who live in the backwash of the Civil War. Inhabiting a fallen world—or one in the midst of that fall—these characters are called upon to impart order to their community, to hold fast to a set of values when all ideals seem called into question. Consequently, a human landscape dominates these films and substitutes for the more iconic geography of his westerns.

Ford's primary interest was always the nature of the human community, and its capacity to endure through the strength of its individual members formed the abiding theme of his films. This communal motif links his famous westerns—*Stagecoach*, *My Darling Clementine*, *The Searchers*—to films as diverse as the Welsh coal-mining saga, *How Green Was My Valley*; the dust-bowl tale, *The Grapes of Wrath*; and his comedy about the South Seas, *Donovan's Reef*. In his southern films he fashioned a mythos that speaks clearly to a traditional concern with the individual and his community that has always marked southern culture.

J. P. Telotte
Georgia Institute of Technology

Peter Bogdanovich, *John Ford* (1978); Tag Gallagher, *John Ford: The Man and His Films* (1986); Andrew Sinclair, *John Ford* (1979).

Freeman, Douglas Southall

(1886–1953) Editor and biographer.

By virtue of his authorship of seven magisterial volumes, Douglas Southall Freeman achieved national fame in the 1940s as the preeminent authority on Confederate military history. He was already a notable figure in his native Virginia as editor of the Richmond *News Leader* (1915–49), a radio newscaster, and a frequent public orator. Though his career broadened in his later life, Freeman steadfastly refused to leave Richmond. As professor of journalism at Columbia University from 1934 to 1941, he fulfilled his teaching obligations there one day each week and commuted overnight from Richmond to New York by Pullman.

Both Freeman's devotion to Virginia and his discipline that allowed him several simultaneous careers followed naturally from the example of his father, a veteran of Lee's army and a strong advocate of order, industry, and perseverance. At 17 Douglas accompanied his father to a Confederate reunion and determined to record for posterity the heroism of his elder's army. After graduation from Richmond College he equipped himself with a doctorate in history from Johns Hopkins University with that specific goal in mind. He also wanted a public career, and only in 1915, the year he assumed the newspaper editorship, did he begin to work on *R. E. Lee.* Twenty years later the four-volume biography received a Pulitzer Prize, but only after Freeman finally assigned himself a weekly stint of 14 hours to ensure its completion. His strict regimen (he allowed himself 17 minutes, precisely, to drive to work) was only possible, Freeman often remarked, because he had a remarkably cooperative wife, Inez Goddin Freeman.

The quality Freeman most admired in his cavalcade of heroes was fortitude, which Lee exemplified almost perfectly in Freeman's view. The commander's subordinates, as *Lee's Lieutenants* (1942–44) would demonstrate, mustered impressive fortitude along with some very human frailties. Freeman considered the three volumes of the *Lieutenants* his best work, and critics have generally agreed.

To embark on an attempted definitive biography of George Washington when Freeman was 58 and still a busy public figure was an ambitious undertaking, but he lived to complete six volumes (1948–54) and to cover all but six years of his subject's life. After his assistants wrote the final volume, the completed work earned Freeman a posthumous second Pulitzer Prize in biography. Not as popular as the Confederate books, *George Washington,* the final tribute from a puritan son to his symbolic ancestors, nevertheless strengthened Freeman's position as one of the foremost American biographers of his time.

John L. Gignilliat
Agnes Scott College

John L. Gignilliat, in *Twentieth Century American Historians: Dictionary of Literary Biography*, vol. 17, ed. Robert E. Morsberger, Stephen O. Lesser, and Randall Clark (1984); Dumas Malone, in *George Washington*, vol. 6, by Douglas Southall Freeman (1954); T. Harry Williams, *Journal of Southern History* (February 1955).

Golden, Harry

(1902–1981) Editor, publisher, and author.

Born Harry Goldhirsch and raised on the Lower East Side of New York City, Harry Golden moved to Charlotte, N.C., to work as a salesman and a reporter during the Depression. In 1941 he founded *The Carolina Israelite*, a one-man newspaper published until 1968 with a national circulation at its peak of 40,000. A collection of his pieces was published in 1958 under the title *Only in America*, which became a national best-seller and was followed by 19 other books. "I got away with my ideas in the South," he said, "because no Southerner takes me—a Jew, a Yankee, and a radical—seriously. They mostly think of a Jew as a substitute Negro, anyway."

A roly-poly American original, he sat in his Kennedy rocker with his feet barely touching the floor, like a Jewish Buddha with a cigar. The office walls were crowded with books and dozens of autographed pictures of famous acquaintances who subscribed to the paper, such as Carl Sandburg, Harry Truman, William Faulkner, John F. Kennedy, Bertrand Russell, Ernest Hemingway, and Adlai Stevenson. In the corner stood his celebrated cracker barrel where he threw finished articles for the paper, which went to press when the barrel was full.

His numerous "Golden plans" infuriated segregationists and delighted southern intellectuals, not because they were absurd but because they were rooted sufficiently in southern myth to work perfectly well should anyone be astute enough to try them. When the South became embroiled in school desegregation and "massive resistance," he proposed the "Vertical Integration Plan," which stated that:

> The white and Negro stand at the same grocery and supermarket counters; deposit money at the same bank teller's window; pay phone and light bills to the same clerk; walk through the same dime and department stores and stand at the same drugstore counters. It is only when the Negro "sets" that the fur begins to fly.
>
> . . . Instead of all those complicated proposals, all the next session needs to do is pass one small amendment which would provide *only* desks in all the public schools of our state—*no seats.* The desks should be those standing-up jobs, like the old-fashioned bookkeeping desk. Since no one in the South pays the slightest attention to a vertical Negro, this will completely solve our problem . . . in fact this may be a blessing in disguise. They are not learning to read sitting down anyway; maybe standing up will help.

His "White Baby Plan" sprang from his mind when he read of two black schoolteachers who wanted to see a revival of Olivier's *Hamlet* in a segregrated movie theater and borrowed the white children of two friends to take in with them. They were sold tickets without hesitation; prompting Golden to suggest:

> . . . People can pool their children at a central point in each neighborhood, and every time a Negro wants to go to the movies all she need do is pick up a white child—and go.
>
> Eventually the Negro community can set up a factory and manufacture white babies made of plastic, and when they want to go to the opera or to a concert, all they need do is carry that plastic doll in their arms. The dolls, of course, should all have blond curls and blue eyes.

Golden punched the paunches of a lot of southern politicians who were taking themselves too seriously and stirring up fears of the black. He had no peer when it came to poking holes in southern segregation and pointing up the South's hypocrisy by manipulating its mores. He proposed a way to solve the problems of busing school children and of prayer in schools in one grand step, by permitting "prayers on the bus instead of the classroom."

With national fame came the revelation that in 1929 he had been sentenced to four years in prison for mail fraud resulting from the misdeeds of a brokerage firm he ran. He had pleaded guilty and had served 18 months, after which he was paroled. After imprisonment Golden had returned to his Irish Catholic wife, the former Genevieve Gallagher, and his four sons, changed his name, and moved to North Carolina to start a new life. In December 1973 President Richard M. Nixon gave Golden a full pardon.

He was often the target of threats of violence, yet his humor seemed to be his armor, leading eventually to his full acceptance by the southern establishment that honored him with degrees and awards. When his home was burned down in 1958, the Charlotte police and the FBI helped him decipher the charred list of *Carolina Israelite* subscribers.

Two years before he died on 2 October 1981, he summed up his life by saying he was "a newspaper man, an American, a Jew, a Democrat and a Zionist, in that order." The Raleigh *News and Observer* added on his death that "he was also a highly literate prophet and satirist whose views and commentary made a beneficial difference in the affairs of the South and the nation."

Eli Evans
Revson Foundation

Eli Evans, *The Provincials: A Personal History of Jews in the South* (1974); *New York Times* (3 October 1981).

Gone with the Wind

Gone with the Wind is the preeminent example of the Civil War and Reconstruction novel. Written by the Atlantan Margaret Mitchell between about 1926 and 1930, it was published in 1936, won the Pulitzer Prize, and has enjoyed unmatched popularity for a novel, becoming part of national and regional folk culture.

The novel tells the story of the rise and fall of the planter class through the fictional histories of southern families. Against this background of chaos and disintegration, Mitchell narrates the history of one woman's survival. Scarlett O'Hara, a giddy belle before the conflict, overcomes the deprivations of war and reconstruction to achieve the wealth and power of a New South entrepreneur. Finally, Mitchell interweaves these themes with the more personal one of unrequited love: Scarlett's for the dreamy aristocrat Ashley Wilkes, and Rhett Butler's for Scarlett.

Especially after David O. Selznick's romanticized film version of 1939, the novel has been taken as the quintessential representation of the moonlight-and-magnolias plantation romance. It does deal with the romantic themes, particularly as represented in southern literature of the late 19th century. It introduces old-school aristocrats and young gallants, stereotypical belles and great ladies; it celebrates faithful slaves and loyal blacks; it condemns worthless field hands and troublemaking freedmen; and political reconstruction is presented as unrelieved violence, corruption, and profligacy.

Yet the novel breaks significantly with the conventional romance and includes major motifs of modernist

Clark Gable and Vivien Leigh as Rhett Butler and Scarlett O'Hara in Gone with the Wind *(1939)*

fiction and 20th-century culture. It debunks and demythologizes: Mitchell represents the planter class as a wildly mixed lot mostly of arrivistes and self-made men who inhabit a crude frontier. The novel also manifests insistent tendencies toward realism: it depicts the horrors of war, the shallowness of wartime propaganda and southern ideology, the prevalence of poor white culture, the greed of wartime profiteers, and the exploitation of postwar southern capitalism. Mitchell's social system rests on a ruthlessly Spencerian struggle for survival in which violence and immorality triumph over grace and decency. Characterization is founded on even more modern psychological values. Thus, conflict in the novel stems less from the Yankees than from Scarlett's ambivalence toward her mother, Rhett's hatred of his father, a broader Oedipal conflict between younger southerners and their ancestors, and a split personality or social schizophrenia pervading the South.

Finally, in sharpest contrast to the traditional romance but in harmony with modernistic values, the novel deals with themes of rebellion, alienation, and irresolution. The narrative is open ended; no happy conclusions cap the novel's bitter struggles. In such ways, Mitchell adapts the "gentle Confederate novel" to the realism and pessimism of post–World War I culture. By this same measure, *Gone with the Wind* fits appropriately into the Southern Literary Renaissance in this period and the effort of southern writers and intellectuals to deal with the conflict between their past and the modernist future.

See also MYTHIC SOUTH: / Mitchell, Margaret; "Moonlight-and-Magnolias" Myth

Darden Asbury Pyron
Florida International University

Richard B. Harwell, *Gone with the Wind as Book and Film* (1983); Darden Asbury Pyron, *Recasting: Gone with the Wind in American Culture* (1983).

Griffith, D. W.

(1875–1948) Film director.

David Wark Griffith was probably the man most responsible for expanding into films the depictions of a mythic, romantic Old South common in fiction. His movie, *Birth of a Nation* (1915), told the story of the Civil War and Reconstruction from the point of view of the defeated South.

Griffith was born in Crestwood, Ky., on 22 January 1875. His father, a colonel in the Confederate army, entertained his children with stories of his exploits in battle; and a cousin added to family folklore with tales of the organization of the Ku Klux Klan. During these family times, the youthful Griffith developed his love of the South. He left Kentucky to begin a career as an actor and playwright; but when that career never bloomed, he reluctantly accepted jobs acting in a new but slightly disreputable medium—motion pictures. He became intrigued by the potential of movies, and by 1908 he was directing films for the American Biograph Company in New York. During the next five years he directed over 400 short films at Biograph and became recognized as the major filmmaker of his time. Often he turned to his native South for plots and settings for his films, 11 of which were set during the Civil War.

In 1912 Griffith joined the Epoch Producing Company and began making a major full-length motion picture. Using Thomas Dixon, Jr.'s emotional novel *The Clansman* as his main source, Griffith produced a film that he believed would tell the truth about the Civil War and the years following it. The story describes two families, one northern and one southern. The young men on both sides go off to fight, but after the war one of the southern men—Little Colonel—returns to his ruined home to find the society he had known in chaos. The narrative portrays the Reconstruction era as a violent period, ending only with the restoration of white rule. Griffith's view of the South in this film is a mixture of his romanticism and realism. He had a romantic view of the Old South's social structure, based on the family and an agrarian way of life, yet his desire to tell the truth and his interest in the photographic qualities of his medium led him to portray battle scenes and other historical vignettes, such as the surrender at Appomattox, with fidelity to history. The war itself was not glorified in Griffith's films, and his most powerful images of it are of soldiers lying dead on the battlefield. The charge of Confederate troops at northern trenches is an emotional moment (James Agee called this "the most beautiful shot I have seen in any movie"), but the bravery of that moment was tempered by the sure defeat soon to follow.

Birth of a Nation caused considerable controversy because of its racial views, but it was to become the most successful movie of its time. Griffith later made two more films with southern settings, *A Romance of Happy Valley* (1919, now lost) and *The White Rose* (1923); neither had the vitality of his earlier southern films. He died in Hollywood in 1948.

See also LITERATURE: / Dixon, Thomas, Jr.

Robert A. Armour
Virginia Commonwealth University

Robert M. Henderson, *D. W. Griffith: His Life and Work* (1972); Russell Merritt, *Cinema Journal* (1972).

Grizzard, Lewis

(b. 1946) Newspaper columnist and humorist.

Born 20 October 1946 in Fort Benning, Ga., Lewis Grizzard grew up in the small Georgia town of Moreland. He and his mother moved there in 1946 after she divorced his father, who was a professional soldier. Grizzard graduated from the University of Georgia and worked as a sportswriter in Athens and Atlanta, Ga., and in Chicago. He returned to Atlanta as a columnist for the Atlanta *Constitution* in 1978. His column is now syndicated to more than 200 newspapers with 9 million readers.

The South has a long tradition of newspaper columnists who have recorded the region's folkways and social manners. These columnists have drawn on and contributed to southern traditions of humor and storytelling. Grizzard is among the most successful and insightful contemporary observers of the changing South. From the New South bastion of Atlanta, Grizzard embodies the traditional southern white male's confrontation with modern America.

Grizzard grew up as a small-town boy, and he often writes of his childhood home and of friends such as Weyman C. Wanamaker ("a great American"), Curtis "Fruit Jar" Hainey (the town drunk), and Hog Phillpot, Cordie Mae Poovey, and Kathy Sue Loudermilk. He tells stories of real-life characters, ordinary people whose stories may be offbeat, nostalgic, sentimental, poignant, or tragic. Called the Faulkner of the common man, Grizzard champions his social class of origin—the plain (often poor) whites. Living in the capital of the new southern upper-middle class, he also is an astute observer of southern Yuppies. He has chronicled, and sometimes protested, the appearance in Atlanta of "hanging fern" restaurants and singles bars, BMWs replacing pickup trucks, and the drinking of wine coolers instead of beer.

Grizzard's significant contribution is his assertion of southern distinctiveness and tradition in the face of a changing South. He defends southern traditions in an age when the small towns of his youth have been enveloped by modern cities such as Atlanta. In his books he tries "to keep the South alive and rekindle it." He writes about country music, trains, pickup trucks, country stores, barbecue, long-necked bottles of beer, fishing, revivals, Sunday schools, saying grace before meals, snuff, pool halls, Vienna sausages, RC Cola, moon pies, juke joints, honky tonks, front porches, dogs, and stock car and dirt track racing. He is a die-hard University of Georgia football fan, often lambasting rival Georgia Tech. He is defined by his sex—a champion of male rights in an age of women's liberation—and his age—a baby boomer who looks back fondly to growing up as part of the Elvis generation.

Lewis Grizzard's books include *Kathy Sue Loudermilk, I Love You* (1979), *Won't You Come Home, Billy Bob Bailey?* (1980), *Don't Sit under the Grits Tree with Anyone Else but Me* (1981), *They Tore out My Heart and Stomped That Sucker Flat* (1982), *If Love Were Oil, I'd Be about a Quart Low* (1983), *Elvis Is Dead, and I Don't Feel So Good Myself* (1984), *Shoot Low, Boys—They're Ridin' Shetland Ponies* (1985), and *My Daddy Was a Pistol and I'm a Son of a Gun* (1986).

Charles Reagan Wilson
University of Mississippi

David C. Foster, *Atlanta* (October 1986); David Treadwell, Los Angeles *Times* (19 June 1986).

Johnson, Gerald

(1890–1980) Journalist, biographer, and historian.

Perhaps best known for his contributions to the *New Republic* over a quarter century, Gerald White Johnson was a leader in the southern critical awakening of the 1920s. Born in Riverton, N.C., and reared in the town of Thomasville in the Carolina Piedmont, Johnson followed other members of his family to Wake Forest College and then into journalism. After serving in World War I, he became an editorial writer for the Greensboro, N.C., *Daily News* and a spokesman for a new, liberal South. In 1922 he caught the eye of notorious South-watcher H. L. Mencken, and Mencken helped him publish in the iconoclastic southern little magazine *The Reviewer* of Richmond and in Mencken's own *American Mercury*. By the mid-1920s Johnson was firmly established as the leading interpreter of the contemporary South. His articles in the *American Mercury* and other magazines described a benighted South of Ku Klux Klansmen, religious fundamentalists, and cotton mill barons and workers. His attitude toward benighted southerners, however, was never so harsh as that of his mentor, Mencken. Partly because of his own southern heritage and Baptist upbringing, he was able to bring an understanding, even a sympathy, to his subject that Mencken rarely displayed.

In 1926 Johnson joined Mencken in Baltimore as an editorial writer and columnist for the Sunpapers, and from that point on his interests were not exclusively southern. He became a serious student of American history, a biographer of Andrew Jackson and numerous other figures, and in the 1930s a fervent supporter of Franklin D. Roosevelt and the New Deal. After he left the Sunpapers in the 1940s, he gained renown as a columnist and commentator, remaining a liberal Democrat until his death. In his later years, he did not forget the South entirely. Some of his most moving essays, appearing largely in the *Virginia Quarterly Review*, were tributes to liberal southerners he had known. But his most important role in southern history was the one he had played in the 1920s as the most perceptive of analysts for national magazines in search of the southern story.

See also LITERATURE: / Mencken, H. L.; MYTHIC SOUTH: / Mencken's South

Fred Hobson
University of Alabama

Fred Hobson, *South-Watching: Selected Essays of Gerald W. Johnson* (1983); Gerald W. Johnson, *America-Watching: Perspectives in the Course of an Incredible Century* (1976).

Kazan, Elia

(b. 1909) Film director.

One of America's most important stage and screen directors and latterly a novelist, Elia Kazan has often used the South as the setting for his vision of the individual identity suppressed or impeded by social pressures.

In *Pinky* (1949) Kazan made one of Hollywood's first approaches to the problems of racial prejudice, but his use of starlet Jeanne Crain as the black female lead never quite succeeded. A more credible mammy-granddaughter bridge was established in *Wild River* (1960), between Jo Van Fleet and Lee Remick. Here Kazan played out the individual-versus-society conflict on two contrary fronts, one between a diehard landholder (Van Fleet) and the Tennessee Valley Authority, the other between the progressive outsider (Montgomery Clift) and the reactionary rural community. The liberated screen of the 1960s enabled Kazan graphically to depict the crust of dead and numbing traditions through which the individual spirit had to break. The moral torpor of the citizenry appeared through either fly-buzzing sleepiness or vigilante violence.

Kazan can take some credit for the matured American cinema through two film adaptations he made with Tennessee Williams—*A Streetcar Named Desire* (1951) and *Baby Doll* (1956). *A Streetcar Named Desire* was the first true adult film in America, though to please the censors it required considerable change. Kazan had no foreknowledge or control of about a dozen small cuts in wording. The ambiguously happy ending in the film, which suggests that Stanley Kowalski will be punished by Stella's desertion for his rape of Blanche DuBois, was a compromise to allow the film to keep even the oblique representations of the rape.

In *Baby Doll* a pathetic dreamer is overcome by a pragmatic realist. Kazan shot this film on location at Benoit, Miss., using many townsfolk as extras, most notably some local blacks as a kind of silent chorus, chortling at the whites' pretensions and frustrations. On this occasion in 1956 Kazan expressed his love for the South and its people: "I'm terribly moved by their problems and their attempts to meet them. Under an onionskin-thin surface is a titanic violence: That is drama. I don't think Northern people, especially Northern intellectuals, know much about it. I didn't until I went to the South and lived there."

Maurice Yacowar
Brock University

Michel Ciment, *Kazan on Kazan* (1973); Toby Cole and Helen Krich Chinoy, eds., *Directors on Directing* (1964); Jim Kitses, *Cinema* (Winter 1972–73).

Kilpatrick, James J.

(b. 1920) Journalist.

James Jackson Kilpatrick, Jr., born in 1920 in Oklahoma City, Okla., is a nationally syndicated newspaper columnist of conservative political outlook who defines his own political affiliation as "Whig." He first achieved national attention in the late 1950s and early 1960s when, as editor of the Richmond *News Leader*, he became one of the leading journalistic advocates of resistance to the U.S. Supreme Court's 1954 *Brown* v. *Board of Education* ruling, which outlawed segregation in the public schools of the South.

A 1941 graduate of the University of Missouri School of Journalism, Kilpatrick joined the staff of the Richmond *News Leader* and between 1941 and 1949 served in virtually every "beat" of a daily newspaper before becoming chief editorial writer for the paper in 1949. In 1951 at age 31 he succeeded Douglas Southall Freeman as editor.

As editor, following the 1954 decision, he argued for "gradualism" in the integration of the races in the South. His 1962 book, *The Southern Case for School Segregation*, summarizes many of his editorial views: "In the South, the acceptance of racial separation begins in the cradle. What rational man imagines this concept can be shattered overnight?" He criticized those who sought integration in the South as "men in high places whose hypocrisy is exceeded only by their ignorance, men whose trade it is to damn the bigotry of the South by day and to sleep in lily-white Westchester County by night."

Kilpatrick in his books and editorials used traditional constitutional arguments and the states' rights principles so effectively that his opponents credited him with stimulating the "massive resistance" legislative measures that were attempted first by Virginia and later by other southern legislatures.

"Patience, the South would ask of its adversaries," Kilpatrick said as he regularly espoused evolutionary change in the 1960s. "If there is ever to be in the South any significant degree of desegregation in public institutions, let alone any significant degree of integration in society as a whole, it can come effectively in one way only: slowly, cautiously, voluntarily, 'some time in the future.'"

Ultimately, Kilpatrick saw change as inevitable. Although he felt that the South would maintain "essential separation of the races for years to come," Kilpatrick also predicted that "doors that have been closed will open one by one. And a South that once would have regarded these innovations with horror will view them at first with surprise, then with regret, for a time with distaste, and at last with indifference."

A syndicated columnist, Kilpatrick became known to wider audiences through television appearances on the "Point-Counterpoint" feature of the CBS program *60 Minutes*. In addition to his earlier books, *The Sovereign States* (1957) and *The Smut Peddlers* (1960), his recent writing includes *The Foxes' Union* (1977); with Eugene McCarthy, *A Political Bestiary* (1978); with William

Bake, *The American South: Four Seasons of the Land* (1980); *The American South: Towns and Cities* (1982); and *The Writer's Art* (1984).

See also LAW: / *Brown* v. *Board of Education*

Jere Real
Lynchburg, Virginia

Neil A. Graver, *Wits and Sages* (1984); William C. Havard, *Virginia Quarterly Review* (Winter 1983); Charles Moritz, ed., *Current Biography* (1981); *Time* (30 November 1970).

King, Henry

(1892–1982) Film director.

Henry King was born near Christiansburg, Va., 24 June 1892. When a teenager, he left the family farm to become a song-and-dance man with a blackface theatrical troupe. Further acting experience on the road led him eventually into films, playing supporting roles with the then-popular Baby Marie Osborne. Like many of his contemporaries, King gravitated to directing as an alternative to acting and found he liked the work. Even he could not recall the number of quickly made films, mostly westerns, for which he served as actor-director before 1920. His big break came in 1921 when he was assigned to direct young matinee idol Richard Barthelmess in *Tol'able David*, a sentimental tale of King's native southern mountains. The Russian director-theorist Pudovkin praised the film for its naturalness, and it remains in circulation today as an outstanding example of silent-film artistry.

Thereafter, as a contract director for Fox Films (subsequently 20th Century Fox), King directed more than 60 films, including some of the studio's major productions of the 1930s and 1940s like *Alexander's Ragtime Band* and *In Old Chicago*. He rarely had a chance to work on stories about the South, but, after D. W. Griffith abandoned rural subject matter in the 1920s, King became the screen's most sympathetic interpreter of such materials. He was assigned such films as the first *State Fair* (1933, starring Will Rogers), *Carolina* (1934), a remake of Griffith's *Way Down East* (1935), *Ramona* (1936), and *Maryland* (1940), on the infrequent occasions that Fox scheduled such productions. He continued working until 1962, when Darryl F. Zanuck, with whom King had collaborated closely, lost control of the studio.

Although he was not highly regarded by film critics, he was twice nominated for Academy Awards—for *The Song of Bernadette* (1943) and *Wilson* (1944). His day came at last when, beginning on 30 June 1978, New York's Museum of Modern Art celebrated his 90th birthday by honoring him with a seven-week retrospective of his films. He died in his San Fernando Valley home on 29 June 1982.

Warren French
Indiana University

New York Times (30 June 1978).

Kuralt, Charles

(b. 1934) Television and radio correspondent.

Charles Bishop Kuralt grew up in Wilmington, N.C., absorbing and observing southern traits. One of his heroes during childhood was Edward R. Murrow, who once read Kuralt's winning entry in the American Legion's "Voice of Democracy" contest over CBS radio. Kuralt pursued his interest in journalism at the University of North Carolina, where he earned a B.A. degree in 1955. He was a reporter and columnist for the Charlotte *News* from 1955 to 1957, and his work won the Ernie Pyle Memorial Award in 1956. He joined CBS news as a writer in 1957 and became a correspondent in 1959. At CBS Kuralt has served as correspondent in Latin America, as West Coast bureau manager, and as anchor. In 1972 he became the host of a CBS radio show called *Dateline America*.

Kuralt's popular series *On the Road*, consisting of stories of his travels throughout America in a van, began in 1967 and appears frequently on the *CBS Evening News*. He offers poignant slices of American life through his musings on his travels and interviews with people he encounters, usually on back roads and often in rural settings. *On the Road* won Emmy Awards in 1969, 1978, and 1981. His unique, folksy, conversational style is key to Kuralt's popularity. In 1979 he took the same style to his job as anchor for the critically successful CBS program *Sunday Morning*. For a short time beginning in 1980 he was also the host of the *CBS Morning News*. Kuralt's first weekly CBS series premiered in the summer of 1983, but it was not renewed. He has been the host of many CBS television specials.

Kuralt is the author of several books that elaborate on his travels in America, including *Southerners: A Portrait of a People* (1986), which explores the southern heritage and traditions in photographs and Kuralt's characteristically personal narration. He draws on his own experiences and North Carolina background frequently in the text. As in all of his work, Kuralt demonstrates the warmth and good humor that prompted *Newsweek* in 1983 to call him "our favorite visiting uncle."

Karen M. McDearman
University of Mississippi

Charles Kuralt, *Dateline America* (1979), *On the Road with Charles Kuralt* (1985), *To the Top of the World: The Adventures and Misadventures of the Plaisted Polar Expedition, March 28–*

May 4, 1967 (1968), with Loonis McGlohan, *North Carolina Is My Home* (1986); *Newsweek* (4 July 1983); William Howard Taft, *Encyclopedia of Twentieth-Century Journalists* (1986).

Leigh, Vivien

(1913–1967) Actress.

Vivien Leigh is known to generations of southerners as Scarlett O'Hara in the movie version of Margaret Mitchell's epic of the Old South, *Gone with the Wind*, and as Blanche DuBois in the movie version of Tennessee Williams's play *A Streetcar Named Desire*. That Leigh, British by birth and upbringing, could have not only convincingly played, but in large part created, these beloved and familiar southern characters is a tribute to her remarkable acting ability.

Born 5 November 1913 in Darjeeling, India, to British parents, Vivian Mary Hartley spent her childhood in Europe. Beginning at age seven, she was educated at convent boarding schools, where she indulged an already passionate interest in plays and the theater. In February 1932 she enrolled in the Royal Academy of Dramatic Art in London, but upon her marriage in December to Herbert Leigh Holman she reluctantly gave up her studies.

Leigh's professional career began with the British film *Things Are Looking Up* (1934). Her first agent suggested she adopt a stage name and Leigh (her husband's middle name) was agreed upon. The producer of her first successful play on the London stage, *The Mask of Virtue* (1935), was responsible for altering the spelling of her first name, because he thought "Vivien" more feminine. Under contract to Alexander Korda, Leigh made several films and performed in several plays before setting her sights on the role of Scarlett O'Hara in *Gone with the Wind*, which was to be made by David O. Selznick in the United States. Reportedly, Selznick and the film's director, George Cukor, almost immediately decided to give Leigh the part upon meeting her. Selznick was concerned about the American public's reaction to his casting an Englishwoman for the part and tried to diffuse negative feelings by referring to Leigh as "the daughter of a French father and Irish mother," emphasizing the parentage that she shared with the character of Scarlett. The British press doubted her ability to disguise her accent and play the part of a fiery southern belle. Certainly, the American public's relatively easy acceptance of Leigh in the role stemmed in part from the traditional association of the southern states with Great Britain. Furthermore, Leigh's performance was so intense and believable that many people agreed with Selznick and Cukor that she was, indeed, the one Scarlett. Her portrayal won her the first of two Academy Awards.

Vivien Leigh as Blanche DuBois in A Streetcar Named Desire *(1951)*

After obtaining a divorce settlement in which she relinquished custody of her daughter, Leigh married Laurence Olivier in October 1940. They made a wartime picture together—*That Mrs. Hamilton* (1941)—and played opposite each other on the stage in Great Britain and the United States many times from 1937 through 1957. Her 1949 portrayal of Blanche DuBois in Tennessee Williams's *A Streetcar Named Desire* on the London stage was directed by Olivier and led to her role in the American screen version of the play. Leigh reportedly became obsessed with the character of Blanche in much the same way as she had with that of Scarlett O'Hara, and attempted to understand her in depth. Indeed, her portrayal of the tragic southern figure of fallen aristocracy, whose fading beauty and vain attempts to regain a life of gentility lead her to madness, was intense on both the stage and the screen. The film, which opened in September 1951, was produced and directed by Elia Kazan and won Leigh her second Academy Award for Best Actress.

Always subject to violent mood swings, Leigh was diagnosed as manic-depressive and schizophrenic in her later years. In addition, she had suffered from tuberculosis since 1945. She made several more films and plays after *Streetcar*, including another Tennessee Williams adaptation, but her work became erratic as she became increasingly ill. She died on 8 July 1967.

Karen M. McDearman
University of Mississippi

Felix Barker, *The Oliviers: A Biography* (1953); Anne Edwards, *Vivien Leigh: A Biography* (1977).

Louisville *Courier-Journal*

Kentucky's leading antebellum newspapers reflected the quandary of the border state. Supportive of union, G. D. Prentice's Louisville *Journal* experienced steadily declining circulation as the sectional crisis took its toll, while the secessionist *Courier* was forced by federal troops to close its offices in 1861.

After the war, *Courier* editor Walter N. Haldeman resumed publication and in 1868 bought the failing *Journal* as well as Louisville's third major paper, the *Democrat*. The consolidation produced the Louisville *Courier-Journal*,and the young journalist Henry Watterson (1840–1921) became the editor. Watterson's flamboyant personality and powerful editorial style extended the paper's influence far outside its region.

Cultivating the physical image of a Kentucky colonel, Watterson was a Confederate veteran who admired Lincoln and advocated the Greeley Liberal Republican ticket; an opponent of carpetbag rule, he was acknowledged by Booker T. Washington as a "liberal concerning the Negro, or any underdeveloped" group. At 28 he had already worked as a music critic for the *New York Times*, a reporter for the Washington *Daily States*, and, after the war, had resuscitated the Nashville *Banner*. By 1880 his editorial leadership had boosted combined circulation of the *Courier-Journal* to 50,000, making it the largest paper west of the Alleghenies.

While never emerging as a "fighting liberal," Watterson, like Henry W. Grady, did much to bridge the postwar gulf between North and South. From his offices just four blocks south of the Mason-Dixon line, he sounded many of the same notes as Grady, proclaiming his version of the New South—"The New Departure." His political enthusiasm set him apart, however. He was unabashed in his support of the 1876 Democratic party nominee, Samuel J. Tilden, "the ideal statesman"; he crossed party lines with ease, and was so vehemently—and unpopularly—opposed to the Democratic free-silver platform in the 1890s that the paper lost half of its circulation in a year.

In 1917 Watterson's prowar editorials made the *Courier-Journal* the first southern paper to win a Pulitzer Prize. In the same year the newspaper and its evening edition, the Louisville *Times*, were sold to Judge Robert Worth Bingham, and in protest over Bingham's support of the League of Nations, Watterson resigned. More conservative and less distinctly a personality newspaper under Bingham's ownership, the *Courier-Journal* continued to increase its readership—73,000 by the 1920s—and to sustain the quality of writing that would result in the award of five more Pulitzers for reporting, public service, and editorials.

Bingham died in 1937 and was succeeded by his son Barry, who shared editorial and publishing responsibilities, as well as a record of government service, with Mississippi native Mark Ethridge. Universally regarded, according to a Chicago *Sun* tribute, "as one of the most forceful, intelligent and progressive newspaper men in America," Ethridge quickly emerged as an archetypical New South editor. Both he and Bingham were sensitive to the responsibilities incumbent upon even the most benign media monopoly and for a time featured syndicated columnists so ideologically disparate that the paper was charged with confusing freedom of the press with columnar chaos.

Retaining its reputation for incisive reporting and high cultural content, the *Courier-Journal* has a current daily circulation of over 175,000 and a Sunday circulation of over 330,000. It is edited and published by Barry Bingham, Jr. The Bingham family, however, sold its interest in the paper in 1986.

See also URBANIZATION: / Louisville

Elizabeth M. Makowski
University of Mississippi

Sidney Kobre, *Development of American Journalism* (1969); Frank Luther Mott, *American Journalism: A History, 1690–1960* (1962) ; Kenneth Stewart and John Tebbel, *Makers of Modern Journalism* (1952); Joseph F. Wall, *Henry Watterson: Reconstructed Rebel* (1956).

McGill, Ralph

(1898–1969) Newspaper editor and publisher.

As associate editor, editor, and publisher of the Atlanta *Constitution* from 1938 to his death in 1969, Ralph McGill campaigned for equal civil rights for blacks. While writing of politics, religion, economics, poetry, poker, bees, the press, farming, war, sports, cooking, and foreign affairs, this Pulitzer Prize winner became recognized for his commentary on southern society.

McGill was a peculiar social reformer, a reluctant crusader with common sense and a good sense of humor.

Ralph McGill (left), editor of the Atlanta Constitution*, 1939*

Showing a deep concern for the "troubles of others," he took on many causes. He enjoyed the give and take of political debate and chided persons who avoided controversial subjects. This restless rebel disliked seeing defenseless people exploited, whether Jew, black, or artist.

Unless a school or synagogue had been bombed or a black person harmed, McGill generally approached social issues "something like a teacher," coaxing and prodding listeners more than berating them, often leaving his audience choices to make. McGill explained that one cannot "get too far ahead of the audience"; otherwise "you find yourself" communicating "to just a small group." So as not to stampede his readers, McGill often softened his persuasion with the claim that he was not arguing "pro or con" but "to create some understanding." But when the deed deserved stronger criticism, McGill was ready: "Not all the perfumes of Araby will wash clean the political hands of Mississippi's Governor Ross Barnett."

Although a Democrat, McGill saw himself politically "just left of center" and "highly idealistic about life." Because of "human limitations," however, he felt that social progress "moves like an inch worm." His moderate and realistic stance on race relations angered racists and segregationists and frustrated some liberals. McGill admitted "there is schizophrenia" in "running with the hare and dropping back . . . to see how the hounds are making out," but "there also is Americanism and good politics as well."

From McGill's moral strength and communicative compromise evolved "a primer of Southern thinking" that he taught friend and foe. He argued that the "old customs" controlling race relations could be resolved permanently only "within the Southern pattern." One more federal law was not the answer; southerners had "to do what is right."

Searching for solutions to racial problems that were both fair and feasible, McGill adapted his arguments and goals to changing conditions between 1940 and 1969. From 1940 to 1950 he "held up and cried aloud" the South's "record of shame" in discriminating against blacks in courts, education, employment, voting, government, housing, religion, and social services. During the 1940s McGill worked for "separate *and equal*" opportunities for blacks and whites. Beginning in 1949 he tried to prepare citizens for the Supreme Court's ultimate ruling against segregation in public schools, a decision for which the region's leaders had no mechanism with which to work. By 1953 McGill declared that "segregation by law no longer fits today's world." From 1954 to 1969 he escalated his criticism of racial evils and his prescriptions for home remedies. "Weary of excuses and evasions," McGill pronounced that "segregation is dead." No longer could a citizen's "rights be compromised." To educate readers and to save the South's public schools, McGill explained that the region could not afford dual school systems. He analyzed historical causes of racial attitudes, including old sectional loyalties, slavery, the Civil War, agrarianism, migration to cities, and the economy. In a highly personable, lucid, and potent style, McGill corrected false negative images assigned to blacks, analyzed other myths of the Solid South, and wrote on such favorite regional topics as the "unconstitutionality of the Constitution," states' rights politics, and racially mixed marriages.

Cal M. Logue
University of Georgia

D. C. Kinsella, "Southern Apologists" (Ph.D. dissertation, University of St. Louis, 1971); Ralph McGill, *The South and the Southerner* (1959).

Mandingo

Mandingo, a novel written by Kyle Onstott (1887–1966) and originally published by Denlinger's, a small Virginia publishing house, significantly recast the portrayal of the antebellum South in American popular fiction. The widely popular 1957 work, which one reviewer called "a slimy mess," eschewed the moonlight-and-magnolias vision of the Old South in favor of an image liberally spiced with violence, racism, and miscegenation. The plot centered on the Maxwells, Warren and his son Hammond, and their interactions with slaves and neighbors. The Maxwell estate, the fictional Falconhurst Plantation, was, to quote from the book, "the most unusual plantation in Alabama." The unique nature of Falconhurst derived from its cash crop: instead of cotton or some other staple, slave breeding provided the Maxwells with a marketable commodity.

The *Mandingo* story line, which became the standard for plantation fiction ever since, had Hammond Maxwell court and marry Blanche Woodford, a stereotype of the belle on the pedestal. Although Blanche was attractive, Hammond continued to lust after young slave women. Rejected by Hammond, Blanche sought sexual gratification with Mede, the pure Mandingo breeding stud whose only responsibilities on the plantation were impregnating slave women and wrestling for the amusement of his owners. When Hammond discovered the liaison between Blanche and Mede, he sadistically murdered both of them. In the world of Falconhurst Plantation it was acceptable for white men to share sexuality with black women, but it remained a sin of the gravest sort for a black man to so much as look at a white woman with desire in his eyes.

Wildly inaccurate from a historical perspective, *Mandingo* nevertheless remains one of the most popular plantation novels of all time. It is still in print (Fawcett paperback), was made into a film in 1975, spawned scores of imitations, and, at last count, had inspired eight sequels. Collectively known as the "Falconhurst Series," *Mandingo* and its sequels sold at least 30 million copies through 1980. Onstott's son once said that *Mandingo* had no significance and that it was "like eating peanuts." Because of the book's overwhelming influence upon popular fiction, however, the mass understanding (or, rather, the mass misunderstanding) of the nature of the

Perry King (center, left) as Hammond and Ken Norton (center, right) as Mede in Mandingo *(1975)*

antebellum South and of the American slave system has been greatly shaped by Onstott's vision of the Old South as a miasmic wasteland of vast plantations on which both masters and slaves engaged in orgiastic sex and sadistic violence.

See also MYTHIC SOUTH: / "Moonlight-and-Magnolias" Myth

Christopher D. Geist
Bowling Green State University

Earl F. Bargainnier, *Journal of Popular Culture* (Fall 1976); Marsha Marks, *Studies in Popular Culture* (Winter 1977); *Time* (13 May 1957); *Washington Post* (21 May 1975).

Memphis *Commercial Appeal*

To maintain the presence of a Democratic newspaper in Memphis, Colonel Henry Van Pelt took over the defunct *Western World and Memphis Banner of the Constitution* in 1840. In 1841 he changed the paper's name to the *Weekly Appeal*, and the first issue appeared on 21 April. With hopes of appealing to "the sober second thought of the people," a phrase adopted as the newspaper's motto, Van Pelt used the paper to promote the Democratic principles of states' rights and a strict interpretation of the Constitution. In 1847 the paper began daily publication, except on Mondays, and published weekly and triweekly editions as well.

As dissension between the North and South increased during the 1850s, the *Appeal* became a strong advocate of southern nationalism. Editors John R. McClanahan, Leonidas Trousdale, and Benjamin F. Dill believed that the Democratic party and southern unity were the South's only hopes for maintaining its rights within the Union. Their stance, in a city with few slaves and many northern commercial ties, was bold. Not until late in 1860, though, did the paper become an exponent of secession, and then it determined to be a voice for the South throughout the war. Fleeing Memphis just hours before occupation by federal troops, Dill and McClanahan (Trousdale left the paper in 1860) settled and published the *Appeal* first in Grenada, Miss., then in Jackson; Atlanta, Ga.; Montgomery, Ala.; and Columbus, Ga. In Columbus, at the war's end, Union soldiers finally captured Dill and destroyed some of the equipment of what one officer called "this defiant rebel sheet." With Dill as sole editor, the *Appeal* reappeared in Memphis on 5 November 1865. Dill's death two months later marked the beginning of a short period of instability; but in 1868 John McLeod Keating began a 21-year term as editor. Under his direction, the paper became an advocate of the New South movement, promoting sanitation reform, agricultural diversification, manufacturing, and political rights (but not social equality) for blacks.

When William Armistead Collier bought the newspaper in 1889, Keating became editor of the newly established Memphis *Daily Commercial*. In 1890 Collier purchased the *Avalanche*, a rival newspaper in the city. By 1893, however, the *Appeal-Avalanche* had fallen victim to financial misfortune. The Commercial Publishing Company bought the paper in 1894 and issued the first edition of the *Commercial Appeal* on 1 July 1894.

Charles Patrick Joseph Mooney edited the paper from 1908 to 1926. Although it gave no support to the cause of racial equality, the *Appeal* won a Pulitzer Prize in 1923 for its coverage and condemnation of Ku Klux Klan activities. J. P. Alley's cartoon "Hambone," featuring a little black man, became a popular feature and appeared regularly until it was discontinued following the assassination of Martin Luther King, Jr., in 1968. One of Mooney's primary local concerns centered upon the Memphis political machine of Edward Hull Crump. "Boss" Crump's control of local politics began with his 1909 election as mayor and continued later through his position as a Shelby County trustee. While the *Appeal* did not favor the state prohibition law, Crump would not even enforce it. Mooney and others used this failure to force Crump's resignation as mayor in 1916, but the principle of one-man rule had been and remained the editor's chief concern.

Before his death, Mooney encouraged the establishment of an evening paper. The first *Evening Appeal* was published on 1 December 1926 but, in June 1933, was absorbed into the morning paper. The *Commercial Appeal* came under chain ownership when the Scripps-Howard news organization, the current owner, acquired it in 1936. Today, the *Appeal* publishes only morning and Sunday editions and no longer officially allies itself with any political party. Its circulation is over 227,500 daily and in excess of 292,000 on Sundays.

Jessica Foy
Cooperstown Graduate Programs
Cooperstown, New York

Thomas Harrison Baker, *The Memphis Commercial Appeal: The History of a Southern Newspaper* (1971); Neil B. Cope, "A History of the Memphis *Commercial Appeal*" (Ph.D. dissertation, University of Missouri, 1969); *The 1986 IMS/AYER Directory of Publications* (1986).

Morris, Willie

(b. 1934) Writer.

Willie Morris, Mississippi-born journalist, editor, essayist, and novelist, continues the long-standing tradition of the southern man of letters as explainer of the South to the rest of the nation, to itself, and to himself. Seeing the South as "the nation writ large," he has probed the complexities of the region and of the country.

When he was six months old, Morris's family moved from Jackson, where he was born in 1934, to Yazoo City, Miss., which, Morris says, "Gave me much of whatever sensibility I now possess." At 17, told by his father "to get the hell out of Mississippi," he entered the University of Texas. As editor of the *Daily Texan*, he battled both the oil and gas interests of Texas and the university's board of regents before graduating as a Rhodes Scholar. After earning the B.A. and M.A. degrees at New College, Oxford University, he returned to Austin in 1960 to edit the liberal *Texas Observer*.

Hired as an editor at *Harper's Magazine* in 1963, Morris became editor-in-chief in 1967. He made *Harper's* probably the most significant magazine in America during a time of fundamental change. In 1965, on the 100th anniversary of Appomattox, his special supplement, *The South Today*, sought to "illuminate for non-Southerners the interaction of North and South, and make it more clear that the assignation of regional guilt or failure is each day becoming a more subtle and complex question" and to provoke for southerners an "awareness of the moral nuances of their own society."

After resigning from *Harper's* in 1971, he settled in Bridgehampton, Long Island. In 1980, perhaps drawn by that "chord of homecoming" that he sensed to be "one of the very threads of my existence as a Southern American of the Twentieth Century," Morris became writer in residence at the University of Mississippi, where he remains.

In all his works, Morris reveals himself "still a son of that bedeviled and mystifying and exasperating region, and sen[sing] in the experience of it something of immense value and significance to the Great Republic." That sense, reconciling in Willie Morris's writings "the old warring impulse of one's sensibility to be both Southern and American," brought Dan Wakefield to write, "In the deepest sense we all live in Yazoo. Mr. Morris' triumph is that he has made us understand that."

William Moss
Clemson University

Willie Morris, *North Toward Home* (1967), *Terrains of the Heart and Other Essays on Home* (1981), *Yazoo: Integration in a Deep-Southern Town* (1971); Dan Wakefield, *New York Times Book Review* (16 May 1971).

Moyers, Bill

(b. 1934) Journalist.

Billy Don Moyers was born 5 June 1934 to a poor farm family in Hugo, Okla., which is in Oklahoma's "Little Dixie" area located in the southeastern corner of the state. His family moved within a few months to Marshall, Tex., where Moyers grew up. A good student active in school affairs, Moyers worked at a local grocery store and became a reporter for the Marshall *News Messenger* while still in high school. Moyers attended North Texas State University and earned his B.A. in journalism from the University of Texas at Austin in 1956. He studied ecclesiastical history at the University of Edinburgh the following year and gained a B.D. degree in 1959 from the Southwestern Baptist Theological Seminary in Ft. Worth, Tex. He became an ordained Baptist minister.

While still an undergraduate, Moyers was involved in Lyndon B. Johnson's 1954 reelection campaign. Johnson later hired Moyers as a personal assistant, and by 1960 he was coordinating Johnson's vice-presidential campaign. Moyers was associate director (1961–62) and then deputy director (1963) of the Peace Corps, special assistant (1963–67) to President Johnson and his press secretary (1965–67), and publisher of *Newsday* (1967–70).

From the early 1970s Moyers has been one of the nation's most respected broadcast journalists, specializing in public affairs programs. He was editor-in-chief of the Public Broadcast System's *Bill Moyers Journal* (1971–76, 1978–81), editor of and chief correspondent for *CBS Reports* (1976–78), and senior analyst for CBS news programming (1981–86). He has produced such innovative series as the 17-part *Creativity with Bill Moyers* and the 21-hour *A Walk through the Twentieth Century*. Moyers is the author of *Listening to America: A Traveler Rediscovers His Country* (1971).

Bill Moyers has extended the long tradition of southern journalism into broadcast media. In his work he explores foreign policy and national political issues, but he has continued to explore the character of his native region as well. He has sought out for interviews such diverse southerners as James Dickey, Maya Angelou, Robert Penn Warren, Jimmy Carter, and Myles Horton. He returned to his hometown of Marshall to study changing race relations for a television show in 1983. *Newsweek* (4 July 1983) has described him as "the journalist as moralist" and a "Texas Populist," and both apt descriptions seem to have origins in his southern background.

Charles Reagan Wilson
University of Mississippi

Katherine Bouton, *Saturday Review* (February 1982); *Current Biography* (1976); *Harper's* (October 1965); *Newsday* (4 June 1974).

Nashville *Tennessean*

Founded in 1812 as the Nashville *Whig*, today's *Tennessean* is the result of 15 consolidations over the years. Throughout most of that time, and particularly in the 20th century, it has been a strong editorial voice in its region.

One of the early ancestors, the Nashville *Union*, was organized as home political organ of Andrew Jackson. For a year after the Civil War another ancestor paper was partially owned by Henry Watterson, who left Nashville to take over the Louisville *Journal*.

The modern history of the newspaper began on 12 May 1907 when Colonel Luke Lea, a colorful politician, organized a new paper, the Nashville *Tennessean*. Grantland Rice was his first sports editor. Within a few years Lea's new paper absorbed a leading competitor, the *Union and American*.

Morning, evening, and Sunday editions were published by Colonel Lea until March 1933, when, as a result of the Depression, the papers were placed under a federal receiver, Lit J. Pardue, an attorney and former newsman. Under Pardue's guidance the papers grew, and in 1937 Silliman Evans, Sr., a Texan, bought the *Tennessean* papers at public auction. Evans revitalized the *Tennessean* and remained its chief executive until his death in 1955. His son, Silliman, Jr., was publisher until his death in 1961, and then the leadership passed to his younger brother, Amon Carter Evans. In 1979 the Evans family sold the *Tennessean* to the Gannett Company of Rochester, N.Y.

John Seigenthaler has edited the *Tennessean* since 1962 and is also president and publisher. In 1982 he assumed an additional role as first editorial director of *USA Today*, the nation's first national, daily, general-interest newspaper.

Some of the brightest names in American journalism have been associated with the *Tennessean*. Those who have worked for the paper over the past 40 years include David Halberstam, Tom Wicker, Will Grimsley, Ed Clark, Wallace Westfeldt, Patrick Anderson, Creed Black, Jesse Hill Ford, Fred Graham, Bill Kovach, Elizabeth Spencer, James Squires, Wendell Rawls, Jr., Reginald Stuart, and U.S. Senator Albert Gore, Jr.

See also URBANIZATION: / Nashville

John Siegenthaler
Nashville, Tennessee

Robert E. Corlew, *Tennessee: A Short History* (2d ed., 1981); *The 1986 IMS/AYER Directory of Publications* (1986).

New Orleans *Times-Picayune*

On 27 January 1837 the first issue of the New Orleans *Picayune* appeared. A morning daily, its name was taken from a local coin worth about six and a quarter cents and reflected its "penny press" format. The founders were Francis Asbury Lumsden of North Carolina and George Wilkins Kendall of New Hampshire.

Lumsden served as the senior editor, and Kendall was the roving reporter who won fame as a Mexican War correspondent. The *Picayune* had its own pony express carrying eastern newspapers to its shop between 1837 and 1839 and bringing news from Mexico and Texas during the Mexican War. By 1839 Alva Morris Holbrook, who had bought into the paper, became its business manager.

In the last half of the 19th century the *Picayune*'s chief rivals were the *Times*, founded in 1863 by Union supporters, and the *Democrat*, begun in 1875 as an organ of the Redeemers. These two were merged into the *Times-Democrat* in 1881. In 1914 that paper, in turn, was absorbed by the *Picayune* to create the *Times-Picayune*.

The last of the original proprietors, A. M. Holbrook, died in 1876, and his widow, Eliza Poitevent, a poet and journalist whose pen name was Pearl Rivers, took over the paper's supervision. Eliza Holbrook later married the *Picayune*'s business manager and part owner, George Nicholson. She was instrumental in presenting society news, a young people's page, and a strong literary section. She also featured women reporters such as the nationally famous lovelorn columnist Dorothy Dix (Elizabeth Gilmer). The Nicholsons both died in 1896.

In 1933 the *Times-Picayune* purchased the *Daily States*, an afternoon paper that used the facilities of the *Times-Picayune* plant but kept its own identity and staff. The *States* was merged in 1958 with the New Orleans *Item*. The *States-Item* continues to put out a separate afternoon paper but shares the Sunday edition with the *Times-Picayune*. The *Times-Picayune* moved into its present plant at 3800 Howard Avenue in 1968 and is under local management, although Samuel I. Newhouse of New York acquired the majority of the paper's stock in 1962. Throughout its existence, the *Times-Picayune* has adhered to a moderately conservative approach to political and social issues.

See also URBANIZATION: / New Orleans

Joy Jackson
Southeastern Louisiana University

Thomas Ewing Dabney, *One Hundred Great Years: The Story of the Times-Picayune* (1944); *Louisiana: A Guide to the State* (rev. ed., 1971).

Page, Walter Hines

(1855–1918) Social reformer, diplomat, and journalist.

Walter Hines Page made cultural improvement of the South his greatest single concern. His birth and upbringing in an antisecessionist North Carolina farmer-businessman's family during the Civil War era exposed him to the effects of both the physical ruin of the Confederate defeat and what he came to regard as the flight from reality in fealty to the Lost Cause. Page's earliest interests and ambitions were literary, and when, after graduate study, teaching, and newspaper work in the North, he returned to Raleigh in 1883 to found a newspaper, *The State Chronicle,* he wanted most to make North Carolina and the South hospitable to the highest forms of art, scholarship, and literature. Although Page became a New South advocate after the manner of Henry W. Grady, he placed his greatest reliance on educational improvement, which he advocated and promoted for the rest of his life. Within two years Page wearied of his native state's backwardness and provinciality and reentered big-city northern journalism, which remained his profession until his ambassadorship to Great Britain during the last five years of his life.

Page did not live in the South after 1885, but his home region was seldom far from his thoughts. Starting with his "Mummy letters" to *The State Chronicle* in 1885, he loosed a stream of criticism and exhortation at southerners, hammering at the basic themes of disenthrallment from the past, hard work in field and factory, and, most important, good schools for all people at all levels. Page usually traveled below the Potomac several times a year and spoke and wrote frequently on southern subjects. His most effective piece of cultural reform advocacy was "The Forgotten Man," originally a speech in Greensboro in 1897, later published in his book *The Rebuilding of Old Commonwealths* (1902). Page also wrote a pseudonymous novel, *The Southerner* (1909), in which he again preached the need to overcome ignorance, sloth, and nostalgia.

Perhaps his two greatest services to southern culture were indirect. One started as participation in the educational and philanthropic crusades, which led to the establishment of the Southern Education Board and General Education Board, on both of which he served. The other was sponsorship as a magazine editor and book publisher of such diverse black and white southern writers as Booker T. Washington, Charles W. Chesnutt, Mary Johnston, Ellen Glasgow, and Thomas Dixon, Jr. Through his myriad activities Page left a strong though not always welcomed mark on the growth of southern culture in the late 19th and early 20th centuries.

See also BLACK LIFE: / Chesnutt, Charles W.; Washington, Booker T.; EDUCATION: / General Education Board; LITERATURE: / Dixon, Thomas, Jr.; Glasgow, Ellen

John Milton Cooper, Jr.
University of Wisconsin
at Madison

John Milton Cooper, Jr., *Walter Hines Page: The Southerner as American, 1855–1918* (1977).

Renoir, Jean

(1894–1979) Film director.

Forced from his homeland by the war, French director Jean Renoir came to America in 1941 to continue his filmmaking career. Because of his international reputation, he found ready employment in Hollywood, although the American system of front-office supervision and control sharply contrasted with the creative freedom he enjoyed in France. He countered the problems of a strange land and a new system, however, by shooting several films on location and by grounding them in a strong sense of the culture. Two of these early projects dealt with the South, a region with which he had no familiarity.

His first film, *Swamp Water* (1941), contrasts the natural world of the Okefenokee swamp—vast, unpredictable, and dangerous—with the human community surrounding it. Despite its dangers, the world of nature is shown to be a place of refuge and even a source of life. The wrongfully accused murderer Keefer finds sanctuary from local "justice" in the swamp and over the years even develops an immunity to its poisonous cottonmouths. After finding Keefer, young Ben Ragan becomes his partner, selling the skins from the old man's trapping. From this partnership, Ben gains an economic independence from his family, finds love with Keefer's daughter Julie, and eventually clears the old man's name. The encounter with this dangerous world thus brings these people a new life and leads to a rejuvenation of their society.

The Southerner (1945) was filmed shortly after Renoir obtained American citizenship. Adapted from George Sessions Perry's novel *Hold Autumn in Your Hand,* the film attempted to capture the rhythms and flavor of life as a southern tenant farmer; adding to this portrait's texture, Renoir consulted William Faulkner on the region's dialects. The resulting "chronicle . . . of soil, seasons and weather," as James Agee described it, stirred much controversy throughout the South. The subject of a Ku Klux Klan–backed boycott, *The Southerner* was ultimately banned in Tennessee because of its supposed exaggerations of the plight of the South's poor.

Hardly indicting the region's poverty, *The Southerner* develops the relationship between the individual, nature, and society explored in *Swamp Water* to disclose a nobility in the human spirit. Tenant farmer Sam Tucker and his family endure storms, disease, hostile neighbors, and a flood in trying to win subsistence from land that had long lain fallow. Although his crop is washed away, Tucker emerges stronger and more resolved to succeed, while his family, too, finds its bonds strengthened. It is this strength of spirit, springing from the encounter with a foreboding but not malevolent nature, that Renoir's film lauds. Like the Agrarians in this respect, Renoir found in the southerner's closeness to the land a significant value, seeing in that contact the potential for fulfilling and even ennobling human nature.

See also MYTHIC SOUTH: / Agrarians, Vanderbilt

J. P. Telotte
Georgia Institute of Technology

Leo Braudy, *Jean Renoir: The World of His Films* (1972); Raymond Durgnat, *Jean Renoir* (1974).

Reynolds, Burt

(b. 1936) Actor.

Compared to Clark Gable by American and European reviewers of his 1973 movie *White Lightning*, Burt Reynolds adds a strong dash of informal virility to the gentility of a late 20th-century Rhett Butler. Born 11 February 1936 in Waycross, Ga., with strong strains of both Italian and Cherokee in his lineage, he grew up there and in Florida. Attending Florida State University gave him as much of a chance to play football as to act, but when injuries ended his gridiron career, he began spending time in both Florida and New York to get whatever stage or television work he could find. Signing with an agent in 1958 started his film career, though his largely uninspiring movies did little to advance his ambitions. But appearances in the early 1970s on late-night talk shows such as Johnny Carson's *Tonight* first gained him national attention as an interesting, amiable person.

Burt Reynolds as "Bandit" in Smokey and the Bandit *(1978)*

After establishing a solid reputation as a decent actor who either got trapped in unsatisfactory vehicles or appeared in decent television shows that were subsequently canceled (*Hawk*, 1967; *Dan August*, 1970), Reynolds became a major entertainment figure in 1972. In that year two important media events occurred: *Deliverance* was released, and Reynolds became the first male nude centerfold when he appeared in *Cosmopolitan* magazine at editor Helen Gurley Brown's request. His role in the movie, adapted from James Dickey's bestselling novel, portrayed Atlanta businessman Lewis as a tough, resourceful, intelligent man pushed to the limits by vicious circumstances. Along with the film image of the strong, attractive southerner on the abortive camping trip came the magazine photograph of an amused sex symbol, wearing a grin and little else. Through numerous films that he has made since then, the image has been consistent: a real "hunk" (the term was first used consistently in describing him), irresistible to ladies and well able to handle himself with other men.

A southern Robin Hood with sex appeal, operating just beyond the law in a car culture whose inhabitants go to drive-in movies, Reynolds can also put on a three-piece suit, Guccis, and a Rolex to deal effectively with big-time crime bosses. The image of the lovable rogue engaged in picaresque journeys across the American landscape (*Smokey and the Bandit* I, 1977, and II, 1980, *Cannonball Run* I, 1981, and II, 1984) is reinforced by those other roles that present him as a natural athlete (*The Longest Yard*, 1975, *Semi-Tough*, 1977, *Stroker Ace*, 1983), or a tough, competent cop/detective (*Hustle*, 1976, *Rough Cut*, 1980, *City Heat*, 1984), or a comedian unafraid to expose his shortcomings or foibles to the world's laughter (*The End*, 1978, *Paternity*, 1985, *Best Friends*, 1983). Reynolds successfully mixes these modes while returning consistently to the southern hero. A revealing clue to Reynolds's identity as a southerner is the sequence in the movie *Best Friends* in which his mother-in-law fixes him a huge bowl of grits as befits a good southern boy. Although he hates grits, he accepts graciously. His persona in popular culture radiates this polite, genteel, good-natured southern charm, as do the public-spirited actions he makes through his contributions to theater in Florida.

See also LITERATURE: / Dickey, James

Peter Valenti
Fayetteville State University

B. Cohen, *New York Times Magazine* (29 March 1981); Richard J. Hurwood, *Burt Reynolds* (1979); Nancy Streebeck, *The Films of Burt Reynolds* (1982).

Richmond *Times-Dispatch*

The Richmond *Times-Dispatch*, with the largest and widest circulation in Virginia, dates its origins from 1850, when its parent paper, the Richmond *Dispatch*, was founded by James A. Cowardin. At the end of a decade it boasted a circulation of 18,000. The *Dispatch* early announced that it was "devoted to the news and eschewing political affiliates." By contrast, the Richmond *Times*, founded in 1886 and purchased soon thereafter by Joseph Bryan, did not hesitate to take strong stands on controversial issues, such as corrupt elections and the free-silver issue of the 1890s.

Joseph Bryan bought the *Dispatch* in 1903 and combined it with the *Times* to constitute the *Times-Dispatch*. Members of the Bryan family have been associated with the paper as publishers off and on ever since. John Stewart Bryan, son of Joseph Bryan, was publisher from 1940, when the paper merged with the Richmond *News Leader*, until his death in 1944. He was succeeded by his son, D. Tennant Bryan, publisher from 1944 to 1977. Tennant Bryan is also chairman of the board of Media General, the recently formed chain that includes both Richmond papers as well as other papers and television stations. His son, John Stewart Bryan III, took over as publisher of the two papers in 1977.

Most editors of the *Dispatch* and the *Times-Dispatch* served only a few years. Joseph Bryan was editor of the *Times* from its acquisition in 1889 until its merger with the *Dispatch*, and then of the *Times-Dispatch* until his death in 1908. The longest tenure in the editorship was that of Virginius Dabney, who served from 1936 until his retirement in 1969. He was awarded the Pulitzer Prize for editorial writing in 1948.

The *Times-Dispatch* led the South in the 1930s in advocating a federal antilynching law and was the first newspaper in the region to urge a significant breach in the segregation front when in 1943 it proposed abolition of segregation on streetcars and buses. It backed Franklin D. Roosevelt the four times he ran for president, but with "diminishing enthusiasm," as the editor stated. Although often supportive of Senator Harry F. Byrd and his political machine, it was sometimes highly critical. The *Times-Dispatch* claimed, with good reason, to be "Virginia's State Newspaper," and its influence was, and is, considerable. In recent years it has been more conservative than in the period 1936 to 1954.

See also URBANIZATION: / Richmond

Virginius Dabney
Richmond, Virginia

Silas Bent, *Newspaper Crusaders: A Neglected Story* (1939); Lester J. Cappon, *Virginia Newspapers, 1821–1935* (1936); Virginius Dabney, *Across the Years: Memories of a Virginian* (1978), *Richmond: The Story of a City* (1976).

Ritt, Martin

(b. 1920) Film director.

Martin Ritt's only connection with the South before he began making the first of his eight films about the region was his brief attendance at Elon College in North Carolina on a football scholarship in the 1930s. Born in New York City on 2 March 1920, Ritt began his acting career in New York in the late 1930s with the Group Theater and directed plays while in the army during World War II. Returning to New York after the war, he worked as an actor and director on stage and also on television until he was blacklisted from that medium in 1951. Ritt directed the first of his 23 films, *Edge of the City*, in 1957 and soon followed it with *The Long Hot Summer* (1958), his first southern movie, loosely adapted from William Faulkner's *The Hamlet*. His other films set entirely or partially in the South are *The Sound and the Fury* (1959), *Sounder* (1972), *Conrack* (1974), *Casey's Shadow* (1978), *Norma Rae* (1979), *Back Roads* (1981), and *Cross Creek* (1983). Except for *The Sound and the Fury*, made on a Hollywood back lot, all were filmed on location in Alabama, Florida, Georgia, and Louisiana.

The most frequent themes in these films involve the relationships among family members; the effects of outsiders on close-knit communities; the isolation of the community, family, or individual; and the place of blacks in the South. (Ritt offers a west Texas variation on many of these themes in his 1963 film *Hud*.) The most successful of Ritt's films, both artistically and commercially is *Sounder*, a loving portrait of a family of black share croppers during the Depression. It was widely praised by contemporaries as easily the best recent movie about blacks and perhaps the best such film ever, though some viewers, both black and white, saw it as patronizing and dishonest. Ritt's most entertaining look at the South is *The Long Hot Summer*, a travesty of its source but a lively, funny, sexy portrayal of a larger-than-life southern family. In his most typical film, *Conrack*, a white liberal arrives in a poor black community, tries to right all its wrongs, and leaves defeated but a better man for the experience. Ritt seems unaware that the blacks the hero has tried to help may be even worse off since their hopes have been raised only to be quashed.

Although some view *Norma Rae* and *Back Roads* as strident and unbelievable, Ritt's movies are generally well acted and are never boring, but they always present an outsider's frequently condescending view of the South. He seems drawn too much to the backward, melodramatic, and sentimental aspects of the region. Almost no signs of progress are evident in Ritt's South. The main virtue of his films is their delineation of the effects of social and economic forces on the family.

Michael Adams
Louisiana State University

Michael Adams, *Southern Quarterly* (Spring–Summer 1981); Bruce Cook, *American Film* (April 1980); Sheila Whitaker, *The Films of Martin Ritt* (1972).

Roots

Roots, a landmark event in the history of television and in the media portrayal of the South, was based on Alex Haley's 1976 best-selling book of "faction" (Haley's word for his blend of fiction and history). Haley recounted his family's descent from Kunta Kinte, an African stolen into slavery in the 1760s. The 12-hour, ABC teleplay was presented on consecutive evenings, 23–30 January 1977.

Roots dramatized the social history of slavery and its impact on both master and slave as seen through the eyes of four generations of Haley ancestors. Never before had a mass audience been treated to such a realistic—and controversial—representation of slavery. Kinte, kidnapped from an Africa too idyllic in portrayal, endured the debilitating passage on a slave ship only to be faced with additional cruelty while adjusting to enslavement on a Virginia plantation. He was viciously whipped until he renounced his African name in favor of "Toby," and, after he made an abortive escape attempt, his foot was severed by poor-white slave catchers. Over the generations, Kinte's progeny faced rape, beatings, family separations, insensitive masters, and numerous instances of degradation and racist brutality. Even after emancipation Haley's ancestors were tormented by sadistic Klansmen and the vagaries of the sharecropping system. Yet in the face of all this, their sense of familial continuity and pride endured and ultimately triumphed.

The success of the "miniseries" was enormous. ABC programming director Fred Silverman had scheduled the series over consecutive evenings for fear of low ratings, but he need not have worried. A. C. Nielsen estimated that about 130 million Americans saw some portion of *Roots*. Astonishingly, the audience for the final episode was nearly half the population of the United States. Each program ranked in the top 13 most-viewed programs of all time, with the 30 January episode ironically unseating the 1976 telecast of *Gone with the Wind* for first place. Thus, *Roots*'s neoabolitionist version of southern history symbolically and literally replaced the romantic and apologetic moonlight-and-magnolias imagery, which undoubtedly reached its zenith in *Gone with the Wind*. There is considerable disagreement over the cause of the unprecedented interest in *Roots*. Coming in the wake of the nation's bicentennial celebrations, *Roots* may have touched a responsive chord in an audience predisposed to an interest in history. Haley's emphasis on tracing his family's origins, and his successful, though painstaking, efforts to uncover a personal heritage clouded by generations of enslavement demonstrated that genealogy is a fruitful and rewarding pursuit; countless thousands of Americans, urged on by *Roots*, began seeking their own family histories. Finally, as several television critics noted, *Roots* was a very gripping drama that synthesized several popular television formulas; the presentation, with its similarities to television soap opera particularly evident, was simply very fine television entertainment.

It is more difficult to assess the cultural meaning of the *Roots* phenomenon. Some, particularly black intellectuals, charged that *Roots* merely provided a rather painless means to expiate white guilt tied to generations of racism without confronting the audience with the complex of issues that continues to bedevil race relations in this country. Others criticized *Roots* as a corrective that went too far, a version of the past in which white characters were stereotyped even as earlier media presentations had stereotyped black characters and had trivialized the situations they faced. Although the audience was certainly treated to vivid and brutal scenes depicting slavery as a dehumanizing institution (*Time* magazine referred to *Roots* as "middle-of-the-road *Mandingo*"), many critics argued that slavery was even worse than the teleplay suggested. For example, slave quarters were depicted as rather more substantial and comfortable than most slaves would have known; then, too, the life of the field hand—the most common of American slaves—was almost totally missing from the presentations.

Still other observers worried that *Roots* had the uncanny impact of strengthening traditional stereotypes of black people, especially those that suggested a tendency toward resignation to misfortune and mistreatment. One black scholar, Robert Chrisman, noted that the final message of *Roots* seemed to suggest that survival by any means is the ultimate goal of life. The episodes certainly demonstrated the manner in which the slaves adopted masks in certain situations (some referred to this as "Tomming"), and it may indeed have been possible for viewers to misinterpret this intentional posturing as personal weakness rather than as attempts to "put one over on the master."

The success of *Roots* led naturally to a sequel. Although Haley's book rapidly skimmed over the post-1880 years, he agreed to cooperate with executive producer David L. Wolper and producer Stan Margulies—both of whom worked on the original project—to develop *Roots: The Next Generations*. This 12-hour continuation, telecast 18–25 February 1979, was not as successful as the original but nevertheless fostered considerable viewer interest. *Roots II* remained the story of one family, but it was a bit more conscious of connecting the Haley history to social and cultural issues. Both miniseries were repeated on network television, were widely viewed in syndicated rerun and as part of college and public school courses, and were distributed in scores of other nations. Together these telecasts represent one of the most important forces in shaping popular images of the American South in media history.

See also BLACK LIFE: / Haley, Alex; MYTHIC SOUTH: / "Moonlight-and-Magnolias" Myth

Christopher D. Geist
Bowling Green State University

Horace Newcomb, ed., *Television: The Critical View* (1979); Frank Rich, *Time* (19 February 1979); Howard F. Stein, *Journal of Popular Culture* (Summer 1977); *Time* (14 February 1977); David L. Wolper and Quincy Troupe, *The Inside Story of T.V.'s Roots* (1978).

Scott, Zachary

(1914–1965) Actor.

Film actor Zachary Thomson Scott, Jr., was born 24 February 1914 in Austin, Tex., the son of a prominent surgeon. He dropped out of the University of Texas after his first year to begin an acting career in provincial British theaters. Returning to complete college, he became a mainstay of the University of Texas's theatrical program before moving on to national stock companies and Broadway. His screen career began most auspiciously when he was put under contract by Warner Brothers to play the lead in the film version of Eric Ambler's popular novel of intrigue, *A Mask for Dimitrios* (1944), featuring the then popular villainous team of Peter Lorre and Sidney Greenstreet.

His greatest opportunity came the following year, however, when the distinguished French director, Jean Renoir, working in exile in Hollywood, chose Scott to replace Joel McCrea in the leading role of *The Southerner*, an adaptation of George Sessions Perry's novel *Hold Autumn in Your Hand*. Even the hypercritical James Agee admired Scott's performance in this tribute to the South. With his next film, *Mildred Pierce* (1945), however, Scott returned to the suavely villainous roles in which he was thereafter typecast. His only subsequent role of importance in a Hollywood film about the South was in another sensational Joan Crawford vehicle, the film version of Robert Wilder's novel *Flamingo Road* (1949). Hoping to escape typecasting, Scott for his next-to-last film went to Mexico to star in Luis Buñuel's *The Young One* (*La Joven*, 1960), the last of 19 surrealistic melodramas that the master made in that country beginning in 1947.

The film has, however, never been distributed in the United States. Scott retired from the screen in 1962, a few years before his death from a malignant brain tumor in his hometown of Austin on 3 October 1965. The new Austin Civic Playhouse was shortly afterward named in his memory.

Warren French
Indiana University

Hart Wegner, in *The South and Film*, ed. Warren French (1981).

Southern Exposure

Southern Exposure is the bimonthly journal of the Institute for Southern Studies, Durham, N.C. A nonprofit educational and research organization, the Institute for Southern Studies was founded in 1970 by journalist Howard Romaine and by Sue Thrasher, then policy studies fellow in Washington, D.C.

With a board of directors headed by legislator and civil rights activist Julian Bond, and a young, biracial staff, many of whom had been actively involved in the freedom movement of the previous decade, the institute launched a variety of projects aimed at preserving and advancing progressive traditions in the South. Acting as a clearinghouse as well as a research center, it helped community organizers formulate policy, conducted seminars and planning sessions, and developed materials for classroom use.

In 1973, partly to assist the institute financially and partly to create a wide audience for its work, director Bob Hall suggested publishing a magazine, and *Southern Exposure* was born. Named after a 1946 muckraking book by Stetson Kennedy, *Southern Exposure* offered an alternative, liberal framework for understanding social and political phenomena in the South. Its first issue, focusing on militarism in the South, included an exposé by a former Lockheed employee, state-by-state statistics on defense spending, essays, book reviews, and a listing of regional antimilitary groups.

Retaining this single-focus format, subsequent issues were organized around topics such as agribusiness and energy cartels; sit-ins and Sunbelt prosperity; histories of the Ku Klux Klan; health care; and organized labor. Concerned that the journal remain a forum for the exchange of ideas from varying perspectives, the editors encouraged submissions from journalists and activists, as well as scholars, and strove for a mix of writing styles. In its 10-year history, *Southern Exposure* has featured investigative reporting by Neal Peirce and Kirkpatrick Sale, interviews by Robert Sherrill, short fiction by Alice Walker, and profiles of congressmen and corporate heads along with the recollections of miners, migrant workers, and prison inmates.

Although primarily concerned with questions of social progress, politics, and the economy, *Southern Exposure* frequently examines the distinctive regional culture. Special issues have celebrated southern literature, black music and art, and folklife. Poetry, graphics, oral history, and feature articles assessing the impact of rapid change on southern traditions appear regularly.

Published six times a year with a circulation of nearly 8,000, *Southern Exposure* now has seven departments including the syndicated *Facing South*—a column that appears in over 80 newspapers, magazines, and newsletters. The journal continues to encourage alternative action and to challenge stereotyped notions by chronicling the richness and diversity of the South.

Elizabeth M. Makowski
University of Mississippi

Katherine Gruber, ed., *Encyclopedia of Associations* (1986); *Southern Exposure*, vols. 1–14.

Southern Living

Established in 1966 as an offshoot of *Progressive Farmer* magazine, *Southern Living* got off to a somewhat uncertain start: one early article was a guide to choosing a daughter's first brassiere. Since then, however, it has flourished as "the acknowledged 'Lifestyle Bible' for the able-to-buy segment of (the southern) market"—that is, the burgeoning southern middle class. By 1980 paid circulation was approaching 2 million, which placed *Southern Living* in every fourth or fifth middle-class household in the South. It was among the top 15 of all U.S. magazines in advertising revenues, a remarkable performance for a magazine published in Birmingham, circulated almost entirely in the South, and priced higher outside the region.

Southern Living's "South," for subscription and promotion purposes, includes 17 states and the District of Columbia, but 1980 circulation exceeded 3 percent of the white population only in a smaller region bounded by Louisiana, Arkansas, Tennessee, and Virginia. Although Texas and Florida supplied the largest numbers of readers, the heart of the magazine's readership, per capita, was found in a band extending from Mississippi east and north to North Carolina.

Most of the magazine's staff and its contents are organized into four departments: travel and entertainment, food, gardening and landscaping, house design and decoration. Many of its features are not conspicuously "southern," but regional emphases are clearly evident, especially in the travel section and in some advertising. Articles often begin with phrases like "A traditional part of Southern hospitality . . ." or "In the South, we have always . . ."—useful information for those readers (and there must be many) who are first-generation southerners, nouveau riche, or both. *Southern Living* is also the only house-and-garden magazine to name an all-star football team, and no other publishes as many recipes for game or as many advertisements for bourbon whiskey.

Never is heard a discouraging word in *Southern Living*, and its relentlessly upbeat treatment of southern life has undoubtedly contributed to its success among readers unaccustomed to seeing their region praised in glossy magazines. In only one area has the magazine even implied a criticism of the southern status quo: it has consistently supported programs of downtown revitalization and historic preservation, despite the overtones of "planning" and government interference. Characteristically, the magazine presents such programs as a matter of preserving traditional amenities and fostering business; it also conducts its campaign not in the abstract but by pointing to successful examples in specific southern towns. A new department called "In the Community" has given this concern officially recognized and continuing standing in the magazine.

Reflections of the South's changing culture and social structure do make their way into several regular editorial columns. "Southerners," for example, presents profiles of accomplished or otherwise praiseworthy individuals from a variety of fields: craftspeople, scholars, community leaders, and "do-gooders" in the best and broadest sense. "Books about the South" each month reviews (favorably) the products of commercial, university, and vanity presses—and provides a real service by reviewing many books that would otherwise pass unnoticed. A more recent addition is the "Southern Journal," a page or two of prose or poetry, usually nostalgic, by southern writers, often distinguished.

Like other "shelter" magazines, *Southern Living* seldom advocates or even implies advocacy of anything other than gracious living. It accurately portrays public life in the South as increasingly biracial; with equal accuracy, it shows at-home entertaining as still lily-white. In this and much else, it reflects its readers' sensibilities and seldom attempts to shape them, except by an occasional nudge (it suggested once, for instance, that evergreen azaleas may have been overused in southern landscaping). Its readers naturally find the magazine's idealized portrayal of their lives agreeable and often flattering; others may find it a valuable resource for understanding the South's new urban and suburban middle class. In 1985 ownership of the magazine passed to Time, Inc., which purchased Southern Progress Corporation from some 200 descendants of its founders for a reported $480 million.

See also AGRICULTURE: / *Progressive Farmer*

John Shelton Reed
University of North Carolina
at Chapel Hill

John Shelton Reed, *One South: An Ethnic Approach to Regional Culture* (1982); Stephen A. Smith, *Myth, Media, and the Southern Mind* (1985); Allen Tullos, *Southern Changes* (July 1979).

Turner, Ted

(b. 1939) Businessman.

Robert Edward Turner III is chairman of the board of Turner Broadcasting System, president of the Atlanta Braves, chairman of the board of the Atlanta Hawks, and a major figure in contemporary southern culture. In January 1970, at the age of 31, Turner bought WTCG, a failing UHF television station in Atlanta; in December 1976 WTCG became the nation's first satellite superstation; and in August 1979 the call letters were changed to WTBS to reflect the station's role as the financial flagship of Turner Broadcasting System. Turner owns 87 percent of the stock of TBS, a holding company comprising Superstation WTBS, Cable News Network (1980), CNN Headline News (1982), and Cable Music Channel (1984), as well as the Atlanta Braves (1976) and Atlanta Hawks (1977) professional sports teams.

Although Ted Turner's acquisitive entrepreneurial activity might suggest to some that he is a modern disciple of Henry W. Grady, others would suggest that he is more akin to Rhett Butler. Variously described as "brash," "outspoken," and "controversial," Turner has been dubbed "The Mouth of the South"—a title intended to describe his personal style as much as his media empire. His flamboyance is often highlighted and his

Ted Turner, media entrepreneur, 1980s

notoriety increased by incidents such as his accompanying Jimmy Carter as an "official guest" aboard Air Force One and in the Presidential Box to watch the Georgia Bulldogs in the Sugar Bowl, and his winning the America's Cup in his yacht, *Courageous*, with a skipper's skill that would have proven valuable in running Union blockades. Media industry analyst Paul Kagan noted that Turner's "style is to go for the next brass ring," and when he announced his 1985 plan for a takeover of Columbia Broadcasting System, an analyst with J. C. Bradford confessed, "he's known for doing things that can't be accomplished." Even Scarlett would be impressed.

Turner's major contribution to shaping southern culture, however, is in his role as the 20th-century storytelling equivalent of Joel Chandler Harris's Uncle Remus. WTBS currently reaches over 31 million homes, and its programming innovations have freed southern storytellers from the bondage of the national media gatekeepers in the studios of New York and Los Angeles. Often dismissed as merely "old movies, reruns, and sports," the TBS cable fare has a deeper meaning. The "Portrait of America" series offers southerners a chance to tell about their own states, as well as the rest of the nation, from a different perspective that is not shackled by old stereotypes; the "Nice People" segments present the good deeds of unsung heroes among the common folk; and even the old movies and reruns serve to offer visions and reinforce traditional values from earlier times. Documentary programming has examined the dangers of nuclear war and such problems as world population, food supply, and youth unemployment, and Turner recently financed a $6 million Jacques Cousteau special on the Amazon, because, as he said, "Someone has to keep Cousteau going."

Whether watching features on the Muscle Shoals recording industry and southern rock bands, the "muscle shows" of Georgia Championship Wrestling (which pit good against evil), stories about historic restoration and neighborhood preservation in southern cities, scenes of southern good old boys on the stock car circuit, or flashbacks on the records of Hank Aaron and Hank Williams, viewers are also listening to the stories of Ted Turner. In the modern media environment of the South, satellite dishes have replaced tire gardens in southern yards, and color televisions have helped to compensate for the absence of front porches on the double-wide mobile homes. Ted Turner's role as a modern storyteller must be seen as a major contribution to the creation, maintenance, and transmission of the public images of contemporary southern culture.

See also INDUSTRY: / Grady, Henry W.; LITERATURE: / Harris, Joel Chandler

Stephen A. Smith
University of Arkansas

Daniel F. Cuff, *New York Times* (5 April 1985); Sandra Salmans, *New York Times* (15 August 1983)

Uncle Tom's Cabin

The most frequently performed stage play in America from 1853 to the late 1920s, *Uncle Tom's Cabin* was an obvious choice for early filmmakers. At least nine separate screen versions appeared between 1903 and 1927. The numerous feature films, short subjects, and cartoons utilizing its characters and themes finally began to fade out in the mid-1960s. The last known "Tom" film, a German-language color production, was issued in 1965.

The earliest films owed more to the Tom shows than they did to the original novel. Sigmund Lubin's May 1903 version preceded by three months Edwin S. Porter's widely admired film for Edison. Lubin promised potential customers that his film would appeal even to those "who opposed the emancipation of the slaves."

Porter used a single camera for his one-reel, 12-minute film. Fourteen scenes performed in front of painted backdrops were announced by a series of titles that replaced the theater curtain. Whites in blackface played the leading black parts, as they were to do until 1914 when a 72-year-old black actor (Sam Lucas) first played Uncle Tom on the screen. Not content merely to photograph a Tom show from a seat in the orchestra, Porter used double exposure for the angels who came to take Little Eva and

Uncle Tom to heaven; added a paddle-wheel steamboat race complete with thunder, lightning, and an explosion; and concluded with various tableaux showing Lincoln the Emancipator and General Lee's surrender.

The appeal of the Tom shows and the films that followed cannot be attributed to their abolitionist sentiments but rather to their stirring melodramatic scenes featuring stock characters who had become part of the national folklore: patient, humble Uncle Tom, the epitome of Christian submission and forbearance; angelic Little Eva, the personification of virtue and innocence; the mischievous, irrepressible Topsy; and the archvillain, the heartless, cruel Simon Legree.

Porter's 1903 film was followed in 1910 by two competing versions. The Vitagraph *Uncle Tom's Cabin* was released in three reels, each shown separately. Both Imp and Kalem issued Tom films in 1913 followed by the World Film version the next year. In a 1918, five-reel version for Paramount, the actress Marguerite Clark played both Topsy and Eva.

In 1927 a 10-reel superproduction was released by Universal. Expected by its sponsors to be the definitive version and "the answer to *Birth of a Nation*," it was directed by Harry Pollard, who himself had played Uncle Tom in blackface for Imp in 1913. James B. Lowe, a black actor, played Uncle Tom but was overshadowed by the histrionics of George Siegmann in the role of Simon Legree. Most of the action concerned the romance of the "nearly white" slaves Eliza and George Harris. The film cost $2 million; took almost two years to make, in the course of which 16,000 separate scenes were photographed on location; and used 5,000 actors as well as 10,000 magnolias. According to *Motion Picture World* (November 1927), "The picture is so constructed that features objectionable South of the Ohio may be eliminated without emasculating the production." This film was reissued in 1958 with a new sound track and Raymond Massey as narrator. Advertisements urged 1958 audiences to "Hate Simon Legree, Pity Uncle Tom, Love Little Eva and Laugh at Topsy."

Some by-products of the Uncle Tom industry include *Uncle Tom's Cabin* (remakes in 1913, 1914), *Death of Simon Legree* (1915), *Uncle Tom's Caboose* (1920), *Little Eva Ascends* (1922), *Uncle Tom's Uncle* (1926), *Topsy and Eva* (1927), and *Uncle Tom's Cabana* (1947). Shirley Temple played three scenes as Little Eva in *Dimples* (1936), Jane Withers the same year sang "Uncle Tom's Cabin Is a Cabaret Now" in *Can This Be Dixie?*, and Judy Garland played Topsy in *Everybody Sing* (1938). Betty Grable and June Haver played twin Topsys in *The Dolly Sisters* (1945), and Abbott and Costello portrayed Eva and Legree in *Naughty Nineties*, also in 1945. In 1956 *The King and I*, a musical remake of the play *Anna and the King of Siam*, featured a ballet called "The Small House of Uncle Thomas."

See also MYTHIC SOUTH: / *Uncle Tom's Cabin*

Joan L. Silverman
New York University

Thomas F. Gossett, *Uncle Tom's Cabin and American Culture* (1985); Lewis Jacobs, *The Rise of the American Film: A Critical History* (1939); Edward Wagenknecht, *The Movies in the Age of Innocence* (1962).

Vidor, King

(1895–1982) Film director.

Descended from Hungarian immigrants, King Wallis Vidor was born in Galveston, Tex., in 1895. As a teenager he worked as an assistant projectionist and used a handmade camera to complete a number of short films. One film, depicting a hurricane that struck Galveston, was shown throughout Texas. With this background, Vidor traveled to Hollywood, where he worked as an extra and a writer before making several independent shorts and then setting up his own small studio, Vidor Village. After moving to MGM Studios, Vidor established a reputation for his ability to handle large projects and his concern with social issues. Following his great success with silent features such as *The Big Parade* (1925) and *The Crowd* (1928), Vidor made the transition to sound films with such successful explorations of poverty and the Depression as *Street Scene* (1931) and *Our Daily Bread* (1934). In his later career he increasingly turned to epic productions that largely lacked the intense social consciousness of the earlier films.

Viewed in the context of his large canon, relatively few of Vidor's films deal with the South. Those that do, however, are among his best and heavily emphasize the geography of the region. His early feature *The Jack Knife Man* (1920) uses the Mississippi River as its backdrop; *Wild Oranges* (1924), based on the Joseph Hergesheimer novel, focuses on the coastal islands and swamps of Georgia; *Hallelujah* (1929), shot on location in the Memphis area, uses an all-black cast to describe rural southern culture; and *So Red the Rose* (1935), a predecessor to *Gone with the Wind*, depicts plantation life during the Civil War. What these and his other southern films demonstrate is Vidor's special concern with nature and its power, a concern that finds particular emphasis in the recurrent images of rivers and swamps in his films.

This emphasis on environment points up a major theme running throughout Vidor's work. His films generally lack real villains, simply because he usually depicts life itself, represented in nature, the land, or human circumstances, as man's greatest challenge. At the same time, Vidor has asserted that "the whole universe springs from the individual." Consequently, his films typically focus on a tension between man and his environment. In both his more personal films, like *Street Scene*, and his epic works, like *War and Peace* (1956), a sense of the individual's struggle with the world he inhabits and of his ability to win a personal victory over it clearly emerges.

J. P. Telotte
Georgia Institute of Technology

John Baxter, *King Vidor* (1976); King Vidor, *A Tree Is a Tree* (1952).

New York Times Magazine (18 November 1973); *Saturday Evening Post* (November 1973).

The Waltons

The Waltons, television's long-running series (1972–81) about a close-knit Virginia mountain family during the Depression, gave viewers a romantically idealized picture of the rural South. This poor but proud three-generation family regularly brought a nostalgic rush to viewers who remembered the Depression and gave many other Americans an ideal family for which to wish and strive. Grandma and Grandpa Walton, the Walton parents, and their seven children reaffirmed weekly the moral uplift of cooperative family effort, intergenerational contact, and the basic values of simple, honest living long associated with the predominant media view of the traditional rural South. Each Walton was the noble southerner personified.

Although *The Waltons* was based on the family life of screenwriter Earl Hamner, Jr., many critics argued that the unfailingly wholesome atmosphere found in the Walton home seldom exists in the real world and that the program stereotyped the southern mountaineer's life. However, *The Waltons* included plots based on common human experiences, examined problems that do not have easy solutions, and explored the value of stability in a rapidly changing society. The show also equated poverty with an elevated moral sense, idealized rural living, and proposed eventual solutions to every family problem that arose. Nowhere in sight were complex issues such as social isolation, divorce, alcoholism, troubled children, lonely elders, or other crises that plague many American families. When crises did emerge among *The Waltons*, positive solutions were written into the script.

The technical excellence and the careful attention to detail by Lorimar Productions, the company responsible for *The Waltons*, along with fine performances by the actors, helped to garner the series numerous awards. The show emerged at a confused time in American social history. Vietnam, drugs, women's liberation, civil rights, divorce, and other elements of rapid social changes left Americans longing for stability and a safe haven at home. The Walton family came from a mythological South to give the nation an idealized security.

The Waltons was one of those rare programs rated highly by young and old alike and has been the only long-running dramatic series presenting a serious, positive portrayal of southerners and life in the South. Although stereotyped, its characters were always portrayed as people whose values, lifestyle, and ideals the rest of the nation would do well to emulate. It presented an idealized, positive view of the American and southern past, and many viewers watched faithfully because they were left with the feeling that it just might still be possible for all to be right with the world.

Marsha McGee
Northeast Louisiana University

WDIA

In the fall of 1948 WDIA in Memphis, Tenn., became the first radio station in the South to adopt an all-black programming format. The station was owned by two white businessmen, but the man most responsible for the format change at WDIA was Nat D. Williams, a local black high school history teacher. Williams was brought into the station to do his own show on an experimental basis; it proved to be an overnight sensation. He was the first black radio announcer in the South to play the popular rhythm-and-blues records of the day over the airways. His show was so successful that within six months of its debut WDIA had changed its format from a classical music station to one appealing solely to black listeners and advertisers.

In addition to initiating an entirely new music format, Williams launched a wide variety of programming innovations at WDIA and recruited other talented blacks onto the airways. His first recruits were fellow high school teachers A. C. Williams and Maurice Hulbert. Both men went on to have long and distinguished careers in black radio. His most famous recruit was a youthful B. B. King, who used the exposure on WDIA to initiate his career as the country's premiere urban blues artist. In addition to these black males, Nat D. Williams also recruited the South's first black female announcers to WDIA's airways; two of the best known were Willa Monroe and Starr McKinney, both of whom did programs oriented toward black women.

Gospel music, religious programs, and black news and public affairs shows were also prominent on WDIA. The most acclaimed public affairs program was called "Brown America Speaks"; it was also created and hosted by Nat D. Williams. The program addressed race issues from a black perspective and won an award for excellence from the prestigious Ohio State Institute for Education in radio in 1949. With the success of WDIA, other radio stations around the country also began to adopt black-oriented formats, and black radio became a fixture in commercial broadcasting nationwide. WDIA still programs for a black audience in Memphis, making it the oldest black-oriented radio station in the country.

See also MUSIC: / Beale Street; URBANIZATION: / Memphis

Bill Barlow
Howard University

Margaret McKee and Fred Chisenhall, *Beale Black and Blue: Life and Music on Black America's Main Street* (1981); Charles Sawyer, *The Arrival of B. B. King: The Authorized Biography* (1980).

Williams, Tennessee, and Film

One of America's greatest dramatists, Tennessee Williams helped American film grow up. The idea of an adult category of film began with the landmark adaptation of Williams's *A Streetcar Named Desire* (1951). The film replaced Jessica Tandy with Vivien Leigh as Blanche DuBois, but otherwise the original Broadway company (Marlon Brando, Karl Malden, Kim Stanley, director Elia Kazan) brought the classic production to the screen. The film was one of the first to use an all-jazz score and brought method acting to the mass audience. Williams and Kazan again collaborated (and ran athwart the censors) on *Baby Doll* (1956), a spirited but now innocuous black comedy against which Cardinal Spellman, without having seen the film, inveighed from the pulpit of St. Patrick's Cathedral.

In addition to the *Streetcar* transfer, two other Williams adaptations rank as great films—John Huston's hearty and humorous *The Night of the Iguana* (1964) and Joseph Losey's sumptuous and sublime parable, *BOOM* (1968). In both cases Williams's material evoked strong, personal responses from brilliant directors.

Otherwise, the Williams film canon reads like an absurd chronicle of bowdlerization. Incredible happy endings were imposed upon the films *The Glass Menagerie* (1950), *The Rose Tattoo* (1955), and *Sweet Bird of Youth* (1962), and Williams's florid characterizations were softened, simplified, and made sentimental. Often the directors tended to literalize Williams's extremely poetic tones, especially in *The Rose Tattoo* (1955), *Cat on a Hot Tin Roof* (1958), *The Fugitive Kind* (1960), and—in Williams's own questioning view—*Suddenly Last Summer* (1959). Happier balances were achieved in *Summer and Smoke* (1961) and *The Roman Spring of Mrs. Stone* (1961). In *Period of Adjustment* (1962) Williams's social vision was trivialized into situation comedy, heedless of its metaphors.

Two minor films are of unusual interest. Sidney Lumet's *Last of the Mobile Hotshots* (1969) is based upon Williams's much underrated play *Kingdom of Earth*. Lumet shifted the focus from the survival of religious instincts to the topic of racism in the decaying South. As the dying heir of the Old South traditions, James Coburn plays a curious variation upon Blanche DuBois. Similarly, Sidney Pollack's *This Property Is Condemned* (1966) starts with a Williams one-act play but develops into a kind of analysis of the Williams canon. The three women in the family represent the three faces of Blanche DuBois: girl-child, glamorous tease, and aging hypocrite. The film develops several other characteristic Williams themes: the heroine's flight into fantasy from the brutish male world, the poetry of the "ghost garden" (i.e., "bone orchard," cemetery), the heroine's full-throated but thwarted desire to "breathe" deep and free, and the passion for life that one wandering spirit can pass on to another. The doomed dreamer, Alva (Natalie Wood), is won and betrayed by the stable, practical company man, Owen Legate (Robert Redford).

In the horde of American films about the South, the Williams works stand out for their magnificent poetry and their charged, psychological realism. Williams presents the southern experience as the nation's neurosis, a culturewide tension between the lusty and poetic energy (an id form) and the cold, suppressive community (an ego form). Williams often brings an outsider, whether a virile Sicilian or a footloose poet/dreamer into a suffocating community, to rouse the lynch mob's dread of freedom and healthy release. In this quintessential vision of Americana, both the dreamer's expansive fantasy and the community's vicious realism exemplify Williams's obsession with man's retreat to fantasy or to mendacity.

Williams's most significant contribution may be his vision of the nation's psychopathology played out in the political-passionate history of the South. Quite understandably, in Jean-Luc Godard's film *La Chinoise* (1967), a young revolutionary writes Williams's name on a blackboard list of heroes who have advanced world freedom and equality. As reservations are raised, some of the names are erased. But Williams remains uncompromised.

See also LITERATURE: / Williams, Tennessee

Maurice Yacowar
Brock University

Foster Hirsch, *Cinema* (Spring 1973); Gene D. Phillips, *The Films of Tennessee Williams* (1980); Maurice Yacowar, *Tennessee Williams and Film* (1977).

WLAC

Founded in 1926, Nashville radio station WLAC is one of the top-ranked AM stations in its home city and among the best known in the South. Billboard Broadcasting Corporation is its owner, having purchased it from the Life and Casualty Insurance Company in 1978. The station serves a population of about 486,000 and is on the air 24 hours every day. A network affiliate of the Columbia Broadcasting System (CBS), WLAC-AM today broadcasts primarily all-talk programming.

From the mid-1940s through the early 1970s, however, WLAC was known widely for its rhythm-and-blues programming. It became known as "Blues Radio" as its nighttime disc jockeys almost exclusively played black music—blues, rhythm and blues, and soul. While the station's 50,000 watts of power brought listeners from most parts of the country, the majority of the audience listened from the South. Many were blacks, and the disc jockeys catered to their preferences, at the same time influencing the musical tastes of the region, the nation, and both white and black artists whose music—rock and roll—would eventually dominate the popular music world.

In the mid-1940s Gene Nobles began playing black music when requested by students at Tennessee State and Fisk universities. Randy Wood, who owned an appliance store in Gallatin, Tenn., then decided to try selling by radio the records he had hoped in vain to sell to his store customers. On 17 February 1947 Nobles advertised records by Eddy Arnold, Nat King Cole, Johnny Mercer, and Ella Mae Morse, and Randy's Record Mart soon became the largest mail-order record store in the world. WLAC flourished, luring advertisers as well as listeners.

The station's most popular feature during this era was disc jockey John Richbourg and his 1:00 to 3:00 A.M. blues show. He became known as "John R." and the "granddaddy of soul." Because he promoted their music and often was the first to play their records or to prerelease a record to test the market, he became a favorite of the black artists. If he liked a record that was not immediately popular, he played it persistently until it became a hit. Such was the case with Otis Redding's "These Arms of Mine," an example of Richbourg's assertion that he and his WLAC colleagues did not just play hits—"We *made* hits." Richbourg broadcast his last show on WLAC on 1 August 1973 and died in 1986.

Of WLAC's blues disc jockeys, Bill "Hoss" Allen was the only one still with the station after rock and roll pushed rhythm and blues out of the programming. He broadcast a late-night, black gospel show in the mid-1980s, when the station had turned otherwise to an all-talk format.

Remembered for its music, its disc jockeys, and its advertisements for sponsors such as Red Top Baby Chicks ("50 percent guaranteed to be alive at the time of delivery"), White Rose Petroleum Jelly, and Royal Crown Hair Dressing, the blues era at WLAC entertained a generation of listeners who probably numbered between 8 and 12 million at its peak. Although programs like "Garden Gate," featuring "The Old Dirt Dobber" Tom Williams, and a talk show conducted by Nashville media personality Ruth Ann Leach have been very successful, WLAC made its biggest impact during the years when the catch phrase "This is John R. comin' at ya from way down in Dixie" could regularly be heard.

Jessica Foy
Cooperstown Graduate Programs
Cooperstown, New York

Walter Carter, *The Tennessee Showcase* (29 November 1981, 20 December 1981); Ron Courtney, *Goldmine* (February 1984); Nelson George, *Billboard* (19 April 1986); Gerry Wood, *Billboard* (18 June 1983); *The Working Press of the Nation*, vol. 3 (1985).

Woodward, Joanne

(b. 1930) Actress.

Joanne Woodward, known for her Academy Award–winning performance in *The Three Faces of Eve* and for other strong performances in movies and films for television, was born 27 February 1930 in Thomasville, Ga., and grew up in Greenville, S.C. She attended Louisiana State University for two years in the late 1940s, returned to Greenville, where she was active in the Little Theatre, and did summer stock for a season before going to New York to study at the Neighborhood Playhouse Dramatic School with Sanford Meisner.

Joanne Woodward as Quentin Compson in The Sound and the Fury *(1959)*

Her first television appearance was in *Penny*, a teleplay produced by Robert Montgomery, and this led to roles in television plays on *Studio One, Kraft Television Theatre, U.S. Steel Hour*, and *Omnibus*. These early appearances attracted the attention of Hollywood, and in 1954 Woodward signed a contract with 20th Century Fox that permitted her to divide her time between films and television. In 1953 she had understudied the two lead roles during the Broadway run of William Inge's *Picnic*, and three years later she made her Broadway debut in the short-lived play *The Lovers*.

The Three Faces of Eve (1957) was not her first film, but it was the film that brought her stardom. She was subsequently cast in films adapted from the works of Tennessee Williams (*The Fugitive Kind*, 1960, in which she costarred with Marlon Brando) and William Faulkner (*The Long Hot Summer*, 1958, and *The Sound and the Fury*, 1959).

Woodward received her second Academy Award nomination for *Rachel, Rachel* (1968) and her third for *Summer Wishes, Winter Dreams* (1973). She won a New York Film Critics Circle Award for *Rachel, Rachel*, which was directed by her husband, actor Paul Newman. In addition to her film awards Joanne Woodward has twice received Emmys. She received the award for outstanding lead actress in a television drama or comedy special for her performance in *See How She Runs* in 1979, and in 1985 for her moving portrayal of a victim of Alzheimer's disease in *Do You Remember Love?*

Charles East
Baton Rouge, Louisiana

Current Biography (1958); Monica M. O'Donnell, ed., *Contemporary Theatre, Film, and Television*, vol. 1 (1984).

WSM

See MUSIC: Grand Ole Opry

Young, P. B.

(1884–1962) Newspaper editor and publisher.

Born on 27 July 1884 in Littleton, N.C., Young received his early education at Reedy Creek Academy and at age 15 went to work as an office boy for a local white newspaper. He enrolled at St. Augustine's College in Raleigh, where he later taught printing and supervised publications from 1903 to 1906.

Young married Eleanor Louise White in 1906, and they soon moved to Littleton, where Young became a foreman at his father's printing shop. In 1907 Young took a new position in Norfolk as a plant foreman for the *Lodge Journal and Guide*, the mouthpiece of a fraternal order; in 1910 he borrowed $3,050 from a local bank and purchased the paper, which became the Norfolk *Journal and Guide*.

Within weeks of its founding, the *Journal and Guide* evolved from a four-page fraternal tabloid of 500 circulation into an eight-page, 40-column weekly. It never missed an issue, and by 1930 Young claimed a circulation of approximately 30,000, a payroll of $50,000, and 45 employees. The *Guide* was the largest and best-edited black weekly in the South.

Although Young never graduated from college, he influenced black education in the South through his membership on various educational boards. From 1930 to 1940 he was a board member of the Anna T. Jeanes Foundation; he also served on the boards of Hampton Institute, Hampton, Va. (1940–44) and St. Paul's Polytechnic Institute, Lawrenceville, Va. (1933–54). Young was first elected as a Howard University trustee in 1933. In 1936 he was elected chairman of the executive committee of this board, and in 1943 he became the school's first black chairman of the board.

Young's concerns extended beyond the boundaries of education. He used his position as chairman of the Norfolk Committee on Negro Affairs, as well as stories in his *Journal and Guide* on dilapidated housing as the incubator of crime and poverty, to pressure city officials to organize a crime conference in 1937. Norfolk soon organized a Housing Authority, with Young as chairman of the Negro Advisory Committee (NAC).

Young founded the Norfolk chapter of the National Association for the Advancement of Colored People (NAACP) in 1917, and during the 1930s he hammered away in defense of the Scottsboro boys. His editorials in defense of William Harper, a convicted black rapist in Virginia, generated a new trial and an acquittal. He vigorously opposed lynching, and his editorials on the deterioration of black schools in Prince George and Surry counties generated a state investigation that resulted in improved schools for blacks. He also worked to equalize teachers' salaries in Virginia.

After Japan attacked Pearl Harbor in December 1941, Young promptly announced his support of President Roosevelt's war initiatives. Throughout the war the *Journal and Guide* often carried front-page articles headlining stories of black heroism, with editorials on the exclusionary policies of the armed forces as well as employment inequities within the defense industry. Young quickly endorsed the Pittsburgh *Courier*'s February 1942 call for a "Double V" campaign—to fight discrimination at home and to promote victory over the enemy abroad. On the other hand, Young opposed A. Philip Randolph's proposed march on Washington by 100,000 blacks to protest discrimination in the defense industry. "What will they think in Berlin?" he asked. Randolph's proposal and increased racial tension prompted Young to organize a meeting of influential southern blacks in Durham, N.C., on 20 October 1942 to outline "what the Negro wants." The conference established Young as the titular head of black leadership in the South. Meanwhile, the *Journal and Guide*'s circulation climbed to 80,000, and its employees numbered approximately 75.

Young remained a firm supporter of the New Deal. His change from a conservative Republican to militant independent during the 1920s and to a moderate Democrat in the 1930s epitomized black politics in the New South. But after the war Young saw that his strategy of conciliation and compromise and his "gentlemen, go slow" approach to race relations were inconsistent with the NAACP's militant crusade against segregation. After the Supreme Court, in *Brown* v. *Board of Education*, declared segregated public schools unconstitutional, he continued to vacillate between the positions of a Bookerite conservative and a liberal statesman. He believed that southerners would "gracefully and calmly" accept desegregation and predicted that "segregated public schools will eventually disappear." He characterized the *Brown* decision as a turning point in stopping the westward march of communism.

P. B. Young died in Norfolk on 9 October 1962.

See also BLACK LIFE: / National Association for the Advancement of Colored People; LAW: / Scottsboro Case

Henry Lewis Suggs
Clemson University

Henry Lewis Suggs, *The Black Press in the South* (1984).

Music

BILL C. MALONE
Tulane University
CONSULTANT

Squatter's son with a new guitar, Shenandoah Valley, Virginia, 1935

Music

For at least a century and a half the South has fired the imagination of musicians and songwriters. As a land of romance and enchantment, and as the home of exotic people—both black and white—the South has inspired a seemingly unending body of songs that speak longingly of old Virginia or the hills of Caroline, while also singing the praises of the region's towns, counties, hills, rivers, bayous, plains, and people. As a source of songs and musical images, the South has spawned a veritable industry of songwriters, from Stephen Foster, Will Hays, and Dan Emmett in the 19th century, to Johnny Mercer, Hoagy Carmichael, Allen Toussaint, Tom T. Hall, Dolly Parton, and Hank Williams, Jr., in our own time. Visions of lonesome pines, lazy rivers, snow-white cotton fields, smoky mountains, and hanging moss have forever ignited the creativity of America's poets and lyricists, while also fulfilling the fantasies of an audience that prefers to believe there is a land where time moves slowly, where life is lived simply and elementally, and whose inhabitants hold clearly-defined values and dearly love to make music.

Southerners *have* made music, and many of them have performed it with distinction, thereby contributing immeasurably to the making and enrichment of American music as a whole. Singers, songwriters, musicians, merchandisers (promoters and record producers), folklorists, and others whose lives in some way intersect with music have proliferated in the South. Some performers, of course—like Mary Martin, Kate Smith, and Ann Miller—have carried little of the South in their styles. Nevertheless, like classical pianist Van Cliburn or opera singer Leontyne Price, many have become internationally famous. The success enjoyed by such musicians has been immensely satisfying to the regional pride of southerners, but these entertainers project little regional identity. On the other hand, such singers as Jimmie Rodgers, Bessie Smith, Mahalia Jackson, Elvis Presley, Hank Williams, Ray Charles, and Charlie Daniels have exhibited southernness in their dialects and lifestyles. And their music has, for the most part, embodied styles of performance that were indigenous to or deeply rooted in the South. A few performers, such as Charlie Daniels and Hank Williams, Jr., have been self-consciously southern in their aggressive "nationalism" or "regionalism." Consequently, many of the dominant American music styles of the 20th century—from country to jazz—have been southern in origin.

The folk South has given the nation much of its music. There are many southern forms of music, from blues to Cajun and Tex-Mex, and each has its own special features. Nevertheless, they share an interrelatedness that reflects the pluralism of the culture. The folk South has been basically biracial; that is, its basic components have been Afro-American and Anglo-American, cultures that in turn were never "pure" but were instead composites of Old World elements. Blacks and whites have shared music with each other since the colonial era. A "common folk pool" of songs and instruments, strongly audible in the 19th century but still exhibiting strength in our own time, reminds one of the mutual interchange that has long occurred among southerners of all racial and ethnic backgrounds.

Although many scholars have argued convincingly that the African admixture has made southern music distinctive and appealing (syncopation, improvisation, blue notes), other groups have contributed much of importance to the shaping of regional music forms. Pockets of "ethnic" music have existed all over the South (Czech, German, Polish, Tex-Mex, Cajun). The Germans made important contributions to music at the folk, popular, and high-art levels through shape-note hymnody in the Shenandoah Valley; folk dances such as "Herr Schmidt," the schottishe, and polka; accordion popularity in Louisiana and south Texas; music publishing houses; music societies; and roles as teachers and classical musicians. Cajuns created a distinctive melange of country, pop, and blues music in southwest Louisiana and exported it to southeast Texas and the Mississippi-Alabama Gulf Coast. French-speaking black people in Louisiana, in turn, created their own exciting fusion, a popular style known as zydeco (a mixture of rhythm and blues and Cajun, with "French" lyrics). Since the 1920s elements of the Cajun style have made their way, via commercial exposure, into the national pop-culture mainstream.

Folk culture was never isolated from the world at large. Music has moved back and forth across the thin and imaginary line that separates folk and popular culture. The folk, in fact, borrowed much from both high-art and popular sources. Some rural dances were of middle- or upper-class origins—the square dance came from the cotillion; the black cakewalk was a burlesque of formal white dancing; the Virginia Reel was a variation of the upper-class dance called the Sir Roger de Coverley. Many fiddle tunes that have become hallowed in the folk-rural tradition, such as "Under the Double Eagle" and "Red Wing," came from marches or pop tunes, and many other "folk" songs came from "popular" composers. The blackface minstrel shows of the mid and late 19th century repeatedly introduced items—such as the five-string banjo, instrumental and vocal styles, songs, dances, comedy—that were preserved in southern rural culture. Some songs collected from black informants in the late 19th century actually began their lives on the minstrel stage. Furthermore, the chautauqua tents, medicine shows, tent-rep shows, vaudeville, and the popular music industry all introduced styles and songs that became part of the southern folk process.

Many songs that rural southerners cherished and preserved started out on Tin Pan Alley and were published on sheet music designed for urban, middle-class consumers. Songs such as "The Letter Edged in Black," "Little Rosewood Casket," "I'll Be All Smiles Tonight," "The Blind Child," and "Wildwood Flower" celebrated the values of family, home, church, and traditional human relationships, or bemoaned their disintegration, and these

Child with phonograph, Transylvania, La., 1939

songs found a welcome reception among rural and small-town southerners. Their descendants still preserve the songs in bluegrass and old-time country music.

Southern music was originally perceived by outsiders as "black" music, and the imagery surrounding the music often projected plantation scenes with happy or doleful "darkeys." The presumption that blacks were musical was made very early in American history. Captains of slave ships, slave traders, plantation masters and overseers, travelers, and others who came in contact with slaves often commented on black musicality, as did Thomas Jefferson in his *Notes on the State of Virginia* (1784). Blackface minstrelsy profited greatly from public perceptions concerning black music, but considerable doubt exists about how much of the minstrel repertoire really came from black or southern sources (the minstrel men, who were mostly northern-born entertainers, borrowed from all kinds of sources, pop and folk, and from cultures outside the South). Whatever the source, minstrel material moved back into the South and permanently influenced the music made there.

Authentic black musicians eventually profited from an association with minstrelsy. Such black groups as the Georgia Minstrels began flourishing after the Civil War. As late as the 1920s many black entertainers still called themselves "minstrels." Both blessings and burdens obviously accompanied the minstrel association. Blacks obtained an entree into the world of show business, but they also carried with them some of the degrading aspects of minstrelsy—the wearing of cork and the depiction of blacks as comic characters (practices that carried over into the "coon song" era).

Black musicians made their first real breakthrough into the realm of American popular culture in the late 19th century, a process that flowed through two important channels—high-art cultivation and sponsorship, and the "underground" movement of black musicians into new geographical regions. The American fine-arts establishment discovered black music in the guise of the famous "spirituals." These songs appeared in print in scattered sources before the 1860's, but their real introduction to the northern literati came through the groundbreaking collection, *Slave Songs from the Southern United States* (compiled by three missionaries to the freedmen and published in 1867). Nevertheless, the songs remained known to only a few people until the 1870s when a small choir of black students from Fisk University in Nashville popularized the spirituals in the North and, eventually, Europe. By the turn of the century such songs as "Go Down, Moses" and "Swing Low, Sweet Chariot" were being performed on the concert stage and in symphonic arrangements. In content and style the spirituals represented a major slice of black folk culture, but they did not tell the whole story of black musical life or even of black religious expression.

Meanwhile, black musicians were insinuating themselves into the popular consciousness of American life, well apart from the activities of the high-art establishment (but certainly not apart from the influence of commercial white culture). Emancipation saw the migration of black musicians from the country to town, from town to town, to other parts of the South, and ultimately to cities all over the North. Southerners, of course, heard black musicians everywhere—on street corners, on work gangs, at public gatherings, and in religious settings. But black musicians who hoped to make money at their trade, or to attain some kind of independence moved into the honky-tonks, saloons, brothels, juke joints, medicine shows, minstrelsy, or black vaudeville. Often, as in the brothels of New Orleans or in the clubs of St. Louis, the audiences were white or mixed. In areas of high black population density, such as the Mississippi Delta, or in institutions where a white presence was rare—such as the black church—musicians were free to be as expressive as they desired. Presumably, a higher percentage of African traits was preserved in such environments than in regions where blacks and whites mingled freely. Most black musicians, however—whether religious or secular—tended to have different repertories, and even performing styles, for white and black audiences.

Black musicians demonstrated a mastery of any instrument with which they came in contact. Pianists, though, made the first big musical impact on American life. Barrelhouse pianists roamed through the Southwest and up the rivers, laying the basis for a variety of modern styles such as "fast western" and "boogie woogie." Piano players proliferated in the "sporting houses" of New Orleans, Kansas City, St. Louis, Sedalia, and other cities, playing a mixture of pop, ragtime, and blues. Some of them, including Ferdinand "Jelly Roll" Morton, became famous.

Black piano styles influenced most musicians who heard them, and they gradually began to make their way into mainstream American music, particularly after World War I when the nation became jazz crazy. Jazz, though, was preceded by ragtime, another piano-based musical phenomenon that took the country by storm at the end of the 19th century. Itinerant piano players,

B. B. King with band, c. 1955, photograph on a wall at Club Paradise, Memphis, Tenn.

mostly black, created the style out of folk forms. Scott Joplin, who was one of them, put many of these "rags" down on paper and tried to convert them into classical forms. His "Maple Leaf Rag" became a national hit, and by 1900 ragtime was the popular rage. White songwriters and musicians, such as Irving Berlin in "Alexander's Ragtime Band," appropriated the name, if not always the true style, of ragtime. Songwriters, both white and black, who wrote for Broadway or Tin Pan Alley, combined the ragtime style with lyrics about "Negro life." The results were the "coon songs"—songs that perpetuated myths and stereotypes of black people (the myth of a childlike but musical people).

By the beginning of the 1920s black musical styles had made major inroads into American cultural life at both the "serious" and "popular" levels. Blues music was also achieving considerable popularity, largely through the work of W. C. Handy and songs like "St. Louis Blues." Mainstream white performers often did ragtime, jazz, or blues numbers, or songs that were influenced by them. White audiences, then, had considerable exposure to "black" forms, although many people heard such music only through "slumming" (visits to black juke joints or to other places of "unrespectable," "naughty," entertainment). Americans associated black music with images of exotic southern life on plantations and in juke joints. Sheet music often reinforced the romance with illustrations of alleged southern scenes, and in the popular mind, black music and southern music were synonymous.

When the full-scale commercialization of southern music came in the 1920s, most Americans already had strong preconceptions about the South and its music. Southern musical styles could not help but be colored by such images, and the musicians and their commercial promoters responded to these southern-spiced images. Commercialization was made possible by major innovations in media dissemination in the United States. Radio and phonograph recording, above all, made possible the maturation and dissemination of southern-born musical styles. The media exploitation of grass-roots music had both positive and negative consequences. Media coverage promoted the standardization and homogenization of styles and weakened local or regional traits. On the other hand, it also presented such styles to a larger audience, encouraged professionalization, and promoted the cross-fertilization of musical styles. Musicians learned from each other, and they became more acutely conscious of audience tastes. Some styles died or remained only locally rooted; others achieved new life, and developed healthy and strong variations.

The 1920s saw the "discovery" and commercialization of a wide variety of "ethnic" music forms, as well as most of the grass-roots genres of the South: jazz, blues, gospel (black and white), Cajun, German, Czech, Tex-Mex, and hillbilly. The first significant southern band to be recorded was done so more or less by accident. The Dixieland Jazz Band, a group of white boys from New Orleans, was playing in clubs in Chicago when they made their first recordings in 1917. They made the nation jazz conscious, while also popularizing the word jazz. Not until 1923 did the first all-black jazz band, that of King Oliver, also playing in Chicago, make its first recordings. By the middle of the 1920s jazz had burgeoned, both in the United States and Europe, and was attracting aficionadoes and musicians elsewhere. The musical form moved away quickly from its folk and southern roots, but southerners continued to play invaluable roles in its development. The first star, for example, was the New Orleans-born trumpeter Louis Armstrong.

Blues also won great popularity during the 1920s, partly through its alliance with jazz. W. C. Handy had earlier contributed greatly to the form's popularity, but radio and recording did most to make Americans conscious of this exciting style. The first blues singers to become highly visible in American popular culture were black women who sang generally to the accompaniment of jazz bands. These classic blues singers, led principally by the "Empress of the Blues," Bessie Smith, were performers who usually had considerable experience in black vaudeville or on medicine shows. In 1926, however, with the recording of the Texas-born Blind Lemon Jefferson, a guitarist with a supple, wailing vocal style, American entertainment received its first strong infusion of rural black music. This has generally been described as the "country blues"—a predominantly masculine style, usually accompanied by guitars or other string instruments, with rural-folk inflections.

The wide variety of black folk styles that became commercialized in the 1920s came to be subsumed under the rubric of *race music*. Not all performers were blues singers. Some were "songsters," that is, entertainers who performed many different styles and songs. But they and the jug bands, string bands, pianists, and gospel singers were advertised in the same record catalogues. And of course most of them shared musical traits because styles flowed freely from entertainer to entertainer. Gospel musicians, for example, might assert their estrangement from the world, but "worldly" musical riffs and phrases constantly intruded into their songs and performances, just as musical ideas born in the church have always affected the performances made by secular black musicians.

Given the reputation for musicianship that white

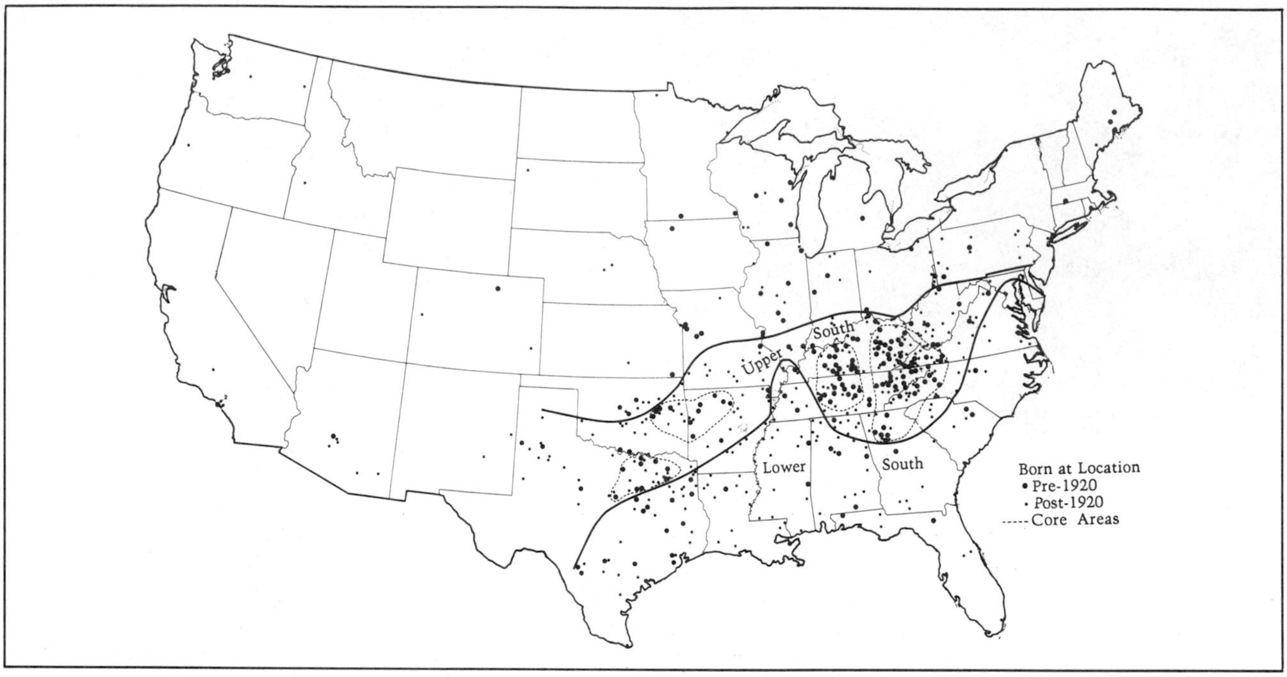

Birthplaces of Country Music Performers, 1870–1970

Map by George O. Carney

Source: John F. Rooney, Jr., Wilbur Zelinsky, and Dean R. Louder, eds., *This Remarkable Continent: An Atlas of United States and Canadian Society and Cultures* (1982).

country entertainers enjoy today, white folk music was discovered remarkably late. When hillbilly music was first recorded in the 1920s, only 20 years or so had elapsed since the first faint glimmers of recognition of "mountain music" or "Anglo-American balladry" occurred. White folk music really went unrecognized until the 20th century. Only an occasional traveler, missionary, or local colorist made reference to frolics, country dances, singing schools, or camp meetings. One receives little understanding from these accounts of how the music was performed or what was performed (even though the social context of such performances is sometimes well described).

The discovery of white folk music came in the years before World War I. The perception that such music was a resource worthy of preservation came in the context of the rapid industrialization of the nation, the "new immigration, the rise of cities, and other related factors that seemed to bode ill for the continued existence of rural, peasant-derived culture. Folklorists and other interested people sought to preserve folk music before it succumbed to modern forces. They viewed such music as a static and pure phenomenon, and the product of a racially homogeneous, i.e., Anglo-Saxon, culture. Some high-art musicians and composers eagerly utilized folk music for artistic purposes, presenting arrangements of it in concerts and recitals and arguing, as did John Powell of Virginia, that it might make the basis of a national music.

Two famous collectors, John A. Lomax and Cecil Sharp, did most to demonstrate the wealth of folk music that still existed in the United States. Lomax's *Cowboy Songs and Other Frontier Ballads* (1910) profited from the popular and romantic perception of cowboys as white knights or Anglo-Saxon heroes—even though cowboy culture was racially and ethnically eclectic, and the songs themselves came from diverse sources. Cowboy songs soon made their way into the larger society, through the high-art concerts of such musicians as Oscar Fox and David Guion, the phonograph recordings of singers like Bentley Ball and Carl Sprague, and performances of a multitude of radio and movie cowboys.

Cecil Sharp was primarily a student of folk dance in his native England. Largely through the influence of Olive Dame Campbell, a settlement schoolteacher in the Kentucky hills, Sharp traveled through much of southern Appalachia between 1916 and 1918, with his assistant Maud Karpeles, collecting ballads and folksongs. Sharp's expedition came after the preoccupation of local color writers and journalists with the southern mountains. Writers of fiction created images of mountaineers in the 19th century that flowed into American popular culture. These images of a "strange and peculiar people" living in a land where "time stood still," a people who preserved "Elizabethan folkways," influenced the attitudes that surrounded the music. The music was perceived as the product of a dying culture—a body of ballads and folksongs that needed to be collected with great urgency.

Although most people had visions of a static culture, Sharp discovered that singing was common to both young and old in the mountain areas that he visited. He noted that many of the oldest British folksongs still en-

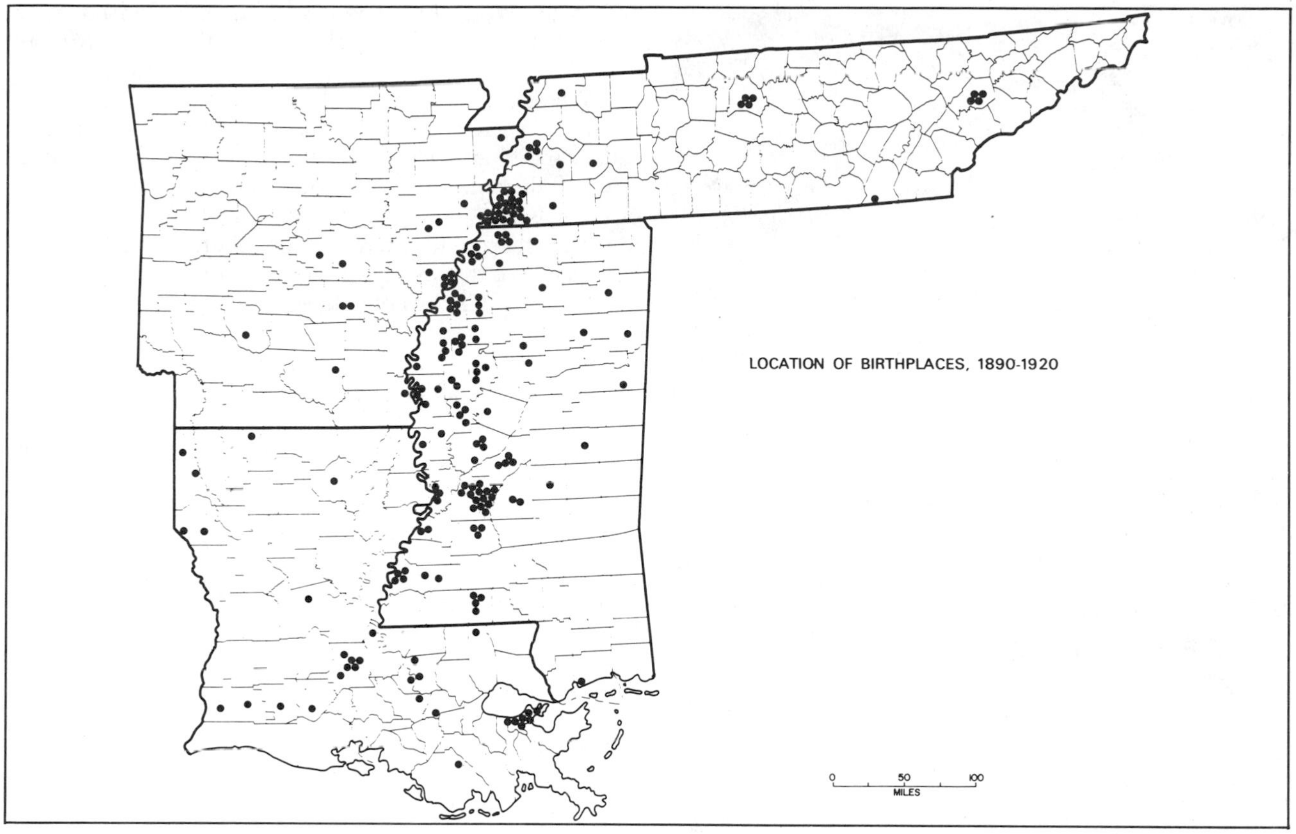

Distribution of Blues People

Map by George O. Carney

Source: John F. Rooney, Jr., Wilbur Zelinsky, and Dean R. Louder, eds., *This Remarkable Continent: An Atlas of United States and Canadian Society and Cultures* (1982).

dured in variant forms. Sharp made great contributions to folk music scholarship, but his work nevertheless had serious omissions. He ignored religious songs and instrumental dance tunes, although both traditions were very strong in the southern hills. The scholarship and song performance (by serious recitalists) that he inspired long reflected Sharp's critical judgments. When the first "hillbilly" records were made in the 1920s, the reactions made to them by scholars, collectors, critics, and the recording men themselves were affected by prior perceptions of mountain folk music.

Radio stations began using live, local talent almost as soon as they opened in the South in the 1920s—string bands, fiddlers, family gospel groups, yodelers, "Hawaiian" bands. Many of the acts appeared on an irregular, unplanned basis, but some stations, led by WBAP in Fort Worth in 1923, created barn dance formats—regular, weekly performances of downhome entertainment. By the middle of the decade phonograph companies also began recording such talent, and the resulting "industry" was described by several terms, the most common of which was hillbilly. The hillbilly music of the 1920s and 1930s reveals a white folk culture far different from that described by Cecil Sharp or by the romantic Anglo-Saxonists. Neither the culture nor the music were ethnically or racially homogeneous, nor were they static. Most crucially, both the music and the culture from which it derived were strongly shaped by commercialization and technology. The music was simultaneously conservative, eclectic, and absorptive; it came from many sources.

All southern forms underwent extensive change and experienced some degree of national expansion during the 1930s and 1940s. Expanded radio coverage introduced southern musicians to audiences in every corner of the United States and in Canada. American business allied itself with grass-roots music, and the resulting advertising was mutually beneficial to both music and commerce. Radio programming also prompted the burgeoning of personal appearances, and promoters and booking agents moved to exploit the developing interest. Hollywood played a major role in making musicians visible to the outside world. Musicians of all types—from Louis Armstrong to Roy Acuff—occasionally appeared in short features or sometimes played roles in full-length films. Singing cowboys, of course—led originally by Gene Autry in 1934—constituted a distinct genre of filmmaking up to the early 1950s. Because of this exposure, Autry may very well have been the best-known southern-born musician in the world.

Guitar on the wall of a house in Tutwiler, Miss., 1968

The heightened commercialization of these decades, along with the consequent competition among musicians, encouraged major stylistic innovations that have ever since been part of the nation's music. Performances in nightclubs, bars, and honky-tonks—all of which proliferated after the repeal of prohibition in 1933—required louder and more percussive sounds. Drums and string basses became common in all kinds of bands, and electric instruments began to make their way into musical organizations by the middle of the 1930s. Pioneering musicians such as steel guitarist Bob Dunn experimented with amplifiers and homemade electric pickups, but by the end of the decade guitar manufacturers were merchandising their own lines of electrified instruments. Fledgling musicians everywhere were introduced to electric guitars through the performances of such great southern performers as Dunn, Charlie Christian, and Aaron "T-Bone" Walker.

World War II and the years immediately following it saw the nationalization of southern music. The migrations made by civilians and servicemen during those years—to the cities, to the North, and around the world—did much to transport southern-born styles to other areas while also bringing southerners in direct contact with other forms of music. Black migration to the North and to the West Coast had begun much earlier but was particularly strong during the World War II era. Migration encouraged a new consciousness among young black people, and life in the American ghettoes inspired musical experimentation. Although both black gospel music and blues had southern rural roots, they achieved new vitality in the segregated neighborhoods of the cities. Georgia-born Tom Dorsey and Louisiana native Mahalia Jackson, for example, contributed greatly to the emergence of modern black gospel music through their work in the churches of Chicago and other cities of the North. Other black migrants in such urban areas as Chicago, Detroit, Los Angeles, and Harlem were far less spiritual than Mahalia, but no less influential and innovative. They created the aggressive, electrified version of blues known as rhythm and blues, as well as its many offshoots, such as rock and roll, soul, and the Motown Sound.

A multitude of small record labels which catered to the grass-roots music styles of the South appeared after the war, in and outside the region. Meanwhile, the big record labels found increasing commercial success with such southern musicians as Hank Williams, Eddy Arnold, Louis Jordan, and Elvis Presley. Although most earlier recordings of southern talent had taken place in such cities as New York, Chicago, or Los Angeles, or in makeshift "studios" hastily assembled by traveling record men in southern towns, postwar recording tended increasingly to be in such southern cities as Dallas, Houston, New Orleans, Memphis, Macon, Muscle Shoals, and Nashville. Nashville became one of the three or four

Jerry Lee Lewis, rockabilly and country singer, 1970s

leading music centers in the nation, first on the strength of the talent affiliated with the Grand Ole Opry and later through the recording of all kinds of music. Memphis did not rival Nashville as a music center, but it was the birthplace of a musical revolution that swept across the world. In 1954 Sam Phillips recorded Elvis Presley for his Sun label and saw that exciting singer become the vanguard of what would soon be known as rock and roll. Elvis, Carl Perkins, Jerry Lee Lewis, Roy Orbison, and other Sun label "rockabillies" joined with such musicians as Buddy Holly and the Everly Brothers to popularize a fusion of hillbilly and rhythm and blues that was redolent of the working-class South and its musical eclecticism.

Since the 1950s southern-born music styles have flowered commercially and have made themselves known around the world. None, however, has remained "pure," and each has spawned a variety of offshoots or substylings that run the gamut from the "traditional" to the "progressive." The Cajun and *música Tejana* (Tex-Mex) styles have moved somewhat out of their ethnic enclaves—away from southwest Louisiana and the barrios of south Texas—to win wider national hearings. Folk festival performances and exposure on the nationally-syndicated television show *Austin City Limits* have permitted such entertainers as the Balfa Brothers, Clifton Chenier, and Flaco Jiménez to attract converts from all regions of the nation. Although these styles have interrelated with other musical forms that lie around them and have both influenced and been influenced by them—the accordion's centrality in Cajun, German, and Mexican *conjunto* bands is illustrative—they nevertheless maintain the imprint of the cultures that gave them birth.

Other southern-born styles have been less successful in maintaining regional identity. Indeed, the promise of national acceptance and prosperity has inspired deliberate efforts by musicians and promoters alike to create products with broad appeal and limited sociocultural identification. The goal is the homogenized mainstream, and vehicles are the crossover record, the top-40 record format, and the television special. Many people in country music (the term that has been used since the early 1950s to describe the hillbilly field), have campaigned for the use of the word *American* to designate their music (seemingly oblivious to the existence of many American styles of music). Only one musical genre, southern gospel, consciously gives itself a southern label, an effort to distinguish its music from the melange of modern pop religious sounds known as *Christian contemporary*. The gospel quartets clearly have been influenced by other forms of music, but they nevertheless still convey the flavor of singing conventions and old-time evangelism. The Christian contemporary musicians, on the other hand, exude the sounds and ambience of pop radio, an ambience that has no regional identification.

Country music has prospered as an industry and has won a respect that scarcely seemed possible back in its hillbilly and honky-tonk days. But no field of music has been more torn by debates concerning loss of identity. Nashville is still the commercial capital of country music, but the city periodically encounters some competition from places such as Austin, Tex., where healthy artistic alternatives are presented. Much of the music now bearing the "country" label has little relationship to southern, rural, or working-class life, but instead is aimed at middle-class urban listeners who presumably have little regional or class identification. Nevertheless, tradition-based sounds and styles still endure—as seen in the growing popularity of the acoustic-oriented bluegrass field, in the proliferation of festivals devoted to homespun or old-time music, and in the commercial success enjoyed by such young "traditionalists" as Ricky Skaggs, Reba McEntire, George Strait, Randy Travis, and Dwight Yoakum.

The Soul Stirrers, southern gospel group, c. 1950

What, then, is the state of southern music in the late 1980s? Southern-born musicians of all varieties still thrive, and they still continue to make major contributions to the nation's cultural life. Their music, however, reflects increasingly the national experience and the powerful communications revolution that has come to dominate our existence and shape our choices. Some musicians, such as Hank Williams, Jr., and Charlie Daniels, are aggressive southern nationalists, and songs like "Dixie on My Mind" and "The South's Gonna Do It Again" sometimes spice their repertories. The South, of course, has never ceased to have exotic appeal for Americans. It still fuels the imaginations of songwriters, and at times the region assumes such a central focus in American life that our popular culture and popular music are dramatically affected.

One such occasion came in the early 1980s during the administration of President Jimmy Carter. This southern president brought country musicians into the White

House and otherwise gave patronage and exposure to entertainers from the South. Considerable media attention was devoted to a group of young entertainers whose music was described as "southern rock"—the Allman Brothers, the Marshall Tucker Band, the Charlie Daniels Band, Lynyrd Skynyrd, Wet Willie, Sea Level, ZZ Top. They were often aggressively southern in attitude and rhetoric, sometimes to the point of jingoism, and a few of them—like Charlie Daniels—projected postures of machismo and hedonism that are generally associated with southern masculinity. Except for the moments when Daniels picked up his fiddle and played a lively hoedown, the music of the southern rock bands seemed little different from that played by rock musicians around the world. Rather than indicating a renewed infusion of originality into the nation's musical mainstream, the success enjoyed by the southern rockers instead demonstrated the all-pervasive influence of the media and the primacy of youth in contemporary popular culture.

Southern music, then, is now American music. Southerners have exported their musical treasures to the world and have in turn absorbed much that the larger world has to offer. The resulting syntheses continue to provide enjoyment and enrichment. Southern styles may not be as distinctive as many people would like, and observers might with good reason bemoan their dilution and disappearance, but one can scarcely ignore the fact that the folk cultures that produced them are undergoing similar dissolution. Happily, much of the best of the older traditions—such as old-time fiddling, clog dancing, and sacred harp singing—are being preserved and revitalized by interested groups, and increasing numbers of young people are being won over to the old-time arts. Within the realm of commercial music young musicians like the blues guitarist Stevie Ray Vaughan and honky-tonk country singer Dwight Yoakum prove it is still possible to create new, exciting, and commercially successful sounds by building on the time-tested musical formulas of the past. Finally, regardless of the directions its musicians may take in the years to come, the South will not soon lose its romantic aura nor its capacity to evoke mythmaking and popular imagery. The South will sing, and it will be sung about.

See also BLACK LIFE: Music, Black; GEOGRAPHY: Migration Patterns; HISTORY AND MANNERS: World War II; INDUSTRY: / Music Industry; MEDIA: Film, Musical; MYTHIC SOUTH: / Carter Era; RECREATION: Traveling Shows; WOMEN'S LIFE: Blues-singing Women

Bill C. Malone
Tulane University

Roger D. Abrahams and George Foss, *Anglo-American Folksong Style* (1968); Bob Artis, *Bluegrass: From the Lonesome Wail of a Mountain Love Song to the Hammering Drive of the Scruggs-Style Banjo, The Story of an American Musical Tradition* (1975); Earl Bargainneer, *Mississippi Quarterly* (Fall 1977); Carl Belz, *The Story of Rock* (1969); Lois S. Blackwell, *The Wings of the Dove: The Story of Gospel Music in America* (1978); Rudi Blesh, *Shining Trumpets: A History of Jazz* (1958), with Harriet Janis, *They All Played Ragtime* (1966); John Broven, *Walking to New Orleans: The Story of New Orleans Rhythm and Blues* (1974); Harry O. Brunn, *The Story of the Original Dixieland Jazz Band* (1960); Robert Cantwell, *Bluegrass Breakdown: The Making of the Old Southern Sound* (1984); Samuel Charters, *The Bluesmen: The Story and the Music of the Men Who Made the Blues* (1967), *The Country Blues* (1959); Ronald Davis, *A History of Opera in the American West* (1965); Bill Ellis, *Journal of American Folklore* (April–June 1978); Dena J. Epstein, *Sinful Tunes and Spirituals: Black Folk Music to the Civil War* (1977); Harry Eskew, "Shape-Note Hymnody in the Shenandoah Valley, 1816–1860" (Ph.D. dissertation, Tulane University, 1966); David Evans, *Big Road Blues: Tradition and Creativity in the Folk Blues* (1981); William Ferris, *Blues from the Delta* (1978); Linnell Gentry, *A History and Encyclopedia of Country, Western, and Gospel Music* (1961); Archie Green, *Only a Miner: Studies in Recorded Coal-Mining Songs* (1972); Douglas B. Green, *Country Roots: The Origins of Country Music* (1976); John Greenway, *American Folksongs of Protest* (1953); Peter Guralnick, *Lost Highway: Journeys and Arrivals of American Musicians* (1979), *Sweet Soul Music: Rhythm and Blues and the Southern Dream of Freedom* (1986); Tony Heilbut, *The Gospel Sound: Good News and Bad Times* (1971); George Pullen Jackson, *White Spirituals in the Southern Uplands* (1933); Henry Kmen, *Music in New Orleans: The Formative Years, 1791–1841* (1966); Ottis J. Knippers, *Who's Who among Southern Singers and Composers* (1937); Alan Lomax, *Folk Songs of North America* (1960); Bill C. Malone, *Country Music, U.S.A.: A Fifty-year History* (1968; rev. ed., 1985), *Southern Music—American Music* (1979), with Judith McCullough, eds., *Stars of Country Music: Uncle Dave Macon to Johnny Rodriguez* (1975); Alan P. Merriam and Robert J. Branford, *A Bibliography of Jazz* (1954); Jim Miller, ed., *The Rolling Stone Illustrated History of Rock 'n' Roll* (1976); Hans Nathan, *Dan Emmett and the Rise of Early Negro Minstrelsy* (1962); Paul Oliver, *Blues Fell This Morning: The Meaning of the Blues* (1960), *Savannah Syncopators: African Retentions in the Blues* (1970), *The Story of the Blues* (1969); Américo Paredes, *A Texas-Mexican Cancionero: Folksongs of the Lower Border* (1975); Jan Reid, *The Improbable Rise of Redneck Rock* (1974); Jim Rooney, *Bossmen: Bill Monroe and Muddy Waters* (1971); Neil V. Rosenberg, *Bluegrass: A History* (1985); Tony Russell, *Blacks, Whites, and Blues* (1970); William J. Schafer and Johannes Riedel, *The Art of Ragtime: Form and Meaning of an Original Black American Art* (1973); Arnold Shaw, *Honkers and Shouters: The Golden Years of Rhythm and Blues* (1978); O. G. Sonneck, *Early Concert-Life in America* (1907); Eileen Southern, *The Music of Black Americans: A History* (1971; 2d ed., 1983); Nicholas Spitzer, in *Long Journey Home: Folklife in the South*, ed. Allen Tullos (1977); Marshall Stearns, *The Story of Jazz* (1956); Frank Tirro, *Jazz: A History* (1977); Jeff Todd Titon, *Early Downhome Blues: A Musical and Cultural Analysis* (1977); Robert C. Toll, *Blacking Up: The Minstrel Show in Nineteenth-Century America* (1974); Nick Tosches, *Country: The Biggest Music in America* (1977); Charles R. Townsend, *San Antonio Rose: The Life and Music of Bob Wills* (1976); Barry Ulanov, *A History of Jazz in America* (1955); D. K. Wilgus, *Anglo-American Folksong Scholarship since 1898* (1959); Mark R. Winchell, *Southern Quarterly* (Spring 1984); Charles K. Wolfe, *Grand Ole Opry: The Early Years, 1925–1935* (1975), *Kentucky Country: Folk and Country Music of Kentucky* (1982), *Tennessee Strings: The Story of Country Music in Tennessee* (1977).

Bluegrass

Bluegrass is a form of country music that grew out of the music of the Grand Ole Opry star Bill Monroe and his Blue Grass Boys during the late 1940s and early 1950s. Bluegrass is frequently associated with southern Appalachia, but the members of Monroe's most influential band were from outside that region (Monroe came from western Kentucky, Lester Flatt from central Tennessee, Chubby Wise from north Florida, and Earl Scruggs from the North Carolina Piedmont) and the music in its definitive form was first heard in Nashville. It did have its strongest early popularity in Appalachia, where such groups as the Stanley Brothers and their Clinch Mountain Boys and Lester Flatt, Earl Scruggs, and the Foggy Mountain Boys, performing at WCYB in Bristol on the Tennessee-Virginia border, emulated Monroe's music and developed his sound into a style. It also gained popularity among Appalachian migrants in Michigan, Indiana, Ohio, Pennsylvania, Maryland, the District of Columbia, and Delaware. The music was popular throughout the South and found receptive listeners among country music fans in every corner of North America—particularly in isolated rural areas.

Like most country music of the postwar era, bluegrass was principally aimed at and consumed by blue-collar workers, farm families, and other working-class people of rural origins. Like most forms of country music, it had roots in the dance, home entertainment, itinerant theater, and religious-musical traditions of the rural South, particularly the highland regions. Hence, it was most familiar to listeners in that part of the country, although it appealed to many non-southerners because of its novelty and because its ingredients were part of a common Anglo-American folk heritage. Bluegrass's popularity is now confined to a relatively small number of avid fans.

A number of musical traits combine to make bluegrass a distinctive type of country music. A typical bluegrass band consists of from four to seven individuals—more often men than women—who sing and accompany themselves with acoustic (rather than electric) string instruments. In comparison with other kinds of country music singing, bluegrass is pitched quite high (particularly for men), often reaching tones an octave above middle C. Many bluegrass vocals involve more than one voice. With duets the second part (tenor) is sung above the melody; trios include a part below the melody (baritone), and in religious quartets a bass part is added. Basically these are harmony parts, but there is a tendency—particularly in duets—toward vocal polyphony. In trios the tenor and baritone parts are sometimes arranged so that the melody is the lowest or highest part. Most bluegrass music is in duple meter; tempos are generally faster than in other kinds of country music. Rhythm is characterized by a stress on the offbeat.

Much attention is paid by musicians and fans alike to the unamplified instruments used in bluegrass. These include two used mainly for rhythm—guitar and string bass—and several others—mandolin, banjo, and fiddle—that play melody ("lead") and provide rhythm and background for vocalists. Lead instrumentalists take solo breaks between verses of songs and provide harmonic and rhythmic background, often in antiphonal relationship to the vocal. Instrumental pieces feature alternating solos, as in many forms of jazz. Certain individuals have initiated basic bluegrass instrumental techniques—notably Earl Scruggs for the banjo and Bill Monroe for the mandolin. Considerable value is placed upon the ownership and use of the proper instruments. Old mandolins, banjos, and guitars of the make and vintage associated with the leading musicians fetch handsome prices, and reproductions of these instruments, both homemade and commercially manufactured, have proliferated. Many publications on bluegrass deal with instruments and instrumental techniques.

The classic bluegrass repertoire resembles that of older (1925–55) country music. A significant number of traditional folksongs and tunes are regularly performed, but recent, newly composed music predominates. Secular songs deal with such topics as memories of the old home and family, love affairs, and the problems of urban life. The religious repertoire reflects a wide range of sources, from old spirituals to newly composed gospel songs, and such songs are performed by virtually every bluegrass band. Forming an important component of bluegrass, instrumentals both demonstrate the virtuosity expected of musicians and symbolize the music's ties to fiddle-dominated dance music of the past.

Through their identification of instrumental styles with earlier traditions, as in their often militant defense of nonelectrified instruments, bluegrass fans stress the essentially conservative form of their music, even though it differs significantly in many aspects from earlier styles. In the late 1940s, when it was a vital new sound, bluegrass was perceived within the country music trade as "backwoods," or old-fashioned, mainly because, despite its musical innovations, the instrumentation, vocal style, and song content were regional, traditional, and familiar. But as with any commercial form, changes and innovations have been essential for bluegrass performers wishing to establish individuality and gain a market; bluegrass fans have debated the propriety of any changes in the music of their favorite bands. Now bluegrass musicians attempt to retain their traditionalist fans while downplaying the bluegrass label for fear it may stereotype them and thereby frighten away others who are potential consumers of their music. The fans, not the professional musicians, named the music, and they are most concerned about maintaining its purity.

Throughout the history of bluegrass, phonograph recordings have provided income and publicity, as well as sources of style and repertoire. In the 1940s most bluegrass groups played on radio and made their living by touring rural communities in the Southeast. The most influential bands were those of Monroe, Flatt and Scruggs, and the Stanley Brothers. By the early 1950s a number of other groups had been organized, including those of Reno and Smiley, Mac Wiseman, and Jim and Jesse. Many of the musicians who started bluegrass bands at this time had, like Flatt and Scruggs, worked in Bill Monroe's band. Today his role as a teacher and perpetuator of this music is reflected in his title, "the father of bluegrass."

Bill Monroe and the Bluegrass Boys, the classic bluegrass group, c. 1950

During the 1950s bluegrass performers appeared increasingly on local television shows, on "package" shows with other country music performers touring large centers, and in urban "hillbilly" bars, which catered to rural immigrants. Among the new groups that emerged as influences in the mid-1950s were the Osborne Brothers and Jimmy Martin.

At the beginning of the 1960s the urban folksong revival opened college concert halls, coffee houses, and folk festivals throughout the nation to bluegrass. For the first time new groups were dependent less upon regular radio or television exposure and more on records and concerts to build their careers. The most important new groups in this era were the Country Gentlemen and the Dillards—located in Washington, D.C., and Los Angeles, respectively. Flatt and Scruggs were, by the 1960s, nationally known, partly because of their exposure via the folk boom, but particularly because of their role in the highly successful television series *The Beverly Hillbillies*, for which they provided theme music and made yearly cameo appearances.

During the 1960s a revival of Bill Monroe's career, then in eclipse, led to his first bluegrass festival, organized near Roanoke, Va., by promoter Carlton Haney in 1965. In the next five years the idea of the bluegrass festival as an annual weekend event slowly spread; a landmark was Monroe's own festival at his country music park in Bean Blossom, Ind., first held in 1967. By the end of the decade few of the pioneering groups, other than Monroe's, were intact. Jim and Jesse, the Osborne Brothers, and the Dillards had "gone electric." Both Flatt and Scruggs and Reno and Smiley had split, Carter Stanley had died, and John Duffey, cofounder of the Country Gentlemen, had retired from that group. In spite of these changes, the bluegrass festival idea had caught on, and by 1971, when Bill Monroe was elected to the Country Music Hall of Fame, the music was better established than ever before, with hundreds of festivals each year, the largest of which attracted audiences in the tens of thousands.

During the 1970s bluegrass music developed in a number of directions across a spectrum ranging from the "traditional" approach of the bands hewing closely to the sound and repertoire of the 1945–55 period to that of "newgrass" groups using rock repertoire and arranging techniques while retaining bluegrass instrumentation and performance styles. By the mid-1970s bluegrass was festival oriented, further outside the country music orbit in some ways, but because of its success in the festival milieu, more highly respected within the country music business. Monroe continued to be an important figure, as did Ralph Stanley and Lester Flatt; Jim and Jesse and the Osborne Brothers returned to the fold; and John Duffey teamed up with other Washington-area musicians to form the influential Seldom Scene. A host of younger musicians were active, including the Louisville-based Newgrass Revival, which mixed country rock with bluegrass in a way that created some controversy among fans, and J. D. Crowe and the New South, which worked toward a country-bluegrass synthesis. At the beginning of the 1980s these and other bands shared the marketplace with individual performers like Earl Scruggs, Ricky Scaggs, and David Grisman, who divided their musical time between bluegrass and other forms.

As the festival movement grew, a bluegrass "establishment" appeared. Specialized record companies—County, Rebel, Rounder, and Sugar Hill are the best-known labels—were established, and regional clubs, often called "area committees," appeared. A few national and many local magazines were initiated, several gaining extensive readerships. The oldest and largest is *Bluegrass Unlimited*, published in northern Virginia, close by the Washington, D.C., area, which is reckoned by most to be the center of bluegrass music activities in the United States today. There are now instrumental instruction books and recorded instruction courses for this once aural-oral style. Spread by festivals and certain types of media exposure (particularly television and movie soundtracks), bluegrass is performed throughout the United States and Canada, though its greatest popularity is in the Southeast. There is interest in the music outside North America, particularly in Japan and Western Europe, where U.S. bands tour regularly and some local bands perform. Although a number of musicians make their living from the music, it is increasingly maintained and perpetuated by amateur and semiprofessional musicians. Today, bluegrass is encountered at fiddle conventions and contests and at other traditional musical gatherings throughout the South. Once a specialized musical style performed only by a few, it has become a standard form of southern musical expression, one, by virtue of its popularity outside the region, that is more accessible and understandable to outsiders than were earlier indigenous forms.

Neil V. Rosenberg
Memorial University
St. Johns, Newfoundland

Thomas Adler, *Folklore Forum*, 7 (1974); Bob Artis, *Bluegrass: From the Lonesome Wail of a Mountain Love Song to the Hammering Drive of the Scruggs-Style Banjo, The Story of an American Musical Tradition* (1975); Fred Bartenstein, *Journal of Country Music* (Fall, 1973); Robert Cantwell, *Bluegrass*

Breakdown: The Making of the Old Southern Sound (1984); George O. Carney, *Journal of Geography* (1974); Neil V. Rosenberg, *Bluegrass: A History* (1985), *Journal of American Folklore* (April–June 1967); L. Mayne Smith, *Journal of American Folklore* (July–September 1965).

Blues

In the 1890s several new musical forms arose in the black communities of the southern and border states. Among the most important of these forms were ragtime, jazz, and blues. The generation that created this new music had been born in the years immediately following the Civil War, the first generation of blacks that did not directly experience slavery. As this generation reached maturity in the 1890s, there arose within it a restlessness to try out new ideas and new courses of action. New economic, social, and political institutions were created to provide a network of mutual support within the black community in the face of a hardening of discriminatory patterns of race relations and Jim Crow legislation. Pentecostal denominations with a more emotional style of worship arose to meet the spiritual needs of many who were trying to improve their lot in life and cope with problems of urban migration, industrialism, and unemployment.

These social changes were reflected in new developments in the arts at all levels—formal, popular, and folk—and in none of the arts was the ferment as intense as in music. In border states like Missouri, Kansas, and Kentucky, where blacks had greater opportunities to obtain formal training in music and were exposed to a variety of popular and even classical music forms, they created ragtime. At this same time the first stirrings of jazz were heard in southern cities along the Atlantic and Gulf coasts, particularly in New Orleans. Blues, on the other hand, was created in the rural areas and small towns of the Deep South, particularly in the areas of large plantations, such as the Mississippi Delta, and in industries that required heavy manual labor, such as mining, logging, levee and railroad construction, and freight loading. Those who sought work as sharecroppers and harvesters on the plantations and in the other industries were hoping to escape the drudgery and hopelessness of life on tiny plots of worn-out farmland and earn some cash for their labor. With little education or property, and no political power in a completely segregated society, they often encountered intolerable working conditions and moved frequently from one plantation or job to another.

Out of this dissatisfaction arose the blues, a music that reflected not only the social isolation and lack of formal training of its creators but also their ability to make do with the most basic of resources and to survive under the most adverse, oppressive circumstances. Blues drew from Western formal music in only the most superficial ways and instead was comprised almost entirely of resources and elements taken from the existing black folk music tradition. Unlike ragtime and jazz, blues has never been fully accepted by mainstream America as a distinct major musical form. Instead it has tended to be viewed as a rather simple and limited, though at times charming and powerfully expressive, type of music, suitable mainly as raw material for jazz, rock and roll, or some other more complex popular music. In the history of these other types of music, blues is viewed as one of the "roots."

Blues introduced a number of new elements into American musical consciousness. The most novel in its initial impact, and now one of the most pervasive elements in American popular music, is the "blue note." Blue notes generally occur at the third and seventh degrees of the scale, though sometimes at other points as well, and can be either flatted notes, neutral pitches, waverings, or sliding tones occurring in the range between the major and minor of these points on the scale. Another primary musical characteristic is the role of the accompanying instrument as a second voice. The musical accompaniment in blues is not simply a rhythmic and harmonic background to the singing. It constantly interacts with, punctuates, and answers the vocal line. Finally, blues introduced a new realism combined with greater individualism into American popular song. During the 1890s most popular songs were either humorous, sentimental, or tragic, dramatizing unusual or exotic situations. The "coon songs" that depicted black life generally portrayed either nostalgic scenes of the old plantation, romantic love, or absurd humor. Blues, on the other hand, dealt with everyday life and met its subjects head-on in an open-ended celebration of life's ups and downs. Although blues focused on relationships between men and women, it did not avoid commenting on such subjects as working conditions, migration, current events, natural disasters, sickness and death, crime and punishment, alcohol and drugs, sorcery, and racial discrimination. As a secular music, blues generally avoided making religious statements, although it could ridicule preachers and discuss the temptations and powers of the devil, and as a highly individualistic statement it seldom mentioned family and organized community life other than the immediate context of the dance or party where the music was performed. Blues developed an extraordinary compactness of form and startling poetic imagery in order to make its points on such a broad range of subjects.

The basic vocal material for early folk blues came from hollers that were sung by workers in the fields and in other occupations requiring manual labor. Hollers were sung solo in freely embellished descending lines employing blue notes and a great variety of vocal timbres. The words tended to be traditional commonplace phrases on the man-woman relationship or the work situation, with successive lines linked to one another through loose thematic associations and contrasts. Hollers appeared to be a direct reflection of the singer's state of mind and feelings poured out in a stream of consciousness. This type of singing had existed long before the 1890s. It was noted by observers during the slavery period and has clear parallels in some singing traditions in Africa and other Afro-American cultures; but it was in the American South that these free, almost formless, vocal expressions were set to instrumental accompaniment and given a musical structure, an expanded range of subject matter, and a new social context.

The accompaniment was most often played on instruments that had been rarely used in older forms of black folk music—the piano, the harmonica, and especially the guitar. For the guitar unorthodox tunings were often used to obtain drone effects. The technique of bending strings helped to achieve blue notes, and sometimes the player would slide a knife, bottleneck, or other hard object along the strings to produce a whining tone, a technique adapted from African stringed instruments. At times the performer established a simple rhythmic pattern behind the singing and then answered the vocal lines with short repeated melodic/rhythmic figures on the guitar. Blues of this sort is basically instrumentally accompanied hollers, and they allow much of the vocal freedom of the older type of song to be preserved. A few rural blues singers still compose and perform blues in this manner. Other performers, however, saw the need for greater structure in their blues and began to fit the vocal lines taken from hollers to existing harmonic patterns. Usually these patterns accommodated stanzas of 8, 12, or 16 measures, but the blues singers left space at the ends of their lines for the instrument to answer the vocal.

The pattern that proved to be predominant by the early 20th century contained three lines of four measures each. The second line repeated the first, and the third line was different but rhymed with the first two. The lines began, respectively, with harmonies in the tonic, subdominant, and dominant chords but always resolved to the tonic. This now-familiar 12-bar AAB pattern derived from 3-line patterns found in such folk ragtime tunes as "Bully of the Town" and blues ballads like "Stagolee" and "Boll Weevil." Blues singers slowed the tempos of these tunes and left room at the ends of the lines for their instrumental response.

As the blues spread in the early 20th century, local and regional performance traditions developed in different parts of the South. At the local level, performers would share a repertoire of traditional verses and melodic and instrumental phrases, recombining these endlessly and often adding further musical and lyrical elements of their own creation to form blues that sounded original yet familiar at the same time. Within broader geographic regions the performers generally shared an overall musical stylistic approach and sometimes variants of certain songs in their repertoires. For instance, in the Mississippi Valley and adjacent areas the folk blues was the most intense rhythmically and emotionally, more modal and less harmonic in conception, often structured upon short repeated melodic/rhythmic phrases, and tending to extract the maximum expression from each note. Variants of tunes like "Catfish Blues" and "Rolling and Tumbling" are familiar to many blues singers throughout this region.

In Texas the guitarists often set up a constant thumping rhythm in the bass, while treble figures were played in a rather free rhythmic style in response to vocal lines that tended more to float over the constant bass rhythm. From Texas guitarists like Aaron "T-Bone" Walker came the contemporary style of lead guitar playing, in which the guitar lines often seem to float over a steady rhythm supplied by the other instruments in the band. In Virginia and the Carolinas, as well as some parts of Georgia and Florida, another style developed featuring lighter, bouncier rhythms, virtuoso playing, a harmonic rather than modal conception, and a pervasive influence of ragtime music on the blues. In whatever region the early folk blues was performed, the contexts were usually the same. Generally this music was played at house parties, roadhouses called juke joints, outdoor picnics for dancing, and for tips from onlookers on sidewalks, railroad stations, store porches, and wherever else a crowd might gather.

In the first decade of the 20th century professional singers in traveling shows began to incorporate blues into their stage repertoires as they worked in the towns and cities of the southern states. W. C. Handy, at that time the leader of a band sponsored by a black fraternal organization in Clarksdale, Miss., encountered folk blues and was so impressed by the music's appeal to both black and white audiences that he began to arrange these tunes for his own group of trained musicians. His success led him to Memphis, and there he published his first blues in sheet music form in 1912. Other blues was published that same year, and soon a flood of new blues compositions appeared from southern songwriters, both black and white, drawing on the resources of folk blues. The songwriters considered folk blues raw material to be extensively reworked and exploited.

At first the general public perceived blues as a novel type of ragtime tune with the unusual features of blue notes and three-line stanzas. The professional singers were generally women accompanied by a pianist or a small jazz combo. They performed in both the North and South in urban cabarets and vaudeville theaters and sometimes in traveling shows that visited small southern towns. This professionalized type of blues first appeared on phonograph records by black singers like Ma Rainey, Bessie Smith, Clara Smith, and Ida Cox, beginning in 1920. By 1926 the record companies began to record folk blues artists, mostly male singers playing their own guitar accompaniments, like Blind Lemon Jefferson from Texas, Charley Patton and Tommy Johnson from Mississippi, and Peg Leg Howell and Blind Willie McTell from Georgia. By the end of the 1920s the companies were also recording many boogie-woogie and barrelhouse pianists such as Pinetop Smith and Roosevelt Sykes.

String bands, brass bands, and vocal quartets had incorporated blues into their repertoires by the first decade of the 20th century, but by the late 1920s there had arisen new types of ensembles created mainly to perform blues. Perhaps the closest to folk blues were the jug bands, which generally consisted of a guitar and harmonica supplemented by other novelty or homemade instruments such as a jug, kazoo, washboard, or one-stringed bass. Jug bands were recorded in Louisville, Cincinnati, Memphis, Birmingham, and Dallas, and similar kinds of "skiffle" bands existed in many other cities and towns in the South and North.

The combination of a full chorded rhythmic piano and guitar playing melodic lead lines also became popular at this time. The chief exponents of this style of blues were pianist Leroy Carr and guitarist Francis "Scrapper" Blackwell, who were based in Indianapolis. Pianist Georgia Tom (Thomas A. Dorsey) and guitarist Tampa Red (Hudson Whitaker) also made many popular recordings at this time, often performing "hokum" blues that contained humorous verses and double entendre refrains. Various combinations of stringed instruments as well as jug bands also performed hokum blues. By the mid-1930s blues bands not uncommonly consisted of a string section made up of blues musicians and a horn-and-rhythm section made up of artists with a jazz background. One of the most popular of such groups, the Harlem Hamfats, featured trumpet, clarinet, piano, guitar, second guitar or mandolin, string bass, and drums.

The continuing influence of jazz and the rise to prominence of the electric guitar served to reshape the sound of the blues in the years following World War II. Small "jump" bands of jazz-influenced musicians became popular in the late 1940s and 1950s, often performing a mixture of blues and sentimental popular songs. Folk blues guitarists in the rural South converted to the new electric guitar, and a new type of blues combo appeared consisting usually of one or two electric guitars, bass, piano or electric organ, drums, and sometimes an amplified harmonica. This type of blues reached its peak of development in Chicago in the 1950s with the bands of artists such as Muddy Waters (McKinley Morganfield) and Howlin' Wolf (Chester Burnett), both originally from Mississippi.

Howlin' Wolf, bluesman, 1970s

A synthesis of the hard down-home style of blues and the sophisticated jump blues was achieved by Aaron "T-Bone" Walker from Texas and B. B. King, a Mississippian who had moved to Memphis. Both men had strong roots in the folk blues tradition and had learned to play electric lead guitar fronting a large band of trained musicians. Their vocals were delivered in an impassioned shouting style showing the influence of gospel singing. This type of blues, developed by Walker in the 1940s and brought to its peak of development by King in the 1950s, remains the most popular blues style.

While blues has had a history of its own, it has also had a profound influence upon other types of popular music in the 20th century. When popular blues began to be published in 1912 and performed by trained musicians, it was perceived as a new type of ragtime tune with a novel three-line verse form and the exotic element of blue notes. The use of blue notes not only helped to loosen up the formalism of ragtime but also soon paved the way for improvisatory jazz performance. The bulk of the repertoire of the early jazz bands consisted of blues tunes and ragtime tunes incorporating blue notes. The blues form has continued to be a staple for jazz compositions, and whenever jazz has seemed to become overly sophisticated, one usually hears calls for a return to the blues.

In the years before World War I, southern Anglo-American folk musicians began performing blues learned from black musicians. By the 1920s "hillbilly" artists from all parts of the South were recording the blues. Beginning in 1927 the Mississippi singer and guitarist Jimmie Rodgers popularized a distinct type of blues by combining folk blues learned from black artists with a yodeling refrain derived from both black field hollers and German/Swiss yodeling that had been popularized on the vaudeville stage. Over the years blues has given to varieties of country music, such as western swing and honky-tonk, not only the blues form but the qualities of improvisation and greater realism as well.

In the 1950s blues-influenced country music combined with black rhythm and blues to produce a new form of music that came to be known as rock and roll. The blues form and blues instrumental techniques were very prominent in most rock-and-roll styles through the 1960s and have continued to be important factors in this music's development up to the present. Blues gave rock and roll not only an important verse form but also its basic instrumentation and instrumental technique as well as a frankness in dealing with themes of love and sex that proved attractive to an adolescent audience.

Finally, blues could even be said to have influenced gospel music. Thomas A. Dorsey, generally considered the "father of gospel music," was a former blues pianist and songwriter. By the early 1930s he was composing gospel songs using blue notes and showing a greater individualism and worldliness in the themes. While gospel has seldom utilized the blues verse form, it has shown blues influence through its use of blues tonality and emphasis on the individual.

Most Americans today are probably more familiar with blues-influenced music than they are with blues itself. Nevertheless, blues is still a thriving form of music, existing in a variety of styles. In the South there are still excellent solo performers of folk blues, while small combos featuring electric lead guitar perform regularly in black communities in the region as well as in northern and West Coast cities. Blues can be heard today in forms close to the earliest folk blues, showing that it is still in touch with its roots, and within modern jazz and rock and roll, showing the enormous impact it has had over the last century.

See also BLACK LIFE: Music, Black; / Johnson, Robert; WOMEN'S LIFE: Blues-singing Women

David Evans
Memphis State University

Bruce Bastin, *Crying for the Carolines* (1971), *Red River Blues: The Blues Tradition in the Southeast* (1986); Samuel Charters, *The Bluesmen: The Story and the Music of the Men Who Made the Blues* (1967); David Evans, *Big Road Blues: Tradition and Creativity in the Folk Blues* (1982), *Tommy Johnson* (1971); John Fahey, *Charley Patton* (1970); William Ferris, *Blues from the Delta* (1978); Paul Oliver, *Conversation with the Blues* (1965), *The Meaning of the Blues* (1963), *The Story of the Blues* (1969); Harry Oster, *Living Country Blues* (1969); Robert Palmer, *Deep Blues* (1981); Jeff Todd Titon, *Early Downhome Blues: A Musical and Cultural Analysis* (1977).

Cajun Music

Cajun music blends elements of American Indian, Scotch-Irish, Spanish, German, Anglo-American, and Afro-Caribbean musics with a rich stock of western French folk traditions. The music traces back to the Acadians, the French colonists who began settling at Port Royal, Acadia, in 1604. The Acadians were eventually deported from their homeland in 1755 by local British authorities after years of political and religious tension. In 1765, after 10 years of wandering, many Acadians began to arrive in Louisiana, determined to re-create their society. Within a generation these exiles had so firmly reestablished themselves as a people that they became the dominant culture in south Louisiana, absorbing other ethnic groups around them. Most of the French Creoles (descendants of earlier French settlers), Spanish, Germans, and Anglo-Americans in the region eventually adopted the traditions and language of this new society, thus creating the south Louisiana mainstream. The Acadians, in turn, borrowed many traits from these other cultures, and this cross-cultural exchange produced a new Louisiana-based community—the Cajuns.

The Acadians' contact with these various cultures contributed to the development of new musical styles and repertoire. From Indians, they learned wailing styles and new dance rhythms; from blacks, they learned the blues, percussion techniques, and improvisational singing; from Anglo-Americans, they learned new fiddle tunes to accompany Virginia reels, square dances, and hoedowns. The Spanish contributed the guitar and even a few tunes. Refugees and their slaves who arrived from Santo Domingo at the turn of the 19th century brought with them a syncopated West Indian beat. Jewish-German immigrants began importing diatonic accordions (invented in Vienna in 1828) toward the end of the 19th century when Acadians and black Creoles began to show an interest in the instruments. They blended these elements to create a new music just as they were synthesizing the same cultures to create Cajun society.

The turn of the 20th century was a formative period in the development of Louisiana French music. Some of its most influential musicians were the black Creoles who brought a strong, rural blues element into Cajun music. Simultaneously, blacks influenced the parallel development of zydeco music, later refined by Clifton Chenier. Although fiddlers such as Dennis McGee and Sady Courville still composed tunes, the accordion was rapidly becoming the mainstay of traditional dance bands. Limited in the number of notes and keys it could play in, it simplified Cajun music; songs that could not be played on the accordion faded from the active repertoire. Meanwhile, fiddlers were often relegated to playing a duet accompaniment or a simple percussive second line below the accordion's melodic lead.

By the mid-1930s, Cajuns were reluctantly, though inevitably, becoming Americanized. Their French language was banned from schools throughout south Louisiana as America, caught in the melting pot ideology, tried to homogenize its diverse ethnic and cultural elements. In south Louisiana, speaking French was not only against the rules, it became increasingly unpopular as Cajuns attempted to escape the stigma attached to their culture. New highways and improved transportation opened this previously isolated area to the rest of the country, and the Cajuns began to imitate their Anglo-American neighbors in earnest.

The social and cultural changes of the 1930s and 1940s were clearly reflected in the music recorded in this period. The slick programming on radio (and later on television) inadvertently forced the comparatively unpolished traditional sounds underground. The accordion faded from the scene, partly because the old-style music had lost popularity and partly because the instruments were unavailable from Germany during the war. As western swing and bluegrass sounds from Texas and Tennessee swept the country, string bands that imitated the music of Bob Wills and the Texas Playboys and copied Bill Monroe's "high lonesome sound" sprouted across south Louisiana. Freed from the limitations imposed by the accordion, string bands readily absorbed various outside influences. Dancers across south Louisiana were shocked in the mid-1930s to hear music that came not only from the bandstand, but also from the opposite end of the dance hall through speakers powered by a Model-T behind the building. The electric steel guitar was added to the standard instrumentation and drums replaced the triangle as Cajuns continued to experiment with new sounds borrowed from their Anglo-American neighbors. As amplification made it unnecessary for fiddlers to bear down with the bow to be audible, they developed a lighter, lilting touch, moving away from the soulful styles of earlier days.

By the late 1940s, the music recorded by commercial producers signaled an unmistakable tendency toward Americanization. Yet an undercurrent of traditional music persisted. It resurfaced with the music of Iry Lejune, who accompanied the Oklahoma Tornadoes in 1948 to record "La Valse du Pont d'Amour" in the turn of the century Louisiana style and in French. The recording was an unexpected success, presaging a revival of the earlier style, and Iry Lejune became a pivotal figure in a Cajun music revival. Dance halls providing traditional music flourished, and musicians such as Lawrence Walker, Austin Pitre, and Nathan Abshire brought their accordions out of the closet and once again performed old-style Cajun music, while local companies began recording them. Cajun music, though bearing the marks of Americanization, was making a dramatic comeback, just as interest in the culture and language quickened before the 1955 bicentennial celebration of the Acadian exile.

Alan Lomax, a member of the Newport Folk Festival Foundation who had become interested in Louisiana French folk music during a field trip with his father in the 1930s, encouraged the documentation and preservation of Cajun music. In the late 1950s, Harry Oster began recording a spectrum of Cajun music ranging from unaccompanied ballads to contemporary dance tunes. His collection, which stressed the evolution of the music, attracted the attention of local activists, such as Paul Tate and Revon Reed. The work of Oster and Lomax was noticed by the Newport Foundation, which sent fieldworkers Ralph Rinzler and Mike Seeger to south Louisiana. Cajun dance bands had played at the National Folk Festival as early as 1935, but little echo of these performances reached Louisiana. Rinzler and Seeger, seeking the unadorned roots of Cajun music, chose Gladius Thibodeaux, Louis "Vinesse" Lejune, and Dewey Balfa to represent Louisiana at the 1964 Newport Folk Festival. Their "gutsy," unamplified folk music made the Louisiana cultural establishment uneasy, for such "unrefined" sounds embarrassed the upwardly mobile Cajuns who considered the music chosen for the Newport festival crude—"nothing but chanky-chank."

The instincts of the Newport festival organizers proved well-founded, as huge crowds gave the old-time music standing ovations. Dewey Balfa was so moved that he returned to Louisiana determined to bring the message home. He began working on a small scale among his friends and family in Mamou, Basile, and Eunice. The Newport Folk Foundation, under the guidance of Lomax, provided money and fieldworkers to the new Louisiana Folk Foundation "to water the roots." With financial support and outside approval, local activists became involved in preserving the music, language, and culture. Traditional music contests and concerts were organized at events such as the Abbeville Dairy Festival, the Opelousas Yambilee, and the Crowley Rice Festival.

In 1968 the state of Louisiana officially recognized the Cajun cultural revival, which had been brewing under the leadership of the music community and political leaders, such as Dudley LeBlanc and Roy Theriot. In that year, it created the Council for the Development of French in Louisiana (CODOFIL), which, under the chairmanship of James Domengeaux, began its efforts on political, psychological, and educational fronts to erase the stigma Louisianans had long attached to the French language and culture. The creation of French classes in elementary schools dramatically reversed the policy that had formerly barred the language from the schoolgrounds.

Domengeaux's efforts were not limited to the classroom. Influenced by Rinzler and Balfa, CODOFIL organized a first Tribute to Cajun Music festival in 1974 with a concert designed to present a historical overview of Cajun music from its origins to modern styles. The echo had finally come home. Dewey Balfa's message of cultural self-esteem was enthusiastically received by an audience of over 12,000.

Because of its success, the festival became an annual celebration of Cajun music and culture, not only providing exposure for the musicians but presenting them as culture heroes. Young performers were attracted to the revalidated Cajun music scene, while local French government officials, realizing the impact of the grass-roots, began to stress the native Louisiana French culture. Balfa's dogged pursuit of cultural recognition carried him farther than he had ever expected. In 1977 he received a Folk Artist in the Schools grant from the National Endowment for the Arts to bring his message into elementary school classrooms. Young Cajuns, discovering local models besides country and rock stars, began to perform the music of their heritage. Yet they did not reject modern sounds totally. Performers such as Michael Doucet and Beausoleil are gradually making their presence known in Cajun music, replacing older musicians on the regular weekend dance hall circuit and representing traditional Cajun music at local and national festivals.

See also ETHNIC LIFE: / Cajuns and Creoles

Barry Jean Ancelet
University of Southwestern Louisiana

Barry Jean Ancelet, *The Makers of Cajun Music / Musiciens Cadiens et Créoles* (1984); Glenn R. Conrad, ed., *The Cajuns: Essays on Their History and Culture* (3d ed., 1983); *J'etais au bal: Music from French Louisiana* (Swallow 6020); *Louisiana Cajun Music* (Old-Timey Records, 108, 109, 110, 111, 114, 124, and 125); *Louisiana French Cajun Music from the Southwest Prairies* (Rounder Records, 6001 and 6002); Lauren Post, *Cajun Sketches from the Prairies of Southwest Louisiana* (2d ed., 1974); Irene Therese Whitfield, *Louisiana French Folk Song* (1969).

Classical Music and Opera

By the 18th century it had become a mark of social distinction for members of the seaboard gentry to demonstrate an appreciation of good music and even play an instrument themselves. Jefferson enjoyed the violin and collected a fine music library, consisting of pieces by Corelli, Bach, Handel, and Haydn, whereas William Byrd's library at Westover included examples of English and Italian opera. Williamsburg emerged as the music center of Virginia, after Peter Pelham began giving recitals there in 1752. Amateur concerts were also held weekly in the drawing room of the Governor's Palace.

Musical life in Charleston became even more sophisticated. The first known concert in that city was presented in April 1732 when John Salter, a local church organist, offered a program in the council chamber. The first ballad opera given in America, *Flora, or, Hob in the Well,* was staged at the courtroom in Charleston three years later. In 1762 the St. Cecilia Society, the oldest musical society in the United States, was founded by 120 Carolina gentlemen who supported a paid orchestra and a yearly series of concerts. Foreign artists were occasionally imported; Maria Storer, perhaps the finest singer to perform in colonial America, was heard in February 1774. The St. Cecilia Society remained in existence until 1912, although the orchestra was eventually reduced to a quintet.

The Moravian settlements of the colonial South, most notably Salem, N.C., held musical festivals, built organs, and were noted for the quality of their choral singing. Other German and French immigrants brought with them a love of serious music and often scores of musical instruments. By the 19th century New Orleans had eclipsed Charleston as a music center, especially in the production of French and Italian opera. By the Civil War violinist Ole Bull and pianist Louis Moreau Gottschalk had played concerts all through the South, while soprano Jenny Lind had been heard in Richmond, Charleston, New Orleans, Natchez, and Memphis.

The first opera known to have been presented in New Orleans was André Grétry's *Sylvain,* given on 22 May 1796, at the St. Peter Street Theater, although there is reason to think earlier productions had been staged there. Later works by Boieldieu, Mehul, Dalayrac, and Monsigny (all stalwarts in Paris) were heard at the St. Peter Street Theater. Throughout the 19th century New Orleans had at least one resident opera company. The Théâtre d'Orléans was built in 1809, rapidly becoming the city's cultural center. The theater burned in 1813, but was quickly rebuilt. Artists were recruited each season from the Paris Opera House, making the staging of works by Rossini, Spontini, Mozart, Gluck, Cherubini, and other European masters possible. Meyerbeer's *Les Huguenots* and Donizetti's *Lucia di Lammermoor* (sung in French) were but two of the many operas to receive American premieres at the Théâtre d'Orléans.

Memphis's Grand Opera House, early 1900s

In 1835 Meyerbeer's *Robert le Diable* was staged for the first time in the United States at James Caldwell's Anglo-American Theater on Camp Street in New Orleans. The following season an Italian troupe presented the American premiere of Bellini's *Il Pirata* at the St. Charles Theater. After 1859 the French Opera House became the city's major lyric theater. Soprano Adelina Patti was engaged for a series of performances during the theater's second season, whereas Massenet's *Herodiade,* Lalo's *Le Roi d'Ys,* and Saint-Säens's *Samson and Delilah* all received their initial American staging there after the Civil War. The well-rehearsed and lavishly mounted productions featured ballet adeptly prepared in the French tradition. Closed during the Civil War, the French Opera House reopened to become "the lyric temple of the South." Not until the close of the century, as New Orleans evolved from a Latin city to a predominantly Anglo-American one, did the theater fall on hard times. The French Opera House burned in 1919, following years of neglect and financial decline.

Although French conductor Antoine Jullien had led concerts in New Orleans before the Civil War, Patrick S. Gilmore rejuvenated a taste for "monster concerts" in 1864, when he assembled a chorus of 5,000 and a band of 500 to perform in Lafayette Square to celebrate Louisiana's return to the Union, a jubilee complete with fife-and-drum corps, church bells, and cannons. Resident orchestras of professional stature were not to return to the South, however, until the 20th century. By 1890, 6 of the 34 symphony orchestras of the United States classified as major orchestras were located in the South. Of those the Dallas Symphony was the first to achieve that status. An orchestra for Dallas had been conceived in 1900 when Hans Kreissig, a German musician stranded in the city, gathered together what local talent he could and organized the Dallas Symphony Club. Five years later a more formal attempt to establish a symphony was made by Walter Fried, who had studied conducting in Germany. The modern Dallas Symphony was launched in 1945 with the appointment of Antal Dorati as conductor. Dorati broadened the standard romantic repertoire to include unusual selections by Schumann and Mendelssohn and introduced both classical and modern compositions, not always to the pleasure of conservative Dallas audiences. When Dorati accepted an offer from the Minneapolis Symphony in 1949, he was replaced by Walter Hendl, formerly associate conductor of the New York Philharmonic. Since 1958 the Dallas Symphony has met with varying success under the leadership of Paul Kletzki, Georg Solti, Donald Johannos, Anshel Brusilow, and Eduardo Mata.

The Houston Symphony, begun in 1913 under Julian

Paul Blitz, reached major status after Efrem Kurtz was made director in 1948. Later a succession of superlative conductors—including Sir Thomas Beecham, Leopold Stokowski, Sir John Barbirolli, and Andre Previn—honed the Houston Symphony into the finest orchestra in the South. On tour under Barbirolli in 1964, the symphony performed at Philharmonic Hall in New York City, winning a prolonged ovation. Two years later the orchestra moved into the resplendent Jesse H. Jones Hall for the Performing Arts; it is currently under the direction of Michael Palmer.

Other major symphony orchestras in the South include the Atlanta Symphony under Robert Shaw, the New Orleans Symphony under Dean Angeles, the North Carolina Symphony under the direction of Gerhardt Zimmerman, and the San Antonio Symphony under the direction of Lawrence Smith. In addition, 10 of the nation's 18 regional orchestras are located in the South. Every southern city of importance has received international concert artists on tour: Paderewski, Caruso, Iturbi, Gigli, Rubinstein, and Heifetz. Pianist Van Cliburn from Kilgore, Tex., who won the International Tchaikovsky Competition in Moscow in 1958, and soprano Leontyne Price from Laurel, Miss., have each achieved world recognition on the concert stage and through recordings.

During the 1920s the Chicago Civic Opera and later the San Carlo Opera toured the larger southern cities, and New York's Metropolitan Opera Company makes annual visits to Atlanta and Dallas. Resident opera returned to New Orleans in 1943, soon evolving into the New Orleans Opera House Association under the direction of Walter Herbert. Unusual French works have occasionally been revived by the New Orleans Opera, and Verdi's *Attila* was staged by the company in 1969 for the first time in this country since 1850. By 1980 the South supported 14 professional opera companies, 3 of them of major importance.

The Greater Miami Opera Association was begun in 1941 on a limited budget under the management of Arturo Di Filippi. The first opera staged by the Florida company was *I Pagliacci*, with Di Filippi himself singing the role of Canio. Under Robert Herman the company expanded its budget, employing singers like Eileen Farrell, Franco Corelli, Joan Sutherland, and Luciano Pavarotti in his American debut. The Houston Grand Opera was formed in 1956, with Richard Strauss's *Salome* its initial work. A mounting of *Die Walküre* in 1959 gave the South a rare look at Wagner's *Ring* cycle, whereas Massenet's *Don Quichotte* in 1969 and Rossini's *La Donna del Lago* in 1981 were both operas rarely presented anywhere in the United States. The company also revived Scott Joplin's long forgotten ragtime opera *Treemonisha* and Gershwin's *Porgy and Bess*, productions that were eventually taken to Broadway and the West Coast.

The Dallas Opera, founded in 1957 by Lawrence V. Kelly, has enjoyed solid financial backing and unusual artistic leadership. Soprano Maria Callas launched the company with a series of performances that included a gala concert, Verdi's *La Traviata*, Cherubini's *Medea*, and Donizetti's *Lucia di Lammermoor*. Nicola Rescigno was named musical director, while Italian stage director Franco Zeffirelli did his first work in America with the Dallas company. Alexis Minotis was imported from the Greek national theater to mount the internationally acclaimed production of *Medea*, which eventually traveled to Covent Garden, La Scala, and Epidaurus. Jean Rosenthal and later Tharon Musser came from Broadway to supervise the company's lighting. Joan Sutherland, Montserrat Caballé, Jon Vickers, Teresa Berganza, Gwyneth Jones, Placido Domingo, Helga Dernesch, and the legendary Italian soprano Magda Olivero all made their American debuts with the Dallas Opera, while the company has staged the American premieres of Handel's *Alcina* and Vivaldi's *Orlando Furioso*.

Charleston reemerged as a music center when Gian Carlo Menotti brought the Spoleto Festival to the New World in May 1977. Since then summer offerings in Charleston have ranged from Tchaikovsky's *The Queen of Spades* (with Olivero as the old Countess) to Haydn's *Creation* to Barber's *Vanessa* to Shostakovich's *Lady Macbeth of the Mtsensk District*. Other southern opera companies include the Charlotte Opera Association, Civic Opera of the Palm Beaches, the Fort Worth Opera, Opera Memphis, and Opera/South in Jackson, Miss.

The South has inspired a variety of serious compositions. Bohemian-born Anton Philip Heinrich immigrated to the United States in 1805, publishing his *The Dawning of Music in Kentucky* 15 years later. Early in the 20th century Henry F. Gilbert wrote *Dance in Place Congo* and a *Negro Rhapsody* based on black folk melodies. George Gershwin spent several months in South Carolina gathering material for his opera *Porgy and Bess*, and Ferde Grofé, Gershwin's orchestrator on *Rhapsody in Blue*, himself wrote *Mississippi Suite* in 1925.

John Powell, a native of Richmond, Va., who studied in Vienna, used Afro-American themes in his *Negro Rhapsody* (1918) and Anglo-American folk tunes in his overture *In Old Virginia* (1921). William Grant Still, born on a plantation near Woodville, Miss., developed into a major spokesman for blacks in serious music. His *Afro-American Symphony* was initially performed by the Rochester Philharmonic in 1931, although opera remained the composer's great love. *A Southern Interlude* and especially *A Bayou Legend*, both dating from the 1940s, have solidified Still's reputation among opera enthusiasts. Carlisle Floyd, a native of Latta, S.C., established himself as an American opera composer of the first order with *Susannah* in 1955 and has continued to write prolifically in that field. *Wuthering Heights* was commissioned by the Santa Fe Opera in 1958, whereas *The Passion of Jonathan Wade*, set in North Carolina during the Civil War, received its premiere four years later at the New York City Opera under a Ford Foundation grant. *Willie Stark*, based on Robert Penn Warren's novel *All the King's Men*, was first staged by Harold Prince in 1981 for the Houston Grand Opera, in a production that combined elements of the operatic and Broadway theater.

Of composers working in a modern idiom, Georgia-born Wallingford Riegger stands at the forefront. Riegger produced a number of dance scores for Martha Graham, then concentrated more on orchestral forms. His *Fourth*

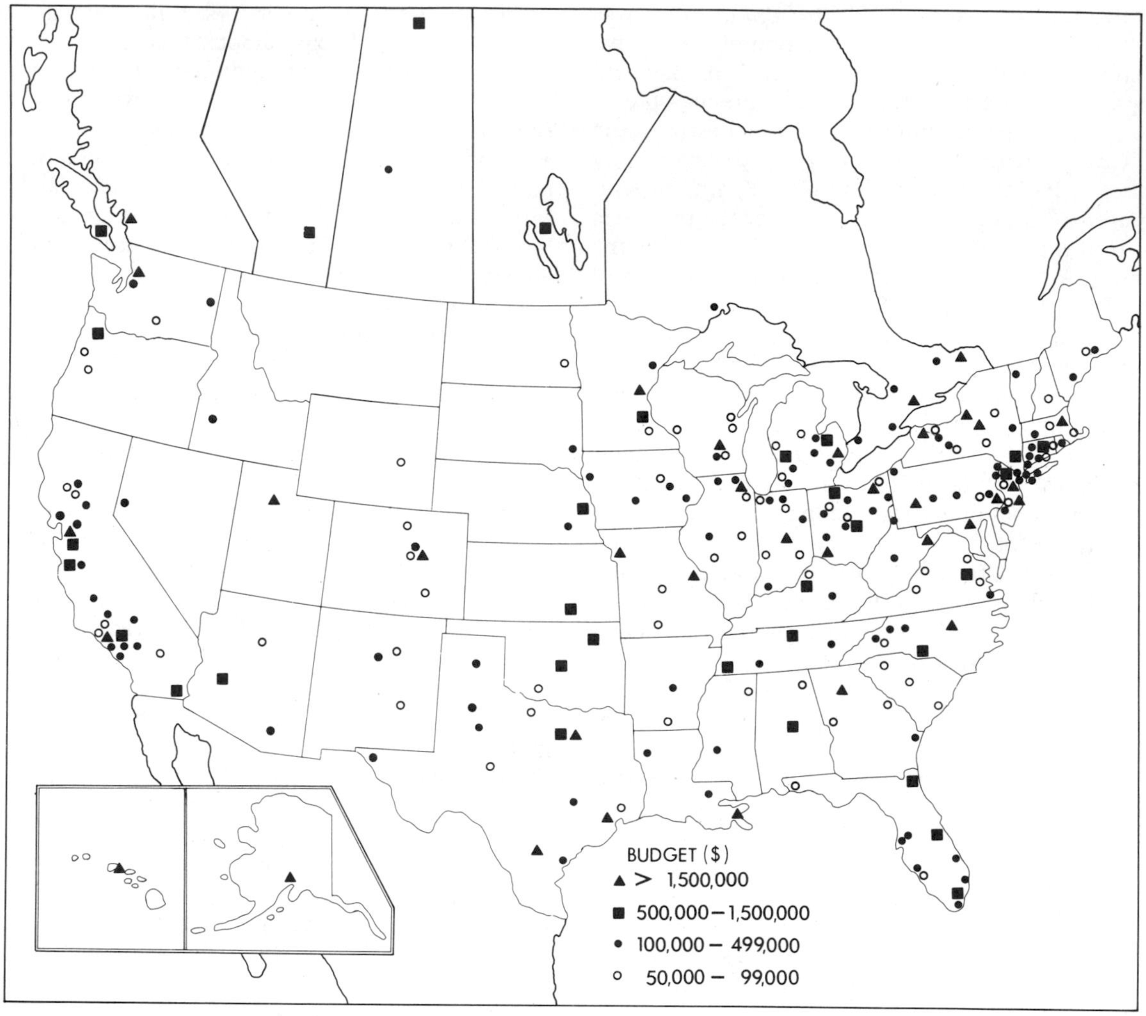

North American Symphony Orchestras

Map by George O. Carney

Source: John F. Rooney, Jr., Wilbur Zelinsky, and Dean R. Louder, eds., *This Remarkable Continent: An Atlas of United States and Canadian Society and Cultures* (1982).

Symphony (1959) was performed by the Boston Symphony Orchestra and judged by national critics to have both head and heart appeal. Other southern art composers include William Levi Dawson from Alabama, Lamar Stringfield from North Carolina, and Don Gillis from Texas.

See also RECREATION: Traveling Shows; / Spoleto Festival U.S.A.; St. Cecilia Ball

Ronald L. Davis
Southern Methodist University

Ronald L. Davis, *A History of Music in American Life*, 3 vols. (1980–82); Quaintance Eaton, *Opera Caravan* (1957); Robert Bartlett Haas, ed., *William Grant Still and the Fusion of Cultures in American Music* (1972); Henry A. Kmen, *Music in New Orleans: The Formative Years, 1791–1841* (1966); Hubert Roussel, *The Houston Symphony Orchestra, 1913–1971* (1972); Albert Stoutamire, *Music of the Old South: Colony to Confederacy* (1972).

Country Music

Although country music is a powerful cultural presence in the United States and an international export of growing magnitude, it is difficult to define. It has been a creation and organic reflection of southern working-class culture, changing as that society has changed, but it has been simultaneously a dynamic element of American popular culture. In the 60 years or so since Texas fiddler Eck Robertson made the first documented phonograph recording by a white rural entertainer, the music has become a massive industry with an appeal that cuts across social, generational, and geographic lines.

The Gully Jumpers, early country music string band, 1920s

Country music had its origins in the folk culture of the South—a diverse culture that drew upon the interrelating resources of Europe and Africa. It was British at its core but eclectic in its borrowing. Long before the decade of the 1920s, when the radio and recording industries made their first exploitations of southern folk talent, fiddlers, banjoists, string bands, balladeers, and gospel singers proliferated throughout the South. Most of their performances were given at house parties or other community functions such as house raisings, fish fries, or corn shuckings, but many were able to function on a broader basis, and in a quasi-professional manner, at fiddle contests or in medicine or vaudeville shows. Musicians drew upon their inherited folk resources for songs and performing styles, but they also picked up any compatible material that was adaptable to their styles and that fit their community aesthetic standards from black entertainers or from the vast panoply of 19th-century popular music. The establishment of radio stations in the South after 1920 (including WSB in Atlanta, WSM in Nashville, WBAP in Fort Worth) and the recording of rural performers after 1922 encouraged further professionalization as well as the development of an "industry."

The early entertainers were rural, for the most part, but not exclusively agricultural. Country music has always been a working-class music (although not self-consciously so until the 1960s). The performers of the early period, who were usually part-time musicians, worked as railroad men, coal miners, textile workers, carpenters, wagoners, sawmill workers, cowboys, and even occasionally as country lawyers, doctors, and preachers. Whatever their occupation, their dialects, speech patterns, and performing styles reflected the rural South. Given the social context of the 1920s, when the rural and socially conservative South seemed greatly out of step with a dynamic nation, and when its rural inhabitants seemed given over to strange oddities and eccentricities, ıch as snake handling, tenantry, and nightriding, it is surprising that a term such as *hillbilly* should be af- to the rural music of the region.

commercialization of southern rural music had both positive and negative consequences. On one hand, folk styles and folksongs received a wider hearing and, presumably, longer leases on life than they otherwise would have had; on the other hand, folk styles were homogenized and diluted, and traditional songs were gradually replaced with newly composed ones. But too much has been made of this change. Folk styles were never pure; folksongs were drawn from a multitude of sources; and folk musicians were never reluctant to accept or seek some kind of reward for their talents.

The string bands of country music's first decade, including such colorful examples of self-parody as the Skillet Lickers, the Fruit Jar Drinkers, the Possum Hunters, and Dr. Smith's Champion Hoss Hair Pullers, as well as the more conventionally named groups such as the North Carolina Ramblers and the East Texas Serenaders, played hoedown tunes and British dance tunes, but they were also receptive to current popular dance tunes and especially to ragtime, which remained a national passion in the World War I period. Songs originally designed for the parlor piano, such as "Chicken Reel," "Redwing," or "Over the Waves," or for marching bands, such as "Under the Double Eagle," made their way into the repertoires of string-band musicians and have become permanently ensconced in the country music repertoire. Singers also ranged far and wide for their songs.

A large percentage of the early hillbilly songs came from 19th-century popular music, the "parlor songs," which had originally been written by professional composers and disseminated on lavishly illustrated sheet music among the nation's urban middle class. Such songs as "The Letter Edged in Black," "Little Rosewood Casket," "Little Old Log Cabin in the Lane," "Listen to the Mockingbird," and "Molly Darling" found a home among rural southerners long after ceasing to be fashionable with their original audience. Many of these sentimental favorites are still performed regularly by bluegrass and old-time country entertainers.

Country entertainers, therefore, were torn between tradition and modernity. They were loyal to their own communities but were eager to build a wider audience. Neither they nor their promoters (radio and recording men, booking agents, advertisers) were quite sure whether the most feasible promotional method would involve a rustic or an urbane approach. Country performers might have preferred conventional suits or even formal attire, but they were encouraged to clothe themselves in rustic or cowboy costumes. The conflict between rusticity and urbanity has been a factor in country music development, in sound as well as in image.

Although string bands and homespun acts predominated on early hillbilly recordings and on radio shows, the star system soon asserted itself and individual talents rose to the top. Vernon Dalhart (born Marion T. Slaughter in Jefferson, Tex.) contributed to the music's commercial acceptance by recording, in 1924, such nationally popular songs as "The Prisoner's Song" and "Wreck of the Old 97." Uncle Dave Macon, a comedian, singer, and five-string banjoist from Tennessee, was one of the first stars of the Grand Ole Opry and a repository of 19th-century folk and popular songs. Although there were a host of pioneer performers, the most seminal, the ones whose impacts are still felt in the music today, were the Carter Family, from Virginia, and Jimmie Rodgers, from Mississippi, both of whom were first recorded in early August 1927 in Bristol, Tenn. No group better embodied the mood and style of the family parlor and country church than the Carters; their three-part harmony, Maybelle's unique guitar style, and their large collection of vintage songs (such as "Wildwood Flower" and "Will the Circle Be Unbroken") still influence country singers today. In Jimmie Rodgers, the former railroad brakeman from Meridian, Miss., the music found its first superstar. Rodgers personified the rambling man, an image in sharp juxtaposition to that which the Carter Family projected. His "blue yodel," his appealing personal style and tragic early death, plus his eclectic repertoire of blues, hobo, train, rounder, and love songs, made him, posthumously, the "father of country music."

Country music not only survived the Great Depression but also solidified its position in American popular culture and greatly broadened its market. The 1930s were the heyday of live radio programming, and cowboy singers, duets, string bands, yodelers, and balladeers could be heard everywhere, even in New York City. Radio barn dances—Saturday-night variety shows with a rural or folk flavor—prevailed in many cities, but none was more important than WLS's National Barn Dance (Chicago) or WSM's Grand Ole Opry in Nashville. The Grand Ole Opry, which first went on the air in 1925, really affirmed its status as a national institution when it gained network affiliation on NBC in 1939. The 50,000-watt, clear-channel stations, such as WSM and KWKH in Shreveport, La., played crucial roles in circulating country music, but no stations had a more profound impact in the national dissemination of country and gospel music than the Mexican-border stations—popularly called X-stations because of their call letters (XERF, XEG, and the like). Their powerful transmission, sometimes surpassing 100,000 watts, blanketed North America with rural music (from the Carter Family to the Stamps Quartet), evangelism, and incessant advertising, which have become part of our national folklore. Radio exposure led to broadened public appearances and the emergence of booking agents and the complex framework of music business promotion.

As the professionalism and commercialization of country music proceeded, the nature of the music also changed. Traditional songs continued to appear with great frequency in the repertoires of such groups as the Blue Sky Boys and Mainer's Mountaineers. Nevertheless, newly composed songs gradually edged the older ones aside, and fledgling performers increasingly sought to find a commercial formula as successful as that of Jimmie Rodgers. Stylistically, the southeastern hoedown-oriented string bands and the "brother duets" (acts such as the Monroe Brothers who usually featured mandolin and guitar accompaniment) relied heavily on old-time songs and ballads and remained conservative in performance and material. On the other hand, musicians from the southwestern part of the South (Texas, Louisiana, and Oklahoma) were more innovative, producing dynamic styles that would revolutionize country music. Very few observers recognized distinctions within country music before World War II, and performers with widely varying styles and repertoires often appeared together on radio shows or on radio barn dances. Whether cowboy singer, mandolin-and-guitar duet, or hot string band, they all conveyed a homespun or down-home feeling, and hillbilly was the rubric that covered them all. Nevertheless, a modern perspective suggests the great differences among them. In 1934 Gene Autry, a radio hillbilly singer from Texas, went to Hollywood, where he became the first great singing cowboy in film. The romance of the cowboy would have been appealing to country singers in any case, but Autry's Saturday afternoon horse operas, his syndicated Melody Ranch radio show, and his very popular recordings magnified the appeal while providing country musicians with an identity much more respectable than that of the hillbilly. The romantic movie-cowboy songs declined significantly after World War II, but singers wearing cowboy costumes endured long after that.

More strongly reflective of evolving southwestern culture than the movie cowboy songs was western swing, the jazz-influenced string-band music popularized by Milton Brown and his Musical Brownies, the Light Crust Doughboys, and Bob Wills and the Texas Playboys. The western swing bands were eclectic in repertories and were receptive to new stylistic ideas, including the use of drums, horns, and electrified instruments. Developing alongside western swing, and drawing its inspiration even more directly from the bars and dance halls of the Southwest, was honky-tonk music. Country music's entrance into white roadhouses, which were called generically "honky-tonks," divested the music of much of its pastoral innocence and tone. The result was a realistic musical sound that documented the movement of country people into an urban industrial environment.

World War II was both the major catalyst for change in country music and the chief agent in its nationalization. The country music industry itself languished under wartime restraints: shellac rationing (which reduced the number of records released), the military drafting of musicians, and the scarcity of gas and tires (which limited personal appearances). On the other hand, jukeboxes became ubiquitous accoutrements in bars, cafés, and penny arcades, and country records began appearing on them in cities like Detroit, Chicago, and Los Angeles (in part, a reflection of the movement of southerners to northern and western industrial centers). The Grand Ole Opry gained its reputation as a mecca for country fans during the 1940s, and Tennessean Roy Acuff, who joined the show in 1938, became the unquestioned king of country music during those years, taking his roadshows to all parts of the United States and holding down the most important time slots on the Saturday night Opry. His versions of "Wabash Cannon Ball" and "The Great Speckled Bird" made both his name and that of the Opry famous throughout America. Above all, in the wa[illegible] time crucible of economic and demographic change [illegible] heightened migration, the mood, style, and appe[illegible] country music were destined to change significant[illegible]

Country music's first great commercial boom came in the years immediately following the war, continuing to about 1955. Postwar prosperity and the ending of wartime restraints generated an unprecedented demand for amusement. Record labels proliferated; new barn dances, such as the Louisiana Hayride, competed with the Grand Ole Opry; and thousands of jukeboxes reverberated with the songs of such country entertainers as Eddy Arnold, Kitty Wells, Lefty Frizzell, and Hank Williams. By the time Williams died on 1 January 1953, pop singers were "covering" his songs, and country music was winning commercial acceptance and respectability that had earlier been scarcely dreamed of. Just a few short years later, country music's "permanent plateau of prosperity" had been shattered by the revolution wrought by Elvis Presley and the rockabillies. All forms of traditional country music suffered temporarily as promoters and recording men began their urgent searches for young and vigorous stylists who could re-create what Elvis had done and who could hold that youthful audience that now dominated American music. One consequence of this quest was the creation of a pop style of country music, known generally as "country pop" or "the Nashville Sound." This form of music was considered to be a compromise that would appeal to both old-time country fans and the newly sought pop audience. By using vocal choruses and a sedate form of instrumentation (vibes, violins, piano, a muted bass), country-pop singers would avoid the extremes of both rockabilly and hillbilly.

Commercially, country music's development since the late 1950s has been one of the great success stories of American popular culture. Country performers now enjoy patronage around the world, and country concerts are regularly presented in the White House and on the Mall of the Smithsonian Institution. Country music's spectacular ascent and expansion have been accompanied by self-doubts and contradictions, and by anguished debates among performers and fans concerning the music's alleged dilution or loss of identity. Many adherents fear that the music may lose its soul as it gains the world. Although the quest for crossover records remains a powerful passion in modern country music, revivals of older country forms have periodically taken place since the rock-and-roll era. Honky-tonk music lives in the performances of men like George Jones, Merle Haggard, Moe Bandy, and the father of the style, Ernest Tubb. Bill Monroe and his fellow bluegrass practitioners have preserved the acoustic style of instrumentation and the "high lonesome" style of singing; bluegrass festivals are held somewhere almost every weekend from May until November. Doc Watson, Grandpa Jones, and Wilma Lee Cooper periodically revive the older country songs, even dipping occasionally into the songbag of ancient British material.

One of the most remarkable manifestations of interest in older songs and styles has come through the performances of youthful entertainers, or through older musicians who have catered to youth. Emmylou Harris, who was raised in Virginia, came to "hard country" through the influence of her friend and mentor, the country-rock singer Gram Parsons. Her fresh, uncluttered style of singing and her choice of material are considerably more traditional than most of the women singers who grew up in the country music world. Willie Nelson, a veteran honky-tonk singer from Texas and one of country music's greatest writers, has probably done most to bridge the gap between the rock-oriented youth audience and country music. He has done so by being receptive to their music and their heroes and by affecting a lifestyle and mode of dress (beard, earring, jogging shoes) that put them at ease. In the process, he has introduced his young fans to the best of older country and gospel songs. The 1980s has seen the emergence of young performers such as Ricky Scaggs, Dwight Yoakum, Randy Travis, Steve Earle, and George Strait, who consciously revive and update traditional forms of country music.

Country music, then, endures in many manifestations. Yet it remains as resistant to definition as it did over 60 years ago when it was first assuming an organized commercial identity. It has become a phenomenon with worldwide appeal, but it maintains its southern identification. Nashville remains its financial hub, the center of a multimillion-dollar music business. Country singers still come from southern working-class backgrounds in surprising numbers, and both they and the lyrics of their songs convey the ambivalent impulses that have always lain at the center of country music and southern culture: puritanism and hedonism, a reverence for home and a fascination with rambling, the sense of being uniquely different and at the same time more American than anyone else. Country songs convey a down-home approach to life and an elemental view of love, home, and patriotism that are absent from other forms of American music. In an age of computerized complexity, country music owes its appeal to the yearning for simplicity and rootedness that permeates modern American society.

See also INDUSTRY: / Music Industry; MEDIA: Film, Musical; WOMEN'S LIFE: Blues-singing Women

Bill C. Malone
Tulane University

Douglas B. Green, *Country Roots: The Origins of Country Music* (1976); Chet Hagan, *Country Music Legends in the Hall of Fame* (1982); Bill C. Malone, *Country Music, U.S.A.: A Fifty-year History* (1968; rev. ed., 1985), *Southern Music—American Music* (1979), with Judith McCullough, eds., *Stars of Country Music: Uncle Dave Mason to Johnny Rodriguez* (1975); Melvin Shestack, *The Country Music Encyclopedia* (1974); Ivan Tribe, *Mountaineer Jamboree: Country Music in West Virginia* (1984); Charles K. Wolfe, *Kentucky Country: Folk and Country Music of Kentucky* (1982), *Tennessee Strings: The Story of Country Music in Tennessee* (1977).

Dance, Development of

Ethnic dance traditions and the latest dances dictated by changing fashions in European high culture were not common in the dispersed settlements of the South. Into the mid-20th century the South's reluctance to adopt popular dance trends and the security afforded it by folk traditions dictated regional dance expressions. No historical studies, however, offer a broad perspective on the development of dance in this region. Folklore studies of dance remain geographically specific and do not deal with issues of time.

Three European nations provided the greatest influence on the development of dance in the Anglo-American South. From the West Indies, Spain penetrated what is now Florida. Spanish court dances such as the *chacona* and *gibao* as well as peasant dances have been described in Mexico and the West Indies. England first settled the Chesapeake and, after 1713, extended its claim to what would become the 13 American colonies and also parts of the West Indies. France occupied the natural harbor of New Orleans and explored the Mississippi River, north and west. The court and folk traditions of England and France thus entered American life. Among black slaves rich dance traditions from Africa via the slaves in the West Indies flourished, bringing to America such dances as the Chica and the Juba.

The predominantly Anglican society of the early and mid-18th-century South did not find the amusement of theatrical and fashionable dancing a social disruption like the Calvinists of the Northeast did. Itinerant dancing masters and musicians, like William Dering, Francis Christian, George Brownell, Peter Pelham, and Charles and Mrs. Stagg, connected the upper and middle classes of townships and plantations in a network of teaching circuits. These teachers brought a western European classical aesthetic, technique, and repertoire of essentially baroque court dances—minuet, rigaudon, allemande, gavotte, and others. As the Northeast diversified and expanded its population, these itinerants moved north to cities like Baltimore, Philadelphia, and Boston. Dancing masters filled a social need for the accomplishments of polite company—conducting oneself gracefully at the many military tributes and encampment celebrations, birthnight balls, and festivities for visiting dignitaries. Urban musical societies and clubs, like the St. Cecilia Society of Charleston, S.C. (1762), sanctioned the private performances of music and dance.

Women dancing, Birmingham, Ala., 1928

Those persons whose daily lives in the South did not allow free time to pursue refinements of high culture retained their traditional dances, which they performed on a seasonal basis and which supported community cohesion. Thus, sailors' competitive jigs, African slaves' tribal dances, and faded variations of 17th-century dances from western Europe (for example, the pavan, allemande, corrante, sarabande, galliard, passapied, and minuet) mixed loosely with less intensely performed popular dances like those English country dances modeled on John Playford's *The English Dancing Master* (1651–1726) and, after 1720, informal French contra dances.

The black slaves' dances served as a mechanism for keeping alive many African traditions, particularly those associated with funerals and with festive occasions. Popular dances with distinct African roots included the Buck, the Ring Dance, and the Cakewalk. Although whites frequently described blacks' dances as wild and offensive, slave owners touted their slaves' dancing abilities, had slaves dance as entertainment for guests, and sponsored dancing contests among slaves from various plantations. In New Orleans many unique black dance traditions developed. Slaves meeting at the city-approved assembly site known as Congo Square enjoyed such popular dances as the Babouille and the Cata, and voodoo traditions from the West Indies also influenced the developing black dance forms in New Orleans.

Economic opportunities presented by the South's climate, fertile land, and raw materials motivated steady trade and settlement. Three centuries of diverse settlement made for a heterogeneous population. However, with the exception of towns like Charleston and New Orleans, whose greater density and economic diversity made them a stage for the display of cultural differences in status and roles, homogeneous communities in which daily life was narrowly focused on agricultural subsistence characterized inland life.

The commitment to an agrarian way of life slowed the development of commerce, manufacturing, and transportation in the South until well into the 20th century. This meant that traditions and styles in physical expression in the South, as in other areas of culture, were generally insular. For example, the conventions of 18th-century public life—dramatized courtesy, elaborate rules of deportment, and formal conduct of events—dominated regional dance. The Northeast and Northwest supported lyceums and established public education in the early 19th century, but the cause of public education was not strongly pursued in the South. Public schools and educational programs typically promoted dance activities. Specifically, physical education programs used dance and helped contribute to the widespread acceptability and appreciation of dance as a useful function of everyday life, something that was lacking in the South except for a few private academies. Furthermore, the emphasis even in private academies was on traditional, 18th-century rationalizations of dance and not on new ideas from physical educators and dancing masters of high fashion. Without a mass communications network afforded by public education and good transportation, the cultural life of the South did not support modern dance.

The growth of southern towns in the late 18th century and of cities in the mid-19th century intensified the contrast between ethnic, social, and theatrical dances and made the nonverbal language of gestures and attitudes in these styles an important aspect of communication. In a city like New Orleans, for example, French, German, Spanish, and English cultures not only met but vied. Dancing cemented participants' and observers' ethnic and national ties. Cajuns, Creoles, mulattoes, and quadroons—representing the infusion of immigrants into the American South—identified performer and observer with dances. Competition and cooperation developed between theaters and opera houses as well as between those individuals involved in the Mardi Gras and other seasonal festivities.

Theatrical tours helped to knit the South together and give it connections to the mass audience and the fashionable dance activities in the rest of the United States. Theatrical managers brought well-known European and American performers of pantomime, the romantic ballet, and other dance forms into all areas of the South. Charleston, S.C., haven for expatriate Frenchmen and emigrants from the West Indies, had been a theatrical center as far back as the 1790s. French dancer and choreographer Alexandre Placide (c. 1750–1812), a multitalented performer whose pantomime productions were the most popular theatrical dance genre of their day, sent southern touring companies north to Richmond. The Louisiana Purchase of 1803 drew theatrical dancers, itinerant dancing masters, and popular and fashionable dance culture west with the settlers. The Ohio and Mississippi rivers provided easy travel, and their shore towns had entertainment-starved audiences. Samuel Drake (1769–1854), James H. Caldwell (1793–1863), Noah Ludlow (1795–1886), and Solomon Smith (1801–69) were the most famous theatrical managers to exploit the southern frontier.

Dancers like the black American William Henry Lane, "Master Juba" (1825–52), minstrel artists like the blackface Thomas Dartmont Rice, who apparently invented the character of Jim Crow in 1828, and later road companies (1843–1908) that used the minstrel theme romanticized the South to audiences all over the country. Depicting contented, artless slaves, minstrel shows usually only parodied black dance traditions and thus shaped long-held views of black dance as shuffling, rhythmic, and comical. Minstrel shows were popular nationwide during the 1800s. River showboats that presented theatrical dancers, music, and dramatic entertainments were popular from 1836 to 1925.

In the early 20th century the Appalachian and Ozark mountain regions and other protected pockets of culture in the American South remained free from the currents of modern commercial and economic development. These areas attracted disciples in the new scholarly disciplines of folklore and anthropology who felt that early American cultural patterns, including those of music and dance, might still survive in the South untouched by modern times. An early noteworthy researcher in this new fieldwork was British musicologist Cecil Sharp, founder of the English Folk Dance Society, who, in 1916–17, believed he had found vestiges of 17th-century dance in rural Kentucky and Tennessee.

The history of dance in the American South offers folklorists and cultural historians a unique challenge. In contrast to 20th-century national trends the South's historical insularity in ethnic culture, high culture, and folk traditions and styles of performance has contributed to regional distinctiveness in ways yet to be fully explored.

See also BLACK LIFE: Dance, Black

Gretchen Schneider
Arlington, Virginia

Norman Arthur Benson, "The Itinerant Dancing and Music Masters of Eighteenth-Century America" (Ph.D. dissertation, University of Minnesota, 1963); John W. Blassingame, *The Slave Community: Plantation Life in the Antebellum South* (1972); Thomas A. Burns and Doris Mack, *Southern Folklore Quarterly* (September–December 1978); Jane Carson, *Colonial Virginians at Play* (1965); Lynne F. Emery, *Black Dance in the United States from 1619 to 1970* (1972); Henry A. Kmen, *Music in New Orleans: The Formative Years, 1791–1841* (1966); Douglas McDermott, *Theatre Survey* (May 1978); Nancy Lee Chalfa Ruyter, *Reformers and Visionaries: The Americanization of the Art of Dance* (1979); Marshall Stearns and Jean Stearns, *Jazz Dance: The Story of American Vernacular Dance* (1968).

Entertainers, Popular

The general public has its own images of southernness: on one hand are images of a graciousness, gentility, politeness, or pride thought to be characteristic of the antebellum elite; on the other hand are images of crudeness, rowdiness, orneriness, or oafishness associated with backwoods rural folk. While some southern-born entertainers strive to capture and project a southern persona, incorporating characteristics often thought of as southern, others work to distance themselves from any regional identification. Entertainers therefore may be from the South but not representative of the South. An overview of entertainers in a variety of categories provides insight on the impact of southernness on performers' careers and popularity.

Various television actors and actresses have been cast in roles that present caricatures of southern personality: for example, Jim Nabors (Alabama) as Gomer Pyle, the goodhearted, inept, hayseed marine; Andy Griffith (North Carolina) and Don Knotts (West Virginia) as Sheriff Andy Taylor and Deputy Barney Fife, folksy small-town law officers; and Polly Holliday (Alabama) as Flo, a spunky diner waitress whose favorite rejoinder is "Kiss my grits!" Tennessee Ernie Ford often portrayed on his own program and in guest roles a gullible, likable, southern hillbilly, though his southern persona has been broader. Ford also conveys a folksy wisdom and is associated with such southern traditions as gospel music, for which he has won a Grammy Award, and good, down-home cooking, an ideal he has promoted through commercials.

Other performers convey their southernness not through characterization but through accents, their personalities, and comments about their roots. For example, Dinah Shore (Tennessee), singer and performer on television, radio, and the stage, conveys vivaciousness coupled with southern graciousness, warmth, and poise, and her soft southern accent is still very evident. Several southern singers who have hosted their own television shows are also good examples, among them Glen Campbell (Arkansas), Mac Davis (Texas), and Bobby Goldsboro (Florida). Devotees of *Star Trek* (created by Texan Gene Roddenberry) no doubt noted DeForest Kelley's (Georgia) southern accent in his role as Dr. McCoy. Charles Kuralt's (North Carolina) *On the Road* vignettes of life in small towns and out-of-the-way places in the United States usually focused on family-centered, slow-paced lifestyles of "common people" and thus celebrated many values associated with the South.

In the early years of television black performers faced tremendous obstacles, and inroads by southern black performers have been recent. Southern television station owners and managers openly objected to appearances of black performers on such variety programs as the *Ed Sullivan Show* and the *Milton Berle Show*, and edited out segments with black performers before airing some shows locally. Early television appearances by black actors and actresses were limited to such roles as the maid played by Butterfly McQueen (Florida), in a variety of programs. In 1956 Nat "King" Cole (born in Alabama but raised in Illinois) hosted his own television show, the first nationwide network program with a black host; but the show lasted only one year because of lack of sponsorship.

Significant changes followed the broad national television coverage of the civil rights movement in the 1960s. Even then, few black entertainers who openly confronted racial issues were accepted as television performers. Two groundbreakers from the South were Moms (Jackie) Mabley (North Carolina) and Nipsey Russell (Georgia). Known almost solely to black audiences for many years, Moms Mabley stands as the grandmother of all black comediennes. She started performing in the black vaudeville circuit, but Mabley did not become widely known until the 1960s, when her record albums became successful and she appeared frequently as a guest or guest host on late-night television talk shows. Nipsey Russell also pioneered the open handling of racial issues, primarily in his nightclub routines. Russell, like Mabley, made appearances on and occasionally hosted late-night talk shows in the 1960s and 1970s, and in the 1970s he became the first black master of ceremonies on nationally televised programs when he cohosted the *Les Crane Show* and *The Wide World of Comedy*. Though inroads have been made, opportunities for black performers on television remain limited and exploration of their southern experience is rare.

In contrast, white "hillbilly" and good old boy/good old girl images have proved popular and easy to handle. The stars of *Hee Haw*, Roy Clark (Virginia), Buck Owens (Texas), and Minnie Pearl (Tennessee), for example, have portrayed stereotyped rural southerners. Minnie Pearl's career, especially, has centered on the distinctive southern hillbilly style of music, costume, and humor. With a price tag dangling from her hat, Minnie salutes audiences with an exaggerated "Howdy," tells down-home yarns, and counsels young women on how to catch and keep a man.

Some southerners are best known for a combination of southern and western traits reflected in their roles. Fess Parker (Texas), for instance, gained popularity by portraying Walt Disney's version of Davy Crockett and later a resourceful, independent, honest, softspoken Daniel Boone. Affable cowboy or western figures have also been played by such actors as Ben Murphy (Arkansas), Andrew Prine (Florida), and Steve Forrest (Texas). Forrest, however, as a recently added character on the immensely popular TV series *Dallas*, contends with the quintessential southern bad guy, the avaricious, power-hungry Texas oil baron J. R. Ewing, played to the hilt by Larry Hagman (Texas).

Known primarily as emcee of the Miss America pageants, Bert Parks (Georgia) has been associated with the promotion of traditional American values. Two former Miss Americas, Mary Ann Mobley (Mississippi) and Phyllis George (Texas), whom many people still think of as classic southern beauties, have translated their pageant successes into varied roles on television. Many actresses famous for their physical beauty are not, however, typically identified by their southern roots. Among them are models-turned-actresses Cybill Shepherd (Tennessee), Lauren Hutton (South Carolina), and Farrah Fawcett (Texas). Fawcett was one of three southern women starring in the highly popular show *Charlie's Angels*, which had no regional theme. Kate Jackson (Alabama) and Jaclyn Smith (Texas) also played in the series.

Other television performers not generally seen as southern are William Conrad (Kentucky); Morgan Fairchild, Linda Day George, and John Hillerman (Texas); Gil Gerard (Arkansas); Earl Holliman (Louisiana); Stacy Keach and Jane Withers (Georgia); Patrick O'Neal (Florida); Gerald McRaney (Mississippi); MacKenzie Phillips (Virginia); and Wayne Rogers (Alabama). *Sesame Street* and Muppet fans probably are not aware that puppeteer and director Jim Henson hails from Greenville, Miss.

Former professional athletes Fran Tarkenton (Virginia), Bill Russell (Louisiana), and Don Meredith (Texas) are now familiar sportscasters and commentators. Other southern-born sportscasters include Keith Jackson (Georgia) and Howard Cosell (North Carolina), known for an acerbic style not usually associated with the South. Meadowlark Lemon (North Carolina) has entertained crowds not only as a key trick-shot basketball player for the Harlem Globetrotters but also as a performer on television and in movies. Likewise, Mohammed Ali (Kentucky) moved from the boxing ring to a variety of entertainment roles.

Newscasters Dan Rather and Bob Schieffer (Texas) are but two southerners currently prominent on network broadcasts, as are game-show hosts Peter Marshall (West Virginia) and Wink Martindale (Tennessee). Comedians

Steve Martin (Texas), Soupy Sales (North Carolina), and Foster Brooks (Kentucky) and comediennes Carol Burnett (Texas) and Pat Carroll (Louisiana) are not usually pictured as southern performers. Fannie Flagg's (Alabama) southern accent is still apparent and is incorporated in her work.

A number of well-known southern movie actors and actresses have played both distinctively southern parts and a range of other roles. A few of these performers and their notable films with southern roles are the following: Ned Beatty (Kentucky) in *Nashville*, Robby Benson (Texas) in *Ode to Billy Joe*, Betty Lynn Buckley (Texas) in *Tender Mercies*, Gary Busey (Texas) in *The Bear*, Ossie Davis (Georgia) in *Gone Are the Days*, Diane Ladd (Mississippi) in *Alice Doesn't Live Here Anymore*, Sondra Locke (Tennessee) in *The Heart Is a Lonely Hunter*, Randy Quaid (Texas) in *The Last Detail*, Burt Reynolds (Georgia) in *Smokey and the Bandit*, Beah Richards (Mississippi) in *Hurry, Sundown*, Sissy Spacek (Texas) in *Coal Miner's Daughter* and *The River*, Rip Torn (Texas) in *Cross Creek*, and Joanne Woodward (Georgia) in *The Sound and the Fury* and *The Long Hot Summer*.

Some southern performers have become associated with southern parts, such as Joe Don Baker (Texas) in *Walking Tall*, Bo Hopkins (South Carolina) in *White Lightning*, and Tommy Lee Jones (Texas) in *Coal Miner's Daughter*. In contrast there are southern actors and actresses very seldom associated with southernness, such as Powers Booth, Shelley Duvall, Valerie Perrine, Paula Prentiss, and Dennis Quaid (Texas); Jim Brown (Georgia); Faye Dunaway (Florida); Louise Fletcher and Dean Jones (Alabama); George Hamilton (Tennessee); and Shirley MacLaine and George C. Scott (Virginia). Of course, some southern-born actors and actresses have not actually grown up in the South. James Earl Jones, for example, was born in Tate County, Miss., but grew up on a farm near Jackson, Mich. A critically acclaimed actor of stage, movies, and television, Jones has maintained ties with his state of birth through such projects as narration of a media presentation on Mississippi for the New Orleans World's Fair and of a film *Painting in the South*.

The southern roots of a number of famous stage performers might surprise audiences. Actress, singer, author, and former United Nations representative Pearl Bailey was born in Newport News, Va., but moved to Philadelphia in her teens. Texans Cyd Charisse, Kathryn Crosby, Mary Martin, Ann Miller, David Purdham, and Debbie Reynolds and South Carolinian Bettye Ackerman have all enthralled audiences. Sultry Eartha Kitt has roots in South Carolina but grew up in New York City.

Musical trends have been strongly influenced by talented southern performers, who have pioneered a wide variety of musical forms. Because musical forms are so varied and markets exist for many types of musical expression, reflections of southern experiences and perspectives have been more forcefully and directly expressed by singers, songwriters, and musicians than by performers in most other realms of popular entertainment.

Jazz is southern in origins, and the South has continued throughout the 20th century to produce great jazz musicians. Louisiana and surrounding areas produced the largest number of early southern performers: Louis Armstrong, King Oliver, Jelly Roll Morton, and Kid Ory were among the giants from Louisiana. Nearby Texas produced keyboard soloist Teddy Wilson and Ornette Coleman; and Mississippi was the birthplace of Lester Young and Mose Allison. But the eastern South produced Fletcher Henderson (Georgia), the "First Lady of Jazz" Mary Lou Williams (Georgia), John Coltrane (North Carolina), and Dizzy Gillespie (South Carolina).

The blues grew from work songs, spirituals, hymns, and field shouts of blacks in the South. A roll call of blues masters abounds with southerners, and the following is only a brief listing: Eddie Boyd, James Cotton, Arthur "Big Boy" Crudup, John Lee Hooker, Robert Johnson, B. B. King, Muddy Waters, and Howlin' Wolf (Mississippi); Albert Collins, Lightnin' Hopkins, and Blind Lemon Jefferson (Texas); Clarence "Gatemouth" Brown and Leadbelly (Huddie Ledbetter) (Louisiana); W. C. Handy (Alabama); the Reverend Gary Davis (South Carolina); "Sleepy" John Estes, Alberta Hunter, and Bessie Smith (Tennessee); Ida Cox, Jesse "Lone Cat" Fuller, and Sonny Terry (Georgia); and Helen Humes (Kentucky). Many of the most popular white blues performers have also been from the South, including Janis Joplin (Texas), Johnny Winter (Mississippi), and Stevie Ray Vaughan (Texas). Some performers combine elements of blues with those of other genres, and one prime example is Ray Charles (Georgia), singer, composer, and pianist, who has combined gospel, blues, country, big-band jazz, rhythm, pop, and rock sounds.

Many of soul's top performers have southern roots, including such masters as "Soul Brother Number One," James Brown (Georgia); "Lady Soul," Aretha Franklin (born in Tennessee, raised in Michigan); and "High Priestess of Soul," Nina Simone (North Carolina). Other leading soul, soul-pop, and soul-folk performers include the Bar-Kays and the Box Tops (Tennessee); Archie Bell and the Drells, and Joe Tex (Texas); Brook Benton (South Carolina); Jerry Butler and Betty Everett (Mississippi); Al Green (Arkansas); Millie Jackson and Otis Redding (Georgia); Wilson Pickett (Alabama); and Bill Withers (West Virginia). Several soul performers also influenced disco trends, most notably, Isaac Hayes (Tennessee), Thelma Houston (Mississippi), and Johnnie Taylor (Arkansas).

Nationally popular rhythm-and-blues performers from the South have included Johnny Ace, and Booker T. and the MGs (Tennessee); Jesse Belvin (Arkansas); Gary "U.S." Bonds (Florida); Ruth Brown (Virginia); Peabo Bryson (South Carolina); The Crusaders, and Barry White (Texas); Roy Hamilton, and Gladys Knight and the Pips (Georgia); Clarence "Frogman" Henry, Ernie K-Doe, The Meters, and The Neville Brothers (Louisiana); David Ruffin (Mississippi); and Eddie Kendricks and Percy Sledge (Alabama).

Southern rock-and-roll greats abound, and some are legendary: Fats Domino (Louisiana), Buddy Holly (Texas), Jerry Lee Lewis (Louisiana), Elvis Presley (Mississippi), and Little Richard (Georgia). Others, too, have gained a wide following, such as Jayne County (Georgia), Bo Diddley (Mississippi), the Dixie Cups (Louisiana), Inez and Charlie Foxx (North Carolina), Jimmy Gilmer and the Fireballs (Texas), Ronnie Hawkins (Arkansas), Brenda Lee (Georgia), Sam the Sham and the Pharaohs (Texas), and Gene Vincent (Virginia).

Founded in 1968 in Macon, Ga., the Allman Brothers Band garnered a large following and set the style for subsequent southern rock groups through their skillful blend of blues, rhythm, country, gospel, and rock. Their style has been described as one that "reflected emergence of the 'New South.'" Other popular groups followed in their footsteps; for example, the Atlanta Rhythm Section, Big Star, Blackfoot, K.C. and the Sunshine Band, the Marshall Tucker Band, Molly Hatchet, .38 Special, Wet Willie, and ZZ Top. Two rock bands that have most conspicuously conveyed a regional identification are the Charlie Daniels Band, with such hits as "The South's Gonna Do It Again" and "Devil Went Down to Georgia," and Lynyrd Skynyrd, with "Sweet Home Alabama." A cocky, rowdy, southern pride has been associated with both groups.

The group Alabama has been one of the nation's most popular country-rock groups during the 1980s. Other famous southern country-rock and country-pop groups and individual performers include the Amazing Rhythm Aces, Rita Coolidge, and Ray Stevens (Tennessee); the Everly Brothers, Crystal Gayle, and Tom T. Hall (Kentucky); Freddy Fender, The Bobby Fuller Four, Johnny Horton, Kris Kristofferson, Barbara Mandrell, Roger Miller, Michael Murphey, Jeannie C. Riley, and Kenny Rogers (Texas); Bobbie Gentry (Mississippi); Emmylou Harris (Alabama); The Outlaws, and Johnny Tillotson (Florida); and Joe South (Georgia).

No discussion of southern performers would be complete without mention of the many outstanding country-and-western artists. A few of these performers are Roy Acuff, the "King of Country Music" (Tennessee); Waylon Jennings, Willie Nelson, and Tanya Tucker (Texas); and Conway Twitty and Tammy Wynette (Mississippi). Loretta Lynn (Kentucky) and Dolly Parton (Tennessee) are particularly famous for their songs about strong, independent, resourceful women, in contrast to the faithful, ever-suffering, role-bound women so often portrayed in country music. Lynn and Parton are excellent examples of performers who convey pride in their rural southern roots both through their music and through interviews.

Perhaps the most aggressively southern performer today in style is Hank Williams, Jr. Songs such as "Dixie on My Mind" and "If Heaven Ain't a Lot Like Dixie, Then I Don't Want to Go" convey a militant regionalism, one that reflects, at times, a traditional southern defensiveness, but, at other times, a self-conscious, good-natured toying with a regional identity. In contrast, though, are various performers who have nurtured a southern image, but a genteel, low-key one, such as Chet Atkins, the "Country Gentleman" (Tennessee), Eddy Arnold, the "Tennessee Plowboy" (Tennessee), and Sonny James, the "Southern Gentleman" (Alabama).

Pop musicians and singers associated generally with mainstream sounds tend not to reflect regional identities. A number of popular entertainers particularly well known during the 1940s and 1950s hail from the South, including Polly Bergen, Pat Boone, and Judy Canova (Florida), Rosemary Clooney (Kentucky), and Kate Smith (Virginia). Other pop entertainers, many of whom have combined such sounds as folk, funk, and rock, include the Classics IV (Georgia), The Commodores (Alabama), the Mike Curb Congregation (Georgia), Tyrone Davis (Mississippi), Jackie DeShannon (Kentucky), the Royal Guardsmen (Florida), Bobby Hebb (Tennessee), Randy Newman (Louisiana), Paul and Paula (Texas), Lionel Ritchie (Alabama), B. J. Thomas (Texas), and Mason Williams (Texas). Big-band leaders Harry James and Fletcher Henderson, both from Georgia, have also played major roles in the popular music trends in America.

Southern folk, folk-pop, and folk-rock artists include, among others, Leo Kottke (Georgia), Phil Ochs (Texas), Odetta Holmes (Alabama), and Loudon Wainwright III (North Carolina), all of whom reflect unique aspects of their southern heritage. Other performers such as gospel greats the Dixie Hummingbirds (South Carolina), Cajun fiddler Doug Kershaw (Louisiana), zydeco master Clifton Chenier (Louisiana), and "harmelody" pioneer Ornette Coleman (Texas) project distinctive southern rhythms through their music, giving glimpses of the wide variety of sounds represented in the South.

An overview of southern performers and the southern persona in popular entertainment shows that in some entertainment realms—particularly television—southernness is encouraged only when a caricature of southerners or southern life serves a need within a program geared to mass appeal. Popular music allows for much greater expression of regional identity. Although stereotyped southerners still abound in movies, in recent decades there have been not only a greater variety of roles but also more multifaceted ones portraying southerners and southernness. This trend may not herald any southern renaissance, though; in most popular media the pressures of homogenization and the emphasis on mass appeal tend to mitigate against nurturance of uniquely southern traits, characterizations, and outlooks.

See also MEDIA articles

Sharon A. Sharp
University of Mississippi

Mike Kaplan, ed., *Variety—International Showbusiness Reference* (1981); W. Augustus Low and Virgil A. Clift, eds., *Encyclopedia of Black America* (1981); Monica O'Donnell, ed., *Contemporary Theatre, Film, and Television*, vol. I (1984); Jon Pareles, ed., *The Rolling Stone Encyclopedia of Rock 'n' Roll* (1983); Harry A. Ploski and James Williams, eds., *The Negro Almanac: The Afro-American* (1983); Charlemae Rollins, *Famous Negro Entertainers* (1967); Melvin Shestack, *The Country Music Encyclopedia* (1974); Mabel M. Smyth, ed., *The Black American Reference Book* (1976).

Festivals, Folk Music

Music festivals have been part of southern cultural experience at least since the fiddlers' contests of the mid-18th century. Prior to 1900, however, most communally shared music was sung and played informally at family reunions, corn shuckings and barn raisings, on court and election days, at house dances, revivals and all-day singings at churches, rent parties, school commencements, county fairs, and on a variety of other occasions that brought families, neighbors, and communities together. Festivals modeled partly on these early forms continue in local benefits and fund-raisers (for volunteer fire companies, rescue squads, and the like) in which food and musical performances are the main attractions.

The hundreds of music festivals currently in evidence mirror both the South's cultural diversity and the complex patterns of cultural development and change the region has undergone. Fiddlers' contests, now in their third century, multiplied especially after the mid-1920s, stimulated by both Henry Ford's national promotional efforts and the growth of commercial country music (and especially its radio barn dances). Camp meetings and sacred harp singings still take place annually at Benton, Ky., Tifton, Ga., Etowa, N.C., and elsewhere. Commercial gospel music of the variety that emanated from the mass revivals of Dwight L. Moody (1837–99) and Billy Sunday (1863–1935), their many successors and local imitators, and the mainly southern-based black and white gospel music industry that grew in their wake (e.g., companies owned by James D. Vaughan and R. E. Winsett in Tennessee) is performed and celebrated weekly either by local congregations, at commemorative anniversary celebrations for gospel quartets, in commercial "all night singings," at state and regional gospel singing conventions (e.g., the Albert E. Brumley sing at Springdale, Ark., and the West Virginia state convention at Nebo). Old-time music festivals such as those at Union Grove, N.C., Galax, Va., and Asheville, N.C., have drawn thousands of visitors annually for many decades. Other older forms, including blues and jazz, are celebrated in festivals such as the Delta Blues Festival in Greenville, Miss., the New Orleans Jazz and Heritage Festival, and jazz festivals at Hampton, Va., and Mobile, Ala.

Festivals styled on older social forms and presenting traditional musical idioms to local audiences exist side by side with those that present more recent idioms in festivals that feature more contemporary music and whose audiences assemble from both near and far. Deriving some of their stimulus from the efforts of educational and cultural missionaries who established industrial, settlement, and folk schools among lowland blacks and upland whites at the turn of the century, these more contemporary festivals proliferated after the mid-1920s, and they received further encouragement from supporters such as Allen Eaton and New Deal agencies.

In the post–World War II period increasing leisure and tourism expanded the market for public cultural presentations, as did the so-called folk revival of the late 1950s and 1960s, some of whose major figures (e.g., the Seegers) had learned about southern music partly by attending earlier festivals. Recently, music festivals have been spurred by the post-1965 growth of federal and state funding for cultural activities (and especially by the advent of state, regional, and federal folklife programs). Further impetus has derived from renewed cultural awareness and pride among minority cultural groups (e.g., the Cajun festival at Abbeville, La., and related observances among Cherokee and Lumbee Indians in North Carolina).

In recent years bluegrass festivals have probably multiplied more rapidly than any other type of music festival in the South. The first one was at Luray, Va., in 1962; scores of them are now held every year, organized by major bluegrass performers (e.g., Mac Wiseman and Carter Stanley), bluegrass promoters such as Carlton Haney (Camp Springs, N.C.), and a variety of local individuals and institutions. Commercial country music is the focus for many other recent festivals, which range from one-time local events headlined by a Nashville star performer, to annual "memorial" festivals (for Hank Williams at Mt. Olive, Ala.; Jimmie Rodgers at Meridian, Miss.; W. C. Handy at Florence, Ala.; and the Carter Family at Hiltons, Va.), to weekly performances at seasonal country music parks (e.g., Hiawassee, Ga.). Entrepreneurial development and promotional efforts—frequently with a dual link to tourism and local agriculture (rice, cotton, sugarcane, peaches, and pecans in the lowlands; apples and tobacco in the uplands)—have produced many music and cultural festivals.

The public "folklife festival," in which music is frequently the most prominent feature, is another important recent form. Drawing distant inspiration from such events as Bascom Lamar Lunsford's Mountain Dance and Folk Festival (Asheville, N.C., 1928), the White Top Folk Festival (White Top, Va., 1931), and the National Folk Festival (1934), but patterned more specifically upon the Smithsonian Institution's Festival of American Folklife (1967), folklife festivals (e.g., the North Carolina Folklife Festival and the Blue Ridge Folklife Festival at Ferrum College [Va.]) tend to emphasize precommercial musical idioms.

In their many forms, folk music festivals in the South bespeak both a deep attachment to local and regional tradition, and a creative and integrative sensitivity to cultural change. In a few cases they also reveal a need to invent (for self, local community, or audience) "traditions" whose authenticity is open to question: festivals at Grandfather Mountain and Red Springs, N.C., and Virginia Beach, Va., present a largely fictitious version of Scottish highland music, and the dulcimer festivals at Birmingham, Ala., and Mountain View, Ark., celebrate a romanticized feature of Appalachian music and culture. Music festivals remain, however, one of the most vital contexts in which southerners celebrate their cultural past and interpret their present cultural identity to others.

See also RECREATION: Festivals

David E. Whisnant
University of Maryland,
Baltimore County

Robert Cantwell, *Bluegrass Breakdown: The Making of the Old Southern Sound* (1984); Archie Green, *John Edwards Memorial Foundation Quarterly* (Spring 1975); Eric Hobsbawm and Terence Ranger, eds., *The Invention of Tradition* (1983); Bill C. Malone, *Southern Music—American Music* (1979); David E. Whisnant, *All That Is Native and Fine: The Politics of Culture in an American Region* (1983), *Folk Festival Issues: Report from a Seminar* (1979); Joe Wilson and Lee Udall, *Folk Festivals: A Handbook of Organization and Management* (1982).

Gospel Music, Black

Despite its immense popularity, widespread appeal, and influence on American popular music, Afro-American gospel music is a comparably recent music phenomenon. Rooted in the religious songs of the late 19th century urban revival, in shape-note songs, spirituals, blues, and ragtime, gospel emerged early in the 20th century.

The term *gospel music* suggests many things to different people. In its most general application, the word simply refers to any religious music, regardless of the music's age or origin. Congregational songs, ring shouts, quartets, sacred harp choirs, sanctified groups, and even some work songs would all qualify. Less broadly, the term *gospel* refers to an innovative, popular style of music combining secular forms, particularly ragtime and blues, with religious texts.

Composed, modern black gospel music became an important style during the 1930s. Thomas A. Dorsey is generally regarded as its "father," although it could be argued that C. A. Tindley should wear that mantle. Tindley was actively composing during the first decade of the 20th century, but his songs did not gain widespread popularity among blacks until the 1920s and 1930s. Dorsey himself was inspired by Tindley's reworkings of older revival songs, blues, and spirituals. Dorsey's own songs, however, made up the first wave of modern gospel music during the Depression.

Thomas A. Dorsey began his career as a blues and gospel singer. He enjoyed an immensely successful stint as a professional blues musician during the 1920s. By the early 1930s he had turned his attention entirely to religious music. During the 1930s and 1940s Dorsey worked with two influential figures, Mahalia Jackson and Sallie Martin. In addition he toured the country as a performer and lecturer and wrote some 500 gospel songs including "There Will Be Peace in the Valley" and "Precious Lord, Take My Hand."

Reverend Herbert W. Brewster, another important composer from this period, was pastor of the East Trigg Baptist Church in Memphis, Tenn. A contemporary of Dorsey, Brewster composed scores of gospel songs beginning in the early 1930s. Many of his compositions were written specifically for his choir of the Brewster Singers, but two of his songs, "Move on up a Little Higher" and "Surely, God Is Able," gained wider popularity.

The music and language of these early gospel songwriters helped to promote an interest in their compositions. Although the compositions of Dorsey and others are formally notated and printed, they almost always undergo a transformation during performance. One of the strong appeals of this music, in fact, is that it encourages participation and improvisation on the part of an audience that feels comfortable with the use of primary chords, standardized chord progression, metaphorical language, and frequent biblical illusions.

By the mid-1930s, the appeal of gospel music within black culture was quite evident, and it was soon embraced by commercial record companies wishing to capitalize on its popularity. Radio stations and the major radio networks featured its music on their live broadcasts. These attempts at mass marketing quickly led to a sense of professionalism among the performers. By the onset of World War II a small but growing cadre of people made their living singing, writing, or promoting black gospel music.

In the decade following 1945 the popularity of groups such as the Spirit of Memphis, Alex Bradford, the Soul Stirrers, Queen C. Anderson, Sallie Martin, and the Famous Blue Jay Singers grew. Dozens of professional and semiprofessional groups appeared on programs throughout the country and recorded for an expanding network of local and regional companies. This interest is well illustrated by Mahalia Jackson's recording of "Move on up a Little Higher" and the Ward Singers's version of "Surely, God Is Able," which both sold a million copies in 1950.

Interest in black gospel music gripped the country and every city and small town in the South staged gospel music programs in churches and auditoriums. New artists such as the Dixie Hummingbirds and Shirley Caesar emerged, initially as second line acts, then as headliners. Soloists such as Ira Tucker of the Dixie Hummingbirds and Claude Jeter of the Swan Silvertones became well known among devotees. Lavish gospel programs were staged by Joe Bostic in New York City and Erskine Fausch of New Orleans. With widespread appeal, groups could afford extravagant costumes and could travel in comfort. Local nonprofessional black gospel groups emulated the dress and singing styles of more popular musicians and even adopted their names. Nearly a half dozen local or semiprofessional groups exploited the "Soul Sisters" name, for instance.

This increasing popularity and professionalism ultimately turned some of the more conservative church members away from contemporary gospel music. By the mid to late 1950s there was something of a backlash against "secularization," most clearly manifested in the opulent manner in which some singers lived.

Black gospel music has changed greatly since the middle 1950s. It has become more sophisticated, particularly in terms of marketing and musical diversity. Popular singers such as William Gaither and Andrae Crouch have had formal musical training and education, which have led to more complicated arrangements.

These changes are part of a natural musical and cultural evolution. Black gospel music changed as the demands of popular culture increased and as Afro-Americans strove toward middle-class status. Black gospel music remains, however, essentially conservative, and its principal mission remains constant—to lift the spirits of its participants and to help them express their religion.

See also BLACK LIFE: Music, Black

Kip Lornell
Ferrum College

Horace Clarence Boyer, *Black Perspectives in Music* (Spring 1979); Harry Eskew and Paul Oliver, in *The New Grove Dictionary of Music and Musicians*, vol. 5, ed. Stanley Sadie (1980); David Evans, *Jazz Forschung/Jazz Research* (1976); Tony Heilbut, *The Gospel Sound: Good News and Bad Times* (1971); Eileen Southern, *The Music of Black Americans: A History* (1971; 2d ed., 1983).

Gospel Music, White

For most people, the term *white gospel music* connotes a type of music characterized not so much by style as by content. Although the sound of different types of white southern gospel can range from that of a sedate vocal quartet to an amplified country band, or from a singing convention assembly of 300 voices to the simple brother duet harmony framed by mandolin and guitar, the message of the music is usually a direct and often optimistic reflection of a working-class Protestant ethos. Since white gospel music emerged as a recognized form in the 1870s and 1880s, it has tended to graft this message onto a rich variety of vernacular musics, both folk and pop; this has given white gospel an ambiguous and confusing stylistic identity. To many southerners, though, white gospel is associated with vocal quartets or family groups, singing in three- or four-part harmony, accompanied by a piano, guitar, or other stringed instruments. Also, for many of them, gospel is not a formal church music to be used in regular Sunday services, but a brand of Christian entertainment to be enjoyed at special church singings, at concerts, on television and radio, and on records.

The roots of gospel music lie in pre–Civil War southern hymnody traditions such as camp-meeting songs, sacred harp singings, and revival music, but the real beginnings of modern southern gospel can be traced to two events occurring in the 1870s—the emergence of the Ruebush-Kieffer publishing business in the Shenandoah Valley of Virginia and the publication and popularity of a series of books of "general hymns" by two northern-based song leaders, Ira D. Sankey and Phillip P. Bliss. Aldine S. Kieffer, the main force behind the Shenandoah Valley tradition, was a Confederate veteran who happened to be the grandson of Joseph Funk, whose 1851 song book *Harmonia Sacra* (or "Hominy Soaker," as it was fondly called in the South) was published in a format using seven shapes for different notes—as opposed to the four shapes in the sacred harp tradition. After the war, as the older four-shape systems lost favor, Kieffer began his company in 1866 with an old friend, Ephraim Ruebush, whom he helped free from a Union prison camp, and began a 50-year campaign to popularize the seven-shape note system. He did this by founding the South's first Normal Singing School at New Market, Va., in 1874; by starting a periodical called *The Musical Million*, to help develop singing conventions and spread news of backwoods singing schools, in 1870; by training and sending across the South singing-school teachers; and by publishing a series of songbooks, such as *The Christian Harp* (1877), a collection of lively, "singable" songs designed for "special singing" rather than for use in regular church services. Not only did the seven-shape notation system of the Ruebush-Kieffer Company take root in the South, but the company provided a training ground for hundreds of later writers and singers; and the company itself, with its multifaceted operation, became a model for dozens of other gospel publishing companies in the South from 1875 to 1955.

The type of song that filled these new books had its prototype in Sankey's and Bliss's 1875 collection *Gospel Hymns and Sacred Tunes*, published in New York and Cincinnati. Although the term *gospel musick* had been used in print as far back as 1644 in London, the intense popularity of the Sankey-Bliss collection, as well as its use by the popular evangelist Dwight L. Moody from 1875 to 1899, was the real source of the term *gospel music* in American culture. The songs in this collection and in others that followed in the 1880s and 1890s derived from the rise of Sunday school songs in the 1850s, songs that were deliberately designed for younger singers; they were more rhythmical than the older hymns, more sentimental, more optimistic, and often patterned on popular secular songs. Though popular nationwide, the new gospel hymns were especially successful in the South, where many of them even entered folk tradition: "Bringing in the Sheaves," "What a Friend We Have in Jesus," "Sweeping through the Gates," and "Let the Lower Lights Be Burning." The rise of southern shape-note publishers in the late 19th century provided outlets for hundreds of amateur songwriters to follow in the gospel song tradition. By the turn of the century graduates of the Ruebush-Kieffer Company had started publishing companies in Georgia (A. J. Showalter, J. B. Vaughan), Texas (Trio Music, Showalter-Patton), Arkansas (Eureka Music Company), and Tennessee (E. T. Hildebrand).

The most successful and influential of these publishers, though, was to be a Giles County, Tenn., native named James D. Vaughan (1864–1941). Early in life Vaughan studied with Ruebush-Kieffer graduate E. T. Hildebrand and later worked with B. C. Unseld, who had been the first teacher in the Ruebush-Kieffer normal schools. Vaughan became a singing-school teacher and composer and by 1903 had settled in Lawrenceburg, Tenn., where he began publishing songbooks using the seven-shape system. By 1909 he was selling 30,000 books a year; by 1912, 85,000 books a year. One or two new books were published each year, often in paperback form and often containing as much as 75 percent new material and 25 percent old standards or favorites. Some rural churches used Vaughan's books in regular services, but most of the books were used in county or statewide singing conventions and specialty singing.

Vaughan's business sense, talent, and personality allowed him to build his company into the South's largest and to establish his own singing schools at Lawrenceburg, making it the citadel of modern gospel music. He also, however, used a number of important innovations to publicize his work. Like Ruebush-Kieffer, he started a magazine, *Vaughan's Family Visitor* (1912–present), to announce singing schools, news, and songbooks; in 1922 he began his own record company, Vaughan Records, to help popularize new songs and saw it become the South's first home-based record company. He bought his own radio station, WOAN, and encouraged his singers to perform on other commercial stations. Most important of all, though, he used quartets made up of his singing teachers to tour the South, giving free concerts of Vaughan's music. The Vaughan quartets were a spectacular success wherever they went, and soon the company had 16 different quartets on the payroll; some of these quartets became popular in their own right and soon eclipsed the company they were representing. By the late 1920s groups like the McDonald Quartet, from southern Missouri, were able to travel independently and make a living with their music. The classic southern gospel quartet—four men and a piano—comes from Vaughan's innovations.

The Vaughan Company continued to publish until 1964, but its alumni set up important rival companies that were even more innovative and aggressive. One of Vaughan's editors, V. O. Stamps, joined forces with J. R. Baxter, Jr., to form the Stamps-Baxter Music and Printing Company in 1926. Using as their theme song, "Give the World a Smile Each Day," Stamps-Baxter sought out the best of the new, younger songwriters; helped get their quartets record contracts with major labels like RCA Victor, Columbia, and Brunswick; and used radio shows to sell their songbooks. With its effective base of operations in Dallas, the company soon shared the dominance of the market with Vaughan; they made an important move toward taking gospel music out of the church and into the realm of pure entertainment when they staged an "all-night sing" in the Cotton Bowl in 1940—thus creating a format that would characterize southern gospel for years.

During the 1930s—when the paperback gospel songbook publishers were at their height—Vaughan claimed cumulative sales of over 5 million books, and some 40 to 50 independent publishers issued such books. In addition to Vaughan and Stamps-Baxter, leaders included Hartford (Arkansas), R. E. Winsett (Tennessee), J. M. Henson (Atlanta), and the Stamps Quartet Company (Texas, formed by Frank Stamps, V. O.'s brother). During this decade, too, independent singing groups arose, and, although not formally associated with the companies, they used their songs for their repertoires. The most successful of these was the Texas family known as The Chuck Wagon Gang, who recorded and broadcasted widely, featuring such tunes as "After the Sunrise," "Jesus Hold My Hand," and "A Beautiful Life."

By the end of World War II the balance of power had shifted away from the song-publishing companies to the quartets and gospel groups; major country radio shows like the Grand Ole Opry had gospel groups as regular members, and in 1946 the Homeland Harmony Quartet of Atlanta saw its "Gospel Boogie" ("Everybody's Gonna Have a Wonderful Time Up There") become a nationwide pop hit. In the late 1940s Georgian Wally Fowler left his country band, formed the Oak Ridge Quartet, and began promoting package tours of new gospel stars, often renting an auditorium for a commercialized version of the "all-night sings." A nationwide fad for pop-gospel music in the early 1950s attracted huge audiences for young groups like the Blackwood Brothers, the Statesmen, the Jordanaires, and the Happy Goodman Family. Country artists like the Bailes Brothers, James and Martha Carson, Molly O'Day, and the Louvin Brothers made gospel a major part of their repertoire, while the newly emerging bluegrass bands often borrowed gospel repertoire and quartet singing styles.

By the end of the 1950s the quartet style no longer dominated southern gospel. Family groups such as the Speer Family and the Rambos injected country and even pop music into their performances, and groups like the Inspirations and the Kingsmen sometimes used five or six singers and a battery of back-up instruments. The 1970s saw the rise of smooth, sophisticated "praise music" by singers like Dallas Holm and "contemporary Christian music" by singers like Amy Grant and Texan Cynthia Clawson, who had more in common with Broadway music and even rock than southern gospel. The southern gospel style was by the mid-1970s being referred to as "traditional gospel" and, although no longer on the cutting edge of American religious music, was still the most popular form of nonprofessional music across the South, still heard in homes, in churches, and at gatherings from Virginia to Texas.

Charles K. Wolfe
Middle Tennessee State University

Clarice Baxter and Vide Polk, *Gospel Song Writers Biography* (1971); Lois S. Blackwell, *The Wings of the Dove: The Story of Gospel Music in America* (1978); Jesse Burt and Duane Allen, *The History of Gospel Music* (1971); Ottis J. Knippers, *Who's Who among Southern Singers and Composers* (1937); Charles K. Wolfe, *American Music* (Spring 1983), in *Folk Music and Modern Sound*, ed. William Ferris and Mary L. Hart (1982).

Honky-Tonk Music

Honky-tonk, also called "hard country" or "beer-drinking music," projects the mood and ambience of its birthplace, the beer joint. Born in the 1930s, honky-tonk became virtually *the* sound of mainstream country music from the late 1940s to about 1955, when rock and roll forced changes in all forms of American popular music. Since then it has endured as a vigorous subgenre of country music, with such important musicians as Ray Price, George Jones, and Moe Bandy making crucial contributions to its development.

Although conditions that contributed to its development prevailed throughout the South and on the West Coast, honky-tonk music experienced its most significant development in the states of Texas, Louisiana, and Oklahoma. There, in the oil-boom atmosphere of the mid-1930s, the combined forces of prohibition repeal and increased professionalization in the still-new hillbilly music field led to the movement of musicians into the taverns and beer joints where their music was welcomed. When country music entered the honky-tonks, its performing styles and thematic content changed significantly. Musicians sought a beat that could be felt even if it could not be heard above the din and merriment of weekend revelers, and they effected instrumental changes that would enhance and diversify their sounds; hence the adoption of electric instruments. Above all, much of the tone of country music changed in this atmosphere of wine, women, and song, where potential danger lurked behind the gay facade and where "honky-tonk angels" lured their men. No force has proved more important in diminishing the pastoral impulse of country music, nor in documenting the transition made by rural southerners to urban industrial culture.

If the 1930s were important as years of nourishment, the war years were absolutely indispensable in both the maturation and popularization of honky-tonk music. As never before in southern history, people fled agriculture and made their way by the thousands to the towns and industrial centers of the South, as well as to cities in the Midwest and on the West Coast. While civilians changed their locales and occupations, their military sons and daughters moved to training camps both in and out of the South and to combat theaters around the world. For a people in transition, who were urban in residence, yet rural in style and outlook, the adjustment was often fraught with frustration and pain. Adjustments were made in diverse ways and with varying degrees of success, but many men sought to reaffirm their identities in a sympathetic setting—over a bottle of beer in a honky-tonk. Servicemen fought the loneliness of enforced separation from loved ones and friends, while their civilian relatives sought relief from the pressures of work and family responsibilities. The music of the honky-tonks, whether performed by live bands or jukeboxes, reflected increasingly the preoccupations of socially and geographically displaced people. Never before had a form of music so effectively mirrored the concerns of the southern working class.

Rustic sounds still thrived in country music during the 1940s; the decade, after all, marked the heyday of Roy Acuff as well as the beginning of the acoustic-based bluegrass style. But sounds introduced and nourished in the honky-tonks of Texas predominated, and names like Bob Wills, Ted Daffan, Cliff Bruner, Moon Mullican, Al Dexter, and Ernest Tubb dominated the jukeboxes. Many of their songs described the world of the honky-tonk itself, detailing the pleasures to be found "Down at the Roadside Inn," or confessing the sorrows that might come from overindulgence ("Driving Nails in My Coffin," "Headin' Down the Wrong Highway"). Al Dexter's "Pistol Packin' Mama," the giant country hit of 1943 and a "crossover" of the first magnitude, grew out of its singer-composer's experiences in the oil-town-honky-tonk atmosphere of east Texas in the 1930s. More often, though, the songs concentrated on matters that had little or nothing to do with the honky-tonk. Instead, they commented on the private concerns of listeners. Voicing the cry-in-your-beer side of honky-tonk, almost to the point of suicidal impulse, were such songs as Rex Griffin's "The Last Letter," Ted Daffan's "Born to Lose," and Floyd Tillman's "It Makes No Difference Now," which poured forth from a thousand jukeboxes and were carried around the world by lonely, homesick southern servicemen. When Ernest Tubb moved to the Grand Ole Opry in 1943, his Texas-born, beer-joint-shaped style gained a national forum. As he won disciples, his style influenced the music of country entertainers from West Virginia to California.

In the prosperous years that followed World War II, as country music enjoyed its first great period of national expansion, the Texas sounds and styles continued to attract the patronage of country fans everywhere. The honky-tonk style never exercised a complete monopoly during the period, but, for all practical purposes, it had become the all-pervasive sound of mainstream country music. The typical band was small and featured a fiddle, a steel guitar, a "takeoff" guitar (one that could take lead, solo passages), a rhythm guitar whose chords were played in closed, percussive fashion, a string bass, and often a piano. The musicians were capable of performing the hot instrumental licks pioneered by the western swing bands of the 1930s, but instrumentation, while crucial and distinctive, was generally subordinated to the needs of a vocalist. A new generation of honky-tonk singers had emerged, men like Hank Thompson, Webb Pierce, and Lefty Frizzell, who were among the most distinctive stylists that the country music field has seen. Surpassing them all, however, was the young singer from Alabama, Hank Williams, whose career marked the greatest commercial flowering of the honky-tonk style.

When Williams died in 1953, few could have anticipated that very soon the honky-tonk style would be driven from recordings and that country music as a whole would be in shambles. As the rock-and-roll wave inundated American music, traditional country music was driven underground to small record labels and back to the bars as promoters and recording men began their frantic search for young, vigorous performers who could imitate Elvis Presley. The rock-and-roll invasion proved temporary, but it left in its wake a continuing consciousness of the youth market and a decision by the Nashville music industry to produce a middle-of-the-road product that would be appealing to both country and pop audiences. Honky-tonk music, of course, did not die, but it could not remain dominant in such a social context. In an industry obsessed with "crossovers," the hard honky-tonk sound was unwelcome and even embarrassing. Furthermore, the temptation among performers to cross over to the more lucrative and respectable country-pop field was irresistible.

Honky-tonk music remains a vigorous subgenre of country music, but few entertainers are consistently faithful to it. In the late 1950s and early 1960s Ray Price, with his band the Cherokee Cowboys, made crucial contributions to the modern honky-tonk sound, featuring duet harmonies on vocal choruses and a thoroughly electrified sound built around a pedal steel guitar, a heavily bowed fiddle, and walking electric bass patterns. But after popularizing the sound among a host of disciples, Price abandoned the style for the country-pop field he had earlier resisted. George Jones, the Texas singer whose supple style resembled the moaning, bent notes of the pedal steel guitar (first introduced on Webb Pierce records), remains faithful to the honky-tonk sound, but his producers often smother him under a barrage of string instruments and vocal choruses. Buck Owens, who claims both Texas and California, became country music's leading vocalist in the early 1960s with an exciting sound that reflected both the honky-tonks of California and the energy of rockabilly music. He too has since abandoned the style.

At the beginning of the 1980s only Moe Bandy (born in Meridian, Miss., and reared in San Antonio, Tex.) seemed able to prosper in the honky-tonk genre. His clean, crisp articulation of lyrics dealing with those staples of honky-tonk music—drinking, cheating, and heartbreak—are complemented perfectly by a fiddle, pedal steel guitar, and walking bass. The mid-1980s witnessed a revival of honky-tonk music with young entertainers such as Randy Travis and George Strait.

Of all country styles honky-tonk has most closely reflected southern working-class culture and has best marked the evolution of the southern folk from rural to urban industrial life. Although intimately associated with the urban adjustment of southern plain folk, honky-tonk music has been ignored by folklorists because it is not pastoral and because it does not protest. It is dismissed by many, perhaps, because it is too real. Honky-tonk instrumentation both attracts and repels: to many, the whine of the pedal steel guitar and bounce of the shuffle beat evoke elemental impulses and emotions. Honky-tonk music conjures up distasteful, seedy images. The lyrics and instrumentation of honky-tonk music evoke emotional pain, isolation, and human weakness that everyone has shared. The songs can be so full of trite self-pity that they drown listeners in their sentimentality. But at its best, honky-tonk music speaks to loneliness and the need for human empathy felt by each person.

See also HISTORY AND MANNERS: World War II; RECREATION: Roadhouses

Bill C. Malone
Tulane University

Bill C. Malone, *Country Music, U.S.A.: A Fifty-year History* (1968; rev. ed., 1985), with Judith McCullough, eds., *Stars of Country Music: Uncle Dave Macon to Johnny Rodriguez* (1975).

Jazz

"Jazz started in New Orleans," Ferdinand La Menthe "Jelly Roll" Morton pronounced confidently to Alan Lomax in 1938. Morton's magisterial oral autobiography-history resounds with invaluable insights into the story of jazz, New Orleans in the 1890s, and southern life and culture. But like many great insights, this is a *mythic* truth.

Jazz was an agglomeration of black and white folk musics, a rich synthesis that occurred in southern, southwestern, midwestern, and eastern urban centers in the last decade of the 19th century. Jazz began in New Orleans as well—but ragtime and blues musicians wandered the Gulf Coast, the Mississippi Delta, the redlight districts of Washington, Baltimore, Kansas City, New York City, and St. Louis. Early black folk music became widely identified as southern in its associations with vaudeville, theater, circuses, as part of a vast cultural myth of the Old South plantation days, building on Stephen Foster's songs, on the spirituals of the Fisk Jubilee Singers, and on the traditions of blackface minstrelsy.

New Orleans, the most cosmopolitan and urbane center in the South before and after the Civil War, provided a hospitable climate for local and itinerant musicians and had a long tradition of musical culture, high and low. In the second half of the 19th century New Orleans mixed a vivid combination of musics—brass band marches, parlor music, Creole and Cajun folksongs, Caribbean musics, church music—and produced a style known as "ragtime," after the spicy, syncopated piano music of the Mississippi River Valley. By about 1915, this new music was often called "jass" or "jazz." Other musical centers flourished at the same time: Memphis, with its bawdy Beale Street district featuring W. C. Handy's dance orchestra; Kansas City, with legions of ragtime writers and publishers; St. Louis, a repository for even more intense ragtime playing, composing, and publishing.

Jazz drew on local scenes and traditions, indigenous southern sensibilities and languages. Handy captured blues songs from the Delta, with resonant lines like "I'm going where the Southern cross the Dog," a near-mystical reference to a Mississippi railroad junction of the Southern and the Yazoo-Delta lines ("Yellow Dog Blues"). Or Jelly Roll Morton could sing, "Michigan water tastes like sherry wine, Mississippi water tastes like turpentine" ("Michigan Water Blues"). Local customs and scenes were paid homage by southern musicians, as Morton hailed the Lake Pontchartrain resort area in "Milenberg Joys" or Louis Armstrong recalled a Basin Street brothel in "Mahogany Hall Stomp."

Jazz in the South was created and exported by blacks and whites, by musicians of every ethnic background—Irish, Italian, French-Spanish-Creole, Jamaican, German, Greek, Protestant, Catholic, and Jewish. This diversity of backgrounds guaranteed variety within the music. Place-name blues celebrated the region: "Atlanta Blues," "Vicksburg Blues," "Memphis Blues," "New Orleans Blues." Other kinds of jazz registered local color: "Beale Street Blues," "South Rampart Street Parade," "Bogalusa Strut," "Chattanooga Stomp," "Ole Miss," "Chef

Menteur Joys." Jazz drew from church music—"Sing On," "When the Saints Come Marching In," "Down by the Riverside"—and from popular exotica—"Big Chief Battle-Ax," "Hindustan," "Lena from Palesteena," "The Sheik of Araby," "Chinatown." The music consciously echoed opera, military bands, call-and-response church singing, ethnic dance music, country blues singing, genteel parlor songs, light classics, and Tin Pan Alley productions.

Southern music absorbed cosmopolitan influences easily and converged with a wide world of vaudeville and minstrel shows, road companies of musicals and operettas, and the long-established French Opera in New Orleans's *Vieux Carré*. The most local and original of New Orleans traditions, Mardi Gras, adopted as its musical theme "If Ever I Cease to Love," a ditty from a New York musical. And another "jazz standard" was created from a New York publisher's arrangement of a novelty march by Yale student Porter Steele—"High Society."

The turn of the century witnessed an explosion of popular music creation and dissemination. Phonograph records, piano rolls, and sheet music made possible a nationwide popular musical culture on a large scale. Scott Joplin's "Maple Leaf Rag" (1899) probably sold a million copies in sheet music form, published first in Sedalia, Mo. Local publishers and artists sprang up everywhere, with important centers in southern and midwestern cities: St. Louis, New Orleans, Kansas City, Indianapolis, and Chicago. Southern music was exported on a grand scale, and local fairs and exhibitions held in Atlanta and New Orleans, the Chicago Columbian Exposition of 1893, and the St. Louis World's Fair of 1904 brought Americans into direct contact with the new southern music.

In New Orleans instrumental music was in constant demand for parties, formal dances, in neighborhood dance halls, cabarets, and social clubs. Popular social dances like the waltz, mazurka, schottische, quadrilles, and reels along with black vernacular dances created a need for a wide range of highly rhythmic accompaniment. By the 1890s strongly syncopated dance music of the sort echoed in piano ragtime was provided by various instrumental combinations. In the regulated redlight district (sardonically nicknamed "Storyville" after the alderman who proposed its legislation), ragtime and blues piano players worked in bordellos. In the rest of the city, bandsmen played for dances and parties.

Jazz performer Bunk Johnson (left) and folk-blues musician Leadbelly (right), late 1940s

Charles "Buddy" Bolden, a black cornetist, was the best-known leader of a rough-and-ready early jazz band of the 1890s. "Papa" Jack Laine, a white drummer-entrepreneur, organized many dance and marching bands around 1900. John Robichaux formed a long-lived "society" orchestra that read popular music scores. Freddie Keppard, another cornet virtuoso, led a group called That Creole Band on extensive vaudeville tours from New Orleans after 1910. But the New Orleans band that created a nationwide (ultimately worldwide) consciousness for a new popular music was the Original Dixieland Jazz Band—five white New Orleanians from Jack Laine's stable who went to Chicago, New York, then London, making in 1917 and 1918 the first New Orleans jazz records and achieving a monumental success in vaudeville and cabaret appearances.

The repertoire of the Original Dixieland Jazz Band was that of New Orleans jazz as it had developed for some 20 years: "Tiger Rag," "Livery Stable Blues," "Clarinet Marmalade," "Ostrich Walk," "Bluin' the Blues," and others became jazz staples and were drawn from the shared traditions of black and white musicians. The Original Dixieland Jazz Band Americanized jazz and jazzified America. Imitations of their music were heard everywhere, and "jazz" passed from the argot of the *demimonde* (where it meant either sexual intercourse or sexual fluids) into the vocabulary of middle America as the name of this new physical, sensual music. The Original Dixieland Jazz Band was followed by a continuous outmigration of southern musicians to Chicago, New York, the West Coast, and Europe. What had been a provincial oddity, a local delicacy like hog's maw, grits, or pralines, a purely regional music, became a significant force in world culture.

A "second generation" of musicians who grew up in the earliest days of New Orleans jazz disseminated it as a complex and sophisticated musical form, a form based on individual improvisational styles blended into an intuitive whole: Jelly Roll Morton (piano-composer); Joseph "King" Oliver (cornet), who took young Louis Armstrong to Chicago in 1922; Sidney Bechet (clarinet, soprano sax), who took jazz genius to Europe in 1919 with the Southern Syncopated Orchestra; Johnny Dodds (clarinet); Edward "Kid" Ory (trombone); Warren "Baby" Dodds (drums). The New Orleans Rhythm Kings, Clarence Williams's bands, and many other New Orleans bands recorded and brought live jazz to the speakeasies of 1920s America.

The impact of the new jazz recordings was catalytic. Jazz was absorbed and imitated by society dance bands everywhere by 1920, with great financial success realized by white bandleaders like Art Hickman, Paul Specht, and Paul Whiteman. "Jazz" to most Americans of the mid-1920s was simply synonymous with "pop music" of any description, and novelist F. Scott Fitzgerald could create the idea of a "Jazz Age." Jazz was identified with youth, excess, exuberance, sin, and license, with gin mills and crime, and with some of the old redlight-district stigma.

In the 1920s and 1930s jazz was established in Chicago and New York, with luminaries like Fletcher Henderson (from Birmingham), Edward "Duke" Ellington (from Washington, D.C.), Jack Teagarden (from Texas), and others rising to the top of the jazz world. Jazz also flourished in the South, especially in so-called "territory" bands that succeeded regionally. Top-flight big bands created their own versions of jazz (now known more frequently as "swing") in Kansas City (Bennie Moten, Harlan Leonard, Walter Page), Missouri (Charlie Creath, Jesse Stone, the Missourians), Memphis (Jimmie Lunceford), Texas (Don Albert, Alphonso Trent), and New Orleans (Sam Morgan, Fate Marable, Armand J. Piron). Some of these groups made the national scene: Bennie Moten's band became the great Count Basie orchestra of the 1930s; the Missourians became Cab Calloway's band; and Jimmie Lunceford created one of the most innovative bands of the era.

Other southern jazz stars became nationally known: blues singers like Gertrude "Ma" Rainey, Bessie Smith, and Ethel Waters rose from backgrounds in minstrelsy and vaudeville to great fame. Jazz virtuosi like Louis Armstrong, Jimmie Noone, Sidney Bechet, and others established exalted standards for playing. Itinerant blues pianists like Pinetop Smith, Jimmy Yancey, Eurreal "Little Brother" Montgomery, Crippled Clarence Lofton, Albert Ammons, Meade Lux Lewis, and Pete Johnson popularized a form of Deep South keyboard style most commonly called "barrelhouse" or "boogie-woogie" piano, which enjoyed a wild vogue in the late 1930s. A rough, powerful form of piano blues, the music was familiar in turpentine camps and rural juke joints a generation before it reached the nation's radios and phonographs.

The South supplied vernacular dances to America after jazz became a national phenomenon in 1918. The brisk one-step "animal dances" of 1910—the Grizzly Bear, Bunny Hug, Turkey Trot, Cubanola Glide—were superseded by the Charleston, the Black Bottom, Varsity Drag, tangos, the Lindy Hop, Suzie-Q, and dozens of variants based on old black social dance patterns. Formalized versions of such dances could be seen at big dance halls, in revues like the famous Cotton Club extravaganzas in Harlem, and in vaudeville routines by such stars as Bill "Bojangles" Robinson, Florence Mills, Snakehips Tucker, and John Bubbles. Jazz was music for dancing, and long before aficionados made it intellectually respectable, America voted with its feet for the new music.

By the 1930s radio had joined with the phonograph to popularize jazz. Radio promotion helped establish bands like those of Duke Ellington and Benny Goodman, while jazz-oriented dance bands like the Coon-Sanders Orchestra, the Casa Loma Orchestra, Paul Whiteman's band, and others brought jazz into the nation's parlors nearly every day over network radio. What started as a provincial cultural phenomenon in one generation became the best-known trademark of America, a symbol for the nation's youthful vitality and melting-pot variety. In Europe, jazz was studied, imitated, and admired to the point of worship by young students and musicians.

The movements of modern jazz after the 1930s have been nationwide, with important centers of activity on the East and West coasts. The South, however, has continued to contribute major jazz artists, such as pianist-composer Thelonious Monk, the Adderly brothers, Nat and Julian ("Cannonball"), and young trumpet virtuoso Wynton Marsalis. Jazz of every variety flourishes in southern cities, from "revivalist" centers like New Orleans's French Quarter, Memphis's Beale Street area, and St. Louis's Gaslight Square to cabarets and concert-hall performances in every major city. Since the 1950s, jazz has moved from the center of popular musical culture to become a kind of "alternative culture" of great vigor and variety.

Jazz was woven into the fabric of southern life. An urban synthesis of rural musics, it reflected the development of the modern South after the turn of the century. Created by black musicians from a multiethnic culture, jazz unified the nation's sensibility. Jazz radically altered its listeners through its feelings about freedom, equality, imagination, joy, and physical vitality.

See also BLACK LIFE: Music, Black; RECREATION: Mardi Gras; WOMEN'S LIFE: Blues-singing Women

William J. Schafer
Berea College

Joachim Ernst Berendt, *The Jazz Book: From Ragtime to Fusion and Beyond* (1982); Rudi Blesh, *Shining Trumpets: A History of Jazz* (1976); Leonard G. Feather, *The Book of Jazz: From Then till Now* (1965); Mark C. Gridley, *Jazz Styles: History and Analysis* (1985); Rex Harris, *The Story of Jazz* (1960); Nat Hentoff, *Jazz Is* (1976); Gunther Schuller, *The History of Jazz* (1968); Marshall Stearns, *The Story of Jazz* (1956); Frank Tirro, *Jazz: A History* (1977); Barry Ulanov, *A History of Jazz in America* (1972); Otto Werner, *The Origin and Development of Jazz* (1984).

Minstrelsy

It is something of a historical paradox that the popular desire for an autonomous cultural tradition in the South—one separating it from the perceived imperfections of the industrial North and of European civilization—should induce the region's white citizenry to turn to the enslaved Afro-Americans for their music, dance, and humor. Blackface minstrelsy is the clearest antebellum example of this contradictory cultural pattern. In the 1820s individual white thespians began doing imitations of Afro-American song and dance in urban theaters. Their performances presented clownlike images of black slaves, portraying them as superstitious, happy-go-lucky "dancing darkies." The actors blackened their faces with burnt cork to accent these caricatures. The most renowned of the early blackface performers were George Washington Dixon, who created a sensation with his "Zip Coon" character, and Thomas D. Rice, who popularized the song and dance, "Jump Jim Crow." Rice copied his famous act from an elderly, crippled, Afro-American stable hand—and even borrowed his suit of ragged clothing for the initial stage performance. His comic rendition of "Jump Jim Crow" was an overwhelming success, catapulting him into a much-heralded tour of the major entertainment halls in the United States and then England. By the 1840s blackface minstrelsy in the South had evolved into a stylized entertainment formula based on the music, dance, and comedy of Afro-Americans and featuring an entire troupe of actors for the show.

From its inception, minstrelsy's characterization of black people was stereotyped. Plantation slaves were depicted as contented, comical, and childlike, while urban house servants were portrayed as dandies and dummies who aped white mannerisms and longed to be white themselves. Most of the popular figures in antebellum minstrel entertainment were from the South and had some knowledge of Afro-American folklore prior to putting on burnt cork. The best known among these performers were Dixon, Rice, Dan Emmett, E. P. Christy, and Stephen Foster. Although its performers reinforced the prevailing racism of the era, both in the South and the North, southern minstrelsy presented a more complex and even varied caricature of African slaves to the American public than had been attempted in previous decades. And even though the characters were terribly distorted, one important effect of the antebellum minstrel tradition was to help force the issues of slavery and emancipation to the forefront of the nation's political agenda. Moreover, the song and dance performed by the white minstrels laid the groundwork for a better appreciation of authentic Afro-American music and humor by white Americans. This trend became more evident in the postbellum era.

After the Civil War black entertainers joined the ranks of minstrelsy, and by the 1870s they dominated the minstrel scene. The more popular and profitable of these troupes, however, were still owned and operated by such white entrepreneurs as Charles Callender, owner of the famous Georgia Minstrels, and W. A. Mahara, owner of the popular Mahara's Minstrels. This select group of white owners and managers, and those who followed in their footsteps, insisted that the material and the format of the shows remain faithful to the content and formulas of early blackface minstrelsy. They required the black entertainers they hired to reproduce the outdated routines of the antebellum minstrel tradition. In essence, they functioned as guardians of the old-culture order, and their collective endeavors resulted in the perpetuation of demeaning racial stereotypes in American show business well into the 20th century. Talented black entertainers who joined the white-owned minstrel troupes often found themselves between the hammer and the anvil with respect to their cultural identity and their artistic integrity. The white entrepreneurs dominated the business; they determined who could work in the most prestigious companies and offered limited fame and fortune in exchange for the Afro-American performers' compliance with the blackface minstrel legacy. Although there was some latitude in negotiating these arrangements, even the most popular—and, therefore, potentially the most powerful—of the black performers in these shows sacrificed their artistic independence in return for stardom and financial gain.

The careers of minstrelsy's most acclaimed Afro-American performers—James Bland, Billy Kersands, and Bert Williams—offer a clear, if disheartening, illustration of the dilemmas of black minstrel entertainers. Bland, known as the "Negro Stephen Foster," was an accomplished musician and composer who wrote over 700 songs in his lifetime, among them "Oh Dem Golden Slippers" and "Carry Me Back to Old Virginny." Although his material included some authentic black folklore, it was overshadowed by a permeating nostalgia for the Old South and slavery. The characters in his songs and his stage performances were replicas of the antebellum minstrel stereotypes—contented plantation slaves, faithful servants, and comic urban dandies being the most prominent. Only during an extended tour of Europe was he able to perform without the customary blackface makeup and routines.

Likewise, Billy Kersands, the most popular Afro-American minstrel entertainer of the postbellum period, based his comedy routines on demeaning racial caricatures of his own people. He portrayed black males as dull-witted and gullible, while burlesquing black women as matronly and unattractive. To his credit, Kersands also made good use of authentic Afro-American folk humor, and he was an excellent dancer who pioneered the use of soft-shoe dancing routines on the minstrel stage. These aspects of his performances may have offset his more self-abasing comedy routines and help to explain his widespread popularity among black people in the South. Billy Kersands's successor to the throne of minstrel comedy was Bert Williams, the last major Afro-American entertainer to perform in blackface. His career began in the 1890s and peaked in the 1910–20 period when he became the first Afro-American to perform with the Ziegfeld Follies. He was a brilliant humorist, but he was also locked into the role of a hapless, antebellum darky, in spite of criticism from his own race. This situation led fellow comic W. C. Fields to comment that "Bert Williams is the funniest man I ever saw, and the saddest man I ever knew."

With the advent of the 20th century, minstrelsy in the South went into a slow but steady decline. Some of the more popular troupes like F. S. Wolcott's Rabbit Foot Minstrels, based in Port Gibson, Miss., and the black-owned Silas Green's Minstrels from New Orleans, La., continued to perform for segregated southern audiences, bolstered by an influx of talented female blues singers such as Ma Rainey and Bessie Smith. But the heyday of southern minstrelsy was over, and it was eventually replaced by other forms of entertainment like vaudeville and motion pictures. The minstrel tradition left behind a conflicting legacy: it was the training ground for many gifted Afro-American entertainers who would not have had the opportunity to develop their talents otherwise, but it was also the spawning ground for many degrading racial stereotypes that found their way into the popular culture of 20th-century America.

See also BLACK LIFE: Dance, Black; Music, Black; / Jim Crow; Silas Green Show

Bill Barlow
Howard University

Gary D. Engle, ed., *This Grotesque Essence: Plays from the American Minstrel Stage* (1978); Hans Nathan, *Dan Emmett and the Rise of Early Negro Minstrelsy* (1962); Ike Simond, *Old Slack's Reminiscence and Pocket History of the Colored Profession from 1865 to 1891* (1974); Robert C. Toll, *Blacking Up: The Minstrel Show in Nineteenth-Century America* (1974).

Música Tejana

Música Tejana, or "Tex-Mex music" as it is sometimes called, is the music of the Texas-Mexicans or *Tejanos*. Inhabiting the same geographic area of south Texas, the *Tejanos* have successively been citizens of a Spanish colony, independent Mexico, the Republic of Texas, the Confederate states, and the United States of America. The development of *música Tejana* is interwoven with the history of the *Tejanos* from the 1700s to the present.

In a cultural sense, from the 1700s until the early 1900s, the *Tejanos* were basically a Mexican provincial people, living in an isolated frontier area of the southern United States. In the past 50 years there has been a steady migration of *Tejanos* from the farms and *ranchos* of south Texas to the urban industrial centers in Texas and throughout the United States. *Tejanos* have incorporated aspects of Anglo-American culture, but overall they have resisted becoming a colonized and absorbed people. They have developed a unique regional Texas-Mexican culture, which is one of the most distinctive subcultures in the South and one that is reflected in the *Tejanos'* own musical styles. Over the course of two centuries *música Tejana* has resulted from a blending of early Spanish and Mexican music; French-European styles filtered through Mexico; Latin-Caribbean music; and now Mexican and American popular music. *Música Tejana* is thus an especially revealing indicator of the subregion of south Texas and the role of music in reflecting broader ethnic patterns within the South.

Little is known about the beginnings of *música Tejana*. Paintings and diaries depict *fandangos*, or dances, held in San Antonio and south Texas through the 1800s, but they give little descriptive information about the sound of the music other than to call it "Spanish" or "Mexican." Violins and *pitos* (wind instruments of various types) usually provided the melody with a guitar for harmonic accompaniment. Sometimes a rustic drum called a *tambora ranchera* was used to accentuate the rhythm.

By the mid to late 1800s, *Tejano* musicians were playing the Spanish and Mexican dance music less and were adopting a new European style that was trickling in from central Mexico. In the 1860s Maximilian, backed by his French army, ruled in Mexico. In his court in Mexico City and in garrisons throughout the country, the European salon music and dances of the time, such as the polka, waltz, mazurka, and schottische, were popular. These styles were enthusiastically embraced in south Texas by the *Tejanos*.

The *Tejanos'* musical culture was also influenced by the Germans who began immigrating to the central Texas area in the 1840s. These German-Texans also favored the European salon music and dances. At times they would hire local *Tejano* musicians to play for their own celebrations.

By the late 1800s the informal *Tejano* bands of violins, *pitos*, and guitars were almost exclusively playing European salon music genres for the local dances. Taking root in this frontier area, far from its European and central Mexican source, this music was being thoroughly adapted to the *Tejano* aesthetic. With French and German styles layered over the base of Spanish and Mexican music, the modern development of *música Tejana* began.

Between 1900 and the 1930s three important *Tejano* styles began to distinguish themselves. The tradition of the *guitarreros*, or singing guitarists, was the first style to become solidified and commercially popular. Using the waltz and polka rhythms with a simple guitar accompaniment, the *guitarreros* imparted stories, news, information, and morals in their songs. They sang primarily in the cantinas and at local male gatherings where listening to and discussing the songs were often combined with drinking and rowdy behavior. Dance music, on the other hand, was always instrumental (until the 1940s). Because of the feeling that words were superfluous to dancing, and partially to separate it from the cantina context, *Tejano* instrumental dance music was kept separate from the *guitarreros'* vocal style.

From the informal ensembles of musicians of the late 1800s, two styles of instrumental dance music emerged as the *Tejanos* entered the 20th century. A new German instrument, the diatonic button accordion, which was perfectly suited to playing the polkas and waltzes, was gaining great popularity among rural *Tejanos* engaged in agricultural labor. Shopkeepers and skilled *Tejanos* working in the small towns, however, were hiring small bands of musicians called *orquestas típicas*. The style of these bands was similar to the earlier violin, *pito*, and guitar dance ensembles, but they had become more organized and sophisticated over time.

From the 1920s to the 1940s, lured by the economic promises of the urban American way of life, many *Tejanos* moved to the cities of south Texas—San Antonio, Corpus Christi, Brownsville, and Laredo. The rural agricultural workers had few skills to advance themselves in their new environment and became employed in low-paying, working-class jobs. The shopkeepers and skilled *Tejanos* from the towns moved into more upwardly mobile, middle-class positions in business and trades. In the cities, the difference between the aspirations and cultural values of the working-class *Tejanos*, on the one hand, and the emerging middle-class *Tejanos*, on the other, became more evident and pronounced. The working class, who suffered from discrimination and received few economic benefits from contact with Anglo-American culture, sought refuge within their own traditional culture. The middle class, encouraged by economic gains, however, saw the adoption of some American culture and values as a passport to greater opportunity and a release from Anglo-American prejudice. Working-class musical groups, or *conjuntos*, developed one distinctive musical tradition, and the middle-class bands, renamed *orquestas Tejanas*, developed another.

By the 1940s and 1950s these two dance music styles were intrinsically tied with the identities of these different segments of the *Tejano* community. Over the basic foundation of the traditional *Tejano* music of 1900, the conservatism and resistance to acculturation of the *conjuntos* and the incorporation of Anglo-American stylistic traits in the *orquestas Tejanas* created two unique Texas-Mexican styles.

Música Norteña, meaning "music of the North" (from the point of view of Mexico), played by *conjuntos*, is synonymous with the sound of the German diatonic button accordion. The instrument may have been brought and popularized by the Germans and Bohemians settling in central Texas or by the Germans working in the mining and brewing industries in northern Mexico. Newspaper accounts nonetheless show that by 1898 *Tejanos* in rural areas of the south Texas *chaparral* were playing their Texas-Mexican polkas, waltzes, and schottisches on a one-row, one-key button accordion.

Norteña accordion music began as a solo tradition. The accordion gradually replaced the violins and *pitos* as the preferred instrument for dance music in the rural areas, but because it was played in the rural areas of the *ranchos* for the laboring people, the button accordion became associated early with working-class *Tejanos*. As more of these *Tejanos* moved from the *ranchos* to the cities, the instrument was heard in the houses and cantinas of the *barrios* (Tejano neighborhoods). By the 1930s the popularity of the *Norteña* style was such that accordionists, paired with guitarists or *bajo sexto* (a 12-string bass guitar, originally from central Mexico) players, began recording their own ranch-style *Tejano* polkas. Following the lead of the *guitarreros* by making "ethnic records" for American companies, the developing *conjuntos* were commercializing their style and bringing the nostalgia for the *rancho* to the city.

Although accordion dance music had been popular for some 30 years in rural areas, two men, Santiago Jiménez from San Antonio and Narciso Martínez, from the lower Rio Grande Valley, were responsible for pioneering the *Norteña* style on recording and radio broadcasts in the 1930s. Because of their popularity and exposure on recordings, their individual accordion styles became models for a generation of musicians. Jiménez had a smooth, fluid style of playing the polkas and waltzes he composed, and he emphasized the bass notes and chords of his instrument. Expanding his *conjunto*, he utilized a guitarist for harmonic accompaniment and added a *tololoche*, or upright bass, for a stronger bass line. Martínez meanwhile had a faster, more ornamented style than Jiménez and emphasized the treble buttons of his accordion. Rarely using the bass notes or chords of his instrument, Martínez delegated the harmonic accompaniment and bass line completely to his accompanying guitarist. Both musicians used the newer two-row, two-key model of accordion.

In the 1940s, taking over the singing tradition of the *guitarreros*, these pioneer accordionists began to add song lyrics with duet harmonies to their previously instrumental dance music. The typical lyrics of lost love, often framed in a rural setting, seemed to reflect the working-class *Tejanos'* ties with the past on the *rancho* and their resistance to adopting urban American culture.

By the 1950s *música Norteña* was crystallizing into a mature style as a second generation of accordionists came to popularity in the working-class cantinas, clubs, and dance halls. Tony de la Rosa, from Kingsville, Tex., became an extremely popular performer in that decade. He used amplification for the four instruments that by this time had become standard in the *conjuntos*—accordion, *bajo sexto*, bass, and drums.

De la Rosa's *conjunto* was also one of the first of a score of groups to perform on what became known as the migrant trail. Areas like Fresno, Calif., and Chicago, Ill., accumulated large communities of transplanted *Tejanos* who paid well to have *conjuntos* from Texas play for their weekend dances.

From the late 1950s to the 1980s the four-member amplified *conjunto* has changed little. *Música Norteña* has continued its conservative stance toward Anglo-American culture by reflecting and reinforcing the identity and values of the working-class *Tejano* public. Despite his recent flirtations with Anglo-American styles, Flaco Jiménez, son of the pioneer accordionist Santiago Jiménez, and his *Norteña* style best exemplify the *conjuntos* of the past 20 years. Like his father, Flaco has been a commercially successful and influential performer within the *Tejano* community.

In the late 1800s *orquestas típicas* (small, genteel orchestras of violins, flutes, clarinets, mandolins, and guitars) formed in south Texas from the earlier informal *Tejano* ensembles. Their audience was primarily a middle-class one, made up of small-town shop owners and skilled employees descended from those tenacious *Tejanos* who had held their land in the face of the Anglo-American economic advance. With more continuous income from their clientele, these bands playing *música Tejana* became better trained and more professional than ever before. When these small-town *Tejano* patrons moved to the cities in the 20th century, the *orquestas* followed.

Orquestas Tejanas developed in an urban environment among those *Tejanos* seeking to balance their traditional culture and the trappings of middle-class American culture. Striving to play in a smoother, more orchestrated style, blending *Tejano*, Latin, and American music, the *orquestas Tejanas* took over in the cities where the *or-*

questas típicas had left off. Paralleling the rise of the *conjuntos*, by the 1930s and 1940s the *orquestas Tejanas* were solidifying their style on recordings and were a necessity for the dances of the more upwardly mobile segment of *Tejano* society.

Beto Ville, a saxophone player from south Texas, is recognized as the father of the *orquesta Tejana* style. Patterning his *orquesta* after American dance bands, like that of Glenn Miller, he used a full horn section, trained musicians, and written musical arrangements. Thus, the flutes and violins of the *orquestas típicas* were replaced by trumpets, saxophones, and trombones. The new *orquestas Tejanas'* choice of repertoire was American foxtrots and swing music and Latin-Caribbean dances popularized in the United States by the orchestras of musicians such as Desi Arnaz and Xavier Cugat. But never straying too far from their ties to *Tejano* culture, they also played highly arranged versions of the same *Tejano* polkas and waltzes played by the *conjuntos*.

In the 1950s the *orquesta Tejana* style crystallized into a well-developed form adding sound reinforcement, complex vocal arrangements, and some new instruments—the electric guitar, the electric bass, and the electric organ. By the 1960s and 1970s two groups, "Little Joe y la Pamilia" and "Sunny Ozuna and the Sunliners," were at the top of popularity. A new generation of *orquestas Tejanas* was playing for a younger, well-educated, more affluent *Tejano* audience. The groups still played American and Latin dance music, but foxtrots were replaced by rock and soul music and earlier Latin dances like the Mambo and Rumba were replaced by New York-Cuban Salsa music. But refusing to lose touch completely with their Texas-Mexican traditions, the newer bands continued to play polkas as the core of the *orquesta Tejana* style.

The tradition of singing troubadours, with a long history in Spain and Mexico, has also shaped *música Tejana*. The *guitarreros* in Texas represented a continuation of that tradition. By the late 1800s and early 1900s many professional *guitarreros* sang in the plazas and cantinas of south Texas towns. Their repertoire consisted of romantic, lyrical songs spawned by the popularity of the operatic style in Mexico and local ballads called *corridos*, which developed from the transplanted Spanish romance ballad tradition. When singing topical *corridos* of local or national events, the *guitarreros* were often the only source of news for the local population.

Lydia Mendoza, Tejana *singer, from the Les Blank film* Chulas Fronteras *(1976)*

La Plaza del Zacate, or "Haymarket Square," in San Antonio was a favorite gathering place for many of these singers through the 1930s. In the 1920s American recording companies such as Vocalion, RCA, Okeh, Bluebird, and Decca came to San Antonio. Setting up makeshift studios in hotels, they made "ethnic records" of local groups to sell to the growing *Tejano* market. The *guitarreros* that performed in Haymarket Square were some of the first to be commercially recorded. Duets such as Pedro Rocha and Lupe Martínez, Juan Gaytán and Timoteo Cantú, and "*Los Hermanos Chavarria*" (the Chavarria Brothers) were well known in the plazas as well as on recordings by the early 1930s. Although the *guitarrero* style was mostly a male tradition, one of the most famous of these singers was a young girl with a beautiful quavering voice—Lydia Mendoza, "*La Alondra de la Frontera*" (The Lark of the Borderlands). She began recording at an early age with her musical family but later enjoyed a solo career with her famed recordings of songs such as "*Mal Hombre*" (Bad Man) and "*Pero Ay Que Triste*" (But Oh How Sad).

The commercial heyday of the *guitarreros* was short-lived, however. The same factors of urbanization that prompted the recording companies to see a commercial value in the style ultimately wrought irrevocable changes in the singing tradition. English- and Spanish-language radio and other mass media were taking over the *guitarreros'* role as the major source of news and information. Also, by the 1940s in the urban environment attitudes about the separate functions of the singing and dance-music traditions had become blurred. The working-class *conjuntos* in the cities gravitated toward performing in the cantinas that had been the domain of the *guitarreros*. In the more permissive urban atmosphere the *conjuntos* could add romantic song lyrics and duet harmonies to their polkas and waltzes without alienating their audience. The *guitarreros* then slowly faded from commercial popularity as their function had been usurped by the media and the dance-music tradition.

Although singing guitarists, or *mariachis* as they are now called, are prevalent today in Texas, their repertoire and style are part of a more general Mexican musical tradition made popular by Mexican movies and records of the past 40 years. Few of the old-style *guitarreros* remain.

Today within the *Tejano* community, one can find an audience for almost any style of *Tejano*, Mexican, or Anglo-American music. Country-and-western music sung in Spanish, *Tejano* rock and jazz, *música tropical* from the Caribbean, *mariachi* music, and the veteran *Tejano* styles can all be heard on radio stations and in dance halls throughout south Texas. Nonetheless, *Tejano* working-class and middle-class economic positions, perspectives, and identities have changed little in the past 25 years, and *música Norteña* and the *orquestas Te-*

janas continue to appeal to the largest segments of the *Tejano* community.

See also ETHNIC LIFE: / Mexicans

Dan W. Dickey
Austin, Texas

Kay Council, "Exploratory Documentation of Texas *Norteño-Conjunto* Music" (M.A. thesis, University of Texas at Austin, 1978), *Texas Observer* (25 March 1977); Dan Dickey, *The Kennedy "Corridos": A Study of the Ballads of a Mexican American Hero* (1978), *Texas Observer* (16 July 1976); Américo Paredes, *A Texas-Mexican Cancionero: Folksongs of the Lower Border* (1976), *With His Pistol in His Hand: A Border Ballad and Its Hero* (1958); Manuel Peña, in *And Other Neighborly Names: Social Process and Cultural Image in Texas Folklore*, ed. Richard Bauman and Roger D. Abrahams (1981), *The Texas-Mexican Conjunto: History of a Working Class Music* (1985); Chris Strachwitz, *Texas-Mexican Border Music* (1974).

Protest

Despite the South's reputation as a conservative region, both protest activities and protest music have flourished at various times in its history. Indeed, southerners have played vital roles in the shaping of the protest genre in this century.

Protest has never been absent from American music. America's revolution against the British was waged in song as well as on the battlefield, and antebellum reformers fought slavery and alcohol in scores of militant songs. In the years surrounding World War I the famous Industrial Workers of the World (IWW) made music an integral part of their struggle with capitalism, and their *Little Red Songbook* continues to be a source of anthems for anyone concerned with labor rights or social justice.

Protest music as a distinct genre, though, developed in the 1930s in the context of the Great Depression and was linked directly to southern workers' struggles for economic dignity. Long presumed to be docile and fatalistic, the southern folk made themselves known in a number of dramatic ways during that period—through their presence in relief offices and hobo jungles, through their migrations (as in the case of the Okies), and, above all, in the wave of strikes that made such names as Gastonia and Marion, N.C., and Harlan County, Ky., well known throughout the United States. The traditional southern habit of ballad making was put to the service of topical songs, which commented on a wide range of social grievances. Such songs even appeared in the repertories of professional country and blues performers, as exemplified by Frank Welling and John McGhee's "The Marion Massacre" (about the shooting of unarmed strikers in North Carolina), the Monroe Brothers' "The Forgotten Soldier Boy" (about the Bonus Marchers of 1932), and Billie Holiday's "Strange Fruit" (about lynching). Even cowboy singer Gene Autry recorded a song of tribute for a radical labor leader—"The Death of Mother Jones."

Most socially conscious songs, however, emerged from areas of worker discontent that dotted the southern landscape. There, "conservative" southern workers often came in contact with ideologically radical labor organizers and political activists, many of whom came from the North, who further fueled the impulse toward song making. In the Mississippi River Delta area of Arkansas, a black sharecropper and preacher named John Handcox supplied songs like "Raggedy" and "There Are Mean Things Happening in This Land" for his fellow farmers and members of the Southern Tenant Farmers' Union who had organized to protect themselves from landlords. At least one of his songs, "Roll the Union On," moved into the possession of union members in other parts of the country.

In Gastonia, N.C., a young mother and millworker named Ella May Wiggins emerged as a spokesperson for the striking cotton-mill workers who walked out of their plants in protest against low pay and the dehumanizing "stretch out" system (a requirement that workers operate additional machines at the same pay). The Gastonia strike attained national notoriety when the Communist-dominated National Textile Workers Union appeared with its policy of "dual unionism," which challenged both the conservative American Federation of Labor and the local power structure. Wiggins's songs lifted the morale of the workers and presented their case to a larger public. They also gave her the reputation of "labor agitator," and when she was shot to death on 14 September 1929, while riding in the back of a truck with other strikers, many people felt that she had been singled out for execution. She became a martyr in the American labor community, and her songs were printed in such liberal and radical journals as the *Nation* and *New Masses* and were sung at northern labor rallies by such activists as Margaret Larkin.

Strikes in the coal-mining district of Harlan and Bell counties, Ky., inspired a similar wave of topical ballad making. One of the most famous labor songs in American history, "Which Side Are You On?," appeared when Florence Reece, the wife of a Harlan County organizer, voiced her anger at the brutality of the company-paid deputy sheriffs. The most famous trio of balladeers, though, to come out of the Kentucky coalfields was Aunt Molly Jackson and her brother and half-sister, Jim Garland and Sara Ogan. Before they were blacklisted and forced to leave Kentucky, each of them turned out a steady stream of songs that graphically portrayed the grim lives of coal miners while also championing their rights. These included Aunt Molly's "Dreadful Memories" and "I Am a Union Woman," Garland's "I Don't Want Your Millions Mister" and "Ballad of Harry Simms" (about a young Communist organizer who was killed by company "gun thugs"), and Ogan's "I Hate the Capitalist System."

These and other songs like them moved north to become the nucleus of an incipient urban folk music movement. They were taken by the northern radicals who recognized their organizing potential, and of course, by such southern singers as Aunt Molly Jackson, Jim Garland, and Woodrow Wilson "Woody" Guthrie. Until he moved in 1940 to New York, where he became part of the labor/radical community, Guthrie had been identified as a hillbilly singer with a storehouse of traditional songs and a guitar style roughly copied after that of Maybelle Carter. The Okemah, Okla., native, though, had been a champion of his fellow Okie migrants ever since he began singing over KFVD in Los Angeles in 1937. With such songs as "Talking Dust Bowl Blues," "Dust Bowl Refugee," and "Do-Re-Mi," Guthrie established his reputation as a champion of the poor and dispossessed. In New York he was welcomed as "the new Joe Hill" and very quickly became the center of a coterie of musicians, which included such fellow expatriate southerners as Aunt Molly Jackson, Brownie McGhee, Sonny Terry, Josh White, Sis Cunningham, Lee Hays, and Huddie "Leadbelly" Ledbetter. He also inspired a host of disciples within his northern audiences, including most notably Cisco Houston, Jack Elliott, and Pete Seeger, who preserved Guthrie's commitment to the use of the folksong as a weapon in the struggle for social justice.

The protest-song movement of the 1930s and 1940s was confined to a narrow segment of Americans—labor activists, radical intellectuals, and some college students. That of the late 1950s and early 1960s, on the other hand, was of a much broader scope and was in fact introduced to virtually every American home through the media of national television and stereophonic sound reproduction. Again, southerners played direct and vital roles in the development of a body of protest material. Although modern protest song making was clearly linked to the traditions and singers of the 1930s, especially through the continued presence of such activists as Pete Seeger, the phenomenon gained most of its inspiration from the civil rights movement. In the aftermath of the Montgomery Bus Boycott in 1956 black people began resurrecting older religious songs to provide moral strength and spiritual sustenance in their marches and demonstrations, and, in the time-tested folk fashion, they attached new words to old folk and religious melodies. Such songs as "Oh Freedom" and "We Shall Not Be Moved" filled the air in places like Selma and Birmingham where black people battled against the entrenched forces of segregation and racial bigotry.

The most famous and stirring song of the civil rights movement, "We Shall Overcome," came from a still-surviving center of 1930s radicalism, the Highlander Folk School in Grundy County, Tenn. Apparently based on a gospel song written by Charles Tindley in 1901, "I'll Overcome Some Day," the song was taken to the folk school by black workers who had sung fragments of it during a 1946 strike. Zilphia Horton, wife of the school's director, Myles Horton, added some verses to it and taught them to the other students. White folk singer Guy Carawan introduced the song to the civil rights movement when he sang it during sit-in workshops at Nashville in 1960. During the first half of the decade students sponsored by the Student Nonviolent Coordinating Committee (SNCC), such as Bernice Reagon and Julius Lester, took the song to every section of the South. By the time President Lyndon B. Johnson quoted the phrase in a speech endorsing the 1964 Civil Rights Act, "We Shall Overcome" had become known, in at least fragmentary form, to most Americans. Indeed, the whole grass-roots phase of protest singing was superseded by the absorption of such songs by American popular culture. Civil rights songs, antiwar songs, and ballads protesting against a wide range of social evils became vital ingredients of a major urban folk music revival that swept the United States in the early 1960s. Southern singers continued to play distinctive roles, but usually on phonograph recordings, in coffee houses and college folk music clubs, in auditorium concerts, or on radio and television broadcasts. Sis Cunningham, an Arkansas-born veteran of 1930s labor struggles, provided a forum for new songwriters with her journal, *Broadside*. Another Arkansas singer and radical, and an alumnus of both the Almanac Singers and Weavers, Lee Hays, functioned as an elder statesman for the new protest musicians. In conservative Dallas, a most unlikely milieu for radical music, singer-writer Lu Mitchell lent encouragement to singers of all kinds and acted as a kind of mentor-patron for the small folk music community there. Among the singers who were active throughout the nation were such southern-born musicians as Odetta Felious (Alabama), Hedy West (Georgia), Carolyn Hester (Texas), Tom Paxton (Oklahoma), and Phil Ochs (Texas). Of course, a very large contingent of singers and musicians received their introduction to music through their participation in the urban folk revival. Among the more important who went on to successful careers in other forms of music were Gram Parsons, from Georgia, and Michael Murphey and Janis Joplin, both from Texas.

Protest music faded perceptibly during the 1970s as national polarization subsided in the aftermath of the Vietnam War. Adult Americans exhibited a growing conservative impulse, and younger people were won increasingly to the more aggressive, electronic sounds of rock music. Nevertheless, some singers and writers have remained faithful to the cause of human rights and social justice and have never wavered in their utilization of music for such purposes. Guy and Candie Carawan and Jane Sapp still promote local folk music resources at the Highlander Education and Research Center in Tennessee; Si and Kathy Kahn sing and write songs as part of their work as community organizers in the north Georgia mountains; Art and Margo Rosenbaum, working in the same area of Georgia, have documented the lives of poor black and white people through sketches, photographs, and traditional songs. In 1966 Anne Romaine and Bernice Reagon, fine singers in their own right, organized the Southern Folk Festival Tour, which provided wider exposure for native folk singers. In the annual tours that followed, audiences saw and heard such powerful singers as Hazel Dickens from West Virginia. Strongly reminiscent of such earlier singers as Aunt Molly Jackson, Dickens sang older material and her own compositions, which dealt with contemporary problems of poverty and social and sexual inequality.

Protest music appears occasionally in the repertories

of professional musicians, and listeners to country music in the late 1960s and early 1970s discovered that protest does not always have an explicit ideological reference. A spate of country songs during those years defended the Vietnam War, protested against protesters and counterculture lifestyles, attacked welfare programs, and identified with establishment values, while others criticized small-town hypocrisy, documented worker alienation and exploitation, commented on environmental waste and pollution, and indicted the mistreatment of Indians and migratory workers.

See also BLACK LIFE: / "We Shall Overcome"; ETHNIC LIFE: / Okies; SOCIAL CLASS: / Highlander Folk School; Southern Tenant Farmers' Union; VIOLENCE: Harlan County, Kentucky; WOMEN'S LIFE: / Jackson, Aunt Molly; Reece, Florence

Bill C. Malone
Tulane University

R. Serge Denisoff, *Great Day Coming: Folk Music and the American Left* (1971), *Journal of American Folklore* (January–March 1969); Lawrence Gellert, *Negro Songs of Protest*, Rounder 4004; Archie Green, *Only a Miner: Studies in Recorded Coal-Mining Songs* (1972), *Sing Out* (July 1966), *Textile Labor* (April 1961); John Greenway, *American Folksongs of Protest* (1953); John W. Hevener, *Which Side Are You On?: The Harlan County Coal Miners, 1931–39* (1979).

Ragtime

In the generation following the Civil War, various elements of southern folk music, especially black-evolved styles from the Mississippi Valley, coalesced to form a piano music known by the 1890s as "ragtime." Marked by an idiomatic syncopation in the treble (right-hand) part against a steady, marchlike bass (left-hand) part, the piano rag developed as a highly formalized music in 2/4 time, built of three or more contrasting strains.

In its origins ragtime drew from blackface minstrel sources, string-band music, sentimental parlor music, brass-band music, and many other heterogenous sources. Called "jig-piano" or "ragged time" by early practitioners, it was transformed at the turn of the century by black composers in the Missouri-Kansas region into a serious, carefully notated musical genre. Among the principal pioneers of piano ragtime were Thomas Turpin (c. 1873–1922), James Scott (1886–1938), Artie Matthews (1888–1958) and, most centrally, Scott Joplin (1868–1917) and his protégés—Arthur Marshall (1881–1968) and Scott Hayden (1882–1915).

In 1897 the first score entitled a "rag" appeared in print—white bandleader-arranger William H. Krell's "Mississippi Rag." Within weeks this was followed by Thomas Turpin's "Harlem Rag." Scott Joplin entered the scene in 1899 with "Original Rags" and "Maple Leaf Rag," the single composition that most epitomized and defined the genre for the public. Other popular artists like Benjamin Harney (1873–1938), Hubert "Eubie" Blake (1883–1983), and James P. Johnson (1894–1954) worked on the East Coast with songs, blues, and other musical materials related to ragtime. Between 1895 and 1905 ragtime spread across the United States via itinerant pianists, mechanical player-piano rolls, gramophone records, published sheet-music scores, and adaptations of the music to bands, orchestras, and every other musical medium. The two decades between 1895 and 1915 can justifiably be called the "ragtime age."

Ragtime became the basis for the whole modern popular music industry. Its infusion of fresh Afro-American musical styles and practices turned the nation from European models and provided a basic matrix of syncopated, contrapuntally voiced, rhythmically sophisticated music from which followed jazz, and rock and roll. It was identified in the public mind with black southern culture, especially through widely popular ragtime songs, which continued the old minstrelsy imagery of the idyllic South of carefree easy living on magnolia-scented plantations. Ragtime also transformed popular social dancing, especially in the years after 1910. One early ragtime song, written by Roberts and Jefferson in 1900, summarized (and satirized) the wild enthusiasm for the new music:

> I got a ragtime dog and a ragtime cat
> A ragtime piano in my ragtime flat;
> Wear ragtime clothes, from hat to shoes,
> I read a paper called the "Ragtime News."
> Got ragtime habits and I talk that way,
> I sleep in ragtime and I rag all day;
> Got ragtime troubles with my ragtime wife,
> I'm certainly living a ragtime life.

The impact must have seemed revolutionary to a generation hitherto unexposed to popular musical fads disseminated by mass media.

The "classic" piano rag developed by Turpin, Scott, Joplin, and others evolved into a simple but effective form: a bisectional construction connecting strains of 16 bars, typically, in an arrangement or sequence of (for example) AA BB A // CC DD. The first section of the rag (AA BB A) always featured a return of the first strain of a cyclical manner. The second section (CC DD) featured two (or more) strains in varied sequences. There are two primary variations in the form: (1) a *linear* construction (e.g., AA BB A // CC DD) or (2) a *rounded* construction, which returns to material from the rag's first section, the A or B strains (e.g., AA BB A // CC DD A or AA BB A // CC A DD). The multirhythmic nature of the "classic" piano rag (so-called by Scott Joplin and his publisher John Stilwell Stark [1841–1927] of Sedalia, Mo.) challenged composers to use a broad variety of compositional creativity.

In the mid-1890s Ben Harney dazzled New York City with ragtime songs like "You've Been a Good Old Wagon" (1895) and "Mr. Johnson, Turn Me Loose" (1896), replete with forceful syncopations, exuberant melody, and racy colloquial lyrics. At the same time, the cakewalk was popularized via vaudeville and minstrelsy. The cakewalk was a stylized "walk-around" dance performed to syncopated march music, livelier and more extroverted than the fast two-step popular since the mid-1880s. Frederick "Kerry" Mills composed "At a Georgia Camp Meeting" (1896) and "Whistlin' Rufus" (1899); Sadie Koninsky had one popular hit in "Eli Green's Cakewalk" (1896); J. Bodewalt Lampe published "Creole Belles" (1899); and ragtimer Charles L. Johnson of Kansas City wrote "Doc Brown's Cakewalk" (1899).

From popular songs and dances ragtime evolved also to purely instrumental music—a highly idiomatic and "pianistic" form invented by the itinerant Mississippi Valley entertainers. Composers like Turpin, Joplin, and Scott served their apprenticeships as pianists in saloons, bordellos, or small theaters with traveling minstrel shows, or aboard riverboats. Their music was lively, loud, and percussive, designed to make a piano sound like a band, to carry over the sounds of high conviviality. It was derived from familiar folk styles and practices, echoing banjo and guitar music, hoedown dance rhythms, and the sentimental strains of popular song.

Traces of the folk origins in *pastiche* construction of early piano rags occur in Joplin's "Original Rags" (1899) and Seymour and Roberts's "St. Louis Tickle" (1904). Joplin's title indicates that he has composed a *set* of original themes (little "rags") that are then assembled in a linear suitelike form of one highly inventive strain after the other. The Seymour and Roberts rag commemorated the St. Louis World's Fair and the "ticklers" (pianists) who lined the "pike" or midway, and it included a very old river-culture folk tune, which Jelly Roll Morton later played and sang as "Buddy Bolden's Blues." The piano-rag form allowed for maximum inventiveness *and* borrowing from the folk culture.

After 1899 the nationwide popularity of Joplin's "Maple Leaf Rag" opened a lucrative market for piano rags, piano rolls, and ragtime "professors" as entertainers. Joplin created dozens of unique, carefully crafted rags—"The Easy Winners" (1901), "The Chrysanthemum" (1904), "The Ragtime Dance" (1906), and "Magnetic Rag" (1914). James Scott, from Neosho, Kan., entered the scene with works like "Sunburst Rag" (1909) and "Climax Rag" (1914). The impact of this new force was so great that a young white composer growing up in New Jersey, Joseph Lamb (1887–1960), could become a major composer in the wake of Joplin and Scott, studying the Stark scores and beginning his own publication in 1908 with "Sensation Rag" and producing a series of deeply felt, black-inspired rags like "Excelsior Rag" (1909), "American Beauty Rag" (1913), "The Ragtime Nightingale" (1915), and "Bohemia Rag" (1919). In a curious postlude to the ragtime era, Lamb would be rediscovered and resume his composing career in the late 1950s, after a 40-year hiatus.

John S. Stark was the disseminator of classic ragtime, printing Joplin, Scott, Lamb, Matthews, Marshall, and other ragtime giants. When he saw the magnitude of his ragtime publishing success, Stark became a champion of "high-class" or "quality" ragtime, which he and Joplin differentiated from popular songs, improvisational folk rags, or ephemeral mass-produced ditties. Stark insisted that rags should be played carefully, at moderate tempos, as written. Stark and Joplin viewed ragtime as a genuine Afro-American art form, and Stark was for his day a remarkably tolerant and fair-minded collaborator with the black composers he sponsored. His large, handsome piano scores are aesthetic prizes of the epoch.

While ragtime became a genuinely national music, composed and published in towns and cities all across the United States, it also achieved international fame, becoming for Europe an indication of America's lively genius. Its roots in the Mississippi Valley remained firm, and Ferdinand "Jelly Roll" Morton (1885–1941) from New Orleans recalled the large numbers of itinerant pianists and composers from New Orleans through Memphis and St. Louis on up to Chicago in the years around 1900. As the music was published and distributed, other "schools" of nonnotated ragtime flourished, with an important East Coast or "stride" piano group including James P. Johnson, Eubie Blake, Charles Luckeyth Roberts (1887–1968), and later Thomas "Fats" Waller (1904–43). Ragtime artists like Joe Jordan (1882–1971), New Orleans's Tony Jackson (1876–1921), and many others made Chicago a base.

Ragtime was not a wholly southern phenomenon, but its taproots were in the Deep South and Southwest, and it reflected an authentic musical culture of the Mississippi Valley and environs. It was a powerful influence on a new instrumental music, later called "jass" or "jazz," which grew in the region in the years around 1900. Early jazz musicians uniformly referred to their music as "ragtime," though it was largely an improvised, unnotated form of syncopated dance music.

The impact of ragtime on American—and world—culture is hard to overstate. The imaginative brilliance, emotional depth, and sheer *joie de vivre* of the music shaped all subsequent popular music. It introduced the black musical imagination and sensibility to a receptive general audience and established high standards for popular composition. When commercial songwriters and arrangers in New York City, in the area dubbed "Tin Pan Alley," took up the thrust of ragtime, around 1910, they were simply passing on a dense, complex, and culturally significant body of musical information and practices. George and Ira Gershwin in 1918 memorialized the ragtime era with "The Real American Folk Song (Is a Rag)." The music that had begun as nobody's music had become everybody's music.

Although the ragtime era seemed dead and gone by 1920, swept away during World War I by the advent of jazz and the new one-step and fox-trot dances, its basic themes and patterns profoundly influenced American music. The lyrics added to Joplin's "Maple Leaf Rag" promised that it would "shake de earth's foundation," and indeed it did.

William J. Schafer
Berea College

Edward A. Berlin, *Ragtime: A Musical and Cultural History* (1980); Rudi Blesh and Harriet Janis, *They All Played Ragtime* (1966); David A. Jasen and Trebor Jay Tichenor, *Rags and Ragtime: A Musical History* (1978); William J. Schafer and Johannes Riedel, *The Art of Ragtime: Form and Meaning of an Origi-*

nal Black American Art (1973); Terry Waldo, *This Is Ragtime* (1976).

Rock, Southern

Southern rock was a self-consciously regional subgenre of rock music that emerged in the early 1970s and reached its commercial and creative peak near mid-decade. It represented the fusion of black and white musical styles and was particularly derivative of black rhythm and blues. It was concert oriented rather than dance oriented, flourishing on FM rather than AM radio, and was best suited to the extended album format (33 rpm) rather than single recordings (45 rpm). Much southern rock evoked explicit images of southern culture and emphasized such traditional themes as masculine aggression, the superiority of rural life, and unbridled individualism. It was highly amplified and electrified—the standard southern rock ensemble featured twin electric lead guitars and dual drum sets as well as various electric keyboards and electric bass. Though it appealed most strongly to white southern working-class teenagers, southern rock also generated a huge and intensely loyal following among white college students.

In the late 1960s, as rock replaced rock and roll as the dominant mode of American popular music and as emphasis shifted from dance to concerts, most southern musicians followed in the wake of such innovative artists as the Beatles, Bob Dylan, and the Rolling Stones. Regional distinctions were all but erased in the rush to emulate the rock heroes and heroines as generational allegiance superseded other forms of affiliation and identification. Many southerners, the overwhelming majority Texans, played minor roles in the crystallization of rock culture—Janis Joplin, Steve Miller, Shawn Phillips, Johnny Winter, Doug Sahm. All of them left the South to pursue careers in San Francisco and Los Angeles. Only Johnny Rivers of Baton Rouge, La., achieved a degree of commercial success to rival the Beatles. Rivers, who began his career as a rockabilly stylist in the manner of Elvis Presley, was one of the nation's most popular recording artists from 1964 to 1967 while retaining a measure of his southern identity.

The only important recordings issued from the South in the 1960s came from Atlanta, Memphis, and Muscle Shoals, Ala. In Atlanta, producer and publisher Bill Lowery oversaw a small but talented corps of artists, which included Billy Joe Royal, Ray Stevens, Jerry Reed, Joe South, and Tommy Roe. Few of the hits produced under Lowery's aegis displayed a distinctive regional sound. From Memphis came the most consistently successful and memorable southern recordings of the 1960s. Stax Records was home to the seminal Memphis studio band, Booker T and the MGs (a biracial group), as well as such pioneer "soul" singers as Sam and Dave, Wilson Pickett, Joe Tex, Carla Thomas, and Otis Redding. The Stax sound, a modification and extension of urban blues, offered no synthesis of southern forms, though it was undeniably southern in style. In the late 1960s former Muscle Shoals sidemen Chips Moman and Dan Penn formed AGP studios and began producing hit recordings by Elvis Presley ("Suspicious Minds") and a local group, the Box Tops. The Box Tops, led by vocalist Alex Chilton, recorded numerous hits in a blues-oriented rock style: "The Letter," "Cry Like a Baby," "Soul Deep," "Sweet Cream Ladies." They were the immediate precursors of the first definitive southern rock group, the Allman Brothers Band. In Muscle Shoals, Fame Records claimed at least two major soul artists—Percy Sledge and Aretha Franklin. Among the highly esteemed Muscle Shoals studio musicians of the late 1960s was the brilliant guitarist, Duane Allman (born in Nashville and reared in Tennessee and Florida).

In 1969 Duane Allman and his brother Gregg, a vocalist and keyboard player, formed the original Allman Brothers Band, which also included guitarist Dicky Betts, bassist Berry Oakley, and drummers Butch Trucks and Jaimoe Johnson. The Allmans were among the first acts to sign with the fledgling Capricorn Records, a Macon, Ga., company established in 1969 by Otis Redding's former manager, Phil Walden. The Allmans soon spearheaded a southern rock movement that centered around Walden and his Capricorn label. Their first and second Capricorn albums, *Live at Fillmore East* (1971) and *Eat a Peach* (1972), established the Allmans as the preeminent southern rock band. They produced a rich body of work informed by both rhythm-and-blues and country music. Unfortunately, the death of both Duane Allman and Berry Oakley in motorcycle accidents in 1971 and 1972, respectively, robbed the group of much of its creative momentum. By 1975 the Allman Brothers Band had ceased to exist in any meaningful sense.

Literally hundreds of groups had arisen in the wake of the Allman Brothers, many of them gaining affiliation with the Capricorn label. Among the most successful southern rock bands were Grinderswitch, the Outlaws, Cowboy, Wet Willie, Molly Hatchet, .38 Special, the Atlanta Rhythm Section, the Amazing Rhythm Aces, Lynyrd Skynyrd, the Marshall Tucker Band, and the Charlie Daniels Band. Of these, only the last four achieved any semblance of the Allmans' commercial and artistic attainments.

The Amazing Rhythm Aces, a Memphis band, employed a light, quasi-pop sound exemplified by their 1976 hit, "Third Rate Romance." The song was a success on both the country and pop record charts.

Lynyrd Skynyrd, from Florida, performed in a hard-rock style strikingly similar to the Allman Brothers. They openly celebrated their southern origins in songs like "Sweet Home Alabama" (1974) and on numerous albums released on the Atlanta-based Sounds of the South label (a subsidiary of the Music Corporation of America). Their most important albums were *Lynyrd Skynyrd* (1973), *Second Helping* (1974), and *One More For the Road* (1975). Like the Allmans, Lynyrd Skynyrd suffered from a tragic accident, an airplane crash that claimed the lives of bandleader and vocalist Ronnie Van Zandt, vocalist Cassie Gaines, and guitarist Steve Gaines in 1977.

The Marshall Tucker Band, from Spartanburg, S.C.,

created probably the most original and eclectic sound of the southern rockers. They drew from such diverse resources as modern jazz and western swing and regularly featured such uncommon rock instruments as the flute and the saxophone. Led by Toy Caldwell, who often played pedal steel guitar, the Marshall Tucker Band has remained closer to country music than blues. Among the group's most notable efforts were such Capricorn albums as *A New Life* (1974), *Searchin' for a Rainbow* (1975), and *Long Hard Ride* (1976). Despite the death of bassist Tommy Caldwell in 1978, the group has continued to perform and record in the 1980s.

The Nashville-based Charlie Daniels Band has been the one southern rock ensemble to be identified primarily with country music. The band has also been the most commercially successful southern rock act. Largely as a result of the group's popularity, southern rock's most enduring influence exists in the country realm. Such artists as Hank Williams, Jr., the Bellamy Brothers, and Alabama have sustained and extended the southern rock legacy into the 1980s.

Stephen R. Tucker
Tulane University

Michael Bane, *White Boy Singin' the Blues: The Black Roots of White Rock* (1982); Steve Cummings, *Southern Exposure* (Spring–Summer 1974); Courtney Haden, *Southern Exposure* (Summer–Fall 1977); Jim Miller, ed., *The Rolling Stone Illustrated History of Rock 'n' Roll* (1980); Norm N. Nite, ed., *Rock On, Volume II: The Illustrated Encyclopedia of Rock 'n' Roll* (1978).

Rock and Roll

Rock and roll is the generic term used to describe the dominant strain of American popular music from 1955 to 1965. In general, rock and roll was teenage-oriented dance music that synthesized elements of black and white folk and popular music styles, specifically and most conspicuously, rhythm and blues and country (or "hillbilly") music. The term *rock and roll* was first popularized by northern disc jockey Alan Freed in the early 1950s, but its widest use came after 1955 when Bill Haley and the Comets released "Rock Around the Clock," the first legitimate rock-and-roll recording to rise to the top of the national pop music charts. Michigan-born Haley (b. 1925) was an anomaly: a rock-and-roll artist from outside the South, though his music was rooted firmly in southern-derived idioms. Haley was soon superseded as the dominant figure in rock and roll by Elvis Presley, born in Tupelo, Miss., and reared in Memphis, Tenn. All of the subsequent rock-and-roll innovators, with the arguable exception of Chuck Berry (born, San Jose, Calif., 1926), were native southerners: Carl Perkins (born, Bermis, Tenn., 1932); Jerry Lee Lewis (born, Ferriday, La., 1935); Buddy Holly (born, Lubbock, Tex., 1936); Fats Domino (born, New Orleans, 1928); Little Richard (born, Macon, Ga., 1932).

From 1955 to 1958 rock and roll remained largely a southern phenomenon. The two principal regional recording centers were Memphis and New Orleans, each of which produced a distinctive idiom of its own.

Memphis, long a cultural crossroads where various southern musical traditions flourished, especially Mississippi Delta blues and hillbilly music, produced a dynamic hybrid known as rockabilly. Rockabilly was firmly rooted in country music but drew heavily from black sources, most notably gospel and rhythm and blues. It was characterized by small ensembles (often a trio), stringed instrumentation, and a persistent yet light beat layered over frenzied vocalizing and an echo produced in the recording studio. The classic rockabilly sound, engineered by Sam Phillips and performed by Elvis Presley (vocal and acoustic rhythm guitar), Scotty Moore (electric lead guitar), and Bill Black (acoustic upright bass) was first recorded at Phillips's Sun Records studio in Memphis in July 1954. Sun soon attracted dozens of aspiring young musicians from across the South who performed in a style similar to Presley's. Important Sun artists after Presley were Carl Perkins, Jerry Lee Lewis, Johnny Cash, Billy Riley, Sonny Burgess, Roy Orbison, Charlie Rich, and Conway Twitty. A definitive rockabilly group from Memphis, which recorded for the New York-based Coral label, was the Rock 'n' Roll Trio (Johnny Burnette, Dorsey Burnette, and Paul Burlison).

After 1955 the basic Memphis rockabilly sound underwent a gradual modification. Elvis Presley moved toward a mainstream rock-and-roll sound after signing with RCA Victor in November 1955. Jerry Lee Lewis introduced his own boogie-woogie-based piano style into rockabilly with his first Sun releases in 1955. Beginning in 1957 Buddy Holly created an original pop-influenced variant of rockabilly, exemplified by such recordings as "That'll Be the Day" (1957), "Peggy Sue" (1957), and "Rave On" (1958). In Louisiana, Dale Hawkins recorded in a strong blues-influenced style, which gained its greatest expression in the hit recording "Suzie Q" (1957). Numerous influential rockabilly artists lived and recorded in Los Angeles after 1955, including Gene Vincent (originally from Virginia), whose best-known song was "Be Bop a Lula" (1956); Wanda Jackson (originally from Oklahoma), the most talented female rockabilly performer; Eddie Cochran, next to Carl Perkins, the finest rockabilly songwriter, who recorded such definitive items as "Summertime Blues" (1958) and "Something Else" (1959); and Ricky Nelson (born in New Jersey), who sold more rockabilly recordings than anyone other than Presley. Nelson and the Nashville-based Everly Brothers followed Presley and Holly in moving rockabilly in the direction of pop music by removing much of the rawness and dynamism from the idiom. The Everly Brothers were especially significant for introducing the traditional hillbilly duet style into rock and roll. Their best recordings, such as "Wake Up Little Susie" (1957) and "Bye, Bye Love" (1957), retained much of the potency of early rockabilly. A few mainstream country performers also recorded in a rockabilly mode, most notably Marty Robbins and Johnny Horton.

The New Orleans sound, which formed the second

major component of southern rock and roll, was infused with the blues. It was characterized by small ensembles (usually five or six pieces) whose central instrument was the piano. Accompaniment usually consisted of saxophones, drums, electric bass, and horns. It was noted for a heavy, rolling beat and Caribbean-derived polyrhythms. New Orleans vocalists, most of whom were black, sang with the thick inflections indigenous to the city. Most of the songs identified with New Orleans rock and roll were exuberant, joyous, and urgent, yet less frenzied than those from rockabilly music. Lyrics were seldom teen oriented.

Though no record label of comparable importance to Sun existed in New Orleans—most of the city's recordings were released by West Coast companies such as Imperial and Specialty—virtually every recording made in the city came from the studio of engineer and producer Cosimo Matassa. Matassa and Dave Bartholomew, a musician, writer, and producer, were key figures in the evolution of a distinctive New Orleans rock-and-roll style.

The quintessential New Orleans rock-and-roll performer was Fats Domino, a musical heir of the great rhythm-and-blues pianist Professor Longhair (Henry Roeland Byrd). Domino was a popular rhythm-and-blues recording artist in the early 1950s, and he made his entry onto the national pop charts in 1955 with "Ain't That a Shame." In the 1955–60 period, Domino produced a remarkable series of hit recordings, including "Blueberry Hill" (1956) and "I'm Walkin'" (1957).

Other important contributors to the New Orleans sound included Lloyd Price, Smiley Lewis, Huey Smith, Clarence "Frogman" Henry, Frankie Ford, Bobby Charles, and Jimmy Clanton. Clanton, a white performer, accomplished the closest approximation of the New Orleans style to a mainstream rock-and-roll sound with recordings like "Just a Dream" (1958). The only non-Louisiana artist to play a significant role in the popularization of the New Orleans style was Little Richard (Penniman) of Macon, Ga. Little Richard became one of the most dynamic and controversial rock-and-roll performers of the 1950s with such hits as "Tutti Frutti" (1955) and "Rip It Up" (1956).

By the early 1960s rockabilly music had largely been subsumed by the rock-and-roll mainstream. The New Orleans sound remained a vital and distinctive regional rock-and-roll form, though it too declined in popularity and experienced a certain degree of accommodation with the mainstream approach. Both Memphis and New Orleans ceased to be important recording centers. Most southern musicians left to work in Los Angeles, New York, or Nashville where, if successful, they tended to produce recordings of minimal regional identity. Southern rock and roll, which, in the forms of rockabilly and New Orleans music, had exerted a formative influence on the creation of a national rock-and-roll style, now merely existed as one element within the broad form as evinced by such representative recordings of the period as Johnny Tillotson's "Poetry in Motion" (1960), Johnny Burnette's "You're Sixteen" (1960), and Elvis Presley's "Return to Sender" (1962).

After 1963 American rock and roll began to succumb to the so-called British Invasion, spearheaded by the Beatles, who were soon followed by such groups as the Rolling Stones, the Animals, and Gerry and the Pacemakers. Ironically, the British invaders were themselves extremely indebted to the southern-derived forms of early rock and roll and thus revived much of the southern character and identity of the music. The most successful American rock-and-roll recording artist of the mid-1960s was Johnny Rivers, a native of Baton Rouge, La. (born 1940), who had begun his musical career as a rockabilly stylist. Rivers's music combined many varied styles, from urban folk music to rockabilly, but retained its essential southern character.

By 1966 the Beatles and Bob Dylan (another musician devoted to southern musical forms) led the way toward "rock," as contrasted to rock and roll. Rock had a general, national (and even international) identity. It was a form oriented more toward concerts than dance and was linguistically and thematically sophisticated and complex. Only in the early 1970s, with the emergence of the Allman Brothers Band and the attendant success of Capricorn Records of Macon, Ga., did a specific, self-conscious, and identifiable southern rock style evolve.

See also URBANIZATION: / Memphis; New Orleans

Stephen R. Tucker
Tulane University

Jason Berry, Jonathan Forse, and Tad Jones, *Up From the Cradle of Jazz: New Orleans Music since World War II* (1987); John Broven, *Rhythm and Blues in New Orleans* (1978); Colin Escott and Martin Hawkins, *Sun Records: The Brief History of the Legendary Record Label* (1980); Charlie Gillett, *The Sound of the City: The Rise of Rock and Roll* (1970); Jim Miller, ed., *The Rolling Stone Illustrated History of Rock 'n' Roll* (1980); Robert Palmer, *A Tale of Two Cities: Memphis Rock and New Orleans Roll* (1979).

Sacred Harp

On most weekends somewhere in the Deep South, one can find a gathering of amateurs singing from *The Sacred Harp*, a tunebook first published in Georgia (but printed in Philadelphia) in 1844. *The Sacred Harp*, one of many tunebooks of the 19th-century South, is the most popular of several that survived, the others being Joseph Funk's *Genuine Church Music* (Harrisonburg, Va., 1832; now entitled *New Harmonia Sacra*); William Walker's *Southern Harmony* (Spartanburg, S.C., printed in New Haven, Ct., 1835, with later editions in Philadelphia), used in an annual singing in Benton, Ky.; Walker's *Christian Harmony* (Spartanburg, S.C.; printed in Philadelphia, 1866), used in Alabama, western North Carolina, and Mississippi; and W. H. and M. L. Swan's *New Harp of Columbia* (Knoxville, Tenn., 1848), used in eastern Tennessee. In contrast to the limited geographical spread of these other tunebooks, *The Sacred Harp* is used in regularly scheduled singings in Georgia, the Florida Panhandle, Alabama, Tennessee, Mississippi, and Texas.

The Sacred Harp is a product of the American singing-school movement, which flourished in New England in the late 18th century and spread to the rural South and Midwest in the early 19th century. As is typical of other tunebooks of its kind, *The Sacred Harp* is oblong in shape and contains an opening summary of the rudiments of music for use in singing schools, followed by an anthology of harmonized music.

The invention of shape notes around 1800 facilitated the learning of music reading and proved so popular in the South and Midwest that practically every singing-school book, including *The Sacred Harp,* used the four-shape notation of William Little and William Smith's *The Easy Instructor* (Philadelphia, 1802), which became standard in the pre–Civil War period. The major scale was notated as shown in Figure 1. In sacred harp singing it has become standard practice to sing through a song first using the fa-sol-la solmization syllables before singing the words; hence the designation "fasola" singing.

The music in *The Sacred Harp* and other shape-note tunebooks, although primarily intended for singing-school use, is predominantly set to religious texts, primarily those of 18th-century English hymn writers, especially those of Isaac Watts (1674–1748). The texts were compiled from the collections of Watts and of numerous other words-only hymnals known in the early 19th-century South, such as South Carolinian Staunton S. Burdett's *Baptist Harmony* (1834) and Georgian Jesse Mercer's *The Cluster* (5th ed., 1835).

Ethel Mohamed stitchery depicting sacred harp singing, photographed in 1977

Figure 1.

fa	sol	la	fa	sol	la	mi	fa
1	2	3	4	5	6	7	8

The texts found in *The Sacred Harp* are strongly Calvinistic in theology with their emphasis on the sovereignty of God and the depravity of mankind. They are also otherworldly, with much emphasis on the vanity of this world and a longing for death and the afterlife, as in Charles Wesley's "Animation" (SH-103).

And let this feeble body fail
And let it faint or die;
My soul shall quit this mournful vale,
And soar to worlds on high.

Broadly speaking, the music in *The Sacred Harp* may roughly be divided into three categories:

1. Psalm or hymn tunes, ranging from those of metrical psalmody and of 18th-century American hymnody to folk hymnody of the early 19th century and even later 19th- and 20th-century tunes essentially in the same earlier styles.
2. Fuging tunes—tunes in which all voices move together in the opening phrases followed by a second section in which the voices enter separately in imitation and then move together once again to approach the final cadence. The second section is normally repeated, making a compact ABB form.
3. Longer pieces—normally designated odes or anthems. These pieces, often with prose texts such as scripture, are multi-sectional and are generally regarded as the most challenging to the singers.

The music of *The Sacred Harp* is printed in open-score format in three (later four) voice parts with the melody in the tenor. In practice, the treble and tenor parts are doubled by men and women, creating a richer, fuller sound.

The type of music most commonly associated with *The Sacred Harp* is folk hymnody in which melodies, and sometimes texts as well, first appeared in oral tradition. These folk hymns are related melodically to Anglo-American secular folksong and are characterized by such traits as the use of gapped scales and the modes. The frontier camp meetings from the early 1800s added simplified folk hymns, termed "revival spirituals" by George Pullen Jackson, to the corpus of folk hymnody, with repeated phrases and often the addition of a refrain. To "On Jordan's Stormy Banks I Stand" (SH-128) was added the following refrain:

I am bound for the promised land,
I am bound for the promised land,
O who will come and go with me?
I am bound for the promised land.

The Sacred Harp was compiled by two Georgia Baptist singing school teachers, Benjamin Franklin White (1800–1879) and Elisha J. King (c. 1821–44). Little is known of King, listed as the composer of more songs in the first edition of *The Sacred Harp* than any other person, for he died in the same year it was published. In contrast, much is known of White, who lived for more than three decades after its publication and was greatly influential in its acceptance. A native of South Carolina, White moved to Harris County, Ga., around 1840. He served as mayor of Hamilton, as clerk of the inferior county court, and as a major in the militia before the Civil War. In addition to composing, compiling, and teaching in singing schools, White in 1847 founded and led for more than two decades the Southern Musical Convention, an important organization in promoting sacred harp singing.

During White's lifetime, *The Sacred Harp* was revised and enlarged under the auspices of the Southern Musical Convention in 1850, 1859, and 1869, increasing the original 263 pages of 1844, respectively, to 366, 429, and 477 pages. With the 1859 and especially the 1869 editions, the fuging tunes received a more prominent place. Indeed, so prominent are fuging tunes in this tradition that they constitute a large portion of the favorites in current sacred harp singings. Another change was the increasing number of tunes in four voice parts rather than three, even though White himself composed in three parts only.

Without attempting to treat all editions of *The Sacred Harp*, which are described in detail by Buell E. Cobb, mention will be made of those that remain in current or recent use:

1. The Cooper revisions, made under the supervision of W. M. Cooper of Dothan, Ala., in 1902 with subsequent editions in 1907, 1919, 1927, 1950, and 1960. The Cooper revision is used in southern Alabama, northern Florida, southern Mississippi, and eastern Texas.
2. The James revision, called the *Original Sacred Harp*, revised by a committee of 23 with Joe S. James of Douglasville, Ga., as chairman and published in 1911. This revision was used for singings in central and south Georgia through 1975, when these singers changed over to the Denson revision.
3. The J. L. White revisions, the fifth edition of *The Sacred Harp*, brought out in 1909 in Atlanta by the son of B. F. White. It was rejected for its concessions to modernity, but White brought out another revision in 1911 omitting objectionable aspects of his earlier edition. Although used at one time in several states, the White book today is restricted to north Georgia.
4. The Denson revision, published by the Sacred Harp Publishing Company in 1936, with later editions in 1960, 1967, and 1971. Although appearing later than the editions of Cooper and White, the Denson revisions are more traditional. In 1933 Thomas Denson organized the Sacred Harp Publishing Company and purchased all legal rights to *The Sacred Harp* from the James family. The Denson revision is by far the edition of *The Sacred Harp* most widely used today.

A sacred harp singing is an informal gathering that emphasizes fellowship and group singing. A typical day's singing begins about mid-morning. Singers are seated facing each other in a square grouped by the four voice parts: tenor (melody), bass, treble, and alto. Each person who wishes to do so leads one or two songs (a turn at leading is called a "lesson" after traditional singing-school terminology). The song is first vocalized by the shape-note syllables and then sung to its words. At the close of the morning the singers adjourn for the traditional dinner on the grounds, a feast of home-cooked food set out on tables for all to enjoy. After lunch the singing continues, normally through at least the middle of the afternoon. When the time comes to close, the final song is often *Parting Hand* (SH-62) by Jeremiah Ingalls.

Sacred harp singing reflects traditional southern culture in terms of its music, its religious outlook, and its sense of community. The sacred harp tradition has preserved styles of music prominent in the pre–Civil War South through the institution of the singing school and many of the rural churches. In addition to the corpus of music from early America, sacred harp singing reflects a traditional southern manner of performance. For example, the tone color of sacred harp singing with its bite and edge contrasts with the sweeter styles of singing found outside the South.

Although sacred harp singings are not church services, they commonly take place in churches. The religious outlook of sacred harp singing is reflected in the piety that is manifested at these gatherings. For example, singings normally open and close with prayer and personal testimonies are often given. Southern religion is also exemplified in the sacred harp singers' use of the parliamentary procedures found in the democratic church business meeting of the rural congregations. The music is from the singing-school tradition, yet it includes the music of Baptists, Methodists, and others in the Upland South before the Civil War. Although these mainline denominations in large measure moved away from the sacred harp tradition, an increasing number of hymn tunes from its pages have appeared in their recent hymnals. The theological perspective of the main denomination to support sacred harp singing—the Primitive Baptists—is expressed in many of the texts of the songs, with their stern Calvinism, their willingness to face death, and their emphasis on the hereafter.

Especially strong in sacred harp singing is the southern sense of community with its focus on the family. The annual reunions of sacred harp singers can be likened to the annual southern family reunions. Furthermore, certain families such as the Densons have played crucial roles in preserving sacred harp singing. These singings are a time for remembering. Some gatherings are memorial singings named after a prominent sacred harp singer. An important feature of many sacred harp singings is the memorial lesson(s), in which the recently deceased are remembered in word and in song. All in all, the conservative values that sacred harp singing embraces and preserves are representative of traditional southern culture.

Harry Eskew
New Orleans Baptist
Theological Seminary

Buell E. Cobb, Jr., *The Sacred Harp: A Tradition and Its Music* (1978); Charles Linwood Ellington, "The Sacred Harp Tradition:

Its Origin and Evolution" (Ph.D. dissertation, Florida State University, 1969); Harry Eskew, in *New Grove Dictionary of Music and Musicians*, ed. Stanley Sadie, vol. 17 (1980); Dorothy D. Horn, *Sing to Me of Heaven: A Study of Folk and Early American Materials in Three Old Harp Books* (1970); George Pullen Jackson, *The Story of the Sacred Harp, 1844–1944* (1944), *White and Negro Spirituals: Their Life Span and Kinship* (1943), *White Spirituals in the Southern Uplands* (1933).

Spirituals

Spirituals are Afro-American sacred folksongs, sometimes also called anthems, hymns, spiritual songs, jubilees, or gospel songs. Distinctions between these terms have not been precise, different terms being used in different communities at different times. The term *spiritual song* was widely used in English and American hymnals and tunebooks during and after the 18th century, but *spiritual* was not found in print before the Civil War. Descriptions of the songs that came to be known by that name appeared at least 20 years earlier, and Afro-American religious singing recognized as distinct from white psalms and hymns was described as early as 1819.

The musical elements that distinguished Afro-American songs from European folksong were described by travelers and traders in Africa in the early 17th century. The elements that appeared exotic and unfamiliar to these Europeans included strong rhythms—accompanied by bodily movement, stamping, hand-clapping, and other percussive devices to accent rhythm—gapped scales, general group participation, improvised texts (frequently derisive or satiric in nature), and the call-and-response form in which leader and responding chorus overlapped. To the European observers the music seemed wholly strange, although later analysts would find elements common to European music. The performance style of African music was one of its unique aspects, one that has survived in many forms of Afro-American music.

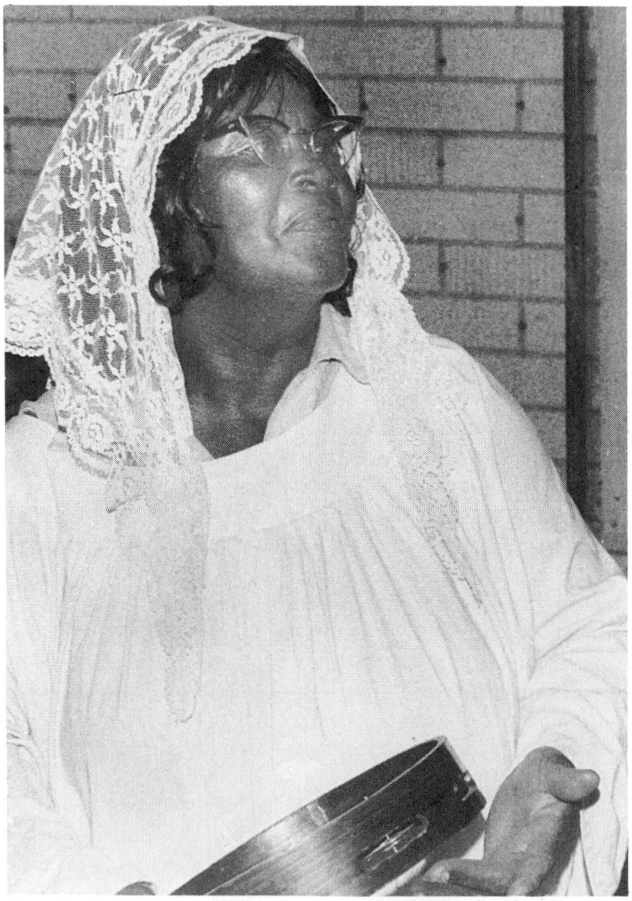

Gospel music singer, Centreville, Miss., 1972

In Africa, song played a prominent role in religion, public ceremonies, and work, in which song was used to regulate the pace. Though scholars do not agree about whether harmony was present, the simultaneous sounding of more than one pitch was common. Vocal embellishments were widely used, and a strong, rasping voice quality was admired. These musical elements continued among the Africans transported to the New World and were reported by numerous witnesses of slave singing throughout the West Indies and the North American mainland during the mid-17th century. Songs to accompany dancing were most frequently reported, with work songs a close second. Not much is yet known about the transmission of African religions to North America, so the relation of the spirituals to African religious song is still largely a matter of conjecture.

The conversion of Africans to Christianity, considered a prerequisite to the development of the spiritual, proceeded slowly. In the 17th century individual slaves were often converted by the families with whom they lived on low country plantations; although in the southern colonies some planters opposed the baptism of their slaves in the belief that baptism might disrupt the master-slave relationship. Where planters permitted religious instruction, the Africans responded with enthusiasm; but the few missionaries sent from England were kept too busy ministering to the widely separated white population to permit much attention to the blacks or the Indians. By the mid-18th century a few Presbyterian ministers, led by Samuel Davies of Hanover, Va., made special efforts to convert blacks within their neighborhoods, using Isaac Watts's hymnbooks shipped from England. The style of singing European hymns may have been influenced by African musical patterns, but scholars have no concrete information about the singing of African songs during this period.

Toward the end of the 18th century Methodist itinerants, such as Bishop Francis Avery, assisted by the black exhorter Harry Hosier, began to hold meetings lasting several days. Large crowds overflowed the meeting rooms, and blacks and whites attended these meetings together. On the frontier, where the population was very widely scattered and organized churches were few, the camp meeting developed, beginning with the Cane Ridge, Ky., meeting in August 1801. Black worshipers attended this meeting, and they participated in white camp meetings throughout the antebellum period. As blacks and whites worshiped and sang together in an atmosphere highly charged with emotion mutual influences were inescapable. The call-and-response style of singing was ideally suited to this kind of participatory service, where vast numbers of people required musical responses they could learn on the spot. The practice of "lining out," in which a leader sang or read two lines of a hymn to the congregation who then repeated them, was widely used in churches with illiterate members or with too few books to go around. The camp meeting provided an introduction for both groups to the sound and style of each other's singing.

The first documented reports of distinctive black religious singing date from the early 19th century, somewhat earlier than the first organized missions to plantation slaves. Spirituals were not transcribed in musical notation until the Civil War, and, when they were, conventional musical notation was inadequate to convey the distinctive features of the music as it was performed. Whatever degree of acculturation may have existed, certain elements in the music could not be represented in a notation developed for European music. The more sensitive transcribers explicitly stated that their transcriptions could not capture all they heard—notes outside the scale system—"blue" notes, swoops, glissandos, growls, rhythmic complexities, and the overlapping of leader and chorus in the call-and-response style.

In the South during the antebellum period spirituals were sung widely and were discussed in letters, diaries, and the periodical press, but they were largely unknown in the North. When wartime conditions brought plantation slaves into contact with northern whites, the songs became known to a wider public. Individual songs were published as sheet music or in magazine articles, and a comprehensive collection was published in 1867, *Slave Songs of the United States,* edited by William Francis Allen, Charles Pickard Ware, and Lucy McKim Garrison. Although the transcriptions had to omit many of the characteristic and distinctive features of the music because of the notational system, the collection was an attempt to preserve songs that otherwise might have been lost. The collection set a pattern for transcribing the songs in conventional musical notation (despite its shortcomings) that was followed in more influential collections of songs as sung by the Fisk Jubilee Singers, the Hampton Singers, and other touring groups from predominantly black schools in the South. The college groups had been trained in European music and were conscious of their mission to herald the emerging black population. After northern and European audiences heard spirituals, their popularity was firmly established. Songs were modified in their arrangement for concert performance, although the extent of this modification has not been determined.

As the spirituals grew more popular, elaborate arrangements that departed still more widely from the folk originals were made, for both solo singers and for choirs. Beginning in 1892 a theory was developed that spirituals were based on European folk hymns and other forms of white popular music, a theory based solely on the examination of the published transcriptions. The elements of improvisation and the performance style were not considered. Only with the advent of sound recording has it been possible to study the performance itself. Current performances cannot fully replicate antebellum ones, but they can capture much of the excitement described by 19th-century listeners. Ethnomusicologists may be able to reconstruct the music as it was performed in earlier eras by utilizing field recordings and contemporary descriptions.

See also BLACK LIFE: African Influences; Creolization; Religion, Black; Slave Culture; EDUCATION: / Fisk University

Dena J. Epstein
University of Chicago

Afro-American Spirituals, Work Songs, and Ballads, Library of Congress Recording AAFSL3; James H. Cone, *The Spirituals and the Blues: An Interpretation* (1972); Dena J. Epstein, *Sinful Tunes and Spirituals: Black Folk Music to the Civil War* (1977); Miles Mark Fisher, *Negro Slave Songs in the United States* (1953); George Pullen Jackson, *Spiritual Folk Songs of Early America* (1964), *White Spirituals in the Southern Uplands* (1933); Lawrence W. Levine, *Black Culture and Black Consciousness: Afro-American Folk Thought from Slavery to Freedom* (1977); A. E. Perkins, *Journal of American Folklore* (July–September 1922).

Square Dancing and Clogging

Square dance in the South has traditionally provided a means to exercise the virtually universal human tendency to move to the accompaniment of music. It is best to think of *square dance* as a generic term for a variety of related dance forms, styles, and occasions. In the popular imagination, traditional square dancing is often associated with the South; in its assorted revivalistic forms the square dance has become a national phenomenon.

Cecil Sharp, the English collector and scholar of folk music and dance, helped bring the square dance to national—and even international—attention after encountering it in Kentucky. In 1918 Sharp wrote, "In the course of our travels in the Southern Appalachian Mountains in search of traditional songs and ballads, we often heard of a dance, called the Running Set, but as our informants had invariably led us to believe that it was a rough, uncouth dance, remarkable only as an exhibition of agility and physical endurance, we had made no special effort to see it." When Sharp and his colleague Maud Karpeles finally did encounter the dance at the Pine Mountain Settlement School in eastern Kentucky, they were captivated by it, and Sharp felt certain that they had found a relic of English dance traditions older than any on record. Actually, they had "discovered" a dance that, although rooted in English and French dance forms, is generally thought to be a 19th-century American development—the southern square dance.

Dancing to the chanted instructions of a caller—one of the major identifying features of square dancing—emerged about the time of the War of 1812. The other common square-dance features—the couple as the basic unit, danced interactions between couples in a bounded group, the group arranged in a simple geometric formation—may be found in any number of British and French antecedent dance forms, folk, popular, and elite. The calling distinguishes the dance.

In the South, couples generally arrange themselves in squares consisting of four male-female couples or in circles made up of as many couples as can be accommodated. Less frequently the dance may take the form of two parallel lines, one for men, one for women, with couples facing each other. The caller may dance, or he or she may stand nearby.

Traditionally the music is provided by a fiddle, fiddle and banjo, or by any of the typical string-band ensemble forms. The fiddle repertoire in the South is, in fact, dominated by square-dance tunes. Although no distributional studies of the square dance in the South exist, the dance-tune repertoire has been played by fiddlers all through the region. It seems reasonable to conclude from this that square dancing may be, or might formerly have been, found wherever there has been an active dance-tune tradition—virtually everywhere in the South.

Square dancing has traditionally been a part of the community life in the South. Moreover, it has often provided one of the major settings for community interaction. Until the World War II era people commonly danced in the homes of their neighbors, particularly in farming areas. Such events were essentially parties for the neighbors, and all were invited. Other community events have also been occasions for dancing. These include communal work activities (corn shuckings and log rollings), picnics and barbecues, holiday observances, and other festivals. A rise in commercially motivated dances in local armories and other halls has, in many instances, kept people dancing despite the declining significance of some of the older community social events. The dance associations themselves seem to encourage friendly interactions between community members, young and old, male and female, and the dancing itself seems to involve the enactment, at some deep level, of community norms and expectations, such as the notion of the couple as a basic social unit.

Each dance typically involves a number of formulaic movements in response to the caller's instructions. Many dance calls, such as "Ocean Wave" and "Cage the Bird," are known widely across the South; others may be limited to subregions. Dance movements will sometimes vary in their execution (in response to the formulaic calls) according to local and regional preferences.

Square dancing is also traditionally a part of southern Afro-American culture, despite its dominant association with Anglo-Americans. Slave narratives describe square dancing among slaves, and recent interviews with black musicians and dancers suggest that square dancing was often a feature of rural life in southern black communities through perhaps the 1930s.

A number of 20th-century revivalistic movements have added to the complexity of the square dance in the South. These range from dance schools and festivals under the sponsorship of southern Appalachian cultural and educational institutions to the efforts of various national square-dance organizations. The latter have tended to emphasize new dance styles based on traditional dances but showing the touch of the choreographer. Typically identified as western dancing, this is generally bound up in a large network of local clubs, whose members dress in stylized cowboy-cowgirl garb and dance to records rather than to live music. A number of publications and supply houses, regional and national, cater to revivalist dancers. As a result of the various dance revivals, many communities in the South typically have a range of square-dance activities, from regionally traditional forms done perhaps weekly at a VFW or sportsman's club, and done occasionally at festivals, to square-dance groups practicing precision dance forms derived from regional models, to clubs that are part of the western square-dance movement. There may well be more people dancing in the South today than ever before.

Clog dancing is a group dance, synthesizing the older square dance and the solo "buck and wing" or "buck dance." Buck dancers traditionally danced on bare earth, front porches, or parlor floors, their arms hanging loose at their sides and their feet close to the floor. The origin of the term *buck and wing* is unclear, but it was used in Lancashire, England, in the early part of this century to describe dancing in wooden shoes. Buck dancing likely has roots in the folk dances of Scotch, Irish, and English immigrants to the Appalachian Mountains, but black dancing patterns also influenced its development through minstrel performers and traveling medicine shows. Ceremonial Indian dances, with their toe-heel, toe-heel movement, also were a likely influence on white mountain buck dancing.

Clog dancing probably originated in the mountains of western North Carolina in the 1920s or 1930s, associated with the Asheville Mountain Dance and Folk Festival. A landmark was a 1939 performance in Washington, D.C., by the Soco Gap Dancers for President Franklin Roosevelt and British King George VI. This was apparently the first time cloggers used costumes, and publicity from the performance helped popularize clogging in the 1940s. Taps were added and costumes became more prominent as the folk dance became increasingly oriented toward public performance. James Kesterson, of Henderson County, N.C., introduced precision clogging in the late 1950s, and his popular Blue Ridge Mountain Dancers won the Ashcville Festival five times in the 1960s.

Precision clogging groups like Kesterson's dance to patterned footwork in unison in set routines. They frequently emphasize colorful costumes and choreography, using both old-time mountain music and popular tunes. The other main type of clogging is freestyle, or traditional. Here the dancers follow time to the music, but each performer has spontaneous footwork, improvising steps as the team moves about the floor. Freestyle clogging is especially associated with older mountain folk culture, but clogging in general remains a not-uncommon practice in mountain areas of the South.

Burt Feintuch
Western Kentucky University

S. Foster Damon, *The History of Square Dancing* (1957); Lynne F. Emery, *Black Dance in the United States from 1619 to 1970* (1972); Burt Feintuch, *Journal of the Folklore Institute* (January–April 1981); Cecil J. Sharp and Maud Karpeles, *The Country Dance Book, Part V* (1918, 1946).

Tex-Mex

See *Música Tejana*

Western Swing

Like so many other forms of American music, western swing is a cultural product of the South. The founders of the music borrowed from other southern styles—ragtime, New Orleans jazz, folk, frontier fiddle music, pop, Tex-Mex, and country and classic blues. In one stage of development, they borrowed heavily from big-band swing. Despite its eclecticism, western swing has remained one of the most distinctive genres in southern musical history. Western swing brought a new vitality and sophistication to the country music of the South.

All three periods in the development of western swing were inextricably interwoven with the career of Bob Wills. The first of these eras was the formative period in Texas; second, the years of experimentation and maturity in Oklahoma; and finally, the years of national recognition and musical influence.

James Robert Wills was born into a family of fiddle players near Kosse in east Texas. He eventually combined folk fiddle music with the blues, jazz, and ragtime from the "black belt" of east Texas. This was the nucleus from which western swing grew. When he was 10, Bob Wills played his first dance as a fiddler at a ranch in west Texas. For the rest of his career he played dance music. The most obvious characteristic of western swing is that the music "swings," or is danceable.

The early fiddle bands often had only a fiddle and an accompanying guitar or mandolin. When Bob Wills moved to Fort Worth in 1929, he started the Wills Fiddle Band featuring only his fiddle and Herman Arnspiger's guitar. In 1929 Wills and Arnspiger recorded on the Brunswick label what may have been the first western swing ever put on record, "Wills Breakdown" and "Gulf Coast Blues." Wills soon added Milton Brown as vocalist and his brother Durwood Brown on guitar. The Wills Fiddle Band became the Light Crust Doughboys in 1930 and eventually played on the Texas Quality Network, originating at WBAP in Fort Worth and broadcasting on the network in Waco, Houston, and Oklahoma City. The Wills group was, if not the first, among the first to play western swing and to perform it on radio.

Between 1929 and 1933 Bob Wills revolutionized popular music in Texas. His success and fame spread throughout the state and inspired the formation of numerous fiddle bands that played his type of swinging dance music. The first and most successful in terms of first-rate western swing was Wills's protégé, Milton Brown, who came into the Wills Fiddle Band with little or no musical experience. He learned quickly from Wills and left the Light Crust Doughboys in 1932 to form a group called Milton Brown and His Musical Brownies. Outside of Wills himself, Brown was the most important figure in the formative years of western swing. The Wills-Brown style could soon be heard in many western-swing bands, in the Light Crust Doughboys, W. Lee O'Daniel's Hillbilly Boys, Cliff Bruner's Texas Wanderers, the True Wranglers, Bill Boyd and His Cowboy Ramblers, The Hi-Flyers, Jimmy Revard and His Oklahoma Playboys, Adolph Hofner and His Texans, Bob Dunn's Vagabonds, Roy Newman and His Boys, the Sons of the Pioneers, the Prairie Ramblers with Patsy Montana, and Shelly Lee Alley and the Alley Cats, to name a few of the better-known recorded groups.

By the time Bob Wills moved the Playboys from Waco, Tex., to Oklahoma in 1934, the formative years of western swing were over. East and west Texas gave birth to his music; Fort Worth was its nursery; and it reached full maturity in Tulsa, Okla., between 1934 and 1942. There the music moved out of its southwestern provincialism to a much broader audience. Wills's experimental spirit led him to take the music far beyond its fiddle-band origins. Shortly after he arrived in Oklahoma, he added enough horns to give him a second front line made up of trumpet, saxophone, and trombone. The reeds and brass played more modern, uptown music and therefore appealed to a broader audience. Wills added drums and began to lay down a solid jazz beat heretofore unheard of in the fiddle-band tradition. In short, he was moving further from his rural roots to jazz, blues, race music, and popular music. Wisely, he kept his front line of fiddles and added more guitars, both amplified and acoustic. By 1938 he could play anything from folk and breakdown fiddle music to a George Gershwin composition and give them a swinging rhythm and solid beat. The recordings from his first session in 1935, for Vocalion (later Columbia), outsold every other artist in the Vocalion catalog.

In April 1940, with an orchestra of 18 members, Wills recorded the song that took the nation by musical storm and introduced western swing to hundreds of thousands of people who otherwise would never have heard it. The song itself revealed much of the evolution and history of western swing. It was originally a breakdown fiddle selection recorded with Wills's heavy 2/4 jazz beat and was called "San Antonio Rose." In 1940 he recorded it with his horn band without the use of any fiddles. It was recorded in the big-band style of the period and was entitled "New San Antonio Rose." Wills sold 3 million recordings of it, and Bing Crosby brought it to a new audience when his recording sold over 1.5 million discs. Crosby had his second gold record, and Bob Wills was soon in Hollywood making movies. His hollering and "Ah haas" and western swing were assured of a place in Americana and the history of American music.

During World War II and in the postwar years, western swing underwent its final stage of development. From the early 1940s to the early 1950s, the music enjoyed its most successful years. As a style, it was so popular that western-swing bands performed in movies, over radio, and on the earliest television shows. At that time the term *western swing* was first used, although historians cannot pinpoint its first usage. Before World War II the bands that performed in the style were labeled everything from "hot dance," "hillbilly," "hot string," "country dance," and "old time" to "novelty hot dance." The musical establishment simply did not know what to call this new hybrid sound, and recording companies listed Wills, the Light Crust Doughboys, and others in "race catalogs" with black artists. Wayne Johnson, who played in the saxophone section of the recording of "New San Antonio Rose," explained in an interview how the terms *western* and *swing* were brought together in the 1930s to describe the Bob Wills style. "That was the swing era, and people were swing dancing. . . . In the Bob Wills band, we did exactly the same thing with a western flavor. We were still playing the same kind of beat, the same kind of arrangements and everything else," but Johnson added, "Bob also had the western flavor, because of the fiddles, the steel guitars, the costumes."

Some authorities believe the term was first used in reference to Spade Cooley and his band on the West Coast. Cooley grew up in Oklahoma and was a fan of Bob Wills and His Texas Playboys. When Cooley organized his band in California in the 1940s, the Wills sound was obvious, but Cooley's band played from written arrangements and produced a clean, rehearsed sound, a sound that was distinctive and very popular. Spade Cooley appeared in films and made many successful recordings. His ability as a musician, bandleader, and showman helped gain new audiences and national acceptance for western swing.

In the postwar years many other musical groups got on the western-swing bandwagon. Bob Wills's brother, Johnnie Lee, formed Johnnie Lee Wills and the Boys and was successful from the war years to 1958. Leon McAuliffe organized the Cimmaron Boys, one of the most popular of all western-swing bands. Luther J. Wills, another of Bob Wills's brothers, had minor success with an excellent band called the Rhythm Busters. In the early 1950s Bob Wills's youngest brother formed Billy Jack Wills and His Western Swing Band in northern California; the band leaned toward rhythm and blues and anticipated the rockabilly style. On the West Coast, Tex Williams performed in a western-swing style and recorded big-selling novelty songs. Hank Penny spread western swing from Alabama to Nashville. Pee Wee King was successful both as a bandleader and as the composer of "Tennessee Waltz." Bob Wills's great singer, Tommy Duncan, left the Texas Playboys in 1948 and hired some of the best musicians in the field for his Western All Stars.

World War II was a watershed in the history of American music. The age of the big bands began to close about the time the war ended. Television soon cut into the audiences that had kept the dance floors hot before and during the war. Dance audiences, though quite large until the late 1940s, began to dwindle and no longer supported the big bands. Western-swing groups, such as Wills's Texas Playboys, took fewer musicians on the road. Stringed instruments dominated western swing as never before. Styles did not change; they continued to play dance music, to produce jazz and swing. Fiddles in particular became more important after the war. There were generally more of them in the bands, and they were used to a greater extent, particularly as an ensemble. The "take off fiddlers" still took jazz choruses. The guitarists, especially in the Cooley, McAuliffe, and Bob Wills bands, continued to use their guitars like traditional jazz or swing instruments. They took choruses and improvised as jazzmen do with trumpets and clarinets. When the western-swing bands no longer had enough reeds and brass to provide the sound of the big-swing bands, they relied on guitars to simulate it. They often combined guitars, steel guitars, and amplified mandolins into a string ensemble to simulate a big-band horn section.

After 1950 television and new entertainment habits shifted popular tastes away from western-swing bands. Young people of that affluent decade, who for the first time dominated record buying and determined the direction of much of American entertainment, began to dance to different drummers. Western swing went into a decline and might well have ended like the big bands in the early 1950s had it not been for the unyielding popularity of Bob Wills and the use of so many stringed instruments by Wills and other western-swing bands. Wills and others in his field influenced rockabillies like Bill Haley, Buddy Holly, and Elvis Presley. The influence of western swing on country music was even greater and continues to this day.

When Bob Wills's health forced him to retire in the mid-1960s, an era ended. Three groups discovered western swing in the 1970s and have kept its sound and history alive. Country-and-western performers claim it as part of their music, and Merle Haggard, Alvin Crow, Red Steagall, Asleep at the Wheel, Waylon Jennings, Willie Nelson, and Ray Price either play it in a pure form or draw from its repertoire. Some rock artists such as Commander Cody, Charlie Daniels, and others perform in the swing style. Finally, many jazz artists performing on strings are continuing what western swing did years ago.

See also GEOGRAPHY: Southwest

Charles R. Townsend
West Texas State University

Bill C. Malone, *Country Music, U.S.A.: A Fifty-year History* (1968), *Southern Music—American Music* (1979); John Morthland, liner notes, *Okeh Western Swing*, Epic EG 37324; Tony Russell, *Blacks, Whites, and Blues* (1970); Chris Strachwitz and Bob Pinson, *Western Swing*, Old Timey T 105; Charles R. Townsend, Brochure notes to *For the Last Time*, United Artists UA-LA216-J2, "Homecoming: Reflections on Bob Wills and His Texas Playboys, 1915–1973," *San Antonio Rose: The Life and Music of Bob Wills* (1976).

Zydeco

Zydeco is a fast, syncopated dance music of Louisiana's black Creole population. Played in urban and rural dance halls from St. Martinville and Lafayette to Houston's black French Fifth Ward, it has evolved in Louisiana over the last 150 years, influenced by Cajun, Afro-American, and Afro-Caribbean cultures. Some zydeco musicians may prefer a more Cajun sound, while other musicians, especially in urban settings, mix blues and soul into the music, reflecting the increasing impact of Afro-American mainstream culture. But nearly all zydeco groups maintain a rhythmic complexity in their music that harkens to their Afro-Caribbean inheritance, an inheritance also found in the early spasm bands of New Orleans jazz and the great "second-line" rhythm-and-blues pianists like Huey "Piano" Smith, Professor Longhair, and Fats Domino.

Zydeco reflects the multicultural and multiracial background of the Creole population on the French Gulf Coast from southern Louisiana into southeast Texas. In French Louisiana and the French Caribbean, the term *Creole* originally referred both to descendants of the French and Spanish colonists from the Old World and to African slaves born in the New World. This original meaning of *Creole*, which refers to the planter class as well as to people from New Orleans and southeastern Louisiana, still persists. The other meaning of *Creole* (the one used here) developed later. It refers to the French-speaking people whose mixed ancestry may include black slaves from the Caribbean and American South, *gens libres de couleur* (free people of color), and Spanish, French, and German planters and merchants, local Indian tribes, Anglo-Americans, and Cajuns.

Many persons in southwestern French Louisiana who identify themselves as Creole or *noir* have some parentage from the Cajuns or Acadians—the peasant farming, fishing, and trapping people who entered the area over a 30-year period (1760s to 1800), following their expulsion from what is now called Nova Scotia. The cultural ties between Creoles and Cajuns are more significant than the genetic ties: the two cultures share, in part, essential features of life, including religion, festivals, foods, language, and music.

The largest numbers of black and *mulâtre* ("mulatto") French-speaking people came to Louisiana either as slaves for French planters in the second half of the 18th century or as *gens libres de couleur* both before and after the Haitian revolution of 1791–1803. In general, to be of "mixed" blood or *mulâtre* carried greater social status. The shift in the use of the term *Creole* may have come from its use by such persons of "mixed" blood claiming their European ancestry, and from an attempt to distinguish the descendants of French culture from the English-speaking *Américains* (Americans), who acquired the territory in 1803.

The word *zydeco* is thought to be a creolized form of the French *les haricots* (snapbeans). Zydeco music is said to take its name from a dance tune in both the Cajun and Creole traditions called *Les Haricots Sont Pas Salés* (The Snapbeans Are Not Salted). The spelling of zydeco used here is one found on posters advertising dances and promoting bands in south Louisiana and southeast Texas. Alternate spellings are *zodico*, *zordico*, and *zologo*. All of these are English spellings used to represent the Creole pronunciation. A closer phonetic spelling would be *zarico* (stress on the last syllable), which preserves the French *a* and *r*.

Zydeco refers not only to the fast, syncopated dance numbers in a Creole band's repertoire, but also to the dance event itself. Old-time musician Bébé Carrière of the Louisiana prairie town of Lawtell says that in the old days word of a dance would be left at the general store or someone would ride around the countryside on horseback yelling, *"Zydeco au soir . . . chez Carrière!"* (Zydeco tonight at the Carrière's place!) Similarly, in urban Houston, the lyrics of *Bon Ton Roulet* by Clarence Garlow describe people going "way out in the country to the zydeco."

Because of the cultural interchange between Cajuns and Creoles in southwest Louisiana, there has been a tendency to overlook the differences between Cajun music and zydeco. Cajun music places more emphasis on developing the melodic line, while zydeco melodies are played much faster and consist of Acadian or Afro-American blues tunes placed in an Afro-Caribbean rhythmic framework. The rhythms are highly syncopated, with accents often shifting to various beats.

Whether the original Cajun tune is a one-step—a "la-la"—or a two-step dance, it can be transformed into a zydeco by the Creole musician, with faster tempo, melodic simplification, and increased syncopation. The rhythm may also change when a Cajun two-step—which accents the first and third beats—is played with the accents on the second and fourth beats. The melody, although simplified to a repeated figure, remains unrecognizable.

Even genres from outside the Afro-Caribbean and Acadian cultural sources, such as Afro-American blues and the Central European polka and mazurka, may be performed in a zydeco style. This is also true of the waltz, which the Creoles probably inherited from the Cajun and other traditions.

The repertoire and style of individual zydeco musicians may be either more Cajun, more Afro-American, or more Afro-Caribbean. For example, Creole musicians such as Fremont Fontenot of Basile and the Carrière brothers of Lawtell often play in a Cajun style because of their strong European cultural affiliations (though these performers do play zydeco and blues). On the other hand, the Lawtell Playboys of Frilot Cove and Sampy and the Bad Habits of Carencro show more Afro-Caribbean and Afro-American inclinations (though they also play waltzes and enjoy "French music"). As young accordionist Clinton Broussard says, "Zydeco bands, they all plays the same tunes, but everybody got their own style to do it."

Although West Indian influences on Louisiana culture can be traced in language, foods, folk beliefs, and in music, a musical form called zydeco or sounding like zydeco did not exist in the French West Indies. This suggests the importance of contact between Cajuns and black Creoles in generating a music form unique to Louisiana.

One item that does survive more directly from the

Afro-French West Indian inheritance (although in modified form) is the dance *Calinda*. A dance called *Calinda*, *Kolenda*, *Kolinda*, and other names is mentioned in travelers' accounts as appearing in the French West Indies—Martinique, Guadeloupe, and Santo Domingo—as well as Trinidad from the late 18th century onward. Recent anthropological studies also note the presence of the dance in contemporary French West Indies in the contexts of *vodoun* (voodoo) worship and social dancing, Mardi Gras, and *Rara* festivities. The *kalinda* may involve such diverse activities as mock stick fighting and erotic courtship gestures.

Slaves gathering in New Orleans's Congo Square in the early 19th century were said to have danced the West Indian style *Calinda*. In rural French Louisiana, *Calinda* was transformed by Cajuns into a two-step and by Creoles into a zydeco. It has become part of the dance band repertoire, and hints of eroticism or extraordinary behavior have been submerged in the lyrics, which refer to dancing the old dances in a way that will make old women mad. Thus, *Calinda* becomes the name of a young woman enticed by her beau to dance too close while her mother is not looking. That *Calinda* may still have Afro-Caribbean influences is indicated by its heavily syncopated beat and by accordionist Delton Broussard's comment that "back toward New Iberia (in the area with more French West Indies influence), they want *Calinda* to dance wild to. You get to Lake Charles, and they want that French waltz." Removed from its West Indies source, *Calinda* is now a part of most Cajun and zydeco bands' repertoires.

At dances in the Creole community today, zydeco musicians usually choose fewer waltzes and more blues and fast two-steps than do Cajun musicians. While Cajun bands make wide use of the violin (an Acadian inheritance), they rarely play the vest *frottoir* (a metal rubbing board worn as a vest and played with spoons, can openers, or thimbles). Played by old-time and rural zydeco groups, the vest *frottoir* has its antecedents in Africa and the Caribbean as a scraped animal jaw, notched stick, and later, a washboard. The current model, made in Louisiana by tinsmiths, became popular in the 1930s when sheet metal was introduced to the area for roofing and barn siding. Also popular is the Cajun *bas trang* or *'tite fer* (triangle).

The accordion, used in both zydeco and Cajun music, was probably introduced to the area by German immigrants in the 1870s. The traditional model, and the one made by a number of local accordion makers, is the *une rangée* (one row) diatonic push-pull instrument. It is used by Cajuns and most rural and old-time zydeco musicians. Urban performers have also experimented with the two- and three-row button accordion, and the chromatic piano accordion.

Cajun music and zydeco are meant for dancing. Indeed, the choice of dance halls and preferred musical style often mark the boundaries of Cajun and Creole communities. Performance of both of these types of Louisiana French music in a club setting is usually highly amplified for dancing, and the lyrics are difficult to hear above the music or noise of the club. In general, lyrics to the dance tunes are not as elaborate as those of the home singing traditions. They are often fragmentary and tend to convey a "feeling" rather than a story.

While Cajun music has been influenced by country and western music in style and instrumentation (the steel guitar), zydeco has been affected more by rhythm and blues and soul music. Urban bands, such as Sampy and the Bad Habits and Mike and the Soul Accordion Band, have dropped the *frottoir* and violin, switching to two- and three-row accordions and sometimes adding a lead guitar. Though these bands play relatively slower zydeco numbers at a dance, the continued impact of the Creole and Cajun repertoire in urban areas is retained, as both bands still play waltzes and highly syncopated numbers.

Afro-American traditions have long existed side by side with the Afro-Caribbean and Cajun traditions in south Louisiana's Creole community. But since World War II they have become heavily integrated with Creole traditions and lifestyles. These changes in zydeco music reflect the acculturation of the Creole population into English-speaking Afro-American culture.

Creole culture remains strongest in the countryside, and here the dance hall is an essential social institution. Men and women come to dances well-dressed in sport coats and ties, pantsuits, carefully set hair, and jewelry. At a rural dance hall like the Ardoins' *Club Morris* in Duralde, entire families, from children to grandparents, come to dance. Zydeco is also performed at church dances, barbecue picnics, occasional *fais-do-do* (house dances), and in a variety of urban clubs that alternate bookings with discjockey and soul bands. The new popularity of such bands as Terrence Semiens and the Mallet Playboys, Buckwheat *Ils Sont Partis Band*, and Fernest Arceneaux and Thunder reflect this change. On the other hand, more traditional groups such as Delton Broussard and the Lawtell Playboys, the Lawrence Ardoin Band, and John Delafose and the Eunice Playboys perform in a more French-influenced style. The new broader range of zydeco styles as projected in films, television programs, records, radio and at the newly formed (1983) Zydeco Festival in Opelousas suggests that Creole music is increasingly a symbol for cultural emergence of the Afro-French people of rural and urban south Louisiana.

Nicholas R. Spitzer
Smithsonian Institution

Amédée Ardoin, *The First Black Zydeco Recording Artist*, Louisiana Cajun Music, vol. 6, ed. Chris Strachwitz with liner notes by Michael Doucet, 1981, Old Timey LP 124; Clifton Chenier, *Louisiana Blues and Zydeco*, record, 1965, ed. with notes by Chris Strachwitz, Arhoolie LP F 1024; Nicholas R. Spitzer, "Zydeco and Mardi Gras: Creole Identity and Performance Genres in Rural French Louisiana" (Ph.D. dissertation, University of Texas at Austin, 1986), *Zydeco: Creole Music and Culture in Rural Louisiana*, film, Center for Gulf South History and Culture, Abita Springs, La., 1984; *Zodico: Louisiana Creole Music*, record, 1978, ed. and booklet Nicholas R. Spitzer, Rounder Records 6009; *Zydeco*, record, 1967, ed. with liner notes by Chris Strachwitz, Arhoolie LP F 1009.

Acuff, Roy

(b. 1903) Country music singer.

Roy Acuff was the dominant country singer of the World War II years and the first living person to be elected to the Country Music Hall of Fame in 1962.

Generally described as "the king of country music," a title first given to him by baseball player Dizzy Dean, Roy Claxton Acuff was born in Maynardville, Tenn., on 15 September 1903. Acuff was a star athlete at Central High School in Knoxville (winning 12 athletic letters), but after suffering a heatstroke in 1929 during a Florida fishing trip, he abandoned a promising baseball career and began perfecting his skills as a fiddler and singer. He joined a medicine show in 1932 as a musician and comedian, and in the following year he began performing with a string band, the Tennessee Crackerjacks, on WROL in Knoxville. From 1934 to 1938 Acuff and his band played, at various times, on both WROL and WNOX in Knoxville and were part of the cast of the Mid-Day Merry Go Round at the latter station. In 1936 Acuff recorded for the Okeh label one of his most famous songs, "The Great Speckled Bird." The performance of this song during an audition at the Grand Ole Opry on 19 February 1938 probably did most to win him a permanent position on that famous show.

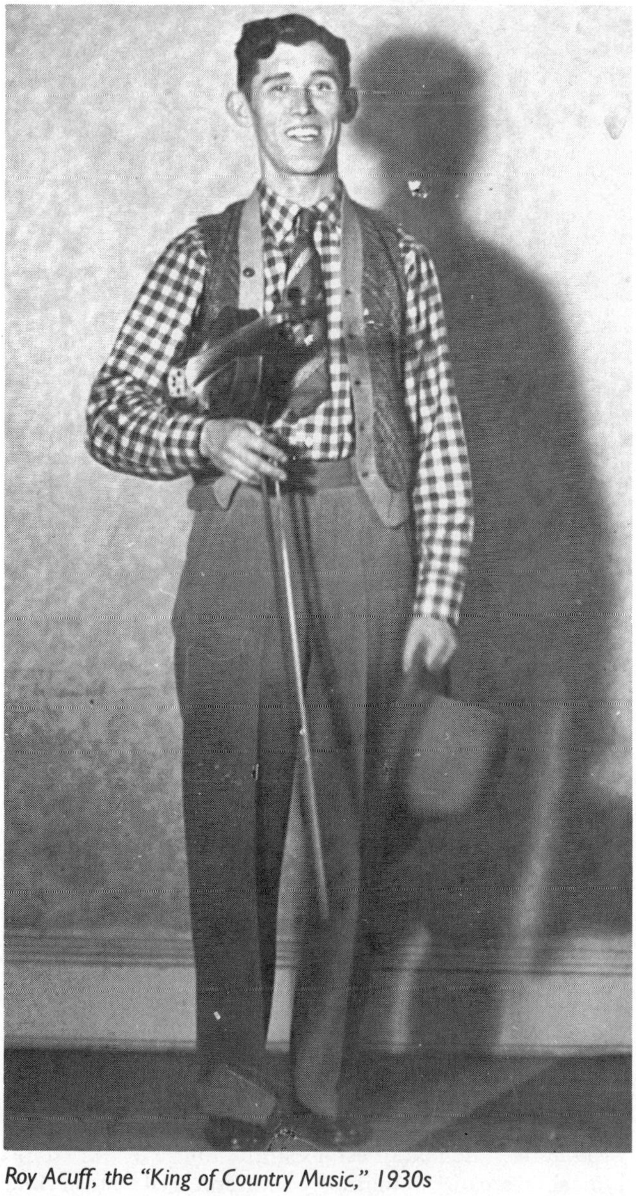

Roy Acuff, the "King of Country Music," 1930s

Acuff's rise to fame in country music paralleled that of the Grand Ole Opry in American entertainment. He was the first host of the show after it attained network status on NBC in 1939. During the war such Acuff songs as "The Great Speckled Bird," "Wabash Cannon Ball," and "Precious Jewel" appeared on jukeboxes all over the nation, and Acuff and his band—now called the Smoky Mountain Boys—drew larger crowds than any other act in country music. Polls indicated that Acuff enjoyed great popularity among American military personnel, and he even outpolled pop vocalist Frank Sinatra in a two-week contest sponsored by the Armed Forces Network. Acuff's earnest, emotional singing style and his preference for religious, sentimental, and old-time songs seemed to make him a fitting symbol of bedrock American values. According to legend, a Japanese banzai charge on Okinawa hurled these taunts at Americans: "To hell with Roosevelt; to hell with Babe Ruth; to hell with Roy Acuff!"

Although his record sales declined significantly after World War II, and his style became increasingly anachronistic amidst the wave of rock, pop, and swing sounds that inundated country music, Acuff maintained a high public visibility. He enjoyed considerable economic affluence as the coowner, along with Fred Rose, of Acuff-Rose Publishing Company, and he ran strongly, though unsuccessfully, as the Republican candidate for governor of Tennessee in 1948. He continued to appear each Saturday night at the Grand Ole Opry, established a souvenir and gift shop at Opryland, remained active in Tennessee Republican politics, and often acted as a spokesman for country music. When the Nitty Gritty Dirt Band made Acuff a central focus of their best-selling album, *Will the Circle Be Unbroken*, in 1972, the young country-rock musicians demonstrated just how far the Smoky Mountain Boys' name and influence had extended into American popular culture.

Bill C. Malone
Tulane University

Elizabeth Schlappi, *Roy Acuff* (1978).

All-Day Singings

All-day singing has long been one of the most cherished social institutions of the rural South. The term has been applied to a wide range of musical affairs and even has its counterpart in the all-night singings of modern gospel quartet music, but it is most closely associated with the shape-note singing convention.

Singing conventions are events that feature the performance of shape-note music, of both the four-shape and seven-shape varieties. The four-shape conventions have always been the more conservative in that they adhere to the use of one songbook, usually the venerable *Sacred Harp*, first published by Benjamin F. White in 1844, and they tend to resist newer songs and innovative styles of performing them (they instead preserve the Fasola style of singing). In short, the four-shape people try to remain faithful to the music and, in some respects, the way of life of their ancestors. The seven-shape conventions, which are by far the most numerous of these events, were originally marked by their acceptance of the do-re-mi system of singing, and they have generally been receptive to innovations in songs and singing style. The singers at such conventions sing not from one book but from a wide variety of paperback shape-note hymnals generally published twice a year by such companies as Vaughan, Winsett, and Stamps-Baxter. The song repertoire therefore includes both the older, familiar religious material and the newest songs "hot off the press." Although everyone in attendance is encouraged to sing, performances are also made by soloists, duets and trios, and often by visiting professional quartets. People clearly attend these conventions not merely to sing but also to be entertained.

Whatever the style of singing, the singing conventions meet regularly throughout the rural and small-town South, often on a monthly basis in the case of the seven-shape singers, but much more infrequently in the case of the Fasola people. Singers gather at a church or at the county courthouse, renew old acquaintances, sing for several hours under the guidance of experienced song leaders, and then sit down at long tables for a sumptuous feast of fried chicken, ham, potato salad, assorted pastries, and other delectables brought by the guests and participants. The practice of combining food and religious music long ago gave rise to the term "all-day singing with dinner on the grounds," which describes one of the most common events in the rural South.

Bill C. Malone
Tulane University

Alan Lomax, *Commentary on All Day Singing from "The Sacred Harp,"* Prestige Records 25007.

Armstrong, Louis

(1900–1971) Jazz musician and entertainer.

Born 4 July 1900 in New Orleans, Daniel Louis "Satchmo" Armstrong achieved acclaim as a jazz emissary to the world. Duke Ellington once called him "the epitome of jazz."

As a child Armstrong played music on the streets of New Orleans and received musical training in the public schools and at the Coloured Waif's Home (1913–14). He heard and was influenced by such early jazz performers

Louis Armstrong, premier jazz musician, c. 1931

as Charles "Buddy" Bolden, William "Bunk" Johnson, and Joseph "King" Oliver, who became his mentor. Armstrong performed briefly in a New Orleans nightclub at age 15 but did not become a full-time professional until he was 17. He joined Edward "Kid" Ory's band in 1918 and thereafter played with other jazz greats and led his own groups, especially the Hot Five and the Hot Seven, in the 1920s. His recording debut was with Oliver in 1923. Recordings made him a celebrity, and he toured widely in the 1930s, including a trip to Europe in 1932. He acquired his nickname "Satchmo" in England from the editor of a music magazine. Armstrong made a historic recording with Jimmie Rodgers, the father of country music, on 16 July 1930. Rodgers sang his "Blue Yodel No. 9" with accompaniment by Armstrong on the trumpet, and his wife, Lillian Hardin Armstrong, on piano.

Armstrong was a popular international figure by the 1940s and thereafter performed around the world; played at major jazz festivals; recorded frequently; performed in Broadway musicals, on radio, and later on television; and appeared in 60 films (including *Cabin in the Sky*, 1943; *New Orleans*, 1947; *High Society*, 1956; *Satchmo the Great*, 1956; *Jazz, the Intimate Art*, 1968; and *Hello, Dolly*, 1969). He died in New York City on 6 July 1971.

Armstrong's powerful trumpet and soulful, gravelly singing voice, as well as his infectious smile and effusive good humor, helped to establish the image of the archetypical jazzman. "Satchmo" communicated to everyone the irrepressible message that jazz was "good-time" music. His nickname, as well as his use of street vernacular for expressions of endearment and cordiality, reflected the communal New Orleans roots of the music.

The jazz personality that Armstrong helped create grew out of the southern urban underclass found most clearly in New Orleans. Armstrong's demeanor was as a loose-mannered, self-assertive (i.e., "bad"), somewhat "hip" good-time person whose music was a refuge from the external world. The jazz personality that emerged with Armstrong from the southern urban world included a bold and flirtatious manner, a zany sense of humor, a familiarity bordering on impertinence in interpersonal contact, a flashy, fancy code of dress, and an open and adventurous attitude toward life. Certainly, all jazz people have not fit this personality mold, but Armstrong—the most influential role model available to early jazz performers—did much to implant that abiding notion in the public mind.

Armstrong's jazz personality reflected certain aspects of the black culture in the South. He found his niche through music entertainment, a common pattern among blacks in southern urban areas. He drew on the vernacular tradition of black street and saloon life. His loose manner reflected an easygoing tolerance essential to the southern black underclass and fit squarely into the laid-back folk tradition. The hip mentality infusing the jazz personality is also a form of pride, validating the jazzman's self-assertiveness ("badness") in musical activities.

Curtis D. Jerde
W. R. Hogan Jazz Archive
Tulane University

Louis Armstrong, *Swing That Music* (1936), *Satchmo* (1954); Robert Goffin, *Horn of Plenty: The Story of Louis Armstrong* (1947); Max Jones and John Chilton, *Louis: The Louis Armstrong Story, 1900–1971* (1971).

Autry, Gene

(b. 1907) Country and western singer.

Though he became known throughout the world as a symbol of the West, Gene Autry's music remained firmly rooted in the southern soil from which it came. Orvon Gene Autry was born on a ranch near Tioga, Tex., on 29 September 1907 and moved to a ranch near Achille, Okla., as a youth. He was interested in a career in entertainment from an early age and even joined a medicine show in his teens; but it was as a guitar-strumming blue yodeler—under the influence of the enormously popular Jimmie Rodgers—that Autry achieved his first success as an entertainer in the late 1920s.

Although he continued to perform blue yodels as late as his 15th film (*The Old Corral*, 1936), he abandoned slavish imitation of Rodgers to adopt a gentler country sound, best exemplified by his first major record success, *That Silver Haired Daddy of Mine* (1931). A pure cowboy period followed, with popular records like *The Last Roundup* and *Tumbling Tumbleweeds* in the early 1930s, followed by standards like *Mexicali Rose, South of the Border*, and *There's a Gold Mine in the Sky* among many others. By the late 1930s his recordings were predominantly country love songs and had settled into an immediately recognizable style: swelling violins and muted trumpet for mainstream appeal, yet with a trademark steel guitar and Autry's straightforward, homespun, laconic voice most prominent. Like all great country singers, he possessed the ability to convey honesty, sincerity, and lack of affectation in his delivery; he sang as though he were speaking with each listener on a one-to-one basis. His recording career reached its apex in the late 1940s, with the multimillion-selling children's records *Here Comes Santa Claus* and *Rudolph the Red-Nosed Reindeer*.

The first singer-actor to popularize the singing cowboy in film, Autry fostered a new musical and film genre of worldwide popularity in a film career that included some 93 films and 91 television programs. He was a country songwriter of consequence; a record seller seldom matched in recording history, with major hits spanning years (1930–51) and styles; an enormously successful businessman and owner of the California Angels baseball club; and a cultural icon who brought an image of the West and western music to the world.

Of primary significance, however, was Gene Autry's adherence to an unabashedly sincere country singing style throughout his career. His stature as a major entertainer in the 1930s and 1940s gave country music a badly needed dignity and respectability, and though he is not often given credit for such a pioneering role, it was largely Autry and the singing cowboys who followed in his footsteps who made millions aware of the sincerity and emotion inherent in the music of the hills and ranges.

Douglas B. Green
Nashville, Tennessee

Gene Autry, with Mickey Herskowitz, *Back in the Saddle Again* (1978); Douglas B. Green, *Journal of Country Music* (May 1978); Bill C. Malone, *Country Music, U.S.A.: A Fifty-year History* (1968, rev. ed., 1985).

Balfa, Dewey

(b. 1927) Cajun folk musician.

Dewey Balfa is one of the nation's most widely respected folk musicians and Cajun cultural activists. His calm, homespun eloquence and sincerity have made him a spokesman for traditional cultures in general, but most of his battles to save his Cajun French culture are fought with a fiddle in south Louisiana, his home.

Balfa's musical heritage is a family affair. "My father, grandfather, great-grandfather, they all played the fiddle, and, you see, through my music, I feel they are all still alive." Balfa's father, Charles, was a sharecropper on Bayou Grand Louis in rural Evangeline Parish near Mamou. He instilled a love of life and music in his children, and Dewey and his four brothers grew up making music for their own entertainment. Born 20 March 1927, Dewey Balfa began playing the fiddle when he was about 13. Dewey had many models to follow, some outside the family, some even outside the culture. "You know, I was influenced by J. B. Fusilier, Leo Soileau, Harry Choates, and I think Bob Wills and the Texas Playboys had a little effect on my fiddling."

Dewey and his brothers soon were playing together for family gatherings and house dances. In the 1940s, when dance halls were at the height of their popularity, the Balfa Brothers band stayed busy, sometimes playing eight dances a week. String bands dominated Cajun music in the 1940s. The traditional music of Balfa's French Louisiana became increasingly Americanized as it was influenced by western swing, bluegrass, and country music. In the years following World War II, musicians such as Iry Lejeune, Nathan Abshire, Alphé Bergeron, and Lawrence Walker dusted off their long-abandoned accordions to perform again and to record traditional Louisiana Cajun French music. Many people were convinced after that of the need for deliberate efforts to encourage the maintenance of the music's traditional form.

In 1964 Balfa played as a last-minute replacement on guitar at the Newport Folk Festival, and after that, national and local interest was focused on traditional south Louisiana music. Balfa was involved in Louisiana contests sponsored by the Newport Folk Festival to discover talented musicians, and in 1967 the Balfa Brothers band performed at the Newport Folk Festival. South Louisiana itself was soon providing greater encouragement to its traditional artists such as Balfa. As a result of the overwhelming response to Lafayette's 1974 "Tribute to Cajun Music," the music festival has become an annual outdoor event. Dewey Balfa saw the festival all along as a way to attract young musicians to Cajun music. Two of Balfa's brothers died in a 1978 automobile accident, but Dewey Balfa and other family members continue to perform and to carry the spirit of the Balfa Brothers.

Barry Jean Ancelet
University of Southwestern Louisiana

Barry Jean Ancelet, *Louisiana Life* (September–October 1981), *The Makers of Cajun Music / Musiciens Cadiens et Créoles* (1984); John Broven, *South to Louisiana: The Music of the Cajun Bayous* (1983).

Banjo

The five-string banjo is a distinctive feature of the indigenous rural music of the South; it is generally not indigenous to rural music elsewhere. But while the banjo has been commonly associated with rural white southern culture, urban and black influences have significantly shaped its history.

The banjo originated in black culture, proto-banjos having been brought by slaves from Africa. Until recently, legend honored Joel Sweeney as the inventor of the five-string banjo. This Virginian, around 1830, allegedly improved the slave instrument by adding a short, high-pitched fifth (or thumb) string to its original four. However, reliable illustrations show that some slave banjos in the Americas had short thumb strings well before Sweeney was born.

Until the 1830s the banjo was strictly a black instrument. The first whites to play it became, like Sweeney, minstrel performers, and it became an essential element in the minstrel show, which was born in the urban North in 1843 and became the most popular entertainment form of the century. Minstrel banjo playing, a downstroking style undoubtedly reflecting preexisting black performance, also became the early style of white rural performers, who called it "frailing" or "clawhammer." By the 1870s the banjo was being played widely by southern rural whites, who probably learned from both black

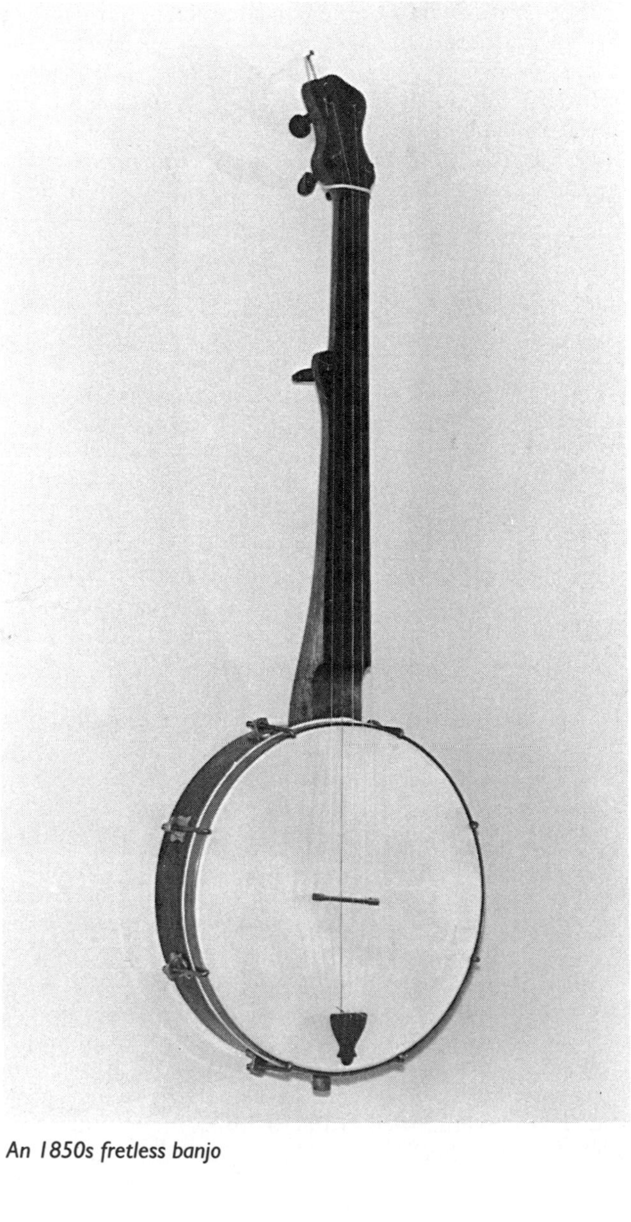

An 1850s fretless banjo

musicians and minstrel players who toured the South with minstrel shows, circuses, and medicine shows. Blacks continued to play the banjo, and until recently musical exchange between white and black players was active; now, however, only a few blacks play.

The first major group of styles, frailing, continues to be used in the South and, through the impetus of Pete Seeger and other figures in the folksong revival of the 1960s and 1970s, has also spread elsewhere. The second major group of styles, finger-picking, entered rural tradition around the turn of the century, apparently in imitation of "classical" banjo, which developed in the 1870s and 1880s as the successor to the minstrel style on the stage and in urban areas. The early, two-finger styles are still used, but in the 1940s Earl Scruggs and other southerners transformed them into the more driving, syncopated, three-finger style known as bluegrass banjo, the most widely heard style at present, as bluegrass gains popularity in rural and urban areas far from the South.

Despite the spread of revivalist "old-time" players and bluegrass, the five-string banjo remains a symbol of the rural South.

Robert B. Winans
Wayne State University

Dena J. Epstein, *Ethnomusicology* (September 1975); Scott Odell, in *New Grove Dictionary of Music and Musicians*, vol. 2, ed. Stanley Sadie (1980); Robert B. Winans, *Folklore and Folklife in Virginia* (1979), *Journal of American Folklore* (October–December 1976).

Beach Music

A treasure of popular culture in the Carolinas, beach music is not historically indigenous to Carolina beaches, where it now finds its greatest popularity, and does not traditionally celebrate beach culture. The origins of beach music lie in both the blues of the mid-20th-century South and the harmonious rhythm and blues of urban black street-corner singing groups like the Clovers, who enjoyed national success in the 1950s. Visitors to the Carolinas often find familiar oldies sanctified as classic "beach music."

The development of beach music as a cultural phenomenon began in the post–World War II era, as whites were attracted to the previously taboo music and dance of blacks. With the expansion of modern roadways and the mass availability of automobiles, this music became accessible in city concert halls and in the developing beach towns.

Beach music prospered in the late 1950s and early 1960s, but submerged somewhat in the Vietnam era, as both musically and thematically it had become traditional and therefore suspect in the social and political climate of the time. Amid the frenzy of hard rock and the earnestness of "message music," rhythm and blues was by no means hip, cool, or relevant for many young people. In this period *beach music* emerged as a cover term for an eclectic assortment of rhythm-and-blues songs. Some people claim the term always existed, but many insist that it did not appear until around 1970 or later. Though the temptation is to credit the Drifters's "Under the Boardwalk" from 1964 with popularizing the term, beach music more likely arose from a nostalgic looking back toward happier tunes in the past, symbolized by the music that permeated them.

With the advent of disco music in the late 1970s, beach music was revitalized and prospered. The return of "touch dancing" at this time contributed to the popularity of the "shag," beach music's dance ritual. Essentially a sophisticated, more refined cousin of the jitterbug (and not related to the shag of the Northeast in the 1940s), the shag became the focal point of beach music. The shag was decreed the state dance by the South Carolina Legislature in 1985, and beach music has become a cultural icon in the Carolinas. Purists seek to preserve it in its earliest, most intricate forms, and a circuit of dance competitions has developed with support from a growing number of teaching professionals.

With the resurgence of beach music in the late 1970s and early 1980s, the beach music scene became self-conscious and lyrically self-glorifying, celebrating itself and the beer-drinking, love-making side of beach culture in regional, independently produced songs such as the Embers's 1979 "I Love Beach Music." Performers now are mostly white, reside principally in the Carolinas, and stress the horns in their rhythm sections.

The resurgence of beach music reached its peak in the early part of the 1980s with two Beach Music Awards shows filmed in 1982 and 1983 in Myrtle Beach, S.C. , a capital for the music. A Society of Stranders (from "The Grand Strand," the popular name for the northeast South Carolina coastal area) meets each year in North Myrtle Beach and brings thousands of beach music fans together for several days of festivities. Some predicted that it would "go national," but this has not occurred. Beach music's true value lies in the regional bonding it inspires in the Carolinas.

Stephen J. Nagle
University of South Carolina,
Coastal Campus

Orin Anderson, *Sandlapper* (June 1981); Bill King, Atlanta *Constitution* (6 June 1981); Steven Levy, *Rolling Stone* (30 September 1982); Stephen J. Nagle, *On The Beach* (Summer 1983).

Beale Street

Beale Street, one of the most celebrated streets in the South, was the black main street of Memphis and of the surrounding rural region, comparable in its heydey to Auburn Avenue in Atlanta and Maxwell Street in Chicago. Beginning at the Mississippi riverfront and extending eastward a mile and a half, the street was lined with commercial buildings, churches, theaters, parks, elegant mansions, everyday dwellings, and apartment houses.

The diversity of its built environment showed that Beale was a mosaic of southern cultures. For more than a century, indigenous white and black southerners, Italian Americans, Greek Americans, Chinese Americans, and Jews lived or worked on Beale.

Unlike its northern counterparts, Beale Street never became a black ghetto. But it was Beale's black culture that gave the street its fame, and the street stood as testimony to the decision of black people to strive to achieve the American Dream in their American homeland, the South, rather than to move North. From the 1830s, when the street was laid out, to the Civil War, black people were present on Beale Street, either as slaves living in quarters behind their masters' homes or as free blacks, some of whom owned Beale Street property. After emancipation, thousands of freed slaves left the declining farms and small towns of the rural South and came to Memphis and to Beale Street in particular, seeking to fulfill the promises of freedom. Alongside white-owned establishments, they founded banks, insurance companies, retail shops, newspapers, schools, churches, fraternal institutions, nightclubs, and political and civil rights organizations. From the 1880s to the 1920s Beale was one of the South's most prosperous black communities. On weekends, thousands of blacks from Memphis and the surrounding countryside came to Beale for shopping and entertainment, crowding the sidewalks so thickly "you had to walk in the street to pass by."

As the urban center of black nightlife for north Mississippi, east Arkansas, and west Tennessee, Beale attracted hundreds of musicians and became one of the nation's most influential centers of Afro-American music. Variety was its hallmark—vaudeville orchestras, marching bands, ragtime, jug bands, blues, jazz, big bands, and rhythm and blues. A meeting place for urban and rural styles, Beale served as a school where young talent was nurtured and it produced musicians who shaped the course of American music. In 1909 W. C. Handy was the first person to pen the blues, a form of music he had first heard in the Mississippi Delta town of Clarksdale, thus enabling it to be played around the world.

Since the 1920s Beale Street has produced a succession of outstanding jazz musicians, such as Jimmy Lunceford, a principal creator of the big-band sound. In the 1940s and 1950s Beale Street musicians like B. B. King and Bobby "Blue" Bland blended traditional blues with jazz arrangements to help produce the new form of music known as rhythm and blues. In the 1950s young white musicians from the region like Elvis Presley were attracted to the music, dance, and dress styles of Beale Street and merged these with their country music traditions to shape a new type of music, rockabilly, and to lay the foundations for rock and roll.

But if Beale Street was a cultural sanctuary, it was a precarious one. Segregation denied blacks effective access to political and economic power beyond their own community, and they were therefore unable to protect their Beale Street haven when hard times came. After World War II, downtown Memphis, like other American inner cities, began to change radically in character; the two most dramatic responses, the civil rights movement and urban renewal, transformed Beale. While the civil rights movement achieved integration of Memphis's public facilities, it ironically damaged Beale by enabling blacks to do business throughout the city. The assassination of Martin Luther King, Jr., near Beale and the turbulent aftermath accelerated the street's decline. Urban renewal then cleared most of the old buildings in its supportive community.

In the late 1970s and 1980s, however, Beale Street like other historic areas in the South has received new recognition as a cultural resource; and governmental, nonprofit, and private organizations have substantially revitalized the street. The resultant preservation of original landmarks together with the establishment of new nightclubs, restaurants, retail stores, and an interpretive center has produced a significant blend of old and new, and the future development of the street will no doubt continue to reflect major trends of urban southern culture.

See also URBANIZATION: / Memphis

George McDaniel
Center for Southern Folklore

Margaret McKee and Fred Chisenhall, *Beale Black and Blue: Life and Music on Black America's Main Street* (1981).

Bechet, Sidney

(1897–1959) Jazz musician and composer.

Like Jelly Roll Morton, Sidney Joseph Bechet, who was born 14 May 1897 in New Orleans, was a black Creole, a member of the group that played a pivotal part in the genesis of jazz. He grew up in the rich musical environment of New Orleans, taught himself clarinet, and later studied sporadically with George Bacquet, "Big Eye" Louis Nelson, and Lorenzo Tio, Jr. By about 1910, he was performing with established New Orleans bands such as Bunk Johnson's. In 1914 he began to tour, settling in Chicago in 1917.

He performed in Europe from 1919 to 1921. He was among the first jazzmen to be critically praised; in 1919 the Swiss conductor Ernest Ansermet called him "an artist of genius." Also in 1919 Bechet began playing the soprano saxophone, and made it his primary instrument the rest of his life. In the mid-1920s, he recorded with Clarence Williams and Louis Armstrong and worked briefly with Duke Ellington. From 1925 to 1928 he toured Germany, France, and the Soviet Union. He returned to the United States with Noble Sissle's band and performed intermittently with it through 1938. During the revival of traditional jazz beginning about 1939, he was praised as one of the master jazz pioneers, and his career rebounded. From 1951 he lived in France, where he became a celebrity as the dominant figure in traditional jazz. He composed both short works (*Petite Fleur*) and longer works (*Nouvelles Orléans*) and appeared in a number of films.

Bechet was one of many jazz pioneers who moved from New Orleans to Chicago during the 1910s and 1920s, and, making records there, spread jazz from its southern beginnings to the nation and beyond. Like Armstrong, Bechet's melodic voice was so strong and original that he came to dominate his ensembles; both musicians helped transform early jazz from an ensemble music to a soloist's art. Bechet made the soprano saxophone into a jazz instrument and set the standard by which all subsequent players have been measured. He developed a strong, individual jazz voice, distinctive for its rhythmic freedom, flowing expressiveness, rich tone, and wide vibrato. He greatly influenced Duke Ellington's saxophonist Jimmy Hodges, who, in turn, perpetuated Bechet's legacy. Bechet was also notable for the longevity of his musical career, which spanned nearly 60 years, and for maintaining his beautiful style almost until his death in Paris, 14 May 1959.

John Edward Hasse
Smithsonian Institution

Sidney Bechet, *Treat it Gentle* (1960); Hans J. Mauerer, *A Discography of Sidney Bechet* (1969); Raymond Mouly, *Sidney Bechet: Notre Ami* (1959); Martin Williams, *Jazz Masters of New Orleans* (1967).

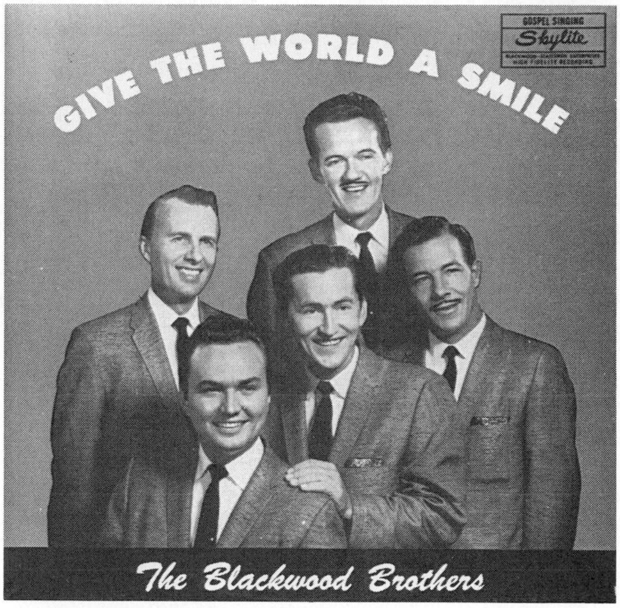

The Blackwood Brothers, gospel music quintet, 1950s

Blackwood Brothers

Gospel music singers.

Perhaps the most popular group in southern gospel music history, the Blackwood Brothers parlayed their rural Mississippi sharecropping background into a million-dollar entertainment empire. For many fans in both the South and the Midwest, the Blackwoods defined the singing quartet style that is the backbone of classic southern gospel music and engineered many of the musical and promotional innovations that permitted gospel singers to professionalize their music. They were among the first to issue their own phonograph records, to break from the songbook publishers that had dominated gospel music for the first four decades of the century, to begin their own radio transcription service, to consciously seek out and adapt new or original songs, to travel by air, and to adapt harmonies and accompaniment appealing to a nationwide popular audience.

The original quartet was formed in 1934 at Ackerman, Miss., by three brothers, Roy, Doyle, and James, sons of a Delta sharecropper and his wife who sang casually in church; the fourth member was Roy's young son, R. W. By 1937 the group found itself broadcasting on radio at Jackson, Miss., doing not only gospel but pop and country tunes, and after April 1939 they performed on a 50,000-watt station, KWKH, recently opened in Shreveport, La. Here they began an affiliation with the songbook publisher V. O. Stamps, who provided them with a car, contracts, a stipend, and a piano player, thus casting them into the format of "four men and a piano" that had become characteristic of earlier gospel quartets. In 1940 Stamps sent them to Shenandoah, Iowa, where they began a decade's stay at KMA that saw them develop their unique style and build a huge following in the Midwest.

At Shenandoah the quartet began to experiment with modern harmonies (built on sixth and ninth chords), developing their precise enunciation and diction and borrowing verve, dynamics, and solo breaks from pop and black gospel music. In 1946 they began to make records, first on the White Church label and then on their own Blackwood label, recording some 49 singles between 1946 and 1951. A move back to Memphis in August 1950 put them in the center of the then-burgeoning gospel movement, where both black and white groups vied for air time and for places at "all-night sings." With their broadcasting base at WMPS, the Blackwoods—now with only two of the original four still singing—became one of the first postwar gospel groups to sign with a major label when they began recording for RCA Victor on 4 January 1952. Hit records and a win on the nationally broadcast *Arthur Godfrey Talent Scouts* show in 1954 followed, but barely two weeks after the Godfrey show two members of the group, R. W. and bass singer Bill Lyles, were killed in a plane crash.

Within a month the Blackwoods had recovered and regrouped and were back on the concert circuit; another Blackwood, Cecil, the brother of R. W., stepped in, as did bass singer J. D. Sumner, who was to play an important role in the group's sound throughout the 1950s. A string of national television appearances and successful record albums followed in the mid-1950s, and the group's promotional activities reached new heights through their founding of the National Quartet Convention in 1957 and of a new all-gospel record company, Skylite, in 1960 as well as through the purchase of several of the old gospel songbook companies, which had fallen on hard times. From 1967 to 1977 the group won numerous Grammy awards and as late as the mid-1970s still featured James Blackwood, his son Jimmy, and his nephew Cecil.

The Blackwood Brothers discography is voluminous. In addition to hundreds of singles, it includes at least 58 long-playing albums on RCA Victor from 1956 to 1973 and at least 42 albums on the Skylite label from 1961 to 1981; probably 20 albums exist on various other labels. Songs the Blackwoods have been most associated with include "Have You Talked to the Man Upstairs" (their first RCA hit and the winning song on the Godfrey show), "Swing Down Chariot," "My Journey to the Sky," "Paradise Island," "In Times Like These," "Looking for a City," and "The Old Country Church."

Charles K. Wolfe
Middle Tennessee State University

James Blackwood, with Don Martin, *The James Blackwood Story* (1975); Kree Jack Racine, *Above All: The Fascinating and True Story of the Lives and Careers of the Famous Blackwood Brothers Quartet* (1967).

Bolden, Buddy

(1877–1931) Jazz musician.

The story of Charles "Buddy" Bolden is part of the earliest history of New Orleans jazz. Bolden was an accomplished cornetist and one of the first musicians to mix ragtime and blues into a sound that would later be called "jazz." He was born in New Orleans on 6 September 1877. His father, a drayman, died of pneumonia when Bolden was six years old. His mother worked to support the family, and Bolden and his sister did not have to work as children. No other members of the Bolden family were interested in music; Bolden learned from religious and various types of street music heard in New Orleans in the late 19th century. His natural musical ability showed itself when he began to play the cornet at age 17.

Bolden played in small string bands for dances and parties and in parades in New Orleans between 1895 and 1900. He achieved citywide fame around 1900 as the leader of his own band. Until 1906 Bolden continued to improvise his music, attracting a considerable following of admirers and being dubbed the "King" of New Orleans jazz. He and his band played in parks and at picnics, in city music halls, lawn parties, and bars. Sometimes they traveled outside New Orleans, playing at train stops along the way. Bolden was immersed in his music, enjoyed drinking, and was said to have hypnotic powers over women.

In the spring of 1906 Bolden began to have severe headaches and reportedly suffered from delusions. He attacked his mother in a fit and was taken into police custody. Once released, Bolden continued to play, but friends said he became increasingly depressed and easily angered. His erratic behavior led to another arrest in September 1906. His condition deteriorated quickly after his release, and in June 1907 Bolden was committed to the Insane Asylum of Louisiana, where he spent the last 24 years of his life. The official cause of his insanity was listed as alcoholism.

Bolden achieved his status as the legendary ancestor of jazz after his death. Jazz fans repeat fictional stories such as the one in which Bolden supposedly blew his cornet so hard that the tuning slide flew out and landed 20 feet away. Most of the stories suggest the remarkable power of Bolden's playing. Even the New Orleans *Times-Picayune* in 1940 reported that Bolden "played with such volume that it is said he could often be heard while playing across the river in Gretna." "King" Bolden's increasing notoriety as a musician is underscored by the tragic nature of his short but inspired career.

Karen M. McDearman
University of Mississippi

Ole Brask, *Jazz People* (1976); Donald M. Marquis, *In Search of Buddy Bolden: First Man of Jazz* (1978).

Brown, James

(b. 1933) Soul music singer.

"Soul Brother No. 1," "The Godfather of Soul," and "Mr. Dynamite" are all names credited to the only black rhythm-and-blues artist of the 1950s to successfully bridge the gap to soul artist in the 1960s and funk artist in the 1970s. Maintaining his popularity through 30 years, James Brown singlehandedly anticipated and shaped 1970s funk and, to a slightly lesser degree, disco music. The repercussions of his aesthetic conceptualizations are heard everywhere on black radio in the 1980s. His influence can be detected in European new wave music, West African Afro-beat, and West Indian reggae.

Brown was born 3 May 1933 near Augusta, Ga., in abject poverty. Twenty-one years later he formed the first version of his Famous Flames. Initially the Flames sang gospel music only. They soon adapted their highly emotional repertoire to secular subjects and started working regularly in and around Macon, Ga. A demo tape of the secularized gospel song "Please, Please, Please" was sent to King Records in Cincinnati (at the time one of the leading independent record labels specializing in black music), and in February 1956 James Brown and the Famous Flames recut the song and attained their first top-10 rhythm-and-blues hit. It would be four years before Brown would cross over to the pop charts and nine years before "Papa's Got a Brand New Bag (Part I)" would go top 10 on the pop charts.

In that nine-year period Brown developed his legendary show-stopping revue with supporting singers, comedians, and dancers. His bands rehearsed meticulously,

James Brown, soul singer, 1960s

achieving a professionalism virtually unknown in rhythm and blues or rock and roll, while Brown exuded nonstop energy replete with dancing, splits, knee drops, microphone acrobatics, and his fabled simulated collapse. The whole package was captured on vinyl in *Live at the Apollo*, a 1962 album, which, although a hardcore rhythm-and-blues album, reached the number-two spot on *Billboard*'s album charts and stayed on the charts for a total of 66 weeks.

Brown began with a style based on gospel intensity and interaction. His early records consist largely of call and response between himself and the Famous Flames. The Flames would echo, shadow, double, and respond to Brown's every nuance. The instrumentalists on these early records largely played a 12/8 triplet feel over a pronounced back beat. By 1959 Brown, originally a drummer, started to change his style, opting for increasingly complex out-front, crack rhythmic arrangements usually consisting of extended one-chord vamps featuring repetitive "groove" vocal figures, choked rhythm guitar, staccato horn bursts, and broken two- and three-note bass patterns. In both styles Brown's singing was marked by a complete lack of inhibition, extensively utilizing gospel devices such as falsetto cries, grunts, hoarse screams, and gasps.

Brown has completely controlled his career. He has written lyrics, produced records, and made all executive decisions, eventually managing himself and forming his own record production company. He also put himself in the vanguard of the black consciousness movement through records such as "Say It Loud, I'm Black and I'm Proud." As a classic example of the rags-to-riches American dream, Brown's importance as a symbol to black youth cannot be overestimated. Forty million-selling records and over one hundred chart entries later, James Brown remains "The Hardest Working Man in Show Business."

Robert Bowman
Memphis, Tennessee

Tony Cummings, in *The Soul Book*, ed. Ian Hoare (1975); Gerri Hirshey, *Nowhere To Run: The Story of Soul Music* (1984); Robert Palmer, in *The Rolling Stone Illustrated History of Rock 'n' Roll*, ed. Jim Miller (1980).

Brumley, Albert

(1905–1977) Gospel music songwriter.

Albert E. Brumley was one of the premier composers of gospel songs and was intimately associated with the rise and expansion of the southern gospel quartet business. Many songs from his repertoire still command the allegiance of musicians in both the gospel and country fields (and particularly in bluegrass music, where his songs are frequently played).

Brumley was born near Spiro, LeFlore County, Okla., on 29 October 1905 into a tenant-farm family that provided inspiration for many of his most popular songs. He began writing songs shortly after attending his first singing school in 1922 at the Rock Island community in eastern Oklahoma, but none were published until 1927 when "I Can Hear Them Singing Over There" appeared in *Gates of Glory*, a convention songbook issued by the Hartford Music Company of Hartford, Ark. Brumley was intimately associated with the Hartford Company from 1926 to 1937, first as a student in its Musical Institute, and then as a traveling teacher in many of its shape-note singing schools, as a bass singer in some of the Hartford Quartets, and as a staff writer. Above all, Brumley profited from the guidance and counsel of Eugene M. Bartlett, the owner of the Hartford Company and the writer of such songs as "Victory in Jesus," "Everybody Will Be Happy over There," and "Take an Old Cold Tater and Wait."

In January 1932 Brumley's most famous song, "I'll Fly Away," was published by the Hartford Company in one of its many paperback songbooks, *Wonderful Message*. Reminiscent of 19th-century camp-meeting songs with its catchy rhythm and repeated chorus, "I'll Fly Away" has since been recorded over 500 times in virtually every field of music and has become one of the standards of white gospel music. Brumley eventually composed over 600 songs, first for the Hartford Company up to 1937, then for the Stamps-Baxter Company from 1937 to 1945, and finally for the Stamps Quartet Publishing Company after 1945. Such songs as "Jesus Hold My Hand," "I'll Meet You in the Morning," "I Found a Hiding Place," "Camping in Canaan's Land" (cowritten with Eugene M. Bartlett), and "If We Never Meet Again" won a wide circulation in homes and churches all over the South through the performances of the quartets. Radio was a prime medium through which his songs were popularized, and Brumley wrote a very popular song, "Turn Your Radio On," which paid tribute to that powerful commercial force while advising listeners to "get in touch with God" by tuning in "the Master's radio."

Although Brumley said that he never consciously wrote a country song, several of his songs (in addition to the purely gospel numbers mentioned previously) have become standards in the country and bluegrass fields. These include "By the Side of the Road," "Dreaming of a Little Cabin," "Did You Ever Go Sailin'," "Nobody Answered Me," and "Rank Strangers to Me." These sentimental and nostalgic songs, which juxtapose memories of a cherished but decaying rural past with visions of a reconciliation with loved ones in heaven, have struck sensitive chords among many southerners who have been conscious of their region's disquieting transition from ruralism and agriculture to urban industrialism. Indeed, all Brumley's songs, both religious and secular, spoke directly to people who often felt discouraged in a world of disappointment and bewildering change. Consequently, his songs were particularly cherished during the Depression when people needed the comfort and assurance of a personal, caring Savior.

Brumley wrote few songs after World War II, but he remained in the music business as the owner of the Hartford Company and Albert Brumley and Sons, and was the promoter of two music festivals, the Sunup to Sundown Sing in Springdale, Ark., and the Hill and Hollow Folk Festival in Powell, Mo. Before his death on 15 November 1977, Brumley was named to the Gospel Music Hall of Fame and the Nashville Song Writers Hall of Fame. He is buried near Powell, Mo., where he had resided since 1931.

Bill C. Malone
Tulane University

Clarence Baxter and Vide Polk, *Gospel Song Writers Biography* (1971); Ottis J. Knippers, *Who's Who among Southern Singers and Composers* (1937); *Music City News* (July 1965).

Byrd, Henry (Professor Longhair)

(1918–1980) Rhythm-and-blues musician.

Professor Longhair, New Orleans rhythm-and-blues musician, 1978

Professor Longhair was a pioneer of the post–World War II New Orleans rhythm-and-blues idiom. Although he made the transition to rock and roll with modest commercial results, his artistic influence on popular music in the Crescent City was immense. Pianist-composer Allen Toussaint dubbed him "the Bach of Rock."

Born in Bogalusa, La., a rural sawmill town, Henry Roeland Byrd moved to New Orleans as a child. He grew up near Rampart Street, then a musical strip connecting black central-city wards to the downtown neighborhoods. His early exposure to music came in church, which he attended with his mother; she played guitar and piano. For the most part, though, Byrd was self-taught, inspired by blues pianists like Kid "Stormy" Weather, Champion Jack Dupree, and Isidore "Tuts" Washington.

As a teenager, Byrd acquired his sense of rhythm by tap dancing. In time, he took the drum-infused movements of his feet and translated them to piano, adding layers of melody to intricate rhythm patterns. Chief among them was boogie-woogie. Another important influence was Sullivan Rock, an obscure honky-tonk pianist about whom little is known.

Byrd—or Fess as fans called him—played with a sizzling left hand, and to this percussive flavor he added "a mixture of mambo, rhumba, and calypso." This fusion resonates in "Go to the Mardi Gras," an anthem that is now a classic and is played on hundreds of jukeboxes during Carnival.

His stage name came in 1947 at the Caldonia Inn. The white proprietor announced, "We'll call you Professor Longhair and the Four Hairs Combo." In the early 1950s, recording with Atlantic Records, he cut the memorable "Tipitina." By the late 1960s he had sunk into obscurity, but the following decade saw a gallant comeback. In 1977 friends opened Tipitina's, a club that served as Byrd's home base in New Orleans.

Byrd's albums include *New Orleans Piano*, *Mardi Gras in New Orleans*, *The Last Mardi Gras*, and *Crawfish Fiesta*, which was being shipped to record stores when he died on 30 January 1980. The jazz funeral in his honor was one of the largest and most exciting in recent memory. An excellent video documentary, *Piano Players Seldom Play Together*, features Toussaint, Tuts Washington, and Professor Longhair, and includes moving scenes at Byrd's funeral.

Jason Berry
New Orleans, Louisiana

Jason Berry, Jonathan Forse, and Tad Jones, *Up from the Cradle of Jazz: New Orleans Music since World War II* (1987); John Broven, *Rhythm and Blues in New Orleans* (1978); Jeff Hannusch, *I Hear You Knockin'* (1985); Robert Palmer, *A Tale of Two Cities: Memphis Rock and New Orleans Roll* (1979).

Carter Family

Country entertainers.

The Carter Family was one of country music's most influential groups and a valuable link to the music's folk origins. The family was composed of Alvin Pleasant (A. P.) Carter, who was born in Scott County, Va., in 1891; his wife Sara Dougherty Carter, who was born in Wise County, Va., in 1898; and A. P.'s sister-in-law Maybelle Addington Carter, who was born at Nickelsville, Va., in 1909. After their marriage on 18 June 1915, A. P. and Sara began singing for friends and relatives who gathered at their home at Maces Spring in the Clinch Mountains of Virginia. After Maybelle married A. P.'s brother Ezra in 1926, she joined the duo, bringing an exceptional talent for the autoharp, banjo, and guitar.

The trio made their first records for the famous talent scout Ralph Peer and the Victor Company in Bristol, Tenn., on 1 and 2 August 1927. Recording at the same session where Jimmie Rodgers made his debut, the Carter Family introduced a style of performing that remained recognizable and appealing for many years, and they began circulating a body of songs that still endures in the repertoire of modern country musicians. From 1927 to 1943 the Carters popularized their large catalog of gospel, sentimental, and traditional songs at personal appearances, on live radio broadcasts, on transcriptions, and on recordings made until 1941 for the Victor, American Record, Decca, and Columbia companies. Most country and folk music fans still know such Carter Family songs as "Wildwood Flower," "Keep on the Sunny Side," "Worried Man Blues," "I'm Thinking Tonight of My Blue Eyes," and "Will the Circle Be Unbroken."

Vocally, the Carter Family featured Sara's strong soprano lead, Maybelle's alto harmony, and A. P.'s baritone. Instrumentally, the family's distinctive sound was centered around Maybelle's much-copied guitar style, which was supported usually by rhythm chords produced by Sara on the autoharp. Although she sometimes played other styles, Maybelle generally used a thumb-brush technique in which the thumb picked the melody on the bass strings while the fingers provided rhythm with a downward stroke of the treble strings. This style was immensely appealing to other guitarists, and her version of "Wildwood Flower" was the model used by most fledgling guitarists when they did their first solo guitar piece.

Although their records circulated widely, the Carter Family was best known to millions of Americans through their performances over the Mexican border station XERA from 1938 to 1941. During these years the Carter children also began performing, and after 1943, when the original trio officially disbanded, new versions of "the Carter Family" began to emerge. Maybelle began performing with her daughters Helen, June, and Anita (as Mother Maybelle and the Carter Sisters), and by 1950 the group had begun a Grand Ole Opry career that would last for 17 years. The Carter Family became more dramatically linked to mainstream country music in 1968 when June Carter married Johnny Cash. Mother Maybelle and her daughters were regular members of Cash's road show until 1973. Neither A. P. nor Sara remained active in music after 1943 (and, in fact, had separated in 1933), but they did join with their children, Joe and Janette, to make records in 1952 and 1956 for the Acme label.

The Carter Family won renewed respect and recognition during the urban folk revival of the early 1960s from a legion of new fans who knew them only through their old records and radio transcriptions. Maybelle, however, became an active participant in the folk scene, and she and Sara in 1967 made one album for Columbia called *An Historic Reunion*. A. P. died in 1960, and Maybelle and Sara died within two and a half months of each other in late 1979. The country music industry paid tribute to the trio in 1970 by naming them to the Hall of Fame.

Bill C. Malone
Tulane University

Bill C. Malone, *Country Music, U.S.A.: A Fifty-year History* (1968; rev. ed., 1985); Irwin Stambler and Grellin Landon, *The Encyclopedia of Folk, Country, and Western Music* (2d ed., 1983); Charles K. Wolfe, *Tennessee Strings: The Story of Country Music in Tennessee* (1977).

Charles, Ray

(b. 1930) Rhythm-and-blues musician.

Charles's recording career has spanned close to 40 years, yet his fame and influence lie with a series of recordings made for Atlantic and ABC-Paramount from 1955 to 1962. These recordings exhibited unprecedented versatility as Charles recorded jazz, blues, gospel, show tunes, and finally country and western music. His significance rests primarily on his fusing of gospel with pop and blues styles and, secondarily, his liberation of country and western as white-only music.

Born 23 September 1930 in Albany, Ga., as Ray Charles Robinson, he and his family moved to Greenville, Fla., where, at the age of six, he developed glaucoma and became blind. His father died when Charles was young, and when his mother passed away in 1945, Charles turned to music full time to provide a living for himself.

Wanting to get away from Florida, he moved to Seattle, Wash., in 1947. There, he dropped his surname to avoid confusion with the boxer Sugar Ray Robinson. In 1948 he made his first records for Bob Geddins's Swingtime label. These first recordings were done with a trio made up of Charles's piano plus guitar and bass. They imitated the recordings of performers such as Nat "King" Cole and Charles Brown. After he made several top-10 rhythm-and-blues hits in this style in 1951 and 1952, Atlantic Records bought his contract.

The recordings for Atlantic gradually exhibited less polish and more blues and gospel influence. In late 1953 Charles arranged and played piano on New Orleans guitarist Guitar Slim's monumental "The Things That I Used to Do." Slim's impassioned gospel-influenced vocal must have set Charles's mind whirring, as his very next sessions were cut in New Orleans without session musicians, and they exhibited a marked gospel feel.

In 1955 in Atlanta Charles hit his stride. Recording at a local radio station, he cut "I Got a Woman." Featuring horns and a churchy piano rather than the "tasteful" jazz guitar heard on the majority of his earlier cuttings and featuring an unrestrained vocal track replete with falsetto shrieks, the record became a number-two rhythm-and-blues hit. Several similar gospel-pop records followed, some written by Charles, many others adapted from extant gospel songs. The Pilgrim Traveler's "I've Got a New Home" became "Lonely Avenue"; Clara Ward's "This Little Light of Mine" became "This Little Girl of Mine"; and the Caravan's "What Kind of a Man Is This, Nobody But You Lord" became simply "Nobody But You."

Charles had effectively created a whole new phase of black pop music, which laid the basis for the unrestrained soul vocalists of the 1960s. This period of his recording career culminated in the 1959 recording of his self-penned "What I Say." The record opens with a blues gospel electric piano hammering out a Latinish rhythm and builds through a series of fragmentary choruses to extended call and response between Charles and his three-piece female backup vocalists, the Raelets. The record sounds like the re-creation of a revival meeting and, at the time, was seen by many as blasphemy. Although consequently banned on several radio stations, it nonetheless became a number-six pop hit and opened a huge white audience for Charles. In the meantime he recorded a number of jazz sessions with vibist Milt Jackson in addition to a number of blues and standards sessions.

"What I Say" prompted ABC-Paramount Records to entice him away from Atlantic. For the first few years at ABC Charles recorded material similar to his Atlantic output, although gradually the Ralph Burns Orchestra increasingly made its presence felt. Hoagy Carmichael's "Georgia" was his biggest hit in this period.

The year 1962 saw the release of a revolutionary album entitled *Modern Sounds in Country and Western Music*, with several ensuing hit singles including "I Can't Stop Loving You" and "You Don't Know Me." At the time, the idea of a black jazz/blues/soul artist recording white country music was extremely daring. Nevertheless, the album went on to sell 3 million copies and further established Charles with a middle-of-the-road white audience.

Since then, Charles's output has been steady but less original. His recordings are generally a heavily orchestrated pastiche of contemporary pop hits, nostalgic sentimental tunes, Broadway standards, and the odd blues. In 1968 he formed his label, Tangerine Records, which was distributed by ABC-Paramount, and in 1973 he formed the independent Crossover Records (an apt name), whose products were later distributed by Atlantic.

Robert Bowman
Memphis, Tennessee

Ray Charles, with David Ritz, *Brother Ray: Ray Charles' Own Story* (1978); Tony Cummings, in *The Soul Book*, ed. Ian Hoare (1975); Gerri Hershey, *Nowhere To Run: The Story of Soul Music* (1984).

Chenier, Clifton

(1925–1988) Zydeco musician.

Born 25 June 1925 near Opelousas in Saint Landry Parish, La., Clifton Chenier was the nation's premier zydeco performer. His father, Joseph, played the accordion, and he took his sons, Clifton and Cleveland, to local parties where he performed. The two boys themselves started playing at a young age—Clifton the accordion his father gave him, and Cleveland his mother's rub board. In the early 1940s they performed with Clarence Garlow's group in clubs around Lake Charles, La., and in 1947 Clifton left home and joined his brother in Lake Charles. The two worked at the oil refineries in Port Arthur, Tex., and formed the Hot Sizzling Band that played along the Texas-Louisiana Gulf Coast in the late 1940s and early 1950s.

J. R. Fulbright, a talent scout for Elko Records in California, met Chenier in 1954 and made the first recording of his music. During the middle and late 1950s Chenier recorded for the Imperial, Specialty, Chess, Argo, Checker, and Zynn labels, and he and his band toured not only in the Southwest but on the West Coast and in Chicago.

Known mostly as a rhythm-and-blues artist in the early 1960s, Chenier returned to his south Louisiana roots after signing with Chris Strachwitz's Arhoolie Records in 1964 and recording zydeco music on such albums as *Louisiana Blues and Zydeco*, *Bon Ton Roulet*, *King of the Bayous*, and *Bogalusa Boogie*. He recorded the classic zydeco song "Oh! Lucille" in 1966 for Crazy Cajun Records in Pasadena, Tex. In the late 1960s Chenier toured widely, including appearances at the Berkeley Blues Festival (1966), the Newport Folk Festival (1969), and in Europe (1967–69). In the 1970s his name became synonymous with the best in zydeco, and he remained a popular performer in rhythm and blues clubs as well.

Known as the "Black King of the South" and the "King of Zydeco," Chenier performed wearing a crown and leading his sometimes-raucous group, the Louisiana Hot Band. Poor health from a kidney infection plagued him in 1979, but he returned to better health in the early 1980s. He continued to play east Texas–southern Louisiana clubs and performed nationally as well, until his death in 1988. Les Blank's *Dry Wood and Hot Peppers* (Flower Films, 1973) captured Chenier in performance and in his off-stage lifestyle.

Charles Reagan Wilson
University of Mississippi

Barry Jean Ancelet, *The Makers of Cajun Music / Musiciens Cadiens et Créoles* (1984); John Broven, *South to Louisiana: The Music of the Cajun Bayous* (1983); Sheldon Harris, *Blues Who's Who: A Biographical Dictionary of Blues Singers* (1979).

Cline, Patsy

(1932–1963) Country singer.

Patsy Cline, born Virginia Patterson Hensley on 8 September 1932, was one of the first country-and-western entertainers to become successful on both the country and popular music charts. Her first big success was winning the *Arthur Godfrey Talent Scouts* contest in January 1957 with her hit song, "Walkin' After Midnight."

Patsy Cline, country music star, 1957

Over the next six years, Cline became the highest-ranked female singer with the Grand Ole Opry and achieved such popular success that Bill C. Malone has called her "the first woman to dethrone Kitty Wells from her position as 'queen of country music.'"

Virginia Hensley grew up in Winchester, Va., where she displayed a talent for music early in life. She played the piano and cultivated an intense interest in country music, dedicating herself to becoming a serious singer when she was a young teenager. Bill Peer, a disc jockey and musician with ties in Nashville, has been credited with giving Patsy Cline her first professional break as well as her first stage name in 1952. In the spring of 1953 Patsy Hensley married Gerald Cline, a contractor she met during one of her performances. Though they divorced in January 1957 and she married Charlie Dick in September of the same year, Cline kept the name under which she had her first commercial success.

Cline's music was characteristic of the traditional style in country music, and also part of the "Nashville Sound," a calculated attempt by the country music industry to attract new listeners from the pop market while retaining the older ones. Innovations included replacing fiddles and steel guitars with background voices and smooth instrumentation. Among Cline's biggest hits were "I Fall to Pieces" (1960), "Crazy" (1961), and "She's Got You" (1961). She received numerous awards, including *Billboard* magazine's Favorite Female Artist and *Cash Box*'s Most Programmed Album in 1962. She was elected to the Country Music Hall of Fame in 1973.

Cline's career was cut short tragically in March of 1963 with her death in a plane crash. She remains a popular country music figure and her records have continued to be released and sold worldwide. She was a prominent character in Loretta Lynn's autobiography, *Coal Miner's Daughter*, the successful screen version of which premiered in 1980. Patsy Cline's own life was portrayed in *Sweet Dreams* (1985), starring Jessica Lange as the legendary vocalist.

Karen M. McDearman
University of Mississippi

Bill C. Malone, *Country Music, U.S.A.: A Fifty-year History* (1968; rev. ed., 1985); Ellis Nassour, *Patsy Cline* (1981).

Daniels, Charlie

(b. 1936) Country-rock singer.

Charlie Daniels, a native of Wilmington, N.C., became one of the leading exponents of southern rock music in the 1970s. In 1967, after more than a decade as an obscure veteran of the southern club circuit, Daniels began working as a studio-session musician in Nashville. His most notable session work occurred in the period from 1969 to 1971, when he backed rock star Bob Dylan on a series of albums.

In 1971 Daniels formed his own band and a year later

experienced substantial record sales with a satirical single release, "Uneasy Rider." The song and the album on which it appeared helped identify Daniels to rock audiences, though he continued to live and record in Nashville. Daniels was a versatile performer who most often played either guitar or fiddle. His dynamic work on the fiddle reinforced his identification as a country artist. From 1973 to 1977 Daniels gained little recognition as a recording artist, due undoubtedly to his marginal position between rock and country. In 1975 he reemerged as a successful recording artist, with a best-selling album, *Fire on the Mountain*, and a hit single, "The South's Gonna Do It Again." By the mid-1970s country rock had become a potent commercial subgenre within country music, and Daniels had established himself as an exemplar of the sound. In addition, "The South's Gonna Do It Again" became a veritable anthem of the southern rock movement. Daniels was perhaps the preeminent musical spokesman of the region.

In 1979 Daniels released *Million Mile Reflections*, an album that rapidly gained platinum status (over 1 million units sold) and also yielded one of the most popular single recordings of the decade, "The Devil Went Down to Georgia." A quintessential Daniels number, it reflected the southern folk tradition in both content and style but tapped the contemporary rock idiom for most of its rhythmic impetus. Other albums include *Night Rider* (1975), *High Lonesome* (1976), and *Saddle Tramp* (1976).

Daniels often generated controversy both for his outspoken political views—he was one of the few Nashville artists to openly oppose the Vietnam War and campaigned ardently for Jimmy Carter in 1976 and 1980—and for his spirited defense of country music against such critics as jazz musician Stan Kenton. Perhaps Daniels's most impressive contribution to southern music has been the Volunteer Jams, a popular series of concerts held annually in Murfreesboro, Tenn. Few individuals have symbolized the South in popular culture as directly and indelibly as Charlie Daniels.

Stephen R. Tucker
Tulane University

Bob Allen, *Country Music* (April 1980); Russell Shaw, *Country Music* (March 1977).

"Dixie"

The word *Dixie* has been a part of the American vocabulary ever since it appeared in the song "Dixie's Land." The song, though closely associated with the history of the South, is not of southern origin. Both tune and text were written by Ohio native Daniel D. Emmett in 1859, shortly before the outbreak of the Civil War. The song immediately attained popularity, first in the North, then as a "battle hymn" in the secessionist Confederate states. The word *Dixie* even became a synonym for the South.

What was compelling about the tune was its blend of incisiveness and exhilaration, giving force to such sentences as "Den I wish I was in Dixie, Hooray! Hooray! In Dixie Land, I'll took my stand, To lib an die in Dixie." The song was commissioned by the Bryant's Minstrel Troupe, a highly successful company, and was performed for the first time in New York on Broadway on 4 April 1859 under the title "Plantation Song and Dance, / Dixie's Land / Introducing the whole Troupe in the Festival Dance." The scene involved voices (solo and group alternating), with instrumental accompaniment, and steps and gestures in imitation of black plantation dances. It was pure entertainment, amply supported by the comedy style of all six stanzas. The protagonist was a black, who, following a minstrel tradition, expressed his yearning for the never-never-land of the southern plantation, a view with special appeal to a white audience.

After the theatrical event came a swift transformation of "Dixie's Land." With the accents and tempo of a quickstep, it became a fierce military statement. Confederate soldiers used new words such as "Southrons, hear your country call you," but sections of the original were retained.

The origin of the word "Dixie" has not yet been clarified; there is no evidence of its existence as a name on southern plantations. Yet it was known to entertainers, for a playbill of 1850 listed a play (probably blackface) "The United States Mail and Dixie [a post-boy] in Difficulty." Continuing a trend of early black minstrel music, the tune of "Dixie's Land" includes elements of British folksong: an Irish hornpipe pattern at the beginning and traces of Scotch tunes in the second part.

Hans Nathan
Arlington Heights, Massachusetts

Hans Nathan, *Dan Emmett and the Rise of Early Negro Minstrelsy* (1962; 2d ed., 1977); John A. Simpson, *Southern Folklore Quarterly* (1981).

Dixie Hummingbirds

Gospel music group.

The Dixie Hummingbirds, a gospel "quartet," most of whose members were from South Carolina, began their long recording career in the late 1930s with the selection "When the Gates Swing Open" (Decca 7645). Ira Tucker, their famous lead singer, joined the group in 1940, soon followed by Willie Bobo, their well-known bass singer. The Birds, as they came to be known, consisted by 1945 of James Walker, Ira Tucker, William Bobo, Beachey Thompson, and James Davis, the original leader. Guitarist Howard Carroll joined the quartet in the early 1950s. All the various male groups were usually referred to as "quartets," even though most of them consisted of five or six members.

The recording of black quartets singing spirituals and gospel songs began with the Dinwiddie Colored Quar-

The Dixie Hummingbirds, gospel music quartet, c. 1950

tet's 1902 Victor recording of "Down on the Old Camp Ground"; so the quartet genre had a considerable history before the Dixie Hummingbirds appeared.

The performing style, the musical structure, and the vocal literature of the quartets changed in the 1930s, and the Birds arrived toward the end of the transitional period, so that they, together with the Blind Boys of Mississippi, the Soul Stirrers of Tyler, Tex., the Blue Jays of Alabama, the Pilgrim Travelers, and the Spirit of Memphis became the first of the more modern gospel quartets.

If one excludes the Golden Gate Quartet, a very popular transitional group, the Birds were the only gospel quartet to achieve a measure of success with white listeners. They have always been regarded by black audiences as among the foremost of the quartets. Their first interracial success came during 1942 at Café Society Downtown in New York City, where they received a standing ovation. Their second such success came in 1966 at the Newport Folk Festival. Finally, a million or more young white listeners became acquainted with them in 1973 when they were included on Paul Simon's "Loves Me Like a Rock" in his successful album *There Goes Rhymin' Simon*.

Tony Heilbut devotes an entire chapter of his book *The Gospel Sound: Good News and Bad Times* (1971) to the Birds, and his study remains the best (and almost only) source of information on the group. Heilbut mentions "Trouble in My Way," "Let's Go out to the Program," and "In the Morning" as perhaps their best recorded performances. To that trio might be added the "Devil Can't Harm a Praying Man," which is on the album *A Christian Testimonial* (Peacock PLP 100).

Those interested in the music and early history and development of the gospel quartet will find the following discs informative: *An Introduction to Gospel Song* (Folkways RF5), *Brighten the Corner Where You Are* (New World Records NW 224), *Birmingham Quartet Anthology* (Clanka Lanka CL 144,001/002; the American distributor is Douglas Seroff, Box 506, Rt. 3, Goodlettsville, Tenn.), and *Jubilee to Gospel* (John Edwards Memorial Foundation JEMF 108).

William H. Tallmadge
Berea College

Barbara Baker, "Black Gospel Music Styles—1942–75" (Ph.D. dissertation, University of Maryland, 1978).

Domino, Fats

(b. 1928) Rock and rhythm-and-blues musician.

Antoine "Fats" Domino is to his home city, New Orleans, what Elvis Presley and B. B. King are to Memphis, and what Roy Acuff is to Nashville—the personification of musical values closely associated with that city. His popular recordings for Lew Chubb's Imperial label—many of which were produced with Dave Bartholomew and engineered by Cosimo Matassa—represent a distillation of the New Orleans sound; piano virtuosity featuring right-hand triplets and a dominant bass line; heavy second-line rhythms from either Domino's left hand or the shuffle of a drummer; and harsh but powerful horn riffs, often featuring tenor saxophone solos from Herb Hardesty or Lee Allen. Domino's mellow, agreeable vocals find a comfortable home within this instrumental context. Taken together, these elements define the sound of New Orleans during the 1950s.

Born in New Orleans on 26 February 1928, Domino inherited the musical sensibility that shaped his music. His father was an accomplished violinist. His older brother-in-law, Harrison Verrett, had played guitar and banjo with Dixieland jazz ensembles led by Kid Ory and Papa Celestin. Verrett tutored young Domino and later served as his advisor and as a member of his band. In New Orleans Domino was surrounded by master pianists like Henry Byrd ("Professor Longhair"), Cousin Joe, Walter "Fats" Pichon, and Leon T. Gross ("Archibald"). He assimilated these local influences, as well as the influences of non–New Orleans pianists like Meade Lux Lewis, Albert Ammons, and Pete Johnson. To his piano, Domino added a gentle and easy vocal style, complete with exotic Creole accent, that stood in contrast to the rawer, darker voices of the gutbucket country blues singers of the Deep South.

Domino has had more commercial success than any other New Orleans musician, and his biggest hits came from 1950 to 1963, when he recorded on the Imperial record label. Twenty of Domino's records have sold over a million copies (the number keeps growing as his records continue to sell), among them such classics as "The Fat Man" (his first record), "Ain't It a Shame," "I'm in Love Again," "Blueberry Hill," "Blue Monday," "I'm Walkin'," and "Walking to New Orleans." White audiences enthusiastically bought his records, and white artists such as Pat Boone, Ricky Nelson, Elvis Presley, and the Beatles either covered his hits or imitated his sound.

Domino made successful transitions from rhythm and blues to rock and roll and now does occasional Las Vegas lounge acts. He continues to play throughout the world to audiences who appreciate his music for its contemporary appeal rather than for its nostalgic value. In 1986 Domino became 1 of only 10 charter inductees into the Rock and Roll Hall of Fame, an institution established by members of the recording industry to honor achievement in that field. That same year he was also featured in a nationally televised special entitled *Fats Domino and Friends*.

Jay Orr
Country Music Foundation
Nashville, Tennessee

John Broven, *Rhythm and Blues in New Orleans* (1978); Peter Guralnick, in *The Rolling Stone Illustrated History of Rock 'n' Roll*, ed. Jim Miller (1980); Robert Palmer, *A Tale of Two Cities: Memphis Rock and New Orleans Roll* (1979).

Dorsey, Thomas

(b. 1899) Blues and gospel musician and composer.

An important figure in both blues and gospel music, Thomas Andrew Dorsey was born in Villa Rica, Ga., on 1 July 1899. His father was a Baptist minister and moved the family to Atlanta, Ga., in 1904. During the years just prior to World War I Dorsey sang and played piano for private parties and at clubs throughout Atlanta. After briefly attending Morehouse College, he moved north and settled in Chicago, Ill., by 1916.

The period between 1916 and 1932 was marked by a deep professional involvement with popular music, especially the blues. He worked with several Chicago-based vaudeville acts and during the mid-1920s toured with a band that worked the TOBA (known colloquially as Tough on Black Artists) circuit across the South and urban North. He and Tampa Red (Hudson Whittaker) formed an extremely popular duo, with Dorsey playing piano, Tampa Red performing on guitar, and both men singing a mixture of blues and risqué numbers. This partnership remained strong for about four years, during which Dorsey also recorded with the Famous Hokum Boys, the Black Hill Billies, and the Hokum Jug Band.

Although much of his early life was spent as a popular entertainer and blues pianist, singer, and composer, Thomas Dorsey always retained an avid interest in and respect for gospel music. In 1932 he decided to give up popular music entirely and devote his talent to sacred music. He met with some resistance initially, both from those who associated Dorsey with "the devil's music" and by the promoters and musicians who prospered because of his popularity.

Thomas Dorsey, gospel music songwriter and performer, 1975

Thomas Dorsey persisted in his gospel music career, however, and the period between 1932 and 1950 is marked by his influence. He worked extensively with Mahalia Jackson and also helped Roberta Martin and Sallie Martin early in their careers. Dorsey's promotion of these and other singers helped to move black gospel music into the realm of popular music after World War II.

Dorsey is perhaps best known as a gospel song composer. An early publication, "Precious Lord, Take My Hand," is one of the most popular gospel songs ever written. Over his lengthy career, Dorsey has composed approximately 500 songs, including "When the Last Mile Is Finished," "Wings over Jordan," "If You See My Savior," and "There Will Be Peace in the Valley."

Kip Lornell
Ferrum College

Arna Bontemps, *Common Ground* (Autumn 1942); Sheldon Harris, *Blues Who's Who: A Biographical Dictionary of Blues Singers* (1979); *Living Blues* (March 1975); Paul Oliver, in *New Grove Dictionary of Music and Musicians*, vol. 5, ed. Stanley Sadie (1980).

Dulcimer

The plucked dulcimer, often called the Appalachian dulcimer, is a southern mountain folk instrument. Its sound is soft and restrained, with a gentle charm and a slight touch of melancholy. Its diatonic scale and heavy drones make it sound like a gentler version of bagpipes. The most common shapes are the "teardrop" and the "figure-eight," but other shapes are sometimes made. Dulcimers usually have three or four strings (although they may have as many as eight) running over a fretboard. The diatonic scale of the fretboard makes the dulcimer an ideal instrument to accompany songs in the various modes. Mountain people have used them for generations to accompany the tragic English and Scots ballads as well as to play sprightly instrumental pieces.

The dulcimer is a lap instrument, played with the tuning pegs to the left (for right-handed musicians). In the traditional style the melody is played on the string nearest the player while the other strings drone. The earliest dulcimers had frets under the first string only. The left hand stops the strings, often with the aid of a "noter" (a small cylinder of very hard wood), while the right hand strums the strings with a quill or plectrum or plucks the strings as though playing a banjo or guitar.

Although the dulcimer first appeared in its American form in the Appalachian South, it is structurally related to the German *scheitholt*, the Swedish *hummel*, and the Norwegian *langeleik*. It may have been introduced to the Appalachians by Pennsylvania Germans.

The folk music revival of the 1960s brought the dulcimer to the attention of the urban audience, especially through the playing of two artists from the southern highlands, Jean Ritchie of Kentucky and Frank Proffitt of North Carolina. A new demand for the instrument created markets for traditional mountain craftspeople and sparked interest in the craft of dulcimer making by disaffected young urbanites. A number of southern craftspeople, such as A. W. Jeffreys of Virginia, Homer Ledford of Kentucky, Jean Schilling of Tennessee, Lynn McSpadden of Arkansas, and Stanley Hicks, Edsel Martin, and Edd Presnell of North Carolina, earned national reputations for their artistry as dulcimer makers.

Charles Joyner
University of South Carolina,
Coastal Campus

R. Gerald Alvey, *Dulcimer Maker: The Craft of Homer Ledford* (1984); Charles Faulkner Bryan, *Tennessee Folklore Society Bulletin* (March 1952, December 1954); Gene DuBey, *Sourwood Mountain Dulcimers* (Appalshop film, 1976); Charles Joyner, *Southern Folklore Quarterly* (December 1975); Jean Ritchie, *The Dulcimer Book* (1963); Charles Seeger, *Journal of American Folklore* (January–March 1958); L. Allen Smith, *A Catalogue of Pre-Revival Appalachian Dulcimers* (1983).

Engel, Lehman

(1910–1982) Composer and conductor.

Time magazine called Lehman Engel "one of the nation's busiest and most versatile men-about-music." He was a composer, conductor, author, and teacher. *A Streetcar Named Desire*, *The Consul*, *Murder in the Cathedral*, and *Li'l Abner* are a few of the many, diverse Broadway shows with which he was associated as a composer or pit conductor. His efforts brought widespread recognition, including two Antoinette Perry ("Tony") awards: one in 1950 for conducting the Menotti opera *The Consul* and one in 1953 for conducting Gilbert and Sullivan operettas and *Wonderful Town*.

Born to Jewish parents in Jackson, Miss., Engel played the piano "by ear" until age 10, when his parents were able to afford piano lessons for him. He wrote that his first piano teacher was an "aristocratic southern lady" whose lessons, like those of his subsequent teachers, he quickly outgrew. He completed his first composition, *The Scotch Highlander*, shortly after he began taking piano lessons, and musical composition for the theater became one of his primary interests. A Jackson movie house, the Majestic Theater, with its small orchestra accompanying the silent movies, impressed the young boy greatly and provided some of his most memorable early experiences.

Although not an extremely talented pianist, Engel entered the Cincinnati Conservatory of Music upon graduation from high school. When he discovered that he had been eligible for a partial scholarship for piano lessons but was the only student not on scholarship, he became angry that his parents had spent so much money unnecessarily and transferred immediately to the Cincinnati College of Music. Two years later he turned down a faculty position at Cincinnati and moved to New York. With a graduate scholarship to the Julliard School, Engel took courses in composition from Rubin Goldmark and studied privately with Roger Sessions.

In New York, Engel worked diligently to make contacts and establish his career. He persisted for several months in an attempt to meet Martha Graham, who encouraged him to write compositions for her dance company and for other concert dancers as well. *Within the Gates* provided his first Broadway credit. When he heard the music already written for the play, he expressed his dislike to director Melvyn Douglas, offering to write a new version by the next morning. Even though the play itself was unsuccessful, Engel's music was praised.

A group of madrigal singers was organized by the Federal Music Project, a subsidiary of the Works Progress Administration (WPA), and Engel was the group's conductor from 1935 to 1939. He composed music for the

Federal Theater Project and the WPA Children's Theater before he began working with Orson Welles and John Houseman at their Mercury Theater. During World War II he joined the U.S. Navy, conducted a military orchestra at the Great Lakes Naval Training Station, and later served as chief composer of the navy's film division in Washington, D.C. His other pursuits included founding (with Aaron Copland, Marc Blitzstein, and Virgil Thompson) the Arrow Music Press, Inc., to publish the work of American composers; conducting more than 60 recordings for major record companies such as Columbia, Decca, and RCA Victor; composing four operas and music for radio, film, and television; writing books about musical theater; and teaching workshops in musical lyrics.

Nicknamed by some the "Poor Man's Lenny Bernstein," Engel became one of the most respected and sought-after musicians on Broadway. He never returned to the South to live but did return to Jackson to conduct the premiere performances of two of his operas. Engel died of cancer in 1982, but his life's accomplishments and honors had been many. With regard to the demands of writing music for the theater, Engel had often spoken of Mozart: "That genius had to write on order. He had no time for the muse to belt him." It seems that the same had been true for Engel himself.

Jessica Foy
Cooperstown Graduate Programs
Cooperstown, New York

Josh Barbanel, *New York Times* (30 August 1982); Lehman Engel, *This Bright Day: An Autobiography* (1974); Walter Rigdon, ed., *The Biographical Encyclopedia and Who's Who of the American Theatre* (1966); Nicolas Slonimsky, *Baker's Biographical Dictionary of Musicians*, (7th ed., 1984); *Time* (8 December 1958).

Fiddler, Tutwiler, Miss., 1967

Fiddle and Fiddlers' Conventions

The fiddle is a four-string, bowed instrument—most often a violin, though resourceful musicians have fashioned facsimiles from cigar boxes and tin cans—upon which are played a variety of folk melodies, primarily for dancing. Some people argue that the fiddle has one string more than the violin—the one used to hang it on the wall. Because of its portability, its common use as dance accompaniment, and its folk heritage extending back to the 18th century in the British Isles and western Europe, the fiddle quickly assumed a role as the primary folk musical instrument of settlers in the New World. In the 19th and early 20th centuries southern fiddlers exhibited subregional variation according to such characteristics as bowing patterns, bowing method, fiddle placement, tunings, repertoire, tune titles, tune texts, tune structure, and instrumental accompaniment. The predominant tune forms in southern fiddling are variously referred to as reels, breakdowns, or hoedowns and are played in double meter to accompany dancing. Southern fiddlers also perform rags, waltzes, blues, and hornpipes, though these forms are less common.

In the second half of the 20th century improved travel conditions, the radio, the phonograph, and the proliferation of fiddle contests whose judges adhere to rigid aesthetic standards have blunted the more pronounced regional distinctions that once characterized southern fiddling. However, the broad stylistic designations of Appalachian or Blue Ridge (further subdivided into Galax, North Georgia, and others), Deep South (including the unique Mississippi fiddle bands, which show an apparent black influence), Ozark, Cajun, and Southwestern (sometimes referred to as "contest" style fiddling for its emphasis on ornate improvisation and precise execution) still have relevance.

Fiddlers' conventions, at which the central event is usually a competition or "contest," have become a primary performance outlet for contemporary fiddlers. As early as 1736, in Hanover County, Va., southern fiddlers competed against one another for prizes and prestige. The most famous contests were held in Atlanta; Union Grove, N.C.; and Knoxville. In the early part of this century Henry Ford sponsored a series of competitions to determine a national champion through his automobile dealerships. Ford felt that fiddlers and fiddle music embodied the moral, conservative values he wanted his contests to inspire in those who attended them. Today, every fiddler in the South lives within easy distance of several of the numerous conventions sponsored by communities, civic groups, state agencies, local businesses, and regional and local fiddlers' associations.

Jay Orr
Country Music Foundation
Nashville, Tennessee

Linda C. Burman-Hall, "Southern American Folk Fiddling: Context and Style" (Ph.D. dissertation, Princeton University, 1973); Alan Jabbour, *American Fiddle Tunes from the Archive of Folk Song* [record and accompanying booklet] (1971); Earl V. Spielman, "Traditional North American Fiddling" (Ph.D. dissertation, University of Wisconsin at Madison, 1975).

Fisk Jubilee Singers

The Fisk Jubilee Singers originally consisted of a black American group of eight singers and a pianist, all students at Fisk University in Nashville, Tenn. This double quartet, together with musical director George L. White; their chaperon, Miss Well; the pianist; and two other students to help with the packing and moving, set off on a tour in 1871 to raise money for their university. By 1880, when the university ended official sponsorship of the group, it had toured the northern United States, England, and Europe and had sung at the White House and for Queen Victoria. From the singing of this organization the world at large first became aware of a body of black music called "spirituals" (they were called "slave songs" in those days).

The term *jubilee* has a number of different meanings. It has been used to designate those black spirituals whose texts refer to freedom—freedom in death from the hardships of life followed by the attainment of heavenly bliss and freedom from slavery. The term has also been used to specify those spirituals having a joyous character, and it has been used to refer to the entire body of black spirituals. It has also been used in reference to special celebrations or annual events such as the Pinkster Jubilee, a celebration of Pentecost Sunday in certain areas of New York, Pennsylvania, and Maryland during the colonial period. At Columbus, Ohio, after the singers had been on the road for several weeks, White thought that the name "Jubilee Singers" would be a good one for the group. He recalled the Old Testament "year of jubilee," a year provided by ancient Hebrew law when slaves were emancipated, and thinking of the students at the university, most of whom had been former slaves, he felt that their year of jubilee had come—"this little band of singers was a witness to it, an outgrowth of it."

Two years after the success of the Fisk choir, the Hampton Institute also sent a choir on tour; they were followed by groups from Tuskegee and Utica institutes, but it was the name of the Fisk Jubilee Singers that remained in the public's memory.

See also EDUCATION: / Fisk University

William H. Tallmadge
Berea College

Alain Locke, *The Negro and His Music* (1936); J. B. T. Marsh, *The Story of the Jubilee Singers; with Their Songs* (1877); G. D. Pike, *The Jubilee Singers, and Their Campaign for Twenty Thousand Dollars* (1873); Thomas Rutling, *Tom: An Autobiography* (1907); William H. Tallmadge, brochure notes to *Jubilee to Gospel: A Selection of Commercially Recorded Black Religious Music, 1921–1953*, John Edwards Memorial Foundation, JEMF 108.

Foster, Stephen

(1826–1864) Composer and songwriter.

Born in Lawrenceville, Penn., and raised in comfortable circumstances in a suburb of Pittsburgh, Stephen Collins Foster began composing for the blackface minstrel theater, where "Oh! Susanna," "Nelly Bly," and "Camptown Races" were popularized by the troupe of E. P. Christy. His ambition, however, was to be a composer of sentimental parlor songs on themes of romantic love and nostalgic yearning. Among his songs of this type are "Old Dog Tray," "Jeanie with the Light Brown Hair," and "Beautiful Dreamer." Although some of his songs achieved commercial success, Foster failed to capitalize on his successes and died in poverty.

In his minstrel songs Foster made no attempt to present realistically the song and speech of southern plantation slaves. In "Oh! Susanna," for example, the dialect, the deadpan irony, the references to southern places and foods, are merely conventions of the minstrel stage. The melody is no more Afro-American than it is English or Irish; the rhythm is that of the European polka. From about 1850 Foster began to modify the conventions of minstrelsy in the direction of middle-class sentimentality. Songs like "Old Folks at Home" and "Old Black Joe" attribute more delicate and varied sentiments to the stage black than had previously been the stereotype. In a few songs, like "My Old Kentucky Home," he omitted the dialect. Many of these less typical minstrel songs were popularized in dramatizations of *Uncle Tom's Cabin*. Indeed, Foster's notebooks reveal that "My Old Kentucky Home" was originally written as "Poor Uncle Tom, Good Night." Ironically, Foster's songs are, with the exception of Dan Emmett's "Dixie's Land," the best-known representatives of minstrelsy today.

Since the late 19th century Foster's songs have been widely accepted as genuine American folksongs. Although Foster never lived in the South, popular myth has associated him with the region. Florida and Kentucky have adopted "Old Folks at Home" and "My Old Kentucky Home," respectively, as official state songs. Bardstown, Ky., and White Springs, Fla., boast shrines to Foster's memory and music; the latter, on the Suwanee River, serves as home of the state's folklife program. Though black critic Alain Locke has observed that "Foster's ballads did more to crystallize the romance of the plantation tradition than all the Southern colonels and novelists put together," adaptations of Foster songs by Ray Charles and Taj Mahal have been sincere portrayals of Afro-American culture and experience. Sung in widely varying arrangements, often with bowdlerized texts, Stephen Foster's songs continue to form part of the musical experience of nearly every American.

David Warren Steel
University of Mississippi

William W. Austin, *"Susanna," "Jeanie," and "The Old Folks at Home"* (1975); John T. Howard, *Stephen Foster: America's Troubador* (1953; rev. ed., 1962); Richard Jackson, ed., *The Stephen Foster Song Book* (1974).

Fountain, Pete

(b. 1930) Jazz musician.

Peter Dewey Fountain was born 3 July 1930 in New Orleans, La. His father was a drummer and violinist who played in local jazz bands in Biloxi, Miss., when Pete was young. Fountain's own musical interest began early, and he played the clarinet in the school band. While still very young, Fountain played with the Junior Dixieland Band, Phil Zito's International Dixieland Express, and the Basin Street Six.

Already an accomplished musician at 16, Fountain replaced Irving Fazola at the Opera House Burlesque Theater. At 19, Fountain joined the Dukes of Dixieland band in Chicago in 1949 and played with them until 1954. Fountain was a member of Lawrence Welk's orchestra from 1957 through 1960. In 1960 he opened his own club, The French Quarter, on Bourbon Street in New Orleans. He played at the club frequently, in addition to appearing on such television programs as the *Ed Sullivan Show*, *Kraft Music Hall*, and specials with Bob Hope and Bing Crosby. He has been an occasional guest on Johnny Carson's program, *The Tonight Show*, where he plays with Doc Severinsen's orchestra. Through television, he has become a prime symbol for Americans of contemporary New Orleans jazz.

In the early 1980s Fountain relocated his club, now called Pete's Place, to the New Orleans Riverside Hilton. He makes frequent appearances at the annual New Orleans Jazz and Heritage Festival. He has recorded nearly 50 records on the Coral label, including *South Rampart Street Parade*, *New Orleans at Midnight*, *Plenty of Pete*, and *Both Sides Now*.

Karen M. McDearman
University of Mississippi

Pete Fountain with Bill Neely, *A Closer Walk: The Pete Fountain Story* (1972); Howard Mandel, *Down Beat* (January 1985); Nicolas Slonimsky, *Baker's Biographical Dictionary of Musicians* (7th ed., 1984).

Gillespie, Dizzy

(b. 1917) Jazz musician.

John Birks "Dizzy" Gillespie was born 21 October 1917 in Cheraw, S.C. Gillespie showed his musical talent at an early age, and he began to play the trumpet when he was 15. He attended Laurinburg Institute in North Carolina, and when he was 18 Gillespie went to Philadelphia, where he joined a local jazz band. He played with the Cab Calloway and Earl Hines bands, and in 1944, when Hines's lead singer, Billy Eckstine, formed his own band, Gillespie joined the group.

Gillespie, along with his friend Charlie "Bird" Parker, who also played with the Eckstine band, was an innovator of the jazz style known as bebop (or bop) beginning in the late 1940s. Bebop introduced revolutionary changes in the traditional rhythmic and harmonic jazz patterns. Gillespie and Parker made a few recordings after leaving Eckstine's band, but had difficulty finding club owners willing to let them play the new style. Club patrons preferred the blues and older style tunes that were danceable. Gillespie still plays in a style directly related to bebop, which eventually came to be heralded as a remarkable original development of jazz.

Gillespie was given the nickname "Dizzy" because of his playing style, which incorporates wild gesturing and grimacing. He is a trumpet virtuoso and has been credited for extending the upper ranges of the instrument and improvising long passages at speed. A brilliant showman, Gillespie has entertained thousands with his stage antics and superior instrumentals. His creativity is demonstrated in albums such as *In the Beginning* and *Oscar Peterson and Dizzy Gillespie*.

Karen M. McDearman
University of Mississippi

Ole Brask, *Jazz People* (1976); Ira Gitler, *Jazz Masters of the Forties* (1974); Marshall Stearns, *The Story of Jazz* (1956).

Gottschalk, Louis

(1829–1869) Classical music composer.

The most renowned American composer of the early 19th century, Gottschalk blended the European romantic tradition with black rhythms and Creole melodies he had experienced as a child in New Orleans. Gottschalk's works possess an individual charm and a spontaneity and verve that draw listeners inside the music. The son of a wealthy English Jew and a titled French Creole, the musician grew up in cultured surroundings and was recognized by age four as a prodigy. Seven years later, his teacher declared the boy must be sent to Paris to study further. In 1842 Gottschalk sailed for France, and a great aunt introduced him to Parisian society.

Having heard French and Italian opera in New Orleans, the youth preferred operatic transcriptions for piano over the German classics. In France he studied both piano and composition. During the revolutionary turmoil of 1848 he was forced to flee Paris, and during that absence he wrote the two piano pieces for which he is best remembered, *La Bamboula* and *La Savanne*. Both were drawn from folk music he had known as a child, and Parisian listeners were enchanted by their rhythmic virtuosity and exotic themes.

In 1849 the composer made his debut as a professional pianist in Salle Pleyel. While in France he performed for Hugo, Chopin, Bizet, and Berlioz, all of whom praised his work. He continued writing and enjoyed special success with *Le Bananier* and *Le Banjo*. He toured Switzerland and Spain, then in 1853 decided to return to the United States. His first New York concert, given in Niblo's Garden, was a triumph he repeated all over the United States. His flamboyant style met sharp criticism, although audiences were attracted by his personality and European reputation.

As Gottschalk became more the entertainer, his compositions grew increasingly sentimental; *The Dying Poet* and *The Last Hope* stand among the more saccharine. He spent six years giving concerts in the West Indies and writing orchestral works like his *Grand Tarantelle* and *A Night in the Tropics*. He returned to the United States, making the most of the fiction that surrounded his life, performing concerts in the thick of the Civil War, and touring the gold fields of California and Nevada. He also staged "monster concerts" in Latin America, but he grew despondent. In Rio de Janeiro he collapsed during a concert and died shortly afterwards. His body was eventually removed to Greenwood Cemetery, Brooklyn.

Ronald L. Davis
Southern Methodist University

Ronald L. Davis, *A History of Music in American Life: The Formative Years* (1982); John G. Doyle, *Louis Moreau Gottschalk, 1829–1869: A Bibliographical Study and Catalog of His Works* (1983); Louis Moreau Gottschalk, *Notes of a Pianist* (1964); Vernon Loggins, *Where the Word Ends: The Life of Louis Moreau Gottschalk* (1958).

Grand Ole Opry

The Grand Ole Opry is America's longest-running radio program. It began in 1925, soon after Nashville station WSM first began broadcasts as the voice of the National Life and Accident Insurance Company. This Nashville-based firm was then expanding rapidly, moving beyond its initial base of sickness and accident policies into the more profitable life insurance field. Along with classical ensembles and pop dance bands, country musicians like Dr. Humphrey Bate's Augmented Orchestra supplied early WSM programming and helped attract prospective policyholders.

The father of the Opry was WSM program director George D. Hay, who came to the station in November 1925, a few weeks after Bate's group arrived. Earlier, Hay had helped announce Chicago's WLS Barn Dance, a program that inspired country radio jamborees nationwide. By the year's end he had organized WSM talent into a regular Saturday-night show known simply as "the barn dance." Early performers included Hawaiian groups, minstrel acts, and military bands, but old-time string bands like Bate's soon prevailed.

Using strategies typical of the genre, Hay shaped the Opry into a folksy but highly commercial production that appealed to a broad-based audience of rural and small-town listeners scattered throughout the nation. He gave string bands names such as "Possum Hunters" or "Fruit Jar Drinkers" and urged them to wear countrified costumes. As master of ceremonies, Hay himself became the Solemn Old Judge, a stage persona with deep roots in American vaudeville and minstrelsy. In short, he made the Opry a variety show with a rural southern accent.

About 1927 Hay named the program the Grand Ole Opry in an impromptu parody of the National Broadcasting Company's *Music Appreciation Hour*, a classical program carried by WSM each Saturday just before the barn-dance show. "For the past hour," he announced, "we have been listening to music taken largely from the Grand Opera, but from now on we will present the Grand Ole Opry." Hay then introduced harmonica player DeFord Bailey, a black man whose musical portrait of a speeding locomotive symbolized the Opry's homespun realism, reminiscent of an authentic rural barn dance or husking bee.

Fan letters, commercial sponsors, and rising insurance income convinced National Life to continue the Opry despite opposition from proper Nashvillians, who saw it as a threat to the city's genteel reputation. As WSM's power climbed from 1,000 watts in 1925 to 50,000 in 1932, the program's radio audience expanded dramatically, and the Opry's position became secure. WSM's clear-channel signal, broadcast through a new, superbly engineered tower built in 1932, blanketed most of the nation, and the show steadily gained supporters in almost every state. By 1936 the Opry generated as much as 80 percent of the station's weekly mail. Southerners were the mainstay of the Opry audience, and WSM naturally played up southern themes in Opry costumes, band names, radio dialogue, and publicity. But the program's national audience increased pressures toward variety: within a decade, cowboys, western swing bands, and honky-tonk singers surpassed old-time string bands as the dominant acts in the Opry roster.

The Opry's listenership widened further after 1939, when the R. J. Reynolds Tobacco Company, makers of Prince Albert smoking tobacco, began sponsoring a half hour of the show on a 26-station NBC network. By 1952 this web had expanded to a coast-to-coast chain of 176

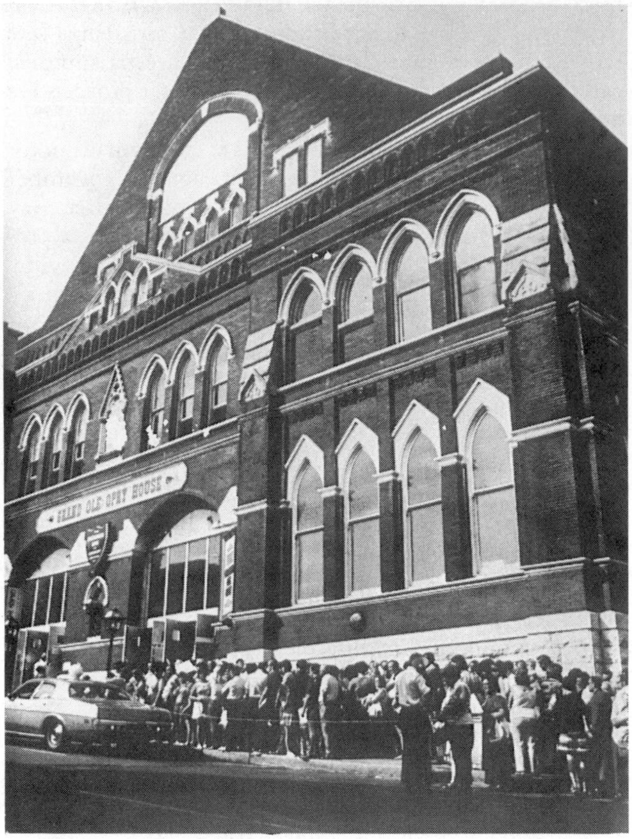

Ryman Auditorium, Nashville, early home of the Grand Ole Opry

stations boasting a weekly audience of 10 million. Although WSM originated many other country or pop programs for network broadcast, the *Prince Albert Show* was by far the most visible and the longest running, lasting until 1961. Network airtime was especially important in sustaining the Opry through the late 1950s, a period in which most other radio barn dances withered in the face of competition from network television and the conversion of country radio stations to rock programming.

Along with the program's network connections, aggressive promotion, stylistic diversification, and the cultivation of a star system, television also helped the Opry thrive. Since the mid-1950s Opry performers have appeared on numerous network TV specials, as well as on syndicated programs produced by WSM or by independent firms. In 1978 the Public Broadcasting System aired portions of the Opry itself for the first time, and in 1985 the Nashville Network began carrying a live, half-hour segment to cable-television viewers across the nation.

Early in the Opry's evolution, a live audience became vital to the broadcast, and a popular stage show developed around the radio program. To gain ever greater seating space, the show moved from WSM's studios (located in the National Life Building in downtown Nashville) to a succession of local halls before settling in the Ryman Auditorium in 1943. The Ryman, which was originally called the Gospel Tabernacle, was built in 1892 with funds raised by riverboat captain Thomas G. Ryman. After a 31-year run there, the Opry shifted to the magnificent new Opry House at Nashville's Opryland theme park, opened in the early 1970s by NLT Corporation, successor to National Life. The Opryland USA complex now embraces a large hotel and serves as headquarters for the Nashville Network; the Music Country Network, a radio web linked by satellite; and the *General Jackson*, a Cumberland River showboat. Since 1983 these enterprises (including WSM radio but not WSMV-TV, now owned by Gillett Broadcasting) have been operated by the Oklahoma Publishing Company, of Oklahoma City. Even in these elegant surroundings, however, the Opry has remained refreshingly informal, belying the planning each show requires. Announcers reading commercials, artists waiting to be introduced, and stagehands moving props all create a complex and entertaining spectacle.

In addition to drawing millions of tourists, the Opry has nurtured Nashville's music industry. About 1934 WSM organized its Artists Service, which booked Opry stars into schoolhouses and theaters, at first mostly in the Southeast. Before long, independent promoters were working with Opry officials to broaden the range of Opry tours throughout the United States and abroad. After World War II, as the Opry began to recruit country music's leading stars, national recording companies began to center their country recording operations in Nashville. Independent recording studios built by WSM engineers or musicians helped produce hits that further established Nashville's reputation as Music City, U.S.A., a name coined by WSM announcer David Cobb about 1950. Capitalizing on the Opry's popularity, Nashville-based music publishers furnished song material for stage shows and recording sessions and helped promote Opry artists' careers.

For more than 60 years the Grand Ole Opry has survived not only changes in media and corporate ownership but also transformations in sounds, styles, and repertoires, reflecting the adaptation of a rural-based music to an increasingly urban society. Today, the Opry is a showcase for almost every type of country music, including honky-tonk, bluegrass, old-time, cowboy, Cajun, and country-pop, all of which continue to enjoy widespread popular favor. As art and as enterprise, the Opry remains country music's most enduring institution and one of the most significant in the history of American popular entertainment.

John W. Rumble
Country Music Foundation

Jack Hurst, *Grand Ole Opry* (1975); John W. Rumble, notes to *Radio Barn Dances*, Franklin Mint Record Society, CW 095/096; Charles K. Wolfe, *The Grand Ole Opry: The Early Years, 1925–35* (1975).

Handy, W. C.

(1873–1958) Blues composer and performer.

In 1909 W. C. Handy's band was engaged by E. H. Crump's forces to deliver the black vote to their man. In his campaign for mayor of Memphis, Crump promised to clean up the city, particularly Beale Street. Though hired by Crump to promote his campaign, Handy wrote a piece called *The Memphis Blues*, which mocked this idea:

> Mister Crump won't 'low no easy riders here.
> Mister Crump won't 'low no easy riders here.
> I don't care what Mister Crump don't 'low.
> I'm gwine bar'l-house anyhow—
> Mister Crump can go an' catch hisself some air!

This was the first time the blues came out of the backwoods and the cotton fields, off the levees, work camps, and lonesome roads to land on main street. Called "Mister Crump" at the time, the piece was an immediate hit, launched W. C. Handy as a local celebrity, and helped elect Crump mayor of Memphis.

Born William Christopher Handy in Florence, Ala., eight years after the Civil War, Handy said he received no musical talent from his parents, nor did he have any encouragement from them when he showed promise in music. In fact, his father, a Methodist minister, hinted that he would rather see him dead than pursue a career in music. But his teacher knew music and taught his pupils to sing. By the age of 10, young Handy could "catalogue almost any sound that came to [his] ears, using the *sol-fa* system."

Handy's inspiration for the blues grew out of his personal experiences and the life around him. But his conscious decision to make the blues his forte was formed in Clarksdale, Miss. One night while playing a dance, he was asked to play some of his native music. He tried to comply. The request then came for a local group to be permitted to play. Three rather ragged young black men began to play, as he recalled in his autobiography, "one of those over-and-over strains that seemed to have no very clear beginning and . . . no ending at all. The strumming attained a disturbing monotony, but on-and-on it went, a kind of stuff that has long been associated with cane rows and levee camps."

Before long, "A rain of silver dollars began to fall around the outlandish, stomping feet. The dancers went wild." After it was over Handy strained his neck and saw "there before the boys lay more money than my nine musicians were being paid for the entire engagement. Then I saw the beauty of primitive music." Seeing that folks would pay money for this unpolished music, Handy concluded "there was no virtue in being blind when you had good eyes."

Handy was cheated out of his profits on the "Memphis Blues" when he published it in 1912. However, he lived long enough to have the copyright revert to him 28 years later. In 1914 Handy wrote the "St. Louis Blues," which became a national anthem and established Handy in the forefront of American composers. He proudly wore the title "Father of the Blues." In 1931 Memphis honored W. C. Handy by naming a park for him, and in 1949 he was named among the 10 outstanding older men in the world.

Handy died of natural causes in 1958. Today the Handy Awards are presented in his honor each year at the Orpheum Theater on Beale Street in Memphis by the Blues Foundation to recognize the nation's outstanding blues musicians.

See also POLITICS: / Crump, E. H.

Leander C. Jones
Western Michigan University

W. C. Handy, ed., *A Treasury of the Blues* (1926), *Father of the Blues: An Autobiography*, ed. Arna Bontemps (1941).

Hays, Will

(1837–1907) Songwriter.

Will Hays was one of America's most popular songwriters in the 19th century. Many of his songs still endure today.

William Shakespeare Hays was born in Louisville, Ky., in 1837. Although most of the details of his early life remain undocumented, he is known to have been the captain of the *Grey Eagle*, a Mississippi River steamboat, and was an authority on the lore and life of this nation's great interior river system. He was the river editor of the Louisville *Democrat* at the age of 19 and was later a columnist for many years on the Louisville *Courier-Journal* and the Cincinnati *Enquirer*. He served briefly during the Civil War as a war correspondent in the South. He was also a poet of popular, sentimental verse, and the writer of over 500 songs.

His first successful song was "The Drummer Boy of Shiloh" (1862), which was popular in both the North and South. Before his death in 1907, Hays achieved a popularity as a songwriter that was unsurpassed. Like most popular songwriters of the mid-19th century, Hays was much influenced by the repertoire and style of blackface minstrelsy, and he wrote both lighthearted and pathetic lyrics, some of which were couched in black dialect. His chief forte lay in the composition of nostalgic laments or tender love songs that breathed Victorian morality and imagery. Some of his popular compositions include "We Parted by the River Side" (1866), "I'll Remember You, Love, in My Prayers" (1869), "Mollie Darling" (1871), "Nobody's Darling on Earth" (1870), and "The Little Old Cabin in the Lane" (1871). He also wrote a poem, "The Faithful Engineer," on which the popular gospel song "Life's Railway to Heaven" was based.

Although music critics and historians have paid little attention to Hays and have never ranked him in the same class with Stephen Foster, in some ways his songs have been more popular than those of the great Pennsylvania composer. Hays never profited from high-art patronage as Foster did (Foster's songs, for example, were warmly endorsed by the Czech composer Anton Dvořák), and his compositions were never anthologized in the songbooks distributed among America's schoolchildren. Nevertheless, Hays's songs endured among the folk and have been collected often "in the field" by folklorists. His "Little Old Cabin in the Lane" inspired the creation of other well-known songs such as "Little Old Sod Shanty," "Little Joe the Wrangler," and "Little Red Caboose behind the Train." Hays's songs also received renewed life, and demonstrated their down-home appeal, in the commercial country music field where they were often performed. "Little Old Cabin" (recorded as "Little Old Log Cabin in the Lane") was one side of Fiddlin' John Carson's historic recording of 1923, the disc that marked the beginning of the country music industry. As late as 1948 the commercial power of Hays's songs was demonstrated when superstar Eddy Arnold recorded a best-selling version of "Mollie Darling" (spelled "Molly" on the label). As is true of much older musical material, Hays's songs have found much acceptance today among bluegrass musicians.

Bill C. Malone
Tulane University

Bill C. Malone, *Southern Music—American Music* (1979).

Hooker, John Lee

(b. 1917) Blues singer.

"The King of the Boogie" began life near the city that spawned so many seminal blues musicians, Clarksdale, Miss. Born 1 of 11 children in a sharecropping family, he followed a familiar pattern of early exposure to both sacred and secular music, experimentation with homemade instruments, and migration first to Memphis and then further north. Arriving in Detroit during 1943, he recorded his first impressions in a song that would become among his most famous, "Boogie Chillen'." "I was walking down Hastings Street / I saw a little place called Henry's Swing Club / Decided I'd stop in there that night / And I got down. . . ." Other well-known Hooker compositions include "Boom Boom" and "House Rent Boogie."

An extremely individual stylist, Hooker speaks with a slight speech impediment that brings a jarring intensity to his vocal phrasing when he sings. He combines this with a guitar technique that is paradoxically repetitious and yet utterly unpredictable. His radically syncopated playing, not constrained by the tyranny of bar lines, complements his own sense of meter. "Word by word, lyric by lyric music—that's from the book: that ain't the way I feel. If I feel some way, I'm gonna let it come out. . . . It might rhyme and it might not. I don't care."

At the height of its popularity among post–World War II black audiences Hooker's work contained another paradox, that of a southern phenomenon flourishing unabated and unmodified in the North. Where other rural

John Lee Hooker, bluesman, 1985

southern musicians yielded to the standardizing, homogenizing forces of the commercial music business, Hooker continued to improvise material freely and pursue a rhythmic and metrical style so unique as to make him difficult to accompany or imitate. Hooker steadfastly maintained the idiosyncrasies of a unique regional and individual stylist, and his success is a testament to the deeply affecting power of this most personal approach.

William A. Cochrane
University of Mississippi

Sheldon Harris, *Blues Who's Who: A Biographical Dictionary of Blues Singers* (1979); Robert Neff and Anthony Connor, *Blues* (1975); Paul Oliver, *Blues Off the Record* (1984); Jim O'Neil and Amy O'Neil, *Living Blues* (Autumn 1979).

Hopkins, Lightnin'

(1912–1982) Blues singer.

Born 15 March 1912 in Centerville, Leon County, Tex., Sam "Lightnin'" Hopkins learned to play a homemade cigar-box instrument when he was eight, picked up a little about playing the guitar later from his brother Joel, sang in the church choir as a youth, and absorbed musical materials from fellow farm workers and in nearby bars. He was a hobo and traveled through Texas in the 1920s doing farm work and playing for small pay in clubs and bars and at dances and parties. He moved to Houston in the 1930s but was unable to find steady work as a musician and soon moved back near Centerville.

In the mid-1940s Hopkins was living in rural east Texas, surviving as a farm laborer and playing music in his free time. He went back to Houston and became a fixture in the blues scene on Dowling Street. A California talent scout arranged a recording session for Hopkins and Wilson Smith, his piano accompanist, in Los Angeles, and in 1946 Hopkins made his first recordings for Aladdin Records. In promoting the release, an Aladdin executive came up with the names of Lightin' Hopkins and Thunder Smith. Hopkins returned to Houston after spending some time in California. He recorded across the nation during the late 1940s and early 1950s, but he performed mostly at clubs around Houston.

Folklorist Mack McCormick met Hopkins in 1959 and promoted him on the folk music circuit of the early 1960s. In 1960 alone, Hopkins played a hootenanny at the Alley Theater in Houston, performed at the California Blues Festival in Berkeley, and debuted at Carnegie Hall on a bill with Bob Dylan and Joan Baez. Television shows were soon being made about him, and many of them appeared on the Public Broadcasting System. Throughout the 1960s and 1970s Hopkins continued recording, and record companies released many of his earlier titles. He recorded in this period on, among others, the Bluesville, Arhoolie, Prestige, and Verve labels, and he appeared throughout the 1960s and the 1970s at major folk festivals, on college campuses, and in clubs. The 1972 film *Sounder* used songs by Hopkins, and Les Blank's documentary film, *The Blues Accordin' to Lightnin' Hopkins*, appeared in 1968. Hopkins died in February 1982 in Houston.

Charles Reagan Wilson
University of Mississippi

Samuel Charters, *The Country Blues* (1959); Sheldon Harris, *Blues Who's Who: A Biographical Dictionary of Blues Singers* (1979); Irwin Stambler and Grellin Landon, *The Encyclopedia of Folk, Country and Western Music* (2d ed., 1983).

Hurt, Mississippi John

(1893–1966) Blues singer.

Born in Teoc, Miss., Hurt was a self-taught guitarist who performed for many years in Avalon, Miss. He made his first recording in 1928. His most noted recorded selections, including "Candy Man," "Avalon Blues," "Spike Driver Blues," and "Stagger Lee Blues," were produced by the Okeh Recording Company. He appeared in public performance very little between 1929 and the early 1960s, but he gained popularity in 1963 through his appearance at the Newport Folk Festival. In 1963 he recorded the album presenting *Mississippi John Hurt: Folk Songs and Blues* for Piedmont Records. This album served as an incentive for the recording of "Worried Blues" in 1964. He toured extensively throughout the United States until his death 2 November 1966 in Grenada, Miss. Two of his most noted concert appearances were at Carnegie Hall and Town Hall. He became one of the most beloved of Mississippi Delta bluesmen, with an almost lyrical musical style.

Lemuel Berry, Jr.
Alabama State University

Samuel Charters, *The Bluesmen: The Story and the Music of the Men Who Made the Blues* (1967); Richard K. Spottswood, *Blues Unlimited* (August 1963).

Jackson, Mahalia

(1911–1972) Gospel singer.

Born in New Orleans 26 October 1911, Mahalia Jackson grew up in the Baptist church, but she was heavily influenced by the music of Holiness congregations and such blues singers as Bessie Smith and Ma Rainey. She moved to Chicago in 1927, joined the choir of Greater Salem Baptist Church, and then in 1928 became a member of the Johnson Gospel Singers, composed of three Johnson brothers—Robert, Prince, and Wilbur—and Louise Lemon, who together were one of the first professional gospel singing groups. The group toured the midwestern states, and their concerts featured religious plays written by the director, Robert Johnson, and starring Johnson and Mahalia in the leading roles. Jackson met Thomas A. Dorsey in the mid-1930s and began a 14-year association with him, first as one of the singers he accompanied and later as the performer of his songs. Through his connection, she secured a recording contract with Decca Records in 1937 and cut four sides for the label, none of which attracted much attention.

Jackson's reputation as a soloist with the National Baptist Convention gained her a wide following, and with her 1947 recording of W. Herbert Brewster's "Move on up a Little Higher" she was catapulted into the limelight as a gospel star and was named the queen of gospel singers by 1950. She had her own radio program in Chicago, appeared on the Ed Sullivan and Dinah Shore television shows, and began a series of concert tours of Europe in 1952. She was invited to perform at one of the inaugural parties for President John F. Kennedy, and she sang at the March on Washington in 1963 and at the funeral of Martin Luther King, Jr. She appeared in several films, including *Imitation of Life* (1959) and *The Best Man* (1964). Jackson was offered huge sums to appear in nightclubs or to switch to a secular repertoire, but she rejected such offers. She did, however, record Duke Ellington's "Come Sunday" with his orchestra in 1958. Her dark, deep, and powerful contralto inspired many singers, including Aretha Franklin, Linda Hopkins, and

Mahalia Jackson, gospel singer, as portrayed on a paper fan produced by the Dillon Funeral Homes and Burial Association, Leland, Vicksburg, Greenville, Indianola, and Cleveland, Miss., 1968

Brother Joe May. Her best-known recordings include "Just Over the Hill," "In the Upper Room," and "He's Got the Whole World in His Hands."

Horace Clarence Boyer
University of Massachusetts, Amherst

Horace Clarence Boyer, "The Gospel Song: An Historical and Analytical Study" (M.A. thesis, Eastman School of Music, University of Rochester, 1964); Lauraine Goreau, *Just Mahalia, Baby* (1975); Tony Heilbut, *The Gospel Sound: Good News and Bad Times* (1971); Mahalia Jackson and Evan Wylie, *Movin' On Up* (1966); William H. Tallmadge, *Ethnomusicology* (May 1961).

Jefferson, Blind Lemon

(1897–1929) Blues singer.

Blind Lemon Jefferson was the South's most renowned country blues oracle in the 1920s. He was born blind into a poor sharecropping family on a farm about 50 miles east of Dallas, in 1897. Like other blind bluesmen, such as Blind Blake, Blind Willie McTell, and Gary Davis, he turned to music at an early age because it was the only way he could make a living. Early in his career, Jefferson became a popular bluesman in the east Texas farming communities around his birthplace. Then he took to the road; throughout the 1920s he made frequent trips outside of Texas to Oklahoma, the Mississippi Delta, Georgia, Virginia, and eventually Chicago, where he recorded for Paramount Records. In the late 1920s, Jefferson recorded over 90 songs. He proved to be the most commercially viable of all the rural blues musicians who made records during this period. His high-pitched voice and eclectic guitar style were especially popular among blacks in the South.

The blues repertoire that he recorded in Chicago reflected the range of themes prevalent in the black oral tradition in the South at the turn of the century. They included travel, work, sexual relationships, poverty, and prison life. His sympathies were always with the downtrodden. The blues he recorded was a mixture of traditional numbers such as "See See Rider" or "Boll Weevil Blues" and his own compositions like "Matchbox Blues"—which ultimately became one of his best-known signature pieces. Taken all together, Jefferson's blues lyrics reconstruct a first-hand account of Afro-American life in the South during the early 1900s. They are humorous and painful, ripe with sexual metaphor and fantasy, skeptical about love, and strikingly blunt in their portrayal of the society from the perspective of those at the bottom.

Blind Lemon Jefferson was in Chicago for a recording session in December 1929 when he was found dead in a snowdrift. Apparently he lost his way after playing at a house party late one night and froze to death. His body was taken back to Texas for burial. Although he died young, he left an impressive blues legacy through the recordings he made in his lifetime. He is still known and respected as one of the greatest rural bluesmen of his era.

Bill Barlow
Howard University

Blind Lemon Jefferson, Milestone Records, M-47022; Samuel Charters, *The Bluesmen: The Story and the Music of the Men Who Made the Blues* (1967); Bob Groom, *Blind Lemon Jefferson* (1970); Sheldon Harris, *Blues Who's Who: A Biographical Dictionary of Blues Singers* (1979).

Jiménez, Flaco

(b. 1939) *Conjunto* musician.

The Jiménez family has established a musical dynasty in the field of *música Norteña*, a south Texas contribution to music in the South. It began with Patricio Jiménez, who worked in San Antonio's Brackenridge quarry and learned the button accordion from local German-Texans in the early 1900s. His son, Santiago Jiménez, pioneered the Texas *Norteña* accordion style in San Antonio by performing on radio broadcasts and recordings beginning in the early 1930s. Since the 1950s Santiago's son, Leonardo "Flaco" (Skinny) Jiménez, now the third generation of the musical family, has developed *música Norteña* to heights of artistic virtuosity and gained international renown.

Flaco Jiménez grew up in an environment enriched by his grandfather's musical status in the community and his father's professional music career. Between the 1940s and early 1950s Santiago and his *conjunto* (group), Los Valedores, played most Saturday nights at the Gaucho nightclub in "el Westside" of San Antonio. On occasion Flaco accompanied his father to the club and sometimes, when Don Santiago took a break to drink a beer, he would let Flaco play a tune or two on the accordion with the band.

Flaco's professional career started in 1955 when, at the age of 16, he began playing with an established *conjunto*, Mike Garza y los Caminantes. By the late 1950s Flaco had formed his own group and was traveling to play at dances in Dallas and other Texas towns and cities.

In the early 1960s Flaco also began recording as his father had done 30 years before. The records were produced by new local San Antonio record companies that specialized in *Norteña* music. Some of his first hit songs such as "Hasta la Vista" (Until I See You), "Los Amores del Flaco" (The Loves of the Skinny One), and "Virgencita de mi Vida" (Little Virgin of my Life) were recorded in these years. In the same years, Flaco, like many other *conjunto* musicians, began to travel and carried *Norteña* music along what was referred to as "the migrant trail." Flaco and his *conjunto* traveled to Fresno, Calif., Chicago, and through the Midwest as well as in Texas, following the trail of Texas migrant farm workers.

Although a recognized artist on the accordion among Mexican Americans throughout the United States, until the early 1970s Flaco remained unknown to the larger American public. This situation changed, however, when he became friends with rock and blues innovators who were interested in *Norteña* music, such as Doug Sahm of San Antonio and Ry Cooder of California. Both musicians recorded on national record labels and helped open the door to Flaco's recognition in Anglo-American society. He has since recorded with these artists and has made several national television appearances. In the past few years, Flaco has also toured Europe and now regularly plays concerts at universities and music halls all over the country. In 1981 he recorded the soundtrack for the movie, *The Border*, with fellow musician Ry Cooder.

Flaco's brother is a well-known accordionist in San Antonio, and his teenage son David has recently made his first recordings, extending the Jiménez tradition into the fourth generation.

Dan W. Dickey
Austin, Texas

Manuel Peña, *The Texas-Mexican Conjunto: History of a Working Class Music* (1985).

Johnson, Bunk

(1879–1949) Jazz musician.

One of the earliest black jazz cornetists, Willie Geary "Bunk" Johnson, who was born in New Orleans, began to study on that instrument at the age of eight and in 1894 joined his first band, the Adam Olivier Orchestra. From 1896 to 1898 he may have played second cornet with Buddy Bolden's band, the first in New Orleans renowned for improvising in a "hot" syncopated style. From 1900 to 1910 he toured in minstrel and circus bands and in ocean-liner orchestras. Returning to New Orleans in the 1910s, Johnson became locally famous as lead cornetist with the Eagle Band, a parade and dance band re-formed from the earlier Bolden band, and with the formal society orchestra of John Robichaux. Johnson resumed touring in the 1920s, but his career rapidly declined with the onset of the Depression. In 1931 he moved to New Iberia, where he worked as a WPA public-school music teacher, a sugarcane field hand, and a Tabasco pepper factory worker. By 1934 dental problems forced him to quit playing altogether, and his career seemed at an end.

In 1938, however, he was rediscovered by jazz critics William Russell and Frederic Ramsey, Jr., who had been directed to him by Louis Armstrong as a source for their book, *Jazzmen* (1939). This renewed attention spurred Johnson to resume playing, and in 1942 he made his first recordings in New Orleans with George Lewis and Jim Robinson. These records generated widespread enthusiasm among jazz critics and listeners, made Johnson a cult figure, and spawned a full-scale revival of "classic" New Orleans jazz, as distinct from later Dixieland styles. As the spearhead of this revival, Johnson's performances and recordings increased during his last years, including appearances in San Francisco with Mutt Carey and Kid Ory (1943) and in New York with Sidney Bechet (1945).

While Johnson's revival revealed much about the schooled proficiency of early black jazz instrumentalists, it also obscured his own contribution to early jazz. Faulty memory and self-aggrandizement have compromised many statements in his recorded interviews, and stylistic accretions in his belated recordings make them an undependable reflection of his early cornet style. One of the oldest of the technically skilled black brassmen in New Orleans, Johnson was a primary participant in the shaping of jazz, whereby vocal devices of rural blues and gospel songs were adapted to the forms, techniques, and rhythms of instrumental band music.

John Joyce
Tulane University

M. Berger, in *Frontiers of Jazz*, ed. Ralph De Toledano (1947); William Russell and S. W. Smith, in *Jazzmen*, ed. Frederic Ramsey, Jr., and Charles E. Smith (1939); Martin Williams, *Jazz Masters of New Orleans* (1967).

Jones, George

(b. 1931) Country music singer.

A native of Saratoga, Tex., George Glenn Jones was born 12 September 1931. His childhood, spent in the area of east Texas known as the Big Thicket, was marked by poverty and abuse. When he was 10, his family moved to Kountze, Tex.; a year later they moved to Beaumont. His father, George Washington Jones, bought him a Gene Autry guitar, and he was soon singing on the streets with a tin cup. Never a serious student, he quit school in the seventh grade and had begun a honky-tonk career by age 16; he entered his first of four marriages at 18.

Upon completing two years of service in the Marine Corps, he returned to Beaumont in November 1953. Less than two months later, he recorded his first single, "No Money in This Deal," and began his 20-year association with Harold W. "Pappy" Daily, his producer and informal manager-advisor. In 1955 George Jones became a country disc jockey on KTRM, Beaumont, and appeared on the Louisiana Hayride; his first hit, "Why Baby Why," entered the charts in 1956, and he was off to Nashville, where he joined the Grand Ole Opry.

George Jones started his transition from an imitator of his idols Roy Acuff, Lefty Frizzell, and Hank Williams to an original vocal stylist whose unique talent would be compared with performers as diverse as Frank Sinatra and Aretha Franklin. Performers such as Waylon Jennings, Tom Petty, and Elvis Costello identify Jones as an important source of influence and inspiration. For many critics, fans, and performers he has become the standard against which "country" is measured. George Jones has produced number-one country songs in each of the past four decades; over 60 of his singles have achieved top-10 status on the country charts.

The authenticity with which Jones sings of heartbreak and headache was validated by news reports of his personal problems, which seemed to intensify in the period between 1975, when he was divorced from his third wife, country star Tammy Wynette, and March 1983, when he married Nancy Sepulveda and moved to Colmesneil, Tex. He struggled with alcohol, drug, and legal problems that threatened his life but not his popularity. In fact, he reached his largest audience at the time his personal life was most disorganized; his 1980 album *I Am What I Am* with Billy Sherrill, his producer since 1972, won both Country Music Association and Grammy recognition. His first video, *Who's Gonna Fill Their Shoes*, won recognition as the country video of 1986.

George Jones's catalog of hits ranges from manic—"White Lightnin'"—to depressive—"The Window Up Above," "The Grand Tour," and "He Stopped Loving Her Today." His songs, performance, and life connect with the large number of southerners separated from traditional communities by migration and modernization. This group provides for him the most loyal fan-following in all of country music.

Larry W. DeBord
University of Mississippi

Bob Allen, *George Jones: The Saga of An American Singer* (1984); Dolly Carlisle, *Ragged But Right: The Life and Times of George Jones* (1984).

Joplin, Scott

(1868–1917) Ragtime composer.

At the peak of his fame (1900–1905), Scott Joplin was billed in vaudeville as "King of Ragtime." His fame rested on the publication in 1899 of "Maple Leaf Rag," a brilliant piano solo in a new popular style called "ragtime." Joplin was a skilled itinerant musician born in 1868 near Texarkana, Tex. He studied piano and composition in Sedalia, Mo., at George R. Smith College (1896) to expand his musical horizons. Playing in saloons and bordellos from Texas to St. Louis, Joplin teamed with other black ragtime composers such as Otis Saunders and Louis Chauvin, helping them notate and sell their compositions. A farsighted publisher, John S. Stark of Sedalia, aided Joplin in his first steps to ragtime, and both men were enriched by this composer-publisher collaboration. Stark expanded his small venture into a fountainhead of "classic" piano ragtime, and Joplin wrote dozens of brilliant rags in the wake of "Maple Leaf Rag."

Joplin experimented with popular songs in a sentimental parlor vein in the mid-1890s, but his ability to compose and notate piano rags led him to ambitious works: "Original Rags" (1899), "The Easy Winners" (1901), "Elite Syncopations" (1902), "The Entertainer" (1902), "Pine Apple Rag" (1908), "Scott Joplin's New Rag" (1912), and some two dozen other published rags. Driven by a desire to make ragtime a respectable musical form, he and Stark admonished sheet-music buyers "DO NOT PLAY FAST," "IT IS NEVER RIGHT TO PLAY RAGTIME FAST," "DO NOT FAKE" (i.e., improvise). Joplin experimented with ragtime in a ballet, "The Ragtime Dance" (1900, published 1906), and a ragtime opera, *A Guest of Honor* (1903), now lost. He tried syncopated waltzes ("Bethena," 1905, and "Pleasant Moments," 1909) and a habañera ("Solace," 1909) and enlarged ragtime's vocabulary in advanced rags like "Euphonic Sounds" (1909) and "Magnetic Rag" (1914).

After traveling from Sedalia to St. Louis, thence to New York City and on vaudeville circuits, Joplin settled in Harlem. He never matched the fame and fortune of "Maple Leaf Rag," though his works were lauded for their consistent gentle genius. From about 1905 Joplin became consumed with ideas for "elevating" ragtime, via symphonic or operatic forms. He wrote an ambitious and unique folk-oriented opera, *Treemonisha*, performed only in rehearsal in 1915. Failure to achieve support for *Treemonisha* may have contributed to Joplin's collapse. He died 1 April 1917, in New York.

Joplin's peers in ragtime composition were Thomas M. Turpin, Charles H. Hunter, Charles L. Johnson, James Scott, and Artie Matthews. His collaborators included Louis Chauvin, Scott Hayden, and Arthur Marshall. He assisted the careers of S. Brunson "Brun" Campbell and

Joseph F. Lamb and scores of other ragtime players who did not leave compositions. Joplin's version of ragtime derived from the playing of Mississippi Valley itinerant composers and from rich late 19th-century folk reservoirs. His contribution to Afro-American music lay in his skill as a composer: he created fluid, lyrical themes, organized them into the coherent multipart form of the piano rag, and forged an individualized, easily recognizable style. His works are marked by a delicacy and grace achieved by few of his contemporaries. Within the form of the piano rag as a serious composition (or "classic," the term he and Stark favored), Joplin fused the vigor of banjo tunes, the swing of country dances, and the limpidity of song. His mark on American popular music is deep and indelible, and interest in his work revived in the 1970s. *Treemonisha* was performed in Atlanta in 1972, and Joplin's compositions were chosen for the soundtrack of the popular 1973 motion picture *The Sting*.

William J. Schafer
Berea College

Rudi Blesh and Harriet Janis, *They All Played Ragtime* (1966); James Haskins and Kathleen Benson, *Scott Joplin* (1978); Vera Brodsky Lawrence, ed., *The Collected Works of Scott Joplin* (1971); William J. Schafer and Johannes Riedel, *The Art of Ragtime: Form and Meaning of an Original Black American Art* (1973).

B. B. King, 1960s, photograph on a wall at Club Paradise, Memphis, Tenn.

King, B. B.

(b. 1925) Blues singer.

Riley B. "B. B." King was born on a plantation between Itta Bena and Indianola, Miss. One of five children, he often sang in local churches as a young child. When his parents separated, King moved with his mother to Kilmichael, Miss., where he sang in a school spiritual quartet from 1929 to 1934. After his mother's death, he returned to Indianola and continued to develop his music while working as a farmhand.

In 1946 King hitched a ride to Memphis and for 10 months lived with noted bluesman Bubba White, his mother's cousin. He returned to the Delta briefly at the end of 1947 and in 1948 harvested a cotton crop. Later that year he returned to Memphis, this time for good, and worked amateur shows at the W. C. Handy Theater/ Palace Theater. He frequently performed with Bobby Bland, Johnny Ace, and Earl Forrest in a group called "the Beale Streeters" and appeared regularly on his own "Pepticon Boy" show on WDIA radio in Memphis. His nickname, the "Beale Street Blues Boy," was shortened to "Blues Boy," then to "B. B." In 1950 his "Three O'Clock Blues" climbed to the top of the rhythm-and-blues charts and stayed there for four months. Its success launched his musical career, and he gave up his disc jockey job to go on the road with his own group, scarcely two years after he had made his last cotton crop in the Delta.

For nearly 20 years he performed some 300 one-night stands a year in black night spots known as the "Chitterlin' Circuit." Once a year he played week-long engagements in large urban black theaters such as the Howard in Washington, the Regal in Chicago, and the Apollo in New York.

In the early 1960s King's career was in a slump, with blacks finding his music uncomfortably close to their "down-home" roots and folk enthusiasts considering him too commercialized. King's return to fame came when the Rolling Stones, Paul Butterfield's Blues Band, and other British and American groups acknowledged him as their idol. After his first European tour in 1968 he was finally recognized by American critics, and since that time his career has steadily grown, with frequent television and film appearances.

King's guitar style is influenced by blues guitarists Lonnie Johnson and T-Bone Walker and by jazz guitarists Django Reinhardt and Charlie Christian. He has always played an electric guitar, which he nicknamed "Lucille." His delicate "bent" notes and powerful vocals echo the blues style of the Mississippi Delta where King first learned his music.

From his early years in rural Mississippi to his international acclaim, B. B. King's blues career is a rare success story. He has issued over 700 recordings and continues to produce and perform at a pace younger musicians would find exhausting. His achievements as a blues performer, composer, and spokesman were recognized in 1977 when Yale President Kingman Brewster awarded him an honorary doctorate of music with the accolade, "In your rendition of the blues you have always taken us beyond entertainment to the deeper message of suffering and endurance that gave rise to the form."

In "Why I Sing the Blues," King explains the meaning of his music:

> When I first got the blues, they brought me over
> on a ship,
> Man was standing over me, and a lot more with
> a whip,
> Now everybody want to know why I sing the
> blues,
> Well I've been around a long time, I've really
> paid my dues.

William Ferris
University of Mississippi

Sheldon Harris, *Blues Who's Who: A Biographical Dictionary of Blues Singers* (1979); Paul Oliver, *The Story of the Blues* (1969); Charles Sawyer, *The Arrival of B.B. King: The Authorized Biography* (1980).

Ledbetter, Huddie (Leadbelly)

(1885–1949) Blues singer.

A singer and composer, Ledbetter was born 21 January 1885, two miles from Mooringsport, La., in the Caddo Lake area near the Texas border, where his parents, Wess Ledbetter and Sallie (Pugh) Ledbetter, owned 65 acres of farmland. Wess Ledbetter's parents in Mississippi had both been slain by the Ku Klux Klan. Huddie Ledbetter's maternal grandmother was a Cherokee, a fact he often mentioned.

Huddie Ledbetter was first exposed to music by his mother, who led her church choir. Two "songster" uncles, Bob and Terrell Ledbetter, encouraged him to become a musician. Huddie Ledbetter was soon known as the best guitar picker and songster in his part of Louisiana. At 16 he started visiting Fannin Street, the red-light district of nearby Shreveport. Here he heard accomplished blues musicians and learned their style and verses. He recalls these early experiences in his song "Fannin Street." Bud Coleman and Jim Fagin were two musicians with whom he worked closely.

Ledbetter soon moved away from Mooringsport. He married a girl named Lethe, and they worked together during summers on farms near New Boston, Tex., in the blackland counties east of Dallas. In the winter they moved to Dallas, where he played his guitar and sang in the red-light district. There he met the Texas bluesman Blind Lemon Jefferson and learned many songs from him.

He received the nickname "Lead Belly" (or "Leadbelly") because his voice was a powerful bass. A handsome, strongly built young man, he had early learned that he was attractive to women. In Marshall, Tex., he attacked a woman who rejected his advances, was sentenced to a year on a chain gang, and escaped from prison three days later. In late 1917 Leadbelly became involved in another fracas over a woman. He was convicted on two counts, murder and assault to murder, on 24 May 1918. Once more he escaped from his cell, but on 7 June 1918, under the alias of Walter Boyd, he entered Shaw State Prison Farm, sentenced to 30 years at hard labor. For the third time he escaped. He was soon recaptured, and in 1920 he was transferred to the Central State Farm near Houston. He worked on labor gangs for 12 to 14 hours a day cutting logs and hoeing cotton, and through his strength and endurance he became the lead man on the fastest work gang.

Leadbelly was also known for his skill as a musician and was asked to sing when visitors came to the prison. When the governor of Texas, Pat M. Neff, came to visit, Leadbelly sang a plea for mercy to him:

> (If I) had you, Governor Neff, like you got me,
> I'd wake up in the mornin', and I'd set you free.

The governor was impressed with the man and his song, and on 15 January 1925 he pardoned Leadbelly, who had then served about six and a half years. After working for a Buick agency in Houston, Leadbelly returned to his home near Mooringsport in 1926. While he worked for the Gulf Refining Company, he continued to develop as a blues singer. In 1930 he was accosted by a group of men who wanted whiskey. Leadbelly wounded five of them with his knife and was sentenced to 10 years at hard labor for assault with intent to murder.

On 28 February 1930 he entered Angola Penitentiary in Louisiana and became the lead man on prison gangs, as he had in Texas. He composed another plea for mercy to Governor O. K. Allen of Louisiana. It was recorded (along with a song that was to become even more famous, "Irene, Good Night") by folklorists John and Alan Lomax in 1934. The Lomaxes played the record for the governor in his office and obtained a reprieve for Leadbelly on 7 August 1934.

The next month Leadbelly joined John Lomax in a journey that helped make both men famous. Lomax recorded folksongs in southern prisons, and Leadbelly accompanied him, telling of his own experiences and singing to encourage the inmates to record for Lomax. Lomax's tapes of Leadbelly's songs were eventually deposited in the Library of Congress. After 6,000 miles of travel, performances, and recording, they arrived in New York City. Leadbelly was given a resounding reception by the New York intellectual and literary scene that embraced him as the "bad nigger."

Leadbelly's repertoire included traditional folk and children's songs, blues, and topical numbers, all of which are an important part of American folklore. His best-known songs include "Boll Weevil," "Rock Island Line," "Old Cottonfields at Home," "Take This Hammer," "Pick a Bale of Cotton," and "Midnight Special." Few other blues musicians have been so studied and appreciated. He died of myotrophic lateral sclerosis on 6 December 1949 at Bellevue Hospital in New York.

William Ferris
University of Mississippi

Richard M. Garvin and Edmond G. Addeo, *The Midnight Special: The Legend of Leadbelly* (1971); John A. Lomax and Alan Lomax, *The Leadbelly Legend* (1965), *Negro Folk Songs as Sung by Lead Belly* (1936), Recordings of interviews and music made with Leadbelly, listed in Recording Division of the Library of Congress; Frederick Ramsey, *Last Sessions* (record), Folkways, FA-2941 and FA-2942.

Lewis, Jerry Lee

(b. 1935) Rock and country singer.

Jerry Lee Lewis of Ferriday, La., one of the most charismatic and controversial musicians of his generation, has long exemplified many of the most profound tensions in southern history.

Born on 29 September 1935 into an extremely talented yet volatile family—two of his cousins are television evangelist Jimmy Swaggart and country musician Mickey Gilley—Lewis's earliest and most indelible influences came from Pentecostal religion. As a child he was also attracted to secular sources, such as a black Ferriday juke joint called Haney's Big House. Lewis has cited Al Jolson, Jimmie Rodgers, Gene Autry, and Hank Williams as vocal influences, but his highly personalized boogie-woogie piano style reflects indigenous black folk sources from his immediate region.

By adolescence Lewis was a skilled entertainer, performing at numerous political rallies, religious services, talent contests, and nightclubs, and on radio in Natchez, Miss. In 1956 he began recording for Sun Records in Memphis and achieved national popularity and notoriety as perhaps the wildest of all rock-and-roll performers. To many observers, Lewis was a public menace, but from 1956 to 1958 he had numerous hit recordings, including "Whole Lotta Shakin' Goin' On" and "Great Balls of Fire," and made several appearances on national television and in movies. Lewis generated copious public criticism in 1958 after marrying his 13-year-old second cousin, Myra Brown. Although he defended his marriage as customary in his native South, Lewis's recording career declined precipitously. Forced to tour incessantly (primarily in the South) for over a decade, he subsequently deepened his already vast repertoire and enhanced his reputation as an unrivaled live performer.

In 1968 Lewis staged a remarkable comeback in the country field, and more than a score of country hits ensued. Despite his success as a country artist, Lewis has continued to perform predominantly in the rockabilly style that had brought him his initial success. He has remained a successful recording artist well into the 1980s despite an uncanny series of financial, physical, and emotional crises.

By the late 1970s Jerry Lee Lewis was widely hailed by both popular journalists and scholars as one of the most creative and important figures in American popular culture. His peculiar resonance as a southern cultural symbol was matched only by Elvis Presley. No one has demonstrated a more thorough command of the South's musical heritage, from minstrelsy and blues to hymns and hillbilly music. His career has operated as a paradigm of the southern experience, dramatizing many of the region's fundamental tensions.

Stephen R. Tucker
Tulane University

Myra Lewis with Murray Silver, *Great Balls of Fire: The Uncensored Story of Jerry Lee Lewis* (1982); Robert Palmer, *Jerry Lee Lewis Rocks!* (1981); Nick Tosches, *Hellfire: The Jerry Lee Lewis Story* (1982).

Little Richard

See Penniman, Richard

Lomax, John A.

(1867–1948) Folksong collector.

Born in Goodman, Miss., on 23 September 1867, John Avery Lomax was one of five sons of James Avery Lomax, a farmer, and Susan Frances (Cooper) Lomax, both natives of Georgia. Although they always worked their own land, Lomax described his family as belonging to the "upper crust of the po' white trash." In 1869 they moved to a farm on the Bosque River near Meridian, Tex. From his country childhood Lomax acquired a love for and appreciation of the rural folklore he later captured on record. He absorbed the popular hymns he heard at the Methodist camp meetings his family attended.

In 1895, at 28, he entered the University of Texas, where he took courses with feverish enthusiasm and received his B.A. degree in two years. From 1897 to 1903, Lomax served the university simultaneously as registrar, secretary to the president, and steward of men's dormitories, for $75 a month. Subsequently, he became instructor and then associate professor of English at Texas Agricultural and Mechanical College (1903–10). Meanwhile, he doggedly pursued graduate studies despite financial constraints. He received the M.A. in literature in 1906 from the University of Texas and an M.A. in English from Harvard the following year.

Since childhood, Lomax had been writing down the cowboy songs he heard. His English professors at Texas had scorned such frontier literature as unworthy, but at Harvard, Barrett Wendell and George Lyman Kittredge strongly encouraged Lomax to continue his collecting. After his return to Texas, Lomax secured three successive fellowships that enabled him to travel through the cattle country with a notebook and a primitive recording machine. Around campfires and in saloon back rooms he persuaded cowboys to sing their songs. Among his findings were the well-known "Git Along Little Dogies" and "Home on the Range," the latter sung to him in San Antonio by a black saloonkeeper who had been a trail cook. The result was Lomax's first published collection, *Cowboy Songs and Other Frontier Ballads* (1910), which he dedicated to Theodore Roosevelt, a firm supporter of his efforts. The book is a landmark in the study of American folklore.

Later in 1932, with a contract from the Macmillan Company for a book of American folksongs and with support from the Library of Congress and the American Council of Learned Societies, he set out on the first of a series of collecting trips that were to occupy the rest of his life. He concentrated on recording songs of the southern black—blues, spirituals, and work chants. Often accompanied by his son, Alan, he visited remote rural black communities, lumber camps, and penitentiaries, where blacks were isolated and where singing softened the pain of prison life. The quality and number of the songs he recorded for the Library of Congress Archive of American Folk Song—more than 10,000 in all—reflect Lomax's unusual skill as a fieldworker. In the Arkansas Penitentiary he came upon two important songs, "Rock Island Line" and "John Henry," the rhythmic ballad of a "steel drivin' man."

Lomax's two collections, *American Ballads and Folk Songs* (1934) and *Our Singing Country* (1941), opened an entirely new area of American folk music to the public and were largely responsible for the folksong movement that developed in New York City and spread throughout the country. One of Lomax's discoveries was an influential figure in that movement: Huddie Ledbetter, nicknamed "Leadbelly" because of his deep bass voice. Lomax and his son found Leadbelly in a Louisiana penitentiary in 1933, arranged for his freedom, brought him to Greenwich Village in New York, and published *Negro Folk Songs as Sung by Lead Belly* (1936).

Lomax died on 26 January 1948 at the age of 80 of a cerebral hemorrhage while visiting in Greenville, Miss., and was buried in Austin, Tex.

William Ferris
University of Mississippi

John A. Lomax, *Adventures of a Ballad Hunter* (1947), *Cowboy Songs* (1922), Recordings at the University of Texas, Harvard University, and the Archives of American Folk Song at the Library of Congress, "The Ballad Hunter: John A. Lomax" (record), AAFS L53; D. K. Wilgus, *Anglo-American Folksong Scholarship since 1898* (1959).

Lunsford, Bascom Lamar

(1882–1973) Music collector, performer, and promoter.

Born on South Turkey Creek in Buncombe County, N.C., and trained as a lawyer, Lunsford worked in a variety of occupations (college teacher, lawyer, newspaperman, seller of fruit trees and war bonds), but achieved local and national renown as a collector, performer, promoter, and interpreter of the old-time music and dance of western North Carolina. During the late 1920s, when mountain music and culture were being stereotyped and exploited for commercial (mainly media and tourism) purposes, Lunsford—who called himself "the squire of South Turkey Creek"—championed their dignity and worth.

In 1928 Lunsford began his Mountain Dance and Folk Festival in Asheville, first as a segment of the Chamber of Commerce-sponsored and booster-oriented Rhododendron Festival, but later as an independent event. During the next half century the festival became a major showcase for traditional Appalachian music and dance. It developed its own traditions, opening each year the first weekend in August, "along about sundown," with the fiddle tune "Grey Eagle." Some of its outstanding performers were banjo players Aunt Samantha Bumgarner and George Pegram, harmonica player Walter "Red" Parham, and the Soco Gap clog team led by Sam Queen.

Lunsford has been criticized for his somewhat idiosyncratic selectivity in presenting mountain music. During his lifetime, for example, no blacks ever performed at the festival, despite the existence of a substantial black population in the area. Nevertheless, as fellow festival promoter Sarah Gertrude Knott observed, Lunsford succeeded better than virtually all of his peers at "finding a way between the old and the new," uncovering and nurturing the oldest levels of tradition; presenting and interpreting traditional music and dance in a dignified manner; respecting the tastes, styles, and choices of the performers themselves; and honoring traditional values and idioms while remaining sensitive to the dynamic quality of tradition.

As a performer and collector, Lunsford recorded both for commercial phonograph companies (Okeh, Brunswick, Columbia, Folkways) and for folklore archives at Columbia University and the Library of Congress. Some of his personal papers and memorabilia are on deposit at Mars Hill College in North Carolina.

David E. Whisnant
University of Maryland,
Baltimore County

Bill Finger, *Southern Exposure* (Spring 1974); Loyal Jones, *Minstrel of the Appalachians: The Story of Bascom Lamar Lunsford* (1984); Harold H. Martin, *Saturday Evening Post* (22 May 1948); David E. Whisnant, *Appalachian Journal* (Autumn–Winter 1979–80).

Mexican Border Stations

Popularly known as X-stations because of their call letters, the Mexican border radio stations in the 1930s and afterwards were powerful disseminators of music and other forms of popular culture throughout North America. Their programming techniques and advertising practices became part of the nation's folklore, and they did much to make the world at large conscious of southern rural folkways.

With transmitters located on the Mexican side of the border and operating with wattage generally far in excess of that permitted in the United States, X-station broadcasts could be heard clearly in this country and Canada. The era of border radio began in 1932 when John R. Brinkley, "the goat-gland doctor" who promoted a cure for male sexual impotence, established XER (later XERA), with offices in Del Rio, Tex., and its transmitter in Villa Acuna, Mexico. XER claimed power of 500,000 watts, and Brinkley advertised his medical ideas and Del Rio hospital on it and also leased time to other American businessmen who sold patent medicines and other products. Additional stations, such as XEPN, XEAW, XENT, and XEG, soon followed, with each of them pursuing a pattern of radio programming similar to that pioneered by Brinkley.

Late-night listeners were introduced to an unforgettable torrent of Americana on the border radio shows. Long-winded announcers incessantly promoted such products as baby chicks, songbooks, records, photographs, prayer cloths, Resurrection plants, Bibles, "genuine simulated" diamonds, laxatives, hair dyes, and other forms of patent medicines (such as Crazy Water Crystals), and "autographed pictures of Jesus Christ." Listeners were constantly solicited for money, asked to send in boxtops and labels, and told to get their orders in the mail immediately for once-in-a-lifetime offers that were due to go off the air forever at midnight.

Border radio advertising was accompanied also by strong doses of southern popular culture: fundamentalist religion, populist politics, and grassroots music of various kinds. Country musicians such as the Carter Family, the Pickard Family, the Callahan Brothers, and the Herrington Trio, cowboy singers like cowboy Slim Rinehart, Jesse Rodgers, and the Utah Cowboy (J. R. Hall), and gospel singers such as the Chuck Wagon Gang and the Stamps Quartet performed on the border stations either in live broadcasts or on transcriptions. They sold their sponsors' products, hawked their own records and picture-songbooks, and disseminated their particular versions of southern music to audiences in the most remote corners of North America. The radio stations still broadcast their southern-influenced programs.

Bill C. Malone
Tulane University

Gerald Carson, *The Roguish World of Dr. Brinkley* (1960); Bill C. Malone, *Country Music, U.S.A.: A Fifty-year History* (1968; rev. ed., 1985).

Monroe, Bill

(b. 1911) Bluegrass musician.

William Smith "Bill" Monroe was born on 13 September 1911 on a farm near the small town of Rosine, Ohio County, in western Kentucky. The youngest of eight children, Monroe had extremely poor sight. He was a shy lad for whom his family's musical traditions afforded comfort and identity. His mother died when he was 10, his father when he was 16. He lived for several years with his Uncle Pen (Pendleton Vandiver), a fiddler who strongly influenced his music and who was later immortalized in song by Monroe. He also learned much from a black guitarist and fiddler, Arnold Shultz, with whom he played at dances. In 1929 he joined two older brothers at industrial jobs near Chicago. In 1932 the three became part of an exhibition square-dance team at the National Barn Dance on Chicago radio station WLS. In 1934 Bill and his brother Charlie became professional "hillbilly" radio singers. By 1938 their duets had become popular throughout the Southeast through their radio broadcasts in Iowa and the Carolinas, their personal appearances, and their Victor Bluebird recordings (1936–38).

In 1938 the brothers parted, and Bill formed his own group, the Blue Grass Boys. In October 1939 he joined the cast of the Grand Ole Opry on WSM, and he has been in Nashville ever since. His recordings for Victor (1940–41), Columbia (1945–49) and Decca/MCA (since 1950) have sold consistently over long periods; many are still in print. His compositions include instrumentals, religious songs, and secular songs on a variety of topics.

During the 1940s Monroe, who plays mandolin and sings in a distinctive high tenor voice, developed an innovative ensemble-band style based on the instrumental and vocal styles of earlier southeastern fiddle-band music. His band's sound, which included the five-string banjo of Earl Scruggs, was copied by a number of groups during the late 1940s. By the mid-1950s it was considered a style and had acquired the name "bluegrass"—taken from his band's name. In the late 1960s Monroe was the central figure in the emergence of bluegrass festivals. Monroe's reputation came not just from his musical ability and his skill as a composer but also from his role as a bandleader and teacher. In his early years he was as an older brother to his band members; he has become later in life a patriarch.

His contributions to country music were recognized in 1971, when he was elected to the Country Music Hall of Fame in Nashville. His national prominence was underscored in July 1982, when he was among the first recipients of the Annual National Heritage Fellowship Awards made by the Folk Arts Program of the National Endowment for the Arts. His award described him as "one of the few living American musicians who can justly claim to have created an entirely new musical style."

Neil V. Rosenberg
Memorial University
St. Johns, Newfoundland

Ralph Rinzler, in *Stars of Country Music: Uncle Dave Macon to Johnny Rodriguez*, ed. Bill C. Malone and Judith McCullough

(1975); Jim Rooney, *Bossmen: Bill Monroe and Muddy Waters* (1971); Neil V. Rosenberg, *Bill Monroe and His Blue Grass Boys: An Illustrated Discography* (1974), *Bluegrass: A History* (1985).

Morganfield, McKinley (Muddy Waters)

(1915–1983) Blues singer.

Muddy Waters was born in Rolling Fork, Miss., and at an early age taught himself to perform on both the guitar and the harmonica. His skills as a young bluesman were widely advertised in north Mississippi and the Memphis, Tenn., area. During the early 1940s he recorded blues selections for folklorists Alan Lomax and John Work. Shortly after his recording session he joined the Silas Green Tent Show. Through his employment with Silas Green, he formed a professional association with William Lee Conley (Big Bill Broonzy). He made his first professional recording in 1946. Two of the musicians with whom he recorded include Andrew Luandrew (Sunnyland Slim) and Leroy Foster.

Morganfield formed his own band, which performed in Chicago for several years and included such noted Chicago bluesmen as Willie Dixon, Otis Spann, Pat Hare, James Cotton, and Little Walter Jacobs. From 1942 to his death he recorded extensively. Among his most celebrated recorded selections are "Caledonia," "Hoochie Koochie Man," "Rolling Stone," "Baby Please Don't Go," and "Mannish Boy." He also toured throughout the United States and in several foreign countries. His foreign tours included appearances in England, Australia, New Zealand, Germany, and France. His peers nicknamed him "Godfather of the Blues."

Muddy Waters, bluesman, 1960s

Muddy Waters bought his first electric guitar in 1944, and he became especially significant in introducing electrified instruments to the blues. It helped make the blues into ensemble music, and the electric blues was a major influence on rock and roll. Waters was a leader in the transformation of Delta blues from southern folk music into a nationally and internationally popular music.

Lemuel Berry, Jr.
Alabama State University

Living Blues (Autumn 1983, March–April 1985); Robert Palmer, *Deep Blues* (1981); James Rooney, *Bossmen: Bill Monroe and Muddy Waters* (1971).

Morton, Jelly Roll (Ferdinand Le Menthe)

(1885–1941) Jazz musician.

Self-proclaimed inventor of jazz, Ferdinand Le Menthe was among the earliest and most prominent of New Orleans jazzmen. Better known on the streets and among the world's musical fraternity as Jelly Roll Morton, he was born in 1885 on the Gulf Coast near New Orleans. His African-Mediterranean-Caribbean ancestry placed him among that city's Creoles of Color, and he drew from their musical traditions. Morton's family moved to New Orleans while the young Ferdinand was quite small, and he grew to manhood there within a community that enjoyed frequent contacts with Mexico and the Caribbean. The young Morton learned on his own to play various musical instruments and was playing on street corners in a band by age eight. He studied piano at age 10, learning from the resident pianist of the local French opera. Much of the European form and attitude long prevalent in jazz has its source in this kind of training received by Creole musicians such as Morton. By age 15 he was regarded as one of New Orleans's leading ragtime-blues pianists.

Morton grew up on the margin of the New Orleans marketplace, struggling to survive within the urban underclass. The street-and-saloon environment fostered the proliferation of flesh parlors and honky-tonk dancehalls where musicians of color often worked. Prevented from performing in formal musical circles, the city's schooled black musicians turned out of necessity to the honky-tonks, cabarets, and sporting houses in places like Storyville.

The honky-tonk culture of the urban underclass in the early 20th century formed a national network, which permitted artists like Morton to take their music to other cities. Between 1910 and 1925 Jelly Roll Morton

Jelly Roll Morton, jazz musician, early 1920s

performed in St. Louis, Los Angeles, San Francisco, Chicago, and New York, in addition to New Orleans. He toured with vaudeville shows operating out of Memphis and later Georgia. In the 1917 to 1923 period he performed mainly on the West Coast. In these and subsequent years Morton composed and recorded a host of songs on the piano, including such jazz classics as "The Pearls," "The Chant," "The Fingerbreaker," "New Orleans Joys," and "Buddy Bolden's Blues."

By the early 1920s Morton's interest, along with that of the rest of the nation, had shifted to jazz bands. He moved to Chicago where he recorded and performed frequently. There he organized and produced the Red Hot Peppers, a seven-piece classic jazz ensemble for which he composed and orchestrated such immortal jazz pieces as "Jungle Blues," "London Blues," "Hello Central, Give Me Doctor Jazz," "Sidewalk Blues," and "Georgia Swing." He moved to New York City in 1928, performing there in nightclubs and ballrooms, recording, working with musical revues, and touring out of town. In 1938 Alan Lomax extensively recorded Morton for the Library of Congress Archive of American Folksong.

See also BLACK LIFE: / Storyville

Curtis D. Jerde
W. R. Hogan Jazz Archive
Tulane University

Alan Lomax, *Mister Jelly Roll* (1950); Martin Williams, *Jelly Roll Morton* (1963).

Muddy Waters

See Morganfield, McKinley

Nelson, Willie

(b. 1933) Country music singer.

Willie Hugh Nelson was born in Fort Worth, Tex., on 30 April 1933 and was reared in the little central Texas town of Abbott, where he was exposed to a wide variety of musical influences. He grew up singing gospel songs in the Baptist church but also played in honky-tonks all over the state. Before he was a teenager, he began playing guitar in the German-Czech polka bands in the "Bohemian" communities of central Texas; he listened to the country music of Bob Wills, Lefty Frizzell, and Floyd Tillman, but he was also an avid fan of jazz and vintage pop music. All of these forms clearly influence the music he plays today.

Despite his skills as a guitarist and unorthodox singer (with his blues inflections and off-the-beat phrasing), Nelson's ticket to Nashville came through his songwriting. In 1960 he moved to Nashville, where he became part of an important coterie of writers that included Hank Cochran, Harlan Howard, and Roger Miller. Nelson made a major contribution to country music's post-rock-and-roll revival with such songs as "Funny How Time Slips Away," "Hello, Walls," "Night Life," and "Crazy," all of which were successfully recorded by other singers.

Recording for RCA Victor in the mid-1960s, Nelson became widely admired by his colleagues as a "singer's singer," but he did not achieve the stardom that he sought. In 1972 he relocated in Austin, Tex., where he became part of an already-thriving music scene that was strongly oriented toward youth who had grown up listening to rock and urban folk music. Nelson made a calculated attempt to appeal to this audience by changing his physical image: he let his hair grow long, grew a beard, began wearing a headband, an earring, jeans, and jogging shoes (a striking contrast to the well-groomed, middle-class appearance he had affected during his Nashville years). He also publicized himself with his huge annual "picnics," first held in Dripping Springs, Tex., in 1972 and 1973, and later staged in a variety of Texas communities, usually on the Fourth of July. These festivals were intended to bridge the gap between youth and adults, while bringing together varied lifestyles and musical forms. The picnics, however, soon lost their appeal to older people or to traditional country fans and instead became havens for uninhibited youth and for musicians who seemed most comfortable with a country-rock perspective.

After winning the youth audience, Nelson then captured the adult market. In 1975 he recorded a best-selling album called *The Red Headed Stranger*, and one song from the album, Fred Rose's "Blue Eyes Crying in the Rain," became the number-one country song of the year

Willie Nelson, outlaw country music singer, 1980s

(it is ironic that the first superhit recorded by this master songwriter was a song written by someone else). Nelson's ascent to superstardom and his building of a large and diverse audience were accomplished without significant departures from his traditional style. Indeed, his repertoire became even more traditional as he reached back to the performance of older gospel, country, and pop songs. No one in American music performed a more eclectic sampling of songs. He also preserved his unorthodox style of singing and sang over a rather spare and uncluttered scheme of instrumentation, which was dominated by his own inventive, single-string style of guitar playing.

While Nelson has won a large array of country music awards since the mid-1970s, including the Country Music Association's Entertainer of the Year award in 1979, his appeal has extended far beyond the country music world. Nelson has received favorable reviews for his role in several movies, such as *The Electric Horseman*; he has been feted constantly by the American media; and he has entertained often at political events, including the Democratic National Convention in 1980, during the Carter presidency. Few country singers have enjoyed such broad exposure.

Bill C. Malone
Tulane University

Jan Reid, *The Improbable Rise of Redneck Rock* (1974); Al Reinert, *New York Times Magazine* (26 March 1978); Lola Scobey, *Willie Nelson* (1982).

Oliver, King

(1885–1938) Jazz musician.

Joseph "King" Oliver was born in or near New Orleans and became an early black jazz cornetist and bandleader. By 1900 he played cornet in a youthful parade band. From 1905 to 1915 Oliver became a prominent figure in various brass and dance bands and with small groups in bars and cafés. He soon gained the title "King" in competition with other leading local cornetists. In 1918 he joined a New Orleans band playing in Chicago and by 1920 was leading his own group there. He toured with this band in California in 1921 and, returning to Chicago the next year, enlarged it as King Oliver's Creole Jazz Band. This handpicked ensemble boasted some of New Orleans's best black instrumentalists, including Johnny and "Baby" Dodds (clarinet and drums, respectively) and Oliver's brilliant young protégé, Louis Armstrong (second cornet). The Creole Band's beautifully drilled performances at Chicago's Lincoln Gardens and its tour through the Midwest created a sensation among northern musicians, and in 1923 it made the most extensive series of recordings (some three dozen) of any early jazz band.

When several members, including Armstrong, left the band in late 1924, Oliver formed a new, larger dance orchestra with saxophones, called the Dixie Syncopators. This sporadically successful orchestra, with changing personnel, played in Chicago from 1925 to 1927 and at New York's Savoy Ballroom in 1927. Between 1926 and 1928 the orchestra made a number of recordings of uneven quality, though a few were popular hits. By 1930 Oliver's career as a soloist ended. From 1930 to 1936 he led a succession of small orchestras across the country, though a severe dental condition prevented him from playing. After 1936 he lived in Savannah with an ailing heart and spent his last year there running a fruit stand and working as a janitor in a pool hall. He died 8 April 1938.

One of the foremost first-generation New Orleans jazz cornetists, Oliver was a central figure in the transfer of ragtime and of the black blues and gospel song from nearby rural areas to the New Orleans urban band tradition. The recordings of his Creole Jazz Band are the best and most extensive documentation of how vocal blues and instrumental ragtime were fused by emerging jazz bands into a new music of distinctively black southern origins.

John Joyce
Tulane University

Frederic Ramsey, Jr., in *Jazzmen*, ed. Frederic Ramsey, Jr., and Charles E. Smith (1939); Martin Williams, *King Oliver* (1960); Lawrence Gushee, in *Jazz Panorama*, ed. Martin Williams (1962).

Parsons, Gram

(1946–1973) Rock singer.

Born 5 November 1946 in Winterhaven, Fla., Gram Parsons was one of the most influential popular musicians of his generation. A devoted follower of Elvis Presley as a teenager, Parsons performed with rock-and-roll bands from 1959 until 1963, when he joined an urban folk music group, the Shilos.

After briefly attending Harvard in 1965, he joined the International Submarine Band and began drawing upon his southern background in an early attempt to synthesize country and rock. Beginning in the mid-1960s, Parsons devoted himself to what he called "cosmic American music"—essentially a dynamic combination of southern-derived styles with a solid country core.

The International Submarine Band dissolved in 1967, just prior to the release of *Safe at Home*, arguably the first complete country-rock album. In 1968 Parsons joined the popular folk-rock group the Byrds, and, in tandem with longtime member Chris Hillman, led the band in the direction of country music. The Byrds's *Sweetheart of the Rodeo*, released in 1969, was a landmark in the evolution of country rock. It also featured one of Parsons's finest compositions, "Hickory Wind," an evocative tribute to his southern childhood.

Both Parsons and Hillman went on to organize what became the definitive country-rock band, the Flying Burrito Brothers. As a Burrito, Parsons began to deepen his vision of the South, which had first emerged with "Hickory Wind." In his songs as well as his lifestyle, Parsons often portrayed himself as a southern country boy set adrift in the contemporary urban maelstrom. His finest song, "Sin City" (1969), was the classic statement of this theme.

After leaving the Burritos in 1970, Parsons produced little significant work until the release of his first solo album, *GP*, in 1973. The album featured Emmylou Harris on vocals and confirmed his mastery of the country-rock idiom. Throughout the album, the South was portrayed as an almost mythical land of stability and steadfastness.

On 19 September 1973 Gram Parsons died in Joshua Tree, Calif. An autopsy was inconclusive as to the cause of death. Several posthumous works, including *Grievous Angel* (1974), *Sleepless Nights* (1976), and *Gram Parsons and the Fallen Angels—Live 1973* (1982), attest to his exceptional gifts as a singer and songwriter. Much of his work continues to inform contemporary popular music, especially in the country field. The principal carrier of his legacy in the 1980s is his former partner, Emmylou Harris.

Stephen R. Tucker
Tulane University

Richard Cusick, *Goldmine* (September 1982); Sid Griffin, *Nashville Gazette* (April–June 1980); Judson Klinger and Greg Mitchell, *Crawdaddy* (October 1976).

Peer, Ralph

(1892–1960) Music publisher and talent scout.

Although he was born in Kansas City, Mo. (22 May 1892), and although he never expressed a great fondness for southern folk music, Ralph Sylvester Peer became the single most important entrepreneur for country and blues recordings. He discovered, or was instrumental in the careers of, dozens of southern artists, both black and white, including Louis Armstrong, the Memphis Jug Band, Jimmie Rodgers, the Carter Family, Mamie Smith, the Georgia Yellow Hammers, Fiddlin' John Carson, Ernest Stoneman, Grayson and Whitter (with their initial recording of the murder ballad "Tom Dooley"), the Reverend J. M. Gates (one of the first black preachers to record extensively), the Reverend Andrew Jenkins (a prolific "event song" composer of items like "The Death of Floyd Collins"), and Gene Autry (who began as an imitator of Jimmie Rodgers). He initiated the practice of bringing recording crews into the South to document black and white folk music; he created the idea of having "blues" and "hillbilly" numerical series on commercial phonograph records; he was one of the first to publish and copyright country and blues songs; and he became in the 1930s and 1940s an innovative and trend-setting publisher of international reputation.

Peer's father was a Columbia Record Company phonograph dealer in Independence, Mo., and by the time he was 20, Ralph Peer was working full time in the retail record business. By 1920 he was in New York working for the Okeh Record Company (actually the General Phonograph Corporation), then one of the smaller of the record companies and one looking for ways to get an edge on their bigger competitors. They found one when, on 10 August 1920, Peer recorded black Cincinnati vaudeville performer Mamie Smith singing "Crazy Blues," a composition by a Georgia native named Perry Bradford. The record sold 7,500 copies a week after its release and became the first in a long line of commercial recordings of blues by black artists. Three years later, in June 1923, Peer stumbled into a similar discovery for white folk music; on a field trip to Atlanta he recorded a millhand and radio personality named Fiddlin' John Carson. Peer thought Carson's singing was "pluperfect awful" but agreed to release his rendition of "The Little Old Log Cabin in the Lane," an 1871 pop song by Will Hays. It duplicated the success of "Crazy Blues," and soon Peer had initiated an "old-time music" record series on Okeh to parallel its blues series.

From 1923 to 1932 Peer made dozens of trips into southern cities such as Dallas, El Paso, Nashville, Memphis, Atlanta, New Orleans, Charlotte, Bristol, and others seeking out and recording on the spot hundreds of blues, gospel, jazz, country, Cajun, and Tex-Mex performers. On one such trip, to the Virginia-Tennessee border town of Bristol in August 1927, he discovered two acts that were to become cornerstones for commercial country music—the Carter Family and "blue yodeler" Jimmie Rodgers.

Dominating all of this, though, was Peer's unusual interest in both black and white music, and his perception of ways in which the two could mutually influence each other. He theorized that both genres were just emerging from their vernacular regional base into the national limelight. He encouraged acts like the Allen Brothers, the Carolina Tar Heels, and Jimmie Rodgers to incorporate blues into their music, and felt that this was one of the reasons that Rodgers enjoyed a wider national appeal than did the Carters.

In 1925 Peer left the Okeh Company and went to work for the Victor Company, trading his huge Okeh salary for more modest gains but an additional incentive: the right to control the copyrights on the new song materials recorded by his artists. Peer began to look for artists who could create original material that he could copyright for them and place in his newly formed Southern Music Publishing Company (1928); such artists would get payment not only for records but for song performance rights as well. The increased emphasis on new material encouraged many blues and part-time country singers to become professionals and prompted the music as a whole to become more commercialized. And throughout the 1930s and 1940s he continued to build a publishing empire (which exists today as one of the country's largest, the Peer-Southern organization) and to excel even at casual hobbies, such as horticulture, for which he received a gold medal for his important work. Though in later years he expressed disdain for the country and blues artists he developed ("I've tried so hard to forget them," he told a reporter), and though some of his artists felt that he had exploited them, Peer laid the foundation for the commercialization of American vernacular music and thrust the rich southern folk music tradition into the mainstream of American popular music.

See also INDUSTRY: / Music Industry

Charles K. Wolfe
Middle Tennessee State University

Nolan Porterfield, *Journal of Country Music* (December 1978); Charles K. Wolfe, in *The Illustrated History of Country Music*, ed. Patrick Carr (1979).

Penniman, Richard (Little Richard)

(b. 1933) Rock-and-roll singer.

Born into a large black family in Macon, Ga., on 5 December 1933, Penniman adopted his nickname, Little Richard, about age eight when he began singing at church and school functions. In his early teens Little Richard was performing on the road all across the South. He sang in minstrel shows, attracting audiences and selling snake oil. He sang the blues in bands following migrant workers as far afield as Lake Okeechobee in Florida, and he journeyed into cities to find gay clubs, where he played Princess Lavonne in the first of his several transvestite acts. Before he was 20 he had recorded, with little profit, for RCA twice and for Peacock Records once. These songs were conventional jump blues that made him sound like a melancholy Dinah Washington.

Success came in New Orleans in September 1955 when he joined Robert "Bumps" Blackwell on Specialty Records and made "Tutti Frutti," one of the first and most important rock records. "Tutti Frutti" was a sublimated version of a bawdy song he had performed in sideshows for years but had never considered recordable. He and Blackwell then followed with a series of influential rock-and-roll hits. "Miss Ann" was about loving a white woman and included a 500-year-old rhyming folk riddle from the English oral tradition. "Long Tall Sally," backed with "Slippin' and Slidin'," narrated the antics of standard black folk figures such as John and Aunt Mary, along with more contemporary ones like Sally, who was "built for speed." "Keep a-Knockin'" and "Good Golly Miss Molly" emerged from the randy lore of prostitutes, circuses, and after-hours clubs and was reshaped as pop and teen lore—as when he purred to Molly, "when you rock 'n' roll, can't hear your mother call."

By 1957, however, Little Richard was called away from rock and roll, entered Bible school, and began preaching. Since then he has made several attempts to return to the world of rock and roll that he helped create, and his performance as a rock-and-roll singer in the 1986 movie *Down and Out in Beverly Hills* brought good reviews and new attention. Nevertheless, he has not regained the power he had in the mid-1950s to mine the underground lore of the American South and fix it in an iconic style for the international youth culture.

W. T. Lhamon, Jr.
Florida State University

W. T. Lhamon, Jr., *Studies in Popular Culture* (1985); Charles White, *The Life and Times of Little Richard: The Quasar of Rock* (1984); Langdon Winner, in *The Rolling Stone Illustrated History of Rock 'n' Roll*, ed. Jim Miller (1976).

Powell, John

(1882–1963) Musician and composer.

Powell was born in Richmond, Va., where his father, a schoolteacher, and his mother, an amateur musician, provided his primary musical education at home. He then studied music with his sister and piano and harmony with F. C. Hahr, a one-time student of Liszt. After receiving his B.A. from the University of Virginia in 1901, he studied piano with Theodor Leschetizky in Vienna (1902–7). There he also was a student of composition with Carl Navratil (1904–7). Powell made his debut as a pianist in Berlin in 1907. After four years of giving concerts in Europe, he returned to the United States, touring the country as a pianist and playing some of his own works. He continued to perform for many years in leading cities of Europe and America.

Powell composed many orchestral works, arrangements of folksongs, and choral settings; he also wrote three piano sonatas, one violin concerto, two piano concertos, and an opera, *Judith and Holofernes*. His other works include *Rhapsodie Negre* (piano and orchestra), 1918; *Sonata Virginianesque* (violin and piano), 1919; *In Old Virginia* (overture), 1921; *At the Fair* (suite for piano, also for orchestra), 1925; *Natchez on the Hill* (three country dances for orchestra), 1932; *A Set of Three* (orchestra), 1935; and *Symphony in A* (orchestra), 1947.

One of Powell's most important achievements lies in the area of ethnomusicology. A methodical collector of the South's rural songs, he was the founder of the Virginia State Choral Festival and the moving spirit behind the annual White Top Mountain Folk Music Festival. A member of the National Institute of Arts and Letters, Powell was honored by his native state when Governor John S. Battle designated 5 November 1951 as John Powell Day. Powell died in Charlottesville, Va., in 1963.

For the most part, southerners have contented themselves with inherited music, folksongs, and contemporary tunes. Apart from John Powell of Virginia, southern composers have remained virtually unknown except to other musicians. During the first half of the 20th century, however, Powell received national recognition and acclaim not only as a virtuoso performer of the classical repertoire at home and abroad but also as a composer of distinctively American music. Although Powell utilized Afro-American elements in his *Rhapsodie Negre* and *Sonata Virginianesque*, his abiding concern was with the cultivation of Anglo-American folk music, of which there existed a rich heritage in the South. His Virginian antecedents and environment had given him a profound sense of intimacy with the founders of the American nation.

Powell felt strongly about the value of those Anglo-Saxon cultural and ethical forces that he believed had motivated the molders of the American past; he wished to preserve them for future generations and insure the persistence of those Anglo-Saxon ideals that he regarded as characteristically American. By the early 1920s patient research and study had convinced Powell that American folk music derived from Anglo-Saxon sources was of fundamental importance to the cultural life of the United States and to the development of a truly national school of American music.

L. Moody Simms, Jr.
Illinois State University

Daniel Gregory Mason, *Music in My Time, and Other Reminiscences* (1983); L. Moody Simms, Jr., *Journal of Popular Culture* (Winter 1973).

Preservation Hall

This New Orleans institution celebrates the emergence of jazz as a popular musical innovation in the South. Philadelphians Allan and Sandra Jaffe founded the hall in the early 1960s at the suggestion of (and in property owned by) artist Larry Borenstein. Endeavoring to revitalize the roots of jazz, it has supported a resurgence of interest and activity in classic New Orleans jazz.

At its outset Preservation Hall provided a stage for fine old black jazz musicians who were unemployed. It also resuscitated a nearly extinct institution of musical life in the Crescent City—the community hall. Figures of the New Orleans revival such as George Lewis, Jim Robinson, and Alvin Alcorn took up musical residence there. Repeatedly throughout the past quarter of a century, classic jazz musicians of the city looked to Preservation Hall to renew the old idiom.

Like Perseverance Hall and San Jacinto Hall before it, Preservation Hall serves a total community. It addresses social and economic problems as well as cultural needs of the city's jazz people. The preservationist impulse itself accounts for the fundamental contribution of Preservation Hall. In an effort to preserve jazz, the Jaffes and their associates have recycled it, establishing for a new era the classic jazz aesthetic. The hall has in fact reinvented and revitalized its community for the future by reaching decisively into the past.

Preservation Hall has succeeded by combining imported, updated marketing techniques with an abiding appreciation for local, traditional lifeways. Its success rests in large part upon the generous life support it has provided to old jazz greats. Preservation Hall emerged as part of a national folk revival in the 1950s and 1960s, and its activities have sought from the beginning to underscore the primal claim to jazz of black Americans.

Curtis D. Jerde
W. R. Hogan Jazz Archive
Tulane University

Jason Berry, Jonathan Forse, and Tad Jones, *Up from the Cradle of Jazz: New Orleans Music since World War II* (1987); Al Rose and Edmond Souchon, *New Orleans Jazz: A Family Album* (1967; rev. ed., 1978).

Presley, Elvis

(1935–1977) Rock-and-roll singer.

Presley is probably the most famous southerner of the 20th century. Born in Tupelo, Miss., and reared in Memphis in near poverty, he became an international celebrity and one of the wealthiest entertainers in history.

In 1954 Presley made his first recordings for Sam Phillips's Memphis-based Sun Records in a style that drew from diverse sources—gospel (black and white), blues (rural and urban), and country. In effect, he and his band forged a dynamic new musical synthesis, which later became known as "rockabilly." In 1955, after joining the Louisiana Hayride, a popular country show broadcast from Shreveport, Presley toured extensively throughout the South and acquired a vast and fervent following. National recognition came in 1956 with the success of his first RCA Victor release, "Heartbreak Hotel,"

Elvis Presley, the "King of Rock and Roll," age 22, 1957

a series of network television appearances, and a movie, *Love Me Tender*. He was often the subject of controversy, both for his frantic performances and his conspicuous adoption of black-derived material and musical styles.

From 1956 to 1966, including his celebrated stint in the army (1958–60), Presley dominated popular music. After a brief decline in popularity during the mid-1960s, he began a sustained comeback in 1968 and 1969 with an acclaimed television special and a return to live performances for the first time since 1961.

In the 1970s Presley again became a major figure in American popular culture. As the decade progressed, he often returned to the southern-rooted material and styles of his youth. Songs like "Amazing Grace" (1971), "Promised Land" (1973), and especially "American Trilogy" (1972) dramatized and reiterated Presley's affinity for the South.

His death in 1977 and the subsequent outpouring of public interest in his life and music served to expose the many tensions and contradictions in southern culture, which he had so vividly symbolized. He was insolent yet courteous; narcissistic yet humble; pious (reflecting the Pentecostalism of his childhood) yet often hedonistic, especially in his final years; extremely wealthy yet ever conscious of his poor origins; his diet, accent, name, and most of all, his music, remained indelibly southern. His Memphis home, Graceland (open to the public since 1982), one of the most popular tourist attractions in the South, is an enduring reminder of the quintessentially southern character of Elvis Presley.

Stephen R. Tucker
Tulane University

Greil Marcus, *Mystery Train: Images of America in Rock 'n' Roll Music* (rev. ed., 1982); Dave Marsh, *Elvis* (1982); Jac Tharpe, ed., *Elvis: Images and Fancies* (1979).

Price, Leontyne

(b. 1927) Grand opera and concert singer.

Leontyne Price was born in Laurel, Miss., where she grew up playing the piano and singing in the church choir. She graduated from Oak Park High School in 1944 and Wilberforce College in Ohio four years later. She then attended Juilliard School of Music on a scholarship, with financial aid from the Alexander F. Chisholm family of Laurel. Virgil Thomson selected her to sing the role of Saint Cecilia in a revival of his *Four Saints in Three Acts* on Broadway and at the 1952 International Arts Festival in Paris. After an audition with Ira Gershwin she won the female lead in an important revival of *Porgy and Bess* opposite William Warfield, playing to packed houses from June 1952 until June 1954 on Broadway and a world tour. Composer Samuel Barber asked her in 1953 to sing the premiere of his *Hermit Songs* at the Library of Congress, and in 1954 she gave a Town Hall recital to enthusiastic reviews.

The NBC Opera Theater's production of *Tosca* in January 1955 marked her professional debut in grand opera, although her first performance in a major opera house came two years later in San Francisco, as Madame Lidoine in Poulenc's *Dialogues of the Carmelites*. In succeeding seasons she returned to San Francisco to interpret the title role of Verdi's *Aïda*, Donna Elvira in *Don Giovanni*, Leonora in *Il Trovatore*, the lead in the American premiere of Carl Orff's *The Wise Maiden*, Cio-Cio-San in *Madame Butterfly*, Amelia in *Un Ballo in Maschera*, Leonora in *La Forza del Destino*, Giorgetta in *Il Tabarro*, and the title role of Richard Strauss's *Ariadne auf Naxos*. With the Lyric Opera of Chicago she first sang Massenet's *Thaïs*, one of her few failures, and the role of Liù in Puccini's *Turandot*. She also appeared in Handel's *Julius Caesar* and Monteverdi's *Coronation of Poppea* in concert form with the American Opera Society.

Her Metropolitan Opera debut came on 27 January 1961, as Leonora in Verdi's *Il Trovatore*. In October of that year she became the first black to open a Metropolitan Opera season, appearing as Minnie in Puccini's *La Fanciulla del West*. She later sang Tatyana in *Eugene Onegin*, Pamina in *The Magic Flute*, and Fiordiligi in *Così Fan Tutte* at the Metropolitan, opening the new house at Lincoln Center in Samuel Barber's *Antony and Cleopatra*. She has performed with the Vienna State

Opera, at the Royal Opera House in London, the Paris Opera, La Scala, the Verona Arena, the Berlin Opera, the Hamburg Opera, and Teatro Colon. In 1961 she sang recitals at the World's Fair in Brussels, and she has given concerts throughout the world. She has recorded extensively, including American popular songs and black spirituals. Leontyne Price often returns to Laurel, Miss., and gave one of the first nonsegregated recitals there. She retired after a final performance on 3 January 1985.

Ronald L. Davis
Southern Methodist University

Sir Rudolf Bing, *5000 Nights at the Opera* (1972); Arthur J. Bloomfield, *50 Years of the San Francisco Opera* (1972); Hugh Lee Lyon, *Leontyne Price: Highlights of a Prima Donna* (1973).

Pride, Charley

(b. 1938) Country singer.

A little over a decade after Jackie Robinson broke the color barrier in baseball, Charley Pride accomplished a similar feat in country music. Born in Sledge, Miss., in the depths of the Great Depression to a family of poor cotton laborers, Pride has not only opened new avenues of acceptance to minorities but has set high standards of excellence in the field of country music.

While many blacks in the Mississippi Delta were drawn to the blues, Pride was interested more in country music, especially the songs of Hank Williams. At night he would listen to country music radio programs, memorizing the words of their songs. The only member of his family with any musical inclination, Pride scraped up enough money when he was 14 to buy his first guitar, which he learned to play by listening to different picking styles. (Pride received only $3 per 100 pounds of cotton he picked with his 10 brothers and sisters.) When Pride left Mississippi three years later, he departed not to pursue a career in music but to try for athletic success through baseball.

Pride's luck with baseball was short-lived. After stints with the Memphis Red Sox and Birmingham Black Barons, teams in the Negro American League, and two years in the army in the late 1950s, Pride eventually made it to the minor leagues, playing in 1960 for a team in Helena, Mont. Pride often sang between innings; the response he received from the venture encouraged him to sing more. Through his landlady in Helena, he found his first musical break, singing in a local country bar. Still hungry to play major league baseball, Pride earned a tryout in 1961 from the California Angels. Unable to make the team, he returned to Helena, where he then worked for a refining plant and sang in area nightclubs. The nightclub performances led to an invitation from Red Sovine in 1963 to do a recording audition in Nashville. Pride auditioned in Nashville for Chet Atkins the following year and signed with RCA Victor after the session.

Charley Pride, country music star, 1980s

Since 1965, when he recorded his first hit single, "Snakes Crawl at Night," he has accumulated numerous gold records and country music awards. His first album, *Country Charley Pride* (1966), garnered the 1967 Most Promising Male Artist Award from the Country Song Roundup. (Fearing the album would not sell well in the racially torn South, RCA released *Country Charley Pride* without Pride's picture on the cover.) In 1971 and 1972 he was named Male Vocalist of the Year by the Country Music Association. During the same period he released six albums that became gold and received three Grammy Awards, the first for Best Sacred Performance ("Did You Think to Pray"), the second for Best Gospel Performance ("Let Me Live"), and a third for Best Country Vocal, Male (*Charley Pride Sings Heart Songs*). *Billboard* gave its Trendsetter Award to Pride in 1970. In 1976 he received *Photoplay*'s Gold Medal Award, and in 1980 *Cash Box* named him its Top Male Country Artist of the Decade.

Pride's gold albums include *Country Charley Pride* (1966), *The Country Way* (1968), *Just Plain Charley* (1970), *Charley Pride 10th Album* (1970), *Charley Pride Sings Heart Songs* (1971), *Did You Think to Pray* (1971), and *The Best of Charley Pride, Vol. 2* (1972). Other top albums recorded by Pride are *Charley* (1975), *I'm Just Me* (1977), *You're My Jamaica* (1979), and *There's a Little Bit of Hank in Me* (1980). Over the past three decades he has released gold and top-10 singles such as "I Know One"

(1967), "Does My Ring Hurt Your Finger" (1967), "Let Me Live" (1971), "Did You Think to Pray" (1971), "Amazing Love" (1973), "We Could" (1974), "I Got a Lot of Hank in Me" (1980), "Roll on Mississippi" (1981), and "Never Been So Loved" (1981).

Elizabeth McGehee
Salem College

Melvin Shestack, *The Country Music Encyclopedia* (1974); Irwin Stambler and Grellin Landon, *The Encyclopedia of Folk, Country and Western Music* (1969; 2d ed., 1983); *Who's Who among Americans* (1982); *Who's Who among Black Americans* (1975).

Redding, Otis

(1941–1967) Soul singer.

Otis Redding epitomized the sound of soul music in the South in the 1960s. The "Big O," as he came to be known, was born in 1941 in Dawson, Ga., and was raised in nearby Macon, one of six children of a Baptist minister. Singing in church throughout his youth, Redding became increasingly fascinated by the rhythm-and-blues and rock-and-roll sounds to be heard on Macon radio, especially those of local luminary Little Richard, the Georgia Peach.

By 1956 Redding was playing locally with Johnny Jenkins and the Pinetoppers; by 1957 he was managed by Phil Walden (later of Allman Brothers and Capricorn Records fame); by 1958 he was married; and by 1960 he had cut his first single, "Shout Bamalama" for Bethlehem Records. The single revealed an exciting singer who had yet to grow beyond Little Richard imitation.

Deciding to try his luck elsewhere, Redding moved to California. He spent six months washing cars and recording two more singles, one for Finer Arts, the other for Alshire, both of which flopped. Back in Macon, Redding hooked up with guitarist Jenkins once again. The latter attracted the attention of Atlantic Records through a local hit entitled "Love Twist." Atlantic arranged for Jenkins to record at the still largely unknown Stax Studio in Memphis in 1962, and Redding was able to record "These Arms of Mine" and "Hey, Hey Baby" at the end of the session. Jenkins's material remains unissued; Redding's recording became his first single and launched a career that was to end on 10 December 1967 when his plane, en route from Cleveland, Ohio, to Madison, Wis., plunged into Lake Minona. All the original members of his band, the Bar Kays, died in the crash with Redding save Ben Cauley and James Alexander. His funeral, held nine days later in Macon, was attended by 6,000 fans and a who's who of soul musicians and singers. He was survived by his wife Zelma and their three children.

Between 1962 and 1967 Redding recorded prolifically. He was able to adapt to almost any material, recording songs as diverse as Bing Crosby's "Try a Little Tenderness" and the Rolling Stones' "Satisfaction," as well as a host of originals that are now standards such as "Respect" and "I've Been Loving You Too Long." In contrast with many of the soul singers of the period, Redding was equally at home with ballads and up-tempo dance numbers. Many of the original compositions were co-written with Steve Cropper, the guitarist for the Stax house band Booker T. and the MG's. Cropper also produced Redding's records and, on most of these, the MG's coupled with the Bar Kays' horns provided the backup. Cropper was white, as were half of the Stax session musicians. This relatively rare musical integration was a large factor in making southern soul from Memphis and Muscle Shoals, Ala., so distinctive in the 1960s.

Redding's single style was immediately recognizable. His voice had a "catch" to it, and he was a master of timbral and dynamic variation and of rhythmic subtlety. In contrast to most soul performers, Redding never employed backup vocalists on his recordings. A typical record such as "Try a Little Tenderness" continually adds instruments as it progresses, with everyone gradually playing louder while the rate of activity increases, Redding's voice becomes strained, the plane of sound gradually shifts upward, the amount of call and responses increases, and, finally, the tension is released through a syncopated drum break over which Redding is so emotionally charged that he is reduced to singing vocables.

Live, Redding was the classic soul performer. He was always in action, continually sweating, discarding superfluous clothes as the performance went on. He generally used Booker T. and the MG's or the Bar Kays as a backup band, but, as with the material, the type or quality of band did not really affect him.

He toured extensively from 1964 to 1967, achieving 17 hits on the rhythm-and-blues charts in the process (seven more Otis Redding records hit after his death). He had formed his own label, Jotis, recording Billy Young, Loretta Williams, and Arthur Conley, and he had also developed his own publishing company, Redwal Music. Redding was successful in Europe and was just starting to break through to the American white audience at the time of his death. Six months prior to that he had had a widely successful performance at the Monterey Pop Festival, and the song he was working on at the time of his death, "(Sittin on) The Dock of the Bay," ironically became his first number-one hit. It reflected a somewhat softer sound and, perhaps, indicated a new direction.

Robert Bowman
Memphis, Tennessee

Clive Anderson, in *The Soul Book*, ed. Ian Hoare (1975); Gerri Hirshey, *Nowhere To Run: The Story of Soul Music* (1984); Jane Schiesel, *The Otis Redding Story* (1973).

Revival Songs

The poetry and music of revivalism have been a major influence in American popular culture, especially in the South. In the first camp meetings around 1800, preachers found the psalms and hymns of congregational worship inadequate: traditional hymns did not sufficiently emphasize the individual's quest for salvation through specific stages (conviction, conversion, assurance) recognized by revival preachers; moreover, hymnbooks were of little use in largely illiterate gatherings, often held at night. In response to the camp-meeting environment, Americans created two major forms of popular religious song during the period from 1810 to 1860.

"Camp-meeting songs," or "spiritual songs," were strophic poems, often in narrative form, stressing the stages of conversion and often referring to various groups at camp meetings: preachers, exhorters, mourners, backsliders, and young converts, as in the following stanza from George Atkin's "Holy Manna":

Is there here a trembling jailer,
Seeking grace, and fill'd with fears?
Is there here a weeping Mary,
Pouring forth a flood of tears?
Brethren, join your cries to help them;
Sisters, let your prayers abound;
Pray, O pray that holy manna
May be scatter'd all around.

Written in a great variety of poetic meters, these songs were often set to secular tunes, including those of folksongs, traditional dances, military marches, and popular theater airs.

"Revival spiritual songs," or "choruses," consisted of couplets or quatrains, often taken from British evangelical hymnody, alternating with refrains:

On Jordan's stormy banks I stand,
And cast a wishful eye,
To Canaan's fair and happy land,
Where my possessions lie. [Samuel Stennant]
CHORUS: I am bound for the promised land,
I'm bound for the promised land,
Oh, who will come and go with me?
I am bound for the promised land.

Often elements of the revival chorus appear between the lines of the original hymn:

I know that my redeemer lives,
Glory, hallelujah.
What comfort that sweet sentence gives,
[Samuel Medley]
Glory, hallelujah,
CHORUS: Shout on, pray on, we're getting ground,
Glory, hallelujah,
The dead's alive, and the lost is found.
Glory, hallelujah.

Revival spiritual songs, with their call-and-response patterns, met the need for a flexible format in which new songs could be created and learned immediately by a large gathering.

Camp-meeting songsters, books containing revival poetry, were first published around 1810. The first southern collection of music for camp-meeting songs was Ananias Davisson's *Supplement to the Kentucky Harmony* (Harrisonburg, Va., 1820). Davisson's book, designed for "his Methodist friends," contained many camp-meeting songs and a few revival choruses. During the 1840s the music of many more revival spiritual songs was printed in southern tunebooks, including B. F. White and E. J. King's *The Sacred Harp* (1844) and William Houser's *The Hesperian Harp* (1848). After the Civil War, the black spiritual emerged, essentially the same as the revival spiritual, despite differences in the date and circumstances of its notation. Indeed, the prevalence of call-and-response forms in Afro-American music and the presence of blacks at early camp meetings suggest that mutual influences may have played a role in the spiritual song traditions of both races.

The revival movements of the late 19th century favored a new style of music based on urban models, especially the sentimental parlor song. "Gospel hymns" like "Sweet By and By" (S. F. Bennett and J. P. Webster) and "Leaning on the Everlasting Arms" (E. A. Hoffman and A. J. Showalter) have reached beyond the revival context. Many have entered the Sunday worship of southern denominations, where they are considered "old standard" hymns, to the virtual exclusion of the camp-meeting genres that preceded them. Late 19th-century gospel hymns were also the model for the flourishing repertoire of shape-note gospel convention and quartet music.

David Warren Steel
University of Mississippi

Dickson D. Bruce, Jr., *And They All Sang Hallelujah: Plain-Folk Camp-Meeting Religion, 1800–1845* (1974); George Pullen Jackson, *White Spirituals in the Southern Uplands* (1933); Ellen Jane Lorenz, *Glory, Hallelujah! The Story of the Camp-meeting Spiritual* (1978).

Rodgers, Jimmie

(1897–1933) Country singer.

Generally acknowledged as "The Father of Country Music," James Charles "Jimmie" Rodgers, who was born 8 September 1897 in Meridian, Miss., was a major influence on the emerging "hillbilly" recording industry almost from the time of his first records in 1927. Although Rodgers initially conceived of himself in broader terms, singing Tin Pan Alley hits and popular standards, his intrinsic musical talent was deeply rooted in the rural southern environment out of which he came, as seen in the titles of many of his songs: "My Carolina Sunshine Girl," "My Little Old Home Down in New Orleans,"

Jimmie Rodgers, the "Father of Country Music," 1929

"Dear Old Sunny South by the Sea," "Mississippi River Blues," "Peach Pickin' Time Down in Georgia," "Memphis Yodel," "In the Hills of Tennessee," the original "Blue Yodel" ("T for Texas"), and others.

In adapting the black country blues of his native South to the nascent patterns of commercial hillbilly music of the day, Rodgers created a unique new form—the famous "blue yodel"—which led the way to further innovations in style and subject matter and exerted a lasting influence on country music as both art form and industry. Through the force of his magnetic personality and showmanship, Rodgers almost single-handedly established the role of the singing star, influencing such later performers as Gene Autry, Hank Williams, Ernest Tubb, George Jones, and Willie Nelson.

The son of a track foreman for the Mobile & Ohio Railroad, Rodgers in his twenties worked as a brakeman for many railroads in the South and West. Stricken by tuberculosis in 1924, he left the rails soon after to pursue his childhood dream of becoming a professional entertainer. After several years of hard knocks and failure, he gained an audition with Ralph Peer, an independent producer who had set up a temporary recording studio in Bristol, Tenn., for the Victor Talking Machine Company (later RCA Victor). There, on 4 August 1927, Rodgers made his first recordings. Within a year he reached national popularity and received billing as "The Singing Brakeman" and "America's Blue Yodeler." In 1929 he built a home in the resort town of Kerrville, Tex., and moved there in an effort to restore his failing health. The onset of the Depression and increasing illness further slowed the progress of his career, but throughout the early 1930s he continued to record and perform with touring stage shows. By the time of his death in New York City at 35 in May 1933, he had recorded 110 titles, representing a diverse repertoire that included almost every type of song now identified with country music: love ballads, honky-tonk tunes, railroad and hobo songs, cowboy songs, novelty numbers, and the series of 13 blue yodels. In November 1961 Rodgers became the first performer elected to Nashville's Country Music Hall of Fame, immortalized as "the man who started it all."

Nolan Porterfield
Cape Girardeau, Missouri

Bill C. Malone, *Country Music, U.S.A.: A Fifty-year History* (1968); Nolan Porterfield, *Jimmie Rodgers: The Life and Times of America's Blue Yodeler* (1979); Mrs. Jimmie Rodgers, *My Husband, Jimmie Rodgers* (1975).

Scruggs, Earl

(b. 1924) Bluegrass musician.

Earl Eugene Scruggs was born on 6 January 1924, in Cleveland County, N.C., on a farm near the small community of Flint Hill. He was the youngest of five children. His father, who played the banjo, died when Scruggs was four; his mother, brothers, and sisters all played music. By the time he was six he was playing string band music with his brothers. Scruggs learned fiddle and guitar but specialized in the five-string banjo. Before he was a teenager he had developed a distinctive three-finger picking style based on that of older men in his neighborhood. In his teens Scruggs played locally with professional bands, but World War II put a temporary end to this; he worked in a textile mill until 1945. In December 1945 he became a member of Bill Monroe's Blue Grass Boys on WSM's Grand Ole Opry. In personal appearances and recordings with Monroe, Scruggs created a sensation with his banjo playing, and he quickly became one of the most emulated instrumentalists in country music.

In 1948 Scruggs left Monroe and teamed up with his partner in the Blue Grass Boys, guitarist-singer Lester Flatt, to form the Foggy Mountain Boys. In 1953, after modest beginnings on small radio stations, their broadcast career was given a considerable boost by the sponsorship of a flour manufacturer, Martha White Mills. In 1955 they joined the cast of the Grand Ole Opry, where they became one of its most popular and widely traveled acts. During the late 1950s they were responsible for popularizing "bluegrass" with folk music audiences outside the South. Their greatest exposure came through their association in 1962 with the popular CBS television series *The Beverly Hillbillies,* for which they recorded the theme and incidental music. Many of their Mercury (1948–50) and Columbia (1951–69) recordings are still available. A key figure in the success of Flatt and Scruggs was Earl's wife, Louise Certain Scruggs, who acted as the band's booking agent and publicist, a role she still performs for her husband.

In 1969 Scruggs and Flatt separated. Earl began performing with sons Gary and Randy, and by 1972 they had organized as the Earl Scruggs Revue. With his banjo amplified, Earl fronted a band that featured country-rock repertoire and sound. The Revue (which eventually included another son, Steve) toured successfully throughout the 1970s, playing to younger, more urban audiences than those for which he and Flatt had performed. They recorded 16 albums for Columbia. By 1980 Scruggs was working as a single act, recording and appearing with various musicians, including the Dillards, Tom T. Hall, and Ricky Skaggs.

In 1971 Scruggs was closely involved with the conception and production of the award-winning album *Will the Circle Be Unbroken* (United Artists UAS 9801), which brought together members of the California rock group the Nitty Gritty Dirt Band with pioneer Nashville musicians. In this and other activities he has shown an interest in bridging the social and musical gaps between the rural South of his youth and the urbanized world of his sons.

Neil V. Rosenberg
Memorial University
St. Johns, Newfoundland

Neil V. Rosenberg, *Bluegrass: A History* (1985), in *Stars of Country Music,* ed. Bill C. Malone and Judith McCullough (1975); Earl Scruggs, *Earl Scruggs and the 5-String Banjo* (1968).

Shape-Note Singing Schools

The singing school was early America's most important musical institution. It offered a brief course in musical sight reading and choral singing, was taught by a singing master according to traditional methods, and used tunebooks that were printed manuals containing instructions, exercises, and sacred choral music. Singing schools arose from British antecedents around 1700 as part of an effort to reform congregational singing in colonial churches. In New England the movement grew quickly and culminated in the first school of American composers and in the publication of hundreds of sacred tunebooks (1770–1810). Singing schools existed in the South as early as 1710, when they are mentioned in the diary of William Byrd II of Virginia. The movement spread during the 18th century as a pious diversion among affluent planters along the Atlantic Seaboard. After the Revolutionary War, itinerant Yankee singing masters established singing schools in the inland and rural South. Both Andrew Law (1749–1821) of Connecticut and Lucius Chapin (1760–1842) of Massachusetts were teaching in Virginia by the 1780s; in 1794 Chapin moved to Kentucky, where he taught for 40 years. Singing schools offered young southerners a rare chance to socialize. Even today, many older southerners associate singing schools with their courting days.

The spread of singing schools through the South was aided by the invention of shape or patent notes. This system, first published by William Little and William Smith in *The Easy Instructor* (Philadelphia, 1801), used four distinctive note heads to indicate the four syllables denoting tones of a musical scale (*fa, sol, la* and *mi*) then employed in vocal instruction, making unnecessary the pupil's need to learn and memorize key signatures. Denounced by critics as uncouth, the simplified notation caught on in the South and West, where it became standard for sacred-music publication. In 1816 Ananias Davisson (1780–1857) and Joseph Funk (1777–1862), both of Rockingham County, Va., became the first southern singing masters to compile and publish their own tunebooks. By 1860 more than 30 sacred tunebooks, all in shape notes, had been compiled by southerners, although many of these were printed outside the South at Cincinnati or Philadelphia. One of the most popular of these was *The Southern Harmony,* by William Walker of Spartanburg, S.C.: 600,000 copies were sold between 1835 and the beginning of the Civil War. *The Sacred Harp* (1844), by Georgia singing masters B. F. White and E. J. King, is still in print and is the basis of a flourishing musical tradition in six southern states.

Southern singing masters continued to teach the music of their Yankee predecessors but also introduced "folk hymns," melodies from oral tradition which they harmonized in a native idiom and set to sacred words. Many, including tunes for "Amazing Grace" and "How Firm a Foundation," have remained popular and have become symbols of rural southern religion. Camp-meeting and revival songs with new refrains also formed part of the southern tunebook repertoire, especially after 1840. Southern singing masters established organizations such as the Southern Musical Association (1845) and the Chattahoochie Musical Association (1852, still active). These and other state and local conventions provided a forum where established teachers met to sing together, to examine and certify new teachers, and to demonstrate the accomplishments of their classes.

After the Civil War, singing schools and shape notes became increasingly identified with the South, while declining in popularity in other regions. Most teachers switched from the four-shape system to a seven-shape system to keep pace with new teaching methods. Leading singing masters established "normal schools" for the training of teachers. Periodicals such as *The Musical Million* (Dayton, Va., 1870–1915) helped to link teachers in many areas of the South. Small, cheap collections of music published every year began to supplant the large tunebooks with their fixed repertoire. Although folk hymns and revival songs continued to be published, gospel hymns derived from urban models entered the southern tradition.

In the 20th century, singing schools have declined over

most of the region but have survived in a few areas. They seldom last more than two weeks of evening classes and may be as brief as one week. Pupils pay at least a token fee, but few teachers, if any, attempt to make a living as singing masters. Contemporary singing schools fall into three categories: (1) "Tunebook" schools are associated with surviving 19th-century books such as *The Sacred Harp* or *The Christian Harmony*. These schools preserve much of the 18th-century American repertoire and performance practice. (2) Denominational schools are sponsored by churches, especially by those (Primitive Baptist, Church of Christ) that prohibit instrumental music in their worship. These schools use denominational hymnals, and, like their 18th-century predecessors, attempt to train skilled sight-readers for congregational singing. (3) Shape-note gospel singing schools are associated with the "little-book" seven-shape gospel repertoire. These schools, often sponsored by local singing conventions or by publishing companies, have declined since mid-century as community "sings" have been replaced by quartet performances. All three types of singing schools are regarded by their adherents as important means of transmitting musical knowledge, skills, and traditions to future generations.

David Warren Steel
University of Mississippi

Buell E. Cobb, Jr., *The Sacred Harp: A Tradition and Its Music* (1978); Harry Eskew, "Shape-Note Hymnody in the Shenandoah Valley, 1816–1860" (Ph.D. dissertation, Tulane University, 1966); George Pullen Jackson, *White Spirituals in the Southern Uplands* (1933).

Smith, Bessie

(1894–1937) Blues singer.

When Bessie Smith made her first recordings, in 1923, she carved for herself a permanent niche in blues and jazz history. By that time, her magnificent voice, captured by the relatively primitive acoustical equipment of the day, was already well known and greatly admired throughout the South.

Born in Chattanooga, Tenn., 15 April 1894, Smith had her first show-business experience when she was about eight: accompanied by her brother Andrew with his guitar, she danced and sang for small change on a Ninth Street corner. Another brother, Clarence, in 1912 arranged for her to join a traveling troupe led by Moses Stokes. With this company, which also included Gertrude "Ma" Rainey, Bessie Smith launched her professional career.

Within a year Bessie Smith had left the Stokes troupe and started to build a faithful following among southern theater audiences, especially in Atlanta, where she became a regular attraction at the "81" Theater. In the 1920s, she rose to the pinnacle of her profession and became the highest-paid black entertainer of her day. So great was her popularity that her appearances caused serious traffic jams around theaters from Detroit to New Orleans. During eight years as an exclusive Columbia Records artist, she made 156 sides, some of which saved that company from bankruptcy, and all of which, over a half century later, are still in catalogs throughout the world.

Promotional hype dubbed her "Empress of the Blues," and the title remains unchallenged, but Bessie Smith was not restricted to that idiom. She was, along with Louis Armstrong, the consummate jazz singer, and her majestic delivery became a major inspiration to such successful and diverse singers as Billie Holiday, Mahalia Jackson, and Janis Joplin.

A victim of the Great Depression, new musical trends, and a changing entertainment scene, Bessie Smith saw her career plummet in the early 1930s, but it was on the upswing as the decade went into its last lap. Sadly, the great singer was not to enjoy the comeback that seemed inevitable in 1937, nor would she ever know the enormous impact of her artistry on American music. On 26 September 1937, as she traveled from Memphis for an appearance in Clarksdale, Miss., a car accident took her life. Her tragic death inspired contemporary playwright Edward Albee's drama, *The Death of Bessie Smith*.

Chris Albertson
New York, New York

Chris Albertson, *Bessie* (1972).

Still, William Grant

(1895–1978) Musician and composer.

Known as the "dean of Afro-American composers," Still spent more than 50 years composing, conducting, and playing music that reflected a fusion of his spiritual and musical imagination, his diverse ethnic ancestry, and 20th-century American culture.

His mother came from black, Spanish, Indian, and Irish stock and his father from black, Indian, and Scotch stock. Still was born on 11 May 1895, on a Woodville, Miss., plantation near the Mississippi River. He lived there only nine months before his father, a teacher and bandleader, died, and his mother moved the family to Little Rock, Ark., where she began teaching. When Still was nine, his mother married a postal clerk who entered Still's life with a Victrola and opera records. The voice of Still's maternal grandmother filled their home with spirituals. He later wrote, "I knew neither wealth nor poverty, for I lived in a comfortable middle class home."

Still left home to study at Wilberforce University. His mother wanted him to be a physician, but Still had already taught himself to play the violin and wanted to be a musician. He left Wilberforce for the navy during World War I, eventually returning, against his mother's wishes, to study music at Oberlin College. He worked as a young musician with W. C. Handy in Memphis and

New York, played the oboe in Eubie Blake's band, and orchestrated for Paul Whiteman and Artie Shaw. In the 1920s he studied composition with George W. Chadwick at the New England Conservatory and in New York with the French ultramodernist Edgar Varèse, who led Still into a dissonant, melodic, and traditional style, reflecting his black heritage. "I made an effort to elevate the folk idiom into symphonic form," Still said. Two Guggenheim Fellowships allowed him to concentrate on composition in the 1930s.

As a black man, Still achieved many "firsts." He wrote the theme for the 1939 New York World's Fair. He conducted WOR's all-white radio orchestra in New York. In 1931, when composer Howard Hanson conducted Still's *Afro-American Symphony* in Rochester, Still became the first black to have written a symphony performed by a major orchestra. In 1936 he was the first black to conduct a major orchestra, the Los Angeles Philharmonic, and two decades later, leading the New Orleans Symphony, he became the first black to conduct a major orchestra in the Deep South.

During the 1940s, when he wrote "And They Lynched Him on a Tree" and "In Memoriam: The Colored Soldiers Who Died for Democracy," his works sounded a social conscience theme. For violin and piano, he wrote Peruvian and Mexican ballads. His operas, with the libretto often written by his wife Verna Arvey, told of Haiti, Spanish colonial America, Africa, and roadside, gas-station life in America. Poet Langston Hughes wrote the libretto for Still's *Troubled Island*. Still lived in Los Angeles, and Hollywood benefited from his presence. He arranged for Columbia and Warner Brothers and wrote the scores for the *Perry Mason* and *Gunsmoke* television series and for the films *Lost Horizons* and *Pennies from Heaven*.

In addition to the Guggenheim Fellowships, Still received honorary degrees and many awards. In 1974 Still's *A Bayou Legend* opera premiered in Jackson, Miss., and Governor Bill Waller named Still a "distinguished Mississippian." Though not a churchgoer, on every composition he wrote, "With humble thanks to God, the Source of inspiration." At age 83, on 3 December 1978, Still died in Los Angeles from a heart ailment.

Berkley Hudson
Providence, Rhode Island

Robert Bartlett Haas, ed., *William Grant Still and the Fusion of Cultures in American Music* (1972); *The Black Perspective in Music* (May 1975).

String Band Tradition

Primarily a mid-19th and 20th century phenomenon, string bands have been, and continue to be, one of the South's major folk musical ensemble forms. They derive from both Anglo- and Afro-American musical cultures, although they are more frequently associated with whites than with blacks. String bands consist of a number of musicians, generally from three to six, most of whom play acoustic stringed instruments. The fiddle, present in the South from the earliest days of colonization, and the banjo, an instrument that developed in the 19th century from African roots, are typically the core instruments, usually joined by at least one guitar, an instrument that grew in popularity during the early years of this century. Although these are the major instruments, it is not at all uncommon to find others, including the mandolin, string bass, and piano. If there are vocalists—and there usually are—they are inevitably also instrumentalists.

A string band usually has in its repertoire a large number of tunes for square dancing, songs generally representative of the broad corpus of southern folksong, and recent country hit songs. The music is infectious, with fiddles speeding through the melody, propelled by a banjo played in an old-time "rapping" or "knocking" style and a guitar or two accentuating the beat with chords and connecting runs. Instrumental styles tend to be regionally defined. Singing is generally solo, although more modern harmonic vocal techniques are used increasingly.

String bands dominated the first decade of country music recordings, indicating the music's deep-seated ties to and familiarity within local communities. Groups had such colorful names as the Skillet Lickers, Dr. Smith's Champion Hoss Hair Pullers, Fisher Hendley and His Aristocratic Pigs, and Seven Foot Dilly and His Dill Pickles. By the mid- and late 1930s, though, the form had become less profitable for the record companies. Bands continued to be part of their communities, playing for such occasions as dances, picnics, and house parties. Their influence continues, providing a substantial foundation for string-based musical styles such as bluegrass and western swing. Many of the old "hillbilly" records from the 1920s and 1930s have been reissued and are available from specialty record dealers.

In recent years young musicians in the United States and abroad have taken up the string-band styles. Ironically, this string-band revival has been slow to come to the South, but its force is being felt increasingly. And the "old" bands, many of which never went away, continue to play.

Burt Feintuch
Western Kentucky University

Bill C. Malone, *Country Music, U.S.A.: A Fifty-year History* (1968), *Southern Music—American Music* (1979); Charles K. Wolfe, *Tennessee Strings: The Story of Country Music in Tennessee* (1977).

Sun Records

Johnny Cash, Jerry Lee Lewis, Roy Orbison, Carl Perkins, and Elvis Presley are among many musicians who first recorded their music at Sun Records. The most successful went on to record for larger companies, such as RCA and Columbia, but it was their early songs on the Sun label that launched their careers and reshaped southern and American popular music.

Sam Phillips was the founder of the Sun Record Company. Born in 1923 in Florence, Ala., he heard black gospel music and blues throughout his childhood. He became a disc jockey at radio station WLAY in Muscle Shoals and then worked in Decatur, Ala., at WLAC in Nashville, and at WREC in Memphis. In 1955 he cofounded the nation's first successful all-female radio station, WHER in Memphis. While he was still in Muscle Shoals, though, he took a correspondence course that led to his certification in radio engineering. This skill, together with his interest in black music, prompted him to open the Memphis Recording Service so that black southern blues artists would have a place to record their music. The studio was in a converted radiator shop on Union Avenue.

Phillips initially stayed in business by recording weddings, funerals, and speeches. When he recorded musicians' performances, he often leased the recordings to Jules and Saul Bihari, who sold them on their Modern and RPM labels, or to Leonard Chess, who owned the Chess label. During this time, Phillips made the first recordings of B. B. King, Howlin' Wolf, and other black singers who later became famous. He also recorded "Rocket 88," a highly successful song that has been called the first rock-and-roll hit. By 1952, however, legal disputes and competition from larger recording companies that lured his talented musicians away frustrated Phillips and convinced him to start his own label.

Early in 1952 the Memphis Recording Service became the Sun Record Company. It released its first record on 1 March 1952 but did not produce a hit until a year later when Rufus Thomas recorded "Bear Cat." The company's second hit was "Just Walkin' in the Rain" sung by the Prisonaires, a group of black inmates at the state penitentiary. During the label's first years, Phillips primarily recorded black artists, but he sought to record black music performed by white singers, who would make the music acceptable to a wider audience. Ultimately, Sun's combination of white country music sung with a black rhythm-and-blues feel broadened the scope of American music and brought Sun Records the sound for which it became famous.

This "rockabilly" music was made most popular by Elvis Presley, whose first recordings were two Ink Spots numbers in 1953. Not pleased with the result, Phillips had Presley work with guitarist Scott Moore and bassist Bill Black and, in 1954, released Presley's first professional record, which contained the songs "That's All Right (Mama)" and "Blue Moon of Kentucky." It was immediately successful, and Presley recorded eight more songs for Sun before Phillips sold Presley's contract to RCA in 1955 for $35,000 plus $5,000 more for back royalties owed to the singer. The sum was an unprecedented amount in the business and provided Sun the financial stability to work with and record other white southern musicians, like Johnny Cash, Jerry Lee Lewis, Roy Orbison, and Carl Perkins.

With a spontaneous feel, an echo effect, and a simple, crisp, aggressive sound, Sun's recordings established several of its unknown artists as stars. Early in 1956 Carl Perkins's "Blue Suede Shoes" became a tremendous success, making the company solvent for the first time. Cash's first hit was "I Walk the Line" in the fall of 1956, and Sun produced Roy Orbison's early recordings during the same year. Then, during 1957 and 1958, Jerry Lee Lewis proved profitable to Sun with his hits "Whole Lotta Shakin' Going On," "Great Balls of Fire," and "Breathless." Sun's subsidiary, the Phillips International label, produced major hits by Carl Mann and Charlie Rich.

In the early 1960s production was much less active and Sun's recordings appealed more to a local audience than to a national one. Cash, Perkins, and Orbison had all moved to larger recording companies, and Lewis left in 1962. Phillips retired in 1968 and, in the following year, sold a controlling interest in Sun to Shelby S. Singleton of Nashville. The sale brought the formation of the Sun International Corporation, headquartered in Nashville, and the transfer of the nearly 3,000 master tapes and the original record catalogs by Sun artists (excluding Presley, whose materials had previously been transferred to RCA).

The landmark Sun era had ended, but not before rejuvenating American popular music. Under the direction of Sam Phillips, Sun's artists established the rockabilly sound and the roots of rock and roll. Phillips and his company made this possible by nurturing the talents of southern artists; by marketing their music through 43 independent record distributors and an overseas distribution affiliate in London; and, most importantly, by concentrating on and developing a southern musical tradition.

Jessica Foy
Cooperstown Graduate Programs
Cooperstown, New York

Colin Escott and Martin Hawkins, *Catalyst: The Sun Records Story* (1975); Peter Guralnick, *Feel Like Going Home: Portraits in Blues and Rock 'n' Roll* (1971), *Lost Highway: Journeys and Arrivals of American Musicians* (1979); Brock Helander, *The Rock Who's Who* (1982); Robert Palmer, *Memphis* (December 1978); Barbara Sims, *John Edwards Memorial Foundation Quarterly* (Autumn 1976); *Variety* (25 June 1969).

Sweeney, Joel Walker

(c. 1810–1860) Musician.

Until recently, "Joe" Sweeney enjoyed legendary status as the "inventor" of the five-string banjo. As a boy, Sweeney learned to play the banjo from slaves on his father's farm, where he was born near present-day Appomattox, Va. According to the legend, he improved their

African-derived instrument by fashioning a wooden hoop to replace the original gourd body, and, more importantly, by adding (around 1831) a short, high-pitched fifth (or thumb) string to the original four. The long-held claim that he thus invented the five-string banjo is supported by little documentary evidence, and recent informed opinion challenges it, primarily on the basis of illustrations clearly showing that some slave banjos had short thumb strings well before Sweeney was born. Slave banjos were undoubtedly quite variable in form, so Sweeney's real claim to fame is that he so popularized the particular form he grew up with that it became the standard. He was certainly the first documented white banjo player.

In the 1830s he traveled widely in the South performing, in blackface, the music of his black mentors; and he became a mentor himself, apparently teaching a number of the early, influential minstrel banjo players. In the 1840s he became a national celebrity, performing first with circuses and then with minstrel shows in northern cities; between 1843 and 1845 he toured and performed in England, reputedly including a performance for Queen Victoria. His brother, Sam, also an accomplished banjo player, was Jeb Stuart's personal minstrel during the Civil War. Joel Sweeney played a critical role in making the banjo an important and permanent part of southern music, especially in initiating and encouraging its widespread use by whites.

Robert B. Winans
Wayne State University

Gene Bluestein, *Western Folklore* (Winter 1964); Burke Davis, *The Iron Worker* (Autumn 1969); Scott Odell, in *New Grove Dictionary of Music and Musicians*, vol. 2, ed. Stanley Sadie (1980); Arthur Woodward, *Los Angeles County Museum Quarterly* (Spring 1949).

Tubb, Ernest

(1914–1984) Country singer.

Ernest Tubb was a major personality in country music from the early 1940s to his death on 6 September 1984. He was a much admired and imitated vocal stylist, a pioneer in the popularization of the electric guitar, a patron of young talent, and one of the leading architects of the popular honky-tonk style of country music.

Tubb was born on 9 February 1914 in the tiny community of Crisp, Tex., about 40 miles south of Dallas. Like many young fledgling musicians of his era, Tubb fell in love with the music of Jimmie Rodgers, and for many years he affected a singing-and-yodeling style that was quite similar to that of the Mississippi Blue Yodeler. He never met his hero, but in 1936 Carrie Rodgers, Jimmie's widow, became Tubb's champion. She loaned him one of Rodgers's guitars, helped him obtain bookings in south Texas, and persuaded the Victor Company to sign Tubb to a contract. The Victor affiliation resulted in eight recordings but brought Tubb little money or fame.

Success did not really come to Tubb until the early 1940s. In 1940 he made the first of his recordings with Decca (an association that lasted until 1975); he began performing on KGKO in Fort Worth and touring for Universal Mills as the Texas Troubadour; and in 1941 he recorded the enduringly popular "Walking the Floor over You." On the strength of the song's popularity, Tubb was invited to join the cast of the Grand Ole Opry, becoming a permanent member of the show in January 1943. Tubb's move to Nashville was symbolic and representative of the growing influence of "western" styles in country music. He was one of the first musicians to bring an electric guitar to the stage of the Grand Ole Opry, an innovation that had already been heard on his records and in his Texas personal appearances. Tubb was a leading record seller and popular concert attraction in country music until the mid-1950s (when rock and roll and country-pop music emerged); and long after that period he continued to be one of the most active in-person performers in country music, averaging close to 300 personal appearances a year until the late 1970s.

Because of his evident commercial viability, Tubb was able to exert great influence in the country music field. He played a prime role in persuading his industry to replace the word "hillbilly" with "country"; he was one of the first country singers to make records with other established performers (such as the Andrews Sisters, Red Foley, and Loretta Lynn); he and his band of musicians, the Texas Troubadours, made crucial contributions to the development of the honky-tonk style of performance; and he provided encouragement and support to many younger entertainers such as Hank Williams, Johnny Cash, Loretta Lynn, Jack Greene, Willie Nelson, and Cal Smith. Tubb's admission to the Country Music Hall of Fame in 1965 was warmly endorsed.

Bill C. Malone
Tulane University

Ronnie Floyd Pugh, *Journal of Country Music* (December 1978, 1981), "The Texas Troubadours: Selected Aspects of the Career of Ernest Tubb" (M.A. thesis, Stephen F. Austin State University, 1978).

Vaughan, James D.

(1864–1941) Gospel music promoter.

James D. Vaughan played a major role in the popularization of gospel music in America during the first half of the 20th century. His promotion company, the James D. Vaughan Company, was founded in 1912 in the middle Tennessee community of Lawrenceburg and remained in operation until 1964.

Vaughan's enterprise began as a singing school and then was expanded to include sales of records, songbooks, and magazines. His first songbook, *Gospel Chimes*, was published under his own name in 1900. His company eventually published 105 songbooks, which enjoyed successful nationwide sales. Vaughan was a creative businessman who sent male vocal quartets to churches around the country to promote his music and books. He started one of the first commercial radio stations in Tennessee, WOAN, to play his music and plug his songbooks. In 1922 one of the Vaughan quartets made a recording of their music, and, although it was not made in the South, the record was one of the first specifically designed for a southern audience.

A devout member of the Church of the Nazarene, Vaughan was influential in the development and spread of gospel music from the 1920s through the 1960s. Vaughan helped preserve the shape-note singing tradition, and his gospel music helped lay the foundation for American country music. The gospel songbooks that Vaughan distributed had a profound impact on southern cultural life. Singing schools and conventions and gospel singing at church-related functions were immensely popular through the 1960s and involved thousands of southerners. Vaughan's books were affordably priced and each sold an average of 117,000 copies.

Karen M. McDearman
University of Mississippi

J. L. Fleming, "James D. Vaughan: Music Publisher, Lawrenceburg, Tennessee, 1912–1964" (Ph.D. dissertation, Union Theological Seminary, 1971); Bill C. Malone, *Southern Music—American Music* (1979); Charles K. Wolfe, *Tennessee Strings: The Story of Country Music in Tennessee* (1977).

Watson, Doc

(b. 1923) Folk musician.

Arthel "Doc" Watson is a unique song stylist, an influential guitarist, and the repository of a vast range of American music originating in the South. Born 2 March 1923 in Deep Gap, N.C., Watson has been blind from birth. He grew up in a farm family oriented toward religion and music. His father was a song leader in the Baptist church, and the Watson family read the Bible and sang hymns most evenings. Watson learned traditional folksongs from his grandparents and his father, and the first instrument he played was the harmonica. He remembers at age six hearing a cousin play the banjo, and a brother-in-law gave him one several years after that.

Throughout Watson's youth, his father guided his musical education. Doc Watson's father gave him a harmonica each Christmas for years when he was a child, helped his young son learn the banjo, and then in 1934 made him a better banjo of hickory, maple, and catskin. His father gave him money to buy his first guitar after the young boy learned to play the Carter Family's "When the Roses Bloom in Dixie." From his father's wind-up gramophone and the radio, Doc Watson remembers hearing songs by the Carter Family, the Skillet Lickers, Mississippi John Hurt, and Barbecue Bob. He still performs and records the songs he listened to growing up. In addition to his early education in traditional music, commercial country, and the blues, he learned jazz, big-band, popular songs, and classical music while attending the North Carolina School for the Blind in Raleigh.

Doc Watson's first stage performance was at age 17 during a fiddlers' convention in Boone, N.C., where he played the "Mule Skinner's Blues." In 1941 he became a member of a group singing for local radio stations, and a woman in a local station gave him his nickname in this period. She suggested calling him "Doc" because "Arthel" was too formal.

Watson worked for nine years in the 1950s playing mostly electric guitar with Jack Williams and the Country Gentlemen, a five-piece dance band, and he continued playing traditional music at home with friends and family. Folklorist Ralph Rinzler came from the Smithsonian Institution in 1960 to record a friend of Watson's, Clarence Ashley, and after Rinzler heard Watson, he encouraged him to seek a solo identity nationally. The Folkways album *Old Time Music at Clarence Ashley's* became Watson's first recording, and he was soon popular on the folk club and college campus circuit. Watson began recording for Vanguard Records in 1964, and the following year his 15-year-old son Merle began recording and touring with his father.

Doc Watson is an influential exponent of guitar flat picking, which involves use of a simple flat pick rather than a thumb pick or finger picking. He is also an engaging storyteller, who explains the background to the songs he performs. Above all, his cultural significance is as an eclectic synthesizer of southern music. Watson absorbed the music of his time and place as a mid-20th-century rural southerner. He performs Jimmie Rodgers ("Miss the Mississippi and You"), the Delmore Brothers ("Blues Stay Away from Me"), Gaither Carleton fiddle tunes, A. P. Carter ("Keep on the Sunny Side"), Mississippi John Hurt ("Spikedriver Blues"), Barbecue Bob ("You Don't Know My Mind Blues"), Bob Wills ("Hang Your Head in Shame"), and Carl Perkins ("Blue Suede Shoes"). In concert he can draw from Ira Gershwin and Bob Dylan if requested. He has recorded over 30 albums.

Watson's son Merle traveled, performed, and recorded with his father and earned praise for his bottleneck slide guitar playing. He died in a tractor accident in 1986. Doc Watson still lives with his wife Rosa Lee a few miles from his birthplace in North Carolina.

Charles Reagan Wilson
University of Mississippi

Irwin Stambler and Grellin Landon, *The Encyclopedia of Folk, Country, and Western Music* (2d ed., 1983).

White Top Folk Festival

Held from 1931 to 1939 on White Top Mountain in southwest Virginia, this festival drew its participants from a tri-state (Tennessee, Virginia, North Carolina) area. It was organized and produced by composer, writer, collector, and clubwoman Annabel Morris Buchanan in collaboration with composer-pianist John Powell, and Abingdon, Va., attorney John A. Blakemore. Folktale collector Richard Chase, composer Lamar Springfield, and white spirituals scholar George Pullen Jackson also played prominent roles.

Featuring such traditional performers as chantey singer Sailor Dad Hunt, ballad singers Horton Barker and Texas Gladden, dulcimer player Sam Russell, clog dancer Harve Sheets, banjo player Jack Reedy, fiddler Jess Johnson, and numerous members of the Wohlford, Blevins, and Cruise families, the festival drew hundreds of performers, thousands of spectators (more than 10,000 when Eleanor Roosevelt made a state visit in 1933), and many nationally known academic folklorists, art critics, composers, and classical musicians. In its later years the festival also included the morris-and-sword dances, Punch 'n' Judy shows, and theatrical presentations (by the Barter Theater) favored by Richard Chase. Each annual event was covered extensively by the local, regional, and national press.

Potential performers were rigorously screened and frequently coached to conform to an image of traditional culture in the southern mountains as the precious vestiges of an ancient English (Anglo-Saxon) cultural heritage, needing protection from the corrupting influences of modernity, and valuable as both raw material for art-music composers and a potential basis for a distinctive American "national culture." John Powell also used the festival to promote the nativist cultural theories upon which he had earlier based his work with the white-supremacist Anglo-Saxon club of America (which he had founded in 1922 and used as a lobbying group for Virginia's antimiscegenation Racial Integrity Law of 1924). Local black musicians were prohibited from performing at the festival.

The festival anticipated hundreds of folk festivals that now exist throughout the South celebrating the region's diverse musical heritage.

David E. Whisnant
University of Maryland,
Baltimore County

John A. Blakemore Papers and Annabel Morris Buchanan Papers, Southern Historical Collection, University of North Carolina, Chapel Hill; John Powell Papers, Alderman Library, University of Virginia, Charlottesville; David E. Whisnant, *All That Is Native and Fine: The Politics of Culture in an American Region* (1983).

Williams, Hank

(1923–1953) Country singer.

Widely acclaimed as country music's greatest singer and composer, Hiram Hank Williams was born on 17 October 1923 at Olive Hill, near Georgiana, Ala., the son of a sawmill and railroad worker. He was introduced to music in the Baptist church, where he was faithfully taken by his mother, and, according to popular legend, learned both songs and guitar chords from a black street singer in Georgiana, Rufus Payne ("Teetot").

Williams's evolution as a professional performer and composer began at the age of 14 when he won a talent show in a Montgomery theater singing "WPA Blues." He obtained his first radio job in the same year, 1937, at WSFA in Montgomery. When World War II—that crucible that integrated country music's disparate regional styles and ultimately nationalized it—came, Williams worked in the Mobile shipyards and sang regularly in the honky-tonks of south Alabama. By the time the war ended Williams had compiled eight hard years of performing experience and had built a style that reflected the composite musical influences of his youth: gospel, blues, and old-time country. Professionally, he acknowledged a debt to the Texas honky-tonk singer Ernest Tubb and to the Tennessee mountain singer Roy Acuff, whose styles Williams fused in a way that reflected a similar synthesis in the larger country field during the war and immediate postwar years.

Williams's ascendance to fame began shortly after the war when he became associated with Fred Rose, the famous Nashville songwriter and publisher. Rose encouraged Williams's natural songwriting abilities and published his songs; he helped him obtain recording contracts with Sterling and MGM Records; he persuaded Molly O'Day, one of the greatest singers of the time, to record some of Williams's compositions; and he helped him get a position on KWKH's Louisiana Hayride in Shreveport. The Hayride, which was then second only to the Grand Ole Opry as a successful country radio show, was the vehicle that launched Williams on the road to performing fame.

Hank Williams's national ascendancy came in 1949 when he recorded an old pop tune, "Lovesick Blues," which featured the yodeling he had learned from another Alabama singer, Rex Griffin. Williams soon moved to the Grand Ole Opry, where he became the most popular country singer since Jimmie Rodgers. In the brief span from 1949 to 1953 Williams dominated the country charts with songs that are still considered classics of country music: "I'm So Lonesome I Could Cry," "Cold Cold Heart," "Your Cheating Heart," "Honky Tonk Blues," "Jambalaya," and many others. With his band, the Drifting Cowboys, Williams played a major role in making country music a national phenomenon. With a remarkably expressive voice that moved with equal facility from the strident yodeling of "Long Gone Lonesome Blues" to the gentle lyricism of "I Just Told Mama Goodbye," Williams communicated with his listeners in a fashion that has only rarely been equaled by other country singers. The word *sincerity* has no doubt been over-

Hank Williams, country music star, c. 1950

used in describing the styles of country musicians, but in the case of Williams it means simply that he as a singer convincingly articulated in song a feeling that he and his listeners shared.

As a songwriter—not as a singer—Williams played a most important role in breaking down the fragile barriers between country and pop music. Williams's singing was quintessentially rural, and his own records never "crossed over" into the lucrative pop market. His songs, though, moved into the larger sphere of American popular music and from there, perhaps, into the permanent consciousness of the American people. Like no earlier country writer's works, Hank's songs appeared with great frequency in the repertoires of such pop musicians as Tony Bennett, Frankie Laine, and Mitch Miller. For good or ill, this popularization in pop music continues.

Commercial and professional success did not bring peace of mind to the Alabama country boy. A chronic back ailment, a troubled marriage, and a subsequent divorce and remarriage accentuated a penchant for alcohol that he had acquired when only a small boy. After being fired by the Grand Ole Opry for drunkenness and erratic behavior, he returned to the scene of his first triumphs—the Louisiana Hayride. He died of a heart attack on 1 January 1953, but his legacy lives on in his songs and in the scores of singers, including his immensely talented son, Hank, Jr., who still bear his influence.

Bill C. Malone
Tulane University

Bill C. Malone, *Country Music, U.S.A.: A Fifty-year History* (1968); Roger M. Williams, *Sing a Sad Song: The Life of Hank Williams* (1981).

Wills, Bob

(1905–1975) Western-swing musician.

James Robert Wills was born near the town of Kosse in the black belt of east Texas on 6 March 1905. From his family he learned to play fiddle music, which had been part of frontier cultural life from the East Coast to west Texas. From the blacks in the black belt he learned blues and jazz. At age 10, Wills played his first dance at a ranch in west Texas; by then he had begun to add blues and jazz idioms to traditional fiddle music. This combination was eventually called "western swing" and became one of the most distinctive sounds in all of American music. There is probably no better example of cultural cross fertilization than Bob Wills's music, which brought together two strains of culture in the American South, one white, one black.

Wills performed his music at country ranch dances in west Texas years before introducing it to the general public on radio stations in Fort Worth. In the early 1930s he organized the Light Crust Doughboys, broadcast over the Texas Quality Network, and soon revolutionized music in Texas. His greatest success was with his Texas Playboys in Tulsa, Okla., between 1934 and 1942. During those years he added brass, reeds, and drums, developing a band that by 1940 numbered 18 members. His recordings sold in the hundreds of thousands and his "San Antonio Rose" in the millions.

After the war he gave up most of the brass and reeds in his band and used more fiddles, guitars, steel guitars, and mandolins. This emphasis on strings helped Wills maintain his popularity even after the passage of the age of the big bands. Because of his use of stringed instruments, Wills influenced two musical forces of the South that have dominated American music to the present—rock and roll and country and western. Western swing left a marked impression on early rockabillies such as Bill Haley and the Comets, Buddy Holly and the Crickets, and Elvis Presley. But Wills's greatest influence was on country and western. The Country Music Association gave him its highest honor in 1968, naming Wills to the Country Music Hall of Fame.

What was it that made Wills's music appeal to the American people for more than 50 years? His music and style had many good qualities, but one quality stood out above all others—his music made people happy. At his dances, during his radio broadcasts, and through his recordings, Bob Wills helped the American people find times of happiness and escape during the Depression and World War II. This was the secret to his success and one of his most direct contributions to humanity.

When Wills died in 1975, he left a rich cultural heritage. His compositions like "Faded Love," "Maiden's Prayer," and "San Antonio Rose" are part of the repertoire of American country and pop artists. He also helped bridge the gap between the black and white musical cultures when he began combining them as a boy. Out of that cultural mix came Bob Wills's richest legacy, the happy, swinging rhythms called "western swing."

Charles R. Townsend
West Texas State University

Ruth Sheldon, *Hubbin' It: The Life of Bob Wills* (1938); Al Stricklin with Jon McConal, *My Years with Bob Wills* (1976); Charles R. Townsend, *San Antonio Rose: The Life and Music of Bob Wills* (1976).

Young, Lester

(1909–1959) Jazz musician.

Lester Willis "Pres" Young was an Afro-American tenor saxophonist whose influential style was viewed as revolutionary when first recorded during the late 1930s. He was a primary influence in the development of modern jazz.

Born in Woodville, Miss., Young was the oldest of three children raised in the vicinity of New Orleans. His parents divorced in 1910, and his father remarried and took his children with him to Minneapolis by 1920. Willis "Billy" Handy Young, Lester's father, was a talented musician who taught his children various instruments and later toured the South with his family in a band that played carnivals. Lester studied violin, trumpet, and drums but turned seriously to the saxophone by age 13. Young left the family band in 1927. He played in the next few years with Art Bronson's Bostonians, Eli Rice's Cotton Pickers, Walter Page's Blue Devils, Eugene Schuck's Orchestra, and Eddie Barefield at the West Club in Minneapolis.

In the fall of 1933 Young moved to Kansas City, where he played with numerous musicians, including Fletcher Henderson's orchestra and its star saxophonist, Coleman Hawkins. Early in 1934, Young joined William "Count" Basie, beginning an association that was to lead eventually to national recognition. During the mid to late 1930s Young was prominently featured on recordings and broadcasts with the Basie band. Although Young gained mixed reviews from critics, younger musicians were wildly enthusiastic. Important recordings included "Lester Leaps In" (1939) and many accompanying Billie Holiday.

Young left the Basie band in December 1940 to start his own group, which performed in New York in early 1941. He was involved with his own bands after that in Los Angeles and New York, before freelancing and then rejoining Basie in late 1943. During this second period with Basie, Young garnered the attention of the general public. In 1944 he won first place in the *Down Beat* poll for best tenor saxophonist. He won many awards thereafter and became popular with a new generation of musicians, among them John Coltrane, Sonny Rollins, and Stan Getz. In 1956 Young was voted "Greatest Tenor Saxophonist Ever" in a list of prominent jazz musicians.

Young's style changed after 1940. His tone was heavier and his vibrato wider. He was more clearly emotional, using wails, honks, and blue notes in his solos. He was inducted into the army in 1944, beginning a nightmarish experience that included time spent at a detention barracks in Georgia. After the war he toured with his own small groups. He continued to develop and modify his style and was generally successful except when his drinking, which was habitual by the early 1950s, weakened him physically. He died in New York in 1959.

Young is a leading example of many great jazz performers who were born and reared in the South but gained fame outside the region. His impact on jazz was profound. His melodic gift and logical phrasing influenced musicians on many instruments, and his personal formulas turned up in countless jazz compositions and improvisations.

Lewis Porter
Rutgers University

Nat Hentoff, in *The Jazz Makers*, ed. Nat Shapiro and Nat Hentoff (1975); J. G. Jensen, *A Discography of Lester Young* (1968); J. M. McDonough, *Lester Young* (1980); Lewis Porter, *The Black Perspective in Music* (Spring 1981), *Lester Young* (1985).

Mythic South

GEORGE B. TINDALL
University of North Carolina at Chapel Hill
CONSULTANT

A 1906 postcard depicting the cotton boll, a symbol of the South

Mythic South

Has the South always been mainly a region of the mind, as many have said, something that exists because people think it exists? Or has it been mainly a region defined by material characteristics of geography, climate, and resources—together with traits it has acquired in the course of its history?

Most would probably say it has been both. Historian U. B. Phillips, for instance, moved from one to the other in two classic definitions of the South. In "The Central Theme of Southern History" (1928), he described the unifying principle of the South as an idea, "a common resolve indomitably maintained" that the South should be and remain "a white man's country." In *Life and Labor in the Old South* (1929), on the other hand, he wrote: "Let us begin by discussing the weather, for that has been the chief agency in making the South distinctive." Geography and climate led in turn to staple crops, the plantation system, chattel slavery, racial problems, sectional conflict, and ultimately the Confederacy. Any serious effort to know the character of a people must confront its mythology, and Phillips's interpretations both belong in some respects to that realm, however matter of fact both may at first appear.

The term *mythology*, of course, conveys variant meanings. While myths are rooted in the religious impulse, they have become in the modern world increasingly secular in character. Some years ago anthropologist Raphael Patai offered a definition: "Myth . . . is a traditional religious charter, which operates by validating laws, customs, rites, institutions and beliefs, or explaining sociocultural situations and natural phenomena, and taking the form of stories, believed to be true, about divine beings and heroes." Later, in his book *Myth and Modern Man* (1972), Patai reaffirmed the definition but deleted the word *religious*. Upon further reflection, he said, he would emphasize more the role of myth in shaping social life: "As I see it, myth not only validates or authorizes customs, rites, institutions, beliefs, and so forth, but frequently is directly responsible for creating them." Thus, the modern world has invented a great variety of myths of both past and future, ranging from Marxist and Nazi myths to myths of planetary escape, with or without theological overtones.

To place the more down-to-earth idea of the South in the realm of social myth is to place it firmly in the region of the mind, where close relatives are such concepts as ideology, symbol, image, and stereotype—the last in the sense that Walter Lippmann gave in his *Public Opinion* (1922), where stereotypes come to mean "pictures in our heads" that have more to do with preconceptions than with reality.

The distinguishing characteristic of social myths is that they develop more or less abstract ideas in concrete and dramatic terms. In the words of Henry Nash Smith, they "fuse concept and emotion into an image." Secular myths, like religious myths, remain true to their origin in a root word meaning "tale."

Historical Myths. The classic myths of the South can be summed up briefly in the oft-quoted statement of Jonathan Daniels: "We Southerners are a mythological people, created half out of dream and half out of slander, who live in a still legendary land." He was referring to the contrary images of the South that grew up in the 19th-century sectional conflict: the plantation idyll versus the abolitionist critique, the "Sunny South" versus the "Benighted South," or to cite the cultural events that have most vividly fixed them in the popular mind, *Uncle Tom's Cabin* versus *Birth of a Nation* and, more recently, *Gone with the Wind* versus *Roots*.

Major myths have given structure to the chronological development of the South. Southern myths have freqently been analyzed as discrete entities, but together their stories tell the story of the South. The myth of a southern garden paradise, a new Eden, provided the initial image of the region for many colonial southerners and northerners. It was a myth rooted in the perception of a bountiful environment. By the late 1700s the democratic, egalitarian South of Thomas Jefferson had become the norm, according to William E. Dodd. Dodd's theme has been reflected in the writing of other historians, largely in depicting a region subjected to economic colonialism by an imperial Northeast. The Jeffersonian image of agrarian democracy has been a favorite recourse of southern liberals.

By the 1830s, though, the myth of the Old South was becoming a dominant literary and cultural construct for northerners and southerners alike, as William R. Taylor has shown. The Old South evokes images of kindly old marster with his mint julep, happy darkies singing in the fields, coquettish belles wooed by slender gallants. It is a romanticized moonlight-and-magnolias world, which yields all too easily to caricature and ridicule. Francis Pendleton Gaines noted, though, that "the plantation romance remains our chief social idyl of the past; of an Arcadian scheme of existence, less material, less hurried, less prosaically equalitarian, less futile, richer in picturesqueness, festivity, in realized pleasure that recked not of hope or fear or unrejoicing labor."

The myth of the Lost Cause focused on the Civil War experience of southerners. It told of noble, virtuous Christian warriors, the highest product of the Old South, defending the southern homeland from rapacious Yankees. Defeat was inevitable because of superior northern resources, but southerners defended their honor and in the process achieved spiritual victories. The Reconstruction era gave birth to a mythic view of southern whites facing the internal and external challenges to their maintenance of an orderly civilization. Exploitive northern carpetbaggers, traitorous southern scalawags, ignorant blacks, and brave but desperate ex-Confederates were the chief characters in this tale of good and evil.

Redemption of the South by the Bourbons brought peace to the region, in the mythic narrative, and promoted the emergence of a New South. Newspaper editors were the prime mythmakers, creating a New South creed that Paul M. Gaston has discussed at some length. New South advocates of the late 19th century promised to make the South as "rich, triumphant, and morally innocent" as the rest of the nation. They looked forward to a region absorbed into the national abundance of progress and equality.

The late 19th century, though, gave birth to a different myth as well—Populism. Despite talk of a New South, the region's people remained predominantly poor farmers, and the Populist myth made them southern heroes. Populist agrarian leaders were defenders of the poor, out to right the wrongs of industrial-commercial exploitation.

In the clever decade of the 1920s a myth of the Benighted South took shape. An older neoabolitionist myth of the Savage South was reinforced by a variety of images in that decade and after: the Scopes Trial, the Ku Klux Klan, lynchings, chain gangs, the Fundamentalist movement, hookworm and pellagra, the Scottsboro trials, labor violence. The response to the civil rights movement in the 1950s and 1960s gave new life to the Benighted South myth.

The Agrarianism of the Nashville Agrarians spoke, like the Populists, in a mythic rhetoric about the virtues of living on the land, although they seemed unclear whether God's chosen people had been southern planters or small farmers. Their manifesto, *I'll Take My Stand*, by Twelve Southerners, appeared by fortuitous circumstance in 1930 when industrial capitalism seemed on the verge of collapse. The ideal of traditional virtues such as, in Donald Davidson's words, "family, bloodkinship, clanship, folkways, custom, community" took on the texture of myth in their image of the agrarian South.

Another image from the Great Depression era was the Problem South, a concept emerging from the writings of sociological regionalists such as Howard W. Odum and Rupert B. Vance at the University of North Carolina. They told of a region with indisputable shortcomings but with potentialities that needed constructive attention and the application of regional social planning.

Contemporary Southern Mythology. "The mythmaking faculty is still active in contemporary America," Max Lerner wrote in *America as a Civilization* (1957). During the 1970s and 1980s a new myth of the South emerged, an ambivalent mixture of extremes, combining elements of the Sunny South and the Benighted South with some ingredients of its own. The new "mythopoets" began to sight on the southern horizons an extended "Sunbelt," stretching from coast to coast, its economy battening on agribusiness, defense, technology, oil, real estate, tourism, and leisure. The geographical definition of the Sunbelt remains uncertain, but it has come more and more often to be synonymous with the South.

Something about the Sunbelt image has a seductive appeal to southerners, so long consigned to the role of underdogs, although the Sunbelt seems to have been, like other myths, less the invention of southerners than of Yankees. The Sunbelt image surfaced first in a book by Kevin P. Phillips, *The Emerging Republican Majority* (1969), but lay dormant until revived by Kirkpatrick Sale in *Power Shift: The Rise of the Southern Rim and Its Challenge to the Eastern Establishment* (1979). Sale's book focused on the Southeast as a likely growth area for investment. The Sunbelt idea, however, is one myth that is subject to a statistical test. One cannot buy into the Sunbelt myth so long as only two southern states (Virginia and Florida) reach the national average per capita income, as the Department of Commerce reported for 1984.

Complexity and Contradictions. The complexity and contradictions of southern mythology, one can argue, make the mythology of the American West seem fairly simple by comparison. Fred Hobson, in his *Tell about the South: The Southern Rage to Explain* (1983), made up a suggestive list of myths with some overlapping, simply by compiling selected titles of books and articles published since 1945: "*The Emerging South, The Changing South,* 'The Disappearing . . . South,' 'The Vanishing South,' *The Enduring South*, 'The Distinctive South,' 'The American South,' 'The World South,' 'The Provincial South,' *The Democratic South*, 'The Embarrassing New South,' 'The South as a Counterculture,' *The Romantic South, The Uncertain South, The Militant South*, 'The Benighted South,' 'The Poetic South,' 'The Backward South,' 'The Progressive South,' *The Lazy South*, 'The Turbulent South,' 'The Squalid South,' 'The Solid South,' 'The Divided South,' 'The Devilish South,' 'The Visceral South,' and 'The Massive, Concrete South.'"

These neglected, among other things, the Jeffersonian yeoman, the Jacksonian frontiersman, chivalrous Southrons, New South boosters, insurgent Populists, the Fighting South, the Liberal South, the Anglo-Saxon (or Scotch-Irish?) South, the Vanderbilt Agrarians, the Chapel Hill Regionalists, the Bible Belt, and a gallery of patricians, rednecks, village nabobs, good old boys, and in general the surfeit of southern fried chic cooked up to celebrate the emergence of Jimmy Carter, the only president to date who was born and bred in the brier patch of the Deep South.

This catalog neither acknowledges nor sorts out the variety of southern black and female stereotypes that have either captivated or shocked the American sensibility. Studies of literature and popular culture, chiefly moving pictures and music, have only begun that process. Nor does the catalog deal with that newer version of the old religious myths that reserved the South for a high destiny—the Integrated South, purged by suffering and prepared to redeem the nation from bias and injustice.

Southern myths have been fostered in a variety of cultural forms. In the antebellum era, writers such as William Gilmore Simms and John Pendleton Kennedy helped create the plantation legend of the Old South as well as creating the tradition of popular literature fostering mythology. In the late 19th century, northern periodicals printed nostalgic articles and stories by southerners about the prewar era, and northerners seemed as taken with them as southerners were. Since the turn of the 20th century, American popular music has been a carrier of southern mythology. Tin Pan Alley's tunes,

Broadway shows, country music, and even rock music have told of Dixie's virtues. Film and television are the most recent sources to create and spread mythic news of the South, drawing on previous symbolism. Throughout southern history, political speeches and religious sermons have spread regional mythology in the South's oral culture.

Mythology, which seemed more than two decades ago a new frontier of southern history, has since been penetrated by a number of scholars. Literary critics have provided perhaps the largest body of scholarship on southern mythology, focusing on the region's writers. Intellectual historians have studied political, economic, religious, military, and journalistic aspects of various myths. There remain many areas that have been little explored and others scarcely touched. Myths continue to appear in modern areas of southern cultural achievement. Popular culture increasingly produces America's celebrities and heroes, and those who come from the South take on aspects of earlier southern mythology. Sports produced Paul "Bear" Bryant, one of the nation's most successful college football coaches and a folksy agrarian hero out of earlier regional tradition. Elvis Presley drew on the region's rich heritage of black and white music and himself became a new symbol (for good or bad) of the modern South.

See also BLACK LIFE: Film Images, Black; Literary Portrayals of Blacks; LITERATURE: Agrarianism in Literature; Popular Literature; MEDIA articles; SOCIAL CLASS: Lower Class, Literary; WOMEN'S LIFE: Belles and Ladies

George B. Tindall
University of North Carolina
at Chapel Hill

David Bertelson, *The Lazy South* (1967); Carl Bridenbaugh, *Myths and Realities: Societies of the Colonial South* (1963); Edward D. C. Campbell, *The Celluloid South: Hollywood and the Southern Myth* (1981); W. J. Cash, *The Mind of the South* (1941); F. Garvin Davenport, Jr., *The Myth of Southern History: Historical Consciousness in Twentieth-Century Southern Literature* (1970); Michael Davis, *The Image of Lincoln in the South* (1972); Carl N. Degler, *The Other South: Southern Dissenters in the Nineteenth Century* (1974); Clement Eaton, *The Mind of the Old South* (1964); Howard R. Floan, *The South in Northern Eyes, 1831 to 1861* (1958); J. Wayne Flynt, *Dixie's Forgotten People: The South's Poor Whites* (1979); John Hope Franklin, *The Militant South* (1956); George Fredrickson, *The Black Image in the White Mind: The Debate on Afro-American Character and Destiny, 1817–1914* (1971); Francis Pendleton Gaines, *The Southern Plantation: A Study in the Development and Accuracy of a Tradition* (1924); Paul M. Gaston, *The New South Creed: A Study in Southern Mythmaking* (1970); Patrick Gerster and Nicholas Cords, eds., *Myth and Southern History*, 2 vols. (1974); Dewey W. Grantham, *The Democratic South* (1963); Fred Hobson, *Tell about the South: The Southern Rage to Explain* (1983); Winthrop D. Jordan, *White over Black: American Attitudes toward the Negro, 1550–1812* (1968); Alexander Karanikas, *Tillers of a Myth: Southern Agrarians as Social and Literary Critics* (1966); Jack Temple Kirby, *Media-Made Dixie: The South in the American Imagination* (1978); Lawrence W. Levine, *Black Culture and Black Consciousness: Afro-American Folk Thought from Slavery to Freedom* (1977); Bernard Mayo, *Myths and Men: Patrick Henry, George Washington, and Thomas Jefferson* (1963); Forrest McDonald and Grady McWhiney, *History Today* (July 1980); Shields McIlwaine, *The Southern Poor-White: From Lubberland to Tobacco Road* (1939); Gary B. Nash, *William and Mary Quarterly* (April 1972); Michael O'Brien, *The Idea of the American South, 1920–1941* (1979); Rollin G. Osterweis, *Myth of the Lost Cause, 1865–1900* (1973), *Romanticism and Nationalism in the Old South* (1949); Raphael Patai, *Myth and Modern Man* (1972); Merrill Peterson, *The Jefferson Image in the American Mind* (1960); David Potter, *The South and the Sectional Conflict* (1968); John Shelton Reed, *The Enduring South: Subcultural Persistence in Mass Society* (1971), *One South: An Ethnic Approach to Regional Culture* (1982); Louis D. Rubin, Jr., *Writers of the Modern South: The Faraway Country* (1963); Anne Firor Scott, *The Southern Lady: From Pedestal to Politics, 1830–1930* (1970); Charles G. Sellers, Jr., *The Southerner as American* (1960); Lewis P. Simpson, *The Dispossessed Garden: Pastoral and History in Southern Literature* (1975); David L. Smiley, *South Atlantic Quarterly* (Summer 1972); Kenneth M. Stampp, *Era of Reconstruction, 1865–1877* (1965), *Journal of Southern History* (August 1971); William R. Taylor, *Cavalier and Yankee: The Old South and American National Character* (1957); George B. Tindall, *The Ethnic Southerners* (1976); Frank E. Vandiver, ed., *The Idea of the South: Pursuit of a Central Theme* (1964); John William Ward, *Andrew Jackson: Symbol for an Age* (1962); C. Vann Woodward, *The Strange Career of Jim Crow* (1955; rev. ed., 1966); Charles Reagan Wilson, *Baptized in Blood: The Religion of the Lost Cause, 1865–1920* (1980); Howard Zinn, *Southern Mystique* (1964).

Appalachian Culture

From the 18th century, "culture" was a process by which the natural was turned into the "cultivated." Beginning in the mid-19th century, however, the unspecified polarities of "natural" and "cultivated," or the "primitive-modern" of common parlance, were elaborated into a variety of schemes that talked of "stages" of development and assumed the inevitability of a people's progress from lower to higher stages. An essential ambiguity toward the primitive persisted, however, throughout the 19th century. A "low" stage of cultural development was frequently valued more highly than any "higher" stage, as maintaining the virtues of the "noble savage" or, in the American context, of "our pioneer ancestors" against the sham sophistication and corrupt usages of modern life. The rise of systematic social science at the turn of the century gave new value to any "low" stage of development, as preserving, like a mammoth in ice, essential evidence for the understanding of social development as a process.

In the context of such a definition of culture, Appalachian culture was called "low" on the scale of development. Appalachia has been routinely defined as "the frontier" and later the "persisting frontier," where primitive patterns of culture prevailed. Both inside and outside

Appalachia, moreover, the undeveloped character of Appalachian culture seemed a spur to development, whether through indigenous effort (including emigration from the region) or intervention by outsiders.

The identification of Appalachia as a distinct region of the nation and the mountaineers as a discrete population during the 1880s and 1890s occurred at the same time that social theory generally was beginning to view culture less as a stage in a universal process of development than as a particular set of beliefs or behavior. It associated culture with the places in which social groups lived. Initially, this took the form of explaining culture either as a response to a particular environment or as the product of environmental conditions in the sense that the environment was either conducive or not conducive to "normal" patterns of development from low to high levels of culture. Early in the 20th century, however, the association through explanation tended to drop out of most discussions of Appalachian culture, which now became the culture of place rather than the culture of people. Appalachia as a distinct region of the nation was now a real place, so most discussions of Appalachian culture in the 20th century began with the assumption that there must be *an* Appalachian culture that—whatever its origins—was as distinct as the region is distinct. Against this vision only John C. Campbell protested (in *The Southern Highlander and His Homeland* [1921]), saying that Appalachian culture was merely a version of rural American culture—no more and no less.

In this context the great campaigns of the early 20th century began to identify the elements of Appalachian culture and then to teach them to the Appalachian people, if they were "desirable" beliefs or behavior, or to replace them with "more desirable" beliefs or behavior. Those engaged in this campaign were usually more familiar with the literature on Appalachia than with the southern mountains and mountaineers themselves, and they frequently misread the beliefs and behavior current in Appalachia. As frequently, they sought to teach the mountaineers patterns of belief and behavior that were essentially alien to them.

Ironically, from the 1890s efforts were made to teach the mountain people their "own" folklore, their "own" folk dance, including the Sword and Morris dances, which they had supposedly forgotten long before their emigration from England and Scotland but which were considered their native tradition nonetheless. As David E. Whisnant has recently shown, a variety of indigenous patterns of culture, like banjo playing and the celebration of "old" Christmas, whether inherited or locally created, were systematically suppressed as being inappropriate to a modern folk culture in Appalachia.

The emergence of cultural pluralism as a conviction in social theory during the 1920s and of cultural relativism as its analogue in anthropological theory changed little. Although these concepts reinforced the legitimation (achieved earlier by the words and work of home missionaries and social workers) of Appalachia as a discrete region with a distinct culture, this culture continued to be viewed as "low," "primitive," "folk"—undeveloped in one way or another and hence unsuited for dealing with the modern world. This view persisted at least through the 1960s, appearing as a continuing theme in the literature on Appalachia and in the construction of social programs like the War on Poverty, which sought to modernize the mountaineer. Efforts were made to create a "viable" folk culture in the region. Many mountain people left the region in search of employment in the industrial centers of the Midwest, while others remained at home—to assimilate to mainstream American culture.

The view of Appalachian culture as low or undeveloped was dominant during the past 150 years and has colored all earlier general discussions of Appalachian culture. As a result, scholars have yet to establish the nature of Appalachian culture in the past, or even whether there *was* an identifiable Appalachian culture distinct from American culture. Nonetheless, the efforts of a new generation of scholars may yet overcome the biases of earlier accounts and by close and careful reading of the evidence develop an accurate picture of life in the past and present.

Henry D. Shapiro
University of Cincinnati

Allen Batteau, ed., *Appalachia and America: Autonomy and Regional Dependence* (1983); William W. Philliber and Clyde McCoy, eds., *The Invisible Minority: Urban Appalachians* (1981); Henry D. Shapiro, *Appalachia on Our Mind: The Southern Mountains and Mountaineers in the American Consciousness, 1870–1920* (1978); David E. Whisnant, *All That Is Native and Fine: The Politics of Culture in an American Region* (1983).

Benighted South

If the 19th-century South was viewed by romantics, North as well as South, as the primal garden, Eden before the Fall, the 20th-century South—at least to many image makers—has often been something quite different. To be sure, the Benighted or Savage South had its origins in the 19th century: William Lloyd Garrison had referred to it as the "great Sodom" and Frederick Law Olmsted, Harriet Beecher Stowe, and other northern writers had written harshly of it. But in the early 20th century—more particularly in the decade of the 1920s—the idea that the South was savage or barbarian took hold even more strongly than before. The new image of the Benighted South was a result partly of actual events in the South during the 1920s and partly of the writings of social critics and novelists who focused attention on the dark side of the contemporary South. The writers did not, as traditional southerners often charged, invent the negative southern image: the events did that. The Scopes evolution trial in Dayton, Tenn., in July 1925; the anti-Catholicism shown during Al Smith's presidential campaign in 1928; textile strikes and violence in Gastonia and Marion, N.C., and in Elizabethton, Tenn., in 1929; the rise of the modern Ku Klux Klan and numerous lynchings, outbreaks of nightriding, and other manifestations of racial injustice—these events drew the attention of national journalists such as H. L. Mencken and Oswald Garrison Villard; of prominent magazines such as the *Nation*, the *New Republic*, and the *Century*; and of social scientists such as Frank Tannenbaum of Columbia University, who wrote the aptly entitled *Darker Phases of the South* (1924). The Yankee crusade against the romantic southern image was carried out on several fronts: Tannenbaum concentrating on social ills; Villard and W. E. B. Du Bois, the black editor of the *Crisis*, focusing on racial matters; and Mencken in general command, attacking intellectual and cultural sterility. Mencken's essay, "The Sahara of the Bozart" (1920), was the most trenchant—and readable—indictment of the South, contributing more than any other work to the popular image of the Benighted South.

But the outsiders were hardly alone in portraying the South of the early 20th century as uncivilized, unsanitary, and violent. A native group of journalists and literary figures was perhaps even more effective in this role, presumably because they, as southerners, knew whereof they spoke. North Carolina newspapermen Gerald W. Johnson and W. J. Cash sent essay after essay to their mentor, Mencken, at the *American Mercury*, and the subjects of their essays were southern racism, religious barbarism, and intellectual sterility. Southern editors took their stands against racism and religious bigotry and won Pulitzers for their courage. As George B. Tindall has written, a "fifth column of native Menckens and Tannenbaums" found "an almost ridiculously simple formula for fame": they revealed "the grotesqueries of the benighted South."

Southern novelists were perhaps even bolder, or at least more graphic. Beginning in the early 1920s, writers such as T. S. Stribling of Tennessee and Clement Wood of Alabama, and slightly later Erskine Caldwell of Georgia, portrayed Dixie as a land of poverty, sloth, ignorance, and racial injustice. Stribling's Tennessee hillbillies and corrupt folk of northern Alabama were depicted in *Birthright* (1922), *Teeftallow* (1926), *Bright Metal* (1928), and his late trilogy, *The Forge* (1931), the Pulitzer Prize-winning *The Store* (1932), and *The Unfinished Cathedral* (1934). Caldwell became famous for his pictures of depraved poor whites in *Tobacco Road* (1932) and *God's Little Acre* (1933). And on their heels came greater, less exclusively regional writers, whose portrait of the South, for all its artistry, was judged by reviewers to be no more flattering. In *Look Homeward, Angel* (1929) Thomas Wolfe—in the words of one reviewer—"spat upon" the South. Wolfe's fictional town of Altamont—based closely on his hometown of Asheville, N.C.—he described as a "barren spiritual wilderness," which maintained a "hostile and murderous intrenchment against all new life." If Wolfe's South was intellectually barren and culturally sterile, that of William Faulkner was downright frightening. Between 1929 and 1936 the young Mississippian burst forth with a series of novels portraying a South of decaying gentry, idiocy, religious fanaticism, murder, rape, and suicide. *The Sound and the Fury* (1929) depicted the decline and fall of the Compson family, antebellum aristocrats who could not cope with the new order. *As I Lay Dying* (1930), Faulkner's tragicomic story of the attempt of a dirt-poor Mississippi family to bury their wife and mother, seemed to reinforce the worst image of southern degradation brought out by the journalists of the 1920s. *Sanctuary* (1931) was even more depraved—and, because it was sold to Hollywood, even more influential in creating the image of a savage South. *Light in August* (1932) presented a gallery of southern grotesques and eccentrics. *Absalom, Absalom!* (1936), perhaps Faulkner's greatest novel, pictured a dark and violent antebellum South. And Faulkner's conniving poor whites, the Snopeses, were yet to come in *The Hamlet* (1940), *The Town* (1957), and *The Mansion* (1959).

By the mid-1930s the depiction of the South in contemporary fiction had become so sordid that even that earlier iconoclast, Gerald W. Johnson, was moved to call this latest Dixie-in-print "The Horrible South." Faulkner, Stribling, Caldwell, and Wolfe were "real equerries of Raw-Head-and-Bloody-Bones . . . the merchants of death, hell, and the grave . . . the horror-mongers-in-chief." *Sanctuary*, Johnson insisted, "put me under the weather for thirty-six hours." Yet, as Johnson maintained, the new picture of the South was a necessary corrective to the romantic picture of the Old, an antidote to Thomas Nelson Page. The South of 1930 was not so bad as its writers suggested—but the South of 1830 had never been so good.

The image of the Benighted South remained firmly entrenched in the national mythology throughout the 1930s. The Scottsboro case of the early 1930s and President Roosevelt's pronouncement in 1938 that the South was "the Nation's No. 1 economic problem" insured that. Events of the next two decades did little to modify the image, and those of the 1960s brought the South the same widespread negative attention it had attracted in the 1920s and 1930s. Now Oxford and Selma and Birmingham were in the news, not Dayton and Gastonia and Scottsboro, but the result was the same: Yankee reporters again flocked South and reported that Dixie remained benighted, savage, somehow out of touch with modern civilization.

Only with the end of the civil rights movement—and the rise of the Sunbelt of the 1970s—did the image of a Benighted South begin to fade. In truth, perhaps the coming of interstate highways and widespread air-conditioning had as much to do with the new positive image of Dixie as the departure of lynching and the decline of racial segregation. In any case, as the South entered the last two decades of the 20th century, it was bolder and more confident than before, possessing shining new cities, a new base of wealth dependent on oil, aerospace, real estate, and leisure, and a working knowledge of the power of public relations. The image of the Benighted South it had consigned, in large part, to its past.

Fred Hobson
University of Alabama

Fred Hobson, *Virginia Quarterly Review* (Summer 1985); Gerald W. Johnson, *Virginia Quarterly Review* (January 1935); H. L. Mencken, *Prejudices, Second Series* (1920); George B. Tindall, *Virginia Quarterly Review* (Spring 1964).

Community

For contemporary southerners the small-town community assumes mythic qualities. Images of community in southern history include plantations in the countryside, a separate black sense of community embodied in the slave quarters, mill villages in the Carolina Piedmont, brush arbor camp meetings, crossroads country stores, the courthouse square, and neighborhoods in cities. The term *community* evokes feelings of warmth and sociability, yet it also summons memories of the violent compulsion of orthodoxy—the lynch mob was a symbol of the white community's consensus on racial mores in the age of segregation.

Pioneering anthropologists and sociologists used the "community approach" in studying small-town southern life in the 1930s. The Institute for Research in Social Science at the University of North Carolina at Chapel Hill, founded by Howard W. Odum in 1924, supported research on southern communities for the next two decades. Most southern community studies from the 1930s and 1940s were concerned with the internal structures and dynamics of community. While studies were done of mill towns, the classic community research of the 1930s dealt with race and class. John Dollard's *Caste and Class in a Southern Town* (1937) was an attempt to understand "the emotional structure" of Indianola, Miss. Dollard set out to study the personality of southern blacks through their life histories and saw a need to study the community in order to understand individuals living there. He called Indianola "Southern town," suggesting the influence of Robert S. Lynd and Helen M. Lynd's *Middletown* (1929). Other community studies in the South at this time include Allison Davis, Burleigh Gardner, and Mary Gardner's *Deep South: A Social Anthropological Study of Caste and Class* (1937), Hortense Powdermaker's *After Freedom: A Cultural Study of the Deep South* (1939), and Allison Davis and John Dollard's *Children of Bondage: The Personality of Negro Youth in the Urban South* (1940). These studies analyzed social classes and racial groups and argued that southern towns and cities formed not one community but several.

Southern community studies of the 1940s and 1950s continued to be strongly influenced by social science. John Gillin (of the University of North Carolina at Chapel Hill) and his students analyzed five representative communities, publishing three of the studies (Morton Rubin, *Plantation County*, 1951; Hylan Lewis, *Blackways of Kent*, 1955; and John Kenneth Morland, *Millways of Kent*, 1958). Researchers used observation, questionnaires, interviews, statistical information, and even Rorschach tests to describe the way of life in each community and to place it in a broader theoretical framework designed by Gillin. Solon T. Kimball and Marion Pearsall's *The Talledega Story: A Study of Community Process* (1954) employed "event analysis," a new technique of southern community research, which explored how the people of Talledega carried out a local study of health needs. Pearsall's *Little Smoky Ridge: The Natural History of a Southern Appalachian Neighborhood* (1959) related a small mountain community to its physical setting, internal dynamics, and surrounding countryside. John Kenneth Morland's 1967 essay "Anthropology and the Study of Culture, Society, and Community in the South" suggested the need for community research dealing with southern values, sociocultural transmission, and educational development, none of which had been the central concerns of these earlier studies.

Recent studies view southern communities as historical processes rather than static institutions. To understand any community, one must observe and analyze its development over time. Although historians have produced numerous studies of colonial New England communities, surprisingly few studies exist of southern colonial communities. Darrett B. Rutman and Anita H. Rutman's *A Place in Time: Middlesex County, Virgina, 1650–1750* (1984) is a model work. Orville Vernon Burton's *In My House Are Many Mansions: Family and Community in Edgefield, South Carolina* (1985) and Randolph B. Campbell's *A Southern Community in Crisis: Harrison County, Texas, 1850–1880* (1983) bridge the antebellum and postbellum eras. Gail W. O'Brien's *The Legal Fraternity and the Making of a New South Community, 1848–1882* (1986) is a careful case study of how an elite group imposed its values on one southern community. Historians have not been alone in studying southern communities over time. Sociologist Elizabeth R. Bethel, in *Promiseland: A Century of Life in a Negro Community* (1981), and folklorist William Lynwood Montell, in *The Saga of Coe Ridge: A Study in Oral History* (1970), study black communities over time. The "community studies" approach today uses interdisciplinary methods and theories to explore southern culture from the grass roots in a way pioneered by the French *Annales* historians.

Modern southern literature preserves the image of small-town community life. Literary critics have linked the declining sense of community to the 20th-century Southern Literary Renaissance. Louis D. Rubin, Jr., wrote that the southern community of the late 19th and early 20th centuries "had been self-sufficient, an entity in itself, with a mostly homogenous population, relatively orderly and fixed in its daily patterns." Southern writers at that time were a part of their communities. They lived spiritually satisfying lives but did not produce great art. White writers of the post–World War I South, members of the generation that witnessed the breakup of cohesive community life, were unable to find "spiritual sustenance and order within community life itself" and became literal or symbolic exiles. Their great art was anchored in the creation of community images—Faulkner's Yoknapatawpha County, Wolfe's Altamont, N.C., and Welty's Morgana, Miss.

The southern sense of community has expressed itself in three important institutions. The courthouse square is perhaps the most potent, distinctive symbol of southern community. It is a center of business, political, and economic life drawing together people from both the small town and surrounding rural areas. The courthouse building and a tall Confederate monument (likely dating from between 1890 and 1920 and facing North) towered over the typical square. Around the square, government offices, jails, and banks were symbols of power. There were lawyers' offices, physicians' offices, hardware stores, department stores, furniture stores, drug stores, hotels, cafés, and by the 20th century, perhaps a funeral home and a dentist's office. The blacksmith was a fixture, succeeded in the 20th century by the gas station. There was often a farmers' market near the courthouse, with fresh vegetables and fruits displayed. John Dollard noted in the 1930s that the movie theater was a major community gathering spot.

Some community institutions around the courthouse square appealed primarily to women, others to men. The beauty parlor was a gathering place for women rich and poor. Eudora Welty's "Petrified Man" captures the conversations of the small-town beauty shop as women exchanged news and gossip. Here, young girls were initiated into the roles expected of women.

The barber shop and the pool hall were equivalent male institutions. The pace in the barber shop, like the beauty parlor, was typically slow, and the shop filled not only with those getting their hair cut but with others simply talking or listening. The pool hall was a rougher place, with aggressive talk. In it young adolescents exchanged opinions on sex, drinking, and gambling, and sometimes the exchange became violent. Playwright Mart Crowley grew up listening to such stories in his father's pool hall, "Crowley's Smoke House," in Vicksburg, Miss. In *Intruder in the Dust* Faulkner portrayed the barber shop and the pool hall as community institutions where one found expression of consensus and orthodoxy. The lynch mob might plot its action and gather up the young men hanging out in those places.

Another typically southern part of community life was the county, an important political and administrative institution. Amateur and professional historians have long used county history to define local history, and the modern "new social history" uses census, tax, court, and voting records to reconstruct life at the county level and relate it to broader regional patterns. As historian Robert C. McMath, Jr., notes, southerners thought of the government and the county as the same. "The seat of the county court also became a center of trade and, to a lesser extent, of organized social life."

Counties are made up of smaller communities or rural neighborhoods, which are often groups of extended kin living within territorial boundaries centered around a country store or church. These small hamlets include a tavern, a church, a store, a mill, a few houses, and, before the days of consolidation, perhaps a school. Post–Civil War sharecroppers and tenants often moved within the bounds of these subcommunities within counties. While county government brought all citizens together for social, economic, and political reasons, pronounced differences existed between townspeople and those living in the nearby rural countryside. Townspeople saw themselves as more sophisticated than country people, often looked down on them, in fact, but depended on them economically.

The church was a third focus for the southern community. Colonial Anglican churches aspired to achieve community but had failed to do so by the mid-1700s. The rise of the evangelical sects in the 1700s established dissenting communities emphasizing personal religious experience, the symbolic ritual of baptism, and church discipline, and separating the chosen from the larger society. Southern evangelical Protestantism is a religion of individual religious experience, but conversion is the entrance to communal church life. Dominant evangelical churches in the South were intensely involved in caring for members of their religious communities. Historian Donald Mathews describes the southern church of the early 19th century as "a redemptive community."

The church building itself does not tower over the southern landscape the way the courthouse has, but the pervasiveness of small churches suggests that religious communities are organized by sect, race, and social class. Neighborhoods were commonly located around church buildings, representing what historian Orville Vernon Burton calls "communities within the larger community." Churches established community values and a rigorous moral code in frontierlike rural areas. The church was also a major focus for women's community concerns. Limited in their public roles in other areas of southern life, women were active in church organizations and groups, and those involvements often led to more extensive community involvement.

Blacks developed their own community in the South. The slave quarters, the Black Belt, the Delta plantation, the Carolina Low Country, and Tuskegee represent images of distinctly black southern communities. Even for migrants out of the region, the South and its local black communities remain "down home." As Robert B. Stepto notes, these places represent "the exhilarating prospect of community, protection, progress, learning, and a religious life while often birthing and even nurturing (usually unintentionally) a sense of enclosure that may reach claustrophobic proportions." Black folk culture has been a prime means for preservation of a distinctive sense of black community. In blues music and in tales of black folk heroes, individual characters symbolize the black community.

The relationship of blacks to *the* overall southern community remains unclear. Blacks had their own subcommunities, but there was also a larger community that had to be dealt with. Until very recently, this community was clearly dominated by whites. Whites controlled the power, set the agenda, and created the myths. James McBride Dabbs noted that blacks "were never a true part of this community," yet "the community was there, in some ways they belonged to it, household servants rather intimately." The South's elaborate rules of interracial etiquette, manners, and customs were designed to facilitate the functioning of communities inhabited by two races. The folk culture of blacks and whites, especially in small towns and rural areas, was a major expression of a shared sense of southern community, beyond ideology. Folktales, folksongs, and folk art all represented the preservation and transmission of a regionally distinct culture.

The civil rights movement was an effort to integrate the southern community. The movement integrated specific public schools and restaurants and developed a broader definition of the community of people who called themselves southerners. A central idea for Martin Luther King, Jr., was the "beloved community," and the title of his last book, *Where Do We Go from Here? Chaos or Community?*, indicated his concern for achieving a sense of community in both the region and the nation.

The civil rights movement occurred in the South in the context of specific communities—Montgomery, Selma, Albany, Birmingham, Memphis, and countless others. Scholars who have begun to explore the origin and development of the movement within specific communities include William H. Chafe, *Civilities and Civil Rights: Greensboro, North Carolina, and the Black Struggle for Freedom* (1980), Aldon D. Morris, *The Origins of the Civil Rights Movement: Black Communities Organizing for Change* (1984), and Robert J. Norrell, *Reaping the Whirlwind: The Civil Rights Movement in Tuskegee* (1985).

A final symbol of community in the contemporary South is the city neighborhood. The 1950s and 1960s were years of urban renewal, which often destroyed older structures and displaced people from their homes. Wealthy white suburbs grew on the edges of southern cities until the 1970s and 1980s, when a new trend developed. The energy crisis of the early 1970s, federal government Community Development Block Grants, and interest in historical preservation led affluent white southerners to look again to urban neighborhoods as residential areas. Ansley Park and Inman Park in Atlanta, Oakwood in Raleigh, Trinity Park in Durham, and the Oakleigh District in Mobile are but a few of the older urban neighborhoods that have been revived as places to live. Sometimes these areas become havens for southern yuppies at the expense of working-class people traditionally living there, but not always. In explaining the trend, Philip Morris of *Southern Living* stressed "the sense of place and community that most residents of reviving districts comment upon. They like the diversity of ages, of interests, of architecture, of viewpoint, that come together as an urban place." This interest in urban neighborhoods represents an attempt by southerners to preserve the regional ideal of community, a small-town southern ideal surviving in the context of big-city living.

Charles Reagan Wilson
University of Mississippi

Orville Vernon Burton and Robert C. McMath, Jr., eds., *Toward a New South?: Studies in Post–Civil War Southern Communities* (1982); James McBride Dabbs, *The Southern Heritage* (1958); Jean E. Friedman, *The Enclosed Garden: Women and Community in the Evangelical South, 1830–1900* (1985); Rhys Isaac, *The Transformation of Virginia, 1740–1790* (1982); John Brinckerhoff Jackson, *The Southern Landscape Tradition in Texas* (1980); Norman K. Johnson, *Southern Living* (January 1980); Lawrence W. Levine, *Black Culture and Black Consciousness: Afro-American Folk Thought from Slavery to Freedom* (1977); Donald Mathews, *The Religion of the Old South* (1977); John Kenneth Morland, in *Perspectives on the American South: Agenda for Research*, ed. Edgar T. Thompson (1967); Philip Morris, *Southern Living* (November 1976); Louis D. Rubin, Jr., *Writers of the Modern South: The Faraway Country* (1967); Stephen A. Smith, *Myth, Media, and the Southern Mind* (1985); Robert B. Stepto, *From Behind the Veil: A Study of Afro-American Narrative* (1979).

Family

Social historian Carl N. Degler identifies part of the South's unique appeal as being "in the human warmth and security of its commitment to family and kin," and he speaks with fascination of "the South—where roots, place, family, and tradition are the essence of identity." Degler says, "It is probable, though the evidence is skimpy, that in the southern English colonies and Southern states, kinship ties beyond the immediate family were more important than in the northern areas. Certainly that has been the traditional view. . . . And to this day Southerners acknowledge a more far-flung and more active kin network beyond the family of origin than people in other regions of the United States. . . . Unfortunately, though, the origins and development of this well-recognized propensity in the South for kin connections has been neither systematically delineated nor adequately explained." Both historical information and social science data about southern families are limited, yet powerful images of the southern family persist in the region's literature, music, and art.

Popular images of the southern family include small-town southerners sitting on a front porch at twilight, swapping stories; Sunday dinner around the table, where the best southern cooking is often served; black maids waiting on the white family and sometimes becoming, in effect, family members; long visits from maiden aunts and distant cousins; genealogists seeking their roots and sometimes engaging in ancestor worship; the reality of bitter family feuds as a counterpoint to sentimental family scenes; and family rituals such as births, weddings, and funerals, each an occasion for homecomings and celebrations of kin. Many movie and television portrayals have incorporated and exaggerated these images, stressing above all clannishness as a southern family trait. Traditionally, images of the region's families have dealt primarily with middle- or upper-class whites, very little with black families, and almost never with the families of any other ethnic or religious groups in the region. Although subgroups and particular families carry their own family-based folklore, myths about the power of the family group in the South rest largely on the experiences of white residents of rural areas or small towns.

Many myths about southern families are rooted in what Richard H. King has termed the "Southern family romance," the vision of the South as long being one huge plantation family ruled by powerful white patriarchs who protected both the gracious white women and the childlike, contented black slaves who were their charges. In this view family position governed social life, and family background was the criterion for judging social worth. This vision dominated the so-called local color literature popular from the late 1860s through the early

1900s, and many of its elements persisted in movies such as *Gone with the Wind*. Only recently have historians shed much light on actual family relations in the antebellum era. For instance, scholars once argued that slavery destroyed the black family, but historians recently have shown that the extended kinship system and the "fictive family," one composed of a wide network of community members who take care of each other, have been an institutional source of black cultural survival since before the antebellum era. The images that characterize the southern family romance have died hard, however, even in the face of historical and sociological findings on family relationships.

In the late 1930s and the 1940s social scientists began to examine the unique nature and power of the family in the social networks of the South. Sociologist and historian Margaret J. Hagood found in her late-1930s interviews with tenant farm wives in Georgia, Alabama, and the Carolinas that family-centered activities dominated their lives. "In the decades after the Civil War the family was the core of southern society; within its bounds everything worth while took place," commented social historian Francis Butler Simkins in 1947. Sociologist Rupert B. Vance wrote in 1948 that southern social life was centered in the home and that family solidarity was stressed so much that a clannishness prevailed. Many subsequent generalizations about the family in the South rested on two notions: (1) that extended kin networks predominate throughout the region and (2) that expectations for contact, mutual support, and affection between family members are high.

During the late 1940s sociologists Ernest Burgess and Harvey Locke provided support for these generalizations through their investigations of *familism*, a term denoting strong identification with one's family group and distrust of outsiders; emphasis on family goals, common property, and mutual support; and a desire to perpetuate the family group and its expectations. Early studies described Ozark and Appalachian highlanders as being highly familistic—as representing one end of a spectrum, with other rural residents generally being somewhat less familistic, and urban residents being considerably less so. As a consequence of being a predominantly rural region for much of its history, the South has been assumed by many to be on the higher-to-middle end of this continuum.

Other researchers have supported the general view of the familistic South. Sociologist Bernard Farber described the South and New England as having an "American-biblical kinship system," which functions in a highly stratified society to meld descent groups, limit the range of potential marriage mates, and solidify one's place in the social structure. Other scholars point to the region's population density, large numbers of kin residing within a given area, and existence of lineages over a long period of time as keys to the family's importance in southern culture. Sociologist John Shelton Reed notes that "the love it or leave it" notion applies even at the level of the family and that southerners identify loyalty to one's family as a characteristically southern trait.

Folklorists have gathered much information on the family's importance in preserving, shaping, and transmitting both the oral and material lore of the region through folk art, music, crafts, and stories. Over time southern families have probably differed not so much in the importance they place on the preservation of family records, mementos, and stories as in their resources for doing so. Wealthy whites, for instance, in the late 1800s and early 1900s often commissioned formal paintings or photographic family portraits; poorer white residents relied more on traveling photographers who worked in the field. Photographs of black and other minority families of the same and earlier eras are rare, as are genealogical records. Other sources of family lore abound, however, such as quilts, toys, and work implements passed down through generations. Southerners have also kept family tales alive through a rich oral heritage.

Some of the most powerful explorations of the nature of the family within the South have been by the region's writers. The local colorists had painted a broad, idealized, highly unrealistic vision of southern families and the South as a plantation family, and the writers of the Southern Literary Renaissance struggled to escape from that vision and formulate new understandings. For example, William Faulkner explored the tension between loyalty to family and allegiance to humanity; Tennessee Williams depicted the twisted personalities and relationships often shaped in families; and Eudora Welty examined the stabilizing but sometimes stultifying nature of family bonds. The compelling visions of these and other writers provide realistic, probing images of the ties that bind families.

Evidence of families as tradition bearers in the South persists in countless forms, yet in recent years southern families have experienced much the same rates of change as families throughout the rest of the nation, with growing numbers of divorces, single-parent families, and two-income couples seeking childcare. Also, the region is no longer predominantly rural, residents are very mobile, and most adults maintain frequent contacts only within the nuclear family and with parents and siblings. The impact of changing lifestyles and family forms on frequency of contact, perceived importance of family bonds, and emphasis on one's ancestry has yet to be seen; thus far scholars have not examined the impact of such changes as much as have writers such as Peter Taylor and country singers such as Loretta Lynn. Although the power of family bonds in the South may be changing, many southerners and non-southerners would agree with anthropologist Carole Hill that "the distinctiveness of the South may not be in empirical differences from other regions, but in its unique belief system." In countless ways the family still lies at the center of that system.

Sharon A. Sharp
University of Mississippi

Bert N. Adams, *Kinship in an Urban Setting* (1968); Carlene F. Bryant, *We're All Kin: A Cultural Study of a Mountain Neighborhood* (1981); Ernest W. Burgess and Harvey J. Locke, *The Family: From Institution to Companionship* (1945); Carl N. Degler, *Place over Time: The Continuity of Southern Distinc-*

tiveness (1977), *At Odds: Women and the Family in America from the Revolution to the Present* (1980); Bernard Farber, *Kinship and Class: A Midwestern Study* (1971); Walter J. Fraser, Jr., R. Frank Saunders, Jr., and Jon L. Wakelyn, eds., *The Web of Southern Social Relations: Women, Family, and Education* (1985); Herbert G. Gutman, *The Black Family in Slavery and Freedom, 1750–1925* (1976); Margaret J. Hagood, *Mothers of the South: Portraiture of the White Tenant Farm Woman* (1939); Peter L. Heller, Gustavo M. Quesada, David L. Harvey, and Lyle G. Warner, in *The Family in Rural Society*, ed. Raymond T. Coward and William M. Smith, Jr. (1981); Carole E. Hill, *Current Anthropology* (June 1977); Richard H. King, *A Southern Renaissance: The Cultural Awakening of the American South, 1930–1955* (1980); Sherry Konter, *Vanishing Georgia* (1982); John Shelton Reed, *One South: An Ethnic Approach to Regional Culture* (1982), *Southerners: The Social Psychology of Sectionalism* (1983), with Daniel J. Singal, eds., *Regionalism and the South: Selected Papers of Rupert Vance* (1982); Louis D. Rubin, Jr., *Writers of the Modern South: The Faraway Country* (1963); Merrill M. Skaggs, *The Folk of Southern Fiction* (1972).

Fatherhood

Historically, sharp divisions between males and females characterized family responsibilities in the South. The man was regarded as the unchallenged patriarch, the strong, respected provider, the mainstay of southern society. The traditional image of the chivalrous southerner, as opposed to the greedy Yankee, was centered in the southern father's devotion to family, tradition, and race; all these restrained the "natural man" that supposedly emerged in the Yankee. At the same time the South has often been celebrated as a region that stressed the so-called masculine traits; a region demarcated by violence, hard-nosed football, stock car racing, a proclivity toward the military, and hawkish attitudes about war and foreign affairs. Yet, in the literature and sometimes in actuality, it is often a Scarlett O'Hara or her mother who ends up running the plantation and the mill.

The patriarchal nature of the southern family has been attributed to slavery. Dependent upon slaves as producers of income, the family head, the southern father, had to maintain control of the peculiar institution, and attempts by family members to assert themselves against the head were thought to threaten slavery itself. As proslavery theorists justified the institution of slavery with every branch of knowledge, from the Bible to science, the rationale for the authority of the father in the household became increasingly the received wisdom of all southerners. Family, church, and community all reinforced patriarchy. Male dominance persisted in the political, cultural, religious, and economic spheres of the South.

Cotton ruled as King, not Queen, in the South. In the early 20th century, powerful U.S. Senator Ben Tillman used a South Carolina law allowing him to deed his grandchildren to himself, thus thwarting their mother's claim to custody. Except for a brief period during Reconstruction, not until after World War II was divorce legalized in South Carolina. Before child labor laws, southern children commonly worked in the textile mill for a family wage, which was paid directly to the father. In the South the father was the family head and considerable legal authority fortified his power.

Bertram Wyatt-Brown has shown that southerners venerated their male ancestors. Naming patterns in the South signified the importance of patriarchy. The tendency to name children after male family elders remains strong in the South where phone books today still show many juniors and thirds after a name. Although individualistic impulses were in some ways influential, duty to family and one's forebears was paramount. The southerner's respect for history and tradition was reinforced by his obedience to his forefathers.

The legendary southern father was much like the myth of the southern gentleman: well-educated and genteel, with a firm and commanding personality, which demanded deference from all family members and from nonaristocratic whites. Thus, the myth of southern fatherhood has a distinct class bias. Eugene D. Genovese's brilliant work showing that slaves had room for cultural autonomy and arguing the patriarchal nature of slavery suggests that the hegemony of the planter class prevented lower-class whites and slaves from being patriarchs themselves. Other scholars, disagreeing, have demonstrated that the planters' status did not prevent less affluent white or slave males from reigning in their own families. The patriarchal values pervaded all levels of the society and culture.

Popular literature, however, has characterized the lower-class white family as a disorderly one led by irresponsible, lazy, drunken fathers. Thus, ironically, in the South, which supposedly counterpoints the North's emphasis on lucre, fatherly success was associated with financial success.

The father in the black family was generally believed to be absent or nonexistent. Studies of urban areas in the North have shown that racism in the occupational structure of modern society has made it difficult for Afro-American men to get jobs in cities. Careful scrutiny of census and other demographic records shows that this is just as true of southern cities and even small towns and villages. Whereas towns and cities offered both protection and domestic jobs for black women, black men there were excluded from jobs other than those associated with farming. Hence, when sociologists studied black families in the cities they found males absent. In the rural South, however, where most blacks lived after slavery, landowning and tenant families were almost always headed by black men. White landowners were not willing to rent to female household heads unless they had nearly grown children to help in the fields. Thus, in the sparsely settled rural areas, not the cities where interviews and records were more easily available, the scholar found the black patriarch ruling his family very much as did his white counterpart.

Scholars have some records suggesting how planter class fathers treated their children. Fathers had intense but ambivalent feelings about their children. They lavished affection on them during infancy but were torn between their love for their children and their desire to see the children—especially the males—become independent. They might be terribly affectionate with the children one day and then completely unavailable the next. One fatherly technique was to alternate providing and withdrawing intimacy in order to teach discipline and right behavior; this technique internalized guilt and shame in the children.

Parents were seen as exemplars. The children were expected to emulate their parents and other worthy relatives as much as possible, to respect adults and to follow their basic moral precepts. Although fathers sought to teach their children independence, they also wanted the children to learn that they were not so much individuals as extensions of their parents. Their every move, therefore, was not only an indication of their own goodness, but just as importantly a reflection of parental worthiness.

One of the most important aspects of behavior that southern fathers could teach their children was aggressiveness. Even young girls were encouraged to be aggressive. But, of course, boys, and particularly the eldest boy, were the focus of this assertiveness training. Many southern fathers thought children should be given freedom to explore their surroundings, thus gaining the confidence needed to assert themselves fully. Sometimes, however, fathers went too far and merely spoiled their children. This mistake could end tragically, with the sons of prominent men often leading short and dissolute lives.

A variety of father images have appeared in southern literature and music, suggesting other dimensions to the role of the father in regional life. Sometimes fathers, like mothers, are sentimentalized, as in the Jimmie Rodgers country songs of the 1930s, "Daddy and Home" and "That Silver Haired Daddy of Mine." This attitude reflected the long Victorian influence in the South. Beverly Lowry's novel, *Daddy's Girl* (1981), offers a humorous contemporary look at one of the most important southern family relationships—father and daughter, an excessively loving, manipulative, and demanding relationship. The nurturing father is an equally strong image and shows the father passing down folk skills and wisdom to sons and daughters.

Fathers have also been portrayed in harsh terms. Religion has contributed a powerful father image: the father as the Calvinist God's patriarch on earth, the person ruling the southern household and the plantation with an iron fist. The father, to Joe Christmas in William Faulkner's *Light in August*, is a stern figure, always judging, ready to mete out justice to wayward children. The poverty of the postbellum and modern eras and the humiliation for blacks in the racial caste system have also shaped cultural attitudes toward fatherhood. One country song says father was "a farmer but all he ever raised was us." The sharecropping father is seen as frustrated, unable to provide a good life for his family. Richard Wright's harsh portrait of his father in *Black Boy* is an extreme version, although Alex Haley's *Roots* gives images of warm, loving, and strong black fathers.

The sociological study of fatherhood is relatively new, and as yet there is little reliable information on regional differences in attitudes toward fathering, degree of involvement of fathers in childcare, or parental authority patterns. In married-couple families with children present, southern fathers have already experienced marked changes in their sole responsibility as breadwinners during the last several decades because over half of their wives work outside the home. In the South, as elsewhere in the nation, the number of divorced fathers who have either sole or joint custody of their children is rising. Increasingly, fathers are emphasizing their nurturant roles, though social class differences, among others, still shape views about fathers as the authority figure in families.

Literary critic Richard H. King argues that the intellectuals and writers of the Southern Literary Renaissance in the 20th century were attempting symbolically to define their relationship with the region's "fathers." He notes the portraits of the "heroic generation" of ex-Confederates, the pictures of "stern, untroubled, and resolute" fathers that hung in southern parlors. Ironic sons and strong fathers have been predominant images in modern southern literature. Allen Tate explored this theme in his one novel, entitled *The Fathers*. Jack Burden in Robert Penn Warren's *All the King's Men* searches for an understanding of his—and through him, the region's—past by defining a complex relationship to his "father," both real and figuratively (in Willie Stark). William Faulkner seemed fascinated with the "father," portraying ruthless, sometimes cruel patriarchs such as Thomas Sutpen, Carothers McCaslin, and the older Sartoris. These powerful figures succeed, yet eventually, through self-centered pride, are brought to earth. Sutpen's downfall, in particular, comes from his failure to acknowledge his son because the son has black blood; issues of race are tied with fatherhood, as in other areas of southern life.

See also BLACK LIFE: Family, Black; FOLKLORE: Family Folklore; VIOLENCE: Honor

Orville Vernon Burton
University of Illinois

Orville Vernon Burton, *In My Father's House Are Many Mansions: Family and Community in Edgefield, South Carolina* (1985); Jane Turner Censer, *North Carolina Planters and Their Children, 1800–1860* (1984); Richard H. King, *A Southern Renaissance: The Cultural Awakening of the American South, 1930–1955* (1980); Daniel Blake Smith, *Inside the Great House: Planter Family Life in Eighteenth-Century Chesapeake Society* (1980); Bertram Wyatt-Brown, *Southern Honor: Ethics and Behavior in the Old South* (1982).

Fighting South

Few dimensions of southern cultural distinctiveness have provoked more comment than the supposed proclivity of Dixie's citizenry toward personal and societal violence. Prior to the Civil War, numerous European and northern travelers reported from the slave states that the southern people enjoyed soldiering and resolved interpersonal disputes with violence to an unusual degree. Twentieth-century scholars have substantiated this im-

The Alamo, a shrine of the fighting South, San Antonio, Tex.

pression, meticulously delineating antebellum southern enthusiasm for wars, the national military establishment, private military academies, filibustering, dueling, and a wide array of other activities indicative of a peculiarly martial/violent regional temperament. The South's martial reputation survived Civil War defeat, won endorsement in the Lost Cause legend, and gained new vitality in the 20th century. It has been a popular concept that southerners have monopolized the army's officer corps, provided disproportionate support for America's role in both world wars and in Vietnam, perpetuated martial instincts with military titles and military preparatory schools, and enshrined violence (high homicide rates, the Ku Klux Klan) within their social mores.

Some recent commentators would relegate unique southern militarism to the realm of myth. The North, it has been discovered, also fostered a plethora of antebellum military academies and volunteer militia companies. Emphasis has been placed upon violence as an American problem rather than as a regional trait. Still, the South's fighting fame persists, encouraged by a tendency of southerners themselves to claim a special military heritage.

If myth, southern militarism has certainly been an operative fiction with considerable impact upon the region's historical experience. Pre–Civil War antislavery capitalized upon perceptions of an aggressive, violent "Slave Power." A mistaken faith that southerners—by virtue of their military traditions—would prove superior to northerners on the battlefield explains much of the risk-taking intrinsic to secession. In the Civil War northern stereotypes of southern warrior propensities retarded the progress of Union army campaigns. Recent evidence of the myth's substantive impact is more elusive, but when President Jimmy Carter in 1980 attributed his commitment to strategic arms limitation to a recognition that his native region had traditionally venerated "the nobility of courage on the battlefield," thus inducing southerners to lead "the rolls of volunteers and also . . . the rolls of casualties" in America's wars, he gave testimony to a lingering influence of perceptions of southern militarism upon the nation's history.

See also EDUCATION: Military Schools; HISTORY AND MANNERS: Military Bases; Military Tradition

Robert E. May
Purdue University

Michael C. C. Adams, *Our Masters the Rebels: A Speculation on Union Military Failure in the East, 1861–1865* (1978); F. N. Boney, *Midwest Quarterly* (Winter 1980); Robert E. May, *Historian* (February 1978).

Garden Myth

Although it is a regional variant of the generalized image of America as "the garden of the world," the pastoral image of the South may best be understood in contrast to that of New England. This contrast originated in the attitudes of the settlers of Massachusetts and Virginia toward the archetypal pastoral dominions of Western culture: the Hebraic Garden of Eden and the Hellenic domain of Arcadia. During their long history in the Western literary imagination these concepts have been interwoven. Eden and Arcadia have been symbols of the replacement of the cosmic (the nonconscious or organic) state of human existence with the consciousness of time and history. Simultaneously they have been symbols of an illusory recovery, through pastoral vision and artifice, of the prehistoric state of harmony among God (or gods), man, and nature.

The Edenic and Arcadian images have also served as metaphors of the poetic consciousness. The poetic consciousness has conceived of itself as a garden that has been invaded by history and dispossessed, as Emerson said, of its "original relation to the universe." For the first and last time the New World settlement, in particular the English settlement along the Atlantic Seaboard, seemed to make possible the inclusion of the pastoral vision in the historical consciousness. This golden prospect of the recovery of the archetypal garden was wholly illogical, since the pastoral vision had arisen in response to the differentiation of history. But in defiance of logic the tension between the fiction of the possible recovery of the garden and the reality of history has been, at least until very recently, at the center of the American literary mind.

In the course of New England settlement, notably in Massachusetts, the prospect of a pastoral restoration was associated primarily with the biblical image of Eden. Under the terms of their covenant with God, the Puritan migrants envisioned making their new home a "pleasure garden of the Lord God of Hosts." Transformed from a "garden of the covenant," a homeland of the Puritan elect, into the homeland of a postrevolutionary line of secular literary spirits (running from Emerson through Robert Lowell), New England remained a coherent symbol of an Edenic and/or Arcadian intervention in history. But in the South the pastoral vision developed differently. Although Edenic and Arcadian images of Virginia emerged in the writings of John Smith in the early 17th century, and these no doubt bear a relation to the vivid pastoral images in Robert Beverley's *History and Present State of Virginia* a century later, they did not constitute a continuous, closely structured vision of the South as the scene of pastoral redemption. The fundamental reason lies in the emphasis on the secular in the planting of the southern colony. In Virginia, as Perry Miller pointed out, historical expediency dictated the propagation of tobacco rather than the propagation of the faith. Increasingly tied to a chattel slave-labor system by the development of a world marketplace economy, tobacco cultivation provided the model for the South's use of land and slaves in the subsequent production of sugarcane and cotton. Although owning slaves was by no means universal among southerners who owned land, slavery, becoming the South's "peculiar institution," frustrated the desire of the literary mind to project the South as a pastoral homeland.

In the mythic rendition of the plantation as a garden, the slave master might be portrayed as a man of letters with his Virgil or Horace in hand while he supervised his slaves, but in truth the gardener was his illiterate African chattel. This knowledge haunted the quest in the South for the image of the pastoral as an intervening force in history. Its disturbing influence may be seen in Thomas Jefferson's turning from his one explicit denunciation of slavery in the *Notes on the State of Virginia* (1785) to a vision of the American yeoman on his freehold as the representative American; in John Pendleton Kennedy's equivocal treatment of slavery in *Swallow Barn* (1832); and in William Gilmore Simms's account of the relationship between Porgy and his slave Tom in *Woodcraft* (1852). Unwittingly, Simms dramatized the insight of Hegel into the master-slave connection. Although he believes he lives in the superiority of his own will, Hegel suggested, the master in actuality has no will and no existence save in the consciousness of his slave. The slave, moreover, knows this. In this symbiotic situation in the South all men of letters, being connected with the figure of the slave master through their involvement in the defense of slavery, were psychically dependent on the unlettered slave.

The repressed tension between the quest for pastoral redemption and historical reality did not become overt in the southern literary expression until the distance between the South of slavery and the South of freed slaves and freed masters (a society still more complex than the antebellum southern society) allowed for the ironic insights of William Faulkner, John Crowe Ransom, Allen Tate, Robert Penn Warren, Eudora Welty, William Styron, Walker Percy, and other white southern writers. Together with a small but significant number of southern black writers—among them Charles W. Chesnutt, Jean Toomer, Richard Wright, Ralph Ellison, and Ernest Gaines—20th-century southern writers have realized the literary possibilities of the drama of the dispossession of the pastoral ethos by the ethos of history. Making this drama their subject, they have made the alienated literary imagination, the dispossessed garden, yield the rich flowering known as the Southern Renaissance.

See also LITERATURE: Agrarianism in Literature

Lewis P. Simpson
Louisiana State University

David Brion Davis, *The Problem of Slavery in the Age of Revolution, 1780–1823* (1975); Leo Marx, *The Machine in the Garden: Technology and the Pastoral Ideal* (1964); Lewis P. Simpson, *The Brazen Face of History: Studies in the Literary Consciousness in America* (1980), *The Dispossessed Garden: Pastoral and History in Southern Literature* (1975); Henry Nash Smith, *Virgin Land: The American West as Symbol and Myth* (1950).

History, Central Themes

The earliest explanation of southern distinctiveness began with the climate. In 1778, when the South Carolina Assembly was debating the ratification of the Articles of Confederation, William Henry Drayton saw the union of the states as a threat to the plantation economy. "From the nature of the climate, soil and produce of the several states," he said, "a northern and a southern interest naturally and unavoidably arise." Meteorological conditions encouraged certain activities among the inhabitants, Drayton declared, and they in turn made possible a particular lifestyle that became characteristically southern.

One hundred and fifty years later U. B. Phillips agreed. "Let us begin by discussing the weather," he said, in a widely quoted statement, "for that has been the chief agency in making the South distinctive." To Phillips, as to Drayton, climate encouraged sectional interests by settlers in the American states.

From tobacco and rice to indigo and cotton and sugarcane, weather and soil imposed an agriculture of semitropical staple crops that yielded quick profits. The large returns induced planters to create ever larger estates, which led to a labor shortage. The availability of land and the lack of people willing to work for someone else together produced the plantation with its system of coerced labor. "The house that Jack built," as Phillips described it, grew inexorably from a determinative weather pattern.

Other interpreters echoed Phillips's views. Clarence Cason defined the South as that part of North America where the Fahrenheit thermometer reached 90 degrees in the shade at least 100 afternoons a year. The oppressive heat compelled cooks to concoct gastronomic delights to tempt sluggish appetites, thus giving rise to the food-and-condiment school of southern analysts. Other students suggested that the humid heat purified and strengthened a Nordic racial strain to engender a superior type of humanity, sometimes called cavalier.

The environmentalists thus explained the central

theme of the South by the plantation and its products, themselves the result of climate and soil conditions. Staple crops, servile laborers, and lordly masters in theory emulated Old World manorial rulers—this was the South of Phillips and his followers.

The climate-determined South was largely mythic, however, and it appeared so self-serving—an excuse for such glaring inequities in the status quo—that it has been under constant attack. The idea was also difficult to defend in a region that extended through 15 degrees of north latitude, and from sea level to the forested heights of Appalachia, from humid woodlands to semiarid plains.

Even as critics questioned the climate theme, other students pursued the possibility that the South might be identified on the basis of behavior patterns. Charles S. Sydnor pointed the way to new paths of investigation, arguing that southern historians must define their subject before proceeding further. The plantation environment of rural farmlands and sparse population provided examples of the social patterns he used to define the region. W. J. Cash agreed, portraying the southern mind as "what happened when the tradition of aristocracy met and married with the tradition of the backwoods." John Hope Franklin identified the South as a violent land still under frontier conditions, with blood feuds, the dueling code, and a strong military tradition.

Earl E. Thorpe perceived a male sheikdom of erotic libertinism in a haremlike world of subjugated and complaisant women. Slavery was, in his view, as much a sexual institution as an economic or a social one. Other students, however, stressed the gynecocracy—the matriarchy—of the isolated estate, in the families of both masters and slaves. That same isolation and underpopulation convinced David Bertelson that the staple-crop society lacked social unity and showed little evidence of community activities, even those as important as road and bridge building. The lazy South was his version of the central theme.

The geographer Wilbur Zelinsky discussed what he called "settlement characteristics" as a way of identifying the South. In house types and urban morphology, including a lack of spatial pattern to farm buildings and a high incidence of abandoned buildings, he found a "constellation of traits" that were coterminous with the South and represented regional characteristics.

Other students of southern society have at one time or another defined their subject in terms of such phenomena as fireworks at Christmas and a quiet Fourth of July, mockingbirds, xenophobia, a chivalric respect for the ladies, a slovenly and dialectical speech pattern, and shoeless, clay-eating poverty. Pellagra, malaria, and hookworm have also provided thematic interpretations.

Subsequent investigators saw significance in the region's religious expression. Known colloquially as the Bible Belt, the Southeast comprised the largest block of Protestant Christian evangelicals to be found anywhere, and at times that faith impelled people to attack the alluring temptations of flesh and mind. Publicity surrounding the 1925 trial of John T. Scopes in Dayton, Tenn., for teaching evolution dramatized the religious attitudes of southerners and made these beliefs an easy explanation for regional distinctiveness.

One-party politics and a preference for a confederated league of semiindependent member states ("states' rights") gave rise to another theme that took its cue from political platforms and voting patterns. Many political observers in more recent times have discussed the Sunbelt South and its implications for government policies.

The presence of black Americans, of course, has been a major guidepost to a definition of southern distinctiveness. The negative side of the region's racial and social relationships—slavery, segregation, violence, and disfranchisement—has provided interpretive themes. An exception came from historian-folklorist Charles Joyner, who wrote that "the transformation of African culture into Afro-American culture has been one of the major themes of American history, with innumerable implications for every aspect of American life."

Twentieth-century efforts by the national government to eradicate racial practices spurred irreconcilable white historians into pursuing still another central theme. The South, they declared, came into existence only under attack from outsiders. Egocentric sectionalism, or the hundred-year effort to reconstruct the South along northern dimensions, required otherwise divided southerners to unite in defense of their interests.

More recent analysts, such as C. Vann Woodward, have found the central theme of southern history to be southern history itself. Prosperity, optimism, and unvarying triumph, said to be the content of the national past, did not describe the aberrant record of southern history. That, went the argument, made the South, and southerners, different. Other students, such as George B. Tindall, sought the essence of the southern character in a preference for myth, the unreal, and the romantic, because reality was too unpleasant.

No single attribute or collection of conditions has succeeded in explaining satisfactorily the continuing awareness of a separate South. It may indeed be necessary to conclude that aside from the idea or belief, the South has no definite existence. That does not detract from its reality or its impact, for ideas are powerful forces in human affairs. The search for the American South is a chapter in the intellectual history of the country, and the idea of the South is one of the most significant facts in making the present what it is.

See also HISTORY AND MANNERS articles

David L. Smiley
Wake Forest University

David Bertelson, *The Lazy South* (1967); W. J. Cash, *The Mind of the South* (1941); Clarence Cason, *90° in the Shade* (1935); Robert S. Cotterill, *The Old South: The Geographic, Economic, Social, Political and Cultural Expansion, Institutions, and Nationalism of the Ante-bellum South* (1936); W. T. Couch, ed., *Culture in the South* (1934); Carl N. Degler, *The Other South: Southern Dissenters in the Nineteenth Century* (1974); John Hope Franklin, *The Militant South* (1956); Charles Joyner,

Down by the Riverside: A South Carolina Slave Community (1984); Michael O'Brien, *The Idea of the American South, 1920–1941* (1979); U. B. Phillips, *American Historical Review* (October 1928); David Potter, *The South and the Sectional Conflict* (1968); Charles S. Sydnor, *Journal of Southern History* (February 1940); William R. Taylor, *Cavalier and Yankee: The Old South and American National Character* (1957); Earl E. Thorpe, *Eros and Freedom in Southern Life and Thought* (1967); Frank E. Vandiver, ed., *The Idea of the South: Pursuit of a Central Theme* (1964); C. Vann Woodward, *The Burden of Southern History* (1961); Wilbur Zelinsky, *Social Forces* (December 1951).

Motherhood

Street slang and graffiti that commonly refer to one's mother in northern cities are less frequently found in the South, even in its urban areas. Call a southern boy a "son-of-a-bitch" and he might break both your legs. Not because you have insulted *him*; you have done far, far worse: you have insulted his *mother*. And to insult any southern mother is to insult Virtue, Piety, Honor, and the South.

Images and popular stereotypes of "southern mothers" have differed along regional, economic, class, and racial lines. Ideals of southern motherhood differ among ethnic and economic subcultures, yet two particular stereotypes of southern motherhood abound in the popular literature and movies—the black mammy and the upper-class white lady, both portrayed to perfection in *Gone with the Wind*.

Although a remarkable group of gifted scholars has written on southern white women, at present less is known about the white southern mother than about the Afro-American mother in the South. This is at least partly because reality is confused with an image central to the development of the southern white identity. Although David Potter argued that women have not participated in the formation of the national character of the United States, William R. Taylor claims that the South adopted essentially feminine characteristics because the region failed in the masculine world of the marketplace. Most recent studies demonstrate that the South did not fail in the chase after wealth but simply took a different and perhaps more lucrative path. After the Civil War, however, both adherents of the Old South legend and advocates of the industrial New South acquiesced in a sentimental portrayal of the plantation South, which held the southern lady at center stage to justify the existing social order.

In its worst forms the idealization of the southern mother, and hence, the southern white woman, was used to justify the barbarism of lynching black men. Winthrop D. Jordan has shown how sexual fantasies of Europeans, especially the English, were projected onto Africans and combined with slavery to foster an intense racism. After slavery ended, protection of southern womanhood became a battle cry for the repression of southern blacks. Many whites portrayed the Afro-American as a destroyer of social order, and they saw the white family, the basis of social stability, as the most obvious point of defense against imagined or real attacks. According to this myth, white women symbolized the family and needed protection from rape or from intermarriage with black men. Thus, such fears expressed both sexual and social concerns.

W. J. Cash called the idolatry of southern white women "downright gyneolatry. . . . Hardly a sermon . . . did not begin and end with tributes in her honor, hardly a brave speech . . . did not open and close with the clashing of shields and the flourishing of swords for her glory. At the last, I verily believe, the ranks of the Confederacy went rolling into battle in the misty conviction that it was wholly for her that they fought."

Despite the romantic plantation literature, the aristocratic southern white wife was not the only figure idealized. All successful southern men owed their accomplishments to their mothers; whatever heights they attained were attributed to their mother's love, teachings, sacrifices, and examples. Two southern leaders identified with the common man were Andrew Jackson of the antebellum South and Ben Tillman of the late 19th-century period of agrarian unrest. Both men's fathers died before the sons were born and both leaders were reared by their mothers—women celebrated for teaching correct patriarchal values to their famous sons. President Jackson praised his mother: "She was as gentle as a dove and as brave as a lioness. . . . The memory of my mother and her teachings were after all the only capital I had to start life with." U.S. Senator Tillman explained that his mother taught "habits of thrift and industry; to be ambitious; to despise shams, hypocrisy, and untruthfulness; to bear trouble and sorrow with resolution." As their nicknames, "Old Hickory" and "Pitchfork Ben," imply, both Jackson and Tillman were celebrated for the so-called masculine traits one might expect from leaders in a patriarchal society.

Historically, the southern woman was the guardian of the family. She had children with remarkable frequency, rarely disclosing the pain and suffering that accompanied almost constant childbearing. Usually she celebrated her childbearing role. When she was not confined to bed in pregnancy or childbirth, environmental, social, and economic conditions dictated her day-to-day routines: gardening, canning, preserving, cooking; spinning, weaving, sewing, knitting; washing, ironing, cleaning; nursing and caring for husband, children, friends, and animals.

Despite the differences between the North and the South, the role of the mother in the 19th century was very similar in both sections. She was the primary rearer of children and the inculcator of domestic moral values. According to the prevailing view, the southern woman was the moral superior of her husband, so upon her fell the burden of making a decent and moral home, providing a good example for her young children and a refuge for the family patriarch from the turmoil of the workplace or the realm of politics.

Because few public schools were available, the southern white matriarch played a substantial role in educating her children. The early education of most southerners therefore depended upon the knowledge of their mothers and the degree to which they took this role seriously. Some southerners were extremely well taught, but others lacked the most rudimentary book learning. Most mothers taught their girls to sew, weave, and care for younger children, while fathers taught their boys to handle responsibility.

As the upholder of key moral values, the woman was also expected to teach the children piety. She did this primarily by example. Although men were active in southern churches, the mother typically was the more constant churchgoer and usually inducted her children into the social order by taking them to church and by reading them the Bible. With religious values so closely allied to family solidarity, the woman's role in introducing the children to religious faith in the South was seen as an effective way for her to strengthen family ties. As keeper of the family's religious flame, the woman made sure her home was a refuge from the meanness of everyday life.

One of the reasons women increasingly took on teaching positions in the North in the 1840s and later in the South was that the female teacher was widely regarded as a sort of classroom surrogate mother who eased the transition of the young child from the home to the community and furthermore prepared the child to take his or her place in the rapidly emerging industrial society. Women assumed an important role in the classroom in the South even though industrial changes occurred very slowly there. Once public schools took hold in the South, the female teacher rapidly became almost universal in elementary schools, carrying out her maternal function of imparting the right values to the young.

Doris Ulmann photograph of a mother and her infant somewhere in the South, c. 1933

The role of southern mother, nonetheless, sometimes conflicted with the southern ideal of womanhood. Whereas the mother was expected to be a preeminent moral guardian and a tower of strength, as well as efficient, protective, and self-reliant, the ideal woman was often seen as gentle, submissive, flighty, independent, and seemingly unfit to rear children. Certainly, southern women, like northern women, struggled under such contradictions and limitations. If there was a resolution to this dilemma for southern women, it emerged with age, the flighty behavior of the southern belle, desirable in young adulthood, changing suitably with the bearing of the first child.

As novelist Gail Godwin recently pointed out, the roles of wife and mother have traditionally given identity to the southern woman. Godwin's fictional composite southern lady responds to the question of identity: "Who am I? I am the wife of a wonderful husband and the mother of four adorable children, that's who I am." Modern writers have been much more unkind about the image and its impact on the South. Among others, Flannery O'Connor, Lillian Smith, and William Faulkner portray the damage done to women and to the South as they tried to live with the requirements of perfectionism that symbolized white southern motherhood. Women struggled to reconcile the expectations and realities of the modern world and the legend of southern motherhood. And southern white men have been accused by many pop psychologists of exhibiting a "madonna-whore" attitude toward women: the southern mother was worshiped and put upon a pedestal, while other women, those of lower economic status, the daughters of white tenants and textile workers, Afro-American or Indian women, were fair game for the South's young bloods.

The sentimentality of the Victorian era helped shape the image of southern white motherhood and has been preserved in modern regional popular culture. Early country singer Jimmie Rodgers sang "Mother, Queen of My Heart" and Hank Williams later wrote and recorded "Message to My Mother," one of a number of poignant country tunes dedicated to mourned dead mothers. Dolly Parton's "Coat of Many Colors" is a tale of the triumph of a mother's love over poverty. Southern popular culture, black and white, conveys images of endlessly toiling, long-suffering mothers. "Mama Tried" is Merle Haggard's tribute to a mother whose good influence was unable to keep her boy from trouble. "I'm the Only Hell My Mama Ever Raised" similarly is Johnny Paycheck's lament of a boy hell-bent for trouble who rejected his mother for questionable friends and fast cars.

The image of the southern black mother has taken a different path altogether. Although most black women worked in the fields and not in the planter's house, the most popular image of the black woman has been the mammy. The black mammy, like the southern lady, was also born in the white mind, a creation of slavery: "the black mammy, that creature of impeccable virtue, administrative skill, power and nurturing ability, who yet inexplicably remained in bondage." Suckling a white baby at one breast and a black child at the other, mammy was simple, religious, strong, practical, and tough enough to knock about male slaves caught with a finger in the pie or scores of home-sacking Yankee "blue-bellies" and poor white trash scalawags. Unlike the mythical southern aristocratic mother, mammies were not ladylike; whereas white women were viewed as unladylike if they worked, black women were considered lazy and impudent if they resisted working long hours at hard labor. The black mammy sweated over boiling cauldrons, toiled with wash, scrubbed the kitchen, and minded the children. The black mother had to take care of herself and she had to teach her children to survive their inferior place in society. Mammy's religious strength was elevated to sainthood by William Faulkner's character Dilsey.

Whereas white mothers were stereotypically submissive to their patriarchal husbands, the strength of the black mother led to the myth of the black matriarchy. The myth that black women were the dominant force within their families and that fathers were often absent originated with well-intentioned reformers and goes back at least to abolitionist literature. Early depictions of slave mothers pointed to the horrors of breaking up the family by selling children and spouses, the arbitrary beatings of slaves by whites, and the sexual exploitation of slave women by white men. Until the 1970s scholars and the public generally accepted the notion of the "weak," meaning fatherless, black home, and this in turn reinforced and influenced white society's attitudes toward black people in general. The concept of black matriarchy dominated scholarly literature and became a political issue in the wake of the controversial 1965 study by Daniel Moynihan, who held that the contemporary black matriarchal family had its principal origins in slavery. In the mid-1980s concerns about the black family gained new attention because of the increase from 29.3 percent in 1970 to 47.2 percent in 1982 in the percentage of black single-parent, female-headed families. Concern has focused particularly on the high percentage of those families who live below the poverty level. For example, in six southern states in 1980 over 60 percent of all the single-parent, female-headed families were black.

Many recent studies have corrected the grosser misconceptions about black family life, including that of the matriarchy. Herbert G. Gutman in particular has proved the Afro-American commitment to the family as an institution, in both slavery and freedom. He and other historians have confirmed for Afro-Americans what is normally assumed for other groups: the two-parent nuclear family was the normal means for organizing primary experience (sex relations, child rearing, and descent). As a result, scholars increasingly concentrate on other questions such as illegitimacy, attitudes toward working wives, influence of religion, and the division of authority in the family. Nevertheless, black leaders are also calling for more attention to the needs of poor, single-parent black families and to means for enhancing the stability of black families.

A certain irony in the study of the black matriarchy suggests, however, a symbiotic relationship between racism and sexism. For over 60 years scholars, mostly male, pointed to the black family and called it matriarchal and therefore deficient. With the civil rights movement young northern white women who came South began to see heroines in strong black women such as Rosa Parks and Fannie Lou Hamer. When the feminist movement needed heroines, it turned to the scholarly literature on the black matriarchy for role models. *Ms.* magazine devoted an issue to black women as historical heroines for modern women, at the same time that mostly white male scholars have been arguing that there was no black matriarchy.

One of the paradoxes within the historical scholarship of the last decade has concerned the place of black and white women within American families. As scholars have "rehabilitated" the male role in the black family, feminist scholars have shown the power of the wife within white middle- and working-class families. Historians are just beginning to understand the images and the roles of black and white mothers in the American South.

See also BLACK LIFE: Family, Black; Race Relations; HISTORY AND MANNERS: Sexuality

Orville Vernon Burton
University of Illinois

Maxine Alexander, ed., *Speaking for Ourselves: Women of the South* (1984); Irving H. Bartlett and Glenn Cambor, *Women's Studies*, vol. 2 (1974); Orville Vernon Burton, *In My Father's House Are Many Mansions: Family and Community in Edgefield, South Carolina* (1985); Walter J. Fraser, Jr., R. Frank Saunders, Jr., and Jon L. Wakelyn, eds., *The Web of Southern Social Relations: Women, Family, and Education* (1985); Herbert G. Gutman, *The Black Family in Slavery and Freedom, 1750–1925*; U.S. Department of Commerce, Bureau of the Census, *Current Population Reports*, Series P-20, no. 380 (1983), *General Social and Economic Characteristics, 1980* (by state) (1981).

New South Myth

Beaten and frustrated, the postbellum South furnished fertile soil for the growth of myth, for grafting the imagined upon the real to produce a hybrid that itself became a force in history. Hardly had Union armies sealed the fate of the Old South in 1865 before some men began to speak of a New South. By the early 1870s optimists were taking hope from defeat, envisioning a society that would be less sumptuous but more substantial than the antebellum plantation order to which they paid homage but which, they believed, had been shown wanting in the ordeal of war.

The advocates of a New South believed that economic regeneration was the region's most pressing need. To solicit the northern capital necessary to effect that regeneration, they encouraged reconciliation between the old enemies. They promised to treat the black man fairly in his sphere, thereby seeking to soothe any northern consciences troubled by the abandonment of Reconstruction and to promote a harmony between the races that would foster the social stability so highly prized by potential northern investors. Racial accommodation and sectional reconciliation would do much to guarantee the *sine qua non* of the New South program, the development of an industrial economy that would restore prosperity and prominence to the region.

During the 1880s, largely because of the untiring labors of publicists such as Henry W. Grady of the Atlanta *Constitution* and Richard H. Edmonds of the Baltimore *Manufacturers' Record*, the New South idea became increasingly popular. To such molders of opinion, the proponents of the industrial ethos were broad-minded and progressive; its opponents, their numbers ever diminishing, narrow and reactionary. In Grady's celebrated "New South" address before an appreciative audience in New York in 1886, he proclaimed that southerners, having been converted to the Yankee way, were rejecting the ideal of leisure, replacing politics with business as their chief endeavor, and sharing liberally with the black man the region's mounting prosperity. Three years later, Edmonds wrote that the South's vast resources were already insuring the recovery of the position the region had held in 1860 as the richest section of the country. For Edmonds, Grady, and others of like mind, the ideal had been transformed into the actual. By 1890 the myth of the New South as a land that was rich, just, and triumphant was perceived as reality by many southerners.

To a great degree the ascendancy of the myth was the result of wishful thinking. In point of fact, at the end of the century, the southern black man existed in circumstances little better than those of slavery; the prosperity vaunted by the New South spokesmen was largely illusory; the industrialization that had occurred—and it was never so prevalent as claimed—was often controlled by northerners. Still the stepchild of the nation, the South was hardly triumphant, rich, or just.

Nevertheless, the New South myth survived not only the challenge of statistics but also the attacks mounted by the desperate agrarians who embraced Populism in the 1890s. With Populism dying, the intellectual temper of the next 30 years, like that of the 1880s, was characterized by a romantic, optimistic faith in progress. By the 1920s the business boosters were excelling their ideological forebears in touting the advance of southern industrialization.

That advance was indeed rapid. As numerous industries underwent significant expansion during the 1920s, the number of manufacturing workers in the South rose by almost 10 percent while the rest of the nation suffered a decline of that same proportion. Yet if the boosterism of the dollar decade had a sounder basis in reality than did the boomerism of the 1880s, there was ballyhoo in generous measure all the way from the Mason-Dixon line to Florida's Gold Coast. The second-generation New South enthusiasts portrayed the region as a land basking in the rays of prosperity, even though the profits of southern industry often wound up outside the region and southern workers labored longer and earned less than did those in the North.

The clouds of the Great Depression eclipsed the myth, but only for a brief time. By the end of the 1930s, lifted by hopes of recovery and by southern indignation over the region's being labeled the nation's primary economic problem, the booster spirit was again ascendant. Moreover, the agrarian myth, which had earlier served as a counterpoise to the New South myth, lost much of its vitality as a force in man's affairs as many of its adherents either abandoned farming as a commercial enterprise or, succumbing to hard times and New Deal policies, left the land altogether.

World War II ushered in a degree of industrialization long dreamed of by southern promoters. Between 1939 and 1972 the number of factories grew by more than 160 percent and the number of workers in them by more than 200 percent. Prosperity accompanied the expansion of industry as per capita income in the South increased by 500 percent between 1955 and 1975—a rate 200 percent higher than that of the nation as a whole. The New South myth grew ever more compelling as the region's economic advance became ever more real. Yet just as important to strengthening the myth were the labors of the region's industrial promoters, who rivaled the boomers of the 1880s and the boosters of the 1920s in the quest for material progress. Intent upon maintaining what was called an excellent business climate, chambers of commerce, development boards, and newspapers often urged local and state governments to offer industrialists a variety of inducements such as public financing of plant construction, "start-up" programs for new industries, tax reductions or exemptions, and courses in "union busting" at public universities to keep labor cheap, docile, and unorganized. Some promoters also encouraged the token integration of the races to help create a proper image elsewhere, which was but a minor variation on a major theme of the New South movement of a century before.

So striking was the region's economic advance and so successful was the selling of the South that by the late 1960s, pundits began referring to the latest New South as part of the Sunbelt, that region spanning the southern portion of the nation and growing rapidly in population, prosperity, and power. Underdogs for so long, southerners sometimes took what they considered well-deserved delight in the discomfiture of residents of the Frostbelt, who lamented the relocation of factories in the South. As had occurred a hundred years earlier, many southerners saw their region as just, triumphant, and rich—just in its treatment of the black man, triumphant in its economic struggle with the North, and rich in material goods.

The myth failed to reflect reality adequately. Despite changes in the law, blacks found that they were often still the victims of segregation and inequality. Despite the hyperbole accompanying the Sunbelt phenomenon, the belief that the South would soon reduce the North to beggary betrayed an ignorance of the facts. Despite increasing prosperity, the South was hardly rich; as of 1981, average annual per capita income in the region lagged behind that of the rest of the country by almost $2,000.

For all the hope that the New South myth has inspired—no mean achievement in itself—it has countenanced complacency toward social ills, resignation to the abuse of the natural environment, and the rise of a mass culture that diminished the personalism in human relations long cherished in the southern folk culture. Unless the New South myth can be more tightly harnessed in order to serve the general welfare, the idea could remain a negative influence.

See also HISTORY AND MANNERS: World War II; INDUSTRY articles; LITERATURE: Agrarianism in Literature; URBANIZATION: Urban Boosterism; Urban Growth; Urban Leadership

Wayne Mixon
Mercer University

James C. Cobb, *The Selling of the South: The Southern Crusade for Industrial Development, 1936–1980* (1982); Paul M. Gaston, *The New South Creed: A Study in Southern Mythmaking* (1970); Richard B. McKenzie, *Tax Review* (September 1982); George B. Tindall, *The Emergence of the New South, 1913–1945* (1967), *The Ethnic Southerners* (1976), *Houston Review* (Spring 1979).

Northern Mythmaking

The southern cultural landscape is surely as diverse as the human, geographical, or economic landscapes that comprise it. Just as surely, southerners remain, as journalist Jonathan Daniels said, "a mythological people . . . who live in a still legendary land." Southern mythology, in turn, is the product of many cultural forces, both interregional and national in character.

The South has had sufficient materials, and certainly the imagination, to shape a fictitious past that its people could regard as true. But regions to the north of the Mason-Dixon line also had an important hand in these legendary creations. Perhaps because of the long-standing desire to discover a central theme for the southern experience, historians have not cultivated enough of a national perspective on the role the Yankee has played in both the original creation and the tenacious upholding of the South's legendary past. Studies of southern myths have too often failed to explore how regional myths attracted a national audience.

As historian Henry Steele Commager has emphasized, "the most familiar of Southern symbols came from the North: Harriet Beecher Stowe of New England gave us Uncle Tom and Little Eva and Topsy and Eliza, while it was Stephen Foster of Pittsburgh who sentimentalized the Old South, and even 'Dixie' had northern origins." Connecticut Yankee Stowe based her impressions of the South on extremely limited firsthand experience and, penning *Uncle Tom's Cabin* (1852) in Brunswick, Maine, gave national narrative strength and attention—to say nothing of credibility—to a kaleidoscope of mythical images and stereotypes, which a good many people even today assume are historically accurate portraits of the South and southerners before the war. She devised the faithful darky (Sambo) image of blacks; graphically portrayed a villainous version of the plantation overseer who uniquely symbolized the acquiescence of the North to southern myth by being of Yankee origins, from Vermont; and indirectly gave vitality to the related ideals of cavalier and southern belle.

To the same effect, Stephen Foster composed "Susanna" (1847) and "Old Folks at Home" (1851) prior to a one-month excursion into the South in 1852, after which he published "Massa's in de Cold, Cold Ground" (1852), "My Old Kentucky Home" (1852), and "Old Black Joe" (1860). These songs not only appealed to the emotions, but their lyrics voiced a strong sense of nostalgia for the old plantation. Immensely popular over the years, Foster's songs fed the American romantic imagination with a sentimentalized view of what life in the South allegedly was like before the Civil War, although most of them were composed in Allegheny County, Pa. Undeniably, Foster's plantation songs have had a legend-creating impact on the American popular mind, conveniently offering succeeding generations easily voiced and recyclable visions of an idealized life in the sunny South.

Three years after the appearance of Harriet Beecher Stowe's faithful old Tom, suffering Eliza, and sadistic Simon Legree, and in the midst of Stephen Foster's mythic musical production, another northerner came forward to offer additional weight to the developing myth of southern antebellum luxury. In 1855 David Christy of Ohio published his book *Cotton Is King*, and in the process he touched off a great deal of discussion both in America and Europe as to the industrial world's dependence upon the raw cotton of the South. The effect of this book was to obscure the realities of the South's diversified economy and create the impression that Dixie was an empire of plantations and slaveholders.

Even considering the influence of Harriet Beecher Stowe, Stephen Foster, and David Christy, perhaps nothing more emotionally captured the flavor of the southern image than the song "Dixie." Symbolic of the southern way of life, it was written in New York City by an Ohioan, Daniel Emmett, in 1859. Though used as a marching tune by both Union and Confederate forces during the Civil War, it soon became the unofficial national anthem of the South and has remained one of the most important sentimental expressions of southern regionalism ever since. By the time Jefferson Davis and Alexander Hamilton Stephens assumed the leadership of the Confederate States of America, the Emmett-inspired romance had already begun to work its magic. Clement Eaton has described the scene in this fashion: "On February 18, 1861, they were inaugurated in the state capitol at Montgomery, and at the ceremonies a band played the new song 'Dixie,' with its pervading nostalgia. Like the candles, coffins, patent medicines, tall silk hats, plows—indeed, most manufactured articles used in the South—the song that was destined to become the unofficial anthem of the Confederacy was also an import from the

Yankee." Even with regard to their regional mythology, apparently, southerners had cause to regard themselves as a colony of the North.

The efforts of northerners to romanticize the South artistically are of course not limited to Stowe, Foster, Christy, and Emmett. Francis Pendleton Gaines has argued that northern drama and northern minstrelsy, to say nothing of northern artistic images of the South such as Eastman Johnson's *My Old Kentucky Home* (1859) and Winslow Homer's *Sunday Morning in Virginia* (c. 1870), gave special consideration to mythical plantation materials. The case can also be made, as William R. Taylor has done, that it was the literary energy of the North as well as the South—the work of James K. Paulding of New York, for example—that seeded the fictional plantation in literature. And not to be forgotten are the numerous sentimental lithographs of Nathaniel Currier at Roxbury, Mass., and James Merrit Ives of New York City, who offered a national audience unblemished images of Americana, both North and South. Collectively, northern works of art from Stowe and Foster to Currier and Ives did much to create an image of southern history the verisimilitude of which was seldom examined by its avid consumers—an image at times at odds with fact, but of critical importance nonetheless to the development of a regional mythology.

But the questions remain: Why did the North find myths of the South so very comfortable and comforting? What caused this fusion of southern and northern sentiment? How was it that so many northerners became so distinctly of the southern persuasion? The South and the North became copartners in the creation of a regional pseudopast for a multitude of reasons: a latent "love of feudalism" and "romantic hunger" (democratic pretense to the contrary notwithstanding); "status anxiety" or "hankering after aristocracy" on the part of northerners being displaced in either the social or political power structures of 19th-century America; a pristine nostalgia for agrarianism while in the throes of national industrialization and urbanization; a need to hide and sustain an emergent national consensus regarding the place of race in American life. For some (Herman Melville and Mark Twain, for example), the mannered South served as an imaginative alternative to the frayed culture of America during the crass inelegance and inarticulateness of the Gilded Age.

Southern mythology has a clearly national as well as regional character. Northern writers such as Henry James and F. Scott Fitzgerald accorded the legends literary respect; disseminators of American values in popular school textbooks—such as the staunch New Englander David Saville Muzzey—adopted the southern mythical perspective in gushing sentimentally about the demise of the great plantation. It may well have been a northern army officer who first coined the term New South, as an expression of only slightly hidden regret for a southern civilization now "gone" and a cause now "lost." The northern regard for the South as "The Enchanted Country," in short, is long-standing. Many of the myths of the South were cultivated by those—North and South—who never owned a slave or planted an acre of cotton. The nation's genuine fondness for both the South and its mythology remains alive in Philadelphia (whether Mississippi or Pennsylvania), and in both Minneapolis and Montgomery. Southern mythology bears, of course, an indelible southern birthmark, but it also stands as testimony to the durable value of seeing the "southerner as American."

See also LITERATURE: North in Literature; MUSIC: / "Dixie"; Foster, Stephen

Patrick Gerster and
Nicholas Cords
Lakewood Community College
White Bear Lake, Minnesota

Howard R. Floan, *The South in Northern Eyes, 1831–1861* (1958); Francis Pendleton Gaines, *The Southern Plantation: A Study in the Development and Accuracy of a Tradition* (1924); Patrick Gerster and Nicholas Cords, eds., *Myth and Southern History* (1974), *Journal of Southern History* (November 1977); William R. Taylor, *Cavalier and Yankee: The Old South and American National Character* (1957); George B. Tindall, in *The Idea of the South: Pursuit of a Central Theme*, ed. Frank E. Vandiver (1964).

Plantation Myth

The plantation myth is a body of tales, legends, and folklore that defines the antebellum plantation and that is frequently extended to explain the social order of the entire South from Jamestown to Fort Sumter. It emphasizes the precapitalistic and essentially feudal characteristics of the plantation, with specific links to an English Cavalier tradition. It makes, for example, the early colonial South a refuge during the Puritan Revolution for royalist and Anglican gentry. In this context the plantation develops primarily as a social or cultural institution rather than an economic one. Money, then, economic self-interest, and capitalistic gain are secondary to a primitive, premodern desire for honor, distinction, and deference. Individuals function less as autonomous figures than as parts of a living social organism extending through time and space.

In the plantation myth, relationships are ordered along hierarchical lines, and the patriarchal family is the central defining device and metaphor. The wellborn father/plantation master and his sons dominate the structure; beneath them are their women, wives and daughters, then children, and finally white dependents and black slaves. The slave order is similarly hierarchical and familial, if with some skewing in the gender roles: house servants rate higher than field-workers, craftsmen higher than unskilled workers, and the fair higher than the dark.

The actors in this social drama perform prescribed roles. Manners, behavior, and deportment lie at the heart of the system. Performance and appearance form its supreme good. The gentleman and the lady represent only the most popular and outstanding of the various roles or forms dictated by the system.

This legendary order centers on the Tidewater of Virginia and South Carolina. These areas constitute the two "mountains of conceit" of the old regional adage (with North Carolina as the "valley of humility"). The system, however, possesses notable outposts in various other localities around the region such as the Mississippi Delta, the Bluegrass counties of Kentucky, central Tennessee around Nashville, and the Piedmont of Georgia—the triangle northwest of Macon and Augusta. Insofar as plantation mythology might affect the entire region, most southern communities would have had a local version or model represented by a particular family or families. In this system, lesser slaveholding families of less prestigious origins defer to the greater, all slaveholders dominate whites without slaves, whites and males prevail over blacks and women, the country rules the cities, and aristocratic values overshadow commercial and business interests.

The plantation legend has four major sources. The first is the pre–Civil War southern impulse to differentiate itself ideologically from the North. A comparable northern attitude exaggerated southern peculiarity. The novels of John Pendleton Kennedy, the poetry of William Grayson, and the sociology of William Fitzhugh illustrate the southern impulse; Harriet Beecher Stowe's *Uncle Tom's Cabin* exemplifies the northern attitude.

The second source of the plantation legend lies in the post–Civil War period and in the southern need to romanticize its past as a means of comprehending its defeat and its radically altered situation after Appomattox. The former Confederates explained their defeat by creating a legendary chivalric past. Summarized in a plantation order, prewar society was too noble, good, and bright to have survived the onslaughts of industrial, middle-class capitalism from the North. In this way, the war itself developed as the capstone of the plantation legend. It became the ultimate knightly adventure: the Quixotic Quest, the Lost Cause, all the more precious because it was foredoomed to failure. The Old South thereby became a place out of time, its inhabitants as immortal as the Olympians. The plantation South became mythology.

The romances of John Esten Cooke and Thomas Nelson Page mirror the nostalgia of the ideal. Even they, however, fail to measure the full power of the mythology as a regional belief system up through the Southern Literary Renaissance. Indeed, that cultural revival stems in considerable measure from the efforts of a new generation to define its own identity in contrast to the heroes of the mythic past. Thus, the myth might be seen to receive its fullest expression as southerners of the 1920s and 1930s tried to exorcise the plantation ghosts, notably in William Faulkner's *Absalom, Absalom!*, in W. J. Cash's *The Mind of the South*, and in realistic and debunking aspects of Margaret Mitchell's *Gone with the Wind*, all of which appeared in a cluster between 1936 and 1941. This defeat-generated mythologizing existed between 1880 and World War II.

Although less chronologically confined, the third source of the plantation myth arose and thrived in the same period. It was a northern phenomenon, and its sources varied. Rooted partially in guilt and ambivalence about the war, especially its racial implications, Yankee celebration of the plantation myth derived a powerful dynamic from a bourgeois impulse to fantasize an alternative to its egalitarian, commercial, materialistic social order. By this means, the plantation legend functioned as a domestic version of the historical novels of Sir Walter Scott that were so popular on both sides of the Atlantic in the early 19th century. The southerners in Henry Adams's works, *Democracy* and *The Education of Henry Adams*, and in Owen Wister's *The Virginian* stand for the northern idealization of the old southerner. The enormous northern popularity of Page's work and the still larger national audiences of the mythologized *Birth of a Nation*, of Margaret Mitchell's book *Gone with the Wind*, and of the film made from the latter represent the same, continuing influences.

Historical reality offers the final source of the plantation myth and its vitality: the existence of some essential, material sources or roots of the mythological belief. This remains its most debated and even polemical aspect. In modern society the very concept of mythology is laden with negative values; "a truth that cannot be proven," the traditional definition of myth, stands in low repute in a modern, scientific world. The linking of a distinctive regional culture with mythology, then, has the effect of discrediting the notion of an essentially premodern order represented in the Plantation South. Pernicious, self-serving uses of plantation mythology (by southerners and northerners alike) have further discredited the concept. Nevertheless, scholars still argue the basic validity and accuracy of the social system suggested in the popular mythology.

Two general lines of thought have emerged among those committed to material accuracy behind plantation mythology. One group, led by Eugene D. Genovese, advances the material reality of a feudal system in the South that arose out of regional peculiarities of demography and economics, such as settlement patterns, mortality and morbidity rates, religious institutions, slavery, and debt and credit structures. Without dismissing these elements, a second group maintains that a value system came first and shaped the material reality toward the form of a feudal order. Bertram Wyatt-Brown leads this line of thought. By analyzing its material bases, both groups illuminate the sources of the plantation myth's persistence and vitality over time, and suggest reasons why even modern southerners perceive their lives and manners in peculiar ways.

See also AGRICULTURE: Plantations; LITERATURE: Popular Literature; / Page, Thomas Nelson; SOCIAL CLASS: Aristocracy

Darden A. Pyron
Florida International University

W. J. Cash, *The Mind of the South* (1941); Francis Pendleton Gaines, *The Southern Plantation: A Study in the Development and Accuracy of a Tradition* (1925); Paul M. Gaston, *The New South Creed: A Study in Southern Mythmaking* (1970); Eugene D. Genovese, *The World the Slaveholders Made: Two Essays in Interpretation* (1969), *Roll, Jordan, Roll: The World the Slaves Made* (1974); Raimondo Luraghi, *The Plantation South* (1975); Darden A. Pyron, *Recasting "Gone with the Wind" in American Culture* (1983); William R. Taylor, *Cavalier and Yankee: The Old South and American National Character* (1957); Frank E. Vandiver, ed., *The Idea of the South: Pursuit of a Central Theme* (1964); C. Vann Woodward, *The Burden of Southern History* (1968); Bertram Wyatt-Brown, *Southern Honor: Ethics and Behavior in the Old South* (1982).

Racial Attitudes

Although it is impossible to measure racial attitudes directly, they may be gauged from written and oral expressions, gestures, and institutional arrangements. Attitudes may be analyzed as discrete entities. As one authority has suggested, the term *attitude* "suggests thoughts and feelings (as opposed to actions) directed toward some specific object (as opposed to generalized faiths and beliefs)." The term also "suggests a wide range in consciousness, intensity, and saliency in the response to the object."

Racial attitudes in the South have primarily involved whites and blacks. Attitudes toward American Indians and toward Asians have been less consistent and less pervasive. In general, both whites and blacks have held less pejorative attitudes toward these groups than toward each other. Nonetheless, both large groups have tended to see Indians and Asians as separate groups with distinguishing characteristics of their own. Blacks have had to deal with the fact that whites usually have less pejorative attitudes toward other non-white groups. Members of these smaller groups, of course, have their own attitudes toward other people whom they perceive as being racially different.

Among both blacks and whites, racial attitudes have hinged on a bipolar system of racial classification. Whites especially have defined all persons with perceptibly African ancestry as "colored," "Negro," or "black." Gradations of intermixed African and European ancestry, based largely on complexion, have carried some meaning. Both groups, while accepting the bipolar system, have accorded some measure of preference to lighter-skinned members of the "Negro" category. The phenomenon of "passing" testifies to the strength rather than the weakness of the bipolar system.

White attitudes toward blacks in America have never been peculiar to the South. Their expression and institutional implementation have indeed been more salient in areas where slavery persisted after the revolutionary era, but the underlying attitudes have always been remarkably similar throughout the country. Pejorative attitudes toward blacks were evident from the period of early settlement in all the English colonies. Regional distinctions within the southern colonies were fully as important as differences between the nascent North and South.

The origins of white racial attitudes may be found in the interaction of two powerful forces: certain important attributes of English culture, and the need for bound labor in land-rich colonies, which needed to export in order to survive. More generally, these origins lay in powerful urges for domination. The content of the attitudes was powerfully molded by the social and psychological insecurities engendered by the Anglo-European migration across the Atlantic into a land that worked to undermine traditional social controls.

Some scholars have held that these attitudes emerged inevitably as the ideology of an oppressive master class. Others have maintained that they were built into English cultural traditions that themselves formed a part of an ancient western European heritage. A third group has viewed these two possibilities as simultaneous forces that interacted with each other to produce racial attitudes that have been remarkable in the history of world cultural contacts for their virulence, consistency, pervasiveness, and persistence through time.

Few scholars dispute these characteristics. From their earliest contacts with West Africans, both in Africa and America, the English regarded them as heathen, uncivilized, brutelike, and oversexed. They also placed great emphasis on physiognomic differences, on hair, facial characteristics, and especially on complexion. In that age, the concept of innateness of human characteristics was itself inchoate, but there was a persistent tendency to ascribe inherency to the black's physiognomy and cultural attributes.

The actual persistence of the Negro's "black" color was matched by the persistence on the part of whites in trying to explain it, in hoping that it might be changed by the American environment, and in using it as a social marker of degraded status. The sexual charge in white attitudes also persisted, showing itself in fears of the sexually potent and aggressive male and in ambivalence toward the black female's sexuality. The sexual fears of white males were evident throughout several hundred years of violent

Stereotypical tobacco advertisement, date unknown

between expressed ideals and actual practice concerning contact between white men and black women.

Racial *stereotypes* may be defined as the bundles of belief carried by the energy of attitudes. Common American stereotypes about blacks are at least two or three hundred years old. There is evidence in the 17th and 18th centuries of virtually all the imputations that can be found today. The reason, or energizing component, underlying the stereotypes varies. Expressions of these beliefs have appeared in such disparate media as jokes; informal and formal speech; symbols—human, bestial, and otherwise; locker-room walls; the Congressional Record; and somber scientific treatises. Any given stereotype may have little, much, or no basis in fact. Such stereotypes and their primary animating energies include the well-hung male and the hot and easy female (sexual aggression), shiftlessness (imposed social role), dark fingernail moons in light-skinned individuals (inherency, the taint of ancestry or "blood"), affinity with apes (sexuality, historical happenstance, and supposed physiognomic attributes), peculiar musicality (cultural reality). The very common imputation of mental inferiority has been heatedly debated for more than two centuries.

The reaction of blacks to this barrage has shown great variability and ambivalence. For many years blacks could not openly or safely express their attitudes. Undoubtedly many blacks acquiesced to or embraced the value whites placed upon a light complexion and straight hair. Some black men welcomed and absorbed the imputation of special sexual potency. While rejecting the charge of mental inferiority as a slur and a fabrication, a great many black children were placed in such positions of inferiority that they could not help but develop a self-negating posture about their own abilities.

Blacks have long displayed and probably actually held a wide and inconsistent range of attitudes toward whites. Black attitudes are especially difficult to assess because American society has discouraged their open expression to whites and even to other blacks, as well as self-acknowledgment. These attitudes are probably more variable and complicated than those of whites toward blacks. In general, black attitudes have not had the shaping and sustaining support that white attitudes have had; they have not been molded into ideologies in defense of existing institutions such as slavery and segregation. As the controlling group, whites have formalized and institutionalized their attitudes through literature, scientific dogma, laws, institutions, the economy, and enforced interracial etiquette. Blacks have in some measure been forced to react to these formulations.

Out of necessity, blacks have been more realistic and more discerning about individual differences among whites, and thus less inclined to think stereotypically. The instinct for sheer survival in American culture has placed a premium on quick and perceptive analysis of white characteristics and behavior. Unable to afford the luxury of misassessment, blacks have been less prone to generalize and ascribe inherency in white people. Sheer rage has animated some blacks, but often this force has been effectively checked by communal values that reject dysfunctional vengefulness. Obviously the imputation of dangerous aggressiveness to whites has a solid basis in fact. Less well known is the black perception of sheer stupidity on the part of whites, a view that for blacks often has a strong moral dimension.

Since 1960 there has been more change in racial attitudes than at any previous time. Some of this change is more apparent than real, for it has involved only the level of formal expression, not underlying attitudes. Thus, it is no longer polite (in the broadest, most potent sense of the term) to institutionalize pejorative attitudes in an obvious way or to express them in more public forums, such as the news media, advertising, political discourse, and directly to members of the other race. How much these changes are affecting actual attitudes is open to question. Certainly there has been some effect, especially among younger people. Yet there is much evidence to show that these attitudes have in some measure merely gone underground. Their presence is still revealed in private conversations, snide allusions, small-group confrontations, and such written media as hate mail and toilet stall doors.

The South has shared in these attitudes and in recent changes. What has distinguished the South has been the more open expression than elsewhere of broadly shared attitudes, through the institutions of prolonged slavery and segregation, and the open frankness of literate and oral expression. In recent years many blacks have voiced a preference for this openness because it permits blacks at least to know where they stand. On the other hand, many southern blacks have hated the institutional and economic results of these attitudes, as well as the implicit and actual violence that they have encouraged. Changing black views on this matter can be partially gauged by the tread of feet northward and now to a lesser extent back "home."

Thus, racial attitudes in the South have been peculiar not for their existence or their content but for their virulence, saliency, pervasiveness, and the predisposition of white people to overt action and of black people to fear, accommodation, resistance, and retaliation. In the South, open expression and implementation of white racial attitudes have been encouraged by the frequent contact between large numbers of blacks and whites over a long period of time. One can still find traces of these racial attitudes in Maine, but they have played a far more important role in the society and culture of Mississippi. And because they have been so long and deeply embedded in southern culture especially, the chances are that they will persist for a very long time. Certainly it is clear that the South has suffered in this respect from tendencies that have long existed in American society as a whole. In this respect, the South seems like the entire nation—only more so.

See also BLACK LIFE: Race Relations; HISTORY AND MANNERS: Manners; Sexuality

Winthrop D. Jordan
University of Mississippi

Gordon W. Allport, *The Nature of Prejudice* (1958); Angus Campbell, *White Attitudes toward Black People* (1971); John

Dollard, *Caste and Class in a Southern Town* (1937); George M. Fredrickson, *The Black Image in the White Mind: The Debate on Afro-American Character and Destiny, 1817–1914* (1971), *White Supremacy: A Comparative Study in American and South African History* (1981); Reginald Horsman, *Race and Manifest Destiny: The Origins of American Racial Anglo-Saxonism* (1981); Winthrop D. Jordan, *White over Black: American Attitudes toward the Negro, 1550–1812* (1969); Hortense Powdermaker, *After Freedom: A Cultural Study in the Deep South* (1939).

Reconstruction Myth

When historians christened the civil rights struggle of the 1960s "the Second Reconstruction," it came as no surprise to anyone. Ever since Rutherford B. Hayes pulled the last federal troops from the southern states in 1877, the specter of renewed national intervention on behalf of racial equality had been the fundamental myth of southern political culture. The events of the Reconstruction period (usually seen as 1865–77), dramatic enough in their own right, took on demonic proportions in the imaginations of southern white conservatives who saw control by the "white supremacy Democrats" as the only road to salvation for their society. It took these "Redeemers" another quarter century to codify and institutionalize segregation and disfranchisement following the defeat of the Populist party—whose political revolt, according to Democratic campaign rhetoric, threatened to return the South to "the evils of Reconstruction." For yet another seven decades every proposal to alter the southern caste system or one-party rule prompted conservative Democrats to parade the great Reconstruction myth before their constituents or on the floor of Congress.

The Republican effort to reconstruct southern society and politics in the 1860s was, to be sure, a radical innovation in the American political tradition. The abolition of slavery during the Civil War was a revolutionary alteration of the southern economic system. In order to preserve a meaningful freedom for the former slaves, the Republican party favored a postwar policy of civil equality for blacks coupled with the establishment of a Freedmen's Bureau that would supervise the establishment of a free labor system in the South. In the political realm, Republicans found it necessary to enfranchise the freedmen after the war in order to prevent the former Confederates from dominating the new civil governments through the Democratic party. The votes of the freedmen, together with the support of a minority of southern whites, gave the Republicans an electoral majority in each state for at least a few years. This brief phase of Republican control in the South, together with the passage of egalitarian federal laws and constitutional amendments, was what conservative whites meant by the term *Reconstruction*.

Reconstruction's mythic cast of characters included the "carpetbaggers," whom southern whites portrayed as greedy interlopers exploiting the South; the "scalawags," who were traitorous native southern whites collaborating with the Yankees; the freedmen, who were sometimes seen as violent and depraved in the myth but mostly seemed ignorant and lost; and the former Confederates, who were the heroes of the story, all honorable, decent people with the South's best interests in mind.

Southern Democrats were willing to use any means necessary to end Republican control of their states, including political violence. Initially through secret organizations such as the Ku Klux Klan and later more openly, as with Wade Hampton's "Red Shirts" in South Carolina, the Democrats resorted to beatings, assassinations, and armed bands of horsemen at the polls to "redeem" the South from "Negro rule." They justified these extreme methods on the grounds that Reconstruction threatened the fundamental stability of their society: economic control by "the better sort," the social elevation of all whites, and the protection of white women from sexual aggression by blacks were at stake.

During the next two decades violence was occasionally used to discourage black political efforts, but the use of large-scale electoral corruption—against both black and white opponents—was a much more common Democratic tactic. Electoral corruption and violence escalated during the 1890s, when the People's party bolted the Democratic party. White conservatives justified both violence and corruption as necessary to prevent a return to black officeholding and Republican rule. By the turn of the century a growing number of northerners (even within the Republican party) had come to agree with the southern view. Ignoring the Fourteenth and Fifteenth Amendments—the "Reconstruction amendments"—the Supreme Court refused to overturn disfranchisement and accepted segregation as constitutional under the separate-but-equal formula.

During the Progressive era the southern view of Reconstruction became enshrined in the popular culture of the nation. Thomas Dixon's *The Clansman* (1905) was a fictional embodiment of the Reconstruction myth, and William A. Dunning's *Reconstruction, Political and Economic, 1865–1877* (1907) was the best example of a series of historical monographs portraying white suffering in the era. In 1915 Woodrow Wilson held an enthusiastic showing of D. W. Griffith's new film, *Birth of a Nation*, at the White House. The president applauded its cinematic tribute to the great Reconstruction myth, complete with the stereotypical rescue of a white damsel from the hands of a black rapist by the heroic Ku Klux Klan. Two decades later *Gone with the Wind* provided a celluloid update of the myth that survives into the age of the VCR.

Whenever the Congress considered a federal antilynching bill in the years between the two world wars, southern Democrats warned of a return to Reconstruction. The same refrain greeted certain New Deal programs, Franklin D. Roosevelt's Fair Employment Practices Commission, and Harry Truman's desegregation of the armed forces. As the Supreme Court began to strike down the white primary, segregated institutions of higher education, and restrictive covenants in the late 1940s, southern conservatives grew concerned that the justices might actually decide to interpret the Reconstruction amendments literally. In *Brown* v. *Board of Education*, which decided the school desegregation cases in 1954, the Court looked seriously at the intent of the framers of the Fourteenth Amendment—ignoring the myth, for once, in favor of serious historical analysis—but concluded that the issue was irrelevant to its unanimous opinion outlawing segregation. In their denunciation of the *Brown* decision, the Citizens' Councils of the Deep South resuscitated the white-supremacy views of the 19th century and warned of the perils of a new Reconstruction.

The myth was not just the shibboleth of the far right. When John F. Kennedy published his *Profiles in Courage* in 1956, he pictured the first Reconstruction as a tragic mistake. Even after he gained the presidency, Kennedy held to the southern view and initially resisted federal intervention on the side of civil rights because he did not want to ignore what he regarded as the lessons of history concerning federal intervention in the South. Displaying an intellectual curiosity rare among chief executives, however, Kennedy actually invited historian David Donald to the White House to lead an after-dinner discussion of what modern historians were saying about the Reconstruction era. Whether this discussion had any impact on the president's thinking is undocumented, but he proceeded to put the federal government behind the enforcement of civil rights in the South to a degree unprecedented since the 1870s.

For white southerners who had grown up believing in the Reconstruction myth, the prospect was terrifying and infuriating. To refer to federal intervention as a Second Reconstruction was, in their eyes, to condemn such an idea out of hand. They characterized northern whites who came south as Freedom Riders, voter registration workers, or demonstrators on picket lines as latter-day abolitionists or carpetbaggers. Southern whites who criticized segregation, disfranchisement, or the jailing of civil rights workers were scalawags. A rejuvenated Ku Klux Klan engaged in savage beatings, bombings, and assassination, only to be acquitted by all-white juries.

The Second Reconstruction was, however, far more successful than the first. This time federal intervention included systematic enforcement of civil rights legislation by the U.S. Justice Department, the Health, Education, and Welfare Department, and the courts. This time southern blacks used civil disobedience, manipulated the national media, won the support of northern public opinion, obtained effective legal representation through public-interest law firms, and created their own heroes in mythic proportions.

By 1970, when a series of political leaders below the Mason-Dixon line were proclaiming a "New South" that turned its back on racial prejudice, a great change had taken place in the region's political culture. Racial prejudice was still alive and well, of course, but for the most part public discussion of the race question was couched in euphemisms and code words of the sort familiar outside of Dixie. No longer could white politicians expect to be taken seriously if they yelled about the evils of Reconstruction. The Second Reconstruction had arrived—and white southerners had learned to live with it. Some, including historians of that first experiment in racial equality, even came to relish being called scalawags.

See also HISTORY AND MANNERS: Reconstruction; MEDIA: / *Birth of a Nation*; VIOLENCE: / Ku Klux Klan

Peyton McCrary
University of South Alabama

Claude G. Bowers, *The Tragic Era: The Revolution after Lincoln* (1929); Carl M. Brauer, *John F. Kennedy and the Second Reconstruction* (1977); John Hope Franklin, *Reconstruction after the Civil War* (1961); Paul M. Gaston, *The New South Creed: A Study in Southern Mythmaking* (1970); William Gillette, *Retreat from Reconstruction, 1869–1879* (1979); V. O. Key, Jr., *Southern Politics in State and Nation* (1949); James M. McPherson, *Ordeal by Fire: The Civil War and Reconstruction* (1982); Robert J. Norrell, *Reaping the Whirlwind: The Civil Rights Movement in Tuskegee* (1985); Kenneth M. Stampp, *Era of Reconstruction, 1865–1877* (1965); C. Vann Woodward, *The Burden of Southern History* (1961; rev. ed., 1968).

Regionalism

The concept of regionalism is a recent adaptation of the cultural theory of romantic nationalism and the lineal descendant of the idea of sectionalism. In the 18th century a *section* meant what today would be called an interest group and was only incidentally geographical in reference, when interests happened to be locally coherent. Romanticism, which became influential in the early 19th century, helped to promote a new and systematic theory of language, race, and geography that transformed the meaning of the word *sectionalism*. Romanticism held that there was an organic relationship between land and people, climate and social custom, which created national groups that, evolving historically, were recognizable by (and manifested themselves in) distinctive and persistent patterns of language, ideology, and religion, from which the individual took his identity. In the southeastern portion of the United States, the doctrine of states' rights became romanticized, whereby the state became a nation in miniature and hence potentially and morally entitled to self-determination. At the same time, the notion of national distinctiveness helped to fashion a conception of southern identity, which many thought should be embodied in political independence. Analytically, nationalism and sectionalism were not distinct, but sectionalism was generally held to be the political expression, energetic and watchful, of southern interests within a perpetuating federal union.

The failure of the Confederacy left the romantic theory of southern nationalism without an integrated political expression, a state, and cast into disfavor the sectional impulse, which was held responsible for the Civil War. Hence developed the transmuted romantic doctrine of *regionalism*, a word first used in the late 19th century. It referred to a depoliticized version of the theory of cultural distinctiveness, whereby portions of the Union retain their special character. This regionalist vision was first developed in literature. Local color writers, who flourished between the 1870s and 1890s, specialized in capturing through the narrative use of dialect and folk stories the pervading spirit of such places as New Orleans (George W. Cable), the Tennessee mountains (Mary N. Murfree), the Virginia Tidewater (Thomas Nelson Page), and Georgia (Joel Chandler Harris). These were students of a depoliticized folk, notably restricted now in scope to small and unintimidating areas. Through their writings a national periodical readership learned about the curious and harmless ways of other and different Americans.

The development of an unpolitical doctrine of regionalism in the United States may be explained by the history and structure of the American union itself. Because of federalism the notion of an American nation-state was slow to develop and a tradition of centralized government did not precede significant modernization. Although the regionalisms of Brittany and Catalonia arose, as did southern regionalism, as a mythic response to the strains of modernization, they were more prone than the South to demands for political autonomy because they had existed as entities before modernization and annexation by the larger nation-state. Southern regionalism had less clarity, being divided between states and variously defined regions within the South, and having been instigated entirely within the framework of the American union.

In the 20th century regionalism became a topic for sociological analysis, especially in the writings of Howard W. Odum and Rupert B. Vance, both of the University of North Carolina. They attempted to develop a sociology for a southern folk, in which the poverty of its colonial economy might be defined and remedied by voluntary action posing no threat to the stability of the nation. Odum was insistent that regionalism was a healthy recognition of diversity, not in conflict with national interests, whereas sectionalism was egocentric and disruptive: this distinction was challenged as spurious, most notably by the poet and social critic Donald Davidson. Odum hoped that regionalism might be advanced by groups of planning experts, with no stake in politics, whose diagnoses might be implemented. With no southern government, however, it was unclear how Odum's plans might be carried out. The strengthening of both the federal government and states by the New Deal undercut this strategy of regional social planning.

Since Odum, regionalism has ceased to be an ambitious political and social theory sympathetic to social change and has become instead implicitly conservative and atomistic. Largely opposed to urbanization and industrialization and to their encouragement of conformity in social customs, regionalism is often concerned now with promoting preindustrial values and habits somewhat in the spirit of William Morris. Regionalism itself, however, has paradoxically arisen because of that same modernization, and thus can be seen as a mythic system of ideological accommodation by which the material advantages of industrialization can still be enjoyed, while preindustrial values are celebrated and, occasionally, invented.

See also EDUCATION: / Odum, Howard W.; Vance, Rupert B.

Michael O'Brien
University of Arkansas

Michael O'Brien, *The Idea of the American South, 1920–1941* (1979); Howard W. Odum, *Southern Regions of the United States* (1936); John Shelton Reed, *One South: An Ethnic Approach to Regional Culture* (1982); Henry D. Shapiro, *Appalachia on Our Mind: The Southern Mountains and Mountaineers in the American Consciousness, 1870–1920* (1978); Anthony D. Smith, *Theories of Nationalism* (1971).

Religion and Mythology

Religion, broadly defined, rests at the heart of southern culture and what it means to be a southerner. Even critics of the region, convinced that the South can be dismissed as the proverbial "buckle on the Bible belt," would concede as much. Unleashing diatribes against the South as was his fashion, H. L. Mencken abrasively declared the South of the 1920s to be "a cesspool of Baptists, a miasma of Methodism, snake charmers . . . and syphilitic evangelists." Southerners, as James McBride Dabbs has said in a more positive vein, are those Americans most "haunted by God." The central theme of southern culture, Samuel S. Hill has added, is religion, at least in the sense that to be southern is most often to see oneself as having "a radical dependence upon God." Protestantism is to the South what Islamism is to Iran or Judaism to Israel. Currently, evangelical Protestantism accounts for 90 percent of the religious loyalty of the region. Public opinion polls disclose that 9 out of every 10 southerners declare themselves Protestant, with nearly four out of every five of these being Baptist, Methodist, or Presbyterian. Thus, most observers of southern culture—sooner or later, and better sooner than later—come to terms with the region's religiosity.

The relationship of southern religion to southern mythology, although not at all patently clear, is nonetheless significant. Religion in almost every society, the South being no exception, stands in service to the process of social integration. The earliest meaning of the word religion is "to bind together." In this sense religion is a bonding agent of culture—it shapes community. Religion makes the business of relating to one's fellows easier by binding all to a common purpose. The sociologist Emile Durkheim said as much in his *Elementary Forms of the Religious Life* (1912). Religion, Durkheim argued, is the most basic of human symbolic systems, the key to culture, the "primal act." Religion renders a cosmology, thereby summarizing the deepest collective experiences of the cultural group. Religion, in this sense, is thick with meaning as it both shapes and expresses cultural ideology.

Myth functions in much the same fashion as religion and is nearly inseparable from it. It is at base a narrative, a "tale of the tribe"—the traditional stories a culture tells itself about itself. In edited, abbreviated form it simultaneously expresses, establishes, and enhances meaning for the cultural group. Myth conveys a culture's collective consciousness. Its function is to provide a society cultural paradigms that codify and structure the group's sense of reality, image of itself, and ultimately collective behavior. The collective dimension of myth serves as bearer of cultural meaning. Myths, psychologically, assure the mind and reaffirm the ancient collective way. In narrative form they act as mechanisms crucial to the dissemination and transmission of tradition and culture. Mythic tales are received and understood with a "religious" seriousness, for they offer an explanation of a culture. Both myth and religion, then, structure community and culture by providing an inner meaning for the group. They both are social facts, not collective fantasies. They offer cultural pictures, which establish group identity by linking past experience, current circumstances, and future expectations.

Southern culture in its formative stages was structured by a blending of religion and myth. The first southerners explored and settled the region in accordance with the religious and mythological premises of their age. Whether articulated in verse, fiction, and sermons, or borne at unconscious levels, myth pictured the region as a new Garden of Eden. Georgia, for example, was early declared to be "that promis'd Canaan." And as early as Robert Beverley's *The History and Present State of Virginia*, published in London in 1705, one witnesses, according to Lewis P. Simpson, "the origin of the plantation in the literary imagination as the fruition of the errand into paradise." Europeans planting themselves in the southern reaches of the New World filtered their experience through an imagination structured by religiously inspired and mythically designed attitudes about the South, and later generations of southerners would see their experience as but an extension of these attitudes. Thus, by the antebellum era there lay a religious substructure to southern culture.

Slavery, as the centerpiece of the South's antebellum pastoral world, not surprisingly took on the character of a religious institution. Southern culture and its peculiar institution became situated, ideologically and imaginatively, within a sacred and cosmic frame of reference at the hands of writers like William Gilmore Simms. Simms, from his plantation, Woodlands, offered the argument that because the black was totally unprepared for freedom, it was only appropriate that white southerners, under a holy contract with God, serve as stewards and "moral conservators" of the African. Early in the southern experience it was believed that European culture was planted in New World soil out of Divine purpose, and later southern generations developed racial myths based on the biblical myth of Ham. The "author" of the southern way of life, it was said, was God. Slavery, grounded in the Bible, was an extension of His law. Stories that explained the southern cultural experience were thus derived from religion and structured by mythology. Such cultural tales framed the white southerner's beliefs and values within a sacred history and functioned as myth. It was predictable that southerners would come to see themselves as being a "people" in the classical and biblical sense of the word.

By the time of the Civil War the South interpreted its historical experience in light of a transcendent religious mythological reality. "We have pulled a temple down," exclaimed the men in Charleston, S.C., as they seceded from the union in December of 1860. The War for Southern Independence carried with it the aura of holy war. A Confederate myth born of the war years stoked the South's social imagination with stories of high purpose, high heroism, and high drama. A Crusade of the Planters bent on the region's salvation stirred the soul of the South as only religious energies could.

As the South emerged from the ashes of Shiloh, Vicksburg, and Chattanooga and discovered its cause to be "lost," it nonetheless carried with it the sense, as Charles Reagan Wilson has aptly suggested, that the region had been "baptized in blood." The myth of the Lost Cause, like earlier southern myths, resonated with religious imagery. Rituals celebrating the Lost Cause exploited the southern talent for ceremonial style. Through the introduction of social rituals such as Confederate Memorial Day and Confederate reunions, the southern past of both religion and myth was reunited with its tragic present. Southern mythology was institutionalized as a civil religion. Protestant churches and their clergy celebrated the Lost Cause, declaring that while the chosen people had lost their holy war, they had been purified and anointed for a yet greater purpose. Heroes such as Robert E. Lee were compared to Moses.

A new set of prophets arose in the South to voice new southern visions. For some, the promised land was destined to be one of racial harmony, economic fulfillment, and political parity with the North—a New South. For others, the Ku Klux Klan, replete with its religious symbolism and religious rituals, offered visions of a recycled South wherein an indomitable commitment to white supremacy would once again prevail. For still others, conservative Democrats—the Redeemers—seemed to represent a higher order of political virtue and to uphold antebellum codes of white rule, pay proper homage to the Lost Cause, and endorse the fiscal policies of the New South. Religion and myth once again came together in reciprocal fashion to structure a new cultural order in a reconstructed South.

Aristotle's *Poetics* long ago defined myth in a general sense as an old story, a traditional tale, but offered the further observation that myth, in essence, is not simply the story told but the plot within it. Herein, perhaps, lies the best clue to the convergence of southern myth and southern religion. Both share a common infrastructure—a patterned plot of paradise, paradise lost, and paradise regained. The Christian myth relates the story of a human destiny born to Edenic perfection, lost to an earthly salvation by the fall, and capable of being born again to a paradise regained. The South, in relation to its historical experience, long has felt itself a participant in much the same pattern of existence.

As initially conceived, the South was an Edenic paradise, its plantation paradise was lost via the Civil War, and the South since has entertained visions of a paradise regained. Southern blacks, as southerners too, also have seen their mythic history tied to a religious, Christian paradigm—a paradise symbolized by their ancestral African heritage. The plantation South was their "time on the cross" and paradise lost. Their recent experience, inspired by Martin Luther King, Jr.'s dream of having seen the Promised Land, was a paradise regained. Jonathan Daniels characterized southerners—both white and black—as "a mythological people . . . who live in a still legendary land" and are Bible centered. The Bible, with its tales of paradise and human destiny, is the South's ultimate text in both a religious and mythical sense.

Patrick Gerster
Lakewood Community College
White Bear Lake, Minnesota

James McBride Dabbs, *Haunted by God: The Cultural and Religious Experience of the South* (1972); Samuel S. Hill, *Southern Churches in Crisis* (1966); John Shelton Reed, *The Enduring South: Subcultural Persistence in Mass Society* (1972); Lewis P. Simpson, *The Dispossessed Garden: Pastoral and History in Southern Literature* (1975); Charles Reagan Wilson, *Baptized in Blood: The Religion of the Lost Cause, 1865–1920* (1980).

Romanticism

Southern self-consciousness emerged in the wake of the Romantic movement, which provided many of the ideological underpinnings for political and cultural nationalism in the Western world. Underlying this growing sense of distinctiveness were the growth of plantation slavery based on cotton, attacks upon this regional commitment to slavery, and the passing of the revolutionary generation of southern leaders committed to Enlightenment ideas and ideals. Thus, the influence of romanticism upon the South coincided with and encouraged the historical development of a separatist mentality in the region.

Romanticism is itself a term applied to certain intellectual and artistic developments in Europe and America between approximately 1790 and 1830. It implies, however, a variety of aesthetic and epistemological positions, theories of society and history, and political visions. This has led Arthur O. Lovejoy, one of the most influential students of romanticism, to suggest that it would be more accurate to speak of "romanticisms" than to suggest a unified phenomenon. The term *romantic* is also associated with certain types and styles of thought, feeling, and behavior. It connotes, for instance, emotionality, passion, high spirits, self-dramatization, and the exotic. More pejoratively, romanticism is often associated with nostalgia, sentimentality, and overidealization.

Certain figures, events, and preoccupations taken to be "southern" have lent themselves to romantic renderings or were themselves by-products of the romantic sensibility. One thinks here of dashing cavaliers and lovely belles, of florid orators and fire-eating politicians, of heroic Hotspurs and melancholic Hamlets, and above all of the plantation legend and lost causes. The romantic perspective has also fastened upon images of the dark, haunted ruins of war-devastated plantations and celebrated the blasted hopes and melancholy despair of a proud but defeated people. On another level, the folk tradition of black and white music, the powerful emotional charge of Protestant revivalism, and the colorful but dangerous tradition of neopopulist demagoguery have also lent themselves to romantic depictions. Still, no matter how exuberant and boisterous the surface manifestations, southern romanticism has been most strongly attracted to nostalgia, loss, and, at a rarified level, to an obsession with time and history. More generally, if romanticism can be defined as the psychology of the extravagant, self-dramatizing, but ultimately futile gesture, then southern culture, whether taken in its "high" or "popular" incarnations, has been incorrigibly romantic.

Southern writers and intellectuals were initially suspicious of this romantic dimension of the southern experience. From their antiromantic point of view, regional romanticism was a smoke screen for inadequacies and deficiencies. As William R. Taylor's *Cavalier and Yankee* makes clear, antebellum southerners were not averse to questioning as well as celebrating the South's romantic impulses. In the 20th century W. J. Cash is perhaps the best known debunker of popular romanticism in the region. By romantic, Cash meant a lack of intellectual complexity and emotional sophistication, expressed in violence, rhetorical excess, and barely submerged feelings of sin and guilt. Cash's hope was that the South's romantic tendencies could be replaced by a realistic and critical habit of mind. Besides Cash, Lillian Smith also analyzed and condemned the southern tendency to mythologize the region's past. Finally, the work of William Faulkner can be seen as a reflection of and an attempt to cope with the tradition of the "family romance."

Romanticism can also be examined as an influence on the formal intellectual and literary life of the South. Where New England Transcendentalism was a romanticism of nature and the self, southern romantic thought focused on tradition and society. Indeed, where Cash saw the antebellum South as an intellectual wilderness, recent historians have detected a coherent intellectual elite in the South, well-schooled in the intellectual trends of the times, particularly in the counterenlightenment and antiliberal social thought.

As it emerged in the 1840s and 1850s romantic social theory rejected the contract theory of society and politics and objected to the utilitarian, materialistic tenor of daily life and of the emerging industrial order. Under the influence of figures such as Herder in Germany and Carlyle and Scott in Britain, southern intellectuals projected an image of the region as historically unique and organic. The South increasingly seemed to resemble the feudal, hierarchical society of medieval Europe more than it did the atomized society of industrial England or the industrializing North in America. At the center of this social and cultural vision stood the plantation system based on chattel slavery. Ideal social relations were based on the model of the family. Change, when it came, should be gradual and not sudden; in all cases it should be guided by an intellectual and political elite.

Though this romantic vision of an organic order never won out over modernizing tendencies and was dealt a serious blow by the abolition of slavery, it found expression later in the romantic fiction of the late 19th century and remained a subterranean impulse among southern intellectuals into this century. Indeed, with the reemergence of concern with regional identity in the 1930s, certain standard motifs of romantic social thought were voiced by groups such as the Vanderbilt Agrarians and took a populist coloring in the work of the regionalists at Chapel Hill. Some historians have even claimed that this was the consequence of direct influence from antebellum romantic social thought.

There is great irony in the resurgence of romantic social theory—at least in its conservative form—in the 1930s. The men who announced its essential themes were literary men whose critical preferences stood at cross-purposes with mainstream romantic poetry and aesthetics. Allen Tate, John Crowe Ransom, and Cleanth Brooks firmly rejected the view that a poem was an "overflow of emotion" or that it was best understood as the personal expression of the poet. Indeed, these "New Critics" rejected most romantic poetry as intellectually shallow and preferred the more structurally and conceptually complex verse of the metaphysical poets of the 17th century. On the other hand, New Critical aesthetics betrayed certain affinities with Coleridge's emphasis upon the deliberate nature of poetic composition and the importance of internal tensions to the organically constructed literary work. One might say that the aesthetics of New Criticism, with its emphasis upon tradition, hierarchy, structure, and organic form, more closely resembled conservative romantic social thought than it did mainstream romantic aesthetics.

Twentieth-century southern fiction also kept alive several aspects of romantic literature, apparent in the work of Edgar Allan Poe, and carried them over into literary modernism. Here one would have to mention the centrality of an alienated, self-conscious protagonist, a proclivity for the grotesque and the surreal, and an exploration of the recesses of the psyche through a kind of psychological gothicism. Besides the obvious example of Faulkner in *The Sound and the Fury* and *Absalom, Absalom!*, there is the work of Tennessee Williams, Carson McCullers, and Flannery O'Connor and, more recently, Cormac McCarthy, Ishmael Reed, and Barry Hannah. Such writers taken together have continued a tradition of extravagance. Even in the work of novelist Walker Percy, as unromantic and unextravagant a writer as is imaginable, the darker strains of southern romanticism occasionally emerge and stand in tension with Percy's ironic vision and philosophical concerns.

Finally, many of the romantic tendencies in the popular culture and mythology of the South endure in the form of defiant gestures against political centralization, support for white supremacy, belief in the cult of Dixie and the Confederate flag, and the lasting popularity of *Gone with the Wind*. The South still remains a kind of exotic cultural "other" for the rest of America, though California is bidding to take its place. Still, these romantic and extravagant characteristics of the South have become a cultural tic or reflex, trotted out on special occasions or in emergencies, but rarely interfering for long with the South's effort to become modern.

See also ART AND ARCHITECTURE: Gothic Revival; HISTORY AND MANNERS: Modernism; Victorianism; LITERATURE: Agrarianism in Literature; New Critics; Popular Literature; Regionalism and Local Color; WOMEN'S LIFE: Belles and Ladies

Richard H. King
University of Nottingham

W. J. Cash, *The Mind of the South* (1941); Drew Faust, *A Sacred Circle: The Dilemma of the Intellectual in the Old South, 1840–1860* (1977); Richard H. King, *A Southern Renaissance: The Cultural Awakening of the American South, 1930–1955* (1980); Arthur O. Lovejoy, *Essays in the History of Ideas* (1948); Michael O'Brien, *The Idea of the American South, 1920–1941* (1979); Rollin G. Osterweis, *Romanticism and Nationalism in the Old South* (1949); William R. Taylor, *Cavalier and Yankee: the Old South and American National Character* (1957); Twelve Southerners, *I'll Take My Stand: The South and the Agrarian Tradition* (1930).

Stereotypes

A stereotype is, in the end, a composite of accurate generalization and dubious belief. The term *stereotype*—introduced to the social sciences by Walter Lippmann's book *Public Opinion* (1922)—refers to those "pictures in our heads" drawn from the proverbial "kernel of truth." Stereotypes are mental overstatements of difference, preconceived beliefs about classes of people, images that are sustained precisely because they contain an image of truth. Stereotypes are, in this sense, mental portraits drawn from a modicum of fact, exaggerated and simplified.

Findings regarding the so-called Contact Hypothesis—alleging that the greater the frequency of interaction between groups the lower the level of prejudice and stereotype—suggest the difficulty of abolishing southern or other stereotypes. Although the findings appear mixed, increased exposure or contact actually works, in some cases, to increase stereotyping. Those with an intermediate degree of interregional experience seem most likely to generalize about regional differences. In short, mod-

Grocery store window, Mebane, N.C., 1939

erate amounts of both direct exposure and education solidify rather than weaken the impulse to stereotype. Regional stereotypes are likely to continue, along with the quest to understand the exact nature of the regional differences—North and South—that pattern these thoughts.

The South is often viewed as a land populated by a succession of predictable stock characters—formerly a land of happy darkies with watermelon or banjo, sadistic overseers, coquettish belles, chivalrous cavaliers, vengeful Klansmen, and more recently a land of rambunctious good old boys, demagogic politicians, corrupt sheriffs, country and western good old girls, nubile cheerleaders, football All Americans with three names, neurotic vixens with affinities for the demon rum, Bible-thumping preachers haunted by God, sugary Miss America candidates of unquestioned patriotism, toothless grizzled "po' white trash," and military "lifers" of considerable spit but little polish.

This stereotyped South is a country on the mental map of the national imagination, its citizenry a distillation of both fact and fiction. To many students of southern culture, the South has sustained its measure of regional distinctiveness because of a long-held and abiding set of cultural values that southerners believe clearly separate them from American culture at large. The South, in this sense, has done much to create and perpetuate its regional stereotypes owing to their usefulness in helping to shape a self-image and a regional consciousness. For northerners the South is seen largely through a kaleidoscope of regional stereotypes and images. To them the South serves as both America at its extreme and as "Uncle Sam's other province."

George B. Tindall suggests that the temptation is to deal mentally with the South in accordance with the generally held categories of a Sunny South versus a Benighted South. Heavily edited cartoons of social reality portray on the one hand an ornamental, utopian, mythic South of gallant cavaliers and beauteous belles (or more recently, a Sunbelt South of the nouveau riche) and on the other a semisavage South of abject poverty feeding moral degeneracy. America's and the world's view of the South seldom transcended these hardened stereotypes. One's mental vision of the South seems either given to the romantic glow of late antebellum plantation splendor (or modernized versions thereof) or the counterimage of what W. J. Cash once saw fit to call the "romantics of the appalling." One must mentally arbitrate between and among the list of supposed southern traits that flow from such stereotyped belief. Southerners, as the story is told, are, at once, conservative, radical, tradition loving, courteous, loyal to family ties, conventional, generous, lazy, faithful, very religious, ignorant, stubborn, excessively nationalistic, jovial, honest, witty, kind, superstitious, naive, revengeful, stolid, and flamboyant. Indeed, the South and southerners have been many things to many people.

The notion of the Sunny South dates from earliest southern history and southern consciousness. The pre-South, or if one prefers, the South of the colonial era, tried to fashion a Sunny South stereotype for public consumption. The discovery and exploration of the New World climaxed a European tradition of grand historical visions of a golden age, of paradise, and of a pure and sacred Eden, and such a view held particularly for the South. For Europeans, America was a mythical land from the beginning, but the South especially was thought destined to be paradise regained. The southern reaches of the fresh, green country of the New World seemed a confirmation of utopian promises. Early settlers in Roanoke Island on the Outer Banks of present-day North Carolina claimed to find "the soil richer, the trees taller, the ground firmer and the topsoil deeper." In 1716 Lieutenant Governor Alexander Spotswood of Virginia argued that the Blue Ridge Mountains shone with the sun's perpetual splendor. The Sunny South inspired the imagination with what Sir Robert Montgomery in 1717 called "natural Sweetness and Beauties." For later generations the South of course became, as W. J. Cash phrased it, "a sort of stage piece out of the eighteenth century, wherein gesturing gentlemen moved soft-spokenly against a background of rose gardens and dueling grounds, through always gallant deeds, and lovely ladies, in farthingales, never for a moment lost that exquisite remoteness which has been the dream of all men and the possession of none." The plantation South of the proverbial moonlight-and-magnolias myth enjoyed, and still enjoys, a career in song and story and was celebrated in various media, from the novel to the musical ballad to the motion picture.

The sectional stereotype of most recent vintage, yet very much in the Sunny South tradition, is the congenial view of the Southland as the Sunbelt. Building upon established mental and narrative conventions, the vision of the region is now said to be one of corporate profits, retirement havens, and salubrious climate. The new, bright image of the Sunbelt South, as with most social stereotypes, is partly based on fact. Although the image of the Sunbelt is a mental caricature of the southern situation, the features it exaggerates are indeed real ones. The South is, as many have reported, closing the economic gap between itself and the non-South. In 1930 the South's income was only 60 percent of the national average, but by 1980 the region had closed the gap to 90 percent plus. Yet, as A. J. Cooper, the black mayor of Pritchard, Ala., aptly put the matter in 1978: "There is a lot of shade in the Sunbelt." The South still has a higher proportion of poor than the rest of the nation. The Sunbelt image is at best a case of "sloppy regionalizing" (its patterns of supposed affluence better fit the West than the South). At worst, it is yet another case of mental shorthand at work—stereotyping on a grand scale, with an impact on public policy.

Scenarios of "another South," populated by rednecks, hillbillies, the prototypical itinerant suspenders-snapping Bible-toting preachers, political demagogues, Klansmen, and degenerate aristocrats, have also been part of the nation's mental image of Dixie. Long ago William Byrd II wrote in the colonial era of the region's "indolent wretches" in his *History of the Dividing Line*, while Augustus Baldwin Longstreet offered a fictional composite of the "bad southerner" in Ransy Sniffle, as did Johnson

Hooper with Simon Suggs. Erskine Caldwell's portrait of the mindless, inarticulate, degenerate southern "yahoo," with chewing-tobacco stains on his beard stubble, contributed to the view of the Sunny South as a region cursed by the ravages of pellagra and hookworm, a land of Baptist barbarians and vigilantes, which South-baiter H. L. Mencken dismissed as a grotesque, a country populated by the peculiar American species, *Homo Boobiens*. This South, of so-called hog-wallow politics and abnormal neuroticism, found additional portrayals in the southern gothic drama of Tennessee Williams (*The Glass Menagerie*, 1945), media advertising (Mountain Dew ads), and television shows and movies (*Dukes of Hazzard*, *Easy Rider*, and *Deliverance*).

Southern stereotypes—ranging from images of a proslavery South, the prosecession South, the agrarian South, the states' rights South, the Confederate South, to the conservative South, the one-party South, the fighting South, the lazy South, the Klanish South, the civil rights South—all offer, in their way, a vision of a monolithic South that is out of keeping with the region's intricate complexity. As a result, southerners seldom have been understood much beyond these sharply etched categories.

See also BLACK LIFE: Film Images, Black; Literary Portrayals of Blacks; MEDIA articles

Patrick Gerster
Lakewood Community College
White Bear Lake, Minnesota

Walter Lippmann, *Public Opinion* (1922); John Shelton Reed, *The Enduring South: Subcultural Persistence in Mass Society* (1974), *One South: An Ethnic Approach to Regional Culture* (1982); Harry Triandis and Vasso Vasiliou, *Journal of Personality and Social Psychology* (November 1967); Frank E. Vandiver, ed., *The Idea of the South: Pursuit of a Central Theme* (1964); Robin M. Williams, *Strangers Next Door: Ethnic Relations in American Communities* (1964).

Agrarians, Vanderbilt

The Vanderbilt (or Nashville) Agrarians were in a sense an extension of the literary circle that came to be known as the Fugitives in the early 1920s. By mid-decade the *Fugitive* magazine of poetry and criticism (1922–25) had ceased publication, and the Fugitives began to disperse. Two of its principal participants, John Crowe Ransom and Donald Davidson, remained on the Vanderbilt faculty and stayed in close touch with other members of the Fugitives, especially Allen Tate and Robert Penn Warren. These four were in large part responsible for planning and seeing into print the "southern book" they and others on the Vanderbilt campus talked about sporadically in the late 1920s.

The book was *I'll Take My Stand: The South and the Agrarian Tradition* (1930), by Twelve Southerners, the basic statement of the social, economic, political, and cultural position of the Agrarians, often referred to as a "Southern Manifesto." Just as the name "Fugitives" was applied to the magazine that launched a major literary movement, so the designation "Agrarians" labeled participants in what many perceived to be a translation of the Fugitive spirit into a related social movement.

The Fugitives had largely ignored politics in their concern with literature, and, according to Donald Davidson, they shifted their focus to social problems because of the Scopes Trial in Dayton, Tenn., in July 1925. The trial involved a contrived violation of a Tennessee statute prohibiting the teaching of evolution in public schools. It was conducted in a circus atmosphere under a powerful spotlight of national publicity designed, in the view of the incipient Agrarians, to ridicule the local culture and humiliate the plain folk of Tennessee. Not until the late 1920s did the conversations and exchanges of letters that followed result in the development of an eclectic manuscript containing contributions by such persons as historian Frank Owsley, psychologist Lyle Lanier, political scientist H. C. Nixon, biographer John Donald Wade, and novelists Robert Penn Warren, Stark Young, and Andrew Lytle. Ransom drafted, and the others subscribed to, a short introductory "Statement of Principles," in which the authors declared themselves southerners, "well acquainted with one another and of similar tastes . . . and perhaps only at this moment aware of themselves as a single group of men."

I'll Take My Stand is a defense of a traditional culture with an agricultural economic base threatened by a modern urban-industrial society. Allen Tate was later to refer to a more universal dimension of the book—a defense of religious humanism. The Agrarians eventually admitted that they were stronger on the critical side than they were in articulating positive values and developing practical ways of realizing their goals. The continuing appeal of the Agrarian manifesto is its critique of the centralized state and the modern mass society produced by an expanding industrial order that reduces man to a functional cog in a production machine, ruthlessly exploits nature, and makes a cash agreement the only binding one. The Agrarians are increasingly recognized as farsighted, even prophetic, observers rather than the reactionary, impractical supporters of the southern romantic moonlight-and-magnolias myth that many of the early critics acccused them of being.

As a movement, Agrarianism made little or no headway, although some effort was made to expand the public's awareness of its main doctrines. In the early 1930s Ransom in particular debated prominent critics of the Agrarians before surprisingly large audiences in several cities. He also devoted himself to the pursuit of economic study with a view to producing a treatise on agrarian economics, but the project never went beyond a draft stage. For several years various members of the group were actively engaged in social and political criticism, much of which appeared in the *American Review*. Their last major group publication was *Who Owns America?* (1936), jointly edited by Herbert Agar and Allen Tate. In this book, essays by a substantial majority of the Agrarians were published with contributions from various English Distributists, whose leading advocates were Hilaire Belloc and G. K. Chesterton—Catholic traditionalists and prominent literary figures in England. Shortly thereafter, Ransom left Vanderbilt, and he and the other Agrarians turned entirely to their literary and academic preoccupations, although a number of them continued to engage in social commentary and political activism on an individual basis. Davidson never ceased to hope for further collective efforts to implement an Agrarian program.

See also LITERATURE: / Davidson, Donald; Lytle, Andrew; Ransom, John Crowe; Tate, Allen; Warren, Robert Penn; Young, Stark

William C. Havard
Vanderbilt University

William C. Havard and Walter Sullivan, eds., *A Band of Prophets: The Nashville Agrarians after Fifty Years* (1982); Thomas Daniel Young, *Waking Their Neighbors Up: The Nashville Agrarians Rediscovered* (1982).

Anglo-Saxon South

The term *Anglo-Saxon* has been more a self-congratulatory and exhortatory banner than a precise definition. Its greatest vogue was after the Mexican War and again from the 1890s through the 1920s. Nationally, it was associated with territorial expansion and ethnic comparison, buttressed by Darwinian racial theorizing and hostility toward southern and eastern European immigration. In the South it came to represent white supremacy and the solidarity of northern European stocks. Although the term initially was used to distinguish the Englishman from the Celt or the Latin, the Huguenots were easily embraced as southern Anglo-Saxons, as were the Scots and the Scotch-Irish countrymen of Andrew Jackson and John C. Calhoun. In her epic of southern suffering and pride, Margaret Mitchell derived her quintessential heroine, Scarlett O'Hara, from well-assimilated Irish seed, without arousing purist complaint.

The pre–Civil War manifest Anglo-Saxon destiny was to absorb and assimilate other lands and peoples, but by the end of the century it had become an exclusionist philosophy. European and American theorists gave it a racial base. Teutonist professors such as Herbert Baxter Adams, the southern labor reformer Alexander McKelway, and others traced American democracy back to early Germany. Georgia's Methodist Bishop Warren A. Candler lauded Anglo-Saxon expansion as God's chosen religious instrument. For naturalist writer Jack London, nature made the choice. The Anglophile North Carolina–born editor and diplomat Walter Hines Page believed that the Anglo-American race held the key to world progress.

The pessimistic side of Anglo-Saxon theorizing was represented by the patrician New England exclusionist Henry Cabot Lodge, who feared that the high birthrate of the new immigrants portended the decay and submergence of the old stock. Southern senators such as Alabama's Tom Heflin picked up the exclusionist refrain.

Although racial theorizing was the particular province of the Northeast, it was easy for southerners to clothe white supremacy in the popular Anglo-Saxon metaphor. Tribunes of white racialism led by South Carolina Senator Ben Tillman called upon Saxon yeomen to enforce black subordination. As the new immigration poured into the rest of the nation, it was popular to picture the South as the remaining bastion of Anglo-Saxon purity.

World War I divided the northern Europeans, and postwar restrictionism diminished the immigrant flow. The vogue of Anglo-Saxonism declined, leaving only the promise of the reborn Ku Klux Klan to protect Anglo-Saxon civilization from submergence by alien people, while the textile mills were lured south by promises of pure Anglo-Saxon labor that would not join unions or strike.

David Chalmers
University of Florida

Thomas F. Gossett, *Race: The History of an Idea in America* (1963); Martin E. Marty, *Righteous Empire: The Protestant Experience in America* (1970).

Appalachian Myth

For the local writers and home missionaries who "discovered" Appalachia during the 1870s, the "otherness" of the region was axiomatic, and it gave shape to their activities. It yielded travel sketches and short stories that identified Appalachia as an exotic "little corner" of the nation, cut off from the more pleasing aspects of modern American life. It yielded home missionary work designed to integrate the mountaineers into the mainstream of American (Protestant) civilization.

Largely as a result of the literary exploitation of Appalachia by local color writers and the publicity generated to support home missionary work in the region, by the mid-1880s the image of Appalachia as a strange land inhabited by a peculiar people had become so well established in the American consciousness as to require both elaboration and explanation. Of what exactly did the otherness of Appalachia consist? Why was a region close to the centers of American population a strange land and its white, native-born, Protestant population of Anglo-Saxon descent a peculiar people? The answers to these questions, framed in a variety of ways and with a variety of possible implications to be drawn from them, comprised the myth of Appalachia, which contained the following assumptions: (1) the mountainous portions of six or more southern states formed a coherent topographic region; (2) the mountain people formed a homogeneous population; (3) social and economic conditions were the same throughout the mountain region; (4) the culture of the mountaineers—both their beliefs and their behaviors—was consistent throughout the region. Which of these was the cause of the others was much debated from the mid-1880s, as were the supposedly real characteristics of the region's topography, population, society, economy, and culture. Also of concern, of course, was the matter of how Americans should feel about the existence of this strange land and peculiar people, and what they should do about it. The myth of Appalachia functioned to normalize and make acceptable Appalachian otherness, even if it did not convince everyone of the wisdom of the situation.

Those who saw Appalachian otherness as a threat to the achievement of national unity, or who identified one or another of the characteristics of mountain life and landscape as undesirable, viewed Appalachian otherness as a problem in need of explanation and the characteristics of mountain life as a fact needing modification. At the same time, however, many argued (beginning about 1895) that Appalachian otherness was legitimate in a nation characterized by regionalism and pluralism, but they wished nonetheless to understand the origin of this otherness. Many were also skeptical about one or another aspect of mountain life. Thus, although the myth of Appalachia has made Appalachian otherness seem normal for Americans, it has not impeded efforts by outsiders to modify some aspects of mountain life. Indeed, since the 1880s it has focused continuing attention on the area and has facilitated the planning (and legitimation) of a variety of schemes for "improving" conditions in the mountains.

The myth of Appalachia emerged as a way of explaining the image of Appalachia as a strange land inhabited by a peculiar people, but the myth itself generated additional images. The most prominent of these have been (in approximate historical sequence): (1) Appalachia is the opposite of America; (2) the mountain economy is primitive; (3) the mountaineers are a survival of America's pioneer population; (4) the mountaineers cannot leave the mountains without becoming deracinated; (5) the mountaineers are a hyper-rural population; (6) the mountaineers are a folk and their culture a folk culture; (7) the mountain economy is based on self-sufficiency in agriculture and manufacturing; (8) Appalachia serves as a model against which American civilization may be evaluated (in a wide variety of ways); (9) Appalachia is a pocket of poverty; (10) Appalachia has been victimized by outside (American) interests; (11) Appalachia has been (is) a colony of America; (12) the mountaineers when leaving the region retain their culture and thus become aliens in a strange land and among a peculiar people. The last three are currently dominant, although most of the others persist in one way or another in contemporary thought and action.

See also ENVIRONMENT: / Appalachian Mountains; ETHNIC LIFE: / Appalachians

Henry D. Shapiro
University of Cincinnati

Harry M. Caudill, *Night Comes to the Cumberlands: A Biography of a Depressed Area* (1962); Ronald D. Eller, *Appalachian Journal* (Autumn–Winter 1983–84), *Miners, Millhands, and Mountaineers: The Modernization of the Appalachian South, 1880–1930* (1981); John Gaventa, *Power and Powerlessness: Quiescence and Rebellion in an Appalachian Valley* (1980); Helen M. Lewis et al., *Colonialism in Modern America* (1978); Henry D. Shapiro, *Appalachia on Our Mind: The Southern Mountains and Mountaineers in the American Consciousness, 1870–1920* (1978), *Appalachian Journal* (Winter 1983); David E. Whisnant, *All That Is Native and Fine: The Politics of Culture in an American Region* (1981), *Modernizing the Mountaineer: People, Power and Planning in Appalachia* (1981).

Carter Era

The 1976 presidential campaign and subsequent election of Jimmy Carter signaled a major change in the South's image. The negative 1960s image of the South as the place of civil rights conflict gave way to the more favorable image of a land of charming eccentricities, a pleasant lifestyle, traditional small-town American values, and a booming Sunbelt economy.

When the 1976 campaign began, Carter was a hopeless long shot, but after he put together a string of primary victories, including capture of the black vote, the national media began to take notice. Carter's southern background became the key element in the national attention focused on the Georgian. Carter was soon being portrayed as a southern version of a Frank Capra film hero, talking about a government "as good and decent as the American people themselves." In the aftermath of Vietnam and Watergate, the nation seemed naturally to choose its presidential candidate from a region that knew the moral complexities of life and yet asserted simple Baptist moralisms and religiosity as a way of dealing with them. Carter played up his southern ties, telling cheering southern audiences, "Come January we are going to have a President in the White House who doesn't speak with an accent."

The Democratic party convention, held in New York City's Madison Square Garden in August of 1976, was a symbolic triumph not only for Carter but for the South as well. In the bicentennial year of the nation's independence, 111 years after the end of the Civil War, another stage of sectional reconciliation occurred, with a national political institution turning over its leadership to a son of the Deep South. The emotional high point was the last day of the meeting, when Martin Luther "Daddy" King led the convention in the singing of "We Shall Overcome."

After the convention, the national media devoted even more attention to understanding this new South that had produced Carter. *Saturday Review* published a symposium on the "South as the New America" in its 4 September 1976 issue; *U.S. News and World Report* did a feature on the "New South" on 2 August 1976; and *Time* magazine provided an in-depth look at the region through the "South Today" special section of its 27 September

1976 issue, which had articles not only on politics but on "The Good Life," "Those Good Old Boys," "Segregation Remembered," "Home-Grown Elegance" (food), football, stock-car racing, honky-tonk music, and an essay, "The South Tomorrow," by historian C. Vann Woodward.

Southern writers, particularly humorists, were kept busy chronicling and interpreting the Carters and the South to the nation. Larry L. King wrote "We Ain't Trash No More" for *Esquire* (November 1976). Roy Blount, Jr., emerged as one of the preeminent southern interpreters of the Carters. Watching Carter's nomination in New York City, Blount had said he felt "like a man who goes from being half eat up with hookworms to catching nice speckled trout with them." Labeling himself a "Crackro-American" writer, he published a series of magazine articles, later collected as *Crackers* (1982), which dealt with country music, opossums, southern women, good old boys, and other topics essential to understanding the region.

The mythology of the Carter era combined various existing images of the South. Interest in the Carter family as a collection of southern eccentrics was particularly pronounced. Wife Rosalyn seemed to be the "iron magnolia," sweet and gentle on the surface but tough underneath; Miss Lillian, the candidate's mother, was a feisty grande dame; sister Ruth Carter Stapleton was a faith-healing evangelist. And, finally, brother Billy was the beer-guzzling good old boy. Writers struggled to determine how "southern" Jimmy himself was. A peanut farmer, a nuclear engineer in the navy, a born-again Baptist, a businessman—Carter embodied paradoxical images of the Old and New South.

Plains, Ga., emerged as a new symbolic center of the southern experience. It appeared in news stories as a typically southern, yet also American, community. Its train depot, café, service stations, pool halls, and its barber shops and beauty parlors could have been midwestern, yet the presence of a seemingly high percentage of stereotypical southerners, as well as the ever-present racial and evangelical religious aspects, set Plains off as a clearly southern landscape. The peaceful quality of life in the rural and small-town South was much praised by observers, many of whom also lauded the bustling cities of the region.

Carter's inauguration day, 20 January 1977, evoked images of Jeffersonian simplicity, as the new president walked to the ceremonies. His inaugural address was a sermon, notable for its explicit use of civil religious "God language," seeing the nation under divine judgment. There were southern touches, such as the presence of James Dickey, the unofficial poet laureate of the administration, who wrote a poem entitled "The Strength of Fields," which he read at the preinaugural gala. "Everybody wants to be a Southerner now," he was quoted as saying. In addition to the seven inaugural balls, the world's largest square dance was staged. Peanut souvenirs were everywhere in the nation's capital. *Newsweek* magazine described "the dawning of a Dixiefied new era." Soon southern writers were being feted in the White House, and musicians such as the Allman Brothers, Charlie Daniels, and Willie Nelson performed there. *Carter Country*, a network television situation comedy featuring an inept white sheriff, a hip black deputy, and assorted small-town Deep South characters (it was set in Georgia), premiered in 1977.

As time passed, though, Carter and his administration were less frequently portrayed by the national media simply in southern terms. On a trip to the South in the summer of 1977, Carter noted that he was pleased to see fewer stories in the national media about his being a southerner. "Now I, like you, am an American," he said. In the 1980 campaign, the South, like the rest of the nation, deserted Carter. Nonetheless, the earlier Carter campaign and presidency helped to focus national attention on the South and led to changes in perception about the region and its people.

See also POLITICS: / Carter, Jimmy; WOMEN'S LIFE: Carter, Lillian; Carter, Rosalyn

Charles Reagan Wilson
University of Mississippi

Robert M. Pierce, in *Perspectives on the American South*, vol. 2, ed. Merle Black and John Shelton Reed (1984); Stephen A. Smith, *Media, Myth, and the Southern Mind* (1985).

Cash, W. J.

(1900–1941) Journalist.

Wilbur Joseph Cash was a Piedmont southerner, born in Gaffney, S.C., in 1900, a graduate of Wake Forest College, a journalist for the Charlotte *News*, who died by his own hand in Mexico City in 1941. His influence rests upon a single work, *The Mind of the South*, published in 1941, an attempt to analyze the relationship between social consciousness and culture in the region. As a prose stylist, Cash was a talented rhetorician, much influenced by H. L. Mencken's slashing, witty, and barbed journalism, but developing his own version, narrower in range of reference and accomplishment, conversational, sentimental, humorous, candid, emotional, and possessed of great impetus of narrative; it is a style, like that of Thomas Wolfe, best relished in youth.

Cash is the leading proponent of the thesis of southern cultural unity, which he argues was fashioned by climate, physical conditions, frontier violence, clannishness, and Calvinist Protestantism, all of which conspired to create a romantic hedonism, a *zeitgeist* of antiintellectualism and prejudice most brutally expressed in racism, which Cash called the "savage ideal." Having evolved before the Civil War, this unity connects the Old and New South. For Cash the South's industrial transformation had failed to create the class consciousness and intellectual flexibility appropriate to such a society, thus the sensibility of the savage ideal had remained the master of southern history. Cash himself was a liberal in racial matters by the standards of his time, that is, he had adjusted his views to deprecate the enemies of blacks, but not yet altered his own opinions to sympathize with black culture and personality. Cash's interpretation has proved most appealing to southern liberals who feel pessimistic about and trapped in southern provincial culture and find an explanation for their fetters in Cash's embittered portrait; his raciness of diction and exposition is the aesthetic counterpoint to, and the vindication of, their unease with southern society.

Michael O'Brien
University of Arkansas

Richard H. King, *A Southern Renaissance: The Cultural Awakening of the American South, 1930–1955* (1980); Joseph L. Morrison, *W. J. Cash: Southern Prophet* (1967); Michael O'Brien, *Journal of Southern History* (August 1978); C. Vann Woodward, *American Counterpoint: Slavery and Racism in the North-South Dialogue* (1971).

Cavalier Myth

The Cavalier myth generally functioned as a prominent aspect of the larger mythic worlds of the plantation and the Lost Cause. According to the myth, the southern Cavalier began his career as a planter or the son of a planter and reached his maturity as a Confederate soldier, generally, but not necessarily, an officer. The Cavalier myth evoked elements of English squirarchy, feudalism, and aristocracy. The Cavalier was courtly, wealthy yet nonmaterialistic, brave, honorable, and gentle. His martial aspects dominated during the war when his conduct was most frequently described as knightly—meaning courageous, devoted to the cause, pure, and still tender. Every Confederate soldier behaved like a Chevalier Bayard without fear and without reproach; he did all that man could do until he was finally overwhelmed. General Robert E. Lee stood as the primary example of the Confederate Cavalier.

The Cavalier began to emerge as a mythic character in plantation novels such as William Alexander Carruthers's *The Cavaliers of Virginia* (1834); he became stock in the plantation domestic novels and polemic writing of the immediate prewar decades; and this ideal reached a stereotypical apex in reminiscences and novels in the first half century after the Civil War, including such works as Thomas Nelson Page's "Marse Chan" (1887) and Thomas Dixon, Jr.'s *The Clansman* (1905). By the 1930s the Cavalier myth was becoming fragmented, as indicated by the Rhett Butler–Ashley Wilkes split in Mar-garet Mitchell's *Gone with the Wind* (1936).

The Cavalier supplied the glamour of wealth, caste, d lineage that Americans envied. He also stood as an ipode to the restless, materialistic society of the th. After the Civil War, he continued to function in e ways as a national ideal, but in the South he had ial meaning as the standard bearer of chivalry's last and as the apotheosis of manly virtue. The Cavalier erved both as an inspiration for those who wanted to push on into the New South and as a consolation for those who embraced the Old South as an unattainable Golden Age. With the coming of the civil rights movement, industrialism, and literary realism to the South, the romantic Cavalier ideal as part of the southern plantation setting no longer seemed a usable ideal, although elements of the cluster of Cavalier traits still lingered. The Cavalier type, however, is still a major ideal in modern romances.

See also HISTORY AND MANNERS: / Lee, Robert E.

Susan S. Durant
University of Kentucky

Francis Pendleton Gaines, *The Southern Plantation: A Study in the Development and the Accuracy of a Tradition* (1925); Jack Temple Kirby, *Media-Made Dixie: The South in the American Imagination* (1978); William R. Taylor, *Cavalier and Yankee: The Old South and American National Character* (1957).

Celtic South

The idea of the Celtic origins of the southern white population is one of the major, but controversial, theories explaining the early development of southern culture. The ethnic polarization of the American colonies, with the English dominating New England and the Celts (Scottish, Irish, Scotch-Irish, Welsh, Cornish) dominating the South, was one factor making the Old South distinctive. By 1790, when the first U.S. census was taken, ethnic sectionalization was firmly established. In New England well over three-quarters of the people were of English origins, and English ways were firmly planted in the region. The Middle Atlantic states had a mixture of peoples, but the further south and west from Philadelphia, the more Celtic the population. In the Upper South, Celts and Englishmen each constituted about two-fifths of the population; in the Carolinas, more than half the people were Celtic, and Celts outnumbered Englishmen two to one. Celts dominated the interior from Pennsylvania southward, ranging in various areas from three-fourths to nearly a hundred percent of the population.

The significance of this distribution lay in its effects on migration patterns during the next six or seven decades. When New Englanders moved westward, most went along the Mohawk River across New York, then fanned out around the Great Lakes. The Celts filled the Ohio Valley and the trans-Appalachian South. In between were Germans and stragglers from the other two major ethnic groups. By the end of the antebellum period, the South's white population was three-quarters or more Celtic, New England and the upper Middle West were three-quarters or more English, and the border areas were mixed. The other major influence on southern culture, which also dated from the early colonial period, was the African heritage.

The Celts who settled in the South brought with them

their non-English ways—including a pastoral economy based upon open-range herding, a leisurely lifestyle and a distaste for hard work, rural values that stressed wasteful hospitality and outdoor sports, the reckless indulgence in food and drink, a touchy and romantic sense of honor, and a strong tendency toward lawlessness and the settlement of disagreements by violent means—and they readily imposed these traditions upon their neighbors. Only a few settlers in the antebellum South, such as determined Yankees and isolated Germans as well as the enslaved Africans, managed to avoid acculturation into the prevailing Celtic cultural patterns.

Forrest McDonald
University of Alabama

Grady McWhiney
Texas Christian University

Rowland Berthloff, *Journal of Southern History* (November 1986); Forrest McDonald and Ellen Shapiro McDonald, *William and Mary Quarterly* (April 1980); Forrest McDonald and Grady McWhiney, *American Historical Review* (December 1980), *History Today* (July 1980), *Journal of Southern History* (May 1975, May 1985), *Names* (1982).

"Crackers"

Americans have long stereotyped poor white southerners with a variety of contemptuous terms including *honky*, *redneck*, *peckerwood*, *linthead*, *hoosier*, *shit kicker*, and *cracker*. The word *crackers* is among the oldest epithets used to describe white southerners, especially those from south Georgia and north Florida. The term extends back at least to the mid-1700s, when it was used in Scotland as a colloquialism for boaster. In Samuel Johnson's famous dictionary of 1755, a *cracker* was defined as a "noisy, boasting fellow."

By the 1760s the word was commonly used by coastal residents as an ethnic pejorative to designate Scotch-Irish frontiersmen in the South. These backcountry folk tended to be herdsmen who depended on an abundance of land for grazing livestock. With diminishing open rangeland in the early 19th century, some of these plain folk moved westward across the Appalachians to the frontier, but others headed into the piney woods of Georgia and Florida, an area that became the Cracker "homeland."

Travelers in this area in the 19th century wrote of the Crackers as poor white farmers, often dismissing them for "cracking," or pounding, corn for food. On the other hand, local histories and other accounts show the existence of a prosperous middle class, whose members typically owned a slave or two, grew corn and other commodities, and grazed cattle and hogs. From this perspective, most of these piney woods folk were not poor "corn crackers" but respectable "whip crackers," who used a long whip with a tip called a "cracker."

After the Civil War, the debt-ridden states of Georgia and Florida sold off much of the public land that Crackers had used for grazing livestock. Their economic lot worsened in the late 19th century, and landless Crackers went to mill towns for work or became sharecroppers or marginal farmers. By the turn of the 20th century the term *cracker* was a pejorative for a poor millworker or rural sharecropper. Some plain folk in south Georgia and north Florida managed, however, to continue a cattle-herding economy until after World War II.

Cracker is also a racial epithet used by black Americans as a contemptuous term for a southern white. In the early 1800s southern slaves and free blacks used the word *buckras*, which is from an African word, to refer to whites. By the 1850s, though, *cracker* was becoming the preferred term. After the Civil War, racial tension rose in the piney woods, as whites blamed freed slaves for their deteriorating economic situation. Mob violence against blacks occasionally occurred there, and the black population declined. Migrant southern blacks took their contempt for "crackers" with them to northern cities in the 20th century, and today the term is often used in ghettoes in referring to all prejudiced whites.

In the 1970s *crackers* became a term of ethnic pride for some southern whites. The election of a south Georgian, Jimmy Carter, to the presidency in 1976 led to media stories about Cracker Chic, and humorist Roy Blount, Jr., used *Crackers* as the title of his book about southerners and the Carter era.

Charles Reagan Wilson
University of Mississippi

Raven I. McDavid, Jr., and Virginia McDavid, *Names* (September 1973); John S. Otto, in *Perspectives on the American South*, vol. 4, ed. James C. Cobb and Charles Reagan Wilson (1987).

Fitzhugh, George

(1808–1881) Slavery advocate.

Fitzhugh, from Port Royal, Va., was the descendant of an old southern family that had fallen on hard times. He practiced law and struggled as a small planter but made a reputation with two books, *Sociology for the South* (1854) and *Cannibals All!* (1857), which alarmed northerners like Abraham Lincoln and roused southerners to take new and higher ground in defense of slavery.

Fitzhugh insisted that all labor, not merely black, had to be enslaved and that the world must become all slave or all free. He defined "slavery" broadly to include all systems of servile labor. These views had become com-monplace in the South by the 1850s. His originality la in the insight that slavery could only survive and prev if the capitalist world market were destroyed. He und stood that organic social relations and attendant val could not survive in a world dominated by capita competition and bourgeois individualism.

His call for war against the modern world, express a harsh polemical style, made him a solitary figur merous others agreed that free labor spelled class war and invited anarchy. They also agreed that slavery overcame the "social question" by establishing a master class that combined interest with sentiment to offer the masses security. But, having no confidence in his utopian vision of a reversal of history, they generally tried, however illogically, to convince the European and northern bourgeoisie to restore some form of slavery in a corporatist order.

Fitzhugh opposed secession until the last minute, arguing that a slaveholding Confederacy could not survive until the advanced capitalist countries had themselves converted. After the war, which once begun he loyally and enthusiastically supported, Fitzhugh sank into obscurity, becoming increasingly negrophobic and idiosyncratic. To all intents and purposes, he died at Appomattox.

Eugene D. Genovese
University of Rochester

Eugene D. Genovese, *The World the Slaveholders Made: Two Essays in Interpretation* (1969); Harvey Wish, *George Fitzhugh: Propagandist of the Old South* (1943).

Good Old Boys and Girls

The terms *good old boy* and *good old girl* are of southern origin. The terms describe social types, persons with particular social characteristics that make them identifiable to others. Although there are similar social types in other regions of the United States, the southern label may make them more obvious in the South.

The good old boy and girl have been pictured most frequently in popular literature. Perhaps the first reference to the social type was in William Byrd's *Histories of the Dividing Line Betwixt Virginia and North Carolina* (1728). W. J. Cash discussed the type in *The Mind of the South* (1941), but the first writer to use the term itself was Tom Wolfe in an essay on stock car racing hero Junior Johnson (*Esquire*, October 1967). William Price Fox, in *Southern Fried* (1962), presented several portraits of the type, including the legendary Georgia politician, Eugene Talmadge. Willie Morris's *Good Old Boy: A Delta Boyhood* (1971) was autobiographical, and Paul Hemphill in *The Good Old Boys* (1974) wrote lovingly of them, mainly because his father was one. Florence King's *Southern Ladies and Gentlemen* (1975) sees the good old boy as mean and nasty. Sharon McKern's *Redneck Mothers, Good Old Girls and Other Southern Belles* (1979) was one of the first literary applications of the concept to women. In *Crackers* (1980), Roy Blount, Jr., suggests that "'good old boy' means pretty much the same as 'mensch.'"

The good old boy frequently appears in such country music songs as "Bar Room Buddies," "If You've Got the Money, I've Got the Time," and "Dang Me," and the term itself was used in Ansley Fleetwood's "Just Good Ol' Boys" (1979). Sometimes the term is used synonymously with "cowboy" in country music. Burt Reynolds embodied the good old boy in a series of movies in the 1970s.

The good old boy is described as blue collar, an outdoorsman, a patriot, something of a populist, basically conservative—a "man's man." He is also somewhat self-centered and scheming, particularly toward out-groups. Yet to his in-group he is an affable comrade and a man of integrity. Billy Carter, the brother of President Jimmy Carter and himself the essence of the type, has defined the good old boy as someone who rides around in a pickup truck, drinking beer and putting his empties in a sack. A redneck, by contrast, rides around in a pickup, drinking and tossing his empties out the window. The "redneck" as a concept describes a more menacing figure.

The good old girl has not been studied as systematically as the good old boy. She has traits of bluffness, camaraderie, and loyalty, which make her more comfortable with men than women. She is usually not seen as a sex object and, in fact, is somewhat asexual in social interaction. She is likely to possess the same affability and integrity as the good old boy and the same ability to manipulate people.

Ingram Parmley
Francis Marion College

Ingram Parmley, in *Perspectives on the American South*, vol. 1, ed. Merle Black and John Shelton Reed (1981); Edgar T. Thompson, *South Atlantic Quarterly* (Autumn 1984).

Hospitality

Hospitality is an intensely real aspect of southern culture, but it has often been misrepresented, as in the oft-told tale of the planter who waylaid travelers and took them at rifle point to visit his home. Other stories, some of them in otherwise accurate historical works, depict southern doors as swinging open to all comers, whatever their rank or degree.

Hospitality in the South was far more restricted than such tales would imply. In the 18th and early 19th centuries some of the most murderous outlaws in American history infested the South, and under such circumstances a householder would have been a fool to welcome some disreputable stranger into his home. Moreover, whatever else the South may have been, it was never a social democracy. The planter whose social aspirations led him to construct a mansion, or even a second story atop his dogtrot cabin, did not extend warm greetings to poor farmers or laborers who barely scratched out a living.

A commercial element also affected hospitality in the Old South. Travelers' accounts make clear that when they sought shelter in private homes travelers were expected to pay for their bed and their food. Frederick Law Olmsted nearly always paid 75 cents or a dollar as he made his way through the rural South, and many others had the same experience.

Southerners normally welcomed neighbors and relatives with open arms, and a stranger might also be joyously greeted if he bore letters of introduction from friends or relatives. Once received, the guest met few limitations; much of the substance of some planters, and some yeoman for that matter, was expended on visitors who often stayed too long. One finds few complaints in the records, however, and more than a little boasting.

The poverty that followed the Civil War curtailed hospitality, but "spending the day" with friends and kin persisted, and widowed or unmarried members of a family often lived by "visiting" their children, nieces, nephews, brothers, and sisters. The southerner is indeed hospitable to this day, loving nothing more than to entertain family and friends with the best food and drink he can afford. The automobile and the telephone make visiting far simpler than in early times; normally only guests who have traveled great distances stay overnight, and the length of such visits is limited by the construction of the modern home. But if the circumstances of southern hospitality have changed, the spirit remains the same.

Joe Gray Taylor
McNeese State University

Joe Gray Taylor, *Eating, Drinking, and Visiting in the South* (1982).

Confederate battle flags draping the Mississippi capitol, 1930s

Lost Cause Myth

The phrase "the Lost Cause," popularized as the title of Edward A. Pollard's 1866 history of the Confederacy, became a common designation for the southern role in the Civil War. Most southerners felt it properly evoked the heroism and nobility of the Confederate armies, but beyond that the term did not symbolize any particular interpretation of the war. Although southerners may not have admitted it, the phrase nevertheless accurately reflected their ambivalence about the outcome of the war. "Lost" acknowledged the defeat of the Confederacy; "Cause" suggested the South had fought less for independence than for philosophical principles that might yet triumph.

The phrase "the Lost Cause" also became identified with the movement within the South to enshrine the memory of the Civil War. As early as a year after Appomattox, Confederate memorial associations were formed to care for the graves of the war dead. A few of the societies placed monuments in the cemeteries they constructed, and all celebrated Confederate Memorial Day every spring. The Southern Historical Society, founded in New Orleans in 1869 but later headquartered in Richmond, sought to preserve a true, i.e., southern, history of the war. In the 1880s this memorialization of the cause gradually became a celebration of the war, which continued into the first decades of the 20th century. During these years, the South dedicated monuments to the wartime leaders Lee and Davis, and many communities placed statues of Confederate soldiers on courthouse lawns or town squares. In 1889 several veterans' groups organized the United Confederate Veterans (UCV), which soon had camps throughout the region. In 1894 the United Daughters of the Confederacy was formed, and two years later a somewhat successful United Sons of the Confederacy appeared. With both veterans and descendants organized, the UCV reunions and monument unveilings attracted huge crowds for public celebrations of the Confederacy.

Historians offer various interpretations of the meaning and significance of the celebration of the war, but two approaches prevail. One stressed the political functions of the idea of the Lost Cause: providing support for states' rights, white supremacy, and the Democratic party. Some adherents of this approach treat the glorification of the Lost Cause as only a diversion from the real issues—another trick by which the Democratic establishment maintained its power. Others consider the Lost Cause notion a widely accepted social myth with a less explicit political role. The second approach emphasizes the cultural functions of the idea—helping southerners assimilate defeat and unifying southern society. Some of the historians who take this view argue that the Lost Cause myth became a civil religion and rendered southerners a people set apart by a special sense of mission. Others, pointing to similar activities in the North, suggest that the celebration of the war owed much to the social tensions of the 1880s and 1890s and did not serve so central a role in forming a southern identity. Most students of the idea of the Lost Cause, however, would agree that its development bestowed cultural authority on Confederate symbols that southerners in the 20th century continued to invoke in defense of various causes from intervention abroad to segregation at home.

See also HISTORY AND MANNERS: / Southern Historical Society; United Confederate Veterans

Gaines M. Foster
Louisiana State University

Susan S. Durant, "The Gently Furled Banner: The Development of the Myth of the Lost Cause, 1865–1900" (Ph.D. dissertation, University of North Carolina at Chapel Hill, 1972); Gaines M. Foster, *Ghosts of the Confederacy: Defeat, the Lost Cause, and the Emergence of the New South, 1865–1913* (1987); Rollin G. Osterweis, *The Myth of the Lost Cause, 1865–1900* (1973); Charles Reagan Wilson, *Baptized in Blood: The Religion of the Lost Cause, 1865–1920* (1980).

"Mammy"

The "mammy" character is a stereotype derived from history and popular culture. She is a black, middle-aged woman who has a strong, loud voice and wears an apron and a kerchief on her head. Her ample body and open, honest expression reveal that she is maternal and reliable. She is the southern archetype of the earth mother. Donald Bogle, who has classified the dominant images of blacks in film, said that the mammy figure is a "desexed, overweight, dowdy, *dark* black woman." Mammy is Aunt Jemima, an icon that recurs often enough to be easily recognized.

The mammy character recurs in fiction. She is William Faulkner's Dilsey in *The Sound and the Fury*, Carson McCullers's Berenice in *The Member of the Wedding*, Fanny Hurst's Delilah in *Imitation of Life*, and Margaret Mitchell's Mammy in *Gone with the Wind*. Actresses who play her in films have become icons of the mammy figure. Ethel Waters, Louise Beavers, and Hattie McDaniel are familiar "mammies" who have even become folk heroines.

Mrs. Wilson's Nurse and Fat Baby, *photographer unknown, late 19th century*

Mammy as a character is the quintessence of strength, constancy, and integrity. She is not only capable, generous, and kind but also very religious, long-suffering, and sometimes scolding. A Christian oracle of wisdom, she passes her knowledge on to white characters whose lives are thereby enriched. She is the all-loving, loyal mainstay to a white family, giving all of herself to the family in this life and asking for nothing in return but heavenly reward.

Mammy is a dominant antebellum black image, personifying the spirit of endurance during the hard times of slavery. Under slavery, white families relied on black slaves to raise their children, nurse their sick, and cook and clean for them. The mammy character is historically derived from the house slave who was the personal servant of the white plantation owners. It was not unusual for the personal slaves of the master and mistress to sleep in the same bedroom with them to be on call should their service be needed during the night. Although they were better fed and dressed than the field slaves, the house slaves were treated as nonpersons. After emancipation, black women were still treated as mammy figures. The mammy image passed from southern plantations to day workers and domestic maids, and thus from the South to the North.

Victoria O'Donnell
North Texas State University

Donald Bogle, *Toms, Coons, Mulattoes, Mammies, and Bucks: An Interpretive History of Blacks in American Films* (1973); Carol Hymowitz and Michaele Weissman, *A History of Women in America* (1978); Victoria O'Donnell, in *The South and Film*, ed. Warren French (1981).

Mencken's South

H. L. Mencken of Baltimore was known in the 1920s as the archenemy of the American South, but in fact Mencken's view of the South was more complex than most of his detractors realized. He was best known for his diatribes against Dixie in "The Sahara of the Bozart" (1920) and other essays; the South, he claimed in the "Sahara," was a cultural and intellectual desert, a land run by poor whites, a colossal paradise of the fourth-rate. But if H. L. Mencken was the graphic realist in cataloging the numerous flaws of southern life in the early 20th century, he was also the most romantic of writers when he envisioned an earlier South. In many of the same essays in which he damned those states below the Potomac and Ohio, he also contended that, up until the Civil War, the South had been the American seat of civilization, a cultivated land "with men of delicate fancy, urbane instinct and aristocratic manner—in brief, superior men." In the antebellum South "some attention was given to the art of living. . . . A certain noble spaciousness was in the ancient southern scheme of things."

What Mencken had in mind when he spoke of an earlier cultivated South was, largely, Virginia of the 18th and early 19th centuries—and even in Virginia the spirit of free inquiry that Mencken prized had begun to decline long before the beginning of the Civil War. But, by his reasoning, the war itself was responsible for the complete "drying up" of southern civilization. After Appomattox, he contended, the aristocrats vanished—died, fled North, or lived out their days in obscurity—and the worthless, depraved poor whites seized control and dominated every aspect of southern life. Fanatical preachers, corrupt politicians, and nostalgic poetasters made the South the laughingstock of the nation. Such was H. L. Mencken's view of southern history, a view which, although not quite historically accurate, was widely circulated in the 1920s and 1930s. The antebellum South, in truth, was never so civilized—nor the postbellum South so barbaric—as the South of H. L. Mencken's imagination.

See also LITERATURE: / Mencken, H. L.

Fred Hobson
University of Alabama

Fred Hobson, *Serpent in Eden: H. L. Mencken and the South* (1974); H. L. Mencken, *Prejudices, Second Series* (1920), *Virginia Quarterly Review* (January 1935).

Mitchell, Margaret

(1900–1949) Writer.

Born 8 November 1900 in Atlanta, Margaret Mitchell was as proud of her long-established Atlanta family as she was of *Gone with the Wind*. She wrote in 1941: "I know of few other Atlanta people who can claim that their families have been associated as long and intimately, and sometimes prominently, with the birth and growth and history of this city."

Mitchell was educated in Atlanta schools and at Smith College. After her mother died in the flu epidemic of 1919, Mitchell returned from Smith to Atlanta to keep house for her father and her brother. She made her debut in 1920 and in 1922 married Berrien Kinnard Upshaw. The marriage lasted barely three months.

In December 1922 Mitchell found a job on the staff of the Atlanta *Journal Sunday Magazine*. On the *Journal* she worked with such writers as Erskine Caldwell and Frances Newman. On 4 July 1925 she married John Robert Marsh, public relations officer of the Georgia Power Company, and in 1926 resigned her job because of ill health. She tried writing short stories but found no market for them, and they were eventually destroyed. Discouraged, she turned to the composition of a long novel for her own amusement during an extended recuperation.

Most of *Gone with the Wind* was completed by 1929. It was still incomplete, however, when in April of 1935 she somewhat quixotically allowed Harold Latham (on a scouting trip for the Macmillan Company) to see the manuscript. Macmillan's almost immediate acceptance was followed by months of checking for historical accuracy, filling gaps in the story, and rewriting. The book was a best-seller the day it was published, 30 June 1936, and dominated its author's life thereafter.

For the next 13 years Mitchell nursed an aging father and later an invalid husband, enthusiastically did war work, and maintained a massive amount of correspondence relating to *Gone with the Wind*. She wrote no more fiction and emerged from private life only occasionally, most notably for the premiere of the film *Gone with the Wind* on 15 December 1939 in Atlanta.

Accident-prone throughout her life, she met her death in an accident on 11 August 1949. Crossing Peachtree Street with her husband, she was struck by a speeding taxicab. She died five days later and was buried in Atlanta's Oakland Cemetery.

See also MEDIA: / *Gone with the Wind*

Richard B. Harwell
Athens, Georgia

Anne Edwards, *The Road to Tara: The Life of Margaret Mitchell* (1983); Finis Farr, *Margaret Mitchell of Atlanta: The Author of Gone with the Wind* (1965); Richard B. Harwell, ed., *Margaret Mitchell's "Gone with the Wind" Letters, 1936–1949* (1976); a collection of over 50,000 items of Miss Mitchell's correspondence, reviews of *Gone with the Wind*, magazine and newspaper articles, pictures, and other memorabilia is in the Manuscript Department of the University of Georgia Libraries, Athens.

"Moonlight-and-Magnolias" Myth

As a phrase, "moonlight and magnolias" has two distinct but related meanings. It is most commonly used as a derogatory epithet for the more excessive manifestations of sentimental cavalier-belle-plantation fiction. In this sense, it is a term of derision, as shown in Margaret Mitchell's defense of *Gone with the Wind*: "I've always been slightly amused by the New York critics who referred to GWTW as a 'moonlight and magnolia romance.' My God, they never read the gentle Confederate novel of the Nineties, or they would know better." Mitchell's statement also implicitly indicates the other less pejorative meaning of the phrase—the myth of an antebellum Golden Age, a myth created in the postbellum world of the 1880s and 1890s and a part of the larger myths of the plantation and the Lost Cause.

The conscious and recognized leader in creating this myth was Thomas Nelson Page, but he had a host of colleagues and imitators who can be found in the 17-volume *Library of Southern Literature* (1907), edited by Edwin Anderson Alderman and Joel Chandler Harris. Page's *In*

Ole Virginia (1887) and *Red Rock* (1898) exhibit all the myth's elements. He fixed the past in time and held on to it. The antebellum South became the romantic "before the war," an Eden, a dream of chivalry; the Civil War became that period of heroism, when the Cause was lost but the South was not beaten on the battlefield; and Reconstruction was the vengeful rape by the vulgar North of the beautiful South. Though this idealized view was simplistic, its popularity with late 19th-century southerners was understandable, for in their economic and political privation they could at least remember, in Page's words, the time when "even the moonlight was richer and mellower." In both its glamour and pathos the myth also appealed to non-southerners and spread a nostalgic image of antebellum southern life across the nation. The anecdote of Union General Higginson's weeping over Page's "Marse Chan," a story apostrophizing the cavalier and belle through the words of an exslave, has often been noted, and rightly so, for it is a symbol of the myth's effect.

The myth has become in the contemporary era an object of parody and an advertising gimmick. By keeping all the plantation paraphernalia, but adding three new elements, it has been transformed in novels and films into a new antebellum myth of sex, sadism, and miscegenation. The present pejorative meaning derives as much from this transformation as from weaknesses inherent in the orginal myth and says much about changes in the way both southerners and non-southerners have looked at the antebellum South for the past 100 years.

See also LITERATURE: / Page, Thomas Nelson

Earl F. Bargainnier
Wesleyan College

Earl F. Bargainnier, *Louisiana Studies* (Spring 1976), in *Icons of America*, ed. Ray B. Browne and Marshall Fishwick (1978), *Southern Quarterly* (Winter 1984).

Nationalism, Southern

Like the American nationalism of which it was an offshoot, southern nationalism attempted to define clearly the circumstances in which 19th-century southerners found themselves. The coming of peace in 1815 allowed all Americans to turn inward and examine those characteristics and institutions that set them apart from other nations. Like Americans in general, southerners were intimately involved in all phases of this quest for nationality: campaigns for economic development, encouragement of a native literature, calls for improved education, state constitutional revisions to broaden the franchise, religious revivals, and territorial expansion.

Giving each of these movements a peculiarly southern twist was a growing sense that in some fundamental way the southern states possessed shared interests that conflicted with those of the nation at large. As this perception grew and spread, increasing numbers of southerners began to agitate for a separate southern nation, which would possess all the cultural and political attributes they as Americans had long desired, but which also would protect that most vital of all southern interests, slavery. By 1860, though only a minority of southerners favored secession, the efforts of southern nationalists had won such an influential following that a southern nation took form.

The unsuccessful career of the short-lived Confederacy has persuaded many historians that southern nationalism never existed. Evidence to support that argument appears abundant. The Constitution of the Confederate States and that of the United States were virtual duplicates. The rival presidents and their governments moved along strikingly similar paths to strikingly similar policies on conscription, finance, and even battlefield strategy. After a brief and moderate Reconstruction, the South resumed full partnership in the Union. Confederate history does indeed show what southern nationalism was not. But it also convincingly shows what it was: an effort to be more fully and more purely American than other Americans, to subscribe more honorably, as southerners saw it, to the meaning of the Constitution.

By 1860 enough southerners perceived that the only way to live up to the definition of America they had been so instrumental in providing was to rebel, as their grandfathers had rebelled. "There is a habit of speaking derisively of going to war for an idea—an abstraction—something which you cannot see," wrote a southern editor in 1861. "This is precisely the point on which we would go to war. An idea is exactly the thing that we would fight for." Southern nationalism was—and is—above all else a state of mind.

John McCardell
Middlebury College

Avery O. Craven, *The Growth of Southern Nationalism, 1848–1861* (1953); John McCardell, *The Idea of a Southern Nation: Southern Nationalists and Southern Nationalism, 1830–1860* (1979); David Potter, *The South and the Sectional Conflict* (1968).

Place, Sense of

"One place comprehended can make us understand other places better," wrote Eudora Welty in "Place in Fiction." The term *sense of place* as used in the South implies an organic society. Until recently southern whites frequently used *place* to indicate the status of blacks. James McBride Dabbs noted in 1957 that southern whites spent much time "keeping the Negro in his place" and foolishly considered themselves "happy because the Negro had a place." But racial "place" was only one aspect of a traditional southern attachment to the region—one had a place in a local community, among a broad kin network, and in history.

Attachment to a place gives an abiding identity because places associated with family, community, and history have depth. Philosopher Yi-Fu Tuan points out that a sense of place in any human society comes from the intersection of space and time. Southerners developed an acute sense of place as a result of their dramatic and traumatic history and their rural isolation on the land for generations. As Welty noted, "*feelings* are bound up with place," and the film title *Places in the Heart* captured the emotional quality that places evoke. *Home* is a potent word for southerners, and the *homeplace* evokes reverence.

The evidence for a deep-seated southern sense of place is extensive. The first settlers in the region, Native Americans, saw the lands of the Southeast as sacred ground, with all happenings in their specific places related to the rest of the cosmos. Native Americans named prominent physical landmarks and plants and animals in their local areas; their place names survive as evocative descriptions of the landscape.

From Mark Twain's Mississippi River to William Faulkner's Yoknapatawpha County, southern writers have created memorable literary landscapes of place. The lyrics of blues singers starkly evoke the Mississippi Delta, and country musicians sing a lyrical version of states' rights with titles such as "My Home's in Alabama," "Mississippi You're on My Mind," "Tennessee Mountain Home," and "Can't Wash the Sands of Texas from My Shoes." Folk artists draw from the long memory of people living in isolated rural areas for generations. They learn from older generations and convey the texture of life in a particular southern place through painting, carving, sewing, and other crafts.

Sociologists use the term *localism* to describe the sense of place in the South. The analysis of public opinion poll results shows that contemporary southern blacks and whites value their states more than non-southern Americans, and they more often emulate local family and neighbors. John Shelton Reed has concluded that "southerners seem more likely than other Americans to think of their region, their states, and their local communities possessively as *theirs*, and as distinct from and preferable to other regions, states, and localities."

Contemporary public policymakers have become aware of the threat economic development poses to preservation of the traditional southern sense of place. In the 1974 Commission on the Future of the South, a group of prominent regional leaders suggested to the Southern Growth Policies Board that an important goal of the modern South should be "to preserve and enhance, in meeting the issues of growth and change, the human sense of place and community that is a vital element of the unique quality of Southern life."

Charles Reagan Wilson
University of Mississippi

William Ferris, *Local Color: A Sense of Place in Folk Art* (1982); Lucinda H. MacKethan, *The Dream of Arcady: Place and Time in Southern Literature* (1980); John Shelton Reed, *The Enduring South: Subcultural Persistence in Mass Society* (1972); Stephen A. Smith, *Myth, Media, and the Southern Mind* (1985); Eudora Welty, *The Eye of the Story: Selected Essays and Reviews* (1978).

Poor Whites

Both outsiders and native southerners helped create and perpetuate myths about the South's poor whites, some of which had a strong basis in fact. Antebellum English and northern travelers described a white South consisting of plantation grandees at the top and wretchedly deprived poor farmers at the bottom. (Both groups, although in fact large, were outnumbered by small yeoman farmers.) The school of antebellum writers known as southwestern humorists were themselves from the upper classes, but the people they described were shrewd, somewhat bizarre, clay eaters who practiced emotional religion and engaged in violent eye gougings. The notion of the two-tiered society later served well the needs of abolitionists who blamed slavery for southern poverty; the comic stereotype of the southwestern humorists, although accurate in many respects, furnished the basis for one of the most enduring myths within American popular culture.

In the late 19th century new layers were added. A region struggling to maintain the values of its agrarian past while at the same time striving for material progress found the poor white useful. New South polemicists noted the breakup of the plantation and the rise of small farms, and they applauded the advent of small-farmer independence and democracy; actually, tens of thousands of whites were descending into tenancy. New South promoters also celebrated the textile mill, which in reality replaced one kind of deprivation with another. When other regions criticized the South for its racial violence or its inclination to elect demagogic politicians, southern apologists absolved themselves and generally blamed poor whites, who unfortunately were often prone to vote for racist demagogues.

In Appalachia a strange and peculiar people challenged America's Gilded Age notions of progress and homogeneity, and missionaries both secular and religious tried to convert the hillbilly primitives from their moonshine, religion, feuds, and culture. Later generations of Americans characterized them as backward hillbillies who were inclined toward incest, fundamentalist religion, laziness, and irresponsibility.

Those who sympathized with poor whites created their own set of myths. In James Agee's classic book, *Let Us Now Praise Famous Men*, the author eulogized poor whites caught in a cosmic dead end. In the novels of Erskine Caldwell the myth of "poor white trash" found its most popular expression. An idealistic generation in the 1960s and 1970s glorified Appalachian poor whites as the finest surviving example of primitive American innocence (a poor but self-contained life lived close to the land in relative isolation, with clean water and air and wonderfully imaginative folk crafts, lore, and music). Each of these descriptions of poor whites contained factual information upon which broad and sometimes unfair or inaccurate generalizations could be built.

Many Americans blame the South's problems on the Jeeter Lesters (of *Tobacco Road*), degenerates and racists, shiftless wanderers, wife-beaters, drunks, and ne'er-do-wells. They believe that such people also furnish the Ernest Angleys, Jerry Falwells, and Marjoe Gortners of American religion. According to the conflicting images of American popular culture, the southern poor white can be the shrewdly innocent Jed Clampett of *The Beverly Hillbillies* or a Pentecostal haunted by incestuous lust, the sodomite of James Dickey's *Deliverance*, or the tough, poor-boy-made-good Paul "Bear" Bryant, who wrestled bears in Fordyce, Ark., because he could make more by fighting the beasts than by chopping cotton. Poor white music furnished many additional themes—the religious, fatalistic poor white or the "second-hand satin ladies" and "honky tonk angels." So far as myth is concerned, the poor white has been a man or woman for all seasons.

J. Wayne Flynt
Auburn University

Sylvia J. Cook, *From Tobacco Road to Route 66: The Southern Poor White in Fiction* (1976); J. Wayne Flynt, *Dixie's Forgotten People: The South's Poor Whites* (1979); Shields McIlwaine, *The Southern Poor-White: From Lubberland to Tobacco Road* (1939); Henry D. Shapiro, *Appalachia on Our Mind: The Southern Mountains and Mountaineers in the American Consciousness, 1870–1920* (1978); Merrill M. Skaggs, *The Folk of Southern Fiction* (1972).

Reb, Johnny

The Confederate soldier's image in regional culture is his cumulative representation in southern novels, poetry, illustration, and statuary, as well as in photography and historiography. Because the manner of this representation suggests popular beliefs about the Civil War and the Confederate experience, Johnny Reb's image is an important factor in southern history and the myths surrounding it.

This image has been eulogistic, reflecting southerners' sentimental attachment to the Confederate soldier. During the war years, patriotic speeches, editorials, and sermons idealized Johnny Reb as defender of morality and American liberty. Poetry by William Gilmore Simms, Paul Hayne, Henry Timrod, and others added romantic elements such as knightly valor to the image. The trials of war and defeat dimmed this early idealism, but developments after Appomattox contributed new elements of eulogy to the soldier's reputation. The elaborate rituals of Confederate Memorial Day, begun in 1866 to venerate the war dead, continued to sanctify the common soldier. Starting in the 1880s, veterans' reminiscences extended the warm glow of nostalgia to the war, and in these writings as well as in the grandiloquent oratory of veterans' reunions, Johnny Reb was exalted for his bravery, endurance, and devotion to duty. Furthermore, southerners' historical writings, begun soon after the war to chronicle—and justify—the Confederate struggle, depicted the fight as a valiant but doomed effort against overwhelming northern resources. This historiography of the Lost Cause ennobled Johnny Reb, particularly when it recounted his victories under Robert E. Lee against numerically superior enemies. "Overpowered by numbers" became a popular means of explaining defeat while maintaining the Confederate soldier's battlefield prowess.

Pictorial representation was an important element of the image. Two notable contributors were William L. Sheppard and Allen C. Redwood, talented illustrators whose drawings of Confederates appeared abundantly after the war in *Scribner's*, *Century*, and other northern periodicals. Their work for *Century* magazine's *Battles and Leaders of the Civil War* (1887) was widely circulated. Memorial statuary provided further visual imagery. Monuments to the Confederate dead were erected on courthouse squares throughout the South, especially during 1880 to 1910, and featured sculpted likenesses of Johnny Reb that endowed him with a perpetual youth. Effusive monument inscriptions underscored his constancy and courage.

One of the surest signs of sectional reconciliation after the 1880s was the increasing similarity of Johnny Reb's image to Billy Yank's, as eulogists hailed both soldiers for their American idealism and pluck. In this century, though, the viewpoints of some southerners tended to undercut Johnny Reb's nationalism and shaped his image as the opponent of progress in modern America. In the 1920s and 1930s the Fugitive poets of Vanderbilt—notably Allen Tate and Donald Davidson—used the Confederate fighting man as a symbol of their protest against contemporary culture, with its cities, cars, and consumer goods that threatened the traditional southern lifestyle. A generation later, segregationists expropriated the Confederate battle flag as their symbol of adherence to "traditional" southern ways. To an extent, each of these developments influenced Johnny Reb's image by characterizing him as a diehard defender of outdated values.

The Confederate soldier's image has consequently aged, as his relevance to modern southerners has waned. By and large, however, the eulogistic tradition remains strong, and Johnny Reb will probably remain a regional folk hero for southerners as well as an enduring reminder of what helps set them apart from the rest of the country.

See also HISTORY AND MANNERS: / Confederate Veteran; United Confederate Veterans

Stephen Davis
Atlanta, Georgia

Stephen Davis, "Johnny Reb in Perspective: The Confederate Soldier's Image in the Southern Arts" (Ph.D. dissertation, Emory University, 1979); Susan S. Durant, "The Gently Furled Banner: The Development of the Myth of the Lost Cause, 1865–1900" (Ph.D. dissertation, University of North Carolina at Chapel Hill, 1972); Rollin G. Osterweis, *The Myth of the Lost Cause, 1865–1900* (1973); Charles Reagan Wilson, *Baptized in Blood: The Religion of the Lost Cause, 1865–1920* (1980).

Rednecks

In modern usage the term *redneck*, which did not come into common usage until the 1930s, is usually a negative expression describing a benighted white southerner. The redneck is any white southerner in the lower or working class, and his image looms large when the media focus on the South in transition. Various critics, whether southern blacks and liberals or northerners, gang up on the redneck and mercilessly dissect him. He is undereducated; he talks funny in a bewildering variety of southern accents, which feature double negatives, jumbled verb tenses, slurred and obsolete words, and all manner of crimes against standard, television English. He is too physical in his approach to life; he sets too high a premium on athletic prowess, and he gets into too many fights. He comes on too strong with women, and he may even scratch when he itches, wherever he or it might be. He eats too much coarse or greasy food like corn bread, grits, fried chicken, chicken-fried steak, and all manner of pork—everything from chops to a wide variety of barbecue. He even likes vegetables like collard greens and turnip greens and string beans cooked with his beloved pork, and worst of all, he seems to infringe on the black monopoly on "soul food." He tends to drink too much whiskey, and he spends too much time in tacky beer halls that play only country music and always on "high." He is noisy but inarticulate. He does not ski and has never seen a psychiatrist. He sometimes smells bad, especially after an eight-hour shift or a hunting trip. He occasionally still repairs his car in the front yard, and he might even leave the engine hanging from a branch of a chinaberry tree for a while. His presence may well depress the local real estate market. He is reactionary but sometimes radical and thus politically unreliable. His women (not ladies) reflect many of the same traits, and, besides, they chew gum vigorously and wear plastic hair curlers in public. And his children act as if they are just as good as anybody else.

Rednecks are known to have peculiar names. Males of the species go by such designations as "Bubba," "Slick," "Ace," "Rusty," Melvin, Leroy, Alvin, T. J., and L. W.; and sometimes grown men, even people in positions of great authority, run around calling themselves Bobby or Billy or Jimmy and insisting that everyone else do the same. Females answer to such names as Billy Jean, Lou Ann, Loretta, Ginny, Sue Ellen, Lawanda Kay, Peggy Joe, LaBelle, Mavis, Flo, Rose, and sometimes in the welter of Jodies, Bobbies, Billies, and Johnnies it is hard to tell whether the names are masculine or feminine. But whatever the name or the sex, you can be sure of one thing: the redneck is, above all else, an incorrigible racist.

The modern critique of the redneck emphasizes style more than substance, but it has some validity. The redneck is a rather plain, direct fellow, and he certainly will fight, especially when pushed. This fighting spirit often embarrasses the nation in normal times, but in wartime it is welcomed, and rednecks are among the first to enlist. The last, major charge against the redneck is certainly true; he is and always has been a racist at heart. But who is not and who was not? The southern redneck fits into the general harsh history of the human race, but given the extreme ethnic mix of his historical environment, he has earned no special distinction as a racist. His record is about par for the rugged course. The redneck's main problem is that he has always been open and candid in his conviction that blacks were inferior to whites. Yet at the same time over the centuries he has blended his culture and his blood with blacks, and in many day-to-day, practical ways he understands blacks perhaps better than his white detractors do. In a rough, earthy kind of way he may be less of a racist than those whites who denounce him so harshly.

In a literal sense the redneck was the average man in the South from the very beginning when white colonists settled along the Virginia and Carolina and finally the Georgia coasts. More commonly known then as "yeoman farmers," they peopled the southern half of the North American continent, moving relentlessly west toward the Pacific Ocean. They and their large families labored on the kind of fertile, cheap new land their European ancestors had not seen for over a thousand years. Under a blazing sun the exposed parts of their bodies tanned and hardened.

A wrinkled, reddened neck was no embarrassment to these proud, independent farmers who were the backbone of a fluid southern society, which allowed some of them to rise into the ranks of the planters. The average antebellum redneck owned his own land and occasionally a few slaves. He read and wrote functionally, voted without restrictions, bore his own arms, worshiped his own God, and generally enjoyed the life, liberty, and pursuit of happiness guaranteed to all free Americans.

Southern rednecks were not people to trifle with. When the Civil War erupted in 1861, they became the backbone of the Confederate armed forces, and they came within an ace of shattering the Union as their forefathers had shattered the British Empire in North America. Indeed, Lee's redneck infantry in Virginia developed into one of the most efficient killing machines of the 19th century.

Finally, the rednecks lost their war but not their pride. They returned to the land they knew so well, the good earth that had nurtured the southern folk for over two centuries. Over the years hard times in agriculture drove many down into some form of sharecropping, and then expanding industries lured many away from the soil. Today not many southern whites actually farm, and the term "redneck," when not used as a crude put-down, vaguely refers to lower- and working-class southern whites. Even so, it designates an important element of contemporary America's population, the most British group by blood and at the same time the group that has lived most closely with American blacks, another sturdy folk whose roots run deep in the soil of the South.

F. N. Boney
University of Georgia

F. N. Boney, *Georgia Review* (Fall 1971), *Southerners All* (1984); Larry L. King, *Of Outlaws, Con Men, Whores, Politicians, and Other Artists* (1980); John Shelton Reed, *Southern Folk, Plain and Fancy: Native White Social Types* (1986).

Sambo

Sambo was a stereotyped character created by whites to denigrate blacks. The stereotype attacked black men by making them the objects of laughter. The Sambo character was probably the most tenacious stereotype of black people in both southern and American culture until the late 20th century.

The name *Sambo* is Hispanic in origin, deriving from a 16th-century word *zambo*, which meant a bowlegged person resembling a monkey. By the 19th century the name had come to refer to a person of mixed ancestry, and the word had derogatory connotations. Descended from court jesters of medieval Europe, the Sambo figure was found in the British colonies of North America from the early 1600s. By the end of the 19th century, according to Joseph Boskin, Sambo's "humorous innocence, reflected in a never-failing grin, was projected everywhere, his natural buffoonery celebrated in every conceivable way."

The Sambo image included such specific types as the Uncle Tom, Coon, Mulatto, Mammy, and Buck. It appeared in oral lore through jokes and stories. It was in newspapers, magazines, travel brochures, diaries and journals, novels, short stories, dime novels, and children's bedtime stories. Joel Chandler Harris's Uncle Remus stories reinforced the stereotype. Graphic expressions of Sambo were, if anything, even more prevalent. Prominent illustrators made Sambo drawings to accompany the text of novels. The figure showed up in sheet music cartoons, calendars, postcards, postage stamps, stereoscopic slides, playing cards, and comic strips; it appeared on billboards and posters and was often featured in popular Currier and Ives prints found in late 19th-century middle-class American homes. Businessmen used Sambo to sell household goods such as soaps, polishes, coffee, jellies, and colas. A national restaurant chain picked Sambo for its name and after World War II used the image for its logo. Sambo appeared in performance routines during minstrel shows, circuses, theatrical shows, and on radio shows, nickelodeon reels, and television programs. Stepin' Fetchit made Sambo the perpetual chauffeur in the movies. Sambo was concretely embodied in the material culture in items such as salt and pepper shakers, place mats, shoehorns, pillows, children's banks, dolls, and whiskey pourers. The ceramic Sambo was found on tables inside homes and as an iron jockey on front lawns.

Scholars even used the Sambo image in textbooks and classrooms as an accurate image of the black personality. Historians in the mid-20th century have explored the Sambo stereotype more critically, focusing on its relationship to the slave period. Stanley Elkins's *Slavery: A Problem in American Institutional and Intellectual Life* (1959) concluded that slavery was a total institution, like a concentration camp, which created a childish, dependent black personality, but John Blassingame's *The Slave Community: Plantation Life in the Antebellum South* (1972) better reflects current consensus, insisting that Sambo was an assumed identity—one of several slave personality types—taken on and used to manipulate whites for survival. Through Sambo's protective foil, blacks were "laughing to keep from crying."

The Sambo stereotype has been severely attacked since the 1950s. James Baldwin declared Sambo dead in *Notes of a Native Son* (1955). Civil rights protests and the threat of violence behind demands for black power made the Sambo image unbelievable. By the 1970s the nation's electronic and print media projected new cultural images of blacks that challenged the older stereotype. The end of Sambo represented the death of a white attempt to define black personality and culture.

Charles Reagan Wilson
University of Mississippi

Joseph Boskin, *Sambo: The Rise and Demise of an American Jester* (1986); Daniel J. Leab, *From Sambo to Superspade: The Black Experience in Motion Pictures* (1975).

Uncle Tom's Cabin

Harriet Beecher Stowe set out to portray slavery as an institution, rather than the South as either a geographical or a cultural entity, in *Uncle Tom's Cabin*. The novel was begun in response to the Fugitive Slave Law of 1850. It was addressed to a national, not a regional, audience to whom Stowe made the argument that it was the educated, well-to-do, Christian gentlemen of the country, the hypocritical readers, in fact, who, through an indifference or cynicism that inhibited active opposition to slavery, were actually responsible for its continuation in American society and for the moral offense inherent in it.

The picture of the South that emerges in the novel is developed through three households, presented as types: the Shelbys of Kentucky, middle-class, kind, but subject to the pressures of a capitalist economy of which slavery is a part; the St. Clares of New Orleans, aristocratic, loving, but ineffectual as guardians of their enslaved servants because a debilitating skepticism undermines both Christian belief and political action; the Legree plantation, low-class, brutal, an example of how bad slavery can become. The Shelbys get very little space after the opening of the novel in which Mr. Shelby's sale of Uncle Tom and of Eliza's son, Harry, to pay some large debts initiates the two main plots. Shelby's predicament, being forced to sell against his own wishes and the strong feelings of his wife, shows the southern slaveholder caught in the grip of economic circumstance that is in no way unique to the South; indeed, Stowe frequently likens American exploitation of slaves to European exploitation of industrial workers. The Legree sequences at the end of the novel, although sensational and meant to provoke outrage at the institution of slavery, are not presented as typical either of it or of southern life. Not only is Legree himself a Yankee, but he also lives virtually beyond the pale of southern society, a day's journey up the Red River to a place described as wild and debauched. The suggestion is that Legree's wild domain is to the west of civilization, a horrible outpost on the Arkansas frontier.

Stowe sets her principal drama of southern life in the St. Clare household. Here, for example, is the kitchen, a place of playful leisure for the servants where the mystery of the cook's ways fosters an easy tolerance and affectionate community not to be found in the scrubbed and strictly managed kitchen of New England. The emotional atmosphere of the kitchen echoes the unruly abundance of southern land. Similarly, the décor of the bedroom belonging to little Eva, the novel's proselytizing child heroine, enhances her deathbed sermon on the gospel of love by suggesting a place of almost heavenly perfection: "The windows were hung with curtains of rose-colored and white muslin. The floor was spread with matting which had been ordered in Paris . . . having round it a border of rosebuds and leaves. . . . Over the head of the bed was an alabaster bracket, on which a beautiful sculptured angel stood, with drooping wings, holding out a crown of myrtle-leaves." A mosquito net made of "light curtains of rose-colored gauze" hung over the bed. The gardens around this summer "villa" by Lake Pontchartrain are also idealized by the fond, and perhaps envious, gardener/novelist from New England. (One must not forget that Stowe invested in a southern plantation after the Civil War and made her winter home in Mandarin, Fla., for many years. Her letters to northern relatives dwell on the floral paradise at her back door.)

The South as portrayed in the St. Clare household, and often contrasted to the northern society of the hero's cousin from Vermont, is a humane culture—disorderly, tender-hearted, distressed about slavery. To be sure, the family does include two destructive types: Augustine St. Clare's arrogant and despotic brother, who raises a son like himself, and Marie St. Clare, the self-indulgent hypochondriac whose pampered childhood led to unmitigated hard-heartedness. Despite the presence of these hateful characters in its midst, the St. Clare family is a loving home for slaves and owners alike. Its greatest weakness, and by implication that of the southern culture it represents, is its vulnerability to abrupt transformations—from the rosy bower of the angelic child Eva and the kind paternalism of her father to the debauchery of the Legree establishment, a transformation brought about by the sudden accidental death of St. Clare. In sum, Stowe sees the South of 1850 as beautiful, elegant, and weak, unable to sustain its gentlemanly ideal, which she values and praises, against the unscrupulous practices of the slave trade or the barbarity represented by the maddened and desperate Legree. In *Uncle Tom's Cabin*, the South is a garden of innocence and delight threatened by the snake of human cruelty; it is a lovely dream hovering on the verge of a nightmare.

See also MEDIA: / *Uncle Tom's Cabin*

Alice C. Crozier
Rutgers University

Alice C. Crozier, *Novels of Harriet Beecher Stowe* (1969); Thomas F. Gossett, *Uncle Tom's Cabin and American Culture* (1985); Moira D. Reynolds, *Uncle Tom's Cabin and Mid-Nineteenth Century United States: Pen and Conscience* (1985).

Watermelon

Watermelon is among the best examples of the mythic significance of food in southern culture. The eating of southern watermelon is one of the most symbolic rituals of southerners. To be sure, watermelon is not a unique possession of the American South. Watermelon seeds have been discovered in Egyptian tombs from thousands of years ago, and Mediterranean peoples have cultivated it for centuries. Northern Americans eat watermelon, although their climate enables them to raise only small-fruited and midget varieties.

An annual called *Citrullus lanatus*, southern watermelon is a member of the gourd family. It grows during

Watermelon vendors, Warren County, Miss., 1975

the South's warm, humid summers, requiring a 120-day growing season. Southern watermelons are called "rampant-growing varieties," and they have regionally meaningful names such as the Dixie Queen, Dixielee, Stone Mountain, Charleston Gray, Alabama Giant, Florida Giant, Louisiana Queen, Carolina Cross, and Africa 8. Africans introduced watermelon to Europe and later North America, and Indians in Florida were cultivating it by the mid-17th century. Thomas Jefferson grew watermelons at Monticello, but they were found more often among the crops of yeoman farmers than planters. Garden patches that fed many an impoverished southerner in the postbellum South often included watermelons. They were a low-cost treat even during the Depression, and some southerners still call the watermelon a Depression ham.

Watermelon has been especially associated in the United States with rural southern blacks. It became a prop identified with the stereotypical Sambo—the childlike, docile, laughing black boy was seen grinning and eating watermelon. This derogatory image was pervasive in popular literature and art, and watermelon-eating scenes later became stock features of films and newsreels. Watermelon has been, nonetheless, a cultural symbol used also in less negative ways as well by southerners and others. Folklore has long told of the proper ways to plant watermelon (by poking a hole in the ground and planting the seed by hand), and the ability to tell a ripe watermelon by thumping it was a legendary rural skill. Literature tells of the simple joys of eating watermelon. Tom Sawyer and Huck Finn (in Mark Twain's *Tom Sawyer, Detective: As Told by Huck Finn*) "snuck off" from Aunt Sally one night and "talked and smoked and stuffed watermelon as much as two hours."

The Skillet Lickers chose a traditional southern folk tune, "Watermelon on the Vine," for one of the earliest recordings of southern country music, and Tom T. Hall celebrated the melon in the more recent "Old Dogs, Children, and Watermelon Wine." The lyrics to the blues song "Watermelon Man" identified the succulent melon with sexual potency, and a 1970 Melvin Van Peebles film about the experiences of a white man who wakes up one morning with a black skin was also called *Watermelon Man*. The watermelon has been used as an advertising symbol, especially on roadsides to direct motorists to stands selling the delicacy. Miles Carpenter, of Waverly, Va., began carving wooden watermelon slices and painting them with enamel decades ago, and today he is recognized as an accomplished folk artist.

In the contemporary South the watermelon remains a part of the summer diet. Cookbooks have recipes not only for the traditional chilled melon, melon balls, pickled watermelon rind, and spiked melon, but also for watermelon and cassis ice, spiced watermelon pie, and watermelon muffins. But the importance of watermelon to southerners transcends its use as food. When popular periodicals discuss symbols of the region, they usually include watermelon (*Southern Magazine*, June 1987; *Texas Monthly*, January 1977). Summer recreation includes festivals, and watermelon is the central feature of festivals at Luling, Tex.; Hampton County, S.C.; Chiefland, Chipley, Lakeland, and Monticello, Fla.; Grand Bay, Ala.; Raleigh, N.C.; and Mize and Water Valley, Miss. The U.S. Watermelon Seed-Spitting Contest is held during the National Watermelon Association's annual convention in Moreven, Ga., the first week of March. Hope, Ark., may be the watermelon capital of the South. The town advertises itself with a logo that has a picture of a watermelon and the claim that Hope offers "a slice of the good life." Hope farmers regularly raise 100–150 pound watermelons.

Southerners would likely still agree with a passage in Mark Twain's *Pudd'nhead Wilson*: "The true southern watermelon is a boon apart and not to be mentioned with commoner things. It is chief of this world's luxuries, king by the Grace of God over all the fruits of the earth. When one has tasted it, he knows what the angels eat. It was not a southern watermelon that Eve took; we know it because she repented."

Charles Reagan Wilson
University of Mississippi

Ellen Ficklen, *Watermelon* (1984).

Yerby, Frank

(b. 1916) Writer.

Frank Garvin Yerby, one of the most popular novelists to set tales in the Old South, was born in Augusta, Ga., on 5 September 1916. He completed degrees at Paine College (A.B., 1937) and Fisk University (M.A., 1938) and did graduate work at the University of Chicago. A black man, Yerby published several excellent short stories from 1944 to 1946 dealing with racial themes. Although he won a major award for his short fiction, Yerby's fame and fortune rest on his widely popular romance novels, the first of which was published in 1946 and sold over 2 million copies. Like many of his novels to follow, *The Foxes of Harrow* was set in the antebellum South and tapped public interest in the Old South that had been fostered by the phenomenal success of Margaret Mitchell's *Gone with the Wind* (1936).

Yerby's southern romances, including such titles as *A Woman Called Fancy* (1951), *Benton's Row* (1954), and *Griffin's Way* (1962), dominated popular fiction set in the Old South for nearly two decades. His works were meticulously researched and included a wealth of elaborate and surprisingly accurate period detail in such areas as costuming, architecture, southern society, and even slave life. One critic termed *Fair Oaks* (1957) a "primer in black history."

The novels were primarily romantic glimpses of the planter elite and were aimed at a predominantly white, female audience. This led many critics to condemn his work as potboiler fiction, and others have often charged that he ignored racial issues. Yerby once countered the latter charge by saying that the novelist does not have the right to "inflict on the public his private ideas on politics, religion or race." In most respects the charges were unfair, for Yerby managed to influence the ideas and values of far more readers through historical romance than could possibly have been reached by other forms of fiction. This point is demonstrated by Yerby's own career, for he did attempt a few novels with racial themes. These included *The Old Gods Laugh* (1964) and *The Dahomian* (1971), both of which sold poorly in comparison to his plantation novels.

Yet Frank Yerby's impact was not in the area of popular and accurate history. His importance rests on his fostering of public interest in the antebellum South and his fiction's impact on extending the romantic ideal of the South as one great plantation. Besides Mitchell's *Gone with the Wind* and Kyle Onstott's *Mandingo* (1957), the novels of Frank Yerby did more to standardize the plantation fiction genre than did the works of any other author. Apart from his careful attention to historic detail, Yerby's major contribution to the fictional portrayal of the Old South was an entrance into the bedrooms of the planters. His incredibly successful fiction helped to solidify the popular impression of the antebellum South as a land of "moonlight and magnolias," of aristocratic lifestyles, of beautiful belles, and of dashing and handsome young gentlemen.

Christopher D. Geist
Bowling Green State University

Jack Temple Kirby, *Media-Made Dixie: The South in the American Imagination* (1978); Jack B. Moore, *Journal of Popular Culture* (Spring 1975); Frank Yerby, *Harper's* (October 1959).

Yoknapatawpha County

"William Faulkner, Sole Owner & Proprietor," states the legend on the map, and no claim to title is any more indisputable, though the reader may wander within the realm identified there by the proprietor for as long as he or she is inclined—and without fear of trespass, for, through one of its paradoxes, Yoknapatawpha County belongs to everyone as well as to the author. It is the setting for all of Faulkner's major fiction and is itself a fictional creation.

Faulkner named his county after the Yoknapatawpha River, which was the old name of the Yocona River, an actual river that runs south of Oxford, Miss. Initially Faulkner used the current name, and it appears as such in *Flags in the Dust*. The *Flags* manuscript was not published until 1973, however, having first been rejected, then edited and published as *Sartoris* (1929). Thus, *Sartoris* was the first published novel in the Yoknapatawpha series, followed in the same year by *The Sound and the Fury*. Faulkner did not employ the old name Yoknapatawpha until *As I Lay Dying* (1930), by which time he had a good start on the chronicle that would ultimately include over a dozen novels and numerous short stories spanning the period from the late 1700s to the middle of the present century.

Faulkner's county is situated in northern Mississippi and consists of 2,400 square miles. It was settled by whites, some with slaves, in the early 1800s, following the Chickasaw Indian cessions. The county seat, Jefferson, originally a Chickasaw Agency trading post dating from the late 1700s, was founded in 1833 with the hasty erection of a log courthouse and named not after the former U.S. president but for a mail rider serving the area. Faulkner's comic rendering of this founding appears in *Requiem for a Nun* (1951), a dramatic work not otherwise known for levity. The families of some of the founders and early settlers figure throughout the entire Yoknapatawpha saga; others die out or disappear. Their genealogies are often elaborate and sometimes confusing. The trajectories of fortune in their lives—and the lives of characters who appear in Yoknapatawpha later—are as varied as those in our own, though more often than not in Faulkner's world the tracings of fortune follow a widely erratic course. They are families at all levels of southern society with names such as Beauchamp, Bundren, Compson, Sartoris, Snopes, and Varner; individuals named Luster, Dilsey, or Ikkemotubbe, the chief of the Chickasaws, whose river gave Faulkner a name for his world.

The two Chickasaw Indian words of which the word *Yoknapatawpha* is constituted mean "split land," though Faulkner said that the two words together mean "water flowing slow through the flatland." And because on one side of the paradox he is the sole owner, Yoknapatawpha means what he said.

In addition to the matter of proprietorship, there are other paradoxes, some specific to all literary creations: Jefferson, the geographic center and county seat of Yoknapatawpha County, Miss., is and is not Oxford, the center and county seat of Lafayette County, Miss., where Faulkner grew up and lived most of his life. He drew on the town and region as a primary source, as many writers draw on a particular place, and there are countless identifiable parallels, geographic and cultural; but in the accounting required with art, Yoknapatawpha exists unto itself.

Similarly, Yoknapatawpha exists both in and out of time. It is timeless in the way that the landscape and human motion arrested on Keats's Grecian urn are timeless, and in the way that Keats's ode itself—which Faulkner refers to in "The Bear," summoning the same idea—exists out of time.

Where temporality does obtain, in the recorded history of Yoknapatawpha, there are discrepancies. (Its sole historian had lapses of memory and changes of heart in the 37 or so years of its progress as a chronicle and admitted as much in his short preface to *The Mansion* [1959].) Yet—the paradox—there is no chronicle any more accurate or rich in information, if one regards the history of Yoknapatawpha as emblematic of the history of the South.

A fanciful way of accounting for these paradoxes would be to observe that Yoknapatawpha County is bordered both to the north and the south by water and is thus mystical (that is, if one accepts Walker Percy's notion that water is the mystical element). Further, these parallel borders—the Tallahatchie River to the north and the Yoknapatawpha River to the south—run east and west, and

Faulkner's map (the one drawn for *Absalom, Absalom!* [1936]) shows that in those directions he left Yoknapatawpha County seemingly borderless. His Yoknapatawpha extends irresistibly toward horizons associated with beginnings and endings, the old and the new, the origins of the world's religions, the myths and archetypes that inform much of the drama of Yoknapatawpha. For the county does indeed exist in a borderless confluence of the mystical and the mythical, the synchronic, the spiritual, and the dramatic.

See also GEOGRAPHY: / Faulkner's Geography; LITERATURE: / Faulkner, William

James Seay
University of North Carolina
at Chapel Hill

Elizabeth M. Kerr, *Yoknapatawpha: Faulkner's "Little Postage Stamp of Native Soil"* (1969).

Politics

NUMAN BARTLEY

University of Georgia

CONSULTANT

Broderick Crawford as Willie Stark (far right) at campaign rally in a scene from All the King's Men *(1949)*

Politics and Ideology

During the 1970s southern political practices came to resemble more closely national norms. The election of a Deep South resident to the presidency in 1976 seemingly confirmed the region's new-found respectability. In earlier years the South's political image was a distinctive and largely negative one. Indeed, the region's long-established reputation as the home of demagogues, Dixiecrats, and disfranchisement contributed to making the region a subject of endless interest, scorn, and puzzlement. V. O. Key's classic study *Southern Politics in State and Nation*, which appeared in 1949, began with the statement: "The South may not be the nation's number one political problem, as some northerners assert, but politics is the South's number one problem." After devoting almost 700 pages to a masterful examination of southern political practices, Key chose to title the final chapter of the book "Is There a Way Out?" Key closely associated southern political problems with three relatively distinctive southern political institutions: the one-party system, disfranchisement, and the pervasive ethos of Jim Crow segregation.

These institutions were crucial to southern electoral politics, particularly during the first half of the 20th century, but more recent scholarship has suggested that southern political problems have been more deeply embedded in the region's social and economic fabric than the statement that "politics is the South's number one problem" would imply. Social and economic developments quite early in southern history were to have long-lasting significance for southern politics. Most important was the creation of an economy based on plantation agriculture and slave labor. Following the perfection of the cotton gin in the late 18th century, the rapid westward expansion of cotton and caste laid the foundation for southern unity. Slavery and plantation agriculture, although profitable for the planters who held the slaves, were not so materially beneficial for southern society as a whole. The purchase of slaves absorbed an enormous amount of southern capital, and the general self-sufficiency of southern agriculture debased the domestic market and hampered economic development. As a result, the antebellum South achieved little in the way of a "modern" economic infrastructure while at the same time it enjoyed a great deal of individual affluence.

Under these conditions agrarian democracy flourished. Popular political participation shot upward during the 1830s, and voter turnout—in terms of the percentage of the eligible electorate that actually appeared at the polls—during the middle years of the 19th century was the highest it has ever been in southern history. Similarly, the South by the 1840s had developed a functioning two-party system. The relatively evenly balanced Whigs and Democrats competed vigorously for the favor of southern voters at all levels of government. It was the most thoroughly developed two-party system the South has ever had.

One of the explanations for such a vigorous assertion of democracy was that white southerners were in general agreement on substantive issues: land should be taken from Indians; agriculture should be promoted; slavery should be advanced; and the South should be defended from the meddling activities of antislavery advocates. A white male consensus on these points tended to promote political democracy and two-party competition.

Herrenvolk Democracy and Paternalism. Southern democracy was herrenvolk—that is, master race democracy with political citizenship limited to white males—and, significantly, its origins were herrenvolk rather than popular. It is of symbolic interest that in August 1619 the first representative assembly to meet in English America convened in Jamestown, Va., where in the same month a Dutch warship sold the first 20 Africans known to have arrived in America, thus providing an early linkage between liberty and slavery. Developments in the South reinforced this paradoxical and symbiotic relationship. Rather early in American history, land hunger fueled growing hostility toward Indians. The need for labor on southern plantations was met by the importation of slaves. Thus, Edmund S. Morgan, in his important study of slavery and freedom in Virginia, concluded: "By lumping Indians, mulattoes, and Negroes in a single pariah class, Virginians had paved the way for a similar lumping of small and large planters in a single master class." Southern democracy not only limited political participation to a master race but rested directly on the exploitation of other races. Indeed, William J. Cooper has observed in *Liberty and Slavery* (1983) that "before 1860, free, white southerners could not conceive of holding on to their own liberty except by keeping black southerners enslaved."

Labor exploitation in the Old South, at least in the direct sense, normally meant whites exploiting blacks rather than each other. Such an arrangement undermined class conflict, encouraged what W. J. Cash termed a "Proto-Dorian" bond between whites, and fostered an autonomous independence that in some ways was conducive to citizenship and republican ideals, as the career of Thomas Jefferson would suggest. But despite generating high voter turnout among white males, herrenvolk democracy had severe inherent limitations. Not only did it rest squarely on racism and exploitation, it also limited the legitimate range of debate. Southern freedom and democracy, even before slavery came under attack from the outside, had tendencies toward "the savage ideal," which Cash described as "that ideal whereunder dissent and variety are completely suppressed."

The paternalistic social values that grew from master-slave relationships further influenced the ideological context of southern politics. Historians continue to disagree over the extent to which the South was capitalist and the extent to which it was a premodern, prebourgeois, traditional society, but, whatever the ultimate resolution of the debate, southern social values were clearly different from those prevalent in the North. In the North Jacksonian democracy marked the coming of age of a laissez-faire society and an ideology of free labor individualism that appealed to independent artisans, farmers, and businessmen; in the South Jacksonian democracy did strengthen the herrenvolk civic concept of autonomous independence, but the region's forced labor system and the mutual dependence of masters and slaves also supported a patriarchal ideology. Southern thought tended to extol a paternal, organic, and hierarchical society, which contrasted with northern ideals of laissez-faire individualism, economic freedom, and legal equality. The southern paternal ethos projected, in the words of Eugene D. Genovese, "an aristocratic, antibourgeois spirit with values and morés emphasizing family and status, a strong code of honor, and aspirations to luxury, ease and accomplishment." Gunnar Myrdal, commenting on conservative southern political thought, pointed out in his epic, *An American Dilemma* (1944): "Slavery was only part of a greater social order which established an ideal division of labor and of responsibility in society between the sexes, the age groups, the social classes and the two races."

Herrenvolk democracy tempered by ideological paternalism produced for a brief period intense partisan competition. During the 1850s the two-party system collapsed under the strain of sectional strife. Following the Civil War and emancipation, the South again experimented with two-party politics. The Fourteenth and Fifteenth Amendments offered citizenship and suffrage to the newly freed blacks, and the black-oriented Radical Republicans in the South accomplished the remarkable feat of politically mobilizing the freedmen. Conservative whites reorganized under the Democratic banner. For varying periods of time, the southern states were battlegrounds for the contending Radical Republicans and conservative Democrats. Conservative whites organized the Ku Klux Klan and other terrorist groups, while the Republicans relied heavily upon federal forces for protection. The Democratic combination of terrorism and political rhetoric that appealed for herrenvolk unity proved successful and Republicanism rapidly declined. The last of the Republican governments in the South collapsed in 1877, when southern Democrats and northern Republicans engineered a historic compromise whereby the southern conservatives accepted northeastern capitalist policies nationally in exchange for federal nonintervention in southern social affairs.

New South Politics. Effectively, the southern leadership tacitly acquiesced to the South remaining economically a colony of the North. The Civil War and emancipation swept away the plantation prosperity that had marked the region's real economic problems. Bereft of capital, bound more closely to the North by postwar railroad construction, overwhelmed by the rapid growth of population and manufacturing above the Potomac, and hampered by northeastern oriented tariff, banking, and other policies, the South provided cotton, lumber products, minerals and other raw materials, and, to a lesser extent, markets for the more advanced northern economy. A fundamental requirement imposed by the South's colonial dependency was cheap labor, and the maintenance of a cheap labor force was an underlying factor in the politics of the New South.

Presiding over these developments were the Bourbon Democrats. By controlling the Democratic party machinery and by manipulating the race issue, the Bourbons were able to maintain themselves in office, and that fact ensured that state power would be exercised on behalf of the employing classes. But if the Bourbon system accomplished the rudimentary goals of those who were most likely to benefit from the South's colonial status, it was not particularly successful in providing political and social stability. The tensions and conflicts in southern society were severe. Civil War, emancipation, and Reconstruction left southern society deeply divided. The failure of plantation agriculture to restore prewar prosperity, the decline of the yeoman farmers, the breakdown of agricultural self-sufficiency, and the economic competition between black and white laborers produced further social stress and helped to explain the growth of lynching and other forms of social violence. The Populist movement of the 1890s grew out of this atmosphere and, indeed, brought to culmination a variety of long-simmering conflicts. So profound were the implications of the Populist radical critique of state and national policy that the conservative Bourbon Democrats responded with violence and with massive fraud in the counting and casting of ballots.

Unlike the antebellum era when the electorate was in general agreement on substantive policies, the New South was rent by social dissension. During the Reconstruction crisis, the conservative Democrats relied upon Ku Klux Klan terrorism to regain control of the southern states; during the post-Reconstruction era, they turned back independent insurgency by using their control of land, credit, and the law to influence the behavior of black voters; and during the Populist crisis they resorted to violence and fraud. Beyond that, they sought more institutionalized methods to ensure the social stability that ultimately rested on white supremacy and cheap labor. The result was the establishment of those institutions so ably described by V. O. Key: disfranchisement, the one-party system, and Jim Crow segregation.

The disfranchisement of black people was such an obvious way to ensure political white supremacy and thereby to bolster the whole southern system of labor relationships that the surprising thing is that conservative white southern political elites did not do it sooner. The explanation for the delay seems to relate to the ability of the Bourbons to manipulate the black vote and to earlier fears that disfranchisement might prompt federal intervention. The Democratic conservatives also demonstrated the willingness to support, often quite openly, the disfranchisement of whites. The president of the Alabama disfranchising convention of 1901 explained: "The true philosophy of the movement was to establish restricted suffrage, and to place the power of government in the hands of the intelligent and virtuous." Although such views were compatible with ideological paternalism, disfranchisement reversed the trend toward the expansion of democracy that had been evident in the antebellum South and the Reconstruction period. The high voter turnout of the antebellum era extended into the postbellum period. Voter turnout remained high after the enfranchisement of blacks, though it did begin to drop off following the end of Reconstruction. Despite this decline, voter participation remained respectable—above 50 percent of the eligible electorate in the former Confederate states—until the disfranchisement movement.

The conservative Democrats' disfranchisement of whites was not at all illogical. After all, inexpensive white labor was as important as black labor, and it was doubtlessly easier to maintain if the electorate were limited to "the intelligent and virtuous." But beyond this, the removal of the lower levels of the white working class from the electorate suggests the extent to which white sharecroppers and mill workers had already been relegated to what J. Wayne Flynt has termed "the Southern poor white caste." Prior to the Civil War southern poor whites were a part of the overall population. In the New South, as Flynt says, "poor whites assumed many aspects of a caste system and were increasingly identifiable within the general population."

It is not entirely surprising that segregation, although having deep roots in southern history, assumed its particularly cruel Jim Crow form at approximately the same time as the disfranchisement movement. The motives for segregationist legislation were complex, but the Jim Crow system contributed substantially to social stability. It virtually guaranteed the continuing existence of cheap black labor, and it further divided the black caste from the poor white caste and encouraged each of them to direct hostility toward the other.

Segregation and disfranchisement not only served as formidable barriers to future Populist heresies but they also strengthened the Solid South. The one-party system discouraged the emergence of divisive issues at home while at the same time unifying southern political power nationally in defense of the region's peculiar social practices. During the first half of the 20th century, few southerners voted and those who did voted overwhelmingly Democratic. When in 1924 Republican Calvin Coolidge received about 1,200 of South Carolina's approximately 50,000 presidential votes, Senator Coleman L. Blease exclaimed: "I do not know where he got them. I was astonished to know they were cast and shocked to know they were counted."

But if these reforms did place southern politics in the hands of "the intelligent and virtuous," there remains the question of just who "the intelligent and virtuous" were. Presumably they were not black southerners, who in the year 1910 made up more than one-third of the population of the former Confederate states. Thus, using 1910 figures, segregation placed 35 percent of the population and even more of the work force in an inferior caste. Not all blacks were poor, of course, but discrimination ensured that most would be. The "intelligent and virtuous" also presumably did not include most of the poor whites. It is difficult to estimate the size of that group or even to define it in statistical terms, but huge numbers of whites labored at occupations not much different from positions held by blacks, and, defined in that manner, a fair estimate would be that the poor white class was probably no smaller than was the black caste around 1910. Thus, the black and white underclass made up approximately two-thirds of the southern population.

During the first four decades of the 20th century, the active southern electorate encompassed between one-fourth and one-third of the adult population, although the figures varied significantly from state to state. The "intelligent and virtuous" made up approximately one-third of the population, and southern election returns indicated that approximately one-fourth of the citizens voted. These figures seem to be compatible because not all people would have necessarily paid their poll taxes and made their way through all the other pitfalls that protected the polls from the voters even though they were otherwise sufficiently white to vote in the white primaries and sufficiently literate to deal with literacy and understanding requirements. Thus, the bulk of southern voters were drawn from that third of southern society that was both whiter and more economically prosperous than the population as a whole; generally speaking, these "intelligent and virtuous" citizens in-

Huey Long image over front steps of the state capitol at the inauguration of Louisiana Governor Richard Leche, Baton Rouge, 1936

cluded three more or less distinct social groups. One might be termed the plantation-oriented county-seat governing class; one could be called the uptown elites; and one was the white common folk.

The Governing Elite and the Common Folk. As the name implies, the county-seat governing class was the South's dominant political group. The Civil War and Reconstruction broke the national power of the planter class, but thereafter southern planters and their allies emerged victorious from the political wars of Reconstruction to become the most powerful social group in southern politics. Geographically concentrated in the region's lowland-plantation counties, the planter-merchant-banker-lawyer governing class set much of the tone for the politics of the region. They were the foremost defenders of the southern way of life, the most devoted proponents of Lost Cause mythology, and the most loyal adherents to paternal social values. They provided the basic hard-core support for Bourbon democracy, marshalled the conservative forces to turn back the Populist threat, and led the disfranchisement movement. V. O. Key was certainly correct when he stated, "The hard core of the political South—and the backbone of political unity—is made up of those counties and sections of the southern states in which Negroes constitute a substantial proportion of the population." At the crucial junctures in the politics of the New South, the plantation–county-seat governing class won the decisive engagements.

The greatest long-term potential threat to the power of the county-seat governing class was the uptown elite in the South's expanding cities. The term *uptown* denotes the leadership of the region's urban areas and suggests a Henry W. Grady New South style of politics. Although lacking the authority and political prestige of the county-seat governing class, uptown elites were the South's most affluent people and in some ways the most strategically placed. They normally controlled the region's larger and more influential newspapers, banks, and other sources of influence. In addition to being the foremost proponents of the New South creed, they were leaders in the drive for segregation. They of course suffered from the South's being for so long so overwhelmingly rural—in 1910 only 2 people of every 10 in the former Confederate states resided in a town of above 2,500 population. Furthermore, the widening economic disparity between the prospering cities and the poverty-ridden country contributed to an increasing rural hostility toward the cities, a fact that further limited uptown influence.

Normally uptown elites were the allies of the county-seat governing class. Not only did the two groups share class interest but southern urban prosperity was closely tied to the overall southern colonial economy. With a few exceptions, most notably Birmingham, southern cities served as the great distributing centers for the products that ultimately appeared on country-store shelves and as the centers for marketing and transporting southern cotton and raw materials to the North. Andre Gunder Frank has observed that Latin America "had a colonial class structure which inevitably gave its dominant bourgeoisie an economic self-interest in freely exporting raw materials and importing manufactured products." This applied equally to New South merchants and businessmen. The prosperity of the cities and towns was deeply enmeshed in existing economic arrangements. As a consequence uptown elites remained only a long-term potential threat to county-seat power in the Solid South.

The largest of the three social groups was the common folk: the farmers, skilled workers, tradesmen, and all the others in southern society who found themselves situated between the black and white underclasses and the county-seat and urban elites. Lacking the ideological and political unity of the county-seat governing class and the strategic and material advantages of uptown, "The Man at the Center" lacked organization and consistent direction. The middle did, however, play a major role in New South politics. The middle was the social base for the southern demagogues. The Baltimore journalist H. L. Mencken lamented on numerous occasions the tragic descent of southern politics from the wise and aristocratic leadership of southern statesmen in the early years of the Republic to the unprincipled buffoonery of the 20th century and always assigned the cause for this catastrophe to the rise of southern poor whites. Mencken's contention that demagoguery was a poor white phenomenon was essentially nonsense. Southern poor whites did not vote, and the great era of the southern demagogues coincided precisely with the period when disfranchisement was most effective.

The common folk were the social base for demagoguery and they were much courted at election time. Their attraction to the demagogues—who at least had redeeming value as spectator entertainment—suggests the extent to which they found the candidates of county seat and uptown inadequate. The demagogues were overwhelmingly antiurban in their politics if not necessarily their policies, a fact that indicates the extent to which the cities of the New South had become alienated from the countryside. To some degree, demagoguery was a politics of protest and insurgency, an antiestablishment thrust that whatever its inadequacies often gave ordinary whites more in the way of program and attention than they were apt to get otherwise. But most of all, demagoguery was a politics of frustration, resulting from the common folk's place in the social structure. The common white folk had the unenviable task of challenging those above while protecting themselves from those below, and any meaningful radical or semiradical assault on the power and pomp of those above would ultimately have involved those below, which incidentally was precisely what happened with Populism. The result was demagoguery, protest, and even on occasion moderate reform without the disruption of the existing social order.

The Conservative Solid South. The South was changing, but in important ways it was still a premodern society with an underdeveloped colonial economy. The unfolding of the region's peculiar and vexing history led to the creation of a politically conservative Solid South that patterned southern political behavior for two-thirds of a century. So enmeshed were its economic, social, and political institutions that the Solid South's longevity is understandable. So undemocratic and exploitive were its arrangements that the criticisms directed against them seem unobjectionable.

Modernizing forces ultimately eroded the economic and social order that underlay the politics of the Solid South. The Great Depression of the 1930s and World War II fundamentally redirected southern development, although several decades were required for the region's people to absorb such a change, and certainly that was true of politics. Franklin D. Roosevelt and the New Deal responded to the Depression with a programic liberalism that won the support of huge numbers of southerners. The Roosevelt Administration's *Report on Economic Conditions of the South* signaled a critical turning point in federal policy. Whereas national governmental policies had usually accepted and often buttressed the South's position as a colonial appendage of the northern economy, the *Report* declared the South to be "the Nation's No. 1 economic problem—the Nation's problem, not merely the South's," thereby justifying the federal government's emerging role as an active sponsor of southern economic development. Although most agricultural historians are sharply critical of New Deal agricultural policies, which contributed so significantly to the depopulation of the southern countryside, the catastrophic condition of southern agriculture made any aid popular; and given the South's huge population of blacks and poor working-class whites, it is little wonder that New Deal liberalism won a very substantial following. Indeed, if public opinion polls are to be believed, the South was the most liberal area of the nation during the 1930s, and the Solid Democratic South became even more solidly Democratic.

Leander Perez, Louisiana political leader, 1950s

But despite the mass appeal of New Deal liberalism in the South, the region's politics was far more conservative than its people. New Deal liberalism was, of course, politically ineffective because a huge percentage of the South's black and white working people were both unorganized and voteless. Beginning in the mid-1930s Solid South political elites increasingly turned away from the New Deal, allying instead with Republicans to form the conservative coalition in Congress. Thus, the area that opinion polls suggested was the nation's most liberal region produced the politicians who most successfully opposed the New Deal. Perhaps understandably, northern liberals chafed under such arrangements and persistently searched for ways to extend the liberal-labor-minority coalition into the South and thereby to transform southern politics.

The most formidable opponents of such a strategy were the Old Guard southern Democrats, who, with their prestige as the defenders of the Southland and their seniority in Congress, remained the most powerful element in southern politics. In Congress, they allied with Republicans in an informal but effective anti–New Deal coalition. The emergence of this coalition protected southern influence in Congress, but it also laid the foundation for an escalating sectional conflict within the Democratic party. New Deal liberals sought to extend the New Deal coalition into the South. Southern conservative elites, while entrenched in Congress, fretted over liberal control of presidential politics and endeavored to restore their influence in national party affairs. This struggle between the northern liberal-labor-minority coalition and the once Solid Democratic South was a crucial factor in American politics from the mid-1930s until the mid-1960s. The conflict escalated when President Truman asked Congress to enact civil rights legislation in 1948 and when later in the year the Democratic national convention endorsed Truman's program.

Outraged southern conservatives responded with the formation of the Dixiecrats, and thereafter third-party movements in presidential politics were common. By depriving the national Democrats of southern electoral votes, southern conservatives hoped to force concessions from the party and to deadlock the electoral college, thereby creating an opportunity to negotiate another sectional compromise as their ideological ancestors had done to end Reconstruction in 1877.

Massive Resistance. The Supreme Court's *Brown* v. *Board of Education* desegregation decision in 1954 further inflamed the southern leadership. Old Guard conservatives launched a determined program of massive resistance to desegregation. If the southern states refused to obey the *Brown* decision, what could the court eventually do but reverse the decision? To accomplish this task, southern conservatives adopted the hoary theory of interposition and sought to interpose state power between the federal courts and southern citizens. In practice that resulted in an astonishing variety of segregationist laws that spewed forth from the malapportioned southern state legislatures.

Like the third party presidential movements, massive resistance began as an elite enterprise. The Old Guard conservative leadership, its ideological roots deeply anchored in Bourbon democracy, placed defense of the southern social system above such things as public education. They had been defending the southern way of life since the Compromise of 1877, and even in the 1950s the planter-merchant-banker-lawyer county-seat governing class that the southern conservatives represented remained a fundamental locus of political power.

During these years, the agenda for both the national liberals and the southern conservatives changed and, indeed, narrowed. Northern New Deal liberals had viewed southern problems within an economic context and had sought to expand political and industrial democracy. During the postwar era, northern liberals moved rather rapidly away from the perception of the South as "the Nation's No. 1 economic problem" to the position that the South was the nation's number one moral problem. Whereas New Deal liberals viewed southern social problems in class terms—as a conflict between haves and have nots—postwar northern liberals tended to see the South in terms of a morality play featuring evil whites and virtuous blacks. A northern liberal agenda, then, which had once defined southern problems in relatively broad terms with profoundly meaningful implications for both southern whites and blacks, became narrowed to race as a moral issue. Similarly, while the southern conservatives defended a paternal order that encouraged such southern virtues as concern for family, kinship, community, church, roots, and place, they, like the liberals, reduced a broad range of values to the one issue of race, a massive resistance to desegregation.

Although originally promoted by conservative elites, the resistance to desegregation did ultimately become a popular reaction. As a result of federal court decisions and other factors, voter turnout steadily increased in the South, and by the late 1950s, the growing restiveness of black southerners and the gradual spread of desegregation made the race issue more salient to southern voters. The group that responded most positively to conservative appeals was the southern white common folk, the people who had often supported demagoguery in the past but who had shown strong proclivities toward New Deal reformism during the 1930s and 1940s. Thus, that social group upon which liberals had based so much hope for the future of liberalism ended up in the camp of the conservatives. The race issue—and the success of both the northern liberals and the southern conservatives in confining the political debate to that issue—completed the rout of the southern political liberals, who found themselves identified with the politically unpopular side of the controversy. Indeed, when the aging and declining southern Old Guard conservatives proved unable to turn back the desegregationist tide, working whites promoted their own spokesmen, the foremost of whom was George Wallace.

The Old Guard conservatives defined the issue as race, branded white liberals as traitors, and propounded a scorched-earth policy of closing the schools. The massive resistance strategy received its test when the schools actually started closing. In the fall of 1958 the governor of Arkansas closed the high schools in Little Rock and the governor of Virginia closed schools in a number of Virginia communities. The schools eventually reopened desegregated, but the process was repeated throughout much of the South. In the state of Georgia the crisis came in 1961 when a federal court ordered the admission of two black students to the University of Georgia. The state legislature had displayed the extent of its wisdom by enacting the usual bevy of massive resistance laws that included measures requiring that any desegregating institution be closed, that state funds be denied, that any instructor who taught mixed black and white students be arrested for felony, that any law enforcement official who failed to arrest a teacher for teaching in a desegregated classroom be himself arrested for felony, and so on. But in Georgia, as elsewhere, state authorities, when faced with the actual consequences of closing down the public schools and state universities, ultimately relented.

Leading the political opposition to closing the schools was the educated and affluent white middle class in the South's rapidly expanding cities and suburbs. Throughout the South it was the urban-suburban middle class, the heirs of the uptown elite, that organized the "save our school" movements in defense of public education. Avoiding the race issue, these campaigns merely insisted that public schools were essential to the continuing economic growth of the region. By endeavoring to avoid the race issue, the urban-suburban middle-class position was perceived as moderate, and in a massive resistance atmosphere their candidates for public office attracted the support of the rapidly expanding black electorate. Thus, the least materially affluent people in the South—the blacks—became the allies of the most affluent people in the South—the white business-professional-metropolitan elites.

Industrialization and Civil Rights. The middle-class uptown moderates provided much of the impetus for the drive to attract new industry. There was little novel in the notion that the South should endeavor to attract outside industry, although, as an important ideological force, its origins were relatively recent. The urban boosterism of the 1920s gained sustained momentum after the Great Depression had exposed the bankruptcy of southern agriculture and the economic thrust generated by World War II had propelled the South in the direction of further rapid economic growth. In 1936 Mississippi created its Balance Agriculture with Industry program, and thereafter all the other southern states created industrial development commissions. In the post–World War II period southern state government competed vigorously with a variety of programs and policies designed to offer services, tax concessions, and public subsidization to national and international corporations that chose to expand into the South. The old-style southern plantations gradually disappeared as agriculture became capital intensive and mechanized, and the diversifying southern economy benefited from labor mobility more than from the coercive forms of labor control that had been such a central factor in the politics and ideology of the New South.

The economic growth ethos had wide appeal. It had been a favored liberal program in earlier years, although the liberals had sought industrialization with industrial democracy. It also appealed to Old Guard conservatives, who hoped to combine industrialization with segregation and paternal social values. While dominating the headlines with their frantic attempts to preserve the southern way of life, conservative governors and legislators also encouraged and funded industrial development programs, though generally taking less interest in them than did such moderate governors as Luther Hodges in North Carolina and Leroy Collins in Florida.

Indeed, the economic growth ethos provided one of the inspirations for the black protest movement. The black sit-in movement, which began in 1960, was in the beginning the work of young, educated, upwardly mobile blacks who wanted an opportunity to participate in the increasingly flourishing southern marketplace. The success of the black freedom movement in capturing the imagination of much of the nation ultimately forced the federal government to override the Congressional Dixieland Band and to enact the 1964 and 1965 Civil Rights Acts, which, when combined with other developments of this period, dismantled the social and political system that had for so long regulated wide areas of southern life. The 1964 act included an equality of economic opportunity provision that came to be interpreted in terms of affirmative action, and Lyndon B. Johnson's Great Society program did include what cynics came to call the skirmish on poverty. These measures broadened enormously the opportunities for better educated, more highly skilled, upwardly mobile black people. Lower-class blacks, while perhaps gaining psychological and even some social benefits from desegregation, remained about where they had always been.

As a result, despite the successes of the civil rights campaign, important elements of the black freedom movement turned steadily leftward. The Student Nonviolent Coordinating Committee, formed in 1960 to coordinate the student sit-ins, became a cadre of professional organizers. Rejecting the race-as-a-moral-issue argument, the SNCC workers developed a radical agenda that fueled their conflict, not only with the conservatives, but with both the southern moderates and the national liberals. Unable to find white allies, they carried their peculiar, semirevolutionary blend of socioeconomic realism and pan-African cultural romanticism into the great metropolitan ghettoes of the nation in an effort to build black power bases from which to negotiate with the white power blocs.

Perhaps more significantly, Martin Luther King, Jr., and the Southern Christian Leadership Conference, which in the beginning stood squarely within the national liberal mainstream in depicting the race issue as a moral question, also moved to the left. Breaking with the Johnson Administration and with many southern moderates, King threw the resources of SCLC into a poor people's campaign that sought to restore a broadly based economic and social liberalism by uniting out-groups behind a demand for a massive Marshall Plan at home. King's assassination in the spring of 1968 was a mortal blow to whatever prospects the campaign may have had. These developments, combined with black rioting mainly in northern ghettoes, contributed to making the decade of the 1960s one of upheaval and conflict.

In the wake of these developments southern Old Guard conservatives declined decisively. It was the county-seat Old Guard who suffered most directly from the demographic and economic transformation of the region, who benefited least from such political reforms as legislative reapportionment and black suffrage, and who most obviously lost prestige when unable to deliver on their massive resistance promises. The southern white common folk also lost in the political battles of the 1960s. Moving beyond the declining appeal of the Old Guard leadership, the white working class rallied under the banners of George Wallace and such lesser lights as Lester Maddox of Georgia. But the Wallace brand of popular resistance was essentially a negative program that was unable to sustain its appeal, at least without its most able practitioner to head it. The Wallace movement was in decline by the early 1970s, and any prospect that the Alabama governor might revive it terminated with the attempted assassination, and permanent crippling, of Wallace at a Maryland campaign rally in 1972. At any rate, white workers remained alienated from a national liberalism that for so long had placed them in the role of the heavies in the moral crusade for black rights, and they found little to applaud in President Johnson's black-oriented Great Society. Black southerners did of course benefit from the upheavals of the 1960s, but the failure of SNCC, the death of King, and the breakup of the civil rights movement left them with few viable options except—like the white working class—to support the southern moderate claim that economic growth would solve southern social problems.

As all this suggests, the basic result of the great political conflicts of the post–World War II years was to transfer the locus of southern political power from plantation-oriented county-seat elites to corporation-oriented metropolitan elites. The Republican party, which was once anathema in the South, attracted increasing support from well-off suburbanites and from white southerners disenchanted with the national Democratic party's liberal racial policies. The southern state elections of the early 1970s swept into office a wave of New South moderates and thereby signaled the triumph of a new political order. Reapportionment, the end of disfranchisement, desegregation, and the decline of the one-party system destroyed the institutional foundations of the old political system. If voter turnout was still low in the South, it was substantial when compared to the recent southern past and it included a far greater range of citizens. The antebellum era and the modern age are the two periods in which southern citizens seem to have been most ideologically united and in which the South has had two-party politics and popular democracy.

The best known of the New South moderates was Jimmy Carter. Like other moderates, Carter welcomed black support and endeavored—especially symbolically—to recognize black aspirations. But most of all he championed continued economic expansion, rationalized governmental procedures, and looked to corporate elites for guidance. By the 1970s the economic growth ethos had come to dominate the formulation of southern state policy, and economic expansion had come to be seen as *the* panacea for southern public problems, in somewhat the same manner that slavery had once been seen as the key to antebellum development. Certainly, differences do exist in southern politics, but the range of debate has vastly narrowed. Whether state governmental policies that favor public aid for industrialists, oppose labor organization, support relatively low taxes and services, and tailor social policies to the needs of land developers and real estate brokers will benefit the region's people as a whole and will alleviate racial and other social problems remains an open question.

See also BLACK LIFE: Politics, Black; / Hancock, Gordon B.; Jackson, Jesse; Lynch, John Roy; EDUCATION: Politics of Education; HISTORY AND MANNERS articles; LAW: States' Rights Constitutionalism; MYTHIC SOUTH: / Carter Era; RELIGION: / Hays, Brooks; SOCIAL CLASS: Politics and Social Class; / Bourbon/Redeemer South; VIOLENCE: Political Violence; WOMEN'S LIFE: Politics, Women in; / Carter, Rosalynn; Johnson, Lady Bird; Mitchell, Martha

Numan Bartley
University of Georgia

Numan Bartley, *The Creation of Modern Georgia* (1983), *The Rise of Massive Resistance: Race and Politics in the South during the 1950s* (1969), with Hugh Davis Graham, *Southern Politics and the Second Reconstruction* (1975); Jack Bass and Walter DeVries, *The Transformation of Southern Politics: Social Change and Political Consequences since 1945* (1976); Dwight B. Billings, *Planters and the Making of a "New South": Class, Politics, and Development in North Carolina, 1865–1900* (1979); Earl Black and Merle Black, *Politics and Society in the South* (1987); W. J. Cash, *The Mind of the South* (1941); James C. Cobb, *The Selling of the South: The Southern Crusade for Industrial Development, 1936–1980* (1982); William J. Cooper, Jr., *Liberty and Slavery: Southern Politics to 1860* (1983); Anthony P. Dunbar, *Against the Grain: Southern Radicals and Prophets, 1929–1959* (1981); J. Wayne Flynt, *Dixie's Forgotten People: The South's Poor Whites* (1979); George M. Fredrickson, *The Black Image in the White Mind: The Debate on Afro-American Character and Destiny, 1817–1914* (1971); Eugene D. Genovese, *The Political Economy of Slavery: Studies in the Economy and Society of the Slave South* (1965), *Roll, Jordan, Roll: The World the Slaves Made* (1974), *The World the Slaveholders Made: Two Essays in Interpretation* (1969); V. O. Key, Jr., *Southern Politics in State and Nation* (1949); Alexander P. Lamis, *The Two-Party South* (1984); Steven F. Lawson, *Black Ballots: Voting Rights in the South, 1944–1969* (1976); Donald R. Matthews and James W. Prothro, *Negroes and the New Southern Politics* (1966); Edmund S. Morgan, *American Slavery, American Freedom: The Ordeal of Colonial Virginia* (1975); Gunnar Myrdal, *An American Dilemma* (1944); Jonathan M. Wiener, *Social Origins of the New South: Alabama, 1860–1885* (1978); Bertram Wyatt-Brown, *Southern Honor: Ethics and Behavior in the Old South* (1982).

Alienation, Political

The idea of political alienation has, at least since the time of Marx, been a major concern of political theorists and analysts. When viewed as a subjective part of the political system, alienation is manifested in at least two different ways: distrust of the political system and apathy toward it, feeling that one can have little impact on political authorities or political outcomes.

Southerners have historically felt alienated from the national political system, especially since the Civil War. Secession, followed by Reconstruction and the Compromise of 1877, reinforced the region's sense of political impotence. In addition, the South suffered economically, consistently trailing the rest of the nation in mean income. Insurgent political movements from the late 19th century to the present, including Huey Long's "Every Man a King" program, the Dixiecrat movement, and the American Independent party, have traditionally appealed to alienated southern voters in their efforts to change the political system. Given such a history, regional differences in alienation might be expected at the individual level, even in recent years.

Nationally, trust in political authority has shown a major drop since the late 1950s, when it was first measured in a national survey by the University of Michigan Survey Research Center. For example, as late as 1964, 76 percent of the national sample said they could "trust the government in Washington to do what is right most of the time" or "always." By 1972 this percentage had dropped to 53 percent and by 1978 to 30 percent. Other questions tapping political trust showed a similar downward trend.

Because of the traditional racial divisions in the South, blacks and whites not surprisingly differed in their degree of political trust. Although aggregate South–non-South differences (defining the South as the states of the Confederacy minus Tennessee and the non-South as the rest of the 48 contiguous states) are small through the 1964–78 period, when election year samples are divided by race as well as by region a clearer picture of regional differences emerges. Whereas southern whites have often perceived themselves to be victims of federal intrusion, southern blacks have seen themselves as the beneficiaries of federal involvement. As a result of these different perspectives, blacks and whites show opposite effects of region on political trust. From 1964 to 1976 southern whites were less trusting on the Political Trust Index than northern whites in every year (the Political Trust Index is derived from a multiitem scale and ranges from 100, when all respondents in a group are trusting, to −100, when all respondents in a group are distrusting),

Figure 1. Political Trust by Region and Race

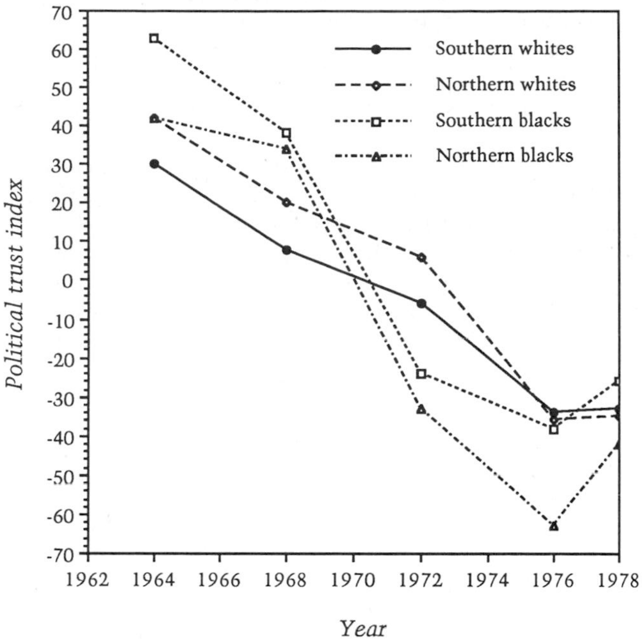

Source: University of Michigan Survey Research Center.

while southern blacks were consistently more trusting of the federal government than nonsouthern blacks (see Figure 1). A second racial difference also shows up. Although regional differences in political trust have been diminishing among whites, there is no evidence of such a nationalization of attitudes among blacks. In fact, the regional difference for blacks in 1978 is actually greater than the average over the entire 1964–78 period.

One basis for nationalization is of course immigration by non-southern whites. Southern migrants (defined here as those currently living in the South, but having spent their childhood outside of the South) were substantially more trusting than native-born southerners over the 1964–72 period. They were, on average, even more trusting than non-southern whites as a whole. Considering that they made up over 25 percent of the white southern sample in every year, their impact was substantial. In contrast, no complementary influx of black southern migrants occurred, so the southern black population remained regionally distinct.

In addition to region and race, trust is related to education. Even controlling for education, though, southern whites were significantly less trusting than non-southern whites ($p<.05$) in 1964; among southern whites, migration continued to have a significant effect ($p<.05$) in 1964, 1968, and 1972, with migrants being more trusting in all years. Strong regional effects for the earlier years, but not the later years, further attest to the nationalization of politics in the South (among whites) and the important role of migrants in that nationalization. For blacks, region's effect on political trust remains strong up to the present. Significant effects of region, controlling for education, existed in 1964, 1976, and 1978.

Although migration does account for a large part of the nationalization that occurred among whites through the mid-1970s, in both 1976 and 1978 the level of trust of native southern whites did not differ significantly from that of either non-southern whites or southern migrants. Perhaps this can be attributed to the presidency of a southerner, Jimmy Carter (the South showed an absolute gain in trust between 1976 and 1978 in distinction to the rest of the country), as well as to continued generational replacement. Neither migration to the South nor age replacement can, of course, explain the continued regional effect on political trust among blacks. Two factors present themselves, however. First, while there was little migration of blacks to the South in the last 30 years, a great deal of migration to the North has occurred. Whereas white migrants to the South are more trusting than either white southerners or white non-southerners, blacks who migrated from the South show levels of trust almost equal to those of native non-southern blacks, born and living outside the South, and substantially lower than current southern blacks. This is due mainly to the youthfulness of non-southern black migrants and the resulting ease of their assimilation and resocialization, compared with the generally older southern migrants.

A second reason for the continued regional effect among blacks is the role of the federal government vis-à-vis state and local governments in the South. The federal government remains a more important guarantor of black rights in the South than in the North. Whereas in 1976 southern blacks were 25 points higher on an index of trust toward federal government than non-southern blacks, they were at the same time less trusting of state government than were non-southern blacks. Every other regional racial group was at least 15 percent more likely to trust the state than the federal government to do what is right most or all of the time; southern blacks were only 1 percent more likely.

Looking at the difference in regional effects on political trust for the two races is a reminder that while the South has become part of a more homogenous nation, southerners have not completely transcended the influence of their past.

Ronald B. Rapoport
College of William and Mary

Joel Aberbach, *American Political Science Review* (March 1969); James Wright, *The Dissent of the Governed: Alienation and Democracy in America* (1976).

Black Politics

See BLACK LIFE: Politics, Black

Congress

Southern concern for protecting distinctive regional interests has often focused on Congress, and the South has sent some of its greatest talent to that institution. South Carolina Congressman and later Senator John C. Calhoun, for example, developed a major American political theory for protection of minority rights in Congress. He maneuvered for decades in Washington, in a losing battle, to protect slave plantation interests. The growing antebellum North-South conflict erupted into outright violence on the floor of Congress in 1856, when South Carolina Congressman Preston Brooks beat Massachusetts Senator Charles Sumner with his cane, as a stunned gallery watched.

Southerners in Congress have displayed a regional love of words through their oratory. John Randolph (1773–1833) of Roanoke, the eccentric Virginian of the early 19th century, was a brilliant extemporaneous speaker, quick witted and frequently acrimonious. Like many later southern congressmen, he defended states' rights. The modern comic image of the southern congressman as "Senator Claghorn"—a verbose, obfuscating, loud speaker—was a satirical distortion of real-life individuals who powerfully used words.

Southerners in Congress also developed unusual skills at procedural maneuvering. Henry Clay (1777–1852) regarded himself as more western than southern, but this Kentucky congressman who served six terms as speaker of the House of Representatives represented a slave state and displayed a seemingly regional talent for mastering the way Congress operates. He put together the Missouri Compromise (1820) and the Compromise Tariff (1833) that ended the nullification crisis, and his ideas became the basis of the Compromise of 1850. Southerners who later rose to prominence as congressional leaders because of unusual legislative skill included speakers of the House John Nance "Cactus Jack" Garner, Sam Rayburn, and William Bankhead, and Senate Majority Leader Lyndon B. Johnson. The filibuster became associated with southern congressional leaders in the mid-20th century, as James Eastland and John Stennis of Mississippi, Richard Russell of Georgia, Strom Thurmond of South Carolina, and others used it as a delaying tactic when Congress considered civil rights legislation.

The file of southern congressional notables would include those from a variety of political positions. Fire-eaters such as William Lowndes Yancey and Robert Barnwell Rhett were extremists in the defense of southern liberty, but Mississippi's Lucius Quintus Cincinnatus Lamar became a famed conciliator between the regions while serving in the House of Representatives (1873–77) and the Senate (1877–85) after the Civil War. Demagogues such as Cole Blease (South Carolina), Jeff Davis (Arkansas), Thomas "Tom-Tom" Heflin (Alabama), and Theodore Bilbo (Mississippi) first achieved notoriety at the state level but then transferred their harsh racial rhetoric to the halls of Congress. Maury Maverick (Texas), though, was a great defender of civil liberties and equality; Lister Hill and John Sparkman of Alabama were famed as racial moderates; and Albert Gore of Tennessee and Ralph Yarborough of Texas were downright liberal on the issue. Southern congressional leaders such as Thomas T. Connally of Texas, J. William Fulbright of Arkansas, and John Tower of Texas have played an active role in foreign affairs, some as "hawks," others as "doves," but most committed to internationalism rather than isolation.

Southern political families such as the Bankheads of Alabama and the Byrds of Virginia have sometimes seemed to claim a genealogical interest in Congress. John Hollis Bankhead, Sr. (1842–1920), for example, served in the House (1887–1907) and Senate (1907), while his sons John Hollis Bankhead, Jr. (1872–1946) and William Brockman Bankhead (1874–1940) played key roles in the Senate and the House in the 1930s.

Southern Democrats have traditionally dominated Congress in the 20th century. Their political longevity, their coalition with northern conservatives, and their ability to act in concert gave them a big advantage over other congressional factions. Southern one-party politics produced long careers in Congress for southern representatives and senators who, once secure as incumbents, rarely faced significant opposition. This factor, working in tandem with the legislature's seniority system, gave southerners the chairmanships of most major congressional committees. They strengthened that advantage in 1946 when many northern representatives and senators of equal seniority went down in defeat at the hands of Republicans. The southern Democrats parlayed their political windfall into a lasting advantage by renewing their cooperation with midwestern conservative Republicans in order to thwart subsequent legislative reform efforts until the Great Society of the 1960s. Congressional southerners acted as a unanimous power bloc, however, only in opposition to civil rights legislation. In the postwar era, civil rights became the keystone of southern congressional unity, as it came to control southern politics generally.

When President Harry Truman made civil rights an important part of his 1948 reelection campaign, he directly threatened customary southern racial relations. Congressional southerners were able to defeat Truman's legislative moves because of their unity of purpose exercised through control of all major committees. Occasionally, civil rights legislation and initiatives did manage to pass through the House of Representatives, where the southerners could be easily outvoted. All these efforts were halted in the Senate, however, where southern senators, led by Richard B. Russell of Georgia, prevented civil rights bills from coming to a vote by waging filibusters and exploiting the chamber's tradition of unlimited debate. This legislative stalemate continued through Truman's term and into the Eisenhower Administration until 1957 when the first civil rights bill since Reconstruction passed both houses. Nevertheless, that act and another approved in 1960 did little to change southern society, and both can be seen as tactical retreats by southern congressmen and senators, providing the illusion of progress while retaining the reality of white supremacy.

Meanwhile, other forces outside Congress were working to transform the South. The Supreme Court's 1954

Brown v. *Board of Education* desegregation decision and the 1957 use of presidential power to achieve integrated education in Little Rock, Ark., were beyond the reach of congressional southerners to stop or alter. In response to the Court, southern senators drafted, and southern House members signed, a 1956 "Declaration of Constitutional Principles," better known as the "Southern Manifesto." The document was little more than a condemnation of the *Brown* decision and a call for legal, peaceful resistance, using states' rights as a justification. Consequently, southerners in Congress were reaching the limits of their power by the early 1960s. With growing nationwide sentiment for a strong civil rights act, marshalled first by President John F. Kennedy and more effectively later by President Lyndon B. Johnson, reformers rammed through legislation in 1964 and 1965 that eventually transformed southern society and politics.

The civil rights acts and urbanization of southern society combined to transform the region's congressional politics. The subsequent decline of civil rights as a political issue encouraged a moderation of the South's political environment, which prompted the emergence of a wider spectrum of political concerns. The section's one-party political society began to weaken as the Republican party gained footholds in a number of states. The advent of ultraconservative southern Republicanism and the attrition of the Old Guard through death and retirement encouraged younger southern Democrats to shift from opposing their party leadership toward cooperation. These older southern Democrats softened their positions on race and other social issues to accommodate the rising numbers of black voters and a growing racial moderation by whites. Although neither a full-fledged two-party system nor a broad political spectrum emerged, the seeds for these vital parts of a political society were laid.

In Congress the South declined from its former position of dominance. As the southern Old Guard passed from positions of power, northerners took their places. The growing political diversity of the region further weakened the cohesiveness of the southerners in acting as a unit to support or oppose legislation. Finally, modifications in the seniority system diluted an important source of their legislative strength, since length of service no longer automatically assured access to positions of power. The distinctive southern identity in Congress consequently declined.

David Potenziani
Memphis State University

Numan Bartley and Hugh Davis Graham, *Southern Politics and the Second Reconstruction* (1975); Jack Bass and Walter DeVries, *The Transformation of Southern Politics: Social Change and Political Consequence since 1945* (1976); James MacGregor Burns, *The Deadlock of Democracy: Four Party Politics in America* (1963); Neil MacNeil, *Forge of Democracy: The House of Representatives* (1963); Robert L. Peabody and Nelson W. Polsby, eds., *New Perspectives on the House of Representatives* (1969); Nelson W. Polsby, *Congress and the Presidency* (3d ed., 1976); Frank Smith, *Congressman from Mississippi* (1964).

County Politics

Few if any popular perceptions of southern politics are more deeply engrained than that of the courthouse "clique" or "ring." Film and fiction, scholarly tomes, and journalistic exposés have united in fostering an image of county governments dominated by self-serving officials closely aligned with business and agricultural wealth and exercising arbitrary, undemocratic control over local affairs. As with other generalizations about the South, this stereotype is more accurate for some eras than others, more applicable to some states and counties than to their neighbors. Nevertheless, a survey of the region's historical experience offers much support for this uncomplimentary appraisal of grassroots political conduct.

The beginnings of the courthouse cliques are readily discernible in the English origins of southern society. Acting for the crown, the king's counsellors appointed militia officers, sheriffs, and justices of the peace in the counties of the mother country during the 1500s and 1600s. The justices of the peace constituted the linchpins of the system. Functioning collectively as members of county courts, they administered governmental affairs in the shires and handled routine judicial matters as well.

These practices exerted an enduring influence. Unlike their dissenting Puritan contemporaries to the north, who fashioned a distinctive amalgam of Calvinist theocracy and town-meeting democracy, the dominant groups in the colonial South willingly adopted the oligarchic governmental forms of Tudor-Stuart England—as modified to accommodate provincial needs and circumstances. Developments in Virginia set the pattern for the region. There the royal governors selected county officials, including justices of the peace. In the Old Dominion—as in England—the justices directed local affairs, establishing tax rates, regulating businesses, overseeing road maintenance, and performing a multitude of other functions. Drawn from the ranks of the plantation gentry and enjoying lifetime tenure on the county courts, the justices soon established a marked degree of independence from gubernatorial control. Most notably, they began to assert the right to fill vacancies in their ranks, and royal governors generally acquiesced in this claim by confirming the justices' nominees (as well as their choices for sheriffs and other county offices). Exercising peremptory control over local administration, members of the county courts also held considerable sway in elections to the House of Burgesses. Rule of, by, and for the planters thus became a fact of political life in Virginia and elsewhere in the region—in spite of sporadic protests by backwoods dissidents and other would-be reformers during the colonial and revolutionary periods.

Indeed, the South's oligarchic county courts escaped significant change until the first decades of the 19th century. By that time various abuses, including the appointment of excessive numbers of new justices and the consequent growth of court membership to unwieldy proportions (ranging upward to 90 men in some counties), demanded public attention. Professional lawyers led the assault by criticizing the planter-justices' lack of legal training, and charges of inefficiency, ineptitude, and corruption proliferated. More importantly, perhaps, democratic ideological currents of the Jacksonian era found obvious targets in the self-perpetuating county courts. This ferment produced dramatic results. Commencing in the new states of the Deep South cotton frontier and spreading throughout the region, legislative enactments and constitutional revisions transformed the tone and conduct of local politics. By the eve of the Civil War voters in most of the southern states could elect their sheriffs, coroners, overseers of the poor, school commissioners, and constables. Life-tenured justices of the peace had given way to county judges chosen by state legislatures or the electorate for limited, specified terms. Although planters still occupied many positions in local government, they could no longer ignore the interests and wishes of ordinary voters.

These democratic trends broadened and deepened during the turmoil of the Reconstruction era, only to experience a stunning reversal during the white supremacist "Redemption" of the 1870s and 1880s. Appalled by the preeminence of scalawags, carpetbaggers, and blacks during the brief heyday of Radical Republicanism, the resurgent planter Democrats and their New South commercial-industrial allies moved inexorably to eliminate or neutralize potentially disruptive influences. Reflecting this antiegalitarian bias, popular election of local officials was replaced by legislative or gubernatorial appointment in Florida, Louisiana, and North Carolina, while violence and ballot box fraud hampered voter participation elsewhere, especially in closely contested Black Belt areas. Entrenched county officeholders provided the organizational cement for long-term Democratic hegemony, and successive generations of Republicans, Populists, and Independents railed against the abuses (real or imagined) of courthouse cliques and rings. Oligarchic control was, once again, the fashion at the grassroots.

One-party rule persisted almost unchallenged through the first half of the 20th century, but county-level politics in the "Solid South" was characterized by considerable diversity. Courthouse cliques generally exerted greater influence in lowland plantation districts than in comparatively egalitarian mountain or piedmont areas. By the 1930s and 1940s, moreover, local officials in Louisiana, Tennessee, and Virginia tended to be closely aligned with dominant machine factions in their respective state Democratic parties, while county officeholders elsewhere in the region formed shifting, ephemeral alliances in state primary races. Courthouse politicos exerted particular influence in Georgia where a county-unit system (similar to the federal electoral college) determined the outcome of statewide primary contests. Exemplifying yet other variations, county seat political dominance in Alabama was typically enjoyed by probate judges; in Virginia, by circuit court judges; in Louisiana and Mississippi, by sheriffs with an abiding interest in the preservation of home rule over gambling and bootlegging in their jurisdictions.

John McCrady, Political Rally *(1935)*

Byzantine in its complexities, sometimes baroque in its manifestations, the courthouse regime constituted a bedrock reality of southern politics until the 1940s and 1950s. Even so, forces of change were omnipresent in the post–World War II years, eroding the authority and imperiling the permanence of the previously invincible cliques and rings. Urbanization, industrial growth, northern migration to the emerging Sunbelt, enhanced educational opportunities, and the advent of mass communications media were fashioning a more cosmopolitan social order, a South less attuned to one-party rule. In the aftermath of the New Deal, state and federal bureaucracies were on the rise and they created alternative centers of power and influence. Most important of all, the civil rights revolution exerted a pervasive impact on the South. Encouraged by federal legislative enactments and judicial decrees, millions of blacks reentered the political process, while the Supreme Court's "one-man, one-vote" rulings bolstered the representation of urban residents at the expense of the old-style crossroads elite. Beset by external antagonists and internal stresses, the cliques and rings were in retreat throughout the region by the 1960s and 1970s. Nevertheless, historical experience suggests that it may be premature, as yet, to write their epitaph.

See also GEOGRAPHY: / Courthouse Square

James Tice Moore
Virginia Commonwealth University

Monroe Billington, *The Political South in the Twentieth Century* (1975); V. O. Key, Jr., *Southern Politics in State and Nation* (1949); Charles S. Sydnor, *Gentleman Freeholders: Political Practices in Washington's Virginia* (1952), *The Development of Southern Sectionalism, 1819–1848* (1948); C. Vann Woodward, *Origins of the New South, 1877–1913* (1951); Ralph A. Wooster, *The People in Power: Courthouse and Statehouse in the Lower South, 1850–1860* (1969), *Politicians, Planters, and Plain Folk: Courthouse and Statehouse in the Upper South, 1850–1860* (1975).

Demagogues

Political demagoguery is at least as old as the early Greek term (from *demos*, for people, and *agog*, for leader) for unscrupulous politicians who gain power by appealing to the electorate's emotions, passions, and prejudices. Throughout Western history, demagogues have symbolized the fear of privileged elites that expanding democracy inevitably degenerates into rabble-rousing. In America, no era or region has been free of demagogues, but the classic southern variety flourished with unusual vigor during the six decades between Reconstruction and World War II.

The term has been applied to successful southern politicians as diverse as Benjamin Tillman, Tom Watson, Jeff Davis, Coleman Blease, James K. Vardaman, Theodore Bilbo, Thomas Heflin, James and Marian Ferguson, W. Lee O'Daniel, Eugene Talmadge, and Huey Long. Their appeals to poor rural whites variously featured irresponsible campaign promises, flamboyant personal styles, violent rhetoric, appeals to racial and religious bigotry and antiintellectualism, and attacks upon the predatory corporate interests. Mississippi's Bilbo denounced from the stump a typical pantheon of enemies of the common people: "farmer murderers, poor-folks haters, shooters of widows and orphans, international well-poisoners, charity hospital destroyers, spitters on our heroic veterans, rich enemies of our public schools, private bankers, European debt cancellors, unemployment makers, Pacifists, Communists, munitions manufacturers, and skunks who steal Gideon Bibles." As for the disfranchised and vulnerable blacks, Blease would "wipe the inferior race from the face of the earth." To Vardaman the Negro was a "lazy, lying, lustful animal which no conceivable amount of training can transform into a tolerable citizen." Bilbo, who shot a black man on a Washington streetcar, called for solving the unemployment problem by shipping 12 million black southern citizens "back" to Africa. Not surprisingly, racial lynching flourished in such an atmosphere—Blease boasted that "whenever the constitution comes between me and the virtues of the white women of the South, I say to hell with the constitution."

These appeals understandably took root in an environment characterized by poverty, illiteracy, racism, Civil War and Populist defeat, agrarian decline, and a small-town and rural cultural barrenness that was only occasionally enlivened by revivals and political campaigns. Reinforcing this socioeconomic and cultural legacy was the South's one-party system and the direct (white) Democratic primary, which strengthened personality-centered stump politics at the expense of issue-focused debates, blurred policy continuities that linked incumbent regimes to policy outcomes, and invited the manipulation of faction-ridden legislatures by organized, well-funded lobbies against the collective interests of the "have-nots." As a result, victorious demagogues rarely implemented such promised and popularly mandated reforms as better schools, hospitals, roads, and pensions, and many of their regimes were riddled with corruption. Richard Hofstadter referred to this phenomenon as the "devolution of reform into reaction," whereby the highly educated Georgia Populist, Tom Watson, was transformed into the embittered baiter of Negroes, Jews, and Catholics, and the modest attempts at reform under the Tillman regime in South Carolina degenerated into the empty promises of Blease, who as governor even opposed compulsory education and child labor laws. As late as the mid-20th century, such common-folk champions as Governor Talmadge in Georgia and the Fergusons and O'Daniel in Texas would attack their state universities while corruption shaped their own administrations and swelled their pockets; as Talmadge explained, "Sure I stole, but I stole it for you." This in turn invited "good government" counterattacks by conservative elites who typically called for slashing both taxes and social services—which amounted, in the classic lament of Gerald W. Johnson, to a dismal choice between a "Live Demagogue or a Dead Gentleman."

Pappy Lee O'Daniel, Texas governor and country-western musician, c. 1940

The dominant stereotype of the southern demagogue masked considerable diversity and irony as well. These masters of the common tongue and taste generally enjoyed a superior education; champions of the downtrodden, they typically lived and retired in material comfort. Although most Deep South demagogues were race-baiters, their Rim South equivalents, such as Jeff Davis of Arkansas and "Pappy" O'Daniel of Texas, generally were not. The most nationally spectacular embodiment of the triumphant demagogue, "Kingfish" Huey Long of Louisiana, staked his presidential bid against Roosevelt on the economic nostrum of "Share Our Wealth." But in Louisiana, Long not only refused to race-bait, he also refused to sell out, once elected, to the corporate interests he had attacked. After seizing near dictatorial control of Louisiana's government, Long taxed the extractive industries and delivered the roads, bridges, hospitals, schoolbooks, and utility regulation that his campaigns had promised.

Many political journalists of the 1930s viewed Long as a forerunner of American fascism, and thereby demonstrated their misunderstanding both of the mainstream American political tradition and of its exaggerated southern variant. Contemporaries of Long watched Europe descend into a fascist nightmare, and with victory in World War II came an understandable surge of domestic social scientific interest in identifying the origin, structure, and location of America's equivalent fascist personality. University-based psychologists generated such test-battery inventories as the "f-scale" (for fascism) to identify the authoritarian personality, and sociologists employed the new tool of survey research to locate its distribution. But southerners proved to be no more inclined toward fascism than other Americans, primarily because America had no fascist tradition.

Southern demagoguery has always confused political analysts, because it tends to appeal simultaneously to the populist left and to the bigoted right. Neither tendency is alien to the American political tradition, but in the prostrate South from Reconstruction through the Great Depression, the bitterness of poverty and defeat was compounded by four warping political institutions—disfranchisement, the one-party system, malapportionment, and de jure Jim Crow—that whiplashed southern politics into a grotesque caricature of the American democratic ideal. Few contemporary observers understood that the pathological environment was temporary, and that its passing would reveal a deeper bedrock of regionally shared American political values.

World War II ushered in a belated surge of prosperity throughout the South, and with it slowly came the improved education and broadened political participation that would relegate the classic post-Reconstruction demagogues to history. Desegregation and the civil rights movement sparked a brief resurgence from the mid-1950s through the mid-1960s of the old demagogic strains, most notably in defiant governors Orville Faubus, Ross Barnett, George Wallace, and Lester Maddox. But the long and circular career of Alabama's Wallace testifies ironically not only to the depth of the South's racial tension, but also to the strength of its populistic tradition and to the liberating effect of a genuinely democratic franchise, of two-party competition, of public education, and ultimately of the South's long submerged but abiding commitment to the norms and goals of American democracy.

Hugh Davis Graham
University of Maryland
Baltimore County

William Anderson, *The Wild Man from Sugar Creek: The Political Career of Eugene Talmadge* (1975); Hugh Davis Graham, ed., *Huey Long* (1970); William F. Holmes, *The White Chief: James Kimble Vardaman* (1970); Gerald W. Johnson, *Virginia Quarterly Review* (January 1936); Albert Kirwan, *Revolt of the Rednecks: Mississippi Politics, 1876–1925* (1951); Reinhard Luthin, *American Demagogues: Twentieth Century* (1954); Daniel M. Robison, *Journal of Southern History* (August 1937); Francis Butler Simkins, *Pitchfork Ben Tillman: South Carolinian* (1944); T. Harry Williams, *Huey Long* (1969), *Journal of Southern History* (February 1960); C. Vann Woodward, *Tom Watson: Agrarian Rebel* (1938).

Government Administration

Government administration in the South has traditionally been considered less professional, less vigorous, less accountable, and more affected by personalized political influences than administration in other regions. To a considerable extent this distinctiveness can be attributed to southern governments' having typically had a much smaller revenue base on which to finance public programs. The administrative establishment had fewer employees per capita, salaries were lower, merit systems were less feasible, and professionalism and administrative effectiveness were less developed. However, much of what is distinctive about southern government administration is not a simple result of the traditionally low level of personal wealth in the South. The special character of partisan and interest-group politics also influences the quality and nature of administration. Consequently, southern government administration may continue to be somewhat distinctive even as the region catches up with the rest of the nation economically.

Perhaps the most important actor in southern government administration is the governor. There is something paradoxical about the way this office has been viewed by political and historical observers. V. O. Key, Jr., classified most southern states as "loose factional systems," because they were characterized by an "issueless politics" and an inability to "carry out sustained programs of action." The absence of a viable, well-defined system of party competition created a situation in which political power was not effectively tied to partisan forces. Thus, southern governors were not normally led to enforce party platforms or to follow party preferences in administrative appointments. Instead, southern governors have often had considerable *personal* control over government jobs, roads, purchasing, and local public improvements. In short, the southern governor was traditionally possessed of notorious personal power, making him highly unpredictable, and yet, in the absence of a cohesive party organization and effective party competition, weak in terms of policy effectiveness.

The institutional weakness of the southern governor is reflected in (1) a lack of exclusive responsibility for budget development (currently a shared responsibility in five southern states, but earlier a shared responsibility in all of them), (2) relatively restricted appointment powers, and (3) the inability, until recently, of governors in many southern states to succeed themselves. In addition to the weakness of the gubernatorial office, the formal administrative procedures of southern state agencies have not traditionally been subject to the kind of "judicialization" accomplished long ago on the federal level and in most other states. Administrative hearing and rule-making procedures were subject to fewer procedural requirements, raising questions about the thoroughness and accountability of administrative activity. Government administration, as a result of all these factors, has often been fragmented, personalized, and unprofessional when compared to administration in non-southern states.

The interest group situation in the South is rather ambiguous. Some researchers have concluded that organized groups are effectively unopposed by countervailing interests, suggesting that interest groups are more powerful in the South than elsewhere. Others, most notably Mancur Olson, Jr., argue that the historically brief period of stable industrialization in the South has prevented the development of groups devoted to collective action. Labor unions, for example, are less numerous and less powerful in the South than elsewhere. One can, therefore, construct and support arguments suggesting that the South is characterized by "strong" or "weak" interest groups, depending upon one's interpretations.

Actually, either view lends support to the idea that southern politics is *not* characterized by persistent, institutionalized conflict among well-established interest organizations to the same degree as are the politics of non-southern states. Government administration is more particularized, less "open," because interest groups do not accumulate broad interests any better than the fragmented one-party political machines. A professional, cohesive, merit-oriented bureaucracy is, in part, a response to the kind of effective, broad-based patterns of political influence that traditionally have not characterized the South. Ironically, such influences should be less developed both in states with weak interest groups *and* in those with organized interests not effectively opposed by others.

Much of what is distinctive about government administration in the South is rapidly disappearing. Southern governors are becoming more powerful. Well over half the states that have recently removed their prohibitions against a governor succeeding himself are southern states. According to a recent study on state party organization, "regional differences in organizational strength have declined . . . as the Republicans in the South developed modern party organizations and the Southern Democrats were forced to follow." As industrialization in the South completes its "catching up" process, the interest group climate should become like that in other states as well. Personality in southern politics and government is so well established a factor, though, it will likely endure for some time to come.

Marcus Ethridge
University of Wisconsin–Milwaukee

Virginia Gray, Herbert Jacob, and Kenneth Vines, eds., *Politics in the American States: A Comparative Analysis* (1983); V. O. Key, Jr., *Southern Politics in State and Nation* (1949); Sarah Morehouse, *State Politics, Parties, and Policy* (1981); Laurence W. Moreland, Tod A. Baker, and Robert P. Steed, eds., *Contemporary Southern Political Attitudes and Behavior: Studies and Essays* (1982); Ira Sharkansky, *The Maligned States: Policy Accomplishments, Problems, and Opportunities* (2d ed., 1978).

Ideology, Political

Not too long ago scholars of southern politics invariably unearthed demagogues, one-party politics based on massive disfranchisement of blacks, malapportionment of representation, factionalism based on issueless friends-and-neighbors politics, a militant and defensive southern bloc in national politics, and, above all else, a politics dedicated to white supremacy. By the end of the 1970s these issues lay dead and the South had conformed to national political ideals. Southern political ideology, though conservative, particularly on social and Cold War issues, is no more conservative than that of the mountain states or even Orange County, Calif. But it has not always been that way.

American political ideology is celebrated in the catchwords of our everyday life—freedom, democracy, and equality. The political culture of the United States includes both the noble ideas of the founding documents, the Declaration of Independence and the Constitution (particularly the first 10 amendments), and the reality of conflict among citizens based on race, ethnicity, class, and region. The development of a distinctive southern political ideology was part of this broader culture. At times in open conflict with theoretical national sentiments, it was based on regional conflict with the North and eventually overrode the subcultures and bands of dissenters within the region.

A distinctive southern political ideology was elusive in the colonial South. The foundations of a system of belief different from that of the nation were there in the beginnings of the plantation system and large-scale black slavery, but the lack of any generalized American nationalism meant no southern regionalism existed either. The years from the Declaration of Independence (1776) to the Missouri controversy (1819–20) were a transitional period in the history of southern political ideology. The South participated fully in the creation of the American system of government and in the political ideals of the new nation. Its greatest leaders—Washington, Jefferson, and Madison—were from southern states, with Jefferson remaining the central figure of American political democracy. But sectionalism lurked everywhere, and the requisite compromises of the 1789 Constitution, particularly those concerning slavery and centralization versus state powers, reflected the South's emerging political differences. Nevertheless, the transitional years left no record of blatant assertion of southern difference or serious calls for a southern polity.

The Missouri controversy was a landmark in the growth of a southern political ideology. The debate gathered up all the bundles of an emerging sectionalism—the division of power between North and South, slavery, the pattern of the growing national economy, and, more significantly, the meaning of American democracy and its values, however compromised they were by intergroup conflict. The debate impelled southerners to define their political views in relationship to the North and to articulate their separate political culture. By the 1830s and 1840s events such as the nullification crisis, the growth of antislavery movements, and the Mexican War overwhelmingly channeled sectional political differences into the single stream of the slavery question. In its defense of slavery the South slid into a political orthodoxy and social conservatism that adjusted the political and social reform movements of the first half of the 19th century to a southern standard. The South's greatest politician of this period, John C. Calhoun, defended southern political differences. Calhoun created a political ideology that attacked democratic values and accepted class- and race-stratified authoritarianism—an ideology that was more distinctive and more at variance with that of the Founding Fathers than any other major American political philosophy of the time.

Recent scholars have shown the importance of paternalism to southern ideology. Defenders of slavery believed that southern society was a hierarchical one, marked by accepted obligations and responsibilities on the part of everyone from the slave to the planter. Eugene D. Genovese has even argued that the personal relationships inherent in paternalism worked against "solidarity among the oppressed by linking them as individuals to their oppressors." The concept of personal honor became closely tied to paternalism as a guiding concept of the antebellum elite.

During the crucial years of the 1850s and 1860s the southern political ideal of orthodoxy and conservatism transformed itself into the radical concept of separate southern nationalism; only the massive defeat of the Confederacy killed the dream. The Old South's political ideals did not wither away in the bitterness of conflict and defeat. The modern political South was born in defeat, and the struggle of Reconstruction only confirmed its distinctive political ideology built around a tense amalgam of rugged, freewill individualism, states' rightsism, white supremacy, social conservatism, a paternalistic class division, and political loyalties to systems that protected these principles.

The values of a white, male-dominated democracy (herrenvolk democracy) and the master-race cultural views of southern planters persisted after the Civil War. The emerging capitalist entrepreneurs in the New South's commerce and industry seemed more captive to this political ideology than such figures elsewhere in the nation, and a distinctive form of conservative politics emerged. It favored a rural county elite ideology that was frankly class centered in the paternalistic ways of the plantation and the cotton mill. As Numan Bartley wrote: "The transfer of political leadership from plantation-oriented county-seat elites to business-oriented metropolitan elites was a long, complex and divisive process."

After Reconstruction, political change came slowly to the South. The ideology of orthodoxy and conservatism weathered the Populist challenge and the subsequent Progressive movement. Southern politicians overwhelmingly supported the Democratic party and used their power to protect all things southern. But the interwar years of the 1920s and 1930s created visible cracks in the foundation of the southern system, and widespread economic changes after the 1940s and 1950s remade southern politics. The civil rights revolution, the impact of a postwar American culture of television, shopping malls, big cities, and major league sports, and the national acceptance of southern music suggested that the Americanization of Dixie had occurred. The result was that southern political ideology began to look suspiciously American. As elsewhere, groups divided or came together by race, income level, lifestyle, occupation, place of residence, transient issues, and education. Southerners now gave ardent homage to all the value words of the American political tradition. By the 1980s journeys to the southern political land revealed fewer exotic, strange, or even different phenomena than earlier. National polling data suggested the South in the 1980s remained the nation's most conservative region on great and small economic and social questions, but its controlling ideologies found ready allies all over the country. At least in terms of political ideology, it no longer appeared to be the "nation within a nation" that V. O. Key described late in the 1940s.

See also HISTORY AND MANNERS: Jacksonian Democracy; SOCIAL CLASS: Politics and Social Class

James A. Hodges
The College of Wooster

Numan Bartley, *The Creation of Modern Georgia* (1983), *Reviews in American History* (December 1982), with Hugh Davis Graham, *Southern Politics and the Second Reconstruction* (1975); Jack Bass and Walter DeVries, *The Transformation of Southern Politics: Social Change and Political Consequences since 1945* (1976); Dwight B. Billings, *Planters and the Making of a "New South": Class, Politics, and Development in North Carolina, 1865–1900* (1979); W. J. Cash, *The Mind of the South* (1941); Eugene D. Genovese, *The Political Economy of Slavery: Studies in the Economy and Society of the Slave South* (1965); Dewey Grantham, *The Democratic South* (1963); V. O. Key, Jr., *Southern Politics in State and Nation* (1949); John McCardell, *The Idea of a Southern Nation: Southern Nationalists and Southern Nationalism, 1830–1860* (1979); John Shelton Reed, *The Enduring South: Subcultural Persistence in Mass Society* (1972); Jonathan M. Wiener, *Social Origins of the New South: Alabama, 1860–1885* (1978); Bertram Wyatt-Brown, *Southern Honor: Ethics and Behavior in the Old South* (1982).

Legislatures, State

Though governors and senators have been famous as individuals, the office of state legislator has best embodied the stereotype of the southern politician. The white male lawyer cum country bumpkin who rants against Yankee capitalists, spouts racial slurs, and is careless toward public policy embodies the stereotype. Whatever the validity of that image in the past, it is far from accurate in the 1980s. Southern legislatures as institutions and legislators as members are in the midst of changes. Although some of these changes reduce regional differences, others underscore the distinctiveness of the South. Much of the change has come as a result of legislatures' gaining the power to counterbalance that of southern governors.

In recent decades similar developments in southern and non-southern legislatures have reduced regional differences. U.S. legislatures in the 1950s, for example, commonly met only in biennial sessions, with the proportion of southern legislatures especially high in this pattern (90 percent to 70 percent). By 1983 the proportion was identical (20 percent) in both the North and the South. The shift to annual sessions has been an important step toward active and informed participation in shaping state public policy.

Southern state legislatures still have more committees than do their northern counterparts, but the number of committees per legislature in both the North and the South has been reduced by over a third. In the process, the disparity between the two regions has lessened. Both changes—increase in frequency of sessions and reduction in the number of committees—were vigorously advanced in the 1960s and 1970s as essential reforms to increase the capacity of legislatures to act. Both trends have been as fully felt in the South as nationally.

Likewise, legislatures throughout the country are now quite similar in the availability of staff support for members and committees. A quarter of the legislatures in each region now provide professional assistance, and close to a majority of states provide only secretarial and other nonprofessional assistance. Another indication of interregional similarities among state legislatures is seen in their attempt to control federal funding. Both state governors and legislatures want control over the disposal of these funds. By the middle of 1982, about a quarter of the states, North and South, had left considerable discretion to their governors, but about 40 percent of the legislatures in each region were taking active steps both to monitor and to decide upon the allocation of such federal funds.

Regional differences, however, still persist. Southern legislatures, for example, on the average consider fewer bills per session but enact a larger number and a higher proportion of all bills introduced than do those outside the South. A higher proportion of southern states lack home rule for municipalities than in other regions, despite the fabled southern belief in localism, and thus a sizable number of bills must be processed to accommodate local requests.

Though the South has traditionally been the locale of strong, flamboyant governors, recent reforms have greatly strengthened the capacity of legislatures to act independently of the governor. The South has adopted, to a greater extent than elsewhere, provisions for "sunset" review of programs and administrative agencies. Over half the southern legislatures may review and terminate the full range of administrative agencies, whereas legislatures elsewhere are much more limited in the scope of their review. Southern state legislatures depend upon regular committees to conduct agency reviews, but legislatures elsewhere tend to rely more upon specialized review bodies.

Perhaps the greatest changes that have taken place in southern legislatures involve membership. Members in the past were almost exclusively white male rural Democrats. The narrowness of representation came not only from strong political ties to the Democratic party, but also from the selection of legislators from multimember districts that were malapportioned to favor rural areas. Judicial decisions on reapportionment combined with Department of Justice rulings under the Voting Rights Act of 1965 have required state legislatures throughout the country to shift to single-member districts drawn in accordance with the location of population. Thus, in keeping with national trends, southern legislatures are becoming more urban and suburban, and less rural, than previously. An integral part of these changes has been an increase in the election of blacks and—to some extent—Republicans to the legislatures.

By 1982 the number of black state legislators in the South was triple that of 1971, while blacks had increased by less than half in legislatures in the rest of the country. In 1971, of all black state legislators in the country, 24 percent sat in southern capitals; by 1982, that proportion had risen to almost 41 percent. The average southern state legislature in 1971 had two black members, but by 1982 the number had grown to six—compared to only three in other states. As a result, legislatures that once fostered Jim Crow laws now have the nation's largest numbers of black representatives.

In spite of the numerous changes cited, the most distinctive feature of southern legislatures remains the partisan dominance of the Democratic party. A southern legislature in the 1950s without a single Republican was not uncommon. In 1951, 7 of the 13 southern states had no Republican solons. In 1961 Democrats controlled on an average 95 percent of the seats in both the upper and lower chambers of southern legislatures. The Democratic dominance in the South during the 1950s and the 1960s was even more pronounced when compared to state legislatures throughout the rest of the country where Democrats averaged only 40 percent of the seats. In 1981, across the 13 states used in this analysis (the 11 states of the Confederacy, plus Oklahoma and Kentucky), the Democrats averaged 80 percent of the House seats and 84 percent of the Senate positions. Though southern states have frequently elected Republicans as both governors and U.S. senators and have supported Republican presidential candidates, Republicanism has not trickled down into the essentially local-district elections of state legislatures.

Although some changes have occurred in this area, any sudden or drastic change in the partisan composition of state legislatures appears unlikely, largely because a substantial number of legislative districts are safe. Over 75 percent of the legislative elections in nine of the southern states were won by the comfortable margin of more than 60 percent of the votes. In two other states over half the elections were safe.

Notable differences exist among the southern state legislatures themselves. Variations within the South in partisanship, structure, and behavior persist in the 1980s. The strong South Carolina Legislature stands in contrast to the gubernatorial-dominated Louisiana Legislature. Still, southern state legislatures are a definable group in contrast with those in the rest of the nation. Having experienced dramatic changes and especially growing power since World War II, they remain distinctive institutions with their southern political outlook.

David M. Olsen
E. Lee Bernick
University of North Carolina
at Greensboro

Council of State Governments, *Book of States* (biennial eds., various years); Virginia Gray, Herbert Jacob, and Kenneth Vines, *Politics in the American States: A Comparative Analysis* (1983); Malcolm E. Jewell, *Legislative Representation in the Contemporary South* (1967), *Representation in State Legislatures* (1982); V. O. Key, Jr., *Southern Politics in State and Nation* (1949); Alan Rosenthal, *Legislative Life* (1981).

National Politics

Alexis de Tocqueville, the oft-quoted French visitor to the young American Republic in the 1830s, observed in *Democracy in America* (1835), "Two branches may be distinguished in the great Anglo-American family, which have hitherto grown without entirely comingling; the one in the South, the other in the North." Politically, that was not entirely true at the time, but it would soon become so. The South had been an integral part of national life in its first half-century, providing talented leaders such as Jefferson, Madison, Jackson, and Marshall, and during the 1840s and early 1850s southern politics were intertwined with the nation's. Whigs and Democrats competed on similar levels in the South as elsewhere and the region's electorate participated at the same high rate as other Americans of that time.

The South's political goals were, of course, somewhat different from those of the rest of the country because of its economy. Madison had stressed in *Federalist* no. 10 how "the possession of different degrees and kinds of property" influences "the sentiments and views of the respective proprietors." This creates "a division of the society into different interests and parties," or factions. The slave economy, a rural and agricultural one, produced a faction of planter elites from the Black Belt areas—where the fertile topsoil was deep and dark—who fought from the constitutional period to Tocqueville's time for a certain agenda. In the Philadelphia Convention of 1787 this influential class shaped several provisions of the new Constitution to their ends, among them the infamous Three-Fifths Compromise, a 20-year protection against halting the importation of slaves, and a $10 tax limit on those brought in, plus a prohibition on direct taxes on personal wealth or income. In ensuing decades they engaged repeatedly in the titanic tariff struggles against the northern manufacturing interests who sought to protect themselves from foreign goods while the planters sought free trade.

Madison had explained in his seminal essay that the federal, republican form of government could effectively rule over an enormous territory through an array of formal checks and balances to fragment elite power and through divided constituencies to do likewise for mass sovereignty. An advantage of this system would be the "security afforded . . . in the greater obstacles to the concert and accomplishment of the majority." By the time of Tocqueville's visit, such protections were becoming increasingly important to the slave-holding elite for a host of reasons.

At the time of the passage of the Constitution the populations of North and South plus their economies and political balance were roughly equal, but that was changing as the nation began its second half-century. The economic advantages of the northern manufacturing and commercial interests grew steadily while the admission of new western states began to alter the political alignment, and by 1850 the North had grown to some 13.5 million, whereas the South grew to only 9.5 million. These and other adverse trends led John C. Calhoun to bemoan to southerners in the 1830s on the Senate floor that "we are here but a handful in the midst of an overwhelming majority." The eminent historian Richard Hofstadter wrote in *The American Political Tradition* of that critical era: "The Southern leaders reacted with the most intense and exaggerated anxiety to every fluctuation in the balance of sectional power. How to maintain this balance became the central concern." It would remain so for the next 150 years.

Thus, the southern planter elite embarked on a futile struggle to maintain a semifeudal, agrarian, and racially stratified society. This eventually made residents of the region the only Americans (until Vietnam) ever to lose a war and the sole ones ever to be governed by a conquering military occupation force. After the war the struggle resumed as the elite, Bourbons or Redeemers as they came to be called, reestablished the state Democratic parties, engineered the removal of the Reconstruction governments in the Compromise of 1877, and moved in the 1880s and 1890s to isolate Republicans to the upland areas that had opposed secession, to squelch the radical Populist uprising of small farmers, and to establish Jim Crow in the turn-of-the-century constitutions. Thus, the Solid South was built on one-party politics, racism, formal and informal disfranchisement of the masses, malapportionment in favor of Black Belt areas, and—perhaps most important of all—regional autonomy from national politics and, in particular, undesirable policies on racial matters.

The foremost scholar of Dixie politics, the late political scientist V. O. Key, Jr., said of this Solid South system in his brilliant study in 1949: "The coin of southern politics has two sides; on one is seen the relations of the South as a whole with the rest of the nation; on the other, the political battle within each state. And the two aspects are, like the faces of a coin, closely connected." He traced how the relatively small white minority of the Black Belt counties ruled Dixie through the unchallenged hegemony of the Democratic party. Democrats won, for example, 113 of 114 gubernatorial elections and 131 of 132 senatorial ones from 1919 to 1948. Also, with the single exception of 1928 when five rim states abandoned the wet, Catholic, urban New York Democrat Al Smith, Dixie gave all its electoral votes to the Democratic ticket in the 17 presidential elections from 1880 to 1944.

Such loyalty provided the region's elite enormous leverage in national politics, particularly in Congress, where the solid bloc of southern Democratic senators consistently controlled the Senate and the overwhelmingly Democratic southern congressional delegations likewise controlled the House. The seniority system adopted in 1910 for choosing chairpersons promoted the South's members into positions of great power, so that by the 1950s Dixie, with some one-fifth of the total population and number of states, commanded approximately 60 percent of the chairs. Because of their power and because of the practice of senatorial courtesy southern senators greatly influenced the federal judiciary, especially at the lower levels. And until 1936 the requirement that Democratic presidential nominees acquire two-thirds of the delegate votes gave the South an effective veto over unacceptable candidates. The thoroughness with which regional autonomy was achieved through these and related devices is highlighted by the observation of W. J. Cash, a full century after Tocqueville, that the South "was not quite a nation within a nation, but the next thing to it."

The use of this power to resist nationalizing, industrializing, and egalitarian trends greatly retarded the economic, political, and social development of the region. In 1938 President Roosevelt assembled a major Conference on Economic Conditions in the South, stating that the "South presents right now the Nation's No. 1 economic problem." Key would write at mid-century, "The cold hard fact is that the South as a whole has developed no system or practice of political organization and leadership adequate to cope with its problems." Racially, the historic gulf between white and black southerners flared into violence often in the civil-rights years, during the Little Rock school crisis in 1958, the University of Mississippi riots in 1962, at Selma in 1965, and in many other locales as well.

The oligarchic, one-dimensional, closed, and inflexible Solid South system that served Black Belt elites so well was shattered in the 1950s and 1960s. These two decades were the watershed years between the politics begun so long ago by Calhoun and his generation and the emerging, as yet undefined politics of the current generation. Many developments in this era transformed the style and substance of southern politics, from the region's increased prosperity to the reemergence of a two-party system with John Tower's election to the Senate from Texas in 1961 on the Republican ticket, victories of the Goldwater forces in 1964, Republican gains in the off-year congressional elections of 1966, and Nixon's wins in 1968 and 1972. The black protest movement was led by a native son, Dr. Martin Luther King, Jr., and the national Democratic party's push for civil rights resulted in the Civil Rights Act of 1964 and the Voting Rights Act of 1965. The seminal court case, *Brown* v. *Board of Education* (1954), ruled segregated schools in violation of the Fourteenth Amendment's "equal protection clause," and another case, *Baker* v. *Carr* (1962), began the process of fair apportionment.

The American nation embarked on its third century with over 4 million southern blacks registered to vote. There were 2,000 black officials in the South; its schools were more desegregated than the rest of the country's; it boasted a rapidly growing population, an expanding economy, and a developing two-party system. Now in the states of Mississippi, Louisiana, and Georgia, blacks constitute approximately 25 percent of the electorate, and they are a force to be reckoned with throughout the

South. In a real sense the election of 1976 was, like that famous one a century earlier, one of redemption. Walker Percy summed up the change nicely in the late 1970s: "The South has entered the mainstream of American life for the first time in perhaps 150 years, that is, in a sense that has not been the case since the 1820s or '30s."

The South's role in contemporary national politics is much more akin to the pre-Calhoun, pre–Civil War era than to the century or more of political resistance and isolation that followed. National issues, from abortion to foreign affairs, educational reform, and budgetary matters, are as important in the South as elsewhere. Presidential elections are now vigorously contested throughout Dixie. In 1984, for example, South Carolina native Jesse Jackson made a credible race for the Democratic nomination, and the 13 March southern primaries in Alabama, Florida, and Georgia proved of crucial importance to him. Jackson's campaign and the primaries, dubbed "Super Tuesday" by the media, received extensive national attention.

Southern political leaders who exercise great national influence include Republican senator Jesse Helms (N.C.), former Senate majority leader Howard Baker (Tenn.), and the current assistant minority leader in the House, Trent Lott (Miss.). Democratic senators Sam Nunn (Ga.), Lloyd Bentson (Tex.), and John Stennis (Miss.) wield significant power on the other side of the aisle, and Jim Wright (Tex.) is speaker of the House. Governor Lamar Alexander of Tennessee, a Republican, assumed the chair of the National Governors' Conference in 1985, while Mayor Ernest Morial of New Orleans, a Democrat, became chairperson of the National Mayors' Conference the following year.

Because of the changing political scene plus population growth—which saw every southern state outstrip the national average of 11.4 percent in the 1970s, thereby giving the region eight additional congressional seats and electoral votes—and an economic performance better than the nation as a whole, some believe America is in the midst of a historic shift in power to the "Sunbelt," the South and West. If this proves true, then the South's role in national politics will be even more critical in the future.

See also BLACK LIFE: Politics, Black; HISTORY AND MANNERS articles; SOCIAL CLASS: Politics and Social Class; WOMEN'S LIFE: Politics, Women in

Jimmy Lea
University of Southern Mississippi

Numan Bartley and Hugh Davis Graham, *Southern Politics and the Second Reconstruction* (1975); Jack Bass and Walter DeVries, *The Transformation of Southern Politics: Social Change and Political Consequences since 1945* (1976); W. J. Cash, *The Mind of the South* (1941); William C. Havard, ed., *The Changing Politics of the South* (1972); V. O. Key, Jr., *Southern Politics in State and Nation* (1949); Alexander P. Lamis, *The Two-Party South* (1984); Donald R. Matthews and James W. Prothro, *Negroes and the New Southern Politics* (1966); T. Harry Williams, *Romance and Realism in Southern Politics* (1961).

One-Party Politics

The disfranchisement of practically all blacks and many white have-nots in the period between 1890 and 1910 decimated the Republican and Populist parties in the South and left the region with only a single important political party. In the era of classic one-party politics, roughly 1910–50, Democrats monopolized state offices and deterred serious opposition in general elections. The national political interests of white southerners were likewise managed exclusively by Democrats; the region regularly cast all of its electoral college votes for Democratic presidential candidates and sent virtually all Democrats to the House of Representatives and the Senate.

As a consequence of the decline in meaningful interparty competition, general elections in the region became empty rituals. Less than one-fifth of the eligible electorate voted in any four-year wave of gubernatorial general elections in the South from 1920 through 1951. Interest in electoral politics, meager as it was, shifted to the relatively new arena of Democratic nominating primaries, which were initially regarded as voluntary organizations open only to whites. In the Democratic primaries, turnout usually exceeded one-fifth of the eligible electorate but never included as many as three-tenths of the potential electorate in the 1920–51 era. One-party politics helped to "anesthetize" or "sterilize" between two-thirds and four-fifths of the region's white adults. As a consequence, politicians representing the interests of more affluent southerners usually triumphed over spokesmen for the region's have-nots.

Until fairly recently the campaigns that counted in the South were conducted as a politics of faction rather than a politics of party, as a struggle among groups of rival Democrats as opposed to a battle between Democrats and Republicans. It is useful to distinguish between *faction* (any subunit of a political party) and *factional system* (the pattern of competition among factions). Students of factional systems have typically followed V. O. Key's lead in identifying three varieties of intraparty

Election posters along a Mississippi roadside, 1968

competition based on the number of factions seeking a particular office and the distribution of the first primary vote among the factions: unifactionalism, where one faction wins a commanding majority of the vote; bifactionalism, where the vote is divided more or less evenly between two factions; and multifactionalism, where the vote is split, not necessarily evenly, among three or more factions.

By far the most common electoral situation in the 1920–49 era was multifactionalism, which appeared in 70 percent of the first gubernatorial primary elections. This outcome was hardly surprising. Because ambitious politicians were plentiful while opportunities to win the governorship were rare, multifactionalism would have been the natural mode of intraparty competition once the Democratic party's dominance in general elections had been established. The most plausible deterrent to multifactionalism is the candidacy of an incumbent governor, whose usual advantages in campaign fundraising, name and face recognition, patronage, and the like should discourage some challengers from running against him. Southern governors, however, were denied by law from succeeding themselves in states with four-year terms; though succession in states with two-year terms was constitutional, most governors limited their aspirations to two two-year terms. Accordingly, most gubernatorial primaries in the South were efforts to fill open seats, which simply reinforced the attractiveness of the governorship to many candidates.

The other patterns of factional cleavage appeared less frequently. Unifactionalism was present in approximately one-fifth of the gubernatorial contests and was the most common form of factional competition in only a single state (Virginia). Bifactional cleavage was even less likely to occur (13 percent of the elections). Tennessee and Georgia provided most of the examples of conflict between two groups of rival Democrats.

When the form of intraparty competition is related to the type of faction that usually won nomination, four central tendencies can be distinguished in intraparty politics in the southern states: bifactional primaries won by successful durable factions (Tennessee), unifactional primaries won by successful durable factions (Virginia), multifactional primaries won by successful durable factions (Louisiana, Mississippi, Alabama, North Carolina, and Georgia), and, as the most chaotic and disorganized of all systems, multifactional primaries won by moderately successful transient factions (Florida, Texas, South Carolina, and Arkansas).

In national presidential politics the Solid South actually ended during the mid-20th-century period covered by Key in *Southern Politics*. Not since 1944 have all 11 former Confederate states voted for the Democratic presidential nominee. The most recent approximation of regional solidarity for the Democrats occurred in 1976, when 10 southern states were carried by Jimmy Carter, but it was short lived and a poor imitation of the real thing. The disintegration of the Solid South has deprived the national Democrats of crucial electoral college votes and has required the Democrats to be disproportionately successful outside the South in order to win the presidency.

Southern congressional delegations remained overwhelmingly Democratic for a longer period. From the late 1930s until the late 1950s most non-southern Senate and House seats were held by Republicans, and only the Democrats' near-monopoly on southern Senate and House seats enabled the Democrats to control both houses of Congress. The weakness of the Democratic party outside the South permitted conservative southern Democrats to exert considerable influence on public policy and, in particular, to prevent passage of meaningful civil rights legislation. Once the white conservatives from the region lost the ability to control the agenda of race relations, the rationale for sending only Democrats to Congress from the South was weakened considerably.

Merle Black
University of North Carolina
at Chapel Hill

Earl Black
University of South Carolina

Earl Black and Merle Black, *Politics and Society in the South* (1987), in *Contemporary Southern Political Attitudes and Behavior*, ed. Laurence W. Moreland, Tod A. Baker, and Robert P. Steed (1982); Bradley C. Canon, *American Journal of Political Science* (November 1978); Malcolm E. Jewell and David M. Olsen, *American State Political Parties and Elections* (1978); V. O. Key, Jr., *Southern Politics in State and Nation* (1949); J. Morgan Kousser, *The Shaping of Southern Politics: Suffrage Restriction and the Establishment of the One-Party South, 1880–1910* (1974).

Partisan Politics

The dominance of a one-party political system in the South after the Civil War and into the mid-20th century belies the existence of earlier two-party systems in the South. Party systems before the Civil War were influenced by the same concerns of personality, ideology, and organization as elsewhere in the country.

The first partisan conflict in the southern United States emerged in the 1790s and led to the appearance of the Federalist party and the Democratic-Republican party. The Federalists in the South were strongest in South Carolina and, to a lesser degree, Virginia and North Carolina. It was a party of merchants, planters, lawyers, editors, speculators, and those, in general, who profited from the national financial politics of Alexander Hamilton in the George Washington Administration. The Federalists declined after 1800, though, as Thomas Jefferson's Democratic-Republicans gained control of the presidency and Congress in that year's elections. Jefferson's party was strong in the South and West from its beginnings and came to stand for local control of government, financial conservatism, and an ideology of individual freedom. The party gradually absorbed Federalist supporters and policies until the South—like the nation—had a virtual one-party system from 1816 to 1828.

After the election of Andrew Jackson as president in 1828, a new party system slowly appeared—the Democratic party of Jackson and the Whig party of Henry Clay and Daniel Webster. Recent studies suggest little philosophical or class difference between the groups, with the personality of Jackson and the organizational techniques of the Democrats at first giving them dominance in the South as elsewhere.

The Reconstruction era after the Civil War witnessed the first partisan conflict between blacks and whites in southern history. Blacks identified with the Republican party—which had emerged as a northern, free-soil political group in the 1850s—while most southern whites moved into the Democratic party. The latter called itself the conservative Democratic party through most of the late 19th century to separate itself, to a degree, from the national Democrats and to attract pre–Civil War Whigs. From the end of Reconstruction in 1877 to the 1960s partisan politics in the South was, in most areas, conducted within a one-party framework.

The annals of American regional partisan change have rarely, if ever, witnessed such a dramatic transformation as occurred in the South from the 1960s to the 1980s. When the national Democratic party effectively advocated equal rights for blacks in the early 1960s, the rationale for the South's unique one-party system collapsed, blacks entered the political process with strong federal support, and the present top-heavy two-party system took hold throughout the 11 states of the former Confederacy.

The overriding purpose of the one-party system was to preserve white supremacy, the argument being that if whites divided their votes blacks would hold the balance of power. This reasoning was destroyed in the mid-1960s when national Democratic leaders "betrayed" the white South and pushed passage of the Civil Rights Act of 1964 and the Voting Rights Act of 1965. The partisan impact of these events was reinforced by the highly publicized opposition to the Civil Rights Act of 1964 by Republican presidential nominee Barry Goldwater. In November 1964 President Lyndon B. Johnson won a landslide Democratic victory nationwide, but Goldwater swept the Deep South, carrying Mississippi, always an extreme case, with 87.1 percent of the vote.

The national Democratic party's civil rights activism unleashed a torrent of Republican activity in the region. The fuel for this GOP spurt was white antagonism toward all things remotely connected with the national Democratic party integrationists. Figure 2 pinpoints the Republican leap forward to the mid-1960s. There was, however, another feature to the GOP's rise that was separable, if not always separated, from the race issue. With the collapse of the one-party system, the economic and philosophical divisions found in party politics outside the South—dating from the class-oriented New Deal realignment—had an opportunity to descend into the region's emerging partisan structure. Thus, in the forefront of the nascent southern GOP movement were well-to-do businessmen and professionals seeking to help along this process in order to give the region's economic conservatives a permanent home. And the southern Republican party made its most faithful converts among those attracted by the party's conservative position on economic-class issues.

Figure 2. The Uneven Growth of the Republican Party in the South, 1948–1986

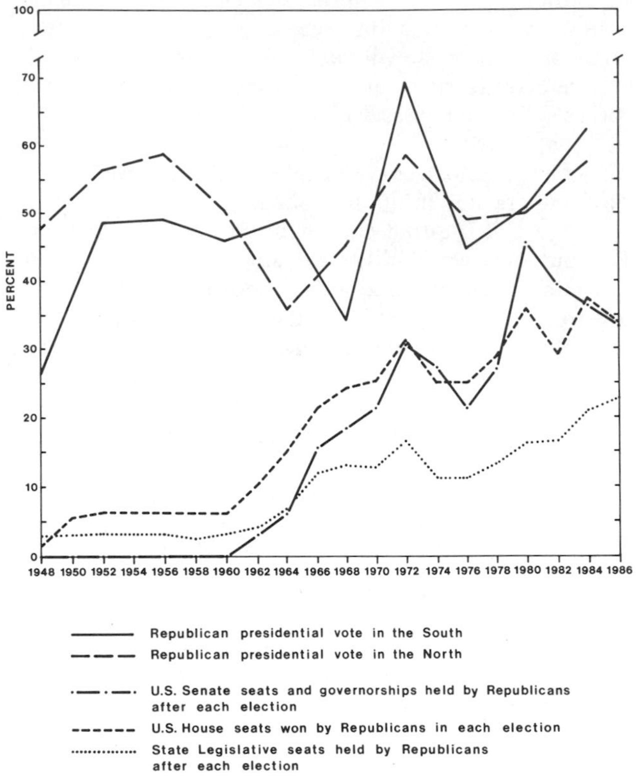

Source: Alexander P. Lamis, *The Two-Party South* (1984).

Simultaneously, however, the race issue became enmeshed in the emerging class-based two-party system that seemed to be taking hold in the post-1964 period. Twisted into the situation was the logical compatibility of conservative economic-class Republicanism with the racial protest. The GOP, as the party philosophically opposed to an activist federal government in economic matters, gained adherents also from those who objected to federal intervention to end racial segregation in the states.

Steady Republican growth ended in the early 1970s when the race issue abated sufficiently to result in a mild resurgence on the part of the region's transformed Democratic party, which had gradually shed its segregationist leaders after blacks entered the electorate in large numbers. Figure 2 reflects this mid-1970s Democratic gain by showing a dip in Republican fortunes in those years. The resurgence was accomplished by clever white Democratic politicians who recognized that the post–civil rights era offered them the potential to put together an effective black-white alliance. This biracial coalition is composed of those traditionally Democratic white voters who returned to their party in the 1970s as the race issue eased *and* of southern blacks, who carried strong Democratic allegiance in gratitude for what the national party did for them during the 1960s. It became a mere matter of arithmetic in some states—especially in the Deep

South—for the Republicans to realize that this black-white Democratic alliance arrayed against them was a powerful one indeed.

The irony present in the situation—namely, that the traditional party of segregation in the South should become the home of, and dependent on, black voters—did not escape Republican notice. One Georgia Republican party chairman ruefully bemoaned the existence of this diverse Democratic coalition that had demolished the once bright GOP potential in his state, complaining that there was "no tie-in" between the twin pillars of the Georgia Democracy—rural, small-town whites of south Georgia and blacks. "They're as far apart as night and day," he noted. And yet, "They're voting hand in hand, and . . . they're squeezing the lives out of us."

This disparate southern Democratic coalition contained serious tensions. Through the early 1980s the alliance held together—although the national victory of Ronald Reagan in 1980 gave the southern GOP a boost—primarily as the result of the canny maneuvers of white moderate leaders, who were its chief beneficiaries. These leaders walked a political tightrope that required Olympian balancing because racial distrust and class antagonisms constantly threatened to divide the coalition's contradictory elements. The alliance's future well-being could be threatened if left-leaning Democratic leaders supplant them and champion the economic interests of, as V. O. Key, Jr., said, "those who have less" of both races. In such an event, more and more white conservative Democrats could be expected to move to the Republican party, a development that would complete the penetration of national party cleavages into the region's once isolated partisan life. The flaring of racial antagonism in the South would also have the same effect of driving white Democrats into the arms of the GOP, although in this case the defecting whites would probably come equally from all economic groups.

See also BLACK LIFE: Politics, Black; WOMEN'S LIFE: Politics, Women in

Alexander P. Lamis
University of Mississippi

Lance Banning, *The Jeffersonian Persuasion: Evolution of a Party Ideology* (1978); Numan Bartley, *The Rise of Massive Resistance: Race and Politics in the South during the 1950s* (1969); Jack Bass and Walter DeVries, *The Transformation of Southern Politics: Social Change and Political Consequences since 1945* (1976); William J. Cooper, Jr., *Liberty and Slavery: Southern Politics to 1860* (1983); Alexander Heard, *A Two-Party South?* (1952); Richard Hofstadter, *The Idea of a Party System: The Rise of Legitimate Opposition in the United States, 1780–1840* (1969); V. O. Key, Jr., *Southern Politics in State and Nation* (1949); Alexander P. Lamis, *The Two-Party South* (1984); Richard P. McCormick, *The Second American Party System: Party Formation in the Jacksonian Era* (1966); C. Vann Woodward, *Origins of the New South, 1877–1913* (1951).

Protest Movements

When Tom Watson, the one-time Georgia Populist, was asked the difference between his campaign and the one run by William Jennings Bryan, he replied, "Bryan had *no everlasting* and overshadowing *Negro Question* to hamper *and handicap his progress*: I HAD." Historians may quarrel about what makes the South different from the rest of the nation—a lost cause, secession, poverty, an agrarian tradition, race. But most would agree, along with Tom Watson, that the issue of race relations has dominated, hindered, and shaped protest movements in southern society.

The South emerged from the Civil War as a region committed politically to the Democratic party. The Democrats had supported both slavery and secession. Moreover, white southerners blamed the Republican party for Reconstruction, which allowed black folks to participate in the political process, an activity that implied racial equality. That was a concept the vast majority of southern whites repudiated. In addition, Reconstruction occurred simultaneously with the first postwar panic (1870–76); Republicans were thus identified with depression and agricultural poverty. By 1877 the "Solid South" stood solidly for the memory of the Confederacy and the Democratic party.

There were, however, cracks in the frame that held the Solid South together. Isolated areas with large black populations elected some Republicans to public offices. Within the Democratic party, both agrarian and conservative—sometimes called Bourbon or Redeemer—constituencies existed. The latter, committed to the New South, warned agrarians that to break with the Democracy would simply bring those black Republicans back into power, destroying both the white man's party and any chance for economic prosperity. Instead, Redeemers argued, the cost of government should be held down, white immigration into the region encouraged, crops diversified, and government stabilized, through the auspices of the Democratic party; eventually, they argued, such acts of austerity and change would bring new industries and prosperity to the New South.

Until 1885 or so, most farmers were willing to heed such pleas. The agrarians, however, always applied pressure to the uneasy alliance between the conservative haves and the farming have-nots. Consequently the Patrons of Husbandry, or the Grange, as it was more popularly called, enlisted 220,000 white southern farmers into its cause. The organization advocated crop diversification, economic cooperatives, and social and educational activities, but eschewed politics. Where possible, it sent representatives to Redeemer constitutional conventions. There Grangers took the lead in defeating poll tax provisions, passing laws that defined railroads as public carriers, and supporting any measure that held down the cost of government. The Patrons of Husbandry opposed both Republicans and third parties. Certainly the issue of race and politics inhibited Granger political protest, yet the organization's limited dissent from the New South orthodoxy was always watched with suspicion by the more conservative Redeemers.

The organization did train potential political protesters. Indeed, some contemporary observers maintained that the Greenback crusade attracted so many Grangers that the Patrons of Husbandry died. The Greenbackers, who wanted to issue legal tender notes to counteract agricultural depressions, organized third parties in Arkansas, Alabama, Texas, Kentucky, West Virginia, and Mississippi—all states with large Granger constituencies. These protest movements ran candidates for local offices in 1876 and for statewide offices in 1878 and 1880, when James B. Weaver was a presidential candidate. The party, although optimistic, ran well only in Texas, Oklahoma, and Kentucky. Tom Watson explained its failure: "The Democrats . . . wrote Greenback platforms, and then said to receding Greenbackers, 'Don't leave your old party; get your reforms inside the party; we white people of the South cannot afford to divide.'" Thus the policy of the Democratic party toward political dissenters in the Solid South was to co-opt, use racial issues to divide, and promise moderate reforms. To a large measure, that policy never changed, and never did it succeed as well as in its defeat of southern Populism.

Populism grew from a sizable number of agricultural societies that appeared as the Grange declined. Historians have designated the Farmers' Alliance, first organized in Lampasas, Tex., in 1875, as the oldest of these voluntary associations. After intermittent stops and starts, the organization began again in 1879 and claimed 50,000 members by 1885. That same period, however, produced organizations throughout the South, such as Reliefmen in Mississippi, Brothers of Freedom and Commonwealth Organizations in Louisiana, the Cross Timbers of Texas, the Arkansas Agricultural Wheel, and the Farmers' Union of Louisiana. In short, southern farmers awaited only a charismatic leader to unite them in an agrarian crusade.

Charles W. Macune of Texas was that man. In 1886 he took over the Texas Farmers' Alliance. Within two years, he joined that organization with the Farmers' Union of Louisiana and the Agricultural Wheel of Arkansas, and the National Farmers' Alliance and Industrial Union, called the Southern Farmers' Alliance, was born. By 1890 the Southern Alliance claimed 3 million members, recruiting not only in all the southern states but in Kansas and the Dakotas as well. In addition, 1.3 million black people joined an affiliate known as the Colored Alliance. These organizations advocated free silver, improved public services, governmental control or regulation of public transportation, no convict leasing, repeal of the national bank act, fairer taxation laws, national and state election reforms, and the subtreasury plan. By 1890 no southern politician could ignore Alliance demands.

Ironically, Macune's organization spun off a political party more radical than most of its members. The key was the subtreasury plan. Macune proposed that subtreasuries be located throughout rural areas and that these government warehouses loan farmers, at 1 percent interest in legal tender notes, up to 80 percent of the value of staple crops. This plan attacked both banks and furnishing merchants and created a flexible currency. Orthodox Democratic politicians could not endorse this scheme, even when radical members of the Alliance demanded that local and state officeholders embrace the subtreasury, warning that failure to do so would mean that farmers would choose an opposition candidate. The result was a third-party movement that spread throughout the South during the depression years of the 1890s. The Populist party would divide and destroy the Alliance, but it became the major challenge on the left to Democratic hegemony in the Gilded Age.

Democratic politicians struck back in two ways. First, the party moved to the left. James S. Hogg of Texas, John B. Gordon of Georgia, James Z. George of Mississippi, Ben Tillman of South Carolina, and Zebulon Vance of North Carolina, for example, all argued that they supported Alliance platforms but opposed such radical measures as government ownership of railroads and the subtreasury. They in turn passed moderate reforms, such as commission regulation, and spoke for free silver. Their slight move to the left prevented a massive switch of dirt farmers from the Democratic to the Populist party.

The second maneuver was even more effective politically, longer lasting, and absolutely devastating to Populist hopes. The Democrats used racism to destroy the third party. Populists called for an alliance between poor blacks and whites. Their platforms denounced lynching and convict leasing and asked for guarantees of black suffrage. White Democrats charged that the unholy alliance of blacks and whites would corrupt southern morality and return the hated Republican party to power. Meanwhile, southern conservatives shamelessly bought and intimidated black voters and used the free machinery of the state to cheat or "count-out" from office many successful Populist candidates.

After the death of Leonidas Polk of North Carolina in June 1892, southern Populists lacked a popular presidential contender. James B. Weaver, the old Greenbacker from Iowa, won the nomination in 1892. Conservatives reclaimed much of what they had lost in 1890, and in no southern state did Weaver win 40 percent of the vote. The panic of 1893 refueled the Populist charge. Democrats defeated their greatest challenge in 1894 by seizing silver as an issue, exploiting racism, proposing moderate reform, and controlling party machinery. In 1896 silver forces controlled the Democratic convention and nominated William Jennings Bryan, who carried the South but not the nation, and Populists saw their victories of 1892 and 1894 melt away, as white, upland farmers returned to the Democratic party.

The Democrats, however, and their opponents needed to chain the unleashed racism. Conservatives and liberals alike argued that politics could not be purified until blacks were disfranchised. Consequently, southern politicians began with poll taxes and continued through Jim Crow laws, carving out a separate and unequal society. The poll tax legislation that disfranchised blacks did the same to most poor whites. Conservatives thus used the specter of Reconstruction to restrict the left in the South. They convinced small farmers to reject third parties and their own economic welfare by threatening "Negro domination," and they convinced the same group to disfranchise part of their own numbers and to remain in support of conservative politics to keep the black in a subordinate position. The left never overcame the myth of "Negro Domination."

Consequently, the two great events of 19th-century southern history, the Civil War and the agrarian revolts, left the Democratic party in control; political wars pitted one faction of that party against another. Occasionally the left would secede briefly and challenge the Democrats. Socialism claimed voting strength ranging from 20 percent of the electorate in Oklahoma to 32 percent in South Carolina in 1912. The xenophobia produced by World War I, however, ended the socialist crusade in the South as elsewhere. Likewise, negrophobia, in particular the outcry in the region against Booker T. Washington's friendship with Teddy Roosevelt, eliminated any appeal that the National Progressive party might have had in the South. The first three decades or so of the 20th century thus saw the left organize the Farmers' Union, voluntary acreage associations, and economic cooperatives, and support such moderate reformers as Hoke Smith of Georgia and Braxton B. Comer of Alabama.

Conservatives retained control of the South until the New Deal. Franklin Roosevelt's policies galvanized southern politics because the region was so poor. Conservative Democrats came quickly to fear that the New Deal threatened their control of the southern economy with legislation like the Tennessee Valley Authority and the activities of the Department of Agriculture. They identified the Congress of Industrial Organizations, the Southern Tenant Farmers' Union, and the Farm Security Administration as political threats. Conservatives believed rightly that these federal and radical organizations sprang from the New Deal reform impulse.

Once more, conservatives turned to race to protect their economic interests. Many southern whites resented the New Deal's drive to win over urban voters, and its consequent appeal to northern blacks. Although certainly not color blind, the New Deal offered economic and social programs that included endorsement of a Fair Employment Practices Commission, antilynching legislation, and repeal of the poll tax; later came Harry Truman's Fair Deal, integration of the armed services, and civil rights legislation. The conservative wing of the Democratic party struck back. In 1944 corporation lawyers, well-to-do businessmen, representatives of industry, and Black Belt conservatives organized the Jeffersonian Democrats in Texas, Mississippi, and South Carolina. In 1948 others in the Deep South joined this group and ran South Carolina Governor Strom Thurmond for president on a Dixiecrat ticket. Dixiecrats carried only South Carolina, Alabama, Mississippi, and Louisiana, but battlelines were once more drawn and race was once more the central issue of southern politics.

As southern conservatives cooperated with the Republican party in the national Congress, supported Dwight D. Eisenhower in 1952 and 1956, and criticized the northern Democrats as being anti-South, the southern left endorsed and fought for the national Democratic party. Liberal southerners created such organizations as the Democrats of Texas, and endorsed such politicians as Senator Ralph Yarborough (Texas) or William Fulbright (Arkansas)—all activities designed to commit southern Democrats to the national party's goals. A major goal after 1954 was, increasingly, an integrated society, and the cause of the southern left became first and foremost integration. Conservatives' goals were to prevent it. Racism was used, as against Populism, as a barrier to any economic or social reform.

In the 1960 presidential race Richard Nixon formulated the "Southern Strategy," implying federal foot-dragging on integration in exchange for a conservative, Republican South. It was not successful in 1960, but in 1972 Nixon succeeded and the Solid South in some places is now more solidly Republican than Democratic.

The Republican party in the South is composed largely of whites. Partially this is in reaction to the civil rights movement of the 1960s, a crusade endorsed by the southern left. As SNCC, CORE, and the SCLC fought for equality, and Dr. Martin Luther King, Jr., Stokely Carmichael, and James Farmer advocated civil rights, their cause dominated all other liberal concerns. The national Democratic party endorsed these goals, and it won the support of southern blacks and other minorities. The 1960s witnessed triumphs for equality: the Civil Rights Act of 1964, the Voting Rights Act of 1965, the end of the poll tax, and an increase in black and brown voters. The left predicted that a political coalition of blacks, browns, feminists, poor whites, liberals, and progressives would seize the South and bring about a myriad of reforms. Then, in the late 1960s, the antiwar movement swept the country and hopes of a broad coalition collapsed, as southern whites rebelled against black power, the student movement, feminism, and reform.

George Wallace led a major southern protest movement in the late 1960s and early 1970s, drawing supporters from a white backlash against the black freedom movement and liberal reform activities in general. Wallace was the charismatic governor of Alabama who first came into office in 1962 vowing "segregation forever." Using populist rhetoric and appealing to rural and working-class voters, Wallace mounted a major third-party effort in 1968, carrying Alabama, Arkansas, Georgia, Louisiana, and Mississippi in the presidential campaign. After an assassin's bullet crippled Wallace in 1972, his influence on national politics waned, but he remained a force in Deep South politics until the late 1970s.

By 1984 the left in the South, as well as in the nation, was in disarray. De jure segregation, but not de facto, had ceased to exist. Civil rights no longer was the bellwether of reform. The left concentrated simply on defeating maneuvers of Republicans to roll back the New Deal, Fair Deal, Great Society, and Supreme Court mandates for civil rights. Most southern blacks were Democrats, and most southern whites were Republicans. Consequently, party battles, in the South as in the nation, revolved around a liberal Democratic versus a conservative Republican party rather than third parties or a Solid South.

See also BLACK LIFE: Freedom Movement, Black; Politics, Black; HISTORY AND MANNERS: Jacksonian Democracy; Jeffersonian Tradition; New Deal; Populism; Progressivism; LAW: Civil Rights Movement; SOCIAL CLASS: Communism;

Marxist History; Politics and Social Class; Religion and Social Class; Socialism

Robert A. Calvert
Texas A&M University

Numan Bartley, *The Rise of Massive Resistance: Race and Politics in the South during the 1950s* (1960); Carl N. Degler, *The Other South: Southern Dissenters in the Nineteenth Century* (1982); Lawrence Goodwyn, *Democratic Promise: The Populist Moment in America* (1976); Dewey Grantham, *Southern Progressivism: The Reconciliation of Progress and Tradition* (1983); James R. Green, *Grass-roots Socialism: Radical Movements in the Southwest, 1895–1943* (1978); John B. Kirby, *Black Americans in the Roosevelt Era: Liberalism and Race* (1980); Robert C. McMath, *The Populist Vanguard: A History of the Southern Farmers' Alliance* (1975); Theodore Saloutos, *Farmer Movements in the South, 1865–1933* (1960); Harvard Sitkoff, *The Struggle for Black Equality, 1954–1980* (1981).

Segregation, Defense of

The 17 May 1954 Supreme Court decision in *Brown* v. *Board of Education* is frequently perceived as the start of both the Second Reconstruction and the white South's struggle to maintain the racial status quo. To be sure, the *Brown* decision had the type of crystallizing impact in the South that the Court's ruling a century earlier in *Dred Scott* v. *Sanford* had had in the North. Both decisions were followed by regional efforts to thwart the law of the land. Still, the perception that the Supreme Court in 1954 inaugurated a new era of federal involvement on behalf of the nation's black citizens is false. Moreover, southern resistance to federal attacks on segregation was ongoing.

During the decade prior to the *Brown* decision, for example, the Supreme Court had invalidated the white primary, ordered blacks admitted to all-white graduate and law schools, struck at racial segregation on interstate carriers, and barred states from enacting legislation designed to enforce racially restrictive property covenants. The President's Committee on Civil Rights was created by President Truman in 1946. Truman also ordered the desegregation of the armed forces.

Although all the aforementioned actions had not occurred prior to the 1948 National Democratic Convention, southern politicians clearly knew by that date the way the wind was blowing. Of special concern to white southerners was the report of the President's Committee on Civil Rights. *To Secure These Rights* (1947) contained 35 recommendations that touched upon virtually every facet of racial discrimination, including education, the armed forces, employment, and voting rights. When a majority of the delegates to the party's 1948 national convention adopted a strong civil rights platform, the entire Mississippi delegation and much of the Alabama delegation bolted the convention. A few days later segregationists from the South held a convention in Birmingham, where they created the States' Rights Democratic Party (Dixiecrats) and nominated Governor J. Strom Thurmond of South Carolina as their presidential candidate. The hope of the Dixiecrats was to secure enough electoral votes to prevent victory by either the Republicans or Democrats; the election would then be decided in the House of Representatives. In the House, according to the plan, the South would be able to negotiate a regional compromise that would protect the southern pattern of race relations. Although the States' Rights Democrats failed, they did focus attention on the "threat from Washington."

In many ways the Supreme Court decisions of the 1940s, the adoption of a civil rights platform by the Democrats in 1948, and the actions of President Truman were a prelude to the events that would follow the *Brown* decision. Indeed, the cumulative effect of the actions of all three branches of the national government was to abolish legal racial discrimination. Such a drastic change over a short time was, of course, resisted by many white southerners. The southern effort to resist change was based on an outdated philosophy and involved legal tactics, economic pressure, and violence.

Southern ideology had at its core the interrelated ideas of racial superiority and the natural order of things. According to the natural order argument, everything in nature had its proper place. In the words of a Florida jurist, "fish in the sea segregate in schools of their kind." The judge, as noted by Numan Bartley in *The Rise of Massive Resistance* (1969), used the example in an opinion that justified segregation. White southerners generally believed that the natural place for blacks was below that of whites. Quite simply, whites believed that blacks were inherently inferior.

The primary disseminators of literature that focused on the alleged inferiority of blacks were the Citizens' Councils of America (CCA) and the various state Citizens' Councils. These organizations had their beginning in Mississippi as part of the reaction to the *Brown* ruling. At first the Citizens' Councils concentrated on the school issue, but as the civil rights protest expanded, council members fought to maintain all forms of segregation. Unlike the Ku Klux Klan, the Citizens' Councils rejected the use of violence.

Convinced that the average white northerner held essentially the same racial beliefs as white southerners, the CCA embarked upon a propaganda campaign designed to demonstrate black inferiority. One tract cited in Neil R. McMillen's *Citizens' Council* (1971) lists the "eleven most essential differences between the two races." As was the case with racist literature of an earlier era, the CCA handbook contended that there were differences between the eyes, ears, hair, lips, noses, cheek bones, jaws, skulls, and voices of whites and blacks. Of special significance was an alleged difference in brain weight. *Racial Facts*, a publication of the Mississippi Council, asserted that the IQ of blacks was between 15 and 20 points below the average for whites.

Segregationists were especially prone to utilize the writings of Carleton Putnam and Carleton Coon. Putnam, a native of the North and a retired airline executive, was the author of *Race and Reason: A Yankee View*

(1961). He first came to the attention of segregationists in 1958 through an open letter to President Eisenhower in which he defended segregation. In *Race and Reason* Putnam asserted that blacks were intellectually inferior and that the American public had been misled by a "pseudo-scientific hoax" put forth by anthropologists who were advocates of "racial equipotentiality."

Coon, a former president of the American Association of Physical Anthropologists, was the author of *The Origin of Races* (1962). In this study Coon concluded that over 500,000 years ago one species of man, *homo erectus*, existed. According to Coon, *homo erectus* evolved into *homo sapiens* at different times and in different geographic locations. Five such evolutionary processes occurred. His research also led Coon to conclude that Caucasoids were about 500,000 years ahead of Negroids in terms of evolutionary development.

Segregationists, both those belonging to Citizens' Councils and those holding political office, frequently cited the writings of Coon and Putnam. Southerners were interested in the two men because of the belief that such individuals gave credibility to the segregationists' perspective. Credibility was essential to any campaign designed to convince northerners that the South should be allowed to continue its way of life.

From a political perspective southerners resorted to the compact theory of government in their effort to overturn the *Brown* decision and to protect regional values. Drawing upon the writings of Jefferson and Calhoun, southern theorists concluded that the *Brown* ruling was unconstitutional. According to this rationale, public education was constitutionally a function of the states and not the federal government. Therefore, the Supreme Court had exceeded its authority by amending the Constitution, rather than merely interpreting it. In the effort to nullify the Court's action, southern politicians proposed to utilize the tools of massive resistance and interposition.

Interposition, a doctrine adopted by eight southern states in 1956 and 1957, was designed to defeat court-ordered desegregation. Under the plan, the sovereignty of the state would be interposed between the federal courts and local school officials. Advocates of the doctrine were convinced that federal judges would not issue contempt of court citations and jail governors and other elected state officials who refused to obey desegregation orders. Critical to the success of the plan was regionwide noncompliance. Total or near-total opposition to desegregation would persuade northerners to abandon efforts to force the South to give up its way of life.

The campaign for massive resistance was encouraged by southerners serving in Congress. In 1956 all but 27 of the southerners in Congress signed a "Southern Manifesto" in which they urged the states to resist integration. Likewise, pressure was brought to bear upon newspaper editors to ensure that they not encourage compliance with the law. And in Orangeburg, S.C., economic pressure was applied to those black parents who had petitioned to have their children attend desegregated schools; the schools in Orangeburg remained segregated. Meanwhile, schools in portions of some states (Prince Edward County, Va., for example) were closed to prevent integration. Several states favored the idea of closing the public schools and providing tuition grants to students who would attend private segregated schools. Finally, in four states (Alabama, Mississippi, Florida, and Georgia) the doctrine of nullification was implemented as legal action was taken to declare the *Brown* decision to be null and void. In these four states, as well as others in the old Confederacy, over 450 new segregation measures were passed. The new laws protected segregation and made desegregation illegal.

With the coming of the sit-in movement and the freedom rides of the 1960s, violence began to characterize part of the resistance to change. In *SNCC: The New Abolitionists* (1964), Howard Zinn describes the violence that confronted civil rights workers. Among the more prominent acts of violence perpetrated upon civil rights workers were the fire-bombing of a bus carrying freedom riders at Anniston, Ala. (1961), the murders in Mississippi of Medgar Evers (1963) and of three civil rights field-workers—Andrew Goodman, James Chaney, and Michael Schwerner (1964)—and the police violence of law enforcement officials in Birmingham, Ala. (1963). In Birmingham police used fire hoses and police dogs against demonstrators, many of whom were children. The use of force against civil rights activists was counterproductive. Each night citizens throughout the land who watched the evening news on television witnessed acts of violence being perpetrated upon fellow Americans. Northerners, as well as many white southerners, were shocked by the tactics of Birmingham officials. Equally disturbing to Americans was the bombing of Birmingham's Sixteenth Street Baptist Church, an incident that killed four black children who were attending Sunday school. Without doubt the acts of violence destroyed any sympathy that southern propagandists had created in the North and stimulated the passage of the Civil Rights Act of 1964.

By the mid-1960s the civil rights movement had moved beyond the limits of the South and into the North's ghettoes. Here the frustrations associated with joblessness, poverty, and hopelessness led to the long hot summers of rioting, burning, and looting. As the nation's great cities burned, a white backlash against blacks became apparent. Governor George Wallace of Alabama exploited this backlash, as well as a growing working-class anger with student demonstrators, antiwar activists, and the nation's welfare system. Using a "law and order" argument that had strong racial overtones, Wallace emerged as a national political force. As the candidate of the American Independent party in 1968, he won 46 electoral votes and 13.5 percent of the popular vote.

In the final analysis, southern attempts to maintain legal segregation failed. Indeed, not one of the tactics employed brought eventual success. Americans rejected the outdated belief that blacks are inherently inferior. Interposition ultimately forced whites to decide that desegregated schools were preferable to no schools. Violence was counterproductive. And even a majority of the South's voters rejected the third party candidacies of Thurmond in 1948 and Wallace in 1968.

Just as there was no clearly defined beginning to the

South's resistance to change, there is no clearly defined end. As legal segregation was abolished, patterns of de facto segregation emerged. Whites fled to the suburbs, argued in favor of neighborhood schools, and opposed court-ordered busing of students to achieve racially balanced schools. In the final analysis, the types of race-related problems that now exist in the South are essentially the same as those that exist elsewhere in the nation.

See also BLACK LIFE: Freedom Movement, Black; Race Relations; / Citizens' Councils; LAW: Civil Rights Movement; / *Brown* v. *Board of Education*; MYTHIC SOUTH: Racial Attitudes

William J. Brophy
Stephen F. Austin State University

Taxing and Spending

Southern state governments have long been distinguished by their relatively low levels of government spending and taxation, and by the often regressive nature of their tax systems. Three examples illustrate: (1) southern states spent an average of $1,657 per pupil for education in 1977–78, while the national average was $2,002; (2) the average southern state spent 0.11 percent of its total expenditures on land and water quality control while the national average was 0.31 percent; (3) the average southern state's Aid to Families with Dependent Children grant received an "adequacy score" of 8.09 percent while the national average was 13.58 percent.

Southern states generally obtain a greater share of their operating revenue from sales taxes than other states do, and their income-tax structures are often less progressive. In fact, one of the few southern governmental innovations was the sales tax itself, pioneered by Mississippi in 1934. These tax patterns help to account for the widely held perception that the southern states are not normally as active, vigorous, or "forward-thinking" as the rest of the country.

Perhaps because governments are often evaluated on the basis of their taxing and spending policies, much research has been devoted to a systematic analysis of the causes and effects of the distinctive southern patterns of taxing and spending. An appreciation of the issues addressed in these studies is necessary to understand the extent to which southern cultural traditions and circumstances are related to the fiscal policies so readily observed.

The most frequently cited explanation for southern taxing and spending patterns is the traditional absence of effective party competition. V. O. Key, Jr., suggested that one-party states spend less on social programs than states with a competitive structure simply because a single dominant party does not have to advocate and implement responsive policies in order to win elections. This notion appeared to have considerable validity when it was advanced in the 1940s, because it was consistent with impressionistic and anecdotal accounts of one-party politics and because it was derived from a straightforward theory of parties and government. The degree of party competition and the level of government spending for various social programs were statistically associated when all states were compared, and this provided additional support for Key's argument.

Key's theory became widely accepted and provided a solid foundation for linking basic southern political characteristics to public policy choices. Certainly, the tradition of Democratic party dominance is a fundamental part of the southern political heritage, and it was not surprising that government expenditures reflected its influence. However, by the 1960s a different view was presented by scholars, particularly Thomas R. Dye. Low government spending and regressive taxation could be explained by economic variables. According to Dye, "when the effects of economic development are controlled . . . almost all of the association between party competition and policy disappears."

This finding, and the voluminous research that it spawned, was unsettling to many students of politics because it suggested that basic political factors, such as party competition, were not important in terms of public policy. It also directly challenged the notion that the special character of southern politics and culture was fundamentally important in explaining why southern governments behaved differently; Dye's research indicated that *any* poor, rural state would adopt the taxing and spending patterns associated with the South.

The most compelling responses to Dye's line of reasoning emphasized political culture. Daniel Elazar suggested that three political subcultures can be identified among the American states—moralistic, individualistic, and traditionalistic. The southern states generally are dominated by traditionalistic subcultures, according to Elazar, which means that their governments should be expected to "maintain traditional patterns" and to be generally conservative in public policy. Conversely, moralistic states, such as Minnesota, Oregon, and Wisconsin, use government to further a representative conception of the good of the "commonwealth." Individualistic states have both moralistic and traditionalistic traits.

In 1969 Ira Sharkansky performed a systematic comparison of the states Elazar identified as moralistic, traditionalistic, and individualistic to determine whether they actually were different in the ways Elazar predicted and, more importantly, to determine whether the differences were simply a result of differences in economic and industrial development. Sharkansky found that the cultural differences were still important after the effects of the economic variables were taken into account. Southern states, with traditionalistic cultures, spent less on certain social programs and had fewer public employees per capita than other states, even those with similar economic circumstances.

The regional norms thus identified have been persistent. Sharkansky reports that "during 1952–1974, per capita personal income in the old Confederacy went from 68 percent of the national average to 83 percent of the national average. Meanwhile, state expenditures per capita moved only slightly, from 87 percent to 88 percent of the national average."

The distinctive southern character identified by novelists, essayists, and journalists apparently has a real effect on the most tangible and concrete aspects of government—taxing and spending. Southerners are not as likely as their northern compatriots to turn to government for various social purposes or to redistribute income, even when their states become economically developed. Analysis of the more simplistic versions of V. O. Key, Jr.'s, ideas indicates, however, that the effect of southern culture on government policy is complicated, and that economic factors are critical in explaining much regional variety.

Marcus Ethridge
University of Wisconsin
at Milwaukee

Thomas R. Dye, *Politics, Economics, and the Public: Policy Outcome in the American States* (1966); Daniel Elazar, *American Federalism: A View from the States* (2d ed., 1972); Virginia Gray, Herbert Jacob, and Kenneth Vines, eds., *Politics in the American States: A Comparative Analysis* (1983); V. O. Key, Jr., *Southern Politics in State and Nation* (1949); Ira Sharkansky, *The Maligned States: Policy Accomplishments, Problems, and Opportunities* (2d ed., 1978).

Voting

"Among the great democracies of the world," V. O. Key, Jr., noted in 1949, "the Southern states remain the chief considerable area in which an extremely small proportion of citizens vote." Yet the South has not always been the most backward, least democratic region in the Western world. Although other countries have, gradually or in sudden spurts, expanded the proportion of their citizens who enjoy and exercise the right to vote, the United States has followed a zigzag, not a linear, path. Born comparatively free, America contracted as well as expanded its suffrage thereafter. In its patterns of voting participation, as in other facets of society, the South exaggerated national trends.

Suffrage theory of the colonial South, like that of the colonial North, mimicked Britain's. "The laws of England," the Virginia Legislature declared in 1655, "grant a voice in such election only to such as by their estates real or personal have interest enough to tie them to the endeavor of the public good." Accordingly, during most of the colonial period, only property holders could vote. Because of the much greater availability of land in the New World, however, freehold suffrage in practice enfranchised a much higher proportion of the free adult males in America than in the mother country. Substantial majorities, in Virginia as well as in Massachusetts, could and did vote. Property restrictions for officeholding, some class deference, and the common interest of large and small planters, in addition to the wider reputations and greater availability of time and money enjoyed by the economic elite, guaranteed men of standing a disproportionate share of the political posts. Yet their tenure existed only at the sufferance of their neighbors (social inferiors, but often political near-equals), and they failed to pay at least rhetorical tribute to white male equality at their peril.

Two factors—legal restrictions on the suffrage and the degree of party competition—have chiefly determined voter turnout levels in the South, and, of these, the former has been much more important. As Figure 3 shows, the pattern of voter participation in the 11 ex-Confederate states was quite similar to that in the other states of the Union from 1840 through the 1880s. The massive divergence that Key noted opened up only after 1892, as southern states passed laws and standardized administrative practices that disfranchised large proportions of blacks and poorer whites. Designed to have a disproportionately adverse impact on the Republican and Populist parties, the restrictive laws virtually ended party competition in most of the South, thereby further discouraging people from voting. Even though literacy tests and other restraints on the suffrage were employed in the North as well as the South, the qualifications were not applied as severely above the Mason-Dixon line. Since 1940, as blacks gradually regained the vote and as Republicans contested more and more elections in the South, participation rates in the two sections have converged. By 1980 the difference in turnout was only 8 percent.

Although the 20th-century sectional gulf in Figure 3 is the most striking, other facets of the graph also deserve attention. In this as in many cases, the choice of the denominator presents a moral problem. Few free black males and no male slaves or women of any status were allowed to vote before 1860. Had black males, slave and emancipated, instead of only adult white males, been included in the antebellum denominators, southern turnout would have been only about two-thirds as high as northern in the antebellum period. Had women been counted, both lines would have shifted downward.

Following convention by calculating turnout on the basis of all males, regardless of race, in the denominator from 1868 to 1908, adding females in a few non-southern states in 1912 and 1916 and in all states thereafter, also hides two shifts that did *not* take place in the South. There were no overall voting declines as a result of the addition of freedmen and women to the voting polls. In 1860, 67 percent of the southern adult white males voted. In 1868, in the seven southern states that held elections, 70 percent of southern adult males, black as well as white, turned out. When compared to the political behavior of the early- or mid-19th-century British or the late-20th-century American voter of lower social status, it seems amazing that such a large portion of the poverty-stricken, largely illiterate, recently slave population should have voted. Just as impressive, they overwhelmingly opposed the wishes of their former owners and then-current landlords. And whereas northern turnout dropped by more than 10 percent with the expansion of women's suffrage, southern women appear to have

Figure 3. Voting Turnout for President, by Region

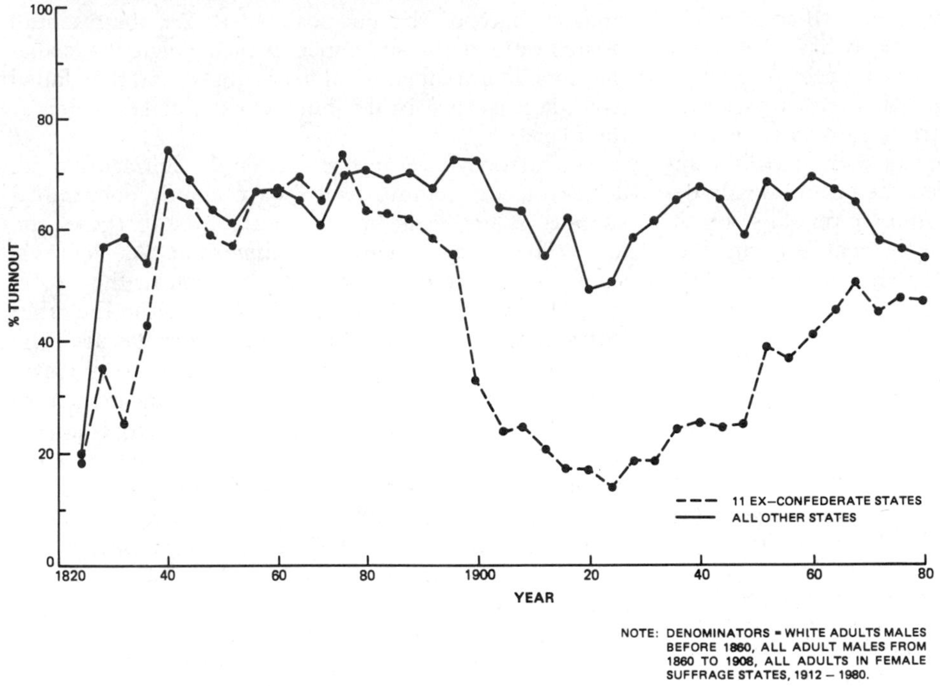

Source: U.S. Commission on Civil Rights, *Political Participation* (1968).

Figure 4. Voting Turnout, Whites Only, in the Eleven Ex-Confederate States

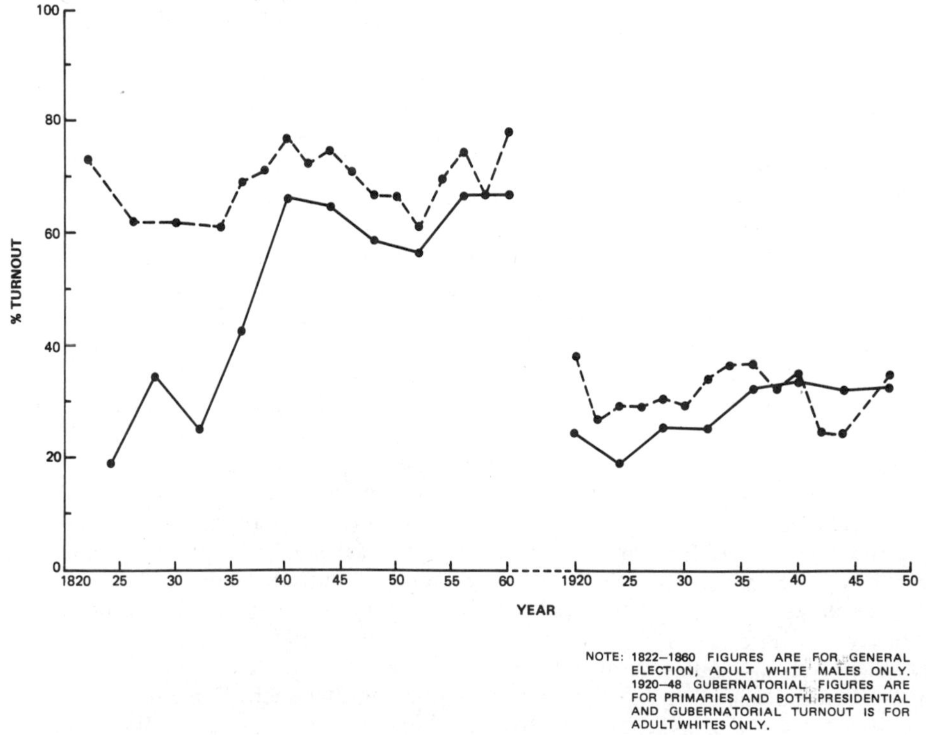

Source: U.S. Commission on Civil Rights, *Political Participation* (1968).

bounded off their pedestals to participate in politics in approximately the same—very low—proportion as the men.

Figure 4 lays to rest two other hoary notions. First, the left section of the graph shows that the high level of antebellum southern turnout was not merely a product of contests for the presidency or of Jacksonian democracy. Southern governors' races attracted large majorities of the adult white males long before battles for the White House did and continued to attract somewhat higher proportions of voters than presidential elections after the Old Hero retired. Second, although the Democratic primaries constituted the real elections in the first half of this century, the right portion of Figure 4 shows that turnout in those races barely exceeded that in southern presidential contests: only about one of three southern white adults generally managed to cast ballots. Competition unstructured by parties did not foster participation; blacks were not the only ones deterred by the post-Populist southern political system.

In 1938 Ralph Bunche estimated that but 4 percent of southern blacks could vote. Legal attacks on the white primary, the poll tax, and other restrictive devices, culminating in the passage of the 1965 national Voting Rights Act, in addition to the return to the South of a Republican party that was almost the negative image of its Reconstruction-era predecessor, vastly increased political activity among all groups, whites as well as blacks and Latinos. The vote brought change, real and symbolic. Public services expanded and were opened more freely to all. Black and Spanish-surnamed southern mayors and congressmen became almost common. Former race baiters kissed black babies and black homecoming queens. Yet in many rural areas and small cities, harsh discrimination persisted; and electoral structures, such as at-large provisions, which had the intent and effect of diminishing minority political power, discouraged blacks and Latinos from voting and diluted the impact of their franchises when they did turn out. The struggle to guarantee equal political opportunity in the South continues.

J. Morgan Kousser
California Institute of Technology

See also BLACK LIFE: Politics, Black

Robert E. Brown and B. Katherine Brown, *Virginia, 1705–1786: Democracy or Aristocracy?* (1964); Ralph J. Bunche, *The Political Status of the Negro in the Age of FDR* (1973); V. O. Key, Jr., *Southern Politics in State and Nation* (1949); J. Morgan Kousser, *The Shaping of Southern Politics: Suffrage Restriction and the Establishment of the One-Party South, 1880–1910* (1974); Steven F. Lawson, *Black Ballots: Voting Rights in the South, 1944–1969* (1976); U.S. Commission on Civil Rights, *Political Participation* (1968), *The Voting Rights Act: Ten Years After* (1975), *The Voting Rights Act: Unfulfilled Goals* (1981); Chilton Williamson, *American Suffrage from Property to Democracy, 1760–1860* (1960).

Women in Politics

See WOMEN'S LIFE: Politics, Women in

Baker, Howard, Jr.

(b. 1925) Politician.

Baker is the heir to a rich tradition of Republican politics. His family has lived in mountainous east Tennessee since the 1700s, and Baker still makes his home in the small town of Huntsville. Both his father and his stepmother served in the House of Representatives, and Baker's father-in-law, Republican Everett Dirksen of Illinois, was Senate minority leader in the 1950s and 1960s. Republicans have won every congressional election since 1858 in Baker's native second district. A World War II veteran, Baker returned from the war to earn a law degree at the University of Tennessee and began a lucrative practice with the law firm his grandfather had established in 1885. Banking, coal, and real estate investments made him a wealthy man.

Baker entered elective politics in 1964 as a candidate for the U.S. Senate. Defeated after a strong campaign, he ran again two years later and became the state's first popularly elected Republican senator. Baker's success heralded a Republican surge in Tennessee that enabled the party to capture the state's other Senate seat and the governor's mansion in 1970. Baker is a bridge between two important sources of Republican strength in the South. Through his family he is linked to the mountain Republicanism that has flourished in Tennessee since the Civil War, but he is also popular with educated, affluent, white business and professional people across the state who have built the southern Republican party into a significant force.

Baker first attracted national attention with his skillful performance as the ranking Republican on the Senate Watergate Committee in 1973. Three years later he won the post of minority leader and became majority leader when the Republicans took over the Senate after the 1980 elections. Ambitious for national office, Baker was frequently considered for a vice-presidential nomination, but his bid for the White House in 1980 fizzled early in the campaign. The hallmark of Baker's Senate career was an emphasis on leadership through consensus. A centrist by instinct, his temperate rhetoric and charming manner made him highly effective in the clubby atmosphere of the Senate, although some conservative members of his own party were skeptical of his ideological leanings. He retired from the Senate in 1985 but returned to the national scene in 1987 as President Reagan's chief of staff. Proud to be called a professional politician, Baker typified the moderate stance long characteristic of Tennessee politics.

David D. Lee
Western Kentucky University

Jack Bass and Walter DeVries, *The Transformation of Southern Politics: Social Change and Political Consequences since 1945*

(1976); Robert Corlew, *Tennessee: A Short History* (1981); Neal Peirce, *The Border South States: People, Politics and Power in the Five States of the Border South* (1975).

Barnett, Ross

(1898–1988) Politician.

Ross Robert Barnett became a symbol of resistance to integration as governor of Mississippi because he precipitated a riot on the campus of the University of Mississippi against federal marshals attempting to register the first black in a "white" Mississippi educational institution. Born the last of a Civil War veteran's 10 children in the Standing Pine community of Leake County, Barnett struggled against poverty to educate himself. While a student at the county agricultural high school, he worked as a janitor and a barber. He continued those occupations and sold aluminum cookware in the summer during his years at Mississippi College. After graduation he taught school and coached in Pontotoc before attending law school at Vanderbilt and the University of Mississippi. Moving to Jackson in 1926, he opened an independent practice. In 1943 he was elected president of the state bar association and by 1951 was secure enough to attempt to fulfill his boyhood dream of becoming governor. Without political experience and never having held a public post, he launched his first campaign for the state's highest office. He lost badly in the primaries of 1951 and 1955. But in 1959 the Citizens' Council wanted an ardent segregationist as its candidate, and Barnett was a complete racist.

While other candidates temporized by calling blacks "niggras," Barnett openly said "nigger" and told audiences, "The Negro is different because God made him different to punish him." Aside from his racism, Barnett was known for his folksy humor, but not all of it was intentional. He once told the Beth-Israel Temple in Jackson that "there is nothing finer than a group of people meeting in true Christian fellowship." Asked what could be done about (the disputed Chinese islands of) Quemoy and Matsu, Barnett responded, "Well, I expect we could find a place for them in the Fish and Game Commission."

The first year of his administration was less than successful. His was "good old boy" style government, and he fought with the legislature for control of state agencies in order to provide the needed jobs. His primary contribution as governor was to promote industrial development through effective, prompt government service to industry, using his sales skills over promotional breakfasts with businessmen at the mansion.

When the federal courts ordered the University of Mississippi to admit James Meredith, a black man, Barnett defied the courts and was found in contempt. He answered Washington's demands with public assertions of state sovereignty while he secretly dealt with President John Kennedy and Attorney General Robert Kennedy. But the secret deal failed because Barnett could not resist playing to the public at an Ole Miss football game just prior to Meredith's enrollment. With over 40,000 people waving Confederate flags and singing "Go Mississippi" to the tune of his campaign song, Barnett said, "I love Mississippi. I love our people. I love our customs." His campaign publicist has written of the moment, "As he stood there, smiling, acknowledging the cheers of the multitude, he was more than just a governor of Mississippi. He was a symbol of the South, with the red blood of his Confederate soldier father running through his veins. He represented the traditions that emerged after Reconstruction, a way of life that white southerners had vowed to continue." After some of the cheering crowd returned to Oxford to riot against federal authority, Barnett surrendered to overwhelming military force.

Despite his surrender, Barnett was enormously popular at the end of his term, a symbol of defeated but unbowed resistance to integration. Political observers predicted that he would dominate state politics for years, but he chose not to run for the U.S. Senate immediately, and as the story of his secret dealings with the Kennedys leaked out, his popularity waned. Another segregationist defeated him in the next gubernatorial primary, and Barnett was reduced quickly to a dated relic of a discredited philosophy. He appeared regularly at the Neshoba County Fair to entertain with stories and songs but had no more role in politics.

Dennis J. Mitchell
Jackson State University

Erie Johnson, *I Rolled with Ross: A Political Portrait* (1980); Robert Sherrill, *Gothic Politics in the Deep South* (1968).

Bilbo, Theodore

(1877–1947) Politician.

Theodore Gilmore Bilbo was born at Juniper Grove in Pearl River County, Miss., on 13 October 1877. He attended public school in Pearl River County and took courses but never earned a degree at Peabody College, Vanderbilt University, and the University of Michigan. He first entered politics in 1903 but was defeated for county clerk by a one-armed Confederate veteran. Displaying a sense of humor that would be a part of his political style, Bilbo confided to friends that he "started to vote for him myself."

Bilbo's 40-year political career was punctuated by victories and defeats. He served as state senator from 1908 to 1912. He became famous statewide for his involvement in "The Secret Causes" of 1910, during which he accepted a bribe in order to gain evidence that James K. Vardaman's opponents were bribing legislators. A vote to expel him from the state senate fell one vote short of the two-thirds necessary. In 1911 he was elected lieutenant governor and thereby became the presiding officer of the senate. Although implicated in a conflict-of-interest scandal while lieutenant governor, Bilbo was elected governor in 1915. His first administration was tainted by charges of sexual improprieties, and he lost a bid for the U.S. Congress in 1918. In 1922 he postponed a bid for a

U.S. Senate seat because he was jailed by a federal judge for refusing to honor a summons to testify in the seduction and breach-of-promise suit filed against Governor Lee Russell by a former secretary. Instead, Bilbo announced his candidacy for governor in 1923 but was defeated. In 1927 he ran again and won.

During his second administration, 1928–32, Bilbo became deeply involved in the governance of higher education. After the legislature refused to restructure the governing boards and relocate the University of Mississippi from Oxford to Jackson, Governor Bilbo, as chairman of the three existing governing boards, ordered extensive personnel changes at most of the state's colleges, but especially at the state university, the agricultural college, and the women's college. Bilbo's intrusion into personnel matters was neither new nor unusual. The state's institutions of higher learning had long been subject to the fury of factional politics. It was the epic sweep of his purge and his disdain for the Southern Association of Colleges and its accrediting standards that prompted several accrediting agencies to censure or withdraw their accreditation from the Mississippi institutions of higher learning.

After Governor Bilbo's second term expired, he organized a campaign for the U.S. Senate. In 1934 he was elected, then reelected in 1940 and 1946. Early in his senatorial career he was an ardent New Dealer, but as relief and recovery gradually gave way to reform his ardor waned. He did, however, strongly endorse President Franklin D. Roosevelt's war policies.

In 1946 Senator Bilbo was confronted by two very serious challenges to his seat. First, a Senate investigating committee had prepared conflict-of-interest charges against him and planned to challenge his right to be sworn in for his third term. Secondly, a group of black Mississippians had filed suit seeking to overturn his reelection in 1946 on the grounds that large numbers of blacks had been systematically denied the right to vote in the Democratic primary.

However, before either of those two challenges could be resolved, Senator Bilbo, whose health had been declining rapidly during the past several months, was admitted to Ochsner's Clinic in New Orleans. He died on 21 August 1947.

David Sansing
University of Mississippi

Theodore Bilbo, Manuscripts, University of Southern Mississippi; A. W. Green, *The Man Bilbo* (1963); Chester M. Morgan, *Redneck Liberal: Theodore G. Bilbo and the New Deal* (1985).

Byrd Machine

The Byrd machine of Virginia (1922–65) was an expression of the unique cultural and political heritage of the Old Dominion, which cherished elitist and traditional values. Created by Harry Flood Byrd, Sr., and other members of the state Democratic party during the 1920s, the machine took advantage of restrictive electoral regulations that made it possible for a small percentage of conservative rural and small-town white voters to control elective offices. Byrd served successively as state party chairman, governor, and U.S. senator (1933–65). At his retirement in 1965, Byrd arranged to have his Senate seat passed to his son, Harry Flood Byrd, Jr.

During the 1930s Byrd joined other southern Democratic and Republican conservatives to oppose the more liberal politics of the New Deal administration of Franklin D. Roosevelt. However, as urban areas in northern and southeastern Virginia developed after World War II, the control of the machine was gradually eroded. The machine's last stand was to organize a "massive resistance" campaign to oppose court-ordered integration of public schools after 1954. By the time Byrd retired from the Senate in 1965, the machine was ill-defined and many of its former loyalists had defected to the growing ranks of the southern Republican party.

Raymond H. Pulley
Appalachian State University

Harry Flood Byrd, Sr., Papers, University of Virginia; Raymond H. Pulley, *Old Virginia Restored: An Interpretation of the Progressive Impulse, 1870–1930* (1968); Francis M. Wilhoit, *The Politics of Massive Resistance* (1973); J. Harvey Wilkinson III, *Harry Byrd and the Changing Face of Virginia Politics, 1945–1966* (1968).

Calhoun, John C.

(1782–1850) Politician and political philosopher.

Born of Scotch-Irish ancestry in the South Carolina upcountry in the wake of the American Revolution, John Caldwell Calhoun traveled north for his education. He graduated from Yale and read law with Federalist judge Tapping Reeve in Litchfield, Conn. Calhoun returned home, practiced law, won a seat in the legislature, and then represented South Carolina in the U.S. Congress from 1811 to 1817. A devout nationalist during this phase of his career, Calhoun was a War Hawk and an avid supporter of the War of 1812. He voted for a protective tariff in 1816 and introduced the bill chartering the Second Bank of the United States in 1817. He served as secretary of war in James Monroe's cabinet and in 1824 won election as vice president of the United States.

Calhoun was elected vice president again in 1828 and entered the administration of Andrew Jackson as heir apparent to the presidency. Within four years, however, Calhoun and Jackson were bitter enemies; Calhoun had resigned his office, and he had become an ardent sectionalist. Calhoun's *South Carolina Exposition and Protest* was the philosophical underpinning of the nullification movement in South Carolina. During the nullification crisis and after, Calhoun devoted his energies and considerable talents to the minority interests of the South. As South Carolina senator and during a brief term as John Tyler's secretary of state (1844–45), Calhoun was the South's political champion and spokesman.

In a sense Calhoun's career in public life embodied southern political behavior. A nationalist during the Virginia Dynasty, he became a sectionalist when he came to believe that nationalism conflicted with southern interests. To his death in 1850 Calhoun fought the South's political battles with considerable skill. His greatest significance, however, lay in his capacity for political thought and analysis. His prime concern was for minority interests in American democracy. He believed the Union to be a compact; southern states had entered the compact when they ratified the Constitution, and they were free to dissolve the compact and leave the Union if they so chose. However, Calhoun revered the Union and attempted to discover some moderate constitutional course that would preserve both southern interests and the Union, and that would offer the minority South some alternatives to submission and secession. He never resolved the dilemma, but in the process of defining and articulating the southern political stance, Calhoun became a constructive critic of American democracy and perhaps the foremost American political thinker of the 19th century.

Emory Thomas
University of Georgia

Gerald M. Capers, *John C. Calhoun, Opportunist: A Reappraisal* (1960); Margaret L. Coit, *John C. Calhoun: American Portrait* (1950); Richard N. Current, *John C. Calhoun* (1963); Charles M. Wiltse, *John C. Calhoun, Nullifier, 1829–1839* (1949).

Carter, Jimmy

(b. 1924) Politician.

"I am a Southerner and an American," Jimmy Carter wrote in his campaign autobiography, *Why Not the Best*? It would be difficult to quarrel with either assertion. Born and reared in the heart of the southwest Georgia Black Belt, James Earl "Jimmy" Carter could trace both his American and southern ancestry back to the early 17th century when the first Carters arrived in Virginia. By the decade of the 1780s ancestors of the future president had made their way to Georgia, eventually settling in Sumter County where Jimmy Carter was born and raised.

The son of a moderately wealthy landowner and businessman, Carter, like many of the other progeny of upper-middle-class southerners, aspired to a military career. After completing his elementary and secondary education in Plains and matriculating for a year at Georgia Southwestern College in nearby Americus, he enrolled in the naval ROTC program at the Georgia Institute of Technology prior to securing an appointment to the U.S. Naval Academy in Annapolis. There the young cadet did well, finishing in the upper 10 percent of his 1946 graduating class. Thereafter, he entered the submarine service after completing his required two years of surface duty.

The young naval officer's promising military career ended in 1953, however, when he returned to Plains to manage the family's business affairs after the death of his father. Within a few years of his return, he was deeply involved in a variety of community affairs and soon was campaigning for the state senate seat once held by his father. After two terms in the Georgia General Assembly, Carter ran unsuccessfully for the Democratic gubernatorial nomination in 1966 before succeeding in the same quest four years later.

On the first day of his governorship, Carter attracted national attention by dramatically proclaiming that the time for racial discrimination in Georgia had ended. During the next four years Carter promoted a moderately liberal, business-progressive reform program, which included state government reorganization, judicial reform, consumer protection, welfare reform, tax reform, and environmental concerns. Following through on earlier commitments, he also appointed numerous black Georgians and women to important positions in state government. Unable to succeed himself in the governorship, Carter in 1974 began laying the groundwork for a successful run for the presidency of the United States. His 1976 campaign focused national attention on changes in the South in the previous decade. Carter played a crucial role within the South in strengthening, at least temporarily, a black-white coalition in the Democratic party. He won black support and also appealed to the white rural South. For the first time since 1964, Democratic politicians across the South enthusiastically supported their party's presidential nominee.

Once installed in the presidential office, Carter, with less success, sought to push the same type of reforms that he had sponsored during his governorship. Domestic economic programs and international crises contributed to Carter's presidential woes, however, and in 1980 he was repudiated by the same voters, many of them southerners, who had supported him four years earlier. Several weeks later he was back in Plains, from which he had launched his meteoric rise to national prominence a few years earlier.

An unorthodox politician in many ways, Carter nevertheless was clearly a product of the southern culture into which he was born and in which he was raised. An inherited sense of noblesse oblige, which he shared with numerous others in the southern elite, combined in Carter with religious convictions (he was a "born again" Baptist) and a sense of history to produce a code of social ethics that permitted him to transcend the race issue that had been the burden of so many other white southerners. Carter's rise to the presidency thus represented, symbolically at least, the ultimate reunification of the South with the rest of the nation.

See also MYTHIC SOUTH: / Carter Era

Gary M. Fink
Georgia State University

Gary M. Fink, *Prelude to the Presidency: The Political Character and Legislative Leadership Style of Governor Jimmy Carter* (1980); David Kucharsky, *The Man from Plains: The Mind and*

Spirit of Jimmy Carter (1975); William L. Miller, *Yankee from Georgia: The Emergence of Jimmy Carter* (1978).

Crump, E. H.

(1874–1954) Politician.

Born and raised in Holly Springs, Miss., Edward Hull Crump moved to Memphis as a young man. His business efforts prospered, especially his insurance firm, and Crump eventually built a sizable personal fortune. Politically active almost from his arrival in Memphis, Crump was elected mayor in 1909, 1911, and 1915, but his refusal to enforce Tennessee's prohibition law prompted the state to initiate legal proceedings, which resulted in his resignation in 1916. Despite the setback, Crump continued to build a political machine that, by the mid-1920s, utterly dominated the large Shelby County vote. In 1932 the Crump-backed candidate for governor won election, and for the next 16 years the Memphis boss and his organization influenced the outcome of most major statewide races. Finally, in 1948, insurgents led by Estes Kefauver and Gordon Browning defeated the Crump choices for senator and governor in the Democratic primary. His power across Tennessee substantially weakened, Crump still controlled Memphis politics until his death in 1954.

A self-described progressive, Crump stressed efficient government and improved public services, policies that generally kept him in good stead with respectable Memphis business leaders, as did his bitter opposition to unions. At the same time, however, the Crump machine was closely linked to the Bluff City's seamy vice trade, a prime source of money and votes for organization candidates. The Crump machine also included the local black community, tied to the boss by his special blend of patronage and coercion. Consequently, Memphis was one of the few places in the South that tolerated black voting during the segregation era. W. C. Handy celebrated Crump in his "Memphis Blues" (1912), a catchy tune that the mayor then used to gain black and white votes. "Mister Crump don't 'low no easy riders here," it said. Crump delighted in conducting well-publicized charity drives to benefit various causes, but he dealt harshly with potential opponents. City bureaucrats and policemen harassed his critics, while curious reporters and persistent labor organizers occasionally encountered strong-arm tactics. Although many Crump policies and practices were generally typical of machine politics in other parts of the country, Crump himself struck the pose of the paternalistic southern gentleman. Dapper and flamboyant, he was an unusually visible political boss who often castigated his enemies in splashy newspaper advertisements. A uniquely skillful politician, Crump wielded more power outside his own city than any other urban boss in the South.

E. H. Crump, mayor of Memphis, Tenn., c. 1940

See also URBANIZATION: / Memphis

David D. Lee
Western Kentucky University

William Miller, *Mr. Crump of Memphis* (1964), *Memphis during the Progressive Era, 1900–1917* (1957); David Tucker, *Memphis since Crump: Bossism, Blacks, and Civic Reformers, 1948–1968* (1980).

Dixiecrats

In 1948 several southern Democrats rejected the liberal leadership of their national party and pursued an independent course. At issue was President Harry Truman's proposal on civil rights that advocated an antilynching law, a permanent fair employment practices commission, desegregation of the armed forces, and elimination of the poll tax. After a special committee of the Southern Governors' Conference unsuccessfully sought concessions on civil rights from the Democratic National Committee, many southerners, fearing the destruction of their regional traditions, considered a revolt against the national party. Under the guidance of Fielding Wright of Mississippi, Frank Dixon of Alabama, Strom Thurmond of South Carolina, and Leander Perez of Louisiana, disgruntled southerners launched a grass-roots organization in the region.

When the South failed to prevent the nomination of Truman at the Democratic national convention in Philadelphia and suffered reversals on civil rights, the rights of states to control tidelands' oil reserves, and the two-thirds rule , several delegates bolted. Six thousand southerners, mainly from Mississippi and Alabama, met later in Birmingham. Influenced by Charles Wallace Collins's *Whither Solid South*? (1947) and seeking to force the presidential election into the House of Representatives, these states' rights supporters "recommended" a separate ticket of Thurmond and Wright. Although race was clearly their key concern, the States' Rights Democrats included, in addition to white supremacists, antiunion industrialist oilmen and constitutional conservatives who abhorred civil rights and communism. Branded "Dixiecrats" by Bill Weisner of the Charlotte *News*, the dissident southerners advanced no positive programs, sought primarily to save the South from the clutches of political modernism, and reflected a historical consciousness that romanticized their regional past and social heritage.

Although States' Rights Democrats generally opposed the creation of a separate southern party, they seized control of the party machinery in Alabama, Mississippi, Louisiana, and South Carolina. Thurmond carried these four states, where he appeared on the ballot as the Democratic nominee and received 1.2 million votes, but Truman triumphed in the remainder of the South and won the election. Throughout the controversy, most prominent southern leaders stayed within the Democratic party. After the election, the Dixiecrat movement evaporated. The South's vocal dissent in 1948, however, forecast the sectional unrest of the following decades, weakened the region's loyalty to the Democratic party, and prepared the way for future political realignment.

Edward F. Haas
Louisiana State Museum
Tulane University

Richard C. Etheridge, "Mississippi's Role in the Dixiecrat Movement" (Ph.D. dissertation, Mississippi State University, 1971); Robert A. Garson, *The Democratic Party and the Politics of Sectionalism, 1941–1948* (1974); Gary C. Ness, "The States' Rights Democratic Movement of 1948" (Ph.D. dissertation, Duke University, 1972).

Faubus, Orval

(b. 1910) Politician.

Six-term governor of Arkansas (1955–67), Orval Eugene Faubus gained notoriety around the world in 1957 for his defiance of the federal government in preventing the integration of Little Rock Central High School. Faubus quickly became one of the powerful symbols of southern resistance to desegregation, embodying in his person—and especially in his rhetoric—much that was of value to the South. Of humble origins, Faubus communicated effectively his distaste for the city and for the "Cadillac brigade" that wielded power there. He was a strong individualist who spoke the language of the states' rights advocates and the opponents of big government. Faubus earned the admiration of many southerners (and others) for standing up to the powerful forces that threatened the traditional values of his region. An ambivalent leader who vacillated in his own mind between liberalism and conservatism, Faubus reflected the southern tension between the forces of continuity and change. His folksy manner, his defiant tone, his regard for the common man, and his orientation toward the past all exemplified a southern cultural style, and all contributed to making Orval Faubus a kind of hillbilly hero.

Born in 1910 in the tiny Ozark Mountain community of Combs, Ark., Orval Eugene Faubus was reared in an environment of poverty and political radicalism (his father was a follower of the Socialist, Eugene V. Debs). After three years of military service the young schoolteacher and newspaperman came to the attention of another GI reformer, the liberal Governor Sid McMath, and landed a job on the Arkansas Highway Commission. In 1954 Faubus ran against an incumbent governor and won in one of the most scurrilous elections in Arkansas history. His opponent labeled him a Communist because of his early association with the Commonwealth College. Faubus's first term was uneventful, and he ran successfully for a second term against an arch-segregationist, whom he characterized as a "purveyor of hate." Hardly a model of political conservatism, Orval Faubus approached 1957 with a solid reputation as a moderate.

As Orval Faubus would say years later, 1957 overshadowed everything. His defiant stand against the forces of change and racial injustice earned him momentary fame, six terms as governor, and tremendous power in his own state, but eventually it left him a captive of his image as a racist and an opportunist.

Elizabeth Jacoway
University of Arkansas at
Little Rock

Orval Eugene Faubus, *Down from the Hills* (1980); Willard B. Gatewood, Jr., and Timothy Donovan, eds., *The Governors of Arkansas: Essays in Political Biography* (1981).

Felton, Rebecca

(1835–1930) Politician and writer.

Rebecca Ann Latimer Felton was a strong-willed, outspoken individual who defied the tradition that women should not become involved in politics. She played an active role in the career of her husband, Dr. William H. Felton, an early leader of Georgia's Independent Democrat party. She managed his campaigns, helped draft bills, advised him on legislative strategy, and responded to his critics with innumerable letters to newspapers. She was perfectly capable of vehemently attacking male opponents, but when they responded she condemned them for criticizing a woman. The extent of her role in her husband's career is illustrated by the comment of one of Dr. Felton's opponents that he had been defeated "by the political she of Georgia" and by a newspaper headline that read "Mrs. Felton and Husband Returned."

Rebecca Latimer Felton, Georgia politician and writer, c. 1920s

Felton supported the temperance movement, worked to abolish the convict lease system, and defended state-supported schools against attacks by denominational colleges. She campaigned for vocational training for poor white girls and agitated for admission of women to state universities. She wrote three books and was a columnist for the rural editions of the Atlanta *Journal*. In her columns she defended working conditions in southern cotton mills and criticized child labor laws, Jews, Catholics, and the theory of evolution. Early in the 1900s she became active in the women's suffrage movement, arguing that giving women the vote was necessary to keep power out of the hands of aliens and blacks. Her attacks on blacks were especially virulent. When the Wilmington, N.C., race riot broke out after she had defended lynching, she responded to criticism of her views by advocating that 1,000 blacks be lynched every week if necessary to prevent rapes. When Georgia's U.S. senator died in office, Felton was appointed to complete his term. She served for one day before resigning in favor of the senator-elect.

Rebecca Latimer Felton defies any simple categorization. Although she shared the conservative economic views and intense racial prejudice of many of her southern contemporaries, her feminism set her apart. Unlike many southern women who were involved in the temperance and suffrage movements, she did not move on to work for improved race relations. A rural woman, she enjoyed her role as one of the two lady managers from Georgia at the World's Columbian Exposition in Chicago. Her dogged determination, energy, and outspoken nature resulted in an unusually active public life and made her a force to be reckoned with in her native state.

Jane Walker
Dekalb Community College

Rebecca Felton, *Country Life in Georgia in the Days of My Youth* (1919), *My Memoirs of Georgia Politics* (1911); John E. Talmadge, *Rebecca Latimer Felton: Nine Stormy Decades* (1960).

Folsom, Jim

(b. 1908) Politician.

James Elisha "Big Jim" Folsom won the Alabama governorship in 1946 and 1954. He introduced classic southern populist campaign techniques to the state, using country music, powerful symbols, and humorous parables to appeal directly to the voters. Folsom used campaigns as a platform from which to educate the electorate about the need to fight for their rights against the "Big Mules," meaning the elite. He spoke of the evils of racial discrimination, the need for reapportionment on a one-person, one-vote basis, women's rights, improved education, and better roads.

His forthright and principled campaign speeches were followed by vigorous but mainly unsuccessful attempts as governor to transform rhetoric into reality. His opponents were entrenched in a gerrymandered legislature controlled by Black Belt and Jefferson County (Birmingham) politicians. His efforts were also inhibited by the image, and often the reality, of corruption that surrounded his administrations and by a drinking problem that sapped his strength and ruined his judgment.

Folsom was born in 1908 in Coffee County, Ala., in the southeastern corner of the state known as the Wiregrass. The Wiregrass had a small-farm economic base, low concentrations of blacks, and a strong populist political tradition. Folsom's many populist-oriented challenges to the state's political elite and his racial moderation had clear origins in his Coffee County upbringing.

His political beliefs were strongly influenced by three people. His father, Joshua Folsom, held many county elective offices and introduced him to courthouse politics. Folsom's uncle, John Dunnavant, a Populist party activist, was a brilliant storyteller who spoke glowingly of Grandfather Dunnavant's freeing of his slaves and of his opposition to the Civil War. Folsom's first father-in-law, Probate Judge J. A. Carnley, was another active and articulate populist advocate, but one who stayed within the Democratic party.

Folsom was not a pure populist. His political views were also influenced by the Great Depression. He received an especially clear perspective on the suffering of that period in his position as Civil Works Administration director in north Alabama's Marshall County. From then on he favored large-scale government assistance programs.

Moving to north Alabama in the later 1930s, Folsom went to a region of the state with a political culture similar to that of the Wiregrass. His election victories united these two very similar regions against the state's Black Belt. In 1962 Folsom was defeated in a reelection bid by George Wallace, who used race-baiting rhetoric to win.

Carl Grafton
Anne Permaloff
Auburn University at Montgomery

Carl Grafton and Anne Permaloff, *Big Mules and Branchheads: James E. Folsom and Political Power in Alabama* (1985).

Helms, Jesse

(b. 1921) Politician.

Jesse Alexander Helms, Jr., was born 18 October 1921 in the Piedmont North Carolina community of Monroe, the son of the town's police and fire chief. Following a Tom Sawyer childhood, a summer at a tiny Baptist college, and a year at Wake Forest, Helms dropped out of college to become a sports reporter with the Raleigh *News and Observer*. During World War II he served with the naval reserve. After the war he was briefly city editor with the *Raleigh Times*, then worked as a reporter with a Roanoke Rapids radio station before returning to Raleigh as news director at WRAL radio station.

While with WRAL, Helms became involved in the successful 1950 Democratic senatorial runoff primary campaign of Raleigh lawyer Willis Smith against Frank Porter Graham, the respected former president of the University of North Carolina, who had been appointed to the Senate in 1949. The Smith-Graham campaign was one of the dirtiest in North Carolina history. Smith literature depicted Graham as a Communist sympathizer and integrationist, exhorting "White People Wake Up!" and warning of "Negroes working beside you, your wife and daughter in your mills and factories," should Graham be elected. In later years, critics claimed that Helms had played a significant role in the Smith campaign—a charge Helms has consistently denied.

Whatever his role in the campaign, Helms became Smith's administrative assistant and served until the senator's death in 1953. Following a brief stint as aide to Smith's successor, Helms returned again to Raleigh and became executive director of the North Carolina Bankers' Association and editor of its conservative monthly bulletin. From 1957 to 1961 he also served on the Raleigh city council.

In 1960 Helms became an executive, editorialist, and minor stockholder with WRAL radio and television stations. Over a 12-year period, he delivered some 2,700 five-minute commentaries over WRAL and the Tobacco Radio Network, a hookup of some 70 rural stations, railing against growing federal power, school desegregation, welfare fraud and waste, and racial "agitators." His *Viewpoint* editorials made Helms a familiar and popular figure in thousands of North Carolina homes. In 1970 he changed his party registration to Republican and in 1972 became the first Republican elected to the Senate from North Carolina since 1894. With the slogan "Elect Jesse Helms—He's One of Us," he won 54 percent of the vote against moderate Durham Congressman Nick Galifianakis, the son of Greek immigrant parents.

During his first term, Helms was little more than a Senate curiosity, opposing abortion and sex education and defending school prayer, curbs on the federal courts, capital punishment, defense spending, and U.S. support for the white minority government of South Africa, but rarely exerting meaningful influence. At the same time, however, his outspoken sympathy for "pro-family" and other religiopolitical causes of the radical right began to attract a national following. Moreover, his Congressional Club, organized initially to retire a 1972 campaign debt, became an extremely successful political action committee, providing funds and technical assistance for a variety of conservative causes and candidates. The club spent over $7 million on Helms's 1978 reelection, outspending his opponent 30 to 1, and over $4 million on Ronald Reagan's 1980 presidential campaign.

The election of President Reagan and a Republican Senate majority in 1980, combined with the conservative national mood the 1980 election results seemed to reflect, gave Helms's movement respectability and the senator considerable national influence. By 1983, however, his position had seriously eroded. Relations with the Reagan Administration—its policies and personalities entirely too moderate for Helms's tastes—had become strained at best. In the Senate, colleagues unsympathetic to his intransigence on "pro-family" issues and opposition to food stamps had countered with attacks on tobacco and other price-support programs important to North Carolina's agricultural economy. At home, every 1982 congressional candidate sponsored by the Congressional Club lost, with that organization's exorbitant spending and negative campaign strategy perhaps the major election issue.

In 1984, however, Helms won reelection over Governor James B. Hunt in the most expensive congressional campaign yet waged. Helms's campaign strategy was reminiscent of that employed so successfully against Frank Graham a quarter-century earlier. Hunt was condemned for supporting a national holiday honoring Martin Luther King, Jr., and depicted as a tax-happy racial and political liberal, the candidate of "the bloc vote," "gays, porno kings, union bosses, and crooks." Campaign leaflets featured photographs of Hunt with Jesse Jackson and Helms with President Reagan, noting the "stark contrast." The ploy worked. Aided by Reagan's lengthy North Carolina coattails, a $15 million campaign chest, and Hunt's liberal image, the senator won 52 percent of the total vote, 63 percent of whites, but less than 1 percent of the black electorate.

Tinsley E. Yarbrough
East Carolina University

Wayne Greenhaw, *Elephants in the Cottonfields: Ronald Reagan and the New Republican South* (1982); Bill Peterson, *Washington Post National Weekly Edition* (3 December 1984); Peter Ross Range, *New York Times Magazine* (8 February 1981).

Hull, Cordell

(1871–1955) Diplomat.

It is a long way from the Tennessee mountains to the State Department corridors, and there was little in Cordell Hull's Overton County roots that prepared him to be the leading diplomat in Franklin Roosevelt's foreign-policy entourage. In fact, in his memoirs Hull mentioned two experiences that prepared him for world affairs; both were outside Tennessee. One was a year and a half of college in Ohio, where he was able to meet people with different habits and ideas; the other was his Spanish-American War service in Cuba where he became aware of the wider world in which the United States would have to exist.

Hull had broad-ranging experience at the state, national, and international levels. A graduate of the law program at Cumberland University, he practiced law briefly before serving two terms in the state legislature. After serving in the Spanish-American War, Hull was a circuit court judge for four years and then was elected to the U.S. House of Representatives, serving from 1907 to 1930 (except for 1921–23). Among his many legislative accomplishments was the proposal of a graduated income tax measure in 1913. In 1930 Hull was elected to the U.S. Senate and served until his appointment as secretary of state.

During his 11 years as secretary of state (1933–44), Hull showed his Tennessee roots. Contemporaries dwelled upon such superficial points as his penchant for telling stories about his days in Tennessee, the colorful profanity that dotted his private conversations when he was angered, and his quiet, almost taciturn demeanor. Like other staunch southern Democrats of his day, Hull worked diligently for a program to lower tariffs. But Secretary of State Hull's views on trade were not those of the local politician who had to protect his constituents. He took a loftier view that a free-trading world would progress while an autarchic world order where nations conquered and hoarded markets and resources would lead to economic stagnation. As secretary of state, Hull engineered the Reciprocal Trade Agreements Act, worked especially to improve Latin American relations, helped shape the Good Neighbor policy, supported strengthening of America's military preparedness, and proposed an international diplomatic organization. Called by President Truman the "Father of the United Nations," Hull received the Nobel Peace Prize in 1945.

If Hull's worldview went beyond the parochial views of most of his fellow Tennesseans, he brought to the Department of State a faith in absoluteness drawn from his early years in the Cumberland Mountains, where certainty mattered above all. To the men of his region during the Civil War, Hull recalled, it made little difference whether you fought in the Confederate or Union armies as long as you fought. His father personified the certainty of right and wrong when he tracked down and publicly killed a man who had informed on him during the war, an act for which his father was neither prosecuted nor chastised.

Even as a law-and-order judge riding circuit in Tennessee, Hull showed he had absorbed this black-white view of life. There were good people and bad people, and it was as simple as that. Similarly, during World War II Secretary Hull saw Nazi Germany and Imperial Japan in this black-white view.

Jonathan G. Utley
University of Tennessee

Harold B. Hinton, *Cordell Hull: A Biography* (1942); Cordell Hull, *The Memoirs of Cordell Hull*, 2 vols. (1948); J. W. Pratt, *American Secretaries of State*, vols. 12, 13 (1964).

Jackson, Andrew

(1767–1845) Politician.

Born near the border of North and South Carolina—the exact spot is in dispute—Andrew Jackson moved to frontier Tennessee in 1788 at the age of 19, an early pioneer in a significant migration pattern that eventually redrew the boundaries of "the South." Tennessee at the time, and throughout Jackson's life, was more western than southern. Although he developed substantial landholdings near Nashville, held slaves, and lived the life of a gentleman planter at "The Hermitage," Jackson as late as the 1840s considered himself a westerner and a nationalist, never a southerner, and he was so perceived by his contemporaries.

Nonetheless Jackson's career was rife with consequences for the South. His defeat of the British at New Orleans and of the Seminoles in Florida nailed down southern borders once and for all. He moved carefully on the issue of expansion into Texas while in office, but his passionate interest in the area eventually resulted in extension of the southern frontier westward.

The Democratic party that he led to the presidency and institutionalized around Jacksonian issues represented an alliance of "Southern Planters and Plain Republicans of the North," as Martin Van Buren put it; it was rooted in the "Old Republican" ideology of Thomas Jefferson and coupled with a strong overlay of western pragmatism. Committed to the Union and to strict construction of the Constitution, the party served for decades as a shield for southern slaveowners against the rising antislavery clamor. Paradoxically, it also embodied and promoted the democratic impulse whose egalitarian values and reform tendencies were ultimately subversive of the southern slavery system.

Although Jackson's Scotch-Irish parents had only recently emigrated at the time of his birth, his formative years in the upcountry Carolinas doubtless contributed

Andrew Jackson, frontier hero and U.S. president, date unknown

to his fierce combativeness, his attraction to the law and the militia, his love of horses and horseracing, and his patrician style. It was as frontier lawyer and politician, militia leader and military hero, that he rose to fame, an ardent unionist and an instinctive democrat.

Richard H. Brown
Newberry Library
Chicago, Illinois

James Curtis, *Andrew Jackson and the Search for Vindication* (1976); Burke Davis, *Old Hickory: A Life of Andrew Jackson* (1977); Robert V. Remini, *The Revolutionary Age of Andrew Jackson* (1976).

Johnson, Lyndon B.

(1908–1973) Politician.

Convinced that a southerner could not be elected to the presidency in his lifetime, Lyndon Baines Johnson sought to minimize his southern credentials. Describing himself as an American, a westerner, a Texan, and, only lastly, a southerner, he attempted to divorce himself from the region and its conservative racial and social image. As a southerner, a congressional leader with a mixed civil rights record, and the successor to a slain president whose reform image loomed larger in death than in life, Lyndon B. Johnson sensed a special need to convince the nation that he too was dedicated to the cause of equality and a decent standard of living for all Americans. Pursuing this goal during the five years of his presidency (1963–69), he pushed through the Congress the most significant civil rights legislation since Reconstruction—the legislation outlawing discrimination in education, public accommodations, voting, employment, and housing. Armed with authority to cut off federal funds to segregated public schools, his administration integrated the schools at a pace that repeated court decisions had largely failed to effect. And his 1965 voting rights legislation produced a 50 percent increase in southern black voter registration by 1966—an increase that facilitated the election of black officeholders (387 in Mississippi alone by mid-1980) and ultimately moderated the region's racial politics.

The administration's War on Poverty attempted to cope, moreover, with the plight of the poor in the South and the rest of the nation. For children, Johnson created the federal school breakfast, Head Start, day care, and foster grandparent programs; for the elderly, Medicare and special housing; for the unemployed, the Job Corps; for the myriad problems confronting the poor, VISTA and the Community Action Program. Nor were such programs intended only for economic relief. They also provided a political base for minorities, especially in the South. Many VISTA volunteers, for example, became heavily involved in southern politics, and the Community Action Program through which federal poverty funds were channeled to largely private, minority-related agencies was designed in part to bypass the traditional federal, state, and local power structures.

While president, Lyndon Johnson was never able to convince most civil rights leaders and social activists of his commitment to reform. For them, as for his critics on the right, he was simply a calculating politician posturing for liberal and minority votes. More critically, urban riots, rising inflation, the growing national preoccupation with Vietnam, the merging of the civil rights movement with the antiwar effort, and the increasingly radical character of the two movements largely derailed Johnson's social programs and dampened public enthusiasm for further civil rights reform. Ironically, too, though he was a creature of the Solid Democratic South, his administration probably did more to drive white southerners into the ranks of the GOP than all the efforts of Republican presidents and presidential aspirants. Whatever its direction, however, his impact on southern politics was to be truly profound. In later years, moreover, liberals would develop a more sympathetic image of his presidency and its role in social reform. That image moved former SNCC leader and caustic Johnson critic Julian Bond to describe the former president in 1972 as "an activist, human-hearted man [who] had his hands on the levers of power and a vision beyond the next election. He was there when we and the Nation needed him, and, oh my God, do I wish he was there now."

Tinsley E. Yarbrough
East Carolina University

Robert A. Divine, ed., *Exploring the Johnson Years* (1981); Eric Goldman, *The Tragedy of Lyndon Johnson* (1968); Doris Kearns, *Lyndon Johnson and the American Dream* (1976).

Kefauver, Estes

(1903–1963) Politician.

Carey Estes Kefauver, U.S. senator from Tennessee for 14 years and Democratic vice-presidential nominee in 1956, is credited with having influenced incorporation of more direct popular appeal in presidential campaign methods, as contrasted with traditional reliance on local political organizations. Less tangible but probably more important was his possible influence on elimination of the customary stance and image of the southern senator.

Before Kefauver's consistently controversial career in the U.S. Senate, the image of the verbose gentleman with flowing hair and tie—like his first Tennessee Senate colleague, K. D. McKellar—was not universally applicable to southern politicians, but it was associated with a solid bloc of Dixie legislators whose votes on certain issues, especially civil rights legislation, were predictable. Kefauver's refusal to conform to that image never lessened his popularity, and his stances probably undermined the assumption that southern senators and congressmen are distinct from—and often opposed to—the mainstream.

Kefauver's almost unheard-of challenge to an incumbent administration of his own party in plunging into the 1952 presidential race against the will of then-President Harry Truman also marked the beginning of the end of the once-traditional axiom that "no southerner can ever become president." He did not make it himself, but two southerners, Lyndon B. Johnson and Jimmy Carter, attained the office after his death. An unacceptable liberal to southern colleagues yet not liberal enough for northern Democratic leaders, Kefauver won successes both in the Senate and on the campaign trail almost exclusively through his ability to appeal directly to the voters, not only in his own state but nationwide.

A Yale graduate who left a successful Chattanooga law practice for a decade in the House of Representatives, Kefauver reached the U.S. Senate in 1948 through a successful challenge to the statewide political hegemony of Memphis's E. H. Crump. He was boosted into the 1952 presidential picture by his televised investigation of organized crime, and his soft voice and unavoidable handshake gave him name recognition second only to that of Dwight D. Eisenhower, according to a Gallup poll. After his second failure, in 1956, to win the Democratic presidential nomination, Kefauver spent the rest of his career leading a series of Senate investigations, the most notable into antitrust violations and prescription drugs.

Charles L. Fontenay
Nashville, Tennessee

Charles L. Fontenay, *Estes Kefauver: A Biography* (1980); Richard Harris, *The Real Voice* (1964); William Howard Moore, *The Kefauver Committee and the Politics of Crime, 1950–1952* (1974).

Long, Huey P.

(1893–1935) Politician.

Governor of Louisiana, U.S. senator, and popular leader during the Great Depression, Huey Pierce Long emerged from the relatively poor hill country of northern Louisiana to transform forever the politics of his state. After eight years as a member of the Public Service Commission, he was elected governor in 1928 as the champion of the common people against the Old Guard, the oil interests, and the planter elite. Although his opponents often decried his radicalism, Long was in many respects a rather conventional progressive reformer. He oversaw a massive public works program, an improvement of state educational and health facilities, and a modest reform of the tax codes. But if Long was relatively moderate in his legislative aims, he was decidedly immoderate in the means he adopted to attain them. In his eight years as leader of Louisiana—four as governor and four as U.S. senator, from which position he continued to control the state through carefully chosen surrogates—he created a political machine without precedent in American history. By skillful use of both his wide popularity and his official powers, he won total mastery of the state legislature; from there, he proceeded to transform state government—through a series of constitutional amendments and other devices—to concentrate virtually all power in his own hands.

After entering the Senate in 1932, Long quickly rose to national prominence as well—first as a supporter and then as a foe of Franklin Roosevelt, but always as an advocate of redistribution of wealth. As leader of his own national political organization—the Share Our Wealth Society—he mobilized a following that alarmed even the president himself. At the peak of his power, positioning himself for a national campaign in 1936, Long was assassinated in September 1935 by a Baton Rouge physician, whose motives remain unknown.

Long was both a classic example of and a radical departure from the southern demagogue. Like others, he rose to power on the basis of explicit, if crudely expressed, class grievances. Like others, he drew from the traditions of populism, defending the sanctity of local communities against the encroachments of powerful interests. But unlike most southern demagogues, Long translated his popular appeal into lasting and far-reaching political power; he compiled a record of substantive accomplishment; and he achieved and maintained authority without exploiting the issue of race. No southern politician of his era, moreover, could match Long's popular appeal outside the region. Long's career exposed in the starkest possible form both the dangers and the opportunities of effective populist appeals to the discontented and dispossessed. He used his popularity to accumulate great and menacing power, but at the same time he turned the gaze of troubled Louisianians (and many others as well) away from the cultural, religious, and racial issues that had dampened economic progress and social reform in the past, and elevated to prominence basic questions of power and wealth. After Huey Long, Louisiana's conservative oligarchy would never rest entirely comfortably again.

Alan Brinkley
Harvard University

Alan Brinkley, *Voices of Protest: Huey Long, Father Coughlin and the Great Depression* (1982); Huey P. Long, *Every Man a King* (1933), *My First Days in the White House* (1935); Allan P. Sindler, *Huey Long's Louisiana* (1956); T. Harry Williams, *Huey Long* (1969).

Maddox, Lester

(b. 1915) Politician.

In January 1967, with the South in the midst of dramatic change initiated by the civil rights movement, Lester Garfield Maddox was elected governor of Georgia. For a decade prior to his election, he had made himself a symbol of white resistance to integration. Each Saturday in the Atlanta newspapers he advertised his fried chicken restaurant, the Pickrick, and purchased space for a political column that attacked liberals as enemies of America, God, individual freedom, and states' rights. His particular brand of right-wing thinking combined religious fundamentalism with racism and classical laissez-faire doctrines. The combination proved to be appealing to many Georgians who shared aspects of his background.

Maddox was born in Atlanta in 1915, one of seven children of parents who had left rural Georgia to seek better employment opportunities in Atlanta. His father worked in a small steel factory and found it difficult to support his family during the Depression. Lester dropped out of high school, married at an early age, and worked at a variety of jobs before starting a small restaurant that he and his wife turned into a highly successful enterprise. Active in the Baptist church and several fraternal orders, Maddox began in the 1950s to challenge the racial moderation that characterized Atlanta's political leadership. In 1964 he attracted national attention when he refused to obey the recently passed Civil Rights Act by denying service to blacks at his restaurant. Brandishing a pistol and distributing ax handles to his supporters, he forcibly turned away blacks from his door. When the federal courts ordered him to end discrimination, he sold the restaurant to friends rather than operate it on an integrated basis.

Maddox's highly visible defiance of federal authority served as a springboard for his pursuit of the governorship in 1966. With little financial support and no assistance from established political leaders, he launched his campaign in rural areas of central and southern Georgia. On fence posts and pine trees he nailed signs announcing, "This Is Maddox Country," and on election day his claims were supported. In the Democratic primary he toppled a former governor, Ellis Arnall, whose moderate stance on racial issues and long-standing opposition to the Talmadge forces in Georgia politics proved to be handicaps. In the general election Maddox was opposed by Republican Howard "Bo" Callaway, a millionaire segregationist who had recently left the Democratic party. Neither man received a majority in the election because 7 percent of the electorate, blacks and white liberals, wrote in the name of Ellis Arnall. The Georgia Legislature convened in January to decide between the two leading candidates; the outcome was not in question as rural Democrats who dominated the proceedings cast their votes for the intrepid Atlanta gadfly, Lester G. Maddox.

As governor, Maddox did not effect any significant changes in the state's institutions. He did not close the public schools nor use the powers of his office to challenge federal authority. White Georgians continued the slow process of adjusting to the end of segregation while their governor delivered regular verbal assaults on those who had brought about the change. In 1968 Maddox made an abortive two-week campaign for the presidential nomination of the Democratic party; afterwards he supported the independent candidacy of George Wallace. When he completed his term as governor and could not succeed himself, he handily won election as lieutenant governor. But in 1974 the voters rejected his bid for the governor's office in favor of a moderate, George Busbee. The majority no longer wanted the state to be led by an extremist defender of the old order of segregation.

James C. Lanier
Rhodes College

Numan Bartley, *From Thurmond to Wallace: Political Tendencies in Georgia, 1948–1968* (1970); Marshall Frady, *Southerners: A Journalist's Odyssey* (1980); Lester Maddox, *Speaking Out: The Autobiography of Lester Garfield Maddox* (1975).

Pepper, Claude

(b. 1900) Politician.

The oldest of four children, Claude Denson Pepper was born on the family farm near Dudleyville, Ala. "Full grown" before he had ever traveled on a paved road, when he accompanied his debate team to Chapel Hill, N.C., as a college freshman, it was the farthest north he had ever been. A southerner, a Baptist, and a lifelong unwavering Democrat, a New Deal liberal who in a 1950 smear campaign was branded a "leader of radicals" and "advocate of treason," Pepper has nevertheless been hailed as a representative American, "the nearest thing this country has to a national congressman."

Pepper's wide ambition and indomitability surfaced early. A schoolteacher for a time in Dothan, Ala., then a steel mill worker, he continued to hold down a part-time job while attending the University of Alabama. He graduated Phi Beta Kappa in 1921 and, after receiving a law degree from Harvard in 1924, taught for a year at the University of Arkansas before setting up practice in Perry, Fla. In 1929 he was elected to the Florida House of Representatives but was defeated two years later and resumed his law practice, this time in Tallahassee.

After an unsuccessful bid for the U.S. Senate in 1934 (lost by only 4,000 votes), Pepper filed for a vacancy two years later and was nominated by his party, unopposed. Committed to Roosevelt's economic programs for the good of the South and the nation, Pepper gained the president's support for election to his first six-year term in 1938. He consistently risked antagonizing both big business and social conservative interests in Florida by opposing racism and by favoring minimum wage laws, national health insurance, old age pensions, and federal aid to education.

Pepper was reelected in 1944 but his postwar record that included such things as encouraging rapprochement with the Soviet Union, early backing of Dwight Eisenhower against Truman, opposition to union-regulating Taft-Hartley legislation, and support for anti–poll tax laws led his enemies to close ranks in 1950. Florida boss Edward W. Ball, assisted with funds gleaned nationally, groomed Representative George A. Smathers to run against Pepper in what has been called "the most elaborate crusade for political annihilation ever conducted in Southern politics." Coupled with slanderous slogans and speeches, a pamphlet, *The Red Record of Senator Claude Pepper*, circulated throughout Florida. On election night, when Pepper had lost by 67,000 votes, people passing his house shouted obscenities and applauded his defeat.

With law offices in Tallahassee, Washington, and Miami, Pepper again returned to a successful private practice, but was discontented out of office. In 1962 he ran for and won a House seat newly created for the Miami congressional district. He has been consistently reelected since.

With nearly four decades of congressional service spanning nine presidential administrations behind him, Pepper is confident that he is "doing more good now" than if he had managed to stay in the Senate. He remains responsive to a diverse constituency that includes Haitian refugees, blacks, Hispanics, and many white retirees. He has introduced legislation to support housing projects and cancer research, crime prevention programs, and economic aid to South Americans. Undaunted by administration pressure to cut social programs, Pepper continues to pursue his maverick policy in an era of conservatism. As chair of the House Select Committee on Aging, he became a particularly staunch defender of government responsibility for the elderly: "I refuse to believe that a country as rich and powerful as ours can't afford to guarantee the basic comfort and security of its older citizens. I know we can do it," he added, characteristically, "and I intend to be long and loud about it."

Elizabeth M. Makowski
University of Mississippi

John Egerton, *New York Times Magazine* (29 November 1981); Lawrence F. Kennedy, compiler, *Biographical Directory of the American Congress, 1774–1971* (1971); Robert Sherrill, *Gothic Politics in the Deep South* (1968); *Time* (25 April 1983).

Radical Republicans

Radical Republicans was a frequently used but often imprecisely defined term applying to one faction of the Republican party in the South after the Civil War. In 1867, at the outset of the congressional program of Reconstruction, the nature of southern Radicalism was reasonably clear: Radicals favored guaranteed equal rights for the freedmen, the establishment of public schools, and fairly sweeping disfranchisement of former Confederates. In some states the Radicals insisted that schools be nonsegregated and that public accommodations be open to both races. The Radicals' opponents, the moderate Republicans, would extend political and civil equality, but nothing more, to the freedmen and hoped to attract part of the native white electorate with a program of economic development. Political alignments and party factionalism make generalization somewhat difficult, but on the whole northern-born white people who came to the South after 1861 (the carpetbaggers), along with the freedmen, were most likely to belong to the Radical faction. However, the majority of the native white Republicans (or scalawags), many with Whig loyalties from the antebellum years, were moderates. Also, as a general rule, the larger the black voting majority in a given district, the greater was the likelihood that Radical candidates—either carpetbaggers or blacks—would be elected.

Southern Radicalism owed much to northern influence, through the power of the carpetbaggers in the party hierarchy and in its commitment both to racial justice and, on occasion, to the social equality of the races. In the 1870s, after some Republican governments had fallen to the Conservatives (or Democrats) and those remaining were under assault, southern Radicals looked to their northern counterparts to intervene once more in southern affairs and salvage their political power, if not the broader goals of Reconstruction. Further intervention, however, was an impossibility after 1872. Finally, the fluidity of political alignments and the serious divisions between moderate and Radical Republicans that weakened the federal government's commitment to Reconstruction also plagued and weakened the southern parties. Radical

Republicanism was an artificial development in the South, introduced by outsiders, and, despite its name, it proved to be less than truly radical in its dedication to the freedmen.

Radical strength varied in the southern states, but it was best embodied in the administrations of Adelbert Ames in Mississippi (1874–76), William P. Kellogg in Louisiana (1873–77), and Edmund J. Davis in Texas (1870–74). On the other hand, Radicalism was fairly weak in Florida, North Carolina, and Georgia, where nearly all prominent Republicans were scalawags, and was almost nonexistent in Virginia. In most states, however, Republican parties were divided and greatly weakened by factional and ideological struggles and found it difficult to combat the increasingly strong challenges from Conservatives. White southerners came to equate Radicalism with Republicanism, thereby rejecting the party of the freedmen, drawing a clear color line in politics, driving most whites into the Democratic party, and helping to create a solidly Democratic South, which lasted until the 20th century.

John M. Matthews
Georgia State University

Warren A. Ellem, *Journal of Southern History* (May 1972); Richard L. Hume, *Journal of American History* (September 1977).

Rayburn, Sam

(1882–1961) Politician.

Rayburn, congressman from a rural northeast Texas district from 1913 until his death in 1961, was one of the most powerful congressmen in the 20th century. Born in Roane County, Tenn., on 6 January 1882, the son of a Confederate soldier, he moved to Fannin County, Tex., at the age of five. He was educated in country schools and attended Mayo College in Commerce, Tex. After a brief stint as a schoolteacher, Rayburn was elected to the Texas House of Representatives in 1906. In 1911 he was elected speaker of the Texas House, and during reapportionment in that year he carved a congressional district that was to elect and reelect him for 25 terms.

In his early years Rayburn was a follower of the charismatic Texas senator Joseph Weldon Bailey. With Bailey's fall from power, Rayburn's ambitions for higher statewide office were thwarted. He became a lieutenant of the influential Texas congressman John Nance Garner and in 1932 directed Garner's campaign for the presidency. Rayburn was heavily involved in the negotiations that led to the Roosevelt-Garner ticket.

After Roosevelt's election Rayburn became a workhorse of the New Deal through his role as chairman of the Interstate and Foreign Commerce Committee. His southern populist leanings led him to support most of Roosevelt's economic policies, and his committee handled such legislation as the Truth-in-Securities Act (1933), the Securities Exchange Act (1934), the Federal Communications Act (1934), the Public Utility Holding Company Act (1935), and the Rural Electrification Act (1936).

In 1937 he was elected majority leader of the House of Representatives, and in 1940, upon the death of William Bankhead of Alabama, he was elected speaker. With the exception of the four years that the Republicans controlled the House, Rayburn was speaker from 1940 to 1961. During those years his primary goal was to serve as a bridge in the House between the southern and northern wings of the Democratic party.

He worked closely with southern committee chairmen, presidents, and his protegé in the Senate, Lyndon B. Johnson, to build the coalitions necessary for national policymaking. Rayburn was a strong supporter of defense preparedness, prolabor legislation, public power, and farm programs. Although a segregationist, he supported the 1957 Civil Rights Act and counseled moderation in the reaction to *Brown* v. *Board of Education*.

Though a national leader, he maintained a strong tie to his district and to the rural South. He died of cancer of the pancreas on 16 November 1961, in Bonham, Tex.

Anthony Champagne
University of Texas at Dallas

Anthony Champagne, *Congressman Sam Rayburn* (1984); C. Dwight Dorough, *Mr. Sam* (1962); H. G. Dulaney, Edward Hake Phillips, and MacPhelan Reese, eds., *Speak, Mr. Speaker* (1978); Alfred Steinberg, *Sam Rayburn: A Biography* (1975).

Russell, Richard B.

(1897–1971) Politician.

Richard Brevard Russell, a dominant force in the U.S. Senate for almost four decades, was born in Winder, Ga., on 2 November 1897. After earning a law degree at the University of Georgia in 1918, he began practicing law in his hometown.

The son of a state legislator who became the chief justice of the Georgia Supreme Court, Russell began his public career in 1921 when he won election to the Georgia House of Representatives. By the time he was 30 he was the speaker of that assembly, and in 1931 he became Georgia's youngest chief executive. His two years as governor are remembered for the reorganization which reduced the number of agencies and departments.

When the incumbent U.S. senator died in 1932, Russell won the special election to replace him. From 1933 until his death on 21 January 1971, he served on the Appropriations Committee, rising through the seniority system to be its chairman during his last two years. Of perhaps greater note was his service on the Naval Affairs Committee and, after the 1947 Legislative Reorganization Act, on the Armed Services Committee, which he chaired for 16 years prior to 1969. From this base Russell developed his reputation as a leading Senate expert on national defense. Although an advocate of a strong military, he opposed the commitment of American troops to Southeast Asia. Nonetheless, once his advice was rejected, he staunchly supported the military action.

The other major feature of Russell's career—the second longest in Senate history—was his leadership of the southern wing of the Democratic party. He was a master of the chamber's rules, which he used to thwart liberal policy initiatives. He was the chief strategist in southern efforts to defeat, or at least weaken, civil rights bills. Although Russell became a leader of the bipartisan Conservative Coalition, he began his career as a New Deal Democrat. Once the economic crisis receded, Russell, like many southern members of Congress, backed away from additional welfare proposals and government regulations.

In 1948 and 1952 Russell's name was placed in nomination for the presidency at the Democratic National Convention. Considered a gifted political leader, Russell was ambitious for the presidency and frustrated by never gaining it. He and many political commentators blamed this failure on his being southern; his opposition to civil rights legislation did, in fact, effectively limit his national appeal. Russell was instrumental in promoting the career of Lyndon B. Johnson, much of whose presidency Russell came to oppose.

Charles S. Bullock III
University of Georgia

Harry Conn, *New Republic* (12 May 1952); Harold H. Martin, *Saturday Evening Post* (2 June 1951); *New Republic* (6 February 1971); *Time* (1 February 1971).

Secession

The politics of secession consisted of the separate actions of individual southern states in late 1860 and early 1861 and did not represent a unified South acting as a concerted whole. Secession was triggered in November 1860 by the election of Lincoln to the presidency, at the head of a sectionalized Republican party that was publicly committed to prohibiting the expansion of slavery into the federal territories and pledged—though recognizing slavery in the states where it already existed—to the ultimate extinction of slavery. Secession itself occurred in two distinct waves; in each it generally received its strongest support from those areas with the heaviest concentrations of slaves.

After a series of hastily called, highly localized, and often closely contested elections, delegates chosen on a countywide basis attended state conventions convened to decide the question of secession. Seven states had left the Union by 1 February 1861. This first wave—South Carolina, Mississippi, Florida, Alabama, Georgia, Louisiana, and Texas—comprised the original Confederate States of America, the provisional constitution for which was adopted in Montgomery, Ala., on 7 February 1861.

In the meantime Unionist sentiment remained dominant in the states of the Upper South. Here the proportion of slaves to the total population was but half that of the Lower South (25 as opposed to 50 percent), fears of slave uprisings were less intense, economic and cultural ties with the free states were deeper, and the prosecessionist wing of the Democratic party did not control local politics. Secession was temporarily halted. Nonetheless, virtually all political factions in the Upper South conceded the legal right of secession and agreed that any effort to coerce a seceded state back into the Union should be resisted.

Lincoln was inaugurated in early March, and any lingering opportunity for reunion floundered over the issue of the expansion of slavery. The second wave of secession was unleashed when Fort Sumter fell to the Confederacy in April and Lincoln called for state militia to put down what the North believed was a rebellion. Four additional slave states from the Upper South—Arkansas, North Carolina, Virginia, and Tennessee—joined the Confeder acy rather than bear arms against fellow southern whites.

The secessionists had appealed successfully to values of individual autonomy, freedom from arbitrary power, and political self-determination. Embedded within America's 19th-century political culture and most often applied to whites only, these values could be used either for or against the Union and either to attack or defend slavery. The politics of secession ensured that this debate would be settled only by a civil war.

William L. Barney
University of North Carolina
at Chapel Hill

David M. Potter, *The Impending Crisis, 1848–1861*, ed. Don E. Fehrenbacher (1976); Ralph A. Wooster, *The Secession Conventions of the South* (1962).

Smith, Frank

(b. 1918) Politician.

Smith represented white southerners who rejected segregation during the 1950s and 1960s. Despite being born (21 February 1918) and reared in the Mississippi Delta where segregation of the races was the unquestioned social system, Smith developed "liberal" social and political attitudes. Educated at Sunflower Junior College and the University of Mississippi, Smith went to war in 1942 as a private and returned a captain, a veteran of General Patton's Third Army. He came back to the Delta, to Greenwood, to help establish the liberal *Morning Star* and entered the state senate in 1947. Leaving the newspaper, he worked in John Stennis's Senate campaign and went to Washington as Stennis's assistant.

In 1950 Smith ran for the Delta's congressional seat and defeated a states' rights candidate. Smith established himself through constituent service and good congressional relationships as a strong representative. Keeping his belief in racial integration secret, he worked to mitigate the effects of segregation. In Congress, he also worked for free-trade and consumer-protection laws such as the act requiring content labeling on clothing. Although he obscured his liberalism as much as possible from Delta voters, voting analysis exposed his record, and following the *Brown* decision in 1954 his "moderation" became more evident as Mississippi withdrew from national politics. Smith's adherence to the national Democratic party's platforms and his backing of John F. Kennedy alienated many supporters. In 1962 the segregationists redistricted Smith into a race that he would not win.

Smith's defeat coincided with the integration crisis at the University of Mississippi. Because Smith publicly condemned the state's segregationist government, he was effectively exiled from the state by a power structure that saw him as a traitor. Kennedy appointed Smith to the TVA board of directors; from that office Smith wrote an autobiography to explain his development into a liberal and advocated integration and voting rights for blacks. During Smith's years at TVA (1962–72) he wrote increasingly about environmental issues. Through his books and his position he worked for intelligent management of natural resources, doing battle with both industry and preservationists.

He continued to work toward leading Mississippi and the South into the American mainstream socially and politically. During his exile from Mississippi, Smith discreetly encouraged a moderate group within the Mississippi Democratic party and worked for cooperation with newly enfranchised black voters. Leaving TVA, Smith ran for Congress in a new district of central Mississippi. Defeated and denied appointive positions in Mississippi, he turned to academic posts in Illinois and Virginia. In the first, he dealt with a plan for environmental education, and in the second, he examined southern politics.

Although Smith published a book of essays outlining his philosophy entitled *Look Away from Dixie*, he did not look away. Instead, he ended his years of public service as special assistant to Governor William Winter of Mississippi (1980–84). In a sense his life's work was realized because metaphorically Mississippi had rejoined the Union.

Smith's personal correspondence is filled with letters from Mississippians praising his defiance of the segregationist power structure and lamenting their forced silence. Smith clearly was spokesman for southern white integrationists and moderates offended by the excesses of the segregationists. He was important as a symbol for whites because he was undeniably a Mississippian. Other integrationists were dismissed as outsiders who did not understand, but Frank Smith was one of their own and an integrationist. Retired from politics, Smith now runs a bookstore in Jackson.

Dennis J. Mitchell
Jackson State University

Frank Smith, *Congressman from Mississippi* (1964), *Look Away from Dixie* (1965), *The Politics of Conservation* (1966), *The Yazoo River* (1954).

Southern Governors' Association

In 1932 President Franklin D. Roosevelt summoned governors from several southeastern states to the Little White House in Warm Springs, Ga., to urge that they establish a regional organization to assist in the development of the South. Within a few weeks the governors of Virginia, Kentucky, North Carolina, South Carolina, Georgia, Florida, Tennessee, Alabama, Mississippi, and Louisiana announced the formation of what was originally called the Southeastern Governors' Association.

Their primary concerns were the economic gap between the South and the rest of the country, how to bring industry to what was at that time a rural economy, and how to raise the overall and individual incomes of the region and its citizens. The first resolution adopted by the conference was directed at changing the territorial freight rate system, which was used to determine costs for transporting goods by rail. Appealing to the courts and to Congress, the governors' efforts were finally successful in ending a system that had forced southerners to pay discriminatory charges.

An equally important result of the early meetings of the governors was the genesis of a permanent organization designed to bring closer cooperation among governors of the southern states, and between these states collectively and the federal government. In the late 1930s a committee for a Balanced Prosperity Program became the forerunner of innumerable committees, task forces, and ad hoc groups, which the governors empowered to attend to the specific details of regional growth and cooperation.

Permanent organizations were set up beginning in the 1940s to address areas of highest priority and ongoing interest to the South. In 1948 the governors formed the Southern Regional Education Board, the oldest interstate compact for higher education and a pioneer in regional planning and action. In 1961 the governors established the Southern Interstate Nuclear Board to encourage proper development of nuclear energy in attaining a balanced, thriving economy in the South. In 1978 the name of the agency was changed to the Southern States Energy Board, reflecting its expanded role in the development of all energy sources and its concern for broad environmental issues. In 1971 the governors launched the Southern Growth Policies Board to give full attention to the problems of economic disparity and unplanned growth. It was authorized to keep a current Statement of Regional Objectives, including recommended approaches to problems and projects deemed to be of regional significance.

In 1982 the Southern Governors' Association voted to move the organization's base of operations to Washington, D.C. Today, the association has 19 member governors, representing the 10 original members plus Arkansas, Delaware, Maryland, Missouri, Oklahoma, Puerto Rico, Texas, the Virgin Islands, and West Virginia. It is the largest and oldest of the regional governors' organizations. Transportation and economic development continue to be important concerns as well as issues ranging from energy and human resources to education and government management.

See also INDUSTRY: / Southern Growth Policies Board

John W. Wilson, Jr.
Southern Governors' Association

Southern Governors' Association, *Annual Report 1984–1985* (1985).

Southern Strategy

In his political dictionary journalist and ex-Nixon aide William Safire defines "Southern Strategy" as "an attack phrase attributing racist or at least political motives toward any position taken on desegregation or busing that would be well received by most Southern whites." William Rusher of the conservative *National Review* has claimed that the term was invented by liberal opponents of Senator Barry Goldwater to suggest that the 1964 Republican presidential candidate was in league with southern bigots, while the senator himself once contended that a journalist actually coined the term in the 1950s to describe Republican efforts to make congressional gains in the South*west*—efforts in no way related to the race issue. Harry S. Dent, former aide to both President Nixon and South Carolina Democrat-Dixiecrat-Republican Senator Strom Thurmond, has traced its origins to John F. Kennedy's 1960 presidential campaign, specifically to Kennedy's selection of Texas Senator Lyndon B. Johnson as a running mate, the candidate's promise to protect the southern textile industry from low-cost imports, and his sympathy call to jailed civil rights leader Martin Luther King, Jr.

Each of these contentions contains some truth. Southern Strategy also encompasses, however, the rhetoric, tactics, and government policies employed by post–World War II Republican presidents and presidential aspirants to lure the southern voter from the traditional Democratic fold. In marshaling southern support Dwight D. Eisenhower did little more than advocate state control of (largely southern) offshore oil deposits and appoint a number of Eisenhower Democrats to patronage positions. Even so, he was able to capitalize on the southern discontent with the Democratic party, which the Dixiecrat movement of 1948 had reflected, and make impressive gains in the South—gains only partially and temporarily deflected by Ike appointee Earl Warren's authorship of the historic 1954 *Brown* decision. The Goldwater movement nudged even more southerners into the GOP ranks in 1964—a disaster year for the Republicans in every other part of the nation but a banner year in the South.

What the Goldwater movement had begun, Richard M. Nixon and Ronald W. Reagan developed and refined. In an effort to woo southerners away, first from Reagan, then from George C. Wallace's third-party candidacy, Nixon complained often and vehemently during the 1968 presidential campaign about court-ordered busing and criminal-coddling judges. As president, moreover, he opposed busing, promoted a federal project to upgrade (segregated) urban ghetto schools, and ordered an IRS tax exemption for segregated private schools that promised—but did not necessarily deliver—an open admissions policy. He also vowed to appoint a "strict constructionist" southerner to the Supreme Court; the liberal Republican Ripon Society, among others, attacked his appointments of social-economic conservatives to the federal bench in the South—including one nominee who, when asked his position regarding segregation, replied, "That's a difficult question to respond to without being put on the spot." During the 1980 presidential campaign, Ronald Reagan promised to get able-bodied "bucks" off the welfare rolls and won every southern state but President Carter's native Georgia. As president, he too has opposed busing, slashed federal welfare budgets, promoted massive increases in defense spending, sought to resurrect the Nixon policy of tax exemptions for segregated private schools, and pushed for a constitutional amendment to restore public school devotional programs—all positions dear to the hearts of conservative southerners. Much in the Nixon-Reagan programs and rhetoric has been a response to a perceived national conservative trend. This national conservative strategy had its origins, however, in a Southern Strategy.

Tinsley E. Yarbrough
East Carolina University

Harry S. Dent, *The Prodigal South Returns to Power* (1978); Reg Murphy and Hal Gulliver, *The Southern Strategy* (1971).

Talmadge, Eugene
(1884–1946) Politician.

Born in Forsyth, Monroe County, Ga., the son of Thomas and Carrie Talmadge and father of U.S. Senator Herman Talmadge, Eugene Talmadge served several terms as governor of Georgia during the period of ferment in which he dominated Georgia politics (1926–46). He was known for his fiery political style that evoked fanatical loyalty from thousands of agrarian supporters who responded to his appeals in celebration and defense of rural Georgia's embattled culture and lifestyle.

As his political style evolved from populistic agrarianism to virulent racism, Talmadge gained notoriety as the stereotype of a southern demagogue, a "Cracker buffoon," a "redneck racist." At the peak of his popularity,

Eugene Talmadge (seated) on the Georgia campaign trail, 1936

Talmadge drew crowds of 20,000 to 30,000 for campaign rallies in small towns throughout Georgia. Country folk from everywhere in the state came to stand in the hot Georgia sun and eat barbecue, sneak a swig or two of corn liquor, listen to "Fiddlin' John" Carson's country music, and take in "Farmer Gene's" political road show. With the appropriate southern drawl and proper quotations from the Scriptures, Talmadge conjured up vivid images of a blessed but embattled rural lifestyle, condemned the farmers' enemies as if he were a country preacher railing against Satan, and promised "he-man" action in the farmers' interests against the minions of such alien forces as "mastadon trusts" and Wall Street.

Talmadge's rural political style represented in many ways a significant agrarian response to the vast changes associated with the emergence of modern America. In a process begun in the late 19th century, the older America of autonomous rural communities was breaking down before the new centralized bureaucratic order, which served "the regulative hierarchical needs of urban-industrial life." "Farmer Gene's" response was similar to the earlier efforts of the Southern Farmers' Alliance and the Populist party led in Georgia by Thomas Watson.

Both Talmadge and Watson made cultural appeals to Georgia farmers at times when their rural lifestyle seemed seriously threatened by circumstances largely beyond their control. In many ways Talmadge's style reflected his support of southern agrarian culture. This can be said about his appeals to his fellow Georgians' fundamentalist religious beliefs, to their habits of "macho" individualism and personal violence, and to their localistic lifestyle centering on long-term attachments to specific places and specific people. Moreover, many of his actions seemed to be designed to preserve Georgia's rural culture in the face of powerful assaults from the outside world, including his attacks on the New Deal federal government. Talmadge always based his defense of rural Georgia on traditional Democratic party principles: the "classical" economic doctrines of Adam Smith and the political doctrines of Thomas Jefferson and the Jacksonian Democrats. When "Farmer Gene" burst upon the Georgia political scene, the Bourbon Democratic establishment supported the New South creed, which celebrated the union in the South of the American pastoral and industrial images described by Leo Marx in *The Machine in the Garden*. Talmadge's political style rejected the Bourbons' ideological synthesis and constructed a sacred mysticism out of the elements of southern rural culture. Earlier, "Farmer Gene's" Populist precursors had called for variation in the traditional principles of the Democratic party when they proposed legislation and other actions requiring significant government power to bring the party's outlook into line with changing realities. Once this effort failed, however, their defense of the rural lifestyle and of the traditional Democratic principles turned into something akin to an irrational emotional response to attacks on a sacred mysticism.

At the zenith of his career, Talmadge was bold enough to muster his agrarian forces against President Franklin D. Roosevelt, but something went awry and "Farmer Gene's" rural political style failed to hold enough supporters firmly to his banner to carry him through the fight. Under normal circumstances his style offered great promise of success. It focused on the cultural issues (tied to rural Georgians' "personally structured value systems"), which, along with purely local concerns, usually dominated American politics before the New Deal. After such a serious crisis as the Great Depression allowed economic issues to capture the voters' attention, however, Talmadge's rural and political style declined in effectiveness from its peak of the mid-1930s. In his later campaigns, "Farmer Gene" focused on the race issue as he tried to find another cultural issue that could earn him votes in rural Georgia.

Karl Rodabaugh
East Carolina University

William Anderson, *The Wild Man from Sugar Creek: The Political Career of Eugene Talmadge* (1975); Sarah Lemmon, "The Public Career of Eugene Talmadge, 1926–1936" (Ph.D. dissertation, University of North Carolina, Chapel Hill, 1952); Karl Rodabaugh, *Southern Studies* (Spring 1982).

Thurmond, Strom

(b. 1902) Politician.

Born in Edgefield, S.C., on 5 December 1902 of a prominent political family, Strom Thurmond has been active in politics for more than half a century. Personifying the conservative nature of the region, Thurmond is an ageless institution reminiscent of W. J. Cash's metaphorical South, "a tree with many age rings . . . bent and twisted by all the winds of the years, but with roots in the Old South."

The formative influences on Thurmond began with his father and were enhanced by the deep political and historical forces of his native Edgefield. William Watts Ball, editor of the Charleston *News and Courier*, once observed that Edgefield "had more dashing, brilliant, romantic figures, statesmen, orators, soldiers, adventurers and daredevils than any [other] county of South Carolina." This rural county has produced 10 governors, half as many lieutenant governors, and a number of U.S. senators. Additionally, Edgefield harbors a deep strain of violence, which originated in the 18th century and has been rather proudly maintained into the 20th. There is also in the area a core of evangelical fundamentalism, which has emerged in Thurmond's personality and value system.

The blood feuds of the 19th century and the *code duello* that characterized much of the South have approached a cultural norm in South Carolina. In 1856 Congressman Preston Brooks of Edgefield caned Massachusetts Senator Charles Sumner into insensibility because of a Sumner speech regarded as slanderous by Brooks. Strom's father "had to kill a man" as a result of a political feud. Senator Benjamin Ryan Tillman, also from Edgefield, and a close personal friend of Thurmond's father, initiated a fistfight on the Senate floor with a colleague. A less spectacular example of the Edgefield tradition occurred when Strom Thurmond twice pinned Senator Ralph Yarborough outside a committee room in order to prevent a quorum.

Thurmond made his national reputation as a presidential candidate in 1948, leading a dissident band of segregationists in their defection from the national Democratic party. Thurmond and his Dixiecrats were manifestations of the stress inherent in the New Deal coalition bequeathed to Harry Truman. Thurmond's secession in 1948 was reminiscent of pre–Civil War tensions when regional candidates bolted the Democracy to close ranks behind defenders of southern values and their peculiar institutions. Not since the days of John C. Calhoun had the South seen such a popular symbolic leader as Thurmond. Indeed, Thurmond as a neo-Calhounite added a fascinating historical dimension as the South faced its "Second Reconstruction."

Strom Thurmond, Dixiecrat leader and Republican U.S. senator, 1980s

By a kind of historic osmosis Thurmond absorbed the ethos of familial and regional values. The development of his personal value system mirrored his social environment. Thurmond's conceptual interaction with the world around him has been essentially fundamentalist. As a literalist he sees things in absolute terms. A Manichaean by nature, Thurmond has a vision of events dominated, as Robert Sherrill put it, by "metaphysical absolutes" where there is "one Eden, one Hell, one Heaven, one Right, one Wrong, and one Strom." The most revealing account of Thurmond's political fundamentalism, vision of history, and analysis of contemporary political events is his book, *The Faith We Have Not Kept*, published in 1966.

To some, Strom Thurmond is nothing more than a segregationist with a penchant for young women. However, deeper analysis shows Thurmond to possess a prism-like quality through which national issues are refracted, making him a symbolic figure of a South in transition. After the Voting Rights Act of 1965 and the increase of black voters in South Carolina, Thurmond ended his overtly segregationist rhetoric and began seeking black votes. The South of 1948 is light years from the South of today, and the evolution of Thurmond and the South stand as twin testaments to a man and a region that have achieved some accommodation with their history.

The appeal of Strom Thurmond is best captured by the reply of a mill worker, when asked why he was voting for Thurmond: "Strom stands up for what he believes in, even when he's wrong." In sum, Thurmond remains the quintessential southern politician: enduring yet resilient, simple but canny, militaristic yet biblical, and always the candidate.

James G. Banks
Cuyahoga Community College

James G. Banks, "Strom Thurmond and the Revolt against Modernity" (Ph.D. dissertation, Kent State University, 1970); Jack Bass and Walter DeVries, *The Transformation of Southern Politics: Social Change and Political Consequences since 1945* (1976).

Wallace, George
(b. 1919) Politician.

George Corley Wallace entered Alabama politics in 1946 when he was elected to the state legislature. Six years later be became a state circuit judge. In 1958 he ran for governor, and when he lost the contest to a blatant racist, Wallace vowed that he was "not goin' to be out-niggahed again." Keeping his promise, he was elected governor in 1962 on a racist platform. In his inaugural address he shouted, "Segregation now! Segregation tomorrow! Segregation forever!" While governor, Wallace criticized the passage of the Civil Rights Act of 1964 and the Voting Rights Act of 1965, unsuccessfully tried to prevent the racial desegregation of the University of Alabama, and had to contend with a voting rights march on the state capitol organized by Martin Luther King, Jr. Wallace entered the national political scene in 1964 when he ran for the Democratic presidential nomination, although he withdrew from that contest before the convention.

When he could not succeed himself as governor, he successfully ran his wife Lurleen for the office in 1966. Two years later Wallace ran for the presidency as the candidate of the American Independent party. He appealed to the latent racism of voters all over the country when he orated for law and order in a racially troubled society and against federal interference in local schools, the liberal Supreme Court, and federal restrictions in regard to racial considerations and the sale of private homes. While his 46 electoral votes came from the South, approximately one-half of his 10 million popular votes were cast by supporters living outside that region.

In 1970, after his wife had died of cancer while in office, Wallace ran for the gubernatorial post again, barely defeating the lieutenant governor who had completed Lurleen Wallace's term. In 1972 Wallace coveted the Democratic nomination for president, billing himself as a national, not a regional, candidate, and as best representing the people's attitudes on the major issues of the day. In the primary contests Wallace called for law and order and opposed busing to achieve racial integration in the schools. Wallace won, or showed great voting strength, not only in the South but also in states such as Wisconsin, Pennsylvania, Indiana, Michigan, and Maryland. His campaign was abruptly sidetracked when he was shot. Paralyzed from the waist down, he was thereafter confined to a wheelchair. The would-be assassin had ended not only Wallace's campaign but also his growing national political power.

George Wallace campaign button

In 1974 Wallace won the Alabama governorship for an unprecedented third term. In 1976 he made another race for the presidency, but when his campaign had no appeal in the southern primaries his national plans collapsed, and he devoted himself to being governor. As in the past, Wallace worked for increased expenditures for education and highways, but also, as in the past, his accomplishments were overshadowed by his stance on civil rights for blacks.

Wallace once again ran for governor in 1982 and won. His campaign was especially noteworthy because he reversed his previous arch-segregationist position and appealed for—and got—black support, an indication of the dramatic racial and political changes in Alabama in the quarter-century of Wallace's career. Citing health problems, Wallace announced on 2 April 1986 that he would not seek a fifth term as governor, thus terminating his active political career. Wallace is perhaps the most influential political figure in Alabama in the 20th century.

Monroe Billington
New Mexico State University

Numan Bartley and Hugh Davis Graham, *Southern Politics and the Second Reconstruction* (1975); Monroe Billington, *The Political South in the Twentieth Century* (1975); Marshall Frady, *Wallace* (1968); Lance Morrow, *Time* (14 April 1986); Robert Sherrill, *Gothic Politics in the Deep South* (1968).

Watson, Tom
(1856–1922) Politician.

Thomas Edward Watson spent most of his life in the village of Thomson, Ga. As a young man he taught in country schools, later becoming a highly successful lawyer who practiced in small towns. He succeeded in part because he knew country people well and spoke in a colorful, rural idiom. For Watson the ideal society embraced the life he had known as a young boy, when his grandfather had owned a valuable plantation. After the Civil War his family lost that estate and sank into poverty. Although Watson became a wealthy lawyer, he knew that many southern farmers—plagued by falling cotton prices and increasing tenancy—faced hard times. He did not believe that the New South creed, with its call for industrialization and urbanization, would help them. Instead, Watson championed the ideal of a South that consisted largely of prosperous farmers.

With the rise of the Farmers' Alliance in the 1880s, Watson hoped that its programs could help country people. In 1890 he won a seat in Congress as an Alliance candidate, and during his one term he introduced a resolution that eventually resulted in free delivery of rural mail. In 1891 Watson joined the People's party and became a leading spokesman for southern Populism, a movement of landowning farmers and tenants who wanted to improve rural life by making reforms in the prevailing economic system. To achieve that, Watson called on blacks and whites to join forces in working for economic reforms. He did not advocate social equality between the races, but his attempt to win black votes caused white Democrats to denounce him and his fellow Populists as threats to white supremacy. During the congressional elections of 1892 and 1894, the Democrats resorted to massive frauds to insure Watson's defeat. In the face of that harsh treatment, Watson remained loyal to the People's party; in 1896 he served as its vice-presidential candidate.

Following his defeat in that election, Watson retired to private life, where he devoted himself to practicing law, writing history, and editing several magazines. Between 1900 and 1920 he continued to use his influence with former Populists to determine the outcome of Georgia elections, and near the end of his life he served for two years in the U.S. Senate. After 1900 he no longer demonstrated the idealism that he had displayed as a Populist leader in the 1890s. Instead of encouraging blacks and whites to work together for common political objectives, he advocated the disfranchisement of blacks. He also became a leading proponent of anti-Catholicism and anti-Semitism. When he died in 1922, the newly revived Ku Klux Klan held him in high esteem.

William F. Holmes
University of Georgia

Charles Crowe, *Journal of Negro History* (April 1970); Robert Saunders, *Georgia Historical Quarterly* (Fall 1970); Thomas E. Watson Papers, Southern Historical Collection, University of North Carolina, Chapel Hill; C. Vann Woodward, *Tom Watson: Agrarian Rebel* (1938).

Young, Andrew

(b. 1932) Minister, civil rights worker, politician, and diplomat.

Andrew Jackson Young, Jr., was born 12 March 1932 in New Orleans to the middle-class household of Andrew Jackson Young, Sr., a dentist, and Daisy Fuller Young. He attended Dillard University (1947–48) and Howard University, where he received his B.S. degree in biology (1951). After leaving Howard, Young attended Hartford Theological Seminary, where he received a degree in divinity (1955). He was ordained by the Congregational church before returning south to pastor churches in Georgia (Beachton and Thomasville) until 1957. That year, unfulfilled with his small-town ministry, he became executive director of the National Council of Churches' New York-based Department of Youth Programs. In that capacity he hosted the nationally televised, youth-oriented series *Look Up and Live*.

Then, captivated by the burgeoning southern civil rights movement, Young returned south again as head of the United Church of Christ's (UCC) voter registration program headquartered in Alabama. While working with the UCC, Young joined the staff of the Southern Christian Leadership Conference (SCLC) in 1961 at the request of its president, Martin Luther King, Jr. Young acquired the reputation of being a moderating force within King's spirited inner circle. While other King lieutenants played firebrand roles during the initial stages of campaigns in such cities as Birmingham and Selma, Young came in later as SCLC's negotiator in meetings with segregationists. Young served as SCLC's executive director and its executive vice president, and he drafted versions of the 1964 and 1965 Civil Rights Acts. He left SCLC in 1970 to make the transition from protest politics to electoral politics.

Young's initial campaign for Georgia's Fifth Congressional District seat was unsuccessful, but he won in 1972. He and Barbara Jordan, who was elected to the House of Representatives from Texas in the same year, thus became the first southern blacks since 1898 to win congressional elections. Young was reelected in 1974 and 1976. During his tenure as congressman, Young opposed the Holt Amendment, which sought to prohibit federal withholding as a means to compel school desegregation. He actively supported the extension of the Voting Rights Act of 1965, citing the increase in black registration (29 percent in 1964 to 56 percent in 1972) in states affected by this law. He also favored the subsequent broadening of

Andrew Young, civil rights activist and mayor of Atlanta, Ga., 1980s

the act to include language minorities, and he served on the committees for Banking and Currency and for Rules.

Young was one of the first nationally known black leaders to support Jimmy Carter's 1976 bid to become the first modern president from the Deep South. Young, as Carter's major advisor, allayed the suspicions of many black leaders and voters about Carter and his southern background. Young came to Carter's defense, nullifying criticism of the former Georgia governor, when he made a campaign blunder by stating his support for the "ethnic purity" of white neighborhoods. When some 90 percent of the more than 6 million black voters cast their ballots for Carter, providing him with his slim margin of victory over Gerald Ford, Young's active support was seen as pivotal by many. In fact, Carter stated that Young was the only person to whom he owed a political debt.

Carter appointed Young U.S. ambassador to the United Nations. In this position, Young was able to create a viable dialogue between the U.S. government and the Third World after a period of intense alienation during the Nixon-Ford years. In particular, relations between Africa and the United States were bettered as a result of Young's efforts to do away with apartheid. His negotiations contributed to the coming of majority rule to Zimbabwe in 1980. Young's time in the United Nations was marked by a bluntness unusual to diplomacy. His statements that Britain had institutionalized racism and that Cuban troops were a stabilizing force in Angola, among others, created much controversy. Young resigned his post in 1979 when an uproar occurred after he met with a Palestine Liberation Organization representative, counter to official U.S. government policy. He came back to Atlanta and was elected its mayor in 1981.

Expressing the conviction that foreign and domestic policies of the Reagan Administration were "clear failures," Young's mayoral career has been characterized by continued support for Atlanta's affirmative action programs ("good business" as well as the law) and attempts to link the gateway city economically with the "new frontier" markets of Latin America, Africa, and the Middle East.

Vincent D. Fort
Morehouse College

Robert H. Brisbane, *Black Activism* (1974); James Gaskins, *Andrew Young: Man with a Mission* (1979); *New York Times* (3 January 1982); Howell Raines, *My Soul Is Rested: Movement Days in the Deep South Remembered* (1977); Eddie Stone, *Andrew Young: Biography of a Realist* (1980).

Recreation

JOHN SHELTON REED
University of North Carolina at Chapel Hill
CONSULTANT

Cajun children fishing, Schriever, La., 1940

Leisure

C. Vann Woodward begins his *American Counterpoint* with a lengthy treatment of southern leisure. He points out that like so many other myths about the South, this one tends to be "Janus-faced," to present contrary aspects that change depending on the observer's point of view. For some, southern leisure has been a gracious thing, involving careful attention to nonpecuniary values and activities in a world mad with materialistic frenzy. Others, looking at the reverse side, see the unattractive countenance, the Lazy South, the "Sahara of the Bozart," with all its blemishes—"idleness, indolence, slothfulness, langor, lethargy, and dissipation."

Leisure/Laziness Myth. These two contrary aspects notwithstanding, the leisure/laziness myth has consistently involved two distinct cultural subjects—work and nonwork—and has represented the typical southerner as less interested in the former than most Americans and more interested in the latter. The myth's Janus-faced quality becomes clear only when values have been assigned to work and to leisure. Some northern observers and proponents of the "new Industrial South" have focused on the South's distaste for work, viewing it as a destructive anachronism that needed to be reformed, and dismissed the various claims about the virtues of free time. But apologists for the South have tended to emphasize the value of leisure as a time for human culture, spiritual reflection, contemplation, friends, family, nature—those things that make life worth the effort—and at the same time to criticize the American preoccupation with busy work, mindless growth, and the resultant spiritual and cultural exhaustion.

This myth, then, has generated two kinds of statements, those about facts and those about values. As such, it may be analyzed on two levels. On the one hand, one may attempt to determine the extent to which the myth is true—the extent to which southern attitudes and behavior correspond to the stereotype. The social scientist, for example, may test southern mass attitudes and behavior and speculate about their causes. On the other hand, the myth may be accepted on its own terms, as an expression of values and as a part of the larger cultural dialogue or "counterpoint" that has existed between the South and the rest of the country. In this regard historians and literary critics may investigate the opinions of articulate and influential writers concerning work and leisure in order to show how at its highest reaches culture emerges in dialogue about questions of values, about what should or might be, rather than about what already exists.

The cultural debate surrounding the leisure/laziness myth goes back a long way. During the mid-18th century southerners such as John Hammond portrayed their region as a land of tropical abundance where tranquility and leisure were the rule. Such idyllic descriptions, echoed by men such as Robert Beverley and William Byrd II, were mainly designed to counter a bad European press and attract settlers. But still these early allurement accounts sounded one major mythic value that by the Civil War was completely developed—that work should be a means to an end, that it should be a way to earn a livelihood and to free oneself from time to time for more important things.

During the antebellum period southern spokesmen expanded, developed, and defended the leisure myth. According to people such as Virginia's Governor Henry Wise, leisure was indispensable for the natural aristocrat, providing the opportunity for learning and public service, freeing him from the servile arts and drudgery for the liberal arts and the creation of new culture, a culture that would benefit all classes. The second part of the myth included an indictment of northern money grubbing, business, and harsh treatment of workers. The North had made money its god, work an end in itself, and had forgotten about human, nonpecuniary needs and the importance of leisure.

But even as the myth developed, critics from both the North and South recognized that the ideal did not match the reality, that the lack of work was more a problem than an opportunity. They pointed out that free time in the South was more the occasion for drunkenness, idleness, and dissipation than for learning, culture, and service. It was work and the discipline of work that held a people together, not the freedom of leisure. It was in the marketplace, not the saloon, that culture grew.

This sort of dialogue, involving a blend of voices, some enthusiastic, others ironic or even cynical, smoldered after the Civil War, especially in the works of southern writers such as Sidney Lanier. It was later rekindled and flared briefly in the 20th century as a response to rapid industrial changes.

Agrarians and the New South. As did many of their contemporaries and the majority of historians who have written about the period, the Twelve Agrarians of *I'll Take My Stand* believed that American industry and business had taken a new direction in the 1920s—had shifted attention from production to consumption. According to the Agrarians, "It [was] an inevitable consequence of industrial process that production [outran] the rate of natural consumption." This overrun had resulted in chronic overproduction and unemployment. But instead of dealing with these consequences of success in a humane fashion, American business had "romanticized" industry and work and developed a "new gospel of consumption." Promoting "the incessant extension of industrialism," the multiplication of luxuries, and the cultivation of fantastic and even lethal desires for them, this new gospel "never proposed a specific goal; it initiated the infinite series"—a squirrel-cage existence where growth was for growth's sake, work purposeless and never ending, and consumption artificial and manipulated.

The Agrarians proposed a traditionally southern alternative to this mindless "progress." Instead of work that was brutal, harried, and meaningless, they offered "a form of labor that [was] pursued with intelligence and leisure"—that was more natural and task oriented, connected to the soil and to a stable social order. Instead of free time that was lost to consumption, satiety, and aimlessness, they suggested a leisure in the "culture of the soil" where art and religion flourished; "a free and disinterested approach to existence" was possible; the amenities of life such as manners, conversation, sympathy, family life, and romantic love were carried on; and the enjoyment of life could be spontaneous. To the Agrarians, leisure should be an integral part of life. It should be a part of work, with a social and economic place. It should not, like industrial free time, alienate more than it brings people together.

Walter Hines Page agreed that leisureliness was a hallmark of regional identity. But unlike the Agrarians, he welcomed industry to the New South because, in addition to its material blessings, it would offer "the inestimable boon of leisure." For Page, leisure was an industrial product as important as consumer goods because it could be used to redeem parts of southern culture even as the traditional forms of work were being lost.

But spokesmen for the New South have generally dismissed these dreams. People such as Henry W. Grady and Richard Edmunds welcomed industry with none of Page's hopes for leisure and saw the South's casual approach to work as a curable weakness. Grady saw the South falling "in love with its work"; Edmunds observed that his compatriots had learned that "time is money." New southern businessmen have been as busy as their northern friends promoting goods and services designed for the "leisure market." City leaders court industry, boasting that the work ethic is stronger in their region than elsewhere. Following the national trend, southerners as a group have lost interest in increased leisure and have remained content with 40 hours' work a week for over 40 years—this after a 20-year period of rapid reduction in the hours of labor.

Even southern historians, while not so much welcoming the Puritan work ethic, have joined in the general condemnation of leisure. W. J. Cash saw the old southern assumptions about leisure—"that the first end of life is living itself"—woefully out of date, a way of degeneration and "incompatible with success." David Bertelson saw leisure as the traditional myth, but laziness as the traditional reality. According to Bertelson, laziness worked against a sense of community because it fragmented southerners and encouraged a preoccupation with self instead of the community.

The discussion has largely ended. Even though a few echoes are heard from time to time, southern life and leisure are no longer seriously proposed as alternatives to industrialism nor is increasing free time offered as a way for the South to accommodate modernism and retain its identity. The lively exchanges about what was more meaningless, work in the industrial squirrel-cage or free time in a disintegrating culture, are mostly forgotten. Yet the perception in its simplest form—that southerners prefer leisure more and work less—remains.

In magazine articles, in newspaper Sunday supplements, and even in advertisements, the region's lazy-leisurely reputation continues to be spread, even internationally. Occasionally a journalist will editorialize and condemn or praise the lazy, leisurely South. But usually, these portrayals are not serious business. Rather they tend to be amusing reports about a charming, regional peculiarity. Public attitudes tend to conform to these popular reports. John Shelton Reed and others have demonstrated that college students North and South still hold on to this regional stereotype. Apparently, the old dialogue produced a vivid enough image in the public awareness to survive its passing.

Watching the bathers at Gulfport, Miss., postcard, early 20th century

But another possibility remains—that the myth is true, and the dialogue, too, about both a reality and an ideal. Those who engaged in the dialogue often thought of themselves as reporters as well as leaders and spokesmen. Even the Agrarians, calling their region back to tradition, made claims about historical truth and existing culture. The extent to which myth matches reality has been approached empirically with some interesting results.

Distinctive Southern Behavior. Statistical evidence for the first three decades of this century indicates that southerners did prefer leisure more and work for wages less than other Americans. For example, in 1920 a typical northern worker making the same hourly wage as his southern brother worked longer hours. If he got a raise he would work even longer hours while the typical southerner would take more time off at higher income levels. But this regional difference disappeared by the 1940s and the South, like the rest of the nation, became content with the 40-hour week.

When investigators study attitudes about work directly, instead of opinions about stereotypes, they have so far failed to find regional variations. There is simply not enough evidence to support or contradict the belief that southerners value work more or less than other Americans. Nor is there much in the way of systematic evidence about southern attitudes toward leisure.

But indications can be found that southerners are distinctive when it comes to leisure behavior. The evidence comes from a variety of sources and it is remarkably consistent. By and large, southerners simply do less in their leisure time than other Americans—or at least less of most things that social scientists and market researchers are interested in.

The U.S. Department of Labor's 1972 survey of consumer expenditures shows that southerners spend a smaller percentage of their incomes on "recreational goods and services" than other Americans—from the lowest to the highest income classification. Research undertaken by private marketing firms also shows that southerners engage in less "commercially relevant behavior" in their leisure than others. In general, these studies have found that the South is not as good a market as its population would suggest and that it is a particularly bad market for recreational products.

Other studies show lower levels of magazine and newspaper circulation, miles driven per year (a stand-in for billboard advertising), television watching and radio listening, memberships in hobby and special interest groups, voting and political activity in general, and what the National Endowment for the Humanities (NEH) called the fine or beaux arts (with the exceptions found by the 1973 Louis Harris Poll of singing in a choir, listening to religious music, and listening to country and western music).

These regional differences are not enormous. Region makes less difference than education does, for instance. But regional differences are about the same size as differences between black and white—about the same size, that is, of some other "cultural" or "ethnic" differences in the United States.

One may reasonably ask at this point what do southerners do when they are not consuming, watching television, reading the newspaper or magazines, or participating in clubs? A Harris Poll in 1978 found a number of these things that were included in the NEH study mentioned above. According to this poll, southerners spend more time fixing things around the house, helping others, having a good time with friends and relatives, resting after work, getting away from problems, taking naps, and "just doing nothing."

One good way to summarize these findings is to point out that the South has a pattern of leisure that is more "time intensive" and less "goods intensive." Southerners are more likely to choose activities that take more time but less money than are other late 20th-century Americans. From all indications the modern South is still holding on to vestiges of a preindustrial folk culture in its leisure. Considering that he wrote over 50 years ago about a South he feared was vanishing, John Crowe Ransom's observations in *I'll Take My Stand* that the arts of the South are the "social arts of dress, conversation, manners, the table, the hunt, politics, oratory, the pulpit, the arts of living and not the arts of escape . . . ; community arts in which every class of society could participate after its kind," are remarkably accurate today.

Since the myth, if not the proven reality, has been around so long, there is certainly no shortage of explanations for the lazy-leisurely South. H. L. Mencken's view, echoed more recently by the Kentucky-born gonzo journalist, Dr. Hunter Thompson, was that white southerners are genetically disposed to idleness and vicious habits. The South Carolina poet Josephine Pinckney, on the other hand, argued that these are innate black traits, somehow spread to whites by contagion. Southerners' favorite explanation—or excuse—has probably been the weather. In its old version, favored by Robert Beverley and William Byrd II, this argument has it that it is too easy to get by where food grows almost by itself and nobody needs many clothes. A version more applicable to the urban, industrial South says that it is just too hot to do much of anything. Another popular theory points to the effects of slavery, producing laziness in slaves and slaveholders alike, and also leading nonslaveholders to believe that exertion was for slaves and beneath their dignity. Still another recalls the earlier, fanciful notion that the South's supposed Cavalier heritage produced individuals fleeing Puritan constraints while pursuing a hedonistic, "long-haired" lifestyle in the southern climes.

C. Vann Woodward, on the other hand, saw a distinctive skepticism emerging in the South after the Civil War about the American dream of endless progress, industrial work, and human perfectibility in general. Resulting from the regional experience of defeat, failure, sin, poverty, and guilt, this skepticism has produced a people less caught up in the fervid rush of modern life and more content with the leisurely enjoyment of the simple present. Finally, the old myth and debate about the defects and virtues of work and leisure may have percolated down through the South, so that the culture comes to resemble what its mythmakers imagined. George B. Tindall has shown how southern myths have a definite way of influencing regional realities. For the lazy-leisurely South, it may be a case of nature imitating art.

Whatever their origins, southern attitudes toward work and leisure are part of the regional culture. Like other cultural traits, these are not things that individuals work out for themselves. *They are learned* from those around us while we are growing up and from each other after we are grown. A large part of any culture is made up of shared views of what is appropriate; success in any culture depends on learning what those views are and, ordinarily, on coming to share them. One is not born knowing what to do with leisure time, nor do individuals make it up as they go along. People learn how to pass the time appropriately. Those who share the same culture—a regional culture, for instance—have learned more or less similar lessons.

See also ART AND ARCHITECTURE: Resort Architecture; BLACK LIFE: Sports, Black; FOLKLIFE: Storytelling; HISTORY AND MANNERS: Manners; INDUSTRY: Industrialization and Change; LANGUAGE: Conversation; LITERATURE: Agrarianism in Literature; MYTHIC SOUTH: New South Myth; / Agrarians, Vanderbilt

John Shelton Reed
University of North Carolina
at Chapel Hill

Benjamin K. Hunnicutt
University of Iowa

David Bertelson, *The Lazy South* (1967); H. C. Brearley, *American Scholar* (Winter 1949); W. J. Cash, *The Mind of the South* (1941); Norval Glenn and Charles Weaver, *Texas Business Review* (November–December 1982); Fred C. Hobson, *Alabama*

Heritage (Summer 1986); Lewis Killian, *White Southerners* (1970); Forrest McDonald and Grady McWhiney, *American Historical Review* (December 1980); Peter Marsden et al., *Social Forces* (June 1982); H. L. Mencken, *Prejudices, Second Series* (1920); Josephine Pinckney, in *Culture in the South*, ed. W. T. Couch (1934); John Shelton Reed, *The Enduring South: Subcultural Persistence in Mass Society* (1974), *North Carolina Historical Review* (April 1983), *One South: An Ethnic Approach to Regional Culture* (1982), *Southerners: The Social Psychology of Sectionalism* (1983); Joe Gray Taylor, *Eating, Drinking, and Visiting in the South: An Informal History* (1982); George B. Tindall, *The Ethnic Southerners* (1976); Twelve Southerners, *I'll Take My Stand: The South and the Agrarian Tradition* (1930); Rupert B. Vance, *Human Geography of the South: A Study in Regional Resources and Human Adequacy* (1935); C. Vann Woodward, *American Counterpoint: Slavery and Racism in the North-South Dialogue* (1964), *The Burden of Southern History* (1960).

Baseball

Throughout baseball history only four former Confederate cities have enjoyed major league baseball status. Richmond was in the American Association for part of a single season in 1884, and the current Houston organization began play in 1962. The move that really counted in southern terms was the move of the Milwaukee Braves to Atlanta in 1966. When the expansion Washington Senators became the Texas Rangers in 1972, the picture was completed.

Exclusion from the big leagues for so long did not mean the South had been divorced from baseball. Far from it. The region had produced many major leaguers, including some of the greatest and most colorful, such as Ty Cobb. The South contributed some of the most influential broadcasters the game has had, including Jay "Dizzy" Dean and Pee Wee Reese, who worked television's game of the week in the 1950s and early 1960s, and radio's Mel Allen and Red Barber. Major southern cities such as Memphis, Nashville, Birmingham, Louisville, and Little Rock have long supported minor league teams and industrial leagues, and southern college teams have dominated competition. The South manufactured the great majority of the game's bats, including the Louisville Slugger, and since 1886 it has been the site of spring training camps.

What then explains the absence of major league membership for so long? The overpowering heat and humidity of the South was one consideration, especially in an age preceding night games, air-conditioning, and summer-weight uniforms. Connie Mack and Clark Griffith, two of the most influential major league owners in the first half of the 20th century, insisted that the weather in St. Louis, Cincinnati, and Washington sapped the strength of players on their teams even before mid-season. Mack stated that those teams "must be 25 percent better than any other in order to win a pennant." Players spoke of soaking their feet, baseball spikes and all, in pails of ice water, then sloshing into the steamy fields in those cities. They bemoaned the nights of fitful sleep in roasting hotel rooms, and recalled soaking their bedsheets in tub water, then wrapping themselves in them for relief. Thoughts of playing in locations farther south were not broadly entertained.

Another basic problem was travel. The population centers of the South that might have supported major league play were too far removed from the long established northern teams. Perhaps even more important, they were separated by great distances from each other. Not until 1958 and the age of convenient and extensive airline travel did the majors open up the West Coast, which was far from populous. In this respect, the South was not far behind.

Until the 1960s southern culture was exported to the nation's baseball fans in the personalities of regional sons who made major league rosters. Often what this meant was little more than an image of Snuffy Smith in the dugout. A short biographical sketch of Mississippian Guy "Joe" Bush appeared in a 1932 issue of the baseball bible, *The Sporting News*, for example. Its opening sentence was: "No lazy bones in the body of this Cub pitcher, his Southern birth notwithstanding." An earlier generation had grown up with the illiteracy of "Shoeless" Joe Jackson, a South Carolinian who had been so frightened of the big cities of the North that he fled from his first train ride en route to the major leagues. He had needed an adult babysitter to ensure his later arrival in Philadelphia. Fans would shout from the grandstands, asking him to spell cat. It was good storytelling and reinforced a powerful stereotype America had of its southern citizens.

Jackson's contemporary, Ty Cobb, epitomized the violent southerner. All big league teams had their sons of the South. They made good copy for baseball writers, many of whom were noted for their cynicism and expertise with one-line putdowns. To be sure, all players from the South were not reported in comic or glaring fashion, but more than enough were. Especially demeaning were instances of players' statements being spelled in dialect. Georgian Luke Appling, a Hall of Fame shortstop who played in the majors for two decades, sometimes referred to in print as a cracker, was repeatedly quoted as saying such words as "jes" (for just), "shucks," "gonna," "'spect," "cain't," "reckon," "uster" (for used to), and "nuthin." "Leg" somehow even became "laig" in Appling's mouth, as reported by the *New York Times*. Fellow Georgian Cecil Travis, another longtime American Leaguer, was once referred to as a "Geawgian."

Yet, a pair of broadcasters from the Deep South—Mel Allen and Red Barber—brought their homespun qualities to New York, the biggest baseball market in the world, and became the most respected of their profession. Both men, extremely fair and balanced in their reportage, represented baseball at its ideal, sportsmanlike best. In doing so their colloquialisms gained undenied respect. Barber's talk about tearing up the pea patch swept Brooklyn. His "catbird seat" was shared by millions of Dodger fans. Nevertheless, the players remained the focus.

Baseball in the South involved nearly every hamlet in the region, though decades went by before the sport was played on a par with the rest of the nation. The game's early history in Dixie featured men from north of the Mason-Dixon line taking leadership. Indeed, quite a few of these early baseball "teachers" carried the label of "carpetbagger." Returning Confederate veterans, many of whom had learned the game from Union soldiers, had preceded them and created a taste for the sport among the white citizenry. Exslaves had learned in the same way and played their own brand of ball on their side of the tracks. Not until Reconstruction ended, however, did baseball expand and improve.

The game, as had already happened elsewhere in the nation, became dominated by community teams, with sponsorship often supplied by businessmen. Jewish merchants, in particular, funded teams in New Orleans, Macon, Atlanta, Augusta, Mobile, Houston, and Birmingham. In the mid-1880s the original Southern League was instituted, and organized professional baseball finally set up shop in the region. Atlanta *Constitution* editor Henry W. Grady, in the forefront in promoting a modern, industrial New South, was key to the establishment of the Atlanta franchise in that league. The team was an obvious example of boosterism.

The Southern League unfortunately led a miserable existence, needing frequent reorganization efforts to prevent its demise. Team rosters had very few players from the South, as locals were not yet talented enough to get contracts with even second-rate minor league clubs. The players who had the contracts performed so poorly that it was believed their ineptness was typical of "northerners sick in the heat."

By the 20th century the sport was extremely significant in southern culture. Wherever there was a mill or mine, that company fielded a team. Competition in the many industrial leagues that developed was fierce, promoting a notable improvement on the ball diamond. Workers who detested the long days and dangerous conditions of their underpaid employment nonetheless were exuberant when their company team was victorious, especially if a championship was at stake. Community spirit was present, at least on game days. Management recognized this and did their utmost to keep their best players and to add the best from other teams. A winning ball club meant a stable work force. Who would want to leave a mill with a title team to take a job with a competitor that fielded losing nines?

Improved skills drew notice from the major league cities to the north. Community and regional pride was enhanced more than ever as increasing numbers of homegrown players advanced to the "bigs." Ty Cobb roared out of Georgia, Joe Jackson came up from South Carolina, Tris Speaker from Texas, Clyde Milan from Tennessee, and the march was on. Throughout the 20th century the lineups of major league clubs have been dotted with such nicknames as "Dixie," "Reb," "Tex," and "Catfish." The South became and remained a chief stomping ground for big league scouts.

Only since the late 1940s, however, when organized baseball was finally desegregated, has that scouting included blacks. Yet black players in the South had been competing on their own fields since the late 1880s. Most of the black semipro players who toured the United States decades later were from the South. Not surprisingly, their struggle was frequently marred by racist insults, even when their playing ability was held to be superior to that of whites.

Even as late as 1953 a Jackson, Miss., team in the Cotton States League refused to play against their Hot Springs opponent because the Arkansas squad was going to use a black pitcher. To compound the situation, the league's officers forfeited the game to Jackson. Hot Springs, to their way of thinking, had no right to expect Jackson to play against a black. Their ruling was overturned by the commissioner of minor league baseball, who made it clear that blacks could not be refused the right to play. In 1955, however, a Pine Bluff, Ark., team in the same Cotton States League signed three blacks to contracts and then released them a few days later, citing the pressure placed on them by other league teams.

The South by the mid-20th century had enthusiastically supported numerous minor league teams, 43 cities in North Carolina alone actually fielding professional teams in seven separate leagues in 1949. Over the years the South had seen play in leagues with names like Texas, Piedmont, Southern, Longhorn, South Atlantic, and Appalachian. Their own sons had graduated to the majors by the many hundreds, often stereotyped in scapegoat images associated with the South. When racism was involved, the term *southerner* assumed an extra burden. Today, black and white southerners such as Dennis "Oil Can" Boyd (Miss.), Ron Guidry (La.), Nolan Ryan (Tex.), and Dwight Gooden (Fla.) remain among the game's best players.

A single major league team declared itself to be "America's Team" in the 1980s. This bold stroke fit nicely into the apparent "southernizing" of the United States. The Atlanta Braves, the only major league baseball franchise ever based in the Deep South, claimed *national* sovereignty because of its owner's extensive television cable system. Fans in all corners of the nation watched the Braves on WTBS-TV and, familiar with that team's personnel because of its frequent television exposure, became supporters of Ted Turner's organization. The Braves, in essence sole baseball representatives of the South, are owned by a white man, utilize the American Indian as their symbol, and had a black, Hank Aaron, as the best player in their history. If anything tells the story of change in America, and particularly in the South, that is it.

See also MEDIA: / Turner, Ted

John E. DiMeglio
Mankato State University

Charles C. Alexander, *Ty Cobb: Baseball's Fierce Immortal* (1984); Alfred Duckett, *I Never Had It Made* (1972); Harvey Frommer, *Rickey and Robinson* (1982); Donald Gropman, *Say It Ain't So, Joe!: The Story of Shoeless Joe Jackson* (1979); John D. McCallum, *The Tiger Wore Spikes: An Informal Biography of Ty Cobb* (1956); Daniel Okrent and Harris Lewine, ed., *The Ultimate Baseball Book* (1979); Lawrence S. Ritter, *The*

Glory of Their Times: The Story of the Early Days of Baseball Told by Men Who Played It (1974).

Basketball

"Basketball is a city game," writes Pete Axthelm in his 1970 book, *The City Game*. "Its battlegrounds are strips of asphalt between tattered wire fences or crumbling buildings; its rhythms grow from the uneven thump of a ball against hard surfaces. . . . Basketball belongs to the cities." Indeed, basketball does belong to the cities. However, the classification of basketball as a "city game" overlooks the tradition of basketball in the South, where the game is played in both urban and rural areas, and where it has for years flourished as a rural game. Basketball courts of all descriptions and designs blanket the South. Salvaged stop signs or sheets of metal or wood often make functional backboards for young players who attach a suitable rim, as their desire to play basketball overrules any prescribed notion of a conventional goal or court.

Shortly after the invention of basketball by James A. Naismith in 1891, southerners began to experiment with the game. As early as the 1920s, high school boys throughout the South played on organized school teams and generally on outdoor courts. The indoor gym was a later addition to the southern game, and it was not uncommon at first for a Mississippi team to dress in spiffy uniforms, patterned after the indoor teams, and play on outdoor courts in subfreezing weather. School systems and towns dedicated to the game could perhaps afford the fancy uniforms, but it would be many years before they could afford the big gymnasium. For high schools and colleges in the South, neither of which had as large a budget as their northern counterparts, the cost of football was often prohibitive. Basketball, on the other hand, required a smaller investment and by the 1950s was earning large revenues for colleges such as Kentucky, North Carolina State, and Western Kentucky. In 1946, North Carolina State "imported" Everett Case, a coach from basketball-rich Indiana; by 1950 the school's annual basketball attendance had reached 230,000, the largest in the country. Part of the increased attendance was the result of increasing postwar college enrollment. College athletic facilities could not hold the crowds, and at a University of North Carolina–North Carolina State game the problem reached crisis proportion. A large crowd of followers, frustrated after being denied admission, tore down the doors of the gym, poured in, and stood around the perimeter of the court. The game eventually was canceled as fans continually spilled onto the court. A similar problem caused cancellation of a game between North Carolina State and Duke in 1948.

Even before World War II, college basketball in North Carolina was very popular. Beginning in 1933, Raleigh hosted the Southern Conference Tournament with Chamber of Commerce support. In 1947 the tournament was shifted to Duke University's 9,000-seat gym, still in use today and a vivid symbol of the richness of basketball tradition in the South. With the catalyst of a $100,000 donation from the Charles Babcock family, the North Carolina Legislature appropriated money for Reynolds Coliseum at North Carolina State, finished in 1951. Not surprisingly, smoking was always permitted in the facility, and R. J. Reynolds tobacco supporters bragged about the ventilation system capable of providing "a complete change of air every 15 minutes." With the new coliseum, North Carolina State dubbed itself the "basketball capital of the South."

North Carolina was also home to a very competitive and successful group of women's basketball teams, led by Hanes Hosiery of Winston-Salem, N.C., the dominant force in the Southern Textile League. Writing about women's basketball in the South in a 1979 issue of *Southern Exposure*, Elva Bishop and Katherine Fulton assert that "high caliber women's basketball wasn't born in the South in the 1970s; it merely got its second wind." Indeed, such teams as Hanes Hosiery and Nashville Business College were very high caliber. By 1947, in large part because of the dominance of Hanes, newspapers in Winston-Salem were hailing the city as the "new women's cage capital." Up until 1947, Hanes had limited competition in the Southern Textile League, made up of company teams formed to induce corporate pride and competition in workers. The dominance of Hanes in that league led the team to compete nationally through the Amateur Athletic Union's (AAU) national playoff. Though Hanes did not win the 1948 tournament, it did reach the quarterfinals where six out of the eight teams were from North Carolina, Georgia, and Tennessee. In 1951 Hanes won the AAU National Championship, defeating the Flying Queens of Wayland College, Tex., 50–34.

North Carolina State and Raleigh may have boasted that, with the completion of Reynolds Coliseum, they were the basketball capital of the South, but one school and one state could lay more legitimate claim to such a title. If there is one team and one region of the South that is most noted for its basketball it is Kentucky. Much of that fame, ironically, is because of a basketball sage from Kansas. Adolph Rupp, who coached the Kentucky Wildcats from 1930 to 1971, came to Kentucky from Kansas where he played under Phog Allen. After 28 seasons at Kentucky, Rupp won his 772nd game, passing the record previously held by Allen, his former coach and teacher. Rupp was to southern basketball what Bear Bryant was to football, though Rupp's longer tenure made him more dominant in his sport. A gruff, determined man, Rupp had the image of a country farm boy turned basketball genius. He became known as a Kentucky gentleman, one who loved his cattle and his bourbon. Dubbed "the Baron," Rupp was a strict father to all of his players. Like other teams in the Southeastern Conference (SEC), Kentucky resisted recruiting black players until the late 1960s, and Rupp's paternal callousness made him seem all the more reluctant to integrate his team. Shy he was not, and in a 1929 interview he claimed he took the job at Kentucky on the advice of a gas station attendant, "because I'm the best damn coach in the country." Such remarks were not uncommon from "the Baron," whose superstitious attachment to wearing brown suits led many to refer to him simply as "the man in the brown suit." In his final years at Kentucky, with his program suffering from lesser talent and from Rupp's genuine fatigue and poor health, he made a modest proposal to the press, again reinforcing his well-earned agrarian image: "The legislature should pass a law that at 3 o'clock every afternoon any basketball coach who is 70 years old gets a shot of bourbon. These damned bouncing, bouncing, bouncing basketballs are putting me to sleep."

Not far from Rupp's Lexington is Bowling Green, Ky., home of the Western Kentucky University Hilltoppers and another coach who embodied southern basketball style and tradition. Edgar Allen Diddle, known as Eddie Diddle, began as the coach of all sports at Western in 1922. A basketball pioneer from outdoor court days, Diddle was a native of Gradyville, in Adair County, where he had played and coached. The son of a lumberman, farmer, and livestock trader, Diddle brought a rural wit and savvy to basketball. Always preferring man-to-man defense, Diddle often said his teams "just play by ear." "Attack is our stock in trade," Diddle once said. "And there are three ways to attack: down one side of the floor, down the middle and down the other side. And you don't even need a play if you get a half-step start on the opposing team." His "half-step" approach bred a very successful fast-break style of basketball at WKU, an approach that after 42 seasons at WKU had won him 759 games.

Fast-break basketball was the backbone of both the Diddle and Rupp games. The success of both of these coaches and schools led many other programs in the South to emulate the "run-and-gun" style of basketball, but not until the mid-1970s could any school approach the success and dominance of Kentucky.

Jim Crow was a member of nearly every major college basketball team in the South, but nowhere was he more visible than in the Southeastern Conference. Perry Wallace of Nashville became the first black player to start for an SEC team when he took the floor for Vanderbilt in 1967. Thinking back on those days he once remarked, "I heard a lot of racial jokes. At Ole Miss they waved the rebel flag. They yelled a lot of things I'd as soon forget." The rebel flag still waves at SEC basketball contests, particularly when the Universities of Mississippi or Georgia play, as a vivid reminder of the history of racial inequality in the South.

By the early 1970s all SEC schools were successfully recruiting black players, but in the mid-1960s many episodes clearly reflected the racial conflict and change on the basketball floor. The strangest of these tales concerns an all-white Mississippi State team that won the SEC in 1963. As champions of the all-white SEC, State was slated to play Loyola University, which started four black players. Mississippi politicians, particularly Governor Ross Barnett, who six months previously had attempted to block James Meredith's entrance to the University of Mississippi, endeavored to make the Bulldogs of State stay home. A Jackson *Clarion-Ledger* editorial said segregationists felt that "if Mississippi State University plays against a Negro outside the state, what would be greatly different in bringing integrated teams into the state? And why not recruit a Negro of special basketball ability to play on the Mississippi State team? This is the road we seem to be traveling." Barnett and his fellow segregationists said "no" to the trip, but white fans, students, and the Mississippi State president let their basketball pride override racial prejudice, claiming loudly that State should make the trip to Ann Arbor, Mich., to play Loyola. Barnett's next tactic, a court injunction prohibiting the team from traveling, was deflected with the help of a local sheriff, also a State basketball rooter. Legend has it that the Oktibbeha County sheriff failed to serve the injunction and turned his back long enough for the players to board a Southern Airlines plane in Starkville for the trip to the National Collegiate Athletic Association (NCAA) tournament. They went on to lose a close, hard-fought game to Loyola, eventual NCAA champions.

As collegiate teams in the South have become integrated in the last two decades, southern schools have "imported" coaches and players from across the country, and the game in the South has lost much of the regional identity it once had. Such college teams as Kentucky and North Carolina, once dominant, are now just two of a large pack of schools that consistently field excellent teams and battle for a trip to the finals of the NCAA tournament. The Atlantic Coast Conference (ACC) and the SEC, the South's two major conferences, are two of the most powerful conferences in the country in the 1980s. Players and coaches on the various SEC and ACC teams, however, hail from all parts of America. The South has recently seen a trend to hire very able coaches with roots in urban areas of the Northeast. Bobby Cremins of Georgia Tech and Jim Valvano of North Carolina State are two examples of the new brash "yankee" coach who recruits as easily on the playgrounds of Brooklyn and Atlanta as he does in rural North Carolina or Georgia. Dean Smith of the University of North Carolina, the "dean" of southern coaches and a product of Kansas, is the current basketball sage of the region. UNC recently completed a new coliseum, named after Smith, that was built just large enough to surpass the capacity of Rupp Arena in Lexington, Ky. While players and coaches battle for victory on the court, the alumni and university officials try to "beat" each other by building the biggest coliseum. The "Dean Dome" is currently the South's basketball showpiece.

The days of Diddle and Rupp have certainly passed, and with them passed an important era of southern basketball. No longer does a coach, with a serious tone, explain that his team, like the Saturday night dance fiddler from western Kentucky, "plays by ear." But throughout the South, especially in Kentucky and North Carolina, the sounds of a basketball, whether dribbled on a steep hillside or a packed-dirt court in the low country, are music to the ears of many. Basketball goals and courts of every description fill the landscape of the South's cities, towns, and rural communities. Television commentator Joe Dean, broadcasting the SEC game of the week, echoes the feelings of many southern fans, players, and coaches.

As a Tennessee forward pushes a soft 20-foot jump shot through the net, Joe Dean typically calls out with excitement: "String music from Tuscaloosa, Alabama."

Tom Rankin
Southern Arts Federation

Pete Axthelm, *The City Game* (1970); Elva Bishop and Katherine Fulton, *Southern Exposure* (No. 2, 1979); Bill Finger, *Southern Exposure* (No. 2, 1979); *Newsweek* (6 January 1947); *Newsweek* (12 February 1968); Harry T. Paxton, *Saturday Evening Post* (10 March 1951); Fred Russell, *Saturday Evening Post* (19 January 1957); *Time* (12 January 1959).

Boxing

Modern boxing grew out of the fairs and gambling rooms of early 18th-century England. A bloody and violent sport that placed a premium on courage and a low price on human life, it also reinforced the class structure of England. Poor men fought and sometimes died for the entertainment of wealthy patrons, who risked only the money they bet. By the Regency period, boxing had achieved remarkable popularity. It excited the imaginations of Lord Byron, William Hazlitt, and Dr. Samuel Johnson, and it received the patronage of members of the royal family.

Wealthy southerners who traveled to England learned the intricacies of boxing. Lovers of English sports and pastimes, and especially of the English class system, planters sometimes staged impromptu matches between slaves, although there were probably fewer of these matches than once believed. In addition, throughout the 19th century the South provided a moral climate conducive to the growth of boxing.

In part, this moral climate was the result of southern attitudes toward leisure. Even before the Revolution, a leisure ethos was apparent in the South. Whereas northerners emphasized the moral importance of work and criticized sport, southerners viewed the enjoyment of leisure as an important aspect of a gentleman's life. Consumption and hospitality, pride and defense of one's honor, were apt to gain more social approval than the pursuit of money and respectability.

The first important American boxer was a southerner. On 18 December 1810 in a field 25 miles from London, Tom Molineaux, an exslave from the South, battled English champion Tom Cribb for title of the world's best fighter. Molineaux was backed by another American black, Bill Richmond, who had fought a few matches himself but spent most of his time running a pub. The fight was close and controversial, but in the end Cribb won. Molineaux stayed in England, engaged in several more important contests, and died young and penniless after a serious bout with dissipation.

Molineaux's career stirred little American interest. Organized boxing was practiced seldom in the South until the 1830s. By that time the sport faced troubles in England. Fixed fights, ring deaths, and Victorian piety and moral earnestness all hurt boxing in England. In 1836 English champion James "Deaf" Burke left the Old Country for America, or, as he referred to it, "Yankeeshire." Searching for an area in which to hold a prize fight, he looked toward the South. In 1837 he fought Sam O'Rourke in New Orleans. The most important result of the fight was to show that New Orleans would tolerate a sport that was barred in most other parts of the country. Even during the opening tense days of the Civil War, patrons of the prize ring were not too busy to journey to Kenner, La., to watch Mike McCool take "the conceit out of big Tom Jennings."

By the time of the Civil War, a pattern in American boxing had emerged. Although promoters staged a number of championship fights in the South, few southerners became important boxers. Most boxing champions came from the cities of the North, and a high percentage of these were immigrants (or sons of immigrants) from England and Ireland. Nevertheless, wealthy southerners enjoyed watching boxing matches and often took lessons in "the manly science of self-defense" at exclusive men's clubs in southern cities.

The "golden age" of southern boxing occurred in the 1880s and early 1890s. On 7 February 1882 John L. Sullivan defeated Paddy Ryan for the American championship in a bout staged in Mississippi. Sullivan soon attracted a large national following, and boxing momentarily came out of the shadows and saloons into the sun of public acclaim. In this dash for quasi-respectability for boxing, New Orleans led the way. The height of 19th-century American boxing occurred during a remarkable three-day period in September 1892. On consecutive days, New Orleans's Olympic Club staged three world championship fights. In the final of the matches, James J. Corbett defeated Sullivan. The triple event was a great critical and financial success.

After 1892 New Orleans declined as the boxing center of the nation. The focus of the ring followed the hands of gamblers, first to the West, then to New York and Chicago, and most recently to Las Vegas and Atlantic City. In the 20th century the South produced some leading fighters and even a few great champions, but the South was never again the center of boxing.

The South produced two of the 20th-century's greatest boxers—Joe Louis and Muhammad Ali. Louis (1914–81) was born to sharecropping parents on a farm near Lafayette, Ala. The young Louis moved with his mother and stepfather to Detroit, where he became active in amateur boxing and had his first professional fight in 1934. The "Brown Bomber" went on to be a legendary heavyweight champion from 1937 to 1949. He was a symbol of the triumph of the underdog, a popular Depression-era figure for many Americans, but his greatest significance was as a symbol for black Americans. He was a soft-spoken, clean-living, God-fearing man, and southern blacks looked on him as one of their greatest heroes.

Muhammad Ali (Cassius Clay) was the preeminent boxer of the 1960s and 1970s. Born 18 January 1942 in Louisville, Ky., to a close-knit, working-class family, Ali won a 1960 Olympic gold medal in boxing, and after 19 victorious professional bouts he defeated Sonny Liston for the heavyweight championship in 1963. Ali became a controversial champion. His refusal to enter the armed services resulted in the World Boxing Association stripping him of his championship. He later became the only person to regain the heavyweight crown twice. A Black Muslim in religion, Ali became one of the best known and most admired Americans in the Third World. He was a colorful champion with his quick wit, graceful style, and dominating personality. He was an appropriate figure in the turbulent 1960s and became a major cultural symbol for the black pride uniting blacks in the South of his birth, in the nation, and in the world.

Randy Roberts
Southwest Texas State
University

Elliot Gorn, "The Manly Art: Bare-Knuckle Fighting and the Rise of American Sports" (Ph.D. dissertation, Yale University, 1983); Randy Roberts, *Papa Jack: Jack Johnson and the Era of White Hopes* (1983); Dale A. Somers, *The Rise of Sports in New Orleans, 1850–1900* (1972).

Cheerleading and Twirling

Cheerleading and twirling are found in a variety of forms in the South, ranging from children's informal playground routines to highly formalized and choreographed performances at high school, college, and professional sports and musical entertainment activities. There are rewards for participants in competitions, including trophies, travel, scholarships, prize money, and prestige. Southern cultural spirit and identity are revitalized through these activities.

Formalized cheerleading seems to have originated in eastern and midwestern colleges at the turn of the century. It quickly spread to high schools and colleges nationwide, taking a particularly strong hold in the South. Cheerleading began as a student extracurricular leadership activity tied to athletics and performed by two to five males to inspire school or class loyalties and good citizenship in the student body.

After World War I more women studied at coed institutions and chose to participate in extracurricular events. By the end of World War II cheerleading had become predominantly a female activity. Squads of 5 to 18 girls were selected on the basis of physical or social characteristics, performance skills, and popularity. The entertainment aspect of cheerleading has grown to rival its original focus on school leadership and has broadened the range of performances.

In the last 15 years male cheerleaders have become more prominent—now representing about 40 percent in the college ranks. The popularity of gymnastics, which grew from the influence of the Olympics, has made cheerleading a true athletic activity and attracted better male and female athletes. Two cheerleading groups—the Dallas-based National Cheerleading Association (NCA) and the Universal Cheerleading Association (UCA)—promote, supply, and generally address the administrative needs of southern cheerleaders. The NCA, for example, trains over 150,000 high-school and college students annually in 350 clinics and workshops. It markets cheerleader goods of all sorts—uniforms, megaphones, and pompons. The modern pompon was invented by a southerner, Lawrence "Herkie" Herkimer, a former Southern Methodist University cheerleader, who applied colored streamers to batons. The NCA, which Herkimer founded, sells crepe, plastic, and metallic pompons. The NCA and the UCA both stage annual nationally televised cheerleading championships.

In 1972 the Dallas Cowboys broke a long tradition of using high school cheerleaders for their games and began the first professional cheerleading squad consisting of seven scantily clad professional dancers. The pattern was soon followed by such National Football League cities as Houston, Atlanta, Washington, D.C., and others in an effort to capitalize on the potent entertainment value of a successful blend of sex with sports. Their style is an extension of the cheerleading and pompon girl traditions, and it has stimulated a revitalization of amateur cheerleading.

Formalized baton twirling also began as a male activity in the early 20th century, but during the 1930s it evolved into performances by groups of beautiful women dressed in skimpy costumes and using smaller, lighter batons than their male counterparts had carried. Best known as an activity for a marching corps in association with marching bands in halftime shows and parades, baton twirling also features solo and team performances in entertainment and competitive settings. Although batons are the most popular of twirled objects, flags, sabres, and flaming batons are among the specialty items used by experienced twirlers.

The dream of becoming a professional cheerleader or a baton-twirling Miss America has inspired many southern girls. By the age of three or four, some girls have begun to perform publicly as mascots with groups of older, more skilled performers as well as with girls their own age. While many girls eventually take private lessons to strengthen their physical coordination skills and to master specific techniques, most begin to learn necessary skills by watching friends or siblings and then attempting to execute various maneuvers in the backyard or on the playground. In many urban and suburban neighborhoods, it is common to find girls gathering to play and practice their skills on a daily basis. They bring these street skills to school and recreation center squads and attend camps and workshops where their skills mature and are refined. Terry Southern in "Twirling at Ole Miss" (1962) discusses the Dixie National Baton Twirling Institute, one of the largest twirling clinics, which is held annually at the University of Mississippi.

Cheerleading and twirling combine African and European cultural elements. Robert Farris Thompson argues for the African source of "the main baton-twirling pose, with left hand on hip," and he believes that cheerleading, in general, was mainly derived from southern black influences. *Time* magazine noted (11 December 1939) that "some of the most versatile cheerleaders" were "at Southern colleges (notably Alabama and Tennessee)." Swiss flag-twirling was another influence, and European-style precision marching provided the context for twirling at football halftimes.

Whatever the origins, Afro-American culture, particularly in the South, has developed these activities into extraordinary art forms drawing on performance principles based in the aesthetics of black American traditional and urban cultures. Syncopation, black dance styles, and soul music have changed the rhythmic character and style of movement for both cheerleading and baton twirling, injecting a new rhythmic energy for black and white performance styles.

Phyllis M. May
Indiana University

Phyllis M. May, "'Uhn! Ain't It Funky Now?' Folkloric and Ethnomusicological Perspectives on Afro-American Cheerleading Performance as Play and Display" (Ph.D. dissertation, Indiana University, forthcoming); Fred Miller et al., *The Complete Book of Baton Twirling* (1978); Randy L. Neil, *The Official Cheerleaders Handbook* (1979); Terry Southern, *Esquire* (February 1963); Robert Farris Thompson and Joseph Cornet, *The Four Moments of the Sun: Kongo Art in Two Worlds* (1981).

Cockfighting

See VIOLENCE: Cockfighting

Fairs

"Step right up! You won't believe your eyes!" Such cries of midway carnies have rung out in the South at state, county, and local fairs, accompanying animal and homemaking exhibitions and a variety of competitions. Southern fairs—like all fairs—have roots in primitive festivities that focused on religious celebrations and bartering. In the Middle Ages fairs were well-established trade mechanisms, evolving by the 1800s toward the grand-scale educational and commercial expositions known as world's fairs. Evolving also in the 1800s in the United States were the agricultural fairs, with their prizes and competitive displays, which most strongly shaped the nature and growth of fairs in the South.

Merging agricultural society exhibitions and traveling carnivals, southern fairs began as mechanisms for promotion of agricultural societies. Planters' clubs were formed in the 18th century for discussion of agricultural problems and stimulation of farm improvements. In 1810 Elkanah Watson organized in Massachusetts the nation's first agricultural fair, and the tradition of annual fairs spread quickly in the eastern seaboard states and more slowly into the South. During the 1840s and 1850s fairs in the livestock states of Kentucky, Tennessee, and Missouri prospered, and by the late 1850s to 1860s most of the southern states boasted annual state fairs. So popular and successful were the fairs that many of the sponsoring agricultural societies—increasingly organized on a statewide basis—purchased permanent fairgrounds and equipment. Georgia's fair in Macon in 1831 stands out as one of the earliest in the Deep South, where fairs were apparently fewer in number than in such states as Virginia and the Carolinas. In most southern states the legislatures readily supported the agricultural societies and fair associations through allocation of state funds; both the societies and fairs promoted commerce and the planters' interests. Businesses and private individuals also offered support.

Child eating cotton candy at the annual Cotton Carnival, Memphis, Tenn., 1940

Fairs have always lured crowds with the exotic, the new, the exciting. Southern farmers and planters in the early to mid-1800s perused the newly imported Cashmere goats and Berkshire hogs in the exhibition stalls, while their children gawked at the two-headed snakes and miniature horses in the sideshows. Fairs served as important mechanisms for transmission of knowledge about improved breeds of domestic animals and innovations in farm machinery. Not only did farmers learn of improvements through local and state fairs; southerners garnered international recognition at the world's fair level, as did one Tennessee livestock baron with his blue-ribbon Saxony sheep at the London World's Fair in 1851.

The South has hosted its share of large expositions. Eight regional expositions, planned mainly to promote cotton and other southern products, had been held in the South by 1907. The Atlanta World's Fair and Great International Exposition in 1881 attracted some 225,000 persons and received considerable financial backing from northerners. In 1883 Louisville's Southern Exposition drew 375,000 people and trumpeted its 15 acres of exhibit floor space. The federal government earmarked approximately $1,300,000 in loans and contributions for the New Orleans World's Industrial and Cotton Centennial Exposition (1884–86), which highlighted the South's industrial prospects. Other successful expositions followed. Despite the economic panic and depression in 1893, Atlanta launched the Cotton States and International Exposition and attracted over 1,200,000 attendees. South American and European countries as well as a variety of states contributed buildings and displays. Booker T. Washington played a prominent role in the exposition's efforts to promote racial reconciliation.

More recently, San Antonio, Tex., dazzled the world in 1968 with HemisFair, an international exposition celebrating the city's 250th anniversary. With a theme of "The Confluence of Civilizations in the Americas," this world's fair contained on its 92.6 acres, among other things, a 622-foot-high observation tower, a multimillion-dollar pavilion, a mile-long lagoon, and a minimonorail train. Twenty-two countries and 19 private corporations participated as exhibitors, and Texas's colorful, multiethnic heritage was the focus of several key exhibits. Knoxville, Tenn., served as the South's next world's fair host in 1982. Congruent with the theme "Energy Turns the World," the Sunsphere, a 266-foot-high tower topped by a restaurant and observation decks, punctuated the skyline and rivaled the six-story, cantilevered, prism-like U.S. Pavilion for attention. In addition to major exhibitions by corporations and foreign nations (most notably the People's Republic of China), the fair featured a variety of shows and displays heralding the culture of the state and the region: a Tennessee music revue, the Stokely Folk Life Festival with southern Appalachian musicians and craftspersons, and a two-barge exhibit on the history of the Tennessee Valley Authority.

Just two years later New Orleans hosted the Louisiana World Exhibition, whose theme was "The World of Rivers: Fresh Water as a Source of Life." The 84-acre site contained a 2,300-foot collage, the Wonder Wall, plus a maze of streams and other water conduits. Displays ranged from an exhibit of Vatican art treasures to a full-scale oil rig. Local flavor on a large scale appeared in the form of jazz and Cajun musical performances, twice-a-day Mardi Gras parades, boat parades on the Mississippi River, and the Louisiana/Gulf South Folklife Festival. Both the Knoxville and New Orleans fairs suffered from disappointingly low attendance and major financial problems, coloring the prospects for the 1992 Miami World's Fair.

To most southerners, though, the character of the fair is embodied in the sights, sounds, and smells of the state, county, or local fair. Usually held in September or October, each state fair is held in one of the larger cities, such as Birmingham, Ala., or Raleigh, N.C. Especially in years past, the location allowed for many rural children's first trip to a big city and for many young city dwellers' first contacts with farm animals. Showmanship, competition, recreation, education, social exchange—all have been inextricably entwined in the history of southern fairs. Exhibitions of prize livestock and displays of award-winning jams and pies stand a room or a building away from school children's science fair entries and artwork. Government agencies' demonstrations show the newest developments in space technology or flood control, and private enterprises promote their wares and distribute literature. Just yards away beckons the other world of the fair—the midway.

Once providing entertainment in the form of horse races, state and county fairs became dependent upon the traveling carnivals that proliferated after the Chicago World's Columbian Exposition in 1893. Within a short time many fairgoers felt that the midway carnival was the heart of a fair. The heyday of the carnival business was in the 1920s, and freak shows were common sideshow entertainment in the 1930s and 1940s. Images of the midways in the 1920s to the 1940s converge with those of today's midways: gaudily and scantily clad women doing a striptease to blaring, bawdy music; carnies shouting "test your skill and win the prize" from booth after booth lined with cheap trinkets and brightly colored stuffed animals; monkeys racing on tiny motorcycles; a tattooed man turning to display a body covered with lines and pictures; children laughing and screaming as they meander through the house of mirrors; teenagers boasting of five turns on the scariest amusement ride; grownups clamoring to lift baubles out of a bin using a toy earth mover. Eudora Welty celebrates these worlds through her photographs of country fairs and in her short story "The Petrified Man."

The excitement of being free of usual social constraints for a few evenings continues to have appeal—if not full approval from the community. Church and civic groups have long protested the lewd shows and gambling practices in carnivals. During the last several decades northern states cracked down both through legislation and enforcement on gambling and other illegal enterprises at fair carnivals, but southern states were somewhat slower to act and have had the reputation for having local authorities more willing to take bribes to overlook illegalities. For this and other reasons certain images are frequently associated with southern fairs: the "rube," or country bumpkin who gets fleeced, and the hotheaded brawler infuriated by losses in rigged carnival games. Although tighter policing now prevails, a certain amount of rigging persists and is considered by some to be part of the risqué character of the fair. The midway dazzle increasingly accompanies performances of musical stars, often country singers, and special events such as car races or tractor pulls.

County fairs often try to emulate the offerings of the state fairs. At county fairs, however, more local color is evident in the activities, the foods, and the participants.

Alongside common fair foods such as hotdogs, cotton candy, and popcorn, fairgoers often find special treats, such as hickory-smoked barbecue, peanut brittle, and fried pork rinds. Many county fairs host a local beauty pageant and competitive activities for local youth, often members of 4-H clubs. The Neshoba County Fair in Philadelphia, Miss., is an unusual but excellent example of down-home southern atmosphere at the county level. About 12,000 people descend on Philadelphia and pack into cabins built for the fair and passed down through generations. The 70,000-plus additional daytime fairgoers hear local and state politicians engaged in old-time stump speaking. Horse races, parties, contests, and a carnival midway offer excitement; but a different revelry marks the night-long songfests, prayer and memorial services, and the hours of play and visiting for scattered family members drawn together for the annual event. Although many county fairs lack the permanent structuring of the Neshoba County Fair and more closely mimic the state fairs, most boast distinctive local touches.

Outstanding among smaller southern fairs are various Native American celebrations, such as the Cherokee Fall Festival at Scottsboro, Ala., and the Choctaw Indian Fair in Philadelphia, Miss. Traditional Native American dances, crafts, games, and foods highlight the festivities. Growing in popularity at the local level are festivals with many features of fairs. Various festivals celebrate the European heritage of area residents, as with the Scottish Festival and Highland Games at Stone Mountain, Ga; the Mexican Heritage Fiesta in Port Arthur, Tex.; and the British Faire in Mobile, Ala. Native products are the focus of countless festivals; for example, the Seafood Festival in Cedar Key, Fla.; the Tobacco Festival in Bloomfield and the Wool Festival in Falmouth, Ky.; the Brushy Mountain Apple Festival in North Wilkesboro, N.C.; the Pumpkin Festival in Pumpkintown, S.C.; and the Sorghum Festival in Springville, Ala. Of note, too, are the festivals and contests centered on southern pastimes, such as the Athens, Ala., Tennessee Valley Oldtime Fiddlers' Contest; the Raleigh, N.C., National Tobacco Spitting Contest; the Yellville, Ark., National Wild Turkey Calling Contest and Turkey Trot; the Buford, Ga., Masters Invitational Clogging Hoedown; and the Jonesborough, Tenn., National Storytelling Festival. Fairs, carnivals, and festivals thrive at all levels in the South, and most actively promote the unique heritage and character of the region.

Sharon A. Sharp
University of Mississippi

Theodore M. Dembroski, *Journal of Popular Culture* (Winter 1973); John Ezell, *The South since 1865* (1978); Lewis C. Gray, *History of Agriculture in the Southern United States to 1860*, 2 vols. (1933); Melton A. McLaurin, *North Carolina Historical Review* (Summer 1982); Wayne C. Neely, *The Agricultural Fair* (1935); *Newsweek* (5 November 1984); Carolyn B. Patterson, *National Geographic* (June 1980); *Southern Living* (May 1982); Don B. Wilmeth, *Variety Entertainment and Outdoor Amusements: A Reference Guide* (1982); Pat Zajac, *Southern Living* (May 1984).

Festivals

The southern festival of today is the direct descendant of the camp meeting and political barbecue, the Saturday night dance and Sunday's "all-day meeting and dinner-on-the-ground." Those were the gatherings that gave southerners the chance to lay aside the plow and pick up the fiddle. Although some fairs and festivals date to those times, most arose in the decades after World War II, when southerners were more educated, better traveled, and one generation removed from the cotton field. The festivals southerners initiated then, and attend today, reflect either that new urbane sophistication or the heritage of the rural past.

Each June in South Carolina, two celebrations, only 80 miles apart in distance but a world apart in content, demonstrate that tradition. While thousands gather in Charleston for Spoleto Festival with its outpouring of fine arts, thousands of others fill the streets of tiny Hampton for the town's watermelon festival, now more than 40 years old. From late May through June, Spoleto Festival, held in Charleston since 1977, may offer a playwright's world premiere, a New York choreographer's newest creation, an orchestra's concert of classical music. Celebrants in Hampton, meanwhile, are listening to gospel music and dancing to country bands, picking among the goods of an arts and crafts fair, watching a parade led by a beauty queen, and, most of all, feasting on the traditional southern delicacy. It is not unlikely that some in Charleston, after getting their fill of Balanchine and Bach, hop in their car and gorge on watermelon a weekend or so later in Hampton. If many southerners hunger for fine arts today, just as many yearn for the tidbits of their inheritance.

Southern festivals provide both. The themes of most small-town festivals center around some aspect of their heritage or livelihood. Even in many urban festivals focusing on the fine arts there are southern features. Spoleto Festival often includes such Dixie-nurtured music forms as jazz and blues, country, and soul and gospel. So does Memphis in May, a monthlong celebration that combines its regional customs of music and food (barbecue) with the cultural characteristics of a different country each year. Heritage Weekends in Louisville, Ky., feature the arts, crafts, food, costumes, and music of Old World ethnic groups that settled in the city.

Southern customs, traditions, and products are most often extolled in the small-town festival. If there is a vegetable that ripens in fall, a plant that blooms in spring, an animal that grazes in pastures, or a food served on local tables, some community has found a way to praise it. Gilmer, Tex., honors the yam; Dothan, Ala., the peanut; Tonitown, Ark., the grape. Towns and cities from Palestine, Tex., to Norfolk, Va., celebrate the arrival of spring in azalea and dogwood festivals. Food festivals often combine cookery with contests. At the Oyster Festival in Leonardtown, Md., the champion of the oyster-shucking contest goes on to international competition. Crawfish races highlight the biannual salute to the local crustacean in Breaux Bridge, La.

Some small-town festivals have helped to preserve a slice of the southern past. In mule festivals, towns like

Columbia, Tenn.; Benson, N.C.; and Calvary, Ga., trot out the legendary but endangered species that plowed farms, scraped out roads, and built river levees. At these gatherings, younger generations hear for the first time words that once sprinkled southern conversation: jack and jenny, hames and singletree, or what it means to "bust the middles" or "lay by a crop."

Although the themes of small-town festivals vary widely, they differ little in form and function. Salley, S.C., may be the only town that honors chitterlings, but its Chitlin' Strut, held one November day malodorous from the aroma of five tons of frying chitterlings, incorporates most all the earmarks of a small-town festival. Along with a lunch of chitlins, gobbled with gusto or tossed away after one nibble, celebrants pick among the tacky and tasteful offerings of the ubiquitous arts and crafts display, listen to country music, and watch a parade led by Miss Chitlin' Strut. Some don t-shirts that may read "I got the guts to strut" or "Chitlin Fever—Catch it!," then enter the chitlin' strut contest. The free-style choreography many create is often determined by the amount of whiskey surreptitiously spiking their soft drinks.

Although most festivals are used for boosterism or fund-raising, they nevertheless offer townspeople a chance to gather and renew acquaintances, a by-product of gatherings since the first southerners gathered in a pioneer forest clearing to help a neighbor raise a new barn.

To renew family and friendship ties is still the main reason residents and former residents of Neshoba County, Miss., have assembled faithfully each year since 1889 in the laying-by time of late July. At the Neshoba County Fair near Philadelphia, families live for a week, many in rude cabins their ancestors built. There is harness racing, a carnival midway, and lots of "visiting around," preaching, and political speech-making at the open-air Founders Pavilion, with its sawdust floor and wooden benches. In recent years the pavilion has provided the last hurrah for old-time southern politicians. As late as 1979 former Mississippi Governor Ross Barnett brought the house down with his stump-speaking, gallus-snapping, "out-seg-your-opponent" brand of rhetoric from a bygone era.

Fairgoers today arrive by Chevrolet instead of mule and wagon, but transportation is about the only ingredient of the fair that has changed since its 19th-century beginning. Certainly the weather is the same, as afternoon rainstorms turn red dirt to mud, and the white heat of midday sun forces fairgoers to the shade of porches. "If you can't take the heat, mud, and dirt, you oughta stay home," says one fairgoer. But at Neshoba County Fair, as in most southern festivals, few stay at home. Festivals offer them a chance to lay aside their work—the pocket calculator now, if no longer the plow; to renew friendships with acquaintances; and, in most cases, to pay homage to a slice of southern life that may be long past. With their festivals, southern towns and cities insure that old times there will not be forgotten.

See also MUSIC: Music Festivals

Gary D. Ford
Southern Living

Alice M. Geffen and Carole Berglie, *Southern Exposure* (January–February 1986); Jane M. Hatch, *The American Book of Days* (3d ed., 1978); *Southern Living* (monthly calendar of festivals); Beverly J. Stoeltje, in *Handbook of American Folklore,* ed. Richard M. Dorson (1983); Paul Wasserman and Esther Herman, eds., *Festivals Sourcebook: A Reference Guide to Fairs, Festivals, and Celebrations* (1977); David E. Whisnant, *All That Is Native and Fine: The Politics of Culture in an American Region* (1983); William Wiggins, in *Discovering Afro-America,* ed. Roger D. Abrahams and John F. Szwed (1975), *Prospects,* vol. 5 (1979).

Fishing

More than one-half of the contiguous U.S. coastline is in the South. Within these limits are the most prolific estuarine complexes in the nation—the Chesapeake Bay, Pamlico Sound, and the Gulf of Mexico. The rich waters of the Gulf Stream pass closest to land in the South, and the barrier islands that shelter the mainland South from the ocean are rich breeding grounds for fish. The rivers draining the southern highlands offer fishing of a different kind. There are few natural lakes in the South, but hydroelectric, flood-control, and irrigation impoundments have created a unique inland fishery.

Fishing thus offers an integral form of recreation and livelihood in this region. Its popularity is part of the legacy of agrarian small-farm existence where every farm needed and often constructed a reliable water source. Fishing followed as a matter of course. Pond fishing today is one of the great pleasures of the region.

Fishing is a predominantly masculine activity, passed along from one generation to the next. It fulfills a need to provide; it is a private challenge—success or failure is the individual's alone; and, most important, failure can quickly be attributed to outside circumstances, beyond the individual's control. Fishing can be relatively inexpensive, but the more you fish, the more likely you are to spend to fish.

According to U.S. Commerce Department annual statistics, the South is one of the most important fisheries in the nation. In 1980–81 Louisiana led the nation in thousands of pounds of live catch, followed by Alaska, California, Virginia, North Carolina, Mississippi, and Massachusetts. The South and Gulf states ranked highest in millions of pounds of fish, netting 2,243 million pounds of all commercial-fishing species taken (the North Atlantic region, which includes Virginia, ranked second with 1,528 million pounds). During 1978–81 four of the top five fishing ports were in Louisiana or Mississippi.

Each regional fishery of the South has a cultural heritage comprised of unique boat styles developed for local waters. The character of these fisheries is based on the available harvest of the offshore waters as well as distinctive cuisine and social customs. Several regions have unique products: Chesapeake Bay blue crab; Lynnhaven oyster of Virginia; Bon Secour oyster of the Gulf; red snapper from Florida; and Georgia and Louisiana shrimp.

(President William Howard Taft consumed seven dozen Lynnhaven oysters at one sitting.)

Through their culture and cuisine, the Cajuns of Louisiana, the Low Country people of South Carolina and Georgia, the watermen of the Chesapeake, and the down-easters of North Carolina have maintained and reinforced a clear identity. These individual groups are clannish and sustain tradition from one generation to the next. They are not open societies—the vehement opposition to Mexican and Vietnamese immigrants and to religious cult–related fishermen by traditional groups bears witness to their strong emotions and fears of economic and social change. Outsiders are warily watched, seldom welcomed, and even when accepted as "fellow fishermen" still remain outsiders.

Sea Grant Research in North Carolina reveals a very precise social network, which distributes fishing information in one typical small coastal North Carolina village. Information and innovation become legitimate only when certain accepted and admired fishermen advocate or legitimize them. This would seem to indicate a traditional subculture, rigidly set in its ways.

Nevertheless, commercial fishing is being forced to change because of circumstances beyond the control of fishermen. Fuel prices, declining and polluted fisheries, and the substantial cost of a vessel (to $250,000) have altered regional patterns. Fishermen have shifted from local water, seasonal fishing to open water, year-round fishing. It is simply not possible to make fishing pay on a local basis unless a monopoly exists, such as legal rights to rich oyster grounds. Fishermen must follow the catch to make ends meet, and this reality, along with foreign competition, is gradually altering the traditional commercial fishing industry.

Southerners are serious about fishing for fun, and no other region works so hard to have a good time at recreational fishing. The numbers are staggering—450,000 fishing licenses were sold in North Carolina in 1981–82, representing almost 8 percent of the population. Only freshwater fishermen must be licensed, so the actual number of fishermen may well top a million individuals.

Across the South, fishermen sustain a fishing publication, *B.A.S.S.* (the magazine of the Bass Anglers' Sportsman's Society), and regional editions of *Field and Stream* and *Sports Afield*. There is a professional fishing circuit, saltwater fishing rodeos, tournaments, invitational fish-offs, derbies, and contests with substantial prizes. North Carolina State University offers a sportfishing short course, and every southern city of any size has an outdoor commercial show, highlighting the latest in outdoor gear and equipment, which includes fishing necessities.

Fishermen with their haul, Bay St. Louis, Miss., early 20th century

State wildlife agencies actively work to develop the fisheries resource through the construction of fishing attractors, artificial reefs, boat ramps, and docking facilities—all of these funded by licensing revenue. Good fishing has a constituency in the South: public works projects as noncontroversial as the Blue Ridge Parkway have been sidetracked because of potential fishing stream pollution by the completion of the roadway as originally proposed.

The two major categories of southern recreational fishing are saltwater and freshwater—everything else is derivative. Within these categories are curious subcategories, many of which are identified by either the technique they use, or the species of fish they pursue.

The three most popular means of catching saltwater game fish are by boat, private or rental; pier fishing; or surf casting. The U.S. Commerce Department statistics confirm that the greatest number of saltwater fish landed are caught within three miles of beachfront, the distance corresponding most frequently to pier fishing, surf casting, and both private and charter (or rental) boating.

Sixty percent of the South's population lives within two hours' driving time of saltwater, so it is not surprising that saltwater fishing is extremely popular. Saltwater fishermen are willing to catch anything and do not simply pursue one species of gamefish to the exclusion of others. They spend extravagant sums of money to achieve their goals. A properly equipped surf fisherman can spend as much as $17,000 for a recreational vehicle that will negotiate the sandy stretches of barrier islands such as the Outer Banks of North Carolina and Padre Island in Texas. In addition to the vehicle cost, there are substantial expenses for tackle and clothing. A serious surf fisherman can justify all of the expense, for only with such equipment can he or she achieve the mobility needed to properly fish the beaches. The expense may make this sport seem an improbable one, but it is commonplace. In 1977 more than 100,000 people drove the sands of Cape Hatteras National Seashore, and the number has increased steadily since.

There is a definite camaraderie among surf fishermen as opposed to private boat owners who fish open and sound waters. A community is created by a shared experience of testy weather conditions and successful fishing "runs." Many fishermen return to the same beaches year after year—indeed, so established are the routines that an element of superstition seems to govern the planning of annual surf-fishing trips.

On the Outer Banks of North Carolina, the surf-fishing mecca in the South if not the nation, motel owners have booked the same rooms to the same fishing parties for many years—often because of the success of a past trip. In 1984 a world record Red Drum, the prized surf gamefish, weighing 94 pounds was landed near Avon, N.C. This catch alone will doubtlessly bring fishermen to the Outer Banks in droves, and there again will be another season of Hatteras Island sunrises, silhouetting shoulder-to-shoulder anglers, and vehicles bristling with poles and as chock-full of equipment as any tackle shop. They will want to better the record of the unfortunate angler who, if he had waited a week later to land his drum, would have pocketed $50,000 during the annual Red Drum Tourney.

Freshwater fishermen tend to pursue one game fish more than others. The fish may be either native or naturalized trout, hybrid and striped bass, crappie, bream and other sunfish, catfish, or the king of all freshwater game fish, the large-mouth bass. The method may be flyrod, spinning tackle, ultralight spinning tackle, bait casting, or cork or bobber fishing with natural bait.

There seems to be a correlation between the economic and social stature of fishermen, the game fish they pursue, and the method they prefer to use. At the bottom of the economic scale, the preferred fishing is catfish/bream by cork or bobber fishing/bait casting, bass/spinner fishing is the choice of blue-collar families, bass flyrod fishing of white-collar workers, and artificial fly fishing for native trout is the preserve of upper-income professionals.

This observation is grounded in economic realities. The expense required for bream and catfish fishing is substantially lower than that for trout fishing. Bream and catfish may be caught from the edge of a lake—a boat is not required; bass fishermen need a boat to fish large impoundments, and trout fishermen must have the means and time to travel and stay in the remote highlands where trout are found.

The large-mouth bass is a southern institution. The fish is widely distributed, easily caught, and a dependable fighter. Bass is also good to eat. Its following is fanatical, almost cultic in devotion. The large-mouth bass may have been placed in the waters of the South so that fishermen have a preordained reason for idleness and spending money.

Bass is frequently used as a verb—"bassin." This is not the same as fishing, but refers to the pursuit of the large-mouth bass with the fire of a crusade. "To bass" is to spend money—on a bass boat with a swivel chair and an outboard motor that could power an aircraft carrier, on a trolling motor, on a fish finder, temperature gauge, fishing maps, boat trailer, docking fees, a suitcase full of tackle, membership in the Bass Anglers' Sportsman's Society (and subscription to their magazine), on beer, on a "gimme cap," but never on suntan lotion. Bass fishermen are always sunburned to the "gimme cap" line.

Magazine articles are devoted to fishing the remote corners of one lake for bass, professional bass fishermen cast for prizes up to $50,000, and substantial multimillion-dollar industries produce equipment for bass fishing. No other fish has such a following in the South, and no other group of fishermen spends so much money as do the Bassers. Indeed, the name is almost synonymous with fishing.

Although smaller in numbers, trout fishermen are equally devoted to their fish. Trout are confined to the pure running water streams and rivers of the mountains and to a few mountain impoundments. This restricted range places the fish out of reach of much of the region's population, but does not diminish its popularity. In 1981 40,000 trout licenses were sold in North Carolina, a state with extensive trout waters.

Trout are wary fish, caught by stalking, rather than fishing. Much of the appeal of trout fishing is in the enjoyment of the fish's environment, and so, to a greater degree than perhaps other game fish, there is an "aesthetic" to trout fishing. The value of catching the fish is often surpassed by the quest for it. This is not a hard and fast rule. For every trout fisherman arduously using an artificially tied fly at the end of a $500 rod, there is a mountain native working the stream with canned corn or worms. Trout fishermen write most often about one single issue: the threatened destruction of a prime trout stream. Indeed, so fragile are the southern waters supporting trout, and so limited is the number of fishable miles, it could very well be the South's most tenuous outdoor recreation.

One further aspect of recreational fishing should be noted—the active stocking of created fisheries funded by wildlife revenues. Money from the sale of licenses has gone to provide a number of "unnatural" prime fishing opportunities, such as inland striped bass fishing on lakes such as the Santee-Cooper in South Carolina. Normally an ocean species, striped bass have adapted very nicely to the all-freshwater habitat of certain reservoirs. This has resulted in a superb inland recreational fishery of an endangered native ocean species. In addition, extensive artificial hybridization has developed cross-specific game fish, which are more readily adapted to the growth conditions of inland impoundments.

Inland fishing is enormously popular in the South. This is a region where the first bream on a worm-baited hook marks a rite of passage in its own way and means passing the love of angling from one generation to the next.

Glenn Morris
Durham, North Carolina

Havilah Babcock, *My Health Is Better in November: Thirty-five Stories of Hunting and Fishing in the South* (1985); William Elliot, *Carolina Sports by Land and Water* (1846); Patrick Mullen, *Southern Exposure* (Summer–Fall 1977); Louis D. Rubin, Jr., *Southern Living* (March 1983); Frank Sargeant, *Outdoor Life* (March 1981); Southeastern Association of Fish and Wildlife Agencies, *Proceedings of Annual Conference* (annual); *Southern Exposure* (May–June 1982); U.S. National Oceanic and Atmospheric Administration, *Fishery Statistics* (annual); Dianne Young, *Southern Living* (July 1983).

Football

More than any other sport, football seems to reflect cultural characteristics of the South. It has a long and noteworthy place in the history of the region. Not long after the inaugural Princeton-Rutgers game of 1869, Washington and Lee played Virginia Military Institute in the first official football game in the South. The year was 1877, and by 1895 John Heisman had instituted the innovation of using offensive guards as blockers for running backs at Auburn University. The infamous, outlawed formation referred to as the "flying wedge" was used by Vanderbilt University as early as 1892 in a game against North Carolina. Southern football's contribution to modern-day football continued with the advent of the forward pass as an offensive weapon in 1906. As early as 1914 Clyde Littlefield of the University of Texas was heralded as one of the best passers in the country. The well-known "Heisman Shift" was introduced by John Heisman at Georgia Tech, and from 1915 to 1917 his Georgia Tech teams were undefeated. Beginning in the 1920s General Bob Neyland introduced the "single-wing" formation at the University of Tennessee with great success. The contributions of these early southern teams, coaches, and players to football were critical for establishing the game as it is played today.

Modern football in the South is characterized by a subcultural passion unrivaled in other regions of the United States. This affinity for the game of football is reflected in the popularity of the sport at the high school, college, and, most recently, professional levels of play. Because the South was predominantly a rural area throughout the first half of the 20th century, community identity with high school teams fostered intense competition. Increased industrial and urban development over the last 50 years has changed the demography of the South; however, high school football remains the most popular Friday night activity in such football-oriented states as Alabama, Florida, Georgia, Louisiana, Mississippi, Tennessee, and Texas.

The regional and community interest in high school football in the South provided a rich pool of talent for the development of this sport at the intercollegiate level. As early as 1921, when tiny Centre College of Danville, Ky., upset a powerful team from Harvard, 6–0, southern teams have been competitors for national titles. A review of the Associated Press National Polls, which began in 1936, reveals the following southern college teams claiming the national title: Texas Christian University (1938); Texas A&M University (1939); Tennessee (1951); Maryland (1953); Auburn (1957); Louisiana State University (1958); Alabama (1961, 1964, 1965, 1978, 1979); Texas (1963, 1969); Georgia (1980); Clemson (1981); and Miami of Florida (1983). In addition, in terms of overall winning percentages, 6 southern teams are ranked in the top 25 all-time winners: Alabama (.732), Texas (.729), Tennessee (.680), Louisiana State (.639), Georgia (.630), and Auburn (.602). These and numerous other outstanding southern football teams have provided many great individual stars.

Eleven southern players have received the Heisman trophy, given to the outstanding college football player in the United States for each year of competition. Southern football players who have achieved such distinction are Davey O'Brien (TCU, 1938), Frank Sinkwich (Georgia, 1942), Doak Walker (SMU, 1948), John David Crow (Texas A&M, 1957), Billy Cannon (LSU, 1959), Steve Spurrier (Florida, 1966), Pat Sullivan (Auburn, 1966), Earl Campbell (Texas, 1977), George Rogers (South Carolina, 1980), Herschel Walker (Georgia, 1982), and Bo Jackson (Auburn, 1985).

Davey O'Brien, the South's first Heisman trophy winner, 1940s

The South has provided college football with some of the most outstanding coaches in the history of the sport. In 1899 Herman Suter coached the famous "iron men" of the University of the South. In a six-day period Suter's Sewanee Tigers defeated Texas, Texas A&M, Houston, Tulane, Louisiana State, and Mississippi. The national attention generated by Coach Suter at Sewanee was continued through Daniel E. McGugin's coaching achievements at Vanderbilt. Coach McGugin's influence on southern football was profound. In his 30-year career at Vanderbilt, McGugin's teams won 13 titles and 196 games. Following McGugin's accomplishments, John Heisman, the person for whom the Heisman trophy was named, succeeded McGugin as the outstanding coach in the Deep South. Heisman's Georgia Tech teams won four straight national titles from 1915 to 1918. His 1916 Georgia Tech team set the record for most points in a game when they defeated Cumberland University 222–0.

Many other coaches in the South made outstanding contributions to the game of football in the early 1900s. Dana X. Bible, in 12 seasons at Texas A&M, won five

Southwest Conference titles and posted a winning percentage of over .77 (1917–28). Frank Bridges of Baylor, who has been characterized as "one of the most original and inventive football coaches who ever lived," experimented with innovative formations during the early 1920s. Wallace Wade's records at Alabama and Duke were outstanding during the late 1920s and early 1930s. However, with the emergence of General Robert Reese Neyland as head coach of the University of Tennessee, one of the first coaching legends of the South emerged. Coach Bob Neyland won 173 games, and his coaching career at Tennessee spanned from 1925 to the modern era of big time football. Coach Neyland's teams were known for outstanding defensive play, and several of his former players—most notably, Bowden Wyatt (Tennessee) and Bobby Dodd (Georgia Tech)—became outstanding college coaches.

Formed in 1953, the Atlantic Coast Conference (ACC) provided football in the South with one of its most colorful and witty coaches in Frank Howard. Coach Howard's Clemson Tigers consistently gained national attention with appearances in the Orange, Sugar, Cotton, and Bluebonnet bowl games. Howard's teams won a total of 165 games, providing the ACC with a team that consistently gained national recognition. The Southwest Conference provided modern football with two coaches who built and maintained football dynasties at Arkansas and Texas. The names of Frank Broyles and Darryl Royal echo legendary achievements on the gridiron from 1959 to the early 1970s. Broyles's teams recorded 74 Southwest Conference victories during his tenure at Arkansas, while Royal's Texas teams won 80 conference games. During the 14-year span in which Broyles and Royal coached in the Southwest Conference, only one other conference team (SMU, 1966) placed in the top 10 of the final national collegiate rankings. The coaching success of Frank Broyles and Darryl Royal consistently focused national attention on the Southwest Conference.

The most legendary southern collegiate football coach, however, was Paul William "Bear" Bryant. Coach Bryant not only established himself as the winningest coach in the history of collegiate football, but he also became a charismatic symbol of success to football fans throughout the world. Bear Bryant's coaching career and incredible record as a major-college coach of 323 victories, 85 losses, and 17 ties spanned 38 years and four southern universities—Maryland, Kentucky, Texas A&M, and Alabama. A true modern hero in the South, Bear Bryant's influence on football in this region and throughout the United States will remain as long as the game is played. The continuing achievements of numerous former players of Coach Bryant in professional football, as well as in collegiate coaching, reflect not only his coaching genius, but also his personal charisma.

There have been many other outstanding football coaches in the South. Ralph Sasse (Mississippi State), Wallace Butts (Georgia), John Vaught (Mississippi), Ralph "Shug" Jordan (Auburn), and Paul Dietzel (Louisiana State) all had winning records and teams in the Southeastern Conference. Among southern teams that were not affiliated with major conferences, Pie Vann (Southern Mississippi), A. C. "Scrappy" Moore (University of Chattanooga), and Bill Peterson (Florida State) had outstanding winning records. Eddie Robinson of Grambling became another coaching legend by achieving more career victories than Bear Bryant. Coach Robinson has been a consistent winner for 44 years at the predominantly black college located in north Louisiana. Both Coach Robinson (324 wins) and Jake Gaither (Florida A&M) have not only had many championship teams, but they also have coached numerous players who have achieved outstanding professional careers.

Professional football arrived in the South in 1960. Both the Dallas Cowboys and the Houston Oilers franchises played their first National Football League (NFL) schedule that year. Six years later, professional teams in Atlanta and Miami were established. The New Orleans Saints franchise had its first season in 1967, and the Tampa Bay Buccaneers (1976) was the last NFL team to be located in a southern city. These six NFL teams have been very competitive in professional football. The Dallas Cowboys have played in five Super Bowl games, winning twice, as have the Miami Dolphins. Tom Landry has been the only coach for the Dallas Cowboys since their beginnings in 1960. Coach Landry has recorded 223 wins, 126 losses, and 6 ties in his 25 years as the head coach of the Cowboys. Often referred to as "America's team," the Cowboys gained wide television coverage in the southern region during the first six years of their franchise. Today they are still one of the most popular teams in the National Football League.

Coach Don Shula of the Miami Dolphins has posted the third highest winning percentage of all coaches in the National Football League (.716). Only the legendary Vince Lombardi (.740) and John Madden (.731) have better winning percentages than Shula. Coach Shula's ultimate achievement as Miami's head coach came in 1972 when the Dolphins compiled the first unbeaten and untied record (17–0) in the league's history. Shula was also the youngest coach to compile 100 victories in the National Football League, and if one included his record while at Baltimore, his six Super Bowl appearances as head coach remain an NFL all-time record.

Texas Stadium, home of the NFL Dallas Cowboys, constructed in 1970s, Arlington Tex.

Many observers claim football has taken on almost religious significance for southerners. As writer Willie Morris has written in *Terrains of the Heart* (1981), "It is no doubt a cliché, yet true, that Southern football is a religion, emanating directly from its bedeviled landscape and the burden of its past." Michael Novak in *The Joy of Sports* (1976) explores the religious implications of southern football. In the Deep South football is "a statewide religion" that celebrates each state and the region itself. The region's dominant evangelical churches "cherish emotion, inspiration, charismatic speaking in tongues, the surges of personal conversion and sudden seizure," and the football of the South reflects such traits. Southern sports are rugged, but football in the region is best described as "fleet, explosive, difficult to contain." Football in the Midwest is closest to that in the South, both driven by a "passional religion," but midwestern sport grows out of its people and their religious style. The churches of the Midwest, says Novak, "are filled by far more orderly and sober folk" than those of the South, and midwestern football is appropriately "hard, orderly, cleanly executed, disciplined, tight."

John Egerton in *The Americanization of Dixie* (1974) suggests that football, "the religion of the masses," is celebrated in the South "with all the ritual and pageantry and spectacle of a High Church ceremony." There is patriotism, militarism, prayer, music, conspicuous consumption, politics, sex, white supremacy, and sport. He believes that southern football has become, though, more a ritual of an American civil religion than of a purely southern faith.

The South as a region has a heritage of great teams, coaches, and fans. It is within such a context that one can claim that football is a very real and vibrant component of the culture of the modern South. Football in the South remains an important source for a variety of social activities. A typical fall weekend includes numerous community activities that are associated with high school, college, and professional football. Friday evening football games involve "pep rallies," band performances, and drill teams. Saturday afternoons and evenings witness tailgate parties, pregame socials, and postgame parties, while on Sunday afternoons professional teams throughout the region draw large crowds, as well as national television coverage.

At the end of the season, the South hosts most of the nation's bowl games, including the All American Bowl (Birmingham), the Bluebonnet Bowl (Houston), the Blue-Gray All-Star Football Classic (Montgomery), the Cotton Bowl (Dallas), the Florida Citrus Bowl (Orlando), the Gator Bowl (Jacksonville), the Independence Bowl (Shreveport), the Liberty Bowl (Memphis), the Orange Bowl (Miami), the Peach Bowl (Atlanta), the Senior Bowl (Mobile), the Sugar Bowl (New Orleans), and the Sun Bowl (El Paso). New Orleans and Miami have been the most frequent sites for pro football's Super Bowl every January.

J. Steven Picou
Duane Gill
Texas A&M University

The Birmingham News, *Remembering Bear* (1983); Clyde Bolton, *Unforgettable Days in Southern Football* (1974); Allison Danzig, *The History of American Football* (1983); D. Stanley Eitzen and George H. Sage, *Sociology of American Sport* (1978); Wilbur Evans and H. B. McElroy, *The Twelfth Man: A Story of Texas A&M Football* (1974); Lawrence Goodwyn, *Southern Exposure* (Fall 1974); Marty Mule, *Sugar Bowl: The First Fifty Years* (1983); Alexander M. Weyand, *The Saga of American Football* (1955); Geoff Winningham and Al Reinert, *Rites of Fall: High School Football in Texas* (1979).

Gambling

Wagering on games of chance has been a recurrent feature of southern social life from the colonial era to modern times. In the 1700s, for example, it offered clues as to social status in the early South. When colonial planters gathered, especially in Virginia, they typically played cards and backgammon or rolled the dice. Wealthy tobacco growers, living in a society with fewer restraints than Puritan New England, were willing to risk much of their wealth on anything involving chance. George Washington kept a list of his gains and losses at gaming and typically preferred large stakes. Above all, southerners bet on horse racing. After 1730 quarter-horse racing was popular, and then at mid-century English thoroughbreds were introduced into the colonies. Races were held in conjunction with fairs, which also brought occasions for gambling. Historian Timothy Breen has argued that gambling on horse racing identified one as a member of the gentry. Honor was gained through victory over one's peers, and this was a safety valve for planters, nurturing structured competition within the group without endangering its hegemony.

The inhabitants of the Old South, proclaimed a foreign visitor, "are universally addicted to gambling." Betting during the antebellum period in the Northeast was "about as common as in England," reported an Englishman, but in the South it was far more prevalent. New Orleans was a major center of gambling, but even rural southerners bet on cards, dice, dominoes, billiards, lotteries, cockfights, horse races, and many other activities. Southerners were such inveterate gamblers, claimed one eyewitness, that many "lost in a night their all."

Professional gamblers frequented riverboats and bars; some got rich and a few got lynched—five in 1835 in Vicksburg alone. But many gamblers considered themselves respectable members of southern society. A Yankee, induced to share his bed at a crowded tavern by the assurance of a landlord that his bedfellow was a gentleman, grew concerned when his heavily armed roommate placed a bowie knife and a pistol by the bedside and a pistol under his pillow. "I shuddered," admitted the Yankee, "having never slept with pistols," but he raised no objection until his bedfellow announced that he was a "gambler *by profession*." Horrified, the Yankee leapt from bed and exclaimed: "The landlord assured me that you were a gentleman, sir, but had he told me of your profession, I would not have consented to share my bed."

The gambler, who failed to understand such squeamishness, "entered into an elaborate argument to prove that his profession was as honest and honorable as that of the physician."

New Englanders, in keeping with their Puritan heritage, were much less tolerant of gamblers and gambling than were southerners, who were as fond of wagers and risks as their Scottish, Irish, and Welsh ancestors. Expressing his objection to horse racing, a Yankee wrote from South Carolina: "Curiosity induced me to go once, which will satisfy me for life." President Timothy Dwight of Yale College boasted: "In New England horse racing is almost and cockfighting absolutely unknown." Both activities enjoyed widespread popularity in the Old South, where spectators frequently gathered at cockpits and racetracks and wagered large sums. Whole seasons were devoted to racing, which so appealed to southerners, noted an observer, that "they have race-paths near each town and in many parts of the country." If gambling was not quite a universal pastime, it had far more adherents, among planters and plain folk alike, in the Old South than in the Old North.

After the Civil War, organized, big-time gaming was rationalized in some southern states as a way to generate money for depleted treasuries or worthwhile charities in hard times. Legal lotteries had existed earlier in some areas, and these were revived. Civic and charitable groups were formed to raise money through lotteries for orphans, widows, crippled Confederate veterans, museums, libraries, schools, and various artistic activities.

The Louisiana Lottery, the largest in the South, was chartered in 1868 in New Orleans, with a 25-year charter. It held daily drawings, with prizes up to $5,000, plus monthly drawings and a six-month drawing, which awarded a grand prize of $600,000. A popular referendum in the 1890s turned down the proposed renewal of the lottery's franchise, but southerners continued, illegally at times, to take part in lotteries of various sorts. New Orleans remained a gambling center, with its activities tied in with boxing promotion and, especially, red-light district prostitution.

Southerners continued in the postbellum era to gamble on horse racing at tracks in places such as New Orleans, Memphis, Nashville, Montgomery, and Little Rock. They won and lost at fairs, carnivals, and circuses, as professional gamblers descended on communities where these shows appeared. Neither could they resist wagering on cockfighting, dogfighting, and other sporting events.

By the 1880s, however, a rising moral consciousness among the South's religious people led to restrictions on gambling. New laws were passed outlawing horse racing, which earlier had been *the* sport of the southern gentleman. Large-scale gambling activities, and particularly wagering on horse racing, came to be concentrated in resort areas such as Hot Springs, Ark., and in coastal towns such as Galveston, Tex., and Miami, Fla., as well as continuing in New Orleans. Though sometimes hidden, gambling continued in other regions of the South. Even where illegal, gambling houses were still found.

Gambling has been celebrated in southern culture from Mark Twain's portrayal of the riverboat gambler on the Mississippi to country music singer Kenny Rogers's 1970s hit song and film, "The Gambler." The early Mississippi country singer, Jimmie Rodgers, who knew the world of small-town gambling as a traveling railroad worker and later as a musical performer, sang such songs as "Gambling Bar Room Blues," "Those Gambler's Blues," and "Gambling Polka Dot Blues."

Georgia gentlemen playing cards and smoking, 1918

The image of the sharp-dressed, successful gambler has been a recurrent one in southern black literature and music, especially in the blues. Lack of economic security and low social status surely encouraged poor blacks to risk gambling as a way to temporary economic betterment. Stuck in oppressive jobs or in the boredom of unemployment, many of the southern poor, black and white, found excitement and thrills in the risk taking of gambling. Blues performers sang the "Poker Woman Blues," "Gambler's Blues," "Dying Crap Shooter's Blues," and "Gambling Man." Card games such as Georgia skin and coon-can are associated with black gamblers, as well as "skin-ball" and shooting craps (the popularity of the latter in the South shown by southerners calling it by such names as Memphis dominoes or Mississippi marbles).

Grady McWhiney
Texas Christian University

Herbert Asbury, *Sucker's Progress: An Informal History of Gambling in America from the Colonies to Canfield* (1938); Timothy H. Breen, *William and Mary Quarterly* (April 1977); George Devol, *Forty Years a Gambler on the Mississippi* (1887); John M. Findlay, *People of Chance: Gambling in American Society from Jamestown to Las Vegas* (1985); Paul Oliver, *Blues Fell This Morning: The Meaning of the Blues* (1960).

Golf

William Faulkner's *The Sound and the Fury* (1929) begins with the idiot Benjy Compson and his young black companion retrieving golf balls. Faulkner himself frequently played golf in the 1920s at the nine-hole University of Mississippi golf course and even acted as chairman of a tournament committee. Faulkner regarded himself as a sportsman, and his interest in golf reflected the South's changing sports scene in the early 20th century. Golf has not traditionally been regarded as a sport particularly associated with the South, yet the region has produced great athletes in that field, and since World War II it has increasingly become a part of the life of middle-class southerners.

The popularity of golf in the United States reflects the British influence on American sport. Golf came to this country from Scotland, with the first organized play here in New York, where country clubs were organized in the 1880s. The U.S. Golf Association appeared in 1894 to provide institutional direction, but at the turn of the century few golf courses had appeared in the South, except for Florida. Before 1900 golf had an elitist air to it and was mainly a pursuit of the leisured classes. Chicago and other cities of the Middle West led in building public courses in the early 20th century, but the appearance of amateur championship golf tournaments and celebrity golfers in the 1920s, along with the prosperity and consumerism of the people of that decade, helped to popularize golf. The South lagged in these developments, although Georgia and Texas were leaders; Georgia Institute of Technology, for example, from the 1920s on fielded successful intercollegiate golf teams, while Texas produced a number of prominent professional golfers.

The country club appeared in many southern communities in the 1920s, although its widespread popularity in the region was a post–World War II phenomenon. Country clubs were organized for social activities, such as dancing, dining, card playing, and drinking, in addition to athletics. Members joined in order to meet influential people and to promote their business interests. The young in small towns especially had a new focus for combining athletic activities and courting. Golf was a social sport well designed to these ends. Unlike urban athletic clubs, country clubs were for both men and women, and golf proved early to be popular among both sexes.

The South has produced some of the most prominent amateur and professional golfers. In a recent survey of the 70 greatest players of all time, 16 were from the South, including 7 from Texas. Prominent golfers have included Jimmy Demaret, Ben Hogan, John Byron Nelson, and Lee Trevino, all from Texas, Cary Middlecoff from Tennessee, and Betsy Rawls from South Carolina. Robert Tyre Jones, Jr., from Atlanta, is generally recognized as the game's greatest performer. The media of the 1920s and 1930s nurtured his image as the modern southern gentleman and helped make him a nationally popular hero. Sammy Snead of Hot Springs, Va., cultivated an image, according to *Golf* magazine, as "a hillbilly type who always had a vast storehouse of pungent jokes." "Slammin' Sammy," who won over 100 tournaments, claimed he had his earnings buried in tin cans back in the hills of home. Mildred "Babe" Didrikson Zaharias, from Port Arthur, Tex., is referred to in virtually all surveys as the greatest American woman athlete. She excelled in every sport she attempted, was a star of the 1932 Olympic Games, and dominated women's golf in the 1930s. Figures from the Professional Golf Association in 1967 showed that southerners have continued to play a prominent role in the game. Of the top 100 money winners for the previous year, 35 were southern natives, with 15 of them coming from Texas.

The South's interest in golf can also be seen in its premier courses. The Augusta National Country Club in Georgia, the Pinehurst Country Club in North Carolina, the Seminole Golf Club in Palm Beach, Fla., the Dunes Golf and Beach Club in South Carolina, and the Ocean Course at Sea Pines Plantation in Hilton Head, S.C., are among the South's nationally recognized courses. The Atlantic shore of the Southeast has been referred to as "The Golf Coast of America." Florida and South Carolina are particularly well known for the number and quality of resorts built around golfing for the region's, and indeed the nation's, vacationing elite. Almost half of the professional tournaments in the United States take place on southern courses.

The Masters Tournament at the Augusta National Country Club is one of the game's four most significant professional championships (along with those of the U.S. Open, the British Open, and the Professional Golf Association). Georgian Robert Tyre "Bobby" Jones, Jr., retired in 1930 from competitive golf, then conceived the idea of creating the Augusta course. Wall Street banker Clifford Roberts became his development partner and Scotland's Alistair Mackenzie was the designer of the course. Its site was 365 acres of rolling Georgia pinelands, which had for 100 years been a nursery. A Belgian baron named Prosper Jules Alphonse Berckmans moved to Augusta in 1857 and established the first nursery in the South. He disseminated hundreds of species of flowers, shrubs, and trees; in his catalogue of items in 1861 were 1,300 varieties of pears, 900 of apples, 300 of grapes, and over 100 each of azaleas and camellias. This natural background has made the Augusta course famed for its beauty, with long lines of magnolias, brilliant colors from azaleas, redbuds, and white dogwoods, and a chorus of sounds from the mockingbirds and cardinals. The architecture at Augusta adds to the stereotypical southern ambience. People sip mint juleps at café tables under huge magnolia trees on the front lawn of the sedate, Georgian-styled clubhouse, which could be from the *Gone with the Wind* set. Despite the southern setting, the Augusta Country Club is a national institution. When the club was organized, only 30 members from Augusta itself were allowed. Most members have always been from outside Georgia, including many outside the South.

As Associated Press sportswriter Will Grimsley has noted, the Masters Tournament "has been called autocratic, arrogant, snobbish, and racist." At the same time it has been lauded as the best organized, most relaxed, and most pleasant of the professional tournaments. As

Florida golfing great Gene Sarazen says, "It's the only tournament with class." Tournament directors carefully regulate the players and spectators, prohibiting cans, tents, and the sale of junk food and programs. CBS television has been televising the tournament since 1956, but even television trucks must be covered in green for camouflage. The key word at the Masters is "tradition," a word not unknown in the South. This emphasis led to conflict in the 1960s, however, when strong press criticism was directed at the tournament directors for never having invited a black to compete. A rule was soon adopted so that any winner of a Professional Golfers' Association tournament could compete, and Lee Elder, winner of the 1974 Monsanto Open, became the first black to receive a bid from Augusta, playing in 1975 without incident.

Charles Reagan Wilson
University of Mississippi

John R. Betts, *America's Sporting Heritage, 1850–1950* (1974); Frank DeFord, *Sports Illustrated* (7 April 1986); John M. Ross, ed., *Golf Magazine's Encyclopedia of Golf* (1979); *Southern Living* (August 1967); Dawson Taylor, *The Masters: An Illustrated History* (1973).

Kentucky Derby, Churchill Downs, Louisville, Ky., 1931

Horses

The distinctive role of horses in the South began in the antebellum era. The plantation economy created sufficient wealth to permit the development of a gentry class and to permit the breeding of horses for pleasure and sport. This resulted in three native American breeds, all developed in significant part in the South: the American Quarter Horse, the American Saddlebred Horse, and the Tennessee Walking Horse.

Prior to the Civil War, the Old South was the center of thoroughbred breeding and racing. Williamsburg, Va., and Charleston, S.C., each claims to be the first community of established racing in America. Virginia was the early center for thoroughbred breeding. Andrew Jackson established an important center for racing at Nashville, Tenn., and for a long time this area was second only to Virginia in thoroughbred breeding. Kentucky became the dominant breeding area in the early 19th century and is still so, although thoroughbreds are bred in other parts of the South, most notably Florida, Virginia, and Maryland.

Horse racing ceased during the Civil War. It came back strongly after the war, but without the dominance of the Old South. Racetracks were widespread and many were disreputable. The establishment of the Jockey Club with legislative, judicial, and executive functions in 1894 commenced the process of cleaning up racing. Racing, nevertheless, declined in the period immediately preceding World War I, probably because of its bad reputation and moral objections of the public to betting. A slow and steady renaissance was led by men of integrity and substance. Since World War I flat racing has steadily increased in popularity and acceptability and is now the largest spectator sport in the United States. The most significant southern tracks operate in Florida, Maryland, Kentucky, Arkansas, and Louisiana. Other states in the South either have, or are about to adopt, active racing programs.

The classic three-year-old thoroughbred races (the Triple Crown) were all instituted in the decade following the Civil War, one in the North and two in border states: the Belmont Stakes (New York), in 1867; the Preakness Stake (Maryland), in 1873; and the best-known horse race in America, the Kentucky Derby, in 1875. These races are regularly contested by southern-bred horses.

Fox hunting (riding to hounds), a natural for the plantation class, developed in the colonies as it was developing in Great Britain and became the principal sport of the planter class prior to the Civil War. (The first pack of hounds was probably imported to southern Maryland in 1650 by Robert Brooks.)

The destruction of the South in the Civil War almost destroyed fox hunting. After the war, the sport was revived and is now very active, with Virginia and Maryland generally considered to be its center. However, almost every state in the South boasts at least one recognized hunt, and the Deep South has produced one of the outstanding fox hunters of all time. Benjamin H. Hardaway III, Master of Foxhounds and Huntsman of the Midland Fox Hounds, Midland, Ga., is a keen student of fox hunting and a worthy successor to Peter Beckford, an early pioneer of modern fox hunting. The world famous Midland Fox Hounds, developed entirely by Hardaway, are deer proof, big mouthed, and aggressive, and will effectively drive a fox. The Midland Hounds hunt continuously in Georgia and Alabama and regularly in Pennsylvania, Maryland, and Virginia.

Hunting is a direct ancestor of steeple chasing. The introduction of jumping horses in the hunt field led to races across the countryside from one landmark to another, usually the steeples of village churches. Early American jump racing was much like the British counterpart. The sport developed in the South where the vast majority of the races are still held.

The horse, necessary for a civilized existence and important for recreation, was an indispensable partner in war. Aside from the mundane, but essential, matter of supply, the horse provided the mobility needed for intelligence gathering and communication, and in battle, the horse made the difference.

Mounted infantrymen who rode to battle and fought on foot appeared in frontier conflicts of the prerevolutionary period. These frontiersmen penetrated deep into enemy territory and appeared where least expected. Horse soldiers flourished in the Revolutionary War, especially in the South where irregular cavalry contributed significantly to the American war effort. Cavalry was a primary factor in the South's early successes in the Civil War and permitted it to last as long as it did. The Confederacy had a brilliant array of cavalry chieftains. Two of the best known of these gifted horse soldiers were the almost invincible Nathan Bedford Forrest and the colorful and dashing James Ewell Brown "Jeb" Stuart.

Today, the cavalry is gone and mules no longer plod the cotton rows or pull the freight and cotton wagons. Churchyards and town squares are not filled with wagons, buggies, and saddle horses. Human existence, with a high level of material comfort, can be maintained without a horse. Nonetheless, the bugle call to the post and the hunting horn are still heard. The Walking Horse and the American Saddlebred Horse are not necessary for plantation management, but throughout the South ringmasters at horse shows are heard to say, "Let your horses walk on" or "Let your horses rack on."

Racing and the breeding of racehorses are large industries. Horse shows range from small one-breed shows to the week-long or more events in large urban centers such as Dallas, Houston, Atlanta, New Orleans, Memphis, and Louisville. Lengthy affairs are devoted to selecting the best of a breed, such as the Walking Horse Celebration in Shelbyville, Tenn., and its counterpart for the American Saddlebred in Louisville, Ky., where annually the champion of the breed is chosen. Many of the contestants at the annual Quarter Horse World Congress in Ohio come from the South. The return of draft horses and mules has led to shows devoted entirely to these animals.

Although a product of the West, the rodeo has become one of the most popular of the horse sports or shows in the South. The roots of rodeo are in the work of the 19th-century cowboys of the West. Ranch life was demanding and tough. Cattle herds were brought in each spring from winter pasture and tended until the autumn trail drives. Each cowboy required a string of horses, and no one could afford the time to train them. Therefore, green and sometimes freshly caught wild horses were roped and ridden. At the end of annual trail drives, when the cowboys gathered in the railroad towns, conversations, particularly with the aid of liquor, soon turned to boasts of prowess with lariat and horse. Impromptu riding and roping contests resulted. Thus, the rodeo was born. Two of the five standard rodeo events, calf roping and saddle bronc riding, grew out of practical cowboy work. The three remaining events, bareback bronc riding, bull riding, and steer wrestling, rose from bragging.

The subject of horses in the South cannot be left without a reference to polo. Polo, a stick-and-ball game that originated in the Orient over 2,000 years ago, was introduced into the United States in 1876 and reached its golden age during the 1920s and 1930s. Once considered the province of the very rich in areas outside the South, it is now played by many people throughout the region on courses ranging from cow pastures to the well-appointed clubs of the wealthy.

Not to be overlooked is the just plain horse of dubious pedigree and faulted conformation found on farms and in backyards. An experienced horse fancier would pass him by, but he can turn a child into a gallant knight, a wild West marshall, or a reincarnation of Jeb Stuart or Nathan Bedford Forrest. Perhaps his real value exceeds that of the blooded horses of the race tracks and show rings.

Frank Hampton McFadden
Pike Road, Alabama

Robert Denhardt, *The Horse of the Americas* (1975); J. Frank Dobie, ed., *Mustangs and Cow Horses* (1940); Kent Hollingsworth, *The Kentucky Thoroughbred* (1976); Robert W. Howard, *The Horse in America* (1965); Kitty Slater, *The Hunt Country of America* (1973).

Hunting

During the South's colonial and antebellum periods, wildlife was abundant and its pursuit provided settlers a diversion from their ordinary work routines as well as supplements to their sometimes meager stocks of food. Settlers also hunted to control the numbers of larger mammals in their vicinity, for their crops were vulnerable to grazing by deer and their free-roaming livestock fell prey to wolves.

Wealthy planters sought to emulate European aristocrats with their privileges and refinements. In some areas, the pursuit of certain wild game became identified with the prerogatives of power and status. For influential, wealthy individuals, hunting was an important social activity. The hunt, the chase, and the shoot are described in the hunting narratives of the antebellum period. Although purported to be factual accounts, these hunting narratives are actually standardized accounts whose recurrent themes provide insights into the ideology of wealthy planters and the ways in which they sought to distinguish themselves.

Many planters believed that hunting enabled them to understand nature and man's place in the world. Southern hunters loved nature for its supposed order and stability, which their own organized social life based on a hierarchical arrangement of people and contingent upon the judicial applicaton of force could only approximate. For these planters, hunting was a socially sanctioned expression of force, and its violence was necessary to participate in the natural world and to appreciate its indestructible order. Southern planters contrasted their modes of hunting with others on the basis of presumed motive and purpose. If most whites and blacks in the South hunted out of necessity, planters insisted they participated for sport and amusement. Although other classes pursued wild animals for meat and for tangible trophies, planters saw the process itself as the most important part of the chase. For them, the end was unimportant and inconsequential. Hunting conventions (sportsmanship) became prerequisites for membership in polite society and provided its participants the opportunity to learn the important lessons of self-discipline and control.

Plantation-style hunting was not for everyone. Outside restricted circles of gentility, most men hunted wildlife for food and for profit. Most subsisted on the land and sold skins and game meat whenever they found buyers.

After the Civil War the processes of urbanization and industrialization gradually concentrated many people in towns and cities. Leisure and wealth for increasing numbers in the cities made a return to nature and the land attractive. These ventures became possible for those owning or leasing large tracts of land, for in the rural areas city hunters came into increasing conflict with rural landowners, market hunters, and game dealers over the declining stocks of wild game. State trespass and federal game laws, with effective enforcement, became the solution to these conflicts and seemed the most democratic way to handle access for those aspiring to hunt. By 1910 most southern states had joined the rest of the nation in enacting trespass and game laws and providing cadres of enforcement officers. With these legal structures in place, market hunting and the sale of wild animals became illegal. State legislatures empowered wildlife agencies to monitor the populations of species now defined by law as game and to determine the ways and means by which these species were to be hunted. Restrictions in the variety of huntable species and the formalization of some hunting norms were the outcome of legal processes begun by urbanites. These statutes and regulations provide the ground rules and boundaries indicating what, where, when, and how species are hunted today. Hunting now is largely for sport and recreation. Nonetheless, a few people continue to hunt for food and to poach.

From organized groups in the cities have come most initiatives affecting field sports—the antihunting leagues, for example, as well as hunting and conservation organizations such as Ducks Unlimited, the National Turkey Federation, and the National Wildlife Federation, to name a few. Each organization publishes its own journal, solicits contributions, and maintains lobbies that seek to influence legislation favorable to their causes. From these journals today hunters glean the latest tips and techniques for tracking their game, learn about the big ones that escaped, and read about current fads in men's games.

Modernization has influenced some types of hunting more than others. Most affected is hunting for which dogs are specially bred and trained. Centered on particular breeds of dogs, a number of national organizations keep breeding records and sponsor an annual series of field trials. The trading, purchase, and breeding of hounds is big business in many rural areas of the South where the various field trials are hosted. The influences of technology and the changing patterns of landownership are apparent in the organization of hunt clubs as well. Hunt clubs began in colonial days when neighbors joined together for game drives. Then their organization was informal, often spontaneous, with no fees or formal membership. Later, when the large estates were divided or sold, individuals joined to lease land for their game and to afford the costs of maintaining the dogs throughout the year. Formal hunt clubs began about 1900. These clubs had a paid and limited membership and set times for hunting. Agribusiness with its mechanized operations on large tracts of land reduced game habitat on the better lands while most of the marginal lands, previously occupied and tilled by tenants, reverted to pine plantations and scrub. With the secondary growth, deer returned to these marginal lands, which now featured a hunt club with its headquarters in a refurbished tenant's shack.

Today precision firearms largely replace the muskets of former times, although a few purists prefer to stalk their deer with primitive weapons such as bows and arrows. Four-wheel-drive vehicles have superseded horses and wagons, dirt roads the foot trails, and CB radios and loudspeakers the hunter's horn. Yet the informal, intimate rituals between close associates and the traditions of time and place continue to make the hunt club a seasonal feature of southern life.

Southern distinctiveness in hunting stems from a peculiar combination of traits found in the region. The myth of a plantation lifestyle continues to inform the traditions of those who can afford them and to influence

Hunters standing over prey, location unknown, c. 1900

many others. The reality persists in the hunting plantations, many purchased and maintained by northern wealth in the 20th century, for quail and deer, and in the colorful pageantries of the exclusive hunt clubs located throughout the region. Extensive landownership, wealth, power, and leisure sustain these plantations and clubs, luring many to join or to observe their seasonal rituals. Still others read about them or participate in regional or national field trials for fox, quail, and coon, species associated with plantation life.

Most hunting in the rural South lacks the pretentiousness of the plantation tradition, yet its contours continue to show the gender, racial, and socioeconomic stratification of the region. Over two-thirds of southern hunters come from small towns or live in rural areas. Most are whites and Indians. Youngsters are taught to hunt by their fathers or close relatives. Guns are often heirlooms passed between generations. Blacks are underrepresented and, in contrast to the other races, they learn to hunt later in life, if at all, and their socialization is more often by peer groups than by their fathers. Hunters tend to be less well educated, make under $15,000 annual income, and are generally under 40 years of age. The expressed motivation for hunting varies, but it is normally for sport rather than for food. However, most game taken is eaten. Hunting continues as a masculine domain with a few inroads by women among either the poor or the wealthy. Because hunting is a masculine activity, game meat falls to the men to clean, to cook, and to serve on special occasions such as for Sunday dinners or at reunions.

Socialization as a hunter begins at an early age, with fathers or within an intimate circle of friends. In these close groups, young boys learn about conceptions of masculinity and their identity with the community, together with skills useful in their transition to manhood. Their maturation and accomplishments are celebrated in coming of age rituals aptly described by William Faulkner in *Go Down, Moses*. For most boys, initial kills are of small game such as squirrels and rabbits, which make relatively easy targets. Youngsters generally pursue a variety of mammals and birds as their time allows, but as they mature, they tend to specialize in one or a few species depending upon their associations with other men, their jobs, and costs of maintaining trained dogs. Men who hunt together are influential in other areas of community social and political life as well. Increasingly, family and work commitments are major disruptions to these male hunting fraternities. Jobs outside of the local community may disrupt these networks temporarily, but some men return religiously for the fall hunting season.

The types of game pursued reflect stratification along socioeconomic and racial lines. Ownership of extensive tracts and trained dogs are the prerequisites for the most prestigious types of game such as quail, deer, fox, and turkey. Access to these species remains difficult for many, although they may be hunted on public lands. Dove shoots, which generally open the fall hunting season, are social occasions. They are generally open to most people because the shoot requires guns positioned in as many places as possible around a recently harvested field to keep the birds flying. (In many northern states, doves are classified as song birds and not hunted.) Blacks and the rural poor generally hunt squirrels, rabbits, raccoons, and possums, species normally avoided by others.

As a region, the South still retains an edge over other areas in numbers of households containing a hunter. According to Gallup polls taken in 1959, slightly over half of southern white households contained a hunter compared to one-third for the rest of the nation. By 1965 these percentages had dropped, but the South still led other regions. White southerners have led the nation in ownership of guns and revolvers. Gallup polls for 1960 showed about two-thirds of white southern households possessing firearms, whereas less than half of those in the non-South did so. In 1968 these polls showed 52 percent for the South and 27 percent elsewhere.

See also VIOLENCE: Guns

Stuart A. Marks
University of Florida

Dickson D. Bruce, Jr., *Violence and Culture in the Antebellum South* (1979); Hennig Cohen and William B. Dillingham, eds., *Humor of the Old Southwest* (2d ed., 1975); William Elliot, *Carolina Sports by Land and Water* (1859); William Faulkner, "The Bear," in *Go Down, Moses* (1942); H. Gibson, "Deer Hunting Clubs in Concordia Parish: The Role of Male Sodalities in the Maintenance of Social Values" (M.A. thesis, Louisiana State University, 1976); C. Gondes, ed., *Hunting in the Old South* (1967); Clifton Paisley, *From Cotton to Quail: An Agricultural Chronicle of Leon County, Florida, 1860–1967* (1968); Robert Ruark, *The Old Man and the Boy* (1957); Louis D. Rubin, Jr., *William Elliot Shoots a Bear: Essays on the Southern Literary Imagination* (1976); Francis Utley, Lynn Bloom, and Arthur F. Kinney, eds., *Bear, Man, and God: Seven Approaches to William Faulkner's "The Bear"* (1964).

Mardi Gras

The celebration of Mardi Gras along the central Gulf Coast portions of Louisiana, Mississippi, and Alabama marks the region's historical and cultural difference from the rest of the South. Mardi Gras ("Fat Tuesday"), or Carnival ("fleshly excess"), is celebrated with costumed float parades, neighborhood marches, informal parties, and formal balls in New Orleans, Biloxi, and Mobile among other Gulf Coast cities. In contrast, a rural Louisiana Cajun and black Creole *courir de Mardi Gras* or Mardi Gras run is carried out by horseback-mounted revelers in over a dozen French-speaking communities of southwest Louisiana.

Mardi Gras is historically associated with French and Spanish populations along the Gulf Coast. However, many ethnic groups now join in the traditional festive occasion, which falls in February or March prior to Ash Wednesday and 40 days before Easter. It has been speculated that the Mediterranean-Latin roots of Mardi Gras are to be found in the pre-Roman rites of spring and later

Roman festival or ritual occasions such as Baccanalia, Lupercalia, and Saturnalia. Over time such occasions became part of the Catholic liturgical calendar. Thus, the Gulf Coast carnival season officially begins on 6 January, the Epiphany and Feast of Kings. On this date in New Orleans "King Cakes"—with a plastic miniature baby inside each and adorned in Mardi Gras colors of gold, purple, and green—are consumed in celebration. The season may be as short as three and a half weeks or as long as two months, depending upon the date of Easter. The culmination of Carnival is Mardi Gras day or Shrove Tuesday (referring to a time to be "shriven of one's sins"). The festive eating, dancing, and drinking associated with Mardi Gras are followed by the relative austerity and penitence of the Lenten period.

Just as Roman Catholicism absorbed earlier pre-Roman carnival elements, so too the worldwide variations on Carnival now reflect regional cultural diversity. Thus, Gulf Coast Carnival, like Carnival in related societies of the Caribbean and Latin America, represents a syncretism of French/Spanish, Native American, and African/Afro-Caribbean performance styles and structures. That the earliest European settlers of the Gulf Coast celebrated Mardi Gras is verified by the explorer D'Iberville's naming of Mardi Gras Bayou along the Mississippi in southern Louisiana. Informal parades and festive masquerades are reported to have occurred in major centers like Mobile and New Orleans throughout the early 19th century; and by midcentury (1857 in New Orleans) officially sanctioned parades began.

The early public parades in New Orleans and Mobile were founded by the Anglo and Creole (French/Spanish) elites of both cities. In New Orleans, such "krewes" as Comus, Momus, Proteus, and Rex have continued from the 19th century into the present. Some krewes still utilize smaller antique floats depicting mythological scenes crafted in *papier-mâché*. These floats were originally drawn by mules, which were eventually replaced by tractors in the 1950s. The artwork found on newer floats is made of plastic.

Today as many as 60 different krewes parade in the roughly two-week period prior to and including Mardi Gras day. Some, such as Arabi and Argus, are quite recent and represent suburban neighborhoods. All parades throw doubloons (introduced in the early 1960s) and other plastic trinkets to the crowds that line such primary parade routes as St. Charles Avenue and Canal Street. The varied krewes both reflect and invert the social structure of New Orleans on a day when the upper classes play at being kings, fools, and mythological beings. Suburban middle classes may likewise assert their right to be royalty for a day. Elite old-line krewes maintain an aura of secrecy about the selection of their royalty and invitation to their balls and affiliated social events. The newer krewes such as Bacchus, on the other hand, charge admission to their open gatherings in the Superdome and elsewhere at the end of parades.

The Zulu parade of New Orleans's black middle class and elite community, founded in 1909 as a reaction to white stereotypes of blacks as "savages," is a Carnival activity rivaled only by the Rex Parade on Mardi Gras day. Zulu members dress in grass skirts and "wooley wigs," put on blackface, and throw rubber spears and decorated coconuts to the delighted crowds. Working-class blacks, particularly those of Creole (French/Spanish) ancestry, also invoke white stereotypes of "wildness" by masquerading pridefully in stylized Plains Indians costumes.

The black "Mardi Gras Indians" are hierarchical groups of men with titles such as Big Chief, Spyboy, Wildman, and Li'l Chief who dress in elaborate bead and feather costumes weighing up to 100 pounds. After months of time and money invested in sewing costumes and practice sessions at local bars, a dozen or more "tribes" appear early on Mardi Gras day to sing, dance, and parade through back street neighborhoods. Some of these black Indians, with "tribe" names such as "Creole Wild West," "White Cloud Hunters," "Yellow Pocahontas," and "Wild Tchoupitoulas," do in fact have partial Native American ancestry and speak in mythological fashion about Indian spirits and customs. Their performance style, however, is essentially Afro-Caribbean, as expressed in competitive dance and song and the call-and-response chants that mark their foot parades. These chants are often based on a secret code language consisting of a group leader's call and responses such as "Hey pocky way" and "Ja ca mo feen non nay." They also use standard tunes such as "Li'l Liza Jane" and "Shoo Fly" to improvise tales of their daring and exploits as they "go to town" on Mardi Gras day.

While the Mardi Gras Indians and the Zulu parade utilize Mardi Gras to make statements about group pride through inverted stereotypes of Indian and African tribes, many blacks also work at the service of whites on Carnival, thereby reflecting the postcolonial social structure of New Orleans. Some, for example, lead horses for major white parades such as Rex and Momus. Others dress in pointed white hoods and cloaks and carry torches called "flambeaux" that light the way for night parades of old elite krewes such as Comus.

Although smaller in scale and less widely known than New Orleans Carnival, Mardi Gras in Mobile has been celebrated in various ways since the beginning of the 19th century. The Cowbellions, an early parading group using cowbells and other noisemakers, formed in the 1830s and later ordered their costumes from Paris. During the Civil War Mobile's public Mardi Gras ceased. It was revived in 1866 by a veteran named Joe Cain, who dressed that year as a mock Chickasaw Indian chief called "Slacabamorinico" and drove through the then-occupied city in a decorated wagon. On Sunday before the Mobile Carnival Joe Cain is now commemorated with a jazz funeral procession. Various other Mobile krewes such as the Comic Cowboys and the Infant Mystics date to the 19th century. The Order of Myths, the oldest krewe (1867), was modeled after the early Cowbellions. The symbol of the Order of Myths, which is the last krewe to parade on Mardi Gras, is Folly chasing Death around a broken neoclassical column and flailing him with a golden pig bladder. Although this imagery symbolizes a general Mardi Gras theme of mirth's triumph over gloom, some suggest that the broken column originally alluded to the broken dreams of the Confederacy.

The large float parades in the Mardi Gras celebrations of Mobile and New Orleans represent Mediterranean and Caribbean traditions. In contrast, the Cajun and black Creole *courir de Mardi Gras* of rural southwest Louisiana reflects country French traditions brought by Acadians of Nova Scotia who came to Louisiana in the latter part of the 18th century. In a manner not unlike Christmas mumming in Europe and the West Indies, a band of masked male revelers goes from house to house on the open prairie land of southwest Louisiana. The men, on horses or flatbed trucks, dress as clowns, thieves, women, and devils. Some wear the traditional pointed *capuchon* hats with bells and streamers. The group is lead by a *capitaine* who may wear an elegant silk costume in the Cajun bands or simple work clothes in some black Creole Mardi Gras bands. The Mardi Gras bands come as quasi-vigilantes and clowns in search of *charité* in the form of live chickens, rice, spices, grease, sausages, and other ingredients for a gumbo supper. The *capitaine,* standing apart from the group as a keeper of the law, tries to prevent the men from getting too disorderly or drunk and sees that they carry out their agreed-upon rounds for the day. At each visited farmstead the *capitaine* or a flagman will visit ahead of the band to see if the household will receive the Mardi Gras. There is usually an affirmative response to the courtly request, *"Voulez-vous recevoir cette band des Mardi Gras?"* ("Do you want to receive the Mardi Gras band?"), whereupon the clowns are waved on to charge the house on horseback. After dismounting and dancing together (which men do only on Mardi Gras), a competitive chase is often held for a live chicken. (This chase is usually preceded by a song of request to the man or lady of the house.) The chicken chase involves a designated bird, or one tossed into the air, and is a hilarious spectacle as men in costume pursue elusive birds through the muddy rice fields of early spring, leaping fences and crossing pig styes. After a chicken is caught, it is killed and put with other spoils in a sack, which is sent back to town where the cooking begins at midday. As the Mardi Gras runners depart a house, they sing a word of thanks and invite the householders to the dance and communal supper to be held in town or at a rural club late in the night.

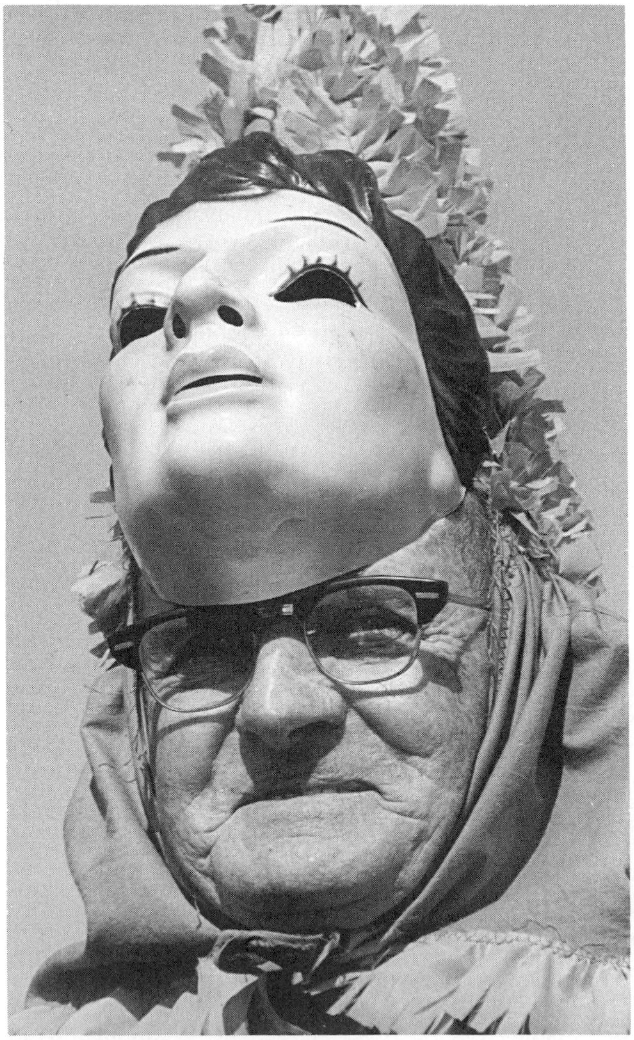

Cajun Mardi Gras celebrant, Church Point, La., 1978

The Mardi Gras song is especially significant because it is sung in a minor modal style reminiscent of Medieval French folk music, generally not found in Cajun music today. The song also contains a description of the Mardi Gras band's activities. Sung in French, the song is usually performed by musicians who ride in a sound truck. The translated song is as follows:

THE MARDI GRAS DANCE

The Mardi Gras riders come from everywhere
All around, around the hub.
They pass once a year
To ask for charity
Even if it's a potato.
A potato and some cracklins.
The Mardi Gras riders are on a long voyage
All around, around the hub.
They pass once a year
To ask for charity
Even if it's a skinny chicken
And three or four corn cobs.
Captain, captain, wave your flag.
Let's go to the other neighbor's place
To ask for charity.
You all come meet us.
You all come meet us.
Yes, at the gumbo tonight.

By the end of the afternoon the band heads back toward "the hub" or their starting point in rice- and soybean-growing and cattleraising towns like Mamou, Church Point, L'Anse Maigre, and Swords. The riders on horseback may enter at a gallop. Those who are sober enough entertain waiting crowds with stunts and various acts of bravado. The gumbo from the day's catch is served to the riders and the general public followed by a large dance ending at midnight and the beginning of the Lenten season.

The parallel black Creole Mardi Gras bands are often

located near the Cajun towns in tiny rural settlements established in the 19th century by manumitted slaves and other people of color. The black Creole Mardi Gras celebrations are usually smaller (10–20 men), more intimate, and more traditional than today's Cajun *courirs*. The cowboy style of Cajun Mardi Gras has not taken hold in the black Creole community. For example, the black bands take great care not to trample house gardens or urinate in public while pursuing the fowl. Elders are helped down from their flatbed trucks by younger men, and the bands present themselves more as polite beggars than as vigilantes. The older Creoles especially take great stock in such details and are critical of young men who do not behave or sing properly. The Creole Mardi Gras song is similar to that of the Cajuns but is often performed in a call-response manner showing Afro-Caribbean influences. The usual response line to the leader's song is "*Ouais mon/bon cher camarade*" ("Yes my/good dear friend").

While old traditions and Carnival groups continue, in recent years new Mardi Gras events and locales have emerged to meet new social concerns and issues. For example, in New Orleans gay krewes and their French Quarter costume contests have become highly visible. In New Orleans and Baton Rouge the Krewe of Clones and the Spanishtown Mardi Gras, respectively, have become avant-garde satires on Carnival itself and on Louisiana topics such as politics and pollution. Suburban Mardi Gras celebrations have sprung up with children included and excessive drunkenness or sexual suggestiveness excluded. Adjacent Anglo-American regions have also started Mardi Gras celebrations. Monroe, La., for example, held its first parade in 1985, and the celebration was criticized by local fundamentalist preachers as "devil worship."

Films such as *Always for Pleasure* (Les Blank, director, Flower Films, 1978) and *Fat Tuesday* (Armand Ruhlman, director, Goofy Gator productions, 1981) offer rich visual documentation of Mardi Gras. Whatever locale and shape Mardi Gras takes in the Gulf Coast region, it will continue to reflect the historical and contemporary cultural traditions of its celebrants.

See also BLACK LIFE: / Mardi Gras Indians; ETHNIC LIFE: Caribbean Influence; / Cajuns and Creoles; Creole; URBANIZATION: / Mobile; New Orleans

Nicholas R. Spitzer
Smithsonian Institution

Always for Pleasure (Les Blank, producer, Flower Films, El Cerrito, Calif., 1978); Erwin Craighead, in *Mobile: Fact and Tradition* (1930); Munro Edmunson, *Caribbean Quarterly* (No. 3, 1956); Arthur La Cour and Stuart Landry, *New Orleans Masquerade: Chronicles of Carnival* (1952); Rosary H. O'Brien, "The New Orleans Carnival Organizations: Theatre of Prestige" (Ph.D. dissertation, University of California at Berkeley, 1973); Harry Oster and Revon Reed, *Louisiana Folklore Miscellany* (No. 1, 1960); Phyllis H. Rabbe, "Status and Its Impact: New Orleans Carnival, The Social Upper Class and Upper Class Power" (Ph.D. dissertation, Pennsylvania State University, 1973); Michael P. Smith, *Spirit World: Pattern in the Expressive Folk Culture of Afro-American New Orleans* (1984); Nicholas R. Spitzer, "Zydeco and Mardi Gras: Creole Identity and Performance Genres in Rural French Louisiana" (Ph.D. dissertation, University of Texas, 1986); Robert Tallant, *Mardi Gras* (1949); Calvin Trillin, *New Yorker* (20 June 1964); Perry Young, *The Mystick Krewe: Chronicles of Comus and His Kin* (1931).

Pets

Keeping domestic animals as pets and as companions is a widespread, almost ubiquitous, pattern in human societies. Pets are of several types: (1) the pet animal kept for pleasure or amusement predominantly, but with no utilitarian function; (2) the food animal, hand- and/or house-raised, which enjoys pet status during some or all of its lifetime; and (3) the companion animal, fulfilling multiple overlapping roles, ranging from comrade to such other roles as work assistant, recreational partner, or surrogate family or household member, any of which meets the key elements described above. In addition, tamed wild animals are sometimes kept as pets.

Earliest evidence of pet or companion animals in the South comes from an A.D. 1100 site in North Carolina. The special pet or companion status of a dog is inferred from a burial site, where careful arrangement of remains indicates a close relationship between the animal and a person or the community. Both pets and companion animals have persisted within southern culture, as have careful burials and memorials for companion animals. Franklin County, Ala., has an elaborate coon dog graveyard, complete with a monument said to have cost $5,000.

Southern pet-keeping practices must be viewed within the larger context of general attitudes toward animals more characteristic of southern culture than of other regions: southerners are more likely to express concern for the practical and material value of animals or their habitat. They are less likely to express concern about the right and wrong treatment of animals or to strongly oppose exploitation or cruelty toward animals. On the other hand, while expressing indifference or incredulity toward the idea of "loving" animals, many southerners form strong affectional attachments to individual animals. This feeling is best expressed in the rural South through the ambivalent relationship between a man and his hound. Other southerners report no such ambivalence in their relationships with their pets and companion animals, readily expressing strong and enduring attachment to them and mourning their loss, whether these companions are household residents or working companions.

The importance of the animal as working companion is reflected in the emergence of several regional dog breeds. The breeds usually derive from stock registered by national breeding registries, but offspring are no longer registered with national bodies. They are identified with the region and local area and are a source of great community pride. Examples are the multiple varieties of coonhounds (many locally recognized as separate pure breeds, with strong local sanctions against breeding back to nonregional stock), the Boykin Spaniel (a variety of Field Spaniel, developed as a hunting spaniel but also suitable as a household companion), and the Catahoula Leopard Dog (a stock dog prized for working ability and companionship, developed from several breeds of stock dogs). Few of these are known or seen outside the South. Small mixed-breed dogs are still routinely referred to as "feist" or "fice" and within local areas may be so similar to one another in appearance and ancestry as to be recognized as the "feist" of a particular area. William Faulkner celebrated the bravery of a "fice" in "The Bear."

The species of pets and companion animals in the South do not differ notably from those in other regions of the United States, especially in urban areas. Dogs are most common, with a greater proportion of the regional purebred and mixed breeds than found in other regions. Some patterns of the dog-human relationship do differ. Individuals and household members develop strong attachments to individual dogs and, while treating them with affection, evaluate them on the basis of their working ability. Once unable to work, however, they still retain a special status within the household. Because their primary function is that of working animal, the special status within the household does not necessarily mean the animal resides inside. This is true for many pets and companion animals in southern culture: The key elements of companion animal status are frequently fulfilled without inside residence for the animal. This remains true when people migrate or obtain animals of other species or breeds. When the need for an animal to assist with work is no longer present, many southerners select an animal solely for companionship purposes. Special status is earned on the basis of satisfaction with fulfillment of companionship function. Country musicians sing sentimental songs of dogs, such as "Old Shep." Writer Willie Morris wrote of the companionship and death of his dog Pete in *The Courting of Marcus Dupree* (1984).

Cats are kept as pets less frequently than in other areas. Most cats kept as pets or companions live in urban areas. In rural areas of the South many barn cats are kept to control rodent populations, with attachments to the territory on which they live and hunt, rather than to people. Breeding cats for companionship functions has occurred only recently. The recency of this is not peculiar to the South, however. Although selective breeding of the dog has occurred for over 2,000 years, selective breeding of cats in most areas of the world has occurred only within the last 100 years.

As in other areas, horses have risen in popularity as companion animals. Previously kept primarily as performance animals by members of the upper and upper middle classes, they are increasingly acquired for companionship and pleasure riding by members of the middle class. Frequently, a strong mutual attachment develops between horse and owner, and the horse spends an entire lifetime with a single owner, rather than being regularly sold and replaced as are many performance animals.

Southerners also keep their share of "pocket pets": guinea pigs, rats, mice, rabbits, gerbils, ferrets, birds, amphibians, and fish. Patterns of keeping these species do not differ notably from those in other regions of the United States; they are more popular in urban areas.

Boy with dog, Vicksburg, Miss., 1972

Another common practice in the South persists even among those who express a utilitarian attitude toward animals: hand raising food animals and selecting an occasional food animal to be kept as a pet. In the past this practice has involved very few animals but has included hogs, dairy and beef cattle, sheep, and poultry. As southern animal agriculture shifts from small operations to large agribusiness, the practice persists, but the types of animals change: goats have become increasingly popular, as have pigs. Both provide food and animal by-products. Both species are also social animals, a fact that increases the probability of becoming a successful companion.

The practices of raising orphaned and keeping tamed wild animals as if they were pets are far more common in the South than in other regions. In many southern towns and rural areas, these are long-standing customs, often considered as much a part of southern culture as nurturing regional breeds or lines of dogs. In the past most of the tamed wild animals have been small and native to the South—raccoons, skunks, possums, squirrels, and birds. They frequently fulfilled some marginal companionship function. Recently, however, there has been a marked increase in the keeping of exotic or endangered animals, including cougars, wolves, buffaloes, wolf-hybrids, parrot-like birds, monkeys, and large snakes. The latter species are kept largely for amusement or as status symbols rather than for utility or companionship. Such practices are currently being actively discouraged in many southern communities as lawsuits against owners of animals that kill or injure people are successfully prosecuted, as the incidence of rabies among wild animals increases, as zoonotic diseases are transmitted from animals to people, and as existing laws that prohibit keeping such animals are more strictly enforced. Efforts to discourage keeping wild animals as pets are usually met with strong resistance and are viewed as attempts of outsiders to interfere with southern rights.

Patterns of keeping companion animals in the South are similar to those in other areas of the United States in many ways. Dogs are still the most popular companion animals, with cats, birds, and other small domestic animals becoming more popular, especially as urbanization increases. But the South has several notable differences from patterns in other regions. Companion animals in the rural South are more likely to be employed actively in some work-assistant role, and they are more frequently kept for herding, hunting, or controlling pests, while enjoying special status within the household or farmstead.

Ownership patterns also differ. The use of the companion animal in its work function is frequently shared by various members in the community; however, the primary figure for attachment, loyalty, affection, and care is an individual rather than a group. Other animals are kept primarily as household companions or working companions during most of the year and employed in communal work-recreational functions (such as raccoon or bird hunting) at intervals throughout the year. In addition, in the South, human companions to companion animals are less likely to be legal owners of the animals than in other regions.

Residence patterns of companions and pets differ from other regions. In the South, many animals are sheltered outside the house. In other regions most are housed in the same structure as their owners. Types of pet animals vary. More wild animals are kept as pets, as are more farm animals. Regional breeds are more highly valued, and animals are more likely to be evaluated on performance of their companionship function than on their status as pure or mixed breed.

Margaret Sery Young
University of North Carolina
at Chapel Hill

David S. Favre and Murray Loring, *Animal Law* (1983); James W. Jordan, *Appalachian Journal* (Spring 1975); Stephen R. Kellert, *Transactions of the 45th North American Wildlife and Natural Resources Conference* (1980); Margaret Sery Young, *Veterinary Clinics of North America: Small Animal Practice* (March 1985).

Resorts

The color photographs in brochures publicizing southern resorts portray romantic luxury in magnificent scenic settings. Handsome couples frolic in the wash of surf, ride bicycles along moss-draped live-oak-lined paths, play golf on green-barbered fairways. They dine by candlelight and enjoy a leisurely breakfast on the terrace of their room, overlooking a sweep of mountains or an expanse of sea. The point of such literature, of course, is to coax the reader to make reservations for a few days in paradise.

Essentially, resorts are rooms with a view, a combination of lodging and nature where the natural beauty of the outdoors, like room service, is offered as an amenity. Resorts are the rich relatives of the poor-cousin interstate motel, inhabiting their own little world on barrier islands and mainland coast, beside lakes and warm springs, in the mountain valleys and in the folds of piedmont. Their guests are mostly middle- and upper-class couples and families who escape home and work for a weekend, a week, even a season to find rest and recreation.

Lodging in most resorts may include both hotel-type rooms for rent and individually owned units, such as condominiums. Through lease agreements, owners permit the resort to rent the property to other guests most of the year. Increasingly popular are timeshare vacation units. In this arrangement, the guest buys a space of time, say a week in June, and the vacation home is theirs for that period each year.

The first southern resorts appeared as early as the late 18th and early 19th centuries and were built around the waters of warm springs. The Greenbrier in White Sulphur Springs, W.Va., and The Homestead in Hot Springs, Va., trace their origins to those times. Early lodging conditions were often no better than the common ordinary (tavern) of that day.

A minister from Charleston in 1838 described White Sulphur Springs as "decidedly the meanest, most nasty place in point of filth, dust, and every other bad quality." Yet, despite the fleas in his bed and the grunting hogs outside his window, the minister paid his money to rub shoulders with the elite of the South and the nation. Southern resorts drew the rich and famous. One of the last photographs of Robert E. Lee, sitting among his Confederate general comrades, was taken at White Sulphur Springs in 1869.

Although southerners used health as an excuse to spend a season at a resort, the purpose of their visit was also pleasure. The resort season glittered with balls, sumptuous meals, music, and gambling. In the late 19th century northerners were also checking into southern resorts and resort towns, not only to bathe in springs, but also to drink the mineral waters. Travel guidebooks, such as *Health Resorts in the South*, published in 1893, were a mixture of boosterism and scholarly treatise, praising the towns and resorts and listing the medical benefits of each locale's water and climate.

Many towns were considered beneficial for specific ailments. Consumptives often headed for mountain towns such as Asheville, N.C. Grove Park Inn, still in operation there today, was built in 1886 by a St. Louis businessman who first came to the area seeking relief from his bronchial ailments.

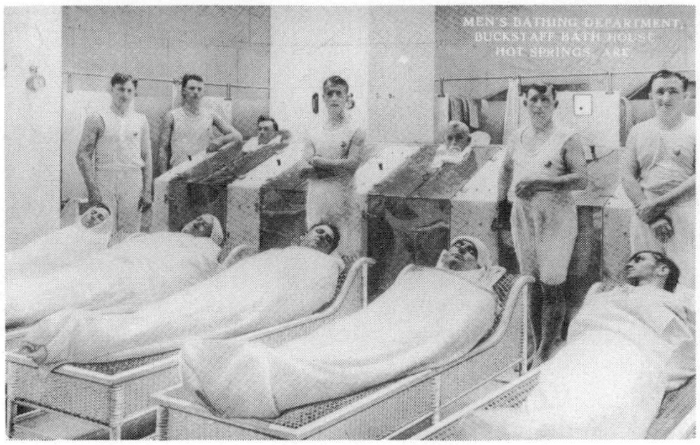

Men's bathing department, Buckstaff Bath House, Hot Springs, Ark., postcard, c. 1900

Railroad transportation provided easier access to resorts and encouraged the building of new ones. In the early 20th century northerners rode the rails further down the southern coastline as these resorts opened. At Jekyll Island, Ga., it is said that one-sixth of the world's wealth gathered each winter on this barrier island. In Florida, Henry Morrison Flagler, the Standard Oil Company magnate, welcomed wintering northerners to a string of coastal resorts he built along his railroad from Jacksonville to Miami.

In the decades after World War II, when the upper class preferred jet travel to Europe, many old resort hotels fell into disrepair. Others, however, survived as oases of grandeur in the neon desert of the chain motel. Such properties as The Breakers in Palm Beach, Fla., The Greenbrier, The Homestead, and Grand Hotel in Point Clear, Ala., constantly upgraded facilities and kept service standards high. They continued to pamper guests with afternoon tea, chamber music, and carriage rides. Ladies and gentlemen dressed for meals prepared by European chefs and served in elegant dining rooms.

Where the upper class goes, the middle class will scrimp and save and surely follow. They, too, took their overseas vacations, but they also trekked to old resorts and to newer ones that began to arise during the early 1960s. These stretch along beaches and huddle in mountain valleys, offering units with kitchens for guests. Property was also sold to families who bought or built vacation or retirement homes.

As stepchildren to the grand old hotels, these nouveau riche resorts attempt to buy instant tradition and class. Many hire European chefs to prepare continental cuisine and offer afternoon tea. They pay handsome sums to top golf course designers to lay out their 18 holes, and hire professional golfers and tennis stars, who represent the resort as "touring pro." These stars drop by for cameo appearances to teach clinics and play exhibition matches. At these new resorts, vacationers may still rub elbows with the rich and famous.

Nearly all offer golf and tennis, water sports, bicycling, and shopping. But despite the similarities, each resort attempts to produce a distinctive ambience. On Greers Ferry Lake, in the foothills of the Arkansas Ozarks, two resorts stretch along opposite shorelines. One, Fairfield Bay, moves with a snappy urbane flair, with rooms as plush as city hotel suites and with entertainment in its nightclub. Red Apple Inn, on the other hand, is flavored with a warm, winesap scent, and is as comfortable as worn tweeds. Its rooms are filled with European antiques, fireplaces, and fresh apples. Guests are expected to dress for dinner, which is served with a view of the sunset over the lake.

To build resorts with views from rooms unencumbered by signs of civilization, developers often shouldered into empty pockets of pristine wilderness. Many were gentle invaders. They attached strict building codes to blend vacation structures with natural surroundings, stilted boardwalks above sacred dunes, and left portions of their property in its natural state. On South Carolina's Hilton Head Island, for example, at least 75 percent of Sea Pines Plantation remains in forest and marshland.

One resort in Pine Mountain, Ga., was built specifically as a caretaker of its land. In the early 1950s Cason Callaway, a retired textile magnate, nursed 2,500 acres of eroded cotton fields into a paradise, Callaway Gardens, which is run by a nonprofit foundation for horticultural and environmental research and preservation. In greenhouses and formal gardens, along woodland paths, or bordering an inn, cottage, condominium, tennis court, or golf course, Callaway Gardens blushes with floral color each season.

Traffic sometimes backs up three miles from Pine Mountain as motorists come in spring to see some 700 varieties of azaleas in bloom. The garden's horticulture and education staffs conduct research in plant life and the local environment and pass that knowledge on to guests in nature walks and seminars. At Callaway Gardens the resort is a backdrop to the land and the flowers that grow upon it.

The land itself is a resort's most important asset, groomed and cared for as meticulously as its rooms and restaurants. Guests come for a resort's outdoor features, first for health and later for recreation. Nature—a woodland path, a sunset-kissed curl of golden beach—comprises the main ingredients visitors need "to get away from it all." Visitors still trek to resorts for their health, if not necessarily for the body, at least for peace of mind and of the soul.

See also ART AND ARCHITECTURE: Resort Architecture

Gary D. Ford
Southern Living

"Callaway Gardens: A Place for Everyone" (information pamphlet published by Callaway Gardens); George H. Chapin, *Health Resorts of the South* (1893); Marshall Fishwick, *Springlore in Virginia* (1978); Jeffrey Limerick, Nancy Ferguson, and Richard Oliver, *America's Grand Resort Hotels* (1979); Donald E. Lundberg, *The Tourist Business* (1974); *Southern Living* (September 1979, August 1982, February 1984).

Restaurants

From the colonial period through Reconstruction, southerners did not care for commercial hospitality. Except in the large cities such as New Orleans, restaurants were unheard of. The word, derived from the French, was not in general use until late in the 18th century, and the word "hotel" was not used until the 19th century. Even in the larger cities, most eating places were operated in conjunction with lodging.

When southerners traveled, they frequently stopped with friends or relations. Roadside taverns and inns were intended primarily for convivial drinking rather than eating. Food that was supplied was meager and unappetizing; some of it, travelers discovered, was tainted or spoiled. However, some of the inns were run by widows or private families wishing to supplement their incomes, and in such establishments, the traveler fared better.

The food on the eastern seacoast tended to be better and more appetizing than that found elsewhere. As the traveler moved westward through the frontier areas, the quality of the food deteriorated rapidly. Too, those states farther north tended to serve better fare than those farther south. In Mississippi and Louisiana (other than New Orleans), food was frequently so bad that it had to be chased down with whiskey. Contemporary reports indicate that the worst accommodations of all were in Arkansas and Texas because of their frontier status. Available food was generally wild game, chicken, or pork served with locally grown vegetables, fruits, and berries when they were in season.

Spas and resorts, which later became popular in the South, did little to improve commercial dining. Food and accommodations at such hotels as Gray Sulfur Springs, Red Sulfur Springs, and White Sulfur left much to be desired. The dining rooms were frequently out of most food, and the straw-stuffed mattresses were hard and uneven. The Englishman J. S. Buckingham commented with some amazement in his study *The Slave States of America* that most Americans accepted bad accommodations and worse food without complaint.

As the southerner traveled to cities such as Mobile, Charleston, and New Orleans, his chances of finding good food served well in commercial settings improved. Buckingham, for example, ate in the dining room of the Saint Charles Hotel in New Orleans, which accommodated some 500 guests—300 men at one table and 200 women at another. Many immigrants brought with them the more sophisticated knowledge of cuisine from Europe. The Creole and French influences in New Orleans cuisine are still strongly felt.

One area of interest regarding commercial hospitality of the time was the river steamer. Here southerners could find food that frequently equalled the quality of that served in the cities. On one such steamer the cabin passengers dined first, followed by the ship's officers, white deck passengers, white waiters, black passengers, and black waiters, in sequence. Steamers seemed to offer more beef and less pork and, when they departed from New Orleans, frequently served seafood, especially shellfish.

The manners and eating habits of southerners of the time left much to be desired. They frequently averaged 10 minutes to eat a meal and left the table while they were still chewing. The knife seemed to be the main utensil they used while eating, and coffee was as frequently sipped from the saucer as from the cup.

The old frontier ways of commercial dining in the South began to change by the middle of the 19th century. More attention was paid not only to the preparation and service of food but also to the environment in which it was served. The Saint Cloud Hotel in Nashville in 1866 had, for example, separate tables for diners, clean and well-appointed surroundings, and, above all, good and appetizing food. The great restaurants continued to appear in the cities, and their reputations spread throughout the area.

In the 20th century urbanization has been perhaps the most notable change in southern life affecting foodways. As late as 1920 only nine southern cities had populations of over 100,000 people; in 1980 there were that many or more with populations over a million. Many of the poorest southerners have migrated to cities in the North and West, and this change has affected their eating habits. Modern conveniences, such as electric refrigeration, have also affected the eating habits of southerners. Mass production of meats such as chicken has forced quality down but increased availability. Fast-food shops have changed the eating patterns of many southerners, although Colonel Sanders's Kentucky Fried Chicken represents the marketing of traditional southern fare. Increasing urbanization has also resulted in more sophisticated tastes for southerners, many of whom now eat out more often than they did in the past.

Family-style buffet restaurants are more popular in the South than elsewhere, according to restaurant trade journals, and five major cafeteria chains—Luby's, based in San Antonio, Morrison's in Mobile, Wyatt's in Dallas, Piccadilly in Baton Rouge, and Furr's, which began in Texas but is now owned by K Mart of Troy, Mich.—provide what has become a distinctive southern form of dining. The *New York Times* reported on 18 August 1985 that while cafeterias had virtually died out in the North, they were steadily expanding in the South. They are, according to the *Times*, "as Southern in spirit as the drawl, wilting heat, and country cooking," the latter of which is the basis of the cafeteria cuisine served to a generally over-40, suburban clientele.

Great restaurants from the past continue to exist and are found primarily in New Orleans—a city that, because of its distinctive European tradition, remains *sui generis* within the region. Antoine's, founded in 1840 and reputed to be the oldest continuously operated restaurant in North America, serves its famous oysters Rockefeller (an original), soufflé potatoes, steak, and seafood dishes in both its public front and its plush private dining rooms in the rear. Galatoire's, also in the French Quarter and also one of New Orleans's oldest restaurants, retains its staunch democratic tradition—no reservations, at any time, for anyone—requiring its hopeful patrons to queue up to sample an original Creole shrimp remoulade, oysters Bienville, or trout Marguery. The city is also home to less historic but no less grand establishments such as the famed Le Ruth's and Paul Prudhomme's Cajun miracle, K-Paul's Louisiana Kitchen.

Outside the Crescent City the South continues to gain national recognition. The Inn at Little Washington, the Trellis in Virginia, Hudson's in South Carolina, and La Residence in North Carolina were listed in *Food and Wine*'s recent "honor roll" of the nation's most promising culinary finds. Southern connoisseurs can now indulge their taste for creme amandine and truffled foie gras in elegant surroundings. They can also visit Doe's Eat Place, a Greenville, Miss., cinderblock shack featuring succulent steaks and sensational tamales prepared with steak suet rather than lard. It is one of a handful of aggressively unpretentious restaurants that have become regional landmarks.

See also GEOGRAPHY: Foodways, Geography of; HISTORY AND MANNERS: Cookbooks; Foodways; INDUSTRY: / Sanders, Colonel Harland; MYTHIC SOUTH: / Hospitality

Curtis C. Whittington
McNeese State University

John Egerton, *Southern Food: At Home, on the Road, in History* (1987); *Food and Wine* (May 1983); Jane Stern and Michael Stern, *Goodfood: The Adventurous Eater's Guide to Restaurants Serving America's Best Regional Specialties* (1983), *Roadfood* (rev. ed., 1980); Joe Gray Taylor, *Eating, Drinking, and Visiting in the South: An Informal History* (1982); *Washington Post* (26 January 1975).

Roadhouses

Southern roadhouses, which are usually called "juke joints" and "honky-tonks," had their origins in the antebellum "groggeries," or taverns, that were found throughout the South. In these establishments, groggery keepers dispensed questionable liquors to local customers and travelers. Consisting of little more than a room for drinking and a room for gambling, these groggeries were the haunts of white farmers, who exchanged their hard-earned cash for "bust-head" whiskey, and black slaves, who traded produce for "red-eye" rum.

Following the Civil War the integrated camaraderie of the antebellum groggeries gave way to racial segregation. In much of the New South, whites claimed the roadside taverns as their own, leaving the newly freed blacks to find their own recreational sites. In response, some rural blacks opened their homes to the public, selling homemade liquors to friends and strangers alike. To entertain their customers, the owners of such houses employed local musicians, who played "jump-ups" and blues for dancing couples and gambling men. Offering entertainment as well as refreshments, these black-owned houses were invariably known as "jukes" or "juke-joints."

"Juke" is the common pronunciation of "joog," a word meaning disorderly, which is found among Gullah-Geechee blacks of coastal South Carolina and Georgia. "Joog," in turn, may ultimately derive from "dzugu," a Bambara African word meaning wicked. The term *juke* is applied to black roadhouses throughout the South, but it can also refer to white taverns, especially in Florida and Georgia. It is not uncommon in those states to hear whites speak of "going jukin" after work.

Most southern whites, however, refer to their roadhouses as "honky-tonks." The etymology of this curious word is unknown, but "honky-tonk" first appeared in print in 1894, when a correspondent for the *Daily Ardmoreite* (Ardmore, Okla.) wrote the following: "The honk-a-tonk last night was well attended by ball-heads, bachelors, and leading citizens." Whatever its origins, the term *honky-tonk* was applied to the roadside taverns that dotted the outskirts of oil boom towns in Oklahoma and Texas. The "honky-tonks" contained little more than a bar, a dance floor, and a tiny stage for the musicians (in some instances shielded by chicken wire to protect the performers from flying objects when the fights broke out). Amid these small but noisy honky-tonk crowds, musicians amplified their guitars and Dobros, overcoming the sounds of shuffling dancers and gambling men to play their mournful ballads about drinking, divorce, and downfall.

Honky-tonks remained a phenomenon associated primarily with the Southwest until 1935, when the Texas-born musician Al Dexter recorded his popular "Honky-Tonk Blues." Within a few years white roadhouses throughout the South were known as "honky-tonks" or "honkies." In the Southwest, it was not uncommon for whites to attend black jukes and for blacks to visit white honky-tonks. But in the Southeast the racial barriers proved more rigid. Although intermingling was not unknown there, black jukes and white honky-tonks remained segregated by custom. Even today southeastern jukes and honky-tonks are segregated at a time when racial integration in public places has become commonplace.

"Honky-tonks" and "juke joints" continue to provide rural southerners with music, recreation, and, all too often, violence. The commercial success of middle-of-the-road country music has given "honky-tonks" a heretofore undreamed of commercial popularity, but even in the midst of commercial boom the rural "honky" survives. The urban migration of blacks has likewise taken its toll on the southern "jukes," but they too remain a part of the southern rural landscape.

See also MUSIC: Blues; Country Music; Honky-Tonk Music

John S. Otto and
Augustus M. Burns
University of Florida

Daniel R. Hundley, *Social Relations in Our Southern States*, ed. William J. Cooper, Jr. (1979); Bill C. Malone, *Country Music U.S.A.: A Fifty-year History* (1968); Mitford M. Mathews, *Americanisms: A Dictionary of Selected Americanisms on Historical Principles* (1966); Paul Oliver, liner notes to "Juke Joint Blues," Blues Classics 23, *Savannah Syncopators: African Retentions in the Blues* (1970); John S. Otto and Augustus M.

Burns, *John Edwards Memorial Foundation Quarterly* (Spring 1974); Nick Tosches, *Country: The Biggest Music in America* (1977).

Sports

During the antebellum period southern sports were distinctive, important parts of the regional culture. With its relative lack of Puritan influence, generous climate, and less work-regulated population, the South tended to play more than other regions. The list of southern sports is long and shows the influence not only of the English sporting tradition, but also influences of Spanish, French, African, and Indian cultures. Southerners before and just after the Civil War amused themselves by riding, hunting, fishing, cockfighting, ninepins, fencing, fives, bowls, billiards, dancing, quoits, boxing, wrestling, animal baiting, cricket, *raquette* (an Indian lacrosse game), pedestrian races, target-shooting matches, medieval-like ring tournaments, bandy, boat races, fistfights, gander pulling, and horseshoes.

Historians have interpreted popular southern sports as reflecting regional values and characteristics—blood sports and militaristic games show the violent penchant, and Sunday prohibitions and sanctions against gambling on games of chance show the South's religious sensibilities. Sports have also embodied the old southern caste system: the leisured planter classes engaging in genteel and mannered pursuits (horse racing, fencing, elaborate hunts), the plain folk amusing themselves in more earthy fashions (cockfighting, wrestling), and slaves finding the rare occasion for their own games (races, hunting, fistfights, fishing, work matches).

During the 20th century southern sports became ever more like the rest of the nation's. Sports were a major influence on the homogenization of American culture as the big three, football, basketball, and baseball, came to dominate, overwhelmingly, interest in games. There was little regional variation to be found in these mass sports, in their rules, styles of play, coaching and organization, and in the passion and pride generated in those who watch them. They had their own structure and even their own histories that have become increasingly exact and unchanging in form, allowing few alterations from sources outside the game. An innovator such as Dean Smith might still initiate the Tarheel "four corners" offense in basketball, but such a change has nothing to do with North Carolina culture—it has to do with the rules and logic of the game. Similarly, erudite discussions of Atlantic Coast Conference versus Big Ten Conference sports and referee styles notwithstanding, the way these games are played is remarkably the same nationwide. It is possible to see differing ethnic playing styles in black ghetto and white suburban "pick-up" basketball, but such stylistic variations have yet to be documented in the South. Organization of sports is also uniform and largely hierarchical, founded in the schools, colleges, and professional teams. Indigenous local teams exist, but do so at the margins of southern sports life.

Certainly local, state, and even regional pride is excited when a winning team comes along, and especially when a winning tradition is established in an Alabama and a folk hero is found in a Bear Bryant. But this is hardly limited to the South. Such emotions are as readily generated in Michigan, Nebraska, and even Boston.

The similarity of watching sports, nationwide, is also striking. A Hawkeye fan in Iowa watches the same kind of game on television or in the stadium, drinks roughly the same kind of beverage, is as limited in his movements and actions—shouting, booing, eating, and arguing the finer points—as the LSU Tiger booster. The art of being a fan, like the skill of the player, has to do with the game itself, not the culture outside the stadium.

Similarly, the hardy, nonprofessional adult who participates in sports at least once a year generally plays one of a handful of regional sports that remain popular. An April 1980 Gallup poll showed that southerners play exactly the same top 20 games as the rest of the nation.

Nevertheless, in the midst of the homogenization of American sports, a few slightly significant regional differences remain. It would be claiming too much to speak of a southern sports culture; rather, these differences point to a faint but apparently resilient tradition existing on the margin of mass, popular sport—vestigial, ethnic-like traces within the dominant culture.

In the first place, the South has been slower than the rest of the nation to embrace popular sports. Though southerners play the same popular sports as everyone else, fewer of them are involved and for shorter periods of time. Southerners are much less involved in bowling, hiking, exercise in a gym, and jogging; only a bit less active in golf, tennis, baseball, volleyball, frisbee, swimming, bicycling, and camping; and about average in fishing, basketball, softball, touch football, and boating. The only sport that they do more of is hunting. They also lead the way in inactivity—about one-third of all southerners participate in no sport, even once a year, a condition that is three or four percentage points above the average.

Southern sports thus follow the general pattern of southern leisure—southerners simply do less. The regional interest in blood sports, and hence in the ownership of sports firearms (well above the average), may have something to do with what many writers have seen as this region's penchant for violence or violent attitudes; on the other hand, it may just be a rural phenomenon.

Racial barriers, although hardly limited to the South, have been a feature of sports history. The South has been slow in lowering these barriers and has done so in gradual, painful ways—taking care to regulate the racial composition of teams and the assignment of positions such as the quarterback and coaches. Most of these restrictions have been removed, and it is no longer uncommon to see all-black southern teams, black quarterbacks, and black superstars. Black coaches are still the exception, but this is true nationwide.

Southern sports, it is sometimes claimed, have even led the way in racial progress, opening up opportunities for blacks and increasing racial respect and understand-

Child with kite, location unknown, 1930s

ing. Herschel Walker's return to his Georgia hometown as a hero, for example, represented a breakthrough in the general recognition of grace and ability that transcends color; Marcus Dupree, born in Neshoba County, Miss., the same month in 1964 as the murder there of three civil rights activists, later became a symbol for racial reconciliation in the community. However, it might also be argued that southerners since the antebellum era have pitted "their" blacks against one another in fistfights and wrestling matches, taking proprietary pride in their champions, a pride similar to that attached to bantam roosters and pit bulldogs. If this alternative interpretation of racial "progress" in sports is true, then there has been little progress indeed, and the South still distinguishes itself as a place apart through its own kind of sports racism.

A few regional sports exist in the South. Cockfighting and pit bulldog fighting may still be found in some of the backwaters of the bayou country and rural areas of Georgia and South Carolina. Traditional kinds of hunting with special rituals, equipment, manners, and styles still exist for raccoon, quail, fox, dove, boar, deer, and even possum. Southerners have also played with technology in unusual ways. Stock car racing and drag racing seem to have originated in the South and remain more popular there. Tom Wolfe attributes much significance to stock car racing, seeing in events like the Charlotte 500 a blending of old and new that produces a distinctive hero—a Junior Johnson, part good old boy, whiskey runner, hell-bent-for-leather adventurer, and cavalier.

But perhaps the most curious regional "sports" have been of very recent origin. In a self-conscious and deliberate way, city fathers and clubs have set about making games or pastimes out of regional peculiarities. Today, the region is full of hollering, cow chip tossing, chili making, watermelon seed and tobacco juice spitting contests; armadillo, turtle, frog, and steamboat "races"; azalea, rose, rhododendron, and magnolia judgings; fiddlers' conventions and bluegrass music competitions; and Civil War battle reenactments. Participants often feel special attachment to their southernness. Whereas the games and sports of the Old South have faded, the "game of the South" flourishes.

Play and games, according to Johan Huizinga and others, keep alive and conserve cultural forms that have lost their usefulness, or which for some reason are no longer taken seriously. Cultural conservation seems especially developed in the South. Some of this region's once distinctive ways of living—agricultural skills, abilities with animals, physical strength, conversational abilities—have been undermined by the modernization and Americanization of the region. Self-conscious southerners have tended to "enframe" some of these things, to keep them alive long after they have lost their original economic or social function. This setting apart and playing with a fading culture is common among other American ethnic groups. Throughout the nation one finds Scandinavian festivals, Bohemian reunions, German Octoberfests, Scottish highland games, Irish parades, all celebrating old cultures.

One might suggest that even renewed scholarly interest in southern history and sociology has traces of play and the sportive. Certainly the amateur southern archaeologist with his metal detector, prowling old battlefields, and the family genealogist, haunting state archives, would admit to some playful, intrinsic motivations. Those who are paid to uncover the "real South" might also admit from time to time that it is, after all, fun; to be southern as well as to write about the South is no longer as serious or as much work as it used to be, and has become in some ways "mere" sport.

See also BLACK LIFE: Sports, Black; GEOGRAPHY: Sports, Geography of; VIOLENCE: Cockfighting

Benjamin K. Hunnicutt
University of Iowa

Dickson D. Bruce, Jr., *Southern Folklore Quarterly*, vol. 41 (1977); S. L. Del Sesto, *Southern Folklore Quarterly* (March 1975); Fred Hobson, *Alabama Heritage* (Summer 1986); John Shelton Reed, *The Enduring South: Subcultural Persistence in Mass Society* (1972); John F. Rooney, *American Demographics* (September 1986), *Geography of American Sport* (1974), *Geographical Review* (October 1969); Dale A. Somers, *Rise of Sports in New Orleans, 1850–1900* (1972); *Southern Exposure* (Fall 1979); Donald Spivey, *Sport in America: New Historical Perspectives* (1985).

Stock Car Racing

Stock car racing is a form of racing with automobiles that resemble standard production passenger cars. Stock car racing has become especially popular in the South where in its most developed forms it takes place in specialized amphitheaters using expensive, powerful, and carefully made machinery.

Automobiles were initially more plentiful in the industrialized parts of the nation, so much early automobile racing was done in the North and Midwest. Informal races were soon moved from the streets onto existing horse racing "tracks," which were surfaced with dirt. Starting around the turn of the century, the brick-surfaced oval track at Indianapolis, Ind., served as a new focus for racing activity.

It took longer for the automobile to reach rural areas, and not until the 1930s did stock car racing as it is known today become popular in the rural Midwest and South. Mass-produced automobiles gave working-class rural southerners more personal mobility than had been provided by horses. Farmers used cars for speedier delivery of their crops to more distant markets. In some cases, they distilled crops into liquor and transported the liquor to market as part of a long-standing family business. Liquor was a compact means of transporting crops and provided a greater return. This trade was opposed by governmental authorities, because most home-liquor makers ("moonshiners") did not pay taxes on their sales. In their efforts to outdistance law officers, some of the liquor runners skillfully modified their cars for greater power and higher speeds. The drivers of these vehicles also participated in informal races between themselves and others interested in automobiles. Liquor runners, although a small minority of those who entered early races, were among the most famous and proficient drivers and race organizers. Some of them became legends.

Alabama International Motor Speedway, Talladega, Ala., late 1970s

With the greater affluence and hence more widespread automobile ownership that followed World War II, racing became more popular than before, especially in the South. However, the rules under which the racing was conducted and the administration of the tracks were often uncertain. A concerted effort to standardize the rules and the administration of racing resulted in the formation in 1947 of the National Association for Stock Car Auto Racing, Inc. (NASCAR). NASCAR has become the largest and best known of such sanctioning organizations in the United States, with wide media coverage of its activities.

Virtually ignored by the national media, the first major paved amphitheater ("superspeedway") built in the South especially for auto racing opened in 1950 in Darlington, S.C. As a result of its success, tracks opened in other parts of the South. At present, stock car races are held from New England to California, although most of the big speedways are in the South. The Carolina Piedmont has the largest concentration of tracks, major races, driver home bases, and driver folk heroes. The heartland goes from central Virginia down to Talledega, Ala.

During the 1950s and 1960s auto makers noticed that successes of a make of car in the races led to increased sales. The auto companies and other sponsors poured money into the sport as a form of advertising. Support for racing has also come from other large corporations. For instance, a cigarette company sponsors several major race series. Individual racers and racing machines also are sponsored by small businesses and individuals.

Throughout its history, stock car racing has been identified with rural white southern males. Blacks and women, although occasional participants, have never made it to the top. Racing has become an accepted way (along with others, including singing and athletics) for a rural white male to achieve fame, money, and the trappings of success. Successful participants in the sport, such as Richard Petty, Junior Johnson, and Cale Yarborough, keep aspects of their southern heritage while they develop an ability to work with big business. Many of the best racers have, along with driving skill and a mechanical genius, a razor-sharp business acumen. They base their racing activities in their hometowns and maintain close family ties. Their "pit crews" tend to be drawn from the local population. They build closeness to their fans through personal appearances and project a "good old boy" image by expressing an interest in such male activities as hunting, fishing, and, of course, tinkering with automobiles. They are folk heroes with whom the average southern male can identify. Stock car racing, with its noise, dirt, powerful cars, and consumption of alcoholic beverages, has become a symbol of the southern way of living.

Stock car racing combines a fascination with technology and a spirit of competition. It has become identified with the South, where it has served both as a sport and as a way for participants to leave rural poverty. At first glance, the cars appear to be like those available to the average person. However, the cars are in fact highly specialized technical accomplishments. The cost of the machinery keeps it from being a widely popular participant sport. As a result, there is mass popular support for a relatively small number of athletes. The drivers epitomize the successful southern male who has managed to retain his "down-home" manner. The average southern male can identify with the racers, both because he drives a car that looks like theirs and because he shares their identification with things southern. At present, many of the prominent drivers are in their 40s, an age by which athletes in many other sports have retired. A few younger drivers are beginning to gain recognition in Winston Cup racing, often through their successes in local competition. Winston Cup racing is the most publicized form of stock car racing.

There are different kinds of racing, varying with the scale of the effort and the technical details of the cars. Categories often are based on the age of the cars and their construction, especially their power plants and wheelbase lengths. Rules also vary with the tracks where the races are run.

There is a continuum of size and complexity in racing tracks. At the amateur level are small tracks (usually oval in shape and ¼ to ½ mile long), which draw spectators and participants from immediately surrounding areas. In these races, older passenger cars are modified for increased safety and speed. As in other sports, there are many participants in local level, dirt track races, which require less money and effort.

At the professional end of the scale are Winston Cup (formerly called Grand National) races on larger speedways. Contestants come from all over the nation. Media reporters jockey for position to interview the winning drivers. At this level, vehicles are usually constructed by specialty builders solely for racing and have little relation to production cars beyond outward appearance.

At all levels of racing, each vehicle has one or more mechanics who build and maintain the vehicle. The "pit crew" services the car during races by refueling, replacing tires, cleaning the windshield, giving the driver refreshments, etc.

Sponsors are individuals or businesses who provide money to support the racing effort. Their names are painted on the sides of the cars (along with each car's number) so that the fans will be encouraged to buy their products. Some drivers have consistently used particular makes of automobiles, endorsing the manufacturer. Fans are fiercely partisan toward particular drivers. Many fans wear clothing and other items imprinted with the car number and name of their driver and belong to fan clubs boosting their favorite.

Track officials work to ensure that the race goes smoothly. There are often also officials from the organization ("sanctioning body") that writes the racing rules. Although NASCAR is the best known of these organizations, smaller, local sanctioning bodies organize most racing events. These bodies write rules to promote safety and competition.

"Technical inspections" of cars are made to ensure that cars conform to the rules. Nevertheless, clever racers try to interpret the rules to their advantage. The emphasis on technical sophistication in the preparation of the vehicles is one of the excitements of the sport, and fans and racers alike are constantly alert to innovations that increase the cars' speeds.

Each driver is involved with several kinds of competition simultaneously. Competition for winning the race by being the first to complete the required number of laps around the track is the most visible. Winning is a combination of driver skill and chance. Winning is also dependent on the speed and efficiency of the pit crew and the ability of the machinery to last as many as 500 laps at speeds up to 200 miles an hour. Behind the scenes, drivers compete for the best sponsors and mechanics.

Before the race, drivers compete in trials designed to see which car can go fastest around the track. The faster a car runs in the trials, the closer it is placed to the front of the pack of 30 to 40 starting cars. The fastest car gets the most advantageous position (the "pole" position) at the front. Drivers compete over a season to accumulate the most "points" from various accomplishments, such as the position of their car in comparison to the winner's at the end of each race, the number of races entered, and the number of laps completed.

See also HISTORY AND MANNERS: Automobile; / Moonshine and Moonshining

David M. Johnson
North Carolina Agricultural
and Technical State University

Patrick Bedard, *Car & Driver* (June 1982); Jerry Bledsoe, *The World's Number One, Flat-Out, All-Time Great, Stock Car Racing Book* (1975); *Handbook of American Popular Culture*, vol. 1, ed. M. Thomas Inge (1979); Jim Hunter, *Official 1982 NASCAR Record Book and Press Guide* (1982); Bill Libby with Richard Petty, *"King Richard": The Richard Petty Story* (1977); Bob Nagy, *Motor Trend* (June 1981); Richard Pillsbury, *Journal of Geography* (1974); Don Sherman, *Car & Driver* (June 1982); *Southern MotoRacing* (biweekly newspaper about stock car racing, Winston-Salem, N.C.); Sylvia Wilkinson, in *American South: Portrait of a Culture*, ed. Louis D. Rubin, Jr. (1980); Tom Wolfe, *Esquire* (March 1965).

Tennis

Lawn tennis in the South shares much of the same general history as golf. Lawn tennis originated in the United States in New York in the 1870s and soon spread through the Northeast, Middle West, and the Pacific Coast. A few southern cities such as New Orleans promoted the sport, but it was not a popular one until well into the 20th century. It lost many of its aristocratic trappings in the 1920s and became a middle-class game. Tennis celebrities such as Big Bill Tilden and Suzanne Lenglen became popular in the South as well as elsewhere. In the South the game was a country club sport, but the 1930s saw an increase in the building of public courts along with community golf courses.

Tennis did not lose its country club image until the 1950s and 1960s. The game became more popular in those years with the emergence of appealing young stars, television coverage of major tournaments, large money payoffs to tournament winners, and the establishment of an open system of competition between amateurs and professionals. Major tournaments are now held in the South. In 1970 Texas millionaire Lamar Hunt financed World Championship Tennis, which sent professional players on tours around the world.

Tennis can now be found as an activity at southern resorts and it can be played on public courts in cities and small towns throughout the region. The South, however, has produced surprisingly few of the game's great players. Chris Evert from Florida is one of those, and Althea Gibson from North Carolina and Arthur Ashe from Virginia were prominent southern black tennis stars. Tennis has not drawn the attention of many southern writers, but Rita Mae Brown's *Sudden Death* (1983) and Barry Hannah's *Tennis Handsome* (1985) have tennis players as the central characters.

Charles Reagan Wilson
University of Mississippi

Will Grimsley, *Tennis: Its History, People and Events* (1971); U.S. Lawn Tennis Association, *Official Encyclopedia of Tennis* (1972).

Theme Parks

Amusement parks, closely related to carnivals, have been an important part of American culture since the beginning of the 20th century. Vacationing families visited the thrilling rides, shows, and concessions of such parks as those at Coney Island in Brooklyn, N.Y., where the concept of the modern amusement park largely was developed. The popularity of amusement parks declined significantly after World War II, and theme parks came to dominate the outdoor amusement business. Disneyland in Anaheim, Calif., has served as a model for the contemporary theme park from its opening in 1954.

Since the Walt Disney cartoon characters came to the South with Disney World in Orlando, Fla., in 1971, southerners have brought their own unique heritage and traditions to theme-park entertainment. Southern theme parks offer the region's history, music, food, religion, art, and humor to attract both southern and non-southern families. Although some people might argue that the picture of southern culture offered in the theme-park setting is often an idealized and stereotypical view of life in the South, millions of visitors flock to the parks every summer, attracted not by their authenticity but by the simple, family entertainment they offer.

The prototype of southern-oriented theme parks is Opryland, U.S.A., in Nashville, which opened in the summer of 1972. Opryland capitalized on Nashville's reputation as the center of the country music industry and on the rise in popularity of the music in the 1970s. Since its opening, the park has continuously broadened its image and now bills itself as "the home of American music." Opryland offers a variety of music, including rock and roll from the 1950s and contemporary tunes, music of the American West (from such musicals as *Annie Get Your Gun*), Dixieland jazz, and folk music. Much of the music is country and western, but it is not the rough sound found in the honky-tonks around Nashville. Many of the music shows at the park, like those at other modern theme parks, are staged in elaborate, air-conditioned theaters and resemble Broadway productions in costuming, music, and choreography. In addition to live musical entertainment, Opryland offers rides, food, shops, games, art, and crafts—all with a southern flavor and often a country or musical theme.

The food at the park, in keeping with the southern image, includes fried chicken, iced tea, and ham and biscuits in establishments such as "The Country Kitchen." Vendors on the sidewalks sell ice cream bars in the shapes of musical instruments. Numerous shops offer tourists a wide assortment of music memorabilia, replicas of frontier clothing and implements, craft items such as handmade dulcimers and carved wooden figures, and various products bearing the Confederate flag. Consistent with Opryland's theme are rides called "The Tennessee Waltz," "Grizzly River Rampage," the "Old Mill Scream," and the "Wabash Cannon Ball." Opryland has even incorporated a carnival midway into its offerings, complete with contest booths and prizes commonly found at county fairs. Opryland is particularly proud of its setting—120 acres of trees and man-made lakes. Approximately 25 percent of the complex, including a roller coaster called the "Timber Topper," is in native woods transplanted when the park was built. Today, the Opryland theme park is one part of the Opryland, U.S.A., complex, which has grown to include the Grand Ole Opry, the Opryland Hotel and Convention Center, and the General Jackson showboat. Opryland's success has inspired other parks (such as Libertyland in Memphis, Tenn.), once simple amusement parks and without clearly defined themes, to incorporate more elaborate shows and music into their offerings.

Since Opryland's success, country music culture has provided the theme for other southern parks such as Dollywood, country music star Dolly Parton's 400-acre park outside Pigeon Forge, Tenn. The park's inspiration is Parton's childhood, which she spent in the Smoky Mountain foothills where the park is located, and her career in music and films. Parton was involved in the planning of the park, which includes a replica of the house in which she was born and an outdoor concert stage that is a copy of the porch where she and her family used to sing together. Like Opryland, Dollywood tries to keep the theme consistent throughout the park. A restaurant called Aunt Granny's Dixie Fixin's serves biscuits and gravy, and cider is served at Apple Jack's Mill. Smoky

Mountain heritage is featured in exhibits of quilting and dulcimer making.

Other country music celebrities have become the focus of southern theme parks, such as Conway Twitty, who lives and works inside an entertainment complex called Twitty City. Twitty City, located just outside Nashville, contains the memorabilia of Twitty and several other country music stars and includes a concession-entertainment pavilion and an audio-visual show that tells Twitty's life story. Open year-round, Twitty City draws hundreds of visitors during the Christmas season, when the park is decorated with 250,000 lights and adds 40 special exhibits, including a life-size nativity scene. Other country music stars who have parks associated with their names include Loretta Lynn (Loretta Lynn's Dude Ranch in Hurricane Mills, Tenn.) and George Jones (George Jones Country Music Park outside Colmesneil, Tex.).

A similar regional theme is portrayed at Arkansas's Dogpatch U.S.A., a park based on the characters from Al Capp's *Li'l Abner* comic strip. The events at Dogpatch feature the hillbilly characters, and the attractions (such as canoe rides) supposedly reflect their lifestyle. The park also highlights the Ozark Mountain culture, offering such exhibits as an authentic gristmill, one of the largest wooden water wheels in the world, and shops specializing in the area's many arts and crafts. The region's natural beauty is also spotlighted here; the park is particularly proud of its huge waterfall and spring-fed lakes.

The newest development in the southern outdoor amusement business is the religious theme park. The biggest of these is Heritage USA, a resort in Fort Mill, S.C., opened in 1977 by Pentecostal television evangelists Jim and Tammy Faye Bakker. The park, which has been called a "spiritual Disneyland," is part of a complex covering 2,300 acres and encompassing time-sharing vacation homes, rental apartments, condominiums, campsites, the five-story Heritage Grand Hotel, a halfway house for exconvicts, and a home for unwed mothers. Heritage USA offers the world's largest wave pool and a 52-foot water slide, evangelist Billy Graham's childhood home, a Passion play staged in Heritage's own 3,000-seat amphitheater, tours of the Christian broadcasting studio on the grounds, amusement rides such as "Jonah in the Belly of the Whale," and shopping at Main Street, USA—designed in turn-of-the-century style with cobblestone streets and quaint storefronts. In 1985 Heritage USA attracted almost 5 million visitors, making it third only to Disneyland and Disney World in attendance. The park has cultivated an image as the preserver of old-time values and old-time southern religion, sometimes calling itself the modern equivalent of camp meetings or Christian campgrounds. Although Heritage USA is by far the largest, other southern theme parks, such as The Living Waters in Johnson City, Tex., also offer biblical messages.

Other theme parks in the South use state histories as the basis for their entertainment, such as Six Flags over Texas in Arlington and Six Flags over Georgia in Atlanta. Busch Gardens (The Dark Continent) in Tampa, Fla., displays the exotic environment of Africa, and Busch Gardens (The Old Country) in Williamsburg, Va., highlights the history and culture of Europe. Both Busch parks feature elaborate animal and plant exhibits and are owned and operated by Anheuser-Busch Co.

Karen M. McDearman
University of Mississippi

Jackson *Clarion-Ledger* (31 August 1986); *Southern Living* (June 1981); Jeff Ulmer, *Amusement Parks of America: A Comprehensive Guide* (1980).

Tourism

Tourist. The word evokes images of Hawaiian shirts and Bermuda shorts, Instamatic cameras and sun-reddened skin, a clay-streaked station wagon, laden with luggage and sacks of Florida oranges. Those millions of wayfarers who hurtle along interstates to bake on sunny beaches and see Rock City pump some $60 billion into the southern economy each year.

That figure alone suggests that traveling in the South is more than a now-and-again whim. Tourism has become as much a part of life for Americans as work in the week and church on Sunday. The modern burst of tourism began in the late 1940s. Veterans, who could not be kept down on the farm after they had seen the world during the war, earned their two weeks of vacation and hit the highways for recreation, relaxation, and entertainment. Nearly every family now marks days off its calendar for a vacation, even two or three a year. Despite oil shortages and the recessions of the 1970s and early 1980s, Americans winced at gasoline prices, dipped into savings, and pointed their cars and campers South.

A century and more before, the purpose of most travels in the South was for health. By the late 1700s travelers eased into hot springs baths to soak their muscles. Modern-day resorts such as The Greenbrier in West Virginia and The Homestead in Virginia trace their origins to those times and still offer bathing facilities.

For more than a century Carolinians who lived along the coast traveled to save their lives. Spring through fall, or "frost to frost," they fled the malarial, soggy low country for the spice of mountain air. Hendersonville, N.C., is still called "Little Charleston in the Mountains," and many of the summer cottages, dating back to the mid-1800s and handed down through the generations, still stand.

In the decades after the Civil War, northerners invaded the South again, but this time as tourists in a campaign for their health. The mineral waters of southern springs and the salubrious southern climate were touted for their curative benefits. Physicians prescribed winter vacations in towns like Thomasville, Ga., which once boasted 15 hotels, 25 boardinghouses, and 50 winter cottages.

From the late 19th century to the mid-20th, pleasure travel evolved from a privilege of a wealthy few to an affordable luxury for the average family. A growing economy was partly the reason, but so also was the increasing ease of transportation—from carriages on dirt roads to railroads to family cars on interstates.

Of all southern states, Florida best symbolizes the rise of tourism. To see Florida in the mid-1800s, when much of the state was still wilderness, travelers had to go by boat. Honeymooners took romantic excursions along the Suwannee River, the St. Johns, and the Oklawaha to Silver Springs. Often the land alongside was scented with orange blossoms in spring, and, at night, the light from burning pine knots played on the overhang of cypress and Spanish moss. By the 1890s railroads were skimming the shoreline of both coasts; Henry Flagler linked Jacksonville to the squat settlement of Miami, building alongside his railroad such palatial hotels as the Ponce de Leon in St. Augustine and The Breakers in Palm Beach.

Down Flagler's railroad came the very rich. But along the increasing miles of paved highways came the families of average means, who, in the flush times of the 1920s, could afford pleasure travel. They fashioned homemade campers on Model-T's, ate store-bought food from tin cans, and camped beside the roads. These "tin-can tourists," as Floridians called them, pioneered the major mode of travel of two decades later—the family car. In the exuberance of release from the Depression, and with a car in every garage, Americans joyously flooded the highways of the South.

With war boom babies in the back seat, they traveled to the beach in summer and the mountains in the fall. Quiet seaside villages like Myrtle Beach, S.C., and mountain towns like Gatlinburg, Tenn., grew into garish neon playgrounds. The family spent nights in tourist courts, stopped at roadside souvenir stands, visited alligator farms, toured Mammoth Cave, walked Civil War battlefields, and yes, saw Rock City. Later, such "attractions" as theme parks offered rides and Broadway-type entertainment in a milk-and-cookies family atmosphere.

Quickly, tourism became an industry with a manufacturing mentality to mass produce. Entrepreneurs like Kemmons Wilson of Memphis, founder of Holiday Inns, stamped one motel after another from the same mold. Fast-food franchises arched their signs above highways. Many of those motels and packaged food restaurants rose at exits of interstates that tie doorsteps to destinations, bypass towns, and hold the countryside at arm's length. Now, in driving 800 interstate miles, travelers may sleep in the same room every night, eat the same hamburger for every meal, and never see a town.

Why and where do tourists today go on vacation? One large segment of the population indicates that three main factors, excluding cost, determine vacation destinations. Readers of *Southern Living* magazine, certainly the epitome of the middle-class southerner, say they travel primarily for scenery. And to most, scenery means mountains and seashore. Second, they go where they will find good restaurants and lodging: to resort condominiums on barrier islands and to quiet country inns in the mountains. And third, they choose routes and destinations to see historical sites. Even on pleasure trips to fish, swim, play golf and tennis, shop, hike, and canoe, southerners will stop a time or two to pay homage to the past.

Tourists who walk the narrow streets of Charleston pour some $460 million annually into the local economy. About 1 million visitors each year walk the battlefield at Vicksburg, Miss., and stroll through the re-created city of Colonial Williamsburg in Virginia. Through travel, southerners continue to learn about life of a century or two ago. In the 1930s garden club ladies in Natchez introduced a new genre of travel when they opened a few antebellum homes each spring to visitors. The name of such tours—pilgrimage—is appropriate for southerners' reverence of the past.

Many historic homes are open for lodging as well as tours, so guests may dream they dwelt in marble halls. At preserved villages like Old Salem in Winston-Salem, N.C., visitors watch costumed docents work at the crafts and cookery of two centuries ago. The Mississippi Museum of Agriculture and Forestry in Jackson moved an entire 100-year-old farm to its premises, where southerners hear words that have almost vanished from the daily vocabulary: singletree, laying-by time, bust the middles. Workers at the farm even plant a tiny patch of cotton and let the visitor try his or her hand at picking.

The flow of tourists' money helps maintain these historic sites, which, in turn, provide the tie that binds the generations and the times of the South. Recently, at Powers Crossroads Arts and Crafts Fair, spread across the old cotton fields of a plantation near Newnan, Ga., a man from Atlanta and his small son strolled up to the mule-powered cane press.

"Look, daddy, a horse," the boy shouted excitedly.

"Mule, son," the father replied.

See also ART AND ARCHITECTURE: Resort Architecture; ETHNIC LIFE: Caribbean Influence; GEOGRAPHY: Roadside; HISTORY AND MANNERS: / Pilgrimage; INDUSTRY: / Flagler, Henry

Gary D. Ford
Southern Living

Ruth Camblos and Virginia Winger, *Shopping Round the Mountains* (1973); Charleston Trident Chamber of Commerce, *Tourism Profile, 1982–83*; John A. Jakle, *The Tourist: Travel in Twentieth-Century North America* (1985); Jeffrey Limerick, Nancy Ferguson, and Richard Oliver, *America's Grand Resort Hotels* (1979); Edward A. Mueller, *Steamboating on the St. Johns, 1830–1885* (1980); *Southern Living* (December 1983, April 1984); *Travel Survey of Southern Living Subscribers* (1984).

Tourism, Automobile

Except for an occasional group of bicyclists who toured the Shenandoah Valley, most 19th-century Americans had only a secondhand knowledge of the South. By the mid-1920s, however, widespread automobile ownership, hard-surfaced roads, and the magnetic attraction of Florida brought droves of tourists into the South from every state in the Union.

Around the turn of the century, automobile manufacturers began to test their fledgling machines in races on the broad, firm beaches of Ormond-Daytona Beach, Fla. These contests, held during the winter months, attracted great attention to the Florida east coast, and in subsequent years more and more northerners entertained the notion of driving—instead of shipping—their automobiles to Florida.

After a group of tourists on a reliability run in 1909 carefully negotiated their way from New York to Atlanta over a route named the "National Highway," the American Automobile Association for the first time mapped a route for motorists wishing to brave a trip into the South. Although it fell short of detailing specific routes and distances, volume three of the AAA's 1910 *Automobile Blue Book* gave adventuresome tourists enough incentive to attempt the trip. As more drivers traveled south and reported their experiences to the AAA and as routing information in popular motoring journals like *American Motorists*, *Motor Travel*, and *Motor Life* improved, the uncertainty of driving a motor vehicle into the uncharted South waned.

With more motorists on the road, southerners began to realize the importance of tourism to local profits. Enterprising boosters of many southern towns went to great lengths to accommodate visiting tourists. In 1910 the first interstate highway association in the South, the Capital Highway Association, was formed. Its purpose was to promote tourism and a route that would link the national capital with the state capitals of Virginia, North Carolina, South Carolina, and Georgia. Leonard Tufts, who was in the initial stages of developing Pinehurst, N.C., as a resort, served as the first president of this organization. Tufts realized the tremendous potential that tourism had for the South.

Floridians were among the first southerners to actively recruit tourists. In 1919 Tampa opened DeSoto Park, located on the banks of the Hillsborough River, to motorists who had come south for the winter. Soon autocamps sprang up throughout Florida and in other southern states along main routes to Florida recommended by the Automobile Club of America. The 1918 *Automobile Blue Book* contained accurate and detailed running information for over 24,000 miles of roads in Virginia, Tennessee, Georgia, North Carolina, South Carolina, Alabama, Mississippi, and Florida.

The motorists who traveled these hazardous routes were a new breed of tourists. They were doctors, lawyers, bankers, dairymen, farmers, building contractors, and retired businessmen who had leisure time to travel. Unlike their 19th-century predecessors, these men and women resisted the comforts of hotel accommodations by carrying everything they needed with them. Tents, suitcases, and mattresses were strapped to running boards, and other necessities like canned goods and cooking utensils were packed wherever they would fit. At night these so-called tin-can tourists pulled into autocamps where they extended their tents over part of their cars, greeted other travelers, fixed supper, and went to bed. For less rustic motorists, it was not difficult to find a tourist home that provided bed, board, and a bath for a nominal fee.

The number of tourists coming into the South increased sharply following World War I. During the winter of 1920–21 so many took advantage of Tampa's free accommodations in DeSoto Park that by the following spring city officials were forced to close the park to out-of-state visitors. That same year the tourist bureau of one of the most active automobile clubs in the South, the Chattanooga Automobile Club, answered approximately 8,000 inquiries from tourists requesting route information. During the winter of 1924–25, however, the volume reached its pre-Depression high. Efforts by southerners to improve their roads, together with federal aid to road construction, bettered travel conditions and led the AAA to recommend as "fascinating" an automobile trip into the South. That advice was well heeded, for in November of 1924, 16,833 automobiles crossed the St. Johns River bridge leading into Jacksonville, Fla. Every state in the United States was represented, and 90 cars came from as far away as Canada.

One writer called this mass migration to Florida a national "pneumatic hegira" and sublimely pronounced its implication to be as far reaching as "the descent of the Goths on Rome, the Mongols on China, the Dutch on South Africa, or the Mormon trek from Illinois to Utah." Another observer, cited in the March 1925 issue of *Hollywood Magazine*, captured the phenomenon in poetry:

> It squeaked and groaned; 'twas rusty, worn;
> Its fenders bent, its curtains torn,
> Its windshield cracked, its wheels not mates
> Caked with mud of seven states,
> Headed South.

Nevertheless, the great influx of motorists gave southerners added incentive to upgrade their roads, and for the first time since the Civil War large numbers of ordinary men and women from the North and South met one another. The cultural isolation of southerners began to end as they came in contact with new ideas, new products, and new ways of doing things. Many southerners saw themselves in a new light and began to sell their region as a place of recreation and relaxation. Tourism became a mainstay of the South's economy, encouraging national companies to seek new markets in southern states. In the view of historian Thomas D. Clark, the migration of tourists to the South amounted to nothing short of a "Yankee invasion that ever disturbed southern complacency. The established way of life in the South was shaken to its very foundation."

See also AGRICULTURE: Good Roads Movement; HISTORY AND MANNERS: Automobile

Howard L. Preston
Spartanburg, South Carolina

American Automobile Association, *The Official 1910 Automobile Blue Book*, vol. 3 (1910); *American Motorist* (1910–1924);

Warren J. Belasco, *Americans on the Road: From Autocamps to Motel, 1910–1945* (1979); *Dixie Highway* (1915–1925); James J. Fink, *America Adopts the Automobile, 1895–1910* (1970), *The Car Culture* (1975); David Gary, *Collier's Weekly* (11 February 1911); Elon Jessup, *The Outlook* (25 May 1921); *Southern Good Roads* (1910–1920).

Traveling Shows

A visit from a traveling show was a major event in the life of the southern small town in the late 19th and early 20th centuries. Colorfully decorated wagons and, later, trucks drove slowly through towns, with jugglers and acrobats drawing children and their parents out of their homes and into a happy procession of people anticipating fun at the show grounds. The coming of traveling shows signaled an unusual period of gaiety, when normal moral restrictions might be loosened and humdrum daily life enlivened. Most of these shows flourished from the end of the Civil War to World War I. After World War I grassroots show business in the South continued to be dynamic, providing the training and experiences for many performers and businessmen in entertainment industries such as country music, jazz, the blues, and gospel. In addition to the circuses, carnivals, Wild West shows, and minstrels that had earlier become staples, there were tent shows, burlesque houses, magicians, freak shows, vaudeville bills, aerial daredevils, water circuses, and medicine shows.

The American circus, with its animal and clown shows, had antecedents in antiquity, but the real beginnings of the modern circus were in England in the mid-1700s. Animal trainers, acrobats, jugglers, and itinerant actors traveled through the American colonies, but the first recorded appearance of the circus in America was in 1791. Early circuses were city shows, and the predominantly rural South had less exposure than the North to circuses in the antebellum era, although circuses did appear along the lower Mississippi River in the 1820s. The basic pattern of the circus was established by the 1850s—circus parades to draw crowds, exhibitions under canvas walls or tents, trained animals, clowns, acrobats and aerialists, jugglers, ventriloquists, and freak shows. Multiple rings were introduced in the 1870s. The golden age of the circus was from 1870 to 1914. Phineas T. Barnum, George F. Bailey, W. C. Coup, and the Ringling brothers were leading circus entrepreneurs. In 1918 a merger brought the appearance of the Ringling Brothers and Barnum and Bailey Combined Shows. As circus audiences became larger in the early 20th century, the circus shows became more elaborate. The Wild West show became part of the event, and stages and rings were added, more dangerous animal acts were encouraged, and money was poured into acts, costumes, and pageants.

Circus owners adapted to the South by advertising their shows as classical and biblical, because they featured chariot races and religious depictions. The most popular circuses touring the South were John Robinson's Circus and Menagerie, W. C. Coup's Monster Shows, and the Grand New Orleans Menagerie and Circus (which had a Mademoiselle Eugene marching ahead of lions and tigers down southern streets to stir interest). In the 1890s almost 40 groups annually toured the region, from April to December, some of them touring only the South. Southerners turned out in large numbers for the circus, with rural people coming into town ahead of the circus in order to camp in or under wagons, watch the circus set up, and view the circus parade and opening ceremonies. Excursion trains brought thousands of people to the cities where the largest circuses were held. The appeal of the circus was universal, but the poor and children were its most fervent enthusiasts. Blacks and whites sat on opposite sides of the same tent. Gamblers and pickpockets frequently accompanied the circus, taking advantage of the rural folk coming out for the show, and the circus always seemed to bring out drinking and fighting. Community and religious leaders objected to them.

Only a dozen or so circuses continue to tour the nation today, but attendance at these is still large. Florida has served as the winter quarters for the Ringling Brothers circus, and Florida State University has become a prominent circus center because of the amateur productions on campus.

The carnival was another traveling show, closely related to the circus. "Pleasure gardens," modelled on London's Vauxhall and Ranelagh, were forerunners of carnivals, appearing in North America near the time of the American Revolution, offering the chance for visitors to stroll, eat, and drink. By the turn of the 20th century, trolley parks had emerged in eastern cities offering more exciting amusements. The beginnings of the American carnival are usually dated from the 1893 World's Columbian Exposition in Chicago, which included outdoor rides, fun houses, and games of chance. Coney Island opened the same year, but even before this, in the 1880s, the traditional state fairs had begun to set aside special areas for outdoor amusements.

Carnivals traveled the South, with their heydey between the world wars. Elaborate shows came to bigger cities, but smaller affairs hit the region's more typical small towns. They included set features: machine rides such as the Ferris wheel, roller coaster, and tunnel of love; the midway featuring food (such as popcorn, cotton candy, corn dogs, and caramel candy), shooting arcades, and gypsy fortune tellers; the freak shows (featuring the Fat Lady, Tattooed Man, or midgets); and the girlie shows with risqué strippers. Gamblers, hustlers, and pickpockets of all sorts frequently accompanied the traveling carnival, as well as the circus. Harry Crews's article "Carny," which appeared in *Blood and Grits* (1979), portrays life on the road for carnival workers in the South; he discusses the distinctive vocabulary of "carny talk" and the social hierarchy among the carnival workers. Those who set up shows rank at the bottom of this society; the hustlers who run the working games rank higher; the "patch man," who exists to patch over conflicts that emerge within the carnival community and between it and the outside world, ranks still higher.

Crews stresses that the farther south the carnival went, the rougher the shows were; a strip show that was relatively tame in Pennsylvania could be gross in Georgia.

The medicine show was a popular aspect of southern entertainment after the Civil War. During the fall, especially, when southern farmers had whatever money they would have to spend during the year, traveling salesmen of cheap patent medicines would appear. Few of these were of much value, as they were typically filled with alcohol or were strong purgatives that usually caused more illness than they cured. To attract attention, medicine salesmen would employ singers, such as the bluesman Sonny Terry or country singer Jimmie Rodgers (who sometimes worked in blackface), to put on a "medicine show" that would draw people together, creating an audience for the salesman to hawk his goods. In normally quiet southern towns and rural areas, this entertainment, no matter how poor in quality, was worth listening to, and people willingly came out to hear it. Performers would pass out Congo oil, liniments, or similar remedies designed to cure whatever ailed anyone with money in hand. Colorful pitchmen with names such as Joe "Fine Arts" Hanks, the Canadian Kid, Doc Zip Hibler, Mad Cody Fleming, Widow Rollins, and Population Charlie were hustlers who went back and forth between medicine shows, carnivals, tent shows, and other forms of grass-roots show business.

The road company theater was another example of the traveling show in the South. Before the Civil War, permanent theaters had existed in southern cities such as Charleston, New Orleans, and Richmond, many of them presenting road show spectaculars featuring exciting stage activities, musical performances, Shakespeare and other dramatic fare, and melodrama. After the war, this continued, with new auditoriums and opera houses appearing. In Atlanta, the 400-seat Davis Hall was built in 1865 as an essential part of the rebuilding of the city. Dallas erected its first opera house in 1872. The new theaters and opera houses were elaborately decorated with balustraded verandas, crimson velvet wall hangings, glass chandeliers, and several tiers of seats for those of different social classes. Blacks and prostitutes were generally restricted to the highest galleries.

In 1869–70 the Wilmington, N.C., theater presented 50 evenings of entertainment, including Shakespearean plays, magicians, and Italian opera. Established theaters in cities presented the best American and European performers and plays, but in smaller places the offerings were less ambitious. The average theatergoer seemed to prefer the extravagant and sentimental, but originality was valued little until after World War I. Italian touring companies performed *Rigoletto*, *Il Trovatore*, and *Mignon* among others; Shakespeare continued to be a favorite; and less uplifting shows, especially melodramas with such titles as *Ten Nights in a Bar Room* and *The Drunkard*, and spectacles with mechanical thrills, as in the chariot race in *Ben Hur* and the railroad crossing the stage in *Under the Gas Lights*, were also popular. Stock companies presenting these programs typically were in a town for a week or so, offering different shows daily. By the 1880s a new star system emerged, leading to shows centered around a celebrity performer giving a single show. Broadway shows from New York—which was the source for many of these performances throughout the period—also went on the road in the early 20th century.

A special aspect of the touring theater was the tent show. The first theater company to tour under canvas was an Illinois group in 1855, and the tent show continued to be mainly a midwestern and southern phenomenon even after permanent theaters proliferated in towns. Rural and small-town audiences seemed especially fond of these shows and continued to support them well into the 20th century. The average tent could hold almost 1,500 people. The tent show presented family-oriented dramatic performances, with three-act plays and specialty entertainers. They were clean shows, avoiding the kind of suggestive material in carnivals and vaudeville. After the movies became popular, the tent shows boasted of offering "a decent alternative to epics, orgies, sex, and horror." Traveling "rep" groups, with such names as Harley Sadler's Own, the Ted North Players, and Swain's Dramatic Show, played a town for three days to a week, offering repertoires of six to nine plays a season. Usually presenting comedies, they also tried to include at least one serious play, sometimes an adaption of a popular novel such as *The Virginian*, *The Trail of the Lonesome Pines*, or *The Shepherd of the Hills*.

The tent shows brought vaudeville to the South. It was not urban entertainment, as in the North, but rather performances designed to appeal to small-town folk. They offered popular singers such as Jimmie Rodgers, who served his apprenticeship in the 1920s in the traveling shows. Black blues singers also performed in this context, as did novelty bands such as Happy Cook's Kentucky Buddies. Impresarios such as W. T. Swain, known as Colonel Swain or "Old Double Eyes" to some who had done business with him, worked the South. Described by Nolan Porterfield as "sort of a cross between P. T. Barnum, William Randolph Hearst, and a snake-oil salesman," Swain typically wore a black suit, set off by a white bow tie and his silver gray hair. For four decades he was a major figure in the traveling theater of the Mid-South and Southwest. Colonel Tom Parker, who eventually struck paydirt as the manager of Elvis Presley, was another typical tent show manager.

Almost 400 tent-show companies traveled the nation in 1925, mostly in the Midwest and South, visiting 16,000 communities and entertaining 76,800,000 people. The Great Depression hit the shows hard, and eventually the competition from radio and television led to their decline. In the 1950s, 30 companies still toured under canvas, but by 1968 only 3 remained.

The tent road show contributed a popular character to show business lore and to regional imagery—Toby. He was the country bumpkin, a humorous figure who appeared in these shows around 1910. One manager, Fred Wilson, built the character into his shows and others copied him, until rural and small-town audiences knew him and looked forward to the character's appearance. A rustic, seemingly backward man, Toby would outwit and confuse the city slickers who tried to take advantage of him. Awkward, bumptious, but shrewd and full of common sense, Toby embodied the southern rural self-imagery of the Arkansas traveler. The character was adapted to different regions—in the Midwest, he was simply a rural hayseed; in the South, a hillbilly from the mountains; in Texas, he was a cowboy. By 1916 some 200 actors traveled specializing in Toby, and always appearing the same—redhaired, freckled, with blacked out tooth and farm clothes.

See also FOLKLIFE: / Arkansas Traveler; LITERATURE; Theater, Contemporary; Theater, Early; MUSIC: Minstrelsy; / Rodgers, Jimmie; SCIENCE AND MEDICINE: Self-Dosage

Charles Reagan Wilson
University of Mississippi

George L. Chindahl, *History of the Circus in America* (1959); Joseph Csida and June Bundy Csida, *American Entertainment: A Unique History of Popular Show Business* (1978); John E. DiMeglio, *Vaudeville U.S.A.* (1973); Neil Harris, *Humbug: The Art of P. T. Barnum* (1973); Joe McKennon, *A Pictorial History of the American Carnival* (1972); Brooks McNamara, *Step Right Up: An Illustrated History of the American Medicine Show* (1976); Russel Nye, *The Unembarrassed Muse: The Popular Arts in America* (1970); Nolan Porterfield, *Jimmie Rodgers: The Life and Times of America's Blue Yodeler* (1979); William L. Slout, *Theatre in a Tent: The Development of Provincial Entertainment* (1972); Marcello Truzzi, *Journal of Popular Culture* (Winter 1972); Don B. Wilmeth, *American and English Popular Entertainment: A Guide to Information Sources* (1980), in *Concise Histories of American Popular Culture*, ed. M. Thomas Ingc (1982).

Wrestling

William Faulkner wrote that Thomas Sutpen, the Old South planter who is the central character of *Absalom, Absalom!*, would watch an evening of slave wrestling. At the end of "the spectacle," he would enter the ring, "perhaps as a matter of sheer deadly forethought toward the retention of supremacy, domination." He and a slave would soon be "naked to the waist and gouging at one another's eyes."

Physical grappling is an old tradition for southern men. In the colonial era well-off gentry planters presided over and sometimes joined in sports such as wrestling, which served as a communal bonding experience between social classes. One of the rituals in frontier areas of the antebellum South, which spawned real-life Thomas Sutpens, was the gouging match. It was a brutal sport where each man tried to pry his opponent's eyes out of their sockets using a thumb for leverage. Brutal though they were, wrestling and eye gouging were not surprising pastimes for men in a society where violence was common. Indians, animals, outlaws, and nature were threats to life; physical labor was long and grueling. Gouging matches tested a man's strength, dexterity, and ferocity. In *Life on the Mississippi* Mark Twain told of an appropriate product of this world, a self-styled Arkansas wrestling champion called "Sudden Death and General Desolation."

Twain's character would have been at home in the contemporary South. Although college football packs southern stadiums, stock car racing is a regional phenomenon, and baseball remains popular, the sport that draws most southerners today is professional wrestling. The National Wrestling Alliance regularly publishes statistics claiming that professional wrestling has a greater paid attendance than college or professional football, basketball, or baseball. The wrestling season, of course, is 52 weeks long, and matches are promoted in countless towns and cities so small other sports would never give them a second thought. An estimated 60 percent of the national attendance is in the South. In 1984 a record 43,000 fans turned out at Texas Stadium in Dallas for a match.

In arenas like that in Dothan, Ala., the setting, wrestlers, and fans are probably typical. The Dothan arena is a drab, barn-like building with a dirt floor and concrete seats, but its center contains a red, white, and blue wrestling ring brilliantly lighted by rows of television lights. Since the 1930s farmers and other Dothan area folk have been coming here for Friday night entertainment. Part athletic competition and part soap opera, professional wrestling is the only sport many of these fans know, and they are intensely loyal and enthusiastic. In the wrestling ring good and evil are distinct, and the fans pour into the arena to cheer the good guys and to jeer and curse the bad ones.

Wrestling promoters say their patrons are predominantly working class, with the average wrestling crowd made up of the kind of people whose pickups in the parking lot wear bumper stickers with messages such as "I Fight Poverty, I Work."

The price of an average wrestling ticket is $4, and the annual paid gate for the industry is estimated at between $100 million and $150 million. Whether sport or entertainment, professional wrestling is big business. It is also a closed business, in many ways a family business. At one time, promoters in almost every city in north Alabama and Tennessee were related by blood or marriage, and many of the wrestlers and promoters active today got into the business through their families or in-laws.

The most frequently asked question by outsiders is whether professional wrestling is *only* entertainment. Are these guys athletes or entertainers? A fair answer is that they are both, that most of them have the skills, stamina, and strength for legitimate wrestling. But the wrestlers say that the fans, especially in the South, want to see "catch as catch can" competition, replete with exaggerated falls, wild punches, and frenzied action.

"A wrestling fan is not like a football fan," says Ox Baker, a well-known wrestler from Texas. "They are more vicious, more sadistic. They want to see the bad guys out there ranting and raving. They won't come to see anything else. You can have the NCAA finals in college wrestling and you can't even get a crowd; it won't even make the papers in most places. People want action and we're professionals, we're geared to it, so we give it to them. But then there's blood out there, it's real blood.

I've had teeth knocked out, my knees are boogered up, my wrist has been broken." (Even fans have been known to get into the action, and wrestlers have been stabbed, punched, and beaten over the head by canes wielded by grandfathers.)

Baker acknowledges that there are limits to the slugging wrestlers can do to one another night after night. "We do have agreement among ourselves. Wrestlers know they have to restrain themselves." Wrestlers say this means not that matches are prearranged and rehearsed, but that to fit the schedule and to please the crowd the wrestling may be mixed with soap opera. "Say we're on TV and it's an hour program. Now I can beat my opponent in 45 seconds," says Baker. "But the promoter may tell me, 'Ox, I need seven minutes.' So I'll entertain the people for seven minutes before I put the man down."

Wrestlers also have an incentive to win consistently and to build up a reputation because their earnings depend on it. A wrestler can do preliminary bouts every night and he may earn as much as $40,000 a year if he is willing to travel enough. But a main event wrestler like Ox Baker will earn $300–$700 for 15 minutes of work in Dothan, Ala.; before a bigger crowd his evening's pay may run as high as $2,000.

There are about 3,000 professional wrestlers in the United States, and only a handful of new performers break in each year. Those who do usually make it with some kind of gimmick to attract either the adoration or the hatred of the fans. It does not matter which, because both sell at the box office. Southern wrestlers sometimes adapt regional imagery for their personas. "Haystack" Calhoun was 600 "pounds of fury" from Dixie, and Hillbilly Jim sometimes still appears on wrestling talk shows while his "Granny" plucks a newly killed chicken in the background. Since the Jimmy Carter era of the late 1970s, the Good Old Boy has been one of the most successful wrestling types. Typically, he takes a physical pounding because he will not engage in dishonorable tactics.

A good promoter instinctively knows what will sell and when to introduce something new. The Dothan promoter, for example, found a pair of strapping black twins. Because they were black, they went over well in heavily black south Alabama, and because they were polite and had "good guy" images (partly because they were matched against known "bad guys") they proved popular with white fans as well.

Keeping the fans excited week after week, however, takes effort. This responsibility belongs partly to the promoter and partly to a "matchmaker," who is employed by the individual or group sponsoring matches in a region. The matchmaker's job is to decide which pairings of wrestlers, because of reputation or chemistry, are likely to please and excite the crowd.

Because the same dozen or so wrestlers compete against each other week after week around the circuit, the pairings have to be adjusted to maintain interest. Once the matchmaker gives the assignment to the wrestlers, they must build up as much interest as possible before the match and then make the match itself as exciting as possible.

The prematch buildup is boosted with television shows taped and shown in each of the cities on the circuit a couple of days in advance of the live wrestling. The promoters pay for the television time, and the show includes some wrestling and a generous amount of interview time in which the wrestlers describe what they are going to do to their next opponents.

The matchmaker will also bring in big-name outside wrestlers like Ox Baker to increase attendance. Baker is well-known around the country partly because of his size and strength—6'5", 318 pounds—and partly because of his legendary heart punch, with which, the promos say, he has killed two wrestlers.

Those in the business who know the facts about Baker's "victims" confide that the story is myth, but the "bad" image nevertheless lives on. Psychologists and sociologists periodically publish treatises on the symbolism and ritual significance of football, but professional wrestling is really the morality play of modern sports. If the good guy wins his match, that is simple justice, and if he loses, that is life.

Baker probably could not change his image if he wanted to because it is so well set in the minds of his fans. Mellonee Kapner is 67 and has been an institution at the Dothan arena for two decades. She gives Ox Baker hell from the minute he enters the arena. She gets up from her ringside seat and walks right up next to the ropes, calling Baker profane names—names she would never utter outside this arena—until he leans over the ropes and shakes his giant fist at her. The sight is almost comical: the huge man towering over the little white-haired woman. Later, Mrs. Kapner is telling some other people what she thinks of Ox Baker: "You know, he's killed two men," she says solemnly.

Randall Williams
Southern Changes

Elliott Gorn, "The Manly Art: Bare-Knuckle Prize Fighting and the Rise of American Sports" (Ph.D. dissertation, Yale University, 1983); John Gutowski, *Keystone Folklore* (1972); Gerald W. Morton and George M. O'Brien, *Wrestling to Rasslin': Ancient Sport to American Ritual* (1986); *Newsweek* (11 March 1985); Randall Williams, *Southern Exposure* (Fall 1979); Mark F. Workman, *Folklore Forum* (1977).

Aaron, Hank

(b. 1934) Baseball player.

Mobile, Ala., has produced several great baseball players, including Willie McCovey, Amos Otis, and Satchel Paige. Perhaps the greatest of them all is Henry Louis "Hank" Aaron. Born 5 February 1934 in Toulminville, a black community in Mobile, he began playing amateur baseball while in high school at the Josephine Allen Institute. Playing first with the Pritchett Athletics, Aaron later played on weekends with a local semiprofessional team, the Mobile Black Bears. An exhibition game between the Bears and the Indianapolis Clowns of the Negro American League proved to be Aaron's breakthrough into professional baseball.

The Clowns were impressed with the young player's performance and offered him $200 a month to join the team. Aaron accepted, playing with the Clowns in 1952 and compiling a .467 batting average with his cross-handed swing. Team owner Syd Pollock attracted attention from the Boston Braves when he ended a letter with the postscript "We've got an eighteen-year-old shortstop batting cleanup for us." On 12 June 1952 the Braves purchased Aaron from the Clowns for $10,000 and sent him to play in the Class C Northern League at Eau Claire, Wis. After being named "Rookie of the Year" there, he was sent to Jacksonville, Fla., where he played second base for the Braves' Class A South Atlantic team. During the off-season he trained in Puerto Rico to play in the outfield and in 1954 won a starting job with the Braves (who had moved to Milwaukee) when outfielder Bobby Thompson was injured during spring training.

No longer a cross-handed hitter, Aaron became best known for his hitting ability and power. In 1956 he won the National League batting championship with a .328 average. Bypassing such stars as Stan Musial and Red Schoendienst, the league gave its Most Valuable Player award to Aaron the following year, the same year he clinched the league pennant for the Braves with an 11th-inning home run against the St. Louis Cardinals. A Milwaukee real estate firm supposedly accepted that home run ball from Aaron as a $1,000 down payment on a home.

When the Braves moved to Atlanta in 1966, Aaron hit 44 home runs and signed a $100,000-a-year contract with the team. In 1972 he signed a contract for $200,000 a year, the largest player salary in baseball history at the time.

During his major league career Aaron steadily approached the record number of home runs set by Babe Ruth, who hit 714. In Cincinnati on 4 April 1974 Aaron hit his 714th home run. Braves officials wanted him to hit his record-breaking home run in Atlanta, so they decided that he would not play in the remaining games in Cincinnati. When Baseball Commissioner Bowie Kuhn objected and threatened to penalize the team, Aaron was put back in the lineup, but he returned to Atlanta without another hit.

The game in Atlanta on 8 April 1974 between the Braves and the Los Angeles Dodgers was sold out and nationally televised. A *New York Times* writer said that "to many Atlantans, it was like the city's festive premier of 'Gone with the Wind' during the 1930s when Babe Ruth was still the hero of the New York Yankees and the titan of professional sports." That evening, Aaron hit his 715th home run, this one on a fastball thrown by pitcher Al Downing.

With a total of 755 home runs and numerous other major league records, "Hammerin' Hank" or the "Hammer," as Aaron was called, retired in 1976, after playing his final years with the Milwaukee Brewers. He was elected to the Baseball Hall of Fame in 1982 and currently serves as vice president and director of player development with the Atlanta Braves.

Jessica Foy
Cooperstown Graduate Programs
Cooperstown, New York

Marjorie Dent Candee, ed., *Current Biography* (1958); *New York Times* (9 April 1974); Edna Rust and Art Rust, Jr., *Art Rust's Illustrated History of the Black Athlete* (1985); Charles Van Doren, ed., *Webster's American Biographies* (1979).

Bryant, Bear

(1913–1983) Football coach.

Born 11 September 1913 to a sharecropping family in Moro Bottom, Ark., Paul "Bear" Bryant became the most successful college football coach in history. The youngest of 11 children of Wilson Monroe and Ida Kilgore Bryant, Paul Bryant was born on a farm and sold farm goods to help his invalid father and his mother. At age 12 he earned his nickname by fighting a bear at the Lyric Theater in Fordyce, Ark. He played football for the Fordyce High School Red Bugs and received a football scholarship to the University of Alabama, where he played end.

Bryant was an assistant coach at the University of Alabama and at Vanderbilt University, then served two years in the U.S. Navy during World War II. He was head coach at Maryland, Kentucky, Texas A&M, and Alabama. After coaching his last game in the Liberty Bowl in Memphis, Tenn., in December 1982, Bryant had a record 323 victories. He died in January 1983, and his funeral was one of the largest in southern history, with an estimated 500,000 people turning out to see the funeral procession from Tuscaloosa to the Birmingham burial site.

Bryant was one of the modern South's preeminent mythic figures. A product of the rural poverty so typical of the South in his youth, Bryant rose to national success. The Bear Bryant story is a rags to riches American tale, told in the southern vernacular. In his origins, Bryant symbolized the poor sharecropping South, but he became a middle-class hero to well-off southerners who made football a part of their lifestyles.

Sportswriters created a legend about Bryant with their stories of his toughness, generosity, compassion, shrewdness, and democratic egalitarianism. "Generations from now they will speak in hushed tones about the back woodsy man from Fordyce whom the city slickers couldn't beat," wrote Memphis sportswriter Al Dunning when Bryant died. The *New Yorker* magazine referred to him as an "actual genius." Observers compared him with Douglas MacArthur, John Wayne, and, most frequently, George Patton.

Although he was a national figure, southerners felt a special claim on Bryant. He was most admired in the South because he was a winning leader. For a people whose heroes sometimes symbolized lost causes, Bryant

Paul "Bear" Bryant, University of Alabama football coach, 1970s

was a change. The Bryant legend was not just one of power and victory. Observers stressed his character and class, his concern for making athletes decent people. In his early career there were recruiting scandals and stories of his meanness, but these were forgotten when sportswriters began his apotheosis in the 1970s. The Bryant legend embodied aspects of earlier regional mythology—the New South hope of education transforming the region; the fighting South, with football as Celtic sublimation; and the Jeffersonian agrarian dream with Bryant as wise rural rustic. The Bryant legend is part of the Sports South myth, which views sports as central to the modern southern identity. Bryant was one of the first Deep South coaches to recruit black athletes. He embodies the hope for a biracial South, in which southern blacks and whites, working together, will achieve great things off the football field as well as on it.

Charles Reagan Wilson
University of Mississippi

The Birmingham News, *Remembering Bear* (1983); James Peterson and Bill Cromartie, *Bear Bryant: Countdown to Glory* (1984); Charles Reagan Wilson, *South Atlantic Quarterly* (Summer 1987).

Cobb, Ty

(1886–1961) Baseball player.

Tyrus Raymond "Ty" Cobb, arguably the greatest of all professional baseball players and the first nationally known southern player, was born on 19 December 1886 in Banks County, Ga. His father was William Herchel Cobb, an itinerant schoolmaster who, after moving his family to Royston in Franklin County, Ga., served as state senator, county school superintendent, and editor of the local newspaper. His mother, Amanda Chitwood Cobb, was the daughter of a prominent Banks County landowner.

Tyrus Cobb showed early signs of being an intelligent, hard-driving youngster, impatient with his own and others' shortcomings. Skinny but fast and well coordinated, he starred on the town baseball team and acquired a burning ambition to pursue the game professionally. That ambition clashed with the wishes of his equally strong-willed father, who intended his elder son to be a lawyer, physician, or career military man. Finally Tyrus won W. H. Cobb's permission to try out with the Augusta team in the South Atlantic League. Although he was a failure at Augusta in 1904, Cobb came back the next year to lead the league in hitting and thus gained the attention of major league scouts. The 18-year-old Cobb was about to join the Detroit Tigers in the American League when he learned that his father had been shot to death by his mother, who claimed she had mistaken him for a prowler.

Arriving in Detroit late in August 1905, "Ty" Cobb (as sportswriters soon dubbed him) finished that season with the Tigers. The next spring, while his mother was tried and acquitted on a charge of voluntary manslaughter, young Cobb struggled to gain a regular place on the Detroit ball club. It was, he said long afterward, "the most miserable and humiliating experience I've ever been through." Cobb was subjected to the customary harassments and petty cruelties that rookies usually had to endure in that day. But as a sensitive, troubled young man, a proud southerner among ballplayers who were mainly Irish-American northerners, Cobb reacted strongly against such treatment and ended up a friendless loner on the Detroit team. The death of his father and his painful early experiences with his teammates largely account for why he became, as he later described himself, "a snarling wildcat," driven to prove himself to everybody, including himself, season after season and game after game.

Prove himself he did. In 1907 Cobb won the American League batting title, in the course of leading the Tigers to the first of three straight league championships. For 11 of the next 12 years he outhit everyone else in the American League and frequently led as well in runs scored and bases stolen. Unquestionably the top star of baseball's "dead-ball" era, Cobb remained an outstanding player after the advent of the "lively ball" in 1920 and the emergence of the power-oriented style of baseball heralded by Babe Ruth's home run exploits. From 1921 through 1926 Cobb managed the Detroit team and continued to play the outfield; his final two years as a baseball player were with Connie Mack's Philadelphia Athletics. He retired with an astonishing lifetime batting average of .367 and some 42 other records.

Already a millionaire by the time he hung up his uniform, Cobb ultimately built his personal fortune to $10 million. A man who had quarreled and brawled with teammates, umpires, opposing players, spectators, and many people off the field, Cobb continued to be a hard man to get along with in his long years of retirement. In 1947 his marriage of 39 years to Charlie Marion Lombard Cobb, an Augusta native, ended in divorce, and nine years later a second marriage, to Frances Fairburn Cass Cobb of Buffalo, N.Y., came to a similar end. Moreover, he became estranged from his surviving three children. By the time of his own death from cancer on 17 July 1961, in Atlanta, few people remained whom Cobb could call his friends. His renown in baseball, however, remains undiminished.

Charles C. Alexander
Ohio University

Charles C. Alexander, *Ty Cobb: Baseball's Fierce Immortal* (1984); Ty Cobb, with Al Stump, *My Life in Baseball: The True Record* (1961); John D. McCallum, *The Tiger Wore Spikes: An Informal Biography of Ty Cobb* (1956); Lawrence S. Ritter, *The Glory of Their Times: The Story of the Early Days of Baseball Told by Men Who Played It* (1974).

Colonial Williamsburg

Something more ubiquitously American than uniquely southern permeates the air about Colonial Williamsburg. What appears to epitomize southern genteel traditions is more a slice of general Americana—a replica of history as all Americans might wish it had been—than a monument to the Tidewater aristocracy that bred generations of influential southerners.

The real Williamsburg, founded in 1699, appeared less tidy and behaved less decorously than today's bewigged guides would have the tourists believe. About 2,000 people lived permanently in what served Virginia more as a political and cultural mecca than as a trading center. At least half those residents were black, slaves who served the wishes of the other half. The pace of life shuffled along leisurely except during the "Publick Times"—generally held once each season during the 1700s, but daily fare for the interpretive 1900s—when either the provincial courts or legislatures held sessions. Williamsburg surged and ebbed to its own social tides through the colonial period, until 1781 when the capital was moved upriver to Richmond. Then, except for the frenzy of the Peninsula campaign in 1862, it declined into dormant insignificance.

Revival came at the hands of the local rector, W. A. R. Goodman, who convinced John D. Rockefeller, Jr., to bequeath part of the family fortune to fund a restoration project. Work began in 1926, and by the 1930s buildings were being opened to the public. Rockefeller spent over $80 million in 40 years as 600 postcolonial structures were demolished, more than 80 existing period buildings restored, and replicas reconstructed over excavated foundations. His success spawned other restoration projects across the South, notably those in Salem and Savannah. Yet Williamsburg has persisted as the most popular "preserved" area. By the 1960s more than 15 million visitors had crowded the 130-acre site, and a second phase of restoration and reinterpretation was instituted to meet demand. Popularity peaked during the American Revolution Bicentennial.

Governor's Palace, built in 1705 and restored in the 1930s to its mid-18th-century appearance, Williamsburg, Va.

A cultural commitment is explicit in the purpose behind Colonial Williamsburg—to interpret American history in light of acknowledged national values. John D. Rockefeller III, son of the restorer, said: "Colonial Williamsburg must help make history—not simply serve as a reminder of history." As such, there is more to the pristine atmosphere than a mere commercialization of a past regional graciousness. The guided tours stress less the lifestyles of the gentry than the values of liberty they came to hold. Journalist Bill Moyers has argued that in a place where "people lived routinely and seldom easily," more modern Americans, from all regions, find cultural significance from a presentation "too tidy to be real," but too encompassing to be missed.

Gary Freeze
University of North Carolina
at Chapel Hill

Taylor B. Lewis, *Window on Williamsburg* (1966); James H. Soltow, *The Economic Role of Williamsburg* (1965).

Dean, Dizzy

(1911–1974) Baseball player.

Jay Hanna "Dizzy" Dean, who was born in Lucas, Ark., in 1911, toiled in cotton fields all over the South as the

Dizzy Dean, Arkansas-born baseball player and sportscaster, 1930s

son of a poor migratory farmer. Dean never advanced past the second grade. Enlistment in the army during the Great Depression gave him comparative stability and a nickname that lasted—"Dizzy."

Dean's return to civilian life brought him a contract in the far-reaching St. Louis Cardinals farm system and a quick advancement to the parent club. It was his first step en route to an eventual place in baseball's Hall of Fame. Dean's fastball became a feared weapon for the Cardinals. Many hitters knew what it was to be knocked down by a loud and proud Dean. A high-and-tight Dean fastball was described very accurately by the opposition as "high neck in."

The boldness of the flame-throwing Dean gained just as much attention as his pitching. His first employer, Branch Rickey, quickly learned this when he confronted Dean, telling the young pitcher he was quite a braggart. Dean's reply, quoted in dialect, was an unblinking "'Tain't braggin' if you kin really do it!" The combination of excellent pitching and colorful personality made Dean one of the sport's greatest gate attractions and, in turn, one of its wealthiest ballplayers. Yet, his eccentricities drove many crazy. In one game, troubled by an umpire's call and what he believed to be poor backing by his own team, he decided to lob the ball to opposing hitters.

One of many high points in Dean's career was the 1934 World Series. After winning the first game, he was put on a shortwave hookup to Antarctica to talk with famed explorer Admiral Richard E. Byrd. "Howdy, Dick Byrd," shouted Dean. In the fourth game of the Series, in a pinch-running role, he was flattened by an infielder's throw and carried off on a stretcher. He reported later, "They X-rayed my head and found nothing." The statement was used to full advantage by the press. Then, in the seventh and final game, he shut out the Detroit Tigers.

A broken toe, the result of a line drive during an all-star game, reduced Dean's efficiency considerably and led to an earlier retirement than desired. Dean had learned well, however, how to take advantage of his uniqueness and was soon entertaining people from the radio booth, doing play-by-play broadcasts. The hillbilly image was played to the hilt—and very profitably. A Dizzy Dean broadcast introduced such terms as *slud, swang, presspecration, airs* (errors), and *spart* (spirit), as well as players called Scorn (Skowron), Bearer (Berra), Mannul (Mantle), and Richison (Richardson), always intermingled with a very liberal sprinkling of "ain't." When his cornpone English brought protests from teachers, among others, Dean candidly assessed, "A lot of people who ain't saying ain't, ain't eating." If he had a favorite word, though, it was "I."

Wealthy and retired, Dean moved "down home" to the Ozarks to live out his life. He is buried in Wiggins, Miss., and the Dizzy Dean Museum displays his memorabilia in Jackson, Miss.

John E. DiMeglio
Mankato State University

Curt Smith, *America's Dizzy Dean* (1978).

Disney World

Walt Disney World, near Orlando, Fla., is a vacation resort complex that ranks as one of the South's most popular holiday spots and draws non-southerners to the region as well. It includes an amusement park (the "Magic Kingdom"), hotels, campgrounds, golf courses, shopping centers, and the EPCOT Center (Experimental Prototype Community of Tomorrow). This complex, which opened in 1971, is on 27,400 acres of land and is run like a municipality, providing many of its own services. It represents the fruition of Walt Disney's ideas, which were first expressed in the opening of "Disneyland," near Anaheim, Calif., in 1955.

Disneyland pioneered as the prototype "theme park," but later parks, such as "Six Flags over Georgia" (Atlanta), "Six Flags over Texas" (Dallas), "Opryland" (Nashville), and even "Dollywood" (Pigeon Forge, Tenn.), which all borrowed heavily from Disney, focused on aspects of the past or present southern experience. Both Disneyland in California and Disney World in Florida originated ideas that relate to city planning and architecture, such as the extensive use of mass transit and the design of spaces to entertain people.

The "Magic Kingdom," Disney World's amusement

park, covers 100 acres, with activities—ranging from exhibits and rides to services such as restaurants—oriented around particular conceptual or historic themes. These themes come from Disney's perceptions of popular ideas about the American experience, and include small-town Midwest America about 1900 in "Main Street USA," American history in "Frontierland," the importance of technology in "Tomorrowland," and literary and mythic figures and themes in "Fantasyland." Despite their location in the South, few of these popularizations embodied in Disney World relate directly to the region. Most of the rides, shows, and performances are given by extremely sophisticated, computer controlled ("audio-animatronics") robots, appropriate perhaps to the high-technology South of Florida. These robots ensure identical presentations for each audience. Numerous forms of mass transit, ranging from a monorail to horse-drawn wagons, move visitors around the park and allow easy access to other parts of the resort. The park has many other architectural and city planning features that make the experience pleasant for visitors as well as serving as models for what humanized technology can do.

Disney's graphics, architecture, and technology blend to create a "magic" aura where visitors can suspend their disbelief and enjoy themselves. The rides, robots, and attractions allow them to return for a moment to their own childhoods and to relive the mythic origins of the nation. The parks, with their own versions of American history, folklore, and technology, serve as a unifying experience for the millions of Americans who have visited them. The parks provide a shared cultural experience, a common interpretation of history (albeit somewhat fantasized), and an attractive vision of the future that will result in greater cultural sameness among southerners as well as among other groups of Americans.

David M. Johnson
North Carolina Agricultural
and Technical State University

Margaret J. King, ed., *Journal of Popular Culture* (Summer 1981); Walt Disney Productions, *The Story of Walt Disney World* (1973).

Gilley's

Gilley's, in Pasadena, Tex., was founded by Sherwood Cryer as "Shelly's." Its success, like its present name, dates from 1971, when Cryer went into partnership with Mickey Gilley, a country music singer and piano player once probably best known as Jerry Lee Lewis's cousin. Billed at one time as "the World's Largest Saloon" (it could accommodate 4,500 customers), it eventually offered, besides the traditional drinking and dancing, such challenging entertainments as a punching-bag machine and "El Toro," a mechanical bull for customers to ride. Dancing at the club was to music supplied by Gilley, by the house band (the Bayou City Beats), or by visiting country music entertainers, and it included group dances like the cotton-eyed Joe (punctuated with rhythmic chants of "Bull-*shit*!") and the schottische.

Despite these attractions, Gilley's was little known outside the Houston area, except in country music circles, before 1978, when *Esquire* published an article by Aaron Latham on the club and some of its patrons. Latham's article was accompanied by a photographic feature on designer Ralph Lauren's new line, "embracing the rugged natural look of the American cowboy." When the movie *Urban Cowboy*, starring John Travolta, was actually filmed in Gilley's, scores of more or less frankly imitative establishments sprang up across the country. These "cowboy" bars sometimes replaced discos that had been inspired by Travolta's performance in "Saturday Night Fever" and catered to much the same clientele, even more urban and less plausibly cowboy than the young oil workers Latham had chronicled. The most bravura of these new establishments was also in Texas, a Fort Worth club called "Billy Bob's" that offered live bull-riding in place of Gilley's machine-simulated version. (Rumors that a patron had been stomped and gored did not hurt at all.) Billy Bob's was even larger than Gilley's, and on one occasion Merle Haggard treated all 5,095 customers to drinks.

The era of "Texas chic" soon faded, but not before Gilley's had become a major tourist attraction with its own magazine, its own brand of beer, and complete line of souvenirs. Mickey Gilley himself had become a major country music singer with a number of hits to his credit, including "Don't the Girls All Get Prettier at Closing Time"—a traditional number at the club.

Southerners themselves have often collaborated in—and occasionally profited from—the marketing of the South. But the story of Gilley's may reflect a new development in the nation's old, on-again/off-again love affair with the South. Gilley's represents, and *Esquire* and Hollywood marketed, a blue-collar South, populated by the same good old boys (and girls) whom the mass media had generally portrayed a decade earlier (in such movies as *Easy Rider* and *Deliverance*, for instance) as vicious rednecks. The increasing national respectability of their music, the popularity of Burt Reynolds and the *Dukes of Hazzard*, and, not least, the "Urban Cowboy" phenomenon all attest to a metamorphosis that was one of the stranger aspects of a strange decade.

John Shelton Reed
University of North Carolina
at Chapel Hill

Bob Claypool, *Saturday Night at Gilley's* (1980); Aaron Latham, *Esquire* (September 1978).

Hilton Head

As a forested refuge for nomadic Indian tribes, as the site for 17th-century Spanish and French fortifications, and as the location of antebellum Sea Island cotton plantations, Hilton Head has lured people through its climate and its geographical diversity.

Now one of the South's most famous resort areas, Hilton Head had historic significance in the 19th century. On 7 November 1861, 17 Union warships blocked South Carolina's Port Royal Sound, capturing the Confederate stronghold of Fort Walker on the island. The Port Royal anchorage remained the principal base of federal naval operations for the duration of the war, and Hilton Head's Port Royal Plantation, quartering some 30,000 troops, was transformed into a boomtown, complete with hotels and a theater. Along with other southern sea islands, Hilton Head became the focus for a social and agrarian experiment, in which large plantations and town property were claimed by the Treasury Department and redistributed to freedmen.

Called a "dress rehearsal for Reconstruction," the Port Royal experiment influenced the formation of federal policy concerning the status of emancipated slaves. Its schools, military training, and wage labor programs acted as a proving ground for freedmen and provided experience for postwar Reconstruction leaders such as General O. O. Howard, head of the Freedmen's Bureau, and Congressman Robert Smalls.

After the war, prosperous northern investors were attracted to the sound. Huge tracts of land, and sometimes whole islands, were purchased for use as hunting preserves and winter havens. The largest of South Carolina's barrier islands—12 miles long and covering about 42 square miles—Hilton Head escaped sole proprietorship and became instead a popular combination of resort and residential development.

Gulf breezes keep temperatures on the island at a semitropical 60° to 80° range year-round. The ocean and networks of freshwater lagoons, meadows, forest area, and marshland support some 260 varieties of birds, as well as bream, bass, and blue marlin. Sea oats and palmetto share the landscape with magnolia, pine, and live oak.

Hilton Head offers its more than 700,000 annual visitors recreational diversity. There are 6 marinas, 17 golf courses, and over 200 tennis courts on the island. Accommodations range from hotel rooms to oceanfront villas with names like Bayberry Dune and Xanadu. Abounding in secluded white sand beaches and quiet nature trails, yet only hours from the urbane charm of Charleston, Hilton Head represents a fusion of society and serenity that has a characteristically southern flavor.

Elizabeth M. Makowski
University of Mississippi

Guion Griffis Johnson, *A Social History of the Sea Islands* (1930); Willie Lee Rose, *Rehearsal for Reconstruction: The Port Royal Experiment* (1964); *Southern Living* (April 1982); David D. Wallace, *South Carolina: A Short History, 1520–1948*.

Johnson, Junior

(b. 1931?) Sports car driver.

Robert Glenn "Junior" Johnson is the most famous resident of Ingle Hollow in Wilkes County, N.C. Neighbors used to admire him for his adeptness at outwitting and outmaneuvering tax agents on moonshine runs. Now they and fans throughout the South and the nation revere him for his accomplishments as a stock car driver.

Johnson's father operated a still in Wilkes County, one of the most productive moonshine regions in the country. The size of his profit often depended on whether or not Junior could deliver the product to customers in nearby cities and towns without getting caught, so Junior learned to drive fast and skillfully, often evading would-be captors by implementing his "bootleg turn," a technique that evolved into the "power slide" he later used as a stock car driver to maintain and accelerate speed coming out of turns on the racetrack. In 1955 agents caught him, not on a delivery, but standing in front of the still. He served just over 10 months in a Chillicothe, Ohio, prison.

At the time of his arrest, Johnson was already well on his way to becoming a successful stock car driver. He had won championships in the Sportsman and Modified classifications and, in 1955, captured the first of his seven Grand National victories. Ten years later he retired as a driver, having won the Daytona 500 and 49 other races. He was one of the sport's most popular figures.

Since 1965 Johnson has been hiring drivers for his cars and, with employees like Bobby Allison, Cale Yarborough, and most recently, Darrell Waltrip, his success has continued. Recognized as a master mechanic, Johnson has been a consultant to General Motors, but he still operates from his home in Ingle Hollow, where he and his staff build parts, make repairs, and work constantly to keep the team's cars among the fastest on the track.

Success has not separated Johnson from his heritage in the rural South. He is a prototypical good old boy who likes coon hunting and chicken farming. He even helped found the Holly Farms Chicken company in North Wilkesboro, N.C. Writer Tom Wolfe called him the "Last American Hero," and Johnson's neighbors would probably agree. His bootlegging days may be well past, but somewhere in Ingle Hollow, he still has his old moonshining car safely stored away.

Jessica Foy
Cooperstown Graduate Programs
Cooperstown, New York

Larry Griffin, *Car & Driver* (April 1982); Charles Leerhsen, *Newsweek* (16 November 1981); Tom Wolfe, *Esquire* (March 1965).

Jones, Bobby

(1902–1971) Golfer.

Born on 17 March 1902 in Atlanta, Ga., Robert Tyre "Bobby" Jones, Jr., was a child prodigy at golf, studying under Stewart Maiden, a Scottish pro who worked at Atlanta's East Lake course. Jones played in the 1916 U.S. Amateur Tournament when he was only 14 years old. He went on to win 13 major championships, climaxed in 1930 by capturing in a single season the "Grand Slam of Golf," which was then the championships of the British Amateur, the British Open, the U.S. Open, and the U.S. Amateur. New York City treated him to an enormous ticker tape parade that year, appropriate to one who had become a national hero. Later, he received a similar outpouring of affection from his hometown in Atlanta. At the height of his fame, at age 28, Jones announced his retirement. He returned to his law practice and business endeavors in Atlanta, starting a long involvement with the A. G. Spalding Company, making a series of instructional film shorts for Warner Brothers studios, and conceiving and assisting in the design of the Augusta National Golf Course in Augusta, Ga., home of the Masters Tournament.

Jones's career reflected the rise of spectator sports in the South and the nation during the 1920s. Although golf was not as popular in the South as in the Northeast and on the West Coast, Jones nonetheless consciously worked to increase its popularity in his home region. He conceived the idea of the Augusta course, because "my native Southland, especially my own neighborhood, had very few, if any, golf courses of championship quality." He regarded it "as an opportunity to make a contribution to golf in my own section of the country."

Jones was frequently referred to as the embodiment of the southern gentleman. Journalist and commentator Alistair Cooke wrote that Jones was "a gentleman, a combination of goodness and grace, an unwavering courtesy, self-deprecation, and consideration for other people." Graceful in his athletic performance, poised at all times, modest in his success, and self-consciously "southern" in his attitudes, Jones symbolized a transitional figure—the traditional regional image of the gentleman in a new 20th-century mass culture context. Through the press and radio in the 1920s, the exploits of "The Emperor Jones" were publicized, and he thereby helped popularize golf with southerners and others who had once dismissed it as an effete game for the wealthy.

Charles Reagan Wilson
University of Mississippi

John R. Betts, *America's Sporting Heritage, 1850–1950* (1974); Robert Tyre Jones, Jr., *Golf Is My Game* (1959).

Kentucky Derby

The Kentucky Derby, America's premier race classic for three-year-old thoroughbreds, showcases some of the South's most established traditions: honorable sporting competition, high fashion, and the love of pageantry. This mile-and-a-quarter test has been run at Churchill Downs in Louisville, Ky., since May 1875. The race originally was proposed as a match between Kentucky's and Tennessee's best three-year-old horses. However, its founder, Colonel M. Lewis Clark of Louisville, after visiting the racecourses of Europe, changed the inaugural to a derby patterned after England's one-and-a-half-mile Epsom Derby.

The names and traditions associated with the Kentucky Derby are a tapestry of American racing history. There was Matt Winn (1861–1949), the colorful track president who had seen every Derby and whose flair for showmanship transformed the race into a national and world event. There was Isaac Murphy (1871–96), the legendary black jockey with three winning rides. And Colonel E. R. "Bet-a-Million" Bradley, whose four winners—Behave Yourself (1921), Bubbling Over (1926), Burgoo King (1932), and Brokers Tip (1933)—like all his horses, had names beginning with the letter "B." The year 1919 produced Sir Barton, the first Triple Crown winner, and 1941, Whirlaway, the chestnut speedster with the flying tail. Then, too, there was "R-r-r-racing fans, this is Clem McCarthy" calling the race on national radio (1928–50); Citation (1948), one of eight horses to carry the devil's red silks of Calumet Stables to victory; and, finally, Penny Tweedy's wonder horse, Secretariat, the race record holder (1.59 2/5, 1973).

Mint juleps, roses, steamboat and balloon races, parades, and southern fashion on display constitute the Kentucky Derby for many. For the thousands that jam into the track infield on Derby Day it is picnic coolers, beer, and lighthearted revelry. Still for others, it is parties, out-of-town guests, good food, and a television or radio tuned to the race.

Run on the first Saturday in May, the Derby is an American tradition, an unofficial holiday that focuses on the spectacle of finely conditioned animals competing in the ultimate two minute test. For the winner, there is racing immortality, a purse in excess of $100,000, and the chance to win America's racing Triple Crown. For the audience, there is an opportunity to enjoy the traditions and to savor a flavoring of timeless culture. When the familiar strains of "My Old Kentucky Home" are sung as the horses are led onto the track, everyone becomes both a Kentuckian and a southerner. In this sense, the Kentucky Derby is more than a race; it is, instead, an expression of national heritage.

James C. Claypool
Northern Kentucky University

Peter Chew, *The Kentucky Derby, the First 100 Years* (1974); Annie Harrison, *The Kentucky Derby: Its Traditions and Triumphs* (1980).

Louisiana State Lottery Company

The Louisiana State Lottery Company had its genesis in 1866 when the legislature, controlled by Confederate veterans, passed an act permitting lottery vending in the state. Two years later a Republican-dominated legislature assisted by Charles T. Howard, a skilled lobbyist, pushed through a bill chartering the Louisiana State Lottery Company. The 25-year charter gave the company a monopoly on the sale of lottery tickets and exempted the organization from state taxes, except for an annual license fee of $40,000. Its capital stock was set at $1 million with 10,000 shares valued at $100 each. Operations began on 31 December 1868.

By the time the Republican government fell in 1877 the company was a lucrative and politically powerful enterprise. Anxious to maintain its privileges and to foil opposition from Louisiana's Redeemers, lotterymen in 1879 allied themselves with the reactionary Bourbon faction of the Democratic party, wrote a new state constitution that ousted unfriendly state officials, installed lottery supporters in key government positions, and gave legal sanction to lotteries until 1 January 1895.

With opposition temporarily stayed, lotterymen improved the image of the organization by undertaking philanthropic endeavors and enshrining their enterprise in the sacrosanct shroud of the Lost Cause. Two ex-Confederate generals, P. G. T. Beauregard and Jubal Early, presided over drawings, thereby ensuring honesty. Yet, with 47 percent of its gross receipts retained as profit, there was little need for chicanery. Conservative estimates of profits accrued in the 1880s range from $8 million to $14 million annually, and by 1890 the company reportedly took in from $20 million to $30 million.

At the peak of its economic and political power, opposition to the company increased locally and nationally. From 1890 to 1892 debates over the renewal of the company's charter raged throughout the state, split both major parties, divided the Populists, and submerged all other issues. The antilottery forces won the battle in Louisiana, but the U.S. Congress, taking direct aim at the Louisiana Lottery, delivered the fatal blow by passing a bill denying the use of the mails to lotteries. Since 90 percent of the Louisiana Lottery's proceeds came from states other than Louisiana, this legislation dried up profits and closed down operations in the state in December 1893. In January diehard lotterymen transferred the company to Honduras, and for some years they sponsored illegal activities in the United States. Federal law enforcement authorities checked these operations, and the company collapsed in 1907.

Carolyn DeLatte
McNeese State University

Berthold C. Alwes, *Louisiana Historical Quarterly* (October 1944); Henry C. Dethloff, *Louisiana History* (Spring 1965); William I. Hair, *Bourbonism and Agrarian Protest: Louisiana Politics, 1877–1900* (1969).

Manning, Archie

(b. 1949) Football player.

Archie Manning was representative of many southern football players who have become heroes in the modern South. They are often identified with a particular university or state, but some are well known throughout the region. Traditional southern military imagery and evangelical religious fervor are applied to them. A few such as Manning transcend the region and become national celebrities, symbolic of their native region. Manning was particularly significant of the few football heroes who played in the South at both the college and professional ranks.

Elisha Archie Manning III was born 19 March 1949 to a Baptist family in the Delta town of Drew, Miss. Young Manning was given a tiny helmet and uniform as soon as he could walk and often slept with a football cradled in his arms. Recruited out of high school by only a few area colleges, Manning accepted a scholarship to play quarterback at the University of Mississippi.

Manning, with his red hair, freckles, and a prominent nose, became known as college football's Huckleberry Finn. The 6′3½″ player could spot receivers over charging linemen, and with his 10.2 seconds' speed in the 100-yard dash he was fast enough to elude the rush. Manning started at quarterback his sophomore year and led his team to a 7-3-1 record.

The next season, 1969, a year of Vietnam protests, Woodstock, and the moon landing, Archie Manning became a folk hero. Mississippi played Alabama in the third game of the season. It was the first nationally televised nighttime broadcast of a college game. Manning and Alabama's Scott Hunter put on a brilliant display of passing as Alabama won the game 33–32. Manning's effort set a Southeastern Conference record for total offense that still stands—540 yards, including 33 completions out of 52 pass attempts. Sportswriters referred to "Super" Manning as "Archie Fever" continued to grow. After the University of Mississippi defeated unbeaten and second-ranked Tennessee 38–0, "The Ballad of Archie Who," written by a postal clerk in Magnolia, Miss., hit the airwaves, and the song quickly sold 35,000 copies.

By his senior year, the quiet boy from Drew with the rifle arm had become a national hero. *Sports Illustrated* called the phenomenon "one of the wildest displays of adulation ever accorded any athlete anywhere, anytime." In 1970 Manning was on the cover of *Sports Illustrated* and *College Football* magazines. Then he broke his left arm in the homecoming game, ruining his chances for the Heisman trophy.

Manning was the second player chosen in the 1971 National Football League draft, going to the lowly New Orleans Saints. His 14-year professional career included two Pro Bowl appearances and selection as the league's most valuable player. Manning never played on a winning team as a professional, but he said "no matter how bad we got beat, in the eyes of Mississippians it was never my fault." He retired in 1985, after brief stays with the Houston Oilers and Minnesota Vikings. Manning lives in New Orleans, where he is a stockbroker and sports announcer for Saints games.

Tom Rieland
University of Mississippi

Pat Putnam, *Sports Illustrated* (24 November 1969); William F. Reed, *Sports Illustrated* (14 September and 12 October 1970).

Paige, Satchel

(1906–1982) Baseball player.

LeRoy "Satchel" Paige was born in Mobile, Ala., on 7 July 1906. As a youngster he was a porter at the railroad station, where he was given the nickname "Satchel" because he built a device that enabled him to carry many more bags than normal. He was in trouble early in life and spent over five years at the Industrial School for Negro Children at Mount Meig, Ala.

As a teenager he attracted attention for his baseball pitching, and he began playing professionally in 1924 for the Mobile Tigers, a black semipro club. By 1928 he had risen to the highest level of black baseball, playing with the Birmingham Black Barons of the Negro National League. He achieved his greatest fame in the Negro Leagues pitching for the Pittsburgh Crawfords during the 1930s and the Kansas City Monarchs during the 1940s, but he pitched for as many as 250 independent ballclubs, usually on a one-game exhibition basis.

His fastball was virtually impossible to hit, and his reputation spread well beyond the world of black baseball, aided by his enormous showmanship and inexhaustible energy. In exhibition games he was frequently advertised as "guaranteed to strike out the first six men," and he was known to call in the outfield or instruct his infielders to sit down.

His reputation was enhanced by a series of historic encounters with white major league players that followed the major league World Series. These games, during the era of segregation, enabled black and white ballplayers to assess each other's skills. Dizzy Dean called Paige the greatest pitcher of his era, and major league testimony to Paige's ability is abundant. Paige's many victories over white major leaguers gave him a symbolic importance to blacks during segregation, and black baseball fans everywhere followed Paige's exploits through the highly developed sports pages of the national black newspapers.

Shortly after the integration of baseball by Jackie Robinson, Paige became the first black pitcher in the American League, with the Cleveland Indians in 1948. He pitched for Cleveland in 1948 and 1949, with the St. uis Browns in 1951–53, and briefly with the Kansas Athletics in 1965, all of which helped qualify him ajor league pension.

was the ultimate barnstorming baseball player, virtually every day. His talent was extraordi- his success was coupled with a flamboyant, comic style that augmented his reputation. Paige's career illustrated the typical Negro League history of southern roots and northern achievement. In 1971 Paige was elected to the Baseball Hall of Fame, the first Negro Leaguer admitted under a new admissions policy. Paige died in 1982 in Kansas City, Mo.

See also BLACK LIFE: / Negro Baseball Leagues

Donn Rogosin
WSWP-TV
Beckley, West Virginia

Donn Rogosin, *Invisible Men: Life in Baseball's Negro Leagues* (1983); Edna Rust and Art Rust, Jr., *Art Rust's Illustrated History of the Black Athlete* (1985).

Petty, Richard

(b. 1937) Sports car driver.

Among modern southern sports legends, few have had as sustained and dedicated a following as Richard Petty, often dubbed "King of the Road" in stock car racing. Petty's dominance of the asphalt ovals in the South has created a following that adores him as much for his traditional lifestyle as for his driving exploits.

His racing record has been impressive. In his first 25 seasons (1958–83), Petty won 198 races, far more than any of his competitors. His earnings exceeded $4.5 million. Although slow to gain prominence—he went winless his first two seasons—Petty dominated the tracks from the early 1960s to the mid-1970s. His peak performances came from 1967 through 1971, when the familiar Petty blue Plymouth was driven into victory lane in 40 percent of the 233 races he entered. Over the course of his career, Petty has won the prestigious Daytona 500 seven times, received seven Winston Cups for the best seasonal performance among drivers, and finished among the first 10 drivers in 70 percent of the 900 races he has entered.

Yet more than simple performance explains the hold of the Petty legend on so many southerners. Intensely personal and familial traits exist in stock car racing. Fans become attached to a particular driver and espouse his cause as if he were kin. Petty's career style has been both an extension of, and a reaction to, such traits. He frequently spends hours after races signing autographs. He has been known, when eliminated early in competition, to use public restrooms to change his clothes. When a movie was made about his life, Petty himself played the lead role. Such closeness to his fans has bred deep loyalties. Through the years those who become Petty fans remain Petty fans.

The depth of such attachments can be best explained by the common origins Petty shares with most of his fans. His background, like theirs, is deeply rooted in the rural South. Petty grew up in the Uwharrie hills of Randolph County, N.C. He has remained there, and, until the late stages of his career, used mostly family members and neighbors to man his pit crew. Racing has been a hereditary trait among the Pettys. Richard succeeded his father Lee and now has a son of his own, Kyle, on the tracks. Much like traditional rural skills such as weaving and smithing, racing is passed along through generations.

Petty fans remain loyal because the racer has remained just like them, even though he achieved uncommon financial success. The Pettys have lived "like folks" even though they have a five-car garage. The Pettys reinforce the ambitions of their fans, who through stock car racing strive to hold on to the identities of their impoverished, rural past as they seek the urbane riches of the Sunbelt. A symbol of this dichotomy is the new Petty brick house, built near the old frame cottage where he grew up. On the dining room wall of the new house is a printed mural of an Old South plantation scene.

Gary Freeze
University of North Carolina
at Chapel Hill

Bill Libby with Richard Petty, *"King Richard": The Richard Petty Story* (1977).

Robinson, Eddie

(b. 1919) Football coach.

Eddie Robinson was born 12 February 1919 in Jackson, La., to sharecropper parents. At age eight he moved with his parents to Baton Rouge, where, according to Robinson, he watched a high school football team practice and decided he wanted to be a coach. Robinson played football at McKinley High School in Baton Rouge and at Leland College. After graduating in 1940, he worked during the day at a Baton Rouge feed mill and at night on an ice truck. In 1941 Grambling hired Robinson as head football coach, and he began his legendary career.

Robinson's success in developing the football program at Grambling was phenomenal. When he first arrived on campus, Robinson assumed chores assigned to support staffs at larger schools, such as mowing the playing field, taping ankles, and even writing game stories for the newspapers. With the support of the Grambling administration, Robinson built the fledgling program into one of the most respected collegiate programs in the country. More than 200 of Robinson's Grambling players have gone on to play on professional teams, a record that testifies to Robinson's success as a coach. Robinson's coaching style has changed little during his years at Grambling. His teams have been characterized by the wing-T formation on offense and a pro-style 4–3 on defense.

During the fall 1985 season, Robinson won his 324th game, surpassing the record previously held by Paul "Bear" Bryant of Alabama. Although some observers charge that Robinson's record meant less than Bryant's because most of his victories came against Division I-AA-caliber teams, others point out that Robinson has had to overcome difficulties Bryant never faced at Alabama, such as low recruitment and operating budgets, and racial discrimination. Robinson remains humble about his victories and characteristically tries to divert attention from the inevitable comparisons between himself and Bryant. "I could win 1,000 games and never replace the Bear," Robinson said about his 324th win.

Karen M. McDearman
University of Mississippi

Paul Hemphill, *Southern Magazine* (December 1986); Rick Reilly, *Sports Illustrated* (14 October 1985); William C. Rhoden, *New York Times* (16 September 1985).

St. Cecilia Ball

A private, exclusive subscription ball, the St. Cecilia is an outgrowth of the oldest musical society in the United States. One of a variety of social, charitable, cultural, and educational organizations in antebellum Charleston, the St. Cecilia Society was founded in 1762. Gentlemen amateurs came together "to indulge a common taste and to pass an agreeable hour" and organized two concerts each month for members, featuring talented musicians from within the city and elsewhere in the nation.

By 1773, when visiting Bostonian Josiah Quincy decreed its first violinist "incomparably better" than any other he had ever heard, the society had a membership of 120 and a professional orchestra comparable in size to European ensembles of the period. Though carefully managed by its officers—the peerage of Charleston—difficulties in obtaining musicians and the increased popularity of dancing led to a gradual change in emphasis. After 1822 subscription balls entirely replaced the concerts.

There were three St. Cecilias during the winter "gay" season: one in January and two in February, the latter cautiously arranged to avoid interfering with Lent. The balls were held on Thursdays (St. Cecilia's day) in St. Andrew's Hall, Broad Street, and, after that hall was destroyed in the fire of 1861, in the Hibernian. Invitations were hand delivered to members; and new membership in the society was strictly limited, typically, to the sons or grandsons of current members. When a man was elected, the names of the ladies of his household were added to "the list." Their names were removed only upon death or departure from the city, "change of fortune affecting them not at all."

When invited as guests, visiting strangers were e pected to follow the traditons of the ball, designed t sure "the greatest decorum." Young ladies always a and returned home with chaperons who, duri course of the ball, sat on a slightly raised platf rounding the dance floor. Men engaged girls f by signing a card. Before each dance, the orc nalled ladies to return to their chaperons to await the next partner.

At midnight the president of the society led the march to supper with the newest bride in the group on his arm. Replete with fine food and wine, silver and monogrammed Irish linen, the elegant suppers were capped by a "scramble of the men for a sugar figure placed on the top of a huge fancy structure of spun sugar," which each tried to secure as a souvenir for his partner.

Still held yearly, the St. Cecilia balls have changed little since the 1800s. In an effort to preserve social distinctions and traditions without, in the words of a former society president, "stirring up jealousies and animosities which seriously impair the goodwill normally existing between members and nonmembers," secrecy continues to surround both rules for admission and customs of the ball, leading outsiders to view the affairs with a mix of awe and incredulity. "It is remarkable," wrote one early 20th-century journalist, "that such exclusive and elective balls, bound by such rigid rules, and so opposed to new members, should exist so long in the whirling change of American life."

Elizabeth M. Makowski
University of Mississippi

Ainslee's Magazine (October 1905); Frederick P. Bowes, *The Culture of Early Charleston* (1942); John J. Hindman, "Concert Life in Ante Bellum Charleston" (Ph.D. dissertation, University of North Carolina, Chapel Hill, 1971); Mrs. St. Julien Ravenel, *Charleston: The Place and the People* (1907).

Showboats

Beginning in the 1830s and reaching a peak from 1870 to 1910, showboats steamed the waterways of the Atlantic Coast and the Mississippi River Valley, bringing spectacular entertainment to people in communities along the way. Some showboats were little more than flatboats with primitive structures on top, but the most elaborate were floating palaces, which had fancy decor and comfortable quarters. Among the most famous showboats were Edwin Price's *Water Queen*, William Chapman's *Floating Theatre*, Norman Thom's *Princess*, Spaulding and Rogers's *Floating Circus Palace*, John McNair's *New Era*, and Augustus French's *New Sensation*. Loud calliopes and brightly colored flags announced the coming of the showboats, and a parade and free concert would be held if the community was big enough. The showboats presented family fare, including musical performances, sentimental melodramas, minstrel routines, acrobatics, fiddlers' contests, humorous speeches, and magic shows. Thousands of people in isolated river towns and on plantations turned out enthusiastically, and uncritically, to see the shows.

In the 20th century showboats declined because of competition from other forms of mass culture, especially the movies. In the early 1900s, though, even more elaborate showboats than before were built, such as the *Cotton Blossom*, the *Goldenrod*, and the *Sunny South*. They were large, sometimes seating almost 1,000 people, and they began specializing in dramatic performances and stage plays from the New York theater. This did not reverse the decline, though, as the number of showboats on the Mississippi fell from 22 in 1910 to 4 in 1938.

Moonlight on Old Man River, *Mississippi River, Greenville, Miss., postcard, c. 1900*

Showboats have become so identified with southern entertainment history that contemporary southerners have shown a renewed interest in them. In 1948 Vicksburg, Miss., for example, purchased the *Sprague*, a huge towboat built in 1901, and converted it into a showboat of sorts. Metro-Goldwyn-Mayer studios used it in 1950 for the musical film *Show Boat*. It then housed a river museum in Vicksburg and served as the stage for a Gay Nineties melodrama, *Gold in the Hills*.

The *Delta Queen* is the most famous paddle-wheel steamer still cruising the Mississippi. The 285-foot-long, 58-foot-wide steamer regularly makes the trip from Cincinnati to New Orleans as well as numerous shorter trips. Its sister ship, the *Mississippi Queen*, is a larger, more modern vessel. Those on their cruises are entertained with presentations of shows such as *The Mississippi Gambler* and Mark Twain's *Huckleberry Finn* and *Tom Sawyer*. The sound of the calliope playing "My Old Kentucky Home," "Are You from Dixie?," or "Way Down in New Orleans" still summons people to river towns to greet the boat as it steams into port. Amusement parks such as Nashville's Opryland use steamboats (the *Andrew Jackson*) as stages for musical entertainment, and museums such as Memphis's Mud Island use riverboat replicas—all evoking memories of an earlier southern form of amusement.

Charles Reagan Wilson
University of Mississippi

Philip Graham, *Georgia Review* (Summer 1958), *Showboats: The History of an American Institution* (1951).

Spoleto Festival U.S.A.

Spoleto Festival U.S.A. is the American equivalent to Gian Carlo Menotti's Festival of Two Worlds, staged annually since 1957 in the Umbrian town of Spoleto, Italy.

With a long tradition of support for theater companies and music societies, such as the venerable St. Cecilia, and unique architectural beauty paralleling its Italian counterpart, Charleston, S.C., was selected in 1977 as the site for this interdisciplinary arts festival. For two-and-one-half weeks each spring, from the end of May to the first week in June, as many as 12 events a day highlight both traditional and experimental forms in the visual arts, music, theater, and dance. Offerings range from Bellini's *La Sonnambula*, Rachmaninoff concerts, and medieval liturgical drama to performances by the Spoleto Express Breakdancers. Pianist Misha Dichter, Dizzy Gillespie (a native South Carolinian), Dance Theatre of Harlem, and members of such distinguished ensembles as the Saint Paul Chamber Orchestra and the Pittsburgh Symphony have appeared on Spoleto stages.

Piccolo Spoleto ("Little Spoleto") supplements these paid-admission events. Emphasizing local and regional talent and children's activities, Piccolo Spoleto holds performances in community centers, schools, and churches throughout Charleston.

Education is an important part of Spoleto. Each year over 800 young musicians from conservatories and universities across the nation are auditioned by music director Christian Baeda. Finalists (106 in 1984) are chosen to join the Festival Orchestra and to perform in Italy at the close of the Charleston program. Opportunities to work with international talents extend to administrators and technicians as well, because in addition to performance, apprentice programs cover most aspects of arts management and production.

More than a showcase for the arts, Spoleto Festival U.S.A. links the established polished performer with the innovative, young artist and European cultural traditions with those of the South.

Elizabeth M. Makowski
University of Mississippi

John Ardoin, *Opera News* (October 1983); Andrew Porter, *New Yorker* (15 July 1985); Harold Rosenthal, *New Grove Dictionary of Music and Musicians*, vol. 18, ed. Stanley Sadie (1980); *Southern Living* (May 1980).

Tournaments

Usually called lancing tournaments in South Carolina and Georgia and ring tournaments elsewhere, these displays of equestrian skill represent survivals in the South of ancient medieval tourneys. Traditionally held on holidays, particularly Independence Day, and sometimes at agricultural fairs in antebellum times, in the New South tournaments lost most of their quality as spectacle and remained largely an entertainment at planter-class family outings. Extant today in their natural form only in much-simplified versions and in a few localities, they have become essentially folk practices, occasionally retaining some hint of their original pageantry.

Originating in France in the mid-11th century, medieval tournaments—exhibitions of military prowess by horsemen in mock battles—were introduced by the Norman Conquest into England, where they flourished for over 300 years. Though the introduction of gunpowder and small arms in the 14th and 15th centuries made knightly skills obsolete in warfare, the popularity of tournaments as spectacle continued through the first half of the 16th century. But after the death of Henry VIII the necessity to economize put such costly shows out of fashion in England, and in 1559 the killing of the French king, Henry II, in a tournament accident blighted the practice everywhere.

Royal tournaments disappeared altogether, but local noblemen in England continued the practice, on a much reduced scale, as private entertainment. In the course of the 17th century the tradition was transplanted to England's American colonies. While in 18th-century England tournaments died out, in the colonies, particularly in the South, they survived.

Still intact in the South at the opening of the 19th century, the tournament tradition got a new lease on life from the Romantic movement and the Gothic revival. Tournaments were incorporated into the southern ideal of chivalry and achieved phenomenal popularity in the Old South. Five thousand people attended an 1856 tournament in Fredericksburg, Va., for example, and 6,000 were at one in Jackson, Miss., in 1859.

Typically, mounted tournament contestants, often military cadets and officers, styled themselves knights—the Knight of the Old Dominion or the Knight of the Black Prince. Each carried a pointed "lance," a long wooden dowel or, in less polished versions, a small pole from which the bark had been carefully stripped. Contestants in turn "ran the rings," charging down a course of 100 or so yards, along which a series of three or more rings, in diameters diminishing from about three inches to half an inch, were hung on wire hooks suspended from bars fixed to the tops of posts lining the course. After finishing the course, each contestant rode before the judges, who counted the rings he had collected on his lance and calculated his time. The winner became the tournament king and crowned a queen.

Tournaments in the New South often lost their medieval trappings and became associated with hunts, particularly with fox hunts. Hence they were often played out in traditional red, white, and black hunting clothes. Very few tournaments in that form remain today, having lost virtually all elements of pageantry.

Jerah Johnson
University of New Orleans

Esther J. Crooks and Ruth W. Crooks, *The Ring Tournament in the United States* (1936); John Hope Franklin, *The Militant South, 1800–1861* (1956).

Walker, Herschel
(b. 1962) Football player.

In 1980 Herschel Walker began a three-year football career at the University of Georgia during which he established himself as the Deep South's first universally acclaimed black collegiate superstar. Having set numerous high-school records in the tiny south Georgia town of Wrightsville, Walker led his team to one national and three Southeastern Conference Championships, claiming for himself not only statistical records and the Heisman trophy, but a unique place in the hearts of his region's white football fanatics.

Despite the often unpleasant experiences of his black predecessors in southern collegiate athletics, most white football fans refused to let several centuries of racial paranoia come between them and an athlete who could run like Herschel Walker. Walker received some racist hate mail, but even his controversial early departure from the University of Georgia for a lucrative contract with the New Jersey Generals of the United States Football League and his challenge of the white South's ultimate racial taboo—dating and marrying a white woman—did little to damage his overall popularity in Georgia and throughout the region. He joined the National Football League Dallas Cowboys in 1986.

Southern whites developed an affection for Walker because of both his physical prowess and the unassuming grace with which he wore their adulation. (Jack Armstrong, the "All-American boy," was a smart-mouthed street punk by comparison.) Walker's conservatism and reticence brought criticism from some black militants and white activists who felt that black athletic heroes should speak out on racial issues. Walker refused to become a social reformer, however, steering clear of civil rights demonstrations in his native Wrightsville and thwarting the efforts of the most determined interviewers to lead him into controversial areas.

Mature and intelligent, Walker realized it was in his best interest to watch what he said and did. He remained, despite his fame, a country boy, profoundly influenced by two determined, God-fearing parents. Walker's mother and father instilled in their children courtesy and humility familiar in the rural and small-town South. The key to Herschel Walker's identity and appeal was his down-to-earth southern upbringing. That upbringing, however, included no color-coded parental instructions to stay in his "place." No one, black or white, doubted that Walker knew what he could do, and his interracial courtship and marriage indicated that he had no qualms about violating southern social norms that he did not accept.

It is difficult to determine whether Herschel Walker parted the waters of racism in the South or simply walked expertly across them. His miracle was primarily a personal one. A decade after Georgia's "Redcoat" marching band had dropped "Dixie" from its title as well as its repertoire, many of the same fans who had lost their hearts to Herschel continued to demand that the band resume playing the song that black southerners saw as the anthem of slavery, segregation, and the Ku Klux Klan. Across the football-mad South, racial epithets still reached the ears of black players and fans, and many whites still objected to starting lineups that were predominantly black. Such evidence suggested that the level of acceptance that Walker achieved would remain exceptional until another uniquely "All-American on-and-off-the-field" black superhero came along to again strike white fans color-blind.

Herschel Walker, football great for the University of Georgia and the Dallas Cowboys, 1980s

James C. Cobb
University of Alabama

Sue Burchard, *Herschel Walker* (1984); Pat Conroy, *Southern Living* (September 1983); Terry Todd, *Sports Illustrated* (4 October 1982).

Religion

SAMUEL S. HILL
University of Florida
CONSULTANT

River baptism in rural Kentucky

Religion

The South's religious life is distinctive in ways that parallel the region's general distinctiveness. Its fervently religious people are frequently described as "born again," their religion as "fundamentalist." There is some accuracy in the use of these terms. But even they refer to complex concepts. Moreover, they do not do justice to the diversity of the South, which includes the religion of white people, the religion of black people, and the varieties of each.

Students of religious movements always do well to ask about the intentions of the religious people themselves. What do they believe? What has powerful meaning for them? What happens to them when they attend church services; what are they seeking to express when they worship and when they support church causes?

Focus on baptism and the Lord's Supper, the two Protestant sacraments, or "ordinances" as they are often called in the South, affords insight into the dynamics of regional faith. Why baptism is such a persistent and public issue tells a great deal about the religious history of the region. It also discloses much about the interaction of religion and culture there. Similarly, such topics as the character of church services, their tone and emphasis, the style of church architecture and the activity that takes place there suggest what the people believe and how their faith is expressed.

Perspectives such as these yield understanding of the humanistic dimensions of the South's religious life. They point to the metaphors in which the message is couched, the mythos on which it is founded, and the system of values that prompts characteristic behavior. They reflect the overall regional culture, in history and in the present, yet they have a life of their own and are not simply byproducts of economic, political, or social forces.

Distinctiveness of Southern Religion. Three features stand out in making the religion of the South different from the patterns that prevail elsewhere. (1) The forms that are common in the region are relatively homogeneous. The range of popular options is narrow. (2) The South is the only society in Christendom where the evangelical family of Christians is dominant. Evangelicalism's dominance is decisive in making the South the "religious region" that it is and in marking off the South from patterns, practices, and perspectives prevalent in other parts of America. (3) A set of four common convictions occupies a normative southern religious position. Movements and denominations in the South are judged for authenticity in the popular mind by how well they support these beliefs: (a) the Bible is the sole reference point of belief and practice; (b) direct and dynamic access to the Lord is open to all; (c) morality is defined in individualistic and personal terms; and (d) worship is informal.

The permeation of religion throughout the southern population continues to puzzle observers imbued with the "modern mind" and a secularist outlook. To a remarkable degree for a modern Western culture, the South adheres to traditional Christianity. It believes in a supernaturalism reminiscent of medieval Europe. Religion is still treated as a vital concern. A majority accept orthodox teachings. And many who are not church members believe they should submit to conversion and expect that some day they will. Traditional faith continues to be the popular form, and its hold on the hearts and minds of people is quite firm.

The identification of Christianity with the "old-time religion" makes believing difficult for other southerners, however. To a sizable and growing segment, the South's traditional religion seems outdated and is untenable. Such people have not abandoned the faith; rather they are unable to respond to it through the typical regional forms. The South is, in Flannery O'Connor's apt phrase, "Christ-haunted." The old-fashioned faith is integral to the regional way of life. Though others resist such a worldview, they cannot give up religion or get away from it. They are so deeply indoctrinated in the orthodox faith that they cannot articulate alternative formulations of it, much as they wish they could.

Few characterizations of the South are more acute than the recognition that it has been a limited-options culture. Historically that has been true, especially in the 75 years following the Civil War. National economic development largely bypassed the region. In hardly any other aspect has the limitation of choices been more pronounced than in religion. Southerners' range of options

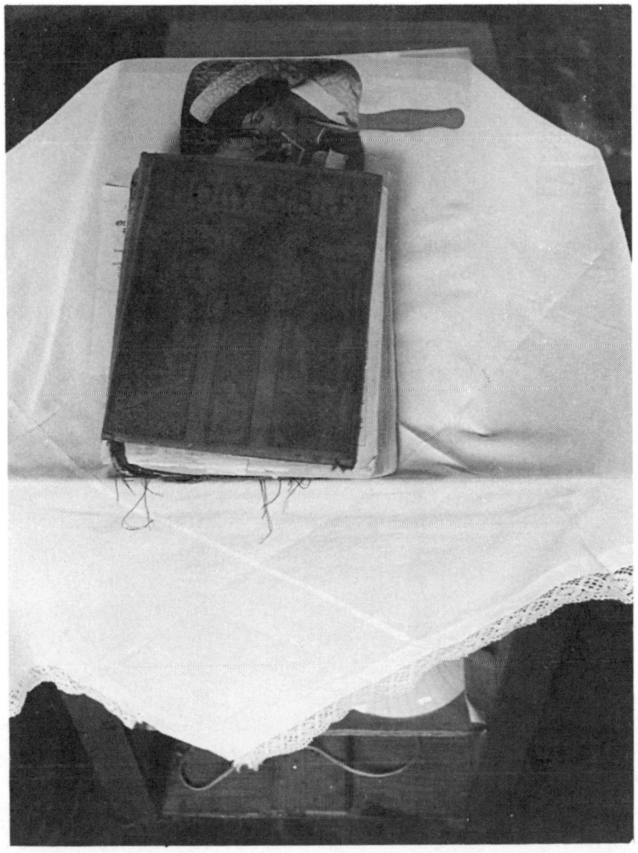

Pulpit of Rose Hill Baptist Church, Vicksburg, Miss., 1974

with respect to personal faith has been narrow. Roman Catholicism has been limited. Such classical Protestant churches as the Episcopal and Lutheran have been viewed as suited to certain classes, families, and tastes, in the former case, and to people of German stock in the latter. Other denominations such as Moravians and the Brethren have been seen as "ethnic." It is only a partial exaggeration to classify the remaining Protestant options as variations on a theme. From Presbyterian to Pentecostal, from Campbellite to Holiness, in black churches and white, there is an insistent preoccupation with the "four common convictions"—the Bible as authority, direct access to the Holy Spirit, traditional morality, and informal worship.

Notable differences in style, teaching, and emphasis differentiate the Presbyterian churches from the Assemblies of God, the Southern Baptists from the United Methodists, the Disciples of Christ from their historic kin in the Churches of Christ, black Methodists from white Methodists, the southern Congregationalists from the independent Baptist congregations. But, all things considered, the impact of a single coherent way of understanding Christianity is extensive and tenacious in the South.

Protestantism can be classified into four major families—liturgical, classical (or Reformation), evangelical, and radical. The evangelical predominates in the South. Even Presbyterianism, which falls within the classical category, takes on features of evangelicalism. Radical Protestantism—Mennonite, Amish, Quaker—has left its stamp on regional forms but has not been prominent in its own right. Its commitment to pacifism has had very little acceptance in the South. At the same time convictions about the possibility and necessity of biblical primitivism have contributed to the popularity of restorationist thought. Prominent among Churches of Christ and Landmark Baptists (some of them members of Southern Baptist churches) especially, restorationism seeks to duplicate church life exactly as it was in New Testament times.

Other families of Protestantism do exist in the South. The Presbyterian presence represents the classical Protestant heritage, even though evangelical influence has modified it somewhat. Radical Protestantism's absence must surprise those who expect to find all kinds of conservativism in the South. A few Mennonite congregations can be found here and there, but even fewer Amish, and no Hutterite. The Episcopal church represents the liturgical family throughout the region. The Lutheran tradition, partly liturgical by classification, is present in selected small areas, sometimes in strength. Episcopalianism's influence has always exceeded its size. It has served as home for certain kinds of regional traditionalists and as an alternative for people dissatisfied with evangelicalism.

Nevertheless, the dominance of the evangelical family is striking. The hold of the four common convictions concerning Bible, Spirit, morality, and worship dramatizes this point. Examples of its effects are finding fault with the Episcopal church because it practices formal worship and with the Presbyterian church because of its understated adherence to the direct access of each Christian to the power of the Holy Spirit.

Black Christianity. The faith of black Christians in the South is both very similar to that of white Christians and quite distinctive from it. Nearly all of what has been discussed about "southern religion" applies to both racial groups in the region. Recent research has shown how co-implicated white religion and black religion were in the antebellum period. At one level, the same denominational traditions, the Methodist and the Baptist especially, but also the Presbyterian, the Episcopalian, and the Roman Catholic, served both groups. The evangelical approach was particularly effective in its appeal to blacks. When white Christians sought to evangelize black people (most of whom were slaves), blacks responded in great numbers and with enthusiasm. The extent of that responsiveness reinforced the white commitment to evangelicalism because (1) it attracted a black following, and (2) in church services where whites and blacks worshiped together the black presence contributed to the music, the theology, and the overall vibrancy of the gathering. Aware of the evangelical faith's power in the daily lives of blacks and in their separate religious services, white Christians had strong incentives to promote it. Also, their own views of evangelicalism were enriched, and somewhat modified, by the participation of blacks in it. The significant differences between the

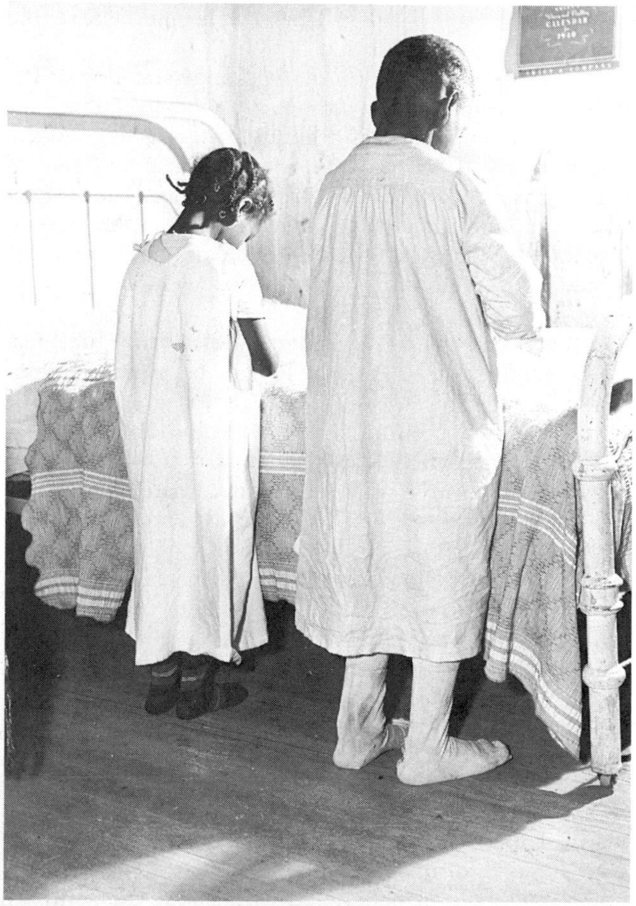

Children saying their prayers, Greene County, Ga., 1941

forms of evangelicalism among the two races came to the fore once blacks had formed independent congregations and denominations in the months and years following the end of the Civil War.

Rituals. In notable ways, the role of the two central rituals of historic Christianity, baptism and the Lord's Supper, reveal the South as a distinctive religious setting. These sacraments, or "ordinances," hold a significant place in regional life and are viewed differently by southerners than by other Christians in the world. For example, baptism outranks Communion in importance. Communion often has a limited importance and place. It is observed just as is baptism. Nevertheless, on a value scale honored by millions of southern Protestants, especially those most vocal about their positions, baptism has primacy.

During most of the colonial period white southerners were practicing Anglicans, nominal Anglicans, or nothing. Few slaves embraced Christianity in any form before the 1790s. An outburst of enthusiastic faith, evangelical in theology and revivalistic in method, altered the denominational profile. The movement developed from Presbyterian beginnings in the 1740s into a "great" awakening in Baptist hands during the 1750s. Soon thereafter Methodist-leaning Anglicans took up the same cause, with the result that there were "Methodists" before the Methodist church was officially organized in 1784.

The southern evangelicals acted on conviction that faith is a relationship one claims in a very personal way. The individual is not born into it, educated into it, or even gradually nurtured into it. Instead, one experiences God's presence and saving power directly, intimately. Thus each life is divided into two periods, life before and after a person receives the gift of salvation. The transition becomes central. Entry into this new condition is life's greatest need and most decisive event.

Baptism understood as a rite of initiation is thus essential. Passage from nominal to genuine practice, from being lost to being saved, from knowing intellectually to experiencing with the heart, becomes a pivotal event. It does not follow, however, that all denominations using revivalism as the technique for introducing people to personal faith have practiced "believer's baptism." Evangelical Presbyterians and Methodists juxtaposed their views of the "new birth" with several other Christian teachings—the family as a covenantal unit, the doctrine of election, and an organic connection between entry and what followed it in a person's spiritual growth. The revivalistic Baptists were more single-minded. Even so, entry, passage, the division of life into a before and an after, came to the fore as a fundamental feature in the southern religious tradition. It was soon to hold an even more prominent position.

The Great Revival on the Kentucky-Tennessee frontier between 1799 and 1805 reinforced and enlarged the role of *entry* into the Christian life. That event assumed primacy and acquired a ritualistic character. One could know, indeed must know, when the passage from death to life occurred. So signal an event ought to be symbolized by an outward sign. These Bible-devout Christians did not have to look far to find one. Indeed, as they read their Bibles, the Lord had intended all along that only people making this transition were subjects for baptism—as the Baptist people had insisted from their English origins about 1610. And as they reproduced the pattern as it existed in the time of Christ, they followed the idea to its logical conclusion, namely, to perform the rite by submerging the new Christian in water, baptism by immersion. Of the three earliest denominations to be both evangelical and revivalistic, only the Baptists insisted upon the straight logic of the position. To their minds, only those personally assured of regeneration in a conscious, willful experience should be baptized; also, proper baptism was by immersion. Presbyterians and Methodists set conversion in a wider context, understanding several doctrines dialectically rather than hierarchically, and seeing entry as having organic continuity with what went before in a person's life and with what was to follow.

Soon the restorationist movement began to develop and take hold. These "Christians" or "Disciples of Christ," those of the Campbellite tradition, were identifiably on the scene by 1830. For them, too, entry into the Christian life was of critical significance. They sought the restoration of New Testament practices in every detail and as a test of faith. Proceeding from somewhat different perspectives, Baptists and "Christians" both seized upon the "rite of initiation" as the distinguishing doctrine in biblical Christianity. The act of entering the saving relationship with Christ and the state of being a Christian claimed first place. Baptism, the badge of entry, thus acquired a dominating significance in the region. It is no wonder that so many denominational squabbles have occurred over the mode of baptism.

Nowhere else is baptism elevated to such eminence—and Communion so deemphasized. Popular southern religion's treatment of the two classic Protestant sacraments adds up to a basic regional distinctiveness, highlighting a unique history. In viewing the place of baptism and the Lord's Supper, one sees the genuine continuity in religious patterns dating from the period 1800–1850. (By contrast, the "North" began to be metamorphosed socially, culturally, and religiously in the 1830s.) Understanding this singular arrangement underscores that the South was cut off from the historical career of the church, Protestant and Catholic, in favor of either a simple repetition of traditional patterns or a deliberately restorationist program.

That the sacraments, their nature and their place, can tell so much about the social history of a region is astonishing. Conventional wisdom would raise doubts that anything so "sacred" could make such a "secular" impact. But their impact has been great. Yet one must take pains not to stretch the truth. For many southern Protestants, Episcopalians and Presbyterians among the larger denominations and Congregationalists and Moravians among the smaller, baptism is not so dominant. Moreover, it is administered to infants by "sprinkling." In addition, Methodists stand as a special case. Some evangelical-revivalistic blood courses through Methodist veins. But the fact of entry, the moment of entry, and the mode of entry do not define Methodist sensibility and practice. That is due to the breadth of its teachings and concerns as well as to the strength of the worship component in its heritage. Within that denomination Communion is granted a large place vis-à-vis baptism.

Communion, the Holy Communion, the Eucharist, or the Lord's Supper—all terms used to refer to taking the bread and the fruit of the vine in celebration of Christ's suffering—is the foremost rite within traditional Christianity. Historically, it has been considered the central act in worship by most branches of the church. In turn, worship has been considered the fundamental act of the church. Thus, worship defines Christian living and Communion is the primary expression of worship.

In the popular religion of southern whites, worship ranks below evangelism and concern with moral uprightness. Converting lost souls, which entails training lay people to engage in that ministry, is the first priority. Not far behind is instruction in and practice of Christian ethical standards. The act of worshiping God, prizing patience and mystery as it does, comes after. In fact, much of the focus in "church services" is on converting the lost, urging members to become involved in soul-winning, and denouncing unrighteous living. Worship as an end in itself, as itself the "work of the people of God," is much less important.

It is not surprising that among Baptists, Pentecostals, Holiness people, and other highly evangelistic groups the Lord's Supper is observed because it is considered a commandment to be obeyed, but is usually observed quarterly and is seen as a departure from the congregation's ordinary rhythm. Whereas exhortation is fast-paced and bent on results, Communion is deliberate and done for its own sake. It simply follows a different cadence. Moreover, a ritual (such as the Lord's Supper) takes some time, makes no person or group of people the primary object (the minister's role being rather minor and passive), and cannot be used to other purposes than its own. It is not the occasion for exhorting or for the preacher to pursue a direction of his own choosing. The service of the Lord's Supper controls; it cannot be controlled. Therefore, following a prescribed course, as it must, it is inevitably liturgical. The cadence is radically different from "preaching service" in which everything moves with vigor and rises to crescendo in the sermon.

The instrumental nature of many white church services and their preference for evangelism over worship offers an interesting comparison with church services of black evangelicals in the South. There is nothing instrumental about black services. The "preaching service," "worship," "going to church" are ends in themselves for the South's black Christians. The gathering is a joyous one, a vital event in the course of the week. Singing is spirited, much of the music coming from the black Christian experience. The congregation actively participates in singing, responds to prayers and the sermon with vocal expressions, contributes its offering to plates that may be passed more than once, and accepts assignments in the choir or in the usher force. The preacher proclaims God's word for the comfort, challenge, and reassurance of the people. The congregation joins their utterances with his in a rhythmic call-and-response. A sermon that does not elicit their vocal participation is regarded as a failure. For the preacher's part, a congregation that does not give back its encouragement and testimony is indifferent.

Thus, what happens in a black church—whatever the denomination—on Sunday or during a revival meeting is the central activity of the church. The service does not focus exclusively on individuals in need of conversion (although they may be led to make that decision). It is an act of worship by all the people present. They praise God for daily blessings and for the forgiveness of sins. They pray to God for strength and courage, for healing, and for the power of the Holy Spirit. The other activities of the congregation, support for mission causes or colleges or appeals for help for those in need, may be mentioned but they are incidental to the singing, praying, testifying, and preaching that are the reasons for the service.

Communion rates well below baptism in the evangelical-revivalistic religion that pervades the American South. Preoccupation with introducing people to faith and the church has proven to be a legacy with staying power. A worship-related, self-contained action, which Communion is, will always have a place but does not quite fit. Nowhere else in Christendom, to repeat, does the ceremony around Christ's final meal with his disciples occupy such a small place. The rhythm is simply different from that of evangelism. What a momentous season it was when southern churches ceased alternating worship services and evangelistic services and turned nearly all into the latter.

The two ordinances are correlated in another way: the affinity between the deemphasis on Communion and the insistence that only conscious, decision-making candidates are suited to baptism. Clearly the stress in this understanding of religion falls on each person's part in the process, on everyone being an active agent. Terms such as the following are in common usage—decide, follow, commit, yield, surrender, give, sacrifice. That is the lexicon of evangelism and believer's baptism (under the conditions of revivalism). It is not the language of Communion. In the Lord's Supper one acknowledges that everything is done for him or her, affirming that grace is raw grace. The rite (and maybe even the elements themselves) suffuses the communicant. Something laden with mystery confronts the dynamic of each person's existence. Its impact cannot be measured. It is not likely to generate immediate activity. Instead its essence is more liquid. Receiving renders one quiet, submissive, reflective, consoled, nourished. A people conditioned to operate in the active voice does not readily shift into that sort of disposition. There is far more affinity between the raw grace of infant baptism and the receptive posture of Communion. (A simple glance at their historical symbiosis would seem to confirm such an interpretation.)

Religion and the Senses. What senses (or faculties) are most prominent in the evangelical-revivalistic nature of southern religion? What are the roles of seeing and tasting, for example? Viewed from a different perspective, what kinds of sense-based achievements emanate from religion of this kind? Standing in the Protestant and

Puritan traditions, popular southern religion maximizes hearing and speaking. The term *Word of God* referring to the Bible is not taken metaphorically. Words are sacred, an utterly reliable guide to reality. Thus, speaking and hearing enable one to participate in reality in the most effective way. Tasting and smelling are simply not considered as potential means of divine revelation. Rites involving bread and wine (regularly grape juice) are deemphasized. The visual sense likewise is not highly cultivated because it too is not regarded as a potential link between the divine and the creation. Art and architecture accordingly do not flow from religious sensibilities. Southern religion rarely generates art, whether paintings or sculpture. One exception is baptistery wall depictions of the River Jordan. Architecture is mostly functional although some surprisingly good forms, classic and modern, sometimes appear in Baptist, Assemblies of God, Seventh-Day Adventist, and other settings.

Speaking and hearing, then, are the senses brought alive by southern religion. It has been remarked that Protestants hear entirely too much, more than they can possibly put into practice. Be that as it may, the Word, words, sermons, exhortations, testimonies, soul-winning conversations, and the like are endemic to this religious style. Relating to the Almighty through seeing, tasting, and smelling—whatever might be the specific forms of such responses—is foreign to this sensibility.

References to the oral and auditory senses suggest music. Singing has a vital place in southern Christianity. The expression of faith through this medium, especially as joy for sin's forgiveness and God's daily blessings, is a regular, natural, and indispensable part of church services, revival meetings, church socials, youth gatherings, and even Sunday school assemblies. Music has to do with the ear and the voice; that makes it a neat fit in the setting of a voice/ear religion.

In a large number of Baptist churches, the music is of diverse sorts, ranging from classical hymnody to gospel songs to choruses and spirituals. In the rest of the denominations that make up popular regional religion, classical hymnody generally disappears. Musical forms include everything from quieter, semiformal gospel songs (or popular-style hymns such as "How Great Thou Art") to simpler choruses. With church services more inclined to the revivalistic and less to worship, musical tastes are predictable. Thus, "living it up," "let's really sing, all together now," and "pulling out all the stops" are representative expressions used by the person leading the singing to arouse the congregation to robust participation.

A glance inside the auditorium—a term far more apt than "sanctuary" when listening is primary and conduct is informal—is revealing. The choir is seated behind and above the rostrum on which the pulpit stands. Its members are facing the congregation and are in the direct vision of most or all of them. The minister of music or song leader typically directs the choir in its special numbers, having turned around from facing the congregation when leading them in the singing of the hymns. In most popular churches of any size, each song is called out by name and number by the "song leader" who directs from the rostrum.

This positioning and these actions afford clues to the understanding of worship prevalent in the popular southern religious tradition. It is not altar-centered. Everything centers on the stand where the Holy Bible rests and from behind which the preacher declares its message. Additionally, in the visual line of the pulpit people seated in the congregation may see the choir and the music director. That central area in the front of the "auditorium" is the focus of attention, by theological intention. The reason for the Word, the words, the congregational and choral music, and the entire event of gathering is the improved spiritual condition of the people in the congregation. They do not move to the special area raised in the front of the building, rather the message of truth and inspiration is projected to them from there.

When this conception of the theological architecture is put into practice, the preacher becomes an exhorter or a persuader, whose aim is to convince members of the error of their ways, to point them to the path of spiritual treasures, such as conversion, power for living, perhaps the gift of tongues, or to rally their support for causes, typically evangelistic in purpose. This approach generates direct response. It takes shape as personal accountability to the Lord—for the salvation of your own soul or as the mandate of dedicated service at His bidding. Closely related is the call to personal responsibility, to follow his commandments concerning your own righteousness and what He wills you to do for others. With the individuals present pressured to respond in active ways, set liturgical forms could hardly be expected to have wide usage in church services. Subtlety and belief that religious growth occurs best at a gradual rate are not features of this approach. Instead, the pace is energetic, the mood urgent, and the manner of approach straightforward.

Seriousness of Southern Religion. The mode of much popular southern religion is rooted in the view that religious issues are enormously significant. The God who has given everything requires a total commitment in return. To fail to heed his commandments, to spurn the pardon he offers to lost humankind is grievous indeed. Behavior in that vein makes no sense; moreover, it entails the direst consequences. A religious animation of this kind instills a keen attitude of guilt, the knowledge that one has defied, disobeyed, and rejected an all-loving and all-requiring God.

Millions of the southern religious are open, even vulnerable, to the message, delivered so forthrightly, that they have fallen short and must conform their lives to God's will. On the positive side, they respond to the appeal of loyalties and causes. They really hear urgings to support their church and its projects. Accordingly, an impressive percentage are involved in the organizational life of the congregation, often attending three or more activities per week. Their generosity with money matches their dedication of time. Many tithe 10 percent of the family's gross income. Concern for the work of the church, evangelistic and mission programs, and charitable institutions runs deep and stimulates much giving.

Some scholars have argued that guilt is a natural by-

Religious sign on roadside, north of Carthage, Miss., 1985

product of the white southerner's treatment of black people. The convincing demonstration of that interpretation is fraught with problems. Guilt is surely much appealed to in southern religious life, and the fundamental injustice of slavery and segregation is equally evident. How they correlate, however, remains a matter of interpretation.

One is struck by the strength revivalistic evangelicalism attained during the period of slavery's tightest hold and of that ideology's rapid growth during the Jim Crow era, when segregation reached its zenith. It would take a thoroughly cynical interpretation to attribute southern religiosity *solely* to guilt. Guilt can be a constructive and appropriate reaction to a religious understanding that divine love should bear the fruits of grateful obedience. Evidence abounds that many of the southern faithful have historically drunk from a wellspring of joy and gratitude for deliverance, not one of terror accompanying visions of an eternal hell.

Black religious attitudes concerning guilt have been somewhat different from white attitudes. Through the age of slavery, the experience of dramatic conversion rooted in the acknowledgment of each sinner's guilt was as much a part of black faith as of white. But the roles of guilt and responsibility shifted somewhat, once southern black Christians had their own churches. Everything came to be seen in communal terms including personal salvation and ethics. Being a part of the worshiping congregation and seeing to the needs of others in the (segregated) black community diffused and redirected the previously more individualistic orientation. Guilt, pardon, and gratitude continue to be elements in black religious practice, but the evangelism-based program of many white churches has been significantly recast.

Church life of the sort that is informal, direct, urgent, and evangelistic remains standard for southern whites. Almost everywhere else in America such an approach to Christianity is viewed by the majority as somewhat strange, a form of faith for extremists. Southern products of this kind of religion may be referred to indiscriminately as "born again" Christians. That ascription, rarely understood in most communities, is what a great many southerners think all Christians, if serious, are. What is mainline in the South is peripheral elsewhere.

To repeat, four common convictions distinguish serious religion in the eyes of the rank-and-file southern religious: (1) the Bible as the sole reference point; (2) direct and intimate access to the Lord; (3) Christian morality defined in the terms of individualistic and personal ethics; (4) informal, spontaneous patterns for worship. The Baptist-like approach scores high on all four tests and is the most popular form of southern religious life. Catholicism, to take the opposite example, fails all four instances and is hence judged deviant. The American South perpetuates a distinctive type of religion. Although different from forms of Christianity found elsewhere only in degree, the degree is decisive. The *standard* form in the South is normative for *all* forms, and the linkage between faith and the regional culture is intimate.

The effects of social change may be seen throughout contemporary southern society. A great many disruptions of the regional culture have occurred in the past 25 years. Urbanization is one major factor making for change; the in-migration of many thousands another. The appearance of new prosperity and the South's significant role in the national economy reflect a dramatic alteration. Racial desegregation of the society is also very important. A secularization of life and thought has accompanied these changes. Many people experience a new freedom to admit that their outlook on life is secular, and far less now distinguishes the South from the rest of the country.

At the same time, fundamentalism grows. The electronic church bases some of its leading programs in the South. The marriage of conservative politics and conservative religion is in evidence and affects elections. The development of evangelicalism in old and modified forms spells a tightening of the four common convictions. Liberal instincts and concerns, and mainline denominations, have been somewhat eclipsed—for how long no one knows.

See also BLACK LIFE: Preacher, Black; Religion, Black; / Jackson, Jesse; King, Martin Luther, Jr.; Mason, Charles Harrison; Southern Christian Leadership Conference; EDUCATION: Religion and Education; / Baylor University; Bob Jones University; Christian Academies; University of the South; FOLKLIFE: Funerals; Voodoo; GEOGRAPHY: Religious Regions; LAW: Religion and Law; MUSIC: Gospel Music, Black; Gospel Music, White; / All-Day Singings; Brumley, Albert; Dixie Hummingbirds; Dorsey, Thomas; Fisk Jubilee Singers; Jackson, Mahalia; Revival Songs; Shape-Note Singing Schools; Vaughan, James; MYTHIC SOUTH: Religion and Mythology; SCIENCE AND MEDICINE: Science and Religion; SOCIAL CLASS: Religion and Social Class; WOMEN'S LIFE: Religion and Women

Samuel S. Hill
University of Florida

David T. Bailey, *Shadow on the Church: Southwestern Evangelical Religion and the Issue of Slavery, 1783–1860* (1985); Kenneth K. Bailey, *Southern White Protestantism in the Twentieth Century* (1964); Tod A. Baker, Robert P. Steed, and Laurence W. Moreland, eds., *Religion and Politics in the South: Mass and Elite Perspectives* (1983); John B. Boles, *The Great Revival, 1787–1805: The Origins of the Southern Evangelical Mind* (1972), *Maryland Historical Magazine* (December 1982); Dickson D. Bruce, Jr., *And They All Sang Hallelujah: Plain-Folk Camp-Meeting Religion, 1800–1845* (1974); Will Campbell, *Brother to a Dragonfly* (1977); John R. Earle, Dean D. Knudsen, and Donald W. Shriver, Jr., *Spindles and Spires* (1975); Jean E. Friedman, *The Enclosed Garden: Women and Community in the Evangelical South, 1830–1900* (1985); David Harrell, *All Things Are Possible: The Healing and Charismatic Revivals in Modern America* (1976), ed., *Varieties of Southern Evangelicalism* (1981); Samuel S. Hill, ed., *Encyclopedia of Religion in the South* (1984), *The South and the North in American Religion* (1980), *Southern Churches in Crisis* (1967); E. Brooks Holifield, *The Gentlemen Theologians: American Theology in Southern Culture, 1795–1860* (1978); C. Eric Lincoln, ed., *The Black Experience in Religion: A Book of Readings* (1974); Anne C. Loveland, *Southern Evangelicals and the Social Order, 1800–1860* (1980); Donald Mathews, *Religion in the Old South* (1977); Robert Moats Miller, *Southern Humanities Review* (Summer 1967); Laurence W. Moreland, Tod A. Baker, and Robert P. Steed, eds., *Contemporary Southern Political Attitudes and Behavior: Studies and Essays* (1982); Albert J. Raboteau, *Slave Religion: The "Invisible Institution" in the Antebellum South* (1978); Charles Reagan Wilson, *Baptized in Blood: The Religion of the Lost Cause, 1865–1920* (1980), ed., *Religion in the South* (1985); Norman Yance, *Religion Southern Style: Southern Baptists and Society in Historical Perspective* (1978).

Appalachian Religion

Using many of the ingredients that historically were part of mainstream Protestant Christianity in the United States, Appalachians imprinted on them a regional particularity. In the Virginias and Carolinas, in eastern Kentucky and Tennessee, in northeastern Alabama, northern Georgia, and western Maryland, the mountains provided a discrete and, for much of American history, isolated landscape in which distinctive religious expression could grow. The earliest contributions to this Appalachian regional religion were made by American Indians, notably the Cherokee, and probably survive in a continuing native tradition of herbal healing (although this was no doubt also influenced by European folk traditions and the "root work" of black conjure). Beginning in the 18th century, however, English, Scotch-Irish, and German immigrants brought left-wing dissenting Protestantism. The English came from Nonconformist (Puritan) roots, and the Scotch-Irish, similarly, were Presbyterians. The Germans included Reformed, Lutheran, and Moravian church members as well as radical sectarians such as Dunkers and Mennonites. By 1850 the regional religion of Appalachia could be clearly discerned; and in its majority expression it became the province of the poor.

Built on prevailing cultural attitudes of Appalachians toward nature, a God beyond nature, and one another, this regional religion was grounded in paradox. There were love and preference for the natural world and, at the same time, awe at the inscrutable and largely Calvinist (and unnatural) God who controlled life. There were strong ties of natural kinship and yet a supernaturally oriented suspicion of the evils that lurked in the human heart. Cast against this background, Presbyterian churches thrived early in the mountains, but with the 19th-century Great Revival and subsequent history, Baptists flourished. Meanwhile, a split from Presbyterian ranks produced the Cumberland Presbytery, which, with the Baptists, preached a modified Calvinism. Methodists, with their efficient network of circuit riders and class system, weakened Calvinism further. The Christian Church (Disciples of Christ) emerged with a doctrine of free grace and an intent to restore the New Testament church, and after 1870 Holiness and then Pentecostalism came. Fundamentalism grew strong (really only a reinforcement of traditional preference for the literal word of God in the Bible), and nondenominational churches made their appearance.

In recent times the traditional churches have continued as a distinctive part of Appalachian culture. Yet in keeping with the history of Appalachian religion, vast portions (probably over half) of the population are unchurched. Thus, understanding the religiousness of this intensely religious people requires more than examining the beliefs and practices of the churches. Even today it is unusual to find a house in the mountains without its Bible—a Bible perhaps not read regularly but quoted often and also at times, in a divinatory way, opened randomly to supply inspired counsel. Folk healers still use specific biblical verses in their cures; and, along with the "root work" of herbal healing, there are shamanistic techniques that perhaps echo the laying on of hands in Holiness churches, and yet independent of it, effect cures for burns, traumatic bleeding, or the perennial children's "thrash." With their enduring nature religion, some Appalachians continue to plant their crops by the signs of the zodiac and rely on other signs for direction in everyday life. Often dismissed as collections of folk sayings or superstitions, these affirmed correspondences (cradle signs, body signs, weather signs, to name some) possess strong implicit religious coherence. All are grounded on a natural occultism that sees the (anciently celebrated) tie between microcosm and macrocosm as contemporary reality.

Meanwhile, the traditional churches, even with their differences, express a more or less identifiable Appalachian religion. At its creedal base is a doctrine of human estrangement from God through sin. Questions of predestination and free will occupy a central place and, although they are answered variously by different churches, constitute a major religious problem. In this Bible Belt territory of the South, the Bible holds the key to its resolution, but the Bible (mostly the King James version) must be unfolded both in everyday and ritual contexts.

The personal moral code formed by a religion of revival and epitomized in the Holiness churches influences the daily lives of the Appalachians. Swearing and Sabbath-breaking, drinking and gambling, cardplaying, dancing, and sexual license—all receive a stern religious rebuke, although with another bow to nature, a practical permissiveness coexists, so that illegitimate children and acts of violence, often in a family context, are accepted realities. With the individualism of mountain character, a social ethic has not been central to Appalachian moral style.

In ritual expression, again shaped by a religion of revival, the felt gap of sin and alienation is overcome in the dramatic experience of conversion. Typically involving a public liturgy of "walking the aisle" in response to an altar call, conversion draws people to the churches. The old style of rhythmic inspired preaching can be found in many of these Appalachian churches today, frequently in one-room buildings in mountain hollows or along country roads. Here men and women sit separately, while in the front, from the amen corner, old Psalms and hymns or new gospel songs are lined out. In Old Regular Baptist congregations, the inherited Anglo-Saxon singing style with its modal scales is employed, but the distinctive southern shape note singing thrives among other groups. Traditional decoration services (honoring the graves of the dead) and funeral preachings (commemorations of death and burial often long after the event) persist. Protracted meetings of annual revival are common. Meanwhile, sacred ordinances—baptism by triple immersion, foot washing, communion (with grape juice or wine and crackers usually)—are typically observed, and, in a few churches, fire and snake handling are practiced. With the awareness of nature that informs the Appalachian religious style, these ordinances take on a sacramental quality in mountain liturgies: they acquire an intensity that is felt as the power of God in people's lives. That some churches experience this power through glossolalia (speaking in tongues) and faith healing provides still further continuity for the theme.

While the Baptist-Methodist establishment dominates this distinctive Appalachian Protestantism, its establishment remains plural and fragmented. Major denominations such as the Southern Baptists and the United Methodists have made inroads, especially in the towns, and the trend for present-day Appalachian religion is to become less distinguishable from Protestantism elsewhere in the United States. Moreover, Roman Catholics now rank after Baptists, Methodists, and Presbyterians among mountain churches. A requiem, nonetheless, would be premature: Appalachian "old-time religion" has proved a tough and enduring expression of tradition in the midst of the modern world.

See also FOLKLIFE: Folk Medicine

Catherine L. Albanese
Wright State University

John C. Campbell, *The Southern Highlander and His Homeland* (1921); Eleanor Dickinson and Barbara Benziger, *Revival!* (1974); Paul F. Gillespie, ed., *Foxfire 7* (1982); Elizabeth R. Hooker, *Religion in the Highlands: Native Churches and Missionary Enterprises in the Southern Appalachian Area* (1933); Emma Bell Miles, *The Spirit of the Mountains* (1905); John D. Photiadis, ed., *Religion in Appalachia: Theological, Social, and Psychological Dimensions and Correlates* (1978); Eliot Wigginton, ed., *The Foxfire Book* (1972).

Architecture, Church

The earliest southern churches, Roman Catholic missions, dotted the East Coast from Florida to Virginia beginning in the 16th century. Although none of these is extant, Roman Catholic missions and chapels built in the 18th century in Texas survive in such places as San Antonio, El Paso, and Goliad. These buildings reflect the then-current styles of Spain, including the elaborate stone carving at San Jose mission, San Antonio, and the Moorish details at St. Francis Espada in San Antonio. The Roman Catholic parish churches of Louisiana, on the other hand, reflect 18th- and 19th-century French classical styles.

The earliest Anglican churches of Virginia reflect a nostalgia for English Gothic (Jamestown, 1627; St. Luke's, Smithfield, 1681). By the end of the 17th century widespread experimentation in building for Anglican worship became evident and continued in the next century. A number of existing buildings scattered throughout the Tidewater region of Virginia and Maryland testify to a willingness to seek new forms and arrangements for Anglican worship. The Anglican churches of South Carolina reflected English sophistication in the Charleston churches of St. Michael's and St. Philip's, but in the backcountry a variety of influences prevailed, including the traditions of the West Indies and Huguenot builders. St. James, Goose Creek (1711), is a marvelous Baroque building arranged around a central pulpit and altar-table.

The 18th century saw the arrival of other groups whose buildings, whether Presbyterian, Methodist, or Baptist, took exterior forms that were rather domestic in appearance. These usually had balconies on three sides and a dominant pulpit raised high on the fourth. Occasionally Congregationalists built distinctive structures as at Midway, Ga., and Lutherans as at Jerusalem, Ga. After the Revolution, new buildings were oriented so that a short side faced the road; a tower, and occasionally a portico, were sometimes added. High pulpits and horseshoe-shaped balconies continued to characterize the interiors throughout most of the 19th century.

Like the rest of the nation, the South was overrun by stylistic revivals in the 19th century. Greek Revival buildings appeared in the 1830s and continued to be popular in neoclassical forms among Methodists and Baptists up through the 1920s. The Gothic Revival appeared a decade later and found expression in such early examples as the Chapel of the Cross, Chapel Hill, N.C. This style flourished off and on until World War II, reaching its apex in the Duke Chapel at Duke University. There were two Gothic revivals—a rather primitive one in the 1840s and a more academic one in the early 20th century. The latter found favor among Methodists and Presbyterians especially. The work of Gothicist Ralph Adams Cram is represented by Trinity United Methodist, Durham, N.C. In the late 19th century the neo-Romanesque styles pioneered by H. H. Richardson gave way in time to eclectic combinations of various styles.

An important factor in 19th-century church architecture was the widespread development of Sunday schools. These led to the addition of classrooms and meeting halls so that today many church plants tend to rival the worship space in size. The scale of buildings increased in time and, by the 20th century, worship space was frequently referred to as the "auditorium."

Changes in the worship space occurred. In many churches, choirs were introduced in the 19th century, necessitating a new liturgical space for them. Revivalism popularized a platform instead of the older tub pulpit. On the platform appeared a desk pulpit plus chairs for preacher, guest preacher, and song leader. A small table for the Lord's Supper stood lower down and, for Baptists and Disciples, a baptismal pool was often built into the wall above the pulpit and hidden by a curtain. The popular Akron Plan—which was designed by an Ohio Methodist Sunday school superintendent to allow easy movement between the congregational worship area and surrounding classrooms—fitted pulpit and choir into a corner of a square building and surrounded them on three sides by semicircular seating. Overflow seating was provided by moving partitions.

The 20th century increased the variety of options. Baptists tended to build a Greek-temple form in the early years but then favored brick Georgian Revival buildings, more reminiscent of New England than the South. Methodists and Presbyterians went through a Gothic phase in the 1920s, but since World War II have favored a whole spectrum of styles. Increasingly the altar-table receives equal emphasis with the pulpit.

Modern architecture appeared slowly in the South. Frank Lloyd Wright pioneered with the chapel at Florida Southern College, Lakeland. More recent monuments have been Paul Rudolph's chapels at Tuskegee Institute and the Bishop William R. Cannon Chapel at Emory University. The Thorncrown Chapel, designed by Fay Jones, opened in a remote area of the Ozark Mountains, near Eureka Springs, in 1981. Roman Catholics and Protestants alike have found contemporary architecture congenial, especially in Florida and such urban centers as Dallas and Houston. Lutheran churches with little connection to Old South traditions have especially embraced modern styles. Important examples of innovative contemporary architecture are St. Richard's Roman Catholic, Jackson, Miss.; First Baptist, Austin, Tex.; St. Michael's and All Angels Episcopal, Dallas; and Temple Emmanual (Jewish), Dallas.

Much of the church architecture of the South is a vernacular architecture, built without the aid of an architect. Countless roadside chapels dot hills and valleys, reflecting local building traditions more than formal architectural skill. The churches of black congregations tend to resemble the white churches in each area. The typical country church is a wooden structure, painted white, often with pointed windows and a small tower. The pulpit dominates the one-room interior, which is usually filled with pews. A cemetery surrounds the building and often there is a space in a grove of trees for homecomings and meals on the grounds. Occasional camp meeting grounds have space for outdoor sessions or provide wooden tabernacles. Such buildings have provided the setting for the South's vital folk religion for generations.

Rural Baptist church, Mississippi Delta, 1975

See also ART AND ARCHITECTURE: Gothic Revival

James F. White
University of Notre Dame

Robert C. Broderick, *Historic Churches of the United States* (1958); Charles M. Brooks, *Texas Missions: Their Romance and Architecture* (1936); Elmer T. Clark, *An Album of Methodist History* (1952); Stephen Dorsey, *Early English Churches in America, 1607–1807* (1952); Carl Julien and Daniel W. Hollis, *Look to the Rock: One Hundred Ante-bellum Presbyterian Churches in the South* (1961); Kenneth Murray, *Appalachia* (October–November 1974); James Patrick, *Winterthur Portfolio* (Summer 1980); James F. White, *Protestant Worship and Church Arthitecture: Theological and Historical Considerations* (1964).

Black Religion

See BLACK LIFE: Religion, Black

Broadcasting, Religious

Religious broadcasting is as old as broadcasting itself. The first wireless voice transmission was an informal religious broadcast. Beamed from Brant Rock, Mass., on Christmas Eve of 1906 to ships within a several-hundred-mile radius, the program content consisted of Bible readings, a violin solo of "O Holy Night," and a vocal recording of Handel's "Largo."

When the first regularly scheduled radio programming

began at station KDKA in Pittsburgh, regularly scheduled religious programs commenced within two months. Radio broadcasting exploded in the 1920s so that by early 1925 there were over 600 stations on the air. Just over 10 percent were owned by churches or religious organizations.

In every city and town in the country with a radio station there were preachers who wanted to broadcast. And many did. But as is still true today, for every mainline church that wanted to broadcast its Sunday worship services, there were a dozen evangelicals trying to get on the air. The current feud between the evangelical and fundamentalist syndicated broadcasters, on the one hand, and the liberal denominations affiliated with the National Council of Churches, on the other, also dates to the early years of broadcasting.

The first religious telecast took place on Easter Sunday, 1940. This was the beginning of two decades of growth that would see television transformed from a laboratory experiment to a consumer commodity that was available in 90 percent of American households.

Bishop Fulton Sheen, who was the first speaker on *The Catholic Hour* presented by NBC in 1930, became the first superstar of religious broadcasting. Bishop Sheen's program, *Life Is Worth Living,* which began in 1952, remains the only regularly scheduled religious program on a network with a commercial sponsor. With an impeccable delivery, a twinkle in his eye, and an angel to clean his blackboard, Sheen attracted millions of viewers.

Sheen's success in television probably was the single most important factor in persuading evangelicals that television—far more than radio—was the medium best suited to their purposes. Television could bring back the evangelistic face-to-face meeting in which a powerful and charismatic preacher could sway audiences and enlist followers.

A few evangelical-fundamentalist preachers saw "televangelism," then, as their great opportunity to spread the Gospel; but getting on television proved to be even more difficult than getting on the radio. Air time for television was a much scarcer resource than was radio air time. Mainline Protestants and Catholics cooperated with Jews and Southern Baptists in sharing the scarce resource of free network time.

For many years evangelicals and fundamentalists believed there was a conspiracy to keep them off the air. Broadcasting stations, under the Communications Act of 1934, are not common carriers and, hence, are not obliged to sell time just because someone wants to buy it. As radio stations grew prosperous, many adopted policies of refusing to sell time for religion and giving it only to ecumenical groups. Most television broadcasters followed the same policy.

But evangelists and fundamentalists were persuaded early that the airways, both radio and television, were a special gift from God that made possible the fulfillment of the great commission to spread the Gospel to every living creature. They persisted. When radio and television stations refused to deal them in on the sharing of free public service time, they offered to buy time. When refused, they offered to pay more. Gradually, station owners recognized that they were passing up a very lucrative market. Little by little, the evangelicals inched their way onto the airwaves.

The cash the evangelists use to pay for air time is raised through audience solicitations. Many styles and gimmicks have been developed to persuade viewers to contribute to radio and television broadcasts, and they work. By the early 1980s the total revenues from religious broadcasting in the United States were estimated at $1 billion.

Technological developments contributed significantly to the expansion of religious television. The first important development was the introduction of videotapes. Lower costs and speed of production made possible wide distribution of the same program for broadcast on the same day all across the country. The number of syndicated programs (those appearing on five or more stations) increased gradually during the 1960s. A big jump occurred during the first half of the 1970s when the number of syndicated programs advanced from 38 in 1970 to 66 in 1975. After leveling off for the remainder of the 1970s, program development increased sharply in the early 1980s to nearly 100 syndicated programs.

Satellite broadcasting promoted the expansion of syndicated programs in the early 1980s. Three religious networks, Christian Broadcasting, PTL, and Trinity Broadcasting, began broadcasting 24 hours, seven days a week around the turn of the decade. Initially, they carried almost exclusively religious programs. None had the capacity to produce more than a few hours of programming daily. Hence, they were in the market for programs. For a while almost anyone who could produce a videotaped program could send it to one of these new networks and be accepted for satellite broadcast. Audiences were very small, but the broadcasts provided good exposure. And once they got on the air via satellite, many evangelists decided to go the syndication route. The quality of many of these programs was not very good, but other technological innovations significantly lowered production costs and made possible the production of technically respectable programs at a cost many preachers could afford.

Audience size, as measured by Arbitron, increased from under 10 million viewers in 1970 to over 22 million by the middle of the decade. Audience size stabilized during the second half of the 1970s and did not appear to expand much during the first half of the 1980s. Religious broadcasters dispute Arbitron and Neilsen ratings, claiming that neither organization has developed adequate methods to accurately measure broadcasts received via satellite on cable channels. There is some evidence to support their position, including various Gallup polls asking people about their viewing of religious programs.

Audience size is clearly much smaller than the claims of many individual "televangelists." Jerry Falwell, for example, has claimed as many as 50 million viewers, but Arbitron and Neilsen have consistently measured the audience for his *Old-Time Gospel Hour* at well under 2 million. Still, the total audience is a sizable minority of the American population. Together with the religious recording and publishing industries, they have forged a new counterculture in America.

Like the youth counterculture of the 1960s, the religious counterculture is hardly monolithic. When Martin Luther King, Jr., led civil rights activists on a march in 1965 from Selma to Montgomery, Ala., Jerry Falwell boldly castigated clergy for involvement in political protest. "Preachers are not called to be politicians," he claimed, "but to be soul winners." By 1976 he had changed his mind, and in 1979 he founded the Moral Majority, a conservative political organization.

In 1980 religious broadcasters were divided over whether it was proper for them to engage in partisan political activity. With the encouragement of Ronald Reagan, who addressed their professional organization, the National Religious Broadcasters, each year during his first term as president, a sizable proportion of radio and television broadcasters by 1984 were on the political bandwagon.

The amount of religious broadcasting available varies by region and metropolitan area of the country. The major "televangelists" claim that they are popular in all regions of the country and that they attract the young and the old, males and females, the educated and the uneducated, the rich and the poor to view their "electronic churches." In one sense these claims are true. Their programs are broadcast on stations across the country and there are some viewers from the various age, education, income, and sex categories.

These claims notwithstanding, the "electronic church" remains uniquely a southern phenomenon. Virtually all the major "televangelists" are from the South or have migrated to the South to establish their ministries: Billy Graham (North Carolina), Oral Roberts (Oklahoma), Rex Humbard (Arkansas), Jerry Falwell (Virginia), Pat Robertson (Virginia), Jim Bakker (North Carolina), Jimmy Swaggart (Louisiana), Richard De Hann (Florida), James Robison (Texas), Kenneth Copeland (Texas), and D. James Kennedy (Florida). Robert Schuller is the only person with a successful television ministry who is neither from the South nor concerned with a southern ministry. Operating out of Orange County in southern California, he is also the only mainline Protestant to develop a successful television ministry.

The audiences of the "electronic church" are also drawn disproportionately from the South. Whereas the South has slightly less than one-third of the nation's population, the major television ministries draw in the range of 45 to 55 percent of their audiences from this region. The Midwest, with roughly a quarter of the nation's population, provides roughly that proportion of the audiences, with the eastern and western regions of the country significantly underrepresented.

These regional figures probably underestimate the extent to which religious broadcasting, especially television, is a southern regional phenomenon. Much of its appeal outside the South is to persons who have migrated from the region. Rex Humbard and Ernest Angley (a lesser light in the "electronic church") both built large congregations in Akron, Ohio, with farm migrants from the South who came to the industrial Midwest in search of blue-collar jobs.

Present migratory patterns into the Sunbelt will reinforce the southern character of the audience. Virtually all the syndicated programs have audiences of which two-thirds to three-quarters are 50 years of age or over. Audiences are also disproportionately female. The Sunbelt movement is a disproportionately older migratory flow and, as females survive males by an average of about seven years, the proportion of females in the region will increase. Only CBN, with its *700 Club* and its soap opera, *Another Life*, seems to be making a systematic effort to attract a broader audience.

Jeffrey K. Hadden
University of Virginia

Charles E. Swann
Union Theological Seminary
Richmond, Virginia

William F. Fore, *Christian Century* (18–25 July 1985); Frye Gaillard, *Race, Rock and Religion: Profiles from a Southern Journalist* (1982); Jeffrey K. Hadden and Charles E. Swann, *Prime Time Preachers: The Rising Power of Televangelism* (1981); Peter G. Horsfield, *Religious Television: The American Experience* (1984); Stephen W. Tweedie, *Journal of Popular Culture* (Spring 1978).

Calvinism

Calvinism designates that way of being Christian that has its roots in the life and work of John Calvin (1509–64), the Protestant reformer of Geneva. Its theology is both Catholic and Protestant. It is Catholic in that Calvin reaffirmed the ancient catholic faith, in particular the Apostles' Creed, the doctrine of the person of Jesus Christ as found in the Nicene Creed and the Chalcedonian Definition, and the doctrine of the Trinity. It is Protestant in that Calvin thought he was continuing the work of Luther. He built upon the affirmations of Luther's writings of 1520: the supreme authority of the Holy Spirit speaking through Scripture, justification by grace through faith, the priesthood of all believers, the sanctity of the common life, and the necessity of personal decision and responsibility. This theology influenced southern religious developments and also found expression in political attitudes, literary works, and the folklore of daily living.

Calvin's greatest work was a comprehensive statement of Christian faith, *The Institutes of the Christian Religion*, which, beginning as a small book in 1536, was continually revised until Calvin found satisfaction with the final Latin edition of 1559. He also prepared a liturgy and a church order for Geneva that was influential in Calvinist churches. He directed the completion of a Psalter in 1562. As a churchman Calvin was in constant contact with Protestant leaders throughout Europe. His letters comprised almost 11 volumes of his collected works.

Calvinism is sometimes used as a synonym for Reformed Protestantism, because Calvin was the latter's dominant personality and, in later history, its most influential figure. Yet the Reformed churches in Zurich under the leadership of Zwingli and Bullinger, in Basel with Ecolampadius, and in the Rhineland all had a part in shaping Reformed Protestantism. In general, the Reformed theology of German-speaking Switzerland and the Rhineland was less passionate and more generous and humanistic, less determined to have an independent church, than Geneva; but each type shared a common perspective in theology.

(1) Calvin's work and theology were shaped by emphases that distinguish it from other forms of Protestantism. Calvin perceived God, the creator of the universe, primarily as energy, activity, power, moral purpose, intentionality. The characteristic response to a God so conceived was not contemplation and the vision of God, but action in service of the Kingdom of God and a life that embodies the purposes of God.

Calvin's understanding of God as energy and purpose found expression in God's lordship in history, in which the sovereign God works as creator, judge, and redeemer. Hence, Calvin understood the Christian life as the embodiment of the purposes of God in history. From the beginning Calvinists were activists engaged in transforming economic, political, and cultural life according to their vision of the Kingdom of God. Calvin sought the coming into being of the holy community in Geneva. The Calvinists carried this vision of the holy community, the embodiment of the purposes of God in society, to Scotland, to Puritan England, and to Massachusetts, where they went on an "errand into the wilderness" to demonstrate the possibility of a Christian society. The Baptists and the Presbyterians embodied Calvinism's influence in the South most clearly, although in neither case so dramatically as with the New England Puritans. Calvinism has always been uneasy with a personal piety defined simply in terms of the relation of the soul to God, but that kind of piety has been the dominant religious form in the evangelical South.

Predestination, the doctrine popularly identified with Calvinism, attributed human salvation to the initiative of God. While Calvinists rejoiced in human freedom, they believed that once the human will becomes sinful it cannot by its own efforts transform itself. A self-centered person can become unself-centered only when divine grace attracts the self away from itself to God.

The Calvinists defined the chief end of life as the glory of God. Calvin, perhaps with Luther in mind, insisted that God's glory, not the salvation of one's own soul, must be the primary human concern. Later Calvinists were skeptical of revivalists who made the salvation of one's soul the center of attention. Calvinism thus represented an important counterforce to the evangelicalism dominant in the South since the early 1800s.

(2) A second characteristic of Calvinism is an emphasis upon sanctification. Luther had rediscovered the primacy of God's mercy over every form of work righteousness: salvation by human merit is beyond human power; our best deeds as well as our worst are flawed by self-interest. As a second generation Protestant, Calvin faced the criticism that this great emphasis on justification by grace undercut the Christian life. Calvin knew that justification, the fact and experience of forgiveness, is the principal hinge on which Christian life hangs, but he also knew that God's grace is power that renews as well as mercy that forgives. He conceived of the Christian life frequently in military terms as a war against the world, the flesh, and the Devil and as the obligation to obey God's command and fulfill his purposes.

(3) Calvinism has also been marked by a distinctive emphasis upon the life of the mind in the service of God and by a skepticism about feelings not subjected to rational scrutiny. Calvinists have always insisted that it is important to know what one believes and to be able to give a reason for one's faith. Catechetical instruction has been characteristic of Calvinistic churches until recent times. Southern Presbyterians and denominations that grew out of that group have especially championed this idea in the region.

(4) Closely related to the emphasis on the life of the mind was a similar emphasis on the task of the minister as teacher and preacher. The Calvinist sermon not only proclaimed the gospel, but also educated people in logical, coherent thought and discourse. Important southern colleges, such as Davidson and Rhodes, founded by Presbyterians reflect this strong belief in education.

(5) A fifth characteristic has been the importance of the organized church and the disciplined life. Order was a basic concept for Calvin. Salvation could be understood as the proper ordering of a life, an order that found primary expression in the church. Order was also a personal virtue. Calvinist asceticism and discipline were not based upon any depreciation of the world, which the Calvinists knew was God's good creation, but upon the need for an economical use of life's resources.

(6) An emphasis upon simplicity was pervasive in Calvin's writings and in the manner of his life. In literary expression he never used two words when one would do. In liturgy he protested against pomp and "theatrical trifle." In manner of life he insisted upon moderation. Calvin and the Calvinists abhorred the pompous, the pretentious, the ostentatious, the contrived, and the artificial. They insisted upon authenticity, clarity, directness, simplicity. The simple for Calvin was closely related to sincerity. It was open to reality. The ostentatious, the contrived, and the pompous covered up reality.

Calvinism was modified and transmitted to later generations through the "school" theology of the 17th century. Scholasticism was a necessary development. Calvin as a preacher did not write theology with care for definition. He left many theological issues poorly defined or unresolved. In addition, Calvinism had to face intellectual challenges from Roman Catholics, from other Protestants, and from later Calvinists whose internal debates had to be resolved. The scholastic theologians with great technical skills gave to Calvinism a clearly defined, logical, coherent form.

Protestant scholasticism also developed a common theological vocabulary, which was carefully defined and generally in the language of ordinary human discourse. This common theological vocabulary, which was influential in the South through the first half of the 20th century, made it possible for people with little formal training to become competent theologians.

Calvinism was mediated to the South largely through

the 17th-century scholastic theology. *Institutio Theologiae Elencticae* by Francis Turretin (1623–87), a Genevan theologian, was used as a textbook at such Presbyterian seminaries as Princeton, Union Theological Seminary in Richmond, Va., Columbia Theological Seminary in Columbia, S.C., and at the Southern Seminary of the Baptists in Louisville, Ky. The Westminster Confession of Faith (1643–47) was the authoritative summary of Calvinism for American Calvinists in Presbyterian, Baptist, and Congregational churches. It was also one of the most influential books of colonial America. The Shorter Catechism, a question-and-answer summary of the Westminster theology, was until World War II the basic text for the education of Presbyterian young people.

The original work of Calvin was not only modified by Protestant scholasticism, but by many other influences as it came to the South. Among these were English Puritanism, the Scottish Common Sense philosophy, and the Scotch-Irish immigrants who constituted the main body of southern Calvinists.

The most influential expressions of Calvinism in the South are to be found in the work of James Henley Thornwell (1812–62), Robert Dabney (1820–98), and Charles Hodge (1797–1878), a Princeton theologian whose influence was widely felt among southern Presbyterians.

Scholastic theology, for all of its technical excellence, was challenged from the late 17th century on by the Enlightenment and by the cultural developments of the 19th century. Yet it maintained a pervasive influence, especially in the South through the first half of the 20th century. The task of giving a statement of Calvinist faith in light of the legacy of the Enlightenment and the social, political, and scientific developments of the 19th and 20th centuries is not yet complete. The most influential 20th-century statements have been the works of the Swiss theologians Karl Barth, *Church Dogmatics* (1932–67), and Emil Brunner, *Dogmatics* (1946–60), and the American theologian Reinhold Niebuhr, *The Nature and the Destiny of Man* (1941–43). No theology now has the pervasive influence that Calvinism had in significant segments of southern society. In a pluralistic society dominated by mass media this may no longer be possible.

Calvinism's influence, however, has extended far beyond its importance as a formal theology. It was one of the fundamental forces creating a distinctive character of the people of the region. W. J. Cash saw popularized Calvinism as part of the major dichotomy of southern psychology—the South was the world's supreme paradox of hedonism in the midst of puritanism. He believed that by the mid-19th century "the whole South, including the Methodists," had moved "toward a position of thoroughgoing Calvinism in feeling if not in formal theology." Arminian free will surely also entered into the character of the region through the large Methodist influence, but the two combined in a peculiar cultural synthesis. Noting Calvinism's part in another cultural combination, James McBride Dabbs talked of "the spiritual pride of the God-selected Calvinist" combining with the pride of "the imperial Englishman" to produce the white southerner. Calvinist belief in human depravity, God's sovereignty, and an ordained universe helped to condition southern enslavement of blacks, he wrote.

Cash called southern Calvinism "puritanism," and so have others. Fred Hobson points out that "Southern 'Puritanism' was vastly different from the New England variety, less structured, less intellectual, more emotional—raw Calvinism, rather than the cerebral Puritanism of the Massachusetts Bay." This faith had a dramatic impact on the southern frontier. Calvinism early became an influence in the region through the prominence of the Scotch-Irish on the frontier. It became a particularly significant aspect of southern culture during the Civil War and its aftermath. Calvinism was one factor that led southerners to expect victory for the Confederacy. The belief in God's sovereignty and His determination of the elect led southern whites to see themselves as God's chosen engaged in holy war. As Daniel Hundley said after hearing of Confederate battle triumphs in Virginia, "When God is for us, who is against us?"

Unreconstructed southerners after the war, however, were frustrated, trying to come to terms with defeat in a holy war. They could see no explanation except for the mysterious will of God. Their popularized Calvinism led them to believe they had sinned and God was punishing them for their sins, preparing his people for a greater destiny. Not only ministers, but teachers and journalists, generals and common soldiers came to believe that God did not fail them; they had rather been unworthy. Stonewall Jackson was the war's supreme incarnation of a Calvinist warrior, but even the aristocratic Robert E. Lee, according to his biographers, had much Calvinism in his soul.

Calvinism was used in a variety of ways by a variety of people, suggesting its pervasive influence in southern culture. Presbyterian Robert Dabney used it to justify a slave society, and others have used the belief in a God-ordained social order to argue against changes in racial customs and against the rights of labor and of women. But George W. Cable, Ralph McGill, Lillian Smith, and other liberals used Calvinism to justify change; as McGill said in *The South and the Southerner*, he became a racial liberal because his "Calvinist conscience was stirred by some of the race prejudice I saw."

Calvinism also influenced the literary development of writers such as William Faulkner. He once noted that he had used religious symbols in his works because they were all around him in north Mississippi, and Calvinism was perhaps the central religious influence he explored. Faulkner disliked what he saw as a puritanical stress on sober living, the discouragement of fleshly pleasures, and a spiritual self-righteousness, all of which he saw stemming from Calvinism. He portrayed characters made authoritarian and repressively violent by a Calvinist outlook. His Calvinists, or Puritans, as he sometimes called them, show little concern for ritual or piety, but believe in God's justice and in human practicality and good works. Characters such as Lucas Beauchamp in *Go Down, Moses* and Mink Snopes in *The Town* believe, for example, less in a divine being of mercy and more in a God of justice. Faulkner did seem to admire especially one emphasis in Calvinism—as it was translated into human behavior in the South—that on the human will and the need for action. *Light in August*, *Absalom, Absalom!*, and "The Bear" in *Go Down, Moses* represent the most thorough explorations of Calvinism's influence in southern literature.

John H. Leith
Union Theological Seminary
Richmond, Virginia

Cleanth Brooks, *William Faulkner: The Yoknapatawpha Country* (1963); W. J. Cash, *The Mind of the South* (1941); James McBride Dabbs, *Who Speaks for the South?* (1964); Fred Hobson, *Tell about the South: The Southern Rage to Explain* (1983); John H. Leith, *Introduction to the Reformed Tradition: A Way of Being the Christian Community* (1977); John T. McNeill, *The History and Character of Calvinism* (1954).

Civil Rights and Religion

The relation of religion and civil rights in the South is as old as southern culture. Black religious experience, forged from oppression, differs from its white counterpart in the South. The oldest black spirituals had political and civil rights overtones imbedded in their religious message. "Wade in the water . . . ," ". . . with my face to the rising sun . . . ," "shall we gather at the river . . . ," and many others had to do with meeting, planning, and escaping. Freedom singing has been a key ingredient in the modern civil rights movement, incorporating gospel music in powerful and moving ways. For instance, the nationally known Freedom Singers were formed out of the often-jailed ranks of the Student Nonviolent Coordinating Committee (SNCC), and their songs in churches greeted protesters returning from jail.

In black churches, preachers constantly compared the plight of black people with the children of Israel. The basic issue of civil rights was seen not in the first instance as legal, sociological, economic, or political, but as moral and spiritual. The black church was the organizational building block of the civil rights movement; its leadership was predominantly clergy, ministerial students, and women of strong religious backgrounds.

Black religious leadership in civil rights in the South came mainly from the clergy and seminary students. Kelley Miller Smith, C. T. Vivian, Martin Luther King, Sr., Fred Shuttlesworth, Metz Rollins, Ralph Abernathy, and Wyatt T. Walker have been key figures. Of course, Martin Luther King, Jr., symbolized most dramatically the mobilizing strength of black religious traditions.

James Lawson was a Vanderbilt Divinity School student when he helped to organize the Nashville sit-ins in 1960 with other seminary students from American Baptist Theological Seminary such as John Lewis, Bernard Lafayette, and James Bevel, all of whom played pivotal roles in SNCC. Andrew Young, a United Church of Christ minister, became Martin Luther King, Jr.'s chief assistant in the Southern Christian Leadership Conference (SCLC), along with several other ministers such as James Orange and Jesse Jackson. Charles Sherrod, a divinity student in Virginia, became a key leader in SNCC.

Strong black women with religious backgrounds were also numerous in the civil rights struggle, and their struggle was often exacerbated by the traditional male clergy leadership. Rosa Parks sat down in the front of the bus in 1955 and started the Montgomery movement that produced Martin Luther King, Jr. Ella Jo Baker wanted to be a medical missionary, and instead became the first full-time executive secretary of the SCLC and founding mother of SNCC. Sharecropper Fannie Lou Hamer joined the civil rights movement in a Mississippi church, became a field secretary for SNCC, and ran for the U.S. Congress.

A common observation is that the civil rights movement in the South lost some of its "soul," or meaning, or heart when it became more secular and popular. Some, such as John Lewis, thought that that happened because of the influx of people from the North, black and white, who had little relationship or kinship to religious foundations or to southern experience.

The white church in the South, overwhelmingly Protestant, at its best experienced guilt and practiced restraint; at its worst, it was the ideological linchpin of racism and segregation. The white southern church has mainly been a conservative, reinforcing agent for traditional values of white southern society. There have been significant exceptions, but often those instances had to do with courageous acts or stands taken by individual white Christians allying themselves to the civil rights movement because of Christian conscience and religious values. Their positions, however, were neither practiced nor condemned by the white institutional church.

Marginal, predominantly white, southern Christian organizations have had an important part in civil rights; among them are United Church Women, the YWCA and YMCA, Councils on Human Relations, the Fellowship of Southern Churchmen, and various churchwomen's and youth groups. Such religiously based organizations, although often ostracized by the southern white church and supported by northern patrons, have served as the "call to conscience" of other southern whites, and often had they not been involved, news organizations might not have paid as much attention to civil rights events. But these marginal organizations, while strategic and courageous, also inadvertently served to help mask the deep differences between black and white religious experience.

Within white southern Christianity the courageous individuals rather than organizations, institutions, or "the beloved community" stood out in support of civil rights. Many protestors had seminary training outside the South and in the 1930s and 1940s were active in farm and labor movements. They were often defrocked, fired by their own churches, and forced to seek employment outside the region. In the 1960s they might have been supported by their national church, while ostracized by the local and regional church; many times they were physically beaten and sometimes murdered.

Southern white religious leadership in civil rights was native and grounded in southern tradition, but also it was conspicuously "against the grain," often isolated, and in danger.

The Commission on Interracial Cooperation was founded in 1919 by Methodist minister Will Alexander. Through the 1920s, 1930s, and 1940s a lineage of Christian-based activists followed, including Alva Taylor, the teacher of many southern organizers at Vanderbilt School of Religion; Don West, a Georgia minister and poet; Myles Horton, a Cumberland Presbyterian from Union Seminary and founder of the Highlander School; Presbyterian Claude Williams; Methodist ministers Ward Rogers and James Dombrowski; YMCA leader and Presbyterian Howard Kester; YWCA's Lucy Mason Randolph; also Sam Franklin, Charles Jones, Winifred Chappell, and Harry and Grace Kroger. Many of these leaders worked with the farm labor movements and were in the Fellowship of Southern Churchmen.

In the 1950s and 1960s southern white religious leadership continued out of the Fellowship of Southern Churchmen and the "Y" with Will Campbell, Nelle Morton, Helen Lewis, and others. Thelma Stevens, in the Methodist church, Hayes Mizell and Connie Curry of the American Friends Service Committee, and Jane Schutt of Church Women United are just a few of the white organizational leaders that emerged in southern civil rights struggles.

Ed King, Mississippi-born chaplain at Tougaloo College, was an important activist in the Jackson Movement and the Mississippi Freedom Democratic party in the 1960s. Bob Zellner, son of an Alabama Methodist minister, was the first white field secretary of SNCC. Jane Stembridge, a Virginian, left Union Theological Seminary to become the first office secretary of SNCC. Maurice Ouillet, a Catholic priest in Selma, Ala., was the only white person there who openly helped the civil rights movement.

Because of continuing black pressures, established religious bodies moved over time to support racial brotherhood, and some even to lend support to ministers persecuted for their stands on civil rights. Nonetheless, the vast majority of white churches in the South remained silent and apart, and many formed the institutional base for evading public school desegregation by founding private "Christian academies" and for promoting reactionary policies through the electronic church and the New Christian Right in the 1970s and 1980s.

In spite of the fundamental role that the southern black church and many southern white Christians played in the struggle for civil rights during the last 50 years, to the present day the southern black church and the southern white church stand far apart. Sunday is still the most segregated day of the week. Ministerial alliances, church boards, and agencies remain segregated, with token representation at best.

Nonetheless, black religion has not become antiwhite, acting on the belief that the liberation of the children of Israel and the teachings of Jesus are universal values. The white religion of the South in its essential Christianity knows that it has no religious basis for racism and oppression, and that the stratified southern society that it has sanctified and defended is itself making accommodations with other forces.

See also BLACK LIFE: Race Relations; Religion, Black; / Hamer, Fannie Lou; Jackson, Jesse; King, Martin Luther, Jr.; Southern Christian Leadership Conference; EDUCATION: / Christian Academies; MYTHIC SOUTH: Racial Attitudes; POLITICS: / Young, Andrew; SOCIAL CLASS: / Highlander Folk School; WOMEN'S LIFE: / Baker, Ella Jo

James Sessions
Commission on Religion in Appalachia
Knoxville, Tennessee

James H. Cone, *Black Theology and Black Power* (1969); James McBride Dabbs, *The Southern Heritage* (1958); Anthony P. Dunbar, *Against the Grain: Southern Radicals and Prophets, 1929–1959* (1981); Samuel S. Hill, ed., *On Jordan's Stormy Banks: Religion in the South: A Southern Exposure Profile* (1983), *Religion and the Solid South* (1972).

Ethnic Protestantism

Southern Protestantism arose, almost entirely, from ethnic roots. During the 18th century nearly a million immigrants entered the southern backcountry—the majority of them of Germanic or Celtic ancestry—as well as numerous Pennsylvania Quakers who formed a special English subcultural, if not ethnic, community. Highland Scots also entered the region through Wilmington and settled the upper Cape Fear Valley in North Carolina, and Salzburgers and Huguenots did so through the ports of Savannah and Charleston respectively. Non-English immigration into the backcountry profoundly shaped the culture of the entire region. In the late 18th century, Presbyterians emerged as the elite in much of the South. Religious pacifism weakened state governments during the Revolution, and Quaker antislavery proved to be a potent witness against human bondage.

Then, suddenly, during the first three decades of the 19th century, ethnic distinctiveness rooted in European heritages became absorbed into a new, dominant southern way of life. Dunkers and many Quakers, who were victims of discrimination, migrated to Indiana, and most Lutheran, Moravian, and Reformed churches and communities adopted the English language. The older coastal aristocracy, largely Episcopalian in affiliation, and newer backcountry elites, almost entirely dissenter in religious preference, tended to coalesce. The spread of evangelicalism blurred differences between denominations, even between Episcopalians and other Protestants, and the preservation of social order and communal purity took precedence over maintenance of traditional liturgy, theology, and polity—further reducing the memory of European origins and ethnic identification. Nonetheless, a handful of ethnic churches can still be found in the South. Infinitesimal in number, they reflect values absent in the dominant culture as well as the persistence of some elements of the region's historical cultural mosaic.

The earliest ethnic Protestants in the South were Huguenots in colonial South Carolina. Part of a diaspora of

French Protestants following the revocation of the Edict of Nantes (in 1685), they comprised an eighth of the white population of South Carolina in 1700. Educated, energetic, commercially skilled, and soon intermarried with the English stock elite, these French Calvinists became Anglicized after 1910. Most of the 10 Huguenot churches in the province became Anglican, and when George Whitefield delivered a controversial sermon in the "French Church" in Charleston in 1740 the Huguenot minister quietly dissociated himself from Whitefield's revivalism. Despite a fire that destroyed the largest French church in Charleston in 1796 and the looting of its successor building by Union troops in 1865, descendants of the early French settlers kept the church alive until 1950. Then, on 17 October 1982, the Huguenot Church of Charleston reopened with a membership that is half former Episcopalian, and the remainder Presbyterian, Baptist, and Methodist. The church continues to be Calvinist in theology and uses a Swiss Protestant liturgy. The minister of the reorganized church is Philip Charles Bryant, a Southern Baptist clergyman and an administrator of the Baptist College of Charleston.

The next oldest ethnic Protestant tradition in the South is that of the Moravians. Dating from the followers of John Hus and organized into the Unity of Brethren (Unitas Fratrum) by Count Nicholas von Zinzendorf in the early 18th century, Pennsylvania Moravians purchased a large tract of land in North Carolina from Lord Granville. There, between 1753 and 1766, they established the towns of Bethabara, Bethania, and Salem and practiced communal management of economic, family, and religious life. Although communalism ceased in the early 19th century and Moravians reluctantly became a Protestant denomination, the churches in North Carolina preserve a wide range of rituals and cultural observances dating to Zinzendorf's practices in Moravia—among them the arrangement of the cemetery into four separate "choirs" for men and women, married and unmarried, using identical flat white grave markers; an Easter sunrise service held in the Old Salem burial ground every year since 1772; lively traditions in Christmas cooking and decorating; and an important musical heritage of brass music and hymnology.

The Waldensians, a dissenting sect founded by the followers of Peter Waldo, a merchant of Lyon in the late 12th century, were among the last ethnic Protestants to reach the South. In 1893, 101 families from nine Alpine Italian towns settled in Burke County, N.C. Their patron in this migration was a Pittsburgh industrialist, Marvin F. Scaife, who owned land in Morganton, N.C. Though at first supported by the Congregationalist church, they chose to affiliate with the southern Presbyterian church in the United States. By the early 1920s the Valdese Presbyterian Church had abandoned several distinctive Old World Waldensian practices—leaving the offering plate at the rear door of the church, receiving communion in pairs at the altar, seating men and women on opposite sides of the church, and worshiping exclusively in French. In 1941 the use of French services ended altogether.

The Lutheran Church–Missouri Synod represented the ethnic tradition of conservative German confessionalism brought to the United States by immigrants in the mid-19th century. In contrast with Lutherans who had been in America since the colonial period and had absorbed evangelical and other Protestant patterns of worship and theology, the Missouri Synod insisted on upholding the hierarchical and legalistic formalism of 17th- and 18th-century continental Lutheranism. The relative isolation of this branch of American Lutherans enabled the Missouri Synod, in a modest way, to serve as an instrument for racial justice in the South. During the late 19th century, the synod's home mission board adopted many black Lutheran churches in the South, which had been denied admission to older Lutheran synods, and in the 20th century it established schools for blacks—Emmanuel College in Greensboro, N.C., and Selma Lutheran Academy and College in Alabama. In 1966 Professor Richard Bardolph, a Missouri Synod layman in Greensboro, drafted the denomination's statement on "Civil Disobedience and the American Constitutional Order," citing biblical and historical support for defiance of law as a tool of the civil rights movement.

The North Carolina Yearly Meeting of the Religious Society of Friends (Conservative), comprising seven Monthly Meetings in North Carolina and one in Virginia, identifies closely with 17th-century English Quakerism. These Quakers broke away from the larger body of evangelical Quakers in the South in 1904. The formal Discipline of the sect (1956) emphasizes parental diligence, harmony and unity with Monthly Meetings, worship under the Holy Spirit without resort to a professional ministry, protection of children from "pernicious books" and "corrupt conversation," pacifism, wholesome diversions and opposition to alcoholic beverages and gambling, living within one's own resources and avoiding business enterprises beyond prudent risk, and care of the poor within each Monthly Meeting.

Mennonites, who settled in Virginia in the 18th century, were pacifists in both the Revolution and the Civil War. At present, they comprise two bodies in the South, the Virginia Mennonite Conference (67 churches, mainly in Virginia and North Carolina) and the Western Conservative Mennonite Fellowship (16 in North Carolina, 6 in South Carolina, 71 in Virginia, and 11 in West Virginia). The Virginia Conference is a part of the Mennonite church and the Conservative Fellowship is an offshoot body culturally close to the Amish in practice and discipline.

The most rapidly growing ethnic Protestant group in the South today is representd by the Korean Presbyterian churches—the product of Presbyterian church (U.S.) missionary activity in Korea, an upsurge of Christianity as an indirect form of opposition to political expression since the 1950s, the migration of Korean professionals to the United States, and the existence of Korean-American families in this country. Twenty Korean Presbyterian congregations can now be found in seven southern states. Finally, there is the Chinese Presbyterian church in New Orleans. Founded in 1882 as a language school and mission for Chinese men, it was until the 1950s operated by four dedicated Presbyterian women. In 1958 Grace Yao came from Hong Kong to become director of Christian education. The service is bilingual.

See also ETHNIC LIFE articles

Robert Calhoon
University of North Carolina
at Greensboro

Peter Brock, *Pacifism in the United States: From the Colonial Era to the First World War* (1968); Jon Butler, *The Huguenots in America: A Refugee People in New World Society* (1983); *Concordia Historical Institute Quarterly* (November 1969, February 1971, Summer 1975, Summer 1977, Fall 1979); Damon Douglas Hickey, "Bearing the Cross of Plainness: Conservative Quaker Culture in North Carolina" (M. A. thesis, University of North Carolina, Greensboro, 1982); Hunter James, *The Quiet People of the Land: A Story of the North Carolina Moravians in Revolutionary Times* (1976); George B. Watts, *The Waldenses in the New World* (1941).

Folk Religion

A leading scholar of American folk religion, William M. Clements, defines it as "unofficial religion," the spiritual experience that exists separate from, but alongside, the theological and liturgical religion of the mainline established churches. Clements has identified 10 traits of the folk church: "general orientation toward the past, scriptural literalism, consciousness of Providence, emphasis on evangelism, informality, emotionalism, moral rigorism, sectarianism, egalitarianism, and relative isolation of physical facilities."

Folk religious events include Sunday school classes, Vacation Bible school meetings in the summer, Bible study gatherings, covered-dish suppers, singing services, devotional hours, and all-day services with dinner on the grounds. The church worship service is perhaps the central ritual of folk religion in the South. Worshipers may clap or wave their hands as they listen to spiritual songs like "Over in Glory Land." Some churches have a cappella services, but many include electric guitars, tambourines, and other instruments. Shouts of "Thank you, Jesus" and "Praise the Lord" are heard, as are extended public prayers, testimonials, and drawn-out invitations by the preacher to come forward. Faith healing and glossolalia sometimes occur. The preacher conveys a message of the need for conversion, controlling and directing the raw emotions of true believers. In the South's well-defined oral culture, the folk preacher is a prime performer of the word, and the religious service is a crucial folk event. Films such as Blaire Boyd's *Holy Ghost People*, which records Appalachian snake handlers; William Ferris's *Two Black Churches*, which shows Sunday morning worship services in rural southern and urban northern churches; and *Joy Unspeakable*, a videotape on southern Indiana Pentecostals, have become important modern tools for studying folk religion.

The relation between southern religion and folk culture is seen in the dynamic of conversion. Born sinful, the individual can be saved by conversion. He accepts the rule of Jesus and God, sometimes through a dramatic conversion experience after which he gives up aspects of folk culture that are regarded as profane. Thus, the hell-raising "good old boy" becomes the "good man," who is a pious member of the church. Drinking and dancing on Saturday night are replaced by temperance and dignified behavior, though in some Pentecostal churches addiction to spirits is transmuted into being possessed by the Spirit and dancing in the flesh to dancing in the Spirit. As one moves from the evangelical/fundamentalist end of the spectrum, which is most identified with folk religion in the South, to the established Southern Baptist, Methodist, and Presbyterian churches, the dramatic conversion syndrome becomes rare, virtually disappearing as one enters the more liturgical churches, such as the Episcopalian (which one southern minister described as "religion in its mildest form").

Some established southern churches, however, include survivals of folk religion. Methodists, for example, may not include in today's services the testimonials and shouts from the day of John Wesley at Aldersgate, but they continue to sing the old Wesleyan hymns as well as hymns from revivals and camp meetings.

After conversion, fundamentalist Christians may stop singing ballads or country music or blues and shift to hymns, spirituals, and gospel songs; or they may keep on doing the old music, but in secular contexts, such as the bluegrass festival, clearly separating that from the sacred song. Lines are thus drawn between folk and sacred music, even though similarity of form may be detected. Folk-

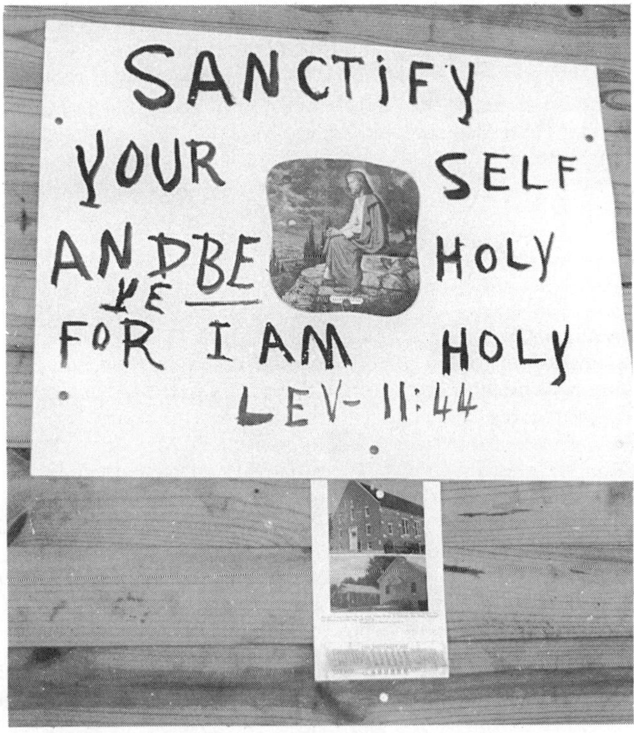

Sign inside Sanctified church, Clarksdale, Miss., 1968

tales do not normally enter the church, but tale-telling forms and the love of telling tales are apparent in southern sermons and testimonies. Religious rhetoric enters secular life through the sermon-speeches of Martin Luther King, Jr., Jesse Jackson, and others.

Folk medicine, as exemplified by the root doctor or herbalist, is rarely drawn explicitly into the church, but folk healers integrate religious symbolism into their systems. Within folk religion faith healing stands in a complementary relationship to the individual folk healers in that faith healing is performed by groups in a church, tent, or prayer band.

Hierarchy creeps into the church as it becomes more institutionalized and mainline, but the overriding emphasis of folk religion is on friendliness, togetherness, hospitality. These qualities have been coded into greeting behaviors, for example, to a greater extent in southern churches than in some of non-southern location or sponsorship. Other values that folk churches in the South share with the wider regional culture include a love of the heroic, the theatrical, the charismatic, and the vivid. Such qualities are exhibited by the most popular southern preachers as well as politicians, by southern sermons and worship services as well as in literature. Often overlooked are the compensating senses of irony and tragedy, and, for some, a Calvinistic puritanism. Behind every Elmer Gantry is a Hazel Motes; but behind them a Cotton Mather and John Bunyan.

Southern familialism finds expression especially in the rural folk churches in family reunions, homecomings, and the decoration of graves. Excepting the family, however, southern folk religion has been remarkably reluctant to identify itself with social units. On the whole, southern folk religion works through preaching and teaching directed at the individual mind, heart, and soul rather than through social or political institutions.

See also BLACK LIFE: Preacher, Black; Religion, Black; FOLKLIFE: Folk Medicine; Folktales; Voodoo; / John the Conqueror Root

James L. Peacock
University of North Carolina
at Chapel Hill

William M. Clements, "The American Folk Church: A Characterization of American Folk Religion Based on Field Research among White Protestants in a Community in the South Central United States" (Ph.D. dissertation, Indiana University, 1974), in *Handbook of American Folklore*, ed. Richard M. Dorson (1983); Robert Coles, *Psychology Today* (January 1972); William Ferris, *Keystone Folklore Quarterly* (1970); Paula H. Anderson Green, *Tennessee Folklore Society Bulletin* (September 1977); Terry G. Jordan, *Southwestern Historical Quarterly* (Spring 1976); Charles Joyner, *Down by the Riverside: A South Carolina Slave Community* (1984); Newbell Niles Puckett, *Folk Beliefs of the Southern Negro* (1926; reprint ed. 1969); Bruce A. Rosenberg, *The Art of the American Folk Preacher* (1970).

Frontier Religion

Three primary phases of southern frontier experience occurred—(1) the colonial frontier; (2) the initial trans-Appalachian frontier; and (3) the frontier created by Indian removals. In each period, the religious life of the Southwest was distinct and in certain respects unique in the nation.

After the first century of southern colonial settlement, which amounted to a frontier experience for Europeans, the southern colonial frontier consisted of the western piedmont and the Great Valley. Settlement of the valley began in earnest in the 1730s, with the massive migration of Scotch-Irish and German settlers, who were attracted by the cheap and plentiful land along the Great Philadelphia Wagon Road. Gradually, these migrants began to spread south and east, so that the westernmost sections of the southern piedmont and the extension of the valley into the Carolinas and Georgia contained perhaps 250,000 settlers by the time of the American Revolution.

These migrants received scant attention from Church of England clergy. The poorly organized established church faced a severe shortage of clergy, the physical barrier of the Blue Ridge, and the non-Anglican background of most of the settlers; it could only watch as the first southern frontier became fertile ground for dissent. Indeed, almost all of the South Carolina backcountry was in one Church of England parish; by 1750 only one Anglican church and two chapels served the upper valley.

The Presbyterian church dominated the first southern frontier, although Dunkers and Moravians found support among the German migrants. By 1768, 21 Presbyterian churches had been built on the South Carolina frontier; Presbyterians were equally successful in northern and southern frontier regions. Southern colonial governments even provided moderate support for the religious freedom of the migrants. In Georgia, the government ignored the wishes of the Privy Council and provided land for 107 Presbyterian settlers on the Great Ogeechee River. In Virginia, Governor Gooch answered a petition of the valley settlers in 1738 by guaranteeing that their religious practices would be tolerated.

These western Presbyterians received the Great Awakening with some suspicion, and most of the frontier response to the religious enthusiasm sweeping the nation took place in the western piedmont, where the settlers of the valley blended with easterners looking for cheaper land. In the piedmont, southwesterners in North Carolina listened to the preaching of Shubal Stearns, a Boston-born Baptist, who led a movement that came to be termed the Separate Baptists. The sometimes radically democratic, highly experiential Separate movement spread north and east, and by the 1760s had influenced much of the western piedmont in Virginia as well.

By the end of the colonial period the settlement of the piedmont and the Great Valley had progressed to the extent that these sections could only very loosely be defined as frontier. Although still dominated by Presbyterians, Baptists—both Regular and Separate—had begun to make inroads, as had Quakers, Moravians, and Dunkers. This first phase of the southwestern frontier experience was unique, because of its religious diversity and the high degree of toleration afforded most faiths.

The second phase of the southern frontier experience was the trans-Appalachian West. Settlers had begun to cross the Appalachian mountain barrier by the 1770s, but the first significant wave of migration into the trans-Appalachian West came at the end of the Revolutionary War. By 1790, 110,000 people lived in these new southwestern settlements; by 1796 both Kentucky and Tennessee were members of the Union; by the first decade of the 19th century most of the best land in the two states was already densely settled.

In the earliest years of this rapidly developing frontier, the most enthusiastic promoters of religion were Baptist preachers who moved with the migrants, settled farms, and became permanent members of the communities. In one of several such instances, 500 members of the "traveling church" followed the lead of the Reverend Lewis Craig from Spottsylvania County in Virginia to the Bluegrass country of Kentucky. Itinerant Methodist preachers, encouraged by the visits of their tireless bishop, Francis Asbury, began to develop small congregations at numerous points along their circuits. Presbyterians remained self-consciously aloof from the other denominations, concentrated as they were in Bourbon County, Ky., the eastern quarter of Tennessee, and the towns and cities springing up on the frontier. Intermingled among these three dominant denominations were scattered Quakers, Episcopalians, and even a few Roman Catholics. Ministers of the leading denominations tried to set themselves up as the moral guardians of the frontier, and some, led by Presbyterian David Rice, even went so far as to propose an end to slavery.

In spite of this religious diversity and activity, ministers in the Southwest of the 1790s complained continually about the lack of piety on the frontier. Most settlers did not attend church, and Deism had begun to be discussed in Nashville and Lexington. Increasingly, preachers began to stress watch-care within their congregations, rather than expansion and evangelism. In the face of real despair, however, a religious fervor began to emerge, first in 1799 in Logan County, Ky., and then by the next year spreading north and south throughout the region. Presbyterians probably served the most important role in the development of this Great Revival, but Methodists joined in many of the services. Although Baptists were reluctant to participate in the interdenominational services, they probably gained the most converts in the awakening.

The Great Revival exerted greatest influence upon southern and national religious development in its stress upon complex revivalistic techniques. The McGee brothers, one a Methodist minister, the other a Presbyterian, served as two of the most innovative leaders of the movement, promoting in particular the concept of the camp meeting. The greatest of these, the 1801 Cane Ridge meeting in Bourbon County, Ky., may have brought 25,000 worshipers together to listen to a flock of preachers, who spoke day and night for a week. The meetings were not segregated by sex, nor in many instances by race, and several black preachers earned their initial reputations speaking at these gatherings.

In the wake of the revival came an inevitable period of reassessment and self-evaluation. In the Presbyterian church the revival had brought a series of schisms, some members following the Shakers, others forming a new denomination, the Cumberland Presbyterians, and still others, under the leadership of Barton W. Stone, taking a long theological odyssey that eventually contributed to the creation of the Disciples of Christ. As Presbyterians and, to a lesser extent, Baptists and Methodists recovered from the social earthquake of the Great Revival, the frontier spirit of the region also began to disappear. Instead, the second decade of the 19th century began to witness the development of a regional culture, a regional economy, and a regional self-consciousness.

This resulted in the third phase of frontier religious development in the Deep South. The area of the trans-Appalachian West, south of the Tennessee River, received some initial settlement by the time of the Great Revival, and sufficient migration had occurred by 1817 to allow Mississippi to enter the Union, followed by Alabama two years later. During the 1820s much of the extremely rich soil of the "Black Belt" began to be exploited with the use of large-scale slave labor. Only in the 1830s, however, with the mass expulsion of the Creek, Cherokee, Chickasaw, and Choctaw Indians, did this section begin to lose its frontier quality and develop both lasting settlement patterns and enduring religious, governmental, and economic institutions. Even as late as the end of the 1830s, according to Joseph Baldwin's account in *The Flush Times of Alabama and Mississippi*, much of the area remained wild, reckless, dangerous, uncivilized—in short, a frontier.

Because this section was at once the frontier for South Carolina and Georgia and an extension of settlement for Kentucky and Tennessee, the religious life of the Deep Southwest was an odd mixture of elements. In the first years a series of missionaries from the three major evangelical denominations visited the region, sometimes risking their lives to endure rough conditions of travel, at other times facing hostile reception from early settlers. Some frontier ministers began to adopt the swaggering, unyielding characteristics of many of the settlers, threatening unruly congregations from the pulpit, fighting when they deemed fighting appropriate. A premium was placed upon a straight-ahead preaching style, and a thundering voice helped drown out any heckling. In these ways, the pioneer preachers faced the same problems they would have found on other frontiers.

Churches of the southwestern frontier were heir to the factionalism and confusion coming out of the Great Revival period. Perhaps no frontier in American history faced so many religious choices. In addition to mainstream Presbyterians, Baptists, and Methodists, the factions, sects, and new denominations of the frontier included the Cumberland Presbyterians, the Shakers, the Stoneites, the Campbellites, the Republican Methodists, and, perhaps most important, the followers of a Baptist preacher, Daniel Parker, variously termed Hardshell, Two-Seed, or Antimission Baptists. This last group, which radically opposed missions and other benevolent actions as well as the education of clergy, disrupted the already difficult work of more conventional Baptist preachers. As a consequence, the first attempt to organize a state convention in Mississippi failed after five years of constant bickering.

Reflecting the confusion of religious life in the region, slaves remained in the white-run churches, participating in watch-care activities, long after Kentucky and Tennessee churches had begun segregating their buildings and their church services. Yet at the same time that this limited measure of equality existed in some Deep Southwest churches, others had begun to encourage the mission to the slaves with its powerful message of social control. Such confusion of purpose could be seen in other aspects of religious life on this frontier; for example, drinking preachers lived nearby those in the same denomination who viewed liquor as diabolic. This religious "split personality" from the frontier era continued to characterize the section for decades after. W. J. Cash and other commentators have even attributed paradoxical 20th-century southern characteristics to the survival of frontier ways, and this seems true in regard to religion.

See also BLACK LIFE: Religion, Black; HISTORY AND MANNERS: Frontier Heritage

David T. Bailey
Michigan State University

Joseph G. Baldwin, *The Flush Times of Alabama and Mississippi: A Series of Sketches* (1853); John B. Boles, *The Great Revival, 1787–1805: The Origins of the Southern Evangelical Mind* (1972); Catharine C. Cleveland, *The Great Revival in the West, 1797–1805* (1916); Wesley M. Gewehr, *The Great Awakening in Virginia, 1740–1790* (1930); Robert D. Mitchell, *Commercialism and Frontier: Perspectives on the Early Shenandoah Valley* (1977); Walter B. Posey, *The Baptist Church in the Lower Mississippi Valley, 1776–1845* (1957).

Fundamentalism

Although much of southern religion has remained conservative into the 20th century and has been popularly characterized as "fundamentalist" in belief, the organized Fundamentalist movement penetrated the South slowly. Broadly defined, the Fundamentalist movement was a reaction of conservatives within most American Protestant churches to the rise of liberal religious beliefs and the social gospel at the beginning of the 20th century. In a narrower sense, the Fundamentalist movement was identified with the spread of dispensational premillennialism, which taught that the various historical eras or dispensations recounted in the Bible were sharply, literally separated into distinct ages, leading to the second coming of Christ before His thousand-year reign on earth. This idea was promoted by a series of prophetic conferences prior to World War I. Perhaps the most important milestones in the early development of the movement were the publication of a series of booklets, *The Fundamentals*, between 1910 and 1915 and the establishment of a number of independent organizations, the most important being the World's Christian Fundamentals Association founded in 1919.

Southerners contributed very little to these developments. The only southerner to contribute to *The Fundamentals* was President E. Y. Mullins of Baptist Theological Seminary in Louisville: his essay was so moderate that he himself was later attacked by fundamentalists. Very few of the early leaders of the Fundamentalist movement were from the South, and only one, J. Frank Norris of Fort Worth, Tex., spent his life working in the South.

In the years immediately after World War I, the fundamentalist-modernist controversy heated up, centering first on battles for control of northern Baptist and Presbyterian churches. Generally, southern churches escaped serious disruption because of their uniformly conservative nature. Militant southern fundamentalists like Norris warned against decay in the southern churches, but a separatist spirit was not strong in the pre–World War II South. On the other hand, when organized fundamentalism, under the leadership of William Jennings Bryan, expanded its attack to include banning the teaching of evolution in the public schools, the South became the movement's stronghold. Between 1921 and 1929, five states, all in the South (Florida, Tennessee, Mississippi, Arkansas, and Oklahoma) passed laws prohibiting the teaching of evolution. The Scopes Trial in Dayton, Tenn., in July 1925, solidified two false notions: that fundamentalism was simply the baroque theology of southern hillbillies and that the movement would soon die under the weight of its own absurdity.

The preeminent southern fundamentalist in the first half of the 20th century was J. Frank Norris. Norris was one of the early leaders of the World's Christian Fundamentals Association, and in 1917 he founded a paper that later became *The Fundamentalist*. From his pulpit and in print he generated a stream of sensational attacks on liberalism, especially censuring his own denomination, the Southern Baptist Convention. Norris's career included a series of stormy confrontations that led to the expulsion of his church from the Texas Baptist Convention in 1923, his indictment and trial on charges of arson and murder, and countless bitter feuds with his closest associates. But in the long run he was the father of southern fundamentalism. In the 1930s and 1940s a generation of young, aspiring Southern Baptist preachers was exposed to the Texas Tornado's flamboyant style and premillennial, separatist teachings; some came to idolize him. In 1939 Norris established a "Bible Institute" at his Fort Worth church, where hundreds of young followers were taught his successful techniques for soul winning and church building.

Scores of other preachers roamed the South in the 1930s, fighting evolution and urging fundamentalist separatism. The most important of these evangelists was Bob Jones, Sr., one of the few Methodist ministers to take up the cause of organized fundamentalism. In 1926 Jones established an interdenominational fundamentalist college and settled permanently in Greenville, S.C., in 1947. In the 1980s Bob Jones University is the educational center of extreme fundamentalism in America. Probably the most widely circulated fundamentalist paper published since the 1930s is *The Sword of the Lord*, founded in 1934 by Independent Baptist evangelist John R. Rice of Murfreesboro, Tenn.

Since World War II, sectarianism and religious conservatism have remained strong in the South, but many southerners could hardly be considered fundamentalists. The Churches of Christ agree with many fundamentalist beliefs, but the movement is militantly antipremillennial. Pentecostals have generally been rejected as heretics by fundamentalists. Many Southern Baptists sympathize with the Fundamentalist movement, but militant fundamentalists refuse to cooperate with them until they separate from the United Southern Baptist Convention.

On the other hand, in the 1940s and 1950s the South became the most fertile breeding ground of separatism—premillennial fundamentalism—especially among Independent Baptists. Hundreds of Independent Baptist churches were founded in the South after World War II, with many sponsoring private schools and scores supporting fundamentalist Bible institutes or colleges. Several important Independent Baptist associations were founded, including the Baptist Bible Fellowship headquartered in Springfield, Mo. Initially dominated by Norris, the movement in 1950 came under the leadership of his two close associates, Noel Smith and G. Beauchamp Vick, who broke with him. Among the generation of fundamentalist church builders trained at Bible Baptist College in Springfield since 1950 was Jerry Falwell, pastor of the Thomas Road Baptist Church in Lynchburg, Va., and founder of Moral Majority. Another important Independent Baptist association was the Southwide Fellowship founded in 1956 and led by the huge Highland Park Baptist Church of Chattanooga, Tenn., and its pastor, Lee Roberson. The post–World War II southern fundamentalists built huge churches; in 1980 Falwell's church claimed over 15,000 members and Roberson's 50,000.

These Baptist fundamentalists once again politicized the movement in the late 1970s. Isolated and ridiculed for a half century after the Scopes Trial, southern fundamentalists had built huge empires in their isolation. By the end of the 1970s they were ready to reassert their influence. At the same time, the success of the movement has deeply divided it. Falwell's political interests have led him to cooperate on public issues not only with Southern Baptists such as James Robison and Bailey Smith but with Roman Catholics and Jews. Separatist fundamentalists, headed by the leaders of Bob Jones University, have openly denounced Falwell as a defector. One fundamentalist recently divided the movement's institutions into three camps: militant, moderate, and modified fundamentalists. These divisions are widely visible in the South in the 1980s and make it increasingly difficult to discuss fundamentalists without additional modifiers.

See also SCIENCE AND MEDICINE: Science and Religion; / Scopes Trial

David Harrell
University of Alabama
at Birmingham

George W. Dollar, *A History of Fundamentalism in America* (1973); Jerry Falwell, ed., *The Fundamentalist Phenomenon* (1981); George M. Marsden, *Fundamentalism and American Culture: The Shaping of Twentieth-Century Evangelicalism, 1870–1925* (1980); Royce Lee Measures, "Men and Movements Influenced by J. Frank Norris" (Th.D. thesis, Southwestern Baptist Theological Seminary, 1976); Clovis Gwin Morris, "He Changed Things: The Life and Thought of J. Frank Norris" (Ph.D. dissertation, Texas Tech University, 1973); Ernest Sandeen, *The Roots of Fundamentalism: British and American Millenarianism, 1800–1930* (1970); Robert Elwood Wenger, "Social Thought of American Fundamentalism, 1918–1933" (Ph.D. dissertation, University of Nebraska, 1973).

Jewish Religious Life

The religious life of the 785,000 Jews currently dispersed throughout the South defies generalization. It ranges from a strict ritualistic definition of Judaism to a purely cultural or philosophical interpretation of the faith. Though a number of southern Jews are not associated with any Jewish religious or philanthropic organization, thriving Jewish communities exist that vary in size and character from the 900-family Reform congregation in Dallas, Tex., to an eight-member Orthodox congregation in Vidalia, Ga. (with the smallest synagogue in the United States), to a "one-man congregation" in a small Louisiana town (he offers a scholarship to a nearby college for a Jewish student to act as a rabbi for his children).

This diversity mirrors the individual responses of Jews—in the absence of a unified higher authority—to the unexpected, widespread, but historically ignored congeniality that has usually greeted them during their more than 300-year residency in the South. As elsewhere in the United States, most Jewish immigrants to the South were from two groups—Sephardic Jews, the earliest to arrive, came from the Iberian Peninsula, whereas the Ashkenazi Jews came in the 19th century from central and eastern Europe. Although New Orleans was one destination for the huge wave of Orthodox Jewish immigrants in the late 19th and early 20th centuries, relatively few stayed there or in the region as a whole. The southern gentile religious outlook, in any event, often acted as a benevolent catalyst allowing the Jews of diverse origins and religious convictions to become far more of an integral part of the southern landscape than has been supposed.

Southern intolerance of Jews, to be sure, did appear at certain times and places. Jews were sometimes portrayed as outsiders. Critics accused them of profiteering during the Civil War and not sacrificing for the southern cause. Over 10,000 Jews, in reality, served the Confederacy, with Judah P. Benjamin, the new nation's secretary of war and secretary of state, the most famous. Some frustrated southerners, though, at the end of the war made Benjamin and Jews scapegoats for defeat. Anti-Semitism in the South seems to have increased in the late 19th century; as Jewish southerners became more prosperous than before as businessmen, commodity brokers, mill owners, and plantation landlords, bigotry toward them increased. The lynching of Leo Frank in 1915 for the alleged murder of Mary Phagan in Georgia was the worst incident of anti-Semitic southern violence. The Ku Klux Klan persecuted southern Jews along with other groups, driving them from political participation by the 1920s.

Southern religion proved, however, a force for Jewish-gentile accommodation. Southern gentiles drew their religious fervor more from piety than from an unswerving doctrinal position. Because piety lends itself more easily to ecumenism than does doctrinalism, southerners were inclined to accept what they perceived as pious Jews. Most southern gentiles, however, did not define Jewish piety solely in the restricted terms of ritual devotion. Their broader understanding of Judaism emphasized the Jewish moral character that manifested itself as an inclination to be socially responsible and unusually charitable, which the gentiles believed was the result of the Jews' religious heritage as "God's chosen Ministers of the Book." As biblical fundamentalists, southern Protestants honored the Jewish Old Testament tradition. This respectful religious stereotype, more than any other, generally proved sufficient to quell bigoted voices and to provide Jews with credentials for acceptance.

Yet, although southern gentiles were willing to accept religious distinction, they generally refused to accept Jewish cultural separatism. Consequently, as gentiles beckoned the Jews to become a part of southern society, they exerted a pressure upon the Jews to forego their old ways and adopt southern lifestyles.

Judaism, nevertheless, developed into an ethnic religion. Its religious traditions were an integral part of a sociocultural system that Old World Jews had developed through the ages as a means of preserving their own identity while coming to terms with the persecutions of the gentile majority. Inescapably, therefore, any process of acculturation in the South automatically required a modification of religious life. Southerners, in fact, became early advocates of the Jewish Reform Movement. Beth Elohim congregation in Charleston, for example, distinguished itself in the 19th century through ritual changes such as organ music in worship, confirmation classes, and the use of family pews.

American Jews evaluated the utility of their Old World religious traditions in two ways. The first was to retain but alter those traditions that allowed them to be different, without appearing to be alien, from their gentile neighbors. Isolated individually and in small groups, the Jews wanted to retain contact with their heritage, from which they could draw a stabilizing sense of identity while shedding what some southerners termed their "outward strangeness." If there was any hesitancy about putting aside the traditions of their forefathers, many Jews overcame it with the excuse that it was impossible to be properly observant: economic and social realities forced severe modifications and even abandonment of Sabbath observance; the unavailability of proper foods and ritual slaughterers seriously weakened resolve to maintain the dietary laws; proper quorums for prayer were often impossible to convene; the proper ritual accoutrements could not be secured; and holidays could not be adequately celebrated.

Jewish religious service, Waco, Tex., 1890s

In those areas where Jews congregated in small communities, they sought to purchase land for a Jewish cemetery, engaged in organized charitable activities, and eventually organized a congregation, all of which were indicators of a communal commitment to their heritage and a devotion to their religion that acted to offset individual ritual laxity. Nevertheless, the form of religious practices often took on a Protestant appearance as Jews tried to minimize outward ritual difference and thereby demonstrate the common religious experience shared with the gentiles. Increasingly, English was substituted for the Hebrew language in the religious service; choirs and musical instruments were introduced into the service and the use of distinctive prayer caps and shawls neglected; the rabbi slowly took on the character of a Protestant clergyman; and even the architecture of later Jewish houses of worship copied Protestant prototypes.

The second criterion Jews used to evaluate the usefulness of their traditions in southern society emphasized the traditional Judaic sense of moral responsibility as a viable substitute to demanding ritual Judaism. In short, if Jews could not be punctiliously ritualistic, their ethical commitment and display of a "good heart" would place them beyond reproach. Thus, often, before congregations were formally organized, a myriad of charitable and social agencies appeared throughout the South: orphan homes, aid societies, relief societies, service clubs for widowed and disabled members, and benevolent societies. It was no accident that Reform Judaism began in the South, nor that early southern Jewry took the lead in transformations that often set the pattern for Jews in other sections of the country.

Jews in the agrarian South could not group together in sufficient numbers to enable them to resist or minimize the lure to acculturate through the creation of ghetto-like communities, as did many of their northern urban counterparts. The receptiveness of the South to the Jewish presence made such resistance less desirable. Though the forces of acculturation that were at work were not uniquely southern, the pressure imposed upon the Jews was greater in the South. The receptiveness of the South to the Jewish presence made it more difficult for the Jews not to be lured into becoming a part of their environment. In addition, the relatively few numbers of Jews who came South imposed a greater sense of vulnerability and isolation on those who did, thereby creating a greater sense of urgency in the minds of these Jews.

The southern Jewish response to the demands of southern gentiles, however, was not uniform. The great diversity of contemporary southern Jewish religious life demonstrates that the process of acculturation has occurred at different stages because southern Jews arrived in different waves over the past 300 years, the last of which ended only in the 1920s. Moreover, the Jews came not only at different times but from different lands, carrying with them varied national, cultural, and religious experiences. Thus, their judgments about what traditions to discard, retain, and alter were not always the same as those of the previous generation of immigrants. Indeed, differing judgments regarding religious celebration, ritual performance, and form of ceremony created a sense of alienation and antagonism among Jews themselves that in some cases was greater than that existing between Jews and gentiles. Migration since World War II of American-born Jews from large northern communities, combined with the absence of any significant number of first-generation immigrants and the formation of Jewish activities into national networks, may be blurring the strong and distinctive sectional religious identities that existed, not too long ago, among southern Jews.

See also ETHNIC LIFE: / Jews

Louis E. Schmier
Valdosta State College

Myron Berman, *Richmond's Jewry, 1769–1976* (1979); Mark Elovitz, *A Century of Jewish Life in Dixie: The Birmingham Experience* (1974); Eli Evans, *The Provincials: A Personal History of Jews in the South* (1973); Steven Hertzberg, *Strangers within the Gate City: The Jews of Atlanta, 1845–1915* (1978); Ben Kaplan, *The Eternal Stranger: A Study of Jewish Life in the Small Community* (1957); Bertram Korn, *The Early Jews of New Orleans* (1969); Louis E. Schmier, *Reflections of Southern Jewry: The Letters of Charles Wessolowsky, 1878–1879* (1982); *Southern Israelite* (1926–).

Literature and Religion

Religion has influenced the imagination of southern writers in fundamental ways. Both aesthetically and thematically, religious practice in the region has helped writers render a particular place and time as a target for their satire and as a prism through which they interpret human experience. Often southern writers' debts to the religious beliefs and practices of their region are unacknowledged, perhaps even unconscious. William Faulkner asserts such influences exist, nonetheless: "The writer must write about his background. He must write out of what he knows and the Christian legend is part of any Christian's background, especially the background of a country boy, a Southern country boy. I grew up with that, took that in without even knowing it. It's just there. It has nothing to do with how much of it I might believe or disbelieve—it's just there." Southern writers, whether or not they expressly address religious issues, engage questions that preoccupy southern culture, questions that often arise in the practice of religion.

The South historically has been more homogeneous and orthodox in its beliefs than other regions. In a recent study by John Shelton Reed, 90 percent of southerners surveyed identified themselves as Protestant as opposed to 60 percent of non-southerners. The same study found more agreement in religious beliefs among these southern Protestants than among non-southern Protestants or Catholics. Within this homogeneity, there is, however, individuality—institutionalized in the many Protestant denominations—producing colorful variants in religious behavior. This individuality within an overwhelmingly Protestant culture resulted from the particular emphasis of the southern church as it parted from the pluralistic patterns of the North. The Baptist and Methodist movements which swept across the largely rural South after 1755 often featured preachers who delivered dramatic, emotional pictures of the struggle to escape sin and achieve salvation. With common roots in the New England Calvinism of the Great Awakening, this expressive religion stressed personal piety and the preeminent importance of achieving one's salvation. Appealing to the often-isolated poor, it cared little for abstract theology or issues of ethical responsibility within the society. No church-state was envisioned. In the hospitable, fertile southern landscape, preachers taught that one must struggle inwardly with an inherent sinfulness. This sense of human frailty and limitation combined with the hedonism of a rich, frontier culture led to what Samuel S. Hill has called a pattern of "confession, purgation, and going out to sin again."

As private morality became more exclusively the domain of the church, engagement with issues of public morality became less frequent. The explanation lies with the South's commitment to slavery. Because the southern church avoided confronting the immorality of the institution of slavery, it could not validly address issues of ethical responsibility in the larger society. Instead, spokesmen of the church defended the institution as consistent with God's plan, vilifying its critics as ungodly in motivation and action and reaffirming the position that the church should concern itself only with issues of personal piety and salvation. Also, the southern church undertook elaborate missionary efforts to teach the slave community to share its outlook.

When writers of the Southern Literary Renaissance looked to the social history of the South for reasons behind its 20th-century ills, they blamed the church's preoccupation with matters of personal behavior and its carefully defended historical blindness to slavery. Writers like Faulkner, Allen Tate, Flannery O'Connor, and Erskine Caldwell created communities of self-righteous churchgoers and hypocritical preachers practicing a narrow, spiritless religion insensitive to the moral issues with which these writers were concerned. Mark Twain had earlier laid the ground for satirizing the formal practice of religion in the South as a fountain of intolerance;

Faulkner tilled the same soil in his depiction of the good Baptist ladies of Jefferson who close the door to those who violate the standards of personal behavior endorsed formally by the church. Once questioned about his own religious beliefs, Faulkner said what other southern writers seemed to be implying in their portrayal of institutional religion: "I think that the trouble with Christianity is that we've never tried it yet." These writers created worlds where issues of public morality had to be engaged; adherence to strict codes of personal piety was insufficient. As Robert Penn Warren wrote at the end of *All the King's Men*, the challenge was to immerse oneself in "the awful responsibility of time."

Yet even as they attack the self-satisfied attitudes of the southern religious establishment, many of these writers accept views basic to regional religious belief. For example, Flannery O'Connor, a writer who makes this gap between belief and practice the focus of her work, finds in the southerner's belief in the Devil, in the reality of evil, an important article of faith. From the perspective of her own orthodox Roman Catholic beliefs, O'Connor keenly perceives the fundamentalist Protestant experiences of the majority of southerners. She introduces her collection of short stories *A Good Man Is Hard to Find* with a quotation from St. Cyril of Jerusalem: "The dragon is by the side of the road, watching those who pass. Beware lest he devour you. We go to the Father of Souls, but it is necessary to pass by the dragon." O'Connor believes she addresses a modern world in which evil is dismissed as sociological or psychological aberration. In the South, particularly the rural Protestant South, this Roman Catholic writer ironically recognizes another point of view.

Episcopal Bishop Robert R. Brown writes that southerners "believe more in the reality of Satan than in the reality of God," and John Shelton Reed's recent study shows that by a significant margin (86 percent to 52 percent) southerners are more likely than non-southerners to say they believe in the Devil. Southern writers, too, insist upon the reality of evil. They present it as active, powerful, inescapable, irreducible, threatening the individual from within as well as from without. They also criticize ideas of social reform dependent upon a view of mankind as essentially good. Writers such as Faulkner, Warren, Katherine Anne Porter, Carson McCullers, and Truman Capote join O'Connor in representing evil as violence, grotesque psychological distortion, selfish pride, or despair. These storytellers find in the individual's confrontation with evil the conflict from which dramatic fiction arises.

Another common theme that reflects the debt of southern writers to their religious environment is closely allied to this acceptance of the existence of evil: humans are flawed, limited, imperfect. "Man is conceived in sin and born in corruption," says Warren's Willie Stark, "and he passeth from the stink of the didie to the stench of the shroud." The viewpoint is essentially conservative, even pessimistic if contrasted with visions of a more idealized human nature. Without explicitly referring to original sin, southern writers create characters more sinning than sinned against. Mr. Thompson of Katherine Anne Porter's "Noon Wine" or Horace Benbow of Faulkner's *Sanctuary* awaken to their own capacity for violence and evil. Individuals resist or succumb to their own selfish pride, their greed, their bestial natures. It is a mistake, however, to label such a vision of human behavior as pessimistic or deterministic. Within the context of the accepted religious beliefs of their culture, southern writers turn their attention to how one conducts life given these imperfections. The measure of the spiritually healthy individual is in his or her ability to recognize limitations and then to involve oneself with the world and its complexities.

In the emotional style of southern evangelical Protestantism lie the clearest connections to the South's creative literature. The southern writer could and often did turn to the preacher for models of imaginative, moving uses of language. Faulkner once speculated about the appeal of the Southern Baptist movement: "It came from times of hardship in the South where there was little or no food for the human spirit—where there were no books, no theater, no music, and life was pretty hard and a lot of it happened out in the sun, for very little reward and that was the only escape they had." The southern preacher dramatized the struggles of good and evil in vivid, concrete stories, enlivened by expressive flourishes, which allowed the congregation to forget for the moment their day-to-day fight to survive. In the competitive world of the itinerant preacher, he who could touch the imagination as well as the conscience of his congregation thrived. Every writer who grew up in the South, then, breathed in this dramatic, emotional atmosphere.

The preacher offered southern writers literary tools and visions that guided them in confronting central questions about life. Writers worked scenes of camp meetings and revivals into their stories. Johnson Jones Hooper, for example, introduces the character Captain Simon Suggs to a camp meeting, where he becomes the object-lesson sinner for the preacher. Mark Twain presents a camp meeting through Huck Finn's eyes as the duke and the king, Huck's con-artist companions, prey on the gullible there assembled. Flannery O'Connor in "The River" shows the preacher Bevel, who baptizes a small boy so that he will "count now." Recently, Lisa Alther has portrayed the modern youth revival and evangelist Brother Buck, who couches his message in extended football metaphors of Christ Jesus Thy Quarterback, the Celestial Coach, and the water boys of life. And Faulkner shows the power of the preacher to raise his audience to new levels of self-recognition in *The Sound and the Fury* with the sermon of the Reverend Shegog.

Faulkner chose to depict a black preacher when he wanted to express a redemptive quality in the religion practiced in the South. Samuel S. Hill has pointed out that the black church developed along lines different from those of white Protestantism, in that "the theology of black people's Christianity was shifting, not away from glorious heaven, to be sure, but away from the threats of hell. It remained a religion of salvation, but less and less from eternal punishment and more from alienation from Jesus. . . . [Black people] created an authentic folk variant of a traditional religion. It featured expressiveness, joy, fellowship, moral responsibility, pious feelings and the hope of heaven." Yet black southern writers, like their white counterparts, respond with ambivalence when portraying religious practice in the region.

Richard Wright in his autobiographical *Black Boy* depicts the women of his family as threatening him with God's punishment for his transgressions. In *Native Son* religion weakens black rebellion with promises that suffering in this life will be rewarded in the next. But in the short story "Fire and Cloud," Wright presents the Reverend Taylor as a man who lives his religious commitment as social action. In his picture of the Reverend Homer Barbee in *Invisible Man*, Ralph Ellison illustrates the rhetorical power of the black preacher even as he suggests it is used to misdirect the attention of the congregation from their exploitation. Alice Walker, however, seems to capture the spirit of what Hill called the joyful folk variant of traditional southern religion in *The Color Purple*. Shug Avery celebrates a personal religion, independent from any formal church, which asks only that one express love for God's creation. It is one of the most positive, albeit unconventional, expressions of religious feeling in southern literature.

H. L. Mencken once characterized the South as the "bunghole of the United States, a cesspool of Baptists, a miasma of Methodism, snake-charmers, phony real-estate operators, and syphilitic evangelists." Southern writers have populated their work with hypocritical preachers, self-righteous congregations, rigid Calvinists, and spiritually twisted fanatics. They have, nevertheless, drawn their vision of human limitation and a world in which good and evil contend from the most basic beliefs of southern religion. Perhaps as the distinctions between the South and other regions fade, the southern writer will become more indistinguishable in his response to his community. In the work of Walker Percy, a southerner and a Catholic, there is attention to philosophical and theological issues that cannot be said to be strictly southern. As long as religion remains a focus within the southern community, it cannot be disregarded by those whose imagination feeds on the southern experience. The ambivalence that has marked writers' responses to the religious beliefs and practices in the South is unlikely to change. Southern religious beliefs will continue to influence the writers' vision.

See also LITERATURE articles

Robert R. Moore
State University of New York
at Oswego

Samuel S. Hill, *The South and the North in American Religion* (1980); C. Hugh Holman, *The Immoderate Past: The Southern Writer and History* (1977); Charles Lippy, ed., *Bibliography of Religion in the South* (1985); Ralph Luker, *Southern Studies* (Summer 1983); Rosemary Magee and Robert Detweiler, in *Encyclopedia of Religion in the South*, ed. Samuel S. Hill (1984); Perry Miller, *Errand into the Wilderness* (1956); John Shelton Reed, *The Enduring South: Subcultural Persistence in Mass Society* (1972); Louis D. Rubin, Jr., in *The Added Dimension: The Art and Mind of Flannery O'Connor*, ed. Melvin J. Friedman and Lewis A. Lawson (1977); Lewis Simpson, in *The Cry of Home: Cultural Nationalism and the Modern Writer*, ed. H. Ernest Lewald (1972); Thomas Daniel Young, in *The American South: Portrait of a Culture*, ed. Louis D. Rubin, Jr. (1980).

Missionary Activities

Religious revivalism swept the South in the early days of the Republic and brought with it an intense belief in the millennium—the thousand-year reign of Christ on earth that would commence when all peoples of the world had been given a chance to accept Christ. By natural extension foreign missions joined domestic missions to Indians in the effort to carry out the great commission: "Go ye therefore, and teach all nations, baptizing them . . . ; [and] teaching them to observe all things whatsoever I have commanded you" (Matthew 28:19–20). Richard Furman, pastor of the First Baptist Church of Charleston, S.C., adjoined nationalism to religion in 1802 when he asserted that the United States would "participate, largely, in the fulfillment of those sacred prophecies which have foretold the glory of Messiah's kingdom. . . . Hence God has prepared this land for a great mission, to lead the world into the millennium." Nationalism thus reinforced religious belief and determined the religio-cultural nature of American foreign missions.

The formal organization of at least one major denomination in the United States resulted from the missionary impulse. Baptists believed so strongly in the autonomy of the individual congregation that they had resisted all efforts to form even statewide organizations. Yet they established a national body when confronted with the need to support foreign missionaries. Adoniram Judson and his wife and Luther Rice, Congregationalists, had been sent to India by the American Board of Commissioners for Foreign Missions (ABCFM) in 1812. During their voyage they became convinced that baptism of believers was scripturally correct, so they requested and received baptism by immersion from a British Baptist upon their arrival. Luther Rice returned to the United States to inform the ABCFM of their actions, whereupon the board severed its connection with them. Rice toured Baptist churches, North and South, requesting support for the Judsons. The need to sustain these missionaries already in the field led to the organization, in 1814, of the General Missionary Convention of the Baptist Denomination in the United States of America for Foreign Missions. Richard Furman, long an advocate of this effort, was elected its first president, and other Baptists from southern states who supported both foreign missions and a national organization for Baptists also served in positions of responsibility.

Frontier Baptists were not as enthusiastic about foreign missions as their eastern brethren. Indeed, in the early 19th century there were more differences between rural and urban Baptists than there were between northern and southern Baptists who lived in cities, and this was most likely true of other denominations as well. Until American sectional issues caused divisions in three

Protestant bodies—Methodists in 1844, Baptists in 1845, and Presbyterians in 1861—southerners were among the early missionary volunteers and worked alongside their colleagues from the North. The three new southern denominations quickly established foreign missions as a major part of their program, with China as one of the first fields to be manned. Each had experienced missionaries who had worked there before the separation, and China loomed large in the millennial view. Here were more people than in any other country; they had to be reached before the millennium could begin.

Several circumstances retarded the southern missionary effort in China. Before the Peking Treaties of 1860 missionaries had been confined to a few treaty ports. Access to the interior, even when obtained, could not be exploited until the financial strains of the Civil War and Reconstruction ended. By that time missionary efforts in India and the Near East, without imperial restrictions on the free movement and activities of foreigners, had become well established and drew heavily on mission budgets. Throughout the 19th century, American support for foreign missions—in expenditure, manpower, and capital construction—went for the most part to the Near East and to the Indian subcontinent.

Qualitatively, if not quantitatively, southern missionaries of the last century made significant contributions to China in particular and to the missionary enterprise in general. A southern Methodist from Georgia, Young J. Allen, arrived in Shanghai in 1860. During his long tenure in China he became one of the most influential American missionaries through his magazine, *The Globe*. Written in Chinese, it became a vehicle to inform readers, non-Christian as well as Christian, of the Western scientific knowledge so many of them sought beginning with the Self-Strengthening Movement of the 1860s and particularly after China's humiliating defeat by Japan in 1895. A young woman from Virginia, Charlotte "Lottie" Moon, served as a missionary to China and became the inspiration for extensive fund-raising activity by the Women's Missionary Union of the Southern Baptist Convention. The Lottie Moon Christmas Offering annually collects millions of dollars, which the Foreign Mission Board uses to maintain the largest number of American Protestant missionaries now in the field.

Perhaps the most influential missionary activity of the late 1800s occurred in the southern United States. In 1880 an American ship's captain, Charles Jones, discovered a young Chinese stowaway on his vessel, and when he docked in Wilmington, N.C., he entrusted the boy to the care of the pastor of the Fifth Avenue Methodist Church there. The lad, named Soong, was converted and took as his Christian name that of the captain. He remained in the United States to receive an undergraduate and ministerial education. In 1886 Charlie Jones Soong returned to China an ordained Methodist minister and became involved in the revolutionary movement of Sun Yat-sen. One of his sons, T. V. Soong, and three of his daughters, Ai-ling, Ching-ling, and Mei-ling Soong, were educated in the United States and became internationally known figures in Chinese political life.

Southern missionaries in the first half of this century generally were indistinguishable from those of other regions of the United States. They volunteered for the same mission fields—Latin America, Africa, the Middle East, South and East Asia—and engaged in the same kinds of activities: evangelization, education, medical missions, and social work. Independence granted to former colonies and the establishment of Socialist governments in the Third World from about 1950 created a divergence between the missionary emphases of southern and northern denominations. The latter mainly joined the National Council of Churches and the World Council of Churches, which stressed the social gospel, with cultural and technological aid projects predominating. Southern denominations have retained a more evangelical focus in their missions overseas. These lines, however, should not be too sharply drawn. As of the early 1980s the evangelical bodies supported more than three times as many foreign missionaries as the "liberal" churches and American Catholics combined. As governments sensitive to foreign presence have discouraged if not forbidden foreign missionary activity, many of today's missionaries seek out the 16,000 tribal groups in remote areas around the world who have not heretofore been reached with the gospel. This may be the greatest change in Protestant missionary strategy of the last decade.

George B. Pruden, Jr.
Armstrong State College

Ecumenical Missionary Conference: New York, 1900, 2 vols. (1900); John K. Fairbank, ed., *The Missionary Enterprise in China and America* (1974); Kenneth Scott Latourette, *A History of the Expansion of Christianity*, vol. 6, *The Great Century in Northern Africa and Asia A.D. 1800–A.D. 1914* (1945); *Time* (27 December 1982).

Modernism and Religion

In American religious studies the term *modernism* describes a style of Christian theology that attempted to adjust traditional religious doctrines to the intellectual demands of the modern world, especially to biological evolution and historical-critical study of Scripture. Although the term is often used to describe the beliefs of all who make such adjustments, it is usually reserved for the liberal theology of the early 20th century (1920–40).

Modernism has not been a significant position among southern theologians. The predominant southern orientation has been theological orthodoxy. Even before the Civil War, southern theologians, especially in the culturally influential Presbyterian church, tended to adopt more traditional theological positions than their northern counterparts. This was partly because of the conviction that the Bible, if interpreted literally, supported the institution of slavery. The Civil War reinforced this preexistent conservatism in two ways. First, the revivals that periodically swept the Confederate armies solidified the evangelical churches as the expression of southern piety. These revivals, often led by lay preachers, stressed biblicism as a key element in religion. Second, the defeat of the South and the subsequent forcible reunion of the country forced the former Confederates to find new ways to express their loyalty to the Lost Cause. An amalgamation of sentimentality, conservatism, and southern identity took place—a southern civil religion—that inhibited intellectual change and adventure.

James Woodrow (1828–1907), Professor of Natural Science in Connection with Revelation at Columbia Presbyterian Seminary in South Carolina from 1861 to 1886, was one of the first southerners to approach the question of the relationship between the new biology and Christian theology. As a result of the publication of his position, controversy arose over the issue from 1884 to 1886, which, although not leading to his conviction for heresy, resulted in his dismissal from the school. Crawford Howell Toy (1836–1919), Professor of Old Testament at Southern Baptist Seminary in Louisville, Ky., had been trained as a biblical critic at the University of Berlin. While teaching the Bible at Southern, he referred to the views current in Europe on such matters as the authorship of the Pentateuch and Isaiah. Fearful of controversy, his colleagues asked for his resignation before the trustees could force the issue by dismissing him. William Whitsitt (1841–1911), president of Southern from 1895 to 1899 was, likewise, persuaded to resign after he applied modern historical techniques to Baptist history.

Among Methodists, a migration of students from Randolph-Macon, Wofford, and other colleges to Germany after the Civil War and to Johns Hopkins after its founding in 1876 created a noticeably larger contingent of progressive thinkers in that denomination than among Presbyterians or Baptists. In 1875 Alexander Winchell was brought to the new Vanderbilt University and within four years came to advocate publicly Darwin's theories. He was dismissed in 1879 after a prolonged controversy. Nonetheless, Vanderbilt became a center for advanced biblical study as well as for the Christian interpretation of evolution. The struggle that separated Vanderbilt from the Methodist church was technically over the issue of who had the right to govern the school, but theological factors were also involved. The elevation of Emory to university status and the establishment of its Candler School of Theology as a response to the Methodist loss of Vanderbilt were also partially antimodernist developments.

During the 1920s the nation as a whole witnessed a battle between modernists and fundamentalists. On the one hand, it was a struggle within various denominations for control of each church's teaching and government. Although these struggles took place primarily in the North, they influenced those southern churches that had miniature fundamentalist-modernist controversies.

In southern Methodism, Bishops Candler, Denny, and DuBose were continually critical of liberal theology, which they saw as a threat to historic Methodist belief, and they were in contact with Harold Paul Slvan, a New Jersey pastor who led the conservative wing in the northern church. In the Southern Baptist Convention, the issue of whether evolution should be taught in the denomination's schools was hotly debated in the twenties, and in 1925 a new confession of faith—*The Baptist Faith and Message*—was adopted to guard against liberal ideas in the church.

The controversy was even more marked in the Presbyterian Church in the United States. This southern denomination had a series of trials in the early 20th century that prepared the way for the major controversy in the 1920s. The Reverend William Caldwell, who moved to Fort Worth from Baltimore, was at the center of a debate on biblical inerrancy that lasted from 1900 to 1909, and F. E. Maddox was suspended from the ministry in 1909 for heresy. Darwinism was continually denounced in the church press, and evolution was an issue before the 1920s made antievolutionism a popular crusade. The internal Presbyterian controversy in the 1920s revolved around The Bible Union of China, which charged that modernism had infected the mission field. Much of the controversy concerned Nanking Theological Seminary, a joint enterprise of the northern and southern churches. In addition, the question of whether a candidate needed to affirm acceptance of biblical inerrancy was also hotly discussed. Feelings on this issue were so high that Walter Moore, president of Union (Richmond), withdrew his nomination of Harris Kirk, a Baltimore pastor, for a faculty position at the denomination's seminaries. By 1930, however, the debate was quieted, although it reemerged from 1938 to 1940 in a controversy over the theology of Ernest Trice Thompson of Union Seminary. When the general assembly declined to investigate the doctrinal views of the faculty of the church's seminaries in 1940, the battle ended.

The other side of the debate in the 1920s was over the teaching of evolution in the public schools. In North Carolina, this debate was particularly hard fought. The presidents of Wake Forest College (Baptist) and Duke University, William Louis Poteat and William Preston Few, took the position that freedom of inquiry was essential to education and resisted the passage of a law preventing the teaching of evolution. For many Baptists and Methodists, their advocacy of academic freedom branded them as modernists and brought them much criticism in the church press. Their alliance, however, helped to block the passage of the act. The issue was fought more dramatically in the neighboring state of Tennessee, whose law prohibiting the teaching of evolution in the public schools resulted in the Scopes Trial in 1925.

The comparatively small number of modernists in the southern churches did not prevent "modernism" from becoming symbolically important in southern religion. The denunciation of modernists became a stock element in much southern preaching, and Bible colleges and similar institutions used the fear of modernism as a way of promoting their own cause. For many southerners, resistance to modernism was a central element of their faith. As part of the system of symbols by which southerners have ordered their religious lives, modernism—real or imagined—has been one of the dominant forces in the 20th century.

See also EDUCATION: / Duke University; Emory University; Vanderbilt University; SCIENCE AND MEDICINE: Science and Religion

Glenn T. Miller
Southeastern Baptist
Theological Seminary

Kenneth K. Bailey, *Southern White Protestantism in the Twentieth Century* (1964); Norman F. Furniss, *The Fundamentalist Controversy, 1918–1931* (1954); Willard B. Gatewood, Jr., ed., *Controversy in the Twenties: Fundamentalism, Modernism, and Evolution* (1969); Robert T. Handy, *Religion in Life* (Summer 1955); William R. Hutchison, *The Modernist Impulse in American Protestantism* (1976); George M. Marsden, *Fundamentalism and American Culture: The Shaping of Twentieth-Century Evangelicalism, 1870–1925* (1980).

Pentecostalism

American Pentecostalism comprises many diverse organizations, some of which are predominantly southern in both membership and influence. Much of the drama of early Pentecostal history occurred in the South, among the socially disinherited whose yearnings for spiritual perfection and otherworldly ecstasy had made them participants in the Holiness movements that had swept the region intermittently for decades.

Pentecostalism became a definable movement after 1901 when a consensus on the evidence of the baptism with the Holy Spirit emerged among the followers of Charles Parham, a Kansas Holiness preacher. The simple assertion that glossolalia (or speaking in tongues) was always the initial evidence of a crisis experience indicating a baptism of the Holy Spirit separated Pentecostals from others who shared the same concern for vital spiritual experience.

For five years this doctrine was preached primarily in Kansas, Oklahoma, and Texas, until in 1906 William Seymour took the message to California. From a warehouse on Azusa Street in Los Angeles the distinctive Pentecostal assertion spread and shaped a movement that would have long-term significance for American religion across the nation, and especially in the South.

Out of the fluid religious culture of the late 19th century came several currents that would converge in 20th-century Pentecostalism. The conviction of some individuals about the imminence of the second advent made them yearn for both "enduement with power for service" and holiness. The focus on restoration that had been a creative force throughout the American religious experience motivated others to desire the contemporary realization of the charismatic experiences of the New Testament church. Others were led through the healing revivalism of people like John Alexander Dowie and Mary Woodworth-Etter to stress the present manifestation of the spiritual gifts cited in I Corinthians 12–14. Another group, influenced by the loosely organized Wesleyan Holiness movement, stressed a "second blessing" of encounter with the Spirit resulting in holiness of heart and life. All these emphases became significant for Pentecostalism. Each stressed intangible blessings and otherworldly benefits and consciously discounted material possessions. Each had a consequent appeal to those who were "dispossessed" in this life.

These approaches to spirituality stressed the Holy Spirit and had some conception of a crisis encounter with the Spirit. There was no consensus among believers, however, as to incontrovertible evidence of the Spirit's special gifts, and those who responded to Parham's assertion of such evidence and thus became Pentecostal were thereby alienated from others in the religious culture whose concerns and heritage most closely resembled their own.

In the South, restorationist and Holiness thinking created a setting favorable to the Pentecostal message. Holiness teaching stressed the necessity of a work of grace, subsequent to the conversion experience, in which the individual would be sanctified. It focused on the Holy Spirit and on a definite religious experience subsequent to conversion. By 1906 outspoken southern Holiness advocates had largely left their original base in the Methodist Episcopal Church, South, to form independent groups, many of which had precise understanding not only of valid spiritual experience but also of appropriate Christian general behavior. Prohibitions against pork, coffee, colas, chewing gum, tobacco, alcohol, dancing, "spectator sports," and mixed bathing were common, as were directives regarding jewelry, short hair for women, and many types of clothing. "Holiness" came to be associated with specific external evidences. Across the South, small Holiness groups, local in character and different in emphasis, struggled to survive. Among those who already claimed a "second blessing" of sanctification were some to whom a "third blessing" of enduement with spiritual power seemed plausible.

Among the hundreds who visited Los Angeles in 1906 to observe the Pentecostal movement were two whose importance to southern Pentecostalism would be central—G. B. Cashwell of the Pentecostal Holiness Church, a Holiness group based in Falcon, N.C., and Charles Harrison Mason of Memphis, Tenn., who shared leadership with Charles Price Jones in the predominantly black Church of God in Christ. Both claimed an experience of Spirit baptism, and returned to the South as advocates of the Pentecostal message. Southern Holiness preachers had already been advised of the Los Angeles Pentecostal revival through articles and letters in such widely circulated Holiness periodicals as *The Way of Faith*, and many responded with interest to the teaching. Cashwell traveled widely, primarily among rural southeastern Holiness groups, with some ministry in urban centers like Memphis and Birmingham. One result of his ministry was the coalescence of several small southern Holiness groups to form the Pentecostal Holiness Church in 1911. Another would be the uniting with the Pentecostalism of Ambrose J. Tomlinson and the restorationist Church of

God that he led. Ultimately, at least three important Pentecostal groups would result from this connection—the Church of God; the Church of God of Prophecy (both with headquarters in Cleveland, Tenn.); and the Church of God, World Headquarters with offices in Huntsville, Ala.

Mason's acceptance of the Pentecostal message divided the Church of God in Christ. Mason assumed leadership of the Pentecostal majority; Jones renamed his Holiness followers the Church of Christ (Holiness) U.S.A. and moved his headquarters to Jackson, Miss.

The earliest division among Pentecostals centered around their understanding of sanctification. Initially Pentecostal leaders had insisted that sanctification was a discreet experience, a "second work," which always preceded the baptism with the Holy Spirit. After 1910 increasing numbers accepted teaching associated with William Durham, a Chicago pastor who understood sanctification as progressive, and perfection as impossible, and who developed his ideas under the heading "the finished work of grace." For several years controversy raged between "two-work" and "one-work" Pentecostals. Southern Pentecostal groups accepted the older "two-work" understanding of sanctification, and the "finished work of grace" became associated with the newer Assemblies of God.

Organized in 1914, the Assemblies of God drew together into a loose association some of the many independent Pentecostal missions across the country. Two important centers of its early strength were Alabama and Texas, but its constituency was always broader than any single geographic region. About 35 percent of its current membership is in the South. The Pentecostal Holiness Church and the several Pentecostal Churches of God, on the other hand, are overwhelmingly southern in membership, essentially Holiness in doctrine, and centralized in polity. These southern Pentecostal groups were scarcely touched by the second dividing crisis in Pentecostal history—the oneness controversy.

Cross atop Sanctified church, Clarksdale, Miss., 1968

Oneness Pentecostalism stresses the name of Jesus, claiming that Jesus is the name of Father, Son, and Spirit. This insistence, with its variant conception of the Trinity, as well as several other doctrinal traits, split the Assemblies of God and gave rise to an array of new Pentecostal groups, none of which has a strong southern base.

One distinct segment of Pentecostalism, then, is an integral part of the southern experience. Wesleyan in theology and centralized in structure, it remains largely confined to the South. The Church of God (Cleveland) and its several offshoots also incorporate a strong restorationist motif that Pentecostalism in other parts of the country does not include. The Church of God in Christ remains predominantly black and maintains its headquarters in Memphis. Its initial southern base has been extended to include outreach in major metropolitan black communities across the nation.

Although Pentecostalism is not exclusively a southern religion, some of its institutions have been shaped by their southern roots and continue to have their principal outreach in the South. Southern Pentecostalism incorporates theology and polity that set it apart, at least to some extent, from the movement at large. It has validity in the culture while perceiving itself as part of a force that transcends culture to provide spiritual vitality to the church.

See also BLACK LIFE: / Mason, Charles Harrison

Edith L. Blumhofer
Evangel College

Robert Mapes Anderson, *Vision of the Disinherited: The Making of American Pentecostalism* (1979); Charles Conn, *Like a Mighty Army Moves the Church of God* (1977); William Menzies, *Anointed to Serve: The Story of the Assemblies of God* (1971); John T. Nichol, *Pentecostalism* (1966); Vinson Synan, *The Holiness-Pentecostal Movement in the United States* (1971).

Politics and Religion

Scholars who have examined the relationship between religion and politics in the South generally agree that the region has identifiable religious patterns that have influenced the conservative political and social attitudes of southerners and promoted cultural beliefs, values, and institutions that can be thought of as distinctively "southern." Religious historian Samuel S. Hill has pointed out that the South, dominated by Baptist and Methodist denominations, remains a distinct religious region, characterized by evangelical, fundamentalist Protestantism.

Geographer James R. Shortridge has asserted that the South should be considered a religious region, arguing that "a religious regionalization is as close to an objective cultural regionalization as we are likely to get in the foreseeable future." Sociologists Joseph Fichter and George Maddox have written that "almost every observer of the South has, sooner or later, recorded impressions about the pervasiveness and peculiarity of religious behavior and institutions in the region." Finally, sociologist John Shelton Reed has analyzed the elements of southern religious beliefs and practices, including overwhelming Protestant dominance, with Baptist-Methodist hegemony; a relatively high level of church attendance for members of all social classes; a greater tendency to "attend" church services conducted by electronic preachers; and adherence to concrete, literal, and orthodox beliefs.

The early history of southern religion gave little indication of these future patterns. The first settlers at Jamestown, to be sure, brought their Anglicanism with them, and a pervasive religious-moral tone, nurtured by government, existed in Virginia's early years, although to a lesser degree than in the Puritan colonies in New England. The first religious-political establishment in the South, then, was Anglican, but it was institutionally weak and grew even more so when colonists moved into the backcountry. With the American Revolution, the Church of England in the new United States became the Episcopal church, and its privileged status ended, replaced by a system of religious freedom and voluntary denominational competition. Evangelical Protestant groups such as the Baptists and Methodists, who had begun as dissenting sects, emerged from recurrent frontier revivals to become the dominant religious groups in the South by the Civil War.

Despite their doctrine of "the spirituality of the church"—which taught that religious institutions should concentrate on purely church matters and stay removed from politics—southern churches in the antebellum period forged close church-state ties. Ministers articulated a biblical defense of slavery, and the southern Baptists, Methodists, and Presbyterians split off from their northern brethren to form distinctly sectional religious bodies, which survived long after the Civil War. Religious leaders justified the Confederacy as a holy war and played a key role in maintaining morale for the war effort. After defeat, the southern churches created a "religion of the Lost Cause," which saw religious meaning in the southern historical experience and discouraged any criticisms of the regional way of life. Ministers and churches in the late 19th century launched a series of moral crusades, using the power of the state to establish laws to prevent gambling (including the end of the popular Louisiana lottery and prevention of horse racing), to honor the Sabbath with blue laws, and, above all, to prohibit the sale of alcoholic beverages. Some ministers were actively involved in the Fundamentalist movement and worked to pass laws regulating textbooks and preventing the teaching of evolution in the schools.

Most of these campaigns were attempts by conservative religious leaders and institutions to shape the South into a moralistic evangelical empire. But religion was also used to promote liberal reform. The Populists of the 1890s used religious rhetoric to justify their call for fundamental reforms in the American economy, although ultimately their efforts proved to be a new "lost cause." In the 20th century, and especially during the Great Depression, reform-minded Christians formed organizations such as the Southern Christian Tenant Farmers' Union, the Fellowship of Southern Churchmen, the Commission on Interracial Cooperation, the Association of Southern Women for the Prevention of Lynching, and the Southern Christian Leadership Conference. Many of those were organized efforts to bring economic reforms in the spirit of a Christian Socialist society, whereas others have aimed at the related goal of racial justice. Southern church women, in particular, launched numerous progressive moral campaigns, including efforts to improve the life of prisoners, the poor, immigrants, industrial workers, and blacks, as well as to end discrimination against women.

Southern religion, nonetheless, has been predominantly a conservative, tradition-oriented influence. Francis Butler Simkins once asserted that "Orthodox Protestantism . . . is a likely explanation of why the section . . . has kept its identity as the most conservative portion of the United States." Charles Roland, in his study of the post–World War II South, noted that in the postwar era southern churches have come out against guaranteed annual income proposals, have denounced the northern churches that promoted such matters as family planning and urban renewal, and have supported American participation in the Vietnam War. And Ted Jelen, in an analysis of National Opinion Research Center data, found that southern fundamentalists tended to be less tolerant of Communists, homosexuals, and atheists than was the case for their non-southern counterparts. In a somewhat broader analysis, published in the early 1960s, W. Seward Salisbury compared religiously orthodox and unorthodox college students in the South and non-South on a number of points. Whereas a rather sharp orthodox-unorthodox distinction existed regardless of region, orthodox students from the South tended to be considerably more opposed to interracial marriage, much more supportive of segregated schools, significantly less willing to extend full pastoral rights to women, and more likely to find some good resulting from war than was the case for their orthodox brethren outside the South.

Scholars agree that southern churches have been closely tied to their culture. I. A. Newby has noted that religious beliefs in the South have tended to reflect secular values rather than to mold them; Fichter and Maddox have pointed out that "the churches seem to employ God to maintain and retain the Old South"; and Reed has stated that "most Southern churches are . . . so much a part of the community as to be indistinguishable from it." Hill has emphasized that "the overall impact of the church leadership has been priestly in that secular traditions and values have been 'baptized' and accorded legitimacy." An important function of religion, thereby, has been to support orthodox and distinctively southern beliefs and values.

Recent research has compared southern whites with

non-southern whites as well as southern whites and southern blacks, and again supported the notion that, religiously, the South does indeed constitute a distinct region. Michael L. Mezey, for example, in assessing the importance of religious beliefs for southern distinctiveness found that religious attitudes divided southerners from those outside the South; however, those differences were not as great as the differences on a number of other issues, such as race, tolerance of deviants, military issues, moral issues, and women's rights issues. Furthermore, considerable variation was found on religious issues, with attitudes toward school prayer showing a great deal of southern distinctiveness and confidence toward the clergy showing none. He concluded, therefore, that religious beliefs tended to have a moderate and mixed effect in distinguishing southerners from people in the rest of the country.

Other research has reaffirmed the religious distinction of the South. Corwin Smidt, who compared the political attitudes and behavior of white evangelicals in the South with those outside the South, found a considerably higher percentage of southerners met the definition for evangelical. A recent study by Robert P. Steed, Laurence W. Moreland, and Tod A. Baker reached much the same conclusion with regard to members of the southern political elite, arguing that the impact of fundamentalism on southern political life was due mainly to the South having more fundamentalists, rather than to qualitative differences between southern and non-southern fundamentalism.

Other research studying the linkages between religion and specific political attitudes has shown, however, that religious beliefs tended *not* to have a *general* conservative effect on political values. Instead, the linkage tended to be limited to social issues, or, perhaps even more specifically, to issues with a moral content. Smidt, for example, found that economic issues divided the respondents in his study along regional lines. However, social issues—including the role of women in society, busing, prayer in schools, and abortion—divided respondents along religious lines, with evangelicals tending to take the more conservative positions. Similarly, Jerry Perkins, Donald Fairchild, and Murray Havens found that, on 8 of the 15 issues they examined, racial differences were greater than religious ones; but on three social issues they examined—abortion, school prayer, and the place of women in society—religious differences were greater. Reaching much the same conclusion, Kenneth Wald and Michael Lupfer sought to determine the causal role of religious beliefs; in their Memphis study, they found that religious orthodoxy was most powerful once again in explaining the effect of moral conservatism on issues such as abortion, women's rights, and drugs.

Research on political activists has also sought to determine the relationship between fundamentalist beliefs and distinctively southern political and social attitudes. In their research on party convention delegates in Virginia and South Carolina, Baker, Steed, and Moreland measured the effects on this relationship of the development of party competition and the movement of blacks into the Democratic elite. They found that on issues such as the Equal Rights Amendment, the SALT II treaty, affirmative action, and increased defense spending, party identification and race divided the party elite much more sharply than religion. However, religious beliefs (along with race) were important in separating their respondents on abortion issues. In short, except for issues with a moral content, changes in the nature of the party system and in the status of blacks seem to have undermined religious beliefs as a principal foundation of southern distinctiveness.

In summary, the most recent research cited above tends to demonstrate the following: first, much of the contemporary impact of religion on the South (as compared with the rest of the nation) is accounted for by the much larger portion of the southern population that considers itself to be fundamentalist; and, second, southern religion's direct impact on political attitudes is greatest on moral and social issues for both the mass public and the political elite.

Inasmuch as the impact of religious beliefs on political and social attitudes must be qualified, as noted above, the research potential of this topic might seem rather limited. Yet, some areas do appear to offer promise. For example, the emergence of blacks in political life could have a profound effect on the nature of evangelicalism in the South and its relation to political life. The white church in the South has historically reflected dominant, orthodox viewpoints in the region and, hence, has been labeled as conservative and as a major support to southern distinctiveness. On the other hand, the black church, also largely evangelical and fundamentalist, has struck a much more progressive note, beginning long before the civil rights movement of the post–World War II period. The black church has a long history of commitment to change and, as a result, could be thought of as constituting a principal mechanism through which blacks have sought to bring about changes in southern mores.

The political attitudes and behavior of black ministers will be of growing interest, just as studies of southern white ministers have contributed to our understanding of religion and politics in the region. For example, James Guth's analysis of data from a survey of white Southern Baptist ministers revealed an association between political ideology and political activism with the politically most conservative being significantly more likely to be politically active. Inasmuch as blacks have now moved into the mainstream of southern political life, comparable studies of black ministers should prove equally useful.

The possibility of evangelical coalitions across racial lines is another potential research focus even though the probability of such a development appears to be low. Perkins and associates concluded that among southern voters race is a considerably more important cleavage than religion; and Baker and associates, in their study of state party activists, found that the cleavages created by party identification and race were more important than the one created by religion. Yet the possibility remains that on the state or local level issues may arise that mobilize people on the basis of religious beliefs. As the South continues its transformation from a rural, small-town society, social issues such as liquor, gambling, and pornography could prompt religious coalitions across racial lines.

The development of party competition could also affect the relationship between religion and politics, particularly with regard to the composition of party elites. Because evangelicalism and fundamentalism are conservative creeds and because members of the political elite tend to be more ideological than the mass of the citizenry, white evangelicals and fundamentalists would likely gravitate to the more conservative party. Steed and associates found that 70 percent of the white fundamentalist party activists in South Carolina and Virginia identified with the Republican party. On the other hand, blacks—both fundamentalist and nonfundamentalist—are overwhelmingly Democratic. Thus, it seems that the Republican party is developing a rather strong white fundamentalist wing whereas the Democratic party is developing a black fundamentalist one. If this is indeed occurring, black fundamentalists within the Democratic elite will tend to take strong conservative positions on moral issues and strong liberal positions on others, with black nonfundamentalists taking more consistently liberal positions. Further, within the Democratic party white nonfundamentalists will tend to take—relative to black Democrats—liberal positions on moral issues and relatively conservative positions on others. Within the Republican party fundamentalists will tend to take strong conservative positions on all issues, with nonfundamentalists taking slightly more liberal positions on moral ones.

Finally, additional research on the role of fundamentalists among political elites may also be useful. Alan Abramowitz, John McGlennon, and Ronald Rapoport have shown that on some occasions fundamentalists have fitted comfortably into southern party organizations, but at other times they found themselves largely isolated and, to a large extent, uncomfortable in the party in which they were active.

See also POLITICS articles; SOCIAL CLASS: Religion and Social Class

Tod A. Baker
Robert P. Steed
Laurence W. Moreland
The Citadel

Tod A. Baker, Robert P. Steed, and Laurence W. Moreland, eds., *Religion and Politics in the South: Mass and Elite Perspectives* (1983); Joseph Fichter and George Maddox, in *The South in Continuity and Change*, ed. John C. McKinney and Edgar T. Thompson (1965); Samuel S. Hill, *Religion and the Solid South* (1972), *Southern Churches in Crisis* (1967), in *Religion in the South*, ed. Charles Reagan Wilson (1985); Laurence W. Moreland, Tod A. Baker, and Robert P. Steed, eds., *Contemporary Southern Political Attitudes and Behavior: Studies and Essays* (1982); Hart M. Nelson and Anne Kusener Nelson, *Black Church in America* (1975); Liston Pope, *Review of Religious Research* (Spring 1963); John Shelton Reed, *The Enduring South: Subcultural Persistence in Mass Society* (1972); Charles Roland, *The Improbable Era: The South since World War II* (1975); W. Seward Salisbury, *Journal for Scientific Study of Religion* (October 1962); James R. Shortridge, *Journal for the Scientific Study of Religion* (June 1977); Joseph R. Washington, *Black Religion: The Negro and Christianity in the United States* (1964).

Preacher, White

White southern religion, once considered a monolithic, unidimensional structure, is now recognized as diverse and filled with ambiguities. Previously accepted stereotypes have been challenged by recent scholarship, which points out the diversity of southern culture in general and of southern religion in particular. Accordingly, the tendency to categorize all southern preachers as overzealous evangelists espousing a fiery brand of fundamentalism must be called into question as well. Ministers of southern white Protestant churches have been represented among the ranks of the theological elite, multimedia practitioners of the Gospel, and country parsons alike. There are as many images as there are preachers, and the effort to discuss *the* image of the southern white preacher seems, at least initially, a futile one. Yet one quality distinguishes the southern white preacher from his neighbors and also from his northern colleagues—and that is precisely his image. Whatever his social situation or professed beliefs, wherever he may live and work, awe and reverence accompany him. His is a powerful image; it is one of authority.

Certainly this distinctiveness is a matter of degree rather than of kind. Protestants in America, Robert S. Michaelsen has pointed out, "have looked to their ministers as the defenders of morality and the representatives of spirituality. They have expected them to stand out as examples of what people ought to be morally and spiritually." If this depiction is accurate in the country as a whole, then it is even more apt as a description of conditions in the South. The centrality of Protestantism in southern culture gives the preacher his legitimacy as an articulator of truths, and he in turn provides religion with its shape and power. For people who are devout believers in God, as large numbers of southerners profess to be, his earthly representative is an awesome figure. Although the preacher's image has consistently been one of authority, his role in southern culture has not been static. Indeed, it is possible to trace certain trends in southern history by examining the unfolding of the image of authority.

During the early days of the South, this sparsely populated region with its scattered outposts demanded a preacher who was an itinerant man of God. As he traveled from place to place, he served as a cultural bonding force. Although southern religion had not yet developed a distinct and separate identity, the region's faith and its self-understanding were gradually becoming inextricably interwoven. Simplicity ruled in those hard times: the minister was one called by God. Educational or professional preparation was incidental to his activities. Peter Cartwright, an early Methodist minister, once explained that when a man went into the ministry he did not seek a seminary; rather he "hunted up a hardy pony of a horse . . . and with his library always at hand, namely Bible, Hymn-Book and Discipline, he started, and with a text that never wore out or grew stale, he cried 'Behold the Lamb of God.'" The sacred works identified him wherever he roamed.

The preacher's image was enhanced as the revivals swept through the South in the early 19th century. Now he had to be a skilled exhorter who could bring sinners into the fold in large numbers and with rapid precision. Although all southerners did not by any means participate in these massive spectacles, the revivals exerted a significant force on southern society. The growth in church membership was impressive, and, though a variety of denominations emerged, within and among the churches there was a strong sense of shared values and beliefs. The feeling of community that evolved contributed to the prestige of the minister in the South; he was the official exponent of religious and regional beliefs. His sphere of power extended beyond the domain of the church steeple. In the words of John Holt Rice, an early 19th-century Presbyterian minister, the preacher's work "embraces every duty, in every situation."

Increasing population density resulted in churches that were established permanently in a particular place, with a wide influence over the inhabitants there. The popular Methodist and Baptist denominations became part of the status quo: the clergy became more educated, church members more affluent, and the churches' attitude toward the world more accepting. As a consequence, the minister of a church with prestigious community members exercised considerable influence over local and regional affairs. His presence at group meetings and political gatherings was not merely perfunctory; he represented the forces of the divine.

With the emergence of the issue of slavery and the subsequent Civil War, the white minister in the South articulated a solid defense of his region's way of life. In so doing he gained even greater prestige and visibility. Although controversies over proper education and appropriate qualifications erupted from time to time, the white preacher—no matter what his background—was an important regional spokesman. At times, however, as villages grew into cities and towns in the antebellum period, his image became fragmented. On the one hand, he was to converse with other professional members of his community and maintain a rational and sophisticated demeanor; on the other hand, he was to represent the simple way of life and belief of the rural past. The result was often a dwindling sense of inner assuredness for individual preachers. All the same, in the days of Reconstruction, the preacher's power expanded significantly as large numbers of southerners turned to churches for a rationale to explain defeat. In 1885 a noted Methodist editor claimed that "there is no part of the world in which ministers of the Gospel are more respected than in the Southern states."

In the first half of the 20th century the white Protestant preacher continued to exercise considerable influence in the South. Erskine Caldwell, the popular southern novelist whose father was a minister, asserted that

Fundamentalist minister, Red Banks, Miss., 1968

"in the 'twenties and 'thirties . . . a Protestant minister was frequently called upon to act as a social welfare worker, a marriage counselor, a financial adviser, an arbitrator between feuding families, a psychiatric consultant, and as a judge to decide what was and what was not moral conduct." In many small towns such expectations continue. But more and more psychologists, college professors, physicians, and other professionals fulfill the tasks traditionally performed by the local minister. The preacher's public role in the South, then, has diminished substantially. Although the national media have brought them increased attention, charismatic exhorters are by no means peculiar to this region. Moreover, in the South, as in the rest of the country, the preacher has repudiated many of the traits that clearly distinguished him in earlier times. Nonetheless, the image of the white preacher as an authority figure, a moral, upright person who represents the divine and speaks the language of the Gospel, still prevails in the South.

See also BLACK LIFE: Preacher, Black

Rosemary M. Magee
Emory University

Erskine Caldwell, *Deep South: Memory and Observation* (1972); Peter Cartwright, *The Autobiography of Peter Cartwright: The Backwoods Preacher* (1856); *Christian Advocate* (17 October 1885); Samuel S. Hill, *Southern Churches in Crisis* (1967); E. Brooks Holifield, *The Gentlemen Theologians: American Theology in Southern Culture, 1795–1860* (1978); Robert S. Michaelsen, in *The Ministry in Historical Perspectives*, ed. H. Richard Niebuhr and Daniel D. Williams (1956).

Protestantism

Southern Protestantism and southern culture are as inseparable as bourbon and fruitcake. The South stands out both as a discernible cultural entity and as an equally unique religious region. Indeed it is the most religious and Protestant area of an extraordinarily religious nation. Southerners tend to be more active in religious organizations and more orthodox in measurable belief than any of their fellow citizens. Evangelical Protestants often make up 80 to 90 percent of the "churched" population, and most call themselves Baptists and Methodists. Yet there is also great diversity—independent churches, all the major organized denominations, and numerous small, proudly independent associations and congregations, which are properly denominations unto themselves.

The South has given rise to distinctively American and even regional styles of religion. This pattern results from a combination of geography (America's early and hence formative frontier), economic conditions (extremes of plantation wealth, slavery, and rural poverty), great mobility (geographic and economic), and a fierce individualism. Protestantism in the South is also nostalgic, smoldering, and languorous. It has an ethos haunted by guilt, defiance, a deep attachment to sacred places and heroes, a strong positive sense of mission, and a painful memory of the bitter combination of chosenness and inexplicable defeat.

The southern Protestant ethos decisively began with the extended period of revivalism that swept in waves over the South from 1799 until 1820. Baptists and Methodists, far more adaptive to frontier conditions than their Presbyterian and Episcopalian competitors, quickly became the dominant organizations and remain so today. The influence of revivalism is everywhere in southern religion. Emotive, rhetorically persuasive preaching designed to produce personal crisis and conversion is central. There are, consequently, traditions of great preaching and great preachers—charismatic leaders whose personalities often serve as the bonding agent of their personal churches. Worship focuses upon the production of palpable religious experiences for congregation-audiences. Christianity tends to be reduced to the simplicity of sin, guilt, conversion, and forgiveness, always centered around individual salvation. An individual's religious life is intensely focused upon the conversion experience. It is an event continually recalled and even relived through revivalistic rededication, the evangelical equivalent to the Catholic sacrament of penance. Additionally there are presumptions of perfectibility or at least thorough transformation. One "gets saved" or is "born again" or "gets right with God."

The shadows of slavery and segregation have fallen heavily across the social gospel, limiting but not eliminating social responsibility. For over 150 years voluntary societies as well as churches have fought for temperance, printed and distributed literature and Bibles, and built settlement houses and educational institutions; yet they were always reluctant to confront the fundamental structure of a society based upon a system of racial oppression. Revivalism insists one attend to the immediate demands of piety; it "verticalizes" one's religion from God above to humans below, enclosing it in what James McBride Dabbs calls "a limited, private world" free from the complexities of social and political life. Additionally, because the revivalistic style takes people out of their normal context and places them as individuals before the righteous God, it has had the power to suspend their usual social rules, including those of hierarchy. This creation of "liminality" (a state "in between" classifications) allowed slaves to instruct their masters in religious matters, urge their conversion, and assume, for the duration of the liminal period, a position of superiority. The "limited world" made possible the experience of socially sage bonds of affection and even friendship between slave and master, black and white. Such a limitation of the ethical dimensions of Christianity required a moralistic ethical style—the connection of specific biblical "principles" to specific individual moral choices, often in an ad hoc and surprisingly legalistic way.

A final and defining characteristic deeply embedded in the evangelical tradition is assurance. This involves a certainty of salvation arising from the varied sources of conversion, Scripture, and experiences of God's presence. It appears almost as an evangelical personality style or perhaps a state of being—warm, confident, immediately and openly religious, intensely yet comfortably intimate with a somewhat domesticated deity, but also quite unquestioning and rather unteachable.

For many white Protestants the line between Christian religion and Christian civilization has often been too fine to discern. Ironically, during the periods of slavery and legal segregation, southerners were in the forefront of those celebrating America's Christian identity and even claiming the achievement of a high degree of social perfection. From this perspective the Civil War was a noble and tragic effort undertaken in defense of a last bastion of Christendom. After the war southern Protestantism became a "suffering servant," a moral and religious preservative with a mission of national salvation. World War I, fought against the German originators of academic biblical criticism and liberal religion, was seen as a triumph of American, Protestant, southern, and Baptist values. This evangelical civil religion continues to inform and motivate numerous southerners and their churches.

For blacks, too, the entwinement of religion and culture has run deep. Slave religion and later the black churches have always served social and political purposes, often providing black people with their primary source for social cohesion and political mobilization. Black churches have given leadership, continuity, and organization to the black community ever since Emancipation. They launched the civil rights movement of the 1950s and 1960s, and a presidential candidacy in 1984, permanently changing southern society at its most basic levels. The enthusiasm of the South's black population for the white vision of a Christian America has been understandably limited. Slaves took the evangelical Protestantism handed them by their captors and adapted it to their own special needs and circumstances. Unlike southern whites, blacks attended to the prophetic dimensions of Christianity, finding the self-esteem and strength necessary to withstand the dehumanization of slavery and segregation in the knowledge that Jesus, too, had felt the oppressor's lash. Christianity confirmed for slaves what they had always known—that slavery was wrong—and what they had always hoped—that it was not permanent. Slaves quickly determined that they were considerably closer to the example established by Jesus than were their owners, and they soon found their own version of Christianity superior to that of the whites. Out of their suffering the slaves created a form of evangelicalism considerably more celebratory than that of white society. Much remained the same—the intensity, experience, simplicity, and informality—but there were crucial differences. Whereas white Protestantism consistently appealed to authority, particularly that of the Scriptures, black religion tended to allow authority to remain tacit while celebrating God's love and deliverance. In the words of Eugene D. Genovese, whites sought forgiveness from Jesus and blacks sought recognition.

As America enters the final decades of the 20th century, southern evangelicalism again stands at the center of action, emerging as the most modern and energetic American religion. In the face of the rather contradictory currents of disintegrating regionalism, growing cultural uniformity, and an ever-increasing social diversity, proponents of Christian civilization have reemerged, creating new voluntary societies aiming to save America for Christendom and the world. This in itself represents a significant secularization of southern evangelicalism as it focuses itself on political questions and mixes hefty amounts of civil religion with its traditional worldview. In related developments, southern evangelicals have discovered that their religious style with its emphasis on ministerial action and congregational consumption translates easily to television, making possible the dawn of evangelical media empires. A growing worldliness, and even a materialistic spirit, is evident in television ministries, which commonly promise tangible transformation—healing or financial success guaranteed for those supporting the ministries. Prophetic voices on the evangelical left warn that idolatry is inherent in the very idea of Christian civilization. Moderates seek areas of compatibility between Christianity and secular republican virtue. Clearly Protestantism in the South is becoming less regional. Geographical and cultural isolation have become impossible to maintain. Rapid population growth, diversification, and continued social and economic mobility promise an immediate future of conflict and realignment. What will emerge is surely in doubt, but it seems likely that the distinctiveness of southern Protestantism and culture will become increasingly difficult to preserve.

See also BLACK LIFE: Religion, Black

Dennis E. Owen
University of Florida

Kenneth K. Bailey, *Southern White Protestantism in the Twentieth Century* (1964); John B. Boles, *The Great Revival, 1787–1805: The Origins of the Southern Evangelical Mind* (1972); John Lee Eighmy, *Churches in Cultural Captivity: A History of the Social Attitudes of Southern Baptists* (1972); Samuel S. Hill, ed., *Encyclopedia of Religion in the South* (1984), *Religion and the Solid South* (1972), *Southern Churches in Crisis* (1967); C. Eric Lincoln, ed., *The Black Experience in Religion: A Book of Readings* (1974); Donald Mathews, *Religion in the Old South* (1977); John Shelton Reed, *The Enduring South: Subcultural Persistence in Mass Society* (1972); Charles Reagan Wilson, *Baptized in Blood: The Religion of the Lost Cause, 1865–1920* (1980).

Restorationist Christianity

Restorationist Christianity, which self-consciously seeks to ignore historic Christian forms and traditions and to reproduce primitive Christianity, has flourished in the American South, but it is not unique to the South. This style of Christianity has deep roots in British Protestantism and appeared with particular vitality in the left wing of that heritage, especially among the Puritans, Baptists, and Quakers, and later among the early Methodists. Thus, restorationist traditions that persist in America today—in addition to the modern heirs of the Swiss and German Anabaptists—include Mormons, various types of Baptists, various Holiness and Pentecostal groups, Christian Churches, and Churches of Christ.

At least two factors influenced the openness of southern Christianity to the restorationist impulse in the 19th century. First, the Baptist and Methodist domination of southern religion created a climate of deference both to the Scriptures and to Christian antiquity. Second, the stubborn persistence of the southern frontier until well into the 20th century in some regions (e.g., Appalachia and the Ozarks) created a cultural situation particularly resistant to modernity and especially amenable to various types of primitivism. When Baptists and Methodists with a primitivist theological orientation settled in large numbers on the southern frontier, it was perhaps inevitable that this potent religious/cultural mix would spawn numerous restorationist movements, some of which would coalesce into lasting denominations.

Four major movements, all with a self-conscious restorationist orientation, emerged in the South after 1800: the Churches of Christ; the Primitive or Antimission Baptists; the Landmark Baptists; and southern Pentecostalists, especially the Church of God (Cleveland, Tenn.) and the snake handlers of southern Appalachia. Interestingly, all these traditions have roots in middle or eastern Tennessee and western North Carolina.

Churches of Christ emerged in Tennessee, Kentucky, and southern Ohio under the leadership of Barton W. Stone in the first decade of the 19th century and by 1825 had made headway into northern Alabama. Reflecting in many ways the quest for liberty that characterized the American Revolution, participants in this movement threw off the yoke of history and bondage to historical traditions, rejected the authority of creeds and clerics, used the primitive church as portrayed in Scripture as a model for their individual and ecclesiastical behavior, and styled themselves simply "Christians" and their congregations "Churches of Christ." Ardently optimistic and utopian, they argued that a universal emulation of the primitive church would bring Christian unity and then the millennium.

Although Stone and some of his "Christian" colleagues

had Presbyterian roots, the vast majority of both members and leaders in the new movement came from the ranks of Separate and Regular Baptists, whose allegiance both to Scripture and to the primitive church made them restorationists in their own right. This was particularly true of the Separate Baptists, who determined to follow the Bible as their only confession of faith in the mid-18th century. They followed Shubal Stearns to North Carolina and Virginia in 1755 and later in the century migrated to Kentucky and Tennessee, where they increased the ranks of the Christian movement. According to one observer in 1812, the Christians in the West had by that time over 13,000 members and at least 117 preachers.

By 1823 Alexander Campbell began to influence both Baptists and the "Christians" of Kentucky and Tennessee, largely through his new periodical, the *Christian Baptist*. Campbell's contribution in this region was essentially twofold. To begin, he was by then a significant link in the growing, nationwide resistance to the new missionary societies of the North and East, viewed by many as flagrant attempts to extend the power of the New England Standing Order throughout the nation in the wake of disestablishment. Campbell's opposition to ecclesiastical societies, clerics, and creeds, and his affirmation of the primitive church as the alternative to modern innovations, greatly strengthened both the restorationist and the antimissionist sentiments already present among both Baptists and Christians. In addition, Campbell superimposed on the primitivist piety of the Stone movement a hard-headed, rational, common sense approach to the restoration ideal that has characterized Churches of Christ ever since. By 1860 the Churches of Christ flourished in middle Tennessee under the leadership of Tolbert Fanning and David Lipscomb.

Due to post–Civil War migration patterns, Churches of Christ are today concentrated not only in southern Kentucky, middle Tennessee, and northern Alabama, but also in other portions of Tennessee, Arkansas, Oklahoma, and Texas, with significant strength in southern California as well.

The Primitive or Antimission Baptists arose out of the same ideological matrix that provided such a fertile field for the growth of Churches of Christ: a passion for liberty, an expectation of the millennium, a rejection of the power of the older ecclesiastical establishments and of their missionary societies, and a consequent affirmation of the freedom and simplicity of the primitive church as a model for Baptists of the 19th century. The antimission agitation, based on a fear of eastern ecclesiastical power and of state-church resurgence, was a nationwide, interdenominational phenomenon in the 1810s and especially the 1820s, led by Deists like Elihu Palmer, Christians like Elias Smith and Alexander Campbell, Baptists like John Leland, Methodists like Peter Cartwright and Lorenzo Dow, and interdenominational figures such as Theophilus Ransom Gates whose *Reformer* (1820–35) was a veritable clearinghouse for antimission sentiment from a wide variety of sources. Antimission arguments from these and other leaders typically contrasted the elaborate extraecclesiastical and interdenominational agencies and societies of that age with the simple, congregational autonomy of the early Christians. The restorationist thrust of this agitation could even be seen in the titles of some of the periodicals, for example, *The Evangelical Restorationist* (Troy, N.Y., 1825) and *Priestcraft Exposed and Primitive Christianity Defended* (Lockport, N.Y., 1828–29).

Although opposition to eastern ecclesiastical power was nationwide, it was especially strong in the Jacksonian South, where rural religionists resented the efforts of eastern missionaries and "dandies" to save the frontier from barbarism. Further, among some Regular Baptists in the South, opposition to missions was buttressed by a rigid predestinarianism: after all, why organize mission societies if the eternal fate of mankind is already determined? These Baptists appealed both to the structure (no societies) and to the theology (predestination) of the primitive church to legitimize their positions, and throughout the 1820s these questions were debated in Regular Baptist churches and associations throughout America and especially in the South.

The key early leaders of Baptist antimissionism were John Leland, Daniel Parker, and John Taylor. By 1820 most Baptist churches in Tennessee and northern Alabama apparently had adopted the primitivist, antimission posture, and the Kehukee Association of North Carolina followed suit in 1827. By 1832 the primitive antimissionists began the process of separating into a distinct denomination. Their greatest early success was in Tennessee and northern Alabama, but they also experienced significant growth in Georgia, Virginia, North Carolina, Kentucky, and Texas.

It is ironic that the Primitive Baptists drank so deeply from the well of optimistic postmillennialism that sustained the early antimission agitation nationwide, for when these Baptists blended their opposition to mission societies with their rigid predestinarianism, they emerged as stridently pessimistic and premillennial—a perspective reflected in their first widely circulated periodical, *Signs of the Times* (1832–35). Their pessimistic and isolationist worldview perhaps accounts for their speedy decline from at least 68,000 members in 1844 to only 45,000 in 1890.

Although Primitive Baptists began as a white denomination, they eventually had even greater strength among blacks than among whites. By 1900 the black church had become more progressive than the white church, employing both Sunday schools and conventions, and by 1936 the black church had considerable strength in Alabama, Florida, Tennessee, Georgia, Texas, and North Carolina. By 1975 the black National Primitive Baptist Convention of the U.S.A. claimed over 1.5 million members. The white church, on the other hand, enjoyed its greatest early success in Tennessee and northern Alabama but also experienced significant growth in Georgia, Virginia, North Carolina, Kentucky, and Texas before experiencing decline.

A third restorationist tradition emerged in 1851 in Tennessee—the Landmark Baptists. Like the Churches of Christ, this tradition drew its greatest strength from the revivalistic Separate Baptists and focused almost exclusively on questions of ecclesiology and particularly on the identity of the "true church." The Landmark leader, James Robinson Graves of Nashville, argued that the true church had existed in an unbroken chain throughout Christian history and had always borne the marks of congregational autonomy, ecclesiastical democracy, and baptism by immersion. Any religious body organized since apostolic days was no church whatsoever, and the true church could be traced by the "trail of blood"—those martyrs who have refused throughout Christian history to be seduced by modernity.

The term *Landmark* was taken from a tract by James Madison Pendleton, "An Old Landmark Reset," which raised and answered negatively the question of whether Baptists should invite pedobaptists to preach in their pulpits. A third significant leader was Amos Cooper Dayton, who articulated fundamental Landmark themes in a two-volume novel, *Theodosia Ernest* (1857). Though Landmarkism had gathered significant strength in Tennessee and parts of the Old Southwest by 1880, it was not organized into a formal denomination until 1905, when Ben M. Bogard and others led in establishing the General Association of Landmark Baptists in Texarkana, Ark., renamed in 1924 the American Baptist Association. By 1980 the American Baptist Association claimed its greatest strength in Arkansas and Texas, with lesser strengths in Oklahoma, Louisiana, and Florida.

Not until the late 19th century would the restoration sentiment again incarnate itself in lasting and major institutional forms and structures in the South. This later development was the Holiness/Pentecostal phenomenon that grew largely, though not exclusively, from Methodist soil and was, like the earlier antimission agitation, a national phenomenon. The restorationist underpinnings of the Holiness revival, which preceded the Pentecostal phase of the movement, were implicit in the Holiness rejection of modern trends in established denominations. But some Holiness denominations, such as the Church of God, Anderson, Ind. (1880), made the restorationist appeal to the primitive church both explicit and fundamental.

During the last two decades of the 19th century, a more radical phase of the Holiness movement was developing—a phase that appealed especially to the poor and disinherited and that emphasized the baptism of the Holy Ghost as a third work of grace (following justification and sanctification), physical healing, and premillennialism. By 1906 and thereafter, most of these more radical churches also accepted glossolalia (speaking in tongues) and emerged as Pentecostalist, separate from the more moderate Holiness movement.

Although Pentecostalism, like the Holiness movement, was a nationwide phenomenon, it is significant that many of the Holiness churches in the South became Pentecostal. A clue to why this occurred lies in the otherwordly rejection of history that was implicit in early Pentecostalism and that appealed powerfully to the disinherited of a still alienated and impoverished South. This otherworldly dimension was evident in two central themes of early Pentecostal theology. First, whereas the Holiness phenomenon had been rooted early in an optimistic postmillennial perspective, Pentecostalism embraced a more pessimistic premillennial theology anticipating an imminent second coming of Christ. Second, implicit in Pentecostalism's emphasis on the baptism of the Holy Ghost and glossolalia was a restorationist perspective that looked beyond the present age to the primitive church and made the power of Pentecost available to disinherited southerners some 19 centuries later. This was true of the four major southern Pentecostal traditions in the early 20th century: the Church of God (Tennessee), the Pentecostal Holiness Church, the Fire-Baptized Holiness Church, and the predominantly black Church of God in Christ.

Although the restoration sentiment was merely implicit in much of Pentecostalism, it was explicitly acknowledged in some of the movement's early literature such as B. F. Lawrence's *The Apostolic Faith Restored* (1916). And it came to full flower especially in the Church of God, Cleveland, Tenn., a major Pentecostal denomination that emerged at the turn of the century in the mountains of southwestern North Carolina. By 1903 the acknowledged leader of the embryonic Church of God was an Indiana Bible salesman, A. J. Tomlinson, who stamped the young church with the conviction that the true church had disappeared in the Dark Ages but was now being recovered in the mountains of Tennessee and North Carolina. The Church of God, Tomlinson taught, had no man-made creed, was not a denomination, and took the Bible as "our only rule of faith and practice." Further, in due time Christ would organize his millennial kingdom at Burger Mountain (North Carolina) and Christians from all denominations would flow into the true Church of God. By 1980 the various factions of the Church of God had particular srength in Georgia, Florida, North and South Carolina, Tennessee, and Alabama, with lesser strength in Texas, Mississippi, Kentucky, Virginia, and West Virginia.

A more radical form of Pentecostalism, but no less restorationist, is the snake-handling tradition that arose in the mountains of southern Tennessee in 1909, under the leadership of George Went Hensley, and then spread throughout southern Appalachia, into other parts of the rural South, and later into industrial centers of Michigan, Ohio, and Indiana where Appalachian folk sought work. Snake handling could be construed as a logical extension of Pentecostal restorationism, which contends that gifts of the primitive church have been restored in these latter days. Most Pentecostals limit these gifts to glossolalia and healing, but snake handlers include "taking up serpents" and drinking poison, according to their reading of Mark 16:17–18, and many snake handlers self-consciously regard their activities as a restoration of primitive Christianity. Steven Kane cites a Tennessee snake handler: "Some people believe that miracles and signs ended with the Apostles. But if I got the same Holy Ghost as John and Peter, then I ought to be able to do the same things they did. Like heal the sick and cast out devils and handle serpents."

The forms of restorationism that have flourished in the South range from the rational and cognitive Churches of Christ to the charismatic and experiential Pentecostals, but all share in common the goal of transcending history and restoring primitive Christianity. Middle and eastern Tennessee and western North Carolina have been a seed-bed where all these forms of restorationist Christianity either have germinated or have taken root to an extraordinary degree.

Richard T. Hughes
Abilene Christian University

Robert Mapes Anderson, *Vision of the Disinherited: The Making of American Pentecostalism* (1979); David Harrell, *Journal of Southern History* (August 1964); Steven Kane, "Snake Handlers of Southern Appalachia" (Ph.D. dissertation, Princeton University, 1979); Byron Cecil Lambert, *The Rise of the Anti-Mission Baptists: Sources and Leaders, 1800–1840* (1980); Vinson Synan, *The Holiness-Pentecostal Movement in the United States* (1971); Robert G. Torbet, *A History of Southern Baptist Landmarkism in the Light of Historical Baptist Ecclesiology* (1980); Earl Irvin West, *The Search for the Ancient Order* (1949, 1950, and 1979).

Revivalism

Revivalism is characterized by an emphasis in religion on a renewal of interest in belief and practice, marked by the conversion of new members and the rededication of existing members to the church. In the South revivalism has set the dominant tone for Protestant Christianity since the early 19th century, informing the main religious concerns of mainstream denominations and smaller organizations alike.

Southern revivalism has occurred at two levels. One is comprised of the spectacular general awakenings of society, which at several periods of the region's history have brought significant numbers of people into connection with various southern denominations. These awakenings have provided the foundation for revivalism at a much less spectacular but more profound level, consisting of an ongoing effort by southern religious organizations to maintain their goal of bringing new members into the church and taking shape most clearly in gatherings called "revival meetings," which are held regularly throughout the South.

Four major periods of general revival have occurred in the South. The first, throughout what were then the English colonies of North America in the mid-18th century, was known as the Great Awakening. It was followed by the Second Awakening, or Great Revival, which centered on the southern frontier between about 1795 and 1805. A third, beginning in the latter part of the 19th century, was also national in scope and involved such noted evangelists as Dwight Moody and Billy Sunday. A fourth began in the mid-20th century and has been strongly identified with the southern evangelist Billy Graham.

The revivalism that is an ongoing phenomenon of southern religion involves a tendency on the part of southern religious organizations to view evangelism as their primary activity, with other aspects of the religious life interpreted in terms of the evangelistic impulse. To a great extent, revivalism at this level has become the religion of the South, for it crosses denominational lines to unite in sympathies and purposes members of most religious organizations, particularly those of the region's dominant communions, the Methodist and Baptist churches.

This revivalistic thrust of southern religion has had major implications for the specific content of religious ideas and practices in the region. Because southerners have understood such a thrust to involve, above all, the conversion and salvation of individual souls, their religion has had an extremely individualistic orientation. Questions of faith, belief, and sinfulness have all been interpreted in terms of the individual's religious state, and the church itself has been considered more a gathering of converted individuals than a community that, as such, has important relationships with God.

The roots of this religious individualism are theological, and may be traced not only to the traditional Protestant concern for salvation but, more specifically, to the triumph in the Second Awakening of an Arminian theology of free and universal grace. According to this theology, God has called everyone to salvation, but each individual must heed and follow God's call. The mission of the church, given this, is to make each individual aware of this call and its significance. Thus, theology not only demands an evangelical focus in religion but also insures that evangelism will be directed toward the individual and individual salvation rather than toward any religious collectivity. Supplanting the older Calvinist notions of predestination and irresistible grace, Arminianism would, by the early 19th century, underlie the practical religion of even such nominally Calvinist bodies as the Presbyterian and Baptist churches and, because of its popularity, would contribute greatly to the growth of the Methodist church, which had embraced it wholeheartedly. Arminianism has, since that time, been the theology of southern Protestantism, the underpinning of its evangelical efforts.

Accompanying a theology that defines the church's duty as reaching individual souls has been an emphasis on personal experience as the most significant element in the religious life. This, too, has its roots in the Second Awakening, when revivalistic denominations made the direct experience of conversion a test for church membership and even sought evidences for such experience in the spectacular physical "exercises" that often accompanied conversion. Although such exercises have become rare in mainstream churches since the middle of the 19th century, the stress on personal experience remains important, and the talented revivalist still tries to bring even the most affluent mainstream congregation to tears. Strong feeling is a significant element in southern revivalistic religion.

This stress on personal experience can be seen in one of revivalism's most important contributions to southern religious practice, the gospel hymns. Composed, for the most part, during the late 19th-century revival, these songs have entered into all the mainstream denominational hymnals, having virtually replaced more traditional hymns for use even in Sunday morning services.

Simple in message and stressing God's love for every individual, these gospel hymns evoke a highly personal and emotional sense of the nature of faith. More spectacularly, the stress on personal experience has contributed to a mid-20th-century charismatic revival. A development in the larger Pentecostal movement, which had its American beginnings around 1905, this revival has adopted traditional techniques and emphases from the southern revival heritage but has elaborated on them through an emphasis on such charismata as divine healing and speaking in tongues. Although most mainstream Protestants tend to desire more decorous forms of experience, the charismatic movement's main concerns are well within the southern revival traditions of evangelism and an individualistic, personal faith.

Southern revivalism has led the region's churches, in general, to adopt a stance toward society that differs markedly from that of religious organizations outside the South. Whereas American religion has been dominated, since the antebellum period, by a liberal Protestantism that has sought to respond to social issues and problems—from temperance and antislavery in the antebellum period to modern problems of race and war—southern churches and religious leaders have tended to avoid questions having deep social roots and to deal mainly with problems that can be addressed from the standpoint of the sinfulness of individuals and their need for conversion and salvation. Thus, southern churches have generally not participated in efforts for social change, even when they have been politically active, as with the conservative efforts of the Virginia-based Moral Majority, but have continued to focus on evangelism as their primary mission in the world.

See also MUSIC: / Revival Songs

Dickson D. Bruce, Jr.
University of California
at Irvine

John B. Boles, *The Great Revival, 1787–1805: The Origins of the Southern Evangelical Mind* (1972); Dickson D. Bruce, Jr., *And They All Sang Hallelujah: Plain-Folk Camp-Meeting Religion, 1800–1845* (1974); David Harrell, *All Things Are Possible: The Healing and Charismatic Revivals in Modern America* (1975); Samuel S. Hill, *Southern Churches in Crisis* (1967); Anne C. Loveland, *Southern Evangelicals and the Social Order, 1800–1860* (1980); William G. McLoughlin, Jr., *Modern Revivalism: Charles Grandison Finney to Billy Graham* (1959); Donald Mathews, *Religion in the Old South* (1977).

Roman Catholicism

From the first Catholic settlers in colonial Maryland to the recent influx of Spanish-speaking and Asian Catholics, "southern" Catholics have traditionally occupied an ambivalent place in the region as they struggled to balance a universal faith with their own peculiar ethnoreligious differences in a social environment that often has been hostile toward them. After the American Revolution the American Catholic church, composed of roughly 35,000 native Catholics located largely in Maryland, Kentucky, and Pennsylvania and under the leadership of John Carroll, the first American bishop (1790), had sought social and cultural assimilation into American life. By the mid-19th century, however, the American Catholic church had veered away from the genteel Anglo-American Catholicism of John Carroll's generation. The annexation of "Latin" Louisiana and the Gulf areas and, more importantly, massive European immigration, chiefly Irish and German, beginning in the 1830s, fixed the multiethnic character of American Catholicism thereafter. Ethnic disputes over liturgical rites, ecclesiastical jurisdictions, and customs came with immigration. They racked Norfolk, Charleston, Richmond, and New Orleans congregations in the early 19th century and prefigured more serious divisions within the American church throughout the century.

With force of numbers and an English-speaking advantage, the Irish gained control of the American church hierarchy. Coming during the devotional revolution underway in Ireland at mid-century, which stressed piety through regular devotions and worship and respect for clerical authority, the Irish had the energy and discipline to impose their ways on the church. Indeed, they largely subdued German elements in Baltimore and New Orleans during the 19th century. In lower Louisiana, however, the European immigrants confronted an entrenched French Catholic population heavily tinged with Continental French liberalism and with Spanish and African cultural strains. The French Creoles lost the contest for control over the church, but enough Creole customs survived in the increasingly austere American church to give Louisiana Catholicism a Mediterranean flavor that exists even today.

Without endorsing ethnic pluralism, the American church muted cultural tensions by establishing nationality parishes, in effect conceding a measure of cultural diversity in parish life while it insisted on greater uniformity in formal church practices and pushed Americanization through education. The cultural development of the church in the South, however, diverged from the national pattern when immigration to the South virtually ceased after the Civil War. A period of relative internal stability in the southern church followed the end of the war and lasted through World War II. Overall, the southern church escaped the cultural and social tremors of the "new immigration" wrenching Catholicism in northern communities, except in Louisiana, where the arrival of southern Italians to work in the sugar fields in the 1890s created fresh cultural tensions in the local church for a generation. By moderating its internal ethnic and ecclesiastical stresses, the southern church slipped into a respectable obscurity in the region until the 1960s.

Catholics remained a religious minority everywhere in the South outside of Louisiana, while Catholicism became the majority religion in the North. Conscious of its minority status in the overwhelmingly evangelical Protestant South, the church assumed a low political and social profile. The Catholic emphasis on personal salvation through the sacramental system tended to deflect Catholic concern from social action, and from John Carroll until Vatican II (1962–65) church leaders preached social and political accommodation with the host society—as much to focus their resources on building a church establishment as to fend off nativism and anti-Catholic prejudices. Southern church leaders provided scriptural justifications for slavery and a conservative social order in the antebellum period, supported secession and the Confederacy, inveighed against Republican rule during Reconstruction, and instituted their own form of Jim Crowism in the 1890s—all in conformity with the dominant regional values and practices. Such actions did not wholly dispel Protestant suspicions concerning Catholic loyalties, however, for nativism and anti-Catholicism flared in the Populist movement in the 1890s and lingered through the 1930s as a political factor in southern life. Effective lay Catholic political resistance—the creation of the Georgia Laymen's League to combat the Ku Klux Klan, for example—and the church's accommodationist policies on race and social issues countered such external threats, but the persistent, if often only latent, anti-Catholic temperament of evangelical Protestantism in the region inclined the Catholic church toward a policy of social enclosure. Concerned about the corrupting influence of the Protestant Bible, hymns, and teaching in public schools, for example, Catholic bishops in the late 19th century began to build a parochial system in their dioceses. Church-sponsored devotional societies, religious and recreational organizations, and the recruitment and training of native-born southerners for religious vocations solidified the southern Catholic culture, although the church's effort to match secular society in social services and schooling led to a proliferation of institutions that sapped the meager financial endowments of an always-poor southern church.

In the 20th century the ideology of southern Agrarianism reduced differences between Protestants and Catholics in the South and, thereby, increased the acceptance of Catholics in southern society. The conservative social views of Catholics increasingly assumed an important place in the region's general critique of modernism. Southern Catholic writers—especially Kate Chopin, Flannery O'Connor, William Alexander Percy, Katherine Anne Porter, and Allen Tate—shared a framework of values that was both Catholic and southern. They distrusted abstraction and modern liberalism, particularly its celebration of the rootless individual in search of the American dream; evidenced a strong sense of place; and praised organic, communal society. Like so many non-Catholic southern writers, they idealized a simpler southern past and decried the insidious secularism of industrial, urban America.

Catholicism, which taught the sanctity of marriage and family, also easily allied with the host society in attacking divorce and abortion—moral positions that contributed to the thawing of relations between Catholics and evangelical Protestant groups. During the 1970s, for example, several regional Southern Baptist/Roman Catholic conferences were held in a mutual effort both to undo generations of stereotypes and mistrust that had separated the two churches and, secondarily, to build a consensus for social action. The improved position of Catholics in the region's public life in recent years further testified to Protestant tolerance of Catholics and to Catholic integration into southern life. If Catholics did not quite belong in the Protestant South, they were no longer universally condemned as wholly antithetical to it.

Yet, even as Catholicism gained acceptance in the South, liberal forces swept into the church and the region to loosen the anchors of social conservatism and political accommodationism. More than anything else, the church's social posture shifted in response to Vatican II, which, among other influences, modified church hierarchical authority by calling for greater lay initiative in devotions and discipline. It also altered the ritual foundation of Catholic conservatism and cultural consensus by modernizing liturgical practices. Tradition gave way to change, and often confusion, in worship and social vision. Catholics reared in a tradition of docility groped to separate new truths from old errors in belief.

In the South, papal denunciation of racism in 1958 and insistence on social justice after Vatican II posed immediate challenges to local Catholic and southern habits. Catholic segregationist policy had begun to crumble in the late 1940s and early 1950s because of the actions of individual prelates in Washington, St. Louis, Raleigh, and Nashville in desegregating parochial schools, but the rush came in the 1960s when Catholic school desegregation moved at a pace faster than that in the public sector. Desegregation of other Catholic institutions soon followed. Desegregation, imposed as it was from above, met stiff resistance from white Catholic laity, particularly in the Deep South, where many persons defied church orders. The continued practice of segregated worship virtually everywhere in the South revealed the fragmented nature of the new Catholic church and the tug between church authority and social norms among southern Catholics. The involvement of Catholic religious leaders in the civil rights movement further alienated southern communicants from the official church, even though many southern bishops opposed civil rights activity.

Similarly, the church's grip on lay thinking weakened as parochial schools became battlegrounds of social change. With fewer nuns, brothers, and priests in teaching positions the influence of lay instructors, who did not always share common social values, increased. The creeping secularism in Catholic education led some pastors to question openly the necessity of parochial schools at all. The floodtide of Spanish-speaking migrants and immigrants in the last few decades, combined with the migration of northern-born and often better-educated Catholics into the southern Sunbelt, introduced new cultural stresses into the church while pulling it toward new, non-southern definitions of social concern. As sections of the South have become "northernized" by industrialization and ethnic pluralism, so too has the southern Catholic church.

On the face of it, the Catholic imprint on the South has been negligible. A small, scattered Catholic population has not developed a regional influence. Within areas of Catholic concentration, however (particularly Louisiana, the lower Gulf region, Florida, Texas, and parts of Maryland and Kentucky), Catholicism continues to inform local cultural and social life. In lower Louisiana, especially, where well over one-third of the population is Catholic, Catholic religious symbols abound in the practice of regular nightly prayers, and in more public, if secularized, expressions such as the annual rice and sugarcane festivals, the Yambilee, the blessing of the shrimp fleets, and even Mardi Gras, which is not without religious overtones.

The contribution of diverse, immigrant Catholic cultures to southern character remains incalculable because it is so elusive and fluid. Catholics have always existed as both outsiders and insiders in southern culture, and the tension between their public and private roles has produced subregional permutations wherever Catholics have lived in significant numbers. On the negative side, cultural differences between Catholic and Protestant reinforced or forged stereotypes and rivalries that have threatened the region's social harmony. The accommodation of the Catholic church and its people to southern social and political norms, in addition to the higher religiosity of southern Catholics compared to their northern counterparts, paradoxically reaffirms the evangelical Protestant core of southern culture with its stress on personal religious accountability and conservative social values.

See also ETHNIC LIFE: Nativism; / French; Germans; Irish; Italians; Mexicans; Spanish; LITERATURE: / O'Connor, Flannery; Porter, Katherine Anne; Tate, Allen; WOMEN'S LIFE: / Chopin, Kate

Randall M. Miller
Saint Joseph's University

John Tracy Ellis, *American Catholicism* (1969); Joseph Fichter, *Southern Parish: Dynamics of a City Church* (1951); John C. McKinney and Edgar T. Thompson, eds., *The South in Continuity and Change* (1965); James Hennesey, *American Catholics: A History of the Roman Catholic Community* (1982); Samuel S. Hill, ed., *Encyclopedia of Religion in the South* (1984); Randall M. Miller and Jon L. Wakelyn, eds., *Catholics in the Old South: Essays on Church and Culture* (1983); William A. Osborne, *The Segregated Covenant: Race Relations and American Catholics* (1967).

Theological Orthodoxy

The theological orthodoxy that permeated the 19th-century South was one expression of a broader pattern of conservative European religious thought then prevailing throughout the United States. It was an eclectic innovation consisting of biblical literalism, 17th-century scholasticism, 18th-century British apologetics and Scottish philosophy, and 19th-century science. It attempted, above all, to confront the Enlightenment on its own terms. The more solicitous the orthodox theologians were about biblical revelation, the more they sought rational proof and explanation. To be orthodox was to assume the unity of truth and therefore to affirm a "natural theology" based on human reason as the corollary of scriptural revelation.

Such a "rational orthodoxy" flourished throughout the region, but its articulate exponents were the pastors of town and city churches and the professors in colleges and seminaries. They were especially attuned to the planter aristocracy and an urban constituency who sought respectability by distancing themselves from the religious and social ineptitude of the unwashed. Almost every college had a required course on "the evidences of Christianity," and between 1795 and 1860 well over 150 ministers from every denomination published treatises and articles exhibiting the logic of rational orthodoxy.

That logic invariably exhibited a threefold pattern: the theologians argued that reason served as a means of preparation, validation, and interpretation of the biblical revelation. To prepare the mind to accept revealed truth, the theologian could assemble all the traditional rational arguments for the existence of God based on the harmony of the natural order, the mutual adaptation of its parts, its complexity, the necessity of a sufficient cause for its existence, and the universality of religious belief. The insights thus garnered constituted a natural knowledge of God, independent of the biblical revelation but clearly congruent with biblical claims. The theologians, therefore, found it necessary to confirm the trustworthiness of rational knowledge; hence they turned to the Scottish philosophy of Thomas Reid and Dugald Stewart, who had seemingly refuted David Hume's skepticism. And they found it equally necessary to maintain a close and optimistic watch over the natural sciences, which, they thought, could become one more weapon in the apologetic armory of Christendom. They admired and tried to emulate the inductive methods favored by Sir Francis Bacon. Scottish philosophy and Baconian method became mainstays of orthodox religious thought.

Having prepared the mind through natural theology to recognize the elementary truths of religion, reason, they thought, could then validate the higher biblical revelation. Therefore, they elaborated endlessly the traditional "evidences of Christianity," which demonstrated that the Bible was the unique word of God. From such English opponents of Deism as Richard Watson and William Paley, they derived the so-called external arguments, designed to show that the validation of the biblical miracles and the fulfillment of its prophecies demonstrated the divine status of the biblical message. From other opponents of Deism—especially Bishop Joseph Butler in England—they took the "internal arguments," which were claims about consistency. The Bible, they hoped to show, was internally consistent: it was consistent with human need and thus capable of transforming the heart; it was consistent with the highest ethical ideals of the race; it was consistent with science. Reason, in short, could determine that the Bible was the authentic word of God; in that sense reason was the criterion for revelation. But the theologians also agreed that reason, having confirmed the Bible, was then to submit itself to Christian truth.

The third task assigned to reason was the interpretation of revelation. The theologians acknowledged that the exegesis of Scripture required the exercise of human understanding. Most interpreters tried to adhere strictly to the "grammatical-historical" methods of interpretation, but their allegiance to the notion of the unity of truth also compelled them to harmonize Scripture with true philosophy and science. They normally argued, for instance, that the Creation account in Genesis referred to seven geological eras rather than seven literal days, or they contended that the Creation in Genesis was but the culmination of aeons of divine creative activity. Such rationalist readings of the biblical text became common among both liberals and conservatives in the South well into the 20th century.

Theological orthodoxy thus reflected the spirit of 17th-century European scholasticism, with its confidence that revelation was above reason though never contrary to it. Southern theologians appealed often, in fact, to such earlier scholastics as Francis Turretin and Jacobus Arminius, and they conducted their quarrels about such doctrines as atonement, predestination, and the sacraments within the conceptual environment formed by the scholastic heritage.

In their adherence to rational orthodoxy, the southern theologians diverged in no significant way from their counterparts in the North, except insofar as they explicitly used theological conclusions to defend the region and its slave economy. Rational orthodoxy dominated the churches, colleges, and seminaries of 19th-century America. It was a commonplace in the nation's churches—as the Methodist Thomas Ralston wrote—that God had "never enjoined upon man the duty of faith, without first presenting before him a reasonable foundation for the same." In their confidence that a rational orthodoxy was compatible both with emotional revivalism and with modern science, the southerners shared in a national consensus.

Rational orthodoxy maintained its hegemony in many southern churches, colleges, and seminaries until late in the 19th century. Theological conservatives have held to its tenets even throughout the 20th century. Indeed, the older orthodoxy stood in the background of both religious modernism and fundamentalism in the South. The later fundamentalists, who merely duplicated the earlier scholasticism within a narrower, more defensive vision, viewed the Bible itself as a rational system of divinely inspired propositions. The modernists still sought to prove the reasonableness of faith. The era of revivalism was also an age of reason in southern religion, and in some respects the rationalism has proved to be as durable as the fervor.

See also SCIENCE AND MEDICINE: Science and Religion

E. Brooks Holifield
Emory University

Theodore Dwight Bozeman, *Protestants in an Age of Science: The Baconian Ideal and Antebellum Religious Thought* (1977); John L. Dagg, *Manual of Theology* (1857); E. Brooks Holifield, *The Gentlemen Theologians: American Theology in Southern Culture, 1795–1860* (1978); George M. Marsden, *Fundamentalism and American Culture: The Shaping of Twentieth-Century Evangelicalism, 1870–1925* (1980); Thomas Ralston, *Elements of Divinity* (1871); James Henley Thornwell, *The Collected Writings of James Henley Thornwell*, ed. John Adger (1971).

Women and Religion

See WOMEN'S LIFE: Religion and Women

Zion, South as

The 17th century saw the crumbling of the old feudal and manorial systems that had dominated the geographic and economic landscape of Europe and had held the landless peasant in virtual bondage, but the modern systems that replaced them did little to elevate the least elements of the general populace. Capitalism was more beneficial to the neophyte capitalists than to the laborers; population pressures, worn-out soil, and problems associated with displacement abounded; unsatisfactory religious conditions paralleled economic woes. Princes in central Europe demanded that their subjects adhere to the religion of their political leaders and religious dissent was not countenanced. When England's King James I promised to "harry them out of the land," he was referring to dissenters to the Church of England who were experiencing both economic hardship and religious intolerance.

Given these Old World conditions, the New World attracted people from the British Isles and mainland Europe. Explorers reported the wonders of the Western Hemisphere, painting America as a land of milk and honey. Dissatisfaction with conditions in Europe combined with the advantages of America—both real and fancied—attracted countless people to the New World. The first Englishmen to settle in Virginia came for multiple reasons: a higher standard of living, a permanent home, a place to worship. These men viewed Virginia and the colonies to the south as a paradise, a utopia, a new Zion. They thought of themselves as descendants of God's chosen people and of America as the new Promised Land.

The Puritans who settled New England attempted to establish a "city upon a hill," but New Englanders did not have a monopoly on religious idealism. It inspired the southern colonists as well. As historian Perry Miller pointed out, southern settlers came out of an English culture that reflected a religious worldview. The Great Awakening, at a later time, affected all the colonies. As English and other Europeans swarmed into the southern colonies, they worked to reap the fruits of the boundless land, at the same time thanking God for their harvests and for the freedom they enjoyed.

As people along the seaboard moved westward, religion and religious ideas permeated southern colonial culture.

Geographic and demographic conditions kept early southerners from joining churches in large numbers, but this fact did not negate the religiosity of the South. The Second Awakening of the early 19th century both grew out of and reinforced this religiosity. It also increased church membership statistics, especially those of the Baptists, Methodists, and Presbyterians. By the mid-19th century, southerners had begun to identify religion and culture so closely that they could not be separated.

The southern religious experience became intertwined with the South's political ideology, both essential elements in what became the southern way of life. Throughout the middle period of American history, when economics, states' rights views, westward expansion, the abolition movement, and a host of other tangible conditions and intangible forces drove wedges between North and South, southerners took umbrage at those who criticized their region and its institutions. The South's intellectual and emotional defense of itself and its ideals, its myths and its realities were to some extent an outgrowth of the impact of religious zeal. When the great sectional crisis reached its climax, the South defended its way of life with fervor imbued with religious convictions. From the southern point of view, the Civil War was a fight between right and wrong, a religious crusade, a holy war, a defense of a beloved Zion. Southerners who died for the cause saw themselves as being like the religious warriors of an earlier era who had defended the Holy Land from the attacks of the infidels.

Once the Civil War was over, southerners surrounded themselves with both old and new myths, as they idealized a society "gone with the wind" and orated about the glories of the "Lost Cause." In the latter years of the 19th century and into the 20th, when powerful social and economic forces racked American society, southerners turned to religion for solace. The church in both hamlet and city was a "solid rock" in an unstable world. Religious revivals stemming from the frontier camp meeting tradition reaped a great harvest of souls. Baptists and Methodists together constituted as much as 90 percent of the church-going population in some states within a region recognized as the most religious in the nation. Religion continued to infiltrate politics, society, and culture, and—despite the Baptists' belief in the doctrine of separation of church and state—the two largest Protestant denominations in the South became essentially the "established" churches of the region. In the 20th century, when denominations like the Southern Baptists and Methodists epitomized and defended the status quo, much of the southern religious commitment continued to be the result of firmly held beliefs (rightly or wrongly) that the South contained the most desirable conditions in the nation. Whatever its shortcomings, for southerners the South continued to be the American Zion.

See also MYTHIC SOUTH: / Lost Cause Myth

Monroe Billington
New Mexico State University

Kenneth K. Bailey, *Southern White Protestantism in the Twentieth Century* (1964); Hunter D. Farish, *The Circuit Rider Dismounts: A Social History of Southern Methodism, 1865–1900* (1938); Samuel S. Hill and Robert G. Torbet, *Baptists: North and South* (1964); Charles A. Johnson, *The Frontier Camp Meeting: Religion's Harvest Time* (1955); Walter B. Posey, *The Baptist Church in the Lower Mississippi Valley, 1776–1845* (1957), *The Development of Methodism in the Old Southwest, 1783–1824* (1933); Rufus B. Spain, *At Ease in Zion: Social History of the Southern Baptists, 1865–1900* (1967); Ernest T. Thompson, *The Presbyterians in the South, 1607–1861* (1963).

African Methodist Episcopal Churches

The African Methodist Episcopal (AME) church and the African Methodist Episcopal Zion (AME Zion) church have never been distinctively "southern" churches, but they have been two of the most popular and powerful religious denominations among southern blacks. Both groups originated in northern cities—Philadelphia and New York City, respectively—in the late 18th century. Blacks were among early converts to Methodism in North America, but segregated church services and discrimination in the ritual of communion led to the withdrawal of black Methodists. Richard Allen, Absalom Jones, and William White were early founders of the AME church, while William Brown, Francis Jacobs, and Peter Williams had incorporated the precursor of the AME Zion church in New York City by 1801. Before the Civil War, the two denominations had established congregations in such border South cities as Louisville, Washington, and Baltimore, and the AME church had even appeared in New Orleans. Both denominations opposed slavery and were therefore closely watched in these locations. Daniel Payne and Morris Brown, both born and reared in Charleston, S.C., became the most prominent antebellum southerners in either denomination, serving as AME church bishops.

The AME churches assumed a new significance in the South with the Civil War and emancipation. Membership expanded as ministers and missionaries came south to work with the freedmen. At the end of the war, the AME Zion church, led by Bishop J. J. Clinton of the Southern Conference, worked vigorously in Alabama, Florida, Louisiana, and, perhaps most effectively, North Carolina. Such colleges and schools of theology as Fayetteville State, Winston-Salem State, and Hood Theological Seminary were formed in this era. Leaders of the AME church organized a state conference in 1865 in South Carolina, and from there ministers expanded throughout the Deep South and into the Southwest. South Carolinian Henry McNeal Turner was among the prominent leaders of the postbellum AME church. He served as bishop of the Georgia Conference from 1880 to 1892 and played a key role in introducing Methodism to Africa. Both AME denominations are currently active in Africa and the Caribbean as well as the United States.

Charles Reagan Wilson
University of Mississippi

David M. Bradley, *A History of the A.M.E. Zion Church*, 2 vols. (1956–70); Harry V. Richardson, *Dark Salvation: The Story of*

Methodism as It Developed among Blacks in America (1976); Clarence E. Walker, *A Rock in a Weary Land: The African Methodist Episcopal Church during the Civil War and Reconstruction* (1982); William J. Walls, *The African Methodist Episcopal Zion Church: Reality of the Black Church* (1974).

Asbury, Francis

(1745–1816) Minister.

Francis Asbury was born four miles from Birmingham, England, 20 or 21 August 1745. As early as age 15, he began to preach, and in 1766 he became one of John Wesley's traveling ministers in the "Methodist" connection. Five years later he volunteered to become a Wesleyan missionary to the colonies. There the greatest interest in the evangelical movement existed in the South, where Asbury took charge of the Baltimore district in 1773. As the only missionary to remain during the Revolution, he became superintendent of the evangelical enterprise throughout the nation. In the first years of the Revolution he began to attract the suspicion of the authorities, who questioned his loyalty to the Revolutionary cause, and he found himself restricted to preaching in Delaware. Such suspicions declined, and by 1779 Asbury had begun to resume control of the American evangelical movement.

Asbury attempted to maintain discipline among the lay preachers, especially the increasingly rebellious southerners, and at the same time he implored Wesley to provide greater support for the American enterprise. Finally, in 1784, Wesley sent representatives who met with Asbury and most of the lay ministers at the "Christmas Conference" in Baltimore, at that point the center of evangelical Anglicanism. Although Thomas Coke, Wesley's main representative, was officially in charge of the meeting, Asbury in fact controlled the events. The members voted to create a new denomination, the Methodist Episcopal church, and, at Asbury's insistence, they voted to invest him with the office of superintendent, a position Wesley had intended to give him without the advice or consent of the American clergy. Again showing his conscious independence of Wesley, Asbury began to call himself "bishop."

As leader of the new denomination, Asbury traveled great distances on horseback and focused most of his attention upon the South and Southwest, where the greatest numbers of Methodists remained during his lifetime. He continually fought minor bureaucratic battles and often ran the denomination with a strong, some said dictatorial, style. He weathered the great crisis of the early years of the denomination, James O'Kelley's movement to democratize Methodism, and only in the last years of his life yielded power to his hand-chosen successor, William McKendree. Never in particularly robust health, Asbury nevertheless continued to travel until his death on 31 March 1816.

Francis Asbury never received acclaim as a great preacher, nor was he a scholarly man. Strongly committed to the necessity of sinless behavior, he vigorously opposed slavery during much of his life, yielding only toward the end of his travels to moderation on the issue. Asbury's greatest strength, and the one that made him one of the most exceptional men in American religious history, was organizational. He had a keen instinct for church politics, managed church expansion with intelligence and remarkable intuition, and built a denomination that became central to 19th century southern religion.

David T. Bailey
Michigan State University

Herbert Asbury, *A Methodist Saint: The Life of Bishop Asbury* (1927); Elmer T. Clark, ed., *The Journal and Letters of Francis Asbury* (1958).

Bible Belt

Bible Belt is a term coined by H. L. Mencken in the 1920s to describe areas of the nation dominated by belief in the literal authenticity of the Bible and accompanying puritanical mores. He did not give the term a specific location, but he did associate it with rural areas of the Midwest and, especially, the "Baptist back-waters of the South." He used the term as one of derision, referring, for example, to "the Bible and Hookworm Belt" and calling Jackson, Miss., "the heart of the Bible and Lynching Belt."

The term has been used by scholars as well. In mapping the geographical range of the Churches of Christ, Edwin Gaustad commented that the denomination's influence represented "perhaps more a Bible Belt than any other region can offer." A 1952 survey by John L. Thomas in *Religion and the American People* (1963) concluded that, based on the prevalence of Bible reading, the Bible Belt was primarily in the West South Central, East South Central, and South Atlantic census areas. Cultural geographer James R. Shortridge analyzed 1971 denominational membership figures and mapped a Bible Belt region of "conservative churches" extending in influence from the Atlantic Seaboard through Texas and eastern New Mexico; its northern boundary was the upper state lines of Virginia, Kentucky, Missouri, and Oklahoma, extending into southern Illinois. "Jackson, Mississippi, could perhaps be called the 'buckle' of the Bible Belt, but Oklahoma City is definitely marginal, and Kansas is not in it," he wrote. Stephen W. Tweedie's study, "Viewing the Bible Belt," analyzed the viewership of evangelical, fundamentalist religious television programming, and concluded that "the Baptist South certainly is a major part of this Bible Belt, but areas of strength also include parts of the Methodist dominated Midwest as well as portions of the predominantly Lutheran Dakotas." These modern studies seem, then, to confirm Mencken's use of the term, although now it is used proudly by those in the Bible Belt to describe their commitments.

Bible Belt is a particularly useful term to describe the importance of the Scriptures in the South. When Hazel Motes in Flannery O'Connor's *Wise Blood* left his hometown of Eastrod, Tenn., he took with him only a black Bible and a pair of glasses belonging to his mother. At his little country school, he "had learned to read and write but that it was wiser not to: the Bible was the only book he read." He was perhaps typical of many southern true believers. On the early frontier and in rural areas throughout southern history, the Bible has been a main source of reading material and intellectual stimulation. Preachers took it as their only text for preaching. Politicians used a campaign language spiced with references to biblical stories and quotes to illustrate their political points, and two favorite southern pastimes—storytelling and conversation—were often filled with biblical references. Writers such as O'Connor and Faulkner used biblical symbols and motifs, artists painted biblical heroes and heroines in their works, and quilters even stitched the stories as themes for their works. Historian Kenneth K. Bailey noted of the South in 1900 that "few Southerners doubted the literal authenticity of the Scriptures or the ever-presence of God in man's affairs," and sociologist John Shelton Reed's studies of southern attitudes in contemporary times suggest the Bible Belt is still literally that.

See also MYTHIC SOUTH: / Mencken's South

Charles Reagan Wilson
University of Mississippi

Kenneth K. Bailey, *Southern White Protestantism in the Twentieth Century* (1964); H. L. Mencken, *Prejudices: Sixth Series* (1927); John Shelton Reed, *The Enduring South: Subcultural Persistence in Mass Society* (1972); James R. Shortridge, *The Geographical Review* (October 1976); Stephen W. Tweedie, *Journal of Popular Culture* (Spring 1978).

Blue Laws

Considered reverential by some, overly puritanical by others, blue laws, or Sunday closing laws, exist in most of the southern states. Based on an English statute passed in 1678 during the reign of Charles II and carried piously into the colonies, blue laws prohibit worldly business and diversion—except when deemed necessary or charitable—on the traditional day of rest.

The term *blue laws* comes from the blue paper used in binding the Massachusetts statutes on moral behavior in the 1600s. The first American colonial law regulating Sabbath activities was passed in Virginia in 1610, requiring Sunday church attendance, and other southern colonies followed suit. In the 19th century Sabbath laws did not require church attendance but did regulate public activities on that day.

Fearing growing secularization after the Civil War, religious groups such as the Baptists, Methodists, and Presbyterians urged their members to refrain from participating in public entertainment, social activities, and recreational travel on Sundays, and eventually they successfully pressured for greater enforcement of blue laws, especially in small towns and rural communities.

Today, stores are closed or merchandising is restricted in honor of holy observance. Realistically, the laws assure merchants of at least one noncompetitive day a week.

The result of such laws, passed by state and local governments, is a chaotic canon of "do's" and "don't's." Hence, the merit of the legislation is challenged constantly. For example, Arkansas's blue law—which permitted the sale on Sunday of film and flashbulbs but not cameras—was deemed unconstitutional in 1982.

In Louisiana there are only a handful of businesses—including ice houses, bookstores, funeral parlors, and steamboats—that can operate legally on Sundays. In South Carolina most commercial endeavors are illegal on Sunday. Exceptions include sanctioned steeplechases, annual harness races, and the sale of fish bait, seeds, swimwear, and ice cream. These anomalous statutes appear on many a code of ordinances, but most communities wink at the law. Enforcement is haphazard and sporadic.

Though probably an endangered species, blue laws linger on most local lawbooks. The one sabbatical restriction that most southern officials insist upon is the prohibition of the sale of alcohol—except in large cities, resort areas, and at private clubs. Because of the irreconcilable differences between whiskey and worship, Sundays in the rural South will be dry for a long time to come.

Linton Weeks
Arkansas Times
Little Rock, Arkansas

Neil J. Dilloff, *Maryland Law Review* (No. 4, 1980); Warren L. Johns, *Dateline Sunday, USA: The Story of Three and a Half Centuries of Sunday-Law Battles in America* (1967); Richard E. Morgan, *The Supreme Court and Religion* (1972).

Campbell, Alexander

(1788–1866) Minister.

Campbell was a major figure in a religious movement that came into being on the American frontier in the early 19th century and continues to thrive in the modern South. Its purpose was to restore the unity of the church on the basis of the Scriptures. Campbell, Thomas Campbell (his father), Barton W. Stone, and Walter Scott were the founders of a movement whose congregations today call themselves Churches of Christ, Christian Churches, and Christian Church (Disciples of Christ). The movement had great appeal to individuals in Virginia, North and South Carolina, Georgia, Tennessee, and Kentucky.

Campbell was born in northern Ireland. His father was a minister in the Anti-Burgher Seceder Presbyterian Church. Accepting the teachings of the Scottish school of Common Sense philosophy, the Campbells were influenced by the evangelical movement led by such men as James and Alexander Haldane, Roland Hill, and John Walker.

Disturbed by the conflict between Protestants and Catholics in northern Ireland, the father in 1807 came to America. His wife and family, led by young Alexander, followed in 1809. When the family reunited in America both father and son had broken with the Presbyterian tradition. Practicing believer's baptism by immersion, the Campbells were in fellowship with the Baptists of western Pennsylvania and northern Virginia between 1815 and 1830, but they soon parted over doctrinal questions.

Alexander Campbell was giving leadership to a growing group of followers, generated in part by a series of debates with such figures as Robert Owen, Bishop John Purcell, and Nathan Rice and William Maccalla of Kentucky. By means of his publications, the *Christian Baptist* and its successor, *The Millennial Harbinger*, Campbell's views were spread throughout the South. In 1829 Campbell served as a delegate to the Virginia Constitutional Convention.

To prepare young men for the ministry, Campbell founded Bethany College in 1840. Located in Brooke County, Va. (now West Virginia), the college was unique in that it was the first college to teach the Bible as a subject along with other studies. Students came to Bethany from most of the southern states but especially from Alabama, Georgia, and Mississippi.

As the slavery controversy grew more heated in the 1850s, Campbell was called upon to take a stand. Always popular with southern audiences, he temporized saying "slavery is a matter of opinion," meaning that it was not central to Christian faith. This position satisfied neither those of the North nor of the South.

Campbell lived near the college, serving as president and teaching several generations of preachers until his death in 1866.

Lester G. McAllister
Christian Theological Seminary

Lester G. McAllister, *Thomas Campbell: Man of the Book* (1954), with William Tucker, *Journey in Faith: A History of the Christian Church* (1975); Robert Richardson, *Memoirs of Alexander Campbell* (1897).

Campbell, Will

(b. 1924) Minister and social activist.

Will Davis Campbell was born 18 July 1924 near Liberty, Miss., a small community in the pine belt of southern Mississippi, which also produced comedian and storyteller Jerry Clower. Educated in local schools at East Fork and ordained a Southern Baptist preacher at the age of 17, he then enrolled in Louisiana College at Pineville (1941–43), intending to be a rural Baptist minister. Campbell was among the several million southerners who migrated during World War II to army camps, munitions factories, and shipyards outside the South. Campbell's own service in the U.S. Army Medical Corps during campaigns in the South Pacific was crucial to his life's work. He became more aware of the injustices suffered by blacks and was strengthened in his new interest in social justice by a reading of Howard Fast's *Freedom Road*.

Returning to the South accompanied by his wife, Brenda, he studied at Wake Forest College (A.B., 1948). After further study at Tulane University, Campbell enrolled at Yale University and received the Bachelor of Divinity degree in 1952. Campbell's first—and only—assignment to the formal ministry paralleled his untraditional training. In his brief 18-month stay as a minister in Taylor, La., Campbell became involved in several human rights issues, an experience that convinced him that his calling was not to assume the role of a traditional minister.

In 1954 he became director of religious life at the University of Mississippi and, after two years, left that post to become head of the Southern Office of the Department of Racial and Cultural Relations for the National Council of Churches.

In 1957 Campbell was among those who escorted black children through jeering mobs during the crisis at Little Rock, Ark. Later, Campbell was the only white man allowed to participate in the organization of the Southern Christian Leadership Conference. He served as a coordinator, troubleshooter, and observer during demonstrations in Clinton and Nashville, Tenn., Greensboro, N.C., Birmingham, Ala., and Albany, Ga. Will Campbell's

Will Campbell, a leader of the Committee of Southern Churchmen, 1980s

resignation in 1963 from his post with the National Council of Churches involved a change in his attitudes toward social reform. The tragic decline and death of his brother, a central theme of the celebrated *Brother to a Dragonfly* (1977), brought Will Campbell back to his Amite County poor white heritage and an awareness that suffering knew no color lines. His association with a liberal Mississippi newspaperman, P. D. East, editor of *The Petal Paper*, influenced Campbell to become aware that he had not allowed southern poor whites the same measure of Christian charity that he had shown to black people. Finally, Campbell became disillusioned with the hostility expressed by some civil rights activists toward southern whites—attitudes he had assumed would have been reserved for white southern views of black people.

A change in Campbell's style was evident in his first book, *Race and Renewal of the Church* (1962). Here Campbell first publicly stated his now-celebrated view that institutions had failed to bring true social change in the South. Campbell suggested it would have been better had the Supreme Court not ruled favorably in 1954 on the segregation issue, because individual Christians would have been forced to resolve the issue. This book was the initial statement of Campbell's continuing belief that the real enemies of human rights in the South were formal institutions, such as government and the business community, which divided downtrodden whites and blacks.

From his farm in Mt. Juliet, Tenn., near Nashville, Campbell devotes himself to writing, speaking engagements, truck farming, and his duties as a leader in the liberal Committee of Southern Churchmen. Campbell became publisher of the group's journal, *Katallagete*, and published a novel, *The Glad River*, in 1982. His concern for southern betterment has become an individualistic guerrilla ministry, which appeals to one's individual conscience rather than to collective action.

Thomas L. Connelly
University of South Carolina

Orley B. Caudill, ed., "An Oral History with Will Davis Campbell, Christian Preacher," vol. 157 of The Mississippi Oral History Program of the University of Southern Mississippi (1980); Thomas L. Connelly, *Will Campbell and the Soul of the South* (1982); Marshall Frady, *Southerners: A Journalist's Odyssey* (1980); Frye Gaillard, *Race, Rock and Religion: Profiles from a Southern Journalist* (1982).

Cannon, James, Jr.

(1864–1944) Minister.

Born in Salisbury, Md., James Cannon, Jr., entered the ministry of the Methodist Episcopal Church, South after a religious conversion experienced while attending Randolph-Macon College. He received training at Princeton Theological Seminary and was given his first charge in 1888 in the Virginia Conference.

Cannon's multifaceted career included educational, editorial, and interdenominational work. He twice served as principal of Blackstone Female Institute in Virginia, substantially adding to that school's funding and enrollment. As the first superintendent of the Junaluska Methodist Assembly in North Carolina, he further demonstrated his administrative talents.

From the beginning of his ministry Cannon was active in ecclesiastical affairs and participated in the annual state and general conferences of his denomination. Cannon's work outside the confines of his church included semiautonomous editorial positions with church newspapers in Virginia and organizational activity with the Federal Council of Churches and Near East Relief. Like many other southern progressives, he adopted prohibition as his primary reform ideal. Helping organize the Virginia Anti-Saloon League in 1901, he also founded a dry publication, the *Richmond Virginian*. Cannon fought against the wet Democratic machine in Virginia, got a wet-dry referendum on the ballot, and then led the state's prohibition forces to victory in 1916. As chairman of the legislative committee of the Anti-Saloon League, he successfully lobbied in Washington for passage of prohibition legislation culminating in the Eighteenth Amendment.

In 1918 the General Conference elected Cannon bishop, a position he held for the next 20 years. His original district included most of the Southwest and part of the Deep South. He also accepted responsibility for Methodist mission fields and made extensive inspection tours of the Belgian Congo, Mexico, and South American countries.

During the 1920s Cannon became chief spokesman for prohibition enforcement. In the tumultuous presidential campaign of 1928, he broke with the Democratic party for the first time and organized the Anti-Smith Democrats. Always a combative personality in both speech and print, Cannon continuously had to answer charges of anti-Catholicism.

Not long after the defeat of Al Smith, Cannon came under relentless attack from the Hearst press and other enemies he had accumulated over the years. The charges against him included wartime hoarding, stock market gambling, misappropriation of campaign funds, and adultery. Much of the early 1930s he spent in seemingly endless legal battles and investigations. On one occasion he shocked the nation by walking out of a congressional hearing. Although never found guilty of any wrongdoing by either court or church tribunal, his image suffered irreparable damage. He spent the remainder of his life after 1938 in retirement, but never relinquished his passion for prohibition.

Perhaps no one in public life exemplified southern mores in the 1920s better than did Cannon. The fall of national Prohibition in 1933 was a watershed for the type of leadership he provided. No southern minister would be as influential until Martin Luther King, Jr., emerged as a civil rights leader in the mid-1950s.

William E. Ellis
Eastern Kentucky University

Virginius Dabney, *Dry Messiah: The Life of Bishop Cannon* (1949); Richard L. Watson, Jr., ed., *Bishop Cannon's Own Story: Life as I Have Seen It* (1955).

Christian Broadcasting Network

The Christian Broadcasting Network (CBN) was founded in 1960 by M. G. (Pat) Robertson and began broadcasting from one-kilowatt station WYAH-TV in Portsmouth, Va., on 1 October 1961. From this modest beginning, CBN grew by the early 1980s to become the largest religious broadcaster and the fourth largest cable network in the United States. In 1984 its programs appeared by syndication on approximately 200 television stations in the United States and on CBN cable network transmitted via satellite to more than 4,000 cable systems. CBN owns and operates television stations in three major markets and has 80 radio affiliates.

Satellite delivery systems permit 24-hour global transmitting capability, and CBN programs are seen or heard in approximately 50 nations. A CBN owned and operated television station in Lebanon transmits to much of the Middle East.

The flagship program of CBN is the *700 Club*, a 90-minute talk, news, and political commentary show, hosted by Robertson. The program took its name from a telethon in 1967 during which participants pleaded for 700 persons to pledge $10 a month to meet the network's budget. From this inauspicious start, the total annual budget for CBN operations by the mid-1980s had reached approximately $100 million.

CBN has initiated a number of religious programs. The most successful to date has been *Another Life*, a soap opera with a Christian outlook. CBN conducts a counseling ministry, which is tied to the *700 Club*. In 1983 the network had 79 domestic and 40 international counseling centers. These centers also administer a program called "Operation Blessing," which provides material assistance for persons in need.

CBN's headquarters are in Virginia Beach, Va., on a 700-acre site that also includes CBN University, which opened in 1978 with 77 students. Focusing on graduate education, student enrollment grew to 570 in 1984. A $13.2 million library was dedicated in October of that year. The CBN master plan calls for 14 schools eventually and projects a student body of 6,000.

Born in Lexington, Va., in 1930, Robertson is the son of the late U.S. Senator A. Willis Robertson. Pat Robertson earned a degree in law at Yale University (1955) and is an ordained Southern Baptist clergyman (1961). He has used the *700 Club* as a platform for his conservative political, as well as religious, views before becoming a Republican presidential candidate during the 1988 campaign.

Jeffrey K. Hadden
University of Virginia

Dick Dabney, *Harper's* (August 1980); Jeffrey K. Hadden and Charles E. Swann, *Prime Time Preachers: The Rising Power of Televangelism* (1981).

Dabbs, James McBride

(1896–1970) Minister, writer, and reformer.

Dabbs was born in 1896 in Sumter County, S.C. He died there in 1970. In the course of his life he was a teacher, a farmer, a poet and essayist, and a symbol of both the past and future. Educated at the University of South Carolina, Clark University (Massachusetts), and Columbia University, he taught English at the University of South Carolina (1921–24) and Coker College (1925–37). In 1937 he returned to the family home where he farmed with an intensity unknown to the academics of the time who extolled the virtues of the agrarian way but remained in the scholarly world.

As a poet, Dabbs was often published, but his mark was made as an essayist. He addressed issues of agrarianism, industrialism, and change in the South. His themes were often similar to those of the Vanderbilt Agrarians, but while he knew the personalities and their work, his relationship to them was not intimate. More significantly, his writing began to address religious issues in the 1940s, and he had become by 1950 a dissenting voice in South Carolina. He tended his garden while the postwar world convulsed. Eventually the convulsions reached Sumter County; the black citizens there and across the South began to march. Dabbs's learning and resulting worldview, his religious insights and commitment to the Presbyterian church, but most importantly his love for the South, made him a formidable spokesman for change. He found his voice in journals such as *The Christian Century* and in organizations like the South Carolina Council on Human Relations and eventually the Southern Regional Council. As president of the Southern Regional Council (1957–63), Dabbs was a spokesman for the view that the South of the future would be integrated.

In his books he reworked themes addressed in his most widely read book, *The Southern Heritage* (1958). He argued that those standing in the mainstream of southern history were the blacks demanding recognition and a place in the body politic. His influence was subtle and far-reaching. He spoke to a generation of young southerners who felt caught between their love of the region and the reality of the postcolonial world. As historian-folklorist Charles Joyner noted, "He was not so much a liberalizing force, but he was a means of reconciling the alienation from the South which I then felt as a result of my hostility to racism. Earlier I had drawn a circle leaving the black folks out, later replacing it with a circle replacing the blacks with the red-necks. Dabbs opened the circle." Representing as he did the revered influences of the region, the church, the university, and the land, Dabbs prepared the way for an era of reconciliation. His other books included *The Road Home* (1960), *Who Speaks for the South?* (1964), *Civil Rights in Recent Southern Fiction* (1969), and *Haunted by God* (1972).

Robert M. Randolph
Massachusetts Institute
of Technology

John Egerton, *New South* (Winter 1969); Richard H. King, in *Perspectives on the American South*, vol. 2, ed. Merle Black and John Shelton Reed (1984); Robert M. Randolph, in *From the Old South to the New: Essays on the Transitional South*, ed. Walter J. Fraser, Jr., and Winifred B. Moore, Jr., (1981).

England, John

(1786–1842) Roman Catholic bishop.

Born in Cork, Ireland, John England won fame there as a preacher, writer, editor, and political agitator against the proposal to allow the British king a veto in the selection of Catholic bishops. When he came to the United States in 1820, he found in his diocese 5,000 Catholics scattered over 140,000 square miles. Most were Irish immigrants or refugees from revolution in Santo Domingo. He had responsibility for Catholics in Georgia and the Carolinas from 1820 to 1842.

England was an active bishop, establishing congregations headed by catechists in the three southern states, where priests visited periodically to say mass. Religious education was his major concern. He wrote a catechism and translated the Roman missal into English for lay use. In 1822 he founded the first Catholic newspaper in the United States, the *United States Catholic Miscellany*, and in 1825 opened the first Roman Catholic seminary in the South. By 1842, 20 priests had been ordained. He founded an orphanage and organized two communities of teaching sisters for the education of whites and free blacks and for the religious instruction of slaves. His effort to establish a school for blacks was blocked. In 1833 he became the first American to serve in the papal diplomatic corps as apostolic delegate to Haiti.

On the national church scene, he was instrumental in persuading Catholic bishops to meet in the series of national councils that began at Baltimore in 1829. A similar collegial sense of the need for shared responsibility in church affairs led him to frame a diocesan constitution and to organize in each parish a lay vestry to share in management of temporal affairs. Organizations representing clergy and laity met in each state and in a general convention of the diocese. In shaping diocesan government he paid explicit attention to the polity of other Christian churches and to the democratic atmosphere of the country, which he tried to integrate with traditional Roman Catholic structures. He opposed John C. Calhoun's nullification doctrine—an extreme version of states' rights—but had an ambivalent approach to slavery. He was "not friendly to the existence or continuation of slavery" but was hostile to abolitionists and in an 1840 exchange with Secretary of State John Forsyth stated that Pope Gregory XVI's condemnation of the slave trade the previous year did not apply to American domestic slavery. In American Roman Catholic annals, John England stands as one of the two or three greatest bishops.

James Hennesey
Boston College

Peter Guilday, *The Life and Times of John England, First Bishop of Charleston, 1786–1842*, 2 vols. (1927, 1969); Sebastian G. Messmer et al., eds., *The Works of the Right Reverend John England*, 7 vols. (1908); Ignatius A. Reynolds, ed., *The Works of the Right Reverend John England, First Bishop of Charleston*, 5 vols. (1849, 1978).

Falwell, Jerry

(b. 1933) Minister.

Born on 11 August 1933 in Lynchburg, Va., Jerry Falwell is the son of a successful businessman and a pious Baptist mother. Falwell did not regularly attend church as a youth, but on Sunday mornings his mother turned on a radio broadcast called the *Old Fashioned Revival Hour*, a pioneering religious broadcast from southern California. His born-again conversion occurred at a Lynchburg Baptist church on 20 January 1952. Two months later, after intensive study of the Bible, he decided to become a minister. Falwell had entered Lynchburg College in 1950 as an engineering student, but after his conversion experience he transferred to Baptist Bible College in Springfield, Mo., earning a Th.G. degree in 1956. He returned to Lynchburg that year and founded the Thomas Road Baptist Church. His ministry soon included a daily radio program, and in late 1956 he launched the *Old-Time Gospel Hour*, a weekly television broadcast of the Sunday morning worship services at his Lynchburg church, which is still on the air.

In 1971 Falwell began Lynchburg Baptist College, now called Liberty University, and a new campus was built in 1977. During the U.S. Bicentennial of 1976, Falwell staged a series of "I Love America" rallies throughout the nation, after which he became increasingly involved in conservative politics. He held "Clean Up America" campaigns in 1978 and 1979 and in the latter year founded Moral Majority, a group that advocated a political agenda focusing on such issues as prayer in school, abortion, homosexuality, and pornography. His 1980 book, *Listen,*

Jerry Falwell, founder of Moral Majority, 1980s

America!, urged that "a coalition of God-fearing moral Americans" reform society. Moral Majority was credited with helping to defeat several liberal senators and to elect Ronald Reagan in the election of 1980. Falwell called that November election "my finest hour," and since 1980 he has been an influential spokesman in New Right politics.

Falwell is the epitome of a middle-class, business-oriented fundamentalist minister in the contemporary South. Dressed in his three-piece suit, Falwell substitutes upbeat lectures for traditional fire-and-brimstone sermons, even when talking about the coming judgment of the Lord. Like other "televangelists," though, Falwell has been accused of financial mismanagement. In 1973 the Securities and Exchange Commission, for example, filed charges against his church for "fraud and deceit" and "gross insolvency," but a federal judge later dismissed the charges. The increasing competition of other electronic churches in the 1980s has taken its toll, and the average viewing audience for his television broadcast has declined from 889,000 households in 1977 to 438,000 in November 1986. *Gospel Hour* contributions fell from $52.6 million in 1983 to $44.3 million in 1986. In early 1987 Falwell replaced Jim Bakker as director of the PTL television network following Bakker's admission of a sexual indiscretion. By 1988, though, Falwell had given up leadership positions in both Moral Majority and PTL.

Charles Reagan Wilson
University of Mississippi

Frances FitzGerald, *Cities on a Hill: Journeys through Contemporary American Cultures* (1986); Julie B. Hairston, *Southline* (6 May 1987); Charles Moritz, ed., *Current Biography* (1981); Jerry Strober and Ruth Tomczak, *Jerry Falwell: Aflame for God* (1979).

Fatalism

In an outlook distinctive to the South, history is viewed as having a predestined outcome. This dark outlook has shaped southern social institutions, literature, and politics, and it has inhibited social reform. In such a view, time and history are not the arena of grand visions and idealistic reconstruction *à la* Thoreau and Emerson. Rather, as Faulkner had Quentin Compson's grandfather say while giving him his pocket watch in *The Sound and the Fury*, time is "the mausoleum of all hope and desire." The battles with time "are not even fought. The field only reveals to man his own folly and despair, and victory is an illusion of philosophers and fools."

Fatalism is manifest in the Stoic romanticism that W. J. Cash saw rooted in the "neo-Catholicism" and "neo-medievalism" of both William Alexander Percy and the Vanderbilt Agrarians. It is evident in Faulkner's sense of doom as the sins of the fathers are visited on the third and fourth generations in *Absalom, Absalom!* It is present in the Calvinistic ordaining of blacks, women, and laborers to their place in the social order (W. J. Cash said the God of the southern mind was "a Calvinist Jehovah"). It is a part of the populist rage, down to George Wallace, that sees the courts and the national media consign the South to a loser status. Journalist Gerald W. Johnson saw a positive side to this outlook in the "sober realism" of southern politics; indeed, Senators Sam Ervin and J. W. Fulbright were good examples of this impulse to resist grand schemes of political salvation.

Stoic fatalism was very much a part of Robert E. Lee's consciousness—as it was for William Alexander Percy. It accented resignation before the forces of fate and death, rather than a struggle with guilt and social responsibility. Percy's melancholy Stoicism led him to write his "Sideshow Gotterdammerung" in 1941 (*Lanterns on the Levee*): "A tarnish has fallen over the bright world . . . my own strong people are turned lotus-eaters: defeat is here again, the last, the most abhorrent."

The Stoic notion of "harmony" was often invoked during the civil rights struggle as a counter to the call for "justice." A deep and continuing conflict abides in the soul of the South between Stoic resignation to fate and death and Christian reconciliation to sin and guilt. The struggle is seen in the fiction of Walker Percy and Flannery O'Connor and is at its height in Faulkner's *Absalom, Absalom!* where Sutpen plays out his tragic role while "behind him Fate, destiny, retribution, irony—the stage manager—was already striking the set." Faulkner portrays the failure of the Stoic tradition in Sutpen. For Faulkner, the human problem is seen as guilt, and when things go wrong, the responsibility is humankind's.

In addition to the Stoic and Calvinist contributions to the sense of fatalism in the South, there is the compounding imprint of history. The Great Defeat, restrictive freight rates, punitive federal legislation, the caricatures portrayed through the media—all hung over the South like "a promissory note" in which everyone had to pay for his past and "fate or luck or chance, can foreclose on you without warning" (Faulkner, *Requiem for a Nun*).

The primary forces working in southern history to counter this sense of fatalism have been Christian affirmations of reconciling hope, liberal idealism that argued history could be bent in more humane and realizable directions, and, more recently, the forces of technological development and capital formation, which suggest the Sunbelt may be the land of fateful promise, rather than defeat and guilt.

See also HISTORY AND MANNERS: Stoicism

Robert L. Johnson
Cornell University

William Faulkner, *Absalom, Absalom!* (1936); John W. Hunt, *William Faulkner: Art in Theological Tension* (1965); William Alexander Percy, *Lanterns on the Levee* (1941).

Graham, Billy

(b. 1918) Evangelist.

Born 7 November 1918 near Charlotte, N.C., William Franklin Graham, Jr., was the firstborn of a fundamentalist Presbyterian couple. His rise to national fame as an evangelist came during the prime of McCarthyism and the early fear of atomic warfare. Graham exploited these two sensations by proclaiming a brand of Christian Americanism that promised to give the United States victory over both internal subversion and external Soviet threat. He perceived the United States as the chosen nation after the order of ancient Israel, with himself as Jehovah's prophet to help save America from spiritual, military, and economic ruin. His favorite Old Testament personality was Daniel, a prophet involved with politicians and politics. Graham befriended presidents and saw himself as their spiritual advisor. He encouraged both Eisenhower and Nixon to run for office, and during the Nixon and Kennedy presidential campaign of 1960, he wrote a magazine article portraying Nixon as a Christian, moral leader. At the last minute, Graham withdrew the article from publication.

The Billy Graham Evangelistic Association represents one of the earliest phases of entrepreneurial religion of the modern South. Despite his rural, small-town upbringing, Graham quickly utilized the most advanced technology and organizational sophistication in transforming the Billy Graham Evangelistic Association into an efficient corporation for exporting southern fundamentalism. Paradoxically, long-range, this-worldly planning for this soul-winning corporation was mingled with the typically southern preoccupation with the apocalypse macabre. His 1983 book *Approaching Hoofbeats: The Four Horsemen of the Apocalypse* represents a throwback to southern revivalism's characteristic preoccupation with "prophecy," including sensational, if not obscene, scenarios of the fate of those outside the circle of the saved. Throughout his ministry Graham struggled to balance his lurid and explicit premillennial apocalyptic vision with his implicit postmillennial drive to transform the United States into a latter-day Christocracy.

In the early 1950s Graham and his fellow southerners in the organization were faced with a consistency crisis. Could they preach to integrated audiences north of the Mason-Dixon line and to segregated audiences in the South and Southwest? In 1953, a year before the U.S. Supreme Court struck its monumental blow against segregation, in *Brown* v. *Board of Education*, Graham had elected to preach only to integrated audiences in the South, beginning with the crusade to Chattanooga, a city made infamous by an earlier race riot. Graham chose, however, to make a weak witness against segregation, which he regarded as much less wicked than either sexual lust or failure to regard Jesus as the Messiah.

The seeds of the New Religious Right of the 1980s are found in Graham's early preaching. He denounced the Supreme Court for removing God from the public schools and called for an American "Christocracy." To date, no other Christian in the world has preached to more people than has Billy Graham. His 1982 trip to preach in the Soviet Union drew considerable fire and misinterpretation from both civil libertarians and fundamentalists. Captured by the vision of proclaiming his evangelical gospel inside the Soviet Union (where communism was the official religion), Graham took the risk of criticism, knowing in advance that he would be falsely accused of becoming a tool of Soviet propaganda regarding religious liberty there.

Billy Graham, the modern South's best-known evangelist, 1980s

In the early 1980s Graham modified his premillennial apocalyptic views sufficiently to entertain plans of nuclear disarmament. Finally, despite the complexity of the Billy Graham Evangelistic Association, it has remained on the whole a model of financial integrity.

Joe E. Barnhart
North Texas State University

Joe E. Barnhart, *The Billy Graham Religion* (1972); Marshal Frady, *Billy Graham: A Parable of American Righteousness* (1979); John C. Pollock, *Billy Graham: The Authorized Biography* (1966).

Great Revival

The series of religious revivals that swept across the southern states between 1800 and 1805 is sometimes called the Second Great Awakening in the South. The movement was more accurately the South's first *great* awakening. It changed the religious landscape of the region, ensuring a Protestant evangelical dominance that continues today.

Small outbreaks of intense religious activity had occurred previously in the South, but these earlier small revivals had been confined to specific locales and to one denomination. Examples were the Presbyterian revival centered in Hanover County, Va., in the 1740s, the Separate Baptist revival beginning in North Carolina in 1755 and soon spreading to Virginia, and the Methodist awakening beginning in Virginia and North Carolina in the 1760s. These smaller awakenings slowly built up a popular evangelical belief system and a network of churches and ministers. Although these are prerequisites for a larger revival, a sense of cultural-religious crisis was required to weld the separate denominations together into common concern and action.

Westward migration in the late 1780s and 1790s, political controversies, and the worrisome news about the radical, deistic tendencies of the French Revolution contributed to a widespread perception of religious crisis in the 1790s. As clerics tried to understand their dilemma, they began to believe that it was a punishment sent by God for their preoccupation with wordly affairs. Recognition of this cause and a willingness to ask God for "deliverance" would, it was argued, end the religious "declension." Through such a religious defense the depressed clergy of the 1790s found reason to expect a miraculous recovery of religious vitality. This sense of expectancy led them to interpret an intensely emotional religious service led by James McGready in Logan County, Ky., in June 1800 as visible evidence that God was ushering in a new season of religious vitality, a second Pentecost. This feeling of heady optimism quickly spread across the South, facilitated by the adoption of camp meetings—huge, outdoor revivals.

In area after area church membership increased markedly, new churches were established, and many young male converts decided to enter the ministry as thousands of laypersons either joined churches for the first time or revived their dormant faith. The resulting religious energy greatly strengthened the popular denominations (especially the Baptists and Methodists) and by 1830 led to an almost complete dominance in the South of evangelical Protestantism, a dominance among blacks as well as whites.

John B. Boles
Rice University

John B. Boles, *The Great Revival, 1787–1805: The Origins of the Southern Evangelical Mind* (1972), in *Religion in the South*, ed. Charles Reagan Wilson (1985); Dickson D. Bruce, Jr., *And They All Sang Hallelujah: Plain-Folk Camp-Meeting Religion, 1800–1845* (1974).

Hays, Brooks

(1898–1981) Politician and religious leader.

Brooks Hays personified, during his more than 50 years in public service, the Christian layman in politics. Born 9 August 1898 near Russellville, Ark., to Sallie Butler and Steele Hays, he graduated from the University of Arkansas (B.A. 1919) and George Washington University (LL.D. 1922). After serving in World War I, he married in 1922, the year he was admitted to the bar.

Hays was an assistant attorney general of Arkansas, twice an unsuccessful reform candidate for governor of that state and once for Congress, before he went to Washington as an attorney for the U.S. Department of Agriculture in 1935. A prominent member of the Southern Baptist Convention, he became an influential religious leader during his years as a member of Congress from Arkansas (1943–59). Washington, D.C., ministers chose him as their Layman of the Year in 1951, and he was later named Churchman of the Year by the Religious Heritage Foundation. He served on the Southern Baptist Christian Life Commission for 15 years and was its chairman in 1957 and 1958. He was president of the Southern Baptist Convention, 1957 through 1959.

His long-standing and widely publicized support of civil rights for southern blacks involved him in his congressional district's 1957 controversy over the integration of Little Rock Central High School. Attempting to moderate the passions on all sides, he was the victim of what was most likely an illegal write-in vote that stripped him of his seat in Congress at the height of the passionate battle in 1958.

The following year, as his prestige grew through what was considered a "political martyrdom," Hays became a director of the Tennessee Valley Authority. With the return of Democrats to the White House in 1961, he became special assistant to President Kennedy and then to President Johnson for "congressional relations, international relations, federal-state relations, and church-state relations." In this capacity he carried his appeal for Christian brotherhood throughout the nation and around the world from 1961 to 1964.

Between 1964 and 1974 Hays taught government at Rutgers and the University of Massachusetts, ran unsuccessfully for governor of Arkansas, directed the first Baptist Ecumenical Institute at North Carolina's Wake Forest University, and ran unsuccessfully for Congress from North Carolina. He died at his home in Chevy Chase, Md., 12 October 1981.

James T. Baker
Western Kentucky University

Brooks Hays, *A Hotbed of Tranquility* (1968), *Politics Is My Parish* (1981), *A Southern Moderate Speaks* (1959), *This World: A Christian's Workshop* (1958).

King, Martin Luther, Jr.

See BLACK LIFE: / King, Martin Luther, Jr.

Merton, Thomas

(1915–1968) Religious figure and writer.

Born in Prades, France, Thomas Merton was the son of Owen Merton, a painter from New Zealand, and Ruth Merton, an American. Thomas Merton settled in the United States in 1935 to attend Columbia University after a tumultuous youth on the Continent and in England where he had attended school after the death of his parents. Converted to the Roman Catholic church while at Columbia, Merton entered the Cistercian (Trappist) monastery at Gethsemani, Ky., in 1941. His spiritual autobiography *The Seven Storey Mountain* (1948) was an immense success. He soon followed this work with a torrent of books, essays, reviews, and articles on subjects that ranged from theology and spirituality to the history of monasticism, belles lettres, and social commentary. He died in 1968. His best-known books include *Seeds of Contemplation* (1949), *The Sign of Jonas* (1952), *Conjectures of a Guilty Bystander* (1966), and *Zen and the Birds of Appetite* (1968). Two posthumous collections are important—*Collected Poems* (1977) and *The Literary Essays of Thomas Merton* (1981).

Merton rarely left his monastery home in Kentucky, but through his writings he became one of the most celebrated Roman Catholic writers of this century. Merton's connection with the South was more than geographical. He was a longtime contributor to the *Sewanee Review* and in the last year of his life edited a little magazine at Gethsemani called *Monk's Pond*. He published widely on the fiction of William Faulkner, Flannery O'Connor, and other southern writers. From his days at Columbia University, Merton had a keen interest in the race question, and, with his admiration for Gandhi, it is no surprise that he was a fervent admirer of Martin Luther King, Jr. In the early days of the civil rights movement, fueled partly by his reading of James Baldwin and his friendship with John Howard Griffin, he championed the movement to a then somewhat skeptical and hostile church public. This interest in racial justice and his long stand as a pacifist made him a natural ally of southern church people of a similar mind. He was a contributor to Will Campbell's *Katallagate*, and through Campbell's association came to know Walker Percy.

Merton lived his life in the comparative solitude of Kentucky's knob country, but his immense intelligence and compassion led him to love and criticize his fellow southerners from the peculiar angle of the contemplative monk.

Lawrence S. Cunningham
Florida State University

Monica Furlong, *Merton: A Biography* (1980); Patrick Hart, ed., *Thomas Merton: Monk* (1974); Elena Malits, *The Solitary Explorer: Thomas Merton's Transforming Journey* (1980); Michael Mott, *The Seven Mountains of Thomas Merton* (1984); Paul Wilkes, ed., *Merton: By Those Who Knew Him Best* (1984).

Methodist Episcopal Church, South

Methodists first entered the South in the 1760s, and by the 1780s most American Methodists were concentrated there. The movement grew dramatically after the revivals of the early 1800s. The Methodist Episcopal Church, South, existed from 1845 until 1939, with most of its membership in the southern states, but with a few churches in the border states and in the West. The precipitating cause of its formation was the slave ownership of one of the bishops of the Methodist Episcopal Church, James O. Andrews, an involvement that led to the division of the church into predominantly northern and southern parts. The church enthusiastically supported the Confederacy, providing chaplains and missionaries and distributing Bibles and religious literature. Methodist leaders such as Atticus G. Haygood later became advocates of a New South.

The Methodist Episcopal Church, South, whose membership was almost 3 million in 1939, reflected a distinctive kind of Methodism. It accepted the Methodist quadrilateral of the Bible, but tended to emphasize the Bible and religious experience more than its northern counterpart. Both branches of Methodism were led by bishops; but, following the southern paternalistic tradition, southern Methodists gave their bishops virtually unlimited power, so that the 58 men who filled the episcopal chairs dominated the life of the southern church, appointing the preachers, presiding over various conferences, and serving as leaders of most of the important boards and agencies.

Southern Methodists limited the mission of the church to the saving of souls, steering clear of most social issues. Bishop James Cannon, Jr., however, led many Methodists

Galloway Memorial Methodist Church, Jackson, Miss., postcard, early 20th century

in support of Prohibition. Entering vigorously into missionary work in Africa, Latin America, and the Far East, they confined their work in these areas, as at home, to evangelism, education, and medical care. A notable exception to this understanding of the mission of the church was the women's home and foreign missionary movement, which, catching a vision of a social gospel, worked to improve the lot of blacks, immigrants, and women and sought to secure world peace.

In many ways, the southern church lagged behind the northern branch of Methodism, not establishing a theological seminary until the 1870s, more than 30 years after northern Methodists had taken the same step, and not admitting women to the General Conference until the 1920s, 20 years after this had been done in the North. Southern Methodists were busy, like northern Methodists, maintaining schools, colleges, and universities, but the southern institutions often lacked both support and academic distinction and generally served as bastions of the white southern way of life. The church established Vanderbilt University in 1873 but withdrew support in 1914. Southern Methodist, Emory, and Duke became prominent Methodist universities.

Having begun its existence with a large number of black members, the Methodist Episcopal Church, South, after the Civil War, pushed most of these free blacks into their own ecclesiastical organization and became an institution devoted primarily to the welfare of white southerners.

Thus, the Methodist Episcopal Church, South, represented an almost perfect example of Richard Niebuhr's "Christ of Culture" Christianity—usually not just following its proclaimed Lord, Jesus Christ, but taking its values from the white South that had helped create it and that it in turn sustained.

See also EDUCATION: / Emory University; Duke University; Vanderbilt University

F. Joseph Mitchell
Troy State University

John Patrick McDowell, *The Social Gospel in the South: The Woman's Home Mission Movement in the Methodist Episcopal Church, South, 1886–1939* (1982); Frederick A. Norwood, *The Story of American Methodism: A History of the United Methodists and Their Relations* (1974).

Moon, Charlotte Digges "Lottie"

(1840–1912) Southern Baptist missionary.

For four decades Lottie Moon was a pioneer China missionary of the Southern Baptist Convention (SBC). Her life is skillfully celebrated by denominational literature, which declares her the most famous individual in Southern Baptist history, as well as the human symbol of her church's ongoing commitment to overseas missionary work.

Growing up on a plantation near Charlottesville, Va., Lottie Moon developed marked interests in religion and in the study of foreign languages and cultures. Following the Civil War she taught school in Kentucky and Georgia until 1873, when deepening spiritual concerns led her to enter missionary service. From that point until her death 40 years later Moon worked as an evangelist and teacher at Tengchow and at other Southern Baptist stations in Shantung province, northeast China. In addition to demonstrating compassion for the Chinese and skill in adapting to their culture, she displayed considerable courage and professional resourcefulness. All these qualities were particularly evident in her life during the late 1880s at P'ingtu, an isolated city in the Shantung interior. Working alone under difficult circumstances, Moon initiated at P'ingtu a successful mission at a time when Baptist efforts in north China were otherwise near collapse.

Moon's unique reputation among Southern Baptists, however, is a product chiefly of the Lottie Moon Christmas Offering for Foreign Missions. Inspired by an 1888 effort to raise money in the United States to help her work at P'ingtu, the Christmas Offering became a churchwide institution and in 1918 was named specifically for her. An extensive promotional literature has developed, idealizing Moon in books, poems, pamphlets, motion pictures and film strips, portraits, photo albums, tape cassettes, dramatic scripts, greeting cards, and even a Lottie Moon Cookbook. The Christmas Offering, with a 1984 goal of $66,000,000, currently accounts for about half the annual funding of the SBC's Foreign Mission Board and is indispensable to American Protestantism's largest foreign missionary program.

Any explanation of Lottie Moon's stature among Southern Baptists is inevitably subjective and arguable. Her story as promoted by the SBC, however, contains at least two themes interesting in terms of southern culture. One is the traditional theme that W. J. Cash called southern gyneolatry or the "pitiful Mother of God" image, centering on white women of intelligence, courage, and high capacity for self-sacrifice. The other theme, also strongly present, is of Lottie Moon as an undeclared feminist—single, self-reliant, wiser and stronger than male associates, pushing in "her own way" (the title of one of her SBC biographies) to advance the Kingdom of God and the status of women both in China and within the Southern Baptist Convention. Rather than being mutually exclusive, these contrasting themes seem instead significantly to have extended Lottie Moon's symbolic range and enduring influence.

Irwin T. Hyatt, Jr.
Emory University

Catherine B. Allen, *The New Lottie Moon Story* (1980); Irwin T. Hyatt, Jr., *Our Ordered Lives Confess: Three Nineteenth Century American Missionaries in East Shantung* (1976); Una Roberts Lawrence, *Lottie Moon* (1927).

Moral Majority

Moral Majority is an educational, lobbying, and fund-raising organization dedicated to conservative Christian causes. Founded in 1979 with the assistance of "New Right" leaders, the Moral Majority has been led by Jerry Falwell, pastor of the 18,000-member Thomas Road Baptist Church in Lynchburg, Va.

Nationally, Moral Majority maintains a legislative office near the Capitol in Washington, D.C., monitors legislation, issues regular appeals to its members for political action through letter-writing, lobbies Congress on behalf of specific legislation, and publishes the *Moral Majority Report*, a small monthly newspaper. Legally, Moral Majority is comprised of three separate organizations: Moral Majority, a lobby; the Moral Majority Foundation, an educational foundation; the Moral Majority Legal Defense Foundation, an organization offering legal assistance and funds to various conservative religious groups such as Christian schools that regularly do battle with secular authorities.

Moral Majority operated a "Political Action Committee" during the 1980 national campaign but abandoned it after spending only $20,000. The national organization is loosely replicated at state and local levels by Moral Majority chapters variously centered in election districts, counties, or major population centers. Lobbying, publication of voting records and newsletters, and organized action are also undertaken at the local level. The national Moral Majority has been active in establishing local chapters and in training their leaders, often by sponsoring regional training programs in conjunction with The Committee for the Survival of a Free Congress. Voter registration, involving participation of local churches, has also been a major concern at all levels.

Although the basic source of support for Moral Majority has been from independent fundamentalist churches, often Baptist, the organization sees its agenda as moral, not religious. It welcomes and cooperates with all who share its views regardless of their religious orientation. Moral Majority seeks to "return the nation to moral sanity," to revitalize those values "which made America great." It opposes abortion, homosexuality, pornography, the exclusive teaching of evolution, feminism, the welfare state, and secularism in general. Issues supported include prayer in public schools, state support for private (particularly religious) education, recognition of parents' and churches' rights to educate children without outside interference, a strong national defense coupled with an aggressively anticommunist foreign policy, and a laissez-faire capitalism at home that subordinates itself to the national interest abroad.

Geographically, Moral Majority has drawn its major support from the South and Midwest and its most effective leadership from the South. It represents a "going public" and an attainment of national influence on the part of southern religion. Moral Majority's political activism constitutes a significant revision of the traditionally separatist and nonworldly tendencies of its supporting churches, but not necessarily a reversal or a sharp break. Moral Majority perpetuates a southern Protestant tradition of selective social activism on a narrow range of issues centered upon personal morality. In so doing, it reflects fundamentalism's holiness roots and the conviction that social well-being is born of individual purity. The call for national repentance as a cure for impending disaster (God's rejection of America) coupled with its Manichaean sense of rigid good and evil in all matters, religious, social, or political, reflects a tradition of revivalism that has moved its converts from total depravity to thorough regeneration.

Moral Majority represents a wedding of fundamentalist religion with a "chosen people" style of civil religion, which represents a major tie between religion and mythology in the region. It is convinced that America's success as a nation depends upon its people rendering obedience to God's law as understood in a fundamentalist reading of the Bible. Moral Majority supporters regard themselves as a saving remnant, calling the nation back to faithfulness, to its covenant with the biblical God who, although once so near to rightfully forsaking America, awaited a sign of repentance that would again allow him to bless that bastion of true religion and return it to its rightful, dominant place in world affairs.

Jerry Falwell's two books, *How You Can Help Clean Up America* (1978) and *Listen, America!* (1980), give a summary of the Moral Majority's aims and its "action programs for decency" in the nation.

Dennis E. Owen
University of Florida

Gabriel Fackre, *The Religious Right and the Christian Faith* (1982); Samuel S. Hill and Dennis E. Owen, *The New Religious Political Right in America* (1982); Peggy Shriver, *The Bible Vote: Religion and the New Right* (1981).

Moravians

The Moravians are a Protestant religious group, known also as the *Unitas Fratrum*, that was founded in the 15th century by followers of John Hus, a Bohemian reformer and martyr. The movement spread to America, and today the headquarters of the Southern Province of the Moravian Church in America are located in Winston-Salem, N.C. Although not representative of predominant southern religious evangelicalism, the Moravians have contributed a distinctive history and aesthetic tradition to the South's culture.

To serve as missionaries to the Indians, as well as to escape German intolerance of their beliefs, a small group of Moravians left Europe and settled in Georgia in 1735. Their settlement was brief, for in 1740, when pressured to fight the Spanish, they moved to Pennsylvania. After the church purchased a 98,985-acre tract of land in the Piedmont of North Carolina, members of the sect again traveled to the South to settle. They called the tract *Wachau* (Wachovia) and settled the villages of Bethabara (1753) and Bethania (1759) before founding, in 1766,

Salem, the town that became the governmental and economic center of the settlement.

The ambitious settlers established in a wilderness a carefully planned, organized community—a theocracy, in which the church was the governing body and their religion a way of life. To ensure the survival of the community and its ideals, the church kept strict control during those early years. Residents did not buy land but leased it from the church, until the lease system was abolished in 1856. Church members were divided according to age, gender, and marital status into choirs, each group having its own officers, living quarters, and burial sites in the congregation cemetery. Trade competition was restricted in favor of a system of monopolies so that each member had opportunity to earn a living.

As a self-sufficient commercial center, Salem, along with the smaller Moravian communities, had skilled craftsmen, trained doctors, fine musicians, and dedicated schoolteachers. The Moravians stressed education and their female academy at Salem, opened to non-Moravians in 1802, quickly gained prominence and operates today as Salem Academy and College. Moravian aesthetic tastes became well known, too, as Moravian craftsmen often produced distinctive work that dominated their cultural region. Fine pottery, needlework, furniture, paintings, metalwork, and architecture remain as evidence of their talents.

Believing that they should, in all endeavors, serve the Lord, early Moravians worked and lived to that end, and in the process they made significant contributions to the ethnic, material, and religious culture of the South. Their unique music is central to church programs, love feasts, and Easter sunrise services that are celebrated by Moravians and non-Moravians alike. The rigid structure of the early Moravian communities dissolved years ago, but the church remains active and dedicated to its missionary efforts.

Jessica Foy
Cooperstown Graduate Programs
Cooperstown, New York

John Bivins and Paula Welshimer, *Moravian Decorative Arts in North Carolina* (1981); Adelaide Fries, K. G. Hamilton, D. L. Rights, M. J. Smith, eds., *The Records of the Moravians in North Carolina*, 11 vols. (1922–69); Kenneth G. Hamilton, *North Carolina Historical Review* (April 1967); Samuel S. Hill, ed., *Religion in the Southern States* (1983).

National Baptists

The National Baptist Convention, U.S.A., Inc., the unincorporated National Baptist Convention, U.S.A., and the Progressive National Baptist Convention have a combined membership of 12 million people in over 50,000 congregations and together form a historic tradition that has dominated southern black Baptist life since the late 19th century. Black Baptists had worshiped in independent congregations and as part of biracial churches before the Civil War, but emancipation quickly brought the establishment of separate black denominations.

From 1865 to 1895 black Baptists worked to achieve a separate religious identity. The Consolidated American Baptist Missionary Convention tried unsuccessfully to unify black Baptists, but it collapsed from internal social divisions in 1879. Black unity received a boost in 1895 with the formation in Atlanta of the National Baptist Convention, U.S.A. The year 1915 brought division, however, as a dispute over control of the National Baptists' publishing house led to the withdrawal of supporters of Robert H. Boyd, the corresponding secretary of the publication board, and establishment of the unincorporated National Baptist Convention, U.S.A. The Progressive National Baptist Convention, Inc., led by L. Venchael Booth, split off from the "incorporated" National Baptists in 1961 as the result of a controversy concerning the process of electing church leaders.

Black Baptist churches represent a vital social, as well as religious, force in the South. The mainstream has been dominated by the ideals of, in James M. Washington's typology, "bourgeois black Baptists." The middle-class ethos of the mainstream has been supplemented by "prophetic black Baptists" who have sought progressive political change. "Black Baptist folk culture" is still a third representation of the faith, stressing the distinctive use of music, prayers, oral testifying, and African rhythms in worship.

Charles Reagan Wilson
University of Mississippi

William D. Booth, *The Progressive Story: New Baptist Roots* (1981); Joseph H. Jackson, *A Story of Christian Activism: The History of the National Baptist Convention, U.S.A., Inc.* (1980); Owen D. Pelt and Ralph Lee Smith, *The Story of the National Baptists* (1960); James M. Washington, *Frustrated Fellowship: The Black Baptist Quest for Social Power* (1986).

O'Connor and Religion

Flannery O'Connor's contribution to the literature of the English-speaking world is widely known. Equally important is her contribution to the knowledge of religion in the South and to contemporary understanding of the Christian faith grounded in southern experience. As a native of Georgia, she knew intimately the dominant Protestant faith of the area and was especially fascinated by the untutored practices and convictions of backwoods religious folk. She often found their religious convictions skewed and desperate and their practice crude; yet she found among them, by her own accounting, a surprising pattern of true Christianity that encompassed the pattern of her own Catholic faith. A Hazel Motes (*Wise Blood*) and a Tarwater (*The Violent Bear It Away*) are eccentric, but through their rough circuitous route they find and claim the Christian God missed by countless reasonable and progressive people.

At an artistic level, O'Connor investigates the concrete, regional scene (a possessed evangelist, a manipulative grandmother, a Bible salesman) in order to touch a deeper, wider reality. The plot of each story therefore climactically focuses on some revealing action or gesture (a blinding of oneself, a reaching out toward one's killer, the theft of an artificial limb) that penetrates the essentials of character and circumstance.

The religious level of her work follows readily upon the artistic because of her sensitivity to the region: "While the South is hardly Christ-centered, it is most certainly Christ-haunted," she stated in a 1960 lecture. Yet a theologically discerning southern writer can disclose, through Christ-haunted chaos, moments that *are* surprisingly Christ-centered. True revelation occurs even amid distortion. The result is pointedly ecumenical: the author's Catholic doctrine comes alive in the actions of backcountry Protestants. Her stories are thereby full of irony and humor, the ultimate comedy of the one true God, who uses outlandish servants in order to reveal himself. As Christian evangel, O'Connor therefore jolts her readers with cultural and Christian reality, sharply distinguished in her work from the conventional and benign Christianity of custom.

See also LITERATURE: / O'Connor, Flannery

William Mallard
Emory University

Robert Bain, Joseph M. Flora, and Louis D. Rubin, Jr., eds., *Southern Writers: A Biographical Dictionary* (1979); Jeffrey Helterman and Richard Layman, eds., *Dictionary of Literary Biography*, vol. 2 (1978); Linn Mainiero and Langdon L. Faust, eds., *American Women Writers: A Critical Reference Guide* (1982).

Presbyterian Church in the United States (PCUS)

Initially known as the Presbyterian Church in the Confederate States of America (PCCSA), the denomination originated as a result of the Civil War. It was organized at Augusta, Ga., in 1861, and it remained separated from the Presbyterian Church in the United States of America (PCUSA) until 1983 when it reunited with the parent body, which had become the United Presbyterian Church in the United States of America (UPCUSA). The PCUS thus no longer has a separate existence, but it was an institutional embodiment of a distinctly regional religious identity. The PCCSA supported slavery and secession, and it continued to exist after the war because of southern concern about an unbiblical and unnatural involvement in political life by the PCUSA, a concern aggravated by the bitterness of the war and Reconstruction. The PCUS established itself in border states, the Southeast, and Texas.

Theologically, the PCUS affirmed with Protestant Christians the belief that the Bible of the Old and New Testaments is the only "rule of faith and practice," and it endorsed the trinitarian and christological decrees of the early Christian councils. In addition the denomination adopted and its officials subscribed to the *Westminster Confession of Faith* (1646) and the Larger and Shorter Catechisms of the 17th century as subordinate standards to the Scriptures. Nineteenth-century theologians James Henley Thornwell (1812–62) and Robert Lewis Dabney (1820–98) shaped a southern Presbyterian mind, and James Woodrow (1828–1907), although disciplined by the denomination, nevertheless helped the South adjust to the evolution hypothesis. Church historian Ernest Trice Thompson (1894–1985) and biblical critic John Bright (b. 1908) led the denomination in facing recent intellectual ferment. Some leaders attempted to modify the theological stand in recent years, with the writing of "A Declaration of Faith." This attempt was defeated by the presbyteries of the church, but the "Declaration" was widely used throughout the church.

Presbyterians believe themselves part of the "one holy catholic and apostolic church." Structurally, however, the PCUS is presbyterian, governed by a representative system with a graded court structure, provisions for the form and discipline of which are found in the *Book of Church Order*. Congregations elect pastors, in cooperation with the presbytery, and also elders and deacons, all ordained in the name of the Trinity by the laying on of hands. Pastors are ordained to the ministry of word and sacrament; elders, to assist in governance; and deacons, to assist in service. Congregations form presbyteries of pastors and elders, and presbyteries are organized in synods and a General Assembly. At first the PCUS controlled its various programs through committees of the various courts and then in 1949 organized education and publishing, domestic and foreign missions, and the pension system under boards. Pastors Stuart Robinson (1814–81), Benjamin M. Palmer (1818–1902), and Moses Drury Hoge (1818–99) and laymen John J. Eagan (1870–1924) and Francis Pickens Miller (1895–1978) gave unusual leadership to the church. Since 1963 women have been ordained to all the offices of the church. Rachel Henderlite (b. 1905) was the first woman ordained.

Liturgically, members of the PCUS have used the *Directory of Worship* of the Westminster Assembly, modified through the centuries, which provided a guide for the public and family worship of God. They have been suspicious of fixed forms, a suspicion reinforced by the revivalist spirit prevalent in the South. They have placed an emphasis on worship (biblically sound, simple, intelligible, and spiritually satisfying) with a focus on reading and interpreting the Bible and the administration of the two sacraments—baptism of children and adults in the name of the Trinity and by sprinkling—and the Lord's Supper, celebrated at least four times a year, and recently, more often. In 1932 the PCUS followed the PCUSA in allowing the "voluntary use" of the *Book of Common Worship* (adopted by the PCUSA in 1903), a collection of services and prayer designed to enrich the worship of congregations. Although Presbyterians were at first Psalms singers only, throughout the years they have broadened their use of hymns of "human composure."

The Hymnbook (1955) is now the most widely used hymnal.

From the beginning the PCUS engaged in the support of education, missions, domestic and foreign, and also showed its social concerns. Four seminaries (Union, Richmond, Va., 1812; Columbia, Decatur, Ga., 1828; Louisville, 1901; Austin, 1902), numerous liberal arts colleges (such as Hampden-Sydney, 1776, Davidson, 1836, Stillman, 1876, and Agnes Scott, 1889, and the Presbyterian School of Christian Education, 1914) serve the church, as do the *Presbyterian Survey* (1911) and the John Knox Press. Presbyterians adopted the Sunday school movement, and in 1963 experimented with a graded Covenant Life Curriculum in cooperation with other denominations and under the leadership of educator Lewis Sherrill (1882–1957). Since the Civil War the PCUS has developed mission work among blacks and Indians, and mission fields in China, Japan, Korea, Colombia, Brazil, Mexico, Africa, Greece, and Italy. Although the denomination thought it had a special mission to preserve the "spirituality" of the church, with the prodding of such persons as Walter L. Lingle (1868–1956), president of Davidson College, and E. T. Thompson, Presbyterians have taken more responsibility for dealing with social, racial, economic, and international problems. A Committee on Moral and Social Welfare was organized in 1934 to care for the moral nurture of Christians and in various forms and ways has continued its mission.

Although at first not ecumenically inclined, gradually the PCUS emerged from its regionalism to participate in the World Alliance of Reformed Churches (1876–77), the Federal Council of Churches (1912), the National Council of Churches (1950), and the World Council of Churches (1948). In 1982 before the reunion with the UPCUSA, the PCUS embraced in its constituency 821,008 communicant members, 4,250 churches, and 6,077 ministers.

James H. Smylie
Union Theological Seminary
in Virginia

A Digest of the Acts and Proceedings of the General Assembly of the Presbyterian Church in the United States, 1861–1965 (1966); Ernest Trice Thompson, *Presbyterians in the South*, 3 vols. (1963–73).

Prohibition

Although closely identified with the southern ethos in the 20th century, the movement to limit the sale and use of alcoholic beverages has never been an exclusively southern endeavor. The areas first touched by this effort were the East and Midwest in the antebellum period. Prohibition, as an ideal, originated in the voluntarism of the early temperance movement. After the Civil War more advocates adopted the policy of abstinence, or "teetotalism," and followed the legislative example of the state of Maine. Such groups as the Woman's Christian Temperance Union and the Anti-Saloon League of America organized for the fight.

In the first decade of this century dry sentiment gained momentum in the South as Georgia enacted statewide prohibition. By 1910 over two-thirds of southern counties were dry. Nationally, the economic exigencies of World War I combined with the denouement of Progressivism to bring about passage of the Eighteenth Amendment and the start of the Prohibition period (1920–33), during which the manufacture and sale of alcoholic beverages were forbidden.

Various interpretations have been offered for this monumental struggle against liquor. Until the early 1970s liberal historiography scorned prohibitionists in general, and the southern variety in particular, as misguided provincials who eschewed genuine reform, advocating prohibition instead, as a panacea for their fears about a changing America.

Recent scholarship has been more sympathetic to the prohibitionist cause, finding a greater degree of diversity among its adherents. For example, not all members of the liturgical churches opposed prohibition. Patrick Henry Callahan, a leading southern Catholic layman, actively supported prohibition. Moreover, studies of individual psychological crises of the late 19th and early 20th centuries indicate that alcohol abuse did, indeed, cause severe economic and social distress. Alcoholism particularly attacked the prevalent middle-class ideal of family autonomy. In effect, the methods now used to study the drug subculture are being applied to alcoholism, past and present.

The presidential election of 1928 solidified the southern consensus favoring prohibition. Many southerners voted against Al Smith because of his lack of support for prohibition, though their votes were read as anti-Catholic. After the repeal of national prohibition in 1933, the South became the bastion of dry support in the nation. While Mississippi opted for statewide prohibition, other southern states adopted some form of local option and allowed municipalities and counties, even precincts, to decide the issue. Will Rogers once commented that "southerners will vote dry as long as they can stagger to the polls." Into the present decade, more southerners live in areas of strict alcohol control than do people in any other region of the United States.

Consequently, the bootlegger and moonshiner have continued to ply their trades, often with the full cooperation of local authorities. Most southern communities have legends about the classic confrontations between moonshiner and revenue agent.

With the development of the Sunbelt South and urbanization, legalization of liquor without restriction has become more common. However, conservative and fundamentalist Christian groups oppose such change in southern mores and often still muster enough votes to win local wet-dry elections.

See also INDUSTRY: / Liquor Industry; SCIENCE AND MEDICINE: Alcohol and Alcoholism

William E. Ellis
Eastern Kentucky University

Paul A. Carter, *Another Part of the Twenties* (1977); Norman H. Clark, *Deliver Us from Evil: An Interpretation of American*

Prohibition (1976); James H. Timberlake, *Prohibition and the Progressive Movement, 1900–1920* (1963).

Protestant Episcopal Church

The earliest English settlers at Jamestown brought their Anglican religion with them. With the American Revolution, though, the Church of England became the Episcopal church and lost its position as the established church of the South. The recovery of the Episcopal church in the South from its near extinction after the Revolution was brought about through the work of strong leaders, many of them southerners, such as Richard Channing Moore, the second bishop of Virginia, who was a New Yorker, and the second and third bishops of South Carolina, Theodore Dehon and Nathanial Bowen, who were New Englanders. Stark Ravenscroft, the first bishop of North Carolina, was born in Virginia but educated in Scotland and England.

The degree to which Episcopalians in the South felt isolated from their northern brethren by cultural factors before the late 1830s is difficult to discern. The American Colonization Society, whose aim was to colonize parts of West Africa with freed black slaves, received active support from such Episcopalians as William Meade, later third bishop of Virginia. The existence of slavery was recognized as a factor of southern culture that the church, per se, was unable to eliminate. The church thus aimed to convert blacks and to influence owners and other whites to treat slaves humanely.

Many southern Episcopalians sent their sons to eastern colleges in the antebellum era but became irritated about the prevalence of antislavery sentiments there. This strengthened the felt need for a first-class collegiate institution under the control of the Episcopal church. Leonidas Polk, bishop of Louisiana, took the lead in promoting the founding of such a college. The site chosen was on Sewanee Mountain in Tennessee, and the name chosen was the "University of the South." Some temporary buildings were erected and the cornerstone of the proposed main building was laid just before the outbreak of the Civil War, which brought all activity to a close.

Southern Episcopalians were not of one mind regarding secession. Polk so strongly supported secession that he accepted a commission as a Confederate general. Bishop Nicholas H. Cobbs of Alabama was strongly opposed, as was Bishop James Hervey Otey of Tennessee, the first chancellor of the university. Some of the clergy strongly opposed to secession left the South, but others stayed. The Protestant Episcopal Church in the Confederate States was organized after the outbreak of hostilities on the principle that the church follows nationality. No desire was expressed to end relations with the church in the North. There was little friction between the churches, and after the surrender of the Confederate forces the church in the South resumed affiliation with the church in the North, beginning with the appearance of southern representatives at the General Convention of 1865. There were problems encountered in this reunion, but resolu-

St. Mark's Episcopal Church, Mississippi City, Miss., postcard, early 20th century

tions condemning the actions of southern Episcopalians were defeated and the fellowship of the church was restored. Sewanee was revived and became an important resource for the southern dioceses.

One of the urgent problems of the Episcopal church in the postbellum South was the situation of its black membership. After Emancipation, many blacks left the church. The need for clergy of their own race was acute. Undergraduate study was afforded in several schools supported by the church's Freedman's Commission, including St. Augustine College, St. Paul's Industrial School, and Voorhees College. In Virginia the Bishop Payne Divinity School was established at Petersburg and for many years provided theological instruction to black candidates. The commission later became the American Church Institute for Negroes and gained backing nationwide. Separate convocations for the black churches were established under the jurisdiction of the diocesan bishop, and the creation of a racial episcopate was proposed but rejected by General Convention several times.

Several dioceses founded missions in outlying areas, attracting children of working-class families lacking transportation to the mother church. Galveston, Dallas, San Antonio, and Houston in Texas furnish examples of such missions. Growing numbers of churches demanded more supervision than bishops of the older dioceses could give, so new jurisdictions were created. The Eastern Shore of Maryland was the first, in 1868; Northern Texas and Western Texas were set apart as missionary jurisdictions in 1874. Later divisions had added 11 new jurisdictions in the South by 1900. In 1985 there were 22 more dioceses in the South than there were in 1865. Along with multiplication of dioceses came increasing differences in social, cultural, theological, and ritualistic emphases, and a diminution of consultation and agreement about them. Migrants from the great urban centers of the North and East have diluted the southern mindset, so that the sense of southern identity in the southern Episcopal church has been muted.

Lawrence L. Brown
Episcopal Theological Seminary
of the Southwest

Lawrence L. Brown, *Historical Magazine of the Protestant Episcopal Church* (March 1966); Arthur Benjamin Chitty, *Recon-*

struction at Sewanee: The Founding of the University of the South and Its First Administration, 1857–1872 (1954); William Wilson Manross, *A History of the American Episcopal Church* (1935); Joseph H. Parks, *General Leonidas Polk, C.S.A.: The Fighting Bishop* (1962); Charles S. Sydnor, *The Development of Southern Sectionalism, 1819–1848* (1948).

Roberts, Oral

(b. 1918) Evangelist.

Born 24 January 1918 in Pontotoc County, Okla., Granville Oral Roberts was the fifth child of Ellis and Claudius Roberts. His father was a minister in the Pentecostal Holiness church, one of the small Pentecostal sects born in the early 20th century. Like many Pentecostal youngsters, Roberts rebelled against the restraints of his religious upbringing, but a series of crises in his life in 1935, culminating in what he believed was a divine healing from a severe case of tuberculosis, led him to decide to become a minister in the Pentecostal Holiness church.

Roberts served his denomination for 12 years both as a pastor and as an itinerant revivalist. In 1938 he married Evelyn Lutman; they had four children, Rebecca Ann, Ronald David, Richard Lee, and Roberta Jean. Roberts was extremely successful as a young preacher, but he nonetheless chafed under the restraints of denominational control and the poverty and social disrepute he shared with other Pentecostal ministers.

Oral Roberts, Pentecostal and Methodist minister, 1980s

In 1947 Roberts made the bold decision to begin an independent healing ministry. A part of a larger revival that brought fame and fortune to numerous other Pentecostal preachers after World War II, he became the ablest and most successful of the tent revivalists who for two decades preached divine healing throughout the country. Roberts became the preeminent spokesman for the Pentecostal message—the availability of God's miracle-working power and a renewed emphasis on the gifts of the Holy Spirit. In 1954 he took this message on television and greatly expanded his national visibility.

The importance of Oral Roberts rests largely on the skill with which he expanded and preserved his ministry when interest in healing revivalism began to wane in the 1960s. In 1965 he opened Oral Roberts University in Tulsa; in 1968 he joined the Methodist church and the following year he returned to television in a modern entertainment format, which had a lasting impact on religious programming. In 1975 Roberts announced the addition of a number of graduate programs at his university, including a medical school, and in 1978 began the construction of a huge hospital and medical research center called the City of Faith. In the mid-1980s the value of the Roberts empire in Tulsa—increasingly managed by Richard Roberts, his son—approached a billion dollars.

While Oral Roberts constantly changed his methods, he insisted that his central call from God, to bring healing to his generation, had remained constant throughout his life. Roberts's grandiose plans, his controversial fund-raising techniques, and his claims of direct divine guidance made him the subject of much attention and criticism in the press. He is, however, probably the most widely known and respected figure in the burgeoning charismatic revival of the late 20th century.

David Harrell
University of Alabama
at Birmingham

David Harrell, *All Things Are Possible: The Healing and Charismatic Revivals in Modern America* (1976), *Oral Roberts: An American Life* (1985); Oral Roberts, *The Call* (1971).

Sacred Places

Does the religious life of the South, centering in evangelical Protestantism, really acknowledge specific sites to which some kind of sacred significance is attached? Not so, of course, if the question assumes a classic Catholic frame of reference. In several other respects, however, it does. In the South, the dominance of center to left-wing Protestantism dictates the particular terms on which certain places are recognized as very special, even sacred.

Four sets of terms exist. The first is places where denominations had their American start, or where momentous events have occurred in their history. The second is locales where indigenous denominations or movements originated. The third is religious "capital cities," that is, headquarters of denominations or clusters of religious institutions. The fourth is major conference or retreat centers. There are many other notable places in the image-life and actual practice of the southern faithful, not least among them churches, rural and urban, to which people return for annual homecomings, and the cemeteries that sometimes adjoin them.

(1) Jamestown, Va., is a notable place to Episcopalians, because of the Church of England's placement there in 1607; Sewanee, Tenn., home of the University of the South, is its modern "capital." Similarly, Bardstown, Ky., for Roman Catholics reflects on their forebears' settlement in the West, and of course St. Augustine, Fla., dates back to 1565. Methodists point with pride to Lovely Lane Chapel in Baltimore, where their church in the United States was officially launched in 1784, and to Frederica and Savannah in Georgia, the initial stopping point for John Wesley in the colonial South. Several groups claim Savannah and Charleston, including Jews who established early settlements in both places, Unitarians in the latter case, and black Catholics in the former. Black Baptists revere Silver Bluff Church near Augusta, the first black church in North America, founded around 1773, and Gillfield Church in Petersburg, Va., which dates to the 18th century and was notable for controlling its internal affairs throughout the slavery era.

(2) The Campbellite Tradition (Disciples of Christ, Churches of Christ), which is a part of Restorationist Christianity, celebrates Bethany, W.Va., and Cane Ridge near Paris, Ky., cooriginating places for that movement. Pentecostalists, a rather diverse family, all take pleasure in memories of Dunn, N.C., Franklin Springs, Ga., and Hot Springs, Ark.

(3) Nashville outranks all other religious "capital cities." Baptists and Methodists have major installations there, especially in the publishing industry. Probably more church people visit Nashville than any other sacred place. Springfield, Mo., in the border South, is a headquarters for Fundamentalist Baptists and Pentecostalists.

(4) In western North Carolina, Presbyterians summer at Montreat, Methodists confer at Lake Junaluska, and Southern Baptists throng to Ridgecrest. Most denominations sponsor regional and state conference and retreat centers across the region.

Pilgrimages, shrines, and holy places as such are not part of southern evangelicalism's outlook. The general religious climate does not provoke their creation or acknowledgement. Yet in ways that accord with the culture, the South has its share of "sacred places."

Samuel S. Hill
University of Florida

Samuel S. Hill, ed., *Encyclopedia of Religion in the South* (1984).

Shakers

The people who took the name of United Society of Believers in Christ's Second Appearing began as a dissenting group among English Quakers. Mother Ann Lee and her followers came to America and founded a settlement in New York in 1774. The Shakers—short for "shaking Quakers"—received their name from the spiritually ecstatic, frenetic whirling and dancing of their religious meetings. They founded the agricultural community of Pleasant Hill in the bluegrass country of Kentucky in 1805 and the South Union community soon after near the Tennessee border with Kentucky. Shaker settlements believed in equality among blacks and whites, women and men; cooperative living; celibacy; nonviolence; and simplicity in living. They depended for continuity on recruiting new members and on raising orphans who one day would become adult members of the group. Members lived in groups of 30 to 100 people called families, each with its own residence, barns, workshops, and industries.

The Shaker communities were the most successful utopian settlements of the antebellum South. They ran well-operated farms. Pleasant Hill pioneered in establishing nurseries and orchards in Kentucky, new crops, the silk industry, experimentation with new seed varieties, and the importation of new breeds of sheep and hogs. They were inventive and not afraid of new technology. They made distinctive pottery, quilts, rugs, bonnets, silk scarves, brooms, cedar pails, and churns. They were noted for an aesthetic tradition favoring simplicity and functionality in design. Shaker furniture was of clean, wooden construction. Northeastern Shakers used pine, but those in Kentucky primarily worked with cherry, walnut, and, to a lesser degree, oak. Architecture stressed solid buildings, of brick and stone, with little embellishment and arranged in symmetrical patterns. Shaker music was an important part of their culture. Hymns were passed along from member to member by letter until the first hymnal appeared in 1813.

The Shaker communities of the South suffered physical and financial damage during the Civil War, as these pacifists cared for both Union and Confederate soldiers. After the war their decline continued, as the Shakers were increasingly unable to recruit new members. Pleasant Hill closed in 1910 and South Union in 1922. Restoration efforts at Pleasant Hill began in 1961, and the restored farm reopened for public tours in 1968.

Charles Reagan Wilson
University of Mississippi

Thomas D. Clark and Gerald Ham, *Pleasant Hill and Its Shakers* (1968); Julia Neal, *The Kentucky Shakers* (1982); Mary Richmond, *Shaker Literature: A Bibliography*, 2 vols. (1976).

Snake Handlers

These religious people are members of various independent Pentecostal Holiness churches who interpret Mark 16:18 ("They shall take up serpents") as an injunction to use poisonous snakes in religious services. At least two nights every week they gather in their one-room frame houses of worship and, to the accompaniment of loud rhythmic music, handle rattlesnakes, copperheads, and other venomous snakes with complete abandon. Sometimes they place the snakes on top of their heads, wrap them around their necks, tread on them with bare feet, or toss them to other worshipers. Bites are surprisingly infrequent and are generally seen as evidence that the victim experienced a wavering of faith or failed to follow the Holy Ghost. Most devotees refuse to consider medical treatment for a bite, preferring to trust the Lord for their healing. Since the start of the snake-handling movement in 1913, at least 63 men and women have died from snakebites suffered in religious meetings. The movement's early leader was George W. Hensley, an illiterate preacher from eastern Tennessee. It began in the coal-mining areas of the Appalachians, at a time when the region was beginning the process of economic modernization.

The great majority of snake handlers live in the southern highlands, in ordinary towns, hamlets, and hollows scattered throughout the region. With very few exceptions they are whites, descendants of English and Scotch-Irish pioneers who settled in the mountains in the period between 1780 and 1840. Their daily lives differ in no essential respects from those of neighboring unbelievers. The men work in the mines, mills, and factories, while the women attend to domestic chores. Snake handlers are people of limited formal education. Some of the older members can neither read nor write.

It would be an error to see the snake-handling religion as a gross aberration in southern religious life. The roots of the snake-handling movement lie deep in the religious heritage of the South—in the Methodism of John Wesley and the frontier revivals and backwoods camp meetings of the early 19th century. Moreover, with the exception of the practices of snake handling, fire handling, and strychnine drinking, there is no element of ritual or belief in the snake-handling religion that is not found in conventional Pentecostal Holiness churches throughout the South. And even these dangerous ritual practices are, after all, based on a literal interpretation of Scripture and on the idea (common to Pentecostal people in the South and everywhere else) that the spirit of God can "move upon" believers and empower them to perform extraordinary and unusual acts.

Snake handlers of eastern Tennessee, date unknown

Despite state and municipal laws prohibiting handling of poisonous snakes, and despite the ever-increasing number of snakebite fatalities, snake handlers remain firm in the conviction that they are "doing the will of the Lord." Their religion continues to draw new adherents even today. Most of these persons are sons and daughters of veteran followers of the movement.

Steven Kane
Connecticut College

Steven Kane, *Appalachian Journal* (Spring 1974), in *Encyclopedia of Religion in the South*, ed. Samuel S. Hill (1984), *Journal of American Folklore* (October–December 1974), *Ethos* 10 (1982).

Southern Baptist Convention

No other major denomination has shaped white southern religion and culture as powerfully or as long as has the Southern Baptist Convention (SBC). Organized in 1845 due to disagreement with northern Baptists over slavery and sectionalism, the SBC became the official "established" church of the South and America's largest Protestant denomination. While retaining a traditional Baptist emphasis on local church autonomy, freedom of conscience, and individualistic conversion, the SBC united a fiercely independent constituency around southern culture, denominational programs, and missional zeal. White southern culture provided a core of values, myths, and symbols that enhanced denominational stability; the denomination itself reinforced them. By sanctioning the southern white way of life—economics, politics, morality, race—Southern Baptists helped preserve regional unity among whites after the Civil War and validated their own continued existence as a distinct Baptist denomination.

The denomination was the means by which a defeated people sought to reclaim their region and to distinguish themselves from their northern counterparts and other "independent" Baptists in the South. Southerners rejected the northern Baptist "society" approach to denominational endeavors for a more centralized "convention" system, which coordinated activities of all agencies. Autonomous local churches united in order to accomplish broader evangelical tasks than their individual resources could facilitate.

While general theological consensus prevails, Southern Baptist churches are heirs of diverse theological traditions. Some represent a Regular Baptist tradition incorporating Calvinism, orderly worship, and a strong commitment to education. Others reflect a Separate Baptist heritage of modified Calvinism, revivalistic worship, and an antieducational bias. Still other segments reveal fundamentalist, Arminian, sectarian, and moderately liberal perspectives. Denominational solidarity and southern cultural stability long provided a sense of "Southern-Baptistness" that held theological diversity in check.

Southern Baptist evangelical zeal has focused primarily on individual conversion and personal morality, often ignoring the corporate sins of southern society. In so doing, the denomination has witnessed significant numerical growth while perpetuating the prevailing mores of white southern culture. Preachers utilized the rhetoric of southern populism and evangelical revivalism to awaken sinners to Christian and white southern values. The denomination sought to dominate southern culture, often without changing it.

This unity of culture and denomination protected the SBC from the doctrinal schisms that have divided many Protestant denominations during the 20th century. As pluralism has overtaken their culture and their denomination, Southern Baptists have experienced a significant identity crisis. Unity and diversity, once protected by cultural and denominational uniformity, have become increasingly difficult to maintain.

Bill J. Leonard
Southern Baptist
Theological Seminary
Louisville, Kentucky

John Lee Eighmy, *Churches in Cultural Captivity: A History of the Social Attitudes of Southern Baptists* (1972); Bill J. Leonard, *Baptist Quarterly* (June 1985); Rufus B. Spain, *At Ease in Zion: A Social History of Southern Baptists* (1961).

Thornwell, James Henley

(1812–1862) Minister and theologian.

Religious educator, editor, and author, James Henley Thornwell was born in Marlboro District, S.C., graduated from South Carolina College in 1831, studied at Andover Theological Seminary, Harvard, and Presbyterian Theological Seminary (Columbia, S.C.), and was licensed to preach in 1834. He served several churches for short periods of time and took part in the affairs of the Presbyterian Church in the United States of America (Old School) beginning in 1837 when he attended his first General Assembly, being elected moderator in 1847. He was elected professor of metaphysics at South Carolina College in 1837 and taught at that institution until 1855, serving as president after 1851. In 1855 he became professor of didactic and polemic theology at the Presbyterian Theological Seminary, a position he held until his death.

Thornwell was known as a careful logician, for his biblicism, and for his Calvinist orthodoxy because of his defense of the Westminster Confession of Faith with ideas of Francis Bacon and the aid of the Scottish philosophy of the 18th-century Enlightenment. As churchman, he held to a strict interpretation of doctrine and structure. He opposed, for example, the development of boards for furthering the church's work because they did not conform to biblical or doctrinal standards of ecclesiastical accountability. As educator he supported the teaching of new scientific knowledge, confident of the harmony of Christian faith and God's created order. He also supported public education in the state of South Carolina. He edited the *Southern Quarterly Review* and the *Southern Presbyterian Review* for a time.

Referred to as the Calhoun of the church, Thornwell used his skills as an author to support the institution of slavery on biblical and natural grounds, calling not for the condemnation of the master-slave relationship, but for its regulation. When the Civil War erupted, he defended the South and accused the General Assembly of the PCUSA of unbiblical and unnatural meddling in the affairs of state, and of thus violating the true "spiritual" character of the church. He encouraged the Synod of South Carolina to endorse political as well as ecclesiastical secession and took part in the organization of the Presbyterian Church in the Confederate States of America, which became the Presbyterian Church in the United States after the war. His pamphlet *The State of the Country* was widely circulated, and he was the principal author of the new denomination's "Address to All the Churches of Jesus Christ throughout the Earth" in 1861. Although he did not write or publish a systematic theology, *The Collected Writings of J. H. Thornwell* (4 vols., 1871–73) were edited and published by J. B. Adger and J. L. Gireadeau, assuring his continued influence among Presbyterians and in the South.

James H. Smylie
Union Theological Seminary
Richmond, Virginia

Theodore Dwight Bozeman, "A Nineteenth Century Baconian Theology: James Henley Thornwell an Enlightenment Theologian" (Th.M. thesis, Union Theological Seminary, Richmond, Va., 1970), *Journal of Presbyterian History* (Winter 1972); James O. Farmer, Jr., *The Metaphysical Confederacy: James Henley Thornwell and the Synthesis of Southern Values* (1986); E. Brooks Holifield, *The Gentleman Theologians: American Theology in Southern Culture, 1795–1860* (1978); Benjamin M. Palmer, *The Life and Letters of J. H. Thornwell* (1875).

Science and Medicine

JAMES O. BREEDEN
Southern Methodist University
CONSULTANT

Physician visiting a patient and her family in a needlework scene by Ethel Mohamed, photographed in 1978

Science and Medicine

Although little noticed by the myriad students of the South, science and medicine have been important and instructive components of southern culture. On one level, they have contributed to social progress. On another, they have been barometers for gauging intellectual life. The South's experience in these areas also sheds valuable light on the question of southern distinctiveness, providing additional support for the contention that regional separateness has had a retarding effect on cultural development.

Colonial South. An interest in science was part of the cultural baggage that the first colonists brought to the South. This interest was fed and intensified by the seemingly insatiable curiosity of Europeans regarding the natural life and products of the New World. Consequently, from the earliest days of colonization the pursuit of science was a prominent feature of southern life.

Throughout the colonial period and into the 19th century, science was generally divided into two broad categories—natural philosophy (the physical sciences) and natural history (the natural sciences). The former was concerned largely with the verification of existing scientific principles and the latter with the observation, collection, and classification of the phenomena of the natural world. Because of the physical and intellectual limitations of their frontier setting, colonial Americans were ill prepared to do much in natural philosophy, but they were ideally situated to excel in natural history. Their research in natural history set a pattern of activity that dominated American science for three centuries.

Motivated by the irresistible appeal of the lush, often exotic, natural world that surrounded them as well as by requests for assistance from English and European students of nature anxious for New World botanical, zoological, and mineral specimens for their research and personal collections, hundreds of early southerners became actively involved in natural history. Most of them served as field collectors for Europeans. By the late colonial period a few became highly competent scientists and as respected members of the international circle of natural historians made contributions to scientific advancement. The most important figures in southern natural history in the 17th century were John Clayton I and John Banister, and in the 18th, Mark Catesby, John Clayton II, John Mitchell, and Alexander Garden. Garden, a Charleston physician, was perhaps the most accomplished and best known of the group.

The activities and accomplishments of the early South's natural historians were highly significant: they made the region, along with the middle colonies, the colonial leader in the study of the American natural world; they played an indispensable role in filling in the New World book of nature; they contributed to the advancement of Western science; and they helped lay the foundation for American science.

The medical story of the early South was not nearly so bright or promising. It was in fact tragic. Disease and death were constant companions of colonists everywhere, but especially in the South. Here health hazards, ranging from endemic "ague" (chills and fever) and "flux" (dysentery) to epidemic outbreaks of smallpox and yellow fever, were at their worst. It is easy to see why the southern colonists were less healthy. "Seasoning," or becoming acclimated to the region's semitropical climate, was the source of extreme morbidity and mortality. Moreover, because of an environment that encouraged insect life, a general disregard for the draining of swamps, and the steady influx of black carriers with the rise of slavery, malaria—early America's most dangerous endemic disorder—tightened its hold on the South in the 18th century as it began to disappear from New England. Southern forms of the disease were more debilitating and deadly than those that prevailed elsewhere in the colonies. Finally, the medical reforms of the late colonial period that improved health—more and better-trained physicians, therapeutic advancements (the use of variolation to prevent smallpox and Cinchona bark to control malaria, for example), and the gradual appearance of regional medical institutions such as schools, societies, and licensing—made less headway in the South than elsewhere.

As the health picture of the South suggests, the American colonies exhibited regional distinctions quite early, because of the diversity of colonizing experiences and New World conditions. But while New England and the middle colonies became recognizable colonial divisions, the southern colonies showed the greatest cultural diversity. Indeed, during the century-and-a-half between the settlement of Jamestown and the outbreak of the Revolution the seeds of southern distinctiveness were planted and the first shoots sent up. A number of influences encouraged a separate southern identity. The region's first European settlers transplanted the social model of the English country gentleman to the New World and tried to follow it. They found favorable climatic and geographic conditions and established a plantation economy based on slavery and a staple-crop system.

Sectional identity had little immediate meaning for the principal areas of regional life, but in the cases of science and medicine the factors that underpinned it boded ill. Agrarianism and the plantation system, for example, fostered ruralism and a sparse pattern of settlement that discouraged and retarded urbanization, with its greater opportunities for intellectual contact and its nurturing environment for societies, journals, and other institutions for the promotion of science. The poor health of the South was in large measure attributable to the social consequences of the region's unswerving devotion to a way of life based on slavery and the plantation economy.

Old South. Southern colonists on the eve of the Revolution were no more devoted to sectionalism than those in New England and the middle colonies. Moreover, following the break with England, they were among the most strident cultural nationalists and celebrated America's special destiny. Independence and nationhood, however, provided the impetus for the transformation of the embryonic South into the sectional South. This unintended, and largely unconscious, historical process was the result of growing inconsistencies between the southern way of life and emerging national patterns that became increasingly obvious after independence. None was more glaring than the South's slave-based economic system and its underlying racism, which stood in contradiction to the philosophy of the Revolution and the idealism of the early Republic. Forced to choose, southerners rejected freedom and equality in favor of slavery and racism. Such unsettling experiences led, by the end of the 18th century, to the emergence of a southern sectional consciousness—the First South. After 1820 a sense of grievance and feelings of defensiveness united southerners as never before and pushed them further out of the national mainstream. This was the Old South, the supreme expression of southern distinctiveness. Science and medicine, like all of southern life, bore the imprint of the South's sectional philosophy.

Reflecting the cultural nationalism of the era, science in the early national period was characterized by the establishment and shaping of institutions and attitudes aimed at ending America's intellectual subservience to Europe. Among the achievements of the period were the establishment of new schools and the improvement of existing ones, the founding of scientific societies and journals, and the building of museums and herbaria. As the result of these steps, the United States by 1830 had become a junior partner with Europe in science and had started down the path that would lead to eventual leadership in the scientific world. The South's leaders of science supported and contributed to the drive for national scientific independence. In fact, Thomas Jefferson, the region's best-known scientist of the early national period, was crucial to the quest for a first-rate American science. Although Jefferson was not a great scientist, his influence permeated the pursuit of science nationwide, and he was a tower of strength to all interested in science.

America's striving for scientific respectability coincided with the maturing of Western science. Indeed, the 19th century was a golden age for science. During this century science came of age and established its utility for social progress. The result was a veritable cult of science that affected every aspect of life. The United States, while overshadowed by the scientific leaders in Europe, was actively involved in the modernization of science.

Between 1820 and 1860, the four decades that are generally associated with the Old South, all parts of the country did not participate equally in the advancement of American science: the Northeast was the clear leader; the West contributed the least; and the South occupied an intermediate position. After performing splendidly in the colonial period, the South fell behind the Northeast in science after the Revolution. The South's comparative lag in science was evident in a variety of ways, including the production of fewer scientists than the northern and middle states, a slower pace of institutional development for the support of science, a lower level of scientific activity, and a less progressive attitude toward science.

Reasons for the region's declining national position ranged from agrarianism to the capitulation of the South to evangelical Protestantism and the defensiveness that accompanied mounting sectional tensions. These forces retarded the growth of institutions for the pursuit of science and created a climate of opinion that inhibited the free inquiry crucial to scientific advancement.

For all its problems, limitations, and comparative lag, science occupied a prominent place in antebellum southern culture. Natural history continued to be the dominant type of scientific activity. Although leadership in this area had shifted to the North by the advent of the Old South, southern contributions to the advancement of natural history were extensive and important. Students of the natural world were to be found throughout the region. Among those of note were William B. Rogers in Virginia, Elisha Mitchell and Moses A. Curtis in North Carolina, Gerard Troost in Tennessee, Charles W. Short in Kentucky, Alvan W. Chapman in Florida, John L. Riddell in Louisiana, and Gideon Lincecum on the Texas frontier.

The greatest activity in natural history was concentrated in the Charleston area. Long the chief center of southern science, this city and its environs were home to some of the most outstanding scientific figures of the Old South, such as Stephen Elliott, John Bachman, John E. Holbrook, and Henry William Ravenel. Its large number of active students of science made Charleston the Old South's most important scientific community. This remarkable group's pursuit of science was nurtured by the Charleston Museum, one of the nation's oldest and most important collections of natural history specimens, and the Elliott Society of Natural History, one of two noteworthy scientific societies in the Old South, the other being the New Orleans Academy of Sciences.

When compared with its outstanding performance in natural history, the Old South's showing in the pure sciences was strikingly lackluster. This situation was the result of a combination of factors: the absence of a tradition of important activity and accomplishment in pure science, the low level of professionalization and institutional development that characterized southern science, and cultural considerations. The cumulative effect of these things was the perpetuation of the South's preoccupation with the collection, description, and classification of natural phenomena and the relegation of experimental research to the periphery of scholarship.

Like Americans everywhere, antebellum southerners were keenly interested in the practical applications of science. Applied science in the Old South largely involved attempts to bring science to bear on the region's mounting agricultural problems toward the end of the era. The highly acclaimed research of Edmund Ruffin in soil chemistry is a case in point.

Like science, medicine in the antebellum South exhibited unmistakable regional characteristics. By the time the Old South emerged, a distinctive southern health picture was evident. It was the worst in the nation. So poor was the state of health in the region that northern life insurance companies charged their southern policyholders higher premiums. Malaria remained endemic and was the principal cause of disability and death. Residents of the southern port cities and the surrounding countryside lived in fear of yellow fever, which became a southern disease in the 19th century. New Orleans, the Old South's largest city, was popularly known as "the graveyard of the Southwest" because of its frightful mortality rate (nearly three times that of Philadelphia and New York). Infant mortality rates in the South were the highest in the nation. In addition, it is estimated that as many as half of all southern children suffered from hookworm infection, a condition not diagnosed until the opening years of the 20th century. Finally, inadequate diets, poor housing, unhealthy quarters, and hazardous working conditions exacted a heavy toll on the health of the South's large slave population.

The Old South's health problems were the result of environmental and cultural factors. Climate and frontier conditions in the developing region, in conjunction with slavery, combined to account for the continued presence of malaria. The insect vectors of yellow fever and typhoid fever also thrived. In addition to fostering insect life, the long, hot summers made the preservation of food difficult, increased sanitary problems, and encouraged going barefoot, a habit associated with the spread of hookworm.

The growing cultural lag that increasingly set the South apart from the more progressive North contributed to regional health problems in a variety of ways. The low level of southern education, the lowest in the nation, clearly complicated the health picture. Nationwide, the "heroic" procedures of physicians were questioned during the first half of the 19th century, a development that encouraged the reliance on traditional healers and self-dosage with patent medicines. The rural and undereducated southerners were particularly prone to resort to these health-threatening practices. The absence of a social conscience on the part of the dominant planter class also had an adverse effect on health. Finally, institutions for the advancement of medicine, such as schools and journals, were, like those in science, slow to appear in the overwhelmingly rural South, and those that were founded faced a difficult struggle for survival. The few that survived were inferior to those in the North. The rise of southern medical nationalism, or states' rights medicine, did little, despite its rhetoric, to change this situation. The product of regional patterns of disease and sectional tensions, states' rights medicine stressed the uniqueness of the South's medical problems and the subsequent need for southern-trained physicians and a southern medical literature. Although the desire to improve the practice of medicine in the region was indisputably one of its goals, southern medical nationalism, like the scientific racism of Josiah C. Nott and others, was primarily a defense of the civilization of the Old South. Consequently, it contributed more to sectionalism than to medical reform.

Although easily overlooked because of the health problems of the region, the antebellum South's strides in surgery contributed significantly to the rise of modern medicine. Two southerners—Ephraim McDowell and J. Marion Sims—achieved international acclaim in operative obstetrics and gynecology. The former, while practicing on the Kentucky frontier in 1808, performed the first successful ovariotomy, pioneering abdominal surgery. The latter, an Alabama surgeon, used slave women as subjects to perfect, in the 1840s, the initial procedure for the treatment of vesicovaginal fistula, a major breakthrough in gynecology. The third southerner who contributed to the birth of American surgery was Crawford W. Long, a small-town Georgia physician who was the first to use ether as a surgical anesthesia in 1842, helping to launch a new age of painless surgery.

Civil War. The culture of the Old South was inhospitable to scientific inquiry and threatening to health, but the region's scientists and physicians closed ranks with their countrymen to defend it against all perceived enemies. In 1861, when the South withdrew from the Union, they pledged their lives and fortunes to the new Confederate nation.

The Civil War was not a scientific war. Neither the North nor the South used scientific talent in ways that led to new or drastically improved weapons that altered tactics and strategy on the battlefield. Still, each side made extensive use of scientists. The North did considerably better than the South in this area. Prominent scientists were consciously incorporated into the northern war effort in an advisory capacity. In the South, they were engaged as problem solvers. The Confederacy's failure to devise a science policy is attributable to the many and pressing problems to be overcome in order to wage war and to the popular perception in the South of scientists as problem solvers.

Scientists in the southern war effort worked in the government-run munitions industry, and the War Department's Ordnance Bureau most especially. Headed by Josiah Gorgas, this agency was responsible for the Confederacy's supply of war materiel. Gorgas and his assistants accomplished the near impossible, building a munitions industry from scratch. It was largely through their efforts that the South was able to keep its armies in the field for four years against a vastly superior enemy. Indeed, the Confederacy ran out of men before it did arms.

Disease, disability, and death stalked the Civil War soldier and made this the costliest conflict in American history. A major reason for the unequaled carnage was the state of contemporary medicine. Indeed, the nation's doctors were plunged without warning into a modern war with its unprecedented medical problems at a critical turning point in American medical history. Out of this era of transition, which saw established beliefs and practices come under attack, was to emerge the beginning of modern American laboratory medicine. In the meantime, a majority of the standard therapeutic measures—puking, purging, bleeding, and giving large doses of potentially dangerous drugs in particular—met with little success in the day-to-day struggle against common complaints and failed miserably when confronted by yellow fever, cholera, and typhoid fever, the great killer epidemics of 19th-century America.

The cruelest blow of all to the Civil War soldier was that the lifesaving antiseptic management of wounds, growing out of the research of Pasteur and Lister, came too late to be of help. Consequently, any serious injury to a limb meant amputation and the distinct possibility of death from one of the so-called surgical fevers—gangrene, erysipelas, or pyemia. Abdominal wounds were especially feared and constituted an almost certain death sentence.

The Civil War's toll of misery and death was most evident in the Confederate army. Like Gorgas and the manufacture of the tools of war, Samuel P. Moore, the southern surgeon general, had to build a medical service from scratch. He also was successful in meeting this challenge. But the efforts of the Confederate medical officers were hampered by an inadequate supply of trained physicians, near-crippling shortages of medicines and medical stores, and a steadily worsening military situation. Still, they faithfully kept at their tasks and provided valiant and commendable service. Few medical lessons, however, emerged from the carnage. For the South, the chief gain was the experience that the war provided in the treatment of the sick and injured and most especially the sharpening of surgical skills.

New South. The civilization of the Old South perished on the battlefields of the Civil War. The legacy of the South's failed bid for independence was frustration, poverty, and obsession with the past. These things supplanted in significance such long-standing cultural determinants as agrarianism and ruralism. Their immediate and lasting effect was to blight life in the region. Indeed, passing time seemed only to worsen matters. Even the much ballyhooed New South movement, with its promise of progress and prosperity based on the northern industrial model, did little to relieve the plight of the southern people. Consequently, as the New South era drew to a close in the opening years of the 20th century, the South was mired in backwardness and misery. Nowhere is this better seen than in science and medicine.

In the North, the Civil War was a catalyst for scientific progress, and American science matured rapidly during the last years of the 19th century, paving the way for domination in the century ahead. In the South, the war produced intellectual stagnation. Consequently, southern scientific leaders were largely sideline observers of Gilded Age and early 20th-century advances in science. The comparative gap separating southern and national science was probably greater at the end of the New South period than ever before.

With life in the South reduced to a scramble for survival and with spiritual malaise rampant in the dark days after Appomattox, there was little opportunity or desire to pursue science. So unbearable were conditions to some scientists, like John and Joseph LeConte, two of the New South's emerging scientific leaders, that they joined the postwar exodus from the region. Yet the beginnings of the revival of southern science date from the immediate postwar period. As the initial shock and agony of defeat began to abate, southern scientists reestablished contact with northern friends, who generously assisted them in rekindling their scientific interests, providing, for example, news of wartime developments in science and copies of recent works.

The first tangible signs of the revival of southern science were predictably found in natural history. The principal figures, men like Henry William Ravenel, Moses A. Curtis, and Alvan W. Chapman, were holdovers from the antebellum period. Natural history would continue to dominate science in the South, but its heyday was at an end. It was giving way to the modern science of botany, and the evolving professional scientist was supplanting the amateur collector.

As before, the southern record in the pure sciences was meager and undistinguished. The fate of this branch of science was inextricably bound up with that of higher education. At the beginning of the period, the South's colleges and universities were paralyzed by the effects of the Civil War and the political turmoil of Reconstruction. By its end, the best of them had made the transition to multipurpose institutions. But the region's continuing poverty, conservative social philosophy, and religious fundamentalism prevented them from becoming true centers for the advancement of learning.

The prospects of applied science in the South were as encouraging as those of abstract science were unpromising. Economic necessity made this the case. A long list of southern scientists sought to bring science to bear in the effort to restore the region's prosperity. In agriculture, the traditional but troubled source of southern wealth, George Washington Carver exemplifies the renewed emphasis on scientific farming and farm management. In industry, Charles Holmes Herty's research on forest products is illustrative of the attempt to use science to create new economic opportunities.

The Civil War and its aftermath had a disastrous effect on health in the South. On the one hand, the hostilities left untold thousands of southerners in precarious or weakened health. On the other, the conflict's legacy of poverty exacerbated the region's tradition of poor health. As a result, old diseases increased in incidence and virulence, and new health problems arose. Malaria, the leading cause of debility and loss of efficiency in the antebellum South, had showed signs of decline in the decade preceding the Civil War. In the postwar period, however, it soared to record levels and reappeared in areas where it had previously been brought under control. Yellow fever, another old and distinctively southern disease, was a recurrent source of terror, death, and economic blight. Tuberculosis was more prevalent in the South than elsewhere. Blacks were especially hard hit. But a higher incidence of tuberculosis was only one indication of the deteriorating health of the former slaves. Left to fend for themselves after the collapse of Reconstruction, freedmen experienced excessively high rates of sickness and death.

Black health problems, as well as those of a growing number of whites, were in large part the result of the rise and spread of tenancy, the cruel backbone of postwar southern agriculture. The proliferation of the mill town, the chief symbol of the New South, further eroded the health of the poor whites. The principal diseases of poverty were hookworm and pellagra. The former, although undetected, was an old health hazard. In the antebellum period, however, it had been limited to slaves and the relatively small class of poor whites. Postwar poverty exposed growing numbers of southerners to hookworm infection, making it a major threat to regional health. Pellagra was the most spectacular and deadly of a number of disorders caused by dietary deficiency that plagued the swelling ranks of the southern poor. Almost exclusively southern in incidence, hookworm and pellagra were widespread by the time they were diagnosed at the turn of the century.

Urbanization in the South was largely a postbellum phenomenon, and New South cities were notoriously unhealthy. Chief among the health hazards were unpaved and poorly drained streets, inadequate or nonexistent sewage arrangements, public garbage heaps, and contaminated water supplies. Conditions were the worst in the segregated quarters into which urban blacks were crowded. With their growth came the multiplication of health problems. Health administrations were virtually nonexistent before the last two decades of the century, so little was done to improve conditions.

The threat of disease did not go unnoticed in the South. But poverty and the inability of the medical profession to combat the principal causes of morbidity and mortality stymied would-be reformers. Toward the end of the century, however, improvement in the southern economy and the acceptance of the new germ theory of disease provided the opportunity for health reform. The result was the genesis of the southern public health movement. Boards of health were established and empowered to investigate and combat health problems. Although the effectiveness of these agencies was limited by inadequate budgets, legislative interference, suspicion and hostility on the part of businessmen, and the ignorance of the masses, they pushed health reform on a broad front. The state boards of health uncovered and attacked a host of health hazards, inspected water supplies, sought to impose quarantines during outbreaks of epidemic disease, supervised vaccines, published reports, and strove to educate the public on health matters.

20th-century South. Still suffering from the physical and emotional effects of the Civil War, the South entered the 20th century with an uncertain future. The years ahead, however, brought slowly improving prospects, the result of the slow transformation of southern society during the interwar years. Indeed, change became the major theme of southern history. The Progressive movement, which flowered after 1910, marked a turning point in the region's reaction to change by making it palatable, indeed desirable, to many southerners. Following World War I, change resumed, stronger than ever.

To the region's traditionalists, however, the prospects of change were not only subversive to the southern way of life but actually threatened to destroy it. The result was social controversy that set southerner against southerner. The struggle for control of the South's destiny was long and often bitter, but the outcome was inevitable—ever so slowly there was an erosion of the South as a distinctive social and cultural entity. Put another way, the South was closing the circle, gradually moving back into the national mainstream, which it had left during the era of the Old South. The consequences of the Americanization of the South were to be immensely beneficial for science and medicine, although they were not to be realized until after World War II. In the meantime, both disciplines faced continued rough sledding.

The maturation of American science accelerated during the interwar years, and by the outbreak of World War II, the United States was poised for world scientific leadership. Owing to its physical, cultural, and intellectual poverty, the South contributed only marginally to national greatness in science.

The state of science during this transitional period in the South's history is best seen through an examination of academic science, for scientific inquiry nationwide was largely university centered. Building on the beginnings from the Progressive era, southern education, from bottom to top, underwent progressive change after 1920. By the outbreak of World War II, the South had experienced a veritable revolution in education. The prospects for the region's colleges and universities, however, were not as bright as the foregoing might seem to indicate. The gap to be closed was great and progress was slow and uneven. Indeed, the perennial problems facing southern schools were numerous and weighty. They included inadequate financial resources, overworked and underpaid faculties, mediocre students, and the desire of communities to control their schools. Such factors severely limited the capacity of the southern schools for intellectual attainment.

The South's institutions of higher learning, however, were not devoid of scholarship. As a matter of fact, there was a general reawakening of the southern intellect in the 1920s. But science fared less well than the social sciences and humanities in the southern intellectual renaissance. To be sure, the South had dedicated scientists. They worked to keep up with developments in their fields of interest, and some engaged in research, the results of which were occasionally noteworthy. Moreover, with the gradual upgrading of student bodies, faculties, and facilities as the 20th century wore on, the general state of science in the region improved. Still, when viewed comparatively, science in the South's institutions of higher learning was undistinguished.

As before, the realities of southern life shed informative light on the reasons for the state of science in the region. The interwar years were the era of the Benighted South. This popular image was the product of the South's long-standing social and economic problems and the unprecedented attention that the raging controversy between the proponents of change and the traditionalists drew to them. Benightedness influenced science in two major ways. First, the region's continuing economic problems, which worsened in the 1920s, meant modest expenditures on education, thereby limiting what could be done in science. Science also found itself embroiled in a conflict with the forces of social and religious fundamentalism. Such a confrontation was perhaps inevitable, for the vital interests of the two were diametrically opposed—free inquiry on the one hand and intellectual conformity on the other. The battleground was evolution, and the celebrated Scopes Trial of 1925 was only the best known of a host of violations of freedom of thought by the crusading fundamentalists. But the proponents of progress refused to yield to the traditionalist onslaught and tenaciously resisted. Their most powerful weapon, however, was time, for try as they might, the traditionalists could not quarantine the South from the formidable and unrelenting winds of change that were buffeting the region.

Owing to a series of medical discoveries around the turn of the century that propelled the southern public health movement into a new stage of activity and accomplishment, medicine made greater progress than science in the South after 1900. Between 1898 and 1906 the insect carriers of malaria (1898) and yellow fever (1899) were identified, and hookworm (1902) and pellagra (1906) were diagnosed as endemic among the southern poor. On the one hand, these developments vividly underscored the South's unique and stigmatizing health problems and focused national attention on them. On the other, they paved the way for the eventual control of the region's principal causes of sickness and death and promoted increased interest in public health reform.

The campaigns against malaria, yellow fever, hookworm, and pellagra, although hindered by regional poverty and the resistance of business and political leaders who were outraged over the embarrassing exposure of the South's myriad and frightful health problems, were landmark victories for southern health. By the end of World War II these scourges had been eradicated (or controlled in the case of pellagra), in large part as the result of the national discovery of the South's health plight after 1900. While publicity about the shocking state of southern health reinforced the stigma of regional backwardness, it also led to crucial assistance from northern philanthropies and the federal government. The indispensable role of the Rockefeller Foundation in the control of hookworm and the U.S. Public Health Service in the fight against pellagra are cases in point.

The nascent southern public health movement was a major beneficiary of the late 19th- and early 20th-century medical advances that stripped the region's principal diseases of their mystery. As increasing numbers of southerners became aware of the modern concept of disease and the lifesaving potential of laboratory medicine, the long-standing belief that an unhealthy climate was the cause of disease was toppled, the importance of sanitation and drainage was recognized, and a lessening of opposition to the recognition of regional health problems and a greater willingness to confront them evolved. These developments coincided with and were influenced by the southern Progressive movement. Chagrined by the South's backward image, the Progressives sought to rid the region of the principal causes of backwardness. Health reform was high on their agenda.

Disease was attacked on a broadening front. Crusades against malaria, yellow fever, hookworm, and pellagra touched off similar campaigns against tuberculosis and syphilis. Sanitaria and hospitals were built. Boards of health were set up in those states that had not already established them. Responding to the stimulus of the Rockefeller Sanitary Commission for the Eradication of Hookworm Disease, which combated this disease at the local level, county health departments mushroomed, propelling the South into the lead in this area. And health department expenditures increased, despite the region's ongoing economic woes. Additional funding for health reform came from philanthropic organizations and federal agencies. The Frontier Nursing Service, established in 1925 by Mary Breckinridge in the mountains of Kentucky, typified the growing concern for the health of the isolated people of southern Appalachia. Finally, southern senators and congressmen began to take a greater interest in health legislation. The cumulative effect of these developments was the gradual improvement of southern health. The narrowing of differences in mortality rates between the regions attests to the gains made.

But as revolutionary as the progress in health reform was, the South remained the nation's sickliest section at the onset of the Depression. Familiar disease forms continued to plague the region. For example, malaria had not been brought under control, and the plummeting of cotton prices in the 1920s led to a resurgence of pellagra. And southern cities remained unhealthy.

The first attempts at a national health program were made during the New Deal, and the South was a major beneficiary of the New Dealers' concern for health. Funds for medical care were provided by the Federal Emergency Relief Administration. Civilian Conservation Corps members received medical attention. The draining of 2 million acres of swamp by the Civil Works Administration, the Federal Emergency Relief Administration, and the Works Progress Administration and studies of the breeding habits of mosquitoes by the Tennessee Valley Authority expedited efforts to eradicate malaria. The control of typhoid fever and dysentery was advanced through the federally sponsored construction of 2.3 million sanitary privies by 1939. New crusades against tuberculosis and venereal disease were launched. The Works Progress Administration built hospitals and sewage plants. The Federal Housing Administration's slum-clearance programs, half of which were in the South, promoted urban health reform. Of far-reaching significance was the Social Security Act of 1935. This historic piece of social welfare legislation provided federal funds for health purposes and created permanent machinery for distributing them.

World War II had major uplifting effects on southern health. The stationing of large numbers of troops in the region brought the resources of the federal government to bear in the fight against disease on an unprecedented scale. As the conquest of malaria illustrates, public health was greatly advanced. The health screenings and medical attention that accompanied military service led to vastly improved health for thousands of southerners. And military instruction in hygiene inculcated in them the importance of good health and taught them how to achieve it. The wartime appearance of enriched flour and bread, containing synthetic vitamins, considerably curtailed the threat of pellagra and other disorders resulting from dietary deficiencies.

Recent South. World War II was a landmark in southern history: it reinvigorated the region's long-troubled economy and swung the battle between the modernists and traditionalists in favor of progressive change, greatly accelerating the Americanization of the South. Indeed, no other period in the South's past has witnessed as much fundamental change as have the years since World War II. The changes in southern life extended across a broad front. Prominent among them were the triumph of industry, the transformation of agriculture, burgeoning urbanization, the breaking of the hold of ruralism, the ending of physical and cultural isolation, the dismantling of the Jim Crow system, the disintegration of the political Solid South, and a revitalized role in national politics. The result, as one historian put it, has been the demise of the "sectional South" and the rebirth of the "American South." Although accomplished at the expense of regional distinctiveness and at times, as in the case of race relations, vigorously opposed, the Americanization of the South has led to unprecedented prosperity, dramatic improvements in the quality of life, growing opportunities for southerners, and renewed respect for the region. Science and medicine have been major beneficiaries of the postwar changes in southern life.

The Americanization of the South has sparked a veritable revolution in the pursuit of science in the region. At the outbreak of World War II, the South was little more than an outpost of American science. At the present, it has risen, at the least, to the status of junior partner in the national scientific establishment. This amazing turnabout is easily demonstrated. The South is producing and using scientists at greater rates than ever before in its history. Institutions of every type for the support of science are unprecedented in quantity and quality. Levels of scientific achievement have soared. Finally, the region's attitude toward science has become increasingly progressive and supportive. The great distance that science in the South has traveled since World War II is clearly seen in the reversal of the South's "brain drain"; the region is now a magnet for scientific talent. To be sure, parity with the national leaders in science, such as the Northeast and the West Coast, has not been achieved, but the prospects for science in the South, especially if the Sunbelt phenomenon is perpetuated, are promising indeed.

With the postwar transformation of the South have also come unparalleled improvements in health. Indeed, the "sickly South" is rapidly becoming a thing of the past as the region moves toward national patterns and norms in health matters. Problems, however, remain to be overcome before it can be said that southerners as a people enjoy good health. These problems include an elevated rate of postnatal mortality, a high incidence of poverty-related diseases, and substandard health care in rural areas. As before, ethnic minorities and the poor are the least healthy southerners.

In retrospect, southern science and medicine have closed the circle. They began on a roughly equal footing with the rest of British North America. With the rise of a distinctive southern culture after the Revolution, they became sectional and second rate. The Civil War and its lingering aftermath perpetuated the South's scientific lag and poor health well into the 20th century. But since World War II national patterns and norms have increasingly prevailed. Indeed, it is appropriate to speak not of southern science and medicine but of science and medicine in the South.

See also BLACK LIFE: Health, Black; EDUCATION: Academic Freedom; Learned Societies; ENVIRONMENT: Naturalists; HISTORY AND MANNERS: Philanthropy, Northern; MYTHIC SOUTH: New South Myth; SOCIAL CLASS: Health, Worker; WOMEN'S LIFE: Healers, Women

James O. Breeden
Southern Methodist University

Wyndham B. Blanton, *Medicine in Virginia in the Eighteenth Century*, 3 vols. (1930–33); James O. Breeden, *Joseph Jones, M.D.: Scientist of the Old South* (1975); Clark R. Cahow, *People, Patients, and Politics: A History of North Carolina Mental Hospitals, 1848–1960* (1982); J. H. Cassedy, *Journal of History of Medicine and Allied Sciences* (April 1973); James X. Corgan, ed., *The Geological Sciences in the Antebellum South* (1982); Horace H. Cunningham, *Doctors in Gray: The Confederate Medical Service* (1958); George Daniels, *American Science in the Age of Jackson* (1968); Richard Beale Davis, *Intellectual Life in the Colonial South, 1585–1763*, 3 vols. (1978); William H. Deaderick and Loyd Thompson, *Endemic Diseases of the Southern States* (1916); John Duffy, *Epidemics in Colonial America* (1953), *The Healers: A History of American Medicine* (1976), *Journal of Southern History* (May 1968), ed., *The Rudolph Matas History of Medicine in Louisiana*, 2 vols. (1958–62); Clement Eaton, *The Mind of the Old South* (1964); Clark A. Elliott, *Biographical Dictionary of American Science: The Seventeenth through the Nineteenth Centuries* (1979); Elizabeth W. Etheridge, *The Butterfly Caste: A Social History of Pellagra in the South* (1972); John Ettling, *The Germ of Laziness: Rockefeller Philanthropy and Public Health in the New South* (1981); Gaines M. Foster, *Journal of Southern History* (August 1982); Brooke Hindle, *The Pursuit of Science in Revolutionary America, 1735–1789* (1956); Howard L. Holley, *A History of Medicine in Alabama* (1982); Thomas Cary Johnson, Jr., *Scientific Interests in the Old South* (1936); Leo J. Klosterman, Loyd S. Swenson, and Sylvia Rose, eds., *100 Years of Science and Technology in Texas* (1986); Dorothy Long, ed., *Medicine in North Carolina: Essays in the History of Medical Science and Medical Service, 1524–1960*, 2 vols. (1972); Edward T. Martin, *Thomas Jefferson, Scientist* (1952); Nancy Smith Midgette, "The Role of the State Academies of Science in the Emergence of the Scientific Profession in the South, 1883–1983" (Ph.D. dissertation, University of Georgia, 1984); Ronald L. Numbers and Janet Numbers, *Journal of Southern History* (February 1982); Nathan Reingold and Marc Rothenberg, eds., *Scientific Colonialism, 1800–1930: A Cross-Cultural Comparison* (1986); Todd L. Savitt, *Journal of Southern History* (August 1982), *Medicine and Slavery: Diseases and Health Care of Blacks in Antebellum Virginia* (1978); Richard H. Shyrock, *South Atlantic Quarterly* (April 1930); Raymond Phineas Stearns, *Science in the British Colonies of North America* (1970); Joseph I. Waring, *A History of Medicine in South Carolina*, 3 vols. (1964–71).

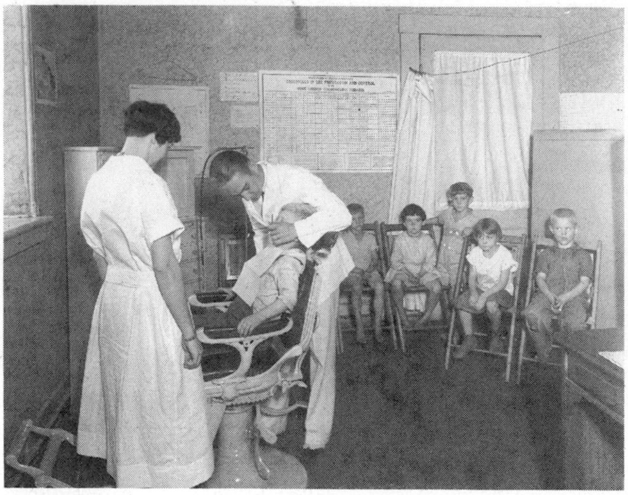

A Red Cross dental clinic in Kentucky, c. 1932

Aerospace

The term *aerospace* gained currency during the 1950s and was a product of U.S. Air Force nomenclature. It evolved in response to the growing interest of aviation manufacturers and the government in space exploration as well as in traditional aeronautics. From the first flight of the Wright brothers at Kitty Hawk, N.C., to the launch of America's first astronauts from Cape Canaveral, Fla., the South has played an active role in aerospace developments.

On 17 December 1903 the Wrights made the world's first flights in a powered airplane. During the years prior to World War I, planes were generally viewed as carnival curiosities, although a number of events in the South gave a hint of future trends and made southerners aware of the coming "air age." In 1911 Cal Rodgers completed the first transcontinental flight, which lasted three months. His route took him across Texas, where good weather and level terrain promised an easier course around the Rocky Mountains. Three years later in Florida promoters launched the country's first commercial airline—a flying boat service across the bay between Tampa and St. Petersburg.

After 1917, when America entered World War I, the attributes of sunny weather and open spaces made the South a center of flight training, a pattern that has persisted across the region. During the 1920s commercial aviation began to expand, especially after the Air Mail Act of 1925, which transferred post office airmail routes to private contractors. Numerous companies launched services, but much consolidation eventually thinned their ranks. On the eve of World War II major airlines with a southern heritage included National and Eastern (in Florida), Delta (in Georgia), and Braniff (in Texas). Also, Pan American had major routes from Florida into the Caribbean and from Brownsville, Tex., into Latin America.

As southern farmers continued their perennial campaign against the cotton boll weevil, aerial crop dusting grew rapidly during the 1920s. Agricultural aviation owed much to pioneering work conducted by Dr. B. R. Coad and the U.S. Bureau of Entomology in Louisiana. Among the many commercial crop-dusting companies, Huff-Daland of Monroe, La., was one of the most successful and grew into Delta Airlines. Aerial crop treatment became even more widespread after World War II; a research and development project at Texas A&M during the 1950s produced a unique design for a crop duster with special safety features that became standard for the industry.

During World War II its even terrain and good flying weather again made the South a major center of flight training; U.S. Army and U.S. Navy facilities turned out thousands of pilots, navigators, and bombardiers. In the postwar era, many of these training fields continued to serve as operational air bases and as centers of flight training. Similarly, aviation manufacturers moved south during the war to take advantage of climate, available land, and a plentiful supply of labor. The Dallas–Fort Worth area continued as a major producer of bombers, fighters, and helicopters; plants in Atlanta, Ga., turned out huge transports and other aerospace hardware. Many cities developed facilities for producing electronics and a variety of aerospace products. Following the creation of the National Aeronautics and Space Administration (NASA) in 1958, the South became known worldwide for its role in America's space program. The John F. Kennedy Space Center in Florida became NASA's principal launch site; the George C. Marshall Space Flight Center in Alabama played a major role in developing launch vehicles and in handling manned operations; and the Lyndon B. Johnson Space Center near Houston, Tex., was the focal point for astronaut training, mission control, and other

Alan L. Bean, astronaut from Texas, 1969

tasks. As one historian noted, these centers represented a "fertile crescent" of advanced technology in the South. The spin-off of their presence was seen in the science-technology activities of neighboring schools, universities, and businesses; they also became major tourist attractions.

Air travel expanded in the postwar years, especially after the introduction of jets in the late 1950s. Certain cities became major hubs of national and international significance. Atlanta's airport (currently handling about 40 million passengers annually) became the second busiest in the nation, trailing only Chicago. The Dallas–Fort Worth regional airport ranked fourth in the United States and was a significant factor in attracting so many national corporations that the Dallas–Fort Worth area ranked third behind New York and Chicago as a location of corporate headquarters. Major southern airports also offered nonstop flights to major cities in Europe, Latin America, and the Pacific, bringing new dimensions of business and vacation travel to southerners. By the 1980s mergers and deregulation left four major airlines in the South—Eastern (Miami), Delta (Atlanta), American (Dallas), and Continental (Houston).

See also AGRICULTURE: / Pest Control; INDUSTRY: Military and Economy; / Delta Airlines

Roger E. Bilstein
University of Houston
at Clear Lake City

Roger E. Bilstein, *Flight in America, 1900–1983: From the Wrights to the Astronauts* (1984); R. E. G. Davies, *Airlines of the United States since 1914* (1972); W. David Lewis and Wesley P. Newton, *Delta: The History of an Airline* (1979); Loyd S. Swenson, *Southwestern Historical Quarterly* (January 1968).

Agriculture, Scientific

Although southerners made remarkable agricultural progress between 1800 and 1860, science contributed comparatively little until the 1870s. Before the Civil War, American agriculturists using empirical methods developed the essentials of modern farming. In the 20th century science and technology built upon this foundation to make American agriculture the most productive in the world.

In the South planters started in the 1790s to cultivate new crops of Sea Island cotton, upland cotton, and sugar with slave labor and primitive farming methods based on spades, hoes, and ox-drawn turning plows. Within the span of a single lifetime they created advanced systems for producing those crops on a vast scale. During the period from 1830 to 1860 they mechanized their farming operations with mule-drawn implements and even used steam engines to power their gins, mills, and presses. By 1850 cotton growers had bred the modern type of upland cotton by crossing varieties imported from the Caribbean Islands, Mexico, and Siam and then refining the resultant cotton with selective breeding. During the 1840s planters adopted horizontal culture of row crops, crop rotation, and elaborate drainage systems in order to preserve the fertility of their farmlands. Finally, they devised effective methods of managing slaves in which rewards replaced threats of punishment. By 1860 southern agriculturists employed almost all the implements and farming methods still in vogue during the 1920s.

In the prewar era chemistry made several useful contributions to southern agriculture. Edmund Ruffin of Virginia demonstrated that marl could renovate worn-out soils by reducing acidity, and Justus Liebig, the German chemist, analyzed soils to discover that cultivation of crops removed important elements from the soil. From him, southerners learned to plow under the stalks of their cotton and corn. Liebig's research also pointed the way to improving soil fertility by adding missing elements.

Many of the South's agricultural achievements were lost as a result of the Civil War. Plantations were subdivided into family-sized farms worked by unsupervised sharecroppers. In the process the economies of large-scale farming disappeared, and the improved management techniques of the 1850s became inapplicable. The prewar trend toward farm mechanization ended and soil-conservation systems were abandoned. Inevitably, the productivity of farmlands and agricultural workers diminished. Had it not been for two contributions made at this time by chemistry, the South's agricultural economy would have declined still further. Newly introduced commercial chemical fertilizers partially offset the loss of soil fertility characteristic of sharecropping, and the first arsenic-based insecticides reduced crop losses.

Around the turn of the 20th century state and federal governments established experiment stations employing chemists, botanists, and entomologists to seek solutions for agricultural problems. In the private sector of the economy, commercial plant breeders who earlier had relied on selective breeding now began to apply the science of botany with noticeable effect.

Between the two world wars gasoline tractors benefitted southern agriculture even more than improvements made in chemical fertilizers and insecticides. Early models assumed the heavy labor of breaking land for planting, and later tricycle types increasingly performed much of the cultivation formerly done with mule-drawn implements. With the coming of tractor-drawn, multirow mechanical implements, landowners regained much authority over farm workers that had been lost with the collapse of slavery. A new system of day labor began slowly to replace sharecropping. By 1940 mechanization had progressed so far that crops of cotton could be planted and cultivated almost entirely with machines. Manual labor was required only for a small amount of hoeing and for harvesting the crop.

Between 1945 and 1950 the mechanization of southern agriculture was completed. Mechanical cotton strippers and cotton pickers now harvested the South's principal crop, and flame-throwing devices and chemical herbicides replaced the last of the hoes. With the advent of these revolutionary machines, the system of sharecropping became obsolete and by 1960 was virtually dead. In the place of sharecropping arose a new system of large landholdings worked as single units, not unlike the old slave plantations, with diesel- and gasoline-powered machines taking the places of slaves and mules.

With the emergence of consolidated mechanized plantations in the 1960s, the age of scientific agriculture finally dawned in the South, decades later than in other sections of the nation. Landowners who had gained full control over their farming operations began effectively to apply modern techniques of management, introducing the new products of science and technology into their system of agriculture. Machines distributed a new generation of chemical fertilizers, insecticides, fungicides, and herbicides with scientific accuracy. Scientific plant breeders supplied farmers with prolific new plants tailored for disease resistance and ease of harvesting by machine. In all major crops yields per acre increased dramatically.

In the post–World War II era, southern agriculturists acquired a new versatility from science and technology. They were able to contend with changes in the market by shifting from cotton to supplementary crops of soybeans or small grains. In some areas cotton was entirely abandoned for rice, corn, or peanuts.

Scientific and technological progress in southern agriculture brought new problems as well as benefits. Millions of farm workers lost their employment, and rural populations declined. With mechanization, the South became dangerously dependent upon the international oil industry for fuel and agricultural chemicals. Insect pests demonstrated a dismaying capability of developing resistance to insecticides, and hybrid plants proved vulnerable to epidemic viral plant diseases. Thus far chemists have overcome insect resistance with new toxic substances, but the future of this approach is clouded because the number of suitable chemical combinations is limited. Agricultural scientists therefore are turning to the control of insects through both natural enemies and sterilization with radiation. In the future southern farmers will undoubtedly find their most serious problem to be obtaining adequate supplies of fertilizers, without which modern scientific agriculture cannot be carried on.

See also AGRICULTURE: Mechanization; / Agricultural Experiment Stations; Fertilizer; Pest Control

John Hebron Moore
Florida State University

Gilbert C. Fite, *Agricultural History* (January 1979, January 1980); John L. Fulmer, *Agricultural Progress in the Cotton Belt since 1920* (1950); Paul W. Gates, *The Farmer's Age: Agriculture, 1815–1860* (1960); Douglas Helms, *Agricultural History* (January 1979, January 1980); Willard Range, *A Century of Georgia Agriculture, 1850–1950* (1954); Charles R. Sayre, *Agricultural History* (January 1979); Richard C. Sheridan, *Agricultural History* (January 1979).

Alcohol and Alcoholism

Anthropologists who describe American drinking practices often use the word "ambivalent" to describe conflicting attitudes toward alcohol. For the South, however, ambivalence is too mild a label; "schizoid" comes closer to the mark. Extremes of opinion and practice can be found in practically any southern community, ranging from teetotalers who condemn all drink to heavy drinkers who swill it in manly ritual. As Will Rogers pointed out, some southerners will "vote dry as long as they can stagger to the polls."

It was not always so. Southern colonists and their descendants in the early years of the Republic had few qualms about alcohol; they drank hard and often. The Virginia Company was plagued by planters who crowded aboard floating taverns in the James River, bartering their tobacco for spirits and sack. They, like later frontiersmen, caroused to escape the loneliness and hardship of wilderness life. Even in well-established towns and plantations, however, drinking was nearly universal among adult white males. Men drank upon arising and retiring; during and between meals; and while celebrating holidays, recuperating from illness, conducting business, and soliciting or pledging votes.

Variety, as well as quantity, characterized southern drinking. Brandies were made from apples, peaches, pears, and other local fruit; cider was also popular, although not as universal as in the North. Imported wines, especially Madeira and claret, graced wealthy planters' tables. All classes drank rum, which was obtained in exchange for southern commodities. Rum fortified most strong drinks of the 18th century, including punch, flip, toddy, grog, and black-strap.

When the Revolution disrupted trade, making supplies of West Indian molasses expensive and uncertain, rum consumption declined. Its place was taken by whiskey, a drink already familiar to Scottish, Irish, and Scotch-Irish immigrants. Their knowledge of making whiskey, combined with improved stills and ample grain, water, and

Paul Newman and Elizabeth Taylor as Brick and Maggie in Cat on a Hot Tin Roof *(1958), in which alcoholism was a prominent theme*

fuel, assured an abundant supply. Distilling was especially important in the corn-growing areas of the Upper South—the word *bourbon* derives from Bourbon County, Ky. Those who were alarmed by the deluge of cheap spirits, such as Thomas Jefferson, proposed viticulture and brewing as more salubrious alternatives, but domestic wines and beer failed to make significant inroads against whiskey in the South, at least until the mid-20th century.

Southerners paid dearly for their indulgence: heavy drinking led to widespread alcoholism and heightened violence. The latter danger arose not only from drinking but from drinking in an environment where weapons were ubiquitous and men shared a homicidal sensitivity about honor. Slaves suffered as well, for there was little they could do to protect themselves from a master turned brutal by drink. Harriet Beecher Stowe capitalized on their plight in *Uncle Tom's Cabin* (1852), which contains several pointed references to Simon Legree's drinking.

The temperance movement in the antebellum South was relatively weak. Although it had 44 percent of the population, the South accounted for only 8 percent of the nation's temperance pledges in 1811; no slave state, save Delaware, had adopted prohibition by the 1850s. A perceived link with antislavery hurt the temperance cause in the South, as did the economic circumstances of isolated farmers, who depended on distilling to retard spoilage, reduce bulk, and enhance the marketability of their crops. Some of the more substantial farmers and aspiring middle-class townsfolk joined temperance societies, but their influence was outweighed by the planter elite, who remained aloof—and conspicuously wet.

The Civil War had mixed consequences for southern drinking. The short-term effects were largely negative: temperance societies were disrupted during the war, and defeat gave many demoralized southerners added cause to resort to the bottle. Yet, in other ways, the war paved the way for the eventual triumph of the drys. First, it set a precedent for prohibition; during 1862 Confederate legislatures sought to preserve grain by outlawing its distillation. As a result, whiskey prices rose sharply. They fell again after 1865, but not to antebellum levels, due to the retention of federal excise taxes on beer and liquor. Bootleggers, of course, did not pay taxes, but trouble and risk necessarily inflated the cost of their product. The net, long-term effect of higher prices was to discourage consumption, at least among nonalcoholics.

In destroying planter hegemony the war also made possible the rise of a new leadership group, the middle class, whose members were much more hostile toward drink. Middle-class reformers were quick to climb aboard the prohibition bandwagon, denouncing alcohol in the name of economy, discipline, and other progressive virtues. They were not alone. Populists also hated the liquor dealers, whom they accused of exploiting the people and (not without evidence) of manipulating their representatives. Ironically, they were joined on this issue by many New South industrialists, who saw liquor as undermining productivity. To this diverse alliance were added the evangelicals, whose numbers and influence were growing rapidly during the postbellum decades. Evangelical ministers admonished their flocks, chided backsliders, and vocally supported antiliquor legislation.

The drys were opposed by conservatives who thought that what a man drank was his own business, as well as by urban machines and the formidable liquor interests. But the wet coalition was fighting, at best, a delaying action. Local-option elections and special legislation dried up more and more territory; 825 of the 994 ex-Confederate counties had some form of prohibition by 1907. Part of the wets' problem was demographic: most of the immigrants with cultural backgrounds favorable to drinking had settled outside of the South during the 19th century. Native-born, lower-class voters of both races were courted as an alternative source of support, but when disfranchisement thinned their ranks, southern drys could no longer be contained. From 1907 to 1909 there was a burst of statewide prohibition victories in Georgia, Oklahoma, Alabama, Mississippi, North Carolina, and Tennessee.

A recurring theme in the southern prohibition debates was control of the lower classes, especially blacks. Before the Civil War, law and custom confined plantation slaves to an occasional holiday spree, but these restraints were loosened by emancipation. Prohibitionists exploited this situation by alleging that atrocities were committed by drunken blacks; "nigger gin" joined "demon rum" as a favored epithet. D. W. Griffith's *Birth of a Nation* (1915) gave cinematic expression to these fears. Drawing upon two earlier novels by Thomas Dixon, Jr., Griffith portrayed freedmen who were drunken, arrogant, and lecherous, in contrast to their sober, docile, and hard-working slave forebears. Not to be outdone, some wets played up stories of cocaine rampages—the implication being that if blacks could not drink, they would turn to more dangerous drugs.

Dry propaganda notwithstanding, postbellum blacks did not have a serious alcohol problem. On the contrary, they drank less than poor whites, especially in rural areas. But as uprooted blacks began drifting to cities, where morals were looser and liquor more abundant, the situation changed. With little prospect of steady employment, many of them settled into a life of drinking and idling; predictably, their alcoholism rate worsened. Today poor black males living in cities (southern or otherwise) are more likely to develop drinking problems, and to develop them sooner, than either the general population or their country relations. In 1974, for example, the District of Columbia, with its large black underclass, had the highest adult alcoholism rate in the nation; however, Alabama and Mississippi, states with large numbers of rural blacks, ranked lowest.

Urban blacks are not the only afflicted group. Alcoholics can be found throughout the South, from Appalachian hollows to the streets of the Vieux Carré. Nevertheless, studies undertaken since World War II have consistently shown that the South, as a region, has the lowest rate of alcoholism and the highest percentage of abstainers in the country. That the South remains disproportionately Protestant, rural, and dry (many areas retaining prohibition long after national repeal) largely accounts for the difference. This may be changing, however, as the sprawling Sunbelt cities attract millions of immigrants with more permissive attitudes toward drink.

See also HISTORY AND MANNERS: / Moonshine; Whiskey; INDUSTRY: / Liquor Industry

David T. Courtwright
University of Hartford

C. C. Pearson and J. Edwin Hendricks, *Liquor and Anti-Liquor in Virginia, 1619–1919* (1967); W. J. Rorabaugh, *The Alcoholic Republic: An American Tradition* (1979); James B. Sellers, *The Prohibition Movement in Alabama, 1702–1943* (1943); Muriel W. Sterne, in *Alcoholism*, ed. David J. Pittman (1967); Joe Gray Taylor, *Eating, Drinking, and Visiting in the South* (1982); Ian R. Tyrell, *Journal of Southern History* (November 1982); Daniel Jay Whitener, *Prohibition in North Carolina, 1715–1945* (1945).

Black Health

See BLACK LIFE: Health, Black

Drug Use

The use of drugs, especially the opiates, cocaine, and marijuana, has deep roots in southern culture. In fact, during the late 19th and early 20th centuries, drug use was more common in the South than in virtually any other region of the country.

The opiates (including opium, laudanum, paregoric, and morphine) comprised the largest part of the problem. These drugs were valued for relieving pain, alleviating anxiety, and checking diarrhea. Widely prescribed by physicians, opiates were also taken as home remedies. "Came home disheartened and miserable," Mary Chesnut confided in her journal. "Was so ill I had to take morphine." Later she wrote, "After several weeks' illness—dawdling on, kept alive by Dr. T's opium—once more I was on my feet."

The trouble with such medication was that it might, if continued for a sufficiently long time, lead to addiction. In this southerners were hardly unique: medical opiate addicts could be found on both sides of the Mason-Dixon line. But what set southerners apart was their higher rate of opiate addiction—perhaps 60 or 70 percent higher than the rest of the country. This in turn reflected the greater prevalence of certain diseases in the South, notably diarrhea, dysentery, and malaria. Simply stated, southerners were ill longer and more frequently than northerners; hence, they resorted to opiates more often. Southerners also suffered, on a per-capita basis, more Civil War casualties; no less than one-fifth of Mississippi's entire 1866 revenue was required to purchase artificial limbs for crippled soldiers. Wounded and shell-shocked veterans, grieving parents and widows, and those afflicted with chronic diseases endemic to the region combined to make up a disproportionately large pool of candidates for addiction. The use of opiates was thus both a manifestation and a symbol of the postbellum South's profound physical and spiritual malaise.

The situation gradually changed during the early 20th century. As addicted veterans and older addicts died off, as the medical profession became more conservative in prescribing, and as opiates were subjected to more stringent legal controls, a new group of users began to emerge. They were typically younger men who began using opiates as a means of sobering up after alcoholic sprees or as a source of pleasure. Although some addicts continued to be created through the treatment of chronic diseases or injuries, their importance was declining relative to the nonmedical type.

Similar changes were observed in other parts of the country. But what set the new breed of southern addicts apart was their continued use of morphine. Even though northern addicts had largely switched to black-market heroin, their southern counterparts injected morphine well into the 1930s. This reflected regional variations in the pattern of drug trafficking, as well as the greater willingness of southern physicians to maintain addicts quietly. When a doctor "wrote scrip" for an addict he prescribed morphine, heroin being illegal after 1924.

In addition to the tendency to use morphine, there was another continuity between 19th- and early 20th-century southern opiate addicts: they were disproportionately white. Studies from states as diverse as Tennessee, Texas, and Florida consistently showed blacks to be underrepresented among known users. This was partly because impoverished blacks often lacked access to doctors. They were thus less likely to receive opiates, especially in the dangerous and tempting form of a hypodermic injection.

This is not to say that southern blacks were without drug problems. Rather than using opiates, they showed a preference for cocaine. Sometime in the late 1880s or 1890s black stevedores in New Orleans began using cocaine as a pick-me-up during long stretches of loading or unloading steamboats. The practice spread to other black laborers scattered across the South; cocaine could be found on cotton plantations, in railroad work camps, and at levee construction sites. Cocaine was also a popular recreational drug among blacks, especially those who lived in or on the fringes of the urban underworld. The drug was generally taken by sniffing or in a patent medicine or a soft drink; cocaine injection was largely confined to those who were also morphine addicts.

Blacks' cocaine use was controversial. "Many of the horrible crimes committed in the Southern States by the colored people can be traced to the cocaine habit," charged Colonel J. W. Watson of Georgia in 1903—an allegation that was repeated by a number of white authorities over the next decade. More recently, scholars have denied these charges, dismissing them as politically or racially motivated. Alternately, it is possible that a handful of genuine incidents, given the prevailing racial climate, were conflated and expanded into a black "cocaine menace." Black cocaine users who committed crimes may have done so for other reasons (such as the need to obtain money), even though white authorities inferred that the deed was inspired by the cocaine itself. In any event, it seems unlikely that cocaine triggered a massive crime wave.

A similar controversy surrounds southern marijuana use. Hemp has long been a cash crop in the South, notably in Kentucky. It was grown, however, for fiber, seed, oil, and medicine; the use of cannabis as an intoxicant seems to have been sporadic and to have elicited no great concern. But during the early 20th century migrant Mexican workers brought the practice of smoking marijuana into the Southwest; by 1924 aroused legislatures in several states, including Texas, Arkansas, and Louisiana, had passed restrictive measures. But by then marijuana use had spread to the native population, especially lower-class and criminal elements in Houston, Galveston, and New Orleans. Residents of these port cities were exposed not only to itinerant Mexican users but also to Caribbean sailors and immigrants who imported and smoked the drug. New Orleans in particular emerged as an important center for its sale and distribution; a sensational 1926 newspaper campaign charged that marijuana smoking was widespread in the city and that it led to behavioral aberrations among the young, including both white and black school children. Although Louisiana passed stricter laws in 1927 and again in 1935, reports of marijuana-inspired crimes persisted. These and other incidents were later used by federal officials to justify the 1937 Marijuana Tax Act, a revenue measure designed to restrict illicit trafficking of the drug.

Although marijuana use was becoming more prevalent in the 1920s and early 1930s and some school-age children undoubtedly experimented with it, there are grounds for skepticism about marijuana's alleged direct link to violent crime. In 1944, for example, Dr. J. D. Reichard debunked the marijuana-crime reports and recounted stories of black field hands in Kentucky who were formerly seen loading their pipes with dried flowering hemp tops and then lighting them up. "There was never the slightest suspicion that this procedure caused abnormal behavior," he noted. "This is particularly important since aggressive behavior by a colored person was, to put it mildly, viewed with alarm." If anything has contributed to the historically high levels of southern violence, it has been alcohol, much more than marijuana or cocaine or any other drug.

The opiates, cocaine, and marijuana are still mainstays of the southern drug culture, although they are presently used mainly in cities and have been supplemented by other substances, such as barbiturates, amphetamines, and methaqualone. The South also remains a focal point for the illicit traffic, with billions of dollars of drugs annually smuggled into Texas, Florida, and other Gulf states.

See also ETHNIC LIFE: Caribbean Influence

David T. Courtwright
University of Hartford

John C. Ball and Carl D. Chambers, eds., *The Epidemiology of Opiate Addiction in the United States* (1970); Richard J. Bonnie and Charles H. Whitebread II, *The Marihuana Conviction: A History of Marihuana Prohibition in the United States* (1974); David T. Courtwright, *Dark Paradise: Opiate Addiction in America before 1940* (1982), *Journal of Southern History* (February 1983); Lester Grinspoon, *Marihuana Reconsidered* (2d ed., 1977); David F. Musto, *The American Disease: Origins of Narcotic Control* (1973); Louis Nyhnanek, *Louisiana History* (Summer 1981); John A. O'Donnell, *Narcotic Addicts in Kentucky* (1969); Charles E. Terry and Mildred Pellens, *The Opium Problem* (1928).

Education, Medical

The idea that southern medical practice was distinctive and that, therefore, southern practitioners ought to be educated through southern medical institutions was common among antebellum southern physicians. Faith in the distinctiveness of southern practice was supported by the principle of specificity, that is, the notion that medical practice had to be matched carefully to such characteristics of patients as gender, ethnicity, and moral status, and to such aspects of locale as climate, topography, and population density. The idea of specificity, which was held by American physicians from all regions, dictated that knowledge appropriate in one context might be inapplicable in another; accordingly, different practices were required for European and American, rural and urban patients, white and black, northern and southern.

Although such basic medical sciences as anatomy and chemistry could be studied anywhere, diagnostic and therapeutic knowledge was best acquired in the region in which it would ultimately be applied. In the South the student's experience with southern patients and diseases assured a training tailored to the region's peculiar climate, diseases, and racial composition. On the other hand, southerners argued that the student educated in the North would be doubtfully fitted to treat southern patients until he had replaced northern precepts with southern experience.

The theory that upheld medical regionalism had been a central part of American medicine from the 18th century, but only from the early 1830s did southern physicians aggressively use it to argue for a distinctive southern medical education. Moreover, as medical theory did not compel arguments for regional medical education in the North or West comparable in force to the southern movement, the animus of southern medical education must be sought elsewhere. In part, it was driven by the strengthening southern commitment to cultural separatism, which southern physicians shared. Economic incentives, made acute by the proliferation of proprietary medical schools in the South from the 1830s, further encouraged the case for southern medical education.

But the argument for a distinctive southern medical education served a deeper function for certain southern physicians. It was the leading expression of a movement for southern medical distinctiveness that many physicians, especially those who held intellectual aspirations, saw as the most promising platform for elevating the profession in the South. Southern physicians, aware of working at the periphery of medical activity, were troubled by the stagnancy of medical inquiry in their region. Their defensive sense of inferiority stemmed from both the profession's failure to cultivate the region's natural medical resources and its educational dependence on northern schools, textbooks, and journals. The institutions of medical education offered physicians a concrete context within which their commitment to southern medical distinctiveness could be objectified, and they were thereby a means of energizing the medical community and satisfying the physician-intellectual's social and cognitive needs.

Both the reform objectives and theoretical underpinnings of the argument for a distinctive southern medical education were expressed in the flourish of new southern medical schools and journals in the 1840s and especially the 1850s. Editorials in journals and inaugural addresses at schools routinely promoted the South's medical distinctiveness as an imperative to professional vigor. The sensitivity of curricula to the South's peculiar medical needs was clearly expressed in the 1850s when a New Orleans school created a separate professorship of the diseases of blacks. Southern medical schools self-consciously stressed that portion of medical education—clinical knowledge—that was specific to region, thereby legitimizing their distinctive regional identity.

More destructive than the Civil War itself to the case for distinctive southern medical education were changes in the structure of medical thought. From the 1870s the gradual ascendance of a new medical epistemology grounded upon experimental science carried with it a commitment to the universalism, not specificity, of medical knowledge. By denying the principle of specificity, this posture undermined the theoretical justification for a distinctive southern medicine, the core of the argument for regional education. Regional differences in practices, other than incidental ones, were no longer legitimate engines of professional improvement, but rather stigmata of inferior practice.

The founding of separate medical schools in the South to educate black physicians, beginning with Howard in 1867 and Meharry in 1876, gave southern medical education what was from that time through the present virtually its only unique feature. The creation of black medical schools was not informed by an allegiance to specificity, but was instead premised on sociopolitically defined racial differences among physicians and driven by white pietism, paternalism, and separatism.

The most pervasive characteristic of medical education in the postbellum South taken as a whole was its inferiority. Persistent poverty made prospects of parity with northern schools unlikely, and through the early 20th century southern physicians attributed a perceived deterioration of the profession's status in the region to its educational deprivations. When the Southern Medical College Association was organized in 1892, the underlying objective of the improvements it endorsed was to make medical education in the South conform to the superior standards of northern schools. Reformation of southern medicine was to be effected not by celebrating its individuality but by effacing it.

In 1910 Abraham Flexner published his influential report on medical education in the United States, and he left no doubt that medical education in the South was inferior to that in any other region. Endowments and organic university affiliations such as that at Tulane, he held, were essential elements of a proper medical school; however, most of the South's schools were proprietary and impoverished. In subsequent years, private endowments at such schools as Baylor, Duke, Emory, and Vanderbilt were principally responsible for elevating standards at a few institutions and forcing the closure of proprietary schools. By the mid-20th century southern medical education was no longer inferior. Moreover, the substance and underlying ideology of medical education in the South and North did not differ in any fundamental way, and through the present such geographically southern schools as Duke, Emory, and Vanderbilt teach virtually the same medicine as Harvard, Michigan, or San Francisco. As of 1982 in the 13 southern states there were 60 medical schools, 37 of which were approved by the American Medical Association.

See also BLACK LIFE: Health, Black

John Harley Warner
Harvard University

AMA *Directory of Physicians in the U.S.* (1982); John Duffy, *Journal of Southern History* (August 1957); Abraham Flexner, *Medical Education in the United States and Canada: A Report to the Carnegie Foundation for the Advancement of Teaching* (1910); Herbert M. Morais, *The History of the Negro in Medicine* (1968); Ronald L. Numbers, ed., *The Education of American Physicians: Historical Essays* (1980); Ronald L. Numbers and John Harley Warner, in *Scientific Colonialism, 1800–1930: A Cross-Cultural Comparison*, ed. Nathan Reingold and Marc Rothenberg (1986).

Health, Mental

Before the mid-19th century there was little publicly supported mental health treatment in the South. By 1825 Virginia, which made the first public attempt to treat the insane before the Revolution, was the only southern state to have a hospital for the insane. The South lagged behind the rest of the nation in this regard: eight other asylums existed in states outside the South. The sufferings of the insane in the South, as elsewhere in the nation, were looked upon as the natural consequences of a stern, unbending Providence, meting out judgment to the wicked and the innately inferior. The shame brought on by such a concept bred an attitude of contempt for, and lack of interest in, the needs of the insane. The families that could afford special accommodations provided strong rooms in attics and barns to shut away the family shame, or they sent the insane member to a neighboring state where institutional care could be purchased. The dependent insane who were not considered violent were allowed to wander through the town begging for food and becoming the butts of children's ridicule. Only those who were considered dangerous to the public welfare or who were a nuisance to the community received any public attention. Motivated by fear, communities used the local jail or almshouse as the common solution to the problem of public protection from the violent.

The South's concern for the insane was awakened by the reform movement of 1825 to 1860. In that period South Carolina, Georgia, Alabama, Louisiana, Tennessee, Missouri, North Carolina, Mississippi, and Texas opened the doors of mental health care to the indigent insane, radically altering the character of the mental hospital movement in the South and bringing it up to par with the rest of the nation. In the early stages of development, moral therapy was employed as the accepted mode of treatment in the new state hospitals. Moral treatment involved removing the patient from the community to an asylum, where therapy of kindness and consideration for physical and emotional needs would lead to a cure. The assumption was that the insane could be cured in institutions removed from local conditions that prompted the onset of insanity. Before the growth of large public mental institutions the insane had been embarrassments to their families, but they had been curiosities to the public. Now removed from the community, the mentally disturbed no longer posed a public embarrassment or a threat to the community, but they were still a public spectacle. For instance, the transfer of patients to the new North Carolina Western Insane Asylum at Morganton created a circus atmosphere in the town when the residents lined the road to watch patients being marched from the train station to the hospital. Likewise, the constant urging by the superintendent at Dorothea Dix Insane Asylum for construction of a fence around the Raleigh, N.C., facility was not for the purpose of protecting the citizens of the town, but rather to control the townspeople who came to the hospital grounds to watch and generally excite the patients.

Although widely heralded in the United States as an effective and successful therapeutic method during the first half of the 19th century, moral therapy fell into disrepute before the end of the century. The failure of moral therapy can be attributed, in large measure, to the exuberance of superintendents who issued reports of high recovery rates to stimulate the founding of new mental institutions and the expansion of existing ones. Superintendents willingly squeezed every patient they could into the hospital. Overcrowding and inadequate financial support made moral treatment impossible to practice. Nevertheless, outside pressures continued to exist to transfer mental patients away from the local community to the central state hospitals. The result of overcrowding and the absence of adequate medical treatment was the creation of warehousing facilities where patients were put out of sight and, therefore, out of mind. No one found it necessary to deal with the profoundly negative attitudes toward mental illness that permeated society.

As the state became increasingly responsible, local government and, more importantly, individual families began to assume that mental illness was not their responsibility alone. Unfortunately, those operating local hospitals were not attuned to the dangers of relegating responsibility for the mentally ill to a central state hospital. A relatively secure and simple hospital routine provided for a patient enabled him or her to avoid facing the more complex problem of life "on the outside" and created, more often than not, a pathological dependence on the institution. Recognition of this particular problem prompted the movement toward community clinics and local mental health programs.

Community responsibility was encouraged after World War II when three major factors combined to reverse the pressures on large state hospitals: (1) the introduction of psychotropic drugs growing out of wartime research, (2) federal support for research and mental health centers prompted by the reports of various presidential and congressional commissions in the 1960s, and (3) civil rights legislation and Supreme Court decisions on behalf of mental patients between 1961 and 1975 that dramatically changed state hospital census patterns. Between 1955 and 1977 patient enrollment in mental hospitals declined from over one-half million to less than 200,000. In the same period over 800 community mental health centers were established. The psychiatric patient has been returned from the large state hospital to his home community. Between 1955 and 1975 psychiatric patient care in state hospitals declined by 50 percent. Outpatient care in community clinics increased 70 percent in the same period.

The South has played a leading role in this movement. No southern state, though, has established a smooth transition from institutional care to community care. Meeting existing needs of the mentally disturbed at the community level rests on three factors: proper distribution of state resources, continuing public support of research and local community acceptance of mental health centers, and establishment of halfway houses and outpatient services. Every southern state has experienced a rapid growth in community mental health centers and comparative declines in state-hospital populations, yet a commensurate shift in the allocation of funds to support local clinics has not occurred. The situation in Texas is typical of the resource distribution of all the states in the South. Between 1965 and 1977 Texas established 28 community centers serving 82 percent of the population of the state. Yet only 9 percent of the state's support for mental health went to community mental health centers. Although the situation has improved since 1959 in the area of research funding, when only four southern states (Florida, Louisiana, Tennessee, and Texas) were allocating more than $25,000 annually for research, every southern state commission cites the shortage of research funds as a deterrent to providing an adequate mental health system.

The return of the mental patient to the local community does not necessarily bode well for the individual. The "Proceedings of the First Robert Lee Sutherland

Seminar on Mental Health" held at the University of Texas in 1978 noted that the movement of chronically ill mental patients away from state hospitals to local communities has "exacerbated the problems faced by the people who most need help." Mental patients and those labeled as mentally ill are still considered to be relatively worthless, dangerous, frightening, and disruptive—all terms that have been used to describe the mentally ill during 100 years of institutional psychiatric care.

Significant studies completed by independent researchers in Virginia, North Carolina, and Louisiana and by state agencies in Texas, Florida, and Georgia have concluded, in the words of the Sutherland seminar proceedings, that "mentally ill persons discharged from hospitals or state institutions face difficulties in being accepted by people in their own community because of the communities' insensitivity, ignorance, fear of mental illness, discrimination and social banishment." Surveys in these states indicate that society ranks the mentally ill below the convicted felon and the alcoholic on the scale of social acceptance. The studies in North Carolina and Virginia during the late 1960s and early 1970s (William C. Butz and J. Wilbert Edgerton, *Social Psychiatry*, 1971) suggest that "the mentally ill are heavily stigmatized, that [community] educational programs have had only a minor effect, and people still respond with the fear, dislike and aversion that traditionally have been manifested toward mental patients in American society." In a 1950s study in Louisiana Charles D. Whatley notes the tendency of the community to "shun or restrict interaction with ex-patients in personal relationships but to generally accept them in relatively impersonal situations."

In this changing pattern of patient care, the fear of being labeled mentally ill may be the reason that the majority of people who receive treatment for mental disorders seek out primary-care facilities and non–mental health professionals in order to avoid being labeled mentally ill. Hence, even mental health services offered by modern community-structured programs are failing to meet existing needs, in large measure because of public apathy toward or opposition to community clinics and the presence of mentally disturbed people in the community.

In spite of the difficulties that the medical profession has experienced in securing research funds or effecting the reallocation of state funds for better support of community mental health centers, significant progress has been made in the South in these areas. Unfortunately, an understanding of the problem of mental illness does not appear to have produced much progress in changing cultural values that affect communities' acceptance or rejection of chronically disturbed people in their midst. Improved clinical services at the community level have not produced a better life for most mentally ill people. Significant research and educational efforts are needed to improve cultural attitudes toward mental illness. Until the social norms that shun the mentally disturbed can be reversed through the joint effort of the medical profession and community leadership, mentally ill people in the South will continue to suffer the same stigma of fear, distrust, and dislike that has persisted for more than a century.

Clark R. Cahow
Duke University

Leopold Bellak, ed., *A Concise Handbook of Community Psychiatry and Community Mental Health* (1974); Clark R. Cahow, *People, Patients, and Politics: A History of North Carolina Mental Hospitals, 1848–1960* (1982); Norman Dain, *Concepts of Insanity in the United States, 1789–1865* (1964); Gerald N. Grob, *Mental Institutions in America* (1973); Jim C. Nunnally, *Popular Concepts of Mental Health: Their Development and Change* (1961); Judith Rabkin, *Schizophrenia Bulletin* (Fall 1974); R. D. Scott, *Schizophrenia Bulletin* (Fall 1974); Charles D. Whatley, *Social Problems* (1958).

Health, Public

The public health experience of the South, at least until the mid-20th century, was in many respects unique in the nation. Perceived as distinctive by northerners—and some southerners—for more than a century, the region's poor health record served as one more defining characteristic, one more peculiar burden added to southern history's extensive list. Although sharing many disease problems with the rest of the country, the South at various times exhibited maladies largely peculiar to itself—yellow fever in the 19th century and hookworm and pellagra in the early 20th century. Furthermore, certain infectious diseases that had afflicted the nation at large (malaria, typhoid fever, and tuberculosis, for example) persisted at serious levels in the South until the 1930s and 1940s, years after having been brought under control elsewhere.

The "Sickly South" was an important facet of the region's image in the 19th century when yellow fever epidemics repeatedly ravaged the Gulf states and lower Mississippi Valley. This "scourge of the South" attracted much negative attention, drained financial and human resources, deterred capital investment and urban population growth, and disrupted commerce and transportation. For much of the 19th century state and local health measures concentrated on epidemic emergencies. With limited knowledge of the nature of diseases and modes of transmission, efforts at control through commercial quarantine and sporadic urban cleanup campaigns had little effect.

A turning point came in the 1870s and 1880s when germ theory and other medical advances brought increased understanding of disease processes. About the same time, the widespread yellow fever epidemic of 1878 led southern urban business interests to support increased public expenditures for such health-promoting, image-improving measures as public water supplies, drainage and sewerage systems, street paving, and garbage collection. These efforts clearly paid off in the improved state of health among whites in the urban South, although blacks showed only slight improvements, as the new urban services rarely extended to poor neighborhoods.

The threat of yellow fever was finally brought under control through discovery of its transmission by the mosquito and the dramatic campaign against New Orleans's last epidemic in 1905. This demonstration of the power of "modern science" applied through the combined efforts of federal, state, and local health authorities, widely viewed as another turning point in southern health history, ended the long reign of "Yellow Jack" and removed what many called the last great obstacle to southern progress.

New obstacles soon appeared, however, as hookworm and pellagra were identified as prevalent ailments in the rural South. These peculiar debilitating disorders together with malaria, a persistent and widespread old malady, served to explain other longstanding features of the stereotyped South—its laziness, its backwardness—at least to the satisfaction of some "progressive" southerners and other Americans who sought in public health improvement a panacea for all the region's problems and a pathway to the modern world. State and local health authorities, assisted by the U.S. Public Health Service, the Red Cross, the Rockefeller Foundation, and other northern philanthropies, set forth to spread the gospel of health and bring modern medicine to the rural South during the next few decades.

Despite substantial achievements in developing health education and institutions, these efforts could provide only a palliative as long as basic conditions remained unchanged. Black and white southerners in the 1930s continued to manifest a remarkably high incidence of malaria, tuberculosis, typhoid fever, diphtheria, smallpox, venereal disease, hookworm, and pellagra, as well as high maternal and infant mortality rates.

Southern public health problems would not be solved by medical knowledge and health crusades alone; lasting solutions required broad social and economic change. Massive federal expenditures and changes associated with the Great Depression and World War II would finally transform the socioeconomic system, ending one-crop agriculture, stimulating urbanization and industrialization, and bringing about a higher standard of living for most of the southern population. With material improvement came the virtual disappearance in the postwar era of many diseases long sustained by the region's poverty. With the decline of nutritional-deficiency and infectious diseases, southern state and local health departments could devote more attention to chronic disorders, environmental and occupational health and safety, and other services. Nonetheless, prevention of communicable diseases remains a central part of public health vigilance.

Southerners now suffer and die from the same major causes as the rest of the country—heart disease, cancer, stroke, and accidents—and they are served by similar state and local agencies. Some parts of the South still

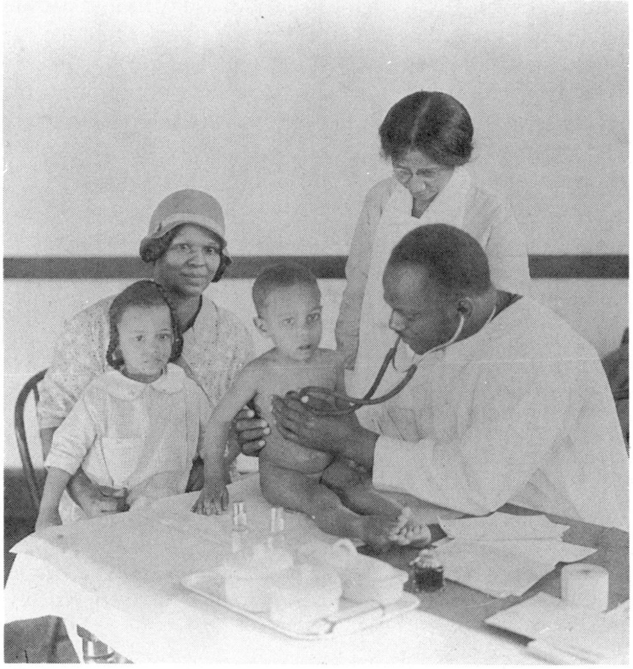

Unidentified physician with child, Kentucky, 1950s

show the nation's highest death rates, infant mortality in particular, and a continuing high incidence of certain diseases—problems closely correlated with poverty and minority populations. Climate and the continued presence of appropriate mosquito vectors make the southern states still receptive to the threat of imported dengue, an infectious tropical disease, and yellow fever. Hence, while southern distinctiveness in health has been substantially diminished, it has not yet been eliminated altogether.

Because of their severity, southern health problems have brought about the establishment of new public health institutions, local, state, and national. Louisiana created the first state board of health in the country in 1855 as a response to several widespread yellow fever epidemics. The epidemic of 1878, affecting the South and the Mississippi Valley interior and threatening the commerce of the nation at large, influenced Congress to establish a National Board of Health, and, after that experiment failed, to assign an expanded federal role in quarantine and inspection service to the U.S. Marine Hospital Service, which became the Public Health Service by 1912. Another distinctive health agency with a southern connection is the National Leprosarium in Carville, La., a state institution in the 1890s that became national in the 1920s. The earliest and most extensive development of county health departments (relying heavily on public health nurses) occurred in the South in the early decades of the 20th century, funded in part by the U.S. Public Health Service and the Rockefeller Foundation. Finally, the Centers for Disease Control are located in Atlanta because of their origins in the Office for Malarial Control in War Areas. Established in 1942, in the center of the region where malaria was still most prevalent, the office sought to protect troops being concentrated and trained in the South, as well as the war industries labor force. The agency's success in coordinating federal and state action led to its postwar continuation and expansion as the Contagious Disease Center, now the Centers for Disease Control.

See also BLACK LIFE: Health, Black; SOCIAL CLASS: Health, Worker; Poverty

Jo Ann Carrigan
University of Nebraska at Omaha

CDC, *Morbidity and Mortality Weekly Report* (22 February 1980); Charles V. Chapin, *Report on State Public Health Work [1915]* (1977); John H. Ellis, *Bulletin of the History of Medicine* (May, August 1970); Elizabeth W. Etheridge, *The Butterfly Caste: A Social History of Pellagra in the South* (1972); Dennis N. Tunnell, "Regional History of Southern Branch, American Public Health Association" (Ed.D. dissertation, University of Alabama, 1977); Margaret Warner, *Journal of Southern History* (August 1984).

Health, Rural

Historically, the southern countryside and the city have differed in almost every way, including health. Although a national homogenization process has changed much of rural culture and social structure, unique qualities still flourish. Low incomes, poor diets, inadequate housing, impure water supplies, poor transportation and communication, and limited medical resources remain key factors in explaining the overall health status of southern rural areas. A particularly important factor in understanding rural health is the problem of access, including the distribution of health services. Throughout rural areas there are shortages of physicians, dentists, and other health care providers. Approximately 49 million people reside in "medically underserved areas" in the nation, with 60 percent being rural.

Until the past decade, public health activities provided the major health services in the rural South unless there happened to be a private doctor in an area. The Rural Sanitation Act of 1916 provided funds to improve such aspects of rural health as disposal of human waste, the protection of water supplies, and the control of insects. In the following years, public health services continued to focus their efforts on malaria control, community sanitation, construction of sanitary privies, and sealing abandoned mines.

In 1935 the Public Health Service began to attack what it deemed the major problem facing rural families—the lack of adequate medical care. As a consequence, new programs for rural rehabilitation provided active medical care personnel to reach more rural residents. After World War II, programs developed in the area of environmental health with a focus on communicable diseases. Increased institutional services were offered by newly constructed hospitals.

More recently, in the 1970s a program called the Rural Health Initiative Projects was begun, administered by the U.S. Public Health Service. Its purpose is to develop and systematize the delivery of health care in rural areas. The several projects included under this act are (1) National Health Service Corps, (2) Community Health Centers, (3) Migrant Health Program, (4) Health Underserved Rural Areas Program, and (5) Appalachian Health Programs. These policies seek to provide primary health care for rural areas, and they have resulted in the construction of clinics in small towns throughout the South.

Whatever is used to measure the health status of rural peoples, one fact is clear: they remain worse off than any other population. Indeed, scholars have identified several predominantly rural groups that have disproportionately severe health needs. They include southern rural blacks, Chicanos, Appalachian and Ozark whites, aged migrant workers, illegal aliens, and residents of environmentally polluted areas. All these groups share several characteristics—they are poor, powerless, and discriminated against because of race, culture, or lifestyle. Many of them live in the South and, as with other rural peoples, have an accident rate four times the national average, infant mortality rates that are 20 percent higher than the urban poor and 50 percent higher than the national average, and limited access to health resources.

The epidemiological patterns of blacks and whites in the rural South reflect serious health problems. The mortality rates are substantially higher than in other regions of the country. Within the South the death rates are significantly higher in the nonmetropolitan South than in the cities. With regard to ethnic differences, infant mortality rates among rural southern blacks are 65 percent higher than among rural southern whites. In addition, the morbidity and disability rates are higher in rural areas, with more disability involving bed confinement among the elderly in rural areas. Although children have a lower incidence of respiratory and infectious disease, adults have a higher rate of acute conditions, especially injury rates. National levels are lower, but the incidence of most chronic conditions (hypertensive heart disease, cerebrovascular heart disease, ulcers, emphysema, arthritis, and rheumatism) is greater in the South.

Most people in rural areas have inadequate water and sewer systems or rely on wells and/or outdoor bathrooms. Consequently, dental problems stemming from the lack of properly fluoridated water are a major problem, as are bacteria and parasitic diseases. Likewise, lack of solid-waste disposal creates a higher risk for injuries and contaminated water supplies. Most rural areas are limited in their economic opportunities and their cultural and recreational resources and, as a consequence, have a high rate of mental health problems such as alcoholism and depression. Furthermore, there are fewer patient-care physicians per capita in the rural areas of the South than elsewhere, and rural southerners obviously receive fewer physician services and incur more hospital stays. Dental visits are 65 percent lower than in the urban South. In general, the health care services in rural areas are inadequate and the health status is poor compared to urban areas in the South.

In 1970, 41.2 percent of southerners were rural. Excluding Florida, more than 47 percent of the South was rural, with the states of Mississippi, North Carolina, and South Carolina having over 50 percent rural population. Poverty is a crucial cause of poor rural health. Over 40 percent of rural people are poor, a factor that contributes substantially to health problems in the South especially. In 1977, 20.7 percent of all households in the rural South had incomes under $5,000, with the average income for all households being $11,591. The median income for the region was $12,562, while the average individual income was $3,765. Furthermore, the percentage of poor families headed by females was higher. Although, in absolute terms, more poor families are headed by white males, the incidence of poverty was highest among black families headed by women. In fact, two out of three of the latter are poor, while 1 out of 10 white male-headed families are poor. Overall, 50 percent of blacks in rural areas are poor, and about 17 percent of whites are poor in the rural South. As Perry B. Rogers states, "the level of family income in a population group is the most influential characteristic which determines whether a population will have health services which are appropriate and accessible."

The rural southern poor, both black and white, use folk medicine and share information about how to alleviate health problems. Middle-class whites often use folk remedies but do not use folk healers as frequently as poor people do. Because of limited access to health services, a unique rural southern culture has developed that not only tries to explain illness but also offers ways to heal the sick. These ideas complement the scientific medical system, and they do not preclude the use of medical services. The poor in rural areas share a sense of community, a worldview that is reflected in their health ideas, many of which are inextricably bound to religious beliefs. Many southern rural people depend on their kin and their friends to help them in times of illness and misfortune. Changes are occurring in rural areas, but traditional ideas of health remain in the face of policy changes that have increased services in the past decade.

See also BLACK LIFE: Health, Black; FOLKLIFE: Folk Medicine; Voodoo; GEOGRAPHY: Population; WOMEN'S LIFE: Healers, Women

Carole E. Hill
Georgia State University

M. C. Ahearn, U.S. Department of Agriculture, *Agriculture Information Bulletin No. 428* (1979); C. L. Beal and Glenn V. Fuguitt, in *Social Demography*, ed. K. L. Taeuber, Larry L. Bumpass, and James A. Sweet (1978); James H. Copp, *Rural Sociology* (December 1972); Karen Davis and Rau Marshall, *Research in Health Economics* (1979); J. Lynn England, Eugene Gibbons, and Barry Johnson, *Rural Sociology* (Spring 1979); Dorothy M. Gilford, *Rural America in Passage* (1981); Carole E. Hill, *Current Anthropology* (June 1977); Olaf F. Larson, in *Rural U.S.A.: Persistence and Change*, ed. Thomas R. Ford (1977); Holly Mathews and Carole E. Hill, *Perspectives on the American South*, vol. 1, ed. Merle Black and John Shelton Reed (1981); Peter A. Morrison and Judith P. Wheeler, *Population Bulletin* (October 1976).

Health, Worker

See SOCIAL CLASS: Health, Worker

Medicine, States' Rights

As slavery came under increasing attack in the 30 years before the Civil War, southerners in all fields closed ranks. The professions, as might be expected, sought to provide the intellectual justification for the South's peculiar institution—lawyers argued on constitutional grounds, ministers cited the Bible, and physicians, as natural scientists, endeavored to demonstrate that blacks were an inferior race and that southern medicine was distinct from northern medicine. The first southern physician to argue the inferiority of the black race was Dr. Josiah C. Nott, a prominent physician in Mobile, Ala., who had learned his medicine in the best northern and European medical schools. In the early 1840s he published an article maintaining that blacks had less endurance, had shorter lives, and were less prolific than whites, and that intermarriage could only result in the destruction of both races. By 1850 he was arguing that "an immutable law of nature" made it impossible for blacks to become civilized. Following his argument to its logical conclusion, he asserted that blacks were "better off in slavery [in] the South than in freedom elsewhere."

Because Nott argued that blacks were an entirely separate race from whites, his views, by conflicting with the biblical account that humans descended from Adam and Eve, ran counter to the religious fundamentalism of the South. Much more to the liking of southerners in general were the ideas of the physiological school, represented by physicians who accepted the biblical view of creation but still maintained that striking anatomical and physiological differences separated whites and blacks. The leading exponent of this school was Dr. Samuel A. Cartwright of Natchez, Miss., and New Orleans. Like Nott, Cartwright was well trained and was widely recognized for his scientific work. He was also a born controversialist who loved to express his views. Beginning in the 1840s he wrote a stream of articles on blacks and southern medicine. In 1850 he was appointed chairman of a committee of the Medical Association of Louisiana to investigate the diseases and physical peculiarities of blacks. His report declared that the "shade of pervading darkness" was present not only in the skin but throughout all parts of the body—even including the "fluids and secretions." The skeletal structure of blacks was distinct from whites, the brain 10 or 11 percent smaller, the vascular system much less developed, and the lungs smaller. Moreover, their brains were so constituted as to produce an excess of "nervous matter," which would have made blacks unmanageable had it not been for the "deficiency of red blood" due to the inefficiency of their lungs.

Cartwright's studies also posited two new diseases among slaves—one was *drapetomania*, a disorder that caused them to run away, and the other was *dyasthesia Aethiopis*, generally known to overseers as rascality. As his studies continued, Dr. Cartwright was led inexorably to the conclusion that the fundamental differences between the two races meant "that the same medical treatment which would benefit or cure a white man, would often injure or kill a Negro." The ideas of Nott, Cartwright, and other medical writers confirmed what many southern physicians had been thinking, and in the ensuing years a flood of articles in southern medical journals cited more and more "scientific" evidence of black inferiority.

Cartwright's argument for a distinctive form of southern medical practice also had a receptive audience. In the quest for causes of disease, physicians had constantly studied the role of climate, meteorology, and topography; southerners believed these factors affected their health. Cartwright insisted not only that the diseases of blacks and their treatment were distinct from those of whites but that southern diseases in general were different from those in the North. Like the anatomical argument, the thesis about southern diseases contained a modicum of truth. Yellow fever was essentially a southern problem at that time, malaria and enteric disorders did tend to be more acute in the South than in the North, and southern blacks did have a greater degree of immunity to certain disorders.

If southern medicine was distinct, it was logical that southern practitioners should be trained in the South. Although American medicine, with some exceptions, generally lagged behind that of Western Europe, medical education in the South was not even up to the level provided by the better northern schools; consequently, southern medical students seeking the best training went first to the North and then to Europe. The South in the antebellum years was trying to gain economic independence from the North, and keeping its medical students at home was financially advantageous. Southern businessmen were acutely conscious of the considerable economic loss entailed by training over half of all southern medical students in the North.

Added to this was the self-interest of southern medical schools. Nearly all medical schools in the United States were proprietary institutions dependent upon student fees for revenue; hence, there was keen competition for students. Southern medical journals and newspapers beginning in the early 1850s constantly emphasized the distinctiveness of southern medicine and the need for southern practitioners to be trained in the South. As the idea of separate southern medicine gained credence, enrollment in southern schools steadily increased and a number of new medical schools appeared on the scene. The campaign to keep southern medical students at home culminated in the mass resignation in the 1859–60 academic year of some 200 students from Jefferson Medical College in Philadelphia and another 100 from the University of Pennsylvania.

By 1860 only a few skeptics in the South questioned the concept of a specific southern medicine. The vast majority of southern physicians never doubted that the diseases they treated and the methods they used differed from those in the North.

See also BLACK LIFE: Health, Black

John Duffy
University of Maryland

James O. Breeden, *Bulletin of the New York Academy of Medicine* (1976); John Duffy, *Journal of Southern History* (May 1968), ed., *The Rudolph Matas History of Medicine* (1962); Mary Louise Marshall, *New Orleans Medical and Surgical Journal* (1940–41).

Professionalization of Science

Although hardly an ordinary man, Andrew Jackson, with his election to the White House in 1828, signaled the "Age of the Common Man" in America. Hard work, determination, and self-improvement were the catchwords of the day, and elitism was out of fashion. Public insistence that knowledge be immediately understandable and useful aroused concern among a growing number of scientists. Scientists resented their need to supplement their meager incomes, usually derived from college professorships, by traveling the popular lecture circuit to which Americans flocked. The root of their discomfort lay in their awareness that rapidly expanding scientific knowledge, and the means by which this knowledge was acquired, could no longer be communicated to a general audience.

As scientific inquiry, fueled by the growth of experimentation, expanded knowledge beyond the realm of the layman's understanding, fields that once belonged in the public domain came to be dominated by small, select groups of scholars with specialized educations. Pleading the necessity of basic research, these scientists maintained that their efforts to advance man's knowledge of his world could proceed only as the result of careful observation and experimentation, free of the financier's watchful eye and the public's preference for utility. These men gained a growing respect for one another as professionals and were anxious that the general public afford them the same professional status as that enjoyed by physicians, lawyers, and clergymen. They struggled to disassociate themselves from technical inventors and, more importantly, from quacks and charlatans who touted miracle cures and regaled the public with outrageous "corrections" of accepted scientific principles.

To foster a spirit of professionalism, American scientists needed contact among themselves. The American Association for the Advancement of Science (AAAS) was founded in 1848 to encourage scientific research, arbitrate scientific disputes, and weed out "pretenders" to the profession. By the end of the century more specialized societies emerged, including the American Chemical Society, the Geological Society of America, and the American Mathematical Society. All of these organizations defined their profession to include a specialized graduate degree, employment as a scientist, and evidence of scholarly research.

Most antebellum southern scientists remained on the periphery of this movement. Although some of them maintained membership in the AAAS, they seldom attended national meetings, usually held in the northeastern region of the nation, because of the distance involved, inadequate transportation, and financial pressures. However, the long-perpetuated notion of the antebellum South as "essentially unscientific" simply is not true. Planters such as Henry William Ravenel, James Hamilton Couper, and Benjamin L. C. Wailes maintained an active correspondence with scientists throughout the world and enjoyed enviable reputations for the specimens, drawings, and descriptions of southern flora and fauna that they provided.

Scientists in the emerging professional sense also inhabited the cotton kingdom. Thomas Cooper, John and Joseph LeConte, Frederick A. P. Barnard, and Elisha Mitchell, all college professors, earned the respect of their colleagues nationwide. Other professionals included Denison Olmsted and Michael Tuomey, who headed the state-sponsored geological surveys of North Carolina and Alabama. Charleston, S.C., the region's major metropolitan area, boasted the greatest concentration of scientific talent. With its relatively large, stable, and wealthy population and intellectual centers such as the Charleston Museum and the College of Charleston, the city sustained such notables as John Bachman, Lewis R. Gibbes, John McCrady, Edmund Ravenel, and Francis S. Holmes.

The move toward professionalization in the South, hardly begun by 1860, suffered in the years following the Civil War. Colleges throughout the region, the primary employers of scientists, closed their doors for a varying number of years during Reconstruction. Some, such as the University of Alabama, lay in smoldering ruins. Libraries and laboratories, ravaged by neglect as much as by war, had to be rebuilt from scratch. Faculty members were scattered. Some chose alternative careers; others, such as John and Joseph LeConte, grew discouraged with Reconstruction politics and moved elsewhere. Young men seeking a science education attended northern or German universities, and many of those who thus imbibed the spirit of research sought positions in schools that would support such work. Southern institutions of higher education, slowly reopening during the 1870s, could scarcely scrape together sufficient funds to pay their faculty members; they provided little in the way of compensated time or financial incentive for research.

Nonetheless, a few well-trained men of science did serve in the postbellum South's colleges, among them Eugene Allen Smith of the University of Alabama, Francis Preston Venable of the University of North Carolina, and William Louis Jones of the University of Georgia. Although pleased that southern colleges were reopening and even expanding their curricula, these men, all products of a graduate education that emphasized the spirit of scientific inquiry through research, suffered from isolation, restricted budgets, and poor communication and transportation facilities. Hoping to "ward off the deadening effect that isolation was bound to have upon our scientific work," Venable and three of his colleagues at the University of North Carolina in 1883 organized the Elisha Mitchell Scientific Society. It met monthly during the academic year to provide North Carolina scientists contact with one another and an opportunity to share research efforts; in addition the society published quarterly the *Journal of the Elisha Mitchell Scientific Society*. However, neither the Mitchell Society nor a similar group in Alabama, the Alabama Industrial and Scientific Society, was able to serve the needs of the relatively few and scattered southern scientists of the late 19th century. Attracting little popular support and receiving almost no institutional financial aid, the societies could not continue their activities. The Alabama organization collapsed completely, and the Mitchell Society survived only as a local university forum.

The pool of southern scientists continued to increase, however, with the growth of southern colleges and universities under the leadership of progressive educators who witnessed the expansion of northern and midwestern universities and coveted for their own region similar educational advantages. The best indicator of the professionalism of this growing body of pre–World War II southern scientists lies once again in their organizations. Still isolated from colleagues in other regions of the nation, they formed state academies of science to provide contact with one another, to foster the spirit of research, and to offer at least a modest outlet for publication. By the mid-1930s every southern state boasted a state academy of science; by 1940 approximately 3,500 scientists throughout Dixie, over 90 percent of whom were college and university faculty members, belonged to these academies. An ever-increasing number of these persons held the doctoral degree, and, if only a handful of them were on the cutting edge of scientific research, many others remained informed and conducted research of local interest and benefit.

Prior to World War II, very few scientists were employed by industry or independent research laboratories. Most southern industry was either extractive, as in the case of the copper mines of Tennessee and the iron-ore mining operations of north Alabama, or labor-intensive, as with the tobacco factories, textile mills, and fertilizer plants that dotted the landscape. With profits more dependent on a labor force willing to work for low wages than on increased efficiency through research and development, management saw no reason to employ professional scientists. Research laboratories such as those at United States Steel and Bell Telephone, an integral part of northern industry by World War I, would not appear in the South for another generation.

World War II and the accompanying financial boom changed the South drastically and permanently. Rapid industrial development brought research-oriented corporations into the region as southern states competed for their attention with such incentives as low taxes and prime locations. Independent research laboratories emerged, as well. Areas such as the Research Triangle Park near Raleigh, N.C., now rival any other region of the nation for productive, scholarly, scientific research. Universities blossomed, too, thanks to greatly increased financial support. Graduate schools attracted highly qualified professors; increasingly, southerners not only chose to remain at "home" for their education but often accepted permanent employment in the region. Modern transportation and communication, coupled with institutional funding for travel and research, meant that these scientists were no longer isolated as they had been earlier. By the 1970s and 1980s black and women scientists represented a growing, previously excluded human resource for the South. Southern scientists have earned the respect of their colleagues, both personally and for the institutions that now support their endeavors.

See also EDUCATION articles

Nancy Smith Midgette
Elon College

George Daniels, *American Science in the Age of Jackson* (1968); John C. Greene, *American Science in the Age of Jefferson* (1984); Brooke Hindle, *The Pursuit of Science in Revolutionary America, 1735–1789* (1956); Thomas Cary Johnson, Jr., *Scientific Interests in the Old South* (1936); Sally Gregory Kohlstedt, *The Formation of the American Scientific Community: The American Association for the Advancement of Science, 1848–1860* (1976); Nancy Smith Midgette, "The Role of the State Academies of Science in the Emergence of the Scientific Profession in the South, 1883–1983" (Ph.D. dissertation, University of Georgia, 1984); Alexander Oleson and Sanborn C. Brown, eds., *The Pursuit of Knowledge in the Early American Republic: American Scientific and Learned Societies from Colonial Times to the Civil War* (1976); Margaret W. Rossiter, *Women Scientists in America: Struggles and Strategies to 1940* (1982).

Racism, Scientific

The history of "scientific racism" before the 20th century is synonymous with the development of the modern scientific study of race. Scientific racism was not "pseudoscience" but an integral part of the intellectual worldview that nurtured the rise of modern biology and anthropology. In the 20th century the paradigm of racial hierarchy based on comparative anatomy came under withering attack from the American anthropologist Franz Boas and his students, but, in the history of race science before the emergence of the Boasian school, almost all the participants were racists, and the insights into human diversity provided by the "culture concept" were not available.

Southerners have always had a strong interest in the scientific discourse on race because the fate of their region has been inextricably tied to questions about the role and capacity of Afro-Americans. According to historian Winthrop D. Jordan, Thomas Jefferson's *Notes on the State of Virginia* (1786) was the strongest formal argument for black inferiority published by any native American before the 19th century. Jefferson's work appeared during the period when prejudice against people of color first became a topic of conscious concern among American intellectuals. Jefferson's description of his native habitat was representative of the international effort by natural philosophers to study systematically the bewildering diversity of plants, animals, and peoples revealed by European expansion. Since Aristotle, Western thinkers had found the metaphor of a hierarchical "great chain of being" useful, and many 18th-century natural philosophers expressed their ethnocentric condescension toward Africans by charting pyramids in which Europeans stood at the apex and blacks below, close to the ape. Jefferson's argument for black inferiority differed from the hardened racism of the 19th century in his regretful and equivocal tone, but *Notes* is one of the documents that marks the general abandonment of the Enlightenment hope that all peoples could achieve "civilization."

By later standards Jefferson's evidence was "soft." He claimed that blacks were less beautiful than whites, judged their emotional life less complex, and compared them unfavorably with Roman slaves, among whom he found many leaders in the arts and sciences despite harsh conditions that he imagined exceeded those endured by Afro-Americans.

Jefferson argued from history and personal experience, but the major 19th-century American contributions to scientific racism depended on advances in classification and morphology. The taxonomic methods that were serving the botanist well might also be used to explain why Cherokees, Mexicans, and Negroes were fated to serve the "Anglo-Saxon race" or disappear. Assuming that human diversity resulted from differences in heredity, a new generation of natural philosophers found great differences in the skulls of white people and black or red people and turned the abstraction of racial type into a fact of nature.

The reification of race through the taxonomic method is well illustrated in the work of the "American School" of anthropology, whose founder, the Quaker physician Samuel G. Morton (1799–1851), developed the first extensive quantitative data in support of "polygenism"—the theory that human races were separate biological species, the descendants of different Adams. Drawing on a collection of over 1,000 human craniums supplied by a vast network of correspondents, Morton published a series of works between 1839 and 1849 that were distinguished by brilliant lithographs of skulls and ingenious measurements of their cavities. He argued that a ranking of races could be established objectively through anthropometric measures, particularly brain size, and, unlike Jefferson, he found the Indian as well as the African absolutely inferior to the white in cranial capacity. In

1981 the Harvard scientist Stephen Jay Gould demonstrated that Morton's statistics were a "patchwork of fudging and finagling" but found "no evidence of conscious fraud."

During Morton's lifetime his work was accepted as a model of methodological sophistication and won an international audience. Morton converted Harvard's Louis Agassiz, the dominant figure in American natural science, to the doctrine that races were separate creations but found his most effective disciple in the Alabama physician Josiah C. Nott (1804–73). Nott's *Types of Mankind* (1854; written with George R. Gliddon) provided the authoritative American text on racial differences until Darwin's work necessitated revision of the racist typology. Nott's argument that races were fixed types "permanent through all recorded time" was intended as a rebuttal of abolitionists and racial equalitarians. With the help of his friend and publisher James D. B. De Bow, Nott enjoyed great notoriety and success, despite the hostility of some southern leaders because of his anticlericalism and the incompatability of polygenism with religious orthodoxy.

Before the Civil War, leadership in scientific racism had passed to Europe, where Paul Broca (1824–80), the French surgeon best known for his discovery of cortical localization in the brain, established himself as Morton's chief scientific heir through painstaking comparative studies of brain weights. By Broca's death in 1880, scientific racism had a well-developed paradigm based on the reification of ideal types and a formidable data base drawn not only from skulls and brains but from the cranial measurements of 25 million living Europeans as well. Although the experts were unable to agree on exactly how many races there were or to produce a living example of any pure type, the faith that these types existed shaped such influential popularizations as William Z. Ripley's *The Races of Europe* (1899) and Madison Grant's *The Passing of the Great Race* (1916).

Thus, white southerners had little need to conduct basic research to justify the competitive racial caste system that emerged after the abolition of slavery. The major southern contributors to the scientific literature on race were physicians who described blacks as a diseased and debauched population that would probably be unable to survive without the paternalism of slavery. The medical claims that liberty would lead to black genocide echoed the antebellum myth of a relentless "Anglo-Saxon race" as the agent of the westward march of civilization, bound to exterminate all other breeds that it did not enslave; but the physical degradation of blacks also fit well with the varieties of Social Darwinism that were becoming fashionable.

Although Charles Darwin was a monogenist, the theory of evolution through natural selection proved compatible with the racial typology established by polygenists. Instead of advocating a series of separate acts of creation, late-19th-century scientific racists artlessly worked the established racial types into explanations of human variation that required longer time and gradual change but still assumed that racial types were the ancient determinants of human history. By the end of the century southern physicians had produced a torrent of abuse in the guise of biomedical studies and had attributed malnutrition, infection, and insanity to a lack of black "fitness" in the struggle for existence. The confidence of white America that the black problem would be solved through extinction of the inferior race was exemplified in the work of Frederick L. Hoffman, a statistician for the Prudential Insurance Company of America, whose *Race Traits and Tendencies of the American Negro* (1896) helped convince most insurance companies that blacks were unacceptable risks.

With white supremacy firmly established in the South by the turn of the century, America's racial anxieties were expressed in campaigns against mass migration from southeastern Europe, and the southern "Negro problem" got relatively little attention. The major development in 20th-century scientific racism in the English-speaking world was the rise of the eugenics movement and its campaigns for sterilization of "defectives," racially discriminatory immigration policies, and tracked school curricula based on intelligence tests. Because most of the immigrants settled in the North and the South's schools were already segregated, the South contributed relatively little to eugenics except for illiterates, dirt eaters, pellagrins, and syphilitics, who served as objects of northern science and philanthropy.

The great public health campaigns that made dramatic contributions to the health of the region were sometimes influenced by scientific racism, most notably in the refusal of many southern physicians to admit that poverty was a better explanation for pellagra than hereditary defect. Many Americans were shocked in 1972 by newspaper headlines describing a U.S. Public Health Service experiment in which over 400 Macon County, Ala., black men were denied treatment for syphilis as part of an experiment to compare the effects of the disease on Negroes and Caucasians. The nightmare that became known as the Tuskegee Syphilis Experiment had its origins in the effort of northern philanthropists to develop model health programs during the 1920s. When the Great Depression erased the funds for a syphilis-treatment project among blacks in Macon County, government scientists decided to salvage something by charting the natural history of syphilis among sharecroppers who were told that they were being treated for "bad blood." The experiment continued until 1972, when public exposure forced the government to reexamine its policies concerning experimentation with humans. In 1974 the United States agreed to pay approximately $10 million to the victims, but there was no public contrition from the scientists involved. Historian James H. Jones concluded: "Had they been given an opportunity to retrace their steps, there is little doubt they would have conducted the experiment again."

The history of scientific racism exemplifies the powerful influence of social values on the development of biomedical science. Southerners have justified their social institutions in the idioms available to them. When revealed religion provided the primary explanation for the social order, southern leaders looked to their Bibles; in the 19th century, when science emerged as an important source of authority, southerners provided an eager audience and offered empirical studies for the new racist science. Long after it had been discredited by the advance of knowledge, racist science influenced medical opinion and helped to legitimate racial injustice. In the case of the Tuskegee Syphilis Experiment, a measure of justice was achieved not through the initiative of the scientific community but as the result of a lawsuit instituted by Fred Gray, a black attorney and native of Alabama, who first gained prominence in 1955 by defending Rosa Parks for refusing to relinquish her bus seat to a white man. Racism had become a liability for the scientist because those alleged to be inferior had endured long enough to command justice.

See also BLACK LIFE: Race Relations; HISTORY AND MANNERS: Philanthropy, Northern; / Jefferson, Thomas; MYTHIC SOUTH: Racial Attitudes

James Reed
Rutgers University

George M. Fredrickson, *The Black Image in the White Mind: The Debate on Afro-American Character and Destiny, 1817–1914* (1971); Stephen Jay Gould, *The Mismeasure of Man* (1981); John S. Haller, Jr., *Outcasts from Evolution: Scientific Attitudes of Racial Inferiority, 1859–1900* (1971); James H. Jones, *Bad Blood: The Tuskegee Syphilis Experiment* (1981); Winthrop D. Jordan, *White over Black: American Attitudes toward the Negro, 1550–1812* (1968); William Stanton, *The Leopard's Spots: Scientific Attitudes toward Race in America, 1815–1859* (1960); Nancy Stepan, *The Idea of Race in Science: Great Britain, 1800–1960* (1982); George W. Stocking, Jr., *Race, Culture, and Evolution: Essays in the History of Anthropology* (1968).

Science and Religion

At the beginning of the 19th century southern theologians and the region's educated clergy entertained optimistic hopes for an alliance between science and religion. They believed that scientific discovery would confirm theological orthodoxy and even improve the methods of theology itself. By the beginning of the 20th century that earlier confidence had eroded, and religious conservatives led a series of statewide crusades against the teaching of evolutionary theory in the public schools. In large part the change resulted from the growing popular awareness of Darwinism, but it also reflected continuing preconceptions formed during the antebellum period.

When John Holt Rice became in 1824 the first professor of theology in the Presbyterian Seminary at Hampden-Sydney, Va., he was officially charged with the task of raising up a generation of scientifically minded clergymen: "that branch of knowledge should form a part of that fund of information, which every minister of the Gospel should possess." The charge embodied a consensus among the educated clergy of the Old South, who were convinced that the scientific investigation of the created order disclosed the existence and nature of the Creator and that the theologian who knew something about natural science could, in the words of Thomas Ralston, "see God . . . mirrored in his works."

The confidence in natural science was an extension of an ancient tradition of natural theology. The antebellum southern theologians—like their northern counterparts—argued that scientific investigation, properly conducted, provided a vast and grand amplification of the traditional argument that design and order in nature demonstrated the reality and trustworthiness of God, and they admired such naturalists as Hugh Miller in Scotland, who had argued that nature was filled with pattern and regularity and therefore with divine intelligence. Some presbyteries and synods required that prospective clergy take examinations on scientific subjects. The southern theological journals carried scores of articles throughout the antebellum period designed to show the harmony of science and religious faith. And the denominational colleges developed courses in chemistry, natural philosophy, geology, and astronomy, confident that they were promoting "the cause of science and religion." For the clerical elite, to become an amateur scientist was to extend and enrich the ministerial calling, and few professional groups in the South exhibited greater enthusiasm for the program of natural science than did the educated antebellum southern clergy.

The clergy did insist, though, that scientists remain within the confines of true scientific method, which they associated with the inductive restraint of Sir Francis Bacon. They opposed scientific materialism, they disliked developmental theories, and they worried about the harmony between scientific conclusions and the book of Genesis. Hence they criticized such scientific skeptics as Thomas Cooper in South Carolina. But most antebellum scientists were themselves pious Christians, and a small number of clergymen—like the Lutheran John Bachman—were respected scientists or amateur naturalists. Few of the educated clergy had much difficulty reconciling Genesis and geology. They simply argued that the seven days in the biblical creation narrative were geological periods, or they assumed that the creation account in Genesis merely described the final stage of a longer creation. So enthusiastic were they, in fact, that a number of southern theologians, including James H. Thornwell in South Carolina, hoped to model theology after the image of the natural sciences.

By the 1850s there were signs of strain. The increased interest in developmental hypotheses after the publication in England in 1844 of the *Vestiges of the Natural History of Creation* troubled some clergymen. When the Tombecbee Presbytery in Mississippi recommended the establishment of chairs in theological seminaries to refute infidel naturalists and to evince the harmony of science and scripture, some ministers favored the plan because they felt defensive about the sciences. But others favored it because they had every expectation of maintaining cordial relations between the disciplines. The leader of the drive for such chairs, James Lyon of Columbus, Miss., felt confident that God's revelation in nature, deciphered by science, was fully as authoritative and inspired as the Bible itself. When a member of Lyon's congregation, Judge John Perkins, donated $50,000 in 1859, the denomination promptly called James Woodrow to the Perkins Professorship at Columbia Seminary. His inaugural address spoke of the "harmony" of science and scripture.

Woodrow soon shifted his language, however, to refer simply to the absence of contradiction between science and religion, and in 1886 he was the defendant in a heresy trial occasioned by his acceptance of evolutionary theory. By that time the churches were increasingly edgy about the new biology: the Methodists had removed Alexander Winchell from a post at Vanderbilt in 1878, partly because of his defense of Darwin. But when the statewide struggles over the teaching of evolutionary theory in the public schools erupted in the 1920s, the churches lined up on both sides of the issue.

The opponents of evolutionary theory were noisy, but only in the Southern Baptist Convention did they succeed, in 1926, in securing an official condemnation of developmental theories of human origins. They also had mixed success in the state legislatures and statewide referenda, passing restrictive laws in Florida, Tennessee, Mississippi, and Arkansas. William Jennings Bryan's appearance at the trial of John Scopes in 1925 strengthened the antievolutionary sentiment in the rural South, but by the end of the 1920s the issue seemed to fade away. A number of prominent religious leaders—men like the Baptist E. Y. Mullins, the Methodist bishops E. D. Mouzon and John M. Moore, and the Presbyterian Hays Watson Smith—had openly opposed the antievolutionary movement, and the opponents of Darwin had failed with the voters and legislatures in all but four states.

Some of the religious opposition to Darwinism reflected a broader opposition to science itself, but many of the fundamentalist opponents of Darwin claimed to be friends of science. They contended only that Darwinism had transcended the bounds of scientific method propounded by Francis Bacon: the evolutionists, they claimed, were insufficiently inductive. Hence with the resurgence of scientific creationism in the 1960s—stimulated in part by the writings of Henry M. Morris of Virginia Polytechnic Institute—southern religious conservatives again tried to compel the schools to teach a biblical science, and only a federal judicial decision in 1982 thwarted them in Arkansas.

Both the 19th-century proponents of natural theology and the later conservative opponents of Darwin usually insisted that the Bible was itself a scientific text and that religious and scientific assertions were therefore equivalent in logical status. The 20th-century southern conservatives have simply held on to the quasi-rationalistic presuppositions of the older 19th-century theological orthodoxy.

See also RELIGION: Fundamentalism; Modernism and Religion; / Thornwell, James Henley

E. Brooks Holifield
Emory University

Theodore Dwight Bozeman, *Protestants in an Age of Science: The Baconian Ideal and Antebellum Religious Thought* (1977); Norman Furniss, *The Fundamentalist Controversy, 1918–31* (1954); Willard B. Gatewood, Jr., *Preachers, Pedagogues and Politicians: The Evolution Controversy in North Carolina, 1920–1927* (1966); E. Brooks Holifield, *The Gentlemen Theologians: American Theology in Southern Culture* (1978); George Marsden, *Fundamentalism and American Culture: The Shaping of Twentieth-Century Evangelicalism, 1870–1925* (1980); James R. Moore, *The Post-Darwinian Controversies: A Study of the Protestant Struggle to Come to Terms with Darwin in Great Britain and America, 1870–1900* (1979); Ronald L. Numbers, *Science* (5 November 1982).

Self-dosage

Self-dosage has traditionally been the first line of prevention and of therapy by which people seek to combat illness; it is rooted in both the natural and the magical-religious facets of folk medicine as conveyed through oral tradition. Popular health guidebooks, reflecting input from both folk and developing scientific medicine, have influenced self-dosage patterns, as has advertising for patented drugs. The most significant distinguishing features of southern self-dosage have arisen from the higher proportion of blacks in the South than elsewhere in the nation and from the region's enduring rural atmosphere.

Immigrant groups brought their respective folk legacies to America, elements of which survived intact or with only minor adjustments. Antecedents and analogues in earlier European experience can be found for many health rituals and herb remedies still used in the South, as recorded in such collections as the Frank C. Brown Collection of North Carolina Folklore at Duke University and the John Q. Anderson Folklore Archives at the University of Houston. An example is a wart cure by magical transference: rub the wart with a stolen dishrag; bury the rag; when the rag rots, the wart disappears. Garlic, one of the most ancient folk medicines, continues to be used.

Local conditions in the New World modified inherited traditions, introducing indigenous flora and fauna learned from the Indians or discovered empirically. In Texas, prickly pear, mesquite, and the roadrunner were used as medical remedies. New amulets—alligator teeth, for instance—might join or replace old cures. Once introduced, newcomers tended to persist. A 1967 study in the environs of Jacksonville, Fla., found several very old remedies still flourishing: a cure-all made with nine rusty nails in a pint of whiskey, clay eating for worms, starch eating for easy pregnancy.

Slaves brought folk traditions from Africa, but it is impossible to tell what parts of black self-treatment represented African survivals and what parts were European modifications. Black folk medicine, in any event, became richly complex, partly because slaves and exslaves possessed few other sources of power and lacked basic medical care. These factors helped folk medical practices retain vitality among blacks after such traditions weakened in white culture. Black folk medicine survived in fullest form, still somewhat linked to its religious roots, in southern Louisiana, because of both Haitian influences and rural isolation. A renaissance of voodoo traditions has occurred in recent years. Voodoo articles are sold in drugstores and through mail-order catalogs. These black practices also penetrated white self-help approaches.

Throughout the 19th century the health manual supplemented oral tradition in guiding self-treatment. Several of the most influential volumes came from southern presses, especially J. C. Gunn's *Domestic Medicine, or Poor Man's Friend*, published in Knoxville in 1830 and going through 100 editions by 1870. Lambasting orthodox physicians and their imported drugs, Gunn praised God for having "stored our mountains, fields and meadows with simples [medicinal plants] for healing our diseases." Despite his condemnation of the regulars, Gunn tended to imitate their heroic prescriptions. Samuel Thomson's botanical school of irregular medicine proved popular in the South, as expounded in his *New Guide to Health* and in southern derivatives like Simon Abbott's *The Southern Botanic Physician* (1844). The popularity of such works declined as patent-medicine advertising expanded.

In colonial days the old English patent medicines were advertised from Baltimore to Savannah. Some of them still survive in a generic form in the rural South. Made-in-America proprietaries, rare until independence, boomed under the impact of cultural nationalism. A few southern entrepreneurs entered the cure-all field, but their wares had a merely local sale. The titans of the trade well through the 19th century came from the North, their bilious pills and worm-destroying lozenges dominating the southern market. During the Civil War, trade interruption and Confederate nationalism combined to stimulate southern brands. In 1862 Augusta, the maker of Broom's Anti-Hydropic Tincture proclaimed in bold type: "DROPSY CURED! NO YANKEE HUMBUG!" But at war's end, northern proprietors sought quickly to recapture their southern markets. Before 1865 was over, a Charleston druggist was shipping southern botanicals to Massachusetts in payment for the packaged remedies of J. C. Ayer. A Columbia, S.C., editor complained that southern newspapers again sold advertising at cut rates to Yankee "patent blood-suckers." Such Yankee bottles far outdistanced southern brands tossed into the moat at Fort Pulaski near Savannah, and Yankee direct-mail ads in a Georgia farm family's papers, filed along with letters from cousins in Arkansas, outnumbered southern nostrum ads.

The New South witnessed a burgeoning of proprietary medicine production. Purgatives were easier to fabricate than cotton textiles, and in this field the South sought to end its colonial subservience. In 1890 Atlanta derived a higher proportion of its gross municipal product from patented drugs than did any other city in the nation, such funds fueling the city's rise to New South leadership. Venturesome pharmacists like John Pemberton and Joseph Jacobs devised, purchased, and promoted a wide variety of brands. Pemberton's Coca-Cola began as a headache remedy and pick-me-up; Asa Candler shrewdly converted the nostrum into a beverage. Other Atlanta brands included Botanic Blood Balm, Swift's Sure Specific, Bradfield's Female Regulator, and Tanlac. Other cities saw similar developments. In Chattanooga, two Union army veterans sought antebellum southern formulas and parlayed Black Draught and Wine of Cardui into fortunes, aided by such salesmen as Huey P. Long.

Advertisements for patented wonder drugs, South Carolina, 1938

In antebellum days northern merchandisers promoted patent medicines as of special value for slaves. Many slaves must have brought the medicine habit with them into freedom. Black entrepreneurs came to share in this market, although whites dominated it. Well into the 20th century, black newspapers—even W. E. B. Du Bois's the *Crisis*—while promoting racial pride in news and editorial columns, were forced, to stay solvent, into accepting advertisements for "skin whiteners" and hair straighteners as well as for purported cures for serious ailments.

Hadacol, the tonic devised by the Louisiana politician Dudley LeBlanc in the early 1950s, demonstrated once again the South's receptivity to patent-medicine appeals. The medicine was promoted with a popular song, the "Hadacol Boogie." A tremendous success within the region, the Hadacol boom collapsed when LeBlanc sought to promote it outside the South.

See also ENVIRONMENT: Plant Uses; ETHNIC LIFE: Indian Cultural Contributions; FOLKLIFE: Folk Medicine; Voodoo; INDUSTRY: / Coca-Cola; WOMEN'S LIFE: Healers, Women

James Harvey Young
Emory University

John Q. Anderson, Elizabeth Brandon, and Bruce Jackson, in *American Folk Medicine: A Symposium*, ed. Wayland D. Hand (1976); John B. Blake, James H. Cassedy, and Ronald L. Numbers, in *Medicine without Doctors: Home Health Care in American History*, ed. Guenter B. Risse et al. (1977); Floyd Martin Clay, *Coozan Dudley LeBlanc: From Huey Long to Hadacol* (1973); Wayland D. Hand, ed., *Popular Beliefs and Superstitions from North Carolina* (1961, 1964, 1981); James Harvey Young, *The*

Toadstool Millionaires: A Social History of Patent Medicines in America before Federal Regulations (1961).

Technology

Southern industry has traditionally included the processing of lumber, coal, and agricultural commodities. Enterprises like these tended to perpetuate low wages and minimal skills. In fact, the agrarian tradition encouraged movement of the work force in and out of these industries on a seasonal basis. Early societal patterns seemed little affected by technology, although Eli Whitney's invention of the cotton gin in 1793 provided a technological foundation for the South's development. Most southerners could easily identify with the position of ardent agriculturalists like Edmund Ruffin, a staunch advocate of the superiority of southern agrarian society in the antebellum era. Rural life was generally believed to be the most wholesome, moral, and virtuous form of existence. At the same time, technological enterprises like the iron industry, dating from the early colonial era, slowly advanced with the western and southern frontiers; by 1860 furnaces, forges, and rolling mills could be found from Delaware south to Georgia and as far west as Texas. Although the Civil War stimulated the growth of iron production in the South, even that industry lay in ruins by 1865.

In the late 19th century many farsighted southern leaders argued that the region needed to industrialize or forever remain a backwater of rural poverty. The agrarian past would not be totally rejected; rather, a New South would have diversified, multicrop agriculture along with diversified manufacturing, lively commerce, and busy citizens. The best-remembered spokesman for the bold new departure was Henry W. Grady, editor of the Atlanta *Constitution*. Grady had watched a revitalized Atlanta emerge from the rubble of the Civil War. Commerce, industry, and urbanization, having worked wonders in Atlanta, could do the same for the Deep South. "The Old South rested everything on slavery and agriculture, unconscious that these could neither give nor maintain healthy growth," he argued in his famous New York address of 1886. The New South, he continued, represented a healthy democracy, "a hundred farms for every plantation, fifty homes for every palace—and a diversified industry that meets the complex need of this complex age." If the realities fell short of this generous ideal, and if overt racism and a patrician style of government still persisted, Grady's vigorous acceptance of urbanism and technology represented a significant shift away from the traditional patterns of culture.

The South's iron industry slowly recovered in the 1880s, especially in areas around Chattanooga, Tenn., and Birmingham, Ala. During World War I and World War II modern techniques for steel production developed, resulting in new plants in Texas; in the postwar era smaller, specialized facilities appeared throughout the South.

Factories and cities became more numerous in the South in the early 20th century, growing even more visible as a result of World War I and its urgent production requirements. Living patterns consistent with a technological society became more commonplace. During World War I and through the mid-1920s, lumbering made a considerable impact. Without completely disrupting rural social patterns, lumbering brought weekly paydays and tended to lessen the uncertainties of sharecropping. When the momentum of the timber industry declined, southern sawmill workers did not return to the farm but moved to newly resurgent southern cities or industrial centers in the North. In order to retain year-round farm labor, farmers in industrial areas were forced to enter into new arrangements. Wages had to come closer to industrial levels, and a day's work came to mean 8 hours, not 16. In many older farming areas, technological society, as represented by industry, encountered stubborn hostility.

The process of industrialization became the catalyst for another technological phenomenon, the automobile. For years, the lack of adequate highways was seen as a serious shortcoming in attracting new industries and expanding existing ones. Just before World War I, surfaced roads were so rare that textbooks in southern elementary schools included pictures of them as wonderful examples of the future. Aggressive highway commissions flourished in the 1920s, with gasoline taxes providing necessary revenues for road construction. Passable in every season, surfaced roads permitted large and small industries to spread throughout the rural South where railroads and rivers were nonexistent. For farmers, trucking brought new economic possibilities in marketing crops and livestock. After 1945 highways carried a flood of northern tourists in search of shrewdly marketed southern charm and a frost-free climate. Collectively, roads, cars, and trucks have helped end rural isolation.

The automobile shielded individual poverty from the public eye. On foot or astride a mule, poverty could be seen in ragged clothes and bare feet, but a car offered a technological cloak. Automobiles provided mobility, opening new horizons of change and opportunity. For poor southerners, the automobile became as significant as medicine or clothing. Following World War II, southerners bought more cars than any other regional market group in the United States. Autos were an expression of individuality, as the prewar novels of William Faulkner and Robert Penn Warren show. In the postwar era, the role of the auto as a popular icon was evident in the huge throngs attracted to stock car races in places such as Darlington, S.C., and Daytona Beach, Fla.

During the 1920s, as the South followed the seemingly irresistible patterns of commerce and industry "up North," there were still dissenters. The most celebrated example was the Agrarian movement at Vanderbilt University in Nashville, Tenn. Although the Agrarian critique was rooted in southern values and directed toward the southern scene, literary critic Louis D. Rubin, Jr., has noted that it was consonant with other contemporary attacks on the materialism and depersonalization of 20th-century industrial society. In general, the Agrarians appealed to the younger generation to resist the onslaught of modern technology and harked back to an earlier era of southern agriculture as more harmonious and reasonable. Their manifesto, *I'll Take My Stand: The South and the Agrarian Tradition* (1930), seems not to have been taken seriously as an antitechnological tract by the great majority of southerners. In truth, the Agrarians did not intend to do away with technology but wanted to keep it within the bounds of a humanistic society. Stark Young, a contributor to *I'll Take My Stand*, asserted that "we can accept the machine, but create our own attitude toward it."

In some respects, the Great Depression of the 1930s was an interlude, a time when industrialization, city building, and technological changes subsided; but only on the surface. The advent of highways and automobiles, the creation of the TVA, the spread of rural electrification, and the onset of World War II set in motion a series of changes of fundamental significance.

In the postwar era inexpensive electricity supported the spread of air-conditioning to rural homes and urban offices alike, and the technology of the military-industrial complex left a pervasive imprint on southern culture. Army, navy, and air force installations dotted the region; Maryland, Georgia, and Texas became major centers of aerospace research and development and of manufacturing. As the nation's space program accelerated during the 1960s, the South achieved international attention due to the location of several key installations of the National Aeronautics and Space Administration in Texas, Alabama, and Florida—a new "fertile crescent." The wartime stimulus of petroleum production and the refining industry was followed by increasing sophistication of the petrochemical industry, electronics, and medical research. These and other commercial/industrial trends have profoundly influenced educational patterns and career choices within an urbanized, industrial society.

The South's fierce attachment to the soil has been altered by an array of interrelated technological factors. Mechanization has changed the pastoral rhythms set by mules and plow horses; ancient landmarks such as boulder-strewn hummocks and fern-lined gullies have been leveled and filled for maximum farm production or for shopping malls. Although postwar industries have often provided the principal income necessary to allow rural families to stay on the "old place," while feeding a few cows and tilling a few acres on the side, much of the rural population has moved into burgeoning urban centers like Atlanta and Houston or to northern cities. More than ever, regional economics became tied to global vagaries of prices for oil, steel, pulpwood, and other commodities.

The spread of technology has contributed to some notable shifts in traditional cultural patterns. Attuned to the realities of the technological world, southern governors within the last few years banded together to urge Congress to raise certain tariffs to protect regional industry, a position that would have outraged southern Populists in the 1890s. The new realities also prompted southern civic leaders to renew criticism of the Ku Klux Klan and other racist groups because such organizations discouraged new industry from moving south.

In past decades, chambers of commerce relied on stock identifications like "Dixie" and "Sunny South," terms that promised pastoral grace of a bygone era, to advertise the region. By the 1970s the preferred term was "Sunbelt," an appellation that, although not excluding the agrarian past, identified a region of commercial opportunity, cosmopolitan services and entertainment, and a hi-tech culture.

See also AGRICULTURE: Mechanization; / Rural Electrification Administration; ENVIRONMENT: Air-Conditioning; Tennessee Valley Authority; HISTORY AND MANNERS: Automobile; Railroads; INDUSTRY articles; LITERATURE: Agrarianism in Literature; MYTHIC SOUTH: New South Myth; / Agrarians, Vanderbilt; RECREATION: Tourism, Automobile

Roger E. Bilstein
University of Houston
at Clear Lake City

Richard M. Bernard and Bradley R. Rice, eds., *Sunbelt Cities: Politics and Growth since World War II* (1983); Blaine A. Brownell and David R. Goldfield, eds., *The City in Southern History: The Growth of Urban Civilization in the South* (1977); Thomas D. Clark, *The Emerging South* (1961); Louis D. Rubin, Jr., ed., *The American South: Portrait of a Culture* (1980); Loyd S. Swenson, *Southwestern Historical Quarterly* (January 1968).

Breckinridge, Mary

(1881–1965) Nurse.

"If you take the unborn child as a focal point," Mary Breckinridge once said, "you will soon be led to a broad program of public health." In this succinct fashion she summarized over five decades of ongoing medical service with a unique health organization, the Frontier Nursing Service (FNS), in the isolated mountains of southeastern Kentucky.

Born in Memphis, Tenn., to a prominent southern family and educated at finishing schools in Switzerland and Connecticut, Breckinridge took a nursing degree from St. Luke's Hospital in New York. Her placid existence as an upper-class southern woman was disrupted by a series of personal tragedies. Twice married (widowed in 1906, divorced in 1920, after which she resumed use of her maiden name), she lost two children in infancy. These misfortunes coupled with a strong family sense of noblesse oblige prompted her to devote the remainder of her life to the cause of child welfare. After service in Europe with the American Committee for Devastated France, she took graduate courses in midwifery at London's British Mothers and Babies Hospital and became a certified midwife.

In 1925, at the age of 44, Mary Breckinridge brought the concept of the professional nurse-midwife to the United States when she established the FNS at Hyden, Leslie County, Ky. She chose the mountains of her family's native region because she could draw on the prestige of the Breckinridge name and the support of numerous relatives. Riding on horseback, "Mrs. Breckinridge's nurses" provided midwifery and general nursing care to some 10,000 people in a 300-square-mile area, where there were few roads and no licensed doctors, telephones, or electricity. World War II brought the departure of most of the British staff and soon prevented American travel abroad for training; Breckinridge then established a graduate school of midwifery at Hyden, which expanded in 1970 to include a family nursing program to train students in primary-care nursing.

Breckinridge's concept of rural southern health care proved prophetic. An early exponent of community involvement, she recognized that the local people themselves should participate in decisions affecting their own welfare. Furthermore, she applied the concept of the family nurse practitioner in Appalachia long before many in the medical profession became cognizant of the idea. She also demonstrated that the health of mothers and babies could be significantly improved through midwifery services. In 1980, after 55 years of operation, the FNS had supervised 18,885 maternity cases with a loss of 11 mothers in childbirth. There have been no maternal deaths since 1952.

Carol Crowe-Carraco
Western Kentucky University

Mary Breckinridge, *Wide Neighborhoods: A Story of the Frontier Nursing Service* (1952); Breckinridge Family Papers, University of Kentucky; Carol Crowe-Carraco, *Register of Kentucky Historical Society* (July 1978).

George Washington Carver, botanist and agricultural researcher, 1906

Carver, George Washington

(c. 1864–1943) Scientist.

Born in the final days of slavery in southwest Missouri, George Washington Carver was raised by his former owners, left home before his teenage years, and wandered until he was almost 30 years old seeking the elusive goal of many black contemporaries—a good education. After a brief career as an art major at Simpson College, he entered Iowa State, where his impressive abilities in botany earned him an invitation to pursue postgraduate studies. He received his master's degree in agriculture in 1896 and immediately accepted the position of director of agricultural studies at Booker T. Washington's Tuskegee Institute in Macon County, Ala. Although he intended to stay only long enough to establish a viable program, Carver remained at Tuskegee until his death in 1943.

For the first 20 years there he labored under the shadow of Washington, endeavoring to improve the conditions of the poor and often landless black farmers of the South. He tried to provide inexpensive alternatives to costly commercial products at the experiment station he founded. His research and varied extension activities placed him in the mainstream, and sometimes the forefront, of agricultural education, but his idea of small-scale technology based on available and renewable resources was increasingly out of tune with the current trends. His efforts therefore brought limited recognition, but they did aid thousands of individuals who were struggling under crushing burdens of debt within the sharecropping and tenancy systems of southern agriculture.

His international fame came after Washington's death in 1915, when much of Carver's most useful work was over. His renown resulted mainly from his symbolic importance to a myriad of causes and was largely based on his essentially unsuccessful attempts to find commercial uses for such southern crops as peanuts and sweet potatoes. The eccentricities of his personality and the romance of his life story provided good copy for the press, and he was adopted as an exemplar by numerous groups—some with contradictory goals. He represented both the beneficence of slavery and segregation and the ability of Afro-Americans. He was also used by the peanut industry, various religious groups, and New South editors preaching agricultural diversification and industrialization.

Although a growing mythology accompanied his rise to prominence, Carver continued to play an important role in the South. His warm, compelling personality led to numerous friendships with southern whites and provided a liberalizing influence on some newspapermen and many students whom he met during his lectures at white colleges. He also remained an inspiration to southern blacks as he was repeatedly hailed as one of Dixie's leading citizens.

Linda O. McMurry
North Carolina State University

George Washington Carver Papers, Tuskegee Institute Archives, Tuskegee, Ala.; Linda O. McMurry, *George Washington Carver: Scientist and Symbol* (1981).

Charleston Museum

Founded in 1670 through land grants to wealthy planters from Barbados, the city of Charles Town, now Charleston, S.C., rapidly became one of the leading cultural centers in British colonial America. A keen interest in the "natural curiosities" of the region soon developed, and in 1773 the Charles Town Library Society "fitted up a Museum for the Reception and Preservation of Specimens of these . . . natural Productions." With those intentions, the first museum in America was established.

In 1778 a disastrous fire destroyed most of its holdings, but the society began anew in temporary quarters and in 1785 moved its collections into the present courthouse. Records of specimens received by the museum from 1798 to 1808 include items from around the globe, reflecting Charleston's importance as a port of call for the growing American merchant fleet.

In 1815 the Library Society gave its collections to the newly formed Literary and Philosophical Society of South Carolina, and by 1825 the museum had made great strides under the leadership of botanist Stephen Elliott. At that time it was located in Chalmers Street and was known as the Museum of South Carolina. In 1828 the museum was moved to the Medical College but made little progress after Elliott's death in 1830.

At the urging of the celebrated naturalist Louis Agassiz, the museum collections were given to the College of Charleston in 1850 and were provided with larger quarters and a full-time curator in the person of Francis S. Holmes, a pioneer in local paleontological studies. Numerous contributions to the collections were made by the Elliott Society of Natural History, formed in 1853 by members of the Charleston scientific community, which included Holmes, John Bachman, Lewis Gibbes, John Holbrook, Edmund and Henry Ravenel, and John McCrady, all of whom published important works in their fields. With men like these, and with the only museum south of Philadelphia, Charleston was the major center of scientific activities in the South prior to the Civil War. But the ruinous defeat of the South in that conflict dealt a devastating blow to scientific progress in South Carolina, the museum's collections being among the only surviving evidence of Charleston's antebellum eminence.

The museum remained at the College of Charleston until its removal to the vacant Thompson Auditorium building on Rutledge Avenue in 1907. In 1915 it became an independent organization administered by a director and a board of trustees and was officially chartered as the Charleston Museum. After more than 70 years in the badly deteriorating Rutledge Avenue building the museum was moved to a modern new building on the corner of John and Meeting streets in 1980. One of the largest museums in the South, its extensive collections in cultural and natural history are used by scholars throughout the nation. Its holdings also include the historically significant Heyward-Washington House, Joseph Manigault House, and William Aiken House.

See also URBANIZATION: / Charleston

Albert E. Sanders
Charleston Museum

Caroline M. Borowsky, *Museum News* (February 1963); Laura M. Bragg, *Charleston Museum Quarterly* (1923); William G. Mazyck, *Charleston Museum Bulletin* (1907); David Ramsay, *The History of South Carolina from its Original Settlement in 1670 to the Year 1808* (1809); *South Carolina Gazette* (22 March 1773).

Country Doctor

Rural doctors have long been viewed as different from their urban counterparts. Although the distinctions well known in Britain between physicians, surgeons, and apothecaries applied occasionally in the colonial South, such distinctions were mostly absent from the later southern rural scene. During the first half of the 19th century a sense of identity among country doctors emerged. Many country doctors wrote to the growing number of medical journals in the 1840s and 1850s. One such Virginia physician commented that "the life of a physician in the country is very different from that of his professional brother who ministers to the ills of humanity in our towns and cities. Whilst the latter can recline at ease in his carriage, during the performance of his daily routine of visits, enjoying all the luxury of practice . . . his country 'confrere' has to undergo a life of constant, frequently *excessive* labor, often riding for hours during the most inclement weather, braving the frost and snows of winter."

While the general fortunes of country doctors throughout the United States were many and varied in the second half of the 19th century, the famous painting *The Doctor* (1891), by British artist Luke Fildes, conveyed an image of benevolence and trust that captured the imagination of physicians and laypersons alike throughout America. More than 1,000,000 engravings of it were to be found in parlors and physicians' waiting rooms.

How accurate is this image for the 19th-century South? The distinctive aura of the country doctor surely owed much to the practitioners' professional concerns, tinged with a negative attitude toward rural life and people. A fear of becoming outdated while living in areas without intellectual stimulation emerges time and time again in country doctors' correspondence and journals from the second half of the 19th century and into the 20th. These attitudes, coupled with the modern transformation of American medicine through rampant specialization and the relentless growth of institutions, contributed to the virtual disappearance of the country doctor by the 1950s.

In many ways the declining numbers encouraged a sense of nostalgia for the "good old country doc" depicted in Luke Fildes's picture. On the other hand, oral testimony can still be gathered—to be added to 19th-century correspondence—that indicates many country doctors provided medical treatment within the context of community needs. They maintained congenial relations with midwives; set flexible arrangements for payment (either in coin or in kind); and prescribed both well-known botanical remedies, which were sometimes collected locally by or for the doctor, and new drugs advertised by pharmaceutical companies.

Once frequently found in the South and elsewhere, such characteristics have become the essence of a romantic stereotype. The rural South provided an ideal location for those doctors who traveled endless miles to carry out their duties.

Paul I. Crellin
Country Doctor Museum
Bailey, North Carolina

Aubrey D. Gates, in *This Is the South*, ed. Robert W. Howard (1959); Arthur E. Hertzler, *Horse and Buggy Doctor* (1970); Paul Starr, *The Social Transformation of American Medicine: The Rise of a Sovereign Profession and the Making of a Vast Industry* (1982).

Creation Science

Creation science, or scientific creationism, supports the biblical story that man and earth were created suddenly by the Supreme Being. Identified with fundamentalist religion in the United States, creation science holds that scientific evidence supports the biblical refutation of Darwinian evolution as an explanation for human existence. In the 1980s the creationism controversy has centered around the argument that creation science should be taught in the public schools as a scientific alternative to evolution.

This argument between religious fundamentalism and public education has repeatedly surfaced in the South, where conservatives and fundamentalists have organized and pressured local and state school districts and legislators. In response to such pressures, the Louisiana Legislature in 1981 passed its Balanced Treatment Act requiring teachers to teach the theory of scientific creationism if they mention evolution. The case challenging the law's constitutionality was brought by the Louisiana Board of Education and the American Civil Liberties Union and supported by some teachers, scientists, and religious groups. It was struck down by the U.S. Supreme Court in 1986. Opponents of the law contended that it was an effort to inject religion into the public schools. The Louisiana Department of Justice and scientific creationists supporting the law, however, argued that creation science is not a religion but a valid scientific theory. On these grounds, they held, the First Amendment requires the presentation of scientific creationism along with evolution.

In a similar case, which has been compared to the Scopes Trial of 1925, a group of Hawkins County, Tenn., families won a court decision against the Tennessee Board of Education for refusing to provide alternative readers for their children. The parents disagreed with several passages in the elementary readers on grounds that they conflicted with their religious views. As in the Louisiana case, fundamentalists cited the First Amendment, arguing that it guarantees their right to free exercise of religion, a right that was being hindered by the state's school system. Powerful national lobbying groups became involved in the case as it attracted attention outside the South.

The recent controversy over scientific creationism differs significantly from the post–World War I battle to outlaw the teaching of evolution of which the Scopes Trial was a part. In the 1920s, also, the South led the fight to take the theory of evolution out of public schools. Four southern states—Arkansas, Florida, Mississippi, and Tennessee—passed restrictive legislation on the issue. The antievolutionists responsible for these laws, led by William Jennings Bryan, openly defended their views as biblically based.

In the 1970s the creationism movement was revived with an entirely different focus, influenced by the efforts of Henry M. Morris, a Texas engineer. Morris, raised a Southern Baptist, argued in *The Genesis Flood* (1961) for a return to the belief in a literal six-day creation and a worldwide flood as described in the Bible. His strict creationism was hotly debated within the scientific community. Morris's book generated arguments that are significant because they appeared to be legitimate scientific ones, rather than judgments of faith based on biblical passages.

In the 1970s Morris joined with fundamentalists outside the scientific world in a renewed effort to propagate creationist ideas. The new fight stressed the scientific aspect of creationism, offered evidence for a worldwide catastrophe, and focused on arguments against evolution. Creationists in the latter part of this century have turned away from attempting to outlaw evolution and have argued that creationism deserves "equal time." The main goal of recent creationists has been to give their ideas scientific legitimacy and to establish intellectual equality with evolutionist theories. Their tactics have included portraying the withholding of alternatives to evolution as "censorship" that violates First Amendment rights.

Karen M. McDearman
University of Mississippi

Melinda Beck, *Newsweek* (28 July 1986); John Hill, Jackson *Clarion-Ledger* (5 October 1986); Ronald L. Numbers, *Science* (5 November 1982).

DeBakey, Michael

(b. 1908) Surgeon.

Dr. Michael Ellis DeBakey, chancellor of the Baylor University College of Medicine in Houston, Tex., ranks among the world's leading authorities in the field of cardiovascular research.

Born 7 September 1908 in Lake Charles, La., the son of a Lebanese immigrant, DeBakey received his M.D. degree from Tulane University, worked for some time under the well-known New Orleans surgeon Dr. Alton Ochsner, then served with the surgeon general during World War II. In 1948 he moved to Baylor and quickly began to earn laurels for himself and the school.

DeBakey's achievements in the world of medical science are legion. In the area of technology he made improvements in the heart-lung machine, developed an artificial ventricle to be used on a temporary basis by heart-surgery patients, and participated in the attempt to design an artificial heart to replace the human organ. A skilled surgeon, he operated successfully on thousands of patients and was a pioneer in heart-transplant surgery. He published hundreds of scholarly articles to report on the results of his research and was granted many scientific and humanitarian awards as well as a number of honorary degrees, both in the United States and abroad.

Michael DeBakey, pioneering heart surgeon, 1970s

In addition to his scientific achievements DeBakey also distinguished himself as an outspoken advocate of government support for various facets of American medicine. He was appointed by Presidents John F. Kennedy and Lyndon B. Johnson to serve on advisory councils that, despite the opposition of organized medicine, recommended that federal funds be used for regional programs to improve patient care for victims of heart disease, cancer, and stroke. He also stressed the need for government sponsorship of pure research and medical education.

During the nearly four decades of his association with Baylor, DeBakey has served in a number of leadership capacities. Moreover, he was also largely responsible for the development of two of the world's leading centers of heart surgery—Methodist Hospital and the Texas Heart Institute, both in Houston. With his work receiving worldwide acclaim and his organizational skill building these lasting institutions, DeBakey has been a significant factor in transforming this southern city into a major international medical center.

Lucie R. Bridgforth
Memphis State University

Saturday Review (16 October 1971); *Time* (28 May 1965).

Dirt Eating (Geophagy)

Geophagy (geophagia), or the conscious consumption of soils, has been observed worldwide for centuries. References to the practice of consuming soils dates back as far as 40 B.C., when Greeks consumed specific clays to combat a variety of illnesses. Wherever the practice has been observed, its specific content has varied according to the local culture.

The practice of geophagy in the United States is decidedly associated with the South. Geophagy was first observed among blacks during slavery. References to clay eating by both black and white females and young children were frequently made in scientific and popular literature of the 1800s. The consumption of soils is not a haphazard practice but a clearly defined one, as only specific clays are extracted and at times prepared (baked) for eating. Although some physiological mechanisms may be involved, clays are consumed mainly because they are identified by the local culture as a food. No overall detrimental health effects from consuming clays have been documented.

The practice of geophagy became more widespread as a result of the mass migration of southern blacks out of the region from 1920 to 1940. However, southern culture and traditions still dominate the practice today. Because many clay eaters prefer southern clays, it is not unusual for these substances to be shipped to the urban North from the rural South. Geophagy today is on the wane with many clay eaters either stopping altogether or switching to commercial products such as laundry starch and baking soda, which have textures similar to clay.

Dennis A. Frate
University of Mississippi

Francis B. Bradley, *North Carolina Folklore* (December 1964); Dennis A. Frate, *Sciences* (November–December 1984); Robert W. Twyman, *Journal of Southern History* (August 1971); Donald E. Vermeer and Dennis A. Frate, *American Journal of Clinical Nutrition* (October 1979).

Disease, Endemic

During the height of southern nationalism (1830–60) some physicians, led by Samuel A. Cartwright of New Orleans, argued for a belief in uniquely southern diseases. In addition to the clear social and political utility of such opinions, epidemiological observations at the time strongly supported the idea. During the 18th century malarial fevers were common in the northern colonies and yellow fever struck northern ports, but, for reasons not fully understood, malaria and yellow fever almost disappeared from the northern states in the 19th century. The latitude of southern ports, and commercial ties with the tropics, gave the South semitropical diseases uncommon in other regions. Most dramatically, during the 19th century the great epidemics of yellow fever were phenomena of southern ports, but three endemic diseases—hookworm, pellagra, and, most importantly, malaria—probably had a more profound, if more difficult to evaluate, role in the shaping of southern life.

Hookworm disease, or uncinariasis, is the result of infestation with the hookworm, *Necator americanus*, identified by Charles Stiles in 1902. Hookworms thrive in areas without snow cover and in sandy soil, conditions common to most of the South. Reports in the 19th-century medical literature frequently show people with symptoms of anemia and physical and mental retardation compatible with the diagnosis of hookworm disease, but only the identification of the parasite made possible precise diagnosis. By 1911 hookworm infections had been scientifically proven by local health authorities in 719 of 884 southern counties. This level of parasitism supported, if it did not largely explain, the characteristic malaise associated with southerners; and, in fact, early in the 20th century the hookworm was widely identified as the southern "germ of laziness." One of the earliest diseases targeted for eradication by scientific public health campaigns, hookworm was the first public health focus of the Rockefeller philanthropies (1909–13). Since World War II, hookworm infection has been controlled by economic improvement, case treatment, and improved public health and sanitation.

Pellagra is a disease that results from an inadequacy of niacin, one of the B vitamins. It is traditionally associated with corn diets because corn is low in niacin and in tryptophan, a metabolic precursor of niacin. Although

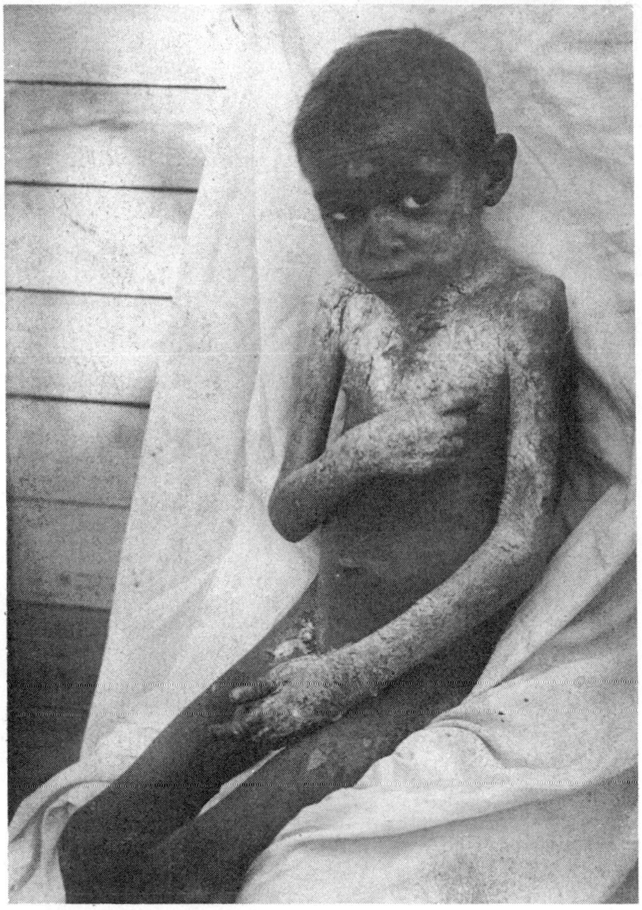

Young boy with pellagra, early 20th-century rural South

reported in 39 states, pellagra was a southern disease because of the traditional southern diet. The early symptoms of pellagra are diverse and nonspecific, but the disease is associated with lassitude and weakness followed by anxiety and irritability. Once quite prevalent—by one estimate, 25,000 cases in 1915—pellagra has declined dramatically with improved nutrition.

Despite the importance of hookworms and pellagra in the New South and probably at other times, the disease that has had the greatest impact on southern culture and life is clearly malaria. Malaria is an infectious disease that classically presents a fever pattern of regular remission and exacerbation with intermittent, remittent, or periodic fever. The disease is spread from person to person via the mosquito and so does not usually appear to be contagious. Its transmission by mosquito also causes a seasonal prevalence of the disease in temperate zones; it is more widespread in the summer and fall when mosquitoes are plentiful. This pattern strongly influenced the pattern of life in the Old South, for planter families would flee the plantations for high country, coastal islands, or northern cities during the sickly season. Although malaria was common in northern Europe and was brought to America by early colonists, a particularly malignant form of the disease was probably introduced into the South by the African slave trade; its widespread incidence made southern fevers much more deadly than the similar fevers of other regions. Furthermore, malaria disappeared with lengthy settlement in the North—during the 18th century in New England and by late in the 19th century in the Midwest. In general, malaria, preeminently a disease of rural poverty, exacerbates the other effects of poverty by physically weakening its victims while making them more susceptible to other diseases.

Numerous other diseases were and are common in the American South, but these three—all diseases of poverty, but all now controlled by public health measures—have exerted a severe physical, mental, and emotional burden on the people of the region. By accidents of geography and history, all were in a very real sense "southern diseases."

Dale C. Smith
Uniformed Services University
of the Health Sciences
Bethesda, Maryland

Daniel Drake, *Malaria in the Interior Valley of North America* (1964); Elizabeth W. Etheridge, *The Butterfly Caste: A Social History of Pellagra in the South* (1972); John Ettling, *The Germ of Laziness: Rockefeller Philanthropy and Public Health in the New South* (1981); Harry Frank Farmer, "The Hookworm Eradication Program in the South, 1900–1925" (Ph.D. dissertation, University of Georgia, 1970); Rockefeller Foundation International Health Board, *Bibliography of Hookworm Disease*, Publication No. 11 (1922); Rockefeller Foundation Sanitary Commission for Eradication of Hookworm, *Annual Reports* (1910–15); Todd L. Savitt, *Medicine and Slavery: The Diseases and Health Care of Blacks in Antebellum Virginia* (1978); Allen Tullos, *Southern Exposure* (Summer 1978).

Disease, Epidemic

Historians of medicine in the South today agree that disease is a central theme in the history of southern culture, a theme at one time punctuated by epidemics related closely to forces that shaped the region. Perhaps the most important force throughout the colonial period and beyond was climate. The rigors of adaptation were much greater in southern than in northern colonies for European immigrants. Among the major epidemic afflictions, malaria (especially in its pernicious or malignant form) and dysentery took a proportionately greater toll of lives in a region where warm weather over a long season fostered the survival of insects that carry disease as well as the transmission of water- and food-borne diseases. Also, the ostensibly greater hardiness of blacks in swampy areas, due to immunological factors including the sickle-cell trait, served in part to support the rationalization of slavery and, thus, the beginnings of a culture of poverty. To some degree epidemics of respiratory diseases, diphtheria, scarlet fever, whooping cough (pertussis), and measles were moderated by relative dispersion of the region's rural population. Colonial Charleston was repeatedly ravaged by violent epidemics of yellow fever and smallpox. And there can be no question that the white man's most potent weapon in warring with southern Indian tribes was smallpox.

During 19th-century regional expansion, a rising agricultural economy, developments in transportation, and urban growth made southern cities and river towns particularly vulnerable to epidemic disease. Cholera and yellow fever were especially significant. Like other parts of the country, southern towns and their nearby countryside were devastated by cholera epidemics in the years following 1832, 1849, and 1866, but in 1873 only communities in the lower Mississippi Valley were stricken. Unlike cholera, whose ancestral home is India, yellow fever came to the Western Hemisphere by way of the African slave trade. By the 1850s, as a result of almost annually recurring epidemics of violent intensity, the name of New Orleans had become virtually synonymous in the North and abroad with sickness and death. However, it was the disastrous Mississippi Valley yellow fever epidemic in 1878, together with postwar poverty, that generated the growth of a widespread and not wholly inaccurate perception of the South as a diseased region, which eventually brought it into the mainstream of the 20th-century American public health movement. Epidemic disease has played a historically continuous and significant role in shaping contemporary southern culture.

John H. Ellis
Lehigh University

Jo Ann Carrigan, *Journal of Southern History* (November 1970); John Duffy, *Epidemics in Colonial America* (1953); John H. Ellis, *Bulletin of the History of Medicine* (May–June, July–August 1970).

Garden, Alexander

(1730–1791) Physician and naturalist.

Alexander Garden was born at Birse, Scotland, near Aberdeen, where his father was a Church of Scotland minister. He attended Marischal College and began the study of medicine as an apprentice to an Aberdeen physician. He served two years in the Royal Navy as a surgeon's mate. After study at the University of Edinburgh, in 1752 he immigrated to South Carolina, becoming one of the leading physicians of Charleston. Although Garden was highly regarded there, his loyalty to Great Britain necessitated that he leave when Loyalists were expelled following the Revolution. He spent the remainder of his life in London.

Although he has sometimes been called the most famous physician of colonial times, Garden made even greater contributions as an untiring student of natural history. Very shortly after his arrival in South Carolina he established himself as one of the small group of men who were eagerly helping European scientists to understand the natural history of North America. He was ambitious for recognition as a scientist of importance. His interests were broad, including plants, animals, medical problems, the health of slaves, climate, minerals, and other aspects of the environment. He sent plant specimens to Charles Alston in Edinburgh, John Ellis in London, and Carolus

Linnaeus in Sweden. Amphibians, fish, insects, and reptiles went to Linnaeus and to John F. Gronovius in Holland. Birds were supplied to Thomas Pennant in England. Garden contributed to the local scene as well, being a stimulus to, and an active participant in, the intellectual and cultural life of Charleston.

His importance was well recognized in his own time. He was elected to membership in the most prestigious scientific societies in both America and Europe, including the American Philosophical Society, the Royal Society of Arts and Science of Upsala, the Royal Society of London, the Royal Society of Arts (London), and the Royal Society of Edinburgh. Linnaeus named the *Gardenia* in his honor.

Garden's publications were few, largely journal articles describing plants and animals. Many of his letters survive and testify to his facility as a writer. His correspondents included all of those persons mentioned above and also John Bartram, Cadwallader Colden, John Clayton, and Benjamin Franklin.

Edmund Berkeley
Dorothy Smith Berkeley
Charlottesville, Virginia

Edmund Berkeley and Dorothy Smith Berkeley, *Dr. Alexander Garden of Charles Town* (1969).

Gorgas, Josiah

(1818–1883) Confederate ordnance officer.

Josiah Gorgas was born 1 July 1818 at Running Pumps, Pa. Graduating sixth in his West Point class in 1841, Gorgas chose the ordnance service and later served in the Mexican War, mostly in depot duty at Vera Cruz. After the war, Gorgas was assigned to duty at a series of arsenals from Maine to Alabama. Ironically, during this period Gorgas strengthened the defenses of Fort Pickens in Pensacola Harbor so effectively that Confederate forces were unable to destroy it during the Civil War.

Upon the organization of the Confederacy Gorgas was offered the post of chief of ordnance. He hesitated, but after receiving word that he had been given an unsatisfactory new assignment in the U.S. Army service he accepted his new Confederate post. That such an important position had been offered to, and accepted by, a "Pennsylvania Yankee" indicates the powerful influence of southern culture, especially in the American military establishment. Gorgas was married to Amelia Gayle of Alabama and through her politically powerful family was drawn into association with prominent southerners. In the army Gorgas had become friends with many military leaders from the South, including P. G. T. Beauregard, who recognized that Gorgas's talents in ordnance administration outshone those of most southerners and persuaded Jefferson Davis to offer him the appointment.

During the Civil War Gorgas supervised one of the most effective technological operations in southern history. By midwar, despite a chronic shortage of skilled workmen, Gorgas's organization was manufacturing most of the ordnance supplies that were not secured through battlefield captures and blockade running. Gorgas was a notable technological innovator, but his strength was a knack for planning ahead. He was also able to find and hold the loyalty of talented specialists, while at the same time staying in the good graces of the secretary of war and the president. By early 1864 Gorgas could survey a vast empire east of the Mississippi: 11 arsenals, a superb powder mill at Augusta, four cannon foundries, rifle and pistol production at four armories, a leather-processing plant, a shot-and-shell foundry, and a research laboratory. Even at the Confederacy's collapse in 1865, Gorgas's bureau was able to supply the ordnance needs of the Confederate armies.

After the war Gorgas formed a company to buy an ironworks at Brierfield, Ala., but the business failed. In 1868 he became master of the junior department and later vice-chancellor of the University of the South. In 1878 he became the president of the University of Alabama, but in 1879 his health began to fail and he was forced to resign the presidency. He lingered in ill health and died on 15 May 1883. His son William entered the medical service of the U.S. Army and became the man chiefly responsible for eradicating yellow fever in Cuba and Panama, making the Panama Canal possible.

Richard D. Goff
Eastern Michigan University

Richard D. Goff, *Confederate Supply* (1969); Frank E. Vandiver, *Ploughshares into Swords: Josiah Gorgas and Confederate Ordnance* (1952), ed., *The Civil War Diary of General Josiah Gorgas* (1947).

Herty, Charles Holmes

(1867–1938) Chemist.

Charles Holmes Herty was a southern chemist whose career as a teacher, researcher, and publicist contributed significantly to the economic development of the South and the growth of chemistry and the organic chemical industry in the United States. Born in Milledgeville, Ga., and educated at Johns Hopkins (Ph.D. 1890), Herty taught at the universities of Georgia and North Carolina from 1891 to 1901 and 1905 to 1916, respectively. Associated with the Bureau of Forestry in the U.S. Department of Agriculture between 1902 and 1904, he patented the Herty Cup and Gutter System of turpentining, which, by supplanting the destructive system of "boxing," then universally practiced in the American South, helped to save the threatened naval stores industry.

Twice elected president of the American Chemical Society (1915–16), Herty attained a national reputation as an expert in wood chemistry and his articulate advocacy of corporate, academic, and governmental cooperation in the establishment of chemical independence from Europe made him a natural for the editorship of the American Chemical Society's *Journal of Industrial and Engineering Chemistry*. He served in that capacity for four years (1917–21), with time out for trips to Europe to advise the American peace commissioners at Versailles on matters regarding German dyestuffs and German patents seized during the war. In 1921 he became president of the Synthetic Organic Chemical Manufacturers' Association, continuing his close relationship with Francis P. Garvan, alien property custodian in the Wilson Administration and president of the Chemical Foundation created in 1919 to administer the development by private American firms of the seized German patents. In 1926 Herty left the manufacturers' association, became a consultant to the Chemical Foundation, and for two years worked closely with Garvan, using foundation funds to promote research in chemotherapy. He also ran his own consulting firm in New York.

Finally, still interested in southern pine trees, conservation, and diversification of the South's stagnant economy, Herty attracted enough funds from the Chemical Foundation, the state of Georgia, and the citizenry of Savannah to establish an experimental pulp and paper laboratory there in 1932. His goal was to prove that sulphite pulp, suitable for the manufacture of fine white newsprint, could be economically made from young southern pines, thereby encouraging reforestation and freeing the U.S. newspaper industry of its dependence on the more expensive and slow-growing spruce pulp imported largely from Canada. At the same time the poor southern farmer, plagued with worn-out fields or no market for his cotton, would be provided with an alternative cash crop. Most important, new industry would be attracted to the region. Herty's papermaking demonstration, conducted under commercial conditions in a Canadian newsprint factory with pulp shipped from the Savannah lab, was a thorough success. Nine southern dailies printed their 20 November 1933 editions on the first run. As a direct result of Herty's efforts, although he did not live to see it, the first southern newspaper plant was erected near Lufkin, Tex. By 1955 an expanded plant at Lufkin, together with two more firms established in Alabama and Tennessee, accounted for 29 percent of all newsprint produced in the United States.

See also AGRICULTURE: / Naval Stores; URBANIZATION: / Savannah

Germaine M. Reed
Georgia Institute of Technology

Charles Holmes Herty Papers, Special Collections, Robert Woodruff Library, Emory University; Jack P. Oden, *Journal of Forest History* (April 1977); Gerry Reed, *Journal of Forest History* (October 1982).

LeConte, John
(1818–1891) Scientist.
LeConte, Joseph
(1823–1901) Scientist.

Natives of Liberty County, Ga., John LeConte and his brother, Joseph, were sons of Lewis and Ann Quarterman LeConte. Descended from a French Huguenot, Lewis operated a large plantation and became an able amateur scientist.

Both John and Joseph graduated from the University of Georgia and earned the M.D. degree from the College of Physicians and Surgeons in New York. After the death of their father, each inherited land and slaves. The brothers operated their plantations through overseers until the end of the Civil War. John practiced medicine in Savannah, Ga., from 1843 until 1846, when he was appointed professor of physics and chemistry at the University of Georgia. Joseph established a medical practice in Macon, Ga., in 1847, but three years later he abandoned it in order to study under Louis Agassiz at the Lawrence Scientific School of Harvard University. Upon completing his studies in 1851, he returned to Georgia and accepted the professorship of science at Oglethorpe University. In 1853 he was appointed professor of natural history at the University of Georgia.

As a result of a dispute with the university president, John resigned in 1855, and Joseph left for the same reason a year later. After serving for one year as a lecturer at the College of Physicians and Surgeons, John, in 1857, accepted a post at South Carolina College, where he was joined by his brother at the same time. Held in high regard, the LeConte brothers gained national recognition as scientists during the antebellum period, but they were severely set back by the Civil War.

Devoted defenders of the South, the LeConte brothers deplored the views of the Radical Republicans, and in 1869 they accepted posts at the newly established University of California, where John served as acting president in the 1869–70 academic year and as president from 1875 to 1881. At the time of his death John was a member of several scientific organizations and had published over 80 articles on medicine and physics. Joseph continued to write and eventually published over 190 articles and nine books. A universalist, he wrote on numerous topics, including education, philosophy, religion, evolution, geology, and physiological optics. His books on vision, geology, and evolution and religion received international notice. Both LeContes were elected to membership in the National Academy of Sciences, and Joseph later served as president of the American Association for the Advancement of Science (1892) and the Geological Society of America (1896). A devoted camper, he was a charter member of the Sierra Club.

Lester D. Stephens
University of Georgia

Joseph LeConte, *Autobiography*, ed. William Dallam Armes (1903); John Samuel Lupold, "From Physician to Physicist: The Scientific Career of John LeConte, 1818–1891" (Ph.D. dissertation, University of South Carolina, 1970); Lester D. Stephens, *Joseph LeConte: Gentle Prophet of Evolution* (1982).

Long, Crawford W.
(1815–1878) Physician.

A general practitioner in the village of Jefferson, Ga., Crawford Williamson Long in March 1842 first used ether to anesthetize a patient, James Venable, prior to the removal of an encysted tumor from the back of his neck. He was thus one of the earliest southern physicians to make a major contribution to medicine.

Born in Danielsville and raised in Jefferson, Long graduated from Franklin College (University of Georgia). After reading medicine with a Jefferson doctor, Long studied at Transylvania, then transferred to the University of Pennsylvania medical school, receiving his M.D. degree in 1839. He gained surgical experience in New York hospitals before returning to Jefferson in 1841. Long thus acquired as sound a medical education as America could offer.

Late in 1841 Jefferson's young set, hearing of antics brought on by nitrous oxide administered to volunteers by an itinerant showman then crisscrossing the country, besought Long to make this gas for their own use. As a student in Philadelphia, Long had seen a showman use sulfuric ether, after which he had joined fellow students in private ether parties. Long superintended such entertainments for the pleasure of his Jefferson friends. His observations led him to use ether as an anesthetic.

The operation, with witnesses present, proved successful. Five times more Long used ether for surgery before publishing his results. In one case Long amputated two injured fingers of a slave boy, employing ether for one operation but not the other. Long explained his delay in publishing by saying he wanted to prove that ether and not the impact of imagination negated pain. Long also had heard a Philadelphia professor condemn premature publication based on isolated experiments.

Long's article in the *Southern Medical and Surgical Journal* (1849) asserted his priority in using anesthesia against the quickly published claims of Harvard surgeon John Collins Warren and Boston dentist William T. G. Morton, who administered his Letheon in 1846. Later, Long also competed with New England claimants for recognition and possible recompense from Congress for discovering anesthesia. Confusing claims and sectional tension kept such a bill from becoming law.

Anesthesia is a classic example of multiple discovery. Long's tardy publication hurt his claim to priority, but he never lacked southern defenders, including J. Marion Sims and his own apprentice, Joseph Jacobs, whose efforts eventually placed Long's statue in the national Capitol. Long made no further discoveries, practicing medicine and operating a pharmacy in Athens for the last 28 years of his life.

James Harvey Young
Emory University

Frank K. Boland, *The First Anesthetic: The Story of Crawford Long* (1950); Crawford W. Long, *Southern Medical and Surgical Journal* (December 1849); Frances Long Taylor, *Crawford W. Long and the Discovery of Ether Anesthesia* (1928); James Harvey Young, *Bulletin of the New York Academy of Medicine* (March 1974).

McDowell, Ephraim
(1771–1830) Physician.

Of Scotch-Irish descent, Ephraim McDowell was born in Rockbridge County, Va., the ninth of 11 children of Samuel and Mary (McClung) McDowell. In 1784 the elder McDowell, a former revolutionary army officer and member of the Virginia Legislature, moved his family to the small community of Danville in the Kentucky district where he served as land commissioner and magistrate. After completing his preliminary education, young Ephraim was apprenticed to Dr. Alexander Humphreys of Staunton, Va., an eminent physician and teacher. Then in 1793 and 1794 he attended medical lectures in Edinburgh, where he was influenced especially by the famous Scottish surgeon-anatomist, John Bell. Returning to Danville in 1795 without a degree (the University of Maryland awarded him an honorary M.D. in 1823), McDowell soon established an extensive practice in the surrounding area. In 1802 the successful young doctor married Sarah Shelby, the daughter of Kentucky's first governor.

In a time before the development of anesthesia and detailed knowledge of the causes of infection, the name of Ephraim McDowell became associated with that of Jane Todd Crawford in one of the most celebrated cases in the annals of surgery. In December 1809 McDowell was called to a village 60 miles from Danville to consult with physicians whose 47-year-old patient appeared to present a complicated pregnancy. Upon examining Jane Todd Crawford, he determined she was not pregnant and that the swelling in her abdomen was a huge ovarian tumor. He advised her of the gravity of the circumstances, explaining that surgery was unprecedented and likely to be fatal; he offered to operate if she would come to Danville. On Christmas Day 1809, assisted by his nephew, McDowell performed the first ovariotomy in his home, removing a 20-pound tumor in the 25-minute operation during which Crawford recited the Psalms. She recovered fully and lived to the age of 78. A delayed report of this first case and two others was received initially by the medical profession with incredulity and harsh criticism, but McDowell's reputation was subsequently vindicated. Ironically, this famous pioneer in abdominal surgery is believed to have died of acute appendicitis. The McDowell house and apothecary in Danville, a national historic site, are owned and maintained by the Kentucky Medical Association.

John H. Ellis
Lehigh University

John Duffy, *The Healers: A History of American Medicine* (1979); J. N. McCormack, ed., *Some of the Medical Pioneers of Kentucky* (1917).

Maury, Matthew Fontaine

(1806–1873) Confederate general and oceanographer.

Born 14 January 1806 near Fredericksburg, Va., and reared on a plantation at Franklin, Tenn., Matthew Fontaine Maury was appointed a U.S. Navy midshipman in 1825. He sailed on three cruises, one being around the world, and rose to the rank of lieutenant before being permanently disabled in a stagecoach accident in 1839.

Maury attended Harpeth Academy, and his mastery of mathematics through calculus is evidenced in *A New Theoretical and Practical Treatise on Navigation*, published in 1836 and adopted by the navy for the instruction of midshipmen. In 1842 he was appointed superintendent of the navy's Depot of Charts and Instruments, and later, upon the completion of the U.S. Naval Observatory in Washington in 1844, he became its head as well.

Lieutenant Maury laid down an agenda for his new bureau and named it the Observatory and Hydrographical Office; soon he called for an astronomical survey of the southern heavens and a scientific study of the twin oceans of water and air. Specifically, he proposed a systematic analysis of wind and current patterns by ships to find "tracks," or the most seaworthy routes. His "abstract logs" required the collection of empirical information about 22 different meteorological and oceanographic conditions such as direction and rate of current, barometric readings, temperature of air and water, and the nature of winds and weather. As Maury explained in the *Southern Literary Messenger* in 1843, "every new fact, however trifling it may seem, that is gathered from nature or her works, is a clue placed in our hands, which assists to guide us into her labyrinth of knowledge." After an international agreement at Brussels in 1853, over 124,000 vessels, constituting over 95 percent of the world's shipping, cooperated in Maury's scientific undertaking.

As millions of daily logs came to Maury's office, his findings were published in the *Wind and Current Charts* with their accompanying *Explanations and Sailing Instructions*. As a result, clipper voyages to Australia, Brazil, and California were shortened by a quarter.

Maury early turned his research toward problems of interest to southern mariners and farmers, including the Isthmian canal, the Tehuantepec railroad, Mississippi River flood lands, and hurricanes. In attendance at various southern commercial conventions, he supported the establishment of direct trade with Europe through the use of steam packets. He found that, due to adverse winds and the Gulf Stream, vessels sailing to the South Atlantic ports made only 133 miles a day while northern ones averaged 162 miles. Nevertheless, he laid out a track for Savannah vessels that required 39 days for European passage, a saving of 20 days over the normal time but still longer than the passage from New York.

Although Maury pursued practical problems of weather and navigation, he also probed the basic mechanics of the sphere. His investigations of the dynamics of the Gulf Stream emphasized the effect of temperature and demolished John Herschel's theories on the trade winds. Maury was the first to chart the Atlantic seabed and to bring up samples of soil for microscopic examination of life forms. These data facilitated the laying of the first transatlantic cable in 1858. In the area of meteorology he concluded that heated air currents and trade winds created hurricanes, and he projected such phenomena as the jet stream.

In 1855 Maury published the first modern work on oceanography, *The Physical Geography of the Sea*, with chapters on the Gulf Stream and Antarctic climatology, among others. Although not all contemporaries accepted his bold interpretations, this book was translated into most European languages and appeared in 20 English editions alone before the turn of the century. After the Civil War, in which Maury served the Confederacy as a technical expert on submarine mines and as a naval purchasing agent in Europe, he continued his writing. He spoke often on science and religion, with emphasis on the earth and its systems as a giant mechanism. In 1867 Maury made a profession of faith and joined the Protestant Episcopal church. He died in 1873, while teaching at Virginia Military Academy.

Harold S. Wilson
Old Dominion University

Matthew Fontaine Maury, *Explanation and Sailing Directions to Accompany the Wind and Current Charts* (1858–59), Papers, Library of Congress, Washington, D.C., *The Physical Geography of the Sea* (1855), *Southern Literary Messenger* (August 1843); Frances Leigh Williams, *Matthew Fontaine Maury: Scientist of the Sea* (1963).

Moore, Samuel P.

(1813–1889) Confederate surgeon.

Samuel Preston Moore, surgeon general of the Confederate army, is among the least appreciated personages of the Civil War.

Born in 1813 in Charleston, S.C., he received his early education in his native state and graduated from the Medical College of South Carolina 8 March 1834. One year later he was commissioned assistant surgeon (with the rank of captain) in the U.S. Army, beginning a 26-year stint of service at military posts in various areas of the country. After serving in the Mexican War, he was made full surgeon in 1849. On 25 February 1861 Moore resigned from the army to avoid fighting against his native state. He entered medical practice in Little Rock, Ark., but on 30 July 1861 Confederate President Jefferson Davis appointed Moore acting surgeon general.

Moore faced an almost insurmountable task—the establishment of a medical department. Physicians, drugs, supplies, and hospitals had to be provided. Starting with only 24 physicians who had resigned from federal service, Moore, during the course of the war, recruited some 3,000 physicians for Confederate service. The medical department cared for 600,000 Confederate soldiers, 270,000 prisoners, and over 3,000,000 wounded or sick persons. Moore soon established an extensive hospital system, ranging from general hospitals to convalescent facilities. He is credited with the introduction of hospital "huts," the forerunner of the pavilion hospital. To replace medical supplies blockaded by the enemy, Moore was responsible for the preparation of drug substitutes from indigenous plants. Moore required regular sick calls, sanitary inspections, and regular reports of all medical activities.

To advance training of his medical officers, Moore encouraged educational meetings, refresher courses, and the publication of practical manuals on military medicine. He was instrumental in organizing in August 1863 the Association of Army and Navy Surgeons of the Confederate States and in the publication of the *Confederate States Medical and Surgical Journal.*

From the outset Moore was a strict disciplinarian, and his rigid enforcement of regulations often seemed to men fresh from civilian life little short of tyranny. Complaints were not wanting, but it was widely agreed that the medical department was among the most efficient in the Confederacy. President Davis accorded the highest praise to Moore and his department.

After the war, Moore remained in Richmond and devoted most of his time to the advancement of precollege education and agriculture. His contributions in both fields were significant.

He died suddenly on 31 May 1889 and is buried in Hollywood cemetery in Richmond.

Harris D. Riley, Jr.
Health Sciences Center
University of Oklahoma

H. R. McIlwane, *Surgery, Gynecology, and Obstetrics* (November 1924).

Reed, Walter
(1851–1902) Physician.

Major Walter Reed, who was one of the foremost bacteriologists and epidemiologists in the nation during the formative years of modern medicine, is best known for his work as chairman of the U.S. Yellow Fever Commission and discoverer of the mode of propagation of the disease.

Reed was born near Gloucester, Va., on 13 September 1851 and spent his childhood moving around the countryside of Virginia and North Carolina with his father, a Methodist minister. He received an M.D. degree from the University of Virginia in 1869 and went on to work for several years in New York hospitals. In 1874 he became a lieutenant in the U.S. Army Medical Corps. Though he was able to study pathology under William H. Welch at Johns Hopkins for a while, he spent most of his army career at isolated and dreary outposts.

He first began to demonstrate his skill as a medical investigator in Washington, D.C., during a virulent outbreak of malaria in 1896. When the Spanish-American War broke out in 1898, Reed was appointed to direct an investigation of typhoid. His findings made it possible to end the deadly epidemic of that disease in army camps.

In 1900 Reed became the head of an army board assigned to investigate the cause of yellow fever, which was rampant in Cuba at that time and also paid regular and deadly visits to the United States, especially the Gulf states and the Mississippi River Valley. Reed and his colleagues traveled to Cuba to search for the origins of the dread disease. Their experiments there led Reed to ascertain that yellow fever was carried by the *Aedes aegypti* mosquito. Once the cause was identified, steps were taken to eradicate the mosquito and thus the disease. The implications of Reed's work for the American South, where yellow fever took devastating tolls in life and productivity throughout the 19th century, were enormous.

Reed died following surgery for a ruptured appendix on 23 November 1902.

Lucie R. Bridgforth
Memphis State University

Century Magazine (October 1903); *New York Times* (2 November 1902); Albert E. Truby, *Memoir of Walter Reed: The Yellow Fever Episode* (1943); Laura N. Wood, *Walter Reed: Doctor in Uniform* (1943).

Ruffin, Edmund
(1794–1865) Agricultural reformer.

The preeminent scientific agriculturist of the Old South and a dedicated southern nationalist, Ruffin was born in Prince George County, Va., the son of a prosperous James River planter. He attended the College of William and Mary, served briefly in the War of 1812, and then embarked upon a nearly half-century career as a gentleman-farmer. Plagued initially by lands impoverished by two centuries of tobacco culture, he set out to improve them. By means of an elaborate series of experiments conducted over the course of 15 years on his Coggin's Point estate, Ruffin demonstrated the useful properties of marl, a shell-like deposit consisting primarily of clay mixed with calcium carbonate, which neutralized soil acidity and rendered sterile soils productive. He published his findings in 1832 under the title *An Essay on Calcarous Manures* and during the following decade spearheaded an agricultural renaissance in the Upper South through his distinguished journal, the *Farmers' Register*. In subsequent years he conducted an agricultural survey of South Carolina, proved the efficacy of his theories by converting his two Virginia farms, Beechwood and Marlbourne, into model estates, and served four terms as president of the Virginia State Agricultural Society.

Although his lasting fame derives from his contributions as an agricultural reformer, Ruffin is significant too as a representative of the planter elite of the slave South. Like others of that class, he exhibited a cultural and intellectual versatility. Thus, quite apart from his pragmatic interest in soil chemistry, he manifested a natural

Edmund Ruffin, agricultural reformer and southern nationalist from Virginia, near the end of his career

curiosity about scientific phenomena ranging from geology to ethnology. Cultured and well-read—he had read all of Shakespeare's plays before he was 11 years old—he was in many respects a true renaissance man. Also typical was Ruffin's consuming interest in politics. Too opinionated and too much a party maverick to stand for elective office—he served only a partial term in the Virginia state senate—Ruffin, nevertheless, immersed himself completely in the secession movement following his retirement from farming. When his labors bore fruit in 1861, he was accorded the honor of firing the first shot at Fort Sumter. Four years later, broken in spirit and fortune by the demise of his beloved Confederacy, the embittered Ruffin, in a gesture that symbolized not only his personal tragedy but that of his region, took his own life rather than submit to the anticipated indignities of Reconstruction.

William K. Scarborough
University of Southern Mississippi

Avery O. Craven, *Edmund Ruffin, Southerner* (1932); Betty L. Mitchell, *Edmund Ruffin: A Biography* (1981); William K. Scarborough, ed., *Diary of Edmund Ruffin* (3 vols. projected; 1972–).

Scopes Trial

No event of the 1920s captured the imagination of the public and the press as did the spectacle of the Scopes Trial. Held in a little Tennessee town, Dayton, during the sweltering month of July 1925, the case of the *People of the State of Tennessee* v. *John Thomas Scopes* is the best-known trial in American history.

With passage of the Butler bill by the Tennessee Legislature—a statute outlawing the teaching of evolution—several Dayton civic boosters accepted the offer of the American Civil Liberties Union to defend any teacher held in violation of the new law. Scopes, having just completed his first year as a science teacher at the local high school, agreed to act as the defendant. Ironically, Scopes probably did not, in fact, teach the theory of evolution.

The main actors in the drama came from outside Dayton. Clarence Darrow, the most famous lawyer of the day, defended Scopes with a staff including Dudley Field Malone and Arthur Garfield Hays. William Jennings Bryan, the three-time presidential hopeful and former secretary of state, led the prosecution team. H. L. Mencken, dubbing the developing spectacle the "Monkey Trial," led a horde of news personnel who descended on Dayton from around the nation and the world.

The trial opened on 10 July 1925 to the whirring of movie cameras and live radio coverage on Chicago station WGN. The courtroom crowd spilled over onto the lawn, and eventually Judge John T. Raulston moved the proceedings to the cooler temperatures outside.

The personalities and objectives of Darrow and Bryan did not, however, allow the trial to lessen its fever pitch. Bryan characterized the trial as a "duel to the death" between unbelievers and Christians. The agnostic Darrow, on the other hand, fully intended to prove that the Butler law was unfair and unconstitutional. The initial subject of all this furor, Scopes himself, became a secondary figure. Judge Raulston did not allow scientific and technical testimony, and the trial degenerated into a personal battle between Darrow and Bryan, a conflict encouraged by an aggressive press corps.

A Darrow challenge to Bryan brought the Great Commoner to the witness stand near the end of the trial. Bryan proved to be conservative in his religious views but not a consistent fundamentalist. For example, he did not espouse a literal meaning for the Creation as taking place in a series of six 24-hour days. Actually Bryan was consistent with his old populist leanings against monopoly, in this instance control of educational processes by educators and scientists. Moreover, his belief in a conservative social gospel scored natural selection as antithetical to reform. Darrow, one of the most clever courtroom orators in American history, was not as consistent in his reasonings. In the case of Leopold and Loeb he defended the young men by arguing that they had been corrupted by naturalistic teachings; at Dayton he defended just such instruction as proper.

The results of the trial proved inconclusive. Some liberals self-righteously believed the immediate posttrial death of Bryan to be fitting justice. The Rhea County jury found Scopes guilty and fined him $100. However, the Tennessee Supreme Court reversed the decision on a technicality, thereby removing the possibility of a test case before the U.S. Supreme Court. Scopes left teaching and entered the oil business as a geologist. His sister was later dismissed from the Paducah, Ky., school system for teaching evolution.

Although only Arkansas and Mississippi followed Tennessee in passage of antievolution statutes, the Scopes Trial undoubtedly led to suppression of evolution instruction across the nation. Most science textbook publishers bowed to the apparent public will and deleted or deemphasized sections on evolution. This trend lasted into the early 1960s. After publication of the Biological Sciences Curriculum Study materials by the American Institute of Biological Scientists in the mid-1960s, a new round of antievolutionist activity began. Self-styled "creationists," who were usually fundamentalists, proposed equal-time statutes. Court decisions in 1982 and 1985 in Arkansas and Louisiana overturned state laws mandating that creation science, which is based on the Genesis account of creation, be given equal time in the classroom if evolution were taught. A study of high school biology instruction in Kentucky, Tennessee, and Indiana in the early 1980s indicated that most instructors placed a "moderate" stress on evolution, a conclusion suggesting that a balance or equilibrium has been reached on the subject of evolution instruction across the nation.

Since the Scopes Trial a plethora of materials has both documented and interpreted this episode in Dayton. Perhaps the most famous of these, *Inherit the Wind*, a McCarthy-era adaptation of the Scopes Trial in play and movie forms, presented a version of the episode distorted by contemporary politics.

William E. Ellis
Eastern Kentucky University

Judith V. Grabiner and Peter D. Miller, *Science* (6 September 1974); Lawrence W. Levine, *Defender of the Faith: William Jennings Bryan; the Last Decade, 1915–1925* (1965); John T. Scopes with James Presley, *Center of the Storm: Memoirs of John T. Scopes* (1967); Ferenc Morton Szasz, *The Divided Mind of Protestant America, 1880–1930* (1982).

Social Class

J. WAYNE FLYNT

Auburn University

CONSULTANT

A Mississippi Delta plantation owner (foreground), 1930s

Social Class

One of America's most cherished ideals is the notion that any person who strives hard can be successful. The possibility of social and economic mobility attracted millions of immigrants and sustained the "American Dream." In no region is this idea more widely believed than in the South, and no section more thoroughly scorns Marxist notions of a society rigidly divided into hostile classes based on economic relationships.

In reality the South exists somewhere between its own idealistic myth of free and easy access to opportunity and the Marxist perception of an impenetrable class structure. Whether phrased in terms of a harsh concept such as "class" or a more acceptable one such as "status," the reality of social differentiation has contradicted the noble ideals of social equality and equal access to opportunity.

Class identification involves a great deal more than one's rank in the economic order. It is related to the entire social structure, although the nature of that relationship is hotly debated. One's status may depend on family, occupation, or self-perception, and it may be expressed in one's education, place of residence, political identification, church, or even depiction in literature.

Interpretations of Social Structure. Attempts to apply class interpretations to the South's social structure may be divided into three categories. The most familiar was expounded by Karl Marx and divided society into two classes engaged in mortal conflict. The prevailing system of economic production created a struggle between those engaged in the production of wealth and those who profited the most from its inequitable distribution. Economic struggle between classes determined all social relationships and political roles. Although some have attempted to apply rigid Marxist interpretations to the South, the more influential studies derive from a modification of Marx that deemphasizes economic determinism in favor of the cultural domination of one ruling elite over all others.

Max Weber, though influenced heavily by Marx, added two elements to the economic notions implicit in "class." "Status," as a concept of social honor or prestige, recognized that one's standing is partly determined by the consciousness of individuals, both of their own position and that of others. "Party" added the idea of political or legal power as a component because Weber observed that social stratification was a manifestation of the unequal distribution of power. Position in society was not determined solely by which economic group one belonged to but by the power that group could command compared to the power held by other groups.

Finally, an American, W. Lloyd Warner, expanded the concept of "status" and applied it specifically to American society. The social position one held depended not so much on economic criteria as on how a person lived, who his family was, and how people in the community judged, interpreted, weighed, and compared these factors. America contained not Marx's simple two-class structure, but a complex six-layer system existing not in mutual hostility and conflict, but in relative harmony.

Complicating all these considerations was the presence of large numbers of blacks in the South. Constituting a caste rigidly divided first by slavery and later by segregation, blacks developed a separate class system sometimes paralleling and at other times conflicting with the white structure.

Colonial Era. The colonial South produced conflicting patterns of landownership and class tension. Earlier historians attributed such conflicts as Bacon's Rebellion in Virginia to class tensions between wealthy seaboard aristocrats and poorer backcountry farmers, although such explanations appear now to be excessively simplistic. Actually the colonial patterns varied from one southern colony to another. For instance, the trustees who established Georgia banned slavery and prohibited ownership of more than 500 acres of land in an attempt to create a democratic region for the "worthy poor." But ambitious Georgia settlers thwarted such noble intentions, pointing to the greater prosperity of South Carolina and Virginia as precedent for introducing slavery and the plantation system. The success of plantation agriculture widened the chasm between classes and created strong antiroyalist sentiments among the upland farmers who would soon earn the title of "crackers." But land policy in Georgia remained generous throughout the colonial period; almost any male head of household could qualify for virtually free land. Although the Revolutionary War had a leveling effect in some ways, it also reflected class tensions. Officers in the state militias came from aristocratic stock. They commanded southern units often composed of unpropertied, poor recruits. South Carolina units contained sharp distinctions in dress, lodging, and food that led to desertions, neglect of duty, insolence toward officers, and general misbehavior.

Antebellum Era. Applying class theories to the antebellum years has produced exciting new interpretations and furious arguments. White society was divided into at least three major groups: planters, yeoman farmers, and poor whites. What united these three classes was a common commitment to the racial superiority of Caucasians, common kinship ties that often existed between planters and yeomen, and belief in the possibility of movement into the upper class if one sought good land, worked hard, and subscribed to community values. Each group also contained substantial variety. Among planters the range extended from small farmers with less than five slaves who lived more like yeomen than feudal lords to legendary barons with thousands of acres who constructed Greek Revival mansions, acquired extensive libraries, and ruled their domains with paternalistic concern for their hundreds of subjects. To those of Marxist persuasion, the planter class appears not to have been so much a capitalist class as precapitalist or even anticapitalist. Planters were hostile to all manufacturing except industry that complemented agriculture, such as the textile industry. They feared the rise of cities because both the urban bourgeoisie and the white working class that would develop there were quite beyond planter control. Moreover, their wealth was concentrated in land and slaves, and credit served their agrarian interests, leaving little money for speculative industries. Their values—honor, gentility, a highly ordered social structure, and an easygoing, relaxed society—were contrary to the capitalist values of northern businessmen and explain the South's inability to sustain manufacturing on any extensive scale. Planters typically belonged to Episcopal churches and were conservative in politics, often supporting the Whig party.

The yeoman class was by far the largest of the three major social groups. Unlike the planter who grew commercially marketable products such as cotton and tobacco, the yeoman was a self-sustaining farmer who worked in his own fields, produced extensive crops of corn and wheat, and maintained herds of livestock that roamed free in woodlands adjacent to his fields. He obtained rudimentary education in one of the hundreds of academies, cast his vote for Jacksonian Democrats, especially the ones who advocated easier access to public lands, and typically belonged to emotional religious sects such as the Baptists or the Methodists. Yeomen were often related to planter families by either kinship or marriage, aspired to enter that class, and were often successful when cotton prices were high and their lands fertile. When unsuccessful, they were a highly mobile group, moving westward in search of better land. Slavery provided them a means of controlling social and economic competition with blacks and a sense of class identification with other whites.

Even poor whites, the most elusive and enigmatic of the classes, generally accepted the plantation ideal, though they participated only peripherally in the economic system. Producing neither commercially marketable staples nor extensive food crops and livestock, they barely existed by hunting, fishing, harvesting sparse crops on poor land that usually did not belong to them, or working for minimal wages as farm laborers or in the cotton mills and urban industrial jobs that began to develop in the late antebellum years. Illiterate, transient, sickly, they were often despised by blacks and other whites alike, stereotyped by the comic southwestern humorists, and dismissed as "po' white trash." Actually poor whites varied from wretched ne'er-do-wells to substantial but landless farmers with stable families. Few of the economic benefits of the plantation system leaked through to them, and their only pride was the color of their skin, praised publicly by planter and yeoman alike, but of little practical value.

The notion that racial solidarity prevented internal dissension between white classes is not supported by the historical facts. Conflict occurred at many points within the social order. There was sectional strife between upcountry farmers, living on small farms with few slaves, and low-country planters. Economically the classes differed about free and easy access to land, taxation, and education. Politically they divided between Whig and Democrat.

Religious divergence according to class inspired a famous description of denominationalism more concerned with social status than theology: a Methodist was a Baptist who wore shoes; a Presbyterian was a Methodist with a bank account; an Episcopalian was a Presbyterian who lived off his investments. Such good-humored stereotyping obscured more fundamental conflicts. During the years immediately following the American Revolution, religious strife developed in the Virginia Tidewater. Separate Baptists held mass gatherings where itinerant preachers proclaimed the depravity of man, the terrors of hell, and the glories of redemption. They denounced finery of dress, cockfighting and gambling, fiddling and dancing—the very values by which the aristocracy demonstrated its superior status. Worse than that, they opposed taxation to support a state church and demanded separation of church and state. Drawn from the lower economic groups, the Separate Baptists created a popular, nonhierarchical, participatory system of association and authority, an "egalitarian world of humble men seeking their own ultimate meaning according to their own lights." In the following years Separate Baptists moderated their fierce Calvinism, but other disputes within the religious community replaced this one. The rise of new sects, such as the Disciples of Christ and the Cumberland Presbyterians, and the bitter struggle between missionary and antimission Baptists had distinctive class aspects.

Literature also reflected the differences in social status. Most southern writers were drawn from the gentry or professional classes, and they created a substantial literary tradition by describing the foibles, eccentricities, shrewdness, and humor of poor whites. Characters such as Augustus Baldwin Longstreet's "Ransy Sniffle" or Johnson J. Hooper's "Yellow-legs" satirized and stereotyped the white lower class.

Daniel R. Hundley, born into the Alabama planter elite, was one of the first southerners to describe systematically the region's class structure. His 1860 volume, *Social Relations in Our Southern States*, devoted chapters to "The Southern Gentleman," "The Middle Classes," "Cotton Snobs," "The Southern Yankee," "The Southern Yeoman," "Poor White Trash," and "The Negro Slaves." His description of poor whites was particularly harsh. Attempting to refute abolitionist charges that poor whites were the inevitable residue of a slave society, Hundley traced the class to paupers, convicts, and indentured servants, people explained by bad blood, not economic environment. Such "lazy vagabonds" preferred to live in rude log cabins on sterile soil where their yellow-faced women dipped snuff, smoked pipes, and raised large broods of "dirty, squalling, white-headed little brats" amid squalor, superstition, and slavish adherence to the Democratic party. Their only redeeming quality was support of slavery and even that was the result of ignoble motives—"downright envy" of the planter and "hatred of the black man."

Although the world of blacks was fundamentally different from that of poor whites, internal variations occurred there also. Standing at the top of the social ladder were free blacks, who in 1860 numbered 262,000 and comprised 12.8 percent of the black population in the Upper South and 1.5 percent in the Lower South. Often of mixed racial ancestry and frequently residing in towns or cities, they developed job skills and relatively independent churches, schools, and fraternal societies. In 1860 one-sixth of Richmond's bricklayers and blacksmiths and half its plasterers and barbers were black. Protected from white competition by the stigma of "nigger work," some free blacks became substantial property holders. In the years following the Civil War many leaders came from this class, including nearly half of the 22 blacks who served in Congress between 1869 and 1900.

Differentiation by class is harder to measure among slaves. Whatever their advantages over their fellows in job skill, skin color, or literacy, free blacks remained bound to the slaves by the "peculiar institution." Nonetheless, a hierarchy did exist, with house servants, ministers, and skilled artisans at the top and field hands at the bottom. Adaptation to white culture also varied, with some slaves maintaining strong African elements and others quickly adopting American forms.

Impact of the Civil War. All class arrangements were affected by the Civil War, but no consensus exists concerning the extent of change. Class tensions—which had been somewhat confined during the antebellum years by common kinship and folkways, the ideology of white supremacy, the availability of land, rapid economic mobility, and the nonelite origins of the planter class—underwent subtle change during the Civil War. In the initial phase of conflict, yeomen and poor whites rallied to the Confederate cause despite frequent hill-country opposition to secession. Most military units contained a cross section of economic classes and elected their own officers, a process considerably more democratic than in the Revolutionary War. But as the war progressed, yeomen and poor whites bore the worst effects. Drought, draft, and taxes-in-kind fell heavily on common whites in hill counties and piney woods. The families soldiers left behind faced grievous problems by 1862–63, causing southern states to levy taxes on wealthy planters in order to distribute food to the poor. But for this relief, unrest would have been even greater. As it was, desertion by yeomen and poor whites increased dramatically by 1863, and southern hill counties experienced growing anarchy. Poverty, desertion, resistance to Confederate policy, and growing peace sentiment were closely related.

The appearance of discontinuity after the Civil War was certainly greater than the reality. Although planters lost their slave work force, they retained control of economic and political life and in some states adjusted quickly to the New South drive for industrialization. In Alabama and North Carolina planters apparently not only survived but participated actively in the manufacturing enterprises that flourished in the Piedmont and in bustling industrial towns such as Birmingham and Anniston. In other states, leaders in the rapidly growing textile industry were urban professionals and businessmen, with planters and farmers playing little role. In South Carolina the rise of upcountry towns had more to do with the development of manufacturing than did the survival of the plantation system.

The New Industrial Order. Whatever the origin of the new industrial order, several elements are clear. The planter class retained a major share of influence and power, although it had to compromise its opposition to towns and factories. Secondly, the promise of emancipation, which offered blacks such bright hope in 1865, dimmed amidst agricultural poverty. Nor was the black dream the only casualty of the last years of the century. New South exponents could proclaim the dawn of a different world, but economic reality defied their pronouncements. In 1900 the South remained the poorest, most technologically backward, most rural, least industrialized region of America.

Because their expectations were so great, blacks were the most disappointed of southerners. As a symbol of their emancipation, tens of thousands of former slaves temporarily left the land, filling towns to overflowing with their tent cities. Wartime devastation not only prevented them from obtaining work but necessitated the Freedmen's Bureau's providing rations to them and to poor whites in order to prevent mass starvation. Gradually most freedmen drifted back to the land, some to purchase their own farms but most to work as day laborers or as tenants. For blacks accustomed to slavery even the sharecropper system represented a step toward freedom. Though often cheated, they could negotiate their own contracts, function at least theoretically as equals, and operate their farms without the constant supervision of owners. But in terms of health, diet, and general economic well-being the status of many black sharecroppers declined even from that of slave.

For whites who had barely survived on the periphery of the antebellum economy, tenancy added social insult to economic injury. Thousands of poor whites left their remote pine barrens and mountain hollows for small plots on former plantations only to discover that falling cotton prices, advancing boll weevils, and sometimes unscrupulous owners and merchants provided no better life. Out of preference or under pressure, tenants often grew cotton because it was one of the few crops that could be marketed for cash. In this way their lot declined from that of the subsistence food producers of the antebellum years. As agricultural conditions worsened, ever larger numbers of yeoman farmers fell through the land tenure system into some form of tenancy: 36.2 percent of all southern farms were operated by tenants in 1880, 49.2 percent in 1920, 55.5 percent in 1930. Poor diet, ill health, and illiteracy doomed one generation after another to sharecropping.

The landless poor searching for a better life were often seduced by the allurements of the industrial South. Although white tenant farmers were vaguely aware that they shared their economic bondage with blacks, some of the new industrial jobs reinforced that knowledge. Many of the industries—notably lumber, iron and steel, and mining—employed a biracial work force in which the major distinction was the white man's pride of race.

Although the intent of employers was not necessarily to exploit workers or create rigid class distinctions, that was the effect of industrialization. Workers of both races lived in company houses, sent their children to company schools, purchased goods from company commissaries, and worshipped in company-built and company-subsidized churches. Newly arrived rural families placed little value on education, barely survived economically, and pressured their children into mines or mills where they often grew up stunted and illiterate. When supplies of free labor lagged, owners contracted with sympathetic state officials to lease convicts.

The notable exception to this new biracial world of lower-class workers was the textile industry. Although blacks held menial jobs as loaders or janitors, cotton mill operatives generally were white. Attracted by the advantages of lower transportation costs, cheap, nonunion labor, and abundant water and steam power, the textile industry moved rapidly south from New England between 1880 and 1930. In 1860 the South contained only 10,152 mill workers, but by 1890 there were 36,415, and by 1900, 110,015. Salaries in the 1890s in North Carolina averaged only 50 cents a day, and 70-hour work weeks were common. By 1900 the industry employed 25,000 children below the age of 15, most of them working in the states of Georgia, Alabama, and the Carolinas.

Child labor owed its existence to pressures both from the family and from industrial society. Farm parents relied heavily on child labor and often put little stock in formal education. Hence, when parents left the land for the mill village, they seldom hesitated to allow young children who chafed under the discipline of the local schoolteacher to enter mill employment. Although 90 percent of working children under 15 were employed in textile mills in 1900, increasing numbers worked in coal mines, glass factories, as Western Union boys, and in various other occupations. Their numbers had tripled in the decade between 1890 and 1900. Other regions shared the problem but none to the extent of the South, and from that region came early organization to abolish child labor. Unfortunately, many of the South's industrialists, though by no means all of them, opposed reform. They had become accustomed to the "family wage," a salary for the male head of family that was so low it required all family members to work. During the textile boom between 1900 and 1915 expansion of the industry required an enormous increase in labor, and much of this addition came from children under the age of 16. Industrialists claimed that children learned factory routine more easily, and their hands were quicker and more agile. Furthermore, idle children were troublesome children, and work at an early age bred habits of thrift and industry. The results frequently were illiteracy and cyclical poverty.

At first the urban middle class felt little threatened by the growth of this large white working class, even praising the conservative religious and family values that made rural Caucasians preferable to either newly arrived European immigrants or recently emancipated blacks. But as industrial conditions worsened and labor unrest increased, they began to view workers as a dangerous and disruptive element.

Organized Labor and Populism. Even though labor unions existed in the urban antebellum South, unionization had made little headway until after the Civil War. The first glimmer of the new direction of labor came in the years from 1873 to 1877 when freedmen, stereotyped as submissive, conducted a series of strikes. The Greenback-Labor party provided the framework for biracial unionization and political action. This early labor activity in the postbellum South was fundamentally different from such disruptions in other regions, not only because it involved a coalition of blacks and whites, which exposed the movement to charges of racial iconoclasm, but also because it was often sustained by a deeply religious perception that cast the conflict more in terms of striving for human justice and right than in Marxist-style confrontation of economic classes.

The failure of the Greenback-Labor party effort in the 1870s was the prelude to a long succession of disappointments for labor. Organizing efforts by the Knights of Labor beginning in 1885 recruited 45,000 members of both races and succeeded in controlling city governments in some southern cities, but these gains were wiped out by the depression of the 1890s.

Organization of farmers proved more immediately successful as the national depression multiplied agricultural problems in the 1880s and 1890s. The Farmers' Alliance at first sought to unite middle-class farmers into marketing collectives. However, rapidly escalating rural poverty carried many farmers further into radical agrarian politics. Primarily a movement of small farmers and rural professionals alarmed by their downward mobility and declining social status, the Populist party also attracted support from lower-class tenants and industrial workers. At the other end of the economic spectrum, prosperous farmers often deserted the Alliance when it moved into the political stage of Populism, frightened by its biracial political appeals and its quasi-socialistic demand for public ownership of railroads. Like the southern labor movement, Populism drew its vision of the impending apocalypse more from the Bible than from Marx or Proudhon. This was a distinctly southern brand of radicalism in which religion played a central role, even furnishing the vocabulary for public debates; Populists seldom used class terms, preferring instead words with moral connotations such as "robbed," "stolen," "injustice," and "evils." Religious imagery and Christian metaphors abounded.

Although Populism ultimately foundered upon a sea of criticism, white and black Populists seldom exceeded the prescribed limits of southern society. White Populists were willing to include blacks in common political efforts, but they were as opposed to racial equality as Democrats. Nonetheless, Populism was a landmark in southern history because it vigorously advocated economic justice for the lower middle class and for poor people of both races.

The demise of Populism forced many whites back into the Democratic party. Together with the return of middle-class farmers, who had left the Alliance earlier, these forces were strong enough to change the Democratic party, which previously had been dominated by large farmers and industrialists. Reform of party rules allowed a direct role for ordinary white voters but also restricted the franchise through the imposition of poll taxes and other strictures.

As a result of these changes, southern politics became democratized whether or not it became more liberal. The Socialist party briefly thrived in the remote farmlands of Oklahoma and Texas and in the cigar factories of Tampa and Key West. Within the increasingly class-conscious populations of mill towns and mining camps, angry voters joined poor rural farmers to elect racial demagogues who promised far more reform than they enacted. Except for the psychic good it did them to abuse the "better classes" symbolically by electing such men as Cole Blease, Sidney Catts, and Theodore Bilbo, they realized few improvements in their lives.

The poor established more enduring patterns in their efforts at unionization. The United Mine Workers conducted organizing drives that resulted in a number of strikes between 1900 and 1921. The Brotherhood of Timber Workers united some 35,000 white and black lumbermen and poor farmers in Louisiana and Texas during the same years. Most strikes were defeated by better organized and financed companies that usually had the support of the state press, the governor and state militia, farmers, and the urban middle class. Frustrated by their defeats, most whites left both unions.

The violence of these strikes alarmed the thriving middle class. Already aware of abuses and injustices thanks to the educational efforts of ministers, social workers, and reform-minded journalists, urban professionals and businessmen sought to slow class polarization. Winning allies from among enlightened businessmen who saw reform to be in their own best interest, this coalition backed political candidates who favored moderate reforms that did not substantially threaten existing class arrangements. Supported by a middle class acting from a variety of motives—economic self-interest, genuine religious and humanitarian concern for economic and social justice, desire for social control of the lower classes—these progressive politicians challenged the more demagogic representatives of poor whites as well as the conservative Bourbons who had dominated the years after Reconstruction. The most advanced reformers endorsed women's suffrage, built settlement houses, favored labor reform, and even organized an interracial movement designed to reduce racial tensions. Their hegemony temporarily broken, conservative landowners and industrialists waited for the reform mood to pass. Their wait was not long.

Sally Field in the title role in Norma Rae *(1978)*

Progressive-era reforms were moderate and often assisted businessmen as much as or more than workers. Disillusioned by the betrayal of politicians whom they elected, by the impotence of their labor unions, and by worsening agricultural and manufacturing conditions in the 1920s, poor whites often directed their frustrations at helpless blacks. The very reform mood that had brought modest progress for whites resulted in worsened conditions for blacks. The American Federation of Labor acquiesced in the exclusion of blacks for skilled jobs. Black workers, abandoned by organized labor and by their white coworkers, became understandably cynical. They desperately sought any jobs available, even if the work involved acting as strike breakers. Natural economic hostility between workers competing for the same jobs was compounded by racial animosity, making the years from 1880 to 1930 the most racially violent in American history. Lynchings, labor violence between strikers and "scabs," and pitched battles between whites and blacks spread across the region. The ideal of working-class solidarity became a mockery in a world where color of skin obscured all other considerations.

Impact of the Great Depression and the New Deal. The maelstrom of the Depression both heightened class divisions and introduced important new elements into southern life. The steady deterioration of agricultural conditions during the 1920s drove many blacks off the land and more and more whites into tenancy. During the 15 years from 1920 to 1935, the number of white tenant families increased by 300,000 while the number of black families in similar circumstances declined by 70,000. Of the South's 1,831,000 tenant families in 1935, nearly two-thirds were white. In Mississippi nearly half the state's total population lived as tenants. Layoffs, wage reductions, and stretchouts propelled textile workers and coal miners into a wave of strikes beginning in 1929. The most famous of these disruptions, the textile strike in Gastonia, N.C., and the miners' strike in Harlan County, Ky., involved Communist organizers and unions, to which workers turned when more conservative unions either deserted them or proved ineffectual. Such actions by white workers who were often among the most religious and traditional people in their communities constituted less a proletarian uprising than a desperate outburst against a society that neither understood nor very much cared for the plight of its lower class.

Although it made few converts, the Communist party established a southern headquarters in Birmingham and even published the *Southern Worker*. It dared to challenge the South's racial taboos by defending nine black boys unjustly accused of raping two white women on a train near Scottsboro, Ala. It also organized a small Sharecroppers Union among black tenants south of Birmingham and gained a foothold in the Mine, Mill, and Smelter Workers Union, which organized Birmingham area iron ore miners of both races.

In the Arkansas Delta H. L. Mitchell, J. R. Butler, and E. B. McKinney began the Southern Tenant Farmers' Union in 1934. A biracial union that enrolled both former white Klansmen and blacks, the STFU attracted national attention and challenged New Deal agricultural policies. Although New Deal reforms were well intentioned, powerful forces in the Farm Bureau, the state agricultural extension agencies, and the U.S. Department of Agriculture administered policies in such a way that most benefits went to landowners who were encouraged to reduce acreage and thereby dislocate thousands of tenants. The extent of such dislocation is uncertain, but early Roosevelt policies obviously did little to improve agricultural conditions among tenant farmers.

Rural rehabilitation through the Resettlement Administration provided temporary assistance, as did state relief administrations that created jobs for the unemployed. Some workers were hired to build new subsistence communities where hard-hit industrial workers could farm small plots and live in decent housing.

The boldest New Deal initiative came in 1937 with the passage of the Bankhead-Jones Farm Tenancy Act. Delayed for two years by Roosevelt's ambivalence and emasculated by intensive conservative opposition, the act provided modest loans to tenants for equipment and seeds. Unfortunately, the most visionary element, federal loans to tenants so they could purchase their own land, was so underfunded and selectively administered that only the most successful, responsible, and promising tenants received loans. Among the millions of southern tenants, only a tiny fraction received land purchase loans, and in the 1940s even this modest effort was destroyed by a conservative Congress.

Other attempts to help were more successful. An internal division within the labor movement and a national administration sympathetic to organized labor created new opportunities for workers. Already aided by New Deal minimum wage legislation, southern workers drew the attention of the Congress of Industrial Organizations (CIO). The CIO attempted to organize all workers within an industry rather than dividing them according to crafts or skills. Its commitment to biracial unions and flirtation with left-wing politics caused middle- and upper-class southerners to brand it a Communist threat to southern institutions. It sent organizers south and trained southern workers, especially at the Highlander Folk School in Tennessee. The result was fierce and often violent struggles to organize Birmingham iron and steel workers, rubber workers in Gadsden, Ala., and textile operatives across the South. Thanks to national publicity and timely help from the federal government, some of these efforts were successful, though the attempt to organize the textile industry was a notable exception.

The descent of many middle-class people into poverty provided tenant farmers and industrial workers with welcome allies. People who had never before faced real want suddenly found themselves quite as helpless as the poorest sharecropper, without job, food, or home. The New Deal provided employment, and frightened middle-class folk joined their impoverished neighbors to elect New Deal congressmen. Conservatives retained enough power to make southern congressmen the least loyal of Democrats to the New Deal, but FDR found the general population of no other region of America more receptive to his programs. Downplaying race and emphasizing economic reforms for all, Roosevelt won the South's affection.

Support for Roosevelt and the New Deal brought together liberals from throughout the region. Liberals, including CIO organizers, state Democratic leaders, social workers, ministers, college professors, and reform journalists, tried to solidify their gains through organizations such as the Southern Conference on Human Welfare. New Democratic leaders, often with strong religious backgrounds, such as Olin Johnson in South Carolina, Brooks Hays in Arkansas and Hugo Black in Alabama, combined white and black, middle- and lower-class support to win office. Unlike earlier candidates elected by poor whites, these men actually advocated significant reform programs in state houses and in Congress.

Impact of World War II. Due both to reforms and to the location of military bases and war industry in the South between 1940 and 1945, unprecedented changes swept through the region. The rate of tenancy, especially among whites, declined as industrial jobs lured tenants off the land. Union strength and federal law raised industrial wages to the point that coal miners and steel workers earned more than schoolteachers and could no longer be categorized as poor whites. Increasingly comfortable in lower-middle-class suburbs or in their own houses

Mechanic at work, Knoxville, Tenn., 1943

newly purchased from mine or mill, they soon forgot about the people left behind. When black outrage erupted among returning Negro servicemen encountering the old racial barriers, such people often became the worst and most violent opponents of change. Shrewd conservative leaders from affluent backgrounds did nothing to prevent such conflict and often fueled it, dividing unions along racial lines and defeating liberal politicians by shackling them with charges of "nigger lovers" or "communists."

Turmoil also occurred within the black community. Older, traditional black elites had coexisted with racism in uneasy but practical compromise. Conservative, upper-class whites had tried to restrain lower-class violence, and blacks had sought economic opportunity without threatening to disturb social inequality. But the small black middle class of teachers, ministers, businessmen, and small-farm owners was swept aside by angry urban residents. The most liberal of the older professional classes, especially ministers, teachers, and labor leaders, provided articulate and courageous leadership, and the modern civil rights movement was born.

Threatened as it was by the aspirations of blacks, the white lower middle class reacted stridently. Rallying to the leadership of conservative politicians who threatened to close integrated public schools or interpose the state between white citizens and unpopular Supreme Court rulings, it posed a primary barrier to implementation of desegregation. As the years passed and black boycotts of businesses and passive disobedience disrupted one community after another, many merchants, newspaper publishers, and business leaders bowed to the inevitable and accepted black demands. But this only unleashed some poor and lower-middle-class whites to a frenzy of violence.

They accepted the leadership of conservative business people when it was available, but angry white workers found their favorite spokesman in the self-proclaimed populist, George C. Wallace of Alabama. Combining a frankly racist rhetoric with a prounion advocacy of the "little man," Wallace proved to be the shrewdest and most enduring southern politician since Louisiana's Huey Long. Although repudiated by AFL-CIO leadership, Wallace remained popular among the white rank and file, especially in the building trades. Capable of changing positions according to altered circumstances, he even survived the racist politics of the 1960s and 1970s, and won the governorship of Alabama in 1982 by class appeals to a biracial constituency of black and white workers and farmers in a state with the nation's second highest rate of unemployment.

Nearly forgotten in the giddy affluence of the war years and after was another South that profited little from the currents of change sweeping south of the Potomac. The mountains of Appalachia proved too stout and high a barrier. Of course changes did occur, particularly in the valleys of the Tennessee River watershed where government dams and cheap power fueled an economic miracle. But higher in the mountains and up the remote hollows poverty persisted. Among a people of immense pride, independence, fierce family loyalty, fatalism, and rich cultural heritage, the new era intensified problems. Technological change in the coal mining industry cost the region 265,000 jobs in just nine years between 1950 and 1959. In some eastern Kentucky counties three of every four miners lost their jobs. In the entire Appalachian region more than 600,000 jobs were lost in mining and farming during this one decade. Internal migration seemed the only solution, and more than 2 million people left the southern highlands for industrial cities between 1940 and 1970. There they carved out ethnic enclaves, established their own storefront churches, and retained their distinctive culture. Stereotyped by local media and citizens, they suffered as badly at the hands of blatant bigots or misguided reformers as blacks had before them. Cynical and bitter, longing for old places and ways, they persisted in their subculture with rare tenacity.

Whatever their woes, migrants were better off than the folks they left behind. Within 340 Appalachian counties in 1960, one of every three families lived on an annual income of less than $3,000; of those over 25 years of age, only 32 of 100 had finished high school. In Kentucky 20 percent of the population was eligible for surplus federal food.

The Appalachian Development Program, the Job Corps, and President Lyndon B. Johnson's War on Poverty made some progress toward resolving the South's enduring poverty. At first middle-class southerners provided lukewarm support for such initiatives, though even this reservoir of good will began to run thin as escalating expenditures and black participation cost the Kennedy-Johnson programs many white allies.

Paradoxically, the success of federal programs and private economic investment swelled the middle and upper classes and reduced concern for the people who remained behind. Even status-conscious, upwardly mobile blacks tended to desert old neighborhoods, churches, and institutions in search of newer and more prestigious environments. For those trapped down the lonely dirt roads or in the urban shacks, life still seemed hard indeed.

See also AGRICULTURE: Sharecropping and Tenancy; / Communal Farms; BLACK LIFE: / Commission on Interracial Cooperation; EDUCATION: Politics of Education; / Berea College; Commonwealth College; HISTORY AND MANNERS: Great Depression; New Deal; Populism; / Byrd, William, II; INDUSTRY: Industrialization and Change; LAW: / Black, Hugo; LITERATURE: / Longstreet, Augustus Baldwin; MUSIC: Protest; MYTHIC SOUTH: Plantation Myth; / "Moonlight-and-Magnolias" Myth; Poor Whites; POLITICS articles; RELIGION: / Hays, Brooks; URBANIZATION: Urban Poor; VIOLENCE: Harlan County, Kentucky; Industrial Violence

J. Wayne Flynt
Auburn University

Fred A. Bailey, *Class and Tennessee's Confederate Generation* (1987); F. N. Boney, *Southerners All* (1984); James C. Cobb, *Industrialization and Southern Society, 1877–1984* (1984); Robert Coles, *Migrants, Sharecroppers, Mountaineers* (1971); Allison Davis, Burleigh Gardner, and Mary Gardner, *Deep South: A Social Anthropological Study of Caste and Class* (1941); John Dollard, *Caste and Class in a Southern Town* (1937); Anthony P.

Dunbar, *Against the Grain: Southern Radicals and Prophets, 1929–1959* (1981); J. Wayne Flynt, *Dixie's Forgotten People: The South's Poor Whites* (1979); Eugene D. Genovese, *The Political Economy of Slavery: Studies in the Economy and Society of the Slave South* (1965); Margaret J. Hagood, *Mothers of the South: Portraiture of the White Tenant Farm Woman* (1939); Daniel R. Hundley, *Social Relations in Our Southern States* (1860); Edward Magdol and Jon L. Wakelyn, *The Southern Common People: Studies in Nineteenth-Century Social History* (1980); Jay Mandle, *The Roots of Black Poverty: The Southern Plantation after the Civil War* (1978); F. Ray Marshall, *Labor in the South* (1967); Marc Miller, ed., *Working Lives: The Southern Exposure History of Labor in the South* (1980); Roger L. Ransom and E. Richard Sutch, *One Kind of Freedom: The Economic Consequences of Emancipation* (1977); John Shelton Reed, *Southern Folk, Plain and Fancy: Native White Social Types* (1986); Leonard Reissman, *Class in American Society* (1959); Robert E. Shalhope, *Journal of Southern History* (November 1971); Tom E. Terrill and Jerrold Hirsch, eds., *Such As Us: Southern Voices of the Thirties* (1978); Jonathan M. Wiener, *American Historical Review* (October 1979), *Social Origins of the New South: Alabama, 1860–1885* (1978).

Appalachia, Exploitation of

In 1884 the West Virginia Tax Commission warned that outside capitalists were rapidly acquiring the state's land. If the process was not halted, the commission charged, West Virginia would "pass into the hands of persons who do not live here and care nothing for our State except to pocket the treasures which lie buried in our hills," and with the state "despoiled of her wealth," the people would be left "poor, helpless, and destitute."

The process was not stopped. By 1900 absentee landowners controlled 90 percent of Mingo, Logan, and Wayne counties in West Virginia. By 1923 nonresidents of West Virginia owned more than half of the state and controlled four-fifths of its total value.

What happened in West Virginia was symptomatic of the Appalachian region. A 1982 survey of 80 Appalachian counties revealed that three-fourths of the surface areas and four-fifths of the region's minerals are absentee-owned. Fifty-three percent of the land and 70 percent of the mineral rights are held by the federal government and by corporations—mostly timber, coal, and other energy companies.

Absentee landownership has spelled a century of exploitation of Appalachia. The monopolization of the land and resources, for example, has weakened the material basis upon which farmers and independent commodity producers operated. By excluding other industries from the area, monopolies have prevented economic diversification, thus rendering the local economies and people liable to the pitfalls of a single industry. The economies of the coal regions of Appalachia fluctuate according to a rise or fall in the coal market; from the rise of petroleum and natural gas industries in the 1920s to the energy shortage of the 1970s, the coal market was one protracted bust, which meant massive unemployment and poverty for large segments of Appalachia. The tourist industry in western Virginia and North Carolina has produced underemployment, low wages, and seasonal employment.

Absentee ownership has polarized the people of Appalachia into those who own the land and those who labor in the logging or mining industries. Having little stake or interest in the land other than the wealth it contains, absentee coal companies have strip-mined it, laying waste to farmland, homes, and hills. In western North Carolina and Virginia tourism has led to a decline in land available for farming; consequently small farms, once of cultural as well as economic importance to Appalachia, have given way to national parks and the damming and flooding of rivers for recreational spots. In Alabama, some lumber companies gained land during Depression-era court-ordered sales, cut down the trees, and then moved to the Northwest, leaving behind ghost towns, exhausted forests, and devastated environments.

Colonial exploitation deprives Appalachians of the wealth that their land contains and that they produce, thus creating the irony of poverty amidst the region's riches. By use of the company-town system and later by establishing a political hegemony over the region (especially in the states of Kentucky and West Virginia), coal owners have maintained a colonial rule. Coal companies have used political clout to prevent the states from imposing much-needed severence taxes (a few states have token ones) and to ensure low property tax rates. Consequently, although Appalachian states are wealthy in resources, they lack locally available capital, adequate infrastructure, and access to the best lands; and there is a lack of income for goods and services. Quality health care, for example, is absent in Appalachia, as is quality education. Kentucky, one of the wealthiest states in the nation in minerals, has the highest high school dropout rate in the nation, a fact largely attributable to its inferior educational facilities. Walker County, Ala., the largest coal-producing county in the state, is periodically forced to borrow money to open its schools.

To be sure, the exploitation of the region has involved local elites working in conjunction with absentee landowners. The building of Shenandoah National Park (dedicated in 1936) pitted the desires of local but nonresident middle- and upper-class entrepreneurs and politicians anxious to promote tourism in the area against the cultural and subsistent needs of a resident, rural population that held the land in private domain. The landowners lost as the elite persuaded the federal government to issue a blanket condemnation and forcibly remove the residents; the Park Service and Civilian Conservation Corps razed their houses.

Americans have responded to the Appalachians' plight with neglect or humor. Television has derided Appalachians in programs such as *The Beverly Hillbillies*. Americans, in general, have dehumanized them with pejorative labels like "hillbillies" and "yesterday's people." In more benevolent yet still condescending moods Americans have attempted to "uplift" Appalachians with missionaries, VISTA workers, and other social redeemers.

In the 1960s the federal government established the Appalachian Regional Commission to solve the region's woes. The commission, however, ignored the absentee-landowner problem as it embarked upon a "prodevelopment" strategy of building roads, supposedly to encourage tourism and industry in Appalachia. Instead, the commission's road building helped depopulate the region, leaving it more open to corporate exploitation.

Appalachians have responded in various ways to colonial exploitation. Some acquiesced with a numbing sense of powerlessness. From the 1920s through the 1940s thousands migrated to Midwest urban-industrial centers such as Chicago, Dayton, Detroit, and Akron. Other Appalachians resisted in a century-long struggle. Labor-management relations in Appalachian coalfields have produced the most intense industrial warfare in American history. "Bloody Harlan," "Bloody Mingo," the "Matewan Massacre," the "Armed March on Logan," the "Black Lung Rebellion" are coalfield struggles that should forever haunt the memories of Americans. The willingness of Appalachian miners to deprive the nation of its energy even during wartime, as in the World War II coal strike, and for lengthy periods as in the 111-day 1977–78 coal strike, which severely disrupted the nation's economy, have caused even non-Marxists to ponder the existence of a class struggle in the Appalachian coalfields.

The miners' struggles are dramatic and visible, but they are not the only episodes of Appalachian militancy. The region's textile and lumber towns have witnessed a century of intense labor strife. Appalachian poor organized and protested their plight, and in November 1971 poverty and welfare rights organizations staged a "March for Survival" in Washington, D.C. During the 1960s and 1970s the so-called anti-strip-mining guerrillas took direct action to prevent their land and homes from being bulldozed. In one year alone more than $2 million worth of strip-mining equipment was dynamited.

In recent decades writers, scholars, and others have added an intellectual dimension to the struggle. Pushing aside the old-time mountain patriarchs who accepted both the plight of Appalachia and the stereotypes of Appalachians, the new Appalachian intellectuals are helping to transform the occupational class consciousness of the workers into a regional identity. Regional publications such as *Mountain Life and Work* and *Mountain Eagle* have exposed corporate abuse of the region's land and people. Educational and cultural institutions such as the Highlander Center in Tennessee, the Appalachian Folklife Center in West Virginia, Appalshop in Kentucky, and the Appalachian centers in the region's colleges and universities are researching the Appalachian past and present, writing about its rich history and culture, and thus promoting pride and confidence in being Appalachian.

See also BLACK LIFE: Appalachians, Black; EDUCATION: / *Foxfire*; ENVIRONMENT: / Appalachian Coal Region; Appalachian Mountains; ETHNIC LIFE: / Appalachians; FOLKLIFE: "Hillbilly" Image; INDUSTRY: / Mining; Timber Industry; MYTHIC SOUTH: Appalachian Culture; / Appalachian Myth; RELIGION: Appalachian Religion; VIOLENCE: Harlan County, Kentucky; WOMEN'S LIFE: Appalachian Women

David A. Corbin
Washington, D.C.

Appalachian Land Ownership Task Force, *Who Owns Appalachia? Landownership and Its Impact* (1983); David A. Corbin, *Life, Work, and Rebellion in the Coal Fields: Southern West Virginia Miners, 1880–1922* (1981); Ronald D. Eller, *Miners, Millhands, and Mountaineers: The Modernization of the Appalachian South, 1880–1930* (1982); John Gaventa, *Power and Powerlessness: Quiescence and Rebellion in an Appalachian Valley* (1980); Helen Lewis, L. Johnson, and D. Askins, *Colonialism in Modern America: The Appalachian Case* (1978); Charles Perdue and Nancy Martia-Perdue, *Appalachian Journal* (Winter 1979–80); David E. Whisnant, *All That Is Native and Fine: The Politics of Culture in an American Region* (1983), *Modernizing the Mountaineer: People, Power, and Planning in Appalachia* (1980).

Aristocracy

Throughout the American experience no group has retained a more unique or enduring image than the southern aristocracy. Still powerful is the *Gone with the Wind* view of dashing gentlemen and spirited ladies—the nation's first "beautiful people"—rushing bravely but foolishly into the holocaust of the Civil War. In recent times a gothic, even grotesque, image surfaces persistently, too. Its roots run back to the abolition crusade, but modern works like *Mandingo* further dramatize a world of miscegenation, incest, violence, and general degeneracy. For three centuries the southern aristocrat has stood tall. Different, and seldom dull, he is often admired as a maverick within an increasingly uniform, middle-class, capitalistic culture.

Southern aristocrats evolved among the Tidewater settlements in Maryland, Virginia, and the Carolinas early in the colonial period. Generally they were a home-grown lot unrelated to the old aristocracy of Europe. Among this early elite were merchants as well as planters, but gradually, when white settlement rolled westward, men of wealth concentrated on staple crop agriculture, especially cotton in the Deep South. Other Americans made money in agriculture, too, and some of the southern elite pursued commercial and industrial profits in the antebellum period—for example, Mary Ann Todd, the southern belle wife of Abraham Lincoln, came from an aristocratic Kentucky family that made its money mainly in banking.

But the South remained predominantly agricultural as the Civil War approached while the North developed a more diversified economy with much industry. The Old South's emphasis—many said overemphasis—on market crops like cotton, rice, tobacco, hemp, and sugar made a difference, but what really set apart the South and its upper class from the rest of the nation was slavery.

While slavery was fading away in most of the rest of the Western world as the 19th century unfolded, it became an increasingly essential part of the Old South. Slave workers produced the profits of the southern aristocracy, and even the masses of southern whites who owned no slaves at all supported the "peculiar institution" as a means of keeping blacks subordinate.

The southern system based on slavery seemed increasingly "peculiar" to the North, and the Civil War loomed on the horizon. Yet in many ways leading southerners, great planters with 50 or even 100 or more slaves, were not as different as they seemed. Dueling faded away more slowly among them than among the northern elite, but such phenomena as race and class consciousness and conspicuous consumption were similar in both upper classes. Like their northern counterparts, elite southerners operated in a very competitive economy based upon bourgeois concepts of private property and free enterprise. As in the North, able, industrious (and lucky) southerners prospered, and in both sections wealth could vanish as rapidly as it had appeared. Bright, aggressive young men like Andrew Jackson, John C. Calhoun, or Henry Clay could work or marry their way into the upper class as readily in the South as in the North; nouveaux riches popped up fairly often in both sections.

Southern aristocrats moved about freely in the North. They often visited the best spots like Saratoga Springs, and they frequently sent their sons to northern schools like Princeton, Yale, and Harvard. Harvard dutifully memorialized her 136 sons who died to preserve the Union, but to this day she has never acknowledged her 64 sons who died for the southern Confederacy.

Slavery made the difference that led to war in 1861. The Confederacy chose Jefferson Davis to lead the great crusade, but, like many other southern aristocrats, he was the son of a dirt farmer. Indeed, the Davises and the Lincolns had lived less than 100 miles apart in frontier Kentucky, and both families were deeply rooted in the southern yeomanry. The Davises moved south to Mississippi and made a fortune in cotton; the Lincolns drifted north to a very different destiny.

The Civil War raged for four years before the South finally crumbled, yet out of this hideous slaughter the southern aristocracy's image emerged grander than ever. The rebel elite had fought well enough, but the real backbone of the Confederacy had been its redneck infantry (farmers like earlier generations of the Davises and the Lincolns) who slugged it out with a numerically superior enemy who were also farmers. Out of the agony of war and defeat rose the aristocratic figure of Robert E. Lee. No matter that his family had been on the economic skids for a generation, that he had no significant stake in slavery until he married into the wealthy Custis family, and that he had never been a planter but rather an officer in the American (Union) army for 32 years; Lee gave the South the hero it needed. More than a century after his death, the somber chapel at Washington and Lee University where he rests still transports the visitor back to a medieval world that never really existed in his native South.

The usual movement into and out of the elite class accelerated considerably after the Civil War, but many wealthy families managed to hold on to their money and status. Despite the optimism of New South spokesmen, the region remained mainly agrarian well into the 20th century, and various sharecropping systems kept many blacks and quite a few whites under the control of postbellum planters. Later, textile mill owners and operators exercised a similar hegemony and paternalism in regard to their employees. The southern aristocracy survived and continued to operate freely and confidently, subtly affecting American society. Through famous sons like Theodore Roosevelt and Douglas MacArthur, a few southern ladies influenced the highest levels of American life long before the nation was prepared to accept southern white male leadership again.

Even in recent decades, as the South has become more and more "Americanized," the influence of the southern aristocracy continues. Wealthy southerners today may sell Chevrolets (or Toyotas) instead of cotton, but they still rule the social roost. Family connections can still be helpful, but, as always, money is the deciding factor. Like many wealthy northerners who either settled in the South or built vacation retreats there, southern aristocrats enjoy great landed estates. Clearly, as long as America maintains a wealthy, visible elite, the southern aristocracy is secure.

F. N. Boney
University of Georgia

F. N. Boney, *Journal of Popular Culture* (Fall 1976), *Midwest Quarterly* (Spring 1974), *Southerners All* (1984); W. J. Cash, *The Mind of the South* (1941); Clement Eaton, *The Growth of Southern Civilization, 1790–1860* (1961); Jack Temple Kirby, *Media-Made Dixie: The South in the American Imagination* (1978); John Shelton Reed, *Southern Folk, Plain and Fancy: Native White Social Types* (1986); William R. Taylor, *Cavalier and Yankee: The Old South and American National Character* (1957).

Communism

Most scholars agree that the Communist party of the United States, despite inspiring much heated controversy, achieved at best only a minor impact on American political and social life. Because the American South lacked both a sizable foreign-born population and large concentrations of industrial workers, from whose ranks the party originally drew most of its members, it is not surprising that the Communist party gained fewer members and exerted less influence in the South than in other regions. Yet it would be an oversimplification to dismiss Communist influence entirely. During the 1930s and 1940s Communists were often in the vanguard of the fight against racism, and they occasionally provided assistance to the struggles of southern workers. A few native southerners even rose to positions of national influence within the party—Benjamin J. Davis of Georgia, Robert Minor of Texas, and James Jackson of Alabama, for example—but only after leaving the South. Eventually the Red Scare and government repression of the late 1940s and 1950s destroyed the party's modest gains in Dixie, just as they did elsewhere in the United States.

Founded in 1919, the Communist party appealed during its first decade mainly to residents of the industrial Northeast and Midwest. With the coming of the Great

Depression and the accompanying crisis of American capitalism, Communists expanded their activities into the South. The first major incident announcing this Communist presence was the famous 1929 textile strike in Gastonia, N.C. During an outbreak of anti-Communist hysteria and violence there, Fred Beal, an organizer for the Communist-dominated National Textile Workers Union, and several strike leaders were arrested and unjustly convicted, in an infamous trial, of the murder of the local police chief. In 1930 the party began publishing the *Southern Worker* and attempted to organize workers in Atlanta, Birmingham, Chattanooga, Tampa, and other industrial centers. In eastern Kentucky in 1931, the Communist-dominated National Miners Union briefly assisted miners in Harlan County, where brutal repression also destroyed the union. These growing activities, as well as the formation of Unemployed Councils in several cities, alerted southern conservatives to an alleged Communist "invasion" of the South and helped link communism and radical ideas with unions in the minds of many southerners.

Even more frightening than Communist overtures to miners and industrial workers, who were mostly white, were the party's attempts after 1929 to recruit black members. The party's Marxist slogans did not inspire much enthusiasm. Communists found instead that what earned respect from blacks were well-organized local protests against specific discriminatory treatment and uncompromising stands against injustice. Still, only a few black (or white) southerners formally joined the party in the 1930s, although many more were affiliated with so-called Communist front organizations. Thus the party's influence was more extensive than membership figures alone would suggest. The new developments that eventually made communism appear a frightening specter in the eyes of white southerners were primarily the activities and aggressive tactics used by the International Labor Defense, a Communist-front legal defense group. In Alabama's famous Scottsboro case in 1931, the ILD vigorously defended the nine black youths accused of raping two white women on a freight train in north Alabama and, along with Communist and non-Communist allies, soon gained international notoriety for the case, thereby dramatizing racism in the South. In 1932 the ILD also represented Angelo Herndon, a young black Communist accused of attempting "to incite insurrection" against the state of Georgia. These and other ILD defense campaigns temporarily gained access to black churches and community institutions for Communists, but the Communist party's extreme left orientation at the time and its rigid Marxist theory nullified these opportunities.

The Communist party also made several efforts to enlist rural workers, especially blacks. In east central Alabama, Communists helped establish the Sharecroppers Union, which attempted to defend the rights of black day laborers, sharecroppers, and tenants against white landlords. Violent clashes in 1931 and again in 1933 resulted in massive repression of the union, but it continued to function underground until later merging with the National Farmers Union.

Communists participated in most Congress of Industrial Organizations (CIO) labor organizing drives, and the party developed a small following in the Birmingham area within the United Steel Workers Union and the Mine, Mill, and Smeltėr Workers Union, primarily among black workers. In the late 1930s and early 1940s chapters of the National Negro Congress and the Southern Negro Youth Congress contained a few black Communists and additional sympathizers, for the party's aggressive attacks on white supremacy particularly appealed to many young black intellectuals. Although a handful of white Communists joined the Southern Conference for Human Welfare, they did not exert any significant influence in the group after 1941.

Following a brief hiatus during World War II, Communists renewed their overtures to industrial workers, blacks, and also veterans. Yet the new climate of opinion shaped by the Red Scare, Cold War, and government repression proved most inhospitable and in time shattered the party. The CIO's purge of left-wing unions and almost anyone accused of Communist sympathies destroyed the limited Communist influence in southern unions. For a few years the Civil Rights Congress, postwar heir to the ILD, generated considerable interest in several legal proceedings dramatizing continued injustice toward blacks, the most prominent of which were the cases of Willie McGee in Mississippi, Rosa Lee Ingram in Georgia, and the so-called Martinsville Seven in Virginia. Many black southerners and occasionally a few whites were concerned about these prosecutions and the apparent racial bias in the application of the death penalty, but the anti-Communist hysteria soon frightened them away from taking direct action.

Despite the virtual collapse of the Communist party in the South and the rest of the nation during the 1950s, a few tiny pockets of interest remained, primarily in Birmingham and Atlanta. In Greensboro, N.C., in 1979, five members of a small splinter group, the Communist Worker's party, which was active in the black community, were killed by alleged Klansmen and neo-Nazis, who were acquitted in 1984 of murder charges. Because of the elimination of the more obvious forms of racial discrimination in the South, the increased opportunities for venting black dissatisfaction through the political system, and the continued conservatism of many white workers, it seems unlikely that the future will bring any serious revival of interest in communism in the South.

See also LAW: / Herndon, Angelo, Case; Scottsboro Case; VIOLENCE: Harlan County, Kentucky

Charles H. Martin
University of Texas at El Paso

Dan T. Carter, *Scottsboro: A Tragedy of the American South* (1969); Angelo Herndon, *Let Me Live* (1937); Charles H. Martin, *The Angelo Herndon Case and Southern Justice* (1976); Nell Irvin Painter, *The Narrative of Hosea Hudson: His Life as a Negro Communist in the South* (1979); Theodore Rosengarten, *All God's Dangers: The Life of Nate Shaw* (1975).

Health, Worker

No concept of occupational health existed in the South or elsewhere in America until after 1910. "It is well known that there is no industrial hygiene in the United States," a Belgian labor expert told the International Congress on Occupational Accidents and Diseases in Brussels that year. In the next decade, however, widespread interest in social justice bore fruit in the recognition of hazards in the workplace. The U.S. Public Health Service was particularly active, and the South was the site of one of its early efforts.

The first disease associated with southern industry was pellagra, a dietary deficiency disease that affected not only southern mill workers but tenant farmers, sharecroppers, and the poor wherever they lived. It was a peculiar and often fatal malady, marking victims with a distinctive rash and sometimes leaving them insane. The disease lost much of its mystery when Dr. Joseph Goldberger of the U.S. Public Health Service proved that pellagra was caused by an inadequate diet, a product of both the peculiar dietary habits of the region and the poor economic conditions under which many southerners lived. The fatback, corn bread, and syrup diet consumed three times a day by tenant farmers and mill workers was a vestige of the frontier past when settlers depended on corn, pork, and cane for their food. Gripped by tradition, many southerners clung to this diet long after the frontier was gone. Their choice was reinforced by economic considerations. Wages, traditionally low in the southern mills, fell even lower in the fall of 1920, and Goldberger predicted a pellagra epidemic. In a brilliant epidemiological study of seven mill villages in South Carolina, Goldberger and his associates had already conclusively linked the incidence of pellagra to poor economic conditions. Irate defenders of the South denounced him and the PHS and refused all offers of aid. Despite their protests pellagra did increase throughout the 1920s and did not vanish until a quarter century later when scientists identified niacin as the missing factor in the diet. A greatly changed economy and an agricultural revolution made southern workers more prosperous and their diets more balanced.

The immediate hazards of the workplace were brought dramatically to the public's attention in the early 1930s by an incident at Gauley Bridge, W.Va. White and black laborers from mountain districts of the South were brought to West Virginia to dig a water-power tunnel through pure sandstone and quartz. The work began in 1929, and by the time it was completed three years later, 500 men had died of silicosis, pneumonia, and tuberculosis. Some dropped dead on the job and were buried within hours, sometimes two or three men in a single grave. Sensational compensation cases were tried in the courts, and Gauley Bridge became a symbol of danger on the job, particularly from dust.

As a result of this tragedy many commissions were formed to study the relationship of dust to health, though some of them may have been more concerned with forestalling massive claims than with improving working conditions. A survey of Virginia industries in 1938 showed that industrial officials believed that if their factories were free of silica dust, they were free of all occupational disease hazards; but as the Virginia study showed, more than a quarter million workers, or one-tenth of the population of the state, were employed in industries where occupational diseases were known to exist. The greatest number were exposed to dust of one sort or another, prolonged exposure to which caused trouble in the upper respiratory tract.

The number of southern workers who became ill as a result of industrial hazards was difficult to ascertain. By 1944 at least six southern states required physicians to report occupational diseases—Alabama, Arkansas, Georgia, Louisiana, Mississippi, and South Carolina—but this requirement did not provide a satisfactory method of getting statistics. The laws were not standardized nor was there any one agency in each state to whom physicians reported. In 1951, when four southern states participated in a pilot study to report occupational diseases, South Carolina found no cases of disease caused by dust in spite of its large textile industry. Nearly all states limited workmen's compensation claims to personal injury by accident, excluding occupational diseases altogether.

The first such disease to attract public attention was black lung, or pneumoconiosis, in the mid-1960s. A prevalence study showed that 1 of 10 miners working in the bituminous coal mines of Appalachia showed radiographic evidence of black lung, a disease marked by black spots on the lungs and greatly impaired breathing. One in five nonworking miners was affected. The study included miners in the southern states of Virginia, Tennessee, and Alabama and refuted the assumption that only miners of anthracite coal were subject to black lung. The disease probably had existed for many years before it became an issue. The danger that dust posed to health was increased with the introduction of mechanical loading equipment in the 1930s. These "man killers" greatly increased the dust level.

For 20 years the United Mine Workers promoted mechanization of the mines, believing that this would lead to higher wages and economic security, but the work force shrank steadily, and the dust, noise, and other hazards increased. The black lung revolt of 1968 was triggered by the refusal of the West Virginia Legislature to make the disease compensable under state law. A strike took 40,000 miners off the job, and a violent explosion in a Farmington, W.Va., mine killed 78 men, setting off a national political debate on black lung disease and resulting in the passage of the Coal Mine Health and Safety Act of 1969. This bill detailed mandatory work practices in the industry and provided compensation for victims of black lung and the widows of those who died from the disease. Activists among the miners contended that the ultimate cause of the disease was economic: mine owners did not spend enough to keep down the dust.

The increasing role of the federal government in protecting workers' health climaxed in the passage of the Occupational Safety and Health Act of 1970. A year later the first health standard was set, a temporary one for asbestos. This standard grew out of a long-range study of asbestos workers in Tyler, Tex., which showed that 39 percent of workers with more than 10 years employment in the company had asbestosis and that 30 percent of those workers who had massive exposure to asbestos fibers would develop cancer. The disclosures were so sensational that the Pittsburgh Corning Corporation, which owned the factory, closed it and buried most of the equipment.

Before the enactment of OSHA, the textile industry was barely aware of problems with cotton dust. Industrial air-conditioning improved the mill environment in the 1950s, but in the next decade speculation grew that raw cotton dust endangered workers' health. It was found to cause byssinosis, or brown lung disease, which is marked by chest tightness, shortness of breath, coughing, and wheezing. The disease begins with "Monday fever," when workers with long-term exposure to cotton dust fall ill every Monday. Later, symptoms last over several days, and finally the disease becomes chronic—the worker is disabled and the effects are irreversible. Industries responded to public pressure and stepped up the installation of dust-cleaning equipment in the 1970s. OSHA set standards for cotton dust exposure in 1978 that were upheld by the U.S. Supreme Court in 1981.

The manufacture of any new product may threaten workers' health. Viscose rayon plants in Virginia, North Carolina, and Tennessee were among those that changed their methods of manufacture in 1937 after it was found that workers were dangerously exposed to carbon disulphide, a poison that affects the central nervous system, causing paralysis in the legs or manic-depressive insanity. More recently, the increase in the number of available chemical compounds has multiplied the danger to workers. The kepone case in Hopewell, Va., in 1976 is illustrative. Workers making insecticides from kepone developed nervous disorders, bodily shakes, and sterility after exposure to the product. Waste from the plant, emptied into the James River, poisoned all the river valley and wiped out fishing there for years.

Labor unions have been important in the struggle for a safer workplace. The textile workers union forced OSHA to establish standards for cotton dust and called for programs of medical surveillance and wage retention for workers too sick to work in dusty areas. Their emphasis has been on forcing industry to modernize, not only to improve working conditions for labor but to make the companies economically viable in a competitive world.

The one constant in the effort to improve working conditions in the South and thus the health of the workers has been economics. From the fight against pellagra to the campaign against brown lung disease more than a half century later, economic factors have been primary. Workers pushed first for higher wages and later pressured industry to spend what was necessary to make the workplace safe.

See also SCIENCE AND MEDICINE: / Disease, Endemic

Elizabeth W. Etheridge
Longwood College

Daniel M. Berman, *Death on the Job: Occupational Health and Safety Struggles in the United States* (1978); Paul Brodeur, *Expendable Americans* (1974); Elizabeth W. Etheridge, *The Butterfly Caste: A Social History of Pellagra in the South* (1972); Joseph Goldberger, George A. Wheeler, Edgar Sydenstricker, and W. I. King, *A Study of Endemic Pellagra in Some Cotton-Mill Villages of South Carolina*, Hygienic Laboratory Bulletin No. 153 (1929); Joseph G. Montalvo, Jr., ed., *Cotton Dust: Controlling an Occupational Health Hazard*, American Chemical Society Symposium Series no. 189 (1982); George Rosin, *Preventive Medicine in the United States, 1900–1975: Trends and Interpretations* (1975); Barbara Ellen Smith, in *Health and Work under Capitalism: An International Perspective*, ed. Vincent Navarro and Daniel M. Berman (1983).

Labor, Organized

Despite the general belief that southern unions are either almost nonexistent or recent arrivals, labor organizations have a long history in the South (defined here as the Confederate states plus Kentucky and Oklahoma). They emerged here about as early as they did elsewhere in the country. Southerners played a major role in the founding of the International Typographical Union, the nation's oldest national union. Indeed, some of the country's strong international unions—like the International Association of Machinists, organized in Atlanta in 1888—were formed in the South. Southerners have played and continue to play important roles in the American labor movement, especially as international union presidents, vice presidents, and international representatives. AFL-CIO president Lane Kirkland, from South Carolina, leads the nation's largest labor federation.

The image of union weakness in the South is due to the well-publicized difficulties unions have had organizing noncraft workers, especially in the textile industry in the Piedmont. These experiences are not typical of the rest of the South, where unions have made more progress and are stronger. The relative weakness of unions among nonagricultural workers in the South, as compared with other areas of the country, is largely attributable to the nature and location of southern industries. Even so, during the 1960s and 1970s unions grew much faster in the South than they did in the rest of the country.

Traditional southern institutions—e.g., the government, the economic structure—have also impeded union growth. Although these institutions could accept the emergence of a nonpolitical craft-oriented movement of skilled white workers (or skilled blacks in segregated locals), they opposed the emergence of a more egalitarian political and economic movement among noncraft workers. This opposition was demonstrated during the late 19th century when efforts to unite black and white workers and farmers in the Knights of Labor failed because of the political and economic powerlessness of blacks and the economic powerlessness of low-income whites. With that failure, racial divisions and disfranchisement of blacks made it difficult for black and white low-income workers to unite before the 1930s.

Since World War II the South has undergone rapid industrialization and what some refer to as "the Americanization of Dixie." South/non-South per capita incomes started converging in the late 19th century with the onset of industrialization. The historical gap between the South's real per capita income and the rest of the country has almost been eliminated, especially for urban white southerners. These trends have eroded the political as well as the economic differences between the South and the rest of the nation. The South is even lumped in with the Southwest as the new "Sunbelt."

The changing character of labor and labor unions has followed this diminishing uniqueness of the South. Most industrial unions either entered the South for the first time or established their present bases during the New Deal period. The most successful was the United Mine Workers, which had support in the South during the 19th century, grew during World War I, was nearly eliminated in the antiunion period of the 1920s, but by 1935 had almost completely organized the southern coalfields. Tobacco, clothing, rubber, oil, automobile, and steel unions also revitalized or expanded their southern bases during this time, and efforts were even made by the Southern Tenant Farmers' Union to establish collective bargaining among the region's sharecroppers.

The greatest growth of southern union membership came during World War II, due to relatively full employment, rapid and stable economic growth, and the activities of the War Labor Board (WLB). The war not only increased total manufacturing in the South, but also changed its composition from the less unionized nondurables (which was two-thirds of total manufacturing before the war) to the more heavily unionized durables group—which made up 46 percent of total manufacturing employment in 1946.

The WLB's influence was due mainly to emergency conditions, which put a premium on the peaceful settlement of labor disputes. The National Labor Relations Board (NLRB), for example, has no power to compel companies to sign contracts after workers vote for the union. The WLB, by contrast, was backed by the armed forces—which took over and operated companies throughout the South when they defied the board's orders to sign contracts with unions. The WLB was especially important in strengthening unions in some industries such as oil, textiles, clothing, and food processing, which had started organizing before the war. Some unions, such as the oil and garment workers, were able to hold their memberships after the war, but the textile unions (in the South's leading industry) had greater difficulty when they had to win strikes to get contracts with intransigent companies. Increased union strength during the war energized antiunion political and business forces, and many southern states countered with antiunion legislation. Southerners were prominent in the passage of the Taft-Hartley Act (1947), which greatly restricted union activity.

Both the American Federation of Labor and the Congress of Industrial Organizations sought to counteract antiunion laws, hold their wartime gains, and organize the South's unorganized workers through campaigns launched in 1946. However, these campaigns were disappointments to both the AFL and the CIO, and labor subsequently suffered a number of important reverses in the South. These were not restricted to the weaker unions, but extended also to such union strongholds as construction, trucking, and coal mining.

Congress of Industrial Organizations pickets in Greensboro, Ga., 1941

An assessment of the sources of union strength and weakness in the South provides some insight into their future prospects. One of the most important forces affecting unions in the South is the strength of the American labor movement, which, except for cyclical fluctuations, has continued to grow absolutely since World War II but has declined relative to the total work force from about 35 percent in the 1950s and 1960s to about 25 percent in 1980. There are many reasons for this relative decline in union strength: employment has been shifting away from the heavily unionized areas of the Midwest and East into the less unionized Sunbelt; away from more heavily unionized black, male, blue-collar workers to less unionized white, female, service, and professional-technical jobs; and away from large, more heavily unionized urban plants into smaller, nonmetropolitan workplaces. Major forces behind these employment shifts have been technological changes, especially the information revolution, and the internationalization of the American economy.

Industrial union strength is closely related to oligopolies in the basic industries, which have been rendered obsolete by intensified international competition from the newly industrialized countries, especially Japan and other nations adopting the highly competitive Japanese management system and export-oriented industrial policies. Unions in the clothing industry became better organized during the 1930s and 1940s because they had highly concentrated geographic bases in the Northeast. Intensified competition from Third World countries and decentralization into the Sunbelt have eroded the strength of these unions. Indeed, a major problem for unions is their inability to match economic strength with multinational corporations (MNCs). The mobility of capital, and high and rising worldwide joblessness, give the MNCs tremendous bargaining advantages. Their superior information bases give the MNCs an important advantage in an internationalized information world.

Although unions probably have reflected their environments more than they have changed them, labor organizations have much more influence on southern political, social, and economic institutions today than they did in the 1950s. Unions as a whole did very little to change race relations in the South before World War II, but in the social ferment of the 1950s and 1960s, the AFL-CIO, the state federations, and some national industrial unions openly supported the more moderate civil rights leaders.

The unions also have challenged conservative domination of southern politics and have provided significant, and sometimes decisive, support for more progressive political candidates, as well as economic and protective legislation favorable to workers. Unions cannot be termed a decisive political force in the South generally, but their influence is very important in a number of states and has increased in all of them. When unions were relatively weak, they tended to reflect their environment; as they gain strength they will do more to change it.

Future union growth in the South will be determined primarily by the changing patterns of industry, and some expected employment changes are generally favorable for union growth. The composition of manufacturing employment is becoming increasingly diversified as the region industrializes. A smaller percentage of southern employment is concentrated in the older textile, tobacco, and lumber and wood products and a larger percentage in newer, better-organized industries. The main exceptions to these trends are the apparel and other finished textile products industries, which have increased rapidly in the South and are not very well organized.

Of the white-collar groups that are expected to continue to grow, the most likely to be organized are clerical and sales groups. The increasing political power of unions in the South has been and should continue to be beneficial to unions among teachers and state, county, and municipal workers. However, the reduction in government employment in the 1970s and 1980s has limited the growth of government employee unions.

Other trends favoring union growth include the following: (1) The migration of workers out of agriculture will help unions by reducing the supply of unskilled labor, and mechanization of farm work and improvement in the farm worker's income will reduce the tendency for farm workers to cross picket lines. (2) The prevailing ideology of the South may be changed with industrialization and become increasingly supportive of collective bargaining, though the prevailing attitude in most states today is still antiunion. (3) The unions' political power probably will grow because of increasing cooperation between unions and blacks (whose political power has increased greatly since the Civil Rights Act and the voter registration drives of 1965), reapportionment in favor of urban areas (where most blacks and most union members are located), the growth of a two-party system in the South, and the growing recognition by unions and workers that they cannot solve their problems in an internationalized information world through collective bargaining alone. (4) The attitudes of southern workers toward unions probably will change also as the region industrializes and their agricultural background recedes into history. In the long run workers probably will turn increasingly to labor organizations to represent their political and economic interests. (5) Pressures within the labor movement may strengthen southern organizing efforts. The unions' main motive will be the growing industrialization of the South and the consequent necessity to protect union conditions elsewhere. (6) Although the trend is very slow, increasing unionization is occurring among important white-collar workers, particularly government employees, and this trend will be accelerated by the unions' growing political power. (7) Inflation impedes union growth by lessening public support for unions and collective bargaining, but, by reducing real wages, inflation strengthens workers' desire to organize in order to catch up with rising inflation.

The trends that will make it more difficult for unions to organize include: (1) Plants tend to be located in smaller communities and rural areas. (2) Workers' homes are dispersed from areas near the plant gates, making it more difficult for union organizers to contact them. (3) Living standards are rising and patterns of living changing, which make the worker more responsive to family, community, and neighborhood influences. Other obstacles to organizing stem from rising educational levels, which make workers more questioning of both management and unions, requiring the latter to change their organizing techniques; technological changes, which increase employment in nonunion areas, small plants, and professional-technical occupations, increasing management's relative bargaining power and its ability to operate during strikes; and management's growing sophistication in avoiding unions when it wishes to.

The most important determinants of union memberships are likely to be those dramatic events, like wars and economic catastrophes, which cannot be predicted but could cause general increases in union membership throughout the region. Projections of membership trends relative to industries suggest that, although union membership in the South probably will continue to increase both absolutely and relative to the rest of the country, unions will have great difficulty bringing their membership up to the proportion of nonagricultural employment (29.4 percent in 1976) outside the region. To do this would require a doubling in southern membership, which would be very difficult in the near future. To do this would also require significant breakthroughs in the unionization of the textile, garment, and other low-wage manufacturing activities, and the service industries.

See also BLACK LIFE: Workers, Black

F. Ray Marshall
University of Texas at Austin

F. Ray Marshall, *Labor in the South* (1967), *The Negro Worker* (1967), *The Negro and Organized Labor* (1965); Marc Miller, ed., *Working Lives: The Southern Exposure History of Labor in the South* (1980); National War Labor Board, *Reports of the Fourth Regional War Labor Board* (1945); George D. Stamer,

Monthly Labor Review (June 1981); U.S. Congress, Joint Economic Committee, *Impact of the Federal Policies on the South*, 81st Congress, 1st Session (1949); U.S. Department of Labor, Bureau of Labor Statistics, *Labor in the South* (1946).

Lower Class, Literary

When aristocratic William Byrd II wrote his *History of the Dividing Line* in 1728, he described "the world where the inhabitants live . . . in North Carolina" as a "Lubberland." Proud of both his Virginia home and his affluent lifestyle, Byrd cataloged the deficiencies of North Carolinians, who would soon be known widely as "Tarheels." The characteristics Byrd listed would become the predictable ingredients in one of the most enduring and productive of all American literary stereotypes—the southern "poor white trash."

From the perspective of his Virginia home, Byrd blamed most North Carolina vices on the "felicity of the climate," which made growing food and finding meat too easy. He did notice that the "poor women" did all the work and therefore conceded in passing that there was a good deal of work to do. But generally, he revealed, the people were slothful; the men slept late, and then, upon rising, stretched and yawned for half an hour, after which they smoked their pipes and leaned upon their shabby fences. "Thus they loiter away their lives," Byrd concluded, "through aversion to labor." He dismissed them by assuming they had an inherent and ineradicable "disposition to laziness." The lazy lowlife everywhere meeting William Byrd's eye included widespread drunkenness, lawlessness, bad manners, incivility, and disrespect.

Once disseminated, Byrd's verbal portrait had the most profound effect on the American imagination and on southern literature in particular. Byrd portrayed a class of southern gentlemen who were unmistakably nonresidents of Lubberland. He also established the southern poor white man as a stock character in southern literature. Mark Twain, almost 150 years later, described him exactly as Byrd had, in the comic opening of *The Gilded Age*.

Out of this character developed the first literature that Americans felt was unique and indigenous. Although lowlife characters were described in the 19th century from Maine to California, the comic poor white tended to be placed in a southern locale. Thus, from the 1830s through the 1860s a body of comic stories and anecdotes came to be written and relished, capitalizing on some variety of southern clown. The most popular settings in which the comic poor were located in this southwestern frontier humor tradition were Deep South states: Georgia, Alabama, and Mississippi. These states could always be described as frontiers or backwoods, when tone demanded, because they could always be said to have backwoods, poor white characters populating them.

Even in the aftermath of Jacksonian democracy, writers creating such characters were encouraged because of the amusingly egalitarian outlook of the poor, the very air of underbred familiarity with which they treated their unrecognized superiors. Before the Civil War the most important writers creating lowlife southern rascals were Augustus Baldwin Longstreet, Johnson Jones Hooper, Thomas Bangs Thorpe, Henry Clay Lewis, Alexander G. McNutt, and George Washington Harris. Hooper's Simon Suggs, McNutt's Chunkey, and Harris's Sut Lovingood represented the southern lower-class mischief maker who lived lustily beyond the pale of social convention. He was never required to obey the rules and existed to explore the improprieties and their laughable consequences.

Thus, in the 19th century the southern lower-class clown became a national literary treasure: he allowed the release of the repressed; laughing at him exploded tensions and restored psychic balance. In the more defensive period of southern literature, after the Civil War and Reconstruction, his economic status was elevated slightly and his antics toned down a little. But as a poor but resilient farmer, he still furnished humor and allowed southern writers to imagine comic characters who were permitted to do and say more than most. His literary progeny thus evolved into several species of nationally recognized stereotypes: Mary Murfree's Tennessee mountaineer; Joel Chandler Harris's or Richard Malcolm Johnston's Georgia cracker; George Washington Cable's Louisiana Cajun. In this late 19th-century period, when such stereotypes were being differentiated under the standard of local color or regionalist writing, poor blacks were also described frequently and stereotypically. But they were separate. "Southern lowlife" was understood to mean either poor white trash or poor white, struggling upward.

With so much vitality embodied in one kind of literary character, 20th-century writers could not ignore the type. William Faulkner, Flannery O'Connor, Eudora Welty—the great southern comic talents of a more recent period—derive much of their most compelling humor from characters descended from 19th-century southern fiction. Faulkner's Anse Bundren and the Snopeses, Welty's Bonnie Dee Peacock and her robber bridegroom, O'Connor's Mr. Shortley and her lewd Bible salesman—all can be related directly to 19th-century, lower-class comic figures.

In the 20th century, however, fiction writers became more sympathetic to the proletariat. After the Gastonia textile mill strike in 1929, at least 10 different novelists based fiction on the plight of the poor southern textile worker. The most popular writer aiming for a political statement, Erskine Caldwell, seemed, however, to dwell most memorably on the sexual irregularities of which such poor were capable. Writers with other political axes to grind described the southern lower class sympathetically. Marjorie Kinnan Rawlings, for example, wrote warmly of Florida backwoods life. Shirley Ann Grau used the Cajuns of the Louisiana bayous and coastal islands. Reynolds Price has explored the emotional intricacies of lower-class life in North Carolina. But perhaps the most impassioned and poetic treatment of this class ever written remains James Agee and Walker Evans's masterful *Let Us Now Praise Famous Men*.

See also ETHNIC LIFE: Mountain Culture; FOLKLIFE: / "Hillbilly" Image; LITERATURE articles; MYTHIC SOUTH: / "Crackers"; Poor Whites

Merrill M. Skaggs
Drew University

John Q. Anderson, ed., *With the Bark On: Popular Humor of the Old South* (1967); Hennig Cohen and William B. Dillingham, eds., *Humor of the Old Southwest* (1964); Sylvia Jenkins Cook, *From Tobacco Road to Route 66: The Southern Poor White in Fiction* (1976); Shields McIlwaine, *The Southern Poor-White from Lubberland to Tobacco Road* (1939); Merrill M. Skaggs, *The Folk of Southern Fiction* (1972).

Marxist History

As a political and social ideology, Marxism has numbered fewer adherents in the South than in the rest of America. Only a handful of white or black southerners ever joined Marxist movements. But in recent years various scholars—historians, economists, sociologists—have used Marxian concepts in an interpretative framework designed to explain the southern past and present.

Few of the scholars who apply Marxist theory to the South could be called "orthodox" Marxists. The fundamental importance that classical Marxism applies to economic (material) forces, and the accompanying class struggle, has been modified or refined in various ways by those social scientists who have examined southern history from a Marxian perspective.

Marxist interpreters of the South have tended to focus on the 19th century. Herbert Aptheker, Eugene Genovese, and Raimondo Luraghi use Marxist theory to analyze the antebellum South and its labor system of racial slavery. Luraghi focuses his research on the Confederate South. W. E. B. Du Bois's pioneering book on Reconstruction (1935) interprets the period as a time of class as well as racial struggle. Recent books by Jay Mandle, Dwight Billings, and Jonathan Wiener use Marxist perspectives to examine economics and class relationships in the South during Reconstruction and beyond. Of these, only Mandle's work extends into the 20th century.

For their analysis of the antebellum plantation South, Luraghi and Genovese were influenced by the Italian Marxist theoretician Antonio Gramsci, who downplayed economic determinism and emphasized the role of cultural domination, or hegemony, by the ruling elite over the underclasses. Luraghi calls the planters a "seigneurial class" and describes the civilization of the Old South as patrician, paternalistic, and precapitalist—indeed, anticapitalist. Luraghi, however, says virtually nothing about the nonslaveholding white majority in southern society. Genovese would agree with some of Luraghi's assumptions, but he views "paternalism" in a more balanced way and devotes less attention to the planter's style of life. In an *Agricultural History* article (1975) Genovese wrestles with the problem of why the southern yeomanry (the nonslaveholding white majority) went against "its own apparent collective interests" by accepting planter hegemony. That question is also briefly dealt with in *Roll, Jordan, Roll.* Genovese asserts that although slavery as a system oppressed nonslaveowners, it did so in a disguised way, whereas the paternalistic spirit that animated the planter's world was extended toward poorer whites in such adroit ways as to minimize class conflict. The slaves responded to paternalism, Genovese suggests, by simultaneous accommodation and resistance; in order to keep peace, slaveowners made informal concessions that allowed slaves some measure of human dignity. But as a Marxist, Genovese maintains that paternalism, wherever it exists, "undermines solidarity among the oppressed" by linking them to their oppressors. Presumably this would apply to the poor whites as well as blacks. Emancipation, however, "meant the end of paternalism as the reigning Southern ideal of social relations," although Genovese adds that paternalism did not totally disappear in the South after 1865.

The most explicitly Marxist analysis of the postwar South is that of Jay Mandle (1978). Mandle asks "what in the historical experience of the black population of the United States is responsible for the deprivation which currently exists?" He seeks the answer in examining "the mode of production," by which he means not only the technology and labor force of the southern economy, but also the power relationships that are established between employers and workers. Mandle concludes that through the devices of sharecropping and tenancy the plantation system was able to survive emancipation; indirect means of labor control replaced the more rigid system of slavery. For blacks, poverty remained the norm, landownership was virtually impossible, and occupational mobility minimal. The grip of the plantation system did not really loosen in the South until World War II. Although the old plantation mode of production has now virtually disappeared, its legacy of poverty for blacks largely remains.

Dwight Billings (1979) deals with North Carolina from 1865 to 1900, and Jonathan Wiener (1978) focuses upon Alabama from 1860 to 1885; yet both their books have implications for the entire South in the late 19th century. Billings concludes that although conservative Democrats controlled North Carolina politics after Reconstruction, their domination was never secure until 1900. He questions North Carolina's reputation as the most progressive of southern states, asserting that the state's leadership continued to work toward reactionary objectives during the late 1800s. The old planter elite simply became the new planter-industrial elite, with the same repressive attitudes toward the labor force.

Wiener's book on Alabama forcefully argues that the old planter elite kept control of the state's economy even during Reconstruction, making fewer concessions to business or industry than was the case in North Carolina. After emancipation, planters and exslaves worked out a reluctant compromise: the blacks, who wanted landownership, had to settle for sharecropping as a better alternative to the gang labor system preferred by planters. But this fragmentation of productive units, Wiener concludes, represented a move away from efficient, cost-intensive agriculture, which would have raised production through improved technology. Instead, planters obtained their profits by passing state laws that gradually (through debt peonage) squeezed more from the laborers. Using a phrase of Barrington Moore's, Wiener concludes that Alabama planters used "the Prussian Road" to modern society. Wiener defines this as "economic development that preserves and intensifies the authoritarian and repressive elements of traditional social relations." But Wiener adds that planter hegemony began to fade toward the end of the 19th century; in Alabama, as elsewhere, the system was increasingly anachronistic in a nation being transformed by bourgeois capitalism.

See also INDUSTRY: Industrialization and Change

William I. Hair
Georgia College

Herbert Aptheker, *American Negro Slave Revolts* (1943); Dwight B. Billings, *Planters and the Making of a "New South": Class, Politics, and Development in North Carolina, 1865–1900* (1979); W. E. B. Du Bois, *Black Reconstruction in America* (1935); Eugene D. Genovese, *Agricultural History* (April 1975), *In Red and Black: Marxist Explorations in Southern and Afro-American History* (1971), *Roll, Jordan, Roll: The World the Slaves Made* (1974); Raimondo Luraghi, *Rise and Fall of the Plantation South* (1978); Jay Mandle, *The Roots of Black Poverty: The Southern Plantation Economy after the Civil War* (1978); Jonathan M. Wiener, *Social Origins of the New South: Alabama, 1860–1885* (1978).

Middle Class

A large, fluid middle class has long dominated America, and the South has shared in this trend, which developed so much more powerfully than in Europe. Southern colonists came mostly from the lower orders of British society with a strong dash of middle-class types, but the New World along the North American coast offered something really new—cheap land weakly held by aboriginal tribes. America was truly the land of opportunity for ordinary emigrants from Europe.

The fertile soil and long growing season in the South gave a special boost to the average farmer who could own his own land, raise subsistence and money crops, and generally do well for himself and his family by hard work—and a little luck with the weather and the market prices of his crops. In many respects he was far better off than his counterpart in Europe. By the time of the American Revolution such farmers, North and South, were relentlessly driving the Indians westward.

The successful rebellion against the British Empire ushered in the world's most exuberant bourgeois democracy, and in the South herrenvolk democracy (for whites and males only) flourished as an integral part of this new order. By the 1840s the new nation had reached the Pacific Ocean, and the increasingly restive South stretched all the way from Virginia to Texas. The southern lower classes were composed of masses of black slaves (owned by a minority of whites) and a much smaller conglomeration of poor whites. At the top of the heap stood the wealthy planters with their gangs of slave laborers, but this agrarian elite composed only a tiny proportion of the white population. In the broad middle was the same sprawling, fluid middle class that dominated the North.

The majority of the southern bourgeoisie owned no slaves at all, and the minority who did owned only a few—generally a white family owning and working alongside a black family. By the eve of the Civil War southern society had matured, and the middle class had become quite complex and diversified. Though many scholars see the middle class as limited in any society to commercial, industrial, and professional people, the antebellum southern middle class was composed primarily of farmers.

Trying to explain his native Southland to a rather puzzled North in the 1860s, Daniel R. Hundley noted that, "the middle classes of the South constitute the greater proportion of her citizens, and are likewise the most useful members of her society. . . . There are among them farmers, planters, traders, storekeepers, artisans, mechanics, a few manufacturers, a goodly number of country school-teachers, and a host of half-fledged country lawyers and doctors, parsons, and the like." Significantly, Hundley included "planters," for most of them, even the so-called aristocrats, had bourgeois attitudes about striving and succeeding in a competitive, capitalistic economy. Hundley felt that planters with some slaves bore "a striking similarity" to prosperous New England farmers and that southern village storekeepers differed "but little" from their northern counterparts. He was especially impressed with middle-class southern women, who generally practiced the old-fashioned art of being the wife and mother, and, as he put it, lived "only to make home happy." Overall, he saw the southern middle class as proud, hospitable, generous, and straightforward; but he decried limited formal education, provincialism, religious bigotry, a pronounced lack of deference, and an abundance of self-confidence. In his view too many southern bourgeois types acted as if they carried "the world in a little private sling" and had all the answers. Grudgingly, Hundley conceded that "intermarriage" with the middle class had diluted his own elite class.

Despite his biases, Hundley drew a basically accurate picture of the dominant southern bourgeoisie. Hardworking, family-oriented folk, they led respectable lives. Generally they obeyed the law, owned property, paid taxes, and attended church (usually an evangelical sect that championed the traditional American work ethic). They remained mobile in order to exploit land that was incredibly cheap by world standards, and a steady trickle continued to filter up into the planter class (and down into the poor white ranks) within a flexible white socioeconomic system. They supported extensive educational efforts that brought functional literacy to a high percentage of citizens (higher than in Britain or France) and firmly held to their belief in progress.

The Civil War brought disaster to the Confederate South. Amidst the chaos of defeat, slavery vanished forever, but the middle-class white society that formed so powerfully in the antebellum era survived the holocaust. Indeed, blacks had felt its influence even as debased slaves, and now as freedmen they sought its fruits: property ("forty acres and a mule"), education, and equality. Leaders like Frederick Douglass and Booker T. Washington who had been shaped in slavery championed the old-fashioned American work ethic and counseled their people to strive and to succeed within the traditional middle-class system. Some blacks, playing by the old rules, made progress. White America, however, was not ready to concede full black equality: in the North, where few blacks lived, whites lost interest in the great crusade called Reconstruction; and in the South, where blacks remained concentrated, whites actively undermined it. Soon most southern blacks found themselves trapped in the sharecropping system or other forms of manual labor, condemned to more generations of discrimination and poverty. Many whites slipped into sharecropping, too, as southern agriculture suffered a long slump after the Civil War.

A middle-class Tennessee couple on vacation, c. 1960

The southern middle class shrank in these prolonged hard times, but it did not disintegrate. Just as important, its optimistic, industrious spirit survived, just waiting for better times to return. Since the post–World War II era the southern middle class has expanded rapidly. The civil rights crusade of the 1960s, a renewal of the first great crusade called Reconstruction, brought many blacks into the southern and American middle class at last. Many women, black and white, have independently achieved middle-class status through educational attainment and pursuit of careers. The old southern bourgeoisie Hundley described in the 1860s has become much more complex and diversified and has generally moved from the country into the growing cities and suburbs and from the farm into office buildings and stores.

Southern cultural imagery in earlier times did not do justice to the middle class. The region's mythology portrayed the white population of the South as either wealthy planters or poor white trash. Middle-class southerners now appear, though, as representatives of the new cultural ideal. They work in white-collar jobs; the South added over 300,000 professional and managerial positions to the middle class each year in the early 1980s. This upper middle class is prosperous, well educated, and well traveled; it is conservative on economic and political issues but increasingly liberal on social issues; and it seems to have a well developed sense of its southern identity. This transformation has been an extension and expansion of that middle-class system that emerged in the South and the rest of the nation before the Civil War. But in the contemporary South the middle class increasingly sets the tone for society and provides cultural models. The southern bourgeoisie has a long history—and a promising future.

F. N. Boney
University of Georgia

F. N. Boney, *Southerners All* (1984); James C. Cobb, *Industrialization and Southern Society, 1877–1984* (1984); Daniel R. Hundley, *Social Relations in Our Southern States* (1860); Frank L. Owsley, *Plain Folk of the Old South* (1949); John Shelton Reed, *One South: An Ethnic Approach to Regional Culture* (1984), *Southern Folk, Plain and Fancy: Native White Social Types* (1986).

Migrant Workers

Poorer than other sections of the United States, the South has historically exported its people by the millions. Whether crossing the Ohio River to flee slavery, following cotton or tobacco away from worn-out soil, or seeking employment in northern industry, the southerner has frequently sought greater opportunity elsewhere.

The "migrant worker," or "migratory laborer," moves from his southern home northward, each year repeating the pattern until he can find permanent work. His domination by his employer, usually a crew leader who furnishes transportation and subsistence, typically of low quality and high price, seems in the 1980s to be reminiscent of the authoritarian standards of earlier times. Even more clearly, the migrant's labor market is nearly as chaotically "free" as it was before World War II. There once were comprehensive planning schemes for consecutive employment in successive harvests, but only vestiges of these remain. Very few migrants follow an entire "stream," working in every state from Texas to Wisconsin or from Florida to New England; more typically, their crew boss haphazardly chooses a few employers for them in one or two other states.

In the 20th century two major southern migratory streams originate in Texas and Florida. The Texas-based movement usually includes about twice as many individuals as the Florida-based pattern; the latter is as completely black as the southwestern one is Mexican and Mexican American. Ethnicity is a key to understanding the lack of access to better employment. The migrant streams, since their origins, have been fed by excess labor from dying peonage and sharecropping systems in Mexico, the Caribbean, and the Deep South. Mechanization, irrigation or drainage, chemical and biological discoveries, and faster refrigerated transport of fruits and vegetables have produced a large-scale agriculture that needs few workers except at peak seasons, such as the harvest period. At that time, however, from the standpoint of the employer who pays by the piece and not the hour, there can never be too much labor on hand: an oversupply guarantees the picking of fruits and vegetables at the peak of perfection, and hand picking is preferable to machine harvesting, except when taste has been sacrificed to toughness in the breeding of new hybrids.

Both southern migrant routes appeared before the turn of the century. The roots of the southwestern stream are the deeper of the two. Mexicans have long traveled north into the Rocky Mountains and Great Plains with cattle drives and at the busier sheepherding seasons. Cotton in Oklahoma and in Texas, sugar beets in the Rockies, vegetables in the upper Midwest, and the wide variety of California crops gradually became major lures out of the South. So huge was Texas that many workers established a migratory pattern within that state alone.

The development of truck farming in New Jersey in the 1890s drew in black harvest workers from Maryland and Virginia, and during World War I Middle Atlantic areas outgrew their local labor supply and attracted Carolina and Old Dominion blacks. During the 1920s, with Upper South agriculture becoming a labor-demand rather than a labor-supply industry, and with corporate agriculture reclaiming Florida swampland so that America could enjoy winter vegetables, the Atlantic Coast stream developed fully. For most of the century, there were four to five times more workers per farm employed in Florida than in other Atlantic Seaboard states, freeing thousands at the end of each winter season. Most went north along the coast, often as far as New England, though a few traveled inland to Ohio and Indiana.

The worldwide Great Depression forced poor Mexicans as well as poor whites onto the highways in a desperate search for jobs. It, and the New Deal programs designed to counteract it, also drove thousands of sharecroppers off cotton plantations into the migrant streams. In this cauldron of misery the only hopeful element was the creation in 1937 of the Farm Security Administration (FSA), which built decent housing for migrants in a few areas and attempted to establish health standards.

A migrant labor camp in Florida, 1930s

World War II brought the first governmental importation of foreign migrant workers. In 1942, to offset the wartime labor shortage, Caribbean workers were imported to the Atlantic states and the first Mexican *braceros*—literally, arm workers—arrived in the Southwest. This program long outlasted the emergency and continued to bring in wage-depressing foreign migrants more than a decade after the war's conclusion. The termination of the program in 1964, once hailed as a victory for American workers, proved to have little if any impact. Immigration laws still permitted thousands of "greencarders" to enter the United States legally, but wages were undoubtedly retarded even more by the incalculably greater number who arrived outside the law. Once known as "wetbacks," later called "illegals," this uncountable army spread from the Southwest to the entire nation, from farm labor to virtually all unskilled and semiskilled work.

At the end of World War II, the Farm Placement Service appeared in the Department of Labor and offered hope that farm workers' as well as farm employers' interests might again be well served. The Farm Placement Service had been a labor-supportive part of the War Manpower Commission until the American Farm Bureau Federation (AFBF) succeeded in placing it under the War Foods Administration and the state extension services, which were generally more sympathetic to employers. The AFBF had also helped kill the FSA during the war, but afterwards the FSA migrant camps were permitted to continue under public as well as private operation.

The President's Commission on Migratory Labor, established by Harry Truman in 1951, and Edward R. Murrow's 1960 television documentary, *Harvest of Shame*, highlighted the decades of greatest public sympathy toward migrant workers. In the Atlantic Coast stream their numbers dropped from a postwar peak in 1949 of well over 50,000 in any one state at a given time to under 30,000 in the 1960s. Social Security coverage was won for some migrants in 1954 and 1956, and most states markedly improved their enforcement of health and housing standards. From World War II to the 1960s, annual migrant wages rose from the $500–$1,000 range to $1,500–$3,000, if the entire family worked, and before the crew chief made his deductions.

The rise and fall of the Annual Worker Plan accompanied, and in some ways explained, the decline of migratory labor conditions after the 1960s. This plan, developed by the Farm Placement Service in 1954, sought to stabilize the harvest labor force, for the benefit of all concerned, by scheduling work crews for consecutive jobs, and by monitoring performance so that substandard workers and employers would not be supplied labor. Participation in the system peaked in about 1967. By the late 1970s the harvest labor market was virtually "free" again, due partially to bureaucratic mismanagement and crew boss chicanery, but largely, however, to employer preference for illegal immigrants and for domestic workers kept cheap and docile by competition with the illegals.

Statistics on such a disorganized labor force range from unreliable to nonexistent, but it appears that tuberculosis, malnutrition, alcoholism, and crew boss dictatorship are rising among 1980s migrants as the degree of law enforcement declines, a development that offsets the drift toward ending agricultural exemptions from labor law. Typical of the trend away from federal enforcement of federal regulations, at a time when state budgets are usually too tight to permit expanded attention to these extremely poor people who are seldom able to vote, was the decision of President Reagan's Environmental Protection Agency to let the individual states enforce pesticide control standards. The historic southern belief in states' rights and minimal government, now at least given lip service at the highest levels of American power, would appear to control the migrant worker's fate for the foreseeable future.

Zora Neale Hurston's novel *Their Eyes Were Watching God* (1937) tells of life among the "eastern stream" of migrant workers in Florida, while John Steinbeck's *The Grapes of Wrath* (1939) is the definitive account of the Depression-era migrants who moved west. Public health physician Earl L. Koos offers a unique perspective on eastern migrants in a 1957 volume entitled *They Follow the Sun* produced for the Florida State Board of Health.

Donald H. Grubbs
University of the Pacific

George O. Coalson, *Migrant Farm Labor System in Texas* (1977); Robert Coles, *Migrants, Sharecroppers, Mountaineers* (1971); Truman E. Moore, *Slaves We Rent* (1965).

Politics and Social Class

Class patterns imported from England took root in the South back in the colonial era. The earliest settlers included few members of the British aristocracy or large landed proprietor class; the organizers of these expeditions were for the most part adventurous, ambitious, talented people from the middle ranks of British society who sought opportunities not open to them at home in 17th-century Britain. A combination of circumstances made large-scale agriculture—or the plantation economy—not only possible, but highly desirable. The planter "aristocrat" (later designated "cavalier") became the southern upper class and was the natural source of political leadership. A pattern of rural-based, planter-dominated politics was established and then extended as the South expanded into the areas south and west of the Chesapeake Bay area. This pattern was not completely broken (despite all the vicissitudes of the region's history) until the 20th century.

At the opposite end of the social scale, of course, was the black slave. Introduced into Virginia by a Dutch trader in 1619 as long-term indentured servants, blacks provided a permanent source of agricultural labor that served the expanding plantation cash-crop system. The enslavement of blacks soon followed, and by the middle of the 17th century the practice was made legal in Virginia. From there slavery moved to other areas, seemed in decline during the relative stagnation of the Tidewater plantations from soil depletion in the late 18th century, and developed and expanded again after 1795 with the invention of the cotton gin and the growth of the Deep South states. Slavery thus provided the plantation system a labor supply that was locked into a permanent state of economic and social immobility, rendered totally dependent, and excluded from the possibility of citizenship and participation in politics. It was ironic that upper-class slaveowners like Thomas Jefferson would, in the 18th century, revolt (in the name of individual freedom and a new order of republican government) against the feudal remnants of inherited privilege. A further irony was the democratization of that republican form of government in the following century, as the South was beginning its self-conscious defense of slavery.

One other social class more or less formally identified as such well before the American revolutionary era and continuously recognized as part of the social structure ever since was the southern "poor white." In 1728 William Byrd II headed a commission to establish the boundary between North Carolina and Virginia. Among other extensive descriptions of places and events in his *History of the Dividing Line* (not published until 1841, but circulated soon after it was produced) Byrd included a graphic account of a singularly unprepossessing group of people in the border backwoods who were referred to as "lubbers." Undernourished and unhealthy, indolent and dirt poor, ignorant and unskilled to the point of surviving only through low native cunning, the "lubber" became the prototype for what, under various derogatory ascriptions, was in effect a declassed, poverty-stricken, rural southern white. Though not clearly fixed by sociological definition, and relatively small in number even when extended to include economically marginal hill farmers, "poor whites" became such a literary convention that many people outside the South (and some inside it) think stereotypically that the South is composed of only three social classes—the planter aristocrat, the poor white, and the black.

In point of fact, through much of southern history the middle class was numerically dominant, because it included the yeoman farmer as well as the small-town merchant and professional person. The planter became both an idealized type and a real wielder of economic, social, and political power, and the economic importance and potential in democratic politics of the middle class was not effectively recognized until the 20th century.

Throughout the colonial period the planter aristocratic tradition continued to hold sway in politics (most notably in Virginia and South Carolina), and public service was considered a part of the continuing obligation of that class. In the more prominent families males prepared for this role by joining a classical education to the study of law. The tradition produced a remarkable collection of early political leaders whose contributions to the American Revolution, the framing and adoption of the Constitution, and the early experience in making the Republic work are incalculable. Out of this class Virginia alone furnished the draftsman of the Declaration of Independence (Jefferson), the chief military commander of the Revolution who was later the presiding officer of the Constitutional Convention (Washington), that convention's most effective recorder and interpreter (Madison), four of the first five presidents of the United States (Washington, Jefferson, Madison, and Monroe), and the chief justice of the U.S. Supreme Court (Marshall) who did most to shape that branch of the national government into the powerful instrument it became. Prominent figures from the South were leaders in developing the Federalist party, and Jefferson and Madison were the founders of the opposition Republican party, which later became the Democratic party. Jefferson's ideas had as much influence on the transition of the American Republic into a constitutional democracy as those of any other single person.

But if it was aristocrats such as Jefferson who provided much of the impetus for American democracy, it was left for the descendants of the "plain folk" settlers of the first American frontier (what are now the states of the Upper South) to make the practical transition in the form of Jacksonian democracy. From roughly the time of Jackson's election to the presidency in 1828 until the breakup of the party system in 1860, the South was part of national two-party politics in which the competition between the Democrats and Whigs was close, and the division in party adherence tended to be along social class lines that are still familiar. The Jacksonian Democrats found support in an expanding electorate moving toward universal white manhood suffrage, and the bulk of its supporters were farmers and laborers. The traditions of Jeffersonian agrarianism and decentralization of political power by way of geographically based pluralism also kept many planters in the Democratic fold. The Whigs, who displaced the moribund Federalists, tended to reflect the growth of the middle class business and professional classes that were part of the incipient industrial development. Early in this period the New England reform movement, of which antislavery was simply one part, combined with the rapid growth of commercial and manufacturing interests in the Northeast to produce increasing sectional tensions in which the issues often turned on the way the North-South political and economic balance was to be maintained in the face of the slave-state, free-state issue.

On the eve of the Civil War, an Alabama lawyer-planter and sometime Chicago businessman, Daniel R. Hundley, published a book entitled *Social Relations in Our Southern States* (1860). The study may well be the first attempt at a systematic analysis of the structure of social classes in the South. Hundley goes beyond the use of basic demographic characteristics in developing his taxonomy, identifying traits of character that affect political behavior and the social types he perceived. Although the southern gentleman is his ideal type, being a planter at a certain economic level is not enough to place one in this category. Two other types may be economically successful, yet never attain the nobility of character, the appropriate sense of honor, and the other virtues that would qualify them as gentlemen. These "cotton snobs" and "southern Yankees" in their respective ways were interested more in getting and spending wealth than in the conduct of individual and social life according to the higher standards of the gentleman. Similarly, Hundley analyzes the middle classes, the primary categories being those in the towns (merchants, et al.) and the yeoman farmer, with considerable ranges in each category in terms of social and economic functions and moral considerations as well. Two other categories that rank low on Hundley's scale of character traits are the "southern bully" (who may range widely in economic status) and "poor white trash"—the extended lubber image. Hundley also includes the "Negro slaves" in his discussion, but mainly for purposes of comparing the social condition of the slaves in the South favorably with the exploited "free" laborers elsewhere.

Hundley's book provided a solid sense of the complexity of the social structure of the pre–Civil War South and revealed the extent to which the South remained traditionally status-based in its social hierarchy rather than moving toward a social structure comparable to that in the northeastern states. The South held to the plantation-agrarian ideal as opposed to contractual foundations of social, economic, and political relations. *Social Relations in Our Southern States* anticipated the restoration in the post-Reconstruction South of something as close to the social structure of the antebellum South as the emerging planter-lawyer-doctor-merchant-banker ruling elite could manage.

The South's "politics as usual" after Reconstruction was a one-party politics in which blacks were, by the end of the 19th century, removed from direct participation. Blacks were used as a symbolic threat to keep white voters in line when economic or other issues that generated divisions along class lines produced electoral challenges to the dominant structures of political power.

Voter participation in elections at all levels declined as large numbers of poor whites (as well as virtually all blacks) were disqualified, and a large portion of those who were qualified did not bother to turn out for elections. Intraparty competition was carried on through various types of factional alignments, with the primary elections for nomination of candidates the point at which the real competition (if any) took place.

From time to time various political movements threatened to break the long-standing pattern of control by the Bourbon-planter class. In the 1890s the "farmer's revolt" made some headway in the South (as it did in the Midwest) when the Populist party challenged the Bourbon-planter hegemony. Although Populism's main source of support was the small farmer and labor classes, it was never able to generate a voter coalition strong enough to sustain the few successes it had at the polls, partly at least because the possibility of uniting blacks and whites in the common effort was diverted by appeals to white racial unity within the Democratic party. Vestiges of Populism appeared in factional form from time to time after 1900, most notably in the case of the Long faction in Louisiana, where economic issues overrode racial ones for a considerable period of time. Southern Progressivism, more of an urban middle-class phenomenon, also constituted reformist challenges to the dominant forces on occasion, but the voter divisions here tended to be less identifiable along class lines than in the case of Populism.

In the 20th century the South began to concentrate more on its economic development, which was interrupted by the Depression but stimulated by the New Deal reforms and by World War II. A new generation of southern political leaders emerged after the war, and the national Democratic party began to take some initiative in advancing both party and national governmental programs against racial segregation.

The actions along these lines in the 1948 Democratic convention led to a walkout on the part of some of the southern states that was the beginning of the breakup of the "old" southern one-party politics and of the social practices that had such an important role in its long perpetuation. The subsequent civil rights movement, the rapid urban-industrial growth in the South, the centralization of governmental power, and all of the related changes have gradually produced political alignments among voters in the South that are more congruent with "normal" American tendencies to vote along economic and social class interest lines than was the case during the era of the solid Democratic South. The nearest thing to a complete political mobilization of a socially identifiable group is the steady support of 90 percent and upwards of the black vote for Democratic candidates in straight contests between regular party candidates. A steady growth has occurred in middle-class, urban-suburban southern Republicanism. It remains to be seen whether the "new" politics will mean continuing movement toward convergence in the social class patterns of support for parties, factions, individual candidates, and issues in the southern and non-southern states or whether new, but still distinctive, ones will emerge.

See also HISTORY AND MANNERS: Populism; Progressivism; POLITICS articles

William C. Havard
Vanderbilt University

Daniel R. Hundley, *Social Relations in Our Southern States* (1860); V. O. Key, Jr., *Southern Politics in State and Nation* (1949); J. Morgan Kousser, *The Shaping of Southern Politics: Suffrage Restriction and the Establishment of the One-Party South, 1880–1920* (1974); Paul Lewinson, *Race, Class, and Party: A History of Negro Suffrage and White Politics in the South* (1932); Rupert B. Vance and Nalia Danilevsku, *All These People: The Nation's Human Resources in the South* (1945).

Poverty

Historian C. Vann Woodward in *The Burden of Southern History* (1960) identified poverty as "a continuous and conspicuous feature of southern experience," one of the central identifying traits of a region that is part of a nation dedicated to material prosperity. If Americans have been a "people of plenty," as David Potter described them, southerners have been a "people of poverty." Historian I. A. Newby has summed up the extent of the problem, noting that "if all the poor could be numbered—the white and black sharecroppers, agricultural laborers, mill villagers, mountaineers, and urban poor—the total would certainly be well over half the population." The South's farm population in the pre-Depression year of 1929 lived on an annual per capita income of $183.

Some historians have traced the beginnings of poverty in the southern region back to the indentured servants of the colonial era. The poor from Europe, and especially England, could come to North America, their passage paid by an employer, and the servant would then work a period of usually five to seven years to pay off the debt. Early accounts of travelers in the South suggested that there were only two classes of whites—the wealthy planters and poor whites. In fact, up to the time of the Civil War, the largest group of southern whites was made up of independent yeoman farmers. Frank L. Owsley, in the 1930s, restored these "plain folk" to their rightful historical place. Moreover, even many landless whites were not poor; they were herdsmen, self-sufficient tenders of livestock, and sometimes practitioners of subsistence farming. Nonetheless, the term *poor white* was used to describe many southerners, and as used it had connotations of moral as well as material impoverishment and even degeneracy. (Mountain people were typically excluded from the category in the antebellum era.) The term *poor white*, then, in the antebellum period described the character of a people, rather than strictly being a term of economic classification.

By the 1850s some southerners were experiencing downward mobility toward poverty. One's ancestors might have been yeoman farmers or slaveowners in the past, but marginal southern farmers were in the process of losing status by the decade before the Civil War. One reason for this was land distribution. Farmers and planters had exhausted the soil with overcultivation. The easy availability of new lands in the early 19th century had encouraged this tendency. Some historians argue that the slave plantation system took the best lands, and poorer whites were shunted aside. Others believe nonslaveowning whites had no significant role in the southern economy. All they had was their labor, but slavery had preempted the market for that. Various observers have attributed the emergence of poverty among large numbers of southern whites to their lack of knowledge of agricultural methods, their refusal to work hard, and even their biological inferiority. Most slaves and free blacks in the Old South lived in conditions perhaps best characterized as those of the working poor.

Southern poverty was institutionalized after the Civil War. During the immediate postwar years virtually all southerners were impoverished. In 1860, 6 of the 10 states with the highest per capita incomes were southern (Louisiana, South Carolina, Mississippi, Georgia, Texas, and Kentucky). In 1880 no southern state ranked in the top 30 in income. The freed slaves were in the worst condition, released from bondage with few resources to prevent their falling into poverty. Despite the aid of the Freedmen's Bureau and church and private charity, they went through terrible suffering in the transition to freedom. The sharecropping-tenant system trapped increasing numbers of blacks and whites in the late 19th century, keeping them at poverty levels. Employment in the textile mills, tobacco factories, and other industries paid such low wages that most southerners remained poor by any definition of that word.

Public efforts to deal with southern poverty began in the 1700s and were always concentrated in urban areas. Early southern public welfare was based on the English poor laws, which required local areas to appropriate money for the needy. There were orphanages for dependent children—at the Ursuline Convent in New Orleans in the 1730s; the Bethesda Orphanage in Savannah, 1738; and a public children's home in Charleston in 1770. Almshouses for the poor appeared before 1800 in Charleston and elsewhere in the South in the early 1800s. Most of the poor, however, preferred begging in the streets to living in the primitive conditions of these institutions. Throughout most of the antebellum era the poor were dealt with through almshouses, poorhouses, work houses, charity hospitals, and orphan asylums. The small number and inadequate nature of the public efforts led to the appearance of private groups, such as the New Orleans Conference of Charities, to try to coordinate efforts between public and private agencies, raise money, provide work for the poor, and in general offer oversight and protection for them. The 1830s brought reform efforts, including the establishment of separate facilities for the mentally and physically ill. The Kentucky School of the Deaf and Mute opened in 1822, the first such institution in the South. The Confederate era launched new welfare programs to care for the children and widows of Confederate soldiers. The defeated Confederate states after the war assumed the full public burden of caring for disabled veterans and their dependents, as they were ineligible for federal aid.

The Progressive era witnessed important improvements in efforts to aid the poor. The Southern Sociological Congress met in 1912 to plot social welfare changes, including an end to child labor and the convict lease system, improved arrangements for orphans and the mentally handicapped, advancement of public health, and better race relations. These efforts received much encouragement and some active support from religious denominations. Communitywide, coordinated campaigns to raise and spend money were launched. By 1915 six states in the region had set up the beginnings of public welfare boards. In this era, though, many cities gave no public welfare to the black poor. In general, a lack of both adequate financing and professional, trained personnel hampered these endeavors. In 1929 the South had only 234 members of the National Conference of Social Work, out of a national membership of 3,487. Colleges and universities in the 20th century have, however, launched programs to train personnel in public health, special education for the handicapped, adult education, and social work. By the post–World War II years, there were both programs and schools in social welfare, and financing for them gradually improved. Nonetheless, the average welfare payment in the southern states has consistently remained lower than elsewhere in the nation. Most states have financed aid for the blind, relief for children and the elderly, and general assistance to the destitute, but even as late as the 1920s most relief for the poor in the South was through such private agencies as churches, benevolent groups, and the community chest.

The Depression hit the South hard because many aspects of the region's economy were depressed even before 1929. Bluesman Lonnie Johnson sang in "Hard Times Ain't Gone Nowhere": "Hard times don't worry me, I was broke when it first started out." The New Deal, though, represented a landmark in efforts to help the southern poor. President Franklin D. Roosevelt identified the South as the "Nation's No. 1 economic problem," noting the large number of its poor. Congress initiated national programs such as the National Youth Administration, Civilian Conservation Corps, Public Works Administration, and Works Progress Administration that had a dramatic effect on the region. Many programs worked specifically to help the rural poor. New Deal relief programs ran into the opposition of southern white administrators desiring to maintain racial segregation, but the laws insisted on including the black poor as well as the white. The Social Security Act was a watershed because for the first time the federal government agreed to send money to the states for distribution to the old, the infirm, and dependent children. This led to the appearance of local public welfare boards to oversee the effort. New Deal "welfare giveaways" became a symbol for conservative southerners who criticized welfare for encouraging laziness, dependency, and the development of a permanent underclass of people living on relief and passing that status on to their children. Eligibility qualification standards and amounts of payments vary from state to state, creating a national problem of fairness and distribution.

Will D. Campbell in his memoir, *Brother to a Dragonfly* (1977), spoke for many on welfare by pointing out the insensitivity of the programs. He said the system was "inefficient, senseless, and began at the wrong end of need." Welfare recipients in 1930s rural Mississippi, where Campbell grew up, had to accept whatever commodities were available for distribution before they could receive needed cash vouchers. Thus, the Campbell family was given massive amounts of grapefruit, a food they had never seen before and would not use. Scientists who came to young Campbell's school to help fight hookworm were arrogant paternalists who treated the students and their families as backward people. "Country people were not impoverished," Campbell notes. "They were simply poor." He reminds one of the relativity of the symbols of poverty, recalling that his schooltime lunch was fried ham on a biscuit. At the time this was a lunch of the poor, eaten while the well-off consumed their bologna sandwiches on white bread.

Scholars began seriously studying the southern poor in the 1920s and 1930s, and their findings gradually replaced the stereotypes created by earlier observers. James Agee and Walker Evans's *Let Us Now Praise Famous Men* (1941) conveys the sensory feeling of living in poverty with a tenant family. Evans and Agee provide extraordinary detail on the material culture of southern rural poverty, describing the unpainted pine houses, smokehouses, barns, and chicken coops; the furniture, fireplace, mantel, and closets; the clothes, eating utensils, the sanitation and lighting; the odors, sights, and smells; the daily rhythms of the rural poor. Walker Evans's photographs made art of this life and reminded viewers that though the rural southern poor have been materially impoverished, they are not spiritually poor.

Novels such as Erskine Caldwell's *Tobacco Road* (1932), through the character of Jeeter Lester, suggested the psychology of white poverty; Dorothy Scarborough's *In the Land of Cotton* (1923) dealt with tenant farmers; Theodore Rosengarten's *All God's Dangers* (1974) was a memoir of an Alabama black sharecropper; and *These Are Our Lives* (1939) and *Such As Us* (1978) were collections of life histories of the southern poor assembled by the Federal Writers' Project during the Depression. Horace Kephart's *Our Southern Highlanders* (1922) explored the lives of southern highland mountaineers, and psychologist Robert Coles studied *Migrants, Sharecroppers, Mountaineers* (1971). John Dollard's *Caste and Class in a Southern Town* (1937), Hortense Powdermaker's *After Freedom* (1939), John Dollard and Allison Davis's *Children of Bondage* (1964), Allison Davis, Burleigh Gardner, and Mary Gardner's *Deep South* (1944), Charles S. Johnson's *Shadow of the Plantation* (1934), Arthur F. Raper's *Tenants of the Almighty* (1943), Herbert J. Lahne's *The Cotton Mill Worker* (1944), and Margaret Hagood's *Mothers of the South* (1939) are classic explorations of the life of different groups of the poor. Howard W. Odum, Rupert B. Vance, Guy Johnson, and other social scientists associated with the University of North Carolina constantly looked at poverty as a part of their broader studies of southern regionalism.

The 1950s and 1960s witnessed a rediscovery of southern poverty. John Kenneth Galbraith's *The Affluent Society* (1958) identified two categories of the poor—"case poverty," those who were poor because of such circumstances as bad health or lack of education; and "insular poverty," those living in pockets of poverty, including rural Appalachia, the Ozarks, the rural South, and urban slums, amidst national prosperity. John F. Kennedy campaigned in the 1960 West Virginia primary, discovering and publicizing poverty. Michael Harrington's *The Other America: Poverty in the United States* (1962) and Dwight Macdonald's article, "Our Invisible Poor" (*New Yorker*, January 1963), both prominently discussed southern poverty and became influential documents for those in the Kennedy administration. Kennedy made fighting poverty a central concern of his New Frontier. The National Advisory Commission on Rural Poverty succinctly explained that "most of the rural South is one vast poverty area." The president launched the first poverty program of the decade in 1961, the Area Redevelopment Administration, to stop the economic decline and social disorganization in Appalachia. It relied on the private business community to design economic programs.

Lyndon B. Johnson launched his War on Poverty in 1964. His Council of Economic Advisers in January of that year had announced that 20 percent of the American population was under the "poverty line," a new classification for a family of four earning less than $3,000 annually. Congress passed the Economic Opportunity Act that set up an administrative agency, the Office of Economic Opportunity (OEO); a Job Corps to provide youth training; job training projects for adults; a work study program for those in school; aid to rural farmers and small businesses; loans for businesses to hire the unemployed; Volunteers in Service to America (VISTA), a program of skilled volunteers to assist the poor; and the Community Action Program, which encouraged the poor to plan and direct programs for their own development.

In May of 1964 Johnson announced that his aim in this was to build a Great Society of "abundance and liberty for all." The goal of this southern-born president would be the end of poverty in the United States. Later programs, such as the Appalachian Regional Development Act (1966), which appropriated $1.1 billion to fight poverty in isolated mountain areas, also assisted the effort, as did programs such as food stamps, medicaid (health insurance for indigents), medicare (health insurance for the elderly), aid for education (especially the Head Start program to help preschoolers), and housing programs.

The War on Poverty represented the national perception that poverty in the South was now part of a broader problem, and the effort had dramatic results in many ways. Between 1960 and 1968 some 14 million people moved above the poverty line. But the War on Poverty did not solve the problem. In 1968 about 25 million people in the nation were still below the poverty line. Southern congressmen had insisted that states be allowed to administer the federal assistance programs, so the system of eligibility and payment standards continued to vary by state. The southern states remained on the low end of payments. Even before the Ronald Reagan-inspired cuts in federal spending, a Mississippi family of four on welfare received only $120 a month. Studies such as David Whisnant's *Modernizing the Mountaineer: People, Power, and Planning in Appalachia* (1981) and Michael Harrington's *The New American Poverty* (1984) studied poverty in the contemporary period and documented the persisting problem.

Many rural poor refused to participate in the federal programs. Bureaucrats who came from outside the South or the rural areas to administer the programs frequently looked at the poor simply in terms of their economic problems and ignored the cultural dimensions of their lives. Many poor whites, for example, would not acknowledge they were poor. They valued their self-respect, which partly came from how others in their communities viewed them. The charge that welfare was socialism prevented many poor from accepting it. The abiding problem of race also worked toward the same end. The admission of blacks to OEO programs led to a loss of support and interest from some poor whites. The attitude of the white working poor was summed up in a line from Merle Haggard's "Working Man Blues," which considers the option of welfare and dismisses it, saying, "that's one place I won't be."

By the 1970s, though, income transfer payments such as welfare and social security were a vital source of economic income in the South. Wealth remained more maldistributed in the region than in the rest of the nation. In 1970 the poorest 20 percent of families in the South received 4.8 percent of the regional income, whereas the top 20 percent got 43.3. A 1968 survey of malnutrition identified 220 counties in the South with authentic hunger out of 256 in the nation. A 1984 study by the Southern Regional Council revealed that 18.2 percent of the 1983 residents in the 11 former Confederate states were below the poverty line, which the Census Bureau now defines as an annual income of $10,178 for a family of four. The South's poverty rate reached a low of 15.6 percent in 1979, but 1984 findings revealed a reversal of a 20-year decline in poverty in the region. The problem, as always, was worse for blacks than whites. The poverty rate among southern blacks in 1983 was 39 percent, and over 60 percent of families headed by a black woman were in poverty.

Oscar Lewis coined the term *culture of poverty* in his studies of the poor of Central America, outlining the traits of physical and spiritual impoverishment. The southern poor surely exemplified the concept, leading lives of unceasing toil in a wearying farm or mill routine. Many southern poor, black and white, lived and continue to live in dilapidated shacks they neither own nor care for. Their yards and surroundings lack any aesthetic touches. There is a general lack of material goods, and there is little sense of the future. A lack of stability and security leads to frequent restlessness and moving about. They give up hope and live drab, unfulfilled lives with few comforts. Nicholas Lemann ("The Origins of the Underclass," *Atlantic Monthly*, June 1986) argued that the hopelessness and welfare dependency found in northern cities should be traced to the culture of poverty existing in the sharecropper South of the post–Civil War period.

The totality of the culture of poverty in the South was especially seen in the way poverty was related to the health of the poor. Joseph Goldberger, a physician with the United States Public Health Service, concluded in 1927 after studying pellagra that it was a poor person's disease. Its development correlated with the cycles of poverty in rural cotton-growing areas. The lack of proper nutrition was partly a cultural matter of food preferences (dating back to a frontier diet), but it was also an economic one. Goldberger blamed the pellagra problem on the "three M Diet" of meat, meal, and molasses—the poor person's menu in the South. Lack of proper nutrition, inadequate sanitation, exposure to the elements because of poor clothing and housing—all promoted disease and ill health and sapped the poor of energy. Health problems of the working poor included black and brown lung and tuberculosis. Inability to afford medical care resulted in lingering health problems that could eventually kill. St. Louis Jimmy's blues song "Bad Condition" captured the slow suffering of the southern poor: "I'm in a bad condition, and I'm still going down slow."

Mississippi roadhouse, 1970s

In spite of all this, the southern poor developed their own culture that transcended the material impoverishment they faced. Much of the culture was created by the working poor, by people who were destitute only in worldly goods. It must be remembered that the southern poor, black and white, were not a hopeless people. Most maintained self-respect and had creative outlets. They shared much with the culture of the yeoman, the subsistence farmer. Theirs was an oral culture of tall tales and drawn-out humorous stories; of fiddle, banjo, and later guitar music; of quilts providing physical warmth and aesthetic beauty; of houses of simple design well adapted to the southern environment. The poor were on the cutting edge of the cultural integration that blended the contributions of the American Indians, Africans, Anglo-Saxons, and Celts into a "southern" culture.

Religion is especially important in understanding southern poverty. The religion of the southern poor is an expressive, emotional, cathartic religion. The unpredictability of life for the economically insecure may have encouraged the fatalism in popular southern religion. The conscious act of conversion in the South's evangelical religion brought the assurance of salvation and relief from the terrors of poverty in this life. Southern theology was otherworldly, appealing to those who sometimes lived truly in a "vale of tears." Religion gave the poor a sense of community, encouraged moral discipline, and provided a sense of purpose to people who might not otherwise have it.

Southern music has documented the cultural significance of poverty. It is a traditional theme of the blues. Lazy Slim Jim sang "Money Blues," Blind Lemon Jefferson did "Broke and Hungry Blues," Ramblin' Thomas recorded "Poor Boy Blues," and Bob Campbell did "Starvation Farm Blues." White country music songs about poverty tend to be of the "poor but proud" type. They provide realistic detail of hard lives, yet frequently are also sentimental. Typical songs of this genre are Dolly Parton's "Coat of Many Colors," Loretta Lynn's "Coal Miner's Daughter," Johnny Cash's "I'm Busted," and Bill Anderson's "Po' Folks." (Anderson has even marketed the "poor but proud" idea in a franchised restaurant chain called Po' Folks that serves southern cooking; in the New South southerners have learned to market poverty.)

These white and black songs show that southerners are aware they are tainted by their background of poverty. They reveal searing incidents of humiliation, of people "looking down at us" because of poverty. But the image of humiliation is counterbalanced frequently by images of the warmth of caring, loving parents, nearby kin, and the shared plight of neighbors.

See also AGRICULTURE: Sharecropping and Tenancy; FOLKLIFE articles; HISTORY AND MANNERS articles; MYTHIC SOUTH: / "Crackers"; Poor Whites; Rednecks; URBANIZATION: Urban Poor

Charles Reagan Wilson
University of Mississippi

James E. Anderson, *Journal of Politics* (February 1967); Lee S. Balliet, "Anglo Poverty in the Rural South" (Ph.D. dissertation, University of Texas at Austin, 1974); J. Wayne Flynt, *Dixie's Forgotten People: The South's Poor Whites* (1979); Gretchen MacLachlan, *The Other Twenty Percent: A Statistical Analysis of Poverty in the South* (1974), *Health Care in the South: A Statistical Profile* (1974); Paul E. Mertz, *New Deal Policy and Southern Rural Poverty* (1978); Dudley L. Poston, Jr., and Robert H. Weller, *The Population of the South* (1981); President's National Advisory Committee on Rural Poverty, *The People Left Behind* (1967); Elizabeth Wisner, *Social Welfare in the South: From Colonial Times to World War I* (1970).

Religion and Social Class

Religion and social class have been intimately related throughout the history of the South. During the early 1700s religious activity was centered in the landed gentry who were Church of England (Anglican). With the movement of Scotch-Irish settlers into parts of the South during the middle 1700s the Presbyterian church began to grow in numbers. The Anglican and Presbyterian churches had limited appeal to the masses, and not until the revival fires of the Baptists and the Methodists began during the early 1800s did the people of the South become noted for their religious enthusiasm. As a general rule the religious group that settled first in a region held a class advantage there. By the beginning of the 1800s religion in the South was stratified along class lines, with the upper classes attending Anglican or Presbyterian churches and the lower classes attending Baptist and Methodist churches.

The relationship between religion and class in the Old South was clearly seen in the emergence of higher education. Unlike settlers in New England, who established the prestigious religious colleges and universities, planters in the southern legislatures established state universities for their sons. The Baptists and Methodists led the way in founding private religious colleges, largely because access to the state universities was denied to them. As an example, in Georgia during the 1840s there was an attempt on the part of Baptists and Methodists to set fire to the University of Georgia because the Anglicans and Presbyterians on the Board of Regents were believed to be discriminating against them. Important exceptions to this pattern were Davidson College, founded in North Carolina by Presbyterians in 1836, and the University of the South at Sewanee, Tenn., founded by Episcopalians in the 1850s.

Questions of social class have also been closely related to sectarian movements. In his classic study of religion and social class in the South, *Millhands and Preachers* (1942), Liston Pope argued that any denomination that did not meet the special needs of the mill workers would soon lose these members to the "ignorant and disreputable" preachers of the newer sects. The growth of sects (the term here is used in a sociological rather than a theological sense), which began in the South during the 1930s, has continued up to the present day, with recruits drawn largely from the "disinherited" lower-class members of society. Through the years, however, many of these sectarian religious groups have achieved middle-class "social respectability." This is especially true of many of the Pentecostal and Holiness groups, of which Oral Roberts and the university that he established in 1965 are the most visible. Many former sects, like the Churches of Christ, Church of God, Foursquare, and Assemblies of God, have become denominations. Even so, continued pockets of poverty in the South are a fertile ground for the emergence of new sectarian movements.

The overwhelming dominance of Protestants in the South has had social class ramifications for non-Protestants. Jews and Roman Catholics occupy a clear religious minority status. Because of their small numbers in most southern communities, Jews and Roman Catholics of all social classes must worship together in the one synagogue or church available to them in the community.

Jews have been excluded from many of the prestigious social organizations (country clubs, lodges, clubs, etc.) found in southern communities. It would not be accurate to say, however, that Jews as a group occupy a lower social class position than Christians in the South. Although discriminated against socially, Jews in the South rank quite high in terms of the traditional criteria of social class—income, education, and occupational prestige.

Race is the most important factor by which religious membership is determined in the South. Except for a few slaves who were baptized into white churches during the colonial period, few blacks were Christians—only 3 percent of their population were church members in 1795. When blacks did convert to Christianity in great numbers, it was into black churches largely Methodist and Baptist in orientation. Segregation in southern churches lasted until the civil rights movement of the 1960s. Even now, however, very few whites or blacks are members of racially integrated local churches.

Black church membership does not seem to be based on social class differences to the same extent as that of whites. This may be in part because stratification within the black community has not been as great as in the white. Since the civil rights movement, certain denominations, most notably the United Methodists, have attempted to place both white and black churches under the same denominational governing body. It is unclear whether blacks who are part of racially integrated denominations, such as the United Methodists, differ significantly in regard to class from those who remain in exclusively black denominations, such as the African Methodist Episcopal church.

The majority of people living in the South belong to either of two denominations. The combined Baptist-Methodist membership in the Deep South states of Mississippi, Alabama, and Georgia is 88 percent, 87 percent, and 87 percent respectively of total church membership. In the five additional states of Texas, Arkansas, Tennessee, South Carolina, and North Carolina, the combined total Baptist-Methodist membership surpasses 70 percent. Such numerical dominance by two denominations suggests that class differentiation exists not only between denominations, but also between local congregations within denominations. This is especially true within the largest southern Protestant denominations. The First Baptist in the typical southern community is made up of members who occupy higher social positions than those in more recently established Southern Baptist Convention churches in the community. Although this pattern also holds true for Methodist churches in the South, the lines of social demarcation are not as clear cut.

See also BLACK LIFE: Religion, Black; LAW: Civil Rights Movement; RELIGION articles

Jack Balswick
Fuller Theological Seminary

David Harrell, *White Sects and Black Men in the Present South* (1971); Samuel S. Hill, *Religion and the Solid South* (1972), *Southern Churches in Crisis* (1966); Thomas Daniel Young, in *The American South: Portrait of a Culture*, ed. Louis D. Rubin, Jr. (1980).

Socialism

Socialism in the South may be appreciated best by considering not only vote tallies and membership lists of historical political parties, but by a look at the influence of Socialist thought and action. In the South, as in the nation, a nominal Socialist presence in electoral politics must be acknowledged. Considered simply in terms of the numbers of votes won by the Socialist Party of America, socialism in the South might be seen as a sentimental, slow fade-out dating from the presidential campaign of Eugene Debs in 1912. If seen, however, as a continually dissenting and engaging critique of social justice in capitalist society, the Socialist vision, Socialist-influenced participants, and full-fledged Socialists of several varieties can be found in every recent and ongoing movement that seeks to eliminate social relations based upon domination.

Certainly, the "foreignness" of socialism to the South has been a consistent and hampering pattern in its history. Throughout the 19th century European immigrants most responsible for bringing Socialist views and organizations to other sections of the United States largely avoided the South. Plantation slavery in the antebellum era stifled the prospects for such immigrants not only to Deep South farms, but also to the South's few cities, limiting occupations in the crafts, industry, and trade. From the end of the Civil War until well into the 20th century, the South remained a section characterized by few decent opportunities for newcomers, by ethnic prejudice, and by the cheap wages paid to its overwhelmingly native-born, black and white work force.

Throughout most of the South's history, suspicion of outsiders and particularly of "Yankee" and "foreign" ideas regarding movements for unionization, racial equality, and women's rights has fed a popular phobia eager to label as socialistic or communistic any striving for democratic social change. The intensity of this reaction reveals an important association of socialism in the South. Abolitionists, Knights of Labor, Populists, feminists, and voting rights and civil rights organizers have all been widely and intensely hated in the South and identified collectively (and for the most part mistakenly) as "Reds."

A stanza of a song written and sung in the 1930s by the Kentucky coalfield Socialist Aunt Molly Jackson reveals the way in which Red-baiting has worked again and again to shift public outrage away from historical scenes of injustice and redirect it against Socialist "agitators":

> I was raised in old Kentucky
> In Kentucky borned and bred,
> And when I joined the union
> They called me a Russian Red.

Among the earliest self-proclaimed Socialists in the South were a number of immigrant Germans who during the 1840s and 1850s published antislavery newspapers in New Orleans and in Texas. A close kin, if not always part of the immediate family of socialism in the South, the communitarian impulse found expression in the antebellum-era Shakers of Pleasant Hill, Ky., the short-lived Owenite Nashoba community near Memphis, the late 19th-century town of Ruskin, Tenn., the mid-1920s colony of New Llano, La., and the current Koinonia Farm in Georgia.

In the late 19th-century South, small numbers of Socialists emerged in the urban industries of New Orleans, Atlanta, and Richmond, and in the mining districts from Birmingham through Tennessee into Kentucky and West Virginia. With the defeat of the Populists in the mid-1890s and the founding of the Socialist Party of America in 1901, Socialists were recruited in the South from the ranks of small farmers, tenants, farm laborers, industrial workers, miners, and immigrant trade unionists. Turn-of-the-century Socialist locals were formed in San Antonio, Houston, Dallas, Bessemer (Ala.), Oklahoma City, and New Orleans.

Despite strong rhetoric and resolutions, such as the one passed in its 1901 founding convention at Indianapolis, and despite the urging of a minority of its members, the Socialist party (until the 1930s) generally backed away from embracing black members in integrated locals. This fear of, and resistance to, racial "social equality" had an especially strong hold in the South. During a tour of the South in 1900, Eugene Debs, who had slowly broken with many of the views of conventional racial prejudice in his own life, confronted white Georgia and Alabama Socialists over the issue of race, often refusing to speak to segregated audiences. Less than eagerly sought by white organizers, southern blacks saw little reason to join segregated Socialist locals. A few blacks did feel the influence of a more indigenous Christian socialism as expounded for a time in the 1890s through publications such as *The Christian Recorder* and the AME *Church Review*, both produced by the African Methodist Episcopal Church.

Although white Socialists' ranks increased with the decline of the Populist party, the movement remained marginal to the experience of most of the South's workers and farmers. An especially effective recruiting technique was the use of the Socialist encampment, which began in Texas in the late summer of 1904 and spread into Oklahoma and the rest of the Southwest. These gatherings joined the traditional southern evangelical camp meeting's emotional style with the urgencies of agrarian revolt. Between 1909 and 1911 Socialist organizers in Oklahoma and Texas began a tenant farmers' Renters Union (or Land League). Building upon an indigenous discontent, they continued the camp meetings and published newspapers that reached tens of thousands of readers. In 1910 the Socialist Party of America counted its largest state membership (almost 10,000) among the cotton farmers in the southernmost part of Oklahoma.

Socialist party opposition to World War I and to U.S. involvement in the war led to a decline in the movement both in the nation and in the South. In 1919 Communists, Socialists, and other American radicals faced severe repression and censorship. Jailed for sedition, Debs ran for the U.S. presidency in 1920 from Atlanta's federal prison.

The 1920s and 1930s saw increasing labor unrest in the textile towns of the Piedmont South and in the Kentucky coal-mining districts. In a few sensational instances, such as those of Gastonia, N.C., and Harlan County, Ky., industrial violence came to be associated in the public mind with the very place names themselves and with Socialist and Communist unionization efforts. In most mill and mining towns, however, workers had little chance to hear any Socialist message except as interpreted by local newspaper editors and industrialists. From the mid-1930s organized Socialist activity faced a general decline due to state, municipal, and business hostility, internal factionalism, the broad appeal of Franklin Roosevelt on one hand, and the attraction of the Communist party on the other.

On the advice of Norman Thomas, the Southern Tenant Farmers' Union (STFU) was begun in the Arkansas Delta in 1934. A year later the new union was carrying out a strike of some 5,000 cotton pickers. Although largely confined to Oklahoma, Arkansas, and eastern Missouri, the STFU, writes scholar James Green, "was the most important organizing project of the Socialist party sponsored anywhere in the country after World War I." The STFU was important not only because of the numbers of grass-roots members involved and the national attention it drew to the plight of sharecroppers, but also for its inclusion of small farm owners together with tenants and farm laborers, its interracial organization, and its recruitment of women members. The STFU gave new life to the southern Socialist tradition.

The Socialist stirrings of the 1930s revealed the significance of a Christian Socialist tradition in the South. A few score renegade preachers and devout church members (ranging from Presbyterian to Holiness) viewed the human devastation of the Depression years and insisted that the biblical gospel be applied in its most egalitarian manner. Among the best known of these Christian radicals were Claude and Joyce Williams, Alice and Howard Kester, Ward Rogers, Don West, Myles Horton, and James Dombrowski.

In 1934 Horton and West began the Highlander Folk School in Grundy County, Tenn.—at that time one of the 10 poorest counties in the United States. Since its founding, Highlander has devoted itself to educational and organizational support for the southern labor movement (in the 1930s and 1940s), the civil rights movement (in the 1950s and 1960s), and the struggle for Appalachian self-determination (during the 1970s and 1980s).

Another route of Socialist influence in the South has come, at least since the mid-1920s, through the presence of a Socialist professor or two, on campus in such places as Chapel Hill, Atlanta, Charlottesville, and Tuscaloosa. Indeed, the late 1970s and early 1980s have seen most major universities in the South hire a number of young scholars—from inside and outside Dixie—intent upon bringing Socialist or Marxist interpretations to the fields of history, political science, literature, and women's studies.

The currents of feminism in the South, emerging from the civil rights and antiwar movements of the 1960s, have been affected by, and have in turn altered, Socialist views. In her 1972 "Open Letter to Southern White

Women," Socialist writer and activist Anne Braden called on white women, "for their own liberation," to refuse complicity with white men in perpetuating the institutions and acts of a racist society.

From their critical but taken-for-granted roles in the 1960s struggles, a number of southern activist women came to question and ultimately resist what historian Sara Evans has described as "the discrepancy between the movement's egalitarian ideology and the oppression [women] continued to experience within it." Out of this contradiction a wave of feminism was born in the South, as well as a feminist critique of socialism capable of producing a more complex and compelling interpretation of culture and society than one limited by a singular preoccupation with class.

See also AGRICULTURE: / Communal Farms; BLACK LIFE: Freedom Movement, Black; HISTORY AND MANNERS: Populism; LAW: Civil Rights Movement; RELIGION: / Shakers; VIOLENCE: Harlan County, Kentucky; Industrial Violence; WOMEN'S LIFE: Feminism and Antifeminism; / Jackson, Aunt Molly

Allen Tullos
Emory University

Anthony P. Dunbar, *Against the Grain: Southern Radicals and Prophets, 1929–1959* (1981); Sara Evans, *Personal Politics: The Roots of Women's Liberation in the Civil Rights Movement and the New Left* (1979); James R. Green, *Grass-roots Socialism: Radical Movements in the Southwest, 1895–1943* (1978); Sue Thrasher, *Southern Changes* (November–December 1982).

Tenant Farmers

The Jeffersonian dream of an America of independent, freeholding farmers never existed in the South. Before the Civil War there was slavery, and afterward the farm tenancy system replaced it as the basis for the southern economic and social order. The system created a new and growing class of permanently poor and suppressed agricultural workers. To call these people a peasantry is to upgrade them, for, unlike the peasants of medieval Europe, they had no guarantees to the land and no rights that the landlord or the government was bound to observe.

When the tenancy system was at its peak in the first three decades of the 20th century it actually resembled slavery, especially on the "tenant plantations" in rich agricultural areas of the South. The tenants there lived in shacks provided by the planter, received their supplies on credit from the plantation commissary, went into the fields each morning at dawn when the plantation bell rang, and came out again at dark when the bell rang again. Their labors were supervised by a riding boss, who was usually a sheriff's deputy and therefore armed and able to inflict physical punishment.

On such plantations women worked in the fields until it was time to prepare the evening meal. Children worked after the age of six and attended school only sporadically. Public schools in rural areas were customarily closed for weeks in the fall so that children might pick cotton.

The upper levels of tenancy, the cash tenants and share tenants, lived better lives and were less under the control of their landlords, but the sad truth is that the system worked to drive more and more people into the lower levels of tenancy. Many different factors could convert an independent farmer into a tenant or a share tenant into a cropper: floods, drought, hail, storms, the boll weevil, soil exhaustion, mechanization, sickness, laziness, injury, ignorance, low prices, or being cheated by the landlord or storekeeper.

Tenancy began in the South as a way of getting former slaves, the freedmen, back to work on the land. But by the end of the 19th century, the system had become the last refuge for the growing class of southern poor whites who had been unable to compete with the cheap labor of black tenancy or who, for other reasons, had lost their farms and equipment. By 1930 there were 1,475,325 white tenant and cropper families in the South. They made up 60 percent of all southern tenants, and their numbers were growing, as was black tenancy, which stood at 1,091,736 families. The situation was so critical that 79 percent of southern farmers owned no land.

Once southern farmers had fallen into the trap of tenancy, they were kept there by ignorance, lack of economic opportunity, disease, social pressures, debt, and state and local law. Their ignorance was a product of poor schools and the inability to attend schools. Also, there was a general distrust of book learning throughout the rural South. Many tenants could not comprehend simple mathematics and had no idea what was coming to them at the end of the crop year on settlement day.

Most tenants were given small tracts to farm, often less than 40 acres and sometimes as little as 10. Clearly, no one, no matter how good a farmer, could make enough money to escape tenancy on such small pieces of land.

Tenants were considered "shiftless and lazy" by other southerners, but often their lack of vigor was caused by pellagra, trichinosis, malaria, venereal disease, tuberculosis, and all the other diseases that went with crowded and unsanitary living conditions and poor diets. Large families of tenants lived in one- and two-room shacks without plumbing, electricity, or much heat. Outhouses were considered a luxury. The staple diet provided by the commissary consisted of corn bread and fatback.

Most tenants not on plantations had their own chickens and pigs, and some had cows and their own vegetable gardens. Their diets were better, but for the lowliest, the sharecroppers, there was little chance to produce food. They were forced by the riding bosses to plant cotton up to the very doorsteps of their shacks, and they were too tired after long days in the fields and too debilitated by disease to tend animals and gardens.

The social pressures on tenant farmers were also a terrible burden. Southerners viewed tenant farmers as a permanent class of lazy, ignorant, immoral subhumans, unfit for a place in normal human society. When the tenants were black, racism added further degradation, but southern social disdain was not confined to blacks. White tenants were often considered "poor white trash," a social status little higher than that of the lowliest blacks. The big difference was that white tenants were not segregated by law in public places.

Debt was a way of life for tenant farmers. When settlement day came in the fall of the year, the tenant had to pay what he owed to the landlord or storekeeper for the "furnish" he had received all year. Often the settlement left the tenant with only a few hundred dollars and he would soon be living on credit again. When they got their hands on any money, the tenants and their families, who had gone without the simplest luxuries for so long, often spent their few dollars on such things as new silk dresses and phonographs.

Most landlords understood clearly that the best way to make profits was through their commissary. Prices there were always higher than in town, and tenants had to pay high interest rates for credit. If it appeared that a landlord might lose money in a given year, he could avoid it by raising prices at the commissary or by cheating the tenants in the settlement. Some of the landlords rationalized their actions by the argument that keeping the tenants in debt was the only way to control them properly. Some even argued that tenants would not work if they were not on the edge of hunger and did not feel that they must go into the fields in order to eat that day.

Faced with such exploitation, tenants had nowhere to turn for justice. State and local law in the South favored the landowner against the tenant. These laws prevented tenants from leaving the landlord as long as they were indebted to him and allowed money owed to tenants to be paid first to the landlord so he might collect what they owed him. In some counties, sheriffs arrested vagrants and placed them in work camps. An unwritten code of civil behavior dictated that a black man never questioned the word of a white man, so black tenants dared not confront a cheating landlord or storekeeper. White tenants could challenge the landlord but the usual result was eviction, which meant being homeless and without credit.

The only escape, if it can be called that, was to move on. Every year after settlement day, the roads and byways of the South were clogged with tenant families on the move, their meager belongings and underfed children piled on wagons and old cars. Southern tenants moved with astounding frequency, especially in hard times. A government study in the 1930s showed that a considerable percentage of tenants had moved six or seven times since they started farming, and a few had been tenants on as many as 15 different farms. They moved because they were evicted or to find a bigger piece of land to work, a kinder landlord, or a better arrangement. But they seldom found what they sought. The tenancy system was the same everywhere and there was no escape.

During the 1930s the plight of the southern tenant farmers came to national attention because of the writings of liberals who used the miserable conditions of the southern tenants to prove that poverty existed in America. John Steinbeck, in *The Grapes of Wrath*, told the tragic story of tenants driven from their farms in Oklahoma by drought, government programs, and mechanization. Erskine Caldwell shocked readers and well-dressed Broadway theater audiences with *God's Little Acre* and *Tobacco Road*, graphic pictures of the ignorance, immorality, and hopelessness of tenancy. James Agee and Walker Evans, in *Let Us Now Praise Famous Men*, told of the wretched lives of three tenant families in Alabama.

The cause of the tenant farmer was taken up by political reformers such as Norman Thomas, the Socialist leader. The Socialists helped in 1934 to form the Southern Tenant Farmers' Union, a biracial labor union that began in Arkansas and spread into neighboring states. In Alabama the Sharecroppers Union, a Communist-backed organization of mostly blacks, got started.

Awareness of the problems of tenancy had its effect on the New Deal. The programs of the Agricultural Adjustment Administration (AAA) were designed to benefit cotton farmers by reducing cotton acreage and raising cotton prices artificially, but these programs necessarily centered on those who owned the land. A small group of liberals in the AAA made an effort to protect the rights of tenants to stay on the land even though they were needed less because of acreage reduction, but the effort failed and most of the liberals were purged from the AAA for their trouble. Rexford Tugwell, a leading brain truster, conceived the idea of relocating tenant farmers to better land, which the government would buy for them. President Franklin Roosevelt bought the idea and set up the Resettlement Administration, which organized dozens of communal and experimental farms for tenants throughout the South. President Roosevelt also appointed a Commission on Farm Tenancy to study the problem. Its work led to the Bankhead-Jones Farm Tenancy Act, which created the Farm Security Administration and set in motion a program to assist worthy tenant farmers in buying their own farms.

None of these actions had a profound effect on tenancy except the AAA acreage reductions. Because of this program, hundreds of thousands of tenants were displaced from the land and the government was helpless to prevent it. The big break for tenants came during World War II when there were jobs in war plants in industrial centers outside the South. Seeking these jobs, southern tenant farmers began a mass exodus that lasted through the war years and continued in the decades that followed. In the South, work that had been done by millions of tenant farmers was taken over by heavy equipment, especially the mechanical cotton picker. Today, only vestiges of the old tenancy system survive, under the combined pressures of economics, changing social values, and the modernization of agriculture.

See also AGRICULTURE: Sharecropping and Tenancy

David E. Conrad
Southern Illinois University
at Carbondale

Sidney Baldwin, *Poverty and Politics: The Rise and Decline of the Farm Security Administration* (1968); David E. Conrad, *The*

Forgotten Farmers: The Story of Sharecroppers in the New Deal (1965); Paul V. Maris, in *Yearbook of Agriculture, 1940* (1940); Paul Mertz, *New Deal Policy and Southern Rural Poverty* (1968); H. L. Mitchell, *Mean Things Happening in This Land: The Life and Times of H. L. Mitchell* (1979); Van L. Perkins, *Crisis in Agriculture: The Agricultural Adjustment Administration 1933* (1969); Arthur F. Raper, *Preface to Peasantry: A Tale of Two Black Belt Counties* (1936); Rupert B. Vance and Nalia Danilevsku, *All These People: The Nation's Human Resources in the South* (1945).

American Federation of Labor (AFL)

The American Federation of Labor, from its 19th-century origins, has always found the South its Achilles' heel. The southern heritage of slavery and peonage, racial divisions within the work force, and the social control exercised by the established governing elite combined to create an inhospitable environment for a working class movement, such as the AFL, which challenged the prevailing socioeconomic order. As a result, the southern ruling elite used its considerable resources—control of local and state police power, the pulpit, and courthouses and statehouses—to contain and, when it was felt necessary, to halt encroachments by the AFL.

Despite the hostile climate, AFL organizers have made significant inroads among skilled workers, particularly building-trades workers, railroad workers, printers, and dock workers. By the early 20th century, central labor unions had been organized in most southern cities and, prior to World War I, state federations of labor had been organized in all of the states in the region. Moreover, a number of the Federation's affiliated unions had first organized in the South, including the Brotherhood of Maintenance of Way Employees (Demopolis, Ala., 1887); the Brotherhood of Painters, Decorators, and Paperhangers of America (Baltimore, 1887); the International Brotherhood of Boilermakers, Iron Shipbuilders, and Helpers (Atlanta, 1888); the International Association of Machinists (Atlanta, 1889); and the International Brotherhood of Blacksmiths, Drop Forgers, and Helpers (Atlanta, 1889).

The limited successes that the AFL had among southern skilled workers, however, were not repeated among the unskilled. Efforts to organize the large southern textile force, for example, were continually frustrated. During the 1930s, the Congress of Industrial Organizations did make some breakthroughs among industrial workers, especially in coal and steel, but these advances came primarily in industries where the union movement could use its power in the North to force concessions in the South. Such leverage was particularly obvious in the organization of the employees of the Tennessee Coal and Iron Company, the southern subsidiary of United States Steel. Meanwhile, the predominant industrial unit in the South, the single plant firm, remained highly resistant to union organization by either the AFL, the CIO, or, after 1955, the AFL-CIO. If, by the fourth quarter of the 20th century, the South has ceased to be, as it had been labeled in the 1930s, "the Nation's No. 1 economic problem," it nevertheless remains the labor movement's "No. 1" organizing problem.

Gary M. Fink
Georgia State University

Gary M. Fink and Merl E. Reed, eds., *Essays in Southern Labor History: Selected Papers, Southern Labor History Conference, 1976* (1977); F. Ray Marshall, *Labor in the South* (1967); Merl E. Reed, Leslie S. Hough, and Gary M. Fink, eds., *Southern Workers and Their Unions, 1880–1975: Selected Papers, the Second Southern Labor History Conference* (1981).

Bourbon/Redeemer South

The Bourbon/Redeemer South refers to the period from the late 1870s until about 1900 when the Democrats returned to power and governed the South after overthrowing Reconstruction. Claiming that they were restoring home rule and good government after the extravagance and corruption of the northern-imposed Republican rule, the Democrats undermined most of the Republicans' innovations, though rarely eliminating them altogether. First, they rewrote the state constitutions that had been created in 1867–68 at the beginning of Reconstruction, thereby reducing drastically the size, scope, and cost of government. Then they rearranged public finance by scaling down or repudiating about $200 million of the state debts incurred during Reconstruction and by reducing state taxation significantly. In the economic sphere, they tightened the control of landlords over their tenants and sharecroppers; they oversaw the creation of a southern textile industry; and they ended state aid to internal improvements and instead encouraged northern capital to develop, and ultimately dominate, the region's burgeoning railroad system as well as most of its iron and steel industry. Finally, by using partisan electoral laws and reapportionment as well as the rallying cry of white supremacy, they consolidated their political hold on the region so that by the end of the century they had successfully implemented wide-scale disfranchisement, primarily of blacks; introduced the white primary; and created a narrowly based, racially exclusive one-party political system.

The terms *Bourbon* and *Redeemer* describe two contrasting interpretations of the men who dominated the post-Reconstruction Democratic party and the regimes they established. Those who at the time and during the early 20th century depicted them as Bourbons believed they were a conservative, even reactionary, element consisting of the planter class and die-hard proponents of the Confederate "Lost Cause" who wanted to restore the values and priorities of the antebellum South. By contrast, those who employ C. Vann Woodward's term and refer to them as Redeemers argue that they represented rather different interests and constituted a rising class of businessmen eager to develop the South's railroads and its manufacturing potential. Their emergence marked a major break, not only with the politics of Reconstruction, but also with the economics of the antebellum South. Despite their claims to be introducing a New South that was economically self-sufficient and diversified, they saddled the region with a dependent, almost colonial, economy and failed to release the grip on the South of the old agrarian and paternalistic values. The Redeemers' limitations were most evident, so these historians argue, in their neglecting the small farmers who finally rose up against them in the Populist revolt of the 1890s and in their allowing the racial gains of Reconstruction to be eroded until a legalized system of segregation arose at the turn of the century. More recently, historians have reemphasized the continuities between the post-Reconstruction era and the antebellum South. They have suggested that the planters and more traditional elements were not replaced by New South businessmen; rather, they persisted and continued to play a major role in the political and economic life of the region.

Michael Perman
University of Illinois at Chicago

Michael Perman, *The Road to Redemption: Southern Politics, 1869–1879* (1984); George B. Tindall, in *The Persistent Tradition in New South Politics* (1975); Jonathan M. Wiener, *Social Origins of the New South: Alabama, 1860–1885* (1975); C. Vann Woodward, *Origins of the New South, 1877–1913* (1951).

Coal Miners

From the beginnings of large-scale commercial coal mining in the South in the 1880s until the 1940s when mechanization of the mines disproportionately displaced blacks, southern coal miners were a polyglot work force. Blacks constituted 50 to 70 percent of the labor force in Alabama while West Virginia coal mines employed roughly one-third native Appalachian white, one-third black, and one-third immigrant. But, despite this diversity, ethnic and racial conflicts have been relatively rare, especially when compared to the interracial turmoil among northern miners and other workers from 1890 to 1945. This has been attributed to the egalitarian policies of the United Mine Workers of America, common occupational hazards, and, most importantly, the predominance of the company town in the southern coalfields. Although oppressive, the standardized and rigidly controlled aspects of these settlements served as a coercive melting pot.

The history of southern miners has been one of struggle and protest. Between 1887 and 1894, for example, one-third of the strikes in the South took place in the coalfields. For 50 years southern miners struggled to unionize in order to end abuses like company stores, payment in scrip, low wages, convict labor, and the mine guard system, which turned company towns into armed camps. In August 1933 the miners got their union, only to begin a 40-year struggle against the autocracy and corruption of the UMWA hierarchy. That effort culminated in 1972 when the Miners for Democracy movement successfully ousted W. A. "Tony" Boyle and elected West Virginia miner Arnold Miller president of the union. Seven years later the miners used the democratic reforms that Miller instituted to throw him out of office.

Southern miners have always shown an independent streak that has made company and union leadership difficult. Often led by legendary figures like John L. Lewis and Mother Jones, whom they allegedly adored, the miners nonetheless continuously rejected the advice of Mother Jones and fought Lewis as tenaciously as they respected him.

In their struggles against both the coal companies and their unions, southern miners developed an intense occupational consciousness that had elements of class tied to it, which partially accounts for the violence that marks their history. The "Coal Creek Rebellion," the Paint Creek-Cabin Creek Strike (1912–13), the "Matewan Massacre" (1920), the "Armed March on Logan" (1921), and the "Bloody Harlan" strikes (1930s) are but a few examples. But, with the exception of Harlan County where the National Miners Union made inroads during the 1930s, southern miners eschewed radical ideologies in favor of a grass-roots brand of "Americanism" that they felt promised life, liberty, and equality regardless of condition of servitude.

The life of the southern miner has been one of resilience amid deprivation, disaster, and tragedy. The protracted depression in the coalfields from the 1920s to the 1970s and the mechanization of the mines in the 1940s produced massive unemployment and poverty. Disasters have always haunted miners in the southern coalfields: 361 died at Monogah, W.Va., in 1907; 90 at Palos, Ala., in 1910; 128 at Littleton, Ala., in 1911; 84 at Cross Mountain, Tenn., in the same year; 181 at Eccles, W.Va., in 1914, and the next year, 112 at Leland, W.Va.; and 119 at Benwood, W.Va., in 1924. During World War I West Virginia miners had a higher casualty rate than the American Expeditionary Force in Europe. Nor have the disasters ended; witness the collapse of a slag dam at Buffalo Creek, W.Va., in 1973 that killed 175 people. Yet the folklore of the coalfields suggests the miners' commitment to their work and life. "Miners' Strawberries" and other humorous songs, for example, are as much a part of miners' culture as are militant songs like "Which Side Are You On?"

A final irony stems from the common perception of the miners' culture as "macho" culture in which women have been subordinate and passive. Women have traditionally played a major role in southern coalfield history and culture, especially as union advocates and activists. The ease with which women entered the mines as miners beginning in 1973 pointed to a long history of women's significance in the southern coalfields.

See also ENVIRONMENT: / Appalachian Coal Region; INDUSTRY: / Mining

David A. Corbin
Washington, D.C.

Harry M. Caudill, *Night Comes to the Cumberlands: A Biography of a Depressed Area* (1963); David A. Corbin, *Life, Work, and Rebellion in the Coal Fields: Southern West Virginia Coal Miners, 1880–1922* (1981); Kai T. Erikson, *Everything in Its Path* (1967); Archie Green, *Only a Miner: Studies in Recorded Coal-Mining Songs* (1972); John W. Hevener, *Which Side Are You On?: The Harlan County Coal Miners, 1931–1939* (1978); George Korson, *Coal Dust on the Fiddle* (1943); F. Ray Marshall, *Labor in the South* (1967).

Company Towns

A company town is a camp, village, or town, usually unincorporated, in which the employer owns the land and houses occupied by the employees. As the South industrialized in the late 19th and early 20th centuries, company towns proliferated, particularly in conjunction with the textile, coal-mining, and lumber industries.

Located adjacent to mineral resources or near water power, industries were often geographically isolated, necessitating the involvement of employers in providing housing and other services. But the company town also gave management greater opportunity for control over the workers. The right to occupancy was dependent upon employment. If out on strike, or ill, or injured, a worker and his family could be evicted on short notice. House leases often contained clauses used to deny union organizers access to the camp: "Lessor may forbid . . . ingress and egress . . . to any and all persons other than Lessee" (Tennessee Coal, Iron and Railroad Co., Birmingham, Ala.). A company deputy, rather than municipal or county law enforcement, provided law and order. Because the company usually furnished a schoolhouse (often subsidizing the teacher's salary) and a church building, opportunity existed for control of the school curriculum and the message from the pulpit.

Housing consisted of double twos (duplex, two rooms each side), double threes, square tops (four rooms), and shotguns, frequently without running water and almost always unsewered. Although textile towns were typically all-white, segregated housing patterns for black and white workers existed in most coal and iron ore camps.

Isolation and lack of transportation made company stores (commissaries) a necessity. In contrast to the low-rental housing, the store often made a profit for the company; however, recent research questions the stereotype of the "pluck me" store. But even if prices were in line with independent merchants and merchandise was of good quality, workers could easily "owe their souls to the company store" because of credit or advances drawn as scrip, a currency redeemable only at the commissary.

Characterizations of exploitation and subservience are an oversimplification. Great variety existed among company towns. A shortage of laborers or the desire to hold a skilled, stable work force could mitigate conditions or the degree of control a company exercised. Some industries (West Point Manufacturing, Tennessee Coal and Iron, Avondale Mills) instituted paternalistic health, welfare, and recreation programs to hold workers and lessen the attraction of unionism. Despite low wages and some loss of personal independence, many southern workers compared their lifestyle in a company town favorably with their former sharecropping existence. They often found, however, that "lintheads" or coal miners were socially ostracized by those residing outside the company town.

For many southerners the company town was a way stop in their rural to urban migration—not quite country, not quite city. Higher wages, unionization, and the automobile have all but eliminated the company town from the South. Industries began selling houses to employees in the 1940s and 1950s. But in some isolated, mountainous regions of West Virginia and Kentucky the company town still survives; in other communities the architectural style of now privately owned homes reveals their lineage as company towns.

Marlene Rikard
Samford University

Ruth A. Allen, *East Texas Lumber Workers: An Economic and Social Picture, 1870–1950* (1961); Harriet L. Herring, *Welfare Work in Mill Villages: The Story of Extra-Mill Activities in North Carolina* (1929); George B. Tindall, *The Emergence of the New South, 1913–1945* (1967).

Congress of Industrial Organizations (CIO)

After breaking with the American Federation of Labor (AFL) in 1937, the Congress of Industrial Organizations (CIO) quickly moved into the South, the nation's staunchest antiunion section. The CIO faced not only intransigent communities and businessmen, but also widespread racism on the part of white industrial workers and their employers. The CIO generated more controversy than the American Federation of Labor because it was determined to organize black as well as white workers and because it did not recoil from the use of Communist organizers, who worked in the most dangerous situations. Although southern workers proved on many occasions that they could behave militantly and form unions as strong as those elsewhere, the CIO encountered much more paternalism, individualism, and apathy in the southern work force than among workers in other regions.

Although they were the most downtrodden workers in the nation, southern tenant farmers and related agricultural hands were offered a glimmer of hope by the CIO, but it was dashed by the depths of their poverty and by other economic, social, and political impediments to effective strikes. Hundreds of thousands of textile workers had been beaten badly in strikes earlier in the 1930s, but the CIO mounted major organizing drives in 1937 and 1940. They won innumerable elections, but few contracts outside the Tri-Cities area of North Carolina. Coal miners and steelworkers were more successful in the late 1930s, and they coped with racism by emphasizing the necessity for economic cooperation and by electing black as well as white officers. The textile, steel, auto, rubber, clothing, packinghouse, and oil workers made their greatest gains during World War II, under the protection of the War Labor Board and a tight labor market. Board policies had some effect on easing racial and North-South wage differentials.

In 1946 the CIO launched a massive organization effort dubbed "Operation Dixie." Perhaps the most celebrated organizer was Lucy Randolph Mason. She utilized her illustrious southern ancestry and her presence as a "little old lady" to explain the requirements of fair treatment provided labor by various New Deal laws. The drive was a disappointment, and by 1953, on the eve of merger with the AFL, the 362,000 CIO members in the South were less than a third of the AFL membership. The social values of union membership in the 1930s and 1940s were almost as important as the economic rewards, and the CIO was undoubtedly among the most vital of the private agencies supporting fair play and justice for black southerners.

George N. Green
University of Texas at Arlington

C.I.O. News, 1937–55; F. Ray Marshall, *Labor in the South* (1967); Lucy Randolph Mason, *To Win These Rights: A Personal Story of the CIO in the South* (1952).

Farmers' Alliance

The southern Farmers' Alliance evolved from local farm organizations established in the 1870s in Texas. In 1886–88 the Alliance spread across the South and into the Great Plains. At its high point in 1891 it had over 1.5 million members. Admission to the organization, officially known by then as the National Farmers' Alliance and Industrial Union, was restricted to whites. However, it maintained ties with a parallel black group, the Colored Farmers' National Alliance.

The Alliance borrowed from the Grange the trappings of a secret society and from Protestant churches techniques for mobilizing rural people into community organizations. The Alliance promised relief for hard-pressed farmers through programs of economic cooperation and political advocacy. Alliance cooperative initiatives ranged from local schemes to buy or sell in bulk (thus bypassing the "middleman") to statewide purchasing and marketing exchanges.

As a political pressure group, the Alliance demanded legal recognition of trade unions and cooperatives, safeguards against land monopolies, federal ownership of railroads, reform of the banking and currency system, and creation of a federal subtreasury system. The subtreasury, conceived by Alliance leader C. W. Macune, would provide for the establishment of commodity storage facilities in rural counties. Farmers could receive legal tender notes with their stored crop as collateral. For southern farmers, the subtreasury plan held promise of breaking the annual cycle of indebtedness to the "furnishing merchant."

In 1890 southern Alliancemen demanded that Democratic candidates for office support the Alliance platform, including the subtreasury. Some prominent officeholders refused, and others reneged on backing the more controversial planks of the platform. Consequently, many Alliancemen bolted the Democratic party and joined their midwestern counterparts in forming the People's (or Populist) party. Southern leaders of this insurgent movement included Leonidas L. Polk of North Carolina, national president of the Farmers' Alliance, and Georgia lawyer Thomas E. Watson. In 1892 the Farmers' Alliance provided the organizational and ideological base for Populism in the South. The Alliance itself quickly faded.

The Farmers' Alliance was not simply absorbed into the People's party. By 1891 membership was declining because Alliance cooperatives could not resolve the massive credit and marketing problems facing southern farmers. Furthermore, the Farmers' Alliance had recruited from a broad spectrum of the rural white southern population, and many of its members had strong ties to the Democratic party. When the Alliance moved from political advocacy to insurgency under the Populist banner, many of its members dropped out.

Some portions of the Alliance platform were later enacted into law, including a form of the subtreasury plan. Additionally, the "movement culture" of the Alliance provided a way of thinking about community organizing and self-determination that lived on in movements ranging from the socialism of the 1910s to the civil rights movement of the 1960s.

Robert C. McMath, Jr.
Georgia Institute of Technology

Lawrence Goodwyn, *Democratic Promise: The Populist Moment in America* (1976); Robert C. McMath, Jr., *Populist Vanguard: A History of the Southern Farmers' Alliance* (1975).

Highlander Folk School

The Highlander Folk School, founded at Monteagle, Tenn., in 1932 by fellow southerners Myles Horton and Don West, has worked for 50 years to develop leadership for democracy in labor unions and community organizations struggling for justice and social change.

The early Highlander staff, working in the poverty and despair of Depression-era Grundy County, were deeply affected by a hard-fought coal miners' strike in nearby Wilder, Tenn. Inspired as much by the determination of the strikers as by the injustices the miners fought, Highlander over the next 15 years became the principal Congress of Industrial Organizations (CIO) training center in the South. Hundreds of shop stewards, organizers, and rank-and-file union members went to Highlander to study labor history, economics, and other topics. More importantly, they learned about union democracy by practicing democracy, taking part in all decisions affecting the program.

The postwar CIO, responding to Cold War pressures, attempted to force Highlander to abandon its work with alleged leftist unions. Highlander resisted the CIO pressure, insisting on its independence. As a result, by the late 1940s Highlander's definition as primarily a labor school came to an end.

Along with the strident anticommunism of the period, it became increasingly clear to the Highlander staff that the principal obstacle to union organizing and union democracy was racism. Asserting that institutionalized racism must be met head-on, the school turned its energies to helping blacks gain full civil rights. In 1953, for example, Highlander sponsored a series of integrated workshops to discuss the anticipated Supreme Court ruling outlawing public school segregation.

Immeasurably aided by two courageous black leaders from the South Carolina Sea Islands, Septima P. Clark and Esau Jenkins, Highlander helped establish "Citizenship Schools" where black adults learned to read in order to register to vote. From a modest beginning on Johns Island with Bernice Robinson, a beautician and seamstress, as the first teacher, the Citizenship Schools spread across the South. Ultimately, tens of thousands of blacks learned to read and registered to vote, profoundly altering the southern political landscape.

As a principal meeting place of the civil rights movement, Highlander became a target and a victim of official repression. After a 1959 raid on the school and protracted legal proceedings, the state of Tennessee in 1961 revoked Highlander's charter and confiscated its Monteagle property. Highlander chose not to contest the seizure, moving instead to Knoxville with a new charter and a new name, the Highlander Research and Education Center, and continued its civil rights work.

The leadership and focus of the civil rights movement changed in the late 1960s and Highlander changed its focus in response, working since that time with the poor and disadvantaged people of Appalachia. At recent workshops, mountain people have addressed such concerns as mining and flood disasters, community-based health clinics, occupational and environmental health, and the economic issues surrounding the control of land and energy resources.

Myles Horton
Lawrence L. Bostian
The Highlander Center

Frank Adams with Myles Horton, *Unearthing Seeds of Fire: The Idea of Highlander* (1975); Dorothy Cotton and Myles Horton, in *Roots of Open Education in America*, ed. Ruth Dropkin and Arthur Tobier (1976); Aimee Horton, "The Highlander Folk School: A History of the Development of Its Major Programs Related to Social Movements in the South, 1932–1961" (Ph.D. dissertation, University of Chicago, 1971).

Kester, Howard Anderson

(1904–1977) Christian activist and educator.

Kester was born in Martinsville, Va. While a student at Lynchburg College and Vanderbilt University's School of Religion, "Buck" Kester became active in the work of the intercollegiate YMCA and the Fellowship of Reconciliation (FOR), serving as youth secretary of the latter organization from 1927 to 1929. As a result of this YMCA and FOR work, he became deeply involved in the nascent interracial student movement in the South. His work as southern secretary of the FOR from 1929 to 1934 was broader in scope than that in which he had engaged earlier, encompassing not only the South's racial but also its economic problems.

Although Kester's initial efforts were largely educational, the Depression, and capitalism's apparent inability to cope with it, persuaded him that political action was necessary. He therefore joined the Socialist party in 1931 and the following year ran unsuccessfully for Congress on the party's Tennessee ticket. In 1933 a dispute developed within the FOR over the role of violence in the class struggle. Kester deplored violence but believed it a likely consequence of the quest for social justice. The pacifist majority of FOR members considered his position too radical and dismissed him from his post as southern secretary. Reinhold Niebuhr and other disaffected Fellowship members who believed that Kester was rendering useful service in the South organized the Committee on Economic and Racial Justice, which supported his work in the region from 1934 until 1941, when the Fellowship of Southern Churchmen assumed responsibility for his activities. During these years Kester investigated lynchings and racial unrest for the NAACP, ACLU, and Workers Defense League; organized and publicized the Southern Tenant Farmers' Union; and, through the Fellowship of Southern Churchmen, sought to awaken southern Protestantism to an awareness of the social dimension of Christianity.

In 1943 he resigned as secretary of the FSC to accept a position as director of the Penn Normal, Industrial and Agricultural School in South Carolina, where he remained until 1948. He then worked for a brief period with the displaced persons program of the Congregational church and the John C. Campbell Folk School in North Carolina. In 1952 he returned to the Fellowship of Southern Churchmen, serving as its secretary from 1952 to 1957. He concluded his career as a teacher and administrator at Eureka College in Illinois and at Christmount Assembly and Montreat-Anderson College in western North Carolina. By the time of his death Kester's work had been largely overshadowed by that of a later generation of reformers, but during the second quarter of the century he was a leading figure among the small band of Christian activists in the South.

Robert F. Martin
University of Northern Iowa

John S. Bellamy, "If Christ Came to Dixie: The Southern Prophetic Vision of Howard Anderson Kester, 1904–1941" (M.A. thesis, University of Virginia, 1977); Anthony P. Dunbar, *Against the Grain: Southern Radicals and Prophets, 1929–1959* (1981); John Egerton, *A Mind to Stay Here: Profiles from the South* (1970).

Knights of Labor

Organized in 1869 by a group of Philadelphia tailors, the Noble Order of the Knights of Labor within a decade had become the nation's largest labor union. Open to all laborers regardless of craft, the Knights stressed education, arbitration, and the development of worker-owned cooperatives rather than direct conflict with management. Shaken by the tumultuous strikes of 1877, the Knights held their first general assembly the following year and adopted a constitution, thus establishing a national organizational structure. Immediately thereafter the Knights began their efforts to organize the South, appointing organizers in Alabama, Georgia, and Florida.

Between 1878 and 1885 the Knights grew slowly in the South, their numbers concentrated in the urban centers, especially Richmond, Atlanta, Birmingham, and New Orleans. The Order experienced rapid growth in 1885, prompted by a visit of the Master Workman, Terence V. Powderly, to the region early in that year and, more significantly, by a successful strike against Jay Gould's southwestern railway system. Southern laborers, black and white, clamored to join the Knights, and organizers could not keep up with the demand. By 1886 the Knights had established district assemblies composed of several locals in Richmond, Nashville, New Orleans, Atlanta, Norfolk, Knoxville, Memphis, Birmingham, Savannah, Augusta, Columbus, Petersburg, Chattanooga, and Key West. Large locals unaffiliated with a district organization existed in several other urban areas. By early 1887 state assemblies had been formed in Florida, Arkansas, Mississippi, and North Carolina. In other states the large district assemblies remained the dominant organizations. Local assemblies were racially segregated, but both white and black locals sent representatives to district and state assemblies.

Although most southern locals contained members representing a variety of occupations, until 1887 membership was concentrated in the mining, textile, lumber, and construction industries. Southern rank-and-file Knights proved as strike prone as members in other sections of the nation. Thousands of workers participated in strikes initiated by the Knights against the cotton mills of Augusta, Ga., in 1886 and the sugarcane growers of Louisiana in 1887. Other strikes involved coal miners, stevedores, typographers, and foundry workers. Inadequate planning, lack of funds, fierce resistance from management, and at best lukewarm support from the Order's national leadership doomed all such actions to failure.

In politics, however, the Knights experienced success, if but briefly. Southern Knights rushed into the political fray in 1886, electing members to city councils, state legislatures, and, in North Carolina and Virginia, to the House of Representatives. Within the year, however, the Order's political influence began to wane as its membership declined. Racial discord, the Order's failure to respond effectively to the membership's needs, failed strikes, and an ineffective national leadership resulted in a swift downfall. By the end of 1888 most urban members had deserted the Knights. Those who remained represented the poorest of the region's yeoman and tenant farmers and day laborers, many of whom were blacks. A few such locals continued to exist into the 20th century.

Melton A. McLaurin
University of North Carolina
at Wilmington

John Abernathy, "The Knights of Labor in Alabama" (M.A. thesis, University of Alabama, 1960); Leon Fink, *Labor History* (Summer 1978); Melton A. McLaurin, *The Knights of Labor in the South* (1978).

Longshoremen

Dockworkers were vital to the port cities of the antebellum South, and they often organized to protect their interests. The New Orleans Screwmen's Benevolent Association (NOSBA), formed in 1850, probably became the South's first longshoremen's union. NOSBA, whose skilled members pressed cotton bales while others loaded ships, immediately began bargaining collectively. During the decade, NOSBA members—600 strong by 1860—waged three successful strikes. After the war, New Orleans longshoremen, with numbers greatly augmented by blacks, endured interracial strife incited by both employers and politicians. Yet, black and white screwmen in 1875 agreed to equalized wages and a quota system that survived into the 20th century.

Elsewhere, southern longshoremen formed unions in Galveston, Pensacola, Jacksonville, and Charleston. Racial friction also characterized their activities. In 1883, when Galveston's whites tried to drive off Afro-Americans, the blacks broke a strike in return for a company promise henceforth to provide them with steady work. Southern blacks, usually unionized, survived under the quota system and sometimes broke it. When the new port of Houston opened in 1917, blacks and whites, in a 99-year compact, agreed to share the work equally.

Many longshoremen's jobs, although avidly sought, provided only sporadic, backbreaking work with low pay. In New Orleans as many as 600 fruithandlers lined up for tickets to unload the banana boats. They earned 75 cents on a good day, but only 25 if just one ship arrived. According to the Marine Transport Workers Union (Industrial Workers of the World), which tried to organize the fruit-handlers in 1913, dock bosses usually dispensed the tickets to favorites, and United Fruit Company paymasters cheated the men out of part of their wages.

By World War I the position of the elite screwmen also eroded as technological changes accelerated ship loading and as the high-density cotton press, operable by the unskilled, weakened the screwmen's bargaining power. With labor in ample supply, employers in 1923 easily defeated the International Longshoremen's Association (ILA) in a disastrous New Orleans strike. By 1931 the ILA had been eliminated from New Orleans and seriously crippled in the Texas Gulf ports.

The passage of the National Industrial Recovery Act strengthened the longshoremen, and in 1935 the ILA struck the Gulf ports west of Pensacola for equal wages and union recognition. Blood flowed as employers armed strikebreakers. A union threat to close all U.S. ports brought representation elections, most of which the ILA won. In 1937, amidst charges by New Orleans longshoremen of corruption and collusion with employers, the ILA-AFL was challenged by a left-wing splinter group, the International Longshoremen and Warehousemen's Union (ILWU-CIO), which advocated racial equality and industrial unionism. In a bitter election, amidst charges of "communism," the ILA won. By 1939 it claimed about 16,611 southern longshoremen.

The ILA was expelled from the AFL in 1959 for gangsterism but continued to dominate southern ports in alliance with the Teamsters. National bargaining, pressed by the ILA but opposed by southern employers and longshoremen, proceeded very slowly. As containerization replaced break-bulk cargoes, however, southern wages and benefits tended to follow trends set by the ILA's master agreement in the Northeast. By 1971 longshoremen in all the southern ports received a standard guaranteed annual income.

Merl E. Reed
Georgia State University

Joseph P. Goldberg, *International Labor Review* (March 1973); F. Ray Marshall, *Labor in the South* (1967); Merl E. Reed, *Labor History* (Winter 1972); Jerrell H. Shofner, *Labor History* (Fall 1972); Philip Taft, *Industrial and Labor Relations Review* (April 1956).

Mine, Mill, and Smelter Workers

The Mine Mill union was initially known as the Western Federation of Miners. In 1916 its name was changed to the International Union of Mine, Mill, and Smelter Workers. The union met with little success in organizing workers before 1933. With the passage of the New Deal legislation, Mine Mill successfully organized in the copper, lead, zinc, iron ore, and precious metal mines of the western, midwestern, eastern, and southern states. Its center of strength in the South was in Alabama.

In Alabama chief support for the organizational efforts of Mine Mill came from the iron ore mines of Red Mountain in Jefferson County. The first local was chartered in July 1933 and eventually led to the union becoming a force to be reckoned with. This power was not realized until the workers had experienced two strikes, prolonged layoffs, harassment, and loss of many jobs. Nonetheless, concrete benefits were won by Mine Mill, for prior to the union coming to Alabama there had been no effective grievance procedures, no seniority clause, few health and safety regulations, no vacation with pay, and no portal to portal pay. In short, prior to Mine Mill arrival there had been no effective mechanism through which the workers could negotiate with management on an equitable basis.

Locally, the International Union of Mine, Mill, and Smelter Workers was termed the "Nigger Union" because it espoused racial equality during a time and in a place where segregation was the law. Its constitution stipulated a 50/50 racial mixture in the locals' leadership. This policy led many white workers to refuse to support the union. In the 1930s Mine Mill gained respectability because of a National Labor Relations Board ruling that awarded back pay to 159 workers who had been fired as a result of their participation in a strike. The union also gained company recognition as sole bargaining agent in the Tennessee Coal, Iron and Railroad Company (TCI) mines.

Prior to 1938 the work force in the iron ore mines was predominately black and the union was also. After 1938 TCI changed its hiring policy and more white workers were employed. Between 1938 and 1948 the complexion of the mines and Mine Mill would change considerably. This would lead to a conflict between the old Mine Mill members and the new members who would be mostly white.

In late 1948 certain white members of the Alabama Mine Mill locals contacted the United Steelworkers of America (USWA) about possible affiliation. This marked the beginning of the successful secessionists' struggle on Red Mountain. Between January and mid-March 1949, the secessionists mounted an intense campaign against the Mine Mill union, and the USWA challenged Mine Mill by calling for a consent election. Mine Mill accused the Steelworkers Union of raiding, and a hotly contested election drive for the loyalty of Red Mountain iron ore miners ensued. Black workers predominated in the effort to retain Mine Mill as sole representative at the workplace, although a few white workers were supportive as well. It appears that only white workers were in support of the USWA. The Steelworkers won the election and replaced Mine Mill as the sole bargaining agent in the TCI mines.

Black miners continually showed strong preference for Mine Mill rather than the USWA. As one miner suggested, "We looked upon Mine Mill not just as another labor union but as a way of life." Nevertheless, the final attempt of Mine Mill to wrest control from the Steelworkers Union was in 1952. This effort failed, and the union continued to decrease in importance on Red Mountain.

What combination made it possible for Mine Mill to organize and sustain itself on Red Mountain for nearly 15 years? First, the federal government and various pieces of labor legislation, including the National Industrial Recovery Act of 1933, the Wagner Act of 1935, and the Fair Labor Standards Act of 1938, enabled the union to achieve victories that would have been otherwise impossible. Second, the international office of Mine Mill was alert enough to recognize the necessity of organization in the iron ore mines, perceptive enough to realize the importance of black workers, and militant enough to organize interracially. Third, the white workers who remained loyal to Mine Mill before and after 1938 were a courageous group, because they and their families were under constant attack by opponents of the "Nigger Union." The fourth ingredient in the success of the Alabama Mine Mill locals was persevering black workers, without whose tenacity Mine Mill would not have survived. The black majority who set the tone and charted the direction of the locals worked heroically from Mine Mill's inception, when it was most unpopular to be a union man on Red Mountain. Eventually the same men would use their knowledge in the wider arena of black protest movements.

Horace Huntley
University of Alabama at Birmingham

H. H. Chapman, *Iron and Steel Industries of the South* (1953); F. Ray Marshall, *Labor in the South* (1967); Philip Taft, in *Organizing Dixie: Alabama Workers in the Industrial Era*, ed. Gary M. Fink (1981).

Mitchell, H. L.

(b. 1906) Reformer.

A champion of the rights of southern tenant farmers and sharecroppers, Harry Leland Mitchell devoted much of his life to promoting and assisting their cause, mostly under the auspices of the Southern Tenant Farmers' Union (STFU). He was instrumental in founding the union, which he believed would help attract government aid and give poor farmers bargaining power with their landlords.

Mitchell was born near Halls, Tenn., and, with his family, lived his first few years in the home of his grandfather, a Baptist preacher. Mitchell did not conform to his grandfather's religious ideals, sympathizing instead with Darwinists and Socialists. In 1933 Mitchell attended a speech by Socialist party leader Norman Thomas, who condemned segregation. The notion had never before occurred to Mitchell, but he agreed and afterward worked for blacks and whites throughout his career. He became the state secretary for the Arkansas Socialist party but turned his allegiance to the Democratic party in 1936.

Having sharecropped with little success, Mitchell moved from Tennessee to Tyronza, Ark., in 1927 to open a dry-cleaning business. He became acquainted with many of the poor farmers in the region and helped unemployed blacks who wanted public work jobs to organize in protest of their situation. In 1934, when plantation owner Hiram Norcross evicted 23 tenant families, Mitchell and Clay East cofounded the STFU. He served as the union's executive secretary from then until 1939, when the STFU withdrew from the Congress of Industrial Organizations (CIO). Mitchell had favored the withdrawal, believing that the STFU should protect itself from the CIO's Communist influence. The issue had been controversial within the STFU, and Mitchell escaped the furor by accepting a job with the National Youth Administration. He also worked with the International Ladies' Garment Workers' Union before he rejoined the STFU in 1941, promptly being reelected to his former position.

Mitchell served as president of the union from 1944 until 1960, during which time the union became the National Farm Labor Union and later, the National Agricultural Workers Union. Until his retirement in 1972, he continued to help organize workers ranging from dairy farmers to sugar mill workers to menhaden fishermen. His greatest influence was in advancing the cause of struggling southern tenant farmers and sharecroppers. Through his efforts for the STFU, he became an important force in the southern labor movement, leading strikes, publicizing agricultural problems in the South, and proving that blacks and whites could indeed work together to protect their rights as laborers.

Jessica Foy
Cooperstown Graduate Programs
Cooperstown, New York

Anthony P. Dunbar, *Against the Grain: Southern Radicals and Prophets, 1929–1959* (1981); Gary M. Fink, ed., *Biographical Dictionary of American Labor Leaders* (1974); H. L. Mitchell, *Mean Things Happening in This Land: The Life and Times of H. L. Mitchell* (1979); Southern Tenant Farmers' Union Papers, University of North Carolina, Chapel Hill.

Murphy, Edgar Gardner

(1869–1913) Clergyman and social reformer.

Murphy was born near Fort Smith, Ark., to Samuel W. and Janie Gardner Murphy. When her husband abandoned the family in 1874, Janie Murphy moved with the children to San Antonio, Tex., where young Murphy received his early formal education. In 1885 he entered the University of the South, where he was heavily influenced by Sewanee's theologian, William Porcher DuBose. After graduating four years later, Murphy studied at New York's General Theological Seminary, married Maud King, and was ordained as a priest in the Protestant Episcopal church.

In 1893 Murphy was called to a parish in Laredo, Tex., where he organized the community's protest of the burning of a black man accused of rape and murder. Although he served parishes in Chillicothe, Ohio, and Kingston, N.Y., Murphy longed to return to the South, and in 1898 the young priest moved to St. John's Episcopal Church in Montgomery, Ala. Thereafter, his liberal theological perspective, largely learned from DuBose and reflected in his own *The Larger Life* (1897), was brought to bear upon the New South's social problems—child labor, public education, and race relations—in two other works, *Problems of the Present South* (1904) and *The Basis of Ascendancy* (1910).

Murphy was instrumental in the formation of the Alabama Child Labor Committee in 1901 and two years later the National Child Labor Committee. Although his commitment to local regulatory initiatives led him to oppose national legislation against child labor, he helped to spark statewide initiatives throughout the South and saw Alabama adopt the strongest regulatory legislation within the region in his lifetime. He resigned from St. John's in 1901 and two years later withdrew from the ministry altogether to serve as executive secretary of the Southern Education Board. In that capacity, Murphy directed public relations campaigns throughout the South, which substantially succeeded in massing public support to strengthen the region's weak public school systems. From 1900, when he organized the Southern Society for the Promotion of the Study of Race Conditions and Problems in the South, until his death, he was a sophisticated spokesman for white racial paternalism. Equally opposed to radical white racists and to black or white racial egalitarians or assimilationists, Edgar Gardner Murphy was a subtle apologist for segregation, but one who gave racism a benign expression.

Ralph E. Luker
Wilmington, Delaware

Hugh C. Bailey, *Edgar Gardner Murphy: Gentle Progressive* (1968); Daniel Levine, *Varieties of Reform Thought* (1964); Ralph E. Luker, *A Southern Tradition in Theology and Social Criticism, 1830–1930: The Religious Liberalism and Social Conservatism of James Warley Miles, William Porcher DuBose, and Edgar Gardner Murphy* (1984).

Oil Workers

Southern oil workers first acted in concert in 1905, when the Guffey Company, predecessor of Gulf, arbitrarily slashed wages. The strike saved the $3 scale, but the men soon allowed their union to disappear. The wage remained at $3 until 1917 while the price of oil increased a hundredfold. Nonunion oil workers thus sacrificed millions of dollars in merited wage increases. Unionism bloomed again during World War I, as the wages and the primitive company camps became intolerable. Ten thousand strikers walked out after the owners of the fields in Texas and Louisiana refused even to meet with their representatives. The major companies utilized martial law and private armies to break the strike, and soon they virtually destroyed the union.

Under the protection of the National Recovery Act (1933–34) oil unionism revived. Dozens of locals were formed and a national agreement was signed with Sinclair. The demise of the NRA, rising company resistance to unions, and relatively high pay scales in the refineries drastically hindered the growth of the oil workers' union. During their renewed organizing efforts of the late 1930s and the war years, members of the Oil Workers International (Congress of Industrial Organizations) were continually labeled as a Communist front by southeast Texas Congressman Martin Dies. And the refineries established company unions, deliberately hired minorities in order to stir racial tensions, and jacked up wages just before organizing drives. Still, the union doubled its membership during the war, winning significant victories at the Texas Company and Gulf in Port Arthur. It failed to crack the nation's largest refinery, Esso at Baton Rouge, or the big Humble plant at Baytown, both of which were Standard Oil operations. In 1944 so many oil workers registered to vote that it was a major factor in convincing Martin Dies not to run for reelection. Despite CIO policy, blacks and whites maintained separate locals in Beaumont and Port Arthur for years, until the Oil Workers International forced them to integrate. The Texas-Louisiana district became the largest branch of the union and took the lead in the 1945 nationwide strike that established oil workers as the highest paid manufacturing hands in the country.

Unlike other CIO unions that "invaded" the South, the Oil Workers International for over 30 years was the only union that maintained its headquarters south of the Mason-Dixon line (in Fort Worth). It did more than any other Texas or Louisiana union in the 1940s and 1950s to obliterate wage differentials among the races.

See also INDUSTRY: / Oil Industry

George N. Green
University of Texas at Arlington

Ruth A. Allen, *Chapters in the History of Organized Labor in Texas* (1941); Clyde Johnson, in *Essays in Southern Labor History: Selected Papers, Southern Labor History Conference, 1976*, ed. Gary M. Fink and Merl E. Reed (1977); James C. Maroney, in *Essays in Southern Labor History: Selected Papers, Southern Labor History Conference, 1976*, ed. Gary M. Fink and Merl E. Reed (1977); Harvey O'Connor, *History of Oil Workers International Union* (1950).

Owsley Thesis

The Owsley thesis is the work of Frank Lawrence Owsley (1890–1956), an Alabama-born historian who spent most of his academic career at Vanderbilt University. Disagreeing with interpretations that portrayed the Old South as a society totally dominated by the planter class, Owsley and his students, most notably Herbert Weaver and Blanche Henry Clark, focused on the role of the southern plain folk. The Owsley thesis, based largely on data from the U.S. census returns for Alabama, Mississippi, Louisiana, and Tennessee, contended that the majority of antebellum southerners were middle-class farmers, that these yeomen (who were often nonslaveholders) owned their fair share of land comparable in quality to that held by planters, and that this middle class prospered and grew during the late antebellum years. Owsley's views were summarized most importantly in *Plain Folk of the Old South*, published in 1949.

The Owsley thesis has always had critics. Even as it was being elaborated, Fabian Linden argued in the *Journal of Negro History* (1946) that Owsley's data and methodology were open to question and that the mere existence of a large middle class did not prove that its members stood on any sort of an equal footing with the planters. Did the plain folk, Linden asked, have a share of southern agricultural wealth and production proportionate to their numbers in the population as a whole? He thought not. Other historians have pointed out that Owsley offered no precise definition of the plain folk, making them nearly indistinguishable from the planters. And the general tendency in the writing of southern history since the 1950s has been a continued, and even greater, emphasis on planter dominance rather than yeoman democracy. Nevertheless, the Owsley thesis constituted a minor revolution in historical interpretation of the Old South. Due primarily to the work of Owsley and his students, it is clear that antebellum society was not a simple three-tiered arrangement of planters, poor whites, and black slaves, and every modern account must at least consider the place and role of the plain folk majority.

Randolph B. Campbell
North Texas State University

Fabian Linden, *Journal of Negro History* (April 1946); Frank L. Owsley, *Plain Folk of the Old South* (1949), with Harriet C. Owsley, *Journal of Southern History* (February 1940).

Railroad Workers

The railroad has been important in the economic and geographic expansion of the United States and certainly so in the South, whose railroad network was rebuilt after the Civil War. Until recently most attention has been paid to the history of railroads as corporate institutions (or to their entrepreneurs) and not to the lives of the individual workers so important to the railroad's development. Particularly through the use of oral history, recent studies have illuminated the lives of railroad workers and illustrated the relationship of the southern railroader to railroaders elsewhere.

Among the common characteristics of railroad life is the counterpoint of hard work and danger and a romantic attachment to railroading. This latter phenomenon bridges the work force from management to labor and contributes to a sense of worker community, a form of corporate family. Railroad workers almost uniformly bemoan the transformation from steam to diesel power and admit a preference for passenger traffic over freight. They share a common store of tales, songs, and poems, which treat the pleasures and problems of railroading, undoubtedly as a means of dealing with the pressures of their occupation.

Some of these are staples of folk culture, such as the story of Casey Jones, the "brave engineer" of the late 19th century who was immortalized in a Tin Pan Alley version of this railroad tale. And there are similar stories passed on by individual railroaders about the brave engineer (the "old hogger") who carried heavy loads at high speeds around dangerous curves and up steep hills, often with the reward being a trip to the "promised land."

Another well-known hero was John Henry, the giant who supposedly weighed 44 pounds at birth and later worked for the Chesapeake & Ohio Railroad laying track and driving tunnels. Legend holds that for a $100 bet he was matched against a steam drill. He won the contest but died the following night from his exertion. Such railroad songs, poems, and fables mix myth and reality. The hard work and danger faced by the railroader often resulted in death or injury, although the folk versions obviously exaggerate the magnitude of the experience.

The role of the union in dealing with management in order to improve working conditions and settle labor disputes weighs heavily on the railroader. Two other topics (which also concern the role of the union) are the status of women in the railroad work group and the treatment of blacks. While these matters are part of a national concern, they also illuminate the more general attitudes of southern society.

Women had to fight for jobs other than the most menial. Even traditional "woman's work"—such as secretarial posts—often went to men on the railroad, for rail secretaries had to travel overnight with their superiors, who were, of course, male.

In the antebellum South black railroad employees dominated most jobs except for managerial and clerical positions and those of conductor. They even drove trains, in violation of state laws. After the Civil War they were relegated to low-level positions such as porters and laborers, a trend that changed (in both North and South) only with late 20th-century fair employment practices. For example, of 136,065 black rail workers in 1924, 115,937 were laborers or porters. (Of these, 86,262 were in the South.)

The black rail worker retained a loyalty to the profession, but also a deep bitterness over the racial attitudes that resulted in crude jokes, separate (and inferior) dining and sleeping conditions on the trains themselves, and the inability to secure food or lodging outside the train yard when runs took a crew away overnight.

Although the Knights of Labor tried unsuccessfully to organize southern railroaders during the 19th century, the American Federation of Labor finally brought unionization to these railroads. Southern locals of the four major operating unions—the Brotherhood of Locomotive Engineers, Order of Railroad Conductors, Brotherhood of Locomotive Firemen and Enginemen, and Brotherhood of Railroad Trainmen—were organized shortly after the creation of their national unions. In addition, some national unions that enrolled many railroaders—Machinists, Blacksmiths, Boilermakers, Telegraphers, and Maintenance of Way—started in the South.

By 1900 most skilled southern railroaders were unionized, and after World War I—due to federal policies—virtually all southern rail employees were union members. But the unsuccessful national shopmen's strike in 1922 caused a decline in nonoperating unions in the South. (In 1925, the operating unions had 6,295 members in Georgia, down from 6,440 in 1920.) The failure to organize blacks after this time was a weakness that also promised an opportunity for potential strikebreaking. Certainly an exception was the Brotherhood of Sleeping Car Porters, a union of black workers whose membership increased (particularly during the late New Deal, under the leadership of A. Philip Randolph).

As the nature of railroading changed—from steam to diesel, passenger to freight, local control to national (often northern)—the railroader retained a sense of nostalgia, but perhaps at the expense of the concept of community.

See also FOLKLIFE: / Henry, John; Jones, Casey; HISTORY AND MANNERS: Railroads; INDUSTRY: / Railroad Industry

Carl Ryant
University of Louisville

Stuart Leuthner, *The Railroaders* (1983); Walter Licht, *Working for the Railroad: The Organization of Work in the Nineteenth Century* (1983); F. Ray Marshall, *Labor in the South* (1967); Carl Ryant, *Register of the Kentucky Historical Society* (Winter 1984).

Sharecroppers Union

In the spring of 1931 the *Southern Worker*, a Communist-party newspaper based in Chattanooga, published letters from "farmer correspondents" in Camp Hill, Ala., stating that landlords and merchants in the area had cut off food advances and reduced day wages for field work. In response to calls for help, the party sent an organizer to form a farm union local. At a first meeting, tenant farmers and sharecroppers drew up a list of demands: food advances through "settlement" time with landowners; the right to sell their own crops and to plant small gardens for home use; cash wages for picking cotton; a three-hour midday rest for day workers; a nine-month school year for black children and a free school bus.

But in 1931 black farmers—and white farmers—had to struggle simply to remain on the land. A confrontation at Camp Hill was characteristic of the Sharecroppers Union's (SCU) early history from 1931 to 1933. Camp Hill farmers had not yet planned how to implement their demands when, on 15 July 1931, their meeting was raided by the high sheriff and his posse. The raid touched off several days of violence. One farmer was killed and his house burned, and 35 black men were jailed on charges ranging from carrying concealed weapons to conspiracy and assault with intent to murder. They were never brought to trial, but their local was effectively suppressed.

In the fall of 1932 the party sent another organizer to Tallapoosa County, this time to Reeltown, 15 miles southwest of Camp Hill. Following a shootout in December between a sheriff's posse and farmers attempting to stop a foreclosure, legal prosecution and vigilante violence curtailed union activity there, too.

Starting in 1933, the SCU concentrated its efforts in Black Belt counties west of Tallapoosa, where the majority of farmers were landless black farm workers whose economic position was suited to industrial-type organizing. In 1935 union-led strikes succeeded in raising wages. But repression was severe, especially in Lowndes County, where white landowners defended their supremacy with armed force. Seeking protection and additional resources, the SCU turned to the New Deal for relief. The union moved its headquarters to New Orleans, where it could maintain an office and publish its newspaper openly. When, in 1936, the Communist party called for a "United Front" of Communist and other "progressive forces," SCU organizers were already preparing to affiliate with national unions. By late 1938 SCU tenants and sharecroppers had transferred to the Farmers Union, an organization modeled on the Grange and the Farmers' Alliance of the 1880s and 1890s. Wageworkers merged into the Agricultural Workers Union, which was chartered by the American Federation of Labor in 1937 as the Farm Laborers and Cotton Field Workers Union.

Affiliation signaled the SCU's shift from a strategy of "national liberation" of the Black Belt to positions squarely in the tradition of American agrarian protest. The union's struggle to secure a livelihood for poor farmers was resolved, in part, by the general "solutions" to the Depression. By the outbreak of World War II, war industries had begun to absorb black and white farmers displaced in the economic crisis, and public agencies were maintaining others who could not or would not leave the land.

Theodore Rosengarten
McClellanville, South Carolina

David E. Conrad, *The Forgotten Farmers: The Story of Sharecroppers in the New Deal* (1965); Donald H. Grubbs, *Cry from the Cotton: The Southern Tenant Farmers' Union and the New Deal* (1971); Theodore Saloutos, *Farmer Movements in the South, 1865–1933* (1960).

Southern Conference for Human Welfare

The Southern Conference for Human Welfare (SCHW) was a controversial liberal organization that advocated sweeping social, economic, and political change in the South from 1938 to 1948. Inspired by President Franklin D. Roosevelt and his New Deal, some 1,200 enthusiastic delegates gathered in Birmingham, Ala., in November 1938 to form the Southern Conference. Hoping to modernize the South and liberalize its Democratic party, the group supported labor's right to organize, endorsed liberal economic policies, advocated repeal of poll tax laws, and criticized racial discrimination.

Frank P. Graham of the University of North Carolina served as the organization's first chairman until 1940, when the Reverend John Thompson, a left-wing Oklahoma minister, succeeded him. Clark Foreman, a New Deal administrator, replaced Thompson and headed the group from 1942 until 1948. Other southern liberals active in SCHW included Lucy Randolph Mason, H. C. Nixon, Virginia Durr, Aubrey Williams, Benjamin Mays, Lillian Smith, James Dombrowski, and the radical activist Joseph Gelders.

During SCHW's early years members sponsored several educational campaigns concerning social problems, devoted special attention to efforts to repeal poll tax laws, and, after World War II, organized numerous voter registration drives. The group's leadership eventually endorsed such liberal congressional legislation as an antilynching law, federal aid to education, and the creation of a Fair Employment Practices Committee.

This controversial support for federal intervention in southern race relations outraged many conservative whites and led to fierce attacks on the organization. Critics also repeatedly charged that SCHW was Communist dominated. Actually, only a handful of Communists ever joined the conference, but the group's leaders stubbornly refused to expel them. This principled but unpopular stand proved quite damaging to the conference during the early years of the Cold War.

The ideological split within American liberalism in the late 1940s between Cold War liberals and Popular Front liberals further divided SCHW, especially when Foreman, Durr, and several others joined Henry Wallace's ill-fated presidential campaign. The communism issue, internal factionalism, and mounting attacks from segregationists eventually combined to destroy the conference, which disbanded in late November 1948. Yet the group's tax-exempt subsidiary, the Southern Conference Education Fund, survived its parent's death and continued to support southern desegregation during the 1950s. Although SCHW failed during its lifetime, its vision was ultimately vindicated in the 1960s when Congress passed extensive civil rights legislation and the Twenty-Fourth Amendment outlawed the poll tax.

Charles H. Martin
University of Texas at El Paso

Clark Foreman, *Phylon* (June 1951); Thomas A. Krueger, *And Promises to Keep: The Southern Conference for Human Welfare* (1967); Charles H. Martin, in *Perspectives on the American South*, vol. 3, ed. James C. Cobb and Charles Reagan Wilson (1985).

Southern Regional Council (SRC)

An Atlanta-based reform agency, the Southern Regional Council (SRC) balances a commitment to social justice with a devotion to rigorous policy analysis. Proud of its native roots yet financially dependent on non-southern foundations, dedicated to the fight against discrimination yet wary of direct action, SRC is unique among southern protest organizations. In contrast to groups like the Southern Organizing Committee for Social and Economic Justice, the council shuns political activity, demonstrations, and radical economic theory. Instead SRC works for equality of opportunity through interracial dialogue, research and publications programs, and the timely influence of "southerners of good will." At times, SRC has taken a more direct approach, notably during the 1960s when it coordinated the black registration drive known as the Voter Education Project. The council prefers, however, to serve as an information clearinghouse, providing community leaders with the knowledge and technical expertise necessary to counter prejudice and promote voluntary change.

Founded in 1944, the SRC grew out of dissatisfaction among moderate blacks and liberal whites with the Commission on Interracial Cooperation (CIC), a race relations betterment group active during the interwar years. During World War II, with racial tensions on the rise, southern blacks like Gordon Hancock and P. B. Young charged the CIC's white leadership with timidity and paternalism. In response, CIC secretary Jessie Daniel Ames convinced white liberals to support a new regional planning agency (an idea advanced by Howard W. Odum as early as 1936), which would appeal to northern foundations, revitalize southern liberalism, and check the growing independence of native blacks. The SRC's white charter members pledged constructive responses to black grievances and assured black leaders of a full partnership in the organization. Yet council leaders were equally committed to winning the support of moderate white professionals and businessmen. Under Executive Director Guy Benton Johnson the SRC avoided a stand on the segregation issue, choosing instead to work for racial progress within the separate-but-equal doctrine. SRC programs, like those of the CIC, reflected a deep respect for regional folkways, especially the white South's antipathy for "racial agitation" and "outside interference."

Critics like Lillian Smith and J. Saunders Redding soon branded the SRC "a defensive holding action" against genuine change. By early 1947, however, as the hope of attracting prominent whites dimmed, the council began to modify its policies in response to the changing racial climate. In 1948, under the leadership of former New Dealer George Mitchell, SRC endorsed the more active federal role proposed by President Harry Truman's Committee on Civil Rights. In 1951, despite an acute financial crisis, SRC renounced segregation as "a cruel and needless penalty on the human spirit." SRC's respected monthly, *New South*, closely monitored the progress of federal desegregation suits. In early 1954, in anticipation of the *Brown* decision and with the help of the first in a series of major Ford Foundation grants, SRC committed itself to the development of a network of state human relations councils. When *Brown* came, SRC officials promptly embraced it, predicting that "the South will go along." By 1956 virulent white resistance forced SRC to place the faltering state councils "on their own mettle" and to refocus on regionwide programs run out of the Atlanta office. Segregationists constantly charged that SRC was a "Communist front" and a threat to the "southern way of life." Yet the council stepped up its analysis of segregationist tactics and even launched new programs, including a race relations consultant service, which sent SRC staff members into racially troubled communities.

In 1960, soon after the Greensboro sit-ins, SRC leaders like Leslie Dunbar and James McBride Dabbs recognized the legitimacy and staying power of the new student activism. In 1961 a report on *The Federal Executive and Civil Rights* caught the attention of the John F. Kennedy Administration. At the suggestion of Martin Luther King, Jr., SRC became the coordinating agent for five major civil rights groups involved in the Kennedy-endorsed but foundation-financed Voter Education Project. Using registration data gathered in the project, SRC threw itself into the fight for the Voting Rights Act of 1965. The council also denounced black separatism and rejected the confrontational tactics some activists thought essential. Tensions between black staff members and white administrators in the Atlanta office threatened SRC's central program. Critics complained that the council had become little more than the voice of an elite white progressivism.

Such charges were symptomatic of the disintegation of the civil rights movement in the late 1960s. SRC's response was to reemphasize its traditional fact-finding role and broaden its range of concern. While SRC researchers documented southern noncompliance with federal civil rights laws, the council published scores of influential reports on such pressing social problems as housing, hunger, public health, prison conditions, and migrant labor. In the 1970s, SRC's "government monitoring project" weighed the social impact of the "new federalism" and a new information service aided southern legislators sympathetic to minorities and the poor. During the 1980s, when SRC became a persistent critic of Reagan Administration policy on voting rights and social welfare issues, the council continued to search for indigenous financial support. Yet SRC had earned a national reputation as an interpreter and advocate of southern change and had become a rallying point for southerners inspired by the council's vision of a "humane and democratic South."

See also BLACK LIFE: / Commission on Interracial Cooperation; Hancock, Gordon Blaine; King, Martin Luther, Jr.; LAW: / *Brown* v. *Board of Education*; MEDIA: / Young, P. B.; WOMEN'S LIFE: / Ames, Jessie Daniel; Smith, Lillian

Anthony Newberry
Jefferson Community College

William C. Allred, Jr., "The Southern Regional Council, 1943–1961" (M.A. thesis, Emory University, 1966); Edwin Lee Plowman, "Analysis of Selective Strategies Used by the Southern Regional Council in Effecting Social Change in the South" (Ph.D. dissertation, Boston University, 1976); The Southern Regional Council Papers, Robert W. Woodruff Library, Atlanta University Center.

Southern Student Organizing Committee

The Southern Student Organizing Committee (SSOC) was a predominantly white organization that encouraged and coordinated student activism on southern campuses from 1964 to 1969. At first the group represented an updated version of liberal interracialism, but eventually many of its members became associated with the New Left. In 1969 the organization disbanded after an internal split resulting from its repudiation on ideological grounds by Students for a Democratic Society (SDS).

In April 1964 some 45 representatives from 15 southern colleges met in Nashville to form SSOC. The organization's major goals, stated in a declaration of principles entitled "We'll Take Our Stand," were to educate well-intentioned but somewhat sheltered southern students at predominantly white schools concerning civil rights, poverty, and other vital national issues, and to sponsor various community and campus projects. The delegates also endorsed such activities as fighting segregation, combating poverty, expanding social services, encouraging peace and disarmament, and ending "man's inhumanity to man."

Elected as officers were Gene Guerrero, Jr., chairman, Sue Thrasher, executive secretary, and Ron Parker, treasurer. As its distinctive symbol the group selected a Confederate flag on which clasped black and white hands had been superimposed. SSOC published several newspapers including *New South Student* and the *Phoenix* and distributed numerous pamphlets on such topics as civil rights, the Vietnam War, and women's liberation.

At first the organization worked closely with the Student Nonviolent Coordinating Committee (SNCC), and the group was even briefly viewed as SNCC's white counterpart. At the same time, SSOC also received recognition as a "fraternal organization" from SDS, and in effect became SDS's southern agent. As ties to SNCC weakened, SSOC leaders moved closer to SDS and its evolving New Left ideology. Meanwhile, SSOC did not seek a mass membership but instead attempted to coordinate local groups' diverse activities while relying on grants from national foundations for its financing. This led to wide variations in local programs and a feeling that the organization lacked direction.

Despite cooperation with SDS, SSOC leaders continued to display a "southern consciousness" and insisted that the unique historical development of the South warranted a special organizing perspective that avoided taking unnecessarily controversial stands. For example, SSOC sponsored various peace activities including antiwar workshops, yet it never adopted a formal resolution condemning the Vietnam War for fear of harming its image. This emphasis on southernness and moderation eventually brought criticism to the group from the New Left.

In March 1969 SDS, racked with bitter internal divisions, unexpectedly condemned these liberal tendencies in SSOC and severed all connections with the group. Taken aback, SSOC activists gathered in Edwards, Miss., in June to discuss the organization's future. Although one faction favored reorganizing and continuing SSOC, pro-SDS members carried the day and voted to disband the group and destroy all records and correspondence.

Charles H. Martin
University of Texas at El Paso

Clayborne Carson, *In Struggle: SNCC and the Black Awakening of the 1960s* (1981).

Southern Tenant Farmers' Union

The Southern Tenant Farmers' Union was founded in Tyronza, Ark., in April 1934 by a handful of black and white sharecroppers, tenants, and small businessmen. Prominent among the latter were cofounders H. L. Mitchell and Clay East, native southerners whose beliefs derived from southwestern Populist, Socialist, and other radical traditions. Responding to growing misery as the Great Depression deepened, Mitchell and East noted that the New Deal's Agricultural Adjustment Administration (AAA) not only created a cotton scarcity but thereby gave planters both the means and the incentive to drive labor off the land. The AAA offered a federal subsidy that could be used to mechanize; the incentive was the easily circumvented requirement to share the subsidy with tenants but not wage laborers. Roosevelt had already explained away his creation of scarcity as a necessary evil, but for the creation of unemployment there could be little justification. With the purge of liberal sharecropper supporters from the AAA and the outbreak of violence against STFU members and leaders, both during the first months of 1935, financial aid began to appear from outside the South. A radical but anti-Communist Virginia clergyman, Howard Kester, and a railroad heir purged from AAA, Gardner Jackson, led a nationwide "sharecropper consciousness" movement that helped produce the LaFollette Civil Liberties Committee, a fact-finding commission on farm tenancy, and generated a degree of visibility that may have saved the STFU from as violent a fate as some other radical, racially mixed organizations. Its membership reached about 35,000 in Arkansas, Oklahoma, and Texas.

Racial integration was common at the larger STFU meetings, although in a few places segregated locals were permitted. The fundamentalist religion of the members furnished inspiration and ritual. Such men as A. B. Brookins and John Handcox, both black, changed gospel music into protest songs, such as "We Shall Not Be Moved," that endured into the 1960s and beyond.

The STFU broke away from a more leftist agricultural union in 1939, exaggerating disagreements over dues and STFU autonomy into one of America's first "Communist rule-or-ruin" controversies. The ruined STFU furnished a base after World War II for cofounder Mitchell's continued efforts to aid farm workers in California and Louisiana.

Donald H. Grubbs
University of the Pacific

Anthony P. Dunbar, *Against the Grain: Southern Radicals and Prophets, 1929–1959* (1981); Donald H. Grubbs, *Cry from the Cotton: The Southern Tenant Farmers' Union and the New Deal* (1971); H. L. Mitchell, *Mean Things Happening in This Land: The Life and Times of H. L. Mitchell* (1979); Southern Tenant Farmers' Union Papers, University of North Carolina and microfilm.

Textile Workers

Southern textile workers, often called "lintheads," have been categorized as a subspecies of "poor whites." Their numbers alone command attention, reaching nearly 600,000 in 1950 and far outnumbering any other group of workers in industrial manufacturing in the South. Nowhere in the United States, save for New England and parts of the Middle Atlantic states, have textile workers had such numerical weight. Southern textile workers lived and worked in the southern Piedmont from southern Virginia to northern Alabama and Mississippi with clusters in Tennessee and into the midlands of the Carolinas and Georgia.

The antebellum southern textile industry worked whites, free blacks, and slaves, sometimes in racially mixed factories. But a shift to using only white workers began before 1865 and became a hallmark of the industry. Although other southern manufacturers, like those in tobacco, iron and steel, or forest products, employed blacks extensively, southern textiles remained a white bastion for more than 100 years.

Textile factories in the Northeast and the Middle Atlantic states also had predominantly white work forces, but that was more the product of demographic factors than overt discrimination. Moreover, these northern factories relied heavily upon immigrant labor from Europe and Canada. By contrast, southern companies used an overwhelmingly white, Anglo-Saxon, Protestant work force drawn from where the industry was located and

Child laborer in a textile mill, North Carolina, early 1900s

from southern Appalachia. Employers found that in the economically underdeveloped South, textiles attracted an adequate supply of labor despite its low pay, its characteristic machine tending, and its slim prospects for promotion and upward mobility.

Southern mills used the "Slater system" of family labor for many years. The heavy reliance upon children under 16 for workers persisted in southern mills longer than elsewhere in the nation. Women always formed a large part of the work force in southern textiles, at times a majority. In fact, textiles probably is unique among manufacturing industries in the United States for employing males and females in nearly equal parts.

Until the selling of most of the company-owned mill villages after the mid-1930s, textile workers lived in company-owned houses. That, plus the power of the companies in local churches, schools, and even stores, gave management great power but not complete control over their labor. Management struggled with high rates of turnover and absenteeism and dealt with workers who often struck even if they were not union builders. Southern textile workers struck as early as the 1870s, and they precipitated the largest strike in American history, the Great Textile Strike of 1934. Southern textile workers even forced management not to reduce its low labor costs further by drawing upon the vast pool of black labor in the South. Management, on the other hand, used the threat of black labor as an effective means for setting limits to worker power, in particular defeating most efforts to unionize.

Individual homeownership, post–World War II economic growth, and the spread of the automobile and of television broke the bounds of the southern textile village. Once virtually the only alternative to farming, the textile industry and the life associated with it began to lose their hold after 1940. Southern textile workers began seeking jobs and futures elsewhere for themselves and their children. Government pressures and economic forces opened the textile industry to blacks after 1960. Once among the most racially segregated of southern laborers, textile workers became some of the most racially integrated, and the transformation occurred largely without violence.

Recent developments suggest that southern textiles will offer fewer jobs for blacks or whites and will play a diminishing role in the regional economy. As in many other manufacturing industries, southern textiles have become less labor-intensive, more capital-intensive, and more dependent upon overseas operations. Textiles and textile workers, the foot soldiers of the New South, are being displaced as a result of the growth of the New South.

See also INDUSTRY: / Textile Industry

Tom E. Terrill
University of South Carolina
at Columbia

Mimi Conway, *Rise, Gonna Rise: A Portrait of Southern Textile Workers* (1979); Herbert J. Lahne, *The Cotton Mill Worker* (1944); J. Kenneth Morland, *Millways of Kent* (1958).

Timber Workers

Laborers from England, Europe, and Africa were the first to exploit colonial southern forests for fuel, building materials, ship timber, and lumber for export. They also cleared trees and tapped and burned stately longleaf pines along the Atlantic and Gulf coasts for naval stores such as pitch, tar, and turpentine. The arduous forest work was done by hand. Originally, the chief tool was the cumbersome European felling ax, unimproved until the 18th century. Woodsmen sawed the felled trees on the spot, dragged the logs with draft animals, or floated them in streams to the sawmills. There others squared logs,

Hauling logs in Heard County, Ga., 1941

and two men, one on the log and the other in a pit, sawed them. When waterpower was available, this hard work could be done by European up-and-down saws until steam-powered mills with circular saws appeared in the 19th century. Working in naval stores was also difficult. Making tar, a sideline to agriculture, occurred in wintertime after summer crops were harvested, but turpentine workers toiled the year round, chopping boxes into the pines, "chipping" the bark so the gum flowed, "dipping" the gum into barrels, and hauling it to the still. This work, performed mostly by blacks, was the least desirable.

After the Civil War, improved technology made some work easier. The woodsman got the double bit ax and crosscut saw; the driver, "caralog" wheels, eight-wheeled log wagons, and tramroads; the rafters, spoke poles, peavys, and jam spikes; and mill workers, improved feeding equipment. But long hours (12 to 14 a day) and low daily pay ($0.66 to $1.25) continued as large corporations began replacing small operators after 1800. Gradually, workers had to move to isolated company towns as the tramroads went deeper into the forests, and submit to the rigid discipline of industrialism. Many faced brutal bosses and exploitation at company stores. Some were held in peonage, especially blacks, who were the majority of the forest workers except in east Texas and western Louisiana. In the late 1880s workers around Pascagoula joined the Knights of Labor and struck for a 10-hour day, but these efforts failed. Labor shortages and spontaneous strikes in western Louisiana led to the formation in 1910 of the Brotherhood of Timber Workers (BTW). The union asked for a 10-hour day, a minimum wage, bimonthly paydays in United States currency, and the end to company-store and hospital-fee abuses. Confronted by organized employers (the Southern Lumber Operators Association), the BTW affiliated with the Industrial Workers of the World but lost their battle in the face of opposition and violence from employers, citizen organizations, and local police. In 1919 Bogalusa timber workers, organized biracially, were also crushed. But wage gains came with the passage of New Deal legislation, and World War II labor shortages brought women of both races into the forests and sawmills. American Federation of Labor and Congress of Industrial Organizations organizing drives after the war were disappointing. Meanwhile, new machines made the workers more insignificant and their economic position less viable. Subsequent gains resulted from increases in the minimum wage.

See also INDUSTRY: / Timber Industry

Merl E. Reed
Georgia State University

Ruth A. Allen, *East Texas Lumber Workers: An Economic and Social Picture, 1870–1950* (1961); James E. Fickle, *The New South and the "New Competition": A Case Study of Trade Association Developments in the Southern Pine Industry* (1980); Nollie Hickman, *Mississippi Harvest: Lumbering in the Longleaf Pine Belt, 1840–1915* (1962).

Tobacco Workers

The first tobacco workers were white indentured servants imported by the Virginia Company of London to work for up to seven years in return for their ocean passage. Tobacco proved so successful, however, that white servants were soon replaced by slaves, and slaves and tobacco spread first to Virginia, then into Kentucky and North Carolina. After the destruction of slavery, tobacco growing continued to spread, and staple-crop agriculture persisted in the South until after World War II.

A traditional and conservative social order with distinguishing attitudes, habits, values, and lifestyles emerged out of slavery, staple-crop agriculture, and the rural economy. After the Civil War, the tobacco culture transmitted rural culture. The tobacco field was a family—men, women, and children working together throughout the long growing season that stretched over almost a year. The tobacco field was a school, a place to learn skills for coping in a society where formal education was an unaffordable luxury and social mobility a distant dream for all except the largest tobacco farmers. Finally, it was a church, a place to inculcate traditional values and to integrate and harmonize these with the realities of inequality, injustice, and a caste system.

Assembly line work in a cigar factory, Louisville, Ky., 1931

The Tobacco Workers' International Union (TWIU) started in 1895 and launched a boycott against the products of the industry giant, the American Tobacco Company. The union did not make a major impact on the industry, though, until signing a closed-shop agreement in December 1933 covering almost 4,600 laborers at the Brown and Williamson factories in Winston-Salem, N.C., Louisville, Ky., and Petersburg, Va. In the summer of 1937 the American Tobacco Company, Philip Morris, and Liggett and Myers signed contracts making the TWIU the bargaining agent for their factories in North Carolina and Virginia. By the beginning of World War II, the South's key tobacco companies were organized by the TWIU or other unions, except for 15,000 R. J. Reynolds employees. Unionization efforts among those workers, and other tobacco workers, would continue to be hampered by black-white tensions.

See also AGRICULTURE: / Tobacco Culture; INDUSTRY: / Tobacco Industry

Crandall Shiflett
Virginia Polytechnic Institute

Anthony J. Badger, *Prosperity Road: The New Deal, Tobacco and North Carolina* (1980); Federal Writers' Project, *These Are Our Lives* (1939); Herbert R. Northrup, *Quarterly Journal of Economics* (August 1942); Crandall Shiflett, *Patronage and Poverty in the Tobacco South: Louisa County, Virginia, 1860–1900* (1982).

Urbanization

BLAINE A. BROWNELL
University of Alabama at Birmingham
CONSULTANT

Street corner in New Orleans, 1940

Urbanization

Until the 20th century most historians of the United States considered cities mere by-products of national settlement or, at best, latecomers to the process. This seemed especially true for the South, the nation's most rural region. Towns and settlements were, however, footholds in a forbidding American wilderness and often precursors of agriculture. They grew up alongside the farm as necessary links in the patterns of regional and international trade, at first along the coast and the rivers and later across the sprawling interior. Such was also the case in the South, though the process of city building along the Chesapeake and the Tidewater was somewhat less pronounced because scores of rivers and thousands of tributaries penetrated the backcountry. Towns grew up everywhere, but few lasted long. In the early colonial era regional peculiarities did not overshadow the broad similarity of urbanization emerging across British North America.

Many southern towns still reflect the varied national legacies of their origins—the Spanish established St. Augustine in Florida and San Antonio in Texas, the French settled in New Orleans and Mobile, and the English founded Jamestown in 1607 and spread settlements inland. Each nation was attempting to exploit the opportunities of a new land and to forge commercial ties with Europe. In port cities such as Charleston and Savannah, merchants clustered around the wharves with an eye on the ocean to which they had consigned their hopes and fortunes.

Throughout history cities have played a pervasive role in nurturing and transmitting culture, from high art to fads and fashions. Traditionally the sites of great institutions and large concentrations of population and resources, urban areas have been inherently more likely to encourage innovation and challenges to authority—a tendency that seemed to be especially pronounced along the frontiers of American settlement. Settlers were escaping from and clinging to an earlier cultural inheritance in the midst of a fresh but sometimes threatening landscape. The earliest southern cities were conduits of European culture, connected by paths of commerce to the Old World and the jumping off point for moves into the interior. They were centers of administrative authority and economic activity.

Antebellum Cities. Cities grew dramatically in the first decades of the 19th century as entrepreneurs, speculators, artisans, and common laborers sought opportunity in new places, usually further inland. As a result, fledgling towns dotted the southern landscape in Tennessee, Alabama, Mississippi, Louisiana, and Texas at the same time that the large plantations played a more prominent role in the region's self-image and its national reputation. The relationship between town and farm was very close, as a largely agricultural economy provided major commercial opportunities and towns competed for rural trade.

A civic elite emerged in antebellum cities and directed every aspect of urban development that mattered as the city strove for recognition and prosperity. Forty percent of Richmond's leadership elite served in posts in the city government, a quarter were stockholders in railroad or canal companies, and a third were involved in charity organizations. Control of the press in the community was the essential ingredient to this leadership group. Newspapers were the main medium for advertising, information, and boosterism. Prominent southern newspapers included the Richmond *Enquirer*, the Charleston *Mercury*, and the New Orleans *Bee*. Editors themselves were boosters. James A. Cowardin, editor of the Richmond *Daily Dispatch*, which was one of the nation's first penny presses, was on the Richmond Board of Trade, vice president of the Virginia Mechanics' Institute, president of a brokerage firm, and a member of the Virginia House of Delegates. Editors like Cowardin defended their cities from accusations by rival cities, as urban areas fought for advantages in the keen competition that led to either success and growth or eventual decline.

Antebellum cities took large steps in providing essential urban services. Major concerns of city governments were crime prevention; fire and police protection; installation of water systems; street lighting, paving, repair, and drainage; and the need for parks and city beautification. Private associations provided relief for the poor, although urban governments gradually became significant sources of financial support for it. Churches operated orphan asylums, and other groups ran houses for widows or the elderly, and provided aid to the poor in general. Local governments established charity hospitals in some locations and almshouses almost everywhere. In locales such as Lexington, Ky., and Natchez, Miss., public education was a tradition by the time of the Civil War, but most city governments remained suspicious of public support for education. Lyceums and libraries encouraged adult education. Disease prevention was a major concern for urban areas throughout the nation, but especially in the South, where the climate made the region's people vulnerable to epidemics, such as the yellow fever plague that devastated Norfolk in 1855. Measures to encourage cleanliness proved to be the main weapon used by urban governments to prevent devastation from disease.

Antebellum cities were a part of the broader context of regional concerns. A considerable debate has taken place, for example, over whether or not southern towns were altogether inimical to chattel slavery, but, in any event, they surely appeared at least to undermine some of the more pronounced plantation features. Urban employers bargained for labor and were less likely than other southerners to inquire about a worker's status. The city provided slaves, and everyone else, a greater measure of anonymity and freedom from strict surveillance than rural areas. Cities attracted communities of free blacks and became magnets for freedmen after emancipation.

Impact of War. The Civil War devastated many southern urban areas. The business districts in Columbia and Charleston, S.C.; Fredericksburg, Petersburg, and Richmond, Va.; Selma, Ala.; and Atlanta, Ga., were all but destroyed. Even before the war the South's percentage of the nation's towns had been declining (in 1830 the 11 southern states that later became the Confederacy had 17.8 percent of the nation's towns; by 1860 the figure was 13.8 percent). The years of warfare spurred this decline. Many cities suffered because of the interruption in normal trade, damage to the surrounding farmlands, financial instability, disruption of public services, and loss of human life. For many cities, however, there were also benefits, such that the war was not the total disaster for urbanization that it has sometimes been portrayed. Cotton merchants in New Orleans and Memphis prospered after federal troops occupied those areas in 1862. Many cities escaped serious destruction, and some that were devastated, such as Atlanta, quickly recovered. The population of urban areas increased significantly during Reconstruction. Although older port cities such as New Orleans, Mobile, and Charleston did face a major recovery job after the war, the spread of the railroad brought the rise of new inland cities such as Atlanta, San Antonio, Houston, Dallas, and Birmingham. Older river towns like Memphis, Richmond, and Nashville continued to expand thanks to the expansion of the railroad system into their communities making them central locations for rail traffic. As before the war and as in other parts of the nation, the railroad was the key to success or failure of an urban area.

Expansion of Cities. Urban governments continued in the postbellum era the expansion of public services that had begun before the war. Advances were made in the growing cities in the installation of sewers, the paving of streets, the expansion of public education, improved law enforcement and fire fighting, city beautification through parks, and the establishment of municipal-owned water companies and city-regulated private utilities. Again, as earlier, disease prevention was a central concern of the governments. Cholera devastated Nashville in 1873, while yellow fever had the same impact on Montgomery in the same year. Fighting diseases emptied city coffers and disrupted trade. New Orleans was most affected of all, though, as yellow fever epidemics hit the city in 1873 and 1878, when 3,977 died. Yellow fever hit Memphis in 1878 and killed 5,800 people, nearly half of them Irish. The well-off, including a large contingent of Germans who moved to St. Louis, fled the city.

The full impact of the Industrial Revolution, registered in the Northeast and Midwest in the last half of the 19th century, was felt in the South, but to a measurably lesser degree. The urban economy remained more commercial than industrial and more tied to agriculture. Major inland cities like Atlanta, Memphis, and Nashville did, to be sure, grow in this era, and New Orleans maintained its role as the region's dominant urban area. Birmingham emerged as a new industrial city and promoters created another new Alabama community, Anniston, as a planned industrial center. Boosterism and an urban-commercial ethos prevailed in all the region's larger cities, as they emphasized economic growth, new technology, strong local loyalty, and "progress." Chambers of commerce appeared in large and small towns. Downtown areas, which symbolized the concentration of urban power, people, and resources, appeared with new buildings and amenities.

Urban architecture at the turn of the century was not, however, on the scale of the northern cities. Large office buildings did not dominate the skylines, but railroad stations, hotels, theaters, YMCAs, government office buildings, and churches did. Two- and three-story commercial buildings were erected after 1880 in business areas such as Second Avenue in Nashville and Commerce Street in Montgomery. Distinctive sections and neighborhoods within the cities, distinguishable by socioeconomic status and by racial composition, emerged. Central cities expanded through annexation and an increasing proliferation of retail and wholesale businesses. Growing suburbs surrounded a relatively dense central core, and urban patterns of trade and influence extended over a large area, perhaps even several counties.

These patterns were altogether like the urban configuration that appeared earlier in the North's largest cities, except that southern metropolises experienced decentralization at earlier stages of their development. At the beginning of the 20th century, in fact, some regional cities manifested arrangements that seemed almost preindustrial in character: a heavy concentration of business activity and upper-class residences near the city core, but with outlying shantytowns and a general mixture of populations and land uses throughout the central city.

Southern cities felt less of an impact in the late 19th century from foreign immigrants than their northern counterparts, but this should not lead to an underestimation of the importance of ethnic groups in southern cities. The Irish were a key part of the work force and the politics of Memphis, New Orleans, and Richmond. Merchants of Jewish ancestry were an important force in business and politics in Atlanta and Montgomery. Near the end of the century, Italian immigrants flocked to New Orleans. To be sure, the percentage of foreign born in southern cities declined in this era, so that by 1900

Alfred R. Waud, Sunday in New Orleans—The French Market *(1866)*

only 3.4 percent of Richmond's population had been born on foreign soil, 4.6 percent of Charleston's, 6.3 percent of Savannah's, and 10 percent of New Orleans's. The proportion of foreign-born citizens declined in all major southern cities in the subsequent years. Between 1900 and 1940 the proportion of foreign residents in the populations of New Orleans and Norfolk dropped from 10.6 to 3 percent, and from 3.7 percent to 1.8 percent, respectively, and Houston (9.9 to 4) and Fort Worth (6.7 to 2) reflected a similar trend. In the Southwest, of course, a considerable number of foreign-born citizens were Mexican Americans. The impact of second- and third-generation members of ethnic groups remained significant, often greater than their numbers suggested.

The streetcar and the motor vehicle made their appearances before most southern urban areas had achieved the population densities characteristic of the largest 19th-century industrial cities. The first practical electric railway system, devised by Frank J. Sprague, was initiated in Richmond in 1888. By 1900 every large city in the South boasted a functioning streetcar system. Exclusive residential areas, such as Ghent in Norfolk and Annesdale Park in Memphis, were generally the first streetcar suburbs to appear in the South. Atlanta developer Joel Hurt pioneered that city's first residential suburb, Inman Park, in 1887 and also built the city's first electric street railway in 1889. Streetcars constituted the foundation of the urban transportation system until about 1920, when they were challenged by the private passenger automobile and the motor bus; but they continued to transport the majority of passengers in and out of central business districts through the 1930s.

The transportation revolution initiated by the trolley was completed by the automobile. In 1920 motor vehicle registrations totaled approximately 20,000 in the Atlanta, New Orleans, and Memphis metropolitan areas, 16,000 in Birmingham, and 12,000 in Nashville. During the decade the increase in registrations ranged from about 192 percent in Memphis to 337 in Birmingham. Atlanta accounted for almost 20 percent of all the automobiles and motor trucks in Georgia in 1920, New Orleans contained a quarter of the registered vehicles in Louisiana, and Memphis and Nashville together accounted for almost a third of Tennessee's vehicle registration in 1920 and for more than a quarter by the end of the decade. Traffic congestion and problems of parking and auto safety loomed larger as automobile registrations mounted, and some local leaders and businessmen began to question the motor vehicle's usefulness in the city even at this early date.

As elsewhere in the country the principal means of increasing city size was annexation of surrounding communities and territory. Significant population growth on the urban fringes was a major impetus for annexation in southern cities. Between 1900 and 1920 Birmingham increased its land area by almost seven times through the "Greater Birmingham" annexation of 1910. In 1909 Fort Worth doubled its land area by acquiring North Fort Worth, and doubled it again in 1922 with the addition of Arlington Heights, Riverside, and other outlying settlements. Atlanta more than doubled its geographic size in the first two decades of the century and added even more territory during the 1920s. Knoxville's geographical size in 1920 was more than five and a half times what it had been 20 years earlier.

The first few years of the century witnessed a significant and growing differentiation between places of work and residence. Certainly, the skylines of 1940 bore little resemblance to those at the turn of the century. New office buildings—reverently identified as "skyscrapers"—hovered over major downtown intersections in the larger southern cities, and cast their shadows over the two- and three-story structures that characterized an earlier time. Together, these monuments to commercial and civic success formed impressive corridors in the heart of downtown, conveying a sense of both permanence and dynamism.

Commercial-Civic Elite. The greatest influence over economic and political affairs in the early 20th-century urban South was exerted by a commercial-civic elite composed of larger merchants, real estate agents, insurance brokers, bankers, contractors, and a variety of other people—attorneys, journalists, doctors, teachers, clergymen, and city officials—who were associated directly or indirectly with the business middle class. The social and economic interests of this elite group were wide ranging, but were concentrated primarily in the local area and specifically in the downtown business district. Perhaps the most important local associations they initiated were the chambers of commerce that took upon themselves the burdens of urban problems and tried to solve them. Besides their function as meeting places and discussion groups for the local elite, chambers usually maintained a lobby in the state legislature, dispatched members into surrounding counties and states to drum up business for the city, raised funds for national advertising drives, promoted more "efficient" forms of government, and advocated comprehensive city planning. In the opinion of some observers, local chambers actually served as quasi governments.

The commercial-civic elite was the most influential group in the southern city, but it did not preside over a monolithic community power structure. Its members did not agree on all matters of public policy, and they did not have anything resembling absolute control over public opinion and the electorate. Competing interest groups often forced commercial and civic organizations to back away from controversial issues, and many municipal governments were not powerful enough to impose specific business goals.

Clearly, though, the commercial-civic elite reigned supreme throughout the early 20th century, reaching its heyday in the business decade of the 1920s when its leadership was virtually unquestioned. The Depression was a genuine crisis for this group: the economy did not respond to any of the old, safe remedies, and enlightened free enterprise was unable to stem the tide of unemployment or even care successfully for its victims. But while the initiative may have passed to the national government in 1932 and 1933, the commercial-civic elite did not fade away. On the contrary, some of its members presided over the administration of government programs and actively solicited federal funds for civic projects.

Urban Change since World War II. World War II was an important dividing line in southern history including the level of urbanization. The war not only brought a flood of GIs to southern ports and training centers, but ushered in probably the most dramatic period of social and demographic change in the region. The economic expansion in the immediate postwar era created new suburban communities and rising demands for more services. The major seaports of New Orleans, Galveston-Houston, Mobile, Charleston, Norfolk-Portsmouth, and Savannah gained increased trade and new shipyards through their strategic locations. Investments in Houston's chemical industry reached $600 million by the end of the war. Even inland cities could profit, as did Huntsville, Ala., where the construction of the Redstone Arsenal brought new prosperity and a final end of the Depression. Growth in such southern cities was often uncontrolled. Mobile, which had two major shipyards and an aluminum factory, grew from a 1940 population of 114,906 to a 1944 figure of 201,369. People from nearby rural areas flocked to the town and overwhelmed existing housing and municipal services. John Dos Passos visited Mobile in 1943 and wrote that it looked "trampled and battered like a city that's been taken by storm." The public schools could not cope with the burgeoning enrollments, and the police force struggled to handle higher levels of juvenile delinquency, robbery, racial conflict, and labor unrest that went with urban growth during the war.

Military installations and defense industries, such as Fort Benning in Columbus, Ga., Eglin Field in Florida, Fort Bragg in Fayetteville, N.C., and Lackland Field in San Antonio, Tex., were vital to the economic growth of their areas. Many bases were established or greatly expanded during the war, and they retained their importance during the Cold War years. Powerful southern politicians, such as Mendel Rivers, who made Charleston into a booming military town, protected the interests of the cities they represented. The national space program proved to be an economic supplement to Houston, New Orleans, and other towns along the Gulf Coast, stretching to Florida.

Increased mobility also promoted economic development of the South's postwar cities. The expansion of the automobile industry, the building of the interstate highway system, and the growth of commercial aviation allowed major corporations to locate large factories in the region, transfer branch offices, and lure retirees to warmer climes. The tourist industry became a major factor. Since the late 1960s Houston, Dallas, Tampa, Shreveport, and Atlanta have built new air terminals to encourage the movement of goods and people.

The 20th century in general has continued to erode the differences between cities in the South and other regions, especially because of the new transportation and communications technologies that transformed all of urban America in this period. As the automobile stimulated new development on the urban fringe, the radio and later television brought national urban tastes and fashions in a most direct way to the urban South, and southern cities increasingly provided to surrounding rural areas the goods and fashions, the music and other entertainment made popular by these media. And air-conditioning may, as much as anything else, have helped pave the way for new migrations from the North and the influx of new businesses and industries that gave rise to the idea of the Sunbelt.

In the 1950s and 1960s the South confronted its legacy of racial injustice through bitter and often violent challenges to the structure and rationale of segregation. These conflicts took place in the major cities as well as in the small towns and reached an apogee in the Birmingham marches and bombings and the passage of the Civil Rights Act of 1964. The fall of segregation did not by any means erase the shadow of racism, but it did open the region for new growth and economic opportunities. By the 1970s blacks were playing an increasingly large role in the urban politics of major cities, leading to the successful mayoral campaigns of Maynard Jackson (1973) and Andrew Young (1981) in Atlanta, Richard Arrington in Birmingham (1979), and Ernest "Dutch" Morial in New Orleans (1977). The success of black politicians has been followed by greater involvement by others traditionally left out of power, symbolized by the victories of Henry Cisneros in San Antonio (1981) and Kathy Whitmire in Houston (1981).

By the 1970s the Old South urban image had given way to that of the Sunbelt, a region generally defined as the southern half of the country from coast to coast. Here interstate highways, satellite relays, lower taxes, the relative absence of labor unions, a good climate, more land, and a "better quality of life" underwrote a shift in population from the Northeast and Midwest to the South and Southwest. Working-class whites fleeing Frostbelt economic problems have migrated south, and white-collar executives have come to the region as managers of branch offices or as part of the transfer of company headquarters.

The middle class is increasingly setting the tone not only for contemporary southern cities but for the region's culture as a whole. Post–World War II prosperity has strengthened the urban middle class, which is made up of professionals, white-collar workers, businesspeople, and blue-collar workers. Since the 1960s middle-class southerners, like other middle-class Americans, have left the cities for suburbs and a commuting lifestyle. These suburbs are much like those in the rest of the nation. The flight from urban areas has meant the loss of revenue sources for urban governments, and the failure of some suburban communities to provide needed schools, recreational areas, and services has strained the resources of nearby cities. The white middle class has recently shown a tendency to move back into southern cities in a gentrification of downtown neighborhoods in places such as Atlanta, Memphis, and Charlotte. The extent and long-range implications of this trend remain to be seen.

Southern cities have worked to create distinctive images. State and metropolitan convention bureaus vigorously promote the advantages of each southern city. Most stress the appeal of a good business climate and a more leisurely lifestyle and milder weather than in the

North. Cities also promote themselves using images from the past—Memphis now attracts middle-class tourists by marketing the blues music that once was mainly for the poor, while Savannah and Charleston promote their historic preservation projects as recreational sites.

Urban growth in the period since World War II has led to social, economic, and cultural changes in the South. The landscape has changed, with shopping malls, apartment complexes, subdivisions, and traffic loops merely the most obvious expression of the new look and expansive spirit. The development of a large urban middle class brought the appearance of major league sports. Viewing the matter in terms of civic pride, southern cities built new stadiums and arenas in order to lure professional teams south. By the 1980s there were major league baseball teams in Houston, Atlanta, and Arlington, Tex., and National Football League franchises in Dallas, Miami, Houston, Atlanta, Tampa, and New Orleans. The short-lived World Football League had clubs in eight southern states, and the now-defunct United States Football League established teams in Birmingham, Tampa Bay, Memphis, Jacksonville, Orlando, San Antonio, and Houston. Professional basketball teams play in Houston, New Orleans, Dallas, San Antonio, Atlanta, and Norfolk–Hampton Roads, Va. Professional hockey is played in Atlanta and Houston. Dallas is the headquarters for World Championship Tennis and a soccer league. Golf tournaments and stock car races occur in dozens of southern cities.

The past two decades have witnessed an expansion of support for the arts in the urban South. Cities built theaters, concert halls, and exhibition centers. New Orleans completed the Rivergate International Exhibition Facility and the Theater for the Performing Arts in the 1970s and renovated its Municipal Auditorium. Shreveport built a new convention center, which opened in 1965. Houston saw the opening of the Jesse H. Jones Hall for the Performing Arts in 1966 and the Alley Theater in 1968. Southern urban leaders oversaw an architectural renaissance that reflected their confidence. Atlanta became the epitome of architectural boosterism. A new airport, civic center, and the Peachtree Center (a downtown redevelopment project) became symbols of Atlanta's progressive spirit in the 1970s. John Portman's Regency-Hyatt House has become a symbol of symbols with futuristic elevators, a dangling cocktail lounge, and a revolving dome, which affords an excellent vantage from which to see what civic boosters have wrought. Other cities have encouraged a similar booster architecture of civic centers, luxury hotels, and domed stadiums, such as in Houston's Astrodome and New Orleans's Superdome.

Higher education expanded to meet the needs of the growing urban populations. Branch campuses of southern universities were opened in major cities such as Little Rock, Birmingham, New Orleans, San Antonio, Arlington, and Dallas. Small state colleges were upgraded to university status. Georgia State College in Atlanta, once a part of Georgia Tech's evening school, became Georgia State University. Southeastern College in Hammond, La., became Southeastern Louisiana University, and McNeese State College in Lake Charles became McNeese State University.

Regional Heritage and Cities. The question of the distinctiveness of southern cities has been a major concern of scholars studying southern urbanization. Southern cities were certainly always more like their counterparts—of comparable age and size—in other regions than they were like the surrounding hinterlands. They were generally affected by major new technologies at about the same time, if not precisely to the same degree, as cities in the North and West. And southern cities hardly had a monopoly on ethnic or racial prejudice, crime and violence, or strong religious inclinations and an orientation to family. But they could not escape the legacies of the region that contained them, and they reflected regional circumstances and tendencies that in some forms persist to this day.

Race—the often noted "key" to understanding southern history—had its urban dimension, and indeed regional cities cannot be comprehended without taking its effects into account. In the American South, ethnicity was overwhelmingly a matter of black or white, with one race in subjugation to the other. Innumerable threads of affection, nuance, and exception ran through this fabric, making it much more complex than it appears at first glance; but, still, the social division of the region into black and white, master and slave, merchant and common laborer determined the pattern. After emancipation blacks were pushed to the lowest rungs of the occupational ladder, and the reign of Jim Crow was firmly established in the statute books by the first decade of the 20th century. Blacks attended segregated schools in cities, lived in mostly segregated housing, were relegated to separate seating in theaters and streetcars, and were either segregated in parks and other public places or denied admittance altogether. Continual police harassment was periodically punctuated by drives to arrest "vagrants" (usually blacks without regular employment), and those arrested might well find themselves acting as conscripted city laborers. Black freedoms were further circumscribed by curfews instituted in black sections and by outbreaks of white vigilantism.

In cities, at least, though, blacks were more likely to find, in whatever period, relatively more opportunity for self-determination, no matter how constricted it might be. Greater opportunity in the urban centers of the North fueled the massive migration of southern blacks to New York, Chicago, Philadelphia, Cleveland, and Detroit in the late 19th and early 20th centuries. But blacks often migrated to southern cities first. As far back as the 1870s black neighborhoods with distinctive institutions such as Shermantown and Summer Hill in Atlanta and Black Bottom and Rocktown in Nashville had appeared on the fringe of southern cities near railroad tracks, industrial sites, and contaminated waterways. At the beginning of this century such black settlements were scattered—huddled next to railroad tracks, warehouses, and factories, along the rivers in Nashville and Memphis, and in alleyways, low-lying places, and even wooded areas along the city's fringe. The prevailing type of housing more closely resembled the small sharecroppers' cabins of the rural South—some divided into duplexes—than the congested tenements and older single-family homes that pre-

Mule with wagon come to town, Columbus, Ga., 1941

dominated in northern ghettoes. In most southern cities, especially New Orleans and Charleston, few census tracts contained populations that were less than 10 or 20 percent white or black. The racial heterogeneity in census districts was, however, misleading. Many blacks living in predominantly white areas were servants who occupied quarters behind their employers' homes, and clusters of black residences contiguous to white sections were like islands set apart. The pattern in all southern cities during the 20th century was one of advancing racial segregation and the increasing concentration of blacks in fewer, larger residential areas near the urban core.

The increasing racial segregation in the early 20th-century South opened the way for a new group of ambitious black entrepreneurs, who pursued the main chance with the vigor of their white counterparts and directed their efforts toward the black consumer. An older elite of clergymen, barbers, contractors, and house servants gave way to a newer elite of skilled laborers, larger merchants, doctors, lawyers, and other professional and business types. The new black elite advocated—as had most of their forebears—a philosophy of thrift, hard work, property ownership, material advancement, and even urban boosterism. Though oriented toward the city rather than the farm, these businessmen supported the goals of Booker T. Washington—especially as they were expressed by the National Negro Business League—and called for an end to ideological conflicts among national black spokesmen and organizations. They were not, however, passive accommodationists. Throughout the period black business and civic leaders protested the economic restrictions and legal sanctions applied to their race and lamented the conditions in their communities.

Indeed, most black residential areas were marked by poor housing, horrendous sanitation facilities, inadequate schools, police harassment rather than protection, and unpaved streets that turned to an impenetrable mire in heavy rains. But southern urban blacks contributed forcefully to the improvement of their communities in a number of ways, and their accomplishments are all the more impressive considering the obstacles cast in their way. As the 20th century advanced, black communities became larger and more complex, economically diverse, and socially organized. Black civic and service organizations proliferated, along with existing religious and fraternal groups, especially in those cities with a significant black middle class.

The impact of Afro-Americans on southern culture has been, of course, both substantial and abiding, and almost impossible to measure with precision. The large black districts in the cities, with their distinct yet related subcultures, are a profound historical fact, comparable to the large communities of foreign immigrants in northern urban centers, and with perhaps even greater cultural influence. The culture of the urban South is thus a biracial product, though whites have not always been inclined to admit it. The relatively greater penchant among southerners for the institutions of family and church, for example, is certainly a shared cultural tendency.

Another aspect of 20th-century regional urban distinctiveness was the rural legacy of the South. It was etched in the urban landscape. Patches of open space, even close to downtown, were more common in southern cities, as were residential plots replete with chickens and pigs (though these were banished by public health ordinances in the 20th century). The old-time religion of the countryside was brought to town embodied by small churches, wandering gospel tents, and strictures against alcohol, gambling, Sabbath activities, and even public dancing.

A quick resort to violence among southern urban dwellers seemed very much a part of the regional heritage. The ancient doctrine of personal honor, once held high by a plantation aristocracy, somehow persisted among the lower classes of urban blacks and whites. If one can believe local newspaper reports, large numbers of men in both races and of all social classes habitually packed sidearms in city streets, and a profusion of weapons would appear on the slightest pretext. Reporters working the downtown sections considered a pencil, a bottle of whiskey, and a revolver standard equipment. Such reports appear to be confirmed by the relatively high murder rates in southern cities in the early 20th century. Memphis was titled the "murder capital of the world" in 1916, when 89 homicides per 100,000 people were recorded. Murder rates in Atlanta, Nashville, and New Orleans rose in the 1920s by 32 percent, 183 percent, and 44 percent, respectively. On the whole, homicide rates in major southern cities have substantially exceeded those in the North and Midwest. The most articulate and persuasive explanation for this phenomenon focuses on the southern "worldview" or on a "feudal agrarian myth" that demanded violence as a perverse cement of community.

The "rural" features of southern cities were not unique: urban America was largely populated by newcomers from the countryside. But the patterns of rusticity were perhaps more distinctive in the South; the region was, after all, largely rural and few migrants came from outside the South. Not surprisingly, some of these cultural tendencies were actually focused, enlarged, and formalized in cities, where larger audiences and better communications encouraged the recording and distribution of folktales, folksongs, and oral traditions. The twangy, plaintive music sung by rural whites and the rolling, mournful sounds of black blues found their ways into southern urban streets and alleyways and from there to a national and international audience. On the other hand, southern cities also fostered a prejudice toward the untutored and unsophisticated countryside, and recent rural newcomers were frequently the subjects of urban humor.

Ambivalence marked the historic role of southern cities as much as irony and tragedy seemed to characterize the history of the region as a whole. As cultural crucibles they provided greater focus for traditional, regional culture at the same time that they introduced new currents from the rest of the nation and the world. They boasted of their regional heritage and simultaneously claimed kinship with larger cities elsewhere. They celebrated the Lost Cause mythology while also calling for new technologies and joking about country bumpkins. In the final analysis southern cities were both southern and urban.

See also EDUCATION: Urbanization and Education; GEOGRAPHY: Towns and Villages; INDUSTRY: Sunbelt South; / Atlanta as Commercial Center; Grady, Henry W.; LANGUAGE: New Orleans English; Urban Speech; MYTHIC SOUTH: New South Myth

Blaine A. Brownell
University of Alabama at Birmingham

Carl Abbott, *The New Urban America: Growth and Politics in Sunbelt Cities* (1981); Richard M. Bernard and Bradley R. Rice, eds., *Sunbelt Cities: Politics and Growth since World War II* (1983); Blaine A. Brownell, *The Urban Ethos in the South, 1920–1930* (1975), with David R. Goldfield, eds., *The City in Southern History: The Growth of Urban Civilization in the South* (1977); James C. Cobb, *South Atlantic Urban Studies*, vol. 1 (1977); Leonard Curry, *Journal of Southern History* (February 1974); David R. Goldfield, *Cotton Fields and Skyscrapers: Southern City and Region, 1607–1980* (1982), in *Perspectives on the American South*, vol. 3, ed. James C. Cobb and Charles Reagan Wilson (1985); David C. Perry and Alfred J. Watkins, eds., *The Rise of the Sunbelt Cities* (1977); Howard N. Rabinowitz, *Race Relations in the Urban South, 1865–1890* (1978); Leonard Reissman, *Journal of Social Issues* (February 1966); William Tabb and Larry Sawyers, eds., *Sunbelt/Snowbelt: Urban Development and Regional Restructuring* (1984); Rupert B. Vance and Nicholas J. Demerath, eds., *The Urban South* (1954); Richard C. Wade, *Slavery in the Cities: The South, 1820–1960* (1964).

Segregation, Residential

Residential segregation has shaped the nature of southern urban life. At times, particularly during the antebellum period, this segregation has had an ethnic foundation. During the mid-19th century Nashville had its Germantown and Little Ireland, by the end of the century there was a pronounced Italian section in New Orleans, and even today there are such ethnic communities as San Antonio's Mexican American westside ghetto and Miami's Little Havana. There also has been economic segregation. On one end of the economic ladder were the factory districts of the mill towns and some of the larger cities, while at the other end were fashionable neighborhoods like Birmingham's South Highland and Atlanta's Buckhead. But the basic form of residential segregation has been racial. The extent of such segregation has always varied from city to city, but southern cities in general have been more racially segregated than their northern counterparts. Although some blacks and whites could always be found living near each other, most southern blacks have historically lived among themselves in dispersed clusters that contained their own institutions and businesses.

Prior to the Civil War, however, segregation was less of a factor in southern residential life. The mass of urban slaves lived within the compounds of their owners, usually above the stable or kitchen, or in other outbuildings at the rear of the property. Yet, even then, the future pattern was already emerging. Some slaves were housed in barracks owned by industrial, commercial, or public employers. Others joined concentrations of free Negroes on the fringes of the antebellum city where they were freer from white surveillance.

In the years immediately after the war, some freedmen remained in the alley dwellings or shacks behind their former master's house and worked as domestics and handymen. This way of life persisted longest in older cities like Charleston and Savannah. In younger cities like Atlanta, Birmingham, and Houston, blacks flocked to the remnants of the old free black enclaves or to the remains of the freedmen camps set up earlier by the victorious Yankees. And in both types of cities new areas on the outskirts were thrown open to black settlement. Rows of shotgun or doublepen cottages spread across the least desirable locations—low-lying areas subject to flooding and epidemics and often adjacent to cemeteries, railroad yards, industrial plants, or other unhealthy sites. Such elemental city services as paved streets, lighting, and water supply were normally absent in these areas and remained so for many years to come. The houses themselves had only the most primitive sanitary facilities, were poorly constructed and therefore subject to frequent fires, and were better suited to rural than urban living. In 1877, for example, the Nashville Board of Health reported that the city's blacks "reside mainly in old stables, situated upon alleys in the midst of privy vaults, or in wooden shanties a remnant of war times, or in huts closely crowded together on the outskirts." Even if the buildings had been structurally sound and healthful, the severe overcrowding in each dwelling, where there was often more than one family per room, would still have made most of them unfit for human habitation.

As the century drew to a close, southern cities exhibited residential patterns more characteristic of preindustrial cities than of the typical city then emerging in the rapidly industrializing North. In the latter, the poor and unskilled tended to live close to downtown, while the middle and upper classes took advantage of transportation breakthroughs that allowed them to flee the increasingly industrialized centers for newly accessible land on the periphery. In contrast, middle- and upper-class white southerners continued to live in large houses on spacious tree-lined streets near the core of cities that remained primarily commercial. When industry did develop in southern cities, it was normally along the railroad tracks on the edges of the city, areas to which blacks and other working-class people were drawn. Furthermore, while the influx of immigrants to northern cities increased, the South's antebellum immigrants were becoming assimilated and dispersed throughout the city. They were joined by a relatively small number of eastern and southern European immigrants who, after some brief initial concentration, were integrated into the community. Such, of course, was not the case with blacks. Although typically found in scattered clusters, rather than the one or two large ghettoes that housed recent immigrants in northern cities and would house a later generation of blacks, southern blacks were segregated to an unprecedented degree within these smaller districts.

Poor white workers of native stock could sometimes be found mixed in among the blacks, together with small businessmen of foreign descent, widows, and others with limited mobility. But there was no question as to "where the niggers lived." Much of the resultant segregation was voluntary as blacks sought out their "own kind," or were attracted by the proliferating number of churches, schools, and places of entertainment established in these new areas. Still other blacks were attracted by the proximity of the unskilled and semiskilled jobs most commonly available for them. Black business streets often formed the spines of these neighborhoods. Here were the shops of black barbers, grocers, and undertakers, cheap hotels and bars, and eventually the offices of black doctors and lawyers. The major streets, as in the case of Atlanta's "Sweet Auburn," might also have the meeting hall of one or more fraternal orders, an office of the black-owned Atlanta Life Insurance Company, several churches, a theater, and perhaps some "high-class" clubs or restaurants. Blacks would still do much of their shopping in the white-owned clothing stores, pawn shops, and groceries on the street, or in the downtown establishments that provided segregated service, but for most southern urban blacks residential segregation clearly meant more than simply the absence of white neighbors—it was the foundation of the region's biracial society. As early as 1881 an Atlanta reporter could conclude that "far the largest proportion of Negroes are never really known to us. They are not employed in private homes nor in the business houses, but drift off to themselves, and are almost as far from the white people, so far as all practicable benefits of associations are concerned, as if the two races never met."

But this situation was not entirely voluntary. After all, an important degree of forced segregation especially affected middle-class blacks. Indeed, segregation in southern cities, to an even greater degree than in the North, was racial rather than economic, at least for blacks. Middle-class blacks were denied opportunities open to either their southern white counterparts or their black counterparts in the North, and they found themselves confined to the least attractive sections of the city with the poorest of their race and kept out of better neighborhoods they could afford to live in. Occasionally, such middle-class blacks might be found in neighborhoods or on blocks that were mostly white, but, as a rule, the whites were far below them in socioeconomic status.

Nevertheless, by the turn of the century enclaves of middle-class black housing emerged, like the one on Atlanta's west side that was built around what became the Atlanta University Center. Yet unlike in the North such neighborhoods were not the products of succession in which blacks moved into areas that once housed large numbers of whites. Instead, as was historically the case for southern blacks in general, such neighborhoods were newly constructed for blacks (often by blacks) on either recently annexed land or land that was deemed unsuitable for whites. The fear of black expansion into white neighborhoods, however, led some cities to substitute de jure housing segregation for their existing de facto system. Baltimore led the way in 1910 with an ordinance requiring separate white and black neighborhoods. Then between 1911 and 1913 other cities, including Richmond and Atlanta, passed similar laws. Between 1913 and 1916 the laws spread westward to Louisville, St. Louis, New Orleans, and Oklahoma City. Such threats to middle-class black interests led the NAACP to challenge the Louisville law. Its efforts were rewarded in 1917 when the U.S. Supreme Court in *Buchanan* v. *Warley* declared legally enforced residential segregation unconstitutional. More laws were in fact passed after 1917, but in every case they were found to be unconstitutional. Yet restrictive covenants and other private arrangements remained in force, and, ironically, the degree of residential segregation increased significantly in both the North and South between 1910 and 1930. This was due partly to the migration of blacks, producing huge ghettoes in northern cities, but it was also due to the rapid growth of newer southern cities that lacked the region's old tradition of "backyard integration."

In the years following World War II, residential segregation continued to increase in southern cities at the same time that it began to decrease elsewhere in the country under the impact of rising black militancy and federal, state, and local antidiscrimination statutes. Few southern cities had the kind of large-scale ghettoes that dominated black life in the North, but a higher percentage of blacks continued to reside in the numerous smaller racial clusters that characterized southern urban life. This was the result of private action as well as municipal manipulation of transportation routes and the choice of sites for segregated public housing. Thus, by 1960 only 5.5 percent of the southern urban population lived in integrated neighborhoods, compared to 31.8 percent in the Northeast. Between 1964 and 1967 the percentage of southern urban blacks living in census tracts that were more than 75 percent black increased from 65 percent to 78 percent in Memphis, 79 percent to 90 percent in Shreveport, and 86 percent to 88 percent in Nashville.

In recent years there has been an increase in class segregation among southern blacks, a process that is historically more identified with northern cities. This change was due to a great surge in the number of middle-class blacks combined with the presence of new opportunities for better housing as whites moved to the suburbs. Such internal segregation continues, however, to be rarer than among whites. Racial discrimination is one obvious cause but so too is the relative homogeneity of the black occupational structure. The persistence of segregation also obscures differences in origins, compared to the past. The extent of neighborhood succession, that is, black migrants moving into once predominantly white areas, long the common road to segregation in the North, has now become more frequent in the South in the wake of more effective enforcement of fair housing legislation and the scarcity of unoccupied land for black housing. Furthermore, so-called displacement, in which whites replace blacks following urban renewal or redevelopment, is also on the rise, though now the North is also moving in this direction. Then, too, the movement of middle- and upper-class whites to the suburbs and the consolidation of many black areas within the center of the city have produced a core-ring pattern more like that of the North, though as late as 1970, 14 percent of the South's metropolitan black population resided on the periphery, frequently in semirural areas, compared to 3 percent in the Northeast.

Patterns of racially determined residential segregation in northern and southern cities are now more similar than they have been at any time in the past, but, in the degree of segregation, its persistence within dispersed clusters, and the rural character of so much black urban housing, the regional uniqueness of southern housing patterns is still evident. The impact of these differences should continue to affect southern urban culture for years to come.

See also BLACK LIFE: Business; Black; Race Relations

Howard N. Rabinowitz
University of New Mexico

Ronald H. Bayor, *Georgia Historical Quarterly* (Winter 1979); Leonard P. Curry, *The Free Black in Urban America, 1800–1850* (1981); John Kellogg, *Geographical Review* (July 1977); Howard N. Rabinowitz, *Race Relations in the Urban South, 1865–1890* (1978); Roger Rice, *Journal of Southern History* (May 1968); Karl Taeuber and Alma F. Taeuber, *Negroes in Cities: Residential Segregation and Neighborhood Change* (1965); Richard C. Wade, *Slavery in the Cities: The South, 1820–1960* (1964).

Urban Boosterism

The southerner's penchant for, and enjoyment of, florid oratorical and literary expression attained its urban apogee in the person of the urban booster. Boosterism, as Sinclair Lewis noted, was a phenomenon of Main Street America. Few boosters, however, surpassed the evangelical fervor, continued popularity, and sense of purpose of the southerners.

The urban booster was an economic and political leader whose immediate objective was to promote a particular program and whose ultimate goal was to unite the citizenry behind his leadership. Surfacing in the late antebellum era, he was a product of the fierce urban competition for markets and internal improvements and of the rise of the penny press, which spread the gospel of progress to unanointed readers. The antebellum urban booster left two legacies to his postwar colleagues—an urban consciousness and huge debts. For the first time citizens were asked to think about "the city" as a distinctive entity possessing a personality and an image of its own. Future boosters utilized this consciousness to implement their projects.

The period between 1865 and 1930 was the golden era for the southern urban booster as he became enshrined along with Civil War heroes in the rhetorical pantheon that historian Paul M. Gaston referred to as the New South creed. The creed emphasized industrialization and urbanization while at the same time paying homage to Old South values. This combination of progressive rhetoric steeped in southern tradition suited the booster perfectly because it linked economic growth with political and social stability. Atlanta journalist Henry W. Grady became the major oracle of the creed, coaxing northern investments and southern stock subscriptions while also promoting white supremacy.

By 1900, despite Grady's proselytizing, southern economic development lagged further behind the North than it had in 1860. But failure was not part of the booster vocabulary and, if anything, boosters redoubled their efforts to obtain elusive growth. As part of the effort to improve their city's image, boosters embarked on extensive public works campaigns in the early decades of the 20th century, including street paving, electric lighting, and sewer and water services. They also avidly sought land accretions through annexation so that population and area figures would swell. Memphis political boss Edward H. Crump became so enraptured with census recordings of Memphis progress through population growth (primarily as a result of timely annexations) that he even recommended the 10-year federal census be taken every five years.

During the 1920s the "commercial-civic elite," as historian Blaine A. Brownell called the boosters of that decade, became more strident as its rhetoric became more hollow. The New South creed's neglect and even vilification of blacks and workers, as well as the evident failures of southern economic development, resulted in challenges to the booster ideal in the late 1920s when much of the South had lapsed into the depression that was soon to engulf the nation. Thomas Wolfe railed against the boosters' "dusty little pint-measure minds" and the conformity they enforced on a naive community slumping perceptibly toward bankruptcy. For Faulkner, the amoral Snopes clan embodied the precepts of booster acquisitiveness, and the Nashville Agrarians took their stand against false prophets and profits by restating the basic humanistic and rural qualities of southern culture.

Despite attacks by Wolfe, Faulkner, and the Agrarians, the boosters weathered the Depression and emerged from the war ready to evangelize a new generation of southern urban residents. In many respects, the religious metaphor is well-taken because boosters and evangelists, especially since 1945, have adopted similar techniques—measuring success in numbers and eschewing social issues. Boosters touted low wages and the absence of unions as regional benefactions, and they received industries appropriate to these attractions—low-wage, low-skill enterprises that exploited natural resources and took profits from the region.

If boosters were not successful during the immediate postwar years in generating quality development, they were successful in projecting positive urban images. Atlanta led the field with campaign slogans such as the "Atlanta Spirit," "Forward Atlanta," "A City too Busy to Hate," and "The International City" to attract growth and investment. More recently, boosters have sold history, as in New Orleans and Charleston, where preservation movements assume the proportions of big business, though the traditional temptation for monumental buildings such as luxury hotels and civic centers persists in these cities as well.

Ironically, when genuine prosperity finally washed over the region in the 1960s and 1970s, urban boosters were caught short as development tended to occur on the periphery while decay and population loss threatened urban vitality. Bankruptcy stalked new development in Atlanta, and deteriorated centers gnawed at Montgomery, Nashville, and Richmond. In spite of such problems southern urban boosters have continued to pursue growth in downtown redevelopment and historic preservation programs. Growing black and Hispanic constituencies have forced social issues on the shallow growth ethic, and contemporary boosters operate in a different political milieu from their predecessors who enjoyed the fruits of economic, political, and racial hegemony.

See also HISTORY AND MANNERS: Historic Preservation; INDUSTRY articles; MYTHIC SOUTH: New South Myth

David R. Goldfield
University of North Carolina
at Charlotte

Blaine A. Brownell, *The Urban Ethos in the South, 1920–1930* (1975); Charles Paul Garofalo, *Journal of Southern History* (May 1976); Paul M. Gaston, *The New South Creed: A Study in Southern Mythmaking* (1970); David R. Goldfield, *Urban Growth in the Age of Sectionalism: Virginia, 1847–1861* (1977); Harold H. Martin, *William Berry Hartsfield: Mayor of Atlanta* (1978); Merl E. Reed, *New Orleans and the Railroads: The Struggle for Commercial Empire* (1966); George B. Tindall, *South Atlantic Quarterly* (Autumn 1965).

Urban Growth

For a century and a half urban growth in the South has held out the expectation of bringing social patterns and values into line with national norms. As the points of contact between agricultural hinterlands and the international economy, the cities of the 19th-century South were strongly drawn toward comparable centers of the North. During the years leading to the Civil War, trading towns of the Mississippi River and the Upper South were reluctant to share the venture of southern independence, with its destruction of internal commerce. In the 1880s and 1890s hopes for a New South were held most strongly by civic leaders in ambitious cities like Atlanta and Birmingham, who hoped to emulate northern industrial cities.

In the 20th century two generations of social scientists have waited for urban growth to undermine the cultural values and social patterns that have set the South apart from the rest of the United States. By the common analysis, the combined forces of industrialization, urbanization, and the expansion of a cosmopolitan middle class would help to close the cultural gap. In the words of sociologist Leonard Reissman, the emergence of large cities should move the South to "a level of modernity comparable to the nation as a whole."

There is no doubt that the South is rapidly attaining the same degree of urban development found in other parts of the country. In technical use, the term "urbanization" refers to the proportion of the population of a state, region, or nation living within urban areas. Table 1 compares the degree of urbanization in the South with that in the remainder of the United States. The surge of urban growth was especially pronounced in the three decades after 1940, with the differential closing at a slower pace during the 1970s.

Urbanization during the past generation has meant new economic roles and influence for established centers and the emergence of new urban rivals. The 16 states of the "Census South" contained 10 metropolitan areas with more than 1 million residents in 1980, compared to 1 in 1940. Their combined metropolitan population of 18,542,000 was three and a half times the total for 1940. At mid-century, independent studies by Vance and Smith and by Duncan and his associates identified Atlanta and Dallas as the only southern cities to rank as high as the

Table 1. *Urbanization in South and Non-South*

	Urbanization South	Urbanization Non-South	Ratio South/Non-South
1900	18.0%	50.0%	.36
1940	36.7	65.7	.56
1950	44.0	65.8	.67
1960	57.7	74.4	.78
1970	64.4	77.2	.83
1980	66.9	77.1	.87

Source: U.S. Bureau of the Census, *Population Reports* (1900, 1940, 1950, 1960, 1970, 1980).

third level in the national urban system. By 1980, however, when a good measure of metropolitan importance was the volume of airline traffic, four southern airports ranked in the top 10 in passenger volume.

At the other end of the urban hierarchy, dozens of small southern cities have grown enough to earn recognition as metropolitan areas (defined as single or adjacent core cities with 50,000 residents along with the counties that have close economic ties to the core). The South counted 58 metropolitan areas in 1950 and 119 in 1980. Additions to the list during the 1970s include Victoria, Tex.; Alexandria, La.; Florence, Ala.; Hickory, N.C.; and Ocala and Bradenton, Fla. Few parts of the South are now more than a two-hour drive from a metropolitan area.

Urbanization has drawn native southerners from the region's farms and small towns and mixed them with a substantial influx of newcomers. In 1979, for example, 8 percent of the southern population had migrated from outside the region in the past four years. Comparable figures for the Northeast and Midwest are 3–4 percent. In Florida and Texas annual in-migration has totaled in the hundreds of thousands.

The movement into southern cities has had an especially important impact on the region's black residents. The level of urbanization for blacks has closely paralleled that for whites, with 17.2 percent of southern blacks in urban places in 1900, 36.5 percent in 1940, and 67.4 percent in 1970. Because the rural South has been a region of extremely limited economic and educational opportunities for blacks, their urbanization has been a vital step in achieving the full benefits of citizenship. Moreover, the newcomers to the South now include significant numbers of blacks. Net in-migration of 14,000 blacks in the years 1970–75 marked the reversal of three generations of black flight. For 1975–80 the net inflow of blacks to the South totaled 195,000.

Many of the new southerners have been attracted by the changing economic base of southern cities. By the middle 1970s three-quarters of the major metropolitan centers in the region were dependent on tertiary activities (trade/finance/transportation) or quarternary activities (services/government/research). A comparison of the 10 largest urban centers in the South in 1940 and in 1980 shows some of the changes (Table 2). Over the 40 years the old river ports and heavy industrial cities of Birmingham, Louisville, Memphis, and Wheeling have dropped off the list, while Baltimore and New Orleans have fallen several places. The replacement cities are three recreation/retirement cities—Miami, Tampa, and Fort Lauderdale—and the military center of San Antonio. Dallas, Houston, and Washington have also increased in relative importance. Another indicator of the emerging postindustrial economy is the list of medium-sized metropolitan areas (500,000 to 1,000,000) that grew by more than 25 percent during the 1970s. Austin and Raleigh-Durham are government and education centers, West Palm Beach and Orlando are recreation cities, and Tulsa is an energy boomtown.

The leading economic sectors in southern cities demand salaried experts and professionals. Military officers, aerospace engineers, tax accountants, medical researchers, university professors, petroleum geologists, and members of corporate publicity departments are members of the footloose middle class. They expect to make their careers in a sequence of cities, and they are more dependent on the judgments of their professional peers than on the attitudes of their neighbors. They constitute not simply the white-collar class anticipated by social theory, but a modern mobile population with little attachment to regional traditions.

One of their impacts has been to homogenize the residential areas of southern cities. Families transferring from city to city tend to look for comparable communities. The taste of a minority of these mobile professionals runs to restored center city neighborhoods—Alexandria, Va., Inman Park in Atlanta, or the Fan District in Richmond. The majority choose suburbs that are indistinguishable from each other or from similar communities outside the South. The sprawl of Houston, the super suburb of Virginia Beach, northside Atlanta,

Table 2. *Largest Southern Metropolitan Areas (rank order)*

1940	1980
Baltimore	Washington
Washington	Dallas–Fort Worth
New Orleans	Houston
Houston	Baltimore
Atlanta	Atlanta
Birmingham	Miami
Louisville	Tampa–St. Petersburg
Dallas	New Orleans
Memphis	San Antonio
Wheeling	Fort Lauderdale–Hollywood

Source: U.S. Bureau of the Census, *Population Reports* (1940, 1980).

The Miami Beach resort area, 1980s

and northside San Antonio offer essentially the same environment.

Indeed, it is arguable whether many of the largest southern cities retain their "southern" character. Baltimore and Washington, which were dominated by local elites with southern orientations as late as the 1930s, have been absorbed within the megalopolis of the Northeast. Houston, Dallas, and Atlanta are high-rise cities, with new downtowns that rise like glass icebergs out of a sea of parking lots. Tampa and Fort Lauderdale serve a national market of vacationers and retirees who know little and care less about the mill towns and cotton crossroads of the historic South. Miami and San Antonio lie within the advancing frontier line of Latin America. If anything defines the uniqueness of the South, it is the patterns and problems of black-white relations. However, Hispanic Americans are the largest minority in metropolitan Miami and San Antonio (as well as in Austin and El Paso).

In the broadest view, urban development is pulling the South into a new regional alignment. Although the Sunbelt is a loosely defined concept, rates of population growth by states and metropolitan areas for the period 1940–80 show two regions of rapid growth in the United States. A Sunbelt-Southeast runs along the South Atlantic coast from Washington to Key West, and a Sunbelt-West angles from Louisiana, Texas, and Oklahoma across the Southwest and Rocky Mountain states to the Pacific. The nine southern states within these Sunbelt zones contain all 21 of the region's metropolitan areas that grew by at least 25 percent during the 1970s. They contain the 10 largest southern metropolitan areas and 24 of the 30 largest.

What remains of the Old South is half a dozen states on the western slope of the Appalachians and central Mississippi Valley. West Virginia, Kentucky, Tennessee, Arkansas, Mississippi, and Alabama have older cities and older manufacturing, a record of slower growth, and limited employment in government and high technology industry.

In summary, urban growth at the end of the 20th century is simultaneously reducing the distinctiveness of the South and drawing it into new regional configurations. The Sunbelt transcends the historic South and links its dynamic sectors to a new, larger region. For most residents, there are now more similarities than differences to life in Anaheim and Orlando, San Diego and Norfolk, Albuquerque, Austin, and Atlanta.

See also INDUSTRY articles

Carl Abbott
Portland State University

Carl Abbott, *The New Urban America: Growth and Politics in Sunbelt Cities* (1981); Blaine A. Brownell and David R. Goldfield, eds., *The City in Southern History: The Growth of Urban Civilization in the South* (1977); Ollinger Crenshaw, in *Historiography and Urbanization: Essays in American History in Honor of W. Stull Holt*, ed. Eric F. Goldman (1941); Otis D. Duncan et al., *Metropolis and Region* (1960); William H. Nichols, in *The American South in the 1960s*, ed. Avery Leiserson (1964); Leonard Reissman, *Journal of Social Issues* (January 1966); Rupert B. Vance and Nicholas J. Demerath, eds., *The Urban South* (1954).

Urban Leadership

Though it was predominantly a rural, agricultural economy until recently, the South required urban centers that spawned their own leadership, frequently at odds with the leaders of agrarian society. During the colonial and antebellum periods the most important cities in the region were mostly coastal trade centers. Baltimore, Norfolk, Charleston, Savannah, Mobile, New Orleans, and other smaller cities provided outlets to northern and European markets for the grain, naval stores, tobacco, rice, and cotton exports produced by the plantation economy. During the colonial era many of the leading merchants and factors who dominated this trade were foreigners, usually Scotch, British, and French. By the 1820s, as the cotton trade expanded and came under the control of New York City, northerners took over the key urban functions of factoring and shipping the lucrative exports of the plantation economy.

Within the local power structure urban merchants and factors used their influence through commercial associations and city government to promote urban growth. Civic improvements in water supply, sanitation, police, and fire control were all subservient to the goal of enhancing the community's commercial prosperity. City governmental agencies were also used to regulate slaves and to guard against their revolt. Though they shared many of the aspirations for urban growth and industrial and commercial development with their counterparts in the North, the leaders of the southern middle class enjoyed less autonomy and less political and economic leverage within a society dominated by large slaveowning planters. Urban merchants and industrial entrepreneurs cooperated with planters in launching new railroads and industrial experiments. During the 1850s these efforts at economic development were linked to plans for sectional independence from the North.

Ultimately, the move toward urban development was contradicted by the commitment to the plantation economy and slavery. Slaveowners realized slave labor could be adapted to industrial work and urban labor markets only at the risk of losing full control over the slaves. Planters feared a large white working class in the cities that might oppose competition from slaves, and they did not wish to encourage the growth of an independent middle class with interests opposed to the slave regime. The strain between the urban middle class and planters became apparent during the secession crisis when urban representatives opposed secession for fear of severing commercial ties with the North. The dominance of the planter class became apparent when urban leaders ultimately capitulated and served the Confederate cause during the war.

During the war urban supply and manufacturing centers like Atlanta, Richmond, and Nashville experienced rapid growth and emerged as powerful components of the postwar economic order. Many entrepreneurs who gained experience during the war took their place in a growing cadre of urban middle class leaders in the New South era. Older seaports like Charleston, Mobile, and New Orleans suffered blockades during the war and continued to stagnate in the decades following it. Along the Piedmont, in northern Alabama, and elsewhere in the interior of the South, towns and cities experienced rapid growth as railroad centers or as textile, tobacco, and iron manufacturing centers. Few of the industrial and commercial leaders who were prominent in the rising cities of the New South came from the planter class. In cities like Atlanta and Nashville they were typically from the yeomanry and small-town merchant and professional classes. Most arrived in their cities after the war as young men and rose to positions of wealth in wholesale commerce, railroads, manufacturing, banking, and insurance. Typically, they were Methodist, Presbyterian, or Baptist, and they celebrated their rise to riches as the reward of hard work and personal piety. By the 1880s representatives of this ascendant middle class "new man" articulated a regional vision of economic development, sectional reconciliation with the North, and interracial cooperation. Though they often paid homage to the Lost Cause of the Confederacy, those who proclaimed this New South creed recognized a departure from the Old South and offered the leadership of a young, progressive urban middle class as an alternative to the defeated planter class.

On the local level prominent merchants, manufacturers, and financiers used their influence through commercial associations, like the chamber of commerce, to direct public policy. Formal control of city government offices was typically held by smaller businessmen whose interests were confined to the local economy. City government continued to serve business interests in efforts to promote urban growth through bonds for railroads, lobbying for federal aid to harbor improvements, tax incentives to new industries, and improved city services. The most visible examples of urban enterprise were the industrial expositions held in Atlanta, Louisville, New Orleans, Nashville, and Charleston in the late 19th and early 20th centuries. Here the New South creed of economic development, national reconciliation, and black progress was displayed in lavish exhibits and reams of publicity. Linked to their vision of New South economic prosperity was a liberal social policy with special application to the black population of the postwar South.

Beginning in the 1880s with religious revivals and temperance campaigns, the reformers of the urban South sponsored a flurry of new private and government-sponsored charitable organizations. Reform moved toward efforts to improve sanitation and public health in the slums, expand and improve public education, and enforce temperance and sexual morality through government regulation. These reforms were linked to goals of economic progress through a healthy, educated, and generally upgraded work force. These policies of social uplift, which gained wide currency in the Progressive era, coincided with a growing tendency toward segregation in the work force, neighborhoods, and public facilities of southern cities. Segregation was approved, if not inspired, by business leaders as a means of assuring social stability in the crowded and competitive cities of the New South.

"Business progressivism," as historian George Tindall has labeled this conservative brand of reform, took firm hold in the early 20th century. Structural reforms in the manner of electing city government officials allowed for "at large" elections of councilmen and the introduction of commission and city manager forms of government. These reforms were intended to model government after the modern corporations and to reduce the influence of ward-level bosses and the poor black and white working-class voters who supported them. In several cities a southern brand of boss politics prevailed despite the efforts of business progressives to undermine their ward-level strength. Edward H. Crump in Memphis, Hilary Howse in Nashville, John Grace in Charleston, and Martin Behrman in New Orleans represented the most durable of such urban bosses. The mobilization effort during World War I and the era of business prosperity that followed gave new strength to "business progressivism." Planning and zoning boards were attached to city government to give the commercial-civic elite additional control over the course of physical growth and residential segregation in their cities. Experts in business and planning expanded the powers of local government to cope with a variety of complex urban problems involving air pollution, traffic control, social welfare, and expanded urban services for the rapidly growing suburban population.

The Depression and the New Deal programs of the 1930s accelerated this growth of public authority as federal funds for highway, park, and airport construction, social welfare, and public housing poured into local agencies. World War II strengthened the federal partnership with southern cities, many of which were grateful recipients of government expenditures for aircraft, ships, weaponry, uniforms, and military bases. After the war a generation of returning veterans and businessmen eager to encourage further federal commitment to southern development began to take over the leadership of their cities. The war against fascism and the cold war against communism made the system of racial segregation a national embarrassment. Business leaders were hesitant, nonetheless, to dismantle the system on their own initiative. Many black business and professional leaders had thrived within a segregated society and were slow to push for desegregation.

A younger generation of college-educated blacks, many of them still in school, began in the 1950s to work through the NAACP and other local organizations to batter down the walls of segregation. Through the courts, public demonstrations, and civil disobedience they forced the leadership of southern cities to put an end to formal segregation in schools, public facilities, and to a lesser degree in the job market. Urban blacks also regained political power lost after Reconstruction and were able to extract concessions from white leaders. In cities like Atlanta black political power was sufficient to win key positions within city government. Whatever their formal positions within local government, however, the white business elites remain the most significant group within the power structure of major southern cities and are a force of growing importance within a region undergoing rapid urbanization.

See also BLACK LIFE: Business, Black; Politics, Black; INDUSTRY articles; MYTHIC SOUTH: New South Myth

Don H. Doyle
Vanderbilt University

Blaine A. Brownell, *The Urban Ethos in the South, 1920–1930* (1975), with David R. Goldfield, eds., *The City in Southern History: The Growth of Urban Civilization in the South* (1977); Eugene D. Genovese, *The Political Economy of Slavery* (1968); Floyd Hunter, *Community Power Succession: Atlanta's Policy-Makers Revisited* (1980).

Urban Planning

The South possesses a rich tradition of urban planning that extends back to the colonial era. Indeed, some of the most innovative town plans of that period were located in the southern colonies. Williamsburg, the small but influential capital of colonial Virginia, introduced baroque civic design to the New World in a plan devised by Theodorick Bland. James Oglethorpe's Savannah plan of 1733 reflected the English philanthropist's commitment to a middle landscape ideal—a cautious blend of city and country. The town's spacious lots, orderly gridiron street pattern, and five squares that served as America's first public parks contrasted sharply with the more exploitative development overtaking northern cities at that time. Southern colonial urban planning also reflected a French cultural influence in the more formal design provided for New Orleans by Jean Baptiste Le Moyne, Sieur de Bienville, in 1722 focusing on the magnificent *place d'armes* dominated by St. Louis Cathedral.

Both the scale and quality of urban planning in the South declined in the 19th century, reflecting a general American trend that emphasized rapid development as opposed to aesthetic layout. The gridiron marched relentlessly over the southern landscape, and paper towns sprang up and folded. Urban planning practice shifted to service delivery and transportation as southern cities participated increasingly in the national economy. The relatively slow rate of urbanization experienced by some southeastern cities such as Charleston and Savannah was a disguised blessing enabling those places to maintain their parks and ready access to the sea and to tree-lined thoroughfares, which later generations of Americans would appreciate greatly.

The aesthetic consciousness of southern urban planning evident in its colonial towns resurfaced in the 1890s as part of the national City Beautiful movement inspired by the 1893 Chicago Columbian Exposition. The movement fitted southern cities well by focusing on cosmetic rehabilitation rather than on more troubling spatial and racial concerns. Further, it was inexpensive and cities in a capital-poor region with a tradition of local government parsimony for services found an economical program that would enhance image at relatively little cost. The activities of the Charlotte Women's Club presenting awards for the best gardens and a similar group in Wilmington encouraging outdoor floral arrangements were typical of southern City Beautiful. Actually, the most innovative urban planning of the era occurred outside the region's cities in fashionable suburbs such as Joel Hurt's Druid Hills development near Atlanta, designed by John C. Olmsted, and Kingsport, Tenn., a planned industrial town creatively laid out by Earle S. Draper.

By the early 1920s, with the rise of a planning profession, planning's traditional physical concerns replaced the superficial activities of City Beautiful. Specifically, transportation and zoning came to characterize urban planning practice in the South, as elsewhere. The ubiquitous Harland Bartholomew, the nation's leading planning consultant at that time, traveled to several southern cities. He eschewed social questions and concentrated on physical planning—expanded road networks and zoning ordinances. Southern urban leaders welcomed the new planning tools as devices to reinforce and solidify traditional patterns of racial residential segregation.

The racial orientation of urban planning persisted after World War II with the rise of urban renewal as the major planning strategy. While cities in other parts of the country evinced disregard for the integrity of black neighborhoods, southern cities were even more thorough in their planning policies, running highways through black districts and replacing demolished black housing with commercial structures to a greater extent than cities elsewhere. Ironically, the planning policies of more and better roads and fewer housing projects (as opposed to civic centers and office buildings) accelerated urban decline. By the 1970s new planning strategies evolved, not necessarily to reduce existing racial inequalities in the built environment, but to capitalize on national trends and legislation designed to conserve rather than to demolish. Cities directed planning resources toward downtown areas and neighborhoods emphasizing historic themes such as Underground Atlanta (which subsequently failed). The objective was to emphasize the southern city's cultural heritage, but the result was frequently a caricature of that past. Charleston and Savannah, perhaps the most authentic southern cities, were among the earliest and best-planned cities, and they are today the least troubled by the destructive forces of growth that other cities are scrambling, with mixed success, to ward off.

The planning profession is enmeshed in a southern dilemma that limits the effectiveness and influence of planners. The trend in professional planning nationally is a greater emphasis on social planning and accompanying measures to avoid or cope with economic decline. The commercial-civic elite, which still wields considerable power in southern cities, remains wedded to the growth ethic and tends to view planning as an interference with the urban land market. The success of historic preservation planning results in great part from its enhancement of downtown property values and the reconstitution (i.e., "whitening") of inner city residential neighborhoods and the investment opportunities such conservation implies.

David R. Goldfield
University of North Carolina
at Charlotte

Blaine A. Brownell, *Journal of Southern History* (August 1975); David R. Goldfield, *Cotton Fields and Skyscrapers: Southern City and Region, 1607–1980* (1982), *Journal of Southern History* (November 1976); Philip Morris, *Southern Living* (January 1978); Howard L. Preston, *Automobile Age Atlanta: The Making of a Southern Metropolis, 1900–1935* (1979); John W. Reps, *Tidewater Towns: City Planning in Colonial Virginia and Maryland* (1972); Dana F. White and Victor A. Kramer, eds., *Olmsted South: Old South Critic/New South Planner* (1979).

Urban Politics

Throughout southern history the mercantile classes have formed the core of urban leadership. In colonial times the business elite dominated the governmental and economic institutions of the South's embryonic cities. For these leaders the key to urban growth was the economic development of regional hinterlands. In early Baltimore, for instance, city expansion depended upon a thriving grain and flour industry that drew directly from the wheat production of the nearby countryside. Enhancement of the local economy was therefore the primary aim of urban government in the southern colonies.

During the antebellum era the bond between the business elite and city government persisted. In New Orleans, the South's largest urban center, directors of local corporations often served simultaneously on the city council. In Richmond 40 percent of the local elite, mainly business and professional men, held governmental offices. Joseph R. Anderson, head of the Tredegar Iron Works, was typical. He became a bank director, an outspoken supporter of various railroad and canal enterprises, and a member of the Richmond city council.

Enlargement of the hinterlands remained important to urban leaders, but many directed greater concern toward developing a regional and national network of cities as well as increasing urban competition. The mercantile elite endorsed railroad subsidies and wharf improvements that would perhaps attract business away from other communities, but they also recognized the importance to urban growth of better fire and police protection, improved street lighting, drainage, and adequate health statutes. Although municipal services infrequently kept pace with local needs, few questioned their usefulness to urban boosterism. At issue in most urban political contests was the cost of municipal improvements, not their value. Voters commonly removed extravagant administrators from office.

The obligation to regulate urban slaves and free blacks won universal acceptance in the South, but other ethnic tensions periodically took political form. In 1836 differences among the French-speaking Creoles, the incoming Americans, and emigrants from Ireland and Germany prompted the city of New Orleans to divide into three separate municipalities. For 16 years three distinct governmental entities directed the affairs of the Crescent City while an inconsequential mayor and general council nominally presided. In 1852 inefficiency, disease, and natural disasters contributed to a reunification that solidified the American sections with the annexation of rapidly growing suburbs. Ethnic animosity, however, continued throughout the decade. In the New Orleans municipal elections of 1854, violent opposition to immigration led directly to the victory of the Know-Nothing party. This organization, with the backing of labor, controlled Crescent City government until the Union conquest in 1862.

Secession sentiment in southern cities was mixed. The commercial leaders in those cities with predominantly northern markets resisted separation. The elite in cities with import trade generally favored disunion. Support for the southern cause, nonetheless, was clearly present in all urban centers.

Urban politics in the Reconstruction South mirrored regional contests that pitted Republicans and their newly franchised black allies against former Confederates and other Conservative Democrats. In New Orleans the White League, a vigorous and ultimately successful foe of the Republican regime and its metropolitan police, helped to spawn a powerful political machine that dominated local affairs for nearly 75 years. A characteristic urban ring, the Regular Democratic Organization used election fraud, patronage, political favors, and violence to maintain control. Its leadership of largely first-generation Americans depended upon labor, new immigrants, and (until 1898) subordinate blacks for electoral support. Businessmen who received lucrative municipal franchises provided financial backing.

The Old Regulars' political opponents were more representative of the leadership in other southern communities. Deemed appropriately the commercial-civic elite by historian Blaine A. Brownell, its members included bankers, real estate entrepreneurs, insurance agents, merchants, and contractors as well as lawyers, journalists, teachers, doctors, and other middle-class, business-oriented professionals. In the Crescent City this group constituted a sporadic opposition that achieved its ends mainly through independent governmental boards. In Atlanta, Birmingham, and other cities the commercial-civic elite dominated municipal offices and generally influenced the disposition of city revenue, services, and regulations. Combining the New South creed with urban boosterism, local leaders sought new industry and greater business development within an atmosphere of municipal stability. Urban growth, often accomplished through annexation, was an acknowledged—though frequently contradictory—goal. The new suburbs, a major source of fresh problems, usually received fewer municipal services than did the central business districts and the industrial neighborhoods.

During the early 20th century the mixing of southern city councils and chambers of commerce intensified. In New Orleans the evolving Old Regulars under Mayor Martin Behrman and in Memphis the powerful machine of Edward H. Crump clearly inclined toward business interests. Business philosophy and the progressive impulse precipitated structural reform in numerous southern city governments. The city commissioner and the city manager forms of municipal administration, created in Dixie, found favor throughout the region. Governmental change, however, rarely altered political structure in the urban South. The New Orleans machine and the Crump organization continued to dominate the new commission councils in their towns.

During the 1920s the link between the commercial-civic elite and city hall raised urban boosterism to higher levels. The "Atlanta Spirit" became the regional model although Miami was perhaps the best example of city boom. City leaders used the automobile revolution and the new interest in municipal planning to promote programs for the economic growth of the central business district, the allocation of adequate land for commercial and industrial use, the improvement of local transportation networks, the separation of the races, and the controlled expansion of the periphery. Although these programs infrequently resolved municipal problems, they established patterns for future development.

During the Depression economic demands forced southern leaders to curtail municipal services and to engage in relief efforts. Many regional chief executives joined with their urban counterparts throughout the nation to plead for federal aid to the cities. After the election of Franklin D. Roosevelt, numerous southern mayors espoused New Deal programs. In Memphis local leaders welcomed cheap electricity from the Tennessee Valley Authority. New Orleans Mayor Robert S. Maestri often joked that the Works Progress Administration was a "money tree" for his community.

World War II brought new growth and added challenges to southern cities. After the conflict, aged political machines in New Orleans and Memphis faltered, and the commercial-civic elite began to reassert itself. New-breed mayors such as De Lesseps S. Morrison of New Orleans, Robert King High of Miami, and William B. Hartsfield and Ivan Allen, Jr., of Atlanta took charge and advanced programs that were in line with commercial expansion and urban development. All facets of municipal administration, particularly building projects, were geared to the enhancement of the urban image in the South. Within this context of city maturation, the financial problems and political tensions of suburbanization began to appear. To cope with these difficulties, Miami and Nashville adopted metropolitan governments.

The civil rights movement contributed to the outward population shift when white southerners fled to the suburbs to escape integration. In Little Rock, New Orleans, and Birmingham resistance to desegregation had a debilitating effect upon the local economies. During these crises governmental and business leadership in the South was sorely lacking until harsh economic reality forced the commercial-civic elite to take a moderate stance on desegregation.

During the 1960s federal legislation on civil rights altered the political structure of the urban South forever and convinced white politicians to reassess their racial views. Candidates who did not address the needs of black voters had little chance for success. An expanding black electorate and white flight to the suburbs increased black political clout in the urban South. By the 1970s blacks commonly populated city councils throughout the region and many of the South's largest cities boasted their first black mayors. Although black governmental leaders often worked with and welcomed the support of the commercial-civic elite, they devoted greater attention to neighborhood needs. Many white governmental leaders also stressed historic preservation and rehabilitation of core areas as a means to offset the population decrease, and accompanying financial drains, of suburban flight. Over the past decade the commercial-civic elite has not surrendered its political power, but it has been forced to vie with other urban interest groups for the allocation of diminishing municipal resources. An increasingly diverse leadership in southern cities has begun to assess the value of economic growth against the importance of metropolitan cooperation, historic renovation, and neighborhood demands.

See also BLACK LIFE: Politics, Black; INDUSTRY: Civil Rights and Business; POLITICS articles

Edward F. Haas
Louisiana State Museum/
Tulane University

Carl Abbott, *The New Urban America: Growth and Politics in Sunbelt Cities* (1981); Blaine A. Brownell and David R. Goldfield, eds., *The City in Southern History: The Growth of Urban Civilization in the South* (1977); Edward F. Haas, *De Lesseps S. Morrison and the Image of Reform: New Orleans Politics, 1946–1961* (1974); Carl V. Harris, *Political Power in Birmingham, 1871–1921* (1977); Christopher Silver, *Journal of Urban History* (November 1983); Eugene J. Watts, *The Social Bases of City Politics: Atlanta, 1865–1903* (1978).

Urban Poor

Historian C. Vann Woodward depicted poverty as one of the burdens of southern history. Poverty, of course, is not a strictly southern phenomenon, but persistent and extensive poverty in the region is distinctive. Southern cities, as inextricable parts of their region, have shared this poverty. Generally, urban southerners have reflected the philosophy of other Americans with regard to poor relief, moving from first viewing poverty as a divine judgment requiring no intervention, to aid only for deserving poor, to work relief programs, to maintenance grants. Three elements have distinguished the southern urban poor and poor relief from poverty and welfare elsewhere: southern cities have generally lacked economic resources for an extensive welfare apparatus, the influence of evangelical sects has tended to limit public intervention, and an overwhelming proportion of blacks among the poor has encouraged official white neglect.

In the antebellum era poor relief tended to be seasonal and private—the needy received wood and food in the winter. The Norfolk Association for the Improvement of the Condition of the Poor typified the attitudes of southern private relief agencies by noting that "*sound discrimination* . . . is the first principle of this Association. It will give to none who will not exhibit evidence of improvement from the aid afforded." The poor, black and white, lived in the least desirable areas, and these locations exposed them to disease.

The decades after the Civil War witnessed an outpouring of literature on the poor and on the causes and relief of poverty. But the dominance of evangelical religion in the South, which emphasized the futility of human solutions to earthly problems, thwarted any investigative impulse in the South. The social gospel, which imbued Protestant churches in the North, was a relatively minor movement in the South. Regional culture reinforced the tendency to neglect and ignore urban poverty. In addition, because of the identification of urban blacks with poverty, the race issue restricted welfare discussions.

If the urban poor could not seek succor from official and even charitable agencies, self-help institutions provided some relief. This was especially so with the growing black community, which swelled with rural freedmen in the decades after the Civil War. The black churches, pooling the meager resources of their congregations, provided relief and burial services to needy families. The churches could do little about the poor's residential environment—typically rented wooden shacks on unpaved streets, devoid of urban services. The few public institutions devoted to poor relief, such as the poorhouse, were usually mismanaged and always underfunded. In New Orleans the poorhouse was administered by the head of the waterworks. In Atlanta the poorhouse consisted of two-room wooden "cottages" without ceiling or heat, where in the middle of winter children dressed "in rags and tatters." Moreover, wide differentials existed with respect to city donations to black and white charitable institutions (though expenditures in both were small). In Richmond in 1900, for example, city contributions to black charities amounted to $550, to white charities, $7,722, despite the greater prevalence of poverty in the black community.

As rural migration to southern cities quickened during the early decades of the 20th century, urban relief efforts failed to keep pace. Birmingham actually abolished its welfare department in the 1920s. The Depression quickly overburdened urban governments and only federal relief efforts relieved a dire situation.

The return of prosperity during and after World War II did not alter the southern philosophy of poor relief or the living conditions of the poor, who remained burdened not only by poverty but by poor housing, an unsanitary environment, and inadequate educational facilities, all of which reinforced that poverty. The poor resided within hailing distance of Houston's or Atlanta's gleaming skyscrapers. In San Antonio in 1970 nearly one out of every three families earned less than $3,000 a year (below the poverty level), and over 6 percent had incomes less than $1,000 a year—a figure that Robert Coles termed "almost incredible for an urban center." No southern city matched or exceeded the national average per capita urban expenditures for public welfare ($11.98), and San Antonio was exceptionally low at 45 cents per capita expenditure.

Race and poverty continued in tandem in southern cities. In Memphis, where blacks comprised 38 percent of the population, they represented 58 percent of all families with annual income less than $1,000 in 1949, and 71 percent of those families in 1969. By 1970 the black median family income in Memphis was only 56 percent of the white family income.

The Sunbelt prosperity of the 1970s did not effect a major transformation in either public poor relief or the decline of poverty. The trickle-down theory of economic development effected no noticeable improvements; in fact, the inflation generated by economic expansion tended to hurt low income groups. Though unemployment rates are lower in southern cities than in cities in the Northeast and Midwest, residents of southern slums are poorer, based on per capita income, than slum dwellers in northeastern cities. While almost one-half of the northeastern poor are unemployed, compared with only one-quarter jobless in poor southern urban neighborhoods, the numbers of those working below a government-defined living wage are significantly higher in southern inner cities than in the North.

See also SOCIAL CLASS: Poverty

David R. Goldfield
University of North Carolina
at Charlotte

Blaine A. Brownell and David R. Goldfield, eds., *The City in Southern History: The Growth of Urban Civilization in the South* (1977); J. Wayne Flynt, *Dixie's Forgotten People: The South's Poor Whites* (1979); Carl Grindstaff, *Social Problems* (Winter 1967); John Kellogg, *Geographical Review* (July 1977); Peter A. Lupsha and William J. Siembieda, in *The Rise of the Sunbelt Cities*, ed. David C. Perry and Alfred J. Watkins (1977); Howard N. Rabinowitz, *Race Relations in the Urban South, 1865–1890* (1978); Edyth L. Ross, *Phylon* (Winter 1976).

Urban Transportation

Cities in the South have undergone tremendous changes as a result of urban transportation, but it was not until the 20th century and the advent of the automobile age that southerners experienced some of the same environmental disruptions that occurred in places like Boston and Philadelphia decades earlier.

Montgomery, Ala., and Richmond, Va., were the first cities nationally to boast the operation of an electric street railway. But the unlikely appearance of this new means of horizontal mobility in the South did not effect dramatic changes as in the North. Although Atlanta, Birmingham, Memphis, Nashville, Tampa, Jacksonville, New Orleans, and Louisville all had streetcar transit, their operations were small and failed to help generate any significant degree of decentralized housing, consumer services, or commercial activities. The increased mobility that streetcars offered southerners certainly resulted in suburban annexations: Atlanta had its Inman Park and Druid Hills; Houston its Houston Heights and Deer Park; Tampa its Tampa Heights; and Memphis its Annesdale Park. But by the conclusion of the 19th century, the urban South was hardly comparable to northern industrial cities where streetcar patronage had helped create the sprawling, fragmented metropolises usually associated with late 19th-century American urban life.

Failure of street railway systems to influence decentralization in southern cities was evident in their size and shape. At the turn of the century, only one city in the South—New Orleans—could claim a population of over 100,000, and for every southerner living in a city in the South with a population of more than 25,000, approximately 15 others remained in smaller cities, towns, or on the farm. Under the influence of street railway transportation many of these provincial capitals retained circular shapes until well into the 20th century. Atlanta, for example, had basically a circular shape enclosing an 11-square-mile area in 1900, but more significantly the Georgia capital closely resembled the size of Boston during the mid-19th century. Thus, southern cities entered the 20th century almost uninfluenced by the dominant means of urban transportation of that era. In fact, at that time these relatively small American cities better fit the mold of a preindustrial walking city than that of a late 19th-century industrial metropolis.

Not until the first three decades of the 20th century did many cities in the South begin to outgrow their provinciality. Most of this growth occurred during the 1920s when the very symbol of that decade—the automobile—overtook the street railway as the most popular means of urban transportation. In Memphis between 1920 and 1930 automobile ownership increased by 192 percent; in Atlanta there were 215 percent more registered motor vehicles in 1930 than in 1920; and in Birmingham the figure climbed to as much as 337 percent.

Most of the changes automobile use brought to cities in the South were no different from those in other parts of the country. Businesses unable to survive in congested downtown locations sought refuge in the suburbs; traffic congestion tarnished the image of city fathers who promoted their cities as havens of business opportunity; and citizens of Atlanta, Birmingham, Charlotte, Nashville, and elsewhere found the amenities of suburban life more attractive than ever before.

Increased racial segregation was perhaps the one change that private use of automobiles wrought in the urban South more dramatically than other places in the country. Writing about Los Angeles, the model automobile metropolis, one urban authority has claimed that the use of motor vehicles created a new land-use structure in which a measure of racial and class justice could be achieved. This was not the case in the urban South. Because whites were generally more affluent than blacks and could better afford private automobiles as well as home mortgages, suburbanization outside southern cities was limited almost exclusively to whites. In fact, the automobile became the means by which whites achieved their desire for separate living. In terms of time and distance, whites and blacks residing in and around southern cities in 1930 were more segregated than ever before.

Ironically, although urban transportation aided the separate-but-equal doctrine in the urban South, it was through that same medium that blacks began to challenge white supremacy. Rosa Lee Parks's refusal to take a seat at the back of a Montgomery, Ala., bus in 1955 and the subsequent successful boycott of the Montgomery City Line buses by blacks not only brought Martin Luther King, Jr., to the attention of Americans as a civil rights activist but, more importantly, gave the civil rights movement credibility and momentum.

The Montgomery bus boycott ended segregation on Montgomery buses in 1956 and eventually led to integration on public transit conveyers in cities across the South. Decades earlier, however, the private use of automobiles in southern cities had established a pattern of racial segregation in suburban housing and educational facilities that integrated public transportation could not dent. Sometime in the 1960s the majority of urban white southerners shifted from central city areas to outlying suburbs. In 1974 the Southern Growth Policy Board's Commission on the Future of the South concluded that heavy reliance on the automobile has caused the urban regions of the South to be "less dense and more diffuse than the centralized cities that developed in other parts of the country in an earlier industrial age." Indeed it had, but perhaps the impact of the automobile on southern cities was even more significant to urban life there than commission members surmised.

See also HISTORY AND MANNERS: Automobile; Railroads

Howard L. Preston
Spartanburg, South Carolina

Rick Beard, in *Olmsted South: Old South Critic/New South Planner*, ed. Dana F. White and Victor A. Kramer (1979); Blaine A. Brownell, *Alabama Review* (April 1972), *American Quarterly* (March 1972), with David R. Goldfield, eds., *The City in Southern History: The Growth of Urban Civilization in the South* (1977); Howard L. Preston, *Automobile Age Atlanta: The Making of a Southern Metropolis, 1900–1935* (1979); Southern Growth Policies Board, *The Future of the South* (1974).

Atlanta

"Gate City of the South," "Capital of the New South," "A City too Busy to Hate," "Black Mecca," and "The World's Next Great City" are all slogans business leaders have coined to promote the growth of Atlanta over the last century and a quarter. Beginning with Atlanta *Constitution* editor Henry W. Grady, whose speeches in northern states in the 1880s carried the message that a reconciled South was a good place for investment, the Chamber of Commerce has actively promoted the potential of the city. The Cotton States and International Exposition of 1895 brought national attention for the somewhat modest imitation of the Chicago World's Fair. Later the Forward Atlanta campaigns of the 1920s and the 1960s utilized national periodicals to advertise the city's attractions for commerce and industry. The business promoters fared far better than Confederate Generals Joseph E. Johnston and John Bell Hood who defended Atlanta during the Civil War: they attracted the investment that has allowed the city not only to rebuild itself from its almost total destruction in 1864 but also to outpace the growth of other cities in the region.

In 1860 Atlanta had a population of slightly more than 10,000; a century later, its metropolitan total topped 1 million. Although this growth enabled the city to outdistance other southern contenders for economic leadership, such as Charleston, Birmingham, and even New Orleans, it still was not equal to the rate of northern rivals. The regional characteristic that did distinguish Atlanta (and other southern cities) well into the 20th century was its high proportion of black citizens, who, until the 1960s, were kept in careful check by the color line. In 1870, 45 percent of the population was black, a portion that declined to one-third by 1900. Metropolitan growth in the last quarter of a century has maintained the overall ratio of blacks to whites at about 33 percent, but the lack of change in corporate limits helped to increase the black percentage in the city to 65 percent in 1980. The end of legal discrimination, coupled with increasing voter concentration in the last decade, led to the election of blacks to positions ranging from mayor (Maynard Jackson, 1973) to U.S. Congressman (Andrew Young, 1974). "A City too Busy to Hate," the Chamber of Commerce's slogan during desegregation in the 1960s, has become the "Black Mecca" of the 1970s.

Margaret Mitchell's *Gone with the Wind*, Stone Mountain's carving of the Confederacy, Cyclorama's diorama of the battle of Atlanta, and calico-dressed black women at popular tourist restaurants represent for many the romantic image of the city as the "Capital of the Lost Cause." Yet few, if any, traces of the Old South can be found in Atlanta. As the "Capital of the New South," its symbols are commercial: railroad stations, warehouses, hotels, and office buildings. In the late 19th century Atlanta pioneered one of the first skyscrapers in the Southeast (the Equitable Building, 1892, by Burnham and Root); in the late 20th century the city popularized the atrium hotel (the Regency-Hyatt House, 1967, by John Portman), the multiuse complex (Peachtree Center, 1967–81, also by John Portman), the suburban mall (Lenox Square, 1959), and the expressway. In fact, construction during the 1960s and 1970s erased many of the symbols of the original New South city, including the rail passenger stations, the Equitable Building, and the turn-of-the-century hotels.

Cultural life in Atlanta has grown with the city. In the 19th century several opera houses were built, the most famous being the DeGive Opera House, which, when it was used later as a movie theater, was the site of the world premiere of *Gone with the Wind*. In 1910 the city fathers succeeded in bringing the Metropolitan Opera of New York for a week's visit, an annual event, which, with an occasional hiatus caused by world wars and the Depression, continues today. The Woodruff Memorial Arts Center has evolved from an Arts Association chartered by families of leading boosters in 1903 into a place to see important regional works of art, the location of traveling exhibitions of national and international importance, and the site of Symphony Hall and a professional theater. University life commenced in Atlanta in 1867 with the founding of Atlanta University, the city's first black institution of higher education. Later, Atlanta's New South promoters financed the establishment of colleges as a means of enhancing the commercial vitality of a growing metropolis. Organized promotions brought, among others, Georgia Institute of Technology in 1888, Emory University in 1915, and Georgia State University in 1955. The population growth of the 1960s was matched by advances in both high and popular culture. The Atlanta Symphony (which was founded in 1944 as a youth orchestra) grew to maturity, while the construction of a stadium and coliseum allowed the city to attract professional sports teams, including the Braves (baseball), the Falcons (football), and the Hawks (basketball).

Atlanta continues to build on its original source of strength—its location in the national transportation network. Beginning in the 1840s when it was the terminus of the state-built railroad linking lines to Charleston and Savannah with an over-the-mountain route to Tennessee and the southern interior, Atlanta grew into the center of a southeastern railroad network. By 1920, 14 lines and four major systems connected through the "Gate City of the South." As auto and truck traffic have supplanted rail since World War II, Atlanta has benefited from the construction of the best interstate highway connections in the Southeast. The city also won over its nearby rivals to become the primary transfer point for air passenger service in the region. So many airline routes to southern cities have Atlanta connections that it is often said, "When you die and go to heaven, you must pass through Atlanta." A thriving convention trade and an uncommonly high number of offices of national corporations are the result of Atlanta's excellent air connections, leading business leaders to dream about being "The World's Next Great City."

See also EDUCATION: / Emory; Georgia Institute of Technology; INDUSTRY: / Atlanta as Commercial Center; Grady, Henry W.; MEDIA: / Atlanta *Constitution*; MYTHIC SOUTH: New South Myth

Timothy J. Crimmins
Georgia State University

Timothy J. Crimmins and Dana F. White, eds., "Urban Structure, Atlanta," a special issue of the *Atlanta Historical Journal* (Summer–Fall 1982); Franklin Garrett, *Yesterday's Atlanta*

(1974); Andrew Hamer, *Urban Atlanta: Redefining the Role of the City* (1980).

Birmingham

Cherokee, Choctaw, and Chickasaw tribesmen roamed Jones Valley before the first white settlers appeared in 1813 in the area that one day would be known as Birmingham. Furnaces and small ironworks were built in the area during the Civil War to provide armaments for the Confederate armies, but they were destroyed by Union forces.

When speculative entrepreneurs founded Birmingham in 1871, they predicted that it would become the "El Dorado of the iron masters" and the "manufacturing center of the habitable globe." Birmingham has never fulfilled that lofty prophecy, but the founders' vision was compelling enough to have attracted a number of major investors by 1880. Within two decades this cadre of New South industrialists, led by Henry Fairchild De Bardeleben, had constructed 28 furnaces, had sunk numerous mines into the rich seams of coal and iron ore nearby, and had constructed railroads and villages throughout the mineral district, of which Birmingham became the center. Due primarily to the development of resources around Birmingham, coal production in Alabama increased from only 17,000 tons in 1872 to 8 million tons in 1900, and pig iron production leaped from just 11,000 tons to more than 1 million tons in the same period. Indeed, by 1898 Birmingham was the largest exporting point for pig iron in the United States, and the third largest in the world. It became known as the "Pittsburgh of the South."

The desires and needs of these early entrepreneurs, however, far outpaced the financial resources available in the capital-poor South. Consequently, investors from outside the district acquired and consolidated the holdings of many smaller and weaker companies. The largest of these new corporations was the Tennessee Coal, Iron and Railroad Company (TCI). Even though TCI inaugurated the production of competitive-grade steel in 1899, it was plagued by financial problems, and by 1900 was almost wholly controlled by absentee owners in the North.

Northern control of Birmingham industry was further consolidated in 1907 when TCI was absorbed by the United States Steel Corporation. To insure that the competitive advantage offered by Birmingham's natural resources and cheap labor supply would not endanger the company's base operations at Pittsburgh, U.S. Steel instituted a series of discriminatory pricing systems for TCI products that remained in force until the late 1930s. Thus, Birmingham became one of the more prominent examples of the South's colonial status in the first half of the 20th century, because the city's economic fortunes were determined largely by policies made in Pittsburgh rather than by decisions made by local business leaders.

Birmingham's population grew from 38,415 to 132,685 between 1900 and 1920, and the place became known as "Magic City." By 1930 the population stood at 259,678. Birmingham's heavy industrial economy assured that its population would be more diverse than that of most southern cities. In addition to native whites, a significant number of first- and second-generation immigrants and an even larger proportion of blacks were attracted by the opportunities in the district. The competition for jobs among these groups was frequently enflamed by racial and cultural differences, and on occasion conflict would escalate into violence. Violence also inevitably accompanied the early, unsuccessful efforts by unions to organize workers at local mines and mills. Meantime, community leaders seeking to mitigate these conflicts could find little support among the industrialists, who wielded the most power but chose either to remain aloof from local affairs or to act solely to protect their economic interests. The city was especially hard hit by the Great Depression, but the increased demand for steel during World War II contributed to the emergence of Birmingham as a major southern industrial center by the 1950s. Today, a 55-foot-high cast-iron statue of Vulcan (the Roman god of fire), which is one of the largest iron statues in the world, stands atop Red Mountain, a symbol of the iron-and-steel-making legacy of the city below.

Birmingham was sometimes called the "Johannesburg of America" in the 1960s because of the racial conflict in the city. Eugene "Bull" Connor was reelected police commissioner in 1957 and did little to discourage the white terrorism of blacks that had already appeared there. The spring of 1963 saw massive civil rights demonstrations and police violence against marchers. News photographs of blacks attacked by snarling dogs and angry police became a large part of the national image of the city. In September 1963 the bombing of the 16th Street Baptist Church, killing four young black girls, initially threatened the racial truce that had ended the demonstrations. Ultimately, however, the tragedy brought blacks and whites closer together. Racial peace appeared in the late 1960s, with the first blacks elected to the City Council in 1968. Richard Arrington became Birmingham's first black mayor in 1979.

In the early 1900s Birmingham's cultural and social life was dominated by a rigid adherence to Protestant moral standards (a city referendum in 1922 resulted in the closing of a public dance pavilion before the den of iniquity ever opened). That era ended long ago, though. Birmingham now supports a symphony orchestra, ballet companies, and theater groups. There are 65 public parks, a professional hockey team, and, until recently, a franchise in the United States Football League. The University of Alabama in Birmingham was established in 1964 as a branch campus of the University of Alabama, including schools of medicine, dentistry, and nursing. Other colleges include Birmingham Southern, Samford University, Miles College, Jefferson State Junior College, and Lawson State Community College.

Robert G. Corley
University of Alabama
at Birmingham

Ethel Armes, *The Story of Coal and Iron in Alabama* (1910); Carl V. Harris, *Political Power in Birmingham, 1871–1921* (1977); Marjorie L. White, *The Birmingham District: An Industrial History and Guide* (1981).

Charleston

Charleston, founded in 1670, became wealthy and prosperous in the early 18th century through its commerce and the shipping of rice, indigo, and backcountry products. The city during its early period contained a mixture of nationalities and religious sects. Sephardic Jews, for example, established one of the largest Jewish communities in North America. Two main groups contributed most to the city's distinctive culture. One was composed of the wealthiest planters and merchants who set the tone for society. They were avid consumers of European culture as well as fashions. Their patronage of the theater helped to make Dock Street Theatre, opened in 1736, one of America's first. Their enjoyment of fine music also led to the founding of the St. Cecilia Society, the earliest American organization sponsoring amateur and professional concerts. Charleston's elite played a large part in the establishment of a private subscription library in 1748 and the erection of private academies and schools. The wealthy also built elegant town houses, the most distinctive of which was the Charleston "single house," which faced not the street but its own side garden and whose width was that of a single room. The city's gentry, self-consciously aristocratic and proud of their social and cultural life, included some of the foremost proponents of a proslavery ideology, southern nationalism, and secession.

Although the wealthy were an important force in Charleston, the city was also a biracial society with a majority black population through much of its history. Most blacks were chattel slaves who as domestics, artisans, market workers, or laborers formed the backbone of the labor force. Less than 10 percent of Charleston's total population was composed of free blacks. Among them was a small but significant group of propertied tradesmen and artisans who created the fraternal and benevolent organizations, the Brown Fellowship and the Humane Brotherhood. But restrictions upon the rights of free blacks, especially after the abortive slave uprising engineered by Denmark Vesey in 1822, probably meant that free blacks maintained many ties with the slave community. A large West African slave trade, which lasted until 1808, helped blacks to maintain a distinctive cultural identity retaining elements from their African origin. Many black Charlestonians spoke Gullah, a dialect that combined African structures with African, Portuguese, and English words. The center of the distinctive black culture lay in religion. Blacks tended to favor the more evangelical sects such as the Methodist and Baptist churches—in the former they outnumbered whites by a margin of around eight to one, in the latter four to one. Charleston blacks founded their own church, Emmanuel African Methodist Episcopal, in 1815, but whites fearful of growing black autonomy suppressed it and forced blacks to rejoin churches with white members.

The Civil War, which began at Fort Sumter in the Charleston harbor, shattered the prosperity that had already begun to wane in Charleston. Through the late 19th century and into the 20th, white Charlestonians of the old elite clung to the symbols of their lost past—their antebellum houses and their cultural societies. Freedom brought black Charlestonians the ability to form separate churches and maintain their cultural identity, but poverty and discrimination continued to limit the roles they could play within the city. Industry slowly gained a foothold in postbellum Charleston, and the two world wars were the harbingers of new economic vitality and population growth. The 1984 population was 69,510.

In the modern period Charleston's culture has retained some of the influence of its elite and black populations but has increasingly become more like that of other Americans. The city has kept its older institutions but new ones have emerged as well so that today a list of Charleston's cultural centers proves formidable. Among the city's many museums are the Charleston Museum, recently relocated to modern quarters, and the Gibbs Art Museum. Charleston today also possesses semiprofessional ballet and theater companies, one of which performs at the historic Dock Street Theatre. Since 1977 the city has gained a richer cultural experience from the increased concentration upon the fine arts at the College of Charleston combined with the creation of the Spoleto Festival by Italian composer Gian Carlo Menotti. Named for its Italian birthplace, this annual summer event includes prominent as well as promising young musicians in areas ranging from opera to jazz.

See also EDUCATION: / Citadel; RECREATION: / Spoleto Festival U.S.A.; St. Cecilia Ball; SCIENCE AND MEDICINE: / Charleston Museum

Jane Turner Censer
The Frederick Law Olmsted Papers

Jack R. Censer
George Mason University

Frederick P. Bowes, *The Culture of Early Charleston* (1942); Erskine Clarke, *Wrestlin' Jacob: A Portrait of Religion in the Old South* (1979); Robert L. Harris, Jr., *South Carolina Historical Magazine* (October 1981); George C. Rogers, Jr., *Charleston in the Age of the Pinckneys* (1969).

Charlotte

Charlotte today is the regional focal point for a continuous network of urban communities in the Carolinas that number over 2 million people—and a far cry from the "trifling place" that visitor George Washington termed the community 200 years ago. At that time Charlotte was a small market town for vegetables, grains, and livestock and had achieved only brief fame as General Cornwallis's North Carolina headquarters. It sank back into relative obscurity until the early 1880s when a gold rush in Mecklenburg County, of which Charlotte is the county seat, revived the town.

By the 1850s cotton was king in Mecklenburg, and Charlotte, like so many other southern cities, developed processing and trade facilities for the region's agricultural products. Future growth of the city was problematic, though, because it did not enjoy the physical advantages of a waterline location so crucial to early 19th-century urban development. The city did occupy a strategic central point in the growing Piedmont agricultural region, and from the 1850s Charlotte became the major railroad center for the Carolinas.

The effective rail connections, as well as the contagious New South creed boosting industrial and urban development, encouraged local entrepreneurs like Daniel A. Tompkins to launch the "Cotton Mill Campaign" in the 1880s. A major objective of the campaign was to provide employment opportunities for rural whites increasingly impoverished by a depressed agriculture. The campaign attempted to alter the economic base of the Carolina Piedmont from predominantly staple agriculture to industry. Its success was seen by 1903, when one-half of the South's looms and spindles were located within a 100-mile radius of the city, most financed with indigenous capital. Charlotte typified southern urban growth of the era with its reliance on basic processing industry, though by the 1940s the city was primarily an administrative center. Charlotte, the "Queen City" (named for George III's wife in 1765), attained economic stability as it gained independence from King Cotton.

Charlotte's strategic rail connections attracted major highway systems beginning in the 1920s, when textile mills began deserting New England for the South. Two major interstate highways—85 ("Textile Highway") and 77—intersect at Charlotte, making automobile pollution an increasing problem in the city. Despite the decline in the textile industry, Charlotte has avoided the economic problems of other Piedmont communities tied to the textile culture through a judicious policy of economic diversification as an administrative and financial center. The city managed to attract IBM and to add to its already-excellent transportation linkages a new airport in 1982.

The city also benefited from a relatively enlightened racial policy as evidenced by the pioneering Charlotte-Mecklenburg school busing plan. Charlotte's diversified economy, relatively high proportion of Yankees, and vibrant and prosperous inner-city neighborhoods make it something of an anomaly in southern urban culture. The future success of Charlotte, a medium-sized city of 331,000 residents in 1984, may very well depend upon the maintenance of its diverse economic base, its image as a city of neighborhoods, and its population diversity.

As Charlotte's economic base has shifted and expanded from an administrative hub for the Piedmont textile empire to the Southeast's major financial and high-tech center, its cultural profile has altered to complement the new demographic (high-salaried, high-skilled, high-educated) and economic trends of the 1980s. The Charlotte Symphony Orchestra attained professional status in 1981; the city's opera company and the recently expanded Mint Museum of Art enjoy a strong financial support from the growing professional population; Spirit Square, a converted church in downtown, has become the location for musical performances ranging from classical to jazz; and another church in the same area will become the Afro-American Cultural Center. Since 1972, the Creative Arts Department at the University of North Carolina at Charlotte has been a community focal point for dance, theater, voice, and fine arts education. The city's cultural centers have recruited actively from the North and even abroad for experienced personnel to direct these activities. There are no contemporary art galleries, however, and patron tastes rarely exceed the conventional in art and music.

David R. Goldfield
University of North Carolina
at Charlotte

LeGette Blythe, *Charlotte and Mecklenburg County, North Carolina Today* (1967); James W. Clay, ed., *Atlas of Charlotte-Mecklenburg* (1981); Mary N. Kraft, *Charlotte, Spirit of the New South* (1980).

Dallas

In the beginning, Dallas had no special advantages in natural resources or geography to favor it over other frontier settlements in north central Texas. Its development has been due in large part to an aggressive civic spirit passed through generations. Somehow, writer Larry L. King has observed, "Dallas attracted men determined to build a great city: go-getters and can-doers, men of ambitious fevers." Each advantage they created became a springboard for other, more ambitious efforts.

The first settler was John Neely Bryan, who established a trading post on the east bank of the Trinity River in 1841 and laid out a townsite half a mile square near a good crossing on the river. Bryan apparently promoted his townsite widely. John B. Billingsley, who arrived at Dallas from Missouri in 1844, recorded in his journal: "We soon reached the place we had heard of so often; but the *town*, where was it? Two small log cabins—this was the town of Dallas; and two families of ten or twelve souls was its population." When Dallas County was created in 1846, Dallas was designated as the temporary county seat; in 1850 it was chosen permanent county seat over Hord's Ridge and Cedar Springs. During the Civil War the town became a Confederate administrative center, with quartermaster, commissary, transportation, and recruiting headquarters. Population reached 1,200 by 1872, and the *Texas Almanac* that year referred to Dallas as one of three north Texas towns already "beginning to put on the airs of a city." In the early 1870s the Houston & Texas Central and Texas & Pacific railroads began operating into Dallas, thus assuring her economic future.

Beginning with the erection of the 15-story Praetorian Building in 1907, the Dallas skyline began to present an urban appearance. Thanks to the popular television program, *Dallas*, a prime-time soap opera about the oil-rich Ewing clan of Southfork Ranch, millions of Americans recognize the modern skyline. New buildings in the 1980s such as the 60-story Allied Bank Tower and the LTV Center, a 50-story skyscraper of stone, gave Dallas a new architectural significance.

"It is the Athens of the Southwest," *Fortune* noted in 1949, "the undisputed leader of finance, insurance, distribution, culture and fashion for this land of the super-Americans." The Chamber of Commerce likes to boast that "Dallas is neither typically Southern or Southwestern, but distinctly cosmopolitan in its outlook." The prevailing political mood is staunchly conservative. Municipal politics is oligarchic, dominated by populous, well-to-do, heavily Republican north Dallas. Blacks represent less than 30 percent of the city's population. Persons of Spanish origin—predominantly Mexican Americans—make up 12.3 percent. Lee Harvey Oswald's assassination of President John F. Kennedy on 22 November 1963 represented the greatest trauma in the city's modern era.

Community enterprises in the cultural field include the Dallas Symphony, the Dallas Civic Opera Company, Summer Musicals, the Dallas Ballet, the Dallas Theater Center, the Dallas Museum of Art, and the Shakespeare Festival. Among the principal institutions of higher education in Dallas County are Southern Methodist University, the University of Texas Health Science Center, Baylor University College of Dentistry, University of Dallas, Bishop College, Dallas Theological Seminary, University of Texas at Dallas, Dallas Baptist College, and Dallas County Community College District. Professional sports in the area are headed by "America's Team"—football's Dallas Cowboys—and include the Texas Rangers in baseball and the Dallas Mavericks in basketball.

Dallas has always been proud of its municipal competence and likes to think of itself as the "City That Works." Agitation by the Cleaner Dallas League (1902) for municipal sanitation, public parks, paved streets, and sidewalks led ultimately to a series of "city plans" and bond issues. Permissive zoning and intensive development, however, have created an office glut downtown, choked major freeways and roads, and caused commercial encroachment into the city's older residential neighborhoods. Its 1984 nonmetropolitan population figure was 974,000. Dallas is now split between residents who want a diverse but stable city and developers and others who prefer to live in a perpetual boom town—"Big D."

See also EDUCATION: / Southern Methodist University

Norman D. Brown
University of Texas at Austin

Sam Acheson, *Dallas Yesterdays* (1977); A. C. Greene, *Dallas: The Deciding Years—A Historical Portrait* (1973); John W. Rogers, *The Lusty Texans of Dallas* (1951).

Houston

Founded in 1836 by two brothers from New York, John and Augustus Allen, Houston is now the nation's fourth largest city with a 1984 population of about 1,706,000. Its metropolitan population recently surpassed 3 million. Houston is located in southeast Texas, about 50 miles from Galveston Bay. The city possesses a humid, semitropical climate, common to the Gulf Coast, which creates lush vegetation during the summer months. The catalyst for Houston's economy is energy, as the city calls itself the energy capital of the United States. Over one-quarter of the refining capacity of the United States and over one-half of the petrochemical capacity of the nation is located in Houston. In addition, over two-thirds of the world's oil tools are produced there. Although the city is 50 miles from Galveston Bay, the port of Houston is ranked among the top three in the country.

In 1900 Houston was a small city consisting of about 44,000 people within a nine-square-mile area. Southern in style and culture, the city called itself the Magnolia City in an attempt to accentuate these roots. But three factors in the 20th century combined to change its character and make it one of the fastest-growing urban areas in the United States. Galveston, its closest rival, was destroyed in 1900 by a hurricane and a flood, and one year later, oil was discovered in nearby Beaumont. With the assistance of the U.S. Army Corps of Engineers, the city dredged and widened Buffalo Bayou, creating the Houston Ship Channel, the shallow narrow waterway that connected the city to Galveston Bay. The result was a deep water port by 1914. The combination of oil and the safe port, plus the destruction of Galveston as a commercial rival, was the basis of Houston's economic boom in the 20th century.

In the 1920s refineries and petrochemical facilities were constructed along the Ship Channel, a process accelerated by the needs of the American military during World War II. The city's growth was also assisted by the mass introduction of air-conditioning after the war, as well as the acquisition of the National Aeronautics and Space Administration (and the title "Space City") in the late 1950s.

Another factor in Houston's rapid growth, and a major characteristic of the city, is a relatively conservative political climate and a concomitant belief in a free enterprise ideology, which has assisted business growth while limiting the size and functions of local government. As a result, the city is the nation's only major metropolis without zoning.

Spatially, the city is a sprawling—over 560 square miles—decentralized, automobile-based and freeway-linked urban region, with a low population density, which averages about 3,300 people per square mile. It is ethnically diverse, approximately 60 percent Caucasian, 25 percent black, and 15 percent Hispanic. A number of large economic and administrative activity centers give it a multicentered land-use pattern rather than the traditional central business district. Although facing a number of service-oriented problems, caused in part by rapid growth that has strained the city's ability to provide services, the city is an exciting and optimistic place in which to live.

Houston likes to call itself the "Third Coast," in reference to its artistic achievements, and supports major ballet, opera, symphony, and theater companies. Numerous exhibits and performances occur regularly in parks, corporate plazas, churches, schools, and even shopping centers. The city's ultra-modern, skyscraper architecture, including landmark buildings by Philip Johnson, is world famous. Support of high culture has been a project of some of Houston's major families including the Cullens, the Hoggs, and the de Menils. There are over 25 colleges and universities in Houston, including Rice University, the University of Houston, and Texas Southern. The city contains a major national medical complex, the 230-acre Texas Medical Center, which was launched in 1943 and now includes 25 institutions. The Astrodome was the world's first domed stadium and is the home for professional baseball, football, and basketball. The mix of high culture and "urban cowboys" makes for an interesting and vital cultural scene.

See also EDUCATION: / Rice University

Barry J. Kaplan
Houston Research Services

Robert Haynes, *A Night of Violence: The Houston Riot of 1917* (1976); David G. McComb, *Houston: A History* (1981); Harold L. Platt, *City Building in the New South: The Growth of Public Services in Houston, Texas, 1830–1915*; Francisco Rosales and Barry J. Kaplan, *Houston: A Twentieth Century Urban Frontier* (1983); Marilyn M. Sibley, *The Port of Houston: A History* (1968).

Little Rock

Quapaw Indian settlement, pioneer trading center, territorial capital, lazy Confederate outpost, western frontier of unreconstructed gentility, Little Rock has emerged in the second half of the 20th century as one of the bustling, dynamic cities of the Sunbelt South. It had a 1984 city population of 170,000.

Suffering under the peculiarly southern burdens of the crop-lien sharecropping system, a one-crop economy, a one-party political system, and widespread poverty, Arkansas experienced limited growth in the years before World War II, and Little Rock reflected the social complacency and the leisurely pace that characterized much of the southern region. Stimulated by their wartime experiences, however, Little Rock businessmen in the 1940s launched a program of planned growth and industrial development based on Little Rock's proximity to the state's wealth of such raw materials as timber, oil, gas, coal, and bauxite. Local leaders initiated a period of growth that altered dramatically the cultural and economic landscape of their city. By the mid-1970s Little Rock had become the major port on the Arkansas River, the chief market for the state's agricultural produce, the second largest manufacturing center in Arkansas, the site of a growing university complex, and the home of a flourishing arts community that includes symphony, theater, opera, and ballet.

In 1957 Little Rock became the focus of international attention in a struggle over the desegregation of Central High School. When Governor Orval Faubus used the Arkansas National Guard to block the entry into the school of nine black children, President Dwight Eisenhower responded by sending the 101st Airborne Division into the city to accomplish the federal court-ordered desegregation. The confrontation was but a temporary impediment to the desegregation process in Little Rock, which was completed within the next decade, but it was a major factor in modifying racial attitudes and practices of the city. The unfavorable publicity and consequent economic stagnation caused a widespread reassessment of racial attitudes and social values in Little Rock and contributed to the growth of a more liberal spirit in this traditionally moderate city.

Little Rock is a blend of both southern and western cultures. In the southern tradition Little Rock is noted for its hospitality to strangers, its neighborliness, and its regard for good manners and good cooks. Its population is approximately 25 percent black. The social hierarchy is not as rigid, however, as those of neighboring states, and it yields easily to the possessors of talent, ambition, and wealth. Little Rock's dramatic growth in the last 40 years and the influx of outsiders from all parts of the globe have given a cosmopolitan outlook and a progressive spirit to the city.

See also LAW: / Little Rock Crisis

Elizabeth Jacoway
University of Arkansas
at Little Rock

Harry Ashmore, *Arkansas: A Bicentennial History* (1976); Leland DuVall, ed., *Arkansas: Colony and State* (1973).

Louisville

Founded in May 1778, Louisville, Ky., first served as a base for George Rogers Clark's ambitious offensive against British-held fortresses in the Northwest during the American Revolution. Clark, a Virginia militia captain, located the settlement at the falls of the Ohio River, the only natural break in navigation on the Ohio-

Bridges over the Ohio River at Louisville, 1964

Mississippi River system, which stretches from Pittsburgh to New Orleans. Soon after Clark established his outpost, the settlers named their new home Louisville in honor of King Louis XVI of France, who pledged aid to the American cause. Two years later, the Virginia Legislature designated Louisville the county seat of its newly formed Jefferson County (part of Kentucky after statehood in 1792).

Louisville thrived as a commercial center after 1830 when the opening of the Louisville and Portland Canal stimulated river traffic by allowing steamboats to bypass the falls. According to the Census of 1850, one of every six of the county's almost 60,000 residents was a slave, but over 1,600 blacks lived in freedom. In 1850 Louisville was the nation's 10th largest city, having first attracted emigrants from France and Great Britain and then from Germany and Ireland. Still influenced by 19th-century demographics, the Falls City is perhaps unique among major southern communities because almost equal numbers of Baptists and Roman Catholics, the area's largest religious denominations, reside there.

Although Louisville was called a "western" town before the Civil War, the city emerged from the conflict as "The Gateway to the South." Most Louisvillians began the war as conservative Unionists, but federal violations of the civil rights of Kentuckians combined with congressional protection for blacks to intensify postwar anti-northern sentiment. At the same time, "Marse Henry" Watterson, the ebullient editor of the Louisville *Courier-Journal*, admonished southerners to follow his city's progressive example by welcoming industry and adopting a more subtle form of racism. Much later, in 1956, the River City, again led by an outspoken press, pioneered southern cities in the successful integration of public schools. In 1975, however, the implementation of court-ordered, countywide busing met with scattered white violence.

By the end of the 19th century Louisville became an important regional manufacturing center, with distilling, meat packing, farm implements, tobacco and wood products, and railroading as its economic mainstays. Subsequently, the Falls City added automobiles and trucks, major appliances, coatings, aluminum products, and chemicals to its industrial constellation. Beginning in the mid-1970s several older industries fell on hard times or built new plants elsewhere, prompting vigorous efforts by community leaders to halt further exodus and to nurture white-collar industries like insurance, banking and finance, law, corporate headquarters, and health care. The city is the center of sophisticated medical research exemplified by the artificial heart experiments conducted by the Humana Heart Institute. Higher education is also important to Louisville's economy with two Catholic colleges, major Southern Baptist and Presbyterian seminaries, and the state-supported University of Louisville, a former municipal institution with schools of medicine (1837) and law (1846) that once drew many students from the South.

Louisville's 1984 city population was 290,000, but in the metropolitan area the figure was nearly 800,000. The city has a strong reputation for the performing arts. It has distinguished itself as a center of informal jazz education, producing well-known stylists like singer Helen Humes, trumpeter Jonah Jones, and guitarist Jimmy Raney. Beginning in 1949 the Louisville Orchestra achieved national recognition for its promotion and newly commissioned music and, more recently, the Actors Theater of Louisville, one of the nation's most successful regional companies, has earned international attention for its annual Festival of New American Plays. Louisville also boasts flourishing professional ballet and opera companies. Most of the city's arts groups perform in a $34.5 million complex that adjoins the Main Street preservation district, a unique collection of 19th-century commercial buildings, many with cast-iron fronts, for which imaginative uses have been found. Nearby, Princeton architect Michael Graves's pyramidal structure, Humana Tower, was completed in 1985. Louisville also has an art museum, a museum of science and history, and a zoo.

Sports are important to the city. In 1983 the Louisville Redbirds, a triple-A baseball team, drew over 1 million fans, an all-time minor league record. The University of Louisville men's basketball team, frequent contenders for the NCAA major college championship, play in a renovated 19,000-seat Freedom Hall. The vintage Kentucky Derby, the first jewel in horse racing's triple crown, draws tens of thousands to Churchill Downs the first Saturday each May. The race is preceded by a week-long festival that has become a major attraction. The Falls City is the fourth largest convention center in the South, ranking behind only Houston, Atlanta, and Dallas. Louisville's Muhammed Ali established a unique record in boxing and is perhaps the city's best-known sports figure.

Because of its strategic river location and proximity to

the North, Louisville early experienced greater economic and social diversity than most of the South. After the Civil War, however, the River City fully identified with Dixie, though sometimes preaching to the region about industrial and racial progress. Louisvillians are still confirmed southerners, despite the fact that their city's progressive image has paled before the Sunbelt's success at building a modern economy and achieving biracial accommodation.

See also MEDIA: / Louisville *Courier-Journal*; RECREATION: / Kentucky Derby

Thomas L. Owen
University of Louisville

Allen J. Share, *Cities in the Commonwealth: Two Centuries of Urban Life in Kentucky* (1982); Samuel W. Thomas, *Louisville since the Twenties* (1978), *Views of Louisville since 1766* (1971); Richard C. Wade, *The Urban Frontier: The Rise of Western Cities* (1959); George Yater, *Two Hundred Years at the Falls of the Ohio* (1979).

Memphis

In 1819 land speculators Andrew Jackson, John Overton, and James Winchester capitalized on the removal of the Chickasaw Indians by founding the city of Memphis on 5,000 acres they had purchased in the 1790s. In its infancy the "Bluff City" was a rough-and-tumble frontier town, a haven for the boisterous flatboatmen bound for New Orleans who "got lickered up" and cavorted in the local fleshpots. The arrival of the steamboat—and later the railroad—helped establish Memphis as a trade center, but of primary importance was the emergence of King Cotton in the Old Southwest. The city's overwhelming dependence upon the crop, as well as the system of labor that produced it, resulted in its reorientation as a southern city; it supported a thriving slave market in the antebellum years and enthusiastically cast its lot with the Confederacy after Fort Sumter.

Prior to the 1870s Memphis sported a heterogeneous population mix in which Germans and Irish figured prominently in the local cultural scene. After that decade's disastrous yellow fever epidemics, which resulted in financial ruin and the surrender of the city charter in favor of a state-administered taxing district, the foreign-born avoided the location. As a result, the arrival of the rural inhabitants—both black and white—fueled the city's population growth.

The steady infusion of native-born farm folk led H. L. Mencken to term Memphis the "most rural-minded city in the South" and the "buckle" of the Bible Belt—a reference to the fundamentalist religion that saturated the community. Memphis also became the economic and cultural center for Mid-South blacks. Robert R. Church, a rural transplant from nearby Holly Springs, Miss., reputed to be the South's first black millionaire, headed the region's largest black business community. His son, Robert E. Church, Jr., went into politics and became the nation's most powerful black Republican by the 1920s. For nearly the first half of the 20th century the city's government was dominated by another native of Holly Springs, Edward H. Crump. Boss Crump presided over a Democratic machine so powerful that he single-handedly ruled not only Memphis but Shelby County and exerted considerable statewide influence as well. The city's reputation and morale received a blow in 1968 when Martin Luther King, Jr., was assassinated there while assisting a garbage workers' strike.

A Crump contemporary, songwriter W. C. Handy, penned "The Memphis Blues" in 1909, and Beale Street, the main thoroughfare of the city's black community, gained the reputation as the birthplace of that distinctive musical form. Memphis later nurtured a host of blues and rock-and-roll performers including B. B. King, Isaac Hayes, Jerry Lee Lewis, and its "father" of rock and roll, Elvis Presley. The opening of Graceland, Presley's mansion, to the public and the restoration of Beale Street reflect the city's attempt in recent years to preserve its rich musical heritage. The Pink Palace Museum and Mud Island Museum emphasize the historic link between the "Bluff City" and the Mississippi River. With Memphis State University, Christian Brothers College, LeMoyne-Owen College, Rhodes (formerly Southwestern at Memphis), and the University of Tennessee Center for the Health Sciences, the city serves as the educational heart of the Mid-South. The 1984 Memphis population was 648,000.

See also MEDIA: / Memphis *Commercial Appeal*; MUSIC: / Beale Street; POLITICS: / Crump, E. H.

Roger Biles
Memphis State University

Gerald A. Capers, *The Biography of a River Town: Memphis, Its Heroic Age* (1966); Margaret McKee and Fred Chisenhall, *Beale Black and Blue: Life and Music on America's Main Street* (1981); Robert A. Sigafoos, *Cotton Row to Beale Street: A Business History of Memphis* (1979).

Miami

Miami is the central city in a southeast Florida metropolitan area with a 1980 population of 1.6 million. The city traces its origins to the 1890s, when urban boosters and land speculators, particularly railroad and hotel man Henry M. Flagler, began promoting tourism in southern Florida. By the 1920s Miami and the nearby suburbs of Miami Beach, Coral Gables, and Hialeah had begun to experience boom conditions. Building on its essential natural resources of seashore, sunshine, and subtropical climate, Miami emerged between 1920 and 1940 as one of the fastest-growing metropolitan areas in the nation. Art Deco buildings popular in that time gave Miami a distinctive look.

Military training activities and the location of several naval and air bases in the area stimulated the Miami economy during World War II. In postwar years the city's economy expanded considerably as construction, light manufacturing, air transportation, and service activities crept up on a still-dominant tourism. The city's population grew rapidly as well, and the urban periphery was subdivided and built up by real estate developers. The rising affluence of Americans and the widespread adoption of air-conditioning in the 1950s strengthened Miami's place as a tourist and retirement haven, pushing the population of the Miami metropolitan area to 935,000 by 1960, almost twice the 1950 amount. Increasing numbers of Miami's newcomers were migrants from the Northeast and Midwest, a demographic development that made Miami more affluent, more Jewish, and more liberal on political and social issues than cities in the rest of the South.

Unlike many other southern cities Miami did not expand its boundaries through annexation after 1925. As a result, numerous small municipalities were incorporated during the 1930s and 1940s, and a rising proportion of Miami-area population resided in unincorporated territory. This fragmentation of local government led "good government" reformers to initiate a decade-long campaign for consolidated metropolitan government. With the beginning of Miami's "Metro" government in July of 1957, the area acquired the nation's first two-tier, or federated, metropolitan government.

The two decades since 1960 have brought dramatic change to Miami. The mass exodus of 800,000 Cubans to the United States between 1959 and 1980, most of whom settled in the Miami area, permanently altered the city's character and culture. As of 1980 Hispanics comprised 56 percent of the population in the city of Miami and over 35 percent in the entire metropolitan area. With Miami's black community growing through the arrival of over 50,000 Haitian exiles in recent years, non-Hispanic whites have become a minority in the Miami area population—a 20-year demographic revolution without precedent in American history.

In the past decade, Miami has emerged as the business and cultural capital of the entire Caribbean basin. Miami was already a major center of international trade and banking by the end of the 1970s. Foreign investment poured into the city, along with the profits from a highly lucrative illegal drug trade. Latin American tourism now surpasses 2 million visitors annually, or about one-sixth of Miami's total tourist business. New skyscraper development in the central business district has transformed Miami's skyline, symbolizing the city's commanding position as the gateway to Latin America. Although Miami shares in the phenomenon of Sunbelt urban growth, the city has always been an anomaly in the American South. Indeed, the patterns of growth and change that have shaped 20th-century Miami demonstrate both the vitality and the cultural diversity of the region. The 1984 nonmetropolitan population figure for Miami was 373,000.

See also ETHNIC LIFE: Caribbean Influence; / Cubans; INDUSTRY: / Flagler, Henry M.

Raymond A. Mohl
Florida Atlantic University

Thomas D. Boswell and James R. Curtis, *The Cuban-American Experience: Culture, Images and Perspectives* (1984); William W. Jenna, Jr., *Metropolitan Miami: A Demographic Overview* (1972); David B. Longbrake and Woodrow W. Nichols, Jr., *Sunshine and Shadow in Metropolitan Miami* (1976); Raymond A. Mohl, *Sunbelt Cities: Politics and Growth since World War II* (1983); Helen Muir, *Miami, U.S.A.* (1953); Arva Parks, *Miami: The Magic City* (1981); Bruce Porter and Marvin Dunn, *The Miami Riot of 1980: Crossing the Bounds* (1984); William Wilbanks, *Murder in Miami: An Analysis of Homicide Patterns and Trends in Dade County (Miami), Florida, 1917–1983* (1984); Reinhold P. Wolff, *Miami: Economic Pattern of a Resort Area* (1945), *Miami Metro: The Road to Urban Unity* (1960).

Mobile

Mobile, founded in 1702 by French naval officer Jean Baptiste Le Moyne, Sieur de Bienville, was named after the nearby Maubila Indians. It has been and continues to be a river-port city largely dependent for its prosperity and even its existence on the economic activity of the hinterland it serves. The Indian trade in colonial times, cotton before and after the Civil War, regional timber, and Birmingham's iron and coal have all flowed through Alabama's only port. Local industries include shipbuilding and chemical plants in addition to the port-related activities.

Mobile's economy boomed in the 1850s thanks to the cotton production of antebellum Black Belt plantations. The city grew rapidly before the war and many fine structures were built, some of which, with their New South cousins, survive to lend an air of southern charm to the modern city. After the defeat of the Confederacy, Mobile languished for several decades. It was almost a century until another war, World War II, brought a second boom, built not on cotton but on defense industries, principally shipbuilding. The city's wartime experience led to considerable expansion and economic growth. Many of the war workers stayed on after 1945 and became an integral part of the city, adopting many of the old town's values and much of its lifestyle for their own.

Alabama's largest city until the end of the 19th century, when Birmingham surpassed it, Mobile has not found the 20th century particularly congenial. A city of promise all too rarely fulfilled, it remains hopeful about the benefits of the Tennessee-Tombigbee Waterway project, coastal oil and natural gas, and a variety of other economic prospects. Its 1984 population was 205,000. Mobile is home to such southern rituals as the annual Azalea Trail, Junior Miss Pageant, and Senior Bowl all-star college football game. The city cultivates its real and imagined colonial and antebellum heritage, celebrating Mardi Gras, whose mother in North America it claims to be, but conscious of the greater success of its age-old rival river city, New Orleans. The University of South Alabama, Spring Hill College, and S. D. Bishop State Junior College are located in Mobile.

See also RECREATION: Mardi Gras

Michael Thomason
University of South Alabama

Harriet Amos, *Cotton City: Urban Development in Antebellum Mobile* (1985); Melton A. McLaurin and Michael Thomason, *Mobile: The Life and Times of a Great Southern City* (1981).

State capitol, Montgomery, Ala., constructed in 1851

Montgomery

Located in the traditional plantation Black Belt, Montgomery sprawls away from a high red bluff overlooking an oxbow bend in the Alabama River, just below the fall line and the end of the Appalachians. It was both the "Cradle of the Confederacy" and the birthplace of the civil rights movement.

Hernando de Soto and his soldiers were the first white men to see the area near present-day Montgomery, stopping at the Indian village of Tawasa on 8 September 1540. For more than 200 years thereafter, Spain, France, and Great Britain struggled for empire there, but Americans finally gained the territory in 1814. Montgomery was founded in 1819 on the site of the Alibamo village of Econchata. The frontier village grew as a transportation center for cotton, and in 1846 the state capital was moved there from Tuscaloosa. Montgomery became a political center and a stronghold of the growing southern states' rights movement. The Deep South states selected Montgomery as the site for their secession convention, and they organized the Confederate States of America in Alabama's Capitol, where Jefferson Davis was inaugurated president on 18 February 1861. The Confederate capital was changed to Richmond later in 1861. After Confederate defeat and Reconstruction, recovery was slow, but Montgomery recovered faster than some other Old South cities because of its continuing importance in government, agriculture, transportation, and some light industry.

In 1917 World War I gave Montgomery another economic boost with the establishment of four military installations, the largest of which was Camp Sheridan. While stationed there, Lieutenant F. Scott Fitzgerald courted debutante Zelda Sayre at the Montgomery country club. On the plantation site where De Soto had camped and where the Wright brothers had run the nation's first civilian pilot-training school in 1910, the War Department established an aviation installation that became a permanent one, Maxwell Field, now one of the 10 oldest U.S. Air Force bases in the country. The Air Corps Tactical School moved there in 1931 and developed the strategic bombardment doctrine later employed in World War II. After that war, Air University, the U.S. Air Force's professional educational center, was placed at Maxwell Air Force Base. In the late 1920s Mayor William A. Gunter pioneered in building America's first planned municipal airport, which is now Gunter Air Force Station, the Air Force's data systems computer center.

In 1955 Montgomery again found itself in the vortex of change with the beginning of the Montgomery bus boycott. A painful 15-year period followed, including the 1961 Freedom Bus Riders' beatings, the Selma to Montgomery march of 1965, and eventually desegregation. In view of that period, the degree of racial accommodation now evident among Montgomery's residents, 40 percent of whom are black, is remarkable.

Cattle and soybeans long ago unseated King Cotton on Montgomery's old plantation lands, and there is some light industry, insurance, banking, and finance. However, Montgomery's economic underpinning is government at all levels, involving both civilian and military positions. Nearly one out of five inhabitants is connected, either directly or indirectly, with the military. Politics remains a favorite sport in between Auburn-Alabama football games, and its chief practitioner was George C. Wallace, Jr., until his recent retirement. There are three public and two denominational institutions of higher learning—traditionally black Alabama State University, Auburn University at Montgomery, Troy State University at Montgomery, Methodist-affiliated Huntingdon College, and the Churches of Christ's Faulkner University—as well as the Air Force's colleges and schools of Air University. The 1984 Montgomery population numbered 185,000.

Montgomery high society maintains its complex circles and hierarchies of elitism, based on bloodlines from an older South. These circles have been revitalized by new people bringing in talent, energy, and new wealth. The new Alabama Shakespeare Festival Theater, the gift of multimillionaire contractor Winton M. Blount, Jr., along with the new Montgomery Museum of Art, promise to make Montgomery flourish as a cultural center. Meanwhile, the city's historic preservation group, the Landmarks Foundation of Montgomery, guards "The

Cradle's" visible past, restoring its historic buildings and attracting many tourists. Folk culture has its shrine at Hank Williams's grave.

John Hawkins Napier III
Cameron Freeman Napier
Montgomery, Alabama

J. Wayne Flynt, *Montgomery: An Illustrated History* (1980); Beth Taylor Muskat and Mary Ann Neeley, *The Way It Was, 1850–1930* (1985); Cameron Freeman Napier, *The First White House of the Confederacy* (1978); John Hawkins Napier III, *Alabama Historical Quarterly* (Fall 1967); Clanton Ware Williams, *The Early History of Montgomery* (1979).

Nashville

Founded as Fort Nashborough in 1780 by North Carolinians under the leadership of James Robertson and John Donelson, this frontier outpost became a center for fur trading and land speculation. Nashville grew rapidly as the major port on the Cumberland River, northern terminus for the Natchez Trace, and trading center for a developing agricultural hinterland of cotton, grain, tobacco, and livestock. The city's bustling western economy thrust upward an ambitious and powerful group of land speculators, planters, politicians, and military leaders, the most notable of whom was Andrew Jackson, the first president elected from trans-Appalachia America. The rise of political leaders Felix Grundy, James K. Polk, and John Bell and the movement of the state capital to Nashville in 1843 reflected the growing importance of the city within Tennessee and the region.

As residents of a commercial city of more than 16,000 in 1860, standing between the heart of the plantation belt and the Midwest, Nashvillians were ambivalent toward secession. It was the first major Confederate city to fall to the Union invasion in February 1862. During federal occupation it flourished as a Union supply center for the western theater of war. Spared the wartime destruction and blockades suffered by other southern cities, Nashville became a major force in transforming the southern economy in the New South era. The Louisville & Nashville Railroad, Tennessee Coal and Iron, and dozens of aggressive commercial and manufacturing firms led the way.

During the late 19th century many of Nashville's colleges were founded, including Fisk University and Meharry Medical College, both for blacks, Vanderbilt University, and George Peabody College for Teachers. All were founded with the support of northern philanthropists intent on reconstructing the minds of southern youth. Along with numerous smaller denominational schools, these colleges bolstered the city's historic claim as the "Athens of the South." Simultaneously, the city became a publishing and administrative center for several major Protestant denominations, a trend that engendered another fanciful name, the "Protestant Vatican."

The Parthenon in Nashville, a replica of the temple in Athens, Greece, constructed in 1896

In the 20th century Nashville's economy shifted to insurance, banking, and brokerage. By the 1920s it boasted of being the "Wall Street of the South," led by the ill-fated financial empire of Caldwell and Company. Nashville's insurance companies, eager to appeal to the new flood of rural white migrants to the cities of the South after World War I, sponsored radio programs with "old timey" music. The "Grand Ole Opry," begun in 1925, became the most famous of these radio shows and formed the nucleus of a nascent recording industry. World War II exposed millions of soldiers and civilians to southern country music, and postwar affluence, along with the continued rural migration to the cities, generated new markets for the music. Recording studios, song writers, musicians, and singers clustered on Nashville's Music Row. In the 1950s Broadcast Music Incorporated broke the New York monopoly on music copyrights and opened the door to a national market for country music. Business leaders in the Athens of the South, initially embarrassed by the image of hillbilly music, came to embrace "Music City, USA," with its flourishing recording and tourist industries, as a major asset. Nashville's 1984 nonmetropolitan population was 462,000.

See also EDUCATION: / Fisk University; Vanderbilt University; MEDIA: / Nashville *Tennessean*; MUSIC: / Grand Ole Opry

Don H. Doyle
Vanderbilt University

Don H. Doyle, *Nashville in the New South, 1880–1930* (1985); John Woolridge, ed., *History of Nashville, Tennessee* (1890).

Natchez

Natchez, one of the oldest settlements on the Mississippi River, was named for the Indian tribe that inhabited the vicinity. The French built a trading post there in 1714 and two years later erected Fort Rosalie; the settlement on

Longwood, at Natchez, built in 1850s

the bluffs passed into the hands of the English (1763) and the Spanish (1779) and in 1798 became a part of the United States with the creation of the Mississippi Territory. Although it was not incorporated until 1803, Natchez was for a time (1798–1802) the capital of the new territory and in 1817 became the first capital of the newly created state of Mississippi. By 1821, however, the legislature had begun the search for a more central location and moved the seat of government to Jackson that year.

During the steamboat era Natchez was an important cotton port, famous up and down the river for the taverns and gambling dives that flourished at Natchez-under-the-Hill, the landing. The city was also the southern terminus of the storied Natchez Trace, an Indian trail running in a southwesterly direction from Nashville that was cleared by General James Wilkinson as a military road in the early 1800s.

Natchez became a center of wealth and culture in the antebellum period, and many of the cotton barons who had extensive landholdings in the surrounding area or across the river in Louisiana built splendid homes for themselves in the city. It is these mansions and the invitation to "Come to Natchez, Where the Old South Still Lives" that every year draws thousands to the Natchez Pilgrimage. Indeed, the Pilgrimage, founded by a local garden club in 1932, is the city's preeminent industry and for its citizens the focus of the social season—a time when descendants of the planter-barons and newcomers open their homes and when many don antebellum dress to attend balls and to appear in the "Confederate Pageant." An annual antiques symposium focuses attention on decorative arts in the South and the city.

Natchez today is especially noteworthy for its architecture, which ranges from the Spanish Provincial style of the late 18th century to the Greek Revival style of the antebellum period and the Oriental style of Longwood, with its bulbiform dome and its Moorish arches, said to be the largest octagonal house in America. Natchez stands alongside Charleston and Savannah as examples of cities that have dedicated themselves to the preservation of their historic architecture. Members of the Hare Krishna religious cult bought one of Natchez's old houses in the early 1980s, but they quickly adapted to the old city's ways. The county seat of Adams County, Natchez had a population of 22,015 in 1984.

See also ENVIRONMENT: / Natchez Trace; HISTORY AND MANNERS: / Pilgrimage

Charles East
Baton Rouge, Louisiana

Mary Wallace Crocker, *Historic Architecture in Mississippi* (1973); Joan W. Gandy and Thomas W. Gandy, *Norman's Natchez: An Early Photographer and His Town* (1978); D. Clayton James, *Antebellum Natchez* (1968); Mary W. Miller and Ronald W. Miller, *The Great Houses of Natchez*, photography by David Gleason (1986).

New Orleans

New Orleans is a multiracial, multiethnic, largely Catholic city located on the fringes of the Bible Belt. Founded by Jean Baptiste Le Moyne, Sieur de Bienville, in 1718 as a French fortification near the mouth of the Mississippi River, the original city (now the French Quarter or Vieux Carré) was modeled after La Rochelle in France. The heart of this area originally was called the *place d'armes* but was renamed Jackson Square in 1849. The mosquito-infested, disease-ridden site combined with French neglect to retard growth and make New Orleans an economic liability for much of the French reign. Ceded to Spain in 1762–63, the city began to prosper as its new administrators spurred colonization by permitting British and American settlers into the region. Spain ceded back New Orleans and the rest of the Louisiana territory to France only to see Napoleon sell it to the United States in 1803. A 1788 fire leveled much of the city, but it was rebuilt using a distinctive mix of Spanish and French architecture. In modern times the city has been an enthusiastic supporter of historic preservation programs for buildings in the French Quarter.

The antebellum era was a golden age for New Orleans. By 1860 it was the largest city in the South (population 168,675) and the fifth largest city in the United States. The War of 1812 brought cooperation between Americans and Creoles against the British, and afterwards the city became an even more important trade center. It remained a predominantly French-speaking city throughout the period, although a large influx of Americans, bolstered by German and Irish immigration, made more heterogeneous an already cosmopolitan populace. The first Mardi Gras parade was in 1857, and it soon became a symbol of the New Orleans spirit. New Orleans was occupied by federal forces between 1862 and 1865, but its white majority later resisted Reconstruction by electing Democratic mayors who were determined not to share power with the freed blacks. In the Gilded Age the city stagnated economically, saw its race relations deteriorate, and succeeded only in adding another layer to its polyglot population through a large-scale Sicilian immigration. Sanitation problems promoted recurrent outbreaks of cholera and yellow fever. Within this troubled context New Orleans demonstrated its cultural vitality, though, by developing jazz as a popular musical form.

In the 20th century New Orleans possessed one of the South's rare urban political machines, which dominated the city from 1904 until its defeat by De Lesseps S. "Chep" Morrison in 1946. Although New Orleans lagged behind its more dynamic Sunbelt competitors after World War II (it ranked fifth among Old South cities with a population of 557,482 in 1980), oil and tourism bolstered a reinvigorated economy. Flood control programs helped the city become a major port in the early 20th century, and shipbuilding industries proliferated in the area during World War II. New Orleans now ranks as the nation's second busiest port. It became a center for National Aeronautics and Space Administration activities in the 1960s. The Voting Rights Act of 1965 transferred political power in the now majority-black city to "progressive" mayors like Moon Landrieu in 1970 and Ernest N. "Dutch" Morial (the city's first black chief executive) in 1978. The 1984 population numbered 559,000.

New Orleans has been a unique cultural center in the American South. A cosmopolitan, Catholic background has made its cultural patterns distinctive through most of southern history. St. Louis Cathedral, completed in 1794, is the oldest one in the United States. The city was an early center of opera with its St. Charles Theater, and the Opera House Association now offers six operas annually. The French Quarter, Fat City, Bourbon Street, Basin Street, and Mardi Gras all evoke images of joyous entertainment and celebration. Storyville used to be a byword for vice and gambling.

In the contemporary era New Orleans has initiated new occasions for good times. The New Orleans Jazz and Heritage Festival is now held in April, a Spring Festival each April or May, the France-Louisiana Festival in July, and the New Orleans Food Festival in July or August (reflecting the importance of cuisine in defining the city's distinctive character). New Orleans has long encouraged sporting activities. It was a center of prizefighting and horse racing in the late 19th century, it now hosts the Sugar Bowl football classic on New Year's Day, and the Superdome is the home for the professional football Saints and the Pride, a women's basketball team. The Cotton Centennial Exposition was held in 1884–85 and the New Orleans World's Fair in 1984. The city, finally, is a medical center, with 22 hospitals, including the Louisiana State University and Tulane medical schools and the Ochsner Foundation Hospital.

See also ART AND ARCHITECTURE: French Architecture; Spanish Architecture; BLACK LIFE: / Mardi Gras Indians; Storyville; EDUCATION: / Tulane University; LANGUAGE: / New Orleans English; MEDIA: / New Orleans *Times-Picayune*; RECREATION: Mardi Gras

Arnold R. Hirsch
University of New Orleans

H. W. Gilmore, *American Sociological Review* (August 1944); Edward F. Haas, *De Lesseps S. Morrison and the Image of Reform: New Orleans Politics, 1946–1961* (1974); John Smith Kendall, *History of New Orleans*, 3 vols. (1922).

Richmond

Founded at the falls of the James River in 1607, Richmond initially served as a crossroads for trade between the Tidewater plantations and the West. When it was incorporated as a town in 1742, Richmond possessed only 250 inhabitants, though its hinterland boasted the estates of some of Virginia's most prestigious families. The city's role as an administrative center—as Virginia's capital beginning in 1779, briefly as capital of the Confederacy, and throughout the 19th and 20th centuries as the nerve center of the state's business community—along with trade and manufacturing, made Richmond one of the South's wealthiest cities.

Old South Richmond was a unique blend of regional traits and features that were decidedly non-southern. The city's rigid gridiron layout adorned by densely packed-in brick town houses, its ethnic diversity, and its extensive industrial sector gave Richmond a look not unlike that of Philadelphia or Baltimore. As the manufacturing hub of the Old South, Richmond excelled in iron, tobacco, and flour processing. Yet the widespread use of slaves as factory laborers, carters, and domestics underscored the city's commitment to "the peculiar institution" and compelled whites to construct an elaborate and rigid system of social controls. The sheer size of Richmond's black community, which in 1860 numbered 14,275 (or 38 percent of the city's population), enabled it to develop an institutional life that flourished in the postwar era and supplied a counterbalance to Jim Crowism.

The process of rebuilding Richmond's ruins following the Civil War fostered visions of urban greatness that exceeded those of Old South entrepreneurs. Building upon the trade and manufacturing base formed in the antebellum era, city promoters vigorously backed canal, railroad, and, by the 20th century, highway connections to an enlarged hinterland. Between 1867 and 1914 Richmond annexed aggressively, thereby incorporating the streetcar suburbs that fanned out from the city center as well as the manufacturing rival of Manchester located on the south side of the James. Prior to 1900, however, city leaders were torn between promotion of urban growth and the desire to forestall change of any sort, and this dilemma was reflected in a marked tendency toward frugality in public expenditures for needed city improvements. Only in the late 1880s, when organized labor through the Knights of Labor temporarily seized the reins of local government, was there serious consideration of civic improvements.

After 1900, however, the vision of Richmond as a New South metropolis gained a broader following. To supply a political foundation for continuous expansion, Richmond experimented with governmental reform, adopting a modified commission government in 1912. This gave way in 1917 to a strong mayoral form committed to progress through public planning for city development. Nevertheless, Richmond retained a bicameral city council (which proved to be a bastion of fiscal conservatism) until 1947, when it shifted to a nine-member, nonpartisan legislative body with a city manager as chief administrator. Spearheaded by downtown business leaders intent on making local government operate as a business, the new political structure proved more amenable to public backing of urban development initiatives, including expressway construction, urban renewal, provision of public housing, and, by the 1960s, development of a civic center complex.

The growing political power of the city's black community, stimulated by white flight to the suburbs during the 1950s and first evidenced in local elections in the 1960s, produced, in 1977, a black majority on the city council and appointment of Henry March as the city's first black mayor. As had been evident since statewide disenfranchisement of blacks in 1902, race was a pivotal issue in local affairs, but Richmond successfully avoided the violent confrontations that rocked other cities especially during the 1960s. Although the 1980 census revealed that the city's population continued a downward trend that had begun in the 1950s, revitalization of housing in inner-city neighborhoods such as the Fan, Jackson Ward, and Church Hill underscored the public and private commitment to preserve portions of Old Richmond as the basis for future growth. The 1984 city population was 219,000.

Ironically, even as the city failed to maintain demographic dominance within the metropolis during the 1960s and 1970s, Richmond retained and enhanced its function as a cultural center. During the past decade the city added museums, theaters, and performing arts companies to its already substantial and diversified cultural base. Indeed, the formation of Virginia Commonwealth University—through the merging of the Richmond Professional Institute and Medical College of Virginia—not only enlarged the educational and cultural opportunities in the city but supplied an impetus to revitalization of adjacent neighborhoods and enlargement of the downtown civic center. The recent creation of a Federated Arts District at the edge of the downtown shopping area underscores Richmond's determination to retain its hegemony over the cultural life of the metropolis and to increase activity in the city center. In higher education (Richmond boasts three universities and numerous professional schools), the performing arts, and in a variety of professional and amateur sports, Richmonders continue to look to the city's center, not to its mushrooming suburbs, for their cultural life.

See also MEDIA: / Richmond *Times-Dispatch*

Christopher Silver
Virginia Commonwealth College

Michael Chesson, *Richmond after the War, 1865–1890* (1981); Virginius Dabney, *Richmond: The Story of a City* (1976); David R. Goldfield, *Urban Growth in the Age of Sectionalism: Virginia, 1847–1861* (1977); Christopher Silver, "Greater Richmond and the Good City: Politics and Planning in a New South Metropolis, 1900–1976" (Ph.D. dissertation, University of North Carolina at Chapel Hill, 1981); Emory M. Thomas, *The Confederate State of Richmond: A Biography of the Capital* (1971).

Savannah

Founded on a bluff overlooking the Savannah River, Savannah developed with deliberation and planning that has had continuing cultural importance since its establishment by James Oglethorpe in 1733. Influenced by the neighborhood developments of late 17th-century London, Oglethorpe envisioned and planned a city of symmetrical squares, gardens, and broad avenues. Even as the military purposes of the colony gave way to the rice and cotton economy of the 18th century, Savannah retained the charm of its origins. British occupation during the Revolution and repeated difficulties with epidemics such as yellow fever did, however, limit early growth.

During the 19th century Savannah joined other southern cities in active boosterism in an effort to enlarge its trade and commercial activity. A modest success resulted, and Savannah emerged as an important cotton and timber port for the Georgia and South Carolina Piedmont. The building of the Central of Georgia Railroad to Macon contributed to this role, and on the eve of the Civil War Savannah's population of 22,292 was large by southern urban standards. During the war years General William Sherman targeted Savannah as his destination for the

Stereoscope view of Savannah harbor, 1870s

March to the Sea, and the city fell to Union forces in December 1864. The destruction was large but the city quickly recovered its prewar fortunes, extended rail lines, and expanded timber and cotton exporting. By 1880 the city could boast the same garden-like charm of its origin and a population of 30,709. In the late 19th and early 20th centuries Savannah joined the state of Georgia in a gradual diversification of economic patterns. The slow transformation temporarily halted Savannah's growth, and the city's relative economic deprivation indirectly contributed to the preservation of its original buildings and plan. Cotton diminished in importance, but timber, particularly pulpwood and turpentine products, remained strong. This has continued into the 20th century as Savannah is now the leading foreign trade port between Baltimore and New Orleans, with primary emphasis on container shipping. Its 1984 population numbered 145,000.

Corresponding to commercial changes, the population of Savannah has experienced a slow but steady growth. Since Savannah is a seaport, immigration played a more important role in its growth than in the growth of most interior southern cities. An early Jewish community developed, and in 1860 the free population of Savannah and surrounding Chatham County was more than 25 percent foreign born. More significant is the continuing large black population. Although free whites outnumbered both slave and free black populations in 1860, Savannah's black population constituted a majority or near majority in the late 19th century and the early 20th. Large black populations (34 percent in 1970 and 36 percent in 1980) remain a part of the modern Savannah profile.

For all its growing commercial importance, Savannah's principal role in the South has been as a leader in the effort to preserve the region's past. Since 1839 the city has been home to the Georgia Historical Society, a most important center for the study of southern history. Telfair Academy of Arts and Sciences, founded in 1920, serves as a museum of the decorative arts, costumes, paintings, and sculpture. As the leading city of coastal Georgia, Savannah has a black land grant college, Savannah State, chartered in 1889, and a predominantly white senior college, Armstrong State. Both are part of the University System of Georgia and have merged many programs in recent years, reflecting a greater interracial cooperation. Although the original plans of Oglethorpe have remained, the city's early architecture sadly deteriorated in the late 19th and early 20th centuries. Since World War II, however, the original area of Savannah has been transformed through the Historic Savannah Foundation (founded in 1955). The restoration of old Savannah is one of the most complete for any American city. Today, visitors can see the restored architecture of William Jay, Charles Clusky, or W. G. Preston featuring wrought iron, gardens, and the Oglethorpe squares. Such domestic restoration has been accompanied by work on public buildings and commercial districts including the city hall, Factor's Walk, the Cotton Exchange Building, Telfair Academy, and a number of churches. The restored charm of Savannah has given the city an important source of revenue through the hosting of small conventions. More importantly it has made Savannah an inspiration for the restoration of other cities and a continuing symbol of the beauty of urban planning in a southern setting.

Thomas F. Armstrong
Georgia College

Federal Writers' Project, WPA, *Savannah* (1937); Richard Haunton, "Savannah in the 1850s" (Ph.D. dissertation, Emory University, 1968); Mills Lane, *Savannah Revisited* (1969).

Tampa

The village of Tampa originated as a civilian settlement adjacent to Fort Brooke, an army post established in 1824 near Tampa Bay on Florida's Gulf Coast. Tampa grew slowly and prospered in the 1850s as a commercial center with a port that dominated the area's cattle trade to Cuba. The town's population of 900 overwhelmingly supported the Confederacy.

After several decades of decline, Tampa's population expanded by 760 percent during the 1880s with the arrival of the cigar industry. Spanish- and Cuban-born entrepreneurs who had fled war-torn Cuba were attracted to Tampa by its port and rail facilities and its proximity to Cuban sources of clear Havana tobacco, which was used to make luxury, hand-rolled cigars. The skilled labor force was composed of Cubans and Spaniards who were later joined by Italian immigrants. The local cigar industry started in the new town of Ybor City, which was annexed by Tampa in 1887.

By 1910 Tampa had become the capital of domestically produced clear Havana cigars, and 45 percent of its residents were first- or second-generation immigrants. Separated from both the native Anglo and black communities, the Latin population lived in Ybor City where mutual aid societies and foreign-language newspapers thrived. The cigar city continued to prosper through the 1920s when its population exceeded 100,000.

The Depression nearly destroyed Tampa's economy, which was based on a luxury product that never regained its former popularity. Moreover, the city's image was sullied by its reputation for political corruption, crime, and violence.

After World War II Tampa broadened its economic base by taking advantage of its location and the growth of the Sunbelt. Military expenditures at MacDill Field stimulated the economy, as did phosphate shipments that made Tampa one of the nation's busiest ports. The biggest boost came from new residents who helped Tampa more than double its population during the 1950s. Tampa's image as a progressive city was advanced by its success in achieving desegregation peacefully in the 1960s. The hundreds of new businesses included medium-sized manufacturing, but service industries predominated with banks and insurance companies locating regional headquarters in Tampa. By 1980 the city's population of

271,523 was at the hub of the third fastest-growing metropolitan area in the country. Its 1984 population had grown to 275,000.

Tampa's emergence as a leading Sunbelt city was marked by the creation of new educational and cultural institutions. The University of South Florida was created by the state legislature in 1956, and a public community college began operating in 1968. The city also has a private college, the University of Tampa (1931). Recently founded cultural institutions include an art museum, a performing arts center, and a museum of science and industry. Since opening in 1959, Busch Gardens has become one of Florida's busiest tourist attractions. Tampa has also gained prominence as the home of a professional football team, the Tampa Bay Buccaneers.

Although originally a southern city with a Latin flavor, Tampa has been "Americanized" and homogenized to the point where today neither its population nor its culture is distinctively southern.

See also ETHNIC LIFE: / Cubans; Spanish

Robert P. Ingalls
University of South Florida

Richard M. Bernard and Bradley R. Rice, eds., *Sunbelt Cities: Politics and Growth since World War II* (1983).

Violence

RAYMOND D. GASTIL

New York, New York

CONSULTANT

Reconstruction violence against blacks portrayed in the film Birth of a Nation, *1915*

Violence, Crime, and Punishment

Violence has been associated with the South since the time of the American Revolution. Connecticut soldiers threatened to leave the front if they were forced to serve alongside those from Virginia, because of the cruelty of the fights among the latter. The attitudes associated with slavery and the warped experiences of young males in this environment were often cited as causes of such cruelty and violence. Historian John Hope Franklin has demonstrated that the South was addicted to violence on every level of society well before the Civil War. Prime evidence for this was the duel, which became widely accepted among "gentlemen" in the South, whereas it died out soon after its introduction in the North. But the duel was only the most formalized means of defending an exaggerated sense of honor with violence. "Honorable" fights were common, and on lower social levels street fights and ambushes were accepted forms of behavior.

Journalist H. V. Redfield pointed out that the tendency to take the law into one's own hands for the sake of honor was reinforced by the weakness of law officers. Patterns thus developed tended to further weaken the state and to support anarchy, for once it became accepted that people had the right to kill for their own purposes, they then took this right to include actions against law officers and jurors who might be so courageous as to get in their way. The shoot-out superseded the law; because the punishments of the law were seldom visited on the murderer, those who felt wronged were often led to bypass it as well. However the process began, the result was a markedly lower regard for human life.

Border or mountain feuding, such as that of the Hatfields and McCoys, was an extreme form of the same tradition, and one bearing little connection to slavery. The immediate cause of many minor mountain wars was the Civil War and the hatreds it engendered in border states. The explosion of the James gang in the West, and the endemic violence of the next generation, had much the same origin. In fact, in the postwar period Kentucky became one of the most violent states in the nation. Exploding again in the labor wars of the 1930s, the coal-mining regions of Kentucky and West Virginia renewed that tradition. Harlan County was the violent center of a violent area.

Southern violence is of a particular kind. Stereotypically, verbal violence has been thought to characterize Mediterranean peoples, fistfighting and other types of physical assault are often associated with the Irish, whereas suicide—internalized violence—may be associated with Scandinavians, Japanese, and other relatively "controlled" peoples. Violence in the South has meant primarily lethal violence, or violence that is cruel and abrupt, designed to punish. This southern type of violence exists in the traditional southern states, but also in an expanding South. Southern attitudes toward violence appear, for example, among southern blacks residing in northern or border cities and among the rural southern white folk who make up a large proportion of the population in the West, particularly the Southwest.

The Study of Southern Violence. The first detailed study of comparative southern homicide rates was conducted by H. V. Redfield. Traveling widely in the South, Redfield in the 1870s compiled extensive files on homicide rates. He found that as one moved south through the counties of Indiana, Ohio, or Illinois, the incidence of homicide rose regularly. He demonstrated that the phenomenon was as characteristic of the Old South as of the New. For example, the homicide rate of South Carolina was 10 times greater than that of Massachusetts, and in the West, that of Texas was 10 times that of Minnesota. Redfield found that assaults on honor, or even political struggles, frequently resulted in murder, because of the almost universal practice of carrying weapons. The street duel, which was later portrayed on movie and television screens as a western phenomenon, was common in South Carolina in his day, as were organized night fights or mob killings—which at that time were not characteristically interracial.

In the 20th century a number of other scholars examined the differences between northern and southern homicide rates. In the early years of the century Frederick Hoffman pointed to the extreme rate in a city such as Memphis. No longer primarily a rural problem—nor solely a white concern—a high homicide rate had become characteristic of black populations, a fact that had not been true in Redfield's day. H. C. Brearley's studies of homicide in the 1920s revealed that the seven states with highest homicide rates were southern. Studies by Lottier, Porterfield, Shannon, and Hackney reported statistics of an equivalent kind up to the 1970s. FBI statistics from 1983 show that, although regional differences are now less extreme, an important North-South differential remains.

Explanations of Southern Violence. On viewing discrepancies such as these, social scientists have often advanced explanations positing poverty, low educational levels, or the oppressive and racist nature of southern life. However, cultural anthropologists see cultural patterns that developed early and still persist in the South as conducive to high homicide rates.

Such a cultural hypothesis was tested in the 1970s by Raymond D. Gastil, a sociologist. Some of the data regarding homicide rates that Gastil examined are reported in Table 1. Because of the movement of people in and out of the South over the last hundred years and the mixing of regional populations, particularly in border states and large cities, the researcher formulated an "Index of Southernness" that attempted to measure the prevalence of certain aspects of southern culture as the observer moves north and west from states such as Mississippi, Alabama, and South Carolina. The result of this study was to reinforce the assumption that the cultural variable of "southernness" represented an important part of the explanation of regional variation.

Table 1. *Criminal Homicides per 100,000 Population by States*

State	White	Non-White	Total	State	White	Non-White	Total
Ga.	4.4	27.3	10.0	Mich.	1.8	20.4	3.6
Ala.	4.2	25.3	10.5	W.Va.	3.1	13.3*	3.6
S.C.	4.9	19.5	10.0	Hawaii	2.5*	3.9*	3.5
Va.	6.9	20.2	9.7	Ohio	1.9	21.3	3.5
Alaska	6.3	19.2*	9.3	N.Y.	1.8	18.7	3.3
Fla.	3.8	34.4	9.3	Ind.	1.8	22.6	3.0
N.C.	3.9	24.9	9.2	Kans.	2.2	18.7*	2.9
La.	3.1	19.1	8.3	S.D.	1.7*	33.3*	2.9*
Nev.	7.2	18.2*	8.1	Pa.	1.5	18.0	2.7
Miss.	2.5	15.5	8.0	N.J.	1.6	13.8	2.6
Tenn.	3.7	27.0	7.6	Wash.	2.2	12.8*	2.6
Tex.	4.3	30.7	7.6	Oreg.	2.0	27.0*	2.5
Ark.	3.7	21.7	7.5	Utah	1.8*	17.6*	2.1*
Ariz.	4.5	27.3	6.8	Conn.	1.2	18.0*	2.0
Ky.	4.5	27.1	6.1	Neb.	.87*	40.5*	1.9
N.M.	4.8	22.9*	6.1	Maine	1.8*	0.0*	1.8*
Okla.	4.0	23.2	5.8	Idaho	1.1*	30.0*	1.5*
Md.	2.5	21.3	5.6	Wis.	1.3	12.9*	1.5
Del.	2.3*	24.2*	5.4	R.I.	1.3*	4.8*	1.4*
Wyo.	4.3*	42.9*	5.2*	N.D.	1.0*	23.1	1.4*
Ill.	2.3	25.1	4.7	Mass.	1.1*	10.4*	1.3*
Mo.	2.8	22.9	4.6	Minn.	1.1*	16.7*	1.3*
Calif.	3.3	18.3	4.5	Iowa	0.9*	10.3*	1.0*
Colo.	3.0	32.1	3.9	N.H.	1.0*	0.0*	1.0*
Mont.	3.1*	25.0	3.9	Vt.	0.0*	0.0*	0.0*

*20 or fewer homicides

Source: *Vital Statistics of the United States, 1964*, vol. 2, pt. B (1966).

This approach has had both critics and defenders. Other factors besides regional origin surely correlate with homicide, most notably youth, sex, and residence in a large city (or other special environment, such as the states of Nevada or Alaska). After allowing for these factors, however, a considerable portion of the variance still appears to come from cultural tradition. The correlations are particularly dramatic for white homicide. Although these separate rates are not published by the FBI along with the other homicide statistics, it is possible to ascertain fairly correct racial statistics because in over 90 percent of recorded homicides, murderer and victim are of the same race.

The very high black homicide rates, often 10 times those of whites, would seem on the one hand to confirm the assumption of a southern "cause" of lethal violence, because of the overwhelming concentration of blacks in the South in the past. On the other hand, the high homicide rates have followed the black migration to large cities, North and South, and therefore have disguised the regional influence. There are many explanations for this particular intensification of the "subculture of violence"; in part, black homicide rates no doubt reflect specifically black experience rather than general southern history, experience that has been reinforced by modern conditions.

The rise of the Ku Klux Klan and its repeated revival; an exaggerated interest in violent sports, such as football, cockfighting, and dogfighting; and the tendency of southerners to regard war as a game, as manifested in the historically greater interest of the South in the military, are all indicative of the region's violent tendencies. This militant, anarchical element in the South is also illustrated by the history of the Texas Rangers, an irregular, border defense force that only gradually became a part of the state's own apparatus.

If the South's attitude toward murder in defense of "rights" or honor has been forgiving, its view of offenders once within the system has tended to be relatively harsh. As Henry Lundsgaarde points out, southerners tend to "publicly approve of the use of lethal violence to settle personal disputes and problems," and judicial officials in the region seem more predisposed "to recommend severe punishment for those wrongdoers who threaten the moral values, beliefs, and social mores of the general public than their counterparts in other parts of the country." Analysis of the latest statistics on the rate of incarceration by state produces a map closely resembling that produced by the attempt to construct the Index of Southernness described above. The South has also tended to be favorably inclined toward capital punishment; most of those facing the death sentence in the 1980s were in the South. In December 1983, for example, 65 percent of the nation's 1,202 individuals awaiting execution were in southern prisons.

Attitudes toward Violence. Attitude studies also confirm the difference between the South and the rest of the country. Southerners have a much more positive attitude toward gun ownership. They are more likely to believe in corporal punishment and more likely to have ex-

University of Alabama student, and later Alabama governor, George C. Wallace, bloodying a Tulane University opponent in a boxing match, 1939

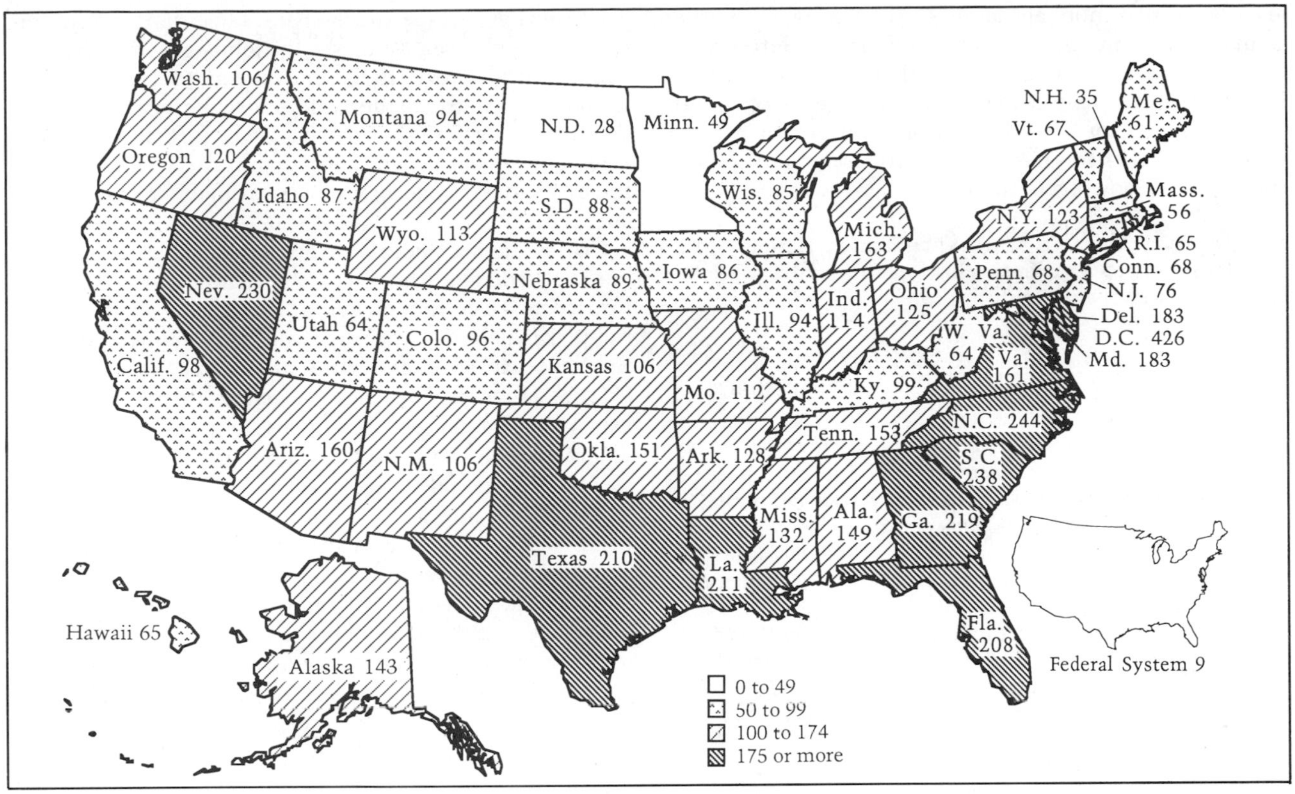

Rate of Sentenced Prisoners in State and Federal Institutions, by Jurisdiction, on December 31, 1980 (per 100,000 Resident Population)

Source: U.S. Department of Justice, Bureau of Justice Statistics, *Prisoners in State and Federal Institutions on December 31, 1980* (1982).

perienced it than people elsewhere in the country. In 1971 sociologist John Shelton Reed, perhaps the most perceptive student of southern violence today, conducted an attitude survey and noted that relatively more southerners than other Americans condone violence; the attitudes of these small subgroups of the sample were characterized as those of warriors, vigilantes, and anarchists.

John Shelton Reed views the culture of violence as a learned trait, and as such, one that is apt to be found in the best "socialized" southerners rather than the least. He points out that the South is not *simply* violent, but that it is violent in certain respects. In many crime categories the South is at or below national averages. If one breaks down homicide data, it is clear that the South is far ahead of the rest of the country in murders of lovers, spouses, or other family adults, as well as other murders resulting from arguments or disputes. But southerners are no more likely than people from other regions to kill their own children, to kill as the result of psychopathy, or to kill as an accompaniment to another crime. Southern homicide is not, in other words, random. This is the reason that a southerner is often astonished to find that the murder rate in his region is higher than in, for example, New York City. "Crime in the streets," including murder, is more common in New York. One is not very likely to be killed in the South as long as cultural rules are obeyed and situations that in the southern ethos "justify" killing are avoided.

Reed suggests that the concept of justifiable homicide is at the heart of the southern tendency to violence. One carries a gun or a knife because one might have to use it, and one uses it because the occasion merits it. Reed points out that much of the literature and popular culture of the South revolves around violence, which is often viewed in a neutral or even laudatory way. Southern humor often involves violent incidents, but not, of course, incidents of psychopathic or "criminal" killings in the ordinary sense. For southerners, murder in defense of honor, after sufficient provocation, is more often tragic rather than simply wrong.

The South developed on the frontier and remained a frontier for a long time. It developed in fear—fear of the Indian, fear of the outsider, fear of the slave (or for the slave, fear of whites). To many southerners over a period of centuries the protection of the law was feeble at best. In this context the southerner developed or maintained ways of coping that were abandoned or never developed in the more densely settled and reliably governed North. The Civil War broke down what were often only poorly institutionalized regulatory measures, and once again the recourse was violence. To a significant extent a propensity for violence continues at two ends of the spectrum in the South. It is part of the life of the most socialized, a part of living the honorable life within society; while at the bottom of the social ladder, the life of the drifter, the outlaw, is an anarchical alternative that has always seemed more appealing to the young southerner than to people in other sections. Only in this latter sense can one perhaps speak of the "southernization" of America as a whole. There seems to be a resurgence of American reverence for a wild, interior frontier, for a purer naturalism; this too has its southern roots as surely as the mythical cowboy of the West.

See also HISTORY AND MANNERS: Frontier Heritage; Military Tradition; LAW: Criminal Justice; Criminal Law; Police Forces; RECREATION: Football

Raymond D. Gastil
Freedom House

Edward L. Ayers, *Vengeance and Justice: Crime and Punishment in the 19th-Century American South* (1984); H. C. Brearley, *Homicide in the United States* (1932); Dickson D. Bruce, Jr., *Violence and Culture in the Antebellum South* (1979); John Hope Franklin, *The Militant South, 1800–1861* (1956); Raymond D. Gastil, *American Sociological Review* (June 1971); Elliot Gorn, *American Historical Review* (February 1985); Sheldon Hackney, in *Violence in America: Historical and Comparative Perspectives*, ed. Hugh Davis Graham and Ted Robert Gurr (1969); Frederick Hoffman, *The Homicide Problem* (1925); Colin Loftin, Robert Hill, and Raymond D. Gastil, *Criminology* (May 1978); Stuart Lottier, *Journal of Criminal Law and Criminology* (June–July 1938); Henry P. Lundsgaarde, *Murder in Space City: A Cultural Analysis of Houston Homicide Patterns* (1977); Thomas Pettigrew and Rosaline Spier, *American Journal of Sociology* (May 1962); Austin Porterfield, *American Sociological Review* (August 1949); H. V. Redfield, *Homicide, North and South: Being a Comparative View of Crime against the Person in Several Parts of the United States* (1880); John Shelton Reed, in *Perspectives on the American South*, vol. 1, ed. Merle Black and John Shelton Reed (1981), *Political Science Quarterly* (September 1971); Lyle Shannon, *Journal of Criminal Law and Criminology* (September–October 1954); U.S. Department of Justice, Federal Bureau of Investigation, *Uniform Crime Reports* (1983); Bertram Wyatt-Brown, *Southern Honor: Ethics and Behavior in the Old South* (1982).

Civil Rights, Federal Enforcement

Prior to 1957 federal intervention to protect the legal rights of black southerners was infrequent at best. Beginning with the Little Rock crisis, the passage of the Civil Rights Act of 1957, and the creation of the U.S. Commission on Civil Rights, however, a new era of federal legal action in the South was born.

From 1957 through the late 1960s federal authorities faced three major and often intertwined legal questions concerning the South: how to ensure southern blacks' right to register and vote; how to secure the desegregation of southern schools and colleges; and how to protect civil rights activists from illegal and often violent harassment of their efforts. On all three fronts federal officials—in the White House, at the Department of Justice, and in the Federal Bureau of Investigation—acted cautiously and conservatively in all but a few instances. That caution of three successive presidential administrations—Eisenhower, Kennedy, and Johnson—was strongly condemned by civil rights movement participants and supporters. At the same time, most white southerners failed to appreciate that the degree of federal action and intervention was much lower than could well have been the case, given the formal powers available to the federal authorities.

Critics of these administrations consistently pointed out that federal authorities were making only the most limited use of certain powers at their disposal: the voting rights provisions of the 1957 and 1960 civil rights acts; the Reconstruction-era criminal statutes codified as 18 U.S.C. 241 and 242; the statute giving the president very expansive federal police powers in any circumstance where state authorities are unable or unwilling to protect constitutional rights (10 U.S.C. 333); and the provisions authorizing all FBI agents and U.S. marshals to make warrantless arrests for any violation of a federal statute that they witnessed (18 U.S.C. 3052, 3053).

The degree of federal restraint was not a matter of happenstance, nor, as some have surmised, was it simply a result of presidential inability to mobilize the resources and energies of the FBI, whose longtime director, J. Edgar Hoover, was accurately regarded as an extreme conservative in matters of race. Instead, in all three areas—schools, voting, and violence—limited federal intervention was based on a straightforward policy supported by all the presidents and attorneys general who were involved: that the racial transformation of southern society would proceed furthest, fastest, and with the fewest scars if federal authorities encouraged maximum voluntary compliance by southern officials and resorted to the coercive use of federal remedies and manpower as little as possible.

Throughout the 1957–64 period Justice Department officials seeking to eliminate racial discrimination from southern voter registration offices made persuasion their first and foremost tool. Only in counties or parishes where registrars rebuffed such approaches and continued to discriminate were federal civil suits brought. Similarly, even in such widely heralded federal-state confrontations as the integration of the University of Mississippi in 1962 and the University of Alabama in 1963, federal officials relied upon private conversations and negotiation and employed actual force only when all other means of obtaining obedience to the law had failed. Furthermore, even in instances where the very lives of civil rights activists were in danger, Justice Department officials moved with caution rather than alacrity. Many movement workers became deeply embittered at the lack of federal response to the shootings, burnings, and beatings that occurred throughout the Deep South between 1961 and 1965.

The summer of 1964 witnessed both a new assertion of federal power in the most violent of the southern states, Mississippi, and passage of the comprehensive Civil Rights Act. Prodded by the murder of three civil rights workers in June 1964, the Johnson Administration established a substantial FBI presence in the state. At the same time, passage of the new law gave the government a powerful new tool for combating racial discrimination,

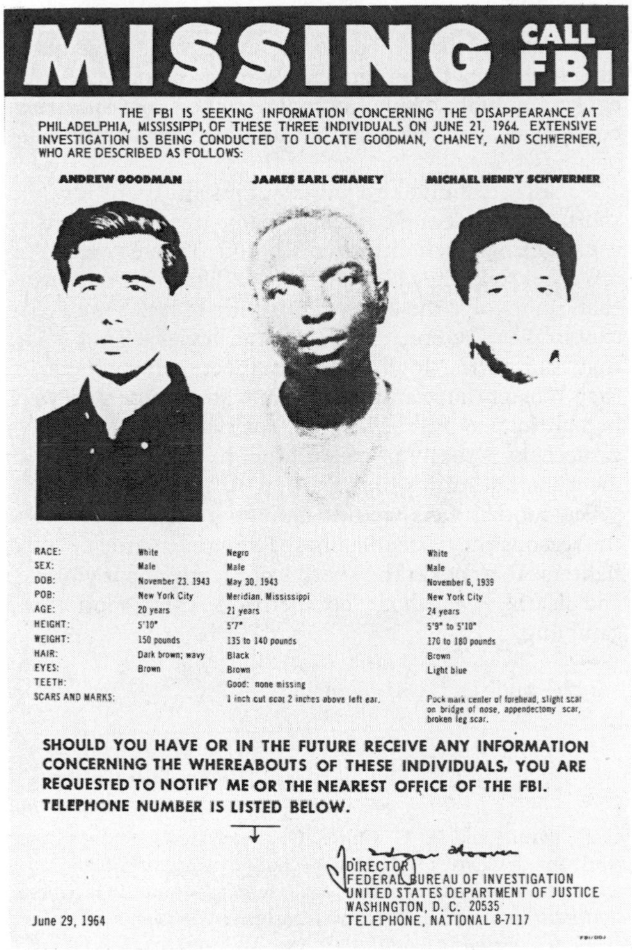

MISSING CALL FBI
THE FBI IS SEEKING INFORMATION CONCERNING THE DISAPPEARANCE AT PHILADELPHIA, MISSISSIPPI, OF THESE THREE INDIVIDUALS ON JUNE 21, 1964. EXTENSIVE INVESTIGATION IS BEING CONDUCTED TO LOCATE GOODMAN, CHANEY, AND SCHWERNER, WHO ARE DESCRIBED AS FOLLOWS:
ANDREW GOODMAN
JAMES EARL CHANEY
MICHAEL HENRY SCHWERNER
RACE: White / Negro / White
SEX: Male / Male / Male
DOB: November 23, 1943 / May 30, 1943 / November 6, 1939
POB: New York City / Meridian, Mississippi / New York City
AGE: 20 years / 21 years / 24 years
HEIGHT: 5'10" / 5'7" / 5'9" to 5'10"
WEIGHT: 150 pounds / 135 to 140 pounds / 170 to 180 pounds
HAIR: Dark brown; wavy / Black / Brown
EYES: Brown / Brown / Light blue
TEETH: Good: none missing
SCARS AND MARKS: 1 inch cut scar 2 inches above left ear. / Pock mark center of forehead, slight scar on bridge of nose, appendectomy scar, broken leg scar.
SHOULD YOU HAVE OR IN THE FUTURE RECEIVE ANY INFORMATION CONCERNING THE WHEREABOUTS OF THESE INDIVIDUALS, YOU ARE REQUESTED TO NOTIFY ME OR THE NEAREST OFFICE OF THE FBI. TELEPHONE NUMBER IS LISTED BELOW.
DIRECTOR
FEDERAL BUREAU OF INVESTIGATION
UNITED STATES DEPARTMENT OF JUSTICE
WASHINGTON, D. C. 20535
TELEPHONE, NATIONAL 8-7117
June 29, 1964

FBI poster seeking information on missing civil rights workers, Mississippi, 1964

particularly in public accommodations. Even in relative "hot spots" such as St. Augustine, Fla., and Selma, Ala., federal officials favored persuasion and conciliation before adopting stronger actions.

Passage of the 1965 Voting Rights Act, which provided for the appointment of federal registration officials in unregenerate southern counties, led many movement activists to expect the kind of extensive federal intervention throughout the South that the movement had sought but previously failed to obtain. To their great disappointment, however, federal officials at the Justice Department again applied the principle they had followed in previous years: direct federal authority should be exerted only where state and local officials failed to show good-faith compliance. Thus, far fewer federal registrars were sent into the South than civil rights proponents requested. A movement initiative to win passage of new federal statutes to eliminate jury discrimination and to specifically forbid any physical harassment of civil rights workers also failed to succeed in 1965–66.

Many movement participants and sympathizers, looking back at the so-called Second Reconstruction years, argue that a more aggressive and forceful federal stance would have meant more racial progress, and at a lesser cost in dead, wounded, and emotionally scarred. Former federal officials, however—those men who served in the Justice Department hierarchy in the 1960s—believe that what many view as the South's tremendous racial progress since the late 1960s would not have occurred and that much of the previous bitterness would not have subsided had not the federal executive branch followed the moderate and restrained path that it did. Had federal authorities employed more heavily the coercive and punitive powers at their disposal, deep racial divisions might well have been further deepened and also prolonged. One's view of how sufficient the changes in southern race relations over the past 15 years have been will in large part determine whether one judges the federal law enforcement stance of the 1960s to have been intelligent or inadequate.

See also BLACK LIFE: Freedom Movement, Black; LAW: Civil Rights Movement; MEDIA: Civil Rights and Media

David J. Garrow
City College of New York
CUNY Graduate Center

Carl M. Brauer, *John F. Kennedy and the Second Reconstruction* (1977); Richard Maxwell Brown, in *Perspectives on the American South*, vol. 1, ed. Merle Black and John Shelton Reed (1981); Haywood Burns, in *Southern Justice*, ed. Leon Friedman (1965); Robert K. Carr, *Federal Protection of Civil Rights: Quest for a Sword* (1947); John Doar and Dorothy Landsberg, U.S. Congress, Senate, Select Committee to Study Governmental Operations with Respect to Intelligence Activities, *Hearings—Federal Bureau of Investigation*, vol. 6, 94th Cong., 1st sess. (1976); John T. Elliff, *Perspectives in American History*, vol. 5 (1971); Allan Lichtman, *Journal of Negro History* (October 1969); Neil R. McMillen, *Journal of Southern History* (August 1977); Burke Marshall, *Federalism and Civil Rights* (1964).

Cockfighting

Ritualized violence is an integral aspect of many sports, and the extreme of recreational violence can be found in the so-called blood sports. In these activities animals are pitted against each other, usually with fatal consequences for the loser, while spectators wager on the outcome. Cockfighting, dogfighting, and bearbaiting were brought to the United States by early settlers from the British Isles where such activities have a long tradition.

Cockfighting is the most common organized blood sport in America and may have as many as several hundred thousand devotees. Fights are regularly scheduled at hundreds of permanent arenas or "pits." Many cockpits are quite elaborate and may be equipped with refreshment stands, public address systems, and tiers of bleachers. There are three national publications for "cockers," as cockfighters call themselves, including the oldest, *Grit and Steel*, founded in 1899. They even have a lobbying group, the United Gamefowl Breeders Association.

Though cockfights occur throughout the country, a disproportionate number of fans are found in the rural South. A recent survey of cockers (Bryant and Capel,

1974) found that 54 percent of respondents resided in the Southeast or Southwest. Also, an examination of a recent issue of *The Gamecock*, a cockfighting magazine, revealed that two-thirds of the more than 200 advertisements originated from southern states. The 1973 film *Feathered Warrior* (Appalshop, Ben Zickafoose, with Gene DuBey and Bill Hatton) documented cockfighting in Appalachia.

In the South, most cockfighters are white, male, middle to lower-middle class, and from rural areas. There is, however, great diversity among cockfight fans. Women and children attend fights with surprising frequency. At some pits blacks regularly attend and participate on apparently equal terms with whites. A sociological study of cockfighters indicated that, as a group, they were not psychopathic, sadistic, or in other ways psychologically disturbed. On the contrary, the values of the individuals studied were not very different from those of comparison groups of noncockers.

Both animal and human violence are associated with cockfighting. Before each match, pointed steel "gaffs" several inches long are attached to the legs of the cocks. Individual matches vary in length from a few seconds to over an hour, and usually the loser dies from injuries sustained during the match. Surprisingly, the fights are not as visually gruesome as one might expect. The steel gaffs inflict puncture wounds that bleed relatively little, and the birds' feathers tend to conceal blood. Cockfighting violence, nonetheless, is reflected in the vocabulary of the sport. "Bayonets" and "slashers" are types of gaffs, and a "butcher" is one of the hundreds of strains of gamecocks.

The general milieu of cockfights provides high potential for violence between the human participants. Drinking, though prohibited in most pits, regularly occurs surreptitiously. Gambling is an inextricable aspect of the sport, and, as in any competitive event, tempers can flare. Some spectators and cockers regularly carry concealed weapons. Despite the possibility of violence, serious disagreements between participants are relatively rare, probably due to strong norms against fighting at pits.

An elaborate structure governs how matches are conducted. The rules are published, and a referee in the pit at all times controls the fight and determines the winner according to the established regulations. (See Ruport, 1949, for sample sets of rules for conducting cockfights.) The referee's word is final in any dispute. Gambling between spectators at fights is informal and consists of accepting odds shouted by others just before each match begins. Bets are promptly paid after each match.

Because the sport is illegal in most areas, cockpits remain in a location only if local authorities look the other way. Police usually crack down on cockpits when there are complaints from the community. Thus, it is in the pit owner's best interest to avoid adverse publicity by preventing violence. Occasionally disputes do occur and fights break out. Disruptive individuals are immediately ejected and may be banned from future attendance.

Cockfighting is deeply rooted in southern culture. The mascot of the University of South Carolina, for example, is the "fighting gamecock." To those outside of the subculture, cockfighting may be synonymous with cruelty, violence, and brutality. To the cocker, however, it is a noble pastime that embodies the values of courage, stamina, and competition, and in many areas of the South, cockers proudly display bumper stickers and special license plates proclaiming their involvement in "the sport of kings."

Cockfighters invoke a variety of justifications for their sport. They link the names of many great Americans to cockfighting, including Washington, Lincoln, and Andrew Jackson. They claim that cockfighting is recreation that can involve the entire family and that the gamecock exemplifies the spirit of valor and bravery. They argue that, unlike the fowl raised in modern factory farms, their roosters have ample room and are treated very well. In addition, cockers argue that the natural aggression of gamecocks actually makes it cruel not to allow them to meet their destinies in the pit.

Few football fans would admit that violence is one of the reasons they attend games. The same is true of cockfighters. To a cocker the sport is not really about violence and death. It is about competition, camaraderie, and gambling.

See also RECREATION: Gambling

Harold A. Herzog, Jr.
Mars Hill College

C. D. Bryant and W. C. Capel, *Grit and Steel* (October 1974; April 1975); Charles R. Gunter, *Tennessee Folklore Society Bulletin* (December 1978); Harold A. Herzog, Jr., and P. B. Cheek, *Southern Exposure* (Fall 1979); Charles H. McGaghy and Arthur G. Neal, *Journal of Popular Culture* (Winter 1974); A. Ruport, *The Art of Cockfighting: A Handbook for Beginners and Old Timers* (1949); G. R. Scott, *The History of Cockfighting* (1957); Eliot Wigginton and Margie Bennett, eds., *Foxfire 8* (1984).

Crime, Attitudes toward

The southern states lead the nation in both the number of violent offenses against persons and the number of people imprisoned for crimes of violence. Southerners generally believe that those who violate criminal laws should be severely punished. Available criminal justice statistics, however, do not provide a clearcut picture of the effects of punishment on the social order.

Southern beliefs concerning proper behavior in interpersonal relations have deep roots in the regional culture. The distinguished southern scholar H. C. Brearley was among the first to call attention to the complex relationship between southern propensities toward lethal violence and regional legacies of personal pride, slavery, racism, lynching, and a castelike social structure. Lynching of both blacks and whites greatly increased after the Civil War, and the practice of collective violence against racial, ethnic, and other minorities continues to this day. The tenacious support of southerners for the right to own and use firearms combines with frontier values of individualism and self-sufficiency to sustain a cultural milieu that admits to both graceful living and judicial self-help.

The available evidence on popular attitudes toward the punishment of crimes compels two conclusions: (1) southerners are more predisposed than others to approve publicly of the use of lethal violence to settle personal disputes and problems; and (2) southern judicial officials are more likely to recommend severe punishment for those wrongdoers who threaten the moral values, beliefs, and social mores of the general public than their counterparts in other parts of the country.

In determining punishment the value of any person's life may be assessed either in terms of his or her social status (the traditional Anglo-Saxon approach) or in terms of the particular characteristics of the offender's act (the modern legalistic approach). The legalistic approach to punishment nominally omits the elements of revenge, reciprocity (an eye for an eye), and restitution benefits. The social costs and benefits associated with any form of behavior are ultimately determined by a combination of public attitudes and values relating to the achievement of the common good. A brief overview of the Texas Penal Code, which shares many characteristics with the penal statutes of other southern states, may serve to illustrate these general points.

Texas homicide statutes define homicide as the destruction of the life of one human being by the act, agency, procurement, or culpable omission of another. Noncriminal homicide, which is not punishable by law, includes a variety of homicides that are classified as justifiable; e.g., killing in self-defense, killing to protect one's property or the property of third persons, or killing in the performance of public duty.

Criminal homicide is subdivided into five major statutory categories. Each one is associated with specific minimum and maximum punishments. Murder is punishable by a minimum prison sentence of five years, by life imprisonment, or by a maximum 99-year prison sentence; capital murder, which specifically applies to anyone who kills a public official, is punishable by life imprisonment or death by execution; voluntary manslaughter imposes a minimum sentence of two years and a maximum prison sentence of 20 years; involuntary manslaughter limits the maximum prison sentence to 10 years; and negligent homicide is treated as a misdemeanor punishable by a fine not to exceed $2,000, imprisonment for one year or less, or a combination of imprisonment and a fine. The individual who kills another citizen in the heat of a personal argument or lethally responds to an injury to pride or property is more likely to escape any official punishment than the person who kills a public official. The slayer who combines killing with a property offense is most likely to be punished with either death or consecutive 99-year life sentences.

Public attitudes imbedded in penal statutes and individual criminal court decisions further reveal their southern regional characteristics if one looks at the available national survey statistics. Survey data from the southern region in the most recent compilation of public attitudes toward criminal justice suggest the following generalizations about popular attitudes: (1) southerners own more handguns than persons in other regions of

Stereotypical redneck southerner, in the film Easy Rider, *1969*

the United States; (2) southerners do not believe that private gun ownership should be subject to legal prohibition; (3) southerners generally believe that the public display and availability of pornographic materials lead individuals to commit rape; (4) southerners favor severe punishment of individuals who either possess or use marijuana. The survey data allow the conclusion that southerners view the possession of both marijuana and pornographic materials as more threatening to life and liberty than either the ready availability of firearms or the continuation of legal statutes that make the private use of firearms permissible in a variety of situations normally prohibited in other cultural regions.

As a result of such attitudes the South has more prison inmates under lock and key than any other region in the United States. The 1979 rate of sentenced prisoners in both state and federal institutions was twice as large for the southern region as for any other region in the nation. An astounding 12 percent of southern prisoners died at the hands of fellow prisoners. As of 31 December 1979, the South had a total of 459 prisoners on death row or the equivalent of 81 percent of the total U.S. death-row population.

Comparative and national statistics reveal that southerners believe strongly that criminals should be punished severely. The statistics fail to reveal why southerners generally believe in this pure form of retributive justice. Forthright acknowledgment of the obvious fact that a disproportionate number of private citizens annually kill or seriously injure others without receiving any form of official punishment also suggests that any understanding or even explanation of popular attitudes toward criminal punishment must begin with an analysis of the regional cultural patterns of the violent South.

See also LAW: Criminal Justice; Criminal Law

Henry P. Lundsgaarde
University of Kansas

H. C. Brearley, in *Culture in the South*, ed. W. T. Couch (1934); James Harmon Chadbourn, *Lynching and the Law* (1933); Timothy J. Flanagan, David J. van Alstyne, and Michael R. Gottfredson, eds., *Sourcebook of Criminal Justice Statistics-1981* (1982); Leon Friedman, ed., *Southern Justice* (1965); Raymond D. Gastil, *American Sociological Review* (June 1971), *Cultural Regions of the United States* (1975); Sheldon Hackney, *American Historical Review* (February 1969); Henry P. Lundsgaarde, *Murder in Space City: A Cultural Analysis of Houston Homicide Patterns* (1977); Arthur F. Raper, *The Tragedy of Lynching* (1933); Milton Rokeach, in *International Encyclopedia of the Social Sciences*, vol. 1, ed. David L. Sills (1968).

Guns

Since the early 1800s the image of southerners with firearms has served as a cliché for the nation and, indeed, the world. The firearm is certainly a secure cultural feature of the South, but that is true of rural groups in other geographical locations. Firearms, generalized violence, and "southernness" have, however, been historically linked in the popular and literary imagination and have served as negative features distorting overall perceptions of the southern reality. Since the 1960s the gun itself has taken on a larger meaning in the context of the American nation, and the traditional identification of southerners with guns has both reinforced stereotypes of regional violence and reaffirmed many southerners' interest in weapons.

The South has traditionally been portrayed as a gun-toting culture. In the last century northern and European travelers frequently remarked on the prevalence of guns and knives in the region. Today many non-southerners, especially urban dwellers, express surprise at gun racks in pickup trucks, the pro-gun-ownership bumper-sticker slogans, and the assertive attitudes of southerners about the right to carry firearms.

Mississippi Delta, 1968

All studies agree that gun ownership and levels of gun usage are relatively high in the South. According to several recent studies, about 65 percent of southerners and about 44 percent of non-southerners own guns. National Opinion Research Center analyses of data for the 1970s compared nine regions, three of which included states generally defined as southern (South Atlantic, East South Central, and West South Central). Residents of Alabama, Kentucky, Mississippi, and Tennessee (the East South Central region) had the highest rate of gun ownership in the nation—74.9 percent of the populace owned guns. The lowest southern rate—57.8 percent—was in the region comprised of Texas, Arkansas, Louisiana, and Oklahoma (although the latter is not usually considered part of the South). The highest non-southern rate, 64.9 percent, found in the Mountain region (e.g., Nevada, Utah), was quite similar to the southern rates; but the lowest rate, 24.3 percent in New England, was markedly lower. Recent studies of college students have shown that far more southern students have fired guns than their northern counterparts, 81 percent and 56 percent, respectively. Of those southern males living in non-gun-owning households, estimates are that 91 percent had fired a gun. Whether the existence of such statistics, coupled with notably high rates of violent crime in the South, constitutes sufficient rationale for the widely held belief that a "southern subculture of violence" exists is problematical.

The belief in such a subculture flourished for many years. Persuasive arguments emanated from politicized campuses and newsrooms of the 1960s, and authors of popular and academic articles asserted that violence was an inherent quality of southerners' worldview. Only in the late 1970s and early 1980s did more balanced, critical views find their way into print. Academicians—not exclusively from the South—pointed out that the South's high rates of gun ownership and violent crime may not be causally related; that is, owning firearms does not necessarily predispose southerners to violent solutions to personal problems. High rates of firearm ownership in the South, they contended, are primarily related to the preponderance of shoulder weapons, i.e., shotguns and rifles, found there among sportsmen. Most firearm-related violence is committed with handguns, a type of weapon whose ownership is, according to an authoritative source, "not very much more prevalent in the South than in other regions." Furthermore, weapon ownership in the South is highest in rural and small-town areas, yet violent crime is primarily an urban phenomenon: a connection between urban crime and regional patterns of weapons ownership has not been proven.

Although regionwide patterns of gun ownership do not provide solid evidence of the South's being a particularly violent milieu, gun ownership in the South has always had symbolic, ritual meaning. The presentation of a series of guns to young males serves as a rite of passage, especially among rurally oriented folk. This progression typically begins with the gift of a BB gun, then a .22 rifle, usually followed by a small-gauge shotgun, often a 20-gauge or, formerly, a 16-gauge. The BB gun is used to develop essential safety skills and to impart basic principles of ballistics. Its use is generally unsupervised, and generations of southern youths have hunted frogs and small birds and have annoyed dogs with these guns. Mock wars fought with BB guns range far and wide in rural southern areas. These are elaborate affairs complete with imaginative scenarios and peculiar etiquette—"don't aim for the face," for example, or "eye shots are unfair."

The next stage of firearm socialization involves the use of the first "real-gun"—the .22 rifle. The first gun of this sort is often a solidly made, bolt-action or pump-action weapon purchased at a catalog store or perhaps handed down from a father, uncle, or grandfather. Use of this more deadly and usually quite accurate weapon is fraught with hazard, and numerous cautionary tales are passed from father to son as to appropriate contexts for its use. The .22 is a small-bore squirrel and rabbit gun that many adult hunters still prefer. Many young people (and young-at-heart adults) take to the woods in the autumn in search of squirrels in the tree tops. For some, the satisfaction of having brought down a moving, elusive "bushytail" transcends the deer-hunting mystique.

Young hunters often learn basic skills at fall dove hunts; one of a youth's first experiences in the field is to learn about frustration from trying his hand at shooting this evasive bird. Sometimes shooting over fields illegally baited with corn, the participants probably use more lead in a day than their grey-clad ancestors did during four years under the Stars and Bars. The number of doves actually shot is, however, almost secondary to the deals consummated, friendships made, and bonds established at these communal rituals. For dove hunting, youths often first receive a 20-gauge shotgun and later graduate to a 12-gauge when their upper-body strength and bulk allow them to master that weapon's recoil.

Once a young person has exhibited field-and-stream know-how and has not committed any major breach of safety or hunting etiquette, he will be lent, then given, a deer rifle of any of a wide variety of calibers. The favored 30–06 has recently declined in popularity because of the introduction and popularization of the more flat-shooting .243 and .270. For use in dense vegetation, "a brush gun," the .44 carbine or .223, often fills the bill. With this proliferation of calibers and weaponry, some hunting enthusiasts now have different guns specifically earmarked for certain types of game—often when one or two all-purpose guns would serve efficiently and much more economically. One wag joked to a gun enthusiast that while he had rifles for rabbit, squirrel, deer, and bear, he was deficient in firearms for hunting armadillos and aardvarks (the latter a nonnative species, and neither a game animal).

Handguns have been anecdotally linked to the South from antebellum times to the present. Recent data show that close to 40 percent of all southerners own handguns, a rate that is about 16 percentage points higher than in non-southern areas, with the exception of the Mountain region. Ownership rates have generally been found to be higher among white Protestant males than among others. Many handgun owners routinely carry revolvers or automatics in their glove compartments, briefcases, or, in the case of women, their handbags. For some southerners (and northern gun enthusiasts) the handgun possesses a certain aesthetic appeal. Most modern handguns are reliable, reasonably safe, and extremely durable. Although some gun enthusiasts claim to use handguns for hunting, their primary function is as a defensive or, frequently, offensive weapon. Some handgun aficionados prefer big-bore "macho" weaponry, such as the .357 and .44 magnums. Others, feeling the pull of tradition, prefer the old reliable .38, .45, or .32 calibers. When in the field or on the water, many outdoorsmen in the South routinely carry .22 magnum pistols in their boats or on their belts as a "kit gun." These are useful for dispatching snakes or other varmints, signaling for help in an emergency, and having "just in case."

Gun shows in the South are a major spectacle. People of all ages troop by long rows of tables covered by a dizzying array of weapons, uniforms, coins, knives, and survival gear. Men and boys dressed for the hunt examine the various weapons, make trades, buy and sell, and renew old friendships. As might be expected, survivalist tracts are much in evidence. The gun show, like the turkey shoot or gander pull of earlier times, is a social occasion that allows a renewal of ties with acquaintances, friends, relatives, and even symbolically with ancestors.

Many southerners possess and prominently display ancestral weaponry from "the war" and subsequent conflicts as well as hunting rifles and shotguns passed down for generations and kept in working order. The preservation and maintenance of these old .44s and .36s suggest that weapons have a totemic significance that trancends the merely decorative and functional. For many rural families in the past, the gun was probably one of the most expensive items they owned and therefore one of the most valuable (next to land) that could be passed on to heirs. The weapons serve as a vital link to ancestors—one of the remaining physical evidences of who they were and of who contemporary southerners are. The weapon links the southerner to a mythic golden age or, alternately, to a hardscrabble, but meaningful existence in the piney woods.

The pronounced cultural interest in weaponry evident in the South may stem from a perceived need for protection from varmints (both the four-legged and two-legged varieties), the enjoyment of hunting and the social constellation surrounding it, and a desire for a link with the past. Although this significant cultural symbolism has become entangled in the broader national debate over crime, attaching too much significance to the role of the gun in the South may be a mistake. The South has been a predominantly rural milieu and continues to hold certain rural values. In this context, to paraphrase Freud, sometimes a gun is just a gun.

See also RECREATION: Hunting

Fred Hawley
Louisiana State University
at Shreveport

Dickson D. Bruce, Jr., *Violence and Culture in the Antebellum South* (1979); Raymond D. Gastil, *Cultural Regions of the United States* (1975); Sheldon Hackney, *American Historical*

Review (February 1969); Lee Kennett and James L. Anderson, *The Gun in America: The Origins of a National Dilemma* (1975); John Shelton Reed, *One South: An Ethnic Approach to Regional Culture* (1982); James D. Wright, Peter Rossi, and Kathleen Daly, *Under the Gun: Weapons, Crime, and Violence in America* (1983).

Harlan County, Kentucky

The 1930s were a time of labor upheaval in the United States. There were strikes, picket lines, lockouts, riots, sit-down strikes, marches, protests, musterings of national guardsmen, and many charges of police brutality. Amid this labor unrest that was truly national in scope, one place caught the attention of the nation and much of the Western world. Previously almost unknown, it accumulated a huge literature in newspapers and magazines and generated a voluminous body of folk music. The place has since been known as "bloody Harlan."

The 1930 census revealed a population of 64,577, nearly all of which was dependent in one way or another on coal mining. John W. Hevener has published a careful study of the county's labor strife in the troubled decade, concluding that the struggle caused 11 deaths and 20 woundings. When viewed against the background of the region's grim history these casualties appear startlingly low—but bloody enough to justify the county's reputation. Harlan County earned its niche in the folklore of American labor violence. However, in considering Harlan's reputation for lawlessness and bloodshed, one can appreciate that the labor struggles mark only a brief and relatively minor facet of its turbulent history.

Harlan County lies between two great barrier walls—the long steep parallel ridges known as the Cumberland and Pine mountains. The area was settled sparsely and late. After the first settlers had built their cabins, forbidding hills kept out new waves of settlers and preserved intact the mores and culture, the ignorance and cunning, the crankiness and suspicion, the narrowness and prejudices, the loyalties and clannishness that marked the pioneer families. Sam Howard, a Revolutionary War veteran, was the county's first permanent settler. His and the 30 or 40 other backwoods families who followed around 1800 had been hardened by decades of warfare. As a people they had been seasoned by two centuries of scrabbling in the backwoods, clearing endless new ground, fighting with the French, struggling over wilderness lands with the British, and countering almost incessant raids from both southern and northern Indians. It was inescapable that the people who stopped off at such places as the Poor Fork and Wallins Creek were a hard-bitten, self-reliant lot who would be quick with knife and gun whenever it appeared to them that they were being "picked on."

The county was established by the legislature in 1819, and the county seat was "established" at Sam Howard's old place, which he called Mount Pleasant. By any standard meaningful to contemporary Americans this backwoods bailiwick was desperately poor. The people there fished, hunted until most of the game was exterminated, and gained such money as came into their hands by bartering ginseng, feathers, whiskey, brandy, hides, and saw logs to stock drovers and backwoods merchants. These settlers became remarkably interrelated, an important circumstance in a society that valued "blood kin."

The county was of the most rudimentary character, with a budget of $6,025.60 in 1857. Data on this period are hard to come by, but there is no reason to believe that the population was unusually violent in those years. During the Civil War, Harlan County residents were Unionists (except for a pro-southern enclave on Clover Fork) and formed strong home guard units to keep the peace. Unlike neighboring Letcher County, which split on the issue and fostered a little war within a big one, Harlan countians did little fighting among themselves. Instead, they relentlessly bushwacked Confederate forces that ventured into their midst between 1862 and 1864.

The struggle left many mountain counties impoverished, divided, and hate filled so that numerous little "wars" followed Appomattox. In the half century after Lee surrendered, scarcely a county was without one of these vendettas that spread from valley to valley until practically the entire population was at peril. Breathitt County was wracked by one struggle after another, as were Clay, Letcher, Pike, Knott, and Bell. The dead were beyond count and included a circuit judge, a U.S. commissioner, a county attorney, a city marshall, a trustee of the State College of Kentucky, a physician, and a witness guarded by a company of state militiamen armed with a Gatling gun.

This bloody record reflected a lingering statewide frontier mentality that endorsed murder as a form of private justice. In that bloody period only Arkansas and Mississippi ranked with Kentucky in violent crime. It was the considered judgment of the *New York Times* (26 December 1878) that Kentucky was "the Corsica of North America," its people considerably less civilized than the Italian Mafia.

Harlan County did not escape these troubles. In April 1882 Wilse Howard won a few dollars from Bob Turner in a card game. Turner drew a gun and compelled Howard to return the money. Three days later Howard killed Turner from ambush. There is no credible tally of the deaths in the ensuing Howard-Turner War. It ended when the Turner faction caught the Howards in "Harlan Town," killed four of them, and wounded seven others.

The whirlwind industrialization of Harlan radically changed its society and economy. In the years from 1900 to 1920 the population increased from 9,838 to 31,546. Subsistence farmers left their hollows and river valleys to mine coal in "company towns." Their dependence on family or "clan" was abandoned for day wages and an erratic coal market. People who had lived all their lives amid "blood kin" and friends found themselves in small houses in communities that were totally dominated by the omnipresent power of coal and iron policemen. When the market for coal evaporated in recurrent depressions, famine and rebellion followed. The rebellions were repressed by a political system that grew directly out of the coal economy: the circuit judge, sheriff, and county chairmen of both political parties were in the coal business. That the men revolted in such uprisings as the "battle of the Evarts" and the "battle of Fork Ridge" is understandable. The only surprise lies in the small number of casualties.

Harlan was never as violent as its sister counties 70 miles away in West Virginia—"Bloody Mingo" and "Bloody Logan." In 1922 the Logan County War saw veritable armies of miners pitted against formations of deputy sheriffs and national guardsmen. Nonetheless it must be conceded that "Bloody Harlan" was not a gratuitous nickname. In 1916 a homicide rate of 0.8 per 100,000 persons was recorded in New Hampshire (a different kind of Appalachian state), and rural America as a whole reported 5.2. Harlan's rate was a horrendous 63.5. Perry reported 30.4. Harlan's neighbor to the south, Wise County, Va., came up with 39.3, and its eastern neighbor, Letcher, led the nation with 77.9—nearly 80 times that of New Hampshire.

See also SOCIAL CLASS: Appalachia, Exploitation of; Labor, Organized; / Coal Miners; Company Towns

Harry M. Caudill
Whitesburg, Kentucky

John W. Campbell, *The Southern Highlander and His Homeland* (1922); Joe Daniel Carr, *Filson Club History Quarterly* (April 1973); Mabel Green Condon, *A History of Harlan County* (1962); David A. Corbin, *Life, Work and Rebellion in the Coal Fields: Southern West Virginia Coal Miners, 1880–1922* (1981); Paul Frederick Cressy, *American Sociological Review* (June 1934); John W. Hevener, *Which Side Are You On?* (1978); G. C. Jones, *Growing Up Hard in Harlan County* (1985); Winthrop Lane, *Civil War in West Virginia* (1922); Howard W. Lee, *Bloodletting in Appalachia: The Story of West Virginia's Four Major Mines Wars and Other Thrilling Incidents of Its Coal Fields* (1969); Elmon Middleton, *Harlan County, Kentucky* (1934); George W. Titler, *Hell in Harlan* (1972).

Honor

Southerners of the antebellum era made it clear that they subscribed to an ethic of honor, but they never specified exactly what honor meant. In large part, this was because the meaning of honor depended on its immediate context, on who claimed and who acknowledged it. In fact, honor might be defined as a system of beliefs in which a person has exactly as much worth as others confer upon him. Antebellum northerners and most 20th-century Americans have some difficulty understanding the idea of honor, for it runs contrary to what has come to be a national article of faith: each person, regardless of race, class, sex, or religion, possesses equal intrinsic worth—regardless of what others think of him. Insult has little meaning to people who share such a faith, but if one takes honor seriously, insult from a respected person can cut to the quick. Accordingly, much of the violence in the South from the 18th century to the present appears to have been sparked by insult, by challenges to honor. Southerners believed a man had to guard his reputation and his honor, by good manners and, if necessary, by violence. Insult literally could not be tolerated.

Women, although traditionally venerated in the South, could have no honor—only virtue. The ultimate protection of honor lay in physical courage, an attribute not considered to be within a woman's sphere. White men also refused to concede that black men could possess honor, although black southerners recognized honor among one another. Further, the honor of wealthy white men could not be damaged by men of lesser rank. Honor came into play only among equals. Contrary to stereotype, though, honor was not restricted to the southern aristocracy. Men of every class felt themselves to be honorable and could not tolerate affront and still enjoy the respect of their peers. The elite alone dueled, of course, but the duel was only the most refined manifestation of honorable conflict, the tip of the iceberg. Fighting, shooting, stabbing, feuding, and shotgun weddings were considered legitimate and inevitable results of honor confronting honor.

An emphasis on honor, concurrently with high homicide rates, prevailed in the 19th-century South, although the cult of honor became less formalized (and probably more dangerous in the process) after the Civil War. Duels faded away; shooting scrapes became more common. The concept of honor also spanned the subregions of the South, lowland and upland, slaveholding and nonslaveholding. It even persisted in southern cities, where volatile rural folkways combined with urban poverty and crowding to make southern cities peculiarly dangerous places to live.

The South was not alone in this culture of honor. In different variations, it has flourished for centuries in Mediterranean cultures such as those of Sicily and Greece. Cultures of honor also flourished among the aristocracy of 17th-century England and among the Scotch- Irish, both of whom exerted decisive influences on southern culture in its formative states. The idea of honor did not prosper among the Puritans, Quakers, or Congregationalists and seems to be at odds with the impersonal relations of a predominantly commercial society. Honor never sank deep roots in the North.

The South, on the other hand, from its very beginnings seemed designed to nurture honor. Slavery and the society it spawned provided the conditions in which the notion of honor could flourish. Honor thrives in a rural society of face-to-face contact, of a limited number of relationships, of one system of values. Honor depends upon a hierarchical society, where one is defined by who is above or below him. Honor grows well in a society where the rationalizing power of the state is weak; an adherence to honor makes the state, at best, irrelevant in settling personal disputes.

Honor found itself increasingly on the defensive in the 19th century, not only from the North and England, but also from within the South. Honor, necessarily a secular system of values, clashed with the ideals of Christian virtue. Evangelical southerners deplored and denounced the violence and pride honor condoned. In their eyes, people who let their actions be dictated by honor allowed themselves to become mere slaves of public opinion. The vast majority of southerners, of course, whatever their religious inclination, killed or assaulted no one, and even those who did resort to violence did so only once or twice in a lifetime—still enough to send many more southerners than northerners to jail and penitentiary for violent crimes, although southerners were notorious for not prosecuting crimes of violence.

Black southerners, when once liberated from slavery, also adapted to southern codes of honor. White observers, particularly those from the North, were appalled that blacks fought and killed each other over the same apparently trivial provocations as white southerners. Indeed, the homicide rate of both races in the South exceeded that of both in the North. Southerners of both races, consciously or not, have held to their notions of honor far into the 20th century, even in northern cities. Those who find that high homicide rates today correlate with southern culture seem to be measuring the fallout of a culture of honor. Those who find a correlation with low literacy rates or poverty are describing the characteristics of a place in which honor can best survive in the present.

See also MYTHIC SOUTH: Militant South; Romanticism; / Hospitality

Edward L. Ayers
University of Virginia

Edward L. Ayers, *Vengeance and Justice: Crime and Punishment in the 19th-Century American South* (1984); Peter Berger, Brigitte Berger, and Hansfried Kellner, *The Homeless Mind: Modernization and Consciousness* (1973); Pierre Bordieu, in *Honor and Shame: The Values of Mediterranean Society*, ed. J. G. Peristiany (1965); Bertram Wyatt-Brown, *Southern Honor: Ethics and Behavior in the Old South* (1982).

Industrial Violence

The United States has earned a reputation for having the most violent labor history of any industrial country, and the South followed the national pattern. The worst violence erupted during strikes, especially ones that involved employer efforts to destroy an existing union or to deny union recognition. In such disputes it is often difficult to determine which side initiated violence, but the results show that both employers (or their supporters) and strikers resorted to violence in the form of physical assaults, some of which were deadly. Company property was also occasionally destroyed, but workers often claimed this was done by employers themselves in an effort to discredit strikers or to encourage the intervention of troops. In any case, no union pursued violence as a systematic policy. Whether labor struggles turned violent was largely determined by the attitude of employers and their response to strike situations. If they hired strikebreakers and/or used armed guards to fight unionization, they created the conditions in which violence was most likely to occur.

Just as the South lagged behind the rest of the country in industrial development and the growth of organized labor, so too it experienced industrial violence somewhat later than other regions. After Reconstruction the first generation of industrialization in the South saw little labor-related violence despite the propensity of southerners to resort to mob violence in other areas of life. Although strikes disrupted textile mills, the South's leading industry, as early as the 1870s, southern textile workers never damaged mill property during this period, and they rarely harmed strikebreakers. The weakness of unions and the control exercised by employers, especially in company towns, help explain the general absence of violence. Moreover, the textile industry relied on a white labor force, which reduced the potential for industrial violence sparked by racial animosities. One of the few southern strikes with fatalities prior to 1910 came in 1894, when Alabama coal miners killed three black strikebreakers and a policeman.

The pace of industrial violence quickened after 1910. During a nationwide railroad strike in 1911–12, the introduction of strikebreakers led to a riot in New Orleans, La., that left six dead. In McComb, Miss., three black strikebreakers were killed, and the violence took the lives of several railway guards and a strikebreaker in Texas. Strikes by Louisiana lumberjacks and longshoremen affiliated with the Industrial Workers of the World resulted in picket-line violence in 1912 and 1913 that killed five strikers. During a 1919 strike by lumber workers affiliated with the American Federation of Labor, vigilantes in Bogalusa, La., killed four union men. Another national walkout by railway shopmen in 1922 resulted in the death of one striker and six black strikebreakers in violence that flared in seven southern states. The next wave of deaths came during the 1929 revolt of textile workers that took the lives of six strikers who were shot by police in a confrontation in Marion, N.C.

During the 1930s industrial violence reached new heights in the entire country. Spurred by union organizing drives and protective New Deal legislation, southern workers struck major industries, especially textiles, seeking recognition. Employers and their defenders responded with deadly force that cost the lives of over 20 strikers, including five shot by deputies in Honea Path, S.C., during the 1934 national textile strike. The decade's toll of strike-related fatalities in the South also included one strikebreaker, four company guards, and four local policemen. During this period antilabor violence was also costly to tenant farmers who organized the Sharecroppers Union of Alabama and the Southern Tenant Farmers' Union.

The record of fatalities in labor disputes shows that the bloodiest battles occurred on picket lines, where police often defended company interests by attacking strikers. Industrial violence did not result in the death of a single employer or company executive in the South. Although strikers sometimes initiated violence, especially in the period before 1929, they usually acted out of frustrated rage, and they failed to advance their cause by resorting to violence. Employers and their supporters used violent tactics to break strikes and intimidate workers, but management possessed so many legal weapons to fight unions that violence alone rarely determined the outcome of strikes.

Antilabor violence, however, made organizing both difficult and dangerous, especially when it was used systematically in southern communities dominated by antiunion industries. In Tampa, Fla., for example, vigilantes consistently employed threats, backed by periodic beatings and forced deportations, to stem the tide of trade unionism in the cigar industry from its establishment in the city during the 1880s to the 1930s when cigarworkers won union recognition. Similar tactics were used in other communities against representatives of the Congress of Industrial Organizations (CIO) after creation of the organization in 1935. Gadsden, Ala., experienced a five-year reign of terror against CIO organizers and rubber workers who attempted to unionize the local Goodyear plant.

Industrial violence went largely unpunished, especially when its victims were trade unionists. Most community leaders and local police tolerated, or abetted, repression in the conviction that southern industrial growth and economic progress depended on preventing the development of unions. When arrests and indictments followed outbreaks of violence, they were usually directed against strikers as an additional method of hampering union activity.

New Deal legislation enhancing the right to organize and bargain collectively shifted labor battles from the streets to courtrooms, and industrial violence declined sharply in most parts of the country after 1937. Some southern cities followed this pattern. In Birmingham, Ala., for example, the violence that had plagued the city abruptly stopped when the Tennessee Coal, Iron and Railroad Company, the city's largest employer, recognized the steelworkers' union in 1937. Gadsden's campaign of threats, beatings, and destruction of union property ended during World War II when Goodyear workers, under the protection of the federal government, voted for a union.

In much of the South, however, industrial violence continued in defiance of the national trend. Between 1947 and 1962, 20 of the nation's 29 strike fatalities occurred in the 11 former Confederate states and Kentucky. The persistence of industrial violence in the South is difficult to explain, but lawlessness plagued labor disputes that pitted militant workers against staunch antiunion employers who dominated local communities and had the backing of police.

Since the 1960s most industrial violence in the South has been limited to sporadic property damage, except in isolated areas, such as Harlan County, Ky. Although resistance to unions remains strong, labor-management battles have become more institutionalized and less violent as they have increasingly taken the form of drawn-out legal disputes over union recognition and contract negotiations. When strikes do occur, they are now usually peaceful as in the rest of the country.

See also INDUSTRY: Industrialization, Resistance to; / Textile Industry; SOCIAL CLASS: Labor, Organized; / American Federation of Labor; Company Towns; Congress of Industrial Organizations; Longshoremen; Textile Workers

Robert P. Ingalls
University of South Florida

Hugh Davis Graham and Ted Robert Gurr, eds., *Violence in America: Historical and Comparative Perspectives* (1969); Melton A. McLaurin, *Paternalism and Protest: Southern Mill Workers and Organized Labor, 1875–1905* (1971); F. Ray Marshall, *Labor in the South* (1967); Charles H. Martin, *Journal of Southern History* (November 1981); Marc Miller, ed., *Working Lives* (1981).

Literature and Song, Violence in Black

Since the mid-19th century the physical and psychological violence of racial oppression has been a prominent concern in the literature of southern blacks. Prior to the 1930s writers were little more than descriptive in their treatment of the subject. This changed, however, in the late 1930s. Writers, to be sure, continued to support the crusade against lynching and other forms of anti-black violence in the South. The technique of their art, however, became more sophisticated. To a large extent, this was a result of the strong influence that the Harlem Renaissance of the 1920s continued to have on southern black literature in the 1930s.

The interracial violence in southern black life stimulated the creative imagination of southern black writers between the late 1930s and the early 1950s. It was a central theme in many poems and short stories; yet the fullest artistic treatment of the subject during this period was in novels of social realism, in problem novels, and in propaganda novels. In these works the lynching scene became a standard symbol of the intensity and pervasiveness of white-on-black violence and often functioned as a major structuring device. Patterns of imagery, narrative voice, thematic structure, character development, and other fictional techniques in the novels of this period reflected the violence that had become ingrained in southern society.

Richard Wright's *Native Son* (1940) is exemplary. Wright uses violence as the novel's primary imaginative idea. Although the novel is set in Chicago, its protagonist, Bigger Thomas, is a composite of various southern black youths for whom violence is the predominant fact of life. Wright demonstrates how the legacy of oppression affects the black psyche. Indeed, *Native Son* remains in the forefront of many southern black novels since the 1930s in which interracial violence undergirds the fictional art. Waters Turpin, William Attaway,

George Wylie Henderson, and George W. Lee are among those southern black novelists in this period whose works have interracial violence at their core. Many of the period's novelists are known as members of the Richard Wright school or the protest school. Protest fiction dominated southern black literature until the 1950s.

Spearheaded by Ralph Ellison's *Invisible Man* in 1952, southern black writers began to concentrate more fully on intraracial violence as a manifestation of the legacy of racial oppression. Intraracial violence gave thematic focus to *Invisible Man*'s first chapter—the battle royal. Representative characterizations, symbolic actions, and generic themes of black life radiate from the intraracial violence of the battle royal. Intraracial violence helps define the novel's thematic structure as the protagonist, a black Everyman, searches for an authentic identity.

The concept of identity and the meaning of the racial past are major concerns in southern black novels published after World War II. Novelists frequently use the violence of the racial past as the context in which their protagonists examine, identify, and affirm their blackness. In their literary treatment of both the recent and the distant past, many contemporary writers use violence as the overriding metaphor for white resistance to any means blacks have used to participate more fully in southern life.

From Wright to Ellison, then, the emphasis on violence shifted from interracial to intraracial. Subsequently fiction writers during and after the 1960s shifted from primary to secondary emphasis on the violence associated with black life (past or present) in the South. Among contemporary writers this shift is evident in rather conventional treatments of a black past laden with violence, such as Margaret Walker's *Jubilee* (1966), as well as in more avant-garde treatments of the slave past, such as Ishmael Reed's *Flight to Canada* (1976). Ernest Gaines's *The Autobiography of Miss Jane Pittman* (1971) is representative of the secondary attention contemporary writers give to violence—interracial or intraracial, physical or psychological—as an index to southern black life. Through the development of a secondary character, Ned, rather than the novel's main character, Jane Pittman, Gaines chronicles the legacy of violence in southern black life from slavery to the 1960s.

The widespread white-on-black violence in the South of the 1960s is reflected primarily in the poetry of this period. The assassinations of civil rights leaders and other incidents of violence are the subjects of numerous poems. Some black poets of southern origin, chiefly Nikki Giovanni and Don L. Lee (Haki R. Mahubuti), became widely known for poems that advocate black-on-white violence as a defense against white oppression. Etheridge Knight became the most popular poet among a group of "prison poets" whose poems concern various kinds of violence affecting black life. During the 1960s poets were in the forefront of an influential group of writers—many of them southern—in whose works black-on-white violence is pervasive. These writers, whom social and literary critics label the Militant Black Writers, wrote as often of the urban North as of the South. The diminishing emphasis on violence in the fiction of southern blacks during the decade is in line with the philosophy of nonviolence that dominated the civil rights movement in the South.

The pervasive social violence of the 1960s did not, however, engender creativity in song as it did in other black arts and as it had done during the antebellum period. Southern blacks in general and vocal artists in particular adopted the slave songs as anthems. The lyrics of many of these songs were easily adaptable to contemporary situations, underscoring the historical continuity of the violence associated with living black in the South. Nina Simone was one of the few vocal artists who popularized songs generated by the physical and psychological violence of the period. Yet even the popularity of her "Mississippi Goddam," for instance, did not supersede that of earlier songs about interracial violence. "Strange Fruit," a song about lynchings in the South, which Billie Holiday had made famous a generation earlier, remained a standard among vocal artists ranging from classical to folk.

Rock, blues, jazz, folk, and popular singers continue to sing and to record songs about intraracial violence. Although several of them are contemporary products, the most popular are products of an earlier time. Since the late 19th century the Mississippi Delta has been the birthplace of numerous songs, especially in the blues, about intraracial violence in southern black life. The area still produces songs with a curious mixture of violence and heroism, such as the "bad men" songs. "Stagolee" (there are various spellings), the legendary prototype, has maintained its popularity since the late 19th century. Many of the songs from the Mississippi Delta have their genesis in the underworld life of gamblers and prostitutes. Others speak of intraracial violence precipitated by unrequited love, love triangles, and other forms of romantic passion. "Frankie and Johnnie," continually popular among contemporary singers, is representative of the type. Contemporary southern black songwriters (unlike the literary artists) seldom indicate in their works that intraracial violence among blacks in the South is a direct consequence of racial oppression.

Interracial violence in the South had been sharply curtailed by the 1970s. Among contemporary southern black songsters and literary artists, the violence of the past, not the present, receives attention. One notable exception is in blues songs, which continue to be written about love conflicts that precipitate intraracial violence. In the main, though, contemporary literature and song by and about southern blacks concentrate on the beauty and spiritual qualities of life among southern blacks.

See also BLACK LIFE: Freedom Movement, Black; Literature, Black; Music, Black; MUSIC: Blues; Jazz

J. Lee Greene
University of North Carolina
at Chapel Hill

Imamu Amiri Baraka (LeRoi Jones), *Blues People: Negro Music in White America* (1963); H. Rap Brown, *Die Nigger Die!* (1969); Charles A. Frye, ed., *Values in Conflict: Blacks and the Ameri-*

can Ambivalence toward Violence (1980); Stephen E. Henderson, *Understanding the New Black Poetry: Black Speech and Black Music as Poetic Reference* (1973).

Literature and Song, Violence in White

Violence has long occupied a significant place in white southern expressive forms of culture. In literature and popular culture white southern writers and performers have made use of violent motifs in order to describe and to come to grips with the region's history and experience. For many writers the South has served as a literary setting in which violence provides an undercurrent to everyday life. Others, however, have gone further, using the violence of southern experience as the key vehicle for conveying their sense of human nature and destiny.

Violence appeared prominently in southern writing with the beginnings of serious southern fiction during the antebellum period. Violence in many of these early works was intimately connected with larger questions of social virtue. This was especially true in the fiction of William Gilmore Simms, the most prominent writer in the antebellum South. Simms used violence in all his works as the main test of his characters' ability to lead lives of virtue and honor. For Simms, human beings were always vulnerable to the evil effects of human passions. He saw the greatest virtue in the man who could confront situations with courage and competence, while maintaining control of his own passions under the terrible stress that violent situations posed. In such tales of heroism as *The Partisan* (1835) Simms explored the character who could remain civilized even in the face of the awful disruptions of war. In such psychological works as *Martin Faber: The Story of a Criminal* (1833), Simms dramatized the tragedy of a man who, dominated by passion, lapsed into the excesses of violence.

Other writers from this period wrote much as Simms did. Such men as Nathaniel Beverley Tucker and William Alexander Caruthers wrote novels of southern chivalry that glorified the heroic characters of gentlemen in a violent world. Virginia-bred Edgar Allan Poe, in his tales of terror, explored the dark souls of individuals who, unable to control their passions, committed acts of unspeakable violence. Though few of Poe's works had a southern setting, their treatment of violence was quite consistent with southern ideas. And his verse-play *Politian* (1835) drew on an actual southern murder for its plot, which Poe chose not to set in the South.

The antebellum period also saw the rise of a significant school of "local color" writers, the southwestern humorists, who looked mainly at life on the southern frontier. Much of the humor in the works of writers such as Augustus Baldwin Longstreet derived from their presentation of the southern frontier as a place of virtual anarchy. Violence was a major manifestation of the lack of concern for social order that characterized the frontier folk in these works.

Violence continued to be important in post–Civil War southern writing. Although much southern literature between the end of the war and the early 20th century was within the bounds of the plantation tradition—glorifying a civilized stability in the Old South and minimizing its violence—at least a few writers stressed the importance of violence in southern life. The most prominent was the southern critic and racial liberal George Washington Cable. Recognizing the need for social change and decrying the effects of southern racism, Cable presented a South in which violence was endemic to social relations, in which men were quick to fight and tragically slow to reconcile social and political differences. From a quite different point of view, Thomas Dixon, Jr., spoke for the white South's fears of black aspirations. He used traditions of black savagery and violence in his most important work, *The Clansman* (1905), to argue the need for white supremacy and even for white violence to thwart black ambitions for equality.

But the most significant use of violence by postbellum southern writers came after 1930 in major works by novelists and poets of the Southern Literary Renaissance. Such writers as William Faulkner and Robert Penn Warren found in southern violence a key vehicle for addressing major social and moral issues. Thus, violence figures prominently in all of Faulkner's major novels. In such works as *Light in August* (1932) and *Absalom, Absalom!* (1936) violent episodes serve to underscore the problems of the South's history and society, and, more deeply, to explore the nature of human freedom and the consequences of human action in a vast, uncontrollable world. Faulkner's world was dense and violent, and he drew on southern historical and racial violence for its construction.

Robert Penn Warren, in both fiction and poetry, has looked directly to southern history for his sources, picking out individual violent episodes, and re-creating them in ways that illuminate both southern history and more general questions of human nature and culture. Warren sees human beings as imperfect creatures in an uncontrollable world and has stressed the importance of original sin in any conception of human nature. His *All the King's Men* (1946), based on the career of Huey Long, describes a political setting filled with violence as Warren explores the meaning of human responsibility in a tormented world. In his long poem *Brother to Dragons* (1953, 1979), Warren focuses on the actual murder of a slave by the nephews of Thomas Jefferson in order to contrast his own pessimistic perspective with more optimistic views of human goodness and perfectibility.

Post–World War II southern writers have continued to use violence to structure their works. Especially significant in this regard is Flannery O'Connor, in whose fiction violence is a key to human nature and a force leading people to confront the demands of religious faith. In his novel *Deliverance* (1970), the poet James Dickey uses a series of brutal murders, set in the wilderness, to force his readers to come to grips with issues of human freedom and social order. The most controversial southern novel of the postwar years, William Styron's *The Confessions of Nat Turner* (1967), is based on the bloody slave rebellion of the 19th century. Through a "meditation" on historical violence, Styron explores the psychological dimensions of southern racism.

Other contemporary writers, though they have not made violence the symbolic focus of their works, have nevertheless maintained a southern literary tradition in which violence seems to underlie regional life. In works as disparate as Shirley Ann Grau's *The Hard Blue Sky* (1958), William Goyen's *Arcadio* (1983), and Barry Hannah's *Ray* (1980), one sees a South in which social relations are usually tense and filled with potential violence. Larry McMurtry's Texas novels similarly present a southern world where violence occurs easily. Violence thus remains an important element in southern writing; many of the key issues associated with violence have remained fairly constant since the antebellum period.

Violence has also been important in another major expressive form in the South, folk song and popular music. During the 19th century, violence was a key element in the plots of the traditional ballads that were current in southern plain-folk communities. These songs, many brought from the Old World but some originating in this country, present a harsh view of human nature and society and keep the human potential for violence clearly in the minds of their hearers. Among the more popular topics are tales of jealous murderers, of faithless and violent lovers, and of cruel betrayals. With the rise of the commercial country music industry in the 1920s, many of these traditional ballads were committed to records by such important early recording artists as Vernon Dalhart and Buell Kazee. A few early commercial songs, written for recording, also made use of structures and motifs from traditional songs—particularly from murder ballads.

In more recent years, most white southern song has focused on the difficulties of life and love, rather than on violence as such, but violence has continued to have a role in country music. This has been particularly true of the balladlike songs of such performers as Johnny Cash, Marty Robbins, and Johnny Horton. In addition, many of the prison songs so popular in country music evoke violent situations from southern life, and several successful pieces, including Kenny Rogers's "Coward of the County," proclaim an ethic in which a readiness to fight is taken as a necessary virtue. Violence has also entered into popular white southern music in some rather distinctive ways. During the Vietnam War era, for example, Merle Haggard gave voice to a violent intolerance familiar to southern tradition in his immensely popular "Fightin' Side of Me." Country music has remained faithful to the view that violence is a necessary part of human life, a natural response to difficult situations. Such a view has long been important in expressive forms of white southern culture.

See also LITERATURE articles; MUSIC: Country Music

Dickson D. Bruce, Jr.
University of California, Irvine

Dickson D. Bruce, Jr., *Violence and Culture in the Antebellum South* (1979); John Hope Franklin, *The Militant South, 1800–1861* (1956); Sheldon Hackney, *American Historical Review* (February 1969); John Shelton Reed, *One South: An Ethnic Approach to Regional Culture* (1982); Jimmie N. Rogers, *The Country Music Message: All About Lovin' and Livin'* (1983).

Mexican Americans, Violence toward

Violence between Anglo-Americans and Mexicans or Mexican Americans has existed since their first contacts in the 1820s, and in the subsequent 160 years Mexican Americans have consistently been on the receiving end of that violence. Texas has continually been at the hub of violence as a meeting ground between the cultures of the southern and eastern United States and the Mexican Southwest. Violence resulted from the Anglo-Americans' conquest of Mexican territory, their taking of lands owned by Mexicans, and their economic subjugation of Mexican Americans. Although Anglo-American economic expansion has been the underlying cause for the ongoing conflict, the rationale for this domination and violence has relied heavily on particular American and southern cultural traditions as well as stereotypes of Mexicans to justify Anglo-American actions and assuage the resultant guilt.

Through the 1800s the mythic idea of Manifest Destiny strongly influenced Americans, and many adventurers coming from the southern and eastern United States felt it was their right to take and develop southwestern lands. They saw themselves as racially, culturally, spiritually, and technologically superior to the Mexicans. Southerners in particular could not understand or tolerate the Mexican's centralized government, authoritative Catholic religion, and undeveloped pastoral economy. Many eastern writers who had never been to Mexican territory wrote popular "dime novels" characterizing Mexicans as lazy, thieving, cowardly, and ignorant, but they were more complimentary of the "dark-eyed *senoritas*." These misinformed stereotypes, coupled with Manifest Destiny and the Mexican's mixed Indian-Spanish racial heritage, were used to create a convenient rationalization for capturing Mexican territory. This process culminated in the Texas War for Independence in the 1830s and the later war with Mexico in 1846, when the United States annexed Texas.

With the political and territorial conquest achieved, Anglo-Americans turned their attention to gaining private lands owned by the Mexican American inhabitants. Settlers and colonizers coming to the slave state of Texas were mostly from the southern United States. Their attitudes about blacks, as well as an economic class structure based on the inequality of races, set the pattern for relations with Mexican Americans. Although Mexicans were not enslaved, they were a conquered and colonized people, and the southern psychology of discrimination and economic exploitation that had applied to blacks easily transferred to the Mexican American. Many Mexican Americans who were now U.S. citizens and supposedly protected by the Treaty of Guadalupe Hidalgo were forced off their property by land-hungry Americans.

If land could not be had by legal means or trickery, then violence and intimidation would often be used by ranchers backed by local law officials, Texas Rangers, or the U.S. military. Frederick Law Olmsted, a northern traveler through Texas in 1853, told, for example, of Anglo-Americans forcing 20 Mexican families from their houses after the mere accusation that Mexicans were horse thieves.

Oral accounts until the early 1900s told of injured or slighted Anglo-Americans roaming the countryside killing any Mexican Americans they could find and then confiscating their property without repercussion from the law.

Many Mexican American *corridos*—ballads of south Texas in the late 1800s and early 1900s—dramatized such occurrences. The case of Gregorio Cortez was probably the most famous of these incidents, as were the *corridos* composed about him. Cortez, a Mexican American farmer, was sitting on his porch in Karnes County, Tex., in June of 1901, when an Anglo-Texan sheriff looking for a horse thief approached him. Existing stereotypes were that all Mexicans were horse thieves and potentially dangerous. A gun battle ensued in which the sheriff was shot, and Cortez was pursued over south Texas by several posses. During the chase many unsuspecting Mexican Americans, who happened to be in the wrong place at the wrong time, were killed by the posses ostensibly because they were members of Cortez's "gang." As it turned out most of the so-called accomplices were laborers walking to and from work through the brush country of the area. Cortez was later captured, but through his exploits he became the hero of many *corridos* and a symbol of resistance for Mexican Americans. After serving a prison term, he was acquitted and pardoned of the crime, which in effect was that of defending himself against Anglo-American economic control and stereotypes.

Since the days of Cortez, violence toward Mexican Americans has been covert but effective in perpetuating their economic subjugation and lower-class status. Stripped of their lands as a source of livelihood, Mexican Americans became a cheap labor pool used in building Texas agriculture and industry. Too often the rationale used by Texas businessmen and ranchers to justify this exploitation has gone back to the old stereotypes, that Mexicans are ignorant, irresponsible, lazy, and content with very little in life. When Mexican Americans have rebelled against these assumptions they have suffered violence and intimidation, the threat of deportation (even if they are American citizens), and economic reprisals.

From the early 1900s any Mexican American effort to unionize or strike in agriculture, mining, and industry, or to protect conditions, has been met with stiff resistance. Laborers were at the mercy of bad bosses, labor contractors, and immigration officials, and they were discriminated against in restaurants, businesses, and public places. As late as 1967 Mexican American efforts to protest and unionize met with violence in the Rio Grande Melon Strike when then governor John Connally sent Texas Rangers to the site.

Since the 1960s many changes have been made through the efforts of the Chicano movement, the Texas Farmworker Union, the United Farmworker Union, and especially through the rise of Mexican American political power. With more Mexican American public officials, the situation has improved, although violence and exploitation have not disappeared. Laborers are still intimidated, and police often shoot first and ask questions later when in the *barrios* (Mexican American neighborhoods). In small Texas towns unexplained killings still occur.

Anglo-American economic expansion in the Southwest has spawned much violence. The rationales—the American and southern cultural traditions and the stereotypes that perpetuate conflict and violence toward Mexican Americans—have been used and reused in different eras for basically the same purpose.

See also ETHNIC LIFE: / Mexicans

Dan W. Dickey
Austin, Texas

Frederick Law Olmsted, *Journey through Texas* (1857); Américo Paredes, *With His Pistol in His Hand: A Border Ballad and Its Hero* (1958); Cecil Robinson, *With the Ears of Strangers: The Mexican in American Literature* (1963).

Organized Crime

In both historical and fictional literature, the South has often been portrayed as a region characterized by crime and violence. The vigilante, the lyncher, the duelist, the race-rioter, and the frontier ruffian have played prominent roles in the region's history. Writers such as W. J. Cash and Sheldon Hackney have described the pervasiveness of violence in southern history, and many writers have concluded that crime and violence assume a distinctive pattern in the region's development. Despite the numerous accounts of a southern propensity for violence, one aspect of it that has received little attention is organized crime in the South.

The term *organized crime* lacks precise definition but is generally employed to describe the illegal enterprises and operations of those underworld organizations commonly called the Mafia, La Cosa Nostra, and the Mob. In the 20th century these organizations have dominated criminal activities such as gambling, prostitution, narcotics, bootlegging, and extortion. Centered in large metropolitan areas throughout the United States, these "families," as they are called, are headed by "bosses," or "godfathers." Each boss is a member of a national organized crime "commission," which dictates overall syndicate policy. Although most of these families are located in large cities in the Northeast, Midwest, and West, three have been assumed to operate from the southern cities of New Orleans, Miami, and Dallas.

According to the organized crime unit of the FBI, the first formal Mafia family in America was established in New Orleans during the Reconstruction era by Italian and Sicilian immigrants who used Mafia organizations in their native country as the basis for a Louisiana family. Recent scholarly studies have shown that this account is not supported by concrete evidence. The earliest publicity given to a Mafia organization in Louisiana came from widespread newspaper coverage of the 1890 assassination of New Orleans police chief David C. Hennessy. In 1891, 16 Italian and Sicilian residents of the city were tried and acquitted of the Hennessy murder. Inflamed by sensational newspaper accounts and stirred to action by anti-Italian remarks made by Mayor Joseph Shakespeare, a mob broke into the Orleans Parish prison and lynched 11 of the defendants. Many writers have described the Hennessy killing as the action of a Mafia vendetta, but an exhaustive study by Humbert Nelli uncovered no evidence to substantiate that version.

The first reliable evidence of organized crime in Louisiana came with the establishment of a slot machine empire in the state by New York mobster Frank Costello in 1935. Costello evidently made a deal with Senator Huey P. Long, whereby the state government would allow the machines in return for a share of the profits for the Long political machine. The Costello operation soon branched into "lotto" (the numbers game), bookmaking, and pinball machines. Shortly after the end of World War II, Costello, Meyer Lansky, the notorious financial wizard of the national syndicate, and Carlos Marcello, a Louisiana entrepeneur, opened two gambling casinos in Jefferson Parish. During the 1948–52 administration of Governor Earl K. Long, casino gambling, slot machines, pinball machines, handbook operations, and lotto flourished openly in the southern half of the state.

Since the early 1950s Carlos Marcello has been reputed to control organized crime in Louisiana and in neighboring states. According to such sources as the Metropolitan Crime Commission of Greater New Orleans and Senator Estes Kefauver's committee on organized crime, Marcello heads an organized criminal empire that takes in almost $1 billion annually from vice, theft, blackmail, extortion, robbery, and political graft. After intensive investigation by the Justice Department under Attorney General Robert Kennedy, Marcello in 1962 was forcibly deported to Guatemala because he had never become a naturalized citizen. Within a few months, Marcello returned to Louisiana and for many years has managed to evade the concerted efforts of law enforcement agencies to uncover concrete evidence of his criminal activities. He did serve a brief sentence in a federal penitentiary for assaulting an FBI agent in 1967, and in 1981 he was convicted of attempting to bribe a federal judge and of conspiracy to influence federal officials. He is currently serving a lengthy term in a federal penitentiary. Despite the many allegations about Marcello's Mafia family in Louisiana, virtually nothing is known about the organization, and little evidence has been produced to support those allegations.

In Florida, Santo Trafficante, Jr., reputedly took over leadership of a Mafia family after his father died in 1954. Originally headquartered in Tampa, the syndicate moved to Miami in the late 1960s. Trafficante reportedly served as the coordinator of Meyer Lansky's casino gambling and wide-open vice, which flourished in Havana during the 1952–59 regime of Cuban dictator Fulgencio Batista. When Fidel Castro came to power in 1959, he jailed Trafficante and closed down the mob's operations on the island. In retaliation, Trafficante, along with Chicago Mafia boss Sam Giancana, conspired with the CIA in several futile attempts to assassinate Castro. Today, the Trafficante organization supposedly dominates the lucrative narcotics trade between Latin America and Florida and is currently engaged in a struggle with Latin American narcotics traffickers.

Little is known about the Dallas family of Joseph Civello. Some accounts depict it as an independent Mafia family; others describe it as the Texas arm of the Marcello empire. Civello allegedly controls illegal vice in Texas and serves as a conduit for communications among various Mafia families. Civello came most prominently into the news when he was identified as one of the 57 mobsters who attended the infamous Appalachian meeting at the upstate New York home of organized crime figure Joseph Barbera, Sr., on 14 November 1957.

Probably the best-known individual in the history of organized crime in the South was Jacob Rubenstein, better known as Jack Ruby. Born in Chicago in 1911, Ruby began his career in the Al Capone organization. He moved to Dallas in 1947, where he joined the Civello organization. Ruby operated several nightclubs, or "striptease joints," handled bookmaking operations and prostitution, and had close contacts with the Dallas police. In 1959 Ruby visited the Havana prison where Santo Trafficante was incarcerated, and he assisted in smuggling arms and supplies to anti-Castro guerrilla fighters in Cuba. Ruby had frequent contacts with close associates of Teamsters union boss Jimmy Hoffa, and he communicated with members of the Civello, Marcello, and Trafficante organizations. During the month prior to the assassination of President John F. Kennedy, he made numerous long-distance telephone calls to known mobsters. When Kennedy was assassinated, Ruby was seen at Dallas police headquarters, where Kennedy's accused assassin, Lee Harvey Oswald, was held in custody. On the morning of 24 November 1963 Ruby shot and killed Oswald in the basement of police headquarters. Convicted of the Oswald killing, Ruby spent the next three years in a Dallas jail. He died in January 1967.

In 1979 the Select Committee on Assassinations of the U.S. House of Representatives issued its final report on the Kennedy assassination, and it concluded that either Marcello or Trafficante may have conspired to kill the president. Kennedy's war on organized crime, his failure to eliminate Castro, and his sexual intimacy with Judith Exner, the girlfriend of Sam Giancana, provided possible motives. The committee found evidence that both Marcello and Trafficante had expressed the desire to be rid of Kennedy and that Lee Harvey Oswald's uncle, as well as several of the people with whom he associated during his stay in New Orleans in 1963, had connections with the Marcello family. The committee, however, could not furnish reliable proof of its speculations.

The subject of organized crime in the South has received scant attention from historians and other scholars. Much of the available material on the subject contains a considerable amount of sensationalism, speculation, and unfounded accusations. Because of its highly controversial nature, organized crime has attracted the attention of journalists and popular writers whose works lack documentation. The reports and studies of congressional committees and government agencies likewise fail to employ the proper techniques of historical inquiry. Much more research into the topic is necessary before an accurate and responsible history of organized crime in the South is possible.

See also ETHNIC LIFE: Caribbean Influence; / Italians

Michael L. Kurtz
Southeastern Louisiana University

G. Robert Blakely and Richard N. Billings, *The Plot to Kill the President* (1981); Michael L. Kurtz, *Louisiana History* (Fall 1983); Humbert S. Nelli, *The Business of Crime: Italians and Syndicate Crime in the United States* (1976); U.S. Congress, House of Representatives, *Investigation of the Assassination of President John F. Kennedy: Hearings Before the Select Committee on Assassinations of the U.S. House of Representatives* (1978–79); U.S. Congress, Senate, *Report on the Select Committee to Investigate Organized Crime in Interstate Commerce* (1951).

Outlaw-Heroes

Southern history and legend have been marked by a procession of outlaws whose illegal behavior in the service of some noble cause or ideal has elevated them to heroic status. Most southern outlaws, like the Harpe brothers who wantonly robbed and murdered across the frontier South, were notorious rather than heroic. But there have always been southern outlaws who fit E. J. Hobsbawm's definition of "social bandits": those who are forced to break the law to avenge a wrong or to defend their honor, family, or community from some oppressive power or circumstance. From the Regulators of colonial South Carolina (1767–69), the first organized vigilantes in America, to Luke and Bo Duke of the *Dukes of Hazzard*, "good old boy" lawbreakers in one of the most popular television programs of the 1980s, honorable outlaws have been celebrated in southern folklore, popular culture, and high arts. Other regions and nations have celebrated them as well.

Southerners have enshrined a wide range of outlaw-heroes in myth and legend. The outlaws' diversity reflects the complexity of a region that embraces the extremes of colonial Virginia and frontier Texas, black and white, planter and mountaineer, yeoman and slave. In 1676 Nathaniel Bacon achieved heroic status by leading an illegal armed rebellion against the legitimate but unresponsive government of Virginia. The South Carolina Regulators stepped outside the law with popular support to control the backcountry in the 1760s. A significant number of southern outlaw-heroes were spawned and found their justification in the events of the Civil War and Reconstruction. In the white southern mind and myth, and eventually in the mythology of other regions, southerners were driven into outlawry by rapacious Yankee armies, corrupt Radical Republican politicians, predatory carpetbaggers, and vindictive former slaves. Guerrilla fighter and bank robber Jesse James protected southern women and children in frontier Missouri from violent northern persecution during the war. For years afterward he protected them from usurious banks and railroads. Similarly, the Ku Klux Klan and other white vigilante/terrorist groups were active in the South during Reconstruction. Harriet Tubman and John Brown were outlaw-heroes to black southerners and abolitionists for their attempts to free slaves.

In the late 19th century the Hatfields and McCoys were two of the well-known feuding mountain clans who ignored points of law and fought over issues of honor and family loyalty. Morris Slater ("Railroad Bill"), the legendary black Robin Hood of Alabama, fought the law and stole for his poverty-stricken people until he was cut down in 1896. During the Depression of the 1930s in the Southwest, Bonnie Parker and Clyde Barrow, "Pretty Boy" Floyd, and other rural outlaws stole from the rich and gave to the poor in the tradition of Jesse James. Junior Johnson was a champion stock car racer in the 1960s who learned his driving skills while running moonshine in the hills of North Carolina, evading the meddling federal agents who put his daddy in jail. Johnson was compared to "Robin Hood or Jesse James" and was called the "last American hero" by Virginia-born writer Tom Wolfe. Since the early 1970s southern actor Burt Reynolds has appeared in a long series of popular movies with Dixie settings in which he has played lovable outlaws who fought corrupt sheriffs, transported illegal beer, and robbed the gas stations of a heartless oil corporation. In the early 1980s cousins Luke and Bo Duke broke the law each week in their stock car "General Lee" while untangling themselves and their down-home kin from the corrupt operations of the judiciary and police in their mythical southern county.

The outlaw-hero's marginal status has defined the limits of acceptable behavior within southern society. He has provided traditional southern culture with a safety valve: honorable models for rebellion. Moreover, southern outlaw-heroes have reflected and reconciled what W. J. Cash called the "social schizophrenia" of the southern character: intense individualism versus a deep sense of responsibility for others; "hedonism" versus "puritanism"; unrestrained violence versus a gentlemanly code of conduct; wanderlust versus a profound sense of place and tradition. Nowhere has this "split" psyche been more apparent than in the southern outlaw-hero and nowhere have these contradictions been so well reconciled. The outlaw-hero is the single figure who can engage with impunity in explosive, illegal behavior because it is justified by some noble purpose.

There has never been unanimity regarding individual outlaw-heroes, especially when race is involved. The knights of the Ku Klux Klan have always had both white and black detractors in the South. And the status of many outlaw-heroes has varied over time. Klansmen enjoyed less heroic status during the "Second Reconstruction" of the 1960s than they had in earlier eras. The outlaw-heroes of the southern black and Mexican American fit the standard southern pattern except that they were seen as mere badmen by the white culture they fought. The 1831 slave revolt led by Nat Turner and the violent struggles of Gregorio Cortez with Texas lawmen were justified in the eyes of their people on the familiar basis of resisting legal but oppressive forces: the cruelties of slavery in Virginia and the uneven hand of justice in the Rio Grande Valley. In some cases no justification was offered for black outlaw-heroes such as the bullying badmen in black folksongs: Stackolee, John Hardy, the Bully of the Town. Their tough defiance and ability to survive in a hostile white world were the stuff of black heroism with no need for moral justification.

There has been a fine line in southern culture between a rebellious hero celebrated for his uninhibited vitality and the true outlaw-hero who is completely beyond the law. Southern frontier heroes like Davy Crockett and Jim Bowie were widely celebrated in folklore and popular southwestern humor for behavior that was often violent and illegal, but they were not generally considered outlaws. Although the southern gentleman who skirted the law to duel for his honor was sometimes seen as a heroic figure representing the best of his culture, this did not make him an outlaw. Heroic Confederate military figures such as Robert E. Lee and Stonewall Jackson were perhaps outlaws in the eyes of the North, but not to southerners. Confederate Partisan Rangers John Hunt Morgan, John Singleton Mosby, and William Clarke Quantrill owed their heroic status to dashing guerilla warfare behind enemy lines. However, only Jesse James and a few other southern guerillas clearly crossed over the line to "outlaw-hero" status by robbing banks and railroads long after the war had ended.

Since the beginnings of commercial country music in the South in the 1920s, some of its most popular figures have celebrated rebellious, rambling behavior in their songs. Much of the popularity and heroic status of Jimmie Rodgers, Hank Williams, Johnny Cash, and Merle Haggard have derived from their legendary participation in this lifestyle. The same was true for southern rockabilly rebels Elvis Presley and Jerry Lee Lewis. In the 1970s Texans Willie Nelson and Waylon Jennings were marketed with great success as "outlaw" country musicians because of their spirited rebellion against straight-laced Nashville's musical and social norms. Yet none of these were traditional outlaw-heroes driven beyond the law. Rather they were rebel-heroes celebrated for their ability to pursue an independent lifestyle while maintaining, like the outlaw-hero, some allegiance to church, home, and mother. Ironically, all these country musicians have used the image of the free-spirited western cowboy to suggest their rugged independence. Despite country music's southern lineage, its performers have often rejected the "hillbilly" image in favor of western motifs that provide more positive and widely accepted images of heroism and rebellion.

A related regional borrowing occurred in the century following the Civil War when the western hero with his personal "code" that transcended the law began to bear a striking resemblance to the southern outlaw-hero with his code of honor. Western heroes of all kinds were fashioned out of real and fictional southerners with outlaw qualities: guerrilla-bandit Jesse James, cowboy-vigilante "The Virginian," farmhand-gunfighter Shane. When such western heroes took the law into their own hands they did it with the southern outlaw-hero's sense of honor and purpose—usually to aid a community besieged by savage forces.

There was a historical basis for this western adaptation of southern characters and traditions; Texas's cowboys and Missouri's outlaws were largely southern in origin and worldview. An equally important reason for this borrowing was the climate of the post–Civil War era. The relatively homogeneous South with its romantic myths of a gracious, agricultural past and noble Anglo-Saxon heroes (outlaws and otherwise), exerted a strong pull on a nation fearful of urbanization, industrialization, and immigration. The nation turned readily to western heroes who embodied traditional qualities of the southern outlaw-hero in a frontier setting free of urbanization and immigration, yet also free of controversial factors associated with the South such as slavery, aristocracy, and defeat.

Regardless of an outlaw-hero's morality as judged by outsiders, or the historical accuracy of the legends surrounding him, glorified "social bandits" like England's Robin Hood have long served significant psychological, sociological, and mythological functions for those who feel frustrated, victimized, and powerless. Southern outlaw-heroes who have demonstrated the continuing utility of the "social bandit" in this century by becoming heroes of national and international proportion include Jesse James, Bonnie and Clyde, Burt Reynolds's outlaw persona, and the fictitious Dukes of Hazzard. These southern outlaw-heroes have a universal appeal in a tumultuous century because they embody the comforting values of a traditional culture yet have the strength and courage to break the law and successfully rebel against the injustices of life.

See also BLACK LIFE: / Turner, Nat; FOLKLIFE: / Murder Legends; Wagner, Kinnie; HISTORY AND MANNERS: / Crockett, Davy; MEDIA: / Reynolds, Burt; MUSIC: / Lewis, Jerry Lee; Nelson, Willie; Presley, Elvis; Rodgers, Jimmie; Williams, Hank; RECREATION: / Johnson, Junior

George B. Ward
Texas State Historical Association

Roger D. Abrahams, *Deep Down in the Jungle: Negro Narrative Fiction from the Streets of Philadelphia* (1970); W. J. Cash, *The Mind of the South* (1941); David Brion Davis, *American Quarterly* (Summer 1954); Hugh Davis Graham and Ted Robert Gurr, eds., *Violence in America: Historical and Comparative Perspectives* (1969); E. J. Hobsbawm, *Primitive Rebels* (1965); John A. Lomax and Alan Lomax, *Folksong U.S.A.* (1947); William A. Settle, Jr., *Jesse James Was His Name* (1966); Tom Wolfe, *The Kandy-Kolored Tangerine-Flake Streamline Baby* (1965).

Political Violence

No other major section of the country can match the South's record of violence, political and otherwise. Southern political violence, like organized violence nationally, has featured repression by social and political elites of those who threatened (or were perceived to threaten) their control. The rare colonial insurrections—Bacon's Rebellion in Virginia (1675–76) and Culpepper's Rebellion in North Carolina (1677–78)—were in the main middle-class or upper-class revolts against ruling factions in their respective colonies and involved very little bloodshed. The Regulator movements of North and South Carolina in the 1760s and 1770s arose out of frontier conditions in the backcountry. The North Carolina movement sought to force the colonial authorities in the east to provide more responsible government in the west. The rebels were defeated on the battlefield of Alamance in 1771, after which six of their leaders were hanged. The South Carolina Regulators were vigilantes organized to suppress anarchy and force the colonial authorities in Charleston to bring government to the frontier. Neither movement aimed seriously to modify the structure of colonial government, much less to overthrow it.

In fact, many backcountry settlers felt a greater kinship with England after 1775 than with the eastern planters who led the movement for independence. Organized North Carolina Loyalists were decisively defeated at the battle of Moore's Creek Bridge in 1776, but partisan warfare raged between Whigs and Tories for several years in some interior districts of the Carolinas and Georgia.

Antebellum vigilantism, aimed at actual or suspected slave insurrections and their white instigators, had not been political, strictly speaking. But the goal of keeping the slaves in subjection, by force if necessary, and the day-to-day requirements of slave discipline conditioned southerners to the use of force as a regular instrument of policy. Even greater discord followed in the wake of southern secession in 1861. Unionist sentiment existed in varying measure throughout the South, reflected in active or passive opposition to the Confederacy. It was strongest in the border states and in the mountain areas of Virginia, North Carolina, Tennessee, Georgia, Alabama, and Arkansas. Opinion was not uniform in these regions, however, and warfare of family against family, even brother against brother, was not unknown. Such hostilities engendered bitterness that lasted for many years, sometimes in the form of blood feuds.

These wartime differences were translated after the war into political party divisions: former Unionists became Republicans, and ex-Confederates affiliated with the Conservative or Democratic party. Federal Reconstruction policy introduced the Republican party to the South in 1867 as the champion of Unionism, black freedom, and civil rights. Regional opposition to these goals drew heavily on prewar precedents.

It was but a short step from the militia musters and the slave patrols of the 1850s to Ku Klux Klans, and the so-called home guards, white leagues, and red-shirt clubs of the Reconstruction era. All were designed to enforce white supremacy. For more than a decade after 1865, therefore, white southerners of a certain age and disposition felt it their duty and privilege to continue the twin struggles against Unionism and for white supremacy, now joined as a crusade against the "Black Republican" party. The crusade took several forms. All were more or less inspired, organized, and led by the middle and upper classes, appearances sometimes to the contrary notwithstanding.

The most spectacular form of resistance, but the least effective in the long run, was the midnight raiding by the Ku Klux Klan and its kindred organizations. Formed in Tennessee in 1866, the Klan spread throughout the South in the spring of 1868 as congressional Reconstruction policies went into effect. It killed, flogged, and intimidated hosts of black and white Republicans in the areas where it flourished, but by 1872 it was put down by a combination of state and federal judicial and military action. The Klan helped to impeach and remove Governor William W. Holden of North Carolina, but it failed to end Reconstruction in any state.

Probably the most successful form of political violence was the urban riot. Seventy-eight have been counted for the years 1865 through 1876 in cities like Memphis and New Orleans and in villages like Camilla, Ga., and Clinton, Miss. Generally planned in advance, they often resulted in the death or banishment of Republican leaders of both races and the demoralization of their followers. Such riots occurred throughout the Reconstruction period and sporadically afterward, the last of them in Wilmington, N.C., in 1898 and Atlanta in 1906.

Closely related to the urban riots were the activities of the white league, red-shirt club, and other paramilitary groups that dispensed with the bizarre disguises of the Ku Klux Klan and operated in broad daylight. They rode about before elections, breaking up Republican meetings and intimidating Republican candidates and voters. Georgians pioneered this tactic in 1870, and it was repeated with increasing sophistication throughout the Deep South from 1874 to 1876. With the urban riots, it was largely responsible for bringing southern Reconstruction to a close by 1877.

From the 1870s to the 1890s southern Democrats controlled their respective states by means of honest electoral victories (where possible) and partial disfranchisement, fraud, and violence (where necessary). Republicans were permitted to vote and to elect candidates in the mountains and the black belts, but only as long as they did not threaten statewide Democratic control. In the 1890s, after a variety of agrarian insurgent movements, sometimes featuring coalitions with Republicans, Democrats began more systematically to disfranchise their opponents through constitutional or legislative action. Henceforth, the law would accomplish peacefully what riots and red shirt campaigns had done through threats and violence. The generation after 1890 saw the climax not only of black disfranchisement but of lynching and enforced racial segregation as well.

The violence of the second Ku Klux Klan in the 1920s was not primarily political, and except for such isolated events as the assassinations of Governor William Goebel of Kentucky in 1900 and Senator Huey P. Long of Louisiana in 1935, substantial political violence did not return until the advent of the civil rights movement, or Second Reconstruction, of the 1950s and 1960s. The civil rights laws of 1957–64, and especially the Voting Rights Act of 1965, helped return millions of black voters to the polls after the lapse of three generations.

The civil rights movement used nonviolent protest as a means of winning public opinion throughout the country to peaceful change. Most of the violence that came was directed by whites against the desegregation of schools, businesses, and public facilities rather than the voting booth. It was not, therefore, specifically political until Martin Luther King, Jr., and his colleagues shifted their emphasis in 1964 to black voter registration. The killing of Michael Schwerner, Andrew Goodman, and James Chaney in the registration drive in Mississippi and other acts of violence in 1964 hastened congressional passage of the Voting Rights Act the following year.

In 1979 members of the Ku Klux Klan and the American Nazi party shot and killed five Communist Worker's party demonstrators at Greensboro, N.C. Unlike most of the political violence since the Civil War, this event had little or no direct racial bearing; the perpetrators and the victims were all white. The incident dramatized the enmity that developed after World War II between political fringe groups of the far left and right. The enmity was most volatile in the South, where violence-prone Klansmen and Nazis were most in evidence.

The reasons for the South's affinity for violence are not easy to pinpoint with assurance, but surely racial dissension has played a central role. So too, perhaps, has the region's rural, scattered population, which traditionally encouraged hunting, self-protection, private settlement of grievances, and attendant carrying of weapons. Politically, the South has experienced more bitter conflict, arising from deep racial and class divisions, than any other section of the country. Even when these conditions change and internal differences abate, old cultural patterns retain a life of their own.

See also BLACK LIFE: Freedom Movement, Black; / King, Martin Luther, Jr.; HISTORY AND MANNERS: Reconstruction; LAW: Civil Rights Movement; SOCIAL CLASS: Communism

Allen W. Trelease
University of North Carolina
at Greensboro

Richard Maxwell Brown, *Strain of Violence: Historical Studies of American Violence and Vigilantism* (1975); William Gillette, *Retreat from Reconstruction, 1869–1879* (1979); Hugh Davis Graham and Ted Robert Gurr, eds., *Violence in America: Historical and Comparative Perspectives* (1969); Steven F. Lawson, *Black Ballots: Voting Rights in the South, 1944–1969* (1976); Allen W. Trelease, *White Terror: The Ku Klux Klan Conspiracy and Southern Reconstruction* (1971); Wilcomb E. Washburn, *The Governor and the Rebel: A History of Bacon's Rebellion in Virginia* (1957); C. Vann Woodward, *The Strange Career of Jim Crow* (1955; 3d rev. ed., 1974).

Prisons

American penitentiaries developed in two distinct phases, and southern states participated in both. Virginia, Kentucky, Maryland, and Georgia built prisons before 1820, and between 1829 and 1842 new or newly reorganized institutions were established in Maryland, Tennessee, Georgia, Louisiana, Missouri, Mississippi, and Alabama. Only the Carolinas and Florida resisted the penitentiary before the Civil War.

Southerners fiercely debated the justice and utility of the penitentiary throughout the antebellum era. Some citizens and legislators argued that the institution constituted an essential part of any enlightened government, whereas other southerners warned that the penitentiary posed a real and direct threat to freedom and republican government. Advocates of the institution believed that the law would be more effective if punishment was less physically brutal; opponents of the institution believed that locking men up out of public sight to "reform" them was a farce and a dangerous precedent. They preferred that their states adhere to the older methods of punishment: fines, branding, imprisonment in local jails, or hanging. In the only two referenda on the penitentiary—in Alabama in 1834 and in North Carolina in 1846—southern voters expressed overwhelming opposition to the institution, but southern states nonetheless created one penitentiary after another. Virtually no reformers championed the cause of penal innovation; rather, obscure state legislators took it upon themselves to keep the South abreast of "progress" made in the rest of the Anglo-American world. The new institutions they created closely resembled one another and their northern counterparts.

Most of the prisoners in these antebellum southern prisons were white men, disproportionately from cities, and of immigrant background. Almost no women received penitentiary terms. After 1818 only Louisiana consistently sentenced slaves to prison. Most states of the Deep South incarcerated exceedingly few free blacks in their prisons, but Virginia and Maryland sent many free blacks to their penitentiaries. Neither state was happy with this situation, however, and both experimented with ways to avoid imprisoning free blacks—including selling them into slavery or leasing them to outside contractors.

Southern governments were not enthusiastic about spending money for any prisoners and always sought ways to make prisons pay for themselves. Pressure mounted for the inmates to be leased to businessmen to make shoes, pails, wagons, and other articles, and leasing was instituted in Alabama, Texas, Kentucky, Missouri, and Louisiana. Often free workers demanded that convict labor be kept out of competition with "honest workmen."

Antebellum southern prisons were not substantially different from northern prisons. Most people in both regions had little faith in reformation, and prison officials North and South dealt out harsh physical punishment, supplied poor food, spent most of their energies on financial matters, became entangled in political patronage, and let contractors or lessees assume real control of the prisons.

The similarity between northern and southern prisons, however, abruptly disappeared with the Civil War and emancipation. Virtually all southern prisons were destroyed or badly damaged in the war, and southern governments had few resources with which to rebuild them. Southerners had become accustomed to the idea of centralized state penal institutions, but they now confronted a radically different situation: postwar prisons would no longer be reserved primarily for white men. Four million exslaves were now liable for incarceration, and the number of defendants who received penitentiary sentences soon outstripped even ambitious attempts by state officials to build penitentiaries. Many southern states, often with reluctance, turned to leasing convicts to work outside the prison walls. More than 9 of 10 prisoners were black men, most of them in their early twenties, most of them convicted of the lesser degrees of larceny. Many of them died in prison, and nearly all were mistreated.

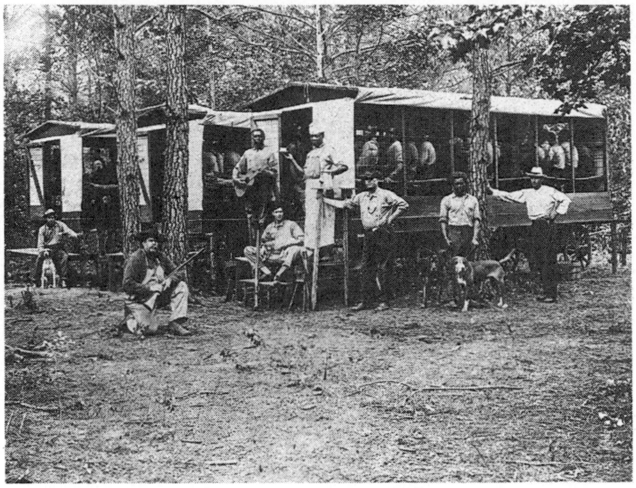

Convict labor chain gang, North Carolina, 1910

No single political group in the postwar South bore sole responsibility for inaugurating the convict-lease system—although the Democrats reaped most of its benefits. Black and white politicians, Republicans and Democrats, tolerated the system. Within 15 years after the Civil War all the ex-Confederate states allowed businessmen to submit bids for the labor of the state's felons.

In the late 1860s and early 1870s, a time of experimentation, leases ran for relatively short periods and convicts worked primarily as agricultural and railroad laborers. Railroad work on an expanded scale absorbed most of the penal labor of virtually every state in the 1870s. In the 1880s and 1890s convicts became increasingly concentrated in mining, especially in the states leasing the largest number of convicts: Alabama, Georgia, Florida, and Tennessee.

The lease system grew not only out of the inertia of the Old South but also the demands of the expanding capitalist system of Gilded Age America. On railroads and then in mines, the convict-lease system served as the only labor force capitalists investing in the South knew they could count on to penetrate swamps and primitive mines. Indeed, as businessmen and officeholders haggled over convict leases, widespread corruption grew up around the system.

Because the New South had so few industries, because those industries were concentrated in relatively small areas, because the products of those industries (especially coal) were so crucial to the growth of the southern economy, and because southern labor was relatively unorganized, convict labor undermined the wage scale and working conditions of entire southern industries. In the early 1890s, after 20 years of suffering at the hands of the convict-lease system, miners in Tennessee and Alabama launched large-scale revolts. Their opposition was joined with that from residents of communities where lessees established camps, cynical politicians of opposition parties, and people of conscience (such as Julia Tutwiler and George Washington Cable) who opposed the lease because it offended their sense of justice.

These protests helped bring the convict-lease system to a very gradual end. Although some southern states—Virginia, Texas, Tennessee, Kentucky, and Missouri—had long used manufacturing prisons in addition to the lease system, as late as 1890 the majority of southern convicts passed their sentences in convict camps run by absentee businessmen. Only three southern states (Mississippi, Tennessee, and Louisiana) completely abolished the convict-lease system before the turn of the century. Even those states that did end the lease system did not build new penitentiaries. Inmates were moved to state-run prison farms, which were considered more healthy and more secure than scattered convict camps. Different classes of prisoners were separated from one another and death rates declined. Reformers continued to agitate for and gradually established juvenile reformatories, as well as prison schools, libraries, and commutation laws. Yet scandals continued to surface throughout the 20th century, highlighting the brutality and corruption of southern prisons.

The South today keeps a far higher percentage of its population in prison than any other part of the country. Although crime rates in the South generally fall below the national average, the region continues to build new prisons at a faster pace than the rest of the United States. The prisons already in operation are usually crowded far beyond their designed capacity. As has been the case since the first decade after the Civil War, blacks make up a disproportionately large percentage of the inmate population in the region and are sentenced for considerably longer terms than their white counterparts. Most southern states spend far less than the national average per convict; training and rehabilitation programs, as well as prison employees, receive only about two-thirds as much funding in the South as in the nation as a whole.

Cultural predispositions lie behind the South's bleak penal history. Southerners have generally held a less optimistic view of human nature than many other Americans and thus have placed less faith in the state in general and "reformatory" institutions in particular. Southerners have tended to adhere to the stern retributive justice of the Old Testament rather than the more compassionate ideals of the New Testament. Southerners in political power long operated in a one-party system that allowed penal corruption and neglect to go unchallenged by other parties. The history of prisons in the South suggests that southern culture is intimately linked with the often tragic history of southern class and race relations.

See also LAW: Criminal Justice; Criminal Law

Edward L. Ayers
University of Virginia

Edward L. Ayers, *Vengeance and Justice: Crime and Punishment in the 19th-Century American South* (1984); *Southern Exposure* (Winter 1978) (special issue on prisons); Hilda Jane Zimmerman, "Penal Systems and Penal Reform in the South since the Civil War" (Ph.D. dissertation, University of North Carolina at Chapel Hill, 1947).

Race Riots

In antebellum times, race riots were called "slave revolts" or "slave insurrections," but even then racial violence was not limited to the South. During the Civil War, draft and labor riots between the races broke out in several northern cities. The most dramatic took place in New York City in mid-July 1863. It raged for five days, and estimates of those killed ranged up to 1,200.

Referring to such violence as a "riot" is not only incomplete but often misleading. Some of the traumatic episodes in the South, as well as the North, were largely one-sided, white massacres of defenseless blacks with a macabre combination of carnage and carnival. *Webster's New Collegiate Dictionary* defines massacre as the killing of a number "of . . . human beings under circumstances of atrocity or cruelty." The terms *pogrom* or *race war* could logically be applied as well.

Beginning with Reconstruction and continuing until the turn of the 20th century, race riots stand out as phenomena of the New South, but they reflect features of the region that go back to the Old South and continue into the 20th century. One cause for racial violence was political; only in the South was the political system openly dependent upon white supremacy. States with black belts—contiguous counties with population ratios of 40 percent black or more—were in constant political turmoil. It was essentially a struggle among white men over who would rule: a white minority (Democrats) was trying to maintain dominance over another white minority (Republicans) who controlled the formidable black voting bloc.

Sometimes economic grievances, rather than partisan politics, led to race riots. This was true of the racial massacre that occurred at Memphis on 1 and 2 May 1866, when whites went on a rampage and tried to destroy the new black community. When peace was restored, two whites and 46 blacks had been slain. The racism of poor whites was far more virulent than that of the wealthier, more conservative white supremacists. After Appomattox, the poor whites found themselves in competition with blacks for the limited economic opportunities in the South. They were perfect tools for the race-baiting political demagogues, who often goaded them into open acts of passion and violence. Racism seemed the only thing poor whites had in common with the landlord and/or planter-merchants.

On 30 July 1866 New Orleans was the scene of the first significant political race riot. Here a mob—supported by the police—assaulted a black suffrage convention. When the smoke cleared, 37 blacks and three of their white supporters had lost their lives. Then between 1868 and 1876, race riots erupted in Pine Bluff, Ark., in the state of Louisiana at Colfax, Opelousas, Coushatta, and again in New Orleans in 1874. Others broke out at Meridian, Vicksburg, and Yazoo City, Miss. In 1876 racial violence flared in South Carolina, a state with a population ratio that exceeded four blacks to each white. In the town of Hamburg an episode escalated into a pitched battle, as 200 whites imported heavy arms and munitions and massacred blacks. Hostilities persisted intermittently throughout the presidential election of 1876.

The compromise of 2 March 1877 and President Hayes's inauguration two days later marked the end of the Reconstruction era. Blacks continued to vote and to hold office, though, and political race riots continued. In 1883 the city of Danville, Va., was the scene of political violence. Here the Democrats exploited the passions of the poor whites with a cry for white supremacy and white solidarity and instigated an election-eve riot on "the color-line issue" to insure the triumph of their party in the legislature.

The Populist revolt of the 1890s presented the South with its greatest challenge since Reconstruction. In some places, the rise of the Populist party in the South divided the white vote to such an extent that the black vote became the balance of power. The revival of the race issue was the Bourbons's answer to this threat. Again the demagogues pulled out their "stock themes" and appealed to the passions of poor whites to do the dirty work of politics for the sake of party unity, white solidarity, and white supremacy. Political riots were to continue until total black disenfranchisement became a fait accompli.

In 1890 Mississippi invented the standard device for voiding the Constitution on a racial basis—an "understanding clause," which required interpretation of written material in addition to literacy as a prerequisite for voting. A modified version of the Mississippi formula was adopted in 1895 by South Carolina. Violence erupted when elitist white factions sought to enforce South Carolina's "grandfather clause," which made it illegal to vote if your grandfather had not voted, thus eliminating descendants of slaves.

The Phoenix riot of November 1898 occurred in the upcountry of South Carolina. At a crossroads country store in the Phoenix community in Greenwood County, and in neighboring communities, election-day riots resulted in the death of one white man and the execution of at least 12 blacks. Included among the wounded were three members of one of the most influential white families, the Tolberts (leading Republican and federal officeholders), who were forced to flee the violence.

The Wilmington, N.C., race riot in 1898 was a watershed; race riots after this were no longer distinctive southern events. During the first decade of the 20th century, riots broke out in the South at New Orleans in 1900 and at Atlanta in 1906. In the North riots occurred at New York in 1900; Springfield, Ohio, in 1904; Greenburg, Ind., in 1906; and Springfield, Ill., in 1908. The worst of these exploded in Atlanta without warning after the Atlanta *Journal* had for months carried on a "nigger-baiting" gubernatorial campaign with Hoke Smith and former Populist Tom Watson on one side and Clark Howell and the regular Democrats on the other. Anarchy reigned for four days.

Race riots in East St. Louis, Ill., and Houston, Tex., in 1917, were the prelude to the period dubbed the "Red Summer." James Weldon Johnson used that name to describe the race riots that bloodied the streets of more than 20 towns and cities—North and South—in the six-month period from April to early October 1919. The riots of the Red Summer first struck at Charleston, S.C., and were followed by those at Longview, Tex.; Washington, D.C.; Omaha, Neb.; Knoxville, Tenn.; and Chester, Pa. The most violent ones occurred at Elaine, Ark., and in Chicago and could be classified as a pogrom and a race war, respectively. Finally, the Tulsa race riot of 1921 was the most serious of the post–World War I era. It had the ingredients of a race war, which propelled this conflict into a new dimension. The city's black community suffered a disaster.

The interim between the Tulsa riot and World War II marked a transitional era from the old-style to the new-style riot. The latter, observed August Meier and Elliot M. Rudwick, "first appeared in Harlem in 1935 and Detroit in 1943, where black attacks were mainly directed against white property rather than white people." They were more likely to occur in the North than in the South. The ghetto riots of the 1960s had no American precedent, and they profoundly shocked both white and black citizens. Beginning in 1964, urban riots swept the Chicago suburb of Dixmoor, Harlem in New York City, the Bedford-Stuyvesant section of Brooklyn, Rochester, Philadelphia, and the New Jersey cities of Jersey City, Elizabeth, and Paterson. "Burn, baby, burn!" was the exultant cry first heard in Watts, the black ghetto of Los Angeles. The following summer witnessed similar chaos in New York, in Cleveland's Hough section, and in Chicago. In 1967 still more violence occurred in Tampa, Cincinnati, and Atlanta, with the most serious riots in Detroit and Newark, where in six days of rioting, 26 were killed and 1,500 were injured, and damage reached $30 million. In April 1968 Dr. Martin Luther King, Jr., was assassinated in Memphis, and this tragedy triggered a new wave of burning and looting in more than a hundred cities.

Urban violence subsided after the riots triggered by the King assassination, yet many of the underlying causes remained at the end of the 1970s. The Miami riot of May 1980 and the renewal of the turbulence there in 1982 demonstrated that the elements that created ghetto riots still exist. Massive racial violence should no longer be viewed, though, as either a southern phenomenon or a northern urban problem, but as a distinct national one.

See also BLACK LIFE: Lynching; Race Relations; MYTHIC SOUTH: Racial Attitudes

H. Leon Prather
Tennessee State University

Scott Ellsworth, *Death in a Promised Land: The Tulsa Race Riot of 1921* (1982); H. Leon Prather, *We Have Taken a City: Wilmington Racial Massacre and Coup of 1898* (1984); Elliot M. Rudwick, *Race War at East St. Louis, July 2, 1917* (1972); William M. Tuttle, Jr., *Race Riot: Chicago in the Red Summer of 1919* (1974).

Southwestern Violence

The roots of the apparently casual mayhem in the wild West can be found in the violence-prone ethic of Texas and the South, specifically in the history of the Scotch-Irish who immigrated to America in the 18th century. Conditioned to border war by generations of fighting first the English across the Tweed and then, as colonists in the province of Ulster, the turbulent Irish, by 1730 they were leaving for America by the thousands. Avoiding existing settlements, these Scotch-Irish headed immediately for the western, Indian frontier.

Independence of thought and action, which was a primary benefit of frontier life, was not without its costs. The threat of Indian hostilities existed for all whites living on the fringe of Anglo-American civilization. The settlers valued the virtues of strength, physical courage, and self-reliance; Augustus Baldwin Longstreet observed in 1833 that to be "the *very best* men in the county . . . in the Georgia vocabulary, means that they could flog any other two men in the county." Life on the Indian frontier was savage, and the frontiersman was familiar with violence.

With the crossing of the Sabine River, new circumstances combined to make frontier conditions even more violent for the Anglo-American pioneer. Texas was the place where western and southern violence overlapped. The brief but bloody revolt against Mexican sovereignty spawned border warfare that lasted for generations and mutual antagonism and mistrust that linger to the present day. In Texas, also, the frontiersman encountered for the first time Indians who were superbly skilled horsemen—Comanche and Kiowa warriors—who fought westward expansion to a standstill until the development of repeating firearms. Finally, the unsettled conditions of a newly won independence and a virtually nonexistent legal system drew like a magnet the derelicts and outlaws of the more developed states in the East. One long-time Texan observed that before 1836 fighting was no more common among the Anglo-American colonists in Texas than in the United States. With the inauguration of the "powder-stained Republic," however, turbulence prevailed in many places. Hundreds of American—mostly southern—soldiers of fortune flocked to the Texas army in 1836, and with its disbanding after San Jacinto, its footloose men stayed on. During the 10 years prior to annexation to the United States, war spirit in Texas continued to run high: legal authority was minimal, bars to immigration were nonexistent, and all sorts of people left the United States for Texas. The western frontier developed too swiftly for its courts of justice.

Texans, like other frontiersmen, commonly settled differences with personal violence, whether by fighting, shooting, stabbing, or dueling. More than two-thirds of the indictments in the district courts of the Republic were for the crimes of assault and battery, affray, assault with intent to kill, or murder. About 60 percent of the assault and battery cases resulted in convictions, but sentences were light—ordinarily 5 or 10 dollars and costs. Prosecutors in trials for more serious offenses encountered great difficulty in obtaining convictions because juries tended to give serious consideration to pleas of self-defense or "unbearable provocation." Only two men, in fact, were executed for murder in the Republic. A Texas doctor wrote that "the killing of a fellow was looked upon with greater leniency than theft," a crime of rare occurrence and harsh punishment on the frontier. Homicide, moreover, was most often a crime without malice. Hot-tempered, armed men, on a sudden and often trivial irritation, killed their fellow men. Personal honor was a thing of great value, and in a raw new land no recourse to the courts existed. The very presence of armed, reckless men, imbued with such an ethic, made any quarrel a potential homicide.

While the middle and lower classes did away with each other in street brawls, barroom shootings, and knife fights, the gentry followed the prescribed form of manslaughter for their class, the formal duel. During the period of the Republic alone, Texas witnessed "affairs of honor" between many officers of the army, including one in which the principals were its general-in-chief, Albert Sidney Johnston, and its acting commander, Felix Huston. Soldiers were not alone in resorting to the "code duello." Numerous Texas senators and representatives exchanged shots on the field of honor, and a fight between President Mirabeau B. Lamar and a member of his cabinet was barely averted.

This heritage of organized and personal violence naturally produced a corps of proficient, if ill-disciplined, soldiers. Ten years of brutal raiding and counterraiding from San Antonio to the Rio Grande followed the Texas Revolution's apparent end at San Jacinto, and as scouts, escorts, and mounted infantry, the Texas Rangers serving under Zachary Taylor and Winfield Scott in Mexico took a full measure of revenge for the Texan dead at the Alamo and Goliad. So ruthlessly efficient was Colonel John Coffee Hays's ranger regiment that General Taylor reportedly said of them, they "are the damndest troops in the world; we can't do without them in a fight, and we can't do anything with them out of a fight." As atrocities attributed to the Texas troops multiplied, the exasperated Taylor sent home all companies but one, Ben McCulloch's spy company, whose daring and precise reconnaissance activities discovered and reported Santa Anna's secret movement toward Taylor's army in February of 1847 just in time to allow the American general to assume a strong defensive position at Buena Vista and thus salvage the United States war effort in northern Mexico.

Not surprisingly, Texas soldiers carried the same ardent martial spirit into the Civil War. As Jefferson Davis observed upon the arrival of the leading elements of the Texas brigade at Richmond in 1861, "the soldiers of the other states have their military reputations to gain, but the sons of the defenders of the Alamo have theirs to uphold." The Texas Brigade of the Army of Northern Virginia, for example, amassed one of the most glorious combat records of any Civil War unit, North or South. They were equally notorious as foragers. Recruited primarily from counties on or near the Indian frontier, this brigade displayed almost superhuman courage and élan at Gaines Mill, Sharpsburg, Gettysburg, Chickamauga, and at the Wilderness, where its decimated regiments are credited with checking the assault of a full Union corps. Despite terrible losses—one of its regiments sustained the highest percentage of casualties of any Civil War unit in a single day at Sharpsburg—the Texas Brigade maintained its formation to Appomattox, with Lee vowing to call upon it "so long as a man remains to wave its flag."

Undoubtedly much of the violence experienced on the frontier was the result of the restlessness engendered by successive wars. The Texas Revolution, the Mexican War, and the Civil War all produced men who had tasted action and could not return to the discipline of the settled world. Jesse James looms largest among this group, but he is only one of scores who continued the war well beyond the passing of the armies.

Many cowboys were also southerners dispossessed by the late war. Among the classic protagonists of western literature are Shane, whose "folks came out of Mississippi and settled in Arkansas," and the model for later cowboys of American fiction, the Virginian of Shiloh Ranch. Like his predecessors on the American frontier, the cowboy valued independence, self-reliance, hard work, austerity in manners and possessions, honesty, bravery, and a rugged stoicism born of life in nature. Like the long rifle and bowie knife of earlier frontiersmen, however, his six-gun was his most enduring icon, and in both legend and fact he was too often quick to react to a real or supposed affront with violence.

Along with the heroic Shane and the Virginian, western fiction also presents the evil Major Tetley of *The Oxbow Incident*, who, dressed in a Confederate uniform and cowboy boots, leads a murderous lynch mob. He represents an undesirable side effect of the frontier imperative of self-reliance and the quest for order—vigilantism and lynch law. Although in the older states of the Deep South both practices flourished well into the 1930s and beyond, long after the development of formal courts of law, it was on the frontier that mob violence, in the name of law and order, took root in America. Nowhere was lynch justice more swift or certain than on the frontier.

Perhaps the most notorious example of vigilante usurpation occurred in east Texas between 1839 and 1844. The so-called Regulator-Moderator War had its background in the influx of lawless characters into the Neutral Ground between the Mexican province of Texas and the state of Louisiana in the first three decades of the 19th century. After 1806 Mexican law forbade the settlement of any lands within 20 leagues of the border of the United States, yet by 1836 the east Texas borderlands had a greater combined population than all other areas of the new Republic combined. These uninvited citizens, largely refugees from justice in the "old states," had become so accustomed to administering their own affairs and giving summary punishment to criminals that they were unwilling to accept the courts of the Texas Republic.

When a killing resulted from a quarrel over fraudulent land certificates, Texas courts acquitted the accused killer. The former defendant quickly organized a posse of 30 "Regulators" to deal with continuing violence. Although their stated purpose was the suppression of crime, this band burned homes and intimidated personal enemies until a rival faction of "Moderators" arose to oppose them. The first act of the Moderators, the murder of the leader of the Regulators, was met with bloody reprisal, and their already inferior numbers were soon further reduced by Regulator guns and ropes. So powerful did these vigilantes become that they openly defied the courts of Shelby County and contemplated overturning the government of the Texas Republic and declaring their new leader dictator.

Regulator excesses, however, strengthened the Moderators' position, and open warfare broke out once again. East Texas experienced a reign of terror while fields went uncultivated, men were shot from ambush, and prisoners were hung without trial. Only when President Sam Houston ordered 600 Texas militiamen into the region to arrest the leaders of the two factions were peace and order restored.

Statehood strengthened civil government in Texas, but it could not erase the effect of generations of summary frontier justice. Too often mixed with vigilantism was an equally malevolent racism, a curious phenomenon on the American frontier. In some ways the frontier was the freest of places, in which a man was judged on the quality of his work and such virtues as honesty, bravery, and shrewdness. The southern frontier was, however, also heir to the Old South's legacy of black slavery. Anglo-Texans never forgot the Alamo and Goliad or forgave the nation that martyred Crockett, Travis, Bowie, and Fannin. Germans, a numerous, prosperous, aloof, and Unionist minority in central Texas, were viewed with great suspicion by their Anglo-Texan neighbors, a prejudice that culminated in the slaughter of German prisoners of war by Confederate irregulars following the battle of the Nueces in 1862. Indians most of all, especially the fiercely imperialistic Comanches, were regarded as a race of savages whose very existence was a bar to the progress of civilization, and raid and counterraid between these mutually antagonistic cultures escalated into a war of attrition, which the Native American could not hope to win. Finally, when an Anglo-Texan was brought before the bar of justice in Langtry, charged with the murder of a Chinese laborer on the Southern Pacific Railroad, Judge Roy Bean freed him, asserting that "nowhere in his lawbook could he find a rule against killing Chinese."

The courage and honor, the militarism and violence of the 19th-century frontiersman, soldier, and cowboy remain part of present-day Texas culture. Texas A&M University provided more general grade officers to the Allied cause in World War II than any other officer-training academy, and Texans received a higher per capita share of Congressional Medals of Honor in Vietnam than servicemen of any other state. Cowboys and would-be cowboys still carry rifles in the gun racks of their pickup trucks, and for recreation the good old boys still enjoy a good free-for-all at the local honky-tonk on a Saturday night. Here, culturally and geographically, the South and the West meet and are one. The only difference, a Texas Ranger once observed, is that to the east of a certain imaginary line running down the middle of the state, roadhouse brawls take place in the parking lot; to the west they are conducted indoors—a vestige, one may suppose, of the southern heritage of order and decorum juxtaposed with the western tradition of experiencing life "with the bark on."

See also GEOGRAPHY: Southwest

Thomas W. Cutrer
University of Texas at Austin

Dickson D. Bruce, Jr., *Violence and Culture in the Antebellum South* (1979); Marcus Cunliff, *Soldiers and Civilians: The Martial Spirit in America, 1775–1865* (1968); John Hope Franklin, *The Militant South, 1800–1861* (1956); Joe B. Frantz, in *Violence in America: Historical and Comparative Perspectives*, ed. Hugh Davis Graham and Ted Robert Gurr (1969); Elliot Gorn, *American Historical Review* (February 1985); William Ransom Hogan, *The Texas Republic: A Social and Economic History* (1946, 1969); Jack K. Williams, *Dueling in the Old South: Vignettes of Social History* (1980).

"Bonnie and Clyde"

Bonnie Parker (1910–1934) and
Clyde Barrow (1909–1934). Outlaws.

On the morning of 23 May 1934 six law officers fired more than 160 shots at a car driving down a road near Arcadia, La. Fifty shots hit the car's passenger and driver—Bonnie Parker and Clyde Barrow, better known as "Bonnie and Clyde." The fatal ambush was the culmination of months in pursuit of the notorious outlaws, who had killed at least 12 people since April of 1932.

Bonnie Parker was high-spirited and intelligent. Her family moved from Rowena, Tex., to Dallas when her father died in 1914. There, she met Clyde Barrow, the quick-tempered, uneducated son of desperately poor parents. By the time they met, Barrow had already been involved in petty crimes. Bonnie's criminal association with him began when she smuggled a gun into a Texas prison where he was being held, thus allowing him to escape.

Often with various other gang members, Bonnie and Clyde drove for miles along the back roads of Texas, Oklahoma, Missouri, Arkansas, and Louisiana. They lived mostly in stolen cars, and they survived on the spoils of their victims. Panic and criminal incompetence characterized Barrow's escapades and often resulted in purposeless killings.

When news spread that Texas Ranger Frank Hamer and his men had killed Bonnie and Clyde, crowds gathered at the scene, tearing off parts of the car, hacking away locks of Bonnie's hair, taking whatever they could that had belonged to the infamous pair. One determined souvenir seeker even tried to amputate Clyde's trigger finger. The desire to possess anything with which Bonnie and Clyde had been associated was compulsive, and it has continued. The death car itself sold at auction in 1973 for $175,000.

For two years, Barrow's gang terrorized residents in and around Texas and, in doing so, sparked the phenomenal growth of a legend. The image of a tiny, cigar-smoking woman and a daring gangster together, living dangerously and outrunning poorly organized pursuers, evoked great excitement. Bonnie's devotion to Clyde and Clyde's successful rise from the anonymity of dire poverty further incited the romanticization of their exploits; and books and movies, such as *Bonnie and Clyde* (1967), have sustained their memory. Many of their contemporaries cheered the outlaws' deaths, but, in a decade when Americans needed heroes, countless others sympathized with and celebrated the careers of Bonnie and Clyde.

Jessica Foy
Cooperstown Graduate Programs
Cooperstown, New York

John Treherne, *The Strange History of Bonnie and Clyde* (1985).

Capital Punishment

Few social issues attract as much public attention as capital punishment. Arguments against capital punishment commonly focus on execution as an amoral or unjust form of legalized homicide. Arguments for the death penalty range from the biblical "an eye for an eye" principle of revenge to the plausible but scientifically unproven theory that capital punishment deters would-be offenders from extreme forms of criminal behavior. While the pros and cons of capital punishment undoubtedly will continue to be debated by both private citizens and public officials in all 50 states, southern states lead the nation in the number of death sentences and executions. Official criminal justice statistics reveal that 3,830 death-row inmates in U.S. state prisons were executed between the years 1930 and 1981. Sixty percent (2,307) of these executions occurred in the South. By comparison, the Northeast accounted for only 16 percent (608), the West for 13 percent (511), and the North Central states for 11 percent (404) of the total number of state-authorized executions.

The 1972 U.S. Supreme Court decision in *Furman* v. *Georgia* resulted in a temporary national moratorium on executions. In response to this landmark decision, which found Georgia's death penalty law to be unconstitutional on grounds that it violated Eighth Amendment protections against "cruel and unusual punishment," individual legislatures revised state criminal statutes to comply with evolving constitutional guidelines. Five additional death penalty cases, all from southern states, were considered by the U. S. Supreme Court in 1976. The tempo-

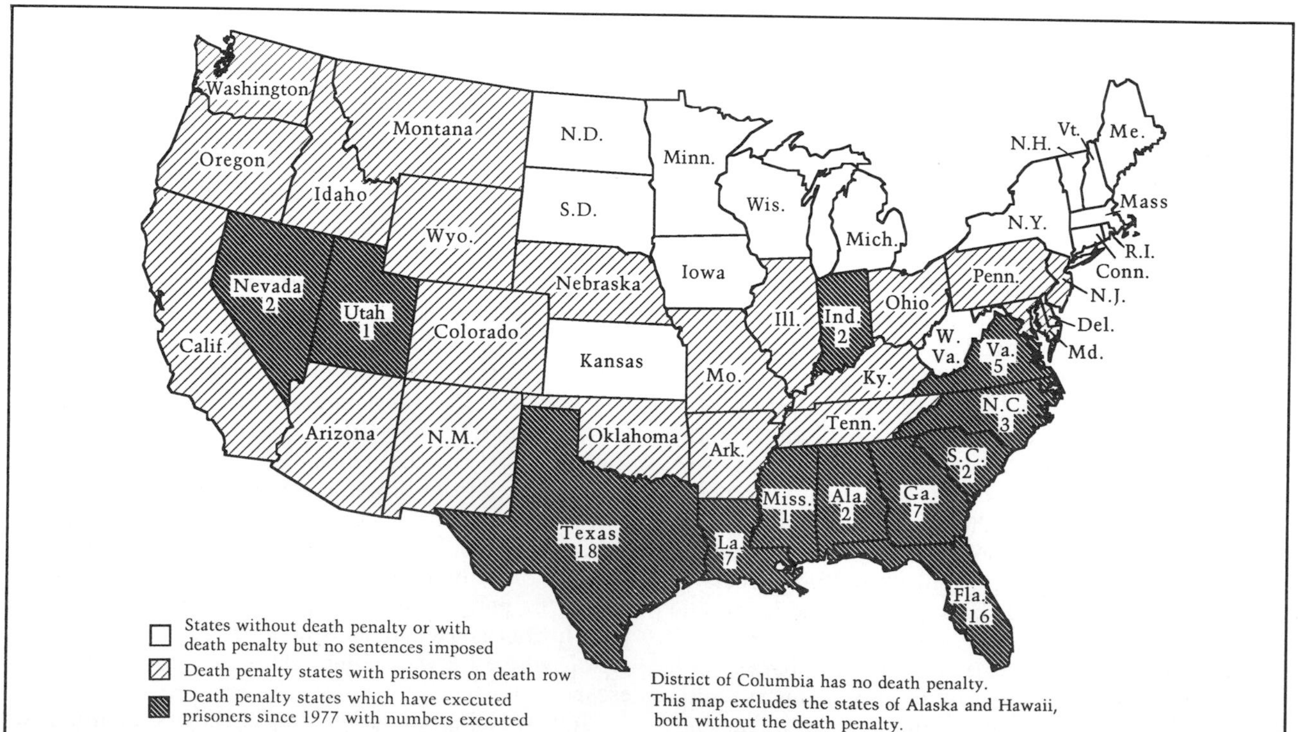

The Death Penalty in the United States, 1977 to October 1986

Source: Adapted from *Southern Changes* (August 1987).

rary national moratorium on capital punishment was finally broken by the widely publicized Utah execution by firing squad of Gary Gilmore in 1977.

Although national public opinion polls do not show significant regional differences in public attitudes toward the death penalty, official statistics as of 31 December 1983 indicate that 777 death-row inmates, or 65 percent of the total number of prisoners (1,202) awaiting execution, were incarcerated in southern correctional institutions (U.S. Department of Justice, 1984). By the end of 1983, 38 states had death penalty statutes. With the sole exception of West Virginia, which abolished its death penalty laws in 1965, all southern states allow capital punishment.

Henry P. Lundsgaarde
University of Kentucky

Edward J. Brown, Timothy J. Flanagan, Maureen McLeod, eds., *Sourcebook of Criminal Justice Statistics* (1984); U.S. Department of Justice, *Capital Punishment 1983: Bulletin* (1984).

Chain Gang

The profit motive and a desire to eliminate tax burdens dominated post–Civil War southern discussions of criminal punishment. The region was impoverished by the war and yet had now to deal judicially with free black as well as white offenders. Convict lease to private contractors and corporations became a standard alternative to government maintenance throughout the southern states. Because convict labor was most profitable when used for large-scale work projects such as levee repair, railroad building, and road construction, the chain gang was closely associated with the lease system. By 1886 it was the chief form of convict labor in eight southern states, and it persisted in these states long after its abolition in the North and West.

Unlike antebellum chattels, chain-gang crews cost lessees little if anything—an 1867 Georgia railroad lease stipulated a $25 annual fee per inmate—and convicts were infinitely expendable since those who died were quickly replaced. Men, women, and often children sentenced for crimes ranging from the theft of a keg of nails and vagrancy to premeditated murder worked as gangs under armed guard, joined together by a long squad chain attached to ankle irons. Escape was further impeded by stride or hobble chains that allowed a span of about eight inches between leg irons. Throughout its history, a disproportionate number of those sentenced to this form of labor were black: 846 out of 952 in an 1878 survey; 2,113 out of 2,221 in Georgia, 1902.

Whether moving the sand and earth required to shore up levees in the Delta mud or "chipping" turpentine in Florida swamps, crews of convicts worked from 10 to 14 hours per day. They were transported to work camps in mule-drawn boxcars or windowless cages with tiers of plank beds on either side. Once at a campsite, these portable cages served as permanent housing when tents or rough-hewn cell houses were not set up. Food, typically fatback, corn bread, and cowpeas, was rationed, often spoiled, and in summer swarmed with flies. Sanitation in the work camps was not even rudimentary. Convicts lacked wash basins, towels, and soap; they slept, secured by a logging chain, in their work clothes, on bare vermin-infested mattresses. No attempt was made to isolate tubercular or syphilitic prisoners.

Medical care was unknown, and entire gangs fell prey to diseases such as meningitis. Shackle poison (an infection caused by the constant friction of ankle irons), malnutrition, overwork, beatings, or self-inflicted mutilations, such as hamstringing, claimed others. Those who tried to escape or who failed to work hard or fast enough were often punished by confinement to a coffinlike sweatbox, flogging, or the riveting of 20 to 50 pound iron weights to leg shackles. At the height of the lease system, the death rate was so appalling (45 percent of the prisoners working the Greenwood to Augusta railroad died annually in the period 1877–79) that leading critics such as the editor of the New Orleans *Daily Picayune* argued that imposing the death sentence on any convict with a term in excess of six years was more humane and expedient.

The hostility of free labor, especially when convict crews were brought in as strikebreakers, led to the abolition of the private lease system in most southern states by the turn of the century. The chain gang, however, did not disappear. Used by state or county officials primarily as road crews, gangs actually became more important, and more visible, with the advent of the automobile. Reformist activity increased in the 1920s, and exposés of abuses culminated in the 1932 Warner Brothers' release of Robert Burns's *I Am a Fugitive from a Chain Gang*—"A gruesome experience" according to *Variety*, "and dynamite for the state of Georgia." Subsequently the use of chain gangs was greatly reduced, although even in the early 1960s small details were still in evidence. Georgia was the last southern state to completely abolish the practice.

Although images of the chain gang in literature (Rich-

Convicts working on a road, Oglethorpe County, Ga., 1941

ard Wright's *Black Boy*) and film (Stuart Rosenberg's film *Cool Hand Luke*) are vivid reminders of the institution, its most enduring legacy is musical. Tunes range from the mournful "holler," a "strange wailing chant" unintelligible to white "walking bosses," to blues lyrics directly inspired by the experience of gang work—such as "Chain Gang Blues" by Ma Rainey and Kokomo Arnold, "Levee Camp Blues" by Robert Pete Williams, and George "Bullet" Williams's "Escaped Convict Blues," with its evocation of tracking hounds. Particularly important is the work song. Supplying a meter for manual labor that required coordination of axes, hoes, and hammers, work songs also provided a partial outlet for frustration and anger. Along with the harsh nonmechanized work that sustained them, the songs have now largely disappeared.

Elizabeth M. Makowski
University of Mississippi

Edward L. Ayers, *Vengeance and Justice: Crime and Punishment in the 19th-Century American South* (1984); Bruce Jackson, *Wake up Dead Man: Afro-American Worksongs from Texas Prisons* (1972); Daniel A. Novak, *The Wheel of Servitude: Black Forced Labor after Slavery* (1978); Paul Oliver, *Blues Fell This Morning* (1960); J. C. Powell, *The American Siberia* (1891); Carl Sifakis, ed., *Encyclopedia of American Crime* (1982); Jesse F. Steiner and Roy M. Brown, *The North Carolina Chain Gang* (1927); Walter Wilson, *Forced Labor in the United States* (1933).

Convict Leasing

Convict leasing provided southern employers with cheap, manageable, and readily available workers for two generations before the last remnants of the system disappeared in the 1930s. Although the practice of hiring out or leasing convicts originated in the pre–Civil War penal systems of Alabama, Kentucky, and Louisiana, the system was not adopted by all southern states until the 1870s.

Prior to emancipation, most southern black offenders were slaves and were punished by their masters as permitted or required by the state slave codes. Thus, penal facilities in the prewar South were largely for "whites only." Some of these offenders were turned over to private contractors, typically textile manufacturers. But, as free persons after 1865, black offenders constituted a sudden and sizable addition to southern prison populations, which the economically depressed states found difficult to handle. The solution was convict leasing on a vast, biracial scale.

The zenith of the brutal and exploitative system lasted from about 1880 to 1910. During those years convict leasing was in reality a legal postwar form of slavery for white and black prisoners alike, although blacks far outnumbered whites (especially in the Deep South) and received much harsher treatment.

Depending on where they had been convicted, postwar southern convicts were leased to cotton, rice, sugarcane, and tobacco planters; levee builders; coal mines; timber companies; and railroad construction firms. Prisoners of both races and sexes, sometimes no more than eight or nine years of age, suffered from overwork, physical abuse, meager diets, and little or no medical care. Death and injury rates were appalling. As the most despised element in the population, convicts had few spokesmen or defenders. Several states had established "penitentiary rings" supported by politicians who favored leasing because it relieved their states of responsibility for maintaining convicts and because the system brought "easy" revenues to public treasuries at no sacrifice to voting taxpayers. Beginning in the 1890s, however, coalitions of political opponents, labor interests, and humanitarian reformers were able to abolish leasing gradually state by state.

Convict leasing should not be considered identical to state or county "chain gangs," which continued to exist in the post–World War II South. "Chain-gang" prisoners were also badly treated, but they were under the custody of public authorities rather than the more insensitive, inhumane, and publicly unsupervised private contractors of the lease system.

See also LAW: / Black Codes; Slave Codes

Mark T. Carleton
Louisiana State University

Mark T. Carleton, *Politics and Punishment: The History of the Louisiana State Penal System* (1971); Dan T. Carter, "Convict Lease" (M.A. thesis, University of Wisconsin, 1964); Hilda Jane Zimmerman, "Penal Systems and Penal Reform in the South since the Civil War" (Ph.D. dissertation, University of North Carolina at Chapel Hill, 1947).

Copeland, James

(1823–1857) Outlaw.

The name of no other outlaw in southern Mississippi and Alabama is more shrouded in mystique and controversy than that of James Copeland, who was hanged 30 October 1857 on the banks of the Leaf River near Augusta in Perry County, Miss. Indeed, Copeland was a household word from Mobile Bay to Lake Pontchartrain not only because his clan had terrorized folks in that region during the flush times of the 1830s and 1840s but also because he dictated his memoirs to a highly literate young sheriff, J. R. S. Pitts. Published first in 1858 with later editions in 1874 and 1909, *The Confession of James Copeland* created a furor that still persists amid the piney woods and coastal counties.

Tales about Copeland, born in Jackson County on the Mississippi Gulf Coast, are still spun. His brutal life of larceny, arson, and murder captivated the imagination of generations who either admired him as a latter-day Robin Hood or scorned him as a contemptible desperado.

His errant ways began as a lad of 12 with the theft of a pocket knife, followed shortly thereafter by grand larceny and the burning of the local courthouse, assisted by an older accomplice, Gale H. Wages, whose clan he soon joined—a clan eventually bearing the name Copeland.

Though the clan operated mainly in south Mississippi and Alabama, Copeland's criminal path took him as far east as the Chattahoochee River, as far west as the Rio Grande, and as far north as the Wabash. In his *Confession* he related crimes committed in the company of his mentor Wages and one Charles McGrath, a quintessential fraudulent frontier preacher. Copeland, who credits himself with only two murders, stole anything readily converted to cash, but he specialized in the theft of horses and slaves. Before the trio split up to avoid capture, Wages supposedly buried their savings of $30,000 in gold in the Catahoula Swamp in southwestern Mississippi. The gold coins are still sought by treasure hunters.

Hoping to escape the grasp of Mississippi officials who had indicted him for murder, Copeland surrendered to Alabama authorities to serve a term for larceny. However, deputies of Sheriff Pitts awaited his release, and after four more years in custody, James Copeland—in the words of Pitts—"expiated his blood stained career on the scaffold" before a massive October crowd in 1857.

John D. W. Guice
University of Southern Mississippi

J. R. S. Pitts, *Life and Confession of the Noted Outlaw James Copeland* (1980).

Cortez, Gregorio

(1875–1916) Outlaw.

Gregorio Cortez was a legendary figure from the Texas-Mexico border. In 1901 Cortez became a fugitive from the law after he killed a sheriff who attempted to arrest him for allegedly having stolen a horse. Details pertaining to the actual shooting are clouded, but significant misunderstanding clearly occurred because of language problems.

For 10 days Cortez managed to elude hundreds of men who chased him throughout the rough country of the Rio Grande region. Finally he was captured and tried in court. He was acquitted of murdering the sheriff but was convicted of killing a member of the posse that sought to capture him. Cortez was pardoned in 1913 and died in 1916 under mysterious circumstances.

The importance of Gregorio Cortez lies in what his story reveals about Mexican American–Anglo-American relations along the United States–Mexican border in the early 1900s. This was a time of marked racial friction influenced by border tensions between Mexico and the United States. The dominant society saw Cortez as a killer and fugitive, but people of Mexican background viewed him as a folk hero who had defied oppressive Anglo lawmen.

Popularized by border balladeers at the time, Cortez's story became the subject of Américo Paredes's *With His Pistol in His Hand: A Border Ballad and Its Hero* (1958). In the early 1980s Jack Young directed the film *The Ballad of Gregorio Cortez*, which played before a national television audience and in theaters across the United States.

Oscar J. Martinez
University of Texas at El Paso

Dueling

Dueling was introduced in America by French and British officers during the Revolution. The practice was outlawed throughout the North after the Alexander Hamilton–Aaron Burr duel in 1804. The death of Hamilton shocked the North, which had already all but abolished the practice. In the South dueling became a criminal offense, with stiff penalties if the duel resulted in a death. Opposition to the practice was one of the few respectable social causes in the antebellum South. Despite statutes, antidueling societies, and public disapproval of the practice, dueling remained an important part of southern culture until the Civil War.

Many southern politicians and editors either engaged in duels or received or issued challenges. A list of such men reads like a "who's who" of the antebellum South, and includes Andrew Jackson, William Clingman, William Yancey, Henry Clay, Cassius M. Clay, Henry Wise, Thomas Hart Benton, Sam Houston, William Crawford, Jefferson Davis, Judah P. Benjamin, John Randolph, George McCuffie, William Graves, Louis T. Wigfall, and Albert Sidney Johnston. Duels were not, however, limited to political and social leaders. Parvenus often used the duel as a vehicle for social advancement. Although it was not considered proper for a true gentleman to accept a challenge from a social inferior, such lines were often unclear, particularly in the Southwest.

Most duels were fought with pistols, although occasionally rifles were used. In New Orleans, swords remained the weapon of choice among some duelists. Duelists were supposed to follow elaborate rules, which were described in John Lyde Wilson's *The Code of Honor* (1838), but duels did not always proceed according to those rules. Indeed, before the publication of Wilson's book most duelists, especially those not living in Charleston or New Orleans, likely knew little of the prescribed rules. The rules of dueling required that a challenge be sent, with an opportunity for the offending party to make amends and avoid a conflict. Nevertheless, spontaneous fights between gentlemen, with knives or canes as weapons, were considered by many a form of dueling. When Congressman Preston Brooks beat Charles Sumner with a cane until the Massachusetts senator was insensible, it was considered the equivalent of a duel by Brooks's Charleston constituents. Northerners, on the other hand, considered this act particularly barbaric because Sumner was seated, with his back to Brooks, when the attack began. Similarly, when Alexander H. Stephens, while unarmed, was attacked and knifed by a political rival, southerners considered the event within the bounds of political behavior.

The duel was one aspect of antebellum southern fascination with chivalry. Most duels were fought over alleged or perceived insults. The cause of a duel could be personal, social, professional, or political. Duels were often fought over the honor of one's family, and particularly of women in the family. Social pressure, a desire to prove one's masculinity, or hotheadedness alone drove innumerable southern men to the field of honor.

Paul Finkelman
University of Texas at Austin

John Hope Franklin, *The Militant South, 1800–1861* (1956); Bertram Wyatt-Brown, *Southern Honor: Ethics and Behavior in the Old South* (1982).

Filibusters

"Filibusters," in the 19th-century meaning of the word, were individuals who led, enlisted in, or helped outfit private military expeditions designed to invade foreign lands. The term came into vogue during the years between the Mexican and Civil wars, when thousands of Americans defied proscriptive clauses in the American Neutrality Act of April 1818 and participated in expeditions to such regions as the Mexican Yucatán, Spanish Cuba, Central America, and Ecuador. This form of filibustering has continued to the present. In 1981 a group of American adventurers drew considerable public notice when they were charged by the FBI with plotting an armed invasion of the island of Dominica, for the purpose of overthrowing its government. Two more times within five years after that, federal agents foiled plots conceived in Louisiana and Mississippi to overthrow a foreign government, the last a 1986 attempt to seize Surinam in Central America.

The United States was by no means the only country to spawn such expeditions in the 19th century, nor was there anything uniquely southern about filibustering. The famous plot of Aaron Burr (1805–7), for instance, occurred during the Jefferson Administration, before the rise of sectional consciousness in the South. It would be misleading, moreover, to simplify even the pre–Civil War expeditions as purely southern endeavors. Men of all regions enlisted in filibuster ranks, for a variety of personal and ideological reasons, including mere adventurism and an ethnocentric belief—sometimes called Manifest Destiny—that Americans had a God-given mission to impose their republican institutions upon peoples presumed to be less fortunate. New York City and California were two of the country's flagrant centers of filibuster activity. On the other hand, many people could be found throughout the United States who opposed filibustering. Several scholars have suggested that filibustering was an expression of antebellum American romanticism.

Nevertheless, when James Stirling, an English visitor to the United States, informed his countrymen in 1857 that filibustering was "essentially a thing of the South" (*Letters from the Slave States*), he was hardly the victim of a far-fetched delusion. Filibustering found its strongest popular support in the Deep South; in several instances federal authorities found it virtually impossible to prosecute blatant violations of the Neutrality Act in the Gulf states because of the force of public opinion. More significantly, several expeditions either began with, or developed, a southern, sectional orientation. Certainly this was the case with former governor John A. Quitman's Cuba conspiracy from 1853 to 1855. Southern governors, congressmen, newspapermen, and even judges and preachers helped Quitman assemble ships, arms, and men to invade Cuba, because they wanted to prevent Spain from "Africanizing" (abolishing slavery in) Cuba and they shared Quitman's belief that new slave states would provide security from the American antislavery movement. The most successful filibuster of the age, a native Tennessean named William Walker, who invaded Nicaragua and became its president in 1856, won widespread southern support when he reestablished slavery in his conquest.

Several commentators, therefore, have presented filibustering as a southern cultural trait. The noted historian John Hope Franklin, for instance, interpreted filibuster expeditions as an element within the general category of southern militarism and violence. However, given northern participation in the filibuster movement, the idea of filibustering as peculiarly southern is a fusion of myth and reality.

Robert E. May
Purdue University

Charles H. Brown, *Agents of Manifest Destiny: The Lives and Times of the Filibusters* (1980); Robert E. May, *The Southern Dream of a Caribbean Empire, 1854–1861* (1973); Edward S. Wallace, *Destiny and Glory* (1957).

Hatfields and McCoys

The Hatfield-McCoy feud, the most famous southern Appalachian vendetta, was one manifestation of general late 19th-century American violence—bloody labor troubles, western lawlessness, and political assassination. It was also part of the cultural milieu of the isolated Tug River Valley along the West Virginia–Kentucky border, an area known for widespread illiteracy, fundamentalist churches, and disrespect for law. Exaggerated family and clan loyalties and acute sensitivity to affronts often mixed with the consumption of moonshine whiskey to produce explosive situations.

Numerous incidents, such as a dispute over ownership of a razorback hog, a romance between "Devil Anse"

Devil Anse Hatfield, Kentucky fighter, 1880s

Hatfield's son Johnse and Randolph McCoy's daughter Rose Anna, and a deadly election altercation, were behind the Hatfield-McCoy feud. Home-guard and bushwhacking activities by the two families during the Civil War had also set the stage for conflict.

Several bloody events in the 1880s drew national attention to the feud: the killing of Ellison Hatfield, a brother of "Devil Anse," at an election in 1882 and the retaliatory murder of three sons of Randolph McCoy by enraged Hatfields; the battle of Grapevine Creek, a pitched battle on the Jug Fork River; and a merciless raid on New Year's night 1888 in which Hatfields burned McCoy's house and killed two more of his children. The feud was elevated to an interstate battle when West Virginia Governor Willis Wilson refused to extradite Hatfield partisans indicted in Pike County, Ky., for the 1882 murders and when he instituted habeas corpus proceedings for return of nine who were seized later by Kentucky authorities in raids into West Virginia. The sensational journalism of large city newspapers provided the nation with gory and sometimes fabricated accounts that did much to encrust the feud with myth and legend.

The hanging of one Hatfield partisan and the sentencing of others to prison terms following an April 1897 trial in Pike County signaled an end to the feud. By then many of the participants, including "Devil Anse," who had become a symbol of the bloodthirsty mountaineer, were weary of the killing. The entry of industry and improved transportation broke the bonds of isolation and fostered a new society that had far less patience with violent feuds. The Hatfields and the McCoys turned to peaceful pursuits, and both families produced important business, industrial, and political leaders for the New South.

Otis K. Rice
West Virginia Institute
of Technology

Virgil C. Jones, *The Hatfields and the McCoys* (1948); Otis K. Rice, *The Hatfields and the McCoys* (1978).

James Brothers

Alexander Franklin James (1843–1915) and
Jesse Woodson James (1847–1882). Outlaws.

Noted outlaws Frank James and Jesse James were born and raised on a western Missouri farm, sons of a prosperous, slaveowning family that had moved from Kentucky in 1842. Like many Missourians, they were southern in origin and outlook. Before and during the Civil War, violence over slavery and secession divided Missouri and consumed the James family. In the absence of regular Confederate troops in Missouri during the war, organizations of pro-southern guerrillas formed to respond to the harsh treatment of southern sympathizers by Union troops and Kansas guerrilla raiders. In 1862 Confederate private Frank James joined guerrilla leader William Clarke Quantrill. Seventeen-year-old Jesse rode with William "Bloody Bill" Anderson's guerrilla band in 1864 after Union militia reportedly attempted to hang Jesse's stepfather, harassed his pregnant mother, and gave him a severe whipping. Both brothers were deeply involved in violent irregular warfare. In this crucible of blood and fire America's best-known outlaws were created.

After the war many guerrillas resumed normal lives though they were denied amnesty and the right to vote. The James brothers, however, did not settle down. Their family had been banished from Missouri, and according to legend, when Jesse attempted to surrender in 1865, he was shot by federal troops. By 1866 Frank and Jesse James had begun their long careers as bank and train robbers. Supporters argued that their treatment during and after the war forced them outside the law and justified their actions. This notion was reinforced when Pinkerton detectives hired by the railroads threw an explosive device into their parents' home, killing their nine-year-old half brother and blowing their mother's arm off.

When the James brothers were involved in an 1869 bank robbery and murder, newspaperman John N. Edwards began an influential 20-year crusade to idealize their lives as guerrillas and outlaws. He portrayed them as dashing southern gentlemen who protected women and children from northern persecution during the war and defended helpless victims of northern banks and railroads afterwards. Many people of southern background agreed that the James brothers were knights of the South's Lost Cause and frontier Robin Hoods.

As people in all regions felt the pinch of big business in the post–Civil War decades, the James brothers were praised nationally in folklore and popular culture as bold western outlaw-heroes who robbed the rich and gave to the poor. This widespread romantic portrayal of the James brothers played a significant role in bringing qualities of the southern gentleman to the western hero. Like later fictional western heroes such as the Virginian and Shane, the James brothers of legend lived on the wild frontier but upheld the chivalrous code of their southern background: they protected the weak and righted wrongs with a fierce sense of honor, pride, and style.

Despite the romantic image of the James brothers, Governor Thomas Crittenden felt they had given Missouri a bad name. In 1881 he offered a $10,000 reward of railroad money for their capture. On 3 April 1882 gang member Robert Ford betrayed Jesse James with a deadly shot from behind while visiting Jesse and his family in their home. Ford was sentenced to hang for murder, but the governor gave him a full pardon. The manner of Jesse's death was the final step in his ascent to the rank of hero. Frank James surrendered his pistol six months later and was tried but acquitted of several crimes.

The James brothers were outlaws for a remarkable 16 years. Thanks to local and public support for their role in the Civil War and their attacks on banks and railroads, they were never apprehended and never convicted of any crimes. A century after the end of their outlaw careers, Frank and Jesse are still celebrated in movies, songs, and novels as heroes of the Lost Cause and Robin Hoods of the West.

George B. Ward
Texas State Historical Association

David Brion Davis, *American Quarterly* (Summer 1954); John Newman Edwards, *Noted Guerrillas, or The Warfare of the Border* (1877); William A. Settle, Jr., *Jesse James Was His Name* (1966).

Knights of the Golden Circle (KGC)

The Knights of the Golden Circle (KGC) was a secret antebellum organization promoted by George W. L. Bickley, a Virginia-born editor, adventurer, and doctor of eclectic medicine. He hoped to create a great slave empire encompassing the West Indies, the southern United States, Mexico, Central America, and part of South America—hence the name Golden Circle. But his main goal was annexation of Mexico, whose relations with the United States were strained in the late 1850s.

Hounded by creditors, "General" Bickley, self-styled "President and Commander-in-Chief of the KGC American Legion," left his Cincinnati base in 1860, toured the East and the South, and promoted a filibustering expedition into Mexico. He received his chief support in Texas, where at least 32 "castles" (lodges) were established under local leadership. Bickley had limited newspaper support elsewhere in the South, and there were rumors that linked prominent southern politicos to the KGC (Jefferson Davis, William L. Yancey, John B. Floyd, John C. Breckinridge), but these were probably fabrications.

Bickley's attempted invasion of Mexico was ineptly handled; he failed to secure the support of Governor Sam Houston, who had seemed interested; and he failed to show up at the appointed time with a large force he claimed he was collecting in New Orleans. In April a number of his disgusted supporters met in New Orleans and expelled Bickley. He retaliated by calling for a convention in Raleigh in May, at which time he was reinstated.

Once more Bickley turned his attention to Mexico. This time he was sidetracked by the 1860 campaign. With Lincoln's election Bickley became an ardent advocate of southern secession and supported it in Tennessee and Kentucky.

The "General" served a stint as a Confederate surgeon, deserted, and for a short time lived with a backwoods woman at Shelbyville, Tenn. In July 1863 Bickley was arrested in Indiana for spying and consequently was imprisoned until October 1865, although nothing was proved. He died a broken man in August 1867.

The KGC was a prime antebellum example of the South's aggressiveness and expansionism. Nevertheless, it was a militancy that failed to achieve its goals. The Republicans in the 1864 campaign tried to link antiwar Democrats to the treasonable plots of the KGC, but, in fact, no "castles" were established in the North. The KGC gained a widespread but unfounded reputation for popularity and it embittered relations between the North and South.

Ernest M. Lander, Jr.
Clemson University

Ollinger Crenshaw, *American Historical Review* (October 1941); Roy S. Dunn, *Southwestern Historical Quarterly* (April 1967); Robert E. May, *The Southern Dream of a Caribbean Empire, 1854–1861* (1973).

Ku Klux Klan, Culture of

Desperate, Dreadful, Desolate, Doleful, Dismal, Deadly, and Dark are the seven days of the Klan Kalendar, and the organization's actual malevolence—past and present—is impossible to ignore. But it would also be a mistake to dismiss the cultural implications of the Hooded Empire in southern society.

Characteristic of most Klansmen are an overwhelming ignorance and a complete alienation from society and its institutions. In the Klan's earlier incarnations thousands of otherwise solid citizens were members, but most Klansmen in the 1980s are powerless people on the fringes of society and the economy. They seem to be filled with hate and anger, going through life manipulated by their employers, by the finance company, by the landlord, by demagogic politicians, and finally by smooth-talking Klan salesmen.

Having been ignored for so long, many of these Klan recruits are attracted by the aroma of power that surrounds the leaders such as the dominant 1960s personality, Robert Shelton, and his 1970s successor, Bill Wilkinson. It must be power, the prospective Klansman reasons, because the Grand Wizards can get on the television talk shows; they can go to city hall and attract half the police and all the press in town; and they have big cars and bodyguards and can even wear a suit that does not look as if it had been bought that morning. Once he joins, the new Klansman gets on the evening news himself, just by standing on the street corner in his robe.

In addition to power, the social side of the Klan, the sense of belonging to something, is a compelling attraction. Many Klansmen have belonged to nothing else. Surprisingly few of them, considering the Klan's lip service to Christianity, even attend church. For such people, the Klavern fills an important though unarticulated role. Frequently, Klan gatherings and rallies have an atmosphere that, for all its perverse weirdness, can be compared to a country camp meeting. There may be music and speeches, children playing in the grass, mama and daddy dressed in their robes, grandma sitting in her folding lawn chair, and plenty of fish and beer.

Increasingly, in the 1980s version of the KKK, women and children are drawn into the fold. The "youth corps" units run by the larger Klan organizations are an unabashed effort to remind the younger generation of the Klan's special place in white southern history while simultaneously insuring that the ranks will continue to be filled in the coming years. Likewise, the role of women in the Invisible Empire is now both social and functional. Whereas the Klans of yesteryear had their auxiliaries, who sewed robes and prepared food for the men, the female Klan member today is likely to take up her semiautomatic rifle and put on her camouflage uniform for exercises at the local paramilitary camp.

The KKK adapts to societal changes while trying to hold fast to an idealized white southern view of race, religion, and history.

Randall Williams
Southern Changes
Montgomery, Alabama

Anne Braden, *Southern Exposure* (No. 2, 1980); Lenwood G. Davis and Janet L. Sims-Wood, *The Ku Klux Klan: A Bibliography* (1984); Patsy Sims, *The Klan* (1979).

Ku Klux Klan, History of

After devoting several decades to the study of southern history, Ulrich B. Phillips ventured one of his few generalizations about southern character. The acid test of a true southerner, he declared in a now-famous essay, was his or her insistence that the South, despite the presence of a sizable black population, "remain a white man's country." No organization so exemplified this credo and carried it to its logical, and often violent, extreme as the Ku Klux Klan.

Begun in May and June of 1866 in the hinterland of postbellum Tennessee, at Pulaski, by six former Confederates eager for amusement and diversion, the Klan soon lost its innocence as its organizers progressed from playing jokes on each other to tricking and frightening blacks. As news of the Klan spread, new groups or "dens" were formed, first in Tennessee and then throughout the South. Despite its official 1867 "prescript" supporting the Constitution of the United States, the Klan's favorite modus operandi became intimidation and violence against those, specifically the freedmen and their white allies, who threatened to upset the carefully crafted southern hierarchical society that placed the white male socially, economically, and politically supreme. Particularly horrifying to Klansmen was any idea of racial equality or so-called black domination. Thus, blacks were whipped for crimes ranging from insolence and voting Republican to making a good crop and becoming prosperous. Others were lynched for alleged rapes and for violating racial norms. Although the Klan was active in only one-quarter of southern counties, it received initial encouragement from the conservative press and the educated elements of society, who eventually became disgusted with the Klan's excesses and withdrew their support by 1870. The combination of the call for disband-

Cover for the music to a Ku Klux Klan song

ment of the Klan by Imperial Wizard Nathan Bedford Forrest in 1869 and the passage and enforcement of the federal Ku Klux Klan Acts in 1870 and 1871 signaled an end to much of the Klan's power, although sporadic outbreaks of violence against blacks continued.

The 19th-century South was largely a closed society, suspicious of anything that threatened its canons of political, religious, and social orthodoxy. To this tradition, the South at the turn of the century joined with much of the North in adding an unhealthy portion of American nativism and its concomitant distrust of Catholics, Jews, and blacks. Thus fertile ground was prepared for the Klan's revival in the wake of D. W. Griffith's sympathetic and successful 1915 movie, *Birth of a Nation*, based on Thomas Dixon, Jr.'s, novel, *The Clansman*. When former preacher, salesman, and history teacher William J. Simmons's reorganization of the Klan in Georgia in 1915 united with the salesmanship of Edward Young Clarke and Elizabeth Tyler, the response was nationwide. The resurgent Klan, numbering at its height over 2 million members, transcended the boundaries of the old Confederacy in its appeal to native-born Americans who feared and distrusted anything they perceived as foreign or inimical to community morality. Also nationwide was the violence that has characterized the Klan from its inception, although most atrocities were still committed in the South. Mob psychology, the anonymity of the hooded costumes, oaths of secrecy imposed by the Klan, and the fears of certain groups conspired to sanction crimes that an individual alone might otherwise never have contemplated. As during Reconstruction, revelations of such excesses destroyed the comparatively widespread support enjoyed by the Klan, and membership declined sharply.

The Klan was never again able to command a membership equal to that of the 1920s. During the push for civil rights by blacks in the 1960s, however, membership in the South rose in response to the perceived threat to accustomed social patterns, and the Klan once more made its influence felt through a reign of terror. Consumed with hatred and fear of social change, Klan members relied on the South's honored tradition of violence for resolving any disagreement—from individual dispute to sectional conflict. Their methods became increasingly sophisticated and deadly. Klansmen added bombing and arson to their familiar repertoire of beating, tarring and feathering, and lynching. Such excesses again brought a backlash from the larger community. It could tolerate and even encourage what it viewed as violence necessary to preserve cultural patterns, but there was a critical line between necessary and wanton violence that the Klan could not overstep without loss of community support. Deprived of this approval and of new issues on which to capitalize, the Klan remains weakened and fragmented by power struggles among its leaders, who are almost as likely to recruit members in New England as in the Deep South.

Mary E. Stovall
Greenville, Mississippi

David M. Chalmers, *Hooded Americanism: The History of the Ku Klux Klan* (1965); John Moffatt Mecklin, *The Ku Klux Klan: A Study of the American Mind* (1924); Allen W. Trelease, *White Terror: The Ku Klux Klan Conspiracy and Southern Reconstruction* (1971).

Mob Violence

Throughout their history Americans have resorted to mob violence in the form of physical assaults, extralegal executions, and riots. Whether spontaneously organized or formally constituted into a more permanent movement, numerous groups have taken the law into their own hands, primarily for the conservative purpose of protecting the existing order against real or imagined threats.

During the 18th century the first vigilante movements appeared on the southern frontier, where law enforcement was ineffective. In 1767 local citizens formed the South Carolina Regulators, who mounted a two-year campaign to rid the area of outlaws through mock trials followed by whippings and/or banishment. "Lynch law," the popular term for this practice, originated in western Virginia in 1780, when settlers—led by Colonel Charles Lynch—dispensed private justice. The practice of "regulating" undesirables through lynch law became a national phenomenon that spread westward with the frontier. Some of the worst outbreaks occurred in Texas, which had more vigilante movements than any other state.

After 1830 collective violence also erupted in well-established communities as a means of summary punishment in both the North and the South. In addition to flogging and sometimes killing whites suspected of opposing slavery, southern mobs occasionally attacked transgressors of local morality, such as five gamblers who were hanged by Vicksburg, Miss., vigilantes in 1835. With the close of the frontier, lynching became increasingly a southern phenomenon, which was used, along with race riots, largely to enforce white supremacy. Although most victims of lynch law were black, mob violence also took the lives of whites, such as immigrants, radicals, and union organizers, who were considered outsiders and a threat. In 1891 a mob executed 11 Italians accused of killing the police chief of New Orleans, La. Anti-Semitism figured in the 1915 lynching of Leo Frank in Atlanta. Industrial violence claimed the life of an Arkansas union leader who was lynched in 1923.

Corporal punishment, often in the form of a flogging and/or the application of tar and feathers, was the most common vigilante method of regulating behavior in the South. Frequently administered by well-organized groups such as the Ku Klux Klan, this type of mob violence claimed thousands of victims from the 1890s through the 1930s. The targets were usually whites whose "offenses" ranged from the violation of local moral codes to support for unpopular causes, such as unions and communism.

People of all classes, including the elite, engaged in mob violence, and many members of the southern press and police endorsed or tolerated vigilantism. As a result, few participants were ever punished. After World War II, mob violence generally declined as changing southern attitudes, outside pressures, and the forces of modernization undermined local support for mob action. During the 1950s and 1960s, however, violence was directed at blacks and whites involved in the civil rights movement. Although infrequent today, collective violence remains a threat as demonstrated by the 1979 killing of five communists by vigilantes in Greensboro, N.C.

See also LAW: / Frank, Leo, Case

Robert P. Ingalls
University of South Florida

Richard Maxwell Brown, *Strain of Violence: Historical Studies of American Violence and Vigilantism* (1975).

Nightriders

If Reconstruction brought a twinkle of progressive thought to the South, it also bred fiery resentment and rabid emotions. Slavery had been demolished, and, overnight, former plantation owners were without labor. A depressed, war-weary southern economy now had an even larger labor force in which poor whites competed for jobs with newly freed blacks. Out of this climate hatred sprouted, and in southern communities throughout the region nightriders and Klansmen rose up in efforts to intimidate blacks psychologically and physically.

In *Night Riders in Black Folk History*, Gladys-Marie Fry discusses the function of the nightrider or "Ku Klux" in controlling blacks before and after the Civil War. This form of intimidation was used before the Civil War to discourage unauthorized movement, to guard against slave insurrections, and, after the war, to repeatedly let blacks know their behavioral boundaries. Black oral history is rich with stories of evil white men joining together to incite the fears of black families and entire towns. Nightrider incidents are stored in the minds of elderly blacks, and although many do not recall the chronological specifics of the events, they well remember acts of intimidation, often having heard tales from older family or community members.

Nightriders were not unique to Reconstruction. Although the practice flourished then, black folk history shows that nightriding existed throughout slavery. The Reconstruction Ku Klux Klan was probably a modern version of the antebellum patrol system. The patrols or "paterollers" set out to check the passes of the slaves, to maintain curfew, and to physically abuse rule breakers. Folklorist William Lynwood Montell writes that slaveowners in the Kettle Creek area of Tennessee relied on the patrol system because they had trouble keeping slaves on the plantation.

Though the stereotype of a masked, robed Klansman was in many cases a true image, many nightriders often traveled without the disguise of a white garment. In the Cumberland plateau community of Free Hill, Tenn., not one resident remembers a Ku Klux disguise or mask; rather, as one resident explained, "these were people that they knew, they knew from down in town." The absence of a mask or hood, however, did not mean that there was no attempt to disguise. Groups of men always came at night and assumed the community would flee out of fear. For them, night itself was some disguise, and there was little risk of recognition.

Tom Rankin
Southern Arts Federation
Atlanta, Georgia

Gladys-Marie Fry, *Night Riders in Black Folk History* (1975); William Lynwood Montell, *The Saga of Coe Ridge: A Study in Oral History* (1970); Elizabeth Peterson and Tom Rankin, *Free Hill: A Sound Portrait of a Rural Afro-American Community* (Tennessee Folklore Society recording, 1985).

Orangeburg Massacre

Violence against blacks in the South erupted on 8 February 1968 when a fusillade of gunfire by state highway patrolmen killed three students and wounded 27 others on the campus of South Carolina State College at Orangeburg. The killings, known in civil rights circles as the "Orangeburg massacre," attracted little national attention at the time, being incorrectly reported by the Associated Press as "an exchange of gunfire." The shooting occurred on the third night of confrontations that had begun when students at the predominantly black college protested the segregation policy of the town's only bowling alley, five blocks from the campus.

The Orangeburg massacre was the first time students on an American college campus had been slain by law enforcement officers. The episode preceded by more than two years an event that became a cause célèbre—the slaying of four white Kent State University students by National Guardsmen in May 1970. A few days later in that same month, Jackson, Miss., city police and state highway patrolmen opened fire on protesting black students at Jackson State University (then Jackson State College), killing two students. A President's Commission on Campus Unrest investigated the Kent State and Jackson State shootings, but its historical section failed to mention the killings two years earlier at Orangeburg.

Jack Bass
University of South Carolina

Jack Nelson and Jack Bass, *The Orangeburg Massacre* (1970).

Parchman

The intervention of convict lease stalemated the penitentiary movement in the postbellum South. Because convicts, most of whom were black, were leased, southern states stopped maintaining existing prisons, and penitentiaries became "mere shells of buildings, depositories for the old, the sick and the most dangerous." The state of Mississippi outlawed convict lease (though not the equally infamous chain gang) by constitutional amendment in 1890 and sought institutional alternatives for using convict labor that would not jeopardize the interests of free labor. Legislators authorized the purchase of several tracts of land on which penal farms were erected to provide convicts with "healthful agricultural labor" and the state with significant profit.

The largest of these farms was established at the turn of the century on some 13,000 acres purchased from a Sunflower County planter, James Parchman. When folksong collector John A. Lomax visited Parchman in the 1930s, more than 2,000 inmates tilled 17,000 acres of rich Delta land, channeling large sums into the state treasury. Lomax found his blues and ballad recording hindered by the length of convict work days and noted that part of the farm's profit came from the "economies" practiced: labor from 4:00 a.m. until dark and a total lack of mechanization.

In 1968 a regional prison report outlined conditions at Parchman and penitentiaries in Arkansas and Louisiana, concluding that "the three states put together could not out of presently available funds and facilities provide the components of one prison which would meet minimum national standards." Parchman's brutality and corruption were not unique. Angola in Louisiana was also infamous, but by the 1960s Parchman had become legendary. Beatings were routinely administered for infractions ranging from failure to address an officer properly to attempted escape. Inmates employed as armed guards—170 out of a total force of 210 guards as late as 1968—abused and often killed fellow prisoners.

In 1971 documented instances of brutality against several hundred incarcerated civil rights workers led to sweeping changes. Within three years, the trusty system was abolished; inadequate, segregated facilities were abandoned; and vocational training was implemented.

Today most of Parchman's 21,000 acres of cotton land are leased to local farmers, and many of its 12,000 prisoners participate in external rehabilitation programs. A stadium, a new $3 million hospital, and apartments for family and conjugal visiting are maintained. Traditional black and white uniforms have been replaced with denim trousers and work shirts. Still, the aura of fear and the reality of punishment remain. Said B. B. King of his childhood visit to his uncle, a fellow bluesman and former Parchman inmate Bukka White: "After that . . . I knew I wanted to stay far away from the place."

Elizabeth M. Makowski
University of Mississippi

L. C. Dorsey, *Cold Steel* (1982); William Ferris, *The New Journal* (25 January 1973); Marvin Hutson, "Mississippi's State Penal System" (M.A. thesis, University of Mississippi, 1939); John A. Lomax, *Adventures of a Ballad Hunter* (1947); Roy Reed, *New York Times* (27 January 1973); Dunbar Rowland, *Mississippi* (1907); Southern Regional Council, *The Delta Prisons: Punishment for Profit* (1968).

Camp B, Parchman Penitentiary, Mississippi, 1975

Peonage

Peonage, a Latin American labor system that entered the United States through Mexican land acquisitions, relies on debt to bind laborers to the land. In 1867 Congress passed a law (14 Stat. 546) that prohibited peonage both in territories recently acquired from Mexico and throughout the United States. The law lay dormant until 1901, when U.S. attorney Fred Cubberly uncovered it and brought a case against Samuel T. Clyatt for using laborers in his turpentine operation to work off debts. During the statute's dormancy, the intricate farm labor system that developed in the South blurred the distinctions between law and custom. State legislatures enacted enticement laws, emigrant agent restrictions, contract laws, vagrancy statutes, the criminal surety system, and convict labor laws, while planters used both laws and rural customs to keep laborers, in most cases black sharecroppers, from leaving their employ. Such labor laws, like discrimination and disfranchisement statutes, became more severe in the 1890s and the first decade of the 20th century.

As the *Clyatt* case (*Clyatt* v. *United States*, 197 U.S. 207) progressed through appeals that ultimately decided the constitutionality of the law, the extent of peonage in the South became more apparent. In Alabama, Judge Thomas G. Jones, experimenting with light sentences and publicity in 1903, dramatized how pervasive peonage had become. In 1906 Booker T. Washington joined with local whites in Alabama and brought another precedent-setting case that exposed, through the plight of Alonzo Bailey, the tight legal framework that trapped men who took cash advances under "false pretenses" and left their jobs before completing the contract. The case also showed the draconian nature of southern rural labor laws. The basic "false pretenses" law had been on the books since 1885, but laborers had won a series of Alabama cases, for employers had been unable to establish the intent of laborers who left their jobs. In 1903 Alabama tightened its law, as did Georgia; Florida followed in 1907. Under the amended law, a laborer's taking the money and failing either to pay it back or work it out was "prima facie evidence of the intent to injure or defraud his employer." A 1907 rule of evidence prohibited the laborer from taking the witness stand to explain his intent. After two appeals, in 1911 the Supreme Court struck down the law (*Bailey* v. *Alabama*, 211 U.S. 452; *Bailey* v. *Alabama*, 219 U.S. 219). Yet other states, particularly Florida and Georgia, persisted with similar laws until the 1940s. The Supreme Court also ruled against the widespread practice of allowing planters to pay off fines of laborers who were facing jail sentences and then working them as criminals (*United States* v. *Reynolds*, 235 U.S. 133). This series of cases successfully unraveled much of the legal net that caught vulnerable farm workers and sucked them into the vortex of peonage. Still, peonage continued outside the law.

Most peonage cases originated in the old cotton belt that ran from South Carolina through the Black Belt of Georgia and Alabama and into the Mississippi and Arkansas deltas. During the first decade of the century many immigrants who were transported to the South became the focus of a series of cases and glaring publicity lasting several years. While successful court cases made southerners aware of the law, peonage continued as evinced in numerous complaints and prosecutions. The vast complaint file in the National Archives suggests not only the extent of involuntary servitude but also the helplessness of barely literate workers who tried to escape. Local law enforcement officials either ignored such conditions or actively supported planters. Most rural laborers did not understand the workings of the law and were caught up in the customary relationship of landlord and tenant; relatively few questioned their conditions. In some cases planters did not understand the law either. Court cases and complaints revealed clearly the bottom rung of the southern rural labor system and showed the confusion in distinguishing freedom from bondage.

Complaints and cases declined during the 1930s, although a landmark Arkansas case in 1936 used an 1866 statute (14 Stat. 50) outlawing slave kidnapping to prosecute lawman Paul Peacher and thus extend federal jurisdiction over any kind of involuntary servitude—not just that which involved debt. In recent years most peonage complaints have come from migrant laborers, and several successful prosecutions have revealed the vulnerability of such agricultural workers. Thus, in a larger sense, peonage has represented continuity with the South's slave past.

See also LAW: / Black Codes

Pete Daniel
Smithsonian Institution

William Cohen, *Journal of Southern History* (February 1976); Pete Daniel, *The Shadow of Slavery: Peonage in the South, 1901–1969* (1972); Daniel A. Novak, *The Wheel of Servitude: Black Forced Labor after Slavery* (1978).

Redfield, H. V.

(1845–1881) Journalist.

Redfield's *Homicide, North and South* was the most careful and extensive study of the differences in regional homicide rates produced in the 19th century. Although the work of a little-known amateur, it is an outstanding example of the American social science of the period.

Horace Victor Eugene Redfield was born about 1845 in Erie County, N.Y., into a family with Vermont origins. However, after his father's early death, he accompanied his mother to the South and in 1860 was residing in Jasper, Marion County, Tenn. A journalist in adult life, he wrote no other known book. Redfield died in 1881 in Washington, D.C., where he had been based for several years as correspondent for the Cincinnati *Commercial*. In the preface to *Homicide* he emphasized his southern upbringing and claimed to have spent most of his life in the South. The author went out of his way to praise southern life and the treatment he had received there. He realized that many would view his work as an attack on the South, but he wished that it could be viewed as friendly criticism that might lead to reform.

Redfield began his book by noting that the rural rates for homicide in England, New England, and the Upper Midwest were very similar, but that rates for the South were much higher than for any civilized country in at least the previous two centuries. He tried to document this remarkable fact and inquire into its causes. He traveled widely throughout the country, collecting data from official sources where it was available (primarily in the North) and developing complete newspaper files where this was possible. He compared rates in the late 1860s and 1870s for "old states" North and South and for frontier states, finding that South Carolina's were as many times greater than New England's as Texas's rates were greater than Minnesota's. In both cases he estimated well over 10 times as many murders per 100,000 population in the South as in the North. He pointed out that Texas was populated largely from the Old South and Minnesota from the North. By comparing homicide rates and population origins in Ohio, Indiana, and Illinois, he demonstrated that the line between North and South ran through these states, whereas Iowa more clearly belonged to the North.

Redfield saw several patterns in southern homicide. Drunken brawls might not be too different from those in the North, yet they more often led to murders, both because of the attitudes of those involved and the general practice of carrying weapons. Murder often occurred to redress insult to personal honor or because of a tough's desire to show off. Groups, whether gangs or clans, often attacked rival groups out of animosity or for political ends. Feuds as such played less of a part in his analysis than one might expect, given his familiarity with Kentucky.

Although very close to the Civil War, he could not see the war as a major cause of southern patterns that greatly antedated it. He saw the most general cause of southern violence as a lack of regard for human life. He thought an exaggerated sense of honor contributed to the high rates of homicide, as did the unnecessary carrying of weapons, particularly concealed weapons. In many rural areas he pointed out that a lone law officer was often powerless or afraid to intervene. Even if caught, the murderer would seldom be convicted or would be given a light sentence. Redfield cited many cases illustrating the difficulty of getting convictions in the South. Convictions were seldom achieved for several reasons: the jurors did not take killing as seriously as in the North; they would be more likely to accept the reasons justifying the killing than would northern jurors; the jurors knew they might themselves later be involved in murder and would not want to meet a juror related to a person they had helped convict; they feared imminent retaliation by relatives of the murderer should they convict.

A great deal has changed since Redfield's study. In his time, for instance, he found whites more involved in murder than blacks. (This may have been because of the availability of weapons, or simply because he did not have sufficient information on black homicide.) Redfield may well have contributed to the amelioration of the situation as he found it, but lethal violence still casts a shadow over southern culture and thus the nation as a whole.

Raymond D. Gastil
Freedom House

New York Times (18 November 1881); H. V. Redfield, *Homicide, North and South: Being a Comparative View of Crime against the Person in Several Parts of the United States* (1880); J. H. Redfield, *Genealogical History of the Redfield Family* (1860).

Texas Rangers

When the first English-speaking colonists moved into Mexican Texas, they brought their own customs, social values, laws, and officials. Among these were the Rangers.

Since the beginnings of the Anglos' westward drive—in the case of Texas settlers, generally through the South—armed, mounted men ranged the line of advancing homesteaders to protect them from Indians and outlaws. These men were usually civilians locally paid, armed with their own guns, and not in uniform.

Rangers may have had their origin hundreds of years ago in English estates in the role of protectors of their employers' lands, patrolling or ranging at will. Once across an ocean and on the southern frontier, they came to deal with whatever trouble could not be appropriately solved by local police, sheriffs, or the army. Rangers were never intended as a substitute for either the police or the army. They were volunteer, but, unlike local lawmen, they were willing to pursue their foe as far as was necessary and were much more mobile than regular army detachments. They would fight on their opponents' terms and settle trouble as they saw it without the delays of formal legal process.

When Stephen F. Austin's Texas colony was threatened by Indian attacks in 1823, he called out a company of rangers for protection. They were not the first such men in the field, but they were probably the first officially called Rangers.

For over 40 years Ranger units in Texas were temporary, raised when necessary and dismissed when not needed. They were called "Rangers," "spies," "volunteer companies," "Corps of Rangers," and "Ranging Companies." Later the term Texas Rangers was commonly used, as in 1866 legislative finance bills.

The duties of the Rangers varied with the times. First, they opposed small groups of hostile Indians. When the Republic of Texas was established in 1836, sporadic conflict between Mexico and Texas continued. The Rangers then faced two enemies, Indians and Mexicans. For a dozen years Rangers were irregular fighting units, riding as scouts, guerrillas, and cavalry support for regular troops. Some groups became virtual border guards on the Rio Grande between Texas and Mexico. Others ranged the northwest frontier of Texas in pursuit of Indians. In time, the Indians were driven from Texas, and the Rio Grande—with exceptions—became a stable, recognized international border.

The next Ranger opponent was the outlaw. Rangers turned to the role of peace officers, serving somewhat as a state police force, though never that in name. They regulated cattle rustling, fence cutting, mob violence—any breach of the law that was too widespread or too violent for local officers.

Of debatable efficiency against Indians, Rangers were demonstrably effective against outlaws. They established a lasting reputation for quick striking power over a vast area. To the Anglo businessman and settler, the Ranger meant courage, peacekeeping, and frontier resourcefulness. To his opponents, he represented unhesitating violence, unrelenting pursuit, and a willingness to use any means, including firepower, to enforce the law.

Over the years, Rangers established a standard of personal bravery that became the basis of myth. The story maintaining that only one Ranger was necessary to quell any riot was certainly myth, but individual acts of courage supported the belief that it just might be true. The Rangers have also attracted considerable criticism. They have been accused of brutality, racism, and illegal arrest. In recent years, Mexican Americans have been especially critical of the Rangers, seeing them as an authoritarian force used against minorities. Rangers have been called strikebreakers and paid assassins. But they have more supporters than critics, as their continued service indicates. The most common feeling is that "as long as there is a state of Texas, there will be Rangers."

Established as a permanent service in 1874, the Rangers were authorized by the Texas Legislature to enlist 450 men. Temporary enlistments in earlier years had risen as high as a thousand. The number of Rangers has since varied from a low of about 20 in 1900 to 94 in 1982.

For many years the Texas Rangers served the state directly under the governor and an adjutant general. In 1935 the service became a division of the Texas Department of Public Safety. Today they are charged with suppressing riots and insurrections, apprehending fugitives, assisting peace officers anywhere in the state, and dealing with major crime on their own initiative.

John L. Davis
Institute of Texas Cultures

John L. Davis, *The Texas Rangers, Their First 150 Years* (1975); James B. Gillett, *Six Years with the Texas Rangers* (1921); Walter Prescott Webb, ed., *The Handbook of Texas* (1952), *The Texas Rangers* (1935).

Wilmington Race Riot

At the entrance of the Cape Fear River, about 30 miles from the east coast of North Carolina, rests the port city of Wilmington. On the morning of 10 November 1898—two days after a statewide election in which terrorized blacks had largely refrained from voting—an armed and angry mob of about 500 white men gathered in front of the headquarters of the Wilmington Light Infantry. From there, in military order and led by Colonel Alfred M. Waddell, they marched to the office of the black newspaper. They forced the door open, broke windows, destroyed furniture, and then burned the building down.

Thus began one of the worst massacres of the Progressive era. In 1898 Wilmington was, ironically, perhaps the most racially tolerant post-Reconstruction southern city. Blacks figured prominently in the city's political and economic life, occupying high positions in government and holding jobs as restaurant owners, barbers, and artisans. The collector of customs at the port of Wilmington, one of the city auditors, the coroner, 30 percent of the aldermen, clerks, firemen, policemen, and justices of the peace were all black. Conspicuous also were black lawyers, a black voting majority, and Alex Manly's black-run newspaper, the Wilmington *Record.*

At the same time, masses of poor whites and blacks lived in abject poverty. Many Democrats were poor, lower-class whites, who scolded employers for giving blacks preference in hiring.

In the 1894 state election the Fusionist forces, a coalition of Populists and Republicans with their black allies, triumphed. Two years later they elected Wilmington's Daniel Russell as the first Republican governor since Reconstruction. In March of 1897 they altered Wilmington's charter, which enabled the Republicans to usurp control of the city government from an office-holding Democratic clique. The old politicians (city bosses) unsuccessfully challenged the victorious allies in the courts.

For a period of months prior to the riot, the "Secret Nine"—a cabal of minor Democrats—clandestinely planned to overthrow the new government. The Wilmington race riot was preceded by a statewide supremacy crusade, which the resurgent Democrats launched to regain political ascendency in 1898. It was abetted by a propaganda campaign, and armed vigilantes terrorized the black population.

During mid-October the Democrats resurrected an Alex Manly editorial that had appeared in the Wilmington *Record* on 18 August. It refuted claims that black men were raping white women and committing other crimes and stated that black men "were sufficiently attractive for white girls of culture and refinement to fall in love with them." Printed out of context and headlined daily in the local papers the article was a catalyst for the riot that exploded on 10 November.

Manly escaped days before a large mob, led by ex-congressman Alfred M. Waddell, burned his press. The wounding of William Mayo (white) roused the whites to a frenzy. A massacre ensued, but no whites were slain, and only three were injured. The large number of blacks killed can never be known.

The Democrats subsequently overthrew the legally elected Republican government and unanimously elected Waddell mayor. The next day, amidst jeering crowds, a militia with "fixed bayonets" banished prominent white Republican and black leaders. After two days the blacks who had hidden in the woods came out to find their property, businesses, artisan trades, municipal jobs, and even the traditionally black-occupied menial vocations taken over by the self-appointed new administration and its supportive clan.

H. Leon Prather
Tennessee State University

H. Leon Prather, *We Have Taken a City: Wilmington Racial Massacre and Coup of 1898* (1984).

Women's Life

CAROL RUTH BERKIN
Baruch College, City University of New York
CONSULTANT

Doris Ulmann photograph of a young woman, Brasstown, N.C., 1930s

Women's Life

"Who was the southern lady?" a serious scholar asked her colleagues. But few historians thought it a serious question. Everyone, of course, knew the answer. In a sea of historical uncertainties, the southern woman has been a cherished constant. Everyone knows her and can call her by name. If she is white, she is Miss Scarlett; if she is black, she is mammy. In either persona, the southern woman radiates mystery, but a comfortable, predictable mystery. Scholars have plumbed, measured, and charted her depths as a cultural figure, and they have learned to recognize her white soul and her black one. They can consign her to the novelists and poets who write, after all, about eternal verities.

Or can they? Since the serious study of American women began in the 1970s, the southern woman has become a troublesome figure. If she is white, she simply will not stay on her pedestal. She keeps stepping down to work in the tobacco fields of 17th-century Maryland; to run taverns and printing presses in 18th-century Carolina; to fight for abolition, and to speak out against slavery; to criticize the very chivalric code that purports to honor her in the antebellum era. In the New South she organizes mission schools, fights for unions in the mill towns, and demands suffrage at the height of her Victorian respectability. In the modern era she organizes antilynching leagues, runs Works Progress Administration agencies, joins in civil rights struggles, and creates political organizations to defeat or defend controversial social legislation like the Equal Rights Amendment.

If she is black, she removes her mammy's apron and her mammy's smile and becomes a member of a vital slave culture, a tobacco and cotton field worker, a midwife, a religious leader among her people. She is not content to be the linchpin of the planter's "domestic patriarchy," but is sometimes a fierce opponent of the peculiar institution. In the New South she resists agricultural oppression, is a union supporter when she is allowed access to a union, and risks her job in a domestic worker's strike. In the 20th century she becomes a segregation fighter, a college educator, and a Democratic party keynote speaker.

Who was the southern woman—and who is she? One cannot be certain anymore. Whoever she is, historians now realize that she is central to the understanding of southern culture—its reality as well as its myths. For, if chivalry became the southern code of behavior, its object and raison d'être was the southern white woman. If slavery became its "peculiar institution," the representative of its most benign aspects was the black mammy and the symbol of its darkest side was the black concubine. If strong family ties came to bind southerner to southerner across the miles and decades, the southern woman was the heart of each family. Everything from the delights of southern hospitality to the modern advantages of cheap southern labor leads one to explore the experiences of the southern woman. Finally, she is also central to understanding American women, for southern women are as distinctive in women's past as the South is in our nation's past.

Women in the Colonial South. Family has always seemed the centripetal force in southern culture. Yet, among white southerners at least, family has undergone more dramatic changes than most southern institutions. So too have the roles women have played in these families.

While patriarchal, nuclear families migrated to 17th-century New England, the Chesapeake colonies filled with kinless, unmarried men. Planters preferred to import young males to work the tobacco fields, and thus they created a society with roughly six men to every woman. For decades, family life of any sort eluded many of these men. Southern males thought of this sexual imbalance as a "paradise for women," but many women may have disagreed. Relentless pressures pushed young, native-born women into the role of wife and mother as early as 16 or 17 years old.

The Chesapeake environment shaped family life and structure also. While the average New England couple lived to raise a large family and become grandparents, a southern couple learned to expect death and disaster. Disease was the villain. Half of all marriages were ended by malaria or related diseases after seven years. The young husband or wife was then left to care for two or three small children. Not surprisingly, remarriage, with the rearing of a new family, was common. Thus, southerners created a unique family structure, with large temporary households made up of stepmothers or fathers, half brothers and sisters. A vocabulary of impermanence developed as children referred to their father's "now-wife" and stepmothers spoke of raising "sons-in-law" rather than sons of their own blood.

Where early and sudden death was a norm, southern women found themselves with greater legal and economic responsibilities than their northern counterparts. For, in a society where adult kin of either sex were rare, isolated farms were more common than towns, and sons were usually minors at their fathers' deaths, husbands tended to entrust their estates to their wives. Many southern women inherited an entire estate, despite the certainty that they would remarry. As relatively young women, they took on the responsibilities of managing their own fortunes and the fortunes of their children. Ironically, a husband's death left southern women with greater familial and social power than long life provided other American women.

The southern white woman's life cycle was different from her New England sister's, yet in their daily household routine all colonial women had much in common. When needed, the southern wife toiled in the fields. But most of her day was spent in domestic duties. She tended gardens, kept a dairy and poultry, baked, preserved foods, sewed, mended, cleaned her home (if a free moment for such a luxury presented itself), fed the family and household servants, and cared for infants and young toddlers alike.

Farm boundaries were a woman's life boundaries in most cases. Yet some women seemed to escape between the cracks in this still fluid, underpopulated, labor-scarce society. Widows ran farms, opened taverns, and kept small shops. Women took their neighbors to court, suing for default on debts or for libel. And, in a society where government would not, and perhaps could not, allocate funds for relief and welfare functions, women left by chance or by choice outside the protection of a male guardian were granted legal rights and social approval to seek economic independence.

By the 18th century the Chesapeake's "demographic disaster" had ended. Perhaps immunities to local diseases developed, or planters learned to locate their families away from the malarial environments. A native-born population came to outnumber immigrants, and their longer life span made the development of a patriarchal, nuclear family possible. Even the sexual imbalance slowly righted itself. Southern women began to marry later, in their early twenties, and to husbands more their own ages. The "American" colonial family had arrived in the South: father, mother, and seven or eight children.

In this family, women's role as surrogate patriarch diminished. Adult sons inherited directly from fathers and were assigned to manage the inheritance of minor siblings. Longer-lived fathers were now able to direct their children's lives, pulling on the key strings of property and dowry. The patriarch was ascendent; the southern wife was eclipsed.

Yet new emphasis on tasks within the home accompanied this shift to a stable nuclear family. Most importantly, across the colonies, a new attitude toward child rearing evolved. Its causes varied—religious imperatives prompting it in the Quaker and Puritan worlds, economic prosperity promoting it in the South. The results were the same: the family became child-centered, and the woman's central role became that of mother. Class was the key to this new emphasis on child care, for only white mothers with household servants could spare the time for children beyond the toddler phase. Beginning as an elite ideal, the nurturant mother was to become "nature's" and "God's" true woman in later decades.

During the early 18th century the marital and familial experiences of women North and South seemed to converge. In truth, however, the regions were on quite different trajectories. The southern family was moving toward its fullest expression of patriarchy in the 19th century; the northern family was undergoing subtle but significant modifications that weakened its patriarchal core. The growth of the black slave system was, of course, central to the intensification of patriarchy in the South.

Southern planters chose to describe the plantation as a single social unit, incorporating slave labor and personal household into one dependency. The planter's authority over the slave and his authority over his wife and children were parts of the whole cloth of his authority over the plantation family. The power over the slave seemed to prepare the way for greater authority with other dependents. At the same time, the need for sexual protection of his wife and other white females of his household came to vindicate his quest for absolute power over the slave.

The rapid increase of slaves in the colonial South dramatically transformed the lives of black women also. Until the 18th century black women's demographic and mortality patterns had paralleled those of their white counterparts. Now, however, in the black population as well as the white, native-born men and women constituted a majority in most of the southern colonies, and by 1740 the sex ratio had begun to even out. For some blacks trapped in slavery, the rise of great plantations provided one small but significant advantage: in slave quarters, population density meant the opportunity to forge tight communities, develop a minority culture, and elaborate a kinship network. Yet for many blacks, isolated or in twos and threes on small farms, family life remained impossible.

The structure of marriage and family was, perforce, different for slaves than for their masters. Patriarchy was not a viable model. Black males could not assert authority over a dependent wife, for both male and female were themselves dependents. Secondly, marriage did not mean the transition for a woman from a father's guardianship and home to a husband's care and household. Indeed, the absence of a physical relocation bespoke the absence of the psychological and legal transference. A slave woman remained on her home plantation even after marriage, for her role as laborer superseded her role as wife.

Slaves did not attempt to emulate the white family structure. The extended family, more than the nuclear family, fit the needs of men and women who might be separated by sale, lease, or transfer to other slave quarters. Like the nuclear family, the extended family had its psychic benefits and costs to all members. Thus far no one has examined them.

The Impact of the American Revolution. The American Revolution, like the Civil War, left different legacies to the North and South. When the war ended and the architects of the Republic had set its cornerstone of republican government in place, women's role in the new nation was examined by northern intellectuals. But the war, fought longer and more fiercely in the South, had devastated much of the region. Renovation, not innovation, was the southern planter's agenda. Thus, "Republican Motherhood," the new idealization of women in northern society, did not take hold in the South as firmly as it did in other regions.

For northern ideologues, Republican Motherhood included an acknowledged role for women in American political life, not as citizens but as the primary educators of future male citizens. Thus, a woman performed a *civic* duty as she performed a familial duty. Republican Motherhood was a rendition of the preindependence trend toward a child-centered family. This emphasis on women as socializing agents did lead to a new and positive evaluation of women's intellectual and moral capacities. It also produced an educational revolution for women in the New England and middle states. Formal schooling for young women flourished there. From Republican Motherhood came a justification for greater participation in public affairs and a greater sense of self-esteem for women. From the women's academies and schools came a knowledge of society, a vocabulary to criticize it, and a shared female experience. The results were soon evident in the reform movements of the 1830s and 1840s.

In the South, however, the reestablishment and entrenchment of the planter patriarchy kept the roles of wife and mother private ones for women. Southern women might have been responsible for their children's morals and values, but their endeavors remained a service within the family rather than a civic function. Indeed, southern male intellectuals and educators did not publicly challenge the notion of female intellectual inferiority until the 1840s. Their hesitant call for formal education of women came 50 years after Benjamin Rush and Susannah Rowson outlined the moral and intellectual potential of the Republican Mother. On the eve of the Civil War, southern women had the highest rate of illiteracy among adult white women in the nation. And black slave women were barred from literacy by law.

Had the idea of the Republican Mother taken root in southern consciousness, southern social and economic realities in the early 19th century would have diffused its impact. White southern women of all classes lived in greater isolation than their northern sisters and had less access to the company of other women. The creation of female voluntary and reform associations, a logical extension of Republican Motherhood, required an urban setting that did not exist in the mainly rural South. In addition, southern women of both races continued to marry earlier, die younger, and bear more children than northerners did. White southern women entered adult roles too quickly to allow the hiatus of the female academy. Finally, southern women did not find the opportunity for participation and leadership within the churches that northern women rushed to accept in the early 19th century. Southern men remained in control of the evangelical churches, church participation remained a family function, and separate women's organizations did not develop within the church.

The Southern Lady. The 1830s did produce a new southern female paradigm—the southern lady. She was, in theory if not in fact, virtuous, modest, pious, and submissive. As a wife, she was "queen of the home"; as a mother, she was devotion and self-denial personified. Historian Anne Firor Scott aptly says that for this model of southern femininity, "life was one long act of devotion."

The southern lady was the logical companion to the idealized southern patriarch, who was himself the kind and protective, stern but just father to both his white and black families. The southern lady's enduring and open respect for, and submission to, her husband was firm evidence of the benign nature of the southern way of life and its peculiar institution. If the pressure of a life on the pedestal was strongest among the elite, the image of a self-sacrificing and devoted wife and mother took firm hold among the ordinary white folk as well.

Even as the pedestal was constructed, however, deep internal fault lines showed themselves. Among the elite class, marriage was prompted as much by a father's consideration of land and slaves and a young girl's fear of spinsterhood as by admiration for a new husband. Reality rather than romance waltzed many a southern belle down the aisle. Daily life on the pedestal was far from romantic or inspirational. All white wives, rich or poor, worked for their daily bread. Plantation mistresses supervised slaves, rationed supplies for the black work force, and acted as medical expert for the white and black community. Poorer women worked in the fields when their labor was needed. The majority of white women spun and sewed, gardened, supervised hog butcherings, made their own lard soap and even their yeast. Urban women were drafted into producing goods or providing services for their husband's shop or trade. Acts of "devotion" were made in the physical rather than the spiritual realm.

Had people been listening, they would have heard southern ladies protesting their lives. Plantation mistresses resented the lack of control over their own sexual lives and reproductive systems, and they objected to their husbands' sexual behavior. Many hated slavery, if not for its immorality and injustice, then for the burden it placed upon them as plantation mistresses. They were exhausted by their duties as arbiters of so many complex and tension-filled interracial and intraracial relationships. They resented their lack of education and the intellectual and physical isolation of their lives. Their discontent challenged the cherished image of boundless maternal devotion.

It is not hard to locate the sources of their discontent. In the South Carolina of 1856, 40.4 percent of all white women were married before their 20th birthday, often to men 10 years their senior. This pattern marked a return to 17th-century models. And, although southern men applauded the fertility of their wives, shouting "well done" to women who bore six children in nine years, southern wives were not cheered by this praise. Two decades of childbearing meant 10 or 11 children. Or, put more graphically, during 180 months of married life, a Louisiana woman was pregnant 90 months and was nursing 70. While Harvard doctors like Horatio Storer bemoaned the decreasing size of New England Protestant families, southern women continued to spend their married lives in reproduction.

Opposition to the sexual double standard, to the morality of specific social institutions, to inequality of male and female education, and to lack of control over fertility was a common theme among American women, North and South. In the North, however, women's reform societies worked to combat such manifestations of the double standard as prostitution. Southern ladies could not use similar methods to promote reform. No existing women's organizations could be called upon to lead campaigns on women's issues. Southern women who wished to be activists made their ways north. Thus, female leadership was drained from the region, as it would be again a century later. Finally, southern plantation patriarchy had so successfully circumscribed women's lives that public protest or reform activity lacked any legitimacy or apparent logic. What, after all, was the point of a reform organization when prostitution or concubinage was not a social but a family affair?

Relations between slave women and slave men were, of course, determined by different rules. Yet historians disagree on the sexual politics of the slave community. They know that husband and wife remained part of an extended network of kin and fictive kin and that work roles were less differentiated because both sexes worked in the fields. In their roles as slaves, men and women enjoyed—or suffered—a rough equality, and they were both dependents of the master or mistress, with no economic ties binding them to each other. Some historians argue, however, that a sexual division of labor was established *within* the slave quarters, where male and female roles were sharply defined.

The Civil War and the New South. The Civil War changed the circumstances of southern women's lives much as the American Revolution had altered the lives of northern women. Military defeat and the dismantling of the slave system weakened the patriarchal power of the planter-husband over his wife. The change was most apparent on mundane levels. Immediately following the war, with many of their men dead or disabled and the economy destroyed, white women were often forced into independence.

For many, the role proved permanent, for the war had created a second southern "demographic disaster." One quarter of a million white men had died in the Civil War. Many who had survived moved west, seeking new land and a new start. By 1870 North Carolina had 25,000 more women than men; Georgia had 36,000 more. Among blacks a similar demographic disaster had occurred. Black female-headed households, now visible as public units rather than private plantation arrangements, were common in the postwar era. Disease and poverty, not the battlefield, took black male lives. For example, in New Orleans, black widows constituted 81 percent of the female heads of households.

Industrialization and urbanization began to transform women's lives also. First, the shift from plantation slavery to systems of sharecropping or tenant farming affected white and black rural women dramatically. Blacks, acting as a family unit, resisted the older work patterns of slavery. A sexual division of labor was the freed black's goal, with women out of the fields and in charge of domestic production. White landowners railed against what they called "female loaferism," but for black men and women this effort to keep one family member's labor outside the grasp of the white landlord and exclusive to the family represented a measure of control over their economic lives.

Often, the desire to free black women from field work could not be fulfilled. As late as 1920, 90 percent of the black women in tenant families did some field work, either with their husbands or for wages off the family farm. Sixty-five percent of the women in black landowning families also did field work.

White tenant farm women shared much in common with these black women. In 1920, 40 percent of all white landowning women worked in the fields and 67 percent of all white tenant women. In all, a far greater percentage of white women worked in the field than did those in other regions of the country.

For women of both races, the crossover into male work was as old as colonial society, North or South. Male crossover to domestic chores or child care was far less common, however. Thus, rural black and white women carried a double duty.

In other basic ways region and class created a uniformity of experience that overshadowed race. Rural women of both races continued to marry young, to have many children, and to spend most of their adult lives in mothering. Like their colonial ancestors, these postwar southern women served as midwives and healers to their communities. And, while farm women in the Midwest reaped the benefits of mechanization and the newest household technologies, southern rural women continued to perform household tasks with primitive tools. A preindustrial women's culture thus remained alive in the South long after Sears and Roebuck catalogs had transformed other regions.

Many of these southern farm women became active participants in agricultural reform movements. In the 1880s and 1890s women were a significant proportion of Alliance and Populist organizations. Although these movements failed, rural women had an experience that set them apart from both northern women and their urban southern sisters. Populist women activists were effective within an organization controlled by men. They were not viewed as isolated eccentrics by their communities. In the New England states this sense of support from men was an urban, not a rural, phenomenon.

In the South, as in New England, the rise of the mill town and factory created a new set of circumstances for women. In the mills and mill-town life, the consequences of sexual divisions of labor within the family and in production became more starkly visible, perhaps because their vocabularies and measurements seem more familiar to the modern eye.

Between 1880 and 1920 southern mill-town development would recapitulate for southern working women the experiences of New England female factory workers before the Civil War. The first southern mill workers were farm daughters, most easily spared from the family farm. Female-headed farm families, highly vulnerable to the ups and downs of the cash-crop economy, were the next source of mill labor. By 1890, 40 percent of the workers in the four leading southern textile states were women or girls.

The agricultural depression after 1900 drew male-headed farm families to the mill towns. These new male workers drove women out of the mills. At the same time, the simple production techniques in the textile factories made child labor profitable. Thus, new family work patterns were established: fathers and children went to the mills, while mothers worked at home. Here, women tended gardens, performed unpaid but essential domestic tasks, and helped to meet living costs by taking in boarders. In these families, female labor became private or "hidden" labor.

By 1920 changes in production and the enforcement of early minimum-wage laws forced another shift in work patterns. Children, paid at a minimum wage, were no longer desirable employees. Married women reentered the mill, where they soon became victims of wage and job discrimination—paid less than males for identical labor and barred from supervisory positions. In this discrimination—as in the double duty of housework and paid work—southern white Protestant women were joined to their northern, ethnic Catholic and Jewish sisters, and like them, they had fewer babies after the first generation in the mill. In their willingness to participate in strikes and to become labor activists, bold southern women matched the careers of northern activists.

The names of Florence Reece, Ella May Wiggins, and Aunt Molly Jackson are familiar to southern workers. Their battles for equal pay, for union rights, and for better working conditions for men and women are legendary. Yet even in activism, a sexual division was evident. Women, one scholar observed, led strikes; men led unions.

Remarkable differences between the experiences of northern and southern working-class women remain. These are largely unexplored. For example, northern industry quickly became urban industry; southern mill production remained rural. Northern urban working-class women thus may have had more job choices (e.g., home piecework versus factory work), a more vigorous and diverse labor-reform movement, and stronger support networks.

Black women made their way to New South towns and cities during this era also. In an urban setting the consequences of racial divisions of labor become more sharply defined. Black women were forced to take domestic jobs, keeping house for white families at rates as low as $3 a week in 1935. The black mammy may have been an imaginary figure before the Civil War, but after it, she definitely existed. She cared for white children, ran white homes, and dominated white kitchens while white mothers worked for wages outside the home or joined the growing numbers of middle-class women's organizations and volunteer societies.

In the South, race cut the same deep chasms through labor solidarity that ethnicity and religion cut in the North. Black women workers in New South factories were often temporary workers; white women held year-round jobs. During layoffs, these black women survived by working as maids in their white co-workers' homes. Thus, women workers met each other both as members of a working classs and across a color line, as employee and employer. Not until the 1940s, when women began to work in offices and education, did black and white women share the same relationship to production.

Change came in the New South in another major area—educational opportunity for southern women. Public school systems were established in the region, and as students, black and white females received the benefits—uneven though they were—of literacy. But the shift of education out of the home and into a public institution had a second significance for women. A maternal function was taken over by the state, and women were drafted to perform that function in the new, public sphere. Thus, a role previously assigned to all married women became an occupation for a small number of women. Teaching provided these women with a respectable and, in the black community, prestigious profession. It also offered some measure of economic independence.

Teacher training became the raison d'être for women's colleges and normal schools. Again, the revolution in education in the South recalled the earlier development in education in the North. The significance of higher education for women was similar, creating for southern women those "bonds of womanhood"—shared experiences based on gender—that historians have described for early 19th-century New England women. These were the first close ties that did not grow out of family relationships. Finally, higher education provided women with the intellectual tools to examine and criticize their society.

Young Florida cowgirls posing in Jacksonville studio, c. 1930s

For many southern women, the most dramatic break with antebellum traditions was their entry into public life. Many factors set the stage for this new visibility: the rise of towns and cities, helping to create a critical mass for collective activity; the entrance of women into the paid work force; improved education; the decline of male participation in and control over religious organizations; and the creation of leisure time for elite white women who traded the responsibilities of the slave system for the less demanding relationship of household servant and mistress.

Without doubt, the first conduit for women into public life was the church. In the aftermath of the Civil War, southern women joined forces to rebuild church buildings and raise emergency funds. By the 1890s female mission societies, especially within the Methodist church, had grown into a major arm of the evangelical order. The Methodist Women's Board of Foreign Missions, for example, owned $200,000 worth of property and ran 10 boarding schools, 31 day schools, and a hospital. From such church-based organizations, southern women, like their northern sisters in the early 19th century, gained training in organization and leadership, self-confidence, and a legitimate public role.

The notion of women as morally superior to men—once a cornerstone of the southern lady's pedestal—was revived, but in a new context and for a new purpose. This time, women, not men, elaborated the ideology. Women's maternal concern and their moral sensitivity, argued activists, propelled them into such projects as the crusade against alcohol, aid for the poor, improvement of working conditions for women, and abolition of child labor. In the South, as in the North, "social housekeeping" moved women's sphere out of the private home and into public and political life.

But southern white women who came to social housekeeping, and later to Progressivism, followed a different timetable from northern women because they responded to very different circumstances. The Civil War defeat, which generated or at least allowed major economic and demographic changes in the South, also demanded a period of basic economic and social recovery. While New England women mounted reform movements in the 1870s and 1880s, southern women were engaged in rebuilding and survival.

A more basic difference, however, lay not in chronology, but in the breadth and reach of social housekeeping, North and South. Northern women operated within the context of a society open to change, but southern reform-minded women struggled within a conservative political and social environment. The energies of southern women were divided by race, despite a shared ideology of "social housekeeping" and the creation of similar organizations. Only occasionally did black and white reformers work together on a project such as school improvement.

Not surprisingly, the women's suffrage movement came late to the South and was less successful there than in any other region. The demand for women's suffrage came at a time when southern political leaders were restricting rather than expanding voting rights in their states, for class and racial ends. Suffragists' support of a federal amendment raised the spectre of new federal "intervention," sincerely or simply rhetorically feared. Finally, in the South women's suffrage was linked with race issues—historically with abolition, more recently with growing black political hopes. Thus, like many of the reforms of the Victorian and Progressive eras, suffrage was filtered through a uniquely southern history and experience.

The American feminist movement, never strong in the South, dissipated after the suffrage victory. Social housekeeping, however, continued to motivate some southern activist women during the 1920s and 1930s. Women could still unite over issues of child welfare, educational reform, and working conditions for women. Often their goals put them on a collision course with southern industrialists. Demands for shorter work days and a ban on night work for women, for example, made the Southern Council on Women and Children in Industry challenge unregulated capitalism in the South and made this women's council a classic Progressive organization.

In the South, as in the North, women's labor reform brought middle-class and working-class women into an uneasy alliance. Too often middle-class women spoke for, rather than with, the working-class beneficiaries of the reform effort. The sharp edges of class frequently severed ties of gender in the northern industrial centers, where vigorous union movements often vied with women's reform organizations for women workers' loyalties. Ironically, in the South such a contest between class and gender rarely occurred because the union movement was too weak to bid effectively for working women's loyalty. Thus, southern experiments in cross-class cooperation such as the Southern Summer School for Women Workers sustained a sense of sisterhood longer than northern organizations such as the Women's Trade Union League.

During the 1920s black and white women activists did come together for a major reform effort. Led by Jessie Daniel Ames, these women launched an antilynching campaign. Ames's vision may have been marred by racial stereotyping, but her "revolt against chivalry" had serious feminist implications. It struck at the remaining underpinnings of southern patriarchy by challenging the myth that racial dominance protected white women's purity and virtue. It challenged sexual stereotypes of black and white women and raised basic questions about sexual and social relations. Such questions went unanswered, yet they were raised again in the 1960s and 1970s.

The Modern South. Today, southern women's lives follow more closely the American mainstream. Yet regional and subregional variations remain. In the rural South, especially in the Mississippi Delta and in the predominantly Catholic areas of Louisiana, rates of fertility and infant mortality are higher than the national norms. From the old cotton belt of the Southeast through the Black Belt of Alabama, larger families and greater risk of infant death are a black phenomenon. In eastern Kentucky, white "hillbilly" women share these conditions. Poverty, not race, is the apparent villain.

The search for work has played havoc with sex ratios in the modern South. Job-seeking Appalachian women, barred from coal mines and timbering, have left a male majority in many of their counties. On the other hand, in the inner Coastal Plain and the Delta, women have remained behind while men have migrated to northern and southern cities. Changes in southern women's rates of employment have paralleled national trends over the last several decades. According to the 1980 census, 50 percent of married women with a husband present were employed. In the 13 southern states in 1980 the percentage of employed married women living with employed husbands ranged from a high of 49 percent in North Carolina to a low of 28 percent in West Virginia. Perhaps more striking are the data on employment of all mothers. In 1980, 58 percent of all females in North Carolina aged 16 or older with children aged 6 or younger worked outside the home, as did the majority of such mothers in seven other southern states. For mothers with children between the ages of 6 and 17, the percentage employed ranged from 70 percent in North Carolina to 46 percent in West Virginia, the only southern state in which a majority of mothers of children aged 17 or younger were not employed.

With higher employment rates have come more varied job opportunities for southern women; but income differentials between women and men, often called the "earnings gap," remain discouraging. As of 1981 the state with the largest earnings gap in the nation was Louisiana, with women's median income being only 50 percent of men's median income. The smallest gap in the South (and the fifth smallest in the nation) was in Tennessee, where women's median income was 64 percent of men's. Interestingly, among the 15 states with the smallest gap

Country storekeeper, Reganton, Miss., 1975

in 1981 were 7 southern states. Economic conditions, changing attitudes about men's and women's roles, and higher divorce rates, among other factors, have dramatically affected southern women's experiences in recent decades.

In the foreseeable future, marriage and employment will continue to be linked since over 90 percent of American women marry at some point in their lives. However, divorce rates in the South and West are higher than in other parts of the country. The crude divorce rate (i.e., the number of divorces and annulments per 1,000 population per year) for the East South Central census division, consisting of Alabama, Mississippi, Tennessee, and Kentucky, has for several decades ranked the fourth highest among the nine census divisions, and Texas and Arkansas are in the nation's so-called divorce belt.

In the South, as elsewhere, female heads of households with children but with no husband present face particularly pressing financial problems, especially black women. According to 1980 census data, in seven southern states 35 percent or more of the single-parent households headed by women had a 1979 income below the poverty level. In 10 southern states 50 percent or more of these households below the poverty level were black. Such figures point to some of the most glaring problems facing southern women.

For blacks and whites, kinship networks remain strong. Thus southern women still operate within a matrix of kin as well as gender, class, or race. Indeed, many black women remain members of, or heads of, extended families, a pattern consistent in southern black culture since the colonial era.

Finally, southern society remains politically and religiously conservative. Whether the southern woman supports or opposes that conservatism, it shapes her political, social, and ideological options.

The choice—to defend or attempt to change their region's conservatism—has been a pressing problem since 1950. Indeed, what distinguishes the modern southern woman from her 19th-century ancestors may be her active role in shaping her own ideologies. This marks an independence from northern women as well as from southern men. During the civil rights movement, for example, young black and white women took as their role models not northern women but middle-aged southern black women. The Fannie Lou Hamers of the rural and small-town South inspired their activism.

Common goals did not necessarily produce common experiences for black and white women, however: for black women, kinship and family and church ties may have provided needed emotional support; for white women activists, commitment to the movement meant a sharp and painful wrenching away from traditional support systems and often led to an awakening of feminist consciousness. As abolition work had led the Grimké sisters to women's rights, SNCC work often led southern college women to feminism. Southern black women, however, have remained more committed to racial than to gender issues.

A number of southern feminist leaders, such as Texas's Liz Carpenter, Sarah Weddington, and Frances Farenthold, have left the southern battlefield to lead national feminist organizations. Today the southern battlefield remains an active one. The attack on traditional southern segregation patterns, followed in the 1970s by the creation of state commissions on women's equality and by ERA ratification drives, led conservative white women to political activism. Thus, the modern feminist movement has become a significant intrasectional women's struggle.

Extremist organizations such as the Ku Klux Klan, John Birch Society, and the National States' Rights party campaign against the ERA. Antifeminist Phyllis Schlafly is not a southern woman, yet her strongest support comes from women of the South. There, antifeminism is also strongly supported by fundamentalist churches. For many southern black women, of course, the church had provided similar support for civil rights activity. Thus, reformist or conservative, southern women's public activities continue to be centered in the church.

To some observers, the battle against the ERA, and its implication of revised sex and gender roles, seems to be a symbolic crusade. By opposing the ERA, southern women—and men—had an opportunity to register their distress at the forces of change still at work upon their region.

This conflict over change, the conflicting values it reflects, the intraregional variations of fertility, wealth, and demographics all suggest that no easily identifiable "southern woman" exists. Yet the dual idealizations of the past—southern lady and black mammy—were never representative either. Class, race, occupation, rural or urban environment, and age have always worked their variations and transformations on any common theme. The powerful images of "Miss Scarlett" and "Mammy" were based on the power of the elite planter class who created these ideals. They were able to maintain an illusion of uniformity. The modern South lacks the agency to perform such an ideological sleight of hand.

See also BLACK LIFE: Family, Black; Race Relations; EDUCATION: Teachers; FOLKLIFE: Childbirth; Family Folklore; Weddings; / Quilting, Afro-American; Quilting, Anglo-American; HISTORY AND MANNERS: Beauty, Cult of; Cookbooks; Debutantes; Fashion; Manners; Patriotic Societies; Sexuality; / United Daughters of the Confederacy

Carol Ruth Berkin
Baruch College
City University of New York

Mary Frances Berry and John Blassingame, *Long Memory: The Black Experience in America* (1982); Catherine Clinton, *The Plantation Mistress: Woman's World in the Old South* (1982), *Journal of the Early Republic* (Spring 1982); Ronald D. Eller, *Miners, Millhands, and Mountaineers: Industrialization of the Appalachian South, 1880–1930* (1982); Mari Evans, ed., *Black Women Writers, 1950–1980* (1985); Sara Evans, *Personal Politics: The Roots of Women's Liberation in the Civil Rights Movement and the New Left* (1979); Jean Friedman, *The Enclosed Garden: Women and Community in the Evangelical South, 1830–1900* (1985); Norval D. Glenn and Beth Ann Shelton, *Journal of Marriage and the Family* (August 1985); Herbert G. Gutman, *The Black Family in Slavery and Freedom, 1750–1925* (1976); Margaret J. Hagood, *Mothers of the South: Portraiture of the White Tenant Farm Woman* (1939); Jacquelyn Dowd Hall, *Revolt against Chivalry: Jesse Daniel Ames and the Women's Campaign against Lynching* (1979); Joanne V. Hawks and Sheila L. Skemp, eds., *Sex, Race, and the Role of Women in the South* (1983); Anne Goodwyn Jones, *Tomorrow Is Another Day: The Woman Writer in the South, 1859–1936* (1981); Jacqueline Jones, *Labor of Love, Labor of Sorrow: Black Women, Work, and the Family from Slavery to the Present* (1985); Kathy Kahn, *Hillbilly Women* (1972); Thelma Kandel, *What Women Earn* (1981); Suzanne Lebsock, *The Free Women of Petersburg: Status and Culture in a Southern Town, 1784–1860* (1983); Mary Beth Norton, *Liberty's Daughters: The Revolutionary Experience of American Women* (1980); Anne Firor Scott, *The Southern Lady: From Pedestal to Politics, 1830–1930* (1970), *Journal of American History* (March 1974); Kathryn L. Seidel, *The Southern Belle in the American Novel* (1985); *Southern Exposure* (Winter 1976); Julia Cherry Spruill, *Women's Life and Work in the Southern Colonies* (1938); Thad W. Tate and David L. Ammerman, eds., *The Chesapeake in the Seventeenth Century: Essays on Anglo-American Society* (1979); U.S. Bureau of the Census, *Current Population Reports*, Series P-20, no. 380 (1983), *General Social and Economic Characteristics, 1980* (by state) (1981).

Appalachian Women

For women of Appalachia, geography is the common denominator; other factors point to diversity. The formative experience for Appalachian women was the frontier process when westward-moving pioneers staked their claims in the region, which includes 13 states or portions thereof. As a group, Appalachian women have frequently fallen victim to caricature. In terms of class, ethnicity, education, vocation, and aspiration, they embody disparate personae contradicting popular images shaped by cartoon characters like Daisy Mae Yokum of Dogpatch, U.S.A., or Aunt Loweezy, wife to moonshining mountaineer Snuffy Smith.

Generally, the Appalachian region has been characterized by a patriarchal family structure and dominated by white, Anglo-Saxon Protestants. Nonetheless, as early as the late 18th century and certainly by the 19th a class system operated, and different ethnic and racial groups coexisted, among them Caucasians, Negroes, and Indians, as well as the mysterious Melungeons. Decades of relative isolation and economic retardation left the region and its people a preindustrial society that began to give way to the modernizing effects of industrialization only in the 20th century. Class structure became even more clearly defined, urban areas increased in number and size, the traditional family lost ground, and cultural pluralism became apparent. The experiences of Appalachian women have been influenced by all these developments.

During the antebellum period Appalachian females seem to have been less fettered by geographical isolation, social conventions, and the patriarchal family than during later decades of the century. Generalizations are dangerous, however, for considerable difference existed between the lives of women in isolated areas and those in small villages and towns—differences intensified by class. Furthermore, reports of early travelers failed to distinguish clearly between Appalachian traits and those of Americans elsewhere, whereas local colorists of the late 19th century labeled Appalachians "peculiar people." Some evidence indicates that Appalachian women of this earlier period asserted themselves at religious and political meetings. Certainly, through their labor on the farms and in the homes, they made a vital contribution to family survival in a preindustrial economy. Some managed to escape the traditional constraints of familial existence by keeping boardinghouses and teaching. Only a minuscule number supervised slaves, for the institution of slavery was far less significant in the mountains than elsewhere in the South. Although an independent spirit is frequently ascribed to Appalachians, the region did not completely avoid the influence of the planter-dominated South with its code of chivalry; and mountain women were not totally removed from the influence of the "southern lady"—an ideal that transcended class lines and challenged topographical barriers.

The turbulent years of Civil War and Reconstruction dealt harshly with Union supporters as well as with Confederate sympathizers in Appalachia. The genuine deprivation of people torn by their own factionalism and plagued by foraging parties from both armies helped shape the national image of Appalachians as needy and the southern mountains as a legitimate missionary field. Judged by northeastern standards, Appalachians seemed poor, but their land harbored tremendous wealth. New

South advocates, some of them native mountaineers, in league with northern investors soon began the irreversible alteration of the mountains and their people. Substantial numbers of poor but proud highland peasants became mill operatives, miners, and coke drawers.

In the early decades of the 20th century scores of Appalachian women moved into the textile factories throughout the Blue Ridge and the Piedmont and exchanged the old, rural, patriarchal family system for the new village paternalism of mill owners. As southern labor stirred, these females, some of them mere girls, led strikes like those in 1929 at Elizabethton, Tenn., and Marion, N.C. A few working-class women were directly influenced by agencies like the Southern Summer School for Women Workers, the Highlander Folk Schools, and the Industrial Department of the Young Women's Christian Association, in turn affecting the lives of other female factory workers. Middle- and upper-class women in Appalachian towns led the work of civic organizations like the YWCA.

New cultural elements had also been introduced into the region during the late 19th and early 20th centuries as coal operators actively recruited "new" immigrants. Substantial numbers of Italian and Hungarian females as well as members of other ethnic groups, mostly Catholics, followed their men into the hollows of West Virginia, southwest Virginia, eastern Kentucky, and northeastern Tennessee. Coal operators also increased the black population as they imported workers from the Deep South after World War I had virtually halted immigration.

During this transition various humanitarian and religious efforts were directed toward the reformation of Appalachia. In the forefront were female outsiders, mostly teachers and nurses, known in the mountain vernacular as "fotched-on" women. Truly outstanding among them was Mary Breckinridge, who hailed from the Kentucky Bluegrass. She established the Frontier Nursing Service in 1925 and devoted the next 40 years to prenatal and postpartum treatment of mothers and infants in eastern Kentucky, meanwhile building a general practice of family medicine.

During the 20th century, portions of the Appalachian region have suffered the boom-bust cycle of the coal industry; other areas with a more diversified economy have enjoyed relative prosperity. Pockets of rural and urban poverty still exist in the region despite massive federal aid programs, and displaced Appalachians can be found in the ghettos of northern and midwestern cities. Nonetheless, women of Appalachia in general have more reason now than ever before to expect a fair share of the nation's goods and services and the opportunity to enjoy a full life. While some have remained trapped at the lowest economic levels, others from humble origins have moved into comfortable middle-class status. Indeed, there are "rags-to-riches" sagas like those of Mother Maybelle and the Carter Sisters, Dolly Parton, and Loretta Lynn. The few women miners have received considerable attention during the last decade. In a less flamboyant way, other young women have written their own success stories by leaving the hillside farms and coal camps for industrial assembly lines, secretarial positions, and college and university campuses; among them was Juanita Morris Kreps, secretary of commerce during the Carter Administration.

A broad spectrum of opinion on feminist issues can be found among mountain females. An attempt to create a network during the 1970s culminated in the establishment of the short-lived Council of Appalachian Women, which purchased the rights to the *Magazine of Appalachian Women* (MAW) and briefly published a journal entitled *Appalachian Women*.

See also ENVIRONMENT: / Appalachian Mountains; Blue Ridge; ETHNIC LIFE: Mountain Culture / Appalachians; FOLKLIFE: / "Hillbilly" Image; INDUSTRY: Industrialization in Appalachia; / Mining; LITERATURE: Appalachian Literature; MUSIC: / Carter Family; MYTHIC SOUTH: Appalachian Culture; New South Myth; / Appalachian Myth; SCIENCE AND MEDICINE: / Breckinridge, Mary; SOCIAL CLASS: Poverty / Coal Miners; Highlander Folk School

Margaret Ripley Wolfe
East Tennessee State University

Carol Crowe-Carraco, *The Register of the Kentucky Historical Society* (July 1978); Ronald D. Eller, *Appalachian Journal* (Winter 1979); Sidney Saylor Farr, *Appalachian Women: An Annotated Bibliography* (1981); Kathy Kahn, *Hillbilly Women* (1973); Henry D. Shapiro, *Appalachia on Our Mind: The Southern Mountains and Mountaineers in the American Consciousness, 1870–1920* (1978); Southern Summer School Papers, American Labor Education Service Collection, Cornell University, Ithaca, N.Y.; *Time* (3 January 1977); David E. Whisnant, *All That Is Native and Fine: The Politics of Culture in an American Region* (1983).

Belles and Ladies

Southern lore has it that the belle is a privileged white girl at the glamorous and exciting period between being a daughter and becoming a wife. She is the fragile, dewy, just-opened bloom of the southern female: flirtatious but sexually innocent, bright but not deep, beautiful as a statue or painting or porcelain but, like each, risky to touch. A form of popular art, she entertains but does not challenge her audience. Instead, she attracts them—the more gentlemen callers the better—and finally allows herself to be chosen by one.

Then she becomes a lady, and a lady she will remain until she dies—unless of course she does something beyond the pale. As a lady she drops the flirtatiousness of the belle and stops chattering; she has won her man. Now she has a different job: satisfying her husband, raising his children, meeting the demands of the family's social position, and sustaining the ideals of the South. Her strength in manners and morals is contingent, however, upon her submission to their sources—God, the patriarchal church, her husband—and upon her staying out of public life, where she might interfere in their formulation. But in her domestic realm she can achieve great if sometimes grotesque power. As a slave mistress, for example, she was capable of enormous cruelty as well as deeply felt kindness; she was a premier manager yet also a slave to the patriarch. Melanie Wilkes was a great, good lady; Marie St. Clare a cruel and narcissistic one; and Scarlett O'Hara, that perpetual adolescent, never made it much past the belle.

Such a description can never satisfy, of course, for it is wrenched out of history, where the attributes of southern womanhood change over time, and it reflects only one out of the immense variety of attitudes about the southern woman. What has changed less than the southern woman's attributes and her reception, however, is her ontology. As the allusion to fiction suggests, southern womanhood exists as more than a historical prescription, job, role, or even source of identity. In fact, to see it as an actual identity is to literalize southern womanhood's function as a symbolic construct within southern ideology, and thus to perpetuate that ideology. Southern girls who assume the roles of belle and lady take on an entire history of the meaning of the South—its class, race, and gender systems, and its past and future. As belle and lady, a woman "becomes" the traditional South; as gentleman and scholar, a man enters into a complex relation *to* the South. He may be idolatrous worshipper, lord and master, dashed and demoralized failure; in any case, he acts as subject to her object, as knower to her known. The gender roles thus work together to prevent change and to obscure reality both between human beings and within the South's conception of itself. Where they fail to work, as is increasingly the case in our time, where southerners of both sexes rebel against the belle (or worse, ignore her), the chance for change finds its place.

Southern men have toasted and celebrated southern womanhood since the South began to think of itself as a region, probably before the American Revolution. The lady, with her grace and hospitality, seemed the flower of a uniquely southern civilization, the embodiment of all it prized most deeply. In truth, southern womanhood has much in common with the ideas of the British Victorian lady and of American true womanhood. All deny to women authentic selfhood; all enjoin that women suffer and be still; all show women sexually pure, pious, deferent to external authority, and content with their place in the home. Yet southern womanhood differs in several ways from other 19th-century images of womanhood. The southern lady has been from the start at the core of a patriotic impulse; the identity of the South is contingent in part upon the persistence of its tradition of the lady. Secondly, the ideal of southern womanhood seems to have lasted longer than the other ideals, even to the present. Thirdly, southern womanhood has from the beginning been inextricably linked to racial attitudes. Its very genesis, some say, lay in the minds of guilty slaveholders who sought an image they could revere without sacrificing the gains of racial slavery. And finally, the class—aristocratic—that the image of the lady represents has deeper ideological roots in the South than elsewhere in the United States.

A belle of the South

Thus, when Lucian Lamar Knight once again, in 1920, toasted the southern woman's "silent influence," "eternal vigil," and "gentle spirit"; when he claimed that the "blood royal of the ancient line" still lives in her daughters, his language suggested her primary ideological functions: to unify the South in its difference; to sustain the desire for British class structure; to protect the racial purity of legitimate white patriarchal inheritance; to provide a container for the conscience that would perpetuate ideals without danger of contact with reality; and thus to keep actual women elevated into perpetual silence and passivity.

Historians speculate variously about the origins and historical function of the concept of southern womanhood in southern ideology. In the knot of region, race, sex, and class, some find one thread clearer than others. In general, they agree that the function of southern womanhood has been to justify the perpetuation of the hegemony of the male sex, the upper and middle classes, and the white race.

Anne Firor Scott sees the base of the pedestal in racial slavery: "Because they owned slaves and thus maintained a traditional landowning aristocracy, southerners tenaciously held on to the patriarchal family structure. . . . Any tendency on the part of any of the members of the system to assert themselves against the master threatened the whole, and therefore slavery itself." Thus, Scott continues, it was "no accident that the most articulate spokesmen for slavery were also eloquent exponents of the subordinate role of women." The threat of violence takes a surprisingly strong role in even the most sophisticated proslavery arguments for women's subordination, as Kent Leslie's work on George Fitzhugh, Chancellor Harper, and Thomas R. Dew shows. Thus, when Louisa McCord argued against women's emancipation, she claimed that, without the protection of the pedestal, women would be intolerably vulnerable to male physical superiority. The argument can still be heard in the South today. W. J. Cash, also, found racial supremacy at the origin of the image. Woman alone could perpetuate white superiority, because of what Cash calls her "remoteness from the males of the inferior group," a remoteness not paralleled in the relationships between white men and black women. "The [white] woman must be compensated, the revolting suspicion in the male that he might be slipping into bestiality got rid of, by glorifying her," argues Cash. Lillian Smith, too, in *Killers of the Dream* (1949), sees the origin of southern womanhood in this "race-sex-sin spiral": "The more trails the white man made to back-yard cabins, the higher he raised his white wife on her pedestal, when he returned to the big house. The higher the pedestal, the less he enjoyed her whom he put there, for statues are after all only nice things to look at."

Insecurities of a more class-related sort led southerners to create the lady, according to William R. Taylor. Despairing at southern social and economic decline and fearing "social dissolution" (particularly in the forms of an open society and a dismembered family), southerners "grasped for symbols of stability and order to stem their feelings of drift and uncertainty and to quiet their uneasiness about the inequities within Southern society." But southern men, Taylor argues, could not associate feeling, introspection, or moral awareness with masculinity. The popular plantation novels solved this problem "without robbing the Southern gentleman of his manhood. The Southern answer to this question lay in the cult of chivalry—in having the Cavalier kneel down before the altar of femininity and familial benevolence."

Yet ultimately, as Sara Evans points out, "it made no sense to place women in charge of piety and morality and then deny them access to the public sphere where immorality held sway." Certain pre–Civil War southern men, Taylor says, "began regretting the moral autonomy which they had assigned to women" and returned full circle, to insist upon a rigid gender, race, and class hierarchy that made woman, slave, and yeoman subject to the Cavalier.

A suggestion that class takes precedence over race and gender in grounding southern womanhood can be found in the incidence of the "lady" in literature by black women. Linda Brent's slave master, for example, promises her he will make her into a "lady" in exchange for sex; clearly the idea was not, even then, limited to white women. And in Zora Neale Hurston's novel *Their Eyes Were Watching God* (1937), Janie becomes a lady, ornamental and silent, within an all-black community, as a sign of class elevation. If a black woman can become a southern lady, then something other than racial exclusion is going on. But can a white lower-class woman climb into ladyhood? Eudora Welty seems to see the lady as a construct that preserves class immobility when she makes it clear in *The Optimist's Daughter* (1972) that Fay's lower-class origins prevent her from attaining the sort of consciousness that makes a "real" lady, that is, a lady in mind and in spirit.

Yet another argument finds the origin of southern womanhood in Western civilization's patriarchal tradition, antedating and then reinforcing racial slavery and class structure. Bertram Wyatt-Brown locates the source of southern womanhood in the South's retention of the ancient code of honor, the system of "patriarchy and womanly subordination." Public reputation, not private guilt, motivates behavior in this system; hence the "enforcement of gender and family conventions [is] community business" rather than personal choice. Men of all classes agreed upon female subordination and docility as a norm. And women participated willingly in their subordination, Wyatt-Brown argues, because southern womanhood meant not simply self-sacrifice and silence, but sacrifice for family honor, in which women took pride, and courage, in accepting fate without complaint. Thus did the patriarchal system of honor simultaneously subordinate its women and reward them for their acquiescence. John Ruoff also argues for the primacy of patriarchy over slavery as the source for southern womanhood. Southern settlers brought with them from England a belief in patriarchal values, says Ruoff. These values made the man the source of family authority, the family the source of societal order and stability, and the planter class the source of authority within society. Then, as early as the 17th century, a native southern aristocracy developed an "ethos of leisure and consumption" that "stipulated that women should perform an essentially ornamental function in society." The development of the master-slave relationship thus reinforced and was reinforced by the prior notion that the husband held absolute authority in the home.

Sara Evans also points to Europe for the myths about women that southern colonists brought along with their patriarchal social and familial assumptions. Those basic myths polarized women into the "virgin, pure and untouchable, and the prostitute, dangerously sexual." The clustering of images—goodness and light with virginity, evil and darkness with sexuality—seemed to be reified and therefore confirmed when white planters owned black slave women. Race and sex thus fused to create in the "white lady" the southern version of the 19th-century's cult of true womanhood.

Whatever the relative importance of class, race, and patriarchy, it is the peculiar relation of patriarchal attitudes toward women with the development of a hierarchical slave society that produced, in the early 19th century, both the South's most intense period of self-definition and the refinement of the images of the lady as the slaveholder's ideal—and the dominant ideal of the South.

How have women fared through all this construction of ideology? Most have, of course, literalized the symbol;

it would be nearly impossible not to. Thus, for most southern women "southern womanhood" has become a very practical and personal concern, a way to be—to reject, to revise, or to adopt.

The rare ones have rejected the necessity even to pretend to conform, have radically criticized their society, and have often left the South, in body if not in mind. The Charleston Grimké sisters moved North—Sarah in 1821 and Angelina in 1820—and, from that "refuge," at times addressing the southern white women at home, directly attacked the "assumptions upon which southern society based its image of women," including, of course, slavery. In fact, Sarah's *Letters on the Equality of the Sexes* were, according to Anne Firor Scott, the "earliest systematic expression in America of the whole set of ideas constituting the ideology of 'women's rights.'" Sara Evans has shown that the 1960s feminist revival found its roots, too, in the South. Once again southern white women—this time in the civil rights movement—saw the connection between racial and sexual oppression, thus providing the initial impulse toward contemporary feminism. Shirley Abbott, in *Womenfolks* (1983), offers herself as a contemporary explanation of why southern girls leave home.

At the opposite extreme from outright rebellion, some women have determined to shape themselves entirely into the ideal. "We owe it to our husbands, children, and friends," wrote Caroline Merrick to a friend in 1859, "to represent as nearly as possible the ideal which they hold so dear." At the extreme, such women blanked out their perceptions and repressed their feelings until they lost, almost entirely, a sense of self. Educated, on the other hand, into the belief that they were perfection itself, some real southern women found it hard to admit and harder to rectify such "besetting sins [as] a roving mind and an impetuous spirit."

More typically, though, southern women neither left home nor attained perfection. Instead, they made for themselves a public persona, a mask of sorts that coexisted with but did not always correspond to an inner self. Such self-division produced guilt both about what they felt was the wolf within and about the inevitable hypocrisy involved in concealing it. In the South the conflict between image and reality took its purest form in the years before the Civil War. Although the ideology depicted them as passive, submissive, and dependent symbols of leisure, these women found that actual experience involved long days of hard active work making administrative decisions that determined how the household ran.

Whereas the image had her needing the economic protection of her husband, reality found her chafing, as did Mary Boykin Chesnut, at her economic dependence. Whereas the ideal southern woman was chaste as a cake of ice, many women felt a natural physical attraction to their husbands and even possessed a "humor so earthy as to contradict the romantic tradition of universal refinement among Southern ladies," says Bell Wiley. Whereas the woman presumably lived in ignorance of it, miscegenation aroused anguish in many. Whereas the ideal woman was a repository of culture and the arts, her actual ignorance of worldly reality (which the image called innocence) was maintained by the low quality of education available for women in the South. The ideal woman, however, remained a pious Protestant, and in fact evidence of any widespread (if private) religious skepticism is rare. Thus each element of the image—leisure, passivity, dependence, sexual purity, submission, ignorance (with the possible exception of piety)—failed to correspond to the reality of women's lives, and for women to undertake to match the ideal must have required creativity and persistence.

The history of woman's specific accommodations to and revisions of the belle and the lady is complicated, fascinating, and ongoing. Anne Firor Scott, Jacquelyn Dowd Hall, and Suzanne Lebsock have notably pieced out parts of that story, a story too long to tell here except in the most generalized way. It seems that most southern women have in their daily lives worked around these conflicts with the ideology of southern womanhood. They have done so in the interests of values and desires that can be called "women's culture" and that subvert, at times, the values of the dominant culture. On the other hand, the fate of the belle in literature, as Kathryn L. Seidel untangles it, has been less hopeful. The belle has moved from the "madonna" of the antebellum period to the narcissistic and masochistic "Magdalen" of, for instance, Faulkner's Temple Drake. These are for Seidel two sides of the same person; they represent the psychosexual distortions inherent in the image itself.

Has southern womanhood died—co-opted by television and trashy passion novels—or metamorphosed into some sort of Sunbelt Total Woman? Long-held images of southern womanhood have not disappeared any more than have the systems that produced them. Perhaps in a place like Sunbelt Atlanta, though, the southern woman has finally found a suitable arena for her skills at manipulating the images.

See also BLACK LIFE: Freedom Movement, Black; Miscegenation; Race Relations; / Hurston, Zora Neale; HISTORY AND MANNERS: Sexuality; LITERATURE: Sex Roles in Literature; / Faulkner, William; Welty, Eudora; MYTHIC SOUTH: Family; Racial Attitudes; Romanticism; / Cash, W. J.

Anne Goodwyn Jones
University of Florida

Irving H. Bartlett and Glenn Cambor, *Women's Studies*, vol. 2 (1974); Linda Brent, *Incidents in the Life of a Slave Girl* (1973); W. J. Cash, *The Mind of the South* (1941); Phyllis Fraley, *Atlanta Magazine* (October 1984); Jacquelyn Dowd Hall, *Revolt against Chivalry: Jesse Daniel Ames and the Women's Campaign against Lynching* (1979); Anne Goodwyn Jones, *Tomorrow Is Another Day: The Woman Writer in the South, 1859–1936* (1981); Suzanne Lebsock, *The Free Women of Petersburg* (1983); Michael O'Brien, *All Clever Men Who Make Their Way* (1982); John C. Ruoff, "Southern Womanhood, 1865–1920: An Intellectual and Cultural Study" (Ph.D. dissertation, University of Illinois, 1976); Anne Firor Scott, *The Southern Lady: From Pedestal to Politics, 1830–1930* (1970); Kathryn L. Seidel, *The Southern Belle in the American Novel* (1986); William R. Taylor, *Cavalier and Yankee: The Old South and American National Character* (1961); Bertram Wyatt-Brown, *Southern Honor: Ethics and Behavior in the Old South* (1982).

Blues-singing Women

In his classic collection of essays, *The Souls of Black Folk* (1903), W. E. B. Du Bois, a northern, black intellectual, expressed the meaning of "sorrow songs" to black people: "They that walked in darkness sang songs in the olden days—sorrow songs—for they were weary at heart. They came out of the South unknown to me, and yet I knew them as of me and mine." In the sorrow songs Du Bois heard "the voices of the past," preserved from generation to generation through oral tradition.

The origins of the blues are in the sorrow songs of the slaves. Both musical forms describe the daily experience of human oppression, while also maintaining a breath of hope that someday, somewhere, human beings will be judged by their souls, their minds, and their acts, rather than their racial background. At the same time, the blues express personal themes and dilemmas that are practically universal. Women who sing the blues sing primarily about love, infidelity, sex, and passion, as they occur in everyday situations and as they are altered by death, liquor, superstition, migration, natural disasters, and loneliness.

Unlike the sorrow songs, which portray the shared oppression of the slave community, the blues portray idiosyncratic and specific experiences in the lives of individuals. This thematic change reflects the social history of southern blacks. In antebellum times slaves sang of their despair, hope, and protest primarily in their work songs and spirituals. After emancipation, black sharecroppers who worked small plots of land sang about the trials and hardships of their individual lives. Early blues developed in the late 19th-century South, as a form of leisure entertainment, a way of communication, and a form of autobiography. In the early blues or "country blues," an individual lament combined with an affirmation of self, representing the black experience in general through an individual life.

By the turn of the century the rural blues were familiar to southerners, black and white, but until a number of black women recorded the "classic blues" during the 1920s most Americans were unfamiliar with the music. The most successful classic blues singers were southern black women, and their themes are written predominantly from a woman's point of view. In their study *Negro Workaday Songs* (1926), Howard W. Odum and Guy B. Johnson noted that "among the blues singers who have gained more or less national recognition, there is scarcely a man's name to be found." Among the more famous women who recorded classic blues are Ma Hunter, Bertha "Chippie" Hill, and Memphis Minnie. Lesser known recording artists include Sara Martin, Lizzie Miles, Trixie Smith, Ada Brown, Eliza Brown, Cleo Gibson, Edmonia and Catherine Henderson, Mary Mack, Ann Cook, Mary Johnson, Lottie Beamon, Lucille Bogan, Georgia White, and Lillian Glinn. These blues-singing women were extremely popular during the 1920s and early 1930s, until the Depression ended the era of classic blues. Born in the late 19th century or the early 20th, a majority of them enjoyed a decade of success and afterward were sadly forgotten. They died poor and unrecognized.

According to historian Bill C. Malone, Americans were gradually introduced to the blues between 1914 and 1920, a period when numerous southern blacks were migrating to the North. Many blues lyrics are a direct response to northern urban life, and blues women who moved to the North were also likely to alter the instrumental style of their music. The blues were not recorded until Mamie Smith (a northern cabaret singer who was probably the first black singer to record a solo performance) sang "Crazy Blues" for Okeh Records in 1920. The record sold well, demonstrating that there was a market for blues music, particularly among black listeners. Following this, Lucille Hegamin ("The Georgia Peach"), Rosa Henderson, and Edith Wilson recorded smooth, refined, professionalized versions of the blues (including "St. Louis Blues" and "He May Be Your Man, But He Comes to See Me Sometimes") in a style influenced by both vaudeville and ragtime.

Ma Rainey and Bessie Smith are primarily responsible for recording and popularizing authentic southern blues and for inspiring the numerous southern women who recorded "classic blues" during the 1920s. Rainey, often called "Mother of the Blues," provided the link between country and classic blues. Like traditional male blues artists, she spent most of her career on the road, attracting large audiences across the South and, less frequently, among southerners who had migrated to the North, particularly in Chicago. According to author and music critic Le Roi Jones (Amiri Baraka), "Ma Rainey's singing can be placed squarely between the harsher, more spontaneous country styles and the smoother, theatrical styles of later blues singers." Born and raised in Columbus, Ga., she retained a rapport with southern audiences. Accompanied by a traditional jug band, she sang country blues including "Counting the Blues," "Jelly Bean Blues," "See See Rider," "Corn Field Blues," "Moonshine Blues," and "Bo-Weevil Blues."

The influence of Ma Rainey upon Bessie Smith is well documented. Often called "Empress of the Blues" or "Queen of the Blues," Smith is probably the best of the recorded classic blues singers. Her life story has become a legend. Born in Chattanooga, Tenn., in 1898 to a large, poor family, Smith enjoyed a decade of success and affluence beginning in 1923. At first, she recorded a number of songs previously sung by others, including "Gulf Coast Blues," "Aggravatin' Papa," and "T'Aint Nobody's Business If I Do." During her career, she recorded over 180 songs, among them "Mama's Got the Blues," "Lady Luck Blues," "See If I'll Care," "Kitchen Man," "Black Mountain Blues," "Nobody Knows You When You're Down and Out," "Nashville Woman Blues," "I Ain't Gonna Play No Second Fiddle," and "Safety Mama." Backed by professional jazz musicians, Smith enjoyed brief success performing for northern urban audiences, yet she was most popular among southerners, black and white. Like other classic blues artists, her success ended during the Depression. She died a tragic and unnecessary death in an automobile accident in 1937.

Although numerous southern women sang and recorded the blues during the 1920s, few are remembered today. A small number continued to record during the 1940s and 1950s, but blues-singing women were never again as popular as they had been during the classic era. A contemporary blues style is exhibited in the recordings of Big Mama Thornton. Backed by electric guitar, she projects a strong, vibrant voice in a style influenced by rock and roll and rhythm and blues. Born and raised in Alabama, Thornton recorded during the early 1950s and 1960s, appealing to audiences in both the United States and Europe. At the same time, countless women who had once sung and performed the traditional or classic blues remained unrecognized. For example, Mary McClain Smith, who is Bessie Smith's half sister and who sings in the classic blues style, was known as "Diamond Teeth Mary" in her heyday. She had performed mostly on the road, traveling by train or bus, spending her money as soon as she earned it. After a career spanning 32 years, performing with Nat King Cole, Duke Ellington, Billie Holiday, and Fats Waller, among others, she retired poor and was never recorded. She lived in obscurity, depending upon social security alone for income, until recently, when she was rediscovered by the Florida Folklife Center.

Whether or not they were recorded, blues-singing women have greatly influenced southern and American music. In the South, blues and white folk music have influenced and enriched one another. Blues themes about love, infidelity, sex, and passion frequently appear in the lyrics of female country stars such as Loretta Lynn, Dolly Parton, and Tammy Wynette, as well as lesser known country artists Alice Garrard and Hazel Dickens. In addition to influencing country lyrics, women who sang classic blues have affected the lyrics and recording styles of rock singers Janis Joplin and Bonnie Raitt. Blues-singing women are also a major influence upon jazz, particularly represented in the delicate voice and music of Billie Holiday. Her recording of "Strange Fruit," for example, clearly illustrates her kinship to the classic blues. By describing the brutality of a lynching, this haunting tune protests the inhumanity of a racist society, as did the sorrow songs of the slaves. An idiosyncratic response to an isolated event becomes representative of the black experience in general.

See also BLACK LIFE: Music, Black; MUSIC: Blues; / Smith, Bessie

Ruth A. Banes
University of South Florida

Chris Albertson, *Bessie* (1972), liner notes for *Bessie Smith: The World's Greatest Blues Singer*, Columbia Records (GP33CV 1040); *Blues Classics by Memphis Minnie*, Blues Classics 1, Arhoolie Records (BC-1); W. E. B. Du Bois, *The Souls of Black Folk* (1903); Peter B. Gallager, St. Petersburg *Times* (6 August 1982); Alberta Hunter, *Amtrak Blues*, Columbia Records (JC 36430); Le Roi Jones, *Blues People* (1963); *Memphis Minnie, vol. 2, Early Recordings with "Kansas Joe" McCoy*, Blues Classics 13, Arhoolie Records (BC-13); Bill C. Malone, *Southern Music/American Music* (1979); Paul Oliver, *Bessie Smith* (1971), *The Story of the Blues* (1969); Harry Oster, *Living Country Blues* (1969); Tony Russell, *Blacks, Whites, and Blues* (1970); *Sippie: Sippie Wallace with Jim Dapogny's Chicago Blues Band*, Arhoolie Records (F-1032); *Bessie Smith: The World's Greatest Blues Singer*, Columbia Records (GP33CV1040); Derrick-Stewart Baxter, *Ma Rainey and the Classic Blues Singers* (1970); Chris Strachwitz, liner notes for *Big Mama Thornton in Europe*, Arhoolie Records (F-1028), liner notes for *When Women Sang the Blues*, Blues Classics 26, Arhoolie Records (BC-26); *Big Mama Thornton in Europe*, Arhoolie Records (F-1028); *Big Mama Thornton, vol. 2, With the Chicago Blues Band*, Arhoolie Records (F-1032); *When Women Sang the Blues*, Blues Classics 26, Arhoolie Records (BC-26).

Child-raising Customs

Like other aspects of southern culture, child-raising customs have been distinctly shaped by rural ways of life and by the conditions of a biracial society. These customs have guided parents in rearing their offspring from infancy to preadolescence, and include habits of nurturing, methods of discipline, values regarding work and play, and means of incorporating a child into the family.

Evidence of these customs is sketchy before the mid-18th century when parents, increasingly literate and intent on leavening folkways with new, Lockeian notions of the importance of early childhood, began to record their methods and expectations. Southern parents in general did not subscribe to the ideas of a child's propensity for evil and ruination that were common in the North. In a century of high infant mortality a healthy child was a boon if not a rarity. Newborns were kept warm, dressed in loosely fitting smocks, and affectionately handled. The vast majority of southern women nursed their own children. But among the elite, breast-feeding was seen as possibly harmful to the mother, and women who could afford to do so made use of wet nurses immediately. It appears that mothers typically were anxious during weaning (usually at 12 to 18 months) and teething periods.

The relatively secular, practical attitude of southern parents also guided them in matters of discipline and work. Women had primary responsibility for child care, but fathers were not uninvolved in bestowing affection and dispensing punishment. At the age of six or seven, boys began to be dressed in long pants rather than the shift worn by both sexes, and parents typically encouraged male children to explore the outdoors, to learn early to ride and hunt, or, in poorer families, to trap and fish. Girls were kept closer to home, but parents clearly valued high-spirited, even boisterous, children of both sexes. Observers agree that southern children were undisciplined and unsupervised compared to children in the North, and evidence suggests that the absence of any systematic attempt to "break the will" of children in the name of duty to God or parents was distinctly southern. Even though physical punishment was used freely, parents also enjoyed their children with equal vigor, having them perform for visitors by singing, reciting, or shooting. In wealthier families this time of free-ranging play lasted until about age 10, when boys began to learn male duties from their fathers and girls took up female chores and skills such as cooking and embroidery. In poorer homes, white and black, work began as soon as children were able to contribute to the sustenance of the family.

As with discipline, a youngster's sense of belonging to

a family was comparatively free from elaborate religious values and heavy emphasis on individual conscience. Southern children were raised into their niche by associating duty and deference with kin. By the late 18th century, with longer life spans permitting contact between three generations, southern children were routinely reared by aunts and grandparents and thus taught that the social world, dispersed by rural distances, was inseparable from the world of family.

These basic patterns of child rearing persisted into the 19th century, although some important shifts occurred. In general, the nurturing of infants among whites kept to established customs, except that elite women were more inclined to breast-feed their own infants, at least in the first few weeks after birth. Afterwards, slave women were used as nurses. Elite mothers also became somewhat more reliant on advice books and physicians. Two significant changes did occur in child-rearing beliefs. First, parents began to attribute a special domain to childhood in which offspring were romanticized as pure and even exemplary. The "little strangers" at birth became in three or four years little angels whose tender natures needed constant tending by all-loving mothers. Second, children were reared into gender differences earlier and more deliberately after the 1820s. Fathers took over the discipline of both sexes until age six or seven, after which time they placed particular emphasis on removing their sons from the maternal world. Especially in the planter class, boys were somewhat separated from girls by the age of 10 and taught to behave in an honorable, "manly" way, while girls had to cast off tomboy ways and assume a mildness of temper deemed feminine.

Children's autonomy was further tempered by teaching them of their forefathers and the importance of family reputation and blood ties. Reprimand or approval was applied in the name of ancestors and continuing family tradition, and the significance of such was supported by unique patterns of cousin intermarriage and preservation of family lore. As sectional differences heightened by the 1850s, the children of slaveowners grew more anxious about the "racial purity" of their ancestry, and tensions grew between the slaveowners and their so-called black family of slaves.

Black children under slavery also were raised with a sense of belonging to two families. More than romantic rhetoric, this contrast between the black family in the quarters and a distant but powerful white paternalism accounted for distinct customs in black child rearing. Although most slave children lived in nuclear families, the constant work demanded of parents kept them apart from offspring who were looked after collectively by women too old for planting and chopping. Older children often took care of those immediately younger, and thus were the dispensers of discipline and values long before they became parents themselves. A child's life under slavery, although perhaps initially as carefree as a white child's, changed sharply about age 10, when boys were put into long pants and both sexes were put to adult work. Black parents, looking toward this trying time, raised their children to be circumspect about life in the quarters and attentive to the strengths of religion. A child was taught that white playmates became masters and that parents, powerful in the quarters, might themselves be punished as children.

The Civil War, the end of slavery, and the penetration of industrial modernity altered child-raising customs but did not completely transform their powerful tradition. Hospital births, improved nutrition, and standardized medical advice by the 1890s began to characterize infant care for families who could afford them. In these families, children were disciplined with less use of corporal punishment. They were less often idealized as angels and seen more as young individuals who would become productive adults. Wealthier white children saw somewhat less of poor black children, and the advent of public education even in many rural areas placed important tasks of child raising under agencies with general standards for self-expression, discipline, reward, and the sense of gender differences.

Many continuities with the past remained, however. Black nurses were much employed in the raising of upper-class white children, and vestiges of white paternalistic "family feeling" persisted. Rural life and its rhythms still informed childhood. Elite children were reared to appreciate the land as the only source of virtue and well-being in the face of urbanization. Well into the 20th century the sense of family membership and ancestry remained a strong factor in the upbringing of these children and was made even sharper by frequent parental emphasis on Old South lore and the cataclysm of war.

For poor, especially black, children childhood remained a time of rural adventure soon encroached upon by work in the fields and work in the homes of whites. Manifold kin connections spread the rearing of children in segregated black communities where an abstract sense of the South was overshadowed by the immediacies of work and racial identity. Here mothers were the dominant child raisers in all aspects of discipline and family continuity, and the church, rather than formal schooling, was for many children the chief force in learning social values and spiritual aspiration. The local church, too, provided such institutional help as day care and food distribution in both ordinary and hard times.

See also BLACK LIFE: Family, Black; FOLKLIFE: Family Folklore; SOCIAL CLASS: Poverty

Steven M. Stowe
New York University

Dorothy Abbott, ed., *Mississippi Writers: Reflections of Childhood and Youth*, 2 vols. (1985–86); James Agee and Walker Evans, *Let Us Now Praise Famous Men* (1941); Eugene D. Genovese, *Roll, Jordan, Roll: The World the Slaves Made* (1976); Chris Mayfield, ed., *Growing Up Southern: Southern Exposure Looks at Childhood, Then and Now* (1981); Anne Moody, *Coming of Age in Mississippi* (1968); William A. Percy, *Lanterns on the Levee* (1941); Daniel Blake Smith, *Inside the Great House: Planter Family Life in Eighteenth-Century Chesapeake Society* (1980); Steven M. Stowe, *Intimacy and Power in the Old South: Ritual in the Lives of the Planters* (1987); Bertram Wyatt-Brown, *Southern Honor: Ethics and Behavior in the Old South* (1982).

Children's Games

Children's play was rarely mentioned by observers of the Old South. Sources that do exist suggest that southern children had active play lives and that games occupied a major portion of their time. Assumptions about social roles, human nature, and conduct were expressed in their play. Many old and popular southern games are remnants of significant events in history and common cultural traditions of the region.

Literature on white middle-class children's games may be found in novels, diaries, and artistic prints. Eighteenth-century prints show a number of games, and below each picture is a statement of the moral lesson the game teaches, reflecting the dominant cultural values. Informal ball games included stoolball, cricket, fives, tip-cat, and baseball. Hop-scotch, leap-frog, and hide-and-seek, all common to American children today, and imitative games such as playing house are also identified in the prints. Board games included chess, fox-and-geese, and checks, which is similar to checkers.

L. Minor Blackford, in *Mine Eyes Have Seen the Glory*, recorded typical games of the Blackford children of Virginia in the mid-1850s. Examples included Anthony over, hickeme dickeme, blindman's bluff, prisoner's base, pull-over-the-bat, kite flying, bull-in-the-pen, cutting jacks, stilt walking, knock, and catch out. The boys often played soldier, perhaps resulting from their awareness of the Mexican War. Additional outdoor play included snowballing, hunting, gymnastics, wrestling, swimming, and skating.

The relationship of play to Old South values was often clear as in the case of representational play or playacting, in which children created small, real-life dramas or imitated everyday life. The dramatic elements of this play, such as in "playing" soldier, were analogous to social roles in antebellum society. Among the more affluent families of the Old South, games emphasized effort and skill, teaching children that outcomes of situations depended on the amount and quality of effort one expended.

Many historical and contemporary games of black children, on the other hand, are most notable for exhibiting an attitude of resistance and assertiveness on the part of the players. Older game songs that date from the days of slavery express an anger against slave masters. The following example of an old game song demonstrates resistance:

Way go, Lily
Way go, Lily
I'm going to rule my ruler
I'm going to rule my ruler
I'm going to rule him with a hickory
I'm going to rule him with a hickory

This song probably originated during slavery and is rarely heard now except in Charleston and Savannah. Blacks have used creative song games in "talking bad" to their oppressors since coming from Africa, allowing them to say what they needed to say without being perceived as a threat.

Another common Afro-American children's game song, played by forming a ring, is "Little Sally Walker." One of a cycle of ring games with African roots, its lyrics encourage a child to "rise":

Little Sally Walker
Sitting in a saucer
Crying and a-weeping
Over all she has done

Rise Sally Rise
Wipe out your eyes
Fly to the east, Sally . . .

Contemporary games of black children show an inherited oral tradition and simultaneously engage in nonverbal behavior that involves body movement and gestures similar to playacting. Clapping games are popular and are primarily nonverbal. Most of the games are rhythmical and allow for improvisation.

Older game songs common along the Georgia and South Carolina coasts have been recorded by Bessie Jones and Bess Lomax Hawes in *Step It Down*. Jones is a black woman born in an area famed for its rich Gullah culture. The book reflects her efforts to preserve remnants of southern tradition and the African heritage. Many of these older game songs may still be heard in black communities and are often taught within organized play times in an effort to preserve cultural traditions. The renewed interest in the preservation of the multiethnic origins of America has stimulated educators to consider traditional games as an instrument for teaching about cultural uniqueness and historical events.

There is limited documentation of games indigenous to the South in the 20th century, and it is likely that southern children's play has become very much like that of other children in the United States. Changes in game preferences of American children were examined by Sutton-Smith and Rosenberg (1961), who compared four studies on games over a 60-year period from 1896 to 1959. They found that formalized games, such as party

Children's Games, *a painting by southern primitive painter Theora Hamblett, 1972*

games, ring games, acting games, singing games, and dialogue games were becoming less important while imitative games and chasing games continued their popularity. This shift away from formalized games is especially significant in relation to the South, where games have been traditionally more decorous and formal than elsewhere in the country.

The uniquely southern aspects of children's games that remain represent traces of ethnic diversity within the dominant American culture and are most likely found within the poorer regions as well as among the larger minority groups. Awakened desire to cultivate multicultural heritage is acting as a stimulus to preserve some traditionally southern children's games as a unique folk art.

See also BLACK LIFE: African Influences; Slave Culture

Rachel D. Robertson
Arizona State University

L. Minor Blackford, *Mine Eyes Have Seen the Glory* (1954); Ruth F. Bogdanoff and Elaine T. Dolch, *Young Children* (January 1979); Dickson D. Bruce, Jr., *Southern Folklore Quarterly* (1977); Jane Carson, *Colonial Virginians at Play* (1965); Bessie Jones and Bess Lomax Hawes, *Step it Down: Games, Plays, Songs, and Stories from the Afro-American Heritage* (1972); B. Sutton-Smith and Bruce G. Rosenberg, *Journal of American Folklore* (January–March 1961).

Clubs and Voluntary Organizations

Somewhat slower than northern women to form clubs and associations, southern women did not participate in social and public affairs through organized groups until after the Civil War and Reconstruction. The loss of one-fourth of the region's males and the accompanying poverty of the late 19th century forced women into the work force and brought increased independence. Release from the burdens of directing large plantation households and supervising the physical care of slaves added to the leisure time of women of means at the same time that the wives of professional and middle-class townsmen also gained added freedom from domestic duties. Moreover, as public colleges stressing industrial and commercial curricula were founded, more southern daughters entered professional fields. Finally, the increasing urbanization of the South facilitated the organization of groups in which women could express their growing sense of social usefulness, self-reliance, and initiative.

Southern women first banded together to further the foreign and home mission work of their churches. Anne Firor Scott has concluded that "the public life of nearly every Southern woman leader for forty years began in a church society." Methodist women formed the Board of Home Missions in 1882, and Baptist women formed the Women's Missionary Union in 1888. The church "circle" was the most accessible and approved institution outside the home through which women were able both to initiate reform through city missions and settlement houses and also to lay the foundation for the interracial cooperation that would come in the 20th century. Concurrently, the Women's Christian Temperance Union (WCTU), organized in the South after Frances Willard visited the region in the 1880s, developed under state leaders such as Caroline Merrick in Louisiana, Belle Kearney in Mississippi, Julia Tutwiler in Alabama, and Rebecca Felton in Georgia. The puritannical foundations of the temperance movement provided a base for allied work of the WCTU in its crusade for the abolition of the convict-lease system, the establishment of industrial schools for girls and homes for youthful offenders, and other reforms.

In the late 1880s and 1890s southern women were drawn into the club movement. Between 1894 and 1907 federations of various cultural and self-improvement groups were formed in every southern state and by 1910 all were members of the General Federation of Women's Clubs (GFWC). Although the initial goal was self-edification, the federated clubs became, in the words of Mrs. Percy Pennybacker, a Texas matron who headed the national GFWC in 1913–14, a "recruiting station in which the unaccustomed women shall be trained to find themselves . . . and [assume] widening responsibilities in the world's work." As a major tool of social change in the South, women's clubs promoted statewide library and adult education programs, guardianship laws for divorced women, marital blood tests, sanitary milk supplies, child labor laws, protective legislation for women, and myriad other reforms. In their "alternative universities" clubwomen kept abreast of current events, mobilized public opinion, and, most importantly, promoted the woman suffrage movement. In the 1920s and 1930s club representatives formed Joint Legislative Councils in most southern states to lobby their club agendas at the statehouse.

Excluded from the GFWC, black women formed their own Southern Association of Colored Women's Clubs after Margaret Murray Washington began the Tuskegee Woman's Club in 1895. Unlike white women, black clubwomen were especially concerned with issues of importance to poor women, working mothers, and tenant wives. Their work was best represented by the community betterment and social service programs of the Atlanta Neighborhood Union initiated by Lugenia Burns Hope in 1908. Also important to southern black women were the mutual aid societies created to provide medical care and burial assistance. Some persisted well into the 20th century.

From the time in 1851 when Ann Pamela Cunningham of South Carolina began the first woman's patriotic society in the United States, the Mount Vernon Ladies' Association, southern white women have responded to organizations commemorating the past. The unique history of the South fostered a high level of interest in genealogy and an attraction to the Colonial Dames of America, the Daughters of the American Revolution (DAR) (its first southern chapter was founded in North Carolina in 1898), and especially the United Daughters of the Confederacy (UDC), founded by Nashville women in 1894 from numerous existing cemetery memorial societies and soldier relief associations. The UDC, like the DAR, was socially glamorous, perpetuating social hierarchies as it strove to glorify the southern war effort, particularly through the creation of libraries on the Confederate past. In recent years, as it has declined in membership, the UDC has shifted its focus to historical preservation.

Reflecting their natural gregariousness and their quest for the "bonds of sisterhood," southern college women founded in the post–Civil War years a number of Greek-letter sororities. Such collegiate groups and related literary societies have remained popular in southern universities. Many women have "graduated" to high-society organizations that flourish in southern towns and cities, best represented by the Junior League and other benefit groups, whose principal functions are to raise funds for community arts and social services. For other women, principally those in small towns, social activities center around the meeting hall of the Order of Eastern Star and other auxiliaries to male fraternal orders.

Academic and professional women in the South created associations patterned after northern organizations. In 1903 the Southern Association of College Women (SACW) was formed in Knoxville and under the strong direction of Elizabeth Avery Colton devoted its energies to raising the standards of institutions of higher education for the region's young women. In 1921 SACW merged with the American Association of University Women. Delta Kappa Gamma, founded in 1929 by Annie Webb Blanton and a charter group of Texas teachers, grew beyond its early southern chapters into an international society for women educators. Altrusa International, begun in Nashville in 1917 as a service club for business and professional women, is one of many such groups that serve to coordinate the leadership and community service of women professionals. Another is Pilot International, founded in 1919 by a Kentuckian, Lena Madesin Phillips.

Rural women in the South, both black and white, are still active in home demonstration clubs organized before World War I by the extension departments of land-grant colleges. They are unique among women's organizations in that from the outset they have had professional leadership salaried through federal and state funds. Organized rural women have devoted their attention almost exclusively to home improvement and rural community development, often working with the American Farm Bureau to stress citizenship, safety, and home and community beautification. Urban women, too, through ubiquitous garden clubs promote memorial plantings, highway beautification, pilgrimages, and the restoration of historic homes and buildings.

Both the economic straits of southern state governments and the general political conservatism of the region's electorate have led women to form associations to institute social change. One of the earliest was the New Orleans Anti-Tuberculosis League formed by Kate Gordon in 1906. Early 20th-century women created societies for village improvement, modern roads, public schoolhouse improvement, and child labor abolition. Reflecting southern emphasis upon maternal responsibilities, the National Congress of Mothers (later the PTA) was founded by a Georgia woman, Alice M. Birney, in 1897, and the National Congress of Colored Parents and Teachers was begun in Atlanta by Selena Sloan Butler in 1926. In 1930 Jessie Daniel Ames of Texas formed the Association of Southern Women for the Prevention of Lynching (ASWPL), which eventually united 40,000 churchwomen to confront the issues of race, lynching, and interracial sex before it met its goals and ceased to exist. The ASWPL is the most distinctive women's voluntary association in southern history.

With the enfranchisement of women in 1920, the eligibility of women to hold public office, and the increasing access of southern women to professions once the exclusive enclave of men, the club and voluntary association work of southern women has declined. Many women have turned from volunteer work to paid jobs. Moreover, women have had less need to pursue education through cultural and literary organizations. As other agencies have arisen to meet society's needs, the federated clubs and reformist associations are no longer major agents for social change. Nonetheless, there is scarcely any southern town or city where women of both races do not still join together in numerous social, professional, and civic organizations.

See also AGRICULTURE: / Agricultural Extension Services; BLACK LIFE: Fraternal Orders, Black; EDUCATION: Fraternities and Sororities; HISTORY AND MANNERS: Historical Preservation; / United Daughters of the Confederacy; Pilgrimage; POLITICS: / Felton, Rebecca; RELIGION: Missionary Activities; SCIENCE AND MEDICINE: Health, Public

Martha H. Swain
Texas Woman's University

Sharon Harley and Rosalyn Terborg-Penn, eds., *The Afro-American Woman: Struggles and Images* (1978); Gerda Lerner, *Journal of Negro History* (April 1974); John Patrick McDowell, *The Social Gospel in the South: The Woman's Home Mission Movement in the Methodist Episcopal Church, South, 1886–1939* (1982); Margaret Nell Price, "The Development of Leadership by Southern Women Through Clubs and Organizations" (M.A. thesis, University of North Carolina, Chapel Hill, 1945); Anne Firor Scott, *The Southern Lady: From Pedestal to Politics, 1830–1930* (1970).

Education of Women

Until recently, the chivalric image of the southern lady supported the hierarchy of race, class, and sex that defined the region's socioeconomic structures. The education of southern white women could proceed only if it did not tamper with that ideal. Translated into social consequences, chivalry blighted educational opportunities for southern white women. From the revolutionary era until recent decades, the South consistently lagged behind other regions of the country in implementing educational reforms for its female population. On the eve of the Civil War, despite the widespread popularity of female academies, the rate of illiteracy among adult white women was highest in the South. Not until World War II did regional differences in female education begin to narrow.

For the majority of southern black women formal education did not begin until the Civil War destroyed the institution of slavery. Black females then took their place beside black males in the schools founded for the freed people by northern missionary societies, the Freedmen's Bureau, and the newly visible black churches. Many of these private schools, specializing in primary instruction, were superseded by segregated public school systems at the end of Reconstruction. After 1877 black private schools increasingly emphasized either an industrial arts or a liberal arts curriculum. Ironically, in the arena of education, the interplay between racism and sexism resulted in what Gerda Lerner termed the "sex loophole in race discrimination": educational achievements did not readily translate into wider economic opportunities for black males but were profitable for black females. The path to upward social mobility for black families turned upon the higher education of their daughters. Educated black women became the mainstay of the teacher corps in the region's segregated public schools.

Throughout the colonial period the education of young white children was a private family concern, largely the privilege of the middle and upper classes. Only in the large urban coastal settlements of the South did one find formal, private schools often called "adventure schools." Generally, southern mothers, like their northern counterparts, tended to the early education of their young sons and daughters. The upper classes employed tutors for their sons once formal instruction began in earnest. A few planters' daughters shared in the classical training made available to their brothers; for the most part, though, female education remained both superficial and ornamental, designed to make them more attractive in the marriage market. Thus, while sons of the upper classes learned Greek, Latin, ancient and modern history, mathematics, and the sciences, their sisters were instructed in the fine arts of conversational French, music, dancing, painting and drawing, fancy needlework, moral training, scripture reading, and the bare rudiments of writing and arithmetic.

Cultural attitudes toward women's education remained surprisingly uniform across the northern, middle, and southern colonies. Intellectual accomplishments were not appropriate for females. A woman's mental and physical capacities supposedly could not "endure" the rigors of a classical training. Higher education "taxed" a woman's brain, defeminizing her and thus rendering her unfit for her role as wife and mother.

In the aftermath of the American Revolution these beliefs increasingly came under attack by American intellectuals. Men such as Benjamin Rush argued that the success of the republican experiment in government depended upon a well-educated citizenry. Because women were responsible for supervising the education of their male as well as female offspring, it became necessary after the Revolution to upgrade women's education, shifting from "style to substance" and, of necessity, from the home to the female academy.

The academy or seminary movement caught fire in the northern and middle states first and then spread to the South. Some scholars contend that planters, their economy disrupted by the Revolution, first attended to economic recovery before investing in their daughters' education. The other interpretation favors a more cultural/ideological explanation: it stresses an emerging plantation culture firmly grounded in patriarchy. This view suggests that although southern elites came to embrace the female academy movement by the second decade of the 19th century, the education of southern women remained more limited than that of their northern and western counterparts. Southern academies remained committed to the ideal of "fitting women for their roles in the plantation culture: a well-read elite serving as wives and mothers to the master class." Although the education of southern white women remained heavily influenced by moral training and scripture reading, definite gains had been made in the quality of women's education. By the late antebellum period plantation daughters also received some of the educational training heretofore reserved for their brothers.

Female academies and seminaries served the interests of the middle and upper classes. Together, the costs of boarding and tuition made academy life a privilege of the well-to-do. During the antebellum period northern and western states moved to combat this inherent class bias by investing in state-supported primary, secondary, and normal schools. Once again, the South lagged behind. Although most southern states created paper systems of free primary schools for whites just before the Civil War, education scholars generally attribute the beginning of free state-supported public education for all southern children to the reforms initiated by Reconstruction governments.

Coeducation was the rule for white boys and girls at the primary level in urban areas. In the secondary institutions that gained popularity in post-Reconstruction southern cities the sexes remained segregated. Southern white girls eagerly availed themselves of public education, especially at the secondary level. Enrollment in female high schools generally surpassed that of male high schools. By World War I, however, high schools were an accepted part of the states' systems of instruction, and coeducation was the norm.

Women seeking education beyond the secondary level had two choices: matriculation at a normal school with its emphasis on teacher training, or enrollment at a women's college offering a liberal arts curriculum. Although the first women's college with degree-granting privileges was founded in Macon, Ga., in 1836, women's colleges came of age in post–Civil War America. Those colleges that existed prior to the war really provided only a seminary education. Northern and western states were first in establishing normal schools and women's colleges on a large scale. Slower to respond to demands for female higher education, six southern states reported no normal schools as late as 1872. White women's colleges were founded in the South during the last two decades of the

19th century: Sophie Newcomb (1887), Goucher (1888), Agnes Scott (1889), and Randolph-Macon (1893) led the way. Black women took advantage of either the private black colleges such as Fisk University or the few state-supported normal and industrial schools such as Florida Agricultural, Mechanical and Normal College.

Judging by entrance requirements, age of admission, standardization of curriculum, and library and laboratory facilities, women's colleges initially were below the standards set for men's colleges. Northern states made the first serious efforts to rectify that situation. The U.S. Commissioner of Education divided institutions of higher learning into A and B divisions, those that offered the classic four-year liberal arts curriculum and those that did not. As late as 1907 between 68 and 75 percent of the women's colleges in division B were located in the South. On the eve of World War I only 6 of the 140 institutions in the South calling themselves women's colleges were regarded as such by the Southern Association of College Women.

The push for coeducation at the collegiate level paralleled the development of women's colleges in the South. Although Trinity College of Duke University accepted three sisters into the 1874 freshman class, coeducation first became policy at Duke in 1896. Almost as soon as women gained entrance to the men's colleges, a backlash occurred. Arguments advanced to discourage female admission to male institutes centered on the notion that women would lower the standards of men's colleges and thus drive away large numbers of male students and faculty. Yet beneath that nagging belief in female inferiority lay the unacknowledged fact that women were in actuality competing successfully with male students for the academic honors offered by the colleges.

The beginning of the 20th century saw the concept of the coordinate college advanced by male educators as a compromise between separate women's colleges and coeducation, although in the South the movement did not gain broad support until the period between the world wars. Under the coordinate college plan women would benefit from their association with men's colleges. The large endowments made to male institutes encouraged distinguished faculties and superior library and laboratory facilities. Women enjoyed these privileges under the coordinate college program, but at the same time they remained "protected" in their separate classes and social organizations.

The period between the two world wars also witnessed a steady increase in the matriculation of southern white women on college campuses. By the end of World War II regional differences in women's education at all levels had diminished sharply. During the 1970s and 1980s, due to the contemporary women's movement, women's higher education shifted again in favor of coeducation. Many of the coordinate colleges have merged with their male institutions, while many separate women's colleges have opened their doors to men or become part of the expanding state college and university systems.

In the study of women's education the focus has been on regions other than the South. To date, no systematic work on southern women's education exists. Scattered evidence suggests that education is a double-edged sword in the hands of southern women, white and black. Black women teachers in the late 19th and early 20th centuries founded schools and colleges that provided an alternative to the inferior segregated schools of the region. Those black institutions contributed vital social services to the local black community. And, as scholars are discovering, the schools often became centers for organized community efforts to promote social change. There is also the recent example of the participation of young southern white college women in the civil rights movement and later in the feminist movement. Young white women from women's colleges first supported black students who challenged segregation and race discrimination. The events of the early 1960s carried those women forward to question the very bedrock of southern society—the patriarchal, racist, and class-based assumptions implicit in the ideal of southern womanhood.

Teacher at Bethune-Cookman College, Daytona Beach, Fla., 1940s

See also BLACK LIFE: Education, Black; Freedom Movement, Black; EDUCATION articles

Kathleen C. Berkeley
University of North Carolina
at Wilmington

Isabella Margaret Elizabeth Blandin, *History of Higher Education of Women in the South Prior to 1860* (1909); Dianne Puthoff Brandstadter, "Developing the Coordinate College for Women at Duke University: The Career of Alice Mary Baldwin, 1924–1947" (Ph.D. dissertation, Duke University, 1977); Catherine Clinton, *The Plantation Mistress: Woman's World in the Old South* (1982); Florence Davis, "The Education of Southern Girls from 1750–1860" (Ph.D. dissertation, University of Chicago, 1952); Sara Evans, *Personal Politics: The Roots of Women's Liberation in the Civil Rights Movement and the New Left* (1979); Gerda Lerner, *The Majority Finds Its Past: Placing Women in History* (1979); Mary Beth Norton, *Liberty's Daughters: The Revolutionary Experience of American Women* (1980); Thomas Woody, *A History of Women's Education in the United States*, 2 vols. (1929).

Elderly

In recent years the South has become a haven for elderly Americans. According to the U.S. census, by 1970 the region led the nation in the number of residents over age 65, and more than 6 million aged individuals lived below the Mason-Dixon line. As of 1980 the median age of Floridians, 34.7 years, was the highest in the nation; and Florida's proportion of residents aged 65 or older, 34.7 percent, was higher than that of any other state.

The growing elderly population in the South is a modern development. Traditionally, both the Northeast and North Central states have had far larger concentrations of elderly persons. In the 19th century, in fact, the South was noted for its young population. Two factors explained this historic condition. First, in contrast to other regions, the South experienced extremely high mortality rates, even among its adult members. One was far more likely to grow old in the North than in the South. Second, many of the southern states were relatively "new" and rural. They attracted the young and mobile, leaving the old to die in the cities of the East Coast.

The South of the 19th century, therefore, provided little in the way of special services for its aged population. Unlike the North, there were relatively few old-age homes or other provisions for those over 65. The status of the old in southern society remained tied—as it traditionally had been in America—to the ownership of property and control of kin.

In the last two decades much of this has changed. Nationwide, demographic trends associated with birthrates, infant mortality, and longevity have led to a higher proportion than ever before of persons aged 65 and over in the population—approximately 11 percent in 1980. Migration of the elderly to the Sunbelt has transformed both the nature of southern old age and the communities in which they live. Although an overwhelming proportion (24.7 percent) of all migrants head for Florida, every southern state has been affected by their numbers. According to census data, the southern states with the highest proportion of elderly residents in 1980 were Florida (17.3 percent), Arkansas (13.6 percent), and West Virginia (12.2 percent). The states with the lowest proportion included Georgia (9.4 percent), South Carolina (9.2 percent), and Virginia (7.5 percent). In Florida a striking 87 percent of the residents aged 65 or over lived in urban areas, as did 26 percent of the elderly in Texas. In most other southern states, however, only a slightly higher percentage were urban rather than rural residents; and in Mississippi, West Virginia, and North Carolina, the majority of the elderly lived in rural areas.

On the whole, these elderly individuals are better educated and wealthier than the natives; yet they come to the region without the traditional status granted by land, occupation, and family. As a result, for the first time the region is developing social services to meet the needs of elderly persons. In places like the peninsula of Florida, the Ozark Mountains, and the Texas hill country the effect is undeniable. In new communities, older cities, and even rural areas, southern culture is being transformed by the politics, recreational demands, and medical and housing needs of their older citizens. Clearly, the growth in attention to the elderly's needs will continue. The future of the South will be one in which the elderly will play an ever larger and more significant role.

Respect for the elderly has long been a southern value, communicated through folklore, literature, and song. "When an old man dies, a library burns," is an old folk saying suggesting the value of the elderly in a rural, peasant, oral culture. Historian C. Vann Woodward has pointed out that while a Hemingway character with a grandfather is "inconceivable," a Faulkner hero without one is also. Welty, Warren, O'Connor, McCullers, and other leading regional writers have filled their stories with old people. Southern whites are respectful, yet the elderly are also portrayed, at times, as a burden, symbols of a noble past that has not been equaled in later times. Faulkner's heroes, for example, are sometimes haunted by their grandparents, as is Gail Hightower in *Light in August*, who confuses his own identity with that of his heroic Confederate ancestor. The image of the snuff-dipping, corncob-puffing granny in the Appalachian and rural white South is also not always favorable, but even this figure is a feisty creature, admirable in tough times.

Elderly blacks have been frequently portrayed, by whites as well as blacks, as repositories of wisdom. From Uncle Tom in Harriet Beecher Stowe's 19th-century novel, to Uncle Remus, to Faulkner's Dilsey in the *Sound and the Fury*, to Ernest J. Gaines's Miss Jane Pittman,

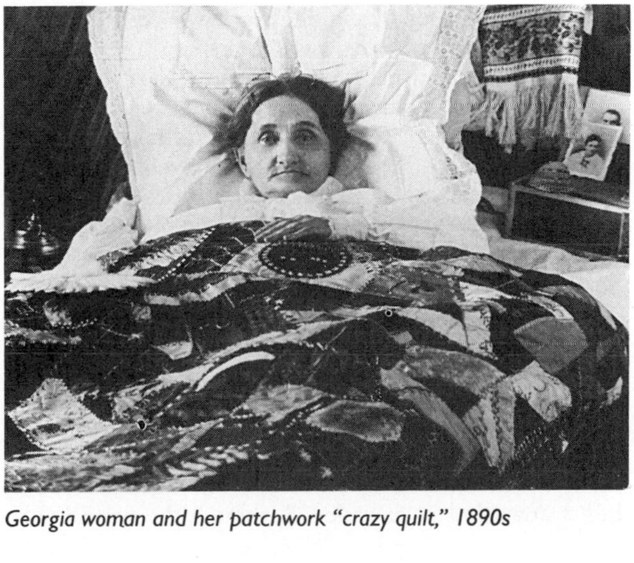

Georgia woman and her patchwork "crazy quilt," 1890s

elderly Afro-Americans have generally been seen as patient, experienced, sober, warm, and perhaps above all, spiritual, as though profiting from their suffering. In contemporary times they are also seen as assertive, willing to speak up eloquently against injustice.

The elderly have been valued in the regional folk culture as a source of specific knowledge and skills and as the embodiment of southern tradition, which had to be orally passed on to survive. Howard W. Odum, in *The Way of the South* (1947), saw grandparents as a key force in inculcating family and regional traditions. "You tell me that I must forget," says one imaginary grandmother to her grandchildren. "But I say unto you, you must remember."

See also FOLKLIFE: Family Folklore; GEOGRAPHY: Population

Carole Haber
University of North Carolina
at Charlotte

Forrest J. Berghorn, Donna E. Shafer et al., *Dynamics of Aging: Original Essays on the Process and Experience of Growing Old* (1980); Charles F. Longino and Jeanne C. Biggar, *The Gerontologist* (June 1981); Daniel Scott Smith, Mark Friedberger, and Michel Dahlin, *Sociology and Social Research* (April 1979); U.S. Bureau of the Census, *Historical Statistics of the United States* (1975); U.S. Senate Special Committee on Aging, *America in Transition: An Aging Society*, 1984–85 ed. (1985).

Family, Modernization of

Although industrialization in the North tended to erode the importance of the family in social life, throughout most of the 19th and well into the 20th century the South resisted those changes that tended to diminish the importance of kinship. In the South more than any other region, the family was at the center of social life, remaining the chief forum for socialization, education, and community.

Industrial development in the South was tied to agriculture. The traditional closeness of the southern agrarian family, its regional persistence, and the clearly defined roles of men and women inhibited economic change. Urbanization rubbed against the grain of deeply rooted agrarianism and conflicted with localist, communal values, a source of strength for so many southern families. A strong anticapitalist, antiindustrial ideology existed in the South, as portrayed in literature from the proslavery writers, Populists, and southern Agrarians (*I'll Take My Stand*) to William Faulkner. Much of this distrust grew out of the desire for personal freedom, but some was the consequence of the nature of the South's industry, which primarily benefited investors from outside the region.

The nuclear family was the norm in the South long before industrialization. Relatives and boarders augmented this basic unit, especially among the affluent, but it nevertheless prevailed. Although the typical farm

Mother, family, and servant in a stitchery by Ethel Mohamed, Belzoni, Miss., photographed in 1978

family in the South was large and primarily an economic unit, during the 19th century the family increasingly became an emotional and spiritual refuge as well. Perhaps the first American family type to be dominated by the emotional intensity associated with modern-day families was that of the wealthy planter. In many plantation families, children were their parents' chief source of pride and satisfaction. In these families, childhood was a time to play, to learn formally from a tutor or private school teacher, and a time to discover one's surroundings.

The offspring of poorer rural families enjoyed fewer of these luxuries and received less concentrated attention from their parents, who had little leisure time. Hardships of making a living from modest farms constricted childhood. At young ages, children were expected to take a hand in the running of the farm; the family members always worked together. But because of the seasonal rhythms of farm life—the rainy days when one could not work in the fields, Sundays, and holidays—the family had playtime together. Thus, close bonds developed, and members of the poorest families demonstrated strong feelings of affection for one another. Children have long been prized among all black and white rural southerners and still today more attention is given to them than in other areas. Fewer children than elsewhere are in day-care arrangements, and more preschoolers are watched by parents or nearby relations, partly for economic reasons and partly for cultural ones.

Historians and sociologists see a standard pattern to industrialization's impact on the family. In the North, for example, as fathers increasingly left home for the workplace, a mother's chief role was to raise children, leading to a deeper attachment between mother and child. As the family became less producer oriented and more consumer oriented, family size decreased.

In the South these developments occurred very slowly, and southern families resisted some of the trends that seemed to characterize the North. Where allegiance to family, community, and patriarchy were strongest, the encroachments of modernization were least likely to be felt. Unlike antebellum New England, where the labors of the youthful Lowell girls were legendary, many southern fathers defied mill owners who sought to hire young women. They felt the work was unsuitable for southern ladies—whether rich or poor—and feared such employment would destroy the harmony of the family. The "Waltham" system, where dormitories and matrons assured the highest morals and guarded the working girls' reputations, failed in the South. When forced by poverty to send his daughters to the mills, the white father was too proud to allow them to leave the patriarchal nest, and, in addition, wanted to retain economic control of their labor. Contracts were made between the mill and the father for working children. Families continued to live together, and although the father may not have worked in the mill, he received the family wage.

In resisting the redistribution of family authority that accompanied industrialization in the North, the southern family also sought to maintain the sharp divisions between males and females that often characterized family responsibilities in the South. The man's role as the unchallenged patriarch, the strong, respected provider, was supported by key elements of southern culture. The woman's inner strength and purity, her social and spiritual superiority, and her political and economic inferiority were also seen as important components of the southern way of life, components to be preserved. This southern romanticism continued to hold sway throughout the 19th century and beyond, slowing down industrialization and urbanization.

When urbanization and industrialization finally developed in the South after World War II, the changes that occurred closely paralleled the transformations that had been occurring in the North for decades. The role of women changed, and Anne Firor Scott suggests that the movement of women into the world of gainful employment was born of necessity and of changing economic conditions. It is possible to argue that when the factories needed cheap labor, it became acceptable for women to work in mills; when businesses needed secretaries, when children needed teachers, whenever economic imperative existed, mores and social barriers gave way.

Once in the work force, women were more readily able to enter public life, though again this development was painfully slow. Correspondingly, the man became less of a patriarch and more of a partner. Post–World War II social and economic change in the South also lessened the importance of the family as an economic unit and a source of emotional satisfaction. Consequently, divorce has become a reality among families, even in rural areas and small towns.

Industrialization also accelerated southern geographic mobility, which now more closely resembles patterns in the North. Southern families traditionally maintained a strong sense of place. They tended to remain in the same region over long periods of time, which meant that families in a southern community had more extensive kinship and social ties than those in the North. Furthermore, southern men and women tended to put a high premium on holding their families together. Offspring often remained within reach of the family circle throughout their adult lives, even attending the same church, and divorce among whites was much rarer in the South than in the North. Although most families did not want to move or split up for the sake of industrial jobs, and mobility was much lower than in other regions, many southerners, both black and white, sought employment and educational opportunities in the North during the early 20th century.

See also BLACK LIFE: Family, Black; FOLKLIFE: Family Folklore; INDUSTRY: Industrialization and Change; Industrialization, Resistance to

Orville Vernon Burton
University of Illinois

Carol K. Bleser, ed., *The Hammonds of Redcliffe* (1981); Orville Vernon Burton, *In My Father's House Are Many Mansions: Family and Community in Edgefield, South Carolina* (1985); James C. Cobb, *Industrialization and Southern Society, 1877–1984* (1985); Carl N. Degler, *At Odds: Women and the Family in America from the Revolution to the Present* (1980); Margaret J. Hagood, *Mothers of the South: Portraiture of the White Tenant Farm Women* (1939); Daniel Blake Smith, *Inside the Great House: Planter Family Life in Eighteenth-Century Chesapeake Society* (1980).

Family Dynasties

When considering the ultimate expression of power in the American South, one thinks of the planter patriarch holding sway over a large plantation worked by gangs of slaves. With one hand the great planter marries off his children to other leading planters in order to augment his landed empire, and with the other hand he serves at the county court or the statehouse to reinforce his political power base.

This image is not without historical foundation, but it is largely the product of a tendency to generalize from a particular moment in the life of the South. For, indeed, there was a golden age of planters in the middle decades of the 18th century, a time when significant parts of the plantation South—especially the Chesapeake and the Carolina Low Country—were governed by a few landed families. These elite members of the southern gentry sat atop the power structure (from the county courts and parish vestries to the lower houses of assembly) setting the tone for virtually all phases of social, economic, and political life. The influence of this elite group of planters was reinforced by ties of blood or marriage that had been first established in the last quarter of the 17th century. In the decades before the Revolution, for example, no less than 70 percent of the 110 leaders of the House of Burgesses were drawn from families resident in Virginia before 1690.

How did these few great planter families manage to extend their influence over the generations? Sons and daughters were carefully, strategically, placed on lands accumulated for them by the economic success and political power of their fathers. This small, homogeneous elite of perhaps no more than 100 wealthy families—English by descent, Anglican in faith, linked to one another by ties of kinship and bonds of economic interest—monopolized political power in 18th-century Virginia. For example, seven members of the Carter family, the richest of all the Virginia clans in the 18th century, owned a total of 170,000 acres of land and 2,300 slaves scattered over seven counties.

The historical prominence of leading planter families such as the Carters, the Byrds, and the Lees should not obscure the relative brevity of their dominance of southern history. In fact, this golden age of great family dynasties flourished only between the early years of the unpredictable, dangerous settlement on the frontier and the 19th-century emergence of a much more diverse, middle-class society.

Younger sons of the English gentry arriving in Virginia in the early years of the 17th century fully expected to establish strong and prosperous family and kin groups. Their power base was to be grounded in the great fortunes they believed would be extracted from gold, precious metals, and (by the 1620s) tobacco. Although a few of these men became wealthy tobacco barons in the early years, most of them failed in finding fortunes and building family lines to perpetuate their status and power.

Most ambitions were stifled by the overwhelming odds against survival in the disease-ridden early South. An endemic malarial environment in the Chesapeake and parts of the Carolina Tidewater created an oppressively high mortality rate that stunted family size, produced a society of orphans and stepparents, and virtually precluded the development of an elderly generation. Perhaps most significant, the high death rates thwarted any tendency toward strong patriarchal authority. Few men who expected to build powerful, multigenerational family dynasties could hope to succeed in an environment where men generally did not live long enough even to see their grandchildren, let alone to nurture and direct their careers. Instead, most gentlemen in this Hobbesian world struggled simply to survive—abruptly finishing their lives with nothing accumulated, nothing permanent to pass on to their heirs. Not until the final decade of the 17th century, when life expectancies gradually lengthened and slave importations increased dramatically, did a few leading families begin to build the large tobacco plantations and powerful family dynasties that would prevail in the 18th-century South.

At the other end of this golden age of southern planters, essentially after 1790, the picture is more difficult to assess. Prominent southern family lines continued well into the 19th century; indeed, scholars consider the antebellum era as the flush time for self-consciously paternalistic planters, men such as George Fitzhugh who intoned the virtues and obligations of the patriarch watching out for all his "people." Some historians, such as Eugene D. Genovese, believe that the paternalism of southern slaveholders reached something of a climax (both politically and ideologically) during the antebellum era. One can surely detect in the writings of these influential planter families an increasing self-consciousness about their patriarchal role—perhaps an indication itself of the minority position they held. They laid great stress on family and kin loyalty, strategically planned marital alliances, a deep attachment to the land, and complete control in managing the slaves, servants, kin, and various hangers-on, who comprised the great planters' "people."

By the 19th century, though, southern society had changed—perhaps not dramatically, for most of it was still based on a staple-crop economy—but clearly the practice of deference to a few leading planters had begun to decline and in some places to disappear altogether. Great wealth was no longer the only road to political power, as scores of middle-class lawyers, teachers, and middling planters found their way into the political arena of the antebellum South.

Clearly, the spread of slaveholding was instrumental in democratizing political leadership among whites in the antebellum South. Slave-based plantations, once the preserve of a relatively few wealthy tobacco and rice planters in the early South, became a much more widely diffused system of labor by the mid-19th century, as cotton spread throughout the Lower South. In some of the most heavily populated slave states (South Carolina, Mississippi, Alabama, Georgia) between one-third and one-half of all white families held slaves in 1860. Most families owned a modest four to six slaves, but, more importantly, at least half the white families in the Deep South had a direct material interest in the protection and perpetuation of slavery. Hence, the number of legitimate spokesmen for slaveholding interests grew rapidly in the 19th century. Wealthy landed families continued to exert political influence; but that influence was increasingly outweighed by an expanding pool of slaveholding lawyers and merchants (particularly the former), who by mid-century controlled the county court in every southern state. By 1850 political power in the South carried a discernibly middle-class connotation.

In the postbellum South the disintegration of family dynasties, especially in the political arena, was even more conspicuous. With the growth of urban centers in the New South, political life became an increasingly diverse affair. Recent studies show that most urban officeholders in the South during the late 19th and early 20th centuries came from new families, not from heirs of old notable families.

More significant was the gradual deterioration of the planters' social and economic hegemony in the New South. According to C. Vann Woodward, the essential drama of the New South was "the story of the decay and decline of the aristocracy, the suffering and betrayal of the poor white, and the rise and transformation of a middle class." As hundreds of textile mills, railroads, and banking institutions emerged in the postwar South, economic power passed from the hands of landowners to manufacturers and merchants. Although some scholars see important family continuity between the elite planter class that prevailed in the antebellum South and the industrialists who dominated the New South, most historians detect an unmistakable fragmentation in planter hegemony during the postwar transformation of the southern economy.

See also AGRICULTURE: Plantations; HISTORY AND MANNERS: Colonial Heritage; MYTHIC SOUTH: / Fitzhugh,

George; Plantation Myth; SCIENCE AND MEDICINE: Disease, Endemic; SOCIAL CLASS: Politics and Class

Daniel Blake Smith
University of Kentucky

Eugene D. Genovese, *Roll, Jordan, Roll: The World the Slaves Made* (1976), *The World the Slaveholders Made* (1971); David Jordan, in *The Chesapeake in the Seventeenth Century: Essays on Anglo-American Society and Politics*, ed. Thad W. Tate and David L. Ammerman (1979); Aubrey Land, *Journal of Economic History* (November 1965); Daniel Blake Smith, *Inside the Great House: Planter Family Life in Eighteenth-Century Chesapeake Society* (1980); Charles S. Sydnor, *Gentlemen Freeholders: Political Practices in Washington's Virginia* (1952); C. Vann Woodward, *Origins of the New South, 1877–1913* (1951).

Feminism and Antifeminism

The South is historically the region of the United States most resistant to changes in the role of women. Of the 10 states that failed to ratify the Nineteenth Amendment by 1920, only one was north of the Mason-Dixon line. More recently, southern legislatures were crucial to the defeat of the proposed Equal Rights Amendment (ERA), as 9 of the 15 states that did not ratify it were former Confederate states. Only Texas and Tennessee approved the amendment, and Tennessee later voted to rescind. Since the 1890s, however, southerners have also played an active role in the women's rights movement. The modern feminist movement, which began in the 1960s and continues today, has made its presence felt in the region, but since the mid-1970s has encountered a powerful antifeminist challenge.

Both the more radical "women's liberation" branch of the feminist movement and the more moderate "women's rights" branch have been active in the South. In the late 1960s women's liberation groups sprang up in many urban centers and university communities. By the early 1970s both the National Organization for Women (NOW) and the National Women's Political Caucus (NWPC) had chapters in every southern state, joining older established women's organizations including the League of Women Voters, the Business and Professional Women's League, and the American Association of University Women as advocates of women's rights. Several southern women rose to positions of prominence in feminist organizations: Liz Carpenter helped organize the NWPC and was a cochairperson of ERAmerica from 1976 to 1979; Frances Farenthold chaired the NWPC from 1973 to 1975; and Sarah Weddington successfully argued *Roe* v. *Wade* (1973) (in which the Supreme Court liberalized abortion laws), and, as an aide to President Jimmy Carter, promoted feminist goals. As first lady, Rosalynn Carter was an enthusiastic advocate of the ERA.

Until 1972, in the South as in the rest of the nation, there seemed to be considerable support for feminist goals and little active opposition. Between 1971 and 1973 all southern states created commissions on the status of women. Both Texas (1972) and Virginia (1971) added equal rights amendments to their state constitutions. In the U.S. Senate Sam Ervin of North Carolina fought to modify or defeat the ERA with little support from his fellow southerners. When Congress voted overwhelmingly in 1972 to submit the amendment to the states, only two southern senators (Ervin and Mississippi's John Stennis) and nine southern congressmen voted against it. Both Texas and Tennessee ratified within two weeks.

The decisive victory of the ERA in Congress and its warm reception in the states (14 ratified within a month) awakened latent antifeminist sentiment; opponents of ratification began to mobilize in the South and throughout the nation. In its 1972 platform the American party denounced "this insidious socialistic plan to destroy the home," as did other right-wing groups active in the South, including the National States' Rights party, the Ku Klux Klan, and the John Birch Society. In the mid-1970s "New Right" groups, including the Conservative Caucus and the National Conservative Political Action Committee, became involved in the ERA controversy in the South, and, through the use of sophisticated direct-mailing techniques, mobilized hundreds of thousands of southerners to write letters to their legislators opposing ratification.

Phyllis Schlafly of Illinois, working through the Eagle Forum and the National Committee to Stop ERA (founded 1972), became the most visible leader of the opposition to the amendment. Along with her native Midwest, the South provided Schlafly her greatest following. She became a cult heroine to her supporters, political and religious conservatives who, sharing her conviction that women were most fulfilled through marriage and motherhood, opposed feminist reforms that they perceived as diminishing these roles and weakening the traditional American family. In the South large numbers of ERA opponents were religious fundamentalists who rejected the whole concept of sexual equality as contrary to biblical teachings. The close cooperation between fundamentalist churches and Stop ERA and other opponents of ratification was a distinctive feature of the ERA controversy in the South.

The antiratification forces in the South faced off against state coalitions composed of state and local chapters of organizations that had endorsed ERA at the national level. In contrast to rank and file Stop ERA activists, these organizations were more often composed of professional women and upper middle-class housewives with greater experience in lobbying. However, the very diversity of the pro-ERA forces, together with the fact that most supporters were involved in other causes, meant that the state coalitions were often loosely coordinated and at a disadvantage against their opponents who pursued with religious intensity the single goal of stopping the ERA.

A majority of southerners favored ratification of the ERA (Gallup 1978), important regional newspapers endorsed the amendment, and prominent southern politicians—e.g., James Hunt (N.C.), Reuben Askew (Fla.), James B. Edwards (S.C.), and President Jimmy Carter—actively supported ratification, but no other southern state ratified after 1972. The reactions of southern state legislators varied from Mississippi (a state eventually written off by ERA supporters), where the amendment never emerged from committee, to North Carolina and Florida, where the ERA succeeded in the house only to be narrowly defeated in the senate. There was also considerable support for ratification among state legislators in South Carolina and Virginia. As proponents searched for the last three states (of the 38 necessary for ratification), they felt frustrated by narrow losses and the skillful political maneuvering of their opponents; Liz Carpenter charged that "a handful of wilful and mischievous men" in Florida, North Carolina, and South Carolina were blocking the ERA.

The most important reason, however, that additional states failed to ratify was that opponents were successful both in raising doubts about the potential effects of ratification and in linking the ERA to such controversial issues as abortion and gay rights. In the South opponents appealed effectively to the southern penchant for chivalry and religious conservatism as well as to the regional antipathy toward expansion of federal power. While proponents argued in vain that the ERA would protect women against discrimination in laws affecting domestic relations, employment, government benefits, and education, opponents insisted American women would lose their right to be supported by their husbands, be driven into the work force, and have to turn over their children to state-run child-care facilities. Fundamentalist ministers throughout the South testified that the amendment represented a direct rejection of God's will. Senator Ervin, whose minority report to the Senate was widely distributed by Stop ERA, lent his authority to the charges that ERA would require sexual integration of prisons, dormitories, and restrooms and compel the military to draft women and use them in combat. This last point proved to be particularly damaging, as many southern legislators proved to be as passionate about the maintenance of a strong defense free of female encumbrances as about the protection of womanhood. The proponents' response, that Congress could draft women even without the ERA, was not particularly reassuring.

Some southern legislators saw the ERA, with its Section II providing for federal enforcement, as yet another infringement upon the rights of states, and insisted that state governments could adequately guarantee equality for women. Still chafing over Supreme Court decisions on school prayer and integration, many southerners feared the outcome of the inevitable court battles over interpretation of the ERA. Others were upset by previous congressional action to protect the rights of blacks and women, and, dismayed by what they perceived as a welter of changes forced upon the South from without, saw a vote against ratification of the ERA as an opportunity to register an objection to rapid social change over which they seemed to have no control.

Having been stirred to action by the ERA controversy, antifeminists went on to form the "Pro-Family Movement" to promote and defend their concept of the family and to repeal feminist-inspired laws and court rulings. By 1977, the year of the United States Conference for International Women's Year (IWY), there were two strong social reform movements in the United States with conflicting ideological perspectives on women and the family. Feminists and antifeminists battled at state conferences leading up to the IWY convention over the election of delegates to the national convention and the right to speak for American women. Most successful in the South and in the heavily Mormon Southwest, the profamily forces elected all of the delegates from Mississippi and a few from Alabama, Georgia, Louisiana, and Texas. But these delegates, together with the delegates from southwestern states, accounted for a scant 20 percent of the total attending the Houston convention. At congressional hearings called by their champion, Senator Jesse Helms of North Carolina, profamily spokesmen testified that their point of view had been deliberately stifled. In Houston feminists celebrated the unity of women of all ages, races, and regions in support of a broad platform of feminist demands, including passage of the ERA; a major federal role in developing child-care programs; gay rights; access to abortion, family planning, and sex education; and a host of issues anathema to the profamily movement. Across town, Schlafly led representatives of Stop ERA, the Eagle Forum, Conservative Caucus, National Right to Life, the Mormon Club, the DAR, and the John Birch Society in a counter-convention attended by 11,000 people. She denounced the IWY conference as a symbol of degeneracy financed by five million federal dollars.

Between 1977 and 1982 feminists gained an extension of the deadline for ratification of the ERA but no new states. Meanwhile, opposition to the amendment and to feminism in general was one of the key issues uniting an increasingly powerful political movement. The Pro-Family Movement helped solve the New Right's search for a constituency by drawing many previously nonpolitical conservatives into political activity. By 1980 the Pro-Family Movement had merged with the New Right to form an effective coalition that influenced the Republican party to drop its support for the ERA and adopt an antiabortion plank. They claimed credit for Reagan's decisive victory over Jimmy Carter, whose party platform endorsed federally funded abortions and the withholding of campaign funds from Democratic candidates who failed to support the ERA. Certainly, the resurgence of antifeminism and social conservatism was only one reason for Carter's defeat, but it helps to explain why Reagan carried the traditionally Democratic South, save only Carter's native Georgia.

When the deadline for ratification of the ERA passed in June 1982, the amendment was immediately reintroduced. Feminists vowed to change their tactics from the defensive to the offensive, to stop trying to persuade "negative politicians" and to elect legislators supportive of their goals. Taking lessons from the New Right, NOW formed its own political action committee (NOWPAC) and claimed to have elected 61 percent of their candidates in the 1982 congressional elections. However, feminists still expend much of their energy defending previous accomplishments against antifeminist opponents who celebrate the defeat of the ERA as the beginning of their effort to restructure America in keeping with "Pro-Family" values.

Marjorie Spruill Wheeler
University of Southern Mississippi

Janet K. Boles, *The Politics of the Equal Rights Amendment: Conflict and the Decision Process* (1979); David W. Brady and Kent L. Tedin, *Social Science Quarterly* (March 1976); Ann Fears Crawford and Crystal S. Ragsdale, *Women in Texas: Their Lives, Their Experiences, Their Accomplishments* (1982); Sara Evans, *Personal Politics: The Roots of Women's Liberation in the Civil Rights Movement and the New Left* (1979); Carol Felsenthal, *The Sweetheart of the Silent Majority: The Biography of Phyllis Schlafly* (1981); Marcia Fram, *National Catholic Reporter* (16 July 1982, 30 July 1982); Nancy Gager, ed., *Women's Rights Almanac* (1974); Susan Harding, *Feminist Studies* (Spring 1981); Jane DeHart Mathews and Donald Mathews, *Organization of American Historians Newsletter* (November 1982); Subject files, Schlesinger Library, Radcliffe College, Cambridge, Mass.

Genealogy

In recent years genealogy has been called "roots mania," referring to Alex Haley's engrossing saga of tracing the origins of a black southern family. Haley's *Roots*, published in 1976, and the television miniseries based on it provided a stimulus for genealogical research as a fulfilling hobby, especially in the South. The North Carolina Department of Archives and History, for instance, reported a 76 percent increase in researchers in its archival services branch between 1974 (9,506 researchers) and 1984 (16,780 researchers). Although not all of these researchers were looking for family data, an estimate was that about two-thirds of them were.

The study of family history is frequently a serious pursuit, both as an intellectual activity and as a profession. The annual Institute of Genealogy and Historical Research offered by the Samford University Library at Birmingham, Ala., has conducted well-attended institutes in genealogy for more than 20 years. Professional genealogists frequently are called upon in the courts to prove or disprove the validity of claims of kinship in the settlement of estates, the Howard Hughes estate in Texas being a recent example. Contemporary group life in the South is marked by the presence of numerous genealogical societies, patriotic organizations, lineage and hereditary groups, to say nothing of the many family associations that hold regular reunions. Patriotic societies based on lineage have long been popular in the southern states. In 1983 the 11 states of the Confederacy accounted for more than one-third of the membership of the National Society, Daughters of the American Revolution, boasting 77,276 members out of the total of 209,624. Among the well-known lineage organizations of southern origin are the Order of the First Families of Virginia, the German Society of New Orleans, Huguenot Descendants of the Founders of Manakin Town in the Colony of Virginia, the Descendants of the Jersey Settlers in Adams County, Miss., and the United Daughters of the Confederacy. These prestigious organizations spawned an ongoing interest in the dynastic families of the South, and the goal of much genealogical research in the 19th century was to prove a relationship to the early immigrants who established themselves in this country before the American Revolution.

The paths of early migration led from the eastern seaboard westward through the South. Today southern research institutions are called upon to provide documentary evidence for descendants of these early migrants as well as those who later settled and remained in the South. Vital records such as wills, marriage bonds, and deeds as well as court records, tax lists, and land records in southern courthouses have been searched, researched, and even removed by zealous genealogists. Through the efforts of the various states and aided by the Church of Jesus Christ of Latter Day Saints, many county records have been microfilmed, and the film is available to researchers in the various state archives departments. Indeed, interest in preservation of records is characteristic of the region: the two earliest state archives departments in the nation were established in Alabama and Mississippi, in 1901 and 1902, respectively.

In the Bible Belt an early acquaintance with the "begats" of the Old Testament contributed to a sense of the importance of family lineages. Pioneer churches provided a means for reinforcing family ties. As the frontier moved southward and westward, these religious ties were strengthened. Churches as well as cemeteries recorded the progress of families from the seaboard states as they moved, generation after generation, slowly and steadily toward the West. The custom developed of having annual reunions at rural churches and cemeteries with the annual cemetery cleaning a feature of the occasion. Family groups, those who had moved on and their children and their children's children, returned and still return to these events.

In addition to church homecomings, reunions of individual family groups or clans bring together several generations. Some reunions are structured organizations with officers, publications, and well-planned meetings. Others are less formal get-togethers planned by round-robin correspondence and telephone calls. A small but well-known group of the descendants of Jefferson Davis meet semiannually on the Davis Plantation in Wilkinson County, Miss. In West Feliciana, La., every 50 years the descendants of Alexander and Anne Stirling meet at the home place, Wakefield Plantation. Most such reunions, however, are conducted annually, often at the rural churches where the family worshiped or at family homes.

Genealogies of American Indians have been compiled since the late 19th century when the southern tribes sought to obtain compensation from the United States for lands that had been their ancestral tribal possessions. The Indian Claims Commission was established to review these claims, and, as it was necessary to prove one's descent from a tribal member, the Indian Claims Commission amassed a store of information on Indian families. This information was augmented by files built up by lawyers who represented the claimants. Due in large part to 20th-century tribal renewal movements, researchers are seeking out the files of these lawyers in order to preserve permanently the information they contain.

An interest in black genealogy is assuming noticeable proportions with the encouragement of studies in black history, the observation of Black History Month, and the stimulus of Alex Haley's *Roots*. Black genealogy is practically all southern based, and blacks wishing to probe into pre–Civil War lineages will need to search church records where baptisms of slaves were listed, cemetery records, recorded manumissions in legislative proceedings and court records, wills in which slaves were involved, estate inventories, lists of slave sales, plantation journals, tax rolls, passports issued (usually by governor or secretary of state) for travel across state and territorial lines, and diaries of plantation mistresses. Military records also provide a rich field for black genealogical research, as blacks have participated in military organizations since the Revolution.

Slaves were first listed by name in the Slave Schedules of the 1850 and 1860 federal censuses. After the Civil War the records of the Freedmen's Bureau documented the families of thousands of blacks, and the 1870 federal census listed black families.

What a boon it would be to black genealogists if every community had numbered among its citizens a black man such as William Johnson, a free man of color and a resident of Natchez. His diary meticulously detailing life in Natchez and mentioning names of slaves and their masters was edited by William Ransom Hogan and Edwin Adams Davis and published by the Louisiana State University Press in 1951.

In addition to the vital records found in county courthouses and archives, newspapers are a valuable source for genealogists. Not only do they provide information on births, deaths, estate settlements, real estate transactions, and marriages, but they furnish valuable social commentary to flesh out statistical material pertaining to families. Reflecting as they do the thoughts and opinions of many minds, newspapers are a cultural catalog of the times. Nowhere is the interest in recording family data more apparent than in the southern country newspaper. Here the genealogist may possibly find records of great-grandfather's birth, his marriage, where he spent his vacation, who came to visit him, the property he bought and sold, his children, his death, and numerous other details of his existence. Newspapers are even more important when local and county records have been lost or destroyed.

A number of union lists are helpful in locating newspaper files, such as Clarence Brigham's *History and Bibliography of American Newspapers, 1690–1820*; Gregory's *American Newspapers, 1821–1926*; and the Library of Congress's *Newspapers on Microfilm* (several editions). The formation of a vast data base of newspaper holdings is currently under way. This is the United States Newspaper Project, an undertaking conceived by the Council of Learned Societies, planned by the National Endowment for the Humanities (which is providing matching funds to the states for its implementation), and assisted by the Library of Congress. At the completion of this project, which is being conducted in three phases, all extant newspapers published since September 1690 will be reproduced in microform, identified in the computer network and made available through interlibrary loan services. The southern regional data entries will be made through SOLINET, the Southeastern Library Network affiliated with OCLC, the Online Computer Center in Dublin, Ohio.

A person conducting genealogical research of southern families will find various compilations and indexes indispensable, such as Earl Gregg Swem's *Virginia Historical Index* (1934 and 1936). The colonial records of Georgia, North and South Carolina, and Virginia have been published and are available in most research libraries.

Important genealogical records are offered in micrographic format, such as North Carolina deeds and wills on microfilm and an index to 170,000 North Carolina marriage bonds on microfiche, both produced by the North Carolina Division of Archives and History. The South Carolina Department of Archives and History has indexed and microfilmed the will transcripts of South Carolina, 1782–1868.

The following list contains a guide to research in the South:

Alabama	M. F. Webb, *National Genealogical Society Quarterly* 57 (1969)
Arkansas	Tom W. Dillard and Valerie Thwing, *Researching Arkansas History: A Beginner's Guide* (1980)
Florida	Diane C. Robie, *Searching in Florida: A Reference Guide to Public and Private Records* (1982)
Georgia	Robert Scott Davis, Jr., *Research in Georgia: With a Special Emphasis upon the Georgia Department of Archives and History* (1981)
Kentucky	Beverly West Hathaway, *Inventory of County Records of Kentucky* (n.d.); George K. Schweitzer, *Kentucky Genealogical Research* (1981)
Louisiana	Donald J. Herbert, *Church and Civil Records*, 31 vols. (n.d.)
Mississippi	Mississippi Genealogical Society, *Cemetery and Bible Records*, 19 vols. (n.d.); *Genealogical Research: Methods and Sources*, vol. 2 (1983)
North Carolina	Helen Leary, F. M. and Maurice R. Stirewalt, *North Carolina Research Genealogy and Local History* (1980)
South Carolina	Brent H. Holcomb, *A Brief Guide to South Carolina Genealogical Research and Records* (1979)
Tennessee	George K. Schweitzer, *Tennessee Genealogical Research* (n.d.)
Texas	G. Winfrey, *Stripes* 9 (1969)
Virginia	Donald J. Martin, *Journal of Genealogy* (February 1979)

See also BLACK LIFE: Family, Black; Genealogy, Black; FOLKLIFE: Cemeteries; Family Folklore; HISTORY AND MANNERS: Patriotic Societies; MEDIA: Newspapers, Country; / *Roots*

Madel Morgan
Mississippi Department of History and Archives

Healers, Women

Women in the South have a long tradition of helping family and friends maintain and restore health. Healing traditions were brought to the South with the early settlers, and they evolved as ideas and procedures were incorporated from European medical practice, African traditions, and American Indian traditions. The passing of remedies and techniques for care of the sick through generations of women is found in many cultures. Distinctive southern healing characteristics stem from the types of rural areas in which folk medicine practices have predominated and from the healers' use of indigenous plants and animals. Because modern techniques for controlling infectious diseases were adopted later in the South than in the North and because many rural southern areas have had shortages of medical personnel, folk healing practices have been particularly important throughout the region.

A mainstay of southern healing has been the use of readily available ingredients. Traditionally, many rural women raised herbs and medicinal plants such as comfrey, ginger, and catnip, along with their flowers and vegetables. They also made use of wild plants and trees, such as cottonwood leaves and fever grass. Household staples—eggs, baking soda, sugar, and whiskey—were also important to the care of the infirm. Teas and syrup were the vehicle for many medicines; other agents were directly applied as poultices to sores, sprains, and pains.

Knowledge and advice about health and healing came also from purveyors of patent medicines, who traveled from town to town attracting a following through shows and testimonials of cures. Mail-order almanacs and manuals were also sources of new information.

The role of women in healing and nursing was strongly supported by tradition. In years when infectious diseases like smallpox, typhoid, and malaria caused much illness and death, women spent long hours alleviating the sickness and suffering. Death was a commonplace occurrence, but religious beliefs and the belief in a joyous afterlife helped to ease the pain associated with death. Before the 20th century medicine was not a well-established profession based on scientific principles. Until the reform of medical education around 1910 almost anyone could claim competence and practice medicine. Mistrust of and disdain for doctors were widespread, as were social movements to restore the art of healing to the domestic sphere. Health-reform movements flourished throughout the country in the mid-19th century because of the failure of medical professionals to cure and because women sought a way to improve the quality of life in a confusing world undergoing major transitions. They were especially prevalent in the South because faith in self-treatment and the home healing arts was in harmony with tradition.

Many health-reform sects such as the Thomsonians, the homeopaths, and the hydropaths prescribed specific remedies and formulas. These prescriptions were added to the already rich base of healing knowledge in the South. Magical cures, formulas for healthful living, medicinal cures derived from local plants and animals, and professional health care coexisted with minimal conflict. Of the many remedies known in the South, some work well and some have proven to be useless or dangerous. Behind them are generations of women who grew and gathered plants, raised animals, treated injuries, prepared barks, herbs, and plants for treatments, applied poultices, and administered medicines. Many of these beliefs and practices, which point out the self-sufficiency and independence of southern women and their families, are preserved in the *Foxfire* books.

Midwifery was another special preserve of women. With the exception of such areas as Appalachia and the Ozarks, southern midwifery was an occupation dominated largely by black women who passed their skills and knowledge down to their mature daughters or nieces. Although the practices of midwives were allegedly a cause of childbed mortality rates higher than those of the North, more recent investigations suggest that other factors, especially nutrition, were responsible.

In the 1920s programs to train midwives in obstetrics were supported in southern states by welfare. Midwives met in the county health departments, and under the supervision of public health nurses learned how to keep germs away during births, fill out birth certificates, and care for the equipment they used. By the 1970s nearly all traditional midwives were retired from practice, although nurse-midwifery training programs continue today.

Nurse-midwifery has increased greatly in importance since Mary Breckinridge began the Frontier Nursing Service in the 1920s. By the 1960s teams of medically supervised nurse-midwives from the University of Mississippi worked in locations throughout the South where infant deaths were disproportionately high. These nurse-midwives have demonstrated that they reduce infant deaths and provide high-quality care that women appreciate.

In recent years the number and availability of physicians and other health professionals have increased, but there is also a greater acceptance of women as healers in roles outside the family. Many southern women became nurses and other health professionals in the 1970s while enrollments of women in medical schools dramatically increased. These changes reflect an increasing involvement of women in healing roles beyond the home and an accompanying belief that women can share economic responsibility without neglecting their traditional roles in healing and caring for their own sick.

See also EDUCATION: / *Foxfire*; ENVIRONMENT: Plant Uses; FOLKLIFE: Folk Medicine; SCIENCE AND MEDICINE:

Health, Public; Health, Rural; Self-dosage; / Breckinridge, Mary; Disease, Endemic; Disease, Epidemic

Molly C. Dougherty
University of Florida

Mary Breckinridge, *Wide Neighborhoods: A Story of the Frontier Nursing Service* (1952); Marie Campbell, *Folks Do Get Born* (1946); Alex Freeman, *Kentucky Folklore Record* (October 1974); Paul F. Gillespie, ed., *Foxfire 7* (1982); Guenter Risse et al., eds., *Medicine Without Doctors: Home Health Care in American History* (1977); Sharon A. Sharp, *Women's Studies International Forum* (October 1986); Karen Shelley and Raymond Evans, in *Appalachia/America: Proceedings of the 1980 Appalachian Studies Conference*, ed. Wilson Somerville (1981); Jack Solomon and Olivia Solomon, compilers, *Cracklin' Bread and Asfidity: Folk Recipes and Remedies* (1979); Wilbur Watson, ed., *Black Folk Medicine: The Therapeutic Significance of Faith and Trust* (1984).

Household

Mint juleps on the veranda, a kettle full of collard greens with corn bread in the oven—whatever the caste or class, from top to bottom of the social ladder, the South is known for its warm and open hospitality. Perhaps this open-door policy developed during the colonial era because taverns for guests were few and far between. Travelers often spent the night in the home of a stranger, as plantations and farmhouses were the only source of shelter in the sparsely settled southern region. By the antebellum era southerners were so well known for their hospitality that this generosity had become proverbial. One southerner described a Sea Island planter so fond of his dinner guests that he insisted they move into his home, whereupon the couple stayed through the births of two children. Although most instances of hospitality in the Old South were not so extreme (indeed this tale tells as much about the art of southern storytelling as it does about hospitality), custom and circumstances combined to make many southern households almost perpetual guesthouses throughout most of the 19th century.

Southern homemakers frequently complained that the virtual parade of family, friends, and strangers would "turn the house into a tavern." Many women, isolated on estates far from town, with infrequent chance for escape, welcomed the company. Most often, though, the wives of wealthier planters, those residing on elaborate estates with lavish reputations, found the tasks associated with hospitality burdensome. Indeed, these plantation mistresses often coped with a crowd of a dozen at breakfast and a score or more for Sunday dinners.

Family members, of course, were universally welcomed into southern homes. For a variety of reasons, kinship ties in the South were strong and extended. During the antebellum era, marriages between cousins occurred with some frequency among whites. Second and even third cousins were frequently childhood playmates and later friends for life, among blacks as well as whites. It was a point of great pride to most southerners that family would never be turned away. As a result "poor relations" became familiar fixtures in the homes of the more prosperous of the clan. The household was a body of persons loosely interconnected by blood and marriage. The head of the household was obviously the all-powerful patriarch, but his wife had great influence on family affairs.

Southern homes of the middle and upper classes always maintained servants. Domestic service in the postbellum period was almost entirely a black occupation. Those of limited means might not have a live-in staff, but it was a mark of financial ease to hire a cook-housekeeper to come into the home daily. During the holidays or at times when guests were expected for longer visits, southern homemakers would often draw on the family of their hired help, binding white households and black families into generational patterns of master-servant relations, which were often hangovers from the slavery era as well. Black mothers often had aspirations that their children should escape the domestic thrall of "workin' for Massa," through education or by migration north. But the majority of southern blacks spent much of their lives "workin' for the man" (a catch-all phrase for whites), and black women encouraged offspring to take advantage of the paternalism built into the southern system of household help.

This paternalism had many drawbacks, some identical to the problems encountered during slavery. Servants were underpaid and subject to long hours and numerous deprivations. If a woman lived in the house of her employer, she was often given basement or attic quarters—the smallest or most unhealthy in the residence. Even if a woman wanted to return home to her family at night, many white employers insisted that their servants live in. Many black cooks bemoaned the fact that they were rarely able to cook for their own families and were sometimes limited to alternate Sundays off. If a cook or a maid did return home, she was privy to "the servant's pan"—leftovers from the white family's table. White homemakers varied in disposition, but most kept close watch over this donation—allegedly to prevent being taken advantage of, although it was obviously the black family who suffered extortion. As late as 1935 the weekly wage for women household servants in the South was $3 a week. Without the servant's pan, many black children would have starved on the combined wages of their parents, who remain underpaid in domestic service occupations even today.

Black women servants complained bitterly of false accusations of stealing—being searched by employers and suffering other humiliations even after years of loyal service—and of being subject to sexual harassment by the husbands in white households. It was not always simple to put a stop to these advances by male employers, for complaint to the white mistress could result in dismissal. And the black woman who called attention to a white man's sexual aggression was branded herself as the cause of the misconduct.

Despite her exploitation and marginal rewards, the black woman was able, in many cases, to wield enormous influence within the white household. In those

Domestic servant tending a child, Atlanta, Ga., 1939

homes where white women were unwilling or unable to manage, magisterial black women often dominated the household. In those homes where men were widowed and children motherless, black women often filled surrogate maternal roles: Carson McCullers's *Member of the Wedding* vividly reflects this touching relationship. Scores of southern novelists have sentimentally explored this subject in their work.

Only recently have authors such as Ann Petry in *The Country Place* and William Melville Kelley in *dem* delved into the subject with a less nostalgic view. These two works are set in the North, where most black novelists live and work in modern America; however, even novelists remaining in the South, such as Louisianian Walker Percy, have begun to alter this early saccharine portrayal. Elgin Buell (*Lancelot*) provides sharp and bitter insight. The master's right-hand man may be daily subject to his employer's demands, but he is acknowledged by the ill-fated Lancelot as perhaps the most intelligent and trustworthy member of the household: the two men act out their roles of master and servant, but the black is playing on white guilt and generosity to insure his escape from the South.

Some may wonder whether in the modern South the traditional virtues of paternalism, hospitality, and a conspicuously languid style can endure. In some cases, the visitor from the North may wonder if this effusive affability is merely for show or genuine. Southern custom has always maintained that what meets the eye is more important than what does not. Thus, a dazzling display of gracious generosity may remain a vital symbol of southern heritage.

See also AGRICULTURE: Plantations; HISTORY AND MANNERS: Sexuality

Catherine Clinton
Harvard University

Jane Carson, *Plantation Housekeeping in Colonial Virginia* (1975); Catherine Clinton, *The Plantation Mistress: Woman's World in the Old South* (1982); Angela Davis, *Women, Race and Class* (1981); Florence King, *Southern Ladies and Gentlemen* (1976); Anne Firor Scott, *The Southern Lady: From Pedestal to Politics, 1830–1930* (1970).

Indian Women

When Europeans first came into contact with Indians in what is today the southeastern United States, native women enjoyed considerable autonomy and personal freedom. Although it would be misleading to apply the term "equality" to the relationship between the sexes in these societies, women certainly were not subservient to men (nor men to women). Men and women merely had different responsibilities, which were equally important to community welfare.

The division of labor in these societies was fundamentally gender based: men hunted and women farmed. Restrictions on pregnant and menstruating women further separated male and female spheres. Yet because southeastern Indians depended on agriculture for subsistence, women had a major economic role. Their contribution was reflected in rituals such as the Green Corn Ceremony, in which women presented the new crop. Domestic chores performed by women included preparing food, gathering wood, carrying water, constructing utensils and furnishings for their houses, and caring for children. These responsibilities stemmed from the matrilineal kinship system and the matrilocal residence pattern, both of which were widespread in the Southeast: men lived in the houses of their wives and mothers, and children were considered to be related to mothers and not fathers. Women regulated their own behavior in most tribes, but their role in political decision making varied among southern tribes. Most influential were Cherokee women, who could speak in council and to whom a specified political position, that of War Women, was ascribed. More commonly, foreign affairs were left to men, whereas matrilineal clans resolved internal controversies.

European contact dramatically altered the status of southern Indian women. In the 18th century the deerskin trade, essential to many southern colonial economies, gave male hunters a disproportionate share of economic power. In the 19th century the U.S. government's "civilization" program and the efforts of missionary societies began to revolutionize Indian sexual roles. Men took up the plow and became dominant economically, politically, and domestically, while women became subservient. Some remnants of traditional female autonomy remained, however. The southern Indians who organized formal governments, for example, attempted to protect property rights of married women and ultimately pointed the way for similar laws adopted by southern states. In 1892 the *Albany Law Journal*, citing the Choctaws in particular, pointed out that the model for such progressive state legislation came from southern Indians.

See also ETHNIC LIFE articles on Indian tribes

Theda Perdue
Clemson University

E. Merton Coulter, *Georgia Historical Quarterly* (March 1927); Rayna Green, *Signs* (Winter 1980); Charles Hudson, *The Southeastern Indians* (1976); Ben Harris McClary, *Tennessee Historical Quarterly* (March 1962); Theda Perdue, *Furman Studies* (December 1980).

Land, Women on the (I)

Like Margaret Mitchell's famed fictional heroine, Scarlett O'Hara, southern women have always had a special attachment to the land. Women of all classes and color, not merely ladies of the planter class, have by preference or necessity been part of the agricultural heritage of the Old South. The romanticization of this association is the mythical facade of southern culture, but the bonds between women and the land formed a foundation for the development of a plantation economy.

Men brought women to the New World as the tamers of the wilderness, a frontier that promised as much danger as it did reward for those who pioneered the interior. Women were needed as settlers of these initial colonies, which many men were content simply to explore. The Earl of Southampton, concerned with the failing Virginia Company, argued "that the plantation can never flourish till families be planted and the respect of wives and children fix the people on the soil." The earliest settlers of the South had great trials with which to contend. Not only did they face an increasingly hostile native population, but the climate of the region was arduous and unhealthy, especially for women who repeatedly hazarded pregnancy. The codification and refinement of chattel slavery further hampered the colonial population, by demoting blacks to a deteriorating status within society and forcing whites to stand guard against those within as well as outside the community.

Although white women might not have been the initiators of southwestward expansion of settlement and the development of a planter aristocracy, they fully participated in the building of the Old South. Judith Giton Manigault, a Huguenot refugee, for example, fled her native France, settling with her husband in Charleston in 1685. Her early years in Carolina were brutal: "I have been six months without tasting bread, working like a ground slave; and I have even passed three and four years without having food when I wanted it." She perhaps savored her family's successes even more due to the harshness of her early struggles.

Life on the seaboard was relatively easy compared with the daily challenges of the frontier. As a young bride, Sally Buchanan, the wife of a pioneer settler of Davidson County, Tenn., lived at a fort near the Cumberland River. She and the other women of the settlement had to be guarded when they went outside the walls of the stockade to tend to the livestock, to do the wash, and to cultivate gardens. Families were crowded into close, uncomfortable quarters for safety. Women had little time to contemplate domesticity when trying to care for their families in these cramped and congested conditions. When the fort was attacked on 30 September 1792 Buchanan was nine months pregnant with her first child. While men fought off the attack from the four guardhouses and women and children cowered under beds, Buchanan kept her husband and his 16 comrades supplied with whiskey and bullets throughout the nightlong battle. Her heroism is celebrated in Cumberland folklore, but her role reflected the demands the southern frontier could and did place upon women.

No matter what the size of the property or the location of the land, white women's contributions to their husband's estates were enormous. Whether her husband's farm was large or small, was planted by slaves, hired hands, or family, or was confined to one plantation or to several, the southern matron was a figure of formidable industry and talent, fulfilling designated and vital responsibilities. Women were not only in charge of the food, shelter, and clothing of all those on the estate; they were also saddled with teaching and doctoring in the absence of professionals. While supplying their families with innumerable services as wives and mothers, black and white women on the plantation were presented with additional burdens associated with slavery. While females of the master and slave classes fulfilled traditional roles as nurturers, they were additionally assigned numerous chores to keep the plantation running.

The white mistress was beset by a veritable barrage of extra duties, not merely supervisory tasks, but work essential to production. Southern matrons grew herbs, blended medicines, planted gardens, spun cloth, knitted socks, sewed clothes, slaughtered pigs, processed and cured meat, plucked chickens, scoured copper utensils, preserved vegetables, churned butter, dipped candles, wove rugs, and performed numerous other harsh and unromantic chores. In addition to this relentless routine, women were often charged with the management of the entire plantation during a husband's absence. Order, efficiency, ability to negotiate, and dispatch in business dealings were expected of the model southern housewife.

Black women were afforded no such power on the plantation; yet their work roles were even more demanding. Slave women were dynamic figures within the black family, working side by side with men in the fields while providing care and affection for their families as well. Black mothers supplied models of strength and endurance for their offspring. Because many men were promoted as artisans on the plantation, field workers were often women. Although the system monopolized and exploited black women's labor, many were able to leave behind testimony to their talents and abilities. Baskets woven in accordance with tribal tradition and gourds decorated with patterns handed down from generation to generation demonstrate survival of African influences. Quilts such as Harriet Powers's masterpiece hanging in the Boston Museum of Fine Arts reflect biblical stories, and other needlework shows how black women were able to weave together the various strands of their lives, despite the obstacles.

The Civil War marked the beginning of a new era for women on the land. The passing of the Old South and the attempt to create a new order marked a traumatic and challenging time for southern women. Both black and white women were tied to the land, although in very different terms following Appomattox. The defeat of the Confederacy brought about the abolition of slavery, but the patterns of exploitation of black women's labor continued. And the crop-lien system incorporated white families into systems of labor expropriation that had previously been restricted by race rather than by class. Many members of the prewar planter class were severely reduced in status. Landownership became a burden to many formerly wealthy whites who faltered in the face of steep taxes and the falling price of cotton. Smaller farmers were especially hard pressed, and rural families were constantly on the move to find better land. Blacks who tried to escape the land, to settle in towns and cities, were often driven back into rural areas by economic necessity. The attempts of freedpeople to achieve autonomy in the postwar South were rejected by the majority of whites, who were dead set against black landowning. Women, struggling to rebuild their war-torn communities, hoping to put the war behind them, and longing to build a new life for their families, were caught in the crossfire.

Women of the Old South were born into a folk culture so rich that modernism held little allure. Although many southern women, especially former slaves, were quick to abandon the shackles of the past, the majority continued their deep and abiding love of the land. The women of the rural South preserve their heritage today, cherishing what enriches and endures. Land provides southern women a vehicle for self-discovery, as author Alice Walker suggests in her essay "In Search of Our Mother's Gardens."

See also AGRICULTURE: Plantations; BLACK LIFE: Family, Black; Landowning, Black; Slave Culture; FOLKLIFE: / Needlework; HISTORY AND MANNERS: Frontier Heritage

Catherine Clinton
Harvard University

Catherine Clinton, *The Plantation Mistress: Woman's World in the Old South* (1982); Jean Friedman, *The Enclosed Garden: Women and Community in the Evangelical South, 1830–1900* (1985); Jacqueline Jones, *Labor of Love, Labor of Sorrow: Black Women, Work, and the Family from Slavery to the Present* (1985); Anne Firor Scott, *The Southern Lady: From Pedestal to Politics, 1830–1930* (1970); Julia Cherry Spruill, *Women's Life and Work in the Southern Colonies* (1938).

Land, Women on the (II)

The Civil War ended one struggle over life and labor in the South and set off another over the nature of the new social order. Women played a vital role in that struggle. After emancipation, for example, black women helped resist gang labor by withdrawing from the fields and devoting their time to caring for their homes and children. But they had to chop and pick cotton again as members of sharecropper families or earn meager wages as farm and domestic workers. Black women's work, though altered, remained necessary to family survival.

Freedmen and the South's yeoman farmers alike were ensnared by the crop-lien system. Furnishing merchants insisted that farmers plant cash crops like cotton and tobacco, and yeoman self-sufficiency was gradually undermined. Tenancy increased, and owners of small farms retained a tenuous hold on the land. Women proved especially vulnerable in the cash-crop economy. Landlords favored families that could muster a large male work force. Tenant widows led insecure lives unless they had sons who could plant, cultivate, and harvest the crops. Daughters were among the most expendable of farm workers. Thus, in the South's Piedmont during the 1870s, women made up the first wave of migrants from farms to the region's fledgling factories.

Farm women, however, were not simply victims of regional social and economic change. In the late 19th century rural southern women were linchpins in the agrarian revolt that exploded in the countryside. Plummeting crop prices, merchant abuse, railroad rate differentials, and government indifference to farm people's plight set the stage for radical reform efforts. Female members of the Southern Farmers' Alliance encouraged the brethren, rallied other women to the cause, and relished the unprecedented opportunity to discuss important economic, social, and political issues. Women were needed on the front lines at the Alliance hall and at home. Within the context of the reform movement, women's domestic tasks were endowed with political significance, for they lessened their families' dependence on merchants. "It won't do," one Texas Alliance sister observed, "for poor farmers to live at home and board at the store." When the Populist party offered farmers a political solution to their economic problems, women continued to support the revolt. Deprived of the vote, rural southern women nonetheless acted on Mary Elizabeth Lease's pithy admonition to "raise less corn and more hell." They used their pens and voices to back the Populists in the reform press and from lecture platforms.

As the 20th century dawned, southern farmers faced both advances and setbacks. Landowners enjoyed prosperity while tenants saw things go from bad to worse. Cotton prices rebounded; credit became more accessible for some farmers; farm bankruptcies declined. The very conditions that favored landowners, however, worked to tenants' disadvantage, for higher land values undercut their chances to climb the agricultural ladder, and the crop-lien system continued to limit their options.

Most southern women remained rooted to the land, but the contours of their lives differed greatly according to their economic circumstances. Wives of prosperous white landowners, like antebellum plantation mistresses, managed their households and often hired black women to relieve them of such backbreaking tasks as the weekly wash. Fieldwork, moreover, was outside their realm of duties.

Middling and tenant farm women of both races mastered and juggled myriad tasks that required physical endurance and skill. They bore and reared the largest families in the nation: 6 children were typical, but 12 or 13 were not uncommon. Repeated pregnancies and the demands of a large farm family often made these farm women old before their time, yet their children were a source of joy and pride. Well into the 20th century poor southern farm women enjoyed few of the household conveniences that were lightening the labors (if not necessarily shortening the workweek) of urban women. With the help of their children, they toted pails of water from a well to the house and cut firewood to heat cookstoves. They supplied the family larder by gardening, preserving fruits and vegetables, raising chickens and gathering eggs, and milking cows and churning butter. Sometimes farm women augmented family finances by bartering or selling surplus produce.

The demands of cash-crop agriculture, furthermore, meant that the wives and daughters of tenants and small-farm owners often had to divide their time between the kitchen and the fields. Although field work was an additional burden, many women preferred the camaraderie of the tobacco barn to the isolation of the house, or the sense of accomplishment at the end of a chopped cotton row to the endless rounds of housework. Many, in fact, took pride in their field prowess and enjoyed the relative fluidity of men's and women's work roles. As one Piedmont North Carolina farm woman testified: "We done men's work. We done women's work. You name it and we done it."

The early 20th century spawned another attempt at agricultural reform in the South. This time the impetus came from agrarian progressives at state and federal departments of agriculture and land-grant colleges. While farm demonstration agents promoted crop rotation, diversification, and soil fertilization, home demonstration agents promoted domestic science and efficient housekeeping. Home economics extension agents, often rural schoolteachers, organized clubs to teach new ways of cooking, sewing, canning, and home decorating and encouraged women to market their produce and handiwork. In addition, professional rural social workers tried to ameliorate the condition of poor farm women who suffered from inadequate health care and the nutritional deficiencies inherent in a meat, meal, and molasses diet.

Two children with a cantaloupe, Mississippi Delta, 1936

Such efforts at reform from the top down, however, could not solve the agricultural problems of the South, where the depression of the 1920s and 1930s took its severest toll. Powerful images of southern tenant farm women entered the national imagination through Depression-era documentary photography. Again, as in the Populist years, farm women joined forces against displacement—through organizations like the Southern Tenant Farmers' Union and the Alabama Sharecroppers Union—and took advantage of the opportunities offered by the Farm Security Administration to gain or hold on to their land.

But New Deal farm policies that encouraged landowners to cut crop production and to mechanize pushed even more farmers off the land and into the cities or the migrant stream. After 1940 the South's farm population declined precipitously. Thousands of southern women, especially blacks and Appalachian mountaineers, joined the post–World War II migration to the North. Severing ties to the land was a heartwrenching experience for many.

Yet the southern population remained one of the most rural in the country. For many women who remained on the land, the next four decades brought enormous changes: electricity, better transportation, and improved communications eroded differences between rural and urban women and their homes. For other rural women, however, the early 20th century seemed little different from the 19th. On the whole, rural women's participation in subsistence farming has declined during the last several decades. Rural women have adapted their traditional roles to the needs of modern agriculture and thereby have reshaped their ties to the land.

See also AGRICULTURE: Garden Patch; Plantations; Sharecropping and Tenancy; / Agricultural Extension Services; Farm Security Administration; BLACK LIFE: Migration, Black; HISTORY AND MANNERS: Great Depression; New Deal; Populism; INDUSTRY: Industrialization and Change; SOCIAL CLASS: Tenant Farmers; / Farmers' Alliance; Sharecroppers Union; Southern Tenant Farmers' Union

Lu Ann Jones
University of North Carolina
at Chapel Hill

Margaret J. Hagood, *Mothers of the South: Portraiture of the White Tenant Farm Woman* (1939); Dolores Elizabeth Janiewski, "From Field to Factory: Race, Class, Sex, and the Woman Worker in Durham, 1880–1940" (Ph.D. dissertation, Duke University, 1979); Julie Roy Jeffrey, *Feminist Studies* (Fall 1975); Joan M.

Jensen, *With These Hands: Women Working on the Land* (1981); Kathy Kahn, *Hillbilly Women* (1972); Marc S. Miller, ed., *Working Lives: The Southern Exposure History of Labor in the South* (1981).

Maiden Aunt

She is a favorite character of fiction and stereotype, but a person who in fact touched the lives of most southerners—the maiden aunt. The demand for marriageable women exceeded the supply during the colonial era, but by the time of the American Revolution the spinster (single women at home were often drafted to the female task of spinning, the origin of the term) was a folkloric figure in southern states. The never-wed woman in southern culture was not only dependent upon men, like her married counterpart, but she was denied the status accorded to matrons and mothers. She was forced to live out her life on the fringes of society, a perpetually lone figure in a culture of tightly knit couples and children. Within the home (usually that of a brother or sister), however, she was often a cherished and fond member of the family circle. Indeed, the maiden aunt became both influential and indispensable.

It was assumed, because of social pressures to marry, that most unmarried women had been rejected, passed over, or never given any opportunity to snare a husband. This promoted several unattractive images of old maids. One antebellum girl described them as "forlorn damsels who made the midnight air echo with their plaintive bewailings, for only bats and owls return their melancholy strains." In southern society the "old" maid ranged anywhere from age 18 to 80. A girl might feel spinsterish if younger sisters married before she did, if she was not married by age 21, or simply if all her friends had "deserted" her for husbands.

Southern women, as a rule, married very young—younger than their northern counterparts and much younger than men. Shortly after puberty, black women often selected a mate, whom they married by folk custom though not by law. Historians of the slave community have found teenaged brides common on the plantation. Studies of planters have confirmed that white women also commonly wed as schoolgirls. In the Old South the average age of marriage for white women was 20, and that of black women was slightly lower. Thus, women who remained unmarried in the South were classified as spinsters at a much earlier age than elsewhere.

The Civil War, of course, greatly reduced the supply of young men to marry. Many southern daughters during the second half of the century were thus demographically deprived of husbands. Strikingly, the Reconstruction era was the first period since early colonial days when interracial sexual relations and even marriage were accepted to any notable extent. However, a large number of the single white women—and especially those of the upper and middle classes—remained unattached, many becoming leaders in shaping new educational and employment opportunities for women. Gradually, career opportunities for females expanded, and the stigma associated with women who lived alone lessened.

Nevertheless, throughout most of the 19th century and well into the 20th, southern society attempted to shelter and confine single women. Those who failed to marry were more often forced by custom or circumstance to spend their time and energy with "other women's families." Spinsters clearly served surrogate roles with the family—single daughters or maiden aunts might be welcome as an extra pair of hands or as substitute mothers—but they were also social outcasts, denied the status a woman could achieve only through her role as matriarch. Few parents, even those of enormous wealth, would bequeath money to an unmarried daughter.

Only in modern times have single women in the South received any of the family resources. Traditionally, a woman was expected to inherit through her dowry. If she did not marry she could only rely on the charity of parents or siblings. Brothers and sisters eagerly provided these spinsters with homes in exchange for valuable domestic services. Maiden aunts were teachers and nurses, confidants and disciplinarians. Indeed, their whole lives were bound up with the strenuous chores of child rearing, but, like servants, they tended children who were not their own.

"Aunt adoption" was a particularly southern phenomenon. Women often singled out a niece for special affection and in many cases quite lavish consideration. This cultivation of a favorite by aunts was traditional and certainly not limited to unmarried or childless females. It was not uncommon for a southern mother to "donate" one of her several daughters to the family of a beloved brother or sister who had no children, or even merely no *female* offspring. This would reduce the burden of the natural parents (costs for living expenses and dower) while maintaining family ties and offering emotional, and sometimes financial, benefits for the adopted child.

Upon occasion a pregnant mother would secure a promise from a favorite sister that if she did not survive the ordeal of childbirth, the surviving sister would look after the orphaned children; in some cases women wanted their husbands to marry these spinsters. With death in childbirth uncommonly high in the South until the 20th century (nearly double that of the North), unmarried women sometimes literally inherited an entire family through marriage to the spouse of a dead sibling. These cases were extreme, yet they reflect the pivotal importance to southern women of the maiden aunt, despite her never-married, childless status.

The stereotypes of these women were most often unflattering exaggerations. Many fictional portraits of maiden aunts painted them as dizzy and foolish, the proverbial "Aunt Pittypat" character of *Gone with the Wind*. A more sympathetic portrayal has been developed by several southern authors who have characterized sturdy, proud females channeling their energies and talents into their nephews and nieces and leading challenging and fulfilling lives: variants on the theme established in one of Faulkner's early novels, *Sartoris*, with the spirited and understanding Miss Jenny. Many of these characters, especially those created by women novelists such as Ellen Glasgow, possess a feminist component: they chose not to enter the ranks of women trapped and trampled by husbands.

Another significant variant for the never-married woman was the portrait of a lady of questionable character. There were women in southern society and southern fiction who chose to lead lives unhampered by spouses but who refused to deny themselves sexual companionship. For some, their reckless behavior at a younger age had supposedly robbed them of their reputation for virtue, leading to a devaluation on the marriage market. Others purportedly were predisposed to this character defect—loose and immoral without hope of redemption. In either case, perpetual singlehood was their fate. This semitragic figure was most poignantly revealed in Tennessee Williams's Blanche DuBois, the fading belle of *A Streetcar Named Desire*.

The plays, films, and novels of the South depict lone women in their variety and complexity, but these myriad roles cannot match the mark these women have made in the great drama of real life. Their impact has been enormous and their contributions monumentally enriching to southern culture.

See also BLACK LIFE: Miscegenation; Slave Culture; FOLKLIFE: Childbirth; Family Folklore; HISTORY AND MANNERS: Civil War; Reconstruction; Sexuality; LAW: Family Law; RELIGION: Missionary Activities

Catherine Clinton
Harvard University

Josephine Carson, *Silent Voices: The Southern Negro Woman Today* (1969); Catherine Clinton, *The Plantation Mistress: Woman's World in the Old South* (1982); Maria Fletcher, "The Southern Heroine in the Fiction of Representative Southern Women Writers" (Ph.D. dissertation, Louisiana State University, 1963); Anne Goodwyn Jones, *Tomorrow Is Another Day: The Woman Writer in the South, 1859–1936* (1981); John C. Ruoff, "Southern Womanhood, 1865–1920: An Intellectual and Cultural Study" (Ph.D. dissertation, University of Illinois, 1976); Lillian Smith, *Killers of the Dream* (1949); Julia Cherry Spruill, *Women's Life and Work in the Southern Colonies* (1938); Alice Walker, *In Love and Trouble: Stories of Black Women* (1973).

Marriage and Courtship

Southern courtship and marriage were most distinctive in the colonial period; the past three centuries have all but erased peculiarly southern patterns. Because 17th-century migration to the southern colonies, unlike that to the North, was predominantly male, women were a particularly valuable commodity. Indeed, an early governor of Virginia would explain that from "the want of wives have sprung up the greatest of hindrances of the encrease of the plantation." In the early decades of settlement, the sexual imbalance and the absence of kin gave white women a great deal of freedom in the choice of a marriage partner. Married typically in her mid-twenties to a somewhat older man and widowed within a decade, an immigrant woman became even more desirable when in the possession of her deceased husband's property. Second-generation women, still outnumbered by men, married earlier than their mothers, probably in their mid- to late-teens; like their mothers, many were pregnant on their wedding day.

Only in the early decades of the 18th century did the population stabilize; then, the demographic pattern that persisted into the 19th century was established: white women in their early twenties (expected to be virgins) married men several years older. Although they almost never chose their children's mates, pre-revolutionary era parents retained a very effective veto in the form of the marriage settlement they were expected to provide (and might withhold). Once a young man and young woman had selected each other, their fathers would enter into negotiations to determine each child's marriage portion. For affluent families, as in the North, such arrangements were crucial to their power and prestige. Young people were trained by their parents in how to make a prudent choice; as one traveler noted, courtship was "the principal business in Virginia."

If, in the years before the American Revolution, material considerations outweighed emotional ones in the selection of a mate, later the balance would be tipped in the other direction. As southerners, like their northern counterparts, came increasingly to expect that their earthly happiness would come from love, and as changes in the economy and custom diminished the importance of the parental settlement, young people became freer to follow the promptings of their own hearts. To be sure, most chose mates from a similar background and of comparable economic standing, but the most important factor was that elusive quality known as "character." Men wanted wives who would be cheerful and affectionate, and women hoped for husbands who would prove kind and even tempered. As a result, southerners tended to find their mates among friends, neighbors, and even cousins, not because of any particular social ideology or strategy, but because in a region that was sparsely settled those who were already known were those who could best be trusted.

In the antebellum period, men and women met and courted at parties, barbecues, church meetings, and other social gatherings. A young man might pay court to a young woman by visiting her at home, or, if separated by great distance, by writing her love letters, to which she would carefully respond. Alexis de Tocqueville noted that American women were especially free before marriage and were more constrained after. The selection of a husband was the most important choice a woman would ever make; consequently, some women played the belle, flirting outrageously and rejecting suitors capriciously (or so it seemed to the men), as if to prolong their final moments of freedom and to assert their greatest power over the opposite sex. Though most couples anticipated intimacy and affection, some women seem to have retreated in the face of so momentous a choice. Once a couple had engaged themselves, they would, out of love and respect, seek the approval of the young woman's father. The marriage ceremony usually took place in the bride's parents' home, in the presence of family and close friends.

Marriage for whites was an institution sanctioned by law, religion, and custom. Slave marriages, however, were protected by custom only. Nonetheless, by the 19th century, most slaves entered into enduring unions, marriages in the eyes of the slave community, if not the law and the church. As with whites, demographic patterns shaped the nature of marriage in the colonial period. Because planters at first preferred to import male Africans, creating sex ratios as high as two to one, and because most slaves were scattered in small groups on small plantations, opportunities to create stable and lasting unions were severely limited. As a result of the similar imbalance in white sex ratios in the 17th century, some African and Afro-American women may have served as white men's concubines or common-law wives. Others became the partners of older slave men, who often lived on other plantations. By the middle of the 18th century importation of slaves began to decline, and the slave population increased naturally. By that time most slave women were marrying in their late teens, slave men perhaps several years older. Larger plantations afforded some couples opportunity to marry and move into their own cabins on the home plantation. Many, however, had to find mates "abroad" on other farms; in that case, a woman and her children would live in their own cabin on her home plantation, and her husband would be allowed to visit on weekends or perhaps some nights.

The postrevolutionary expansion of the South and the establishment of large cotton and sugar plantations created a different pattern of slave marriage. Increasing numbers of slaves could hope to find mates on their own plantations. Moreover, the federal prohibition of slave imports after 1808 gave masters added incentive to encourage slave fertility. By her early twenties, the typical slave woman had entered into a union that would endure, usually, until death or the master severed it. That slaves themselves regarded such unions as binding is given ample testimony by the great number of couples who took advantage of emancipation to register their marriages, thus obtaining civil sanction for their unions and official legitimacy for their children.

Slave marriages were always contingent upon the approval of the master. Sometimes he performed the ceremony, reading an edited version of the standard Christian marriage service. At other times, the slaves might follow their own customs, such as jumping over the broomstick, with a respected slave officiating. Some masters allowed their slaves great latitude or even feted favored slaves; others cruelly mocked the slaves' behaviors. Often masters complied with their slaves' wishes, recognizing that a contented labor force was in their own best interest. Others, however, intent upon encouraging slave reproduction, would select or purchase particular slave men as husbands for particular slave women. At other times, a slave whose mate had been sold away would likewise be forced to acquire a new mate. There are even scattered but largely unsubstantiated references to slave breeding, using selected slave men as "studs."

Scholars have not yet examined post–Civil War southern courtship and marriage with as much care as they have devoted to the antebellum period. Patterns for the majority of whites do not appear to have been different from those in the North, for in the decades preceding the Civil War the main differences were those related to a lower social density: a greater tendency toward marriage between cousins, friendly involvement of family and friends in courtship, and perhaps less privacy for courting couples. Time has probably erased such differences. For blacks, emancipation eliminated the restrictions of slavery, allowing them to participate in civil and religious marriage ceremonies as a prelude to enduring unions.

Regionally as well as nationally, patterns of dating have changed since the World War II era. Courting visits by the young man in the woman's home, formally or informally chaperoned by parents or other family members, and outings approved by the girl's family were once common. Cars provided a new degree of autonomy and privacy and helped reshape courtship practices. Dating in the 1940s and 1950s became more stylized, traditional sex roles governed interactions, and the double standard for sexual behavior prevailed. In the last several decades, however, southern courtship patterns have loosened, and informal groups of couples dating have become more popular. Among upper-middle and upper classes and some social groups such as sororities, courtship rituals associated with going steady, being pinned, and announcing engagements are still formalized and highly valued. In recent years cohabitation in the South has increased at rates comparable to those of other regions, though within the South, as elsewhere, there are variations associated with religious affiliation and other factors.

Marriage rates in the South have followed national patterns of fluctuation. In 1983, for example, the marriage rate, or number of marriages per 1,000 persons in the population, fell nationwide. Mississippi and Texas were among the 10 states in which marriage rates declined more than 5 percent that year. As of 1983 the highest marriage rate in the South was 16.4 percent in South Carolina (also the state with the lowest divorce rate, 4.2 percent), and the lowest was 8.1 percent in West Virginia.

Marriage rates are tied to many demographic and social variables, among them the sex ratio and social definitions of eligible and desirable mates. Increased mobility throughout the post–World War II South and the influx of young people into colleges have decreased the likelihood that one will marry a hometown sweetheart, but many

Catholic wedding, Louisville, Ky., c. 1950

clear-cut expectations about marrying someone similar in family background, race, religion, and educational level still hold. In the mid-1980s much attention focused on a nationwide shortage of eligible men in proportion to women over age 25, and recent research on selected cities has shown that for southern females aged 20–34 the number of potential mates is higher in Houston and New Orleans than Atlanta or Miami. In all of these states, however, the number of eligible men exceeds the number of eligible women among 20- to 24-year-olds, but the imbalance reverses—and increases—in all age groups above 25. Partly as a result of the so-called marriage squeeze, there will probably be an increasing number of adults in the region who never marry, though most southerners—about 90 percent—will probably marry at some time in their lives.

See also FOLKLIFE: Family Folklore; Weddings

Jan Lewis
Rutgers University, Newark

Sharon A. Sharp
University of Mississippi

John Blassingame, *The Slave Community: Plantation Life in the Antebellum South* (1972); Lois Green Carr and Lorena Walsh, *William and Mary Quarterly* (October 1977); Jane Turner Censer, *North Carolina Planters and Their Children, 1800–1860* (1984); Herbert G. Gutman, *The Black Family in Slavery and Freedom, 1750–1925* (1976); Allan Kulikoff, *Law, Society, and Politics in Early Maryland* (1977); Jan Lewis, *The Pursuit of Happiness: Family and Values in Jefferson's Virginia* (1983); National Center for Health Statistics, *Monthly Vital Statistics Report*, vol. 32, no. 13 (21 September 1984); Ellen Rothman, *Hands and Hearts: A History of Courtship in America* (1985).

Marriage and Divorce Laws

Chivalry—the romantic ideal of male-female relationships—was as much a legal doctrine as a social prescription in the antebellum South. No statute or code used the term, but its underlying assumptions about the weakness of women and the protective authority of men ran through southern domestic law. From the first colonial statutes and case law on marriage and divorce, women were accorded an inferior status. "Reform" of this status—liberalization of divorce law, passage of married women's property acts, and adoption of equal rights amendments—neither arose from nor carried forward any general program of equality for men and women under the law.

Marriage and divorce law in the colonial South mixed ecclesiastical and civil procedures. Marriage made a single woman into a *femme covert*, whose legal person and property are merged with her husband's. Coverture originated in English common law and was widely adopted in all the colonies. The wife lost the right to sue and be sued, to use or manage the common property, and to arrange for her children's estates without the consent of her husband, unless arrangements were made prior to marriage or the courts intervened upon a suit of equity. At her husband's death, a wife possessed a life interest in a part of the common property (dower). Divorce was uncommon. Where they functioned, church courts could order an annulment (a declaration that the marriage had never been valid) or a separation with division of property but without the right to remarry. This, again, was the English practice, as well as being common in Roman Catholic countries. A third form of divorce, by specific legislative decree, was not adopted in the colonial South, though it was quite common in New England.

The demography of the early southern settlements, marked by early death for women from childbirth, epidemic diseases, and overwork, ironically countered, in a limited way, the detriments imposed upon women by the law. The value of wives and mothers, particularly in frontier communities, was a matter of supply and demand, not legal formulas. Southern colonial women were administrators of estates, heirs, heads of families, and substantial property holders. As *femmes sole*, they ran businesses, sued, and were sued. In the absence of other forms of divorce, these women obtained redress by petitioning the local courts.

During the revolutionary era divorce laws were liberalized (partly in response to the expansion of women's educational opportunities) to the extent that women with grievances against their spouses gained access to courts under general divorce laws. But postrevolutionary chivalric ideals of personal conduct (and of offenses justifying divorce) were everywhere apparent. An Alabama code provision of 1852 spelled these out: "The legal responsibilities of a wife are to live in the home established by her husband; to perform the domestic chores (cleaning, cooking, washing, etc.) necessary to help maintain that home; to care for her husband and children. The legal responsibilities of a husband are to provide a home for his wife and children; to support, protect and maintain his wife and children." In cases of conflict, the rights of the husband remained paramount, so long as he provided for the family. Indeed, it was neither a crime nor grounds for divorce for a man to force his wife against her will to engage in sexual relations.

Southern states introduced divorce by legislative decree at the end of the 18th century. In 1839 the Maryland Legislature passed the first general divorce law in the South (much like the general incorporation acts promulgated in the same era), and it was soon copied by other southern general assemblies. The Virginia statute of 1853 was typical—allowing divorce in cases of adultery, impotency, felony, abandonment (of three years or more in duration), prostitution, and cohabitation. When women appealed disputed lower court divorce rulings to supreme courts, judges counted the submissiveness of the wife-plaintiff in her favor. The court protected the wife, the weaker partner, from the erring husband, under the unwritten law of chivalry. Divorce remained relatively uncommon in the pre–Civil War era, though the rate steadily increased and would continue to increase throughout the next century and a half. Marital separation by consent or necessity was far more common.

The most notorious of the marital separations explicitly sanctioned by the law involved slave families. Masters might encourage, or even officiate at, slave marriages (which had little or no legal sanction), but married slave women had no legal remedy for dissolution of their marriage by sale, gift, or devise. Slave women were chattel, and whether they were trusted members of the family circle, field hands, or breeding stock, chivalry played no part in their lives.

The mid-19th century did bring genuine reform in the legal status of free southern married women. For a decade before the Civil War, and then with added vigor in the years of Reconstruction, southern state legislatures enacted married women's property acts. As in their contemporaneous northern counterparts, these laws allowed married women to dispose of their own property, including that property obtained during marriage. Such property, after divorce or widowhood, remained theirs. Although these laws were never absolute guarantees of entitlement (in some of them the wife did not have sole possession of wages and rents even if they were earned only by her), they did elevate the legal status of the *femme covert*. In practice, such women often already managed family and business finances. The new laws protected a part of the family assets against a husband's creditors, no mean advantage in the boom-and-bust economy of the antebellum South and in the hard times following the Civil War. At the same time, proponents of these bills in legislatures rarely showed any sympathy for more sweeping reform of domestic law. Women were still protected by men. Political rights, as well as recognition of women as heads of households or as independent participants in the marketplace, did not immediately follow upon the married women's property acts. Georgia, for example, officially recognized women as heads of households in 1982.

Over the past century southern legislators and courts have redressed some of the inequities of domestic law, while retaining the prerogatives of chivalric protectors of wives and mothers. Women's participation in public affairs has not destroyed such prejudices, though the oppressive weight of discrimination in the law has lessened. Divorce laws in 8 of the 13 southern states no longer require proof of fault or immorality. Recognition in divorce settlements of nonmonetary contribution to family life in the form of homemaking and child rearing is now standard practice in Arkansas, Florida, Kentucky, Maryland, Mississippi, and Virginia, as it is in almost all the northern states. Nevertheless, local courts throughout much of the South continue to regard themselves as the protectors of traditional roles in the family. State equal rights amendments (in the few southern states that have them) have not brought an end to this latter-day expression of chivalry, despite husbands' suits claiming reverse discrimination.

Although a historical and sentimental tie can thus be discerned between chivalric attitudes among southern lawmakers and judges and the simultaneous protection and debasement of women under the law, it is not so clear that this relationship is purely southern. Women were denied equal access to education, professional occupations, wealth, political activity, and public expression in the North, under rationales very similar to those given in the South. Married women's property laws had a very similar economic (rather than egalitarian) basis in North and South. The post–Civil War movement to prohibit, or at least curtail, divorce had its origins in New England and New York, not the South. Indeed, the South was an innovator in liberalizing some domestic and economic restrictions upon married women. To be sure, southern women were not so well organized, vocal, or successful in the drive for autonomy as their northern sisters—allowing southern lawmakers the chance to loosen domestic restrictions without fear of militancy among the recipients of their largesse. Perhaps for this reason—a mixture of tacit consent and continuing disorganization—southern women are still waging the legal fight against chivalry.

See also BLACK LIFE: Family, Black; HISTORY AND MANNERS: Sexuality; LAW: Family Law

N. E. H. Hull
University of Georgia

Barbara A. Babcock et al., *Sex Discrimination and the Law: Causes and Remedies* (1975); Jane Turner Censer, *American Journal of Legal History* (January 1981); Carl N. Degler, *At Odds: Women and the Family in America from the Revolution to the Present* (1980); Doris J. Freed and Henry H. Foster, Jr., *Family Law Quarterly* (Winter 1981); George E. Howard, *A History of Matrimonial Institutions*, 2 vols. (1904); Leo Kanowitz, *Sex Roles in Law and Society* (1973); Paul M. Kurtz, *Family Law Quarterly* (Summer 1977); Suzanne Lebsock, *Journal of Southern History* (May 1977); Peggy A. Rabkin, *Fathers to Daughters: The Legal Foundations of Female Emancipation* (1980); Max Rheinstein, *Marriage Stability, Divorce, and the Law* (1972).

Matriarchy, Myth of

A matriarch is a woman who maintains the authority to make major decisions and to control the property as well as the political environment of the family. In some traditional African societies, like the Ashanti, lineage was traced through the female; however, her power was limited by male members of her line. Similar lineage patterns could be found in North America among Indians such as the Cherokee. Nonetheless, truly matriarchal societies have been rare throughout world history.

During the colonial period in the United States, slavery was found everywhere. Not all enslaved Africans came from matriarchal or even matrilineal societies, but many of them were familiar with these family patterns. Typically, African women were socialized to be self-reliant, to be the center of family activity, and to contribute to family income or food production. Once enslaved, African women were valued by their masters for their labor and as producers of additional slaves. Healthy family development was not a priority among slaveowners, so black family survival was always precarious. In some communities, such as the Maryland plantation where Frederick Douglass was born, mothers were not allowed to take care of their own children, because the value of their labor was preferred; child rearing was left to older women, like Douglass's grandmother.

Despite the challenges, family life among slaves managed to continue in various forms. By the early 19th century most slaves lived in the South, many of them working on plantations. Family survival often depended upon slave mothers, who were usually allowed to provide care for their young children. Moreover, in some slave communities, like the Cedar Vale plantation in Virginia, family life was encouraged. Slave parents lived together with their offspring and perhaps other kin, who made up an extended family. Members other than parents helped to care for children; grandmothers, in particular, played an important role in child rearing. Extended families are common in traditional African societies. Slavery in the New World accommodated well to this familial arrangement, which promoted family survival for generations after slavery. Following emancipation, black women often found work as live-in domestic servants. Grandmothers who were at home cared for the children of their daughters, who worked and lived elsewhere.

Extended familial organization was only one of the similarities between Africans and Indians during the slavery era. As a result of similar worldviews, Africans and Indians could relate well in the New World environment that Europeans often found alien. Although slavery fostered self-reliant mothers and female-centered families, Europeans dominated North America by the 17th century and attempted to discredit non-European culture, promoting a negative view of African women. In modern times, this negative view has been misinterpreted as black matriarchy.

Black women, who have been victims of the heritage of slavery and economic exploitation, have, nevertheless, been blamed for causing family disruption and deterioration. The 1965 U.S. Labor Department report, *The Negro Family: The Case for National Action*, strengthened the myth of black matriarchy. This document, referred to as the "Moynihan Report," was built upon earlier theories of black family development put forth by black sociologist E. Franklin Frazier. Frazier blamed slavery for destroying the African patriarchal family, which he believed to be the common form of family authority. The conclusions of the Moynihan study, on the other hand, led to indictments of black women for usurping authority in the family by dominating black men in employment, achieving higher educational levels, and making family decisions. One of the suggested solutions to the problem of so-called black matriarchy was for black men to throw off female control and to reorganize families along patriarchal lines. Patriarchy was deemed the panacea for all the ills created by dominant black women. This solution seemed natural in a society where Western values embrace the traditional values of patriarchy.

In Western societies income and education are prerequisites for achieving authority and power outside, as well as inside, the home. Curiously, the myth of black matriarchy never has taken into consideration that black women have not attained power in American society; they consistently remain at the bottom of income scales

Woman washing clothes by hand, Vicksburg, Miss., 1968

that compare men and women by race. Black status in the U.S. economy has been determined by racism and sexism, not by black female ascendency as the authority figure in the home or the community. When necessary, black women have been forced to become the foundation for family survival.

Nevertheless, female-headed households have not been the dominant structure in black families since emancipation. The growing rate of single-parent households in the late 20th century is high among blacks, but it is not exclusive to black families. In 1970, 29.3 percent of black families and 7.8 percent of white families were headed by women. In 1982 the respective figures were 47.2 percent and 15.3 percent. The increasing divorce rate in American society has promoted this situation among women, and the death rate for black men, always the highest among men and women, blacks and whites, contributes to the high number of black female heads of families, many of whom face poverty. As of 1983 over one-third of all single-parent, female-headed families lived below the poverty level, and of these, 56.2 percent were black. In five southern states in 1980, 70 percent or more of the single-parent, female-headed families below the poverty level were black. Recently the needs of such families have received increasing attention, particularly from black leaders.

Self-reliance and willingness to assume family responsibilities are values learned by black females early in life. These values, which can be found in rural and urban communities, across regional lines, and among the educated and noneducated, are essential to family and personal survival in a society that has historically placed little value on the quality of black life.

See also BLACK LIFE: Family, Black

Rosalyn Terborg-Penn
Columbia, Maryland

Agnes Ahosua Aidoo, in *The Black Woman Cross-Culturally*, ed. Filomina C. Steady (1981); John Blassingame, *The Slave Community: Plantation Life in the Antebellum South* (1972); Frederick Douglass, *Narrative of the Life of Frederick Douglass* (1963); E. Franklin Frazier, *The Negro Family in the United States* (1939); Herbert G. Gutman, *The Black Family in Slavery and in Freedom, 1750–1925* (1979); Bernice Reagon Johnson, *Feminist Studies* (Spring 1982); U.S. Bureau of the Census, *Current Population Reports*, Series P-20, no. 380 (1983), *General Social and Economic Characteristics, 1980* (by state) (1981); U.S. Department of Labor, *The Negro Family: The Case for National Action* (1965).

Mexican Women

Mexicans living in the South have traditionally resided in Texas, and the historical and contemporary experiences of *las Tejanas*—the Mexican women of Texas—offer a unique perspective on life in the westernmost realm of the South. Beginning in 1659 with the founding of El Paso del Norte, Mexican pioneers attempted to carve out a prosperous province called *Tejas* despite hostile American Indians and apparent neglect from the colonial government in Mexico City. Mexican women on the frontier performed various tasks in addition to nurturing children and maintaining a home. They cleaned the mission sacristy, made candles, tended the sick, and taught domestic arts (such as cooking and knitting) to the small numbers of American Indian women living at the mission. In addition, they worked alongside their fathers or husbands feeding livestock and tending crops. Under the Spanish and Mexican legal systems, women possessed community property rights and owned land in their own names.

Because of Indian raids, a shortage of colonists, and indifference from the colonial government, *Tejas* was a struggling outpost. In 1820 the Mexican government decided to take action; it invited Anglo settlers to Texas. At first Anglo and Mexican pioneers enjoyed cordial relations. *Tejanos* offered help and hospitality to the new arrivals. However, as the Anglo population swelled, cultural differences, misunderstandings, and prejudice eroded the goodwill between Anglos and Mexicans. From 1830 onward the new arrivals viewed Mexicans as inferior beings. Expedition reports, diaries, and journalistic accounts characterized Mexicans as lazy, greasy, dumb, superstitious, sneaky, and morally degenerate. Mexican women, in particular, were deemed sensual, wanton creatures—a stereotype that has survived to the present. As Texas pioneer Susan Magoffin recorded in her diary, "The women go around with their arms and neck bare—perhaps their bosoms exposed (and they are none of the prettiest or whitest)."

These pejorative observations held tragic implications. After the Texas Revolution and the United States–Mexican War, Anglos took over property they coveted, and Mexicans had no legal recourse. For instance, in 1830 Doña Patricia de Leon was one of the wealthiest women in the Southwest. She and her husband owned large, prosperous landholdings in south Texas worth over $500,000. Although Doña de Leon had been a principal financial supporter of the Texas Revolution, she and her family fled the state in 1836. Eight years later she returned in poverty to her home in Victoria. Moreover, the only woman ever executed in the history of Texas was of Mexican descent. Convicted of murder based on circumstantial evidence, Chepita Rodriguez was executed in 1863.

From 1836 to the 1950s Texas was a segregated state with segregated schools, restaurants, theaters, and jobs. Mexicans were relegated to the lowest occupational levels with little opportunity for advancement. Whether in urban or rural areas, several members of a family labored to put food on the table. As farm workers, Mexicans have usually been paid as a family unit rather than as individuals. During the early decades of the 20th century, a rural *Tejana* had few occupational choices outside of laboring in the fields with her husband and children. Sometimes unmarried daughters worked as clerks in stores that catered to Mexican clientele, but more often women worked as domestic servants for Anglo landowners. Urban women faced similar circumstances. They were typically employed by laundries, garment factories, canneries, and packing houses. Moreover, stores that served Hispanics hired *Mexicanas* as sales clerks and office help. They also served as maids in private homes, hotels, and businesses.

The economic participation of Mexican women was not overlooked in their communities. During the early 1900s Spanish-language newspapers, such as *El Cronista del Valle* of Brownsville, editorialized that the industrial employment of *Tejanas* posed a threat to the family. Newspapers argued that factory labor would turn women into "robots with no emotion or sense of home responsibilities." Although this blanket prohibition against female employment was an extreme in Mexican communities, most Hispanic families did accept the notion that, while unmarried daughters could work for wages, wives were to stay within the confines of the home unless financially desperate. Many mothers, however, supplemented their families' incomes by taking in sewing, laundry, and boarders.

In addition to home and work duties, many 20th-century *Tejanas* have been involved in labor and political struggles. Examples of trade-union activism include the El Paso Laundry Strike of 1919, the San Antonio Pecan Shellers' Strike of 1938, and the recent two-year dispute at Farah, one of the largest clothing manufacturers in the state. These women have also been involved in various political and community activities. Groups of *Tejanas* raised funds for Ricardo Flores Magon and the *Partido Liberal Mexicano* during the era of the Mexican Revolution (1910–26). Magon, one of the first proponents of political and economic equality for Mexican women, enjoyed considerable popularity among Hispanic women. In 1911 Magon supporters Andrea and Teresa Villarreal published the first feminist newspaper in Texas, *La Mujer Moderna.*

Tejanas also helped organize *El Primer Congreso Mexicanista,* held on 11–12 September 1911 in Laredo. Addressing a number of civil rights issues, the Congress protested lynchings of Mexicans and called for an end to inferior, segregated schools. The education of women was also an important issue. As Soledad Pena declared, "the best way . . . is to educate woman; to instruct her, and to encourage and to give her due respect." Pena and other women involved in the meetings founded the *Liga Feminist Mexicanista.*

In addition, *Tejanas* have participated in *mutualistas* and patriotic societies. *Mutualistas* provided insurance and charitable services to their members and to residents of the local Mexican community. Some organizations became involved in trade-union activities. For example, *Mexicana* labor organizer Sara Estela Ramirez worked for *La Sociedad de Obreros, Igualdad y Progreso.* During the 1970s *La Raza Unida,* an incipient Hispanic political party, actively recruited women both as precinct workers and candidates. Mexican women have also made inroads in the Democratic party, as well as in nonpartisan civic groups such as the League of United Latin American Citizens. *Tejanas,* however, are still clustered in the lower socioeconomic brackets. According to the 1980 census, the median income of Mexican women in Texas averaged $7,750. (The figures for Anglo and black women reached $10,586 and $8,503, respectively.) In fact, their average earnings were 43.7 percent of those garnered by Anglo males. These economic disparities can be explained, in part, by the low levels of education characteristic of Mexican-American women. Fifty-five percent of *Tejanas* in the labor force have eight years or less of formal education while only 4 percent have attained college degrees. Although not a panacea, an expansion of educational opportunities for Hispanic women holds exciting possibilities for the future.

From the frontier period to the present, *Tejanas* have displayed remarkable resiliency and resourcefulness. Whether establishing a settlement in a hostile land or working in the factories and fields, they have been survivors and innovators. As political organizers, labor activists, teachers, blue-collar workers, and as wives and mothers, *Tejanas* have been important, creative forces shaping Texas and southern history.

See also ETHNIC LIFE: / Mexicans; HISTORY AND MANNERS: Mexican War; SOCIAL CLASS: Labor, Organized

Vicki L. Ruiz
University of California, Davis

Martha P. Cotera, *Diosa y Hembra: The History and Heritage of Chicanas in the U.S.* (1976); Arnoldo De Leon, *They Called Them Greasers: Anglo Attitudes toward Mexicans in Texas, 1821–1900* (1983); Mario T. Garcia, *Proceedings of the National Association for Chicano Studies* (1979); Magdalena Mora and Adelaida R. Del Castillo, eds., *Mexican Women in the United States: Struggles Past and Present* (1980); Vicki L. Ruiz, *Southwest Institute for Research on Women, Working Paper No. 19* (1984); Paul S. Taylor, *Mexican Labor in the United States,* 2 vols. (1930–32).

Politics, Women in

The South has added distinctive connotations to the definition of women's "proper sphere" in the United States. An examination of southern politics confirms that, even though constrained by powerful cultural, legal, social, economic, and psychological forces, women have steadily moved from a predominantly private family role into public political activities.

The culture of the Old South, although never monolithic, generally restricted women to a narrow orbit circumscribed by the ascendant symbol of "the lady." Inspired by a variety of literary and historical sources, as well as by practical considerations, the complex image of "the lady" magnified the prevalent 19th-century national "cult of true womanhood," which prescribed piety, purity, submissiveness, and domesticity as preeminent female virtues and consigned women to the special province of the home. Southern shibboleths about women created an elaborate rationale dedicated to the defense of the peculiar institution of slavery and infatuated with the medieval code of chivalry. Submissiveness translated into inferiority, polemics superseded reason, myth obscured reality, and idealization became repression.

Disfranchised and denied orthodox political influence, women developed unconventional methods to challenge the male-dominated system. In time southern women proved particularly ingenious in their devices, but few opportunities existed in the society before 1860. In South Carolina, the Grimké sisters represented the dilemma of antebellum dissenters, who frequently took the path of imposed or self-imposed exile.

After 1865 southerners were compelled by education, industrialization, and urbanization to reconsider women's proper place. Voluntary associations, often affiliated with the authoritative institution of the church, enabled southern women to gain confidence as administrators and public speakers. From the 1870s they participated openly if not powerfully in state political organizations.

The campaign for women's suffrage and the crusade against lynching epitomized the strengths and weaknesses of the political efforts of southern women. To avoid the abusive epithet "short-haired women," they painstakingly displayed ladylike demeanor and selectively deferred to tradition in their appearances and actions. Racism, states' rights, and pragmatic elitism compromised both the Southern States Woman Suffrage Conference created in 1913 by Kate Gordon of New Orleans and the Association of Southern Women for the Prevention of Lynching launched in 1930 under the leadership of Jessie Daniel Ames of Texas. Torn between the desire for change and the perceived need for social control, southern reformers acquiesced in the dogma of white supremacy. The failure, except for ephemeral and fragile coalitions, to transcend the race question prevented the achievement of gender solidarity. Although Arkansas, Tennessee, and Texas among the former Confederate states secured partial woman suffrage through legislative enactment and also ratified the Nineteenth Amendment, only the dreaded federal intervention brought full citizenship in 1920. Many veterans of the suffrage wars competed successfully for state political positions, but inexperience and prolonged socialization impeded the acquisition of real power. Toleration, not equality, most accurately described the condition of southern women.

The political culture after 1920 accentuated three southern phenomena: women as appointed male successors, women as male proxies, and women as mirrors of male political authority. Occasionally a successor has established her own political identity, but most women appointed to office have exerted marginal influence. Appointed U.S. senators, Rebecca Felton of Georgia, Hattie Caraway of Arkansas, Rose Long of Louisiana, and Dixie Graves of Alabama upheld the accepted image of southern women. Caraway won two complete terms in the elections of 1932 and 1938, but the precedents she set in the Senate had limited significance. The classification of "gracious southern lady" has survived in the career of Representative Corinne "Lindy" Boggs of Louisiana, who initially triumphed in 1973 in a special election for her missing husband's congressional seat.

Two dramatic examples typify the southern woman as male proxy. Elected governor in Texas in 1924 and 1932 as a substitute for her disqualified husband, Miriam "Ma" Ferguson unabashedly offered voters two Fergusons for the price of one. Lurleen Wallace's brief administration as nominal governor of Alabama caricatured women in politics. Exploited by her ineligible husband, Governor George C. Wallace, who emerged victorious in her name in 1966, she stoically endured subordination until her death in 1968.

An exceptional model of women who are mirrors of male political authority, Rosalynn Carter attracted unusually intense scrutiny during her husband's presidency. All presidents' wives derive prestige from their relationships, but Carter's southern background marked her as the "steel magnolia," a superficial but telling delineation that popularly symbolized the contradictory impact of southern culture on women in politics.

In the era of the Second Reconstruction after World War II, organized attacks on race and sex discrimination reappeared. Awareness of racism stimulated consciousness of sexism, and again the South figured prominently in the battle. Women activists in student and civil rights groups publicized the common injustices, but the struggles allied women temporarily rather than permanently and expectations of fairness and equality remained unmet.

Southern women have played a part in their own victimization by their equivocal attitudes. Both enthralled by and at odds with the stereotypical claims of their peculiar morality and virtue, they tailored their arguments to gain maximum advantage. Conflicting demands for liberation and the preservation of special protection negated each other.

Alteration, not transformation, has distinguished the political status of southern women. Evolutionary and revolutionary, conservative and radical, conformist and iconoclastic, pragmatic and idealistic, racist and egalitarian, their causes have embodied many of the paradoxes of the regional heritage that have influenced contemporary cultural patterns. Ambivalent about women's roles, the South sanctions sexual politics and the illusion of change, while the southern cultural tradition continues to inhibit genuine participation by women in its politics.

See also BLACK LIFE: / Hamer, Fannie Lou; POLITICS: / Felton, Rebecca

Betty Brandon
University of South Alabama

Sara Evans, *Personal Politics: The Roots of Women's Liberation in the Civil Rights Movement and the New Left* (1979); Jacquelyn Dowd Hall, *Revolt against Chivalry: Jessie Daniel Ames and the Women's Campaign against Lynching* (1979); Sharon Harley and Rosalyn Terborg-Penn, eds., *The Afro-American Woman: Struggles and Images* (1978); Julie Roy Jeffrey, *Feminist Studies* (Fall 1975); Gerda Lerner, *The Majority Finds Its Past: Placing Women in History* (1979); Anne Firor Scott, *The Southern Lady: From Pedestal to Politics, 1830–1930* (1970); A. Elizabeth Taylor, *The Woman Suffrage Movement in Tennessee* (1957).

Race Relations and Women

Antebellum plantation society made manifest the South's dual caste system based on race and sex. During the era of slavery white women and black women and men occupied an overtly subordinate position compared to white men, but the forms and functions of racial and sexual oppression differed in each case. Blacks of both sexes served as the primary labor force within a staple-crop economy, and slave women, as childbearers and nurturers, were integral to the reproduction and sustenance of that labor force. In contrast, white women had primary responsibility for household management and bore the heirs who would eventually oversee the geographical expansion and increasing politicization of the region's "peculiar institution." Thus, although their inferior legal and social position derived from physical characteristics that differentiated them from white men, blacks and white women held statuses that were not strictly analogous. Certainly, white women's class prerogatives and material advantages derived from the exploitation of slaves, both male and female. For these reasons, relations between women of the two races, whether conducted in white households or in the public arena, were fraught with tension.

Together with their menfolk, black women helped to create a distinctive Afro-American culture that rejected the white (male) middle-class values of aggressive individualism and personal ambition. A cooperative ethos informed the slaves' religious beliefs, kin relations, and day-to-day resistance to bondage. Despite this sense of racial separateness, however, black people never lost sight of the goal of equality, defined first as freedom from slavery and then, after emancipation, as full legal rights and economic opportunity. The black scholar-activist W. E. B. Du Bois termed this double consciousness "twoness." For black women, twoness meant that their relations with white women would be problematic in both cultural and political terms. Moreover, conflict between the two groups of women was exacerbated by the South's social divisions of labor, which dictated that the most arduous and disagreeable household chores were labeled not so much women's work as black women's work. Well into the 20th century, black women scorned white women as lazy and condemned the time-honored tradition that allowed one group of women to play a direct role in the economic exploitation of another.

White women brought quite different perspectives to bear on the issue of race relations. Individual white women throughout southern history have represented a wide spectrum of attitudes. In the 19th century Sarah and Angelina Grimké, daughters of a Charleston slaveholder, devoted much of their adult lives to the abolitionist cause in the North, and the two sisters showed special sensitivity to the plight of slave women. During the civil rights revolution, Anne Braden, Lillian Smith, and Virginia Durr joined the struggle initiated by blacks against disfranchisement and segregation. In contrast, vengeful slave mistresses quick to unleash their anger on slave women and white housewives who, in the 1960s, clawed the faces of black freedom riders or sprayed peaceful civil rights demonstrators with insecticides demonstrated the ways in which the white supremacist imperative could turn woman against woman.

Nevertheless, exclusive attention to these extreme forms of behavior obscures the complexity of women's roles in race relations. For example, the female relatives of a Birmingham Ku Klux Klan member who bombed a black church in that city and killed four black girls in 1963 cooperated in the 14-year investigation that led to his conviction and imprisonment for life. Their clandestine activities as FBI informants sprang from feelings that were not altogether clear—either personal dislike for the man's tyrannical nature, their own sympathy and concern for the victims, or a combination of these motives. Upper middle-class white women figure prominently in accounts of racial liberalism in the South, but perhaps only because their public pronouncements have been better documented than more modest challenges to the racial caste system carried out by their less well-to-do sisters. In fact, it would be exceedingly difficult to correlate white women's sense of racial egalitarianism with their class standing; privileged white women, in their roles as employers, landlords, and voter registrars, often upheld the tenets of racial inequality.

Indeed, a focus on nonelite white and black women after slavery reveals an irony in the history of southern race relations—that these two groups exhibited mutual suspicion and hostility toward one another despite their very similar material condition. For example, tenant farm wives from the late 19th century through the 1930s followed the same daily and seasonal household routines. They lived in similarly dilapidated cabins (in some cases the same dwelling alternately housed black and white families) and reared equal numbers of children with little in the way of cash or modern conveniences. These women took pride in their large families and in their ability to work in the fields "like a man." Their domestic responsibilities, combined with petty trade activities, set them apart from their husbands, who labored exclusively in the realm of the larger commercial economy.

Nevertheless, female tenants of the two races had few occasions to explore these common bonds. In the late 1930s the sociologist Margaret Hagood told the story of the white Piedmont mother who, when asked directions to a nearby schoolhouse, persisted in declaring that there was no such place in the vicinity. When the woman finally realized that the school in question was for black children, she felt vindicated in her original assertion; a black school simply did not enter into her view of the world, though it was just down the road from her own house. Women had fewer opportunities to see each other in the course of routine tasks, compared to black men and white men, who, together, more often frequented public places like general stores, banks, post offices, or county buildings. One can only speculate about the significance of a poor white woman attended in childbirth by a black midwife (this kind of encounter apparently occurred once in a while); whether the two had any consciousness of the forces that united as well as divided them remains an intriguing question.

Thus far, major themes in the history of women's roles in southern race relations suggest certain northern counterparts—for example, attitudes on the part of northern women toward the issues of de facto housing and school segregation, and the degrading conditions under which both black women and female Eastern European immigrants toiled in factories and in the homes of middle-class white women. Nevertheless, the southern pattern is unique for several reasons, including the violence directed at black women in the form of rape, punishment, and terrorism, not only during slavery, but up through the first half of the 20th century as well. This form of institutionalized violence had no northern counterpart, and it guaranteed that the white South would remain entangled in a web of, in Lillian Smith's words, "hate and guilt and sex and fear."

The brutalization of slave women, the terrorizing of freedwomen, and the persistent sexual harassment of black domestics over the generations constituted direct attacks upon the integrity of black family life, as well as assaults on the dignity of the victims themselves. The sexual abuse of black women by white men served as a warning to all black men that they protected their wives, daughters, and sisters only at great risk to themselves, and as a reminder to all white women that paeans to their tender virtue were hollow indeed. This is not to deny that northerners perfected their own techniques of exploiting black female labor, but accounts of the whipping of pregnant black field hands, for example, come only from the South.

By the mid-20th century several developments signaled cause for a new hopefulness in relations between black and white southern women. Desegregation of public school systems and institutions of higher learning helped to facilitate interracial contact and friendships. Title VII of the Civil Rights Act of 1964 opened up the way for black women to enter "white women's jobs"—clerical, sales, and textile factory work—for the first time. Henceforth, growing numbers of women would share a workplace outside the home and the hardships associated with building low-wage unionism.

The women's liberation movement that emerged in the late 1960s was biased in favor of middle-class white women, but a decade later it had broadened its perspectives to become more sensitive to the issues of class and race. At the same time, an articulate group of black feminists, representing a wide range of professional interests and personal backgrounds, began to write and speak on their own behalf, citing the bruised knees and calloused hands of their mothers (and in some cases their own) as symbols of their doubly disadvantaged status in American society. Black feminists sought to create a form of "identity politics" that would advance their unique interests. In the mid-1980s it was still unclear whether or not their priorities would include a coalition with white women, young and old, rich and poor, southern and northern. But it was clear that white women's best efforts to combat inequality in all its forms would avail little without the insights of resourcefulness that southern black women had to offer.

See also BLACK LIFE: Freedom Movement, Black; RELIGION: Civil Rights and Religion; SOCIAL CLASS: Tenant Farmers

Jacqueline Jones
Wellesley College

William H. Chafe, *Women and Equality: Changing Patterns in American Culture* (1977); W. E. B. Du Bois, *The Souls of Black Folk* (1903); Margaret J. Hagood, *Mothers of the South: Portraiture of the White Tenant Farm Woman* (1939); Gloria T. Hull, Patricia Bell Scott, and Barbara Smith, eds., *All the Women Are White, All the Blacks Are Men, But Some of Us Are Brave: Black Women's Studies* (1982); Jacqueline Jones, *Labor of Love, Labor of Sorrow: Black Women, Work, and the Family from Slavery to the Present* (1985); *New York Times Magazine* (24 July 1983); George P. Rawick, ed., *The American Slave: A Composite Autobiography*, 19 vols. (1972), *Supplement Series I*, 12 vols. (1978), *Supplement Series II*, 10 vols. (1979); Lillian Smith, *Killers of the Dream* (1949); Alice Walker, *In Search of Our Mothers' Gardens: Womanist Prose* (1983).

Religion and Women

Three factors help explain the place of women in religious movements and institutions in the American South. The first is the overwhelming dominance of evangelical Protestantism among whites since the turn of the 19th century and among blacks since emancipation. Secondly, the white South is more ethnically homogeneous than other regions. Third, the South has been slower to abandon the traditional family structure, which is reflected in the patriarchal nature of all southern institutions.

The distinctive religious history of the South began with the two Great Awakenings. Although the revivals of the mid-18th century had some small impact on the seaboard South, the religious fervor inspired by the camp meetings around the turn of the 19th century changed the spiritual topography of the South for all time. Evangelical Protestantism, with its emphasis on the individual conversion experience, came to dominate the region by the 1850s. Finding its institutional expression primarily in the Methodist and Baptist churches, the movement had a twofold impact on white women. Evangelical religion was family oriented. Women and children were as lost in sin as were the family patriarchs, and however steadfastly the fathers were able to dominate the institutions of the South, they could not control the souls of their womenfolk. Conversion was not a gender-specific experience. Women were free to give their souls to Jesus, whatever the men did with theirs, and give they did. They outnumbered the men in church membership, and, although denied positions of authority in the institutional structure, their prayerful presence and domestic support for a largely itinerant ministry were critical to a sense of successful mission.

The nature of evangelical religion also encouraged the gathering together of women and their families for religious services. Out of this gathering rapidly grew societies of women working together to pursue certain spiritual goals, missionary work, religious education of children, and various aid societies. Joint religious activities have been central to the organized social life of southern white women since that time.

Where Afro-Americans, slave or free, were Christian, they tended to follow the same pattern as white evangelicals. Black women were not permitted to take roles of institutional leadership but had the same freedom of religious expression as did the whites, although the circumscribed nature of their social lives did not permit them to form as extensive a network of female societies. In the folk religion of the South, on the other hand, some black women held positions of power. On the plantations they often acted as spiritual leaders—prophetesses or witches—called upon for assistance by blacks and whites alike. Black women often took the lead in organized voodoo activities, particularly in New Orleans, where the two Marie Laveaus, mother and daughter, were widely celebrated priestesses during a 50-year period in the middle of the 19th century.

The continued dominance of evangelical Protestantism after the Civil War and the failure of people with strikingly different religious orientations to migrate into the South tended to reinforce patterns established earlier. Institutional religious leadership would go to the men; the women would find their role in the ladies' auxiliary. As the South became increasingly middle class, the women sought ways in which they could spend their increased leisure time in projects allowing them to use their intelligence and energy in the service of others. The church organizations provided that opportunity.

The women in the largest white denominations organized their activities along similar lines. Baptist, Methodist, and Presbyterian women all developed missionary societies. The task of these organizations was to develop support, both financial and spiritual, for foreign missionaries. Although women were barred from the clergy of these major religious groups, they were encouraged to become foreign missionaries. Many unmarried women went abroad under the auspices of the missionary societies. Wives were also commissioned along with their husbands in missionary activities—not as clergy, but as nurses, teachers, social service workers, and, above all, witnesses to Christ's saving grace. There was probably no role available to southern women that so enabled them to use their courage, intelligence, initiative, and resourcefulness as that of spinster missionary. One of the most widely known religious figures among Southern Baptists is Charlotte "Lottie" Moon, a genuine cultural heroine, who served as a missionary in China for many years and whose exemplary life is used by Baptists to symbolize the entire missionary enterprise.

Unlike the Baptist women who focused almost exclusively on foreign missions, the Methodists began to look closer to home as well for fields of service. As Methodist women began to seek and be denied positions of leadership in the denomination, they developed progressive societies to address the evils in the culture around them. They organized social settlements and a variety of services for poor and working women. It was Methodist women's organizations that represented the social gospel movement in the South. These women also formed a vanguard in the struggle to establish some basis for racial cooperation.

Even before the Civil War the evangelical denominations provided education for their women. These women, after all, managed the homes in which the next generation of evangelicals would be raised. After the war, in both white and black denominational schools and colleges, women were given an education that sometimes led them to reject the principle on which the education was based. Many of those black and white women who challenged the religious, social, and political status quo got their inspiration from the very tradition they opposed.

In recent years, as women have increasingly insisted that they be allowed to provide ministerial leadership in their churches, the South continues to lag behind the rest of the nation in ordaining women. The largest number of female clergy to be found in the South is in the growing Pentecostal movement.

Whereas women have been influential in founding new religious movements in other parts of the United States, rarely, if ever, has a woman been instrumental in the formation of such a movement in the South. The religious homogeneity of the region, as well as the patriarchal emphasis of the culture, has tended to restrict religious innovation of any kind. Southern women have channeled their spiritual energies into the traditional religious structure. Those who have been unable to fit into the cultural mold have either left the region or turned inward upon themselves and nurtured their spiritual lives. The stifling of southern women's spiritual insights has led some of these women to seek self-fulfillment in areas outside the life of the churches, an enterprise that only today is meeting with any degree of success.

See also BLACK LIFE: Religion, Black; FOLKLIFE: Voodoo; RELIGION articles

Thomas R. Frazier
Baruch College,
City University of New York

Jean E. Friedman, *The Enclosed Garden: Women and Community in the Evangelical South, 1830–1900* (1985); Samuel S. Hill, *The South and the North in American Religion* (1980); Donald Mathews, *Religion in the Old South* (1977); Albert J. Raboteau, *Slave Religion: The "Invisible Institution" in the Antebellum South* (1978); Anne Firor Scott, *The Southern Lady: From Pedestal to Politics, 1830–1930* (1970); Noreen Dunn Tatum, *Crown of Service: A Story of Woman's Work in the Methodist Episcopal Church, South, from 1878–1940* (1960).

Suffrage and Antisuffrage

Prior to the Civil War the South showed little interest in woman's enfranchisement. During Reconstruction the issue was raised in several constitutional conventions, but in no state were women granted the right to vote. After Reconstruction woman suffrage became associated with the South's desire to reduce the importance of the black male vote. A widely discussed proposal was the enfranchisement of women with educational and/or property qualifications.This extension of the franchise would include black as well as white women. Fewer black women would be able to meet these requirements, so the proportion of white voters would be increased. The strength of the black vote would be diluted, and white control of southern politics would be assured.

Proposals to enfranchise women meeting certain qualifications were introduced in constitutional conventions in Mississippi (1890), South Carolina (1895), and Alabama (1901). None of these proposals was adopted, however. Involving women in politics was contrary to southern cultural traditions, and southern men were unwilling to use this stratagem even for the purpose of coping with the vexing race issue.

In 1892 the National American Woman Suffrage Association established a special committee on southern work. This committee was composed of southern women and was chaired by Laura Clay of Kentucky. It endeavored to influence public opinion through the distribution of literature and the sponsoring of lectures. Due largely to its efforts, suffrage organizations were formed in all the southern states before the end of the decade.

When crusading for the ballot, southern women followed the guidelines of the National American Woman Suffrage Association. They conducted their agitation with dignity and restraint. They avoided the militant tactics advocated by Alice Paul's National Woman's party. The National Woman's party organized branches in the southern states, but its following there was small. It conducted no militant agitation in the area, but some southern women participated in such activities in the nation's capital. The oldest of the White House pickets and suffrage prisoners, for example, was a southern woman, 73-year-old Mary C. Nolan of Jacksonville, Fla.

The suffragists assured the public that enfranchisement would enable women to be better wives, mothers, citizens, and taxpayers. They would use their votes for the general betterment of society. The antisuffragists countered by arguing that enfranchisement would constitute a threat to the home and the family. Participation in politics would coarsen women and cause them to lose their femininity. It would also cause them to neglect their household duties and would lead to quarrels between husbands and wives.

The "antis" did little organizing in the South and can hardly be considered to have had a movement there. Their strength lay in their appeal to traditional prejudices and to generally established values. They were endeavoring to maintain the status quo while the suffragists were working for change.

The suffragists established lobbies in state capitals. Bills to enfranchise women were introduced in state legislatures, but they were seldom passed. In only three states were significant gains made. In Arkansas in 1917 the legislature passed a law permitting women to vote in primary elections. The following year Texas passed a similar law. In 1919 Tennessee granted women the right to vote for presidential electors and also the right to vote in municipal elections. No southern state, however, allowed full enfranchisement.

When the federal woman suffrage amendment was submitted to the states for ratification, it encountered its strongest opposition in the South. Many southerners considered suffrage a state, not a federal, matter and

Suffragists in early 20th-century Kentucky

feared that ratification would mean federal control of elections. Others held that the enfranchisement of black women would reopen the entire issue of the Negro's role in politics. Some predicted that it would usher in another era of Reconstruction.

In June 1919 Texas became the first state in the South to ratify the Susan B. Anthony Amendment. A few weeks later, Arkansas followed. Kentucky ratified in January 1920. In July 1919 Georgia became the first state in the Union to reject the proposed amendment. Georgia's example was soon followed by Alabama, South Carolina, Virginia, Mississippi, and Louisiana.

Thirty-five states had ratified by August 1920. The approval of only one more was needed. The governor of Tennessee submitted the question to a special session of the legislature. A bitter controversy ensued. Those opposing ratification called the proposed amendment a peril to the South and urged its rejection. Those in favor maintained that eventual ratification was a certainty and that Tennessee's refusal could only delay it. After much emotional debate and political maneuvering, both houses of the legislature approved, and on 26 August 1920 the Nineteenth Amendment became part of the U.S. Constitution.

Two southern states refused to accept woman suffrage as the supreme law of the land. Mississippi and Georgia did not allow women to vote in the general election of 1920, claiming that the Nineteenth Amendment had been ratified too late to permit women to comply with state election laws. Georgia's leading suffragist, Mary Latimer McLendon of Atlanta, telegraphed the secretary of state in Washington and asked his opinion in regard to her eligibility to vote. Her effort was in vain, however, because the secretary refused to become involved.

During the months that followed, Mississippi and Georgia yielded, and woman suffrage prevailed throughout the South. Women voted and held office. The fears of the "antis" were not realized, however. Women did not lose their femininity, nor did they neglect their homes for politics. Only a few aspired to political careers.

The South's strong opposition to woman suffrage was due to its basic conservatism, its devotion to the ideal of the patriarchal family, and its fear of federal interference in elections. Having no alternative, the South accepted enfranchisement, but remained conservative in its attitude toward women and the family. The advent of woman suffrage apparently resulted in no appreciable change in the fundamental nature of southern culture.

See also POLITICS: Voting

A. Elizabeth Taylor
Texas Woman's University

Clement Eaton, *Georgia Review* (Summer 1974); Paul E. Fuller, *Laura Clay and the Woman's Rights Movement* (1975); Kenneth R. Johnson, *Journal of Southern History* (August 1972); Anne Firor Scott, *The Southern Lady: From Pedestal to Politics, 1830–1930* (1970); A. Elizabeth Taylor, *Journal of Mississippi History* (February 1968), *South Carolina Historical Magazine* (April 1976, October 1979), *The Woman Suffrage Movement in Tennessee* (1957).

Workers' Wives

Although attention has been given to upper-class southern women (e.g., the "southern belle") and slave women (e.g., the "black mammy"), the wife of the southern worker has been neglected. Not bound by the restrictions of racism or the social demands to appear "ladylike," the worker's wife has been a significant contributor to southern history and society.

On the southern colonial farm, work was divided along gender lines. In addition to cooking, cleaning, and rearing children, women had responsibility for small animals, the dairy, gardening, and the orchard. Men cared for large animals, planted and harvested crops, and did general field work. But, in times of need, for example during harvest season, sex roles on the colonial farm merged as children and wife helped the husband bring in the crops.

The preindustrial work patterns continued into the antebellum South. As Frank L. Owsley noted in *Plain Folk of the Old South*, the wife of the yeoman farmer "hoed the corn, cooked the dinner or plied the loom, or even came out and took up the ax and cut the wood with which to cook the dinner." The Civil War revealed both her productivity and her endurance; after her husband went off to fight, often with her encouragement, she took over the farms and shops, and women provided the bulk of the urban labor force.

As scholars have recently discovered, southern women have had a more active and important role in southern politics than has been traditionally assumed. The Women's Christian Temperance Union (WCTU), antilynching crusades, and the progressive reform movements of the 19th and 20th centuries involved wives of southern workers, as well as middle- and upper-class women. But their role as political activists dates back even further. Workers' wives, for example, were politically active in the 1600s in Bacon's Rebellion in Virginia, and women such as Harriet Tubman were later involved in resistance to the slave system.

The industrialization of the South transformed to some extent the economic and social functions of women as well as men. In order to support their families, both husband and wife left farms and took factory jobs. In Alabama, while the number of men drawn into industry between 1885 and 1895 increased 31 percent, that of women increased 75 percent. In 1890 women constituted 40 percent of the work force in the four largest southern textile plants. But their political activity did not change. Women, particularly wives of workers, were active in protesting child labor, and, like Ella May Wiggins of the Gastonia strike, they were heavily involved in southern industrial struggles.

Rural married couple, Batesville, Miss., 1968

Nowhere were the importance and influence of workers' wives more vividly revealed than in the southern coalfields. By law and superstition (a mine would supposedly explode if a woman entered it), women were prohibited from industrial work, that is, working in the coal mines. And because southern coal towns were usually in isolated, rural areas, women were not able to find employment in other industries as did miners' wives in northern coalfields. They hardly submitted, however, to the life of Victorian domesticity.

In the era before unions (1880–1933) men worked in the mines 10–14 hours a day, 6 days a week. Hence, their wives essentially controlled the domestic economy and ran the family. To assist the husband in supporting the family, wives continued their preindustrial roles of caring for the family garden, taking in boarders, and doing the laundry of company officials and single miners. And it was the wife who dealt with the daily frustration of keeping the house clean and sanitary in a town filled with coal dust and grime because the company refused to install sanitary facilities such as running water and sewers.

In the company towns that predominated in the southern coalfields, the home was hardly a "separate sphere" sheltering women from the cruelties of the competitive, "public" world, as was said to have been the case in northern urban areas. With her husband down in the coal mines, a wife dealt with the company store and had direct, day-to-day contact with company officials. Consequently, she most keenly and intensely felt the coal company's abuse of power, especially its exploitation in the form of low wages, monopolistic prices, and the lack of sanitary facilities.

Women expressed their anger toward the coal operators in a number of ways. One was in song; Florence Reece, who wrote the classic labor song, "Which Side Are You On?" after company police had driven her husband out of their company town, was but one of a multitude of female coalfield troubadors, a list that also includes the likes of Aunt Molly Jackson, Sarah Gunning, and more recently Hazel Dickens.

Women expressed their desire for improved living and working conditions in the coalfields, as well as their anger, by becoming major advocates for unionization. The exploits of the legendary union organizer Mother Jones are well known. But Ralph Chaplin (author of "Solidarity Forever") captured Jones's appeal when he wrote, after hearing her speak: "She might have been any coal miner's wife filled with righteous fury." The miner's wife helped offset the rigors of labor strife by planting larger gardens and canning more food. With wages stopped, the usual source of food and clothing (the company store) cut off, and shelter denied (miners were thrown out of company houses during strikes), miners could not have succeeded in any coal strike without this extensive preparation.

Miners' wives formed auxiliaries to the United Mine Workers of America to promote the union cause. These organizations, sometimes denigrated as separate, sexist, and unequal, nevertheless increased social awareness and camaraderie among coalfield women and provided needed moral and financial support for organizing the southern coalfields. And wives of miners fought, often violently, for the union. After witnessing a gun battle during a coal strike in West Virginia in 1912 a San Francisco journalist reported, "In West Virginia women fight side-by-side with the men." Indeed, the wife's hostility to the company and her role in strikes were so important that coal company officials often took elaborate measures to try to co-opt them into the company-town system.

As the Academy Award-winning movie *Harlan County, USA* revealed, wives of miners still play a significant role in the unionization of the coalfields. The relative ease with which women have entered the coal mines as workers suggests that the coalfields may be a less "macho" culture than once assumed. Wives of workers in other southern industries and occupations have faced obstacles similar to those faced by miners' wives and have made similar contributions.

See also INDUSTRY: Industrialization and Change; / Mining; SOCIAL CLASS: Labor, Organized; / Coal Miners; Company Towns; Textile Workers

David A. Corbin
Washington, D.C.

David A. Corbin, *Life, Work, and Rebellion in the Coal Fields: Southern West Virginia Miners, 1880–1922* (1981); Margaret J. Hagood, *Mothers of the South: Portraiture of the White Tenant Farm Woman* (1939); Anne Firor Scott, *The Southern Lady: From Pedestal to Politics, 1830–1930* (1970); Julia Cherry Spruill, *Women's Life and Work in the Southern Colonies* (1938).

Working Women

From the colonial period to the present the work performed by southern women has varied according to race and class. Upper- and middle-class white women rarely worked in the public sphere before the 20th century; white working-class women and black women, before and after emancipation from slavery, worked for many generations in agricultural labor and became the South's first industrial workers. Changes in the patterns of women's work in the South resulted from industrialization, the decline of agricultural labor, and increased urbanization. Southern women have a long history of working to support themselves and their families and of struggling to gain fundamental rights within their workplaces. In 1985 southern women, like women throughout the United States, continued to resist occupational segregation in the lowest-paid sectors of the economy and sought to maintain their jobs in a rapidly changing economy.

Women's work in the southern colonies was performed by slaves, indentured servants, and free white women. Like men's work, women's labor was home based and geared toward life in an economy dependent on agricultural production. The work performed by women in the southern colonies varied widely according to class and race. In Virginia, for example, Indian women built houses, farmed, and provided the principal means of production. As white women came into the colonies in greater numbers, they managed households on plantations or smaller farms. Provided with limited education and training, white southern women in colonial towns worked as retail dealers, monopolized the millinery and dressmaking trades, and sold foodstuffs and liquor.

In the early 17th century most southern domestic workers were female white indentured servants. Later in the century these workers were replaced by black slave women who performed myriad skilled and unskilled jobs in antebellum southern society. Slave women worked as children's nurses, cooks, seamstresses, housekeepers, midwives, dairy maids, and agricultural laborers. Forced to spend most of their time working for others, slave women were only occasionally allowed to garden and raise poultry for consumption by their own families or for sale to their masters. During the period between 1775 and 1812 slave women were trained as skilled spinners and weavers, and their labor changed the South from a region that imported all manufactured goods to one in which home manufacturing was widespread.

Work for women in the early 19th-century South continued to be defined by an agricultural, slave-based economy. Slave women worked in agriculture and domestic service. Wealthy white women, dependent on slave labor, administered large plantations or ran large homes in southern cities. Wives of yeoman farmers managed much smaller farms, with the help of their children. The dominance of staple-crop agricultural production affected the lives of all southern women, regardless of their social or economic status.

After the Civil War exslave women responded to freedom by refusing to work in white homes and for the first time demanding the right to work for their own families. Within a few years, however, economic imperatives compelled large numbers of black women to perform domestic work for white southerners, although day work replaced the live-in arrangement reminiscent of slavery. In the decades after the Civil War, increasing numbers of black and white southern farm families lost their land, mortgaged future cotton or tobacco crops to obtain money for supplies, and struggled for survival in a cashless, debt-dominated economy. Gradually, the women in these families, those most easily spared from agricultural labor, began to work as spinners and weavers in newly built southern cotton mills. Female mill workers, and frequently their children, became the region's first industrial workers and provided farm families with cash wages, which were increasingly necessary for survival. Urban and commercial development was slow in the South in the late 19th century, and only a few women from southern middle-class families had the opportunities to work in urban areas as teachers and clerical workers.

In the 20th century the occupational distribution of women workers varied dramatically between the North and the South. In 1910, 83 percent of the southern female work force was in agriculture and domestic service, compared to 33 percent in the North. As late as 1950 manufacturing employed fewer than 18 percent of the region's women workers but 34 percent of those in the North. In the 1920s, with the onset of agricultural depression in the region, farm tenancy increased for both white and black women. White women had the option of industrial work more frequently than black women, who were usually denied manufacturing jobs, except for seasonal handwork in the tobacco industry. The large number of southern women in agriculture and domestic service constituted a reserve pool of workers waiting to "move up" to manufacturing work. This labor surplus reduced the job security of female industrial workers and increased the leverage manufacturers had over them.

The margin of survival for southern women workers was always much thinner than for their northern sisters. Before 1940 southern wages were substantially lower than the national average, while the cost of living in the South was only 5 percent lower than in other regions. In 1946 southerners made up 25 percent of the nation's population but received only 8 percent of the national income. Because wage rates were low for all workers, southern families often depended on the wages of two or more family members, and women's wages were more critical to the family economy than in the North. Southern women working in cotton textiles, for example, typically provided 30–40 percent of the family income.

The biracial composition of the female work force in the South and rigid occupational segregation by race have affected both black and white women workers. Sixty percent of the southern female work force was black in 1910, and the figure was 40 percent as late as 1940. White women workers feared being replaced by black workers as managers repeatedly threatened to hire black workers in the place of white employees. Black women migrated north and west to obtain the industrial work denied them within the region or moved into urban areas within the South to toil as domestic workers for an increasingly prosperous white middle class. Only with the civil rights movement of the 1960s did black southern women gain access to work in the textile industry, the South's largest employer, and to clerical positions. This racial shift within southern industry was also important because of its impact on unions. Black women, many of whom had gained organizing experience in the civil rights movement, often proved to be more willing supporters of unions and more active union members than their white counterparts.

Black domestic workers were among the first southern women to participate in organized resistance to existing working conditions. Their locally organized and self-financed efforts were modest in scale, rarely involving an entire community or municipal area. In 1880, for example, black washerwomen in Atlanta organized an association in a black church, and a year later 3,000 washerwomen, cooks, servants, and child-nurses struck for higher wages. For each publicized protest of this type there were no doubt hundreds of similar, even smaller efforts of which no record has survived.

Student training in mechanics at Bethune-Cookman College, Daytona Beach, Fla., 1940s

The history of southern women and unions began with the response of black and white women workers, including homemakers and farmers' wives, to the Knights of Labor. Women who had been active in the Grange and Populist movements responded to the Knights and joined locals in communities across the South. In 1889 over 50 women's local assemblies were already in the region—10 of which had been organized by black women—and southern women's locals comprised 30 percent of the Knights' women's assemblies in the United States. After the demise of the Knights in 1890, American Federation of Labor (AFL) craft unions concentrated on organizing male workers and ignored the needs and concerns of female workers, who turned to middle-class reform groups for support.

Throughout the 1920s the plight of women workers in the South drew the attention of the Young Women's Christian Association, the National Women's Trade Union League, and the Southern Summer School. These groups emphasized the importance of organizing all the workers within a given industry, focused on the needs of the thousands of southern female workers, and offered direct assistance to striking southern workers. These efforts provided a crucial transitional form of organizing, which transcended the limited goals of the AFL and later encouraged the emergence of the Congress of Industrial Organizations (CIO) in the South.

In 1937 the clothing unions joined with the Textile Workers' Organizing Committee to launch the CIO's first major campaign in the South. Female organizers, especially native southerners, were now hired to work throughout the region. After World War II the CIO launched "Operation Dixie," a far more intensive effort to organize southern workers than the union drives of the 1930s. As the CIO focused on the textile industry, in which women made up over 50 percent of the work force, organizers emphasized union benefits for women workers. The drive brought 400,000 new members into southern locals, over half of them women.

Southern women workers faced strike defeats and declining union membership during the 1950s and 1960s. After the civil rights movement and the opening of industrial jobs for black southerners, however, new efforts in southern union-organizing drives have come increasingly from black women. Long denied access to jobs in the industrial sector, black women in the 1980s hold over 50 percent of the operative positions in many southern plants.

By 1989 the southern female work force reflected national trends more than regional differences. A total of 48 percent of all southern women work outside the home, compared to 50 percent nationally. Among black women, representing 18 percent of the southern female work force in 1980, 52 percent held paid jobs. Southern women are still the lowest-paid workers; in 1980, 65 percent of southern female workers were employed in either manufacturing, clerical, or service occupations. Contemporary southern working women have had to deal with the adverse consequences of deep recessions in the region's basic industries—textiles, tobacco, furniture, and steel—and simultaneously to confront the rapid job shifts resulting from the development and use of new technologies in the clerical and service sectors.

See also AGRICULTURE: Sharecropping and Tenancy; / Grange; BLACK LIFE: Freedom Movement, Black; Slave Culture; Workers, Black; EDUCATION: Teachers; INDUSTRY: Industrialization and Change; / Textile Industry; SOCIAL CLASS: Labor, Organized; Tenant Farmers; / American Federation of Labor; Congress of Industrial Organizations; Knights of Labor; Textile Workers; Tobacco Workers

Mary Frederickson
University of Alabama
at Birmingham

Mary Frederickson, *Women, Work and Protest: A Century of Women's Labor History* (1985); Margaret J. Hagood, *Mothers of the South: Portraiture of the White Tenant Farm Woman* (1939; 1977); Dolores Elizabeth Janiewski, *Sisterhood Denied: Race, Gender, and Class in a New South Community* (1985); Jacqueline Jones, *Labor of Love, Labor of Sorrow: Black Women, Work, and the Family from Slavery to the Present* (1985); Alice Kessler-Harris, *Out to Work: A History of Wage-Earning Women in the United States* (1982); Tobi Lippin, ed., *Southern Exposure* (Winter 1981); Julia Cherry Spruill, *Women's Life and Work in the Southern Colonies* (1972).

Ames, Jessie Daniel

(1883–1972) Social reformer.

Jessie Daniel Ames, born 2 November 1883, had moved three times in Texas by the time she was a teenager. Her father, a stern Victorian eccentric, migrated from Indiana to Palestine, Tex., where he worked as railroad station master, and in 1893 the Daniels moved to Georgetown, Tex., the site of Southwestern University, from which Ames later graduated.

The brutal Indian Wars and vigilantism of the period created a violent atmosphere, which strongly affected the sensitive young Jessie. A strong-willed child, she had resisted the perfect table manners expected of her and often was sent to the kitchen. In the Daniel kitchen young Jessie heard about a lynching nearby in Tyler, an event she remembered for years and that influenced her lifelong efforts to abolish lynching.

In June 1905 Jessie Daniel married a handsome army surgeon, Roger Post Ames, who later died in Guatemala. In 1914 she rose to prominence in Texas as an advocate of southern progressivism and women's suffrage. Unlike most suffragists in the early 1920s, she understood the grave injustice against blacks in this country. She served as a vital link between feminism and the 20th-century struggle for black civil rights.

In 1924 she became field secretary of Will Alexander's Atlanta-based Commission on Interracial Cooperation. She immediately began organizing against lynching in Texas, Arkansas, and Oklahoma. Alexander brought her to Atlanta in 1929 as Director of Women's Work for the Commission, and in 1930 she began Southern Women for the Prevention of Lynching, which in nine years had 40,000 members. Alerted by friendly law officers and her contacts in the press when a lynching threatened, Ames contacted women in that county who had pledged to work against violence. Her work was not always appreciated. Opposition came from women as well as men. The Women's National Association for the Preservation of the White Race claimed that Ames's women "were defending criminal Negro men at the expense of innocent white girls."

Ames did not support the federal antilynching law in 1940 as being practical. She said the bill would pass the House and southern senators would then defeat it. She was soon at odds with her boss, Dr. Alexander, as well as her old allies in the NAACP.

From May 1939 to May 1940 in the South, for the first time since records had been kept, not a single lynching occurred. World War II, however, dealt a death blow to Southern Women for the Prevention of Lynching, just as it did to the attempt to abolish the hated poll tax in the South. The alliance between women and victimized blacks, which Ames hoped for, was postponed.

In 1943 Southern Women for the Prevention of Lynching was absorbed by the newly formed Southern Regional Council, as was the Interracial Commission. Ames wanted to work for the new agency but found her services were not needed.

In the foothills of the Blue Ridge Mountains Ames set out to rebuild her life. Elected superintendent of

Christian Social Relations for the Western North Carolina Conference of the Methodist Church, she welcomed the opportunity "to get back into public life and be remembered." She later returned to Texas and was honored in the 1970s as a pioneer who combined feminism with civil rights activism. Jessie Daniel Ames died on 21 February 1972 at the age of 88.

See also BLACK LIFE: / Commission on Interracial Cooperation; SOCIAL CLASS: / Southern Regional Council

Marie S. Jemison
Birmingham, Alabama

Jessie Daniel Ames Papers, Texas Historical Society, Dallas, Texas State Library, Austin, and Southern Historical Collection, University of North Carolina, Chapel Hill; Association of Southern Women for the Prevention of Lynching and The Commission on Interracial Cooperation Papers, Trevor Arnett Library, Atlanta University; Jacquelyn Dowd Hall, *Revolt against Chivalry: Jessie Daniel Ames and the Women's Campaign against Lynching* (1979).

Atkinson, Ti-Grace

(b. 1939) Feminist.

Ti-Grace Atkinson captured public attention between 1966 and 1972 as one of the most articulate and radical speakers for the women's movement in the United States. She was a protégé of Betty Friedan, who promoted her in the National Organization for Women (NOW) because her "lady-like blond image would counter-act the man-eating specter." Yet Atkinson, who was described by the media as "softly sexy," "tall," and "elegantly feline," came to stand for all that Friedan saw as most damaging to the movement: total separation from men, advocacy of abortion on demand, and the destruction of marriage and the family.

Atkinson was born in 1939 to an established Baton Rouge family. Had she remained at home, she might have become simply the family eccentric, an acceptable, though not desirable, role for southern women of her class. But she was one of those southerners whom Roy Reed described as "born afire" and who spend their days looking elsewhere for something to ease the burning. Although Atkinson virtually disowned and never discussed her southern upbringing, she always insisted that interviewers record her name as the Cajun "Ti-Grace."

Married at 17, Atkinson went to Philadelphia. By the time she was divorced five years later, she had taken a B.F.A. at the University of Pennsylvania and was establishing a career as an art critic, writing for *Art News* and acting as the founding director of the Philadelphia Institute for Contemporary Art. Then, Simone de Beauvoir's *The Second Sex* converted her to a new philosophy. In 1966 Atkinson joined the nascent NOW, where her appearance, manners, and genteel Republican connections were put to use in national fund-raising.

A year later, Atkinson moved to New York City to pursue graduate study in political philosophy at Columbia University. As president of the local NOW chapter, she generated conflict within the group with her demands for changes not only in the organization's goals and programs but also in its internal structure. Failing to achieve her aims within NOW, she resigned in 1968 to start The October 17th Movement, later modestly renamed the Feminists. Acting on her fierce drives for constant purification, Atkinson and a small group of 15 to 20 women created a mechanically egalitarian group, within which women were to separate totally from men. Although frequently cited as a lesbian, Atkinson was in fact an advocate of celibacy. It was, she acknowledged, a model for which most women were not ready.

Atkinson's distinctive position in the women's movement was characterized by her exceptional intelligence, her uncompromising radicalism, and a willingness to follow any position to its logical conclusion. She took the Mafia as a model of resistance, living outside the law, and formed an alliance with reputed mobster Joseph Colombo's Italian-American Civil Rights League. This affiliation was widely attacked, and on 6 August 1971 Atkinson divorced herself from the rest of the women's movement.

Despite this breach, in November 1971 she helped organize the Feminist party, which attempted to get the major political parties to incorporate feminist positions into their 1972 platforms. After publication in 1974 of *Amazon Odyssey*, a collection of her speeches and other writings from 1967 to 1972, Atkinson faded from public view. She continues to live in New York City.

Jordy Bell
Croton-on-Hudson, New York

Ti-Grace Atkinson, *Amazon Odyssey: Collection of Writings* (1974); Maren Lockwood Carden, *The New Feminist Movement* (1974); Betty Friedan, *New York Times Magazine* (4 March 1973); Martha Weinman Lear, *New York Times Magazine* (10 March 1968); *Newsweek* (23 March 1970).

Baker, Ella Jo

(b. 1903) Civil rights activist.

Ella Jo Baker, the daughter of Georgianna and Blake Baker, was born in 1903 in Norfolk. When she was seven, Baker's family moved to Littleton, N.C., to live with her maternal grandparents, who owned a plantation where they had previously worked as slaves. The absence of adequate public school for blacks in rural North Carolina and her mother's concern that she be properly educated resulted in Baker's attending Shaw University in Raleigh. There, she received both her high school and college education. Following her graduation in 1927, she moved to New York City to live with a cousin, where she worked as a waitress and, later, in a factory.

The product of a southern environment in which caring and sharing were facts of life, and of a family in which her grandfather regularly mortgaged his property in order to help neighbors, Baker soon became involved in various community groups. In 1932 she became the National Director of the Young Negroes Cooperative League and the office manager of the *Negro National News*. Six years later, she began her active career with the National Association for the Advancement of Colored People (NAACP), working initially as a field secretary in the South. In 1943 she was appointed National Director of the Branches for the NAACP. In both capacities Baker spent long periods in southern black communities, where her southern roots served her well. Her success in recruiting southern blacks to join what was considered a radical organization in the 1930s and 1940s may be attributed, in part, to her being a native of the region and, therefore, best able to approach southern people. Baker, who neither married nor had children of her own, left active service in the NAACP in 1946 in order to raise a niece. A short while later she reactivated her involvement with the NAACP, becoming president of the New York City chapter of the NAACP in 1954.

In 1957 Baker went south again, this time to work with the Southern Christian Leadership Conference (SCLC), a newly formed civil rights organization. The student sit-in movement of the 1960s protested the refusal of public restaurants in the South to serve blacks and resulted in Baker's involvement in still another civil rights group. As the coordinator of the 1960 Nonviolent Resistance to Segregation Leadership Conference, which brought together over 300 student sit-in leaders and resulted in the formation of the Student Nonviolent Coordinating Committee (SNCC), Baker is credited with playing a major role in SNCC's founding. Severing a formal relationship with SCLC, she worked with the Southern Conference Educational Fund. In recognition of her contribution to improving the quality of life of southern blacks and to the founding of the Mississippi Freedom Democratic party, Ella Baker was asked to deliver the keynote address at its 1964 convention in Jackson, Miss.

Currently, Ella Baker resides in New York City, where she serves as an advisor to a number of community groups. Prior to the recent release of the film *Fundi: The Story of Ella Baker*, few people outside of the civil rights movement in the South knew about Baker's long career as a civil rights activist. She is probably less well known than many other civil rights workers because she was a woman surrounded by southern men, primarily ministers, who generally perceived women as supporters rather than as leaders in the movement, and because of her own firm belief in group-centered rather than individual-centered leadership.

See also BLACK LIFE: / National Association for the Advancement of Colored People; Southern Christian Leadership Conference; Student Nonviolent Coordinating Committee.

Sharon Harley
University of Maryland

Ellen Cantarow and Susan Gushee O'Malley, *Moving the Mountain: Women Working for Social Change* (1980); Clayborne Carson, *In Struggle: SNCC and the Black Awakening of the 1960s* (1981); Transcript of a Recorded Interview with Miss Ella Baker, 19 June 1968, The Civil Rights Documentation Project, Moorland Spingarn Research Center, Howard University, Washington, D.C.

Bankhead, Tallulah

(1902–1968) Actress.

Born in Huntsville, Ala., 31 January 1902, Tallulah Bankhead, actress and legend, dazzled outraged audiences in a career spanning 50 years, 51 plays, 18 films, numerous radio and television appearances, lectures, and nightclub extravaganzas. Her name, like her image, evoked contradictions. Bankhead stood for a respected Alabama family engaged in national and state Democratic politics. Tallulah remained conscious of her southern heritage and family position while transforming her given name into a synonym for flamboyance and excess.

Bankhead was a well-mannered belle who expected to be treated as a lady, yet she threw temper tantrums, drank to excess, and used drugs. To say her speech was scatological is an understatement. Married once to actor John Emery, from 1937 to 1941, she was first seduced by and then

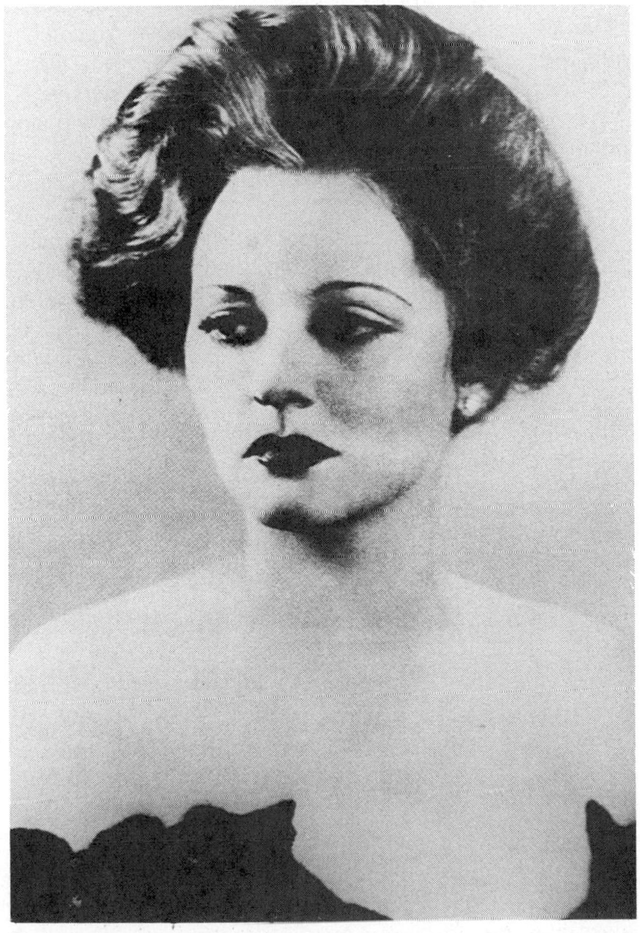

Tallulah Bankhead, Alabama-born actress

seduced untold numbers of men and women. Nevertheless, she prudishly rejected plays that Tennessee Williams wrote with her in mind because the language and the conjunction of sex and religion were objectionable.

Although her career was chronicled and celebrated, it was not always illustrious. From the moment she arrived in New York in 1917 at the age of 15, Tallulah discovered that it was more difficult to find satisfactory roles than it was to exploit her beauty and boldness to gain notoriety as a flapper in the postwar era. The vivacious rebel captivated London, where she lived from 1923 to 1931. Although the social, political, and artistic elite there pursued her, working-class young women constituted the fanatical cult that made Bankhead's mediocre plays box-office successes.

Bankhead's attempt to repeat her London triumphs in Hollywood in the early 1930s resulted in six forgettable films with such titles as *Tarnished Lady* and *My Sin*. The studios foolishly promoted this child/woman as a femme fatale à la Dietrich while criticizing her offscreen antics as offensive. Hollywood failed to provide the desired critical and financial success, and the role of Scarlett O'Hara went to a younger woman.

Not until the 1940s did Tallulah win acclaim and awards for her performances in two plays and one film: in *The Little Foxes*, as Regina Giddens; in *The Skin of Our Teeth*, playing Sabina; and in Alfred Hitchcock's *Lifeboat*. A two-year stint, beginning in 1950, as the mistress of ceremonies of *The Big Show* on NBC radio completed what 30 years of performance and press coverage had begun. Her first name, husky voice, and the word "Dahling," an appellation for both intimates and strangers, were recognized as the unofficial trademarks of a major personality known nationally and internationally.

During the last 20 years of her life, Tallulah Bankhead increasingly exploited, and was victimized by, the tension between being a legend and being a professional actress. The Tallulah persona had always been inclined to dominate any character she attempted to represent. In her later years she fell back on self-caricature, disrupting serious performances with a camp version of "Tallulah, Dahling," incited by a new cult following composed primarily of gays. Thus, when she finally attempted to render Tallulah-inspired protagonists in Tennessee Williams's *A Streetcar Named Desire* and *The Milktrain Doesn't Stop Here Anymore*, it was too late. The legend had eclipsed the actress and woman.

Ida Jeter
Saint Mary's College of California

Tallulah Bankhead, *Tallulah* (1952); Brendan Gill, *Tallulah* (1972); Lee Israel, *Miss Tallulah Bankhead* (1972).

Carter, Lillian

(1898–1983) Public figure.

Born in Richland, Ga., on 15 August 1898, Lillian Jackson Carter was the daughter of James Jackson, a Richland postmaster from whom she inherited an active interest in social justice and liberal politics. She remembers, for example, her father bringing meals from the local hotel, which served whites only, to blacks who waited at the post office.

In 1923 Jackson married James Earl Carter. The Carters had four children: James Earl, Jr.; Gloria; Ruth; and William Alton. A trained nurse, Lillian Carter worked in a Plains, Ga., hospital during the 1920s and 1930s, helped with the Carter family business, served as housemother to an Auburn University fraternity during the 1950s, later managed a nursing home, and served in the Peace Corps in India from 1966 to 1968. In 1978 she and Gloria Carter Spann published *Away from Home: Letters to My Family*.

Devotion to family characterized Lillian Carter. She never disguised her ambitions for Jimmy Carter nor her pride in his accomplishments. She campaigned for his elections, from the Georgia Legislature to the presidency. She had earlier helped in her husband's race for the state legislature. When James Earl Carter died in 1953, she was offered his legislative seat but declined. She later claimed that she might have accepted had she not been so grief stricken.

A staunch supporter of civil rights, Lillian Carter stood firmly with the national Democratic party throughout the 1960s. In 1964 she served as cochairman of President Lyndon Johnson's Americus, Ga., campaign office and suffered harassment for her leadership. In explaining her actions, Lillian stated: "I just couldn't stand to see a Negro mistreated." In 1977 the Synagogue Council of America awarded her its Covenant of Peace award, and in 1980 she was named honorary chairman of the Peace Corps National Advisory Council. Religious but not puritanical, Lillian Carter preferred small-town life, hated to dress up, liked bourbon, and admitted that the only luxury she wanted was "a good-looking car." She died of cancer in Americus–Sumter County hospital at the age of 85.

Julia Kirk Blackwelder
University of North Carolina
at Charlotte

Good Housekeeping (April 1977); *Ms.* (October 1976); *Newsweek* (4 and 26 July 1976); *New York Times* (1977–80); *Redbook* (October 1976); *Time* (3 January, 28 February 1976); *Who's Who of American Women*, 12th ed. (1981–82).

Carter, Rosalynn

(b. 1927) Former first lady of the United States.

Like First Lady Eleanor Roosevelt, Rosalynn Smith Carter played a major role in national affairs during her tenure in the White House. Since then, she has acted as a partner in many of former President Jimmy Carter's political and business endeavors, and she has strongly promoted mental health and women's rights issues. Her au-

Rosalynn Carter, First Lady of the United States, 1977–81

tobiography, *First Lady from Plains* (1984), has been warmly received by political analysts and literary critics.

Born in Plains, Ga., 18 August 1927, Rosalynn Smith enjoyed a relatively carefree childhood until her father died of leukemia when she was 13. The following years were lean ones for her family; her mother, Allie Smith, was forced to make ends meet by taking in sewing and selling extra eggs and butter from the family's farm. Rosalynn helped her mother by working part-time after school in a beauty salon. After her graduation from Plains High School as valedictorian of her class, Rosalynn Smith entered Georgia Southwestern College, a two-year college in Americus, Ga. In 1944 while visiting her best friend, Ruth Carter, Rosalynn spied and admired a picture of Ruth's brother Jimmy, a U.S. Naval Academy student. The couple married two years later. Ambitious and intelligent, she viewed her husband's naval career as her ticket out of Plains. Jimmy Carter's career took the young couple as far as Hawaii before his father died in 1953, when he resigned his commission to return to Plains to take over the family peanut business. Although she opposed his decision to return to Plains, Rosalynn Carter soon plunged into keeping books for the business, raising her family, and, eventually, taking accounting courses.

Politics has been the lifeblood of the Carter family. Rosalynn Carter's first taste of public life occurred in the early 1960s during her husband's membership on the local schoolboard. His liberal political stances often brought threats to her family and the peanut business from area residents. In Jimmy Carter's 1962 bid for the Georgia state senate Rosalynn Carter handled all of his campaign correspondence. By 1970, when Carter was elected governor of Georgia, she had gained experience and, thereby, a reputation as a "steel magnolia"—a warm, gracious woman who was also politically astute. Eager to move beyond the boundaries of the governor's mansion, she worked with the Georgia Governor's Commission to Improve Service for the Mentally and Emotionally Handicapped, as a volunteer at the Georgia Regional Hospital in Atlanta, and as honorary chairman of the Georgia Special Olympics; over the next four years she helped establish 134 day-care centers for the mentally retarded.

From 1973 to 1976 Rosalynn Carter campaigned independently in 96 cities and 36 states in Governor Carter's bid for the presidency. Once the Carters reached the White House, the new first lady took an active interest in national policymaking, attending Cabinet meetings, holding weekly working lunches with President Carter, heading a diplomatic mission to South America, and attending the Camp David Mideast Peace Summit. She continued to pursue mental health reform on a national level while serving on the President's Commission on Mental Health and on the Board of Directors of the National Association of Mental Health. Her support of the Equal Rights Amendment won her a merit award from the National Organization for Women.

Rosalynn Carter again took to the campaign trail in President Carter's reelection drive of 1980. His defeat was particularly devastating for her; after two decades of public service she initially found it difficult to adjust to private life. Since her return to Plains she has renewed her focus on mental health and women's rights. Numerous speaking engagements and promotions of her autobiography have allowed Rosalynn Carter to talk publicly and candidly about her life as first lady and to raise social and political issues of concern to her.

Elizabeth McGehee
Salem College

Patricia A. Avery, *U.S. News and World Report* (25 June 1984); Rosalynn Carter, *First Lady from Plains* (1984); Phil Gailey, *New York Times Book Review* (15 April 1984); Charles Moritz, ed., *Current Biography* (1978); *Who's Who in America*, 11th ed. (1980–81).

Chesnut, Mary Boykin

(1823–1886) Diarist and author.

Mary Boykin Miller Chesnut was born 31 March 1823 in Stateboro, S.C., eldest child of Mary Boykin and Stephen Decatur Miller, who had served as U.S. congressman and senator and in 1826 was elected governor of South Carolina as a proponent of nullification. Educated first at home and in Camden schools, Mary Miller was sent at 13 to a French boarding school in Charleston, where she remained for two years broken by a six-month stay on her father's cotton plantation in frontier Mississippi. In 1838 Miller died and Mary returned to Camden. On 23 April 1840 she married James Chesnut, Jr. (1815–85), only surviving son of one of South Carolina's largest landowners.

Chesnut spent most of the next 20 years in Camden and at Mulberry, her husband's family plantation. When James was elected to the Senate in 1858, his wife accompanied him to Washington where friendships were begun with many politicians who would become the leading figures of the Confederacy, among them Varina and Jefferson Davis. Following Lincoln's election, James Chesnut returned to South Carolina to participate in the drafting of an ordinance of secession and subsequently served in the Provisional Congress of the Confederate States of America. He served as aide to General P. G. T. Beauregard and President Jefferson Davis, and he achieved the rank of general. During the war, Mary accompanied her husband to Charleston, Montgomery, Columbia, and Richmond, her drawing room always serving as a salon for the Confederate elite. From February 1861 to July 1865 she recorded her experiences in a series of diaries, which became the principal source materials for her famous portrait of the Confederacy.

Following the war, the Chesnuts returned to Camden and worked unsuccessfully to extricate themselves from heavy debts. After a first abortive attempt in the 1870s to smooth the diaries into publishable form, Mary Chesnut tried her hand at fiction. She completed but never published three novels, then in the early 1880s expanded and extensively revised her diaries into the book now known as *Mary Chesnut's Civil War* (first published in truncated and poorly edited versions in 1905 and 1949 as *A Diary From Dixie*).

Although unfinished at the time of her death on 22 November 1886, *Mary Chesnut's Civil War* is generally acknowledged today as the finest literary work of the Confederacy. Spiced by the author's sharp intelligence, irreverent wit, and keen sense of irony and metaphorical vision, it uses a diary format to evoke a full, accurate picture of the South in civil war. Chesnut's book, valued as a rich historical source, owes much of its fascination to its juxtaposition of the loves and griefs of individuals against vast social upheaval and much of its power to the contrasts and continuities drawn between the antebellum world and a war-torn country.

Elisabeth Muhlenfeld
Florida State University

Elisabeth Muhlenfeld, *Mary Boykin Chesnut: A Biography* (1981); C. Vann Woodward, ed., *Mary Chesnut's Civil War* (1981), with Elisabeth Muhlenfeld, eds., *The Private Mary Chesnut: The Unpublished Civil War Diaries* (1985).

Chopin, Kate

(1851–1904) Writer.

Although Katherine O'Flaherty Chopin was a native of St. Louis (born 8 February 1851) and spent barely 14 years in Louisiana, her fiction is identified with the South. At 19, Kate O'Flaherty married Oscar Chopin, a young cotton broker, and moved with him to New Orleans and later to his family home in Cloutierville, La., near the Red River. After Oscar died in 1882, she returned with their six children to St. Louis; but when, eight years later, she began to write, it was the Creoles and 'Cadians of her Louisiana experiences that animated her fiction.

Distinctly unsentimental in her approach, she often relied on popular period motifs, such as the conflict of the Yankee businessman and the Creole, a theme that informs her first novel, *At Fault* (1890), and several of her short stories. These vivid and economical tales, richly flavored with local dialect, provide penetrating views of the heterogeneous culture of south Louisiana. Many of them were collected in *Bayou Folk* (1894) and *A Night in Acadie* (1897). Chopin's second novel, *The Awakening* (1899), also strongly evokes the region, but is primarily a lyrical, stunning study of a young woman whose deep personal discontents lead to adultery and suicide. Praised for its craft and damned for its content, the novel was a scandal, and Chopin, always sensitive to her critics, gradually lost confidence in her gift and soon ceased to write.

Chopin died of a brain hemorrhage after a strenuous day at the St. Louis World's Fair, where she had been a regular visitor. She was remembered only as one of the southern local colorists of the 1890s until *The Awakening* was rediscovered in the 1970s as an early masterpiece of American realism and a superb rendering of female experience.

Barbara C. Ewell
Loyola University

Barbara C. Ewell, *Kate Chopin* (1986); Per Seyersted, *Kate Chopin: A Critical Biography* (1969); Peggy Skaggs, *Kate Chopin* (1985); Marlene Springer, *Edith Wharton and Kate Chopin: A Reference Guide* (1976).

Durr, Virginia

(b. 1903) Social reformer.

Born on 6 August 1903, Virginia Foster Durr spent childhood summers on her grandmother's plantation in Union Springs, Ala., where antebellum customs were preserved virtually intact. Her father had been destined to inherit the mantle of the slaveowning aristocracy; instead he was reduced to genteel poverty, first as a Presbyterian minister, then as an insurance salesman in Birmingham. Although an inheritance from her grandmother eventually allowed the family to pursue a fashionable social life in Birmingham, they were never altogether secure. "You see," she recalls, "we lived in this half way stage between being benevolent despots . . . and trying to make a living . . . and the poorer we got, the more snobbish we became." By the time she reached adolescence, Virginia Foster had absorbed the lessons of ladyhood: the sexual inhibitions, aristocratic pretensions, and racial taboos that went along with good manners and noblesse oblige.

The events of the 1920s and 1930s, however, exposed what Durr calls "the contradictions, the total contradictions" in her parents' world and set her on a profoundly different path. In 1920 she went North for two years of college at Wellesley where, for the first time, she met black students as equals. In 1926 she married a young lawyer named Clifford Judkins Durr; a year later their first daughter was born. Working for the Red Cross and the Junior League during the Depression, Virginia saw Birmingham's unemployed iron ore and steel workers "literally starving to death" because the city fathers refused to provide adequate relief.

Meanwhile, Virginia Durr's sister Josephine had married Hugo Black, who was elected to the U.S. Senate in 1920 and appointed to the Supreme Court in 1936. Black's recommendation helped Clifford secure a job in Washington, where he became assistant general counsel of the Reconstruction Finance Corporation and then a member of the Federal Communications Commission (FCC). In Washington, the Durrs joined a lively circle of like-minded young southerners. She had four more children during these years and reveled in the excitement of the early New Deal. Attending the La Follette Committee hearings on antilabor violence in Birmingham, her compassion for the poor turned to outrage at the Tennessee Coal and Iron Company, the U.S. Steel subsidiary that dominated her hometown. After the death of her only son, she became increasingly involved in politics in her own right, first in the Woman's National Democratic Committee and then in the Southern Conference for Human Welfare (SCHW).

Virginia Durr was a founding member of the SCHW and director of its Washington Committee, the most vital of its local organizations. The committee raised funds, united the capital's southern contingent for action on issues affecting the South, and conducted a vigorous congressional lobbying campaign. As executive vice-president of the National Committee to Abolish the Poll Tax, she helped lay the groundwork for eliminating a major device by which blacks and poor whites were barred from the polls.

The postwar years brought a swing to the right and the beginning of the Cold War. In the 1948 presidential campaign Virginia Durr left the Democratic party to serve on Henry Wallace's platform committee and to run for governor of Virginia on the Progressive party ticket. Clifford refused reappointment to the FCC because of his objections to President Harry Truman's loyalty program. Smeared as a "Communist sympathizer," he soon gave up his effort to practice law in the capital and moved to Denver to take a job with the Farmers Union. When Virginia Durr signed a petition critical of the Korean War, Clifford was forced to leave that job, too. Reluctantly, the Durrs moved back to Alabama, where Clifford established a law practice in Montgomery and Virginia worked as his secretary.

Living with Clifford's parents in Montgomery, then moving to their own home in Wetumpka, the Durrs struggled to overcome their isolation and integrate themselves into the community they had left two decades before. In 1954, however, Virginia was pulled back into the political limelight when she was subpoenaed to appear at Senate Internal Security Commission hearings, presided over by Mississippi's James Eastland, on Communist influence in the Southern Conference Education Fund (an offshoot of the SCHW). A year later the civil rights movement began in earnest when Rosa Parks, a friend of the Durrs and a longtime stalwart of the NAACP, set the Montgomery bus boycott in motion. "It was a terrifically thrilling period," Virginia Durr recalls. "I wouldn't have missed it for anything." Clifford took civil rights cases. Virginia joined Dorothy Tilley's "Fellowship of the Concerned" and published articles on the movement. The Durr home became a mecca for lawyers, journalists, and civil rights workers. In the late 1960s Virginia brought her political experience to bear once more in the Alabama National Democratic party, founded in opposition to the George Wallace-controlled regular Democrats.

Rosa Parks, Virginia Durr once observed, is "a remarkable woman . . . really what you would call the perfect Southern lady." And so, to be sure, is Virginia Foster Durr. Peeling away ladyhood's repressive conventions, she has kept its informing spirit: gracious, generous, and attuned to the nuances of individual lives even as she pursued justice and gloried in the rough and tumble of a political fight. In that sense she is part of a little-known tradition—the southern lady as radical, embodying the past while fighting for a different future.

See also SOCIAL CLASS: / Southern Conference for Human Welfare

Jacquelyn Dowd Hall
University of North Carolina
at Chapel Hill

Hollinger F. Barnard, ed., *Outside the Magic Circle: The Autobiography of Virginia Foster Durr* (1985); Virginia Durr Papers, Schlesinger Library, Radcliffe College; Tom Gardner, *Southern Exposure* (Spring 1981); Sue Thrasher and Jacquelyn Dowd Hall, Southern Oral History Program, University of North Carolina, Chapel Hill, 1975.

Edelman, Marian Wright

(b. 1939) Civil rights lawyer.

Marian Wright Edelman is founder and president of the Washington, D.C.-based Children's Defense Fund. Born 6 June 1939 to a Bennettsville, S.C., Baptist minister and his wife (who also raised her four brothers, her sister, and 14 foster children), Edelman in 1983 was named by *Ladies' Home Journal* one of the "100 most influential women in America." In 1985 she received a MacArthur Foundation award of $228,000 which she promptly devoted to her Children's Defense Fund to make the needs of children—especially poor children—a top priority on America's agenda. She is a voice for children who cannot vote, lobby, or speak out for themselves. Edelman is concerned with every aspect of childhood health and education, infant mortality, teenage pregnancy, and child abuse. Her work graphically details the effect of poverty on the minds and future of America's children.

Awards and accolades for Marian Wright Edelman have cascaded in a steady stream since her undergraduate days at Spelman College in Atlanta, where a Merrill Scholarship afforded her a year's study at the universities of Paris and Geneva. She now serves as chair of Spelman's Board of Trustees.

In the intervening years, she has fulfilled her early promise as one of *Mademoiselle* magazine's "four most exciting young women in America" (1965) and as *Vogue*'s "Outstanding Young Woman of America (1965–66)." During those years, many pieces of civil rights legislation were forged under the force of her determination and penchant for detail. Her brilliant congressional testimony, her lobbying for and drafting of legislation, and her highly focused intellect and energy led former Vice President Walter Mondale to call Marian Wright Edelman "the smartest woman I have ever met."

Marian Wright grew up in a close-knit southern family, for whom civil rights represented an American ideal. Her father's final days in 1954 were spent with a radio at his side, listening to news of the school desegregation decision (*Brown* v. *Board of Education*) being argued before the Supreme Court. His last words to Marian, a week before the decision came down, were, "Don't let anything get between you and your education."

Edelman graduated from Spelman as valedictorian in 1960, won a John Hay Whitney Fellowship to Yale University Law School, received her LL.B. in 1963, and joined the NAACP Legal and Education Defense Fund as staff attorney in New York. From 1964 to 1968 she served as director of the Fund's Jackson, Miss., office, where in 1965 she became the first black woman admitted to the Mississippi Bar.

In Mississippi during the thick of the civil rights movement, she organized Head Start programs throughout the state for the Child Development Group of Mississippi (CDGM) and developed a keen awareness of the effect of poverty and hunger on the lives of young children. Her advocacy drew national attention to children suffering from hunger and malnutrition in America. As a Field Foundation Fellow and partner in the Washington research project of the Southern Center for Public Policy, she became a principal architect of and successful lobbyist for the Food Stamp Act of 1970. That year she became an honorary fellow at the University of Pennsylvania Law School and won the Louise Waterman Wise Award. In 1971 *Time* magazine named her one of 200 outstanding young American leaders. From 1971 to May 1973 she served as director of the Center for Law and Education at Harvard University—a position she left to form the Children's Defense Fund.

Edelman's research on the plight of children in America is quoted in the major media, cited by congressional committees, and used in state and federal programming. She is the author of three books, *Children Out of School in America* (1974), *School Suspensions: Are They Helping Children?* (1975), and *Portrait of Inequality: Black and White Children in America* (1980), all published by the Children's Defense Fund, as well as numerous articles and scholarly papers.

Mary Lynn Kotz
Washington, D.C.

Harry A. Ploski and James Williams, eds., *The Negro Almanac* (1983); *Psychology Today* (June 1975); *Who's Who in America*, 43d ed. (1984–85); *Who's Who in Black America*, 4th ed. (1985).

Family Reunions

"Next week be the fourth of July and us plan a big family reunion outdoors here at my house," says Celie, the main character in Alice Walker's *The Color Purple*. On the day of the reunion family members analyze the custom this way: "'Why us always have family reunion on July 4th,' say Henrietta, mouth poke out, full of complaint. 'It so hot.'" . . . "'White people busy celebrating they independence from England July 4th,' say Harpo, 'so most black folks don't have to work. Us can spend the day celebrating each other.'" Among the other attendees are two women who sip lemonade and make potato salad, noting that barbecue was a favorite food for them even while they were in Africa. The reunion day is especially joyful for the two women, who had been thought lost until their appearance at the reunion, where they are joyfully reunited with Celie and the other family members.

Southern family reunions are characteristic of extended and elaborated families, who plan the occasions around celebration, abundant good food, shared reunion

Dinner on the grounds, Houston, Miss., 1967

responsibilities, simple recreational activities, and, above all, talk.

Although summer is the most popular season and the Fourth of July a popular date for family reunions for both black and white southern families, family reunions can happen at any time. Some families have them annually, others have them on a schedule best described as "every so often," and still others have them only once or twice in a generation's lifetime, depending on some member's initiative in getting the reunion organized.

Like the indefinite date for family reunions, there is an inexactness as to who constitutes "family" for each gathering. Some families invite only the descendants of a given couple and those descendants' spouses and children. Others invite the eldest couple's brothers and sisters and their children plus in-laws and some of the in-laws' relatives. Some gather households that have only a vague bond of kinship—those who are "like family" because of strong friendships. There is inevitably a logic of kinship and affection to each family reunion, and such a party is hard indeed to crash.

The impetus for a family reunion, if it is not an annually scheduled event, may be a late-decade birthday party for one family member, a holiday, a wedding anniversary, or the celebration of an achievement such as paying off a home mortgage. Sometimes a family holds a reunion for a homecoming of one of its members, as in Eudora Welty's novel *Losing Battles*, which is a family reunion story focused around the day a son and husband return from a stay at Parchman, the Mississippi state prison.

Families often gather in someone's home, though summer picnic versions are commonly held in state or city parks. Motels, hotels, or restaurants host them, as do club houses or community centers, but by far the most popular settings after homes are churches. "Dinner-on-the-grounds" in the churchyard, with food burdening tablecloth-covered makeshift tables set on sawhorses, is a happy memory of family reunions in the minds of many southerners.

The occasion for catching up on the relatives' news and gossip, perhaps for transacting a little family business, for settling or even stirring up family disputes, and for generally getting in touch again, a family reunion in the South usually has no program. There might be an occasional game or swim or boat ride, but the main activities are conversation and eating. The time span may be overnight or even several days, but it is most frequently only over one meal.

The food might be barbecue with baked beans and coleslaw or fried fish with hush puppies, fried potatoes, and a salad. A restaurant meal might be ordered, but in a great many cases family reunion food is a large and generous potluck dinner where each participating household brings versions of its best offerings of food and drink—fried chicken, ham, meat casseroles, rice dishes, cooked garden vegetables, fresh raw vegetables, potato salad, gelatin salad, seafood salad, homemade rolls and breads, cakes, pies, cookies, jams, preserves, pickles, watermelons, iced tea, and lemonade. A time for eating, conversing, and sharing each other's company, a southern family reunion is a special occasion for reaffirming family ties.

Gayle Graham Yates
University of Minnesota

Alice Walker, *The Color Purple* (1982); Eudora Welty, *Losing Battles* (1970).

Gibson, Althea

(b. 1927) Tennis player.

Althea Gibson was the first black tennis player to win a major national tournament. She dominated women's tennis in 1957 and 1958 and was later elected to the National Lawn Tennis Hall of Fame (1971) and the Women's Sports Hall of Fame (1980).

Gibson was born in Silver, N.C., on 25 August 1927. Her parents, Daniel and Annie Washington Gibson, sharecropped cotton and corn. Seeking a better living, the family moved to New York City when Althea was three years old. When she was a schoolgirl, Gibson's success in city paddle tennis tournaments caught the attention of sponsors, who financed her tennis lessons. Her backers also arranged for Gibson to attend high school in Wilmington, N.C., where she competed on the black tennis circuit. From 1947 to 1956 Gibson won 10 straight national singles championships in competitions for black women sponsored by the American Tennis Association.

In 1953 Gibson graduated from Florida Agricultural and Mechanical University in Tallahassee and thereafter began her rapid rise in the U.S. Lawn Tennis Association. Her first invitations to important USLTA tournaments received nationwide comment because her participation integrated the previously all-white women's competitions.

Gibson became internationally known in 1956, when she won tennis titles in France, Great Britain, and Italy. The next year she was ranked as the number one woman tennis player in the United States. In 1957 and 1958 Gibson won the women's singles and doubles events at Wimbledon, England, as well as the women's singles championships in the United States. The Associated Press named her outstanding woman athlete for those years.

Gibson's autobiography, *I Always Wanted to Be Somebody*, was published in 1958. In it she recalled her father's fondness for the small, "three-store town" in South Carolina that he and his family left to go north. He always wanted to return there "and raise chickens on the old farm place." Gibson herself hesitantly returned south to attend high school, having heard stories of the terrible brutalities under Jim Crow segregation. Looking back on the experience, she wrote that "it wasn't a Ku Klux Klan nightmare like I'd been afraid it might be," but she "hated every minute of it" and determined "that I was never going to live any place in the South, at least not as long as those laws were in existence." Gibson won the women's professional singles championship in 1960 but subsequently focused on golf and toured as a professional golfer. She married William Darben in 1965. In 1975 Gibson became athletic commissioner of the state of New Jersey.

Lynn Weiner
Roosevelt University

Althea Gibson, *I Always Wanted to Be Somebody* (1958); *Who's Who of American Women, 1983–84* (1983).

Grimké Sisters

Sarah Grimké (1793–1874) and
Angelina Grimké (1805–1879). Abolitionists.

The Grimké sisters, Sarah and Angelina, were unique in the American antislavery movement. They were southerners, women, and members of a family known to own slaves. Sarah was born in 1793 and Angelina in 1805, the last of 11 Grimké children. Sarah virtually adopted her new baby sister, and they remained close throughout their lives. The Grimké family belonged to Charleston's elite upper class, whose children were reared in luxury and served by many slaves. They were city dwellers, but their large plantation in upper South Carolina and its numerous slaves were an important source of family wealth. The sisters' education in a select girls' academy stressing the social graces was slight and superficial. They were expected to marry well, bear children, and become successful matrons. However, the sisters lost interest in conventional life as each grew into adulthood.

Religion led them both to reject slavery. Though the Grimké family church was St. Philip's Episcopal, each sister, in her early twenties, experienced conversion in revivals of other churches. Sarah in time became a member of the Society of Friends, Angelina an enthusiastic Presbyterian. Sarah came to know Friends during her father's final illness. In 1821, following his death, she moved to Philadelphia and joined the Friends' Society. She accepted their firm tenet opposing slavery as a sin and eventually won her sister to the Quaker faith and the antislavery conviction. After her efforts failed to convert family and friends, Angelina left Charleston to make her home with Sarah in Philadelphia.

In early 1853 the more activist Angelina began to make contact with the antislavery movement. After William Lloyd Garrison published a letter of hers in the *Liberator*, Angelina began to write her first tract, *Appeal to the Christian Women of the South*. The American Anti-Slavery Society rushed it into print. The society then urged her to aid the cause by addressing women's groups in "parlor meetings"; Sarah went with her and remained at her side.

They were the only women asked to the "Convention of the Seventy," which met in October of 1836, for the training of new agents to spread abolitionism. Theodore Weld, whom Angelina later married, was the leader in the sessions and gave the sisters special training for their coming lecture tours. They went from this convention to their crowded "parlor meetings," held in churches, and they accepted invitations from other localities. They were swept into preparations for a forthcoming "Convention of American Anti-Slavery Women," held in March of 1837. When it ended, the Grimkés had come to know most of the abolitionist leaders in the East, men and women, and were themselves regarded as belonging to the circle of female leaders. The Grimkés arrived in Boston in May of 1837 and began their historic antislavery crusade. They also increasingly spoke out in favor of women's rights, despite criticism from antislavery leaders.

The spring months of 1838 saw Angelina Grimké's greatest triumphs. Twice in a crowded Massachusetts legislative hall she addressed a committee of the legislature, a sensational occasion headlined in the press. Also, Boston's antislavery women rented the Odeon Theater, and for five meetings, one a week, Angelina addressed an overflowing hall on abolition of slavery. In Philadelphia, she calmly addressed a mass meeting of a Convention of American Anti-Slavery Women with a threatening mob outside.

Angelina and Weld were married the day before the convention. When the sessions ended, Sarah accompanied them to their new home, and she stayed with them for the remainder of her life. Angelina fully expected to return to her work for the antislavery cause, but did not do so. She and Sarah assisted Weld on his best-known tract, *American Slavery as It Is* (1839). Three children were born between 1839 and 1844, two boys and a girl.

In the late 1850s both sisters taught in the Eagleswood School, which Weld headed. Later the family lived near Boston, where Weld and Angelina continued to teach. When war came in 1861, Angelina Grimké, at the age of 56, returned to part-time public life. Garrison had persuaded Weld to lecture again, this time in aid of the war effort. Angelina now rejoined her old friends in forming an organization, "Loyal Women of the Republic," and once again she was speaking for freedom of the slaves. Sarah was over 70 when the end of the war brought full emancipation. She died in 1874. Angelina suffered two strokes, the first in 1875, and was ill until her death in 1879.

Katherine Du Pre Lumpkin
Chapel Hill, North Carolina

Gerda Lerner, *The Grimké Sisters from South Carolina: Rebels against Slavery* (1967); Katherine Du Pre Lumpkin, *The Emancipation of Angelina Grimké* (1974); Weld-Grimké Collection, Clements Library, University of Michigan, Ann Arbor.

Jackson, Aunt Molly

(1880–1960) Labor activist and composer.

Aunt Molly Jackson is known for writing over 100 songs about the lives and struggles of Kentucky coal miners and their families. She was born Mary Magdalene Garland in Clay County, Ky., to Oliver and Deborah Robinson Garland in 1880. Her father was a coal miner, minister, and labor organizer. By the age of five Mary Garland was assisting her father at union meetings, leading picket lines, and composing songs. At 14 she married Jim Stewart, a coal miner. Within four years she had borne two children and completed training in nursing and midwifery—a career she would follow for the next 30 years.

Jim Stewart was killed in a mine rockfall in 1917. While married to her second husband, a miner named Bill Jackson, "Molly" Jackson was given the nickname "pistol packin' mama." She carried a gun for protection while traveling through the hills as a midwife and while riding to her husband's still, hidden deep in the mountains. Her husband's brother drafted a song about her that was later made into a popular hit.

During the early years of the Depression, while campaigning throughout Appalachia for the rights of coal miners, Jackson became widely known as "Aunt Molly." In 1931 she was "discovered" by a delegation (which included Theodore Dreiser and John Dos Passos) that visited Harlan County to investigate reports about starvation and the denial of civil liberties. Jackson, who had been blacklisted by the mine operators, was persuaded to come north and tour the country to raise funds for the miners. She first appeared before 21,000 people in New York City and eventually visited 38 states. Her impassioned speeches and songs widely publicized the labor struggles in Kentucky while raising thousands of dollars, which she sent south.

Aunt Molly Jackson was divorced from Bill Jackson in 1931. She later married Gustavos Stamos and settled in New York City by 1936. There she continued to eke out a living as a composer, working as a labor activist on behalf of industrial workers. She died in Sacramento, Ca., in 1960.

Aunt Molly Jackson's best-known songs include "Harlan County Blues," "Kentucky Miner's Wife's Hungry, Ragged Blues," and "I Am a Union Woman." Like other women composers of the South, including Florence Reece ("Which Side Are You On?"), Ella May Wiggins ("Mill Mother's Lament"), and Sarah Ogan Gunning ("I Am a Girl of Constant Sorrow"), Jackson is credited with boosting the morale of striking workers while bringing nationwide attention to the living and working conditions in the South. Jackson also contributed to the growing interest in American folk music, especially through her influence on the American composer Elie Siegmeister.

Lynn Weiner
Roosevelt University

Philip S. Foner, *Women and the American Labor Movement*, 2 vols. (1979–80); John Greenway, *American Folksongs of Protest* (1953); Edward Jablonski, *Encyclopedia of American Music* (1981); *New York Times* (3 September 1960).

Johnson, Lady Bird

(b. 1912) Former first lady of the United States and conservation advocate.

Claudia Alta Taylor Johnson was born on 22 December 1912 near Karnack, a small east Texas town. Her parents were Thomas Jefferson Taylor, a landowner and country storekeeper, and Minnie Lee Pattillo, both Alabama natives. Lady Bird, so named by a nursemaid, was the youngest of three children and the only daughter. When she was five her mother died and her Aunt Effie Pattillo, a genteel Alabamian, moved to "The Brick House," the family home in Karnack, to care for her. Lady Bird Taylor was educated in local public schools, graduating from Marshall High School in 1928. She attended St. Mary's Episcopal School for Girls in Dallas and then received two bachelor degrees (liberal arts and journalism) from the University of Texas at Austin. In 1934 she married Lyndon Baines Johnson, the secretary of a Texas congressman, after a two-month courtship. Washington, D.C., was home for the Johnsons almost continuously from 1934 until 1969. They had two daughters, Lynda Bird on 19 March 1944 and Luci Baines on 2 July 1947.

Lady Bird Johnson emerged as a public figure when her husband became vice president in 1961. As the nation's "second lady" she earned a reputation as a gracious hostess who skillfully combined superb good taste with down-home southern hospitality. Her role as national hostess and decorator was enlarged when she became first lady in November 1963. As a political helpmate she made a special appeal to the Deep South, which she traversed in a whistle-stop tour during her husband's campaign in 1964. Aware of the importance of her position, she began to record on tape aspects of her personal and public life; one-seventh of the resulting transcript has been published in the 800-page *A White House Diary* (1970). The journal is a testament to Lady Bird Johnson's keen sense of family, devotion to the principles espoused by her husband, and commitment to her own special concerns—national beautification, conservation, education, and children.

Lady Bird Johnson attributes her love of land, nature, and nation to her early years of growing up in the east Texas piney woods and Alabama cotton lands and to her later life in the Texas hill country, where the ancestral Johnson family home is located. For her First Lady's Committee for a More Beautiful Capital she tapped prominent architects, conservationists, and philanthropists who landscaped Washington with seasonal plantings and groves, refurbished memorials, and improved parks and school yards in the inner city. The Highway Beautification Act of 1965 translated into public policy her programs for control of billboards, the screening of junkyards, and highway plantings. Following the retirement of President Johnson in 1969 and his death in 1973, Lady Bird Johnson has devoted her time to her daughters and seven grandchildren and to her extensive holdings in Texas television and other media, begun in the 1940s with the purchase of station KTBC in Austin. She has continued to focus her public work on roadside beautification, conservation, and the arts.

In 1982 more than 100 historians who rated first ladies on the basis of their leadership, intelligence, value to country, and independence ranked Lady Bird Johnson third, following Eleanor Roosevelt and Abigail Adams.

See also POLITICS: / Johnson, Lyndon Baines

Martha H. Swain
Texas Woman's University

Elizabeth Carpenter, *Ruffles and Flourishes: The Warm and Tender Story of a Simple Girl who Found Adventure in the White House* (1970); Lady Bird Johnson Papers, Lyndon Baines Johnson Library, Austin, Tex.; Lady Bird Johnson, *Texas—A Roadside View* (1980), *A White House Diary* (1970); Ruth Montgomery, *Mrs. LBJ* (1965); Marie Smith, *The President's Lady: An Intimate Biography of Mrs. Lyndon B. Johnson* (1964).

Jordan, Barbara

(b. 1936) Lawyer and politician.

Barbara Charline Jordan holds the Lyndon B. Johnson Centennial Chair in National Policy, LBJ School of Public Affairs, the University of Texas at Austin. She first came to national prominence in November 1972 when she was elected to the U.S. House of Representatives from the 18th Congressional District in Houston, Tex. She and Andrew Young, who was elected that same year from Atlanta, Ga., were the first two blacks from the Deep South to win national office since the turn of the century.

Barbara Jordan, U.S. representative from Texas and educator, 1980s

Born 21 February 1936, the youngest of three daughters, to the Ben Jordans in Houston, Barbara Jordan grew up in a devoutly religious environment. Her parents and grandparents were lifelong members of the Good Hope Baptist Church in Houston's predominantly black Fifth Ward. As a child, she was a bright student with a natural flair for speaking. Her high school teachers encouraged her to develop her talent by participating in various oratorical contests. Although the Houston school system was segregated, the precocious youngster took many honors in citywide matches. She graduated magna cum laude from Texas Southern University and earned her law degree at Boston University in 1959.

Returning to Houston, the fledgling barrister worked three years before being able to open her law office, but the lure of politics was already beckoning her. She became active in the local Democratic party. In 1966, following redistricting, Barbara Jordan was elected to the Texas Senate, the first woman to win a seat in the upper chamber of that legislature. During her six years in the senate, she earned the admiration of her white male colleagues for her ability to get along well with others and to influence the passage of such legislation as the Texas Fair Employment Practices Commission, improvement of the Workmen's Compensation Act, and the state's first minimum wage law. In 1972 Barbara Jordan made history when the senate unanimously elected her president pro tempore. On 10 June 1972, in the traditional "Governor for a Day" ceremonies, she became the first black woman governor in U.S. history.

In 1971 her supporters in the state senate carved out a new congressional district to include a majority mixture of blacks and Hispanics. In November 1972 that electorate gave her a sweeping victory as their representative to Congress from the 18th District. She was assigned to the important House Judiciary Committee. In the wake of the scandals growing out of the Watergate break-in on 17 June 1972, the Senate Select Committee on Presidential Campaigning, under the chairmanship of Sam Ervin of North Carolina, began holding hearings in May of 1973. One year later, on 9 May 1974, the House Judiciary Committee under Peter Rodino opened impeachment hearings against President Richard Nixon.

During the House hearings, Barbara Jordan became a household name throughout America. As *Time* magazine said, "She voiced one of the most cogent and impassioned defenses of the Constitutional principles that emerged from the Nixon impeachment hearings." Opinion polls soon listed her as among the 10 most influential members of Congress, and Democratic party leaders chose her, along with Senator John Glenn, to give a keynote address to its 1976 national convention.

Always realistic, Barbara Jordan firmly resisted all efforts to draft her as a candidate for the vice-presidential nomination that year. She believed the country was not ready for such a development, although it was slowly inching toward the goal of equality in race relations. For personal reasons, Jordan retired from politics in 1978. She accepted a position as professor at the University of Texas. In 1982 she was one of the 100 professors honored with chairs established in commemoration of the centennial year of the institution. Barbara Jordan has left a legacy of great accomplishments in public service, both legislatively and personally. She resides today in Austin, Tex.

Ethel L. Payne
Washington, D.C.

Ira B. Bryant, *Barbara Charline Jordan: From the Ghetto to the Capitol* (1977); *Ebony* (February 1975); *Houston Post* (21 July 1976).

Lynn, Loretta

(b. 1937) Entertainer.

Country music is an essential accompaniment to contemporary images of the South and is the source for an emergent regional mythology. Loretta Lynn is a rural southerner who celebrates the traditional values of the South through her original compositions and her authentic folk style. She has created and portrayed the "coal miner's daughter," a popular myth of the working-class southern woman that may become as pervasive as the myth of the antebellum southern belle, Scarlett O'Hara.

Born in the small community of Butcher Holler, Ky., 14 April 1937, Loretta Lynn is the second of eight children born to Clara Butcher and Ted Webb. When she was 13, she married Mooney Lynn, a soldier who had recently returned from World War II. The first of her six children was born when she was 14, and she was a grandmother by 28. Loretta Lynn had been married over 10 years before she began singing for audiences other than her family. She was successful almost immediately after the release of her first record, "I'm a Honky Tonk Girl" (1960), which was her own composition. Neither the small recording company, Zero, nor the Lynns could finance promotion of "I'm a Honky Tonk Girl," so Loretta and Mooney mailed copies of the record, along with a short letter of explanation, to disc jockeys across the nation. When they realized that the record was a hit, the Lynns sold their home in Washington state and drove to Nashville in a 1955 Ford to sign a contract.

Since then, Loretta Lynn has released over 60 singles and 50 albums for Decca and MCA, including many of her own compositions. Based upon *Billboard*'s year-end charts of hit songs, her most successful singles have been "Success" (1962), "Wine, Women, and Song" (1964), "Blue Kentucky Girl" (1965), "Happy Birthday" (1965), "You Ain't Woman Enough" (1966), "Dear Uncle Sam" (1966), "If You're Not Gone Too Long" (1967), "Fist City" (1968), "You've Just Stepped In (From Stepping Out on Me)" (1968), "Woman of the World—Leave My World Alone" (1969), "That's a No, No" (1969), "You Want to Give Me a Lift" (1970), "I Know How" (1970), "I Wanna Be Free" (1971), "You're Looking at Country" (1971), "One's On the Way" (1972), "Rated X" (1973), "Hey, Loretta" (1974), "She's Got You" (1977), and "Out of My Head and Into My Bed" (1978). Loretta Lynn has won a number of awards, including a Grammy, 12 nominations and three awards from the Country Music Association for top female artist, two awards from *Record World*, three from *Billboard*, and four from *Cash Box*. In 1961 she received an award as "The Most Promising Female Artist" and by 1972 she had become the first woman to be honored as the Country Music Association's "Entertainer of the Year." In 1980 the album soundtrack of the film *Coal Miner's Daughter*, which featured Loretta's hit songs sung by actress Sissy Spacek, was named "Album of the Year" by the Country Music Association.

Loretta Lynn is popular regionally, nationally, and internationally. She received an honorable mention in the 1973 Gallup Poll list of the world's 10 most admired women. In addition to creating southern regional mythology, Loretta Lynn's lyrics and life history reflect the social history of working-class southern women and reinforce the American values of individualism, patriotism, and freedom. She embodies the American "rags to riches" story within a southern setting.

Ruth A. Banes
University of South Florida

Ruth A. Banes, *Canadian Review of American Studies* (Fall 1985); Dorothy A. Horstman, *Stars of Country Music*, ed. Bill C. Malone and Judith McCulloh (1975); Loretta Lynn with George Vecsey, *Coal Miner's Daughter* (1976); Vertical file on "Loretta Lynn," Country Music Foundation Library and Media Center, Nashville, Tenn.

Martin, Maria

(1796–1863) Painter and naturalist.

Maria Martin collaborated with John James Audubon in the production of *Birds of America*. Born in Charleston, S.C., the youngest of four daughters, little is known of her early life, although she appears to have been self-educated. Two events shaped her life: first, the marriage in 1816 of her sister, Harriet, to the Reverend John Bachman, amateur naturalist and Lutheran pastor of St. John's Church in Charleston, and second, a long friendship with Audubon.

After her marriage, Harriet Martin Bachman, who bore 13 children, secured the help of her sister, and by 1827 Maria Martin was living in the airy, verandaed Bachman home. After Harriet became a semiinvalid, her sister assumed the tasks of running the large house, including organizing and managing slaves. One of John Bachman's guests, John James Audubon, who visited Charleston in 1831, helped her develop her artistic talents.

Audubon taught Maria Martin to paint from life, and her natural but underdeveloped talent was sharpened until her skills as a painter of exquisite flowers, insects, butterflies, and landscapes became substantial. The flamboyant and often difficult Audubon began a collaboration with Martin in which she contributed backgrounds for the Audubon paintings. Audubon's vagueness in his attributions makes it unclear precisely which plates in the "Elephant folio" edition of *Birds of America* and in the Octavo edition published later contain her work. Audubon's *Ornithological Biography* credits her with 11 of the engravings in *Birds of America*, but she probably did more. Approximately 30 of the Octavo plates can be attributed to her. Audubon named "Maria's Woodpecker" (*picus martinae*) after her and he clearly considered her work superior.

In 1842 Audubon began illustrations for *The Vivaporous Quadrupeds of North America* for which Bachman would write the text. When John Bachman's eyesight failed, Maria Martin became what he called his "amanuensis." She measured and described specimens sent to them, took down Bachman's dictation, and edited it. "She corrects, criticises, abuses and praises," wrote Bachman. In 1846 Harriet Bachman died, and two years later John Bachman and Maria Martin married. From then until 1856, when she was incapacitated with paralysis of the right arm and subsequent failing health, Maria and John Bachman continued their work. Strong supporters of secession, the Bachman family fled to Columbia to avoid the fighting in the countryside, and soon after the Christmas of 1863 Maria Martin died there. She was buried in Ebenezer Church.

Martin's work was not publicly recognized, nor was the extent of her contributions to the understanding of southern flora and fauna realized, because of the circumstances of her life as a white southern woman. She combined within her character the elements of the southern lady, as set forth by tradition and contemporary mores, and an internal strength of will. She was supportive, dutiful, and reportedly good-tempered and amiable. Prevented from the public exercise of her talents and dependent upon others for her livelihood, Maria Martin's artistic abilities could only be pursued after the demands of her roles as housekeeper, aunt, and wife had been fulfilled. Despite these barriers, much knowledge of the natural environment of the antebellum South came from Maria Martin and her colleagues in Charleston.

See also ENVIRONMENT: / Audubon, John James

Marion Roydhouse
University of Delaware

C. L. Bachman, ed., *John Bachman D.D.* (1888); Annie Roulhac Coffin, *New-York Historical Society Quarterly* (January 1965); Howard Corning, ed., *Letters of John James Audubon, 1826–1840* (1930).

Mitchell, Martha

(1918–1976) Public figure.

Martha Elizabeth Beall Jennings Mitchell, a well-known and controversial figure in recent American politics, was born in Pine Bluff, Ark. Her mother, Arie Ferguson Beall, was the daughter of a prominent South Carolina and Arkansas business leader. Her father, George Virgil Beall, was a cotton broker who suffered financial reverses after the stock market crash of 1929 and deserted his wife and daughter. Because Arie Beall was busy as an elocution teacher and very active in local affairs, Martha Mitchell was reared by her black nurse, Mary Byas Walker, from whom she received constant love and attention.

Mitchell briefly attended Stephens College in Columbia, Mo., transferred to the University of Arkansas, and graduated from the University of Miami in 1942. After teaching school and serving as a Red Cross volunteer, she worked at the Pine Bluff Arsenal. In mid-1945 she was transferred to Washington, D.C., an event she later regretted: "I would have been all right if I'd never left the South."

She married Clyde Jennings, Jr., of Lynchburg, Va., in 1946 and bore a son, Clyde Jay Jennings, in 1947. The marriage ended in divorce after 11 years. In 1957 she married John Newton Mitchell, a successful Wall Street lawyer. After living in New York City and Darien, Conn., the Mitchells purchased a large mansion in Rye, N.Y. Martha Mitchell was a gracious and charming hostess who maintained a southern gentility and femininity in her dress and hairstyle. A daughter, Martha Elizabeth Mitchell, was born in 1961. In 1969 John Mitchell became presidential campaign manager for Richard M. Nixon. He was appointed attorney general upon Nixon's election.

Because she was open and frank about happenings in Washington, Martha Mitchell soon became a media celebrity much loved by Middle America for her forthright comments and genuine good humor. Following her husband's resignation as attorney general in 1972 to head the Committee for the Re-Election of the President, the Watergate burglary occurred. Martha Mitchell later claimed that she was drugged and forcibly prevented from speaking out concerning the involvement of high-ranking Nixon Administration officials in the affair. There followed a growing estrangement from her husband during which she resorted to liquor and drugs to allay her fears. She died of cancer in 1976. Her spontaneity, sense of humanity, and heroic efforts to alert the country to the danger of political repression were reflected in an anonymous floral tribute at her funeral in Pine Bluff that read: "Martha Was Right."

Dorothy D. DeMoss
Texas Woman's University

Winzola McLendon, *Martha: The Biography of Martha Mitchell* (1979); Jonas Robitscher, *Journal of Psychohistory* (Winter 1979); Helen Thomas, *Dateline: White House* (1975).

Mobley, Mary Ann

(b. 1939) Beauty queen and actress.

Mary Ann Mobley was born 17 February 1939 in Brandon, Miss., and grew up in a small town where her social life centered around church, school, and family. A childhood dream was to be a missionary. She had years of piano, dance, and voice lessons and won an academic award, the Carrier Scholarship, to the University of Mississippi. At the university she became involved in beauty contests. In 1956 Bing Crosby selected her the most beautiful among 40 contestants in the Ole Miss Parade of Beauties, and the following year actor Fred McMurray, the contest judge, ranked her among the top five beauties. Her first national beauty title was National College Football Queen of 1957. In 1959 she reached the pinnacle of the beauty contest world, winning the Miss America Pageant.

Southerners tend to take their beauty queens seriously and to see them as models. Mary Ann Mobley translated her beauty pageant fame into a career as an actress. Her Broadway debut was as an ingenue in the play *Nowhere to Go But Up*, a role she landed shortly after finishing her year as Miss America. She has appeared in off-Broadway productions of *Oklahoma*, *The King and I*, *Hello, Dolly*, and *Cabaret*. She went to Hollywood in the early 1960s, appearing with another Mississippian, Elvis Presley, in *Girl Happy*. Other movies followed; she was named one of the 10 stars of the future by the United Theater Owners of America and received a Golden Globe Award as the International Female Star of Tomorrow from the Hollywood Foreign Press in 1965.

Most recently, Mary Ann Mobley has appeared on television, ranging from frequent appearances on talk shows and game shows to a starring role in *Different Strokes*, where she plays the surrogate mother of two black children. Married to actor Gary Collins and mother of a daughter, Clancy, Mobley has been active in humanitarian causes such as the March of Dimes, United Cerebral Palsy Association, Exceptional Children's Foundation for the Mentally Retarded, and World Vision's feeding and medical centers around the world. A 1985 trip to Nairobi to shoot a documentary film on hunger in the Third World helped to dramatize that horror.

Brenda West
University of Mississippi

Jane Ardmore, *View Magazine* (8–14 February 1986); Mary Ann Mobley Collins file, Alumni Association, University of Mississippi.

Mary Ann Mobley, a Miss America from Mississippi, 1959

Newcomb, Josephine

(1816–1901) Philanthropist.

Josephine Louise Newcomb was the founder of H. Sophie Newcomb Memorial College, the first degree-granting college for women established within a previously all male major university. Born in Baltimore, Md., 31 October 1816, she was the daughter of Alexander Le Monnier, a prominent Baltimore businessman. Orphaned in 1831, Josephine Louise moved to New Orleans to live with her only sister. While summering in Louisville, Ky., she met and married Warren Newcomb, a successful businessman who lived in New Orleans most of the summer because his wholesale business was located there.

In 1866 Warren Newcomb died, leaving to his wife and a daughter, Harriott Sophie, born to the couple in 1855, an estate valued at between $500,000 and $850,000. Under her own direction Josephine Newcomb's inheritance increased to over $4 million by her death in 1901. In 1870, at age 15, Harriott Sophie died of diphtheria. Devastated by the loss of her child, Newcomb began to search for a suitable memorial to her daughter. An Episcopalian, she donated generously to the support of her church. A native southerner, she gave to numerous causes to assist the recovery of the war-torn South. She contributed to the library of Washington and Lee University. She founded a school for sewing girls and supported a Confederate orphans' home, both in Charleston, as well as a school for deaf children in New York. In 1886, at the behest of Ida Richardson, a wealthy New Orleans woman, and Colonel William Preston Johnson, president of the recently established Tulane University of Louisiana, Newcomb agreed to found a college for women as a memorial to her daughter.

Although coeducational colleges and independent women's colleges existed, the H. Sophie Newcomb Memorial College was a unique experiment, the design of which influenced Barnard at Columbia, Radcliffe at Harvard, and the Women's College of Western Reserve. Part of, and yet separate from, Tulane University, the college had a separate administration and faculty, empowered to formulate its own academic policy. The college's stated aim to offer a liberal arts education for women equal to that available for men represented a departure in the history of female education in the South. In an age when higher education for women was viewed with indifference, Josephine Louise Newcomb initiated significant change in the patterns of women's education.

See also EDUCATION: / Tulane University

Sylvia R. Frey
Tulane University

Brandt V. B. Dixon, *A Brief History of H. Sophie Newcomb Memorial College, 1887–1919* (1928); John P. Dyer, *Tulane: The Biography of a University, 1834–1965* (1966).

Parks, Rosa

(b. 1913) Civil rights activist.

The burden of 100 years of discrimination added to the weariness of a difficult day was just too much for the gentle black woman that early December day in 1955. Asked to give up her seat on a crowded Montgomery, Ala., bus to allow whites to sit down, Rosa Parks, once dubbed the civil rights movement's "most mannerly rebel," flatly refused.

Recalling that a year earlier a black teenager, Claudette Colbert, had been removed in handcuffs, kicking and screaming, for a similar offense, she felt sure the authorities would not repeat such a disgraceful performance. She was wrong. Summoned by the bus driver, the police arrested her and placed her in a cell with two other black women, one of whom would not speak to her. The other had attacked a man with an ax.

Born 14 February 1913 in Tuskeegee, Ala., Parks was one of two children, and the only daughter, of Leona Curlee. Her mother was born on a tenant farm in Montgomery County. Raised in Montgomery, Parks attended Alabama State College, then worked as a clerk and an insurance saleswoman before becoming a tailor's assistant at the Montgomery Fair Department Store, where she was employed when the bus incident occurred. A former secretary of the Montgomery chapter of the NAACP, Parks also served as a "stewardess" (an assistant at communion services) at that city's African Methodist Episcopal Church.

"Rosa Parks was just the right person at the right time," civil rights activist E. D. Nixon later remarked. Nixon, an old friend of Parks and former president of the Alabama NAACP, paid her bail and asked if she would be willing to serve as a test case to challenge the legality of Montgomery's segregation ordinances. After receiving the support of her husband Raymond, a barber at Maxwell Air Force Base, and her mother, she agreed and thereby stepped into history as the "mother of the civil rights revolution."

The real challenge to white supremacy came not from judicial action, however, but from the leadership of Martin Luther King, Jr., the 26-year-old pastor of the Dexter Avenue Baptist Church, who launched the year-long boycott of the bus system in Montgomery's black Protestant churches. The bus boycott, with its attendant violence on the part of the police and the white community and its hundreds of arrests, was the crucible from which King emerged as a nationally known leader.

After a 381-day boycott the bus company capitulated and ended segregation on the city's public transporation network. On 13 November 1956 the U.S. Supreme Court ruled that bus segregation was unconstitutional.

Fired from her job as a result of her notoriety, Parks worked as a volunteer for the Montgomery Improvement Association, which was formed to coordinate the bus boycott. In 1957 she moved to Detroit, where she is still employed by Representative John Conyers of Michigan. Parks's husband Raymond, whom she married in 1932, died in 1977. The couple had no children.

The catalyst that sparked the militant phase of the modern civil rights movement, Parks has often expressed embarrassment at the adulation she has received as the symbol of black resistance to injustice. Honored at the White House by President Jimmy Carter in February 1979, along with other notable elderly blacks including Jesse Owens and the Reverend Martin Luther King, Sr., she was also awarded the Martin Luther King, Jr., Nonviolent Peace Prize in Atlanta in January 1980. Detroit has named a street and a school after her. Rosa Parks embodies the idea of the individual who is willing to stand up and be counted.

Helen C. Camp
New York City

Ebony (November 1980); *Los Angeles Times* (15 January 1980); *New York Times* (6 December 1955; 5 April 1978; 14 February, 24 February, 25 November 1979; 15 January 1980; 5 June 1982); *Southern Exposure* (Spring 1981).

Parton, Dolly

(b. 1946) Entertainer.

Dolly Parton is often described as a contemporary "Cinderella," a fairy-tale princess, or a country gypsy—a platinum blonde heroine who escapes poverty in the foothills of the Great Smoky Mountains, achieves fame

Dolly Parton, country music singer and actress, 1987

and fortune in Nashville and later Hollywood, and lives happily ever after. More realistically, she is a talented and creative artist and businesswoman.

Dolly Parton was born 19 January 1946 in Locust Ridge in Sevier County, Tenn., the fourth of 12 children, to Avie Lee Owens and Randy Parton. Her grandfather Owens was a minister, and her early life with family and community centered around religion and the church. She learned to love storytelling, music, and singing, as well as to adhere to a rigid Christian moral code. Her mother sang the traditional folksongs she had learned from a harmonica-playing grandmother Owens. By the time she was five years old Parton was imagining lyrics and tunes, and when she was seven she had written her first song. An exceptionally intelligent child, Dolly Parton used the rich southern folk environment surrounding her to create poetry and music.

She began her singing career as a child on the Cas Walker Radio Show, broadcast from Knoxville, and she released her first record, "Puppy Love," in her early teens. At 18, after she graduated from high school, she moved to Nashville, and, despite a difficult beginning, which she describes in her song "Down on Music Row" (1973), she became a popular recording and television partner for country artist Porter Wagoner. Together, they recorded 13 albums and won awards for "Vocal Duo of the Year" in 1968, 1970, and 1971. In 1967 Dolly Parton released her first solo album, and since then, she has recorded over 30 albums for Monument and RCA. She has written and recorded hundreds of her own compositions, which are usually autobiographical songs, work songs, or sentimental, moralistic ballads, often sung in a traditional country style reminiscent of the Carter Family, an authentic southern folk group that was among the first to record country music during the early 20th century.

Based upon *Billboard*'s year-end hit charts, her most successful singles have been "Mule Skinner Blues" (1970), "Joshua" (1971), "Jolene" (1974), "I Will Always Love You" (1974), "The Seeker" (1975), "All I Can Do" (1976), "Here You Come Again" (1978), "Heartbreaker" (1978), "Two Doors Down" (1978), "You're the Only One" (1979), "Baby, I'm Burning" (1979), "Starting Over Again" (1980), and "But You Know I Love You" (1981). She was "Female Vocalist of the Year" in 1975 and 1976 and was the Country Music Association's "Entertainer of the Year" in 1978. In 1980 *Billboard* listed her among the top female artists in country music and *Dolly, Dolly, Dolly* and *Nine to Five* among the top albums.

Dolly Parton achieved celebrity status by appealing to both country and pop music audiences and by entering the fields of television, film, and freelance writing. She has been featured in numerous periodicals and has appeared on the cover of *Playboy* (1978), *The Saturday Evening Post* (1979), *Parade* (1980), and *Rolling Stone* (1980). In 1976 she became the first woman in country music history to acquire her own syndicated television show, and she has since starred in three films, *Nine to Five* (1981), *The Best Little Whorehouse in Texas* (1982), and *Rhinestone* (1984). She published a book of poems titled *Just the Way I Am* (edited by Susan P. Shultz, 1979) and is also writing a novel, *Wild Flowers*, for Bantam Books. Parton and Herchend Enterprises in 1986 opened Dollywood, a theme park based on Parton's life and located at Pigeon Forge, Tenn.

Dolly Parton has demonstrated the strength of a southern cultural and musical background, and she retains a loyalty to her homeplace and her people. The lyrics she writes in songs like "Jolene," "My Tennessee Mountain Home," and "Coat of Many Colors" portray strong women who hail from the working-class South. Moreover, in film, television, and music, Parton herself is a country woman with stamina, intelligence, independence, and a sense of humor. She has popularized the idea that mountain women in particular are not the stereotypical hillbillies viewed in comic strips or popular situation comedies, but rather complex, intelligent, articulate, and loving. Dolly Parton's music and personality will have a lasting impact upon popular images of women in the South.

Ruth A. Banes
University of South Florida

Chet Flippo, *Rolling Stone* (December 1980); Alanna Nash, *Dolly* (1978); *Playboy* (October 1978); Vertical files on "Dolly Parton," Country Music Foundation Library and Media Center, Nashville, Tenn.

Peterkin, Julia Mood

(1880–1961) Writer.

Julia Mood Peterkin was a southern writer best known for her sympathetic portrayals of black folklife in the

South Carolina Low Country, where she was born 31 October 1880. Her novel *Scarlet Sister Mary* won the Pulitzer Prize for literature in 1929.

Early reviewers focused on her depiction of black culture rather than on her literary techniques. Black intellectuals in particular, such as Countee Cullen, Langston Hughes, Paul Robeson, and Walter White, praised her avoidance of the racist stereotypes common at the time among white writers, North and South. W. E. B. Du Bois said of her, "She is a Southern white woman, but she has the eye and the ear to see beauty and know truth."

Scholars continue to find in her delineation of the worldview of a black community and in her depiction of its creole language, Gullah, a near-native sensitivity and richness of texture. She may, in fact, be regarded as a native speaker of the language. Raised by a Gullah-speaking nurse after the death of her mother, she wrote, "I learned to speak Gullah before I learned to speak English."

Folklorists have praised Peterkin's "primary knowledge" of Afro-American folk culture. Her explanation was that "I have lived among the Negroes. I like them. They are my friends, and I have learned so much from them."

The literary establishment, after its initial enthusiasm, ignored her writings for more than a generation. Not until the late 1970s were the literary aspects of her work—its scope and themes, characterization and narrative techniques—examined. Now literary scholars rank her fiction high, and recognize that she, like Joyce and Faulkner, was more interested in individual human beings in timeless and universal struggles than in local color. Although many of the incidents in her books she had personally witnessed on her plantation, Lang Syne (near Orangeburg, S.C.), the physical setting—Sandy Island, Heaven's Gate Church, and "Blue Brook" (Brookgreen) plantation—is often the Waccamaw region of Georgetown County, her summer home.

Peterkin's narrative technique grew out of the southern storytelling tradition (with the Gullah necessarily simplified to accommodate the limitations of her readers). She did not attempt, as did Hemingway, Dos Passos, Faulkner, and many of her other contemporaries, to borrow experimental styles from such modern European masters as Joyce. Unlike those of most writers, her male and female characters are equally well drawn and credible. Her vivid characterization owes much more to reality and the burdens of the immoderate past than to literary influences. There are no literary counterparts to her God-haunted, courageous, and compassionate black heroes and heroines—Scarlet Sister Mary, Black April, Cricket, Maum Hannah, and Killdee Pinesett, whom a modern critic calls "one of the most moving, one of the most admirable characters in modern fiction."

Among her most important works are the mythic *Green Thursday* (1924), a story-cycle like *Go Down Moses* and *Dubliners*; her classical tragedy *Black April* (1927), which has been called "perhaps her most powerful work of fiction"; her feminist comedy *Scarlet Sister Mary* (1928), whose sexually demanding heroine not merely endures but prevails over all men and circumstances; her lyrical but disappointing *Bright Skin* (1932); and her magisterial work of nonfiction, *Roll, Jordan, Roll* (1933).

See also LANGUAGE: Gullah

Charles Joyner
University of South Carolina,
Coastal Campus

Thomas H. Landess, *Julia Peterkin* (1976); Noel Polk, in *South Carolina Women Writers*, ed. James B. Meriwether (1979).

Pringle, Elizabeth Allston

(1845–1921) Plantation mistress.

Elizabeth Allston Pringle exemplified the resourcefulness of elite southern women during and after the Civil War. She was born 29 May 1845 near Pawley's Island, S.C., to Robert Allston, a successful rice planter and future governor of the state, and Adele Petigru Allston. In her memoir, *Chronicles of Chicora Wood,* Pringle devoted no fewer than 100 pages to her family background, demonstrating the concern with lineage and heritage characteristic of wealthy 19th-century southerners.

Initially taught at home by a governess, Pringle was sent at age nine to join her sister at a small, select Charleston boarding school, which "finished off" young ladies by teaching them the fine arts and French, as well as basic subjects. The Allstons displayed considerable ambivalence about the education of their daughters, insisting that the girls study at home during the summer, yet acknowledging that by age 16 "balls, receptions, and dinners" made it "impossible" for a young girl to "keep her mind on her studies." Elizabeth Pringle was too young to attend social events before the Civil War, but she recalled her sister's gowns and beaus and parties with keen interest.

The war, of course, was a central experience in Pringle's life. Through her youthful eyes, the excitement of seeing the men march off with banners waving was a dominant early impression. But she also recalled her father's death, the steady reduction in food and clothing, the looting of the family residence, and tense confrontations with the now-free blacks on the family's various plantations. Clearly Elizabeth Allston derived much of her later strength and independence from watching her mother cope with these trying circumstances and from facing up to them herself.

In the fall of 1865 Elizabeth Allston's mother decided to support herself by opening a school in Charleston. Initially afraid to teach, her daughter was ashamed of her weakness. "Am I really just a butterfly?" she asked herself. "Is my love of pleasure the strongest thing about me? What an awful thought." After three months of teaching, she was ecstatic about her work and confident in her abilities.

In 1868 she accompanied her family back to Chicora

Wood, where she married John Julius Pringle two years later. Her memoir is characteristically discreet on the subject of their relationship, but the marriage appears to have been a happy one until Pringle's untimely death in 1876. In a bold move, Elizabeth Pringle acquired her husband's plantation and elected to run it herself, growing rice, fruit, and raising livestock. When her mother died in 1896, she took over Chicora Wood as well. Thus, she became a substantial rice planter, a rare venture for a woman to undertake alone.

Elizabeth Allston Pringle pursued this occupation with vigor. She became deeply involved in agricultural techniques and in the often frustrating management of her workers. While she enjoyed years of prosperity, she succumbed to failure early in the 20th century, when severe weather and competition from other regions ruined many Low Country rice planters. But she voiced no regrets. "I have so loved the freedom and simplicity of the life, in spite of its trials and isolation," she asserted, noting too "the exhilaration of making a good income myself." In the last two decades before her death in 1921, she turned to writing, and her gracefully penned recollections add much to the understanding of southern womanhood and southern life during the important transitional period in which she lived.

Laura L. Becker
University of Miami

Patience Pennington, *A Woman Rice Planter* (1961); Elizabeth A. Pringle, *Chronicles of Chicora Wood* (1922).

Reece, Florence

(1907–1986) Writer and social activist.

Florence Reece is the author of several poems, short stories, and songs. A coal miner's daughter from Sharp's Chapel, Tenn., she is best known for her struggle song "Which Side Are You On?," written to rally support for the 1930 United Mine Workers' strike in Harlan County, Ky. No political ideologue, Reece wrote her song out of a sense of desperation when her husband, Sam, was blacklisted, beaten, and driven from their home because of his activities as a union organizer among his fellow miners. As she watched her children and others in the community suffer hunger and deprivation, Reece attempted to deal with her anger by writing these lyrics on the back of a calendar, reflecting the centuries-old southern folk tradition of articulating and simplifying complex personal and social problems through songs and storytelling. Along the picket lines across the South, her simple statement, rising out of a great frustration with the unfair exploitation of laborers and identifying the need for solidarity among all workers, quickly became a familiar chant sung to the tune of the old hymn, "I Am Going to Land On That Shore":

If you go to Harlan County
There is no neutral there.
You will either be a union man,
Or a thug for J. H. Blair.

Which side are you on?
Which side are you on?

Reece's militant assertion that the poor and the powerless "had to be for themselves, or against themselves" is the message that made "Which Side Are You On?" as meaningful to civil rights workers in Harlem during the 1960s as to the miners of Harlan County during the 1930s.

Reece, who came from the same impoverished section of Tennessee as Roy Acuff, continued to write prose and verse, finding her voice in the traditional themes of country and western music—motherhood, home, and country. In 1981 she published a collection of her work, *Against the Current*, which shows her abiding concern with social commentary and the problems of her people:

If you take away their food stamps,
And all their other means,
What're you going to feed them on?
They can't live on jelly beans.

Barbara L. Bellows
Middlebury College

John W. Hevener, *A New Deal for Harlan: The Roosevelt Policies in a Kentucky Coal Field, 1931–1939* (1978), *Which Side Are You On?: The Harlan County Miners, 1931–39* (1978); Loyal Jones, *Appalachian Journal* (Fall 1984).

Smith, Lillian

(1897–1966) Writer and social critic.

Internationally acclaimed as author of the controversial novel *Strange Fruit* (1944) and the autobiographical critique of southern culture *Killers of the Dream* (1949, rev. 1961), Lillian Eugenia Smith was the most outspoken white southern writer in areas of economic, racial, and sexual discrimination during the 1930s and 1940s. When other southern liberals—Ralph McGill, Hodding Carter, Virginius Dabney, and Jonathan Daniels—were charting a cautious course on racial change, Smith boldly and persistently called for an end to racial segregation. Furthermore, her work for social justice continued throughout her life. In 1955 she wrote *Now Is the Time* urging support for the Supreme Court's decision on school desegregation. Her last published book, *Our Faces, Our Words* (1964), reflects her personal knowledge and experience with the young black and white civil rights activists of the 1950s and 1960s.

Lillian Smith was born 12 December 1897, the seventh of nine children of Anne Hester Simpson and Calvin Warren Smith, and grew up in Jasper, Fla., where her father was a prominent business and civic leader. Some of the richness of that childhood is portrayed in *Memory of a Large Christmas* (1962). Her life as daughter of upper-class whites in the small-town Deep South ended rather abruptly when her father lost his turpentine mills in 1915 and moved the family to their summer home near Clayton, Ga. Financially on her own, Smith attended the nearby Piedmont College one year, was principal of a two-room mountain school, and helped her parents manage a hotel before she was able to pursue her interest in music. During the school terms of 1916–17 and 1919–22 she studied piano at Peabody Conservatory in Baltimore, spending summers working in the family's summer lodge and teaching music at Laurel Falls Camp for Girls, opened by her father in 1920.

In the fall of 1922 Smith accepted a three-year position as director of music at Virginia School in Huchow, China. But her ambitions for a career in music ended when her parents' ill health necessitated her return to direct Laurel Falls Camp. Under her direction from 1925 through 1948, the camp became an outstanding innovative educational institution, known for its instruction in the arts, music, theater, and modern psychology. It was also a laboratory for many of the ideas informing Smith's analysis of southern culture, especially her understanding of the effects of child-rearing practices on adult racial and sexual relationships.

Through the camp Smith also met Paula Snelling and began the lifelong relationship that encouraged and sustained her writing career. From 1936 to 1946 Smith and Snelling coedited a magazine, first called *Pseudopodia*, then *North Georgia Review*, and finally *South Today*, which quickly achieved acclaim as a forum for liberal opinion in the region.

A record-breaking best-seller, *Strange Fruit* was translated into 15 languages, banned for obscenity in Boston, and produced as a Broadway play. But *Killers of the Dream*, an even more insightful exploration of the interrelationship of race, class, and gender in southern society, brought strong criticism from more moderate southerners. Though widely reviewed, none of her subsequent works achieved the popularity or financial success of her first novel.

Her more philosophical works, *The Journey* (1954) and *One Hour* (1959), demonstrate the extent to which Smith's concerns extended beyond race relations to encompass all aspects of human relationships in the modern world. In *The Journey* she wrote, "I went in search of an image of the human being I could be proud of." *One Hour*, Smith's response to the McCarthy era, is a complex psychological novel about the inevitable destruction unleashed in a community when the reality and power of the irrational are unacknowledged in human life.

Two collections of her work have been published posthumously: *From the Mountain* (1972), a selection of pieces from the magazine, edited by Helen White and Redding Sugg; and *The Winner Names the Age* (1978), selected speeches and essays, edited by Michelle Cliff with an introduction by Paula Snelling.

See also MEDIA: / Carter, Hodding; Dabney, Virginius; Daniels, Jonathan; McGill, Ralph

Margaret Rose Gladney
University of Alabama

Louise Blackwell and Frances Clay, *Lillian Smith* (1971); Margaret Rose Gladney, *Southern Studies* (Fall 1983); Fred Hobson, *Tell about the South: The Southern Rage to Explain* (1983); Jo Ann Robinson, in *Notable American Women: The Modern Period*, ed. Barbara Sicherman and Carl Hurd Green (1980).

Walker, Maggie Lena

(1867–1934) Banker.

Walker, born 15 July 1867 in Richmond, Va., founded the Saint Luke Penny Savings Bank in Richmond in 1903, becoming the first woman bank president in the United States. Before her death she helped to reorganize it as the present-day Consolidated Bank and Trust Company, the oldest continuously existing black bank in the country. The bank, like most of Walker's activities, was the outgrowth of the Independent Order of Saint Luke, which she served as Right Worthy Grand Secretary for 35 years. Under her leadership this female-founded but previously male-run mutual benefit association established a juvenile department, an educational loan fund for young people, a department store, and a weekly newspaper. Growing to include 80,000 members in 2,010 Councils and Circles in 28 states, the order demonstrated a special commitment to expanding the economic opportunities within the community in the face of racism and sexism. It sought to develop interdependence among black women as a positive response to their problems and a step toward collective well-being.

Walker believed that black women had a "special duty and incentive to organize." And her work as a founder or leading supporter of the Richmond Council of Colored Women, the Virginia State Federation of Colored Women, the National Association of Wage Earners, the International Council of Women of the Darker Races, the National Training School for Girls, and the Virginia Industrial School for Colored Girls was a positive representation of that belief. Additionally, Walker and others of the Saint Luke women were instrumental in political activities of the black community including the struggle for women's suffrage, voter registration campaigns after the passage of the Nineteenth Amendment, and the formation of the Virginia Lily-Black Republican party, which nominated Walker for State Superintendent of Public Instruction in 1921. Throughout the 1920s Walker handled the finances of the National League of Republican Colored Women.

As a contributor to the ideological perspectives and political strategies of the black community, Walker symbolizes the growing belief in the early 20th century in economic development and self-help. All of her activities were motivated by a profound belief in the necessity to create an independent, self-sustaining community. Walker also helped direct the NAACP, the National Urban League, and the Negro Organization Society of Virginia.

Throughout her life and career this daughter of a washerwoman developed a distinct understanding of what it meant to be wife, mother, businesswoman, and female activist. It was this perspective that shaped her struggle to expand notions within the black community of the proper role of women and within the larger society of the proper place of blacks.

Elsa Barkley Brown
Emory University

Wendell P. Dabney, *Maggie Walker and the I.O. of Saint Luke: The Woman and Her Work* (1927); Sadie Iola Daniel, in *Women Builders*, ed. S. Daniel (1931); Maggie Lena Walker Papers, Maggie Walker National Historic Site, Richmond, Va.

Index of Contributors

General Index

Page numbers in boldface type refer to articles; page numbers in italic type refer to illustrations.

Picture Credits

Agriculture

Page
1 William Ferris Collection, Archives and Special Collections, University of Mississippi Library, Oxford
7 Ann Rayburn Paper Americana Collection, Archives and Special Collections, University of Mississippi Library, Oxford
9 Photographic Archives, University of Louisville (Kentucky)
11 Arthur Rothstein, Library of Congress (LC-USW-3-4061-D), Washington, D.C.
13 Gold Kist Corporation, Atlanta, Georgia
17 William Ferris Collection, Archives and Special Collections, University of Mississippi Library, Oxford
19 Georgia Department of Archives and History, Atlanta
25 William Ferris Collection, Archives and Special Collections, University of Mississippi Library, Oxford
26 Marion Post Wolcott, Library of Congress (LC-USF-34-53810D), Washington D.C.
29 Walker Evans, Library of Congress (LC-USF-342-8147-A), Washington, D.C.
36 Marion Post Wolcott, Library of Congress (LC-USF-51099F), Washington, D.C.
43 Jack Delano, Library of Congress (LC-USF-34-440054D), Washington, D.C.
49 Howard Odum Papers, Southern Historical Collection, University of North Carolina, Chapel Hill

Art and Architecture

51 Brooks Museum of Art, Memphis, Tennessee
57 National Trust for Historic Preservation, Washington, D.C.
59 Colonial Williamsburg, Inc., Virginia File, Library of Congress (LC-USW-33-26180-ZC), Washington, D.C.
65 Jack Delano, Library of Congress (LC-USF-34-44484-D), Washington, D.C.
67 William Ferris Collection, Archives and Special Collections, University of Mississippi Library, Oxford
70 Valentine Museum, Richmond, Virginia
74 David J. Kaminsky, photographer, Historic American Buildings Survey, Library of Congress, Washington, D.C.
75 Photographer not given, Historic American Buildings Survey, Library of Congress, Washington, D.C.
76 Trinity Episcopal Church, Mobile, Alabama
77 Marion Post Wolcott, Library of Congress (LC-USF-34-54827-D), Washington, D.C.
86 Benjamin Henry Latrobe Collection, Maryland Historical Society, Baltimore
88 Cook Collection, Valentine Museum, Richmond, Virginia
92 Walter Anderson Family, Ocean Springs, Mississippi
96 Marion Post Wolcott, Library of Congress (LC-USF-33-30740-M3), Washington, D.C.
97 Frances Benjamin Johnston, Library of Congress (number unavailable), Washington, D.C.
98 Todd Webb, Historic New Orleans Collection (1978.90.13), New Orleans, Louisiana
104 The Greenbrier, White Sulphur Springs, West Virginia
113 M. B. Newton, Baton Rouge, Louisiana
120 William Christenberry, University Museums, University of Mississippi, Oxford
124 Patrons Art Fund, 1944, Carnegie Museum of Art, Pittsburgh, Pennsylvania

Black Life

131 William Ferris Collection, Archives and Special Collections, University of Mississippi Library, Oxford
137 William Ferris Collection, Archives and Special Collections, University of Mississippi Library, Oxford
138 Ernest C. Withers, photographer, Memphis, Tennessee
140 Victor Howard Collection, Archives and Special Collections, University of Mississippi Library, Oxford
149 *The Century Magazine*, vol. 31, February 1886, p. 525
156 Film Stills Archives, Museum of Modern Art, New York, New York
161 Birmingham (Alabama) *News*
162 William Ferris Collection, Archives and Special Collections, University of Mississippi Library, Oxford
162 William Ferris Collection, Archives and Special Collections, University of Mississippi Library, Oxford
175 Georgia Department of Archives and History, Atlanta
179 Film Stills Archives, Museum of Modern Art, New York, New York
179 Cheryl Thurber, photographer, Memphis, Tennessee
189 Archives and Manuscripts, Birmingham (Alabama) Public Library
206 Sophia Smith Collection, Smith College, Northampton, Massachusetts
210 Robert Jordan, photographer, University of Mississippi, Oxford
214 Esther Bubley, Library of Congress (LC-USW3-37939-E), Washington, D.C.
217 William Ferris Collection, Archives and Special Collections, University of Mississippi Library, Oxford
218 Michael P. Smith, photographer, Brazos Films/Arhoolie Records, Los Cerrito, California
228 William Ferris Collection, Archives and Special Collections, University of Mississippi Library, Oxford
229 Photographer and number unavailable, Library of Congress, Washington, D.C.

Education

233 R. G. Potter Collection, Photographic Archives, University of Louisville (Kentucky)
239 Russell Lee, Library of Congress (number unavailable), Washington, D.C.
241 William Ferris Collection, Archives and Special Collections, University of Mississippi Library, Oxford
256 Archives and Manuscripts, Birmingham (Alabama) Public Library
261 Photographic Archives, University of Louisville (Kentucky)
270 Auburn (Alabama) University Archives
271 Archives and Special Collections, University of Mississippi Library, Oxford
279 University Archives, Swem Library, College of William and Mary, Williamsburg, Virginia
282 Duke University Archives, Durham, North Carolina
287 Southern Historical Collection, University of North Carolina, Chapel Hill
291 William Garver, Kappa Alpha Order, Lexington, Virginia
293 E. C. Boynton, photographer, Archives and Special Collections, University of Mississippi Library, Oxford
296 North Carolina Collection, University of North Carolina, Chapel Hill
298 Ann Rayburn Paper Americana Collection, Archives and Special Collections, University of Mississippi Library, Oxford

303 Barker Texas History Center, University of Texas at Austin

Environment

311 Virginia Museum of Fine Arts, Richmond
316 Maier Museum of Art, Randolph-Macon Woman's College, Lynchburg, Virginia
318 William Ferris Collection, Archives and Special Collections, University of Mississippi Library, Oxford
326 William Ferris Collection, Archives and Special Collections, University of Mississippi Library, Oxford
328 William Ferris Collection, Archives and Special Collections, University of Mississippi Library, Oxford
337 Ann Rayburn Paper Americana Collection, Archives and Special Collections, University of Mississippi Library, Oxford
358 Photographic Archives, University of Louisville (Kentucky)
361 William Ferris Collection, Archives and Special Collections, University of Mississippi Library, Oxford
363 Soil Conservation Service, U.S. Department of Agriculture, Washington, D.C.
373 Historic New Orleans Collection (1979.338i-vi), New Orleans, Louisiana
388 Doug Marlette, Atlanta (Georgia) *Journal-Constitution*
390 Uncredited engraving in A. B. Strong, editor and compiler, *Illustrated Natural History of the Three Kingdoms* (1849)
394 Marion Post Wolcott, Library of Congress (LC-USF-34-54302-D), Washington, D.C.

Ethnic Life

397 Hargrett Rare Book and Manuscript Library, University of Georgia, Athens
402 Historic New Orleans Collection (1985.41), New Orleans, Louisiana
407 New Orleans Museum of Art (56.34), New Orleans, Louisiana
410 From a drawing by Du Pratz, Louisiana, 1718–34, National Anthropological Archives, Smithsonian Institution, Washington, D.C.
412 Deaconness Bedell Collection, National Anthropological Archives, Smithsonian Institution, Washington, D.C.
420 William Ferris Collection, Archives and Special Collections, University of Mississippi Library, Oxford
422 Philip Gould, photographer, Lafayette, Louisiana
425 Eudora Welty, Mississippi Department of Archives and History (12.31.86), Jackson
430 University of Texas Institute of Texan Cultures, San Antonio
431 Library of Congress (LC-USW-3-43130-KC), Washington, D.C.
435 Louis Schmier Collection, Valdosta, Georgia
441 National Museum of American Art, Smithsonian Institution, Washington, D.C.

Folklife

447 Doris Ulmann, Art Department, Berea College, Berea, Kentucky
454 William Ferris Collection, Archives and Special Collections, University of Mississippi Library, Oxford
459 William Ferris Collection, Archives and Special Collections, University of Mississippi Library, Oxford
462 William Ferris Collection, Archives and Special Collections, University of Mississippi Library, Oxford
468 Russell Lee, News and Information Service and Barker Texas History Center, University of Texas at Austin
474 Amon Carter Museum, Fort Worth, Texas
486 Private collection, Winston-Salem, North Carolina
499 William Ferris Collection, Archives and Special Collections, University of Mississippi Library, Oxford
501 William Ferris Collection, Archives and Special Collections, University of Mississippi Library, Oxford
503 William Ferris Collection, Archives and Special Collections, University of Mississippi Library, Oxford
509 William Ferris Collection, Archives and Special Collections, University of Mississippi Library, Oxford
511 William Ferris Collection, Archives and Special Collections, University of Mississippi Library, Oxford
513 William Ferris Collection, Archives and Special Collections, University of Mississippi Library, Oxford
522 William Ferris Collection, Archives and Special Collections, University of Mississippi Library, Oxford
526 William Ferris Collection, Archives and Special Collections, University of Mississippi Library, Oxford

Geography

539 Marion Post Wolcott, Library of Congress (LC-USF-34-55745-D), Washington, D.C.
550 William Ferris Collection, Archives and Special Collections, University of Mississippi Library, Oxford
560 Georgia Department of Archives and History, Atlanta
562 San Antonio (Texas) Conservation Society
569 Ann Rayburn Paper Americana Collection, Archives and Special Collections, University of Mississippi Library, Oxford
570 Marion Post Wolcott, Library of Congress (LC-USF-34-51787-D), Washington, D.C.
574 Russell Lee, Library of Congress (LC-USF-33-11410-MS), Washington, D.C.

History and Manners

579 Marion Post Wolcott, Library of Congress (LC-USF-34-54814-D), Washington, D.C.
584 Gift of Edgar Williams and Bernice Chrysler Garbisch, 1963 (63.210.3), Metropolitan Museum of Art, New York, New York
588 Georgia Department of Archives and History, Atlanta
598 Marion Post Wolcott, Library of Congress (LC-USF-34-54195-E), Washington, D.C.
601 Tom Rankin, photographer, Atlanta, Georgia
602 Florida State Archives, Tallahassee
606 Slide and Photography Library, Virginia Museum of Fine Arts, Richmond
610 Jack Delano, Library of Congress (LC-USF-34-46448-D), Washington, D.C.
616 Odum Photographic Survey, Southern Historical Collection, University of North Carolina, Chapel Hill
631 John Collier, Library of Congress (LC-USW-3-22785-C), Washington, D.C.
642 Audie Murphy Collection, Baylor University, Waco, Texas
645 Walker Evans, Library of Congress (LC-USF-342-8083-A), Washington, D.C.
657 Photographic Archives, University of Louisville (Kentucky)
674 Standard Oil Collection, Photographic Archives, University of Louisville (Kentucky)
682 Dementi-Foster Studios, Richmond, Virginia
683 Shelby County Public Office
684 Mathew B. Brady, National Portrait Gallery, Smithsonian Institution, Washington, D.C.
685 Photographer and number unavailable, Library of Congress, Washington, D.C.
690 Charles Reagan Wilson Collection, University of Mississippi, Oxford
692 Rembrandt Peale painting, New-York Historical Society, New York, New York
693 Mathew B. Brady, National Archives (111-B-1564), Washington, D.C.

695 Manuscripts Department, University of Virginia Library, Charlottesville
697 Filson Club, Louisville, Kentucky
700 Ann Rayburn Paper Americana Collection, Archives and Special Collections, University of Mississippi Library, Oxford
705 William Ferris Collection, Archives and Special Collections, University of Mississippi Library, Oxford

Industry

711 Walker Evans, Library of Congress (LC-USZ62-34372), Washington, D.C.
717 Lewis Hine, Albin O. Kuhn Library and Gallery, University of Maryland, Baltimore County
728 John Vachon, Library of Congress (LC-USF-34-62666-D), Washington, D.C.
731 Ann Rayburn Paper Americana Collection, Archives and Special Collections, University of Mississippi Library, Oxford
738 Coca-Cola Company Archives, Atlanta, Georgia
739 Duke University Archives, Durham, North Carolina
748 Seley Collection, Baylor University, Waco, Texas
753 Ann Rayburn Paper Americana Collection, Archives and Special Collections, University of Mississippi Library, Oxford
754 Photographic Archives, University of Louisville (Kentucky)
755 John Vachon, Library of Congress (LC-USW-3-21955-D), Washington, D.C.
755 Wal-Mart, Bentonville, Arkansas

Language

757 Tennessee State Library and Archives, Nashville, Tennessee
766 Jack Delano, Library of Congress (LC-USF-33-20841-2), Washington, D.C.
768 William Ferris Collection, Archives and Special Collections, University of Mississippi Library, Oxford
770 Historic New Orleans Collection (1980.205.35), New Orleans, Louisiana
791 McDonald County Library, Pineville, Missouri

Law

793 Paul Kwilecki, photographer, Bainbridge, Georgia
799 Jack Delano, Library of Congress (LC-USF-34-43941-D), Washington, D.C.
803 Ann Rayburn Paper Americana Collection, Archives and Special Collections, University of Mississippi Library, Oxford
819 Archives and Manuscripts, Birmingham (Alabama) Public Library
820 Southern Historical Collection, University of North Carolina, Chapel Hill
821 Film Stills Archives, Museum of Modern Art, New York, New York
823 Jack Moebes, photographer, Greensboro (North Carolina) *News and Record*
825 Frank M. Johnson, Jr., Office, Montgomery, Alabama
829 Lewis Powell Office, Washington, D.C.

Literature

835 Jack Cofield, Oxford, Mississippi
842 Joe Rudis, Photographic Archives, Vanderbilt University Library, Nashville, Tennessee
855 Film Stills Archives, Museum of Modern Art, New York, New York
858 William Ferris Collection, Archives and Special Collections, University of Mississippi Library, Oxford
863 Charles Reagan Wilson Collection, University of Mississippi, Oxford
874 James Agee Film Project, Knoxville, Tennessee
875 George W. Cable Collection, Manuscript Section, Tulane University Library, New Orleans, Louisiana
877 A. E. Bradley, Library of Congress (LC-USZ-62-28844), Washington, D.C.
879 Photographic Archives, Vanderbilt University Library, Nashville, Tennessee
880 Jim Cleveland, photographer, Public Relations Department, University of Mississippi, Oxford
882 Random House book edition, Archives and Special Collections, University of Mississippi Library, Oxford
884 Ellen Glasgow Papers (#5771), University of Virginia Library, Charlottesville
892 Jerry Bauer, photographer, Farrar, Straus and Giroux photo, New York, New York
894 Photographic Archives, Vanderbilt University Library, Nashville, Tennessee
896 Nancy Crampton, photographer, Random House, New York, New York
897 Photographic Archives, Vanderbilt University, Nashville, Tennessee
898 William Ferris Collection, Archives and Special Collections, University of Mississippi Library, Oxford
900 William Ferris Collection, Archives and Special Collections, University of Mississippi Library, Oxford
901 Thomas Wolfe Collection, Pack Memorial Public Library, Asheville, North Carolina
903 Archives and Special Collections, University of Mississippi Library, Oxford

Media

905 Paul Culp, WOPI, Bristol, Tennessee, and Archives of Appalachia, East Tennessee State University, Johnson City, Tennessee
917 Film Stills Archives, Museum of Modern Art, New York, New York
922 Film Stills Archives, Museum of Modern Art, New York, New York
923 Film Stills Archives, Museum of Modern Art, New York, New York
931 Photographic Archives, University of Louisville (Kentucky)
943 Texas Tourist Development Agency, Austin
945 WLOS-TV, Asheville, North Carolina
952 Southern Historical Collection, University of North Carolina, Chapel Hill
958 Film Stills Archives, Museum of Modern Art, New York, New York
963 Film Stills Archives, Museum of Modern Art, New York, New York
964 Special Collections Department, Robert W. Woodruff Library, Emory University, Atlanta, Georgia
966 Film Stills Archives, Museum of Modern Art, New York, New York
970 Film Stills Archives, Museum of Modern Art, New York, New York
975 Ted Turner Enterprises, Atlanta, Georgia
979 Film Stills Archives, Museum of Modern Art, New York, New York

Music

981 Arthur Rothstein, Library of Congress (LC-USF-33-2184-M5), Washington, D.C.
986 Russell Lee, Library of Congress (LC-USF-34-31941-D), Washington, D.C.
987 William Ferris Collection, Archives and Special Collections, University of Mississippi Library, Oxford
990 William Ferris Collection, Archives and Special

Collections, University of Mississippi Library, Oxford
990 Country Music Foundation, Library and Media Center, Nashville, Tennessee
991 Ray Funk Collection, Fairbanks, Alaska
994 Country Music Foundation, Library and Media Center, Nashville, Tennessee
997 Diane Allmen, photographer, Living Blues Archival Collection, University of Mississippi Blues Archive, Oxford
1000 Ann Rayburn Paper Americana Collection, Archives and Special Collections, University of Mississippi Library, Oxford
1003 Country Music Foundation, Library and Media Center, Nashville, Tennessee
1006 Woodward Iron Company Collection, Special Collections, University of Alabama Library, Tuscaloosa
1017 Hogan Jazz Archive, Tulane University, New Orleans, Louisiana
1022 Brazos Films/Arhoolie Records, El Cerrito, California
1030 William Ferris Collection, Archives and Special Collections, University of Mississippi Library, Oxford
1032 William Ferris Collection, Archives and Special Collections, University of Mississippi Library, Oxford
1039 Country Music Foundation, Library and Media Center, Nashville, Tennessee
1040 Hogan Jazz Archive, Tulane University, New Orleans, Louisiana
1042 Robert Winans, photographer, Gettysburg College, Gettysburg, Pennsylvania
1045 Skylite Records photograph, Cheryl Thurber Collection, Memphis, Tennessee
1047 Solid Smoke Records photograph, Living Blues Archival Collection, University of Mississippi Blues Archive, Oxford
1048 Hogan Jazz Archive, Tulane University, New Orleans, Louisiana
1051 Country Music Foundation, Library and Media Center, Nashville, Tennessee
1053 Ray Funk Collection, Fairbanks, Alaska
1054 Amy Van Singel, photographer, Living Blues Archival Collection, University of Mississippi Blues Archive, Oxford
1056 William Ferris Collection, Archives and Special Collections, University of Mississippi Library, Oxford
1060 Country Music Foundation, Library and Media Center, Nashville, Tennessee
1062 Michael Stachnik, photographer, Living Blues Archival Collection, University of Mississippi Blues Archive, Oxford
1064 William Ferris Collection, Archives and Special Collections, University of Mississippi Library, Oxford
1067 William Ferris Collection, Archives and Special Collections, University of Mississippi Library, Oxford
1072 Ray Flerlage, photographer, Living Blues Archival Collection, University of Mississippi Blues Archive, Oxford
1073 Hogan Jazz Archive, Tulane University, New Orleans, Louisiana
1074 Columbia Records, New York, New York
1078 Graceland, Inc., Memphis, Tennessee
1079 16th Avenue Records, Nashville, Tennessee
1082 Jimmie Rodgers Museum, Meridian, Mississippi
1090 Country Music Foundation, Library and Media Center, Nashville, Tennessee

Mythic South

1093 Ann Rayburn Paper Americana Collection, Archives and Special Collections, University of Mississippi Library, Oxford
1108 Texas Tourist Development Agency, Austin
1112 Doris Ulmann, Southern Historical Collection, University of North Carolina, Chapel Hill
1118 Brown and Williamson Tobacco Company Archives, Louisville, Kentucky
1125 Southern Historical Collection, University of North Carolina, Chapel Hill
1134 Eudora Welty, Mississippi Department of Archives and History, Jackson
1135 Everhard Collection, Amon Carter Museum, Fort Worth, Texas
1142 William Ferris Collection, Archives and Special Collections, University of Mississippi Library, Oxford

Politics

1147 Film Stills Archives, Museum of Modern Art, New York, New York
1153 Louisiana State Library, Baton Rouge
1155 Louisiana State Library, Baton Rouge
1162 Mr. and Mrs. Jack M. McLarty, Jackson, Mississippi
1164 Texas State Library, Austin
1170 William Ferris Collection, Archives and Special Collections, University of Mississippi Library, Oxford
1185 Tennessee State Library and Archives, Nashville
1187 No photographer given, Library of Congress (LC-USZ-62-20175), Washington, D.C.
1190 Tennessee State Library and Archives, Nashville
1198 Georgia Department of Archives and History, Atlanta
1199 Senate Office, Strom Thurmond, Washington, D.C.
1200 Charles Reagan Wilson Collection, University of Mississippi, Oxford
1201 Mayor's Office, Atlanta, Georgia

Recreation

1203 Marion Post Wolcott, Library of Congress (LC-USF-54259-D), Washington, D.C.
1208 Ann Rayburn Paper Americana Collection, Archives and Special Collections, University of Mississippi Library, Oxford
1216 Marion Post Wolcott, Library of Congress (LC-USF-33-30905-M3), Washington, D.C.
1220 Ann Rayburn Paper Americana Collection, Archives and Special Collections, University of Mississippi Library, Oxford
1222 National Football League Hall of Fame, Canton, Ohio
1223 Dallas Cowboys, Dallas, Texas
1225 Georgia Department of Archives and History, Atlanta
1227 Photographic Archives, University of Louisville (Kentucky)
1229 Ann Rayburn Paper Americana Collection, Archives and Special Collections, University of Mississippi Library, Oxford
1232 Philip Gould, photographer, Lafayette, Louisiana
1234 William Ferris Collection, Archives and Special Collections, University of Mississippi Library, Oxford
1236 Ann Rayburn Paper Americana Collection, Archives and Special Collections, University of Mississippi Library, Oxford
1240 Eudora Welty, Mississippi Department of Archives and History, Jackson
1241 Alabama International Motor Speedway, Talladega
1252 Sports Information Office, University of Alabama, Tuscaloosa
1253 Edward R. Hollen, Library of Congress (LC-USW-3-24585C), Washington, D.C.
1254 National Baseball Library, Cooperstown, New York
1261 Ann Rayburn Paper Americana Collection, Archives and Special Collections, University of Mississippi Library, Oxford
1263 Dallas Cowboys, Dallas, Texas

Religion

1265 Photographic Archives, University of Louisville (Kentucky)
1269 William Ferris Collection, Archives and Special Collections, University of Mississippi Library, Oxford
1270 Jack Delano, Library of Congress (LC-USF-34-46523-D), Washington, D.C.
1274 Tom Rankin, photographer, Atlanta, Georgia
1277 William Ferris Collection, Archives and Special Collections, University of Mississippi Library, Oxford
1285 William Ferris Collection, Archives and Special Collections, University of Mississippi Library, Oxford
1290 Waco Jewry Collection, Baylor University, Waco, Texas
1297 William Ferris Collection, Archives and Special Collections, University of Mississippi Library, Oxford
1301 William Ferris Collection, Archives and Special Collections, University of Mississippi Library, Oxford
1314 Al Clayton, photographer, Peachtree Publishers, Atlanta, Georgia
1317 Thomas Road Baptist Church, Lynchburg, Virginia
1319 Billy Graham Evangelistic Association, Minneapolis, Minnesota
1321 Ann Rayburn Paper Americana Collection, Archives and Special Collections, University of Mississippi Library, Oxford
1327 Ann Rayburn Paper Americana Collection, Archives and Special Collections, University of Mississippi Library, Oxford
1328 Oral Roberts University, Tulsa, Oklahoma
1330 National Archives, Washington, D.C.

Science and Medicine

1333 Jane Moseley, photographer, Center for Southern Folklore, Memphis, Tennessee
1344 Wolff, Gretter, Cusick, Hill Collection, Kentucky Historical Society, Frankfort
1344 National Aeronautics and Space Administration, Houston, Texas
1346 Film Stills Archives, Museum of Modern Art, New York, New York
1353 Photographic Archives, University of Louisville (Kentucky)
1362 Marion Post Wolcott, Library of Congress (LC-USF-34-50583-D), Washington, D.C.
1365 Frances Benjamin Johnston, Library of Congress (LC-J694-302), Washington, D.C.
1368 Texas Collection, Baylor University, Waco, Texas
1369 National Archives, Washington, D.C.
1376 Virginia State Library and Archives (45.9232), Richmond

Social Class

1379 Dorothea Lange, Library of Congress (LC-USF-34-9599C), Washington, D.C.
1387 Film Stills Archives, Museum of Modern Art, New York, New York
1388 Esther Bubley, Library of Congress (LC-USW-3-38103E), Washington, D.C.
1396 Jack Delano, Library of Congress (LC-USF-33-20926-M2), Washington, D.C.
1401 Frank Collection, Mississippi Valley Collection, Memphis (Tennessee) State University Library
1402 Marion Post Wolcott, Library of Congress (LC-USF-34-51178E), Washington, D.C.
1408 William Ferris Collection, Archives and Special Collections, University of Mississippi Library, Oxford
1428 Lewis Hine, Albin O. Kuhn Library and Gallery, University of Maryland, Baltimore County
1428 Jack Delano, Library of Congress (LC-USF-34-43995D), Washington, D.C.
1429 Photographic Archives, University of Louisville (Kentucky)

Urbanization

1431 Marion Post Wolcott, Library of Congress (LC-USF-34-57018-D), Washington, D.C.
1436 Historic New Orleans Collection (1951.68), New Orleans, Lousiana
1440 Jack Delano, Library of Congress (LC-USF-33-20850-M5), Washington, D.C.
1445 Metropolitan Dade County, Florida
1459 Filson Club, Louisville, Kentucky
1462 Ann Rayburn Paper Americana Collection, Archives and Special Collections, University of Mississippi Library, Oxford
1463 Nashville (Tennessee) Area Chamber of Commerce
1464 Natchez (Mississippi) Pilgrimage Garden Club
1466 Charles East Collection, Baton Rouge, Louisiana

Violence

1469 Film Stills Archives, Museum of Modern Art, New York, New York
1474 University of Alabama Library, Tuscaloosa
1477 Mississippi Department of Archives and History, Jackson
1479 Film Stills Archives, Museum of Modern Art, New York, New York
1480 William Ferris Collection, Archives and Special Collections, University of Mississippi Library, Oxford
1495 Jack Delano, Library of Congress (LC-USF-33-20863-M3), Washington, D.C.
1501 Photographer not given, Library of Congress (LC-USF-344-7541-2B), Washington, D.C.
1505 West Virginia Department of Archives and History, Charleston
1507 Texas Sheet Music Collection, Baylor University, Waco, Texas
1510 William Ferris Collection, Archives and Special Collections, University of Mississippi Library, Oxford

Women's Life

1515 Doris Ulmann, Art Department, Berea College, Berea, Kentucky
1523 Florida State Archives, Tallahassee
1525 William Ferris Collection, Archives and Special Collections, University of Mississippi Library, Oxford
1528 Ann Rayburn Paper Americana Collection, Archives and Special Collections, University of Mississippi Library, Oxford
1534 Jane Moseley, photographer, Center for Southern Folklore, Memphis, Tennessee
1538 Gordon Parks, Library of Congress (LC-USW-3-17125C), Washington, D.C.
1539 Georgia Department of Archives and History, Atlanta
1540 Jane Moseley, photographer, Center for Southern Folklore, Memphis, Tennessee
1549 Marion Post Wolcott, Library of Congress (LC-USF-34-51738D), Washington, D.C.
1552 Marion Post Wolcott, Library of Congress (LC-USF-34-9610C), Washington, D.C.
1555 Photographic Archives, University of Louisville (Kentucky)
1558 William Ferris Collection, Archives and Special Collections, University of Mississippi Library, Oxford
1565 Photographic Archives, University of Louisville (Kentucky)
1566 William Ferris Collection, Archives and Special Collections, University of Mississippi Library, Oxford
1568 Gordon Parks, Library of Congress (LC-USW-3-14883C), Washington, D.C.

1571 Theater Collection, New York Public Library
1573 Carter Presidential Library, Atlanta, Georgia
1576 William Ferris Collection, Archives and Special Collections, University of Mississippi Library, Oxford
1580 News and Information Service, University of Texas at Austin
1583 Alumni Association, University of Mississippi, Oxford
1585 Columbia Records, New York, New York